THE STATESMAN'S YEARBOOK
2000

Nations are fast losing their nationality. The great
and increasing intercourse, the exchange of fashions
and uniformity of opinions by the diffusion of
literature are fast destroying those peculiarities
that formerly prevailed. We shall in time grow to
be very much one people, unless a return to barbarism
throws us again into chaos.

Washington Irving, *Journals and Notebooks*.
October 1822

Credits

Publisher	Sara Lloyd (London)
	Garrett Kiely (New York)
Editor	Dr Barry Turner
Editorial Assistant	Jill Fenner
Research	Nicholas Heath-Brown
	Daniel Smith
	Michèle Roche
	Lorraine Roche
	Kenneth Hadley
	Bridget Kinnersley
	Faith Clark
	Linus Nordquist
	Sally Page
	Richard Evans
Index	Gary Hall
Marketing	Alex Lankester
	Catherine Jones
Production	Jeremy Macdonald
Database Development/ Administration	Philip Meldrum
	Mark Wharram

THE
STATESMAN'S
YEARBOOK

THE POLITICS, CULTURES, AND
ECONOMIES OF THE WORLD

2000

EDITED BY

BARRY TURNER

ST.MARTIN'S
PRESS

First published in 1864
136th edition 1999

For information, write:
ST. MARTIN'S PRESS, INC.
175 Fifth Avenue, New York, N.Y. 10010

Library of Congress Catalog Card No. 4-3776

ISBN 0-312-22519-9

Printed in the UK by
Polestar Wheatons, Exeter

CONTENTS

CONTENTS

CONTENTS

Part II: Countries of the World A–Z

CONTENTS

CONTENTS

CONTENTS

CONTENTS

CHRONOLOGY

CHRONOLOGY

CHRONOLOGY

March 1998–March 1999

Week beginning 29 March, 1998

A national emergency in Guyana was declared after a prolonged drought had destroyed crops and caused forest fires.

Radu Vasile became prime minister of Romania.

Ukraine's Communist Party triumphed in the general election.

Robert Kocharian was elected president of Armenia.

Botswana's President Ketumile Masire retired. He was succeeded by Festus Mogae.

Week beginning 5 April, 1998

In the week in which France and Britain ratified a treaty banning the testing of nuclear weapons, Pakistan tested a surface-to-surface missile with a range of 1,500 km.

Yugoslavia announced a referendum to decide the future of Kosovo with its largely Albanian population. Separatist leaders rejected the proposal and demanded international mediation.

The OECD forecast for growth in member countries in 1998 and 1999 was cut to 2·5% while the IMF looked to worldwide growth of 3·1% for 1998.

Week beginning 12 April, 1998

A breakthrough in peace talks on the future of Northern Ireland opened the way for an elected assembly for the Province and for closer relations between northern and southern Ireland. A referendum on the proposals was announced for 22 May.

Direct talks between North and South Korea, the first since 1994, broke up without agreement on humanitarian aid to citizens of the north threatened with starvation.

A 'prison cleansing' campaign in Iraq had added up to 1,500 executions according to a UN Human Rights Commission report.

Romania's parliament backed plans for faster economic reform.

A Summit of the Americas, involving 34 countries, met in Santiago to negotiate pan-American free trade.

Week beginning 19 April, 1998

After a year's stalemate in the Middle East peace effort, Binyamin Netanyahu and Yasser Arafat agreed to talks in London with Madeleine Albright, US secretary of state.

The new government in Armenia promised to speed up economic reforms.

In France, a parliamentary vote on joining the single European currency was won by 334 to 49.

Relations between Iraq and the UN on the question of weapons inspectors deteriorated to the point of breakdown as Iraq demanded the lifting of sanctions.

The situation in Yugoslavia worsened as Albania was accused of supporting separatists in Kosovo with armed infiltrators.

Week beginning 26 April, 1998

New sanctions were threatened against Yugoslavia as violence mounted in Kosovo.

Sergei Kiriyenko was confirmed as prime minister by the Russian Duma.

Belgium's government survived a vote of no confidence but two ministers resigned after an alleged child killer escaped from custody.

Violence accelerated in Algeria after the army had launched an offensive against Islamist rebels in the west of the country. The death toll for April was over 200.

In Guatemala, a human rights report listed 55,000 atrocities committed, mostly by the army, in 36 years of civil war. Bishop Juan José Geradi, chief architect of the report, was murdered two days after completing the investigation.

Week beginning 3 May, 1998

The official inauguration of the European Single Currency, with 11 of the 15 EU members agreeing to adopt the EURO from the beginning of 1999, was overshadowed by a row over who was to run the European Central Bank. It was suggested by France that Wim Duisenberg, its first president, should stand down halfway through his eight-year term to make way for the head of France's central bank, Jean-Claude Trichet. Whether or not a deal had been struck remained unclear.

The London session of Middle East peace talks failed to persuade Israel to agree to a partial withdrawal from the West Bank.

In the Netherlands general election, the outgoing coalition government led by Wim Kok, was returned to office.

Week beginning 10 May, 1998

Fears of a nuclear arms race in Asia were prompted by India's decision to carry out five nuclear tests. The US response was to cut off economic and military aid.

Social unrest in Indonesia persuaded President Suharto to cut short his visit to Egypt.

Week beginning 17 May, 1998

Guido di Tella, Argentina's foreign minister, ordered the expulsion of 7 Iranians, including 3 diplomats, amid growing suspicions of Iranian involvement in the 1994 bombing of a Buenos Aires Jewish cultural centre in which 86 people died.

Congressional and municipal elections in the Dominican Republic were won by the main opposition left centre Democratic Revolutionary Party which promised to curtail drug trafficking and to modernize the economy. The Democratic Revolutionary Party won 23 of the 30 Senate seats that were at stake and achieved a comfortable margin in the lower house of congress. The party also won the most important mayoral race, in the capital, where the singer Johnny Ventura swept to victory.

Indonesia was on the verge of civil war after several days of rioting and looting had left large areas of the capital, Jakarta, in ruins. By the time President Suharto arrived home, more than 1,000 buildings and shops had been destroyed. The speaker of the parliament announced that the leaders of the 5 factions in the assembly would ask Mr Suharto to step down. On 20 May, President Suharto announced his resignation. His proclamation followed a further day of protest demonstrations under tight army control and growing criticism from abroad at his failure to deliver reforms required under the multi-billion dollar rescue package led by the International Monetary Fund. Vice president B.J. Habibie was sworn in as Mr Suharto's successor, promising to push through political and economic reforms, including those agreed with the IMF as part of its $43bn. rescue package.

Alexander Lebed, the tough-talking paratroop general, shocked the Russian political establishment by winning the regional election for governor of the Siberian province of Krasnoyarsk. General Lebed, a veteran of the Afghan war who campaigned for the restoration of 'order' in Russia, had 57% of the vote, against 38% for the Kremlin-backed incumbent, Valery Zubov.

A bomb exploded in a packed market in an Algiers suburb, killing at least 16 people and wounding more than 60.

The people of Northern Ireland voted for the Good Friday peace agreement with 71% in favour. In the Irish Republic there was an overwhelming 94·4% in support. The result paved the way for the creation of an administration based on cross-community consensus and power sharing. The result suggested that a majority of Unionists had endorsed the agreement, together with almost all nationalist voters. The referendum result cleared the way for the first power-sharing administration since the collapse of the Sunningdale government of 1974. A fundamental overhaul of Northern Ireland's justice and policing systems, together with the early release of prisoners whose paramilitary groups maintain ceasefires, was expected to follow.

Week beginning 24 May, 1998

In response to India's nuclear tests, Pakistan carried out 6 nuclear tests of its own. The response from the US was the same; sanctions were imposed.

A right-wing coalition defeated the Socialist-led government of Hungary in a general election.

Interest rates in Russia hit 150% after a collapse of the currency and stock market.

Amidst accusations of fraud, Senegal's ruling Socialist party was returned in a general election.

Week beginning 31 May, 1998

In Yugoslavia, Serbian attacks on separatist guerrillas in Kosovo intensified as thousands of refugees fled to Albania.

Meanwhile, in Montenegro, the smaller of Yugoslavia's 2 republics, the general election was won by reformers opposed to Yugoslav president, Slobodan Miloševic.

Week beginning 7 June, 1998

As economic troubles in Asia intensified, the Japanese yen dropped to a 7-year low against the dollar. The US responded with a $2bn. spending pledge to boost the yen.

The military boss of Nigeria, General Sani Abacha, died of a heart attack. He was replaced by General Abdulsalam Abubakar, who promised a return to civilian rule.

An attempted coup in Guinea-Bissau was led by Ansumane Mane, a dismissed army chief. Gambia offered to mediate but talks soon broke down.

Javier Valle Riestra became prime minister of Peru.

Week beginning 14 June, 1998

At a summit of European leaders, Germany demanded a cut in its contribution to the EU budget. The meeting failed to reach agreement on a trade deal with South Africa.

NATO threatened retaliation against Yugoslavia if Serbian repression continued in Kosovo.

Week beginning 21 June, 1998

The IMF advanced $6bn. to Indonesia bringing the total Indonesian loan to $47bn. and released $670m. to Russia as part of a 3-year agreement. Russia sought an extra $1·15bn. to keep its economy afloat.

Andrés Pastrana was elected president of Colombia.

The Czech general election was won by the centre left Social Democrats but with a majority so marginal as to lead to a coalition with the right-wing Civil Democrats.

Bill Clinton visited China, the first American president to do so since the Tiananmen Square repression in 1989. The authorities allowed live coverage of President Clinton's speech on political rights.

Week beginning 28 June, 1998

An assembly for Northern Ireland set up under the recent peace agreement held its first meeting. The first minister designate was the Ulster Unionist leader David Trimble, his deputy Seamus Mallon of the nationalist SDLP.

China's president Jiang Zemin opened Hong Kong's new airport at Chek Lap Kok.

Promising a crackdown on corruption, Joseph Estrada took over the presidency of the Philippines.

Week beginning 5 July, 1998

The first steps of opening up the government of Nigeria was marred when Moshood Abiola, the imprisoned winner of the 1993 presidential election, died while talking to American officials who were negotiating his release. His supporters claimed he had been murdered.

As fighting between government and rebels continued in Sudan, UN agencies reported that 1·2m. people in the south of the country faced starvation.

Week beginning 12 July, 1998

Ryutoro Hashimoto, prime minister of Japan, resigned after his party's defeat in elections for the upper house of parliament.

A ceasefire was agreed in Sudan allowing aid convoys to get through to the south.

The US lifted the ban on some food exports to India and Pakistan while insisting that sanctions remained in place.

A $22bn. loan to Russia was agreed by the IMF and World Bank but payments were subsequently delayed when the Duma refused to implement reforms.

Week beginning 19 July, 1998

Representatives from 160 countries meeting in Rome agreed to set up an international criminal court to try individuals accused of crimes against humanity. Initial opposition from the US was overcome by majority vote.

General Abubakar, Nigeria's military ruler, promised a return to civilian rule in May 1999 after an internationally monitored election.

Fighting in Kosovo intensified in and around the towns of Orahovac and Maliesvo. A Serb offensive recaptured large areas held by the Kosovo Liberation Army.

Week beginning 26 July, 1998

Keizo Obuchi became prime minister of Japan. Kiichi Miyazawa, a former prime minister, was made finance minister.

Floods along China's Yangzi river killed up to 2,500 people. A massive effort to hold back the water, said to involve 5m. helpers, was not enough to prevent widespread devastation.

In Cambodia's general election, victory was claimed by Hun Sen amidst charges by his opponents of electoral fraud.

An IMF loan of $74m. was secured by Georgia after President Eduard Shevardnadze replaced most of his cabinet with economic reformers.

Week beginning 2 August, 1998

Share prices in Hong Kong plunged to a 3-year low on news that the economy had contracted by 2·8% in the first quarter of the year.

The Japanese government attempted to give some impetus to the economy by promising extensive tax cuts.

Civil war threatened in the Democratic Republic of the Congo where former supporters of President Laurent Kabila accused him of reneging on his promises.

Government forces in Colombia suffered a serious defeat when rebels launched a concerted attack on army bases and oil installations.

Week beginning 9 August, 1998

Islamic militants were blamed for attacks on American embassies in Nairobi and Dar es Salaam which killed 250 and injured 5,000.

As floods in China spread north, some 140,000 were dispossessed in South Korea when their homes were destroyed by mud slides.

Javier Valle Riestra resigned as prime minister of Peru only two months after taking on the job. His predecessor, Alberto Pandolfi Arbulú, was reappointed.

CHRONOLOGY

Week beginning 16 August, 1998

Beset by rumours of sexual scandal, President Bill Clinton, having testified to a grand jury, admitted that he had had a relationship with a White House intern. Opinion polls seemed to back the President against Republican calls for his impeachment.

The peace accord in Northern Ireland was stretched to the limit when a bomb planted by a splinter group of the IRA went off in the centre of Omagh, killing 28 people. It was the worst single atrocity in 30 years of violence.

Disruption in the Congo grew worse as Zimbabwe and Angola forces were brought in to support President Kabila against Rwandan-backed rebels.

Week beginning 23 August, 1998

As Russia suspended payments on foreign debt and the central bank gave up trying to support the rouble, President Yeltsin dismissed Sergei Kiriyenko, his prime minister of five months, and reappointed Viktor Chernomyrdin.

The US used cruise missiles to destroy an Islamist guerrilla training centre in Afghanistan and a supposed chemical weapon factory in Sudan.

Week beginning 30 August, 1998

Erratic trading on the world's stock markets followed hard upon fears that economic troubles in Asia and Russia would lead to world recession.

The Russian Duma rejected President Yeltsin's nominee for prime minister.

In Malaysia, the prime minister Mahathir Mohamad dismissed his reformist deputy, Anwar Ibrahim and imposed tight capital controls.

North Korea test fired a ballistic missile over Japanese territory.

Poland abolished the death penalty.

Week beginning 6 September, 1998

A report on President Clinton's alleged misconduct was delivered to Congress by special prosecutor Kenneth Starr.

American investigators revealed 'horrendous human rights violations' committed by government forces in Kosovo.

The 5 countries participating in the civil war in the Congo failed to negotiate a ceasefire.

Yevgeniy Primakov, Russia's acting foreign minister and former head of the central bank, became prime minister with Communist support.

The death toll from floods in Bangladesh rose to 1,300 with millions of homes lost and damage estimated at $900m.

Week beginning 13 September, 1998

Basque guerrillas (ETA) declared a 'total and indefinite' truce after 30 years of violent opposition to rule from Madrid.

CHRONOLOGY

Zimbabwe backed down on its policy of redistribution of white-owned farms. Instead, of the 1,470 farms originally designated, only 118 would be taken over.

There were riots in Albania and Indonesia but anti-government protests in Cambodia died down after opposition leaders called for restraint.

Week beginning 20 September, 1998

A videotape was released of President Clinton's testimony to the grand jury in which he admitted a relationship with White House intern Monica Lewinsky but claimed that oral sex did not amount to an affair within the normal meaning of the term.

South African troops crossed into Lesotho to support the government against an army mutiny.

Sweden's Social Democrats were returned to power in the general election but with their lowest share of votes in 40 years.

Week beginning 27 September, 1998

After 16 years as German Chancellor, Helmut Kohl and his Christian Democrat Party were ousted in the general election. The Social Democrats, led by Gerhard Schröder began negotiations with the Greens to form a coalition government.

The IMF scaled down its forecast for world economic growth in 1998 from 3·1% to 2%.

Malaysia's former deputy prime minister, Anwar Ibrahim, was accused of corruption and sexual misconduct.

India and Pakistan agreed in principle to abide by a nuclear test ban treaty.

At 30, Pandeli Majko, Albania's latest prime minister, became Europe's youngest leader.

Week beginning 4 October, 1998

President Milošević of Yugoslavia was warned that unless he obeyed a UN resolution to withdraw Serb troops from Kosovo, he would face NATO air strikes.

Brazil's president, Fernando Henrique Cardoso, was elected for a second 4-year-term.

Italy's government led by Romano Prodi faced defeat after the withdrawal of Communist support.

In Australia's general election, the ruling Liberal National government was returned to power but with a sharply reduced majority.

Latvia's general election was indecisive with no single party winning a majority.

Week beginning 11 October, 1998

The threat of NATO air strikes against Yugoslavia was lifted when President Milošević agreed to the withdrawal of Serb forces from Kosovo, to be checked by unarmed observers, and talks on greater autonomy for the province.

China and Taiwan held their first official talks in 5 years.

A dispute between Eritrea and Yemen over the Hanish islands was resolved by the international court in The Hague.

In Italy, the Socialist government of Romano Prodi collapsed after losing a confidence motion by one vote. The crisis was brought about by tough budget proposals designed to limit government spending to single currency criteria.

Week beginning 18 October, 1998

In Italy, a coalition including Communists, Greens and one-time Christian Democrats came together under the leadership of Massimo D'Alema to form a government.

General Pinochet, in London for an operation, was arrested on a warrant from a Spanish judge investigating crimes committed when he was dictator of Chile between 1973 and 1990.

Syria agreed not to give further help to Turkey's separatist Kurds.

The Middle East peace process advanced a step when Israel agreed to withdraw from a further 13% of the West Bank on condition that the Palestinians cracked down on terrorism.

Week beginning 25 October, 1998

The report of South Africa's Truth and Reconciliation Commission was presented to President Mandela.

Having agreed to accept arbitration to settle a long-standing border dispute, Peru and Ecuador signed a pact which confirmed Peru's assertion that the border lies along the high peaks of the Condor. Ecuador gained navigation rights on the Amazon.

A 4-party coalition took over as the government of Slovakia. It was led by Mikuláš Dzurinda, a Christian Democrat.

Week beginning 1 November, 1998

Mid-term Congressional elections in the US brought unexpected gains for the Democrats who reduced the Republican majority in the House of Representatives by 5 seats. The risk of impeachment of President Clinton receded.

Hurricane Mitch devastated Honduras and Nicaragua killing thousands and wrecking their economies.

The prospect for government finances in Brazil improved markedly with lower house approval of pension reform.

Iraq withdrew co-operation with UN arms inspectors.

Vilis Krištopans became prime minister of Latvia, heading a coalition government.

Week beginning 8 November, 1998

Further intransigence from Iraq increased the likelihood of American air attacks. The military buildup in the Gulf continued as UN personnel withdrew from Iraq.

Economic sanctions imposed on India and Pakistan in response to nuclear tests were lifted.

Tajikistan suffered renewed violence between army and rebels in the Leninabad region.

Israel's cabinet accepted the Wye Accord but imposed conditions on its implementation.

Week beginning 15 November, 1998

Air strikes against Iraq were called off at the last moment when Saddam Hussein agreed to co-operate with UN inspectors.

Troops opened fire on demonstrators in Jakarta killing 14.

An agreement between four parties led to a coalition government for Cambodia with Hun Sen as prime minister and Prince Norodom Ranariddh as president.

In Zimbabwe, 841 white-owned farms were designated for compulsory purchase.

The IMF led a rescue of the Brazilian economy with a $41·5 billion package.

Week beginning 22 November, 1998

After 16 months in office, Turkey's government was defeated by a vote of censure.

Jiang Zemin became the first head of a Chinese government to make a state visit to Japan and Tony Blair became the first British prime minister to address the Irish parliament.

Galina Starovoitova, a leading Russian politician, was shot dead in St. Petersburg.

As a first stage towards implementing the Wye Accord, Israeli troops withdrew from another 2 per cent of the northern west bank.

Week beginning 29 November, 1998

India's Congress party made big gains in state elections.

Christmas day was restored as a public holiday in Cuba.

Lebanon's prime minister, Rafiq Hariri, resigned. He was succeeded by Selim al-Hoss.

The price of oil dropped to its lowest level in 25 years.

Week beginning 6 December, 1998

Ruth Dreifuss was confirmed as Switzerland's first female president.

The ruling party in Taiwan was returned to power in the general elections.

Hugo Chávez was elected president of Venezuela and Omar Bongo was re-elected president of Gabon.

There was violence in Comoros as rebels tried to take control of the island of Anjouan.

CHRONOLOGY

Week beginning 13 December, 1998

After further obstruction of UN arms inspectors, American and British forces launched air attacks on Iraq.

Having refused to accept the latest EU accounts, the European Parliament moved to censure the Commission.

Puerto Rico rejected American statehood in a referendum.

Argentina and Chile settled their last territorial dispute in the Andes.

Week beginning 20 December, 1998

Tension in Kosovo built up as NATO warned of civil war within weeks.

Week beginning 27 December, 1998

The US increased defence spending.

Peace talks between government and rebels started in Colombia.

Week beginning 3 January, 1999

The impeachment trial of President Clinton began.

The Euro made its debut on world markets.

Rebel forces in Sierra Leone reached the capital, Freetown. The president fled.

Amidst accusations of fraud and mismanagement, pressure built up on a number of European commissioners to resign.

Week beginning 10 January, 1999

The European Commission narrowly escaped censure by the European Parliament by promising to investigate allegations of fraud and mis-management.

Government forces made a comeback in Sierra Leone, recapturing Freetown.

Brazil devalued against the dollar after one state declared a debt moratorium.

Bülent Ecevit became Turkey's prime minister, heading a caretaker government to rule up to the April elections.

Week beginning 17 January, 1999

NATO renewed threats against Yugoslavia after 45 Albanians were massacred in Kosovo.

UN peacemakers began pulling out of Angola as violence accelerated.

Colombian peace talks broke down.

Boris Yeltsin, Russia's president, cancelled a visit to France and went back into hospital.

CHRONOLOGY

Week beginning 24 January, 1999

Indonesia raised the possibility of independence for East Timor.

King Hussein of Jordan, mortally ill with cancer, named his son as heir.

Arab League foreign ministers refused to condemn American air attacks against Iraq.

Serb forces attacked guerillas in northern Kosovo.

Brazil introduced a tough budget to restore confidence in its currency.

Week beginning 31 January, 1999

American and British air attacks were stepped up against military targets in Iraq.

Separatists in Kosovo agreed to attend peace talks in Paris.

India held out the probability of signing the nuclear test ban treaty.

Week beginning 7 February, 1999

King Hussein of Jordan died.

War broke out between Ethiopia and Eritrea over a border dispute.

Venezuela introduced economic measures to reduce the state deficit.

Germany's Social Democrats lost to the Christian Democrats in Hessen depriving Chancellor Schröder of his majority in the upper house.

Week beginning 14 February, 1999

The US Senate cleared President Clinton of charges of perjury and obstruction of justice.

Abdullah Ocalan, the Kurdish rebel leader, was captured in Kenya and taken to Turkey to face charges of murder and terrorism.

Fierce fighting broke out yet again between government forces and rebels in the Congo.

Week beginning 21 February, 1999

Talks on the future of Kosovo ended in Paris with the Serbs rejecting the plans for a NATO maintaining force and the separatists unable to decide on limited autonomy.

India and Pakistan signed an agreement to reduce the tension between the two countries.

Wuo Yonggak, a North Korean commander and the world's longest serving political prisoner, was released by South Korea after serving 41 years.

Week beginning 28 February, 1999
Olusegun Obasanjo was elected president of Nigeria in the first big step towards civilian rule.

A trade war over bananas threatened between America and Europe as the US imposed duties on a wide range of products. America claimed that the EU deal on imports of bananas from its former colonies offended world trade rules.

Ion Sturza became prime minister of Moldova, heading a coalition government.

Local elections in Iran saw the victory for reformist candidates.

Week beginning 7 March, 1999

Separatists in Kosovo agreed a peace deal giving them limited autonomy but the Serbian government refused concessions.

Shaikh Hamad became ruler of Bahrain after the death of his father, Sheikh Isa.

Ecuador declared a state of emergency after a run on its currency.

EU agriculture ministers agreed a modest packet of reforms in the hope of reducing the Community farm budget.

Week beginning 14 March, 1999

The entire team of European commissioners resigned after a report on fraud and nepotism came out strongly against particular individuals. The commissioners remained as caretakers while the European government decided on the next move.

Oskar Lafontaine resigned as Germany's finance minister and chairman of the Social Democratic Party. Hans Eichel replaced him at finance while Gerhard Schröder succeeded to the party chair.

Ecuador lifted its state of emergency.

Indonesia promised a referendum on independence for East Timor.

Poland, Hungary and the Czech Republic joined NATO.

Week beginning 21 March, 1999

After Serbian forces renewed their offensive in Kosovo, NATO fighters bombed military targets in Yugoslavia. Russia protested and called for renewed efforts to negotiate a settlement.

European first ministers nominated Romano Prodi, former Italian prime

minister, to succeed Jacques Santer as the EU commission president.

A general election in Finland left the leftish coalition government in power but with a reduced majority.

South Africa and the EU concluded a free trade agreement.

Paraguay's vice president was assassinated. President Raúl Cubas was blamed.

General Augusto Pinochet, former dictator of Chile who was under house arrest in Britain waiting a law lords ruling on an application to have him extradited to Spain, heard that his claim to immunity had been rejected but that any charges must relate to events after 1988.

ADDENDA

ADDENDA

All dates are 1999 unless stated otherwise

ALGERIA. In presidential elections on 15 April Abdelaziz Bouteflika gained 73·8% of the votes cast. All of the other candidates had withdrawn the previous day alleging fraud.

AUSTRALIA. Northern Territory *Chief Minister* Shane Stone resigned on 8 Feb. and was replaced by Denis Burke.

CANADA. The new Province for Inuit people, Nunavut, became self-governing under the rule of its first Premier, Paul Okalik, 34, the first and only Inuit lawyer in Nunavut. The name means 'our land' and the province is as big as Western Europe but home to only 25,000 people, 85% of them Inuits.

COMOROS. President Tadjiddine Ben said Massounde and Prime Minister Abbas Djoussouf were ousted in a coup on 30 April by Col. Azaly Assouamani, who was sworn in as head of state on 6 May. In the new government, he gave himself the posts of *Prime Minister* and *Defence Minister*.

DJIBOUTI. Ismail Omar Guelleh won the presidential election on 9 April, with 74·1% of the votes cast.

FIJI. In parliamentary elections held on 8 and 15 May the Indian-dominated Labour Party won 37 of 71 seats, ahead of the Fiji Association Party with 10 seats. Mahendra Chaudhry, the Labour Party leader, became the country's first Indian *Prime Minister*.

FRANCE—NEW CALEDONIA. In elections to the Territorial Congress on 9 May, the Rally for Caledonia in the Republic won 24 seats and the National Liberation Front of the Socialist Kanaks 18, with other parties and independents winning 4 seats or fewer.

GERMANY. The revamped Reichstag in Berlin was formally inaugurated as the national seat of the German parliament on 19 April. Parliament was scheduled to move permanently from Bonn to Berlin in Sept.

GUINEA-BISSAU. President João Bernardo Vieira was ousted on 7 May in a military coup led by former chief of staff Gen. Ansumane Mané, who the president had dismissed in 1998. National Assembly Speaker Malam Bacai Sanhá was installed as *acting President* on 14 May.

ICELAND. In the parliamentary election held on 8 May, the conservative Independence Party of Prime Minister Davíð Oddsson won 27 of the 64 seats with 40·7% of the votes cast, the People's Alliance 17 with 26·8%, the Progressive Party 12 with 18·4%, the Left-Green Alliance 6 with 9·1% and the Liberal Party 2 with 4·2%.

INDIA. On 17 April Prime Minister Atal Behari Vajpayee lost a confidence motion by one vote and the coalition government was removed from power. Elections were scheduled for Sept.

ISRAEL. Ehud Barak of Avoda (the Labour Party) won the election for *Prime Minister* on 17 May with 55·9% of the vote, against 43·9% for incumbent Binyamin Netanyahu of Likud. In the parliamentary elections of the same day, the Yisrael Ahat (One Israel) alliance of Avoda, Gesher and Meimad won 27 of the 120 seats with 20·2% of the votes cast, Likud won 19 with 14·0% and Shas won 17 with 13·1%. Other parties won fewer than 10 seats.

ITALY. Treasury and Budget Minister Carlo Azeglio Ciampi was elected *President* on 13 May.

KUWAIT. The Amir dissolved parliament on 4 May and called for elections on 3 July. The move followed a feud between MPs and the cabinet about misprints in a free state-published edition of the Koran.

KYRGYZSTAN. Prime Minister Zhumabek Ibraimov died on 4 April. Boris Silayev, the first Deputy Prime Minister, took over temporarily and was in turn succeeded on 12 April by Amangeldy Muraliyev.

LIBERIA. President Charles Taylor dismissed 11 members of the cabinet on 14 May, including Monie Captan, the *Foreign Minister*; Daniel Chea, the *Defence Minister* and Philip Kammah, the *National Security Minister*. The ministers had failed to attend a church service in memory of 8 people killed in a border clash. The service was held to mark the end of a 3-day fast and prayer.

LITHUANIA. President Valdas Adamkus named Irena Degutiene *acting Prime Minister* on 3 May, following the resignation of Gediminas Vagnorius. On 18 May Parliament approved the nomination of Rolandas Paksas as *Prime Minister*.

MALAYSIA. The sultan of the state of Selangor, Tunku Salahuddin Abdul Aziz Shah ibni Al-Marhum Sultan Hisamuddin 'Alam Shah Al-Haj, took office as Malaysia's *yang di-pertuan agong* (head of state) on 26 April.

MALTA. Guido de Marco took office as *President* on 4 April following his election by parliament.

MICRONESIA. Former *Vice-President* Leo A. Falcam was elected *President* by the Congress on 11 May, and Redley Killian as *Vice-President*.

MOROCCO. Mohamed Benaissa was appointed *Foreign Minister* on 8 April.
NAURU. Rene Harris was elected *President* on 27 April, defeating the incumbent President Bernard Dowiyogo by 10 votes to 7.

NEPAL. In parliamentary elections held on 3 and 17 May the Nepali Congress Party won an absolute majority, winning 107 of the 205 seats and bringing an end to a succession of weak coalition governments.

NEW ZEALAND. *Tourism Minister* Murray McCully resigned on 28 April.

NIGER. President Daouda Mallam Wanké announced a new cabinet on 16 April, including Aïchatou Mindaoudou as *Foreign Minister*, Col. Moussa Moumouni Djermakoye as *Defence Minister* and Lt. Col. Moumouni Bouraima as *Interior Minister*. Elections intended to return the country to civilian rule were to take place in Nov.

PANAMA. Mireya Moscoso de Gruber of the conservative Arnulfist Party won the presidential election on 2 May, obtaining 44·9% of votes cast against 2 other candidates. She was set to take office in Sept. In the Legislative Assembly elections on the same day the Revolutionary Democratic party won 33 seats, the Arnulfist Party 11, the Papá Egoró Movement 6 and the Liberal Republican Nationalist Movement also 6, with other parties winning 4 seats or fewer.

PERU. President Alberto Fujimori dismissed several ministers on 14 April, including *Defence Minister* Gen. Julio Salazar. The next day Gen. Carlos Bergamino was named *Defence Minister*.

RUSSIA. President Boris Yeltsin dismissed Prime Minister Yevgeniy Primakov and the government on 12 May and appointed Sergey Stepashin as acting *Prime Minister*. An attempt to impeach President Yeltsin failed on 15 May.

SPAIN. Jésus Posada was appointed *Agriculture Minister* on 3 May as replacement for Loyola de Palacio del Valle-Lersundi, who had been chosen to head the ruling Popular party's campaign for the European Parliament elections in June.

SWEDEN. *Finance Minister* Erik Åsbrink resigned on 12 April, and was replaced by Bosse Ringholm.

TUNISIA. In a cabinet reshuffle announced on 22 April, Taoufik Baccar moved from the post *of Economic Development Minister* to replace Mohamed Jeri as *Finance Minister*, Abdellatif Saddam *became Economic Development Minister*, and Faiza Kefi replaced Mohamed Mehdi Mlika as *Environment and Land Use Management Minister*.

TURKEY. In parliamentary elections on 18 April, Prime Minister Bülent Ecevit's Democratic Left Party won 136 of the 550 seats with 22·3% of the votes cast, the Nationalist Movement Party 129 with 18·1%, the Virtue Party 111 with 15·5%, the Motherland Party 86 with 13·3% and the True Path Party 85 with 12·1%. 3 seats went to non-partisans.

TUVALU. Ionatana Ionatana was elected *Prime Minister* on 27 April after Bikenibeu Paeniu had lost a no-confidence vote.

ADDENDA

UGANDA. Apolo Nsibambi became *Prime Minister* on 5 April, replacing Kintu Musoke.

UNITED KINGDOM. In elections to the new Scottish Parliament on 6 May, Labour won 56 of 129 seats, against 35 for the Scottish National Party, 18 for the Conservatives, 17 for the Liberal Democrats and 2 for others. Turn-out was 59%. Donald Dewar was elected as First Minister on 13 May. In the elections to the Welsh Assembly, also on 6 May, Labour won 28 of 60 seats, followed by Plaid Cymru with 17, the Conservatives with 9, and the Liberal Democrats with 6. Turn-out was 46%. Local government elections for 362 councils on 6 May resulted in Labour having control of 137 councils, the Conservatives 61, the Liberal Democrats 20, Ind 20, Plaid Cymru 3 and the Scottish National Party 1, with no overall control in 122. The Conservatives gained 1,391 seats and Labour lost 1,239, but with Labour having 4,802 councillors against 3,766 Conservatives, it was the first time in the 20th century that the party in government had been ahead after mid-term local elections. On 17 May *Minister for Transport* John Reid was appointed *Secretary of State for Scotland*.

UNITED KINGDOM—BRITISH VIRGIN ISLANDS. In parliamentary elections on 17 May the Virgin Islands Party won 7 of the 13 seats, ahead of the National Democratic Party with 5.

UNITED STATES OF AMERICA. Secretary of the Treasury Robert Rubin resigned on 12 May and was to be replaced by Lawrence Summers.

VENEZUELA. 90% of votes cast in a referendum on 25 April were in favour of the plan to rewrite the constitution proposed by President Chávez. As a result, on 25 July the public was to elect a constituent assembly to write a new constitution, which in turn was to be voted on in a national referendum in early 2000.

PART I

INTERNATIONAL ORGANIZATIONS

NERVOUS BREAKDOWN: AMERICA AND UN REFORM

Rosemary Righter

On February 26, 1999 in San Francisco, Bill Clinton delivered an address on 'America's role in the century to come'. It was a high profile occasion. Beside him on the podium sat Madeleine Albright, his Secretary of State, and Sandy Berger, his National Security Adviser; the audience consisted of such concerned and knowledgeable groups as the World Affairs Council. The President's theme was the need for post-Cold War America to resist the perennial temptation of isolationism, its tendency to 'rise to great causes, [yet] to believe that we can go back to minding our business when we're done'.

Americans, he argued, must instead 'embrace the inexorable logic of globalisation—that everything, from the strength of our economy to the safety of our cities, to the health of our people, depends on events not only within our borders, but half a world away'. It was easy 'to say that we really have no interests in who lives in this or that valley in Bosnia, or who owns a strip of brushland in the Horn of Africa, or some piece of parched earth by the Jordan River'; but Americans should understand the consequences for their security of letting conflicts fester, and remember that 'the real challenge of foreign policy is to deal with problems before they harm our national interests'. And he recalled how, after World War II, Harry Truman had come to San Francisco to pledge the US to work for a world in which 'right has might', and that 'he and his allies and their successors built a network of security alliances to preserve the peace, and a global financial system to preserve prosperity'

But what brought Truman to San Francisco in 1945 was the landmark conference which created an organization that Clinton did not list: the United Nations. Too much should never be read into one political speech; yet it is remarkable that in what was a grand survey of American foreign policy goals in the new century, and one which robustly confronted the unilateralist as well as the isolationist camps in American politics with a firm insistence on the need to work with America's friends and allies, the only reference to the UN was buried at the end in a half sentence. Clinton expressed the 'hope' that Congress would 'finally pay both our dues and our debts to the United Nations'. But about why an effective UN mattered to the US, he had not a word to say.

The uncomfortable truth is that to leave the UN virtually out of the picture has become politically prudent for an American president making the case for global engagement. Ordinary Americans tell pollsters that they support the goals of the United Nations, and like most people are ready to give it the benefit of the doubt; but they do not give it much thought. Those who do, in Congress and thinktanks, are at best critical of its slipshod management, inflated agendas, bureaucratic sprawl and ritual sparring between the 'North' and a 'South' that no longer exists, outside the UN General Assembly, as a unified bloc. At worst, they view it either as an irrelevance or, even, as an impediment to US interests. The critics are not confined to the Republican right; and many who do not share the Right's more preposterous allegations that the UN undermines US sovereignty share what Sir John Weston, the UK's permanent representative until 1998, describes as 'a deeper unease that the whole institutional and organizational approach at the international level is obsolete'.

For Kofi Annan, who started as UN Secretary-General in 1997 with strong American backing and a pledge to make the UN better managed, more open and accountable and focussed on the areas where it is indispensable, this is hugely frustrating. Sensibly, he has put more effort both into management reforms and into courting American public opinion than any of his predecessors. For the UN, American disaffection is potentially disastrous—and not only because of the impact on its finances.

The huge backlog of unpaid US dues to the UN dates back to 1985, when

NERVOUS BREAKDOWN: AMERICA AND UN REFORM

Congress decided to use the power of the purse to obtain much needed UN reform—as in fact it did for some years. By the end of the 1990s, the law of diminishing returns had set in. Non-payment was hobbling American influence at the UN and exasperating even its closest allies, while the hitherto patient Mr Annan grumbled, unwisely, about 'the constant harassment of **reform, reform, reform**'. But, to the embarrassment of both the Bush and Clinton Administrations—and Mrs Albright worked the Hill pretty persistently—the US dues remained mostly unpaid for a more ominous reason: indifference among all but a handful of Congressmen, which the Right was able to exploit.

Determined to avoid the fate of the League of Nations, the UN's founders sited the UN headquarters in the US so as to be sure of keeping the US in the UN. That paid off. Down the decades, while the US was often fiercely critical of the UN, particularly and understandably in the 1970s and 1980s when Third World ideologues in the General Assembly made America their whipping boy, it took the battles there more seriously than many worldly-wise West Europeans. The UN's future depends on the organization's capacity to regain the attention and support of the world's only remaining superpower. Any discussion of the UN's patchy attempts to drag itself into the 21st century has to consider that dimension.

Most governments know this; but it is not a *Realpolitik* that appeals to the General Assembly. The most basic changes—such as 'sunset' rules to free the Secretariat to drop pointless or outdated activities or 'results-based' budgeting, which is the bedrock of any strategy of securing value for money in UN spending—meet resistance because they are seen as American-driven and thus part of an assault on the sovereign equality enshrined in the UN Charter. As always, there is a gulf between the real world and the politics of rhetoric practised in UN forums.

Kofi Annan claims to be effecting 'a quiet revolution'. He has streamlined the management structures in New York—the only bit of the sprawling UN empire over which he has direct executive control—devolving responsibilities, creating a more collegial cabinet system at the top and planning systems of incentives and penalties for staff performance which truly would constitute a revolution in this sleepiest of bureaucratic cultures.

He is also trying to get the UN's specialized agencies to work together better under his overall leadership: but this is ground that has been trod many times before, always to a dead end. The UN is not a centralized system, but a polycentric cluster of legally autonomous agencies; the barons who head these fiefdoms have no intention of being co-ordinated; and, however appalling the record of some of these agencies may be, they have a point when they argue that New York should first clean its own stables of the great accretion of overlapping bodies.

There is also a cogent argument to be made that co-ordination is a red herring, when what the UN needs is a healthy blast of competition. Agency-by-agency reform is much more likely to succeed; their chief executives should be encouraged to innovate, in the knowledge that governments intend to shift funding, as some of them are already doing, to the agencies that work best and provide services which they indisputably need. Finally, any attempt to fold the Bretton Woods financial institutions under New York's umbrella deserves to fail; controversial the IMF and the World Bank may sometimes be, but they are relatively well managed, unpoliticized organizations of undoubted consequence. Governments would never consent to risk exposing them to the 'UN disease'. The UN will never conform to a 'system-wide' master plan; and anyway, the best reforms are not always top down.

But in another sense, if Mr Annan is to rescue the UN from its midlife slough of despond, he has to be much bolder. Tactically, he must work round, not through the member states. With 185 of them, it is no wonder that they have never agreed to scrap a single pointless programme or agency: each will be some nation's pet pork barrel. Trying to obtain consensus for reform is self-cancelling; as Mr Annan has already discovered, the most innocuous reforms get watered down or sabotaged. But the very unwieldiness of the membership is an opportunity for a Secretary-General prepared to exercise his managerial responsibilities to the hilt; many changes, including results-based budgeting, do not formally even have to be laid before the UN's inter-governmental committees and should not be. Like most of his predecessors, Mr Annan, a long-serving UN career officer, was picked partly because he was seen more as a 'Secretary' than a 'General'; but the task before him requires generalship. Putting the broader global interest ahead of keeping sweet the often unruly delegates governments send to New York, he will need to use his moral authority to push through changes without waiting for universal assent.

Strategically, he must go beyond moving the office furniture around, to work out where, in a world where the UN no longer has a monopoly on intergovernmental co-operation, its comparative advantages lie. Mr Annan started by promising 'to achieve more with less'; but the UN's real need is to do less altogether. He may be unable to close down the least worthwhile of the hundreds of UN funds, programmes and organizations that have multiplied, since 1945, like a galactic accident. But some will quietly wither on the vine because governments are reluctant to waste money supporting them. He should be relaxed about that; it will help him to concentrate the UN's moral authority and slender resources on those areas where it has a distinctive, irreplaceable contribution to make, and where the extra margin of effort at global level can make all the difference.

That means focusing on the UN's core political and humanitarian mandates. For most people, that begins with collective security. But the experience of the past decade suggests that, although the UN will not be able to turn its back on ethnic and civil conflicts, it will have to be rigorous about where and how it acts, and to distinguish more clearly between the UN as legitimator and guardian of international law, and the UN as enforcer. Collective security does not necessarily imply, and may not even be compatible with, *collectively organized* security. International bureaucracies cannot run modern wars.

But security has dimensions beyond enforcement or even peacekeeping. These include the effective defence of basic human rights, workable judicial procedures to deal with crimes against humanity and civilian humanitarian interventions, and the indispensable work of the overburdened Office of the UN High Commissioner for Refugees. There are also holes to be plugged in the global machinery. Post-chaos assistance is one example. The task lies somewhere between emergency relief and standard development aid. Stabilization and reconstruction need to be made a priority, and seen as central to peace-building. For the UN, this is a difficult area, not just because it requires speed and flexibility, but because it can run up against the taboo against intervening in a state's internal affairs. But tackled it will have to be—inside or outside the UN.

Conversely, and controversially, the UN's sprawling development activities, which consume 60 per cent of its spending, are largely redundant. Most of its programmes are so tiny and scattershot as to make no impact. The World Bank is the only really serious intergovernmental actor, mainly because its expertise, even in 'specialized' areas such as education, now exceeds that of the UN and its agencies. The Secretary-General's plans for an 'integrated development assistance framework' are, conceptually as well as organizationally, a blast from the past. With more than 90 per cent of investment in the developing world now flowing through corporations and non-governmental agencies, rather than directly from the public purse, the UN needs instead to concentrate on its original functions as a talking shop.

This is an aspect of global organization that has often been derided. Properly run, it should not be. Consciousness-raising is an area where universal membership is a precious asset. The UN has an important role as a clearing house for ideas, helping governments and specialists to learn from best practice on a range of problems, from environmental management to population and drug-trafficking and providing a negotiating space for specific agreements on tackling frontier-spanning threats. The convention on the ozone layer was a model for this kind of global diplomacy. The more the UN can draw not just NGOs, but the business world into these deliberations—as Mr Annan wishes to do—the better.

Would such rethinking at the UN bring the US back into the multilateral arena as a committed player? The answer is yes, although there will continue to be arguments about funding until the American share is reduced from the current 25 per cent of the regular budget and 31 per cent of peacekeeping—which is fiercely resisted but would politically be no bad thing. Congress has ended its long stand-off with the World Bank and the International Monetary Fund; and the US is the largest user of the World Trade Organisation's trade disputes mechanisms. The lesson may be that the future lies with rule-based organization where the lines of management are clear and the objectives focussed. But a transformation of the institutional culture at the UN, accompanied by greater modesty about what it can attempt and a clearer sense of purpose, could turn the political climate in the US. One lesson of the crisis in US-UN relations is, however, that the UN will need to justify public affection and respect for what it does in the new century, because for many purposes, governments are free, far freer than they were in 1945, to look elsewhere. And that applies not only to the great powers. Multilateral co-operation is in fact a growth industry; but the UN is no longer a monopoly global provider. Mr Annan's challenge is to adapt it to a crowded and competitive multilateral world.

Rosemary Righter is Chief Leader Writer and an Assistant Editor of The Times. *Her latest book is* Utopia Lost: the United Nations and World Order *(New York, Twentieth Century Fund, 1995).*

THE UNITED NATIONS (UN)

Origin and Aims. The United Nations is an association of states which have pledged themselves to maintain international peace and security and co-operate in solving international political, economic, social, cultural and humanitarian problems towards achieving this end. The name 'United Nations' was devised by United States President Franklin D. Roosevelt and was first used in the Declaration by United Nations of 1 Jan. 1942, during the Second World War, when representatives of 26 nations pledged their Governments to continue fighting together against the Axis Powers.

The United Nations Charter, the constituting instrument of the UN, was drawn up by the representatives of 50 countries at the United Nations Conference on International Organization, which met in San Francisco from 25 April to 26 June 1945. Those delegates deliberated on the basis of proposals worked out by the representatives of China, the Soviet Union, the United Kingdom and the United States at Dumbarton Oaks (Washington, D.C.) from 21 Aug. to 28 Sept. 1944. The Charter was signed on 26 June 1945 by the representatives of the 50 countries. Poland, which was not represented at the Conference, signed it later and became one of the original 51 Member States. Nothing contained in the Charter authorizes the organization to intervene in matters which are essentially within the domestic jurisdiction of any state.

The United Nations officially came into existence on 24 Oct. 1945, with the deposit of the requisite number of ratifications of the Charter with the US Department of State. United Nations Day is celebrated on 24 Oct. each year.

Over the past five decades, international co-operation has brought advances in every area of the United Nations Charter but the post-cold war era brings new challenges to the UN. Peacekeeping operations, for which demand has increased sharply, now operate under greatly expanded mandates in response to the bitter conflicts which menace societies from within. Today, 80% of the UN's work is devoted to helping developing countries build the capacity to help themselves. This includes promoting the creation of independent and democratic societies, which it is hoped will offer vital support for the Charter's goals in the 21st century; the protection of human rights; saving children from starvation and disease; providing relief assistance to refugees and disaster victims; countering global crime, drugs and disease; and assisting countries devastated by war and the long-term threat of landmines.

Members. Membership is open to all peace-loving nations which accept the obligations of the Charter and, in the judgement of the Organization, are willing and able to carry them out. New Member States are admitted by the General Assembly on the recommendation of the Security Council. The Charter provides for the suspension or expulsion of a Member for violation of its principles, but no such action has ever been taken. It has 185 member states. (For a list of these, see below.)

Finance. Assessments on member states constitute the main source of funds. These are in accordance with a scale specified by the Assembly, and determined primarily by the country's share of the world economy and ability to pay, in the range 25%–0·01%. The Organization is prohibited by law from borrowing from commercial institutions.

A Working Group on the Financial Situation of the United Nations was established in 1994 to address the long-standing financial crisis which has come about because of the non-payment of assessed dues by many Member States, severely threatening the Organization's ability to fulfil its mandates. Member States owed the UN a total of US$2,300m. in 1997.

INTERNATIONAL ORGANIZATIONS

Official languages. Arabic, Chinese, English, French, Russian and Spanish.

Structure. The UN has six principal organs established by the founding Charter. All have their headquarters in New York except the International Court of Justice, which has its seat in The Hague. These core bodies work through dozens of related agencies, operational programmes and funds, and through special agreements with separate, autonomous, intergovernmental agencies, known as Specialized Agencies, in order to provide an increasingly cohesive programme of action in the fields of peace and security, justice and human rights, humanitarian assistance, and social and economic development. The six principal UN organs are as follows:

1. **The General Assembly**, composed of all members, is the main deliberative body; each member has 1 vote. It meets once a year, commencing on the first Tuesday following 1 Sept., and the general debate is organized over a period of 2 weeks, beginning the 3rd week of Sept. (The 53rd Session opened on 9 Sept. 1998.)

At the start of each session, the Assembly elects a new President, 21 vice-presidents and the chairmen of its seven main committees, listed below. To ensure equitable geographical representation, the presidency of the Assembly rotates each year among the five geographical groups of states: African, Asian, Eastern European, Latin American, and Western European and other States. Special sessions may be convoked by the Secretary-General if requested by the Security Council, by a majority of members, or by 1 member if the majority of the members concur. Emergency sessions may be called within 24 hours at the request of the Security Council on the vote of any 9 Council members, or a majority of United Nations members, or 1 member if the majority of members concur. Decisions on important questions, such as peace and security, new membership and budgetary matters, require a two-thirds majority; other questions require a simple majority of members present and voting.

The work of the General Assembly is divided between 6 Main Committees, on which every member state is represented. These are: Disarmament and International Security Committee (First Committee); Economic and Financial Committee (Second Committee); Social, Humanitarian and Cultural Committee (Third Committee); Special Political and Decolonization Committee (Fourth Committee); Administrative and Budgetary Committee (Fifth Committee); Legal Committee (Sixth Committee).

There is also a General Committee charged with the task of co-ordinating the proceedings of the Assembly and its Committees; and a Credentials Committee. The General Committee consists of 29 members: the president and 21 vice-presidents of the General Assembly and the chairmen of the 6 main committees. The Credentials Committee consists of 9 members appointed by the Assembly on the proposal of the President at each session. In addition, the Assembly has 2 standing committees—an Advisory Committee on Administrative and Budgetary Questions, and a Committee on Contributions; and may establish subsidiary and *ad hoc* bodies when necessary to deal with specific matters. These include: Special Committee on Peacekeeping Operations (34 members), Human Rights Committee (18 members), Committee on the Peaceful Uses of Outer Space (61 members), Conciliation Commission for Palestine (3 members), Conference on Disarmament (38 members), International Law Commission (34 members), Scientific Committee on the Effects of Atomic Radiation (21 members), Special Committee on the Implementation of the Declaration on the Granting of Independence to Colonial Countries and Peoples (25 members), and Commission on International Trade Law (36 members).

The General Assembly has the right to discuss any matters within the scope of the Charter and, with the exception of any situation or dispute on the agenda of the Security Council, may make recommendations on any such questions or matters. While it has no power to compel action by any Government, its recommendations are seen to carry the weight of world opinion. Occupying a central position in the UN, the Assembly receives reports from other organs, admits new members, directs activities for development, sets policies and determines programmes for the Secretariat, appoints the Secretary-General, who reports annually to it on the work of the Organization, and approves the UN budget.

UNITED NATIONS

Under the "Uniting For Peace" resolution adopted by the General Assembly in Nov. 1950, the Assembly is also empowered to take action if the Security Council, because of a lack of unanimity of its permanent members, fails to exercise its primary responsibility for the maintenance of international peace and security in any case where there appears to be a threat to the peace, breach of the peace or act of aggression. In this event, the General Assembly may consider the matter immediately with a view to making appropriate recommendations to members for collective measures, including, in the case of a breach of the peace or act of aggression, the use of armed force when necessary, to maintain or restore international peace and security.

2. **The Security Council** has primary responsibility, under the Charter, for the maintenance of international peace and security. It is so organized as to be able to function continuously. A representative of each of its members must be present at all times at UN Headquarters, but it may meet elsewhere as best facilitates its work.

The Presidency of the Council rotates monthly, according to the English alphabetical order of members' names. The Council consists of 15 members: 5 permanent and 10 non-permanent elected for a 2-year term by a two-thirds majority of the General Assembly. Each member has 1 vote. Retiring members are not eligible for immediate re-election. Any other member of the United Nations may participate without a vote in the discussion of questions specially affecting its interests.

Decisions on procedural questions are made by an affirmative vote of at least 9 members. On all other matters, the affirmative vote of 9 members must include the concurring votes of all permanent members (subject to the provision that when the Council is considering methods for the peaceful settlement of a dispute, parties to the dispute abstain from voting). Consequently, a negative vote from a permanent member has the power of veto, and all five permanent members have exercised this right at one time or other. If a permanent member does not support a decision but does not wish to veto it, it may abstain. Under the Charter, the Security Council alone has the power to take decisions which member states are obligated to carry out.

The Council has 2 standing committees at present—the Committee of Experts on Rules of Procedure and the Committee on the Admission of New Members. In addition, as needed, it may establish *ad hoc* committees and commissions, such as the Committee on Council Meetings away from Headquarters.

When a threat to peace is brought before the Council, its first action is usually to recommend to the parties agreement by peaceful means. It may undertake mediation and set forth principles for a settlement, and may take measures to enforce its decisions by ceasefire directives, economic sanctions, peacekeeping missions, or in some cases, by collective military action. For the maintenance of international peace and security, the Council can, in accordance with special agreements to be concluded, call on the armed forces, assistance and facilities of the member states. It is assisted by a Military Staff Committee consisting of the Chiefs of Staff of the permanent members of the Council or their representatives.

The Council also makes recommendations to the Assembly on the appointment of the Secretary-General and, with the Assembly, elects the judges of the International Court.

Permanent Members. China, France, Russian Federation, UK, USA (Russian Federation took over the seat of the former USSR in Dec. 1991).

Non-Permanent Members. Bahrain, Brazil, Gabon, Gambia, Slovenia (until 31 Dec. 1999), Argentina, Canada, Malaysia, Namibia, Netherlands (until 31 Dec. 2000).

Finance. The total cost of all UN peacekeeping operations in 1997 was US$1·3bn. Assessments for 1998 were expected to total US$900m. All Member States are obligated to pay their share of peacekeeping costs, but at 15 Sept. 1998, Member States owed the UN US$1·75bn. in current and back peacekeeping dues.

3. **The Economic and Social Council (ECOSOC)** is responsible under the General Assembly for co-ordinating the functions of the UN with regard to international economic, social, cultural, educational, health and related matters. The year-round

work of the Council is carried out by related organizations, specialized agencies, and subsidiary bodies, commissions and committees, which meet regularly and report back to it.

It consists of 54 member states elected by a two-thirds majority of the General Assembly for a 3-year term. Members are elected according to the following geographic distribution: Africa, 14 members; Asia, 11; Eastern Europe, 6; Latin America and Caribbean, 10; Western Europe and other States, 13. A third of the members retire each year. Retiring members are eligible for immediate re-election. Each member has 1 vote. Decisions are made by a majority of the members present and voting.

The Council holds one 5-week substantive session a year, alternating between New York and Geneva, and one organizational session in New York. The substantive session includes a high-level special meeting attended by Ministers, to discuss major economic and social issues. Special sessions may be held if required. The President is elected for 1 year and is eligible for immediate re-election.

The subsidiary machinery of ECOSOC is as follows.

Nine Functional Commissions. Statistical Commission; Commission on Population and Development; Commission for Social Development; Commission on Human Rights (and Subcommission on Prevention of Discrimination and Protection of Minorities); Commission on the Status of Women; Commission on Narcotic Drugs (and Subcommission on Illicit Drug Traffic and Related Matters in the Near and Middle East); Commission on Science and Technology for Development; Commission on Crime Prevention and Criminal Justice; Commission on Sustainable Development.

Five Regional Economic Commissions. ECA (Economic Commission for Africa, Addis Ababa, Ethiopia); ESCAP (Economic and Social Commission for Asia and the Pacific, Bangkok); ECE (Economic Commission for Europe, Geneva); ECLAC (Economic Commission for Latin America and the Caribbean, Santiago, Chile); ESCWA (Economic Commission for Western Asia, Amman, Jordan).

Nine Standing Committees and Subsidiary Expert Bodies. Committee for Programme and Co-ordination; Commission on Human Settlements; Committee on Non-Governmental Organizations; Committee on Natural Resources; Committee for Development Planning; Committee on Economic, Social and Cultural Rights; Committee on New and Renewable Sources of Energy and on Energy for Development; Ad Hoc Group of Experts on International Co-operation in Tax Matters; Committee of Experts on the Transport of Dangerous Goods.

Other related operational programmes, funds and special bodies, which report to ECOSOC (and/or the General Assembly) include: The United Nations Children's Fund (UNICEF); Office of the United Nations High Commissioner for Refugees (UNHCR); United Nations Conference on Trade and Development (UNCTAD); United Nations Development Programme (UNDP) and Population Fund (UNFPA); United Nations Environment Programme (UNEP); World Food Programme (WFP); International Research and Training Institute for the Advancement of Women (INSTRAW); United Nations International Drug Control Programme (UNDCP).

In addition, the Council may make arrangements for consultation with international non-governmental organizations (NGOs) and, after consultation with the member concerned, with national organizations. There are over 1,500 non-governmental organizations which have consultative status with the Council. Non-governmental organizations may send observers to the Council's public meetings and those of its subsidiary bodies, and may submit written statements relevant to its work. They may also consult with the UN Secretariat on matters of mutual concern.

Members. (1998): Algeria, Argentina, Bangladesh, Belarus, Belgium, Brazil, Canada, Cape Verde, Central African Republic, Chile, China, Colombia, Comoros, Cuba, Czech Republic, Djibouti, El Salvador, Finland, France, Gabon, Gambia, Germany, Guyana, Iceland, India, Italy, Japan, Jordan, Korea (Republic of), Latvia, Lebanon, Lesotho, Mauritius, Mexico, Mozambique, New Zealand, Nicaragua, Oman,

Pakistan, Poland, Romania, Russia, St Lucia, Sierra Leone, Spain, Sri Lanka, Sweden, Togo, Tunisia, Turkey, United Kingdom, USA, Vietnam, Zambia.

Finance. The UN has US$6,300m. a year to spend on economic and social development.

4. **The Trusteeship Council** was established to ensure that Governments responsible for administering Trust Territories take adequate steps to prepare them for self-government or independence. It consists of five permanent members of the Security Council. The task of decolonization was completed in 1994, when the Security Council terminated the Trusteeship Agreement for the last of the original UN Trusteeships (Palau), administered by the USA. All Trust Territories attained self-government or independence either as separate States or by joining neighbouring independent countries. Since 1994 the Council's role has been under review.

The proposal from UN Secretary-General Kofi Annan, in the second part of his reform programme, in July 1997, is that it should be used as a forum to exercise their "trusteeship" for the global commons, environment and resource systems.

Members. China, France, Russia, UK, USA.

5. **The International Court of Justice** is the principal judicial organ of the UN. It has a dual role: to settle in accordance with international law the legal disputes submitted to it by States; and to give advisory opinion on legal questions referred to it by duly authorized international organs and agencies.

It operates under a Statute, which is an integral part of the United Nations Charter. All UN members are *ipso facto* parties to the Statute of the Court. Parties to the Statute who are not members of the UN are Switzerland and Nauru. The Court is composed of 15 judges, each of a different nationality elected with an absolute majority to 9-year terms of office by both the General Assembly and the Security Council. The composition of the Court must also reflect the main forms of civilization and principal legal systems of the world. Elections are held every 3 years for one-third of the seats, and retiring judges may be re-elected. Members do not represent their respective governments but sit as independent magistrates in the Court, and must possess the qualifications required in their respective countries for appointment to the highest judicial offices, or be jurists of recognized competence in international law.

Candidates are nominated by the national panels of jurists in the Permanent Court of Arbitration established by the Hague Conventions of 1899 and 1907. The Court elects its own President and Vice-President for a 3-year term, and is permanently in session.

Decisions are taken by a majority of judges present, subject to a quorum of 9 members, with the President having a casting vote. Judgement is final and without appeal, but a revision may be applied for within 10 years from the date of the judgement on the ground of a new decisive factor. When the Court does not include a judge possessing the nationality of a State party to a case, that State has the right to appoint a person to sit as judge *ad hoc* for that case, on equal terms with Members.

While the Court normally sits in plenary session, it can form chambers of 3 or more judges to deal with specific matters. Judgements by chambers are considered as rendered by the full Court. In 1993, in view of the global expansion of environmental law and protection, the Court formed a 7-member Chamber for Environmental Matters.

Judges. The present composition of the Court, which holds office until 5 Feb. 2000, is as follows: Stephen M. Schwebel, President (USA), Christopher G. Weeramantry, Vice-President (Sri Lanka), Rosalyn Higgins (UK), Gilbert Guillaume (France), Gonzalo Parra-Aranguren (Venezuela), Raymond Ranjeva (Madagascar), Shigeru Oda (Japan), Géza Herczegh (Hungary), Shi Jiuyong (China), Carl-August Fleischhauer (Germany), Abdul G. Koroma (Sierra Leone), Mohammed Bedjaoui (Algeria), Pieter H. Kooijmans (Netherlands), José F. Rezek (Brazil), Vladlen S. Vereshchetin (Russian Federation), Eduardo Valencia-Ospina, Registrar (Colombia).

Competence and Jurisdiction. In contentious cases, only States may apply to or appear before the Court, which is open only to parties to its Statute, which automatically includes all Members of the UN. The conditions under which the Court will be open to other states are laid down by the Security Council. The jurisdiction of the Court covers all matters which parties refer to it, and all matters provided for in the Charter or in treaties and conventions in force. Disputes concerning the jurisdiction of the Court are settled by the Court's own decision. The Court may apply in its decision:

(a) international conventions;
(b) international custom;
(c) the general principles of law recognized by civilized nations;
(d) as subsidiary means for the determination of the rules of law, judicial decisions and the teachings of highly qualified publicists. If the parties agree, the Court may decide a case *ex aequo et bono.*

Since 1946, the Court has delivered 67 judgements on disputes concerning inter alia land frontiers and maritime boundaries, territorial sovereignty, the non-use of force, non-interference in the internal affairs of States, diplomatic relations, hostage-taking, the right of asylum, nationality, guardianship, rights of passage and economic rights.

The Court may also give advisory opinions on legal questions to the General Assembly, the Security Council, certain other organs of the UN and 16 specialized agencies of the UN family.

Since 1946, the Court has given 23 advisory opinions, concerning inter alia admission to United Nations membership, reparation for injuries suffered in the service of the United Nations, territorial status of South-West Africa (Namibia) and Western Sahara, judgements rendered by international administrative tribunals, expenses of certain United Nations operations, the applicability of the United Nations Headquarters Agreement, the status of human rights informers and the threat or use of nuclear weapons.

Finance. The expenses of the Court are borne by the UN. No court fees are paid by parties to the Statute.

Official languages. English, French.

Headquarters: The Peace Palace, 2517 KJ The Hague, Netherlands.
Website: http://www.icj-cij.org
Registrar: Eduardo Valencia-Ospina (Colombia).

6. **The Secretariat** services the other 5 organs of the UN, administering their programmes and carrying out the Organization's day-to-day work with its increasingly streamlined staff of some 8,900 at the UN Headquarters in New York and all over the world.

At its head is the Secretary-General, appointed by the General Assembly on the recommendation of the Security Council for a 5-year, renewable term. The Secretary-General acts as chief administrative officer in all meetings of the General Assembly, Security Council, Economic and Social Council and Trusteeship Council. An Office of Internal Oversight, established in 1994 under the tenure of former Secretary-General Boutros Boutros-Ghali (Egypt), pursues a cost-saving mandate to investigate and eliminate waste, fraud and mismanagement within the system. The Secretary-General is assisted by Under-Secretaries-General and Assistant Secretaries-General. A new appointment of Deputy Secretary-General was agreed in principle by the General Assembly in 1997 and was announced in Jan. 1998.

A Quiet Revolution. The agenda of the UN's 52nd General Assembly (1997) was dominated by the Secretary-General's reform plans to make the UN leaner, more efficient and more effective, cutting administrative costs by as much as a third by the year 2000. Initiatives included the rationalization and consolidation of the UN's bureaucratic machinery by merging overlapping programmes and departments, and streamlining management, in an attempt to shift resources from administration to development work for the poorest nations. The proposals included the establishment of a new, less-personal, cabinet-style administration; the appointment of a Deputy

UNITED NATIONS

Secretary-General; and a Millennium Assembly in 2000 with a companion People's Assembly to focus on defining the UN's role for the 21st century.

Finance. The Secretariat had a zero-growth budget of US$2,600m. for the 2-year period 1996–97. This represented over US$250m. in savings achieved through efficiency gains and a 25 % cut in staff (from a 1984 high of more than 12,000 to 8,900 by 1998). The budget proposed for 1998–99 cuts a further US$120m., bringing it to US$2,480m.

Headquarters: United Nations Plaza, New York, NY 10017, USA.
Website: http://www.un.org.
Secretary-General: Kofi Annan (app. 1 Jan. 1997, Ghana). *Deputy Secretary-General:* Louise Fréchette (app. 12 Jan. 1998, Canada).

MEMBER STATES OF THE UN

The 185 member states, with percentage scale of contributions to the 1998 Regular Budget and year of admission:

	% contribution	Year of admission		% contribution	Year of admission
Afghanistan	0·004	1946	Colombia[1]	0·108	1945
Albania	0·003	1955	Comoros	0·001	1975
Algeria	0·116	1962	Congo, Rep. of the	0·003	1960
Andorra	0·004	1993	Congo,		
Angola	0·010	1976	Dem. Rep. of the[3]	0.008	1960
Antigua and Barbuda	0·002	1981	Costa Rica[1]	0·017	1945
Argentina[1]	0·768	1945	Côte d'Ivoire	0·012	1960
Armenia[1]	0·027	1992	Croatia	0·056	1992
Australia[1]	1·471	1945	Cuba[1]	0·039	1945
Austria	0·935	1955	Cyprus	0·034	1960
Azerbaijan	0·060	1992	Czech Republic[4]	0·169	1993
Bahamas	0·015	1973	Denmark[1]	0·687	1945
Bahrain	0·018	1971	Djibouti	0·001	1977
Bangladesh	0·010	1974	Dominica	0·001	1978
Barbados	0·008	1966	Dominican Republic[1]	0·016	1945
Belarus[1,2]	0·164	1945	Ecuador[1]	0·022	1945
Belgium[1]	1·096	1945	Egypt[1,5]	0·069	1945
Belize	0·001	1981	El Salvador[1]	0·012	1945
Benin	0·002	1960	Equatorial Guinea	0·001	1968
Bhutan	0·001	1971	Eritrea	0·001	1993
Bolivia[1]	0·008	1945	Estonia	0·023	1991
Bosnia-Hercegovina	0·005	1992	Ethiopia[1]	0·007	1945
Botswana	0·010	1966	Fiji Islands	0·004	1970
Brazil[1]	1·514	1945	Finland	0·538	1955
Brunei	0·020	1984	France[1]	6·494	1945
Bulgaria	0·045	1955	Gabon	0·018	1960
Burkina Faso	0·002	1960	Gambia	0·001	1965
Burundi	0·001	1962	Georgia	0·058	1992
Cambodia	0·001	1955	Germany[6]	9·630	1973
Cameroon	0·014	1960	Ghana	0·007	1957
Canada[1]	2·825	1945	Greece[1]	0·386	1945
Cape Verde	0·001	1975	Grenada	0·001	1974
Central African Rep.	0·002	1960	Guatemala[1]	0·019	1945
Chad	0·001	1960	Guinea	0·003	1958
Chile[1]	0·113	1945	Guinea-Bissau	0·001	1974
China[1]	0·901	1945	Guyana	0·001	1966

	% contribution	Year of admission		% contribution	Year of admission
Haiti[1]	0·002	1945	Palau	0·001	1994
Honduras[1]	0·004	1945	Panama[1]	0·016	1945
Hungary	0·119	1955	Papua New Guinea	0·007	1975
Iceland	0·032	1946	Paraguay[1]	0·014	1945
India[1]	0·305	1945	Peru[1]	0·085	1945
Indonesia[7]	0·173	1950	Philippines[1]	0·077	1945
Iran[1]	0·303	1945	Poland[1]	0·251	1945
Iraq[1]	0·087	1945	Portugal	0·368	1955
Ireland, Rep. of	0·223	1955	Qatar	0·033	1971
Israel	0·329	1949	Romania	0·102	1955
Italy	5·394	1955	Russia[1,11]	2·873	1945
Jamaica	0·006	1962	Rwanda	0·002	1962
Japan	17·981	1956	St Kitts and Nevis	0·001	1983
Jordan	0·008	1955	St Lucia	0·001	1979
Kazakhstan	0·124	1992	St Vincent		
Kenya	0·007	1963	and Grenadines	0·001	1980
Korea (North)	0·031	1991	Samoa	0·001	1976
Korea (South)	0·955	1991	San Marino	0·002	1992
Kuwait	0·154	1963	São Tomé		
Kyrgyzstan	0·015	1992	e Príncipe	0·001	1975
Laos	0·001	1955	Saudi Arabia[1]	0·594	1945
Latvia	0·046	1991	Senegal	0·006	1960
Lebanon[1]	0·016	1945	Seychelles	0·002	1976
Lesotho	0·002	1966	Sierra Leone	0·001	1961
Liberia[1]	0·002	1945	Singapore[12]	0·167	1965
Libya	0·160	1955	Slovakia[4]	0·053	1993
Liechtenstein	0·005	1990	Slovenia	0·060	1992
Lithuania	0·045	1991	Solomon Islands	0·001	1978
Luxembourg[1]	0·066	1945	Somalia	0·001	1960
Macedonia[8]	0·005	1993	South Africa[1]	0·365	1945
Madagascar	0·003	1960	Spain	2·571	1955
Malawi	0·002	1964	Sri Lanka	0·013	1955
Malaysia[9]	0·168	1957	Sudan	0·009	1956
Maldives	0·001	1965	Suriname	0·004	1975
Mali	0·003	1960	Swaziland	0·002	1968
Malta	0·014	1964	Sweden	1·099	1946
Marshall Islands	0·001	1991	Syria[1,13]	0·062	1945
Mauritania	0·001	1961	Tajikistan	0·008	1992
Mauritius	0·009	1968	Tanzania[14]	0·004	1961
Mexico[1]	0·941	1945	Thailand	0·158	1946
Micronesia	0·001	1991	Togo	0·002	1960
Moldova	0·043	1992	Trinidad and Tobago	0·018	1962
Monaco	0·003	1993	Tunisia	0·028	1956
Mongolia	0·002	1961	Turkey[1]	0·440	1945
Morocco	0·041	1956	Turkmenistan	0·015	1992
Mozambique	0·002	1975	Uganda	0·004	1962
Myanmar[10]	0·009	1948	Ukraine[1]	0·678	1945
Namibia	0·007	1990	United Arab		
Nepal	0·004	1955	Emirates	0·177	1971
Netherlands[1]	1·619	1945	UK[1]	5·076	1945
New Zealand[1]	0·221	1945	USA[1]	25·000	1945
Nicaragua[1]	0·002	1945	Uruguay[1]	0·049	1945
Niger	0·002	1960	Uzbekiston	0·077	1992
Nigeria	0·070	1960	Vanuatu	0·001	1981
Norway[1]	0·605	1945	Venezuela[1]	0·235	1945
Oman	0·050	1971	Vietnam	0·010	1977
Pakistan	0·060	1947	Yemen[15]	0·010	1947

	%contribution	Year of admission		%contribution	Year of admission
Yugoslavia[1,16]	0·060	1945	Zimbabwe	0·009	1980
Zambia	0·003	1964			

[1]Original member. [2]As Byelorussia, 1945-91. [3]As Zaïre, 1960-97. [4]Pre-partition Czechoslovakia (1945-92) was an original member. [5]As United Arab Republic, 1958-71, following union with Syria (1958-61). [6]Pre-unification (1990) as two states: The Federal Republic of Germany and the German Democratic Republic. [7]Withdrew temporarily, 1965-66. [8]Pre-independence (1992), as part of Yugoslavia, which was an original member. [9]As the Federation of Malaya till 1963, when the new federation of Malaysia (including Singapore, Sarawak and Sabah) was formed. [10]As Burma, 1948-89. [11]As USSR, 1945-91. [12]As part of Malaysia, 1963-65. [13]As United Arab Republic, by union with Egypt, 1958-61. [14]As two states: Tanganyika, 1961-64, and Zanzibar, 1963-64, prior to union as one republic under new name. [15]As Yemen, 1947-90, and Democratic Yemen, 1967-90, prior to merger of the two. [16]Excluded from the General Assembly 1992.

The USA is the leading contributor to the Peacekeeping Operations Budget, with 30·3648% of the total for 1999, followed by Japan (19·9840%), Germany (9·8080%), France (7·9434%), UK (6·1823%), Italy (5·4320%), Canada (2·7540%) and Spain (2·5890%). All other countries contributed less than 2%.

Publications. Yearbook of the United Nations. New York, 1947 ff.—*United Nations Chronicle. Quarterly.—Monthly Bulletin of Statistics.—General Assembly: Official Records: Resolutions.—Reports of the Secretary-General of the United Nations on the Work of the Organization.* 1946 ff.—*Charter of the United Nations and Statute of the International Court of Justice.—Official Records of the Security Council, the Economic and Social Council, Trusteeship Council and the Disarmament Commission.—Demographic Yearbook.* New York.—*Basic Facts about the United Nations.* New York, 1995.—*Statistical Yearbook.* New York, 1947 ff.—*Yearbook of International Statistics.* New York, 1950 ff.—*World Economic Survey.* New York, 1947 ff.—*Economic Survey of Asia and the Far East.* New York, 1946 ff.—*Economic Survey of Latin America.* New York, 1948 ff.—*Economic Survey of Europe.* New York, 1948 ff.—*Economic Survey of Africa.* New York, 1960 ff.—*United Nations Reference Guide in the Field of Human Rights.* UN Centre for Human Rights, 1993.

Further Reading

Arnold, G., *World Government by Stealth: The Future of the United Nations.* Macmillan, 1998
Baehr, P. R. and Gordenker, L., *The United Nations in the 1990s.* 2nd ed. London, 1994
Bailey, S. D. and Daws, S., *The United Nations: a Concise Political Guide.* 3rd ed. London, 1994
Baratta, J. P., *United Nations System* [Bibliography]. Oxford and New Brunswick (NJ), 1995
Beigbeder, Y., *The Internal Management of United Nations Organizations: the Long Quest for Reform.* London, 1996
Carnegie Commission on Preventing Deadly Conflict, *Preventing Deadly Conflict: Final Report.* New York, 1997
Durch, W. J., *The Evolution of UN Peacekeeping: Case Studies and Comparative Analysis.* New York, 1993
Ginifer, J. (ed), *Development Within UN Peace Missions.* London, 1997
Hoopes, T., and Brinkley, D., *FDR and the Creation of the UN.* Yale Univ. Press, 1998
Luard, E., *The United Nations: How It Works and What It Does.* 2nd ed. London, 1994
Meisler, S., *United Nations: The First Fifty Years.* Atlantic Monthly Press, 1998
New Zealand Ministry of Foreign Affairs, *UN Handbook.* 1997
Osmanczyk, E., *Encyclopaedia of the United Nations.* London, 1985
Parsons, A., *From Cold War to Hot Peace: UN Interventions, 1947–94.* London, 1995
Pugh, M., *The UN, Peace and Force.* London, 1997
Ratner, S. R., *The New UN Peacekeeping: Building Peace in Lands of Conflict after the Cold War.* London, 1995
Righter, R., *Utopia Lost: the United Nations and World Order.* New York, 1995
Roberts, A. and Kingsbury, B. (eds.) *United Nations, Divided World: the UN's Roles in International Relations.* 2nd ed. Oxford, 1993.
Simma, B. (ed.) *The Charter of the United Nations: a Commentary.* OUP, 1995
Williams, D., *The Specialized Agencies of the United Nations.* London, 1987

UNIVERSAL DECLARATION OF HUMAN RIGHTS

On 10 Dec. 1948 the General Assembly of the United Nations adopted and proclaimed the Universal Declaration of Human Rights.

Preamble

Whereas recognition of the inherent dignity and of the equal and inalienable rights of all members of the human family is the foundation of freedom, justice and peace in the world,

Whereas disregard and contempt for human rights have resulted in barbarous acts which have outraged the conscience of mankind, and the advent of a world in which human beings shall enjoy freedom of speech and belief and freedom from fear and want has been proclaimed as the highest aspiration of the common people,

Whereas it is essential, if man is not to be compelled to have recourse, as a last resort, to rebellion against tyranny and oppression, that human rights should be protected by the rule of law,

Whereas it is essential to promote the development of friendly relations between nations,

Whereas the peoples of the United Nations have in the Charter reaffirmed their faith in fundamental human rights, in the dignity and worth of the human person and in the equal rights of men and women and have determined to promote social progress and better standards of life in larger freedom,

Whereas Member States have pledged themselves to achieve, in co-operation with the United Nations, the promotion of universal respect for and observance of human rights and fundamental freedoms,

Whereas a common understanding of these rights and freedoms is of the greatest importance for the full realization of this pledge,

Now, Therefore THE GENERAL ASSEMBLY proclaims THIS UNIVERSAL DECLARATION OF HUMAN RIGHTS as a common standard of achievement for all peoples and all nations, to the end that every individual and every organ of society, keeping this Declaration constantly in mind, shall strive by teaching and education to promote respect for these rights and freedoms and by progressive measures, national and international, to secure their universal and effective recognition and observance, both among the peoples of Member States themselves and among the peoples of territories under their jurisdiction.

Article 1. All human beings are born free and equal in dignity and rights. They are endowed with reason and conscience and should act towards one another in a spirit of brotherhood.

Article 2. Everyone is entitled to all the rights and freedoms set forth in this Declaration, without distinction of any kind, such as race, colour, sex, language, religion, political or other opinion, national or social origin, property, birth or other status. Furthermore, no distinction shall be made on the basis of the political, jurisdictional or international status of the country or territory to which a person belongs, whether it be independent, trust, non-self-governing or under any other limitation of sovereignty.

Article 3. Everyone has the right to life, liberty and security of person.

Article 4. No one shall be held in slavery or servitude; slavery and the slave trade shall be prohibited in all their forms.

Article 5. No one shall be subjected to torture or to cruel, inhuman or degrading treatment or punishment.

Article 6. Everyone has the right to recognition everywhere as a person before the law.

Article 7. All are equal before the law and are entitled without any discrimination to equal protection of the law. All are entitled to equal protection against any discrimination in violation of this Declaration and against any incitement to such discrimination.

Article 8. Everyone has the right to an effective remedy by the competent national tribunals for acts violating the fundamental rights granted him by the constitution or by law.

Article 9. No one shall be subjected to arbitrary arrest, detention or exile.

Article 10. Everyone is entitled in full equality to a fair and public hearing by an independent and impartial tribunal, in the determination of his rights and obligations and of any criminal charge against him.

Article 11. (1) Everyone charged with a penal offence has the right to be presumed innocent until proved guilty according to law in a public trial at which he has had all the guarantees necessary for his defence.

(2) No one shall be held guilty of any penal offence on account of any act or omission which did not constitute a penal offence, under national or international law, at the time when it was committed. Nor shall a heavier penalty be imposed than the one that was applicable at the time the penal offence was committed.

Article 12. No one shall be subjected to arbitrary interference with his privacy, family, home or correspondence, nor to attacks upon his honour and reputation. Everyone has the right to the protection of the law against such interference or attacks.

Article 13. (1) Everyone has the right to freedom of movement and residence within the borders of each state.

(2) Everyone has the right to leave any country, including his own, and to return to his country.

Article 14. (1) Everyone has the right to seek and enjoy in other countries asylum from persecution.

(2) This right may not be invoked in the case of prosecutions genuinely arising from non-political crimes or from acts contrary to the purposes and principles of the United Nations.

Article 15. (1) Everyone has the right to a nationality.

(2) No one shall be arbitrarily deprived of his nationality nor denied the right to change his nationality.

Article 16. (1) Men and women of full age, without any limitation due to race, nationality or religion, have the right to marry and to found a family. They are entitled to equal rights as to marriage, during marriage and at its dissolution.

(2) Marriage shall be entered into only with the free and full consent of the intending spouses.

(3) The family is the natural and fundamental group unit of society and is entitled to protection by society and the State.

Article 17. (1) Everyone has the right to own property alone as well as in association with others.

(2) No one shall be arbitrarily deprived of his property.

Article 18. Everyone has the right to freedom of thought, conscience and religion; this right includes freedom to change his religion or belief, and freedom, either alone or in community with others and in public or private, to manifest his religion or belief in teaching, practice, worship and observance.

Article 19. Everyone has the right to freedom of opinion and expression; this right includes freedom to hold opinions without interference and to seek, receive and impart information and ideas through any media and regardless of frontiers.

Article 20. (1) Everyone has the right to freedom of peaceful assembly and association.

(2) No one may be compelled to belong to an association.

Article 21. (1) Everyone has the right to take part in the government of his country, directly or through freely chosen representatives.

(2) Everyone has the right of equal access to public service in his country.

(3) The will of the people shall be the basis of the authority of government; this will shall be expressed in periodic and genuine elections which shall be by universal and equal suffrage and shall be held by secret vote or by equivalent free voting procedures.

Article 22. Everyone, as a member of society, has the right to social security and is entitled to realization, through national effort and international co-operation and in accordance with the organization and resources of the State, of the economic, social and cultural rights indispensable for his dignity and the free development of his personality.

Article 23. (1) Everyone has the right to work, to free choice of employment, to just and favourable conditions of and to protection against unemployment.

(2) Everyone, without any discrimination, has the right to equal pay for equal work.

(3) Everyone who works has the right to just and favourable remuneration ensuring for himself and his family an existence worthy of human dignity, and supplemented, if necessary, by other means of social protection.

(4) Everyone has the right to form and to join trade unions for the protection of his interests.

Article 24. Everyone has the right to rest and leisure, including reasonable limitation of working hours and periodic holidays with pay.

Article 25. (1) Everyone has the right to a standard of living adequate for the health and well-being of himself and his family, including food, clothing, housing and medical care and necessary social services, and the right to security in the event of unemployment, sickness, disability, widowhood, old age or other lack of livelihood in circumstances beyond his control.

(2) Motherhood and childhood are entitled to special care and assistance. All children, whether born in or out of wedlock, shall enjoy the same social protection.

Article 26. (1) Everyone has the right to education. Education shall be free, at least in the elementary and fundamental stages. Elementary education shall be compulsory. Technical and professional education shall be made generally available and higher education shall be equally accessible to all on the basis of merit.

(2) Education shall be directed to the full development of the human personality and to the strengthening of respect for human rights and fundamental freedoms. It shall promote understanding, tolerance and friendship among all nations, racial or religious groups, and shall further the activities of the United Nations for the maintenance of peace.

(3) Parents have a prior right to choose the kind of education that shall be given to their children.

Article 27. (1) Everyone has the right freely to participate in the cultural life of the community, to enjoy the arts and to share in scientific advancement and its benefits.

(2) Everyone has the right to the protection of the moral and material interests resulting from any scientific, literary or artistic production of which he is the author.

Article 28. Everyone is entitled to a social and international order in which the rights and freedoms set forth in this Declaration can be fully realized.

Article 29. (1) Everyone has duties to the community in which alone the free and full development of his personality is possible.

(2) In the exercise of his rights and freedoms, everyone shall be subject only to such limitations as are determined by law solely for the purpose of securing due recognition and respect for the rights and freedoms of others and of meeting the just requirements of morality, public order and the general welfare in a democratic society.

(3) These rights and freedoms may in no case be exercised contrary to the purposes and principles of the United Nations.

Article 30. Nothing in this Declaration may be interpreted as implying for any State, group or person any right to engage in any activity or to perform any act aimed at the destruction of any of the rights and freedoms set forth herein.

UNITED NATIONS SYSTEM

Operational Programmes and Funds. The total operating expenses for the entire UN system, including the World Bank, IMF and all the UN funds, programmes and specialized agencies, come to US$18,200m. a year. Some 53,300 people work in the UN system, which includes the Secretariat and 28 other organizations.

Social and economic development, aimed at achieving a better life for people everywhere, is a major part of the UN system of organizations. In the forefront of efforts to bring about such progress is the United Nations Development Programme (UNDP), the world's largest agency for multilateral technical and pre-investment co-operation. It is the funding source for most of the technical assistance provided for sustainable human development by the UN system, and in 1997 helped people in 174 countries and territories, supporting some 6,000 projects, which focus on poverty elimination, environmental regeneration, job creation and the advancement of women.

UNDP assistance is provided only at the request of governments and in response to their priority needs, integrated into overall national and regional plans. Its activities are funded mainly by voluntary contributions outside the regular UN budget. 87% of the UNDP's core programme funds go to countries with an annual per capita GNP of US$750 or less, which are home to 90% of the world's poorest peoples. Headquartered in New York, the UNDP is governed by a 36-member Executive Board, representing both developing and developed countries.

Administrator: James Gustave Speth (USA).

UN development programmes include the *United Nations Children's Fund (UNICEF).* Established in 1946 to deliver post-war relief to children, UNICEF now concentrates its assistance on development activities aimed at improving the quality of life for children and mothers in developing countries. Working in some 150 countries, its programmes focus on immunization, primary healthcare, nutrition and basic education. *The State of the World's Children Report,* published annually by UNICEF, has helped to spread acceptance by local and national leaders of a strategy for child health and nutrition which UNICEF estimates could save the lives of 7m. children. UNICEF has focused on popularizing 4 primary healthcare techniques which are low in cost and produce results in a relatively short time. These include: oral rehydration therapy to fight the effects of diarrhoeal infections, which kill some 4m. children each year; expanded immunization against the 6 most common childhood diseases; child growth monitoring; and promotion of breastfeeding. UNICEF works closely with the World Health Organization (WHO), providing training, equipment and the services of healthcare professionals. It is the world's largest supplier of oral rehydration salts and vaccines, and of the 'cold chain' equipment needed to deliver them.

Executive Director: Carol Bellamy (USA).

The UN *Population Fund (UNFPA),* established in 1969, carries out development programmes in over 130 countries and territories, and is the largest international provider of population assistance to developing countries. In 1996, it provided support to 168 countries. The Fund's aims are to build up capacity to respond to needs in population and family planning; to promote awareness of population problems in both developed and developing countries and possible strategies to deal with them; to assist developing countries at their request in dealing with population problems.

The Fund provides assistance for sustainable reproductive healthcare and family planning; for population data collection, analysis and demographic research; and for population policy formulation, as well as for special programme interests, such as gender issues, ageing and HIV/AIDS. In addition, it provides most of the funding for the *United Nations Population Information Network (POPIN),* a decentralized community of population institutions, whose objectives are to identify, establish, strengthen and co-ordinate information activities at international, national and regional levels; and to facilitate the availability and exchange of population information and related issues. *UNFPA's State of the World Population Report* is published annually.

Executive Director: Dr Nafis Sadik (Pakistan).

The UN Environment Programme (UNEP), established in 1972, works to encourage sustainable development through sound environmental practices everywhere. Its activities cover a wide range of issues, from atmosphere and terrestrial ecosystems to the promotion of environmental science and information, which is central to its role. It seeks to establish an early warning mechanism and emergency response capacity to deal with environmental disasters and emergencies. Information networks and monitoring systems established by the UNEP include: the Global Environment Monitoring System (GEMS); Global Resource Information Database (GRID); INFOTERRA, with focal points in 170 countries; and the International Register of Potentially Toxic Chemicals (IRPTC). Its research and synthesis of environmental information has generated a number of *State-of-the-Environment Reports,* the latest of which was the Global Environment Outlook or GEO-1 published in 1997. GEO-2000 was due for publication mid-1999.

Its 1992 Conference (the Earth Summit) in Rio de Janeiro broke new ground in reversing environmental deterioration, with a comprehensive blueprint for action on global sustainable development in the adoption of Agenda 21 by the then largest-ever gathering of world leaders, with more than 100 Heads of State or Government in attendance. At the request of the Earth Summit, a Commission on Sustainable Development was established by the General Assembly to oversee activities to combat problems such as desertification, the global depletion of fish, and issues affecting small islands. The most important funding mechanism towards this end is the Global Environment Facility (GEF) which is managed jointly by UNDP, UNEP and the World Bank.

Executive Director: Klaus Toepfer (Germany).

Other UN programmes working for development include: the *UN Conference on Trade and Development (UNCTAD),* which promotes international trade, particularly by developing countries, in an attempt to increase their participation in the global economy; and the *World Food Programme (WFP),* the world's largest international food aid organization, which is dedicated to both emergency relief and development programmes.

The *UN Centre for Human Settlements (Habitat),* which assists over 600m. people living in health-threatening housing conditions, was established in 1978. The 58-member *UN Commission on Human Settlements (UNCHS),* Habitat's governing body, meets every 2 years. The Centre serves as the focal point for human settlements action and the co-ordination of activities within the UN system.

In addition to its regular programmes, the UNDP administers various special-purpose funds, such as the *UN Capital Development Fund (UNCDP),* a multilateral donor agency working to develop new solutions for poverty reduction in the least developed countries; the *United Nations Volunteers (UNV)* and the *UN Development Fund for Women (UNIFEM),* whose mission is the empowerment of women and gender equality in all levels of development planning and practice. Its 3 areas of immediate concern are: strengthening women's economic capacity; engendering governance and leadership; and promoting women's rights. Together with the World Bank and UNEP, the UNDP is one of the managing partners of the Global Environment Facility (GEF), a US$2,000m. fund to help countries translate global concerns into national action so as to help fight ozone depletion, global warming, loss of biodiversity and pollution of international waters. The UNDP is also one of 6 UN sponsors of a global programme on HIV/AIDS.

The United Nations Development Programme has a network of 134 country offices. At country level, it is responsible for all UN development activity. The head of each country office acts as Resident Co-ordinator for UNDP.

The United Nations International Drug Control Programme (UNDCP), established 1991 and headquartered in Vienna, has 22 field offices around the world. UNDCP spearheads international efforts at fighting drug abuse and trafficking. Its annual budget is in the region of US$70m. At the core of its activities are 3 internationally agreed conventions (treaties) on policy. The Commission on Narcotic Drugs, the body which oversees UNDCP, meets once a year. UNDCP is now an integral part of the UN Office for Drug Control and Crime Prevention (ODCCP), together with the Centre for International Crime Prevention (CICP).

Executive Director: Pino Arlacchi (Italy).

The UN work in crime prevention and criminal justice aims to lessen the human and material costs of crime and its impact on socio-economic development. The UN Congress on the Prevention of Crime and Treatment of Offenders has convened every 5 years since 1950 and provides a forum for the presentation of policies and progress. The Ninth Congress (Cairo, 1995) also reviewed practical measures aimed at combating corruption among public officials. The *Commission on Crime Prevention and Criminal Justice*, a functional body of ECOSOC, established 1992, seeks to strengthen UN activities in the field, and meets annually in Vienna. The interregional research and training arm of the UN crime and criminal justice programme is the *United Nations Interregional Crime and Justice Research Institute (UNICRI)* in Rome. An autonomous body, it seeks through action-oriented research to contribute to the formulation of improved policies in crime prevention and control.

Humanitarian assistance to refugees and victims of natural and man-made disasters is also an important function of the UN system. The main refugee organizations within the system are the *Office of the United Nations High Commissioner for Refugees (UNHCR)* and the *United Nations Relief and Works Agency for Palestine Refugees in the Near East (UNRWA)*.

UNHCR, created in 1951, was charged primarily with resettling 1·2m. European refugees left homeless in the aftermath of the Second World War, and was envisioned as a temporary office with a projected lifespan of 3 years. Today, with more than 27m. people in over 140 countries under its concern, it has become one of the world's principal humanitarian agencies. Headquartered in Geneva, its Executive Committee comprises 53 member states. It has offices in 115 countries, with a 5,000 member staff, and has twice been awarded the Nobel Peace Prize. The High Commissioner is elected by and reports annually to the UN General Assembly through ECOSOC.

The work of UNHCR is humanitarian and non-political. International protection is its primary function. Its main objective is to promote and safeguard the rights and interests of refugees. In so doing UNHCR devotes special attention to promoting a generous policy of asylum on the part of Governments and seeks to improve the legal status of refugees in their country of residence. Crucial to this status is the principle of *non-refoulement*, which prohibits the expulsion from or forcible return of refugees to a country where they may have reason to fear persecution. UNHCR pursues its objectives in the field of protection by encouraging the conclusion of intergovernmental legal instruments in favour of refugees, by supervising the implementation of their provisions and by encouraging Governments to adopt legislation and administrative procedures for the benefit of refugees. UNHCR is often called upon to provide material assistance (i.e. the provision of food, shelter, medical care and essential supplies) while durable solutions are being sought. Durable solutions generally take one of 3 forms: voluntary repatriation, local integration or resettlement in another country.

UNHCR works in tandem with governmental and non-governmental organizations, and within the UN framework its closest partnership is with the World Food Programme. Other partners include UNICEF, WHO, UNDP and the Department of Humanitarian Affairs. The Red Cross (ICRC and IFRC) and the International Organization for Migration (IOM) are also close allies. Financial institutions such as the World Bank are also likely to increase their involvement with UNHCR in addressing the social and economic conditions underlying many refugee movements. At present, UNHCR is funded almost entirely by voluntary contributions. UNHCR expenditure amounted to over US$1,000m. in 1997.

High Commissioner: Sadako Ogata (Japan).

UNRWA was created by the General Assembly in 1949 as a temporary, non-political agency to provide relief to the nearly 750,000 people who became refugees as a result of the disturbances during and after the creation of the State of Israel in the former

British Mandate territory of Palestine. 'Palestine refugees', as defined by UNRWA's mandate, are persons or descendants of persons whose normal residence was Palestine for at least 2 years prior to the 1948 conflict and who, as a result of the conflict, lost their homes and means of livelihood. UNRWA has also been called upon to help persons displaced by renewed hostilities in the Middle East in 1967. The situation of Palestine refugees in south Lebanon, affected in the aftermath of the 1982 Israeli invasion of Lebanon, was of special concern to the Agency in 1984. Over 2m. refugees are registered with UNRWA. Education and basic healthcare account for over 80% of the Agency's budget, financed by voluntary contributions from Governments. Its mandate is renewed at intervals by the UN General Assembly.

The UN's activities in the field of human rights are the primary responsibility of the *High Commissioner for Human Rights*, a post established in 1993 under the direction and authority of the Secretary-General and held, currently, by Mary Robinson (Ireland). The High Commissioner is nominated by the Secretary-General for a 4-year term, renewable once. The principal co-ordinating human rights organ of the UN is the *Commission on Human Rights*, set up by ECOSOC in 1946. It has 53 members elected for 3-year terms, meets for 6 weeks in Geneva each year, and is aided in its task by a Subcommission on Prevention of Discrimination and Protection of Minorities, composed of 26 experts from all over the world. The implementation of international human rights treaties is monitored by 6 committees (also called treaty bodies): the Human Rights Committee; the Committee against Torture; Committee on the Rights of the Child; Committee on Economic, Cultural and Social Rights; Committee on the Elimination of Racial Discrimination; Committee on Elimination of Discrimination against Women.

Training and Research Institutes. There are 6 training and research institutes within the UN, all of them autonomous.

United Nations Institute for Training and Research (UNITAR). Established in 1963 to enhance the effectiveness of the UN in achieving its major objectives. Recently, its focus has shifted to training, with basic research being conducted only if extra-budgetary funds can be made available. Training is provided at various levels for personnel on assignments under the UN, its specialized agencies or related organizations. By 1996, more than 24,000 participants from 180 countries had attended UNITAR courses, seminars or workshops.

Address: Palais des Nations, 1211 Geneva 10, Switzerland.

United Nations Institute for Disarmament Research (UNIDIR). Established by the General Assembly in 1980 to undertake research on disarmament and related problems, particularly international security issues, its programme is reviewed annually subject to approval by its Board of Trustees, and its Director reports to the General Assembly.

Address: Palais des Nations, 1211 Geneva 10, Switzerland.

United Nations Research Institute for Social Development (UNRISD). Established in 1963 to conduct multidisciplinary research into the social dimensions of contemporary problems affecting development, it aims to provide governments, development agencies, grassroots organizations and scholars with a better understanding of how development policies and processes of economic, social and environmental change affect different social groups.

Address: Palais des Nations, 1211 Geneva 10, Switzerland.

United Nations International Research and Training Institute for the Advancement of Women (INSTRAW). Established by ECOSOC and endorsed by the General Assembly in 1976, INSTRAW provides training, conducts research, and collects and disseminates information to stimulate and assist women's advancement and integration into the development progress. Its 11-member Board of Trustees, which reports to ECOSOC, meets annually to review its programme and to formulate the principles and guidelines for INSTRAW's activities.

Address: POB 21747, Santo Domingo, Dominican Republic.

United Nations University (UNU). Sponsored jointly by the UN and UNESCO, UNU is guaranteed academic freedom by a charter approved by the General Assembly in 1973. It is governed by a 28-member Council of scholars and scientists, of whom 24 are appointed by the Secretary-General of the UN and the Director-General of UNESCO. Not traditional in the sense of having students and awarding degrees, it works through networks of collaborating institutions and individuals to undertake multidisciplinary research on problems of human survival, development and welfare; and to strengthen research and training capabilities in developing countries. It also provides postgraduate fellowships to scholars and scientists from developing countries.

Address: 53-70 Jingumae 5-chome, Shibuya-ku, Tokyo 150, Japan.

University for Peace. Founded in 1980 to conduct research on, *inter alia,* disarmament, mediation, the resolution of conflicts, preservation of the environment, international relations, peace education and human rights. The University has a European centre in Belgrade.

Address: POB 138, Ciudad Colon, Costa Rica.

Information. *The UN Statistics Division* in New York provides a wide range of statistical outputs and services for producers and users of statistics worldwide, facilitating national and international policy formulation, implementation and monitoring. It produces printed publications of statistics and statistical methods in the fields of international merchandise trade, national accounts, demography and population, gender, industry, energy, environment, human settlements and disability, as well as general statistics compendiums including the *Statistical Yearbook* and *World Statistics Pocketbook.* Many of its databases are available on CD-ROM, diskette, magnetic tape and the Internet.

Website: http://www.un.org/Depts/unsd

UN Information Centres. Millbank Tower, 21st Floor, London SW1P 4QH; Public Inquiries Unit, Department of Public Information, Room GA-57, United Nations Plaza, New York, NY 10017.

Website: http://www.un.org

CHEMICAL AND BIOLOGICAL WEAPON PROLIFERATION

Dr Jean Pascal Zanders

The use of chemical weapons (CW) in the war between Iraq and Iran in 1980-88 revealed that several countries outside the East-West confrontation had acquired chemical and possibly biological weapons (BW). At the same time, the likelihood of outside military intervention into regional conflicts, such as the 1990-91 Gulf War, increased after the end of the cold war. The realization that expeditionary forces could face an army with chemical or biological weapons heightened international awareness of the dangers of proliferation. The dimension of sub-state proliferation was added to after the first large-scale indiscriminate terrorist attack with CW in the Tokyo underground system in March 1995.

Although the issue may appear to be of relatively recent origin, the spread of chemical weapons actually started in World War I and has continued ever since. The Allies, whose chemical industry was generally less developed than that in Imperial Germany, soon began sharing knowledge and expertise on offensive and defensive aspects of chemical warfare and exchanging production capabilities for certain chemicals. In addition, France and Great Britain supplied other Allies whose territory was occupied, such as Belgium, or who had an insufficiently developed CW production base, such as the United States, with chemical warfare munitions.

After World War I most major belligerents scaled back their offensive CW programmes. But it was not the number of states with a chemical capacity, but the size of the CW arsenals that was the chief security concern. A significant imbalance offered the CW possessor the prospect of a swift, decisive victory and therefore contributed to the likelihood of war. For this reason some major powers viewed the sale of chemicals, technology and factories to smaller or less-advanced states as beneficial to their own national security. The transactions involved direct government-to-government dealings. On the eve of World War II many European second-tier powers maintained limited offensive CW programmes and, in doing so, contributed to the continent-wide patchwork of overlapping balances of power. In addition, Italy's use of CW in Abyssinia (1935-36) and the worsening political climate in Europe gave a major impetus to offensive and defensive CW programmes. At no other point in history have so many countries been known to possess chemical weapons.

Biological weapons took a little longer to gain credibility. The only experience from the Great War was German sabotage with pathogens against livestock in the United States destined for Europe and the Middle East. Thereafter, a better understanding of disease transmission in the 1920s and 1930s combined with the dramatic experiences of the Spanish Flu epidemic at the end of World War I increased concerns about biological warfare. Based on essentially faulty intelligence and fears of vulnerability, several countries began to look seriously at the feasibility of biological warfare and the suitability of certain pathogens for weaponization. Germany's research and development remained splintered throughout World War II and did not lead to a useful weapon. More concerted efforts in Canada, Great Britain and the United States led to the three countries pooling their resources. However, apart from a limited British capability to retaliate with anthrax against German cattle, the Allies failed to produce an operational offensive biological weapon. The only country with a dedicated long-term offensive BW programme was Japan. Its research and development of agents and dissemination devices began in the early 1930s and lasted until the end of the war. The programme was also based on human experimentation in occupied China. On several occasions Japanese troops released biological warfare agents against Chinese villages and soldiers.

Post-war research and production of offensive CBW was continued in the Soviet Union and the USA. The new nerve agents, which the Germans had discovered in the late 1930s while researching pesticides, rekindled their interest in chemical warfare. Most secondary powers, however, gradually abandoned their offensive CBW programmes to concentrate on chemical and biological defence, protection and prophylaxis. The number of countries with offensive CW capabilities thus dropped considerably from the pre-World War II high and few countries other than those which had begun BW-related investigations during the inter-war years were known to have started up new biological warfare programmes.

It therefore came as something of a shock to the major powers when, in the 1980-88 Gulf War, Iraq breached the only international legal norm against chemical warfare then in force, the 1925 Geneva Protocol, by attacking Iranian forces and Kurdish guerrillas and civilians in Iraq with CW. It soon emerged that Western companies had been or were supplying Iraq with the technology and know-how to manufacture these weapons. Active CW programmes were reported in several other countries and in many instances Western companies were found to be heavily involved. Most of these programmes were located in politically volatile regions and led to fears of rapid escalation of violence as military leaders contemplated preemptive strikes against production and storage facilities.

While there is always a degree of uncertainty as to the number of countries engaging in chemical or biological warfare programmes, we are even less confident in assessing the level of development and whether the programmes are offensive or defensive. At what point should a country enter the league of chemical or biological weaponry? Should it be when it has the scientific, technological and industrial base to support a CBW programme, when it has a research and development programme, when it produces chemical or biological weapons, when it stockpiles them, when it deploys them with troops, or when there is clear evidence that they have been assimilated into military doctrine? An important factor here is that whatever country is making the assessment is liable to use different criteria depending on whether a state is hostile or friendly. Perceived intent is a major subjective component in threat assessment.

Recent US analyses have tended to converge on a figure of at least 20 to 25 countries that have or may have been developing nuclear, biological or chemical weapons, or their missile delivery systems. As the figures now usually comprise four categories of weapons, it has become more difficult to isolate the CBW threat assessment. The 1997 edition of *Proliferation: Threat and Response* by the US Department of Defense listed nine countries as having a CW programme in various stages of development: China, India, Iran, Iraq, North Korea, Libya, Pakistan, Russia and Syria. It also named seven countries as have a BW programme: China, India, Iran, Iraq, North Korea, Pakistan and Russia. Some countries, however, are conspicuously absent from these lists. Egypt, Israel, South Korea and Taiwan, for instance, were named in the August 1993 Office of Technology Assessment report, *Proliferation of Weapons of Mass Destruction: Assessing the Risks*.

Under the 1993 Chemical Weapons Convention (CWC) signatories are required to declare CW programmes initiated after 1 January 1946. These declarations are subject to verification and inspections by personnel of the Organization for the Prohibition of Chemical Weapons (OPCW) in The Hague. In case of doubt, any party to the convention may request a challenge inspection to ascertain the veracity of submissions. The United States and Russia, as successor state to the Soviet Union, have declared large CW stockpiles (30,000 and 40,000 agent tonnes respectively), which are in the process of being destroyed. They have also declared production facilities, which are either being destroyed or converted. China, France, India, South Korean and the United Kingdom are known to have made declarations of CW production facilities. Japan has declared and destroyed the Aum Shinrikyo sarin factory. Following the hearings of the Truth and Reconciliation Commission in June 1998 and the publication of the report in October, South Africa is now also known to have had a major CW armament programme in the 1980s.

The 1972 Biological and Toxic Weapons Convention (BTWC) does not require states parties to declare past programmes but they are encouraged to volunteer information. Few countries have submitted details of offensive biological warfare activities. International inspections in Iraq, conducted as part of the cease-fire agreement ending the 1990-91 Gulf War, have uncovered a vast and advanced biological warfare programme although its full scope has not yet been determined. There is still some doubt as to whether Russia has totally abandoned its offensive BW research and development despite decrees by President Boris Yeltsin ordering its termination. Negotiators in Geneva are currently considering a protocol to the BTWC with verification measures, but until the conclusion of these talks no formal procedures to verify compliance with the convention are available.

CHEMICAL AND BIOLOGICAL WEAPON PROLIFERATION

Addressing the CBW proliferation threat: export controls and disarmament

Most of the technologies and materials necessary for the manufacture of chemical or biological weapons are dual-use in nature. They have important civilian applications, but can easily be diverted for CBW programmes. One way of controlling the way they are used is to impose export controls. Few countries, whether industrialized or industrializing, object to the principle of export controls. Export controls are embedded in the CWC and will become part of the BTWC treaty regime once the negotiations on an additional protocol to that convention have been concluded. In each case they allow the right of access to the controlled technologies and goods for purposes not prohibited by either convention. Far more controversial in North-South relations is the existence of an export control regime outside both conventions, namely the Australia Group. Several developing countries see it as an attempt to undercut their right of access to certain commodities under the disarmament treaties.

Specific CBW-related export controls emerged in the mid-1980s, when it became clear that Western companies were aiding Iraq's CW programmes. Previously, trade regulations to prevent the diversion of dual-use goods were either non-existent or easily circumvented. The need to co-ordinate national export controls led to the formation of the Australia Group as an informal consultative forum in 1985. Its original objective was to prevent CW proliferation while the negotiations to complete the CWC were being undertaken. Subsequently, it has also acted to prevent BW proliferation while improved measures to ensure compliance with the BTWC are introduced. Today, the control lists of the Australia Group comprise chemical precursors, equipment used in the production of CBW, and biological warfare agents and organisms. The participants - 30 states plus the European Commission, which attends as an observer - have agreed to apply decisions taken collectively through their national export control systems. In 1992 the Missile Technology Control Regime (MTCR) extended its scope to include missiles capable of delivering chemical and biological warheads. The Australia Group list of controlled goods is incorporated into other export control regimes, such as the Wassenaar Arrangement and the European Union regulations on exports of dual-use goods.

So far, we have dealt with strategies to control the supply of biological and chemical weapons. But what of controlling demand? A disarmament treaty is the ultimate demand-side non-proliferation policy, because it involves a conscious decision to renounce these weapons under all circumstances. The BTWC and the CWC contain an absolute prohibition to develop or otherwise acquire chemical or biological weapons and the obligation never to assist anybody under any circumstances to acquire such weapons. In addition, parties also have a disarmament obligation: they must reduce existing stockpiles of chemical or biological weapons to zero.

At present, the CWC generates a far higher degree of confidence, because it contains elaborate verification and inspection mechanisms as well as procedures to restore compliance in case of a breach. The BTWC does not have similar provisions simply because in the early 1970s there was widespread consensus that BW had little military utility. In view of the rapid progress in biotechnology and genetic engineering, concerns about designer biological warfare agents and their antidotes have risen sharply. Hopefully, the states parties to the BTWC will reach agreement on verification and compliance measures in additional protocol to the convention before the 5th Review Conference of States Parties to the BTWC in 2001.

Dr Jean Pascal Zanders is CBW Project Leader at the Stockholm International Peace Research Institute

SPECIALIZED AGENCIES
OF THE UN

The intergovernmental agencies related to the UN by special agreements are separate autonomous organizations which work with the UN and each other through the co-ordinating machinery of the Economic and Social Council. 16 of them are 'Specialized Agencies' within the terms of the UN Charter, and report annually to ECOSOC.

FOOD AND AGRICULTURE ORGANIZATION OF THE
UNITED NATIONS (FAO)

Origin. In 1943, the International Conference on Food and Agriculture, at Hot Springs, Virginia, set up an Interim Commission, based in Washington, with a remit to establish an organization. Its Constitution was signed on 16 Oct. 1945 in Quebec City. Today, membership totals 175 countries. The European Union was made a member as a 'regional economic integration organization' in 1991.

Aims and Activities. The aims of FAO are to raise levels of nutrition and standards of living; to improve the production and distribution of all food and agricultural products from farms, forests and fisheries; to improve the living conditions of rural populations; and, by these means, to eliminate hunger. Its priority objectives are to encourage sustainable agriculture and rural development as part of a long-term strategy for the conservation and management of natural resources; and to ensure the availability of adequate food supplies, by maximizing stability in the flow of supplies and securing access to food by the poor.

In carrying out these aims, FAO promotes investment in agriculture, better soil and water management, improved yields of crops and livestock, agricultural research and the transfer of technology to developing countries; and encourages the conservation of natural resources and rational use of fertilizers and pesticides; the development and sustainable utilization of marine and inland fisheries; the sustainable management of forest resources and the combating of animal disease. Technical assistance is provided in all of these fields, and in nutrition, agricultural engineering, agrarian reform, development communications, remote sensing for climate and vegetation, and the prevention of post-harvest food losses. In addition, FAO works to maintain global biodiversity with the emphasis on the genetic diversity of crop plants and domesticated animals; and plays a major role in the collection, analysis and dissemination of information on agricultural production and commodities. Finally, FAO acts as a neutral forum for the discussion of issues, and advises governments on policy, through the convention of international conferences like the 1996 World Food Summit in Rome.

Special FAO programmes help countries prepare for, and provide relief in the event of, emergency food situations, in particular through the setting up of food reserves. The *Special Programme for Food Security through Food Production in Low-Income Food-Deficit Countries*, launched in 1994, is designed to assist target countries to increase food production and productivity as rapidly as possible, primarily through the widespread adoption by farmers of available improved production technologies, with the emphasis on high-potential areas. FAO provides support for the global co-ordination of the programme and helps attract funds. The *Emergency Prevention System for Transboundary Animal and Plant Pests and Diseases (EMPRES)*, established in 1994, strengthens FAO's existing contribution to the prevention, control and eradication of diseases and pests, with locusts and rinderpest among its priorities. *The Global Information and Early Warning System* provides current information on the world food situation and identifies countries threatened by shortages to guide potential donors. The *People's Participation Programme* promotes the involvement of rural people in decision-making, and the policy-making and activities affecting their lives. Together with the UN, FAO sponsors *the World Food Programme (WFP)*.

Finance. The budget for the 1998–99 biennium is US$650m. FAO's Regular Programme budget, financed by contributions from member governments, covers the cost of its secretariat and Technical Co-operation Programme (TCP), and part of the costs of several special programmes.

The technical assistance programme is funded by extra-budgetary sources. Its single largest contributor is the UN Development Programme (UNDP), which in 1997 accounted for US$46·4m., or 18% of field project expenditures. Increasingly important are the trust funds that come from donor countries and international financing institutions, totalling some US$165·9m., or 64% of technical assistance funds. In 1997 FAO's contribution under its TCP and Special Programme for Food Security was US$47·8m., or 18%. Its total field programme expenditure for 1997 was an estimated US$260·2m. In 1997, there were 2,320 field projects in operation: 33% in Africa, 22% in Asia and the Pacific, 10% in Latin America and the Caribbean, 12% in the Near East, 4% in Europe, and 19% interregional or global.

Organization. The FAO Conference, composed of all members, meets every other year to determine policy and approve the FAO's budget and programme. The 49-member Council, elected by the Conference, serves as FAO's governing body between conference sessions. Much of its work is carried out by dozens of regional or specialist commissions, such as the Asia-Pacific Fishery Commission, the European Commission on Agriculture and the Commission on Plant Genetic Resources. The Director-General is elected for a renewable 6-year term.

Headquarters: Viale delle Terme di Caracalla, 00100 Rome, Italy.
Website: http://www.fao.org
Director-General: Jacques Diouf (Senegal).

Publications. Unasylva (quarterly) 1947 ff; *The State of Food and Agriculture* (annual), 1947 ff.; *Animal Health Yearbook* (annual), 1957 ff.; *Production Yearbook* (annual), 1947 ff.; *Trade Yearbook* (annual), 1947 ff.; *FAO Commodity Review* (annual), 1961 ff.; *Yearbook of Forest Products* (annual), 1947 ff.; *Yearbook of Fishery Statistics* (in two volumes); *FAO Fertilizer Yearbook; FAO Plant Protection Bulletin* (quarterly); *Environment and Energy Bulletin; Food Outlook* (monthly); *The State of World Fisheries and Aquaculture* (annual); *The State of the World's Forests; World Watch List for Domestic Animal Diversity.*

INTERNATIONAL BANK FOR RECONSTRUCTION AND DEVELOPMENT (IBRD) — THE WORLD BANK

Origin. Conceived at the UN Monetary and Financial Conference at Bretton Woods (New Hampshire, USA) in July 1944, the IBRD, frequently called the World Bank, began operations in June 1946, its purpose being to provide funds, policy guidance and technical assistance to facilitate economic development in its poorer member countries. The Group comprises 4 other organizations (see below).

Activities. The Bank obtains its funds from the following sources: capital paid in by member countries; sales of its own securities; sales of parts of its loans; repayments; and net earnings. A resolution of the Board of Governors of 27 April 1988 provides that the paid-in portion of the shares authorized to be subscribed under it will be 3%.

The Bank is self-supporting, raising most of its money on the world's financial markets. In the fiscal year ending 30 June 1997, it achieved a net income of US$1,285m.; medium- and long-term borrowing equivalent of US$15,100m. in 18 currencies; average medium- to long-term borrowing costs, after swaps, of 5·01%; financial returns on its investment folio of 5%; a reserves-to-loan ratio of 14%; and decline in its net administrative expenditure in real terms to a figure set at $1,177m.

The Bank lends in the region of US$22,000m. a year. At 30 June 1997, it had lent a total of US$106,000m. to member countries. 89% of borrowers took advantage of the new single-currency loans which became available in June 1996 to provide borrowers with the flexibility to select IBRD loan terms that are consistent with their debt-managing strategy and suited to their debt-servicing capacity. In order to eliminate wasteful overlapping of development assistance and to ensure that the funds available are used to the best possible effect, the Bank has organized consortia or consultative groups of aid-giving nations for many countries. These include Bangladesh, Belarus, Bolivia, Bulgaria, Egypt, Ethiopia, Jordan, Kazakhstan, Kenya, Kyrgyzstan, Macedonia, Malaŵi, Mauritania, Moldova, Mozambique, Nicaragua, Pakistan, Peru, Romania, Sierra Leone, Tanzania, the [Palestinian] West Bank and Gaza Strip, Zambia, Zimbabwe and the Caribbean Group for Co-operation in Economic Development.

For the purposes of its analytical and operational work, in 1996 the IBRD characterized economies as follows: low-income (average annual *per capita* GNP of $785 or less); middle-income (between $786 and $9,635); and high-income ($9,636 or more).

A wide variety of technical assistance is at the core of IBRD's activities. It acts as executing agency for a number of pre-investment surveys financed by the UN Development Programme. Resident missions have been established in 64 developing member countries and there are regional offices for East and West Africa, the Baltic States and South-East Asia which assist in the preparation and implementation of projects. The Bank maintains a staff college, the *Economic Development Institute* in Washington, D.C., for senior officials of member countries. In 1997, the institute held training workshops on anti-corruption strategies and public integrity in more than 10 countries as part of IBRD's initiative to combat corruption.

The Strategic Compact. Unanimously approved by the Executive Board in March 1997, the Strategic Compact set out a plan for fundamental reform to make the Bank more effective in delivering its regional programme and in achieving its basic mission of reducing poverty. Decentralizing the Bank's relationships with borrower countries is central to the reforms. The effectiveness of devolved country management and the bank's promotion of good governance and anti-corruption measures to developing countries are likely to be key policies of the new strategy.

Organization. As of July 1997, the Bank had 180 members, each with voting power in the institution, based on shareholding which in turn is based on a country's economic growth. The president is selected by the Bank's Board of Executive Directors. The Articles of Agreement do not specify the nationality of the president but by custom the US Executive Director makes a nomination, and by a long-standing, informal agreement, the president is a US national (while the managing director of the IMF is European). The initial term is 5 years, with a second of 5 years or less.

European office: 66 avenue d'Iéna, 75116 Paris, France. *London office:* New Zealand House, Haymarket, London SW1Y 4TE, England. *Tokyo office:* Kokusai Building, 1–1, Marunouchi 3-chome, Chiyoda-ku, Tokyo 100, Japan.
Headquarters: 1818 H St., NW, Washington, D.C., 20433, USA.
Website: http://www.worldbank.org
President: James D. Wolfensohn (USA).

Publications. World Bank Annual Report; Summary Proceedings of Annual Meetings; The World Bank and International Finance Company, 1986; *The World Bank Atlas* (annual); *Catalog of Publications,* 1986 ff; *World Development Report* (annual); *World Bank Economic Review* (thrice yearly); *World Bank and the Environment* (annual); *World Bank News* (weekly); *World Bank Research Observer; World Tables* (annual); *Social Indicators of Development* (annual); *ICSID Annual Report; ICSID Review: Foreign Investment Law Journal* (twice yearly); *Research News* (quarterly).

INTERNATIONAL DEVELOPMENT ASSOCIATION (IDA)

A lending agency established in 1960 and administered by the IBRD to provide assistance on concessional terms to the poorest developing countries. Its resources consist of subscriptions and general replenishments from its more industrialized and developed members, special contributions, and transfers from the net earnings of IBRD.

In 1997 the IDA lent a total of US$101,600m. for 2,780 development projects in around 100 countries. The same year, however, saw overall loan commitments for the poorest countries fall by almost a third, to US$4,600m., with commitments 15% down on the lower end of its US$5,300-6,600m. planning range for that year. The biggest shortfall has been in lending to Africa.

Officers and staff of the IBRD serve concurrently as officers and staff of the IDA at the World Bank headquarters.

INTERNATIONAL FINANCE CORPORATION (IFC)

Established in July 1956 to help strengthen the private sector in developing countries, through the provision of long-term loans, equity investments, guarantees, standby financing, risk management and quasi-equity instruments such as subordinated loans, preferred stock and income notes. It helps to finance new ventures and assist established enterprises to expand, improve or diversify, and provides a variety of advisory services to public and private sector clients. To be eligible for financing, projects must be profitable for investors, must benefit the economy of the country concerned, and must comply with IFC's environmental guidelines.

About 80% of its funds are borrowed from the international financial markets through public bond issues or private placements, 20% from the IBRD. Its authorized capital is US$2,450m.; paid-in capital at 30 June 1996 was US$2,076m. The IFC invested US$6,700m. in project financing in 1997 and approved 276 private-sector projects in around 80 countries. It has 172 members.

Headquarters: 1850 I St., NW, Washington, D.C., 20433, USA.
Website: http://www.ifc.org

Publications. Annual Reports; What IFC Does, 1988; How to Work with IFC, 1988; Emerging Stock Markets Factbook (annual); *Global Agribusiness Series; Lessons of Experience* (series).

MULTILATERAL INVESTMENT GUARANTEE AGENCY (MIGA)

Established in 1988 to encourage the flow of foreign direct investment to, and among, developing member countries, MIGA is the insurance arm of the World Bank. It provides investors with investment guarantees against non-commercial risk, such as expropriation and war, and gives advice to governments on improving climate for foreign investment. It may insure up to 90% of an investment, with a current limit of US$50m. per project. In 1997 it issued 293 guarantees for US$3,400m. in coverage. By 1999 it had 149 member countries and a further 16 countries in the process of fulfilling membership requirements. Located at the World Bank headquarters (see above).

INTERNATIONAL CENTRE FOR SETTLEMENT OF INVESTMENT DISPUTES (ICSID)

Founded in 1966 to promote increased flows of international investment by providing facilities for the conciliation and arbitration of disputes between governments and foreign investors. It does not engage in such conciliation or arbitration. This is the task of conciliators and arbitrators appointed by the contracting parties, or as otherwise provided for in the Convention. Recourse to conciliation and arbitration by members is entirely voluntary.

At 31 Oct. 1997, its Convention had been signed by 143 countries. 47 cases had been registered by it (3, conciliation; 44, arbitration) and 12 arbitrations were pending. Disputes involved a variety of investment sectors: agriculture, banking, construction, energy, health, industrial, mining and tourism.

ICSID also undertakes research, publishing and advisory activities in the field of foreign investment law. Like the IDA and MIGA, it is located at the World Bank headquarters in Washington (see above).

Secretary-General: Ibrahim F. I Shihata (Egypt).

Publications. ICSID Annual Report; News from ICSID; ICSID Review: Foreign Investment Law Journal; Investment Laws of the World; Investment Treaties.

Further Reading

Caufield, C., Masters of Illusion: The World Bank and the Poverty of Nations. London, 1997
Nelson, P. J., The World Bank and Non-Government Organizations: The Limits of Apolitical Development. London, 1995
Salda, A. C. M., World Bank: *[Bibliography]. Oxford and New Brunswick (NJ), 1994*
Wilson, C. R., The World Bank Group: A Guide to Information Sources. *New York, 1991*

INTERNATIONAL CIVIL AVIATION ORGANIZATION (ICAO)

Origin. The Convention providing for the establishment of the ICAO was drawn up by the International Civil Aviation Conference held in Chicago in 1944. A Provisional International Civil Aviation Organization (PICAO) operated for 20 months until the formal establishment of ICAO on 4 April 1947. The Convention on International Civil Aviation superseded the provisions of the Paris Convention of 1919 and the Pan American Convention on Air Navigation of 1928.

Functions. It assists international civil aviation by establishing technical standards for safety and efficiency of air navigation and promoting simpler procedures at borders; develops regional plans for ground facilities and services needed for international flying; disseminates air-transport statistics and prepares studies on aviation economics; and fosters the development of air law conventions. As an administrative arm of the UN Development Programme, it provides technical assistance to states in developing civil aviation programmes.

Organization. The principal organs of ICAO are an Assembly, consisting of all members of the Organization, and a Council, which is composed of 33 states elected by the Assembly for 3 years, which meets in virtually continuous session. In electing these states, the Assembly must give adequate representation to: (1) states of major importance in air transport; (2) states which make the largest contribution to the provision of facilities for the international civil air navigation; and (3) those states not otherwise included whose election would ensure that all major geographical areas of the world were represented. The ICAO's main subsidiary bodies are: 15-member Air Navigation Commission appointed by the Council; Committee on Joint Support of Air Navigation Services; Personnel Committee; the Finance Committee; Committee on Unlawful Interference; Technical Co-operation Committee; Air Transport Committee (all open to Council members); and the Legal Committee, on which all 185 of the Organization's members may be represented. The budget approved for 1998 was US$54·6m.

Headquarters: 999 University St., Montreal, PQ, Canada H3C 5H7.
Secretary-General: Renato Claudio Costa Pereira (Brazil).

Publications. Annual Report of the Council; ICAO Journal (10 yearly; quarterly in Russian); ICAO Training Manual; Aircraft Accident Digest; Procedures for Air Navigation Services.

INTERNATIONAL FUND FOR AGRICULTURAL DEVELOPMENT (IFAD)

The idea for an International Fund for Agricultural Development arose at the 1974 World Food Conference. An agreement to establish IFAD entered into force on 30 Nov. 1977, and the agency began its operations the following month. IFAD's purpose is to mobilize additional funds for improved food production and better nutrition among low-income groups in developing countries through projects and programmes directly benefiting the poorest rural populations while preserving their natural resource base. In line with the Fund's focus on the rural poor, its resources are made available in highly concessional loans and grants. By 1999 the Fund had invested US$5,670m. in financing 489 projects in 111 developing countries.

Organization. The highest body is the Governing Council, on which all 160 member countries are represented. Operations are overseen by an 18-member Executive Board (with 17 alternate members), which is responsible to the Governing Council. The Fund works with many co-operating institutions, including the World Bank, regional development banks and financial agencies, and other UN agencies; many of these co-finance IFAD projects.

Headquarters: 107 Via del Serafico, Rome 00142, Italy.
President: Fawzi H. Al-Sultan (Kuwait).

Publications. Annual Report; IFAD Update (thrice yearly); *Staff Working Papers* (series); *The State of World Rural Poverty.*

INTERNATIONAL LABOUR ORGANIZATION (ILO)
Origin. The ILO was established in 1919 under the Treaty of Versailles as an autonomous institution associated with the League of Nations. An agreement establishing its relationship with the UN was approved in 1946, making the ILO the first Specialized Agency to be associated with the UN. An intergovernmental agency with a tripartite structure, in which representatives of governments, employers and workers participate, it seeks through international action to improve labour and living conditions, to promote productive employment and social justice for working people everywhere. On its fiftieth anniversary in 1969, it was awarded the Nobel Peace Prize. In June 1998, it numbered 174 members.

Functions. One of the ILO's principal functions is the formulation of international standards in the form of International Labour Conventions and Recommendations. Member countries are required to submit Conventions to their competent national authorities with a view to ratification. If a country ratifies a Convention it agrees to bring its laws into line with its terms and to report periodically how these regulations are being applied. More than 6,544 ratifications of 181 Conventions had been deposited by 30 Oct. 1998. Procedures are in place to ascertain whether Conventions thus ratified are effectively applied. Recommendations do not require ratification, but Member States are obliged to consider them with a view to giving effect to their provisions by legislation or other action. By 2 Dec. 1998, the International Labour Conference had adopted 189 Recommendations.

Activities. In addition to its research and advisory activities, the ILO extends technical co-operation to governments under its regular budget and under the UN Development Programme and Funds-in-Trust in the fields of employment promotion, human resources development (including vocational and management training), development of social institutions, small-scale industries, rural development, social security, industrial safety and hygiene, productivity, etc. Technical co-operation also includes expert missions and a fellowship programme.

In 1994 the technical services offered by the ILO to its tripartite constituents came under scrutiny leading to a re-affirmation of technical co-operation as one of the principal means of ILO action. Since 1994 the process of implementing the new Active Partnership Policy made significant progress and today 16 multidisciplinary advisory teams are engaged in a dialogue with ILO constituents centred on the identification of Country Objectives to form the basis of the ILO's contribution.

In June 1998 delegates to the 86th International Labour Conference adopted a solemn ILO Declaration in Fundamental Principles and Rights at Work, committing the Organization's 174 member States to respect the principles inherent in 7 core labour standards: the right of workers and employers to freedom of association and the effective right to collective bargaining, and to work toward the elimination of all forms of forced or compulsory labour, the effective abolition of child labour and the elimination of discrimination in respect of employment and occupation.

The Conference also adopted a Resolution on Youth Employment, which calls on member States to take specific measures to increase employment opportunities for young persons, while ensuring employment protection for them. These measures include investment and education, vocational training, counselling, flexible work arrangements, and the creation of small and medium-sized enterprises.

Finance. In 1997, expenditure on operational activities, under all sources of funding, totalled US$108·4m. The 3 leading programmes (representing 64% of total expenditure) were in employment and training (US$24·6m.), enterprise and co-operative development (US$23·4m.) and development policies (US$21·2m.). Other programmes dealt with working conditions and environment (US$13·1m.), including an International Programme for the Elimination of Child Labour (US$8·6m.).

Interregional and global activities accounted for some US$18·6m. In terms of regional distribution, Africa accounted for 39% of total expenditure (US$42m.), Asia and the Pacific for 22% (US$23·5m.), and Latin America and the Caribbean for 12% (more than US$13·3m.). Expenditure in Europe was US$6·8m. in 1997; in the Arab States programmes rose from US$2·6m in 1996 to US$4m. in 1997.

The ILO's *International Institute for Labour Studies* promotes the study and discussion of policy issues. The core theme of its activities is the interaction between labour institutions, development and civil society in a global economy. It identifies emerging social and labour issues by opening up new areas for research and action; and encourages systematic dialogue on social policy between the tripartite constituency of the ILO and the international academic community, and other public opinion-makers. It achieves its mandate through research networks; courses and seminars; social policy forums; internships; visiting scholar and internship programmes; and publications.

The *International Training Centre* of the ILO, in Turin, was set up in 1965 to lead the training programmes implemented by the ILO as part of its technical co-operation activities. Member States and the UN system also call on its resources and experience, and a UN Staff College was established on the Turin Campus in 1996.

Organization. The International Labour Conference is the supreme deliberative organ of the ILO; it meets annually in Geneva. National delegations are composed of 2 government delegates, 1 employers' delegate and 1 workers' delegate. The Governing Body, elected by the Conference, is the Executive Council. It is composed of 28 government members, 14 workers' members and 14 employers' members. 10 governments of countries of industrial importance hold permanent seats on the Governing Body. These are: Brazil, China, Germany, France, India, Italy, Japan, Russia, UK and USA. The remaining 18 government members are elected every 3 years. Workers' and employers' representatives are elected as individuals, not as national candidates. The International Labour Office serves as secretariat, operational headquarters, research centre and publishing house. The ILO has a branch office in London (for UK and Republic of Ireland), and regional offices in Abidjan (for Africa), Bangkok (for Asia and the Pacific), Lima (for Latin America and the Caribbean) and Beirut (for Arab States). The ILO budget for 1998–99 was US$481m.

Headquarters: International Labour Office, CH-1211 Geneva 22, Switzerland.
London Office: Vincent House, Vincent Square, London, SW1P 2NB, UK.
Website: http://www.ilo.org
Director-General: Michel Hansenne (Belgium).
Governing Body Chairman: Nobutoshi Akao (Japan).

Publications. (available in English, French and Spanish) include: *International Labour Review; Bulletin of Labour Statistics; Official Bulletin* and *Labour Education; Yearbook of Labour Statistics* (annual)*; World Labour Report* (annual)*; World Employment Report* (annual)*; Encyclopaedia of Occupational Health and Safety.*

INTERNATIONAL MARITIME ORGANIZATION (IMO)

Origin. The International Maritime Organization (formerly the InterGovernmental Maritime Consultative Organization) was established as a specialized agency of the UN by a convention drafted in 1948 at a UN maritime conference in Geneva. The Convention became effective on 17 March 1958 when it had been ratified by 21 countries, including 7 with at least 1m. gross tons of shipping each. The IMCO started operations in 1959 and changed its name to the IMO in 1982.

Functions. To facilitate co-operation among governments on technical matters affecting merchant shipping, especially concerning safety at sea; to prevent and control marine pollution caused by ships; to facilitate international maritime traffic. The IMO is responsible for convening international maritime conferences and for drafting international maritime conventions. It also provides technical assistance to countries wishing to develop their maritime activities, and acts as a depositary authority for international conventions regulating maritime affairs. *The World Maritime University (WMU)*, at Malmö, Sweden, was established in 1983; the *IMO International Maritime Law Institute (IMLI)*, at Valletta, Malta and the *IMO International Maritime Academy*, at Trieste, Italy, both in 1989.

Organization. The IMO has 156 members (and 2 associate members). The Assembly, composed of all member states, normally meets every 2 years. The 32-member Council acts as governing body between sessions. There are 4 principal committees (on maritime safety, legal matters, marine environment protection and technical co-operation), which submit reports or recommendations to the Assembly through the Council, and a Secretariat. The budget for 1996–97 amounted to £36·6m.

Headquarters: 4 Albert Embankment, London, SE1 7SR, UK.
Secretary-General: William A. O'Neil (Canada).

Publications. IMO News.

INTERNATIONAL MONETARY FUND (IMF)
The International Monetary Fund was established on 27 Dec. 1945 as an independent international organization and began financial operations on 1 March 1947; its relationship with the UN is defined in an agreement of mutual co-operation which came into force on 15 Nov. 1947. The first amendment to the IMF's Articles creating the special drawing right (SDR) took effect on 28 July 1969. The second amendment took effect on 1 April 1978. The third amendment came into force on 11 Nov. 1992; it allows for the suspension of voting and related rights of a member which persists in its failure to settle its outstanding obligations to the IMF.

Aims. To promote international monetary co-operation, the expansion of international trade and exchange rate stability; to assist in the removal of exchange restrictions and the establishment of a multilateral system of payments; and to alleviate any serious disequilibrium in members' international balance of payments by making the financial resources of the IMF available to them, usually subject to economic policy conditions to ensure the revolving nature of IMF resources.

Activities. Each member of the IMF undertakes a broad obligation to collaborate with the IMF and other members to ensure orderly exchange arrangements and to promote a system of stable exchange rates. In addition, members are subject to certain obligations relating to domestic and external policies that can affect the balance of payments and the exchange rate. The IMF makes its resources available, under proper safeguards, to its members to meet short-term or medium-term payment difficulties. The first allocation of SDRs was made on 1 Jan. 1970 with 5 SDR allocations since then. SDRs totalled SDR 21,400m. in March 1998.

To enhance its balance of payments assistance to its members, the IMF established a compensatory Financing Facility on 27 Feb. 1963; temporary oil facilities in 1974 and 1975; a Trust Fund in 1976; and an Extended Fund Facility (EFF) for medium-term assistance to members with special balance of payments problems on 13 Sept. 1974. In March 1986, it established the Structural Adjustment Facility (SAF) to provide assistance to low-income countries. In Dec. 1987, it established the Enhanced Structural Adjustment Facility (ESAF) to provide further assistance to low-income countries facing high levels of indebtedness. In Aug. 1988, the Compensatory and Contingency Financing Facility was established, succeeding the Compensatory Financing Facility. The new facility provides broader protection to members pursuing IMF-supported adjustment programmes. Because of the importance of continuing concessional ESAF support, the IMF in 1996 endorsed proposals for a continuation of ESAF operations beyond the year 2000, when current ESAF resources are expected to be fully committed. There is to be an interim period of operations from 2001–04 for which new financing would be mobilized. This would be followed in 2005, or earlier, by a self-sustained ESAF. In Dec. 1997, the Supplemental Reserve Facility (SRF) was established to provide short-term assistance to countries experiencing exceptional balance of payments problems owing to a large short-term financing need resulting from a sudden disruptive loss of market confidence, reflected in pressure on the capital account and the member's reserves.

Capital Resources. In April 1997, the Interim Committee of the Fund's Board of Governors endorsed the concept of an amendment that would make the promotion of capital account liberalization one of the Fund's purposes and would give the Fund the appropriate jurisdiction over capital movements. The capital resources of the IMF comprise SDRs and currencies that the members pay under quotas calculated for them when they join the IMF. A member's quota is largely determined by its economic position relative to other members; it is also linked to their drawing rights on the IMF under both regular and special facilities, their voting power, and their share of SDR allocations. Every IMF member is required to subscribe to the IMF an amount equal to its quota. An amount not exceeding 25% of the quota has to be paid in reserve assets, the balance in the member's own currency. The members with the largest quotas are: 1st, the USA; joint 2nd, Germany and Japan; joint 4th, France and the UK.

An increase of almost 60% in IMF quotas became effective in Nov. 1992 as a result of the 9th General Review of Quotas. Quotas were not increased under the 10th General Review. In the 11th General Review, the IMF's Executive Board adopted a resolution at its 1997 annual meeting, approving a one-time equity allocation of SDRs of SDR 21,400m., which would equalize all members' ratio of SDRs to quota at 29·3%. The Board also agreed to recommend a 45% increase in IMF quotas, which would raise total quotas from SDR145,300, in Sept. 1997, to SDR 209,500m. As of Sept. 1998, 21 member countries (representing 19·53% of total current quotas) had consented to their quota increase; an 85% majority of member countries is required for the quota increase to take effect.

Borrowing Resources. The IMF is authorized under its Articles of Agreement to supplement its resources by borrowing. In Jan. 1962, a 4-year agreement was concluded with 10 industrial members (Belgium, Canada, France, Germany, Italy, Japan, Netherlands, Sweden, UK, USA) who undertook to lend the IMF up to US$6,000m. in their own currencies, if this should be needed to forestall or cope with an impairment of the international monetary system. Switzerland subsequently joined the group. These arrangements, known as the General Arrangements to Borrow (GAB), have been extended several times. In early 1983, agreement was reached to increase the credit arrangements under the GAB to SDR 17,000m.; to permit use of GAB resources in transactions with IMF members that are not GAB participants; to authorize Swiss participation; and to permit borrowing arrangements with non-participating members to be associated with the GAB. Saudi Arabia and the IMF have entered into such an arrangement under which the IMF will be able to borrow up to SDR 1,500m. to assist in financing purchases by any member for the same purpose and under the same circumstances as in the GAB. The changes became effective by 26 Dec. 1983. In view of the expected continuing high demand for IMF's resources, a doubling of borrowed resources under the GAB to SDR 34,000m. was endorsed through the development of New Arrangements to Borrow in Jan. 1997, with 25 member countries agreeing to make loans to the IMF when supplementary resources are needed to forestall or cope with an impairment of or threat to the international monetary system.

In order to oversee the compliance of members with their obligations under the Articles of Agreement, the IMF is required to exercise firm surveillance over members' exchange rate policies. In conjunction with the need for up-to-date reliable data to support its surveillance activities, it encourages member countries to make available to the public and to financial markets core financial and economic data. In April 1996, the IMF established the Special Data Dissemination Standard (SDDS) to improve access to reliable economic statistical information for member countries that have, or are seeking, access to international capital markets. In Dec. 1997, it established the General Data Dissemination Standard (GDDS), which applies to all member countries and focuses on improved production and dissemination of core economic data. Information on both are available on the IMF's website.

The IMF works with the IBRD (World Bank) to address the problems of the 41 most heavily indebted poor countries (33 in Sub-Saharan Africa) through their Initiative for the Heavily Indebted Poor Countries (HIPCs). It is designed to ensure that HIPCs with a sound track record of economic adjustment receive debt relief sufficient to help them attain a sustainable debt situation over the medium term.

Organization. The highest authority is the Board of Governors, on which each member government is represented. Normally the Governors meet once a year, and may take votes by mail or other means between meetings. The Board of Governors has delegated many of its powers to the 24 executive directors in Washington, who are appointed or elected by individual member countries or groups of countries. Each appointed director has voting power proportionate to the quota of the government he or she represents, while each elected director casts all the votes of the countries represented. The managing director is selected by the executive directors and serves as chairman of the Executive Board, but may not vote except in case of a tie. The term of office is for 5 years, but may be extended or terminated at the discretion of the executive directors. The managing director is responsible for the ordinary business of the IMF, under the direction of the executive directors, and supervises a staff of about 2,200. Under a long-standing, informal agreement, the managing director is European (while the President of the World Bank is a US national). There are 3 deputy managing directors. In Dec. 1998, the IMF had 182 members.

The *IMF Institute* is a specialized department of the IMF providing training in macroeconomic analysis and policy, and related subjects for officials of member countries, at the Fund's headquarters in Washington and at the Joint Vienna Institute (JVI). Since its establishment in 1964, the Institute has trained more than 10,900 officials from 181 countries. Courses in Washington are in Arabic, English, French and Spanish; at the JVI, in English, with Russian interpretation.

Headquarters: 700 19th St. NW, Washington, D.C., 20431. Offices in Paris and Geneva.

Website: http://www.imf.org

Managing Director: Michel Camdessus (France).

Publications. Annual Report; International Financial Statistics (monthly); *IMF Survey* (2 a month); *Balance of Payments Statistics Yearbook*; *Staff Papers* (4 a year); *IMF Economic Reviews* [of the economies of member countries]; *Direction of Trade Statistics* (quarterly); *Government Finance Statistics Yearbook; World Economic Outlook* (2 a year); *The International Monetary Fund, 1945-65: Twenty Years of International Monetary Co-operation,* 3 vols. Washington, 1969; de Vries, M. G., *The International Monetary Fund, 1966–1971: The System Under Stress,* 2 vols. Washington, 1976; *The International Monetary Fund 1972–1978: Co-operation on Trial.* 3 vols. Washington, 1985.

Further Reading

Humphreys, N. K., *Historical Dictionary of the International Monetary Fund.* Metuchen (NJ), 1994

James, H., *International Monetary Cooperation since Bretton Woods.* OUP, 1996

Salda, A. C. M., *The International Monetary Fund.* [Bibliography] Oxford and New Brunswick (NJ), 1993

INTERNATIONAL TELECOMMUNICATION UNION (ITU)

Origin. Formed from the merger, in 1932, of the Telegraph Convention (1865) and the Radiotelegraph Convention (1906) under the new name of the International Telecommunication Union, the ITU became a Specialized Agency of the UN in 1947 and is governed by a new Constitution and Convention which came into force on 1 July 1994.

Functions. To maintain and extend international co-operation for the improvement and rational use of telecommunications of all kinds, and promote and offer technical assistance to developing countries in the field of telecommunications; to promote the development of technical facilities and their most efficient operation to improve the efficiency of telecommunication services, increasing their usefulness and making them, so far as possible, generally available to the public; to harmonize the actions of nations in the attainment of these ends.

Organization. The supreme organ of the ITU is the Plenipotentiary Conference, which normally meets every 4 years. A 46-member Council, elected by the Conference, meets annually in Geneva and is responsible for ensuring the co-ordination of the 4 permanent organs at ITU headquarters: the General Secretariat; Radiocommunication Sector; Telecommunication Standardization Sector; and Telecommunication Development Sector. The Secretary-General is also elected by the Conference. ITU has 187 member countries; a further 363 scientific and technical companies, public and private operators, broadcasters and other organizations are also ITU members.

Headquarters: Place des Nations, CH-1211 Geneva 20, Switzerland.
Website: http://www.itu.ch
Secretary-General: Dr Pekka Tarjanne (Finland).

UNITED NATIONS EDUCATIONAL, SCIENTIFIC AND CULTURAL ORGANIZATION (UNESCO)

Origin. UNESCO's Constitution was signed in London on 16 Nov. 1945 by 37 countries and the Organization came into being in Nov. 1946 on the premise that: "Since wars begin in the minds of men, it is in the minds of men that the defences of peace must be constructed". In Jan. 1998, UNESCO had 187 members including the UK, which rejoined in 1997. They include 4 Associate Members with no single member status in the UN (Aruba; British Virgin Islands; Macau; Netherlands Antilles). The USA is not a member.

Aims and Activities. UNESCO's primary objective is to contribute to peace and security in the world by promoting collaboration among the nations through education, science, communication and culture in order to further universal respect for justice, the rule of the law, human rights and fundamental freedoms, affirmed for all peoples of the world by the UN Charter.

Education. Various activities support and foster national projects to renovate education systems and develop alternative educational strategies towards a goal of lifelong education for all. The 4 main areas of focus, today, are: to provide basic education for all; expand access to basic education; improve the quality of basic education; and education for the 21st century. There are regional and sub-regional offices for education in 53 countries.

Science. UNESCO seeks to promote international scientific co-operation and encourages scientific research designed to improve living conditions. Science co-operation offices have been set up in Cairo, Jakarta, Nairobi, New Delhi, Montevideo and Venice. A *Sciences in the Service of Development* programme aims to provide support to member states in the fields of higher education, advanced training and research in natural and social sciences, and in the application of these sciences to development. It focuses on questions concerning issues such as peace, human rights, youth, the management of social transformations, the human genome, and man and the biosphere.

Communication. Here, activities are geared to promoting the free flow of information, freedom of expression, press freedom, media independence and pluralism. In this way, UNESCO endeavours, by disseminating information, carrying out research and providing advice to increase the scope and quality of press, film and radio services throughout the world.

Culture. In the cultural field, UNESCO's focus areas are research on the link between culture and development, and action to conserve and protect the world's cultural inheritance, by assisting member states in studying and preserving both the physical and the non-physical heritage of their societies.

Organization. The General Conference, composed of representatives from each member state, meets biennially to decide policy, programme and budget. A 58-member Executive Board elected by the Conference meets twice a year and there is a Secretariat. In addition, national commissions act as liaison groups between UNESCO and the educational, scientific and cultural life of their own countries. The budget for 1996–97 was over US$455m.

Headquarters: UNESCO House, 7 Place de Fontenoy, 75352 Paris, France.
Website: http://www. unesco.org
Director-General: Federico Mayor (Spain).

Periodicals. Museum International (quarterly); *International Social Science Journal* (quarterly); *Impact of Science on Society* (quarterly); *Unesco Courier* (monthly); *Prospects* (quarterly); *Copyright Bulletin* (twice-yearly); *Nature and Resources* (quarterly); *Unesco Sources* (monthly); *World Education Report* (biennial); *World Science Report* (biennial).

INTERNATIONAL BUREAU OF EDUCATION (IBE)
The International Bureau of Education is a centre for information and research in the field of comparative education. It focuses on the renewal of education curricula, contents, methods and materials, with particular emphasis on human and civic values. Founded in 1925, it became an intergovernmental organization in 1929 and since 1969 has been an integral part of UNESCO.

The IBE has three main activities: (i) Educational information and documentation; (ii) Comparative research in education; (iii) Policy dialogue among ministers of education.

Since 1934, the IBE has organized the International Conference on Education (ICE), which provides a forum for debate on common concerns, to define policy agreements, strategic approaches and normative instruments to the ministers of education in all countries.

Address: C.P. 199, CH-1211 Geneva 20, Switzerland.
Website: http://www.unicc.org/ibe/
Director: Jacques Hallak.

UNITED NATIONS INDUSTRIAL DEVELOPMENT ORGANIZATION (UNIDO)
Origin. UNIDO was established by the UN General Assembly in 1966 and became the 16th UN specialized agency in 1985.

Aims. UNIDO is dedicated to promoting sustainable industrial development in countries with developing and transition economies. It harnesses the joint forces of government and the private sector to foster competitive industrial production and raise capacity; to develop international industrial partnerships and provide technical co-operation services; and to promote socially equitable and environmentally friendly industrial development. UNIDO's ultimate goal is to create a better life for people by laying the industrial foundations for long-term prosperity and economic strength.

Activities. The 1993 General Conference approved a recommendation for the reform and revitalization of the Organization. The reform process concentrated on the re-orientation of UNIDO's activities to adjust to the economic environment of the 1990s, and was completed in Dec. 1995.

In Dec. 1997, the 7th session of the General Conference endorsed the *Business Plan on the Future Role and Functions of UNIDO*, which defines future programmes and activities of the Organization. The Conference also approved the regular budget for the biennium 1998–99, reflecting the new programme priorities.

Organization. The General Conference meets every 2 years to determine policy and approve the budget. It consists of representatives of all member states. The 53-member governing body (33 members from developing countries) is the Industrial Development Board, elected for 4 years by the General Conference. The General

Conference also elects a 27-member Programme and Budget Committee for 2-year terms of office, and appoints a Director-General for 4 years.

In March 1999, UNIDO had 168 members. The USA withdrew from the Organization at the end of 1996 and Australia on 1 Jan. 1997.

Finance. UNIDO's financial resources come from regular and operational budgets, as well as contributions for technical co-operation activities. Derived from Member States' assessed contributions, the regular budget of UNIDO for 1998-99 amounts to US$129·5m. The operational budget of US$27·4m. is earned from overheads on projects implemented by UNIDO. Administrative costs represent less than 15% of the regular budget.

Technical co-operation, which in 1997 amounted to US$97·3m., is funded from various sources. These include voluntary contributions from donor countries and institutions; allocations by the United Nations Development Programme (UNDP); the Multilateral Fund for the Implementation of the Montreal Protocol on Substances that Deplete the Ozone Layer; the regular programme of technical co-operation financed from UNIDO's regular budget; and the Common Fund for Commodities.

Headquarters: POB 300, A-1400 Vienna, Austria.
Website: http://www.unido.org
Director-General: Carlos Alfredo Magariños.

Publications. International Yearbook of Industrial Statistics; UNIDO Annual Report; Emerging Technologies series; The Globalization of Industry: Implications for Developing Countries beyond 2000; Industrial Economics for Countries in Transition; Evidence from Eastern Europe and Asia Pacific; Guidelines for Infrastructure Development through BOT Projects; Guidelines for Project Evaluation; World Information Directory of Industrial Technology and Investment Support Services; Manual on Technology Transfer Negotiations; Fertilizer Manual; Pesticide Formulation.

UNIVERSAL POSTAL UNION (UPU)

Origin. The UPU was established in 1875, when the Universal Postal Convention adopted by the Postal Congress of Berne on 9 Oct. 1874 came into force. It has 189 member countries.

Functions. The aim of the UPU is to assure the organization and perfection of the various postal services, and to promote the development of international collaboration in the field. To this end, UPU members are united in a single postal territory for the reciprocal exchange of correspondence. A Specialized Agency of the UN since 1948, the UPU is governed by its Constitution, adopted in 1964 (Vienna), and subsequent protocol amendments: (1969, Tokyo; 1974, Lausanne; 1984, Hamburg; 1989, Washington; 1994, Seoul).

Organization. It is composed of a Universal Postal Congress which meets every 5 years; a 41-member Council of Administration, which meets annually and is responsible for supervising the affairs of the UPU between Congresses; a 40-member Postal Operations Council; and an International Bureau which functions as the permanent secretariat, responsible for strategic planning and programme budgeting. The budget for 1999 is 35·7m. Swiss francs.

Headquarters: Weltpoststrasse 4, 3000 Berne 15, Switzerland.
Website: http://www.upu.int
Director-General: Thomas E. Leavey (USA).

Publications. The UPU Looks to the Future: Seoul Postal Strategy, 1994; Postal Statistics (annual); *UPU Annual Report; Union Postale* (quarterly); *Universal Postal List of Localities,* 1997 (also on CD-ROM); *Post 2005: Core Business Scenarios,* 1997.

WORLD HEALTH ORGANIZATION (WHO)

Origin. An International Conference convened by the UN Economic and Social Council to consider a single health organization resulted in the adoption on 22 July 1946 of the Constitution of the World Health Organization, which came into force on 7 April 1948.

Functions. WHO's objective, as stated in the first article of the Constitution, is 'the attainment by all peoples of the highest possible level of health'. As the directing and co-ordinating authority on international health, it establishes and maintains collaboration with the UN, specialized agencies, government health administrations, professional and other groups concerned with health. The Constitution also directs WHO to assist governments to strengthen their health services; to stimulate and advance work to eradicate diseases; to promote maternal and child health, mental health, medical research and the prevention of accidents; to improve standards of teaching and training in the health professions, and of nutrition, housing, sanitation, working conditions and other aspects of environmental health. The Organization is also empowered to propose conventions, agreements and regulations, and make recommendations about international health matters; to revise the international nomenclature of diseases, causes of death and public health practices; to develop, establish and promote international standards concerning foods, biological, pharmaceutical and similar substances.

Methods of work. Co-operation in country projects is undertaken only on the request of the government concerned, through the 6 regional offices of the Organization. Worldwide technical services are made available by headquarters. Expert committees, chosen from the 55 advisory panels of experts, meet to advise the Director-General on a given subject. Scientific groups and consultative meetings are called for similar purposes. To further the education of health personnel of all categories, seminars, technical conferences and training courses are organized, and advisors, consultants and lecturers are provided. WHO awards fellowships for study to nationals of member countries.

Activities. The main thrust of WHO's activities in recent years has been towards promoting national, regional and global strategies for the attainment of the main social target of the Member States for the coming years: 'Health for All by the Year 2000', or the attainment by all citizens of the world of a level of health that will permit them to lead a socially and economically productive life. Almost all countries indicated a high level of political commitment to this goal; and guiding principles for formulating corresponding strategies and plans of action were subsequently prepared.

The 50th World Health Assembly which met in 1997 adopted numerous resolutions on public health issues. *The World Health Report, 1997: Conquering suffering, enriching humanity* focused on 'non-communicable diseases'. It warned that the human and social costs of cancer, heart disease and other chronic diseases will rise unless confronted now.

The number of cancer cases is expected to double in most countries over the next 25 years. There will be a 33% increase in lung cancers in women and a 40% increase in prostate cancers in men in European Union countries alone by 2005. The incidence of other cancers is also rising rapidly, especially in developing countries. Heart disease and stroke, the leading causes of death in richer nations, will become more common in poorer countries. Globally, diabetes will more than double by 2025, with the number of people affected rising from about 135m. to 300m., and there is likely to be a huge rise in some mental disorders, especially dementias and particularly Alzheimer's disease. Already an estimated 29m. people suffer from dementia, and at least 400m. suffer from other mental disorders ranging from mood and personality disorders to neurological conditions like epilepsy, which affects some 40m. worldwide.

These projected increases are reported to be due to a combination of factors, not least population ageing and the rising prevalence of unhealthy lifestyles. Average life expectancy at birth globally reached 65 years in 1996. It is now well over 70 years in many countries and is approaching 80 years in some. There are today an estimated 380m. people over 65 years or more. By 2020 that number is expected to rise to more than 690m.

The report warns that many countries will increasingly come under the double burden of both infectious (the focus of the 1996 World Health Report) and non-communicable diseases, and recommends that the 2 should be fought simultaneously on a global scale.

The 10 leading killer diseases in the world are: coronary heart disease, 7·2m. deaths annually; cancer (all sites), 6·2m.; cerebrovascular disease, 4·6m.; acute lower respiratory infection, 3·7m.; perinatal conditions, 3·6m.; tuberculosis, 2·9m.; chronic obstructive pulmonary disease, 2·9m.; diarrhoea and dysentery, 2·5m.; HIV/AIDS, 2·3m.; malaria, 2·1m. Tobacco-related deaths, primarily from lung cancer and circulatory disease, amount to 3m. a year. Smoking accounts for 1 in 7 cancer cases worldwide, and if the trend of increasing consumption in many countries continues, the epidemic has many more decades to run.

In response, WHO has called for an intensified and sustained global campaign to encourage healthy lifestyles and attack the main risk factors responsible for many of these diseases: unhealthy diet, inadequate physical activity, smoking and obesity.

Priorities for Action. These were summarized by the Report as follows:

1. Integration of disease-specific interventions in both physical and mental health into a comprehensive chronic disease control package that incorporates prevention, diagnosis, treatment and rehabilitation, and improved training of health professionals.

2. Fuller application of existing cost-effective methods of disease detection and management, including improved screening, taking into account the genetic diversity of individuals.

3. A major intensified but sustained global campaign to encourage healthy lifestyles, with an emphasis on the health development of children and adolescents in relation to risk factors such as diet, exercise and smoking.

4. Healthy public policies, including sustainable funding, and legislation on pricing and taxation, in support of disease prevention programmes.

5. Acceleration of research into new drugs and vaccines, and into the genetic determinants of chronic diseases.

6. Alleviation of pain, reduction of suffering and provision of palliative care for those who cannot be cured.

Other issues reported on to the Assembly included tropical diseases, violence, the sale of medical products through the Internet, persistent organic pollutants and cloning in human reproduction.

Cloning in human reproduction. The 1997 Assembly adopted a resolution affirming that the use of cloning for the replication of human individuals is ethically unacceptable and contrary to human integrity and morality. In accepting the resolution delegates recognized the need to respect the freedom of ethically acceptable scientific activity and to ensure access to the benefits of its applications.

Joint UN Programme on HIV/AIDS (UNAIDS). In 1996 the Assembly reviewed implementation of the global strategy for the prevention and control of AIDS, and progress of the Joint UN Programme on HIV/AIDS (UNAIDS), which became operational in 1996. The impact of the HIV/AIDS epidemic is seen to be expanding and intensifying, particularly in developing countries, and new resource mobilization mechanisms were called for to support countries in combating HIV/AIDS. The Assembly requested WHO to facilitate the incorporation of UNAIDS-specific policies, norms and strategies into the activities of WHO at global, regional and country levels, and to collaborate in all aspects of resource mobilization for HIV/AIDS activities.

World Health Day is observed on 7 April every year. The 1999 theme for World Health Day was Active Aging Makes the Difference; the theme for 1998 was Safe Motherhood. World No-Tobacco Day is held on 31 May each year; International Day Against Drug Abuse on 26 June; World AIDS Day on 1 Dec.

Organization. The principal organs of WHO are the World Health Assembly, the Executive Board and the Secretariat. Each of the 192 member states has the right to be represented at the Assembly, which meets annually in Geneva. The 32-member Executive Board is composed of technically qualified health experts designated by as many member states as elected by the Assembly. The Secretariat consists of technical and administrative staff headed by a Director-General, who is appointed for not more than two 5-year terms. Health activities in member countries are carried out through regional organizations which have been established in Africa (Brazzaville), South-East Asia (New Delhi), Europe (Copenhagen), Eastern Mediterranean (Alexandria) and Western Pacific (Manila). The Pan American Sanitary Bureau in Washington serves as the regional office of WHO for the Americas.

Finance. The global programme budget for 1998-99 adopted by the World Health Assembly in May 1997 was US$842·7m.

Headquarters: Avenue Appia, CH-1211 Geneva 27, Switzerland.
Website: http://www.who.int
Director-General: Gro Harlem Brundtland (Norway).

Publications. Annual Report on World Health; *Bulletin of WHO* (6 issues a year); *International Digest of Health Legislation* (quarterly); *Health and Safety Guides; International Statistical Classification of Diseases and Related Health Problems; WHO Technical Report Series; WHO AIDS Series*; *Public Health Papers; World Health Statistics Annual*; *Weekly Epidemiological Record*; *WHO Drug Information* (quarterly).

WORLD INTELLECTUAL PROPERTY ORGANIZATION (WIPO)

Origin. The roots of the World Intellectual Property Organization go back to the Paris Convention for the Protection of Industrial Property, adopted in 1883, and the Berne Convention for the Protection of Literary and Artistic Works (adopted 1886). The Convention establishing WIPO was signed at Stockholm in 1967 by 51 countries, and entered into force in April 1970. WIPO became a UN specialized agency in 1974.

Aims. To promote the protection of intellectual property throughout the world through co-operation among Member states; and to ensure administrative co-operation among the intellectual property Unions created by the Paris and Berne Conventions.

Intellectual property comprises two main branches: industrial property (inventions, trademarks and industrial designs) and copyright and neighbouring rights (literary, musical, artistic, photographic and audiovisual works).

Activities. There are three principal areas of activity: the progressive development of international intellectual property law; global protection systems and services; and co-operation for development. WIPO seeks to harmonize national intellectual property legislation and procedures; provide services for international applications for industrial property rights; exchange intellectual property information; provide training and legal and technical assistance to developing and other countries; facilitate the resolution of private intellectual property disputes; and marshal information technology as a tool for storing, accessing and using valuable intellectual property information.

New approaches to the progressive development of international intellectual property law. The development and application of international norms and standards is a fundamental part of WIPO's activities. It administers 21 treaties (15 on industrial property, 6 on copyright). With a view to making the system more responsive to change in the intellectual property domain, The Standing Committee of Member States has been formed to examine questions of substantive law or harmonization in WIPO's main fields of activity.

Global protection systems and services. The most successful and widely used treaty is the Patent Co-operation Treaty (PCT), which implements the concept of a single international patent application that is valid in many countries. Once such application is filed, an applicant has time to decide in which countries to pursue the application, thereby streamlining procedures and reducing costs. In 1997 the PCT system recorded 54,422 applications (the equivalent of nearly 3·5m. national applications for inventions). In March 1999, there were 98 countries party to the PCT.

The treaties dealing with the international registration of marks and industrial designs are, respectively, the Madrid Agreement (and its Protocol) and the Hague Agreement. In 1997, there were 19,070 registrations of marks under the Madrid System (equivalent to 220,000 national applications) and 6,223 deposits, renewals and prolongations of industrial designs under the Hague System.

Co-operation for development. On 1 Jan. 2000, many developing and other countries are due, as members of the World Trade Organization, to bring their national legislative and administrative structures into conformity with the Agreement on Trade-Related Aspects of Intellectual Property Rights (TRIPS). WIPO and WTO agreed on a joint technical co-operation initiative to provide assistance to developing countries to meet their obligations to comply with the TRIPS Agreement. This represents a major step in the international harmonization of the scope, standards and enforcement of Intellectual Property rights, and will require WIPO to provide the necessary technical assistance to the countries concerned.

The newly created WIPO Worldwide Academy co-ordinates training activities, originates new approaches and methods to expand the scope, impact and accessibility of WIPO programmes, and creates more effective training tailored for diverse-user groups.

Impact of digital technology on intellectual property law. WIPO takes a range of initiatives to tackle the implications of modern digital and communications technology for copyright and industrial property law, and in electronic commerce transcending national jurisdictions. The WIPO Arbitration and Mediation Centre was established in 1994 to provide online dispute-resolution services.

Organization. WIPO has 3 governing bodies: the General Assembly, the Conference and the Co-ordination Committee. Each treaty administered by WIPO has one or more Governing Bodies of its own, composed of representatives of the respective member states. In addition, the Paris and Berne Unions have Assemblies and Executive Committees. There are also a number of Permanent Committees, such as the Permanent Committee on Industrial Property Information. The executive head of WIPO is the Director-General, who is elected by the General Assembly. In Jan. 1999, WIPO had 171 member states, with an international staff of around 650 in 67 countries. The budget for 1998-99 was 383m. Swiss Francs, 85% of which is covered by revenue earned by the Organization's international registration and publication activities, with the other 15% coming primarily from contributions made by member states.

Official languages. Arabic, Chinese, English, French, Russian and Spanish.

   Headquarters: 34, chemin des Colombettes, 1211 Geneva 20, Switzerland.
   Website: http://www.wipo.int
   Director-General: Dr Kamil Idris (Sudan).

Periodicals. Industrial Property and Copyright (monthly, bi-monthly, in Spanish); *PCT Gazette* (weekly); *PCT Newsletter* (monthly); *International Designs Bulletin* (monthly); *WIPO Gazette of International Marks* (fortnightly); *Intellectual Property in Asia and the Pacific* (quarterly).

WORLD METEOROLOGICAL ORGANIZATION (WMO)

Origin. A 1947 (Washington) Conference of Directors of the International Meteorological Organization (est. 1873) adopted a Convention creating the World Meteorological Organization. The WMO Convention became effective on 23 March 1950 and WMO was formally established on 19 March 1951, when the first session of its Congress was convened in Paris. It was recognized as a Specialized Agency of the UN in 1951.

Functions. (1) To facilitate worldwide co-operation in the establishment of networks of stations for the making of meteorological observations as well as hydrological or other geophysical observations related to meteorology, and to promote the establishment and maintenance of meteorological centres charged with the provision of meteorological and related services; (2) to promote the establishment and maintenance of systems for the rapid exchange of meteorological and related information; (3) to promote standardization of meteorological and related observations and ensure the uniform publication of observations and statistics; (4) to further the application of meteorology to aviation, shipping, water problems, agriculture and other human activities; (5) to promote activities in operational hydrology and to further close co-operation between meteorological and hydrological services; and (6) to encourage research and training in meteorology and, as appropriate, to assist in co-ordinating the international aspects of such research and training.

Organization. WMO has 179 member states and 6 member territories responsible for the operation of their own meteorological services. Congress, which is its supreme body, meets every 4 years to approve policy, programme and budget, and adopt regulations. The Executive Council meets at least once a year to prepare studies and recommendations for Congress, and supervises the implementation of Congress resolutions and regulations. It has 36 members, comprising the President and 3 Vice-Presidents, as well as the Presidents of the 6 Regional Associations (Africa, Asia, South America, North and Central America, South-West Pacific, Europe), whose task is to co-ordinate meteorological activity within their regions, and 26 members elected in their personal capacity. There are 8 Technical Commissions composed of experts nominated by members of WMO, whose remit includes the following areas: basic systems, climatology, instruments and methods of observation, atmospheric sciences, aeronautical meteorology, agricultural meteorology, hydrology, marine meteorology. A permanent Secretariat is maintained in Geneva, and there are 3 regional offices for Africa, Asia and the Pacific, and the Americas. The budget for 1996-99 was 255m. Swiss francs.

Headquarters: Case Postale 2300, CH-1211 Geneva 2, Switzerland. *Secretary-General:* Prof. G. O. P. Obasi (Nigeria).

Publications. WMO Bulletin. (quarterly); *WMO Annual Report.*

OTHER ORGANS RELATED TO THE UN

INTERNATIONAL ATOMIC ENERGY AGENCY (IAEA)

Origin. An intergovernmental agency, the IAEA was established in 1957 under the aegis of the UN and reports annually to the General Assembly. Its Statute was approved on 26 Oct. 1956 at a conference at UN Headquarters.

Functions. To accelerate and enlarge the contribution of atomic energy to peace, health and prosperity throughout the world; and to ensure that assistance provided by it or at its request or under its supervision or control is not used in such a way as to further any military purpose. In addition, under the terms of the Non-Proliferation Treaty, the Treaty of Tlatelolco, the Treaty of Rarotonga, the Pelindaba Treaty and the Bangkok Treaty: to verify states' obligation to prevent diversion of nuclear fissionable material from peaceful uses to nuclear weapons or other nuclear explosive devices.

Activities. The IAEA gives advice and technical assistance to developing countries on nuclear power development, nuclear safety, radioactive waste management, legal aspects of atomic energy use, and prospecting for and exploiting nuclear raw materials. In addition, it promotes the use of radiation and isotopes in agriculture, industry, medicine and hydrology through expert services, training courses and fellowships, grants of equipment and supplies, research contracts, scientific meetings and publications. During 1998 there were over 1,000 operational projects for technical co-operation. These activities involved 3,610 expert assignments while 1,718 persons received training abroad.

Safeguards are the technical means applied by the IAEA to verify that nuclear equipment or materials are used exclusively for peaceful purposes. IAEA safeguards cover more than 95% of civilian nuclear installations outside the 5 nuclear-weapon states (China, France, Russia, UK and USA). These 5 nuclear-weapon states have concluded agreements with the Agency which permit the application of IAEA safeguards to all their nuclear activities. Installations in non-nuclear-weapon states under safeguards or containing safeguarded material at 1 Jan. 1998 were 194 power reactors, 159 research reactors and critical assemblies, 13 conversion plants, 42 fuel fabrication plants, 6 reprocessing plants, 13 enrichment plants, and 359 other installations. In 1997, 2,499 inspections were conducted under the safeguard agreements at 931 nuclear installations in 63 non-nuclear-weapon states, and 3,038 samples of uranium and plutonium were analyzed. By Jan. 1998 a total of 221 safeguard agreements were in force with 137 states. A programme designed to prevent and combat illicit trafficking of nuclear weapons came into force in April 1996.

Organization. The Statute provides for an annual General Conference, a 35-member Board of Governors and a Secretariat headed by a Director-General. The IAEA had 128 member states in Nov. 1998.

There are also research laboratories in Austria and Monaco. *The International Centre for Theoretical Physics* was established in Trieste, in 1964, and is operated jointly by UNESCO and the IAEA.

Headquarters: Vienna International Centre, PO Box 100, A-1400 Vienna, Austria.
Website: http://www.iaea.or.at/worldatom
Director-General: Mohamed El Baradei (Egypt).

Publications. Annual Report; IAEA Bulletin (quarterly); *IAEA Newsbriefs* (bi-monthly); *IAEA Yearbook; INIS Atomindex* (twice monthly); *INIS Reference Series; Legal Series; Nuclear Fusion* (monthly); *Nuclear Safety Review* (annual); *Technical Directories; Technical Reports Series.*

INTERNATIONAL SEABED AUTHORITY (ISA)

The ISA is an autonomous international organization established under the UN Convention on the Law of the Sea (UNCLOS) of 1982 and the 1994 Agreement relating to the implementation of Part XI of the above Convention. It came into existence on 16 Nov. 1994 and became fully operational in June 1996.

Following its initial financing from the UN budget, its administrative expenses were to be met by assessed contributions from its members. Membership currently numbers 130 and the budget for 1998 was US$4·7m.

The Convention on the Law of the Sea covers almost all ocean space and its uses: navigation and overflight, resource exploration and exploitation, conservation and pollution, fishing and shipping. It entitles coastal states and inhabited islands to proclaim a 200-mile exclusive economic zone or continental shelf (which may be larger). Its 320 Articles and 9 Annexes constitute a guide for behaviour by states in the world's oceans, defining maritime zones, laying down rules for drawing sea boundaries, assigning legal rights, duties and responsibilities to States, and providing machinery for the settlement of disputes.

Organization. The Assembly, consisting of representatives from all member States, is the supreme organ. The 36-member Council, elected by the Assembly, includes the 4 largest importers or consumers of seabed minerals, 4 largest investors in seabed minerals, 4 major exporters of the same, 6 developing countries representing special interests and 18 members from all the geographical regions. The Council is the executive organ of the Authority. There are also two subsidiary bodies: the Legal and Technical Commission (22 experts) and the Finance Committee (15 experts). The Secretariat serves all the bodies of the Authority and under the 1994 Agreement is in charge of the Enterprise organ (until such time as it starts to operate independently of the Secretariat). The Enterprise is the organ through which the ISA carries out deep seabed activities directly or through joint ventures.

Activities. The ISA is currently finalizing rules and regulations governing the exploration of polymetallic nodules (the Mining Code). Upon adoption of the Mining Code, it will issue contracts to seven registered pioneer investors who have submitted plans of work for deep seabed exploration. These include: the government of India;

the Institut Français de Recherche pour l'Exploitation de la Mer (IFREMER) and Association Française pour l'Etude de la Recherche des Nodules (AFERNOD); Deep Ocean Resources Development Co. Ltd (DORD), Japan; Yuzhmorgeologiya (Russian Federation); China Ocean Minerals Research and Development Association (COMRA); Interoceanmetal Joint Organization (IOM) Bulgaria, Cuba, Czech Republic, Poland, Russian Federation and Slovakia; and the government of the Republic of Korea.

In 1998 the ISA organized a workshop in China to develop guidelines for the assessment of possible environmental impacts arising from the exploration of polymetallic nodules. Two other workshops are envisaged: one on the technologies for exploration and exploitation and for the protection of the environment, in 1999; the second on the available knowledge on mineral resources other than polymetallic nodules, in 2000. The Authority is also developing a database on mineral resources of the seabed (POLYDAT).

The *International Tribunal for the Law of the Sea (ITLOS)*, founded in Oct. 1996 and based in Hamburg, adjudicates on disputes with respect to the ISA's activities. It comprises 21 judges elected by signatories from 5 world regional blocs: 5 each from Africa and Asia; 4 from Western Europe and North America; 4 from Latin America; and 3 from Eastern Europe. Judges serve for 9 years, but 7 of the inaugural judges will serve for 3 years only and another 7 will serve for 6. Disputing parties may also take their case to the International Court of Justice in The Hague, or to a temporary arbitration tribunal.

Headquarters: 14-20 Port Royal St., Kingston, Jamaica.
Secretary-General: Satya N. Nandan (Fiji Islands, elected 1996).
Website: http://www.isa.org.jm

Publications. Handbook 1998; plus selected decisions and documents from the Authority's first three sessions.

WORLD TRADE ORGANIZATION (WTO)

Origin. The WTO is founded on the General Agreement on Tariffs and Trade (GATT), which entered into force on 1 Jan. 1948. Its 23 original signatories were members of a Preparatory Committee appointed by the UN Economic and Social Council to draft the charter for a proposed International Trade Organization. Since this charter was never ratified, the General Agreement remained the only international instrument laying down trade rules. In Dec. 1993, there were 111 contracting parties, and a further 22 countries applying GATT rules on a *de facto* basis. On 15 April 1994, trade ministers of 123 countries signed the Final Act of the GATT Uruguay Round of negotiations at Marrakesh, bringing the WTO into being on 1 Jan. 1995. As of Nov. 1998, the WTO had 132 members.

The object of the Act is the liberalization of world trade. By it, member countries undertake to apply fair trade rules covering commodities, services and intellectual property. It provides for the lowering of tariffs on industrial goods and tropical products; the abolition of import duties on a variety of items; the progressive abolition of quotas on garments and textiles; the gradual reduction of trade-distorting subsidies and import barriers; and agreements on intellectual property and trade in services. Members are required to accept the results of the Uruguay Round talks in their entirety, and subscribe to all the WTO's agreements and disciplines. There are no enforcement procedures, however; decisions are ultimately reached by consensus.

Functions. The WTO is the legal and institutional foundation of the multilateral trading system. Surveillance of national trade policies is an important part of its work. At the centre of this is the *Trade Policy Review Mechanism (TPRM)*, agreed by Ministers in 1994 (Article III of the Marrakesh Agreement). The TPRM was broadened in 1995 when the WTO came into being, to cover services trade and intellectual property. Its principal objective is to facilitate the smooth functioning of the multilateral trading system by enhancing the transparency of members' trade policies. All members are subject to review under the TPRM, which mandates that 4 members with the largest share of world trade (European Union, USA, Japan, Canada) be reviewed every 2 years; the next 16, every 4 years; and others every 6, with a longer period able to be fixed for the least-developed members. Also, in 1994, flexibility of up to 6 months was introduced into the review cycles, and in 1996, it was agreed that every second review of each of the first 4 trading entities should be an interim review. Reviews are conducted by the Trade Policy Review Body (TPRB) on the basis of a policy statement by the member under review and a report by economists in the Secretariat's Trade Policy Review Division.

The *International Trade Centre* (since 1968 operated jointly with the United Nations through UNCTAD) was established by GATT in 1964 to provide information and training on export markets and marketing techniques, and thereby to assist the trade of developing countries. In 1984 the Centre became an executing agency of the UN Development Programme, responsible for carrying out UNDP-financed projects related to trade promotion.

Organization. A 2-yearly ministerial meeting is the ultimate policy-making body. The 132-member General Council has some 30 subordinate councils and committees. The *Dispute Settlement Body* was set up to deal with disputes between countries. Appeals against its verdicts are heard by a 7-member *Appellate Body*. In 1997, it was composed of representatives of Egypt, European Union, Japan, New Zealand, Philippines, USA and Uruguay. Dispute panels may be set up *ad hoc*, and objectors to their ruling may appeal to the Appellate Body whose decision is virtually binding. Refusal to comply at this stage results in the application of trade sanctions. Each appeal is heard by 3 of the Appellate Body members. Before cases are heard by dispute panels, there is a 60-day consultation period. The previous GATT Secretariat now serves the WTO, which has no resources of its own other than its operating budget. The budget for 1997 was 116m. Swiss francs.

Headquarters: Centre William Rappard, 154 rue de Lausanne, CH-1211 Geneva 21, Switzerland.
Website: http://www.wto.org
Director-General: Renato Ruggiero (Italy).

Publications. Annual Report; International Trade: Trends and Statistics (annual); *WTO Focus* (10 a year).

Further Reading
Croome, J., *Reshaping the World Trading System.* WTO, 1996
Preeg, E., *Traders in a Brave New World.* Chicago Univ. Press, 1996

NORTH ATLANTIC TREATY ORGANIZATION (NATO)

Origin and History. On 4 April 1949 the foreign ministers of Belgium, Canada, Denmark, France, Iceland, Italy, Luxembourg, the Netherlands, Norway, Portugal, the UK and the USA signed the North Atlantic Treaty, establishing the *North Atlantic Alliance.* In 1952, Greece and Turkey acceded to the Treaty; in 1955 came the Federal Republic of Germany; in 1982 Spain; in 1999 the Czech Republic, Hungary and Poland, bringing the total to 19 member nations.

Functions. The Alliance was established as a defensive political and military alliance of independent countries in accordance with the terms of the UN Charter. It provides common security for its members through co-operation and consultation in political, military and economic as well as scientific and other non-military fields. The Alliance links the security of North America to that of Europe. NATO is the organization which enables the goals of the Alliance to be implemented.

Reform and Transformation of the Alliance. Following the demise of the Warsaw Pact in 1991, and the improved relations with Russia, NATO has undertaken a fundamental transformation of structures and policies to meet the new security challenges in Europe. Attention has focused in particular on the need to reinforce the political role of the Alliance.

An essential component of this transformation has been the establishment of close security links with the states of Central and Eastern Europe and those of the former USSR through the North Atlantic Co-operation Council (NACC), established in Dec. 1991 as an integral part of NATO's new Strategic Concept, which was adopted by heads of state and government at a summit in Rome earlier that year.

The Partnership for Peace Programme. The PfP builds on the momentum of co-operation created by the North Atlantic Co-operation Council. It was launched at the 1994 Brussels Summit and is expanding and intensifying political and military co-operation throughout Europe. Its core objectives are: the facilitation of transparency in national defence planning and budgeting processes; democratic control of defence forces; members' maintenance of capability and readiness to contribute to operations under the authority of the UN; development of co-operative military relations with NATO (joint planning, training and exercises) in order to strengthen participants' ability to undertake missions in the fields of peacekeeping, search and rescue, and humanitarian operations; development, over the longer term, of forces better able to operate with those of NATO member forces. NATO will consult with any active Partner which perceives a direct threat to its territorial integrity, political independence or security; and active participation in the Partnership is to play an important role in the process of NATO's expansion.

PfP has been a key factor in promoting the spirit of practical co-operation and commitment to the democratic principles which underpin the Alliance. One of the most tangible aspects of the PfP has been the holding of joint peacekeeping exercises. PfP exercises take place on a regular basis in both NATO and Partner countries. A large number of nationally sponsored exercises in the spirit of PfP have also been set up. In 1998 NATO had 27 PfP partners: Albania, Armenia, Austria, Azerbaijan, Belarus, Bulgaria, Czech Republic, Estonia, Finland, Georgia, Hungary, Kazakhstan, Kyrgyzstan, Latvia, Lithuania, Macedonia, Malta, Moldova, Poland, Romania, Russia, Slovakia, Slovenia, Sweden, Turkmenistan, Ukraine and Uzbekiston. Many of these countries have accepted the Alliance's invitation to send liaison officers to permanent facilities at NATO Headquarters in Brussels and to the Partnership Co-ordination Cell in Mons, Belgium, where the Supreme Headquarters Allied Powers Europe (SHAPE) is located.

Other key reforms undertaken include a reduced and more flexible force structure, development of increased co-ordination and co-operation with other international institutions (EU, UN, WEU), implementation of the concept of Combined Joint Task Forces (CJTFs), development of the European Security and Defence Identity (ESDI), and the agreement to make NATO's assets and experience available to support international peace enforcement operations.

In 1997, Allied Foreign and Defence Ministers launched a wide range of enhancement measures to PfP, which have strengthened it in political, security, military and institutional fields. The establishment of the Euro-Atlantic Partnership Council (EAPC) as a new co-operative mechanism replacing the former 44-member North Atlantic Co-operation Council (NACC) was itself a significant enhancement of the consultation element in PfP.

In Jan. 1994, NATO heads of state and government welcomed the Maastricht Treaty which allows for the development of a common European foreign policy to strengthen the European Pillar of Combined Joint Task Forces (CJTFs) and the separable capabilities of NATO and the WEU. At the meeting of NATO Foreign Ministers in Berlin in June 1996, agreement was reached on the implementation of CJTF policy. The agreement will facilitate NATO's new missions in crisis management and peace support operations by providing the flexibility needed to deploy at short notice forces specifically tailored to a particular contingency. The agreement also enables CJTFs to be made available for operations undertaken by the WEU, and represents a decisive and effective step towards the emergence of the new European Security and Defence Identity (ESDI) within the Alliance.

NATO's military capabilities and its adaptability to include forces of non-NATO countries were decisive factors in the Alliance's role in implementing the Bosnian Peace Agreement. Following the signing of the Agreement in Paris on 14 Dec. 1995, and on the basis of the UN Security Council's Resolution 1031, NATO commenced implementation of the military aspects of the accord through the NATO-led multinational force, the Implementation Force (IFOR), under an operation code-named Joint Endeavour. Its task was to help the parties implement the peace accord to which they had freely agreed and create a secure environment for civil and economic reconstruction. IFOR in Bosnia was the largest-ever military operation undertaken by the Alliance.

In March 1999, following the collapse of negotiations with President Milošević of Yugoslavia on a settlement to the Kosovan crisis, NATO forces launched a series of attacks on Serb military targets.

Enlargement. In Dec. 1994, NATO foreign ministers initiated a study on enlargement, which was followed by intensified individual dialogues with interested partner countries and by an analysis of the relevant factors associated with the admission of new members. The conclusion was that, subject to agreed criteria, the accession of new members would enhance security and extend stability throughout the Euro-Atlantic area.

On 27 May 1997, in Paris, NATO and Russia signed the Founding Act on Mutual Relations, Co-operation and Security, committing them to build together a lasting peace in the Euro-Atlantic area, and establishing a new forum for consultations and co-operation called the NATO-Russia Permanent Joint Council.

Two days later, in Sintra, Portugal, a NATO-Ukraine charter was drawn up and initialled, to be signed in Madrid the following July. At the same time, Foreign Ministers agreed to enhance their dialogue, begun in 1995, with 6 countries of the Mediterranean (Egypt, Israel, Jordan, Mauritania, Morocco, Tunisia), and a new committee, the Mediterranean Co-operation Group was established to take the Mediterranean Dialogue forward.

At the July 1997 meeting of Heads of State and Government in Madrid it was decided to invite 3 countries (Czech Republic, Hungary and Poland) to begin accession negotiations. On 16 Nov. 1997, 85·6% of Hungarians endorsed that initiative and voted in favour of joining NATO. By Dec. 1997, the 3 had signed accession agreements, and subsequently joined NATO early in 1999.

Organization. The North Atlantic Council (NAC) is the highest decision-making body and forum for consultation within the Atlantic Alliance. It is composed of Permanent Representatives of all 19 member countries meeting together at least once a week. The NAC also meets at higher levels involving foreign ministers or heads of state or government, but it has the same authority and powers of decision-making, and its decisions have the same status and validity at whatever level it meets. All decisions are taken on the basis of consensus, reflecting the collective will of all member governments. The NAC is the only body within the Atlantic Alliance which derives its authority explicitly from the North Atlantic Treaty. The NAC has responsibility under the Treaty for setting up subsidiary bodies. Committees and planning groups have since been created to support the work of the NAC or to assume responsibility in specific fields such as defence planning, nuclear planning and military matters.

The *Military Committee* is responsible for making recommendations to the Council and the Defence Planning Committee on military matters and for supplying guidance to the Allied Commanders. Composed of the Chiefs-of-Staff of member countries (Iceland, which has no military forces, may be represented by a civilian), the Committee is assisted by an International Military Staff. It meets at Chiefs-of-Staff level at least twice a year but remains in permanent session at the level of national military representatives. The area covered by the North Atlantic Treaty is divided into 2 commands: European and the Atlantic.

Finance. The co-ordination of military plans and defence expenditures rests on detailed and comparative analysis of the capabilities of member countries. In 1997, the cost of enlargement sparked a potentially damaging dispute between the USA and

European members of the Alliance following Pentagon estimates that the cost would be in the region of US$27,000–35,000m. over a 12-year period. Later assessments, taking into account the fact that Britain, France and Germany are already engaged in improving and increasing the mobility of their rapid-reaction or crisis forces, reduced the estimate to current members to US$1,300m. over 10 years, with the cost of improved military capability in line with NATO standards in new member countries being the responsibility of new members.

Under the terms of the Partnership for Peace strategy, partner countries undertake to make available the necessary personnel, assets, facilities and capabilities to participate in the programme, and share the financial cost of any military exercises in which they participate.

Headquarters: NATO, 1110 Brussels, Belgium.
Website: http://www.nato.int
Secretary-General: Javier Solana (Spain).

Publications. NATO Basic Fact Sheets; NATO Facts and Figures; NATO Handbook; NATO Review (6 a year).

Further Reading
Carr, F. and Infantis, K., *NATO in the New European Order.* London, 1996
Cook, D., *The Forging of an Alliance.* London, 1989
Heller, F. H. and Gillingham, J. R. (eds.) *NATO: the Founding of the Atlantic Alliance and the Integration of Europe.* London, 1992
Smith, J. (ed.) *The Origins of NATO.* Exeter Univ. Press, 1990
Williams, P., *North Atlantic Treaty Organization* [Bibliography]. Oxford and New Brunswick (NJ), 1994

BANK FOR INTERNATIONAL SETTLEMENTS (BIS)

Origin. Founded in 1930 to settle the question of German First World War reparations, the BIS now functions as the central banks' bank. Its assets are owned by 45 central banks.

Aims. To promote co-operation between central banks; provide facilities for international financial operations, monetary and economic research; and act as agent or trustee in international financial settlements.

Finance. The authorized share capital of the Bank is 1,500m. gold francs, divided into 600,000 shares of equal nominal value (2,500 gold francs per share), and at the close of the financial year, in 1998, 517,165 shares were in issue. In 1998, it held US$104,900m. (about 7% of world foreign exchange reserves) on behalf of some 120 central banks and international financial institutions.

Organization and Membership. The 17-member Board of Directors consists of the governors of the central banks of the following member countries: Belgium, Canada, France, Germany, Italy, Japan, the Netherlands, Sweden, Switzerland, the UK and the USA. The Chairman of the Board acts as President.

3 Standing Committees operate within the BIS: the Basle Committee on Banking Supervision (the Basle Committee); Committee on the Global Financial System (CFGS); Committee on Payment and Settlement Systems (CPSS); and a number of specialized Groups have been set up such as the Group of Experts on Monetary and Economic Databank Questions, and the Co-ordinating Service for Central Banks and International Organizations.

Since Jan. 1998 the BIS has hosted the Secretariat of the International Association of Insurance Supervisors (IAIS). The Secretariat operates in full independence of the BIS but has its offices at the Bank.

The Joint Year 2000 Council, comprising members nominated by the Basle Committee, CPSS, IAIS and the International Organization of Securities Commissions (IOSCO) and supported by the CPSS Secretariat, is also located at the BIS. It was formed in April 1998 to maintain a high level of attention within the supervisory community and to support and encourage private-sector efforts with regard to the Year 2000 issue.

The Financial Stability Institute, a joint initiative of the BIS and the Basle Committee on Banking Supervision, was set up in 1998 in response to the need to strengthen financial systems worldwide. Interaction between the private sector, central banks and supervisory authorities will play an important role in the Institute's activities.

As at 31 March 1998, the Bank's balance sheet stood at 62·5bn. gold francs (US$124,800m.), with funds (capital and reserves) at 2·6bn. gold francs (US$5,200m.).

The BIS has had a long and close association with the Group of Ten (G10) and participates at G10 meetings.

Headquarters: Centralbahnplatz 2, 4002 Basle, Switzerland.
Website: http://www.bis.org
Chairman: Urban Bäckström (Sweden).
Representative Office for Asia and the Pacific: 8th Floor, 3 Garden Road, Central, Hong Kong SAR, People's Republic of China.

Further Reading
Deane, M. and Pringle, R., *The Central Banks.* London and New York, 1995
Fleming, *Who's Who in Central Banking.* London, 1997
Goodhart, C. A. E., *The Central Bank and the Financial System.* London, 1995

ORGANISATION FOR ECONOMIC CO-OPERATION AND DEVELOPMENT (OECD)

Origin. Founded in 1961 to replace the Organisation for European Economic Co-operation (OEEC), which was linked to the Marshall Plan and was established in 1948. The change of title marks the Organisation's altered status and functions: with the accession of Canada and USA as full members, it ceased to be a purely European body, and at the same time added development aid to the list of its priorities. The aims of the organization are to promote policies designed to achieve the highest sustainable economic growth and employment and a rising standard of living in Member countries, while maintaining financial stability, and thus to contribute to the development of the world economy; to contribute to sound economic expansion in Member as well as non-member countries in the process of economic development; and to contribute to the expansion of world trade on a multilateral, non-discriminatory basis in accordance with international obligations.

Members. Australia, Austria, Belgium, Canada, Czech Republic, Denmark, Finland, France, Germany, Greece, Hungary, Iceland, Ireland, Italy, Japan, Korea (Republic of), Luxembourg, Mexico, Netherlands, New Zealand, Norway, Poland, Portugal, Spain, Sweden, Switzerland, Turkey, UK and USA.

Activities. The OECD's main fields of programming in 1999 were: economic policy; statistics; energy; development co-operation; sustainable development; public management; international trade; financial, fiscal and enterprise affairs; food, agriculture and fisheries; territorial development; environment; science, technology and industry; education, employment, labour and social affairs.

Relations with non-member countries. The *Centre for Co-operation with Non-Members (CCNM)* was established in Jan. 1998 when the OECD's *Centre for Co-operation* with Economies in Transition (CCET) was merged with the Liaison and Co-ordination *Unit (LCU)*. The CCNM, in combining the functions of these two entities, serves as the focal point for the development of policy dialogue between the OECD and non-member economies.

The CNNM manages multicountry thematic, regional and country programmes. The Emerging Market Economy Forum (EMEF), the Transition Economy Programme (TEP) and the Special Programme on financial instability in East Asia provide the framework for these programmes. The programmes are linked to the core generic work areas of the Organisation, such as trade and investment, taxation, labour market, social policies and the environment. Country and regional programmes, with specially focused dialogue and assistance, are in place for Bulgaria, China, Romania, Russia, the Slovak Republic, Slovenia, South America and the Baltic States.

Relations with developing countries. The OECD's Development Assistance Committee (DAC) is the principal body through which the Organisation deals with issues related to co-operation with developing countries and is one of the key forums in which the major bilateral donors work together to increase the effectiveness of their common effort to support sustainable development. Guided by the 'development partnership strategy' (OECD, 1996), the DAC's mission is to foster co-ordinated, integrated, effective and adequately financed international efforts in support of sustainable economic and social development. In addition, the Development Centre researches social and economic issues in the developing world and the Club du Sahel acts as a forum between the countries of West Africa and OECD assistance agencies.

Relations with other international organizations. Under a protocol signed at the same time as the OECD Convention, the European Commission generally takes part in the work of the OECD. EFTA may also send representatives to attend OECD meetings. Formal relations exist with a number of other international organizations, including the ILO, FAO, IMF, IBRD, UNCTAD, IAEA and the Council of Europe. A few non-governmental organizations have been granted consultative status enabling them to discuss subjects of common interest and be consulted in a particular field by the relevant OECD Committee or its officers, notably the Business and Industry Advisory Committee to the OECD (BIAC) and the Trade Union Advisory Committee (TUAC).

Organization. The governing body of OECD is the Council, on which each member country is represented. It meets from time to time (usually once a year) at the level of government ministers, with the chairmanship at ministerial level being rotated among member governments. The Council also meets regularly at official level, when it comprises the Secretary-General (chairman) and the Permanent Representatives to OECD (ambassadors who head resident diplomatic missions). It is responsible for all questions of general policy and may establish subsidiary bodies as required to achieve the aims of the organization. Decisions and recommendations of the Council are adopted by agreement of all its members.

The Council is assisted by an Executive Committee which prepares its work and is also called upon to carry out specific tasks where necessary. Apart from its regular meetings, the Committee meets occasionally in special sessions attended by senior governments officials. The greater part of the work of the OECD is prepared and carried out by about 200 specialized bodies (Committees, Working Parties, etc). All members are normally represented on these bodies, except those of a restricted nature. Delegates are usually officials coming either from the capitals of member states or from the Permanent Delegations to the OECD. They are serviced by an International Secretariat headed by the OECD Secretary-General. Funding is by contributions from member states, based on a formula related to their size and economy.

3 other bodies are part of the OECD system: the International Energy Agency (IEA), the Nuclear Energy Agency (NEA) and the Centre for Educational Research and Innovation (CERI).

Headquarters: 2 rue André Pascal, 75775 Paris Cedex 16, France.
Website: http://www.oecd.org
Secretary-General: Donald J. Johnston (Canada).
Deputy Secretaries-General: Joanna R. Shelton (USA), Kumiharu Shigehara (Japan), Thorvald Moe (Norway), Herwig Schogl (Germany).

Publications. OECD Policy Briefs (10 a year); *Environmental Performance Reviews* (by country); *The Agricultural Outlook 1997-2001* (annual); *Energy Balances* (quarterly); *Financial Market Trends* (3 a year); *Foreign Trade Statistics* (monthly); *Main Developments in Trade* (annual); *Main Economic Indicators* (monthly); *Microfinance for the Poor?; OECD Economic Outlook* (2 a year); *OECD Economic Surveys* (annual, by country); *OECD The Employment Outlook* (annual); *Oil, Gas, Coal and Electricity Statistics* (quarterly statistics); *Quarterly Labour Force Statistics; Education at a Glance 1997, OECD Indicators; The Future of Food: Long-term Prospects for the Agro-Food Sector; The World in 2020; From War to Wealth: 50 Years of Innovation.*

Further Reading

Blair, D. J., *Trade Negotiations in the OECD: Structures, Institutions and States.* London, 1993

A CAPITAL FOR EUROPE

Barry Turner

Fast forward twenty, maybe thirty years. The European Union has progressed from a hands-off association of neighbouring countries to a fully-fledged United States of Europe. The system of government is a mélange of the US and German models with the old nation states retaining control over essentially regional matters including all the social services. A central administration, the real power centre, watched over by the European Parliament is based in .... Well, where is it based?

If the Europhile's dream is realised (and even the sceptics acknowledge it as an odds-on possibility) it will need a metropolitan focus. Current wisdom would nominate Brussels. Nearly all that is presently essential to the working of the European Union is already based there. But in its European guise, the city is essentially a weak compromise between German and French aspirations. Notwithstanding the superb quality of its restaurants (better than Paris, say the gourmets) Brussels still has a provincial feel about it. Then, looking ahead to one Europe, Brussels is likely to lose status as Belgium splits into its French and Flemish sectors, each having its own regional government within the European framework.

Strasbourg is even less likely to measure up to its European pretensions. With their triumph over the Commission, MEPs are getting a taste for genuine parliamentary democracy. But once we have a European assembly in more than name, this charming yet unexciting border city will fade from the political scene.

The culmination of European unity will need a capital with a recognisable face. Paris has many of the essential qualities including a universally respected cultural tradition. But Paris is too French to be properly European. The enduring attractions of the city cannot disguise an underlying hostility towards outsiders. Parisians are keen Europeans as long as they call the shots.

London? A world class city without question and one that is not too full of self regard to resist change. But London is on the edge of Europe. So too, it may be argued, is Washington on the edge of the United States. The difference, of course, is that Washington set the pace for the American Union while London has consistently dragged its feet over Europe. There is no reason to doubt the Blair government's eagerness to re-establish Britain's European credentials. Even so, the weight of post-war antipathy towards Europe puts London out of the running.

Others are disqualified by a tradition of erratic politics (Rome, Athens), relative inexperience in democratic management (Madrid, Lisbon) or a reluctance to take on the job (Stockholm, Copenhagen, The Hague). Dublin might appeal (Ireland is, after all, a notable beneficiary of EU largesse) but not while Belfast remains an aggravation.

That leaves Berlin. Those of a certain age will be shocked at the idea. Berlin as the capital of Europe? Isn't that why two great wars were fought, to prevent such a thing happening? But the days of the Kaiser and the Fuhrer are long past. Post-1945 Germany is Europe's success story. The democracy created by the Federal Republic proved itself as the begetter of a succession of enlightened leaders. Social welfare went hand in hand with economic prosperity.

The current fashion is to belie Germany as a lumbering giant in drastic need of rejuvenation. But this is the same Germany that absorbed the costs of reunification. It was not achieved without pain. It came as no surprise to find that the Communists had left behind them not so much a workers' paradise as a workers' nightmare. But the miracle is that reunification was achieved at all.

So what about Berlin?

Its geographical advantage is undeniable. If not quite at the centre of the Union it soon will be as Hungary, Poland and other countries to the East sign up for membership. Berlin is a cosmopolitan city, well accustomed to coping with English, the only language to qualify as the *lingua franca* of Europe. The link with the US is important here. Britain prides herself on the 'special relationship' but Germany's handshake across the Atlantic is every bit as firm and has been so ever since the late forties when America decided that free market Germany was better able than socialist Britain to lead the economic revival of Europe. Also, of course, Berlin has a symbolic significance for Americans as a beacon of democracy in the dark days of the Cold War.

A CAPITAL FOR EUROPE

High school students of middle America may not know much of Hitler (or Churchill for that matter) but they are able to tell you about the Berlin airlift of 1948-49 when some 280,000 flights carried 2 million tons of supplies to the beleaguered western sector. They also know that President Kennedy promised to stand by the city come what may, a pledge that was reinforced by the ugly reality of the Berlin Wall. Such collective memories, let it not be forgotten, are the stuff of practical diplomacy.

Berlin is a new city built on old foundations. First impressions are of glass and concrete, generously landscaped. (Berlin sprawls. Spread over 39 square miles, its area is six times that of Paris.) Starting with a pile of rubble in 1945, Berliners acquired a passion for building and rebuilding. They are still at it today, their vigour renewed by the need to wipe clean the Communist desecration of much of the east side and to make ready for the imminent restoration of the city as host to the government of a united Germany.

And that is the excitement of Berlin. It is taking shape before your eyes. There may be arguments as to the quality of the architecture (traditional it is not) and the planners' scale of priorities but for the visitor there is the ever present sensation of history in the making.

Reconstruction has opened the way to new ideas, maybe even a return to the glory days of the 1920s when Berlin was synonymous with modernism. The arts thrive in old East Berlin north of Unter den Linden where the cafes and bars are crowded with young people who feel themselves part of a renaissance. Potsdamer Platz, once the hub of Berlin, later, with the Wall slicing its centre, the symbol of divided Germany, now regeneration made manifest in a frenzy of construction, has attracted the world's leading architects to match their powers of invention.

Recent history may count against Berlin. The discovery by construction workers of a bunker used by Joseph Goebbels prompted the acid comment that the trouble with burying the past is that every now and then someone comes along and digs it up again. It came as a shock to Berliners that their bid to host the 2000 Olympics was sunk by the weighty image of 1936 when the Games were turned into an instrument of Nazi propaganda.

But the city should not be judged purely by association. In 1932, when the Nazis became the biggest single party in the Reichstag, Berlin was alone in resisting the trend. Three out of four Berliners voted against Hitler. Their traditional and deep-rooted irreverence for authority—especially when dressed up in uniform—also explains why Bismark disliked the place so intensely, refusing ever to buy a home there.

Much will depend on how Berlin adapts to its role as capital of a united Germany. The costs of updating the infrastructure have been huge. After reunification it was found that the sewage system on the east side was near collapse, that electricity supply was dependent on seventy-year-old equipment and that 500 miles of gas piping needed to be replaced. There was only one telephone for every ten people. Closing down uneconomic industries has pushed up the unemployment rate while borrowing to support and retrain the jobless has inflated the budget deficit.

But in the context of Berlin's eventful history, no crisis is beyond solution. Having measured up to its latest challenge, Berlin should be better equipped than any other city to take on the European mantle.

Siren voices will warn of Germany hegemony. And, yes, it could happen. Germany is and will remain by far the largest economy in the Union. But no one now seriously suggests that Germany is a military threat to the rest of Europe. Or, that in the progress towards union, Germany has not been sensitive to the interests of other member states. Partnership has proved its worth, as even Britain has come to recognise. The question is, can the spirit of partnership be maintained by this and the next generation. The answer will determine whether Berlin becomes the capital of Europe on German or on European terms.

Further Reading.
Read, Anthony and Fisher, David, *Berlin: The Biography of a City*, Pimlico, 1994.
Richie, Alexandra, *Faust's Metropolis*, HarperCollins, 1998.
Taylor, Ronald, *Berlin and Its Culture*, Yale, 1997.

EUROPEAN UNION (EU)

Origin. The Union is founded on the existing European communities set up by the Treaties of Paris (1951) and Rome (1957), supplemented by revisions, the Single European Act in 1986, the Maastricht Treaty on European Union in 1992, and the draft Treaty of Amsterdam in 1997.

Members (15). As at March 1999: Austria, Belgium, Denmark, Finland, France, Germany, Greece, Republic of Ireland, Italy, Luxembourg, the Netherlands, Portugal, Spain, Sweden and the UK.

History. On 19 Sept. 1946, in Zürich, Winston Churchill called for a 'united states of Europe'. Two years later, the Congress of Europe (the meeting in The Hague of nearly 1,000 Europeans from 26 countries calling for a united Europe) resulted in the birth in 1949 of the Council of Europe, a European assembly of nations whose aim (Art. 1 of the Statute) was: 'to achieve a greater unity between its members for the purpose of safeguarding and realizing the ideals and principles which are their common heritage'.

On 18 April 1951, subsequent to a proposal by the French foreign minister Robert Schuman (Schuman Declaration), Belgium, France, the Federal Republic of Germany, Italy, Luxembourg and the Netherlands signed the Treaty of Paris establishing the *European Coal and Steel Community (ECSC).* The treaty provided for the pooling of coal and steel production and was regarded as a first step towards a united Europe. Encouraged by the success of the ECSC, plans were laid down for the establishment of 2 more communities. *The European Economic Community (EEC)* and *the European Atomic Energy Community (EAEC or Euratom)* were subsequently created under separate treaties signed in Rome on 25 March 1957. The treaties provided for the establishment by stages of a common market with a customs union at its core, the approximation of economic policies, and the promotion of growth in the nuclear industries for peaceful purposes.

To this end, Euratom was awarded monopoly powers of acquisition of fissile materials for civil purposes EUROPEAN UNION (EU) (it is not concerned with the military uses of nuclear power). Subsequently, the various powers of the 3 communities (ECSC, EAEC, EEC, sometimes referred to collectively as the European Community or EC) were transferred by a treaty signed in Brussels in 1965 to a single Council and single Commission of the European Communities, today the core of the EU. The Commission is advised on matters relating to EAEC by a Scientific and Technical Committee.

Enlargement. On 30 June 1970, membership negotiations began between the European Community and the UK, Denmark, Ireland and Norway. On 22 Jan. 1972, all 4 countries signed a Treaty of Accession, and with the exception of Norway which later rejected membership in a referendum in Nov. that year, the UK, Denmark and Ireland became full members on 1 Jan. 1973 (though Greenland exercised its autonomy under the Danish Crown to secede in 1985). Greece joined on 1 Jan. 1981; Spain and Portugal on 1 Jan. 1986. The former German Democratic Republic entered into full membership on reunification with Federal Germany in Oct. 1990, and following referendums in favour, Austria, Finland and Sweden became members on 1 Jan. 1995. In a referendum in Nov. 1994, Norway again rejected membership.

Single European Act. The enlarging of the Community resulted in renewed efforts to promote European integration, culminating in the signing in Dec. 1985 of the Single European Act. The SEA represented the first major revision of the Treaties of Rome and provided for greater involvement of the European Parliament in the decision-making process.

Maastricht Treaty on European Union. Further amendments were agreed at the Maastricht Summit of Dec. 1991 in the draft Treaty on European Union whereby moves to a common currency were agreed subject to specific conditions (including an opt-out clause for the UK) and the social dimension was recognized in a protocol (not applicable to the UK) allowing member states to use EC institutions for this purpose. Ratification by member states of the Maastricht Treaty proved unexpectedly controversial. In June 1992, the Danish electorate in a referendum voted against it, then reversed the decision in a second referendum in May 1993. Ratification was finally completed during 1993, with the UK ratifying on 2 Aug., and the European Union (EU) officially came into being on 1 Nov. that year.

Further Enlargement. On 16 July 1997, Jacques Santer presented *Agenda 2000*, the European Commission's detailed strategy for consolidating the Union through enlargement as far eastwards as Ukraine, Belarus and Moldova. It recommended the early start of accession negotiations with Hungary, Poland, Estonia, the Czech Republic and Slovenia under the provision of Article 0 of the Maastricht Treaty whereby 'any European State may apply to become a member of the Union' (subject to the Copenhagen Criteria set by the European Council at its summit in 1993). The first accession could be as early as 2001 though Agenda 2000 assumes 2003 to be more likely.

Meanwhile, other central and eastern European applicants (Bulgaria, Latvia, Lithuania, Romania and Slovakia) enjoy associate agreements to help speed up their preparations for membership. Applications to join the EU have been received by Cyprus (already favourably received), Turkey, Malta and Switzerland; and the Prince of Liechtenstein has made it known that he wishes his government to apply.

Objectives. The ultimate goal of the EU is 'an ever closer union among the peoples of Europe, in which decisions are taken as closely as possible to the citizen'. Priorities include the implementation of the Treaty of Amsterdam (new rights for citizens, freedom of movement, strengthening the institutions of the EU, employment); economic and monetary union; further expansion of the scope of the Communities; implementation of a common foreign and security policy; and development in the fields of justice and home affairs.

Structure. The institutional arrangements of the EU provide for an independent policy-making executive with powers of proposal (European Commission), various consultative and advisory bodies, and a decision-making body drawn from the Governments (Council of Ministers).

Website: http://www.europa.eu.int

1. **European Commission** consists of 20 members appointed by the member states (one from each small country, two from each big one) to serve for 5 years. The President of the Commission is selected by a consensus of prime ministers and serves a 5-year term. In addition to its power of proposal, the Commission acts as the EU executive body and as guardian of the Treaties. In this it has the right of initiative (putting proposals to the Council of Ministers for action) and of execution (once the Council has decided); and it can take the other institutions or individual countries before the European Court of Justice should any of these renege upon its responsibilities. Decisions on legislative proposals made by the Commission are taken in the Council of the European Union. Members of the Commission swear an oath of independence, distancing themselves from partisan influence from any source. The Commission operates through 23 Directorates-General.

The Commission first took office on 23 Jan. 1995. Members, their nationality and political affiliation (CD, Christian-Democrat; Cons, Conservative; Ind Lib, Independent Liberal; Lab, Labour; Lib, Liberal; R, Radical; Ri, Rightist; S, Socialist; SD, Social-Democrat) in Feb. 1999 (prior to the entire Commission resigning in March) were as follows.

President: Jacques Santer (Luxembourg, CD; app. 1994), to be succeeded by Romano Prodi (Italy); responsible for monetary and institutional affairs, foreign policy and common security.

Having resigned in March 1999, in the wake of a Parliamentary motion of censure, the following Commissioners acted in a caretaker capacity:

Vice-president: Sir Leon Brittan (UK, Cons) Trade policy and relations with industrialized countries of America and the Pacific Zone.

Vice-president: Manuel Marin (Spain, S) Relations with the Southern Mediterranean, Near East, Latin America and part of Asia.

Agriculture and rural development: Franz Fischler (Austria, Cons).

Budget, personnel and administration: Erkki Liikanen (Finland, S).

Competition: Karel van Miert (Belgium, S).

Consumers, fisheries and humanitarian aid: Emma Bonino (Italy, R).

Environment and nuclear safety, and Cohesion Fund: Ritt Bjerregaard (Denmark, S).

Domestic market, financial services and taxation: Mario Monti (Italy, Ind Lib).

Economic, financial and monetary affairs: Yves Thibault de Silguy (France, Ri).

Energy and primary materials: Christos Papoutsis (Greece, S).

External relations with central and eastern Europe, the CIS and other European countries; common foreign security policy and human rights (with the President): Hans van den Broek (Netherlands, CD).

Immigration, internal and judicial affairs: Anita Gradin (Sweden, S).

Industrial affairs, information and telecommunications: Martin Bangemann (Germany, Lib).

Institutional questions and relations with the European Parliament: Marcelino Oreja (Spain, CD).

Regional policies and funding: Monika Wulf-Mathies (Germany, SD).

Relations with South Africa and ACP Countries: João de Deus Pinheiro (Portugal, Lib).

Science, research and development, education and training: Edith Cresson (France, S).

Social affairs and employment: Pádraig Flynn (Ireland, Cons).

Transport and the Cohesion Fund: Neil Kinnock (UK, Lab).

Official languages. Danish, Dutch, English, Finnish, French, German, Greek, Italian, Portuguese, Spanish and Swedish.

Headquarters: 200 rue de la Loi, B-1049 Brussels, Belgium.

Secretary-General: David Williamson.

2. **The European Council.** Since 1974, Heads of State or Government meet at least twice a year (in the capital of the member state currently exercising the presidency of the Council of European Union) in the form of the European Council or European Summit as it is commonly known. Its membership includes the President of the European Commission, and the President of the European Parliament is invited to make a presentation at the opening session. The European Council has become an increasingly important element of the Union, setting priorities, giving political direction, providing the impetus for its development and resolving contentious issues that prove too difficult for the Council of the European Union. It has become directly responsible for common policies within the fields of foreign and security policy, justice and home affairs. Though there was no provision made for its existence in the original Treaty of Rome, its position was later acknowledged and formalized in the Single European Act.

3. **Council of the European Union (Council of Ministers)** Consists of foreign ministers from the 15 national governments and is the only institution which directly represents the member states' national interests. It is the Union's principal decision-making body. Here, members legislate for the Union, set its political objectives, co-ordinate their national policies and resolve differences between themselves and other institutions. The presidency rotates every 6 months. Meetings are held in Brussels, except in April, June and Oct. when all meetings are in Luxembourg. In 1994-95, the Council held around 100 formal ministerial sessions during which it adopted some 300 regulations, 50 directives and 160 decisions.

Decisions are taken either by qualified majority vote or by unanimity. Since the adoption of the Single European Act, an increasing number of decisions are by majority vote, though some areas such as taxation are reserved to unanimity. 27 votes are needed to veto a decision, and member states carry the following vote weightings: France, Germany, Italy and the UK, 10; Spain, 8; Belgium, Greece, the Netherlands and Portugal, 5; Austria and Sweden, 4; Denmark, Finland and the Republic of Ireland, 3; Luxembourg, 2. Each member state has a national delegation in Brussels known as the Permanent Representation, headed by Permanent Representatives, senior diplomats whose committee (Coreper) prepares ministerial sessions. Coreper meets weekly and its main task is to ensure that only the most difficult and sensitive issues are dealt with at ministerial level. Coreper is also the point of reference for many of the Council's working groups of national experts. Specialist Councils such as the Agriculture Council meet to discuss matters related to individual policies.

The Secretariat provides the practical infrastructure of the Council at all levels.

Legislation. The Community's legislative process starts with a proposal from the Commission (either at the suggestion of its services or in pursuit of its declared political aims) to the Council. The Council generally seeks the views of the European Parliament on the proposal, and the Parliament adopts a formal Opinion after consideration of the matter by its specialist Committees. The Council may also (and in some cases is obliged to) consult the Economic and Social Committee which similarly delivers an opinion. When these opinions have been received, the Council will decide. Most decisions are taken on a majority basis, but will take account of reservations expressed by individual member states. The text eventually approved may differ substantially from the original Commission proposal.

Provisions of the Treaties and secondary legislation may be either directly applicable in Member States or only applicable after Member States have enacted their own implementing legislation. Community law, adopted by the Council (or by Parliament and the Council in the framework of the co-decision procedure) may take the following forms: (1) *Regulations*, which are of general application and binding in their entirety and directly applicable in all member states; (2) *Directives*, which are binding upon each Member State as to the result to be achieved within a given time, but leave the national authority the choice of form and method of achieving this result; and (3) *Decisions*, which are binding in their entirety on their addressees. In addition the Council and Commission can issue recommendations and opinions which have no binding force.

Transparency. The Council is making strong efforts to make more of its work accessible to its citizens. Votes on legislative matters, as well as the explanations of these votes, are now automatically made public. Other attempts to improve transparency include briefings for journalists and the provision of background notes on subjects under discussion. Europe Day is celebrated on 9 May each year.

Headquarters: 170 rue de la Loi, B-1048 Brussels, Belgium.
Secretary-General: Jürgen Trumpf.

4. **European Parliament** Consists of 626 members, 542 elected by proportional representation, 84 (British) by single-seat constituencies for 5-year terms. 567 members were elected from 12 member states on 9 and 12 June 1994.

All EU citizens may stand or vote in their adoptive country of residence. Germany returned 99 members, France, Italy and the UK 87 each, Spain 64, the Netherlands 31, Belgium and Portugal 25, Greece 24, Denmark 16, Ireland 15 and Luxembourg 6. Seats allocated to countries which joined in Jan. 1995, and where elections were subsequently held, were: Sweden (1995) 22, Austria 21 and Finland 16 (1996).

Political groupings. Party of European Socialists (PES) 215 seats; European People's Party (EPP) 182; Union for Europe (UE) 56; European Liberal Democratic and Reformist Group (ELDR) 43; European Unitary Left (EUL) 33; Greens (GR) 27; European Radical Alliance (ERA) 20; Independents (I) 32; Europe of the National States (ENS) 18.

The Parliament has a right to be consulted on a wide range of legislative proposals and forms one arm of the Community's Budgetary Authority. Under the Single European Act, it gained greater authority in legislation through the 'concertation' procedure under which it can reject certain Council drafts in a second reading procedure. Under the Maastricht Treaty, it gained the right of 'co-decision' on legislation with the Council of Ministers on a restricted range of domestic matters. The President of the European Council must report to the Parliament on progress in the development of foreign and security policy. It also plays an important role in appointing the President and members of the Commission. It can hold individual commissioners to account and can pass a motion of censure on the entire Commission, a prospect that was realized in March 1999 when the Commission, including the President, Jacques Santer, was forced to resign following an investigation into mismanagement and corruption. Parliament's seat is in Strasbourg where the 1-week plenary sessions are held each month. In the Chamber, members sit in political groups, not as national delegations. All the activities of the Parliament and its bodies are the responsibility of the Bureau, consisting of the President and 14 Vice-Presidents elected for a two-and-a-half year period. The Conference of Presidents is responsible for organizing Parliament's work and drawing up the agenda for plenary sessions.

Parliamentary committees generally meet for 2 weeks a month in Brussels for ease of contact with the Commission and Council of Ministers.

Location: Brussels, but meets at least once a month in Strasbourg.
President: José Gil-Robles Gil-Delgado (Spain; EPP).

5. The **Court of Justice of the European Communities** composed of 13 judges and 6 advocates-general is responsible for the adjudication of disputes arising out of the application of the treaties, and its findings are enforceable in all member countries. A Court of First Instance (est. 1989) handles certain categories of cases, including cases arising under the competition rules of the EC and cases brought by Community officials.

Address: Palais de la Cour de Justice, Kirchberg, Luxembourg.
President: Gil Carlos Rodríguez Iglesias (Spain).

6. The **Court of Auditors of the European Communities** was established by a treaty of 22 July 1975 which took effect on 1 June 1977. It consists of 12 members and was raised to the status of a full EU institution by the 1993 Maastricht Treaty. It audits all income and current and past expenditure of the EU.

Address: 12, rue Alcide de Gasperi, L-1615 Luxembourg.
President: Bernhard Friedmann (Germany).

Major Policy Areas. The major policy areas of the EU were laid down in the Treaty of Rome of 25 March 1957 which guaranteed certain rights to the citizens of all member states, including the outlawing of economic discrimination by nationality, and equal pay for equal work as between men and women.

The single internal market. The single internal market represents the core of the process of economic integration and is characterized by the removal of obstacles to the 4 fundamental *freedoms of movement for persons, goods and capital.* Under the Treaty, individuals or companies from 1 Member State may establish themselves in another country (for the purposes of economic activity) or sell goods or services there on the same basis as nationals of that country. With a few exceptions, restrictions on the movement of capital have also been ended. Under the Single European Act the member states bound themselves to achieve the suppression of all barriers to free movement of persons, goods and services by 31 Dec. 1992.

The *Schengen Accord* abolished border controls on persons and goods between those EU and non-EU states which have signed it. It came into effect on 26 March 1995 and was signed by Austria, Belgium, Denmark, Finland, France, Germany, Greece, Iceland, Italy, Luxembourg, Netherlands, Norway, Portugal, Spain and Sweden.

Economic and Monetary Union. The establishment of the single market provided for the next phase of integration: economic and monetary union. The *European Monetary System (EMS)* was founded in March 1979 to control inflation, protect European trade from international disturbances and ultimately promote convergence between the European economies. At its heart was the *Exchange Rate Mechanism (ERM).* The ERM is run by the finance ministries and central banks of the EU countries on a day-to-day basis; monthly reviews are carried out by the EU Monetary Committee (finance ministries) and the EU Committee of Central Bankers. Greece and Sweden are not in the ERM; the UK suspended its membership on 17 Sept. 1992. In Jan. 1995, Austria joined the ERM. Finland followed in 1996, and in Nov. that year the Italian lira, which had been temporarily suspended, was re-admitted.

Members are obliged to restrict the fluctuations in the value of their currencies to a variation 'band', of 15% (2·25% for Germany and the Netherlands) higher or lower than a central rate established by comparing all the currencies in the ERM and the European Currency Unit, the ecu. If a currency reaches its top or bottom limits, central banks are obliged to buy or sell currency on the foreign exchanges. Further stabilization measures would involve adjustment of national interest rates, central bank borrowing from other central banks or withdrawal of reserves from the European Monetary Co-operation Fund. The adjustment of last resort is re- or devaluation. In July 1993, following intensive currency speculation on European financial markets, forcing the weaker currencies to the edge of their permitted bands, the ERM almost collapsed. In response the fluctuation margins were widened. The ecu's value in national currencies is calculated and published daily.

Under the Maastricht Treaty the second stage in economic and monetary union began with the establishment of the European Monetary Institute (see below) in order to prepare for the implementation of a single monetary policy and single currency. A future European Central Bank (ECB) will take over the tasks of the EMI once a single policy and currency are in place.

European Monetary Union (EMU). The single European currency with 11 member states came into operation in Jan. 1999 although it will be another 2 years before the currency is in general circulation. The euro-zone is the world's second largest economy after the USA in terms of output and the largest in terms of trade. EMU currency will consist of the euro of 100 cents, with coins of 1, 2, 5, 10, 20 and 50 cents and 1 and 2 euros and notes of 5, 10, 20, 50, 100, 200 and 500 euros. From 1 July 2002 it will be the only legal currency in EMU countries. EU member countries not in EMU will select a central rate for their currency in consultation with members of the euro bloc and the European Central Bank. The rate is set according to an assessment of each country's chances of joining the euro zone.

An agreement on the legal status of the euro and currency discipline, the Stability and Growth Pact, was reached by all member states at the Dublin summit on 13 Dec. 1996. Financial penalties will be applied to member states running a GDP deficit (negative growth) of up to 0·75%. If GDP falls between 0·75% and 2%, EU finance ministers will have discretion as to whether to apply penalties. Members running an excessive deficit will be automatically exempt from penalties in the event of a natural disaster or if the fall in GDP is at least 2% over 1 year.

In economic and financial terms, the euro-11 countries are a close match for the USA. Their combined GDP in 1997 was US$6·5 trillion, compared with America's $6·1 trillion. Their share of international trade outside the euro area (19%) is a shade larger than that of the USA (17%). Taken together, bond markets in euro countries are somewhat smaller than America's, although Europe's equity markets are much smaller than Wall Street.

The dollar's role in international finance is, however, far bigger. It is the main currency used for the world's trade and investment. Roughly half of world trade is invoiced in dollars. Almost all commodities are priced in dollars. According to a recent survey by the Bank for International Settlements, the dollar features in at least one side of 87% of all foreign-exchange transactions, the D-mark in 30%, and other euro-member currencies in only 24%.'

Environment. The Single European Act gave environmental policy its place with the view of making the protection of the environment an integral part of economic and social policies. Community policy aims at preventing pollution (the Prevention Principle), rectifying pollution at source, and imposing the costs of prevention or rectification upon the polluters themselves (the Polluter Pays Principle). The European Environment Agency (see below) was established to ensure that policy was based on reliable scientific data.

The Common Agricultural Policy (CAP). The objectives set out in the Treaty are to increase agricultural productivity, to ensure a fair standard of living for the agricultural community, to stabilize markets, to assure supplies, and to ensure reasonable consumer prices. In Dec. 1960 the Council laid down the fundamental principles on which the CAP is based: a single market, which calls for common prices, stable currency parities and the harmonizing of health and veterinary legislation; Community preference, which protects the single Community market from imports; common financing, through the European Agricultural Guidance and Guarantee Fund (EAGGF), which seeks to improve agriculture through its Guidance section, and to stabilize markets against world price fluctuations through market intervention, with levies and refunds on exports. At present, common market organizations cover over 95% of EU agricultural production.

Following the disappearance of stable currency parities, artificial currency levels have been applied in the CAP. This factor, together with over-production due to high producer prices, meant that the CAP consumed about two-thirds of the Communities' budget. It was finally agreed in May 1992 to reform CAP and lessen over-production by reducing the price supports to farmers by 29% for cereals, 15% for beef and 5% for dairy products. In June 1995, the guaranteed intervention price for beef was decreased by 5%. In July 1996, agriculture ministers agreed a reduction in the set-aside rate for cereals from 10% to 5%. Fruit and vegetable production subsidies were fixed at no more than 4% of the value of total marketed production, rising to 4·5% in 1999. Compensatory grants are made available to farmers who remove land from production or take early retirement. The CAP reform aims in the long term to make the agricultural sector more responsive to the level of supply and demand. Farm spending currently absorbs 50% of the EU budget but accounts for only 1·8% of Europe's GDP.

The Beef Crisis. In July 1994 Community ministers adopted measures to prevent the spread of bovine spongiform encephalopathy (BSE) by imposing strict controls on carcass beef trade. In March 1996, owing to increased fears about possible links between BSE and Creutzfeldt-Jakob Disease (CJD) and a collapse in consumer confidence in the beef market, the Commission accepted that member countries could unilaterally stop imports of beef on health grounds. By 22 March, 12 EU countries had taken the step of banning UK beef, and on 27 March the Commission agreed a ban on exports from the UK of live cattle, beef and beef products. The UK responded to the crisis with a programme of selective slaughter to eradicate BSE from the national herd, then later repudiated the agreement and applied for the ban to be suspended. This was duly rejected by the European Court of Justice in July 1996 and an additional cull on the UK herd was requested. In Aug. 1996, the Beef Assurance Scheme for specialist grass reared beef herds which had not been affected by BSE or come into contact with meat and bonemeal was introduced. A report criticizing the UK handling of the BSE problem was published by the European Temporary Committee of Inquiry. The ban on beef exports from Northern Ireland was lifted on 1 June 1998. On 25 Nov. 1998, the European Commission adopted a proposal for a Date Based Export Scheme, for the export of deboned beef and beef products from the UK. The Commission is to undertake an inspection of the UK's procedures for implementing the Scheme and, if satisfied, they will set a date for exports to begin.

Customs Union and External Trade Relations. Goods or Services originating in one Member State have free circulation within the EU, which implies common arrangements for trade with the rest of the world. Member States can no longer make bilateral trade agreements with third countries; this power has been ceded to the EU. The Customs Union was achieved in July 1968.

In Oct. 1991 a treaty forming the *European Economic Area (EEA)* was approved by the member states of the then EC and European Free Trade Association (EFTA). Association agreements which could lead to accession or customs union have been made with Cyprus, Estonia, Latvia, Lithuania, Israel, Malta, Morocco and Turkey. The customs union with Turkey came into force on 1 Jan. 1996. Commercial, industrial, technical and financial aid agreements have been made with Algeria, Egypt, Jordan, Lebanon, Morocco, Russia, Syria, Tunisia and the former Yugoslavia. In 1976 Canada signed a framework agreement for co-operation in industrial trade, science and natural resources, and a transatlantic pact was signed with the USA in Dec. 1995. Co-operation agreements also exist with a number of Latin American countries and groupings, and with Arab and Asian countries, and an economic and commercial agreement has been signed with the Association of South East Asian Nations (ASEAN). Partnership and co-operation agreements were signed with Ukraine in June 1994, Kazakhstan in Jan. 1995, Kyrgyzstan in Feb. 1995 and with Uzbekiston in June 1996. In the Development Aid sector, the EU has an agreement (the Lomé Convention, originally signed in 1975 but renewed and enlarged in 1979 and 1984) with some 60 African, Caribbean and Pacific (ACP) countries which removes customs duties without reciprocal arrangements for most of their imports to the Community.

The application of common duties has been conducted mainly within the framework of the *General Agreement on Tariffs and Trade (GATT),* which was succeeded in 1995 by the establishment of the World Trade Organization.

Fisheries. The Common Fisheries Policy (CFP) came into effect in Jan. 1983, according to which all EU fishermen have equal access to the waters of member countries (a zone extending up to 200 nautical miles from the shore around all its coastlines), with the total allowable catch for each species being set and shared out between member countries according to pre-established quotas, with in some cases 'historic rights' applying, as well as special rules to conserve stock, preserve marine biodiversity, and the sustainable pursuit of fishing.

A number of agreements are in place with other countries (Canada, Norway, USA and some African countries) allowing reciprocal fishing rights. When Greenland withdrew from the Community in 1985 EU boats retained their fishing rights subject to quotas and limits, which were revised in 1995 owing to concern about overfishing of Greenland halibut. Agreements were initialled with Estonia, Latvia, Lithuania and Argentina in 1992.

Transport. Under the Maastricht Treaty, the Community must contribute to the establishment and development of trans-European networks in the areas of transport, telecommunications and energy infrastructures.

Competition. The Competition (anti-trust) law of the EU is based on 2 principles: that businesses should not seek to nullify the creation of the common market by the erection of artificial national (or other) barriers to the free movement of goods; and against the abuse of dominant positions in any market. These two principles have led among other things to the outlawing of prohibitions on exports to other Member States, of price-fixing agreements and of refusal to supply; and to the refusal by the Commission to allow mergers or takeovers by dominant undertakings in specific cases. Increasingly heavy fines are imposed on offenders.

A number of structural funds have been established in an attempt to counter specific problems within and across the Community. These include:

European Social Fund. Provides resources with the aim of combating long-term unemployment and facilitating integration into the labour market of young people and the socially disadvantaged. The 1996 budget included an allocation of around ecu 7,146m. for the Fund's commitments.

European Regional Development Fund. Intended to compensate for the unequal rate of development among different regions of the EU by encouraging investment and improving infrastructure in 'problem regions'.

Finances. The general budget of the EU covers all EEC and Euratom expenditure, and the administrative expenditure of the ECSC.

EU revenue in ecu 1m.:

	1997
Own resources	81,754
Miscellaneous Community taxes, levies and dues	476
Administrative operation of the institutions	97
Contributions to EU programmes	16
Borrowing and lending	18
Miscellaneous	5
Total	82,366

Expenditure for 1996 was ecu 85,094m.

The resources of the Community (the levies and duties mentioned above, and up to a 1·4% VAT charge) have been surrendered to it by Treaty. The Budget is made by the Council and the Parliament acting jointly as the Budgetary Authority. The Parliament has control, within a certain margin, of non-obligatory expenditure (where the amount to be spent is not set out in the legislation concerned), and can also reject the Budget. Otherwise, the Council decides. An agreement of 1992 fixed the permissible ceiling of expenditure at 1·2% of EC GDP in 1993 and 1994, rising to 1·27% in 1999. In Dec. 1994, taking into account the enlargement of the EU to 15 countries (from 1 Jan. 1995), it was agreed to set a level of maximum expenditure at ecu 75,500m., in 1995, increasing to ecu 87,000m., in 1999.

The Consultative Bodies There are 3 main consultative committees whose members are appointed in a personal capacity and are not bound by any mandatory instruction.

1. *Economic and Social Committee.* The 222-member committee is consulted by the Council of Ministers or by the European Commission, particularly with regard to agriculture, free movement of workers, harmonization of laws and transport. It is served by a permanent and independent General Secretariat, headed by a Secretary-General.

Secretary-General: Adriano Graziosi.

2. *ECSC (European Coal and Steel Community) Consultative Committee.* A 108-member committee representing producers, workers, consumers and traders in the coal and steel industry. Appointed by the Council for a 2-year term and attached to the Commission, it plays an advisory role on the coal and steel sectors.

3. *Committee of the Regions.* A new advisory body established by the Maastricht Treaty and consisting of 222 full members and an equal number of alternate members appointed by the Council for a 4-year term. The Committee must be consulted on matters regarding education, culture, public health, trans-European networks, economic and social cohesion, and on any issue with regional implications.

President: Pasqual Maragall I. Mara (Spain).

In addition to these, there are many advisory committees dealing with all aspects of EU policy and several hundred special interest groups, which may hold unofficial talks with the Commission.

EU General information. Available as free-of-charge publications. The Official Journal, other official documents, specialized publications and databases addressing professional needs can be ordered from the EUR-OP network.

Address: Jean Monnet Building, rue Alcide de Gasperi, L-2920 Luxembourg.

The **EU Ombudsman** was inaugurated in 1995. The present incumbent is Jacob Söderman (Finland).

EUROPEAN INVESTMENT BANK (EIB) Created in 1958 by the 6 founder member states of the EEC under the Treaty of Rome to which its statute is annexed, its role was reaffirmed in a protocol to the Maastricht Treaty. Its governing body is the Board of Governors, consisting of ministers designated by member states. Its main task is to further regional development within the Community by financing capital projects; modernizing or converting undertakings; or developing new activities. To this end, it raises on the markets substantial volumes of funds which it directs on favourable terms.

Address: 100 Bd Konrad Adenauer, L-2950 Luxembourg.
President: Sir Brian Unwin.

EUROPEAN MONETARY INSTITUTE Established by the Maastricht Treaty on 1 Jan. 1994 as the precursor of a European Central Bank (ECB). Its purpose is to strengthen the co-ordination of monetary policies of member states with a view to ensuring price stability, and to make the necessary preparations required for the establishment of the European System of Central Banks (ESCB), for the conduct of a single monetary policy and creation of a single European currency, the euro. The EMI was to be replaced by the ESCB at the start of Stage II of the process of economic and monetary union in 1999, when the changeover to the euro began.

Address: 29 Kaiserstrasse, 60311 Frankfurt-am-Main, Germany.
President: Willem Duisenberg (Netherlands).

EUROPEAN ENVIRONMENT AGENCY Launched by the EU in 1993 with a mandate to orchestrate, cross-check and put to strategic use information of relevance to the protection and improvement of Europe's environment. Based in Copenhagen, it has a mandate to ensure objective, reliable and comprehensive information on the environment at European level to enable its members to take the requisite measures to protect it. The Agency carries out its tasks through the European Information and Observation Network (EIONET). Membership is open to countries outside the EU that share the Agency's concerns. Current membership includes all EU countries, Iceland, Liechtenstein and Norway.

EUROPOL Founded in 1994 to exchange criminal intelligence between EU countries. Its precursor was the European Drug Unit whose field of operations was extended in 1994 to include traffic in nuclear and radioactive substances, illegal immigration and stolen vehicles. All EU states are represented by liaison officers (ELOs) working for their national police, gendarme or customs services. The 1995 budget was ecu 4·5m. Member countries subscribe in proportion to their GNP.

Co-ordinator: Jürgen Storbeck (Germany).

STATISTICAL OFFICE OF THE EUROPEAN COMMUNITIES (EUROSTAT) Eurostat's mission is to provide the EU with a high-quality statistical service. It receives statistical data collected according to uniform rules from the national statistical institutes of member states, then consolidates and harmonizes the data, before making them available to the public as printed or electronic publications. The data are directly available from the Data Shop network and from EUR-OP distribution networks.

Address: Jean Monnet Building, L-2920 Luxembourg.
Data Shop: Rue de la Loi 120, B-1049 Brussels, Belgium.

Further Reading

Official Journal of the European Communities.—General Report on the Activities of the European Communities (annual, from 1967).—*The Agricultural Situation in the Community.* (annual).—*The Social Situation in the Community.* (annual).—*Report on Competition Policy in the European Community.* (annual).—*Basic Statistics of the Community* (annual).—*Bulletin of the European Community* (monthly).—*Register of Current Community Legal Instruments.* 1983

Europe (monthly), obtainable from the Information Office of the European Commission, 8 Storey's Gate, London, SW1P 3AT; European Parliament. *Members of the European Parliament, 4th Electoral Period, 1994–99.* 1995

Brittan, L., *The Europe We Need.* London, 1994

Cox, A. and Furlong, P., *A Modern Companion to the European Community: a Guide to Key Facts, Institutions and Terms.* Aldershot, 1992

Crawford, M., *One Money for Europe: the Economics and Politics of EMU.* 2nd ed. London, 1996

Davies, N., *Europe: A History.* London, 1997

Delors, J., *Our Europe: the Community and National Development*. London, 1993

Dinan, D., *Ever Closer Union? An Introduction to the European Community*. London, 1994.

Dod's European Companion. Hurst Green, East Sussex. Occasional

Hitiris, T., *European Community Economics: a Modern Introduction*. London, 1991

Hurwitz, L. and Lequesne, C. (eds.) *The State of the European Community: Policies, Institutions and Debates in the Transition Years*. Harlow, 1992

Kirschner, E. J., *Decision-Making in the European Community: the Council Presidency and European Integration*. Manchester Univ. Press, 1992

Leonardi, R., *Convergence, Cohesion and Integration in the European Union*. London, 1995

Lewis, D. W. P., *The Road to Europe: History, Institutions and Prospects of European Integration, 1945–1993*. Berne, 1994

Mazower, M., *Dark Continent: Europe's 20th Century*. London, 1998

Newman, M., *Democracy, Sovereignty and the European Union*. Farnborough, 1996

Nugent, N., *The Government and Politics of the European Union*. 3rd ed. London, 1994

Nuttall, S. J., *European Political Co-operation*. Oxford, 1992

Paxton, J., *European Communities* [Bibliography]. Oxford and New Brunswick (NJ), 1992

Weigall, D. and Stirk, P., *The Origins and Development of the European Community*. Leicester Univ. Press, 1992

Westlake, M., *Modern Guide to the European Parliament*. London, 1994

Williams, A. M., *The European Community: the Contradictions of Integration*. 2nd ed. Oxford, 1994

Winters, L. and Venables, A. (eds.) *European Integration: Trade and Industry*. CUP, 1991

COUNCIL OF EUROPE

Origin and Membership. In 1948, the Congress of Europe, bringing together at The Hague nearly 1,000 influential Europeans from 26 countries, called for the creation of a united Europe, including a European Assembly. This proposal, examined first by the Ministerial Council of the Brussels Treaty Organization, then by a conference of ambassadors, was at the origin of the Council of Europe, which is, with its 41 member States, the widest organization bringing together all European democracies. The Statute of the Council was signed at London on 5 May 1949 and came into force 2 months later.

The founder members were Belgium, Denmark, France, Ireland, Italy, Luxembourg, the Netherlands, Norway, Sweden and the UK. Turkey and Greece joined in 1949, Iceland in 1950, the Federal Republic of Germany in 1951 (having been an associate since 1950), Austria in 1956, Cyprus in 1961, Switzerland in 1963, Malta in 1965, Portugal in 1976, Spain in 1977, Liechtenstein in 1978, San Marino in 1988, Finland in 1989, Hungary in 1990, Czechoslovakia (after partitioning, the Czech Republic and Slovakia rejoined in 1993) and Poland in 1991, Bulgaria in 1992, Estonia, Lithuania, Romania and Slovenia in 1993, Andorra in 1994, Albania, Latvia, Macedonia, Moldova and Ukraine in 1995, Croatia and Russia in 1996, and Georgia in 1999.

Membership is limited to European states which 'accept the principles of the rule of law and of the enjoyment by all persons within [their] jurisdiction of human rights and fundamental freedoms'. The Statute provides for both withdrawal (Article 7) and suspension (Articles 8 and 9). Greece withdrew during 1969–74.

Aims and Achievements. Article 1 of the Statute states that the Council's aim is 'to achieve a greater unity between its members for the purpose of safeguarding and realizing the ideals and principles which are their common heritage and facilitating their economic and social progress'; 'this aim shall be pursued... by discussion of questions of common concern and by agreements and common action'. The only limitation is provided by Article 1 (d), which excludes 'matters relating to national defence'.

The main areas of the Council's activity are: human rights, the media, social and socio-economic questions, education, culture and sport, youth, public health, heritage and environment, local and regional government, and legal co-operation. 167

Conventions and Agreements have been concluded covering such matters as social security, cultural affairs, conservation of European wildlife and natural habitats, protection of archaeological heritage, extradition, medical treatment, equivalence of degrees and diplomas, the protection of television broadcasts, adoption of children and transportation of animals.

Treaties in the legal field include the adoption of the European Convention on the Suppression of Terrorism, the European Convention on the Legal Status of Migrant Workers and the Transfer of Sentenced Persons. The Committee of Ministers adopted a European Convention for the protection of individuals with regard to the automatic processing of personal data (1981), a Convention on the compensation of victims of violent crimes (1983), a Convention on spectator violence and misbehaviour at sport events and in particular at football matches (1985), the European Charter of Local Government (1985), and a Convention for the Prevention of Torture and Inhuman or Degrading Treatment or Punishment (1987). The European Social Charter of 1961 sets out the social and economic rights which all member governments agree to guarantee to their citizens.

European Social Charter. The Charter defines the rights and principles which are the basis of the Council's social policy, and guarantees a number of social and economic rights to the citizen, including the right to work, the right to form workers' organizations, the right to social security and assistance, the right of the family to protection and the right of migrant workers to protection and assistance. Two committees, comprising independent and government experts, supervise the parties' compliance with their obligations under the Charter. A revised charter, incorporating new rights such as protection for those without jobs and opportunities for workers with family responsibilities, was opened for signature on 3 May 1996 and signed by 13 members.

Human rights. The promotion and development of human rights is one of the major tasks of the Council of Europe. The European Convention on Human Rights, signed in 1950, set up special machinery to guarantee internationally fundamental rights and freedoms. The European Commission of Human Rights investigates alleged violations of the Convention submitted to it either by States or, in most cases, by individuals. Its findings can then be examined by the European Court on Human Rights (est. 1959), whose obligatory jurisdiction has been recognized by all the 40 States, or by the Committee of Ministers empowered to take binding decisions by two-thirds majority vote. In Oct. 1997, leaders of the 40 members of the Council of Europe met in Strasbourg to reinforce and extend the organization's watchdog role on human rights in Europe, turning its human rights court into a full-time body and appointing a human rights mediator, and to encourage more members, particularly in Eastern Europe, to sign the Council's social charter. The summit, only the second in the Council's 48-year history, also endorsed the idea of a continent-wide ban on human cloning, and closer co-operation to combat corruption, organized crime and money laundering.

President of the European Commission of Human Rights: Stefan Trechsel (Switzerland).

President of the European Court on Human Rights: Rudolf Bernhardt (Germany).

The Social Development Fund, formerly the Resettlement Fund, was created in 1956. The main purpose of the Fund is to give financial aid in the spheres of housing, vocational training, regional planning and development. Since 1956 the Fund has granted loans totalling ecu 10,000m.

The *European Youth Foundation* provides money to subsidize activities by European youth organizations in their own countries.

Structure. Under the Statute, 2 organs were set up: an intergovernmental *Committee of [Foreign] Ministers* with powers of decision and recommendation to governments, and an interparliamentary deliberative body, the *Parliamentary Assembly* (referred to in the Statute as the Consultative Assembly)—both served by the Secretariat. A Joint Committee acts as an organ of co-ordination and liaison between the two and gives members an opportunity to exchange views on matters of important European interest. In addition, a number of committees of experts have been established. On municipal matters the Committee of Ministers receives recommendations from the Congress of Local and Regional Authorities of Europe. The Committee usually meets twice a year and has a rotatory chair; their deputies meet for several days each month.

The *Parliamentary Assembly* consists of 286 parliamentarians elected or appointed by their national parliaments (Albania 4, Andorra 2, Austria 6, Belgium 7, Bulgaria 6, Croatia 5, Cyprus 3, the Czech Republic 7, Denmark 5, Estonia 3, Finland 5, France 18, Germany 18, Greece 7, Hungary 7, Iceland 3, Ireland 4, Italy 18, Latvia 3, Liechtenstein 2, Lithuania 4, Luxembourg 3, Macedonia 3, Malta 3, Moldova 5, Netherlands 7, Norway 5, Poland 12, Portugal 7, Romania 10, Russia 18, San Marino 2, Slovakia 5, Slovenia 3, Spain 12, Sweden 6, Switzerland 6, Turkey 12, Ukraine 12, UK 18). It meets 3 times a year for approximately a week. The work of the Assembly is prepared by parliamentary committees. Since June 1989 representatives of a number of central and East European countries have been permitted to attend as non-voting members ('special guests'), namely Armenia, Azerbaijan, Bosnia-Hercegovina and Georgia.

Although without legislative powers, the Assembly acts as the powerhouse of the Council, initiating European action in key areas by making recommendations to the Committee of Ministers. As the widest parliamentary forum in Western Europe, the Assembly also acts as the conscience of the area by voicing its opinions on important current issues. These are embodied in Resolutions. The Ministers' role is to translate the Assembly's recommendations into action, particularly as regards lowering the barriers between the European countries, harmonizing their legislation or introducing, where possible, common European laws, abolishing discrimination on grounds of nationality, and undertaking certain tasks on a joint European basis.

Official languages. English and French.
Headquarters: Council of Europe, F-67075 Strasbourg Cedex, France.
Secretary-General: Daniel Tarschys (Sweden).

Publications. European Yearbook, The Hague; *Yearbook on the Convention on Human Rights,* Strasbourg; *Catalogue of Publications* (annual); *Sports Information Bulletin* (quarterly); *Activities Report* (annual); *Naturopa* (3 a year); *European Heritage* (bi-annual); *Strategy Bulletin* (6 a year).

Further Reading

Cook, C. and Paxton, J., *European Political Facts, 1900–1996.* London, 1998

WESTERN EUROPEAN UNION (WEU)

Origin. In March 1948, the signing of the Brussels Treaty of Economic, Social and Cultural Collaboration and Collective Defence by Belgium, France, Luxembourg, Netherlands and the UK opened the way for the establishment of the Western European Union. Six years later, the Paris Agreements, signed in Oct. 1954, which amended the Brussels Treaty, gave birth to WEU as a new international organization and provided for the Federal Republic of Germany and Italy to join. WEU came into being in 1955. Today, as an international defence and security organization, it brings together 18 nations that are also members of the European Union and/or NATO and 10 Central European countries which are closely involved in the work of the organization. Its primary role is to enable Europeans to undertake the politico-military management of crises in which the North Americans would not wish to become directly involved. WEU will probably act following a political decision by the European Union and may, depending on the circumstances, call on NATO assets and capabilities.

Members. Belgium, France, Germany, Greece, Italy, Luxembourg, Netherlands, Portugal, Spain and the UK. Spain and Portugal became members in 1990; Greece in

1995. In 1991 at Maastricht the WEU decided to extend invitations to other members of the EU to accede to the WEU or seek observer status, and to European members of NATO to become associate members. In Jan. 1998, Austria, Denmark, the Republic of Ireland, Finland and Sweden had observer status; the Czech Republic, Hungary, Iceland, Norway, Poland and Turkey are associate members; Bulgaria, Estonia, Latvia, Lithuania, Romania, Slovakia and Slovenia are associate partners.

Reform. A joint meeting of the foreign and defence ministers within the WEU framework, held in Rome on 26–27 Oct. 1984, was marked by the adoption of the founding text of WEU's reactivation: the *Rome Declaration.* Work on the definition of a European security identity and the gradual harmonization of its members' defence policies were among the stated objectives. Ministers recognized the 'continuing necessity to strengthen western security, and that better utilization of WEU would not only contribute to the security of Western Europe but also to an improvement in the common defence of all the countries of the Atlantic Alliance'.

In 1987, WEU foreign and defence ministers adopted the *Hague Platform on European Security Interests,* defining the conditions and criteria for European security, and the responsibilities of WEU members to provide an integrated Europe with a security and defence dimension. In 1987 and 1988, following the laying of mines in the Persian Gulf during the Iran-Iraq war, minesweepers dispatched by WEU countries helped secure free movement in international waters. Operation Cleansweep helped to complete the clearance of a 300-mile sea lane from the Strait of Hormuz, and was the first instance of a concerted action in WEU. During the Gulf Crisis, at the end of 1990 and early 1991, co-ordinated action took place among WEU nations contributing forces and other forms of support to the coalition forces involved in the liberation of Kuwait.

In Maastricht, on 10 Dec. 1991, WEU ministers stated that: 'WEU will be developed as the defence component of the European Union and as the means to strengthen the European pillar of the Atlantic Alliance. To this end, it will formulate common European defence policy and carry forward its concrete implementation through the further development of its own operational role.' The Declaration then proposed ways of strengthening WEU's relations with the European Union and NATO, as well as measures to develop its operational role. A number of practical decisions were taken, including the transfer of the WEU headquarters from London to Brussels, which was completed in Jan. 1993.

At a meeting in Bonn in June 1992, they went on to adopt the *Petersberg Declaration,* agreeing that the WEU should have a military capability in order to conduct humanitarian and rescue tasks, peacekeeping tasks and tasks of combat forces in crisis management, including peacemaking (the so-called 'Petersberg tasks') at the initiative of the WEU Council or following a request by the European Union, the OSCE or the UN.

At the Alliance Summit of Jan. 1994, NATO leaders gave their full support to the development of a European Security and Defence Identity (ESDI) and to the strengthening of the WEU. They declared their readiness to make collective assets of the Alliance available for WEU operations. The Alliance leaders also endorsed the concept of Combined Joint Task Forces (CJTFs) with the objective not only of adapting Alliance structures to NATO's new missions but also of improving co-operation with the WEU, and in order to reflect the emerging ESDI. Work on the CJTF concept came to fruition at the NATO Ministerial meeting in Berlin in June 1996. One of the fundamental objectives of the Alliance adaptation process identified by NATO Ministers in Berlin was the development of the European Security and Defence Identity within the Alliance.

With the agreement on the Treaty of Amsterdam revising the Treaty on European Union, WEU has drawn closer to the EU. In particular, the European Council's guidelines for the Common Foreign Security Policy (CFSP) 'shall obtain in respect of WEU for those matters for which the Union avails itself of the WEU'; and the Petersberg tasks have been incorporated into the EU Treaty. It is stated that WEU is an integral part of the development of the European Union, giving the Union access to an operational capability, notably in the context of the Petersberg tasks. In the WEU Ministerial Declaration of 22 July 1997 responding to the Treaty of Amsterdam,

WEU confirmed its readiness to develop WEU's relations with the EU and work out arrangements for enhanced co-operation.

In the context of the Yugoslav conflict, WEU has undertaken 3 operations, 2 of them to help in the enforcement of sanctions imposed by the UN Security Council (the WEU/NATO operation SHARP GUARD in the Adriatic and the WEU Danube operation) and one to assist in the European Union administration of the town of Mostar. Since 1997, WEU has deployed a Multinational Advisory Police Element (MAPE) in Albania to assist in the reorganization of the Albanian Police.

Organization. Since the 1984 reforms, the Council, supreme authority of the WEU, meets twice a year at ministerial level (foreign and defence) in the capital of the presiding country. The presidency rotates biannually. The Permanent Council, chaired by the Secretary-General, meets weekly at ambassadorial level, at the WEU headquarters in Brussels. The WEU Military Committee is responsible to the WEU Council for the general conduct of WEU's military affairs. It provides military advice on military and operational matters to the Council. The WEU has a satellite centre at Torrejon de Ardoz in Spain, and a *WEU Institute for Security Studies* was set up in Paris in 1990. The WEU Assembly, located in Paris, comprises 115 parliamentarians of member states and meets twice a year, usually in Paris. There are Permanent Committees on: defence questions and armaments; general affairs; scientific questions; budgetary affairs and administration; rules of procedure and privileges; and parliamentary and public relations.

Headquarters: WEU, B-1000 Brussels, Belgium.
Secretary-General: José Cutileiro (Portugal).

ORGANIZATION FOR SECURITY AND CO-OPERATION IN EUROPE (OSCE)

The OSCE is a pan-European security organization of 55 participating states. It was established as a primary instrument in its region for early warning, conflict prevention, crisis management and post-conflict rehabilitation in Europe.

Origin. Initiatives from both NATO and the Warsaw Pact culminated in the first summit Conference on Security and Co-operation in Europe (CSCE) attended by heads of state and government in Helsinki on 30 July–1 Aug. 1975. It adopted the *Helsinki Final Act* laying down 10 principles governing the behaviour of States towards their citizens and each other, concerning human rights, self-determination and the interrelations of the participant states. The CSCE was to serve as a multilateral forum for dialogue and negotiations between East and West.

The Helsinki Final Act comprised 4 main sections: 1) security in Europe, including commitments to non-aggression and respect for human rights; 2) co-operation in the fields of economics, science, technology and the environment; 3) co-operation in humanitarian and related fields, including promotion of cultural exchange and free movement of peoples; 4) a commitment to the process of consultation and increased co-operation.

From CSCE to OSCE. The Paris Summit of Nov. 1990 set the CSCE on a new course. In the Charter of Paris for a New Europe, the CSCE was called upon to contribute to managing the historic change in Europe and respond to the new challenges of the post-Cold War period. At the meeting, members of NATO and the Warsaw Pact signed an important Treaty on the Reduction of Conventional Forces in Europe (CFE) and a declaration that they were 'no longer adversaries' and did not intend to 'use force against the territorial integrity or political independence of any state'. All 34 participants adopted the Confidence and Security-Building Measures (CSBMs), which pertained to the exchange of military information, verification of military installations, objection to unusual military activities etc., and signed the Charter of Paris. The Charter sets out principles of human rights, democracy and the rule of law to which all the signatories undertake to adhere, and lays down the bases for east-west co-operation and other future action. In July 1992, member nations unanimously agreed to set up an armed peace-keeping force. The 1994 Budapest Summit recognized that the CSCE was no longer a conference and on 1 Jan. 1995, the CSCE changed its name to the Organization for Security and Co-operation in Europe (OSCE). The 1996 Lisbon Summit elaborated the OSCE's key role in fostering security and stability in all their dimensions. It also stimulated the development of an OSCE Document-Charter on European Security.

Members. Albania, Andorra, Armenia, Austria, Azerbaijan, Belarus, Belgium, Bosnia-Hercegovina, Bulgaria, Canada, Croatia, Cyprus, the Czech Republic, Denmark, Estonia, Finland, France, Georgia, Germany, Greece, Holy See, Hungary, Iceland, Ireland, Italy, Kazakhstan, Kyrgyzstan, Latvia, Liechtenstein, Lithuania, Luxembourg, Macedonia, Malta, Moldova, Monaco, Netherlands, Norway, Poland, Portugal, Romania, Russian Federation, San Marino, Slovak Republic, Slovenia, Spain, Sweden, Switzerland, Tajikistan, Turkey, Turkmenistan, Ukraine, UK, USA and Uzbekiston. Currently suspended: Yugoslavia (Serbia and Montenegro). *Partners for co-operation:* Japan and the Republic of Korea. *Mediterranean partners for co-operation:* Algeria, Egypt, Israel, Jordan, Morocco, Tunisia.

Organization. The OSCE's regular body for political consultation and decision-making is the Permanent Council. Its members, Permanent Representatives of the OSCE participating States, meet weekly in the Hofburg Congress Center in Vienna to discuss and take decisions on all issues pertinent to the OSCE. The Forum for Security Co-operation (FSC), which deals with arms control and confidence and security-building measures, meets weekly in Vienna. In addition, a Senior Council is convened for periodic political deliberations. It also meets once a year as the Economic Forum. The Chairman-in-Office has overall responsibility for executive action. The chair rotates annually. The Secretary-General acts as representative of the Chairman-in-Office and manages OSCE structures and operations.

The Secretariat is based in Vienna and includes a *Conflict Prevention Centre* which provides operational support for OSCE missions. There are some 200 staff employed in OSCE institutions, and about 2,500 professionals, seconded by OSCE-participating states, work at OSCE missions and other field operations. The Secretariat is assisted by the Prague Office.

The *Office for Democratic Institutions and Human Rights* is located in Warsaw. It is active in monitoring elections and developing national electoral and human rights institutions, providing technical assistance to national legal institutions, and promoting the development of NGOs.

The budget for 1999 (not including the budget for the Kosovo Verification Mission) was EUR104m.

Headquarters: Kärntner Ring 5-7, A-1010 Vienna, Austria.
Website: http://www.osce.org
Chairman-in-Office: Knut Vollebæk (Norway).
Secretary–General: Giancarlo Aragona (Italy).

Further Reading

Freeman, J., Security and the CSCE Process: the Stockholm Conference and Beyond. London, 1991

EUROPEAN BANK FOR RECONSTRUCTION AND DEVELOPMENT (EBRD)

History and Membership. A treaty to establish the EBRD was signed in May 1990; it was inaugurated on 15 April 1991. The EBRD has 60 members (58 countries, the European Community and the European Investment Bank), including 26 countries of operations in central and eastern Europe and the CIS.

Capital. Its subscribed capital is ecu 20bn., of which 30% is paid in. The Bank borrows in various currencies on world capital markets.

Objectives. The EBRD was set up to foster the transition towards market-oriented economies in central and eastern Europe, to lend funds at market rates to companies and countries 'committed to, and applying, the fundamental principles of multiparty democracy, pluralism and market economics'. Facilities were extended to the countries of the former USSR in 1992.

A policy statement of May 1991 placed initial emphasis on programmes: to support the creation and strengthening of infrastructures; privatization and reform of the financial sector, including development of capital markets and privatization of commercial banks; development of productive competitive private sectors of small and medium-sized enterprises in industry, agriculture and services; restructuring industrial sectors to put them on a competitive basis; encouraging foreign investment; and the promotion of sustainable and environmentally sound development.

Activities. Under a phased programme, countries which fulfil certain development criteria graduate out of the Bank's sphere of operations. By 30 Sept. 1998, the Bank had approved 603 projects, involving ecu 13·9bn. of EBRD's own funds, which were expected to mobilize an additional ecu 32·2bn. Of the approved projects, 525 had been signed, committing ecu 11·2bn. of EBRD funds. 84% of total committed funding was for private-sector projects.

Project-related technical co-operation is a major part of EBRD's activities. By 1997, 53 co-operation fund agreements with bilateral donors, totalling ecu 512m. had been made with the Bank for this purpose; 1,808 projects, with a total estimated cost of ecu 500m. had been committed.

Organization. There is a Board of Governors with full management powers, and a 23-member Board of Directors elected for a 3-year term, which is involved in day-to-day operations. The President is elected by the Board of Governors for a 4-year term. The EBRD's headquarters are in London with 29 Resident Offices or other offices in 22 of its countries of operations.

Headquarters: 1 Exchange Square, London, EC2A 2JN, UK.
Website: http://www.ebrd.com
Secretary-General: Antonio Maria Costa.

EUROPEAN FREE TRADE ASSOCIATION (EFTA)

History and Membership. The Stockholm Convention establishing the Association entered into force on 3 May 1960. Founder members were Austria, Denmark, Norway, Portugal, Sweden, Switzerland and the UK. With the accession of Austria, Denmark, Finland, Portugal, Sweden and the UK to the EU, EFTA was reduced to 4 member countries: Iceland, Liechtenstein, Norway and Switzerland.

Activities. Free trade in industrial goods among members was achieved by 1966. Co-operation with the EU began in 1972 with the signing of free trade agreements and culminated in the establishment of a *European Economic Area (EEA),* encompassing the free movement of goods, services, capital and labour throughout EFTA and the EU countries. The Agreement was signed by all members of the EU and EFTA on 2 May 1992, but was rejected by Switzerland in a referendum on 6 Dec. 1992. Entry into force took place on 1 Jan. 1994.

The main provisions of the EEA Agreement are: free movement of products within the EEA from 1993 (with special arrangements to cover food, energy, coal and steel); EFTA to assume EU rules on company law, consumer protection, education, the environment, research and development and social policy; EFTA to adopt EU competition rules on anti-trust matters, abuse of a dominant position, public procurement, mergers and state aid; EFTA to create an EFTA Surveillance Authority and an EFTA Court; individuals to be free to live, work and offer services throughout the EEA, with mutual recognition of professional qualifications; capital movements to be free with some restrictions on investments; EFTA countries not to be bound by the Common Agricultural Policy (CAP) or Common Fisheries Policy (CFP).

The EEA-EFTA states have established a Surveillance Authority and a Court to ensure implementation of the Agreement among the EFTA-EEA states. Political direction is given by the EEA Council which meets twice a year at ministerial level, while ongoing operation of the Agreement is overseen by the EEA Joint Committee. Legislative power remains with national governments and parliaments.

EFTA has formal relations with several other states. Declarations on co-operation were signed with Hungary, former Czechoslovakia and Poland (1990), Bulgaria, Estonia, Latvia, Lithuania and Romania (1991), Slovenia and Albania (1992), Egypt, Morocco and Tunisia (1995), the former Yugoslav Republic of Macedonia and the Palestine Liberation Organization (1996), Jordan and Lebanon (1997). Co-operation with Yugoslavia was suspended in Nov. 1991. Free trade agreements have been signed with Turkey (1991), Israel and Czechoslovakia (1992, with protocols on succession with the Czech Republic and Slovakia in 1993), Poland and Romania (1992), Bulgaria and Hungary (1993), Estonia, Latvia, Lithuania and Slovenia (1995), Morocco (1997). Contacts with the Gulf Co-operation Council have also been established.

A Central European Free Trade Area (CEFTA) has also now been established between the Czech Republic, Hungary, Poland, Slovakia and Slovenia.

Organization. The operation of the free trade area among the EFTA states is the responsibility of the EFTA Council which meets regularly at ambassadorial level in Geneva. The Council is assisted by a Secretariat and standing committees. Each EFTA country holds the chairmanship of the Council for 6 months. For EEA matters there is a separate committee structure.

Brussels Office (EEA matters, press and information)*:* 74 rue de Trèves, B-1040 Brussels.

Headquarters: 9–11 rue de Varembé, 1211 Geneva 20, Switzerland.
Website: http://www.efta.int
Secretary-General: Kjartan Jóhansson (Iceland).
Deputy Secretary-General, Brussels: Guttorm Vik (Norway).

Publications. Convention Establishing the European Free Trade Association; EFTA Annual Report; EFTA Fact Sheets; Information Papers on Aspects of the EEA.

CERN – THE EUROPEAN LABORATORY FOR PARTICLE PHYSICS

Founded in 1954, CERN is the world's leading particle physics research centre. By studying the behaviour of nature's fundamental particles, CERN aims to find out what our Universe is made of and how it works. CERN's biggest accelerator, the large Electron Positron collider (LEP) recreates conditions at the birth of the Universe. A yet more powerful accelerator, the large Hadron Collider (LHC), is due for completion in 2005. One of the beneficial byproducts of CERN activity is the Worldwide Web, developed at CERN to give particle physicists easy access to shared data. One of Europe's first joint ventures, CERN now has a membership of 19 Member States: Austria, Belgium, Czech Republic, Denmark, Finland, France, Germany, Greece, Hungary, Italy, The Netherlands, Norway, Poland, Portugal, Slovak Republic, Spain, Sweden, Switzerland, United Kingdom. Some 6,500 scientists, half of the world's particle physicists, use CERN's facilities.

Address: CH-1211 Geneva 23, Switzerland.
Website: http://www.cern.ch
Director-General: C.H. Llewellyn Smith.

CENTRAL EUROPEAN INITIATIVE (CEI)

In Nov. 1989 Austria, Hungary, Italy and Yugoslavia met on Italy's initiative to form an economic and political co-operation group in the region.

Members. (1998) Albania, Austria, Belarus, Bosnia-Hercegovina, Bulgaria, Croatia, Czech Republic, Hungary, Italy, Macedonia, Moldova, Poland, Romania, Slovakia, Slovenia, Ukraine.

Address: Executive Secretariat, Via Genova 9, 34132 Trieste, Italy.
Website: http://www.cei-es.org
e-mail: cei-es@cei-es.org

THE NORDIC COUNCIL

Founded in 1952 as a co-operative link between the parliaments and governments of the Nordic states. The co-operation focuses on Intra-Nordic co-operation, co-operation with Europe/EU/EEA and co-operation with the adjacent areas. The Council consists of 87 elected MPs and the committees meet several times a year, as required. Every year the Nordic Council grants prizes for literature, music, and nature and environment.

Members: Denmark (including the Faroe Islands and Greenland), Finland (including Åland), Iceland, Norway, Sweden.

Address: Postboks 3043, DK-1021 Copenhagen K, Denmark.
Website: http://www.norden.org/
President: Berit Brørby Larsen.

COUNCIL OF BALTIC SEA STATES

Established in 1992 in Copenhagen following a conference of ministers of foreign affairs.

Members. Denmark, Estonia, Finland, Germany, Iceland, Latvia, Lithuania, Norway, Poland, Russia, Sweden and the European Commission.

Aims. To promote co-operation in the Baltic Sea region in the field of trade, investment and economic exchanges, combating organized crime, civil security, culture and education, transport and communication, energy and environment, human rights and assistance to democratic institutions.

The Council meets at ministerial level once a year, chaired by rotating foreign ministers; it is the supreme decision-making body. Between annual meetings the Committee of Senior Officials meets once a month. A number of action programmes have already been adopted and are now implemented.

Headquarters: Strömsborg, PO Box 2010, S-103 11 Stockholm, Sweden.
Website: http://www.baltinfo.org
Director: Jacek Starosciak.

EUROPEAN BROADCASTING UNION (EBU)

The EBU is the world's largest professional association of national broadcasters with 66 active members in 49 European and Mediterranean countries and 51 associate members in 30 countries elsewhere in Africa, the Americas and Asia. One of the EBU's best-known television activities is Eurovision which has a permanent network comprising 13 channels on a Eutelsat satellite, plus 5,500 km of permanently rented terrestrial circuits.

Headquarters: C.P. 67, CH-1218 Grand Saconnex, Geneva, Switzerland.
Website: http://www.ebu.ch

BLACK SEA ECONOMIC CO-OPERATION GROUP (BSEC)

Founded 1992 to promote economic co-operation in the region. Priority areas of interest include: transport and communications, energy, environmental protection, tourism, trade and industrial co-operation, agriculture and agro-industry, healthcare and pharmaceutics, science and technology, finance administration.

Members. Albania, Armenia, Azerbaijan, Bulgaria, Georgia, Greece, Moldova, Romania, Russia, Turkey, Ukraine.

Observers. Austria, Egypt, Israel, Italy, Poland, Slovakia, Tunisia.

There is a *BSEC Business Council*, and a *Black Sea Trade and Development Bank* was established in Thessalonika, Greece, in 1993, with a founding capital of US$300m. In May 1994, members met to try and create a mechanism for the solution of conflicts in the region, under the auspices of the Group's Interparliamentary Legal and Political Affairs Committee.

Headquarters: İstinye Cad., Müşir Fuad Paşa Yalısı, Eski Tersane 80860, İstinye, İstanbul, Turkey.
Secretary-General: Vassil Baytchev (Russia).

DANUBE COMMISSION

History and Membership. The Danube Commission was constituted in 1949 according to the Convention on the regulation of shipping on the Danube signed in Belgrade on 18 Aug. 1948. The Belgrade Convention declared that navigation on the Danube from Ulm to the Black Sea (with access to the sea through the Sulina arm and the Sulina Canal) is equally free and open to the nationals, merchant shipping and merchandise of all states as to harbour and navigation fees as well as conditions of merchant navigation. The Commission holds annual sessions and is composed of 1 representative from each of its members countries: Austria, Bulgaria, Hungary, Romania, Russia, Slovakia, Ukraine and the Federal Republic of Yugoslavia. Croatia, Germany and Moldova have observer status.

Functions. To ensure that the provisions of the Belgrade Convention are carried out; to establish a uniform buoying system on all navigable waterways; to establish the basic regulations for navigation on the river and ensure facilities for shipping; to co-ordinate the regulations for river, customs and sanitation control as well as the hydrometeorological service; to collect relevant statistical data concerning navigation on the Danube. Recent events, including the emergence of newly independent states with justified interests in the region, will require a new multilateral agreement on management of the river. The scope of the original Convention may also be broadened to include new areas such as energy production and environmental protection.

Official languages. French, Russian.
Headquarters: Benczúr utca 25, H-1068 Budapest, Hungary.
Director-General: Hellmuth Strasser (Austria).

THE COMMONWEALTH

The Commonwealth is a free association of sovereign independent states. It numbered 54 members in 1998. With a membership of 1·7bn. people, it represents over 30% of the world's population. There is no charter, treaty or constitution; the association is expressed in co-operation, consultation and mutual assistance for which the Commonwealth Secretariat is the central co-ordinating body.

Origin. The Commonwealth was first defined by the Imperial Conference of 1926 as a group of 'autonomous Communities within the British Empire, equal in status, in no way subordinate one to another in any aspect of their domestic or external affairs, though united by a common allegiance to the Crown, and freely associated as members of the British Commonwealth of Nations'. The basis of the association changed from one owing allegiance to a common Crown, and the modern Commonwealth was born in 1949 when the member countries accepted India's intention of becoming a republic at the same time as continuing 'her full membership of the Commonwealth of Nations and her acceptance of the King as the symbol of the free association of its independent member nations and as such the Head of the Commonwealth'. In 1998 the Commonwealth consisted of 33 republics and 21 monarchies, of which 16 are Queen's realms. All acknowledge the Queen symbolically as Head of the Commonwealth. The Queen's legal title rests on the statute of 12 and 13 Will. III, c. 3, by which the succession to the Crown of Great Britain and Ireland was settled on the Princess Sophia of Hanover and the 'heirs of her body being Protestants'.

A number of territories, formerly under British jurisdiction or mandate, did not join the Commonwealth: Egypt, Iraq, Transjordan, Burma (now Myanmar), Palestine, Sudan, British Somaliland, South Cameroons and Aden. 4 countries, Ireland in 1948, South Africa in 1961, Pakistan in 1972, and Fiji (now Fiji Islands) in 1987 have left the Commonwealth. Pakistan was re-admitted to the Commonwealth in 1989, South Africa in 1994, Fiji Islands in 1997. Nigeria was suspended in 1995 for violation of human rights. Mozambique, admitted in Nov. 1995, is the first member state not to have been a member of the former British Commonwealth or Empire. Nauru and Tuvalu are special members, with the right to participate in all functional Commonwealth meetings and activities but not to attend meetings of Commonwealth Heads of Government.

MEMBER STATES OF THE COMMONWEALTH
The 54 member states, with year of admission:

	Year of admission		Year of admission
Antigua and Barbuda	1981	Mauritius	1968
Australia[1]	1931	Mozambique	1995
Bahamas	1973	Namibia	1990
Bangladesh	1972	Nauru[4]	1968
Barbados	1966	New Zealand[1]	1931
Belize	1981	Nigeria[5]	1960
Botswana	1966	Pakistan[6]	1989
Brunei[2]	1984	Papua New Guinea	1975
Britain	1931	St Kitts and Nevis	1983
Cameroon	1995	St Lucia	1979
Canada[1]	1931	St Vincent and Grenadines	1979
Cyprus	1961	Samoa	1970
Dominica	1978	Seychelles	1976
Fiji Islands[3]	1997	Sierra Leone	1961
Gambia	1965	Singapore	1965
Ghana	1957	Solomon Islands	1978
Grenada	1974	South Africa[7]	1994
Guyana	1966	Sri Lanka	1948
India	1947	Swaziland	1968
Jamaica	1962	Tanzania	1961
Kenya	1963	Tonga[2]	1970
Kiribati	1979	Trinidad and Tobago	1962
Lesotho	1966	Tuvalu	1978
Malawi	1964	Uganda	1982
Malaysia	1957	Vanuatu	1980
Maldives	1982	Zambia	1964
Malta	1964	Zimbabwe	1980

[1]Independence given legal effect by the Statute of Westminster 1931.
[2]Brunei and Tonga had been sovereign states in treaty relationship with Britain.
[3]Fiji left 1987; but rejoined in 1997. It changed its name to 'Fiji Islands' in 1998.
[4]Nauru was first a Mandate, then a Trust territory.
[5]Membership suspended 1995. [6]Left 1972, rejoined 1989. [7]Left 1961, rejoined 1994.

United Kingdom Overseas Territories and Associated States. There are 13 United Kingdom overseas territories, 6 Australian external territories, 2· New Zealand dependent territories and 2 New Zealand associated states. A dependent territory is a territory belonging by settlement, conquest or annexation to the British, Australian or New Zealand Crown.

United Kingdom Overseas Territories administered through the Foreign and Commonwealth Office comprise, in the Indian Ocean: British Indian Ocean Territory; in the Mediterranean: Gibraltar; in the Atlantic Ocean: Bermuda, Falkland Islands, South Georgia and South Sandwich Islands, British Antarctic Territory, St Helena and Dependencies (Ascension and Tristan da Cunha); in the Caribbean: Montserrat, British Virgin Islands, Cayman Islands, Turks and Caicos Islands, Anguilla; in the Western Pacific: Pitcairn Group of Islands.

The Australian external territories are: Coral Sea Islands, Cocos (Keeling) Islands, Christmas Island, Heard and McDonald Islands, Australian Antarctic and Ashmore and Cartier Islands. The New Zealand dependent territories are: Tokelau Islands and the Ross Dependency. The New Zealand associated states are: Cook Islands and Niue.

British Government Department. With effect from 17 Oct. 1968, the Secretary of State for Foreign and Commonwealth Affairs is responsible for the conduct of relations with members of the Commonwealth as well as with foreign countries. While constitutional responsibility to Parliament for the government of the United Kingdom overseas territories rests with the Secretary of State for Foreign and Commonwealth Affairs, the administration of the territories is carried out by the Governments of the territories themselves.

Aims and Conditions of Membership. Membership involves acceptance of certain core principles, as set out in the Harare Declaration of 1991, and is subject to the approval of other member states. The Harare Declaration charts a course to take the Commonwealth into the 21st century and affirms members' continued commitment to the Singapore Declarations of 1971, by which members committed themselves to the pursuit of world peace and support of the UN.

The core principles defined by the Harare Declaration are: political democracy, human rights, good governance and the rule of law, and the protection of the environment through sustainable development. Commitment to these principles was made binding as a condition of membership at the 1993 Heads of Government meeting in Cyprus.

The Millbrook Action Programme of 1995 aims to support countries in implementing the Harare Declaration, providing assistance in constitutional and judicial matters, running elections, training and technical advice. Violations of the Harare Declaration will provoke a series of measures by the Commonwealth Secretariat, including: expression of disapproval, encouragement of bilateral actions by member states, appointment of fact-finders and mediators, stipulation of a period for the restoration of democracy, exclusion from ministerial meetings, suspension of all participation and aid and finally punitive measures including trade sanctions. An 8-member *Ministerial Action Group* may be convened by the Secretary-General as and when necessary to deal with violations. The Group held its first meeting in Dec. 1995. Its terms of reference are as set out in the Millbrook Action Programme.

The *Commonwealth Parliamentary Assembly* was founded in 1911. As defined by its constitution, its objectives are to 'promote knowledge of the constitutional, legislative, economic, social and cultural aspects of parliamentary democracy'. It meets these objectives by organizing conferences, meetings and seminars for members, arranging exchange visits between members, publishing books, newsletters, reports, studies and a quarterly journal and providing an information service. Its principal governing body is the General Assembly, which meets annually during the Commonwealth Parliamentary Conference and is composed of members attending that Conference as delegates. The Assembly elects an Executive Committee comprising a Chair, President, Vice-President, Treasurer and 27 regional representatives, which meets twice a year. The Chair is elected for 3-year terms. The Assembly is financed by membership fees levied on each branch and based on the number of delegates entitled to attend the Commonwealth Parliamentary Conference. The Secretariat is headed by the Secretary-General, with access to Heads of Government; the Secretariat is staffed by officers from member countries and is financed by contributions from member governments.

Commonwealth Secretariat. The Commonwealth Secretariat is an international body at the service of all 54 member countries. It provides the central organization for joint consultation and co-operation in many fields. It was established in 1965 by Commonwealth Heads of Government as a 'visible symbol of the spirit of co-operation which animates the Commonwealth', and has observer status at the UN General Assembly.

The Secretariat disseminates information on matters of common concern, organizes and services meetings and conferences, co-ordinates many Commonwealth activities, and provides expert technical assistance for economic and social development through the multilateral Commonwealth Fund for Technical Co-operation. The Secretariat is organized in divisions and sections which correspond to its main areas of operation: international affairs, economic affairs, food production and rural development, youth, education, information, applied studies in government, science and technology, law and health. Within this structure the Secretariat organizes the biennial meetings of Commonwealth Heads of Government (CHOGMs), annual meetings of Finance Ministers of member countries, and regular meetings of Ministers of Education, Law, Health, and others as appropriate. To emphasize the multilateral nature of the association, meetings are held in different cities and regions within the Commonwealth. Heads of Government decided that the Secretariat should work from London as it has the widest range of communications of any Commonwealth city, as well as the largest assembly of diplomatic missions.

Commonwealth Heads of Government Meetings (CHOGMs). Outside the UN, the CHOGM remains the largest intergovernmental conference in the world. Meetings are held every 2 years. The theme for the 1997 CHOGM in Edinburgh was the promotion of interCommonwealth trade, investment and development. At the Commonwealth Business Forum 2 days before the CHOGM, Tony Blair announced the British Government's decision to sell its majority holding in the Commonwealth Development Corporation and introduce private capital to the Corporation, which would effectively become a public-private partnership. The CDC has £1·6bn. invested in over 400 businesses in 54 countries worldwide. The hope is that this will allow the CDC to raise money in financial markets, which it is banned from doing under Treasury rules as a state-owned company. The proceeds from the sale will go back into development aid. A host of Commonwealth organizations and agencies are dedicated to enhancing interCommonwealth relations and the development of the potential of Commonwealth citizens. A list of these can be obtained from the *Commonwealth Institute* in London.

Commonwealth Day is celebrated on the second Monday in March each year. The theme for 1999 was music.

Headquarters: Marlborough House, Pall Mall, London, SW1Y 5HX, UK.
Website: http://www.thecommonwealth.org
Secretary-General: Emeka Anyaoku (Nigeria).

Selected publications. Commonwealth Yearbook; The Commonwealth Today; Commonwealth Currents (quarterly); *Directory of Commonwealth Organizations.*

Further Reading

The Cambridge History of the British Empire. 8 vols. CUP, 1929 *ff.*

Austin, D., *The Commonwealth and Britain.* London, 1988

Chan, S., *Twelve Years of Commonwealth Diplomatic History: Summit Meetings, 1979-1991.* Lampeter, 1992

Hall, H. D., *Commonwealth: A History of the British Commonwealth.* London and New York, 1971

Judd, D. and Slinn, P., *The Evolution of the Modern Commonwealth.* London, 1982

Keeton, G. W. (ed.) *The British Commonwealth: Its Laws and Constitutions. 9 vols.* London, 1951 ff.

Larby, P. and Hannam, H., *The Commonwealth* [Bibliography]. Oxford and New Brunswick (NJ), 1993

McIntyre, W. D., *The Significance of the Commonwealth, 1965–90.* London, 1991

Moore, R. J., *Making the New Commonwealth.* Oxford, 1987

COMMONWEALTH OF INDEPENDENT STATES (CIS)

The Commonwealth of Independent States, founded on 8 Dec. 1991 in Viskuli, home of the Belarussian government, is a community of independent states which proclaimed itself the successor to the Union of Soviet Socialist Republics in some aspects of international law and affairs. The member states are the founders, Russia, Belarus and Ukraine, and 9 subsequent adherents: Armenia, Azerbaijan, Georgia, Kazakhstan, Kyrgyzstan, Moldova, Tajikistan, Turkmenistan and Uzbekiston.

History. Extended negotiations in the Union of Soviet Socialist Republics (USSR) in 1990 and 1991, under the direction of President Gorbachev, sought to establish a 'renewed federation' or, subsequently, to conclude a new union treaty that would embrace all the 15 constituent republics of the USSR at that date. According to a referendum conducted in March 1991, 76% of the population (on an 80% turn-out) wished to maintain the USSR as a 'renewed federation of equal sovereign republics in which the human rights and freedoms of any nationality would be fully guaranteed'. In Sept. 1991, the 3 Baltic republics—Estonia, Latvia and Lithuania—were nonetheless recognized as independent states by the USSR State Council, and subsequently by the international community. Most of the remaining republics reached agreement on the broad outlines of a new 'union of sovereign states' in Nov. 1991, which would have retained a directly elected President and an all-union legislature, but which would have limited central authority to those powers specifically delegated to it by the members of the union.

A referendum in Ukraine in Dec. 1991, however, showed overwhelming support for full independence, and following this the 3 Slav republics (Russia, Belarus and Ukraine) concluded the Minsk Agreement on 8 Dec. 1991, establishing a Commonwealth of Independent States (CIS), headquartered in Minsk. The USSR, as a subject of international law and a geopolitical reality, was declared no longer in existence, and each of the 3 republics individually renounced the 1922 treaty through which the USSR had been established.

The CIS declared itself open to other former Soviet republics, and to states elsewhere that shared its objectives, and on 21 Dec. 1991 in Alma-Ata, a further declaration was signed with 8 other republics: Armenia, Azerbaijan, Kazakhstan, Kyrgyzstan, Moldova, Tajikistan, Turkmenistan and Uzbekiston. The declaration committed signatories to recognize the independence and sovereignty of other members, to respect human rights including those of national minorities, and to the observance of existing boundaries. Relations among the members of the CIS were to be conducted on an equal, multilateral, interstate basis, but it was agreed to endorse the principle of unitary control of strategic nuclear arms and the concept of a 'single economic space'. In a separate agreement the heads of member states agreed that Russia should take up the seat at the United Nations formerly occupied by the USSR, and a framework of interstate and intergovernment consultation was established. Following these developments Mikhail Gorbachev resigned as USSR President on 25 Dec. 1991, and on 26 Dec., the USSR Supreme Soviet voted a formal end to the 1922 Treaty of Union, and dissolved itself. Georgia decided to join on 9 Dec. 1993 and on 1 March 1994 the national parliament ratified the act.

The Charter, adopted on 22 Jan. 1993 in Minsk, proclaims that the Commonwealth is based on the principles of the sovereign equality of all members. It is not a state and does not have supranational authority.

Activities and Institutions. The principal organs of the CIS, according to the agreement concluded in Alma-Ata on 21 Dec. 1991, are the *Council of Heads of States*, which meets twice a year, and the *Council of Heads of Government*, which meets every 3 months. Both councils may convene extraordinary sessions, and may hold joint sittings. There is also a *Council of Defence Ministers*, established Feb. 1992, and a *Council of Foreign Ministers* (Dec. 1993). The Secretariat is the standing working organ.

At a summit meeting of heads of states (with the exception of Azerbaijan) in July 1992, agreements were reached on a way to divide former USSR assets abroad; on the legal cessionary of state archives of former Soviet states; on the status of an Economic Court; and on collective security. In 1992 an *Inter-Parliamentary Assembly* was established by 7 member states (Armenia, Belarus, Kazakhstan, Kyrgyzstan, Russia, Tajikistan and Uzbekiston).

At a subsequent meeting in Jan. 1993, Russia, Belarus, Armenia, Kazakhstan, Kyrgyzstan, Tajikistan and Uzbekiston agreed on a charter to implement co-operation in political, economic, ecological, humanitarian, cultural and other spheres; thorough and balanced economic and social development within the common economic space; interstate co-operation and integration; and to ensure human rights and freedoms. Three participants (Ukraine, Moldova and Turkmenistan) agreed only to a declaration that the decision would be open for signing in the future. For the purpose of the maintenance and development of multilateral industrial, trade and financial relations, Heads of State established an *Inter-State Bank* and adopted a Provision on it. Its charter was signed by 9 Heads of State (Armenia, Belarus, Kazakhstan, Kyrgyzstan, Moldova, Russia, Tajikistan, Turkmenistan, Uzbekiston, Ukraine) on 22 Dec. 1993.

The *CIS Inter-State Bank* was set up with a starting capital of 5,000m. roubles, to facilitate multilateral clearing of CIS interstate transactions. Members' contributions (by %), based on their share of foreign trade turnover in 1990, were as follows: Russia, 50%; Ukraine, 20·7%; Belarus, 8·4%; Kazakhstan, 6·1%; Uzbekiston, 5·5%; Moldova, 2·9%; Armenia, 1·8%; Tajikistan, 1·6%; Kyrgyzstan, 1·5%; Turkmenistan, 1·5%. The bank is an international settlement and financial-credit institution, established in accordance with the rules of international public law. The authorized capital on 1 Jan. 1999 was 20,000m. roubles. Members' contributions are the same as in 1993. The bank's highest management body is a Bank Council.

In accordance with the Agreement on Armed Forces and Border Troops, concluded on 30 Dec. 1991, it was decided to consider and solve the issue on the transference of the management of the General-Purpose Armed Forces in accordance with the national legislation of member states. On 14 Feb. 1992 the *Council of Defence Ministers* was established. In 1993, the Office of Commander-in-Chief of CIS Joint Armed Forces was reorganized in a Staff for Co-ordinating Military Co-operation. Its Chief of Staff is appointed by the Council of Heads of State. On 24 Sept. an Agreement on collective peacekeeping was concluded. Peacekeeping operations in intra-CIS conflicts could be implemented at the request of member states, and with the consent of parties to the conflict. CIS members contribute to this force in proportion to the size of their armed forces and are responsible for the conditions, training and supply of military and civil personnel to the conflict region; the commander is appointed on each occasion by the Council of Heads of State.

At the same meeting, Azerbaijan, Armenia, Belarus, Kazakhstan, Kyrgyzstan, Moldova, Russia, Tajikistan and Uzbekiston signed an agreement to form an *Economic Union*. Georgia and Turkmenistan signed later (14 and 23 Jan. 1994). Ukraine became an associated member on 15 April 1994. In Oct. 1994, a summit meeting established the *Inter-State Economic Committee (MEK)* to be based in Moscow. Members include all CIS states except Turkmenistan. The Committee's decisions are binding if voted by 80% of the membership. Russia commands 50% of the voting power; Ukraine 14%. The Committee's remit is to co-ordinate energy, transport and communications policies. The leading MEK organs are the Presidium and Collegium. There are 60 inter-state bodies within the CIS, 40 of them dealing with issues of economic or social policy. One of the MEK's main tasks is the co-ordination of the work of these councils or bodies. A *Customs Union* to regulate payments between member states with non-convertible independent currencies and a regulatory *Economic Court* have also been established.

On 29 March 1996, Belarus, Kazakhstan, Kyrgyzstan and Russia signed an agreement increasing their mutual economic and social integration by creating a *Community of Integrated States* (Tajikistan signed in 1998). The agreement established a Supreme Inter-Governmental Council comprising heads of state and government and foreign ministers, with a rotatory Chair, an integration committee of Ministers and an Inter-Parliamentary Committee.

On 2 April 1996, the Presidents of Belarus and Russia signed a treaty providing for political, economic and military integration, creating the nucleus of a *Community of Russia and Belarus*. The agreement establishes a Supreme Council comprising the Presidents, Prime Ministers and Speakers of both countries and the Chairman of the Executive Committee. A further treaty was signed on 22 May 1997, instituting common citizenship, common deployment of military forces and the harmonization of the 2 economies with a view to the creation of a common currency. The Community was later renamed the *Union of Belarus and Russia* and signed subsequent agreements on equal rights for its citizens and equal conditions for state and private entrepreneurship.

In March 1994, the CIS was accorded observer status in the UN.

Headquarters: 220000 Minsk, Kirava 17, Belarus.
Website: http://www.cis.minsk.by
Executive Secretary: Boris A. Berezovsky.

Further Reading

Brzezinski, Z. and Sullivan, P. (eds.) Russia and the Commonwealth of Independent States: Documents, Data and Analysis. Armonk (NY), 1996

ORGANIZATION OF AMERICAN STATES (OAS)

Origin. On 14 April 1890, representatives of the American republics, meeting in Washington at the First International Conference of American States, established an International Union of American Republics and, as its central office, a Commercial Bureau of American Republics, which later became the Pan-American Union. This international organization's object was to foster mutual understanding and co-operation among the nations of the western hemisphere. This led to the adoption on 30 April 1948 by the Ninth International Conference of American States, at Bogotá, Colombia, of the Charter of the Organization of American States. This co-ordinated the work of all the former independent official entities in the interAmerican system and defined their mutual relationships. The Charter of 1948 was subsequently amended by the Protocol of Buenos Aires (1967) and the Protocol of Cartagena de Indias (1985).

Members. This is on a basis of absolute equality, with each country having 1 vote and there being no veto power. Members (1998): Antigua and Barbuda, Argentina, Bahamas, Barbados, Belize, Bolivia, Brazil, Canada, Chile, Colombia, Costa Rica, Cuba (suspended 1962), Dominica, Dominican Republic, Ecuador, El Salvador, Grenada, Guatemala, Guyana, Haiti, Honduras, Jamaica, Mexico, Nicaragua, Panama, Paraguay, Peru, St Kitts and Nevis, St Lucia, St Vincent and the Grenadines, Suriname, Trinidad and Tobago, USA, Uruguay, Venezuela.

Permanent Observers. Algeria, Angola, Austria, Belgium, Bosnia-Hercegovina, Croatia, Cyprus, Czech Republic, Egypt, Equatorial Guinea, EU, Finland, France, Germany, Ghana, Greece, Holy See, Hungary, India, Israel, Italy, Japan, Kazakhstan, Republic of Korea, Latvia, Lebanon, Morocco, the Netherlands, Pakistan, Poland, Portugal, Romania, Russia, Saudi Arabia, Spain, Sri Lanka, Sweden, Switzerland, Tunisia, UK, Ukraine.

Aims and Activities. To strengthen the peace and security of the continent; promote and consolidate representative democracy, with due respect for the principle of non-intervention; prevent possible causes of difficulties and ensure the peaceful settlement of disputes among member states; provide for common action in the event of aggression; seek the solution of political, juridical and economic problems; promote by co-operative action economic, social and cultural development; and achieve an effective limitation of conventional weapons in order to devote maximum resources to economic and social development.

The Santiago Commitment to Democracy and the Renewal of the Inter-American System. With the emergence of democratically elected governments throughout the continent, the OAS has been increasingly concerned with the preservation, protection and promotion of democracy. At its 21st Regular Session (Santiago, Chile, 1991) the OAS General Assembly adopted the Santiago Commitment to Democracy and the Renewal of the Inter-American System as well as the Protocol of Washington (1992) to amend the Charter by provisions of the Resolution 1080 on representative democracy. The latter calls for collective action in the event of a 'sudden or irregular interruption of the democratic political institutional process or of the legitimate exercise of power by the democratically elected government in any of the Organization's member states'. Specifically, the Assembly approved an Article which provides that a member of OAS whose democratically constituted government has been overthrown by force may be suspended from the exercise of the right to participate in the sessions of OAS organs, and spells out the way such suspension shall be applied.

The Protocol of Washington also incorporates among the essential purposes of the OAS the eradication of extreme poverty which constitutes an obstacle to the full democratic development of the peoples of the hemisphere. This commitment was further strengthened by amendments under the Protocol of Managua the following year, with measures designed to improve the delivery of technical co-operation to such member states. At its 20th Special Session (Feb. 1994, Mexico City), the OAS General Assembly approved a resolution on a commitment to a partnership for development and struggle to overcome extreme poverty.

Declaration of Belém do Pará. At its 24th Regular Session (June 1994, Belém do Pará), the General Assembly adopted the Declaration of Belém do Pará, in which the Ministers of Foreign Affairs and Heads of Delegation of Member States declared their commitment to strengthening the OAS as the main hemispheric forum of political consensus, so that it may support: the realization of the aspirations of member states in promoting and consolidating peace, democracy, social justice, and development, in accordance with the purposes and principles of the Charter; their decision to promote and deepen co-operative relations in the economic, social, educational, cultural, scientific, technological and political fields; their commitment to continue and further the dialogue on hemispheric security in order to consolidate and strengthen mutual confidence; their determination to continue to contribute to the objective of general and complete disarmament, under effective international control; their determination to strengthen regional co-operation to increase the effectiveness of efforts to combat the illicit use of narcotic drugs and traffic therein; their decision to co-operate in a reciprocal effort towards preventing and punishing terrorist acts, methods and practices, and the development of international law in this matter; and their commitment to promote economic and social development for the indigenous populations of their countries.

The OAS also carries out programmes to promote the economic and social development of its member states. Specialized training is provided for Latin American and Caribbean citizens each year in development-related fields; and development projects are executed each year in response to requests from member governments.

Organization. Under its Charter the OAS accomplishes its purposes by means of:
 (a) The General Assembly, which meets annually.
 (b) The Meeting of Consultation of Ministers of Foreign Affairs, held to consider problems of an urgent nature and of common interest.
 (c) The Councils: The Permanent Council, which meets on a permanent basis at OAS headquarters and carries out decisions of the General Assembly, assists the member states in the peaceful settlement of disputes, acts as the Preparatory Committee of that Assembly, submits recommendations with regard to the functioning of the Organization, and considers the reports to the Assembly of the other organs. The Inter-American Council for Integral Development (CIDI) (formed from the merger of two previous councils, the Inter-American Economic and Social

Council and the Inter-American Council for Education, Science and Culture) directs and monitors OAS technical co-operation programmes.

(d) The Inter-American Juridical Committee which acts as an advisory body to the OAS on juridical matters and promotes the development and codification of international law. 11 jurists, elected for 4-year terms by the General Assembly, represent all the American States.

(e) The Inter-American Commission on Human Rights which oversees the observance and protection of human rights. 7 members elected for 4-year terms by the General Assembly represent all the OAS member states.

(f) The General Secretariat, which is the central and permanent organ of the OAS.

(g) The Specialized Conferences, meeting to deal with special technical matters or to develop specific aspects of inter-American co-operation.

(h) The Specialized Organizations, intergovernmental organizations established by multilateral agreements to discharge specific functions in their respective fields of action, such as women's affairs, agriculture, child welfare, Indian affairs, geography and history, and health.

The Secretary-General is elected by the General Assembly for 5-year terms. The General Assembly approves the annual budget which is financed by quotas contributed by the member governments. The budget in 1996 amounted to US$100·6m.

Headquarters: 17th Street and Constitution Avenue, NW, Washington, D.C., 20006, USA.

Secretary-General: César Gavíria Trujillo (Colombia).

Publications. Charter of the Organization of American States. 1948.—As Amended by the Protocol of Buenos Aires in 1967 and the Protocol of Cartagena de Indias in 1985; The OAS and the Evolution of the Inter-American System; Annual Report of the Secretary-General; Status of Inter-American Treaties and Conventions (annual).

Further Reading

Sheinin, D., *The Organization of American States* [Bibliography]. Oxford and Metuchen (NJ), 1995

INTER-AMERICAN DEVELOPMENT BANK (IDB)

The IDB, the oldest and largest regional multilateral development institution, was established in 1959 to help accelerate economic and social development in Latin America and the Caribbean. The Bank's original membership included 19 Latin American and Caribbean countries and the USA. Today, membership totals 46 nations, including non-regional members.

Members. Argentina, Austria, Bahamas, Barbados, Belgium, Belize, Bolivia, Brazil, Britain, Canada, Chile, Colombia, Costa Rica, Croatia, Denmark, Dominican Republic, Ecuador, El Salvador, Finland, France, Germany, Guatemala, Guyana, Haiti, Honduras, Israel, Italy, Jamaica, Japan, Mexico, Netherlands, Nicaragua, Norway, Panama, Paraguay, Peru, Portugal, Slovenia, Spain, Suriname, Sweden, Switzerland, Trinidad and Tobago, USA, Uruguay, Venezuela.

In carrying out its mission, the Bank has mobilized some US$206,000m. for project financing, and its lending has increased dramatically from the US$294m. approved in 1961 to US$6,700m. in 1996.

Current lending priorities include poverty reduction and social equity, modernization and integration, and the environment. The Bank has a Fund for Special Operations for lending on concessional terms for projects in countries classified as economically less developed. An additional facility, the Multilateral

Investment Fund (MIF), was created in 1992 to help promote and accelerate investment reforms and private-sector development throughout the region.

The Board of Governors is the Bank's highest authority. Governors are usually Ministers of Finance, Presidents of Central Banks or officers of comparable rank. The Board of Directors is the Bank's executive body. The IDB has country offices in each of its borrowing countries, and in Paris and Tokyo.

Headquarters: 1300 New York Avenue, NW, Washington, D.C., 20577, USA
Website: http://www.iadb.org.
President: Enrique V. Iglesias (Uruguay).

CENTRAL AMERICAN COMMON MARKET (CACM)

In Dec. 1960, El Salvador, Guatemala, Honduras and Nicaragua concluded the General Treaty of Central American Economic Integration under the auspices of the Organization of Central American States (ODECA) in Managua. Long-standing political and social conflicts in the area have repeatedly dogged efforts to establish integration towards the establishment of a common market.

Members. Costa Rica, El Salvador, Guatemala, Honduras, Nicaragua and Panama.

A protocol to the 1960 General Treaty signed by all 6 members in Oct. 1993 reaffirmed an eventual commitment to full economic integration with a common external tariff of 20% to be introduced only voluntarily and gradually.

A Treaty on Democratic Security in Central America was signed by all 6 members at San Pedro Sula, Honduras in Dec. 1995, with a view to achieving a proper 'balance of forces' in the region, intensifying the fight against trafficking of drugs and arms, and reintegrating refugees and displaced persons.

In addition, the CACM countries signed a new framework co-operation agreement with the EC in Feb. 1993, revising the previous (1985) failing agreement between them, to provide support to CACM's integration plans.

Headquarters: 4a Avda 10–25, Zona 14, Apdo 1237, Guatemala City, Guatemala.
Secretary-General: Haroldo Rodas Melgar.

LATIN AMERICAN INTEGRATION ASSOCIATION (ALADI/LAIA)

The ALADI was established to promote freer trade among member countries in the region.

Members. (12) Argentina, Bolivia, Brazil, Chile, Colombia, Ecuador, Mexico, Paraguay, Peru, Uruguay, Venezuela and Cuba, subject to the receipt by ALADI of the Instrument of Ratification.

Observers. (23) China, Commission of the European Communities, Costa Rica, Dominican Republic, El Salvador, Guatemala, Honduras, Inter-American Development Bank, Italy, Nicaragua, Organization of American States, Panama, Portugal, Spain, UN Development Programme, UN Economic Commission for Latin America and the Caribbean (ECLAC), Romania, Russia, Switzerland, Inter-American Institute for Cooperation on Agriculture (IICA), Andean Development Corporation (CAF), Latin-American Economic System (SELA).

Headquarters: calle Cebollati 1461, Casilla de Correo 577, 11000 Montevideo, Uruguay.

THE ANDEAN COMMUNITY

On 26 May 1969, an agreement was signed by Bolivia, Chile, Colombia, Ecuador and Peru establishing the Cartagena Agreement (also referred to as the Andean Pact or the Andean Group). Chile withdrew from the Group in 1976. Venezuela, which was initially actively involved, did not sign the agreement until 1973. In 1997, Peru announced its withdrawal for 5 years; and Panama joined.

The Act of Caracas signed at the Group's 5th meeting in May 1991 established a free trade zone between member states to come into effect on 1 Feb. 1993 as the first step towards the creation of a common market. Bolivia, Colombia, Ecuador and Venezuela have fully liberalized the trade among them, while Peru is still implementing its liberalization process, due to end by 2005. A Common External Tariff for imports from third countries has been in effect since Feb. 1, 1995.

In March 1996 at the Group's 8th summit in Trujillo in Peru, member countries (Bolivia, Colombia, Ecuador, Peru, Venezuela) signed a reform protocol to the Agreement, according to which the Group would be superseded by the Andean Community, in order to promote greater economic, commercial and political integration between member countries under a new Andean Integration System (SAI).

Organization. The Andean Presidential Council, composed of the presidents of the Member States, is the highest-level body of the Andean Integration System (SAI). The Commission and the Andean Council of Foreign Ministers are legislative bodies. The General Secretariat is the executive body and the Andean Parliament is the deliberative body of the SAI. The Court of Justice, which began operating in 1984, resolves disputes between members and interprets legislation. The SAI has other institutions: Andean Development Corporation (CAF), Latin American Reserve Fund (FLAR), Simon Bolivar Andean University, Andean Business Advisory Council, Andean Labour Advisory Council and various Social Agreements.

Headquarters: Avda Paseo de la República 3895, San Isidro, Lima 17, Peru.
Website: http://www.comunidadandina.org
e-mail: contacto@comunidadandina.org
Secretary-General: Sebastián Alegrett.

SOUTHERN COMMON MARKET (MERCOSUR)

Founded in March 1991 by the Treaty of Asunción between Argentina, Brazil, Paraguay and Uruguay, the treaty committed the signatories to the progressive reduction of tariffs culminating in the formation of a common market on 1 Jan. 1995. This duly came into effect as a free trade zone affecting 90% of commodities. A common external tariff averaging 14% applies to 80% of trade with countries outside Mercosur. Details were agreed at foreign minister level by the Protocol of Ouro Preto signed on 17 Dec. 1994.

In 1996, Chile negotiated a free-trade agreement with Mercosur which came into effect on 1 Oct. Two weeks later, Bolivia signed the same. In Dec. that year, an agreement conferring associate membership on Bolivia was also endorsed.

Organization. The member states' foreign ministers form a Council responsible for leading the integration process, the chairmanship of which rotates every 6 months. The permanent executive body is the Common Market Group of member states, which takes decisions by consensus. There is a Trade Commission and Joint Parliamentary Commission, an arbitration tribunal whose decisions are binding on member countries, and a secretariat in Montevideo.

Headquarters: Rincon 575 P12, 11000 Montevideo, Uruguay.
Administrative Secretary: Manuel Olarreaga.

ASSOCIATION OF CARIBBEAN STATES (ACS)

The Convention establishing the ACS was signed on 24 July 1994 in Cartagena de Indias, Colombia, with the aim of promoting integration among all the countries of the Caribbean, comprising 25 full Member States and a number of potential Associate Members.

Members. Antigua and Barbuda, Bahamas, Barbados, Belize, Colombia, Costa Rica, Cuba, Dominica, Dominican Republic, El Salvador, Grenada, Guatemala, Guyana, Haiti, Honduras, Jamaica, Mexico, Nicaragua, Panama, St Lucia, St Kitts and Nevis, St Vincent and the Grenadines, Suriname, Trinidad and Tobago, Venezuela.

The CARICOM Secretariat, the Latin American Economic System (SELA), the Central American Integration System (SICA) and the Permanent Secretariat of the General Agreement on Central American Economic Integration (SIECA) were declared Founding Observers of the ACS.

Functions. The ACS is an organization for consultation, co-operation and concerted action in the context of economic integration and functional co-operation. Its objectives are enshrined in the Convention and are focused around the following: the strengthening of the regional co-operation and integration process, with a view to creating an enhanced economic space in the region; preserving the environmental integrity of the Caribbean Sea which is regarded as the common patrimony of the peoples of the region; and promoting the sustainable development of the Great Caribbean.

Organization. The main organs of the Association are the Ministerial Council and the Secretariat. There are also Special Committees on: Trade Development and External Economic Relations; Protection and Conservation of the Environment and the Caribbean Sea; Natural Resources; Tourism; Budget and Administration; Science and Technology; Health; and Education and Culture.

Headquarters: ACS Secretariat, 11-13 Victoria Ave., POB 660, Port of Spain, Trinidad and Tobago.
Website: http://www.acs-aec.org
Secretary-General: Dr Simón Molina Duarte (Venezuela).

CARIBBEAN COMMUNITY (CARICOM)

Origin. The Treaty of Chaguaramas establishing the Caribbean Community and Common Market was signed by the Prime Ministers of Barbados, Guyana, Jamaica and Trinidad and Tobago at Chaguaramas, Trinidad, on 4 July 1973, and entered into force on 1 Aug. 1973.

6 additional countries and territories (Belize, Dominica, Grenada, St Lucia, St Vincent and the Grenadines, Montserrat) signed the Treaty on 17 April 1974, and the Treaty came into effect for those countries on 1 May 1974. Antigua acceded to membership on 4 July that year; St Kitts and Nevis on 26 July; the Bahamas on 4 July 1983 (not Common Market); Suriname on 4 July 1995.

Members. Antigua and Barbuda, Bahamas, Barbados, Belize, Dominica, Grenada, Guyana, Haiti, Jamaica, Montserrat, St Kitts and Nevis, St Lucia, St Vincent and the Grenadines, Suriname and Trinidad and Tobago. The British Virgin Islands and Turks and Caicos Islands are associate members.

Activities. The Caribbean Community has 3 areas of activity: (i) economic co-operation through the Caribbean Common Market; (ii) co-ordination of foreign policy; (iii) functional co-operation in areas such as health, education and culture, labour and manpower development, and women's affairs.

In 1998 the Region moved closer to putting the necessary legal instruments in place for the achievement of a CARICOM Single Market and Economy with the signing of 2 additional Protocols amending the Treaty of Chaguaramas. These were Protocol III: Industrial Policy—the objectives of which are international competitive and sustainable production of goods and services for the promotion of the Region's economic and social development; and Protocol V: Agricultural Policy—the transformation of the agricultural sector towards market-oriented, internationally competitive and environmentally sound production of traditional and non-traditional primary agricultural products, and efficient management and sustainable exploitation of the Region's natural resources.

The Treaty of Chaguaramas is in the process of being revised by means of 9 Protocols. By March 1999, Protocols I, II, III and V had been signed.

Agreement was reached for the setting up of a Caribbean Court of Justice. Issues that were addressed during the year included the policy implications of investing the Caribbean Court of Justice with original jurisdiction in respect of the interpretation and application of the Treaty establishing the Caribbean Community, as amended, and in particular the issues relating to exclusive jurisdiction of the Court; parties to be accorded *locus standi* in proceedings before the Court; the doctrine of precedent in respect of decisions of the Court and privileges and immunities of the Court; Rules of the Court; the Regional Judicial and Legal Services Commission; and judges and counsel enjoying the right of audience before the Court.

Structure. The Conference of Heads of Government is the principal organ of the Community, and its primary responsibility is to determine and provide the policy direction for the Community. It is the final authority on behalf of the Community for the conclusion of treaties and for entering into relationships between the Community and international organizations and States. It is responsible for financial arrangements to meet the expenses of the Community.

The Community Council of Ministers is the second highest organ of the Community and consists of Ministers of Government responsible for Community Affairs. The Community Council has primary responsibility for the development of Community strategic planning and co-ordination in the areas of economic integration, functional co-operation and external relations.

Ministerial Councils established by the Conference of Heads of Government to assist the principal organs are: Council for Trade and Economic Development (COTED); the Council for Foreign and Community Relations (COFCOR); the Council for Human and Social Development (COHSOD); and the Council for Finance and Planning (COFAP).

The Bureau of the Conference of Heads of Government which is recognized as a Committee of the Conference has the authority to initiate proposals, update consensus, facilitate implementation of Community decisions and provide guidance to the Community on policy issues. The Bureau comprises the current Chairperson of the Conference of Heads of Government, the outgoing and incoming chairpersons, as well as the Secretary-General.

The Secretariat is the principal administrative organ of the Community. The Secretary-General is appointed by the Conference (on the recommendation of the

Community Council) for a term not exceeding 5 years, and may be re-appointed. The Secretary-General is the Chief Executive Officer of the Community and acts in that capacity at all meetings of the Community Organs.

Institutions of the Community: Caribbean Disaster Emergency Response Agency (CDERA); Caribbean Meteorological Institute (CMI); Caribbean Meteorological Organization (CMO); Caribbean Food Corporation (CFC); Caribbean Environmental Health Institute (CEHI); Caribbean Regional Centre for the Education and Training of Animal Health Assistants; Association of Caribbean Community Parliamentarians (ACCP); Caribbean Centre for Development Administration (CARICAD); Caribbean Food and Nutrition Institute (CFNI).

Associate Institutions. Caribbean Development Bank (CDB); University of Guyana (UG); University of the West Indies (UWI); Caribbean Law Institute (CLI)/Caribbean Law Institute Centre (CLIC).

Headquarters: Bank of Guyana Building, PO Box 10827, Georgetown, Guyana.
Secretary-General: Edwin W. Carrington (Trinidad and Tobago).

Publications. CARICOM Perspective. (2 a year); *Annual Report; Treaty Establishing the Caribbean Community.*

Further Reading

Parry, J. H., et. al. A Short History of the West Indies. Rev. ed. London, 1987

ORGANIZATION OF EASTERN CARIBBEAN STATES (OECS)

Founded 1981 when 7 eastern Caribbean states signed the Treaty of Basseterre agreeing to co-operate with each other to promote unity and solidarity among the members.

Members. (1998) Antigua and Barbuda, Dominica, Grenada, Montserrat, St Kitts and Nevis, St Lucia, and St Vincent and the Grenadines. The British Virgin Islands and Anguilla have associate membership.

Functions. As set out in the Treaty of Basseterre: to promote co-operation among members and to defend their sovereignty, territorial integrity and independence; to assist member states in the realization of their obligations and responsibilities to the international community with due regard to the role of international law as a standard of conduct in their relationships; to assist member states in the realization of their obligations and responsibilities to the international community with due regard to the role of international issues, and to establish and maintain, where possible, arrangements for joint overseas representation and common services; to promote economic integration among members; to pursue these through its respective institutions by discussion of questions of common concern and by agreement on common action.

OECS's work is carried out through a number of specialized institutions, work units or projects in 7 countries. Main areas of interest include: natural resources and solid waste management; education reform, technical and vocational education; pharmaceuticals; trade and agricultural diversification; investment promotion; and civil aviation.

Headquarters: Morne Fortune, PO Box 179, Castries, St Lucia.
Director-General: Swinburne Lestrade.

ASIAN DEVELOPMENT BANK

A multilateral development finance institution established in 1966 to promote economic and social progress in the Asian and Pacific region, the Bank's strategic objectives in the medium term are to foster economic growth, reduce poverty, improve the status of women, support human development (including population planning) and protect the environment.

The bank's capital stock is owned by 56 member countries, 40 regional, 16 non-regional. The bank makes loans and equity investments, and provides technical assistance grants for the preparation and execution of development projects and programmes; promotes investment of public and private capital for development purposes; and assists in co-ordinating development policies and plans in its developing member countries (DMCs).

The bank gives special attention to the needs of smaller or less developed countries, giving priority to regional, subregional and national projects which contribute to the economic growth of the region and promote regional co-operation. Loans from ordinary capital resources on non-concessional terms account for about 70% of cumulative lending. Loans from the bank's principal special fund, the Asian Development Fund, are made on highly concessional terms almost exclusively to the poorest borrowing countries.

Regional members. Afghanistan, Australia, Bangladesh, Bhutan, Cambodia, China, Cook Islands, Fiji Islands, Hong Kong, India, Indonesia, Japan, Kazakhstan, Kiribati, Republic of Korea, Kyrgyzstan, Laos, Malaysia, Maldives, Marshall Islands, Micronesia, Mongolia, Myanmar, Nauru, Nepal, New Zealand, Pakistan, Papua New Guinea, Philippines, Samoa, Singapore, Solomon Islands, Sri Lanka, Taiwan, Thailand, Tonga, Tuvalu, Uzbekiston, Vanuatu and Vietnam.

Non-regional members. Austria, Belgium, Canada, Denmark, Finland, France, Germany, Italy, Netherlands, Norway, Spain, Sweden, Switzerland, Turkey, UK, USA.

Organization. The bank's highest policy-making body is its Board of Governors, which meets annually. Its executive body is the 12-member Board of Directors (each with an alternate), 8 from the regional members, 4 non-regional.

The ADB also has seven resident missions: in Dhaka, Bangladesh; Phnom Penh, Cambodia; New Delhi, India; Jakarta, Indonesia; Káthmandu, Nepal; Islamabad, Pakistan; Hanoi, Vietnam; and a regional mission in Port Vila, Vanuatu. There are also 3 representative offices: in Tokyo, Frankfurt and Washington; and resident missions are being set up in Kazakhstan, Uzbekiston and Sri Lanka.

Headquarters: 6 ADB Avenue, Mandaluyong, Metro Manila, Philippines.

ECONOMIC CO-OPERATION ORGANIZATION (ECO)

An intergovernmental organization established in 1985 by Iran, Pakistan and Turkey for the purpose of promoting regional economic co-operation among member states. Afghanistan, Azerbaijan, Kazakhstan, Kyrgyzstan, Tajikistan, Turkmenistan and Uzbekiston joined in 1992, bringing the total of member states to 10.

The principal objectives of the Organization are to promote conditions for sustainable economic development and raise the standard and quality of living in Member States through mobilization of the region's economic and social potentials. Areas of co-operation include trade, industry, agriculture, environment, transport and communications, energy, drug abuse control, human resource development, social, cultural, technical and scientific fields.

At a conference in Tehran in Feb. 1992, it was agreed to introduce preferential tariffs between member states, set up a development bank in Istanbul, and co-operate in the modernization of transport, communications, industry and agriculture. In 1993, a protocol on Preferential Tariff Arrangements was signed between Turkey, Iran and Pakistan.

At the 1995 summit of heads of state, it was agreed to set up 4 regional institutions: a trade and development bank, a shipping line, an airline and a reinsurance company. The fifth summit meeting was held in Almaty, Kazakhstan in May 1998. The Council of Ministers was to meet in Baku, Azerbaijan, in May 1999. The sixth summit will take place in Bishkek, Kyrgyzstan in 2000.

The long-term perspectives and priorities of ECO are defined in the form of 2 Action Plans: the Quetta Plan of Action, and the Istanbul Declaration and Economic Co-operation Strategy, which was adopted in 1996, with concrete targets to be achieved by 2005.

The highest policy and decision-making body is the Council of Ministers (COM) which meets at least once a year by rotation among Member States. The Council of Permanent Representatives (CPR) meets regularly in Tehran to formulate issues requiring decision by Member States and to implement decisions taken by COM. The Regional Planning Council (RPC) meets annually to review and evaluate programmes and evolve new programmes of action for submission to and approval by COM. In addition there are two specialized agencies (the Cultural Institute and the Science Foundation) and six regional institutions. ECO has observer status at the UN General Assembly and the Organization of Islamic Conference (OIC).

Headquarters: 1 Goulbou Alley, Kamranieh, PO Box 14155-6176, Tehran, Islamic Republic of Iran.
Secretary-General: H. E. Mr. Onder Ozar (Turkey).

COLOMBO PLAN

History. Founded in 1950 to promote the development of newly independent Asian member countries, the Colombo Plan has grown from a group of 7 Commonwealth nations into an organization of 24 countries. Originally the Plan was conceived for a period of 6 years. This was renewed from time to time until the Consultative Committee gave the Plan an indefinite lifespan in 1980.

The Plan is multilateral in approach, bilateral in operation: multilateral in that it takes cognizance of the problems of development of member countries in the Asia and Pacific region and endeavours to deal with them in a co-ordinated way; bilateral because negotiations for assistance are made direct between a donor and a recipient country.

Members. (Permanent Member Countries) Afghanistan, Australia, Bangladesh, Bhutan, Cambodia, Fiji Islands, India, Indonesia, Islamic Republic of Iran, Japan, South Korea, Lao People's Democratic Republic, Malaysia, Maldives, Myanmar, Nepal, New Zealand, Pakistan, Papua New Guinea, Philippines, Singapore, Sri Lanka, Thailand and USA; *(Provisional member country)* Mongolia.

Aims. The aims of the Colombo Plan are: (1) to provide a forum for discussion, at local level, of development needs; (2) to facilitate development assistance by encouraging members to participate as donors and recipients of technical co-operation; and (3) to execute programmes to advance development within member countries. The Plan currently has the following programmes:

Programme for Public Administration (PPA). Initiated in 1995 to provide developing member country officials training in all sectors of public administration in the context of market-oriented economies, drawing on the experience of more developed economies in the region.

South-South Technical Co-operation Data Bank Programme (SSTC/DB). Published a report in December 1997 entitled South-South Technical Co-operation in Selected Member Countries covering technical co-operation activities of India, Indonesia, Malaysia, Pakistan, Philippines, Singapore and Thailand.

Drug Advisory Programme (DAP). Initiated in 1972, it works with governments, international bodies and NGOs in the region to deliver more effective anti-narcotics programmes. It works both in supply (controlling availability of drugs) and demand (helping counter the culture and providing assistance to addicts).

Programme for Private Sector Development (PPSD). In 1998 the PPSD conducted training programmes co-sponsored by the Asian Development Bank (ADB), the Malaysian Technical Co-operation Programme (MTCP) and the Pakistan Industrial Technical Assistance Centre (PITAC).

Colombo Plan Staff College for Technician Education (CPSC). Established in 1973, it trains management and technical staff from member countries. It is separately financed by most member countries and functions under the guidance of its own Governing Board, consisting of the heads of member countries' permanent diplomatic missions in the Philippines.

Structure. The Consultative Committee is the principal policy-making body of the Colombo Plan. Consisting of all member countries, it meets every 2 years to review the economic and social progress of members, exchange views on technical co-operation programmes and generally review the activities of the Plan. The Colombo Plan Council represents each member government and meets several times a year to identify development issues, recommend measures to be taken and ensure implementation.

Headquarters: 12 Melbourne Avenue, PO Box 596, Colombo 4, Sri Lanka.
Secretary-General: Dr Hak-Su Kim.
e-mail: cplan@slt.lk

Publications. Consultative Committee Meeting – Proceedings and Conclusions (biennial); *Report of the Colombo Plan Council* (annual); *The Colombo Plan* (brochure); *Drug Advisory Programme – Report of the Panel of Experts* (quadrennial); *The Colombo Plan Focus* (quarterly newsletter); *South-South Technical Co-operation in Selected Member Countries.*

ASIA-PACIFIC ECONOMIC CO-OPERATION (APEC)

Origin and Aims. Founded in 1989 in response to the growing interdependence among Asia-Pacific economies. Begun as an informal dialogue group, APEC has since become the primary regional vehicle for promoting open trade and practical economic co-operation in the region. It aims to promote free and open trade in the Asia-Pacific region through trade and investment liberalization and facilitation. Also, to promote economic and technical co-operation among its members. APEC's 21 member economies had a combined GDP of over US$16 trillion in 1996 and 45 per cent of global trade. New Zealand is the APEC Chair for 1999. Membership consists of economies rather than countries. Peru, Russia and Vietnam joined the community at the 10th APEC Ministerial Meeting held in Kuala Lumpur, Malaysia, in Nov. 1998.

Members. Australia, Brunei, Canada, Chile, China, Hong Kong, Indonesia, Japan, Korea (Republic of), Malaysia, Mexico, New Zealand, Papua New Guinea, Peru, Philippines, Russia, Singapore, Taipei (Taiwan), Thailand, USA and Vietnam.

Activities. At Blake Island near Seattle in Nov. 1993, Economic Leaders envisaged a community of Asia-Pacific economies based on the spirit of openness and partnership, of co-operative efforts to solve the challenges of change, of free exchange of goods, services and investment, of broadly based economic growth and higher living and educational standards, and of sustainable growth that respects the natural environment. In 1994, in Bogor, Indonesia, Ministers translated the vision of an open trading system into the goal of free and open trade and investment in the Asia-Pacific by 2010 for developed member countries and 2020 for developing ones.

In Osaka, 1994, Leaders adopted the Osaka Action Agenda, establishing the three pillars of APEC activities: trade and investment liberalization, business facilitation and economic-technical co-operation. The Manila Action Plan for APEC (MAPA), adopted by Economic Leaders in Nov. 1996, includes the individual joint activities of all APEC economies to achieve the objectives outlined in Bogor. Attention was focused on the following 6 areas of economic and technical co-operation: developing human capital; fostering safe and efficient capital markets; strengthening economic infrastructure; harnessing technologies of the future; promoting environmentally sustainable growth; and encouraging the growth of small and medium-sized enterprises.

In Vancouver, in 1997, Economic Leaders recognized members' efforts to improve the commitments in their Individual Action Plans and reaffirmed their intention to update these annually. Leaders endorsed their Ministers' agreement that action should be taken with respect to early voluntary sectoral liberalization (EVSL) in 15 sectors, with 9 to be advanced through 1998 and implementation to begin in 1999. At the same time, they endorsed the Vancouver Framework for Enhanced Public-Private Partnership for Infrastructure Development.

In Kuala Lumpur, in 1998, Leaders reaffirmed their commitment to co-operative growth strategy. They resolved to strengthen social safety nets, financial systems, trade and investment flows, the scientific and technological base, human resources development, economic infrastructure, and business and commercial links, so as to provide the base for sustained growth into the 21st century. They also adopted the Kuala Lumpur Action Program on Skills Development, which seeks to encourage greater participation of the private/business sectors in skills development in APEC through public-business 'smart partnership'.

Headquarters: 438 Alexandra Road, 14-00 Alexandra Point, Singapore 119958.
Website: http://www.apecsec.org.sg
Executive Director: Timothy Hannah.

THE PACIFIC COMMUNITY (SPC)

Until Feb. 1998 known as the South Pacific Commission, this is a regional intergovernmental organization founded in 1947 under an Agreement commonly referred to as the Canberra Agreement. It is funded by assessed contributions from its 22 members and by voluntary contributions from member and non-member countries, international organizations and other sources.

Members. American Samoa, Australia, Cook Islands, Fiji Islands, France, French Polynesia, Guam, Kiribati, Marshall Islands, Federated States of Micronesia, Nauru, New Caledonia, New Zealand, Niue, Northern Mariana Islands, Palau, Papua New Guinea, Pitcairn Islands, Samoa, Solomon Islands, Tokelau, Tonga, Tuvalu, UK, USA, Vanuatu, and Wallis and Futuna.

Functions. The SPC has 3 main areas of work: land resources, marine resources and social resources. It conducts research and provides technical assistance and training in these areas to member Pacific Island countries and territories of the Pacific.

Organization. The Conference of the Pacific Community is the governing body of the Community. Its key focus is to appoint the Director-General, to consider major national or regional policy issues and to note changes to the Financial and Staff Regulations approved by the CRGA, the Committee of Representatives of Governments and Administrations. It meets every 2 years. The CRGA meets once a year and is the principal decision-making organ of the Community. There is also a regional office in Fiji Islands.

Headquarters: BP D5, 98848 Nouméa Cedex, New Caledonia.
Website: http://www.spc.org.nc
e-mail: spc@spc.org.nc
Director-General: Robert Dun (Australia).

SOUTH PACIFIC FORUM (SPF)

The South Pacific Forum held its first meeting of Heads of Government in New Zealand in 1971. The SPF provides an opportunity for informal discussions to be held on a wide range of issues. It meets annually or as necessary. The Forum has no written constitution or international agreement governing its activities nor any formal rules relating to its purpose, membership or conduct of meeting. Decisions are reached by consensus. In Oct. 1994, the Forum was granted observer status to the UN.

Members. (1998) Australia, Cook Islands, Fiji Islands, Kiribati, Marshall Islands, Micronesia, Nauru, New Zealand, Niue, Palau, Papua New Guinea, Samoa, Solomon Islands, Tonga, Tuvalu and Vanuatu.

Functions. The Secretariat's mission is to enhance the economic and social well-being of the South Pacific peoples, in support of the efforts of the national governments. Its particular responsibility is to facilitate, develop and maintain co-operation and consultation between and among its 16 member countries. Its mandate includes the identification of opportunities for the modification of trade patterns; investigation of development methods which are in keeping with the concept of regional enterprise and free and open trade; establishment of an advisory service on technical assistance, aid and investment finance; provision of economic expertise and assistance.

Activities. The Secretariat has 4 core divisions: Trade and Investment; Political and International Affairs; Development and Economic Policy; Corporate Services. Its focus is on providing a policy advisory role on issues which cannot be fully assessed on a national basis, and on providing high-level policy advice on trade and investment to members.

The *South Pacific Nuclear-Free Zone Treaty* (of Rarotonga) was signed in 1985, prohibiting the acquisition, stationing or testing of nuclear weapons in the region. The major nuclear powers were to sign a protocol to the treaty. Russia and China signed in 1987; France, the UK and USA did not. In July 1995, when the French government decided to resume testing in French Polynesia, pressure was brought to bear on the 3 governments to sign. All 3 announced their intention to accede by mid-1996. In Jan. 1996 France announced its intention to cut short its programme, and all 3 countries signed up to the Treaty in March 1996.

Organization. The South Pacific Bureau for Economic Co-operation (SPEC) was established by the Agreement of 17 April 1973 at the 4th meeting of the SPF. In 1988 at its 19th meeting, SPEC was reorganized and renamed the South Pacific Forum Secretariat. The Secretariat has been headed (since 1977) by a Secretary-General and a Deputy Secretary-General. They form the Executive. It is governed by an executive committee, the Forum Officials Committee, which acts as intermediary between it and the Forum.

Headquarters: Ratu Sukuna Road, Suva, Fiji Islands.
Secretary-General: Ieremia Tabai.

ASSOCIATION OF SOUTH EAST ASIAN NATIONS (ASEAN)

History and Membership. ASEAN is a regional intergovernmental organization formed by the governments of Indonesia, Malaysia, the Philippines, Singapore and Thailand through the Bangkok Declaration which was signed by their foreign ministers on 8 Aug. 1967. Brunei joined in 1984, Vietnam in 1995, Laos and Myanmar in 1997. The decision on whether to admit Cambodia, which has for some time enjoyed observer status in ASEAN, was deferred in July 1997 due to civil unrest there. Papua New Guinea also has observer status. In 1998, the combined GDP of member countries was estimated to be US$500,000m.

Objectives. The main objectives are to accelerate economic growth, social progress and cultural development, to promote active collaboration and mutual assistance in matters of common interest, to ensure the political and economic stability of the South East Asian region, and to maintain close co-operation with existing international and regional organizations with similar aims.

Activities. Principal projects concern economic co-operation and development, with the intensification of intra-ASEAN trade, and trade between the region and the rest of the world; joint research and technological programmes; co-operation in transportation and communications; promotion of tourism, South East Asian studies, cultural, scientific, educational and administrative exchanges. The decision to set up an *ASEAN Free Trade Area (AFTA)* was taken at the Fourth Summit meeting, in Singapore in 1992, with the aim of creating a common market in 15 years. The first step towards this was the Common Effective Preferential Tariff (CEPT) Scheme Agreement, setting a common tariff regime for manufactured and processed agricultural goods.

In Dec. 1995, heads of government meeting in Bangkok signed a treaty establishing a South-East Asia Nuclear-Free Zone, which was extended to cover offshore economic exclusion zones. Individual signatories were to decide whether to allow port visits or transportation of nuclear weapons by foreign powers through territorial waters. The *ASEAN Regional Forum (ARF)* was proposed at a meeting of foreign ministers in July 1993 to discuss security issues in the region. Its first formal meeting took place in July 1994 attended by all 7 members and its dialogue partners (Australia, Canada, the EU, Japan, Republic of Korea, New Zealand and the USA) and observers (People's Republic of China, Laos, Papua New Guinea, Russia and Vietnam).

Organization. The highest authority is the meeting of Heads of Government, which takes place on a formal basis every 3 years, with informal meetings each year in between. The highest policy-making body is the annual Meeting of Foreign Ministers, commonly known as AMM, the ASEAN Ministerial Meeting, which convenes in each of the member countries on a rotational basis in alphabetical order. The AEM (ASEAN Economic Meeting) meets formally or informally each year to direct ASEAN economic co-operation. The AEM and AMM report jointly to the heads of government at summit meetings. The ASEAN Standing Committee (ASC) is the policy arm and organ of co-ordination between the AMMs. An advisory body to the permanent committees, the ASC reviews the work of committees with a view to implementing policy guidelines set by the AMM. There are 5 economic committees under the AEM, and 5 non-economic committees that recommend and draw up programmes for co-operation. These committees are responsible for the operation and implementation of projects in their respective fields. Each capital has its own national secretariat. The central secretariat in Jakarta is headed by the Secretary-General, a post that revolves among the member states in alphabetical order every 3 years.

Headquarters: POB 2072, Jakarta 12110, Indonesia.
Website: http://www.asean.or.id
Secretary-General: Rodolfo C. Severino (Philippines).

ASEAN MEKONG BASIN DEVELOPMENT CO-OPERATION (MEKONG GROUP)

The ministers and representatives of Brunei, Cambodia, China, Indonesia, Laos, Malaysia, Myanmar, Philippines, Singapore, Thailand and Vietnam met in Kuala Lumpur on 17 June 1996 and agreed the following basic objectives for the Group. Its principal objectives are to co-operate in the economic and social development of the Mekong Basin area and strengthen the link between it and ASEAN member countries, through a process of dialogue and common project identification.

Priorities include: development of infrastructure capacities in the fields of transport, telecommunications, irrigation and energy; development of trade and investment-generating activities; development of the agricultural sector to enhance production for domestic consumption and export; sustainable development of forestry resources and development of mineral resources; development of the industrial sector, especially small to medium enterprises; development of tourism; human resource development and support for training; co-operation in the fields of science and technology.

Further Reading

Broinowski, A., *Understanding ASEAN*. London, 1982;—(ed.) *ASEAN into the 1990s*. London, 1990

Tran Van Hoa (ed), *Economic Developments and Prospects in the ASEAN*. London, 1997

Wawn, B., *The Economics of the ASEAN Countries*. London, 1982

SOUTH ASIAN ASSOCIATION FOR REGIONAL CO-OPERATION (SAARC)

SAARC was established to accelerate the process of economic and social development in member states through joint action in agreed areas of co-operation. The foreign ministers of the 7 member countries met for the first time in New Delhi in Aug. 1983 and adopted the Declaration on South Asian Regional Co-operation whereby an Integrated Programme of Action (IPA) was launched. The charter establishing SAARC was adopted at the first summit meeting in Dhaka in Dec. 1985.

Members. Bangladesh, Bhutan, India, Maldives, Nepal, Pakistan, Sri Lanka.

Objectives. To promote the welfare of the peoples of South Asia; to accelerate economic growth, social progress and cultural development; to promote and strengthen collective self-reliance among members; to promote active collaboration and mutual assistance in the economic, social, cultural, technical and scientific fields; to strengthen co-operation with other developing countries, and among themselves through international forums on matters of common interest. Co-operation within the framework is based on respect for the principles of sovereign equality, territorial integrity, political independence, non-interference in the internal affairs of other states, and mutual benefit. Agreed areas of co-operation under the *Integrated Programme of Action (IPA)* include agriculture; communications; education, culture and sports; environment and meteorology; health, population activities and child welfare; prevention of drug trafficking and drug abuse; rural development; science and technology; tourism; transport; and women in development.

The eradication of poverty in South Asia by the year 2002 was accorded the highest priority at the 1991 Colombo Summit, which established an Independent South Asian Commission on Poverty Alleviation (ISACPA) to study the problem and report back with recommendations.

SAARC has taken important steps to expand co-operation among member countries in core economic areas. The completion of the Regional Study on Trade, Manufactures and Services (TMS) in 1991 was the first significant step towards strengthening co-operation in the field. A high-level Committee on Economic Co-operation (CEC), comprising the Commerce Secretaries of member states, was established in July 1991 to act as the forum for addressing trade and economic issues. Members signed a Preferential Trading Agreement (SAPTA) on 7 Dec. 1995 and are working towards the realization of a South Asian Free Trade Area by 2000, and no later than 2005.

Organization. The highest authority of the Association rests with the heads of state or government, who meet annually at Summit level. The Council of Foreign Ministers, which meets twice a year, is responsible for formulating policy, reviewing progress and deciding on new areas of co-operation and the mechanisms deemed necessary for that. The Council is supported by a Standing Committee of Foreign Secretaries, and by the Programming Committee and 11 Technical Committees. There is a secretariat in Káthmandu, headed by a Secretary-General, who is assisted in his work by 7 Directors, appointed by the Secretary-General upon nomination by member states for a period of 3 years which may in special circumstances be extended.

Decisions at all levels are taken on the basis of unanimity. Bilateral and contentious issues are excluded from deliberations.

Headquarters: PO Box 4222, Káthmandu, Nepal.
Secretary-General: Naeem U. Hasan (Pakistan).

THE LEAGUE OF ARAB STATES

Origin. The League of Arab States is a voluntary association of sovereign Arab states, established by a Pact signed in Cairo on 22 March 1945 by the representatives of Egypt, Iraq, Saudi Arabia, Syria, Lebanon, Jordan and Yemen. It seeks to promote closer ties among member states and to co-ordinate their economic, cultural and security policies with a view to developing collective co-operation, protecting national security and maintaining the independence and sovereignty of member states, in order to enhance the potential for joint Arab action across all fields.

Members. Algeria, Bahrain, Comoros, Djibouti, Egypt, Iraq, Jordan, Kuwait, Lebanon, Libya, Mauritania, Morocco, Oman, Palestine, Qatar, Saudi Arabia, Somalia, Sudan, Syria, Tunisia, United Arab Emirates and Republic of Yemen.

Joint Action. In the political field, the League is entrusted with defending the supreme interests and national causes of the Arab world through the implementation of joint action plans at regional and international levels, and with examining any disputes that may arise between member states with a view to settling them by peaceful means. The Joint Defence and Economic Co-operation Treaty signed in 1950 provided for the establishment of a Joint Defence Council as well as an Economic Council (renamed the Economic and Social Council in 1977). Economic, social and cultural activities constitute principal and vital elements of the joint action initiative.

Arab Common Market. The Arab Common Market came into operation on 1 Jan. 1965. The agreement, reached on 13 Aug. 1964 and open to all the Arab League states, has been signed by Iraq, Jordan, Syria and Egypt. The agreement provides for the abolition of customs duties on agricultural products and natural resources within 5 years, by reducing tariffs at an annual rate of 20%. Customs duties on industrial products are to be reduced by 10% annually. The agreement also provides for the free movement of capital and labour between member countries, the establishment of common external tariffs, the co-ordination of economic development and the framing of a common foreign economic policy. In May 1997, in a move to finance economic reforms, 2 funds totalling US$900m. were set up.

Organization. The machinery of the League consists of a Council, 11 specialized ministerial committees entrusted with drawing up common policies for the regulation and advancement of co-operation in their fields (information, internal affairs, justice, housing, transport, social affairs, youth and sports, health, environment, telecommunications and electricity), and a permanent secretariat. On the Council each state has 1 vote. Councils may meet in any of the Arab capitals. Its functions include mediation in disputes between members or a member and a country outside the League. The Secretariat is the executive organ of the Council and ministerial councils. There are also 22 specialized agencies.

The League is considered to be a regional organization within the framework of the United Nations at which its Secretary-General is an observer. It has permanent delegations in New York and Geneva for the UN, in Addis Ababa for the Organization of African Unity (OAU), as well as offices in Bonn, Vienna, Brussels, Athens, Madrid, Washington D.C., New Delhi, Beijing, Moscow, Rome, London and Paris.

Headquarters: Al Tahrir Square, Cairo, Egypt.
Secretary-General: Ahmed Esmat Abdel-Meguid (Egypt).

Further Reading

Clements, F. A., *Arab Regional Organizations* [Bibliography]. Oxford and New Brunswick (NJ), 1992
Gomaa, A. M., The Foundation of the League of Arab States. London, 1977

GULF CO-OPERATION COUNCIL (CCG)

Origin. Also referred to as the Cooperation Council for the Arab States of the Gulf (CCASG), the Council was established on 25 May 1981 on signature of the Charter by Bahrain, Kuwait, Oman, Qatar, Saudi Arabia and the United Arab Emirates.

Aims. To assure security and stability of the region through economic and political co-operation; promote, expand and enhance economic ties on solid foundations, in the best interests of the people; co-ordinate and unify economic, financial and monetary policies, as well as commercial and industrial legislation and customs regulations; achieve self-sufficiency in basic foodstuffs.

In June 1997 the 6 member states, together with Egypt and Syria, agreed to consolidate national markets into a larger regional market by the abolition of national tariffs and the adoption of a minimum and maximum customs duties on non-national products imported from outside the region.

Organization. The Supreme Council is formed by the heads of member states and is the highest authority. Its presidency rotates, based on the alphabetical order of the names of the member states. It holds 1 regular session every year. The Cooperation Council has a commission, called 'Commission for the Settlement of Disputes', which is attached to the Supreme Council. The Ministerial Council is formed of the Foreign Ministers of the member states or other delegated ministers and meets quarterly. The Secretariat-General is composed of Secretary-General, Assistant Secretaries-General and a number of staff as required. The Secretariat consists of the following sectors: Political Affairs, Military Affairs, Economic Affairs, Information Centre, Information Department, Secretary-General's Office, GCC Delegation in Brussels, Technical Telecommunications Bureau in Bahrain.

Finance. The annual budget of the GCC Secretariat is shared equally by the 6 member states.

Headquarters: P.O. Box 7153, Riyadh-11462, Saudi Arabia.
Secretary-General: HE Shaikh Jamil Ibrahim Alhejailan (Saudi Arabia).

Publications. GCC News (monthly, in English); *Attaawun* (quarterly, in Arabic); *GCC Economic Bulletin* (annual).

Further Reading

Twinam, J. W., The Gulf, Co-operation and the Council: an American Perspective. Washington, 1992

ORGANIZATION OF THE PETROLEUM EXPORTING COUNTRIES (OPEC)

Origin and Aims. Founded in Baghdad in 1960 by Iran, Iraq, Kuwait, Saudi Arabia and Venezuela. The principal aims are: to unify the petroleum policies of member countries and determine the best means for safeguarding their interests, individually and collectively; to devise ways and means of ensuring the stabilization of prices in international oil markets with a view to eliminating harmful and unnecessary fluctuations; and to secure a steady income for the producing countries, an efficient, economic and regular supply of petroleum to consuming nations, and a fair return on their capital to those investing in the petroleum industry. It is estimated that OPEC members possess 75% of the world's known reserves of crude petroleum, of which about two-thirds are in the Middle East.

Members. (1998) Algeria, Indonesia, Iran, Iraq, Kuwait, Libya, Nigeria, Qatar, Saudi Arabia, United Arab Emirates and Venezuela. Membership applications may be made by any other country having substantial net exports of crude petroleum, which has fundamentally similar interests to those of member countries. Gabon became an associated member in 1973 and a full member in 1975, but in 1996 withdrew owing to difficulty in meeting its percentage contribution.

Organization. The main organs are the Conference, the Board of Governors and the Secretariat. The Conference, which is the supreme authority meeting at least twice a year, consists of delegations from each member country, normally headed by the respective minister of oil, mines or energy. All decisions, other than those concerning procedural matters, must be adopted unanimously.

Headquarters: Obere Donaustrasse 93, A-1020 Vienna, Austria.
Website: http://www.opec.org.
Public Relations and Information Dept. fax: +43 1 214 9827.
e-mail: prid@opec.org
Secretary-General: Dr Rilwanu Lukman (Nigeria).

Publications. Annual Statistical Bulletin; Annual Report; OPEC Bulletin (monthly); *OPEC Review* (quarterly); *Facts and Figures* (occasional); *OPEC General Information and Chronology.*

Further Reading
Al-Chalabi, F., *OPEC at the Crossroads.* Oxford, 1989
Skeet, *OPEC: 25 Years of Prices and Policies.* CUP, 1988

OPEC FUND FOR INTERNATIONAL DEVELOPMENT
The OPEC Special Fund was established in 1976 to provide financial aid on advantageous terms to developing countries (other than OPEC members) and international development agencies whose beneficiaries are developing countries. In 1980 the fund was transformed into a permanent autonomous international agency and renamed the OPEC Fund for International Development. It is administered by a Ministerial Council and a Governing Board. Each member country is represented on the Council by its finance minister.

The initial endowment of the fund amounted to US$800m. At the start of 1999, pledged contributions totalled US$3,435m., and the fund had extended 778 loans totalling US$3,982·7m. of which US$2,953·1m. or 74·1% was for project financing, US$724·2m. (18·2%) for balance-of-payments support and US$305·3m. (7·7%) for programme funding. The Fund has recently been authorized by its governing bodies to participate in the financing of private-sector activities involving entities located in eligible beneficiary countries.

Headquarters: POB 995, A-1011 Vienna, Austria.
Website: http://www.opec.org
Director-General: Dr Yesufu Seyyid Abdulai (Nigeria).

ARAB MAGHREB UNION

Founded in 1989 to promote political co-ordination, co-operation and 'complementarity' across various fields, with integration wherever and whenever possible.

Members. Algeria, Libya, Mauritania, Morocco, Tunisia.

By late 1996, joint policies and projects under way or under consideration included: the establishment of the Maghreb Investment and Foreign Trade Bank to fund joint agricultural and industrial projects; free movement of citizens within the region; joint transport undertakings, including railway improvements and a Maghreb highway; creation of a customs union; and establishment of a common market.

A Declaration committing members to the establishment of a free trade zone was adopted at the AMU's last summit in Tunis. In Nov. 1992, members adopted a charter on protection of the environment.

Headquarters: 27 rue Okba, Agdal, Rabat, Morocco.
Secretary-General: Mohamed Amamou (Tunisia).

ORGANIZATION OF AFRICAN UNITY (OAU)

History. On 25 May 1963, the heads of state or government of 32 African countries, at a conference in Addis Ababa, signed a charter establishing an Organization of African Unity. Membership comprises 53 of the 54 African countries. The only state that is not a member is Morocco, which withdrew in 1985 following admittance of the disputed state of Western Sahara as a member in 1982. In Nov. 1995, the following countries were suspended from voice and vote for failure to pay their dues: Central African Republic, Chad, Comoros, Equatorial Guinea, Guinea-Bissau, Niger, São Tomé e Príncipe, Seychelles and Sierra Leone.

Aims. OAU's chief objectives are the furtherance of African unity and solidarity; the co-ordination of political, economic, cultural, health, scientific and defence policies; the elimination of colonialism in Africa; and the defence of sovereignty, territorial integrity and independence.

Activities. In June 1991, the heads of state of member countries signed a treaty to create an Africa-wide economic community by 2000, and in 1993, a mechanism was adopted for conflict prevention, management and resolution by the OAU.

Organization. The Assembly of the Heads of State and Government is the principal policy-making organ, and meets annually. The Council of Ministers meets twice a year, with each session electing its own chairperson. There is also a permanent secretariat headed by the Secretary-General elected for a 4-year term by the Assembly.

The Commission of Mediation, Conciliation and Arbitration is a 21-member body (no state may have more than 1 member) elected by the Assembly for a 5-year term, to hear and settle disputes between member states by peaceful means. There are also specialized commissions for economic, social, transport and communication, education, science, culture and health, defence, human rights and labour affairs. The biennial budget for 1996-98 was US$61·45m.

Official languages. Arabic, French, Portuguese and English.
Headquarters: POB 3243, Addis Ababa, Ethiopia.
Secretary-General: Dr Salim Ahmed Salim (Tanzania).

Further Reading
El-Ayouty, Y. (ed.) *The Organization of African Unity after Thirty Years.* New York, 1994
Harris, G., *The Organization of African Unity* [Bibliography]. Oxford and New Brunswick (NJ), 1994

AFRICAN DEVELOPMENT BANK

Established to promote economic and social development in the region.

Regional Members. (53) Algeria, Angola, Benin, Botswana, Burkina Faso, Burundi, Cameroon, Cape Verde, Central African Republic, Chad, Comoros, Congo (Rep. of), Congo (Dem. Rep. of), Côte d'Ivoire, Djibouti, Egypt, Equatorial Guinea, Eritrea, Ethiopia, Gabon, The Gambia, Ghana, Guinea, Guinea-Bissau, Kenya, Lesotho, Liberia, Libyan Arab Jamahiriya, Madagascar, Malaŵi, Mali, Mauritania, Mauritius, Morocco, Mozambique, Namibia, Niger, Nigeria, Rwanda, São Tomé e Príncipe, Senegal, Seychelles, Sierra Leone, Somalia, South Africa (Rep. of), Sudan, Swaziland, Tanzania, Togo, Tunisia, Uganda, Zambia, Zimbabwe.

Non-regional Members. (25) Argentina, Austria, Belgium, Brazil, Canada, China, Denmark, Finland, France, Germany, India, Italy, Japan, Korea (Rep. of), Kuwait, Netherlands, Norway, Portugal, Saudi Arabia, Spain, Sweden, Switzerland, UK, United Arab Emirates, USA.

Headquarters: 01 BP 1387, Abidjan 01, Côte d'Ivoire.
Website: http://www.afdb.org
e-mail: Afdb@afdb.org

ECONOMIC COMMUNITY OF WEST AFRICAN STATES (ECOWAS)

Founded 1975 as a regional common market, it has now become involved in political disputes, and in 1993 amended its charter to assume responsibility for the regulation of regional armed conflicts. Its military arm is Ecomog.

Members. Benin, Burkina Faso, Cape Verde, Côte d'Ivoire, Gambia, Ghana, Guinea, Guinea-Bissau, Liberia, Mali, Mauritania, Niger, Nigeria, Senegal, Sierra Leone, Togo.

Organization. It meets at yearly summits which rotate in the different capitals of member states. There is a secretariat in Abuja.

Headquarters: 60 Yakubu Gowon Crescent, Asokoro, Abuja, Nigeria.

COMMON MARKET FOR EASTERN AND SOUTHERN AFRICA (COMESA)

COMESA is a grouping of 21 countries who are committed, over the long term, to the creation of a Common Market for Eastern and Southern Africa. It was established in 1994 as a building block for the African Economic Community and replaces the

Preferential Trade Area for Eastern and Southern Africa, which had been in existence since 1981.

Membership: Angola, Burundi, Comoros, Democratic Republic of Congo, Djibouti, Egypt, Eritrea, Ethiopia, Kenya, Madagascar, Malaŵi, Mauritius, Namibia, Rwanda, Seychelles, Sudan, Swaziland, Tanzania, Uganda, Zambia and Zimbabwe.

Objectives: To establish a Free Trade Area by 2000 by eliminating tariff and non-tariff barriers to intra-COMESA Trade; to establish a Customs Union with Common External Tariff by 2004.

Activities: COMESA is already on its way to achieving a Free Trade Area and a Customs Union. By 1999, 8 of its Member States had reduced their tariffs by 80%, another 4 members had reduced by 60–70%. All Member States are committed to reducing their tariffs to zero by 2000. Currently, the conventional non-tariff barriers (quantitative restrictions, licensing, import permits and restrictive foreign exchange controls) have been largely eliminated. As a result of trade liberalization and transport facilitation measures taken by COMESA, Intra-COMESA trade is now growing at the rate of 15% while overall trade has been growing at about 10%. Furthermore, the cost of transporting goods within the region has reduced by about 25%.

In addition to creating the policy environment for freeing trade, COMESA has also created specialized institutions like the Trade and Development Bank of Eastern and Southern Africa, the Re-Insurance Company, the Clearing House and the Court of Justice, to provide the required financial infrastructure and service support.

Headquarters: COMESA Secretariat, COMESA Centre, Ben Bella Road, PO Box 30051, 10101 Lusaka, Zambia.
Website: http://www.comesaint

SOUTHERN AFRICAN DEVELOPMENT COMMUNITY (SADC)

History and Membership. The Declaration and Treaty establishing the SADC was signed at the summit of heads of state or government on 17 July 1992 in Windhoek, Namibia. It replaces the South African Development Co-ordination Conference (SADCC), established in 1980 on the adoption of the Lusaka Declaration to reduce the region's economic dependence on South Africa and combat the effects of sanctions.

Members. The 10 founder member countries are Angola, Botswana, Lesotho, Malaŵi, Mozambique, Namibia, Swaziland, Tanzania, Zambia and Zimbabwe. South Africa joined in 1994; Mauritius in 1995. Each member state has responsibility for co-ordinating a sector or sectors on behalf of all other members.

Aims and Activities. To promote economic integration and strengthen regional solidarity, peace and security. The founding treaty provides for the establishment of an arbitration tribunal.

At the Johannesburg summit in Aug. 1995, an agreement was reached committing members to the sharing of water resources. A treaty to eliminate internal trade barriers by 2000 is also being drawn up; and in 1994, SADC ministers of defence meeting in Arusha, Tanzania, approved the establishment of a regional rapid deployment peacekeeping force to contain regional conflicts or civil unrest in member states.

Official languages. English, Portuguese.
Headquarters: Private Bag 0095, Gaborone, Botswana.
Executive Secretary: Kaire Mbuende (Namibia).

LAKE CHAD BASIN COMMISSION

Established by a Convention and Statute signed on 22 May 1964 by Cameroon, Chad, Niger and Nigeria, and later by the Central African Republic, to regulate and control utilization of the water and other natural resources in the Basin; to initiate, promote and co-ordinate natural resources development projects and research within the Basin area; and to examine complaints and promote settlement of disputes, with a view to promoting regional co-operation.

In Dec. 1977, at Enugu in Nigeria, the 3rd summit of heads of state of the commission signed the protocol for the Harmonization of the Regulations Relating to Fauna and Flora in member countries, and adopted plans for the multidonor approach towards major integrated development for the conventional basin. An international campaign to save Lake Chad following a report on the environmental degradation of the conventional basin was launched by heads of state at the 8th summit of the Commission in Abuja in March 1994.

The Commission operates an annual budget of CFA 400m., and receives assistance from various international and donor agencies including the FAO, and UN Development and Environment Programmes.

Headquarters: BP 727, N'Djaména, Chad.
Executive Secretary: Bobboi Jauro.

WORLD COUNCIL OF CHURCHES

The World Council of Churches was formally constituted on 23 Aug. 1948 in Amsterdam. Today, member churches number over 330 from more than 100 countries.

Origin. The World Council was founded by the coming together of diverse Christian movements, including the overseas mission groups gathered from 1921 in the International Missionary Council, the Faith and Order Movement founded by American Episcopal Bishop Charles Brent, and the Life and Work Movement led by Swedish Lutheran Archbishop Nathan Söderblom. On 13 May 1938, at Utrecht, a provisional committee was appointed to prepare for the formation of a World Council of Churches, under the chairmanship of William Temple, then Archbishop of York.

Membership. The basis of membership (1975) states: 'The World Council of Churches is a fellowship of Churches which confess the Lord Jesus Christ as God and Saviour according to the Scriptures and therefore seek to fulfil together their common calling to the glory of the one God, Father, Son and Holy Spirit.' Membership is open to Churches which express their agreement with this basis and satisfy such criteria as the Assembly or Central Committee may prescribe. Today, more than 330 Churches of Protestant, Anglican, Orthodox, Old Catholic and Pentecostal confessions belong to this fellowship.

Activities. WCC programmes are organized by a range of supervisory committees drawn from member churches. The 4 programme units are: Unity and Renewal; Churches in Mission: Health, Education Witness; Justice, Peace and Creation; and Sharing and Service.

In Aug. 1997, the WCC launched a Peace to the City campaign, as the initial focus of a programme to overcome violence in troubled cities.

Organization. The governing body of the World Council, consisting of delegates specially appointed by the member Churches, is the Assembly, which meets every 7 or 8 years to frame policy. It has no legislative powers and depends for the implementation of its decisions upon the action of member Churches. The 8th Assembly in Harare, in 1998, had as its theme, 'Turn to God, Rejoice in Hope'. A

150-member Central Committee meets annually to carry out the Assembly mandate, with a smaller 28-member Executive Committee meeting twice a year. The General Secretariat includes Offices for Church and Ecumenical Relations, Interreligious Relations, Programme Co-ordination, Department of Communication, Office of Management and Finance, and the *Ecumenical Institute* at Bossey.

The budget in 1996 amounted to 103m. Swiss francs, funded by the churches and their agencies, and other project-related organizations.

Headquarters: PO Box 2100, 150 route de Ferney, 1211 Geneva 2, Switzerland.
Website: http://www.wcc-coe.org
General Secretary: Rev. Dr Konrad Raiser.

Publications. Annual Reports; Dictionary of the Ecumenical Movement, Geneva, 1991; *Directory of Christian Councils,* 1985; *A History of the Ecumenical Movement,* Geneva, 1993; *Ecumenical Review* (quarterly); *Ecumenical News International* (weekly); *International Review of Mission* (quarterly).

Further Reading

Castro, E., *A Passion for Unity.* Geneva, 1992
Potter, P., *Life in all its Fullness.* Geneva, 1981
Raiser, K., *Ecumenism in Transition.* Geneva, 1994
Van Elderen, M., *Introducing the World Council of Churches.* Geneva, 1991
Vermaat, J. A. E., *The World Council of Churches and Politics.* New York, 1989
Visser 't Hooft, W. A., *The Genesis and Formation of the World Council of Churches. Geneva, 1982; Memoirs.* Geneva, 1987

UNREPRESENTED NATIONS AND PEOPLES ORGANIZATION (UNPO)

UNPO is an international organization created by nations and peoples around the world who are not represented as such in the world's principal international organizations, such as the UN. Founded in 1991, UNPO has over 50 members representing over 100m. people.

Membership. Open to all nations and peoples unrepresented, subject to adherence to the 5 principles which form the basis of UNPO's charter: equal right to self-determination of all nations and peoples; adherence to internationally accepted human rights standards; to the principles of democracy; promotion of non-violence; and protection of the environment. Applicants must show that they constitute a 'nation or people' as defined in the Covenant.

Functions and Activities. UNPO offers an international forum for occupied nations, indigenous peoples, minorities and oppressed majorities, who struggle to regain their lost countries, preserve their cultural identities, protect their basic human and economic rights, and safeguard their environment.

It does not represent those peoples; rather it assists and empowers them to represent themselves more effectively. To this end, it provides professional services and facilities as well as education and training in the fields of diplomacy, international and human rights law, democratic processes and institution building, conflict management and resolution, and environmental protection. The Organization is funded by members, private foundations and voluntary contributions.

5 former members of UNPO (Armenia, Belau, Estonia, Georgia and Latvia) subsequently achieved full independence and gained representation in the UN. Belau is now called Palau.

Headquarters: 40A Javastraat, NL-2585 AP The Hague, Netherlands.
Website: http://www.unpo.ee
General Secretary: Michael van Walt.

INTERNATIONAL ORGANIZATION FOR MIGRATION (IOM)

Established in Brussels in 1951 to help solve European population and refugee problems though migration, and to stimulate the creation of new economic opportunities in countries lacking certain manpower. IOM is committed to the principle that humane and orderly migration benefits migrants and society.

Members. Albania, Angola, Argentina, Armenia, Australia, Austria, Bangladesh, Belgium, Bolivia, Bulgaria, Canada, Chile, Colombia, Costa Rica, Croatia, Cyprus, Czech Republic, Denmark, Dominican Republic, Ecuador, Egypt, El Salvador, Finland, France, Germany, Greece, Guatemala, Guinea-Bissau, Haiti, Honduras, Hungary, Israel, Italy, Japan, Kenya, Liberia, Lithuania, Luxembourg, Mali, Morocco, Netherlands, Nicaragua, Norway, Pakistan, Panama, Paraguay, Peru, Philippines, Poland, Portugal, Republic of Korea, Romania, Senegal, Slovak Republic, Sri Lanka, Sudan, Sweden, Switzerland, Tajikistan, Thailand, Uganda, United Republic of Tanzania, USA, Uruguay, Venezuela and Zambia. Some 48 governments and a large number of government agencies and NGOs have observer status.

Activities. As an intergovernmental body, IOM acts with its partners in the international community to: assist in meeting the operational challenges of migration; advance understanding of migration issues; encourage social and economic development through migration; work towards effective respect of human dignity and the wellbeing of migrants. Since 1952 the IOM has assisted over 10m. refugees and migrants. The operational budget in 1997 was US$238·1m.

Headquarters: Route des Morillons 17, POB 71, 1211 Geneva 19, Switzerland.
Website: http://www.iom.ch
Director-General: James N. Purcell Jr (USA).

INTERNATIONAL COMMITTEE OF THE RED CROSS (ICRC)

Origin: Founded in Geneva in Feb. 1863. From its outset the ICRC saw that volunteers could act effectively on the battlefield, without risking rejection by officers and soldiers, only if they could be told apart from ordinary civilians by a distinctive emblem and were protected from fighting.

Mission Statement: The ICRC acts to help all victims of war and internal violence, attempting to ensure implementation of humanitarian rules restricting armed violence.

The ICRC's mission arises from the basic human desire, common to all civilizations, to lay down rules governing the use of force in war and to safeguard the dignity of the weak. With a mandate from the international community to help victims of war and internal violence and to promote compliance with international humanitarian law, the ICRC's activities are aimed at protecting and assisting the victims of armed conflict and internal violence so as to preserve their physical integrity and their dignity and to enable them to regain their autonomy as quickly as possible.

* The ICRC is independent of all governments and international organizations. Its work is prompted by the desire to promote humane conduct and is guided by empathy for the victims. The ICRC is impartial: its only criterion for action is the victims' needs. The ICRC is neutral and remains detached from all political issues related to conflict.

* By applying these principles strictly, the ICRC is able to act as an intermediary between the parties to armed conflict and to promote dialogue in situations of internal violence, with a view to finding solutions for matters of humanitarian concern.

* Through its work, the ICRC helps to prevent the worsening of crises and even at times to resolve them.

* The ICRC systematically reminds all military and civilian authorities directly involved in armed conflict or internal violence of their obligations under international humanitarian law and the other humanitarian rules by which they are bound.

* The ICRC has the duty to remind all States of their collective obligation to ensure respect for international humanitarian law.

* In all societies and cultures, the ICRC endeavours to promote international humanitarian law and the fundamental human values underlying the law.

* As the founding member of the International Red Cross and Red Crescent Movement, the ICRC directs and co-ordinates the international work of the Movement's components in connection with armed conflict and internal violence.

* The ICRC gives priority to co-operation with the National Red Cross and Red Crescent Societies and their Federation. It acts in consultation with all other organizations involved in humanitarian work.

Finance. The ICRC relies for its financing on voluntary contributions from signatories to the Geneva Conventions, supranational organizations such as the European Union; and public and private sources. To obtain the necessary funding the ICRC launches annual appeals.

In 1997, the ICRC maintained a permanent presence in 54 countries but conducted operations in around 80. It also stepped up its drive to raise awareness of the banning of landmines, lobbying at international, national and regional levels.

Headquarters: 19 avenue de la Paix, CH-1202 Geneva, Switzerland.
Website: http://www.icrc.ch

Further Reading
Moorehead, Caroline, *Dunant's Dream: War, Switzerland and the History of the Red Cross.* HarperCollins, London, 1998

AMNESTY INTERNATIONAL (AI)

Origin: Founded in 1961 by British lawyer Peter Beneson as a 1-year campaign for the release of prisoners of conscience, Amnesty International has grown to become a worldwide organization, winning the Nobel Peace Prize in 1977. As defined by AI, 'prisoners of conscience' are people imprisoned solely because of their political or religious beliefs, gender, or their racial or ethnic origin, who have neither used nor advocated violence. The organization's mandate is based on the United Nations Universal Declaration of Human Rights.

AI has over 1m. members, subscribers and regular donors in more than 100 countries. The organization is governed by a 9-member International Executive Committee (IEC). It comprises 8 volunteer members elected every 2 years by an International Council comprising representatives of the worldwide movement, and an elected member of the International Secretariat. During the 12 months to 31 March 1998 the International Secretariat had expenditure of £16,312,000.

Each year, AI produces a global report detailing human rights violations in all regions of the world. The 1998 report, which detailed abuses during 1997, included the fact that executions were carried out in 40 countries, people were arbitrarily arrested and detained, or in detention without charge or trial in 53 countries, and in 117 countries people were reportedly tortured or ill-treated by security forces, police or other state authorities.

International Secretariat: 99-119 Rosebery Avenue, London, EC1R 3RE, UK.
Website: http://www.amnesty.org
Secretary General: Pierre Sané.

ORGANIZATION FOR THE PROHIBITION OF CHEMICAL WEAPONS (OPCW)

The OPCW is responsible for the implementation of the Chemical Weapons Convention (CWC), which became effective on 29 April 1997. The principal organ of the OPCW is the Conference of the States Parties, composed of all the members of the organization.

Given the relative simplicity of producing chemical warfare agents, the verification provisions of the CWC are far-reaching. The routine monitoring regime involves submission by States Parties of initial and annual declarations to the OPCW, initial visits and systematic inspections of declared weapons storage, production and destruction facilities. Verification is also applied to chemical industry facilities which produce, process or consume, above certain thresholds, chemicals listed in the three Schedules of the Convention.

Headquarters: Johan de Wittlaan 32, 3517 JR The Hague, The Netherlands.
Website: http://www.opcw.org

ANTARCTIC TREATY

Antarctica is an island continent some 15·5m. sq. km in area which lies almost entirely within the Antarctic Circle. Its surface is composed of an ice sheet over rock, and it is uninhabited except for research and other workers in the course of duty. It is in general ownerless: for countries with territorial claims, *see* ARGENTINA; AUSTRALIA: Australian Antarctic Territory; CHILE; FRANCE: Southern and Antarctic Territories; NEW ZEALAND: Ross Dependency; NORWAY: Queen Maud Land; UNITED KINGDOM: British Antarctic Territory.

12 countries which had maintained research stations in Antarctica during International Geophysical Year, 1957-58 (Argentina, Australia, Belgium, Chile, France, Japan, New Zealand, Norway, South Africa, the USSR, the UK and the USA) signed the Antarctic Treaty (Washington Treaty) on 1 Dec. 1959. Austria, Brazil, Bulgaria, Canada, China, Colombia, Cuba, Czechoslovakia, Denmark, Ecuador, Finland, Germany, Greece, Hungary, India, Italy, South Korea, North Korea, the Netherlands, Papua New Guinea, Peru, Poland, Romania, Spain, Sweden, Switzerland and Uruguay have subsequently acceded to the Treaty. The Treaty reserves the Antarctic area south of 60° S. lat. for peaceful purposes, provides for international co-operation in scientific investigation and research, and preserves, for the duration of the Treaty, the *status quo* with regard to territorial sovereignty, rights and claims. The Treaty entered into force on 23 June 1961. The 39 nations party to the Treaty (26 full voting signatories and 13 adherents) meet biennially. Decisions taken by the signatories of the 1959 Washington Treaty must be unanimous.

An agreement reached in Madrid in April 1991 and signed by all 39 parties in Oct. imposes a ban on mineral exploitation in Antarctica for 50 years, at the end of which any one of the 26 voting parties may request a review conference. After this the ban may be lifted by agreement of three quarters of the nations then voting, which must include the present 26. The agreement demilitarizes the continent, establishes the right to scientific research for all countries and creates a procedure for monitoring the environment.

Further Reading

Elliott, L.M., *International Environmental Politics: Protecting the Antarctic.* London, 1994
Jørgensen-Dahl, A. and Østreng, W., *The Antarctic Treaty System in World Politics.* London, 1991
Meadows, J. *et al., The Antarctic* [Bibliography]. Oxford and New Brunswick (NJ), 1994

INTER-PARLIAMENTARY UNION (IPU)

Founded in 1889 by William Randal Cremer (UK) and Frédéric Passy (France), the Inter-Parliamentary Union was the first permanent forum for political multilateral negotiations. The Union is a centre for dialogue and parliamentary diplomacy among legislators representing every political system and all the main political leanings in the world. It was instrumental in setting up what is now the Permanent Court of Arbitration in The Hague.

Activities: The IPU fosters contacts, co-ordination and the exchange of experience among parliaments and parliamentarians of all countries; considers questions of international interest and concern, and expresses its views on such issues in order to bring about action by parliaments and parliamentarians; contributes to the defence and promotion of human rights—an essential factor of parliamentary democracy and development; contributes to better knowledge of the working of representative institutions and to the strengthening and development of their means of action.

Membership: The IPU had 137 Members and 3 Associate Members in March 1999.

Headquarters: C.P. 438, 1211-Geneva 19, Switzerland
Website: http://www.ipu.org
Secretary General: Anders B. Johnsson (Sweden)

ORGANIZATION OF THE ISLAMIC CONFERENCE (OIC)

Founded in 1969, the objectives of the OIC are to promote Islamic solidarity among Member States; to consolidate co-operation among Member States in the economic, social, cultural, scientific and other vital fields of activities, and to carry out consultations among Member States in international organizations; to endeavour to eliminate racial segregation, discrimination and to eradicate colonialism in all its forms; to take the necessary measures to support international peace and security founded on justice; to strengthen the struggle of all Muslim peoples with a view to safeguarding their dignity, independence and national rights; to create a suitable atmosphere for the promotion of co-operation and understanding among Member States and other countries.

Members: Afghanistan, Albania, Algeria, Azerbaijan, Bahrain, Bangladesh, Benin, Bosnia-Hercegovina, Brunei, Burkina Faso, Cameroon, Chad, Comoros, Djibouti, Egypt, Gabon, Gambia, Guinea, Guinea-Bissau, Indonesia, Iran, Iraq, Jordan, Kuwait, Kyrgyzstan, Lebanon, Libya, Malaysia, Maldives, Mali, Mauritania, Morocco, Mozambique, Niger, Nigeria, Oman, Pakistan, Palestine, Qatar, Saudi Arabia, Senegal, Sierra Leone, Somalia, Sudan, Suriname, Syria, Tajikistan, Tunisia, Turkey, Turkmenistan, Uganda, United Arab Emirates, Uzbekiston, Yemen.

Secretary General: H.E. Dr Ezzeddine Laraki
Website: irna.com/oic/index.html

WORLD CUSTOMS ORGANIZATION

Established in 1952 as the Customs Co-operation Council, the World Customs Organization is an intergovernmental body with worldwide membership, whose mission it is to enhance the effectiveness and efficiency of customs administrations throughout the world. It has 145 member countries or territories.

Headquarters: Rue de l'Industrie 26-38, B-1040 Brussels, Belgium.
Secretary-General: J. W. Shaver (USA).

INTERPOL (INTERNATIONAL CRIMINAL POLICE ORGANIZATION)

Organization: Founded in 1914 and composed of 177 member countries, INTERPOL provides assistance to the law enforcement community. The police of any Member State can communicate with the police of any other Member State using INTERPOL's 4 official languages: English, Arabic, French and Spanish.

Aims: Under Article 2 of the Organization's Constitution, INTERPOL's aims are:
   (a) 'To ensure and promote the widest possible mutual assistance between all criminal police authorities, within the limits of the laws existing in the different countries and in the spirit of the Universal Declaration of Human Rights.
   (b) To establish and develop all institutions likely to contribute effectively to the prevention and suppression of ordinary law crimes.'
The limits of its actions are laid down in Article 3:
   'It is strictly forbidden for the Organization to undertake any intervention or activities of a political, military, religious or racial character.' A political offence is one which is considered to be of a predominantly political nature because of the surrounding circumstances and underlying motives, even if the offence itself is covered by the ordinary criminal law in the country in which it was committed. But offences are not considered to be political when they are committed outside a 'conflict area', and when the victims are not connected with the aims or objectives pursued by the offenders.
   Co-operation with INTERPOL is based on actions taken by the police forces in the various Member States, operating within their own national boundaries and in accordance with their own national laws. All Member States are provided with the same services and have the same rights, irrespective of the size of their financial contributions to the Organization.
   Although governed by principles designed to ensure regularity and continuity, working methods are flexible enough to take account of the wide variety of structures and situations in different countries. Respect for these principles means that INTERPOL cannot have teams of detectives with supranational powers who travel around investigating cases in different countries. International co-operation has to depend on co-ordinated action on the part of the Member States' police forces, all of which may supply or request information or services as needed.

Headquarters: Quai Charles de Gaulle, 69006 Lyon, France.
Website: http://193.123.144.14/interpol-pr/
Secretary-General: Raymond E. Kendall, QPM MA.

INTERNATIONAL MOBILE SATELLITE ORGANIZATION (IMSO)

Founded in 1979 as the International Maritime Satellite Organization (Inmarsat) to establish a satellite system to improve maritime communications for distress and safety and commercial applications. Its competence was subsequently expanded to include aeronautical and land mobile communications. Privatization, due to be completed in April 1999, transfers the business to a newly created company and the Organization remains as a regulator to ensure that the company fulfils its public services obligations. The company is to take the Inmarsat name and the Organization is to use the acronym IMSO. In March 1999 the Organization had 86 member Parties.

Organization. The Assembly of all Parties to the Convention meets every 2 years. There is also a 22-member Council of representatives of national tele-communications administrations as well as an executive Directorate.

Headquarters: 99 City Road, London, EC1Y 1AX, UK.
Director of the Secretariat, IMSO: Jerzy Vonau.
Chief Executive, Inmarsat Ltd: Warren Grace.

INTERNATIONAL TELECOMMUNICATIONS SATELLITE ORGANIZATION (INTELSAT)

Intelsat was founded in 1964 to own and operate the worldwide commercial satellite communications system. Costs are borne by members in proportion to their usage of the system. 19 Intelsat satellites in geosynchronous orbit provided a global communications service, including most of the world's overseas traffic in 1998. It has 143 member states.

Objectives. To provide international telephone and TV services, a digital data transmission service (Intelnet), a business service (IBS) and domestic telecommunications services.

Organization. The Assembly of Parties attended by representatives of member governments meets every 2 years to consider policy and long-term aims, and matters of interest to members. Practical aspects of the system are dealt with at the annual Meeting of Signatories. There is a 27-member Board of Governors.

Headquarters: 3400 International Drive, NW, Washington, D.C., 20008–3098, USA.
Director-General: Irving Goldstein (USA).

INTERNATIONAL AIR TRANSPORT ASSOCIATION (IATA)

Founded in 1945 for inter-airline co-operation in promoting safe, reliable, secure and economical air services, IATA has over 230 members from more than 130 nations worldwide. IATA is the successor to the International Air Traffic Association, founded in the Hague in 1919, the year of the world's first international scheduled services.

Main offices: IATA Centre, Route de l'Aeroport 33, PO Box 416, CH-1215 Geneva, Switzerland. 800 Place Victoria, PO Box 113, Montreal, Quebec, Canada H4Z 1M1. 77 Robinson Road, #05-00 SIA Building, Singapore 068896.
Website: http://www.iata.org
Director-General: Pierre Jeanniot.

INTERNATIONAL ROAD FEDERATION (IRF)

The IRF is a non-profit, non-political service organization whose purpose is to encourage better road and transportation systems worldwide and to help apply technology and management practices to give maximum economic and social returns from national road investments.

Founded following the second world war, over the years the IRF has led major global road infrastructure developments, including achieving 1,000 km of new roads in Mexico in the 1950s, and promoting the Pan-American Highway linking North and South America. It publishes *World Road Statistics*, as well as road research studies, including a 140-country inventory of road and transport research in co-operation with the US Bureau of Public Roads.

Headquarters: 2 chemin de Blandonnet, CH-1214 Vernier/GE, Switzerland.
Website: http://www.irfnet.org

INTERNATIONAL CONFEDERATION OF FREE TRADE UNIONS (ICFTU)

Origin. The founding congress of the ICFTU was held in London in Dec. 1949 following the withdrawal of some Western trade unions from the World Federation of Trade Unions (WFTU), which had come under Communist control. The constitution, as amended, provides for co-operation with the UN and the ILO, and for regional organizations to promote free trade unionism, especially in developing countries. By 1999 the ICFTU represented some 124m. workers across 213 national trade union centres in 143 countries.

Aims. The ICFTU aims to promote the interests of working people and to secure recognition of workers' organizations as free bargaining agents; to reduce the gap between rich and poor; and to defend fundamental human and trade union rights. In 1996, it campaigned for the adoption by the WTO of a social clause, with legally binding minimum labour standards.

Organization. The Congress meets every 4 years. It elects the Executive Board of 50 members nominated on an area basis for a 4-year period; 5 seats are reserved for women, nominated by the Women's Committee; and the Board meets at least once a year. Various committees cover economic and social policy, violation of trade union and other human rights, trade union co-operation projects and also the administration of the International Solidarity Fund. There are joint ICFTU–International Trade Secretariat committees for co-ordinating activities.

The ICFTU has branch offices in Geneva and New York, and regional organizations in America (Caracas), Asia (Singapore) and Africa (Nairobi).

Headquarters: Bd. Emile Jacqmain 155, Brussels 1210, Belgium.
Website: http://www.icftu.org
General Secretary: Bill Jordan (UK).

Publications. Free Labour World (monthly); *Occupational Health and Safety Bulletin; Survey of Violations of Trade Union Rights* (annual); *World Economic Review* (annual).

WORLD FEDERATION OF TRADE UNIONS (WFTU)

Origin and History. The WFTU was founded on a worldwide basis in 1945 at the international trade union conferences held in London and Paris, with the participation of all the trade union centres in the countries of the anti-Hitler coalition. The aim was to reunite the world trade union movement at the end of the Second World War. The acute political differences among affiliates, especially the east-west confrontation in Europe on ideological lines, led to a split. A number of affiliated organizations withdrew in 1949 and established the ICFTU. The WFTU now draws its membership from the industrially developing countries like India, Vietnam and other Asian countries, Brazil, Peru, Cuba and other Latin American countries, Syria, Lebanon, Kuwait and other Arab countries, and it has affiliates and associates in more than 20 European countries. It has close relations with the International Confederation of Arab Trade Unions, the Organization of African Trade Union Unity as well as the All-China Federation of Trade Unions, all of which participated at its Congress in Damascus in 1994. Its Trade Unions Internationals (TUIs) have affiliates in Russia, the Czech Republic, Poland and other East European countries, Portugal, France, Spain, Japan and other OECD countries.

The headquarters of the TUIs are situated in Helsinki, New Delhi, Budapest, Paris and Moscow. The WFTU and its TUIs have 130m. members, organized in 92 affiliated or associated national federations and 6 Trade Unions Internationals, in 130 countries. It has regional offices in New Delhi, Havana, Dakar, Damascus and Moscow and Permanent Representatives accredited to the UN in New York, Geneva and Rome.

Headquarters: Branicka 112, CZ-14701 Prague 4, Czech Republic.
Website: http://www.wftu.org
President: Indrajit Gupta (India)
General Secretary: Aleksandr Zharikov (Russia).

Publications. Flashes From the Trade Unions (fortnightly, published in English, French, Spanish and Arabic), reports of Congresses, etc.

WORLD CONFEDERATION OF LABOUR (WCL)

Founded in 1920 as the International Federation of Christian Trade Unions, it went out of existence in 1940 as a large proportion of its 3·4m. members were in Italy and Germany, where affiliated unions were suppressed by the Fascist and Nazi regimes. Reconstituted in 1945 and declining to merge with the WFTU or ICFTU, its policy was based on the papal encyclicals *Rerum novarum* (1891) and *Quadragesimo anno* (1931), and in 1968 it became the WCL and dropped its openly confessional approach.

Today, it has Protestant, Buddhist and Moslem member confederations, as well as a mainly Roman Catholic membership. In its concern to defend trade union freedoms and assist trade union development, the WCL differs little in policy from the ICFTU above. A membership of 11m. in about 90 countries is claimed. The biggest group is the Confederation of Christian Trade Unions (CSC) of Belgium (1·2m.).

Organization. The WCL is organized on a federative basis which leaves wide discretion to its autonomous constituent unions. Its governing body is the Congress, which meets every 4 years. The Congress appoints (or re-appoints) the Secretary-General at each 4-yearly meeting. The General Council which meets at least once a year, is composed of the members of the Confederal Board (at least 22 members, elected by the Congress) and representatives of national confederations, international trade federations, and trade union organizations where there is no confederation affiliated to the WCL. The Confederal Board is responsible for the general leadership of the WCL, in accordance with the decisions and directives of the Council and Congress. There are regional organizations in Latin America (Caracas), Africa (Banjul, Gambia) and Asia (Manila), and a liaison centre in Montreal.

Headquarters: 33 rue de Trèves, Brussels 1040, Belgium.
Secretary-General: Carlos Luís Custer (Argentina).

Publications. Annual Report; Labour Press and Information Bulletin (6 a year).

THE FRANCOPHONIE INSTITUTIONNELLE

The Francophonie Institutionnelle is an intergovernmental organization representing 52 states (including 3 with observer status) using French as the official language. Objectives include the exchange of information and the holding of ministerial conferences to promote economic and social development. The Secretary-General is based in Paris.

Members: Belgium, Benin, Bulgaria, Burkina Faso, Burundi, Cambodia, Republic of Cameroon, Canada (New Brunswick, Quebec), Cape Verde, Central African Republic, Comoros, Republic of the Congo, Democratic Republic of the Congo, Côte d'Ivoire, Djibouti, Dominica, Egypt, Equatorial Guinea, France, Gabon, Guinea, Guinea-Bissau, Haiti, Laos, Lebanon, Luxembourg, Madagascar, Mali, Mauritius, Mauritania, Moldova, Monaco, Morocco, Niger, Romania, Rwanda, St Lucia, Senegal, Seychelles, Switzerland, Chad, Togo, Tunisia, Vanuatu, Vietnam.

Headquarters: 13 quai André-Citroën, 75015 Paris, France.
Website: http://www.francophonie.org
Secretary General: Boutros Boutros-Ghali.

INTERNATIONAL ORGANIZATION FOR STANDARDIZATION (ISO)

Established in 1947, the International Organization for Standardization is a non-governmental federation of national standards bodies from some 130 countries worldwide, one from each country. ISO's work results in international agreements which are published as International Standards. The first ISO standard was published in 1951 with the title 'Standard reference temperature for industrial length measurement'.

Mission: To promote the development of standardization and related activities in the world with a view to facilitating the international exchange of goods and services, and to developing co-operation in the spheres of intellectual, scientific, technological and economic activity.

Headquarters: 1 rue de Varembé, Case postale 56, CH-1211 Geneva 20, Switzerland.
Website: http://www.iso.ch

WORLD WIDE FUND FOR NATURE (WWF)

Origin: WWF was officially formed and registered as a charity on 11 Sept. 1961. The first National Appeal, with HRH The Duke of Edinburgh as President, was launched in the United Kingdom on 23 Nov. 1961, shortly followed by the United States and Switzerland.

Organization: WWF is the world's largest and most experienced independent conservation organization with over 4·7m. supporters and a global network of 24 National Organizations, 5 Associates and 26 Programme Offices.

The National Organizations carry out conservation activities in their own countries and contribute technical expertise and funding to WWF's international conservation programme. The Programme Offices implement WWF's fieldwork, advise national and local governments, and raise public understanding of conservation issues.

Mission: preserving genetic, species and ecosystem diversity; ensuring that the use of renewable natural resources is sustainable now and in the longer term, for the benefit of all life on Earth; promoting actions to reduce to a minimum pollution and the wasteful exploitation and consumption of resources and energy; WWF's ultimate goal is to stop, and eventually reverse, the accelerating degradation of our planet's natural environment, and to help build a future in which humans live in harmony with nature.

Address: Avenue du Mont-Blanc, CH-1196 Gland, Switzerland.
Website: http://www.panda.org
Director General: Dr Claude Martin.
President Emeritus: HRH The Prince Philip, Duke of Edinburgh.
President: S. Barbar Ali.

INTERNATIONAL UNION AGAINST CANCER (UICC)

Founded in 1933, the UICC is an international non-governmental association of more than 260 member organizations in about 80 countries.

Objectives: The UICC is devoted exclusively to all aspects of the worldwide fight against cancer. Its objectives are to advance scientific and medical knowledge in research, diagnosis, treatment and prevention of cancer, and to promote all other aspects of the campaign against cancer throughout the world. Particular emphasis is placed on professional and public education.

Membership: The UICC is made up of voluntary cancer leagues, associations and societies as well as cancer research and treatment centres and, in some countries, ministries of health.

Activities: The UICC creates and carries out programmes around the world in collaboration with several hundred volunteer experts, most of whom are professionally active in UICC member organizations. It co-operates with other organizations, societies and governmental bodies engaged in promoting cancer control and research. The international Cancer Congress is held by the UICC every 4 years; the most recent took place in Aug. 1998 in Rio de Janeiro.

Address: 3 rue du Conseil General, 1205-Geneva, Switzerland.
Website: http://www.uicc.ch
Executive Director: Archie Turnbull.

COUNTRIES OF THE WORLD

A— Z

COUNTRIES OF THE WORLD

—— A ——

AFGHANISTAN

Islamic State of Afghanistan

Capital: Kabul
Population estimate, 2000: 25·59m.
Estimated GDP: $18·1bn.

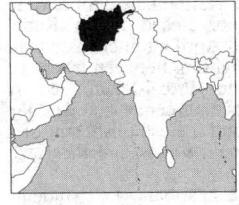

KEY HISTORICAL EVENTS

Ahmad Sháh Durráni consolidated Afghanistan as a kingdom, ruling with an advisory council of tribal chiefs from 1747 until his death in 1773. His frontiers extended into modern Kir and Pakistan, although by 1770 he had suffered reversals at the hands of the Sikhs in the Punjab. After 1773 the unity of Afghanistan was threatened by internal quarrels. In 1816–24 there was civil war, ending in victory for the Barakzay clan, whose leader Dost Mohammed became Amir in 1826. His capital was Kabul.

By then the Punjab and Kashmir had been lost, the British had become dominant in India and the Russian empire was ambitious to expand southwards. The British, believing that Dost Mohammed was unwilling or unable to resist Russia, invaded Afghanistan in 1839 in an attempt to replace him with their own protégé, Shah Shoja. An apparent British victory in 1840 was followed by actual defeat when the Afghans murdered Shah Shoja, and British forces were forced to retreat from Kabul with heavy losses.

Dost Mohammed was restored in 1843 and made friendship treaties with Britain in 1855 and 1857; he died in 1863 and was succeeded by his third son Shír 'Ali Khan. There was then civil war between two branches of the family and once more the Russians and the British tried to exploit instability. There was a second war with Britain (1878–79). In 1879 Shír 'Ali Khan fled leaving his son Ya'qúb Khan on the throne. In 1880 the British recognized the rival 'Abdor Rahmán Khan, in return for his undertaking to accept British control of his foreign policy. He defeated internal uprisings and in 1893 he accepted the Durand Line as his frontier with Russia.

Habíbolláh Khan (1901–19) continued the relationship with Britain in return for a subsidy. During the First World War he succeeded in remaining neutral. However, there was popular support in Afghanistan for the Ottoman Turks, and Habíbolláh's refusal to ally himself with them against Britain led to his assassination in 1919. His son and successor Amánolláh declared total independence from Britain at his coronation. Fighting broke out, but Britain then recognized the independence of Afghanistan at the Treaty of Rawalpindi, 1919.

Amánolláh was a reforming Khan who antagonized the conservatives of traditional society. Tribal revolt and banditry reached a climax in 1928 and the Khan abdicated in 1929 to be replaced first by Habíbolláh (soon murdered) and then by Mohammed Nadir (1929–33). The latter signed a friendship treaty with Russia. He was murdered in 1933 and succeeded by Mohammed Záhir who (like Nadir towards the end of his reign) took the title of Shah. Záhir Shah ruled with the advice, and under the influence, of his family for 40 years. In 1964 he was able to overcome opposition and put through a constitution establishing parliamentary democracy (effective 1965). In 1973 there was a military *coup* led by his cousin and brother-in-law Mohammed Daoud who abolished the 1964 constitution and declared a republic. Záhir Shah abdicated on 24 Aug. 1973.

The republic inherited pressure for tribal autonomy and economic crises mainly brought about by drought and famine. In April 1978 President Daoud was overthrown and killed in a further *coup* which installed a pro-Soviet government led by the People's Democratic Party. The new president was Noor Mohammad Taraki who signed a new treaty of friendship with the Soviet Union. In Sept. 1979 Taraki was overthrown, whereupon the Soviet Union invaded Afghanistan in Dec., deposed his successor and placed Babrak Karmal at the head of government.

In Dec. 1986 Sayid Mohammed Najibullah became president amid continuing civil war between government and rebel Moslem forces. Whereas in the 1960s both the USSR and the USA had financed government projects, in 1987 the USSR provided considerable military support and development aid to the pro-Soviet administration while the USA extended more limited support to the rebels. In the mid-1980s the UN began negotiations on the withdrawal of Soviet troops and the establishment of a government of national unity. Soviet troops began withdrawing from Afghanistan in early 1988.

After talks in Nov. 1991 with Afghan opposition movements ('mujahideen'), the Soviet government agreed to transfer its support from the Najibullah regime to an 'Islamic Interim Government'. As mujahideen insurgents closed in on Kabul President Najibullah stepped down on 16 April 1992. On 28 April an interim council received power from the outgoing government. Factional fighting between troops of the Minister of Defence, Ahmed Shah Massoud, and the Hezb-i-Islami, led by Gulbuddin Hekmatyar, continued until the signing of a peace agreement on 21 May providing for the withdrawal of armed forces from Kabul and the establishment of a neutral zone. On 11 Aug. 1992 fighting between government forces and the Hezb broke out again.

Late in 1994 a newly formed militant Islamic movement, 'Taliban' (i.e. 'students of religion'), took possession of Kandahar and routed Hekmatyar's Hezb-i-Islami at Kabul in Feb. 1995, apparently with Pakistani support. They were in turn defeated by the troops of President Rabbani, who regained possession of Kabul by 11 March 1995, but had rallied by Sept. 1995 and captured Herat, carrying out air and rocket raids on Kabul in Nov. 1995. On 13 May 1996 Hekmatyar and President Rabbani formed an alliance against the Taliban.

On 26 Sept. 1996 Taliban forces captured Kabul and set up an interim government under Mohamed Rabbani. Former President Najibullah and his brother were hanged, and Afghanistan was declared a complete Islamic state under Sharia law.

Government forces which had retreated to the north of Kabul, in alliance with an Uzbek warlord, Abdul Rashid Dostam, and a pro-Iranian Sh'ite faction, Hezb-i-Wahdat, then counter-attacked.

A new Taliban offensive, launched on 27 Dec. 1996, gave Taliban control of 90% of the country. In Aug. 1998 the Taliban seized control of Mazar i Sharif, and it now controls all but a small part of the country in the north. However, only three countries—Pakistan, Saudi Arabia and the United Arab Emirates—recognize Taliban as the legal government. In early 1999, hopes were raised of a broad based government to include representatives of the opposition coalition.

On 20 Aug. 1998 the USA launched cruise missile attacks against a camp at Khowst, 150 km south of Kabul, which the USA claimed was one of the most active terrorist bases in the world. The attack was carried out in response to the bombings of the US embassies in Kenya and Tanzania earlier in the month in which a total of 263 people had been killed.

Early in 1999, hopes were raised of a broad-based government to include representatives of the opposition coalition.

TERRITORY AND POPULATION
Afghanistan is bounded in the north by Turkmenistan, Uzbekiston and Tajikistan, east by China, east and south by Pakistan and west by Iran.

The area is 251,773 sq. miles (652,090 sq. km). Population according to the last (1979) census was 15,551,358, of which some 2·5m. were nomadic tribes. Estimate (1995) 23·5m. Population density, 31 per sq. km. The UN gives a projected population for 2000 of 25·59m. In 1995 an estimated 19·9% of the population lived in urban areas. There remained 3·5m. refugees in Pakistan and Iran in 1995.

The capital, Kabul, had an estimated population of 0·7m. in 1993. Other towns (with UN population estimates, 1988): Kandahar (225,500), Herat (177,300), Mazar i Sharif, (130,600), Jalalabad (55,000).

Main ethnic groups: Pashtuns, 35–38%; Tajiks, 25–30%; Hazaras, 10–15%; Uzbeks, 10%; Turkman, 5%; Others, 2%. The official languages are Pashto and Dari.

SOCIAL STATISTICS
Infant mortality, 1990–95, 163 per 1,000 live births; fertility rate (number of births per woman), 6·9; annual growth rate, 2·6%. Expectation of life at birth, 43 years for men and 44 for women over the period 1990–95.

AFGHANISTAN

CLIMATE
The climate is arid, with a big annual range of temperature and very little rain, apart from the period Jan. to April. Winters are very cold, with considerable snowfall, which may last the year round on mountain summits. Kabul, Jan. 27°F (−2·8°C), July 76°F (24·4°C). Annual rainfall 13" (338 mm).

CONSTITUTION AND GOVERNMENT
After the removal of President Najibullah, power was exercised by a 10-member Ruling Council chaired by Burhanuddin Rabbani who became interim President of the country on 28 June 1992. In Dec. 1992 a Grand Council of 1,335 national delegates convened and re-elected Burhanuddin Rabbani president. The Grand Council was wound up after 205 of its members had been designated a constituent assembly. President Rabbani's mandate expired in June 1994 but he remained in office.

CURRENT ADMINISTRATION
The *de facto* government is formed by the Taliban movement. The *de jure* government is led by President Burhanuddin Rabbani.
  President: Burhanuddin Rabbani, b. 1942; (Jamiat Party; sworn in 2 Jan. 1993).
  Prime Minister: Arsala Rahmani.

Local Government. There are 32 provinces, each administered in theory by an appointed governor.

DEFENCE
In 1997 military expenditure totalled US$209m. (US$10 per capita), representing 12·5% of GDP.

Army. Army organization disintegrated into factional groups after the deposition of President Najibullah in April 1992. Equipment included 700 T-54/-55/-62 main battle tanks. Strength was (1993) about 40,000, mainly conscripts, but most units of the Army are well below strength, largely as a result of desertions.

Air Force. Prior to the overthrow of the regime of President Najibullah in 1992, the Air Force had about 180 combat aircraft and 5,000 officers and men. Since then, the service has also been broken into various factions and few combat aircraft remain airworthy; the helicopters and transport aircraft fleet are also largely grounded.

INTERNATIONAL RELATIONS
Relations between Iran and Afghanistan have deteriorated as Taliban militants gain ground against government forces supported by Iran. Threats of war were provoked in Oct. 1998 after the Taliban allegedly killed 6 Iranian diplomats and a journalist during the capture of Mazar i Sharif, Afghanistan's 4th largest city, and Bamiyan, one of the last strongholds of the Iranian-backed Shia Muslims. Border clashes were reported on 8 Oct. near the north-eastern city of Torbat-e-Jam. 1·5m. Afghan refugees, mostly from the Shia minority, have fled to Iran.
  Afghanistan is a member of the UN and Colombo Plan.

ECONOMY
Performance. Real GDP growth was 26·2% in 1995, after many years of negative growth (−3·0% in 1994 and −10·8% in 1993).

Currency. The unit of currency is the *afghani* (AFA) of 100 *puls*.

Banking and Finance. The Afghan State Bank is the largest of the 3 main banks and also undertakes the functions of a central bank, holding the exclusive right of note issue. Foreign banks have been permitted to operate since 1990.

Weights and Measures. The metric system is in increasingly common use. Local units include: 1 *khurd* = 0·244 lb; 1 *pao* = 0·974 lb; 1 *charak* = 3·896 lb; 1 *sere* = 16 lb; 1 *kharwar* = 1,280 lb or 16 maunds of 80 lb each; 1 *gaz* = 40 inches; 1 *jarib* = 60 x 60 kabuli yd or ½ acre; 1 *kulba* = 40 jaribs (area in which 2½ kharwars of seed can be sown); 1 jarib yd = 29 inches.

ENERGY AND NATURAL RESOURCES

Electricity. Most generating plant is hydroelectric. Installed capacity was 371,000 kW in 1993. Production was 670m. kWh in 1994; consumption per capita was an estimated 35 kWh in 1995.

Oil and Gas. Oil reserves are estimated at 100m. tonnes; gas at 100,000m. cu. metres. A consortium of oil and gas companies led by Unocal plans a US$2bn. natural gas pipeline from Turkmenistan through Afghanistan to Pakistan.

Minerals. There are deposits of coal, copper, barite, lapis-lazuli, emerald, talc and salt.

Agriculture. The greater part of Afghanistan is mountainous but there are many fertile plains and valleys. In 1994 there were 7·91m. ha of arable land, 0·14m. ha of permanent cropland and 30m. ha of pasture; 2·8m. ha were irrigated in 1994. 69·2% of the economically active population were engaged in agriculture in 1995. Principal crops include grains, rice, fresh and dried fruits, vegetables, cotton seed and potatoes.

Production, 1992, in 1,000 tonnes: Wheat, 1,650; barley, 150; maize, 300; rice, 300. Livestock (1996): Cattle, 1·65m.; horses, 300,000; camels, 265,000 (1995); sheep, 14·3m.; goats 2·15m. (1995); asses, 1·16m.; chickens, 9m. (1995).

Forestry. In 1995 forests covered 2·1% of the total land area (3·1% in 1990). Timber production in 1995 was 7·68m. cu. metres.

Fisheries. In 1995 total catches were estimated to be 1,300 tonnes, exclusively from inland waters.

INDUSTRY

Major industries include natural gas, fertilizers, cement, coalmining, small vehicle assembly plants, building, carpet weaving, cotton textiles, clothing and footwear, leather tanning, sugar manufacturing and fruit canning.

Labour. The workforce was 8,851,000 in 1996 (65% males). In 1995 the unemployment rate was estimated at 8%.

INTERNATIONAL TRADE

Imports and Exports. Total exports (1995), US$153m.; imports US$344m. Main exported products: non-edible crude materials (excluding fuels), manufactured goods (raw material intensive), machinery and transport equipment, fruits, nuts, hand-woven carpets, wool, hides, precious and semi-precious gems. Main imports: foodstuffs and live animals, beverages and tobacco, mineral fuels, manufactured goods, chemicals and related products, machinery and transport equipment. Main trading partners : Kyrgyzstan, Pakistan and Russia.

COMMUNICATIONS

Roads. There were an estimated 21,000 km of roads in 1996, of which 2,800 km were paved. All roads, particularly outside the towns, are in a very poor state of repair as a result of military action. Approximately 31,000 passenger cars (1·4 per 1,000 inhabitants) and 25,000 trucks and vans were in use in 1996.

Rail. There are no railways in the country, but the Oxus bridge—opened in 1982—brought a short section of 1,524 mm gauge track into the country from Uzbekistan. A Trans-Afghan Railway was proposed in an Afghan-Pakistan-Turkmen agreement of 1994.

Civil Aviation. There is an international airport at Kabul (Khwaja Rawash Airport). The national carrier is Ariana Afghan Airlines, which in 1998 operated direct flights from Kabul to Amritsar, Dubai and Jeddah. In 1995 scheduled airline traffic of Afghanistan-based carriers flew 5·8m. km, carrying 250,000 passengers (107,000 on international flights).

Shipping. There are practically no navigable rivers. A port has been built at Qizil Qala on the Oxus and there are 3 river ports on the Amu Darya, linked by road to Kabul.

Telecommunications. In 1997 there were 29,000 telephone main lines, or 1·3 per 1,000 inhabitants. There is telegraphic communication between all the larger towns and with other parts of the world.

Postal Services. In 1995 there were 352 post offices.

SOCIAL INSTITUTIONS

Justice. A Supreme Court was established in June 1978. If no provision exists in the Constitution or in the general laws of the State, the courts follow the Hanafi jurisprudence of Islamic law.

Religion. The predominant religion is Islam. An estimated 84% of the population are Sunni Moslems, and 15% Shi'ites.

Education. Adult literacy was 31·5% in 1995 (male, 47·2%; female, 15·0%). Afghanistan has the biggest difference in literacy rates between the sexes in favour of males of any country outside Africa. There are elementary schools throughout the country, but secondary schools exist only in Kabul and provincial capitals. Both elementary and secondary education are free. In 1995 there were 1,312,197 pupils (20,055 teachers in 1994) in primary education and 512,851 pupils (17,548 teachers in 1994) in secondary education. During the period 1990–95 only 8% of females of primary school age were enrolled in school (the lowest percentage in the world).

In 1995–96 there were 5 universities, 1 university of Islamic studies, 1 state medical institute and 1 polytechnic. Kabul University had 9,500 students and 500 academic staff.

Health. In 1991 there were 2,233 doctors, 267 dentists, 1,451 nurses, 510 pharmacists and 338 midwives.

CULTURE

Broadcasting. Radio and TV Afghanistan is government-controlled. In 1995 there were 2·4m. radio receivers and 200,000 television receivers (colour by PAL and SECAM).

Press. In 1995 there were 15 daily newspapers with a combined circulation of 200,000, at a rate of 10 per 1,000 inhabitants.

Tourism. In 1996 there were 4,000 foreign tourists.

DIPLOMATIC REPRESENTATIVES
Of Afghanistan in Great Britain (31 Prince's Gate, London, SW7 1QQ)
Chargé d'Affaires: Ahmad Wali Masud.

Of Great Britain in Afghanistan (Karte Parwan, Kabul)
Ambassador: Vacant.

Of Afghanistan in the USA (360 Lexington Ave., 11th Floor, New York, NY 10017)
Chargé d'Affaires: Dr Ravan A. G. Farhadi.

Of the USA in Afghanistan (Wazir Akbar Khan Mina, Kabul)
Ambassador: Vacant.

Of Afghanistan to the United Nations
Ambassador: Dr Ravan A. G. Farhadi.

Of Afghanistan to the European Union
Ambassador: Vacant.

FURTHER READING
Amin, S. H., *Law, Reform and Revolution in Afghanistan.* London, 1991
Arney, G., *Afghanistan.* London, 1990
Hyman, A., *Afghanistan under Soviet Domination, 1964–1991.* 3rd ed. London, 1992
Jones, S., *Afghanistan.* [Bibliography]. Oxford and Santa Barbara (CA), 1991
Roy, O., *Islam and Resistance in Afghanistan.* 2nd ed. CUP, 1990
Rubin, B.R., *The Fragmentation of Afghanistan: State Formation and Collapse in the International System.* Yale Univ. Press, 1995.—*The Search for Peace in Afghanistan: from Buffer State to Failed State.* Yale Univ. Press, 1996
Sykes, P. M., *A History of Afghanistan.* 2 vols. New York, 1975

ALBANIA

Republika e Shqipërisë

Capital: Tirana
Population estimate, 2000: 3·49m.
Estimated GDP: $4·4bn.
HDI/world rank: 0·656/105

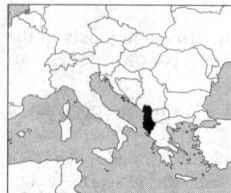

KEY HISTORICAL EVENTS

Of Illyrian origin, the Albanian clans were compelled to recognize the suzerainty of the expanding Ottoman empire in 1385. Split since 1054 between Rome (Catholics) and Constantinople (Orthodox), many Albanians converted to Islam and were able to rise high in the Ottoman administration. One such was Gjergj Kastrioti (1405–68), surnamed Skanderbeg, who defected from his Turkish commandership in 1443, reconverted to Christianity and maintained, with help from Naples, Venice and the Papal States, a guerrilla resistance to the Turks. In 1431 the Turks introduced a fiefdom system, whereby land was held in return for military or civil service. These fiefdoms became hereditary estates, and a class of large landowners developed. With the decline of central power, some lords acquired a wide measure of local autonomy.

After the Russo-Turkish war of 1877–78, an Albanian League was set up at Prizren to resist the cession of Albanian territory ordered by the Treaty of San Stefano and the Congress of Berlin. Demands grew for autonomy from the Turkish government, and although the League was suppressed by force in 1881, revolts continued. Expectations of reform from the Young Turk government of 1909 were disappointed. After the defeat of Turkey in the Balkan war of 1912, Albanian nationalists under the leadership of Ismail Kemal, a liberal opposition deputy in the Turkish parliament, proclaimed Albania's independence at Vlorë on 28 Nov. 1912 and set up a provisional government with Kemal at its head.

The London conference of 1912–13 recognized Albania's independence and chose the German, Prince William of Wied, as ruler, aided by a government of landowners and an international control commission. Weid's 6-month reign was bedevilled by subversion. During the First World War Albania became a battlefield for warring occupation forces. By the secret Treaty of London (26 April 1915), Britain, France and Russia offered Italy large tracts of Albania as an inducement to enter the war; and on 3 June 1917 the Italian commander in Albania declared Albania's independence under Italian protection. Such clandestine arrangements, however, were in conflict with the US President Woodrow Wilson's 'Fourteen Points' which emphasized self-determination and open treaties. In Jan. 1920, 50 Albanian regional delegates met at Lushnjë to protest to the peace conference against partitioning. They set up a regency council of 4 (representing the religious denominations) and formed a government under Sulejman Delvina. Irregular forces ejected the Italians who, however, retained the island of Sazan. Albania was admitted to the League of Nations on 20 Dec. 1920. In Nov. 1921 the conference of ambassadors confirmed her 1913 frontiers with minor alterations.

A parliament was elected in April 1921 in which 2 factions emerged led respectively by Ahmet Zogu, representing conservative landowners, and the Orthodox Bishop Fan Noli, representing the intelligentsia and urbanized middle class. Zogu became prime minister in 1922 and secured 40 out of 95 seats in the elections of Dec. 1923, but his government's harshness and corruption provoked a military *coup* on 10 June 1924. Zogu fled to Yugoslavia and Fan Noli set up a government which was idealistic but ineffective and made the fatal step of recognizing the Soviet Union. In Dec. 1924, with Yugoslav help, Zogu drove Noli into exile and set up a personal authoritarian régime. On 1 Sept. 1928 he proclaimed himself King Zog I.

Italian influence grew from the mid-1920s. A friendship pact was signed with Italy in 1926 and a defence treaty in 1927. In April 1939 Mussolini invaded Albania outright and set up a puppet state, uniting the Italian and Albanian crowns. Zog went into exile.

During the Second World War Albania suffered first Italian and then German occupation. Resistance was carried on by royalist, nationalist republican and communist movements, often at odds with each other. The latter enjoyed the support of Tito's partisans, who were instrumental in forming the Albanian Communist Party on 8 Nov. 1941. Communists dominated the Anti-Fascist National Liberation Committee which became the Provisional Democratic Government on 22 Oct. 1944 after the German withdrawal, with Enver Hoxha, a French-educated school teacher and member of the Communist Party Central Committee, at its head. Large estates were broken up and the land distributed, though full collectivization was not brought in until 1955–59. Britain, the USA and the USSR recognized the provisional government on condition that free elections were held, but at the elections of 2 Dec. 1945 only communists and their sympathizers were allowed to stand. The new national assembly met in Jan 1946, proclaimed a people's republic and promulgated a Soviet-type constitution.

In 1946 Yugoslav plans to incorporate Albania were set in motion with a customs union and Treaty of Mutual Aid. Hoxha emerged as an opponent, and managed to delay the tactics of the pro-Yugoslav faction until the Stalin-Tito rift of 1948 gave him a chance to espouse the Moscow line. Close ties were forged with the USSR, but following Khrushchev's reconciliation with Tito in 1956 China replaced the Soviet Union as Albania's powerful patron from 1961 until the end of the Maoist phase in 1977. The régime then adopted a policy of 'revolutionary self-sufficiency'. In Dec. 1981 Mehmet Shehu, then prime minister, allegedly committed suicide. Hoxha died on 11 April 1985.

Following the collapse of the Soviet empire, there were demonstrations against the government, often led by students. In Dec. 1990 the People's Assembly adopted a decree legalizing opposition parties. A Communist government was elected in March 1991, but following a general strike resigned in June. A successor government was itself replaced by a non-party interim government in Dec. 1991. A non-Communist government was elected in March 1992.

In 1997 Albania was disrupted by financial crises caused by the collapse of fraudulent pyramid finance schemes. A period of violent anarchy, with many fatalities, led to the fall of the administration led by President Berisha (Democratic Party) and to fresh elections which returned a Socialist-led government. A UN peacekeeping force withdrew in Aug. 1997 but sporadic violence continued, with the opposition calling for new elections.

On 12 Sept. 1998 a close aide of former President Berisha was assassinated in what the Socialist government claimed was a failed coup attempt. Violence erupted, bringing with it 2 days of rioting, the resignation of the Interior Minister and on 28 Sept. the resignation of Prime Minister Fatos Nano. The Socialist Party nominated 30-year-old Pandeli Majko as his replacement.

In April 1999 the Kosovo crisis which led to NATO air attacks on Yugoslavian military targets set off a flood of refugees into Albania.

TERRITORY AND POPULATION

Albania is bounded in the north by Yugoslavia, east by Macedonia, south by Greece and west by the Adriatic. The area is 28,748 sq. km (11,101 sq. miles). At the census of 1989 the population was 3,184,417; density, 111 per sq. km.

The UN gives a projected population for 2000 of 3·49m.

In 1995, 62·8% of the population lived in rural areas. The capital is Tirana (population in 1,000 in 1991, 251); other large towns are Durrës (86·9), Shkodër (83·7), Elbasan (83·2), Vlorë (76), Korçë (67·1), (populations in 1990) Fier (37), Berat (37), Lushnjë (24), Kavajë (23) and Gjirokastër (Argyrocastro) (21).

The country is administratively divided into 26 districts, 66 towns, 306 town boroughs, 537 village unions and 2,844 villages.

Districts	Area (sq. km)	Population (1990)	Districts	Area (sq. km)	Population (1990)
Berat	1,027	180,489	Korçë	2,181	218,219
Dibrë	1,568	153,775	Krujë	607	109,876
Durrës	848	251,029	Kukës	1,330	104,731
Elbasan	1,481	248,676	Lezhë	479	63,505
Fier	1,175	251,115	Librazhd	1,013	73,871
Gjirokastër	1,137	67,392	Lushnjë	712	137,830
Gramsh	695	44,791	Mat	1,028	78,754
Kolonjë	805	25,291	Mirditë	867	51,701

ALBANIA

Districts	Area (sq. km)	Population (1990)	Districts	Area (sq. km)	Population (1990)
Permet	929	40,419	Skrapar	775	47,605
Pogradec	725	73,333	Tepelenë	817	51,022
Pukë	1,034	50,286	Tirana	1,238	374,483
Sarandë	1,097	89,456	Tropojë	1,043	45,965
Shkodë	2,528	241,549	Vlorë	1,609	180,725

Districts are named after their capitals; exceptions: Tropojë, capital—Bajram Curri; Mat—Burrel; Mirditë—Rrëshen; Skrapar—Çorovodë; Dibrë—Peshkopi; Kolonjë—Ersekë.

At the 1989 census, members of ethnic minorities totalled 64,816, including 58,758 Greeks and 4,697 Macedonians.

The official language is Albanian.

SOCIAL STATISTICS
1996 estimates: Births, 76,000; deaths, 26,000. Rates (per 1,000, 1996 est.): Births, 22·2; deaths, 7·6. Infant mortality, 1990–95, was 32 per 1,000 live births, the highest in Europe. Fertility rate (number of births per woman), 2·9 in 1990–95, also the highest in Europe. Life expectancy at birth, 1990–95, 68·0 years for males and 74·0 years for females. Annual growth rate, 1990–95, 2·3%. Abortion was legalized in 1991.

CLIMATE
Mediterranean-type, with rainfall mainly in winter, but thunderstorms are frequent and severe in the great heat of the plains in summer. Winters in the highlands can be severe, with much snow. Tirana, Jan. 44°F (6·8°C), July 75°F (23·9°C). Annual rainfall 54" (1,353 mm). Shkodër, Jan. 39°F (3·9°C), July 77°F (25°C). Annual rainfall 57" (1,425 mm).

CONSTITUTION AND GOVERNMENT
A new constitution was promulgated on 26 April 1991. The supreme legislative body is the single-chamber *National Assembly* of 155 deputies, 115 directly elected and 40 elected by proportional representation, for 4-year terms. Where no candidate wins an absolute majority, a run-off election is held. Senior members of the former Communist Party, or members of parliament before May 1991, are not permitted to stand in national or local elections until 2002.

A draft new constitution, submitted to a referendum in Nov. 1994, was rejected by 53·8% of votes cast; turn-out was 75%.

The *President* is elected by Parliament for a 5-year term.

National Anthem. 'Rreth Flamurit të për bashkuar' ('The flag that united us in the struggle'); words by A. S. Drenova, music by C. Porumbescu.

RECENT ELECTIONS
On 2 March 1997 President Berisha dismissed the government of Alexander Meksi (Democratic Party of Albania) and declared a state of emergency. On 3 March Sali Berisha was re-elected President for a second term. In an agreement between the Government and opposition brokered by Italy, President Berisha promised a general amnesty, the formation of a government of national reconciliation and elections in June. On 11 March he appointed Bashkim Fino (Socialist Party of Albania) prime minister. On 11 May the government adopted an electoral law, approved by the Organization for Security and Co-operation in Europe, setting up a mixed system of 2 rounds of first-past-the-post voting and proportional representation. These elections took place on 29 June and 6 July 1997. The Socialist Party of Albania won 99 of the 155 seats with 52·8% of votes cast, the ruling Democratic Party of Albania 29 with 25·7%, Social Democratic Party of Albania 8 with 2·5%, Human Rights' Unity Party 4 with 2·8%, National Front 3 with 2·3%. Non-partisans won 3 seats and 5 other parties won 7 seats between them. There were also 2 seats vacant.

The newly elected parliament chose Rexhep Mejdani (Socialist Party of Albania; PSS) as President on 24 July 1997.

ALBANIA

CURRENT ADMINISTRATION
President: Rexhep Mejdani (PSS), elected 24 July 1997.
In March 1999 the government comprised:
Prime Minister: Pandeli Majko (PSS).
Deputy Prime Minister: Ilir Meta. *Foreign:* Paskal Milo (Social Democratic Party of Albania; SDP). *Defence:* Luan Hajdaraga. *Public Sector Economy and Privatization:* Ulli Bufi (PSS). *Labour and Social Affairs:* Kadir Rrapi. *Food and Agriculture:* Lufter Xhuveli (Agrarian Party). *Finance:* Anastas Angjeli. *Public Works and Transport:* Ingrid Shuli. *Education:* Et'hem Ruka (PSS). *Culture, Youth and Sport:* Edi Rama. *Health:* Leonard Solis (Human Rights Union). *Information:* Musa Ulqini. *Economic Co-operation and Trade:* Ennelinda Meksi (PSS). *Governmental Co-ordination:* Ilir Meta. *Justice:* Thimio Kondi (Independent). *State Secretary for European Integration:* Maqo Lakrori (PSS). *Local Government:* Arben Demeti. *Minister of State for Legislative Reform and Relations with Parliament:* Arben Imami (Democratic Alliance).

Local Government. There are 12 prefectures, each under a prefect nominated by the Prime Minister, subdivided into 36 districts. Elected councils function at district, municipal and commune level. There are 64 city and 310 commune mayoralties. Elections were held on 20 and 26 Oct. 1996; turn-out was 72%. The Democratic Party gained 58 city and 267 commune mayoralties. The OSCE refused to monitor the elections because it was not permitted sufficient observers.

DEFENCE
Conscription is for 15 months. In 1997 defence expenditure totalled US$94m. (US$26 per capita), representing 6·7% of GDP.

Army. The Army consists of 9 infantry divisions. Equipment includes 138 T-34 and 721 T-59 main battle tanks. Strength (1996) 60,000 (including 20,000 conscripts). There is an internal security force of 5,000; frontier guards number 5,000. There is a People's Militia of 3,500.

Navy. The combatant navy includes 2 submarines, 2 offshore patrol craft, 24 hydrofoil torpedo boats, 11 inshore patrol craft and 4 inshore minesweepers. Auxiliaries include 2 tankers and about 10 service craft. Navy personnel in 1996 totalled 2,500 officers and ratings, including 350 coastal defence guards. There are naval bases at Durrës and Vlorë.

Air Force. The Air Force, controlled by the Army, had (1997) about 7,000 personnel (1,400 conscripts), and operated 70 combat aircraft, mostly Chinese. There are 5 aviation regiments, 3 with fighters, 1 with transport aircraft and 1 with helicopters. In 1997 the USA agreed to supply Cessna T-37 trainers.

INTERNATIONAL RELATIONS
Albania is a member of the UN, the Council of Europe, the Central European Initiative and the NATO Partnership for Peace.

ECONOMY
Policy. Priority is given to the development of agriculture and the exploitation of tourism and natural resources. Privatization of land, small businesses and housing was effected in 1991–93. A privatization programme for large enterprises was initiated in 1995 under the aegis of the National Privatization Agency. Sales are at auction or through vouchers.
Towards the end of 1997 Prime Minister Fatos Nano succeeded in raising US$600m. from foreign donors (more than had been requested) to help rebuild the country's economy.

Performance. GDP fell by 6% in 1997 after the collapse of pyramid finance schemes.

Budget. The fiscal year is the calendar year.
In 1995 revenue amounted to 49,068m. leks and expenditure to 69,687m. leks.

Currency. The monetary unit is the *lek* (ALL), notionally of 100 *qindars*. In Aug. 1965 a new *lek* was introduced: 10 old *leks* = 1 new *lek*. In Sept. 1991 the lek was pegged to the ecu at a rate of 30 leks = 1 ecu. In June 1992 it was devalued from 50 to 110 to US$1. Annualized inflation was 14·5% in 1995 (85% in 1993), but in Feb. 1998 was reported to be nearing 50%. In Feb. 1996 the UK restored 1,574 kg of gold which had been held in compensation under a French-UK-US trusteeship for the mining of 2 British warships in the 'Corfu incident' of 1946. Foreign exchange reserves were US$317m. in Feb. 1998 and gold reserves 120,000 troy oz. Total money supply was 87m. leks in Nov. 1997.

Banking and Finance. The central bank and bank of issue is the formally independent Bank of Albania, founded in 1925 with Italian aid as the Albanian State Bank and renamed in 1993. Its *governor* is Qarmil Tusha. In 1996 there were 3 state-owned commercial banks, 1 foreign bank and 2 joint ventures.

A stock exchange opened in Tirana in 1996.

Weights and Measures. The metric system is in force.

ENERGY AND NATURAL RESOURCES

Electricity. Albania is rich in hydro-electric potential. Electricity capacity was 1·53m. kW in 1995. Production was 3·86bn. kWh in 1994. Consumption per capita in 1995 was an estimated 1,221 kWh.

Oil and Gas. Offshore exploration began in 1991. Oil has been produced onshore since 1920. Oil reserves are some 540m. tonnes. Output of crude in 1992, 0·99m. tonnes. Natural gas is extracted. Reserves, 8,000m. cu. metres. Output, 1993, 100m. cu. metres. Oil investment includes the building of a 40 km pipeline to the Adriatic coast.

A consortium led by Premier Oil, an independent UK company, signed an agreement in Dec. 1997 to develop Albania's biggest onshore oilfield, Patos Merinze, by investing US$250m. Production is to increase from 6,000 bbls. a day to more than 25,000 within 4 years as a result of the venture, which represents the largest single foreign investment made in Albania.

Minerals. Mineral wealth is considerable and includes lignite, chromium, copper and nickel. Production, 1994 (in 1,000 tonnes): Lignite, 169; chromium ore, 223; copper ore, 178; iron-nickel ore (1991), 931. Nickel reserves are 60m. tonnes of iron containing 1m. tonnes of nickel, but extraction had virtually ceased by 1996. A consortium of British and Italian companies is modernizing the chrome industry with the aim of making Albania the leading supplier of ferrochrome to European stainless steel producers.

Agriculture. In 1996, 60% of the population depended upon agriculture, which contributed 56% of GDP. No other European country is dominated by agriculture to such an extent. The country is mountainous, except for the Adriatic littoral and the Korçë Basin, which are fertile. Only 25% of the land area is suitable for cultivation. In 1994 there were 0·58m. ha of arable land, 0·13m. ha of permanent cropland and 0·4m. ha of pasture. 0·35m. ha were irrigated in 1994.

A law of Aug. 1991 privatized co-operatives' land. Families received allocations according to their size made by village committees. In 1994 there were 0·42m. private farms; holdings averaged 1·4 ha. Since 1995 owners have been permitted to buy and sell agricultural land. In 1994 there were 9,000 tractors in use.

Production (in 1,000 tonnes), 1994: Total grains, 508 (including maize, 151); sugar-beet, 60; potatoes, 86; barley, 3; sunflower seeds, 2; tobacco, 13; dried beans, 16; soya beans, 1; fodder, 20; vegetables (including water melons), 585.

Livestock, 1996: Cattle, 0·85m.; sheep, 2·45m.; goats, 1·28m. (1995); pigs, 1·1m.; horses 58,000; asses, 113,000; chickens, 3m. (1995). Livestock products, 1994 (in 1,000 tonnes): Beef and veal, 50; pork, 20; mutton and goat, 33; chicken, 4; wool, 3; milk, 764,000 litres; 285m. eggs.

Forestry. Forests covered 1,046,000 ha in 1995 (38·2% of the total land area), mainly oak, elm, pine and birch. Timber production in 1995 was 409,000 cu. metres.

Fisheries. The total catch in 1995 amounted to an estimated 3,100 tonnes (1,850 tonnes from sea fishing).

ALBANIA

INDUSTRY
Output is small, and the principal industries are agricultural product processing, textiles, oil products and cement. Closures of loss-making plants in the chemical and engineering industries built up in the Communist era led to a 60% decline in production by 1993. Output, 1994 (in 1,000 tonnes): Rolled steel, 17; phosphate fertilizer, 11; ammonium nitrate, 6; sulphuric acid, 4; cement, 240; cigarettes, 1; soap, 3; vegetable oil, 6; 40m. bricks; 3m. articles of knitwear; beer, 7·2m. litres; wine, 0·5m. litres.

Labour. In 1994 the workforce was 1·54m., including 0·6m. in the private sector. Nearly half of the active labour force is engaged in agriculture. Unemployment was 15·8% in 1997.

Minimum wages may not fall below one-third of maximum. Hours of labour: 8-hour day, 6-day week and 12 days yearly paid holiday. Retirement age is 60 for men and 55 for women.

Trade Unions. Independent trade unions became legal in Feb. 1991.

INTERNATIONAL TRADE
Foreign investment was legalized in Nov. 1990. Foreign debt was some US$781m. in 1996. Remittances from Albanians working abroad totalled US$334m. in 1993.

Imports and Exports. Exports in 1996 totalled US$211m.; imports, US$938m. In 1994 exports included 45·3% manufactures, 26·7% fuels and lubricants, 14·3% foodstuffs, tobacco and live animals, 4·6% raw materials, 3·4% machinery and transport equipment; imports: 31·8% machinery and transport equipment, 25·5% foodstuffs, tobacco and live animals, 18·9% manufactures, 10·9% fuels and lubricants, 6·5% chemical products.

Main export markets, 1995 (% of total trade): Italy, 51·1%; Greece, 9·7%; Germany, 6·1%; Turkey, 6%. Main import suppliers: Italy, 36·8%; Greece, 26·1%; Germany, 4·8%; Turkey, 3·9%.

COMMUNICATIONS

Roads. In 1995 there were 2,900 km of paved main roads, 5,000 km of unpaved secondary roads and 9,500 km of rural tracks. 160,000 vehicles were registered in 1996.

Rail. Total length in 1996 was 742 km. 4m. passengers and 0·6m. tonnes of freight were carried in 1995.

Civil Aviation. The national carrier is Albanian Airlines, a joint venture with a Kuwaiti firm. It began operations in Oct. 1995. In 1998 it flew services to Bologna, Frankfurt, Istanbul and Rome. Tirana (Rinas Airport) was also served in 1998 by Ada Air, Adria Airways, Alitalia, Austrian Airlines, Hemus Air, Lufthansa, Malév, Olympic Airways, SABENA, Swissair and Turkish Airlines. 200,000 passengers used Rinas in 1995 (30,000 in 1990). In 1995 scheduled airline traffic of Albanian carriers flew 0·2m. km, carrying 13,000 passengers (all on international flights).

Shipping. In 1995 merchant shipping totalled 80,954 GRT. The main ports are Durrës, Vlorë, Sarandë and Shëngjin.

Telecommunications. A state-owned mobile telephone network was set up in 1996, initially serving 8,000 subscribers. There were 86,800 telephone main lines in 1997, or 23·3 per 1,000 inhabitants (the lowest telephone provision of any European country).

Postal Services. In 1995 there were 698 post offices.

SOCIAL INSTITUTIONS

Justice. A new criminal code was introduced in June 1995. The administration of justice is presided over by the *Council of Justice*, chaired by the President of the Republic, which appoints judges to courts. A Ministry of Justice was re-established in 1990 and a Bar Council set up. In Nov. 1993 the number of capital offences was reduced from 13 to 6 and the death penalty was abolished for women.

ALBANIA

Religion. The population is 70% of Moslem origin, mainly Sunni with some Belaktashi, 7% Albanian Orthodox, 5% Roman Catholic and 18% others. The Albanian Orthodox Church is autocephalous; it is headed by an Exarch and 3 metropolitans. In 1993 there were 47 priests. The Roman Catholic cathedral in Shkodë has been restored. In 1993 there were 4 Roman Catholic bishops. Percentages of the population actively practising were estimated in 1996 as Moslems, 20%; Orthodox, 6%; Roman Catholics, 3%.

Education. Primary education is free and compulsory in 8-year schools from 7 to 15 years. Secondary education is also free and lasts 4 years. Secondary education is divided into 3 categories: General; technical and professional; vocational. There were, in 1995–96, 2,670 nursery schools with 84,536 pupils and 4,416 teachers; in 1994–95, 1,782 primary schools with 550,737 pupils and 30,893 teachers; and in 1995–96, 89,895 pupils and 6,321 teachers at secondary schools. In 1995–96 there were 4 universities, 1 agricultural university, 1 technological university, 1 polytechnic, 1 academy of fine arts and 1 higher institute of physical education. There were 14,699 university students and 1,138 academic staff in 1994–95. Adult literacy is 85%.

In 1994 total expenditure on education came to 3% of GNP.

Health. Medical services are free, though medicines are charged for. In 1993 there were 40 hospitals, 6,308 doctors and 6,801 nurses. In 1995 there were about 10,000 hospital beds.

CULTURE

Broadcasting. Broadcasting is regulated by the National Council for Radio-Television, 1 member of which is appointed by the president, and the other 6 by the permanent Commission on the Media, which is composed equally of representatives of government and opposition parties. The National Council broadcasts a national radio programme and a second radio programme from 14 stations. There are also regional programmes and an external service. In 1995 there were 700,000 radio and 350,000 TV receivers (colour by PAL). Albania has the fewest TV receivers per 1,000 population in Europe, with 103 per 1,000 in 1995.

Cinema. In 1990 there were 108 cinemas with an attendance of 3·3m.

Press. In 1995 there were 4 national dailies (combined circulation of 180,000, at a rate of 53 per 1,000 inhabitants), 2 owned by political parties; and 45 other newspapers.

Tourism. In 1996 there were 56,000 foreign tourists, spending US$11m. In 1995 there were 3,000 hotel beds.

DIPLOMATIC REPRESENTATIVES
Of Albania in Great Britain (4th Floor, 38 Grosvenor Gdns., London, SW1W 0EB)
Ambassador: Agim Besim Fagu.

Of Great Britain in Albania (Rruga Skenderberg 12, Tirana)
Ambassador: Mr. S. Nash.

Of Albania in the USA (1150 18th St., NW, Washington, D.C., 20036)
Ambassador: Petrit Bushati.

Of the USA in Albania (Tirana Rruga Elbasanit 103, Tirana)
Ambassador: Marisa R. Lino.

Of Albania to the United Nations
Ambassador: Agim Nesho.

Of Albania to the European Union
Ambassador: Idriz Basha.

FURTHER READING
Bland, W. B., *Albania*. [Bibliography] Oxford and Santa Barbara (CA), 1988
Hutchings, R., *Historical Dictionary of Albania*. Lanham (MD), 1997
Sjoberg, O., *Rural Change and Development in Albania*. Boulder (CO), 1992
Vickers, M., *The Albanians: a Modern History*. London, 1997
Vickers, M. and Pettifer, J., *Albania: from anarchy to a Balkan Identity*. Farnborough, 1997
Winnifrith, T. (ed.) *Perspectives on Albania*. London, 1992

National statistical office: Statistical Institute of Albania, Tirana.

ALGERIA

Jumhuriya al-Jazairiya
ad-Dimuqratiya ash-Shabiya

(People's Democratic Republic
of Algeria)

Capital: Algiers
Population estimate, 2000: 31·6m.
GNP per capita: (PPP$) 4,620
HDI/world rank: 0·746/82

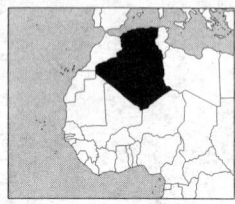

KEY HISTORICAL EVENTS

The first Algerian kingdom emerged from the Punic Wars. Massinissa reigned over his kingdom of Numidia from 202–148 BC and his dynasty lasted until 106 BC when his grandson Jugurtha became a Roman client. As part of the Roman Empire, Numidia flourished, becoming known as the 'granary of Rome'.

With the decline of the Roman Empire, Algeria became part of the powerful Berber empires of the Almoravids and Almohads. Tlemcen became the eastern capital of the Almohads and flourished as a centre of Islam. During this period Algerian seaports like Algiers, Annaba and Bijaya thrived on trade with European markets. The demise of the Almohad empire created a power vacuum which led to the rise of piracy along what became known as the Barbary Coast. Coastal cities hired corsairs to seize merchant vessels and gain an advantage in the fierce competition for trade on the high seas. It was not until late in the 18th century that Europeans were able to challenge the Barbary pirates of Algeria with superior naval power and artillery. In 1815 a US naval squadron under Captain Stephen Decatur attacked Algiers and forced its governor to sign a treaty banning piracy against US ships.

Persistent attacks on European shipping caused the British and Dutch to combine their forces against the Algerians and almost totally destroyed their fleet in 1816. The French took Algiers in 1830 and, despite formidable resistance, by 1857 the whole country was in French control. The French settlers who subsequently arrived developed political and economic power at the expense of the indigenous Moslem population. In Nov. 1954 the *Front de Libération Nationale* (FLN), representing the Moslem majority, sought national independence by open warfare against the French administration and armed forces. There was extensive loss of life and property during the fighting which continued unabated until in March 1962 a ceasefire was agreed between the French government and the nationalists. The conflict marked the only successful challenge to colonialism by a Middle Eastern country. Against the wishes of the French in Algeria, Gen. de Gaulle conceded Algerian independence on 3 July 1962.

The Political Bureau of the FLN took over the functions of government, a National Constituent Assembly was elected and the Republic was declared on 25 Sept. 1962. The founder of the FLN, Ahmed Ben Bella, became prime minister, becoming president the following year. On 15 June 1965 the government was overthrown by a junta of army officers, who established a Revolutionary Council under Col. Houari Boumédienne. After 10 years of rule, Boumédienne proposed that elections should be held for a president and a National Assembly. The proposed new constitution was accepted in a referendum in Nov. 1976 and Boumédienne was elected president (unopposed), securing more than 99% of the votes cast. A National Assembly was elected in Feb. 1977, only FLN members being allowed as candidates.

On the death of the president in Dec. 1978 the Revolutionary Council again took over the government. Col. Bendjedid Chadli was proposed president, and a referendum accepted him. When he stood for re-election in 1984, as the sole candidate, he was chosen for a further 5 years. But in Dec. 1991, when the Islamic Salvation Front (FIS) won the first round, the President resigned and his functions were assumed by a High Committee of State. The second round of elections was cancelled. In March 1992 the FIS was dissolved by court order. The head of state, Mohamed Boudiaf, was assassinated on 29 July 1992, and a campaign of terrorism was launched by Moslem fundamentalists which has continued to the present day. It is estimated that over 100,000 lives have been lost since the war between the Government and the Islamists began in 1992. Additionally, more than 1,000 Algerians have 'disappeared' after being arrested by government forces.

Liamine Zeroual was appointed State President in Jan. 1994 and elected President on 16 Nov. 1995. Hopes that violence would be brought to an end by the parliamentary poll of June 1997 were disappointed and local elections in Oct. 1997 brought opposition accusations of ballot rigging. 1998 began with reports of over 1,000 deaths in the previous 2 weeks. The Algerian government blamed the slaughter on fanatical Islamists.

TERRITORY AND POPULATION
Algeria is bounded in the west by Morocco and Western Sahara, south-west by Mauritania and Mali, south-east by Niger, east by Libya and Tunisia, and north by the Mediterranean Sea. It has an area of 2,381,741 sq. km (919,595 sq. miles). Population (census 1987) 22,971,558; estimate (1998) 29,300,000. Population density (1995), 12 per sq. km.

The UN gives a projected population for 2000 of 31·6m.

2·5m. Algerians live in France.

83% of the population speak Arabic, 17% Berber; French is widely spoken. A law of Dec. 1996 made Arabic the sole official language.

The estimated populations (1993-94) of the 48 *wilayat* (provincial councils) were as follows:

Adrar	279,000	Mila	598,000
Ain Defla	634,000	Mostaganem	605,000
Ain Témouchent	308,000	M'Sila	737,000
Algiers	1,866,000	Naâma	134,000
Annaba	522,000	Ouahran (Oran)	1,089,000
Batna	922,000	Ouargla	346,000
al-Bayadh	178,000	al-Oued	459,000
Béchar	222,000	Oum al-Bouaghi	466,000
Béjaia	826,000	Qacentina (Constantine)	790,000
Biskra	492,000	Relizane	671,000
Bordj Bou Arreridj	501,000	Saida	266,000
Bouira	631,000	Sétif	1,222,000
Blida	839,000	Sidi-bel-Abbès	530,000
Boumerdes	803,000	Skikda	722,000
Chlef	813,000	Souk Ahras	341,000
Djelfa	611,000	Tamanrasset	118,000
Guelma	399,000	at-Tarf	332,000
Ghardaia	251,000	Tébessa	477,000
Illizi	24,000	Tiaret	692,000
Jijel	559,000	Tindouf	20,000[1]
Khenchela	282,000	Tipaza	733,000
Laghouat	257,000	Tissemsilt	265,000
Mascara	670,000	Tizi-Ouzou	1,088,000
Médéa	770,000	Tlemcen	830,000

[1]Excluding Saharawi refugees (170,000 in 1988) in camps.

The capital is Algiers (1995 population, 2,168,000). Other major towns (with 1987 census populations): Oran, 609,823; Constantine, 440,842; Annaba, 222,518; Batna, 181,601; Sétif, 170,182; Sidi-bel-Abbès, 152,778; Skikda, 128,747; Biskra, 128,280; Blida, 127,284; Béjaia, 114,534; Mostaganem, 114,037; Tlemcen, 107,632; Tébassa, 107,559; Béchar, 107,311.

SOCIAL STATISTICS
1998 estimates: Births, 806,000; deaths, 164,000; marriages, 151,467; stillbirths, 17,190. Rates (1998): Births, 27·5 per 1,000; deaths, 5·6 per 1,000; growth, 2·14%. Expectation of life (1992), 65·6 years.

ALGERIA

CLIMATE
Coastal areas have a warm temperate climate, with most rain in winter, which is mild, while summers are hot and dry. Inland, conditions become more arid beyond the Atlas Mountains. Algiers, Jan. 54°F (12·2°C), July 76°F (24·4°C). Annual rainfall 30" (762 mm). Biskra, Jan. 52°F (11·1°C), July 93°F (33·9°C). Annual rainfall 6" (158 mm). Oran, Jan. 54°F (12·2°C), July 76°F (24·4°C). Annual rainfall 15" (376 mm).

CONSTITUTION AND GOVERNMENT
A referendum was held on 28 Nov. 1996. The electorate was 16,434,527; turn-out was 79·6%. The electorate approved by 85·81% of votes cast a new Constitution which defines the fundamental components of the Algerian people as Islam, Arab identity and Berber identity. It was signed into law on 7 Dec. 1996. Political parties are permitted, but not if based on a separatist feature such as race, religion, sex, language or region. The terms of office of the President are limited to 2, but the President's powers of nomination are widened (General-Secretary of the Government, governor of the national bank, judges, chiefs of security organs and prefects). Parliament is bicameral: A 380-member *National Assembly* elected by direct universal suffrage using proportional representation, and a 144-member *Council of the Nation*, one-third nominated by the President and two-thirds indirectly elected by the 48 local authorities. The Council of the Nation debates bills passed by the National Assembly which become law if a three-quarters majority is in favour.

National Anthem. 'Qassaman bin nazilat Il-mahiqat' ('We swear by the lightning that destroys'); words by M. Zakaria, tune by Mohamed Fawzi.

RECENT ELECTIONS
At the presidential elections on 16 Nov. 1995 the electorate was 15,969,904; turn-out was 74·92%. Liamine Zeroual was elected for a second term with 61·34% of votes cast against 3 opponents.

Elections for the National Assembly were held on 5 June 1997. There were 7,486 candidates from 39 parties. The electorate was 16·8m. Turn-out was officially put at 65·4%. The National Democratic Rally (RND) gained 155 seats, the Society for Peace Movement (MSP) 69, the National Liberation Front (FLN) 64, Ennahda 34, FFS 19, Rally for Culture and Democracy 19, Labour Party 4 and others 16. In the elections to the Council of the Nation on 25 Dec. 1997 the National Democratic Rally won 80 of the 96 seats, the National Liberation Front 10, FFS 4 and MSP 2.

CURRENT ADMINISTRATION
President and Minister for National Defence: Liamine Zeroual (b. 1941; sworn in 27 Nov. 1995).

In March 1999 the government comprised:
Prime Minister: Ismail Hamdani.

Agriculture and Fisheries: Boulahouadjeb Benalia. *Commerce:* Belaid Bakhti. *Communication, Culture and Government Spokesman:* Abdelaziz Rahabi. *Energy and Mines:* Youcef Yousfi. *Equipment, Urban and Rural Development:* Abderrahmane Belayat. *Finance:* Abdelkrim Harchaoui. *Foreign Affairs:* Ahmed Attaf. *Health and Population:* Yahia Guidoum. *Higher Education and Scientific Research:* Amar Tou. *Housing:* Abdelkader Bounekraf. *Industry and Restructuring:* Abdelmadjid Menasra. *Interior, Local Communities and Environment:* Abdelmalek Sellal. *Justice:* Ghaouti Mekamcha. *Labour, Social Protection and Vocational Training:* Hacene Laskri. *National Education:* Boubakeur Benbouzid. *National Solidarity and Family:* Rabea Mechernene. *Posts and Telecommunications:* Mohamed Salah Youyou. *Religious Affairs:* Bouabdallah Ghoulemallah. *Small and Medium-sized Enterprises:* Bougerra Soltani. *Tourism and Handicrafts:* Abdelkader Bengrina. *Transportation:* Sid Ahmed Boulil. *Veterans Affairs:* Mohamed Said Abadou. *Youth and Sports:* Mohamed Aziz Derouaz.

Local Government. There are 48 provincial (*wilayat*) councils, headed by prefects (*walis*) appointed by the President, and 1,539 local authorities.

DEFENCE
Conscription is for 18 months (6 months basic training and 12 months civilian tasks) at the age of 19.

Military expenditure totalled US$2,114m. in 1997 (US$73 per capita), representing 4·6% of GDP.

Army. There are 6 military regions. The Army had a strength of 107,000 (75,000 conscripts) in 1996, organized in 2 armoured and 2 mechanized divisions, 5 motorized infantry brigades, 1 airborne division, and 7 artillery and 5 air defence battalions. Equipment includes 330 T-54/-55, 330 T-62 and 300 T-72 main battle tanks. The Ministry of the Interior maintains National Security Forces of 20,000. The Republican Guard numbers 1,200 personnel and the Gendarmerie 25,000.

Navy. The Naval combatant force consists of 2 modern Russian-built diesel-powered patrol submarines, 3 frigates, 3 missile-armed corvettes, 11 fast missile craft, 8 other patrol craft, 1 ocean minesweeper, 2 tank landing ships, and 1 tank landing craft. There are some 10 auxiliaries. An associated coastguard 500-strong operates 28 fast cutters. Naval personnel in 1997 totalled 7,000. There are naval bases at Algiers, Annaba, Mers el Kebir and Jijel.

Air Force. The Air Force in 1997 had about 200 combat aircraft and 10,000 personnel. There are 8 squadrons of MiG-21s, 5 squadrons of MiG-23 variable-geometry interceptors and fighter-bombers, 3 squadrons of Su-20 variable-geometry attack aircraft, more than 30 Mi-24 assault helicopters and gunships, 17 C-130H Hercules, 3 F.27, 4 Il-76 and 5 An-12 transports and a variety of smaller transports, a wing of helicopters mainly operating Mi-8/17s, and training units equipped with CM.170 Magister and L-39 Albatros armed jet counter-insurgency/trainers, and two-seat versions of operational types. Surface-to-air missile units have Soviet-built 'Guidelines', 'Goas', 'Gainfuls' and 'Gaskins'.

INTERNATIONAL RELATIONS
Algeria is a member of UN, OAU, the Arab League, UMA (Maghreb Arab Union) and OPEC.

ECONOMY

Policy. A law on privatization of July 1995 envisages the creation of small- and medium-size businesses in commerce, tourism and transport. Strategic industries (gas and oil) and large industrial complexes are to remain state-owned. Some 1,200 small and 50 large businesses were offered for sale to Algerian citizens; 30% of the shares are reserved for employees (5% free of charge).

Performance. GDP growth was 4% in 1995 (0·6% in 1994; –1·2% in 1993).

Budget. The fiscal year starts on 1 Jan. In 1996 (1995 in brackets) revenue was DA 825,157m. (DA 600,847m.) and expenditure DA 749,009m. (DA 625,695m.).

Currency. The unit of currency is the *Algerian dinar* (DZD) of 100 *centimes*. Foreign exchange reserves were US$8,803m. in Feb. 1998, with gold reserves 5·58m. troy oz. Total money supply was 584,695m. dinars in Sept. 1996. Inflation was 15·1% in 1996. The dinar was devalued by 28·6% in April 1994.

Banking and Finance. The central bank and bank of issue is the Banque d'Algérie. The *Governor* is Abdelwahab Keramane. In 1996 there were 5 state-owned commercial banks. Private banking recommenced in Sept. 1995.

Weights and Measures. The metric system is in use.

ENERGY AND NATURAL RESOURCES

Electricity. Installed capacity was 6·01m. kW in 1994. 7% is hydro-electric. Production in 1994 was 18·7bn. kWh. Consumption per capita was estimated to be 583 kWh in 1995.

Oil and Gas. A law of Nov. 1991 permits foreign companies to acquire up to 49% of known oil and gas reserves. Oil and gas production accounted for 23·2% of GDP in 1994. Oil production in 1995 was 1·21m. bbls. a day. Production of natural gas in 1995 was 150,000m. cu. metres. Proven reserves are 3,700,000m. cu. metres.

Minerals. Output in 1992 (in tonnes): Iron ore 2,565,300; lead, 1,507; phosphates, 1,173; zinc, 7,488. There are also deposits of mercury, silver, copper, antimony, kaolin, marble, onyx, salt and coal.

Agriculture. In 1996 agriculture accounted for 13% of GDP. Much of the land is unsuitable for agriculture. The northern mountains provide grazing. There were 7·48m. ha of arable land in 1994, 0·57m. ha of permanent crops and 31·6m. ha of permanent pasture. 0·55m. ha were irrigated in 1994. In 1987 the government sold back to the private sector land which had been nationalized on the declaration of independence in 1962; a further 0·5m. ha, expropriated in 1973, were returned to some 30,000 small landowners in 1990. In 1995 the agricultural population was 6·57m. There were 98,800 tractors and 10,000 harvester-threshers in 1994.

The chief crops in 1993 were (in 1,000 tonnes): Wheat, 1,350; barley, 800; dates, 265; potatoes, 1,200; oranges, 270; mandarins and tangerines, 96; watermelons, 395; wine, 65; tomatoes, 515; olives, 130; onions, 232; oats, 40.

Livestock, 1996: Horses, 67,000; mules, 82,000; asses, 230,000; cattle, 1·28m.; camels, 115,000 (1995); sheep, 17·56m.; goats, 2·55m. (1995), chickens, 80m. (1995).

Forestry. Forests covered 1·86m. ha. in 1995, or 0·8% of the total land area. The greater part of the state forests are brushwood, but there are large areas with cork-oak trees, Aleppo pine, evergreen oak and cedar. The dwarf-palm is grown on the plains, alfa on the tableland. Timber is cut for firewood and for industrial purposes, and for bark for tanning. Timber production in 1995 was 2·52m. cu. metres.

Fisheries. There are extensive fisheries for sardines, anchovies, sprats, tunny fish and shellfish. The total catch in 1995 amounted to 106,246 tonnes (105,902 tonnes from marine waters).

INDUSTRY

1992 output of state enterprises (in 1,000 tonnes): Pig iron, 930; crude steel, 768; rolled steel, 439; steel tubes, 106; concrete bars, 134; cement, 7,093; bricks, 1,776; ammonitrates, 193; phosphate fertilizers, 154; tobacco, 24; (in units) tractors, 3,009; lorries, 2,434; TV sets, 218,000.

Labour. In 1996 the workforce numbered about 5·4m. (75% males) of whom 1m. were engaged in agriculture. Some 1·2m. non-agricultural workers were employed in the private sector; 2m. workers were unemployed.

INTERNATIONAL TRADE

Foreign debt was US$32,940m. in May 1996. Foreign investors are permitted to hold 100% of the equity of companies, and to repatriate all profits.

Imports and Exports. In 1996 exports were valued at US$12,652m. and imports at US$8,709m.

Main trading partners in 1995, with percentages of total trade: France (imports, 24·9%; exports, 14·1%); USA (13·2%; 16·7%); Italy (9·6%; 22·4%).

1994 exports included (in US$1m.): Crude oil, 1,980; gas, 2,270; condensates, 2,190; refined products, 1,670.

COMMUNICATIONS

Roads. There were, in 1996, an estimated 25,840 km of motorways and national highways, 23,900 km of regional roads and 53,700 km of other roads. There were approximately 1,505,000 vehicles registered in 1996, of which 725,000 were passenger cars (24·7 cars per 1,000 inhabitants). In 1991, 55m. passengers and 6·2m. tonnes of freight were conveyed by public transport.

Rail. In 1995 there were 3,210 km of 1,432 mm route (301 km electrified) and 1,156 km of 1,055 mm gauge. In 1995 the railways carried 8·6m. tonnes of freight and 44·2m. passengers.

Civil Aviation. There is an international airport at Algiers (Houari Boumédienne). The national carrier is the state-owned Air Algérie. In 1998 Algeria was also served by Balkan, Egyptair, Royal Air Maroc, Saudia, Syrian Arab Airlines and Tunis Air. In 1996 the 4 principal airports handled 4·84m. passengers and 19,500 tonnes of freight. In 1995 Air Algérie flew 30·6m. km, carrying 3,478,000 passengers (1,352,000 on international flights).

Shipping. In 1995 vessels totalling 88,502,000 NRT entered ports and vessels totalling 88,865,000 NRT cleared. The state shipping line, Compagnie Nationale Algérienne de Navigation, owned 70 vessels in 1994. The merchant shipping fleet totalled 980,000 GRT in 1995, including oil tankers, 35,000 GRT.

Telecommunications. In 1997 there were 1,400,300 telephone main lines, or 47·5 per 1,000 inhabitants. In Jan. 1998 there were approximately 500 Internet users. There were 85,000 PCs in use in 1995 and 4,700 cellular phone subscribers.

Postal Services. There were 3,145 post offices in 1995.

SOCIAL INSTITUTIONS

Justice. The judiciary is constitutionally independent. Judges are appointed by the Supreme Council of Magistrature chaired by the President of the Republic. Criminal justice is organized as in France. The Supreme Court is at the same time Council of State and High Court of Appeal. The death penalty is in force for terrorism.

Religion. The 1996 Constitution made Islam the state religion, established a consultative *High Islamic Council*, and forbids practices 'contrary to Islamic morality'. Over 98% of the population are Sunni Moslems. There are also around 110,000 Ibadiyah Moslems and 150,000 Christians, mainly Roman Catholics. In 1995 the latter had an archbishop, 130 priests and 250 nuns.

Education. Adult literacy was 61·6% in 1995 (73·9% among males and 49% among females). In 1995 there were 17,186 state primary schools with 169,010 teachers and 4,617,000 pupil; 3,934 middle and secondary schools with 150,397 teachers and 2,844,864 pupils, of whom 43·9% were female.

In 1995–96 there were 6 universities, 2 universities of science and technology, 5 university centres, 1 agronomic institute, 1 telecommunications institute, 1 veterinary institute, 1 school of architecture and town planning and 1 *école normale supérieure*. In 1996 there were 160,000 university students and 7,947 academic staff.

In 1994 total expenditure on education came to 5·6% of GNP and represented 17·6% of total government expenditure.

Health. In 1994 there were 25,796 doctors, 7,763 dental surgeons and 3,425 pharmacists. In 1990 there were 284 hospitals (with 60,124 beds), 1,309 health centres, 510 poly clinics, 475 maternity clinics and 3,344 care centres.

Welfare. Welfare payments to 7·4m. beneficiaries on low incomes were introduced in March 1992.

CULTURE

Broadcasting. The state-controlled Radiodiffusion Algérienne and Entreprise Nationale de Télévision broadcast home services in Arabic, Kabyle (Berber) and French, and an external service. There are 18 TV transmitting stations (colour by PAL). In 1995 there were 6·7m. radio and 2·5m. TV receivers.

Press. Algeria had 6 daily newspapers in 1995, with a combined circulation of 1·4m.

Tourism. In 1996 there were 605,000 foreign tourists, spending US$16m.

DIPLOMATIC REPRESENTATIVES

Of Algeria in Great Britain (54 Holland Park, London, W11 3RS)
Ambassador: Ahmed Benyamina.

Of Great Britain in Algeria (Résidence Cassiopée, Bâtiment B, 7 Chemin des Glycines, Algiers)
Ambassador: J. François Gordon.

Of Algeria in the USA (2118 Kalorama Rd., NW, Washington, D.C., 20008)
Ambassador: Ramtane Lamamra.

Of the USA in Algeria (4 Chemin Cheich Bachir Ibrahimi, Algiers)
Ambassador: Cameron R. Hume.

Of Algeria to the United Nations
Ambassador: Abdallah Baali.

Of Algeria to the European Union
Ambassador: Mohamed Lamari.

FURTHER READING
Ageron, C.-R., *Modern Algeria: a History from 1830 to the Present*. London, 1991
Bennoune, M., *The Making of Contemporary Algeria, 1830–1987*. CUP, 1988
Eveno, P., *L'Algérie*. Paris, 1994
Heggoy, A. A. and Crout, R. R., *Historical Dictionary of Algeria*. Metuchen (NJ), 1995
Horne, A., *A Savage War of Peace: Algeria 1954–1962*. London, 1977
Lawless, R. I., *Algeri*. [Bibliography]. 2nd ed. Oxford and Santa Barbara (CA), 1995
Pazzanita, A. G., *The Maghreb* [Bibliography]. Oxford and Santa Barbara (CA), 1998
Ruedy, J., *Modern Algeria: the Origins and Development of a Nation*. Indiana Univ. Press, 1992
Stone, M., *The Agony of Algeria*. Columbia University Press, 1997
Stora, B., *Histoire de l'Algérie depuis l'Indépendance*. Paris, 1994
Willis, M., *The Islamist Challenge in Algeria: A political history*. New York, 1997

National statistical office: Office National des Statistiques, 8 rue des Moussebiline, Algiers.

ANDORRA

Principat d'Andorra

Capital: Andorra-la-Vella
Population estimate, 2000: 80,000
Estimated GDP: $1·2bn.

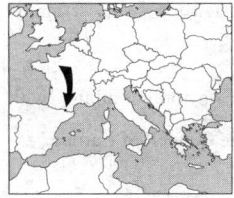

KEY HISTORICAL EVENTS
The political status of Andorra was regulated by the *Paréage* of 1278 which placed Andorra under the joint suzerainty of the Comte de Foix and of the Bishop of Urgel. The rights vested in the house of Foix passed by marriage to that of Bearn and, on the accession of Henri IV, to the French crown. A democratic constitution was adopted in 1993.

TERRITORY AND POPULATION
The co-principality of Andorra is situated in the eastern Pyrenees on the French–Spanish border. The country is mountainous. Area, 450 sq. km. In lieu of a census, a register of population is kept. The registered population on 1 July 1996 was 72,766; 0–14 years, 16%; 15–64 years, 73%; 65 and over, 11%. Density, 162 per sq. km.

In 2000 the population is projected to be 80,000.

In 1995, 95·4% of the population lived in urban areas.

The chief towns are Andorra-la-Vella, the capital (population, 22,387) and its suburb Escaldes-Engordany (13,177). 30% of the residential population are Andorran, 61% Spanish and 6% French. Catalan is the official language; Spanish is widely spoken.

SOCIAL STATISTICS
Births (1995, per 1,000 inhabitants), 11·0; deaths, 3·4. Life expectancy (1997): male, 80·5 years; female, 86·5 years.

CLIMATE
Escaldes-Engordany, Jan. 36°F (2·3°C), July 67°F (19·3°C). Annual rainfall 32" (808 mm).

CONSTITUTION AND GOVERNMENT
The joint heads of state are the President of the French Republic and the Bishop of Urgel, the co-princes.

A new democratic constitution was approved by 74·2% of votes cast at a referendum on 14 March 1993. The electorate was 9,123; turn-out was 75·7%. The new Constitution, which came into force on 4 May 1993, makes the co-princes a single constitutional monarch and provides for a parliament, the *General Council of the Andorran Valleys*, elected by universal suffrage. The General Council has 28 members elected, 2 from each of the 7 parishes and 14 elected from the single national constituency, for 4 years. In 1982 an *Executive Council* was appointed and legislative and executive powers were separated. The General Council elects the President of the Executive Council, who is the head of the government

There is a *Constitutional Court* of 4 members who hold office for 8-year terms, renewable once.

National Anthem. 'El Gran Carlemany, mon pare' ('Great Charlemagne, my father'); words by Enric Marfany, tune by D.J. Benlloch i Vivò.

RECENT ELECTIONS
Elections to the General Council were held on 15 Feb. 1997. Electorate, 10,837; turn-out was 82%. The Liberal Union gained 18 seats.

CURRENT ADMINISTRATION
In March 1999 the government comprised:

President, Executive Council: Marc Forné Molné (Liberal Union).

Minister for Presidential Affairs and the Interior: Estanislau Sangrà Cardona. *Foreign Affairs:* Albert Pintat Santolària. *Finance:* Susagna Arasanz Serra.

Economy: Enric Casadevall Medrano. *Land Management:* Càndid Naudi Mora. *Health and Social Affairs:* Josep Maria Goicoechea Utrillo. *Education, Youth and Sports:* Josep Cervós Cardona. *Tourism and Culture:* Enric Pujal Areny. *Agriculture and Environment:* Olga Adellach Coma.

Local Government. Andorra is divided into 7 parishes, each of which is administered by a Communal Council. Councillors are elected for 4-year terms by universal suffrage.

INTERNATIONAL RELATIONS
The 1993 Constitution empowers Andorra to conduct its own foreign affairs, with consultation on matters affecting France or Spain.

Andorra is a member of the UN, UNESCO, WIPO and the Council of Europe.

ECONOMY
Performance. Real GDP growth was 3·9% in 1995 (2·1% in 1994).

Budget. 1993: Revenue, US$138m. Expenditure, US$177m.

Currency. French and Spanish currency are both in use. *Diner* coins are minted for collectors.

Banking and Finance. The banking sector, with its tax-haven status, contributes substantially to the economy.

ENERGY AND NATURAL RESOURCES
Electricity. Installed capacity was 35,000 kW in 1992. Production in 1992 was 140m. kWh.

Agriculture. In 1992 there were some 1,000 ha of arable land (2% of total) and 25,000 ha of pasture (56%). Tobacco and potatoes are principal crops. The principal livestock activity is sheep raising.

Forestry. In 1992 there were some 10,000 ha of forests (22% of the total area).

INDUSTRY
Labour. Only 1% of the workforce is employed in agriculture, the rest in tourism, commerce, services and light industry. Manufacturing consists mainly of cigarettes, cigars and furniture.

INTERNATIONAL TRADE
Andorra is a member of the EU Customs Union for industrial goods, and is a third country for agricultural produce. There is a free economic zone.

Imports and Exports. 1997 exports, US$46·2m.; imports, US$920·2m.

COMMUNICATIONS
Roads. There are 269 km of roads (198 km paved). Motor vehicles (1993): motor cars, 36,660; trucks and vans, 4,343.

Civil Aviation. There is an airport for Andorran traffic at Seo de Urgel.

Telecommunications. In 1997 there were 32,000 telephone main lines, or 431·4 per 1,000 inhabitants. There were 2,800 cellular phone subscribers and 1,300 fax machines in 1995.

SOCIAL INSTITUTIONS
Justice. Justice is administered by the High Council of Justice, comprising 5 members appointed for single 6-year terms. The independence of judges is constitutionally guaranteed. Judicial power is exercised in civil matters in the first instance by Magistrates' Courts and a Judge's Court. Criminal justice is administered by the *Corts*, consisting of the judge of appeal, 2 *rahonadors* elected by the General Council of the Valleys, a general attorney and an attorney nominated for 5 years alternately by each of the co-princes.

Religion. The Roman Catholic is the established church, but the 1993 Constitution guarantees religious liberty. In 1997 around 79% of the population were Catholics.

Education. Free education in French- or Spanish-language schools is compulsory: 6 years primary starting at 6 years, followed by 4 years secondary. A Roman Catholic school provides education in Catalan. In 1993–94 there were 18 schools altogether with 9,163 pupils.

Health. In 1994 there were 2 hospitals and 132 doctors.

CULTURE

Broadcasting. Servei de Telecomunicacions d'Andorra relays French and Spanish programmes. Radio Andorra is a commercial public station; Radio Valira is commercial. Number of receivers, 1995: radio, 14,000 (212 per 1,000 inhabitants); TV, 24,000 (368 per 1,000 inhabitants). The dominance of TV receivers over radio receivers per 1,000 inhabitants is greater in Andorra than anywhere else in Europe.

Press. In 1995 there were 3 daily newspapers with a combined circulation of 4,000, at a rate of 59 per 1,000 inhabitants

Tourism. Tourism is the main industry, averaging 13m. visitors a year and accounting for 80% of GDP.

DIPLOMATIC REPRESENTATIVES
Of Great Britain in Andorra
Ambassador: Mr. P. J. Torry (resides in Madrid).

Of Andorra in the USA and to the United Nations (2 United Nations Plaza, 25th Floor, N.Y. 10017)
Ambassador: Juli Minoves Triquell.

US interests in Andorra are represented by the Consulate General's office in Barcelona.

Of Andorra to the European Union
Ambassador: Meritxell Mateu i Pi.

FURTHER READING
Taylor, B., *Andorra.* [Bibliography]. Oxford and Santa Barbara (CA), 1993

ANGOLA

República de Angola

Capital: Luanda
Population estimate, 2000: 12·78m.
GNP per capita: (PPP$) 1,030
HDI/world rank: 0·344/156

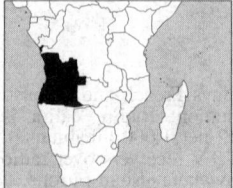

KEY HISTORICAL EVENTS

The earliest people in Angola, as in most of sub-Saharan Africa, were hunter-gatherers. They were displaced by Bantu-speaking farmers who by the 14th century were organized in several powerful states such as the kingdoms of Kongo and Mbundu. The rulers of Mbundu were called *ngola*, from which the Portuguese derived the name Angola. The Portuguese first made contact with Kongo in 1491, and for some time thereafter its kings were Catholic and their capital was renamed São Salvador.

Only brief Dutch occupation in the 1640s interrupted 4 centuries of Portuguese rule along the coast, from which hundreds of thousands of slaves were shipped and where, by the 19th century, a small Portuguese-speaking African and *mestiço* (half-European) élite had emerged. Inland, African states remained independent until the 19th century.

The Portuguese founded Luanda in 1875, and from the 1870s gradually occupied the interior of Angola, often called Portuguese West Africa. The occupation was slow in the face of strong African resistance (such as the Bailundo rising of 1902), and Portuguese rule was only fully established about 1920. Angola remained a Portuguese colony until 11 June 1951, when it became an Overseas Province of Portugal.

After the coup d'état in Portugal in April 1974, negotiations between Portugal, the MPLA (People's Movement for the Liberation of Angola), the FNLA (National Front for the Liberation of Angola) and UNITA (National Union for the Total Liberation of Angola) resulted in the signing of the Alvor Agreement in Jan. 1975, under which a quadripartite transitional government was formed, with a view to elections in Oct. and independence on 11 Nov The FNLA tried to seize power by force, but was driven out of the capital. As independence approached, the invasion from the north was combined with a South African invasion in support of UNITA. The MPLA declared independence and, subsequently, with the help of Cuban troops, defeated the FNLA in the north and drove the invading South African army out of the country. South African invasions and the occupation of large areas of Angola continued until the signing of the New York Agreement in Dec. 1988, under which South Africa agreed to withdraw its forces from Angola and Namibia (and grant independence to Namibia), while Angola and Cuba agreed to the phased withdrawal of Cuban troops.

After many abortive attempts to end the internal conflict with UNITA, a peace agreement was signed on 31 May 1991 under which the government and UNITA armies were to be disbanded, a single national army formed and multi-party elections held. In Sept. 1992 the MPLA won the elections and José Eduardo dos Santos was re-elected President against UNITA leader Jonas Savimbi. But the latter rejected the election results, withdrew his generals from the unified army and went back to war, seizing an estimated 70% of the country.

On 15 Sept. 1993 the UN Security Council unanimously adopted an embargo on arms and fuel supplies to UNITA. On 20 Nov. 1994 an agreement was signed in Lusaka, but not at presidential level because Jonas Savimbi failed to turn up. The Lusaka Protocol provided for the quartering and disarming of UNITA troops, the integration of 26,300 of them into the single national army, and the demobilization of the remainder. The government also agreed to offer UNITA a substantial number of posts in central and local government. The settlement required the extension of central administration to all UNITA-held areas and free movement of people and goods throughout the country. Elections were to be held when the UN deemed that conditions permitted. Despite the fact that the military aspects of the Protocol were not completed 70 elected UNITA deputies took their seats in the National Assembly in April 1997. A Government of Unity and

National Reconciliation included officials from UNITA and all other parties with seats in the National Assembly. The mandate of the third UN peacekeeping force, UNAVEM III, expired on 30 June 1997. It was replaced by a smaller mission of 86 military and 345 police known as MONUA. There were continued delays in the completion of the registration and demobilization of UNITA troops and on 29 Oct. 1997 the UN Security Council imposed a further package of sanctions on UNITA including the closure of its offices abroad and restrictions on travel abroad by its officials.

On 9 Jan. 1998 a breakthrough in negotiations between the government and UNITA rebels was announced. Jonas Savimbi, UNITA's leader, met with President dos Santos but talks soon foundered and serious fighting resumed in the north, raising fears of a major new offensive by the Angolan Armed Forces against the UNITA rebels. Meanwhile, Angolan troops fought in the Republic of the Congo alongside the forces of President Kabila in his efforts to quash a Rwandan-backed rebellion in the east of his country.

TERRITORY AND POPULATION
Angola is bounded in the north by the Republic of the Congo, north and north-east by the Democratic Republic of the Congo, east by Zambia, south by Namibia and west by the Atlantic Ocean. The area is 1,246,700 sq. km (481,354 sq. miles) including the province of Cabinda, an exclave of territory separated by 30 sq. km of territory of the Democratic Republic of the Congo. The population at census, 1970, was 5,646,166, of whom 14% were urban. Official estimate, 1995, 11·5m. (31% urban); density, 9·2 per sq. km. Population figures are rough estimates because the civil war has led to huge movements of population.

There were 0·3m. Angolan refugees in the Democratic Republic of the Congo, Zambia and the Republic of the Congo in 1995.

The UN gives a projected population for 2000 of 12·78m.

Area, population and chief towns of the provinces:

Province	Area (in sq. km)	Population estimate, 1992 (in 1,000)	Chief town
Bengo	31,371	196·1	Caxito
Benguela	31,788	656·6	Benguela
Bié	70,314	1,119·8	Kuito
Cabinda	7,270	152·1	Cabinda
Cuando-Cubango	199,049	139·6	Menongue
Cuanza Norte	24,190	385·2	Ndalatando
Cuanza Sul	55,660	694·5	Sumbe
Cunene	89,342	241·2	Ondjiva
Huambo	34,274	1,521·0	Huambo
Huíla	75,002	885·1	Lubango
Luanda	2,418	1,588·6	Luanda
Lunda Norte	102,783	305·9	Lucapa
Lunda Sul	45,649	169·1	Saurimo
Malanje	97,602	906·0	Malanje
Moxico	223,023	319·3	Luena
Namibe	58,137	107·3	Namibe
Uíge	58,698	802·7	Uíge
Zaire	40,130	237·5	Mbanza Congo

The most important towns (populations) are Luanda, the capital (1995, 2·25m.), Huambo (1995, 0·4m.), Lobito (1970, 59,258), Benguela (1970, 40,996), Lubango (1984, 105,000), Malanje (1970, 31,559) and Namibe (formerly Moçâmedes, 1981, 0·1m.).

The main ethnic groups are Umbundo (Ovimbundo), Kimbundo, Bakongo, Chokwe, Ganguela, Luvale and Kwanyama.

Portuguese is the official language. Bantu and other African languages are also spoken.

SOCIAL STATISTICS
Life expectancy at birth, 1990–95, 44·9 years for males and 48·1 years for females. 1995 births (estimates), 567,000; deaths, 217,000. Birth rate in 1995 was 49·3 per

ANGOLA

1,000 population; death rate, 18·9. Annual growth rate, 1990–95, 2·0%. Infant mortality, 1990–95, 124 per 1,000 live births; fertility rate, 7·2 births per woman.

CLIMATE
The climate is tropical, with low rainfall in the west but increasing inland. Temperatures are constant over the year and most rain falls in March and April. Luanda, Jan. 78°F (25·6°C), July 69°F (20·6°C). Annual rainfall 13" (323 mm). Lobito, Jan. 77°F (25°C), July 68°F (20°C). Annual rainfall 14" (353 mm).

CONSTITUTION AND GOVERNMENT
Under the Constitution adopted at independence, the sole legal party was the MPLA. In Dec. 1990, however, the MPLA announced that the Constitution would be revised to permit opposition parties. The supreme organ of state is the 220-member *National Assembly*. There is an executive *President* elected for renewable terms of 5 years, who appoints a *Council of Ministers*.

National Anthem. 'O Pátria, nunca mais esqueceremos' ('Oh Fatherland, never shall we forget'); words by M. R. Alves Monteiro, tune by R. A. Dias Mingas.

RECENT ELECTIONS
At the presidential and parliamentary elections of 29–30 Sept. 1992 the electorate was 4,862,748. Turn-out was about 90%. Eduardo Dos Santos (MPLA) was re-elected as President with 49·5% of votes cast against 40·7% for his single opponent, Jonas Savimbi (UNITA). The latter refused to accept the result. The MPLA gained 129 seats in the National Assembly with 53·74% of votes cast, UNITA 70 with 34%.

On 11 April 1997 a Government of National Unity was installed, with 3 ministerial posts going to UNITA. Jonas Savimbi, UNITA's leader, received the specially created position of Chief of the Principal Opposition Party.

CURRENT ADMINISTRATION
President: José Eduardo dos Santos, b. 1943 (since 10 Sept. 1979; re-elected 9 Dec. 1985 and 29–30 Sept. 1992).

In March 1999 the Government comprised:
Minister for Agriculture and Rural Development: Gilberto Lutucuta. *Assistance and Social Reintegration:* Albino Malungo. *Commerce:* Victorino Domingos Hossi. *Education and Culture:* Antonio Burity da Silva Neto. *Energy and Water:* Luis Filipe da Silva. *External Relations:* Joao Bernardo de Miranda. *Family and Women's Affairs:* Candida Celeste da Silva. *Finance:* Joaquim Duarte da Costa David. *Fisheries and Environment:* Maria de Fatima Monteiro Jardim. *Geology and Mines:* Manuel Gunjo. *Health:* Adelino Manacas. *Hotels and Tourism:* Jorge Alicerces Valentim. *Industry:* Albina Faria de Assis 'Africano'. *Interior:* Fernando Dias dos Santos da Piedade 'Nando'. *Justice:* Paulo Tjipilica. *National Defence:* Kundi Paihama. *Petroleum:* Jose Maria Botelho de Vasconcelos. *Planning:* Ana Dias Lourenco. *Posts and Telecommunications:* Licinio Tavares Ribeiro. *Public Administration, Employment and Social Welfare:* Antonio Domingos Pitra Costa Neto. *Public Works and Urban Affairs:* Antonio Henriques da Silva. *Science and Technology:* Joao Baptista Nganda Gina. *Social Communication:* Pedro Hendrick Vaal Neto. *Territorial Administration:* Fernando Faustino Muteka. *Transport:* Andre Luis Brandao. *War Veterans:* Pedro Jose van Dunem. *Youth and Sports:* Jose Marcos Barrica.

Local Government. The 18 provinces, each under a Governor appointed by the President and an elected legislative of from 55 to 85 members, are subdivided into 139 districts.

DEFENCE
Conscription is for 2 years. Defence expenditure totalled US$658m. in 1997 (US$58 per capita).

Army. In 1997 the Army had 25 regiments. Total strength 98,000. Equipment includes Soviet 100 T-34, 100 T-54/55 and some T-62 and T-72 main battle tanks.

ANGOLA

Navy. The Navy, almost all Soviet-built, includes 5 inshore patrol craft, 1 mine-hunter, 1 landing ship and 6 landing craft, together with 10 auxiliary vessels. Naval personnel in 1997 totalled about 1,500. Naval bases are at Luanda, Lobito and Namibe.

Air Force. The Angolan People's Air Force (FAPA) was formed in 1976 and had (1996) about 5,000 personnel. Since the elections in 1992 and the relative calm, the Air Force has been run down and serviceability of combat aircraft is low. There are 5 combat squadrons, 2 with MiG-23s and 1 each with Mig-21s, Su-22s and Su-25s. The transport force, including An-26s, An-32s and Aviocars, is still active, as are the helicopter formations, mainly equipped with Mi-8/17s and Mi-25s. Pilatus PC-7 and PC-9 trainers are equipped for counter-insurgency operations.

INTERNATIONAL RELATIONS
Angola is a member of the UN, OAU, SADC and is an ACP member state of the ACP-EU relationship.

ECONOMY

Policy. Reforms are under way to introduce a market economy and restore private property. An Economic and Social Programme covered 1995–96.

Performance. GDP growth was 5% in 1995 (8·6% in 1994). 70% of Angola's population live below the poverty line. Although Angola has experienced an uneasy peace since the end of the civil war, there are few signs of the economy reviving.

Budget. The 1995 budget envisaged recurrent revenue (in 1,000m. former kwanzas) of 3,765·3 (of which taxes, 2,257·6; royalties, 1,159); capital revenue of 15·8 (mainly from privatization); recurrent expenditure of 2,515·6 and capital expenditure of 2,177·2.

Currency. The unit of currency is the *readjusted kwanza* (AOK) of 100 *lwei*, which replaced the former new kwanza at Kzr1 = Nkz1,000 in July 1995. In Jan. 1994 a 2-tier system was replaced by a single floating exchange rate. Foreign exchange reserves were US$163m. in 1995; gold reserves, 46,500 troy oz. in 1990. Inflation was an annualized 7,500% in 1996.

Banking and Finance. Banking was re-opened to commercial competition in 1991. The Banco Nacional de Angola is the central bank and bank of issue (*Governor*, Aguinaldo Jaime). All banks remain state-owned, though the government is progressively reducing its stake in them. An agricultural bank and a commercial and industrial bank were founded in 1991. 5 Portuguese banks have branches, as well as the French Banque Paribas, the Equator Bank, and the African Development Bank.

Weights and Measures. The metric system is in force.

ENERGY AND NATURAL RESOURCES

Electricity. Installed capacity was 620,000 kW in 1994. Production in 1994 was 1·82bn. kWh, with consumption per capita an estimated 171 kWh in 1995.

Oil and Gas. Oil is produced mainly in the Cabinda exclave and contributed 49·9% of Angolan GDP in 1994. Total production (1992) 25·57m. tonnes.

Minerals. Production of diamonds in 1992 totalled 1,235,000 carats; the illegal export of diamonds is the chief source of income for UNITA. Other minerals produced include (1991) granite, 635,000 cu. metres; marble, 244,000 cu. metres; salt, 6,600 tonnes. Iron ore, phosphate, manganese and copper deposits exist.

Agriculture. Agriculture contributed 7% of GDP in 1996. In 1994 there were 3m. ha of arable land, 0·5m. ha of permanent crops and 54m. ha of permanent pasture. The agricultural population in 1995 was 8·17m., of whom 3·78m. were economically active. The principal cash crops (with 1993 production, in 1,000 tonnes): Sugar-cane (290), coffee (5), bananas (280), palm oil (40), palm kernels (12), seed cotton (12); others include tobacco, citrus fruit and sisal. Food crops (1993, in 1,000 tonnes) include cassava (1,870), maize (274), sweet potatoes (170) and dry beans (36).

Livestock (1996): 3·1m. cattle, 245,000 sheep, 1,570,000 goats (1995), 810,000 pigs.

Forestry. In 1995, 222,000 sq. km, or 17·8% of the total land area, was covered by forests (18·8% in 1990), including mahogany and other hardwoods. Timber production in 1995 was 7m. cu. metres.

Fisheries. In 1993 the fishing fleet had 73 vessels over 100 GRT totalling 17,332 GRT. Total catch in 1995 came to 93,847 tonnes, mainly from sea fishing.

INDUSTRY

The principal manufacturing branches are foodstuffs, textiles and oil refining. Output, 1991 (in tonnes): Maize flour, 21,200; wheat flour, 18,900; bread, 25,100; soap, 4,700; plate glass, 6,900; plastic bags, 1,600; pesticides, 46; zinc sheets, 6,012; cable, 112; 52,000 radio sets; 15,600 TV sets.

Labour. In 1996 the total labour force numbered 5,144,000 (54% males). In 1994, 2,762,000 people out of an economically active population of 4,053,000 were engaged in agriculture.

INTERNATIONAL TRADE

In 1996 total foreign debt was US$10,612m.

Imports and Exports. Imports and exports for calendar years in US$1m.:

	1991	1992	1993	1994	1995
Imports	1,347	1,988	1,463	1,633	1,700
Exports	3,449	3,833	2,900	3,002	3,880

Main exports, 1994 (in US$1m.): Crude oil, 2,821; diamonds, 96; refined oil, 61; gas, 14. Chief import suppliers (1991 trade in US$1m.): Portugal, 587; USA, 207; France, 194; Japan, 153; Brazil, 144. Chief export markets: USA, 1,751; France, 328; Germany, 174; Brazil, 152; Netherlands, 131.

COMMUNICATIONS

Roads. There were, in 1996, 72,626 km of roads (7,955 km highways and 25% of all roads surfaced), and approximately 207,000 passenger cars and 25,000 commercial vehicles. Many roads remain mined as a result of the civil war; a programme of de-mining and rehabilitation is under way.

Rail. The length of railways open for traffic in 1987 was 2,952 km, comprising 2,798 km of 1,067 mm gauge and 154 km of 600 mm gauge. The Benguela Railway runs from Lobito to the Democratic Republic of the Congo border at Dilolo where it connects with the National Railways of the Democratic Republic of the Congo. Other lines link Luanda with Malanje; Gunza with Gabela; and Namibe with Menongue. In 1993 railways carried 4m. passengers and 2·8m. tonnes of freight.

Civil Aviation. There is an international airport at Luanda (Fourth of February). The national carrier is Linhas Aéreas de Angola (TAAG). In 1998 there were also services by Aeroflot, Air France, Air Gabon, Air Namibia, Ethiopian Airlines, SABENA, South African Airways and TAP. In 1995 scheduled airline traffic of Angola-based carriers flew 13·4m. km, carrying 545,000 passengers (148,000 on international flights).

Shipping. There are ports at Luanda, Lobito and Namibe, and oil terminals at Malongo, Lobito and Soyo. 1·24m. tonnes of cargo were discharged in 1994. There are 3 state shipping companies. In 1995 the merchant fleet totalled 120,000 GRT, including oil tankers, 2,665 GRT.

Telecommunications. There were 62,300 telephone main lines in 1997, or 5·4 per 1,000 inhabitants. In Jan. 1998 there were approximately 1,500 Internet users, and in 1995, 2,000 cellular phone subscribers.

Postal Services. In 1995 there were 62 post offices, or 1 for every 162,000 persons.

SOCIAL INSTITUTIONS

Justice. The Supreme Court and Court of Appeal are in Luanda. The death penalty was abolished in 1992.

Religion. In 1997 there were 5·39m. Roman Catholics, 1·56m. Protestants, 460,000 African Christians, and most of the remainder follow traditional animist religions.

Education. The education system provides 3 levels of general education totalling 8 years, followed by schools for technical training, teacher training or pre-university studies. Enrolment (in 1,000) in 1991–92: Pre-school, 188; general education first level, 923; second level, 141; third level, 42; technical training, 12·7; teacher training, 109; pre-university studies (1990–91), 6·1. There is 1 university. Private schools have been permitted since 1991. The University of Luanda has campuses at Luanda, Huambo and Lubango. It had 8,954 students in 1991–92. The adult literacy rate is 42·5%.

Health. In 1990 there were 662 doctors, 10 dentists, 9,334 nurses, 4,165 medical auxiliaries and 266 hospitals and health centres with 11,857 beds. There were 1,339 medical posts.

In the period 1990–96 only 32% of the population had access to safe drinking water.

CULTURE

Broadcasting. In 1995 there were 80,000 TV receivers and 370,000 radio receivers in Angola. The government-controlled Rádio Nacional de Angola broadcasts 3 programmes and an international service. There are also regional stations. Televisão Popular de Angola transmits from 7 stations (colour by PAL).

Press. The government daily is the *Jornal de Angola*. The *Diário da República* is the official gazette. There is a weekly called the *Correio da Semana*, and there are around 100 specialized and independent publications.

Tourism. In 1996 there were 8,000 foreign tourists, bringing revenue of US$9m.

DIPLOMATIC REPRESENTATIVES
Of Angola in Great Britain (98 Park Lane, London, W1 3TA)
Ambassador: António da Costa Fernandes.

Of Great Britain in Angola (Rua Diogo Cão 4, Luanda)
Ambassador: Miss Catherine Elmes.

Of Angola in the USA (1615 M Street, NW, Suite 900, Washington, D.C., 20036)
Ambassador: António Dos Santos Franca.

Ambassador Of the USA in Angola (32 rua Houari Boumédienne, Miramar, Luanda): Donald K. Steinberg.

Of Angola to the United Nations
Ambassador: Afonso Van Dunem 'Mbinda'.

Of Angola to the European Union
Ambassador: José Guerreiro Alves Primo.

FURTHER READING
Anstee, M. J., *Orphan of the Cold War: the Inside Story of the Collapse of the Angolan Peace Process, 1992–93*. London, 1996
James, W. M., *Political History of the War in Angola*. New York, 1991
Roque, F., *Económia de Angola*. Lisbon, 1991
Somerville, K., *Angola: Politics, Economics and Society*. London and Boulder, 1986

National statistical office: Instituto Nacional de Estatística, Luanda.

ANTIGUA AND BARBUDA

Capital: St John's
Population estimate, 2000: 68,000
GNP per capita: (PPP$) 8,660
HDI/world rank: 0·895/29

KEY HISTORICAL EVENTS

Antigua and Barbuda make up the island nation of the lesser Antilles in the Eastern Caribbean. Most of the population is descended from African slaves brought in during colonial times to work on sugar plantations.

The country was sighted by Christopher Columbus on his second voyage to the West Indies in 1493. The Spaniards attempted to settle on the island in 1520 as did the French in 1629. Antigua was eventually colonized in the year 1632 and in 1667, under the Treaty of Breda, it became a British Colony. Barbuda was colonized in 1628 and leased to the Codrington Family in 1680. By the late 19th century, however, it had reverted to the British Crown.

Antigua and Barbuda formed part of the Leeward Islands Federation from 1871 until 30 June 1956 when Antigua and Barbuda became a separate Crown Colony. It was part of the West Indies Federation from 3 Jan. 1958 until 31 May 1962 and became an Associated State of the UK on 27 Feb. 1967. Antigua and Barbuda gained independence on 1 Nov. 1981.

TERRITORY AND POPULATION

Antigua and Barbuda comprises 3 islands of the Lesser Antilles situated in the Eastern Caribbean with a total land area of 442 sq. km (171 sq. miles); it consists of Antigua (280 sq. km), Barbuda, 40 km to the north (161 sq. km) and uninhabited Redonda, 40 km to the south-west (1 sq. km). The population at the census of 1991 was 65,962 (1,400 on Barbuda). Estimate, 1995, 63,900 (1,500 on Barbuda); density, 145 per sq. km; urban population, 35·8%.

In 2000 the population is projected to be 68,000.

The chief towns are St John's, the capital on Antigua (30,000 inhabitants in 1995) and Codrington (1,200), the only settlement on Barbuda.

English is the official language; local dialects are also spoken.

SOCIAL STATISTICS

Expectation of life, 1993: Males, 71·1 years, females, 75·3. Annual growth rate, 1990–95, 0·6%. Births, 1994, 1,217 (rate of 19·0 per 1,000 population); deaths, 415 (6·5 per 1,000 population). Infant mortality in 1998 was 18 per 1,000 live births.

CLIMATE

A tropical climate, but drier than most West Indies islands. The hot season is from May to Nov., when rainfall is greater. Mean annual rainfall is 40" (1,000 mm).

CONSTITUTION AND GOVERNMENT

H.M. Queen Elizabeth, as Head of State, is represented by a Governor-General appointed by her on the advice of the Prime Minister. There is a bicameral legislature, comprising a 17-member Senate appointed by the Governor-General and a 17-member House of Representatives elected by universal suffrage for a 5-year term. The Governor-General appoints a Prime Minister and, on the latter's advice, other members of the Cabinet.

Barbuda is administered by a 9-member directly elected council.

National Anthem. 'Fair Antigua and Barbuda, we thy sons and daughters stand'; words by N. H. Richards, tune by W. G. Chambers.

RECENT ELECTIONS

At the elections to the House of Representatives of 9 March 1999 the Antigua Labour Party (ALP) gained 12 seats, the United Progressive Party 4, and the Barbuda People's Movement 1.

ANTIGUA AND BARBUDA

CURRENT ADMINISTRATION
Governor-General: Sir James Carlisle, GCMG.

In March 1999 the government comprised:

Prime Minister, Minister of Defence, External Affairs, Information, Telecommunications, Civil Aviation, International Transportation, and Gaming: Lester Bird (ALP).

Finance and Social Security, Agriculture, Lands and Fisheries: John E. St. Luce.

Justice, Legal Affairs and Attorney-General: Radford Hill. *Public Utilities, Public Works, Local Transportation and Energy:* Robin Yearwood. *Trade, Industry and Consumer Affairs:* Hilroy Humphries. *Education, Youth and Sports:* Bernard Percival. *Labour, Home Affairs and Citizens' Services:* Adolphus Eleazer Freeland. *Tourism and Culture:* Dr Rodney Williams. *Health and Home Affairs:* Samuel Aymer. *Planning, Implementation and Environment:* Molwyn Joseph.

DEFENCE
The Antigua and Barbuda Defence Force numbers 150. A coastguard service has been formed.

In 1997 defence expenditure totalled US$3m. (US$39 per capita).

INTERNATIONAL RELATIONS
Antigua and Barbuda is a member of the UN, the Commonwealth, CARICOM, ACS, OAS, OECS and is an ACP member state of the ACP-EU relationship.

ECONOMY
Performance. There has been strong economic growth of late despite 4 hurricanes in 4 years. The economy grew by 9·95% in 1996, 7% in 1997 and 4·5% in 1998. GDP was EC$1·4bn. in 1996.

Budget. The budget for 1996 envisaged recurrent revenue of EC$284·8m. and recurrent expenditure of EC$305·9m.

Currency. The unit of currency is the *Eastern Caribbean dollar* (XCD), issued by the Eastern Caribbean Central Bank. Foreign exchange reserves in Feb. 1998 were US$56m. Total money supply was EC$263,000 in Nov. 1997.

Banking and Finance. In 1993, 9 commercial banks were operating (6 foreign). There is also the Antigua Co-operative Bank and a government savings bank. Total national savings were EC$1,320·4m. in Sept. 1998.

In 1981 Antigua established an offshore banking sector which in 1997 had 52 banks registered and operating.

ENERGY AND NATURAL RESOURCES
Electricity. Capacity in 1993 was 54,000 kW. Production was 95m. kWh in 1993 and consumption per capita an estimated 5,145 kWh in 1994.

Water. Water shortages are frequent. There is a desalination plant with a capacity of 0·6m. gallons per day.

Agriculture. In 1994 there were 8,000 ha of arable land and 4,000 ha of permanent pasture. Cotton and fruits are the main crops. Production (1993) of fruits, 9,000 tonnes.

Livestock (1996): Cattle, 16,000; pigs, 2,000; sheep, 12,000; goats (1995), 12,000.

Forestry. Forests covered 9,000 ha, or 20·5% of the total land area, in 1995.

Fisheries. Total catch in 1995 came to 470 tonnes, exclusively from sea fishing.

INDUSTRY
Manufactures include toilet tissue, stoves, refrigerators, blenders, fans, garments and rum (molasses imported from Guyana).

Labour. The unemployment rate in 1998 was the lowest in the Caribbean, at 4·5%. Between 1994 and 1998, 2,543 jobs were created. The average annual salary in 1998 was US$8,345 per head of population.

INTERNATIONAL TRADE
Foreign debt was US$260m. in 1994.

Imports and Exports. Imports in 1996 were estimated at US$351m. and exports US$45m. The main trading partners were the USA, the UK and Canada.

COMMUNICATIONS
Roads. In 1995 there were 384 km of main roads, 164 km of secondary roads, 320 km of rural roads and 293 km of other roads. 15,100 passenger cars and 5,700 commercial vehicles were in use in 1995. More than EC$64m. was spent to rebuild major roads and highways in the 3 years following damage caused by hurricanes Luis and Marilyn in 1995.

Civil Aviation. V. C. Bird International Airport is near St John's. Antigua is served by Air Canada, Air France, American Airlines, British Airways, BWIA, Cardinal Airlines, Condor Flugdienst, Continental Airlines, LIAT, Société Nouvelle Air Guadeloupe and Virgin Atlantic. There are flights to Anguilla, Barbados, Bogotá, Cali, Caracas, Dominica, Frankfurt, Georgetown, Grenada, Guadeloupe, Kingston, London, Martinique, Medellín, Miami, the Netherlands Antilles, New York, Paris, Puerto Rico, St Kitts and Nevis, St Lucia, St Vincent, Toronto, Trinidad, the UK, the British and US Virgin Islands and Washington, D.C. A domestic flight links the airports on Antigua and Barbuda.

Shipping. The main port is St John's Harbour. The merchant shipping fleet totalled 1,842,000 GRT in 1995.

Telecommunications. Main telephone line supply, 1998: 50 per 100 inhabitants (the highest in the Caribbean). There is a mobile phone system.

Postal Services. The Post Office is located in St John's. There is another one at the airport.

SOCIAL INSTITUTIONS
Justice. Law is based on UK common law as exercised by the Eastern Caribbean Supreme Court (ECSC) on St Lucia. There are Magistrates' Courts and a Court of Summary Jurisdiction. Appeals lie to the Court of Appeal of ECSC, or ultimately to the UK Privy Council.

Religion. In 1997, 73% of the population were Protestants and 11% Roman Catholics.

Education. Adult literacy was 90% in 1995. There were 72 government primary and secondary schools in 1992–93. Other schools were run by religious organizations.

Health. In 1997 there were 3 hospitals. A new one was being built at Mount St John's (1998).

Welfare. The state operates a Medical Benefits Scheme providing free medical attention, and a Social Security Scheme, providing age and disability pensions and sickness benefits.

CULTURE
Broadcasting. The government-owned Antigua and Barbuda Broadcasting Service broadcasts a radio and TV programme (colour by NTSC). There are 2 commercial radio and a commercial TV station, a religious radio station and relay stations. In 1995 there were estimated to be 29,000 radio and 28,000 TV receivers.

Press. The main newspapers are The Observer, The Outlet Newspaper and the Antigua Sun. The Chamber of Commerce has a monthly publication.

Tourism. Tourism is the main industry, contributing about 90% of GDP and 80% of foreign exchange earnings and related activities. In 1995 there were 191,401 staying visitors and 227,443 cruise ship arrivals.

Festivals. Of particular interest are the Annual Tennis Championship; International Sailing Week (April–May); Mid-Summer Carnival (July–Aug.); International Hot Air Balloon Festival (Oct.).

Museums and Galleries. The main attractions are the Museum of Antigua and Barbuda; Coates Cottage; Aiton Place; Harmony Hall; Cedars Pottery; SOFA (Sculpture Objects Functional Art); Pigeon Point Pottery; Harbour Art Gallery.

DIPLOMATIC REPRESENTATIVES
Of Antigua and Barbuda in Great Britain (15 Thayer St., London, W1M 5LD)
High Commissioner: Ronald M. Sanders, CMG.

Of Great Britain in Antigua and Barbuda (Price Waterhouse Centre, 11 Old Parham Rd, St John's, Antigua)
High Commissioner: Mr. G. M. Baker (resides in Barbados).

Of Antigua and Barbuda in the USA (3400 International Dr., NW, Washington, D.C., 20008)
Ambassador: Lionel Alexander Hurst.

The US Embassy is based in Barbados.
Ambassador: Jeanette Hyde.

Of Antigua and Barbuda to the United Nations
Ambassador: Dr Patrick Albert Lewis.

Of Antigua and Barbuda to the European Union
Ambassador: Edwin Laurent.

FURTHER READING
Berleant-Schiller, R., et al., *Antigua and Barbuda*. [Bibliography] Oxford and Santa Barbara (CA), 1995

ARGENTINA

República Argentina

Capital: Buenos Aires
Population estimate, 2000: 37·03m.
GNP per capita: (PPP$) 9,530
HDI/world rank: 0·888/36

KEY HISTORICAL EVENTS

In 1515 Juan Diaz de Solis discovered the Río de le Planta. In 1534 Pedro de Mondoza was sent by the King of Spain to take charge of the 'Gobernación y Capitania de las tierras del Río de la Plata', and in Feb. 1536 he founded the city of the 'Puerto de Santa María del Buen Aire'. In 1810 the population rose against Spanish rule, and in 1816 Argentina proclaimed its independence. Civil wars and anarchy followed until, in 1853, stable government was established.

In this century there have been a succession of military *coups*. The first took place in 1930, the second in 1943 when Gen. Juan Domingo Perón won control. His regime was autocratic but popularist and nationalistic and propagated some social reforms. His wife Eva (Evita), played a major role, giving the regime an almost cult-like following. She died in 1955 and a civilian administration followed until 1966 when the next military *coup* led to seven years of government by the military. However, a political party had established itself around the Peróns, and when elections were held in 1973 the Peronists were the victors; Gen. Perón was elected president. When he died in 1974, his widow Isobel succeeded him as president. She was deposed in 1976 following another military *coup*, which established a three-man junta with Gen. Jorge Videla, C.-in-C. of the army, as president. The new government instituted a savagely repressive attitude towards any opposition.

Videla was succeeded as president first by Gen. Viola and then by Gen. Leopoldo Galtieri, the army C.-in-C. In April 1982 Galtieri, in an effort to distract attention from domestic failings, invaded the Falkland Islands (Islas Malvinas). The subsequent military defeat helped to precipitate the fall of Galtieri and the junta in July 1982. Return to civilian rule took place on 10 Dec. 1983. A new Constitution was adopted in Aug. 1994 since when Argentina has reinforced its commitment to democratic rule and restructured its economy to allow for greater market freedom.

TERRITORY AND POPULATION

The second largest country in South America, the Argentine Republic is bounded in the north by Bolivia, in the north-east by Paraguay, in the east by Brazil, Uruguay and the Atlantic Ocean, and the west by Chile. The republic consists of 23 provinces and 1 federal district with the following areas and populations at the 1991 census:

Provinces	Area (sq. km)	Population (1991 census)	Capital	Population (1991 census)
Federal Capital	200	2,965,403	Buenos Aires	–
Buenos Aires	307,571	12,594,974	La Plata	542,567
Corrientes	88,199	795,594	Corrientes	258,103
Entre Ríos	78,781	1,020,257	Paraná	277,338
Chaco	99,633	839,677	Resistencia	292,350
Santa Fé	133,007	2,798,422	Santa Fé	406,388
Formosa	72,066	398,413	Formosa	148,074
Misiones	29,801	788,915	Posadas	210,755
Jujuy	53,219	512,329	San Salvador de Jujuy	180,102
Salta	155,488	866,153	Salta	370,904
Santiago del Estero	136,351	671,988	Santiago del Estero	263,471
Tucumán	22,524	1,142,105	San Miguel de Tucumán	622,324
Córdoba	165,321	2,766,683	Córdoba	1,208,713
La Pampa	143,440	259,996	Santa Rosa	80,592
San Luis	76,748	286,458	San Luis	110,136
Catamarca	102,602	264,234	Catamarca	132,626
La Rioja	89,680	220,729	La Rioja	103,727
Mendoza	148,827	1,412,481	Mendoza	121,696
San Juan	89,651	528,715	San Juan	352,691

ARGENTINA

Provinces	Area (sq. km)	Population (1991 census)	Capital	Population (1991 census)
Neuquén	94,078	388,833	Neuquén	243,803
Chubut	224,686	357,189	Rawson	19,161
Rio Negro	203,013	506,772	Viedma	57,473
Santa Cruz	243,943	159,839	Rio Gallegos	64,640
Tierra del Fuego	21,571	69,369	Ushuaia	29,166

Argentina also claims territory in Antarctica.

The area is 2,780,400 sq. km excluding the claimed Antarctic territory and the population at the 1991 census was 32,615,528 (16,677,548 females); 1996 estimate, 34·6m., giving a density of 12 per sq. km. The official census included the 'sovereign territories of Argentina in the Antarctic': Population 3,300.

The UN gives a projected population for 2000 of 37·03m.

In 1995 an estimated 88·1% of the population were urban.

In April 1990 the National Congress declared that the Falklands and other British-held islands in the South Atlantic were part of the new province of Tierra del Fuego formed from the former National Territory of the same name. 1991 census data for Tierra del Fuego above do not include these territories. The 1994 Constitution reaffirms Argentine sovereignty over the Falkland Islands.

The population of the principal metropolitan areas in 1992 (provisional) was: Buenos Aires, 11,662,050; Córdoba, 1,179,420; Rosario, 1,157,372; Mendoza, 801,920; La Plata, 676,128; Tucumán, 642,473.

95% speak the national language, Spanish, while 3% speak Italian, 1% Guaraní and 1% other languages.

SOCIAL STATISTICS
1996 births, 664,000; deaths, 269,000. Rates, 1996 (per 1,000 population): birth, 19·2; death, 7·8; infant mortality, 20·9 per 1,000 live births. Estimated life expectancy at birth, 1995–2000, 69·7 years for males and 76·8 years for females. Annual growth rate, 1995–2000, 1·3%; fertility rate, 2·6 children per woman.

CLIMATE
The climate is warm temperate over the pampas, where rainfall occurs at all seasons, but diminishes towards the west. In the north and west, the climate is more arid, with high summer temperatures, while in the extreme south conditions are also dry, but much cooler. Buenos Aires, Jan. 74°F (23·3°C), July 50°F (10°C). Annual rainfall 37" (950 mm). Bahía Blanca, Jan. 74°F (23·3°C), July 48°F (8·9°C). Annual rainfall 21" (523 mm). Mendoza, Jan. 75°F (23·9°C), July 47°F (8·3°C). Annual rainfall 8" (190 mm). Rosario, Jan. 76°F (24·4°C), July 51°F (10·6°C). Annual rainfall 35" (869 mm). San Juan, Jan. 78°F (25·6°C), July 50°F (10°C). Annual rainfall 4" (89 mm). San Miguel de Tucumán, Jan. 79°F (26·1°C), July 56°F (13·3°C). Annual rainfall 38" (970 mm). Ushuaia, Jan. 50°F (10°C), July 34°F (1·1°C). Annual rainfall 19" (475 mm).

CONSTITUTION AND GOVERNMENT
On 10 April 1994 elections were held for a 230-member constituent assembly to reform the 1853 constitution. The Justicialist National Movement (Peronist) gained 38·8% of votes cast and the Radical Union, 20%. On 22 Aug. 1994 this assembly unanimously adopted a new Constitution. This reduces the presidential term of office from 6 to 4 years, but permits the President to stand for 2 terms. The President is no longer elected by an electoral college, but directly by universal suffrage. A presidential candidate is elected who gains more than 45% of votes cast, or 40% if at least 10% ahead of an opponent; otherwise there is a second round. The Constitution attenuates the President's powers by instituting a *Chief of Cabinet*. The *National Congress* consists of a Senate and a Chamber of Deputies: The Senate comprises 72 members, 3 nominated by each provincial legislature and 3 from the Federal District for 9 years (one-third retiring every 3 years). The Chamber of Deputies comprises 257 members directly elected by universal suffrage (at age 18).

National Anthem. 'Oid, mortales, el grito sagrado Libertad' ('Hear, mortals, the sacred cry of Liberty'); words by V. López y Planes, 1813; tune by J. Blas Parera.

RECENT ELECTIONS

Elections for half the seats in the Chamber of Deputies were held on 3 Oct. 1993. The ruling Justicialist Party (JP; Peronist) gained 42% of votes cast, the Radical Civil Union 31%. Representation in the Chamber of Deputies following the 1993 elections was: JP, 126 seats; Radicals, 83; others, 50. Elections for the remaining seats were held on 14 May 1995. The JP gained 132 seats (and 38 in the Senate). In the presidential elections held on 14 May 1995 Carlos Saúl Menem was re-elected in the first round by 49% of votes cast.

On 6 Aug. 1997 the Radical Union and centre-left Frepaso parties joined together to form the Alliance to fight against the Peronists in the lower house of Congress elections in Oct. 1997. 127 of the 257 seats were up for election. On 26 Oct. 1997 the JP suffered its first legislative defeat since 1983. The Alliance received 36·5% of votes cast and in the 10 provinces where no coalition existed the two parties separately collected an additional 9·6%, bringing the opposition tally to 46·1%. The JP received nearly 36% of votes cast, losing 12 seats and its absolute majority in Congress (it remains the largest single political bloc). The Alliance has no agreed candidate or method of choosing one for the 1999 Presidential elections on 17 Oct. Menem's main Justicialist rival and leading hopeful for the presidential candidacy, Eduardo Duhalde, suffered a setback when his wife, Hilde Duhalde, was defeated in the 1997 Congress elections in the province of Buenos Aires, a previous Peronist bastion of power.

Parliamentary elections are due to take place on 17 Oct. 1999.

CURRENT ADMINISTRATION

President: Carlos Saúl Menem, b. 1930 (JP; sworn in 8 July 1989 and re-elected in 1995).

Vice-President: Dr Carlos Ruckauf.

The Cabinet comprised in March 1999:

Defence: Jorge Dominguez. *Economy, Public Works and Services:* Roque Fernández. *Education and Culture:* Susana Decibe. *Foreign Affairs, International Trade and Worship:* Dr Guido José Maria di Tella. *Interior:* Dr Carlos Corach. *Justice:* Raúl Granillo Ocampo. *Labour and Social Security:* Antonio Erman González. *Public Health and Social Action:* Dr Alberto Mazza.

Local Government. 23 provincial gubernatorial elections were held Aug.–Dec. 1991. Peronists won 14 governorships.

DEFENCE

Conscription was abolished in 1995. In 1997 defence expenditure totalled US$4,687m. (US$134 per capita), representing 1·7% of GDP.

Army. There are 5 military regions. The Army is organized in 3 corps, 1 with 1 armoured, 1 mechanized and 1 training brigade; 1 with 1 infantry and 1 mountain brigade, and 1 with 1 armoured, 1 mountain and 2 mechanized brigades. Equipment in 1996 included 96 M-4 Sherman and 200 TAM main battle tanks and about 100 aircraft, including 23 Mohawks for reconnaissance and 35 UH-1H Iroquois transport helicopters. In 1996 the Army was 41,000 strong. The trained reserve numbers about 250,000, of whom 200,000 belong to the National Guard and 50,000 to the Territorial Guard.

There is a paramilitary gendarmerie of 18,000 run by the Ministry of Defence.

Navy. The light aircraft carrier *Veinticinco de Mayo* remains in reserve. Combatant forces include 3 German-built diesel submarines with 1 more in major refit, 4 modern German-built destroyers, 2 British-built guided missile destroyers (Type 42), 4 German-designed and 3 French-built frigates, 2 old training frigates, 2 fast torpedo craft, 5 patrol ships, 4 coastal minesweepers, 2 minehunters and 1 tank landing ship. Auxiliaries include 1 survey ship, 2 training ships, 3 transports, 1 ice-breaker and numerous harbour and service craft. Serviceability is reported as very poor.

The new construction programme includes 2 diesel submarines (both building—but slowly) and 2 small frigates nearing completion but being offered for sale.

The Naval Aviation Service has some 32 combat aircraft and 15 helicopters with (1996) 3,500 personnel, in 5 wings. Aircraft include 8 Super-Etendard strike aircraft, 7 EMB-326 and 5 EMB-339A light jet armed trainers, 2 Lockheed Electra maritime surveillance aircraft and 6 S-2E carrier-adapted Tracker anti-submarine aircraft, as well as varied training, transport and general purpose aircraft. There is a squadron of 7 SH-3 anti-submarine helicopters, 4 Alouettes and 4 S-61 transport helicopters. The remaining Super-Etendards and Trackers as well as Sea King and Alouette helicopters could operate from the aircraft carrier if she is re-activated.

Personnel 1997, 20,000 including 3,500 marines, 4 reinforced battalions equipped with armoured personnel carriers and about 40 artillery pieces.

Main bases are at Buenos Aires, Puerto Belgrano (HQ and Dockyard), Mar del Plata, Ushuaia and Puerto Deseado.

The Prefectura Naval Argentina (PNA) for Coast Guard and rescue duties was 13,000 strong in 1996 and operates 5 910-tonne corvettes with helicopter and hangar, an ex-whaler of 700 tonnes, and 23 patrol vessels.

Air Force. The Air Force is organized into Air Operations, Air Regions, Materiel and Personnel Commands. Air Operations Command, responsible for all operational flying, is made up of air brigades, each with 1 to 4 squadrons, usually operating from a single base. No. I Air Brigade is a military air transport service, with responsibility also for airline operations into areas of Argentina not served by civilian companies. Its equipment includes 9 C-130 Hercules and 10 F.27 Friendship/Troopship turboprop transports, 2 KC-130H Hercules tanker/transports, 3 twin-turbofan F.28 Fellowship freighters, 15 Guarani IIs, the Presidential Boeing 757, 4 707s, 2 VIP Fellowships, and many older or smaller types. No. II Air Brigade comprises a photographic squadron with Guarani IIs and Learjets. No. III Air Brigade has 2 squadrons of IA 58 Pucara twin-turboprop COIN aircraft. No. IV Air Brigade comprises 2 ground attack squadrons, one equipped with about 20 Paris light jet combat and liaison aircraft, and the other with 15 IA 63 Pampas. No. V Air Brigade comprises 2 squadrons with a total of about 18 A-4 Skyhawk strike aircraft. No. VI Air Brigade has 30 Dagger (Israeli-built Mirage III) fighters, equipping 2 squadrons, 1 squadron of Mirage 5 fighter-bombers, and 1 squadron with 15 Mirage IIIE fighter-bombers and 4 Mirage IIID trainers. No. VII Air Brigade has 2 helicopter squadrons with 12 armed Hughes 500M, 6 Bell 212, 4 Bell UH-1 and 2 Chinook helicopters. There is a flying school at Córdoba, equipped with turboprop-powered Embraer Tucanos and Paris jets. There were (1997) 12,000 personnel and 220 combat aircraft.

INTERNATIONAL RELATIONS

Argentina is a member of the UN, OAS and Mercosur and is set to apply for membership of the OECD. Diplomatic relations with Britain broken since the 1982 Falklands War were re-opened in 1990. Praising Argentina's 'call to peace' US President Clinton plans to give the country 'major non-NATO ally' status (Nov. 1997). The alignment with US foreign policy comes after years of anti-American sentiment and a policy of neutrality.

ECONOMY

Policy. In 1990, the government introduced a programme privatizing some 40 public enterprises. An economic plan entering into force on 1 April 1991 guaranteed the convertibility of the currency, lowered interest rates and opened the economy to foreign imports. Agricultural export taxes were abolished in March 1991. Argentina suffered a severe recession in 1995 but since then privatization and deregulation have improved the economy's prospects into the medium term. Tax evasion and fraud remain a major occurrence but tighter controls are being instituted. In Feb. 1998 the IMF approved a 3-year US$2·8bn. extended fund facility for Argentina. The accord set a target for the 1998 fiscal deficit of US$3·5bn., just over 1% of GDP, against the 1996 US$4·5bn. target.

Performance. The economy grew by 4·4% in 1996, after falling 4·6% in 1995, and was estimated to have grown by 8·6% in 1997. Consumer spending is recovering gradually from the 1995 recession. GDP growth in 1997 totalled 8·4%. GDP per capita has more than tripled since 1989, to US$9,010 in 1997, and was forecast to rise still further to US$9,520 in 1998.

Budget. The financial year commences on 1 Jan. Estimated revenue in 1997 was US$55bn. and expenditure, US$59bn.

Currency. The monetary unit is the *peso* (ARP) which replaced the austral on 1 Jan. 1992 at a rate of 1 peso = 10,000 australs. Inflation was 0·3% in 1997 and was estimated at 0·8% in 1998. Gold reserves were 360,000 troy oz. in Feb. 1998. In 1999 foreign exchange reserves were estimated at US$20·0bn. Total money supply was 22,263m. pesos in Feb. 1998.

Banking and Finance. In 1996 there were 20 government banks, 100 private banks, 28 foreign banks and 27 other financial institutions. Bank and non-bank total monetary resources totalled US$67,449m. as at Dec. 1996. The *Governor* of the Central Bank is Pedro Pou. Convertibility regulations of April 1991 require the Central Bank to back the entire currency in circulation with its foreign currency reserves. The current account balance in 1999 was forecast to be US$–16·0bn.

There is a stock exchange at Buenos Aires.

Weights and Measures. The metric system is legal.

ENERGY AND NATURAL RESOURCES

Electricity. Electric power production (1995) was 62,478m. kWh (7,066m. kWh nuclear). In 1995 there were 2 nuclear plants. Installed capacity in 1995 was 20·21m. kW, with consumption per capita in 1995 an estimated 1,606 kWh.

Oil and Gas. Crude oil production (1996) 46m. cu. metres. Reserves were estimated at some 416m. cu. metres in 1997. The oil industry was privatized in 1993. Natural gas production (1996) 34,650m. cu. metres. Reserves were about 684,000m. cu. metres in 1997. The main area in production is the Neuquen basin in western Argentina, with over 40% of the total oil reserves and nearly half the gas reserves.

Minerals. An estimated 215,000 tonnes of washed coal were produced in 1996. Other minerals (with estimated production in 1996) include iron ore (3,388 tonnes of metal), gold (837 kg in 1995), silver (47,787 kg), tungsten, beryllium, clays (3·3m. tonnes), marble, lead (10,521 tonnes of metal), zinc (36,697 tonnes of metal), borates (244,933 tonnes), bentonite (0·11m. tonnes) and granite. Production from the US$1·1bn. Alumbrera copper and gold mine, the country's biggest mining project, in Catamarca province in the north-west, started in late 1997. In 1993 the mining laws were reformed and state regulation was swept away creating a more stable tax regime for investors. In Dec. 1997 Argentina and Chile signed a treaty laying the legal and tax framework for mining operations straddling the 5,000 km border, allowing mining products to be transported out through both countries.

Agriculture. In 1996 there were 23·5m. ha of arable land, 2·1m. ha of permanent crops and 142m. ha of permanent pasture. The agricultural population was 3·82m. in 1995, of whom 1·49m. were economically active. 1·7m. ha were irrigated in 1994.

Livestock (1998): Cattle, 47,075,156; sheep, 22,408,681; pigs, 3,341,652; horses, 1,994,241. In 1997 wool production was 45,120 tonnes; milk, 9,167m. litres.

Crop production (in 1,000 tonnes) in 1997: wheat, 15,914; sugar-cane, 9,949; rice, 1,205; maize, 15,537; potatoes, 2,275; tobacco, 123; sunflower seed, 5,450. Cotton, vine, citrus fruit, olives, soya and yerba maté (Paraguayan tea) are also cultivated.

Forestry. The woodland area was 44,975,115 ha in 1994. Production in 1996 included 1·71m. cu. metres of sawn wood, 6.6m. tonnes of round logs and 63,000 tonnes of tannin.

Fisheries. Fish landings in 1997 amounted to 1,339,615 tonnes.

INDUSTRY

Production (1996 in tonnes): Paper, 1,123,000; primary iron, 3,388,000; crude steel, 4,065,000; primary aluminium, 184,533; sulfuric acid, 219,562; cement, 5,117,000; synthetic rubber, 57,994; polyethylene, 180,849; sugar, 1,290,000; vegetable oils, 4,044,000. Motor vehicles produced totalled 313,150; tractors, 5,589; tyres, 7,593,000. In Feb. 1998 it was forecast that industrial production would grow by about 6% over the year.

ARGENTINA

Labour. The labour force in 1996 totalled 13,809,000. 2·12m. persons were registered unemployed at July 1996. Unemployment in 1998 was 11·0% of the workforce, down from 18·4% in 1995.

INTERNATIONAL TRADE
External debt was US$99,708m. in 1996.

Imports and Exports. Foreign trade (in US$1m.):

	1991	1992	1993	1994	1995	1996
Imports	8,275	14,872	16,784	21,590	20,122	23,762
Exports	11,978	12,235	13,118	15,839	20,963	23,811

Principal exports in 1996 (in US$1m.) were cereals (2,560), residues and waste from the food industry (2,367), oils and fats (1,890), fuels, mineral oils and distillates (3,089), oilseeds and fruits (964) and fish, shellfish and molluscs (945).

Principal imports in 1996 (in US$1m.) were boilers, machines and mechanical equipment (4,576), electrical machinery and equipment (2,976), land vehicles (3,095), organic chemical products (1,387), plastic materials (1,106) and cast iron and steel (424).

In 1996 imports (in US$1m.) were mainly from Brazil (5,326), USA (4,749), Germany (1,427), Italy (1,503), Japan (725), Chile (559) and France (1,181); exports went mainly to Brazil (6,615), USA (1,973), Netherlands (1,225), Germany (565), Chile (1,766), Italy (721) and Spain (724).

In 1997 exports grew by 7%, but imports rose by 27%. In 1999 imports were forecast to rise to US$35·2bn. and exports to US$30·5bn.

The trade balance deteriorated to a deficit of almost US$4·9bn. in 1997, and around US$5·0bn. in 1998, but was projected to rise back to US$4·9bn. in 1999.

In Jan. 1998 Canadian and Argentine business leaders signed 70 contracts worth $200m. in mining, atomic energy and finance sectors.

COMMUNICATIONS

Roads. In 1996 there were 37,704 km of motorways and national and provincial highways, plus 180,572 km of secondary roads. The 4 main roads constituting Argentina's portion of the Pan-American Highway were opened in 1942. Vehicles in use in 1996 totalled 5,414,000, of which 4,459,000 were passenger cars, 943,000 trucks and vans, and 12,000 buses and coaches.

Rail. Much of the 33,000 km state-owned network (on 1,000 mm, 1,435 mm and 1,676 mm gauges; 210 km electrified) was privatized in 1993–94. 30-year concessions were awarded to 5 freight operators; long-distance passenger services are run by contractors to the requirements of local authorities. Metro, light rail and suburban railway services are also operated by concessionaires.

In 1996 railways carried 16,980,000 tonnes of freight and 419,455,000 passengers.

The metro and light rail network in Buenos Aires extends to 46 km.

Civil Aviation. There is an international airport at Buenos Aires (Ministro Pistarini). The national carrier, Aerolíneas Argentinas, is 15% state-owned. In 1998 services were also operated by Aeroflot, Aeroperú, Air France, Alitalia, ALTA, American Airlines, Austral, Avianca, British Airways, Canadian Airlines International, Cubana, Ecuatoriana, Iberia, KLM, Lan-Chile, Lloyd Aéreo Boliviano, Lufthansa, Malaysia Airlines, Mexicana, Pluna, SAS, South African Airways, Swissair, Transbrasil, Transportes Aereos del Mercosur, United Airlines, VASP and Varig.

In 1996, 5,559,000 passengers and 139,467 tonnes of freight were carried on international flights, and 5,904,000 passengers and 16,447 tonnes of freight on internal flights.

Shipping. The merchant shipping fleet totalled 595,000 GRT in 1995, including oil tankers totalling 107,000 GRT.

Telecommunications. The telephone service Entel was privatized in 1990. The number of lines in service in 1997 totalled 6,824,425. In June 1997 there were approximately 170,000 Internet users. In 1995 there were 341,000 cellular phone subscribers, 850,000 PCs (25 per 1,000 persons) and 50,000 fax machines.

Postal Services. In 1995 there were 5,676 post offices.

SOCIAL INSTITUTIONS

Justice. Justice is administered by federal and provincial courts. The former deal only with cases of a national character, or those in which different provinces or inhabitants of different provinces are parties. The chief federal court is the Supreme Court, with 5 judges whose appointment is approved by the Senate. Other federal courts are the appeal courts, at Buenos Aires, Bahía Blanca, La Plata, Córdoba, Mendoza, Tucumán and Resistencia. Each province has its own judicial system, with a Supreme Court (generally so designated) and several minor chambers. The death penalty was re-introduced in 1976 for the killing of government, military police and judicial officials, and for participation in terrorist activities.

The police force is centralized under the Federal Security Council.

Religion. The Roman Catholic religion is supported by the State; affiliation numbered 31·06m. in 1997. There were 2·66m. Protestants of various denominations in 1997, and 520,000 Moslems. There were 267,000 Latter-day Saints (Mormons).

Education. Adult literacy was 96·2% in 1995 (males and females both 96·2%). In 1996, 1,116,951 children attended pre-school institutions, 5,250,329 primary schools, 2,594,329 secondary schools and 391,778 tertiary colleges. Numbers of teachers in 1994–95: Pre-school, 63,751; primary, 277,064; secondary, 228,289; tertiary, 40,160.

In 1996, in the public sector, there were 33 universities; 1 technical university; and university institutes of aeronautics, military studies, naval and maritime studies and police studies. In the private sector, there were 15 universities; 7 Roman Catholic universities; 1 Adventist university; universities of business administration, business and social science, the cinema, notarial studies, social studies, and theology; and university institutes of biomedical science, health and the merchant navy. In 1996, there were 790,775 university students and 128,478 academic staff.

In 1994 total expenditure on education came to 3·8% of GNP and represented 14% of total government expenditure.

Health. Free medical attention is obtainable from public hospitals. In 1996 there were 7,243 beds available in public health care institutions.

Welfare. Until the end of 1996 trade unions had a monopoly in the handling of the compulsory social security contributions of employees, but private insurance agencies are now permitted to function alongside them.

CULTURE

Broadcasting. There are state-owned, provincial, municipal and private radio stations overseen by the Secretaria de Comunicaciones, the Comité Federal de Radiodifusión, the Servicio Oficial de Radiodifusión (which also operates an external service and a station in Antarctica) and the Asociación de Teleradiodifusoras Argentinas. In 1995 there were 23,500,000 radio and 7,600,000 TV (colour by PAL) receivers.

Cinema. In 1997 there were 598 cinemas with an audience of approximately 26,565,000.

Press. In 1995 there were 190 daily newspapers with a combined circulation of 4,700,000, a rate of 135 per 1,000 inhabitants.

Tourism. In 1997, 4,540,215 tourists visited Argentina. Receipts totalled US$4·57bn. in 1996.

DIPLOMATIC REPRESENTATIVES

Of Argentina in Great Britain (65 Brook St., London, W1Y 1YE)
Ambassador: Rogelio Pfirter.

Of Great Britain in Argentina (Dr Luis Agote 2141/52, 1425 Buenos Aires)
Ambassador: William Marsden, CMG.

ARGENTINA

Of Argentina in the USA (1600 New Hampshire Ave., NW, Washington, D.C., 20009)
Ambassador: Diego Guelar.

Of the USA in Argentina (4300 Colombia, 1425 Buenos Aires)
Ambassador: Vacant.

Of Argentina to the United Nations
Ambassador: Fernando Enrique Petrella.

Of Argentina to the European Union
Ambassador: Juan Uranga.

FURTHER READING

INDEC. *Statistical Yearbook of Argentina*
Bethell, L. (ed.) *Argentina since Independence.* CUP, 1994
Biggins, A., *Argentina* [Bibliography]. Oxford and Santa Barbara (CA), 1991
Lewis, P., *The Crisis of Argentine Capitalism.* North Carolina Univ. Press, 1990
Manzetti, L., *Institutions, Parties and Coalitions in Argentine Politics.* Univ. of Pittsburgh Press, 1994
Rock, D., *Argentina 1516–1982.* London, 1986
Shumway, N., *The Invention of Argentina.* California Univ. Press, 1992
Wynia, G. W., *Argentina: Illusions and Realities.* 2nd ed. Hoddesdon, 1993

National statistical office: Instituto Nacional de Estadística y Censos (INDEC). Av. Presidente Julio A. Roca 609, 1067 Buenos Aires. *Director:* Dr Hector E. Montero.
Website: http://www.indec.mecon.ar/default.htm

ARMENIA

Hayastani Hanrapetoutiun

(Republic of Armenia)

Capital: Yerevan
Population estimate, 2000: 3·66m.
GNP per capita: (PPP$) 2,160
HDI/world rank: 0·674/99

KEY HISTORICAL EVENTS

The early history of Armenia was one of foreign domination with, at various times, the Turkish, Persian and Russian empires claiming control. In the early part of this century the Armenians under Turkish rule suffered brutal persecution. Armenia enjoyed a brief period of independence after the First World War but in 1920 the country was proclaimed a Soviet Socialist Republic. The Soviet-Turkish Treaty of Kars (March 1921) confirmed the Turkish possession of the former Government of Kars and of the Surmali District of the Government of Yerevan. From 1922 to 1936, Armenia formed part of the Transcaucasian Soviet Federal Socialist Republic. In 1936 it was proclaimed a constituent republic of the USSR.

With the dramatic changes in Soviet politics initiated by Mikhail Gorbachev after 1985, Armenia began to assert its cultural and political identity, though a territorial dispute with Azerbaijan over Nagorno-Karabakh was the big issue until the 1991 referendum on independence when 99% of voters supported a breakaway from the Soviet Union. A declaration of independence in Sept. 1991 was followed by presidential elections after which President Ter-Petrosyan came to an agreement on economic co-operation with the other Soviet republics and joined the CIS. A new constitution adopted in July 1995 led to National Assembly elections, in which the Pan-Armenian National Movement (PANM) won 119 seats with 42·66% of votes cast; President Ter-Petrosyan was re-elected in Sept. 1996. OSCE observers noted 'very serious irregularities' in the conduct of the election.

Hostilities with Azerbaijan were brought to an end with a 1994 ceasefire but negotiations on a territorial settlement continue.

TERRITORY AND POPULATION

Armenia covers an area of 29,800 sq. km (11,490 sq. miles). It is bounded in the north by Georgia, in the east by Azerbaijan and in the south and west by Turkey and Iran. The 1989 census population was 3,304,776 (density, 111 per sq. km.), of whom Armenians accounted for 96·0% (1996), Azerbaijanis 2·6%, Kurds 1·7% and Russians 1·6%.

The UN gives a projected population for 2000 of 3·66m.

In 1995 an estimated 68·6% of the population lived in urban areas.

The capital is Yerevan (1·2m. population in 1994). Other large towns are Kumairi (formerly Leninakan) (120,000) and Kirovakan (159,000).

The official language is Armenian.

SOCIAL STATISTICS

1994 births, 58,000; deaths, 27,000, marriages, 17,074. Rates, 1994 (per 1,000 population): Births, 15·8; deaths, 7·4; marriage, 4·6; infant mortality (per 1,000 live births), 17·1. Annual growth rate, 1990–95, 1·2%. Life expectancy at birth, 67·2 years for men and 74·0 years for women, 1990–95; fertility rate, 2·2 children per woman.

CLIMATE

Summers are very dry and hot although nights can be cold. Winters are very cold, often with heavy snowfall. Yerevan, Jan. –9°C, July 28°C. Annual rainfall 318 mm.

CONSTITUTION AND GOVERNMENT

The head of state is the *President*, directly elected for 5-year terms. Parliament is a 190-member *National Assembly*, of which 150 members are directly elected on a first-past-the-post system, and 40 by proportional representation, distributed among those parties gaining more than 5% of votes cast. The government is nominated by the President.

National Anthem. 'Mer Hayrenik azat, ankakh' ('Land of our fathers, free and independent'); words by M. Nalbandyan, tune by B. Kanachyan.

RECENT ELECTIONS

President Ter-Petrosyan resigned in Feb. 1998 in a row over the disputed Armenian-inhabited enclave of Nagorno-Karabakh in Azerbaijan. In the election which resulted, Robert Kocharian, the Prime Minister, won, obtaining 59·7% of the votes in the second round on 30 March 1998 in a run-off against Karen Demirchyan, the former Communist Party leader, having previously obtained 38·8% in the first round of voting on 16 March against 4 other candidates. Parliamentary elections were scheduled for May 1999.

CURRENT ADMINISTRATION

President: Robert Kocharian, formerly President of Nagorno-Karabakh, the Armenian-inhabited enclave in Azerbaijan.

In March 1999 the government comprised:

Prime Minister: Armen Darbinian.

Minister of Foreign Affairs: Vartan Oskanian. *Defence:* Vazgen Sarkissian. *Justice:* David Artyunyan. *Education and Science:* Levon Mkrtchyan. *Health:* Hayk Nikosyan. *Culture:* Roland Sharoyan. *Environmental Protection:* Gevork Vardanyan. *Industry and Trade:* Hayk Gevorkyan. *Post and Telecommunications:* Artak Vardanyan. *Agriculture:* Vladimir Movsisian. *Transportation:* Yervan Zakaryan. *Finance and Economy:* Eduard Sandoyan. *Economic and Structural Reforms:* Vahram Avanesian. *Statistics:* Stepan Mnatsakanyan. *Energy:* Meruzhan Mikaelyan. *Internal Affairs and National Security:* Serzhik Sarkissian. *Social Security:* Gagik Yeganyan. *Urban Planning and Construction:* Felix Pirumian. *Privatization:* Pavel Ghaltakhchian. *Territorial Administration:* David Zadoyan.

The *Speaker* is Babken Ararktsyan.

DEFENCE

There is conscription for 18 months. Paramilitary Forces at the disposal of the Ministry of the Interior are estimated at 30,000. Most personnel are from local militia or police forces.

Defence expenditure in 1997 totalled US$138m. (US$37 per capita), representing 8·9% of GDP.

Army. Current troop levels are 32,682. There are approximately 300,000 Armenians who have received some kind of military service experience within the last 15 years. The Defence Ministry is aiming for a standing army of 70,000.

Army organization: 4 Motorized Rifle Brigades, 1 Special Forces Regiment, 1 Artillery Brigade, 1 Artillery Regiment, 1 Anti-tank Regiment, 2 Surface-to-Air Missile (SAM) Brigades, 1 Independent Helicopter Squadron.

INTERNATIONAL RELATIONS

There is a dispute over the mainly Armenian-populated enclave of Nagorno-Karabakh, which lies within Azerbaijan's borders.

Armenia is a member of the UN, CIS and the NATO Partnership for Peace. It is the biggest recipient of US government aid, per head of population, after Israel.

ECONOMY

Policy. A privatization scheme was launched on 1 March 1995 under the auspices of a Privatization Commission.

Performance. Real GDP growth was 3·3% in 1997. The conflict with Azerbaijan is a serious brake on economic development.

Budget. Budgetary revenue in 1995 was US$237m.; expenditure in 1995 was US$318m.

Currency. In Nov. 1993 a new currency unit, the *dram* (AMD) of 100 *lumma*, was introduced to replace the rouble. Inflation was 17·4% in 1997. Foreign exchange reserves (including gold) were US$127·5m. in June 1996.

Banking and Finance. The *Chairman* of the Central Bank (founded in 1993) is Tigran Sarkisyan. In 1997 there were 33 commercial banks (1 state-owned).

ENERGY AND NATURAL RESOURCES

Electricity. Output of electricity in 1996 was 6,300m. kWh. Capacity was 2·77m. kW in 1994. Consumption per capita was an estimated 1,462 kWh in 1995. A nuclear plant closed in 1989 was re-opened in 1995 because of the blockade of the electricity supply by Azerbaijan; it was anticipated that domestic supply would be raised from 4 to 12 hours daily.

Minerals. There are deposits of copper, zinc, aluminium, molybdenum, marble and granite.

Agriculture. Agriculture accounts for approximately 44% of GDP. The chief agricultural area is the valley of the Arax and the area round Yerevan. Here there are cotton plantations, orchards and vineyards. Almonds, olives and figs are also grown. In the mountainous areas the chief pursuit is livestock raising. In 1994 there were 483,000 ha of arable land, 90,000 ha of permanent crops and 688,000 ha of permanent pasture. Private and commercial agriculture accounted for 96% of the value of agricultural output in 1993. Livestock (1996): Cattle, 497,000; sheep, 548,000; pigs, 79,000; horses, 8,000; chickens, 3m. (1995).

Forestry. In 1995 forests covered 334,000 ha, or 11·8% of the total land area (10·4% in 1990).

Fisheries. Total catch in 1995 came to an estimated 4,500 tonnes, exclusively from inland waters.

INDUSTRY

Among the chief industries are the chemical, producing mainly synthetic rubber and fertilizers, the extraction and processing of building materials, ginning- and textile-mills, carpet weaving and food processing, including wine-making.

Labour. In 1997 the population of working age was 1·98m., of whom 1·5m. were employed: 36% in agriculture, 22% in industry. The registered unemployment rate was 9% of the workforce in Oct. 1996. The average monthly income in 1996 was 6,000 drams.

INTERNATIONAL TRADE

External debt was US$552m. in 1996.

Imports and Exports. In 1996 imports were valued at US$856m. and exports at US$290m. The main import suppliers were Iran (17·5%), Russia (14·7%), USA (12·1%) and Turkmenistan (10·1%). Principal export markets were Russia (33·1%), Belgium-Luxembourg (15·4%), Iran (15·1%) and the Southern African Customs Union (12·5%).

COMMUNICATIONS

Roads. There were 11,300 km (10,500 km with hard surface) of motor roads in 1996. In 1995 there were 300 road deaths.

Rail. Total length in 1996 was 840 km of 1,000 mm gauge (590 km electrified). Passenger-kilometres travelled in 1995 came to 166m.

There is a tramway in Yerevan.

Civil Aviation. There is an international airport at Yerevan (Zvartnots). The state-owned Armenian Airlines has been operational since 1995. In 1998 it operated services to Adler/Sochi, Aleppo, Amman, Amsterdam, Anapa, Ashgabat, Athens, Beirut, Delhi, Dubai, Ekaterinburg, Istanbul, Kharkiv, Krasnodar, Kyiv, London, Milan, Mineralnye Vody, Moscow, Nizhny Novgorod, Novosibirsk, Odesa, Paris, Rostov, St Petersburg, Samara, Saratov, Simferopol, Sofia, Stavropol, Tbilisi, Teheran, Toshkent, Vladikavkaz and Volgograd. Services were also provided in

1998 by Aeroflot, Air Enterprise, Arax Airways, Belavia, British Airways, Crimea Air, Donavia, Odessa Airlines, Samara Airlines, Siberia Airlines, Swissair and Volga Aircompany.

Telecommunications. Telephone main lines numbered 568,500 in 1997 (149·5 per 1,000 inhabitants). There were 300 fax machines in 1995.

SOCIAL INSTITUTIONS

Justice. In 1994, 9,923 crimes were reported, including 201 murders or attempted murders.

Religion. Armenia adopted Christianity in 301 AD, thus becoming the first Christian nation in the world. The Armenian Apostolic Church is headed by its Catholicos (Karekin II, b. 1932) whose seat is at Etchmiadzin, and who is head of all the Armenian (Gregorian) communities throughout the world. In 1995 it numbered 7m. adherents (4m. in diaspora). The Catholicos is elected by representatives of parishes. The Catholicos of the diaspora is Kachechyan of Cilicia, with seat at Antelias. In 1997, 70% of the population belonged to the Armenian Apostolic Church.

Education. Armenia has more than 99% literacy. In Jan. 1994, 0·1m. children, 23% of those eligible, attended pre-school institutions. In 1995–96 there were 249,872 pupils and 11,341 teachers in primary schools and, in 1994–95, 343,096 pupils and 32,674 teachers in secondary schools. In 1994–95 there were 69 technical colleges with 25,200 students and 14 higher educational institutions with 46,500 students. Yerevan houses the Armenian Academy of Sciences, 43 scientific institutes, a medical institute and other technical colleges, and a state university. In Jan. 1989, 33 institutions with 3,330 scientific staff were under the Academy of Sciences; scientific workers in 101 institutions totalled 21,800.

In 1995–96 there were 2 universities (including the American University), an engineering university, 10 other institutes of higher education and a conservatory.

Health. In Jan. 1994 there were some 14,000 doctors, 36,200 junior medical personnel and 183 hospitals with 31,000 beds.

Welfare. In Jan. 1995 there were 437,000 age, and 202,000 other, pensioners.

CULTURE

Broadcasting. The state-owned Armenian Radio broadcasts 2 national programmes and relays of Radio Moscow and Voice of America, and a foreign service, Radio Yerevan (Armenian, English, French, Spanish, Arabic, Kurdish, Russian). Television broadcasting is by the state-controlled Armenian Television (colour by SECAM).

Press. In 1997 there were 80 daily publications.

DIPLOMATIC REPRESENTATIVES

Of Armenia in Great Britain (25A Cheniston Gdns, London, W8 6TG)
Ambassador: Dr Armen Sarkissian.

Of Great Britain in Armenia (28 Charents St., Yerevan 375010)
Ambassador: Dr John Mitchiner.

Of Armenia in the USA (122 C St., NW, Washington, D.C., 20001)
Ambassador: Rouben Robert Shugarian.

Of the USA in Armenia (18 Gen. Bagramian, Yerevan)
Ambassador: Peter Tomsen.

Of Armenia to the United Nations
Ambassador: Dr Movses Abelian.

Of Armenia to the European Union
Ambassador: Viguen Tchitetchian.

FURTHER READING

Brook, S., *Claws of the Crab: Georgia and Armenia in Crisis.* London, 1992

Hovannisian, R. G., *The Republic of Armenia.* 4 vols. Univ. of California Press, 1996

Lang, D.M., *Armenia: Cradle of Civilization.* London, 1978. *The Armenians: a People in Exile.* London, 1981

Malkasian, M., *Gha-Ra-Bagh: the Emergence of the National Democratic Movement in Armenia.* Wayne State Univ. Press, 1996

Nersessian, V. N., *Armeni.* [Bibliography]. Oxford and Santa Barbara (CA), 1993

Walker, C. J., *Armenia: The Survival of a Nation.* 2nd ed. London, 1990

AUSTRALIA

**Commonwealth
of Australia**

Capital: Canberra
Population estimate, 2000: 18·84m.
GNP per capita: (PPP$) 19,870
HDI/world rank: 0·932/15

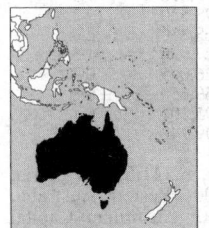

KEY HISTORICAL EVENTS

Various dates are given for the discovery of Australia, including 1522 in which year it was sighted by Magellan's followers. Capt. Cook discovered the east coast in 1770 and initially the British planned to establish a colony there; instead, however, the government decided to set up a penal settlement. In 1801 Matthew Flinders, a British naval officer, completed the charting of Australia. He suggested that the name Australia replace New Holland, and this took place in 1817.

The appointment of Lachlan Macquarie as Governor in 1809 began a period of development in which Australia ceased primarily to be a penal settlement. The crossing of the Blue Mountains in 1813 was the first of many expeditions which led to discovery and use of vast areas of good grazing land.

On 1 Jan. 1901 the 6 separately constituted colonies of New South Wales, Victoria, Queensland, South Australia, Western Australia and Tasmania were federated under the name of the Commonwealth of Australia, the designation of 'colonies' being at the same time changed into that of 'states'—except in the case of Northern Territory which was transferred from South Australia to the Commonwealth as a 'territory' on 1 Jan. 1911.

In 1911 the Commonwealth acquired from the State of New South Wales the Canberra site for the Australian capital. Building operations were begun in 1923 and a Federal Parliament was opened at Canberra in 1927. A further area at Jervis Bay was acquired in 1915.

Territories under the administration of Australia are Norfolk Island, the territory of Ashmore and Cartier Islands, and the Australian Antarctic Territory (acquired on 24 Aug. 1936), the latter comprising all the islands and territory, other than Adélie Land, situated south of 60° S. lat. and between 160° and 45° E. long. The Coral Sea Islands became an External Territory in 1969.

The British Government transferred sovereignty in the Heard and McDonald Islands to the Australian Government on 26 Dec. 1947. Cocos (Keeling) Islands on 23 Nov. 1955 and Christmas Island on 1 Oct. 1958 were also transferred to Australian jurisdiction.

Since the Second World War, Australia has played an increasingly important role in Asia and the Pacific. For most of this period central government has been in the hands of the Australian Labor Party (ALP) which, in the last decade, has shifted its stance on state control and economic planning to allow for an ambitious programme of privatization. In March 1986 the Australia Act abolished the remaining legislative, executive and judicial controls of the British Parliament.

TERRITORY AND POPULATION

Australia, excluding external territories, covers a land area of 7,682,300 sq. km, extending from Cape York (10° 41' S) in the north some 3,680 km to Tasmania (43° 39' S), and from Cape Byron (153° 39' E) in the east some 4,000 km west to Western Australia (113° 9' E). External territories under the administration of Australia comprise the Ashmore and Cartier Islands, Australian Antarctic Territory, Christmas Island, the Cocos (Keeling) Islands, the Coral Sea Islands, the Heard and McDonald Islands and Norfolk Island. For these *see below.*

Growth in census population has been:

1901	3,774,310	1961	10,508,186	1981	15,053,600
1911	4,455,005	1966	11,599,498	1986	15,763,000
1921	5,435,734	1971	12,755,638	1991	16,852,258
1947	7,579,358	1976	13,915,500	1996	17,892,423

Of the 1996 census population, 9,043,199 were females. Estimated population at 30 June 1998 was 18,751,000.

The UN gives a projected population for 2000 of 18·84m.

Areas and populations of the States and Territories at the 1996 census:

States and Territories	Area (sq. km)	Population	Per sq. km
New South Wales (NSW)	801,600	6,038,696	7·5
Victoria (Vic.)	227,600	4,373,520	19·2
Queensland (Qld.)	1,727,200	3,368,850	2·0
South Australia (SA)	984,000	1,427,936	1·5
Western Australia (WA)	2,525,500	1,726,095	0·7
Tasmania (Tas.)	67,800	459,659	6·8
Northern Territory (NT)	1,346,200	195,101	0·1
Australian Capital Territory (ACT)	2,400	299,243	124·7

Estimated population at 30 June 1998: New South Wales, 6,341,600; Victoria, 4,660,900; Queensland, 3,456,300; South Australia, 1,487,300; Western Australia, 1,831,400; Tasmania, 471,900; Northern Territory, 190,000; Australian Capital Territory, 308,400.

In 1996 density was 2·3 per sq. km. 86% of the population lived in urban areas. Resident population (estimate) in capitals and other statistical districts with more than 150,000 population at 30 June 1996:

Capital	State	Population	Capital	State	Population
Canberra[1]	ACT	344,800	Darwin	NT	82,400
Sydney	NSW	3,879,400	*Statistical district*		
Melbourne	Vic.	3,283,000	Newcastle	NSW	463,700
Brisbane	Qld.	1,520,600	Wollongong	NSW	255,700
Adelaide	SA	1,079,200	Gold Coast[2]	Qld.	354,200
Perth	WA	1,295,100	Geelong	Vic.	152,400
Hobart	Tas.	195,800	Sunshine Coast	Qld.	156,100

[1]Includes Queanbeyan. [2]Includes part of Tweed Shire (in NSW).

The median age of the 1996 census population was 34 years.

Australians born overseas (census 1996), 3,901,900, of whom 1,124,000 were from the UK and Ireland, and 291,400 from New Zealand.

Aboriginals have been included in population statistics only since 1967. At the 1996 census 352,970 people identified themselves as being of indigenous origin. A 1992 High Court ruling that the Meriam people of the Murray Islands had land rights before the European settlement reversed the previous assumption that Australia was *terra nullius* before that settlement. The Native Title Act setting up a system for deciding land claims by Aborigines came into effect on 1 Jan. 1994.

Overseas arrivals and departures:

	1994	1995	1996
Arrivals	5,886,200	6,450,600	7,121,700
of whom long-term	221,910	253,930	261,340
(including settlers)	(77,940)	(96,970)	(92,500)
Departures	5,810,200	6,344,600	7,001,100
of whom long-term	114,660	121,490	158,260

The 1994–95 quota for settlers was 86,000. The Migration Act of Dec. 1989 sought to curb illegal entry and ensure that annual immigrant intakes were met but not exceeded. Provisions for temporary visitors to become permanent were restricted.

The national language is English.

SOCIAL STATISTICS

Life expectancy at birth, 1996, 75·2 years for males and 81·1 years for females.

Statistics for 1996:

States and Territories	Marriages	Divorces	Births	Deaths	Infant deaths
New South Wales	37,716	15,984	86,595	45,141	499
Victoria	26,074	12,491	61,143	32,726	308
Queensland	20,913	10,996	47,769	22,281	304
South Australia	8,011	4,358	19,056	11,606	94
Western Australia	10,294	4,959	24,793	11,027	160

AUSTRALIA

States and Territories	Marriages	Divorces	Births	Deaths	Infant deaths
Tasmania	2,654	1,582	6,457	3,872	29
Northern Territory	787	486	3,562	758	41
ACT	1,654	1,610	4,396	1,300	25
Total	106,103	52,466	253,834	128,719	1,460
Rate (per 1,000)[1]	5·9	12·9[2]	14·2	7·2	5·8[3]

[1]Resident (estimate). [2]Per 1,000 married couples. [3]Per 1,000 live births registered.

Growth rate in the year ending 30 June 1998 was 1·22%.

In 1995 the most popular age range for marrying was 25–29 for males and 20–24 for females. Fertility rate, 1996, 1·9 children per woman.

Suicide rates (per 100,000 population, 1996): 13·1 (men, 21·2; women, 5·0).

CLIMATE

Over most of the continent, four seasons may be recognized. Spring is from Sept. to Nov., Summer from Dec. to Feb., Autumn from March to May and Winter from June to Aug., but because of its great size there are climates that range from tropical monsoon to cool temperate, with large areas of desert as well. In Northern Australia there are only two seasons, the wet one lasting from Nov. to March, but rainfall amounts diminish markedly from the coast to the interior. Central and southern Queensland are subtropical, north and central New South Wales are warm temperate, as are parts of Victoria, Western Australia and Tasmania, where most rain falls in winter. Canberra, Jan. 68°F (20°C), July 42°F (5·6°C). Annual rainfall 25" (635 mm). Adelaide, Jan. 73°F (22·8°C), July 52°F (11·1°C). Annual rainfall 21" (528 mm). Brisbane, Jan. 77°F (25°C), July 58°F (14·4°C). Annual rainfall 45" (1,153 mm). Darwin, Jan. 83°F (28·3°C), July 77°F (25°C). Annual rainfall 59" (1,536 mm). Hobart, Jan. 62°F (16·7°C), July 46°F (7·8°C). Annual rainfall 23" (584 mm). Melbourne, Jan. 67°F (19·4°C), July 49°F (9·4°C). Annual rainfall 26" (659 mm). Perth, Jan. 74°F (23·3°C), July 55°F (12·8°C). Annual rainfall 35" (873 mm). Sydney, Jan. 71°F (21·7°C), July 53°F (11·7°C). Annual rainfall 47" (1,215 mm).

CONSTITUTION AND GOVERNMENT

Federal Government. Under the Constitution legislative power is vested in a Federal Parliament, consisting of the Queen, represented by a Governor-General, a Senate and a House of Representatives. Under the terms of the constitution there must be a session of parliament at least once a year.

The *Senate* comprises 76 Senators (12 for each State voting as one electorate and as from Aug. 1974, 2 Senators respectively for the Australian Capital Territory and the Northern Territory). Senators representing the States are chosen for 6 years. The terms of Senators representing the Territories expire at the close of the day next preceding the polling day for the general elections of the House of Representatives. In general, the Senate is renewed to the extent of one-half every 3 years, but in case of disagreement with the House of Representatives, it, together with the House of Representatives, may be dissolved, and an entirely new Senate elected. Elections to the Senate are on the single transferable vote system; voters list candidates in order of preference. A candidate must reach a quota to be elected, otherwise the lowest-placed candidate drops out and his or her votes are transferred to other candidates.

The *House of Representatives* consists, as nearly as practicable, of twice as many Members as there are Senators, the numbers chosen in the several States being in proportion to population as shown by the latest statistics, but not less than 5 for any original State. Elections to the House of Representatives are on the alternative vote system; voters list candidates in order of preference, and if no one candidate wins an overall majority, the lowest-placed drops out and his or her votes are transferred. The Northern Territory has been represented by 1 Member in the House of Representatives since 1922; the Australian Capital Territory by 1 Member since 1949 and 2 Members since May 1974. The Member for the Australian Capital Territory was given full voting rights as from the Parliament elected in Nov. 1966. The Member for the Northern Territory was given full voting rights in 1968. The House of Representatives continues for 3 years from the date of its first meeting, unless sooner dissolved.

AUSTRALIA

Every Senator or Member of the House of Representatives must be a subject of the Queen, be of full age, possess electoral qualifications and have resided for 3 years within Australia. The franchise for both Houses is the same and is based on universal (males and females aged 18 years) suffrage. Compulsory voting was introduced in 1925. If a Member of a State Parliament wishes to be a candidate in a federal election, he must first resign his State seat.

Executive power is vested in the *Governor-General*, advised by an Executive Council. The Governor-General presides over the Council, and its members hold office at his pleasure. All Ministers of State, who are members of the party or parties commanding a majority in the lower House, are members of the Executive Council under summons. A record of proceedings of meetings is kept by the Secretary to the Council. At Executive Council meetings the decisions of the Cabinet are (where necessary) given legal form, appointments made, resignations accepted, proclamations, regulations and the like made.

The policy of a ministry is, in practice, determined by the Ministers of State meeting without the Governor-General under the chairmanship of the Prime Minister. This group is known as the *Cabinet*. There are 11 Standing Committees of the Cabinet comprising varying numbers of Cabinet and non-Cabinet Ministers. In Labour Governments all Ministers have been members of Cabinet; in Liberal and National Country Party Governments, only the senior ministers. Cabinet meetings are private and deliberative, and records of meetings are not made public. The Cabinet does not form part of the legal mechanisms of Government; the decisions it takes have, in themselves, no legal effect. The Cabinet substantially controls, in ordinary circumstances, not only the general legislative programme of Parliament but the whole course of Parliamentary proceedings. In effect, though not in form, the Cabinet, by reason of the fact that all Ministers are members of the Executive Council, is also the dominant element in the executive government of the country.

The legislative powers of the Federal Parliament embrace trade and commerce, shipping, etc.; taxation, finance, banking, currency, bills of exchange, bankruptcy, insurance; defence; external affairs, naturalization and aliens, quarantine, immigration and emigration; the people of any race for whom it is deemed necessary to make special laws; postal, telegraph and like services; census and statistics; weights and measures; astronomical and meteorological observations; copyrights; railways; conciliation and arbitration in disputes extending beyond the limits of any one State; social services; marriage, divorce etc.; service and execution of the civil and criminal process; recognition of the laws, Acts and records, and judicial proceedings of the States. The Senate may not originate or amend money bills. Disagreement with the House of Representatives may result in dissolution and, in the last resort, a joint sitting of the two Houses. The Federal Parliament has limited and enumerated powers, the several State parliaments retaining the residuary power of government over their respective territories. If a State law is inconsistent with a Commonwealth law, the latter prevails.

The Constitution also provides for the admission or creation of new States. Proposed laws for the alteration of the Constitution must be submitted to the electors, and they can be enacted only if approved by a majority of the States and by a majority of all the electors voting.

The Australia Acts 1986 removed residual powers of the British government to intervene in the government of Australia or the individual states.

In Feb. 1998 an Australian Constitutional Convention voted for Australia to become a republic. A national referendum was to be held in 1999.

State Government. In each of the 6 States (New South Wales, Victoria, Queensland, South Australia, Western Australia, Tasmania) there is a State government whose constitution, powers and laws continue, subject to changes embodied in the Australian Constitution and subsequent alterations and agreements, as they were before federation. The system of government is basically the same as that described above for the Commonwealth—i.e., the Sovereign, her representative (in this case a Governor), an upper and lower house of Parliament (except in Queensland, where the upper house was abolished in 1922), a cabinet led by the Premier and an Executive Council. Among the more important functions of the State governments are those relating to education, health, hospitals and charities, law, order and public safety, business undertakings such as railways and tramways, and public utilities such as water supply and sewerage. In the domains of education, hospitals, justice, the police, penal establishments, and railway and tramway operation, State government activity predominates. Care of the public health and recreative activities are shared with local government authorities and the Federal Government, social services other than those referred to above are now primarily the concern of the Federal Government; the operation of public utilities is shared with local and semi-government authorities.

Administration of Territories. Since 1911, responsibility for administration and development of the Australian Capital Territory (ACT) has been vested in Federal Ministers and Departments. The ACT became self-governing on 11 May 1989. The ACT House of Assembly has been accorded the forms of a legislature, but continues to perform an advisory function for the Minister for the Capital Territory.

On 1 July 1978 the Northern Territory of Australia became a self-governing Territory with expenditure responsibilities and revenue-raising powers broadly approximating those of a State.

National Anthem. 'Advance Australia Fair' (adopted 19 April 1984; words and tune by P. D. McCormick). The 'Royal Anthem' (i.e. 'God Save the Queen') is used in the presence of the British Royal Family.

RECENT ELECTIONS
The 39th Parliament was elected on 3 Oct. 1998.

House of Representatives: Liberal Party (LP), 64 seats and 34·1% of votes cast; Australian Labor Party (ALP), 67 (40·0%); National Party of Australia, 16 (5·3%); ind, 1.

Senate. Following elections of 3 Oct. 1998 the make-up of the Senate was: Australian Labor Party, 29; Liberal Party, 31; Australian Democratic Party, 9; National Party of Australia/Country Liberal Party, 4; Greens, 1; One Nation,1 ; Northern Territory Country Liberal Party, 1.

CURRENT ADMINISTRATION
Governor-General: Sir William Deane, AC, KBE (assumed office 16 Feb. 1996).

The *President* of the Senate is Margaret Reid.

An LP-NP coalition government was formed on 21 Oct. 1998, which in March 1999 comprised:

Prime Minister: John Winston Howard (LP).

Deputy Prime Minister and Minister for Trade: Tim Fischer (NP). *Treasurer:* Peter Costello. *Environment and Heritage, Leader of the Government in the Senate:* Robert Hill. *Communications, Information Technology and the Arts, Deputy Leader of the Government in the Senate:* Richard Alston. *Employment, Workplace Relations and Small Business, Leader of the House:* Peter Reith. *Foreign Affairs:* Alexander Downer. *Industry, Science and Resources:* Nick Minchin. *Immigration and Multicultural Affairs, Minister Assisting the Prime Minister for Reconciliation:* Kay Patterson. *Agriculture, Fisheries and Forestry:* Mark Vaile. *Defence:* John Moore. *Health and Aged Care:* Dr Michael Wooldridge. *Education, Training and Youth Affairs, Minister Assisting the Prime Minister for the Public Service:* Trish Worth. *Finance and Administration:* John Fahey. *Transport and Regional Services:* John Anderson. *Family and Community Services, Minister Assisting the Prime Minister for the Status of Women:* Jocelyn Newman. *Attorney General:* Daryl Williams AM, QC.

Outer Ministry: Assistant Treasurer: Rod Kemp. *Community Services:* Warren Truss. *Justice and Customs:* Amanda Vanstone. *Veterans' Affairs, Minister Assisting the Minister for Defence:* Bruce Scott. *Aboriginal and Torres Strait Islander Affairs:* John Herron. *Sport and Tourism, Minister assisting the Prime Minister for the Sydney 2000 Games:* Warren Entsch. *Special Minister of State:* Chris Ellison. *Regional Services, Territories and Local Government:* Ian Macdonald. *Financial Services and Regulation:* Joe Hockey. *Arts and the Centenary of Federation, Deputy Leader of the House:* Peter McGauran. *Employment Services:* Tony Abbott. *Aged Care:* Bronwyn Bishop. *Forestry and Conservation, Minister Assisting the Prime Minister:* Wilson Tuckey.

The *Speaker* is John Neil Andrew.

Leader of the Opposition: Kim C. Beazley (ALP). *Deputy Leader of the Opposition:* Simon Crean.

Local Government. The system of municipal government is broadly the same throughout Australia, although local government legislation is a State matter.

Each State is sub-divided into areas known variously as municipalities, cities, boroughs, towns, shires or district councils, totalling about 900. Within these areas the management of road, street and bridge construction, health, sanitary and garbage services, water supply and sewerage, and electric light and gas undertakings, hospitals, fire brigades, tramways and omnibus services and harbours is generally part of the functions of elected aldermen and councillors. State governments may also be responsible for some services.

In some instances, *e.g.* in New South Wales, a number of local government authorities combine to conduct a public undertaking such as the supply of water or electricity. State and territory taxation revenue was $A30,298m. in 1995–96; local governments, $A5,522m.

Howard, C., *Australia's Constitution*. Melbourne, 1985

Lucy, R., *The Australian Form of Government*. Melbourne, 1985

DEFENCE

The Minister for Defence has responsibility under legislation for the control and administration of the Defence Force. The Chief of Defence Force Staff is vested with command of the Defence Force. He is the principal military adviser to the Minister. The Secretary, Department of Defence is the Permanent Head of the Department. He is the principal civilian adviser to the Minister and has statutory responsibility for financial administration of the Defence outlay. The Chief of Defence Force Staff and the Secretary are jointly responsible for the administration of the Defence Force except with respect to matters falling within the command of the Defence Force or any other matter specified by the Minister.

The Chief of Naval Staff, the Chief of the General Staff and the Chief of the Air Staff command the Navy, Army and Air Force respectively. They have delegated authority from the Chief of Defence Force Staff and the Secretary to administer matters relating to their particular Service.

The structure of Defence is characterized by 3 organizational types: *(i)* A Central Office comprising 5 groups of functional orientated Divisions: Strategic Policy and Force Development; Supply and Support; Manpower and Financial Services; Management and Infrastructure Services; and, Defence Science and Technology; *(ii)* the 3 Armed Services of the Defence Force, each having a Service Office element in addition to the command structure; and *(iii)* a small number of outrider organizations concerned with such specialist fields as intelligence and natural disasters.

Defence Support. The Department of Defence Support purchases goods and services for defence purposes; provides technical expertise and other assistance to the defence industry; involves Australian industry in defence equipment to the maximum practical extent; administers the Australian Offsets Program so as to stimulate technological advancement and broaden the capabilities of strategic industries; within overall defence policies helps the capacity, efficiency and capability of Australian industry to design and export defence materiel; manages the Government's munitions and aircraft factories, and dockyards; markets defence and allied products and services to help maintain strategic industries.

In 1997 defence expenditure totalled US$8,501m. (US$456 per capita) and represented 2·2% of GDP.

Army. Overall organization and financial control of the Army is vested in the Chief of General Staff. The Army is organized in a Land Headquarters and a Northern Command.

The strength of the Army was 25,885, including 2,783 women, at 30 June 1997. There was 1 infantry division, 1 armoured regiment, 1 armoured reconnaissance regiment, 1 armoured personnel carrier squadron, 4 infantry battalions, 2 artillery regiments, 1 air defence regiment, 2 combat engineer regiments, 1 special forces regiment and 2 aviation regiments. Equipment included 90 Leopard 1A3 main battle tanks. The Army Aviation Corps has 4 fixed-wing transports and 120 helicopters.

The effective strength of the Army Reserve at 30 June 1997 was 25,100.

Women have been eligible for combat duties since 1993.

Navy. The Chief of Naval Staff is assisted by the Deputy Chief of Naval Staff and Assistant Chiefs for Personnel and for Materiel. The command, operation and

AUSTRALIA

administration of the Fleet is vested in the Maritime Commander, Australia headquartered at Sydney.

The fleet includes 1 new Swedish-designed Collins class and 3 UK-built Oxley class diesel submarines, 3 US-built guided missile destroyers, 1 new ANZAC class German-designed frigate, 4 US- and 2 Australian-built guided missile frigates and 1 older frigate, 6 mine countermeasure vessels, 2 ex-US landing ships being converted for helicopter operations, 5 tank landing craft and 16 inshore patrol craft. Major auxiliaries include 2 fleet replenishment tankers and 2 survey ships, and there are some 80 minor auxiliaries and service craft.

A further 5 Collins class submarines and 5 ANZAC class frigates are under construction.

The Fleet Air Arm operates a shore-based anti-submarine helicopter squadron of 7 Sea Kings and 16 S-70B Seahawk helicopters for the guided missile frigates. There are additionally 2 transport and 1 survey aircraft, and 9 transport and utility helicopters.

The fleet main base is at Sydney, with subsidiary bases at Cockburn Sound (Western Australia), Cairns and Darwin.

The all-volunteer Navy was (1997) 14,701-strong including 990 Fleet Air Arm.

Air Force. Command of the Royal Australian Air Force (RAAF) is vested in the Chief of the Air Staff (CAS) assisted by the Deputy Chief of the Air Staff, Chief of Air Force Operations and Plans, Chief of Air Force Materiel, Chief of Air Force Personnel, Chief of Air Force Technical Services, Director-General Supply—Air Force and Assistant Secretary Resources Planning.

The CAS administers and controls RAAF units through two commands: Operational Command and Support Command. Operational Command is responsible to the CAS for the command of operational units and the conduct of their operations within Australia and overseas. Support Command is responsible to the CAS for training of personnel, and the supply and maintenance of service equipment.

Flying establishment comprises 16 squadrons, of which 2 are equipped with 22 F-111 strike/reconnaissance aircraft. Of the others, 3 are equipped with missile-armed F-18 Hornet interceptors and 3 with Orion maritime reconnaissance aircraft. There are 5 transport squadrons, 2 with Hercules turboprop transports, 1 with Caribou STOL transports, 1 with Boeing 707 tanker and transport aircraft, and 1 with Falcon 900 VIP transports. There were (1997) 125 combat aircraft.

Primary training has been transferred to a civilian school. Training aircraft include Pilatus PC-9 turboprop-powered basic trainers, Aermacchi MB 326H jets for pilot training, and HS 748 aircraft for navigator training. A training unit has F-18 Hornets for crew conversion.

Training for commissioned rank is carried out at the RAAF Academy and Officers' Training School, both located at Point Cook, Victoria. Other major training activities which lead to commissioned rank include basic aircrew training, and technical and commercial cadet schemes. Basic ground training to tradesman level is conducted at RAAF technical training schools. Higher command and staff training is, in the main, carried out at the RAAF Staff College, Fairbairn, ACT.

Personnel (30 June 1997) 16,650, including 2,645 women. There is also an Australian Air Force Reserve, 4,400-strong.

INTERNATIONAL RELATIONS

Australia is a member of the UN, the Commonwealth, OECD, Colombo Plan, the South Pacific Forum and the Pacific Community.

ECONOMY

Policy. Since 1942 the Federal Government alone has levied taxes on incomes. In return for vacating this field of taxation, the State Governments are reimbursed by grants from the Federal Government out of revenue received. Payments to the States represent about one-third of Federal Government outlays, and in turn the payments State Governments receive from the Federal Government account for nearly half of their revenues.

The Financial Agreement of 1927 established the Australian Loan Council which represents the Federal and six State Governments, and co-ordinates domestic and overseas borrowings by these governments, including annual borrowing programmes. The Federal Government acts as a central borrowing agency in raising loans to finance the major part of those programmes. The Loan Council in 1984 agreed upon arrangements for the co-ordination of borrowings by semi-government and local authorities, and government-owned companies.

Reforms were initiated at a special Premiers' Conference in Oct. 1990 to form a partnership between the Commonwealth, States, Territories and local government, with a view to improving national efficiency and international competitiveness, and enhancing delivery and quality of government services. In July 1991 the premiers agreed a programme of inter-state standardization and integration in such areas as the railway system, electricity grid, product control and professional qualifications.

Performance. There was strong growth of real domestic demand, 6%, in 1997–98, the seventh year of the current upswing. GDP was $A529,408m. for 1997 ($A433,688m. in 1995–96) with GDP growth of 4·0% in 1997–98. Over the past 7 years, real GDP expanded at an annual rate of 3·5% while inflation was brought down and kept low; this makes the Australian economy's performance one of the best in the OECD area.

Budget. In 1929, under a financial agreement between the Federal Government and States, approved by a referendum, the Federal Government took over all State debts existing on 30 June 1927 and agreed to pay $A15·17m. a year for 58 years towards the interest charges thereon, and to make substantial contributions towards a sinking fund on State debt. The Sinking Fund arrangements were revised under an amendment to the agreement in 1976.

In Aug. 1998, the Commonwealth Government introduced a tax reform package which is intended to come into effect in July 2000. The package includes: the introduction of a General Savings Tax (GST) at a 10% rate, with all the revenues going to states provided that they agree to abolish a range of other indirect taxes; the abolition of Financial Assistance Grants to states; the abolition of wholesale sales tax (which is levied by the Commonwealth Government); cuts in personal income tax; and increases in social security benefits, especially for families. In all, the package reduces the budget surpluses of the Commonwealth and States in the financial year 2000–01 by $A4·8bn. (0·7% of GDP) and $A0·7bn. (0·1% of GDP), respectively.

Outlays and revenue of the Commonwealth Government for years ending 30 June (in $A1m.):

	1994–95	1995–96	1996–97[1]
Total outlays	121,877	126,694	129,686
including			
Defence	9,795	10,011	10,027
Education	10,093	10,590	11,064
Health	17,134	18,583	19,408
Social security and welfare	43,302	46,744	48,897
Housing	1,116	1,201	1,122
Culture and recreation	1,263	1,425	1,390
Economic services	8,505	8,661	7,767
Public services	7,713	7,796	8,689
Payments to States, NT and local government	15,074	13,798	16,797
Public debt interest	8,005	9,135	9,781
Total revenue	110,247	121,649	130,160
including			
Customs duty	3,474	3,124	3,010
Excise duty	12,001	12,849	13,360
Sales tax	11,624	12,955	13,890
PAYE income tax	50,928	56,442	61,470
Other individual tax	9,178	10,078	10,930
Prescribed payments	2,169	2,179	2,340
Company tax	15,588	18,252	19,700
Superannuation	1,913	1,634	1,800
Withholding tax	903	1,349	1,170
Fringe benefits tax	2,740	3,031	3,180
Interest, rent and dividends	...	5,254	5,132

[1]Estimate.

Currency. On 14 Feb. 1966 Australia adopted a system of decimal currency. The currency unit, the Australian dollar (AUD), is divided into 100 *cents*.

Foreign exchange reserves were US$15,627m. in Feb. 1998 and gold reserves 2·56m. troy oz. Total money supply was A$105,781m. in Feb. 1998.

Underlying inflation is projected to pick up from an estimated 1·75% in 1999 to a little over 3% in 2000.

Banking and Finance. The banking system comprises:

(a) The Reserve Bank of Australia is the central bank. It is responsible for the objectives of monetary policy, overall financial system stability and regulation of the payments system. It is also banker to the Commonwealth Government and several state governments. A wholly owned subsidiary of the Reserve Bank (Note Printing Australia) manufactures Australia's currency notes and other security products. The *Governor* is a statutory appointee (present incumbent, Ian Macfarlane, appointed 1996 for a 7-year term). Within the Reserve Bank there are two Boards: the Reserve Bank of Australia Board and the Payments System Board; the Governor is the Chairman of each.

As at 30 June 1998, total assets of the Reserve Bank of Australia were $A47,310m., including gold, $A1,237m., foreign exchange, $A24,197m. and domestic government securities, $A21,012m. Main liability items were capital and reserves, $A9,829m.; Australian notes on issue, $A21,651m.; and deposits, $A11,073m. Responsibilities derive principally from the Reserve Bank Act 1959 and Banking Act 1959.

Inflation rate for year ended June 1998 (Consumer Price Index—All Groups) was +0·7%.

(b) 4 major banks: (i) The Commonwealth Bank of Australia; (ii) The Australia and New Zealand Banking Group Ltd; (iii) Westpac Banking Corporation; (iv) National Australia Bank.

(c) Other banks: (i) 3 State Government banks—The State Bank of New South Wales, The State Bank of South Australia, and the Rural and Industries Bank of Western Australia; (ii) one joint stock bank—The Bank of Queensland Ltd, formerly The Brisbane Permanent Building and Banking Co. Ltd, which has specialized business in one district only; (iii) The Australian Bank Ltd; (iv) branches of 17 overseas banks—the restrictions on foreign banks operating in Australia, and on foreign investment in the merchant banks, were lifted in 1984-85.

(d) The Commonwealth Development Bank of Australia commenced operations on 14 Jan. 1960. Its function is to provide finance for primary production and small business.

(e) The Australian Resources Development Bank Ltd opened on 29 March 1968 to assist Australian enterprises in developing Australia's natural resources, through direct loans and equity investment or by re-financing loans made by trading banks. The bank is jointly owned by the 4 major Australian trading banks.

(f) The Primary Industry Bank of Australia Ltd commenced operations on 22 Sept. 1978. The equity capital of the bank consists of eight shares. Seven shares are held by the Australian Government and the major trading banks while the eighth share is held equally by the 4 State banks. The main objective of the bank is to facilitate the provision of loans to primary producers on longer terms than are otherwise generally available. The role of the bank is restricted to re-financing loans made by banks and other financial institutions.

(g) The Banking Legislation Amendment Act of 1989 removed the legislative differences between savings and trading banks. In June 1995 there were 49 authorized banks under 44 banking groups. In June 1995 there were 6,655 branches and 5,897 agencies.

Total deposits in Oct. 1996 were $A295,940m. (including $A8,380m. of non-residents' deposits).

(h) In March 1992 there were 45 building societies. Assets were $A10,576m. at 30 June 1997. Building societies are permitted to have up to 50% of their assets in non-home loans.

There is an Australian Stock Exchange (ASX).

Weights and Measures. The metric system is in use.

ENERGY AND NATURAL RESOURCES

Electricity. Electricity supply is the responsibility of the State governments. At 30 June 1994 total installed capacity was 37·3m. kW. Production 1996–97, 168,370m. kWh (11% hydro-electric). Total consumption at 30 June 1996 was an estimated 144·3m. kWh.

Oil and Gas. The main fields are Gippsland (Vic.) and Carnarvon (WA). Crude oil production was 30,763m. litres in 1995-96; natural gas, 29,985m. cu. metres.

Minerals. Australia is the world's largest producer of bauxite (39% of total world production) and diamonds (38%). Coal is Australia's major source of energy. Reserves are large (1996 estimate: 68,000m. tonnes) and easily worked. The main fields are in New South Wales and Queensland. Production in 1995-96 was 195·5m. tonnes. Brown coal (lignite) reserves are mainly in Victoria and were estimated at 41,700m. tonnes in 1990. Production, 1995-96 was 54·3m. tonnes.

Production of other major minerals in 1995-96 (1,000 tonnes): Bauxite, 50,724; copper concentrate, 1,297; iron ore, 137,267; manganese ore, 1,298; uranium concentrate, 3,200 tonnes; gold bullion, 291,965 kg.

Agriculture. At 31 March 1996 there were 143,202 establishments mainly engaged in farming. Agricultural land in 1997 covered an estimated 471·1m. ha, representing about 60% of total land area with 19·41m. ha sown to crops. The most important are (1995-96): wheat (16·5m. tonnes from 9·22m. ha); sugar-cane (35·89m. tonnes from 0·38m. ha); barley (5·8m. tonnes from 3·1m. ha); oats (1·88m. tonnes from 1·14m. ha); rice (0·97m. tonnes from 0·14m. ha). In 1995-96, 782,566 tonnes of grapes were harvested from 64,858 ha of vines.

Gross value of agricultural production in 1995-96, $A27,451·9m., including (in $A1m.): Crops, 15,396·7; livestock slaughtering, 6,192·7; wool, 2,548·5; other livestock products, 3,302·9.

Livestock (in 1,000) in 1996:

	NSW	Vic.	Qld	SA	WA	Tas.	NT	ACT	Australia
Cattle	6,390	4,396	10,214	1,219	1,924	718	1,503	13	26,377
Sheep	41,100	22,000	10,700	13,600	29,800	3,900	...	...	121,100
Pigs	710	458	603	412	314	26	...	...	2,526[1]

[1]Includes Northern Territory and ACT

Total poultry, 1996: 71,028,000.

In 1996 Australia was overtaken by China as the country with the greatest number of sheep.

Livestock products (in 1,000 tonnes) for the year ending 30 June 1996: Beef, 1,711; veal, 34; lamb and mutton, 575; pigmeat, 334; poultry meat, 516; wool, 726; milk, 8,716m. litres.

Williams, D. B. (ed.) *Agriculture in the Australian Economy*. 3rd ed. Sydney Univ. Press and OUP, 1991

Forestry. The Federal Government is responsible for forestry at the national level. Each State is responsible for the management of publicly owned forests. Total native forest cover was 155·84m. ha at 30 June 1997, made up of (in 1,000 ha): Public forest, 112,631, privately owned, 42,018. The major part of wood supplies derives from coniferous plantations, of which there were 883,840 ha in 1995. Production was 3·43m. cu. metres of sawn timber and 986,000 tonnes of wood pulp in 1995–96.

Fisheries. The Australian Fishing Zone covers an area 16% larger than the Australian land mass and is the third largest fishing zone in the world, but fish production is insignificant by world standards due to low productivity of the oceans. The major commercially exploited species are prawns, rock lobster, abalone, tuna, other fin fish, scallops, oysters and pearls. Total catch in 1996 came to 214,205 tonnes, mainly from marine waters.

INDUSTRY

Manufacturing industries at 30 June 1996: Persons employed, 923,100; salaries paid, $A29,902m.; turnover, $A197,963m. (excludes small single-establishment enterprises employing fewer than 4 persons).

Manufacturing by sector, 1995-96:

	Persons Employed	Salaries in $A1m.	Turnover in $A1m.
Food, beverages and tobacco	162,700	5,175	43,067
Textiles, clothing, footwear and leather products	75,900	1,857	9,832
Wood and paper products	60,400	1,858	11,446
Printing, publishing and recording media	90,800	3,073	13,675
Chemical, petroleum, coal and associated products	89,500	3,383	30,058
Non-metallic mineral products	37,700	1,315	8,599
Metal products	147,700	5,206	36,918
Machinery and equipment	204,700	6,766	38,704
Other manufacturing	53,700	1,269	5,664

Manufactured products in 1995–96 included: Bricks, 1,468m.; portland cement, 6·7m. tonnes; ready-mixed concrete, 15·4m. sq. metres; confectionery, 181,059 tonnes; electric motors, 2·7m.; washing machines, 268,000; refrigerators, 398,000; pig iron, 7·3m. tonnes; tobacco and cigarettes, 22,192 tonnes; woven fabric, 209·1m. sq. metres; woollen yarn, 18,284 tonnes; motor cars, 304,000; beer, 1,735m. litres.

Labour. In June 1997 the total workforce (persons aged 15 and over) numbered 9,185,600, of whom 8·4m. (3,623,900 females) were employed. Since 1992-93, employment has increased by over 11%. In Sept. 1997 there were 8,415,400 employed persons and the unemployment rate was 8·6%. In 1996-97 the labour force included 354,100 employers, 6,676,500 wage and salary earners and 821,300 self-employed. The majority of wage and salary earners have had their minimum wages and conditions of work prescribed in awards by the Industrial Relations Commission, which in April 1991 awarded a 2·5% rise, making the minimum weekly wage about $A442, but in Oct. 1991 the Commission decided to allow direct employer-employee wage bargaining, provided agreements reached are endorsed by the Commission. In some States, some conditions of work (e.g., weekly hours of work, leave) are set down in State legislation. Average weekly wage, May 1997, $A577·50 (men, $A686·30; women, $A457·40). Average working week, 1996-97: 35·8 hours. 4 weeks annual leave is standard.

Employees in all States are covered by workers' compensation legislation and by certain industrial award provisions relating to work injuries.

During 1996 there were 543 industrial disputes in progress which accounted for 928,500 working days lost. In these disputes 577,700 workers were involved.

The following table shows the distribution of employed persons by industry in 1996-97, by sex and average weekly hours worked:

Industry	Numbers (in 1,000)		Hours worked	
	Persons	(Females)	Per person	(Females)
Agriculture, forestry, fishing	427·0	(130·1)	43·2	(30·3)
Mining	86·7	(10·8)	42·8	(35·5)
Manufacturing	1,129·8	(298·8)	38·6	(32·9)
Electricity, gas and water supply	66·7	(10·1)	36·8	(34·2)
Construction	586·8	(80·1)	38·4	(21·6)
Wholesale trade	492·5	(151·0)	38·7	(32·1)
Retail trade	1,237·7	(628·1)	31·4	(25·3)
Transport and storage	393·3	(91·1)	39·8	(32·0)
Property and business services	827·5	(371·8)	37·0	(30·9)
Education	581·9	(381·2)	34·4	(32·0)
Cultural and recreation services	192·5	(95·9)	32·3	(27·9)
Accommodation, cafés and restaurants	399·1	(226·6)	32·5	(28·1)
Communication	163·0	(52·2)	36·7	(31·3)
Finance and insurance	316·8	(177·3)	36·3	(32·0)
Government administration and defence	369·1	(159·6)	34·7	(31·8)
Health and community services	771·6	(596·7)	30·7	(28·4)
Personal and other services	317·4	(155·2)	33·7	(29·4)
Totals	8,362·9	(3,616·3)	35·8	(29·4)

AUSTRALIA

In Feb. 1997, 1,457,700 wage and salary earners worked in the public sector and 5,307,300 in the private sector.

The following table shows the distribution of employed persons in 1994 according to the *Australian Standard Classification of Occupations (2nd edition)*:

Occupation	Employed persons (in 1,000) Persons	(Females)
Managers and administrators	682·2	(149·8)
Professionals	1,413·6	(695·1)
Associate professionals	889·3	(328·2)
Tradespersons	1,149·1	(106·9)
Advanced clerical and service workers	390·9	(352·6)
Intermediate clerical, sales and service workers	1,397·2	(1,000·3)
Labourers and related workers	842·9	(315·5)
Intermediate production and transport workers	788·5	(107·4)
Elementary clerical, sales and service workers	863·6	(560·7)
	8,362·9	(3,616·3)

In June 1997, 796,500 persons (8·8% of the labour force) were unemployed, (including 334,300 females) of whom 403,800 persons were seeking full-time work. In June 1997, 233,100 persons had been unemployed for more than one year. In Aug. 1997 there were 63,900 job vacancies.

Trade Unions. In June 1996 there were 132 trade unions with 2,800,500 members. About 37·4% of wage and salary earners (35·5% females) were estimated to be members of unions. There were 62 unions with fewer than 1,000 members and 15 unions with 50,000 or more members. Many of the larger trade unions are affiliated with central labour organizations, the oldest and by far the largest being the Australian Council of Trade Unions formed in 1927. In July 1992 the Industrial Relations Legislation Amendment Act freed the way for employers and employees to negotiate enterprise-based awards and agreements.

INTERNATIONAL TRADE

In 1990 Australia and New Zealand completed a Closer Economic Relations agreement (initiated in 1983) which establishes free trade in goods. Net foreign debt was $A203·7m. as at 30 June 1997. The effect of the Asian meltdown on exports became apparent towards the end of 1997. But in 1998 shipments of commodities and exports of manufactures and some services were increasingly redirected to other destinations, notably the USA and Europe. As a result, the volume of exported goods and services increased by 4·25%, well below the 10% increase of the year before.

Imports and Exports. Merchandise imports and exports for years ending 30 June (in $A1m.):

	Imports	Exports
1993–94	64,470	64,574
1994–95	74,634	67,063
1995–96	77,792	76,043
1996–97	78,977	78,885

The Australian customs tariff provides for preferences to goods produced in and shipped from certain countries as a result of reciprocal trade agreements. These include the UK, New Zealand, Canada and Ireland.

Merchandise exports and imports, 1996-97 (in $A1m.):

	Exports	Imports
Live animals	704	103
Meat and preparations	2,952	67
Dairy goods and eggs	1,759	195
Fish, shellfish and their preparations	1,087	604
Cereals and preparations	5,952	178
Vegetables and fruit	1,142	588
Sugar and honey	1,695	85
Coffee, tea, cocoa, spices and their manufactures	190	502
Animal feed (excl. unmilled cereal)	530	122
Miscellaneous edible products	282	543

AUSTRALIA

	Exports	Imports
Beverages	712	351
Tobacco and manufactures	67	152
Raw hides and skins	504	2
Oil seeds and oleaginous fruit	201	95
Crude rubber (incl. synthetic and reclaimed)	10	136
Cork and wood	616	430
Pulp and waste paper	13	136
Textile fibres and their wastes	4,605	151
Crude fertilizers, minerals (not coal, petroleum, gems)	377	140
Metal ores and scrap	9,025	174
Crude animal and vegetable materials	219	223
Coal, coke and briquettes	8,006	11
Petroleum and products	3,805	5,047
Gas, natural and manufactured	1,895	97
Animal oils and fats	184	8
Fixed vegetable oils and fats	10	235
Processed oils and fats, waxes thereof	38	23
Organic chemicals	116	2,040
Inorganic chemicals	317	700
Dyeing, colouring and tanning materials	407	408
Medicinal and pharmaceutical products	978	1,996
Essential oils, perfume and cleansing preparations	295	636
Manufactured fertilizers	24	706
Plastics in primary forms	296	854
Plastics in non-primary forms	154	720
Chemical materials and products	452	969
Leather and manufactures, dressed furskins	469	162
Rubber manufactures	149	1,115
Cork and wood manufactures (not furniture)	102	333
Paper, board and pulp	392	1,770
Textile yarn, fabrics, made-up articles and related products	577	2,284
Non-metallic mineral goods	714	1,245
Iron and steel	1,618	1,296
Non-ferrous metals	4,433	613
Metal manufactures	804	1,908
Power generators	917	1,896
Special machinery, industrial	1,155	4,044
Metalworking machinery	205	609
General machinery and parts, industrial	1,189	4,649
Office machines and data-processing equipment	1,616	5,983
Telecommunications and sound equipment	628	3,669
Electrical machinery and parts	1,292	4,914
Road vehicles (inc. air-cushion vehicles)	1,828	8,579
Other transport equipment	1,805	2,441
Sanitary, plumbing, heating and lighting fittings, pre-fabricated buildings	84	234
Furniture and parts	96	532
Travel goods, handbags etc.	15	339
Clothing and accessories	353	1,842
Footwear	65	623
Professional, scientific and controlling instruments	629	1,944
Photographic and optical goods, watches and clocks	578	1,252
Miscellaneous manufactured articles	1,013	4,588
Other commodities and transactions	513	32
Gold and other coin	116	9
Non-monetary gold	4,717	561
Confidential items	1,194	80
Total trade	78,885	78,977

AUSTRALIA

Trade by bloc or country in 1996–97 (in $A1m.):

	Exports	Imports
APEC	59,239	52,190
ASEAN	12,235	8,301
EU	8,163	19,669
OPEC	5,780	3,828
China	3,581	4,205
Japan	15,373	10,242
South Korea	7,129	2,521
New Zealand	6,177	3,686
Singapore	3,396	2,620
Taiwan	3,620	2,522
Indonesia	3,308	1,858
Malaysia	2,325	1,892
Germany	1,057	4,558
UK	2,354	5,182
USA	5,517	17,649

COMMUNICATIONS

Roads. There are 803,075 km of roads (18,700 km of National Highways).

At 31 May 1995, 8,628,800 cars, 2,022,100 vans, trucks and buses, and 296,600 motor cycles were registered. New registrations, 1996–97, included 557,962 cars, 663,852 vans, trucks and buses, and 22,842 motor cycles.

In 1996, 1,942 persons were killed in road accidents (2,014 in 1995).

Rail. There are 7 government-owned railway systems. In 1991 the National Rail Corporation was set up to market inter-state freight service. Statistics for the year ended 30 June 1996:

State	Route length in km[4]	Passenger journeys, 1,000[5]	Goods carried, (1,000 tonnes)	Freight earnings, ($A1,000)
New South Wales	7,451	258,800	63,800	810,500
Victoria	4,872	116,256	6,877	121,210
Queensland	9,442	40,068	96,120	1,297,000
South Australia[3]	120	8,273	...	...
Western Australia	5,369	23,286	31,081	254,704
Australian National[1,2]	6,118	244	7,905	73,578
National Rail	...	...	9,941	475,747
	33,372	446,927	215,724	3,032,739

[1]The Australian National Railways operates services of the former Commonwealth Railways, the non-metropolitan South Australian Railways and the Tasmanian Railways.
[2]Excludes Adelaide metropolitan rail passenger services and the Tasmanian Region.
[3]The South Australian State Transport Authority operates services in the Adelaide metropolitan area.
[4]*Source: Australasia Railway Association, Inc.*
[5]Inter-system traffic is included in the total for each system over which it passes.

The State railway gauges are: New South Wales, 1,435 mm; Victoria, 1,600 mm (325 km, 1,435 mm); Queensland, 1,067 mm (111 km, 1,435 mm); South Australia, 1,600 mm for 2,533 km plus 1,435 mm for 1,824 km and the rest 1,067 mm; West Australia, 137 km, 1,435 mm and the rest 1,067 mm, and Tasmania, 1,067 mm. Australian National Railways comprises 3,530 km of 1,435 mm ('standard') gauge, 1,173 km of 1,600 mm ('broad') gauge and 1,532 km of 1,067 mm ('narrow') gauge routes. Under various Commonwealth–State standardization agreements, all the State capitals are now linked by standard gauge track (except Darwin—the Central Australia railway extends only as far north as Alice Springs).

The National Rail Corporation operating as 'National Rail' was incorporated in Sept. 1991; terminal operations commenced in 1993. It is scheduled to take over inter-state rail freight operations and the ownership of rail assets.

There are also private industrial and tourist railways, and tramways in Adelaide, Melbourne and Sydney.

AUSTRALIA

Civil Aviation. Qantas Airways is Australia's international airline. In 1992 Qantas merged with Australian Airlines, and in 1993, 25% of the company was purchased by British Airways. The remainder is government-owned. Ansett Australia is the second largest airline after Qantas. There are 12 international airports, the main ones being Adelaide, Brisbane, Cairns, Darwin, Melbourne, Perth and Sydney. In 1998 services were also provided by Aerolíneas Argentinas, Air Calédonie International, Air China, Air Facilities, Air Mauritius, Air Nauru, Air New Zealand, Air Niugini, Air Pacific, Air Vanuatu, Air Zimbabwe, Airlines of South Australia, Airnorth Regional, Alitalia, All Nippon Airways, American Airlines, AOM French Airlines, Asiana Airlines, British Airways, Canadian Airlines International, Cathay Pacific Airways, China Eastern Airlines, Continental Airlines, Country Connection Airlines, Eastland Air, Egyptair, Emirates, EVA Airways, Flight West Airlines, Garuda Indonesia, Gulf Air, Hazelton Airlines, Impulse Airlines, International Aviation, JAL, Kendell Airlines, KLM, Korean Air, Lauda Air, Lufthansa, Macair, Malaysia Airlines, Mandarin Airlines, MBA Pty Ltd, Merpati Nusantara Airlines, National Jet, O'Connor-Mount Gambier Airline, Olympic Airways, Par Avion, Philippine Airlines, Polynesian, Royal Brunei Airlines, Royal Tongan Airlines, Rottnest Airlines, Shepparton Airlines, Singapore Airlines, Skywest Airlines, Solomon Airlines, South African Airways, Tamair, Thai Airways International, Transtate Airlines, United Airlines, Vietnam Airlines, Virgin Atlantic, Western Airlines, Whyalla Airlines and Yanda Airlines.

Sydney (Kingsford Smith) handles most passengers (20,337,000 in 1996), followed by Melbourne International (13,104,000 in 1996) and Brisbane (9,578,000 in 1996).

Internal airlines carried 21,465,300 passengers in 1993–94 and 217,900 tonnes of freight. Domestic airlines were deregulated in Oct. 1990.

At 30 June 1994 there were 400 Commonwealth or licensed aerodromes in Australia and its Territories. At 14 Dec. 1995, 9,633 aircraft were registered in Australia.

Shipping. The chief ports are Sydney, Newcastle, Port Kembla; Melbourne, Geelong, Westernport; Hay Point, Gladstone, Brisbane; Port Hedland, Dampier, Port Walcott, Fremantle. At 30 June 1996 the trading fleet comprised 82 vessels totalling 3,303,294 DWT, 2,267,719 GRT.

Coastal cargo handled at Australian ports in 1994–95 (in gross weight tonnes): Loaded, 49,190,000; unloaded, 50,466,000.

Telecommunications. Complete deregulation of the Australian telecommunications market occurred on 1 July 1997. The market is supervized by an independent regulatory authority, the Australian Telecommunications Authority (AUSTEL). Internal telecommunications used to be operated by Telecom Australia, while services to other countries were operated by the Overseas Telecommunications Corporation. In 1991 these merged to form Telstra, a general carrier providing both domestic and international services in competition with other licensed general carriers. Telstra was partly privatized in 1997, in the most successful flotation in Australia's history. In Sept. 1997 there were 12 licenced carriers operating under the Telecommunications Act 1997. Under this Act, carriers must have been able to provide digital data capability to at least 96% of the population by 31 Dec. 1998.

Telephone main lines numbered 9,350,000 in 1997 (504·5 per 1,000 inhabitants). Subscribers to digital mobile services increased from 309,000 in 1994-95 to 2,246,000 in 1996-97.

Three telecommunications satellites are in orbit covering the entire continent.

Nearly 4·2m. people accessed the Internet in the 12 months to Aug. 1998. In 1995, 4,979,000 PCs were in use, or 276 per 1,000 persons. There were 475,000 fax machines in use in 1995.

Postal Services. Postal services are operated by Australia Post, operating under the Australian Postal Corporation Act, 1989 as a government business enterprise. Revenue was $A3,109·7m. in 1996–97, expenditure $A2,763·1m. There were 4,468 post offices and other agencies in 1997, and 4,205·7m. postal items were handled.

SOCIAL INSTITUTIONS

Justice. The judicial power of the Commonwealth of Australia is vested in the High Court of Australia (the Federal Supreme Court), in the Federal courts created by the Federal Parliament (the Federal Court of Australia and the Family Court of Australia) and in the State courts invested by Parliament with Federal jurisdiction.

High Court. The High Court consists of a Chief Justice and 6 other Justices, appointed by the Governor-General in Council. The Constitution confers on the High Court original jurisdiction, *inter alia*, in all matters arising under treaties or affecting consuls or other foreign representatives, matters between the States of the Commonwealth, matters to which the Commonwealth is a party and matters between residents of different States. Federal Parliament may make laws conferring original jurisdiction on the High Court, *inter alia*, in matters arising under the Constitution or under any laws made by the Parliament. It has in fact conferred jurisdiction on the High Court in matters arising under the Constitution and in matters arising under certain laws made by Parliament.

The High Court may hear and determine appeals from its own Justices exercising original jurisdiction, from any other Federal Court, from a Court exercising Federal jurisdiction and from the Supreme Courts of the States. It also has jurisdiction to hear and determine appeals from the Supreme Courts of the Territories. The right of appeal from the High Court to the Privy Council in London was abolished in 1986.

Other Federal Courts. Since 1924, 4 other Federal courts have been created to exercise special Federal jurisdiction, i.e. the Federal Court of Australia, the Family Court of Australia, the Australian Industrial Court and the Federal Court of Bankruptcy. The Federal Court of Australia was created by the Federal Court of Australia Act 1976 and began to exercise jurisdiction on 1 Feb. 1977. It exercises such original jurisdiction as is invested in it by laws made by the Federal Parliament including jurisdiction formerly exercised by the Australian Industrial Court and the Federal Court of Bankruptcy, and in some matters previously invested in either the High Court or State and Territory Supreme Courts. The Federal Court also acts as a court of appeal from State and Territory courts in relation to Federal matters. Appeal from the Federal Court to the High Court will be by way of special leave only. The State Supreme Courts have also been invested with Federal jurisdiction in bankruptcy.

State Courts. The general Federal jurisdiction of the State courts extends, subject to certain restrictions and exceptions, to all matters in which the High Court has jurisdiction or in which jurisdiction may be conferred upon it.

Industrial Tribunals. The chief federal industrial tribunal is the Australian Conciliation and Arbitration Commission, constituted by presidential members (with the status of judges) and commissioners. The Commission's functions include settling industrial disputes, making awards, determining the standard hours of work and wage fixation. Questions of law, the judicial interpretation of awards and imposition of penalties in relation to industrial matters are dealt with by the Industrial Division of the Federal Court.

In March 1997 the prison population averaged 16,871.

Total police force personnel at 1 July 1997: 42,092.

Religion. Under the Constitution the Commonwealth cannot make any law to establish any religion, to impose any religious observance or to prohibit the free exercise of any religion. The following percentages refer to those religions with the largest number of adherents at the census of 1996. The census question on religious adherence was not obligatory, however.

Christian, 71% of population: Catholic, 27·0%; Anglican, 22·0%; Uniting Church, 7·5%; Presbyterian and Reformed, 3·8%; Orthodox, 2·8%; Baptist, 1·7%; Lutheran, 1·4%; Pentecostal, 1·0%; Churches of Christ, 0·4%; Jehovah's Witnesses, 0·5%; Salvation Army, 0·4%; other Christian, 2·4%. Religions other than Christian 3·4%; no religion, 16·6%; no statement, 9·0%.

The Anglican Synod voted for the ordination of 10 women in Nov. 1992.

Thompson, R. C., *Religion in Australia, a History.* OUP, 1995

Education. The Governments of the Australian States and the Northern Territory have the major responsibility for education, including the administration and substantial funding of primary, secondary, and technical and further education. In most States, a single Education Department is responsible for these three levels, but in New South Wales and South Australia there is a separate department responsible solely for technical and further education, and in Victoria, a Technical and Further Education Board. Furthermore, in New South Wales an Education Commission advises the Minister on primary, secondary and post-secondary education.

The Australian Government is responsible for education in Norfolk Island, Christmas Island and the Cocos (Keeling) Islands. It also provides supplementary finance to the States and is responsible for the total funding of universities and colleges of advanced education. It has special responsibilities for student assistance, education programmes for Aboriginal people and children from non-English-speaking backgrounds, and for international relations in education.

The Australian Constitution empowers the Federal Government to make grants to the States and to place conditions upon such grants. The National Board of Employment, Education and Training was established in 1988 to advise the Federal Government on the financial needs of educational institutions. It is assisted by 4 councils: The Schools Council, the Higher Education Council, the Employment and Skills Formation Council, and the Australian Research Council.

The Commonwealth has been working with the states to develop a national perspective for schools and a common curriculum. The Curriculum Corporation has been established under the auspices of the Australian Education Council.

School attendance is compulsory between the ages of 6 and 15 years (16 years in Tasmania), at either a government school or a recognized non-government educational institution. Many children attend pre-schools for a year before entering school (usually in sessions of 2-3 hours, for 2-5 days per week). Government schools are usually co-educational and comprehensive. Non-government schools have been traditionally single-sex, particularly in secondary schools, but there is a trend towards co-education. Tuition is free at government schools, but fees are normally charged at non-government schools.

Primary and secondary schools at Aug. 1996:

	Schools		Teachers[1]		Pupils[2]	
	Govern-ment	Non-govern-ment	Govern-ment schools	Non-govern-ment schools	Govern-ment schools	Non-govern-ment schools
States and Territories						
New South Wales	2,186	867	49,202	19,892	760,078	305,269
Victoria	1,700	679	34,045	17,295	517,062	259,393
Queensland	1,314	410	25,898	9,876	411,686	155,448
South Australia[3]	660	193	12,053	4,172	178,471	66,321
Western Australia[4]	704	276	14,335	5,649	226,075	85,007
Tasmania	226	69	4,206	1,389	62,776	21,406
Northern Territory[4]	144	29	2,089	551	28,294	8,172
ACT[4]	98	42	2,738	1,281	40,031	21,708

[1]Full-time teachers plus the full-time equivalent of part-time teaching.
[2]Full-time pupils only. [3]1995 totals. [4]1997 totals.

In post-secondary education, tuition fees were abolished in 1974 and student allowances are provided for full-time students subject to a means test. Universities are autonomous institutions. From 1 Jan. 1989 the university and college of advanced education sectors were merged by the Federal Government. The resulting institutions are self-governing, though funded by the Federal Government. A private university sector is developing (e.g. Notre Dame University in Western Australia and Bond University in Queensland). The major part of technical and further education is provided in government-administered technical and further education institutions (TAFE).

In 1996 there were 36 universities in the Unified National System which receive Commonwealth funding. These operate under state legislation. Outside this system, the Australian National University, Canberra University and the Australian Maritime College receive Commonwealth funding on a contract basis. There were 634,094 university students in 1996. Academic students by university within each State or Territory (1996): NSW: Sydney, 30,369; New South Wales, 27,348; New England, 16,433; Newcastle, 17,407; Macquarie, 17,827; Wollongong, 12,081; Southern Cross, 8,612; Sydney University of Technology, 21,397; Western Sydney, 24,997;

AUSTRALIA

Charles Sturt, 20,123; Vic.: Melbourne, 31,499; Monash, 39,516; La Trobe, 20,975; Deakin, 28,232; Ballarat, 4,166; Victoria University of Technology, 14,290; Swinburne University of Technology, 9,775; Royal Melbourne Institute of Technology, 26,499; Qld.: Queensland, 26,407; James Cook, 7,951; Griffith, 19,542; Queensland University of Technology, 28,855; Central Queensland, 10,080; Southern Queensland, 15,340; SA: Adelaide, 14,000; Flinders, (1998) 11,850; South Australia, 24,156; WA: Western Australia, 13,132; Curtin University of Technology, 21,240; Edith Cowan, 18,458; Murdoch, 8,524; Tas.: Tasmania, 12,611; NT: Northern Territory, 4,203; ACT: Canberra, 8,541; Australian National, 9,925; Australian Catholic University, (1997) 648.

Teacher education usually takes place in colleges of advanced education, though a substantial number of secondary teachers and a few primary teachers receive their pre-service education in a university.

The Australian Government provides assistance for students. The Assistance for Isolated Children Scheme provides special support to families whose children are isolated from schooling or are handicapped. AUSTUDY is a means-tested scheme to assist students aged 16 years and over enrolled for full-time study in approved courses at secondary and post-secondary institutions. Allowances are also available for postgraduate study and overseas study. Aboriginal students are eligible for assistance under the ABSTUDY scheme. Federal government expenditure on these schemes was $A1,602m. in 1994. In addition, under the Higher Education Contribution Scheme, students may be funded by a government loan repaid interest-free later through the tax system. The Federal Government introduced a supplementary loans scheme for eligible students in 1993. The States also offer various schemes of assistance, principally at the primary and secondary levels.

National bodies with a co-ordinating, planning or funding role include: the Australian Education Council, comprising the Federal and State Ministers of Education, the Conference of Directors-General of Education, the Australian Council for Educational Research and advisory bodies, the National Aboriginal Education Committee, and the Vocational Education Employment and Training Advisory Committee.

Total government expenditure on education (public and private sectors) in 1995–96 was $A23,778m. (4·9% of GDP).

Health. In 1995–96 there were 45,800 physicians, 9,100 dentists, 160,500 nurses, 705 public acute hospitals and 1,104 hospitals (general); there were an average 4·5 hospital beds per 1,000 population. The Royal Flying Doctor Service serves remote areas. Total government expenditure on health services (public and private sectors) in 1995-96 was $A41,742m. ($A2,300 per person), representing 8·5% of GDP and 24·9% of total government expenditure.

Welfare. All Commonwealth Government social security pensions, benefits and allowances are financed from the Commonwealth Government's general revenue. In addition, assistance is provided for welfare services.

Expenditure on social security and welfare, 1995–96, $A49,534m., representing 29·3% of total government outlays.

The following summarizes the conditions of the major benefits:

Age and Disability Pensions—age pensions are payable to men 65 years of age or more and women 60 years and 6 months of age or more who have lived in Australia for a specified period and, unless permanently blind, also satisfy an income test. Persons over 16 years of age who are permanently blind or permanently incapacitated for work to the extent of at least 85% may receive an invalid pension. Invalid pension is paid subject to a residence qualification, income and assets test, unless the person is permanently blind. Additional amounts are paid to pensioners with dependent children. Supplementary assistance may be paid to a pensioner paying rent or private lodging subject to an income test. Remote area allowance is payable to pensioners living in certain remote areas, except for those aged 70 or more receiving the special rate of age pension. Supplementary assistance, additional pension for children, mother's/guardian's allowance and remote area allowance are not taxable.

In the year ending 30 June 1997, 1,680,214 age pensioners received a total of $A13,204,658, and 527,514 disability support pensioners received $A5,299,148.

182

Wife Pension—payable to the wife of an age or invalid pensioner if she is not eligible for a pension in her own right. The maximum rate and the income test are identical to those for age and invalid pensioners. Wife Pension is being phased out; new grants have ceased since 1 July 1995.

Carer Pension—payable to a person who is providing constant care and attention at home for a severely disabled age or invalid pensioner living in the same house, where the carer is not eligible for pension in his own right. Since March 1996 Carer Pension has been extended to carers of non-pensioners meeting the Basic Family Payment assets and income criteria. The maximum rate and the income test are identical to those for age and invalid pensions.

Sole Parent Pensions—sole parents who have custody, care and control of any dependent children may, if they satisfy a residence requirement and an income test, receive sole parent pensions. Mother's/guardian's allowance, additional pension for each dependent child, supplementary assistance and remote area allowance are also payable.

In 1996–97, 358,893 beneficiaries received a total of $A2,992,322.

Rehabilitation Allowance—persons undertaking a rehabilitation programme with the Commonwealth Rehabilitation Service who are eligible for a social security pension or benefit are eligible to receive a non-taxable rehabilitation allowance during treatment or training and for up to 6 months thereafter. The allowance is equivalent to the invalid pension and is subject to the same income test. There have been no new grants of Rehabilitation Allowance since 12 Nov. 1991.

Maternity Allowance—was introduced from 1 Feb. 1996 to assist families with the costs associated with a new baby (including forgone income). It is paid for each new child to families meeting the Family Payment residence, income and assets criteria. Since 1 Jan. 1998, Maternity Allowance is paid in 2 stages as part of the initiative to boost immunization rates. A lump sum of $A750 is paid within 13 weeks of the birth and an additional $A200 after the child reaches 18 months upon proof of age-specific immunization. Families are not disadvantaged in cases where children are not immunized for medical reasons, or where parents conscientiously object to immunization.

Family Payment—is paid subject to an income and assets test to assist families with children under 16 years or dependent full-time students aged 16 years to 18 years. Since July 1996 payments to students age 16 and over are paid by the Department of Employment, Education and Training through the AUSTUDY system. It is not subject to income tax.

In 1996–97, 1,811,745 families comprising 3,491,160 children received a total of $A6,284,731.

Child Disability Allowance—payable to parents or guardians of severely physically or mentally handicapped children in the family home and needing constant care and attention. The allowance is free of an income test but is subject to a residence qualification similar to that for family allowance.

Allowances totalling $A233·1m. were paid in 1996–97.

Double Orphan's Pension—the guardian of a child under 16 years of age or of a full-time student under 25, both of whose parents are dead, or one of whose parents is dead and the whereabouts of the other parent unknown, and for refugee children where both parents are outside Australia or in prison, may receive double orphan's pension. The payment is not subject to an income test, nor is it taxable. The amount paid out in 1996–97 was $A1·7m.

Unemployment and Sickness Allowances—are paid, subject to an income test, to persons between the ages of 18 and 16 respectively and age pensioners, who are unemployed, able and willing to work and making efforts to obtain work, or temporarily unable to work because of sickness or injury. Unemployment benefit was replaced in July 1991 by a two-payment structure under the 'Newstart Strategy': Jobsearch Allowance (JA) and Newstart Allowance (NSA). In Sept. 1996, JSA and NSA were amalgamated into a single payment called NSA, payable to those who are unemployed and capable and willing to undertake suitable paid work. Eligibility is

AUSTRALIA

subject to income and assets tests. To be granted benefit a person must have resided in Australia for at least 12 months preceding his or her claim or intend to remain in Australia permanently. For unemployment benefit purposes unemployment must not be due to industrial action by that person or by members of a union to which that person is a member. Special benefits may be granted to persons not qualified above. 769,859 unemployment beneficiaries received a total of $A6,048m. in the year to June 1997. A total of $A144·3m. was paid in sickness benefit and $A472·5m. in mature age allowance in the year ended June 1997.

Service Pensions—are paid by the Department of Veterans' Affairs, similar to the age and invalid pensions provided by the Department of Social Security. Male Veterans who have reached the age of 60 years or are permanently unemployable, and who served in a theatre of war, are eligible subject to an income test. Female Veterans who served abroad and who have reached the age of 55 or are permanently unemployable, are also eligible. Wives of service pensioners are also eligible, provided that they do not receive a pension from the Department of Social Security. Disability pension is a compensatory payment in respect of incapacity attributable to war service. It is paid at a rate commensurate with the degree of incapacity and is free of any income test. A separate allowance may be paid to dependants. In 1996–97, $A2,664m. of service pensions and $A1,819m. of disability and dependants' pensions were paid out; in 1997 there were 328,748 eligible veterans.

In addition to cash benefits, welfare services are provided either directly or through State and local government authorities and voluntary agencies, for people with special needs.

Medicare—On 1 Feb. 1984 the Commonwealth Government introduced a universal health scheme known as Medicare. This covers: Automatic entitlement under a single public health fund to medical and optometrical benefits of 85% of the Medical Benefits Schedule fee, with a maximum patient payment for any service where the Schedule fee is charged; access without direct charge to public hospital accommodation and to inpatient and outpatient treatment by doctors appointed by the hospital; the restoration of funds for community health to approximately the same real level as 1975; a reduction in charges for private treatment in shared wards of public hospitals, and increases in the daily bed subsidy payable to private hospitals.

The Medicare programme is financed in part by a 1·5% levy on taxable incomes, with low income cut-off points, which were $A13,127 p.a. for a single person in 1996-97 and $A22,152 p.a. for a family with an extra allowance of $A2,100 for each child. A levy surcharge of 1% was introduced from 1 July 1997 for single individuals with taxable incomes in excess of $A50,000 p.a. and couples and families with combined taxable incomes in excess of $A100,000 who do not have private hospital cover through private health insurance. The Commonwealth Government subsidizes registered health insurance organizations by contributing to the Health Benefits, and makes an annual contribution to the Reinsurance Trust Fund of $A20m. for payments of benefits to patients with hospital treatment in excess of 35 days.

Medicare benefits are available to all persons ordinarily resident in Australia. Visitors from the UK, New Zealand, Italy, Sweden, the Netherlands and Malta have immediate access to necessary medical treatment, as do all visitors staying more than 6 months.

Medical Benefits. The Health Insurance Act provides for a Medical Benefits Schedule which lists medical services and the Schedule (standard) fee applicable in each State in respect of each medical service. Schedule fees are set and updated by an independent fees tribunal appointed by the Government. The fees so determined are to apply for Medicare benefits purposes.

Home and Community Care Program—was introduced in 1985 to provide support services to enable aged and disabled persons to live at home. It is jointly funded by the Commonwealth and State or Territory Governments. Commonwealth funding was $A451·6m. in 1996–97.

AUSTRALIA

CULTURE

Australia is preparing for a massive influx during the year 2000 as between 100,000 and 200,000 spectators, athletes, officials and journalists come to Sydney for the Olympic Games. The opening ceremony will be on 15 Sept. 2000, and the Games themselves from 16 Sept. to 1 Oct.

Broadcasting. Broadcasting is regulated by the Australian Broadcasting Authority, established in 1992 under the Broadcasting Services Act 1992. Foreign ownership of commercial radio and TV companies is restricted to 20%. The national broadcasting service is provided by the Australian Broadcasting Corporation (ABC), an independent statutory corporation receiving 85% of its funding from sales and other revenues, and the Special Broadcasting Service. The latter's function is to provide radio and TV services in more than 60 languages, reflecting a multicultural society. There are also commercial radio and TV services operated by companies under licence, subscription TV services, public radio services operated on a non-profit basis and a parliamentary radio service to state capitals, Canberra and Newcastle. The short-wave international service Radio Australia broadcasts in English, Bahasa Malay, Cantonese, Chinese, French, Khmer, Thai, Tok Pisin and Vietnamese. Radio Australia had an audience of 10m. in 1997.

In 1997 there were almost 30m. radios in use; 99% of Australian homes had TV sets with an average of 1·8 sets per household. In Aug. 1997 it was estimated that 16% of households subscribed to pay-TV.

Cinema. In 1995 there were 1,137 cinemas. In the year ending March 1995, attendance at cinemas by people aged 15 years and over was 8,734,000. 30 feature films were produced in 1995-96.

Press. There were 50 daily newspapers in 1997 (12 metropolitan and 38 regional). 30 magazines have a circulation of between 80,000 and 1m. copies per issue.

Tourism. Overseas visitors totalled 4·29m. in the year to Aug. 1997, an increase of 6·8% on the previous year. A total of $A17m. was spent. The figures are expected to double by 2006. The top source countries for visitors in the year to Sept. 1997 were Japan (810,000); New Zealand (675,000); UK (395,000); USA (330,000) and South Korea (253,000).

Festivals. Attendance at festivals between Nov. 1995 and Sept. 1996 totalled 4·1m.

Libraries. In the year ending March 1995, 5,403,100 people visited a national, State or local library at least once. In 1996 the number of books in public lending libraries was 30·4m.

National Theatre and Opera. At March 1995, 2,722,100 people aged 15 years and over had attended at least one performance of musical theatre in the past year; 2,336,300 people, other theatre; 2,634,400 people, other performing arts; 1,407,500 people, dance performances. Popular music concerts were attended by 3,790,700 people and classical music concerts by 2,634,400.

Museums and Galleries. In 1993 there were 1,765 museums and art museums operating in Australia. 3·9m. people aged 15 years and over visited a museum at least once in the year ending March 1995, while 3·1m. visited an art museum.

DIPLOMATIC REPRESENTATIVES

Of Australia in Great Britain (Australia House, Strand, London, WC2B 4LA)
High Commissioner: Philip Flood, AO.

Of Great Britain in Australia (Commonwealth Ave., Yarralumla, Canberra)
High Commissioner: Mr. A. C. S. Allan.

Of Australia in the USA (1601 Massachusetts Ave., NW, Washington, D.C., 20036)
Ambassador: Andrew S. Peacock.

Of the USA in Australia (Moonah Pl., Canberra, A.C.T. 2600)
Ambassador: Genta Hawkins Holmes.

Of Australia to the United Nations
Ambassador: Penelope Anne Wensley.

185

Of Australia to the European Union
Ambassador: Donald Kenyon.

FURTHER READING

Australian Bureau of Statistics (ABS). *Year Book Australia.—Pocket Year Book Australia.—
Monthly Summary of Statistics.* ABS also publish numerous specialized statistical digests.
Australian Encyclopædia. 12 vols. Sydney, 1983
Blainey, G., *A Short History of Australia.* Melbourne, 1996
The Cambridge Encyclopedia of Australia. CUP, 1994
Clark, M., *Manning Clark's History of Australia*; abridged by M. Cathcart. London, 1994
Concise Oxford Dictionary of Australian History. 2nd ed. OUP, 1995
Docherty, J. D., *Historical Dictionary of Australia.* Metuchen (NJ), 1993
Emy, H. and Hughes, O., *Australian Politics: Realities in Conflict.* Sydney, 1991
Gilbert, A. D. and Inglis, K. S. (eds.) *Australians: a Historical Library.* 5 vols. CUP, 1988
Hancock, K. (ed.) *Australian Society.* Cambridge Univ. Press, 1990
Hocking, B. (ed.) *Australia towards 2000.* London, 1990
Kepars, I., *Australia.* [Bibliography] 2nd ed. Oxford and Santa Barbara (CA), 1994
Oxford History of Australia. vol 2: 1770–1860. OUP, 1992. vol 5: 1942–88. OUP, 1990
The Oxford Illustrated Dictionary of Australian History. OUP, 1993
Serle, P., *Dictionary of Australian Biography.* 2 vols. Sydney, 1949
Turnbull, M., *The Reluctant Republic.* London, 1994
Who's Who in Australia. Melbourne, 1906 to date

For other more specialized titles see under CONSTITUTION AND GOVERNMENT *and*
AGRICULTURE, *above.*

National library: The National Library, Canberra, ACT.
National statistical office: Australian Bureau of Statistics (ABS), Belconnen, ACT. The
statistical services of the states are integrated with the Bureau.
ABS Website: http://www.statistics.gov.au/

AUSTRALIAN TERRITORIES AND STATES

AUSTRALIAN CAPITAL TERRITORY

KEY HISTORICAL EVENTS

The area, now the Australian Capital Territory (ACT), was explored in 1820 by
Charles Throsby who named it Limestone Plains. Settlement commenced in 1824.
Until its selection as the seat of government, it was a quiet pastoral and agricultural
community with a few large holdings and a sprinkling of smaller settlers.

In 1901 the Commonwealth constitution stipulated that a land tract of at least 260
sq. km in area and not less than 160 km from Sydney be set aside from New South
Wales and reserved as a capital district. The Canberra site was adopted by the Seat
of Government Act 1908. The present site, together with an area for a port at Jervis
Bay, was surrendered by New South Wales and accepted by the Commonwealth in
1909. By subsequential proclamation the Territory became vested in the
Commonwealth from 1 Jan. 1911. In 1911 an international competition was held for
the city plan. The plan chosen was that of W. Burley Griffin, of Chicago.
Construction was delayed by the First World War and it was not until 1927 that
Canberra became in fact the seat of government.

In 1989 self-government was proclaimed and the first ACT assembly was elected
in May of that year.

TERRITORY AND POPULATION
The total area is almost 2,400 sq. km of which 60% is hilly or mountainous. Timbered mountains are located in the south and west, and plains and hill country in the north. The ACT lies within the upper Murrumbidgee River catchment, in the Murray-Darling Basin. The Murrumbidgee flows throughout the Territory from the south, and its tributary, the Molonglo, from the east. The Molonglo was damned in 1964 to form Lake Burley Griffin. As at 30 June 1997 the estimated resident population was 309,800. The growth rate for 1996-97 was 0·5%, compared with a growth rate of 1·13% in the previous year. Population (1996 census), 299,243.

SOCIAL STATISTICS
1996: Births, 4,396; deaths, 1,300; marriages, 1,654; divorces, 1,610. Infant mortality (per 1,000 live births), 5·7.

CLIMATE
ACT has a continental climate, characterized by a marked variation in temperature between seasons, with warm to hot summers and cold winters.

CONSTITUTION AND GOVERNMENT
The ACT became self-governing on 11 May 1989. It is represented by 2 members in the Commonwealth House of Representatives and 2 senators.

The parliament of the ACT, the *Legislative Assembly*, consists of 17 members elected for a 3-year term. Its responsibilities are at State and Local Government level. The Legislative Assembly elects a Chief Minister and a 4-member cabinet.

RECENT ELECTIONS
At the elections of 21 Feb. 1998 the Liberal Party won 7 seats, Labor 6, Greens 1 and ind. 3. 1 Liberal member subsequently resigned from the Liberals to become an independent member. The Liberals formed a coalition government with the minority parties.

CURRENT ADMINISTRATION
Chief Minister: Kate Carnell.

Deputy Chief Minister, Minister Assisting the Treasurer, Attorney General, Justice and Community Safety: Gary Humphries. *Urban Services:* Brendan Smyth. *Education:* Bill Stefaniak. *Health and Community Care:* Michael Moore.

Speaker: Greg Cornwell.

ECONOMY
Budget. In 1987–88 the ACT was given its own budget. It is treated equitably with the States regarding local revenue raising, expenditure and assistance by the Commonwealth government. In 1996–97 current consolidated Territory outlays were $A1,218m., capital outlays $A128m., and revenue $A1,262m.

Banking and Finance. Bank Deposits and Loans, June 1997: Deposits, $A5,120m.; other lending, $A5,998m.; Credit Union loans, $A215m. Housing Finance for Owner Occupation (all lenders), total commitments 1996–97, $A925·1m.

ENERGY AND NATURAL RESOURCES
Water. The Australian Water Resources Council has estimated the ACT has around 175 gigalitres of surface water resources. 106 gigalitres (60·6%) has been developed for use and is currently sourced from 4 water supply dams. 3 are within the ACT, while the largest, Googong Dam, is on the Queanbeyan River.

Agriculture. Farming is mainly in grazing: Livestock (1995-96 estimate), 13,689 cattle, 72,670 sheep, and 210,500 poultry. In 1995-96, 675 tonnes of beef and veal, and 430 tonnes of greasy wool were produced.

Forestry. Outside Canberra, the Territory is mainly reserved for forestry and nature conservation (Namadgi National Park is 105,000 ha). A considerable amount of reafforestation (mostly pine) has been undertaken, the total area of coniferous plantations at 30 June 1997 being 21,600 ha.

INDUSTRY

Labour. In Oct. 1998 there were an estimated 156,800 employed persons and an estimated 10,200 unemployed persons.

25·6% of the ACT labour force were employed in public administration and defence; 13·1% in retail trade; 13·1% in property and business services.

Trade Unions. As at 30 June 1996 there were 32 separate trade unions registered in the ACT. Financial membership made up 33% of total employees. The number of unions fell by 40% from 1992 to 1996 due, in part, to amalgamations.

INTERNATIONAL TRADE

Imports and Exports. In 1996-97, 80% of imports came from 4 countries: Germany, $A4·3m. (36%); USA, $A3·2m. (27%); India, $A1·2m. (10%); UK, $A1m. (8%). In the same year 74% of exports went to 4 countries: USA, $A3·5m. (40%); UK, $A1·6m. (18%); New Zealand, $A0·9m. (10%); Belgium-Luxembourg, $A0·6m. (7%).

COMMUNICATIONS

Roads. At 16 June 1998 there were 2,583 km of road.

SOCIAL INSTITUTIONS

Religion. At the time of the 1996 census, 66·6% of the population were Christian. Of these, 44·5% were Roman Catholic and 29·5% Anglican. Non-Christian religions accounted for 3·4%, the largest groups being Buddhism, Islam and Hinduism.

Education. In Feb. 1997 there were 185 government schools comprising 82 pre-schools, 98 primary and secondary schools (including colleges) and 5 special schools. There were 44,066 students in government schools, 4,035 in pre-schools, 21,762 in primary schools, 11,058 in high schools, 6,815 in colleges and 396 in special schools. Non-government schools numbered 46 comprising 4 pre-schools and 42 primary and secondary schools (including colleges). There were 21,795 students in non-government schools: 87 in pre-schools, 10,637 in primary schools, 8,229 in high schools and 2,842 in colleges. Vocational education and training is provided by the Canberra Institute of Technology and the ACT Schools Authority, which had an estimated total of 18,700 students in 1997. There are 4 higher education institutions: The Australian National University (9,694 students in 1997); the University of Canberra (8,651); the Australian Defence Force Academy (1,675); the Australian Catholic University (648).

Health. The ACT is serviced by 2 public and 6 private hospitals.

CULTURE

In March 1995 a survey of attendance at selected cultural/leisure venues showed participation rates as follows: art gallery, 41·6%; museum, 45·4%; cinema, 72·9%; theatre, 23·0%; classical music, 14·2%; popular music, 39·6%; dance, 15·2%; opera or musical, 25·0%; other performing arts, 25·3%.

Tourism. Tourism is an important sector in the economy, attracting considerable numbers of national and international visitors.

Libraries. A survey conducted in Oct. 1996 showed that the ACT had a high level of library usage (54·4% of respondents were classified as library users). 6·4% of all households had at least 1 person who was a library user.

National Theatre and Opera. The Canberra Playhouse opened in 1998.

Museums and Galleries. The Canberra Museum and Gallery opened in 1998.

FURTHER READING

Australian Capital Territory in Focus (formerly *Statistical Summary*). Australian Bureau of Statistics. Annual.

Wigmore, L., *Canberra: A History of Australia's National Capital.* 2nd ed. Canberra, 1971

NORTHERN TERRITORY

KEY HISTORICAL EVENTS
The Northern Territory, after forming part of New South Wales, was annexed on 6 July 1863 to South Australia and in 1901 entered the Commonwealth as a corporate part of South Australia. The Commonwealth Constitution Act of 1900 having made provision for the surrender to the Commonwealth of any territory by any state, an agreement was entered into on 7 Dec. 1907 for the transfer of the Northern Territory to the Commonwealth. It formally passed under the control of the Commonwealth Government on 1 Jan. 1911. On 1 Feb. 1927, the Northern Territory was divided for administrative purposes into two territories but in 1931 it was again administered as a single territory under the control of an Administrator in Darwin. The Legislative Council for the Northern Territory, constituted in 1947, was reconstituted in 1959. In that year, citizenship rights were granted to Aboriginal people of 'full descent'. On 1 July 1978, self-government was granted to the Northern Territory.

TERRITORY AND POPULATION
The Northern Territory is bounded by the 26th parallel of S. lat. and 129° and 138° E. long. Its total area is 1,346,200 sq. km and includes adjacent islands. It has 5,100 km of mainland coastline and 2,100 km of coast around the islands. The greater part of the interior consists of a tableland rising gradually from the coast to a height of about 700 metres. On this tableland there are large areas of excellent pasturage. The southern part of the Territory is generally sandy and has a small rainfall, but water may be obtained by means of sub-artesian bores.

The population of the Territory at the 1996 census was 195,101. The capital, seat of Government and principal port is Darwin, on the north coast; population 69,400 in June 1997. Other main centres include Katherine (9,800), 330 km south of Darwin; Alice Springs (25,700), in Central Australia; Tennant Creek (3,856), a rich mining centre 500 km north of Alice Springs; Nhulunbuy (3,800), a bauxite mining centre in the Gove Peninsula Province in eastern Arnhem Land; and Jabiru, a model town built to serve the rich Uranium Province in eastern Arnhem Land. Palmerston is a Darwin satellite town and Yulara is a resort village serving Uluru National Park and Ayers Rock. There also are a number of large self-contained Aboriginal communities. People identifying themselves as Aboriginal numbered 44,486 and Torres Strait Islanders 714 at the 1996 census.

SOCIAL STATISTICS
1996: Births, 3,562; deaths, 758; marriages, 797; divorces, 432. Infant mortality per 1,000 live births, 11·5. Life expectancy, 1996: 69·2 years for males, 75·0 for females.

CLIMATE
See AUSTRALIA: Climate.

The highest temperature ever recorded in the NT was 118·9°F (48·3°C) at Finke in 1960, while the lowest recorded temperature was 18·5°F (−7·5°C) at Alice Springs in 1976.

CONSTITUTION AND GOVERNMENT
The Northern Territory (Self-Government) Act 1978 established the Northern Territory as a body politic as from 1 July 1978, with Ministers having control over and responsibility for Territory finances and the administration of the functions of government as specified by the Federal Government. Regulations have been made conferring executive authority for the bulk of administrative functions. At 31 Dec. 1979 the only important powers retained by the Commonwealth related to rights in respect of Aboriginal land, some significant National Parks and the mining of uranium and other substances prescribed in the Atomic Energy Act. Proposed laws passed by the Legislative Assembly require the assent of the Administrator. The Governor-General may disallow any law assented to by the Administrator within 6 months of the Administrator's assent.

The Northern Territory has federal representation, electing 1 member to the House of Representatives and 2 members to the Senate.

The Legislative Assembly has 25 members, directly elected for a period of 4 years. The Chief Minister, Deputy Chief Minister and Speaker are elected by, and from, the members. The *Administrator* (Dr Neil Conn) appoints Ministers on the advice of the Leader of the majority party.

RECENT ELECTIONS
The Legislative Assembly elected in 1997: Country Liberal Party, 18; Australian Labor Party, 7.

CURRENT ADMINISTRATION
The Country Liberal Party Cabinet was as follows in Jan. 1999:

Chief Minister, Attorney-General, Minister for Young Territorians, Women's Policy, Constitutional Development: Shane I. Stone.

Deputy Chief Minister, Treasurer, Police, Fire and Emergency Services, Tourism, Public Employment, Industrial Relations, Minister Responsible for the Territory Insurance Office: Mike A. Reed. *Leader of Government Business, Vice President Executive Council, Health, Family and Children's Services, Senior Territorians, Industries and Business, Regional Development, Racing, Gaming and Licensing, Defence Support:* Denis Burke. *Transport and Infrastructure Development, Territory Ports, the AustralAsia Railway, Essential Sevices:* Barry F. Coulter. *Aboriginal Development, Housing, Local Government, Lands, Planning and Environment:* Tim D. Baldwin. *Resource Development, Parks and Wildlife, Central Australia:* Eric Poole. *Asian Relations and Trade, Arts and Museums, Corporate and Information Services, Communications, Science and Advanced Technology:* Daryl W. Manzie. *Primary Industry and Fisheries, Ethnic Affairs, Correctional Services:* Mick Palmer. *School Education, Sport and Recreation, Tertiary Education and Training:* Peter F. Adamson.

Local Government. Local government was established in Darwin in 1957 and later in 3 regional centres. These are each managed by a mayor and a municipal council elected at intervals of not more than 4 years by universal adult franchise. Provision has been made for a limited form of local government for smaller communities. In 1998 there were 6 municipal and 32 community government councils and 25 other incorporated community associations responsible for local government.

ECONOMY

Budget. Revenue and expenditure in $A1m.:

	1992–93	1993–94	1994–95	1995–96	1996–97
Revenue	1,372	1,451	1,512	1,645	1,718
Expenditure	1,482	1,844	1,584	1,601	1,697

Using uniform presentation standards, total revenue in 1996–97 was $A1,718m. of which $A1,237m. were grants to the Northern Territory from the Commonwealth, and $A348m. was raised by the Northern Territory Government, which included $A309m. through state-like taxes.

Expenditure during 1996–97 included $A345m. for education; $A54m. for housing and community amenities; $A305m. for health; $A167m. for public order and safety, and $A136m. for transport and communication.

$A81m. of Territory borrowings were repaid in 1996–97, while other financing transactions of $A9m. (consisting mainly of cash balances) were used. Net debt declined by $A42m. to $A1,311m.

ENERGY AND NATURAL RESOURCES

Electricity. Electric power is supplied by the Power and Water Authority (PAWA).

Oil and Gas. Significant oil and gas reserves have been discovered and developed offshore in the Joseph Bonaparte Gulf and Timor Sea areas, and onshore in the Amadeus Basin. In 1995–96, 1,547 megalitres of crude oil and 407bn. litres of natural gas were produced. Total value of oil and gas production in 1995–96 was $A259·6m., and in 1996–97 about $A229m. Natural gas is piped from the Amadeus

Basin to Darwin. In 1998, 15 offshore oil and gas fields had been discovered in the previous 4 years (7 of them in 1997), with a success rate of about 30%, and development and exploration programmes were under way.

Water. The Power and Water Authority (PAWA) is responsible for providing water supply (also electric power and sewerage services) throughout the NT. The Aboriginal Essential Services Branch of PAWA maintains water supply to the 85 remote communities and Aboriginal outstations.

Minerals. The most important natural resources are minerals, and mining is one of the largest industries. At 30 June 1997 there were 30 mining establishments employing 1,911 people. Value of production (including uranium) in 1996–97 was estimated at $A1,438m., including (in $A1m.): Gold bullion, 347; manganese ore, 226; bauxite, 131; alumina, 356; base metals, 221; uranium oxide, 110. In 1995–96 the Territory produced 100% of Australia's manganese, 15·9% of its bauxite and 7·8% of gold bullion. In terms of value it produced 12·9% of its uranium. In the financial year 1996–97 mining contributed 10·7% ($A536m.) of Gross State Product.

Agriculture. Cattle production constitutes the largest farming industry. Livestock, 1997: Cattle, 1,608,846; domesticated buffalo, 9,440; pigs, 2,467; horses, 6,414. In 1996 the total value of the cattle industry was $A133·7m., from which 199,044 head were exported live at a value of $A84·8m. The value of other animal industries including buffalo, pigs, poultry, eggs, milk and crocodiles was estimated at $A154m. in 1996. In 1997 there were 8 crocodile farms: Production at 2 with abattoir facilities comprised 4,595 animals slaughtered and 15,689 kg of meat sold in the period 1 Jan.–30 June 1997.

At March 1997 there were 357 agricultural producers with a total area under holding of 70,768,932 ha, representing just over half of the Territory's land mass.

Horticultural production was valued at $A47·9m. in 1996–97 for fruit and vegetables. The main crops were mangoes, bananas, melons and grapes.

In 1995–96, 3,894 ha were used for grain crops, seed and hay production with an industry value of $A24m.

Forestry. Total area at 30 June 1997 was 35·39m. ha.

Environment. There are 93 parks and reserves covering 43,709 sq. km. Twelve of the parks are classified as national parks, including the Kakadu and Uluru-Kata Tjuta National Park.

Fisheries. The total value of the fishing industry in 1996-97 was $A118·4m. The expanding aquaculture industry (producing crayfish, prawns, giant clams and beta carotene extracts) made the largest contribution, generating $A58m. The production value of crustaceans was $A49·6m., with prawns comprising 81·3% ($A40·3m.). The value of fish caught was $A10·2m., with barramundi comprising 27·9% ($A2·8m.).

INDUSTRY

At June 1997 turnover was $A915·6m. 3,400 persons were employed in manufacturing in 1997. In the financial year 1996–97 manufacturing contributed 4·9% of Gross State Product.

Labour. The labour force totalled 91,100 in June 1998, of whom 87,500 were employed. The unemployment rate was 4·0%, the lowest of any State or Territory in Australia.

Trade Unions. At June 1996, 26 trade unions had 19,300 members.

INTERNATIONAL TRADE

Imports and Exports. In 1997-98 the Territory's exports, valued at $A1,198·3m., accounted for 1·4% of all Australia's exports. Major export destinations were the USA, Japan and China, accounting for 47·7% of all exports from the Territory.

1997-98 imports, valued at $A656·9m., accounted for 0·7% of all Australia's imports. Major sources of imports were the USA, Japan and Singapore, accounting for 82·8% of all Northern Territory imports.

COMMUNICATIONS

Roads. There were (in 1997) 6,573 km of sealed road. They include three major interstate links: The Stuart Highway from Darwin to the South Australian border (1,787 km), the Barkley Highway, Three Ways to the Queensland border (434 km), and the Victoria Highway, Katherine to the Western Australian border (470 km). In addition to this there were 6,573 km of gravel roads and 4,724 km of formed roads. Total roads, excluding township and municipal, 20,541 km. Registered motor vehicles at 1 July 1997 numbered 113,554, including 93,894 light vehicles (less than 4·5 tonnes). There were 73 fatalities in road accidents in 1996.

Rail. In 1980 Alice Springs was linked to the Trans-continental network by a standard (1,435 mm) gauge railway to Tarcoola in South Australia (831 km). In 1998 the governments of the Northern Territory and South Australia were seeking the participation of the private sector to complete the construction of the AustralAsia Railway. The completion of the railway between Darwin and Alice Springs (1,410 km) will be a strategic link in the seamless AustralAsia Trade Route.

Civil Aviation. Darwin and most regional centres in the Territory are serviced by daily flights to all State capitals and major cities. In 1998 there were direct international services connecting Darwin to Bali, Brunei, Kuala Lumpur, Kupang and Singapore. In 1996–97 Darwin airport handled 0·84m. domestic and 165,000 international passengers, Alice Springs 864,000 domestic passengers, and Ayers Rock 265,000.

Shipping. Regular freight shipping services connect Darwin with both the east and west coasts of Australia, South East Asia and the rest of the world. In 1998 there were 10 shipping lines making regular calls, and cruise ships and naval vessels also include Darwin as a port of call.

The Port of Darwin is equipped to handle bulk, container and roll-on-roll-off traffic. 3,654 vessels visited the port and it handled 1,289,849 tonnes of cargo in 1996–97. There is a sheltered morning basin which provides 85 non-tidal berths.

Commercial and pleasure vessels also call at the ports of Melville Bay (Gove) and Milner Bay (Groote Eylandt), and at Seven Spirit Bay on a regular basis.

SOCIAL INSTITUTIONS

Justice. Voluntary euthanasia for the terminally ill was legalized in 1995. However, the federal Prime Minister stated that the High Court of Australia would consider cases of euthanasia as murder, and the law was overturned by the Federal Senate on 24 March 1997. The first person to have recourse to legalized euthanasia died on 22 Sept. 1996.

Police personnel at 30 June 1997, 819. At June 1997 the Territory had 3 prisons with a daily average of 541 prisoners held. In 1996-97, 19,821 crimes were reported to the police.

Education. In 1998 there were 3,177 children and 80 full-time teachers in 62 government and private pre-schools. Education is compulsory from the age of 6 to 15 years. There were (1997) 36,466 full-time students enrolled in 144 government primary, secondary and special education schools with 2,089 full-time equivalent teaching staff, and 8,172 full-time students enrolled in 29 private primary and secondary schools with 551 full-time equivalent teaching staff. The proportion of migrant and of Aboriginal and Torres Strait Islander students in the Territory is high, with the 2 latter comprising 34·6% of all full-time enrolments in 1997 (9,432 primary and 3,172 secondary students). Schools range from single classrooms and transportable units catering for the needs of small Aboriginal communities and pastoral properties to urban high schools and secondary colleges (years 11–12), catering for about 7,500 students. Bilingual programmes operate in some Aboriginal communities where traditional Aboriginal culture prevails. Secondary education extends from school years 8 to 12 (7 to 12 in Alice Springs).

The Northern Territory University (NTU) was founded in 1989 by amalgamating the existing University College of the Northern Territory and the Darwin Institute of Technology, with the technical and further education courses hitherto offered by the latter to be conducted by an Institute of Technical and Further Education within the new University. At 31 March 1997, 4,203 students were enrolled in a total of 4,294 higher education courses at the NTU. Batchelor College, a multi-purpose institution of Aboriginal tertiary education, had 1,315 students enrolled in higher education or TAFE courses in 1995. There are 5 colleges of higher education. In 1997 there were 107 registered Vocational Education and Training (VET) course providers in the Territory, offering 101 courses. At 31 Dec. 1997, 22,321 students enrolled in VET courses.

Health. In 1997 there were 6 hospitals (5 public and 1 private) with 703 beds. Community health services are provided from urban and rural Health Centres including mobile units. Remote communities are served by the Aerial Medical Service and by resident Aboriginal health workers.

Welfare. The number of pensions current at Dec. 1997 was: Age, 4,981; wives' (due to be phased out), 639; carers', 179; disability, 4,195; widows' allowance, 90; sole parent, 4,928. Number of unemployed being paid benefit, 12,105. Youth Allowance, which commenced on 1 July 1998, supports the unemployed under the age of 21 years and students under 25 years.

CULTURE

Broadcasting. Darwin's radio services include 4 ABC stations, 1 SBS station, 2 commercial stations and a community station.
Darwin has 2 commercial, 1 ABC and 1 SBS TV service.
Alice Springs radio services include 4 ABC stations, 2 commercial and 2 community stations. It has 2 commercial, 1 ABC and 1 SBS TV service.
Most other Northern Territory centres have 1 commercial and 1 national radio service, with 1 each of ABC, SBS and commercial television, many of these being provided by self-help projects.

Tourism. In 1996–97 nearly 1·3m. people visited the Territory, with tourist expenditure totalling $A715·9m. Largest proportion of visitors in 1996–97 were from mainland Europe, 34%; UK, 23%; Japan, 21%; North America, 14%.

FURTHER READING
Profile of Australia's Northern Territory—1997/98. Protocol and Public Affairs Branch, Dept. of the Chief Minister, GPO Box 4396, Darwin
The Northern Territory: Annual Report. Dept. of Territories, Canberra, from 1911. Dept. of the Interior, Canberra, from 1966–67. Dept. of Northern Territory, from 1972
Australian Territories, Dept. of Territories, Canberra, 1960 to 1973. Dept. of Special Minister of State, Canberra, 1973–75. Department of Administrative Services, 1976
Northern Territory in Focus (formerly *Statistical Summary*). Australian Bureau of Statistics, Canberra, from 1960
Donovan, P. F., *A Land Full of Possibilities: A History of South Australia's Northern Territory 1863–1911.* 1981.—*At the Other End of Australia: The Commonwealth and the Northern Territory 1911–1978.* Univ. of Queensland Press, 1984
Heatley, A., *The Government of the Northern Territory.* Univ. of Queensland Press, 1979.— *Almost Australians: the Politics of Northern Territory Self-Government.* Australian National Univ. Press, 1990
Mills, C. M., *A Bibliography of the Northern Territory.* Canberra, 1977
Powell, A., *Far Country: A Short History of the Northern Territory.* Melbourne Univ. Press, 1996

NEW SOUTH WALES

KEY HISTORICAL EVENTS
The name New South Wales was applied to the entire east coast of Australia when Capt. James Cook claimed the land for the British Crown on 23 Aug. 1770. The separate colonies of Tasmania, South Australia, Victoria and Queensland were proclaimed in the 19th century. In 1911 and 1915 the Australian Capital Territory around Canberra and Jervis Bay was ceded to the Commonwealth. New South Wales was thus gradually reduced to its present area. The first settlement was made

at Port Jackson in 1788 as a penal settlement. A partially elective council was established in 1843 and responsible government in 1856.

Gold discoveries from 1851 had brought a large influx of immigrants, and responsible government was at first unstable, with 7 ministries holding office in the 5 years after 1856. The times were somewhat lawless and bitter conflict arose from loose land laws enacted in 1861. Lack of transport hampered agricultural expansion.

New South Wales federated with the other Australian states to form the Commonwealth of Australia in 1901.

TERRITORY AND POPULATION
New South Wales is situated between the 29th and 38th parallels of S. lat. and 141st and 154th meridians of E. long., and comprises 309,433 sq. miles (801,600 sq. km), inclusive of Lord Howe Island, 6 sq. miles (17 sq. km), but exclusive of the Australian Capital Territory (911 sq. miles, 2,359 sq. km) and 28 sq. miles (73 sq. km) at Jervis Bay.

Lord Howe Island, 31° 33' 4" S., 159° 4' 26" E., which is part of New South Wales, is situated about 702 km north-east of Sydney; area, 1,654 ha, of which only about 120 ha are arable; resident population, estimate (30 June 1989), 320. The Island, which was discovered in 1788, is of volcanic origin. Mount Gower, the highest point, reaches a height of 866 metres.

The Lord Howe Island Board manages the affairs of the Island and supervises the Kentia palm-seed industry.

Census population of New South Wales (including full-blood Aboriginals from 1966):

	Males	Females	Persons	Population per sq. km	Average annual increase % since previous census
1901	710,264	645,091	1,355,355	2	1·86
1911	857,698	789,036	1,646,734	2	1·97
1921	1,071,501	1,028,870	2,100,371	3	2·46
1933	1,318,471	1,282,376	2,600,847	3	1·76
1947	1,492,211	1,492,627	2,984,838	4	0·99
1954	1,720,860	1,702,669	3,423,529	4	1·98
1961	1,972,909	1,944,104	3,917,013	5	1·94
1971	2,307,210	2,293,970	4,601,180	6	1·66
1981	2,548,984	2,577,233	5,126,217	6	1·42
1986	2,684,570	2,717,311	5,401,881	7	1·05
1991	2,844,532	2,886,415	5,730,947	7	1·22

The 1996 census population was 6,038,696. At 30 June 1996 the estimated resident population was 6,203,900 (3,123,200 females); population density, 7·7 per sq. km. Although NSW comprises only 10·4% of the total area of Australia, over 33·9% of the Australian population live there.

The state is divided into 12 *Statistical Divisions*. The estimated population of these (in 1,000) in 1996 was: Sydney, 3,879·4; Hunter, 555·5; Illawarra, 373·0; Richmond-Tweed, 200·7; Mid-North Coast, 262·6; Northern, 178·6; North Western, 117·3; Central West, 172·5; South Eastern, 179·0; Murrumbidgee, 149·2; Murray, 110·9; Far West, 25·3. Population of the Statistical Subdivisions Newcastle (within Hunter) and Wollongong (within Illawarra) was 463·7 and 255·7 respectively.

SOCIAL STATISTICS
Statistics for calendar years:

	Live births	Marriages	Divorces	Deaths
1994	87,977	38,814	13,999	44,763
1995	87,849	37,828	14,945	44,773
1996	86,595	37,716	15,984	45,141

The annual rates per 1,000 of mean estimated resident population in 1996 were: Births, 14·0; deaths, 7·3; marriages, 5·8; infant mortality, 5·8 per 1,000 live births. Expectation of life in 1996: Males, 74·97 years, females, 80·88.

CLIMATE
See AUSTRALIA: Climate.

CONSTITUTION AND GOVERNMENT
Within the State there are three levels of government: The Commonwealth Government, with authority derived from a written constitution; the State Government with residual powers; the local government authorities with powers based upon a State Act of Parliament, operating within incorporated areas extending over almost 90% of the State.

The Constitution of New South Wales is drawn from several diverse sources; certain Imperial statutes such as the Commonwealth of Australia Constitution Act (1900); the Australian States Constitution Act (1907); an element of inherited English law; amendments to the Commonwealth of Australia Constitution Act; the (State) Constitution Act; the Australia Acts of 1986; the Constitution (Amendment) Act 1987 and certain other State Statutes; numerous legal decisions; and a large amount of English and local convention.

The Parliament of New South Wales may legislate for the peace, welfare and good government of the State in all matters not specifically reserved to the Commonwealth Government.

The State Legislature consists of the Sovereign, represented by the Governor, and two Houses of Parliament, the Legislative Council (upper house) and the Legislative Assembly (lower house).

Australian citizens aged 18 and over, and other British subjects who were enrolled prior to 26 Jan. 1984, men and women aged 18 years and over, are entitled to the franchise. Enrolment and voting is compulsory. The optional preferential method of voting is used for both houses.

The Legislative Council has 42 members elected for a term of office equivalent to 2 terms of the Legislative Assembly, with 21 members retiring at the same time as the Legislative Assembly elections. The whole State constitutes a single electoral district.

The Legislative Assembly has 99 members elected in single-seat electoral districts for a maximum period of 4 years.

CURRENT ADMINISTRATION
In 1995, the Legislative Council consisted of the following parties: Australian Labor Party (ALP), 17; Liberal Party of Australia (Lib), 12; National Party (NP), 6; Call to Australia Group (CTA), 2; Australian Democrats (AD), 2; A Better Future for Our Children,1; Shooters' Party, 1; Greens, 1.

The Legislative Assembly elected in 1995 consisted of the following parties: ALP, 50; Lib, 29; NP, 17; ind, 3.

Governor: Gordon J. Samuels, AC, QC, MA.

The New South Wales ALP Ministry, in Feb. 1999, was as follows:

Premier, Minister for Arts and Ethnic Affairs: Robert John Carr (b. 1948).

Deputy Premier, Minister for Health and Aboriginal Affairs: Dr Andrew John Refshauge. *Treasurer, State Development, Vice President of Executive Council:* Michael Rueben Egan. *Police:* Paul Francis Patrick Whelan. *Olympics:* Michael Steven Knight. *Transport and Roads:* Patrick Scully. *Education and Training, Minister assisting the Premier on Youth Affairs:* John Joseph Aquilina. *Environment:* Pamela Diane Allan. *Public Works and Services:* Ronald David Dyer. *Community Services, Ageing, Disability Services and Women:* Faye Lo Po'. *Attorney-General, Industrial Relations, Fair Trading:* Jeffrey William Shaw. *Agriculture, Land and Water Conservation:* Richard Sanderson Amery. *Urban Affairs and Planning, Housing:* Craig John Knowles. *Regional Development, Rural Affairs:* Harry Francis Woods. *Energy, Tourism, Corrective Services, Emergency Services, Minister assisting the Premier on the Arts:* Robert John Debus. *Gaming and Racing, Minister assisting the Premier on Hunter Development:* Richard Face. *Mineral Resources and Fisheries:* Robert Douglas Martin. *Sport and Recreation:* Gabrielle Mary Harrison. *Local Government:* Ernest Thomas Page. *Information Technology, Forestry, Ports, Minister assisting the Premier on Western Sydney:* Kimberley Yeadon.

Local Government. A system of local government extends over most of the State, including the whole of the Eastern and Central land divisions and almost three-quarters of the sparsely populated Western division. Since 1 July 1993, an area established for local government purposes is known as a council or city council, and the terms municipality or shire have been abandoned (except for Sutherland Shire). At 1 July 1993 there were 39 city councils and 138 councils. In addition there is one unincorporated area in the far west of the State. Local government councils most importantly provide the general services of administration, health, community amenities, recreation and culture, roads and debt servicing. County councils administer electricity or water supply or render other local services of common benefit in districts which comprise a number of councils.

ECONOMY

Budget. State Government outlays (in $A1m.) for financial years ending 30 June:

	1993–94	1994–95	1995–96
General public services	1,281	1,302	1,400
Public order and safety	1,754	1,885	2,082
Education	6,506	6,851	7,081
Health	4,098	4,406	4,695
Social security and welfare	1,358	1,464	1,573
Housing and community amenities	1,084	1,601	1,189
Recreation and culture	641	228	608
Fuel and energy	730	770	581
Agriculture, forestry and fishing	516	515	523
Mining, manufacturing and construction	39	42	45
Transport and communications	3,131	2,923	2,893
Other economic affairs	808	825	509
Other purposes	3,581	2,904	3,179
Total	*25,526*	*25,716*	*26,357*

State Government receipts for 1995–96 included taxes, fees and fines, $A11,226m., and Commonwealth Government grant, $A10,574m.

State Government taxes, fees and fines, by type:

	1993–94	1994–95	1995–96
Employers' payroll taxes	2,422	2,658	2,843
Taxes on property—			
Taxes on immovable property	596	537	601
Taxes on financial and capital transactions	2,479	2,395	2,391
Taxes on provision of goods and services—			
Excises and levies	31	30	42
Taxes on gambling	988	1,071	1,178
Taxes on insurance	727	755	765
Taxes on goods and performance of activities—			
Motor vehicle taxes	1,113	1,241	1,260
Franchise taxes	1,397	1,437	1,700
Other taxes on use of goods etc.	34	35	37
Fees and fines—			
Compulsory fees	206	200	213
Fines	182	170	195

Banking and Finance. Banking business is transacted chiefly by the Commonwealth Bank of Australia, the State Bank of New South Wales (government banks) and 3 private banks. At June 1997, there were 42 banking groups (comprised of 50 banking companies, of which 17 were domestic owned and 33 foreign owned). Banks operated 2,089 branches and 2,019 agencies in New South Wales.

Lending activity of financial institutions in New South Wales in 1995–96 comprised (in $A1m.): Business loans, 78,288·8; personal, 12,377·6; house purchase, 21,200·3; lease financing, 3,130·2.

ENERGY AND NATURAL RESOURCES

Electricity. In 1995–96, 60,006m. kWh were produced.

Oil and Gas. No natural gas is produced in NSW. All is imported from the Moomba field in South Australia.

Water. Ground water represents the largest source with at least 130 communities relying on it for drinking water.

Minerals. New South Wales contains extensive mineral deposits. For the year ended 30 June 1996, turnover from 120 mining establishments in the coal and metal ore mining industries, employing 15,509 people, was $A4,808m. The value of selected metallic minerals produced in 1995–96 was $A653m.; industrial minerals, $A203·4m.; construction materials, $A429m. Output of principal products:

	1993–94	1994–95	1995–96
Antimony concentrates (tonnes)	812	1,129	1,380
Coal (1,000 tonnes)	84,014	88,588	91,900
Copper concentrates (tonnes)	157,584	155,714	170,815
Gold (kg)	10,049	30,128	11,274
Lead concentrates (tonnes)	319,697	320,469	302,146
Construction sand (1,000 tonnes)	11,030	10,645	8,670
Zinc concentrates (tonnes)	599,258	604,879	557,876

Agriculture. In 1995–96 GDP at factor cost for agriculture, forestry, hunting and fishing was $A3,800m. Farm income (including Australian Capital Territory) was $A116m. At 31 March 1996 there were 42,497 farming establishments with a net worth of $A32,008m. These had an area of 61,008,553 ha, of which 4,756,721 ha were used for cropping.

Principal crops in the years ended 31 March 1996 with production in 1,000 tonnes: Wheat for grain, 4,508; barley for grain, 1,074; oats for grain, 711; rice, 965; cotton (raw and seed), 868; oilseeds, 339; sugar-cane, 1,922. (Data relates to farms whose estimated value of agricultural operations was $A5,000 or more at the census.)

The total area under grapes at 31 March 1996 was 16,883 ha (including 3,115 ha not bearing); the production of table grapes was 10,841 tonnes; of wine grapes, 167,556 tonnes; for drying, 46,687 tonnes (fresh weight).

In 1996, there were 3,625 ha of banana plantations; production, 38,708 tonnes. In 1995, there were 4·16m. citrus fruit trees; production (1994), 260,491 tonnes.

At 31 March 1996 there were 41·09m. sheep and lambs, 6·02m. beef cattle, 0·37m. dairy cattle and 0·71m. pigs. The production of shorn and crutched wool in 1996–97 was 194,897 tonnes (greasy). In 1996–97 production (in tonnes) of butter was 4,560; cheese, 21,552; beef and veal, 486,500; mutton, 109,280 and lamb, 66,909; pig meat, 88,530.

Forestry. State forests (timber reserves) represent 5% of land area.

INDUSTRY

A wide range of manufacturing is undertaken in the Sydney area, and there are large iron and steel works near the coalfields at Newcastle and Port Kembla. Around one-third of Australian manufacturing takes place in NSW.

Manufacturing establishments' operations, 1995–96:

Industry	No. of persons employed	Wages and salaries ($A1m.)	Turnover ($A1m.)	Industry gross product ($A1m.)
Food, beverages and tobacco	47,509	1,582·9	12,994·5	3,293·0
Textiles, clothing, footwear and leather	22,673	568·5	3,103·0	1,001·2
Wood and paper products	19,622	583·1	3,495·3	1,223·2
Printing, publishing and recorded media	34,234	1,282·4	6,076·8	2,828·5
Petroleum, coal, chemical and associated products	32,348	1,255·7	11,353·1	3,108·0
Non-metallic mineral products	11,125	383·2	2,607·6	884·2
Metal products	51,241	2,018·6	13,855·8	4,495·1
Machinery and equipment	63,091	2,210·0	10,446·6	3,665·5
Other manufacturing	15,246	376·3	1,779·3	668·8
Total manufacturing	297,089	10,260·7	65,712·0	21,167·5

Some of the principal articles manufactured in 1996–97 were: 850,000 tonnes of plain wheat flour; 630m. clay bricks; 69·72m. sq. metres of man-made fibre woven fabric; 2,986,000 pairs of footwear; 4,456,000 men's and boys' shirts; 620,000 tonnes of hardwood chips; 346,000 tonnes of plastics in primary forms.

Labour. In May 1997 the labour force was estimated to number 3,049,200 persons, of whom 2,804,000 were employed: 487,600 as intermediate clerical, sales and service workers; 495,500 as professionals; 282,000 as labourers and related workers; 366,700 as tradespersons and related workers; 208,200 as managers and administrators; 250,500 as production and transport workers, and 129,500 as advanced clerical and service workers. There were 245,300 unemployed.

Industrial tribunals are authorized to fix minimum rates of wages and other conditions of employment. Their awards may be enforced by law, as may be industrial agreements between employers and organizations of employees, when registered.

The principal State arbitration and conciliation tribunal is the Industrial Commission of New South Wales. The Commission is empowered to exercise all the powers conferred on subsidiary tribunals, and has in addition authority to determine any widely defined 'industrial matter', to adjudicate in case of illegal strikes and lockouts, to investigate union ballots when irregularities are alleged, and to hear appeals from subsidiary tribunals. Subsidiary tribunals are Conciliation Committees for various industries, each having an equal number representing employers and employees and a Conciliation Commissioner as chairman.

Trade Unions. Registration of trade unions is effected under the New South Wales Trade Union Act 1881, which follows substantially the Trade Union Acts of 1871 and 1876 of England. Registration confers a quasi-corporate existence with power to hold property, to sue and be sued, etc., and the various classes of employees covered by the union are required to be prescribed by the constitution of the union. For the purpose of bringing an industry under the review of the State industrial tribunals, or participating in proceedings relating to disputes before Commonwealth tribunals, employees and employers must be registered as industrial unions, under State or Commonwealth industrial legislation respectively. At 30 June 1996 there were 71 trade unions with a total membership of just over 1m.

INTERNATIONAL TRADE

Imports and Exports. External commerce, exclusive of interstate trade, is included in the statement of the commerce of Australia. Overseas commerce of New South Wales in $A1m. for years ending 30 June:

	Imports	Exports		Imports	Exports
1991-92	23,296	11,700	1994-95	33,280	15,201
1992-93	26,418	13,156	1995-96	34,891	16,684
1993-94	28,491	14,651	1996-97	34,194	17,710

The major commodities exported in 1996-97 (in $A1m.) were coal, not agglomerated (3,396·5), wheat (including spelt) and meslin (unmilled) (1,115·0), aluminium (992·7), wool and other animal hair (858·2), cotton (614·2), meat (508·9) and parts and accessories for office machines and computers (403·9). Principal imports were computers (2,925·9), parts and accessories for computers (1,523·8), telecommunications equipment, parts and accessories of radio, TV, video, etc. (1,548·2), and private motor vehicles (1,714·8).

Principal destinations of exports in 1996-97 (in $A1m.) were Japan (3,929·0), New Zealand (1,668·3), South Korea (1,242·7), USA (1,050·1), Hong Kong (937·7) and Indonesia (820·5). Major sources of supply were USA (8,304·1), Japan (3,862·6), UK (2,467·4), China (1,819·5), Germany (1,811·6), New Zealand (1,459·2) and Taiwan (1,307·0).

COMMUNICATIONS

Roads. At June 1997 there were 180,849 km of public roads of all sorts. The Roads and Traffic Authority of New South Wales is responsible for the administration and upkeep of major roads. In 1997 there were 20,368 km of roads under its control, comprising 3,010 km of national highways, 14,387 km of state roads and 2,971 km of regional and local roads.

The number of registered motor vehicles (excluding tractors and trailers) at 30 June 1996 was 3,448,900, including 2,775,700 passenger vehicles, 451,700 light commercial vehicles, 128,400 trucks, 15,200 buses and 77,900 motor cycles. There were 543 fatalities in road accidents in 1996–97.

Rail. In 1996 the Rail Access Corporation was formed to own and maintain the railway infrastructure. It leases trackage rights to the State Rail Authority, which operates passenger trains, and to the Freight Rail Corporation. At 30 June 1996, 8,851 km of government railway were open (618 km electrified). In 1996–97, 270·7m. passengers were carried and 76·62m. tonnes of freight. Also open for traffic are 325 km of Victorian Government railways which extend over the border; 68 km of private railways (mainly in mining districts), and 53 km of Commonwealth Government-owned track.

A tramway opened in Sydney in 1996. There is also a small overhead railway in the city centre.

Civil Aviation. Sydney Airport (Kingsford Smith) is the major airport in New South Wales and Australia's principal international air terminal. In 1996 it handled 20,237,000 passengers (13,684,000 on domestic and 6,553,000 on international flights). It is also the leading airport for freight, handling 372,500 tonnes in 1995.

Shipping. The main ports are at Sydney, Newcastle, Port Kembla and Botany Bay. Visits by vessels to the ports of New South Wales in 1992–93 totalled 4,245 (97·43m. GRT). The number of overseas vessels which entered in 1992–93 was 3,091.

Postal Services. At June 1997, a total of 1,320 post offices, post office agencies and community mail agencies provided Australia Post services throughout NSW and the ACT.

SOCIAL INSTITUTIONS

Justice. Legal processes may be conducted in Local Courts presided over by magistrates or in higher courts (District Court or Supreme Court) presided over by judges. There is also an appellate jurisdiction. Persons charged with the more serious crimes must be tried before a higher court.

Children's Courts have been established with the object of removing children as far as possible from the atmosphere of a public court. There are also a number of tribunals exercising special jurisdiction, *e.g.,* the Industrial Commission and the Compensation Court.

As at 2 June 1996 there were 6,300 persons in prison.

Religion. At the 1996 census of those who stated a religion, 29% were Roman Catholic and 25% Anglican. These 2 religions combined had almost 3·3m. followers.

Education. The State Government maintains a system of free primary and secondary education, and attendance at school is compulsory from 6 to 15 years of age. Non-government schools are subject to government inspection.

In 1996 there were 2,186 government schools with 760,078 pupils (452,117 primary and 307,961 secondary) and 49,202 teachers, and 867 non-government schools with 305,269 pupils (159,546 primary and 145,723 secondary) and 19,892 teachers.

There were 195,240 students in higher education in 1996. The largest number of students (23%) were enrolled in arts, humanities and social sciences.

The University of Sydney, founded in 1850, had 30,369 students in 1996. There are 7 colleges providing residential facilities at the university. The University of New England at Armidale, previously affiliated with the University of Sydney, was incorporated in 1954, and in 1996 had 14,154 students.

The University of New South Wales was established in 1949. Enrolments in 1996 numbered 27,348. There are 7 colleges providing residential facilities at the university. The University of Newcastle, previously affiliated with the University of New South Wales, was granted autonomy from 1965, and in 1996 had 17,407 students. The University of Wollongong, also previously associated with the University of New South Wales, became autonomous in 1975, and in 1996 had 12,081 students. Macquarie University in Sydney, established in 1964, had 17,827 students in 1996. In 1996 the University of Technology, Sydney, had 21,397 students, the University of Western Sydney, 24,997, and Charles Sturt University, 20,123.

Colleges of advanced education were merged with universities in 1990.

Post-school technical and further education is provided at State TAFE colleges. Enrolments in 1996 totalled 417,873 (87% being part-time).

Health. At 30 June 1996 there were 22,231 medical practitioners, 3,979 dentists and 74,131 nurses. There were 18,953 beds in public hospitals, and 89 private hospitals with 5,987 beds.

Welfare. The Commonwealth Government makes provision for social benefits, such as age and disability pensions, widows' pensions, supporting parents' benefits, family allowances, and unemployment, sickness and special benefits.

The number of age and disability pensions (including wives' and carers' pensions) in New South Wales on 30 June 1996 was: Age, 546,499; carers/wives, 58,331; disability support, 172,352; sole parent, 114,778.

Under the Basic Family Payment scheme, which commenced in 1993, at 30 June 1996, 1,136,126 children and students in 587,757 families were receiving payments.

246,883 unemployment, 11,675 sickness and 8,688 special benefits were paid.

Direct State Government social welfare services are limited, for the most part, to the assistance of persons not eligible for Commonwealth Government pensions or benefits, and the provision of certain forms of assistance not available from the Commonwealth Government. The State also subsidizes many approved services for needy persons.

CULTURE

Broadcasting. In addition to national broadcasting, at Sept. 1997 there were 11 commercial television services broadcasting in NSW and a total of 39 AM and 24 FM commercial radio services. The first cable-pay television service commenced in Sept. 1995, and satellite-delivered services in Nov. 1995.

Cinema. In the year ended March 1995, 2,836,900 people attended cinema screenings. Construction of a major film studio development for Fox Studios, valued at $A120m., began in 1997.

Tourism. In the year ended 30 June 1996, 1,719,900 overseas visitors arrived for short-term visits. At 30 June 1996 there were 1,743 hotels and motels providing 57,920 rooms; and 791 caravan parks.

Museums and Galleries. In the year to March 1995, 2,389,700 people visited museums and galleries.

FURTHER READING

Statistical Information: The NSW Government Statistician's Office was established in 1886, and in 1957 was integrated with the Commonwealth Bureau of Census and Statistics (now called the Australian Bureau of Statistics). *Deputy Commonwealth Statistician:* Denis Farrell. Its principal publications are:

New South Wales Year Book (1886/87–1900/01 under the title *Wealth and Progress of New South Wales*). Annual.—*Regional Statistics.—New South Wales Pocket Year Book.— Monthly Summary of Statistics.—New South Wales in Brief.*

State Library: The State Library of NSW, Macquarie St., Sydney.

QUEENSLAND

KEY HISTORICAL EVENTS

Queensland was first visited by Capt. Cook in 1770. From 1778 it was part of New South Wales and was formed into a separate colony, with the name of Queensland, by letters patent of 8 June 1859, when responsible government was conferred. Although by 1868 gold had been discovered, wool was the colony's principal product. The first railway line was opened in 1865. Queensland federated with the other Australian states to form the Commonwealth of Australia in 1901.

TERRITORY AND POPULATION

Queensland comprises the whole northeastern portion of the Australian continent, including the adjacent islands in the Pacific Ocean and in the Gulf of Carpentaria. Estimated area 1,727,200 sq. km.

The increase in the population as shown by the censuses since 1901 has been as follows (including Aboriginals from 1966):

		Census counts		Intercensal increase	
Year	Males	Females	Total	Numerical	Rate per annum %
1901	277,003	221,126	498,129	—	—
1911	329,506	276,307	605,813	107,684	1·98
1921	398,969	357,003	755,972	150,159	2·24
1933	497,217	450,317	947,534	191,562	1·86
1947	567,471	538,944	1,106,415	158,881	1·11
1954	676,252	642,007	1,318,259	211,844	2·53
1961	774,579	744,249	1,518,828	200,569	2·04
1966	849,390	824,934	1,674,324	144,857	1·84
1971	921,665	905,400	1,827,065	152,741	1·76
1976	1,024,611	1,012,586	2,037,197	210,132	2·20
1981	1,153,404	1,141,719	2,295,123	257,926	2·41
1986	1,295,630	1,291,685	2,587,315	292,192	2·43
1991	1,482,406	1,495,404	2,977,810	390,495	2·60
1996	1,673,220	1,695,630	3,368,850	391,040	2·63

At the 1996 census there were 95,518 Aboriginals and Torres Strait Islanders.

Since the 1981 census, official population estimates are according to place of usual residence and are referred to as estimated resident population. Estimated resident population at 30 June 1997, 3,338,690.

Statistics on birthplaces from the 1996 census are as follows: Australia, 78·4% (83·6% in 1986); UK and Ireland, 5·6% (6·1%); other countries, 12·4% (14·4%); at sea and not stated, 3·6% (1·4%).

Brisbane, the capital, had at 30 June 1997 (estimate) a resident population of 1,548,346 (Statistical Division). The estimated resident populations of the other major centres (Statistical Districts) at 30 June 1997 (preliminary) were: Gold Coast-Tweed, (including that part in New South Wales) 367,722; Townsville, 123,575; Sunshine Coast, 162,099; Cairns, 109,516; Rockhampton, 64,477; Mackay, 62,442; Bundaberg, 54,809 and Gladstone, 38,141.

SOCIAL STATISTICS

Statistics (including Aboriginals) for calendar years:

	Total births	Marriages	Divorces	Deaths
1993	46,778	20,704	9,935	19,972
1994	46,578	20,798	9,762	21,655
1995	46,484	20,610	10,192	20,663
1996	47,769	20,913	10,996	22,281

The annual rates per 1,000 population in 1996 were: Marriages, 6·3; births, 14·3; deaths, 6·7. The infant death rate was 6·3 per 1,000 live births.

CLIMATE

A typical subtropical to tropical climate. High daytime temperatures during Oct. to March give a short spring and long summer. Centigrade temperatures in the hottest inland areas often exceed the high 30s before the official commencement of summer on 1 Dec. Daytime temperatures in winter are quite mild, in the low- to mid-20s. Average rainfall varies from about 150 mm in the desert in the extreme south-western corner of the State to about 4,000 mm in parts of the sugar lands of the wet north-eastern coast, the latter being the wettest part of Australia.

CONSTITUTION AND GOVERNMENT

Queensland, formerly a portion of New South Wales, was formed into a separate colony in 1859, and responsible government was conferred. The power of making laws and imposing taxes is vested in a parliament of one house—the *Legislative Assembly*, which comprises 89 members, returned from 4 electoral zones for 3 years, elected from single-member constituencies by compulsory ballot.

Queensland elects 26 members to the Commonwealth House of Representatives.

The Elections Act, 1983, provides franchise for all males and females, 18 years of age and over, qualified by 6 months' residence in Australia and 3 months in the electoral district.

RECENT ELECTIONS

Following a by-election to the Legislative Assembly in Dec. 1998 the Australian Labor Party (ALP) held 45 seats, the National Party (NP) 23, One Nation 10, the Liberal Party (LP) 9, and ind 2.

CURRENT ADMINISTRATION

Governor of Queensland: Maj. Gen. Peter Arnison, AO.

An NP-LP coalition government was formed in June 1996, with the support of independent Peter Wellington, comprising as at Feb. 1999:

Premier: Peter Douglas Beattie.

Attorney-General, Justice and Arts: Matthew Joseph Foley. *Deputy Premier, Minister for State Development and Trade:* James Peter Elder. *Aboriginal and Torres Strait Islander Policy, Women's Policy and Fair Trading:* Judith Caroline Spence. *Communication and Information, Local Government, Planning, Regional and Rural Communities:* Terence Michael Mackenroth. *Education:* Dean MacMillan Wells. *Emergency Services:* Merri Rose. *Employment, Training and Industrial Relations:* Paul Joseph Braddy. *Environment and Heritage, Natural Resources:* Rodney Jon Welford. *Families, Youth and Community Care, Disability Services:* Anna Maria Bligh. *Health:* Wendy Marjorie Edmond. *Mines and Energy, Minister assisting the Deputy Premier on Regional Development:* Anthony McGrady. *Police and Corrective Services:* Thomas Alfred Barton. *Primary Industries:* Heinrich Palaszczuk. *Public Works and Housing:* Robert Evan Schwarten. *Tourism, Sport and Racing:* Robert James Gibbs. *Transport and Main Roads:* Stephen Dominic Bredhauer. *Treasurer:* David John Hamill.

Local Government. In 1997, there were 125 local governments made up of 18 city councils (including Brisbane), 3 town councils and 104 shire councils. Queensland local governments own and manage public infrastructure worth at least $A50,000m. They provide water, sewerage and cleansing services, and are responsible for land use planning, building control and waste management. Facilities for recreational and sporting activities, including parks and gardens, libraries, child care and aged care, as well as a range of community development programmes covering areas such as arts, cultural heritage and youth activities, are also maintained.

The 1997 local government triennial elections were held on 15 March. In all, 349 Councillors were elected out of the almost 1,200 Councillor positions contested, and 36 new Mayors.

In addition to government grants and subsidies, local authority revenue is derived from general rates, paid by landowners on the unimproved capital value of land, and by charging for some specific services. For the year ended 30 June 1997, total outlays for all Queensland local government authorities were $A2,020m., while revenue totalled $A1,817m.

ECONOMY

Budget. In 1996–97 current outlays by the state totalled $A12,174m., of which $A7,097m. were general government final consumption expenditure, and capital outlays totalled $A2,171m. Revenue and grants received totalled $A13,390m.

Banking and Finance. In June 1996 deposits at all banks in Queensland totalled $A38,137m., of which $A10,107m. were current, $A21,171m. were term deposits and $A3,628m. were investment savings. Other lending totalled $A51,206m. In 1995–96 permanent building societies had total assets of $A6,625·7m.

QUEENSLAND

ENERGY AND NATURAL RESOURCES

Electricity. Installed capacity in 1991–92 was 5,285 MW. Output 1993–94, 31,831m. kWh, of which 24,001m. kWh was consumed by 1,355,793 customers. Some 0·9% of production is hydro-electric; most power stations are coal-fired.

Water. In the western portion of the State water is comparatively easily found by sinking artesian bores. Monitoring of water quality in Queensland is carried out by the Department of the Environment (estuarine and coastal waters) and the Department of Natural Resources (fresh water).

Minerals. Principal minerals produced during 1995–96 (in tonnes): Bauxite, 9,179,000; copper concentrates, 1,007,000; lead concentrate, 359,000; mineral sands, 208,000; nickel ore, 3,000; tin, 82,000; zinc concentrate, 446,000; zinc-lead concentrate, 48,000; gold bullion, 38,108 (kg); silver, 520,000. Total value of output, at the mine, in 1995–96 was $A6,053·5m.

Agriculture. In 1995–96 there were 32,186 agricultural establishments farming 149,748,000 ha. Livestock on farms and stations at 31 March 1996 numbered 10,214,000 cattle, 10,707,000 sheep and lambs and 603,000 pigs. Total wool production in the year ended 31 March 1995, 51,935 tonnes. The total area under crops during 1995–96 was 2,495,000 ha.

	Area (1,000 ha)		Production (tonnes)	
Crop	1996	1997	1996	1997
Sugar-cane, crushed	358	371	33,897,600	36,231,800
Wheat	626	980	519,500	1,979,500
Maize	31	34	113,600	129,900
Sorghum	596·8	423·9	1,115,600	1,003,300
Barley	169	180	195,000	428,600
Potatoes	5	5	103,845	115,434
Pumpkins	3	3	43,266	38,688
Tomatoes	3	4	102,643	109,911
Peanuts	20	23	37,600	45,900
Apples[1]	501	545	28,362	28,045
Grapes[2]	1	1	3,984	4,530
Bananas[2]	5	6	165,639	143,747
Pineapples[2]	3	3	127,835	122,980
Cotton (raw)	120	129	302,800	457,700

[1]Number of trees 6 years and over (in 1,000). [2]Bearing area only.

The gross value of agricultural commodity production in 1995–96 amounted to $A5,370m., which comprised crops, $A3,244m.; livestock disposals, $A1,552m., and livestock products, $A575m.

Forestry. A considerable area consists of natural forest, eucalyptus, pine and cabinet woods being the timbers mostly in evidence; a large quantity of ornamental woods is utilized by cabinet makers. The amount of sawn timber processed in 1994–95 was 651,979 cu. metres of pine and 238,310 cu. metres of other wood.

INDUSTRY

In 1995–96, manufacturing establishments recorded $A28,801m. in turnover, paid $A3,966m. in wages and salaries, and (at 30 June 1996) employed 133,855 persons. The largest manufacturing sector was food, beverages and tobacco with 30·1% of turnover, 25·8% of wages and salaries paid and 24·8% of employment.

Labour. In May 1997 the labour force numbered 1,713,900, of whom 1,546,500 (669,100 females) were employed. Unemployment was 9·7%.

Trade Unions. There were 51 trade unions in June 1996 with 477,400 members.

INTERNATIONAL TRADE

Imports and Exports. Total value of direct overseas imports and exports (in $A1,000) f.o.b. port of shipment for both imports and exports:

	1991–92	1992–93	1993–94	1994–95	1995–96
Imports	5,626,715	6,334,175	6,869,158	7,771,035	21,433,600
Exports	10,865,144	11,798,170	11,984,172	12,510,814	19,844,300

In 1995–96 interstate exports totalled $A6,220,000 and imports $A13,381,40. Chief sources of imports in 1995–96 (in $A1m.): Japan, 1,427·4; USA 1,427·1; EU, 1,360·9; Papua New Guinea, 816·0; New Zealand, 558·8. Exports went chiefly to: Japan, 4,140·1; EU, 1,736·8; Korea, 1,119·4; USA, 612·6; Taiwan, 595·1.

The chief exports overseas in 1995–96 (in $A1m.) were: Coal, 4,481·5; sugar, 1,628·4; meat and meat preparations, 1,399·5; non-ferrous metals, 927·7; metalliferous ores and metal scrap, 811·2; machinery and transport equipment, 750·0. Principal overseas imports were: Road vehicles, 1,550·5; petroleum and petroleum products, 1,088·1; machinery, specialized for particular industries, 646·6; non-monetary gold, 400·9.

COMMUNICATIONS

Roads. At 30 June 1996 there were 177,032 km of roads open to the public. Of these, 65,129 km were surfaced with sealed pavement. At 31 Oct. 1996 motor vehicles registered (in 1,000) totalled 2,082, comprising 1,567·3 passenger vehicles, 353·1 light commercial vehicles, 82·8 trucks, 12·4 buses and 66·4 motor cycles. There were 385 fatalities in road accidents in 1996.

Rail. Queensland Rail is a State government-owned corporation. Total length of line at 30 June 1996 was 9,442 km, of which 1,820 km were electrified. In 1995–96, 40·1m. passengers and 96·2m. tonnes of freight were carried.

Civil Aviation. Queensland is well served with a network of air services, with overseas and interstate connections. Subsidiary companies provide planes for taxi and charter work, and the Flying Doctor Service operates throughout western Queensland. In 1993 there were 134 licensed airports. In 1995-96 Brisbane handled 2,064,592 passengers and 56,102 tonnes of freight; Cairns, 694,348 passengers and 14,603 tonnes of freight. No international passenger services were recorded for Townsville during the year. The number of aircraft registered at 30 June 1995 was 2,186.

Shipping. Queensland has 14 modern trading ports, 2 community ports and· a number of non-trading ports. In 1995–96, cargo discharged was 25,124,000 mass tonnes and cargo loaded was 105,842,000 mass tonnes.

Telecommunications. There were 1·45m. telephones in 1993.

Postal Services. At 30 June 1997 there were 440 post offices and postal agencies.

SOCIAL INSTITUTIONS

Justice. Justice is administered by Higher Courts (Supreme and District), Magistrates' Courts and Children's Courts. The Supreme Court comprises the Chief Justice and 21 judges; the District Courts, 34 district court judges. Stipendiary magistrates preside over the Magistrates' and Children's Courts, except in the smaller centres, where justices of the peace officiate. A parole board may recommend prisoners for release.

The total number of appearances in the Higher Courts resulting in convictions in 1995–96 was 4,983; appearances resulting in convictions in Magistrates' Courts totalled 171,708, and proven offences in Children's Courts totalled 5,137. At 30 June 1996 there were 12 correctional centres with 3,538 prisoners (172 females). The total police force was 6,582 at 30 June 1996.

Religion. Religious affiliation at the 1991 census: Roman Catholic, 25·4%; Anglican, 25·2%; Uniting Church, 10·4%; Presbyterian, 5·4%; Lutheran, 2·3%; Baptist, 1·9%; other Christian, 6·4%; non-Christian, 1%; no religion, 11·6%; not stated, 10%.

Education. Education is compulsory between the ages of 6 and 15 years and is provided free in government schools.

Primary and secondary education comprises 12 years of full-time formal schooling, and is provided by both the government and non-government sectors. In 1997 the State administered 1,309 schools with 267,147 primary students and 148,116 secondary students. In 1997 there were 26,720 teachers in government schools. There were 417 private schools in 1997 with 80,537 primary students and

79,306 secondary students. Educational programmes at private schools were provided by 10,290 teachers in 1997.

In 1996 there were 24,039 full-time students at TAFE institutes. The 6 publicly funded universities had 108,175 full-time students in 1996. Teaching staff totalled 12,523.

Health. In 1995-96 there were 195 hospitals (148 public with over 9,900 beds), 7 psychiatric institutions. At 30 June 1997 there were 6,390 doctors, 3,147 specialists, 2,062 dentists and 34,278 registered nurses.

Welfare. Welfare institutions providing shelter and social care for the aged, the handicapped and children, are maintained or assisted by the State. A child health service is provided throughout the State. Age, invalid, widows', disability and war service pensions, family allowances, and unemployment and sickness benefits are paid by the Federal Government. At 30 June 1996, age pensioners in the State numbered 276,448 and invalid/disability support pensioners, 109,563 (including wife and carer pensioners); disability pensioners, 68,127; and service pensioners, 68,499 (including dependants).

There were 7,916 widows' and 69,341 sole parent pensions current at 30 June 1996, and basic family payment was being paid for 678,148 children under 16 years and eligible students aged 16 to 24 years in 349,799 families.

CULTURE

Broadcasting. In addition to the national networks Queensland is served by 13 public radio stations (non-profit-making), 44 commercial radio stations and 3 commercial TV channels.

Tourism. Overseas visitors to Australia who specified Queensland as their primary destination numbered 1,279,700 in 1996 with the main source being from Asia with 62% of the State visitor total, of which Japanese made up 35·2% and other Asians 26·8%. Visitors from New Zealand accounted for 18·8%; Europe, 9·8% (including UK and Ireland, 5·1%) and North America, 4·5%.

Festivals. The Brisbane Festival in 1997 featured 238 performances in 37 venues across the city.

Libraries. The State Library of Queensland aims to provide equitable access to high-quality State Library and public library services. The Library received about 150,000 requests for information during 1996-97 and more than 450,000 people visited the State Library at South Bank.

National Theatre and Opera. The Queensland Performing Arts Complex at South Bank comprises a Concert Hall, Lyric Theatre, the Cremorne Theatre and, in 1998, a drama theatre: the Southbank Playhouse. During 1996-97, 850 performances and activities were presented in the 3 main auditoria of the Complex, with attendances totalling 730,000.

Museums and Galleries. The Queensland Museum focuses on science and human achievement. 492,874 people visited the museum during 1996-97. The Queensland Art Gallery is located at South Bank. Over 35,000 people attended the Gallery's travelling exhibitions in regional Queensland.

FURTHER READING

Statistical Information: The Statistical Office (now Australian Bureau of Statistics, 313 Adelaide St., Brisbane) was set up in 1859. *Deputy Commonwealth Statistician:* R. A. Crockett. *A Queensland Official Year Book* was issued in 1901, the annual *ABC of Queensland Statistics* from 1905 to 1936 with exception of 1918 and 1922. Present publications include: *Queensland Year Book.* Annual, from 1937 (omitting 1942, 1943, 1944, 1987, 1991). —*Queensland Pocket Year Book.* Annual from 1950.—*Monthly Summary of Statistics, Queensland.* From Jan. 1961. Selected statistics available at *website:* http://www.abs.gov.au

Australian Sugar Year Book. Brisbane, from 1941
Johnston, W. R., *A Bibliography of Queensland History.* Brisbane, 1981.—*The Call of the Land: A History of Queensland to the Present Day.* Brisbane, 1982
Johnston, W. R. and Zerner, M., *Guide to the History of Queensland.* Brisbane, 1985

AUSTRALIA

State Library: The State Library of Queensland, Queensland Cultural Centre, South Bank, South Brisbane.
Website: http://www.slq.qld.gov.au

SOUTH AUSTRALIA

KEY HISTORICAL EVENTS
South Australia was surveyed by Tasman in 1644 and charted by Flinders in 1802. It was formed into a British province by letters of patent of Feb. 1836, and a partially elective legislative council was established in 1851. From 6 July 1863, the Northern Territory was placed under the jurisdiction of South Australia until the establishment of the Commonwealth of Australia in 1901.

TERRITORY AND POPULATION
The total area of South Australia is 380,070 sq. miles (984,377 sq. km). The settled part is divided into counties and hundreds. There are 49 counties proclaimed, covering 23m. ha, of which 19m. ha are occupied. Outside this area there are extensive pastoral districts, covering 76m. ha, 49m. of which are under pastoral leases.

Estimated resident population at 30 June 1998 was 1,487,294, including (30 June 1997) 747,887 females and 22,503 Aboriginal and Torres Strait Islander people, of whom 11,499 were female. The 1996 census population was 1,427,936.

The Adelaide Statistical Division had 1,045,854 persons at the 1996 census in 25 councils and 4 municipalities and other districts. Cities outside this area (with 1996 census populations) are Whyalla (23,644), Mount Gambier (22,047), Port Augusta (14,244), Port Pirie (13,960) and Port Lincoln (12,182).

SOCIAL STATISTICS
Statistics for calendar years:

	Live Births	Marriages	Divorces	Deaths
1995	19,336	8,547	4,199	11,218
1996	19,056	8,011	4,358	11,606
1997	18,362	7,945	4,115	11,658

The infant mortality rate in 1997 was 4·7 per 1,000 live births.

CONSTITUTION AND GOVERNMENT
South Australia was formed into a British province by letters of patent of Feb. 1836, and a partially elective Legislative Council was established in 1851. The present Constitution dates from 24 Oct. 1856. It vests the legislative power in an elected Parliament, consisting of a Legislative Council and a House of Assembly. The former is composed of 22 members. Every 4 years half the members retire, and the resulting vacancies are filled at a general election on the basis of proportional representation with the State as one multi-member electorate. The qualifications of an elector are, to be an Australian citizen, or a British subject who on 25 Jan. 1984 was enrolled on a Commonwealth electoral roll and/or at some time between 26 Oct. 1983 and 25 Jan. 1984 inclusive was enrolled on an electoral roll for a South Australian Assembly district or a Commonwealth electoral roll in any State. The person must be at least 18 years of age and have lived continuously in Australia for at least 6 months, in South Australia for at least 3 months, and in the sub-division for which he is enrolled at least 1 month. War service may substitute for residential qualifications in some cases. By the Constitution Act Amendment Act, 1894, the franchise was extended to women, who voted for the first time at the general election of 25 April 1896. The qualifications for election as a member of both Houses are the same as for an elector. Certain persons are ineligible for election to either House.

SOUTH AUSTRALIA

The House of Assembly consists of 47 members elected for 4 years, representing single electorates. Election of members of both Houses takes place by preferential secret ballot. Voting is compulsory for those on the Electoral Roll.

Electors enrolled (2 March 1996) numbered 989,885.

The executive power is vested in a Governor appointed by the Crown and an Executive Council, consisting of the Governor and the Ministers of the Crown. The Governor has the power to dissolve the House of Assembly but not the Legislative Council, unless that Chamber has twice consecutively with an election intervening defeated the same or substantially the same Bill passed in the House of Assembly by an absolute majority.

CURRENT ADMINISTRATION

The House of Assembly, elected on 27 Oct. 1998, consists of the following members: Liberal Party of Australia (LP), 23; Australian Labor Party (ALP), 21; Independent (IND), 2; National, 1. The Legislative Council consists of 10 LP, 8 ALP, 1 IND and 3 Australian Democrat members.

Governor: Sir Eric James Neal, AC, CVO.

In Feb. 1999 the Liberal Ministry was as follows:

Premier, Minister for Multicultural Affairs: John Wayne Olsen.

Deputy Premier, Minister for Primary Industries, Natural Resources and Regional Development: Robert Gerard Kerin. *Treasurer:* Kenneth Trevor Griffin. *Human Services:* Dean Craig Brown. *Government Enterprises, Information, Economy:* Dr Michael Harry Armitage. *Transport, Urban Planning and the Arts:* Diana Vivienne Laidlaw. *Environment and Heritage, Aboriginal Affairs:* Dorothy Christine Kotz. *Education, Children's Services and Training:* Malcolm Robert Buckby. *Local Government, Employment, Youth:* Mark Kennion Brindal. *Industry and Trade, Recreation, Sport and Racing:* Iain Frederick Evans. *Tourism:* Joan Hall. *Year 2000 Compliance:* Wayne Matthew. *Disability Services, Ageing, Administrative Services, Information Services:* Robert Lawson. *Police, Correctional and Emergency Services:* Robert Brokenshire.

Ministers are jointly and individually responsible to the legislature for all their official acts.

Local Government. The closely settled part of the State (mainly near the sea-coast and the River Murray) is incorporated into local government areas, and sub-divided into district councils (rural areas only), municipal corporations (mainly metropolitan, but including larger country towns) and cities (more densely populated areas with a qualification of 15,000 residents in the Adelaide metropolitan area, and 10,000 in the country). At 1 Jan. 1996 there were 118 local government authorities. The main functions of councils are the construction and maintenance of roads and bridges, sport and recreational facilities, and garbage collection and disposal.

The number and area of the sub-divisions, together with expenditure (in $A1,000) for the year ended 30 June 1996, were:

	No.	Area (1,000 ha)	Roads and bridges	Recreation and culture	All other	Total expenditure
Adelaide statistical division	24	189·3	89,750	87,935	74,905	531,032
Other municipal corporations and district councils	64	15,220·0	72,403	32,914	46,163	266,822
Total	88	15,409·3	162,153	138,562	120,258	797,854

ECONOMY

Budget. Public sector revenue and outlays (in $A1m.) for years ended 30 June:

	1990	1991	1992	1993	1994
Revenue	4,787	5,154	5,324	6,139	6,433
Outlays	5,516	6,172	7,040	6,611	6,681

Banking and Finance. In March 1993 the average weekly balance of deposits held by all banks was $A14,651m. The average weekly balance of loans, advances and bills discounted was $A17,240m.

AUSTRALIA

ENERGY AND NATURAL RESOURCES

Minerals. The value of minerals produced in 1994–95 was $A1,186·0m. (metallic minerals, $A323·4m.; opals, $A38·6m.; natural gas, $A339m.; crude oil, $A114·4m.; condensates, $A86·3m.; liquefied petroleum gas, $A92·5m.; coal, $A72·7m.; construction materials, $A64·7m.). The principal metallic minerals produced are iron ore, copper, uranium oxide, gold and silver.

Agriculture. Total area of agricultural establishments, at 31 March 1995, was 56,100,961 ha.

Soil Conservation. A Department of Agriculture programme to deal with the problems of erosion and soil conservation includes the planting of cereal rye, perennial rye and other grasses to check sand drifts; contour furrowing and contour banking; contour planting with vines and fruit trees; and several water-diversion schemes.

Gross value of agricultural production (in $A1,000), 1994–95: Crops, 1,493,100; livestock slaughtering, 466,200; livestock products, 505,300. Total gross value, $A2,464,600.

Sown area (in ha) and output (in tonnes) of the chief crops in 1994–95: Wheat, 1,534,900 and 2,794,900; barley, 1,023,310 and 1,008,900; oats, 120,600 and 155,800; hay, 103,200 and 383,000; vines, 38,545 and 374,589.

Fruit culture is extensive, and in 1996–97, 210,393 tonnes of citrus and 65,343 tonnes of other orchard fruit were produced. Other products, in addition to root crops and vegetables, are grass seeds and oil seeds.

Livestock, 31 March 1995: 1,216,020 cattle, 13,249,100 sheep and 422,903 pigs. In 1994, 87,313 tonnes of wool clip and (1994–95) 484m. litres of milk were produced.

Irrigation. For the year ended 31 March 1994, 112,177 ha were under irrigated culture, being used as follows: Vineyards, 23,667; fruit (excluding grapes), 16,008; vegetables, 8,940; other crops, 10,872; and pasture, 52,688.

INDUSTRY

The turnover for manufacturing industries for 1996–97 was $A18,449m.

Industry sub-division	Establish-ments (No.)	Persons employed (1,000)	Wages and salaries ($A1m.)	Turnover ($A1m.)
Food, beverages and tobacco	474	14·9	481	3,988·5
Textiles, clothing, footwear and leather manufacturing	275	4·9	134	779·2
Wood and paper products manufacturing	312	5·5	182	907·7
Printing, publishing and recorded media	422	5·8	180	809·8
Chemical, petroleum, coal and associated products	247	6·6	245	1,372·9
Non-metallic mineral products	217	2·6	94	610·4
Metal products manufacturing	681	11·1	401	2,510·9
Machinery and equipment	836	28·1	1008	6,889·1
Other manufacturing	588	5·1	123	571·0
Total	4,052	84·5	2,847	18,449·5

Practically all forms of secondary industry are to be found, the most important being motor vehicle manufacture, saw-milling and the manufacture of household appliances, basic iron and steel, meat and meat products, and wine and brandy.

Labour. Two systems of industrial arbitration and conciliation for the adjustment of industrial relations between employers and employees are in operation—the State system, which operates when industrial disputes are confined to the territorial limits of the State, and the Federal system, which applies when disputes involve other parts of Australia as well as South Australia.

The industrial tribunals are authorized to fix minimum rates of wages and other conditions of employment, and their awards may be enforced by law. Industrial agreements between employers and organizations of employees, when registered, may be enforced in the same manner as awards.

INTERNATIONAL TRADE

Imports and Exports. Overseas imports and exports in $A1m. (year ending 30 June):

	1991–92	1992–93	1993–94	1994–95	1995–96
Imports	2,396·9	3,068·1	2,803·4	3,099·5	3,113·8
Exports	3,505·1	3,756·3	3,889·8	3,829·3	4,496·9

Principal exports in 1995–96 were (in $A1m.): Cereals and cereal preparations, 712·9; road vehicles, parts and accessories, 249·2; meat and meat preparations, 244·4; wool and sheepskins, 239·6; metals and metal manufacture, 610·4; petroleum and petroleum products, 220·4; wine, 317·3; fish and crustaceans, 196·3.

Principal imports in 1995–96 were (in $A1m.): Road vehicles, parts and accessories, 546·5; machinery, 675·9; petroleum and petroleum products, 346·4.

In 1995–96 the leading suppliers of imports were (in $A1m.): Japan (709·8), USA (439·1), UK (223·5), New Zealand (117·9). Main export markets were Japan (678·5), USA (278·8), New Zealand (374·3), UK (287·6), China (293·1), Hong Kong (201·5).

COMMUNICATIONS

Roads. At 30 June 1996, of the roads customarily used by the public, there were 2,753 km of national highways, 9,560 km of arterial roads and 83,020 km of local roads, totalling 95,333 km. Lengths of road classified by surface were as follows: Sealed, 25,900 km; unsealed, 69,433 km. Costs of construction and maintenance are shared by the State and Commonwealth governments and by the councils of the local areas. Motor vehicles registered at 30 June 1995: Passenger and other motor vehicles, 908,400; motorcycles, 26,600. In 1995 there were 182 fatalities in road accidents.

Rail. At 30 June 1996, Australian National Railways operated 4,415 km of railway in country areas. TransAdelaide operated 120 km of railway in the metropolitan area of Adelaide, which carried 8·4m. passengers in 1994–95.

There is a tramway in Adelaide.

Civil Aviation. There is an international airport at Adelaide. In 1996 it handled 3,653,000 passengers (220,000 on international flights), and in 1995, 21,200 tonnes of freight. In July 1996 there were 27 licensed aerodromes.

Shipping. There are 10 state and 5 private deep-sea ports. In 1995, 770 vessels conducting overseas trade entered South Australia with 3·12m. import tonnes of cargo and left with 4·93m. export tonnes. In 1995–96 the state-owned ports handled 12·5m. tonnes of cargo out of a total of 20·1m. tonnes.

Telecommunications. Telephone services in operation totalled 805,478 at 30 June 1994.

Postal Services. At 30 June 1997, there were 527 post offices.

SOCIAL INSTITUTIONS

Justice. There is a Supreme Court, which incorporates admiralty, civil, criminal, land and valuation, and testamentary jurisdiction; district criminal courts, which have jurisdiction in many indictable offences, and magistrates courts, which include the Youth Court. Circuit courts are held at several places. In the year ended 31 Dec. 1994, there were 1,456 appearances in the higher criminal courts. In 1,324 of those cases, the defendant was found guilty of the major charge. In 1996 the police force numbered 3,586. There were 4,540 prisoners received under sentence in 1995.

Religion. Religious affiliation at the 1996 census: Catholic, 296,048; Anglican, 228,151; Uniting Church, 180,604; Lutheran, 70,970; Orthodox, 42,053; Baptist, 26,251; Presbyterian, 23,994; other Christians, 74,868; non-Christians, 25,236; indefinite, 4,885; no religion, 310,908; not stated, 138,554.

Education. Education is secular and is compulsory for children 6–15 years of age. Primary and secondary education at government schools is free. In 1995 there were

19,461 children in 421 pre-school centres. In 1995 there were 853 schools operating, of which 193 were non-government and 660 government schools, the latter comprising 60 junior primary, 407 primary, 3 primary-secondary, 84 secondary, 51 area, 21 special, 16 rural, 16 Aboriginal schools; 1 English as Second Language and 1 Open Access College. There were 122,582 children in government and 39,355 in non-government primary schools, and 55,889 children in government and 26,966 in non-government secondary schools. 10 Institutes of Vocational Education were formed in 1993 by a merger of the former 19 TAFE colleges. There were 49,432 students at the 3 universities in 1995.

Welfare. The number of pensioners at 30 June 1995 was: Age, 155,569; disability support, 43,247; wife's/carer's pension, 17,462; widow's, 4,034; sole parent, 27,646; rehabilitation, 33.

CULTURE

Broadcasting. Apart from the national services, there were in 1997, 92 radio stations (22 AM and 70 FM) and 4 commercial TV stations.

Tourism. In June 1998 there were 226 hotels, motels, guest houses and serviced apartments with 9,900 rooms.

FURTHER READING

Statistical Information: The State branch of the Australian Bureau of Statistics is at 55 Currie St., Adelaide (GPO Box 2272). *Regional Director:* I. Crettenden. Although the first printed statistical publication was the *Statistics of South Australia, 1854*, with the title altered to *Statistical Register* in 1859, there is a written volume for each year back to 1838. These contain simple records of trade, demography, production, etc. and were prepared only for the use of the Colonial Office; one copy was retained in the State.

The publications of the State branch include the *South Australian Year Book* and a *Monthly Summary of Statistics, South Australian Economic Indicators*, a quarterly bulletin of building activity, a quarterly bulletin of tourist accommodation and approximately 40 special bulletins issued each year as particulars of various sections of statistics become available.

Gibbs, R. M., *A History of South Australia: From Colonial Days to the Present*. Adelaide, 1984
Whitelock, D., *Adelaide, 1836–1976: A History of Difference*. Univ.of Queensland Press, 1977

State Library: The State Library of S.A., North Terrace, Adelaide. *State Librarian:* Frances H. Awcock.

TASMANIA

KEY HISTORICAL EVENTS

Abel Janszoon Tasman discovered Van Diemen's Land (Tasmania) on 24 Nov. 1642. The island became a British settlement in 1803 as a dependency of New South Wales; in 1825 its connection with New South Wales was terminated; in 1851 a partially elected Legislative Council was established; and in 1856 responsible government came into operation. On 1 Jan. 1901 Tasmania was federated with the other Australian states into the Commonwealth of Australia.

TERRITORY AND POPULATION

Tasmania is a group of islands separated from the mainland by Bass Strait with an area (including islands) of 68,049 sq. km, or 6·8m. ha, of which 6,408,600 ha form the area of the main island. The population at 10 consecutive censuses (including full-blood Aboriginals from 1966) was:

	Population		Population
1947	257,078	1976	402,868
1954	308,752	1981	418,957
1961	350,340	1986	436,353
1966	371,435	1991	452,837
1971	390,413	1996	459,659

TASMANIA

At the census of 6 Aug. 1996, 23,103 were born in the UK or Ireland, 11,120 in other European countries and 394,774 in Australia. Estimated resident population at 31 Dec. 1997, 471,789 (240,100 females).

The largest cities and towns (with populations at the 1996 census) are: Hobart (189,944), Launceston (95,982), Devonport (23,814) and Burnie (19,283).

SOCIAL STATISTICS
Statistics for calendar years:

	Marriages	Divorces	Births	Deaths
1994	2,887	1,544	6,844	3,911
1995	2,840	1,279	6,558	3,739
1996	2,654	1,582	6,419	3,884
1997	2,672	1,321	6,007	3,809

CLIMATE
Mostly a temperate maritime climate. The sea, never more than 115 km distant, suppresses temperature extremes. The prevailing westerly airstream leads to a marked variation of cloudiness, rainfall and temperature. The result is a west coast and highlands that are cool, wet and cloudy, and an east coast and lowlands that are milder, drier and sunnier.

CONSTITUTION AND GOVERNMENT
Parliament consists of the Governor, the Legislative Council and the House of Assembly. The Council has 19 members, elected by adults with 6 months' residence. Members sit for 6 years, 3 retiring annually and 4 every sixth year. There is no power to dissolve the Council. Vacancies are filled by by-elections. The House of Assembly has 35 members; the maximum term for the House of Assembly is 4 years. Women received the right to vote in 1903. Proportional representation was adopted in 1907, the method now being the single transferable vote in 7-member constituencies. Casual vacancies in the House of Assembly are determined by a transfer of the preference of the vacating member's ballot papers to consenting candidates who were unsuccessful at the last general election.

A Minister must have a seat in one of the two Houses.

RECENT ELECTIONS
At the elections of Aug. 1998 the Australian Labor Party won 14 seats in the House of Assembly, the Liberal Party 10 and the Tasmanian Greens 1.

CURRENT ADMINISTRATION
The Legislative Council is predominantly independent without formal party allegiance; 4 members are Labor-endorsed and 1 Liberal.

Governor: Sir Guy Stephen Montague Green, AC, KBE.

A majority Labor government was formed in Oct. 1998, which in Jan. 1999 comprised:

Premier, Minister for State Development: James Bacon.
Deputy Premier, Minister for Infrastructure Energy and Resources, Racing and Gaming: Paul Lennon. *Chair of Committees:* James Cox. *Secretary to Cabinet:* Fran Bladel. *Health and Human Services:* Judith Jackson. *Primary Industries, Water and Environment, Minister for Police:* David Llewellyn. *Attorney General, Justice and Industrial Relations:* Peter Patmore. *Education:* Paula Wriedt.

Local Government. The State is divided into 29 municipal areas comprising the cities of Hobart, Launceston, Glenorchy, Clarence, Burnie and Devonport and 23 municipalities. The number of municipalities was reduced from 46 in 1993 because of the amalgamation of smaller into larger municipalities. The cities and municipalities are managed by elected aldermen and councillors, respectively, with reference to local matters such as sanitation and health services, domestic water supplies and roads and bridges within each particular area. The chief sources of revenue are rates (based on assessed annual value) levied on owners of property and government grants.

Tasmanian Islands. Two inhabited Tasmanian islands (King and Flinders) are organized as municipalities. Nearly 1,360 km south-east lies Macquarie Island (123 sq. km), part of the State, and used only as a research base and meteorological station.

ECONOMY

Budget. The revenue is derived chiefly from taxation (pay-roll, motor, lottery and land tax, business franchises and stamp duties), and from grants and reimbursements from the Commonwealth Government. Customs, excise, sales and income tax are levied by the Commonwealth Government, which makes grants to Tasmania for both revenue and capital purposes.

Specific Purpose Grants are mainly used to provide essential services such as hospitals, housing, roads and educational services, while General Purpose Revenue Funds have been paid since 1942 to compensate the State for the loss of income tax to the federal government.

Consolidated Revenue Fund receipts and expenditure, in $A1m., for financial years ending 30 June:

	1994–95	1995–96	1996-97
Revenue	2,157	2,220	2,269
Expenditure	2,228	2,377	2,427

Net State and local government debt, 1996–97, $A3,260m.

In 1996–97 State Government revenue from taxes, fees and fines amounted to $A670m., of which pay-roll tax provided $A148m.; motor tax, $A92m.; taxes on property, $A141m.; taxes on gambling and insurance, $A90m. and franchise taxes, $A150m.

Banking and Finance. Trading bank activity in Tasmania is divided between 3 private banks and the Commonwealth Trading Bank. The 5 savings banks operating in Tasmania are the Commonwealth Savings Bank, the Trust Bank (a trustee savings bank formed by the amalgamation of 2 smaller trustee banks) and 3 private savings banks operated by trading banks. The total value of deposits at 30 June 1997 was $A3,719m. (1996: $A3,615). The value of loans at 30 June 1997 was $A4,500m. (1996: $A4,529m.).

ENERGY AND NATURAL RESOURCES

Electricity. Installed capacity was 2,502 MW in 1997–98. Energy generated in 1997–98, 9,675 GWh. Tasmania has good supplies of hydro-electric power because of assured rainfall and high level water storages (natural and artificial). The disaggregation process has created the new Hydro Electric Commission, Aurora Energy and Transend Networks.

Minerals. Output of principal metallic minerals in 1996–97 was (in tonnes): Zinc, 186,406; iron ore pellets, 809,359; copper, 24,759; lead, 37,974; tin, 8,732; tungsten, 2; gold, 2·43; silver, 165. Coal production, 545,820 tonnes. Value of output, 1996–97 (in $A1,000): Metallic minerals, 460,907; non-metallic and fuel minerals, 48,451; construction materials, 26,962.

Agriculture. The estimated gross value of recorded production from agriculture in 1996–97 was (in $A1m.): Livestock products, 225·8; livestock slaughterings and other disposals, 117·1; crops, 317·2; total gross value, 660·1. There were 4,536 agricultural establishments in 1996–97, occupying a total area of 1,920,000 ha. Area (in 1,000 ha) and production (in 1,000 tonnes) of the principal crops:

	1994–95		1995–96		1996–97	
	Area	Production	Area	Production	Area	Production
Wheat	1·3	2·8	1·1	4·1	1·9	7·5
Barley	14·0	27·1	14·0	38·5	14·5	35·2
Oats	8·3	11·3	10·1	18·4	8·1	14·0
Green peas	6·0	37·9	6·1	30·0	6·3	32·4
Potatoes	6·1	255·7	7·6	302·0	7·4	317·5
Hay	50·6	190·0	64·4	281·6	54·2	225·9
Hops (bearing) (dry)	0·8	1·8	0·7	1·9	0·7	1·8

Livestock at 31 March 1997: Sheep, 3,976,200; cattle, 725,200; pigs, 23,900.

Wool produced during 1996–97 was 18,876 tonnes, valued at $A82·1m.; butter, 10,869 tonnes; cheese, 25,589 tonnes. In 1996–97, 55,649 tonnes of apples and 1,497 tonnes of grapes were produced.

Forestry. Indigenous forests cover a considerable part of the State, and the sawmilling and woodchipping industries are very important. Production of sawn timber in 1997–98 was 344,200 cu. metres. 4,878,300 cu. metres of logs were used for milling and chipping in 1997–98. Newsprint and paper are produced from native hardwoods, principally eucalypts.

Fisheries. Estimated gross value of fisheries production was $A215·3m. in 1996–97. The volume of fisheries production in 1996–97 was 26,426 tonnes.

INDUSTRY
The most important manufactures for export are refined metals, woodchips, newsprint and other paper manufactures, pigments, woollen goods, fruit pulp, confectionery, butter, cheese, preserved and dried vegetables, sawn timber, and processed fish products. The electrolytic-zinc works at Risdon near Hobart treat large quantities of local and imported ore, and produce zinc, sulphuric acid, superphosphate, sulphate of ammonia, cadmium and other by-products. At George Town, large-scale plants produce refined aluminium and manganese alloys. During 1997–98, 4,440,100 tonnes (green weight) of woodchips were produced. In 1996–97 employment in manufacturing establishments was 21,600; wages and salaries totalled $A744m.; turnover, $A4,745m.

Labour. In Nov. 1998, 217,000 persons (58·9% of the civilian population aged 15 and over) were in the workforce, of whom 194,600 were employed.

Trade Unions. In 1998 Tasmania had the highest rate of trade union membership of any Australian State, 34·6%. This compared with 39·3% in Aug. 1996 and 42·9% in Aug. 1994.

INTERNATIONAL TRADE
Imports and Exports. In 1997–98 exports totalled $A2,134·1m. to overseas countries. The principal countries of destination in 1997–98 (with values in $A1m.) for overseas exports were: Japan, 549·0; USA, 176·3; Taiwan, 150·4; Denmark, 135·7; Hong Kong, 132·6; Thailand, 110·8; Malaysia, 108·7; Indonesia, 82·9. Exports to the European Community totalled $A338·7m. In 1997–98 direct imports into Tasmania totalled $A385·4m. from overseas countries. The principal countries of origin in 1997–98 (with values in $A1m.) for overseas imports were: USA, 70·6; Japan, 45·8; New Zealand, 37·4; UK, 36·5.

The main commodities by value (in $A1m.) exported to overseas countries in 1997–98 were: Non-ferrous metals, 556·0; cork and wood, 311·3; metalliferous ores and metal scrap, 254·4; transport equipment (except road vehicles), 273·1; fish, crustaceans and molluscs, 141·2; dairy products, 133·7; iron and steel, 76·5; meat and meat preparations, 71·9; vegetables and fruit, 55·2. The main imports from overseas countries in 1997–98 (in $A1m.) were: Power generating machinery and equipment, 44·0; road vehicles, 41·6; pulp and waste paper, 28·8; coffee, tea, cocoa and spices, 28·1; general industrial machinery and parts, 24·3.

COMMUNICATIONS
Roads. In 1998 there were approximately 24,000 km of roads open to general traffic, of which 370 km were National Highway and 3,350 km were arterial State roads. Motor vehicles registered at 30 June 1997 comprised 240,460 cars and station wagons, 74,244 commercial vehicles and 7,581 motor cycles.

Rail. A 733 km freight-only rail network services many of the State's principal industries via links with all major ports and cities. 1,942,700 tonnes of freight were carried in 1993–94.

Civil Aviation. Regular passenger and freight services connect the south, north and north-west of the State with the mainland. Air New Zealand provides a direct international service to Christchurch between Oct. and March. For the year ended 30

AUSTRALIA

June 1996 the 6 main airports handled 1,725,000 passengers and 9,004 tonnes of freight.

Shipping. In 1995–96, 10,783,576 mass tonnes of cargo were carried through the 4 major ports. Passenger ferry services connect Tasmania with the mainland and offshore islands.

Telecommunications. At 30 June 1997 there were 34 post offices and 152 licensees. There were 4 TV broadcasters and 27 radio stations.

SOCIAL INSTITUTIONS

Justice. The Supreme Court of Tasmania, with civil, criminal, ecclesiastical, admiralty and matrimonial jurisdiction, established by Royal Charter on 13 Oct. 1823, is a superior court of record, with both original and appellate jurisdiction, and consists of a Chief Justice and 6 puisne judges. There are also inferior civil courts with limited jurisdiction, licensing courts, mining courts, courts of petty sessions and coroners' courts.

In 1995–96 there were 52,330 recorded offences, of which 47,737 were against property, 2,661 against the person and 1,791 fraud and similar offences. The total police force at June 1995 was 1,049. There is one prison, with 1,138 imprisonments in 1995–96.

Religion. At the census of 1996 the following numbers of adherents of the principal religions were recorded:

Anglican Church	156,192	Other Christian	28,515
Roman Catholic	89,156	Indefinite and not stated	45,606
Uniting Church	34,901	No religion	76,859
Presbyterian	13,977	Non-Christian	3,661
Baptist	9,727		
		Total	458,594

Education. Education is controlled by the State and is free, secular and compulsory between the ages of 6 and 16. In 1997, government schools had a total enrolment of 62,921 pupils, including 27,258 at secondary level; 63 private schools had a total enrolment of 21,236 pupils, including 10,428 at secondary level.

Technical and further education is conducted at technical and community colleges in the major centres throughout the state. In 1996 there were 26,588 students enrolled in the Division of Technical and Further Education and almost 30,000 students in the Division of Adult Education.

Tertiary education is offered at the University of Tasmania in Hobart and Launceston and the Australian Maritime College in Launceston. The University (established 1890) had (1996) 12,611 students (68% full-time) and 1,653 academic staff. The Maritime College had 904 student enrolments in June 1995.

Welfare. The number of pensioners in Tasmania on 30 June 1996 was: Age (including wife and carer pensioners), 43,483; disability support, 16,993; war (service), 14,852; widows, 1,061.

CULTURE

Press. There are 3 daily papers with a combined circulation of 117,199. The largest circulation for a Tasmanian daily is for the Saturday edition of *The Mercury*, with a circulation of 64,067.

Tourism. In 1997, 946,114 passengers arrived (799,108 by air from other Australian states or New Zealand and 147,006 by sea).

Festivals. The Australian Wooden Boat Festival takes place biennially in Nov. Boat owners exhibit craft and maritime skills around Hobart's waterfront. At the inaugural Festival in 1994, 40,000 people attended.

Libraries. The State Library of Tasmania delivers its services through a Statewide network of 49 public libraries; 4 Bookmobiles and 6 reference specialist libraries. These include the Tasmaniana Library, the W. L. Crowther Library, and the Allport Library and Museum of Fine Arts.

VICTORIA

National Theatre and Opera. The Theatre Royal in Hobart, established in 1834, has resumed its pre-eminent position in the city's cultural scene following extensive renovation.

Museums and Galleries. The Tasmanian Museum and Art Gallery (TMAG) houses collections in the fields of fine and applied art, zoology, geology, botany, history, anthropology and applied science. The Queen Victoria Museum and Art Gallery was established in 1891.

FURTHER READING
Statistical Information: The State Government Statistical Office (200 Collins St., Hobart), established in 1877, became in 1924 the Tasmanian Office of the Australian Bureau of Statistics, but continues to serve State statistical needs as required.
Regional Director and Government Statistician of Tasmania: Glenn Appleyard.
Main publications: Annual Statistical Bulletins (e.g., *Demography, Agriculture, Government Finance, Manufacturing Industry* etc.).—*Tasmanian Pocket Year Book.* Annual (from 1913).—*Tasmanian Year Book.* Annual (from 1967; biennial from 1986).—Monthly *Tasmanian Statistical Indicators* (from July 1945).
E-mail address: Sales and Inquiries: client.services@abs.gov.au
Website: http://www.abs.gov.au

Kepars, I., *Tasmania* [Bibliography]. Oxford and Santa Barbara (CA), 1997
Robson, L., *A History of Tasmania. Vol. 1: Van Diemen's Land from the Earliest Times to 1855.* Melbourne, 1983
Robson, L., *A History of Tasmania. Vol. 2: Colony and State from 1856 to the 1980s.* Melbourne, 1990

State Library: The State Library of Tasmania, 91 Murray St., Hobart. *State Librarian:* Robyn Collins, BA, MLibSc.
Website: http://www.tased.edu.au/library/stateref/stateref.htm

VICTORIA

KEY HISTORICAL EVENTS
The first permanent settlement in the area was formed at Portland Bay in 1834. Regular government was first established in 1839. Victoria, formerly a portion of New South Wales, was proclaimed a separate colony in 1851 at much the same time as gold was discovered . A new constitution giving responsible government to the colony was proclaimed on 23 Nov. 1855. This event had far-reaching effects, as the population increased from 76,162 in 1850 to 589,160 in 1864. By this time the main impetus behind the search for gold had waned and the new arrivals availed themselves of the opening of the pastoral and agricultural lands to smaller holders and the gradual development of manufacturing industries. Victoria federated with the other Australian states to form the Commonwealth of Australia in 1901.

TERRITORY AND POPULATION
The State has an area of 227,600 sq. km, and a resident population (estimate) of 4,560,100 at 30 June 1996; density, 20·0 per sq. km. The 1996 census population was 4,373,520. Victoria has the greatest proportion of people from non-English-speaking countries of any State or Territory, with (1996) 2·3% from Italy, 1·4% from Greece and 1·3% from Vietnam.

Estimated population at 30 June 1995, within 11 'Statistical Divisions': Melbourne, 3,218,051; Barwon, 238,767; Western District, 101,550; Central Highlands, 133,969; Wimmera, 52,840; Mallee, 88,932; Loddon, 156,081; Goulburn, 184,731; Ovens-Murray, 88,696; East Gippsland, 82,254; Gippsland, 155,812.

Population of urban centres with over 10,000 inhabitants at the 1996 census: Melbourne, 2,865,329; Geelong, 125,382; Ballarat, 64,831; Bendigo, 59,936; Shepparton-Mooroopna, 31,945; Melton, 30,304; Warrnambool, 26,052; Albury-Wodonga (Wodonga Part), 25,825; Mildura, 24,142; Cranbourne, 24,752; Sunbury,

22,126; Traralgon, 18,993; Wangaratta, 15,527; Moe-Yallourn, 15,512; Morwell, 13,823; Sale, 13,366; Horsham, 12,591; Craigieburn, 12,919; Bacchus Marsh, 11,279; Ocean Grove-Barwon Heads, 11,272; Bairnsdale, 10,890; Echuca-Moama (Echuca part), 10,014.

SOCIAL STATISTICS
Statistics for calendar years:

	Births	Marriages	Divorces	Deaths
1994	63,974	26,974	11,228	32,353
1995	62,591	26,607	11,838	32,425
1996	61,143	26,074	12,491	32,726

The annual rates per 1,000 of the mean resident population (estimate) in 1996 were: Marriages, 5·8; births, 14·0; deaths, 7·3; divorces, 2·6. Infant mortality rate, 1996, 5·0 per 1,000 live births. Expectation of life, 1996: Males, 75·6 years; females, 81·2 years.

CLIMATE
See AUSTRALIA: Climate.

CONSTITUTION AND GOVERNMENT
Victoria, formerly a portion of New South Wales, was, in 1851, proclaimed a separate colony, with a partially elective Legislative Council. In 1856 responsible government was conferred, the legislative power being vested in a parliament of two Houses, the Legislative Council and the Legislative Assembly. At present the Council consists of 44 members who are elected for 2 terms of the Assembly, one-half retiring at each election. The Assembly consists of 88 members, elected for 4 years from the date of its first meeting unless sooner dissolved by the Governor. Members and electors of both Houses must be aged 18 years and Australian citizens or those British subjects previously enrolled as electors, according to the Constitution Act 1975. No property qualification is required, but judges, members of the Commonwealth Parliament, undischarged bankrupts and persons convicted of an offence which is punishable by life imprisonment, may not be members of either House. Single voting (one elector one vote) and compulsory preferential voting apply to Council and Assembly elections. Enrolment for Council and Assembly electors is compulsory. The Council may not initiate or amend money bills, but may suggest amendments in such bills other than amendments which would increase any charge. A bill shall not become law unless passed by both Houses.

In the exercise of the executive power the Governor is advised by a Cabinet of responsible Ministers. Section 50 of the Constitution Act 1975 provides that the number of Ministers shall not at any one time exceed 22, of whom not more than 6 may sit in the Legislative Council and not more than 17 may sit in the Legislative Assembly.

At the elections of 23 March 1996 the Liberal and National Party coalition was re-elected, with 34 seats in the Legislative Council and 58 in the Legislative Assembly.

CURRENT ADMINISTRATION
Governor: Sir James Augustine Gobbo, AC, QC.

The Liberal-National coalition Cabinet was as follows in Feb. 1999:

Premier, Minister for Multicultural Affairs and for the Arts: Jeffrey Gibb Kennett. *Deputy Premier, Minister for Agriculture and Resources:* Pat McNamara. *Small Business, Tourism:* Louise Asher. *Industry, Science and Technology:* Mark Birrell. *Transport:* Robin Cooper. *Roads and Ports:* Geoff Craige. *Education:* Phil Gude. *Finance, Gaming:* Roger Hallam. *Housing, Minister responsible for Aboriginal Affairs:* Ann Henderson. *Tertiary Education, Minister assisting the Premier on Multicultural Affairs:* Phil Honeywood. *Police and Emergency Services, Corrections:* Bill McGrath. *Planning and Local Government:* Rob Maclellan. *Youth, Community Services:* Dr Denis Napthine. *Sport, Rural Development:* Tom Reynolds. *Treasurer, Minister for Information Technology and Multi-Media:* Alan Stockdale. *Conservation and Land Management:* Marie Tehan. *Attorney-General, Fair Trading, Women's Affairs:* Jan Wade. *Health and the Aged:* Rob Knowles.

VICTORIA

Local Government. At 30 June 1997 the state was divided into 78 municipal districts, comprising 31 cities (including 4 greater cities), 6 rural cities, 40 shires and 1 borough. The unincorporated areas (not part of a municipality) include French Island (154 sq. km), Lady Julia Percy Island (1·3 sq. km), Bass Strait Islands (3·8 sq. km) and part of the Gippsland Lakes (309 sq. km). The constitution of cities, towns, boroughs and shires is based on statutory requirements concerning population, rate revenue and net annual value of rateable property.

ECONOMY

Budget. State and local government outlays and receipts (excluding financial enterprises, e.g. government savings banks, insurance offices, etc.) in $A1m.:

State 1995–96: Current outlays, 16,606; capital outlays, 7,992. Revenue, 19,026. State expenditure included: Education, 4,884; health, 3,271; general public services, 1,358; transport and communications, 1,380; public order and safety, 1,183. Revenue included: Property taxes, 2,254; payroll taxes, 1,994; taxes on uses of goods and performance of activities, 2,312; taxes on provision of goods and services, 1,864.

Local 1995–96: Outlays, 1,474, including transport and communications, 452; recreation and culture, 416; general public services, 268; housing and community amenities, 317; social security and welfare, 295. Revenue, 1,953, including taxes, fees and fines, 1,287; Commonwealth and State grants, 589.

Banking and Finance. The State Bank of Victoria, the largest bank in the State, provides domestic and international services for business and personal customers and is the largest supplier of housing finance in Victoria. In 1990 it ran into debt and was acquired by the Commonwealth from the Victorian government in Sept. 1990.

The 11 major trading banks in Victoria are the Commonwealth Bank of Australia, the Australia and New Zealand Banking Group, the Westpac Banking Corporation, the National Australia Bank, the Bank of Melbourne, the St George Bank, the Challenge Bank, the Metway Bank, the State Bank of New South Wales, Bendigo Bank and Citibank. Banks had a total of 1,546 branches and 1,785 agencies between them at 30 June 1997.

In June 1997 bank deposits repayable in Australia totalled $A79,483m.; other lending, $A80,783m.

There were 4 permanent building societies in 1995-96 (8 in 1992-93).

ENERGY AND NATURAL RESOURCES

Electricity. Electricity production in 1993-94 was 35,442m. kWh.

In 1993 the State Government began a major restructure of the government-owned electricity industry along competitive lines. The distribution sector was privatized in 1995, and 4 generator companies in 1997.

About 90% of power generated is supplied by 4 brown-coal fired generating stations. There are 2 other thermal stations and 3 hydro-electric stations in north-east Victoria. Victoria is also entitled to approximately 30% of the output of the Snowy Mountains hydro-electric scheme and half the output of the Hume hydro-electric station, both of which are in New South Wales.

Oil and Gas. Crude oil in commercially recoverable quantities was first discovered in 1967 in 2 large fields offshore, in East Gippsland in Bass Strait, between 65 and 80 km from land. These fields, with 10 other fields since discovered, have been assessed as containing initial recoverable reserves of more than 2,930m. bbls. of treated crude oil. Estimated reserves of crude oil (1994) 113,000m. litres; gas, 139,000m. cu. metres.

In 1995-96 Victoria produced 41·4% of Australia's crude oil and 32·9% of its natural gas. Production of crude oil (1995-96), 12,732m. litres.

Natural gas was discovered offshore in East Gippsland in 1965. The initial recoverable reserves of treated gas are 220,400m. cu. metres. Production of natural gas (1995-96) was 6,299bn. litres. Natural gas is distributed to residential and industrial consumers through a network of 23,400 km of mains.

Liquefied petroleum gas is produced after extraction of the propane and butane fractions from the untreated oil and gas. In 1995-96, 1,275m. litres of propane were produced and 1,037m. litres of butane.

Brown Coal. Major deposits of brown coal are located in the Central Gippsland region and comprise approximately 94% of the total resources in Victoria. In 1993 the resource was estimated to be 0·2m. megatonnes, of which about 52,000 megatonnes was economically recoverable. It is young and soft with a water content of 60% to 70%. In the Latrobe Valley section of the region, the thick brown coal seams underlie an area from 10 to 30 km wide extending over approximately 70 km from Yallourn in the west to the south of Sale in the east. It can be won continuously in large quantities and at low cost by specialized mechanical plant.

The primary use of these reserves is to fuel electricity generating stations. Production of brown coal in 1995-96 was 54,281,000 tonnes, value $A465m.

Minerals. Production, 1995-96: Gold, 4,838 kg; (in 1,000 tonnes): Copper concentrate, 8; zinc concentrate, 14; bauxite, 1.

Land Settlement. Of the total area of Victoria (22·76m. ha), 13,973,915 ha on 30 June 1984 were either alienated or in the process of alienation. The remainder (8,786,085) constituted Crown land as follows: Perpetual leases, grazing and other leases and licences, 2,160,352; reservations including forest and timber reserves, water, catchment and drainage purposes, national parks, wildlife reserves, water frontages and other reserves, plus unoccupied and unreserved including areas set aside for roads, 6,625,733.

Agriculture. In 1995-96 there were 36,905 agricultural establishments with a total area of 12,768,000 ha; the gross value of agricultural commodities produced was $A6,388,943,000. The following table shows the area under the principal crops and the produce of each for 2 seasons (in 1,000 units)[1]:

	Total crop area	Wheat		Oats		Barley		Potatoes		Hay	
Season	Ha	Ha	Tonnes	Ha	Tonnes	Ha	Tonnes	Ha	Tonnes	Ha	Tonnes
1994-95	2,163	822	944	148	201	492	448	10	280	419	1,605
1995-96	2,190	853	1,921	187	392	628	1,342	11	356	511	1,971

[1]Excluding establishments with an estimated value of agricultural operations less than $A5,000.

In 1995-96 there were 23,104 ha of vineyards with 19,834 ha of bearing vines, yielding 199,325 tonnes of grapes for wine-making and 227,677 tonnes for drying or table use. Other produce (in tonnes), 1995-96: Almonds, 2,907; pears, 141,275; apples, 78,988; oranges, 72,358; kiwi fruit, 2,063; strawberries, 3,279; tobacco (dry), 3,214; tomatoes, 171,805.

Livestock (in 1,000), 1995-96: Beef cattle, 2,714; dairy cattle, 1,682; sheep, 21,944; pigs, 458.

Animal products (in tonnes), 1995-96: Wool clip, 115,672; poultry, 128,000; mutton, 50,910; lamb, 110,172; honey, 4,415; milk, 5,482m. litres; 40·1m. dozen eggs.

Forestry. Of Victoria's 7·3m. ha of native forest (June 1997), 6·2m. ha (85%) were publicly owned and 1·0m. ha (14%) were on private land.

Fisheries. Total live weight production in 1996-97 was 8,438 tonnes with a value of $A78,018,000.

INDUSTRY

The manufacturing industry accounts for 18·7% of production in Victoria with an annual turnover of $A62bn. At 30 June 1996, there were 292,600 persons employed in the manufacturing sector. Selected articles manufactured (in tonnes), 1996–97: Butter and butter oil, 120,041; cheese, 164,079; wheat flour, 227,170; wool yarn, 15,692; wool cloth, 2,674,000 sq. metres; 13,000 vehicles for goods and materials; plastics in primary forms, 825,000; 264m. clay bricks; ready mixed concrete, 3,169,000 cu. metres.

Labour. At May 1997 there were 2,299,200 persons in the labour force (63·3% of the civilian population aged 15 years and over), of whom 2,090,800 were employed: Agriculture, forestry and fishing, 103,400; mining, 3,000; manufacturing, 348,700; electricity, gas and water supply, 14,500; construction, 119,000; wholesale and retail trade, 442,600; transport and storage, 102,300; accommodation, cafes and restaurants, 85,100; communication, 93,100; finance, insurance, property and business services, 309,000; government administration and defence, 75,100;

education, 136,800; health and community services, 180,700; culture, recreation, personal and other services, 131,400. There were 208,400 unemployed persons in May 1997 (9·1% of the labour force).

Trade Unions. There were 57 trade unions with a total membership of 680,000 at 30 June 1996.

INTERNATIONAL TRADE

Imports and Exports. The total value of the overseas imports and exports of Victoria, including bullion and specie, was as follows (in $A1m.):

	1991–92	1992–93	1993–94	1994–95	1995–96	1996–97
Imports	15,353	18,147	20,770	23,967	24,663	25,190
Exports[1]	9,545	11,044	12,349	13,006	15,410	16,288

[1]Includes re-exports.

The chief exports in 1996–97 (in $A1m.) were: Dairy products and birds' eggs, 1,427; textile fibres and their wastes, 1,193; non-ferrous metals, 887; meat and meat preparations, 554; petroleum, petroleum products and related materials, 757; road vehicles, 816; cereals and cereal preparations, 589. Exports in 1996–97 (in $A1m.) went mainly to New Zealand, 2,134; Republic of Korea, 2,098; Japan, 1,525; USA, 956; Singapore, 891; Hong Kong, 811; Taiwan, 799; Malaysia, 667.

The chief imports in 1996–97 (in $A1m.) were: Road vehicles, 2,924; general industrial machinery and equipment and machine parts, 1,711; electrical machinery, apparatus and appliances and parts, 1,572; miscellaneous manufactured articles, 1,460; machinery for particular industries, 1,175; telecommunications and sound recording and reproducing apparatus and equipment, 1,052; textile yarns, fabrics, made-up articles and related products, 1,066. Imports in 1996–97 (in $A1m.) came mainly from the USA, 5,945; Japan, 3,097; Germany, 1,922; China, 1,756; the UK, 1,634; New Zealand, 1,247; Italy, 832; Taiwan, 695.

COMMUNICATIONS

Roads. At Jan. 1997 there were 150,468 km of roads open for general traffic, consisting of 1,005 km of National Highways, 6,739 km of state highways and freeways, 14,406 km of main, tourist and forest roads (30 June 1996), and 128,318 km of other roads and streets. The number of registered motor vehicles (other than tractors) at 31 Oct. 1996 was 2,819,174. There were 417 fatalities in road accidents in 1996.

Rail. All the railways are the property of the State and are under the management of the Public Transport Corporation, responsible to the Victorian Government. In 1998 the Victorian Government planned to privatize the V/Line Passenger and V/Line Freight, and Met Trains (providing rail services in metropolitan Victoria) are to be split into 2 separate businesses and offered for sale.

At 30 June 1995, 4,917 km of government railway were open, comprising 3,716 km of 1,600 mm gauge (385 km electrified) and 1,201 km of 1,435 mm gauge. In 1996–97, 8·19m. tonnes of freight were carried and there was a total of 127·2m. passenger boardings (7·3m. non-urban). Melbourne's tramway and light rail network extends to 240 km.

Civil Aviation. There were 11,072,000 domestic and regional passenger movements and 2,421,000 international passenger movements in 1996–97 at Melbourne (Tullamarine) airport. Total freight and mail handled was 340,000 tonnes.

Shipping. The 4 major commercial ports are at Melbourne, Geelong, Portland and Hastings. Together, these ports serviced 3,762 ships with a total trade of 37,329,000 mass tonnes in 1996–97.

Telecommunications. In 1996, almost 97% of households had a telephone connected; 262,000 households used computers to access the Internet.

Postal Services. Postal items handled by Australia Post in Victoria (1996-97): Letters, 1,315·6m.; parcels, 31·1m.

SOCIAL INSTITUTIONS

Justice. There is a Supreme Court with a Chief Justice and 21 puisne judges. There are a county court, magistrates' courts, a court of licensing and a bankruptcy court.

The New Prisons Project (NPP) involves replacing the State's ageing prisons with new facilities developed, owned and operated by the private sector. When all 3 private prisons are commissioned, approximately 45% of Victoria's prison population will be accommodated in them.

At March 1997, the average daily number of prisoners was 2,310, with around 85% of these being sentenced prisoners.

Religion. There is no State Church, and no State assistance has been given to religion since 1875. At the 1991 census the following were the enumerated numbers of the principal religions: Catholic, 1,237,399; Anglican, 772,632; Uniting, 342,493 (including Methodist); Orthodox, 199,063; Presbyterian, 193,300; other Christian, 255,375; Moslem, 49,617; Jewish, 33,882; Buddhist, 42,350; no religion, 612,074; not stated, 474,921.

Education. In 1996 there were 1,700 government schools with 517,062 pupils and 34,045 full-time teaching staff plus full-time equivalents of part-time teaching staff: 303,769 pupils were in primary schools and 213,293 in secondary schools. As from 1990 students attending special schools have not been identified separately and have been allocated to either primary or secondary level of education. They are integrated where possible into mainstream education. There were, in 1996, 679 non-government schools, excluding commercial colleges, with 17,295 teaching staff and 259,393 pupils: 130,053 pupils at primary schools and 127,340 pupils at secondary schools.

All higher education institutions, excluding continuing education and technical and further education (TAFE), now fall under the Unified National System, and can no longer be split into universities and colleges of advanced education. In addition, a number of institutional amalgamations and name changes occurred in the 12 months prior to the commencement of the 1992 academic year. In 1996 there were 9 higher education institutions with 175,038 students, and 4 universities: Deakin (founded 1974), La Trobe (1964), Melbourne (1853) and Monash (1958).

Health. In 1995–96 there were 91 public hospitals with 12,332 beds, and 104 private hospitals; 18,1471 nurses were employed.

Welfare. Victoria was the first State of Australia to make a statutory provision for the payment of Age Pensions. The Act providing for the payment of such pensions came into operation on 18 Jan. 1901, and continued until 1 July 1909, when the Australian Invalid and Old Age Pension Act came into force. The Social Services Consolidation Act, which came into operation on 1 July 1947, repealed the various legislative enactments relating to age (previously old-age) and invalid pensions, maternity allowances, child endowment, unemployment, and sickness benefits and while following in general the Acts repealed, considerably liberalized many of their provisions; it has since been amended. On 30 June 1996 there were 410,122 age and 115,580 invalid pensioners. In 1994–95, the amounts paid in age and invalid pensions (including payments to 12,177 wives and spouse carers of age pensioners and 31,394 of invalid pensioners) were \$A3,035,432,000 and \$A1,056,769,000 respectively.

Under the Australian Unemployment and Sickness Benefit Act 1944, payments were made to (1995–96): 205,458 unemployment claimants, 8,796 sickness, 75,144 supporting parents and 5,682 special benefits.

At 30 June 1996, there were 12,982 widow pensioners.

In 1995–96, 441,065 received family allowance and there were 22,730 recipients of child disability allowance.

CULTURE

Broadcasting. In 1993–94 there were 77 businesses providing television services and radio services. There were 3 public broadcasters in radio and 2 in television.

Cinema. During the year ended March 1995, 2,220,200 people attended cinema screenings.

Tourism. In 1996, the number of short-term overseas visitors to Australia who specified Victoria as their main destination was 543,094 (13% of total overseas visitors to Australia), with 379,515 nominating 'holiday' or 'visiting friends' as purpose of their visit. New Zealand represented the major source of international visitors with 19·3%; UK and Ireland (10·7%), USA (9·9%) and Japan (8·5%).

Libraries. During the year ended March 1995, 1,288,700 people visited national, State or local libraries. The largest category of cultural funding for Victorian Local Government was libraries and archives, accounting for 43% of total funding.

Museums and Galleries. In the year to March 1995, 1,679,200 people visited museums and galleries.

FURTHER READING

Australian Bureau of Statistics Victorian Office. *Victorian Year Book.—Summary of Statistics (annual).*

State library: The State Library of Victoria, 328 Swanston St., Melbourne, 3000.
State statistical office: Victorian Office, Australian Bureau of Statistics, 525 Collins Street, Melbourne 3000. *Deputy Commonwealth Statistician:* Stuart Jackson.

WESTERN AUSTRALIA

KEY HISTORICAL EVENTS

In 1791, the British navigator George Vancouver took formal possession of the country around King George Sound. In 1826 the Government of New South Wales sent 20 convicts and a detachment of soldiers to King George Sound and formed a settlement then called Frederickstown. The following year, Capt. James Stirling surveyed the coast from King George Sound to the Swan River, and in May 1829 Capt. Charles Fremantle took possession of the territory. In June 1829, Capt. Stirling founded the Swan River Settlement (now the Commonwealth State of Western Australia) and the towns of Perth and Fremantle and was appointed Lieut.-Governor.

Large grants of land were made to the early settlers and agricultural and pastoral occupations were pursued by a small population with varying success until, in 1850, with the colony languishing, the inhabitants' petition that it be made a penal settlement was acceded to. Between 1850 and 1868 (in which year transportation ceased), 9,668 convicts were sent out. In 1870, partially representative government was instituted, and in 1890 the administration was vested in the Governor, a legislative council and a legislative assembly. The legislative council was, in the first instance, nominated by the Governor but in 1893 it became elective. Western Australia federated with the other Australian states to form the Commonwealth of Australia in 1901.

In the 1914-18 war, Western Australia provided more volunteers for overseas military service in proportion to population than any other State (possibly because Western Australia had a higher proportion of British migrants and single men).

The worldwide depression of 1929 brought widespread unemployment (30% of trade union membership), and in 1933, over two-thirds voted to leave the Federation. While there were modest improvements in the standard of living through the 1930s, it was the 1939-45 war which brought regular employment for all.

Japanese aircraft attacked the Western Australia coast in 1942. Talk of a 'Brisbane line', which would abandon the West to invasion only served to reinforce Western Australia's sense of isolation from the rest of the nation. The post-war years saw increasing demand for wheat and wool but the 1954-55 decline in farm incomes led to diversification. Work began in the early 1950s on steel production and oil processing. Oil was discovered in 1953 but it was not until 1966 that it was commercially exploited. The discovery of deposits of iron ore in the Pilbara, bauxite in the Darling scarp, nickel in Kambalda and ilmenite from mineral sands led to the State becoming a major world supplier of mineral exports by 1965.

AUSTRALIA

TERRITORY AND POPULATION
Western Australia lies between 113° 09' and 129° E. long. and 13° 44' and 35° 08' S. lat.; its area is 2,525,500 sq. km.

The population at each census from 1947 was as follows[1]:

	Males	Females	Total		Males	Females	Total
1947	258,076	244,404	502,480	1976	599,959	578,383	1,178,342
1954	330,358	309,413	639,771	1981	659,249	642,807	1,300,056
1961	375,452	361,177	736,629	1986	736,131	722,888	1,459,019
1966	432,569	415,531	848,100	1991	793,626	792,767	1,586,393
1971	539,332	514,502	1,053,834	1996	862,645	863,450	1,726,095

[1]1961 and earlier exclude persons of predominantly Aboriginal descent; from 1966 figures refer to total population (*i.e.*, including Aborigines). Figures from 1971 are based on estimated resident population.

The population at the 1996 census was 1,726,095. Of the total 1996 census population, 1,178,331 were born in Australia. Married persons numbered 710,468 (355,594 males and 354,874 females); widowers, 13,656; widows, 59,635; divorced, 39,624 males and 48,986 females; never married, 233,048 males and 186,081 females. Estimated resident population at 30 June 1997 was 1,798,129 (893,720 females).

Perth, the capital, had an estimated resident population of 1,318,974 at 30 June 1997.

Principal local government areas outside the metropolitan area, with population at 30 June 1997 (estimate): Mandurah, 42,072; Kalgoorlie-Boulder, 30,488; Bunbury, 27,664; Geraldton, 20,295; Busselton, 19,188; Albany, 15,503; Roebourne, 13,985; Port Hedland, 12,823.

SOCIAL STATISTICS
Statistics for calendar years[1]

	Births	Marriages	Divorces	Deaths
1993	25,081	10,382	4,654	10,318
1994	25,138	10,366	5,024	10,293
1994	25,139	10,366	5,024	10,293
1995	25,139	10,404	5,040	10,364
1996	24,793	10,294	4,959	11,027

[1]Figures are on state of usual residence basis.

CLIMATE
Western Australia is a region of several climate zones, ranging from the tropical north to the semi-arid interior and Mediterranean-style climate of the south west. Most of the State is a plateau between 300 and 600 metres above sea level. Except in the far south west coast, maximum temperatures in excess of 40°C have been recorded throughout the State. The normal average number of sunshine hours per day is 8·0 hours.

CONSTITUTION AND GOVERNMENT
In 1870 partially representative government was instituted, and in 1890 the administration was vested in the Governor, a Legislative Council and a Legislative Assembly. The Legislative Council was, in the first instance, nominated by the Governor, but it was provided that in the event of the population of the colony reaching 60,000, it should be elective. In 1893 this limit of population being reached, the Colonial Parliament amended the Constitution accordingly.

The *Legislative Council* consists of 34 members elected for a term of 4 years. There are 6 electoral regions for Legislative Council elections. 4 return 5 members and 2, 7 members. Each member represents the entire region.

There are 57 members of the *Legislative Assembly*, each member representing one of the 57 electoral districts of the State. Members are elected for the duration of the Assembly which may be for a period of up to 4 years. The qualifications applying to candidates and electors are identical for the Legislative Council and the Legislative Assembly. A candidate must be at least 18 years of age and free from legal incapacity, be an Australian citizen, and be enrolled, or qualified for enrolment, as an elector. A member of the Commonwealth Parliament or of the legislature of a territory or another state, an undischarged bankrupt or a debtor against whose estate there is a subsisting receiving order in bankruptcy, or a person who has been attainted or convicted of treason or felony is disqualified from membership of the legislature. No person may hold office as a member of the Legislative Assembly and the Legislative Council at the same time. An elector must be at least 18 years of age, be an Australian citizen (or a British subject who was at some time within the 3 months preceding 26 Jan. 1984 an elector of the Assembly or the Commonwealth parliament), be free from legal incapacity, and must have resided in Western Australia for 3 months continuously, and in the electoral district for which he or she claims enrolment for a continuous period of 1 month immediately preceding the date of his or her claim. Enrolment is compulsory for all qualified persons. Voting at elections is on the preferential system and is compulsory for all enrolled persons. A system of proportional representation is used to elect members of the Legislative Council.

Ordinary members of the legislature were paid (1998) a salary of $A82,663 a year with an additional electorate allowance, ranging from $A19,512 to $A36,099 a year according to location of the electorate. All members of Parliament also receive a basic postage and lettergram allowance of $A6,000.

In addition to the basic member's salary, electorate and postage allowances, the Premier receives (1998) a salary and expense of office allowances of $A108,289. On the same basis the Deputy Premier receives $A80,183; the Leader of the Government in the Legislative Council $A74,397; and other ministers $A66,130.

RECENT ELECTIONS

Legislative Assembly representation after the Dec. 1996 election: Liberal Party, 29; Australian Labor Party, 19; National Party of Australia, 6; Independent, 3. Legislative Council: Liberal Party, 14; Australian Labor Party, 12; National Party of Australia, 3; Greens (Western Australia), 3; Australian Democrats, 2.

CURRENT ADMINISTRATION

Governor: Maj.-Gen. Philip Michael Jeffery, AC, AO, MC.
 Lieut-Governor: David Kingsley Malcolm, AC.
 In Feb. 1999 the Cabinet comprised:
 Premier, Treasurer, Minister for Public Sector Management, and for Federal Affairs: Richard F. Court.
 Deputy Premier, Minister for Commerce and Trade, Regional Development and Small Business: Hendy Cowan. *Resources Development and Energy, Education, Leader of the House in the Legislative Assembly:* Colin James Barnett. *Primary Industry and Fisheries:* Monty House. *Mines, Tourism, Sport and Recreation:* Norman Moore. *Transport:* Murray Griddle. *Environment, Labour Relations:* Cheryl Edwardes. *Finance, Racing and Gaming:* Max Evans. *Lands, Fair Trading, Parliamentary and Electoral Affairs:* Doug J. Shave. *Police, Emergency Services:* Kevin Prince. *Attorney-General, Justice, the Arts:* Peter Foss. *Planning, Employment and Training, Heritage:* Graham Kierath. *Housing, Aboriginal Affairs, Water Resources:* Kim D. Hames. *Health:* John H. Day. *Works, Services, Citizenship and Multicultural Interests, Youth:* Mike F. Board. *Family and Children's Services, Seniors' and Women's Interests:* Rhonda K. Parker. *Local Government, Disability Services:* Paul Omodei.

Local Government. Including the lord mayoralty of the City of Perth, there were 20 cities, 12 towns and 112 shires as at 30 Jan. 1999. The executive body in each of these authorities is an elected council, consisting of councillors and presided over by a mayor (city and town) or a president (shire). The mayor or president can be elected by the people or by their fellow councillors. The Western Australian *Local Government Act 1995* prescribes that an elected council, including the mayor or president, cannot be less than 6 members nor more than 15. In extraordinary circumstances, the Governor may appoint commissioners to perform the decision-making functions of a local government. The functions of local government include the provision of community services, sporting and recreation facilities, the upkeep of parks, road construction, town planning, building control and refuse removal. Finance is derived largely from rates levied on property owners. Funds are also derived from Commonwealth Government grants as well as charges for council services.

ECONOMY

Budget. Revenue and expenditure (in $A1m.), as reported in the Consolidated Revenue Fund, in years ended 30 June:

	1995	1996	1997	1998
Revenue	6,020·6	7,152·9	7,023·6	7,095·8
Expenditure	5,998·1	7,152·9	6,864·7	7,613·9

Main items of revenue in 1997–98: Departmental ($A1,339·6m.), taxation ($A2,383·2m.), timber and mining ($A661·5m.), from Commonwealth funds ($A3,069·2m.). Western Australia had a gross operating surplus of $A1,385·4m. on 30 June 1998 (including $A229·3m. from Public Trading Enterprises, $A640·0m. from General Government). The Financial Enterprises Sector had a deficit of $A141·6m.

Banking and Finance. At 30 June 1998, there were 18 banks operating in Western Australia.

ENERGY AND NATURAL RESOURCES

Electricity. The Office of Energy was established to administer energy policy and regulatory functions previously managed by the State Electricity Commission of Western Australia (SECWA), which was split into 2 corporate utilities in 1995 (Western Power and AlintaGas). The Office of Energy reports directly to the Minister of Energy and provides advice on policy and coordinates economic and commercial issues in the Western Australian energy sector. Deregulation of the energy industry was passed by the Office of Energy during 1996-97. The gradual introduction of the Electricity Transmission Open Access Plan commenced on 1 July 1997, allowing independent generators to supply associated loads by utilizing Western Power's transmission system. Electricity users now have the option of obtaining power from Western Power or private sector operators.

Oil and Gas. Petroleum has been the State's most valuable contributor to the resource sector for the second year, with a record production rate for oil, gas and condensate, increasing the value of output by 24% to $A4,693m. in 1996. The State accounted for approximately 51% of Australia's total crude oil and condensate, and 48% of gas production in 1996, making Western Australia the main producer of petroleum in Australia. In 1996, 45% of Western Australia's crude oil production was exported overseas. Of this proportion, most went to Asia.

The value of Liquefied Natural Gas (LNG) output increased just over 0·5% in 1996, to $A1,391m. Almost all LNG was exported to Japan; however, new markets are opening up within other Asian countries. The value of natural gas production increased 11% in 1996 to $A495m. This was due to the commencement of production from the East Spar subsea gas gathering system. The first full year's production from a new $A300m. liquefied petroleum gas (LPG) plant occurred in 1996, with approximately 310,000 tonnes of LPG worth $A41m. produced.

Water. The administration of Western Australia's water resources is the responsibility of the Water and Rivers Commission, and the Water Corporation is the primary provider of services. The operation and activities of the Water Corporation are monitored by the Office of Water Regulation. According to the Water Corporation Annual Report 1997, there were 460,739 metropolitan and 157,121 country services connected to the water supply system.

Minerals. Mining is a significant contributor to the Western Australia economy. Until the mid-1960s the major mineral produced was gold. It was then replaced by iron ore in terms of value, and has at various times fallen behind nickel concentrates, bauxite, oil, mineral sands and salt. In the latter half of the 1980s gold enjoyed a resurgence and has continued to exceed iron ore in value terms (with the exception of 1991-92 and 1992-93).

The total ex-mine value of minerals from mining and quarrying in 1996 was $A15,956m. Principal minerals produced in 1996 were: Gold, 221,033 kg (value $A3,526·3m.); iron ore, 133·7m. tonnes ($A2,924·5m.); crude oil, 16,255 megalitres ($A2,732·5m.); bauxite-alumina, 8·2m. tonnes ($A1,974·4m.); liquefied natural gas, 377,819m. gigajoules ($A1,391·2m.); nickel concentrates, 0·8m. tonnes ($A1,033·9m.); heavy mineral sands concentrates, 2·0m. tonnes ($A598·1m.);

natural gas, 6,623 gigalitres ($A494·7m.); diamonds, 47·4m. carats ($A442·0m.); coal, 5·8m. tonnes ($A268·4m.); salt, 7·2m. tonnes ($A143·3m.).

Agriculture.

| | 1996 | | 1997 | |
| | Area | Production | Area | Production |
Crop	1,000 ha	1,000 tonnes	1,000 ha	1,000 tonnes
Wheat	3,892·4	6,826·7	4,263·7	7,516·0
Oats	300·4	584·8	316·3	546·1
Barley	744·5	1,322·8	909·3	1,635·3
Lupins	1,100·3	1,290·0	1,080·4	1,271·7

Production, 1997 (in tonnes), apples, 38,217·9; pears, 9,931·7; oranges, 5,307·5.

Livestock at 31 March 1997 (in 1,000): Cattle, 1,786·8; sheep and lambs, 27,821·1; pigs, 297·4.

The wool clip in 1997 was 159,981 tonnes.

Forestry. The area of State forests and timber reserves at 30 June 1997 was 1,725,036 ha; production of sawn timber was 1,036,466 cu. metres in 1994-95. Jarrah and Karri hardwoods account for 69·0% and pine accounts for 28·9% of sawn timber production.

Fisheries. The total fisheries production in 1996–97 was 44,673 tonnes and was worth $A568·5m. Of this, over half was from crustaceans, with a total catch of 14,699 tonnes and a value of $A308·3m. Pearling was also a significant contributor, producing $A171·4m. worth of pearls, or 30% of the total value of Western Australia's fishing production.

INDUSTRY
Heavy industry is concentrated in the south-west, and is largely tied to export-orientated mineral processing, especially alumina and nickel. Other significant manufacturing industries include meat and seafood processing, production of timber and wood products, metal fabrication and production of industrial and mining machinery. The North West Shelf development has stimulated recent growth in industries involved in providing materials and equipment during the construction phase, as well as in new and existing industries using gas in processing.

The following table shows manufacturing industry statistics for 1996–97:

Industry sub-division	Number of establishments operating at 30 June	Persons employed[1] 1,000	Wages and salaries $A1m.	Turnover $A1m.
Food, beverages and tobacco	498	164·0	5,610·2	44,978·4
Textiles, clothing and leather products	333	77·0	2,012·6	9,935·4
Wood and paper products	422	61·5	2,019·9	11,481·2
Printing and publishing and recorded media	581	96·7	3,335·3	14,867·6
Petroleum, coal, chemical and associated products	373	93·4	3,805·7	32,862·9
Non-metallic mineral products	330	371·1	1,373·2	8,622·3
Metal products	1,002	150·2	5,567·8	37,894·0
Machinery and equipment	1,295	207·5	7,497·0	41,260·3
Other manufacturing	826	57·9	1,412·1	6,445·8
Total	5,660	945·3	32,634·0	208,348·0

[1]At 30 June. Includes working proprietors.

Labour. The labour force comprised 886,700 employed and 69,600 unemployed persons in June 1998. The average weekly wage in May 1998 was $A572·00 (males $A741·30, females $A406·10).

The Western Australian Industrial Appeal Court consists of 3 Judges, one of whom is the Presiding Judge. The members are nominated by the Chief Justice of Western Australia. An appeal lies to the Court from decisions of the President of the Western Australian Industrial Commission, the Full Bench or the Commission in Court Session. The Western Australian Industrial Commission consists of a

AUSTRALIA

President (who must be a judge), a Chief Industrial Commissioner, a Senior Commissioner, and 'such number of other Commissioners as may, from time to time, be necessary'. The President or a Commissioner sitting or acting alone constitutes the Commission and may exercise the appropriate powers of the Commission. The Commission can inquire into any industrial matter and make an award, order or declaration relating to such matter. The Commission may also make inquiries where industrial action has occurred or is likely to occur. The Commission in Court Session is constituted by not less than 3 Commissioners sitting or acting together, and may make General Orders, hear matters referred by the Commission, and hear appeals from decisions of Boards of Reference.

The Full Bench is constituted by not less than 3 members of the Commission, 1 of whom is the President, and may hear matters referred by the Commission on questions of law, and appeals from decisions of the Commission and Industrial Magistrates.

The following table shows details of the number of industrial awards, unions and members registered with the Western Australian Industrial Commission.

At 30 June	1995	1996	1997	1998
Awards in force	887	1,315	1,661	1,899
Employee organizations:				
Number	61	59	60	57
Membership	187,208	186,163	177,844	170,578
Employer organizations:				
Number	17	18	18	18
Membership	3,122	3,418	3,290	3,180

During 1997, 30,900 workers were directly involved in 69 industrial disputes. A total of 60,100 working days were lost.

Trade Unions. In 1996 there were 54 trade unions with a total of 135,200 male members and 86,500 female members.

INTERNATIONAL TRADE

Imports and Exports. Foreign commerce is comprised in the statement of the commerce of the Commonwealth of Australia.

Value of foreign imports and exports (i.e. excluding inter-state trade) for years ending 30 June (in $A1m.):

	1995–96	1996–97	1997–98
Imports	6,289·5	6,815·2	8,608·6
Exports[1]	18,843·5	19,332·1	22,767·2

[1]Including ships' stores.

Selected overseas exports (in $A1m.) for 1997–98: Iron ore and concentrates, 3,765·9; petroleum, petroleum products and related materials, 2,046·8; meat and meat preparations, 193·0; fish, crustaceans, molluscs, etc., 337·2; cereals and cereal preparations, 1,651·1; textile fibres and other work, 655·3.

Selected overseas imports (in $A1m.) for 1997–98: Petroleum, petroleum products and related materials, 799·0; machinery and transport equipment, 3,657·1; road vehicles, 1,051·9; miscellaneous manufactured articles, 712·9.

The chief countries exporting to Western Australia in 1997–98 were (in $A1m.): USA, 1,247·8; Japan, 1,012·5; South Korea, 952·0; Indonesia, 884; South Korea, 255·76; Singapore, 603; South Korea, 255·79; UK, 471·9; Main export markets in 1997–98 (in $A1m.): Japan, 5,391·2; South Korea, 2,340·9; USA, 1,877·0; China, 1,499·8; Singapore, 1,308·5; Taiwan, 1,011·3.

COMMUNICATIONS

Roads. At 30 June 1997 there were 142,001 km of sealed and unsealed roads comprising 10,780 km of highways, 6,548 km of main roads and 124,672 km of local roads. Of these, 45,459 km are sealed. In addition, there are 29,169 km of unsealed roads in forests and national parks.

New motor vehicles registered during the year ended 30 June 1998 were 81,455.

In 1996 there were 241 fatalities in road accidents.

WESTERN AUSTRALIA

Rail. At 30 June 1998 the State had 5,369 km of State government railway. In 1997–98 state railways carried 32·8m. tonnes of paying goods and 250,000 passengers on country rail.

Civil Aviation. An extensive system of regular air services operates for passengers, freight and mail. In 1996 Perth International handled 4,448,000 passengers (1,365,000 on international flights), and in 1995, 62,500 tonnes of freight.

Shipping. In 1997–98, the Port of Fremantle handled 1,910 vessels; Port Hedland, 634. The gross weight (in tonnes) of overseas cargo through those ports was: Port of Fremantle, 9,019,000 discharged, 12,606,000 loaded; Port Hedland, 346,484 discharged, 69,486,555 loaded.

Postal Services. In 1995, the Australia Post Corporation had 441 outlets and 722,114 delivery points in Western Australia.

SOCIAL INSTITUTIONS

Justice. Justice is administered by a Supreme Court, consisting of a Chief Justice, 16 other judges and 2 masters; a District Court comprising a chief judge and 20 other judges; a Magistrates Court, a Chief Stipendiary Magistrate, 37 Stipendiary Magistrates and Justices of the Peace. All courts exercise both civil and criminal jurisdiction except Justices of the Peace who deal with summary criminal matters only. Juvenile offenders are dealt with by the Children's Court. Overall responsibility for the Children's Court is vested in a President, who has the status of a District Court Judge. A children's court may be constituted by a judge, a magistrate or 2 lay members. Each has different sentencing powers. For certain offences involving first offenders under the age of 16 years who have pleaded guilty, such cases may be dealt with by the Children's (suspended Proceedings) Panel which comprises a representative from the Department for Community Services and one from the Police Department. The Family Court also forms part of the justice system and comprises a Chief Judge, 4 other judges, 7 magistrates/registrars, and exercises both State and Federal jurisdictions.

In 1997–98 (1996–97), 254,543 (242,757) crimes were reported and 78,498 (72,593) were cleared.

Religion. At the census, 6 Aug. 1996, the principal denominations were: Catholic, 427,848; Anglican, 410,233; Uniting, 87,549; Presbyterian and Reformed, 45,761; Baptist, 27,618; other Christian, 126,041. There were 48,294 persons practising non-Christian religions and 367,491 persons had no religion.

Education. School attendance is compulsory from the age of 6 until the end of the year in which the child attains 15 years. A non-compulsory year of education is available to children from the beginning of the year in which they reach 5 years of age, at pre-primary centres attached to most government primary schools, or at community-based and privately owned pre-school centres, and at some non-government schools. Children may be enrolled during their fourth year where vacancies exist. In 1997 there were 767 government primary and secondary schools (with 14,335 teaching staff) providing free education to 226,075 students, and 276 non-government primary and secondary schools (with 5,649 teaching staff) providing education, for which fees are charged, to 85,007 students.

Technical and Further Education (TAFE) is offered by the Department of TAFE, a sub-department of the Ministry of Education, and by three independent regional colleges. The latter also provide higher education facilities. Additionally, higher education is available through 4 state universities and 1 private (Notre Dame).

Tertiary education (1996): University of Western Australia (13,132 students); Murdoch University (8,524); Curtin University of Technology (21,240); Edith Cowan University (18,458).

State and local government current outlay on education during the year ended 30 June 1997 amounted to $A1,120,392.

Health. At Jan. 1999 there were 91 acute public hospitals, 28 acute private hospitals and 11 day hospitals.

Welfare. The Department for Community Development is responsible for the provision of welfare and community services throughout the State. Operations and planning are managed through a decentralized structure of 5 regions and 21 districts. There are 8 directorates (2 support, 1 special services and 5 regional).

Direct services provided to the community include emergency financial assistance, family and substitute care, and counselling and psychological services. The Department supervises children's Day Care Centres. There is a 24-hour emergency welfare service provided through the Crisis Care Unit. Specialist units work in the areas of child abuse, adoptions, youth activities and Family Court counselling.

The Department provides residential facilities for the temporary accommodation, care and training of children, is responsible for young offenders recommended for detention or remand by a Court, and also supervises young offenders subject to non-custodial court orders.

Age, invalid, widows', disability and service pensions, and unemployment benefits, are paid by the Federal Government. The number of pensioners in Western Australia at 30 June 1997 was: Age, 135,182; widows, 2,971; disability, 44,160; service, 31,731 (1996); sole parents, 35,316. There were 75,528 recipients of unemployment benefits at 30 June 1997, comprising 4,892 recipients of Mature Age Allowance, 2,723 of Youth Training Allowance and 65,913 of Newstart Allowance.

Funding of $A16·84m. was provided to 108 services throughout the State to assist people in crisis due to domestic violence or youth/adult homelessness. Of this, $A9·9m. was allocated to provide supported accommodation and assistance.

CULTURE

Tourism. In 1997–98 there were 402,400 short-term overseas visitors. Of these, 81,390 were from the UK and Ireland, and 73,140 from Singapore. Nearly a quarter of the 205,550 short-term visitors who arrived by air for holidays were from Singapore. In June 1998, there were 293 hotels, motels, guest houses and serviced apartments.

Festivals. The Festival of Perth is the oldest and largest annual international arts festival in the southern hemisphere. It is held annually for 3½ weeks in Feb. and March.

Libraries. The Libraries and Information Service of Western Australia (LISWA) within the Ministry for Culture and the Arts is responsible for delivering library archival and information services to the people of Western Australia. The State Reference Library is situated in the Alexander Library in the Perth Cultural Centre. Also located in the Alexander Library Building is the J. S. Battye Library of Western Australian History.

The provision of public library services is a partnership between LISWA and local government authorities. Through its Public Library Services Program, LISWA provides and maintains the bookstock and other resource materials for public libraries throughout the State.

Museums and Galleries. The Western Australian Museum was established in the early 1890s, and its headquarters and principal exhibition centre is located in the Perth Cultural Centre, with branches in Fremantle (Fremantle History Museum including Samson House, and the Western Australian Maritime Museum incorporating the Historic Boats Museum), Albany, Geraldton and Kalgoorlie. During 1996, a total of 836,303 visitors, of which 81,984 were school students, visited the various museum sites. The Art Gallery of Western Australia is the oldest visual arts organization in the State, having acquired its first work of art in 1895. The Gallery is located in the Perth Cultural Centre and is housed in 2 buildings: the Main Galleries and the adjoining Centenary Galleries. The Gallery collects for, and maintains, the State Art Collection, comprising Western Australian, Australian and international works, with a particular emphasis on Western Australian and Aboriginal art.

FURTHER READING

Statistical Information: The State Government Statistician's Office was established in 1897 and now functions as the Western Australian Office of the Australian Bureau of Statistics (Level 16 Exchange Plaza, 2 The Esplanade, Perth). *Deputy Commonwealth Statistician and*

Government Statistician: William McLennan. Its principal publications are: *Western Australia: Facts and Figures* (from 1989). *Monthly Summary of Statistics* (from 1958)

Broeze, F. J. A. (ed.) *Private Enterprise, Government and Society.* Univ. of Western Australia, 1993
Crowley, F. K., *Australia's Western Third: A History of Western Australia from the First Settlements to Modern Times.* (Rev. ed.) Melbourne, 1970
Stannage, C. T. (ed.) *A New History of Western Australia.* Perth, 1980

State Library: Alexander Library Building, Perth.

AUSTRALIAN EXTERNAL TERRITORIES

AUSTRALIAN ANTARCTIC TERRITORY

An Imperial Order in Council of 7 Feb. 1933 placed under Australian authority all the islands and territories other than Adélie Land situated south of 60° S. lat. and lying between 160° E. long. and 45° E. long. The Order came into force with a Proclamation issued by the Governor-General on 24 Aug. 1936 after the passage of the Australian Antarctic Territory Acceptance Act 1933. The boundaries of Adélie Land were definitively fixed by a French Decree of 1 April 1938 as the islands and territories south of 60° S. lat. lying between 136° E. long. and 142° E. long. The Australian Antarctic Territory Act 1954 declared that the laws in force in the Australian Capital Territory are, so far as they are applicable and are not inconsistent with any ordinance made under the Act, in force in the Australian Antarctic Territory.

The area of the territory is estimated at 6,119,818 sq. km (2,362,875 sq. miles).

There is a research station on MacRobertson Land at lat. 67° 37' S. and long. 62° 52' E. (Mawson), one on the coast of Princess Elizabeth Land at lat. 68° 34' S. and long. 77° 58' E. (Davis), and one at lat. 66° 17' S. and long. 110° 32' E. (Casey). The Antarctic Division also operates a station on Macquarie Island.

COCOS (KEELING) ISLANDS

GENERAL DETAILS
The Cocos (Keeling) Islands are 2 separate atolls comprising some 27 small coral islands with a total area of about 14·2 sq. km, and are situated in the Indian Ocean at 12° 05' S. lat. and 96° 53' E. long. They lie 2,768 km north-west of Perth and 3,685 km west of Darwin.

The main islands are West Island (the largest, about 10 km from north to south), on which there is an airport and an animal quarantine station, and most of the European community; Home Island, occupied by the Cocos Malay community; Direction, South and Horsburgh Islands, and North Keeling Island, 24 km to the north of the group. The islands were discovered in 1609 by Capt. William Keeling but remained uninhabited until 1826. In 1857 the islands were annexed to the Crown; in 1878 responsibility was transferred from the Colonial Office to the Government of Ceylon, and in 1886 to the Government of the Straits Settlement. By indenture in 1886, Queen Victoria granted all land in the islands to George Clunies-Ross and his heirs in perpetuity (with certain rights reserved to the Crown). In 1903 the islands were incorporated in the Settlement of Singapore and in 1942–46 were temporarily placed under the Governor of Ceylon. In 1946 a Resident Administrator, responsible to the Governor of Singapore, was appointed.

On 23 Nov. 1955 the Cocos Islands were placed under the authority of the Australian Government as the Territory of Cocos (Keeling) Islands. An Administrator, appointed by the Governor-General, is the Government's representative in the Territory and is responsible to the Minister for Territories and Local Government. The Cocos (Keeling) Islands Council, established as the elected body of the Cocos Malay community in July 1979, advises the Administrator on all issues affecting the Territory.

In 1978 the Australian Government purchased the Clunies-Ross family's entire interests in the islands, except for the family residence. A Cocos Malay co-operative was established to take over the running of the Clunies-Ross copra plantation and to engage in other business with the Commonwealth in the Territory, including construction projects. In 1993 the Australian Government took control of the Clunies-Ross family residence also.

The population of the Territory (1994) was 670, distributed between Home Island (75%) and West Island (25%).

The islands are low-lying, flat and thickly covered by coconut palms, and surround a lagoon in which ships drawing up to 7 metres may be anchored, but which is extremely difficult for navigation.

There is an equable and pleasant climate, affected for much of the year by the south-east trade winds. Temperatures range over the year from 68° F (20° C) to 88° F (31·1° C) and rainfall averages 80" (2,000 mm) a year.

The Cocos (Keeling) Islands Act 1955 is the basis of the Territory's administrative, legislative and judicial systems. Under section 8 of this Act, those laws which were in force in the Territory immediately before the transfer continued in force there.

CURRENT ADMINISTRATION
Administrator: Bill Taylor.

COMMUNICATIONS

Roads. There are 15 km of roads.

Civil Aviation. In 1998 National Jet operated scheduled flights to Christmas Island and Perth.

SOCIAL INSTITUTIONS

Religion. About 85% are Moslems and 15% Christians.

Education. In 1992 there were 2 primary schools (on Home Island and West Island) with 98 pupils and 7 teachers and 1 teaching assistant, 2 secondary schools with 70 pupils and 9 teachers and 1 teaching assistant, and 29 students in a technical school.

Health. In 1992 there was 1 doctor and 7 nursing personnel, with 5 beds in clinics.

CHRISTMAS ISLAND

GENERAL DETAILS
Christmas Island is an isolated peak in the Indian Ocean, lat. 10° 25' 22" S., long. 105° 39' 59" E. It lies 360 km S. 8° E. of Java Head, and 417 km N. 79° E. from Cocos Islands, 1,310 km from Singapore and 2,623 km from Fremantle. Area about 135 sq. km. The climate is tropical with temperatures varying little over the year at 27° C. The wet season lasts from Nov. to April with an annual total of about 2,673 mm. The island was formally annexed by the UK on 6 June 1888, placed under the administration of the Governor of the Straits Settlements in 1889, and incorporated

with the Settlement of Singapore in 1900. Sovereignty was transferred to the Australian Government on 1 Oct. 1958. The population at the 1991 census was 1,275; 1994 estimate, 2,500 of whom 1,300 were of Chinese, 400 of Malay and 800 of Australian/European origin.

The legislative, judicial and administrative systems are regulated by the Christmas Island Act, 1958–73. They are the responsibility of the Commonwealth Government and are operated by an Administrator. The Territory underwent major changes to its legal system when the Federal Parliament passed the Territories Law Reform Bill of 1992; Commonwealth and State laws applying in the state of Western Australia now apply in the Territory as a result, although some laws have been repealed to take into account the unique status of the Territory. The first Island Assembly was elected in Sept. 1985, and is now replaced by the elected members of the Christmas Island Shire Council.

Extraction and export of rock phosphate dust is the main industry. The Government is also encouraging the private sector development of tourism.

CURRENT ADMINISTRATION
Administrator: Bill Taylor.

ENERGY AND NATURAL RESOURCES
Electricity. Production (1994–95) 20m. kWh.

COMMUNICATIONS
Roads. In 1993 there were 205 km of roads, 917 passenger cars and 362 commercial vehicles.
Civil Aviation. In 1998 National Jet operated scheduled flights to Perth and Cocos Island.
Shipping. In 1991, 40,000 tonnes of cargo were loaded and 45,600 tonnes discharged at the port. 2,000 cu. metres of general cargo were also discharged.
Postal Services. There was one post office in 1992.

SOCIAL INSTITUTIONS
Religion. About 50% are Buddhists or Taoists, 16% Moslems and 30% Christians.
Education. In 1995 there was a district high school with 50 pre-primary, 369 primary and 73 secondary level pupils.
Health. In 1994 there were 2 doctors, a visiting dentist, a pharmacist, and 1 hospital with 10 beds.

CULTURE
Broadcasting. In 1992 there were 1,500 radio receivers. A local radio and television station operate 24 hours per day.

NORFOLK ISLAND

KEY HISTORICAL EVENTS
The island was formerly part of the colony of New South Wales and then of Van Diemen's Land. It was a penal colony between 1788–1814 and 1825–55. In 1856 it received all 194 descendants of the *Bounty* mutineers from Pitcairn Island. It has been a distinct settlement since 1856, under the jurisdiction of the state of New South Wales; and finally by the passage of the Norfolk Island Act 1913, it was accepted as a Territory of the Australian Government. The Norfolk Island Act 1957 is the basis of the Territory's legislative, administrative and judicial systems.

TERRITORY AND POPULATION
Situated 29° 02' S. lat. 167° 57' E. long.; area 3,455 ha; population (June 1993), 1,896. Descendants of the *Bounty* mutineer families constitute the 'original' settlers

and are known locally as 'Islanders', while later settlers, mostly from Australia, New Zealand and the UK, are identified as 'mainlanders'. Over the years the Islanders have preserved their own lifestyle and customs, and their language remains a mixture of West Country English, Gaelic and Tahitian.

CLIMATE
Sub-tropical. Summer temperatures (Dec.-March) average about 75°F (25°C), and 65°F (18°C) in winter (June-Sept.). Annual rainfall is approximately 50" (1,200 mm), most of which falls in winter.

CONSTITUTION AND GOVERNMENT
An Administrator, appointed by the Governor-General and responsible to the Minister for Territories and Local Government, is the senior government representative in the Territory. The Norfolk Island Act 1979 gives Norfolk Island responsible legislative and executive government to enable it to run its own affairs to the greatest practicable extent. Wide powers are exercised by the Norfolk Island Legislative Assembly of 9 members, elected for a period of 3 years, and by an Executive Council, comprising the executive members of the Legislative Assembly, who have ministerial-type responsibilities. The seat of administration is Kingston, the only major settlement. The Act preserves the Commonwealth's responsibility for Norfolk Island as a Territory under its authority, indicating Parliament's intention that consideration would be given to an extension of the powers of the Legislative Assembly and the political and administrative institutions of Norfolk Island within 5 years. Some powers were transferred in 1985 and further transfers are being considered.

RECENT ELECTIONS
At the last elections, on 30 April 1997, only non-partisans were elected.

CURRENT ADMINISTRATION
Governor-General: A. J. Messner. *Administrator:* Alan Gardner Kerr.

ECONOMY
The office of the Administrator is financed from Commonwealth expenditure which in 1991–92 was approximately $A493,000; local revenue for 1990–91 totalled $A6,411,000; expenditure, $A6,222,000. Public revenue is derived mainly from tourism, the sale of postage stamps, customs duties, liquor sales and company registration and licence fees. Residents are not liable for income tax on earnings within the Territory, nor are death and personal stamp duties levied.

Currency. Australian notes and coins are the legal currency.

Banking and Finance. There are 2 banks, Westpac and the Commonwealth Bank of Australia.

COMMUNICATIONS

Roads. There are 80 km of roads (53 km paved), some 2,000 passenger cars and 100 commercial vehicles.

Civil Aviation. In 1998 there were scheduled flights to Auckland, Brisbane and Sydney, with Air New Zealand, Ansett Australia, Flight West Airlines and National Jet.

Postal Services. There is one post office located in Burnt Pines.

SOCIAL INSTITUTIONS

Justice. The island's Supreme Court sits as required and a Court of Petty Sessions exercises both civil and criminal jurisdiction.

Religion. 40% of the population are Anglicans.

Education. A school is run by the New South Wales Department of Education covering pre-school to 10th year. It had 322 pupils at 30 June 1990.

Health. In 1985 there were 2 doctors, a pharmacist and a hospital with 20 beds.

CULTURE

Broadcasting. In 1984 there were 400 television receivers and, in 1987, 1,500 radio receivers.

Press. There is one weekly with a circulation of 1,200.

Tourism. In 1991–92, 27,351 visitors travelled to Norfolk Island.

HEARD AND McDONALD ISLANDS

These islands, about 2,500 miles south-west of Fremantle, were transferred from UK to Australian control as from 26 Dec. 1947. Heard Island is about 43 km long and 21 km wide; Shag Island is about 8 km north of Heard. The total area is 412 sq. km (159 sq. miles). The McDonald Islands are 42 km to the west of Heard. In 1985–88 a major research programme was set up by the Australian National Antarctic Research Expeditions to investigate the wildlife as part of international studies of the Southern Ocean ecosystem. Subsequent expeditions followed from June 1990 through to 1992.

TERRITORY OF ASHMORE AND CARTIER ISLANDS

By Imperial Order in Council of 23 July 1931, Ashmore Islands (known as Middle, East and West Islands) and Cartier Island, situated in the Indian Ocean, some 320 km off the north-west coast of Australia (area, 5 sq. km), were placed under the authority of the Commonwealth. Under the Ashmore and Cartier Islands Acceptance Act, 1933, the islands were accepted by the Commonwealth as the Territory of Ashmore and Cartier Islands. It was the intention that the Territory should be administered by the State of Western Australia but owing to administrative difficulties the Territory was deemed to form part of the Northern Territory of Australia (by amendment to the Act in 1938). On 16 Aug. 1983 Ashmore Reef was declared a National Nature Reserve. The islands are uninhabited but Indonesian fishing boats fish within the Territory and land to collect water in accordance with an agreement between the governments of Australia and Indonesia.

TERRITORY OF CORAL SEA ISLANDS

The Coral Sea Islands which became a Territory of the Commonwealth of Australia under the Coral Sea Islands Act 1969 comprises scattered reefs and islands over a sea area of about 1m. sq. km. The Territory is uninhabited apart from a meteorological station on Willis Island.

FURTHER READING
Australian Department of Arts, Sport, the Environment, Tourism and Territories. *Christmas Island: Annual Report.—Cocos (Keeling) Islands: Annual Report.—Norfolk Island: Annual Report.*

AUSTRIA

Republik Österreich

Capital: Vienna
Population estimate, 2000: 8·29m.
GNP per capita: (PPP$) 21,650
HDI/world rank: 0·933/13

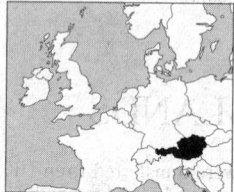

KEY HISTORICAL EVENTS

Governed by the Hapsburgs from 1282, Austria served thereafter as the centre of their expanding power and empire, an empire which lasted until 1918. At their greatest extent under Charles V (1519-55) the Hapsburg dominions included part of Hungary (wholly conquered from the Turks in 1688), Belgium, Italian territories, Spain and its vast empire. Spain was soon separated, and the Hapsburgs struggled to gain international recognition of their dynastic holdings. The Pragmatic Sanction of 1713 was only partially successful in this, but the Empire survived the War of the Austrian Succession (1740-63). Polish territory was annexed in 1772 and 1795. The Empire, represented by Prince Metternich at the Congress of Vienna, in 1815, recovered the influence in Germany and Italy it had lost during the French Revolutionary and Napoleonic Wars. It remained the major power in Central Europe till defeated in 1866 by Prussia and her German allies, a position confirmed by the unification of Germany in 1870-71 under Prussian leadership. Hungarian nationalism, the main obstacle to the integration of the Empire, was in 1867 appeased by the *Ausgleich* or Compromise; the state became known as the Dual Monarchy of Austria-Hungary.

As national feeling spread to the other peoples in the Empire, politics turned increasingly on national rivalries and aspirations. Tension was particularly high among the Serbs of Bosnia (annexed 1908) who looked to the independent state of Serbia. It was at Sarajevo in Bosnia on 28 June 1914 that the heir to the throne, Archduke Franz Ferdinand, was assassinated by Serbian nationalists, an event that triggered the First World War. The Empire, allied with Germany, suffered severely in the war, with 1·2m. dead out of a population of 52m. In 1918 the Empire disintegrated into its national units.

The Treaty of St Germain (1919) left substantial populations of German speakers in Italy and Czechoslovakia. The federal constitution of 5 Oct 1920 introduced proportional representation; Christian Socialists dominated the governments (except for 1929-30) until 1938. But the Socialists were strong, and the general strike of July 1927 and the rising of Feb. 1934 induced Chancellor Dolfuss to end parliamentary democracy and introduce Fatherland Front backed by the paramilitary Heimwehr. The Nazis who assassinated Dolfuss on 25 July 1934 helped to bring about the *Anschluss* or Union with Germany, which was achieved by a German invasion on 12 March 1938. Until 1945 Austria was Ostmark, a province of the Third Reich.

Although the 1943 Moscow Conference of Allied Foreign Ministers regarded Austria as the first victim of German aggression, Austria was occupied by Britain, France, USA and USSR (and paid reparations over a ten-year period). Independence came with the Austrian State Treaty of 15 May 1955.

Austria became a member of the European Union on 1 Jan. 1995.

TERRITORY AND POPULATION

Austria is bounded in the north by Germany and the Czech Republic, east by Slovakia and Hungary, south by Slovenia and Italy, and west by Switzerland and Liechtenstein. It has an area of 83,858 sq. km (32,378 sq. miles). Population (1997) 8,072,000; density, 96 per sq. km. Previous population censuses: (1923) 6·53m., (1934) 6·76m., (1951) 6·93m., (1971) 7·49m., (1981) 7·56m., (1991) 7·80m. In 1997 an estimated 64·3% of the population lived in urban areas. In 1990 the percentage had been higher, at 64·5%. Austria and Italy are the only European countries to have had a decline in the proportion of the population living in urban areas in the period 1990-95.

AUSTRIA

In 1991, 93·4% of residents were of Austrian nationality and 94% were German-speaking, with linguistic minorities of Slovenes (29,000), Croats (60,000), Hungarians (33,000) and Czechs (19,000).

The UN gives a projected population for 2000 of 8·29m.

The areas, populations and capitals of the 9 federal states:

Federal States	Area (sq. km)	Population (1996)	(1997)	State capitals
Vienna (Wien)	415	1,595,000	1,600,000	Vienna
Lower Austria (Niederösterreich)	19,174	1,524,000	1,530,000	St Pölten
Burgenland	3,965	275,000	276,000	Eisenstadt
Upper Austria (Oberösterreich)	11,980	1,381,000	1,378,000	Linz
Salzburg	7,154	509,000	511,000	Salzburg
Styria (Steiermark)	16,388	1,207,000	1,206,000	Graz
Carinthia (Kärnten)	9,533	563,000	564,000	Klagenfurt
Tyrol	12,648	660,000	662,000	Innsbruck
Vorarlberg	2,601	344,000	345,000	Bregenz

The populations of the principal towns at the census of 1991: Vienna, 1,539,848; Graz, 237,810; Linz, 203,044; Salzburg, 143,978; Innsbruck, 118,112; Klagenfurt, 89,415; Villach, 54,640; Wels, 52,594; St Pölten, 50,026.

The official language is German. For orthographical changes agreed in 1996 *see* GERMANY: Territory and Population.

SOCIAL STATISTICS
Statistics, 1997: Live births, 84,000 (rate of 10·4 per 1,000 population); stillbirths, 363; deaths, 79,400 (rate of 9·8 per 1,000 population); marriages, 41,400; divorces, 18,000. Suicide rates in 1996 (per 100,000 population): 22·1; men 34·2, women 10·7. Annual growth rate, 1997, 0·2%. Life expectancy at birth, 1997, 80·6 years for women and 74·3 years for men. In 1995 the most popular age range for marrying was 25–29 for both males and females. Infant mortality, 1990–95, was 7 per 1,000 live births; fertility rate, 1·5 children per woman.

CLIMATE
The climate is temperate and from west to east in transition from marine to more continental. Depending to the elevation, the climate is also predominated by alpine influence. Winters are cold with snowfall. In the eastern parts summers are warm and dry.

Vienna, Jan. –0·6°C, July 20·1°C. Annual rainfall 607 mm. Graz, Jan. –1·5°C, July 19·3°C. Annual rainfall 838 mm. Innsbruck, Jan. –1·1°C, July 18·7°C. Annual rainfall 864 mm. Salzburg, Jan. –1·3°C, July 18·3°C. Annual rainfall 1,169 mm.

CONSTITUTION AND GOVERNMENT
The Constitution of 1 Oct. 1920 was restored on 27 April 1945. Austria is a democratic federal republic comprising 9 states *(Länder)*, with a federal *President (Bundespräsident)* directly elected for not more than 2 successive 6-year terms, and a bicameral National Assembly which comprises a National Council and a Federal Council.

The National Council *(Nationalrat)* comprises 183 members directly elected for a 4-year term by proportional representation in a 3-tier system by which seats are allocated at the level of 43 regional and 9 state constituencies, and 1 federal constituency. Any party gaining 4% of votes cast nationally is represented in the National Council.

The Federal Council *(Bundesrat)* has 64 members appointed by the 9 states for the duration of the individual State Assemblies' terms; the number of deputies for each state is proportional to that state's population. In Dec. 1998 the ÖVP held 27 seats, the SPÖ, 22 and the FPÖ, 15.

The head of government is a *Federal Chancellor*, who is appointed by the President (usually the head of the party winning the most seats in National Council elections). The *Vice-Chancellor* and *Council of Ministers* are appointed by the President at the Chancellor's recommendation.

National Anthem. 'Land der Berge, Land am Strome' ('Land of mountains, land on the river'); words by Paula Preradovic; tune attributed to Mozart.

RECENT ELECTIONS

Elections were held on 17 Dec. 1995; in 4 constituencies they had to be repeated on 13 Oct. 1996 which led to the re-allocation of 1 seat. The electorate was 5·8m; turn-out was 86%. The Social Democratic Party (SPÖ) won 71 seats with 31% of votes cast (65 with 34·9% in 1994); the People's Party (ÖVP), 52 with 28·2% (52 with 27·7%); the Freedom Party (FPÖ), 41 with 16·8% (42 with 22·5%); the Liberal Forum (LIF), 10 with 11·4% (11 with 6%); the Greens, 9 with 11·4% (13 with 7·3%). Parliamentary elections are scheduled for Oct. 1999.

In the second round of the presidential elections on 24 May 1992 Thomas Klestil was elected against a single opponent by 56·85% of votes cast. In the presidential election held on 19 April 1998 The was elected to another six-year term, obtaining 63·5% of the votes cast, with his nearest rival, Gertraud Knoll, polling 13·5% of votes cast. There were 5 candidates in total.

In Dec. 1998 the party composition of the National Council was: SPÖ, 71; ÖVP, 52; FPÖ, 41; Greens, 9; LIF, 9; ind, 1.

European Parliament. Austria has 21 representatives. At the Oct. 1996 elections turn-out was 67·21%. The ÖVP won 7 seats with 29·7% of votes cast; the SPÖ, 6 with 29·2%; the FPÖ, 6 with 27·5%; the Greens, 1 with 6·8%; the LIF, 1 with 4·3%.

CURRENT ADMINISTRATION

Federal President: Dr Thomas Klestil, b. 1933 (ÖVP; re-elected 19 April 1998; previously elected 24 May 1992 and sworn in 8 July 1992).

Following the Dec. 1995 elections, the SPÖ and ÖVP agreed in March 1996 to form a coalition government, which in March 1999 consisted of the following members:

Chancellor: Dr Viktor Klima (b. 1947; SPÖ).

Vice-Chancellor, Minister of Foreign Affairs: Dr Wolfgang Schüssel (ÖVP). *Minister of the Environment, Youth and Family:* Martin Bartenstein (ÖVP). *Economic Affairs:* Johann Farnleitner (ÖVP). *Interior:* Karl Schlögl (SPÖ). *Defence:* Werner Fasslabend (ÖVP). *Labour, Health and Social Affairs:* Lore Hostasch (SPÖ). *Education and Culture:* Elisabeth Gehrer (ÖVP). *Science and Transport:* Caspar Einem (SPÖ). *Women's Affairs and Consumer Protection:* Barbara Prammer (SPÖ). *Justice:* Nikolaus Michalek (ind). *Agriculture and Forestry:* Wilhelm Molterer (ÖVP). *Finance:* Rudolf Edlinger (SPÖ).

The *President of the Nationalrat* (Speaker) is Heinz Fischer (SPÖ).

Local Government. Each state (*Land*) has its assembly. Seats gained by parties at the latest state elections:

Burgenland (June 1996): SPÖ, 17; ÖVP, 14; FPÖ, 5.
Carinthia (March 1999): SPÖ, 12; FPÖ, 16; ÖVP, 8.
Lower Austria (May 1998): ÖVP, 27; SPÖ, 18; FPÖ, 9; Greens, 2.
Salzburg (March 1999): ÖVP, 15; SPÖ, 12; FPÖ, 7; Citizens' List, 2.
Styria (Dec. 1995): ÖVP, 21; SPÖ, 21; FPÖ, 10; Greens, 2; LIF, 2.
Tyrol (March 1999): ÖVP, 19; SPÖ, 8; FPÖ, 7; Greens, 4.
Upper Austria (Oct. 1997): ÖVP, 25; SPÖ, 16; FPÖ, 12; Greens, 2.
Vienna (Oct. 1996): SPÖ, 43; FPÖ, 29; ÖVP, 15; Greens, 7; LIF, 6.
Vorarlberg (Sept. 1994): ÖVP, 20; FPÖ, 7; SPÖ, 6; Greens, 3.

Every community has a Council, which chooses one of its members to be head of the Community (Mayor) and a committee for the administration and execution of its resolutions. The provincial assemblies of the former Tyrol meet as the Regional Provincial Parliament of North Tyrol, South Tyrol and Trentino.

DEFENCE

The Federal President is C.-in-C. of the armed forces. Conscription is for a 7-month period, with liability for at least another 30 days' reservist refresher training spread over 8 to 10 years. Since 1992 the total 'on mobilization strength' of the forces has been reduced from approximately 200,000 to 110,000 troops. In 1998 approximately 1,000 personnel from so-called 'prepared units' were deployed in peace support operations in places such as Bosnia, the Golan Heights, Cyprus, etc.

Defence expenditure in 1997 totalled US$1,786m. (US$222 per capita), representing 0·8% of GDP.

Army. The army is structured in 2 corps with combat brigades and battalion- or regimental-sized combat support units. The artillery units are corps-directed. Towed artillery was phased out, and upgraded M-109 armoured self-propelled guns equip the artillery regiments. Corps I in the east of Austria comprises 3 brigades and a number of corps-directed units. A mechanized brigade is equipped with 'Leopard 2/A4' main battle tanks. One of 2 infantry brigades is earmarked for airborne operations, the second is equipped with 'Pandur' wheeled armoured personnel carriers. Corps II in the west comprises a number of corps-directed combat support units, a mechanized brigade with 'Leopard' tanks and an infantry brigade which is specialized in mountain operations. Enhanced armoured fighting vehicles for the 2 mechanized brigades are on the shopping list. In addition, some 20 infantry battalions which are under the direction of the provincial military commands are available on mobilization. Active personnel, 1998, 45,500. Women started to serve in the armed forces on 1 April 1998.

Air Force. The air service (*Luftstreitkräfte*) actually forms part of the army. The division comprises 3 aviation and 3 air-defence regiments with about 6,500 personnel, more than 150 aircraft and a number of fixed and mobile radar stations. Some 24 Draken interceptors equip a surveillance wing responsible for the defence of the Austrian air space, and a fighter-bomber wing operates SAAB 105s. Helicopters equip 6 squadrons for transport/support, communication, observation, search and rescue duties. Fixed-wing aircraft such as PC–6s, PC–7s and Skyvans are operated as trainers and for transport. The procurement of a fourth generation fighter, armed helicopters and medium-range air-defence missiles is planned for the beginning of the 21st century.

INTERNATIONAL RELATIONS
Austria is a member of the UN, EU, Council of Europe, the Central European Initiative, OECD and NATO Partnership for Peace. Austria is a signatory to the Schengen Accord abolishing border controls between Austria, Belgium, Denmark, Finland, France, Germany, Greece, Iceland, Italy, Luxembourg, Netherlands, Norway, Portugal, Spain and Sweden.

ECONOMY
Policy. In 1991 some 50% of production derived from the state-owned or state-protected sector, but a privatization programme in accordance with EU directives had largely been completed by 1995.

Performance. Real GDP growth was 2·5% in 1997 (2·0% in 1996 and 1·7% in 1995). Growth was projected to be 3·3% in 1998 and 2·8% in 1999.

Budget. The federal budget for calendar years provided revenue and expenditure (ordinary and extraordinary) as follows (in 1m. schilling):

	1993	1994	1995	1996
Revenue	601,445	626,629	646,678	665,422
Expenditure	699,685	731,447	764,581	754,788

VAT is 20% (10% reduced rate).

Currency. On 1 Jan. 1999 the euro (EUR) became the legal currency in Austria and the *schilling* became a subdivision of it; irrevocable conversion rate 13·7603 schillings to 1 euro. The euro, which consists of 100 cents, will not be in circulation until 1 Jan. 2002. There will be 7 euro notes in different colours and sizes denominated in 500, 200, 100, 50, 20, 10 and 5 euros, and 8 coins denominated in 2 and 1 euros, then 50, 20, 10, 5, 2 and 1 cents. Even though notes and coins will not be introduced until 1 Jan. 2002 the euro can be used in banking; by means of cheques, travellers' cheques, bank transfers, credit cards and electronic purses. Banking will be possible in both euros and schilling until the schilling is withdrawn from circulation—which must be by 1 July 2002.

The *schilling* (ATS) consists of 100 *groschen*. The schilling is linked to the German Mark at DM1 = 7 schillings. Inflation was 0·9% in 1998 and 1·3% in 1997, compared to 4·1% in 1992. In Oct. 1998 it was 0·7%, the lowest rate in 11 years. In Feb. 1998 foreign exchange reserves were US$18,594m. and gold reserves 8·23m.

troy oz. Note circulation in Oct. 1997 amounted to 171,125m. schilling. The schilling has been pegged to the German Mark for 20 years.

Banking and Finance. The National Bank of Austria, opened on 1 Jan. 1923, was taken over by the German Reichsbank on 17 March 1938. It was re-established on 3 July 1945. Its *President* is Klaus Liebscher. Bank accounts up to 0·2m. schilling are anonymous for Austrians, but foreign depositors must declare their identity.

There were 1,042 banks in June 1996. The 10 principal banks with total assets (in 1m. schilling, June 1996): Bank Austria, 700,052 (merger of Zentralsparkasse and Länderbank in Oct. 1991; the state retains a 21·7% stake); Creditanstalt-Bankverein, 653,714 (the state has a 49·4% stake in it); Girocredit Bank AG der Sparkassen, 321,662; Österreichische Kontrollbank AG, 257,480; Bank für Arbeit und Wirtschaft AG, 237,944; Bank der Österreichischen Postsparkasse, 227,016; Raiffeisen Zentralbank Österreich AG, 230,623; Die Erste Österreichische Spar-Casse-Bank, 223,042; Bank für Oberösterreich und Salzburg (Oberbank), 81,298; Österreichische Volksbanken AG, 72,583.

There is a stock exchange in Vienna (Börse).

Weights and Measures. The metric system is in force.

ENERGY AND NATURAL RESOURCES

Electricity. Electricity is supplied by the United Enterprise (Verbundkonzern) and by a regional company for each of the 9 states, 4 of which are partly privatized. There are also some 270 municipal and private electricity companies. Capacity was 17·86m. kW in 1997. Electric energy produced (1m. kWh): 1997, 56,851. Consumption per capita: 6,768 kWh (1995 estimate).

Oil and Gas. The commercial production of petroleum began in the early 1930s. Production of crude oil (in tonnes): 1997, 972,340.

Production of natural gas (in 1,000 cu. metres): 1997, 1,427,893.

Minerals. The most important minerals are dolomite (1997 production, 9,196,726 tonnes), quartz and arenacious quartz (7,885,148 tonnes), basalt, clay and kaolin, limestone and marble.

Agriculture. In 1997, 200,699 persons were employed in agriculture as their main occupation. The total area cultivated in 1997 amounted to 3,422,449 ha. There were 267,000 farms in 1998. Agriculture accounts for 1·1% of GDP, 6·5% of exports and 8·2% of imports.

The chief products (area in 1,000 ha, yield in tonnes) were as follows:

	1995 Area	1995 Yield	1996 Area	1996 Yield	1997 Area	1997 Yield
Wheat	255·9	1,301,310	247·6	1,239,723	259·8	1,352,281
Rye	76·8	313,835	51·2	156,227	57·8	207,238
Barley	229·1	1,065,188	259·6	1,082,789	260·6	1,257,800
Oats	40·8	161,645	41·6	152,705	46·1	196,684
Potatoes	27·0	724,426	26·3	768,973	23·5	676,872

Livestock (1997): Cattle, 2,197,940; pigs, 3,679,876; sheep, 383,655; goats, 58,340; horses, 74,170; poultry, 14,759,995.

Forestry. Forested area in 1996, 3·9m. ha (47% of the land area), of which 76% was coniferous. Felled timber, in 1,000 cu. metres: 1994, 14,359·6; 1995, 13,805·8; 1996, 15,010·2; 1997, 14,725·8.

Fisheries. Total catches in 1996 came to 4,500 tonnes, and in 1997, 4,700 tonnes, exclusively from inland waters.

INDUSTRY

Output (in tonnes if not stated otherwise):

	1996	1997		1996	1997
Raw steel	1,082,643	1,349,687	Glass (flat)		
Rolled steel	2,787,121	3,206,794	(1,000 sq. metres)	1,791	1,885
Cellulose	793,755	742,902	Cement	3,899,972	...
Paper			Salt (unrefined)	785,835[1]	833,516[2]
and cardboard	3,565,474	3,793,664	Sugar (refined)	458,693	501,421
Sawnwood			Margarine	47,195[1]	48,536[2]

238

	1996	1997		1996	1997
(1,000 cu. metres)	6,443	7,334	Milk (1,000 litres)	1,334,362	1,360,597
Synthetic fibre yarn	48,672	46,939	Fertilizers	758,445	773,348
		[1]1994. [2]1995.			

In 1997, 8,265 industrial establishments employed 571,749 persons, producing a value of 1,115bn. schillings (excluding VAT).

Labour. Austria has the second highest per capita income among the euro-11 countries and the second lowest unemployment rate (6·1% in June 1998).

In 1997 there were 3,757,400 employed persons. There were 19,000 job vacancies. In June 1998 there were 202,200 registered unemployed.

The number of foreigners who may be employed in Austria is limited to 9% of the potential workforce. There were 2 strikes in 1997, with 25,800 participants (total strike hours, 153,000). There were no strikes in 1996.

Austria has one of the lowest average retirement ages but reforms passed in 1997 now make it less attractive to retire before 60.

INTERNATIONAL TRADE

The budgetary external debt was 296,474m. schillings in 1996.

Imports and Exports. Imports and exports are as follows (excluding coined gold):

	Imports		Exports	
	1996	1997	1996	1997
Quantity (1,000 tonnes)	55,390	54,805	28,745	31,893
Value (1m. schillings)	712,760	790,251	612,190	715,016

Main export markets (% of total exports) in 1997: Germany, 35·1%; Italy, 8·3%; Switzerland, 4·9%; Hungary, 4·9%. Main import suppliers: Germany, 41·7%; Italy, 8·5%; USA, 5·4%; France, 4·7%.

COMMUNICATIONS

Roads. On 31 Dec. 1997 federal roads had a total length of 10,269 km: 1,613 km Autobahn; provincial roads, 23,472 km. On 31 Dec. 1997 there were registered 5,162,243 motor vehicles, including 3,782,544 passenger cars, 300,726 trucks, 9,718 buses, 425,710 tractors and 575,744 motor cycles.

Rail. The major railways are nationalized. Length of route in 1997, 5,672 km, of which 3,418 km were electrified. There are also 19 private railways with a total length of 594 km. In 1997, 188m. passengers and 74m. tonnes of freight were carried by Federal Railways.

There is a metro and tramway in Vienna, and tramways in Gmunden, Graz, Innsbruck and Linz.

Civil Aviation. The national airline is Austrian Airlines, which is 51·9% state-owned. There are international airports at Vienna (Schwechat), Linz, Salzburg, Graz, Klagenfurt and Innsbruck. In 1998 services were provided by 64 other airlines. In 1997, 232,483 commercial aircraft and 12,980,558 passengers arrived and departed (8·95m. at Vienna in 1996); 121,396 tonnes of freight, 8,740 tonnes of transit freight and 7,493 tonnes of mail were handled. In 1995 Austrian Airlines carried 2,563,800 passengers (2,559,800 on international flights), Tyrolean Airways 972,400 passengers (697,800 on international flights) and Lauda Air 528,100 passengers (all on international flights).

Shipping. The Danube is an important waterway. Goods traffic (in 1,000 tonnes): 7,706 in 1994; 8,791 in 1995; 9,303 in 1996; 9,204 in 1997 (including the Rhine-Main-Danube Canal). The merchant shipping fleet totalled 92,000 GRT in 1995.

Telecommunications. In 1997 postal, telegraph and telephone services were mainly state-owned; there were 3,725,800 telephone main lines. In Aug. 1998 there were 442,000 Internet users. Cellular phone subscribers numbered 384,000 in 1995 and there were 1m. PCs in use (124 per 1,000 persons).

Postal Services. In 1995 there were 2,634 post offices; 3,627m. postal items were handled.

AUSTRIA

SOCIAL INSTITUTIONS

Justice. The Supreme Court of Justice *(Oberster Gerichtshof)* in Vienna is the highest court in the land. In addition, there were in 1995 4 higher state courts *(Oberlandesgerichte)*, 16 state courts *(Landesgerichte)* and 187 local courts *(Bezirksgerichte)*.

Religion. In 1997 there were 6,310,000 Roman Catholics (78·3%), 390,000 Evangelical Lutherans (4·8%), 700,000 without religious allegiance (8·6%) and 690,000 others (8·6%). The Roman Catholic Church has 2 archbishoprics and 7 bishoprics.

Education. In 1997–98 there were 5,027 general compulsory schools (including special education) with 74,180 teachers and 685,208 pupils. Secondary schools totalled 1,185 with 507,525 pupils.

There were also 122 commercial academies in 1997–98 with 39,290 pupils and 5,396 teachers; 318 schools of technical and industrial training (including schools of hotel management and catering) with 6,885 teachers and 65,944 pupils; 62 higher schools of women's professions (secondary level) with 20,214 pupils; 8 training colleges of social workers with 1,333 pupils; 126 trade schools with 14,018 pupils.

The dominant institutions of higher education are the 12 universities and 6 colleges of arts, which are publicly financed. In 1994 Higher Technical Study Centres *(Fachhochschul-Studiengänge,* FHS) were established, which are private, but government-dependent, institutions. In the winter term 1997–98 there were 212,247 students enrolled at the universities, 6,915 at the colleges of arts and 5,773 at 40 FHS. About 15,000 teachers (full-time equivalent) provide tertiary-level education.

In 1996 government expenditure on education came to 131·5bn. schillings.

Health. In 1997 there were 32,720 doctors, 329 hospitals and 75,281 hospital beds.

Welfare. Maternity/paternity leave is for 18 months.

CULTURE

Broadcasting. The 'Österreichische Rundfunk' (Austrian Broadcasting Corporation) is state-controlled. It transmits 4 national and 9 regional radio programmes. An additional programme in English and French can be received all over the country; there is also a 24-hour foreign service (short wave). Broadcasting is financed by licence payments and advertisements. There were 2·77m. registered listeners and 2·64m. television licenses (colour by PAL) issued in Dec. 1997.

Cinema. In 1997 there were 419 fixed cinemas, 1 drive-in cinema and 21 mobile units. Audience numbers totalled 13,716,900 in 1997.

Press. There were 17 daily newspapers (6 of them in Vienna), 151 non-daily newspapers and 2,637 other periodicals in 1997.

Tourism. Tourism is an important industry. In 1997, 18,000 hotels and boarding houses had a total of 640,200 beds available; 17,090,000 foreigners visited Austria. Tourist receipts were 134,691m. schillings in 1997.

Festivals. The main festivals in 1997 were Salzburger Festspiele (218,000 visitors), Bregenzer Festspiele (199,200 visitors) and Wiener Festwochen (172,800 visitors).

Libraries. In 1996 there were 5,706,000 library users and 28,648,000 volumes in scientific and special libraries, and 1,063,800 users and 10,634,800 volumes in public libraries.

National Theatre and Opera. The attendance at federal theatres was 1,431,600 in 1997/98.

Museums and Galleries. In 1997 there were 22,684,800 visitors to museums, exhibitions and similar attractions (9,527,700 in Vienna).

DIPLOMATIC REPRESENTATIVES
Of Austria in Great Britain (18 Belgrave Mews West, London, SW1X 8HU)
Ambassador: Eva Nowotny.

Of Great Britain in Austria (Jaurèsgasse 12, 1030 Vienna)
Ambassador: Sir Anthony Figgis, KCVO, CMG.

Of Austria in the USA (3524 International Court, NW, Washington, D.C., 20008)
Ambassador: Dr Helmut Türk.

Of the USA in Austria (Boltzmanngasse 16, A-1091 Vienna)
Ambassador: Cathryn Walt-Hall.

Of Austria to the United Nations
Ambassador: Dr Ernst Sucharipa.

FURTHER READING

Austrian Central Statistical Office. *Main publications: Statistisches Jahrbuch für die Republik Österreich.* New Series from 1950. Annual.—*Statistische Nachrichten.* Monthly.—*Beiträge zur österreichischen Statistik* (1,104 vols.).—*Statistik in Österreich 1918–1938.* [Bibliography] 1985.—*Veröffentlichungen des Österreichischen Statistischen Zentralamtes 1945–1985.* [Bibliography], 1990.—*Republik Österreich, 1945–1995.*

Brook-Shepherd, G., *The Austrians: a Thousand-Year Odyssey.* London, 1997
Peniston-Bird, C. M., *Vienna,* Oxford, 1997
Salt, D., *Austria* [Bibliography]. Oxford and Santa Barbara (CA), 1986
Sully, M. A., *A Contemporary History of Austria.* London, 1990
Wolfram, H. (ed.) *Österreichische Geschichte.* 10 vols. Vienna, 1994

National statistical office: Austrian Central Statistical Office, POB 9000, A-1033 Vienna.
Website: http://www.oestat.gv.at/index.htm
National library: Österreichische Nationalbibliothek, Josefsplatz, 1015 Vienna.

AZERBAIJAN

Azarbaijchan Respublikasy

Capital: Baku
Population estimate, 2000: 7·83m.
GNP per capita: (PPP$) 1,490
HDI/world rank: 0·623/110

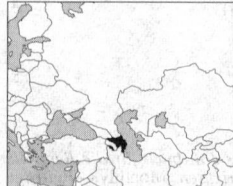

KEY HISTORICAL EVENTS
The 'Mussavat' (Nationalist) party, which dominated the National Council or Constituent Assembly of the Tatars, declared the independence of Azerbaijan on 28 May 1918, with a capital first at Ganja (Elizavetpol) and later at Baku. On 28 April 1920 Azerbaijan was proclaimed a Soviet Socialist Republic. From 1922, with Georgia and Armenia, it formed the Transcaucasian Soviet Federal Socialist Republic. In 1936 it assumed the status of one of the Union Republics of the USSR. In 1990 it adopted a declaration of republican sovereignty, and on 18 Aug. 1991 the Supreme Soviet of Azerbaijan passed a constitution act on independence and the Republic re-established its full sovereignty; this was approved by 99·6% of votes at a referendum in Jan. 1992. Under the presidency of Heydar Aliyev, parliament ratified its adhesion to the CIS on 20 Sept. 1993. A treaty of friendship and co-operation was signed with Russia on 3 July 1997.

TERRITORY AND POPULATION
Azerbaijan is bounded in the west by Armenia, in the north by Georgia and the Russian Federation (Dagestan), in the east by the Caspian sea and in the south by Turkey and Iran. Its area is 86,600 sq. km (33,430 sq. miles), and it includes the Nakhichevan Autonomous Republic and the largely Armenian-inhabited Nagorno-Karabakh.

In 1997 there were 7,625,200 inhabitants of whom 52·4% lived in urban areas. Density, approximately 88 per sq. km. There are 65 towns (1 in each region), 8 of which have over 50,000 people. The population breaks down into 82·7% Azerbaijanis, 5·6% Russians, 5·6% Armenians and 2·4% Lezgis (1989 census).

The UN gives a projected population for 2000 of 7·83m.

Chief cities: Baku (1997 population, 1·7m.), Gandja (0·3m.) and Sumgait (0·3m.). The official language is Azeri.

SOCIAL STATISTICS
In 1997: Births, 132,052 (159,761 in 1994); deaths, 46,962 (54,921 in 1994); marriages, 46,999; divorces, 5,806. Rates, 1997 (per 1,000 population): Births, 17·4 (21·4 in 1994); deaths, 6·2 (7·4 in 1994); infant mortality (per 1,000 live births), 19·3 (25·2 in 1994); deaths of children under 1 year, 2,589 (4,180 in 1994). Life expectancy in 1997: 74·0 years for women and 66·5 years for men. Annual growth rate, 1990–95, 0·9%; fertility rate, 2·6 children per woman.

CLIMATE
The climate is almost tropical in summer and the winters slightly warmer than in regions north of the Caucasus. Cold spells do occur, however, both on the high mountains and in the enclosed valleys. Baku, Jan. –6°C, July 25°C. Annual rainfall 318 mm.

CONSTITUTION AND GOVERNMENT
Parliament is the 125-member *Melli-Majlis*. 100 seats are contested on a majority basis, and 25 distributed proportionally among political parties. For the majority seats there is a minimum 50% turn-out requirement. There is an 8% threshold. A constitutional referendum and parliamentary elections were held on 12 Nov. 1995. Turn-out for the referendum was 86%. The new Constitution was approved by 91·9% of votes cast.

National Anthem. 'Azerbaijan! Azerbaijan!'; words by A. Javad, tune by U. Hajibayov.

AZERBAIJAN

RECENT ELECTIONS
At elections on 3 Oct. 1993 Heydar Aliyev was elected President unopposed, with 98·8% of votes cast; he was re-elected on 11 Oct. 1998 with 76·1% of votes cast against 5 other candidates.

At the parliamentary elections held on 12 Nov. 1995, 386 candidates from 8 parties and independents stood; turn-out was 79·5%. Run-off elections were held on 26 Nov. The New Azerbaijan Party (NAP) gained 67 of the 125 seats and 70% of votes cast. (The OSCE declared these elections 'not in accordance with international standards.')

The next parliamentary elections are due before Nov. 2000.

CURRENT ADMINISTRATION
President: Heydar Aliyev (b. 1924; NAP; sworn in 10 Oct. 1993, re-elected Oct. 1998).

In March 1999 the government comprised:

Prime Minister: Artur Rasizade (NAP).

Foreign Affairs: Tofiq Zulfiqarov. *Interior:* Ramil Usubov. *Culture:* Polad Byulbyulogly. *Education:* Misir Mardanov. *National Security:* Namig Abbasov. *Defence:* Lt-Gen. Safar Abiev. *Media and Information:* Siruz Tebrizli. *Communications:* Nadir Ahmedov. *Agriculture:* Ershad Aliyev. *Economy:* Namik Nasrullaev. *Justice:* Sudaba Hasanova. *Health:* Ali Insanov. *Finance:* Fikret Usifov. *Labour and Social Protection:* Ali Nagiyev. *Youth and Sport:* Abulfaz Karaev.

DEFENCE
Conscription is for 17 months. Defence expenditure in 1997 totalled US$146m. (US$19 per capita), representing 4·0% of GDP.

Army. The Army is organized in 1 tank, 12 motor rifle, 1 air assault, 2 motor rifle training and 2 artillery brigades; and 2 motor rifle, 2 mountain infantry and 1 anti-tank regiment. Equipment includes 325 T-55 and T-72 main battle tanks. Personnel, 1997, 53,300. There is also a paramilitary Ministry of the Interior militia of about 20,000.

Navy. The flotilla is based at Baku on the Caspian Sea and numbered about 2,200 in 1997. It operates 34 miscellaneous vessels, including 2 small frigates, 3 missile craft, 18 fast patrol craft, 14 mine-countermeasure vessels and 1 tank landing craft.

Air Force. How many ex-Soviet aircraft are usable is not known, but MiG-21 fighters, Su-25 close support aircraft and Mi-24 armed helicopters are in use, as well as L-29 Delfin armed trainers. Personnel, 11,200 in 1997.

INTERNATIONAL RELATIONS
Total foreign debt in 1997 amounted to US$567m.

Azerbaijan is a member of the UN, CIS, the NATO Partnership for Peace, OSCE, IMO, WB, IMF, EBRD, BSEC and OEC. There is a dispute with Armenia over the status of the chiefly Armenian-populated Azerbaijani enclave of Nagorno-Karabakh. Fighting more or less ended in 1994 with about 16% of Azerbaijan's land in Armenian hands.

ECONOMY
Performance. Total GDP was US$4·1bn. in 1997, up from US$3·4bn. in 1996. Real GDP growth was 5·0% in 1997 compared to 1·3% in 1996. This was largely thanks to foreign investment into the country in anticipation of the forthcoming oil boom. Between 1990 and 1996 the average annual real growth in GNP per capita was –18·7%.

Budget. The 1998 budget envisaged revenue of 3,071,729·8m. manats (of which profits tax accounted for 498,000m. manats and VAT 800,000m. manats), and expenditure of 3,796,847·3m. manats (of which social welfare accounted for 88,275·4m. manats, education 825,842·9m. manats, health 290,143m. manats and social protection 340,000m. manats). In 1997 revenue was 2,525,300m. manats and expenditure was 2,913,700m. manats.

AZERBAIJAN

Currency. The *manat* (AZM) of 100 *gyapiks* replaced the rouble in Jan. 1994. Inflation was 4·0% in 1997 (19·0% in 1996). Foreign exchange reserves were US$457m. in 1997.

Banking and Finance. The central bank and bank of issue is the National Bank (*Chairman*, Elman Rustamov). In 1996 there were 112 commercial and 4 state-owned banks. With capital requirements increasing, the number of commercial banks is rapidly decreasing.

Reserves, excluding gold, totalled US$457m. in 1997, up from US$214m. in 1996.

ENERGY AND NATURAL RESOURCES

Electricity. Capacity in 1994 was 5·24m. kW. Output was 17,005m. kWh in 1996. Consumption per capita in 1996 was estimated to be 2,200 kWh.

Oil and Gas. The most important industry is crude oil extraction. An estimated average of 9·0m. tonnes of oil and 6·0 bn. cu. metres of gas are produced annually (1997). Baku is at the centre of oil exploration in the Caspian. Partnerships with Turkish, Western European and US companies have been forged.

Minerals. The republic is rich in natural resources: Iron, bauxite, manganese, aluminium, copper ores, lead, zinc, precious metals, sulphur pyrites, nepheline syenites, limestone and salt. In 1991, 1·6m. tonnes of iron ore were produced. Cobalt ore reserves have been discovered in Dashkasan, and Azerbaijan has the largest iodine-bromine ore reserves of the former Soviet Union (the Neftchala region has an iodine-bromine mill).

Agriculture. In 1997, the total area devoted to agriculture was 4·5m. ha, of which 1·7m. ha was under crop and 223,747 ha were orchards and vineyards. In 1997, 34% of the economically active population was engaged in agriculture; in 1996 it accounted for 23% of GDP. In 1994 there were 1·6m. ha of arable land, 400,000 ha of permanent crops and 2·2m. ha of permanent pasture. Principal crops include grain, cotton, rice, grapes, citrus fruit, vegetables, tobacco and silk. The Mexican rubber plant *grayule* has been acclimatized. A new kind of high-yielding winter wheat has been produced for use in mountainous parts of the republic.

Livestock (1996): Cattle, 1·66m.; sheep, 4·4m.; goats, 182,000 (1995); chickens, 23m. (1995).

Output of main agricultural products (in 1m. tonnes) in 1997: Grain, 1·1; cotton, 0·1; grapes, 0·1; vegetables, 0·5; fruit and berries, 0·3; meat, 0·09; milk, 0·9; and 491m. eggs.

Forestry. In 1995 forests covered 990,000 ha, or 11·4% of the total land area.

Fisheries. About 10 tonnes of caviar from the Caspian sturgeon are produced annually. Total catches in 1995 came to an estimated 37,000 tonnes, exclusively from inland waters.

INDUSTRY

There are oil extraction and refining, oil-related machinery, iron and steel, aluminium, copper, chemical, cement, building materials, timber, synthetic rubber, salt, textiles, food and fishing industries. Output (1993), valued at 123,000m. manats, was (in tonnes): Rolled ferrous metals, 0·2m.; mineral fertilizers, 30,000; cement, 0·6m.; processed meat, 16,500; milk products, 48,000; fabrics, 116m. sq. metres; footwear, 4·1m. pairs; 200 lathes; 90 lorries; 8,700 TV sets; 229,000 refrigerators, freezers and air conditioners.

Labour. In 1997 the population of working age was 4·5m. of whom 2·9m. were employed, 67·5% in the state sector and 17·2% in co-operatives (in 1991). There were 31,900 registered unemployed in 1996 (11% of the labour force), of whom 4,400 were receiving benefits. The average monthly salary in 1997 was 125,500 manats.

INTERNATIONAL TRADE

Imports and Exports. In 1997 imports were valued at US$794·3m. (1996, US$960·6m.) and exports at US$781·3m. (1996, US$631·2m.).

AZERBAIJAN

Fuel and oil accounted for approximately 61% of exports in 1997. Cotton, chemicals, tobacco, beverages, air-conditioners, wool and refrigerators are also important exports. The main imports were power, grain meal, steel tubes, sugar and sweets.

The main export markets in 1997 were Iran (24%), Russia (23%), Georgia (17%) and Turkey (5%). Leading import suppliers were Turkey (23%), Russia (19%), Ukraine (11%) and Iran (6%).

COMMUNICATIONS

Roads. There were 48,670 km of roads (24,335 km highways and main roads) in 1996. Passenger cars in use in 1996 totalled 273,656 (36·2 per 1,000 inhabitants). In addition, there were 77,710 trucks and vans, 28,000 road tractors and 12,925 buses and coaches.

Rail. Total length in 1994 was 2,118 km of 1,520 mm gauge (1,310 km electrified). In 1994, 10·6m. passengers and 12·9m. tonnes of freight were carried.

There is a metro and tramway in Baku and a tramway in Sumgait.

Civil Aviation. There is an international airport at Baku. Azerbaijan Airlines had international flights in 1998 to Aleppo, Ankara, Antalya, Ashgabat, Chelyabinsk, Delhi, Ekaterinburg, Istanbul, Kazan, Kharkov, Kiev, London, Moscow, Nakhichevan, Nizhny Novgorod, Orenburg, Perm, St Petersburg, Samara, Tbilisi, Tehran, Tel Aviv, Trabzon, Turkmanbashi, Volgograd, Voronezh and Zaporozhye. In 1995 Azerbaijan Airlines flew 21·3m. km, carrying 1,156,000 passengers (119,400 on international flights).

Shipping. In 1995, merchant shipping totalled 480,000 GRT, including oil tankers, 230,000 GRT.

Telecommunications. Telephone main lines numbered 663,200 in 1997 (86·9 per 1,000 inhabitants). In 1995 there were 6,000 cellular phone subscribers and 2,500 fax machines.

Postal Services. There were 1,857 post offices in 1995.

SOCIAL INSTITUTIONS

Justice. The number of reported crimes in 1997 was 16,402 (compared to 18,533 in 1994), including 449 murders or attempted murders (605 in 1994). There were 219 crimes per 1,000 inhabitants (249 in 1994) and 80% of crimes were solved (69·3% in 1994).

Religion. In 1997 the population was 92% Moslem (mostly Shia), the balance being mainly Russian Orthodox and Armenian Apostolic.

Education. In 1995–96 there were 697,510 pupils and 34,201 teachers at 4,462 primary schools, and 812,610 pupils with 105,656 teachers at secondary schools. There were 103,608 children enrolled at pre-school institutions. In 1997 there were 111,382 students at 25 institutes of higher education and 73 specialized secondary schools. There is a state university at Baku, with 94,300 students in 1993–94 (including correspondence students). The Azerbaijan Academy of Sciences, founded in 1945, has 30 research institutes. Adult literacy is more than 99%.

In 1994 total expenditure on education came to 5·5% of GNP and represented 13·7% of total government expenditure.

Health. In 1997 there were 29,300 doctors, 65,500 paramedics and 762 hospitals with 72,000 beds.

Welfare. In Jan. 1994 there were 797,000 age pensioners and 454,000 other pensioners.

CULTURE

Broadcasting. The government-controlled Azerbaijan Radio broadcasts 2 national and 1 regional programme, a relay of Radio Moscow and a foreign service, Radio Baku (Azeri, Arabic, Iranian and Turkish). There are a number of private TV and radio stations. In 1995 there were 250,000 TV receivers and 150,000 radio receivers.

Cinema. In 1997 there were 696 cinemas.

Press. In 1997 Azerbaijan published 270 different newspapers and 45 magazines. In 1995, 422 newspapers were registered with the Ministry of Justice, but only about 50 were actually appearing. There is 1 daily, published by parliament, with a circulation of 5,000, and 2 independent thrice-weeklies with a combined circulation of 30,000. 73 journals were registered in 1995, but only 12 were appearing. 80% of all newspapers circulate in the Baku area.

Tourism. In 1996 there were 145,000 foreign tourists, spending US$158m.

Libraries. There are 4,647 public libraries (1997).

National Theatre and Opera. Azerbaijan has 26 professional theatres (1997).

Museums and Galleries. There were 145 museums including a National Museum of History in 1997.

DIPLOMATIC REPRESENTATIVES
Of Azerbaijan in Great Britain (4 Kensington Court, London, W8 5DL)
Ambassador: Mahmud Mamed-Kuliyev.

Of Great Britain in Azerbaijan (2 Izmir St., Baku 370065)
Ambassador: D. R. Thomas.

Of Azerbaijan in the USA (Temporary: 927–15th Street, NW, Suite 700, 20005; P.O. Box 28790, Washington, D.C., 20038)
Ambassador: Hafiz Mir Jalal Pashayev.

Of the USA in Azerbaijan (83 Azadliq Prospekt, Baku 37007)
Ambassador: Stanley Escudero.

Of Azerbaijan to the United Nations
Ambassador: Eldar G. Kouliev.

Of Azerbaijan to the European Union
Ambassador: Mir-Gamza Efendiev.

NAKHICHEVAN

This territory, on the borders of Turkey and Iran, forms part of Azerbaijan although separated from it by the territory of Armenia. Its population in 1989 was 95·9% Azerbaijani. It was annexed by Russia in 1828. In June 1923 it was constituted as an Autonomous Region within Azerbaijan. On 9 Feb. 1924 it was elevated to the status of Autonomous Republic. The 1996 Azerbaijani Constitution defines it as an Autonomous State within Azerbaijan.

Area, 5,500 sq. km (2,120 sq. miles); population (Jan. 1994), 315,000. Capital, Nakhichevan (66,800).

70% of the people are engaged in agriculture, of which the main branches are cotton and tobacco growing. Fruit and grapes are also produced.

In 1989–90 there were 219 primary and secondary schools with 60,200 pupils, and 2,200 students in higher educational institutions.

In Jan. 1990 there were 381 doctors and 2,445 junior medical personnel.

NAGORNO-KARABAKH

Established on 7 July 1923 as an Autonomous Region within Azerbaijan, in 1989 the area was placed under a 'special form of administration' subordinate to the USSR government. In Sept. 1991 the regional Soviet and the Shaumyan district Soviet jointly declared a Nagorno-Karabakh republic, which declared itself

NAGORNO-KARABAKH

independent with a 99·9% popular vote (only the Armenian community took part in this vote as the Azeri population had already been expelled from Nagorno-Karabakh) in Dec. 1991. The autonomous status of the region was meanwhile abolished by the Azerbaijan Supreme Soviet in Nov. 1991, and the capital renamed Khankendi. A presidential decree of Jan. 1992 placed the region under direct rule. Azeri-Armenian fighting for possession of the region culminated in its occupation by Armenia in 1993 (and the occupation of 7 other Azerbaijani regions outside it), despite attempts at international mediation. Since May 1994 there has been a ceasefire. Negotiations on settlements are conducted within the OSCE Minsk Group.

Area, 4,400 sq. km (1,700 sq. miles); population (Jan. 1990), 192,400. Capital, Khankendi (33,000). Populated by Armenians (76·9% at the 1989 census) and Azerbaijanis (21·5%).

Main industries are silk, wine, dairying and building materials. Crop area is 67,200 ha; cotton, grapes and winter wheat are grown. There are 33 collective and 38 state farms.

In 1989–90, 34,200 pupils were studying in primary and secondary schools, 2,400 in colleges and 2,100 in higher educational institutions.

BAHAMAS

**Commonwealth of
The Bahamas**

Capital: Nassau
Population estimate, 2000: 302,000
GNP per capita: (PPP$) 10,180
HDI/world rank: 0·893/32

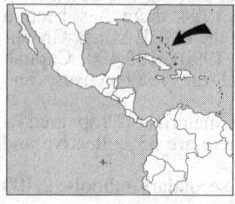

KEY HISTORICAL EVENTS

The Bahamas were discovered by Columbus in 1492 but the Spanish did not make a permanent settlement. After British settlers arrived in the 17th century the islands were occupied by Britain, except for a short period in the 18th century, until they gained independence. Internal self-government with cabinet responsibility was introduced on 7 Jan. 1964 and full independence achieved on 10 July 1973.

TERRITORY AND POPULATION

The Commonwealth of The Bahamas consists of over 700 islands and inhabited cays off the south-east coast of Florida extending for about 260,000 sq. miles. Only 22 islands are inhabited. Land area, 5,382 sq. miles (13,939 sq. km).

The areas and populations of the major islands in 1990 were as follows:

	Area (in sq. km)	Popu-lation		Area (in sq. km)	Popu-lation
Grand Bahama	1,373	40,898	Exuma Islands	290	3,556
Abaco	1,681	10,003	San Salvador	163	465
Bimini Islands	23	1,639	Rum Cay	78	53
Berry Islands	31	628	Long Island	448	2,949
New Providence	207	172,196	Ragged Island	23	89
Andros	5,957	8,177	Crooked Island	238	412
Eleuthera, Harbour Island			Acklins Island	389	405
and Spanish Wells	518	10,584	Mayaguana	285	312
Cat Island	388	1,698	Inagua Islands	1,671	985

1990 census population, 255,049 (130,091 females). 1996 estimate, 284,000; density, 20 per sq. km.

The UN gives a projected population for 2000 of 302,000.

In 1995 an estimated 86·5% of the population were urban. The capital is Nassau on New Providence Island (178,000 in 1996); the other large town is Freeport (45,000) on Grand Bahama.

English is the official language. Creole is spoken among Haitian immigrants.

SOCIAL STATISTICS

1997 estimates: Births, 6,300; deaths, 1,600. Rates, 1997 (per 1,000 population): Birth, 21·47; death, 5·45; marriage (1994), 9·3; infant mortality (per 1,000 live births), 1997, 19·6. Expectation of life was 69·3 years for males and 76 for females in 1990–95. Annual growth rate, 1990–95, 1·7%; fertility rate, 2·0 children per woman.

CLIMATE

Winters are mild and summers pleasantly warm. Most rain falls in May, June, Sept. and Oct., and thunderstorms are frequent in summer. Rainfall amounts vary over the islands from 30" (750 mm) to 60" (1,500 mm). Nassau, Jan. 71°F (21·7°C), July 81°F (27·2°C). Annual rainfall 47" (1,179 mm).

CONSTITUTION AND GOVERNMENT

The Commonwealth of The Bahamas is a free and democratic sovereign state. Executive power rests with Her Majesty the Queen, who appoints a Governor-General to represent her, advised by a Cabinet whom he appoints. There is a bicameral legislature. The *Senate* comprises 16 members all appointed by the Governor-General, 9 on the advice of the Prime Minister, 4 on the advice of the Leader of the Opposition, and 3 after consultation with both of them. The *House of*

Assembly consists of 40 members elected from single-member constituencies for a maximum term of 5 years.

National Anthem. 'Lift up your head to the rising sun, Bahamaland'; words and tune by T. Gibson.

RECENT ELECTIONS

At the election for the House of Assembly of 14 March 1997, the Free National Movement gained 34 seats and the Progressive Liberal Party, 6. In a subsequent by-election the Free National Movement won a further seat from the Progressive Liberal Party.

CURRENT ADMINISTRATION

Governor-General: Sir Orville Turnquest, GCMG, QC.

The Cabinet was composed as follows in March 1999:

Prime Minister: Hubert Alexander Ingraham.

Deputy Prime Minister and Minister of National Security with responsibility for the Public Service and Public Utilities: Frank H. Watson. *Agriculture and Fisheries:* Earl Deveaux. *Attorney General and Justice:* Tennyson R. G. Wells. *Consumer Welfare and Aviation:* Pierre V. Dupuch. *Foreign Affairs:* Janet Gwenneth Bostwick. *Education:* Dame Ivy Leona Dumont. *Finance and Planning:* William C. Allen. *Health and Environment:* Ronald Knowles. *Labour, Immigration and Training:* Theresa Moxey-Ingraham. *Public Works:* O. A. Tommy Turnquest. *Social Development and Housing:* Algernon S. P. B. Allen. *Transport:* James F. Knowles. *Minister of State for Public Enterprises:* Anthony Rolle. *Youth, Sports and Culture:* Zhivargo Laing. *Education:* Dion Foulkes. *Economic Development:* Carl Bethel. *Public Service Commission:* David Thompson.

Secretary to the Cabinet: Basil O'Brien.

Local Government. The Local Government Act came into effect on 25 June 1996. Elections were held on 26 July 1996. The Act divides the Family Islands into 23 local government districts administered by a popularly elected district council.

DEFENCE

The Royal Defence Force is a primarily maritime force tasked with naval patrols and protection duties in the extensive waters of the archipelago. Equipment comprises 4 coastal defence vessels, 2 auxiliary vessels, 2 Dauntless search and rescue craft, and 10 assorted coastal and inshore patrol craft for harbour and shallow water operations. There are also 2 cabin-class fixed-wing aircraft, a Cessna Golden Eagle 421C and a Cessna Titan 404. Personnel in 1996 numbered 850, and the base is at Coral Harbour on New Providence Island.

In 1997 defence expenditure totalled US$22m. (US$82 per capita).

INTERNATIONAL RELATIONS

The Commonwealth of The Bahamas is a member of the UN, OAS, the Commonwealth, CARICOM, FAO, IBRD, ICAO, ILO, IMF, Intelsat, ITU, UNESCO, UNIDO, WHO, WIPO and is an ACP member state of the ACP-EU relationship.

ECONOMY

Policy. The Government of the Commonwealth of The Bahamas is committed to building an economic environment in which free enterprise can flourish; where the Government assumes its proper role as regulator and facilitator of economic development; where the ideals of transparency, fair play and equality of treatment are paramount; and a policy that maintains a stable society in which all people are afforded the opportunity to realize their maximum potential. In this regard, the National Investment Policy is designed to support an investment-friendly climate; guarantees the complementarity of Bahamian and overseas investments; fosters appropriate linkages with all sectors of the economy, in particular, the tourism and financial services sectors; encourages the exploitation of the country's natural resources in an environmentally sound and sustainable manner; provides for the

BAHAMAS

maximum level of employment; guarantees an acceptable level of economic security and generally foster the economic growth and development of The Bahamas.

Performance. The Bahamas experienced a recession during the period 1988–94; this was mainly due to the recession in the USA leading to a fall in the number of American tourists. The economy has been growing since, and there are continuing efforts to diversify. Freeport's tax-free status was extended by 25 years in 1995, and import duties were reduced in the 1996–97 budget. 1996 saw an increase in growth; but the budget deficit is increasing; an overall deficit of US$190m. was projected for 1997–98, 3 times the 1996–97 deficit, and 5% of GDP.

Real GDP growth was 1·0% in 1995 (0·3% in 1994).

Budget. (in B$1m.):

	1995-96	1996-97
Revenue	665·2	725·2
Expenditure	725·4	767·5

The main sources of revenue are customs duties and receipts from fees, post office and public utilities. There is no direct taxation.

Currency. The unit of currency is the *Bahamian dollar* (BSD) of 100 *cents*. American currency is generally accepted. Inflation was 1·6% in 1996. Foreign exchange reserves were US$337m. in Dec. 1998. Total money supply was B$517m. in Dec. 1997.

Banking and Finance. The Central Bank of The Bahamas was established in 1974. Its *Governor* is Julian Francis. The Bahamas is an important centre for offshore banking. Financial business produces about 20% of GDP. In Dec. 1996, 425 banks and trust companies were licensed, about half being branches of foreign companies.

Weights and Measures. The Bahamas follows the USA in using linear, dry and liquid measure.

ENERGY AND NATURAL RESOURCES

Electricity. In 1996, installed capacity was 424 MW, all thermal. Output, 1996, 1,290m. kWh. Consumption per capita was 2,717 kWh in 1993.

Oil and Gas. The Bahamas does not have reserves of either oil or gas, but oil is refined in the Bahamas. The Bahamas Oil Refining Company (BORCO), in Grand Bahama, operates as a terminal which trans-ships, stores and blends oil.

Minerals. Aragonite is extracted from the seabed.

Agriculture. In 1996 there were some 8,444 ha of arable land, 3,921 ha of permanent crops and 2,230 ha of pasture. Production (in 1,000 tonnes), 1993: Sugar-cane, 200; vegetables and melons, 28; fruit, 12.

Livestock (1995): Cattle, 2,000; sheep, 37,000; goats, 17,000; pigs, 13,000; chickens, 2m.

Forestry. In 1995 forests covered 158,000 ha or 15·8% of the total land area (18% in 1990). Timber production in 1995 was 117,000 cu. metres.

Fisheries. The total catches in 1995 amounted to 9,638 tonnes, mainly lobsters, and exclusively from sea fishing. Total value was B$59·7m.

INDUSTRY

Tourism and offshore banking are the main industries. Two industrial sites, one in New Providence and the other in Grand Bahama, have been developed as part of an industrialization programme. The main products are pharmaceutical chemicals, salt and rum.

Labour. The workforce was estimated at 146,635 in 1996. Around 30% of the economically active population work in trade, restaurants and hotels. Unemployment was 11·5% in 1996.

Trade Unions. In 1996 there were 43 unions, the largest being The Bahamas Hotel Catering and Allied Workers' Union (5,000 members).

BAHAMAS

INTERNATIONAL TRADE
Public-sector foreign debt was US$372,862 in Dec. 1997. There is a freeport zone of Grand Bahama. Although a member of CARICOM, the Bahamas is not a signatory to its trade protocol.

Imports and Exports. In 1996 imports were valued at US$1,262m. and exports at US$202m.

The principal exports are oil products and trans-shipments, chemicals, fish, rum and salt.

In 1996 the main export markets were: USA, 81%; Canada, 1·9%; Sweden, 7%; Singapore, 7%. The main import suppliers were: USA, 90·3%; Japan, 0·3%; France, 1·1%.

COMMUNICATIONS

Roads. There were about 2,500 km of roads in 1996 (1,400 paved). In 1996, 84,234 motor vehicles were registered on New Providence.

Civil Aviation. There are international airports at Nassau, Freeport (Grand Bahama Island) and Moss Town (Andros). The national carrier is the state-owned Bahamasair, which in 1998 flew to Fort Lauderdale, Miami, Newark, Orlando and West Palm Beach as well as providing services between different parts of The Bahamas. Scheduled flights were also operated in 1998 by Air Canada, Air Jamaica, American Airlines, AOM, British Airways, Condor Flugdienst, Continental Airlines, Delta Air Lines, United Airlines and USAir. In 1995 scheduled airline traffic of Bahamas-based carriers flew 4·3m. km, carrying 937,000 passengers (449,000 on international flights).

Shipping. The Bahamas' shipping registry consists of a fleet of 25m. GRT. There are more than 1,500 vessels, making the fleet the fourth largest in the world.

Telecommunications. New Providence and most of the other major islands have automatic telephone systems in operation, interconnected by a radio network, while local distribution within the islands is by overhead and underground cables. In 1997 there were 96,300 telephone main lines in use. International telecommunications service is provided by a submarine cable system to Florida, USA, and an INTELSAT Standard 'A' Earth Station and a Standard 'F2' Earth Station. International operator-assisted and direct dialling telephone services are available to all major countries. There is an automatic Telex system and a packet switching system for data transmission, and land mobile and marine telephone services. In 1995 there were 2,400 cellular phone subscribers and 500 fax machines.

Postal Services. In 1997 there were over 120 post offices.

SOCIAL INSTITUTIONS

Justice. English Common Law is the basis of the Bahamian judicial system, although there is a large volume of Bahamian Statute Law. The highest tribunal in the country is the Court of Appeal. New Providence has 15 Magistrates' Courts and Grand Bahama has 3.

The strength of the police force (1995) was 2,223 officers.

Religion. Religious adherents as at the 1996 census: Baptist, 32%; Anglican/Episcopalian, 20%; Roman Catholic, 19%; Protestant, 12%; Church of God, 6%; Methodist, 6%.

Education. Education is compulsory between 5 and 16 years of age. The adult literacy rate in 1995 was 98·2% (98·5% among males and 98% among females). In 1996 there were 210 schools (49 independent). Total school enrolment, Sept. 1996, 61,118. Courses lead to The Bahamas General Certificate of Secondary Education (BGCSE). Independent schools provide education at primary, secondary and high school levels.

The 4 institutions offering higher education are: The Government-sponsored College of The Bahamas, established in 1974; the University of the West Indies (regional), affiliated with The Bahamas since 1960; the Bahamas Hotel Training College, sponsored by the Ministry of Education and the hotel industry; and The Bahamas Technical and Vocational Institute, established to provide basic skills. Several schools of continuing education offer secretarial and academic courses.

BAHAMAS

Health. In 1996 there was a government general hospital (436 beds) and a psychiatric/geriatric care centre (502 beds) in Nassau, and a hospital in Freeport (82 beds). The Family Islands, comprising 20 health districts, had 13 health centres and 107 main clinics in 1996. There were 2 private hospitals (86 beds) in New Providence in 1993.

Welfare. Social Services are provided by the Department of Social Services, a government agency which grants assistance to restore, reinforce and enhance the capacity of the individual to perform life tasks, and to provide for the protection of children in The Bahamas.

The Department's divisions comprise: community support services, child welfare, family services, senior citizens, Family Island and research planning, training and community relations.

CULTURE

Broadcasting. The Broadcasting Corporation of The Bahamas is a government-owned company which operates 5 radio broadcasting stations and a TV service with 1 channel, ZNS TV 13. In 1998, 5 independent radio stations were operating. In 1996 there were 58,000 television and 0·2m. radio receivers. TV colour is by NTSC. There is cable TV on Grand Bahama, New Providence and the majority of the Family Islands.

Cinema. In 1998 there were 4 cinemas.

Press. There were 3 national dailies and 1 weekly in 1998.

Tourism. Tourism is the most important industry, accounting for about 70% of GDP. In 1997 there were 1,617,595 stop-over and 1,743,736 cruise-ship visitors. Tourist expenditure was B$1,416m. in 1997.

Festivals. Junkanoo is the quintessential Bahamian celebration, a parade or 'rush-out', characterized by colourful costumes, goatskin drums, cowbells, horns and a brass section. It is staged in the early hours of 26 Dec. and the early hours of 1 Jan.

Libraries. There were 8 libraries in The Bahamas in 1998.

National Theatre and Opera. The Bahamas had 1 National Theatre in 1998, the Dundas Centre for the Performing Arts.

Museums and Galleries. In 1998 there were 4 museums and 13 art galleries.

DIPLOMATIC REPRESENTATIVES
Of The Bahamas in Great Britain (10 Chesterfield St., London, W1X 8AH)
High Commissioner: Arthur Foulkes.

Of Great Britain in The Bahamas (3rd Floor, Ansbacher House, East St., Nassau)
High Commissioner: Peter M. H. Young, OBE.

Of The Bahamas in the USA (2220 Massachusetts Ave., NW, Washington, D.C., 20008)
Ambassador: Sir Arlington Griffith Butler.

Of the USA in The Bahamas (Mosmar Bldg., Queen St., Nassau)
Ambassador: Arthur Schechter.

Of The Bahamas to the United Nations
Ambassador: Maurice E. Moore, JP.

Of The Bahamas to the European Union
Ambassador: Arthur Foulkes.

FURTHER READING
Albury, P., *The Story of The Bahamas.* London, 1975.—*Paradise Island Story.* London, 1984
Boultbee, P. G., *Bahamas.* [Bibliography] Oxford and Santa Barbara (CA), 1989
Cash, P., et al., *Making of Bahamian History.* London, 1991
Craton, M. and Saunders, G., *Islanders in the Stream: a History of the Bahamian People.* 2 vols. Univ. of Georgia Press, 1998
Hughes, C. A., *Race and Politics in The Bahamas.* Univ. of Queensland Press, 1981
Hunte, G., *The Bahamas.* London, 1975

BAHRAIN

Dawlat al Bahrayn
(State of Bahrain)

Capital: Manama
Population estimate, 2000: 618,000
GNP per capita: (PPP$) 13,970
HDI/world rank: 0·872/43

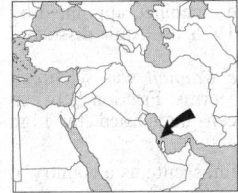

KEY HISTORICAL EVENTS

Bahrain was controlled by the Portuguese from 1521 until 1602. The Khalifa family gained control in 1783 and has ruled since that date, rejecting claims of suzerainty from Persia (Iran) and the Ottoman Empire. British assistance was sought to retain independence and in 1861 Bahrain and Britain signed a treaty of peace and friendship. From 1861 until 1971 Bahrain was in all but name a British protectorate. Treaties signed in 1882 and in 1892 gave Britain responsibility for defence and foreign policy. In 1970 a Council of State was established, so that the ruling family was no longer the sole executive power.

On 15 Aug. 1971 a new treaty of friendship was signed with Britain. This replaced all earlier treaties, and at the same time Bahrain declared its independence. Shaikh Isa bin Salman Al-Khalifa became the Amir with the Council of State as a cabinet. A constitution was ratified in June 1973 providing for a National Assembly of 30 members, together with all members of the cabinet (appointed by the Amir). Elections took place in Dec. 1973. However, the relationship between the National Assembly and the Khalifa family was not successful and in 1975 the National Assembly was dissolved and the emir began ruling by decree. In 1987 the largest island was joined to the Saudi mainland by a causeway. In 1994, demands for the restoration of democracy led to the arrest and expulsion of prominent dissidents.

TERRITORY AND POPULATION

The State of Bahrain forms an archipelago of 36 low-lying islands in the Arabian (Persian) Gulf, between the Qatar peninsula and the mainland of Saudi Arabia. The total area is 706·6 sq. km.

The island of Bahrain (578 sq. km) is connected by a 1·5-mile causeway to the second largest island, Muharraq to the north-east, and by a causeway with the island of Sitra to the east. A causeway links Bahrain with Saudi Arabia. From Sitra, oil pipelines and a causeway carrying a road extend out to sea for 3 miles to a deep-water anchorage.

Population (1996 est.) 598,600 (males, 349,100; females, 249,500), of which 369,200 were Bahraini and 229,400 non-Bahraini. 90·3% of the population lived in urban areas and population density was 850 per sq. km.

The UN gives a projected population for 2000 of 618,000.

There are 12 regions: Central, Eastern, Hamad Town, Hidd Town, Isa Town, Jidhafs, Manama, Muharraq, Northern, Rifa'a, Sitra, Western. Manama, the capital and commercial centre, had a 1991 census population of 136,999. Other towns are Muharraq (74,254), Rifa'a (45,596), Jidhafs (44,769), Sitra (36,755) and Isa Town (34,509).

Arabic is the official language. English is widely used in business.

SOCIAL STATISTICS

Statistics 1995: births, 13,469 (Bahraini, 10,366); deaths, 1,910 (Bahraini, 1,580). Rates (per 1,000) for Bahrainis in 1994: birth, 29·2; death, 3·4; natural increase, 3·9; infant mortality (per 1,000 live births), 20·4. For non-Bahrainis: birth, 15·9; death, 1·5; natural increase, 14·4; infant mortality, 16·3. Life expectancy at birth, 1990–95, was 69·8 years for men and 74·1 years for women. Fertility rate, 1990–95, 3·4 children per woman. In 1996 there were 3,632 marriages and 730 divorces.

The Shia make up 70% of the national population, half of whom are under 15.

253

BAHRAIN

CLIMATE

The climate is pleasantly warm between Dec. and March but from June to Sept. the conditions are very hot and humid. The period June to Nov. is virtually rainless. Bahrain, Jan. 66°F (19°C), July 97°F (36°C). Annual rainfall 5·2" (130 mm).

CONSTITUTION AND GOVERNMENT

The ruling family is the Al-Khalifa who have been in power since 1783.

A Constitution was ratified in June 1973 providing for a National Assembly of 30 members, popularly elected for a 4-year term, together with a cabinet, appointed by the Amir. Elections took place in Dec. 1973, but in Aug. 1975 the Amir dissolved the Assembly and has since ruled through the cabinet alone.

By decree of the Amir on 20 Dec. 1992 a *Consultative Council* was set up. It consists of 30 members nominated by the Amir for 4-year terms. Friction between Bahrain's Shia Moslems and their Sunni rulers has been intensified by high unemployment.

National Anthem. 'Bahrain ona, baladolaman' ('Our Bahrain, secure as a country'); words by M. S. Ayyash, tune anonymous.

CURRENT ADMINISTRATION

The present Amir, HH Shaikh Hamad bin Isa Al-Khalifa, KCMG (b. 1950) succeeded on 6 March 1999.

In March 1999 the cabinet was composed as follows:

Prime Minister: Shaikh Khalifa bin Salman Al-Khalifa (b. 1935). He is currently the longest-serving Prime Minister of any sovereign country.

Defence: Shaikh Khalifa bin Ahmed Al-Khalifa. *Transport and Communications:* Shaikh Ali bin Khalifa bin Sulman Al-Khalifa. *Housing, Municipalities and Environment:* Shaikh Khalid bin Abdulla Al-Khalifa. *Cabinet Affairs and Information:* Mohammed bin Ibrahim Al-Mutawa. *Education:* Abdul-Aziz bin Mohammed Al-Fadhil. *Health:* Dr Faisal Radhi Al-Musawi. *Justice and Islamic Affairs:* Shaikh Abdullah bin Khalid Al-Khalifa. *Labour and Social Affairs:* Abdul-Nabi al-Shoala. *Power and Water:* Abdullah bin Mohammed Jumaa. *Interior:* Shaikh Mohammed bin Khalifa bin Hamad Al-Khalifa. *Foreign Affairs:* Shaikh Mohammed bin Mubarak Al-Khalifa. *Finance and National Economy:* Ibrahim Abdul Karim Mohammed. *Oil and Industry:* Shaikh Isa bin Ali Hamad Al-Khalifa. *Commerce:* Ali Saleh Abdullah Al-Saleh. *Works and Agriculture:* Majid Jawad Al-Jishi. *Amiri Court Affairs:* Ali bin Isa bin Salman al-Khalifa. *Minister of State:* Jawad Salim al-Urayid.

DEFENCE

The Crown Prince is C.-in-C. of the armed forces. An agreement with the USA in Oct. 1991 gave port facilities to the US Navy and provided for mutual manoeuvres.

Military expenditure totalled US$364m. in 1997 (US$608 per capita), representing 6·5% of GDP.

Army. The Army consists of 1 infantry brigade, 1 artillery brigade and 1 air defence battalion. Equipment includes 106 M-60A3 main battle tanks. Personnel, 1998, 8,500. There is a paramilitary police force of 9,000 with 5 helicopters.

Navy. The Naval force based at Mina Sulman consists of 2 West German-built missile corvettes with helicopter facilities, 4 fast missile craft, 6 fast patrol craft and 4 small amphibious transports. Personnel in 1998 numbered 1,000. There is also a Coast Guard of 250 with 20 coastal patrol craft, 4 other vessels and 1 hovercraft.

Air Force. 1 fighter squadron operates 12 F-5E/F Tiger IIs, while a second unit has 12 F-16s. 6 AH-64 Apache; 3 MBB BO 105 helicopters are also in use as well as an S-70 VIP helicopter. Personnel (1998), 1,500.

INTERNATIONAL RELATIONS

Bahrain is a member of the UN, the Arab League, the Gulf Co-operation Council and OAPEC (Organization of Arab Petroleum Exporting Countries).

BAHRAIN

ECONOMY

Performance. GDP in 1996 was BD2,015·8m.; GNP was BD1,691·8m. Real GDP growth was 2·3% in 1995 (2·2% in 1994).

Budget. 1997: revenue, BD600m.; expenditure, BD602m. Bahrain is suffering from low oil prices, as it relies on oil for 50% of government revenue.

Currency. The unit of currency is the *Bahraini dinar* (BHD), divided into 1,000 *fils*. Annualized inflation was 0·9% in 1994. Foreign exchange reserves were US$1,147m. in Feb. 1998 and gold reserves were 150,000 troy oz. In Sept. 1997 total money supply was BD294m.

Banking and Finance. The Bahrain Monetary Agency (*Governor*, Abdullah Hassam Saif) has central banking powers. In 1998 Bahrain hosted 180 different financial institutions including 46 offshore banking units. In 1994, 38 foreign banks had representative offices. Offshore banking units may not engage in local business; their assets totalled US$62,503m. in March 1996.

There is a stock exchange linked with those of Kuwait and Oman.

Weights and Measures. The metric system is in use.

ENERGY AND NATURAL RESOURCES

Electricity. In 1996 installed capacity was 986 MW, and 5,016·07m. kWh were produced. Electricity consumption per capita, in 1996, was 4,226 kWh.

Oil and Gas. In 1931 oil was discovered. Operations were at first conducted by the Bahrain Petroleum Co. (BAPCO) under concession. In 1975 the government assumed a 60% interest in the oilfield and related crude oil facilities of BAPCO. Oil reserves in 1988 were 150m. bbls. Crude oil runs to refinery in 1996 amounted to 14·2m. bbls. Production (1996) was around 39,000 bbls. a day.

There were known natural gas reserves of 7·1m. cu. ft in 1987. Production in 1996 was 10,211·11m. cu. metres. Gas reserves are government-owned.

Water. Water is obtained from artesian wells and desalination plants and there is a piped supply to Manama, Muharraq, Isa Town, Rifa'a and most villages. In 1996 total water production was 24,066m. gallons; daily consumption 65·9m. gallons.

Agriculture. There are about 900 farms and smallholdings (average 2·5 ha) operated by about 2,500 farmers who produce a wide variety of fruits (23,000 tonnes in 1993) including dates (19,000 tonnes). In 1996 an estimated 11,912 tonnes of vegetables were produced. The major crop is alfalfa for animal fodder.

Livestock (1996): Cattle, 17,000; camels, 1,000; sheep, 29,000; goats, 18,000 (1995); chickens, 1m. (1995).

In 1996 an estimated 119·8m. eggs were produced and 22·1m. litres of fresh milk.

Fisheries. In 1990 the government operated a fleet of 2 large and 5 smaller trawlers totalling 1,004 GRT. The total catch in 1996 was estimated at 12,940·2 tonnes.

INDUSTRY

Industry is being developed with foreign participation: Aluminium smelting (and ancillary industries), shipbuilding and repair, petrochemicals, electronics assembly and light industry. Aluminium production was 450,749 tonnes in 1995.

Traditional crafts include boatbuilding, weaving and pottery.

Labour. The workforce (estimate 1996) was 272,100 of which 103,500 were Bahraini. There were 5,100 unemployed persons in 1995.

INTERNATIONAL TRADE

Totally foreign-owned companies have been permitted to register since 1991. Foreign debt was US$3,106m. in 1993.

Imports and Exports. In 1996 imports totalled US$4,093m. and exports US$4,602m. (approximately two-thirds of which was oil). In 1994, the principal exports were (in US$1m.): Petroleum products, 2,225; manufactures, 885. Principal imports: Mineral fuels, 1,248; machinery and transport equipment, 807; manufactures, 587; chemicals, 321.

BAHRAIN

In 1994 the main export markets were: India, 21·5%; Japan, 12·2%; Saudi Arabia, 5·8%; USA, 5·6%; UAE, 4·8%. Main import suppliers: Saudi Arabia, 40%; USA, 13·1%; UK, 6·8%; Japan, 5·2%; Switzerland, 4·6%.

COMMUNICATIONS

Roads. A 25-km causeway links Bahrain with Saudi Arabia. In 1996 there were 3,013 km of roads (2,284 km hard-surfaced), including 411 km of main roads and 441 km of secondary roads. In 1996 there were 174,425 vehicles in use, including 143,878 passenger cars (240 per 1,000 inhabitants). The average distance covered by a passenger car in the year 1996 was 25,720 km (18,280 km in 1992). There were 57 deaths in road accidents in 1996.

Civil Aviation. Bahrain has a 25% share (with Oman, Qatar and UAE) in Gulf Air. Services were also operated in 1998 by Air India, Air Lanka, Air Malta, Alitalia, American Airlines, Balkan, Biman Bangladesh Airlines, British Airways, Cathay Pacific Airways, Cyprus Airways, Czech Airlines, Egyptair, Gulf Air, Indian Airlines, Iran Air, KLM, Kuwait Airways, Northwest Airlines, Pakistan International Airlines, Royal Jordanian, Saudia, Syrian Arab Airlines, Turkish Airlines and Yemenia Yemen Airways. In 1996 Bahrain International Airport handled 2,806,777 passengers (all on international flights) and 115,997 tonnes of freight.

Shipping. In 1995 the merchant fleet totalled 240,000 GRT, including oil tankers, 98,297 GRT. The port of Mina Sulman is a free transit and industrial area; about 800 vessels are handled annually. In 1994, 3,864 passengers arrived and 3,963 departed by sea.

Telecommunications. The government has a 37% stake in Bahrain Telecommunications (BATELCO). In 1996 there were 144,391 telephone lines and 5,678 fax machines. There were 28,000 cellular phone subscribers and 29,000 PCs in use in 1995.

Postal Services. There were 12 post offices in 1995.

SOCIAL INSTITUTIONS

Justice. Criminal law is codified, based on English jurisprudence. The death penalty is authorized. In 1994, 189 cases were dealt with by summary and cassation courts, 820 by sharia courts, 8,051 by civil courts, 3,616 by executive courts, 2,967 by appeal courts and 8,061 by criminal courts (including 5,315 traffic offences). 2,965 crimes (5 murders) were registered and 4,015 sentences passed (excluding traffic offences).

Religion. Islam is the state religion. In 1997, 84% of the population were Moslem (63% Shia and 21% Sunni). There are also Christian, Jewish, Bahai, Hindu and Parsee minorities.

Education. Adult literacy was 85·2% in 1995 (89·1% among males and 79·4% among females). Government schools provide free education from primary to technical college level. Schooling is in 3 stages: Primary (6 years), intermediate (3 years) and secondary (3 years). Secondary education may be general or specialized.
Government school statistics for 1993–94:

	Pupils		Schools		Teachers	
	Boys	Girls	Boys	Girls	Male	Female
Primary	29,533	29,148	50	47	1,203	1,343
Intermediate	13,380	13,143	22	25	944	1,143
Secondary	10,413	10,982	12	11	1,120	799

In 1993–94 there were also in the private sector 86 nurseries; and 33 schools with 4,046 Bahraini and 19,554 non-Bahraini pupils, and 144 Bahraini and 1,435 non-Bahraini teachers. There were 2 universities (1994–95) with 7,019 students in attendance; as well as 3,711 persons attending adult education centres.

Health. There is a free medical service for all residents. In 1994 there were 278 doctors in government service and 96 in private practice, and 49 dentists. In 1996 there were 7 general hospitals (4 government; 3 private), 5 maternity hospitals, 19 health centres, and a total of 669 physicians.

Welfare. In 1976 a pensions, sickness benefits and unemployment, maternity and family allowances scheme was established. Employers contribute 7% of salaries and Bahraini employees 11%. In 1994, 36,612 persons received state benefit payments totalling BD3,715,158. BD5,975,700 was paid out to pensioners, and BD306,600 to recipients of social insurance.

CULTURE

Broadcasting. Radio Bahrain is government-controlled, Bahrain Television part-commercial. In 1995 there were 320,000 radio and 260,000 TV receivers (colour by PAL).

In 1998 there were 6 television channels—2 in English and 4 in Arabic—as well as a satellite channel.

Cinema. There were 10 cinemas in 1998—3 of which screened English films. In 1996 the total attendance was 833,000.

Press. In 1996 there were 2 official daily newspapers.

Tourism. In 1996 there were 1,757,000 foreign tourists, spending US$300m. In 1994 there were 44 hotels with 5,175 beds.

Libraries. In 1996 there were 10 public libraries; a total of 242,573 books were borrowed in that year.

DIPLOMATIC REPRESENTATIVES
Of Bahrain in Great Britain (98 Gloucester Rd., London, SW7 4AU)
Ambassador: Shaikh Abdul Aziz bin Mubarak Al Khalifa.

Of Great Britain in Bahrain (21 Government Ave., Manama 306, P.O. Box 114, Bahrain)
Ambassador: Ian Lewty.

Of Bahrain in the USA (3502 International Dr., NW, Washington D.C., 20008)
Ambassador: Muhammad Abdul Ghaffar.

Of the USA in Bahrain (Building No. 979, Road No. 3119, Block 331, Zinj District, Manama)
Ambassador: Johnny Young.

Of Bahrain to the United Nations
Ambassador: Jassim Mohammed Buallay.

FURTHER READING
Bahrain Monetary Authority. *Quarterly Statistical Bulletin.*
Central Statistics Organization. *Statistical Abstract.* Annual.

Al-Khalifa, A. and Rice, M. (eds.) *Bahrain through the Ages.* London, 1993
Al-Khalifa, H. bin I., *First Light: Modern Bahrain and its Heritage.* London, 1995
Lawson, F. H., *Bahrain: The Modernization of Autocracy.* Boulder, 1989
Rumaihi, M. G., *Bahrain: Social and Political Change since the First World War.* New York and London, 1976
Unwin, P. T. H., *Bahrain.* [Bibliography]. London and Santa Barbara (CA), 1984

National statistical office: Central Statistics Organization, Council of Ministers, Manama.

BANGLADESH

Gana Prajatantri Bangladesh
(People's Republic of
Bangladesh)

Capital: Dhaka
Population estimate, 2000: 128·31m.
GNP per capita: (PPP$) 1,010
HDI/world rank: 0·371/147

KEY HISTORICAL EVENTS
In the first half of the 18th century, the eastern territory of the Bengali people was ruled by the Nawab of Bengal. His defeat by the British East India Company in 1757 and the company's assumption of control of the area marked the beginning of the British Empire in India.

The first formal partition of Bengal was made by the Government of India in 1905. East Bengal, which was predominantly Moslem and also rural and poor, was united with Assam to form a new province. The partition was extremely unpopular with Bengali Hindus who claimed that their Bengali nationality was more important than their religious diversity. In 1912 East and West Bengal were reunited—a move unpopular with the Moslems.

Independent India was partitioned according to religion in 1947. West Bengal became part of India while East Bengal elected to join Pakistan as East Pakistan. The province, however, was separated from West Pakistan physically and ethnically; it was still poor and it continued to be neglected. Differences became unmanageable when East Pakistan's Awami League, campaigning for greater autonomy, won the majority of seats in the federal parliament in Dec. 1970. There was civil war from March to Dec. 1971. With the help of Indian troops, the Pakistani forces were defeated and the East broke away as an independent state to become the Republic of Bangladesh. The Awami League leader, Sheikh Mujibur Rahman was its first president. The constitution of 1972 provided parliamentary democracy, but in Jan. 1975 the president banned political parties and began to rule with an advisory parliament. In Aug. 1975, he was murdered and martial law was introduced. His successor as head of state, Maj.-Gen. Ziaur Rahman, was murdered by a group of army officers in May 1981. In March 1982, there was a further army *coup* after a short period of ineffective civilian government. Lieut.-Gen. Ershad was installed at the head of a military government and assumed the presidency in Dec. 1983. He was re-elected on 15 Oct. 1986. Following popular unrest President Ershad declared a state of emergency on 27 Nov. 1990, but was forced to resign on 4 Dec. and was arrested on 12 Dec. He was later sentenced to 20 years imprisonment.

Democratic parliamentary elections were held in Feb. 1991 and a new President, Abdur Rahman Biswas, was elected on 8 Oct. Continuing unrest reflected the increasing strength of Islamic fundamentalism. Sheikh Hasina Wajed was sworn in as Prime Minister in June 1996 (one of her first acts was the release of former President Ershad) and in July a former Chief Justice, Shahabuddin Ahmed, was elected president.

TERRITORY AND POPULATION
Bangladesh is bounded in the west and north by India, east by India and Myanmar and south by the Bay of Bengal. The area is 57,295 sq. miles (148,393 sq. km). In 1992 India granted a 999-year lease of the Tin Bigha corridor linking Bangladesh with its enclaves of Angarpota and Dahagram. At the 1991 census the population was 111,455,000 (54,141,000 females). Estimate, July 1997: 125,430,000. Population density, 845 per sq. km.

The UN gives a projected population for 2000 of 128·31m.

In 1995 an estimated 81·7% of the population lived in rural areas. The country is administratively divided into 5 divisions, subdivided into 64 *zila*. Area (in sq. km) and population (in 1,000) in 1994 of the 5 divisions:

	Area	Population
Barisal division	13,297	7,757
Chittagong division	46,367	29,015

BANGLADESH

	Area	Population
Dhaka division	31,119	33,940
Khulna division	22,274	13,243
Rajshahi division	34,513	27,500

The populations of the chief cities (1991 Census) were as follows:

Dhaka[1]	3,397,187	Mymensingh	185,517	Nawabganj	121,205
Chittagong[2]	1,363,998	Barisal	163,481	Pabna	104,479
Khulna[3]	545,849	Jessore	160,198	Tangail	104,387
Rajshahi[4]	299,671	Tongi	154,175	Saidpur	102,030
Narayanganj	268,952	Comilla	143,282	Jamalpur	101,242
Rangpur	203,931	Dinajpur	126,189	Naogaon	100,794

[1]Metropolitan area 6,105,160. [2]Metropolitan area 2,040,663. [3]Metropolitan area 877,388. [4]Metropolitan area 517,136.

The official language is Bengali. English is also in use for official, legal and commercial purposes.

SOCIAL STATISTICS
1995 births, 3,168,000; deaths, 1,229,000. In 1995 the birth rate was 26·8 per 1,000 population; death rate, 10·4; marriage rate, 1994, 10·7; infant mortality, 1994, 77 per 1,000 live births. Life expectancy at birth, 1990–95, 55·6 years for both males and females. The annual population growth rate by the late 1990s was almost half the 3·1% of the early 1970s. The fertility rate dropped from 6·2 births per woman in 1980–85 to 3·4 births per woman in 1990–95. No other country saw such a large reduction in its fertility rate over the same period.

CLIMATE
A tropical monsoon climate with heat, extreme humidity and heavy rainfall in the monsoon season, from June to Oct. The short winter season (Nov.–Feb.) is mild and dry. Rainfall varies between 50" (1,250 mm) in the west to 100" (2,500 mm) in the south-east and up to 200" (5,000 mm) in the north-east. Dhaka, Jan. 66°F (19°C), July 84°F (28·9°C). Annual rainfall 81" (2,025 mm). Chittagong, Jan. 66°F (19°C), July 81°F (27·2°C). Annual rainfall 108" (2,831 mm). In mid-1998 the Ganges and other rivers flowing into Bangladesh burst their banks causing a deluge that covered two-thirds of the country. More than 22m. were made homeless and 700 died in the floods.

CONSTITUTION AND GOVERNMENT
Bangladesh is a unitary republic. The Constitution came into force on 16 Dec. 1972 and provides for a parliamentary democracy. The head of state is the *President*, elected by parliament every 5 years, who appoints a *Vice-President*. A referendum of Sept. 1991 was in favour of abandoning the executive presidential system and opted for a parliamentary system. Turn-out was low. There is a *Council of Ministers* to assist and advise the President. The President appoints the government ministers. Presidential elections were held on 23 July 1996; Shahabuddin Ahmed was elected unopposed.

Parliament has one chamber of 300 members directly elected every 5 years by citizens over 18. There are additionally 30 seats reserved for women members elected by Parliament.

National Anthem. 'Amar Sonar Bangla, ami tomay bhalobashi' ('My golden Bengal, I love you'); words and tune by Rabindranath Tagore.

RECENT ELECTIONS
At the elections of 12 June 1996 the electorate was 57m.; turn-out was 70%. The Awami League gained 146 seats, the Bangladesh National Party (BNP) 116, the Jatiya Party 32. A coalition was formed between the Awami League and the Jatiya Party, but in March 1998 the Jatiya Party quit the 'national consensus' government.

CURRENT ADMINISTRATION
President: Justice Shahabuddin Ahmed (b. 1930; Awami League; elected 23 July 1996, sworn in 8 Oct. 1996).

In March 1999 the government included:

Prime Minister and Minister of Establishment, Cabinet Division, Special Affairs, and Defence with responsibility for Armed Forces: Sheikh Hasina Wajed (b. 1947; Awami League; sworn in 23 June 1996).

Agriculture and Food: Matia Chowdhury. *Civil Aviation and Tourism:* Mosharraf Hossain. *Commerce and Industries:* Tofail Ahmed. *Communications:* Anwar Hossain Manju. *Education:* A. S. H. K. Sadeque. *Finance:* S. A. M. S. Kibria. *Foreign Affairs:* Abdus Samad Azad. *Health and Family Welfare:* Salahuddin Yusuf. *Home Affairs, Post and Telecommunications:* Mohammad Nasim. *Law, Justice and Parliamentary Affairs:* Syed Ishtiaq Ahmed. *Labour and Manpower:* M. A. Mannan. *Local Government, Rural Development and Co-operatives:* Zillur Rahman. *Information:* Mohammad Habibur Rahman. *Religious Affairs:* Maj. Gen. (rtd) Abdur Rahman Khan. *Housing and Public Works:* Afsaruddin Ahmed Khan. *Shipping:* A. Abdur Rob. *Water Resources:* Abdur Razzak. *Without portfolio:* Kalparanjan Chakma.

Local Government. The country is divided into 6 divisions, each headed by a Divisional Commissioner, and subdivided into 64 districts administered by Deputy Commissioners and elected District Council. The districts are divided into 490 *thana*, of which 30 are urban.

DEFENCE
The supreme command of defence services is vested in the President. Defence expenditure in 1997 totalled US$593m. (US$5 per capita), representing 1·9% of GDP.

Army. There are 7 infantry divisional headquarters, with 16 infantry brigades, 1 armoured brigade, 5 artillery brigades, 1 Engineer brigade and 4 armoured regiments. Strength (1996) 101,000. There are also an armed police reserve, 5,000 strong, 20,000 security guards (Ansars) and the Bangladesh Rifles (border guard) numbering 30,000. Equipment includes 60 Soviet T-54 and 80 Chinese Type-59 main battle tanks.

Navy. Naval bases are at Chittagong, Kaptai, Khulna and Dhaka. The fleet comprises 1 new Chinese-built missile-armed frigate, 3 old ex-British frigates, 8 Chinese-built fast missile craft, 8 Chinese-built fast torpedo boats, 1 ex-British offshore patrol vessel, 15 other patrol craft, 5 inshore minesweepers, 5 locally-built 70-tonne river gunboats, 1 oiler, 1 repair vessel and 12 auxiliaries. Personnel, 1996, 9,000.

Air Force. There are 11 squadrons, 2 with F-7M interceptors, 2 with A-5 fighter-bombers, 1 with F-6 fighter-bombers, 3 with JetRanger Bell 212 and Mi8/17 helicopters, 2 with AN-32 transports, 1 with BT-6 basic trainers and 1 with Magister jet trainers. The US Government is supplying T-37s to replace the Magisters, while the Czech Republic has delivered L-39 trainers. Personnel strength (1996) 6,500. There were 70 combat aircraft in 1995.

INTERNATIONAL RELATIONS
Bangladesh is a member of the UN, the Commonwealth, the Colombo Plan, D-8, Organization of Islamic Countries, SAARC and the Non-Aligned Movement.

ECONOMY
Policy. The National Economic Council is responsible for policy. The prospective development of large natural gas reserves is expected to push up annual growth to 7·8%. Alongside the 5-year plan are 3-year rolling plans and annual development plans.

Performance. Real GDP growth was 5·4% in 1996 and 5·8% in 1997. Corporate earnings grew by 9% in 1997. Trade liberalization measures were introduced 1994–96.

Budget. The fiscal year ends on 30 June. Budget, 1996–97: revenue, US$3·6m.; expenditure, US$5·3m.

BANGLADESH

Currency. The unit of currency is the *taka* (BDT) of 100 *poisha,* which was floated in 1976. Total money supply was Tk.152,633m. in Dec. 1997. Foreign exchange reserves in Feb. 1998 were US$1,714m. and gold reserves were 100,000 troy oz. Inflation was 5·8% in 1997.

Banking and Finance. Bangladesh Bank is the central bank. There are 3 nationalized commercial banks, 11 private commercial banks, 4 specialized banks and 7 foreign commercial banks. In May 1992 the Bangladesh Bank had Tk.22,402m. deposits, Tk.33,612m. foreign liabilities and Tk.57,619m. assets. The scheduled banks had Tk.244,533m. deposits, Tk.53,442m. assets and Tk.36,289m. borrowings from the Bangladesh Bank. Post office savings deposits were Tk.6,265·7m. in 1994.

There is a stock exchange in Dhaka.

Weights and Measures. The metric system was introduced from July 1982, but some imperial and traditional measures are still in use. 1 *maund* = 37·32 kg = 40 *seers*; 1 *seer* = 0·93 kg.

ENERGY AND NATURAL RESOURCES

Electricity. Installed capacity, June 1994, 2,608 MW; electricity generated, 1994, 10·01bn. kWh. Consumption per capita was an estimated 76 kWh in 1995.

Oil and Gas. There are 17 natural gas fields with recoverable reserves of 10,438,700m. cu. ft. Production, 1993–94, 6,338m. cu. metres; consumption, 5,964m. cu. metres. It is believed that Bangladesh may have world-class gas reserves, although the results of the country's latest exploration round in 1998 are still not known. It is estimated that the reserves may be anything between 4 and 7 times as much as the current proven reserves.

Water. A Ganges water-sharing accord was signed with India in 1997, ending a 25-year dispute which had hindered and dominated relations between the two countries.

Minerals. The principal minerals are lignite, limestone, china clay and glass sand. There are reserves of good-quality coal of 300m. tonnes. Production, 1992–93: Limestone, 23,209m. tonnes (value Tk.13·93m.); china clay, 1,637m. tonnes (Tk.12·48m.).

Agriculture. In 1995 the agricultural population was 74·13m., of whom 37·18m. were economically active. Agriculture contributed 30% of GDP in 1996. There are 8·8m. ha of arable land and 0·6m. ha of pasture. About 3·25m. ha is irrigated.

Bangladesh is a major producer of jute: Production, 1994, 806,000 tonnes.

Rice is the most important food crop; production in 1995 (in 1m. metric tonnes), 16·83. Other crops (1,000 tonnes): Sugar-cane, 7·45; wheat, 1·24; tobacco, 3·7; pulses, 0·53; tea, 4·7; potatoes, 1·95.

Livestock in 1996: Cattle, 24,340,000; goats, 30,330,000 (1995); sheep, 1,155,000; buffalo, 882,000 (1995); chickens, 123,000,000 (1995). Livestock products in 1994 (tonnes): Beef and veal, 145,000; cow milk, 774,000; buffalo milk, 24,000; goats' milk, 1,048,000; eggs, 102,000.

Forestry. In 1995 the area under forests was 10,000 sq. km, or 7·8% of the total land area (8·1% in 1990). Timber production in 1995 was 32·04m. cu. metres.

Fisheries. Bangladesh is a major producer of fish and fish products. There are 500,000 sea- and 800,000 inland-fishermen, with 1,249 mechanized boats, including 52 trawlers, and 3,317 motor boats. The total catches in 1995 amounted to an estimated 1,170,365 tonnes, mainly from inland waters.

INDUSTRY

Manufacturing contributes around 11% of GDP. The principal industries are jute and cotton textiles, tea, paper, newsprint, cement, chemical fertilizers and light engineering. Production, 1994–95 (in 1,000 tonnes unless otherwise stated): Jute goods, 550,000; cotton yarn, 57·59m. kg; cotton cloth, 31·73m. metres; cement, 316; sugar, 270; vegetable oil, 13; fertilizer, 1,981; paper, 83; bicycles (1992–93) 12,965; motor vehicles, 610; television sets, 22,916.

Labour. In 1996 the labour force totalled 60·4m. (58% males). In 1990-91 it was 51·2m. (20·1m. females), of whom 50·2m. (19·7m.) were employed (5·7m. children between 10 and 14 years were also employed). Employment (in 1,000) by industry: Agriculture, forestry and fishing, 33,303; manufacturing, 5,925; trade and catering, 4,285; services, 1,909; transport and communications, 1,611. Average daily industrial wages, 1992–93, by division: Dhaka, skilled Tk.80·61, unskilled Tk.51·68; Rajshani, skilled Tk.61·88, unskilled Tk.47·60; Khulna, skilled Tk.80·61; unskilled Tk.59·10; Chittagong, skilled Tk.61·79, unskilled Tk.49·95. On average, wage rates (US$0·23 an hour, 1997) are among the lowest of developing countries. Labour unrest was widespread in 1996.

INTERNATIONAL TRADE
Foreign companies are permitted wholly to own local subsidiaries. Tax concessions are available to foreign firms in the export zones of Dhaka and Chittagong. Foreign debt was US$17·1m. in 1996.

Imports and Exports. The main exports are jute and jute goods, tea, hides and skins, newsprint, fish and garments, and the main imports are machinery, transport equipment, manufactured goods, minerals, fuels and lubricants. In 1996 exports were valued at US$3,297m., and imports at US$6,621m.

32·1% of exports went to the USA in 1996, 11·4% to the UK, 10·2% to Germany and 6·9% to France. 16·2% of imports in 1996 came from India, 10·3% from China, 8·6% from Japan and 5·9% from Singapore.

Since the early 1980s the garment industry has developed from virtually nothing to earn some 70% of the country's hard currency. Garment exports in 1997 earned US$3·5bn.

COMMUNICATIONS
Roads. There were 8,862 km of main roads and 6,742 km of paved secondary roads in 1994, but some 10,000 km of roads were destroyed in the floods of 1998. In 1995 there were 27,243 buses, 34,936 trucks, 2,235 taxis, 46,561 motorized rickshaws and 39,454 private cars. There were also 411,000 rickshaws and 727,000 bullock carts.

Rail. In 1993 there were 2,706 km of railways, comprising 884 km of 1,676 mm gauge and 1,822 km of metre gauge. Passenger-km travelled in 1995-96 came to 4·04bn. and freight tonne-km to 760m.

Civil Aviation. There are international airports at Dhaka (Zia) and Chittagong, and 8 domestic airports. Biman Bangladesh Airlines is state-owned. In addition to domestic routes, in 1998 it operated international services to Abu Dhabi, Bahrain, Bangkok, Bombay, Brussels, Calcutta, Delhi, Doha, Dubai, Frankfurt, Hong Kong, Jeddah, Karachi, Káthmandu, Kuala Lumpur, Kuwait, London, Manchester, Muscat, New York, Paris, Rangoon (Yangon), Riyadh, Rome, Singapore and Tokyo. Services were also operated in 1998 by Aeroflot, British Airways, Dragonair, Druk-Air, Emirates, GMG Airlines, Gulf Air, Indian Airlines, Iran Air, Kuwait Airways, Lufthansa, Malaysia Airlines, Oman Air, Pakistan International Airlines, Qatar Airways, Saudia, Singapore Airlines and Thai Airways International. In 1996 Dhaka's Zia International Airport handled 2,105,665 passengers (1,625,853 on international flights) and 72,364 tonnes of freight.

Shipping. There are sea ports at Chittagong and Mongla, and inland ports at Dhaka, Chandpur, Barisal, Khulna and 5 other towns. There are 8,000 km of navigable inland waterways. The Bangladesh Shipping Corporation owned 18 ships in 1994. Total tonnage registered, 1995, 0·53m. GRT, including oil tankers, 86,388 GRT. In 1993–94 the 2 sea ports handled 8·20m. tonnes of imports and 1·66m. tonnes of exports. In 1994-95 vessels entering totalled 6,013,000 net registered tons, and vessels totalling 3,094,000 NRT cleared. The Bangladesh Inland Water Transport Corporation had 288 vessels in 1994. 70·29m. passengers were carried in 1992–93.

Telecommunications. Telephone main lines numbered 316,100 in 1996 (2·6 per 1,000 inhabitants). International communications are by the Indian Ocean Intelsat IV satellite. In Sept. 1997 there were approximately 7,500 Internet users. There were 2,500 cellular phone subscribers and 4,000 fax machines in 1995.

Postal Services. There were 8,312 post offices in 1994.

BANGLADESH

SOCIAL INSTITUTIONS

Justice. The Supreme Court comprises an Appellate and a High Court Division, the latter having control over all subordinate courts. Judges are appointed by the President and retire at 65. There are benches at Comilla, Rangpur, Jessore, Barisal, Chittagong and Sylhet, and courts at District level.

Religion. Islam is the state religion. In 1997 the population was 88% Moslem and 11% Hindu.

Education. In 1993–94 there were 95,886 primary schools, with 16·7m. pupils and 312,186 teachers. In 1992–93 there were 11,382 secondary schools, with 4·7m. pupils and 129,655 teachers; 1,031 colleges of further education (797 private), with 912,895 students and 26,263 teachers. In 1993–94 there were 80 professional colleges with 43,503 students and 2,752 teachers.

In 1995–96 there were 5 universities, an Islamic university, an open university and universities of agriculture, engineering and technology, and science and technology; there were 5 teacher training colleges, 5 medical, 3 law and 2 fine arts colleges, an institute of ophthalmology and a rehabilitation institute. In 1994–95 there were 92,654 university students and 2,217 academic staff. Adult literacy was 38·1% in 1995 (49·4% among males and 26·1% among females).

Health. In 1994 there were 639 state and 280 private hospitals with a total of 35,795 beds, equivalent to just 3 beds for every 10,000 persons. There were 24,911 doctors, 9,630 nurses, 7,713 midwives and 75,567 other medical personnel.

CULTURE

Broadcasting. The government-controlled Bangladesh Betam and part-commercial Bangladesh Television transmit a home service and an external service radio programmes and a TV programme (colour by PAL). In 1995 there were 5·6m. radio and 0·7m. TV receivers.

Cinema. In 1994 there were 946 cinemas with 420,000 seats. 130 full-length films were made.

Press. In 1994 there were 179 daily newspapers in Bengali with a circulation of 1·86m. and 13 in English with a circulation of 0·18m. There were 235 other periodicals (18 in English) with a circulation of 1·26m. In 1994, 1,258 book titles were published (122 in English).

Tourism. In 1996 there were 166,000 foreign tourists. Receipts totalled US$32m.

Libraries. Dhaka is home to The United States Information Centre, The British Council, and The Central Public Library (which also has branches outside the capital).

National Theatre and Opera. The principal theatres are the Dhaka Theatre and the Nagorik Theatre.

Museums and Galleries. The main museums are: The National Museum; Muktijuddha Judughar (War of Liberation Museum); and The Bangabandhu Memorial Museum.

DIPLOMATIC REPRESENTATIVES
Of Bangladesh in Great Britain (28 Queen's Gate, London, SW7 5JA)
High Commissioner: A. H. Mahmood Ali.
(There are also Assistant High Commissioners in Birmingham and Manchester)

Of Great Britain in Bangladesh (United Nations Rd., Baridhara, Dhaka 12)
High Commissioner: David C. Walker, CMG., CVO.

Of Bangladesh in the USA (2201 Wisconsin Ave., NW, Washington, D.C., 20007)
Ambassador: K. M. Shehabuddin.

Of the USA in Bangladesh (Madani Ave., Baridhara, Dhaka 1212)
Ambassador: David N. Merrill.

Of Bangladesh to the United Nations
Ambassador: Anwarul Karim Chowdhury.

Of Bangladesh to the European Union
Ambassador: Asm Khairul Anam.

FURTHER READING
Bangladesh Bureau of Statistics. *Statistical Yearbook of Bangladesh.—Statistical Pocket Book of Bangladesh.*

Baxter, C., *Bangladesh: a New Nation in an Old Setting.* Boulder (CO), 1986
Chowdhury, R., *The Genesis of Bangladesh.* London, 1972
Hajnoczy, R., *Fire of Bengal.* Bangladesh Univ. Press, 1993
O'Donnell, C. P., *Bangladesh: Biography of a Muslim Nation.* Boulder (CO), 1986
Ziring, L., *Bangladesh from Mujib to Ershad: an Interpretive Study.* OUP, 1993

National statistical office: Bangladesh Bureau of Statistics, Ministry of Planning, Dhaka

BARBADOS

Capital: Bridgetown
Population estimate, 2000: 269,000
GNP per capita: (PPP$) 10,510
HDI/world rank: 0·909/24

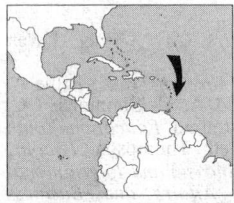

KEY HISTORICAL EVENTS
Barbados was settled by the British during the 1620s. In 1627 a Governor was appointed with a legislative council. In 1639 a House of Assembly was created. Barbados was developed as a sugar plantation economy, initially on the basis of slavery until its abolition in the 1840s. In the 19th century an executive council with ministerial powers was established. In 1951 universal suffrage was introduced, followed in 1954 by a complete ministerial system with cabinet government. Full internal self-government was attained in Oct. 1961. From 1958–62 Barbados was a member of the short-lived Federation of the West Indies. On 30 Nov. 1966 Barbados became an independent sovereign state within the Commonwealth.

TERRITORY AND POPULATION
Barbados lies to the east of the Windward Islands. Area 166 sq. miles (430 sq. km). In 1990 the census population was 260,491; 1997 estimate, 266,100 giving a density of 619 per sq. km.

The projected population for 2000 is 269,000.

In 1995 an estimated 52·7% of the population were urban. Bridgetown is the principal city: Population, 6,720 in 1990.

The official language is English.

SOCIAL STATISTICS
1997 births, 3,800; deaths, 2,300. Birth rate, 1997, 14·3 per 1,000 population; death rate, 8·7; infant mortality, 1997, 13·2 per 1,000 live births. Expectation of life, 1990–95, males 72·9 years and females 77·9. Growth rate, 1997, 0·6%; fertility rate, 1·7 children per woman.

CLIMATE
An equable climate in winter, but the wet season, from June to Nov., is more humid. Rainfall varies from 50" (1,250 mm) on the coast to 75" (1,875 mm) in the higher interior. Bridgetown, Jan. 76°F (24·4°C), July 80°F (26·7°C). Annual rainfall 51" (1,275 mm).

CONSTITUTION AND GOVERNMENT
The Governor-General is the head of state. Parliament consists of a Senate and a House of Assembly. The *Senate* comprises 21 members appointed by the Governor-General, 12 being appointed on the advice of the Prime Minister, 2 on the advice of the Leader of the Opposition and 7 in the Governor-General's discretion. The *House of Assembly* comprises 28 members elected every 5 years. In 1963 the voting age was reduced to 18.

The *Privy Council* is appointed by the Governor-General after consultation with the Prime Minister. It consists of 12 members and the Governor-General as chairman. It advises the Governor-General in the exercise of the royal prerogative of mercy and in the exercise of his disciplinary powers over members of the public and police services.

Following the victory of the Barbados Labour Party in the Jan. 1999 elections, the severing of links with Britain is expected to proceed, with amendments to the constitution allowing for the replacement of the Queen as head of state by a Barbadian president.

National Anthem. 'In plenty and in time of need'; words by Irvine Burgie, tune by V. R. Edwards.

RECENT ELECTIONS
In the general election of 20 Jan. 1999, the Barbados Labour Party (BLP) gained 26 seats (65·4% of the total vote), the Democratic Labour Party (DLP) 2 seats (34·6%). There were 2 independent candidates but neither gained a seat.

CURRENT ADMINISTRATION
Governor-General: Sir Clifford Husbands, GCMG, KA.

In March 1999 the government comprised:

Prime Minister, Minister of Finance and Economic Affairs, Civil Service: Owen S. Arthur (b. 1950; BLP).

Deputy Prime Minister, Minister of Foreign Affairs and Foreign Trade: Billie A. Miller. *Attorney-General, Minister of Home Affairs:* David A. C. Simmons, QC. *Environment, Energy and Natural Resources:* Rawle C. Eastmond. *Education, Youth Affairs and Culture:* Mia A. Mottley. *Health:* H. Elizabeth Thompson. *Labour, Sports and Public Sector Reform:* Rudolph N. Greenidge. *Tourism and International Transport:* George W. Payne. *Commerce, Consumer Affairs and Business Development:* Ronald Toppin. *Industry and International Business:* Reginald R. Farley. *Transport and Public Works:* Sen. Phillip C. Goddard. *Housing and Lands:* Gline Arley Clarke. *Social Transformation:* Hamilton Lashley. *Agriculture and Rural Development:* Anthony Wood. *State, Prime Minister's Office:* Sen. Glyne Murray.

DEFENCE
The Barbados Defence Force has a strength of about 1,000. A small maritime unit numbering 110 (1996) operates 5 lightly armed coastal patrol vessels.

In 1997 defence expenditure totalled US$14m. (US$49 per capita).

INTERNATIONAL RELATIONS
Barbados is a member of UN, OAS, CARICOM, the Commonwealth and is an ACP member state of the ACP-EU relationship.

ECONOMY
Performance. Real GDP growth was 2·7% in 1995 (3·8% in 1994).

Budget. The financial year runs from April. Capital expenditure for 1998–99 was BDS$328·4m., current expenditure for the same period was BDS$1,536·3. The budget for 1995–96 put total revenue at 1,150 (BDS$ m.) and recurrent expenditure at 1,264 (BDS$ m.).

VAT at 15% was introduced in Jan. 1997.

Currency. The unit of currency is the *Barbados dollar* (BDS$) of 100 *cents*. Inflation was 2·4% in 1996. Total money in circulation was BDS$252,443,000 in Oct. 1998. Foreign exchange reserves were US$273m. in Feb. 1998.

Banking and Finance. The central bank and bank of issue is the Central Bank of Barbados, which had total assets of BDS$679·6m. in Oct. 1998. In July 1998 the provisional figures for the total assets of commercial banks were BDS$3,931·2m. and savings banks' deposits, BDS$1,660·3m. Barbados is of growing importance as an offshore banking centre. In 1997 there were 2,632 international business companies, 2,291 foreign sales corporations, 339 exempt insurance companies and 44 offshore banks.

There is a stock exchange which participates in the regional Caribbean exchange.

Weights and Measures. Both Imperial and metric systems are in use.

ENERGY AND NATURAL RESOURCES
Electricity. Production in 1997, 692·4m. kWh. Capacity in 1995 was 153,000 kW. Consumption per capita was an estimated 2,208 kWh in 1995.

Oil and Gas. Crude oil production in 1997 was 327,806 bbls. (453,427 bbls. in 1994) and reserves, 2·3m. bbls. (3·2m. bbls. in 1994). Output of gas (1997) 28·3m. cu. metres, and reserves 200m. cu. metres.

Water. In 1995 water consumption was 10·6m. cu. metres (metered), 29·6m. cu. metres (non-metered). The number of metered consumers was 28,096; non-metered, 62,734.

Agriculture. The agricultural sector accounts for approximately 5% of GDP (24% in 1967). In 1994, 5·1% of the total labour force was employed in agriculture. Of the total area of 42,995 ha, about 16,000 ha are arable land, which is intensively cultivated. In 1994, 7,800 ha were under sugar-cane cultivation and 1,280 ha were planted with vegetables and root crops, of which 34·9% were sweet potatoes, yams and carrots. Cotton was successfully replanted in 1983. Production, 1994 (in tonnes): Sugar-cane, 0·5m.; sweet potatoes, 2,553·2 (1997); yams, 1,319·4 (1997); carrots, 1,047; onions, 480·0 (1997); tomatoes, 565; cucumbers, 367; cabbages, 637·6 (1997); beets, 699; cotton 49·9. Meat and dairy products, 1994 (in tonnes): Pork, 1,688; mutton, 55; beef, 866; veal, 13; poultry, 10,152; milk, 7,297; eggs, 1,322.

Livestock (1996): Cattle, 28,000; sheep, 41,000; pigs, 30,000; chickens (1995), 3m.

Forestry. Timber production in 1995 was 5,000 cu. metres.

Fisheries. In 1994 there were 740 fishing vessels employed during the flying-fish season. Large numbers of these boats are laid up from July to Oct. The catch in 1995 was 3,284 tonnes, exclusively from sea fishing.

INDUSTRY
Industrial establishments in 1994 numbered 442 and ranged from the manufacture of processed food to small specialized products such as garment manufacturing, furniture and household appliances, electrical components, plastic products and electronic parts. In 1994, 51,396 tonnes of sugar were produced.

Labour. In 1994 the workforce was 128,800 (60,800 females), of whom 96,900 were employed (46,500 females). In 1995 there were 26,900 unemployed people, or 19·7% of the total workforce.

Trade Unions. About one-third of employees are unionized. The Barbados Workers' Union was founded in 1938 and has the majority of members. There are also a National Union of Public Workers and 2 teachers' unions.

INTERNATIONAL TRADE
External debt was US$581m. in 1996.

Imports and Exports. In 1996 exports were valued at US$279m. (US$238m. in 1995), and imports at US$829m. (US$766m. in 1995). The main import suppliers in 1996 were the USA (43·5%), Trinidad and Tobago (10·8%), UK (8·4%), Canada (5·1%) and Japan (5·1%). Principal export markets were UK (16·6%), USA (14·1%), Jamaica (9·0%) and Venezuela (8·7%).

The main exports are electrical components, sugar, chemicals, petroleum products, foodstuffs and clothing. Main imports are foodstuffs, cars, chemicals, mineral fuels and lubricants.

COMMUNICATIONS
Roads. There were 1,650 km of roads in 1996 (1,580 paved). In 1994 there were 40,120 private cars, 2,442 hired cars and taxis, 865 buses including minibuses and 10,797 other vehicles including motor cycles.

Civil Aviation. The Grantley Adams International Airport is 16 km from Bridgetown, and was served in 1998 by Aeropostal Alas de Venezuela, Air Canada, Air Caribbean, Air Jamaica, American Airlines, BWIA, British Airways, Cardinal Airlines, Condor Flugdienst, Delta Air Lines, Helenair Corporation, LIAT, Martinair Holland, Region Air Caribbean, Surinam Airways and Virgin Atlantic. In 1996 Grantley Adams International handled 1,394,013 passengers (all on international flights) and 13,401 tonnes of freight.

Shipping. There is a deep-water harbour at Bridgetown. 665,595 tonnes of cargo were handled in 1994. Shipping registered in 1995 totalled 0·11m. GRT, including oil-tankers, 76,219 GRT. The number of merchant vessels entering in 1994 was 1,956, of 17·3m. net tons.

Telecommunications. In 1997 telephone main lines numbered 108,500 (404·3 per 1,000 inhabitants). There were 4,600 cellular phone subscribers, 1,800 fax machines and 15,000 PCs in use in 1995.

Postal Services. There is a general post office in Bridgetown and 16 branches on the island.

SOCIAL INSTITUTIONS

Justice. Justice is administered by the Supreme Court and Justices' Appeal Court, and by magistrates' courts. All have both civil and criminal jurisdiction. There is a Chief Justice, 3 judges of appeal, 5 puisne judges of the Supreme Court and 9 magistrates. The death penalty is authorized. Final appeal lies to the Privy Council in London.

In 1995, the police force numbered 1,200.

Religion. In 1997, 65% of the population were Protestants, 4% Roman Catholics and the remainder other religions.

Education. The adult literacy rate was 97·4% in 1995 (98% among males and 96·8% among females). In 1991-92 there were 26,921 primary, 21,261 secondary and 202 vocational pupils in government schools and 2,573 pre-primary/primary and 3,818 secondary pupils in private schools. There were 22 secondary schools altogether in 1994-95. Education is free in all government-owned and -maintained institutions from primary to university level.

In 1994-95 the University of the West Indies in Barbados (founded 1963) had 2,883 students and the Samuel Jackman Prescod Polytechnic 1,311.

Health. In 1995 there was 1 general hospital, 1 geriatric hospital, 1 psychiatric hospital, 1 leprosy hospital, 5 district hospitals and 8 health centres. In 1992 there were 1,966 hospital beds and 312 doctors.

Welfare. The National Insurance and Social Security Scheme provides contributory sickness, age, maternity, disability and survivors benefits. Sugar workers have their own scheme.

CULTURE

Broadcasting. The Caribbean Broadcasting Corporation is a government-owned commercial TV and radio service. There are 2 other commercial services. In 1995 there were 235,000 radios and 74,000 television sets (colour by NTSC).

Cinema. There were (1997) 2 cinemas and 1 drive-in cinema for 600 cars.

Press. In 1995 there were 2 daily newspapers, 5 weeklies and a monthly.

Tourism. There were 447,000 foreign tourists in 1996, bringing revenue of US$712m. In 1994 tourism contributed 15·51% of GDP.

DIPLOMATIC REPRESENTATIVES
Of Barbados in Great Britain (1 Great Russell St., London, WC1B 3JY)
High Commissioner: Peter Patrick Simmons.

Of Great Britain in Barbados (Lower Collymore Rock, Bridgetown)
High Commissioner: Mr. G. M. Baker .

Of Barbados in the USA (2144 Wyoming Ave., NW, Washington, D.C. 20008)
Ambassador: Courtney Blackman.

Of the USA in Barbados (PO Box 302, Bridgetown)
Ambassador: Jeanette Hyde.

Of Barbados to the United Nations
Ambassador: Carlston B. Boucher.

Of Barbados to the European Union
Ambassador: Michael King.

BARBADOS

FURTHER READING

Beckles, H., *A History of Barbados: from Amerindian Settlement to Nation-State.* Cambridge Univ. Press, 1990

Hoyos, F. A., *Barbados: A History from the Amerindians to Independence.* 2nd ed. London, 1992.—*Tom Adams: a Biography.* London, 1988

Potter, R. B. and Dann, G. M. S., *Barbados* [Bibliography]. Oxford and Santa Barbara (CA), 1987

National statistical office: Barbados Statistical Service, Fairchild Street, Bridgetown.

BELARUS

Respublika Belarus

Capital: Minsk
Population estimate, 2000: 10·28m.
GNP per capita: (PPP$) 4,380
HDI/world rank: 0·783/68

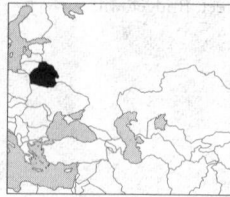

KEY HISTORICAL EVENTS

Though part of the Russian Empire since the late 18th century, national sentiment remained strong. War with Germany and revolution in Russia provided the opportunity for a declaration of independence (25 March 1918) but with the defeat of Germany, Soviet forces reasserted control. The Belorussian Soviet Socialist Republic was set up on 1 Jan. 1919. Under the Treaty of Riga (18 March 1921), Western Belarus became part of Poland. Integration with Russia was close until the Gorbachev reforms of the mid-1980s encouraged demands for greater freedom. On 25 Aug. 1991, Belarus declared its independence and in Dec. it became a founder member of the CIS. The failure to win compensation for the Chernobyl nuclear disaster on the Ukrainian border caused friction with Moscow. The Communists retained power in Belarus despite formidable opposition and it was not until a new constitution was adopted in March 1994 and the following presidential election which brought Alyaksandr Lukashenka to power that the economic reformers began to influence events. Even so, by 1996 only 11% of state enterprises had been privatized and the government remains pro-Russian.

A referendum held over 9–24 Nov. 1996 extended the President's term of office from 3 to 5 years; increased the President's powers to rule by decree; and created a parliamentary upper house.

In June 1998, the ambassadors of France, USA and Japan were withdrawn after President Lukashenka locked them out of their embassies.

TERRITORY AND POPULATION

Belarus is situated along the Western Dvina and Dnieper. It is bounded in the west by Poland, north by Latvia and Lithuania, east by Russia and south by Ukraine. The area is 207,600 sq. km (80,134 sq. miles). The capital is Minsk (1·7m. population in 1994). Other important towns are Homel, Vitebsk, Mahilyou, Bobruisk, Hrodno and Brest. On 2 Nov. 1939 western Belorussia was incorporated with an area of over 108,000 sq. km and a population of 4·8m. The total population in 1995 was estimated at 10·3m; density, 50 per sq. km.

The UN gives a projected population for 2000 of 10·28m.

In 1995 an estimated 71·1% of the population lived in urban areas. Major ethnic groups: 78% Belarussians, 13% Russians, 4% Poles, 3% Ukrainians, 1% Jews, 1% others.

Belarus comprises 6 provinces. Areas and populations, Jan. 1991:

Province	Area sq. km	Population 1991	Capital	Population 1991
Brest	32,300	1,483,700	Brest	277,000
Homel	40,400	1,628,400	Homel	503,300
Hrodno	25,000	1,188,700	Hrodno	284,800
Minsk	40,800	3,256,000	Minsk	1,633,600
Mahilyou	29,000	1,269,400	Mahilyou	363,000
Vitebsk	40,100	1,434,200	Vitebsk	369,200

Belarussian is the national language. Russian is also spoken.

SOCIAL STATISTICS

Annual growth rate, 1990–95, –0·2%. Life expectancy at birth, 1990–95, was 64·4 years for men and 74·8 years for women. 1995 births, 101,444 (rate of 9·8 per 1,000 population); deaths, 133,775 (rate of 13·0 per 1,000 population). Infant mortality, 1990–95, 16 per 1,000 live births; fertility rate, 1·7 children per woman.

CLIMATE
Moderately continental and humid with temperatures averaging 20°F (–6°C) in Jan. and 64°F (18°C) in July. Annual precipitation is 22-28" (550-700mm).

CONSTITUTION AND GOVERNMENT
A new Constitution was adopted on 15 March 1994. It provides for a *President* who must be a citizen of at least 35 years of age, have resided for 10 years in Belarus and whose candidacy must be supported by the signatures of 70 deputies or 100,000 electors.

There is an 11-member *Constitutional Court*. The chief justice and 5 other judges are appointed by the President.

4 referendums held on 14 May 1995 gave the President powers to dissolve parliament; work for closer economic integration with Russia; establish Russian as an official language of equal status with Belorussian; and introduce a new flag.

At the referendum of 9–24 Nov. 1996 turn-out was 84·05%. 79% of votes cast were in favour of the creation of an upper house of parliament nominated by provincial governors and 70% in favour of extending the presidential term of office by 2 years to 5 years. The Supreme Soviet was dissolved and a 110-member lower *House of Representatives* established.

National Anthem. The music is that of the former Soviet anthem. 2 competitions for a new anthem have been held without a result.

RECENT ELECTIONS
The first 2 rounds of parliamentary elections were held on 14 and 28 May 1995, as a result of which 120 deputies were elected. At the third round on 29 Nov. 1995 for 141 constituencies not elected in May, turn-out was 61·8%; 20 candidates were elected. A fourth round was held on 10 Dec. 1995 when enough deputies were elected to form a quorum. Presidential elections were held on 23 June 1994. The electorate was 7·2m.; turn-out was 79%. Alyaksandr Lukashenka gained 45% of votes cast against 5 opponents, and was elected President at a run-off on 11 July 1994 by 80·1% of votes cast against 1 opponent. Turn-out was 69·9%.

CURRENT ADMINISTRATION
President: Alyaksandr Lukashenka (b. 1955; sworn in 20 July 1994).

In March 1999 the government comprised:

Prime Minister: Syarhei Linh (b. 1949).

First Deputy Prime Minister: Vasily Dolgolev. *Deputy Prime Ministers:* Alexander Popov, Valery Kokorev, Leonid Kozik, Gennady Novitskiy, Uladzimir Zamyatalin, Ural Latypov (also *Minister for Foreign Affairs*).

Minister of Defence: Alyaksandr Chumakau. *Interior:* Yuriy Sivakov. *Justice:* Gennady Vorontsov. *Trade:* Petr Kozlov. *Economy:* Uladzimir Shimov. *Finance:* Nikolai Korbut. *Health:* Igor Zelenkevich. *Education:* Vasil Strazher. *Culture:* Alexander Sosnovsky. *Social Security:* Volga Dargel. *Business and Investment:* Alexander Sazonov. *Architecture and Construction:* Viktor Vetrov. *Communications:* Vladimir Goncharenko. *Emergency Situations:* Valery Astapov. *Forestry:* Valentin Zorin. *Housing and Municipal Services:* Boris Batura. *Industry:* Anatoliy Kharlap. *Labour:* Ivan Lyakh. *Natural Resources and Environmental Protection:* Mikhail Rusaga. *Sports and Tourism:* Nikolay Ananyev. *State Property and Privatization:* Vasiliy Novak.

Local Government. Elections were held in 1995.

DEFENCE
Conscription is for 18 months. A treaty with Russia of April 1993 co-ordinates their military activities. All nuclear weapons had been transferred to Russia by Dec. 1996.

Defence expenditure in 1997 totalled US$381m. (US$37 per capita), representing 2·9% of GDP.

Army. In 1996 ground forces numbered 50,500 and were organized in Ministry of Defence troops comprising 2 motor rifle, 1 airborne, 1 artillery and 1 rear defence division, 1 independent airborne brigade, and 2 artillery and 2 multiple rocket launcher regiments; 1 surface-to-surface missile, 1 anti-tank, 1 special forces and 2 surface-to-air missile brigades; and 3 corps (1 with 3 mechanized, 1 surface-to-surface missile and 1 surface-to-air missile brigade, and 1 artillery and 1 multiple rocket launcher regiment; 1 with 1 mechanized, 1 surface-to-surface missile and 1 surface-to-air missile brigade, and 1 artillery and 1 multiple rocket launcher regiment; and 1 non-combatant). Equipment includes 2,348 main battle tanks (381 T-55, 170 T-62 and 1,797 T-72), 419 medium-range launchers, 60 surface-to-surface and 350 surface-to-air missiles.

Air Force. The Air Force operates 3 fighter regiments with MiG-23s, MiG-29s and Su-27s, 2 ground attack regiments equipped with Su-25 aircraft and 1 bomber regiment with Su-24s. Helicopter assets are divided among 4 regiments with 300 machines, and 1 transport regiment has over 40 aircraft. Personnel, 1996, 25,700 with about 200 combat aircraft.

INTERNATIONAL RELATIONS

A treaty of friendship with Russia was signed on 21 Feb. 1995. A further treaty signed by the respective presidents on 2 April 1997 provides for even closer integration.

Belarus is a member of the UN, CIS, IMF, World Bank, European Bank, the Central European Initiative and the NATO Partnership for Peace.

ECONOMY

Policy. Subsidies were removed in Jan. 1992 but under a reform programme of Jan. 1993, 53% of retail prices were state-controlled. An economic programme for 1994 limited credit, linked the National Bank's base rate to inflation and abolished subsidies on dairy products and bread. Some 50% of state enterprises were scheduled for privatization under a scheme initiated in April 1994.

Performance. Real GDP growth was –12·6% in 1995 (–10·0% in 1994).

Budget. The 1996 budget envisaged revenue of 56,950,000m. roubles, and expenditure of 62,940,000m. roubles. Budget income in 1993 (in 1,000m. roubles), 3,624·9, including profits tax, 1,065·4; VAT, 998·3; excise duty, 437·7; income tax, 258·3. Expenditure in 1992 was 314·1, including subsidies to state enterprises, 131·5; welfare, 96·2.

Currency. The rouble was retained under an agreement of Sept. 1993 and a treaty with Russia on monetary union of April 1994. Foreign currencies ceased to be legal tender in Oct. 1994. The average annual inflation rate during the period 1990–96 was 715%. In Feb. 1998 total money supply was 32,318m. roubles, compared to just 17,075m. in Feb. 1997.

Banking and Finance. The central bank is the National Bank (*Chair*, Tamara Vinnikova). In 1996 there were 36 commercial banks (3 specialized), 1 development bank and 1 commercial savings bank. (The State Savings Bank merged with a commercial bank in 1995).

In early 1998 Belarus experienced a major currency collapse, and within the space of a month the value of the rouble dropped from around 45,000 to the dollar to 67,000 to the dollar.

ENERGY AND NATURAL RESOURCES

Electricity. Installed capacity was 7·21m. kW in 1994. Production was 23·7bn. kWh in 1996. Consumption per capita in 1995 was estimated to be 2,553 kWh.

Oil and Gas. In 1993, 2m. tonnes of crude oil (including gas concentrate) and 300m. cu. metres of natural gas were produced.

Minerals. Particular attention has been paid to the development of the peat industry with a view to making Belarus as far as possible self-supporting in fuel. There are over 6,500 peat deposits. There are rich deposits of rock salt and of iron ore.

Agriculture. Belarus is hilly, with a general slope towards the south. It contains large tracts of marshland, particularly to the south-west.

Agriculturally, it may be divided into 3 main sections—Northern: Growing flax, fodder, grasses and breeding cattle for meat and dairy produce; Central: Potato growing and pig breeding; Southern: Good natural pasture land, hemp cultivation and cattle breeding for meat and dairy produce. Agricultural output was valued at 10,500m. roubles (in constant 1983 prices) in 1993. In 1996 agriculture accounted for 16% of GDP, with 19·6% of the workforce employed in agriculture.

Output of main agricultural products (in 1m. tonnes) in 1993: Grain, 7·5; meat and fats, 0·8; milk, 5·6; potatoes, 11·6; vegetables, 1; sugar-beet, 1·6; and 3,505m. eggs. In 1996 there were 5·05m. cattle; 3·89m. pigs; 264,000 sheep and (1995) 45m. chickens.

Since 1991 individuals may own land and pass it to their heirs, but not sell it. In 1994 there were 6·19m. ha of arable land, 140,000 ha of permanent crops and 2·92m. ha of permanent pasture. There were 2,700 farms in 1993. The private and commercial sectors accounted for 38% of the value of agricultural output in 1993 (particularly potatoes and vegetables).

Forestry. Forests occupied 74,000 sq. km, or 35·5% of the land area in 1995 (33·9% in 1990). There are valuable reserves of oak, elm, maple and white beech. Timber production in 1995 was 10·01m. cu. metres.

Fisheries. The total catches in 1995 amounted to approximately 15,000 tonnes, exclusively from inland waters.

INDUSTRY
Industrial production was valued at 16,868,000m. roubles in current prices in 1993, or 90% of the 1992 figure. There are food-processing, chemical, textile, artificial silk, flax-spinning, motor vehicle, leather, machine-tool and agricultural machinery industries. Output in 1993 (in tonnes): Rolled ferrous metals, 0·7m.; mineral fertilizers, 2·5m.; paper, 58,800; cement, 1·9m.; milk products, 1·4m.; artificial fabrics, 293,000; fabrics, 372m. cu. metres; footwear, 33·4m. pairs; 10,000 lathes; 30,800 lorries; 82,400 tractors; 609,000 TV sets; 738,000 refrigerators and freezers.

Most industry is still state-controlled.

Labour. In 1996 the labour force totalled 5,351,000. In 1994, out of 4,696,000 economically active people, 1,245,600 were in manufacturing and 1,099,700 in community, social and personal services. In 1995 there were 131,000 unemployed persons, or 2·7% of the workforce.

Trade Unions. Trade unions are grouped in the Federation of Trade Unions of Belarus.

INTERNATIONAL TRADE
Foreign debt was US$1,071m. in 1996.

Imports and Exports. In 1995 imports were valued at US$4,644m. and exports at US$4,156m. The main import suppliers in 1996 were Russia (50·8%), Ukraine (12·8%), Germany (8·7%) and Poland (2·8%). Principal export markets were Russia (53·2%), Ukraine (8·8%), Poland (5·9%) and Latvia (4·4%).

COMMUNICATIONS
Roads. In 1996 there were 51,000 km of motor roads (50,100 km hard-surfaced). There were estimated to be 1,036,000 passenger cars in use in 1996 (100 per 1,000 inhabitants). In 1993, 1,702m. passengers and 209m. tonnes of freight were carried.

Rail. In 1995 there were 5,523 km of 1,520 mm gauge railways (889 km electrified). In 1995, 125m. passengers and 73·4m. tonnes of freight were carried.

Civil Aviation. The main airport is Minsk International 2. The national carriers are Belavia and Minskavia. In 1998 Belavia flew on domestic routes and operated international services to Adler/Sochi, Beijing, Berlin, Chelyabinsk, Chişinau, Ekaterinburg, Frankfurt, Istanbul, Kyiv, Krasnodar, Larnaca, London, Moscow, Nizhnevartovsk, Prague, Rome, Samara, Shannon, Stockholm, Toshkent, Tbilisi, Tel Aviv, Vienna, Warsaw and Yerevan. Minskavia flew to Chişinau, Kyiv, Moscow and Stockholm. In 1998 scheduled flights were also operated by Armenian Airlines, Austrian Airlines, El Al, Estonian Air, Imair Airline, LOT, Lufthansa, MDA Airlines and Samara Airlines. In 1995 scheduled airline traffic of Belarus-based carriers flew 36·0m. km, carrying 805,000 passengers (42,000 on international flights).

Shipping. In 1993, 0·3m. passengers and 8·9m. tonnes of freight were carried on inland waterways.

Telecommunications. In 1997 there were 3,969,400 telephone main lines (226·6 per 1,000 inhabitants). There were 5,900 cellular phone subscribers and 8,900 fax machines in 1995.

Postal Services. In 1994 there were 3,894 post offices.

SOCIAL INSTITUTIONS

Justice. The death penalty is retained following the constitutional referendum of Nov. 1996.

120,254 crimes were reported in 1994. In 1996 there were 52,200 prisoners; Belarus had one of the highest rates of imprisonment in the world, with 505 prisoners per 100,000 population.

Religion. The Orthodox is the largest church. There is a Roman Catholic archdiocese of Minsk and Mahilyou, and 5 dioceses embracing 455 parishes. In 1997, 31% of the population were Belarussian Orthodox and 18% Roman Catholics.

Education. Adult literacy rate in 1995 was over 99%. There were 349,500 children and 5,558 teachers at 5,558 pre-school institutions in 1995–96, 636,300 pupils and 32,200 teachers at 5,000 primary schools in 1994–95, and 313,800 students and 40,000 teachers at institutions of higher education in 1995–96.

In 1995–96 there were: 4 universities; specialized universities of agriculture, culture, economics, informatics and radio-electronics, linguistics, teacher training and transport; academies of agriculture, arts, music, physical culture and sport, and a polytechnical academy; 4 medical, 3 polytechnical and 3 teacher training institutes, and institutes of agriculture, co-operation, light industry technology, machine-building and veterinary science.

In 1994 total expenditure on education came to 6·1% of GNP and represented 17·3% of total government expenditure.

Health. In 1995 there were 45,000 doctors, 117,000 nurses and midwives, and 880 hospitals. There were 122 beds per 10,000 population.

Welfare. In Jan. 1994 there were 1,987,000 age, and 0·6m. other, pensioners.

CULTURE

Broadcasting. The government-controlled Belarus Radio broadcasts 2 national programmes and various regional programmes, a foreign service (Belorussian, German) and a shared relay with Radio Moscow. Belarus Television broadcasts on 1 channel (colour by SECAM). In 1995 there were 2,350,000 TV receivers and 2,950,000 radio receivers.

Press. There were 10 dailies in 1995, with a combined circulation of 1,800,000, a ratio of 174 per 1,000 inhabitants

Tourism. In 1996 there were 234,000 foreign tourists. Receipts totalled US$48m.

DIPLOMATIC REPRESENTATIVES

Of Belarus in Great Britain (6 Kensington Court, London, W8 5DL)
Ambassador: Uladzimir Shchasny.

Of Great Britain in Belarus (37 Karl Marx St., Minsk 220030)
Ambassador: Miss Jessica M. Pearce.

Of Belarus in the USA (1511 K Street NW, Washington, D.C., 20005)
Chargé d'Affaires: Valery V. Tsepkalo.

Of the USA in Belarus (46-220002 Starovilenskaya, Minsk)
Ambassador: Daniel V. Speckhard.

Of Belarus to the United Nations
Ambassador: Alyaksandr Sychov.

Of Belarus to the European Union
Ambassador: Vladimir Labunov.

FURTHER READING
Marples, D. R., *Belarus: from Soviet Rule to Nuclear Catastrophe*. London, 1996
Zaprudnik, J., *Belarus at the Crossroads in History*. Boulder (CO), 1993

BELGIUM

Royaume de Belgique

Koninkrijk België

(Kingdom of Belgium)

Capital: Brussels
Population estimate, 2000: 10·26m.
GNP per capita: (PPP$) 22,390
HDI/world rank: 0·933/12

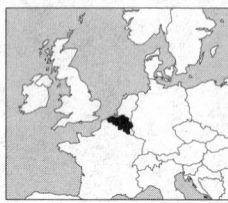

KEY HISTORICAL EVENTS

The Netherlands became part of the duchy of Burgundy in the late 14th century and through dynastic marriage came under the control of the Spanish Hapsburgs in 1504. When the northern provinces rebelled against Spanish rule in the 1570s, the southern provinces pledged their allegiance to Catholicism and the Spanish crown. The War of the Spanish Succession (1701–14) ended with the cession of Belgium to the Austrian Hapsburgs. Briefly annexed to France during the Napoleonic war, Belgium and Holland were reunited by the Treaty of Paris (1815) to form one state. The Belgians rose in revolt against this arrangement, and the kingdom of Belgium was formed as an independent state in 1830. A National Congress elected Prince Leopold of Saxe-Coburg as King of the Belgians, and he ascended the throne as Leopold I on 21 July 1831. By the Treaty of London, 15 Nov. 1831, the neutrality of Belgium was guaranteed by Austria, Russia, Great Britain and Prussia. It was not until after the signing of the Treaty of London, 19 April 1839, which established peace between Leopold I and the King of the Netherlands, that all the states of Europe recognized the kingdom of Belgium.

In 1914 Belgian neutrality was violated by the German invasion. As a consequence, Britain declared war on Germany.

In the Second World War Belgium was again invaded by Germany. On this occasion the king, Leopold III, immediately surrendered, although an exiled Belgian Government operated from Britain during the war. In 1950 Leopold III abdicated in favour of his son, Baudouin.

In the post-war years, linguistic problems have caused persistent quarrelling between the Flemish (Dutch)-speaking north of the country and the French-speaking Walloons of the south. This animosity has been accentuated by increasing industrialization and consequent population movements. Following constitutional reforms voted by Parliament in May 1993, Belgium became a federal state.

Recent events have tarnished central government. Revelations of corruption and incompetence accompanied the arrest of Marc Dutroux, a paedophile murderer in 1996. Then in Sept. 1998, Willy Claes, former NATO secretary general, and others went on trial accused of taking bribes for the allocation of defence contracts. The money was said to have been channelled towards the Socialist party. In Jan. 1999 Claes was found guilty of corruption and given a 3-year suspended prison sentence.

TERRITORY AND POPULATION

Belgium is bounded in the north by the Netherlands, north-west by the North Sea, west and south by France, and east by Germany and Luxembourg. Its area is 30,528 sq. km. The Belgian exclave of Baarle-Hertog in the Netherlands has an area of 7 sq. km, and a population (1996) of 2,702. Population (1998 estimate) 10,192,264m., (5,209,592 females); density, 333 per sq. km. There were 903,120 resident foreign nationals in 1998. In 1995 an estimated 97% of the population lived in urban areas.

The UN gives a projected population for 2000 of 10·26m.

Dutch (Flemish) is spoken by the Flemish section of the population in the north, French by the Walloon south. The linguistic frontier passes south of the capital, Brussels, which is bilingual. Some German is spoken in the east. Each language has official status in its own community. (Bracketed names below signify French or Dutch alternatives.)

BELGIUM

Area, population and chief towns of the 10 provinces on 1 Jan. 1998:

Province	Area (sq. km)	Population	Chief Town
Flemish Region			
Antwerp	2,867	1,637,857	Antwerp (Anvers)
Flemish Brabant	2,106	1,007,882	Leuven (Louvain)
East Flanders	2,982	1,357,576	Ghent (Gand)
West Flanders	3,144	1,125,140	Bruges (Brugge)
Limbourg	2,422	783,927	Hasselt
Walloon Region			
Walloon Brabant	1,091	344,508	Wavre
Hainaut (Henegouwen)	3,786	1,282,783	Mons (Bergen)
Liège (Luik)	3,862	1,016,762	Liège (Luik)
Luxembourg	4,440	243,790	Arlon (Aarlen)
Namur (Namen)	3,666	438,864	Namur (Namen)

Population of the regions on 1 Jan. 1998: Brussels Capital Region, 953,175; Flemish Region, 5,912,382; Walloon Region, 3,326,707 (including the German-speaking Region, 70,119).

The most populous towns, with estimated population on 1 Jan. 1998:

Brussels	953,175	Hasselt	67,772
Antwerp (Anvers)	449,745	Tournai (Doornik)	67,651
Ghent (Gand)	224,545	Ostend	67,595
Charleroi	203,853	Genk	62,524
Liège (Luik)	188,568	Seraing	61,038
Brugge (Bruges)	115,573	Roeselare (Roulers)	53,821
Namur (Namen)	104,986	Verviers	53,303
Mons (Bergen)	91,460	Mouscron (Moeskroen)	52,638
Leuven (Louvain)	87,907	Turnhout	38,412
La Louvière	76,665	Herstal	36,501
Aalst (Alost)	76,291	Lokeren	36,354
Mechelen (Malines)	75,429	Vilvoorde (Vilvorde)	34,130
Kortrijk (Courtrai)	75,408	Lier (Lierre)	31,815
St Niklaas (St Nicolas)	68,034		

SOCIAL STATISTICS
Statistics for calendar years:

	Births	Deaths	Marriages	Divorces	Immigration[1]	Emigration[1]
1995	115,638	105,993	51,402	34,983	514,093	500,714
1996	116,208	105,322	50,552	28,402	511,095	486,247
1997	116,244	104,190	47,759	26,748	511,934	492,405

[1]Including internal.

Annual growth rate, 1990–95, 0·3%. Life expectancy at birth, 1995–97, was 74·3 years for men and 80·9 years for women. 1997 birth rate (per 1,000 population): 11·4; death rate: 10·2. Infant mortality, 1990–95, 8 per 1,000 live births; fertility rate, 1·6 children per woman.

CLIMATE
Cool temperate climate influenced by the sea, giving mild winters and cool summers. Brussels, Jan. 36°F (2·2°C), July 64°F (17·8°C). Annual rainfall 33" (825 mm). Ostend, Jan. 38°F (3·3°C), July 62°F (16·7°C). Annual rainfall 31" (775 mm).

CONSTITUTION AND GOVERNMENT
According to the constitution of 1831, Belgium is a constitutional, representative and hereditary monarchy. The legislative power is vested in the King, the federal parliament and the community and regional councils. The King convokes parliament after an election or the resignation of a government, and has the power to dissolve it in accordance with Article 46 of the Constitution.

The reigning King is **Albert II,** born 6 June 1934, who succeeded his brother, Baudouin, on 9 Aug. 1993. Married on 2 July 1959 to Paola Ruffo di Calabria, daughter of Don Fuleo and Donna Luisa Gazelli de Rossena. *Offspring:* Prince Philippe, Duke of Brabant, b. 15 April 1960; Princess Astrid, b. 5 June 1962; Prince

Laurent, b. 19 Oct. 1963. Princess Astrid married Archduke Lorenz of Austria, 22 Sept. 1984. *Offspring:* Prince Amedeo, b. 21 Feb. 1986; Princess Maria Laura, b. 26 Aug. 1988; Prince Joachim, b. 9 Dec. 1991; Princess Luisa Maria, b. 11 Oct. 1995.

The Dowager Queen. Queen Fabiola de Mora y Aragón, daughter of the Conde de Mora y Aragón and Marqués de Casa Riera; married to King Baudouin on 15 Dec. 1960. *Sister of the King.* Josephine Charlotte, Princess of Belgium, b. 11 Oct. 1927; married to Prince Jean of Luxembourg, 9 April 1953. *Half-brother and half-sisters of the King.* Prince Alexandre, b. 18 July 1942; Princess Marie Christine, b. 6 Feb. 1951; Princess Maria-Esmeralda, b. 30 Sept. 1956. *Aunt of the King.* Princess Marie-José, b. 4 Aug. 1906; married to Prince Umberto (King Umberto II of Italy in 1946) on 8 Jan. 1930.

A constitutional amendment of June 1991 permits women to accede to the throne.

The King receives an annual tax-free sum from the civil list of BEF244m. for the duration of his reign; Prince Philippe receives BEF13·5m.; Queen Fabiola, BEF45m.

Constitutional reforms begun in Dec. 1970 culminated in May 1993 in the transformation of Belgium from a unitary into a 'federal state, composed of communities and regions'. The communities are 3 in number and based on language: Flemish, French and German. The regions also number 3, and are based territorially: Flemish, Walloon and the Capital Brussels.

Since 1995 the federal parliament has consisted of a 150-member *Chamber of Representatives*, directly elected by obligatory universal suffrage from 20 constituencies on a proportional representation system for 4-year terms; and a *Senate* of 71 members (excluding senators by right, i.e. certain members of the Royal Family). 25 senators are elected by a Flemish, and 15 by a French, electoral college; 21 are designated by community councils (10 Flemish, 10 French and 1 German). These senators co-opt a further 10 senators (6 Flemish and 4 French).

The federal parliament's powers relate to constitutional reform, federal finance, foreign affairs, defence, justice, internal security, social security and some areas of public health. The Senate is essentially a revising chamber, though it may initiate certain legislation, and is equally competent with the Chamber of Representatives in matters concerning constitutional reform and the assent to international treaties.

The number of ministers in the federal government is limited to 15. The Council of Ministers, apart from the Prime Minister, must comprise an equal number of Dutch- and French-speakers. Members of parliament, if appointed ministers, are replaced in parliament by the runner-up on the electoral list for the minister's period of office. Community and regional councillors may not be members of the Chamber of Representatives or Senate.

National Anthem. 'La Brabançonne'; words by C. Rogier, tune by F. van Campenhout. The Flemish version is 'O Vaderland, o edel land der Belgen' ('Oh Fatherland, noble land of the Belgians').

RECENT ELECTIONS
Elections to the 150-member Chamber of Representatives were held on 21 May 1995. The electorate was 7,199,440; turn-out was 6,562,149. Flemish Christian Social Party (CVP) won 29 seats with 17·18% of votes cast; Flemish Liberal and Democratic Party (VLD) 21 with 13·15%; Francophone Socialist Party (PS) 21 with 11·87%; Flemish Socialist Party (SP) 20 with 12·56%; Francophone Liberal Reform Party-Democratic Front of Francophones (PRL-FDF) 18 with 10·26%; Francophone Christian Social Party 12 with 7·73%; Vlaams Blok (VB) 11 with 7·83%; Francophone Ecology Party (ECOLO) 6 with 4·01%; Volksunie (VU) 5 with 4·67%; Flemish Ecology Party (AGALEV) 5 with 4·43%; National Front (FN) 2 with 2·28%.

European Parliament. Belgium has 25 representatives. At the June 1994 elections turn-out was 90·7%. The CVP won 4 seats with 17% of votes cast (group in European Parliament: Popular European Party); the Flemish Liberal and Democratic Party, 3 with 11·4% (Liberal, Democratic and Reformist Group); the PS, 3 with 11·4% (European Socialist Party); the SP, 3 with 11% (European Socialist Party); the PRL, 3 with 9% (Liberal, Democratic and Reformist Group); the Vlaams Blok, 2 with 7·8% (Radical European Alliance); the PSC, 2 with 7% (Popular European Party); Agalev, 1 with 6·7% (Greens); the Ecology Party, 1 with 4·8% (Greens);

Volksunie, 1 with 4·4% (Europe of Nations); the National Front, 1 with 2·9% (Radical European Alliance); PSC, 1 with 0·2% (Popular European Party).

Elections to the European Parliament, Chamber of Representatives, the Senate, Walloon Council, Flemish Council, Council of the Brussels Capital Region and the German-speaking Community were due to be held on 13 June 1999.

CURRENT ADMINISTRATION

A 4-party coalition government was formed in June 1995, which in March 1999 comprised:

Prime Minister: Jean-Luc Dehaene (CVP).

4 Deputy Prime Ministers: Elio di Rupo (PS) *(Communications, Economic Affairs and Foreign Trade)*; Luc Van den Bossche (PS) *(Interior)*; Jean-Jacques Viseur (PSC) *(Finance)*; Herman Van Rompuy (CVP) *(Budget)*.

Cabinet Ministers; Science Policy: Yvan Ylieff (PS). *Health and Pensions:* Marcel Colla (SP). *Foreign Affairs:* Eric Derycke (SP). *Employment and Work, with responsibility for Equality of the Sexes:* Miet Smet (CVP). *Social Affairs:* Magda De Galan (PS). *Agriculture and Small Business:* Karel Pinxten (CVP). *Transport:* Michel Daerden (PS). *Justice:* Tony Van Parys (CVP). *Civil Service:* André Flahaut (PS). *Defence:* Jean-Paul Poncelet (PSC).

There are 2 *Secretaries of State* who are not members of the Council of Ministers: Reginald Moreels (CVP) *(Foreign Aid)*; Jan Peeters (SP) *(Security, Social Integration and Environment)*.

Local Government. Communities and Regions elect parliaments ('councils') which in turn form governments. The Flemish Community and the Flemish Region are represented by a single council, whereas the French Community and the Walloon Region have a council each. There are also councils for the Brussels Capital Region and the German-speaking Region.

The areas of competence of Community Councils are culture, education, the media, medicine, protection of young people, the use of languages, some branches of scientific research, and international relations affecting any of these areas.

Regional Councils have responsibility for land use, town planning, the environment, conservation and rural renewal, housing, water resources, overseeing provincial and local authorities, labour, public works, transport, the economy, credit, foreign trade, agriculture, energy, some branches of scientific research, and international relations affecting any of these areas. Regions raise their own revenues and also have a right to draw upon central government funds in some cases. Grants are available from the federal budget when the regional average product is lower than the national level.

Community and Regional Councils and Governments in 1995:

Community/Region	Seat	No. of Council members	No. of Government members	Chief Minister
Flemish Council	Brussels	124[1]	11[3]	Luc van den Brande
French Community	Brussels	94[2]	4	Laurette Onkelinx
Walloon Region	Namur	75	7	Robert Collignon
Brussels Capital Region	Brussels	75	8	Charles Picqué
German-speaking Community	Eupen	25	3	Joseph Maraite

[1]Including 6 representatives of Flemish-speakers in Brussels.

[2]Includes 19 representatives of French-speakers in Brussels.

[3]11 is the maximum number; the actual number in 1998 was 9.

There are 10 provinces and 589 communes, with elected councils under a governor and burgomaster, respectively. The 19 communes of the Brussels Capital Region stand outside the provincial administrative structure. They are administered by a governor appointed by the King. Governors and burgomasters are appointed by the King. Last elections held on 9 Oct. 1994.

DEFENCE

Conscription was abolished in 1995 and the Armed Forces were restructured, with the aim of progressively reducing the size, making more use of civilian personnel. The Interforces Territorial Command is responsible for assignments to assure the safety of the National Territory and for logistic support in those fields which are mutual for the different forces. In 1998 the unit totalled 3,870 personnel, comprising a Staff and three Groups: General Support (including engineers), Infrastructure and Signals.

In 1997 defence expenditure totalled US$3,769m. (US$373 per capita), representing 1·6% of GDP. The budget for 1999 is BEF100·8bn. (US$2,700m.).

Army. The Army consists of 3 divisions. The first, the Intervention Force, comprises 3 mechanized brigades, 1 paracommando brigade, 1 light aviation group (helicopter battalions) and support troops. The second, the Combat Support Division, comprises 5 branch training schools and 10 schools. The third, the Logistical Support Division, comprises 1 supply group, 1 maintenance group and 1 logistical battalion. Total strength (1998–99) 28,250.

Equipment includes 132 Leopard 1A5 main battle tanks, 211 combat reconnaissance tracked vehicles, 123 howitzers, 1,039 armoured personnel carriers and 28 Epervier remotely-piloted vehicles. Aircraft operated: 10 Islander aircraft, 32 Alouette II helicopters and 46 Agusta A109 helicopters.

Navy. The naval forces, based at Ostend and Zeebrugge, include 3 frigates with 1 in reserve, 2 ocean minehunters, 7 coastal tripartite minehunters, 1 research ship and 1 training sailing vessel. Naval personnel (1998–99) totalled 2,600.

The naval air arm comprises 3 Alouette SA-318 general utility helicopters.

Air Force. The Belgian Royal Air Force has a strength of (1998–99) 11,600 personnel and comprises a Tactical Air Force and a Training and Support Command (schools and logistical units). The Tactical Air Force includes 2 tactical wings (each has 36 F-16s), an operational reserve of 18 F-16s, 1 transport wing (equipped with 11 C-130s, 2 Airbus A310 and 11 smaller passenger aircraft), 1 training wing (equipped with 33 Marchetti, 31 Alpha Jet and 11 Fouga Magister) and 5 Sea King helicopters for search and rescue missions.

INTERNATIONAL RELATIONS
Belgium is a member of the UN, EU, Council of Europe, NATO, OECD and WEU. Belgium is a signatory to the Schengen Accord abolishing border controls between Austria, Belgium, Denmark, Finland, France, Germany, Greece, Iceland, Italy, Luxembourg, the Netherlands, Norway, Portugal, Spain and Sweden.

ECONOMY
Performance. The *OECD Economic Survey of 1999* reports: 'The Belgian economy has performed fairly well over the past couple of years, with buoyant growth and low inflation... As business fixed investment has remained buoyant and private consumption and residential investment have strengthened, the driving force of the expansion has progressively shifted from net exports to domestic demand. The revival of private consumption has reflected not only stronger job creation and an acceleration in disposable personal income, but also a fall in the saving ratio, as consumer confidence has rebounded, possibly as a result of remarkable progress in fiscal consolidation and better prospects in the labour market.'

Real GDP growth was 2·8% in 1998, with a forecast of 2·5% for 1999. The OECD projects a moderate slowing to around 2·25% in 1999 and 2000.

Wage-price performance has remained relatively good during this upswing. According to the OECD: 'The end of the 1995–96 real wage freeze was followed by modest acceleration in wage increases and compensation per employee. Contributing factors to this include the introduction of the law on employment and competitiveness, which limits on an *ex ante* basis the maximum increase in compensation per employee in the private sector to the expected weighted average increase in Germany, France and the Netherlands.'

Budget. In 1997 federal revenue (in BEF1,000m.) was 1,444·6 and expenditure 1,619·8; regional and community revenue was 1,037·2, and expenditure 1,039·5.

The budget deficit hit a record low of 1·3% of GDP in 1998, compared with an original target of 1·7% (down from around 7% in the early 1990s). Government debt fell from 121·9% in 1997 to 116·5% in 1998, beating the target of 118%. The projected figure for end 1999 has been revised down from 115 to 113·8%.

VAT is 21% (reduced rate, 6%).

Currency. On 1 Jan. 1999 the euro (EUR) became the legal currency in Belgium and the *Belgian franc* became a subdivision of it; irrevocable conversion rate BEF40·3399 to EUR1. The euro, which consists of 100 cents, will not be in circulation until 1 Jan. 2002. There will be 7 euro notes in different colours and sizes denominated in 500, 200, 100, 50, 20, 10 and 5 euros, and 8 coins denominated in 2 and 1 euros, then 50, 20, 10, 5, 2 and 1 cents. Even though notes and coins will not be introduced until 1 Jan. 2002, the euro can be used in banking, by means of cheques, travellers' cheques, bank transfers, credit cards and electronic purses. Banking will be possible in both euros and Belgian francs until the Belgian franc is withdrawn from circulation—which must be by 1 July 2002. The *Belgian franc* (BEF) consists of 100 *centimes*. On 30 June 1997 the notes in circulation totalled BEF482bn. Total money supply in Dec. 1997 was BEF1,510bn. In Feb. 1998 gold reserves were 15·32m. troy oz. and foreign exchange reserves US$15,124m. Inflation in 1998 was 1·1% (1999 forecast, 1·4%).

In 1990 Belgian authorities decided to peg the franc to the EMS currencies considered to be stability anchors. In the present case this is the German mark.

Banking and Finance. The National Bank of Belgium was established in 1850. The *governor*—in 1998, Alfons Verplaetse—is appointed for a 5-year period. The Bank's independence is guaranteed by the law of 22 March 1993 regarding the status and the supervision of credit institutions. The national Bank of Belgium is in charge of the issue of banknotes, the execution of exchange rate policy and the conduct of monetary policy. Furthermore, it is the Bank of banks and the cashier of the federal state.

The law of 22 March 1993 defines the legal provisions governing banking activity. It transposes into Belgian legislation the European Directive of 15 Dec. 1989 on the co-ordination of laws, regulations and administrative provisions relating to the taking up and pursuit of the business of credit institutions; and the Directive of 6 April 1992 on the supervision of credit institutions on a consolidated basis.

The term 'credit institutions' covers the Belgian credit institutions and those which come under the law of another country, be it a member of the European Union or not, with a registered office in Belgium. The activity of credit institutions must consist of receiving deposits and other repayable funds from the public, and granting credit on their own account.

The law of 4 Dec. 1990 on financial transactions and financial markets defines the legal framework for collective investment institutions, the sole object of which is the collective investment of capital raised from the public. It transposes into Belgian legislation the European Directive of 20 Dec. 1985 on the co-ordination of laws, regulations and administrative provisions, relating to undertakings for collective investment in transferable securities.

The law of 6 April 1995 relating to secondary markets, status and supervision of investment firms, intermediaries and investment consultants, provides the credit institutions with direct access to securities' stock exchanges. Stock exchange legislation was also subject to an important reform. The law fundamentally modifies the competitive environment and strengthens exercise conditions for securities' dealers.

On 30 June 1998, 129 credit institutions with a balance sheet totalling BEF30,065bn. were established in Belgium: 88 governed by Belgian law and 41 by foreign law. 353 collective investment institutions (109 Belgian and 244 foreign) were marketed and supervised by the Banking and Finance Commission; and 55 investment firms were operating, with the approval of the Banking and Finance Commission.

Weights and Measures. The metric system is in force.

ENERGY AND NATURAL RESOURCES

Electricity. The production of electricity amounted to 75,079m. kWh in 1997. 59% of production in 1995 was nuclear-produced. Capacity (1994) was 13·59m. kW; consumption per capita (1995 estimate) was 6,823 kWh.

Oil and Gas. Production of gas in 1997 was 372,095m. cu. metres.

Water. Total capacity for 1997 was 1,065·46m. cu. metres.

Minerals. Output (in tonnes) for 4 calendar years:

	1994	1995	1996	1997
Coke	3,735,744	3,696,076	3,549,789	3,401,431
Cast iron	8,979,387	9,198,831	8,626,651	8,076,475
Wrought steel	11,265,234	11,539,883	10,751,711	10,717,603
Finished steel	10,979,804	11,035,293	10,962,985	12,044,923

Agriculture. There were, in 1997, 1,383,000 ha under cultivation, of which 300,992 ha were under cereals, 31,658 ha vegetables, 126,264 ha industrial plants, 189,872 ha root crops and 621,784 ha pastures and meadows. There were 76,000 farms in 1998. Agriculture accounts for 2·6% of GDP, 11·9% of exports and 12·9% of imports. The agricultural sector employs 2·7% of the workforce.

Chief crops	Area in ha		Produce in tonnes		
	1996	1997	1995	1996	1997
Wheat	196,393	201,995	1,452,824	1,795,709	1,617,004
Barley	50,468	50,319	356,408	382,374	372,544
Oats	5,387	6,162	28,319	28,443	34,939
Rye	1,844	1,685	9,129	8,741	7,671
Potatoes	61,043	55,510	2,153,221	2,643,202	2,643,202
Beet (sugar)	97,990	95,789	6,080,767	6,079,300	6,544,716
Beet (fodder)	9,333	8,871	851,653	892,795	915,044
Tobacco	384	376	1,253	1,356	1,271

In 1997 there were 27,445 horses, 3,157,095 cattle, 154,700 sheep, 12,276 goats and 7,313,223 pigs.

Forestry. In 1996 forest covered 608,151 ha (19·9% of the total land area).

Fisheries. In 1995 the fishing fleet had a total tonnage of 23,031 GRT. Total catch, 1995, 20,519 tonnes.

INDUSTRY
Output (1997) of sugar factories and refineries, 1,034,202 tonnes; 11 distilleries, 11,063 hectolitres of alcohol; breweries, 17,871,920 hectolitres of beer; margarine factories, 341,533 tonnes.

Labour. Retirement age is flexible for men and 60–65 years for women. In 1997 (Labour Force Survey), 1,051,000 persons worked in industry and 2,806,000 in other sectors. There were 425,000 registered unemployed in June 1998. The rate of 'broad unemployment' has fallen from 25% of the broad labour force in 1994 to 23% in 1998.

INTERNATIONAL TRADE
In 1922 the customs frontier between Belgium and Luxembourg was abolished; their foreign trade figures are amalgamated.

Imports and Exports. Trade by selected countries (in BEF1m.):

	Imports from			Exports to		
	1995	1996	1997	1995	1996	1997
Argentina	7,415	10,870	10,790	6,458	8,500	11,960
Australia	10,292	14,070	20,630	17,548	19,390	23,320
Brazil	22,443	23,690	31,920	28,542	22,900	30,110
Canada	30,349	27,250	34,650	14,220	17,230	22,730
Congo (Dem. Rep)	20,384	23,270	22,530	5,609	6,580	4,810
Denmark	29,364	30,100	31,800	45,199	48,100	54,600
France	691,754	771,200	802,000	860,889	948,100	1,026,800
Germany	942,388	998,300	1,047,200	1,022,159	1,081,200	1,164,500
India	32,895	37,270	42,270	75,977	77,970	102,780
Italy	192,536	212,100	221,400	241,124	288,200	333,400
Netherlands	799,812	935,800	1,008,800	632,989	710,000	761,100
Russia	39,654	41,510	51,170	30,673	41,110	56,210
South Africa	22,427	24,210	29,170	15,746	19,300	21,410
Switzerland	65,573	61,170	62,660	88,189	94,990	105,070
UK	398,740	454,200	510,100	388,045	481,600	610,200
USA	252,651	300,880	422,110	184,798	229,490	305,890

BELGIUM

Imports and exports for 6 calendar years (in BEF1m.):

	Imports	Exports		Imports	Exports
1992	4,023,736	3,967,859	1995	4,618,800	5,041,100
1993	4,021,200	4,191,900	1996	4,995,700	5,273,260
1994	4,288,600	4,666,500	1997	5,575,200	6,017,890

COMMUNICATIONS

Roads. Length of roads, 1997: Motorways, 1,679 km; other state roads, 12,509 km; provincial roads, 1,326 km; local roads, about 129,400 km. The number of motor vehicles registered on 1 Aug. 1998 was 5,454,056, including 4,491,734 passenger cars, 14,588 buses, 453,122 trucks, 42,342 non-agricultural tractors, 159,993 agricultural tractors, 241,110 motor cycles and 51,167 special vehicles. In 1997 there were 50,078 road accidents, with 1,257 fatalities.

Rail. The main Belgian lines were a State enterprise from their inception in 1834. In 1926 the *Société Nationale des Chemins de Fer Belges (SNCB)* was formed to take over the railways. The State is sole holder of the ordinary shares of SNCB, which carry the majority vote at General Meetings. The length of railway operated in 1997 was 3,422 km (electrified, 2,507 km). Revenue in 1997 was BEF77,012m.; expenditure, BEF74,248m. In 1997, 59·0m. tonnes of freight and 144m. passengers were carried.

The regional transport undertakings *Société Régionale Wallonne de Transport* and *Vlaamse Vervoermaatschappij* operate electrified light railways around Charleroi (19 km) and from De Panne to Knokke (68 km). There is also a metro and tramway in Brussels (165 km), and tramways in Antwerp (180 km) and Ghent (29 km).

Civil Aviation. There are international airports at Brussels and Antwerp (Deurne). In 1994, 5·73m. passengers departed and 5·61m. arrived. The national airline SABENA (*Société anonyme belge d'exploitation de la navigation aérienne*) was set up in 1923. It was announced in Nov. 1990 that it was to be partially privatized, the state retaining a 25% stake. SABENA operates routes to other parts of Europe, North and South America, North, Central and South Africa and to the Near, Middle and Far East. In 1997 its fleet comprised 33 aircraft. In 1997 SABENA flew 73m. km, carrying 6,872,146 passengers and 341 tonne-km of freight. 61 other airlines operate services. In 1996 Brussels National Airport handled 13,359,813 passengers (13,358,163 on international flights) and 450,710 tonnes of freight.

Shipping. On 1 Jan. 1998 the merchant fleet was composed of 27 vessels of 429,554 tonnes. There were 8 shipping companies in 1997. In 1996, 14,628 vessels entered, and 14,653 cleared, the port of Antwerp. In 1994, 33·8m. tonnes of cargo were loaded and 65·5m. tonnes discharged at Belgian ports.

The length of navigable inland waterways was 1,493·3 km in 1995. 107·8m. tonnes of freight were carried on inland waterways in 1996.

Telecommunications. In 1997 telephone main lines numbered 4,768,900 (468·1 per 1,000 inhabitants). There were 235,000 cellular phone subscribers, 165,000 fax machines and 1,400,000 PCs in use in 1995. There were around 558,000 Internet users in Aug. 1998.

Postal Services. In 1995 there were 1,635 post offices, with a gross revenue totalling BEF50,540m.

SOCIAL INSTITUTIONS

Justice. Judges are appointed for life. There is a court of cassation, 5 courts of appea,l and assize courts for political and criminal cases. There are 27 judicial districts, each with a court of first instance. In each of the 222 cantons is a justice and judge of the peace. There are also various special tribunals. There is trial by jury in assize courts. The death penalty, which had been in abeyance for 45 years, was formally abolished in 1991.

The Gendarmerie ceased to be part of the army in Jan. 1992.

Religion. There is full religious liberty, and part of the income of the ministers of all denominations is paid by the State. In 1997 there were 8·96m. Roman Catholics. Numbers of clergy, 1996: Roman Catholic, 3,899; Protestant, 84; Anglican, 9; Jews,

283

26; Greek Orthodox, 39. There are 8 Roman Catholic dioceses subdivided into 260 deaneries. The Protestant (Evangelical) Church is under a synod. There is also a Central Jewish Consistory, a Central Committee of the Anglican Church and a Free Protestant Church.

Education. Following the constitutional reform of 1988, education is the responsibility of the Flemish and Walloon communities. There were (1996–97) 4,107 pre-primary schools, with 424,521 pupils; 4,401 primary schools, with 737,823 pupils and 82,168 teachers; and 1,727 secondary schools, with 796,945 pupils and 115,262 teachers. In higher education, there were 229,749 students and 38,014 teachers in 17 university and 134 non-university colleges and institutes. There are 5 royal academies of fine arts and 5 royal conservatoires at Brussels, Liège, Ghent, Antwerp and Mons.

Total expenditure on education in 1996 amounted to 3·3% of GNP and represented 7·0% of total government expenditure.

Health. On 1 Jan. 1998 there were 39,240 physicians, 7,360 dentists and 14,597 pharmacists. Hospital beds numbered 75,360 in 1995. Total health spending (around BEF600bn.) accounted for 7·6% of GDP in 1997.

Welfare. Expenditure in 1994 (in BEF1m.): Sickness and injury benefit (wage-earners) 511,259, (self-employed) 38,792; unemployment benefit, 247,623; retirement and survivors' (wage-earners) 437,819, (self-employed) 67,206; family allowances, 163,712.

CULTURE

Brussels is one of nine European Cities of Culture in the year 2000, along with Avignon (France), Bergen (Norway), Bologna (Italy), Helsinki (Finland), Kraków (Poland), Prague (Czech Republic), Reykjavík (Iceland) and Santiago de Compostela (Spain). The title attracts large European Union grants.

Broadcasting. Broadcasting is organized according to the language communities. VRT, RTBF and BRF fulfil the public service of broadcasting in Dutch, French and German respectively.

VRT (*Vlaamse Radio en Televisieomroep*) is organized by decree as a public-sector public-limited company, which has concluded a management contract with the Flemish Government. It has 6 radio and 3 TV services: Radio 1 (news), Radio 2 (regional stations), Radio 3 (cultural), Studio Brussels (youth emphasis), Radio Donna (entertainment) and RVI (world service); TV1 (broadening channel), Canvas (deepening channel) and KetNet (youth programmes).

RTBF has 5 radio and 3 TV services: La Première (news and general), FW (local and regional news and entertainment), Musique 3 (classical music and culture), Bruxelles Capitale (local and regional news and entertainment), Radio 21 (youth emphasis); RTBF International (general, broadcasting in Central Africa), La Une (general), La Deux (culture, sport and documentaries).

BRF transmits a radio programme from 3 stations.

TV colour is by PAL. There are also 4 commercial networks: VTM (Dutch, cable only), VT4 (under British licence; Dutch, cable only), RTL-Tvi (French, 1 station), Canal Plus (pay TV; French, 3 channels; Dutch, 2 channels).

Number of receivers (1997): radios, 8m., including car radios, 2,952,832; TVs, 3·4m.

Cinema. In 1997 there were 438 cinemas, with a seating capacity of 103,617.

Press. In 1995 there were 32 daily newspapers (17 in French, 14 in Dutch and 1 in German) with a combined circulation of 3,200,000, at a rate of 316 per 1,000 inhabitants.

Tourism. *Internal Tourism.* In 1997, 28,522,674 tourist nights were spent in 3,602 establishments in accommodation for 639,272 persons. The number of overnight stays accounted for by leisure, holiday and recreation was 22,100,275, with 1,965,672 for congresses and conferences, and 3,864,189 for other business purposes. The total number of tourists reached 9,981,982 (6,857,004 leisure, 925,652 conference and 1,841,268 other business purposes). Receipts totalled BEF189·4m.

National Tourism. In 1996, 5,216,250 Belgians went on holiday for 4 nights or more. They spent 5,644,896 nights abroad and 1,562,549 in Belgium. The Belgian tourist tends to organize holidays themselves. They prefer to travel by car to France for long holidays and stay in hotels. In 1996 they spent on average BEF19,651 per holiday of 4 nights and more.

DIPLOMATIC REPRESENTATIVES

Of Belgium in Great Britain (103–105 Eaton Sq., London, SW1W 9AB)
Ambassador: Lode Willems.

Of Great Britain in Belgium (Rue d'Arlon 85, 1040 Brussels)
Ambassador: David H. Colvin, CMG.

Of Belgium in the USA (3330 Garfield St., NW, Washington, D.C., 20008)
Ambassador: Alex Reyn.

Of the USA in Belgium (Blvd. du Régent 27, 1000 Brussels)
Ambassador: Alan J. Blinken.

Of Belgium to the United Nations
Ambassador: André Adam.

FURTHER READING

The Institut National de Statistique. *Statistiques du commerce extérieur* (monthly). *Bulletin de Statistique.* Bi-monthly. *Annuaire Statistique de la Belgique* (from 1870).—*Annuaire statistique de poche* (from 1965).
Service Fédéral d'Information. *Guide de l'Administration Fédérale.* Occasional

Deprez, K., and Vos, L., *Nationalism in Belgium – Shifting Identities, 1780-1995,* London 1998
Fitzmaurice, J., *The Politics of Belgium: a Unique Federalism.* Farnborough, 1996
Hermans, T. J. et al. (eds.) *The Flemish Movement: a Documentary History.* London, 1992
Riley, R. C., *Belgium.* [Bibliography] Oxford and Santa Barbara (CA), 1989

National statistical office: Institut National de Statistique, Rue de Louvain 44, 1000 Brussels.
Service Fédérale d'Information: POB 3000, 1040 Brussels 4.

BELIZE

Capital: Belmopan
Population estimate, 2000: 242,000
GNP per capita: (PPP$) 4,170
HDI/world rank: 0·807/63

KEY HISTORICAL EVENTS
A low-lying country on the Central American mainland, Belize was the home of the Mayan civilization, which flourished from about 300 BC to 900 AD. In 1502 Columbus sailed into a bay which he named the Bay of Honduras, although he did not actually visit the area later known as British Honduras. European settlement was established in 1638 by shipwrecked British sailors. These were later joined by British soldiers and sailors disbanded after the capture of Jamaica from Spain in 1655. Spain claimed sovereignty over the entire New World except for certain Portuguese possessions and so there were numerous attacks from nearby Spanish settlements during the next century. Victory was won by the settlers in the Battle of St George's Caye in 1798. In 1862 British Honduras was formally declared a British colony, subordinate to Jamaica.

From an early date the settlers had governed themselves under a system of democracy by public meeting. A constitution was granted in 1765 and, with some modification, continued until 1840 when an executive council was created.

In 1853 the public meeting was replaced by a legislative assembly with the British Superintendent, an office created in 1786 at the settlers' request, as chairman. British settlers began to penetrate the interior as coastal timber became exhausted. The Indians resisted this penetration and the 19th century was punctuated by clashes between the two. When the settlement became a colony in 1862, the Superintendent was replaced by a Lieut.-Governor under the Governor of Jamaica. The frontier with Guatemala was agreed by Convention in 1859 but was declared invalid by Guatemala in 1940.

The Crown Colony system of government was introduced in 1871, and the legislative assembly by its own vote was replaced by a nominated legislative council with an official majority, presided over by the Lieut.-Governor. The administrative connection with Jamaica was severed in 1884 when the title of Lieut.-Governor was changed to that of Governor. Universal suffrage was introduced in 1964 and thereafter the majority of the legislature were elected rather than appointed. The ministerial system was adopted in 1971. In June 1974 British Honduras became Belize. Independence was achieved on 21 Sept. 1981 and a new constitution introduced.

TERRITORY AND POPULATION
Belize is bounded in the north by Mexico, west and south by Guatemala and east by the Caribbean. Fringing the coast there are 3 atolls and some 400 islets (cays) in the world's second longest barrier reef (140 miles) which was declared a world heritage in 1997. Area, 22,963 sq. km.

There are 6 districts as follows, with area, population at the 1991 census and chief city:

District	Area (in sq. km)	Population	Chief City	Population
Corozal	1,860	28,217	Corozal	7,062
Belize	4,307	56,131	Belize City	44,087
Orange Walk	4,636	29,462	Orange Walk	10,966
Cayo	5,196	35,194	San Ignacio	8,962
Stann Creek	2,554	18,061	Dangriga	6,435
Toledo	4,413	17,275	Punta Gorda	3,458

Population (1996 census, est.), 219,296; density, 10 per sq. km.
The UN gives a projected population for 2000 of 242,000.

In 1995 an estimated 53·5% of the population were rural. The proportion of the population considered as rural had been 52·5% in 1990. No other country saw such a considerable percentage swing away from urbanization in the same 5-year period. In 1995 some 45,000 Belizeans were working abroad.

The capital Belmopan had a population of 3,852 in 1993. Other towns (with 1993 population) are: Belize City (47,724), Orange Walk Town (11,922), San Ignacio (9,701), Corozal Town (7,645), Dangriga (6,966).

English is the official language. Spanish is widely spoken. At the 1996 census (est.) the main ethnic groups were Mestizo (Spanish-Maya), 44%; Creole (African descent), 30%; Mayans, 11%; and Garifuna (Caribs), 7%.

SOCIAL STATISTICS
1996 births, 7,200; deaths, 1,250. In 1996 (est.) the birth rate per 1,000 was 32·8 and the death rate 5·7; infant mortality in 1996 (est.) was 33·9 per 1,000 births and there were 1,138 marriages. Life expectancy was 68·5 years in 1996. Fertility rate, 1990–95, 4·2 children per woman.

CLIMATE
A tropical climate with high rainfall and small annual range of temperature. The driest months are Feb. and March. Belize, Jan. 74°F (23·3°C), July 81°F (27·2°C). Annual rainfall 76" (1,890 mm).

CONSTITUTION AND GOVERNMENT
The Constitution, which came into force on 21 Sept. 1981, provided for a National Assembly, with a 5-year term, comprising a 29-member *House of Representatives* elected by universal suffrage, and a *Senate* consisting of 8 members, 5 appointed by the Governor-General on the advice of the Prime Minister, 2 on the advice of the Leader of the Opposition and 1 on the advice of the Belize Advisory Council.

National Anthem. 'O, Land of the Free'; words by S. A. Haynes, tune by S. W. Young.

RECENT ELECTIONS
At the general election of 27 Aug. 1998 the opposition People's United Party (PUP) won 26 seats with 59·4% of the votes cast against just 3 for the ruling United Democratic Party (UDP). Turn-out was 78·1%.

CURRENT ADMINISTRATION
Governor-General: Sir Colville Young, GCMG.

The cabinet in March 1999 comprised as follows:

Prime Minister and Minister of Finance and Foreign Affairs: Said Musa (PUP).
Senior Minister: George Price.
Deputy Prime Minister, Minister of Natural Resources: John Briceno. *Budget Planning and Management:* Ralph Fonseca. *Economic Development:* Manuel Esquivel. *Trade and Industry:* Alfredo Martinez. *Commerce and Public Services:* José Coye. *Works:* Henry Canton. *Health:* Servulo Baeza. *Tourism and the Environment:* Mark Espat. *Agriculture and Fisheries:* Daniel Silva. *Energy, Science, Technology and Transport:* Joseph Cayetano. *Public Utilities and Communications:* Maxwell Samuels. *Education and Sports:* Cordel Hyde. *Housing, Urban Development and Co-operatives, Home Affairs and Labour:* Hubert Elrington. *Rural Development and Culture:* Marcel Mes. *Youth Development, Women's Affairs and Human Resources:* Dolores Balderamos García. *National Co-ordination and Mobilization:* Ruben Campos. *National Security:* Jorge Espat. *Sugar Industry, Local Government and Latin American Affairs:* Florencio Marin.

The *Speaker* is B. Q. Pitts.

Local Government. At elections to 7 municipalities in March 1991 the electorate was 23,215 and 19,527 votes were cast. The PUP gained control of 5 town boards and the UDP of 2.

DEFENCE
The Belize Defence Force consists of 1 infantry battalion, with 5 active and 3 reserve companies. The Air Wing operates 2 Islander patrol aircraft and a T.67 Firefly trainer. There is also a Maritime wing. In 1996 it numbered 50 and operated

1 fast patrol craft and 10 boats and support craft. Total personnel (1996) 1,050, with a reserve militia of 700.

In 1997 defence expenditure totalled US$16m. (US$69 per capita).

INTERNATIONAL RELATIONS

While asserting a longstanding territorial claim on Belize, Guatemala recognized Belize's independence in Sept. 1991. In return Belize reduced its maritime zones to 3 miles in the south, subject to final agreement on a maritime boundary.

Belize is a member of the UN, the Commonwealth, OAS, CARICOM and is an ACP member state of the ACP-EU relationship.

ECONOMY

Policy. The National Social and Economic Council was set up in 1993 to provide a forum for discussion between the public and private sectors. There are national economic plans.

Performance. Real GDP growth was 3·7% in 1995 (6·0% in 1994).

Budget. The 1997 budget (forecast) had revenues of $B283·36m. and expenditure of $B362·26m.

Currency. The unit of currency is the *Belize dollar* (BZD) of 100 *cents*. Since 1976 $B2 has been fixed at US$1. Total money supply was $B170m. in Feb. 1998. The average annual inflation rate over the period 1990–96 was 3·9%. Foreign exchange reserves in Feb. 1998 were US$54m.

Banking and Finance. A Central Bank was established in 1981 (*governor*, Keith Arnold). There were (1993) 4 commercial banks of which 2 were locally owned, and a Government Savings Bank. The Development Finance Corporation provides long-term credit for development of agriculture and industry. Amendments to the Banking Ordinance permit offshore banking.

ENERGY AND NATURAL RESOURCES

Electricity. Installed capacity in 1995 was 34,000 kW. Production was 110m. kWh in 1994 and consumption per capita in 1994 was 524 kWh. Supply, 110 and 220 volts; 60 Hz. A rural electrification unit was set up in 1991.

Agriculture. In 1994 there were 45,000 ha of arable land, 12,000 of permanent crops and 48,000 ha of permanent pasture. Agriculture accounted for 21% of GDP in 1996. The main crops are sugar-cane, citrus fruits and bananas. Maize, rice and kidney beans are grown for domestic consumption. Livestock (1996): Cattle, 60,000; pigs, 22,000; horses, 5,000; chickens (1995), 1m.

Forestry. In 1995, 1,962,000 ha (86·1% of the total land area) were under forests, which include mahogany, cedar, Santa Maria, pine and rosewood and many secondary hardwoods, as well as woods suitable for pulp. Timber production in 1995 was 188,000 cu. metres.

Fisheries. There were (1995) 13 registered fishing co-operatives. The total catches in 1995 amounted to 2,094 tonnes, mainly from sea fishing.

INDUSTRY

Manufacturing is mainly confined to processing agricultural products and timber. There is also a clothing industry. Sugar production was 105,397 tonnes in 1993-94 (100,200 tonnes in 1992-93).

Labour. The labour market alternates between full employment, often accompanied by local shortages in the citrus and sugar-cane harvesting (Jan.–July), and under-employment during the wet season (Aug.–Dec.), aggravated by the seasonal nature of the major industries. In 1996 the labour force totalled 73,000 (78% males), of whom 13% were unemployed.

Trade Unions. There were 14 accredited unions in 1997.

INTERNATIONAL TRADE

External debt was US$288m. in 1996.

BELIZE

Imports and Exports. In 1996 imports amounted to US$256m., exports US$168m. Main exports are sugar and molasses, citrus products, clothes, fish products and bananas. Main imports are machinery and transport equipment, basic manufactures, and food and live animals.

Main export markets in 1995: UK (42·4%), USA (36·6%), Germany (5·2%) and Canada (4·3%). Main import suppliers in 1995 were USA (54·1%), Mexico (11·0%), UK (6·3%), Netherlands (5·8%).

COMMUNICATIONS

Roads. In 1995 there were 416 km of main roads and 1,834 km of other roads. In 1996 there were 9,282 passenger cars in use and 9,846 trucks and vans.

Civil Aviation. There is an international airport (Philip S. W. Goldson) in Belize City. The national carrier is Maya Airways, which in 1998 operated domestic services and international flights to Flores (Guatemala). American Airlines, Aviateca, Caribbean Air, Continental Airlines, Mexicana, Taca International Airlines and Tropic Air also operated services in 1998. In 1996 Philip S. W. Goldson International handled 360,220 passengers (261,965 on international flights) and 1,325 tonnes of freight.

Shipping. The main port is Belize City, with a modern deep-water port able to handle containerized shipping. There are also ports at Commerce Bight and Big Creek. In 1995 the merchant marine totalled 0·43m. GRT, including oil tankers, 0·11m. GRT and container vessels, 17,641 GRT. 9 cargo shipping lines serve Belize, and there are coastal passenger services to the offshore islands and Guatemala.

Telecommunications. Number of telephone main lines (1997), 30,700 (about half in Belize City). Belize Telecommunications Ltd has instituted a countrywide fully automatic telephone dialling facility. There were 1,200 mobile telephones in 1995, 1,000 paging users, 300 voice mail users, 200 Internet customers, 6,000 PCs and 500 fax machines.

Postal Services. In 1995 there were 113 post offices.

SOCIAL INSTITUTIONS

Justice. Each of the 6 judicial districts has summary jurisdiction courts (criminal) and district courts (civil), both of which are presided over by magistrates. There is a Supreme Court, a Court of Appeal and a Family Court. There is a Director of Public Prosecutions, a Chief Justice and 2 Puisne Judges.

In 1995 the police force was 450 strong.

Religion. In 1997, 59% of the population was Roman Catholic and 37% Protestant.

Education. The adult literacy rate in 1991 was 70·3% (70·3% among both males and females). Education is in English. State education is managed jointly by the government and the Roman Catholic and Anglican Churches. It is compulsory for children between 6–14 years and primary education is free. In 1994–95, 277 primary schools had 51,377 pupils with 1,976 teachers; there were 10,272 pupils and 758 teachers at secondary schools; in 1992 there were 8 other post-secondary schools, with, in 1987, 932 students and 69 teachers. There are 2 government-maintained special schools for disabled children. There is a Technical College offering craft and technical courses, a vocational Training Centre providing courses for primary school leavers, a Youth Development Centre and a College of Agriculture. There is a teachers' training college. The University College of Belize opened in 1986. The University of the West Indies maintains an extramural department in Belize City.

Health. In 1995 there were 7 government hospitals (1 in Belmopan, 1 in Belize City and 1 in each of the other 5 districts) and an infirmary for geriatric and chronically ill patients, with 139 doctors and (1993) 300 nurses and 233 midwives. Medical services in rural areas are provided by health care centres and mobile clinics.

CULTURE

Broadcasting. The Broadcasting Corporation of Belize operates a national broadcasting service. Proportion of programmes, 60% in English, the remainder in

Spanish and the Amerindian languages. There is also a commercial radio station. There are 2 commercial TV channels (colour by NTSC). There are satellite links with Bermuda, the USA and the UK, and radio links with Central America. In 1995 there were some 125,000 radio and 38,000 TV sets in use.

Press. There were 4 weekly newspapers and several monthly magazines in 1995.

Tourism. In 1996 there were 143,000 foreign tourists. Receipts totalled US$75m.

DIPLOMATIC REPRESENTATIVES
Of Belize in Great Britain (22 Harcourt House, 19 Cavendish Sq., London, W1M 9AD)
High Commissioner: Vacant.

Of Great Britain in Belize (P.O. Box 91, Belmopan, Belize)
High Commissioner: Mr T. J. David.

Of Belize in the USA (3400 International Dr., NW, Washington, D.C., 20008)
Ambassador: James S. Murphy.

Of the USA in Belize (Gabourel Lane, Belize City)
Ambassador: Carolyn Curiel.

Of Belize to the United Nations
Ambassador: Vacant.

FURTHER READING
Dobson, D., *A History of Belize.* Belize, 1973
Fernandez, J., *Belize: Case Study for Democracy in Central America.* Aldershot, 1989
Grant, C. H., *The Making of Modern Belize.* CUP, 1976
Wright, P. and Coutts, B. E., *Belize.* [Bibliography] 2nd ed. Oxford and Santa Barbara (CA), 1993

National statistical office: Central Statistical Office, Belmopan.

BENIN

République du Bénin

Capital: Porto-Novo
Population estimate, 2000: 6·22m.
GNP per capita: (PPP$) 1,230
HDI/world rank: 0·378/145

KEY HISTORICAL EVENTS

The People's Republic of Benin is the former Republic of Dahomey. Dahomey was called after the historic kingdom of Dahomey or Abomey, conquered by the French in 1892–94. The new name given to the country on 30 Nov. 1975 came from the Bight of Benin and the former 'French Bight of Benin Settlements', themselves called after the ancient kingdom of Benin in modern Nigeria. The kingdom of Dahomey was a powerful, well-organized state from the 17th century, trading extensively in slaves through the port of Whydah with the Portuguese, British and French. On the coast an educated African elite grew up in the 19th century.

After the defeat of Dahomey, whose monarchy was abolished, the French occupied territory inland up to the River Niger, and created the colony of Dahomey as part of French West Africa. Subsequently, there were several African revolts, a number occurring during the First World War. The African elite protested frequently at French rule and, as African nationalism blossomed after the Second World War, Dahomey saw lively political activity and the formation of several parties.

Dahomey became independent on 1 Aug. 1960 with a coalition of 3 parties in power and Hubert Maga as president. Opposition to his rule led to a military coup by Gen. Christophe Soglo in Oct. 1963. Soglo handed over power to another political leader, Sourou-Migan Apithy, but returned to power in late 1965. Two years later he was deposed and replaced by another military regime, led by Col. Alphonse Alley. Alley handed over in 1968 to a civilian president, Emile Derlin-Zinsou. In Dec. 1969 a 3-man military junta took control; elections were held in early 1970, after which a Presidential Council was installed in power, consisting of Maga, Apithy and Justin Ahomadegbe. Maga chaired the Council until May 1972 when he handed over to Ahomadegbe.

In Oct. 1972 Gen. Mathieu Kérékou seized power and installed a new left-wing regime committed to socialist policies. A constitution was adopted in 1977, based on a single Marxist-Leninist party, the *Parti de la Révolution Populaire du Bénin* (PRPB). Despite persistent economic problems, factional fighting within its ranks and frequent plots and attempts at its overthrow, the regime has retained power.

TERRITORY AND POPULATION

Benin is bounded in the east by Nigeria, north by Niger and Burkina Faso, west by Togo and south by the Gulf of Guinea. The area is 112,622 sq. km, and the population, census 1992, 4,855,349. Estimate (1996) 5·71m.; density, 50·7 per sq. km.

The UN gives a projected population for 2000 of 6·22m.

In 1995 an estimated 61·6% of the population were rural.

The areas, populations and capitals of the 6 provinces are as follows:

Province	Sq. km	Census 1992	Capital	Census 1992
Atakora	31,200	648,330	Natitingou	57,535
Borgou	51,000	816,278	Parakou	106,708
Zou	18,700	813,985	Abomey	65,725
Mono	3,800	646,954	Lokossa	52,909
Atlantique	3,200	1,060,310	Cotonou	533,212
Ouéme	4,700	869,492	Porto-Novo	177,660

Other large towns (with 1992 census population): Djougou (132,192), Bohicon (81,121), Kandi (74,169), Ouidah (64,068).

In 1992 the main ethnic groups numbered (in 1,000): Fon, 1,930; Yoruba, 590; Adja, 540; Bariba, 420; Aizo, 420; Somba, 320; Fulani, 270. The official language is French. Over half the people speak Fon.

SOCIAL STATISTICS

1996 (estimates) births , 267,000; deaths, 77,000. Rates, 1996 estimates (per 1,000 population): Births, 46·8; deaths, 13·5. Infant mortality (per 1,000 live births), 105·1. Expectation of life in 1996 was 52·7 years (50·7 for males and 54·7 for females). Annual growth rate (1997 est.), 3·3%. Fertility rate, 1990-95, 6·3 children per woman.

CLIMATE

In coastal parts there is an equatorial climate, with a long rainy season from March to July and a short rainy season in Oct. and Nov. The dry season increases in length from the coast, with inland areas having rain only between May and Sept. Porto-Novo, Jan. 82°F (27·8°C), July 78°F (25·6°C). Annual rainfall 52" (1,300 mm). Cotonou, Jan. 81°F (27·2°C), July 77°F (25°C). Annual rainfall 53" (1,325 mm).

CONSTITUTION AND GOVERNMENT

The Benin Party of Popular Revolution (PRPB) held a monopoly of power from 1977 to 1989.

In Feb. 1990 a 'National Conference of the Vital Elements (*'Vives forces'*) of the Nation' proclaimed its sovereignty and appointed Nicéphore Soglo Prime Minister of a provisional government. At a referendum in Dec. 1990, 93·2% of votes cast were in favour of the new constitution, which has introduced a presidential regime. The *President* is directly elected for renewable 5-year terms. Parliament is the 83-member *National Assembly*, elected by proportional representation for 4-year terms.

A 30-member advisory *Social and Economic Council* was set up in 1994. There is a *Constitutional Court*

National Anthem. 'L'Aube Nouvelle' ('New Dawn'); words and tune by Gilbert Dagnon.

RECENT ELECTIONS

Presidential elections were held in 2 rounds on 3 and 18 March 1996. The electorate was 2,524,262; turn-out was 77·6%. There were 7 candidates for the first round, won by President Nicéphore Soglo with 35·69% of votes cast. At the run-off on 18 March Mathieu Kérékou was elected with 52·49% of votes cast.

Parliamentary elections were held on 28 March and 28 May 1995. Some 2,600 candidates, representing 50 parties, stood. The electorate was 2,531,122. Benin Renaissance (BR) gained 21 seats; the Democratic Renewal Party, 18; Action Front for Renewal and Development, 14; the Social Democratic Party, 8; Our Common Cause, 4; Rally of Liberal Democrats, 4; Alliance for Democracy and Progress, 3; Impulse to Progress and Democracy, 2; others, 1 each.

CURRENT ADMINISTRATION

President: Mathieu Kérékou (b. 1934; elected 18 March 1996; sworn in 4 April 1996).

In March 1999 the government comprised:

Minister Delegate to the President responsible for National Defence and Relations with Institutions: Pierre Osho.

Minister of Justice, Legislation, Human Rights and Guardian of the Seals: Joseph Gnonlonfoun. *Foreign Affairs and Co-operation:* Antoine Kolawole Idji. *Culture and Communication:* Severin Adjovi. *National Education and Scientific Research:* Damien Zinsou Alahassa. *Mines, Energy and Hydraulics:* Felix Dansou. *Environment, Housing and Urbanism:* Sylvain Adekpedjou Akindes. *Finance:* Abdoulaye Bio Tchane. *Public Health:* Marina d'Almeida-Massougbodji. *Social Welfare and Women's Condition:* Ramatou Baba-Moussa. *Industry, Small and Medium Enterprises:* Pierre John Igue. *Interior, Security and Territorial Administration:* Daniel Tawema. *Planning, Economic Restructuring and Promotion of Employment:* Albert Tevoedjre. *Public Works and Transport:* Joseph Souru Attin. *Rural Development:* Saka Saley. *Youth, Sports and Leisure:* Christian Enock Lagniede. *Civil Service, Labour and Administrative Reform:* Ousmane Batoko. *Commerce, Handicrafts and Tourism:* Marie-Elise Gbedo.

The *Speaker* of the National Assembly is Bruno Amoussou (Social Democratic Party).

BENIN

Local Government. The 6 provinces are divided into 84 districts. In Nov. 1990 elections were held for mayors and district chiefs.

DEFENCE
There is selective conscription for 18 months. Defence expenditure totalled US$27m. in 1997 (US$5 per capita).

Army. The Army consists of 3 infantry, 1 para-commando and 1 engineer battalions, 1 armoured squadron and 1 artillery battery. Equipment includes 20 PT-76 light tanks. Strength (1996) 4,500, with an additional 2,500-strong paramilitary gendarmerie.

Navy. The flotilla comprises 1 French-built inshore craft and 4 Soviet-built inshore patrol craft reported in reserve. There is 1 tug. Personnel in 1996 numbered 150, and the force is based at Cotonou.

Air Force. The Air Force has suffered a shortage of funds and in 1995 operated only 1 Twin Otter and 2 Ecureuil helicopters. Personnel, 1996, 100.

INTERNATIONAL RELATIONS
Benin is a member of the UN, OAU and is an ACP state of the EU.

ECONOMY
Policy. The Second Structural Adjustment Programme began in 1991; it seeks to provide resources for priority social and economic goals by economies, reforms and rationalization. An action plan envisages some privatization. Price controls were imposed in 1994.

Performance. Real GDP growth was 5·7% in 1995 (3·4% in 1994).

Budget. The fiscal year is the calendar year. In 1994 revenue was 127,100m. francs CFA and expenditure 161,800m. francs CFA, of which 108,400m. francs CFA were current expenditure. The 1995 budget balanced at 204,000m. francs CFA.

Currency. The monetary unit is the *franc CFA* (XOF), with a parity value of 100 francs CFA to 1 French franc. Total money supply was 193bn. francs CFA in Dec. 1997. Foreign exchange reserves were US$250m. in Dec. 1997. Gold reserves in 1993 were US$2·8m. Annualized inflation was 25% in 1995 (54% in 1994).

Banking and Finance. The bank of issue and the central bank is the regional West African Central Bank (BCEAO). There are 5 private commercial banks. Total deposits were 182,000m. francs CFA in May 1995.

ENERGY AND NATURAL RESOURCES
Electricity. Installed capacity in 1992 was 28,000 kW. In 1994 production was 10m. kWh with 238m. kWh imported. A solar energy programme was initiated in 1993. Consumption per capita in 1994 was estimated to be 45 kWh.

Oil and Gas. The Semé oilfield, located 10 miles offshore, was discovered in 1968. Production commenced in 1982 and was 195,000 tonnes in 1992.

Agriculture. Benin's economy is underdeveloped, and is dependent on subsistence agriculture. In 1992, 2·93m. persons depended on agriculture, of whom 1·35m. were economically active. In 1996 agriculture accounted for 38% of GDP. Small independent farms produce about 90% of output. In 1994, 1·43m. ha were arable, 0·45m. ha permanent crops and 0·44m. ha permanent pasture. The chief food products, 1994–95 (in 1,000 tonnes) were: Cassava, 1,145·8; yams, 1,250·5; maize, 491·5; sorghum and millet, 137·6; beans, 64; rice, 13·7; cash crops were: Groundnuts, 77·6; cotton, 251·2; sugar-cane, 34·6.

Livestock 1996: Cattle, 1,350,000; sheep, 601,000; goats (1995), 1,180,000; pigs, 584,000; poultry (1995), 20m.

Forestry. In 1995 there were 4·62m. ha of forest (41·8% of the total land area), mainly in the north. In 1990 the area under forests had been 4·92m. ha. Timber production in 1995 was 5·9m. cu. metres.

Fisheries. In 1991 there were 8 fishing boats totalling 1,078 GRT. Total catch, 1995, approximately 37,000 tonnes, of which fresh fish, 30,000 tonnes and marine fish, 7,000 tonnes.

INDUSTRY
Only about 2% of the workforce is employed in industry. The main activities include palm-oil processing, brewing and the manufacture of cement, sugar and textiles. Also important are cigarettes, food, construction materials and petroleum. Firms by product in 1994: Printing, paper, publishing, 33; chemicals, 22; wood, 16; foodstuffs, 11.

Labour. The labour force numbered 2,490,000 in 1996 (52% males). Approximately half of the economically active population is engaged in agriculture, fishing and forestry.

Trade Unions. In 1973 all trade unions were amalgamated to form a single body, the *Union Nationale des Syndicats des Travailleurs du Bénin*. In 1990 some unions declared their independence from this Union, which itself broke its links with the PRPB. In 1992 there were 3 trade union federations.

INTERNATIONAL TRADE
Commercial and transport activities, which make up 36% of GDP, are extremely vulnerable to developments in neighbouring Nigeria, with which there is a significant amount of illegal trade. Foreign debt was US$1,594m. in 1996.

Imports and Exports. Imports in 1996, US$635m.; exports, US$424m. The main exports in 1994 were cotton (US$132m.) and crude oil (US$12m.). Other exports include cocoa, palm oil, palm kernel cake and oil, and cotton cake.

Principal export markets, 1994: Morocco, 37·6%; Portugal, 13·8%; Libya, 7·9%; Italy, 5·8%; USA, 5·3%. Principal import suppliers: France, 24·3%; Thailand, 11·9%; Netherlands, 7%; China, 6·4%; Hong Kong, 6%; USA, 5·6%.

Main imports include foodstuffs, beverages, tobacco, petroleum products, intermediate goods, capital goods and light consumer goods.

COMMUNICATIONS

Roads. There were 6,787 km of roads in 1996, of which 20% were surfaced. Passenger cars in use in 1996 totalled 37,772, and there were also 7,554 buses and coaches plus approximately 250,000 motor cycles and mopeds.

Rail. There are 578 km of metre-gauge railway. In 1994, 0·6m. passengers and 250m. tonne-km of freight were carried.

Civil Aviation. The international airport is at Cotonou (Cadjehoun), which in 1996 handled 193,000 passengers (all on international flights) and 4,300 tonnes of freight. Benin is a member of Air Afrique. In 1998 services were are also provided by Aeroflot, Air Burkina, Air France, Air Gabon, Cameroon Airlines, Ghana Airways, Nigeria Airways and SABENA.

Shipping. There is a port at Cotonou. In 1995 the merchant fleet totalled 1,000 GRT. In 1994 vessels entering totalled 1,163,000 NRT.

Telecommunications. There were, in 1997, about 36,500 main telephone lines (6·4 per 1,000 persons). There were approximately 1,750 Internet users in Jan. 1998, and in 1995, 1,100 cellular phone subscribers and 800 fax machines.

Postal Services. In 1995 there were 159 post offices.

SOCIAL INSTITUTIONS

Justice. The Supreme Court is at Cotonou. There are Magistrates Courts and a *tribunal de conciliation* in each district. The legal system is based on French civil law and customary law.

Religion. Some 62% of the population follow traditional animist beliefs. In 1997 there were 1·24m. Roman Catholics and 710,000 Moslems.

Education. Adult literacy rate was 37% in 1995 (48·7% among males and 25·8% among females). There were, in 1995–96, 722,161 pupils in 3,088 primary schools

BENIN

with 13,889 teachers and, in 1991–92, 76,672 pupils in secondary and high schools with 2,178 teachers. The University of Benin (Cotonou) had 9,000 students and 240 academic staff in 1994–95.

Health. In 1993 there were 363 doctors and 1,236 nurses. Hospital bed provision was just 2 for every 10,000 persons in 1993.

CULTURE

Broadcasting. The media are overseen by the 9-member Haute Autorité de l'Audiovisuel et de la Communication. The government-controlled Office de Radiodiffusion et Télévision du Bénin broadcasts a radio programme from Cotonou and a regional programme from Parakou, and a TV service (colour by SECAM) from Cotonou. In 1995 there were 500,000 radio and some 32,000 TV sets.

Press. In 1995 there was 1 daily newspaper with a circulation of 3,000, at a rate of 1 per 1,000 inhabitants.

Tourism. In 1996 there were 147,000 foreign tourists. Receipts totalled US$29m.

DIPLOMATIC REPRESENTATIVES
Of Benin in Great Britain
Ambassador: Vacant (resides in Paris).

Of Great Britain in Benin
Ambassador: G. S. Burton, CMG (resides in Nigeria).

Of Benin in the USA (2737 Cathedral Ave., NW, Washington, D.C., 20008)
Ambassador: Lucien Tonoukouin.

Of the USA in Benin (Rue Caporal Bernard Anani, Cotonou)
Ambassador: John M. Yates.

Of Benin to the United Nations
Ambassador: Fassassi A. Yacoubou.

Of Benin to the European Union
Ambassador: Saliou Aboudou.

FURTHER READING
Eades, J. S. and Allen, C., *Benin* [Bibliography]. Oxford and Santa Barbara (CA), 1997

BHUTAN

Druk-yul

(Kingdom of Bhutan)

Capital: Thimphu
Population estimate, 2000: 2·03m.
Estimated GDP: $1·3bn.
HDI/world rank: 0·347/155

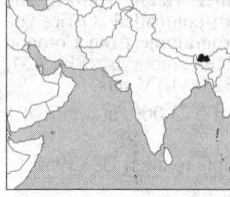

KEY HISTORICAL EVENTS

A sovereign kingdom in the Himalayas, Bhutan was governed by a spiritual ruler and a temporal ruler—the Dharma and Deb Raja—from the 17th century. The capital was Funakha. The interior was organized into districts for defence. Districts were controlled by governors and each district's central fort (*dzhong*) by a fort commander. These officials formed the electoral council appointing the Deb Raja. The British East India Company made a treaty with Bhutan in 1774 but relations were uneasy and there were violent incidents. The British annexed a number of borderland areas in an attempt to contain Bhutanese raiders.

During the 19th century civil wars were fought between district governors for the office of the Deb Raja. The governors of Tongsa and Paro were the most frequently chosen because they were the strongest. The appointment of new governors was likewise settled by force. By 1860 the British in India were disturbed by the instability of Bhutan. An attempt to interfere in 1863 resulted in a short frontier war, ending with a treaty in 1865. The British annexed part of Dewangiri and agreed to pay the rulers of Bhutan an annual subsidy.

In 1907 the office of Dharma Raja came to an end. The governor of Tongsa, Ugyen Wangchuk, was then chosen Maharajah of Bhutan, the throne becoming hereditary in his family (the title is now King of Bhutan). He concluded a further treaty with the British in 1910 allowing internal autonomy but British control of foreign policy. The treaty was renewed with the Government of India in 1949; the subsidy was further increased and the annexed area of Dewangiri returned to Bhutan.

India concluded a fresh treaty with Bhutan on 8 Aug. 1949 under which Bhutan continues to be guided by India in its external relations while India undertakes not to interfere in the internal administration of Bhutan. The subsidy paid to Bhutan was increased to Rs 0·5m. In the early 1990s, tens of thousands of 'illegal immigrants', mostly Nepali-speaking Hindus, were forcibly expelled. A decade on, there are still nearly 90,000 people claiming to be Bhutanese refugees in camps set up by UNHCR in eastern Nepal.

TERRITORY AND POPULATION

Bhutan is situated in the eastern Himalayas, bounded in the north by Tibet and on all other sides by India. In 1949 India retroceded 32 sq. miles of Dewangiri, annexed in 1865. Area about 18,000 sq. miles (46,500 sq. km); population estimate, 1997, 1·87m; density, 40 per sq. km.

The UN gives a projected population for 2000 of 2·03m.

In 1995 an estimated 6·0% of the population lived in urban areas. Only Rwanda has a larger proportion of its population living in rural areas. A Nepalese minority makes up 30–35% of the population, mainly in the south. The capital is Thimphu (1993, 30,340 population).

The official language is Dzongkha.

SOCIAL STATISTICS

1995 (estimates) births, 74,000 (rate of 41·4 per 1,000 population); deaths, 25,000 (rate of 14·4 per 1,000 population). Life expectancy at birth, 1990–95, was 49·1 years for men and 52·4 years for women. Infant mortality, 1990–95, 117 per 1,000 live births; fertility rate, 5·9 children per woman.

BHUTAN

CLIMATE
The climate is largely controlled by altitude. The mountainous north is cold, with perpetual snow on the summits, but the centre has a more moderate climate, though winters are cold, with rainfall under 40" (1,000 mm). In the south, the climate is humid sub-tropical and rainfall approaches 200" (5,000 mm).

CONSTITUTION AND GOVERNMENT
There is no formal constitution. The monarchy acts in consultation with a National Assembly (*Tshogdu*), which was reinstituted in 1953. But King Wangchuck is leaning towards democracy. In July 1998 the National Assembly was given the right to dismiss him. This has 150 members and meets at least once a year. Two-thirds are representatives of the people and are elected for a 3-year term. All Bhutanese over 30 years may be candidates.

The reigning King is **Jigme Singye Wangchuck**, who succeeded his father Jigme Dorji Wangchuck (died 21 July 1972).

In 1907 the Trongsa Penlop (the governor of the province of Trongsa in central Bhutan), Sir Ugyen Wangchuk, GCIE, KCSI, was elected as the first hereditary Maharaja of Bhutan. The Bhutanese title is *Druk Gyalpo*, and his successor is now addressed as King of Bhutan. Educated in Britain, King Wangchuk is opposed to certain Western influences such as television and jeans.

12 monastic representatives are elected by the central and regional ecclesiastical bodies, while the remaining members are nominated by the King, and include members of the Council of Ministers (the Cabinet) and the Royal Advisory Council.

National Anthem. 'Druk tsendhen koipi gyelknap na' ('In the Thunder Dragon Kingdom'); words by Dasho Shinkar Lam, tune by A. Tongmi.

CURRENT ADMINISTRATION
In March 1999 the government comprised:

Minister of Agriculture, Education and Health: Kinzang Dorji. *Finance:* Hishey Zimba. *Foreign Affairs:* Jigme Thinly. *Home Affairs:* Thinley Gyamtso. *Law:* Sonam Tobgye. *Trade and Industry:* Khandu Wangchuck. *Chairman, Royal Advisory Council:* Kungang Tsangbi. *Chairman, Third Committee (Social, Humanitarian, Cultural):* Ugyen Tsering.

Local Government. There are 20 districts, each under a district officer (*dzongda*) responsible to the Royal Civil Service Commission through the Home Ministry.

DEFENCE
Army. There was (1996) an Army of 6,000 men. 3 to 5 weeks militia training was introduced in 1989 for senior students and government officials, and 3 months training for some 10,000 volunteers from the general population in 1990 and 1991. Since 1992 only refresher training has been implemented.

INTERNATIONAL RELATIONS
Bhutan is a member of the UN.

ECONOMY
Policy. The 8th development plan (1997–2002) allows for expenditure of Nu35,169m. Hydro-electric power and industries are stressed. The 7th plan (1992–97) emphasized forest and mineral exploitations, education and medical facilities.

Performance. Real GDP growth was 8·0% in 1995 (6·0% in 1994).

Budget. The budget for 1996–97 envisaged current expenditure of Nu2,198m. and internal domestic revenue of Nu1,950m.

Currency. The unit of currency is the *ngultrum* (BTN) of 100 *chetrum*, at parity with the Indian rupee. Indian currency is also legal tender. Total money supply in Nov. 1997 was Nu2,078m.

Banking and Finance. The Bank of Bhutan was established in 1968. The headquarters are at Phuentsholing with 26 branches throughout the country. The

BHUTAN

Royal Monetary Authority (founded 1982) acts as the central bank. Deposits (Dec. 1995) Nu2,816·3m. Foreign Exchange reserves: US$120m.

ENERGY AND NATURAL RESOURCES

Electricity. Installed capacity at June 1995 was 342,000 kW (of which 336,000 kW were hydro-electric). Production (1994) was 1,685m. kWh. In 1995, 38 towns and 297 villages had electricity. Consumption per capita in 1995 was estimated to be 79 kWh. Bhutan exports electricity to India.

Minerals. Large deposits of limestone, marble, dolomite, slate, graphite, lead, copper, coal, talc, gypsum, beryl, mica, pyrites and tufa have been found. Most mining activity (principally limestone, coal, slate and dolomite) is small-scale.

Agriculture. Agriculture accounts for approximately 42% of GDP. The area under cultivation in 1996 was 0·36m. ha. The chief products (1990 production in 1,000 tonnes) are rice (43), millet (7), wheat (5), barley (4), maize (40), potatoes (31), oranges (58), apples (5), handloom cloth, timber and cardamom.

Livestock (1996): Cattle, 435,000; pigs, 75,000; sheep, 59,000; goats (1995), 42,000; horses, 30,000.

Forestry. In 1996, 2·98m. ha were forested. Timber production in 1995 was 1·4m. cu. metres.

Fisheries. The total catches in 1995 amounted to an estimated 340 tonnes, exclusively from inland waters.

INDUSTRY

In 1995 there were 3,206 licensed industrial establishments, of which 1,785 were service, 1,085 construction and 336 manufacturing industries. Of the latter, 167 were forest-based, 81 agriculture-based and 35 mineral-based.

Labour. In 1996 the labour force totalled 888,000 (60% males).

INTERNATIONAL TRADE

The cumulative outstanding convertible currency debt at 30 June 1996 was US$81m. To the same date, cumulative debt service payments totalled US$7m.

Financial support is received from India, the UN and other international aid organizations.

Imports and Exports. Trade with India dominates but oranges and apples, timber, cardamom and liquor are also exported to the Middle East, Singapore and Europe.

Exports in 1994–95 were estimated at US$71m. and imports at US$114m.

COMMUNICATIONS

Roads. In 1996 there were about 3,285 km of roads, of which 1,543 km were highways and main roads, and 10,384 cars, buses, coaches, trucks and vans plus 5,959 motor cycles and mopeds. In the entire kingdom there is only one set of traffic lights.

Civil Aviation. In 1998 Druk-Air made 2 weekly flights to Delhi via Káthmandu and 4 weekly services to Bangkok via Dhaka and Rangoon (Yangon) or Calcutta. In 1995 scheduled airline traffic of Bhutan-based carriers flew 300,000 km, carrying 9,000 passengers (all on international flights).

Telecommunications. In 1997 there were 6,400 telephone main lines (10·4 per 1,000 inhabitants).

An international microwave link connects Thimphu to the Calcutta and Delhi satellite connections. A telecommunications link between Thimphu and London by Intelsat-satellite was inaugurated in 1990. Thimphu and Phuentsholing are connected by telex to Delhi. There were 300 fax machines in 1995.

Postal Services. In 1995 there were 103 post offices.

SOCIAL INSTITUTIONS

Justice. The High Court consists of 8 judges appointed by the King. There is a Magistrate's Court in each district, under a *Thrimpon*, from which appeal is to the High Court at Thimphu.

BHUTAN

Religion. Government estimates, 1995: 70% of the population are Mahayana Buddhists, 25% Hindu and 5% Moslem.

Education. In April 1996 there were 9,257 pupils and 225 teachers in community schools, 53,097 pupils and 1,374 teachers in primary schools, 18,762 pupils and 650 teachers in 20 junior high and 10 high schools, and 1,795 pupils and 203 teachers in technical, vocational and tertiary-level schools. There were 1,248 students and 61 teachers in 7 private schools. Many students receive higher technical training in India, as well as under the UN Development Programme and the Colombo Plan, in Australia, Germany, New Zealand, Japan, Singapore, the USA and the UK. In Oct. 1990, 140 students were receiving university education in India. Adult literacy was 42·2% in 1995 (56·2% among males and 28·1% among females).

Health. There were (1996) 27 hospitals, 32 dispensaries, 97 basic health units, 10 indigenous dispensaries, 454 outreach clinics, 19 malaria centres and 3 training institutes. In 1994 beds totalled 970; there were 100 doctors and 578 paramedics in 1994. Free health facilities are available to 90% of the population.

CULTURE

Broadcasting. In 1994 there were 52 radio stations for internal administrative communications, and 13 hydro-met stations. Bhutan Broadcasting Service (autonomous since 1992) broadcasts a daily programme in English, Sharchopkha, Dzongkha and Nepali. There is no local television station. Satellite and cable television are illegal. In 1995 there were 10,000 TV receivers and 30,000 radio receivers.

Cinema. There are 2 in Thimphu and 4 others.

Press. There is 1 weekly newspaper, published in English, Dzongkha and Nepali. Total circulation (1996) about 12,000.

Tourism. Tourism is the largest source of foreign exchange. In 1996, 5,150 tourists visited Bhutan (4,765 in 1995), bringing revenue of US$5m.

DIPLOMATIC REPRESENTATIVES
Of Bhutan to the United Nations
Ambassador: Om Pradhan.

Of Bhutan to the European Union
Ambassador: Jigmi Thinley.

FURTHER READING
Bhutan, Himalayan Kingdom. Bhutan Government, Thimphu, 1979

Aris, M., *Bhutan: The Early History of an Himalayan Kingdom.* Warminster, 1979.— *The Raven Crown: the Origins of Buddhist Monarchy in Bhutan.* London, 1994
Chakravarti, B., *A Cultural History of Bhutan.* 2nd rev. ed., 2 vols. Chitteranjan, 1981
Collister, P., *Bhutan and the British.* London, 1987
Das, B. N., *Mission to Bhutan: a Nation in Transition.* New Delhi, 1995
Dogra, R. C., *Bhutan* [Bibliography]. Oxford and Santa Barbara (CA), 1991
Edmunds, T. O., *Bhutan: Land of the Thunder Dragon.* London, 1988
Hickman, K., *Dreams of the Peaceful Dragon: a Journey through Bhutan.* London, 1987
Hutt, M., *Bhutan: Perspectives on Conflict and Dissent.* London, 1994
Mehra, G. N., *Bhutan: Land of the Peaceful Dragon.* Rev. ed. New Delhi, 1985
Misra, H. N., *Bhutan: Problems and Policies.* New Delhi, 1988
Parmanand, *The Politics of Bhutan: Retrospect and Prospect.* Delhi, 1992
Rahul, R., *Royal Bhutan.* New Delhi, 1983
Rose, L. E., *The Politics of Bhutan.* Cornell Univ. Press, 1977
Rustomji, N., *Bhutan: The Dragon Kingdom in Crisis.* OUP, 1978
Savada, A. M. (ed.) *Nepal and Bhutan: Country Studies.* Washington, D.C., 1993
Sinha, A. C., *Bhutan: Ethnic Identity and National Dilemma.* Delhi, 1991
Strydonck, G. van, et al., *Bhutan: a Kingdom of the Eastern Himalayas.* Geneva and London, 1984
Verma, R., *India's Role in the Emergence of Contemporary Bhutan.* Delhi, 1988

National statistical office: Central Statistical Organization, Thimphu

BOLIVIA

República de Bolivia

Capital: Sucre
Seat of Government: La Paz
Population estimate, 2000: 8·33m.
GNP per capita: (PPP$) 2,860
HDI/world rank: 0·593/116

KEY HISTORICAL EVENTS

Bolivia was part of the Inca Empire until conquered by the Spanish in the 16th century. In 1776 it became part of the viceroyalty of Buenos Aires. Independence was won and the Republic of Bolivia was proclaimed on 6 Aug. 1825. During the first 154 years of its independence, Bolivia had 189 governments, many of them installed by coups. Largely civilian governments from 1880 gave way to mainly military ones after 1936. In 1952 a revolution led by the MNR (National Revolutionary Movement) brought about agrarian reform and nationalization of the tin mines, Bolivia's chief source of wealth. In the 1960s the Argentinian revolutionary and former minister of the Cuban government, Ernesto 'Che' Guevara, was killed in Bolivia while fighting with a left-wing guerrilla group. In 1971, Bolivian instability reached a peak with the brief establishment of a revolutionary Popular Assembly during the regime of Gen. Torres. Later repression under Gen. Hugo Banzer took a heavy toll on the left-wing parties. An attempt to hold elections in July 1978 led to Gen. Juan Pereda Asbún (supported by the army) carrying out a military coup. In Nov. he was in turn overthrown by Gen. David Padilla Arancibia, the army commander. Elections in July 1979 proved indecisive, and an interim government was formed until it was overthrown in Nov. by yet another army coup, which won power for a mere two weeks.

The 1980 elections were as inconclusive as those of the previous year and a coup followed, led by the army C.-in-C. Gen. Luis Garcia Meza. However in 1981 he was forced to resign in favour of Gen. Celso Torrelio Villa. When the new president tried introducing civilians to the Cabinet and adopting a liberal attitude to trade unions, he was superseded by Gen. Guido Vildoso Calderón. Civilian rule was restored in Oct. 1982 when Dr Siles Zuazo (who had won a small majority in the two previous elections) became president. There followed a period of economic reform embracing free markets and open trade. The minister responsible for economic changes, Gonzalo Sanchez de Lozada, was elected president in 1993. In 1997 he was succeeded by Gen. Hugo Banzer Suarez.

TERRITORY AND POPULATION

Bolivia is a landlocked state bounded in the north and east by Brazil, south by Paraguay and Argentina, and west by Chile and Peru, with an area of some 424,165 sq. miles (1,098,581 sq. km). A coastal strip of land on the Pacific passed to Chile after a war in 1884. In 1953 Chile declared Arica a free port and Bolivia has certain privileges there.

Population estimate, 1998: 7,949,933 (60·3% urban); density, 6·9 per sq. km.

The UN gives a projected population for 2000 of 8·33m.

Area and population of the departments (capitals in brackets) at the 1992 census and as estimated in 1998:

Departments	Area (sq. km)	Census 1992	Estimate 1998
La Paz (La Paz)	133,98	1,900,786	2,313,877
Cochabamba (Cochabamba)	55,631	1,110,205	1,445,990
Potosí (Potosí)	118,218	645,889	755,895
Santa Cruz (Santa Cruz)	370,621	1,364,389	1,703,901
Chuquisaca (Sucre)	51,524	453,756	562,917
Tarija (Tarija)	37,623	291,407	379,704
Oruro (Oruro)	53,588	340,114	386,980
Beni (Trinidad)	213,564	276,174	346,180
Pando (Cobija)	63,827	38,072	54,489
Total	1,098,581	6,420,792	7,949,933

BOLIVIA

Population (1992 census) of the principal towns: La Paz, 711,036; Santa Cruz, 694,616; Cochabamba, 404,102; El Alto, 404,367; Oruro, 183,194; Sucre, 130,952; Potosí, 112,291; Tarija, 90,000.

Spanish is the official and commercial language. The Amerindian languages Aymará and Quechua are spoken exclusively by 22% and 5·2% of the population respectively; Tupi Guaraní is also spoken.

SOCIAL STATISTICS
The population growth rate has been estimated at 2·3% for the years 1995-2000; in 1996 births totalled an estimated 258,000 (birth rate of 34·0 per 1,000 population); deaths totalled an estimated 71,000 (rate, 9·4 per 1,000); infant mortality, 64·6 per 1,000 live births, the highest in South America. Expectation of life was 61·65 years in 1998. Fertility rate, 1990–95, 4·8 children per woman, also the highest in South America.

CLIMATE
The varied geography produces different climates. The low-lying areas in the Amazon Basin are warm and damp throughout the year, with heavy rainfall from Nov. to March; the Altiplano is generally dry between May and Nov. with sunshine but cold nights in June and July, while the months from Dec. to March are the wettest. La Paz, Jan. 53°F (11·7°C), July 47°F (8·3°C). Annual rainfall 23" (574 mm). Sucre, Jan. 55°F (13°C), July 49°F (9·4°C). Annual rainfall 27" (675 mm).

CONSTITUTION AND GOVERNMENT
Bolivia's first constitution was adopted on 19 Nov. 1826. The *President* is elected by universal suffrage for a 5-year term. If 50% of the vote is not obtained, the result is determined by a secret ballot in Congress amongst the leading 2 candidates. The President appoints the members of his Cabinet. There is a bicameral legislature; the *Senate* comprises 27 members, 3 from each department, and the *Chamber of Deputies* 130 members, all serving terms of 5 years. A constitutional amendment of 1996 introduced direct elections for 65 deputies; the remainder are nominated by party leaders. Voting is compulsory.

National Anthem. 'Bolivianos, el hado propicio' ('Bolivians, the propitious fate'); words by I. de Sanjinés; tune by B. Vincenti.

RECENT ELECTIONS
Presidential and parliamentary elections were held on 1 June 1997. The electorate was 3·2m. Gen. Hugo Banzer Suarez gained 22·3% of the votes cast, and Juan Carlos Durán 17·7%. As no candidate gained an absolute majority, Congress elected Gen. Hugo Banzer Suarez President on 4 Aug. 1997.

Presidential and parliamentary elections are scheduled for June 2002.

CURRENT ADMINISTRATION
President: Gen. Hugo Banzer Suarez (ADN; sworn in Aug. 1997).

Vice-President: Jorge Quiroga (ADN).

The Cabinet was composed as follows in March 1999:

Foreign Affairs and Worship: Dr Javier Murillo de la Rocha (ADN). *Finance:* Herbert Muller Costas. *Economic Development:* Jorge Pacheco. *Sustainable Development and Planning:* Erick Alberto Reyes Villa (NFR). *Presidency:* Carlos Iturralde Ballivian (ADN). *Health:* Dr Tonchi Marinkovic Uzqueda (MIR). *Defence:* Fernando Kieffer Guzman (ADN). *Government:* Guido Nayar Parada (ADN). *Labour and Microbusiness:* Leopoldo López Cossio (MIR). *Justice and Human Rights:* Dr Ana Maria Cortes de Soriano (ADN). *Education, Culture and Sports:* Tito Hoz de Vila (ADN). *Housing and Basic Services:* Dr Maria Amparo Ballivian. *International Trade and Investment:* Dr Jorge Crespo Velasco (MIR). *Agriculture:* Oswaldo Antezana Vaca Diez.

Parties represented: Acción Democrática Nacionalista (ADN), Movimiento de Izquierda Revolucionaria (MIR), Unidad Cívica Solidaridad (UCS), Conciencia de Patria (CONDEPA), Nueva Fuerza Republicana (NFR).

Local Government. The republic is divided into 9 departments, with 94 provinces administered by sub-prefects, and 1,713 cantons administered by *corregidores*. Each department has a prefect appointed by the President and a legislature elected by municipal councillors. There are 312 municipalities. Elections are held every 5 years.

DEFENCE
There is selective conscription for 12 months at the age of 18 years. There has been optional pre-military training for high school pupils since 1998.

In 1997 defence expenditure totalled US$155m. (US$18 per capita).

Army. There are 6 military regions. The Army consists of 2 armoured battalions, 1 mechanized cavalry regiment and a Presidential Guard infantry regiment under direct Headquarters command; and 10 divisions comprising altogether 8 cavalry groups, 1 motorized infantry regiment, 22 infantry, 1 artillery, 1 armoured, 1 airborne and 6 engineer battalions. Equipment includes 36 Kuerassier SK-105 light tanks. There are 1 King Air 90, 1 Super King Air 200 and 2 C-212 Aviocar transports. Strength (1997) 25,000 (18,000 conscripts).

Navy. A small force exists for river and lake patrol duties, comprising 9 small patrol craft operating on Lake Titicaca and in the 6,000-mile Beni and Bolivia-Paraguay river systems, and also 1 Cessna 402 transport and 1 Cessna 206 for patrol duties. 1 ocean-going transport for use to and from Bolivian free zones in Argentina and Uruguay and 2 17-tonne hospital craft on Lake Titicaca complete the inventory.

Personnel in 1996 totalled 4,500, including 2,000 marines.

Air Force. The Air Force, established in 1923, has 6 combat-capable Groups, 4 equipped with T-33 armed jet trainers, 1 with armed PC-7s and 1 with Hughes 500 helicopters, for counter-insurgency operations. A search and rescue helicopter Group has 6 Brazilian-assembled Lamas and 20 UH-1 Iroquois. Other types in service include Brazilian T-23 Uirapuru and American T-41 primary trainers and Italian SF-260 basic trainers, 1 Electra transport, 6 Fokker F.27 and 2 Israeli-built Arava twin-turboprop light transports, 5 Convair transports, 2 Learjet VIP aircraft, 11 C-130/L-100 Hercules, 3 C-47s, 15 Turbo-Porters and some single- and twin-engined light aircraft, some confiscated from drug smugglers. Personnel strength (1996) about 4,000 (2,000 conscripts).

INTERNATIONAL RELATIONS
Bolivia is a member of the UN, OAS, LAIA, the Andean Group and the Amazon Pact, and is an associate member of Mercosur.

ECONOMY
Policy. Following the collapse of the international tin market in 1985 and severe inflation, a New Economic Policy was introduced de-restricting foreign trade, ending price controls and subsidies and freezing public-sector wages. A privatization programme affecting some 60 state-owned enterprises was instituted in June 1992. A programme of capitalization aims to attract foreign investment into state enterprises in oil, telephones, electricity supply, railways, airlines and smelters, while distributing 50% of the shares to adult citizens, to be held in retirement accounts.

Performance. Real GDP growth was estimated at 4·0% in 1996.

Budget. In 1m. bolivianos:

	1993	1994	1995	1996	1997
Revenue	3,993	4,446	5,256	6,565	7,467
Expenditure	5,876	6,400	6,802	8,720	9,490

Currency. The unit of currency is the *boliviano* (BOB) of 100 *centavos*, which replaced the *peso* on 1 Jan. 1987 at a rate of 1 boliviano = 1m. pesos. Inflation was an annualized 4·4% in 1998. Foreign exchange reserves were US$903m. in Feb. 1998 and gold reserves 940,000 troy oz. Total money supply was 5,692,000 bolivianos in Dec. 1997.

BOLIVIA

Banking and Finance. The Central Bank (*governor*, Juan Antonio Morales) is the bank of issue. In 1998 there were 14 commercial banks operating, including 5 foreign and 8 specialized development banks.

There are stock exchanges in La Paz and Santa Cruz.

Weights and Measures. The metric system is legal, but the old Spanish system is also employed.

ENERGY AND NATURAL RESOURCES

Electricity. Installed capacity was estimated to be 1,010,520 kW in 1997. Estimated production from all sources (1995), 3·02bn. kWh. Consumption per capita was estimated to be 334 kWh in 1995.

Oil and Gas. There are petroleum and natural gas deposits in the Santa Cruz-Camiri areas. Production of crude oil in 1996 was 10,682,314 bbls. Work has begun on a US$1·9 bn. pipeline from eastern Bolivia to São Paulo in Brazil. National gas output was 117,573 cu. ft in 1996.

Minerals. Mining accounts for 5·76% of GDP (1996 estimate). Tin-mining had been the mainstay of the economy until the collapse of the international tin market in 1985. Production, 1997 (in tonnes): Zinc, 154,491; lead, 18,608; tin, 12,898; antimony, 5,999; wolfram, 647; silver, 387; gold, 13,291 fine kg.

Agriculture. In 1996 agriculture contributed 14·95% of GDP (estimate). The rural population was estimated at 3,012,260 in 1996, 39·70% of total population. Output in 1,000 tonnes in 1996 (estimate) was: Sugar-cane, 4,120; rice, 343; coffee, 22; maize, 613; potatoes, 715; wheat, 98. In 1992, 77,000 tonnes of coca (the source of cocaine) were grown. Since 1987 Bolivia has received international (mainly US) aid to reduce the amount of coca grown, with compensation for farmers who co-operate.

Livestock, 1996: Cattle, 6,118,000; horses, 322,000; asses and mules, 712,000 (1995); pigs, 2,482,000; sheep, 8,039,000; goats (1995), 1,496,000; chickens (1995), 56m.

Forestry. Forests covered 48·3m. ha (44·6% of the land area) in 1995, down from 51·2m. ha in 1990. Tropical forests with woods ranging from the 'iron tree' to the light balsa are exploited. Timber production in 1995 was 2·57m. cu. metres.

Fisheries. In 1995 total catches were 6,308 tonnes, exclusively from inland waters.

INDUSTRY

At the 1992 census there were 14,389 factories employing a total of 76,718 persons. The principal manufactures are foodstuffs and tobacco, and textiles.

Labour. Out of 1,256,000 people in employment in 1995, 348,000 were in wholesale and retail, 231,000 in manufacturing, 106,000 in construction and 95,000 in transport, storage and communications. The unemployment rate in 1995 was 3·6%. In 1998 the minimum wage was 300 bolivianos a month.

Trade Unions. Unions are grouped in the Confederación de Obreros Bolivianos.

INTERNATIONAL TRADE

An agreement of Jan. 1992 with Peru gives Bolivia duty-free transit for imports and exports through a corridor leading to the Peruvian Pacific port of Ilo from the Bolivian frontier town of Desaguadero, in return for Peruvian access to the Atlantic via Bolivia's roads and railways. The mining code of 1991 gives tax incentives to foreign investors. Foreign debt was US$5,174m. in 1996.

Imports and Exports. The value of imports and exports in US$1m.:

	1992	1993	1994	1995	1996	1997
Imports	1,130·50	1,176·95	1,196·35	1,433·59	1,656·61	1,909·36
Exports	742·07	786·71	1,091·00	1,139·07	1,216·19	1,255·64

Main exports, 1996 (in US$1m.): Soya beans, 201; zinc, 151; gold, 119; natural gas, 94; jewellery, 88; timber, 83; tin, 83.

Main export markets, 1996: USA, 26·1%; EU (especially UK, Germany and Belgium), 22·3%; Argentina, Peru and Colombia, 39·3%. Main import suppliers:

Brazil, Argentina and Chile, 36·8%; EU (Germany, Belgium and Italy), 36·8%; Japan, 12%.

Imports and exports pass chiefly through the ports of Arica and Antofagasta in Chile, Mollendo-Matarani in Peru, through La Quiaca on the Bolivian-Argentine border, and through river-ports on the rivers flowing into the Amazon.

COMMUNICATIONS

Roads. The total length of the road system was 53,153 km in 1996, of which 3,200 km were hard-surfaced. Estimated total vehicles in use in 1997 was 397,112.

Rail. In 1994, the state railway ENFE network totalled 3,697 km of metre gauge, comprising unconnected Eastern (1,423 km) and Andina (2,274 km) systems, and carried 0·8m. passengers and 1·4m. tonnes of freight.

Civil Aviation. The 2 international airports are La Paz (El Alto) and Santa Cruz (Viru Viru). The national airlines are the state-owned Aerosur (domestic services only) and Lloyd Aéreo Boliviano (97·5% state-owned), which in 1998 ran scheduled services between La Paz and Arica, Buenos Aires, Guayaquil, Lima, Miami, Montevideo and Trinidad, as well as many internal services. Other airlines serving Bolivia in 1998 were Aerolíneas Argentinas, Aeroperú, American Airlines, Lan-Chile, SAETA and Varig. In 1994 Lloyd Aéreo Boliviano flew 13·8m. km, carrying 1,175,000 passengers (424,000 on international flights).

Shipping. Lake Titicaca and about 19,000 km of rivers are open to navigation.

Telecommunications. In 1997 there were 535,000 telephone main lines (68·8 per 1,000 inhabitants). In Oct. 1997 there were approximately 8,000 Internet users; in 1995 there were 7,200 cellular phone subscribers.

Postal Services. In 1995 there were 159 post offices, or 1 for every 46,600 persons.

SOCIAL INSTITUTIONS

Justice. Justice is administered by the Supreme Court, superior department courts (of 5 or 7 judges) and courts of local justice. The Supreme Court, with headquarters at Sucre, is divided into two sections, civil and criminal, of 5 justices each, with the Chief Justice presiding over both. Members of the Supreme Court are chosen on a two-thirds vote of Congress.

Religion. The Roman Catholic church was disestablished in 1961. It is under a cardinal (in Sucre), an archbishop (in La Paz), 6 bishops and vicars apostolic. It had 7·16m. adherents in 1992.

Education. Adult literacy was 83·1% in 1995 (male, 90·5%; female, 76%). The female literacy rate is the lowest in South America. Primary instruction is free and obligatory between the ages of 6 and 14 years. In 1993 there were 11,878 schooling facilities; 10,485 public and 1,393 private. The national rate of school attendance (6–19-year-olds) reaches 74·3%.

In 1994-95 there were 7 universities, 2 technical universities, 1 Roman Catholic university, 1 musical conservatory, and colleges in the following fields: Business, 6; teacher training, 4; industry, 1; nursing, 1; technical teacher training, 1; fine arts, 1; rural education, 1; physical education, 1. There were 103,900 university students in 1995-96 and 4,920 academic staff.

In 1994 total expenditure on education came to 5·4% of GNP and represented 11·2% of total government expenditure.

Health. In 1993 there were 3,392 doctors, 1,869 nurses and 336 hospitals.

Welfare. Retirement pensions are funded by the state out of its share of the capitalization of enterprises. Previously established funds covered only some 10% of the workforce, and are being allowed to run down. A second compulsory contributory pension fund was started in 1997 for all workers aged 21 or over.

CULTURE

Broadcasting. The broadcasting authority is the Dirección General de Telecomunicaciones. There were (1987) about 85 radio stations, the majority of which were local and commercial. There is a commercial government television

BOLIVIA

service. There are 4 private television stations and 1 university station (educational channel) in La Paz. In 1995 there were 4,980,000 radio and 850,000 TV (colour by NTSC) receivers.

Cinema. In 1993 there were 129 cinemas.

Press. There were 11 daily newspapers in 1995 with a combined circulation of 500,000, at a rate of 67 per 1,000 inhabitants.

Tourism. In 1996 there were 375,000 foreign tourists. Receipts totalled US$160m.

DIPLOMATIC REPRESENTATIVES
Of Bolivia in Great Britain (106 Eaton Sq., London, SW1W 9AD)
Ambassador: Jaime Quiroga Matos.

Of Great Britain in Bolivia (Avenida Arce 2732, La Paz)
Ambassador: Mr G. Minter.

Of Bolivia in the USA (3014 Massachusetts Ave, NW, Washington, D.C., 20008)
Ambassador: Marcelo Perez Monasterios.

Of the USA in Bolivia (Avenue Arce, No. 2780, La Paz)
Ambassador: Donna J. Hrinak.

Of Bolivia to the United Nations
Ambassador: Roberto Jordán-Pando.

Of Bolivia to the European Union
Ambassador: Vacant.

FURTHER READING
Fifer, J. V., *Bolivia: Land, Location and Politics since 1825.* CUP, 1972
Klein, H., *Bolivia: The Evolution of a Multi-Ethnic Society.* OUP, 1982
Yeager, G. M., *Bolivia.* [Bibliography] Oxford and Santa Barbara (CA), 1988

National statistical office: Instituto Nacional de Estadistica, Casilla Postal 6129, La Paz.
Website: http://www.ine.gov.bo/

BOSNIA-HERCEGOVINA

Republika Bosna i
Hercegovina

Capital: Sarajevo
Population estimate, 2000: 4·34m.
Estimated GDP: $1·9bn.

KEY HISTORICAL EVENTS

Settled by Slavs in the 7th century, Bosnia was conquered by the Turks in 1463 when much of the population was gradually converted to Islam. At the Congress of Berlin (1878) the territory was assigned to Austro-Hungarian administration under nominal Turkish suzerainty. Austria-Hungary's outright annexation in 1908 generated international tensions which contributed to the outbreak of the First World War.

After 1918, Bosnia Hercegovina became part of a new kingdom of Serbs, Croats and Slovenes under the Serbian monarchy. Its name was changed to Yugoslavia in 1929. (See YUGOSLAVIA for developments up to and beyond the Second World War.)

On 15 Oct. 1991 the National Assembly adopted a 'Memorandum on Sovereignty', the Serbian deputies abstaining. This envisaged Bosnian autonomy within a Yugoslav federation. A referendum on independence was held on 29 Feb.–1 March 1992. Turn-out was 63·04%, the Serbian population largely boycotting it; 99·78% of votes cast were in favour. In March 1992 an agreement was reached under EC auspices by Moslems, Serbs and Croats to set up 3 autonomous ethnic communities under a central Bosnian authority.

Bosnia-Hercegovina declared itself independent on 5 April 1992, and was recognized by the EC and USA on 7 April. The 2 Serbian members of the Bosnian collective presidency resigned. Fighting broke out between the Serb, Croat and Moslem communities, with particularly heavy casualties and destruction in Sarajevo, leading to extensive Moslem territorial losses and an exodus of refugees. UN-sponsored ceasefires from June on were repeatedly violated. On 29 June the UN Security Council unanimously voted for the deployment of UN forces to secure the functioning of Sarajevo Airport and protect humanitarian aid missions.

On 13 Aug. 1992 the UN Security Council voted by 12 to nil with 3 abstentions (China, India and Zimbabwe) to authorize the use of force if necessary to ensure the delivery of humanitarian aid to besieged civilians. Internationally sponsored peace talks were held in Geneva in Jan. and at the UN in Feb. 1993, but Serb-Moslem-Croat fighting continued.

A NATO ultimatum of 10 Feb. 1994 gave Bosnian Serbs 10 days to withdraw their artillery from around Sarajevo. NATO forces used air strikes for the first time against Serb forces at Gorazde on 10 April. In Aug. Yugoslavia ceased supplying Bosnian Serbs and sealed the frontier.

An upsurge in fighting began in Oct. with Moslem-Croat attacks in the Bihać area. The Moslem advance was beaten back by Serb forces which bombed Bihać with napalm on 18 Nov. NATO air forces retaliated with a raid on the Serbian airfield, but Serb forces occupied Bihać. On 12 Nov. 1994 the USA ended its embargo on the supply of arms to Bosnian forces.

On 23 Dec. Bosnian Serbs and Moslems signed a countrywide interim ceasefire. Bosnian Croats also signed on 2 Jan. 1995. However, Croatian Serbs and the Moslem secessionist forces under Fikret Abdić did not sign the agreement, and fighting continued.

On 28 May 1995 Bosnian Serb forces took some 400 UN peacekeeping troops hostage. Under pressure from Serbian President Milošević all had been released by 18 June.

On 16 June 1995 Bosnian government forces launched an attack to break the Bosnian Serb siege of Sarajevo. On 11 July Bosnian Serb forces began to occupy UN security zones despite retaliatory NATO air strikes, and on 28 Aug. shelled Sarajevo.

BOSNIA-HERCEGOVINA

To stop the shelling of UN safe areas, more than 60 NATO aircraft attacked Bosnian Serb military installations on 30-31 Aug. Further air strikes on military targets began on 5 Sept. after Bosnian Serbs failed to comply with demands that they withdraw heavy weapons from around Sarajevo.

On 26 Sept. in Washington the foreign ministers of Bosnia, Croatia and Yugoslavia (the latter negotiating for the Bosnian Serbs) agreed a draft Bosnian constitution under which a central government would handle foreign affairs and commerce and a Serb Zone, and a Moslem-Croat Federation would run their internal affairs. The Bosnian Presidency and Parliament would be elected, one third from the Serb Republic (i.e. the Serb zones of Bosnia) and two thirds from the Moslem-Croat Federation. A ceasefire came into force on 12 Oct. 1995.

In Dayton (Ohio) on 21 Nov. 1995 the prime ministers of Bosnia, Croatia and Yugoslavia initialled a US-brokered agreement to end hostilities in Bosnia, and this was signed by the respective presidents on 14 Dec. in Paris. The Bosnian state was divided into a Serb Republic containing 49% of Bosnian territory and a Croat-Moslem Federation. A central government authority representing all ethnic groups with responsibility for foreign and monetary policy and citizenship issues was established, and free elections held. On 20 Dec. 1995 a 63,000-strong NATO contingent (IFOR) took over from UN peacekeeping forces to enforce the Paris peace agreements and set up a 4-km separation zone between the Serb and Moslem-Croat territories. Some 1,500 advisers were sent by the UN to help in the formation and training of local civil police units.

Following the expiry of the mandate of IFOR on 20 Dec. 1996, a new NATO 30,000-strong Stabilization Force (SFOR) took over peacekeeping duties until mid-1998. Czech, Polish and Russian troops were also attached to SFOR. In Dec. 1997 NATO defence ministers decided that troops would stay on after the 1998 deadline.

TERRITORY AND POPULATION
The republic is bounded in the north and west by Croatia and in the east and south-east by Yugoslavia. It has a coastline of only 20 km with no harbours. Its area is 51,129 sq. km. The capital is Sarajevo.

Population at the 1991 census: 4,377,033 (34·2% urban), of which the predominating ethnic groups were Moslems (1,905,829), Serbs (1,369,258) and Croats (755,892). Estimate, 1995, 4,484,000; density, 88 per sq. km.

The UN gives a projected population for 2000 of 4·34m.

In 1995 an estimated 58·9% of the population lived in rural areas. By 1996, 1,319,250 Bosnians had taken refuge abroad, including 0·45m. in Yugoslavia, 0·32m. in Germany, 0·17m. in Croatia and 0·12m. in Sweden.

Population (1991 census) of the principal cities: Sarajevo, 415,631 (est. 1993, 383,00); Banja Luka, 142,644; Zenica, 96,238.

In 1998 some 800,000 Bosnians were still displaced in the country following the war.

The official language is Serbo-Croat.

SOCIAL STATISTICS
Annual growth rate, 1990–95, 0·0%. Life expectancy at birth, 1990–95, was 69·5 years for men and 75·1 years for women. Infant mortality, 1990–95, 15 per 1,000 live births; fertility rate, 1·5 children per woman.

CLIMATE
The climate is generally continental with steady rainfall throughout the year, although in areas nearer the coast it is more Mediterranean.

CONSTITUTION AND GOVERNMENT
On 18 March 1994, in Washington, Bosnian Moslems and Croats reached an agreement for the creation of a federation of cantons with a central government responsible for foreign affairs, defence and commerce. It is envisaged that there will be a president elected by a 2-house legislature alternating annually between the nationalities.

On 30 March 1994 a 123-member constituent assembly adopted the constitution by 112 votes in favour. On 31 May 1994 the National Assembly approved the creation of the Moslem Croat federation. Alija Izetbegović remained the unitary states' President. An interim government with Hasan Muratović as Prime Minister was formed on 30 Jan. 1996.

Following the Dayton agreement the government structure was established in 1996 as follows:

Heading the state is a 3-member *Presidency* (1 Croat, 1 Moslem, 1 Serb) with a rotating president. The Presidency is elected by direct universal suffrage, and is responsible for foreign affairs and the nomination of the prime minister. There is a 2-chamber parliament: The *Chamber of Representatives* (which meets in Sarajevo) comprises 42 directly elected deputies, two-thirds Croat and Moslem and one-third Serb; and the *Chamber of Peoples* (which meets in Lukavica) comprises 5 Croat, 5 Moslem and 5 Serb delegates.

Below the national level the country is divided into 2 self-governing entities along ethnic lines.

The **Croat-Moslem Federation** is headed by a President and Vice-President, alternately Croat and Moslem, a 140-member Chamber of Representatives and a 74-member Chamber of Peoples. The **Serb Republic** is also headed by an elected President and Vice-President, and there is a National Assembly of 140 members, elected by proportional representation.

Central government is conducted by a *Council of Ministers*, which comprises Moslem and Serb Co-Prime Ministers and a Croat Deputy Prime Minister. The Co-Prime Ministers alternate in office every week.

RECENT ELECTIONS

Elections were held on 12 and 13 Sept. 1998 for all the institutions outlined under 'Constitution and Government' above for a 2-year term of office.

Elected to the national *Presidency* were Živko Radišić (Serb, Sloga); Alija Izetbegović (Moslem, Party of Democratic Action—SDA); Ante Jelavić (Croat, Croat Democratic Union—HDZ).

Elections in the Serb Republic in Sept. 1998 brought a swing against the moderates and in favour of hardline nationalists. Nikola Poplasen, a Serb nationalist hardliner, defeated Biljana Plavšić, the President of the Serb Republic, who supported co-operation with the West. Milorad Dodik, who had been the prime minister of the Serb Republic under Biljana Plavšić, remained in office. Controlling only 11 of the 83 seats in the Bosnian Serb Parliament, Poplasen tried to oust his western-backed prime minister Milorad Dodik. Instead, Poplasen himself was dismissed by the representative of the international community, Carlos Westendorp.

In the elections to the Chamber of Representatives (*Zastupnički dom*) on 12 and 13 Sept. 1998, the Coalition for a Unified and Democratic Bosnia-Hercegovina (KCD) obtained 32·7% of the votes cast and 17 of the 42 seats; 6 seats went to the Croation-nationalist Croatian Democratic Community, with other parties winning 4 seats or fewer.

CURRENT ADMINISTRATION

In March 1999 the government consisted of:

Presidency Chairman: Živko Radišić (Serb, Sloga). *Presidency Members:* Ante Jelavić (Croat, HDZ). Alija Izetbegović (Moslem, SDA).

Co-Chairmen of the Council of Ministers: Haris Silajdžić (Moslem, SBiH); Svetozar Mihajlović (Serb, Sloga).

Deputy Chairman: Neven Tomić. *Chairman, House of Peoples:* Momir Tosić. *Minister of Foreign Affairs:* Jadranko Prlić. *Foreign Trade and Economic Relations:* Mirsad Kurtović. *Civil Affairs and Communications:* Marko Asanin. These 3 ministries are also jointly controlled by 2 deputy ministers from each community.

Local Government. In the Croat-Moslem Federation there are 10 cantons with elected local assemblies.

DEFENCE

Defence expenditure in 1997 totalled US$327m. (US$74 per capita), representing 5·0% of GDP.

Army. In 1998 the Army numbered some 40,000 and was organized in 5 corps headquarters. There were 40 infantry, 1 reconnaissance, 1 special forces brigades and 19 artillery regiments. Equipment included 80 T-34 and T-35 main battle tanks. The Croatian Defence Council also had personnel of some 16,000 active in the country, with 50 main battle tanks, while the forces of the Serb Republic were estimated at up to 30,000, with 500 main battle tanks. The USA supplied 16 UH1 Iroquois helicopters in 1996 to join 3 Mi-8s and is assisting in training and equipping the armed forces.

INTERNATIONAL RELATIONS
The Serb Republic and Yugoslavia signed an agreement on 28 Feb. 1997 establishing 'special parallel relations' between them. The agreement envisages co-operation in cultural, commercial, security and foreign policy matters, allows visa-free transit of borders and includes a non-aggression pact. A customs agreement followed on 31 March.

ECONOMY
Performance. Real GDP growth was –20·0% in 1995 (–12·1% in 1994).

Budget.
(In 1m. Deutsche Marks)

	1994	1995
Revenue	535·7	874·3
Expenditure	668·4	1,051·4

Currency. Dinars are issued by the National Bank of Bosnia-Hercegovina in Sarajevo in denominations up to 100,000. The new dinar, introduced in Aug. 1994, has an official value fixed at 100 BHD = 1 Deutsche Mark.

Banking and Finance. The Dayton agreement stipulated that the governor of the Central Bank must not be a Bosnian citizen. The present governor is Serge Robert (France). In 1998 there were 59 commercial banks.

ENERGY AND NATURAL RESOURCES
Electricity. Capacity was 3·99m. kW in 1991. Production in 1994 was 1·87bn. kWh. In 1995 consumption per capita was an estimated 475 kWh.

Agriculture. In 1994 there were 600,000 ha of arable land, 200,000 ha of permanent crops and 1·2m. ha of permanent pasture. 1993 yields (in 1,000 tonnes): Wheat, 350; maize, 750; potatoes, 230; cabbages, 36; sugar beets, 55; plums, 50. Livestock in 1996: Cattle, 314,000; sheep, 276,000; pigs, 165,000; poultry (1995), 3m.

Forestry. In 1995 forests covered 27,100 sq. km, or 53·1% of the total land area.

Fisheries. Estimated total catch of freshwater fish in 1995 (in 1,000 tonnes), 2·5.

INDUSTRY
In 1991 there were 7,823 enterprises (4,563 private, 1,882 social, 655 limited companies, 322 co-operatives and 157 public). Production (in 1,000 tonnes) 1994: Lignite, 1,400; aluminium, 89; cement, 797; 1990, crude steel, 1,421. Cars (1990), 38,000; tractors, 34,000; lorries, 16,000; TV receivers, 21,000.

Labour. The labour force totalled 1,719,000 in 1996 (62% males).

INTERNATIONAL TRADE
External debt was US$815m. in 1996.

Imports and Exports. 1997 external trade (in US$1m.): Exports, 570; imports, 2,199. 1994 figures were: Exports, 91; imports, 894.

COMMUNICATIONS
Roads. In 1996 there were 21,846 km of roads, 3,722 km of which were highways or main roads. There were 96,182 passenger cars in use in 1996 (23 per 1,000 inhabitants) and 9,783 vans and trucks.

Rail. There were 1,021 km of railways in 1991 (795 km electrified); they carried 554m. passenger-km and 1,946m. tonne-km of freight.

Civil Aviation. There are international airports at Sarajevo and Banja Luka. Services were operated in 1998 by Adria Airways, Air Bosna, Austrian Airlines, Croatia Airlines, JAT, Lufthansa, Swissair and Turkish Airlines, with direct flights to Belgrade, Istanbul, Ljubljana, Munich, Tivat, Vienna, Zagreb and Zürich.

Telecommunications. There were 302,900 telephone main lines in 1997, equivalent to 80 per 1,000 inhabitants.

Postal Services. In 1995 there were 159 post offices.

SOCIAL INSTITUTIONS

Religion. At the 1991 census 40% of the population were Moslem, 31% Orthodox and 15% Roman Catholic.

Education. In 1990–91 there were 543,500 pupils in primary schools, 173,100 in secondary schools and 2,400 in tertiary schools. In 1995 there were 4 universities.

Health. In 1996 there were 4,500 doctors, 550 dentists and 11,900 nurses.

Welfare. There were 380,000 pensions in 1990 (including 140,000 old age).

CULTURE

Broadcasting. In 1995 there were 840,000 radio receivers.

Press. There were 2 daily newspapers in 1995 with a combined circulation of 520,000, at a rate of 146 per 1,000 inhabitants.

DIPLOMATIC REPRESENTATIVES

Of Bosnia-Hercegovina in Great Britain (4th Floor, Morley House, 320 Regent St., London, W1R 5AB)
Ambassador: Osman Topcagić.

Of Great Britain in Bosnia-Hercegovina (8 Tina Ujevića, Sarajevo)
Ambassador: Mr G. Hand.

Of Bosnia-Hercegovina in the USA (2109 E Street, NW, Washington, D.C., 20037)
Ambassador: Sven Alkalaj.

Of the USA in Bosnia-Hercegovina (Alipasina 43, 71000, Sarajevo)
Ambassador: Richard D. Kauzlarich.

Of Bosnia-Hercegovina to the United Nations
Ambassador: Muhamad Saćirbey.

Of Bosnia-Hercegovina to the European Union
Ambassador: Vacant.

FURTHER READING

Bert, W., *The Reluctant Superpower: United States Policy in Bosnia, 1991-1995.* New York, 1997
Cigar, N., *Genocide in Bosnia: the Policy of Ethnic Cleansing.* Texas Univ. Press, 1995
Fine, J. V. A. and Donia, R. J., *Bosnia-Hercegovina: a Tradition Betrayed.* Farnborough, 1994
Friedman, F., *The Bosnian Muslims: Denial of a Nation.* Boulder (CO), 1996
Garde, P., *Journal de Voyage en Bosnie-Herzégovine.* Paris, 1995
Holbrooke, R., *To End a War.* Random House, London, 1998
Malcolm, N., *Bosnia: a Short History.* 2nd ed. London, 1996
O'Ballance, E., *Civil War in Bosnia, 1992-94.* London, 1995
Rieff, D., *Slaughterhouse: Bosnia and the Failure of the West.* New York, 1997
Sells, M. A., *The Bridge Betrayed: Religion and Genocide in Bosnia.* California Univ. Press, 1996

BOTSWANA

Republic of Botswana

Capital: Gaborone
Population estimate, 2000: 1·62m.
GNP per capita: (PPP$) 7,390
HDI/world rank: 0·678/97

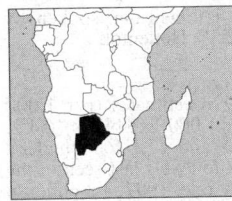

KEY HISTORICAL EVENTS

The Tswana or Batswana people are the principal inhabitants of the country formerly known as Bechuanaland and now called Botswana. The 8 main communities of the Batswana are the Bakgatla, Bakwena, Bangwaketse, Bamalete, Bamangwato, Barolong, Batawana and Batlokwa.

Dominant in the area from the 17th century, the Batswana were disturbed in the early 19th century by invasions of Nguni peoples fleeing from Shaka in the mass immigration called the *Mfecane*, and by Boers moving east in the Great Trek. They clashed with the Boers, but obtained the support of British missionaries (including David Livingstone). King Khama III, a Christian who became ruler of the Bamangwato in 1872, appealed with other chiefs to Britain because of the Boer danger. In 1885 Britain took control and the territory was formally declared a protectorate in 1895. Britain ruled through her High Commissioner in South Africa and a Resident Commissioner whose office was at Mafeking. When the post of South African High Commissioner was abolished in 1964, the British representative was restyled Commissioner and placed directly under the Colonial Secretary in London. The seat of government was moved to Gaborone in 1965. Frequent suggestions for the addition of Bechuanaland and the other two High Commission Territories to South Africa were rejected, the Africans being strongly against the idea. Economically, however, the country was very closely tied to that of South Africa and has remained so.

The British left much day-to-day administration in the hands of the Tswana chiefs. They set up an African Advisory Council in 1920 and a European Advisory Council for the (never very numerous) white residents in 1921; a Joint Advisory Council was created in 1950.

Seretse Khama, ruler of the Bamangwato since 1923 when he was 4 years old, was deposed in 1950 because of South African opposition to his marriage to a white woman. He returned in 1956 and joined the African Advisory Council in 1957. In Dec. 1960 Bechuanaland received its first constitution. Elections followed in 1961 for African members of the Legislative Council, of whom Seretse was one. In 1962 he formed the Bechuanaland Democratic Party, now the Botswana Democratic party (BDP). Further constitutional change brought full self-government in 1965 and full independence on 30 Sept. 1966. Sir Seretse Khama became president.

The BDP easily won elections in 1969, 1974 and 1979. President Khama died on 13 July 1980 and was succeeded by Dr Quett Masire, without any change of policy. For years Botswana had great difficulties with the neighbouring settler regime in Rhodesia, until that country became Zimbabwe in 1980. Such difficulties continued with South Africa; Botswana supported African resistance to the Pretoria regime but at the same time it was economically dependent on South Africa. Many border clashes and other incidents between Botswana and South Africa culminated in South African raids on African National Congress offices in Gaborone. Improved relations between the two countries had to wait on the ending of apartheid.

TERRITORY AND POPULATION

Botswana is bounded in the west and north by Namibia, north-east by Zambia and Zimbabwe, and east and south by South Africa. The area is 581,730 sq. km. Population (1991 census), 1,326,796 (45·7% urban). Estimate, 1996, 1,478,000; density, 2·3 per sq. km.

The UN gives a projected population for 2000 of 1·62m.

In 1995, 60% of the population were urban. Between 1990 and 1995 there was a 10% rise in the urban population every year, the largest percentage increase anywhere in the world in the same period.

BOTSWANA

The country is divided into 10 districts (Central, Chobe, Ghanzi, Kgalagadi, Kgatleng, Kweneng, Ngamiland, Ngwaketse, North East and South East).

The main towns (with population, 1991 census) are Gaborone (133,468), Francistown (65,244), Selebi-Phikwe (39,772), Molepolole (36,931), Kanye (31,354), Serowe (30,260), Mahalapye (28,079), Maun (26,769), Lobatse (26,052) and Mochudi (25,542).

The official language is English; the national language is Setswana, spoken by 75% of the population. 12% speak Sishona, 3·4% San and 2·5% Hottentot.

SOCIAL STATISTICS
1996 (estimates) births, 49,000; deaths, 25,000. Rates, 1996 estimates (per 1,000 population): Births, 33·3; deaths, 17·0. Infant mortality (per 1,000 live births), 54·2. Expectation of life in 1996 was 46·0 years (44·9 for males and 47·1 for females). The impact of AIDS has caused life expectancy to sink back to levels last seen in the mid-1960s. Growth rate, 1990–95, 2·3% per annum. Fertility rate, 1997, 4·3 children per woman.

CLIMATE
In winter, days are warm and nights cold, with occasional frosts. Summer heat is tempered by prevailing north-east winds. Rainfall comes mainly in summer, from Oct. to April, while the rest of the year is almost completely dry with very high sunshine amounts. Gaborone, Jan. 79°F (26·1°C), July 55°F (12·8°C). Annual rainfall varies from 650 mm in the north to 250 mm in the south-east. The country is prone to droughts.

CONSTITUTION AND GOVERNMENT
The Constitution adopted on 30 Sept. 1966 provides for a republican form of government headed by the President with 3 main organs: The Legislature, the Executive and the Judiciary. The executive rests with the President who is responsible to the National Assembly. The President is elected for 5-year terms by the National Assembly.

The *National Assembly* consists of 47 members, 40 elected by universal suffrage, and 7 elected by itself. Elections are held every 5 years. Voting is on the first-past-the-post system.

The President is an *ex-officio* member of the Assembly.

There is also a *House of Chiefs* to advise the Government. It consists of the Chiefs of the 8 tribes who were autonomous during the days of the British protectorate, plus 4 members elected by and from among the sub-chiefs in 4 districts; these 12 members elect a further 3 politically independent members.

National Anthem. 'Fatshe leno la rona' ('Blessed be this noble land'); words and tune by K. T. Motsete.

RECENT ELECTIONS
At the elections of 15 Oct. 1994 the Botswana Democratic Party gained 27 seats and the Botswana National Front 13. Presidential and parliamentary elections are scheduled for Oct. 1999.

CURRENT ADMINISTRATION
President: Festus Mogae (sworn in on 1 April 1998).
In March 1999 the Cabinet was as follows:
Vice-President and Minister for Presidential Affairs and Public Administration: Lieut.-Gen. Seretse Khama Ian Khama. *Finance and Development Planning:* Hon. Ponatshego Horatius Kedikilwe. *Foreign Affairs:* Lieut.-Gen. Mompati Merafhe. *Health:* Chapson Butale. *Works, Transport and Communications:* Hon. David N. Magang. *Commerce and Industry:* George Kgoroba. *Mineral Resources and Water Affairs:* Hon. Margaret N. Nasha. *Education:* Dr Gaositwe Chiepe. *Labour and Home Affairs:* Bahiti Temane. *Agriculture:* Ronald Sebego. *Local Government, Land and Housing:* Hon. Daniel K. Kwelagobe.

Local Government. Local government is carried out by 10 district, 1 city (Gaborone), 3 town and 3 township councils. Revenue is obtained mainly from sales

BOTSWANA

taxes, from rates in the towns and from central government subventions in the districts.

DEFENCE
In 1997 defence expenditure totalled US$241m. (US$153 per capita).

Army. The Army is organized in 2 brigades comprising 4 infantry, 2 field artillery and 2 air defence battalions, 1 engineer regiment and 1 commando unit. Personnel (1997), 7,000.

Air Force. Equipment includes 5 BAC Strikemaster light strike aircraft, 5 Britten-Norman Defender armed light transports for border patrol, counter-insurgency and casualty evacuation duties, 13 second-hand CF-5 fighters, 7 PC-7 basic trainers, 2 CN-235 turboprop-powered medium transports, 2 C-212 turboprop passenger/cargo transports, 4 Islander, 5 Ecureuil and 6 Bell 412 helicopters and 2 Cessna 152 light aircraft. Personnel (1997), 500.

INTERNATIONAL RELATIONS
Botswana is a member of the UN, the Commonwealth, OAU, SADC and is an ACP state of the EU.

ECONOMY
Policy. The Eighth National Development Plan is running from 1997 to 2003. It is intended to stimulate industries and economic activities that can take over from mines and create jobs.

Performance. In 1997 the economy grew by 7%, compared with a projected 5·7%.

Budget. The fiscal year begins in April. Budgets for recent years (in P1m.):

	1991–92	1992–93	1993–94	1994–95	1995–96
Revenue	3,969·0	4,503·6	5,103·0	4,352·9	5,377·7
Expenditure	2,691·3	3,209·3	3,924·5	4,017·8	4,760·8

1993–94 revenue (in P1m.) included: Mineral taxes, 2,456; customs pool, 830; other revenue, 1,858. Expenditure: Recurrent, 3,470; development and capital transfer, 1,735.

Currency. The unit of currency is the *pula* (BWP) of 100 *thebe*. Inflation was 9·8% in Oct. 1996. Foreign exchange reserves were US$5,906m. in Feb. 1998. Total money supply was P1,042m. in Jan. 1998.

Banking and Finance. There were 4 commercial banks at 1 Jan. 1996 with 46 branches. Total assets were P3,729m. at 30 Nov. 1995. The Bank of Botswana (*Governor*, H. C. L. Hermans), established in 1976, is the central bank. The National Development Bank, founded in 1964, has 6 regional offices, and agricultural, industrial and commercial development divisions. The Botswana Co-operative Bank is banker to co-operatives and to thrift and loan societies. The government-owned Post Office Savings Bank operates throughout the country.

There is a stock exchange.

Weights and Measures. The metric system is in use.

ENERGY AND NATURAL RESOURCES
Electricity. Installed capacity was 197,000 kW in 1993. Production (1994–95) 916·6m. kWh. Consumption per capita was an estimated 747 kWh in 1993. The coal-fired power station at Morupule supplies cities and major towns.

Water. Surface water resources are about 18,000m. cu. metres a year. Nearly all flows into northern districts from Angola through the Okavango and Kwando river systems. The Zambezi, also in the north, provides irrigation in the Chobe District. In the south-east, there are dams to exploit the ephemeral flow of the tributaries of the Limpopo. 80% of the land has no surface water, and must be served by some 6,000 boreholes.

Minerals. Botswana is the world's biggest diamond producer; in 1997 the total value was estimated to be US$1·82bn. Debswana, a partnership between the government and De Beers, runs 3 mines producing around 17·5m. carats a year, with plans to double the capacity of the largest mine from 6m. to 12m. carats a year. Coal reserves are estimated at 17,000m. tonnes. There is also salt and soda ash. Mineral production, 1994: Diamonds, 15,547,178 carats (value P1,807m.); copper–nickel ore, 3,462,823 tonnes; coal, approximately 0·94m. tonnes.

Agriculture. 70–80% of the total land area is desert. 80% of the population is rural, 71% of all land is 'tribal', protected and allocated to prevent over-grazing, maintain small farmers and foster commercial ranching. Agriculture provides a livelihood for over 80% of the population, but accounts for only 4–5% of GDP.

Cattle-rearing is the chief industry after diamond-mining, and the country is more a pastoral than an agricultural one, crops depending entirely upon the rainfall. In 1995, 258,000 persons were economically active in agriculture. In 1990, 128,000 ha were sown to sorghum. In 1995 there were: Cattle, 1·9m.; goats, 1·9m.; sheep, 250,000; asses, 235,000; chickens, 2m. 80% of the cattle were owned by traditional farmers, about half owning fewer than 20 head. A serious outbreak of cattle lung disease in 1995–96 led to the slaughter of around 300,000 animals.

Production (1993, in 1,000 tonnes): Maize, 4·3; sorghum, 16·5; (1992) millet, 1; roots and tubers, 8; pulses, 12; seed cotton, 3; vegetables, 16; fruit, 11.

17% of the land is set aside for wildlife conservation and 20% for wildlife management areas, with 4 national parks and game reserves.

Forestry. Forests covered 139,000 sq. km, or 24·6% of the total land area, in 1995 (25·2% in 1990). There are forest nurseries and plantations. Concessions have been granted to harvest 7,500 cu. metres in Kasane and Chobe Forestry Reserves, and up to 2,500 cu. metres in the Masame area. In 1995, 1·58m. cu. metres of roundwood were cut.

Fisheries. In 1995 total catches were estimated to be 2,000 tonnes, exclusively from inland waters.

INDUSTRY

Meat is processed, and textiles, foodstuffs and soap manufactured. 565 companies were registered at the end of 1992. Rural technology is being developed and traditional crafts encouraged.

Labour. In March 1994, 321,200 persons were in formal employment. At the 1991 census there were 276,950 paid employees (including informal employment) and 28,764 self-employed. A further 76,101 persons worked on a non-cash basis, e.g. as family helpers. 60,757 were seeking work. In March 1994 there were 12,342 Botswana nationals employed in the mines of South Africa. In 1991 there were 57,001 building workers, 34,322 in trade and 29,325 in domestic service. Average earnings in 1994 in the formal sector were P807 per month. Botswana's biggest individual employer is the Debswana Diamond Company, with a workforce (1997) of nearly 6,000. In April 1998 the unemployment rate was 21%.

INTERNATIONAL TRADE

Botswana is a member of the Southern African Customs Union (SACU) with Lesotho, Namibia, South Africa and Swaziland. There are no foreign exchange restrictions. External debt in 1996 totalled US$613m. in 1996.

Imports and Exports. In 1994 imports totalled P4,392m. More than three-quarters of all imports are from the SACU countries, the main commodities being machinery and electrical equipment, foodstuffs, vehicles and transport equipment, textiles and petroleum products.

In 1994 export earnings totalled P4,962m., including diamonds (P3,727m.), copper and nickel (P266m.) and beef (P215m.).

In addition to the SACU countries, other significant trading partners are Switzerland and the UK; and for imports, the USA.

COMMUNICATIONS

Roads. In 1996 some 4,600 km of road were bitumen-surfaced out of a total of 18,327 km. In 1996 there were 66,540 motor vehicles in use (22,540 cars and 44,000 trucks and vans).

BOTSWANA

Rail. The main line from Mafeking in South Africa to Bulawayo in Zimbabwe traverses Botswana. With 3 branches the total was (1994) 971 km. In 1993–94 railways carried 0·3m. passengers, and in 1995 freight tonne-km came to 687m.

Civil Aviation. There is an international airport at Gaborone (Sir Seretse Khama) and 6 domestic airports. The national carrier is the state-owned Air Botswana. In 1998 services were also operated by Air Zimbabwe, British Airways, South African Airways and Zambian Express. Direct flights are operated to the UK, South Africa and Zimbabwe. In 1995 Air Botswana flew 2·1m. km, carrying 99,900 passengers (70,300 on international flights). In 1996 Gaborone handled 181,629 passengers (135,382 on international flights).

Telecommunications. There were 85,600 main telephone lines in 1997, 3,100 fax machines in 1995, and in Jan. 1998 approximately 500 Internet users.

Postal Services. There are 109 post offices and 65 agencies.

SOCIAL INSTITUTIONS

Justice. Law is based on the Roman-Dutch law of the former Cape Colony, but judges and magistrates are also qualified in English common law. The Court of Appeal has jurisdiction in respect of criminal and civil appeals emanating from the High Court, and in all criminal and civil cases and proceedings. Magistrates' courts and traditional courts are in each administrative district. As well as a national police force there are local customary law enforcement officers.

Religion. Freedom of worship is guaranteed under the Constitution. About 50% of the population is Christian. Non-Christian religions include Bahais, Moslems and Hindus.

Education. Adult literacy rate (1995) 69·8% (male, 80·5%; female, 59·9%). Basic free education, introduced in 1986, consists of 7 years of primary and 3 years of junior secondary schooling. In 1994 enrolment in 670 primary schools was 310,128 with 11,371 teachers, and 93,250 pupils at secondary level with 5,678 teachers. In 1993 there were 1,261 students in teacher training colleges. 'Brigades' (community-managed private bodies) provide lower-level vocational training. The Department of Non-Formal Education offers secondary-level correspondence courses and is the executing agency for the National Literacy Programme. There is 1 university (6,673 students in 1995–96).

In 1994 total expenditure on education came to 8·5% of GNP.

Health. In 1994 there were 16 general hospitals, a mental hospital, 13 health centres, 200 clinics and 310 health posts. There were also 701 stops for mobile health teams. In 1994 there were 339 doctors and 3,329 nurses. The health facilities are the concern of central and local government, medical missions, mining companies and voluntary organizations.

CULTURE

Broadcasting. The government-controlled Radio Botswana broadcasts daily on 2 channels in English and Setswana. A commercial television company transmits on a 50 km-radius from Gaborone (colour by SECAM). There were 190,000 radio and 27,000 TV sets in 1995.

Press. In 1995 there was 1 government newspaper (distributed free) and 5 independent newspapers, with a total circulation of about 100,500, and 6 other periodicals.

Tourism. There were 770,000 foreign visitors in 1997. Receipts totalled US$178m in 1996.

DIPLOMATIC REPRESENTATIVES

Of Botswana in Great Britain (6 Stratford Pl., London, W1N 9AE)
High Commissioner: Roy Warren Blackbeard.

Of Great Britain in Botswana (Private Bag 0023, Gaborone)
High Commissioner: John Wilde.

Of Botswana in the USA (4301 Connecticut Ave., NW, Washington, D.C., 20008)
Ambassador: Archibald Mooketsa Mogwe.

Of the USA in Botswana (PO Box 90, Gaborone)
Ambassador: Robert C. Krueger.

Of Botswana to the United Nations
Ambassador: Legwaila Joseph Legwaila.

Of Botswana to the European Union
Ambassador: Sasara George.

FURTHER READING

Central Statistics Office. *Statistical Bulletin* (Quarterly).

Ministry of Information and Broadcasting. *Botswana Handbook.* — *Kutlwano* (monthly).

Colclough, C. and McCarthy, S., *The Political Economy of Botswana.* OUP, 1980

Harvey, C. (ed.) *Papers on the Economy of Botswana.* London and Nairobi, 1981

Molomo, M. G. and Mokopakgosi, B. (eds.) *Multi-Party Democracy in Botswana.* Harare, 1991

Parson, J., *Botswana: Liberal Democracy and Labour Reserve in Southern Africa.* Aldershot, 1984

Perrings, C., *Sustainable Development and Poverty Alleviation in Sub-Saharan Africa: the Case of Botswana.* London, 1995

National statistical office: Central Statistics Office, Private Bag 0024, Gaborone.
Website: http://www.gov.bw

BRAZIL

República Federativa do
Brasil

Capital: Brasília (Federal District)
Population estimate, 2000: 169·2m.
GNP per capita: (PPP$) 6,340
HDI/world rank: 0·809/62

KEY HISTORICAL EVENTS

Brazil, South America's largest country, was colonized by the Portuguese following the arrival of Admiral Pedro Alvares Cabral on 22 April 1500. In 1815 the colony was declared 'a kingdom'. When, in 1822, the Portuguese king João VI returned home after using Rio de Janeiro as his capital during the French occupation of Portugal, his eldest surviving son, Dom Pedro, was chosen 'Perpetual Defender' of Brazil by a National Congress. He proclaimed the independence of the country on 7 Sept. 1822, and was chosen 'Constitutional Emperor and Perpetual Defender' on 12 Oct. 1822, with the title Emperor Pedro I. He abdicated in 1831 and was succeeded in 1840 by his son, Pedro II. Pedro ruled for nearly 50 years. His policies were liberal and included the gradual abolition of slavery.

Under the dictatorship of President Vargas from 1930 to 1945, some areas (such as São Paulo) saw considerable economic development. Vargas was succeeded by Presidents Kubitschek and Quadros.

Juscelino Kubitschek, popularly known as JK, was elected president in 1956. Promising '50 years progress in five' he brought 40 years inflation in four. A big spender, he created roads and hydroelectric plants. Brasília, supposed to be the catalyst for development of Brazil's huge interior, was built.

Janio Quadros became the next president in 1961 on a wave of public euphoria. But when he decorated Che Guevara in a public ceremony, he upset the right wing military. A few days later Quadros resigned after only six months in office. João Goulart, his vice-president, took over. His leftist policies led to his overthrow by the military in 1964. This was followed by 20 years of single party rule and censored press.

Brazil's military regime was not as brutal as those of Chile or Argentina, but at its height, around 1968 and 1969, the use of torture was widespread. The generals benefited from the Brazilian economic miracle in the late '60s and '70s when the economy was growing more than 10% every year. Brazil became one of the biggest industrial nations in the world, but uncoordinated growth made bureaucracy, corruption and inflation explode.

In 1980 a militant working-class movement sprung up under the charismatic leadership of a worker called Lula. The popular opposition, together with economic problems, forced the military slowly to announce the so-called 'abertura' (opening)—a slow process of returning the government to democracy.

Tancredo Neves surprised his military opponents by winning the 1985 elections, but tragically died shortly before assuming power. José Sarney, his vice-president, took over. With a new finance minister every three months, the country drifted into economic chaos and foreign debt reached Cr$115,000m.

In 1989 Fernando Collor de Mello, governor of a forgotten state in the north-east, won a hard-fought victory over the Labour Party candidate, Lula. One of the main promises of the incoming government was to cut inflation and attack corruption. When he assumed control in March 1990, Collor took drastic measures. In an attempt to reduce inflation caused by excess liquidity in the market, he confiscated 80% of every bank account worth more than US$1,200, promising to release it 18 months later with interest. He announced the privatization of state-owned companies and the opening of Brazilian markets to foreign competition and capital.

By 1992 few promises had been met, most of the popular goodwill was gone and Collor found his government shaken by scandals and corruption linked directly to his family. Inflation was heading again into astronomical figures. The parliament,

BRAZIL

under public pressure, forced an impeachment. Itamar Franco, Collor's vice-president, took office for three years.

Fernando Henrique Cardoso, former finance minister responsible for the 'Plano Real', the economic plan to end inflation, was elected president at the end of 1994. He instituted an economic revolution which included a radical privatization programme and a lowering of trade barriers; but in 1997-98 economic turbulence in the Far East spread to Brazil, which had to be kept afloat by IMF loans. In Jan. 1999, the *real* was devalued, thereafter losing 35% of its value against the dollar in two months.

TERRITORY AND POPULATION

Brazil is bounded in the east by the Atlantic and on its northern, western and southern borders by all the Latin American countries except Chile and Ecuador. The area is 8,547,403·5 sq. km including 55,457 sq. km of inland water. Population as at censuses of 1991 and 1996:

Federal Unit and Capital	Area (sq. km)	Census 1991	Census 1996
North	3,869,639		
Rondônia (Porto Velho)	238,513	1,132,692	1,229,306
Acre (Rio Branco)	153,150	417,718	483,593
Amazonas (Manaus)	1,577,820	2,103,243	2,389,279
Roraima (Boa Vista)	225,116	217,583	247,131
Pará (Belém)	1,253,165	4,950,060	5,510,849
Amapá (Macapá)	143,454	289,397	379,459
Tocantins (Palmas)	278,421	919,863	1,048,642
North-East	1,561,177[1]		
Maranhão (São Luís)	333,366	4,930,253	5,222,183
Piauí (Teresina)	252,378	2,582,137	2,673,085
Ceará (Fortaleza)	146,348	6,366,647	6,809,290
Rio Grande do Norte (Natal)	53,307	2,415,567	2,558,660
Paraíba (João Pessoa)	56,585	3,201,114	3,305,616
Pernambuco (Recife)	98,938	7,127,855	7,399,071
Alagoas (Maceió)	27,933	2,514,100	2,633,251
Sergipe (Aracajú)	22,050	1,491,876	1,624,020
Bahia (Salvador)	567,295	11,867,991	12,541,675
South-East	927,287		
Minas Gerais (Belo Horizonte)	588,384	15,743,152	16,672,613
Espírito Santo (Vitória)	46,184	2,600,618	2,802,707
Rio de Janeiro (Rio de Janeiro)	43,910	12,807,706	13,406,308
São Paulo (São Paulo)	248,809	31,588,925	34,119,110
South	577,214		
Parana (Curitiba)	199,709	8,448,713	9,003,804
Santa Catarina (Florianópolis)	95,443	4,541,994	4,875,244
Rio Grande do Sul (Porto Alegre)	282,062	9,138,670	9,634,688
Central West	1,612,078		
Mato Grosso (Cuiabá)	906,807	2,027,231	2,235,832
Mato Grosso do Sul (Campo Grande)	358,159	1,780,373	1,927,834
Goiás (Goiânia)	341,290	4,018,903	4,514,967
Distrito Federal (Brasília)	5,822	1,601,094	1,821,946
Total	8,547,395	146,825,475	157,070,163

[1]Including disputed areas between states of Piauí and Ceará (2,977 sq. km).

Population density, 18 per sq. km. The 1996 census showed 77,442,865 males and 79,627,298 females. The urban population comprised 78·4% in 1996.

The UN gives a projected population for 2000 of 169·2m.

BRAZIL

The official language is Portuguese.
Population of principal cities (1996 census):

City	Pop.	City	Pop.	City	Pop.
São Paulo	9,839,066	São Luis	780,833	Feira de Santana	450,487
Rio de Janeiro	5,551,538	Maceió	723,142	Niterói	450,364
Salvador	2,211,539	Duque de Caxias	715,089	Uberlândia	438,986
Belo Horizonte	2,091,371	São Bernardo do		São João de Meriti	434,323
Fortaleza	1,965,513	Campo	660,396	Cuiabá	433,355
Brasília	1,821,946	Natal	656,037	Sorocaba	431,561
Curitiba	1,476,253	Teresina	655,473	Aracaju	428,194
Recife	1,346,045	Santo André	624,820	Juiz de Fora	424,479
Porto Alegre	1,288,879	Osasco	622,912	Londrina	421,343
Manaus	1,157,357	Campo Grande	600,069	Santos	412,243
Belém	1,144,312	João Pessoa	549,363	Joinville	397,951
Goiânia	1,003,477	Jaboatão	529,966	Campos dos	
Guarulhos	972,197	Contagem	492,214	Goytacazes	389,547
Campinas	908,906	São José dos		Olinda	349,380
São Gonçalo	833,379	Campos	486,167	Diadema	323,116
Nova Iguaçu	826,188	Ribeirão Preto	456,252	Porto Velho	294,227

The principal metropolitan areas (census, 1996) were São Paulo (16,583,234), Rio de Janeiro (10,192,097), Belo Horizonte (3,803,249), Porto Alegre (3,246,869), Salvador (2,709,084), Recife (3,087,967), Fortaleza (2,582,820), Curitiba (2,425,361) and Belém (1,485,569).

SOCIAL STATISTICS
1998 estimates: Births, 3,451,000 (rate of 20·9 per 1,000 population); deaths, 1,404,000 (8·5 per 1,000 population). Life expectancy was 66·85 years in 1998 (63·2 years for males and 70·6 for females). 1996 growth rate, 1·4%; infant mortality, 37·5 per 1,000 live births; fertility rate, 2·3 children per woman.

CLIMATE
Because of its latitude, the climate is predominantly tropical, but factors such as altitude, prevailing winds and distance from the sea cause certain variations, though temperatures are not notably extreme. In tropical parts, winters are dry and summers wet, while in Amazonia conditions are constantly warm and humid. The north-east *sertão* is hot and arid, with frequent droughts. In the south and east, spring and autumn are sunny and warm, summers are hot, but winters can be cold when polar air-masses impinge. Brasília, Jan. 72°F (22·3°C), July 68°F (19·8°C). Annual rainfall 63" (1,603 mm). Belém, Jan. 78°F (25·8°C), July 80°F (26·4°C). Annual rainfall 102" (2,315 mm). Manaus, Jan. 79°F (26·1°C), July 80°F (26·7°C). Annual rainfall 110" (2,842 mm). Recife, Jan. 80°F (26·6°C), July 77°F (24·8°C). Annual rainfall 94" (2,474 mm). Rio de Janeiro, Jan. 83°F (28·5°C), July 67°F (19·6°C). Annual rainfall 67" (1,758 mm). São Paulo, Jan. 75°F (24°C), July 57°F (13·7°C). Annual rainfall 71" (1,800 mm). Salvador, Jan. 80°F (26·5°C), July 74°F (23·5°C). Annual rainfall 90" (2,315 mm). Porto Alegre, Jan. 75°F (23·9°C), July 62°F (16·7°C). Annual rainfall 67" (1,775 mm).

CONSTITUTION AND GOVERNMENT
The present Constitution came into force on 5 Oct. 1988, the eighth since independence. The *President* and *Vice-President* are elected for a 4-year term and are not immediately re-eligible. To be elected candidates must secure 51% of the votes, otherwise a second round of voting is held to elect the President between the two most voted candidates. Voting is compulsory for men and women between the ages of 18 and 70, and optional for illiterates, persons from 16 to 18 years old and persons over 70. A referendum on constitutional change was held on 21 April 1993. Turn-out was 80%. 66·1% of votes cast were in favour of retaining a republican form of government, and 10·2% for re-establishing a monarchy. 56·4% favoured an executive presidency, 24·7% parliamentary supremacy.

A constitutional amendment of June 1997 authorizes the re-election of the President, state governors and mayors for a second term.

Congress consists of an 81-member *Senate* (3 Senators per federal unit) and a 513-member *Chamber of Deputies*. The Senate is two-thirds directly elected (50% of these elected for 8 years in rotation) and one-third indirectly elected. The

Chamber of Deputies is elected by universal franchise for 4 years. There is a *Council of the Republic* which is convened only in national emergencies.

Constituição da Republica Federativa do Brasil. Brasília, 1988

Baaklini, A. I., *The Brazilian Legislature and Political System.* London, 1992

Martinez-Lara, J., *Building Democracy in Brazil: the Politics of Constitutional Change.* London, 1996

National Anthem. 'Ouviram do Ipiranga. . .' ('They hear the river Ipiranga'); words by J. O. Duque Estrada; tune by F. M. da Silva.

RECENT ELECTIONS

At the presidential elections of 4 Oct. 1998, Fernando Henrique Cardoso was re-elected President by 53·1% of votes cast against 4 other candidates, his closest rival, Luiz Inacio Lula da Silva, backed by a coalition of the left, obtaining 31·7%. Cardoso thus became the first Brazilian president to win a second successive term in office. Turn-out was 80%.

Parliamentary elections were also held on 4 Oct. 1998 for both the Chamber of Deputies and the Senate.

In the elections to the Chamber of Deputies the government coalition gained 347 seats (Liberal Front, 106; Brazilian Social Democratic Party, 99; Party of the Brazilian Democratic Movement, 82; Progressive Party, 60); their ally the Brazilian Labour Party gained 31 seats and the opposition gained 135 (Workers' Party, 58; Democratic Labour Party, 25; others, 52).

In the Senate elections the Party of the Brazilian Democratic Movement won 68 of the 81 seats; Liberal Front, 20; Brazilian Social Democratic Party, 16; Progressive Party, 5.

CURRENT ADMINISTRATION

President: Fernando Henrique Cardoso, b. 1931 (Social Democrat; sworn in 1 Jan. 1995, re-elected 4 Oct. 1998).

Vice-President: Marco Maciel.

In March 1999 the government comprised:

Justice: José Renan Calheiros. *Foreign Affairs:* Luiz Felipe Lampreia. *Finance:* Pedro Sampaio Malan. *Transport:* Eliseu Padilha. *Development, Industry and Commerce:* Celso Lafer. *Agriculture:* Francisco Sérgio Turra. *Education:* Paulo Renato de Souza. *Culture:* Francisco Corrêa Weffort. *Labour and Employment:* Francisco Dornelles. *Social Security:* Waldeck Vieira Ornélas. *Health:* José Serra. *Mines and Energy:* Rodolpho Tourinho. *Communications:* João Pimenta de Veiga. *Science and Technology:* Luis Carlos Bresser Pereira. *Environment:* José Sarney Filho. *Budget and Administration:* Paulo Paiva. *Sports and Tourism:* Rafael Greca. *Defence:* Elcio Alvares. *Land Policy:* Raul Jungmann. *Special Programmes:* Ronaldo Sardenberg.

Local Government. Brazil consists of 27 federal units (26 states and 1 federal district). Each has its distinct administrative, legislative and judicial authorities, and its own constitution and laws, which must, however, agree with federal constitutional principles. The governors and members of the legislatures are elected for 4-year terms. The country is sub-divided into 5,507 municipalities, each under an elected mayor and municipal council, and then further sub-divided into districts. The Federal District is the national capital, inaugurated in 1960; it is divided into 12 administrative Regions, the first Region being Brasília. Gubernatorial elections were held for all 27 federal units etc. in Oct.–Nov. 1994. Municipal elections were held on 30 Oct. 1996 and, for municipalities with at least 0·2m. electors, on 15 Nov. 1996.

DEFENCE

Conscription is for 12 months, extendable by 6 months.

In 1997 defence expenditure totalled US$13,944m. (US$84 per capita). In 1985 expenditure was US$3,347m.

Army. There are 7 military commands and 11 military regions. The Army consists of 8 divisions, 1 armoured cavalry, 3 armoured infantry, 4 mechanized cavalry, 13 motor infantry, 1 mountain, 4 jungle, 1 frontier, 1 airborne, and 2 coast and air defence brigades, 3 cavalry guard regiments, 28 artillery and 2 engineer groups.

Equipment includes 60 Leopard I main battle tanks and 287 light tanks. Strength, 1998, 195,000 (125,000 conscripts). A helicopter brigade has 76 Dauphin, Ecureuil, Fennec and UH-60 helicopters.

There are paramilitary state militias under Army control considered an Army reserve, totalling about 385,000 personnel.

Navy. The principal ship of the Navy is the 20,200-tonne Light Aircraft Carrier *Minas Gerais*, formerly the British *Vengeance*, completed in 1945 and purchased in 1956, which normally operates an air group of 8 S-2E Tracker anti-submarine aircraft and 8 ASH-3H anti-submarine Sea King helicopters.

There are also 5 diesel submarines (1 built in Germany, 1 in Brazil and 3 British Oberon-class) and 16 frigates including 4 Type 22 Batch 1 (Broadwood class) bought from the UK in 1995 and 1996. The fleet still includes 1 old ex-US Gearing class destroyer and 2 Sumner class, but these are decommissioning. There are 3 offshore and 6 inshore minesweepers and a patrol force numbering about 30 including 9 tug trawler types, 6 ex-US inshore craft, 2 locally-built and a number for work on the rivers. Major auxiliaries include 2 oilers, 1 repair ship, 4 transports, 4 survey and rescue, 1 training frigate and 5 tugs. There are some 70 minor auxiliaries. Amphibious forces consist of 2 ex-US landing ships (dock) and 1 tank landing ship. A further diesel submarine is being built.

Fleet Air Arm personnel only fly helicopters, the 6 S-2E Tracker anti-submarine aircraft held for carrier operations and the 20 shore-based maritime patrol EMB-111 being operated by the Air Force. Naval aircraft include 7 ASH-3 Sea King for carrier service, 5 Lynx, and 17 Esquilo for embarkation in the smaller ships. Utility and search-and-rescue duties are performed by 16 Bell 206B Sea Ranger and 6 Super Puma helicopters. Naval bases are at Rio de Janeiro, Aratu (Bahia), Belém, Natal, Rio Grande do Sul and Salvador, with river bases at Ladario and Manaus.

Active personnel, 1998, totalled 68,250, including 15,100 well-equipped Marines and 1,200 in Naval Aviation.

The Brazil navy is preparing to buy 20 McDonnell Douglas A-4 Skyhawk fighter-bombers from Kuwait for US$70m. (£43m.) as part of a long-term project to increase its ability to protect military and civilian shipping. The jets will be the Brazilian navy's first fixed-wing aircraft and will be operated from its single aircraft carrier, the Minas Gerais.

Air Force. The Air Force is organized in 6 zones, centred on Belém, Recife, Rio de Janeiro, São Paulo, Porto Alegre and Brasília. The 1a GDA (Air Defence Group) has 12 Mirage IIIE fighters and 4 Mirage IIID trainers, integrated with Roland mobile short-range surface-to-air missile systems deployed by the Army, and a radar/communications/computer network. Two fighter groups have 3 squadrons of F-5E Tiger II supersonic fighter-bombers and two-seat F-5B/Fs; 3 others operate AT-26 (Aermacchi MB 326G) Xavante light jet attack/trainers, licence-built by Embraer in Brazil, and 2 squadrons operate the AM-X fighter-bomber, jointly developed by Italy and Brazil; 79 AM-Xs are being delivered. Counter-insurgency squadrons are equipped with armed Ecureuil helicopters for liaison and observation. 2 air-sea rescue units are equipped with Bandeirantes. Equipment of transport units includes 1 squadron of C-130E/H Hercules transports; 1 squadron of Boeing 707 tanker/transports; 1 group made up of a squadron of HS 748 and a second squadron of Bandeirante turboprop transports; 2 troop-carrier groups with DHC-5 Buffaloes; 1 group with Bandeirantes; 1 group with UH-1 Iroquois and Super Puma helicopters; and 7 independent squadrons with Bandeirantes. Light aircraft for liaison duties include 30 Embraer U-7s (licence-built Piper Senecas), 30 Neiva Regente lightplanes and 7 Cessna Caravans. The VIP transport group has 2 Boeing 737s, 11 HS 125 twin-jet light transports, 4 Embraer Brasilias, 6 Embraer Xingu (VU-9) twin-turboprop pressurized transports, and Ecureuil and JetRanger helicopters. Training is performed primarily on locally built T-25 Universal and turboprop T-27 Tucano (EMB-312) basic trainers, and AT-26 Xavante armed jet basic trainers. Personnel strength (1998) 50,000 (5,000 conscripts).

INTERNATIONAL RELATIONS
Brazil is a member of the UN, OAS, LAIA and Mercosur.

ECONOMY

Policy. In 1991 a National Reconstruction Plan was introduced to promote growth and investment and reduce the role of the state. State monopolies in ports, communications and fuels were reduced and agricultural and industrial subsidies ended. A sixth economic plan was introduced in 1993 to cut spending and accelerate privatization. Since Oct. 1994 the government has authorized privatization of the energy, electricity, petrochemicals and telecommunications sectors. The programme is the largest privatization drive in the world. After an initial stage in which steel, petrochemicals, fertilizers and mining industries were privatized, the programme was headed by roads, railways, sea ports, electricity and telecommunications in 1997. During 1990–95, 22 state-owned and 19 partly state-owned companies were privatized. The Real Plan (*Plano Real*), a monetary and economic stability programme, was launched in July 1994. In Nov. 1997 the government announced a package of proposed spending cuts and tax rises worth R$20,000m. to reduce the long-standing fiscal and balance-of-payments deficits.

Revenue from privatization (US$1m.): 1991, 1·99; 1992, 3·38; 1993, 4·19; 1994, 2·32; 1995, 1·63; 1996, 4·75.

In 1997 the Asian financial crisis put the *real* under pressure, forcing up interest rates to 50%. A US$18bn. package of tax rises and spending cuts was intended to cut the budget deficit by 2·5% of GDP. Even so, Brazil's borrowing requirement had climbed from 4·5% of GDP in 1997 to 7·8% in 1998. In Nov. 1998 the IMF announced a US$41bn. financing package to help shore up the Brazilian economy.

Performance. Real GDP growth was estimated to be 1·5% in 1998, with a forecast of 3·1% in 1999. In March 1999 an IMF agreement introduced a tight monetary policy with an emphasis on reducing the ratio of debt to GDP.

Budget. 1995–96 (in R$1,000): revenue was 229,722,437 and expenditure 173,992,572. Internal federal debt, July 1996, was R$176,478m. Internal states and municipalities (main securities outstanding), R$49,672m.

Currency. The unit of currency is the *real* (equal to 100 *centavos*) which was introduced on 1 July 1994 to replace the former *cruzeiro real* at a rate of 1 real (R$1) = 2,750 cruzeiros reais (CR$2,750). The real was devalued in Sept. 1994, March 1995 and June 1995. Inflation fell from 2,500% in 1993 to 22% in 1995 and 11·1% in 1996, and was forecast to be 2·3% in 1998. In Feb. 1998 foreign exchange reserves were US$56,656m. and gold reserves 3·22m. troy oz. Total money supply in Jan. 1998 was R$45,056m.

Banking and Finance. On 31 Dec. 1964 the Banco Central do Brasil (*President*, Arminio Fraga Neto) was founded as the national bank of issue.

The Bank of Brazil (founded in 1853 and reorganized in 1906) is a state-owned commercial bank; it had 3,125 branches in 1995 throughout the republic. On 31 Dec. 1996 deposits were R$33,604m. In 1994 there were 6 public-sector banks and 24 banks controlled by state governments.

There are 9 stock exchanges of which Rio de Janeiro and São Paulo are the most important. All except São Paulo are linked in the National Electronic Trading System (Senn).

Lees, F. A. et al. (eds.) *Banking and Financial Deepening in Brazil.* London, 1990

Weights and Measures. The metric system has been compulsory since 1872.

ENERGY AND NATURAL RESOURCES

Electricity. Hydro-electric potential capacity was estimated at 255,000 MW per year in Dec. 1990, of which 41% belonged to the Amazon hydro-electric basin. Installed capacity (1995) 55,512 MW, of which 50,687 MW were hydro-electric. There is 1 nuclear power plant, supplying some 0·2% of total output. Production (1995) 260,678m. kWh (231,389m. kWh hydro-electric in 1993). Consumption per capita in 1995 was an estimated 1,572 kWh.

Oil and Gas. There are 13 oil refineries, of which 11 are state-owned. Crude oil production (1996), 45,605,631 cu. metres. In 1997 domestic production of 1m. bbls. a day met 55% of demand. The state petroleum company Petrobrás was negotiating joint ventures with up to 70 interested foreign companies to develop some of its oilfields, many off-shore. Crude oil reserves were estimated at 11,600m. bbls. in 1997.

Gas production (1996) 9,167,427,000 cu. metres. The World Bank has approved the financing for the construction of the 3,150-km Bolivia-Brazil gas pipeline, one of Latin America's biggest infrastructure projects. The cost of the project is put at around US$2bn. (£1·2bn.). The pipeline runs from the Bolivian interior across the Brazilian border at Puerto Suarez-Corumbá to the far southern port city of Porto Alegre.

Minerals. The chief minerals are bauxite, gold, iron ore, manganese, nickel, phosphates, platinum, tin and uranium. Brazil is the only source of high-grade quartz crystal in commercial quantities; output, 1992, 38,148 tonnes raw, 27,275 tonnes processed. It is a major producer of chrome ore: Output, 1992, 948,788 tonnes; reserves, 1992, 14·2m tonnes. Other minerals, with 1992 output in tonnes, are mica, 14; zirconium, 15,017; beryllium 1,412; graphite, 685,850; and magnesite, 1,161,200. Along the coasts of the states of Rio de Janeiro, Espírito Santo and Bahia are found monazite sands containing thorium: Output, 1991, 560 tonnes; estimated reserves, 1991, 772,000 tonnes. Manganese ores of high content are important: Output, 1995, 3,395,078 tonnes; estimated reserves, 1992, 81·2m tonnes. Output, 1996 (in tonnes) of bauxite, 11m. Output, 1992 (in tonnes), mineral salt, 1,230,608; tungsten ore, 28,767, unrough, 205; lead, 334,426; asbestos, 3,895,805; coal, 9,241,099. Primary aluminium production in 1989 was 888,000 tonnes. Deposits of coal exist in Rio Grande do Sul, Santa Catarina and Paraná. Total reserves were estimated at 5,190·2m. tonnes in 1988.

Iron is found chiefly in Minas Gerais, notably the Cauê Peak at Itabira. The government is opening up iron-ore deposits in Carajás, in the northern state of Pará, with estimated reserves of 35,000m. tonnes, representing a 66% concentration of high-grade iron ore. Total output of iron ore, 1996, mainly from the Vale do Rio Doce mine at Itabira, was 180m. tonnes. Brazil is the second largest producer of iron ore after China.

Production of tin ore was 20,304 tonnes in 1996; output of barytes, 1992, 72,171 tonnes, and of phosphate rock, 15·5m. tonnes.

Gold is chiefly from Pará (18,837 kg in 1992), Mato Grosso (18,009 kg) and Minas Gerais (23,120 kg); total production (1992), 80,543 kg processed. Silver output (processed in 1992) 20,042 tonnes. Diamond output in 1992 was 1,285,402 carats (157,805 carats from Minas Gerais, 1m. carats from Mato Grosso).

Agriculture. In 1996 agriculture contributed 14% of GDP. In 1995, 30·22m. people depended on agriculture, of whom 13·57m. were economically active. There were 4·86m. farms in 1995. Arable land covered 5% of the total area of the country in 1994, permanent crops just under 1% and meadows and permanent pasture 22%. 3m. ha were irrigated in 1994.

Production (in tonnes):

	1996	1997		1996	1997
Bananas			Grapes	733,585	900,979
(1,000 bunches)	561,932	595,344	Coconut		
Beans	2,822,340	2,989,637	(1,000 fruits)	1,011,705	1,015,359
Cassava	24,583,971	24,310,049	Coffee	2,685,641	2,342,635
Castor-beans	43,391	95,860	Cotton	1,011,080	835,561
Oranges			Maize	32,185,179	34,601,865
(1,000 fruits)	109,324,530	114,891,259	Soya	23,562,279	26,430,782
Potatoes	2,702,942	2,756,618	Sugar-cane	325,929,067	337,255,203
Rice	9,989,839	9,293,498	Wheat	3,359,447	2,440,863
Sisal	129,247	145,049	Cocoa	256,751	285,029
Tomatoes	2,674,833	2,602,038			

Harvested coffee area, 1996, 1,989,890 ha, principally in the states of Minas Gerais, Espírito Santo, São Paulo and Paraná. Harvested cocoa area, 1996, 683,544 ha. Bahia furnished 82% of the output in 1994. 2 crops a year are grown. Harvested castor-bean area, 1996, 121,178 ha. Tobacco output was 470,888 tonnes in 1996, grown chiefly in Rio Grande do Sul and Santa Catarina.

Rubber is produced chiefly in the states of Acre, Amazonas, Rondônia and Pará. Output, 1996 (preliminary), 53,437 tonnes (natural). Brazilian consumption of

BRAZIL

rubber in 1996 was 150,676 tonnes. Plantations of tung trees were established in 1930; output, 1995, 993 tonnes.

Livestock, 1996: Cattle, 165m.; pigs, 36·6m.; sheep, 18m.; goats (1995), 12·2m.; horses, 6·3m.; mules, 1·95m.; asses, 1·3m.; chickens (1995), 700m. Livestock slaughtered for meat in 1994 (in 1,000): Cattle, 15,512; pigs, 14,575; sheep and lambs, 763; goats, 729; poultry, 1,447,525. Livestock products, 1995: Milk, 16,474m. litres; wool, 24,959 tonnes; honey, 18,123 tonnes; hen's eggs, 18,252m.

Forestry. With forest lands covering 5,511,000 sq. km in 1995, only Russia had a larger area of forests. In 1995, 65·2% of the total land area of Brazil was under forests, down from 66·7% in 1990. In 1990 the total area under forests was 5,639,000 sq. km. The loss of 128,000 sq. km of forests between 1990 and 1995 was the biggest in any country in the world over the same period, and more than twice the area lost in Indonesia, the country with the second biggest reduction in forest area. Nevertheless, an independent study commissioned by NASA found that the rate of deforestation was on the decline and stated that the government had been extremely active since 1990 in reducing the rate of illegal deforestation.

In 1996 the government ruled that Amazonian landowners could log only 20% of their holdings, instead of 50%, as had previously been permitted. Timber production in 1995 was 285·3m. cu. metres.

In 1997 the government's environmental agency, Ibama, levied fines of nearly US$11m. on illicit loggers.

Environment. Brazil has the world's biggest river system and about a quarter of the world's primary rainforest. Current environmental issues are deforestation in the Amazon Basin, air and water pollution in Rio de Janeiro and São Paulo (the world's third-largest city), and land degradation and water pollution caused by improper mining activities. Contaminated drinking water causes 70% of child deaths.

Fisheries. The fishing industry had a 1995 catch of 800,000 tonnes (75% sea fishing and 25% inland).

INDUSTRY
The main industries are textiles, shoes, chemicals, cement, lumber, iron ore, tin, steel, aircraft, motor vehicles and parts, and other machinery and equipment. The National Iron and Steel Co. at Volta Redonda, State of Rio de Janeiro, furnishes a substantial part of Brazil's steel. Total output, 1997: crude steel, 26,154,000 tonnes. Cement output, 1997, was 38,097,000 tonnes. Output of paper, 1994, was 5,653,517 tonnes. Production of rubber tyres for motor vehicles (1994), 33,820,000 units; motor vehicles (1997), 2,058,724.

Labour. The workforce in 1997 numbered 69,331,507, of whom 16,770,675 worked in agriculture and 13,864,785 worked in industry (including the construction industry). A constitutional amendment of Oct. 1996 prohibits the employment of children under 14 years. In 1996 there was a minimum monthly wage of R$120. Unemployment was 5·7% in 1997, against 5·4% in 1996.

Trade Unions. The main union is the United Workers' Centre (CUT).

INTERNATIONAL TRADE
In 1990 Brazil repealed most of its protectionist legislation. Import tariffs on some 13,000 items were reduced in 1995. Since 1991 direct foreign investment on equal terms with domestic has been permitted. Foreign investment nearly tripled in 1996, reaching US$9,900m., much of it as a result of the privatization programme. In 1991 the government permitted an annual US$100m. of foreign debt to be converted into funds for environmental protection. Total foreign debt, 1996, US$173,900m. (the highest of any country in the world).

Imports and Exports. Imports and exports for calendar years in US$1m.:

	1994	1995	1996	1997
Imports	35,997	53,783	56,947	65,007
Exports	43,558	46,506	47,762	52,987

Estimate for 1997 trade deficit: US$783m.

BRAZIL

Principal imports in 1996 were (in US$1m.): Machinery and electrical equipment, 15,671; chemical products, 6,840; transport equipment, 5,512; crude oil, 2,576; foodstuffs, 3,459; coal and coke, 755; fertilizers, 860; cast iron and steel, 792.

Principal exports in 1996 were (in 1,000 tonnes): Soya, 3,646; iron, manganese and other ores, 987; coffee, 833; orange juice, 1,180; sugar, 5,989; tobacco, 282; cocoa beans, 33; (in US$1m.) transport equipment, 3,720; machine tools, 187.

Main export markets, 1995 (in US$1m.): USA, 8,798; Argentina, 4,041; Japan, 3,102; Netherlands, 2,918; Germany, 2,158. Main import suppliers: USA, 11,873; Argentina, 5,446; Germany, 5,139; Italy, 2,725; Japan, 2,543.

COMMUNICATIONS

Roads. There were (1994) 1,824,363 km of highways, of which 1,660,352 km were in operation. Less than 10% of roads are paved. In 1997 there were 15m. cars and 1·1m. active trucks. Some 56% of freight is carried by truck.

Rail. Public railways are operated by two administrations: the Federal Railways (RFFSA) formed in 1957, and São Paulo Railways (Fepasa) formed in 1971, which is confined to the state of São Paulo. They are in process of being privatized: all 6 branches of the RFFSA network were under private management by the end of Aug. 1997. RFFSA had a route-length of 22,069 km (65 km electrified) in 1994, and Fepasa 4,344 km (1,044 km electrified). An RFFSA subsidiary, CBTU (the Brazilian Urban Train Company), runs passenger services in some cities, while others are in the hands of the local authorities. Principal gauges are metre (24,720 km) and 1,600 mm (5,419 km). Passenger-km travelled in 1995-96 came to 14·5bn. and freight tonne-km to 136·44bn.

There are several important independent freight railways, including the Vitoria à Minas (898 km in 1993), the Ferroeste (238 km), the Carajas (opened 1985, 1,076 km in 1991) and the Amapa (194 km). There are metros in São Paulo (44 km), Rio de Janeiro (23 km), Belo Horizonte (14 km), Porto Alegre (28 km) and Brasília (38·5 km).

Civil Aviation. There are international airports at Rio de Janeiro and São Paulo (Guarulhos). The 3 main airlines are Viação Aérea Rio Grande do Sul (Varig), with 49% of the domestic market, Transbrasil and Viação Aérea São Paulo (Vasp; 38% state-owned). In 1995 scheduled airline traffic of Brazilian carriers flew 382·8m. km, carrying 19,510,000 passengers (3,703,000 on international flights). In 1998 Brazil was also served by Aeroflot, Aerolíneas Argentinas, Aeromexico, Aeroperú, Air France, Alitalia, American Airlines, Avianca, Brasil Central, British Airways, Canadian Airlines International, Continental Airlines, Cubana, Delta Air Lines, Ecuatoriana, Iberia, JAL, KLM, Korean Air, Lan-Chile, Lloyd Aéreo Boliviano, Lufthansa, MEA, Nordeste, Olympic Airways, Pluna, Rio-Sul Servicos Aereos Regionais, SABENA, SAS, South African Airways, Spanair, Swissair, TAAG, TAP, Transportes Aereos del Mercosur, Transportes Aereos Regionais, United Airlines and Yagon Airways.

Brazil's busiest airport is São Paulo (Guarulhos), which handled 12,205,872 passengers in 1996 (6·45m. in 1992), followed by Rio de Janeiro International, with 5,202,997 passengers in 1996.

Shipping. Inland waterways, mostly rivers, are open to navigation over some 43,000 km. Santos and Rio de Janeiro are the 2 leading ports; there are 19 other large ports. During 1996, 26,387 vessels entered and cleared the Brazilian ports; 336·3m. tonnes of cargo were loaded and unloaded. In 1997 Santos handled 0·85m. container units. In 1995 the merchant fleet comprised 249 vessels totalling 10·22m. DWT, representing 1·55% of the world's total fleet tonnage. 16 vessels (14·67% of tonnage) were registered under foreign flags. Total tonnage registered, 5·3m. GRT, including oil tankers, 2·12m. GRT, and container ships, 192,777 GRT.

Telecommunications. Telephone services are provided by a state-owned company and 27 federally controlled companies operating in individual states. Mobile phone services were opened to the private sector in 1996. There were 17,038,900 telephone main lines in 1997 (106·6 per 1,000 inhabitants). There were approximately 1·3m. Internet users in May 1998. Cellular phone subscribers totalled 1,286,000 in 1995 (8·2 per 1,000 inhabitants), PCs numbered 2m. (13 per 1,000 persons), and there were 200,000 fax machines.

Postal Services. In 1995 there were 10,905 post offices, equivalent to 1 for every 14,300 persons. A total of 6,009,791,111 items were handled in 1996.

SOCIAL INSTITUTIONS

Justice. There is a Supreme Federal Court of Justice at Brasília composed of 11 judges, and a Supreme Court of Justice; all judges are appointed by the President with the approval of the Senate. There are also Regional Federal Courts, Labour Courts, Electoral Courts and Military Courts. Each state organizes its own courts and judicial system in accordance with the federal Constitution.

The prison population was 0·13m. in 1996. In 1995 there were 511 prisons. In 1997 a further 55 were under construction.

Religion. In 1997 there were estimated to be 115,500,000 Roman Catholics (including syncretic Afro-Catholic cults having spiritualist beliefs and rituals) and 37,000,000 Evangelical Protestants, with 7,200,000 followers of other religions. Roman Catholic estimates in 1991 suggest that 90% were baptized Roman Catholic but only 35% were regular attenders. In 1991 there were 338 bishops and some 14,000 priests. There are numerous sects, some evangelical, some African-derived (e.g. *Candomble*).

Education. Elementary education is compulsory from 7 to 14. Adult literacy was 85·3% in 1996 (male, 85·5%; female, 85·2%). There were 50,646 literacy classes in 1993 with 1,584,147 students and 75,413 teachers. In 1996 there were 77,740 pre-primary schools with 4,270,376 pupils and 219,517 teachers; 195,767 primary schools, with 33,131,270 pupils and 1,388,247 teachers; 15,213 secondary schools, with 5,739,077 pupils and 326,827 teachers; and 851 higher education institutions, with 1,661,034 students and 141,482 teachers.

The tertiary education sector includes 114 universities (53 private, 37 federal, 20 state and 4 municipal), 85 private and 3 municipal college faculty federations, and 671 other higher education institutions (514 private, 80 municipal, 57 state and 20 federal).

Extensive education reforms are under way to increase the average length of schooling, which in 1997 was 5½ years.

In 1995 total expenditure on education came to 5·2% of GNP.

Health. In 1992 there were 49,676 hospitals and clinics (22,584 private), of which 7,430 were for in-patients (5,316 private). In 1993 there were 222,658 doctors, 160,000 dentists and (1992) 57,047 pharmacists.

CULTURE

Broadcasting. In 1995 there were 2,033 radio and 119 television stations (colour by PAL). In 1996 there were 70m. radio and 36m. television receivers.

Cinema. There were 3,737 cinemas in 1988.

Press. Daily sale of newspapers in 1996 was 6·5m.

Tourism. In 1996, 1,991,416 tourists visited Brazil. 657,942 were Argentinian, 224,577 US citizens, 200,423 Uruguayan, 102,106 German, 90,716 Paraguayan, 84,001 Italian, 63,900 Chilean, 59,502 Spanish, 55,257 French, 52,183 Portuguese, 38,520 UK citizens, 33,505 Swiss and 30,219 Japanese. Receipts totalled US$2·47bn.

Festivals. New Year's Eve in Rio de Janeiro is always marked with special celebrations, with a major fireworks display over the bay at Copacabana Beach. On 31 Dec. 1999 there are proposals for a spectacular laser show too. Immediately afterwards, preparations start for Carnival, which in 2000 will be held in the week leading up to 5 March, when the parade of samba schools take place.

Libraries. In 1993 Brazil had a National Library with 5·28m. volumes, and in 1994 a total of 2,739 public libraries.

DIPLOMATIC REPRESENTATIVES

Of Brazil in Great Britain (32 Green St., London, W1Y 4AT)
Ambassador: Rubens Antonio Barbosa.

Of Great Britain in Brazil (Setor De Embaixadas Sul, Quadro 801, Conjunto K, CP70.408-900, Brasília, DF *or* Av. das Nações, CP07-0586, 70.359, Brasília, DF)
Ambassador: Donald Keith Haskell, CMG, CVO.

Of Brazil in the USA (3006 Massachusetts Ave., NW, Washington, D.C., 20008)
Ambassador: Paulo-Tarso Flecha de Lima.

Of the USA in Brazil (Av. das Nações, Lote 03, Quadra 801, CEP: 70403-900, Brasília, D.F.)
Ambassador: Vacant.

Of Brazil to the United Nations
Ambassador: Celso L. N. Amdriim.

Of Brazil to the European Union
Ambassador: Jório Dauster Magalhães e Silva.

FURTHER READING

Instituto Brasileiro de Geografia e Estatística. *Anuário Estatístico do Brasil.—Censo Demográfico de 1991.—Indicadores IBGE*. Monthly
Boletim do Banco Central do Brasil. Banco Central do Brasil. Brasília. Monthly
Baer, W., *The Brazilian Economy: Growth and Development*. 4th ed. New York, 1995
Burns, E. B., *A History of Brazil*. 2nd ed. Columbia Univ. Press, 1980
Dickenson, John, *Brazil*. [Bibliography] Oxford and Santa Barbara (CA), 1997
Eakin, Marshall C., *Brazil: The Once and Future Country*. New York, 1997
Falk, P. S. and Fleischer, D. V., *Brazil's Economic and Political Future*. Boulder (CO), 1988
Font, M. A., *Coffee, Contention and Change in the Making of Modern Brazil*. Oxford, 1990
Guirmaraes, R. P., *Politics and Environment in Brazil: Ecopolitics of Development in the Third World*. New York, 1991
Mainwaring, S., *The Catholic Church and Politics in Brazil, 1916–86*. Stanford Univ. Press, 1986
Stepan, A. (ed.) *Democratizing Brazil: Problems of Transition and Consolidation*. OUP, 1993
Welch, J. H., *Capital Markets in the Development Process: the Case of Brazil*. London, 1992

For other more specialized titles see under CONSTITUTION AND GOVERNMENT *and* BANKING AND FINANCE, *above*.

National library: Biblioteca Nacional, Avenida Rio Branco 21939, Rio de Janeiro, RJ.
National statistical office: Instituto Brasileiro de Geografia e Estatística (IBGE), Rua General Canabarro 666, 20.271-201 Maracanã, Rio de Janeiro, RJ.
Website: http:/www.ibge.gov.br/

BRUNEI

Negara Brunei Darussalam—
State of Brunei Darussalam

Capital: Bandar Seri Begawan
Population estimate, 2000: 326,000
Estimated GDP: $4·6bn.
HDI/world rank: 0·889/35

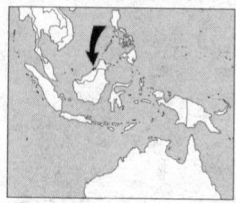

KEY HISTORICAL EVENTS

Situated on the northern coast of Borneo, Brunei was trading with China during the 6th century, and through allegiance to the Javanese Majapahit Kingdom in the 13th-15th centuries, it came under Hindu influence. In the early 15th century, with the decline of the Majapahit Kingdom and widespread conversion to Islam, Brunei became an independent Sultanate.

When Magellan anchored his ships off Brunei in 1521, Bolkiah (the fifth Sultan) controlled most of Borneo, its neighbouring islands and the Suhi Archipelago. By the end of the 16th century, however, the power of Brunei was on the wane. Cessions were made to Great Britain, the Rajah of Sarawak and the British North Borneo Company until by the middle of the 19th century the State had been reduced to its present limits.

Brunei became a British protectorate in 1888 and in 1906 accepted a British Resident, who exercised control over all matters except the Islamic faith and Malay custom. The discovery of major oilfields in the western end of the State in the 1920s brought economic stability to Brunei and created a new style of life for the population. Brunei was occupied by the Japanese in 1941 and liberated by the Australians in 1945.

Self-government was introduced in 1959 but Britain retained responsibility for foreign affairs. In 1962 an attempt was made by a section of the community to overthrow the Sultan, Sir Omar Ali Saifuddin. In 1965 constitutional changes were made which led to direct elections for a new Legislative Council. In 1967 Sultan Sir Omar Ali Saifuddin abdicated in favour of his eldest son, Sultan Sir Muda Hassanal Bolkiah, who was crowned in 1968.

The sultan negotiated a new treaty with the British in 1979, and full independence and sovereignty was gained on 1 Jan. 1984.

TERRITORY AND POPULATION

Brunei, on the coast of Borneo, is bounded in the north-west by the South China Sea and on all other sides by Sarawak (Malaysia), which splits it into two parts, the smaller portion forming the Temburong district. Area, 2,226 sq. miles (5,765 sq. km). Population (1991 census) 260,482; 1996 estimate, 299,900, giving a density of 52 per sq. km.

The UN gives a projected population for 2000 of 326,000.

In 1995 an estimated 69·2% of the population lived in urban areas. The 4 districts are Brunei/Muara (1993: 181,600), Belait (56,000), Tutong (30,700), Temburong (about 8,000). The capital is Bandar Seri Begawan (census 1991: 45,867); other large towns are Seria (1991: 21,082) and Kuala Belait (21,163). Ethnic groups include Malays 64%, and Chinese, 20%.

The official language is Malay but English is in use.

SOCIAL STATISTICS

1996 births, 7,600; deaths, 1,500. Rates, 1996: Birth per 1,000 population, 25·5; death, 5·1. There were 1,874 marriages in 1993. Life expectancy in 1996: Males, 69·8 years; females, 73·1. Annual growth rate, 1990–95, 2·4%. Infant mortality, 1990–95, 9 per 1,000 live births; fertility rate, 3·0 children per woman.

CLIMATE

The climate is tropical marine, hot and moist, but nights are cool. Humidity is high and rainfall heavy, varying from 100" (2,500 mm) on the coast to 200" (5,000 mm) inland. There is no dry season. Bandar Seri Begawan, Jan. 80°F (26·7°C), July 82°F (27·8°C). Annual rainfall 131" (3,275 mm).

CONSTITUTION AND GOVERNMENT
The Sultan and Yang Di Pertuan of Brunei Darussalam is HM Paduka Seri Baginda Sultan Haji Hassanal Bolkiah Mu'izzadin Waddaulah. He succeeded on 5 Oct. 1967 at his father's abdication and was crowned on 1 Aug. 1968. On 10 Aug. 1998 *his* son, Oxford-graduate Prince Al-Muhtadee Billah, was inaugurated as Crown Prince and heir apparent.

On 29 Sept. 1959 the Sultan promulgated a Constitution, but parts of it have been in abeyance since Dec. 1962. There is no legislature and supreme power is vested in the Sultan.

National Anthem. 'Ya Allah, lanjutkan lah usia' ('O God, long live His Majesty'); words by P. Rahim, tune by I. Sagap.

CURRENT ADMINISTRATION
The Council of Ministers was composed as follows in March 1999:
   Prime Minister, Minister of Defence and of Finance: The Sultan.
   Foreign Affairs: Prince Haji Mohammad Bolkiah. *Home Affairs:* Pehin Dato Haji Isa bin Ibrahim. *Education, Health (Acting):* Pehin Dato Haji Abdul Aziz bin Umar. *Industry and Primary Resources:* Pehin Dato Haji Abdul Rahman bin Mohammad Taib. *Religious Affairs:* Pehin Dato Dr Haji Mohammad Zain bin Serudin. *Development:* Pengiran Dato Dr Haji Ismail bin Damit. *Culture, Youth and Sports:* Pehin Dato Haji Hussain bin Mohammad Yusof. *Communications:* Dato Haji Zakaria bin Sulaiman.

DEFENCE
In 1997 military expenditure totalled US$353m. (US$1,141 per capita).

Army. The armed forces are known as the Task Force and contain the naval and air elements. Only Malays are eligible for service. Strength (1997) 3,900. Military units include 3 infantry battalions, 1 armoured reconnaissance squadron, 1 engineer squadron, 1 special forces squadron and 1 surface-to-air missile battalion. Equipment includes 16 Scorpion light tanks.

There is a paramilitary Gurkha reserve unit 2,300-strong.

Navy. The Royal Brunei Armed Forces Flotilla comprises 3 fast missile-armed attack craft of 200 tonnes and 3 coastal patrol boats. There are also 2 landing craft, 2 utility craft and 3 small patrol boats. The River Division operates 24 fast-assault boats. Personnel in 1996 numbered 700.

3 coastal patrol craft operate with 7 smaller boats for the Marine Police.

Air Wing. The Air Wing of the Royal Brunei Armed Forces was formed in 1965. Current equipment includes 6 MBB BO 105, 2 Bell 206B JetRanger, 1 Bell 214, 1 S-70 Black Hawk and 11 Bell 212 helicopters, and 2 SF.260M piston-engined trainers. Personnel (1996), 400.

INTERNATIONAL RELATIONS
Brunei is a member of the UN, the Commonwealth, APEC and ASEAN.

ECONOMY
The fall in oil prices in 1997-98 led to the setting up of an Economic Council to advise the Sultan on reforms. An investigation was mounted into the affairs of the Amedeo Corporation, Brunei's largest private company run by Prince Jefri, the Sultan's brother.

Performance. Real GDP growth was 1·8% in 1995 and 1994.

Budget. Revenues in 1995 were an estimated US$2·5bn. and expenditure US$2·6bn.

Currency. The unit of currency is the *Brunei dollar* (BND) *of 100 cents*, which is at parity with the Singapore dollar (also legal tender).

Banking and Finance. The Brunei Currency Board is the note-issuing monetary authority. In 1993 there were 7 banks (1 incorporated in Brunei), with a total of 33 branches. Savings deposits totalled B$999·3m. in 1993 and fixed time deposits B$1,935·4m. Total bank assets in 1993 were B$6,567·7m.

ENERGY AND NATURAL RESOURCES

Electricity. Installed capacity was 344,000 kW in 1995. Production in 1995 was 1·56bn. kWh. Consumption per capita was an estimated 4,003 kWh in 1995.

Oil and Gas. The Seria oilfield, discovered in 1929, has passed its peak production. The high level of crude oil production is maintained through the increase of offshore oilfields production. There were 735 producing wells at 31 Dec. 1993. Production was 8·85m. tonnes in 1992. The crude oil is exported directly, and only a small amount is refined at Seria for domestic uses.

Natural gas is produced (9,789m. cu. metres in 1993) at one of the largest liquefied natural gas plants in the world and is exported to Japan.

Agriculture. In 1994 there were 3,000 ha of arable land, 4,000 ha of permanent crops and 6,000 ha of permanent pasture. The main crops produced in 1994 were (estimates) rice (1,000 tonnes), vegetables (8,000 tonnes), cassava (1,000 tonnes) and fruit (5,000 tonnes).

Livestock in 1996: Cattle, 2,000; pigs, 4,000; buffaloes, 5,000 (1995); chickens, 3m. (1995).

Forestry. Forests covered 448,000 ha, or 82·4% of the total land area, in 1995 (down from 85% in 1990). Most of the interior is under forest, containing large potential supplies of serviceable timber. Timber production in 1995 was 295,000 cu. metres.

Fisheries. The 1995 catch totalled 4,812 tonnes, of which 4,786 tonnes were from marine waters.

INDUSTRY

Brunei depends primarily on its oil industry. Other minor products are rubber, pepper, sawn timber, gravel and animal hides. Local industries include boatbuilding, cloth weaving and the manufacture of brass- and silverware.

Labour. The labour force totalled 131,000 in 1996 (66% males).

INTERNATIONAL TRADE

Imports and Exports. In 1995 (and 1994) imports totalled US$1,915m. (US$1,695m.); exports US$2,273m. (US$2,296m.). Crude oil accounts for approximately 48% of revenue from exports, and liquefied natural gas 43%. In 1994 Singapore supplied 29% of imports, the UK 19% and the USA 13%. Japan took 50% of all exports.

COMMUNICATIONS

Roads. There were in 1996 approximately 1,150 km of roads, of which 400 km are surfaced. The main road connects Bandar Seri Begawan with Kuala Belait and Seria. In 1996 there were 149,738 private cars, 15,797 vans and trucks, and 4,366 road tractors. There were 65 fatalities in road accidents in 1996.

Civil Aviation. Brunei International Airport serves 0·8m. passengers annually. The national carrier is the state-owned Royal Brunei Airlines (RBA). In 1998 RBA operated services to Abu Dhabi, Balikpapan, Bangkok, Beijing, Brisbane, Calcutta, Darwin, Denpasar Bali, Dubai, Frankfurt, Hong Kong, Jakarta, Jeddah, Kota Kinabalu, Kuala Lumpur, Kuching, Labuan, London, Manila, Miri, Mulu, Osaka, Perth, Singapore, Surabaya and Taipei. Other airlines operating to Brunei in 1998 were Bouraq Indonesia, Lufthansa, Malaysia Airlines, Philippine Airlines, Singapore Airlines and Thai Airways International. In 1995 RBA flew 22·1m. km, carrying 916,200 passengers (all on international flights).

Shipping. Regular shipping services operate from Singapore, Hong Kong, Sarawak and Sabah to Bandar Seri Begawan, and there is a daily passenger ferry between Bandar Seri Begawan and Labuan. 97 sea-going vessels were licensed in 1993. In 1995, merchant shipping totalled 366,000 GRT.

Telecommunications. There is a telephone network (78,800 telephone main lines in 1996) linking the main centres. In 1996 there were 36,000 cellular phone subscribers (126 per 1,000 persons), 8,000 PCs and 2,000 fax machines.

Postal Services. There were 17 post offices in 1993.

SOCIAL INSTITUTIONS

Justice. The Supreme Court comprises a High Court and a Court of Appeal and the Magistrates' Courts. The High Court receives appeals from subordinate courts in the districts and is itself a court of first instance for criminal and civil cases. The Judicial Committee of the Privy Council in London is the final court of appeal. Shariah Courts deal with Islamic law. 25,310 crimes were reported in 1993.

The Royal Brunei Police numbers 1,750 officers and men (1997). In addition, there are 500 additional police officers mostly employed on static guard duties.

Religion. The official religion is Islam. In 1991, 67% of the population were Moslem (mostly Malays), 13% Buddhists and 10% Christian.

Education. The government provides free education to all citizens from pre-school up to the highest level at local and overseas universities and institutions. In 1994 there were 165 kindergartens and schools, with 10,717 children and 506 teachers in kindergartens. In 1994 there were 158 primary schools with 42,270 pupils and 2,772 teachers. There were 2,413 teachers in secondary schools for 28,851 pupils. In 1993 there were 7 technical and vocational colleges with 1,593 students and 371 teachers, and a teacher training college with 418 students and 28 teachers.

In 1993 the University of Brunei Darussalam (founded 1985) had 1,138 students and 207 teachers. An institute of advanced education had 310 students and 71 teachers.

Adult literacy rate, 1995, 88·2% (male, 92·6%; female, 83·4%).

Health. Medical and health services are free to citizens and those in government service and their dependants. Citizens are sent overseas, at government expense, for medical care not available in Brunei. Flying medical services are provided to remote areas. In 1995 there were 10 hospitals; there were 251 doctors, 38 dentists, 15 pharmacists, 278 midwives and 1,228 nursing personnel.

CULTURE

Broadcasting. Radio Television Brunei operates on medium- and shortwaves in Malay, English, Chinese and Nepali. Number of receivers (1995): Radio 80,000 and television 70,000 (colour by PAL).

Press. In 1995 there was 1 local newspaper with a circulation of 20,000.

Tourism. In 1996 there were 837,000 foreign tourists. Receipts totalled US$38m.

DIPLOMATIC REPRESENTATIVES
Of Brunei in Great Britain (19/20 Belgrave Sq., London, SW1X 8PG)
High Commissioner: Pehin Dato Jaya Abdul Latif.

Of Great Britain in Brunei (2/01 2nd Flr. Block D, Komplexs Bangunan Yayasan, Sultan Haji Hassanal Bolkiah, Jalan Pretty, Bandar Seri Begawan 1921)
High Commissioner: Mr. S. Laing.

Of Brunei in the USA (2600 Virginia Ave., NW, Washington, D.C., 20037)
Ambassador: Pengiran Anak Dato Puteh.

Of the USA in Brunei (3rd Floor, Teck Guan Plaza, Jalan Sultan, Bandar Seri Begawan 2085)
Ambassador: Glen R. Rase.

Of Brunei to the United Nations
Ambassador: Jemat Haji Ampal.

Of Brunei to the European Union
Ambassador: D. S. L. Jasa Awang Mohd Daud.

BRUNEI

FURTHER READING

Ministry of Finance Statistics Department. *Brunei Darussalam Statistical Yearbook.*
Cleary, M. and Wong, S. Y., *Oil, Economic Development and Diversification in Brunei.* London, 1994
Horton, A. V. M., *A Critical Guide to Source Material Relating to Brunei with Special Reference to the British Residential Era, 1906-1959.* Bordesley, 1995
Krausse, S. C. E. and G. H., *Brunei.* [Bibliography] Oxford and Santa Barbara (CA), 1988
Saunders, G., *History of Brunei.* OUP, 1996

National statistical office: Ministry of Finance Statistics Department.

BULGARIA

Republika Bulgaria

Capital: Sofia
Population estimate, 2000: 8·31m.
GNP per capita: (PPP$) 4,280
HDI/world rank: 0·789/67

KEY HISTORICAL EVENTS

The Bulgarians take their name from an invading Asiatic horde (Bulgars) and their language from the Slav population, with whom they merged after 680. From 681 to 1018 and 1185 to 1389 the Bulgarians carved out empires against a background of conflict with Byzantium and Serbia, establishing a civilization of which the Orthodox missionaries Cyril and Methodius, credited with the invention of the Slavonic alphabet, are noteworthy exemplars.

After the Serb-Bulgarian defeat at Kosovo in 1389 Bulgaria finally succumbed to Ottoman encroachment. The Bulgar landowners were replaced by military and civil officials who held land in return for state service. The Ottoman empire's decline, however, engendered corruption and exactions, uprisings and reprisals.

The 1876 rebellion met with brutal repression which provoked great power intervention. Russia invaded Turkey in 1877 and imposed the Treaty of San Stefano (March 1878) which established a 'big Bulgaria' extending into Macedonia and Thrace. Conceiving this as a threat to the balance of power, Britain and Austria-Hungary pressurized Russia into revising these boundaries by the Treaty of Berlin (July 1878): Macedonia and Thrace reverted to Turkey, Eastern Rumelia became semi-autonomous and Bulgaria proper became a principality under Turkish suzerainty.

Under the Treaty, a constituent assembly at Turnovo voted a liberal constitution which provided for a single-chamber parliament elected by male suffrage. The throne was offered to the German Prince Alexander of Battenberg. In 1885 Eastern Rumelia was united to Bulgaria by a *coup d'état.* Alexander accepted the unification against the wishes of Russia, who forced his abdication in 1886. He was replaced by Ferdinand of Saxe-Coburg-Gotha, who did not gain Russian recognition until 1896. Prime Minister Stefan Stambolov achieved a period of prosperity but Ferdinand engineered his resignation in 1894, and thenceforth ruled personally through manipulation of the political parties.

After Austria annexed Bosnia in 1908, Bulgaria declared itself independent. To block Austrian expansion into the Balkans, Russia encouraged Greece, Serbia, Montenegro and Bulgaria to form a Balkan League in 1912. The League successfully attacked Turkey (First Balkan War, 1912), but in the dispute which followed over the territorial spoils (principally in Macedonia) Bulgaria failed to secure her claims against her formal allies by force (Second Balkan War, 1913). Territorial aspirations led Bulgaria to join the First World War on the German side in Oct. 1915 and the peace settlement (Neuilly, 1919) left her with little gained.

Economic decline caused by the war produced social unrest. Ferdinand was forced to abdicate in favour of his son, Boris III, in Oct. 1918, and the radical Agrarian Party took office, headed by Alexander Stamboliiski. The latter's reformism, friendship with Yugoslavia (a contender for Macedonia) and high-handed behaviour generated various currents of opposition and he was assassinated after a *coup* in June 1923. The Communist Party launched an abortive rising in Sept. 1923, and bombed Sofia cathedral in April 1925, killing 120 people. This led to a reign of government terror against all radicals. Bedevilled by Macedonian terrorism and the effects of the world economic depression, parliamentary government was ended by a military *coup* in May 1934. In 1935 Boris established a royal dictatorship under which political parties were banned. Boris died in 1943 and was succeeded by a regency.

Increasingly drawn into the German economic orbit, and in pursuit of the San Stefano territories, Bulgaria joined the Nazis against Britain in March 1941, but retained diplomatic relations with the Soviet Union. In Sept. 1944 the Soviet Union declared war and sent its troops across the frontiers. Wartime opposition to the government had centred round the Communist-dominated Fatherland Front, which formed a government on 9 Sept. A referendum abolished the monarchy and a people's republic was proclaimed in Sept.1946. In 1947 the Soviet-type 'Dimitrov' constitution replaced the Turnovo constitution of 1879. Georgi Dimitrov, a veteran Communist leader who had secured acquittal from a Nazi court after charges of complicity in the arson of the Reichstag, was Prime Minister until his death in 1949. The 'Titoist' purges of late Stalinism were presided over by Vulko Chervenkov, but he was soon eclipsed by Todor Zhivkov, who became leader of the BCP in 1954 and Prime Minister in 1962.

In May 1971 a new constitution led to Zhivkov's election as first President of the newly formed State Council. He was re-elected in 1976, 1981 and 1986. When demonstrations in Sofia in Nov. 1989, occasioned by the Helsinki Agreement ecological conference, broadened into demands for political reform, Todor Zhivkov was replaced as Communist Party leader and head of state by the foreign minister Petur Mladenov. In Dec. the National Assembly approved 21 measures of constitutional reform, including the abolition of the Communist Party's sole right to govern. The government was succeeded in Feb. 1990 by the Communist government of Andrei Lukanov. Attempts at economic reform led to demonstrations and a general strike. Lukanov's government was replaced by a caretaker government in Nov. 1990. A new constitution and fresh elections produced a non-Communist government in Oct. 1991 but strikes and unrest continued, while political divisions virtually paralyzed government. Elections in Dec. 1994 were won by an alliance led by Zhan Videnov, a former Communist-turned-Socialist, who failed to deliver on his promise of painless reform. In 1996 Petar Stoyanov was elected as an anti-Communist pro-reform President. In the election the following April the anti-Communist Union of Democratic Forces (UDF) coalition, led by Ivan Kostov and Alexander Bozhkov, swept back to power.

TERRITORY AND POPULATION
The area of Bulgaria is 110,993 sq. km (42,855 sq. miles). It is bounded in the north by Romania, east by the Black Sea, south by Turkey and Greece, and west by Yugoslavia and the Republic of Macedonia. The country is divided into 9 regions.

Area and population in 1996:

Region	Area (sq. km)	Pop. (1,000)	Region	Area (sq. km)	Pop. (1,000)
Bourgas	14,724	847	Rousse	10,843	760
Haskovo	13,824	889	Sofia (city)	1,311	1,192
Lovech	15,150	990	Sofia (region)	19,021	967
Montana	10,607	616	Varna	11,929	901
Plovdiv	13,585	1,214			

The capital, Sofia, has regional status.

The population of Bulgaria at the census of 1992 was 8,472,724 (females, 4,515,936); population density 76·3 per sq. km.

The UN gives a projected population for 2000 of 8·31m.

Population of principal towns (1996 estimate): Sofia, 1,141,712; Plovdiv, 344,326; Varna, 301,421; Bourgas, 199,470; Rousse, 168,051; Stara Zagora, 151,218; Pleven, 127,945; Sliven, 107,267; Dobrich, 104,074; Shumen, 97,126; Pernik, 90,460; Yambol, 90,239; Pazardzhik, 82,295; Khaskovo, 80,972; Vratsa, 77,069; Gabrovo, 75,220.

Ethnic groups at the 1992 census: Bulgarians, 7,271,185; Turks, 800,052; Gypsies, 313,396.

Bulgarian is the official language.

SOCIAL STATISTICS
1996: Live births, 72,743; deaths, 117,056. Rates per 1,000 population, 1996: Birth, 8·6; death, 14·0; marriage, 4·3; infant deaths, 15·6; growth per 1,000 live births, –5·4. Abortions, 1996, 93,540, of which 9,389 were spontaneous. In 1994 the most popular age range for marrying was 20–24 for both males and females. Expectation of life in 1996 was 70·6 years (males, 67·1; females, 74·9). Fertility rate, 1990–95, 1·5 children per woman.

BULGARIA

CLIMATE
The southern parts have a Mediterranean climate, with winters mild and moist and summers hot and dry, but further north the conditions become more Continental, with a larger range of temperature and greater amounts of rainfall in summer and early autumn. Sofia, Jan. 28°F (−2·2°C), July 69°F (20·6°C). Annual rainfall 25·4" (635 mm).

CONSTITUTION AND GOVERNMENT
A new constitution was adopted at Turnovo in July 1991. The *President* is directly elected for not more than two 5-year terms. Candidates for the presidency must be at least 40 years old and have lived for the last 5 years in Bulgaria. American-style primary elections were introduced in 1996; voting is open to all the electorate.

The 240-member *National Assembly* is directly elected by proportional representation. The President nominates a candidate from the largest parliamentary party as Prime Minister.

National Anthem. 'Gorda stara planina' ('Proud and ancient mountains'); words and tune by T. Radoslavov.

RECENT ELECTIONS
A primary was held on 11 June 1996 for the opposition presidential candidate; turn-out was 12%. There were 2 candidates. Presidential elections were held in 2 rounds on 27 Oct. and 3 Nov. 1996. Petar Stoyanov won the first round against 12 opponents with 44·1% of votes cast; turn-out was 62·7%. He also won the run-off round with 59·7% of votes cast; turn-out was 61·5%.

At the elections of 19 April 1997 a United Democratic Forces coalition was elected, obtaining 137 seats with 52·26% of votes cast; the BSP, 58 with 22·07%; the Union of National Salvation (a coalition of the Turkish Movement for Rights and Freedom and monarchists), 19 with 8%; Euroleft, 14 with 6%; the Bulgarian Business Bloc, 12 with 5%. On 14 May 1997 Ivan Kostov (UDF) became Prime Minister.

CURRENT ADMINISTRATION
President: Petar Stoyanov (b. 1948; Union of Democratic Forces; sworn in 19 Jan. 1997).

Vice-President: Todor Kavaldjiev.

In March 1999 the government comprised:

Prime Minister: Ivan Kostov.

Deputy Prime Ministers: Aleksandur Bozhkov, Evgeniy Bakurdzhiev, Veselin Metodiev.

Minister of Agriculture, Forests and Agrarian Reform: Ventsislav Vurbanov. *Culture:* Ema Moskova. *Defence:* Georgi Ananiev. *Education and Science:* Veselin Metodiev. *Environment and Water:* Evdokiya Maneva. *Finance:* Muravey Radev. *Foreign Affairs:* Nadezhda Mikhaylova. *Health:* Dr Petur Boyadzhiev. *Industry:* Aleksandur Bozhkov. *Interior:* Bogomil Bonev. *Justice and Legal Euro-Integration:* Vasil Gotsev. *Labour and Social Policy:* Ivan Neykov. *Regional Development and Urbanization:* Evgeniy Bakurdzhiev. *State Administration:* Mario Tagarinski. *Trade and Tourism:* Valentin Vasilev. *Transportation:* Wilhelm Kraus.

The *Speaker* is Iordan Sokolov (UDF).

Local Government. Local authorities for the 9 regions and 278 districts within them are elected for 30 months. Elections were held for mayors and councillors on 29 Oct. and 12 Nov. 1995. Turn-out was 54·7% for the former and 53·1% for the latter. A large majority of mayorships were won by the BSP and its allies. In the elections for councillors, the BSP and its allies won 41% of votes cast, the UDF 24·1%, the PU 12·3%, the Movement for Rights and Freedom 8·2% and the Bulgarian Business Bloc 5%.

DEFENCE
Conscription was reduced from 18 to 12 months in 1992.

Defence expenditure in 1997 totalled US$339m. (US$41 per capita), representing 3·4% of GDP. In 1985 the total had been US$2,331m., equivalent to US$276 per capita and representing 14·0% of GDP.

Army. There are 3 military districts based on Sofia, Plovdiv and Sliven. In 1997 the Army had a strength of 51,600, including 33,300 conscripts, and is organized in 4 tank, 1 mechanized, 1 surface-to-air missile and 1 airborne brigade, 3 motor rifle divisions and 3 artillery, 3 anti-tank, 1 surface-to-air missile and 3 air defence brigades. Equipment includes 177 T-34, 1,276 T-55 and 333 T-72 main battle tanks. There are 12 regiments of border guards numbering 12,000.

Navy. The Navy, all ex-Soviet or Soviet-built, comprises 2 'Romeo' class old diesel submarines, 1 Koni class small frigate, 4 'Poti', 1 'Tarantul' and 2 'Pauk' class corvettes, 6 'Osa' class missile craft, 10 patrol vessels, 4 coastal and 16 inshore minesweepers. There are 2 medium landing ships and 20 craft. Major auxiliaries include 2 oilers, 2 research ships, 1 electronic intelligence gatherer, 2 training ships and 1 tug. There are some 20 minor auxiliaries and service craft. There are 2 regiments of coastal artillery including some missile-armed, and some 10 shore-based Ka-25 and Mi-14 helicopters. The naval headquarters is at Varna, and there are bases at Atiya and at Vidin on the Danube. Personnel in 1996 totalled 6,000.

Air Force. The Air Force had (1996) 20,100 personnel (16,000 conscripts). There are 3 wings of MiG-21/23/29 interceptors; 3 wings of fighter/ground attack MiG-23s and Su-20/25s; 1 regiment of Mi-24 helicopter gunships; a total of about 20 Tu-134, L-410, An-2 and An-24/26 transport aircraft; some 45 Mi-2 and Mi-8/17 helicopters; and Yak-18T, L-29 Delfin and L-39 Albatros trainers. Soviet-built 'Guideline', 'Goa' and 'Ganef' surface-to-air missiles have also been supplied to Bulgaria.

INTERNATIONAL RELATIONS

Talks began with international financial institutions in Feb. 1998 on the question of a 3-year recovery and restructuring programme, and in Oct. 1998 the International Monetary Fund approved a US$850m. loan to help cover the balance of payments deficit and support market reforms.

Bulgaria is a member of the UN, the Council of Europe, the Central European Initiative and the NATO Partnership for Peace, and is an Associate Member of the EU and an Associate Partner of the WEU.

ECONOMY

Policy. At the beginning of 1992, 95% of enterprises were still in state ownership. A plan to privatize a further 500 large and medium-sized firms was introduced in 1993. Mining, energy, oil processing, railways and munitions production remain in state hands. A law of April 1992 allocates 10% of the proceeds of privatization to agricultural development, 20% to the compensation of former owners, 30% to social funds and 40% to local management councils to cover irrecoverable debts. A Centre for Mass Privatization was set up in 1994 to supervise a new stage of privatization in an attempt to speed it up.

Privatized firms enjoy a 5-year tax exemption. 67 loss-making public enterprises were wound up in 1996.

Performance. In 1996 GDP was 1,660,237m. leva. Real GDP growth in 1997 was −7·5% (−10·7% in 1996), but was estimated to be 4·5% in 1998. In 1997–98 the country pulled itself back from the abyss of economic and financial disaster. Its success in stabilizing the economy, in the wake of the collapse of the banking system and the lurch into hyperinflation in early 1997, has exceeded most expectations.

Budget. The fiscal year is the calendar year. In 1998 budget revenue was envisaged at 4,416,000m. leva, and expenditure at 5,411,000m. leva. VAT was first introduced in 1995. In 1996 there was an increase in VAT from 18% to 22%. The current account deficit was estimated to be US$−161m. in 1998.

Currency. The unit of currency is the *lev* (BGL) of 100 *stotinki*. Foreign exchange reserves were estimated to be US$2·65bn. in 1998. Gold reserves were 36·5m. tonnes. Runaway inflation (123·0% in 1996 rising to 1,082·6% in 1997) forced the closure of 14 banks in 1996. However, by the end of 1998 it was forecast to drop to

BULGARIA

9%. In June 1997 the new government introduced a currency board financial system which stabilized the lev and renewed economic growth. Under it, the lev is pegged to the German mark at DM1 = 1,000 leva. In May 1996 the lev was devalued by 68%.

Banking and Finance. The National Bank (*Governor*, Svetoslav Gavriiski, b. 1948) is the central bank and bank of issue. There is a commercial bank, Bulbank (founded 1964) and a State Savings Bank, the latter serving local enterprises as well as the public. In 1996, there were savings accounts totalling 81,606m. leva. There were 41 commercial banks in 1996.

There is a stock exchange in Sofia.

Weights and Measures. The metric system is in general use. On 1 April 1916 the Gregorian calendar came into force.

ENERGY AND NATURAL RESOURCES

Electricity. Bulgaria has little oil, gas or high-grade coal, and energy policy is based on the exploitation of its low-grade coal and hydro-electric resources. But the country is a major distribution centre for energy in the Black Sea region, a fact underlined by the 1997 deal with Russia which guarantees gas supplies to Bulgaria, while clearing the way for the construction of a transit gas pipeline between Russia and western Turkey. There is 1 nuclear power station. Installed capacity was 12·09m. kW in 1994. Output, 1996, 42,710m. kWh (thermal, 21,714m. kWh; nuclear, 18,082m. kWh; hydro-electric, 2,914m. kWh). Consumption per capita: 4,491 kWh (1995 est.)

Oil and Gas. Oil is extracted in the Balchik district on the Black Sea, in an area 100 km north of Varna, and at Dolni Dubnik near Pleven. There are refineries at Bourgas (annual capacity 5m. tonnes) and Dolni Dubnik (7m. tonnes). Crude oil production (1996) was 32,000 tonnes; gas, 18·75m. cu. metres.

Minerals. Production in 1996: Manganese ore, 13,100 tonnes; iron ore, 282,000 tonnes; lignite, 28·10m. tonnes; brown coal, 3·06m. tonnes; hard coal, 31·30m. tonnes.

Agriculture. Agriculture accounted for around 23·4% of GDP in 1997. Agricultural land covered 6,164,000 ha in 1996, of which 4,693,000 ha were arable. In 1996 sown area was 2,902,000 ha; there were 277,000 ha of meadows and 1,471,000 ha of commons and pastures. By 1999, 60% of Bulgarian households worked a plot of land, often on a part-time basis.

Legislation of 1991 and 1992 provided for the redistribution of collectivized land to its former owners up to 30 ha. Landless peasants received state land or compensation in lieu. Bulgarians resident abroad may acquire such land, as may legal bodies with up to 50% foreign ownership. It may be rented out, but not sold for 3 years. There were 2,073 agricultural collectives and firms in 1992; and 2,435 private farms in 1996.

Production in 1996 (in 1,000 tonnes, with percentage from private holdings): Wheat, 1,786 (27·2%); maize, 1,089 (67·3%); barley, 456 (27·6%); sugar beet, 87 (35·6%); sunflower seed, 530 (15·5%); seed cotton, 11 (4·5%); tobacco, 31 (96·8%); tomatoes, 325 (90·2%); potatoes, 320 (96·6%); grapes, 660 (63·9%). Bulgaria is a leading producer of attar of roses (rose oil). In 1993 an estimated 3,000 ha were under rose cultivation, with an annual output of over 1,500 kg. Other products (in 1,000 tonnes, with percentage from private holdings) in 1996: Meat, 578 (86·8%); wool, 9 (92·1%); honey, 4·60 (98·0%); eggs, 1,734m. (74·8%); litres of milk 1,387m. (88·0%)

Livestock (1996, in 1,000): Cattle, 582 (milch cows, 358) (in private holdings, 473 and 309); sheep, 3,020 (2,843); pigs, 1,500 (1,173); poultry, 16,227 (13,478).

There were 24,293 tractors in use in 1995.

Forestry. Forest area, 1996, was 3,878,000 ha, or nearly 35% of the total land area (1·29m. ha coniferous, 2·58m. ha broad-leaved). 16,000 ha were afforested in 1996 and 1·931m. cu. metres of building timber were cut.

Fisheries. In 1996 total catches were 15,300 tonnes. As recently as 1988 the catch amounted to 118,000 tonnes.

BULGARIA

INDUSTRY

In 1996 there were 342,261 registered economic units. Units by ownership: State, 9,682; municipal, 9,820; joint-stock companies, 3,588; co-operatives; 5,410; social organizations, 6,306; associations, 2,483; foreign ventures, 9,005; resident, 307,448. In 1996 the private sector accounted for 45·9% of production.

Production, 1996 (in 1,000 tonnes): Pig iron and ferro-alloys, 1,513; steel, 2,457; rolled steel, 1,898; artificial fertilizers, 559; sulphuric acid, 518; cement, 2,132; paper, 174; cotton fabric, 69·2m. metres; woollen fabric, 12m. metres. 10,000 TV sets (5,900 colour) and 36,200 refrigerators.

Labour. In Nov. 1996, 646,600 employees worked in the private sector. There is a 42½-hour 5-day working week. Retirement is at 55 for women and 60 for men, or 52 and 57 after 25 years in the last employment. The average wage (excluding peasantry) was 13,269 leva per month in 1996; minimum wage was 1,200 leva per month. Population of working age (males 16–59; females 16–54), 1996, 4,746,790 (47·6% females). At the end of 1996 the economically active population was 3,576,200 (1,681,000 females), of whom 3,085,400 were employed. Unemployment was around 11% in Dec. 1998.

Trade Unions. An independent white-collar trade union movement, Podkrepa, was formed in 1989. It claimed 100,000 members in July 1990. The former official Central Council of Trade Unions reconstituted itself in 1990 as the Confederation of Independent Trade Unions.

INTERNATIONAL TRADE

Legislation in force as of Feb. 1992 abolished restrictions imposed in 1990 on the repatriation of profits and allows foreign nationals to own and set up companies in Bulgaria. Western share participation in joint ventures may exceed 50%. Total foreign debt was US$10,500m. in Jan. 1996.

Imports and Exports. In 1996 exports totalled US$4·6bn. and imports, US$4·3bn. Principal exports in 1996 (in tonnes): meat, (pork and poultry), 6,700; tomatoes, 22,500; cheese, 5,700; wine, 214,500; tobacco, 21,200; soda ash, 631,200; carbamide, 733,000; ammonium nitrate, 746,800; polyethylene, 49,800; footwear, 5·51m. pairs; rolled iron and steel products, 819,600 (1994); zinc, 57,800 (1994); electric motors, 486,800 items. Principal imports: Pepper, 397,000; newsprint, 32,600; cotton, 18,500; wool, 4,700,000; iron and steel tubes, 22,800; buses, 743 items; motor cars, 35,100 items; lorries, 3,000 items; sugar, 312,700; coal, 231,300; anthracite, 2,006,100; crude oil, 5·9m. (1994); petrol, 107,100 (1992); natural gas, 5,261·5m. cu. metres (1994).

Main export markets in 1996 (trade in 1m. leva): Russian Federation, 76,938; Germany, 74,722; Greece, 61,384; Italy, 78,951. Main import suppliers: Russian Federation, 337,121; Germany, 98,418; Italy, 53,352; Greece, 30,793.

COMMUNICATIONS

Roads. In 1996 there were 37,300 km of hard-surfaced roads, including (1994) 277 km of motorways and 2,935 km of main roads. 817m. passengers and 40·67m. tonnes of freight were carried in 1996. Vehicles in use in 1996 numbered 1,955,716, of which 1,707,023 were passenger cars (204 per 1,000 inhabitants). There were 6,351 road accidents in 1996 with 1,014 fatalities.

Rail. In 1996 there were 4,293 km of 1,435 mm gauge railway (2,655 km electrified). 66·1m. passengers and 30·1m. tonnes of freight were carried.

There is a tramway in Sofia.

Civil Aviation. There is an international airport at Sofia (Vrazhdebna). The state-owned Balkan is the national carrier. In 1996 it carried 1·22m. passengers and 10,000 tonnes of freight. In 1998 services were also operated by Aeroflot, Air France, Air Koryo, Air Moldova, Air Ukraine, Alitalia, Armenian Airlines, Austrian Airlines, British Airways, Czech Airlines, El Al, Hemus Air, JAT, Lauda Air, LOT, Lufthansa, Malév, Olympic Airways, Swissair, Tarom and Turkish Airlines.

Shipping. In 1995 the merchant fleet totalled 1·84m. GRT, including oil tankers, 0·42m. GRT, and container ships, 63,305 GRT. Bourgas is a fishing and oil-port. Varna is the other important port. There is a rail ferry between Varna and Ilitchovsk

(Ukraine). In 1996, 20,000 passengers and 17·07m. tonnes of cargo were carried. There were 74,000 km of inland waterways in 1996. 11,000 passengers and 1m. tonnes of freight were carried.

Telecommunications. BTC, the national telecommunications company, was scheduled for privatization during 1999, with the 51% holding expected to be valued at between US$1bn. and US$1·5bn. Only about 15% of local exchanges had been digitalized by early 1999. In 1997 there were 2,681,100 telephone main lines (322·6 per 1,000 inhabitants). There were approximately 10,000 Internet users in 1995, 180,000 PCs in use, 21,000 cellular phone subscribers and 15,000 fax machines.

Postal Services. In 1996 there were 3,502 post and telecommunications offices.

SOCIAL INSTITUTIONS

Justice. A law of Nov. 1982 provides for the election (and recall) of all judges by the National Assembly. There are a Supreme Court, 28 provincial courts (including Sofia) and regional courts. Jurors are elected at the local government elections.

The maximum term of imprisonment is 20 years. 'Exceptionally dangerous crimes' carry the death penalty.

The Prosecutor General and judges are elected by the Supreme Judicial Council established in 1992.

In 1996 there were 13,097 crimes reported (227 murders) and 16,376 convicted persons (1,076 females, 1,188 juveniles under 17).

Religion. The traditional church of the Bulgarian people' (as it is officially described) is that of the Eastern Orthodox Church. It was disestablished under the 1947 Constitution. In 1953 the Bulgarian Patriarchate was revived. The Patriarch is Maksim (enthroned 1971). The seat of the Patriarch is at Sofia. There are 11 dioceses (each under a Metropolitan), 10 bishops, 2,600 parishes, 1,700 priests, 400 monks and nuns, 3,700 churches and chapels, one seminary and one theological college.

Anti-Maksim schismatics set up a rival synod in 1992 and elected Pimen as Patriarch in 1996.

In 1992 there were some 70,000 Roman Catholics with 53 priests, in 3 bishoprics. In 1987 there were 10,000 Uniates with 20 priests. At the 1992 census, 7,349,544 Christians were recorded and 1,110,295 Moslems (Pomaks). There is a Chief Mufti elected by regional muftis.

Education. Adult literacy rate, 1995, 98·3% (male, 98·9%; female, 97·7%). Education is free, and compulsory for children between the ages of 7 and 16.

In 1996 there were 3,713 kindergartens with 247,000 children and 23,353 teachers; 3,286 primary schools with 71,431 teachers and 944,733 pupils; 129 special needs schools with 2,336 teachers and 13,849 pupils; 7 vocational technical schools with 125 teachers and 3,384 pupils; 203 secondary vocational technical schools with 5,113 teachers and 77,299 pupils; 337 technical colleges and schools of art with 13,943 teachers and 125,887 students; 46 post-secondary institutions with 3,018 teachers and 24,981 students; 42 institutes of higher education with 23,285 teachers and 235,701 students. There are 4 state universities, an American university, and universities of mining and geology, architecture, civil engineering and geodesy. The Academy of Sciences was founded in 1869.

There were also 62 private schools with 5,874 pupils in 1996–97.

In 1996 total expenditure on education came to 3·3% of GNP.

Health. All medical services are free. Private medical services were authorized in Jan. 1991. In 1996 there were 289 hospitals and clinics with 86,160 beds. There were 29,529 doctors, 5,467 dentists, 1,736 pharmacists, 6,576 midwives, 6,910 medical auxiliaries and 51,269 nurses.

Welfare. Retirement and disability pensions and temporary sick pay are calculated as a percentage of previous wages (respectively 55–80%, 35–100%, 69–90%) and according to the nature of the employment. Free medical treatment is available to all, but private practice also exists. Medicines are free to people with chronic conditions or on low incomes.

In 1996 there were 2,381,128 recipients of pensions; disbursements were 121,191m. leva. The average annual pension was 49,681 leva.

BULGARIA

CULTURE

Broadcasting. Broadcasting is under the aegis of the state-controlled Bulgarian National Radio and Bulgarian Television. There are 4 national and 6 regional radio programmes. A service for tourists is broadcast from Varna. There are 2 TV programmes; Bulgaria also receives transmissions from the French satellite channel TV5. There are 2 independent TV channels—Nova TV (New Television) and 7 Dni (7 Days). Colour programmes are by SECAM system. Radio receiving sets in 1996, 4,070,000; televisions, 3,540,000.

Cinema. There were 219 cinemas in 1996 (attendance, 3·69m.).

Press. In 1996 there were 1,053 newspapers with an annual circulation of 454m., and 635 other periodicals. 5,100 book titles were published in 22·9m. copies in 1996.

Tourism. There were 6,810,688 foreign visitors in 1996, of whom 2,191,911 were tourists. Most came from Russia and Ukraine as well as traditional Western markets such as Germany, Britain and Scandinavia. 3,006,292 Bulgarians made visits abroad in 1996. Direct earnings from tourism were US$490m. in 1997.

Festivals. From May to July 1999, Plovdiv, the second largest city, plays host to a major international cultural festival.

DIPLOMATIC REPRESENTATIVES

Of Bulgaria in Great Britain (186-188 Queen's Gate, London, SW7 5HL)
Ambassador: Valentin Dobrev.

Of Great Britain in Bulgaria (38 Blvd. Vassil Levski, Sofia)
Ambassador: Richard Stagg.

Of Bulgaria in the USA (1621 22nd St., NW, Washington, D.C., 20008)
Ambassador: Philip Dimitrov.

Of the USA in Bulgaria (1 Saborna St., Sofia)
Ambassador: Avis Bohlen.

Of Bulgaria to the United Nations
Ambassador: Vacant.

Of Bulgaria to the European Union
Ambassador: Nikola Karadimov.

FURTHER READING

Central Statistical Office. *Statisticheski Godishnik.—Statisticheski Spravochnik* (annual).— *Statistical Reference Book of Republic of Bulgaria* (annual).
Kratka Bulgarska Entsiklopediia (Short Bulgarian Encyclopaedia), 5 vols. Sofia, 1963–69

Crampton, R. J., *A Short History of Modern Bulgaria.* CUP, 1987.—*Bulgaria.* [Bibliography] Oxford and Santa Barbara (CA), 1989.—*A Concise History of Bulgaria.* CUP, 1997

National statistical office: Natsionalen Statisticheski Institut, Sofia. *Chairman:* Zakhari Karamfilov.
Website: http://www.acad.bg/BulRTD/nsi/index.htm

BURKINA FASO

República Démocratique
du Burkina Faso

Capital: Ouagadougou
Population estimate, 2000: 12·06m.
GNP per capita: (PPP$) 950
HDI/world rank: 0·219/172

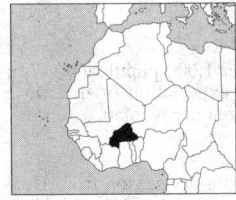

KEY HISTORICAL EVENTS

Formerly known as Upper Volta, the country's name was changed in 1984 to Burkina Faso, meaning 'the land of honest men'. The area it covers was settled by farming communities until their invasion by the Mossi people in the 11th century, who set up several powerful kingdoms—Ouagadougou, Yatenga and Tenkogodo. These successfully resisted Islamic crusades and attacks by neighbouring empires for seven centuries until conquered by the French between 1895 and 1903.

France made Upper Volta a separate colony in 1919, only to abolish it as such in 1932, dividing its territory between the Ivory Coast (now Côte d'Ivoire), French Sudan (now Mali) and Niger. In 1947 the territory of Upper Volta was reconstituted. For much of the colonial era the people of Upper Volta suffered from military and labour conscription, forced labourers being often sent to the Ivory Coast. After the abolition of forced labour in 1946, Voltaic men continued to emigrate to the Ivory Coast and Ghana, this time voluntarily. Upper Volta remained a desperately poor country often hit by drought, particularly in 1972-74 and again in 1982-84.

After independence, President Maurice Hameogo and his *Union Démocratique Voltaique* (UDV) ruled until 3 Jan. 1966 when the army took power under Gen. Sangoule Lamizana. His régime surrendered some power to civilians in 1971 under a new constitution allowing for an elected assembly and with a government consisting of two-thirds civilians and one-third military officers. But after three years Lamizana, who had remained president, and his military colleagues again took power.

Their régime created a new governmental political party in 1975. A new constitution was drawn up and approved by referendum in 1977, and elections were held to a new national assembly in 1978. Joseph Conombo, as prime minister, formed a coalition government. Gen. Lamizana was elected president.

In 1980 a *coup d'état* overthrew this new régime and Col. Saye Zerbo, at the head of a *Comité Militaire de Redressement pour le Progrés National* (CMRPN), held power for two years. Then, on 7 Nov. 1982, the CMRPN was overthrown in another *coup* and replaced by the *Conseil du Salut de Peuple* (CSP), headed by Jean-Baptiste Ouedraogo. Younger and more radical officers now came to the fore, but there was serious tension within the CSP, leading to the arrest of the leading radical Capt. Thomas Sankara on 17 May 1983, and then, on 4 Aug. 1983, to a new *coup d'état* which put him in power.

Sankara and his radical military colleagues formed a *Conseil National de la Révolution* (CNR) and installed a left-wing régime, with Revolutionary Defence Committees (*Comités de Défense de la Révolution*, CDR) operating at local level. The régime aimed at ending exploitation, and sought to curb food traders. Although it established close relations with the similar régime in Ghana, and with Libya, it also maintained fairly normal relations with France and remains in the franc zone.

A border dispute between Burkina Faso and Mali led to fighting in 1974 and again in Dec. 1985. A year later, on 22 Dec. 1986, the International Court of Justice ruled on the dispute, dividing the contested area into roughly equal shares for each; both countries accepted the judgement. Sankara was overthrown and killed in a *coup* on 15 Oct. 1987, the fifth since 1960, led by his friend Capt. Blaise Compaoré.

TERRITORY AND POPULATION

Burkina Faso is bounded in the north and west by Mali, east by Niger and south by Benin, Togo, Ghana and Côte d'Ivoire. Area: 274,122 sq. km; population (census, 1985) 7,967,019 (3,846,518 males). 1996 estimate, 10,623,300 (15·9% urban in 1995); density, 38·8 per sq. km.

The UN gives a projected population for 2000 of 12·06m.

BURKINA FASO

The largest cities (1985 census) are Ouagadougou, the capital (442,223), Bobo-Dioulasso (231,162), Koudougou (51,670), Ouahigouya (38,604), Banfora (35,204), Kaya (25,799), Fada N'Gourma and Tenkodogo.

The principal ethnic groups are the Mossi (49%), Fulani (8%), Mandé (7%), Bobo (7%), Gourounsi (7%), Gourmantché (7%), Bissa (4%), Lobi-Dagari (4%), Sénoufo (2%).

French is the official language.

SOCIAL STATISTICS

Births, 1996, 499,000; deaths, 212,000. Birth rate (1996) per 1,000 population, 47·0; death, 20·0; infant mortality, 117·8 per 1,000 live births; expectation of life, 43·2 years; growth rate, 2·53%. Fertility rate, 1990–95, 7·1 children per woman.

CLIMATE

A tropical climate with a wet season from May to Nov. and a dry season from Dec. to April. Rainfall decreases from south to north. Ouagadougou, Jan. 76°F (24·4°C), July 83°F (28·3°C). Annual rainfall 36" (894 mm).

CONSTITUTION AND GOVERNMENT

At a referendum in June 1991 a new constitution was approved; there is an executive presidency. Parliament consists of the 111-member *Assembly of People's Deputies*, elected by universal suffrage, and the 178-member *Chamber of Representatives*, a consultative body representing social, religious, professional and political organizations. There is also a 90-member *Economic and Social Council*. *National Assizes* of about 2,000 representatives from a broad spectrum of government, public, social and professional bodies may be convened by the President ad hoc to discuss public issues. A constitutional amendment of 1997 permits the President an indefinite number of terms of office.

National Anthem. 'Contre la férule humiliante' ('Against the shameful fetters'); words by T. Sankara, tune anonymous.

RECENT ELECTIONS

At the presidential elections of 15 Nov. 1998 Blaise Compaoré was re-elected by 87·5% of votes cast against 2 other candidates.

At the parliamentary elections of 11 May 1997 there were 569 candidates representing 13 parties. The Congress for Democracy and Progress (CDP) won 101 seats; the Party for Democracy and Progress (PDP), 6; the African Democratic Rally (UDV/RDA), 2, and the Alliance for Democracy and Federation, 2. The electorate was 5m. and turn-out was 50%.

CURRENT ADMINISTRATION

President, Head of Government: Capt. Blaise Compaoré (since 1987; most recently re-elected on 15 Nov. 1998).

In March 1999 the government comprised:

Prime Minister: Kadre Desire Ouedraogo.

Ministers of State: Salif Diallo, Bongnessan Arsene Ye. *Agriculture:* Michel Koutaba. *Animal Resources:* Alassane Sere. *Civil Service and Institutional Development:* Juliette Bonkoungou. *Culture and Communications:* Mahamoudou Ouédraogo. *Defence:* Albert D. Millogo. *Economy, Finance and Government Spokesman:* Tertius Zongo. *Employment, Labour and Social Security:* Elie Sarre. *Energy and Mines:* Elie Ouédraogo. *Foreign Affairs:* Youssouf Ouédraogo. *Health:* Ludovic Alain Tou. *Commerce, Industry and Crafts:* Idrissa Zampalegre. *Justice, Keeper of Seals:* Yarga Larba. *Basic Education and Mass Literacy:* Baworo Seydou Sanou. *Infrastructure, Housing and Town Planning:* Joseph Kaboré. *Relations with Parliament:* Cyril Goungounga. *Higher Education and Scientific Research:* Christophe Dabiré. *Social Affairs and the Family:* Bana Ouandaogo. *Territorial Administration and Security:* Yero Boly. *Transport and Tourism:* Bedouma Alain Yoda. *Youth and Sport:* Joseph André Tiendrébéogo. *Regional Integration:* Viviane Yolande Compaoré. *Promotion of Women:* Alice Tiendrébéogo.

Local Government. Following administrative reform in 1997, Burkina Faso is divided into 45 provinces.

DEFENCE
There are 6 military regions. All forces form part of the Army. Defence expenditure totalled US$67m. in 1997 (US$6 per capita).

Army. The Army consists of 8 infantry companies, 1 airborne company and tank, artillery and engineer support units. Equipment includes 83 armoured cars. Strength (1997), 5,600 with a paramilitary Gendarmerie of 4,200.

Air Force. Equipment comprises 1 Super King Air 200, 1 Aero Commander 500 and 1 Reims/Cessna Super Skymaster for transport and liaison duties, 1 Cessna 172 trainer, and 1 Dauphin and 2 Alouette III helicopters. Personnel total (1997) 200.

INTERNATIONAL RELATIONS
Burkina Faso is a member of the UN, OAU and is an ACP state of the EU.

ECONOMY
Policy. A development programme for 1994–96, based mainly on agriculture and costing 62,000m. francs CFA, was being financed largely by foreign aid. It is proposed to privatize and restructure the banking and industrial sectors. 11 enterprises had been privatized by Nov. 1994. A second phase of privatization was then initiated.

Price controls were imposed on basic items following the devaluation of the franc CFA in Jan. 1994.

Performance. Real GDP growth was 4·5% in 1995 (1·2% in 1994).

Budget. Total revenues in 1995 were an estimated US$277m. and expenditure US$492m.

Currency. The unit of currency is the *franc CFA* (XOF) with a parity rate of 100 francs CFA to 1 French franc. Total money supply was 269bn. francs CFA in Dec. 1997. Foreign exchange reserves were US$333m. in Dec. 1997; gold reserves were 11,000 troy oz. in 1993. The average annual inflation rate during the period 1990–96 was 7·1%.

Banking and Finance. The bank of issue which functions as the central bank is the regional West African Central Bank (BCEAO; *Governor*, Boukary Ouédraogo). There are 3 commercial banks, 4 specialized development institutions, a savings bank, 5 non-bank credit institutions and an investment company.

Weights and Measures. The metric system is in use.

ENERGY AND NATURAL RESOURCES
Electricity. Production of electricity (1994) was 216m. kWh. There are 5 thermal power stations with a total capacity in 1995 of 38·9 MW. Hydro-electric capacity in 1994 was 15 MW. Consumption per capita was 22 kWh in 1994.

Minerals. There are deposits of manganese, zinc, limestone, phosphate and diamonds. Gold production was 1·8 tonnes in 1992.

Agriculture. In 1996 agriculture accounted for 35% of GDP. In 1994 there were 3·55m. ha of arable land and 6m. ha of permanent pasture. 24,000 ha were irrigated in 1994. 9·54m. persons depended on agriculture in 1994, of whom 5m. were economically active. Production (1992, in 1,000 tonnes): Sorghum, 1,292; millet, 784; sugar-cane, 340; maize, 341; groundnuts, 143; rice, 47; cotton, 172; sesame, 8. Rice and groundnuts are of increasing importance.

Livestock (1996): Cattle, 4·35m.; sheep, 5·8m.; goats (1995), 7·24m.; pigs, 560,000; asses, 455,000; chickens (1995), 19m.

Forestry. In 1995 forests covered 42,700 sq. km, or 15·6% of the total land area (down from 16·2% in 1990). Timber production in 1995 was 10·03m. cu. metres.

Fisheries. In 1995 total catches were approximately 8,000 tonnes, exclusively from inland waters. There is some fish farming.

INDUSTRY
In 1994 manufacturing contributed 14% of GDP, mainly food-processing and textiles. Plant is primitive, and employs only about 1% of the workforce. There are about 100 firms, most publicly owned.

Labour. In 1996 the labour force was 5,419,000 (53% males). Over 80% of the economically active population are engaged in agriculture, fishing and forestry.

Trade Unions. There were (1998) 4 federations: the CGTB, USTB, CNTB and ONSL.

INTERNATIONAL TRADE
Foreign debt was US$1,294m. in 1996.

Imports and Exports. In 1996 imports totalled US$545m. and exports US$305m. Value of main exports (in US$1m.), 1994: Cotton, 59; gold, 22. Principal export markets, 1994: France, 13·2%; Côte d'Ivoire, 10·8%; Thailand, 10·2%; Italy, 7·8%; Taiwan, 7·2%. Principal import suppliers: Côte d'Ivoire, 25·6%; France, 15·6%; Niger, 3·5%; Nigeria, 3%; Japan, 2·3%.

COMMUNICATIONS

Roads. The road system comprised an estimated 12,100 km in 1996, of which 5,720 km were national, 3,030 km regional and 3,350 km other roads. Only 1,900 km are asphalted. There were an estimated 56,430 vehicles in use in 1996, including 38,220 passenger cars (3·6 per 1,000 inhabitants).

Rail. The railway from Abidjan in Côte d'Ivoire to Kaya (622 km of metre gauge within Burkina Faso) is operated by the mixed public-private company Sitarail, a concessionaire to both governments. The railways carried 0·6m. passengers and 0·2m. tonnes of freight in 1993.

Civil Aviation. The international airports are Ouagadougou and Bobo-Dioulasso. The national carrier is Air Burkina (66% state-owned) which in 1998 flew to Abidjan, Bamako, Cotonou, Lomé and Niamtougou in addition to operating on domestic routes. In 1998 services were also operated by Air Afrique, Air Algérie, Air France, Air Ivoire, Ghana Airways and SABENA. In 1995 scheduled airline traffic of Burkina Faso-based carriers flew 3·4m. km, carrying 137,000 passengers (111,000 on international flights).

Telecommunications. There were about 36,300 telephone main lines in 1997, or 3·3 per 1,000 inhabitants. Approximately 700 people were Internet users in Jan. 1998.

SOCIAL INSTITUTIONS

Justice. Civilian courts replaced revolutionary tribunals in 1993. There is a Supreme Court in Ouagadougou and Courts of Appeal at Ouagadougou and Bobo-Dioulasso.

Religion. In 1991 there were 4·81m. Moslems and 1·9m. Christians (mainly Roman Catholic). Many of the remaining population follow traditional animist religions.

Education. In 1995 adult literacy was 19·2% (male, 29·5%; female, 9·2%), the second lowest in the world after Niger. The 1994–96 development programme established an adult literacy campaign, and centres for the education of 10–15-year-old non-school-attenders. In 1995 there were 3,233 primary schools with 12,754 teachers and 650,195 pupils. During the period 1990–95 only 24% of females of primary school age were enrolled in school. In 1992 there were 115,753 pupils in secondary schools, and in 1994 there were 9,452 students in higher education.

In 1994 total expenditure on education came to 3·6% of GNP and represented 11·1% of total government expenditure.

Health. In 1993 there were 78 hospitals.

CULTURE

Broadcasting. Radio and television services (colour by SECAM) are provided by the state-controlled Radiodiffusion-Télévision Burkina. Radio Bobo is a regional service and there is a commercial radio station. In 1995 there were estimated to be 290,000 radio and 60,000 television receivers.

Press. There were 3 dailies (1 government-owned) with a combined circulation of 15,000 and 2 weeklies in 1995.

Tourism. In 1996 there were 136,000 foreign tourists. Receipts totalled US$23m.

DIPLOMATIC REPRESENTATIVES
Of Burkina Faso in Great Britain
Ambassador: Youssouf Ouédraogo (resides in Brussels).

Of Great Britain in Burkina Faso
Ambassador: Mr. H. B. Warren-Gash (resides in Abidjan).

Of Burkina Faso in the USA (2340 Massachusetts Ave., NW, Washington, D.C., 20008)
Ambassador: Bruno Zidouemba.

Of the USA in Burkina Faso (PO Box 35, Ouagadougou)
Ambassador: Sharon P. Wilkinson.

Of Burkina Faso to the United Nations
Ambassador: Michel Kafando.

Of Burkina Faso to the European Union
Ambassador: Youssouf Ouédraogo.

FURTHER READING
Decalo, S., *Burkina Faso* [Bibliography]. Oxford and Santa Barbara (CA), 1994
Nnaji, B. O., *Blaise Compaoré: Architect of the Burkina Faso Revolution.* Lagos, 1991

BURUNDI

Republika y'Uburundi

Capital: Bujumbura
Population estimate, 2000: 6·97m.
GNP per capita: (PPP$) 590
HDI/world rank: 0·241/170

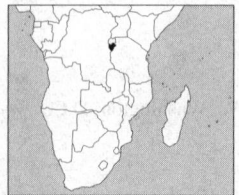

KEY HISTORICAL EVENTS
Tradition recounts the establishment of a Tutsi kingdom in the 16th century. German military occupation in 1890 incorporated the territory into German East Africa. From 1919 Burundi formed part of Ruanda-Urundi administered by the Belgians, first as a League of Nations mandate and then as a UN trust territory. Internal self-government was granted on 1 Jan. 1962, followed by independence on 1 July 1962.

On 8 July 1966 Prince Charles Ndizeye deposed his father Mwami Mwambutsa IV, suspended the constitution and made Capt. Michel Micombero Prime Minister. On 1 Sept. Prince Charles was enthroned as Mwami Ntare V. On 28 Nov., while the Mwami was attending a Head of States Conference in incorporated Kinshasa (Congo), Micombero declared Burundi a republic with himself as president.

On 31 March 1972 Prince Charles returned to Burundi from Uganda and was placed under house arrest. On 29 April 1972 President Micombero dissolved the Council of Ministers and took full power; that night heavy fighting broke out between rebels from both Burundi and neighbouring countries and the ruling Tutsi, apparently with the intention of destroying the Tutsi hegemony. Prince Charles was killed during the fighting in which it was estimated that up to 120,000 died. On 14 July 1972 President Micombero reinstated a Government with a Prime Minister. On 1 Nov. 1976 President Micombero was deposed by the Army, as was President Bagaza on 3 Sept. 1987. Pierre Buyoya assumed the presidency on 1 Oct. 1987.

On 1 June 1993 President Buyoya was defeated in elections by Melchior Ndadaye, who thus became the country's first elected president and the first Hutu president, but on 21 Oct. President Ndadaye and 6 ministers were killed in an attempted military coup. A wave of Tutsi-Hutu massacres broke out, and it is generally accepted that over 100,000 people have been killed since then. On 6 April 1994 the new president, Cyprien Ntaryamira, was also killed, possibly assassinated, together with the President of Rwanda.

On 25 July 1996 the army seized power, installing Maj. Pierre Buyoya as president for the second time, after deposing President Sylvestre Ntibantunganya, dissolving parliament and prohibiting political parties. Parties were permitted to function again in Sept. 1996, but the rebel movement has grown in strength and the civil war between Tutsi and Hutu groups shows no sign of ending. A single attack in Jan. 1998 by a group of rebels left more than 280 Hutus dead.

In June 1998 Maj. Buyoya drew up a settlement for a power-sharing transitional government with 11 opposition ministers in a 22-strong government and the replacement of the prime minister by two vice-presidents, one Hutu and one Tutsi. The National Assembly was to be enlarged from 81 members to 121. Extremists on both sides denounced the agreement which is still under negotiation.

TERRITORY AND POPULATION
Burundi is bounded in the north by Rwanda, east and south by Tanzania and west by the Democratic Republic of the Congo, and has an area of 27,834 sq. km (10,759 sq. miles). The population at the 1990 census was 5,292,793; estimate (1996) 5,356,000; population density, 192·4 per sq. km.

The UN gives a projected population for 2000 of 6·97m.

Since 1994 there have also been some 0·3m. Rwandan refugees, mainly Hutu. Only 7·5% of the population was urban in 1996.

There are 15 regions, all named after their chief towns. Area and population:

Region	Area (in sq. km.)	Population (1990 census)
Bubanza	1,093	222,953
Bujumbura	1,334	608,931
Bururi	2,515	385,490

BURUNDI

Region	Area (in sq. km.)	Population (1990 census)
Cankuzo	1,940	142,707
Cibitoke	1,639	279,843
Karuzi	1,459	287,905
Kayanza	1,229	443,116
Kirundo	1,711	401,103
Kitega	1,989	596,174
Makamba	1,972	223,799
Muhinga	1,825	373,382
Muramuya	1,530	441,653
Ngozi	1,468	482,246
Rutana	1,898	195,834
Ruyigi	2,365	238,567

The capital, Bujumbura, had an estimated population of 0·3m. in 1996.

There are 3 ethnic groups—Hutu (Bantu, forming over 83% of the total); Tutsi (Nilotic, less than 15%); Twa (pygmoids, less than 1%). The local language is Kirundi. French is also an official language. Kiswahili is spoken in the commercial centres.

SOCIAL STATISTICS
1995 births, 268,000; deaths, 111,000. Rates, 1995 (per 1,000 population): Birth, 44·2; death, 18·3. Life expectancy at birth, 1990–95, was 43·0 years for men and 46·1 years for women. Infant mortality, 1990–95, 120 per 1,000 live births; fertility rate, 6·8 children per woman.

CLIMATE
An equatorial climate, modified by altitude. The eastern plateau is generally cool, the easternmost savanna several degrees hotter. The wet seasons are from March to May and Sept. to Dec. Bujumbura, Jan. 73°F (22·8°C), July 73°F (22·8°C). Annual rainfall 33" (825 mm).

CONSTITUTION AND GOVERNMENT
The Constitution of 1981 provided for a one-party state. In Jan. 1991 the government of President Buyoya, leader of the sole party, the Party of Unity and National Progress (Uprona), proposed a new constitution which was approved by a referendum in March 1992 (with 89% of votes cast in favour), legalizing parties not based on ethnic group, region or religion and providing for presidential elections by direct universal suffrage.

There used to be a *National Assembly* with 81 members elected from 16 constituencies by proportional representation. There was a 5% threshold. On 16 July 1998 the *National Assembly* was reformed into a *National Transition Assembly*, whereby 40 additional members were appointed from a mix of political parties and civil society. Government activities are overseen by a 10-member *National Security Council*, of which the President and Prime Minister are members.

National Anthem. 'Uburundi Bwacu' ('Dear Burundi'); words by a committee, tune by M. Barengayabo.

RECENT ELECTIONS
At the presidential elections of 1 June 1993 the electorate was 2·36m.; turn-out was 97·18%. Melchior Ndadaye was elected against former President Buyoya and one other opponent with 64·79% of votes cast, and was sworn in on 10 July 1993.

Following his assassination Cyprien Ntaryamira was elected President by the National Assembly on 13 Jan. 1994 to serve out President Ndadaye's 5-year term of office. After the latter's death and possible assassination, Sylvestre Ntibantunganya (b. 1956; Frodebu) was elected *President* by the National Assembly on 5 Sept. 1994 against 5 opponents.

At the parliamentary elections of 29 June 1993, 740 candidates stood representing 6 parties. The Front for Democracy in Burundi (Frodebu) gained 65 seats with 71·4% of votes cast, and Uprona, 16 with 21·4%. A number of Frodebu MPs elected in June 1993 have been killed in the meantime.

CURRENT ADMINISTRATION

On 25 July 1996 Maj. Pierre Buyoya (b. 1950; Uprona) was installed as *Interim President* after a military coup, and sworn in as *President* on 27 Sept. The *First Vice-President* is Frederic Bamvuginyumvira; the *Second Vice-President* is Mathias Sinamenye.

Pascal-Firmin Ndimira became *Prime Minister* and formed a 'transitional government of national unity'.

Most countries do not recognize either Maj. Pierre Buyoya as President or the government that was formed, which in March 1999 comprised:

Prime Minister: Pascal-Firmin Ndimira.

Minister of Agriculture and Livestock: Salvator Ntihabose. *Civil Service, Labour and Vocational Training:* Emmanuel Tungamwese. *Commerce, Industry and Tourism:* Nestor Nyabenda. *Communal Development and Handicrafts:* Gaspard Ntirampeba. *Defence:* Lt.-Col. Alfred Nkurunziza. *Development and Reconstruction:* Leon Nimbona. *Education:* Prosper Mpawenayo. *Energy and Mines:* Bernard Barandereka. *External Relations and Co-operation:* Severin Ntahomvukiye. *Finance:* Astere Girukwigomba. *Health:* Dr Juma Mohamed Kariburyo. *Human Rights, Institutional Reform and Relations with the National Assembly:* Eugene Nindorera. *Information and Government Spokesman:* Dr Luc Rukingama. *Internal Affairs and Security:* Col. Ascension Twagiramungu. *Justice:* Terence Sinunguruza. *Land and Environment:* Jean-Pacifique Nsengiyumva. *Peace Process:* Ambroise Niyonsaba. *Public Works and Housing:* Denis Nshimirimana. *Reintegration of Refugees, Displaced Persons and Repatriates:* Pascal Nkurunziza. *Transport, Post and Telecommunications:* Col. Epitace Bayaganakandi. *Women, Welfare and Social Affairs:* Romaine Ndorimana. *Youth, Sports and Culture:* Gerard Nyamwiza.

Local Government. The 15 regions are each under a military governor, and are subdivided into 114 districts and then into communes.

DEFENCE

The Army had a strength (1997) of 18,500, plus some 3,500 in paramilitary units. Equipment includes a small naval flotilla and air force flight of 6 SF 260, 3 Cessna 150 and 1 DO27 liaison aircraft, 3 Alouette III and 1 armed Gazelle helicopter. The Army comprises 5 infantry and 2 light-armed battalions. There were 100 air force personnel in 1997.

Defence expenditure totalled US$60m. in 1997 (US$9 per capita).

INTERNATIONAL RELATIONS

Burundi is a member of the UN and OAU and is an ACP member state of the ACP-EU relationship.

ECONOMY

Performance. Real GDP growth was 6·6% in 1995 (−6·3% in 1994, at the height of the civil conflict in the area).

Budget. In 1997 (with 1996 in brackets) total revenue (in 1m. Burundi francs) was 46,253 (46,601); expenditure was 80,800 (75,405).

Currency. The unit of currency is the *Burundi franc* (BIF) of 100 *centimes*. The average annual inflation rate over the period 1990–96 was 14·3%. In Feb. 1998 gold reserves were 20,000 troy oz. and foreign exchange reserves US$97m. Total money supply was 47,953m. Burundi francs in Dec. 1997.

Banking and Finance. The Bank of the Republic of Burundi is the central bank and bank of issue. There are 3 commercial banks; a state development bank, a savings bank and a property investment bank.

Weights and Measures. The metric system operates.

ENERGY AND NATURAL RESOURCES

Electricity. Installed capacity was 55,000 kW in 1991. Production was an estimated 149m. kWh in 1994. Consumption per capita in 1994 was an estimated 31 kWh.

Minerals. Gold is mined on a small scale. Deposits of nickel (280m. tonnes) and vanadium remain to be exploited. There are proven reserves of phosphates of 17·6m. tonnes.

Agriculture. The main economic activity is agriculture, which contributed 57% of GDP in 1996. Beans, cassava, maize, sweet potatoes, groundnuts, peas, sorghum and bananas are grown according to the climate and the region.

The main cash crop is coffee, of which about 95% is arabica. It accounts for 90% of exports, and taxes and levies on coffee constitute a major source of revenue. A coffee board (OCIBU) manages the grading and export of the crop. Production (1992) 34,000 tonnes. The main food crops (production 1992, in 1,000 tonnes) are cassava (597), yams (8), bananas (1,645), dry beans (346), maize (178), sorghum (67), groundnuts (99) and peas (37). Other cash crops are cotton (8) and tea (6).

Livestock: 920,000 goats (1995); 390,000 cattle, 320,000 sheep, 72,000 pigs (all 1996); and 4m. chickens (1995).

Forestry. Forests covered 317,000 ha, or 12·3% of the total land area, in 1995 (324,000 ha and 12·6% in 1990). Timber production (1995) was 4·97m. cu. metres, the majority of it for fuel.

Fisheries. There is a small commercial fishing industry on Lake Tanganyika. In 1995 total catches were 21,101 tonnes, exclusively from inland waters.

INDUSTRY
In 1994 manufacturing contributed 20% of GDP. Textile and leather industries constituted 20% of production, foodstuffs 13% and agricultural industries 9%. In 1992 production of sugar totalled 17,302 tonnes.

Labour. In 1996 the labour force was 3,337,000 (51% males).

INTERNATIONAL TRADE
With Rwanda and the Democratic Republic of the Congo, Burundi forms part of the Economic Community of the Great Lakes. Foreign debt was US$1,127m. in 1996.

Imports and Exports. The total value of exports in 1996 was US$40m.; imports, US$130m. Main exports are coffee, manufactures and tea. Main imports are producer goods, equipment and consumer goods. Main export markets, 1992: Belgium, 33·7%; Germany, 27·4%; USA, 7·8%; France, 4·9%. Main import suppliers, 1993: Belgium-Luxembourg, 16·5%; France, 11·6%; Japan, 9·2%.

COMMUNICATIONS
Roads. In 1996 there were 14,480 km of roads of which approximately 1,030 km were paved. An estimated 37,200 vehicles were in use in 1996, including 19,200 passenger cars (2·8 per 1,000 inhabitants).

Civil Aviation. Regular services to Johannesburg and Sharjah are provided by Shuttle Air Cargo. In 1995 scheduled airline traffic of Burundi-based carriers flew 200,000 km, carrying 9,000 passengers (8,000 on international flights). Bujumbura International airport handled 64,000 passengers and 6,400 tonnes of freight in 1995.

Shipping. There are lake services from Bujumbura to Kigoma (Tanzania) and Kalémie (Democratic Republic of the Congo). The main route for exports and imports is via Kigoma, and thence by rail to Dar es Salaam.

Telecommunications. In 1997 there were 15,900 main telephone lines. In 1995 there were 300 cellular phone subscribers and 100 fax machines, and in Jan. 1998 approximately 75 Internet users.

Postal Services. In 1994 there were 27 post offices, equivalent to 1 for every 219,000 persons.

SOCIAL INSTITUTIONS
Justice. There is a Supreme Court, an appeal court and a court of first instance at Bujumbura, and provincial courts in each provincial capital.

BURUNDI

Religion. In 1993 there were 3·69m. Roman Catholics with an archbishop and 3 bishops. About 3% of the population are Pentecostal, 1% Anglican and 1% Moslem, while the balance follow traditional tribal beliefs.

Education. Adult literacy rate was 35·3% in 1995 (49·3% among males and 22·5% among females). In 1992–93 there were 651,086 pupils in 1,418 primary schools with 10,400 teachers, 55,713 pupils in 97 secondary schools with 2,652 teachers and 4,256 students in 8 higher education institutes with 556 teachers. In 1995–96 there were 3,750 students and 170 academic staff at the university.

Health. In 1993 there were 354 doctors and 1,270 nurses.

CULTURE

Broadcasting. Broadcasting is provided by the state-controlled *Radiodiffusion et Télévision du Burundi*. In 1995 there were estimated to be 410,000 radio and 12,000 TV (colour by SECAM) receivers.

Press. There was (1995) one daily newspaper *(Le Renouveau)* with a circulation of 20,000.

Tourism. There were 27,000 foreign tourists in 1996.

DIPLOMATIC REPRESENTATIVES
Of Burundi in Great Britain (26 Armitage Road, London, NW11 8RD)
Ambassador: Leonidas Ndoricimpa (resides in Brussels).

Of Great Britain in Burundi
Ambassador: Mr. G. Loten (resides in Kigali).

Of Burundi in the USA (2233 Wisconsin Ave., NW, Washington, D.C., 20007)
Chargé d'Affaires a.i.: Thomas Ndikumana.

Of the USA in Burundi (PO Box 1720, Ave. des Etats-Unis, Bujumbura)
Ambassador: Morris N. Hughes.

Of Burundi to the United Nations
Ambassador: M. Gamaliel Ndaruzaniye.

Of Burundi to the European Union
Ambassador: Vacant.

FURTHER READING
Daniels, M., *Burundi* [Bibliography]. Oxford and Santa Barbara (CA), 1992
Lemarchand, R., *Burundi: Ethnic Conflict and Genocide*. CUP, 1996
Weinstein, W., *Historical Dictionary of Burundi*. Metuchen (NJ), 1976

National statistical office: Service des Etudes et Statistiques, Ministère du Plan, Bujumbura.

CAMBODIA

Preah Reach Ana Pak Kampuchea

(Kingdom of Cambodia)

Capital: Phnom Penh
Population estimate, 2000: 11·21m.
Estimated GDP: $7·7bn.
HDI/world rank: 0·422/140

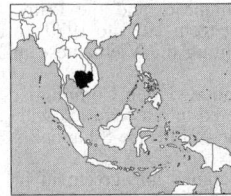

KEY HISTORICAL EVENTS

The recorded history of Cambodia starts at the beginning of the Christian era with the Kingdom of Fou-Nan, whose territories at one time included parts of Thailand, Malaya, Cochin-China and Laos. The kingdom was absorbed at the end of the 6th century by the Khmers. Attacked on either side by the Vietnamese and the Thai from the 15th century onwards, Cambodia was saved from annihilation by the establishment of a French protectorate in 1863. Thailand eventually recognized the protectorate and renounced all claims to suzerainty in exchange for Cambodia's north-western provinces of Battambang and Siem Reap, which were, however, returned under a Franco–Thai convention of 1907, confirmed in the Franco–Thai treaty of 1937. In 1904 the province of Stung Treng, formerly administered as part of Laos, was attached to Cambodia.

A nationalist movement began in the 1930s, and anti-French feeling strengthened in 1940–41 when the French submitted to Japanese demands for bases in Cambodia and allowed Thailand to annex Cambodian territory. On 9 March 1945 the Japanese suppressed the French administration and King Norodom Sihanouk proclaimed Cambodia's independence. British troops occupied Phnom Penh in Oct. 1945, and the re-establishment of French authority was followed by a Franco–Cambodian *modus vivendi* of 7 Jan. 1946, which promised a constitution embodying a constitutional monarchy. Elections for a National Consultative Assembly were held on 1 Sept. 1946 and a Franco–Thai agreement of 17 Nov. 1946 ensured the return to Cambodia of provinces annexed by Thailand in 1941.

In 1949 Cambodia was granted independence as an Associate State of the French Union. The transfer of the French military powers to the Cambodian government on 9 Nov. 1953 is considered in Cambodia as the attainment of sovereign independence. In Jan. 1955 Cambodia became financially and economically independent, both of France and the other two former Associate States of French Indo-China, Vietnam and Laos.

Anti-French guerrilla bands had operated in the jungle from 1945, the most important being a nationalist group known as the Khmer Issarak led by Son Ngoc Thanh. By 1953 Communist bands drawn from the Vietnamese minority and controlled by the Vietminh were active, and in 1954 regular Vietminh forces invaded Cambodia.

Fighting came to an end on 21 July 1954, with the Geneva Agreement. This led to the withdrawal of French and Vietminh troops. Most of the Khmer Issarak bands then surrendered. The International Control Commission responsible for the implementation of the Geneva Agreements was withdrawn in Dec. 1969 at the request of Prince Sihanouk.

Cambodia gained independence in 1953 and in 1967 the Khmer Rouge took up arms to support peasants against a rice tax. An American-backed coup ousted King Sihanouk in 1970 and there followed a five-year civil war with the Khmer Rouge who aimed to establish a communist rice-growing dynasty, a combination of Maoism and ancient xenophobic nationalism. From 1970 hostilities extended throughout most of the country involving North and South Vietnamese and US forces as well as republican and anti-republican Khmer troops. During 1973 direct US and North Vietnamese participation in the fighting came to an end, leaving a civil war situation which continued during 1974 with large-scale fighting between the Khmer Republic, supported by US arms and economic aid, and the United National Cambodian Front including 'Khmer Rouge' communists, supported by North Vietnam and China.

After unsuccessful attempts to capture Phnom Penh in 1973 and 1974, the Khmer Rouge defeated the American backed leader Lon Nol in April 1975, when the remnants of the republican forces surrendered the city.

From April 1975 the Khmer Rouge instituted a harsh and highly centralized regime. They cut the country off from normal contact with the world and expelled all foreigners. All cities and towns were forcibly evacuated and the population were set to work in the fields.

In late 1978, in response to repeated border attacks, Vietnam invaded Cambodia. On 7 Jan. 1979 Phnom Penh was captured by the Vietnamese, and the Prime Minister, Pol Pot, fled. Over 2m. Cambodian lives were lost from 1975 to 1979. In Dec. 1985 the Khmer Rouge still had 30,000 guerrillas fighting the Vietnamese in Cambodia.

In June 1982 the Khmer Rouge (who claimed to have abandoned their Communist ideology and to have disbanded their Communist party) entered into a coalition with Son Sann's Kampuchean People's National Liberation Front and Prince Sihanouk's group.

On 23 Oct. 1991 the warring factions and 19 countries signed an agreement in Paris instituting a ceasefire in Cambodia to be monitored by UN troops. On 31 Oct. the UN Security Council unanimously agreed to establish a UN Transitional Authority in Cambodia (UNTAC), and on 28 Feb. 1992 the Security Council voted to send a force of 22,000 soldiers, police and officials to disarm the factions and organize elections. Following the election of a constituent assembly in May 1993, a new constitution was promulgated on 23 Sept. 1993 restoring parliamentary monarchy.

During 1993–94 the Khmer Rouge continued hostilities against the government in disregard of the 1991 Paris Agreement, refusing to take part in the 1993 elections. They were formally banned by the National Assembly in June 1994. By 1996 the Khmer Rouge had split into two warring factions. The leader of one, Ieng Sary, who had been sentenced to death in his absence for genocide, was pardoned by the King in Sept. 1996. In early Nov. 1996 Ieng Sary and some 4,000 of his forces threw in their lot with government forces.

In July 1997 Hun Sen, the second prime minister, engineered a coup which led to the ousting of first prime minister, Prince Norodom Ranariddh. Prince Ranariddh went into exile and was later convicted in his absence by 2 military courts of security crimes. However, on 30 March 1998 he returned as guest of a Japanese-brokered plan to ensure 'fair and free' elections. These took place on 26 July 1998 against a background of violence and general intimidation. Hun Sen's Cambodian People's Party declared victory but the opposition parties alleged fraud and threatened to boycott the new National Assembly. King Norodom Sihanouk offered to mediate while Hun Sen tightened his grip on the country. Cambodian refugees in Thailand total 87,000 according to the UN. Other after-effects of war include the clearing of landmines which take their daily toll on innocent civilians.

TERRITORY AND POPULATION
Cambodia is bounded in the north by Laos and Thailand, west by Thailand, east by Vietnam and south by the Gulf of Thailand. It has an area of about 181,035 sq. km (69,898 sq. miles).

Population, 5,756,141 (census, 1981), of whom 93% were Khmer, 4% Vietnamese and 3% Chinese. Estimate, based on the UN's electoral roll (1996), 9,857,000; density, 54 per sq. km. Approximately 20% of the population in 1995 lived in urban areas.

The UN gives a projected population for 2000 of 11·21m.

The capital, Phnom Penh, had an estimated population of 0·92m. in 1994. Other cities are Kompong Cham and Battambang. Ethnic composition, 1994: Khmer, 89%; Vietnamese, 6%; Chinese, 3%; Cham, 2%; Lao-Thai, 1%.

Khmer is the official language.

SOCIAL STATISTICS
1996 estimated births, 429,000; deaths, 156,000. Rates, 1996 estimates (per 1,000 population): Births, 43·5; deaths, 15·8. Infant mortality (per 1,000 live births), 107·8. Expectation of life in 1996 was 49·9 years (48·4 for males and 51·4 for females).

CAMBODIA

Annual growth rate, 1990–95, 2·8%. Fertility rate, 1990–95, 4·9 children per woman.

In the Human Development Index, or HDI (measuring progress in countries in longevity, knowledge and standard of living), Cambodia and Namibia were the countries which made the most progress in 1995 compared to 1994—both recording increases of 0·074. Cambodia's HDI value was 0·422 out of a maximum of 1·0 in 1995, up from 0·348 in 1994, resulting in a rise from 153rd in the world to 140th.

CLIMATE
A tropical climate, with high temperatures all the year. Phnom Penh, Jan. 78°F (25·6°C), July 84°F (28·9°C). Annual rainfall 52" (1,308 mm).

CONSTITUTION AND GOVERNMENT
A parliamentary monarchy was re-established by the 1993 constitution. Prince Norodom Sihanouk (b. 31 Oct. 1922) regained the throne (which had been abolished in 1955) as King on 23 Sept. 1993. He had previously reigned from 1941 to 1955. The protocol of succession is to be determined by a Throne Council consisting of the Speaker and 2 Deputy Speakers, the First and Second Prime Ministers and 2 Buddhist patriarchs. In Jan. 1996 King Sihanouk's wife, Queen Monineath, was dubbed 'First Lady'.

There is a 122-member constituent assembly, which on 14 June 1993 elected Prince Sihanouk head of state. On 21 Sept. it adopted a constitution (promulgated on 23 Sept.) by 113 votes to 5 with 2 abstentions making him monarch of a parliamentary democracy. The constitution converted the constituent assembly into a legislature sitting for a 5-year term.

National Anthem. 'Jham kraham cral' ('Bright red blood was spilt'); words and tune anonymous.

RECENT ELECTIONS
Parliamentary elections were held on 27 July 1998. Under the UN-brokered constitution, a party had to win two-thirds of seats in the 122-member Parliament in order to form a government. With a 90% turn-out, the Cambodian People's Party (KPK) won 64 seats with 41·4% of the vote, the royalist FUNCINPEC party of Prince Norodom Ranariddh won 43 seats with 31·7%, and the party of the government critic Sam Rainsy won 15 seats with 14·1%. Opposition parties claimed a wide range of irregularities and there were re-counts in a number of districts.

CURRENT ADMINISTRATION
The Cabinet comprised in March 1999:
Prime Minister: Hun Sen, b. 1951 (KPK; sworn in on 30 Nov. 1998).
Deputy Prime Ministers: Sar Kheng, Tol Lah. *National Defence, Co-ministers:* Tea Banh, Sisowath Sirirath. *Interior, Co-ministers:* Sar Kheng, You Hockry. *Parliamentary Affairs and Inspection:* Khun Hang. *Foreign Affairs and International Co-operation:* Hor Nam Hong. *Economy and Finance:* Keat Chhon. *Information and Press:* Lu Lay Sreng. *Health:* Hong Sun Huot. *Industry, Mines and Energy:* Suy Sem. *Planning:* Chhay Than. *Commerce:* Cham Prasidh. *Education, Youth and Sports:* Tol Lah. *Agriculture, Forestry and Fisheries:* Chhea Song. *Culture and Fine Arts:* Norodom Bopha Devi. *Environment:* Dr Mok Mareth. *Rural Development:* Chhim Seak Leng. *Social Affairs, Labour, Vocational Training and Youth Rehabilitation:* Ith Sam Heng. *Post and Telecommunications:* So Khun. *Religions and Cults:* Chea Savoeurn. *Women's Affairs and Veterans:* Mov Sok Huor. *Public Works and Transport:* Khy Taing Lim. *Justice:* Uk Vithun. *Tourism:* Veng Sereyvuth. *Territorial Organization, Urbanization and Construction:* Im Chhun Lim. *Water Resources and Meteorology:* Lim Kean Hor.

Local Government. There are 21 provinces administered by governors.

DEFENCE
The King is C.-in-C. of the armed forces. Defence expenditure in 1997 totalled US$254m. (US$25 per capita).

CAMBODIA

Army. Conscription is for 5 years. Strength (1997) 36,000, including 7 infantry divisions, 3 independent infantry brigades, and 9 independent infantry and 3 armoured regiments. Equipment includes 250 T-54/-55/-59 main battle tanks. There are also provincial (50,000) forces and paramilitary local forces.

Navy. The navy is believed to include 2 ex-Soviet hydrofoil patrol craft, 10 inshore patrol craft and a miscellany of riverine and support craft. Naval personnel in 1996 totalled about 1,200.

Air Force. Aviation operations were resumed in 1988 under the aegis of the Army; equipment includes a squadron of 10 MiG-21 fighters being refurbished with Israeli help, 15 Mil Mi-8/17 transport helicopters and 2 Ecureuil helicopters. At least 4 An-24 and 2 Yak-40 transports are in use as well as 6 L-39 trainers. Personnel (1996), 500.

INTERNATIONAL RELATIONS
In Jan. 1998 the European Union agreed to provide the Cambodian government with over US$11m., primarily to fund voter registration for the election which was held in July 1998.

Cambodia has failed to secure a seat at the UN or membership of ASEAN (deferred because of the coup in July 1997).

ECONOMY
Performance. In 1997, GDP was US$3,177m. Real GDP growth was 7·6% in 1995 (5·3% in 1994).

Budget. In 1995 revenues were estimated to be US$261m. and expenditures US$496m.

Currency. The unit of currency is the *riel* (KHR) of 100 *sen*. Inflation was 6% in 1995. Foreign exchange reserves were US$293m. in Feb. 1998. Total money supply in Dec. 1997 was 384,761m. riels. Inflation in 1997 stood at 11·8%.

Banking and Finance. The banking system consists of the National Bank of Cambodia, which is the bank of issue; the Central Bank and 28 commercial banks (2 state-owned; 17 privately-owned; 6 foreign and 3 joint venture banks). The National Bank of Cambodia is studying the possibility of setting up a stock market and a capital market for stimulating the flow of capital from foreign countries.

ENERGY AND NATURAL RESOURCES
Electricity. Installed capacity was 100,000 kW in 1995. Production (1994) was 180m. kWh. Consumption per capita in 1995 was estimated to be 17 kWh. A long-term plan for hydro electricity has been issued by the government.

Water. In 1995, 65% of the urban and 26% of the rural population had access to safe water.

Minerals. There are phosphates and high-grade iron-ore deposits. Some small-scale gold panning and gem (mainly zircon) mining is carried out.

Agriculture. The majority of the population is engaged in agriculture, fishing or forestry. In 1996 agriculture accounted for 51% of GDP. In 1994 there were 3·82m. ha of arable land, 19,000 ha of permanent crops and 1·5m. ha of permanent pasture. Before the spread of war, the high productivity provided for a low but well-fed standard of living for the peasant farmers, the majority of whom owned the land they worked before agriculture was collectivized. A relatively small proportion of the food production entered the cash economy. The war and unwise pricing policies led to a disastrous reduction in production so much so that the country became a net importer of rice. Private ownership of land was restored by the 1989 Constitution.

A crop of 1·8m. tonnes of rice was produced in 1994. Production of other crops, 1994 (in tonnes): Maize, 64,000; dry beans, 14,000; soybeans, 40,000.

Livestock (1996): Cattle, 2·8m.; pigs, 2·05m.; buffaloes, 839,000 (1995); poultry, 11m. (1995).

Forestry. Some 9·8m. ha, or 55·7% of the land area, were covered by forests in 1995, nearly half of which is reserved by the Government to be awarded to concessionaires. Such areas are not at present worked to any extent. The remainder is available for exploitation by the local residents, and as a result some areas are over-exploited and conservation is not practised. Timber exports have been banned since Dec. 1996. In 1990 the area under forests was 10·65m. ha. There are substantial reserves of pitch pine. Rubber plantations are a valuable asset with production at around 40,000 tons per year. There are plans to expand the area under rubber cultivation from 50,000 ha to 800,000 ha. Timber production in 1995 was 7·76m. cu. metres. In 1997 forestry represented 43% of foreign trade.

Fisheries. 1995 catch, 112,510 tonnes (81,279 tonnes from inland waters).

INDUSTRY
Some development of industry had taken place before the spread of open warfare in 1970, but little was in operation by the 1990s except for rubber processing, sea-food processing, jute sack making and cigarette manufacture. In the private sector small family concerns produce a wide range of goods. Apart from rice mills, about 70 factories were functioning in 1994. Light industry is generally better developed than heavy industry.

Labour. In 1996 the labour force was 5,322,000. Females constituted 53% of the labour force in 1996—the highest proportion of women in the workforce anywhere in the world. More than 60% of the economically active population are engaged in agriculture, fishing and forestry.

INTERNATIONAL TRADE
Foreign investment has been encouraged since 1989. Legislation of 1994 exempts profits from taxation for 8 years, removes duties from various raw and semi-finished materials and offers tax incentives to investors in tourism, energy, the infrastructure and labour-intensive industries. External debt was US$2,111m. in 1996.

Imports and Exports. Imports in 1995, $630·5m.; exports, $240·7m. The main exports are timber, rubber, soybeans and sesame. Main imports include cigarettes, construction materials, petroleum products, machinery and motor vehicles. The principal partners for exports are Singapore, Japan, Thailand, China (in particular Hong Kong), Indonesia and Malaysia; and for imports, Singapore, Vietnam, Japan, Australia, China (again, in particular Hong Kong) and Indonesia.

COMMUNICATIONS

Roads. There were an estimated 35,800 km of roads in 1996, of which 2,700 km were paved. 46,800 passenger cars were in use in 1996 (up from 20,085 in 1992) and 397,800 motor cycles and mopeds.

Rail. Main lines link Phnom Penh with Sisophon near the Thai border and the port of Kompong Som (total 603 km, metre gauge). After a long period of disruption due to political unrest, limited services were restored on both lines in 1992, when 1·2m. passengers and 0·1m. tonnes of freight were carried.

Civil Aviation. Pochentong airport is 8 km from Phnom Penh. Royal Air Cambodge was reconstituted in Jan. 1995 with 60% of the equity government-owned. There are regular domestic services, and in 1998 there were international flights to Bangkok, Chongqing, Guangzhou, Ho Chi Minh City, Kuala Lumpur, Singapore, Taipei and Vientiane. Services were also operated in 1998 by Angkor Airlines, Bangkok Airways, DRAGONAIR, Kampuchea Airlines, Lao Aviation, Malaysia Airlines, President Airlines, Silk Air, Thai Airways International and Vietnam Airlines.

Shipping. There is an ocean port at Kompong Som; the port of Phnom Penh can be reached by the Mekong (through Vietnam) by ships of between 3,000 and 4,000 tonnes. In 1995, merchant shipping totalled 60,000 GRT.

Telecommunications. There are telephone exchanges in all the main towns. Number of telephone main lines in 1997 totalled 19,000 (1·8 per 1,000 persons). In 1995 cellular phone subscribers numbered 15,000 and there were 600 fax machines.

Postal Services. In 1995 there were 30 post offices, or 1 for every 328,000 persons.

SOCIAL INSTITUTIONS

Religion. The Constitution of 1989 reinstated Buddhism as the state religion; it had 8·2m. adherents in 1994. About 2,800 monasteries were active in 1994. There are small Roman Catholic and Moslem minorities.

Education. In 1994–95 there were 1,703,316 pupils and 37,827 teachers in 4,617 (1990–91) primary schools, and in general secondary education 16,349 teachers for 297,555 pupils. In 1990–91 there were 8,095 students in vocational establishments. There is a university (with 8,400 students and 350 academic staff in 1995–96) and a fine arts university. Adult literacy rate was 66% in 1994 (80% among males and 54% among females).

Health. In 1993 there were 5,642 doctors, 9,950 nurses and 3,235 midwives.

CULTURE

Broadcasting. Broadcasting is provided by the state-owned Voice of the People of Cambodia and Cambodian Television (colour by PAL). In 1995 there were an estimated 85,000 TV and 1·1m. radio sets.

Press. There are 21 newspapers, 2 of which are in English.

Tourism. In 1997 there were 218,000 foreign visitors, up from 25,000 in 1991. Of these, 28,116 were from Taiwan; Japan, 25,362; USA, 20,291; France, 17,538; China, 17,282; Australia, 7,237; UK, 9,193. Tourist numbers in the 1990s have increased at a faster rate in Cambodia than in any other country. Receipts in 1996 totalled US$118m.

DIPLOMATIC REPRESENTATIVES

Of Great Britain in Cambodia (29 Street 75, Phnom Penh)
Ambassador: C. G. Edgar.

Of Cambodia in the USA (4500 16th Street, NW, Washington, D.C., 20011)
Ambassador: Huoth Var.

Of the USA in Cambodia (27 EO Street 240, Phnom Penh)
Ambassador: Kenneth M. Quinn.

Of Cambodia to the United Nations
Ambassador: Vacant.

Of Cambodia to the European Union
Ambassador: Namhong Hor.

FURTHER READING

Ablin, D. A. and Hood, M. (eds.) *The Cambodian Agony.* London and New York, 1987
Barron, J. and Paul, A., *Murder of a Gentle Land.* New York, 1977
Chandler, D. P., *A History of Cambodia.* 2nd ed. Boulder (CO), 1996
Jarvis, Helen, *Cambodia* [Bibliography]. Oxford and Santa Barbara (CA), 1997
Martin, M. A, *Cambodia: A Shattered Society.* California Univ. Press, 1994
Peschoux, C., *Le Cambodge dans la Tourmente: le Troisième Conflit Indochinois, 1978–1991.* Paris, 1992.—*Les 'Nouveaux' Khmers Rouges.* Paris, 1992

CAMEROON

République du Cameroun—

Republic of Cameroon

Capital: Yaoundé
Population estimate, 2000: 15·13m.
GNP per capita: (PPP$) 1,760
HDI/world rank: 0·481/132

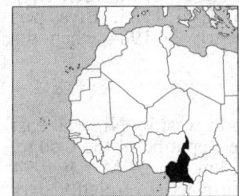

KEY HISTORICAL EVENTS

The name Cameroon is derived from the Portuguese *camaráes* (prawns), introduced by Portuguese navigators who from 1472 came for the crayfish in the Wouri river estuary. Called Kamerun in German and Cameroun in French, the estuary was later called the Cameroons River by British navigators. The Duala people living there were important traders, selling slaves and later palm oil to Europeans. On 12 July 1884 they signed a treaty establishing German rule over Kamerun. Originally covering the Duala's territory on the Wouri, this German colony later expanded to cover a large area inland, to which the name Kamerun was also applied.

The area occupied was home to a large number of African peoples; Betis, Bassas, Bamilekes, Bamouns, Tikars, Fulanis and many others. Some, like the Betis and Bassas, had only small traditional states; others had larger ones notably, in the 19th century, the kingdom of Bamoun and the Moslem Fulani state of Adamawa. Their territory was largely incorporated in German Kamerun although the capital, Yola, was included in Nigeria. Resistance to German colonization was strong, and it was about 20 years before German rule was established over the whole territory. In 1911, France ceded large adjoining areas of its neighbouring colonies (Chad, Ubangi-Shari, Middle-Congo and Gabon) to the Germans, who called this new territory Neu-Kamerun. The Duala people, advanced in education and important traders, planters and junior government officials, became increasingly critical of German rule, especially when many were evicted from their homes in Douala City in 1914 and one Duala paramount chief, Rudolf Duala Manga Bell, was executed.

In the First World War Allied forces rapidly occupied Douala and then fought the Germans over a wide area, until the last Germans left in early 1916. The occupied territory was provisionally partitioned between France and Britain in 1916, a division confirmed in 1919 when each obtained a League of Nations mandate over its section. British Cameroons consisted of 2 areas, British Southern Cameroons and British Northern Cameroons, adjoining Nigeria. France's mandated territory of Cameroun occupied most of the former German colony. Its capital was at first at Douala, and then, from 1921, at Yaoundé. The Dualas continued to take the lead in anti-colonial protest and in 1929 their paramount chiefs signed a petition calling for self-government.

In the Second World War French Cameroun was occupied at an early stage by the Free French. From 1944, reforms in the French colonial empire allowed African trade unions and parties and nationalism spread rapidly. In 1946, the French and British territories became Trust Territories of the UN. Africans in British Cameroons joined in the nationalist politics of Nigeria and for some years British Southern Cameroons was represented in the parliament and government of Nigeria's Eastern Region. In French Cameroun the *Union des Populations du Cameroun* (UPC), founded in 1948, became the major nationalist party, calling for independence and 'reunification' with British Cameroons and appealing for UN support.

In the 1950s other parties emerged, encouraged by the French to rival the radical UPC, notably the *Bloc des Democrates Camerounais* led by André Mbida. In 1955, after rioting, the UPC was banned. In Dec. 1956, when elections were held prior to self-government, the UPC began guerilla war but other parties took part in the elections and Mbida became prime minister in 1957. In Feb. 1958, Ahmadou Ahidjo, leader of the northern-based *Union Camerounais* (UC), became prime minister, while the UPC remained illegal and fought against the French and the new Cameroonian government. On 1 Jan. 1960 French Cameroun gained independence; elections were held, and Ahidjo became president. The UPC guerillas were largely defeated by 1963.

CAMEROON

On 11 Feb. 1961, British Southern Cameroons voted in a referendum to join ex-French Cameroun, while British Northern Cameroons chose to join Nigeria. On 1 Oct. 1961, the Republic of Cameroon and British Southern Cameroons were united to form the Federal Republic of Cameroon. On 2 June 1972, the limited powers of the West and East Cameroon governments were ended when the country became the United Republic of Cameroon. Ahidjo resigned on 6 Nov. 1982 and was succeeded as president by Paul Biya, previously prime minister. After a crisis between Biya and his predecessor in 1983, and a *coup* attempt on 6 April 1984, Biya was confirmed in power. He was elected without opposition early in 1984 when the country's name was changed to the Republic of Cameroon.

TERRITORY AND POPULATION
Cameroon is bounded in the west by the Gulf of Guinea, north-west by Nigeria, east by Chad and the Central African Republic, and south by the Republic of the Congo, Gabon and Equatorial Guinea. The total area is 475,440 sq. km. On 29 March 1994 Cameroon asked the International Court of Justice to confirm its sovereignty over the Bakassi Peninsula, occupied by Nigerian troops. Population (1987 census) 10,494,000. Estimate (July 1996) 14,261,600 (7,150,400 females); density, 30·0 per sq. km.

The UN gives a projected population for 2000 of 15·13m.

In 1995, 44·7% of the population were urban.

The areas, populations and chief towns of the 10 provinces were:

Province	Sq. km	Census 1987	Chief town	Estimate 1981
Adamaoua	63,691	495,185	Ngaoundéré	47,508
Centre	68,926	1,651,600	Yaoundé	649,000[1]
Est	109,011	517,198	Bertoua	18,254
Extrême-Nord	34,246	1,855,695	Maroua	124,000[1]
Littoral	20,239	1,354,833	Douala	810,000[1]
Nord (Bénoué)	65,576	832,165	Garoua	142,000[1]
Nord-Ouest	17,810	1,237,348	Bamenda	110,000[1]
Ouest	13,872	1,339,791	Bafoussam	113,000[1]
Sud	47,110	373,798	Ebolowa	22,222
Sud-Ouest	24,471	838,042	Buéa	29,953[1]
		[1]1991		

The population is composed of Sudanic-speaking people in the north (Fulani, Sao and others) and Bantu-speaking groups, mainly Bamileke, Beti, Bulu, Tikar, Bassa, Duala, in the rest of the country. The official languages are French and English.

SOCIAL STATISTICS
1995 births, 526,000 (rate of 39·9 per 1,000 population); deaths, 164,000 (rate of 12·4 per 1,000 population). Growth rate (1996): 2·89%; infant mortality, 78·7 per 1,000 live births; expectation of life (1996 est.): Males, 51·5 years; females, 53·7. Fertility rate, 1990–95, 5·7 children per woman.

CLIMATE
An equatorial climate, with high temperatures and plentiful rain, especially from March to June and Sept. to Nov. Further inland, rain occurs at all seasons. Yaoundé, Jan. 76°F (24·4°C), July 73°F (22·8°C). Annual rainfall 62" (1,555 mm). Douala, Jan. 79°F (26·1°C), July 75°F (23·9°C). Annual rainfall 160" (4,026 mm).

CONSTITUTION AND GOVERNMENT
The 1972 Constitution, subsequently amended, provides for a *President* as head of state and government. The President is directly elected for a 5-year term, and there is a Council of Ministers whose members must not be members of parliament.

The *National Assembly*, elected by universal adult suffrage for 5 years, consists of 180 representatives. After 1966 the sole legal party was the Cameroon People's Democratic Movement (RDPC), but in Dec. 1990 the National Assembly legalized opposition parties.

National Anthem. 'O Cameroon, Thou Cradle of our Fathers/O Cameroun, Berceau de nos Ancêtres'; music by S. M. Bamba, tune by M. Nkoro.

RECENT ELECTIONS

Presidential elections were held on 12 Oct. 1997. The electorate in 1992 was 4,195,687. Paul Biya was elected against 2 opponents by 92·6% of votes cast.

The most recent National Assembly elections were held on 17 May 1997. The conservative Rassemblement Démocratique du Peuple Camerounais (RDPC) won 109 seats, the Social-Democratic Front (SDF) 43, the Union Nationale pour la Démocratie et le Progrès (UNDP) 13, the Union Démocratique du Cameroun (UDC) 5 and others won 3 seats. 3 constituencies (7 seats) were cancelled by the Supreme Court because of claims of fraudulent practices.

CURRENT ADMINISTRATION

President: Paul Biya (assumed office 6 Nov. 1982, elected 14 Jan. 1984, re-elected 24 April 1988, re-elected 10 Oct. 1992 and sworn in 3 Nov. 1992, and once again re-elected 12 Oct. 1997).

Peter Musonge Mafani became *Prime Minister* in Sept. 1996 and formed a new government which in March 1999 comprised:

Minister for Agriculture: Zacharie Perevet. *Communication:* Rene Ze Nguele. *Culture:* Ferdinand Oyono. *Economy and Finance:* Edouard Mfoumou. *Employment, Labour and Social Insurance:* Pius Scurity Ondoua. *Environment and Forests:* Sylvestre Naah Ondoua. *External Relations:* Augustin Kontchou Kouomegni. *Industrial and Commercial Development:* Maigari Bello Bouba. *Justice and Keeper of the Seals:* Laurent Esso. *Livestock, Fisheries and Animal Industries:* Adjoudi Hamadjoda. *Mines, Water Resources and Energy:* Dr Yves Mbele. *National Education:* Charles Etoundi. *Public Health:* Gotlieb Monekosso. *Social Affairs:* Madeleine Fouda. *Tourism:* Claude Joseph Mbafou. *Transport:* Joseph Tsanga Abanda. *Women's Affairs:* Aissatou Yaou. *Youth and Sport:* Joseph Owona. *Higher Education:* Antangana Mebara. *Posts and Telecommunication:* Mounchipou Seidou. *Public Works:* Jerome Etah. *Scientific and Technical Research:* Henri Hogbe Nlend. *Town Planning and Housing:* Pierre Hele. *Towns:* Antoine Zanga. *Public Investments and Territorial Development:* Justin Ndioro. *Public Service and Administrative Reform:* Sali Dairou. *Superior State Control:* Joseph Owona. *Territorial Administration:* Samson Ename Ename.

Local Government. The 10 provinces are each administered by a governor appointed by the President. They are sub-divided into 49 departments (each under a prefect) and then into 336 communes (each under an under-prefect). Elections for councillors were held on 21 Jan. 1996. The electorate was 4·5m. 38 parties presented candidates. The RDPC gained a majority overall.

DEFENCE

The President of the Republic is C.-in-C. of the armed forces. Defence expenditure totalled US$240m. in 1997 (US$17 per capita).

Army. There are 8 military regions. The Army consists of a Presidential Guard, 5 infantry battalions, 1 para-commando, 1 engineer, 1 artillery and 1 anti-aircraft battalion. Total strength (1997) 11,500; there is a Gendarmerie 9,000 strong.

Navy. The Navy, all French-built, operates 1 missile craft and 1 inshore patrol vessel. There are 2 landing craft and about 30 boats and service craft. Personnel in 1997 numbered 1,300. The marine wing of the Gendarmerie operates 10 inshore patrol craft.

Air Force. The Air Force has 2 Hercules turboprop transports, 4 Buffalo short-take-off-and-landing transports, 1 Puma and 1 Super Puma transport helicopters, 5 Magister armed jet basic trainers, 4 Alpha Jet close support/trainers, and 5 Alouette and 2 Bell 206 helicopters. Some of 4 Gazelle light helicopters are armed with anti-tank missiles. A small VIP transport fleet, maintained in civil markings, comprises 1 Boeing 727 jet aircraft, 1 Gulfstream III and 4 Aerospatiale helicopters. Radar-equipped Dornier 128-6 twin-turboprop aircraft serve for offshore patrol. Aircraft availability is low because of funding problems. Personnel (1997), 300.

INTERNATIONAL RELATIONS

Cameroon is in dispute with Nigeria over both its land and its maritime boundary. The two countries are in conflict on the question of sovereignty over the Bakassi Peninsula and also territory which Cameroon claims in the area of Lake Chad.

Cameroon is a member of the UN, the Commonwealth and the OAU and is an ACP state of the EU.

ECONOMY

Policy. The Technical Commission for the Rehabilitation of Public Enterprises is overseeing both privatization and the restructuring of all state-owned companies. 18 companies were scheduled for privatization in 1997.

Performance. Real GDP growth was 3·3% in 1996.

Budget. The financial year ends on 30 June. Revenues in 1995 were an estimated US$2·23bn. and expenditure also US$2·23bn.

Currency. The unit of currency is the *franc CFA* (XAF), with a parity rate of 100 *francs CFA* to 1 French *franc*. Gold reserves were 30,000 troy oz. in 1993; in Jan. 1998 foreign exchange reserves were US$2m. Total money supply was 404bn. francs CFA in Jan. 1998. Annualized inflation was 6% in 1996.

Banking and Finance. The Banque des Etats de l'Afrique Centrale is the sole bank of issue. There are 10, including 3 foreign, commercial banks.

Weights and Measures. The metric system is in use.

ENERGY AND NATURAL RESOURCES

Electricity. Installed capacity in 1994 was 630,000 kW. Total production in 1994 was 2·7bn. kWh (95% hydro-electric). Consumption per capita was an estimated 186 kWh in 1995.

Oil and Gas. Oil production (1992 estimate), mainly from Kole oilfield, was 7·46m. tonnes.

Minerals. Tin ore and limestone are extracted. There are deposits of bauxite, uranium, nickel, gold, cassiterite and kyanite. In 1993, 6·2m. metric tonnes of crude petroleum were produced.

Agriculture. In 1996 agriculture contributed 40% of GDP. In 1994 there were 5·96m. ha of arable land, 1·08m. ha of permanent crops and 2·0m. ha of permanent pasture. 21,000 ha were irrigated in 1994. The main food crops (with 1992 production in 1,000 tonnes): Cassava, 1,230; sorghum, 380; millet, 55; maize, 380; plantains, 860; yams, 80; groundnuts, 100; bananas, 520. Cash crops include: Palm oil, 107; palm kernels, 53; cocoa, 94 (126 in 1997-98 season); coffee, 85; rubber, 48; cotton lint, 48. Banana cultivation is being redeveloped.

Livestock (1996): 4·9m. cattle; 3·6m. sheep; 3·8m. goats (1995); 1·41m. pigs; 20m. chickens (1995).

Livestock products (in 1,000 tonnes), 1990: Beef, 78; pork, 16; mutton, 14; goat meat, 13; poultry meat, 14; cow's milk, 50; eggs, 12; honey, 2·7.

Forestry. Forests covered 19·6m. ha in 1995 (42·1% of the total land area), ranging from tropical rain forests in the south (producing hardwoods such as mahogany, ebony and sapele) to semi-deciduous forests in the centre and wooded savannah in the north. The area under forests in 1990 had been 20·3m. ha (43·5% of the land area). Timber production in 1995 was 15·71m. cu. metres.

Fisheries. In 1995 the total catch was estimated to be 64,000 tonnes (40,000 tonnes from sea fishing).

INDUSTRY

Manufacturing is largely small-scale, with only some 30 firms employing more than 10 workers. Aluminium production in 1993 was 86,500 metric tonnes. There are also factories producing shoes, beer, soap, oil and food products, cigarettes. 1994 output included: sugarcane, 1·3m. tonnes; palm kernels, 54,000 tonnes; cassava, 1·3m. tonnes; cigarettes, 5m.

Labour. In 1996 the workforce numbered 5,500,000 (62% males) of whom over 50% were occupied in agriculture.

Trade Unions. The principal trade union federation is the *Organisation des syndicats des travailleurs camerounais* (OSTC) established on 7 Dec. 1985 to replace the former body, the UNTC.

INTERNATIONAL TRADE
Foreign debt was US$6,000m. in 1997.

Imports and Exports. Imports and exports in US$1m.:

	1993	1994	1995
Imports	1,106	1,090	1,245
Exports	1,901	1,496	2,047

Principal exports (in 1,000m. francs CFA), 1991: Oil, 262·1; logs, 37·5; cocoa, 31·7; coffee, 31·5; aluminium, 24·1; timber products, 23·9; cotton, 17·4; bananas, 13·2.

Main export markets, 1996: Spain, 21·2%; Italy, 20·4%; France, 17·7%; Netherlands, 10·3%. Main import suppliers, 1996: France, 27·0%; Nigeria, 9·7%; USA, 8·5%; Germany, 7·3%.

COMMUNICATIONS

Roads. There were about 64,626 km of classified roads in 1997, of which 2,666 km are paved. In 1996 there were 98,000 passenger cars and 64,350 commercial vehicles.

Rail. Cameroon Railways (*Regifercam*), 1,104 km in 1995, link Douala with Nkongsamba and Ngaoundéré, with branches M'Banga–Kumba and Makak–M'Balmayo. In 1992-93 railways carried 1·9m. passengers and 1·2m. tonnes of freight.

Civil Aviation. There are 45 airports including 3 international airports at Douala, Garoua and Yaoundé (Nsimalen). In 1998 Cameroon Airlines (Camair), the national carrier, operated on domestic routes and provided international services to Abidjan, Brazzaville, Cotonou, Harare, Jeddah, Johannesburg, Kigali, Lagos, Libreville, Lomé, London, Malabo, Nairobi, N'Djaména and Paris. In 1998 Cameroon was also served by Air Afrique, Air France, Air Gabon, Kenya Airways, Nigeria Airways, SABENA and Swissair. In 1995 Cameroon Airlines flew 7·2m. km and carried 345,000 passengers.

Shipping. In 1995 the merchant marine totalled 40,194 GRT. In 1993 vessels totalling 5,279,000 net registered tons entered. The main port is Douala; other ports are Bota, Campo, Garoua (only navigable in the rainy season), Kribi and Limbo-Tiko.

Telecommunications. In 1997 there were 75,200 telephone main lines. There were approximately 2,800 cellular phone subscribers in 1995 and 2,000 Internet users in Jan. 1998.

Postal Services. There were 261 post offices in 1995.

SOCIAL INSTITUTIONS

Justice. The Supreme Court sits at Yaoundé, as does the High Court of Justice (consisting of 9 titular judges and 6 surrogates all appointed by the National Assembly). There are magistrates' courts situated in the provinces.

Religion. In 1992 there were 4·43m. Roman Catholics, 2·79m. Moslems and 2·23m. Protestants. Some of the population follow traditional animist religions.

Education. In 1995, there were 1,061 pre-primary schools with 3,778 teachers for 91,242 pupils and 6,801 primary schools with 40,970 teachers for 1,896,722 pupils. In 1993–94 there were 550,480 secondary level pupils at general secondary and tertiary schools and technical schools.

In 1991, 33,177 students were in higher education at 33 teacher training colleges and 5 new institutions of higher education. Total staff: 1,086. In 1994-95 there were 6 universities and 1 Roman Catholic university, 4 specialized *Ecoles Nationales*, an

Ecole Supérieure for posts and telecommunications, 6 specialized institutes, a national school of administration and magistracy and a faculty of Protestant theology. In 1995-96 there were 15,220 university students and 830 academic staff. The adult literacy rate in 1995 was 63·4% (75·0% among males and 52·1% among females).

In 1994 total expenditure on education came to 3·1% of GNP.

Health. In 1988 there were 629 hospitals. In 1989 there were 945 doctors, 55 dentists, 206 pharmacists and 6,053 nurses.

CULTURE

Broadcasting. The state-controlled Cameroon Radio Television provides home, national, provincial and urban radio programmes and a TV service (colour by PAL). In 1995 there were about 2m. radio and 320,000 TV receivers.

Press. There was (1997) 1 national government-owned daily newspaper with a circulation of 66,000 and about 100 other periodicals, including 20 weeklies.

Tourism. In 1996 there were 101,000 foreign tourists, bringing revenue of US$52m.

DIPLOMATIC REPRESENTATIVES
Of Cameroon in Great Britain (84 Holland Pk., London, W11 3SB)
Ambassador: Samuel Libock Mbei.

Of Great Britain in Cameroon (Ave. Winston Churchill, BP 547, Yaoundé)
High Commissioner: Mr. G. P. R. Boon.

Of Cameroon in the USA (2349 Massachusetts Ave., NW, Washington, D.C., 20008)
Ambassador: Jerome Mendouga.

Of the USA in Cameroon (Rue Nachtigal, BP 817, Yaoundé)
Ambassador: Charles Twining.

Of Cameroon to the United Nations
Ambassador: Martin Belinga-Eboutou.

Of Cameroon to the European Union
Ambassador: Isabelle Bassong.

FURTHER READING
DeLancey, M. W., *Cameroon: Dependence and Independence.* London, 1989
DeLancey, M. W. and Schraeder, P. J., *Cameroon.* [Bibliography] Oxford and Santa Barbara (CA), 1986

National statistical office: Direction de la Statistique et de la Comptabilité Nationale, Ministère du Plan et de l'Aménagement du Territoire, Yaoundé

CANADA

Capital: Ottawa
Population estimate, 2000: 30·68m.
GNP per capita: (PPP$) 21,380
HDI/world rank: 0·960/1

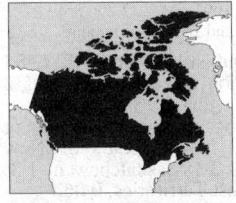

KEY HISTORICAL EVENTS

The first European in Canada was John Cabot in 1497. France claimed possession in 1534. The territories which now constitute Canada came under British power at various times by settlement, conquest or cession. For the most part such efforts were directed at gaining advantage over the indigenous Indian and Eskimo communities as well as displacing French colonial rule. Conflict also broke out, however, with the fledgling United States in the Anglo-American war of 1812–14. Since then, Canada and the USA have maintained the world's longest undefended border. Nova Scotia was occupied in 1628 by settlement at Port Royal, was ceded back to France in 1632 and was finally ceded by France in 1713 by the Treaty of Utrecht. The Hudson's Bay Company's charter, conferring rights over all the territory draining into Hudson Bay, was granted in 1670. Canada, with all its dependencies, including New Brunswick and Prince Edward Island, was formally ceded to Great Britain by France in 1763; Vancouver Island was acknowledged to be British by the Oregon Boundary Treaty of 1846; and British Columbia was established as a separate colony in 1858. As originally constituted, Canada was composed of the provinces of Upper and Lower Canada (now Ontario and Quebec), Nova Scotia and New Brunswick. They were united under the British North America Act, 1867. The Act provided that the constitution of Canada should be 'similar in principle to that of the United Kingdom'; that the executive authority should be vested in the Sovereign and carried out by a Governor-General and Privy Council; and that the legislative power should be exercised by a Parliament of two Houses: the Senate, membership of which is by appointment, and the House of Commons, whose members are elected.

In 1931 the Statute of Westminster emancipated the Provinces as well as the Dominion from the operation of the Colonial Laws Validity Act, thus removing any remaining limitations on Canada's legislative autonomy.

Provision was made in the British North America Act for the admission of British Columbia, Prince Edward Island, the Northwest Territories and Newfoundland into the Union. In 1869 Rupert's Land, or the Northwest Territories, was purchased from the Hudson's Bay Company; the province of Manitoba was erected from this territory and admitted into the confederation on 15 July 1870. On 20 July 1871 the province of British Columbia was admitted and Prince Edward Island on 1 July 1873. The provinces of Alberta and Saskatchewan were formed from the provisional districts of Alberta, Athabaska, Assiniboia and Saskatchewan, and were admitted on 1 Sept. 1905. Newfoundland formally joined Canada as its 10th province on 31 March 1949.

In Feb. 1931 Norway formally recognized the Canadian title to the Sverdrup group of Arctic islands. Canada thus holds sovereignty in the whole Arctic sector north of the Canadian mainland.

In 1982 an amended constitution replaced the British North America Act to give Canada prerogative over all future constitutional changes. At the same time a charter of Rights and Freedoms was introduced recognizing the nation's multi-cultural heritage, affirming the existing rights of native peoples and the principle of equality of benefits to the provinces.

TERRITORY AND POPULATION

Canada is bounded in the north-west by the Beaufort Sea, north by the Arctic Ocean, north-east by Baffin Bay, east by the Davis Strait, Labrador Sea and Atlantic Ocean, south by the USA and west by the Pacific Ocean and USA (Alaska). The area is 9,970,610 sq. km, of which 755,180 sq. km are fresh water. Census population, 1996, 28,846,761. Estimate, July 1997, 30,286,596 (15,286,919 females), giving a density of 3 per sq. km.

The UN gives a projected population for 2000 of 30·68m.

An estimated 76·7% of the population were urban in 1995.
Population at previous censuses:

1851	2,436,297	1901	5,371,315	1951	14,009,429
1861	3,229,633	1911	7,206,643	1961	18,238,247
1871	3,689,257	1921	8,787,949	1971	21,568,311
1881	4,324,810	1931	10,376,786	1981	24,343,181
1891	4,833,239	1941	11,506,655	1991	27,296,859[1]

[1]Excludes data from incompletely enumerated Indian reserves and Indian settlements.

Of the total population in 1996, 23,390,340 were Canadian-born and 5,137,785 foreign-born. British Columbia had the biggest population increase with 13·5% whilst Newfoundland had the biggest population reduction with −2·9%.

The population (1991) born outside Canada in the provinces was in the following ratio (%): Newfoundland, 0·19; Prince Edward Island, 0·09; Nova Scotia, 0·89; New Brunswick, 0·55; Quebec, 13·6; Ontario, 54·6; Manitoba, 3·1; Saskatchewan, 1·3; Alberta, 8·8; British Columbia, 16·7; Yukon, 0·07; Northwest Territories, 0·06.

In 1996, figures for the population, according to ethnic origin, were[1]:

Single origins	18,303,625	*Multiple origins*	10,224,500
British Isles	3,267,525	British Isles only[3]	1,606,445
French[1]	2,683,840	British Isles and French	856,985
European	3,742,895	British Isles and Canadian	1,179,725
Arab	188,430	British Isles and Other	2,217,370
West Asian	106,865	British Isles, Canadian	
South Asian	590,150	and Other	598,635
East and Southeast Asian	1,271,450	French only[1]	12,430
African	137,315	French and Canadian	597,605
Pacific Islands	5,765	French and Other	435,205
Latin, Central and		French, Canadian	
South American	118,635	and Other	121,805
Caribbean	305,290	Canadian and Other	579,045
Aboriginal	477,635	British Isles, French	
Canadian	5,326,995	and Canadian	280,595
Other single origins[2]	80,485	British Isles, French	
		and Other	518,480
		British Isles, French,	
		Canadian and Other	121,870
		Other multiple origins[2]	1,098,295

[1]Includes the single origins of French, Acadian and Québécois. The 'French only' multiple category includes respondents who reported French and Acadian.
[2]Includes American, Australian, New Zealander, Québécois and Other. The 'Other multiple origins' category includes respondents who reported 2 or more origins other than a British Isles origin, French, Acadian or Canadian.
[3]The 'British Isles only' multiple category includes respondents who reported more than one of the following origins: English, Scottish, Irish, Welsh and British.

In 1991, 60·5% of the population gave their mother tongue as English, 23·8% as French.

The total aboriginal population (single origins) numbered 470,615 in 1991 and the Inuit population was 30,085.

Populations of Census Metropolitan Areas (CMA), 1996 census, and Cities (proper), 1991 census:

	CMA	City proper		CMA	City proper
Toronto	4,263,757	635,395	Kitchener	382,940	168,282
Montreal	3,326,510	1,017,666	St Catharines-		
Vancouver	1,831,665	471,844	Niagara	372,406	—
Ottawa-Hull	1,010,498	—	St Catharines	—	129,300
Ottawa	—	313,987	Niagara Falls	—	75,399
Hull	—	60,707	Halifax	332,518	114,455
Edmonton	862,597	616,741	Victoria	304,287	71,228
Calgary	821,628	710,677	Windsor	278,685	191,435
Quebec	671,889	167,517	Oshawa	268,773	129,344
Winnipeg	667,209	616,790	Saskatoon	219,056	186,058
Hamilton	624,360	318,499	Regina	193,652	179,178
London	398,616	303,165	St John's	174,051	95,770

CANADA

	CMA	City proper		CMA	City proper
Sudbury	160,488	92,884	Sherbrooke	147,384	76,429
Chicoutimi-			Trois Rivières	139,956	49,426
Jonquière	160,454	—	Saint John	125,705	113,946
Chicoutimi	—	62,710	Thunder Bay	125,562	74,969
Jonquière	—	57,933			

In 1995-96 there were 219,183 immigrants, of whom 142,535 were from Asia (including 28,317 from Hong Kong, 20,542 from India and 10,180 from the Philippines), 37,936 from Europe (including 5,483 from the UK), 13,962 from Africa, 8,295 from the West Indies, 5,657 from South America and 5,448 from the USA. In 1995 there were 46,416 emigrants.

English and French are both official languages.

SOCIAL STATISTICS
Statistics for calendar years:

	Live births	Deaths
1995–96	372,444	209,746
1996–97	365,048	218,188
1997–98	355,290	217,860

Annual growth rate, 1993–96, 1·3%. Birth rate, 1995 (per 1,000 population), 12·8 (13·2 in 1994); death arte, 7·1 (7·1 in 1994); marriage rate, 5·4. Life expectancy at birth, 1990–95, was 75·6 years for men and 81·4 years for women. Marriages, 1995, numbered 160,616. In 1994 the most popular age range for marrying was 25–29 for both males and females, followed by 30–34 for males and 20–24 for females. Infant mortality, 1995, 6·1 per 1,000 live births; fertility rate, 1·7 children per woman.

CLIMATE
The climate ranges from polar conditions in the north to cool temperate in the south, but with considerable differences between east coast, west coast and the interior, affecting temperatures, rainfall amounts and seasonal distribution. Winters are very severe over much of the country, but summers can be very hot inland. *See* individual provinces for climatic details.

CONSTITUTION AND GOVERNMENT
In Nov. 1981 the Canadian government agreed on the provisions of an amended constitution, to the end that it should replace the British North America Act and that its future amendment should be the prerogative of Canada. These proposals were adopted by the Parliament of Canada and were enacted by the UK Parliament as the Canada Act of 1982. This was the final act of the UK Parliament in Canadian constitutional development. The Act gave to Canada the power to amend the Constitution according to procedures determined by the Constitutional Act 1982. The latter added to the Canadian Constitution a charter of Rights and Freedoms, and provisions which recognize the nation's multi-cultural heritage, affirm the existing rights of native peoples, confirm the principle of equalization of benefits among the provinces, and strengthen provincial ownership of natural resources.

Under the Constitution legislative power is vested in Parliament, consisting of the Queen, represented by a Governor-General, a Senate and a House of Commons. The members of the *Senate* are appointed until age 75 by summons of the Governor-General under the Great Seal of Canada. Members appointed before 2 June 1965 may remain in office for life. The Senate consists of 104 senators: 24 from Ontario, 24 from Quebec, 10 from Nova Scotia, 10 from New Brunswick, 4 from Prince Edward Island, 6 from Manitoba, 6 from British Columbia, 6 from Alberta, 6 from Saskatchewan, 6 from Newfoundland, 1 from the Yukon Territory and 1 from the Northwest Territories. Each senator must be at least 30 years of age and reside in the province for which he or she is appointed. The *House of Commons* is elected by universal secret suffrage, by a first-past-the-post system, for 5-year terms. Representation is based on the population of all the provinces taken as a whole with readjustments made after each census.

The Special Joint Committee of the Senate and the House of Commons on a Renewed Canada released a unanimous report on 28 Feb. 1992 (Beaudoin-Dobbie Report). Another constitutional document was released on 16 July 1992 by the provincial premiers which summarized the multilateral meetings on the Constitution. A final constitutional accord was arrived at by the provinces and the federal government in Aug. 1992. At a national referendum on 26 Oct. 1992 proposed constitutional reforms were rejected by 54·4% of votes cast.

Indians have representation in the *Assembly of First Nations* (Chief, Ovide Mercredi).

The office and appointment of the Governor-General are regulated by letters patent of 1947. In 1977 the Queen approved the transfer to the Governor-General of functions discharged by the Sovereign. The Governor-General is assisted by a *Privy Council* composed of Cabinet Ministers.

Canadian Parliamentary Guide. Annual. Ottawa
Federalism and the Charter: Leading Constitutional Decisions. Edited and with an introduction by Peter H. Russell, 5th ed. Carleton Univ. Press, Ottawa, 1989
Laskin's Canadian Constitutional Law. 5th ed., Vol. 2, Neil Finkelstein. Toronto: Carswell, 1986
Bayefsky, A. F., *Canada's Constitution Act 1982 and Amendments: A Documentary History.* 2 vols. Toronto, 1989
Bejermi, J., *Canadian Parliamentary Handbook.* Ottawa, 1993
Cairns, A. C., *Charter versus Federalism: the Dilemmas of Constitutional Reform.* Montreal, 1992
Canada: The State of the Federation. Queen's Univ., annual
Cheffins, R. I. and Johnson, P. A., *The Revised Canadian Constitution: Politics as law.* Toronto, 1986
Forsey, E. A., *How Canadians Govern Themselves.* Ottawa, 1991
Fox, P. W. and White, G., *Politics Canada.* 7th ed. Toronto, 1991
Franks, C. E. S., *The Parliament of Canada.* Univ. of Toronto Press, 1987
Hogg, P. W., *Constitutional Law of Canada.* 3rd ed. Toronto, 1992
Kaplan, W. (ed.) *Belonging: the Meaning and Future of Canadian Citizenship.* McGill-Queen's Univ. Press, 1993
Kernaghan, K., *Public Administration in Canada: a Text.* Scarborough, 1991
Mahler, G., *Contemporary Canadian Politics, 1970–1994: an Annotated Bibliography.* 2 vols. Westport (CT), 1995
Osbaldston, G. F., *Organizing to Govern.* Toronto, 1992
Reesor, B., *The Canadian Constitution in Historical Perspective.* Scarborough, 1992
Tardi, G., *The Legal Framework of Government: a Canadian Guide.* Aurora, 1992
White, W. L., *Introduction to Canadian Politics and Government.* 5th ed. Toronto, 1990

National Anthem. 'O Canada, our home and native land'/'O Canada, terre de nos aïeux'; words by A. Routhier, tune by C. Lavallée.

RECENT ELECTIONS

At the elections of 2 June 1997 the Liberal Party (Lib) gained 155 seats (177 in 1993) with 38·4% of votes cast; the Reform Party 60 (52) with 19·3%, thus becoming the official opposition; the Bloc Québécois (BQ) 44 (54) with 10·7%; the New Democratic Party 21 (9) with 11·0%; the Progressive Conservative Party 20 (2) with 18·9%; ind 1.

CURRENT ADMINISTRATION

Governor-General: Roméo Leblanc (b. 1928; term of office 1994–99).

The thirty-sixth Parliament, elected on 2 June 1997, comprised 301 members.

State of the parties in the Senate (1995): Progressive Conservatives, 51; Liberals, 42; Bloc Québécois, 8; Reform Party, 1; Independent Conservatives, 1; Vacant, 1.

The *Speaker* of the Senate is Gildas L. Molgat.

The following is the list of ministers in the Liberal Cabinet in March 1999:

Prime Minister: The Rt. Hon. Jean Chrétien.

Deputy Prime Minister: Herbert Eser Gray. *Foreign Affairs:* Lloyd Axworthy. *Transport:* David Michael Collenette. *Fisheries and Oceans:* David Anderson. *Natural Resources and Minister responsible for The Canadian Wheat Board:* Ralph E. Goodale. *Canadian Heritage:* Sheila Copps. *International Trade:* Sergio Marchi. *Industry:* John Manley. *International Co-operation and Minister responsible for Francophonie:* Diane Marleau. *Finance:* Paul Martin. *National Defence:* Arthur C. Eggleton. *President of the Treasury Board and Minister responsible for Infrastructure:* Marcel Massé. *Justice and Attorney General of Canada:* Anne McLellan. *Health:* Allan Rock. *Labour:* Claudette Bradshaw. *Environment:* Christine Stewart. *Public Works and Government Services:* Alfonso Gagliano.

CANADA

Citizenship and Immigration: Lucienne Robillard. *Veterans Affairs, Atlantic Canada:* Fred J. Mifflin. *Indian Affairs and Northern Development:* Jane Stewart. *President of the Queen's Privy Council for Canada and Intergovernmental Affairs:* Stephané Dion. *Human Resources Development:* Pierre Pettigrew. *Leader of the Government in the House of Commons:* Don Boudria. *Leader of the Government in the Senate:* Bernard Alasdair Graham. *Agriculture and Agri-Food:* Lyle Vanclief. *National Revenue:* Herb Dhaliwal. *Solicitor General of Canada:* Andy Scott.

The *Speaker* is Gilbert Parent (Lib).

The *Leader of the Opposition* is Michel Gauthier (BQ).

DEFENCE
The armed forces are unified and organized in functional commands: Mobile Command (land forces), Air Command (air forces) and Maritime Command (naval and naval air forces). There is a Tactical Air Group under the control of Mobile Command. In 1997 the armed forces numbered 61,600 (6,500 women); reserves, 72,100.

Military expenditure totalled US$7,757m. in 1997 (US$270 per capita), representing 1·3% of GDP.

Army. The Land Forces numbered 21,900 in 1997 and were organized in 1 Task Force Headquarters, 3 mechanized infantry brigade groups (each with 1 Armoured regiment, 2 infantry battalions, 1 mechanized infantry battalion, 1 artillery regiment, 1 engineer regiment and 1 air defence battery), 1 Independent air defence regiment and 1 independent engineer support regiment. Reserves comprise a Militia of 20,100 and the Canadian Rangers, 3,250. Equipment includes 114 Leopard C-1 main battle tanks and 130 surface-to-air missiles.

Navy. The naval combatant force, which forms part of the Maritime Command of the unified armed forces, is headquartered at Halifax (Nova Scotia), and comprises 3 diesel submarines, 4 guided-missile destroyers and 16 helicopter-carrying frigates. Major auxiliaries include 3 helicopter-carrying replenishment tankers, 2 survey research ships, 2 tugs and a diver support ship, and there are some 40 Minor auxiliaries, tenders and service craft. The Maritime Air Group includes 28 Sea King for embarked service. Naval personnel in 1997 numbered about 9,400, with 4,000 reserves. The main bases are Halifax, where about two-thirds of the fleet is based, and Esquimault (British Columbia).

The Coast Guard numbers 4,000, and operates 17 icebreakers, numerous search-and-rescue and support craft, together with 2 fixed-wing aircraft, 37 helicopters and 5 hovercraft.

Air Force. The air forces numbered 17,600 in 1997 (825 women) with 190 combat aircraft and 150 helicopters. They are organized in the Air Combat and Mobility Group, the Maritime Air Group and Air Command HQ. The first controls air defence, tactical transport and helicopter units; the second oversees patrol, search-and-rescue and electronic countermeasures units; the third is responsible for training and logistics transports. Combat units include 5 squadrons of F-18 Hornet fighters, 4 of P-3 Orion patrol aircraft and 3 with Sea King anti-submarine helicopters.

INTERNATIONAL RELATIONS
Canada is a member of the UN, the Commonwealth, OAS, OECD, OSCE, APEC and NATO.

ECONOMY
Performance. GDP at market prices was $830,828m. in 1998 ($806,737m. in 1997). Real GDP growth was 3·8% in 1997 and 2·98% in 1998.

Budget. Federal government revenue and expenditure for fiscal years ending 31 March (in $1m.):

	1994-95	1995-96	1996-97	1997-98
Revenue	137,269	143,498	153,875	166,051
Expenditure	173,403	175,388	167,538	162,866

In 1997-98 revenue included (in $1m.): Income taxes, 100,275; consumption taxes, 33,789; contributions to Social Insurance Plans, 18,882; sales of goods and income, 6,171. Expenditure included social services, 48,632; debt charges, 43,971; and general purpose transfers, 20,101.

On 31 March 1994 the net public debt was $409,100m.

On 1 Jan. 1991 a 7% Goods and Services Tax (GST) was introduced, superseding a 13·5% manufacturers' sales tax.

Currency. The unit of currency is the *Canadian dollar* (CAD) of 100 *cents*. In Feb. 1998 gold reserves were 3·09m. troy oz., and foreign exchange reserves totalled US$18,451m. Total money supply was $170bn. in Jan. 1998. Inflation was 0·9% in 1998.

Banking and Finance. The Bank of Canada (established 1935) is the central bank and bank of issue. The *governor* (in 1997, Gordon G. Thiessen) is appointed by the Bank's directors for 7-year terms. The Minister of Finance owns the capital stock of the Bank on behalf of Canada. Banks in Canada are chartered under the terms of the Bank Act, which imposes strict conditions on capital reserves, returns to the federal government, types of lending operations, ownership and other matters. In Aug. 1994 there were 60 chartered banks—7 domestic and 53 foreign. The 6 biggest domestic banks had 7,971 branches serving over 1,600 communities in all provinces and both territories in Canada, and 259 branches in 56 other countries. The foreign bank subsidiaries operate 269 offices in Canada. The First Nations Bank was founded in Dec. 1996 to provide finance to Inuit and Indian entrepreneurs.

Bank charters expire every 10 years which gives the federal government an opportunity to review and amend sections of the Bank Act. Extensive changes were brought into force in June 1992. As a result of the substantial revision, bank charters were only renewed for 5 years. The chartered banks make regular detailed returns to and are subject to periodic inspection by the Superintendent of Financial Institutions, an official appointed by the Government.

The Bank Act of 1980 required chartered banks to maintain a statutory primary reserve of 10% on demand deposits, 3% on foreign-currency deposits and 2% on notice deposits, with an additional 1% on the portion of notice deposits exceeding $500m. This reserve is required to be maintained in the form of notes and deposits with the Bank of Canada. A secondary reserve of 4% in the form of treasury bills, government bonds, etc., is also required.

There are stock exchanges at Calgary (Alberta Stock Exchange), Montreal, Toronto, Vancouver and Winnipeg.

Weights and Measures. The legal weights and measures are in transition from the Imperial to the International system of units. The Metric Commission, established in June 1971, co-ordinates Canada's conversion to the metric system.

ENERGY AND NATURAL RESOURCES

Electricity. Generating capacity, 1995, 113m. kW. Net electricity generation in 1995 was 544m. MWh. 503m. MWh was to meet domestic demand. Of the total generated, 62% was from hydrogeneration, 21% from thermal generation and 17% from nuclear generation. Production, 1996, 440·06m. MWh. Consumption per capita was an estimated 16,137 kWh in 1995.

Oil and Gas. Oil reserves at the beginning of 1995 were 656·1m. cu. metres (4,100m. bbls.); gas, 1,898,000m. cu. metres. Production of petroleum crude and equivalent, 1996, 318,600 cu. metres a day; natural gas (1995), 149,600m. cu. metres. Canada's first off-shore field, 250 km off Nova Scotia, began producing in June 1992.

Minerals. Mineral production in 1995 (in 1,000 tonnes): Coal (1996), 75,675; iron ore (1996), 36,000; copper, 705; lead, 203; zinc, 1,094; nickel, 167; uranium, 10·09; silver, 1·19; gold, 149,027 kg; salt, 10,772; asbestos, 511; cobalt, 2; lime, 2,516; gypsum, 7,974; peat, 1,010; sand and gravel, 239,871.

Agriculture. According to the census of 1991 the total land area was 2,278·6m. acres of which 167·4m. acres was agricultural.

Grain growing, dairy farming, fruit farming, ranching and fur farming are all practised. In 1995, 2·5% of the economically active population was engaged in agriculture. Total farm cash receipts (1997) $29,585,697.

CANADA

The following table shows the value of farm cash receipts for 1997, for selected agricultural commodities, in $1m.:

Crops		Livestock	
Wheat	13,933	and products	14,581
Barley	3,593	Beef	5,222
Canola	732	Hogs	2,985
Oats	2,038	Poultry	1,298
Deferred grain receipts	274	Dairy	3,710
Other cereals	102		
and oilseeds	1,962		
Other crops	4,507		

Average farm size, 598 acres. In 1996, 252,839 farms (of which 67,531 were beef cattle farms; 24,411 dairy; 29,526, wheat; 51,577 other grain and oilseed) reported total gross farm receipts of $2,500 or more.

Output (in 1,000 tonnes) and sown area (in 1,000 ha) of crops:

	Output		Sown Area	
	1992	1993	1992	1993
Wheat	29,871	27,825	13,830	12,626
Barley	10,919	13,342	3,790	4,240
Maize	4,883	6,300	858	950
Rye	265	314	138	159
Oats	2,823	3,615	1,238	1,357
Potatoes	3,588	3,333	124	125
Beans	53	120	54	82
Peas	505	1,000	277	482
Lentils	349	300	267	332
Soya beans	1,455	1,900	623	725
Sunflowers	65[1]	79[1]	74	85
Rape	3,872[1]	5,400[1]	3,045	4,027
Tomatoes	474	475	11	12
Carrots	299	310	7	8
Sugar beet	776	1,050	23	22
Hops	480	490	300	305
Tobacco	65	76	30	30

[1]Seeds

Livestock. 1996: Cattle, 13,186,000; pigs, 12,097,000; sheep, 677,000; horses, 350,000; chickens, 1995, 132m.; turkeys, 6m. In parts of Saskatchewan and Alberta, stockraising is still carried on as a primary industry, but the livestock industry of the country at large is mainly a subsidiary of mixed farming. The following table shows the numbers of livestock (in 1,000) by provinces in July 1992:

Provinces	Milch cows	Total cattle and calves	Sheep and lambs	Pigs
Newfoundland	4·9	8·6	8·9	15·0
Prince Edward Island	18·5	94·0	3·2	103·0
Nova Scotia	28·3	128·0	30·0	126·0
New Brunswick	22·8	104·0	8·5	83·0
Quebec	505·0	1,430·0	116·0	3,068·0
Ontario	433·0	2,175·0	250·0	3,092·0
Manitoba	55·0	1,176·0	35·0	1,452·0
Saskatchewan	45·0	2,442·0	92·0	879·0
Alberta	105·0	4,866·0	311·0	1,868·0
British Columbia	75·0	773·5	72·5	213·5
Total	1,292·5	13,197·1	927·1	10,900·0

Livestock products. Slaughterings in 1993: Cattle, 3·37m.; sheep, 0·53m.; pigs, 15·4m. Production, 1993 (in 1,000 tonnes): Beef, 930; pork, 1,200; mutton, 11; horsemeat, 22; poultry meat, 735; cow's milk, 7,045; hens' eggs, 315; honey, 31; greasy wool, 1·52; rinsed wool, 0·96; hides, 85·84.

Fruit production in 1993 (and 1992), in 1,000 tonnes: Apples, 482 (553); pears, 16 (21); peaches and nectarines, 43 (40); plums, 3 (3); strawberries, 28 (29); raspberries, 15 (15).

Forestry. Forestry is of great economic importance, and forestry products (pulp, newsprint, building timber) constitute Canada's most valuable exports. As of 1986, the total area of land covered by forests was estimated at 453·3m. ha. In 1995, the area classed as productive forest land was estimated at 2,446 sq. km, or 26·5% of the total land area, up from 2,437 sq. km in 1990 as a result of afforestation.

In 1995 the net merchantable volume (in 1,000 cu. metres) of roundwood harvested was 188,433; logs and bolts, 148,837; plywood, 31,089; fuelwood and firewood, 5,319; other industrial roundwood, 3,189.

Fur Trade. In 1996, 1,467,500 wildlife pelts valued at $34,541,000, and 948,800 ranch-raised pelts valued at $41,265,300 were produced.

Fisheries. In 1993, the fishing fleet comprised 432 vessels totalling 169,900 GRT.

In 1995 total catches were 880,891 tonnes (877,238 tonnes from sea fishing). Atlantic landings totalled 633,413 tonnes; Pacific landings totalled 243,852 tonnes. Value of sea fisheries landed in 1996 totalled $1,536m.

INDUSTRY

Principal manufactures in 1993 (in 1,000 tonnes): Cement, 9,396; crude iron and alloys, 9,391; crude steel, 14,387; aluminium, 2,309; copper, 562; lead, 220; nickel, 141; zinc, 662; cadmium, 2; synthetic rubber, 199; passenger cars, 1·17m. units; lorries, 0·84m. Other products, 1992 (in 1,000 tonnes unless otherwise stated): Petroleum products, 31,293; heating oil, 28,336; mechanical wood pulp, 22,830; paper and cardboard, 16,585; newsprint, 8,931; sugar, 114; sawn timber, 56·3m. cu. metres; plywood, 1·84m. cu. metres; chipboard, 3·26m. cu. metres.

Labour. In 1996 the labour force was (in 1,000) 15,145·4 (6,844 females), of whom 13,676·2 (6,197·3) were in employment (2,589 part-time), distributed as follows: Business and personal services, 2,786·4; trade, 2,361·2; manufacturing, 2,082·5; health and social services, 1,425·7; educational services, 929; transport, storage and communication, 872·6; public administration, 820·1; finance, insurance and real estate, 799·9; primary industries, 733·2 (including agriculture, 453·3); construction, 718·6; utilities, 147. Unemployed, 1996, 1,469·2 (646·7 females). Unemployment rate, 1997, 9·2% (1996, 9·7%). By Sept. 1998 the rate had fallen to 8·1%, the lowest for 8 years.

Average weekly earnings in industry in Oct. 1996 were $592·64.

In 1995, 1,607,000 working days were lost in industrial disputes.

Trade Unions. Union membership in 1994 was 4,077,987, 29·2% of the workforce. 60·8% of the membership was affiliated to the Canadian Labour Congress, 6·3% to the Confédération des Syndicats Nationaux and 4·9% to the Canadian Confederation of Labour. 19·4% of unions were unaffiliated.

It is generally established by legislation, both federal and provincial, that a trade union to which the majority of employees in a unit suitable for collective bargaining belong, is given certain rights and duties. An employer is required to meet and negotiate with such a trade union to determine wage rates and other working conditions of employees. The employer, the trade union and the employees affected are bound by the resulting agreement. If an impasse is reached in negotiation, conciliation services provided by the appropriate government board are available. Generally, work stoppages do not take place until an established conciliation or mediation procedure has been carried out, and are prohibited while an agreement is in effect.

INTERNATIONAL TRADE

A North American Free Trade Agreement (NAFTA) between Canada, Mexico and the USA was signed on 7 Oct. 1992 and came into force on 1 Jan. 1994.

Imports and Exports. In 1998 exports totalled $323,400·3m.; merchandise imports totalled $303,983·8m.

Main export markets, 1998 (in $1m.): USA, 270,560·5; Japan, 9,635·5; EU, 17,837·3; other OECD countries, 7,487·0; other countries, 17,879·9. Main import suppliers: USA, 234,177·3; Japan, 9,657·0; EU, 25,424·0; other OECD countries, 11,377·3; other countries, 23,348·2.

Main categories of exports, 1998 (in $1m.): Vehicles and parts, 79,246·8 (of which passenger cars and chassis, 43,599·9; motor vehicle parts, 21,621·4); machinery and equipment, 78,770·2 (industrial and agricultural machinery, 16,598·1; aircraft and other transport equipment, 16,245·6); industrial goods and materials, 57,356·1 (metals and alloys, 19,720·2; chemicals, plastics and fertilizers, 17,513·7); forestry products, 35,464·6 (lumber and sawmill products, 16,569·6; newsprint and other paper and paperboard products, 12,761·9). Imports (in $1m.): Machinery and equipment, 101,599·2 (of which industrial and agricultural machinery, 28,200·9; office machines and equipment, 16,037·9); vehicles and parts, 66,753·0 (motor vehicle parts, 39,459·5); industrial goods and materials, 60,295·6 (chemicals and plastics, 21,502·0; metals and metal ores, 15,344·6).

COMMUNICATIONS

Roads. In 1995 there were 912,200 km of roads, of which 16,600 km were motorways, 15,000 km highways and main roads, 224,800 km secondary roads and 655,800 km other roads.

In general, highways are controlled and maintained by the provinces who also have the responsibility of providing assistance to their municipalities and townships. Federal expenditures are directed largely to the maintenance of national park highways, Indian Reserve roads and designated provincial/territorial highway construction projects. The Alaska Highway is part of the Canadian highway system.

In 1991 intercity and rural bus services carried 15·3m. passengers 163·6m. vehicle-km, earning $408·2m.

Registered motor vehicles totalled 17,794,703 in 1994; they included 13,639,358 passenger cars and taxis, 3,697,792 trucks and truck tractors, 65,138 buses and 329,809 motor cycles and mopeds.

There were 3,347 fatalities in road accidents in 1995.

Rail. Canada has 2 great trans continental systems: The Canadian National Railway system (CN), a body privatized in 1995 which operated 32,500 km (1994) of routes, and the Canadian Pacific Railway (CP), a joint-stock corporation operating 30,039 km (1994). A government-funded organization, VIA Rail, operates passenger services; 3·6m. passengers were carried in 1995. There are several provincial and private railways.

There are metros in Montreal, Toronto and Vancouver, and tram/light rail systems in Calgary, Edmonton and Toronto.

Civil Aviation. Civil aviation is under the jurisdiction of the federal government. The technical and administrative aspects are supervised by Transport Canada, while the economic functions are assigned to the National Transportation Agency.

In 1996 the 8 principal Canadian airports handled 52,923,000 passengers (40,876,000 in 1992) and 729,700 tonnes of freight, with Toronto (Lester B. Pearson International) handling 20,922,000 passengers and 336,600 tonnes of freight, and Vancouver International 11,947,000 passengers and 190,800 tonnes of freight.

The 2 major airlines are Air Canada (privatized in July 1989) and Canadian Airlines International. In 1995 Air Canada flew 261·1m. km and carried 12,569,000 passengers, and Canadian Airlines International flew 188m. km and carried 7,722,000 passengers.

Shipping. In 1993 the merchant marine comprised 1,049 vessels over 100 GRT, including 31 oil tankers. Total tonnage, 1995, 0·66m. GRT, including oil tankers, 0·2m. GRT and container ships, 1,910 GRT. In 1994 vessels totalling 60,417,000 net registered tons entered ports and vessels totalling 116,279,000 NRT cleared.

The major canals are those of the St Lawrence–Great Lakes waterway. In 1992, traffic on the Montreal–Lake Ontario Section of the Seaway numbered 2,493 transits carrying 31·4m. cargo tonnes; on the Welland Canal Section, 3,140 transits with 33·2m. cargo tonnes.

Telecommunications. In Oct. 1996 there were 18,459,500 telephone main lines in use (609·5 per 1,000 persons); telephone provision was delivered in 1996 by about 100 companies to 98·7% of households. There were 0·5m. fax machines in 1997. There were approximately 6·3m. Internet users in Nov. 1998, or nearly 21% of the population. In 1995 there were 2,590,000 cellular phone subscribers (88 for every

1,000 persons), 5,700,000 PCs (193 for every 1,000 persons) and 525,000 fax machines.

Postal Services. At the end of the fiscal year 1995–96 Canada Post Corporation's retail network consisted of 18,500 retail locations. During fiscal year 1995–96, 11,800m. pieces of mail were processed. Total revenue (1995–96) was $4,900m.; income after expenditure, $28m.

SOCIAL INSTITUTIONS

Justice. There is a Supreme Court in Ottawa, having general appellate jurisdiction in civil and criminal cases throughout Canada. The Exchequer Court (established in 1875) was replaced by the Federal Court in 1971. This has a Trial Division, consisting of the Associate Chief Justice and 9 other judges, and an Appeal Division, consisting of the Chief Justice and 3 other judges. Its seat is in Ottawa, but each Division may sit in any place in Canada. Decisions of the Trial Division may be appealed to the Appeal Division, those of the latter to the Supreme Court. There is a Superior Court in each province and county courts, with limited jurisdiction, in most of the provinces, all the judges in these courts being appointed by the Governor-General. Police, magistrates and justices of the peace are appointed by the provincial governments.

For the year ended 31 Dec. 1997, 2,632,082 Criminal Code Offences (excluding traffic) were reported, including 517 homicides. 203,900 cases were heard in Youth Courts in 1995. By the end of 1996 there were 14,143 inmates in federal custody.

Royal Canadian Mounted Police (RCMP). The RCMP is a civil force maintained by the federal government. Established in 1873 as the North-West Mounted Police, it became 'Royal' in 1904. Its sphere of operations was expanded in 1918 to include all of Canada west of Thunder Bay. In 1920 the force absorbed the Dominion Police, its headquarters was transferred from Regina to Ottawa, and its title was changed to Royal Canadian Mounted Police. The force is responsible to the Solicitor-General of Canada and is controlled by a Commissioner who holds the rank of Deputy Minister. The Commissioner is empowered to appoint peace officers in all the provinces and territories of Canada.

The responsibilities of the RCMP are national in scope. The administration of justice within the provinces, including the enforcement of the Criminal Code of Canada, is the responsibility of provincial governments, but all the provinces except Ontario and Quebec have entered into contracts with the RCMP to enforce criminal and provincial laws under the direction of the respective Attorneys-General. In addition, in these 8 provinces the RCMP is under agreement to provide police services to municipalities. The RCMP is also responsible for all police work in the Yukon and Northwest Territories, enforcing federal law and territorial ordinances. The 13 Divisions, alphabetically designated, make up the strength of the RCMP across Canada; they comprise 52 sub-divisions which include 723 detachments. Headquarters Division, as well as the Office of the Commissioner, is located in Ottawa.

Assisting the criminal investigation work of the RCMP is the Directorate of Identification Services; its services, together with those of divisional and sub-divisional units, and of 8 Crime Detection Laboratories, are available to police forces throughout Canada. The Canadian Police Information Centre at RCMP Headquarters, a national computer network, is staffed and operated by the RCMP. Law Enforcement agencies throughout Canada have access via remote terminals to information on stolen vehicles, licences and wanted persons.

In Feb. 1993 the Force had a total strength of 21,311 including regular members, special constables, civilian members and public service employees. It maintained 6,992 motor vehicles, 92 police service dogs and 156 horses.

The Force has 13 divisions actively engaged in law enforcement, 1 Headquarters Division and 1 training division. Marine services are divisional responsibilities and the Force currently has 402 boats at various points across Canada. The Air Directorate has stations throughout the country and maintains a fleet of 21 fixed-wing aircraft and 8 helicopters.

CANADA

Total police personnel in Canada at the end of 1994 numbered 74,902. Apart from the RCMP, Ontario and Quebec have police forces, as do most municipal centres. In 1995, 9% of police officers were women.

Religion. The most recent statistics available in 1997:

Religious body	Inclusive membership	Number of churches	Number of clergy
Anglican Church of Canada	780,897	2,499	3,240
Canadian Baptist Ministries	138,000	1,136	1,107
Evangelical Lutheran Church	290,846	1,006	1,230
Pentecostal Assemblies of Canada	226,678	1,075	...
Presbyterian Church	152,425	1,026	1,169
Roman Catholic Church	12,498,605	5,878	11,838
Ukrainian Greek Orthodox	120,000	270	...
United Church of Canada	2,018,808	4,044	3,939

Membership of other denominations: Latter-day Saints (Mormons), 146,000; Jehovah's Witnesses (1996), 110,659; Mennonites (1995), 114,000; Moslems (1996), 0·35m.; Jews (1996), 0·35m; Salvation Army (1996), 92,330.

Education. Under the Constitution the provincial legislatures have powers over education. These are subject to certain qualifications respecting the rights of denominational and minority language schools. School board revenues derive from local taxation on real property, and government grants from general provincial revenue.

In 1996–97 there were 16,096 elementary and secondary public and private schools and 198 community colleges. There were 541,650 children in pre-elementary institutions; 4,969,317 children in elementary and secondary schools with 306,498 teachers; and 388,976 students in community colleges.

Enrolment for Indian and Inuit children, 1992–93: Federal schools, 5,096; band-operated schools, 49,426; provincial schools, 44,418; private schools, 1,950.

In 1995–96 there were 48 universities, 1 technical university, 4 university colleges, 10 colleges, 1 Dominican college, 1 college of agriculture, 1 college of art and design, 2 open universities, 2 polytechnics, higher schools of business, public administration, and technology, and institutes of education, microbiology and virology, and scientific research. In 1996–97 there were 572,179 full-time and 248,231 part-time university students with 36,035 teachers.

The adult literacy rate in 1995 was 98·8% (99% among males and 98·7% among females). In 1994, total public education expenditure was $49,932m.

Health. Constitutional responsibility for healthcare services rests with the provinces and territories. Accordingly, Canada's national health insurance system consists of an interlocking set of provincial and territorial hospital and medical insurance plans conforming to certain national standards rather than a single national programme. These national standards, which are set out in the Canada Health Act, include: Provision of a comprehensive range of hospital and medical benefits; universal population coverage; access to necessary services on uniform terms and conditions; portability of benefits; and public administration of provincial and territorial insurance plans.

Provinces and territories satisfying these national standards are eligible for federal financial transfer payments. The provinces and territories are entitled to receive equal-per-capita federal health contributions escalated annually by the 3-year average increase in nominal GNP. These federal contributions, estimated at $3,734m. in 1993–94, are paid in the form of a combination of tax point and cash transfers. Over and above these health transfers, the federal government also provides financial support for such provincial and territorial extended healthcare service programmes as nursing-home care, certain home care services, ambulatory healthcare services and adult residential care services. These supplementary equal-per-capita cash payments were estimated at $1,475m. in 1993–94.

The national health insurance programmes were introduced in stages. The Hospital Insurance and Diagnostic Services Act was passed in 1957, providing prepaid coverage to all Canadians for in-patient and, at the option of each province and territory, out-patient hospital services. The Medical Care Act was introduced in 1968 to extend universal coverage to all medically equipped services provided by

CANADA

medical practitioners. The Canada Health Act, which took effect on 1 April 1984, consolidated the original federal health insurance legislation and clarified the national standards provinces and territories are required to meet in order to qualify for full federal health contributions.

The approach taken by Canada is one of state-sponsored health insurance. Accordingly, the advent of insurance programmes produced little change in the ownership of hospitals, almost all of which are owned by non-government non-profit corporations, or in the rights and privileges of private medical practice. Patients are free to choose their own general practitioner. Except for a small percentage of the population whose care is provided for under other legislation (such as serving members of the Canadian Armed Forces and inmates of federal penitentiaries), all residents are eligible, regardless of whether they are in the workforce. Benefits are available without upper limit so long as they are medically necessary, provided any registration obligations are met.

In addition to the benefits qualifying for federal contributions, provinces and territories provide additional benefits at their own discretion. Most fund their portion of health costs out of general provincial and territorial revenues. There are no co-charges for medically necessary short-term hospital care or medical care. Most provinces and territories have charges for long-term chronic hospital care geared, approximately, to the room and board portion of this OAS–GIS payment mentioned under Social Welfare. In 1991, total health expenditures were about $66·77m., representing 10·2% of GNP. Public sector spending accounts for about 72·2% of total national health expenditure.

In 1995 there were estimated to be 63,700 doctors, giving a rate of 465 persons per doctor.

Welfare. The social security system provides financial benefits and social services to individuals and their families through a variety of programmes administered by federal, provincial and municipal governments, and voluntary organizations. Federally, Human Resources and Labour is responsible for research into the areas of social issues, provision of grants and contributions for various social services, and the administration of several income security programmes. These services are: The Old Age Security programme, introduced in 1952 and to which were added the Guaranteed Income Supplement in 1967 and the Spouse's Allowance in 1975; and the Canada Pension Plan and Canada Assistance Plan which came into being in 1966.

The Old Age Security (OAS) pension is payable to persons 65 years of age and over who satisfy the residence requirements stipulated in the Old Age Security Act. The amount payable, whether full or partial, is also governed by stipulated conditions, as is the payment of an OAS pension to a recipient who absents himself from Canada. OAS pensioners with little or no income apart from OAS may, upon application, receive a full or partial supplement known as the Guaranteed Income Supplement (GIS). Entitlement is normally based on the pensioner's income in the preceding year, calculated in accordance with the Income Tax Act. The spouse of an OAS pensioner, aged 60 to 64, meeting the same residence requirements as those stipulated for OAS, may be eligible for a full or partial Spouse's Allowance (SPA). SPA is payable, on application, depending on the annual combined income of the couple (not including the pensioner spouse's basic OAS pension or GIS). In 1979, the SPA programme was expanded to include a spouse, who is eligible for SPA in the month the pensioner spouse dies, until the age of 65 or until remarriage (Extended Spouse's Allowance). Since Sept. 1985, SPA has also been available to low income widow(er)s aged 60–64 regardless of the age of their spouse at death. For the third quarter of 1993, the basic OAS pension was $383·51 monthly; the maximum Guaranteed Income Supplement was $455·76 monthly for a single pensioner or a married pensioner whose spouse was not receiving a pension or a Spouse's Allowance, and $296·87 monthly for each spouse of a married couple where both were pensioners. The maximum Spouse's Allowance for the same quarter was $680·38 monthly (equal to the basic pension plus the maximum GIS married rate), and $751·13 for widow(er)s. Total OAS/GIS/SPA benefit expenditures for 1991–92 were $18,921m.; in July 1992, over 3m. Canadians received benefits through these programmes.

CANADA

The Canada Pension Plan (CPP) is designed to provide workers with a basic level of income protection in the event of retirement, disability or death. Benefits may be payable to a contributor, a surviving spouse or an eligible child. As of 1 Jan. 1992, payment of actuarially adjusted retirement benefits may begin as early as age 60 or as late as age 70. Benefits are determined by the contributor's earnings and contributions made to the Plan. Contribution is compulsory for most employed and self-employed Canadians 18 to 65 years of age. The CPP does not operate in Quebec, which has exercised its constitutional prerogative to establish a similar plan. In 1993, the maximum retirement pension payable under CPP was $667·36; the maximum disability pension was $812·85; and the maximum surviving spouse's pension was $400·42 (for survivors 65 years of age and over). For survivors under 65 years of age CPP pays a reduced flat rate. In 1993 CPP was funded by equal contributions of 2·5% of pensionable earnings from the employer and 2·5% from the employee (self-employed persons contribute the full 5%), in addition to the interest on the investment of excess funds. In 1993, the range of yearly pensionable earnings was from $3,300 to $33,400; a person who earned and contributed at less than the maximum level receives monthly benefits at rates lower than the maximum allowable under CPP. In July 1993, over 3·8m. Canadians received Canada or Quebec Pension Plan benefits. Total expenditure in 1992–93 for CPP was about $13,100m.

Social security agreements co-ordinate the operation of the Old Age Security and the CPP with the comparable social security programmes of certain other countries.

The Federal Government passed legislation in Nov. 1992 which replaced the Family Allowances programme with a new Child Tax Benefit, administered jointly by Human Resources and Labour and Revenue Canada. The programme delivered Canada its first payments in Jan. 1993.

Ismael, J. S. (ed.) *Canadian Welfare State: Evolution and Transition.* Univ. of Alberta Press, 1987

CULTURE

Broadcasting. The Canadian Radio-Television and Telecommunications Commission is an independent authority established by parliament in 1968 to regulate public and private radio and television. The Canadian Broadcasting Corporation operates 2 national TV networks, one in English and one in French, and there are 3 private TV networks. In 1995, there were 2,245 cable TV systems, and in 1997 there were 7,867,000 subscribers to cable television. In 1996 there were 21,200,000 TV receivers and 32,000,000 radio receivers (714 and 1,078 per 1,000 population).

There were 841 originating radio stations operating in 1996, of which 333 were AM and 508 FM. There were also 968 radio re-broadcasters.

Cinema. There were 620 cinemas and 103 drive-in theatres in 1991–92.

Press. In 1996 there were 107 daily papers (total circulation, 4·72m., giving a rate of 159 per 1,000 inhabitants). There were 1,071 non-daily papers with a circulation of 21,235,000 or 715 per 1,000 inhabitants.

Tourism. In 1996 there were 17,286,000 foreign tourists, around 90% of whom were from the USA. Revenue from visitors was US$8,868m.

Festivals. There are numerous festivals planned for the Millenium including a Millenium Eve Vigil and Music Canada 2000, which will showcase Canadian artistic and cultural resources.

Libraries. In 1995 there was 1 National Library and 3,672 public libraries with 76,464,000 volumes.

Museums and Galleries. In 1994 there were 1,347 museums with over 27m. visitors.

DIPLOMATIC REPRESENTATIVES

Of Canada in Great Britain (Macdonald House., 1 Grosvenor Sq., London, W1X 0AB)
High Commissioner: Roy Maclaren, PC.

Of Great Britain in Canada (80 Elgin St., Ottawa, K1P 5K7)
High Commissioner: Sir Anthony Goodenough, KCMG.

Of Canada in the USA (501 Pennsylvania Ave., NW, Washington, D.C., 20001)
Ambassador: Raymond A. J. Chrétien.

Of the USA in Canada (100 Wellington St., Ottawa, K1P 5TI)
Ambassador: Gordon D. Giffen.

Of Canada to the United Nations
Ambassador: Robert R. Fowler.

Of Canada to the European Union
Ambassador: Jean-Pierre Juneau.

FURTHER READING

Statistics Canada. *The Canada Year Book.*
Cambridge History of the British Empire. Vol.VI. Canada and Newfoundland. Cambridge, 1930
Canadian Annual Review. From 1960
Canadian Encyclopedia. 2nd ed. 4 vols. Edmonton, 1988
Brown, R. C., *An Illustrated History of Canada.* Toronto, 1991
Cook, C., *Canada after the Referendum of 1992.* McGill-Queens Univ. Press, 1994
Dawson, R. M. and Dawson, W. F., *Democratic Government in Canada.* 5th ed. Toronto Univ. Press, 1989
Granatstein, J. L., *Twentieth-Century Canada.* Toronto, 1983
Harris, R. C. (ed.) *Historical Atlas of Canada.* Vol 1. Univ. of Toronto, 1987
Ingles, E., *Canada.* [Bibliography] Oxford and Santa Barbara (CA), 1990
Jackson, R. J., *Politics in Canada: Culture, Institutions, Behaviour and Public Policy.* 2nd ed. Scarborough (Ont.), 1990
Leacy, F. H. (ed.) *Historical Statistics of Canada.* Government Printer, Ottawa, 1983
Longille, P., *Changing the Guard: Canada's Defence in a World in Transition.* Toronto Univ. Press, 1991
McCann, L. D. (ed.) *Heartland and Hinterland: A Geography of Canada.* Scarborough, Ontario, 1982
Silver, A. I. (ed.) *Introduction to Canadian History.* London, 1994
Smith, D. L. (ed.) *History of Canada: an Annotated Bibliography.* Oxford and Santa Barbara (CA), 1983

Other more specialized titles are listed under CONSTITUTION AND GOVERNMENT *and* WELFARE, *above.*

National library: The National Library of Canada, Ottawa, Ontario. *Librarian:* Marianne Scott.
National statistical office: Statistics Canada, Ottawa, K1A 0T6.
Website: http://www.statcan.ca/

CANADIAN PROVINCES

GENERAL DETAILS

The 10 provinces each have a separate parliament and administration, with a Lieut.-Governor, appointed by the Governor-General in Council at the head of the executive. They have full powers to regulate their own local affairs and dispose of their revenues, provided only that they do not interfere with the action and policy of the central administration. Among the subjects assigned exclusively to the provincial legislatures are: The amendment of the provincial constitution, except as regards the office of the Lieut.-Governor; property and civil rights; direct taxation for revenue purposes; borrowing; management and sale of Crown lands; provincial hospitals, reformatories, etc.; shop, saloon, tavern, auctioneer and other licences for local or provincial purposes; local works and undertakings, except lines of ships, railways, canals, telegraphs, etc., extending beyond the province or connecting with other provinces, and excepting also such works as the Canadian Parliament declares are for the general good; marriages, administration of justice within the province; education. On 18 July 1994 the federal and provincial governments signed an agreement easing inter-provincial barriers on government procurement, labour mobility, transport licences and product standards. Federal legislation of Dec. 1995 grants provinces a right of constitutional veto.

For the administration of the 2 territories *see* Northwest Territories, Yukon Territory *below*.

Areas of the 10 provinces and 2 territories (Yukon and Northwest Territory) (in sq. km) and population at recent censuses:

Province	Land area	Total land and fresh water area	Population, 1986	Population, 1991[1,2]	Population, 1996
Newfoundland (Nfld.)	371,634	405,720	568,349	568,474	551,792
Prince Edward Island (PEI)	5,660	5,660	126,646	129,765	134,557
Nova Scotia (NS)	52,840	55,490	873,199	899,942	909,282
New Brunswick (NB)	71,569	73,440	710,442	723,900	738,133
Quebec (Que.)	1,357,811	1,540,680	6,540,276	6,895,963	7,138,795
Ontario (Ont.)	916,733	1,068,580	9,113,515	10,084,885	10,753,573
Manitoba (Man.)	547,703	649,950	1,071,232	1,091,942	1,113,898
Saskatchewan (Sask.)	570,113	652,330	1,010,198	988,928	990,237
Alberta (Alta.)	638,232	661,190	2,375,278	2,545,553	2,696,826
British Columbia (BC)	892,677	947,800	2,889,207	3,282,061	3,724,500
Yukon Territory (YT)	531,843	483,450	23,504	27,797	30,766
Northwest Territories (NWT)[3]	3,246,389	3,426,320	52,238	57,649	64,402

[1]Excludes data from incompletely enumerated Indian reserves and Indian settlements.
[2]Comparison of the 1991 census data with data from earlier censuses is affected by a change in the definition of the 1991 census population. Persons in Canada on student authorizations, Minister's permits, and as refugee claimants were enumerated in the 1991 census but not in previous censuses. These persons are referred to as non-permanent residents.
[3]For data on the new territory of Nunavut *see* NORTHWEST TERRITORIES: Constitution and Government.

Local Government. Under the terms of the British North America Act the provinces are given full powers over local government. All local government institutions are, therefore, supervised by the provinces, and are incorporated and function under provincial acts.

The acts under which municipalities operate vary from province to province. A municipal corporation is usually administered by an elected council headed by a mayor or reeve, whose powers to administer affairs and to raise funds by taxation and other methods are set forth in provincial laws, as is the scope of its obligations to, and on behalf of, the citizens. Similarly, the types of municipal corporations, their official designations and the requirements for their incorporation vary between provinces. The following table sets out the classifications as at the 1991 census:

	Federal electoral districts	Sub-provincial regions	Census divisions
Nfld.	7	4	10
PEI	4	1	31
NS	11	5	18[1]
NB	10	5	15[1]
Que.	88	16	99[2]
Ont.	95	5	49[3]
Man.	14	8	23
Sask.	14	6	18
Alta.	21	8	19
BC	28	8	30[4]
YT	1	1	1[5]
NWT	2	1	5[5]

[1]Counties.
[2]4 Census divisions, 3 communautés urbaines, 92 municipalités régionales de comté.
[3]24 counties, 10 districts, 1 district municipality, 1 metropolitan municipality, 10 regional municipalities, 3 united counties.
[4]1 region, 29 regional districts.   [5]Regions.

SOCIAL INSTITUTIONS

Justice. The administration of justice within the provinces, including the enforcement of the Criminal Code of Canada, is the responsibility of provincial governments, but all the provinces except Ontario and Quebec have entered into contracts with the Royal Canadian Mounted Police (RCMP) to enforce criminal and provincial law. In addition, in these 8 provinces the RCMP is under agreement to provide police services to municipalities.

ALBERTA

KEY HISTORICAL EVENTS

The southern half of Alberta was administered from 1670 as part of Rupert's land by the Hudson's Bay Company. Trading posts were set up after 1783 when the North West Company took a share in the fur trade. In 1869 Rupert's land was transferred from the Hudson's Bay Company (which had absorbed its rival in 1821) to the new Dominion and in the following year this land was combined with the former Crown land of the North Western Territories to form the Northwest Territories. In 1882 'Alberta' first appeared as a provisional 'district', consisting of the southern half of the present province. In 1905 the Athabasca district to the north was added when provincial status was granted to Alberta.

TERRITORY AND POPULATION

The area of the province is 661,185 sq. km; 644,389 sq. km being land area and 16,796 sq. km water area. The population at the 1996 census was 2,696,826; estimate, July 1997, 2,847,006. The urban population (1996), centres of 1,000 or over, was 79·5% and the rural 20·5%. Population (14 May 1996) of the 14 cities, as well as the 2 specialized municipalities (*see below under* Local Government for definition): Calgary, 768,082; Edmonton, 616,306; Lethbridge, 63,053; Red Deer, 60,075; St Albert, 46,888; Medicine Hat, 46,783; Grande Prairie, 31,140; Airdrie, 15,946; Leduc, 14,305; Spruce Grove, 14,271; Camrose, 13,728; Fort Saskatchewan, 12,408; Lloydminster (Alberta portion), 11,317; Wetaskiwin, 10,959; Specialized Municipality of Wood Buffalo (Fort McMurray), 35,213; Specialized Municipality of Strathcona County (Sherwood Park), 64,176.

SOCIAL STATISTICS

See CANADA: Social Statistics.

CLIMATE

A continental climate: long, cold winters and mild summers. Rainfall amounts are greatest between May and Sept. Edmonton, Jan. 5°F (−15°C), July 63°F (17°C). Annual rainfall 13·6" (345·6 mm).

CONSTITUTION AND GOVERNMENT

The constitution of Alberta is contained in the British North America Act of 1867, and amending Acts; also in the Alberta Act of 1905, passed by the Parliament of the Dominion of Canada, which created the province out of the then Northwest Territories. All the provisions of the British North America Act, except those with respect to school lands and the public domain, were made to apply to Alberta as they apply to the older provinces of Canada. On 1 Oct. 1930 the natural resources were transferred from the Dominion to provincial government control. The province is represented by 6 members in the Senate and 26 in the House of Commons of Canada.

The executive is vested nominally in the Lieut.-Governor, who is appointed by the federal government, but actually in the Executive Council or the Cabinet of the legislature. Legislative power is vested in the Assembly in the name of the Queen.

Members of the Legislative Assembly are elected by the universal vote of adults over the age of 18 years.

RECENT ELECTIONS

There are 83 members in the legislature (elected 11 March 1997): 63 Progressive Conservative, 18 Liberal and 2 New Democrat.

CURRENT ADMINISTRATION

Lieut.-Governor: H. A. Olson.

The members of the Ministry were as follows in March 1999:

Premier, President of Executive Council: Ralph Klein (b. 1942; Progressive Conservative).

Minister of Advanced Education and Career Development: Clint Dunford.
Energy: Stephen C. West. *Family and Social Services:* Dr Lyle Oberg. *Provincial
Treasurer:* Stockwell Day. *Science, Research and Information Technology:* Lorne
Taylor. *Environmental Protection:* Ty Lund. *Health:* Halvar Jonson. *Community
Development:* Shirley McClellan. *Agriculture, Food and Rural Development:* Ed
Stelmach. *Intergovernmental and Aboriginal Affairs:* David Hancock, QC.
Municipal Affairs: Iris Evans. *Transportation and Utilities:* Walter Paszkowski.
Economic Development and Tourism: Patricia Nelson. *Justice and Attorney
General, Government House Leader:* Jon Havelock. *Education:* Gary G. Mar, QC.
Labour: Murray Smith. *Public Works, Supply and Services:* Stan Woloshyn.
Without Portfolio responsible for Children's Services: Pearl Calahasen.

Local Government. The local government units are City, Town, New Town,
Village, Summer Village, County, Municipal District and Improvement District.

There are 14 cities (*see* TERRITORY AND POPULATION, *above*). These cities
operate under the Municipal Government Act. The governing body consists of a
mayor and a council of from 6 to 20 members. A city can be incorporated by order
of the Lieut.-Governor-in-Council. A population of 10,000 is required on
incorporation.

There are no limits of area specified in the statutes for any of the different local
government units. The population requirement for a Town as specified in the
Municipal Government Act is 1,000 people, and the area at incorporation is that of
the original village.

A Village must contain 75 separate and occupied dwellings. The Municipal
Government Act requires each dwelling to have been occupied continuously for a
period of at least 6 months. A Summer Village must contain 50 separate dwellings.

A rural county area is an area incorporated through an order of the Lieut.-
Governor-in-Council under the provisions of the County Act. One board of
councillors deals with both municipal and school affairs.

A rural Municipal District is an area which has been incorporated under the
Municipal Government Act. In Municipal Districts separate boards control
municipal and school affairs.

Areas not incorporated as counties or Municipal Districts are termed
Improvement Districts or Special Areas. Sparsely populated, such districts are
administered and taxed by the Department of Municipal Affairs of the provincial
government. There are no requirements as to the minimum number of residents of a
County or Municipal District.

ECONOMY

Banking and Finance. The budgetary revenue and expenditure (in $1m.) for years
ending 31 March were as follows:

	1992–93	1993–94	1994–95	1995–96	1996–97
Revenue	14,173	15,308	16,082	15,504	16,651
Expenditure	17,497	16,679	15,144	14,353	14,162

Personal income *per capita* (1996), $23,511.

ENERGY AND NATURAL RESOURCES

Oil and Gas. In 1996, 90,353,000 cu. metres of crude oil were produced with gross
sales value of $14,914,615,000. Alberta produced 76·8% of Canada's crude
petroleum output in 1996.

Oil sands underlie some 60,000 sq. km of Alberta, the 4 major deposits being: The
Athabasca, Cold Lake, Peace River and Buffalo Head Hills deposits. Some 7%
(3,250 sq. km) of the Athabasca deposit can be exploited through open-pit mining.
The rest of the Athabasca, and all the deposits in the other areas, are deeper reserves
which must be developed through in situ techniques. These reserves reach depths of
760 metres. Oil sands mining plants produced 16,317,500 cu. metres of synthetic
crude oil in 1996.

Natural gas is found in abundance in numerous localities. In 1996, 127,903,000
cu. metres valued at $7,533,487,000 were produced. Production of natural gas by-
products was 25,960,600 cu. metres, valued at $2,747·95m.

Minerals. Coal reserves are estimated at 2,300,000m. tonnes, of which 720,000m. tonnes are recoverable. Production in 1996 was 41·93m. tonnes.

Value of total mineral production increased from $20,700m. in 1995 to $26,000m. in 1996.

Agriculture. Total area of farms (1996), 51,964,360 acres; improved land, 35,617,109 acres (under crops, 23,590,033; improved pasture, 4,731,087; summer fallow, 3,550,265; other improved land, 3,745,724); unimproved land, 16,347,251 acres. Number of farms (1996), 59,007.

For particulars of agricultural production and livestock *see* CANADA: Agriculture. Farm cash receipts in 1996 totalled $6,391·74m., of which crops contributed $2,921·85m., livestock and products, $3,318·32m. and direct payments $151·57m.

Forestry. Forest land in 1991 covered some 203,000 sq. km. In Jan. 1995, 22,750,434 cu. metres was the net allowable cut from land managed by the Crown.

Fisheries. The largest catch in commercial fishing is whitefish. Perch, tullibee, walley, pike and lake trout are also caught in smaller quantities. In 1984 a provincial fish marketing policy was implemented, and a new commercial fishery licensing system was implemented in 1987. Commercial fish production in 1990–91 was 2,210 tonnes, value $2·49m.

INDUSTRY

The leading manufacturing industries are food and beverages, petroleum refining, metal fabricating, wood industries, primary metal, chemical and chemical products and non-metallic mineral products. In 1995 there were 2,509 manufacturing establishments, in which were employed 99,225 persons who earned salaries and wages of $3,702,100,000.

Manufacturing shipments had a total value of $30,771·9m. in 1996. Chief among these shipments were (in $1m.): Food, 6,257·6; beverages, 584·2; chemicals and chemical products, 5,392·8; refined petroleum and coal products, 5,268·4; primary metals, 938·2; fabricated metal products, 1,578·4; wood, 1,915·1; printing, publishing and allied products, 882; machinery, 1,709; paper and allied products, 1,678·1; non-metal mineral products, 1,709; furniture and fixtures, 396·6; other, 350·7.

Total retail sales (1996) $23,141m.

Labour. In 1996 the labour force was 1,519,700 (681,000 females), of whom 1,412,700 (633,200) were employed.

COMMUNICATIONS

Roads. In 1997 there were 158,388 km of roads and highways, including 110,891 km gravelled and 23,146 km paved.

At 31 March 1997 there were 1,962,789 motor vehicles registered, including 1,549,662 passenger vehicles.

Rail. In 1997 the length of main railway lines was 8,395 km. There are light rail networks in Edmonton (12·8 km) and Calgary (29·3 km).

Telecommunications. The telephone system is owned and operated by the Telus Corporation (in which the Alberta Government holds 44% of the shares), except in the city of Edmonton (owned and operated by the City Council). There were 1,904,038 telephone subscriber lines in service in 1997.

SOCIAL INSTITUTIONS

Justice. The Supreme Judicial authority of the province is the Court of Appeal. Judges of the Court of Appeal and Court of Queen's Bench are appointed by the Federal Government and hold office until retirement at the age of 75. There are courts of lesser jurisdiction in both civil and criminal matters. The Court of Queen's Bench has full jurisdiction over civil proceedings. A Provincial Court which has jurisdiction in civil matters up to $2,000 is presided over by provincially appointed judges. Youth Courts have power to try boys and girls 12–17 years old inclusive for offences against the Young Offenders Act.

The jurisdiction of all criminal courts in Alberta is enacted in the provisions of the Criminal Code. The system of procedure in civil and criminal cases conforms as nearly as possible to the English system. In 1996, 248,296 Criminal Code offences were reported, including 46 homicides.

Education. Schools of all grades are included under the term of public school (including those in the separate school system which are publicly supported). The same board of trustees controls the schools from kindergarten to university entrance. In 1996–97 there were about 0·56m. pupils enrolled in grades 1-12, including private schools and special education programmes.

In 1998 Alberta had 35 post secondary institutions, 4 universities and 2 technical colleges with a total of approximately 80,000 students. The University of Alberta (in Edmonton), founded in 1907, had, in 1996–97, 26,130 full-time students; the University of Calgary, formerly part of the University of Alberta and autonomous from April 1966, had 19,714; and the University of Lethbridge, founded in 1966, had 5,160. The Athabasca University had in 1996–97, 11,689 part-time students.

CULTURE

Tourism. Tourism is important and in 1996 contributed an estimated $3,000m. to the economy.

FURTHER READING

MacGregor, J. G., *A History of Alberta.* 2nd ed. Edmonton, 1981
Masson, J., *Alberta's Local Governments and their Politics.* Univ. of Alberta Press, 1985
Richards, J., *Prairie Capitalism: Power and Influence in the New West.* Toronto, 1979
Wiebe, R., *Alberta: a Celebration.* Edmonton, 1979

Statistical office: Alberta Treasury, Statistics, Room 259, Terrace Bldg, 9515-107 St., Edmonton, AB T5K 2C3.

BRITISH COLUMBIA

KEY HISTORICAL EVENTS

British Columbia, formerly known as New Caledonia, was first administered by the Hudson's Bay Company. In 1849 Vancouver Island was given crown colony status and in 1853 the Queen Charlotte Islands became a dependency. The discovery of gold on the Fraser river and the following influx of population resulted in the creation in 1858 of the mainland crown colony of British Columbia, to which the Strikine Territory (established 1862) was later added. In 1866 the two colonies were united.

TERRITORY AND POPULATION

British Columbia has land area of 892,677 sq. km. The capital is Victoria. The province is bordered westerly by the Pacific Ocean and Alaska Panhandle, northerly by the Yukon and Northwest Territories, easterly by the Province of Alberta and southerly by the USA along the 49th parallel. A chain of islands, the largest of which are Vancouver Island and the Queen Charlotte Islands, affords protection to the mainland coast.

The 1996 census population was 3,724,500; estimate, July 1998, 4,014,329.

The principal cities and their 1996 census populations are as follows: Metropolitan Vancouver, 1,831,665; Metropolitan Victoria, 304,290; Abbotsford (amalgamated with Matsqui), 105,403; Kelowna, 89,442; Kamloops, 76,394; Prince George, 75,150; Nanaimo, 70,130; Chilliwack, 60,186; Vernon, 31,817; Penticton, 30,987; Mission, 30,519; Campbell River, 28,851; North Cowichan, 25,305; Port Alberni, 18,468; Cranbrook, 18,131.

SOCIAL STATISTICS

See CANADA: Social Statistics.

CLIMATE
The climate is cool temperate, but mountain influences affect temperatures and rainfall very considerably. Driest months occur in summer. Vancouver, Jan. 36°F (2·2°C), July 64°F (17·8°C). Annual rainfall 58" (1,458 mm).

CONSTITUTION AND GOVERNMENT
The British North America Act of 1867 provided for eventual admission into Canadian Confederation, and on 20 July 1871 British Columbia became the sixth province of the Dominion.

British Columbia has a unicameral legislature of 75 elected members. Government policy is determined by the Executive Council responsible to the Legislature. The Lieut.-Governor is appointed by the Governor-General of Canada, usually for a term of 5 years, and is the head of the executive government of the province.

The Legislative Assembly is elected for a maximum term of 5 years. There are 75 electoral districts. Every Canadian citizen 18 years and over, having resided a minimum of 6 months in the province, duly registered, is entitled to vote. The province is represented in the Federal Parliament by 33 members in the House of Commons, and 6 Senators.

RECENT ELECTIONS
At the Legislative Assembly elections of 28 May 1996 the New Democratic Party (NDP) gained 39% of votes cast and 39 seats, the Liberal Party gained 34 seats, the Progressive Democratic Alliance 1 and independents 1.

CURRENT ADMINISTRATION
Lieut.-Governor: His Honour the Hon. Garde B. Gardom, QC.

The NDP Executive Council comprised in Jan. 1999:

Premier, Minister Responsible for Youth: Glen Clark.

Deputy Premier, Minister of Energy and Mines and Minister Responsible for Northern Development: Dan Miller. *Aboriginal Affairs and Labour:* Dale Lovick. *Advanced Education, Training and Technology and Intergovernmental Relations:* Andrew Petter. *Agriculture and Food:* Corky Evans. *Attorney General and Minister responsible for Multiculturalism, Human Rights and Immigration:* Ujjal Dosanjh. *Children and Families:* Lois Boone. *Education:* Paul Ramsey. *Employment and Investment and Minister responsible for Housing:* Michael Farnworth. *Environment, Lands and Parks:* Cathy McGregor. *Finance and Corporate Relations:* Joy K. McPhail. *Fisheries:* Dennis Streifel. *Forests:* David G. Zirnhelt. *Health and Minister responsible for Seniors:* Penny Priddy. *Human Resources:* Jan Pullinger. *Municipal Affairs:* Jenny Kwan. *Public Service:* Moe Sihota. *Small Business, Tourism and Culture:* Ian Waddell. *Transportation and Highways:* Harry Lali. *Women's Equality:* Sue Hammell.

Local Government. Vancouver City was incorporated by statute and operates under the provisions of the Vancouver Charter of 1953 and amendments. This is the only incorporated area in British Columbia not operating under the provisions of the Municipal Act. Under this Act municipalities are divided into the following classes: (a) a village with a population between 500 and 2,500, governed by a council consisting of a mayor and 4 aldermen; (b) a town with a population between 2,500 and 5,000, governed by a council consisting of a mayor and 4 aldermen; (c) a city where the population exceeds 5,000, governed by a council consisting of a mayor and 6 or 8 aldermen depending on population; (d) a district where the area exceeds 810 hectares and the average density is less than 5 persons per hectare, governed by a council consisting of a mayor and 6 or 8 aldermen depending on population; (e) an Indian government district.

There are 2 other forms of local government: the Regional District covering a number of areas both incorporated and unincorporated, governed by a board of directors; and the improvement district governed by a board of 3 trustees.

Revenue for municipal services is derived mainly from real-property taxation, although additional revenue is derived from licence fees, business taxes, fines, public utility projects and grants-in-aid from the provincial government.

ECONOMY

Budget. Current provincial revenue and expenditure in $1m. for fiscal years ending 31 March:

	1995-96	1996-97	1997-98	1998-99[1]
Revenue	20,401·6	20,209·0	20,285·0	20,441·0
Expenditure	20,170·0	20,546·0	20,437·0	20,536·0

[1]Estimate.

The main sources of current revenue are income taxes, sales taxes, contributions from the federal government, licences and fees, and natural resource taxes and royalties.

The main items of expenditure in 1998 (estimate) were as follows: Health, $7,271·3m.; education, $5,774·2m.; transportation, $789·9m.; natural resources and economic development, $866·5m.; protection of persons and property, $1,030·6m.; general government, $232·0m.

Banking and Finance. At Oct. 1997, Canadian chartered banks maintained 925 branches and had total assets of $146·3bn. in British Columbia. In 1997, credit unions at 96 locations had total assets of $20·4bn. Several foreign banks have Canadian head offices in Vancouver and several others have branches.

ENERGY AND NATURAL RESOURCES

Electricity. Generation in 1998 totalled 66,693m. kWh, of which 12,114m. kWh were exported. Available within the province was 71,009m. kWh (with imports 4,316m. kWh).

Minerals. Copper, coal, natural gas, crude oil, gold and molybdenum are the most important minerals produced. The 1997 value of mineral production was estimated at $4,695m. Total value of mineral fuels produced in 1997 was estimated at: Coal, $1,191m.; oil and gas, $1,533m.

Agriculture. Only 2·4m. ha, or 4% of the total land area, is arable or potentially arable. Farm cash receipts, in 1997, were $1,765m., of which livestock and products $992m.; crops, $773m.

Forestry. About 55% of British Columbia's land is productive forest land, with 51·8m. ha bearing commercial forest. Over 90% of the forest area is owned or administered by the provincial government. The total timber harvest in 1997 was 68·8m. cu. metres. Output of forest-based products, 1997: Lumber, 31·6m. cu. metres; plywood, 1·48m. cu. metres; pulp, 7·1m. tonnes; newsprint, paper and paperboard, 2·57m. tonnes.

Fisheries. In 1997 the total landed value of the catch was $594m.; wholesale value $982m.

INDUSTRY

The value of shipments from all manufacturing industries reached $34,672m. in 1997.

Labour. In 1997 the labour force averaged 2,012,400 persons (913,300 females) with 1,837,700 (836,300) employed, of whom 754,000 were in service industries, 323,000 in trade, 201,000 in manufacturing, 146,000 in transportation and communications, 106,000 in finance, insurance and real estate, 91,000 in public administration, 129,000 in construction, 33,000 in agriculture, 30,000 in forestry, 17,000 in mining and 7,000 in fishing and trapping.

INTERNATIONAL TRADE

Imports and Exports. Exports in 1997 totalled $26,748m. in value, while imports amounted to $23,236·4m. The USA is the largest market for products exported through British Columbia customs ports ($14,865m. in 1997), followed by Japan ($6,005m.) and South Korea ($953m.).

The leading exports in 1997 were: Wood products, $9,759m.; pulp, $3,099m.; machinery and equipment, $2,638m.; coal, $2,016m.; metallic minerals, $1,790m.

COMMUNICATIONS

Roads. In 1996 there were 42,500 km of provincial roads and rights of way in the province, of which 21,500 km were paved. At 31 Dec. 1997, 1·651m. passenger cars and 573,166 commercial vehicles were registered.

Rail. The province is served by two transcontinental railways, the Canadian Pacific Railway and the Canadian National Railway. Passenger service is provided by VIA Rail, a Crown Corporation and the publicly owned British Columbia Railway. In 1995 the American company Amtrak began operating a service between Seattle and Vancouver after a 14-year hiatus. British Columbia is also served by the freight trains of the B.C. Hydro and Power Authority, the Northern Alberta Railways Company and the Burlington Northern and Southern Railways Inc. The combined route-mileage of mainline track operated by the CPR, CNR and BCR totals 6,800 km. The system also includes CPR and CNR wagon ferry connections to Vancouver Island, between Prince Rupert and Alaska, and interchanges with American railways at southern border points. A metro line was opened in Vancouver in 1986 (29 km). A commuter rail service linking Vancouver and the Fraser Valley was established in 1995 (69 km).

Civil Aviation. International airports are located at Vancouver and Victoria. In 1997, total passenger arrivals and departures on scheduled services at Vancouver were 14·82m., and at Victoria 1·1m. Daily interprovincial and intraprovincial flights serve all main population centres. Small public and private airstrips are located throughout the province.

Shipping. The major ports are Vancouver, Prince Rupert and the Fraser River. Other coastal harbours include Nanaimo, Port Alberni, Campbell River, Powell River, Kitimat, Stewart and Squamish. Total cargo shipped through the port of Vancouver during 1996 was 71·7m. tonnes; from the port of Prince Rupert (1997), 12·5m. tonnes. 289 cruise ship voyages with 0·7m. passengers visited Vancouver in 1996.

The British Columbia Ferries connect Vancouver Island with the mainland and also provide service to other coastal points; in 1997, 22·0m. passengers and 8·1m. vehicles were carried. Service by other ferry systems is also provided between Vancouver Island and the USA. The Alaska State Ferries connect Prince Rupert with centres in Alaska.

Telecommunications. The British Columbia Telephone Company had (1997) approximately 2·5m. customers. In July 1997 there were 130 radio and 12 television stations originating in British Columbia. In addition there were 218 radio and 35 television re-broadcasting stations in the province.

SOCIAL INSTITUTIONS

Justice. The judicial system is composed of the Court of Appeal, the Supreme Court, County Courts, and various Provincial Courts, including Magistrates' Courts and Small Claims Courts. The federal courts include the Supreme Court of Canada and the Federal Court of Canada.

In 1997, 504,703 Criminal Code offences were reported, including 114 homicides.

Education. Education, free up to Grade XII levels, is financed jointly from municipal and provincial government revenues. Attendance is compulsory from the age of 5 to 16. There were approximately 623,317 pupils enrolled in 1,733 public schools from kindergarten to Grade 12 in the 1996-97 school year.

The universities had a full-time enrolment of approximately 53,012 for 1997-98. As of 1 Nov. 1996 they were: the University of British Columbia, Vancouver; University of Victoria, Saanich; Simon Fraser University, Burnaby, and the University of Northern British Columbia, Prince George. The regional colleges in 1996 were: Camosun College, Victoria; Capilano College, North Vancouver; Cariboo College, Kamloops; College of New Caledonia, Prince George; Douglas College, New Westminister; East Kootenay Community College, Cranbrook; Fraser Valley College, Chilliwack/Abbotsford; Kwantlen College, Surrey; Malaspina College, Nanaimo; North Island College, Comox; Northern Lights College, Dawson Creek/Fort St John; Northwest Community College, Terrace/Prince Rupert; Okanagan College, Kelowna with branches at Salmon Arm and Vernon; Selkirk

College, Castlegar; Vancouver Community College, Vancouver; Langara College, Vancouver.

There are also the British Columbia Institute of Technology, Burnaby; Emily Carr College of Art and Design, Vancouver; Open Learning Institute, Richmond. A televised distance education and special programmes through KNOW, the Knowledge Network of the West, is provided.

Health. The Government operates a hospital insurance scheme giving universal coverage after a qualifying period of 3 months' residence in the province. The province has come under a national medicare scheme which is partially subsidized by the provincial government and partially by the federal government.

CULTURE

Tourism. In 1997, 21·3m. tourists spent $8,499m.

FURTHER READING
Barman, J., *The West beyond the West: a History of British Columbia.* Toronto Univ. Press, 1991
Morley, J. T., *The Reins of Power: Governing British Columbia.* Vancouver, 1983

Statistical office: BC STATS, Ministry of Finance and Corporate Relations, P.O. Box 9410, Stn. Prov. Govt., Victoria, V8V 1X4.

MANITOBA

KEY HISTORICAL EVENTS
Manitoba was known as the Red River Settlement before it entered the dominion in 1870. During the 18th century its only inhabitants were fur-trappers, but a more settled colonization began in the 19th century. The area was administered by the Hudson's Bay Company until 1869 when it was purchased by the new dominion. In 1870 it was given provincial status. It was enlarged in 1881 and again in 1912 by the addition of part of the Northwest Territories.

TERRITORY AND POPULATION
The area of the province is 250,946 sq. miles (649,947 sq. km), of which 211,721 sq. miles are land and 39,225 sq. miles water. From north to south it is 1,225 km, and at the widest point it is 793 km.

The 1996 census population was 1,113,898; estimate, July 1997, 1,142,100. Population (estimate 1996) of Winnipeg, the capital, 667,209; other municipalities with over 10,000 inhabitants: Brandon, 39,175; Thompson, 14,385; Portage la Prairie, 13,077; Springfield, 12,162; St Andrews, 10,144.

SOCIAL STATISTICS
See CANADA: Social statistics.

CLIMATE
The climate is cold continental, with very severe winters but pleasantly warm summers. Rainfall amounts are greatest in the months May to Sept. Winnipeg, Jan. –3°F (–19·3°C), July 67°F (19·6°C). Annual rainfall 21" (539 mm).

CONSTITUTION AND GOVERNMENT
The provincial government is administered by a *Lieut.-Governor* assisted by an *Executive Council* (Cabinet), which is appointed from and responsible to a *Legislative Assembly* of 57 members elected for 5 years. Women were enfranchised in 1916. The Electoral Division Act, 1955, created 57 single-member constituencies and abolished the transferable vote. There are 26 rural electoral divisions, and 31 urban electoral divisions. The province is represented by 6 members in the Senate and 14 in the House of Commons of Canada.

RECENT ELECTIONS

Elections to the Legislative Assembly were held on 25 April 1995. Party standings in late 1998: Progressive Conservative Party, 31 seats; New Democratic Party, 23; Liberal Party, 3.

CURRENT ADMINISTRATION

Lieut.-Governor: Yvon Dumont (appointed 1993).

The members of the Progressive Conservative Ministry in Jan. 1999 were:

Premier, President of the Executive Council, Minister of Federal-Provincial Relations: Gary Albert Filmon.

Deputy-Premier, Minister of Industry, Trade and Tourism: Merv Tweed. *Family Services:* Bonnie Mitchelson. *Natural Resources:* Glen Cummings. *Education and Training:* James McCrae. *Culture, Heritage and Citizenship:* Rosemary Vodrey. *Finance:* Eric Stefanson. *Highways and Transportation:* Glen Findlay. *Justice and Attorney General:* Victor Eric Toews, QC. *Consumer and Corporate Affairs:* Michael Radcliffe. *Agriculture:* Harry Enns. *Rural Development:* Leonard Derkach. *Health:* Eric Stefanson. *Environment:* Linda McIntosh. *Labour:* Harold Gilleshammer. *Urban Affairs and Housing:* Jack F. Reimer. *Energy and Mines and Northern Affairs:* David Newman. *Emergency Management Organization:* Franklin Pitura.

Local Government. Rural Manitoba is organized into rural municipalities which vary widely in size. Some have only 4 townships (a township is 6 sq. miles), while the largest has 22 townships. The province has 116 rural municipalities, as well as 49 incorporated towns, 26 incorporated villages and 8 incorporated cities.

On 1 Jan. 1972, the cities and towns comprising the metropolitan area of Winnipeg were amalgamated to form the City of Winnipeg. A mayor and council are elected to a central government, but councillors also sit on 'community committees' which represent the areas or wards they serve. These committees are advised by non-elected residents of the area on provision of municipal services within the community committee jurisdiction. Taxing powers and overall budgeting rest with the central council. The mayor is elected at the same time as the councillors in a city-wide vote. Revisions to the City of Winnipeg Act came into effect with the municipal elections held in Oct. 1977.

Since Jan. 1945, 17 Local Government Districts were formed in the less densely populated areas of the province. In 1997, only two remained. They are administered by a provincially appointed person, who acts on the advice of locally elected councils.

In the extreme north, many communities have locally elected councils, while others are administered directly by the Department of Northern Affairs. This department provides most of the funding in all these northern settlements.

ECONOMY

Performance. Real GDP growth was 3% in 1998, and was forecast at 2·7% for 1999.

Banking and Finance. Provincial revenue and expenditure (current account, excluding capital expenditures) for fiscal years ending 31 March (in Canadian $1m.):

	1995–96	1996–97	1997–98[1]	1998–99[2]
Revenue	5,517	5,499	5,602	5,600
Expenditure	5,505	5,408	5,448	5,502

[1]Forecast.   [2]Budgeted figure.

ENERGY AND NATURAL RESOURCES

Electricity. In the year ending 31 March 1998, almost 35,000m. kWh of electricity was generated. The Manitoba Hydro System (generating capacity about 5m. kW), owned by the province, produced 34,000m. kWh, of which 19,100m. kWh was delivered to its 394,328 customers throughout the province. The city-owned Winnipeg Hydro (generating capacity about 140,000 kW) generated about 930m. kWh in 1997. It also bought about 1,582 kWh of power from Manitoba Hydro to serve its 102,984 customers. Total sales of Manitoba electricity in 1997 were more than $1,100m. Exports accounted for 26% of total sales. In the year ending 31 March 1998 about 13,600 kWh was exported, primarily to the USA.

Oil and Gas. Crude oil production in 1997 was valued at $103m.

Minerals. Total value of mineral production in 1997 was about $1,129m, a 12·6% increase on 1996. Principal minerals mined are nickel, copper, zinc, gold, and small quantities of silver. It was predicted that the value would decline in 1998.

Agriculture. Rich farmland is the main primary resource, although the area in farms is only about 14% of the total land area. In 1997 the total value of agricultural production was $3,029m., with more than $1,720m. from crops and more than $1,179m. from livestock, and the rest coming from direct payments. These figures represented a 9·9% increase on 1996. Wheat was the most important crop with canola the 2nd most valuable. Hogs were the most valuable livestock, then cattle and calves. 22,456 census farms reported total gross farm receipts of $2,500 or more in 1996.

Forestry. About 51% of the land area is wooded, of which 334,460 sq. km is productive forest land. In 1997–98 there were about 184 primary wood producers with 2,800 direct employees. In 1995–96 primary wood producers were responsible for $440m. in shipments, including $300m. in export sales.

Fur Trade. The value of fur production to the trapper was $3·3m. in the year ending 31 Aug. 1998; the estimated overall contribution of trapping to the provincial economy was about $18m.

Fisheries. From 57,000 sq. km of rivers and lakes, the value of fisheries production to fishers was about $17m. in 1996–97. Whitefish, sauger, pickeral and pike are the principal varieties of fish caught.

INDUSTRY
Goods-producing industries accounted for about 25% of GDP in 1996. In 1997, the value of Manitoba's manufacturing shipments grew to a record $10,000m. Of this, food and beverages was the largest sector, followed by transport equipment (primarily aerospace parts and buses) and machinery (mainly farm equipment). Other industries with strong growth in 1997 included electrical equipment, furniture and fixtures, and clothing and textiles.

Labour. In 1997 the labour force was 576,400, of whom 538,300 were employed. This 6·6% unemployment rate was the lowest since 1981.

INTERNATIONAL TRADE
Products grown and manufactured in Manitoba find ready markets in other parts of Canada, in the USA, particularly the upper Midwest region, and in other countries. Export shipments to foreign countries from Manitoba in 1997 were valued at $7,000m.

Imports and Exports. Exports rose by 13·6% in 1997 to around $7·08bn. Motor vehicles and parts were the main export commodity, followed by cereal grains and oil seeds. The major export markets were the USA, Japan, Belgium and China.

COMMUNICATIONS
Roads. Highways and provincial roads totalled 18,500 km, with 2,800 bridges and other structures, in 1997. In 1998 there were 777,222 motor vehicles registered, including 446,415 passenger cars.

Rail. The province has about 5,650 km of commercial track, not including industrial track, yards and sidings. Most of the track belongs to the country's 2 national railways. Canadian Pacific owns about 1,950 km and Canadian National about 2,400 km. The Hudson Bay Railway, operated by Denver–based Omnitrax, has about 1,300 km of track. Fort Worth-based Burlington Northern's railcars are moved in Manitoba on CN and CP tracks and trains.

Civil Aviation. There are 64 domestic commercial aviation operators flying from bases in Manitoba. 5 are designated private; 50 air taxi companies are licensed to carry less than 10 passengers; and 5 computer operations are licensed to carry up to 19 passengers. 4 airlines are licensed to carry more than 19 passengers, and 9

CANADA

foreign airlines land in the province. In addition, 37 aerial services are licensed (largely for agricultural chemical spraying).

Telecommunications. The Manitoba System provided service to over 450,000 residential customers in Sept. 1998.

SOCIAL INSTITUTIONS

Justice. In 1997, 125,043 Criminal Code offences were reported (a ratio of 10,948 per 100,000 people), including 30 homicides (a ratio of 2·63 per 100,000 people).

Education. Education is controlled through locally elected school divisions. There were 209,718 children enrolled in the province's nursery, kindergarten, elementary, secondary, independent (private) and home school system in the 1997–98 school year. Public school operating cost expenditure per pupil for 1997–98 was expected to be about $6,033. The ratio of teachers to students in Sept. 1997 averaged 1:18·9. Manitoba has 4 universities with an enrolment (full- and part-time) of about 30,000 for the 1998–99 year: they are the University of Manitoba, founded in 1877, in Winnipeg; the University of Winnipeg; Brandon University; and the Collegiate University of Saint Boniface.

Community colleges in Brandon, The Pas and Winnipeg offer 2-year diploma courses in a number of fields, as well as specialized training in many trades. They also give a large number and variety of shorter courses, both at their campuses and in many communities throughout the province. Expenditure (estimate) on education in the 1997–98 fiscal year was $1,076m.

CULTURE

Tourism. In 1997, tourists staying 1 or more nights in Manitoba numbered an estimated 1m. Tourism contributed an estimated $1,121m. to the economy.

Festivals. Folklorama is a celebration of Canadian culture that takes place in over 40 multicultural pavillions each July. The Festival du Voyageur takes place in St Boniface each Feb. and is Western Canada's biggest winter festival. Canada's National Ukrainian Festival takes place over a long weekend each August, and in mid-July there is the 4-day Manitoba Stampede and Exhibition, one of Canada's largest rodeos.

National Theatre and Opera. The Royal Winnipeg Ballet is Canada's oldest ballet company.

Museums and Galleries. The Manitoba Museum of Man and Nature has 7 galleries showing the inter-relationship between man and the environment.

FURTHER READING
General Information: Inquiries may be addressed to Information Services, Room 29, Legislative Building, 450 Broadway, Winnipeg, Manitoba R3C 0V8 (Website: Government of Manitoba Home Page: http://www.gov.mb.ca).
The Department of Agriculture publishes: *Manitoba Agriculture Year Book, The Manitoba Agricultural Review* and *Manitoba Agricultural Statistics* (all annual).
Manitoba Statistical Review. Manitoba Bureau of Statistics, Quarterly

Jackson, J. A., *The Centennial History of Manitoba.* Toronto, 1970
Morton, W. L., *Manitoba: A History.* Univ. of Toronto Press, 1967

NEW BRUNSWICK

KEY HISTORICAL EVENTS
Visited by Jacques Cartier in 1534, New Brunswick was first explored by Samuel de Champlain in 1604. With Nova Scotia, it originally formed one French colony called Acadia. It was ceded by the French in the Treaty of Utrecht in 1713 and became a permanent British possession in 1759. It was first settled by British colonists in 1764 but was separated from Nova Scotia, and became a province in June 1784 as a result of the great influx of United Empire Loyalists. Responsible government came into

being in 1848 and consisted of an executive council, a legislative council (later abolished) and a House of Assembly. In 1867 New Brunswick entered the Confederation.

TERRITORY AND POPULATION
The area of the province is 28,354 sq. miles (73,440 sq. km), of which 27,834 sq. miles (72.090 sq. km) is land area. The population at the 1996 census was 738,133; estimate, Oct. 1998, 752,486. Based on the 1996 census, 25% of New Brunswick's total population were of British Isles only ancestry, 24% were of 'Canadian' origin and 17% had French only ancestry. Other significant ethnic groups were German, Dutch and Scandinavian. In 1996 there were 10,250 North American Indian, Métis or Inuit people in New Brunswick. Census 1996 population of urban centres: Saint John, 125,705; Moncton, 113,491; Fredericton (capital), 78,950; Bathurst, 25,415; Edmundston, 22,624; Campbellton, 16,867. The official languages are English and French.

SOCIAL STATISTICS
See CANADA: Social Statistics.

CLIMATE
A cool temperate climate, with rain at all seasons but temperatures modified by the influence of the Gulf Stream. Precipitation ranges from 889 mm in the north to 1,143 mm in the south. The average summer temperature for Saint John is 22°C, –3.9°C in the winter.

CONSTITUTION AND GOVERNMENT
The government is vested in a Lieut.-Governor and a Legislative Assembly of 55 members, each of whom is individually elected to represent the voters in one constituency or riding. A simultaneous translation system is used in the Assembly. Any Canadian subject of full age and 6 months' residence is entitled to vote.

RECENT ELECTIONS
The last provincial election was held on 11 Sept. 1995. As of Oct. 1998, the Legislative Assembly consisted of 45 Liberals, 9 Progressive Conservatives and 1 from the New Democratic Party. The province has 10 members in the Canadian Senate and 10 members in the federal House of Commons.

CURRENT ADMINISTRATION
Lieut.-Governor: Dr Marilyn Trenholme Counsell (appointed April 1997).
   The members of the Liberal government were as follows in Jan. 1999:
   Premier, President of Executive Council: Camille H. Thériault.
   Minister of Justice, Attorney General, Services NB: Greg Byrne. *Finance, Quality:* Edmond Blanchard. *Supply and Services:* Gregory O'Donnell. *Transportation:* Sheldon Lee. *Natural Resources and Energy:* Doug Tyler. *Agriculture and Rural Development:* Stuart Jamieson. *Health and Community Services:* Ann Breault. *Human Resources Development:* Georgie Day. *Labour:* Joan Kingston. *Education:* Bernard Richard. *Municipalities and Housing, Status of Women:* Marcelle Mersereau. *Environment:* Gene Devereux. *Economic Development, Culture and Tourism:* Roland MacIntyre. *Fisheries and Aquaculture:* Danny Gay. *Solicitor General:* James Lockyer. *Regional Development Corporation and Northern Development:* Jean-Paul Savoie. *Minister of State for Seniors:* Reginald MacDonald. *Minister of State for Tourism and Culture:* Jean-Camille DeGrâce. *Minister of State for Intergovernmental and Aboriginal Affairs:* Bernard Thériault. *Minister of State for Youth and Literacy:* Harry Doyle.

Local Government. Under the reforms introduced in 1967 the Province has assumed complete administrative and financial responsibility for education, health, welfare and administration of justice. Local government is now restricted to provision of services of a strictly local nature. Under the new municipal structure, units include existing and new cities, towns and villages. Counties have disappeared as municipal units. Areas with limited populations have become local service

CANADA

districts. The former local improvement districts have become towns, villages or local service districts depending on their size.

ECONOMY

Banking and Finance. The ordinary budget (in Canadian $1m.) is shown as follows (financial years ended 31 March):

	1995	1996	1997	1998
Gross revenue	4,300·0	4,426·3	4,470·5	4,459·4
Gross expenditure	4,368·6	4,375·1	4,355·8	4,397·7

Funded debt and capital loans outstanding (exclusive of Treasury Bills) as of 31 March 1998 was $6,685·1m. Sinking funds held by the province at 31 March 1998, $2,440·0m. The ordinary budget excludes capital spending.

ENERGY AND NATURAL RESOURCES

Electricity. Hydro-electric, thermal and nuclear generating stations of NB Power had an installed capacity of 4,116 MW at 31 March 1998, consisting of 15 generating stations. The Mactaquac hydro-electric development near Fredericton has a name plate capacity of 672 MW. The largest thermal generating station, Coleson Cove, near Saint John, has 1,006 MW of installed capacity. Atlantic Canada's first nuclear generating station, a 635 MW plant on a promontory in the Bay of Fundy, near Saint John, went into operation in 1982. New Brunswick is electrically inter-connected with utilities in neighbouring provinces of Quebec, Nova Scotia and Prince Edward Island, as well as the New England States of the USA. The sale of out-of-province power accounted for 21% of revenue in 1997–98. Total revenue amounted to $1,140·4m. A 350 MW power plant at Belledune is planned.

Minerals. In 1997 approximately 15 different metals, minerals and commodities were produced. These included lead, zinc, copper, cadmium, bismuth, gold, silver, antimony, potash, salt, lime, stone, gas, coal, sand and gravel, clay, peat and marl. The total value of minerals produced in 1997 reached $936·6m. The top 3 contributors to mineral production are zinc, silver and lead, accounting for 65·4% of total value in 1997. In Canada, in 1997, New Brunswick ranked first in the production of zinc, bismuth and lead, second in silver, and fifth in the production of copper. Not all of the province's minerals have been explored sufficiently and research continues.

Agriculture. The total area under crops is estimated at 135,008 ha. Farms numbered 3,405 and averaged 129 ha each (census 1996). Potatoes accounted for 20·9% of total farm cash income in 1997. Mixed farming is common throughout the province. Dairy farming is centred around the larger urban areas, and is located mainly along the Saint John River Valley and in the south-eastern sections of the province. Income from dairy products provides 21·0% of farm cash income. New Brunswick is self-sufficient in fluid milk and supplies a processing industry. For particulars of agricultural production and livestock, *see* CANADA: Agriculture. Farm cash receipts in 1997 were $301·2m.

Forestry. New Brunswick contains some 61,000 sq. km of productive forest lands. The value of manufacturing shipments for the wood-related industries in 1997 was $3,115·7m., representing 37·4% of total shipments in the province. The paper and allied industry group is the largest component of the industry, contributing 62·6% of forestry output. In 1997 wood industries employed about 16,929 people for all aspects of the forest industry, including harvesting, processing and transportation. Practically all forest products are exported from the province's numerous ports and harbours, near which many of the mills are located, or sent by road or rail to the USA.

Fisheries. Commercial fishing is one of the most important primary industries of the province, employing 7,233 in 1997. Nearly 50 commercial species of fish and shellfish are landed, including scallop, shrimp, crab, herring and cod. Landings in 1997 (101,572 tonnes) amounted to $124·1m. In 1998 there were 107 fish processing plants, employing an average of 6,570 people. In 1997 molluscs and crustaceans ranked first with a value of $107·4m., 86·5% of the total landed value;

pelagic fish second, 10·9%; and groundfish third, 2·0%. Exports (1997) $435·6m., mainly to the USA and Japan.

INDUSTRY
In 1998 there were 1,417 manufacturing and processing establishments, employing on average 43,300 persons. New Brunswick's location, with deepwater harbours open throughout the year and container facilities at Saint John, makes it ideal for exporting. Industries include food and beverages, paper and allied industries, and timber products. Nearly 20% of the industrial labour force work in Saint John.

Labour. New Brunswick's labour force increased 2·4% in 1997 to 362,400 (163,400 females). Of the 316,100 employed, 144,100 were females. The participation rate rose to 60·1% (67·4% for males and 53·1% for females).

INTERNATIONAL TRADE

Imports and Exports. The main exports of New Brunswick are forest products, such as lumber, woodpulp, newsprint, and energy products which include petroleum oils, other than crude, and electricity. In 1997, the major trading partners of the province were the USA with 78·1% of total exports, followed by Brazil with 4·4% and Japan with 3·9% of total exports. Exports reached $5,463·7m. while imports totalled $3,894·1m. in 1997.

COMMUNICATIONS

Roads. There are over 15,000 km of collector and local roads which provide access to most areas. The main highway system, including 596·4 km of the Trans-Canada Highway, links the province with the principal roads in Quebec, Nova Scotia and Prince Edward Island, as well as the Interstate Highway System in the eastern seaboard states of the USA. A new 4-lane access highway is under construction between Fredericton and Moncton. At 31 March 1998, total road motor vehicle registrations numbered 442,283 of which 299,367 were passenger automobiles, 131,841 were truck and truck tractors, 10,519 motor cycles and mopeds, and 556 other vehicles.

Rail. New Brunswick is served by main lines of both Canadian Pacific and Canadian National railways.

Telecommunications. In 1996 the New Brunswick Telephone Co. Ltd had 542,887 access lines in service.

SOCIAL INSTITUTIONS

Justice. In 1997, 54,060 Criminal Code offences were reported, including 8 homicides.

Education. Public education is free and non-sectarian.
There were, in Sept. 1997, 131,586 students (including kindergarten) and 7,772 full-time equivalent/professional educational staff in the province's 356 schools. There are 18 school districts.
There are 4 universities. The University of New Brunswick at Fredericton (founded 13 Dec. 1785 by the Loyalists, elevated to university status in 1823, reorganized as the University of New Brunswick in 1859) had 7,569 full-time students at the Fredericton campus and 2,040 full-time students at the Saint John campus (1997–98); Mount Allison University at Sackville had 2,146 full-time students; the Université de Moncton at Moncton, 3,565 full-time students, with 380 and 648 full-time students respectively at its satellite campuses at Shippagan and Edmundston; St Thomas University at Fredericton, 1,970 full-time students.

CULTURE

Broadcasting. The province is served by 28 radio stations, of which 3 are owned by the Canadian Broadcasting Corporation, 10 broadcast in French, and 3 are bilingual. The province is served by 7 television stations, 2 of which broadcast in French.

Press. New Brunswick had (1998) 5 daily newspapers, 1 in French, and 16 weekly newspapers, 3 in French and 2 bilingual.

Tourism. Tourism is one of the leading contributors to the economy. In 1997, tourism revenues reached $790m. Popular attractions include Magnetic Hill (Moncton), the Reversing Falls (Saint John) and the Rocks formation. There are 2 national parks as well as a number of provincial parks.

Libraries. The Harriet Irving Library and Legislative Library are in Fredericton.

National Theatre and Opera. Theatre New Brunswick is based at the Playhouse in Fredericton, and Symphony New Brunswick are at Saint John.

Museums and Galleries. The Beaverbrook Art Gallery and the Provincial Archives are 2 of the most notable galleries and museums.

FURTHER READING
Industrial Information: Dept. of Economic Development and Tourism, Fredericton. *Economic Information:* Dept. of Finance, New Brunswick Statistics Agency, Fredericton. *General Information:* Communications New Brunswick, Fredericton.

Thompson, C., *New Brunswick Inside Out.* Ottawa, 1977
Trueman, S., *The Fascinating World of New Brunswick.* Fredericton, 1973

NEWFOUNDLAND AND LABRADOR

KEY HISTORICAL EVENTS
Archaeological finds at L'Anse-au-Meadow in northern Newfoundland show that the Vikings established a colony here in about AD 1000. This site is the only known Viking colony in North America. Newfoundland was discovered by John Čabot on 24 June 1497, and was soon frequented in the summer months by the Portuguese, Spanish and French for its fisheries. It was formally occupied in Aug. 1583 by Sir Humphrey Gilbert on behalf of the English Crown but various attempts to colonize the island remained unsuccessful. Although British sovereignty was recognized in 1713 by the Treaty of Utrecht, disputes over fishing rights with the French were not finally settled till 1904. By the Anglo-French Convention of 1904, France renounced her exclusive fishing rights along part of the coast, granted under the Treaty of Utrecht, but retained sovereignty of the offshore islands of St Pierre and Miquelon. Self-governing from 1855, the colony remained outside of the Canadian confederation in 1867 and continued to govern itself until 1934, when a commission of government appointed by the British Crown assumed responsibility for governing the colony and Labrador. This body controlled the country until union with Canada in 1949.

TERRITORY AND POPULATION
Area, 143,501 sq. miles (371,690 sq. km), of which freshwater, 13,139 sq. miles (34,030 sq. km). In March 1927 the Privy Council decided the boundary between Canada and Newfoundland in Labrador. This area, now part of the Province of Newfoundland and Labrador, is 102,699 sq. miles. The coastline is extremely irregular. Bays, fiords and inlets are numerous, and there are many good harbours with deep water close to shore. The coast is rugged with bold rocky cliffs from 200 to 400 ft high; in the Bay of Islands some of the islands rise 500 ft, with the adjacent shore 1,000 ft above tide level. The interior is a plateau of moderate elevation, and the chief relief features trend north-east and south-west. Long Range, the most notable of these, begins at Cape Ray and extends north-east for 200 miles, the highest peak reaching 2,673 ft. Approximately one-third of the area is covered by water. Grand Lake, the largest body of water, has an area of about 200 sq. miles. The principal rivers flow towards the north-east. On the borders of the lakes and water-courses, good land is generally found, particularly in the valleys of the Terra Nova River, the Gander River, the Exploits River and the Humber River, which are also heavily timbered.

Census population, 1996, was 551,792; estimate, July 1997, 563,641.

The capital of Newfoundland is the City of St John's (1991 population, 171,859, metropolitan area). The other cities are Mt Pearl (23,689) and Corner Brook

(22,410); important towns are Conception Bay South (17,590), Grand Falls-Windsor (14,693), Gander (10,339), Labrador City (9,061), Happy Valley-Goose Bay (8,610), Stephenville (7,621), Marystown (6,739), Channel-Port aux Basques (5,644), Bay Roberts (5,474), Carbonear (5,259).

SOCIAL STATISTICS
See CANADA: Social Statistics.

CLIMATE
The cool temperate climate is marked by heavy precipitation, distributed evenly over the year, a cool summer and frequent fogs in spring. St. John's, Jan. –4°C, July 15·8°C. Annual rainfall 1,240 mm.

CONSTITUTION AND GOVERNMENT
Until 1832 Newfoundland was ruled by the Governor under instructions of the Colonial Office. In that year a Legislature was brought into existence, but the Governor and his Executive Council were not responsible to it. Under the constitution of 1855, which lasted until its suspension in 1934, the government was administered by the Governor appointed by the Crown with an Executive Council responsible to the House of Assembly of 27 elected members, and a Legislative Council of 24 members nominated for life by the Governor in Council. Women were enfranchised in 1925. At the Imperial Conference of 1917 Newfoundland was constituted as a Dominion.

In 1933 the financial situation had become so critical that the Government of Newfoundland asked the Government of the UK to appoint a Royal Commission to investigate conditions. On the strength of their recommendations, the parliamentary form of government was suspended and Government by Commission was inaugurated on 16 Feb. 1934.

A National Convention, elected in 1946, made recommendations to H. M. Government in Great Britain in 1948 as to the possible forms of future government to be submitted to the people at a national referendum. Two referenda were held. In the first referendum (June 1948) the three forms of government submitted to the people were: Commission of government for 5 years; confederation with Canada; and responsible government as it existed in 1933. No one form of government received a clear majority of the votes polled, and commission of government, receiving the fewest votes, was eliminated. In the second referendum (July 1948) confederation with Canada received 78,408 and responsible government 71,464 votes.

In the Canadian Senate on 18 Feb. 1949 Royal assent was given to the terms of union of Newfoundland and Labrador with Canada, and on 23 March 1949, in the House of Lords, London, Royal assent was given to an amendment to the British North America Act, made necessary by the inclusion of Newfoundland and Labrador as the tenth Province of Canada.

Under the terms of union of Newfoundland and Labrador with Canada, which was signed at Ottawa on 11 Dec. 1948, the constitution of the Legislature of Newfoundland and Labrador as it existed immediately prior to 16 Feb. 1934 shall, subject to the terms of the British North America Acts, 1867 to 1946, continue as the constitution of the Legislature of the Province of Newfoundland and Labrador until altered under the authority of the said Acts.

The franchise was in 1965 extended to all male and female residents who have attained the age of 19 years and are otherwise qualified as electors.

The House of Assembly (Amendment) Act, 1979, established 52 electoral districts and 52 members of the Legislature.

The province is represented by 6 members in the Senate and by 7 members in the House of Commons of Canada.

RECENT ELECTIONS
Elections were held on 9 Feb. 1999. In March 1999 there were 32 Liberals, 14 Progressive Conservatives and 2 New Democrats.

CURRENT ADMINISTRATION
Lieut.-Governor: Arthur Maxwell House (assumed office 5 Feb. 1997).

The Liberal Executive Council was, in March 1999, composed as follows: *Premier:* Brian Tobin.
Development and Rural Renewal (Acting): John Efford. *Education:* Judy Foote. *Environment and Labour:* Oliver Langdon. *Finance, and Justice and Attorney General:* Paul Dicks. *Fisheries and Aquaculture:* John Efford. *Forest Resources and Agrifoods:* Kevin Aylward. *Government Services and Lands:* Ernest McLean. *Health:* Joan Aylward. *Human Resources and Employment:* Julie Bettney. *Industry, Trade and Technology:* Sandra Kelly. *Mines and Energy:* Roger Grimes. *Municipal and Provincial Affairs:* Lloyd Matthews. *Tourism, Culture and Recreation:* Charles Furey. *Works, Services and Transportation:* Rick Woodford.

ECONOMY

Banking and Finance. Budget in Canadian $1,000 for fiscal years ended 31 March:

Current account:

	1992–93	1993–94	1994–95[1]	1995–96[2]
Gross revenue	3,044,401	3,071,526	3,243,602	3,398,268
Gross expenditure	3,124,001	3,125,222	3,218,471	3,270,412

[1]Revised estimates. [2]Estimates.

Capital account:

	1992–93	1993–94	1994–95[1]	1995–96[2]
Gross revenue	149,215	86,920	149,841	146,892
Gross expenditure	330,664	238,474	311,275	272,804

[1]Revised estimates. [2]Estimates.

Public debenture debt as at 31 March 1995 (estimate) was $5,623m.; sinking fund, $1,538m.

ENERGY AND NATURAL RESOURCES

Electricity. The electrical energy requirements of the province are met mainly by hydro-electric power, with petroleum fuels being utilized to provide the balance. The total amount of energy generated in the province in 1993 was 40,849,949 MWh, of which 96% was derived from hydro-electric facilities. The greater part of the energy produced in 1993 came from Churchill Falls, of which 29,942,214 MWh was sold to Hydro-Quebec under the terms of a long-term contract. Energy consumed in the province during 1993 totalled 10,907,775 MWh, with 9,251,443 MWh, or 85%, coming from hydro-electric facilities. At Dec. 1994 total electrical generating capacity in the province was 7,343 MW, with hydro-electric plants accounting for 6,601 MW, or 90%. It is estimated that potential additional hydro-electric generating capacity of up to 4·5m. kW can be developed at various sites in Labrador.

Oil and Gas. Since 1965, 140 wells have been drilled on the Continental Margin of the Province. Only the Hibernia discovery had commercial capability with production starting in the early 1990s. In Sept. 1990 the governments of Canada and Newfoundland and a development consortium signed an agreement to start developing the Hibernia discovery from Oct. 1990.

Minerals. The mineral resources are vast but only partially documented. Large deposits of iron ore, with an ore reserve of over 5,000m. tonnes at Labrador City, Wabush City and in the Knob Lake area are supplying approximately half of Canada's production. Other large deposits of iron ore are known to exist in the Julienne Lake area. There are a variety of other minerals being produced in more limited amounts. The Central Mineral Belt, which extends from the Smallwood Reservoir to the Atlantic coast near Makkovik, holds uranium, copper, beryllium and molybdenite potential.

There is a gold mine at Hope Brook on the south coast, east of Port aux Basques.

In 1994 a rich nickel, copper and cobalt discovery was made at Voisey's Bay, Labrador, with defined reserves of 31·7m. tonnes. Production in 1994 (preliminary): Iron ore, 20·9m. tonnes ($747,038,000); gold, 2,799,360 grammes ($47,219,000); sand and gravel, 3,128,000 tonnes ($14,202,000); stone ($5,939,000); cement, 56,882 tonnes ($7,395,000); dolomite, 267,145 tonnes ($2,885,000).

Agriculture. The estimated value of agricultural products sold, including livestock, 1994, was $62·2m. In 1996, 573 census farms reported total gross farm receipts of $2,500 or more.

NEWFOUNDLAND AND LABRADOR

Forestry. The forestry economy in the province is mainly dependent on the operation of 3 newsprint mills. In 1994 the gross value of newsprint exported from these 3 mills totalled $472m. Lumber mills and saw-log operations produced 57m. flat bd ft in 1994–95.

Fisheries. The principal fish landings are cod, flounder, redfish, Queen crabs, lobster, salmon and herring. In 1994 (preliminary) a yearly average of some 2,800 persons were employed by the fish-processing industry, and there were 22,045 licensed full-, part-time and casual fishermen engaged in harvesting operations. 207 processing operations were licensed in 1994. The production of fresh and frozen fish products was $490m. in 1994.

The total catch in 1993 was 245,942 tonnes valued at $197,125,873, including (in tonnes): Cod, 37,177 ($24,771,725); flounder and sole, 22,128 ($8,863,274); herring, 21,355 ($3,012,684); redfish, 26,284 ($7,253,497); capelin, 48,469 ($19,298,947); crab, 23,160 ($32,058,472); other, 41,612 ($31,499,911).

INDUSTRY
The total value of manufacturing shipments in 1993 was $1,324m. This consists largely of first-stage processing of primary resource products, with two of the largest components being paper and fish products.

Labour. In 1996 the labour force was 235,500 (102,900 females), of whom 189,700 (85,600) were employed.

Trade Unions. There were 35 unions in 1993 representing 75,627 members of international and national unions, and government employee associations.

COMMUNICATIONS
Roads. In 1993 there were 8,895 km of roads, of which 6,356 were paved. In 1994 there were 322,652 motor vehicles registered, including 216,760 passenger cars.

Rail. In 1993 the Quebec North Shore and Labrador Railway operated 576 km of standard-gauge main railway track. The route runs from Sept-Iles, Quebec, to Schefferville, Quebec, with a branch at Ross Bay Junction to Wabush, Labrador. In 1995, 22m. tonnes of freight were carried.

Civil Aviation. The province is linked to the rest of Canada by regular air services provided by Air Canada, Canadian Airlines International, Quebecair and a number of smaller air carriers.

Shipping. At 21 Dec. 1995 there were 1,624 ships on register in Newfoundland. In 1993 Marine Atlantic provided a freight and passenger service all year round to the south of the island and during the ice-free season as far north as Nain. There is a year-round ferry from Port-aux-Basques to North Sydney, Nova Scotia; and seasonal ferries connect Argentia with North Sydney, and Lewisporte with Goosebay, Labrador.

Telecommunications. There were 430 post offices in 1995. Telephone access lines numbered 262,856 in 1993 (193,987 private). There were 3,384 public pay phones.

SOCIAL INSTITUTIONS
Justice. In 1996, 33,828 Criminal Code offences were reported, including 7 homicides.

Education. The number of schools in 1994–95 was 479. The enrolment was 114,010; full-time teachers numbered 7,331. The Memorial University, offering courses in arts, science, engineering, education, nursing and medicine, had 17,226 full- and part-time students in 1994 (calendar year). Total expenditure for education by the government in 1995–96 (estimate) was $716m.

FURTHER READING
Horwood, H., *Newfoundland*. Toronto, 1969
Perlin, A. B., *The Story of Newfoundland, 1497–1959*. St John's, 1959
Taylor, T. G., *Newfoundland: A Study of Settlement*. Toronto, 1946

Statistical office: Newfoundland Statistics Agency, POB 8700, St. John's, A1B 4J6.

NOVA SCOTIA

KEY HISTORICAL EVENTS
Nova Scotia was visited by John and Sebastian Cabot in 1497-98. In 1605 a number of French colonists settled at Port Royal. The old name of the colony, Acadia, was changed in 1621 to Nova Scotia. The French were granted possession of the colony by the Treaty of St-Germain-en-Laye (1632). In 1654 Oliver Cromwell sent a force to occupy the settlement. Charles II, by the Treaty of Breda (1667), restored Nova Scotia to the French. It was finally ceded to the British by the Treaty of Utrecht in 1713. In the Treaty of Paris (1763) France resigned all claims and in 1820 Cape Breton Island united with Nova Scotia. Representative government was granted as early as 1758 and a fully responsible legislative assembly was established in 1848. In 1867 the province entered the dominion of Canada.

TERRITORY AND POPULATION
The area of the province is 21,425 sq. miles (55,000 sq. km), of which 20,401 sq. miles are land area, 1,024 sq. miles water area. The population (census 1996) was 909,282; estimate (Oct. 1998) 937,000.

Population of the principal cities (census 1996): Halifax, 113,910; Dartmouth, 65,629. Principal towns (census 1996): Bedford, 13,638; Truro, 11,938; New Glasgow, 9,812; Amherst, 9,669; Yarmouth, 7,568; Bridgewater, 7,351; Kentville, 5,551.

SOCIAL STATISTICS
See CANADA: Social Statistics.

CLIMATE
A cool temperate climate, with rainfall occurring evenly over the year. The Gulf Stream moderates the temperatures in winter so that ports remain ice-free. Halifax, Jan. 23·7°F (−4·6°C), July 63·5°F (17·5°C). Annual rainfall 54" (1,371 mm).

CONSTITUTION AND GOVERNMENT
Under the British North America Act of 1867 the legislature of Nova Scotia may exclusively make laws in relation to local matters, including direct taxation within the province, education and the administration of justice. The legislature of Nova Scotia consists of a Lieut.-Governor, appointed and paid by the federal government, and holding office for 5 years, and a House of Assembly of 52 members, chosen by popular vote at least every 5 years. The province is represented in the Canadian Senate by 10 members, and in the House of Commons by 11.

The franchise and eligibility to the legislature are granted to every person, male or female, if of age (19 years), a British subject or Canadian citizen, and a resident in the province for 1 year and 2 months before the date of the writ of election in the county or electoral district of which the polling district forms part, and if not by law otherwise disqualified.

RECENT ELECTIONS
At the provincial elections of 24 March 1998, Premier Russell MacLellan's Liberals won 19 seats (35·3% of the vote), the New Democratic Party 19 seats (34·7%), and the Progressive Conservatives 14 (29·7%). Turn-out was 69·2%. State of the parties in Dec. 1998: 19 Liberals, 13 Progressive Conservatives, 19 New Democrats and 1 Independent.

CURRENT ADMINISTRATION
Lieut.-Governor: John James Kinley.
The members of the Liberal Ministry were as follows in Jan. 1999:
Premier, President of the Executive Council, Minister of Intergovernmental Affairs: Russell MacLellan, Q.C.
Deputy Premier, Deputy President of the Executive Council, Minister of Finance, Minister responsible for Aboriginal Affairs, for the administration of Part I of the Gaming Control Act: Donald R. Downe. *Economic Development and Tourism,*

Minister responsible for the Petroleum Directorate, for the Innovation Corporation Act, for the Business Development Corporation, for the Nova Scotia Marketing Agency and for the Sydney Steel Corporation Act: Manning MacDonald. *Health, Chair of Priorities and Planning Committee, Minister responsible for Communications Nova Scotia:* James A. Smith M.D. *Justice and Attorney General, Business and Consumer Services, Minister responsible for the Technology and Science Secretariat, for the administration of the Human Rights Act, in charge of the Regulations Act, responsible for the Nova Scotia Sport and Recreation Commission, for the Residential Tenancies Act:* Robert Harrison. *Education and Culture, Minister responsible for Acadian Affairs:* Wayne Gaudet. *Agriculture and Marketing:* Edward Lorraine. *Natural Resources, Minister responsible for the administration of the Liquor Control Act, for the Emergency Measures Act, for the Nova Scotia Boxing Authority:* Kenneth MacAskill. *Community Services, Human Resources, Chair of the Senior Citizens Secretariat, Minister responsible for the administration of the Advisory Council on the Status of Women Act, for the Disabled Persons' Commission Act:* Francene Cosman. *Labour, Minister responsible for the Workers' Compensation Act:* Russell MacKinnon. *Transportation and Public Works:* Clifford B. Huskilson. *Fisheries and Aquaculture, Minister responsible for the administration of Part II of the Gaming Control Act:* Keith W. Colwell. *Housing and Municipal Affairs, Minister in charge of the administration of the Heritage Property Act:* Raymond J. White. *Environment, Minister responsible for the administration of the Youth Secretariat Act:* Michel P. Samson.

Local Government. In 1995 the new Cape Breton Regional Municipality was formed to amalgamate the former City of Sydney, the rural municipality of Cape Breton and 6 towns within the county. On 1 April 1996 a new Regional Municipality of Halifax incorporated the cities of Halifax and Dartmouth, the town of Bedford and the rural municipality of Halifax County. The other main divisions of the province for governmental purposes are 32 towns and 22 rural municipalities, each governed by a council and a mayor or warden. The cities have independent charters; and the various towns take their powers from and are limited by The Towns Act, while the various municipalities take their powers from and are limited by The Municipal Act as revised in 1967. The majority of municipalities comprise 1 county, but 6 counties are divided into 2 municipalities each. In no case do the boundaries of any municipality overlap county lines. The 18 counties as such have no administrative function.

Any incorporated town (of which there are 32) that lies within the boundaries of a municipality is excluded from any jurisdiction by the municipal council and has its own government.

ECONOMY

Performance. GDP (factor cost) was $16,495m. in 1997, an increase of just under 2% on 1996.

Budget. Revenue, expenditure and debt (in $1,000) for fiscal years ending 31 March:

	1996-97[1]	1997-98[2]	1998-99[3]
Ordinary Revenue	4,246,045	4,240,674	4,382,718
Net Programme Expenditures	3,550,555	3,509,422	3,690,824
Net Current Account	3,347,486	3,305,270	3,539,857
Restructuring Costs	35,627	31,510	3,129
Net Capital Account	167,442	172,642	147,838
Debt Servicing Costs	811,082	855,180	821,942
−Sinking Fund Earnings	123,868	127,900	131,200
Net Debt Servicing Costs	687,214	727,280	690,742
Budgetary surplus (Deficit)	8,276	3,972	1,152

[1]Actual. [2]Estimate. [3]Forecast.

Banking and Finance. Revenue is derived from provincial sources, payments from the federal government under the Federal-Provincial Fiscal Arrangements and Established Programs Financing Act. Recoveries consist generally of amounts received under various federal cost-shared programmes. Main sources of provincial revenues include income and sales taxes.

CANADA

In the fourth quarter of 1995 total deposits with chartered banks totalled $7,951m.

Weights and Measures. The metric system was officially adopted in 1983, but measurement in the imperial system is still widespread.

ENERGY AND NATURAL RESOURCES

Electricity. In 1997, production was 10,175,370 kWh, of which 88% came from thermal sources and the rest from hydroelectric, wind and tidal sources.

Oil and Gas. Significant finds of offshore natural gas are currently under development. A gas pipeline to serve markets in Canada and the USA is scheduled for completion in late 1999.

Minerals. Principal minerals in 1997 were: Coal, 2·6m. tonnes, valued at $152m.; gypsum, 6·9m. tonnes, valued at $73·7m.; sand and gravel, 4·2m. tonnes, valued at $16·1m. Total value of mineral production in 1997 was $487·7m.

Agriculture. Dairying, poultry and egg production, livestock and fruit growing are the most important branches. Farm cash receipts for 1997 were estimated at $374·2m., with an additional $4·3m. going to persons on farms as income in kind. Cash receipts from sale of dairy products were $86·3m., with total milk and cream sales of 171,689,000 litres. The production of poultry meat in 1997 was 30,904 tonnes, of which 27,555 tonnes were chickens and 3,349 tonnes were turkeys. Egg production was 16·8m. dozen.

The main 1997 fruit crops were apples, 45,042 tonnes; blueberries, 10,385 tonnes; strawberries, 1,721 tonnes.

Forestry. The estimated forest area of Nova Scotia is 15,830 sq. miles (40,990 sq. km), of which about 28% is owned by the province. The principal trees are spruce, balsam fir, hemlock, pine, larch, birch, oak, maple, poplar and ash. 6,568,223 cu. metres of roundforest products were produced in 1997.

Fisheries. The fisheries of the province in 1997 had a landed value of $479m. of sea fish; including scallop fishery, $66·4m., and lobster fishery, $206·1m. In 1997 there were 8,700 employees in the fish-processing industry; the value of shipment of goods was $804m.

INDUSTRY

The number of manufacturing establishments was 748 in 1996; the number of employees was 34,402; wages and salaries, $1,110m. The value of shipments in 1996 was $6,894·4m., and the leading industries were food, paper and allied products, and beverage production.

Labour. In 1997 the labour force was 446,600 (205,400 females), of whom 391,900 (183,000) were employed.

Trade Unions. Total union membership in 1997 was 102,352, belonging to 78 unions comprised of 653 individual locals. The largest union membership was in the service sector, followed by public administration and defence.

INTERNATIONAL TRADE

Imports and Exports. Total of imports and exports to and from Nova Scotia (in $1m.):

	1995	1996	1997
Imports	4,130	3,932	5,218
Exports	2,977	3,117	3,160

COMMUNICATIONS

Roads. In 1997 there were 26,000 km of highways, of which 13,600 km were paved. The Trans Canada and 100 series highways are limited access, all-weather, rapid transit routes. The province's first toll road opened in Dec. 1997. Acadian Lines provides a bus link to most major communities in the province and there are also a number of regional and local bus services. In the fiscal year 1996–97, vehicle registrations numbered 363,534 passenger cars and 169,746 trucks and truck tractors. Over 550,000 persons had road motor vehicle operators licences.

Rail. The province has a 700 km network of mainline track operated predominantly by Canadian National Railways. The Cape Breton and Central Nova Scotia Railway operates between Truro and Cape Breton Island. The Windsor and Hantsport Railway operates in the Annapolis Valley region. VIA Rail operates the Ocean for 6 days a week, a transcontinental service between Halifax and Montreal.

Civil Aviation. There is direct air service to all major Canadian points, and international scheduled services to Boston, New York, Bermuda, London, Glasgow and Amsterdam. There are winter charter services to Florida and the Caribbean. In 1997, airlines providing national and international service from the major airports included Air Canada, Canadian Airlines International, Icelandair, Air Nova, Air Atlantic, Air St Pierre and Business Express. Charter air service is provided by Canada 3000, Air Transat, Royal Airlines, Air Europa and Can Air. Halifax International Airport is the largest airport, and there are also major airports at Yarmouth and Sydney.

Shipping. Ferry services connect Nova Scotia to the provinces of Newfoundland, Prince Edward Island and New Brunswick as well as to the USA. The deep-water Port of Halifax handles about 14m. tonnes of cargo annually. Direct container service is provided to the USA, Europe, Asia, Australia/New Zealand and the Caribbean. There are numerous smaller ports.

Telecommunications. In 1996 there were 565,874 access lines (372,794 residential and 193,080 business). There were 59·8 access lines per 100 population and 98·3% of households had telephones.

Postal Services. The postal service is provided by the Federal Crown Corporation Canada Post.

SOCIAL INSTITUTIONS

Justice. The Supreme Court (Trial Division and Appeal Division) is the superior court of Nova Scotia and has original and appellate jurisdiction in all civil and criminal matters unless they have been specifically assigned to another court by Statute. An appeal from the Supreme Court, Appeal Division, is to the Supreme Court of Canada. The other courts in the Province are the Provincial Court, which hears criminal matters only, the Small Claims Court, which has limited monetary jurisdiction, Probate Court, County Court, which has jurisdiction in criminal matters as well as original jurisdiction over actions not exceeding $50,000, and Family Court. Young offenders are tried in the Family Court or the Provincial Court.

For the year ending 31 March 1997 there were 3,932 adult admissions to provincial custody; of these, 2,113 were sentenced. In 1997, 80,848 Criminal Code offences were reported, including 24 homicides.

Religion. The population is predominantly Christian. In 1991, 37·2% were Roman Catholic, 17·2% were United Church, 14·4% Anglicans, 11·1% Baptist and 3·5% Presbyterian.

Education. Public education in Nova Scotia is free, compulsory and undenominational through elementary and high school. Attendance is compulsory to the age of 16.

There were 522 elementary-secondary public schools, with 9,333 full-time teachers and 169,194 pupils, in 1997–98, plus the Nova Scotia Youth Centres for young offenders in Shelburne and in Waterville; and the Nova Scotia Youth Training Centre in Truro for mentally handicapped children. The province has 12 degree-granting institutions, of which the largest is Dalhousie University in Halifax. The Nova Scotia Agricultural College is located at Truro. The Technical University of Nova Scotia at Halifax grants degrees in engineering and architecture. Through the Nova Scotia Community College, the Department of Education administers 19 college campuses, including 2 adult vocational training centres, 2 institutes of technology, a nautical institute, plus the College de l'Acadie, the French component of the Nova Scotia Community College. There are also 7 teaching hospitals.

The Nova Scotia government offers financial support and organizational assistance to local school boards for provision of weekend and evening courses in academic and vocational subjects, and citizenship for new Canadians. It also provides local authorities with specialist support services to assist them in providing community workshops, and it operates a correspondence study service for children and adults.

Health. A provincial retail sales tax of 8% provides funds for free hospital in-patient care up to ward level and free medically required services of physicians. Health service programmes in the province are administered by the Department of Health and operated in conjunction with Maritime Medical Care Inc. Prescription service is available to those over 65 years for a minimum fee. The Queen Elizabeth II Hospital in Halifax is the overall referral hospital for the province and, in many instances, for the Atlantic region. The Izaak Walton Killam Hospital provides similar regional specialization for children.

Welfare. General and specialized welfare services in the province are under the jurisdiction of the Department of Community Services. The provincial government funds all of the costs. The Family Benefit Act provides financial assistance to individuals or families in need where the cause of need is likely to be of a prolonged nature. Qualifying groups include the aged, disabled, unemployable, foster parents and disabled parents.

CULTURE

Broadcasting. In 1996 there were 12 business organizations with licences for stations. There were 5 television stations, 16 AM radio stations and 8 FM radio stations. There were a further 85 operating cable television systems with 243,683 subscribers.

Tourism. Tourism revenues exceeded $1bn. for the first time in 1997. This figure translated into employment for 33,000 with a payroll of $400m.

FURTHER READING
Nova Scotia Fact Book. N. S. Department of Economic Development, Halifax, 1993
Nova Scotia Statistical Review. N. S. Department of Finance, Halifax, 1998
Nova Scotia Facts at a Glance. N. S. Department of Finance, Halifax, 1998

Atlantic Provinces Economic Council. *The Atlantic Vision, 1990*. Halifax, 1979
Beck, M., *The Evolution of Municipal Government in Nova Scotia, 1749–1973*. 1973
McCreath, P. and Leefe, J., *History of Early Nova Scotia*. Halifax, 1982
Vaison, R., *Nova Scotia Past and Present: A Bibliography and Guide*. Halifax, 1976

Statistical office: Statistics Division, Department of Finance, POB 187, Halifax, Nova Scotia, B3J 2N3.

ONTARIO

KEY HISTORICAL EVENTS
The French explorer Samuel de Champlain explored the Ottawa River from 1613. The area was governed by the French, first under a joint stock company and then as a royal province, from 1627 and was ceded to Great Britain in 1763. A constitutional act of 1791 created there the province of Upper Canada, largely to accommodate loyalists of English descent who had immigrated after the United States war of independence. Upper Canada entered the Confederation as Ontario in 1867.

TERRITORY AND POPULATION
The area is 412,580 sq. miles (1,068,580 sq. km), of which some 344,100 sq. miles (891,190 sq. km) are land area and some 68,480 sq. miles (177,390 sq. km) are lakes and fresh water rivers. The province extends 1,050 miles (1,690 km) from east to west and 1,075 miles (1,730 km) from north to south. It is bounded in the north by the Hudson and James Bays, in the east by Quebec, in the west by Manitoba, and in the south by the USA, the Great Lakes and the St. Lawrence Seaway.

The census population, 1996, was 10,753,573; estimate, July 1998, 11,404,750. Population of the principal cities (1996 census):

Toronto[1]	653,734	Windsor	197,694	Thunder Bay	113,662
North York[1]	589,653	Kitchener	178,420	East York[1]	107,822
Scarborough[1]	558,960	Markham	173,383	Gloucester	104,022
Mississauga	544,382	York[1]	146,534	Richmond Hill	101,725
Etobicoke[1]	328,718	Burlington	136,976	Cambridge	101,429
London	325,646	Oshawa	134,364	Guelph	95,821
Ottawa	323,340	Vaughan	132,549	Sudbury	92,059
Hamilton	322,352	St Catharines	130,926	Brantford	84,764
Brampton	268,251	Oakville	128,405	Sault Ste Marie	80,054

[1]Municipality of Metropolitan Toronto.

There are over 1m. French-speaking people and 0·25m. native Indians. An agreement with the Ontario government of Aug. 1991 recognized Indians' right to self-government.

SOCIAL STATISTICS
See CANADA: Social Statistics.

CLIMATE
A temperate continental climate, but conditions can be quite severe in winter, though proximity to the Great Lakes has a moderating influence on temperatures. Ottawa, Jan. –10·8°C, July 20·8°C. Annual rainfall (including snow) 911 mm. Toronto, Jan. –4·5°C, July 22·1°C. Annual rainfall (including snow) 818 mm.

CONSTITUTION AND GOVERNMENT
The provincial government is administered by a *Lieut.-Governor*, a cabinet and a single-chamber 130-member *Legislative Assembly* elected by a general franchise for a period of no longer than 5 years. The minimum voting age is 18 years.

RECENT ELECTIONS
At the elections on 8 June 1995 to the *Legislative Assembly*, the Progressive Conservative Party won 82 seats (20 in 1990), the Liberal Party, 31 (36), the New Democratic Party (NDP), 16 (74) and Independents, 1. At 3 by-elections on 4 Sept. 1997, the Liberals won 2 seats and the NDP won 1 seat. At 1 by-election on 1 Oct. 1998, the Liberals won 1 seat. 1 Liberal member joined the NDP. The Party standings are currently: Progressive Conservative Party, 82; Liberals, 30; NDP, 17; Independents, 1.

CURRENT ADMINISTRATION
Lieut.-Governor: Right Hon. Hilary Weston (b. 1942; appointed Dec. 1996).
In Feb. 1999 the Executive Council comprised:
Premier and President of the Council: Michael Harris.
Deputy Premier, Minister of Finance: Ernie Eves. *Agriculture, Food and Rural Affairs, Minister responsible for Francophone Affairs:* Noble Villeneuve. *Consumer and Commercial Relations:* David Tsubouchi. *Environment and Government House Leader:* Norman Sterling. *Correctional Services and Solicitor-General:* Robert Runciman. *Education and Training:* David Johnson. *Attorney-General, Minister responsible for Native Affairs:* Charles Harnick. *Energy, Science and Technology:* Jim Wilson. *Northern Development and Mines, Chair of the Management Board of Cabinet:* Chris Hodgson. *Health:* Elizabeth Witmer. *Intergovernmental Affairs, Minister responsible for Women's Issues:* Dianne Cunningham. *Natural Resources:* John Snobelen. *Economic Development, Trade and Tourism:* Al Palladini. *Community and Social Services:* Janet Ecker. *Transportation:* Tony Clement. *Labour:* James Flaherty. *Long-Term Care (responsible for Seniors):* Cameron Jackson. *Municipal Affairs and Housing:* Allan Leach. *Citizenship, Culture and Recreation:* Isabel Bassett. *Ministers without portfolio:* Rob Sampson *(responsible for Privatization)*; Margaret Marland *(responsible for Children)*; David Turnbull *(Chief Government Whip)*.

Local Government. There are 2 levels of municipal government in the southern, settled part of Ontario. The upper level consists of 23 counties plus 10 regional municipalities, 1 district municipality and 1 restructured county. In addition, there are 5 single-tier governments. As of 1 Jan. 1998, metropolitan Toronto and its area municipalities became the City of Toronto, a single-tier municipality. The local level comprises more than 600 cities, towns and townships. Cities with one exception in the traditional county system function independently of the county in which they lie, as do 4 towns and 1 township which have been separated for municipal purposes. There are no separated municipal units in regional governments.

Ontario's local municipalities are governed by councils elected by popular vote.

Lower-tier municipal councils are composed of a head of council (mayor or reeve) and councillors. In the case of regional municipalities, one or more regional councillors represent the area municipalities on the regional council. Niagara and Ottawa-Carleton have their own directly elected upper-level councils. Waterloo, Hamilton-Wentworth, Ottawa-Carleton and Sudbury have directly elected regional chairs.

County councils are federations. A county council consists of at least 1 representative of each local municipality. The head of the county council is the warden, who is elected by the council from among its own members.

A regional council may include the heads of council of the local municipalities, as well as a varying number of regional councillors, who are elected on the basis of representation, either directly or indirectly.

No municipality may incur long-term debts over a reasonable level without the sanction of the tribunal created by the Provincial Legislature and known as the Ontario Municipal Board. Debenture obligations incurred by municipalities for utility undertakings are discharged out of revenues derived from the sale of utility services and do not fall upon the general property tax rate.

Municipal councils have no jurisdiction for education beyond the collection of taxes for school purposes. Responsibility for providing, operating and maintaining school facilities, and for the supply of teachers, rests with elected local education authorities known as Boards of Education or School Boards. These Boards are now generally organized on a large regional basis.

Municipal institutions come under the jurisdiction of the Provincial Ministry of Municipal Affairs and Housing. One of the principal functions of the Ministry is to ensure municipalities have the legislative authority to respond to local needs and offer management and administrative support along with financial assistance to Ontario's 586 municipalities. Educational support and guidance at the provincial level is the responsibility of the Ministry of Education and Training, which deals with the training of teachers and the formulation of curriculum.

There are areas in the north where there is little or no settlement of population. Administration of such areas, for the most part, remains in the hands of the Provincial Government. Where there are municipalities in the north they are single lower tier, with the exception of the regional municipality of Sudbury.

ECONOMY

Banking and Finance. Provincial revenue and expenditure (in $1m.) for years ending 31 March:

	1993–94	1994–95	1995–96	1996–97	1997–98
Gross revenue	43,674	46,039	49,473	49,450	52,488
Gross expenditure	54,876	56,168	58,273	56,355	56,454

Gross revenue and expenditure figures reflect accrual and consolidation accounting as recommended by the Public Sector Accounting and Auditing Board of the Canadian Institute of Chartered Accountants. Transactions on behalf of Ontario Hydro are excluded.

Personal income per capita, 1997–98, was $24,949.

ENERGY AND NATURAL RESOURCES

Electricity. Ontario Hydro recorded for the calendar year 1997 an installed generating capacity of 30,284 MW. Primary energy made available 145,000m. kWh. In 1997 there were 69 hydro-electric, 5 nuclear and 6 fossil-fuel stations operating. Ontario Hydro served 106 direct industrial customers, almost 1,000,000 retail customers (homes, farms and small businesses) and 305 municipal utilities, who in turn serve over 2,946,000 customers.

Minerals. The total value of mine production in 1997 was $5,530,754,000. The top 10 commodities (in $1m.) were: Nickel, 1,334·7; gold, 1,170·6; copper, 752·4; cement, 407·7; sand and gravel, 328·3; stone, 288·3; salt, 282·1; zinc, 213·3; cobalt, 119·8; platinum group, 138·6. Direct employment in the mining industry was 18,500 in 1997.

Agriculture. In 1996, 67,118 census farms operated on 5,617,059 ha, with total farm receipts of $7·78bn.

Forestry. In 1996 the total area of productive forest was 60·9m. ha, of which the inventoried area was 40·3m. ha, comprising: Softwoods, 27·1m. ha; hardwoods, 13·1m. ha. The growing stock equals 5·34m. cu. metres.

INDUSTRY

Ontario is Canada's most industrialized province, with GDP in 1997 at $346,871m., or 40·6% of the Canadian total. Manufacturing accounts for 23·6% of Ontario's GDP.

Leading manufacturing industries include: Motor vehicles and parts; office and industrial electrical equipment; food processing; chemicals; and steel.

In 1997 Ontario was responsible for about 52% ($154,442m.) of Canada's merchandise exports; motor vehicles and parts accounted for about 45·1%.

Labour. In 1997 the labour force was 5,914,900 (2,692,700 females), of whom 5,412,900 (2,450,200) were employed. Total labour income was $185,099m.

COMMUNICATIONS

Roads. There were, in 1998, 159,456 km of roads (municipal, 143,000; provincial MTO, 16,456). Motor licences (on the road) numbered (1997) 8,324,830, of which 5,222,698 were passenger cars, 1,127,015 commercial vehicles, 27,293 buses, 1,490,377 trailers, 94,886 motor cycles and 362,561 snow vehicles.

Rail. In 1998 there were 14 provincial short lines plus the provincially owned Ontario Northland Railway and 12 federal railways. The Canadian National and Canadian Pacific Railways operate in Ontario. Total track miles, approximately 12,500 km. There is a metro and tramway network in Toronto.

Telecommunications. The telephone service in 1998 was provided by 30 independent systems and Bell Canada.

SOCIAL INSTITUTIONS

Justice. In 1996, 893,824 Criminal Code offences were reported, including 174 homicides.

Education. There is a provincial system of publicly financed elementary and secondary schools as well as private schools. In 1997–98 publicly financed elementary and secondary schools had a total enrolment of 2,103,586 pupils.

There are 18 universities (Brock, Carleton, Dominicain, Guelph, Lakehead, Laurentian, McMaster, Nipissing, Ottawa, Queen's, Ryerson, Toronto, Trent, Waterloo, Western Ontario, Wilfred Laurier, Windsor and York) and 1 institute of equivalent status (Ontario College of Art and Design) with full-time enrolment for 1997–98 of 226,886. All receive operating grants from the Ontario government. There are also 25 publicly financed Colleges of Applied Arts and Technology (CAAT), with a full-time enrolment of 136,170 in 1997–98.

Operating expense (including capital expense) by the Ontario government on education for 1997–98 was $9,470m.

FURTHER READING

Statistical Information: Annual publications of the Ontario Ministry of Finance include: *Ontario Statistics; Ontario Budget; Public Accounts; Financial Report.*

PRINCE EDWARD ISLAND

KEY HISTORICAL EVENTS
The first recorded European visit was by Jacques Cartier in 1534, who named it Isle St-Jean. In 1719 it was settled by the French, but was taken from them by the English in 1758, annexed to Nova Scotia in 1763, and constituted a separate colony in 1769. Named Prince Edward Island in honour of Prince Edward, Duke of Kent, in 1799, it joined the Canadian Confederation on 1 July 1873.

TERRITORY AND POPULATION
The province lies in the Gulf of St Lawrence, and is separated from the mainland of New Brunswick and Nova Scotia by Northumberland Strait. The area of the island is 2,185 sq. miles (5,660 sq. km). Total population (census, 1996), 134,557; estimate, July 1997, 137,244. Population of the principal cities (1991): Charlottetown (capital), 15,396; Summerside, 7,474.

SOCIAL STATISTICS
See CANADA: Social Statistics.

CLIMATE
The cool temperate climate is affected in winter by the freezing of the St. Lawrence, which reduces winter temperatures. Charlottetown, Jan. 3·4°C, July 23°C. Annual rainfall 869 mm.

CONSTITUTION AND GOVERNMENT
The provincial government is administered by a Lieut.-Governor-in-Council (Cabinet) and a Legislative Assembly of 27 members who are elected for up to 5 years.

RECENT ELECTIONS
As of Dec. 5 1997 parties in the Legislative Assembly were: Progressive Conservatives, 18; Liberals, 8; Island New Democrats, 1.

CURRENT ADMINISTRATION
Lieut.-Governor: Gilbert R. Clements (sworn in 30 Aug. 1995).
The Executive Council was composed as follows in Jan. 1999:
Premier and President of the Executive Council, Minister Responsible for Intergovernmental Affairs: Patrick G. Binns.
Agriculture and Forestry: J. Eric Hammill. *Community Services and Attorney-General:* J. Weston MacAleer. *Development:* Donald G. MacKinnon. *Education:* J. Chester Gillan. *Fisheries and Tourism:* Kevin J. MacAdam. *Health and Social Services:* Mildred A. Dover. *Provincial Treasurer:* Patricia J. Mella. *Technology and Environment:* P. Mitchell Murphy. *Transportation and Public Works:* Michael F. Currie.

Local Government. The Municipalities Act provides for the incorporation of Towns and Communities. The City of Charlottetown, the Town of Cornwall and the Town of Stratford are incorporated under the Charlottetown Area Municipalities Act. The City of Summerside is incorporated under the City of Summerside Act.

ECONOMY
Banking and Finance. Revenue and expenditure (in Canadian $1,000) for 5 financial years ending 31 March:

	1992–93	1993–94	1994–95	1995–96	1996–97
Revenue	676,028	738,855	812,461	802,579	801,143
Expenditure	793,328	810,199	821,422	797,937	818,747

Per capita personal income was $18,708 in 1996.

ENERGY AND NATURAL RESOURCES

Electricity. In 1996, Prince Edward Island received 73,867 MWh of electricity from other provinces via an underwater cable which spans the Northumberland Strait. Net generation on Prince Edward Island was 483 MWh.

Agriculture. Total area of farmland occupies approximately half of the total land area of 566,177 ha. Farm cash receipts in 1996 were $294m., with cash receipts from potatoes accounting for about 50% of the total. Cash receipts from dairy products, cattle and hogs followed in importance. For particulars of agricultural production and livestock, *see* CANADA: Agriculture.

Forestry. Forests cover some 280,000 ha. or 48·6% of Prince Edward Island. In 1996 the forest produced 557,000 cu. metres of products, with the commercial softwood component being 379,000 cu. metres. Sawlogs accounted for 65·2% of the commercial softwood harvest, with pulpwood the other component. 70% of the sawlogs were processed on Prince Edward Island. The pulpwood shipments were to Quebec (40%), Newfoundland (26%), New Brunswick (20%), Nova Scotia (9%) and a small quantity was exported internationally. The rest of the forest products were primarily firewood (144,000 cu. metres) and wood chips for energy.

Fisheries. The total catch of 107m. lbs in 1996 had a landed value of $118m. Lobsters accounted for $79m., over two-thirds of the total value; other shellfish, $32m.; pelagic and estuarial, $5·2m.; groundfish, $0·8m.; seaplants, $1·7m.

INDUSTRY

Value of manufacturing shipments for all industries in 1996 was $641·6m.

In 1996, provincial GDP in constant prices for manufacturing was $166·0m.; construction, $133·0m. In 1996 the total value of retail trade was $956·0m.

Labour. The average weekly wage (industrial aggregate) rose from $466·91 in 1995 to $491·04 in 1996. The labour force averaged 70,400 in 1995, while employment averaged 60,100.

COMMUNICATIONS

Roads. At the end of 1995 there were 5,308 km of road, including 3,806 km of paved highway. A bus service operates twice daily to the mainland.

Civil Aviation. In 1998 Air Canada provided daily services between Charlottetown and Boston, Fredericton, Halifax and Toronto. Canadian Airlines International operated daily sevices to Boston and Halifax, and there were also services to Moncton, Montreal and St John.

Shipping. Modern car ferries link the Island to New Brunswick and Nova Scotia. Service is provided year-round to New Brunswick on schedules which vary from 14 to 20 return crossings daily, with ice-breaking ferries maintaining the service during the winter months. Ferry service is operated to Nova Scotia from late April to mid-Dec. on schedules ranging from 9 to 19 return crossings daily. A third ferry service, to the Magdalen Islands (Quebec), operates from 1 April to 31 Jan. There is also a substantial water movement of certain commodities, primarily through the ports of Summerside and Charlottetown.

Telecommunications. At the end of 1995 there were 83,104 telephone lines in service.

SOCIAL INSTITUTIONS

Justice. In 1996, 10,247 Criminal Code offences were reported, including no homicides.

Education. Under the regional school boards there were in 1995-96 a total of 65 public schools, 1,434 teaching positions and 24,422 students. There is one undergraduate university (2,401 full-time and 7,477 part-time students), a veterinary college (197 students), and a Master of Science programme (25 students), all in Charlottetown. Holland College provides training for employment in business, applied arts and technology, with approximately 2,300 full-time students in post-secondary and vocational career programmes. The college offers extensive academic and career preparation programmes for adults.

Government expenditure on education, 1994–95, $174·7m.

CULTURE

Tourism. The value of the tourist industry was estimated at $150·8m. in 1996, with 298,693 tourist parties.

FURTHER READING

Baldwin, D. O., *Abegweit: Land of the Red Soil*. Charlottetown, 1985
Bolger, F. W. P., *Canada's Smallest Province*. Charlottetown, 1973
Clark, A. H., *Three Centuries and the Island*. Toronto, 1959
Hocking, A., *Prince Edward Island*. Toronto, 1978
MacKinnon, F., *The Government of Prince Edward Island*. Toronto, 1951

QUEBEC—QUÉBEC

KEY HISTORICAL EVENTS

Quebec was known as New France from 1534 to 1763; as the province of Quebec from 1763 to 1790; as Lower Canada from 1791 to 1846; as Canada East from 1846 to 1867, and when, by the union of the four original provinces, the Confederation of the Dominion of Canada was formed, it again became known as the province of Quebec (Québec).

The Quebec Act, passed by the British Parliament in 1774, guaranteed to the people of the newly conquered French territory in North America security in their religion and language, their customs and tenures, under their own civil laws.

In a referendum on 20 May 1980, 59·5% voted against 'separatism'. At a further referendum on 30 Oct. 1995, 50·6% of votes cast were against Quebec becoming 'sovereign in a new economic and political partnership' with Canada. The electorate was 5m.; turn-out was 93%.

On 20 Aug. 1998 Canada's supreme court ruled that Quebec was prohibited by both the constitution and international law from seceding unilaterally from the rest of the country, but that a clear majority in a referendum would impose a duty on the Canadian government to negotiate. Both sides claimed victory.

TERRITORY AND POPULATION

The area of Quebec (as amended by the Labrador Boundary Award) is 1,667,926 sq. km (594,860 sq. miles), of which 1,315,134 sq. km is land area and 352,792 sq. km water. Of this extent, 911,106 sq. km represent the Territory of Ungava, annexed in 1912 under the Quebec Boundaries Extension Act. The population (census 1996) was 7,138,795; estimate, July 1997, 7,419,890.

Principal cities: (1991 census populations): Quebec (capital), 167,517; Montreal, 1,017,666; Laval, 314,398; Longueuil, 129,874; Montreal North, 85,516; Sherbrooke, 76,429; Saint-Hubert, 74,027; LaSalle, 73,804; Sainte-Foy, 73,133; Saint-Laurent, 72,402, Charlesbourg, 70,788; Beauport, 69,158; Chicoutimi, 62,670; Verdun, 61,307; Hull, 60,707; Jonquière, 57,933.

SOCIAL STATISTICS

See CANADA: Social statistics.

CLIMATE

Cool temperate in the south, but conditions are more extreme towards the north. Winters are severe and snowfall considerable, but summer temperatures are quite warm. Quebec, Jan. −12·5°C, July 19·1°C. Annual rainfall 1,123 mm. Montreal, Jan. −10·7°C, July 20·2°C. Annual rainfall 936 mm.

QUEBEC—QUÉBEC

CONSTITUTION AND GOVERNMENT
There is a Legislative Assembly consisting of 125 members, elected in 125 electoral districts for 4 years.

RECENT ELECTIONS
At the elections of 30 Nov. 1998, the Parti Québécois won 75 seats with 42·7% of votes cast, the Liberal Party 48 with 43·7%.

CURRENT ADMINISTRATION
Lieut.-Governor: The Hon. Lise Thibault.
Members of the Council of Ministers in Jan. 1999 included:
Premier and President of Executive Council: Lucien Bouchard.
Deputy Premier, Finance, Industry, Trade, Science and Technology, Revenue, and Minister of State for the Economy and Finance: Bernard Landry. *Education:* François Legault. *Child and Family Welfare:* Pauline Marois. *Culture and Communications:* Agnès Maltais. *Justice:* Linda Goupil. *Transport, and Canadian Inter-Governmental Affairs:* Guy Chevrette. *Natural Resources:* Jacques Brassard. *Environment and Wildlife:* Paul Bégin. *Agriculture, Fisheries and Food:* Rémy Trudel. *Public Security:* Serge Ménard. *Labour:* Diane Lemieux. *Health and Social Services:* Gilles Baril. *Social Solidarity:* André Boisclair. *International Relations, Minister responsible for Relations with French-Speaking Communities:* Louise Beaudoin. *Municipal Affairs, Minister responsible for Independent Community Action and for the Status of Women:* Louise Harel. *Administration and Public Service, Chairman of the Treasury Board:* Jacques Léonard. *Industry and Trade:* Guy Julien. *Electoral and Parliamentary Reform, and Government House Leader:* Jean-Pierre Jolivet. *Relations with the Citizens and Immigration:* Robert Perreault. *Revenue:* Rita Dionne-Marsolais. *Research, Science and Technology:* Jean Rochon. *Minister responsible for Regional Development:* Guy Chevrette.

ECONOMY

Budget. Ordinary revenue and expenditure (in Canadian $1,000) for fiscal years ending 31 March:

	1991–92	1992–93	1993–94	1994–95	1995–96
Revenue	34,457,600	35,445,600	36,056,000	36,437,000	38,254,000
Expenditure	38,649,000	40,377,000	40,953,000	42,236,000	42,220,000

The total net debt at 31 March 1996 was $60,842m.

ENERGY AND NATURAL RESOURCES

Electricity. Water power is one of the most important natural resources of Quebec. Its turbine installation represents about 40% of the aggregate of Canada. At the end of 1994 the installed generating capacity was 38,909 MW. Production, 1994, was 193,000 GWh.

Minerals. For 1995 the value of mineral production (metal only) was $2,158,132,564. Chief minerals: Iron ore (confidential); copper, $458,756,897; gold, $681,547,351; zinc, $242,782,635.

Non-metallic minerals produced include: Asbestos ($233,747,031; about 97% of Canadian production), titanium-dioxide (confidential), industrial lime, dolomite and brucite, quartz and pyrite. Among the building materials produced were: Stone, $197,833,920; cement, $172,687,663; sand and gravel, $82,735,967; lime (confidential).

Agriculture. In 1995 the agricultural area was 3,445,000 ha. The yield of the principal crops was (1995 in 1,000 tonnes):

Crops	Yield	Crops	Yield
Tame hay	5,800	Fodder corn	760
Oats for grain	173	Corn for grain	2,000
Potatoes	429	Barley	350
Mixed grains	92	Buckwheat	88

About 38,000 farms were operating in 1995. Cash receipts, 1995, $4,382m. (dairy products, 31·9%; livestock, 30·1%; crops, 26·3%; poultry and eggs, 10·8%). In 1996, 33,906 census farms reported total gross farm receipts of $2,500 or more.

Forestry. Forests cover an area of 757,900 sq. km. 516,601 sq. km are classified as productive forests, of which 447,541 sq. km are provincial forest land and 65,991 sq. km are privately owned. Quebec leads the Canadian provinces in pulp and paper production, having nearly half of the Canadian estimated total.

In 1995 production of lumber was: Softwood and hardwood, 13,688,000 cu. metres; pulp and paper, 9,097,000 tonnes.

Fisheries. The principal fish are cod, herring, red fish, lobster and salmon. Total catch of sea fish, 1996, 47,070 tonnes, valued at $122,747m.

INDUSTRY

In 1994 there were 10,164 industrial establishments in the province; employees, 461,056; salaries and wages, $15,717·9m.; cost of materials, $51,774·34m.; value of shipments, $94,458·3m. Among the leading industries are petroleum refining, pulp and paper mills, smelting and refining, dairy products, slaughtering and meat processing, motor vehicle manufacturing, women's clothing, sawmills and planing mills, iron and steel mills, commercial printing.

Labour. In 1996 the labour force was 3,642,500 (1,614,000 females), of whom 3,212,600 (1,434,000) were employed.

INTERNATIONAL TRADE

Imports and Exports. In 1996 the value of Canadian exports through Quebec custom ports was $34,417·72m.; value of imports, $27,583·15m.

COMMUNICATIONS

Roads. In 1995 there were 28,898 km of roads and 4,275,429 registered motor vehicles.

Rail. There were (1996) 6,570 km of railway. There is a metro system in Montreal (64 km).

Civil Aviation. There are 2 international airports, Dorval (Montreal) and Mirabel (Montreal).

Telecommunications. Telephones numbered 4·1m. in 1994.

SOCIAL INSTITUTIONS

Justice. In 1996, 510,375 Criminal Code offences were reported, including 143 homicides.

Education. Education is compulsory for children aged 6-16. Pre-school education and elementary and secondary training are free in some 2,670 public schools, which were managed by 156 school boards (135 Catholic, 18 Protestant and 3 serving mainly Native students) in 1996–97. Instruction is given in French only in 100 school boards, in French and English in 46, in English only in 7, and in French, English and aboriginal languages in 3. Just under 10% of the student population attends private schools: In 1996–97, 286 establishments were authorized to provide pre-school, elementary and secondary education. After 6 years of elementary and 5 years of secondary school education, students enter Cegeps, a post-secondary educational institution. In 1996–97, college, pre-university and technical training for young and adult students was provided by 47 Cegeps, 11 government schools and 70 private establishments.

In 1994–95, in pre-kindergartens, there were 14,023 pupils; in kindergartens, 89,912; in primary schools, 547,395; in secondary schools, 498,105; in colleges (post-secondary, non-university), 180,977; and in classes for children with special needs, 134,621. The school boards had a total of 65,541 teachers.

Expenditure of the Departments of Education for 1995–96, $9,176·41m. net. This included $1,709·01m. for universities, $5,329·95m. for public primary and secondary schools, $302·57m. for private primary and secondary schools and $1,190·99m. for colleges.

In 1994–95 the province had 10 universities: 3 English-language universities, McGill (Montreal, founded 1821), Bishop (Lennoxville, founded 1845) and the Concordia University (Montreal, granted a charter 1975); 6 French-language universities: Laval (Quebec, founded 1852), Montreal University (opened 1876 as a branch of Laval, independent 1920), Sherbrooke University (founded 1954), University of Quebec (founded 1968) and 2 others; 1 French- and English-language university. In 1994 there were 134,933 full-time university students and 109,792 part-time students.

CULTURE
Broadcasting. In 1994 there were 29 television and 171 radio stations.

Press. In 1996 there were 11 French- and 2 English-language daily newspapers.

FURTHER READING
Dickinson, J. A. and Young, B., *A Short History of Quebec.* 2nd ed. Harlow, 1994
Gagnon, A.- G., *Québec* [Bibliography]. Oxford and Santa Barbara (CA), 1998
Jacobs, J., *The Question of Separatism: Quebec and the Struggle for Sovereignty.* London, 1981
McWhinney, E., *Quebec and the Constitution.* Univ. of Toronto Press, 1979
Wade, F. M., *The French Canadians, 1760–1967.* Toronto, 1968
Young, R. A., *The Secession of Quebec and the Future of Canada.* McGill-Queen's Univ. Press, 1995

Statistical office: Bureau de la Statistique du Québec, 117 rue Saint-André, Québec, G1K 3Y3

SASKATCHEWAN
KEY HISTORICAL EVENTS
Saskatchewan derives its name from its major river system, which the Cree Indians called 'Kis-is-ska-tche-wan', meaning 'swift flowing'. It officially became a province when it joined the Confederation on 1 Sept. 1905.

In 1670 King Charles II granted to Prince Rupert and his friends a charter covering exclusive trading rights in 'all the land drained by streams finding their outlet in the Hudson Bay'. This included what is now Saskatchewan. The trading company was first known as The Governor and Company of Adventurers of England; later as the Hudson's Bay Company. In 1869 the Northwest Territories was formed, and this included Saskatchewan. In 1882 the District of Saskatchewan was formed. By 1885 the North-West Mounted Police had been inaugurated, with headquarters in Regina (now the capital), and the Canadian Pacific Railway's transcontinental line had been completed, bringing a stream of immigrants to southern Saskatchewan. The Hudson's Bay Company surrendered its claim to territory in return for cash and land around the existing trading posts. Legislative government was introduced.

TERRITORY AND POPULATION
Saskatchewan is bounded in the west by Alberta, in the east by Manitoba, in the north by the Northwest Territories and in the south by the USA. The area of the province is 251,700 sq. miles (570,113 sq. km), of which 220,182 sq. miles is land area and 31,518 sq. miles is water. The population, 1996 census, was 990,237; estimate, July 1998, 1,025,595. Population of cities, 1996 census: Regina (capital), 180,400; Saskatoon, 193,647; Prince Albert, 34,777; Moose Jaw, 32,973; Yorkton, 15,154; Swift Current, 14,890; North Battleford, 14,051; Estevan, 10,752; Weyburn, 9,723; Lloydminster, 7,636; Melfort, 5,759; Melville, 4,646.

SOCIAL STATISTICS
See CANADA: Social Statistics.

CLIMATE

A cold continental climate, with severe winters and warm summers. Rainfall amounts are greatest from May to Aug. Regina, Jan. 0°F (−17·8°C), July 65°F (18·3°C). Annual rainfall 15" (373 mm).

CONSTITUTION AND GOVERNMENT

The provincial government is vested in a Lieut.-Governor, an Executive Council and a Legislative Assembly, elected for 5 years by universal suffrage.

RECENT ELECTIONS

State of parties in Jan. 1998: New Democratic Party, 42; Saskatchewan Party, 8; Liberal Party, 6; Independent, 3.

CURRENT ADMINISTRATION

Lieut.-Governor: Jack Wiebe.

The New Democratic Party Ministry in Jan. 1999 comprised as follows:

Premier, President of the Executive Council: Roy Romanow, QC (b. 1939).

Deputy Premier, Minister of Crown Investment Corporation: Dwain Lingenfelter. *Intergovernmental and Aboriginal Affairs, Provincial Secretary:* Bernhard Wiens. *Labour, Minister responsible for Women's Secretariat:* Joanne Crofford. *Economic and Co-operative Development, Minister responsible for Information Highway:* Janice MacKinnon. *Education:* Clay Serby. *Social Services, Minister responsible for Seniors and for Disabilities Directorate:* Harry Van Mulligan. *Energy and Mines:* Eldon Lautermilch. *Northern Affairs:* Keith Goulet. *Post-Secondary Education and Skills Training:* Maynard Sonntag. *Municipal Government:* Carol Teichrob. *Agriculture and Food:* Eric Upshall. *Finance:* Eric Cline. *Environment and Resource Management:* Lorne Scott. *Justice and Attorney General:* John Nilson, QC. *Health:* Pat Atkinson. *Highways and Transportation:* Judy Bradley. *Public Service Commission, Minister responsible for Gaming, for SPMC:* Doreen Hamilton.

Local Government. The organization of a city requires a minimum population of 5,000 persons; that of a town, 500; that of a village, 100 people. No requirements as to population exist for the rural municipality. Cities, towns, villages and rural municipalities are governed by elected councils, which consist of a mayor and 6–20 aldermen in a city; a mayor and 6 councillors in a town; a mayor and 2 other members in a village; a reeve and a councillor for each division in a rural municipality (usually 6).

ECONOMY

Budget. Budget and net assets (years ending 31 March) in Canadian $1,000:

	1994–95	1995–96	1996–97	1997–98
Budgetary revenue	4,841,700	5,165,200	5,345,400	5,073,400
Budgetary expenditure	5,030,424	5,140,849	4,987,602	5,049,267

ENERGY AND NATURAL RESOURCES

Agriculture used to dominate the history and economics of Saskatchewan, but the 'prairie province' is now a rapidly developing mining and manufacturing area. It is a major supplier of oil, has the world's largest deposits of potash and the net value of its non-agricultural production accounted for (1997 estimate) 88·0% of the provincial economy.

Electricity. The Saskatchewan Power Corporation generated 16,383m. kWh in 1997.

Minerals. 1997 mineral sales were valued at $5,584m., including (in $1m.): Petroleum, 2,896·4; natural gas, 283·5; coal and others, 757·4; potash, 1,504·8; salt, 29·7; uranium (1996), 666·2; sodium sulphate, 31·9. Other major minerals included potassium sulphate, ammonium sulphate, bentonite, coal, gold and base metals.

Agriculture. Saskatchewan produces normally about two-thirds of Canada's wheat. Wheat production in 1997 (in 1,000 tonnes) was 12,236 from 16m. acres; oats, 1,743 from 2·3m. acres; barley, 4,180 from 4·0m. acres; rye, 156 from 0·23m. acres;

canola, 3,175 from 6m. acres; flax, 686 from 1·4m. acres. Livestock (1 July 1998): Cattle and calves, 2·7m.; swine, 924,700; sheep and lambs, 79,500. Poultry in 1997: Chickens, 12·5m.; turkeys, 719,000. Cash income from the sale of farm products in 1997 was $5,902m. At the June 1996 census there were 56,995 farms in the province, each being a holding of 1 acre or more with sales of $250 or more during the previous year.

The South Saskatchewan River irrigation project, whose main feature is the Gardiner Dam, was completed in 1967. It will ultimately provide for an area of 0·2m. to 0·5m. acres of irrigated cultivation in Central Saskatchewan. As of 1997, 226,430 acres were intensively irrigated. Total irrigated land in the province, 322,091 acres.

Forestry. Half of Saskatchewan's area is forested, but only 115,000 sq. km are of commercial value at present. Forest products valued at $655m. were produced in 1997–98.

Fur Production. In 1996–97 wild fur production was estimated at $2,990,893 ($1,947,951 in 1995–96). Ranch-raised fur production amounted to $42,244 in 1996 and $44,834 in 1997.

Fisheries. The lakeside value of the 1996–97 commercial fish catch of 3·1m. kg was $4·1m.

INDUSTRY

In 1996 there were 800 manufacturing establishments, employing 16,998 persons. Manufacturing contributed $1,390·4m. and construction $1,512·2m. to total GDP at factor cost of $23,199·3m. in 1997.

Labour. In 1997 the labour force was 504,200 (224,600 females), of whom 474,200 (211,900) were employed.

COMMUNICATIONS

Roads. In 1997 there were 25,477 km of provincial highways and 195,930 km of municipal roads (including prairie trails). Motor vehicles registered totalled (1996) 779,801. Bus services are provided by 2 major lines.

Rail. There were (1997) approximately 10,057 km of railway track.

Civil Aviation. There were 2 major airports, 176 airports and landing strips in 1997.

Telecommunications. There were 626,924 telephone network access services to the Saskatchewan Telecommunications system in 1997.

Postal Services. In 1996 there were 458 post offices (excluding sub-post offices).

SOCIAL INSTITUTIONS

Justice. In 1996, 118,961 Criminal Code offences were reported, including 27 homicides.

Education. The Saskatchewan education system in 1997–98 consisted of 107 school divisions and 5 comprehensive school boards, of which 21 were Roman Catholic Separate School Divisions, serving 130,587 elementary pupils, 58,580 high-school students and 3,341 students enrolled in special classes. In addition, the Saskatchewan Institute of Applied Science and Technology (SIAST), established on 1 Jan. 1988, had 11,890 full-time and 34,255 part-time students in 1997–98. There are also 9 regional colleges with an enrolment of approximately 37,830 students in 1997–98.

The University of Saskatchewan was established at Saskatoon in 1907. In 1997–98 it had 14,849 full-time students, 3,565 part-time students and 967 full-time academic staff. The University of Regina was established in 1974; in 1997–98 it had 8,413 full-time and 3,169 part-time students and 317 full-time academic staff.

CULTURE

Broadcasting. In 1997 there were 51 TV and re-broadcasting stations, and 33 AM and FM radio stations.

Tourism. An estimated 1·7m. out-of-province tourists spent $325m. in 1997.

FURTHER READING
Archer, J. H., *Saskatchewan: A History*. Saskatoon, 1980
Arora, V., *The Saskatchewan Bibliography*. Regina, 1980

Statistical office: Bureau of Statistics, 2350 Albert St., Regina, SK, S4P 4A6.

THE NORTHWEST TERRITORIES

KEY HISTORICAL EVENTS
The Territory was developed by the Hudson's Bay Company and the North West Company (of Montreal) from the 17th century. The Canadian Government bought out the Hudson's Bay Company in 1869 and the Territory was annexed to Canada in 1870. The Arctic Islands lying north of the Canadian mainland were annexed to Canada in 1880.

A plebiscite held in March 1992 approved the division of the Northwest Territories into 2 separate territories. (For the new territory of Nunavut *see* CONSTITUTION AND GOVERNMENT, *below*).

TERRITORY AND POPULATION
The total area of the Territories is 3,426,320 sq. km, divided into 5 administrative regions: Fort Smith, Inuvik, Kitikmeot, Keewatin and Baffin. The population at the 1991 census was 57,649, 37% of whom were Inuit (Eskimo), 16% Dene (Indian) and 7% Metis. The population at the 1996 census was 64,402; estimate, July 1997, 67,528. The capital is Yellowknife, population (1991): 15,179. Other main centres (with population in 1991): Iqaluit (3,552), Hay River (3,206), Inuvik (3,206), Fort Smith (2,480), Rankin Inlet (1,706), Rae-Edzo (1,521) and Arviat (1,323).

CLIMATE
Conditions range from cold continental to polar, with long hard winters and short cool summers. Precipitation is low. Yellowknife, Jan. mean high –24·7°C, low –33°C; July mean high 20·7°C, low 11·8°C. Annual rainfall 26·7 cm.

CONSTITUTION AND GOVERNMENT
The Northwest Territories comprises all that portion of Canada lying north of the 60th parallel of N. lat. except those portions within the Yukon Territory and the provinces of Quebec and Newfoundland. It also includes the islands in Hudson Bay, James Bay and Ungava Bay except those within the provinces of Manitoba, Ontario and Quebec.

The Northwest Territories is governed by a Premier, with a cabinet (the Executive Council) of 8 members including the Speaker, and a Legislative Assembly. The Assembly is composed of 24 members elected for a 4-year term of office. A Commissioner of the Northwest Territories acts as a lieutenant-governor and is the federal government's senior representative in the Territorial government. The seat of government was transferred from Ottawa to Yellowknife when it was named Territorial Capital on 18 Jan. 1967. On 10 Nov. 1997 the Governments of Canada and the Northwest Territories signed an agreement so that the territorial government could assume full responsibility to manage its elections.

Legislative powers are exercised by the Executive Council on such matters as taxation within the Territories in order to raise revenue, maintenance of justice, licences, solemnization of marriages, education, public health, property, civil rights and generally all matters of a local nature.

The Territorial Government has assumed most of the responsibility for the administration of the Northwest Territories but political control of Crown lands and non-renewable resources still rests with the Federal Government. On 6 Sept. 1988, the Federal and Territorial Governments signed an agreement for the transfer of management responsibilities for oil and gas resources, located on- and off-shore, in

THE NORTHWEST TERRITORIES

the Northwest Territories to the Territorial Government. In a Territory-wide plebiscite in April 1982, a majority of residents voted in favour of dividing the Northwest Territories into two jurisdictions, east and west. In a plebiscite held in March 1992 residents voted in favour of an east-west boundary line. Constitutions for an eastern and western government have been under discussion since 1992. A referendum was held in Nov. 1992 among the Inuit on the formation of a third territory, **Nunavut** ('Our Land'), in the eastern Arctic, and comprising the present administrative regions of Kitikmeot, Keewatin and Baffin. The electorate was 9,648; turn-out was 80%. 69% of votes cast were in favour. An agreement was signed on 25 May 1993 by the federal Prime Minister beginning the process of establishing this territory. It was scheduled to become Canada's 3rd territory on 1 April 1999. Its area of 2,201,400 sq. km was to be made over to the population of 22,000, of which some 80% are Inuit. The remainder will remain federal property. The capital is Iqaluit (formerly Frobisher Bay) with a 1991 population of 3,552. Rankin Inlet had 1,706 inhabitants in 1991.

CURRENT ADMINISTRATION
Commissioner: Helen Maksagak.
  Premier: Don Morin.
  Executive Council ministers in Jan. 1999:
  Education: Charles Dent. *Finance, Intergovernmental Affairs:* John Todd. *Health and Social Services:* Kelvin Ng. *Justice:* Goo Arlooktoo. *Municipal and Community Affairs:* Manitok Thompson. *Transportation, Public Works and Services:* Floyd Roland. *Aboriginal Affairs:* Jim Antoine. *Resources, Wildlife and Economic Development:* Stephen Kakfwi.

ENERGY AND NATURAL RESOURCES
Oil and Gas. As of July 1993, 13 licences for oil and gas exploration were held for 1·4m. ha, 20 production licences were held for 64,578 ha and 108 significant discovery licences were retained on 695,473 ha.
  Crude oil is produced at Norman Wells and piped to Alberta. Value of crude oil production in 1992 was $142·5m.

Minerals. Mineral production in 1992 was valued at $476·2m., 4·7% of Canada's total. The Northwest Territories yielded 12·3% of lead, 15·1% of zinc, 8·8% of gold, and 2% of silver produced in Canada in 1992.

Forestry. Forest land area in the NWT consists of 61·4m. ha, about 18% of the total land area. The principal trees are white and black spruce, jack-pine, tamarack, balsam poplar, aspen and birch. In 1990–91, 56,000 cu. metres of timber, valued at $1·83m., was produced.

Trapping and Game. The 39,629 pelts, furs and hides sold by 1,838 Northwest Territories hunters and trappers in the 1991–92 season were valued at $2,325,814. The pelts of highest value are those of the polar bear, black and brown bear, wolf, wolverine and lynx. There are some 1·3m. barren-ground caribou, 113,000 muskox and 12,700 polar bears. There are 2 protected herds of wood bison.

Fisheries. Commercial fishing, principally on Great Slave Lake, in 1991–92 produced 1,431,000 kg of fish valued at $912,000, principally trout, whitefish and pickerel.

INDUSTRY
Co-operatives. There are 39 active co-operatives, including 2 housing co-operatives and one central organization to service local co-operatives, in the Northwest Territories. They are active in handicrafts, furs, fisheries, retail stores, hotels and print shops. Total revenue in 1991 was about $41m.

COMMUNICATIONS
Roads. The Mackenzie Route connects Grimshaw, Alberta, with Hay River, Pine Point, Fort Smith, Fort Providence, Rae-Edzo and Yellowknife. The Mackenzie

Highway extension to Fort Simpson and a road between Pine Point and Fort Resolution have both been opened.

Highway service to Inuvik in the Mackenzie Delta was opened in spring 1980, extending north from Dawson, Yukon as the Dempster Highway. The Liard Highway connecting the communities of the Liard River valley to British Columbia opened in 1984.

In 1994 there were 26,721 motor vehicles registered, including 9,582 passenger cars and 14,890 trucks and truck tractors.

Rail. There is one small railway system in the north which runs from Hay River, on the south shore of Great Slave Lake, 435 miles south to Grimshaw, Alberta, where it connects with the Canadian National Railways, but it is not in use.

Civil Aviation. In 1993 there were 9 certified airports operated by the federal Department of Transport and 33 certified and 9 uncertified airports operated by the Government of the Northwest Territories. Numerous certified and uncertified airports are operated privately in support of military operations, mining and resource exploration, and tourism. There are also privately owned float plane bases. Major communities receive daily jet service to southern points. Most smaller communities are served by scheduled turboprop air service several times weekly.

Shipping. A direct inland-water transportation route for about 1,700 miles is provided by the Mackenzie River and its tributaries, the Athabasca and Slave rivers. Subsidiary routes on Lake Athabasca, Great Slave Lake and Great Bear Lake total more than 800 miles.

Communities in the eastern Arctic are resupplied by ship each summer via the Atlantic and Arctic Oceans or Hudson Bay.

Telecommunications. Telephone service is provided to nearly all communities in the Northwest Territories. Those few communities without service have high frequency or very high frequency radios for emergency use.

Postal Services. There is a postal service in all communities.

SOCIAL INSTITUTIONS

Education. In 1993–94 there were 8 divisional boards of education, which provide for more local and regional control of education. There were also 3 boards of education operating in Yellowknife: A separate school board, a public school board and a board of secondary education.

In 1993–94 there were 80 schools operating with 1,091 teachers for 16,089 enrolled students. Residences in regional larger communities provide accommodation for students from smaller communities that cannot provide all education services up to grade 12. There is a full range of courses available in the school system: Academic, French immersion, native language and culture, commercial, technical and occupational training, post-secondary programmes, along with a first-year general arts university programme. Financial assistance (from the territorial government) is available to qualifying students for post-secondary studies.

Health. In 1988 complete responsibility for health services was transferred to the Territorial Government by the Government of Canada. There are (1993) 8 Boards of Management established to operate, manage and control the health services and programmes in their respective service regions. The health system is comprised of: 6 hospitals, providing both acute and long-term care; 6 public health clinics; 43 community health centres; 8 lay dispensaries; 6 boarding homes for patients and escorts travelling.

Welfare. Welfare services are provided by professional social workers. Facilities included (1993) for children: 7 group homes and 2 residential treatment centres.

CULTURE

Broadcasting. In 1993 the CBC northern service operated radio stations at Yellowknife, Inuvik, Iqaluit and Rankin Inlet. All communities receive television via satellite.

FURTHER READING
Annual Report of the Government of the Northwest Territories
Government Activities in the North, 1983–84. Indian and Northern Affairs, Canada
NWT Data Book 90/91. Yellowknife, 1991

Dawson, C. A., *The New North-West.* Toronto, 1947
MacKay, D., *The Honorable Company.* Toronto, 1949
Zaslow, M., *The Opening of the Canadian North 1870–1914.* Toronto, 1971

YUKON TERRITORY

KEY HISTORICAL EVENTS
The territory owes its fame to the discovery of gold in the Klondike at the end of the 19th century. Formerly part of the Northwest Territories, the Yukon was joined to the Dominion as a separate territory on 13 June 1898.

TERRITORY AND POPULATION
The Yukon is situated in the extreme north-western section of Canada and comprises 483,450 sq. km. of which 4,480 sq. km is fresh water. The census population in 1996 was 30,766; estimate, June 1997, 33,586. Principal centres (with 1997 populations) are Whitehorse, the capital, 24,031; Watson Lake, 1,791; Dawson City, 2,151; Faro, 1,266; Haines Junction, 862.

SOCIAL STATISTICS
See CANADA: Social Statistics.

CLIMATE
A cold climate in winter with moderate temperatures in summer provide a considerable annual range of temperature and moderate rainfall. Whitehorse, Jan. $-5°F$ ($-20°C$), July $56°F$ ($14·1°C$). Annual rainfall 10" (261 mm). Dawson City, Jan. $-22°F$ ($-30°C$), July $57°F$ ($15·6°C$). Annual rainfall 13" (306·1 mm).

CONSTITUTION AND GOVERNMENT
The Yukon was constituted a separate territory in June 1898. It is governed by a Cabinet (Executive Council) appointed from the majority party in the 17-member elected Legislative Assembly. The members are elected for terms not to exceed 4 years.

The seat of government is at Whitehorse. A federally appointed Commissioner serves in a similar capacity to the provincial lieutenant governors.

The Yukon government consists of 12 departments, as well as a Women's Directorate and 4 Crown corporations, each taking direction from a responsible Cabinet Minister and generally from Cabinet. Government departments and agencies are responsible for a similar range of activities as found in Canadian provinces, including education, economic development, municipal affairs, housing, social services, transportation, tourism, justice, renewable resources, and finance. The administration of certain programmes, mostly in the natural resources field, remains under federal control. The Yukon government is, however, involved in negotiations with the federal government on the transfer of further responsibilities to its jurisdiction.

RECENT ELECTIONS
In the territorial elections on 30 Sept. 1996 the New Democratic Party gained 11 seats, the Yukon Party 3 and the Liberal Party 3.

CURRENT ADMINISTRATION
Commissioner: Judy Gingell (appointed 12 June 1995).
Government Leader: Piers McDonald.

ECONOMY

Performance. GDP at market prices increased by 9·6% in 1996 to $1,037m. The key sectors of the economy are mining, tourism and government. Renewable resource industries' production was estimated at $9m. in 1995. Processing of renewable resources is an important source of economic diversification. In the manufacturing sector, manufacturers' shipments were valued at $47m. in 1995.

Banking and Finance. The Territorial Government's revenue and expenditure (in $1,000) for years ended 31 March was:

	1994–95	1995–96	1996–97[1]	1997–98[1]
Revenue	489,894	509,570	466,732	447,431
Expenditure	481,388	480,780	501,272	457,385

[1]Projected.

ENERGY AND NATURAL RESOURCES

Electricity. Hydro-generated power is supplied through plants at Whitehorse Rapids, Aishihik Lake, Fish Lake and Mayo. Diesel-generated power is supplied from plants at several communities (including Whitehorse, Faro, Haines Junction, Ross River, Dawson City, Mayo and Watson Lake). Current capacity is 78 MW hydro and 52 MW diesel-generated power. Production, 1995, 390,035 MWh, of which 319,399 MWh hydro-electric.

Oil and Gas. In 1997, the Yukon Oil and Gas Act was passed, replacing the federal legislation. This Act provides for the transfer of responsibility for oil and gas resources to Yukon jurisdiction.

Minerals. Mining is the main industry. Lead, zinc and gold are the chief minerals. Production in tonnes (and value) in 1996 (preliminary): Gold, 5 ($76·9m.); zinc, 145,335 ($202·2m.); lead, 90,019 ($95·7m.); silver, 112 ($25·6m.).

Agriculture. Many areas have suitable soils and climate for the production of forages, cereal grains and vegetables, domestic livestock and game farming. In 1996 there were 160 farms operating full- and part-time. There were about 24,000 acres associated with farm operations, of which 13,000 acres were in production or under development. Farm receipts in 1996 were estimated at $3·5m. Total farm capital, 1996, was $45m.

Forestry. The forests, which cover 281,030 sq. km of the territory, are part of the great Boreal forest region of Canada, which stretches from the east coast of Canada into Alaska and north well above the Arctic Circle. Vast areas are covered by coniferous stands in the southern portion of Yukon, with white spruce and lodgepole pine forming pure stands on wet sites, and in northern aspects. Deciduous species form pure stands or occur mixed with conifers throughout forest areas.

Production from forestry was 420,600 cu. metres in 1994–95.

Game and Furs. The country abounds with big game, such as moose, goat, caribou, mountain sheep and bear (grizzly and black). The fur-trapping industry is considered vital to rural and remote residents and especially First Nations people wishing to maintain a traditional lifestyle. Fur production in 1996 (mostly beaver, lynx, marten, wolf and wolverine) was valued at $274,540.

Fisheries. Commercial fishing concentrates on chinook salmon, chum salmon, lake trout and whitefish.

Environment. The Yukon is recognized as a critical habitat for many species of rare and endangered flowers, big game animals, birds of prey and migratory birds. Three national parks (total area 36,572 sq. km), 3 territorial parks (297 sq. km), 3 protected areas (7,917 sq. km) and 2 wildlife sanctuaries (8,150 sq. km) had been established by 1996 to protect fragile and significant areas for the future.

COMMUNICATIONS

Roads. The Alaska Highway and branch highway systems connect Yukon's main communities with Alaska and the provinces, and with adjacent mining centres. Interior roads connect the mining communities of Elsa (silver–lead), Faro (lead–zinc–silver) and Dawson City (gold) and mineral exploration properties (lead–zinc and tungsten) north of Ross River. The 735-km Dempster Highway north of Dawson

City connects with Inuvik, on the Arctic coast; this highway, the first public road to be built to the Arctic Ocean, was opened in Aug. 1979. The South Klondike Highway links the tidewater port of Skagway, Alaska with the Yukon. It was opened in May 1979, providing a new access to the Pacific Ocean. In 1996-97 there were 4,680 km of roads maintained by the Yukon Territorial Government, of which 260 km were paved. The other major roads, including the Alaska Highway, have received a new surface treatment which resembles pavement, and the rest are all-weather gravel, of which 700 km are accessible during the summer months only. Vehicles registered in 1996 totalled 42,228, including 11,035 passenger cars and 21,027 trucks and truck tractors.

Rail. The 176-km White Pass and Yukon Railway connected Whitehorse with year-round ocean shipping at Skagway, Alaska, but was closed in 1982. A modified passenger service was restarted in 1988 to take cruise ship tourists from Skagway to Carcross, Yukon, over the White Pass summit.

Civil Aviation. In 1997, Canadian International Airlines provided regular daily service between Whitehorse and Vancouver. Regular air service also extended beyond the Yukon to Yellowknife and Inuvik, Northwest Territories, and Juneau and Fairbanks, Alaska, with connecting service to other points in Alaska and other states in the USA. Regularly scheduled air services extend from Whitehorse to the Yukon communities of Dawson City, Old Crow and Watson Lake, with limited air service to Mayo. Commercial operations offering charter services are located throughout the Territory.

Shipping. The majority of goods are shipped into the Territory by truck over the Alaska and Stewart–Cassiar Highways. Some goods are shipped through the ports of Skagway and Haines, Alaska, and then trucked to Whitehorse for distribution throughout the Territory. The majority of goods are transported by road within the Territory, while a modest amount is shipped by air. Although navigable, the rivers are no longer used for shipping.

Telecommunications. All telephone and telecommunications are provided by Northwestel, a subsidiary of Bell Canada Enterprises. Microwave stations, satellite ground stations and radio-telephone facilities provide most of the telephone transmission services to the communities.

SOCIAL INSTITUTIONS

Education. The Yukon Department of Education operates (with the assistance of elected school councils) the Territory's 27 schools, both public and separate, from kindergarten to grade 12. There is also 1 private school and 1 French First Language school, which is under the governance of a school board. In Dec. 1996 there were 457 teachers and 6,241 pupils. French immersion is offered from kindergarten through grade 12. Yukon College provides adult education for young and mature students, 26% of whom are of First Nations ancestry. Ayamdigut Campus in Whitehorse is the administrative and programme centre for 13 other campuses located throughout the territory. In 1996–97 a total of 758 full-time and 4,318 part-time students enrolled in programmes and courses. The Yukon government provides financial assistance to students for post-secondary education whether they study at Yukon College or outside the Territory. Financial assistance is provided to First Nations students by the federal Department of Indian Affairs and Northern Development.

Health. In Dec. 1996 there were 2 hospitals with 69 staffed beds, 4 nursing stations, 8 health treatment centres, 3 public health centres, 112 doctors and 18 dentists. The territorial government operates a medical travel programme to send patients to Edmonton or Vancouver for specialized treatment not available in the Territory.

CULTURE

Broadcasting. There are 3 radio stations in Whitehorse and 15 low-power relay radio transmitters operated by CBC, and 6 operated by the Yukon Government. CHON-FM, operated by Northern Native Broadcasting, is broadcast to virtually all Yukon communities by satellite. Dawson City has its own community-run radio station, CFYT-FM. There are also 27 basic and 36 extended pay-cable TV channels

CANADA

in Whitehorse, and private cable operations in Faro and Watson Lake. Live CBC national television and TVNC is provided by satellite and relayed to all communities.

Press. In 1997 there were 1 daily and 1 semi-weekly newspaper in Whitehorse, and semi-weekly and monthly papers in Dawson City. Other communities with local newspapers include Stewart Crossing, Haines Junction and Faro. There is also a monthly newspaper for francophones.

Tourism. In 1996 there were 244,960 foreign visitors.

FURTHER READING
Annual Report of the Government of the Yukon.
Yukon Executive Council, *Statistical Review.*

Berton, P., *Klondike.* (Rev. ed.) Toronto, 1987
Coates, K. and Morrison, W., *Land of the Midnight Sun: A History of the Yukon.* Edmonton, 1988
McClelland, C., *Part of the Land, Part of the Water.* Vancouver, 1987
Minter, R., *White Pass: Gateway to the Klondike.* Toronto, 1987

There is a Yukon Archive at Yukon College, Whitehorse.

CAPE VERDE

República de Cabo Verde

Capital: Praia
Population estimate, 2000: 437,000
GNP per capita: (PPP$) 2,640
HDI/world rank: 0·591/117

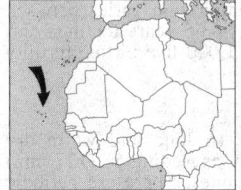

KEY HISTORICAL EVENTS

The Cape Verde Islands were uninhabited, except perhaps by some Lebou fishermen from Senegal, when first visited by the Portuguese in 1456. During centuries of Portuguese rule the islands were gradually peopled with Portuguese, slaves from Africa, and people of mixed African-European descent who became the majority. While retaining some African culture, the Cape Verdians came to speak Portuguese or the Portuguese-derived Crioulo (Creole) language, and became Catholics.

Cape Verde included Portuguese Guinea until 1879, when that mainland territory was separated. Ruled as a colony and then, from 1951 to 1974, as an Overseas Territory of Portugal, Cape Verde had a governor, a government council, and latterly a partly elected legislative council. While many Cape Verdians were taken to São Tomé as labourers on cocoa plantations, because of their Portuguese culture and some degree of education, Cape Verdians were in some ways privileged among Portuguese-ruled Africans; they held subordinate government positions in other colonies, such as Portuguese Guinea.

In 1956 nationalists from Cape Verde and Portuguese Guinea formed the *Partido Africano da Independência da Guiné e Cabo Verde* (PAIGC). In the 1960s the PAIGC led by Amilcar Cabral waged a successful guerilla war. While armed resistance was not possible in the Cape Verde Islands, the PAIGC won control there after the Portuguese revolution of 1974. On 5 July 1975 Cape Verde became independent, ruled by the PAIGC, which was already the ruling party in ex-Portuguese Guinea-Bissau. Aristides Pereira became president of the new republic.

On 14 Nov. 1980 Luis Cabral, brother of the PAIGC's founder and president of Guinea-Bissau since 1974, was overthrown in a *coup d'état* caused partly by resentment at Cape Verdians' privileged position in Guinea-Bissau. Ensuing tension led to the end of the ties between the two countries' ruling parties. Although the PAIGC retained its name in Guinea-Bissau, in Jan. 1981 it was renamed the *Partido Africano da Independência do Cabo Verde* (PAICV), in Cape Verde. The Constitution of 1981 made the PAICV the sole legal party, but in Sept. 1990 the National Assembly abolished its monopoly and free elections were permitted.

TERRITORY AND POPULATION

Cape Verde is situated in the Atlantic Ocean 620 km off West Africa and consists of 10 islands (Boa Vista, Brava, Fogo, Maio, Sal, Santa Luzia, Santo Antão, São Tiago and São Vicente) and 5 islets. The islands are divided into 2 groups, named Barlavento (windward) and Sotavento (leeward). The total area is 4,033 sq. km (1,557 sq. miles). The population was 341,491 at the census of 1990. Estimate (1996) 417,000; density, 103·3 per sq. km; 54·2% urban, 1995.

The UN gives a projected population for 2000 of 437,000.

About 600,000 Cape Verdeans live abroad.

Areas and populations of the islands:

Island	Area (sq. km)	Population Census 1980	Population Census 1990
Santo Antão	779	43,321	43,845
São Vicente[1]	227	41,594	51,277
São Nicolau	388	13,572	13,665
Sal	216	5,826	7,715
Boa Vista	620	3,372	3,452
Barlavento	*2,230*	*107,685*	*119,954*
Maio	269	4,098	4,969
São Tiago	991	145,957	175,691
Fogo	476	30,978	33,902
Brava	67	6,985	6,975
Sotavento	*1,803*	*188,018*	*221,537*

[1]Including Santa Luzia island, which is uninhabited.

CAPE VERDE

The main towns (1990 census) are Praia, the capital, on São Tiago (61,644) and Mindelo on São Vicente (47,109). Ethnic groups: Mixed, 71%; Black, 28%; White, 1%. The official language is Portuguese; a creole (Crioulo) is in ordinary use.

SOCIAL STATISTICS
1995 births, 13,000; deaths, 3,000. 1995 birth rate, 32·8 per 1,000 population; death rate, 7·8. Annual growth rate, 1990–95, 2·8%. Annual emigration varies between 2,000 and 10,000. Life expectancy at birth, 1990–95, was 63·5 years for men and 65·5 years for women. Infant mortality, 1990–95, 50 per 1,000 live births; fertility rate, 3·9 children per woman.

CLIMATE
The climate is arid, with a cool dry season from Dec. to June and warm dry conditions for the rest of the year. Rainfall is sparse, rarely exceeding 5" (127 mm) in the northern islands or 12" (304 mm) in the southern ones. There are periodic severe droughts. Praia, Jan. 72°F (22·2°C), July 77°F (25°C). Annual rainfall 10" (250 mm).

CONSTITUTION AND GOVERNMENT
The Constitution was adopted in Sept. 1992.

A constitutional referendum was held on 28 Dec. 1994; turn-out was 45%. 82·06% of votes cast favoured a reform extending the powers of the presidency and strengthening the autonomy of local authorities. The President is elected for 5-year terms by universal suffrage.

The National Assembly is elected for 5-year terms.

National Anthem. 'Sol, suor, o verde e mar' ('Sun, sweat, the green and the sea'); words and tune by A. Lopes Cabral.

RECENT ELECTIONS
Elections for the *National Assembly* of 72 members elected domestically and 3 from Cape Verdeans living abroad were held on 17 Dec. 1995. The electorate was 190,000; turn-out was 70%. 5 parties stood. The Movement for Democracy (MPD) won 50 seats with 61·3% of votes cast, the PAICV 21 with 29·8% and the Party of Democratic Convergence 1 with 6·7%.

In the presidential elections which took place on 17 Feb. 1991, Antonio Mascarenhas Monteiro (b. 1943; MPD) was elected by 72% of votes cast, defeating the incumbent President Pereira. On 18 Feb. 1996 he was re-elected unopposed.

CURRENT ADMINISTRATION
President: Antonio Mascarenhas Monteiro, b. 1943 (MPD; sworn in 22 March 1991).

An MPD government was formed in Dec. 1995, which in March 1999 comprised:
Prime Minister: Carlos Wahnon Veiga (b. 1949).

Deputy Prime Minister, Economic Co-ordination: António Gualberto do Rosário. *Foreign Affairs and Communities:* José Luis Jesus. *Health and Social Progress:* João Baptista Medina. *Education, Science, Youth and Sport:* José Luis Livramento Monteiro de Brito. *Agriculture, Food, Environment and Food Safety:* José Antonio Pinto Monteiro. *Infrastructure and Housing:* Antonio Joaquim Rocha Fernandes. *Justice and Internal Administration:* Simão Rodrigues Monteiro. *Defence, Adjunct Minister to the Prime Minister:* Ulpio Napoleao Fernandes. *Tourism, Transport and Sea:* Maria Helena Semedo. *Presidency of the Council of Ministers:* Rui Figueiredo Soares. *Culture:* Antonio Jorge Delgado. *Employment, Training and Social Integration:* Orlanda Maria Duarte Santos Ferreira. *Finance:* José Ulysses Correia Silva. *Trade, Industry and Energy:* Alexandre Dias Monteiro.

Local Government. There are 16 municipal councils. Local elections were held in Jan. 1996.

DEFENCE
There is selective conscription. Defence expenditure totalled US$4m. in 1997 (US$9 per capita).

CAPE VERDE

Army. The Army is composed of 2 battalions and had a strength of 1,000 in 1997.

Navy. The coast guard numbered 50 in 1997 and has 2 inshore patrol craft.

Air Force. The Air Force has 2 An-26 transport and 1 DO228 patrol aircraft and fewer than 100 personnel.

INTERNATIONAL RELATIONS
Cape Verde is a member of the UN, OAU, ECOWAS and is an ACP member state of the ACP-EU relationship.

ECONOMY
Policy. The third National Development Plan (1992–95) emphasized rural development, balanced regional development and promoted private enterprise.

Performance. Real GDP growth was 3·5% in 1995 (2·6% in 1994).

Budget. The budget for 1996 envisaged revenue of 21,110m. escudos and expenditure of 21,020m. escudos.

Currency. The unit of currency is the *Cape Verde escudo* (CVE) of 100 *centavos*. Foreign exchange reserves were US$42m. in Nov. 1997. The average annual inflation rate during the period 1990–96 was 3·6%. Total money supply was 14,117m. escudos in Nov. 1997.

Banking and Finance. The Banco de Cabo Verde is the central bank (*Governor*, Amaro Alexandre da Luz) and bank of issue, and was also previously a commercial bank. Its latter functions have been taken over by the Banco Comercial do Atlántico, mainly financed by public funds. Another bank has been opened recently in Cape Verde (Tota Acores) and the Caixa Economica has been upgraded into a Bank. Two foreign banks have also been established there.

Weights and Measures. The metric system is in use.

ENERGY AND NATURAL RESOURCES
Electricity. Installed capacity is 17,000 kW. Production was 63·6m. kWh in 1994. Consumption per capita in 1994 was 102 kWh.

Minerals. Salt is obtained on the islands of Sal, Boa Vista and Maio. Volcanic rock (pozzolana) is mined for export. There are also deposits of kaolin, clay, gypsum and basalt.

Agriculture. In 1996 agriculture contributed 7% of GDP. Some 10–15% of the land area is suitable for farming. Approximately 37,000 ha are cultivated, mainly confined to inland valleys. About 2,500 ha are irrigated. The chief crops (production, 1993, in 1,000 tonnes) are: Coconuts, 10; sugar-cane, 19; bananas, 6; potatoes, 3; cassava, 2; sweet potatoes, 4; maize, 6; beans, groundnuts and coffee. Bananas and coffee are mainly for export.

Livestock (1995): 130,000 goats, 19,000 cattle, 450,000 pigs, 14,000 asses and 1m. chickens.

Forestry. In 1995 the woodland area was 47,000 ha, or 31% of the total land area (16,000 ha and 11·7% in 1990). Cape Verde is one of only two developing countries to have increased its area under forests between 1990 and 1995, the other being India.

Fisheries. In 1993 there were 64 large and 1,400 small fishing vessels. In 1995 total catches were 7,081 tonnes (mainly tuna), exclusively from marine waters. About 200 tonnes of lobsters are caught annually.

INDUSTRY
In 1993 industry accounted for 17·2% of GDP, services for 81%.

Labour. In 1996 the workforce was 157,000 (62% males).

INTERNATIONAL TRADE
Foreign debt was US$211m. in 1996.

Imports and Exports. Imports in 1995 totalled US$252m.; exports, US$9m. Main exports: Fish, salt, pozzolana (volcanic rock) and bananas.

Main export markets, 1994: Portugal, 50%; Spain, 16·7%; UK, 16·7%. Main import suppliers: Portugal, 37·3%; France, 14·5%; Netherlands, 6·6%; Côte d'Ivoire, 5·4%.

COMMUNICATIONS

Roads. In 1995 there were 1,100 km of roads (858 km paved) and there were 2,860 private cars and 870 commercial vehicles.

Civil Aviation. Amilcar Cabral International Airport, at Espargos on Sal, is a major refuelling point on flights to Africa and Latin America. Transportes Aéreos de Cabo Verde (TACV), the national carrier, provided services to most of the other islands in 1998, and internationally to Amsterdam, Basle, Bissau, Bologna, Lisbon, Munich, Paris and Vienna. Scheduled flights were also provided in 1998 by Aeroflot, Aerolíneas Argentinas, American Airlines, Condor Flugdienst, South African Airways, TAAG and TAP. In 1996 Amilcar Cabral International Airport handled 227,000 passengers (104,000 on international flights) and 2,100 tonnes of freight.

Shipping. The main ports are Mindelo and Praia. In 1995, the merchant marine totalled 32,320 GRT. There is a state-owned ferry service between the islands.

Telecommunications. There were 33,200 telephone main lines in 1997 (81·9 per 1,000 persons). In 1995 there were approximately 500 fax machines.

Postal Services. In 1995 there were 55 post offices.

SOCIAL INSTITUTIONS

Justice. There is a network of People's Tribunals, with a Supreme Court in Praia. The Supreme Court is composed of a minimum of 5 Judges, of whom 1 is appointed by the President, 1 elected by the National Assembly, and the other by the Supreme Council of Magistrates.

Religion. At the 1990 census 93·2% of the population were Roman Catholic and 6·8% were mainly Protestant (Nazarene Church).

Education. Adult literacy was 71·6% in 1995 (male, 81·4%; female, 63·8%). Primary schooling is followed by lower (13-15 years) and upper (16-18 years) secondary education options. In 1994, there were 370 primary schools with 2,657 teachers for 78,173 pupils; in 1993 there were 14,097 pupils at secondary schools. In 1990 there were 531 students and 52 teachers at a technical school, 211 students and 53 teachers in 3 teacher-training colleges and about 500 students at foreign universities.

Health. Medical provision, 1992: 1 doctor per 4,270 inhabitants, 1 nurse per 670 inhabitants. In 1996 there were 2 central and 3 regional hospitals, 15 health centres, 22 dispensaries and 60 community health clinics.

CULTURE

Broadcasting. There are 2 national radio stations and a national TV service. Portuguese and French international radio and TV services also broadcast to Cape Verde. There were (1995) 69,000 radio receivers and 1,000 television receivers.

Press. In 1996 there were 3 national newspapers—a state-owned bi-weekly, and a weekly and a fortnightly, owned by political parties. Total circulation approximates 12,000, but publication is suspended from time to time due to shortage of paper.

Tourism. Tourism is in the initial stages of development. In 1996 there were 37,000 foreign tourists, bringing revenue of US$10m. Some 50% of tourists originate from Portugal, 15% from Germany and 7% from France.

DIPLOMATIC REPRESENTATIVES
Of Cape Verde in Great Britain
Ambassador: Vacant (resides in The Hague).

Of Great Britain in Cape Verde
Ambassador: David R. Snoxell (resides in Dakar).

CAPE VERDE

Of Cape Verde in the USA (3415 Massachusetts Ave., NW, Washington, D.C., 20007)
Chargé d'Affaires a.i.: Manuel De Matos.

Of the USA in Cape Verde (Rua Abilio Macedo 81, Praia)
Ambassador: Lawrence N. Benedict.

Of Cape Verde to the United Nations
Ambassador: José Luis Barbosa Leão Monteiro.

Of Cape Verde to the European Union
Ambassador: José Rocha.

FURTHER READING
Carreira, A., *The People of the Cape Verde Islands.* London, 1982
Foy, C., *Cape Verde: Politics, Economics and Society.* London, 1988
Shaw, C., *Cape Verde Islands:* [Bibliography]. Oxford and Santa Barbara (CA), 1990

National statistical office: Direcção Geral de Estatística, Praia.

CENTRAL AFRICAN REPUBLIC

République Centrafricaine

Capital: Bangui
Population estimate, 2000: 3·64m.
GNP per capita: (PPP$) 1,430
HDI/world rank: 0·347/154

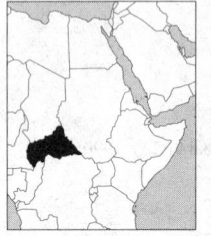

KEY HISTORICAL EVENTS

Central African Republic became independent on 13 Aug. 1960, after having been one of the 4 territories of French Equatorial Africa (under the name of Ubangi Shari) and from 1 Dec. 1958 a member state of the French Community. A Constitution of 1976 provided for the country to be a parliamentary democracy to be known as the Central African Empire. President Bokassa became Emperor Bokassa I. He was overthrown in a coup on 20–21 Sept. 1979 and the empire was abolished. On 15 March 1981 David Dacko was re-elected President, but Army Chief General André Kolingba took power in a bloodless coup on 1 Sept. 1981 at the head of a Military Committee for National Recovery (CMRN), which held supreme power until 21 Sept. 1985 when President Kolingba dissolved it and initiated a return towards constitutional rule.

On 5 June 1996 following a mutiny in the army, President Patassé accepted an agreement brokered by France which amnestied the mutineers and led to the formation of a government of national unity. In Jan. 1997 mutineers demanded the replacement of President Patassé and killed 2 French soldiers. French forces retaliated, taking prisoner some 50 mutineers. France chaired a mediation committee of various neighbouring French-speaking states, and an agreement to end the mutiny was signed on 24 Jan. 1997 in Bangui and a peacekeeping force of neighbouring states, MISAB, was set up. Conflicts between the mutineers and MISAB continued well into 1997 despite a ceasefire concluded on 21 June 1997. A further ceasefire was concluded on 2 July 1997.

TERRITORY AND POPULATION

The republic is bounded in the north by Chad, east by Sudan, south by the Democratic Republic of the Congo and the Republic of the Congo, and west by Cameroon. The area covers 622,436 sq. km (240,324 sq. miles). The population at the 1988 census was 2,568,426; estimate, 1996, 3,274,000, giving a density of 5 per sq. km.

The UN gives a projected population for 2000 of 3·64m.

In 1995 an estimated 39·1% of the population were urban.

The areas, populations and capitals of the prefectures are as follows:

Prefecture	Sq. km	1988 census	Capital
Bangui[1]	67	451,690	Bangui
Ombella-M'poko	31,835	180,857	Bimbo
Lobaye	19,235	169,554	M'baiki
Sangha M'baéré	19,412	65,961	Nola
Mambere Kadéi	30,203	230,364	Berbérati
Nana-Mambere	26,600	191,970	Bouar
Ouham-Pendé	32,100	287,653	Bozoum
Ouham	50,250	262,950	Bossangoa
Nana Gribizi	19,996	95,497	Kaga-Bandoro
Bamingui-Bangoran	58,200	28,643	Ndele
Vakaga	46,500	32,118	Birao
Kemo	17,204	82,884	Sibut
Ouaka	49,900	208,332	Bambari
Basse-Kotto	17,604	194,750	Mobaye
Haute-Kotto	86,650	58,838	Bria
M'bomou	61,150	119,252	Bangassou
Haut-M'bomou	55,530	27,113	Obo

[1]Autonomous commune.

There are a number of ethnic groups, the main ones being Baya (34%) and Banda (27%).

French and Sango are the official languages.

SOCIAL STATISTICS
1996 births, 131,000; deaths, 58,000. Rates, 1996 estimates (per 1,000 population). Births, 40·0; deaths, 17·6. Infant mortality (per 1,000 live births), 111·7. Expectation of life in 1996 was 45·9 years (45·0 for males and 46·7 for females). Annual growth rate, 1990–95, 2·5%. Fertility rate, 1990–95, 5·3 children per woman.

CLIMATE
A tropical climate with little variation in temperature. The wet months are May, June, Oct. and Nov. Bangui, Jan. 31·9°C, July 20·7°C. Annual rainfall 1,289·3 mm. Ndele, Jan. 36·3°C, July 30·5°C. Annual rainfall 203·6 mm.

CONSTITUTION AND GOVERNMENT
Under the Constitution adopted by a referendum on 21 Nov. 1986, the sole legal political party was the *Rassemblement Démocratique Centrafricaine*. In Aug. 1992 the Constitution was revised to permit multi-party democracy. Further constitutional reforms followed a referendum in Dec. 1994, including the establishment of a *Constitutional Court*. The President is elected by popular vote for not more than 2 terms of 6 years, and appoints and leads a Council of Ministers. There is a 109-member *National Assembly*.

National Anthem. 'La Renaissance' ('Rebirth'); words by B. Boganda, tune by H. Pepper.

RECENT ELECTIONS
At the presidential elections held in 2 rounds on 22 Aug. and 19 Sept. 1993 there were 8 presidential candidates. Turn-out was 68·47%. Ange-Félix Patassé gained 37·8% of votes cast in the first round and 52·24% in the second.

In National Assembly elections on 22 Nov. and 13 Dec. 1998 the Central African People's Liberation Movement (MLPC) gained 47 seats, the Central African Democratic Rally (RDC) 20, the Movement for Democracy and Development (MDD) 8, Patriotic Front for Progress 7, Social Democratic Party 6, Alliance for Democracy and Progress 5, National Unity Party 3, the Liberal Democratic Party 2, FODEM 2, ind 7. 2 other parties gained 1 seat each.

CURRENT ADMINISTRATION
President: Ange-Félix Patassé (MLPC; sworn in 22 Oct. 1993).

On 5 June 1996 an agreement was concluded between the government and opposition parties to form a government of national unity.

In March 1999 the government comprised:

Prime Minister, Minister of Economy, Finance, Planning and International Co-operation: Anicet Georges Dologuele.

Minister of Agriculture: Dr Joseph Kalite. *Communication, Postal and Telecommunications:* Desire Pendemou. *Economy, Planning and International Co-operation:* Christophe Bremaidou. *Environment, Waters, Forestry, Hunting and Fishing:* Thierry Ignifolo Vanden-Boss. *Social Welfare for the Promotion of the Family and the Handicapped:* Anne-Marie Ngouyombo. *Foreign Affairs and Francophonie:* Marcel Metefara. *Higher Education and Research:* Theophile Touba. *Housing, Town Planning and Public Building:* Armand Sama. *Culture:* Marie Joseph Songomali Toungovala. *Industry, Commerce and Tourism:* Germain Nadjibe. *Justice:* Laurent Gomina Pampali. *Mining and Energy:* Jean Serge Wafio. *National Defence:* Dr Pascal Kado. *Education and Scientific Research:* Agba Oktikpo Mezode. *Parliamentary Relations:* Juliette Nzekou. *Posts and Telecommunications:* Michel Bindo. *Public Health:* Dr Prosper Timossa. *Public Works:* Jacquesson Mazette. *Tourism, Arts and Culture:* Gaston Beina Gbandi. *Transportation and Aircraft:* Timothee Aguene. *Youth and Sports:* Cyrus Emmanuel Sandy. *Territory Administration and Public Security:* Theodore Bicko. *Civil Service and Professional Training:* Denis Wangao-Kizimale.

Local Government. The Republic is divided into 16 prefectures (subdivided into 67 sub-prefectures and 2 administrative control posts) comprising 65 urban and 102 rural communes and 7 cattle-grazing communes. The 8 *arrondissements* of Bangui, the capital, have the status of communes. Local elected assemblies were inaugurated by the constitutional reforms of Dec. 1994.

DEFENCE
Selective national service for a 2-year period is in force. Some 1,200 French military personnel were stationed in 1993.

Defence expenditure totalled US$39m. in 1997 (US$11 per capita).

Army. The Army consisted (1997) of about 2,500 personnel, comprising a Republican Guard, 1 territorial defence, 1 combined arms and 1 support HQ regiment. Equipment includes 4 T-55 tanks. There are some 2,300 personnel in the para-military Gendarmerie.

Navy. The naval wing of the army has 9 river patrol craft and (1997) about 80 personnel.

Air Force. The Air Force has 2 Rallye light aircraft, 2 C-47 transports, 1 Falcon 20 VIP aircraft and 1 Ecureuil helicopter. Personnel strength (1997) about 150.

INTERNATIONAL RELATIONS
The Central African Republic is a member of the UN, OAU, Lake Chad Commission, and is an ACP member state of the ACP-EU relationship.

ECONOMY
Performance. Real GDP growth was 0·0% in both 1994 and 1995.

Budget. The budget for 1994 provided for expenditure of 54,406m. francs CFA, and for revenue of 43,904m. francs CFA.

Currency. The unit of currency is the *franc CFA* with a parity of 100 francs CFA to 1 French franc. Total money supply in Jan. 1998 was 110bn. francs CFA. Foreign exchange reserves were US$176m. in Jan. 1998. During the period 1990–96 the average annual inflation rate was 6·6%.

Banking and Finance. The Banque des Etats de l'Afrique Centrale (BEAC) acts as the central bank and bank of issue.

Weights and Measures. The metric system is in use.

ENERGY AND NATURAL RESOURCES
Electricity. Installed capacity was 40,000 kW in 1991. Production in 1995 totalled 100·22m. kWh (100·16m. kWh hydro-electric). Consumption per capita in 1994 was 31 kWh.

Minerals. In 1994, 531,992 carats of gem diamonds, 95,957 carats of industrial diamonds and 138·18 kg of gold were mined. There are significant regions of uranium in the Bakouma area.

Agriculture. In 1994, the agricultural population numbered 3·32m. persons, of whom 1·25m. were economically active. In 1996 agriculture accounted for 56% of GDP. The main crops (production 1993, in 1,000 tonnes) are cassava, 610; groundnuts, 43; bananas, 96; plantains, 68; millet, 7; maize, 55; seed cotton, 20; coffee, 11; rice, 7.

Livestock, 1996: Cattle, 2·8m.; goats, 1995, 1·35m.; sheep, 170,000; pigs, 550,000.

Forestry. There were 29·9m. ha of forest in 1995, or 48% of the total land area (down from 49·1% in 1990). The extensive hardwood forests, particularly in the south-west, provide mahogany, obeche and limba. Timber production in 1995 was 3·86m. cu. metres.

Fisheries. The catch in 1995 was approximately 13,300 tonnes, all from inland waters.

CENTRAL AFRICAN REPUBLIC

INDUSTRY
The small industrial sector includes factories producing cotton fabrics, footwear, beer and radios. Output in 1994: Beer, 258,149 hectolitres; cotton fabrics (1992), 5·32m. metres; soap, 1,896 tonnes; leather, 19 tonnes.

Labour. In 1996 the labour force was 1,623,000 (53% males).

INTERNATIONAL TRADE
External debt was US$928m. in 1996.

Imports and Exports. Tarde in 1m. francs CFA:

	1991	1992	1993	1994	1995
Imports	44,770	43,211	35,559	73,263	94,582
Exports	30,750	28,328	31,073	79,541	96,981

Main export markets, 1996: Belgium-Luxembourg, 60·1%; France, 30·9%; UK, 3·5%; Democratic Republic of the Congo, 1·7%. Main import suppliers, 1996: France, 39·5%; Japan, 8·7%; Cameroon, 3·9%; Republic of the Congo, 1·9%. Main exports are coffee, diamonds, timber and cotton. Main imports include food, textiles, petroleum products, machinery, electrical equipment and motor vehicles.

COMMUNICATIONS
Roads. There were 24,000 km of roads in 1996, including 4,280 km of highways or main roads. In 1995 there were 8,900 passenger cars and 3,500 commercial vehicles.

Civil Aviation. There is an international airport at Mpoko, near Bangui. The country is a member of Air Afrique, the regional carrier, with services to Paris and African capitals. In 1995 scheduled airline traffic of Central African Republic-based carriers flew 3·4m. km, carrying 131,000 passengers (74,000 on international flights). Air France also operates services.

Shipping. Timber and barges are taken to Brazzaville (Republic of the Congo).

Telecommunications. There were 9,800 main telephone lines in 1997, equivalent to 2·9 per 1,000 persons. In Jan. 1998 there were approximately 200 Internet users, and in 1995 around 100 cellular phone subscribers and 200 fax machines.

Postal Services. In 1995 there were 31 post offices.

SOCIAL INSTITUTIONS
Justice. The Criminal Court and Supreme Court are situated in Bangui. There are 16 high courts throughout the country.

Religion. In 1992 there were 1·44m. Protestants and 0·97m. Roman Catholics. Traditional animist beliefs are still current.

Education. A national education plan was initiated in 1994 to fund capital educational projects. Adult literacy rate was 60% in 1995. In 1991–92 there were 277,961 pupils at primary schools and 43,740 at secondary schools. The pupil/teacher ratio at primary school level was 77 pupils per teacher in 1990–91, the highest ratio in any country in the world. There is a university at Bangui. It had 3,590 students and 140 academic staff in 1995–96.

Health. In 1990 there were 255 hospitals and health centres with 4,120 beds; in 1992 there were 157 doctors; in 1990, 8 dentists, 1,353 nurses and 166 midwives.

CULTURE
Broadcasting. Broadcasting is provided by the state-controlled Radiodiffusion-Télévision Centrafricaine. There were 245,000 radio and 16,000 TV (colour by SECAM) sets in 1995.

Cinema. In 1992 there were 5 cinemas.

Press. In 1995 there was 1 daily newspaper with a circulation of 2,000, giving a rate of 1 per 1,000 inhabitants.

Tourism. In 1996 there were 29,000 foreign tourists, bringing revenue of US$5m.

DIPLOMATIC REPRESENTATIVES

Of Central African Republic in Great Britain
Ambassador: Vacant (resides in Paris).

Of Great Britain in Central African Republic
Ambassador and Consul-General: Mr. G. P.R. Boon (resides in Yaoundé).

Of Central African Republic in the USA (1618 22nd St., NW, Washington, D.C., 20008)
Ambassador: Henri Koba.

Of the USA in Central African Republic (Ave. David Dacko, Bangui)
Ambassador: Mosina Jordan.

Of Central African Republic to the United Nations
Ambassador: Antonio Deinde Fernandez.

Of Central African Republic to the European Union
Ambassador: Vacant.

FURTHER READING

Kalck, P., *Central African Republic* [Bibliography]. Oxford and Santa Barbara (CA), 1993

CHAD

République du Tchad

Capital: N'Djaména
Population estimate, 2000: 7·27m.
GNP per capita: (PPP$) 880
HDI/world rank: 0·318/163

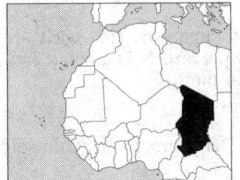

KEY HISTORICAL EVENTS

France proclaimed a protectorate over Chad on 5 Sept. 1900, and in July 1908 the territory was incorporated into French Equatorial Africa. It became a separate colony in 1920, and in 1946 one of the 4 constituent territories of French Equatorial Africa. On 28 Nov. 1958 it became an autonomous republic within the French Community and achieved full independence on 11 Aug. 1960.

Conflicts between the government and secessionist groups, particularly in the Moslem north and centre, began in 1965 and developed into civil war. In 1982 forces led by Hissène Habré gained control of the country. In June 1983 the Libyan-backed forces of former President Goukouni Oueddei re-occupied some territory, but by April 1987 they were forced back into the Aozou Strip in the north, occupied by Libyan forces since 1973. A ceasefire took effect in Sept. 1987. There was an attempted coup on 1 April 1989.

Rebel forces of the Popular Salvation Movement led by Idriss Déby entered Chad from Sudan in Nov. 1990 and, meeting little resistance, overcame the government forces of President Hissène Habré, who took refuge in Cameroon. On 4 Dec. 1990 Déby declared himself President.

TERRITORY AND POPULATION

Chad is bounded in the west by Cameroon, Nigeria and Niger, north by Libya, east by Sudan and south by the Central African Republic. In Feb. 1994 the International Court of Justice ruled that the Aozou Strip along the Libyan border, occupied by Libya since 1973, was part of Chad. Area, 1,284,000 sq. km. At the 1993 census the population was 6,279,931 (5,929,192 settled, of whom 1,327,570 were urban and 359,069 nomadic). 1996 population estimate, 6,977,000; density, 5 per sq. km.

The UN gives a projected population for 2000 of 7·27m.

In 1995 an estimated 77·8% of the population were rural. The capital is N'Djaména with 530,965 inhabitants (1993 census), other large towns being Moundou (282,103), Sarh (193,753), Bongor (196,713), Abéché (187,936) and Doba (185,461).

The areas, populations and chief towns of the 14 prefectures were:

Prefecture	Area sq. km	Population (1993 census)	Capital
Borkou-Ennedi-Tibesti	600,350	73,185	Faya (Largeau)
Biltine	46,850	184,807	Biltine
Ouaddaï	76,240	543,900	Abéché
Batha	88,800	288,458	Ati
Kanem	114,520	279,927	Mao
Lac	22,320	252,932	Bol
Chari-Baguirmi	82,910	1,251,906	N'Djaména
Guéra	58,950	306,253	Mongo
Salamat	63,000	184,403	Amtiman
Moyen-Chari	45,180	738,595	Sarh
Logone Oriental	28,035	441,064	Doba
Logone Occidental	8,695	455,489	Moundou
Tandjilé	18,045	453,854	Laï
Mayo-Kebbi	30,105	825,158	Bongor

The official languages are French and Arabic, but more than 100 different languages and dialects are spoken. The largest ethnic group is the Sara of southern Chad.

SOCIAL STATISTICS
1996 births, 308,000; deaths, 121,000. Rates, 1996 estimates (per 1,000 population): Births, 44·2; deaths, 17·4. Infant mortality (per 1,000 live births), 120·4. Annual rate of growth, 1990–95, 2·2%. Expectation of life in 1996 was 47·6 years (45·2 for males and 50·0 for females). Fertility rate, 1990–95, 5·9 children per woman.

CLIMATE
A tropical climate, with adequate rainfall in the south, though Nov. to April are virtually rainless months. Further north, desert conditions prevail. N'Djaména, Jan. 75°F (23·9°C), July 82°F (27·8°C). Annual rainfall 30" (744 mm).

CONSTITUTION AND GOVERNMENT
After overthrowing the regime of Hissène Habré, Idriss Déby proclaimed himself *President* and was sworn in on 4 March 1991.

A law of Oct. 1991 permits the formation of political parties provided they are not based on regionalism, tribalism or intolerance. There were 59 parties in 1996.

At a referendum on 31 March 1997 a new Constitution was approved by 63·5% of votes cast. It defines Chad as a unitary state. The head of state is the *President*, elected by universal suffrage.

The *National Assembly* has 125 members, elected for a four-year term in 25 single-member constituencies and 34 multi-member constituencies.

National Anthem. 'Peuple tchadien, debout et à l'ouvrage' ('People of Chad, arise and to the task'); words by L. Gidrol, tune by P. Villard.

RECENT ELECTIONS
A first round of presidential elections was held on 2 June 1996. There were 15 candidates. President Déby won 43·8% of votes cast, and was re-elected at the second round on 3 July by 69·09% of votes cast against 1 opponent. Turn-out was 76% in the first round, but less than 50% in the second.

At the National Assembly elections on 5 Jan. and 23 Feb. 1997 Idriss Déby's party, the Patriotic Salvation Movement, won 63 seats, the Union for Renewal and Democracy won 29 and the National Union for Democracy and Renewal won 15. Of the other 18 seats, 16 were won by 7 different parties and 2 were vacant. A new government was formed on 21 May 1997.

CURRENT ADMINISTRATION
President: Idriss Déby (b. 1954; re-elected 3 July 1996).

In March 1999 the government comprised:

Prime Minister: Nassour Ouad'dou.

Minister of Agriculture: Mohktar Moussa. *Civil Service and Employment:* Mahamout Hissein Mahamout. *Commercial and Industrial Development and Promotion of Crafts:* Djitanger Djibangar. *Communication, Parliamentary Affairs and Government Spokesman:* Moussa Dago. *Culture, Youth and Sports:* Nagoum Yamassoum. *Environment and Water:* Pascal Yoadimnadji. *Finance and the Economy:* Bichara Cherif Daoussa. *Foreign Affairs and Co-operation:* Mahamat Saleh Annadif. *Higher Education and Scientific Research:* Adoum Goudja. *Interior, Security and Decentralization:* Sallah Abderahmane. *Justice and Keeper of the Seals:* Limane Mahamat. *Livestock:* Mahamat Nouri. *Mines, Energy and Petroleum:* Abdoulaye Lamana. *National Defence and Reinsertion:* Oumar Boukar Kadjallami. *Planning and Territorial Development:* Mahamat Ali Hassane. *Posts and Telecommunications:* Salibou Garba. *Elementary and Secondary Education and Literacy:* Abderahim Breme Hamit. *Public Health:* Kedellah Younouss Hamit. *Public Works, Housing and Urban Affairs:* Ahmat Lamine. *Social Affairs and Family:* Agnes Allafi. *Tourism Development:* Sekimbaye Bessane.

Local Government. The 14 prefectures are divided into 54 sub-prefectures and the Aozou Strip.

DEFENCE
There are 8 military regions. Conscription is for 3 years. Defence expenditure totalled US$43m. in 1997 (US$6 per capita).

CHAD

Army. In 1996 the strength was 25,000 and there was a paramilitary Gendarmerie of 4,500, and a Republican Guard of 5,000. Equipment included 60 T-55 main battle tanks.

Air Force. The Air Force has 2 C-130 Hercules, 2 Turbo-Porters, 2 armed PC-7 aircraft and 2 Alouette helicopters.

Personnel (1995) about 350.

INTERNATIONAL RELATIONS
Chad is a member of the UN, OAU, Lake Chad Basin Commission, and is an ACP member state of the ACP-EU relationship.

ECONOMY
Performance. Real GDP growth was 1·1% in 1995 (4·1% in 1994).

Budget. Revenues in 1998 were an estimated US$198m. and expenditure US$218m.

Currency. The unit of currency is the *franc CFA* with a parity value of 100 francs CFA to 1 French franc. The average annual inflation rate during the period 1990–96 was 8·6%. Total money supply was 109bn. francs CFA in Jan. 1998.

Banking and Finance. The Banque des Etats de l'Afrique Centrale is the bank of issue, and the principal commercial banks are the Banque de Développement du Tchad, the Banque Tchadienne de Crédit et de Dépôts and the Banque Commerciale du Chari.

ENERGY AND NATURAL RESOURCES
Electricity. Installed capacity was 40,000 kW in 1991. Production in 1994 amounted to 84·78m. kWh. Consumption per capita was 14 kWh—the lowest in the world—in 1994.

Oil and Gas. The oilfield in Kanem préfecture has been linked by pipeline to a new refinery at N'Djaména but production has remained minimal. There is a larger oilfield in the Doba Basin.

Minerals. Salt (about 4,000 tonnes per annum) is mined around Lake Chad, and there are deposits of uranium, gold, iron ore and bauxite. There are small-scale workings for gold and iron.

Agriculture. Some 80% of the workforce is involved in subsistence agriculture and fisheries. In 1996 agriculture accounted for 46% of GDP. Cotton growing (in the south) and animal husbandry (in the central zone) are the most important branches. Production, 1994 (in 1,000 tonnes): Millet, 320; sugar-cane, 336; yams, 245; seed cotton, 160; groundnuts, 207; gum arabic, 7; dry beans, 24; sweet potatoes, 48; mangoes, 32; dates, 25; maize, 159; cotton lint, 39.

Livestock, 1996: Cattle, 4,539,000; goats, 3,271,000 (1995); sheep, 2,219,000; camels, 600,000 (1995); chickens, 4m. (1995).

Forestry. In 1995 the area under forests was 11·02m. ha, or 8·8% of the total land area (11·5m. ha and 9·1% in 1990). Timber production in 1995 was 4·53m. cu. metres.

Fisheries. Total catches, from Lake Chad and the Chari and Logone rivers, were approximately 60,000 tonnes in 1995.

INDUSTRY
Output, 1994: Cotton fibre, 38,600 tonnes; edible oil, 5·41m. litres; sugar, 26,800 tonnes; beer, 1·1m. litres; cigarettes, 23·16m. packets; soap, 2,801 tonnes; bicycles, 1,827.

Labour. In 1996 the labour force was 3,145,000 (56% males). In 1994 approximately 70% of the economically active population were engaged in agriculture, fishing and forestry.

INTERNATIONAL TRADE
External debt was US$997m. in 1996.

Imports and Exports. Trade (in 1m. francs CFA):

	1992	1993	1994	1995
Imports	127,700	126,560	173,870	223,450
Exports	62,400	52,890	105,590	124,570

The main trading partners are France, Nigeria and Cameroon. Cotton exports in 1994, 28,857m. francs CFA; cattle, 15,401 francs CFA. Apart form cotton and cattle, other important exports are textiles and fish. The principal imports are machinery and transportation equipment, industrial goods, petroleum products and foodstuffs.

COMMUNICATIONS

Roads. In 1996 there were 33,400 km of roads, of which 0·82% were surfaced. Approximately 10,560 passenger cars were in use in 1996, plus 14,550 trucks and vans, and 3,640 motor cycles and mopeds.

Civil Aviation. There is an international airport at N'Djaména, from which Air Afrique, Air France, Cameroon Airlines, Ethiopian Airlines and Sudan Airways run services to Abidjan, Abu Dhabi, Addis Ababa, Bamako, Bangui, Bissau, Brazzaville, Douala, El Fasher, Garoua, Jeddah, Khartoum, Lomé, Niamey, Paris and Yaoundé. In 1995 scheduled airline traffic of Chad-based carriers flew 2·9m. km, carrying 92,000 passengers (77,000 on international flights).

Telecommunications. In 1997 there were 7,500 telephone main lines (1·1 per 1,000 persons). Only the Democratic Republic of the Congo had a lower penetration rate in 1997. There were 200 fax machines in use in 1995 and 50 Internet users in Jan. 1998.

Postal Services. In 1994 there were 34 post offices, or 1 for every 200,000 persons.

SOCIAL INSTITUTIONS

Justice. There are criminal courts and magistrates courts in N'Djaména, Moundou, Sarh and Abéché, with a Court of Appeal situated in N'Djaména.

Religion. The northern and central parts of the country are predominantly Moslem. At the 1993 census there were 3,335,869 Moslems, 2,151,996 Christians and 456,064 animists.

Education. In 1995–96 there were 591,784 pupils in primary schools with 9,404 teachers; in 1994–95 there were 85,836 pupils in secondary schools with 2,203 teachers, 2,108 in technical schools and 2,000 at the university, with 120 academic staff. Adult literacy rate was 48·1% in 1995 (62·1% among males and 34·7% among females).

In 1994 total expenditure on education came to 2·2% of GNP.

Health. In 1994 there were 3,962 hospital beds, 217 doctors, 878 nurses, 130 midwives and 10 pharmacists.

CULTURE

Broadcasting. The state-controlled Radiodiffusion Nationale Tchadienne broadcasts a national and 3 regional services in French, Arabic and Sara. There were estimated to be 1·57m. radio sets in 1995. Television is being developed (colour by SECAM) by the state-controlled Télé-Tchad, and there were 9,000 TV receivers in 1995.

Press. In 1995 there was 1 daily newspaper with a circulation of 2,000, giving a rate of 1 per 2,500 inhabitants.

Tourism. There were 8,000 foreign tourists in 1996, bringing revenue of US$10m.

DIPLOMATIC REPRESENTATIVES
Of Chad in Great Britain
Ambassador: Vacant.

Of Great Britain in Chad
Ambassador: Mr. G. P. R. Boon (resides in Yaoundé).

Of Chad in the USA (2002 R. St., NW, Washington, D.C., 20009)
Ambassador: Ahmat Mahamat-Saleh.

Of the USA in Chad (Ave. Felix Eboue, N'Djaména)
Ambassador: David Halsted.

Of Chad to the United Nations
Ambassador: Ahmat A. Haggar.

Of Chad to the European Union
Ambassador: Ramadane Barma.

FURTHER READING
Joffe, G. and Day-Viaud, C. (eds.) *Chad* [Bibliography]. Oxford and Santa Barbara (CA), 1995

National statistical office: Direction de la Statistique des Etudes Economiques et Démographiques, Ministère du Plan et de la Cooperation, N'Djaména.

CHILE

República de Chile

Capital: Santiago
Population estimate, 2000: 15·21m.
GNP per capita: (PPP$) 11,700
HDI/world rank: 0·893/31

KEY HISTORICAL EVENTS

Magellan sighted what is now Chile in 1520. Subsequently Spaniards colonized the land in the 1530s and 1540s, defeating the Incas in the north and subjugating the Araucanian Indians in the South. Santiago, the capital, was founded in 1541, and Chile, as a colony, was attached to the viceroyalty of Peru.

In 1810 the Republic of Chile threw off allegiance to the Spanish crown, establishing a national government on 18 Sept. 1810. However, there were seven years of fighting before Chile was recognized as an independent republic in 1818. A constitution was adopted in 1883, and the country enjoyed stable government. Peru and Bolivia, which had been in dispute with Chile over their boundaries, were defeated in the War of the Pacific, 1879–84. In 1925 the constitution was amended so as to strengthen the executive at the expense of the legislature.

1964 saw the election of the first Christian Democrat president, Eduardo Frei Montlava; but in 1970 Dr Salvador Allende Gossens was elected president as the Marxist leader of five left-wing parties which formed a coalition, the Popular Unity, to speed up social reform. This government was overthrown in 1973 by a *coup* of the three armed services and the *cabineros* (paramilitary police). These forces formed a government headed by a four-man junta. Gen. Augusto Pinochet Ugarte, C.-in-C. of the Army took over the presidency. President Allende died in the course of the *coup*. Tens of thousands of Popular Unity supporters were massacred and all political activities banned. The new government assumed wide-ranging powers, but the 'state of siege' ended in March 1978. A new constitution came into force on 11 March 1981 and provided for a return to democracy after a minimum period of eight years. Anti-government protests increased over the years while relations with the Roman Catholic church deteriorated. However, Gen. Pinochet continued as head of state until 1989 when elections brought victory for the opposition. He remained army commander until March 1998 when he claimed his right, under the constitution, to become a senator for life (and hence immune from prosecution). While clearing the way for much-needed economic reforms, the Pinochet regime was responsible for wholesale human right abuses, a legacy which had its consequences in 1999 when Augusto Pinochet, in Britain for medical treatment, was held on human rights charges instigated by Spain.

TERRITORY AND POPULATION

Chile is bounded in the north by Peru, east by Bolivia and Argentina, and south and west by the Pacific Ocean. The area is 736,905 sq. km (284,520 sq. miles) excluding the claimed Antarctic territory. Many islands to the west and south belong to Chile: The Islas Juan Fernández (179 sq. km with 516 inhabitants in 1982) lie about 600 km west of Valparaíso, and the volcanic Isla de Pascua (Easter Island or Rapa Nui, 118 sq. km with 1,867 inhabitants in 1982), lies about 3,000 km west-northwest of Valparaíso. Small uninhabited dependencies include Sala y Goméz (400 km east of Easter Is.), San Ambrosio and San Félix (1,000 km north-west of Valparaíso, and 20 km apart) and Islas Diego Ramírez (100 km south-west of Cape Horn).

In 1940 Chile declared, and in each subsequent year has reaffirmed, its ownership of the sector of the Antarctic lying between 53° and 90° W. long., and asserted that the British claim to the sector between the meridians 20° and 80° W. long. overlapped the Chilean by 27°. Seven Chilean bases exist in Antarctica. A law of 1955 put the governor of Magallanes in charge of the 'Chilean Antarctic Territory' which has an area of 1,269,723 sq. km. and a population (1982) of 1,368.

The population at the census of 1992 was 13,231,803 (6,730,478 females). Estimate, 1997, 14,656,200 (83·9% urban in 1995; 7,416,500 females in 1997); density, 20 per sq. km.

The UN gives a projected population for 2000 of 15·21m.
Area, population and capitals of the 13 regions:

Region	Sq. km	Population (1992 census)	Capital	Population (1992 census)
Tarapacá	58,786	341,112	Iquique	152,654
Antofagasta	125,253	407,409	Antofagasta	226,749
Atacama	74,705	230,786	Copiapó	100,946
Coquimbo	40,656	502,460	La Serena	120,336
Valparaíso	16,396	1,373,967	Valparaíso	276,736
Metropolitan	15,549	5,170,293	Santiago	5,180,757[1]
Libertador	16,456	688,385	Rancagua	187,134
Maule	30,518	834,053	Talca	171,467
Bíobío	36,939	1,729,920	Concepción	330,448
Araucanía	31,946	774,959	Temuco	240,880
Los Lagos	67,247	953,330	Puerto Montt	130,737
Aysén	108,997	82,071	Coihaique	31,167[2]
Magallanes	132,034	143,058	Punta Arenas	113,661

[1]Metropolitan area; city proper, 4,385,481. [2]1982 census.

Other large towns (1992 census population) are: Viña del Mar (302,765), Puente Alto (254,534), Talcahuano (246,566), San Bernardo (188,850), Arica (169,217), Chillán (158,731), Los Angeles (142,136), Osorno (128,709), Coquimbo (122,872), Valdívia (122,436), Calama (120,602), Curicó (103,919) and Quilpué (102,824). 79% of the population is mixed or *mestizo*, 20% are of European descent and 1% are indigenous Amerindians of the Araucanian, Fuegian and Chango groups. Language and culture remain of European origin, with the 675,000 Araucanian-speaking (mainly Mapuche) Indians the only sizeable minority.

The official language is Spanish.

SOCIAL STATISTICS
1996 births, 253,000; deaths, 80,000; 1995 marriages, 87,205. Rates, 1996 (per 1,000 population): Birth, 18·1; death, 5·7; infant mortality (per 1,000 live births), 13·6. Growth rate, 1996, 1·24%. In 1995 the most popular age range for marrying was 20–24 for both males and females. Expectation of life at birth (1996), 74·59 years; males 71·3 years, females 77·8 years. Chile has the highest life expectancy in South America. Fertility rate, 1990–95, 2·5 children per woman.

CLIMATE
With its enormous range of latitude and the influence of the Andean Cordillera, the climate of Chile is very complex, ranging from extreme aridity in the north, through a Mediterranean climate in Central Chile, where winters are wet and summers dry, to a cool temperate zone in the south, with rain at all seasons. In the extreme south, conditions are very wet and stormy. Santiago, Jan. 67°F (19·5°C), July 46°F (8°C). Annual rainfall 15" (375 mm). Antofagasta, Jan. 69°F (20·6°C), July 57°F (14°C). Annual rainfall 0·5" (12·7 mm). Valparaíso, Jan. 64°F (17·8°C), July 53°F (11·7°C). Annual rainfall 20" (505 mm).

CONSTITUTION AND GOVERNMENT
A new Constitution was approved by 67·5% of the voters on 11 Sept. 1980 and came into force on 11 March 1981. It provided for a return to democracy after a minimum period of 8 years. Gen. Pinochet would remain in office during this period after which the Government would nominate a single candidate for President. At a plebiscite on 5 Oct. 1988 President Pinochet was rejected as a presidential candidate by 54·6% of votes cast.

The *President* is directly elected for a non-renewable 6-year term. Parliament consists of a 120-member *Chamber of Deputies* and a *Senate* of 48 members.

National Anthem. 'Dulce patria, recibe los votos' ('Sweet Fatherland, receive the vows'); words by E. Lillo, tune by Ramón Carnicer.

RECENT ELECTIONS
Elections were held on 12 Dec. 1993 for the presidency. Eduardo Frei Ruiz-Tagle was elected President by 58% of votes cast against 5 other candidates. In elections to

the Chamber of Deputies on 11 Dec. 1997 the Christian Democratic Party (PDC) won 39 seats, National Renewal 23 (RN), the Independent Democratic Union (UDI) 17, Party for Democracy 16 (PPD), the Socialist Party (PS) 11, the Radical Social Democratic Party (PRSD) 4 and ind 8. 2 other parties won 1 single seat each. Member parties of Eduardo Frei's Concertación alliance (PDC, PPD, PS and PRSD) won 70 of the 120 seats.

The next presidential elections are due in Dec. 1999.

CURRENT ADMINISTRATION
In March 1999 the government comprised:

President: Eduardo Frei Ruiz-Tagle, b. 1943 (PDC; sworn in 11 March 1994).

Minister of Agriculture: Carlos Mladinic Alonso (ind). *Defence:* José Florencio Guzman. *Economy, Development and Reconstruction:* Jorge Leiva. *Public Education:* José Pablo Arellano Marín (PDC). *Energy:* Alejandro Jadresic (ind). *Finance:* Eduardo Aninat Ureta (PDC). *Foreign Affairs:* José Miguel Insulzá (PS). *Health:* Alex Figueroa (PDC). *Housing and Urbanization:* Sergio Henriquez Diaz. *Interior:* Raul Troncoso. *Justice:* Soledad Alvear (PDC). *Labour:* German Molina. *Mining:* Sergio Jimenez Moraga. *National Resources:* Adriano del Piano Puelma (PPD). *Planning and Co-operation:* Roberto Pizarro Hofer (PS). *Public Works:* Jaime Toha. *Transportation and Telecommunications:* Claudio Hohmann Barrientos (PDC). *General Secretary of the Government:* Jorge Arrate. *General Secretary of the Presidency:* John Biehl del Rios.

Local Government. There are 340 municipalities. Mayors and the 2,126 councillors are elected jointly and directly from the same list for 4-year terms, the most preferred candidate becoming mayor. Elections were held on 27 Oct. 1996. Concertación won 56·02% of votes cast; the Union for Chile coalition, 33%.

DEFENCE
Military service is for 1 year in the Army and 2 in the Navy and Air Force. Plans for weapons' modernization amounting to nearly US$2bn., which would benefit both the army and the air force, were announced in April 1998.

In 1997 defence expenditure totalled US$2,148m. (US$147 per capita).

Army. A modernization plan of 1995 provided for the transformation of the 7 Army divisions into 3 garrisons—North, Centre-South and Austral—independent and adapted to the terrains in which they operate. Equipment includes 100 M4-A3 and 19 AMX-30 main battle tanks. The service operates 17 transport and 15 training aircraft and 7 helicopters. Strength (1997) 51,000 (28,000 conscripts) with 50,000 reserves. There is a 31,000-strong para-military force of Carabineros.

Navy. The principal ships of the Navy are the 4 ex-British 'County'-class guided missile armed destroyers of which 2 have had the missile launcher removed and replaced with an extended helicopter hangar and flight deck to operate 2 Super-Puma helicopters. There are also 2 small modern West German-built diesel submarines, 2 British Oberon class submarines, 1 other British-built destroyer, 4 British Leander class frigates, 4 fast missile craft, 4 torpedo boats, 2 offshore patrol vessels and 8 coastal and 10 fast inshore patrol craft. There are 2 ex-US and 3 French-built landing ships. Major auxiliaries include 2 tankers, 1 submarine support vessel, 1 survey ship, 2 transports, and 1 Antarctic patrol ship. There are 11 service craft and numerous boats.

The Naval Air Service numbering 800 personnel operates 5 squadrons: 16 maritime patrol aircraft, 6 transport utility aircraft, 12 anti-submarine helicopters and 10 training aircraft.

Naval personnel in 1997 totalled 29,800 (3,800 conscripts) including 3,200 marines equipped with 30 light tanks and 60 artillery pieces, and 1,500 Coast Guard who operate 15 patrol craft and 1 helicopter.

Air Force. Strength (1997) is 13,500 personnel (1,000 conscripts), with over 100 first-line and 150 second-line aircraft, divided among 13 groups, each comprising 1 squadron, within 4 combat and support brigades. Group 12 has twin-jet A-37Bs, and Groups 1 and 3 have C-101CC Aviojets, all for strike duties. Group 2 is equipped for photo-reconnaissance with 3 Canberras. Group 4 has 14 Mirage 50 fighters.

Group 5 has 14 Twin Otters for light transport and survey duties. Group 7 has 12 F-5E Tiger II fighter-bombers and 2 F-5F trainers. Group 8 fighter-bomber unit has 25 Mirage 5s. Group 10 is a transport wing, with 4 C-130 Hercules, 4 Aviocars, 4 Boeing 707s, including 1 equipped for airborne early warning, and various helicopters. Group 9 has UH-1 Iroquois transport helicopters and Black Hawks. An aerial survey unit has 2 Learjets and 3 Beech twin-engined aircraft. Training aircraft include piston-engined Piper Dakota and T-35 Pillan basic trainers, and licence-built CASA C-101BB Aviojets.

INTERNATIONAL RELATIONS

Chile is a member of the UN, OAS and LAIA, and is an associate member of Mercosur.

ECONOMY

Performance. Real GDP growth averaged 7·7% between 1991 and 1997, leading to Chile being labelled the 'tiger of South America'. Between 1990 and 1996 the average annual real growth in GNP per capita was 6·4%.

Budget. The fiscal year is the calendar year. Revenues in 1997 (1996 in brackets) were 7,366·764bn. pesos (6,633·84bn. pesos) and expenditure 6,695·35bn. pesos (5,982·77bn. pesos). VAT is 16-18%.

Currency. The unit of currency is the *Chilean peso* (CLP) of 100 *centavos*. The peso was revalued 3·5% against the US dollar in Nov. 1994. Inflation was 7·4% in 1996. Total money supply in Feb. 1998 was 2,608m. pesos. In Jan. 1998 gold reserves were 1·86m. troy oz. Foreign exchange reserves were US$381m. in Feb. 1998.

Banking and Finance. Banking is regulated by legislation of 1995. There is a Central Bank and a State Bank. The Central Bank was made independent of government control in March 1990. There were 12 domestic and 23 foreign banks in 1996. In May 1995, deposits in domestic banks totalled 8,623,323m. pesos; in foreign banks, 1,771,057m. pesos, and in other finance companies, 347,415m. pesos.

There are stock exchanges in Santiago and Valparaíso.

Weights and Measures. The metric system has been legally established since 1865, but the old Spanish weights and measures are still in use to some extent.

ENERGY AND NATURAL RESOURCES

Electricity. Installed capacity was 5·96m. kW in 1995. Production of electricity was 26,742m. kWh in 1995, of which 18,688m. kWh were hydro-electric. Consumption per capita in 1995 was an estimated 1,662 kWh.

Oil and Gas. Production of crude oil, 1995, was 605,100 cu. metres. Gas production, 1995, was 3,783·2m. cu. metres.

Minerals. The wealth of the country consists chiefly in its minerals. Copper is the most important source of foreign exchange and government revenues. Production, 1995, 2,448,100 tonnes. Coal is low-grade and difficult to mine, and mining is made possible by state subsidies. Production, 1995, 1,330,637 tonnes.

Output of other minerals, 1995 (in tonnes): Iron, 8·1m. (1996); iron pellets, 3,859,700; limestone, 4,834,927; molybdenum, 16,694; zinc, 34,457; manganese, 70,450; gold, 44,233 kg; silver, 1,037,847 kg. Lithium, nitrate, iodine and sodium sulphate are also produced.

Agriculture. Agriculture and forestry contributed 6·9% of GDP in 1995. In 1994, 3·98m. ha of land was arable, 0·27m. ha permanent crops and 13·6m. ha pasture. 1·27m. ha were irrigated in 1994. Some 41,000 tractors were in use in 1994.

Principal crops were as follows:

Crop	Area harvested, 1,000 ha 1995	Production, 1,000 tonnes 1994	Crop	Area harvested, 1,000 ha 1994	Production, 1,000 tonnes 1992
Wheat	390	1,322	Potatoes	58	1,023
Oats	65	202	Dry beans	44	91

CHILE

	Area harvested, 1,000 ha	Production, 1,000 tonnes		Area harvested, 1,000 ha	Production, 1,000 tonnes
Barley	25	84	Lentils	10	16
Maize	104	899	Sugar-beet	52	2,978
Rice	30	131			

Fruit production, 1993 (in 1,000 tonnes): Apples, 870; grapes, 880; pears, 230; peaches and nectarines, 160; plums, 130; oranges, 112; lemons and limes, 100. 0·32m. tonnes of wine were produced in 1992.

Livestock, 1996: Cattle, 3,858,000; horses, 550,000; sheep, 8,039,000; goats, 600,000 (1995); pigs, 1,486,000; poultry (1995), 62m. Livestock products, 1994 (in 1,000 tonnes): Beef, 247; mutton, 13; pork, 158; poultry, 310; milk, 1,222; eggs, 1,856m.

Since 1985 agricultural trade has been consistently in surplus. Wine exports rose from US$50m. in 1990 to US$400m. in 1996.

Forestry. In 1995 nearly 14% of the total land area was under forests. There were 9m. ha of natural forest and woodland (eucalyptus, pine and poplar are important species) and 1·3m. ha of planted forest. Deforestation between 1990 and 1995 had resulted in an average loss of 29,000 ha each year. Timber production in 1995 was 31·36m. cu. metres.

Fisheries. Chile has 4,200 km of coastline and exclusive fishing rights to 1·6m. sq. km. There are 220 species of edible fish. In 1990 the fishing fleet comprised 250 vessels over 100 GRT, totalling 111,140 GRT. Catch in 1995 was 7·59m. tonnes, almost entirely from sea fishing. Only China and Peru had higher annual catches in 1995. Exports of fishery commodities in 1995 were valued at US$1·7bn., against imports of US$45·88m. Fish farms produced 60,728 tonnes of salmon in 1992.

INDUSTRY
Manufacturing contributed 16·8% of GDP in 1995.

Output of major products in 1995 (in 1,000 tonnes): Fishmeal, 877; cellulose, 1,219·8; newsprint, 201·5; paper and cardboard, 198·7; motor tyres, 2,329,900 items; cement, 2,885·2; iron or steel plates, 294·1; copper wire, 5·6; beer, 331·7m. litres; motor vehicles, 21,574 items.

Labour. In 1996 the workforce numbered 5,294,100, of whom 240,100 were unemployed. In June 1996, 1,338,500 persons were employed in social or personal services, 770,900 in agriculture, forestry and fisheries, 907,900 in trade, 847,200 in manufacturing, 389,400 in transport and communications, and 401,600 in building. In 1992 there was a monthly minimum wage of 38,600 pesos.

Trade Unions. Trade unions were established in the mid-1880s.

INTERNATIONAL TRADE
In Sept. 1991 Chile and Mexico signed the free trade Treaty of Santiago envisaging annual tariff reductions of 10% from Jan. 1992. On 1 Oct. 1996 Chile joined the Mercosur free trade zone, but continues to act unilaterally in trade with third countries.

Foreign debt was US$20,877m. on 30 June 1996.

Imports and Exports. Trade in US$1m.:

	1991	1992	1993	1994	1995	1996
Imports	8,094	10,129	11,125	11,825	15,914	17,828
Exports	8,942	10,007	9,199	11,604	16,137	15,353

In 1995 the principal exports were (in US$1m.): Agricultural products, 1,562; minerals, 7,984 (of which copper, 6,487); manufactures, 6,847. Major export markets (in US$1m.), 1995: Japan, 2,906; USA, 2,375; UK, 1,076; Brazil, 1,056; South Korea, 896; Germany, 837. Major import suppliers: USA, 3,793; Argentina, 1,385; Brazil, 1,195; Japan, 1,013; Germany, 790.

COMMUNICATIONS

Roads. In 1997 there were about 80,000 km of roads, but only 20% were hard-surfaced. There were 65 km of motorways and 10,255 km of main roads. In 1996

CHILE

there were 1,017,052 private cars, 538,443 trucks and vans, 34,734 buses and coaches and 32,179 motor cycles and mopeds.

Rail. The total length of state railway (EFE) lines was (1995) 3,447 km, including 1,317 km electrified, of broad- and metre-gauge. EFE is now mainly a passenger carrier, and carried 10·1m. passengers in 1995. Freight operations are in the hands of the semi-private companies Ferronor, which carried 1·5m. tonnes in 1995, and Pacifico, which carried 4·3m. tonnes in 1995. The Antofagasta (Chili) and Bolivia Railway (728 km, metre-gauge) links the port of Antofagasta with Bolivia and Argentina, and carried 1·8m. tonnes in 1995.

There is a metro in Santiago (37·5 km).

Civil Aviation. There are 344 airports, with an international airport at Santiago (Comodoro Arturo Merino Benítez). The largest airline is Línea Aérea Nacional Chile (Lan-Chile), which in 1995 carried 1,427,000 passengers (611,000 on international flights), followed by Línea Aérea de Colore (Ladeco), with 1,397,000 passengers in 1995 (546,000 on international flights). In 1996 Comodoro Arturo Merino Benítez handled 4,215,646 passengers and 200,981 tonnes of freight. In 1998 services were also provided by Aerolíneas Argentinas, Aeromexico, Aeroperú, Air France, Air New Zealand, American Airlines, Avant Airlines, Avianca, British Airways, Canadian Airlines International, Continental Airlines, COPA, Cubana, Ecuatoriana, Iberia, KLM, LACSA, Lloyd Aéreo Boliviano, Lufthansa, Mexicana, National Airlines, Pluna, SAS, Swissair, Tame Linea Aerea del Ecuador, Transbrasil, Transportes Aereos del Mercosur, United Airlines and Varig.

Shipping. The mercantile marine in 1995 totalled 0·98m. GRT, including oil tankers, 71,150 GRT, but most of the fleet operates under flags of convenience. The 6 major ports, the largest being Valparaíso, San Antonio, Antofagasta, Arica and Iquique, are state-owned; there are 11 smaller private ports. In 1990, 28·56m. tonnes of cargo were loaded, and 19·19m. unloaded.

Telecommunications. In 1997 there were 2·63m. telephone main lines. There were approximately 200,000 Internet users in June 1997. Cellular phone subscribers numbered 197,000 in 1995, there were 540,000 PCs in use and 15,000 fax machines.

Postal Services. In 1995 there were 587 post offices.

SOCIAL INSTITUTIONS

Justice. There are a High Court of Justice in the capital, 12 courts of appeal distributed over the republic, courts of first instance in the departmental capitals, and second-class judges in the sub-delegations.

Religion. In 1990 there were 10·63m. Roman Catholics with 1 cardinal archbishop, 5 archbishops, 22 bishops and 2 vicars apostolic. 15% of the population defined themselves as evangelical. There were 0·13m. Jews in 1991.

Education. In 1995 there were 4,779 pre-primary schools with 9,576 teachers for 283,061 pupils; 8,702 primary schools with 80,155 teachers for 2·1m. pupils; and 51,042 teachers in secondary schools for 679,165 pupils. Adult literacy rate, 95·2%; male 95·4%, female 95·0% (1995).

In 1996 there were 367,094 students in higher education. In the public sector there were 12 universities, 5 Roman Catholic universities, 2 universities of educational science and 1 technological university. In the private sector there were 33 universities, 2 Roman Catholic universities, 1 Adventist university, 2 technical universities, 2 maritime universities, 1 IndoAmerican university, 1 international university and 1 university for each of the following: arts, science and communications; arts and social science; Christian humanism; computer science; science and arts; teaching. There were also 83 other institutes of higher education.

In 1994 total expenditure on education came to 2·9% of GNP and represented 13·4% of total government expenditure.

Health. There were 198 hospitals and 16,000 doctors in 1994, and 5,200 dentists and 5,653 nurses in 1993.

Welfare. The Pension Fund Administration was founded in 1981. Employees are required to save 13% of their pay. In Oct. 1995 it had 5,193,590 members and assets of 9,974,787m. pesos. In 1995 about 25% of adults had private health insurance.

CULTURE

Broadcasting. There are 168 radio stations grouped in the Asociación de Radiodifusores de Chile. There are 131 television broadcast stations. The state-controlled Televisión Nacional de Chile transmits from 23 stations (colour by NTSC). 4 universities also transmit programmes. In 1995 there were 4·95m. radio and 3m. TV sets.

Cinema. Cinemas numbered 133 in 1993. Total attendance, 1993, 7,733,407.

Press. In 1995 there were 32 national daily newspapers with a combined circulation of 1·4m.

Tourism. There were 1·5m. foreign visitors in 1996. Tourist receipts were US$918m. in 1996.

DIPLOMATIC REPRESENTATIVES

Of Chile in Great Britain (12 Devonshire St., London, W1N 2DS)
Ambassador: Mario Artaza.

Of Great Britain in Chile (Av. El Bosque 0125, Casilla 72-D, Santiago 9)
Ambassador: Glynne Evans.

Of Chile in the USA (1732 Massachusetts Ave., NW, Washington, D.C., 20036)
Ambassador: Genaro Arriagada.

Of the USA in Chile (Ave. Andres Bello 2800, Santiago)
Ambassador: Gabriel Guerra-Mondragon.

Of Chile to the United Nations
Ambassador: Juan Somavia Altamirano.

Of Chile to the European Union
Ambassador: Eduardo Gonzalo Arenas Valverde.

FURTHER READING

Banco Central de Chile. *Boletín Mensual.*

Bethell, L. (ed.) *Chile since Independence.* CUP, 1993
Blakemore, H., *Chile.* [Bibliography] Oxford and Santa Barbara (CA), 1988
Collier, S. and Sater, W. F., *A History of Chile, 1808–1994.* CUP, 1996
Garretón, M. A., *The Chilean Political Process.* London and Boston, 1989
Hickman, J., *News From the End of the Earth: A Portrait of Chile.* Hurst, London, 1998
Hojman, D. E., *Chile: the Political Economy of Development and Democracy in the 1990s.* London, 1993.—(ed.) *Change in the Chilean Countryside: from Pinochet to Aylwin and Beyond.* London, 1993
Oppenheim, L. H., *Politics in Chile: Democracy, Authoritarianism and the Search for Development.* Boulder (CO), 1993

National statistical office: Instituto Nacional de Estadísticas (INE), Santiago.

CHINA

Zhonghua Renmin Gonghe Guo

(People's Republic of China)

Capital: Beijing (Peking)
Population estimate, 2000: 1,276·3m.
GNP per capita: (PPP$) 3,330
HDI/world rank: 0·650/106

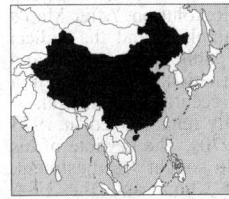

KEY HISTORICAL EVENTS

The Han dynasty (216 BC–220 AD) made Confucianism a state philosophy and instituted the system of civil service recruitment by public competitive examination. Buddhism was introduced from India. The Han dynasty collapsed amid intrigues and was followed by centuries of division and disorder. Unity was restored under the T'angs (618–906), but was lost again until the Sung period (960–1279). Mongol invaders succeeded in imposing a foreign dynasty (Yuan) and were quickly assimilated to the higher cultural and technological level of the Chinese. A peasant rising drove the last Mongol from the throne in 1368 and ushered in the Ming dynasty.

Although unity and tradition were restored, the Ming empire was not as efficient as the T'ang nor as enlightened as the Sung. A new imperial capital was built at Beijing only 40 miles from the Wall and thus vulnerable to attack; preoccupation with the defence of this frontier contributed to a neglect of the defence of the sea, whence came the Portuguese in 1516, the Dutch in 1622, and the English in 1637. A wave of nomad invaders, the Manchus, breached the Wall to capture Beijing in 1644 and founded the Ch'ing dynasty, which lasted until 1912. The Manchus, who used Dutch ships to subdue Taiwan in 1683, were not sea-going and confined foreign trade to Canton after 1757. The court would not enter into diplomatic relations with Europe, and would receive foreigners only if they paid homage. Catholic missionaries were tolerated and even employed in state service, but outside ideas made little impression on the ossified and complacent traditionalism of the court and mandarins. Though gradually assimilated, the Ch'ing did not forget they were a foreign dynasty in an occupied country. A quota of posts was reserved for Manchus and a system of garrison governorships was set up, which degenerated into sinecures doing nothing to modernize the armed forces.

A British expeditionary force sent to overturn a Chinese ban on imports of opium forced the empire to cede Hong Kong and grant Britain economic and diplomatic privileges. Other western nations followed suit. Foreigners established concessions in 'treaty ports' administered by their own officials. In 1851 a neo-Protestant *T'ai P'ing* rebellion broke out, which was put down with Western help in 1864. The British and French seized Beijing in 1860 and burnt the imperial palace. In 1895 China was defeated by a modernized Japan and forced to cede Korea and Taiwan. The emperor became converted to the necessity for reforms, but these were blocked by court intrigue. An anti-foreigner *Boxer* rebellion was suppressed by Western forces in 1900.

Sun Yat-sen founded the Kuomintang (Nationalist Party) in 1905. When troops at Hangchow mutinied in Oct. 1911 and proclaimed a republic, the emperor's mediator Yuan went over to them and made himself president; the infant emperor abdicated. Yuan attempted to make himself emperor but was overthrown in 1916 after acceding to Japan's demands which would have made China a virtual protectorate. The Beijing government lost all real authority and the country disintegrated into the hands of squabbling warlords. At Versailles the Allies failed to restore territory seized by Japan. Sun Yat-sen, who had formed a separatist government in Canton, turned to the Soviet regime. The Communist Party (founded in 1921) co-operated with the Kuomintang, led after 1926 by Chiang Kai-shek, in attacking both warlords and foreign concessionaries, but in 1937 Chiang turned on the Communists and suppressed them. Communism was then carried on by Mao Zedong's rural 'Soviet', at first in Kiangsi, and then, after the Long March, in Yenan. Chiang came to terms with the warlords and foreign concessionaries, but his aims to create a modern state were thwarted by Japanese invasions in 1931 and 1937 and by his campaign against the Communists. In 1936 he was forced (after being kidnapped) to declare a joint front with them against Japan, but hostilities continued.

After the Second World War full-scale civil war broke out. Chiang was defeated and took refuge on Taiwan where the Republic of China was set up. Mao proclaimed a People's Republic on 1 Oct. 1949. The Maoist period was marked by innovatory excesses: the agricultural communes (now abolished); the conscription of intellectuals to till the fields; the disastrous 'Great Leap Forward' with its backyard blast furnaces; the Thought (and cult) of Mao; the Cultural Revolution. After Mao's death in 1976 moderates within the Communist Party triumphed, and the radical Gang of Four led by Mao's wife Chang Ch'ing were first publicly denounced and then arrested. China has since emerged as a major international power with a liberalized economy, firstly under Deng Xiaoping and more recently Jiang Zemin.

Denounced in the Cultural Revolution, Deng was formally rehabilitated in 1973 and became one of Mao's vice-premiers for a time in the 1970s. The keynote of his administration was political and economic pragmatism. He sought 'readjustment, restructuring, consolidation and improvement'. In 1979 China and the USA established full diplomatic relations. From that time contacts with the west have grown considerably. Deng Xiaoping resigned from the Politburo in Nov. 1987 and from the chairmanship of the Military Commissions in Nov. 1989.

The funeral of the Communist party General Secretary Hu Yaobang on 15 April 1989 sparked off mass student demonstrations which escalated into a popular 'pro-democracy' movement in Beijing, Shanghai and other provincial centres, demanding reforms. The demonstrations gathered strength during the summit visit of the Soviet President Gorbachev (15–17 May) and culminated in a sit-in in Tiananmen Square, Beijing. This was confronted by army units, at first peacefully. However, on 4 June troops opened fire on the demonstrators and tanks were sent in to disperse them. The official casualty figures were: 'over 200' demonstrators and 'dozens' of soldiers killed, and some 9,000 injured. A hard-line faction assumed control in the Party Politburo which appointed Jiang Zemin as General Secretary. Martial law was imposed from May 1989 to Jan. 1990. Since then, however, China has moved cautiously towards a more open society, with an economy that makes allowance for market principles.

For the background to the handover of Hong Kong in 1997, see p. 455.

TERRITORY AND POPULATION
China is bounded in the north by Russia and Mongolia; east by North Korea, the Yellow Sea and the East China Sea, with Hong Kong and Macao as enclaves on the south-east coast; south by Vietnam, Laos, Myanmar, India, Bhutan and Nepal; west by India, Pakistan, Afghanistan, Tajikistan, Kyrgyzstan and Kazakhstan. The total area (including Taiwan) is estimated at 9,572,900 sq. km (3,696,100 sq. miles). A law of Feb. 1992 claimed the Spratly, Paracel and Diaoyutasi Islands. An agreement of 7 Sept. 1993 at prime ministerial level settled Sino-Indian border disputes which had first emerged in the war of 1962.

At the 1991 census the population was 1,130,510,638 (548,690,231 females). Population estimate, 1996: 1,223·89m. (601·89m. female; 359·5m., or 29·3%, urban); density, 128 per sq. km.

The UN gives a projected population for 2000 of 1,276·3m.

China is set to lose its status as the world's most populous country to India by 2050.

1979 regulations restricting married couples to a single child, a policy enforced by compulsory abortions and economic sanctions, have been widely ignored, and it was admitted in 1988 that the population target of 1,200m. by 2000 would have to be revised to 1,270m. Since 1988 peasant couples have been permitted a second child after 4 years if the first born is a girl, a measure to combat infanticide.

43·2m. persons of Chinese origin lived abroad in 1993.

A number of widely divergent varieties of Chinese are spoken. The official 'Modern Standard Chinese' is based on the dialect of North China. The ideographic writing system of 'characters' is uniform throughout the country, and has undergone systematic simplification. In 1958 a phonetic alphabet (*Pinyin*) was devised to transcribe the characters, and in 1979 this was officially adopted for use in all texts

CHINA

in the Roman alphabet. The previous transcription scheme (Wade) is still used in Taiwan and Hong Kong.

China is administratively divided into 22 provinces, 5 autonomous regions (originally entirely or largely inhabited by ethnic minorities, though in some regions now outnumbered by Han immigrants) and 4 government-controlled municipalities. These are in turn divided into 335 prefectures, 666 cities (of which 218 are at prefecture level and 445 at county level), 2,142 counties and 717 urban districts.

Government-controlled municipalities	Area (in 1,000 sq. km)	Population (1990 census, in 1,000)	Density per sq. km (in 1987)	Population (1996 estimate, in 1,000)	Capital
Beijing	17·8	10,870	644	12,590	—
Tianjin	4·0	8,830	777	9,480	—
Shanghai	5·8	13,510	2,152	14,190	—
Provinces					
Hebei[2]	202·7	60,280	301	64,840	Shijiazhuang
Shanxi	157·1	28,180	183	31,090	Taiyuan
Liaoning[2]	151·0	39,980	261	41,160	Shenyang
Jilin[2]	187·0	25,150	132	26,100	Changchun
Heilongjiang[2]	463·6	34,770	76	37,280	Harbin
Jiangsu	102·2	68,170	654	71,100	Nanjing
Zhejiang[2]	101·8	40,840	407	43,430	Hangzhou
Anhui	139·9	52,290	402	60,700	Hefei
Fujian	123·1	30,610	244	32,610	Fuzhou
Jiangxi	164·8	38,280	229	41,050	Nanchang
Shandong	153·3	83,430	551	87,380	Jinan
Henan	167·0	86,140	512	91,720	Zhengzhou
Hubei[2]	187·5	54,760	288	58,250	Wuhan
Hunan[2]	210·5	60,600	288	64,280	Changsha
Guangdong[2]	197·1	63,210	319	69,610	Guangzhou
Hainan[2]	34·3	6,420	191	7,340	Haikou
Sichuan[2]	569·0	106,370	188	114,300	Chengdu
Guizhou[2]	174·0	32,730	186	35,550	Guiyang
Yunnan[2]	436·2	36,750	85	40,420	Kunming
Shaanxi	195·8	32,470	168	35,430	Xian
Gansu[2]	366·5	22,930	61	24,670	Lanzhou
Qinghai[2]	721·0	4,430	6	4,880	Xining
Autonomous regions					
Inner Mongolia	1,177·5	21,110	18	23,070	Hohhot
Guangxi Zhuang	220·4	42,530	192	45,890	Nanning
Tibet[1]	1,221·6	2,220	2	2,440	Lhasa
Ningxia Hui	170.0	4,660	70	5,210	Yinchuan
Xinjiang Uighur	1,646·8	15,370	9	16,890	Urumqi

[1]See also Tibet below.
[2]Also designated minority nationality autonomous area.

Population of largest cities in 1993: Shanghai, 8·76m.; Beijing (Peking), 6·56m.; Tianjin, 4·97m.; Shenyang, 3·86m.; Wuhan, 3·86m.; Chongqing, 3·78m.; Guangzhou (Canton), 3·56m.; Harbin, 3·1m.; Chengdu, 2·67m.; Zibo (1991), 2·46m.; Nanjing, 2·43m.; Changchun, 2·4m.; Xian, 2·36m.; Dalian, 2·33m.; Qingdao, 2·24m.; Jinan, 2·05m.; Hangzhou, 1·74m.; Taiyuan, 1·68m.; Zhengzhou, 1·53m.; Kunming, 1·45m.; Tangshan (1990), 1·5m.; Changsha, 1·48m.; Nanchang, 1·42m.; Anshan (1991), 1·39m.; Qiqihar (1991), 1·38m.; Fushun (1991), 1·35m.; Lanzhou, 1·32m.; Fuzhou, 1·29m.; Jilin (1991), 1·27m.; Shijiazhuang (1991), 1·21m.; Baotou (1991), 1·2m.; Huainan (1991), 1·2m.; Luoyang (1991), 1·19m.; Urumqi (1991), 1·11m.; Datong (1991), 1·11m.; Handan (1991), 1·11m.; Guiyang, 1·07m.; Ningbo, 1·07m.

The autonomous regions and 14 provinces (*see table above*) have non-Han components in their populations, ranging from 97·2% (in 1994) in Tibet to 9·9% in Zhejiang. Total minority population, 1994, 72,818,100. 55 ethnic minorities are identified. At the 1990 census the largest were: Zhuang, 15,555,820; Manchu, 9,846,776; Hui, 8,612,001; Miao, 7,383,622; Uighur, 7,207,024; Yi, 6,578,524; Tujia, 5,725,049; Mongolian, 4,802,407; Tibetan, 4,593,072.

Li Chengrui, *The Population of China.* Beijing, 1992
The Population Atlas of China. OUP, 1988
Song, J. *et al., Population Control in China.* New York, 1985

Tibet

After the 1959 revolt was suppressed, the Preparatory Committee for the Autonomous Region of Tibet (set up in 1955) took over the functions of local government, led by its Vice-Chairman, the Banqen Lama, in the absence of its Chairman, the Dalai Lama, who had fled to India in 1959. In Dec. 1964 both the Dalai and Banqen Lamas were removed from their posts and on 9 Sept. 1965 Tibet became an Autonomous Region. 301 delegates were elected to the first People's Congress, of whom 226 were Tibetans. The Chief of Government is Gyaincain Norbu. The senior spiritual leader, the Dalai Lama, is in exile. He was awarded the Nobel Peace Prize in 1989. The Banqen Lama died in Jan. 1989. The borders were opened for trade with neighbouring countries in 1980. In July 1988 Tibetan was reinstated as a 'major official language', competence in which is required of all administrative officials. Monasteries and shrines have been renovated and reopened. There were some 15,000 monks and nuns in 1987. In 1984 a Buddhist seminary in Lhasa opened with 200 students. A further softening of Beijing's attitude towards Tibet was shown during President Bill Clinton's visit to China in June 1998. Jiang Zemin, China's president, said he was prepared to meet the Dalai Lama providing he acknowledged Chinese sovereignty over Tibet and Taiwan.

In 1996 the population was 2·49m. In 1994 there were 2·22m. Tibetans living in Tibet out of a total population of 2·36m. Birth rate (per 1,000), 1996, 24·7; death rate, 8·5; growth rate, 16·2. Population of the capital, Lhasa, in 1992 was 124,000. Expectation of life was 65 years in 1990. 2m. Tibetans live outside Tibet, in China, and in India and Nepal.

Chinese efforts to modernize Tibet include irrigation, road-building and the establishment of light industry. In 1991 there were 328 township and 123 village enterprises employing 21,168 persons; 12,000 persons worked in heavy industry, 16,000 in state-owned enterprises. 1990 output included 136,300 metres of woollen fabrics, 1,000 tonnes of salt, 1,900 tonnes of vegetable oil, 208,200 cu. metres of timber and 132,300 tonnes of cement.

Electricity production in 1990 was 330m. kWh, of which 323m. kWh were hydro-electric.

In 1996 there were 953,000 rural labourers, including 886,000 in farming, forestry and fisheries. The total sown area was 220,100 ha, including 52,500 ha sown to wheat, 18,300 ha to rapeseed, 18,300 ha to oil-bearing crops and 14,500 ha to soya beans. Output (in 1,000 tonnes), 1996: Wheat, 261; soya beans, 41; oil-bearing crops, 35; rapeseeds, 35. There were 5·10m. cattle, 1·21m. draught animals, 0·36m. horses, 0·22m. pigs, 11·10m. sheep and 5·83m. goats in 1996.

In 1991 there were 21,842 km of roads, of which 6,240 km were paved. There are airports at Lhasa and Bangda providing external links. 30,000 tourists visited Tibet in 1986.

In 1988 there were 2,437 primary schools, 67 secondary schools, 14 technical schools and 3 higher education institutes. The total number of primary school pupils in 1990–91 was 101,000. A university was established in 1985.

In 1990 there were some 9,000 medical personnel and 1,006 medical institutions, with a total of about 5,000 beds.

Barnett, R. and Akiner, S. (eds.) *Resistance and Reform in Tibet.* Farnborough, 1994
Batchelor, S., *The Tibet Guide*. London, 1987
The Dalai Lama, *My Land and My People* (ed. D. Howarth). London, 1962:—*Freedom in Exile.* London, 1990
Grunfeld, A. T., *The Making of Modern Tibet.* London, 1987
Levenson, C. B., *The Dalai Lama: A Biography.* London, 1988
Pinfold, J., *Tibet:* [Bibliography]. Oxford and Santa Barbara (CA), 1991
Schwartz, R. D., *Circle of Protest: Political Ritual in the Tibetan Uprising.* Farnborough, 1994
Shakabpa, T. W. D., *Tibet: A Political History.* New York, 1984
Sharabati, D., *Tibet and its History.* London, 1986
Smith, W. W., *A History of Tibet: Nationalism and Self-Determination.* Oxford, 1996

SOCIAL STATISTICS

Births, 1996, 20,780,000 (more than the total population of Australia); deaths, 8,030,000. 1996 birth rate (per 1,000 population), 16·98; death rate, 6·56. There were 9,339,615 marriages and 1,132,215 divorces in 1996. Life expectancy at birth, 1990–95, was 66·7 years for men and 70·5 years for women. Annual growth rate, 1990–95, 1·1%. Infant mortality, 1990–95, 44 per 1,000 live births. The average number of live births per woman (married or otherwise) in 1996 was 1·42. The lowest and highest averages by region were Beijing with 0·84 and Hainan with 1·78. Only Beijing and Shanghai had averages less than 1. In 1996 the average Chinese woman had 1·39 living children.

CLIMATE
Most of China has a temperate climate but, with such a large country, extending far inland and embracing a wide range of latitude as well as containing large areas at high altitude, many parts experience extremes of climate, especially in winter. Most rain falls during the summer, from May to Sept., though amounts decrease inland. Beijing (Peking), Jan. 24°F (−4·4°C), July 79°F (26°C). Annual rainfall 24·9" (623 mm). Chongqing, Jan. 45°F (7·2°C), July 84°F (28·9°C). Annual rainfall 43·7" (1,092 mm). Shanghai, Jan. 39°F (3·9°C), July 82°F (27·8°C). Annual rainfall 45·4" (1,135 mm). Tianjin, Jan. 24°F (−4·4°C), July 81°F (27·2°C). Annual rainfall 21·5" (533·4 mm).

CONSTITUTION AND GOVERNMENT
On 21 Sept. 1949 the *Chinese People's Political Consultative Conference* met in Beijing, convened by the Chinese Communist Party. The Conference adopted a 'Common Programme' of 60 articles and the 'Organic Law of the Central People's Government' (31 articles). Both became the basis of the Constitution adopted on 20 Sept. 1954 by the 1st National People's Congress, the supreme legislative body. The Consultative Conference continued to exist after 1954 as an advisory body. Its 9th session was convened in 1998. It has 2,093 members.

New Constitutions were adopted in 1975, 1978, 1982 and 1993, the latter embodying the principles of a 'Socialist market economy'.

The *National People's Congress* can amend the Constitution and nominally elects and has power to remove from office the highest officers of state. The Congress elects a *Standing Committee* (which supervises the State Council) and the *President* and *Vice-President* for a 5-year term. Congress has 2,978 deputies and is elected for a 5-year term, and meets once a year for 2 or 3 weeks. When not in session, its business is carried on by its *Standing Committee*. It is composed of deputies elected on a constituency basis by direct secret ballot. Any voter, and certain organizations, may nominate candidates. Nominations may exceed seats by 50–100%.

The *State Council* is the supreme executive organ and comprises the Prime Minister, Deputy Prime Ministers and State Councillors.

National Anthem. 'March of the Volunteers'; words by Tien Han, tune by Nieh Erh.

RECENT ELECTIONS
The 9th *National People's Congress* was elected in March 1998.

CURRENT ADMINISTRATION
President: Jiang Zemin (b. 1926; elected 27 March 1993 and sworn in April 1993).
  Deputy President: Hu Jintao.
  In March 1999 the government comprised:
  Prime Minister: Zhu Rongji.
  Deputy Prime Ministers: Li Lanqing, Qian Qichen, Wu Bangguo, Wen Jiabao.
  Minister of Agriculture: Chen Yaobang. *Civil Affairs:* Doje Cering. *Communications:* Huang Zhendong. *Construction:* Yu Zhengsheng. *Culture:* Sun Jiazheng. *Education:* Chen Zhili. *Finance:* Xiang Huaicheng. *Foreign Affairs:* Tang Jiaxuan. *Foreign Trade and Economic Co-operation:* Shi Guangsheng. *Information Industry:* Wu Jichuan. *Justice:* Gao Changli. *Labour and Social Security:* Zhang Zuoji. *Land and Natural Resources:* Zhou Yongkang. *National Defence:* Chi Haotian. *Personnel:* Song Defu. *Public Health:* Zhang Wenkang. *Public Security:* Jia Chunwang. *Railways:* Fu Zhihuan. *Science and Technology:* Zhu Lilan. *State Security:* Xu Yongyue. *Supervision:* He Yong. *Water Resources:* Wang Shucheng.
  Ministers heading State Commissions: *Economics and Trade*, Sheng Huaren. *Family Planning*, Zhang Weiqing. *Nationalities Affairs*, Li Dezhu. *Development Planning*, Zeng Peiyan. *Science, Technology and Industry for National Defence*, Liu Jibin.

De facto power is in the hands of the Communist Party of China, which had 57m. members in 1997. There are 8 other parties, all members of the Chinese People's Political Consultative Conference.

The members of the Standing Committee of the Politburo in March 1998 were Jiang Zemin (*General Secretary*), Li Peng, Zhu Rongji, Hu Jintao, Li Ruihuan, Li Lanqing and Wei Jianxing.

Local Government. There are 4 administrative levels: (1) Provinces, Autonomous Regions and the municipalities directly administered by the Government; (2) prefectures and autonomous prefectures (*zhou*); (3) counties, autonomous counties and municipalities; (4) towns. Local government organs ('congresses') exist at provincial, county and township levels; and in national minority autonomous prefectures, but not in ordinary prefectures which are just agencies of the provincial government. Up to county level congresses are elected directly. Elections take place every 3 years. Any person proposed by 10 electors may stand after political vetting. There are quotas for Party members and women. Multiple candidacies are permitted at local elections.

DEFENCE

President Jiang Zemin is chairman of the State and Party's Military Commissions. China is divided into 7 military regions. The military commander also commands the air, naval and civilian militia forces assigned to each region.

Conscription is compulsory but for organizational reasons selective: only some 10% of potential recruits are called up. Service is 3 years with the Army; and 4 years with the Air Force and Navy. A military academy to train senior officers in modern warfare was established in 1985.

Defence expenditure in 1997 totalled US$36,551m. (US$30 per capita) and represented 5·7% of GDP, down from 7·9% of GDP in 1985.

Nuclear weapons. Having carried out its first test in 1964, there have been 45 tests in all. The nuclear arsenal consisted of approximately 395 warheads in Jan. 1998 according to the Stockholm International Peace Research Institute. China has been helping Pakistan with its nuclear efforts.

Army. The Army (PLA: 'People's Liberation Army') is divided into main and local forces. Main forces, administered by the 7 military regions in which they are stationed, but commanded by the Ministry of Defence, are available for operation anywhere and are better equipped. Local forces concentrate on the defence of their own regions. There are 24 Integrated Group Armies comprising 78 infantry, 10 armoured and 5 artillery divisions; and 15 engineer regiments. Equipment includes some 700 T-34/85 and T-54, 6,000 T-59 and 200 T-69 main battle tanks. Land-based missile forces consisted of (1995 estimate): 17 intercontinental and 70 intermediate range. Military aviation has 8 Gazelle armed helicopters, 20 S-70 Black Hawk and 24 Mi-17 transport helicopters. Total strength in 1997 was 2·09m. including some 1·07m. conscripts.

There is a para-military People's Armed Police force of 0·6m. under PLA command.

Joffe, E., *The Chinese Army after Mao*. London, 1987

Navy. The naval arm of the PLA comprises 1 nuclear-powered ballistic missile armed submarine, 5 nuclear-propelled fleet submarines, 1 diesel-powered cruise missile submarine and some 40 patrol submarines. Surface combatant forces include 18 missile-armed destroyers, 36 frigates, some 185 missile craft and 150 torpedo craft. There is a mixed coastal and inshore patrol force of some 500 vessels and 50 riverine craft. The mine warfare force consists of 40 ex-Soviet offshore mine-sweepers, some 12 inshore, and about 60 unmanned drones. There are 55 landing ships of various types and some 150 craft. Major auxiliaries number over 100, including 2 underway replenishment oilers and 1 fleet stores ship, and there are several hundred minor auxiliaries, yard craft and service vessels.

The land-based naval air force of about 620 combat aircraft, primarily for defensive and anti-submarine service, is organized into 3 bomber and 6 fighter divisions. The force includes some 120 H-5 torpedo bombers, about 100 Q-5 fighter/ground attack aircraft and 600 fighters, including J-5 (MiG-17), J-6 (MiG-19), and J-7 (MiG-21) types. Maritime patrol tasks are performed by 15 Be-6 and a small number of PS-5 flying boats, and anti-submarine operations by 40 Z-5 and 15 Super Frelon helicopters from shore and about 10 Z-9 afloat. There are also about 60 communications, training and transport aircraft.

Main naval bases are at Qingdao (North Sea Fleet), Shanghai (East Sea Fleet), and Zhanjiang (South Sea Fleet).

In 1997 personnel numbered some 280,000, including 25,000 in the naval air force, 29,000 coastal defence troops and 5,000 naval infantry.

Air Force. The Air Force has an estimated 3,500 front-line aircraft, organized in 100 regiments of jet-fighters and about 12 regiments of tactical bombers, plus reconnaissance, transport and helicopter units. Each regiment is made up of 3 or 4 squadrons (each 12 aircraft), and 3 regiments form a division.

Equipment includes about 500 J-7 (MiG-21) and 2,000 J-6 (MiG-19) interceptors and fighter-bombers, with about 500 H-5 (Il-28) jetbombers, about 120 H-6 Chinese-built copies of the Soviet Tu-16 twin-jet strategic bomber, plus 500 Q-5 twin-jet fighter-bombers, evolved from the MiG-19, while 50 Su-27 fighters have been supplied by Russia. About 100 of a locally-developed fighter designated J-8 (known in the West as 'Finback') are in service. Transport aircraft include about 500 Y-5 (An-2), Y-8 (An-12), Y-12, An-24/26, Il-76, Challenger and Il-14 fixed-wing types, plus 300 Z-5 (Mi-4) and Z-6 (Mi-8) helicopters, as well as 6 Super Puma VIP transport helicopters. Total strength (1997) 470,000 (160,000 conscripts), including 220,000 in air defence organization.

INTERNATIONAL RELATIONS
The People's Republic of China is a member of UN (and its Security Council).

ECONOMY
Policy. A ninth 5-year plan covers 1996–2000; there is also a 15-year strategic plan 'Long-Term Target for 2010'. These plans envisage a continued opening to the outside world, an enhanced development of agriculture, the reduction of tariff barriers and the development of the poorer regions.

A Communist Party statement of Nov. 1993 declared that public ownership should remain the mainstay of the economy, but alongside a modern enterprise system suited to the demands of a market economy in which government control is separated from management.

The new cabinet appointed in March 1998 was composed of technocrats chosen for their ability to solve problems and push through a series of reforms. The new Prime Minister Zhu Rongji stressed the urgency of reforming the debt-ridden state industrial sector consisting of some 370,000 enterprises, and its central bureaucracy. Zhu Rongji stated that the number of civil servants in the central bureaucracy would be halved in 1998.

Performance. In 1997 GDP growth was 8·8%, with a forecast for 1998 of 8%. Between 1990 and 1996 the average annual real growth in GNP per capita was 11%—the second highest in the world after Equatorial Guinea.

Budget. 1996 revenue was 740,799m. yuan; expenditure, 793,755m. yuan. Of this, local government revenue accounted for 374,692m. yuan and local government expenditure, 578,628m. yuan. Total debt incurred, 1996, 196,728m. yuan, of which 119,510m. yuan were foreign debts. The current account surplus was running at US$29,718m. in 1997.

Sources of revenue, 1996 (in 1m. yuan): Taxes, 690,982; industrial and commercial taxes, 527,004. Expenditure: Economic construction, 285,578 (1995); culture and education, 175,672 (1995); national defence, 63,672 (1995); government administration, 99,654 (1995); agriculture, 51,007; pensions and social welfare, 12,803; debt payments, 131,191.

Currency. The currency is called Renminbi (*i.e.,* People's Currency). The unit of currency is the *yuan* (CNY) which is divided into 10 *jiao*, the *jiao* being divided into 10 *fen*. The yuan was floated to reflect market forces on 1 Jan. 1994 though remaining state-controlled, and the official rate of exchange was abolished. It became convertible for current transactions from 1 Dec. 1996. Total money supply in Dec. 1997 was 3,834bn. yuan. In Feb. 1998 foreign exchange reserves were

CHINA

US$140,333m. (only Japan, with US$209,778m., had more). Gold reserves were
12·7m. troy oz. in Feb. 1998. Annualized inflation was 6·1% in 1996, but was
forecast to be around 80% in 1998.

Banking and Finance. The People's Bank of China is the central bank and bank of
issue (*Director:* Dai Xianglong, b. 1945). There are a number of other banks, the
largest of which are Agricultural Bank of China, Industrial and Commercial Bank of
China, Construction Bank of China, Bank of China, Bank of Communications and
Agricultural Development Bank of China. Legislation of 1995 permitted the
establishment of commercial banks; credit co-operatives may be transformed into
banks, mainly to provide credit to small businesses. Insurance is handled by the
People's Insurance Company. There were (1994) 350,813 credit co-operatives. The
Bank of China is responsible for foreign banking operations.

Savings bank deposits were 2,151,880m. yuan in 1994.

611,566m. yuan was loaned from State Banks in 1996. It is estimated that up to
20% of outstanding loans are bad debts (about US$145bn. at the end of 1996).

There are stock exchanges in the Shenzhen Special Economic Zone and in
Shanghai. A securities trading system linking 6 cities (Securities Automated
Quotations System) was inaugurated in 1990 for trading in government bonds.

Weights and Measures. The metric system is in general use alongside traditional
units of measurement.

ENERGY AND NATURAL RESOURCES

Electricity. Installed capacity, 1996, 0·2m. MW. 1996 electricity output was
1,081,310m. kWh. Consumption per capita was an estimated 684 kWh in 1995.
Sources of energy in 1996 as percentage of total energy production: Coal, 74·8%;
crude oil, 17·1%; hydro-electric power, 6·2%; natural gas, 1·9%. Generating is not
centralized; local units range between 30 and 60 MW of output.

Oil and Gas. There are on-shore fields at Daqing, Shengli, Dagang and Karamai,
and 10 provinces south of the Yangtze River have been opened for exploration in
co-operation with foreign companies. Crude oil production was 157·33m. tonnes in
1996.

Natural gas is available from fields near Canton and Shanghai, and in Sichuan
province. Production was 20,114m. cu. metres in 1996.

Minerals. Most provinces contain coal, and there are 70 major production centres,
of which the largest are in Hebei, Shanxi, Shandong, Jilin and Anhui. Coal reserves
were estimated at 1,000,850m. tonnes in 1996. Coal production was 1,397m. tonnes
in 1996.

Iron ore reserves were 47,560m. tonnes in 1996. Deposits are abundant in the
anthracite field of Shanxi, in Hebei and in Shandong, and are found in conjunction
with coal and worked in the north-east. Production in 1996 was 249·6m. tonnes,
making China the world's leading iron ore producer.

Tin ore is plentiful in Yunnan, where the tin-mining industry has long existed. Tin
production was 40,000 tonnes in 1989.

China is a major producer of wolfram (tungsten ore). Mining of wolfram is
carried on in Hunan, Guangdong and Yunnan.

Salt production was 29·96m. tonnes in 1994; gold production was 110 tonnes in
1992; output of other minerals in 1989 (in 1,000 tonnes): Aluminium, 770; copper,
540; nickel, 30; lead, 270; zinc, 430. Other minerals produced: Barite, bismuth,
graphite, gypsum, mercury, molybdenum, silver. Reserves (in tonnes) of phosphate
ore, 15,766m.; sylvite, 458m.; salt, 402,400m.

Agriculture. Agriculture accounts for approximately 21% of GDP. In 1996 the
sown area was 152·4m. ha comprising (in 1m. ha): rice, 31·41; wheat, 29·61; corn,
24·50; beans, 10·54; tubers, 9·8; oil-bearing crops, 12·56m. Intensive agriculture and
horticulture have been practised for millennia. Present-day policy aims to avert the
traditional threats from floods and droughts by soil conservancy, afforestation,
irrigation and drainage projects, and to increase the 'high stable yields' areas by
introducing fertilizers, pesticides and improved crops. In spite of this, 18·1m. ha of
land were flooded in 1996 and 20·1m. ha were covered by drought. 50·38m. ha were

irrigated in 1996. In Aug. 1998 more than 21m. ha, notably in the Yangtze valley, were under water as China experienced its worst flooding in recent times.

'Township and village enterprises' in agriculture comprise enterprises previously run by the communes of the Maoist era, co-operatives run by rural labourers and individual firms of a certain size. There were 24·95m. such enterprises in 1994, employing 120·18m. persons. There were 2,157 state farms in 1994 with 5·18m. employees. In 1996 there were 234·38m. rural households. The rural workforce was 452·88m., of whom 322·6m. were employed in agriculture, fishing or land management. Net per capita annual peasant income, 1996: 1,926 yuan.

In 1992 there were 25,023 agricultural technical stations. There were 670,848 large and medium-sized tractors in 1996.

Agricultural production (in 1m. tonnes), 1996: Rice, 195·10; wheat, 110·57; corn, 127·47; beans, 17·90; tubers, 35·36; tea, 0·59; cotton, 4·20; oil-bearing crops, 22·11; sugar-cane, 66·88; fruit, 46·53. The gross value of agricultural output in 1996 was 2,342,866m. yuan.

Livestock, 1996: Draught animals, 91,920,000; cattle, 139,813,000 (including 4,470,000 milch cows); goats, 170,680,000; pigs, 457,360,000; sheep, 132,690,000; horses,10,038,000; chickens (1995), 2·8bn.; ducks (1995), 463m. China has more goats, pigs, sheep, horses and chickens than any other country, having overtaken Australia in 1996 as the country with the greatest number of sheep. China also has more than half of the world's ducks. Meat production in 1996 was 59·15m. tonnes; milk, 7·36m. tonnes; eggs, 19·54m. tonnes.

Powell, S. G., *Agricultural Reform in China: from Communes to Commodity Economy, 1978–1990*. Manchester Univ. Press, 1992

Forestry. In 1995 the area under forests was 133·32m. ha, or 14·3% of the total land area (133·76m. ha in 1990). Total roundwood production in 1995 was 300·36m. cu. metres, making China the second largest producer after the USA.

Fisheries. Total catch, 1996: 32·88m. tonnes, of which 12·75m. tonnes were freshwater produce. China's annual catch is the largest in the world, and accounts for more than 20% of the world total every year. In 1986 the annual catch had been just over 8m. tonnes.

INDUSTRY

Cottage industries persist into the 21st century. Modern industrial development began with the manufacture of cotton textiles, and the establishment of silk filatures, steel plants, flour mills and match factories. In 1996 there were 7,986,500 industrial enterprises. 113,800 were state-owned, 1,591,800 were collectives and 6,210,700 were individually owned. A law of 1988 ended direct state control of firms and provided for the possibility of bankruptcy.

Output of major products, 1996 (in tonnes): Cotton yarn, 5·12m.; paper, 26·38m.; sugar, 6·40m.; salt, 29·03m.; steel, 101·24m.; rolled steel, 93·38m.; cement, 491·1m.; chemical fertilizers, 28·09m.; aluminium ware, 159,100; silk, 94,900; woollen fabrics, 459·5m. metres; bicycles, 33·61m. units; TV sets, 35·41m. units; radios, 56·50m. units; cameras, 41·20m. units; refrigerators, 9·79m. units; motor vehicles, 1,470,000 units; locomotives, 1,050 units.

The gross value of industrial output in 1996 was 9,959,500m. yuan.

Labour. The employed population at the 1990 census was 647·2m. (291·1m. female). By 1996 it was estimated to have risen to 688·5m., of whom 490·3m. were in rural areas and 198·2m. in urban areas. There were 329·1m. people working in agriculture, 97·6m. in manufacturing, 45·1m. in commerce, 34·1m. in construction and 20·1m. in communications. 109·4m. worked in state-owned enterprises, 29·5m. in urban collectives, and 50·2m. were self-employed. In 1994 there were 446·54m. working as individual rural labourers or in rural collectives and there were 15·57m. individual urban labourers.

At the 1990 census there was a floating population of 21m. internal migrants who tour the country seeking seasonal employment. There were 5·53m. urban unemployed in 1996 (3% of the urban population). Almost one-third of unemployed people had not worked for a year. Only a quarter of the unemployed in 1996 were registered at employment services and only 1·7% received unemployment relief payments. In early 1998 the official unemployment rate was 3%, but was thought to be much higher.

The average non-agricultural annual wage in 1996 was 6,210 yuan. 4,302 yuan, urban collectives; 6,280 yuan, state-owned enterprises; 8,261 yuan, other enterprises. There is a 6-day 48-hour working week. Minimum working age was fixed at 16 in 1991. There were 19,098 labour disputes in 1994.

Trade Unions. The All-China Federation of Trade Unions is headed by Wei Jianxing. In 1991 there were 614,000 union branches with a total membership of 103·89m. (39·92m. female).

INTERNATIONAL TRADE

Foreign debt was US$116,275m. in 1996. Actual foreign investment totalled US$33,800m. in 1994. Direct foreign investment (in US$1m.) in 1995 by major countries of origin: Taiwan, 11,600; USA, 10,900; Japan, 10,500; Singapore, 3,900; South Korea, 2,300; UK, 2,200.

There are 6 Special Economic Zones at Shanghai and in the provinces of Guangdong and Fujian, in which concessions are made to foreign businessmen. The Pudong New Area in Shanghai is designated a special development area. Since 1979 joint ventures with foreign firms have been permitted. A law of April 1991 reduced taxation on joint ventures to 33%. There is no maximum limit on the foreign share of the holdings; the minimum limit is 25%. Contracts between Chinese and foreign firms are only legally valid if in writing and approved by the appropriate higher authority.

In June 1998 the US president extended most-favoured-nation status to China for a further year.

Imports and Exports. 1996: Imports, US$138,944m.; exports, US$151,197m.

Major exports in 1996 (in 1,000 tonnes): Crude oil, 20,330; silk and satin, 147m. metres; coal, 29,030; cotton cloth, 3,043m. metres; cement, 11,800. Imports: Wheat, 8,250; steel products, 15,840; chemical fertilizers, 18,570; iron ore, 43,870.

Exports to (and imports from) major trade partners in 1995: Hong Kong, 24·2% (6·5%); Japan, 19·1% (22·0%); USA, 16·6% (12·2%); Taiwan, 2·1% (11·2%), South Korea, 4·5% (7·8%); Germany, 3·8% (6·1%); Singapore, 2·4% (2·6%). Customs duties with Taiwan were abolished in 1980.

Lardy, N. R., *Foreign Trade and Economic Reform in China, 1978–1990.* CUP, 1992
Pearson, M. M., *Joint Ventures in the People's Republic of China: the Control of Foreign Direct Investment under Socialism.* Princeton Univ. Press, 1991
Wong, K. and Chu, D. (eds.) *Modernization in China: the Case of the Shenzhen Special Economic Zone.* OUP, 1986

COMMUNICATIONS

Roads. The total road length was 1,185,800 km in 1996. In 1994, 998,077 km were hard-surfaced. In 1996 there were 5·75m. trucks and 4·8m. passenger vehicles. 2·89m. vehicles were privately owned. The use of bicycles is very widespread. In 1996, 9,838m. tonnes of freight and 11,221m. persons were transported by road.

There were 253,537 traffic accidents in 1994, with 66,362 fatalities.

Rail. In 1996 there were 56,700 km of railway including 10,100 km electrified. Gauge is standard except for some 600 mm track in Yunnan. In 1996 the railways carried 1,668m. tonnes of freight and 941m. passengers.

Civil Aviation. There are international airports at Beijing and Shanghai (Hongqiao). Altogether there were 142 civil airports in 1996, 106 of which can accommodate Boeing 737s or larger aircraft. The national and major airlines are state-owned, except Shanghai Airlines (75% municipality-owned, 25% private) and Shenzhen Airlines (private). Chinese airlines operating scheduled services in 1998 were China Southern Airlines (10,767,000 passengers carried in 1995), Air China (6,274,000 passengers in 1995), China Eastern Airlines (6,240,000), China Southwest Airlines (5,071,000), China Northern Airlines (4,442,000), China Northwest Airlines (2,488,000), Xiamen Airlines (2,403,000), China Yunnan Airlines (1,854,000), Xinjiang Airlines (1,159,000), Changan Airlines, China National Aviation, Fujian Airlines, Hainan Airlines, Shandong Airlines, Shanghai Airlines, Shanxi Airlines, Shenzhen Airlines, Sichuan Airlines and Xiamen Airlines.

In 1996 airlines carried 55·55m. passengers (4·40m. international) and 1·15m. tonnes of freight. In 1995 the busiest airport was Beijing, with 15,045,000 passengers (11,804,000 on domestic flights), followed by Guangzhou (Baiyun), with 12,575,000 passengers (12,204,000 on domestic flights) and Shanghai (Hongqiao), with 11,076,000 passengers (9,361,000 on domestic flights).

In 1998 services were also provided by Aeroflot, Air France, Air Kazakhstan, Air Koryo, Air Macau, Air Ukraine, Alitalia, All Nippon Airways, Ansett Australia, Asiana, Austrian Airlines, Belavia, British Airways, Canadian Airlines International, Chita Avia, DRAGONAIR, El Al, Ethiopian Airlines, Finnair, Iran Air, JAL, JAT, KLM, Korean Air, LOT, Lufthansa, Malaysia Airlines, Malév, Mongolian Airlines, Pakistan International Airlines, President Airlines, Qantas Airways, Royal Brunei Airlines, Royal Nepal Airlines, SAS, Singapore Airlines, Swissair, Tarom, Thai Airways International, United Airlines and Uzbekiston Airways.

Shipping. In 1995 the ocean-going fleet consisted of 1,826 vessels totalling 34·27m. DWT, representing 5·18% of the world's total fleet tonnage. 308 vessels (35·22% of tonnage) were registered under foreign flags. Total tonnage registered, 15·83m. GRT, including oil-tankers, 2·28m. GRT, and container ships, 1·35m. GRT.

Cargo handled by the major ports in 1996 (in tonnes): Shanghai, 164m.; Qinhuangdao, 83m.; Ningbo, 76m.; Guangzhou (Canton), 75m.; Dalian, 64m.; Tianjin, 62m.; Qingdao, 60m. In 1993, 125·08m. tonnes of freight were carried.

Inland waterways totalled 110,593 km in 1994. 1,070·91m. tonnes of freight and 261·65m. passengers were carried.

Telecommunications. In 1997 there were 70,310,000 telephone main lines (55·8 per 1,000 persons), and in 1995, 270,000 fax machines. At the end of 1996 there were 6·85m. mobile telephone subscribers (3·62m. at end of 1995). There were approximately 1·5m. Internet users in Dec. 1998, of whom 92·8% were male and 83·2% under 35 years of age. At the beginning of the year there had only been around 500,000 users. In 1996 there were 2·6m. PCs in use (2·1 per 1,000 inhabitants).

Postal Services. There were 72,496 post offices in 1996. The use of *Pinyin* transcription of place names has been requested for mail to addresses in China (*e.g.*, 'Beijing' *not* 'Peking').

SOCIAL INSTITUTIONS

Justice. Six new codes of law (including criminal and electoral) came into force in 1980, to regularize the legal unorthodoxy of previous years. There is no provision for *habeas corpus.* The death penalty has been extended from treason and murder to include rape, embezzlement, smuggling, drug-dealing, bribery and robbery with violence. There were 4,376 reported executions in 1996. 'People's courts' are divided into some 30 higher, 200 intermediate and 2,000 basic-level courts, and headed by the Supreme People's Court. The latter tries cases, hears appeals and supervises the people's courts.

People's courts are composed of a president, vice-presidents, judges and 'people's assessors' who are the equivalent of jurors. 'People's conciliation committees' are charged with settling minor disputes.

There are also special military courts.

Procuratorial powers and functions are exercised by the Supreme People's Procuracy and local procuracies.

Religion. The government accords legality to 5 religions only: Buddhism, Islam, Protestantism, Roman Catholicism and Taoism. Confucianism, Buddhism and Taoism have long been practised. Confucianism has no ecclesiastical organization and appears rather as a philosophy of ethics and government. Taoism—of Chinese origin—copied Buddhist ceremonial soon after the arrival of Buddhism two millennia ago. Buddhism in return adopted many Taoist beliefs and practices. A more tolerant attitude towards religion had emerged by 1979, and the Government's Bureau of Religious Affairs was reactivated.

Ceremonies of reverence to ancestors have been observed by the whole population regardless of philosophical or religious beliefs.

CHINA

Moslems are found in every province of China, being most numerous in the Ningxia–Hui Autonomous Region, Yunnan, Shaanxi, Gansu, Hebei, Honan, Shandong, Sichuan, Xinjiang and Shanxi. They totalled 18m. in 1997.

Roman Catholicism has had a footing in China for more than 3 centuries. In 1992 there were about 3·5m. Catholics who are members of the Patriotic Catholic Association, which declared its independence from Rome in 1958. In 1979 there were about 1,000 priests. In 1977 there were 78 bishops and 4 apostolic administrators, not all of whom were permitted to undertake religious activity. This figure included 46 'democratically elected' bishops not recognized by the Vatican. A bishop of Beijing was consecrated in 1979 without the consent of the Vatican and 2 auxiliary bishops of Shanghai in 1984. Archbishop Gong Pinmei, arrested in 1955, was freed in 1988. Protestants are members of the All-China Conference of Protestant Churches. 2 Protestant bishops were installed in 1988, the first for 30 years. In 1997 there were an estimated 73,000,000 Christians in total.

In 1997 there were also estimated to be 247,000,000 Chinese folk-religionists, 147,000,000 atheists, 104,000,000 Buddhists, 1,000,000 advocates of traditional beliefs and 637,000,000 non-religious persons.

Legislation of 1994 prohibits foreign nationals from setting up religious organizations.

Education. In 1996, 82·18% of the adult population were literate (89·88% of men and 74·46% of women). In 1994, 98·4% of school-age children attended school. In 1993 maximum school fees were 10 yuan a term, to which other charges might be added. In 1996 there were 187,324 kindergartens with 26·66m. children and 889,000 teachers. An educational reform of 1985 planned to phase in compulsory 9-year education consisting of 6 years of primary schooling and 3 years of secondary schooling, to replace a previous 5-year system. In 1996 there were 645,983 primary schools with 5,736,000 teachers and 136·15m. pupils; 79,967 secondary schools, with 3,465,000 teachers and 57·39m. pupils; and 10,049 vocational schools with 308,000 teachers and 4·73m. students. There were 1,032 institutes of higher education, including universities, with 403,000 teachers and 3·02m. students. One-third of all higher education students study engineering.

There is an Academy of Sciences with provincial branches. An Academy of Social Sciences was established in 1977.

In 1995–96 in the private sector there were 3 general universities and 9 specialized universities (aeronautics and astronautics; agricultural engineering; agriculture; chemical technology; foreign studies; labour; medicine; traditional Chinese medicine; polytechnic). In the public sector there were 60 general universities, 2 for ethnic minorities and the following specialized universities: Agriculture, 12; agriculture and land reclamation, 1; land reclamation, 1; architecture, 2; architecture and technology, 1; chemical technology, 1; coal and chemical technology, 1; electronic science and technology, 1; engineering, 1; fisheries, 1; foreign languages, 1; forestry, 1; hydraulic and electrical engineering, 1; international business and economics, 1; international studies, 1; iron and steel technology, 1; maritime studies, 1; medicine, 11; traditional Chinese medicine, 2; mining and technology, 1; petroleum, 1; pharmacology, 1; political science and law, 1; polytechnic, 8; radio and television, 1; science and technology, 5; surveying and mapping, 1; teaching, 4; technology, 6; textiles, 1.

In 1996 there were also 893 teacher training schools. In 1994, 19,000 students were studying abroad. Fees were introduced for university students in 1996–97.

In 1996 total expenditure on education came to 155,611m. yuan (2·3% of GNP), around 11·9% of total government expenditure.

Health. Medical treatment is free only for certain groups of employees, but where costs are incurred they are partly borne by the patient's employing organization. In 1996 there were 1·94m. doctors, of whom 0·35m. practised Chinese medicine, and 1·16m. nurses. About 10% of doctors are in private practice.

In 1996 there were 67,964 hospitals (with 2·87m. beds), 528 sanatoria (with 109,000 beds) and 103,472 clinics. There were 24 beds per 10,000 population in 1996.

Welfare. In 1996 there were 42,821 social welfare institutions with 769,348 inmates. Numbers (in 1,000) of beneficiaries of relief funds: Persons in poor rural households, 30,790; in poor urban households, 2,610; persons in rural households entitled to 'the 5 guarantees' (food, clothing, medical care, housing, education for children or funeral expenses), 2,675; retired, laid-off or disabled workers, 535. The major relief funds (in 1,000 yuan) in 1996 were: Families of deceased or disabled servicemen, 5,187,970; poor households, 712,270; orphaned, disabled, old and young persons, 1,856,680; welfare institutions, 1,551,000.

CULTURE

Broadcasting. In 1994 there were 1,107 radio and 766 TV stations. The Central People's Broadcasting Station provides 2 central programmes, regional services, special services, a Taiwan service and external services. China Central Television (colour by PAL) transmits 3 programmes from Beijing, a programme from Shanghai, and an English-language programme. There are 29 regional programmes transmitted from 361 local stations. By 1995 about 600 cable TV systems had been licensed. In 1995 there were 225·5m. radio receivers (only the USA has more) and 250m. TV receivers (the greatest number in any country in the world). In 1980 there had been just 9m., representing an increase of nearly 241m. between 1980 and 1995, or more TV sets than were in use in the USA (the country with the second highest number of sets) in 1995. In urban areas 96%, and in rural areas 48·5%, of households possessed a TV set in 1994. The use of satellite receiving dishes was prohibited in 1993.

Cinema. There were 4,639 cinemas in 1995. 148 feature films were made in 1994. In 1992 there were some 10,600m. cinema attendances.

Press. In 1994 there were 1,635 newspapers with a combined circulation of 125,200m. and 7,325 periodicals with 2,210m. The Party newspaper is *Renmin Ribao* (People's Daily), which had a daily circulation of 3m. in 1994. 103,836 book titles were produced in 6,007·75m. copies in 1994. There were 2,596 public libraries in 1993.

Tourism. 51,128,000 tourists visited in 1996, including 44,229,000 from Hong Kong, Taiwan and Macao, and 155,000 other overseas Chinese. The World Tourism Organization predicts that China will overtake France as the world's most visited destination by 2020 and become the world's 4th most important source of tourists to other countries. Income from tourists in 1996 was US$10,200m.

Libraries. In 1993 there were 2,579 public libraries and 5,000 higher education libraries with a combined 720,571,000 volumes and 11,401,724 registered users.

DIPLOMATIC REPRESENTATIVES

Of China in Great Britain (49-51 Portland Pl., London, W1N 4JL)
Ambassador: Ma Zhengang.

Of Great Britain in China (11 Guang Hua Lu, Jian Guo Men Wai, Beijing 100600)
Ambassador: A. C. Galsworthy, CMG.

Of China in the USA (2300 Connecticut Ave., NW, Washington, D.C., 20008)
Ambassador: Li Zhao Xing.

Of the USA in China (Xiu Shui Bei Jie 3, 100600 Beijing)
Ambassador: James Sasser.

Of China to the United Nations
Ambassador: Qin Huasun.

Of China to the European Union
Ambassador: Mingjiang Song.

FURTHER READING
State Statistical Bureau. *China Statistical Yearbook*
China Directory [in Pinyin and Chinese]. Tokyo, annual

CHINA

Baum, R., *Burying Mao: Chinese Politics in the Age of Deng Xiaoping*. Princeton Univ. Press, 1994

Boorman, H. L. and Howard, R. C. (eds.) *Biographical Dictionary of Republican China*. 5 vols. Columbia Univ. Press, 1967–79

Brugger, B. and Reglar, S., *Politics, Economics and Society in Contemporary China*. London, 1994

The Cambridge Encyclopaedia of China. 2nd ed. CUP, 1991

The Cambridge History of China. 14 vols. CUP, 1978 ff.

De Crespigny, R., *China This Century*. 2nd ed. OUP, 1993

Deng Xiaoping, *Speeches and Writings*. 2nd ed. Oxford, 1987

Dreyer, J. T., *China's Political System: Modernization and Tradition*. 2nd ed. London, 1996

Dietrich, C., *People's China: a Brief History*. OUP, 1986

Evans, R., *Deng Xiaoping and the Making of Modern China*. London, 1993

Fairbank, J. K., *The Great Chinese Revolution 1800–1985*. London, 1987.—*China: a New History*. Harvard Univ. Press, 1992

Fathers, M. and Higgins, A., *Tiananmen: the Rape of Peking*. London and New York, 1989

Glassman, R. M., *China in Transition: Communism, Capitalism and Democracy*. New York, 1991

Goldman, M., *Sowing the Seeds of Democracy in China: Political Reform in the Deng Xiaoping Era*. Harvard Univ. Press, 1994

Goodman, D., *Deng Xiaoping and the Chinese Revolution: a Political Biography*. 2nd ed. London, 1994.—and Segal, G., (eds.) *China in the 90s: Crisis Management and Beyond*. Oxford, 1991

Gray, J., *Rebellions and Revolutions: China from the 1800s to the 1980s*. CUP, 1990

Hayford, C. W., *China*. [Bibliography] 2nd ed. Oxford and Santa Barbara (CA), 1997

Hinton, H. C. (ed.) *The People's Republic of China 1949–1979*. 5 vols. Wilmington, 1980

Huang, R., *China: a macro History*. 2nd ed. Armonk (NY), 1997

Jenner, W. J. F., *The Tyranny of History: the Roots of China's Crisis*. London, 1992

Lichtenstein, P. M., *China at the Brink: the Political Economy of Reform and Retrenchment in the Post-Mao Era*. New York, 1991

Lieberthal, K. G., *From Revolution through Reform*. New York, 1995.—and Lampton, D. M. (eds.) *Bureaucracy, Politics and Decision-Making in Post-Mao China*. California Univ. Press, 1992

Lippit, V. D., *The Economic Development of China*. Armonk, 1987

Loewe, M., *The Pride that was China*. London, 1990

McCormick, B. L., *Political Reform in Post-Mao China: Democracy and Bureaucracy in a Leninist State*. California Univ. Press, 1990

MacFarquhar, R. (ed.) *The Politics of China: the eras of Mao and Deng*. 2nd ed. CUP, 1997.—*The Origins of the Cultural Revolution*. 3 vols. Columbia University Press, 1998

Mackerras, C. et al., *China since 1978: Reform, Modernization and Socialism with Chinese Characteristics*. New York, 1994.—and Yorke, A., *The Cambridge Handbook of Contemporary China*. CUP, 1991

Moise, E. E., *Modern China: A History*. London, 1986

Nathan, A. J., *Chinese Democracy*. London, 1986:—*China's Crisis: Dilemmas of Reform and Prospects for Democracy*. Columbia Univ. Press, 1990

Nolan, P., *State and Market in the Chinese Economy: Essays on Controversial Issues*. London, 1993

Phillips, R. T., *China since 1911*. London, 1996

Riskin, C., *China's Political Economy: The Quest for Development since 1949*. OUP, 1987

Rodzinski, W., *A History of China*. Oxford, 1981–84

Schram, S., (ed.) *Mao's Road to Power: Revolutionary Writings 1912–1949*. 4 vols. Harvard, 1998

Sheng Hua, et al., *China: from Revolution to Reform*. London, 1992

Shirk, S. L., *The Political Logic of Economic Reform in China*. Univ. of California Press, 1993

Spence, J. D., *The Chan's Great Continent: China in Western Minds*. Norton, New York, 1998

Spence, J. D., *The Search for Modern China*. London, 1990

White, G. (ed.) *The Chinese State in the Era of Economic Reform: the Road to Crisis*. London, 1991.—*Riding the Tiger: the Politics of Economic Reform in Post-Mao China*. London, 1993

Womack, B. (ed.) *Contemporary Chinese Politics in Historical Perspective*. CUP, 1992

Other more specialized titles are listed under TERRITORY AND POPULATION; TIBET; DEFENCE; AGRICULTURE; INTERNATIONAL TRADE.

National statistical office: State Statistical Bureau, 38 Yuetan Nanjie, Beijing.

HONG KONG

KEY HISTORICAL EVENTS

Hong Kong island and the southern tip of the Kowloon peninsula were ceded by China to Britain after the first and second Anglo-Chinese Wars by the Treaty of Nanking 1842 and the Convention of Peking 1860. The New Territories were leased to Britain for 99 years by China in 1898. Talks began in Sept. 1982 between Britain and China over the future of Hong Kong after the lease expiry in 1997. On 19 Dec. 1984, the two countries signed the Joint Declaration of the British and Chinese Governments on the Question of Hong Kong which entered into force on 27 May 1985. By the terms of this Hong Kong became, with effect from 1 July 1997, a Special Administrative Region of the People's Republic of China enjoying a high degree of autonomy, and vested with executive, legislative and independent judicial power, including that of final adjudication. It was agreed that the laws currently in force in Hong Kong would remain basically unchanged. The existing social and economic systems, and the present lifestyle, were to remain unchanged for another 50 years. This 'one country, two systems' principle, embodied in the Basic Law, which was enacted by the National People's Congress of the People's Republic of China in 1990, became the constitution for the Hong Kong Special Administrative Region.

TERRITORY AND POPULATION

Hong Kong island is situated off the southern coast of the Chinese mainland 32 km east of the mouth of the Pearl River. The area of the island is 79·99 sq. km. It is separated from the mainland by a fine natural harbour. On the opposite side is the peninsula of Kowloon (46·27 sq. km). Total area of the Territory is 1,091 sq. km, a large part of it being steep and unproductive hillside. Country parks and special areas cover over 40% of the land area. Since 1945, the Government has reclaimed over 5,400 ha from the sea, principally from the seafronts of Hong Kong and Kowloon, facing the harbour. The 'New Territories' are on the mainland, north of Kowloon.

The population was 5,674,100 at the 1991 census. Estimate (1998) 6,805,600. Some 43,100 persons emigrated in 1995. The British Nationality Scheme enables persons to acquire citizenship without leaving Hong Kong. There were 45,986 legal immigrants from China in 1995. 60% of the population was born in Hong Kong, 34% in China (1991 census). The population of Vietnamese migrants ('boat people') in Oct. 1996 was 12,710. All remaining 'boat people' were repatriated by Jan. 1997.

The official languages are Chinese and English.

SOCIAL STATISTICS

Annual growth rate, 1998, 2·8%. Vital statistics, 1998 (provisional): Known births, 53,100; known deaths, 32,200; registered marriages, 31,700. Rates (per 1,000): Birth, 7·9 death, 4·8; marriage, 4·7; infant mortality, 3·2 (per 1,000 live births). Life expectancy, 1998: Males, 76·9 years; females, 82·3. The most popular age for marrying was 30 for males and 27 for females. Fertility rate, 1990–95, 1·9 children per woman.

CLIMATE

The climate is sub-tropical, tending towards temperate for nearly half the year, the winter being cool and dry and the summer hot and humid, May to Sept. being the wettest months. Normal temperatures are Jan. 60°F (15·8°C), July 84°F (28·8°C). Annual rainfall 87" (2,214·3 mm).

THE BRITISH ADMINISTRATION

Hong Kong was administered by the Hong Kong Government. The Governor was the head of Government and presided over the *Executive Council*, which advised the Governor on all important matters. The last British Governor was Chris Patten. In Oct. 1996 the Executive Council consisted of 3 ex-officio members and 10 appointed members, of whom 1 was an official member. The chief functions of the *Legislative Council* were to enact laws, control public expenditure and put questions to the administration on matters of public interest. The Legislative Council elected in Sept. 1995 was, for the first time, constituted solely by election. It comprised 60 members, of whom 20 were elected from geographical constituencies, 30 from functional constituencies encompassing all eligible persons in a workforce of 2·9m., and 10 from an election committee formed by members of 18 district boards. A president was elected from and by the members.

At the elections on 17 Sept. 1995 turn-out for the geographical seats was 35·79%, and for the functional seats (21 of which were contested), 40·42%. The Democratic Party and its allies gained 29 seats, the Liberal Party 10 and the pro-Beijing Democratic Alliance, 6. The remaining seats went to independents.

CONSTITUTION AND GOVERNMENT
In Dec. 1995 the Standing Committee of China's National People's Congress set up a Preparatory Committee of 150 members (including 94 from Hong Kong) to oversee the retrocession of Hong Kong to China on 1 July 1997. In Nov. 1996 the Preparatory Committee nominated a 400-member Selection Committee to select the Chief Executive of Hong Kong and a provisional legislature to replace the Legislative Council. The Selection Committee was composed of Hong Kong residents, with 60 seats reserved for delegates to the National People's Congress and appointees of the People's Political Consultative Conference. On 11 Dec. 1996 Tung Chee-hwa was elected Chief Executive by 80% of the Selection Committee's votes.

On 21 Dec. 1996 the Selection Committee selected a provisional legislature which began its activities in Jan. 1997 while the Legislative Council was still functioning. In Jan. 1997 the provisional legislature began repealing some civil rights legislation.

Theoretically Hong Kong is a Special Administrative Region of the People's Republic of China. It is supposed to retain a high degree of autonomy, and the legislative, judicial and administrative systems which were previously in operation are to remain in place. The Special Administrative Region Government is also empowered to decide on Hong Kong's monetary and economic policies independent of China.

In July 1997 the first-past-the-post system of electing the Legislative Council was replaced by proportional representation.

RECENT ELECTIONS
In the Legislative Council election held on 25 May 1998 pro-democracy candidates won 63% of the popular vote, compared to 51% in the 1995 election. However, under an electoral system which allows only a third of the seats to be chosen by the entire electorate, the pro-democracy members remained a minority political force. Of the 20 seats elected by universal suffrage, 9 went to the Democratic Party, 3 to Frontier and 1 to Citizens (all pro-democracy), 5 to the Democratic Alliance for the Betterment of HK and 2 to independents. The other 40 seats were elected by committees and professional associations. The make-up of the Legislative Council following the elections was: Democratic Party, 13; DAB (pro-China, populist), 9; Liberals (pro-business), 9; HK Progressive Alliance (pro-China), 5; Frontier, 3; Citizens, 1; Non-affiliates, 20.

CURRENT ADMINISTRATION
Chief Executive: Tung Chee-hwa (b. 1937; elected 11 Dec. 1996).
  Chief Secretary: Anson Chan, CBE, JP.
  Financial Secretary: Donald Tsang, OBE, JP.
  The Chief Executive is aided by the Executive Council consisting of the Chief Secretary, the Financial Secretary and 12 other members.

Local Government. There are 2 municipal councils, the Urban Council and the Regional Council. With all appointed seats abolished in 1995, 59 of 80 seats were open to direct election in the March 1995 elections. Turn-out was 25·8%. Elections to the 18 Consultative District Boards set up in 1982 were held in Sept. 1994; turn-out was 33·1%.

At local council elections on 18 Sept. 1994 for 346 council seats, turn-out was 33·1%. The United Democratic Party gained 77 seats; the Alliance for Democracy, 28; the Democratic Alliance for a Better Hong Kong (pro-Beijing), 37; the Liberal

HONG KONG

Party, 30; the United Democrats of Hong Kong won 11 out of 27 seats; independents 11; the Liberal Democratic Federation 3; and Communists 2.

ECONOMY

Performance. Hong Kong was second behind Singapore in the World Economic Forum's Global Competitiveness Reports, which assesses countries on their potential for economic growth and their income levels, in both 1997 and 1998. Following real GDP growth of 5·7% in 1997, the economy was expected to contract by around 4% in 1998, representing Hong Kong's most severe recession since the 1970s.

Budget. The total Government revenue and expenditure for financial years ending 31 March were as follows (in HK$1m.):

	1996	1997	1998
Revenue	180,045	208,400	275,200
Expenditure	191,338	173,600	194,200

Public expenditure, 1998, was divided as follows (HK$1bn.): Education, 47·0; support, 30·2; health, 28·0; housing, 24·7; security, 23·8; social welfare, 21·7; infrastructure, 21·5; economic, 17·8; community and external affairs, 13·1; environment, 7·0.

Currency. The unit of currency is the *Hong Kong dollar* (HKD) of 100 *cents*. Banknotes are issued by the Hongkong and Shanghai Banking Corporation and the Standard Chartered Bank, and, from May 1994, the Bank of China. Total money supply was HK$174m. in Jan. 1998. Fiscal reserves at 31 March 1997 stood at HK$163,000m. In Feb. 1998 gold reserves were 70,000 troy oz. and foreign exchange reserves US$78,617m.

Banking and Finance. As at Dec. 1995 there were 185 banks licensed under the Banking Ordinance, of which 31 were locally incorporated, 63 restricted licence banks and 154 representative offices of foreign banks. Licensed bank deposits were HK$2,601,971m. in June 1997; restricted licence bank deposits were HK$62,033m. There were 132 deposit-taking companies registered under the Banking Ordinance with total deposits of HK$18,419m. as at Nov. 1995.

There is a stock exchange. The summer of 1997 saw record highs on the Hang Seng index (16,365 in July 1997 compared with 10,681 in July 1996). In July 1997 the average daily turnover was HK$19,500m.

Weights and Measures. Metric, British Imperial, Chinese and US units are all in current use in Hong Kong. However, Government departments have now effectively adopted metric units; all new legislation uses metric terminology and existing legislation is being progressively metricated. Metrication is also proceeding in the private sector.

ENERGY AND NATURAL RESOURCES

Electricity. Installed capacity was 10·32m. kW in 1994. Production in 1994 was 25·14bn. kWh. Consumption in 1998 was 35·4bn. kWh.

Water. Reservoirs are needed to store the summer rainfall in order to meet supply requirements. There are 17 impounding reservoirs with a total capacity of 586m. cu. metres. Water is also purchased (720m. cu. metres in 1996). Consumption in 1996 was 928m cu. metres.

Agriculture. Agriculture supplies about a quarter of domestic demand. Only 3·4% of the total land area is suitable for crop farming and most produce derives from intensive market gardening: 1,350 ha were under cultivation in 1995. In 1995, 88,000 tonnes of vegetables and 4,820 tonnes of fruit and nuts were produced. Poultry production was 24,921 tonnes; milk, 407 tonnes; eggs, 1,112 tonnes. There were 109,000 pigs in 1996.

Forestry. Timber production in 1995 was 200,000 cu. metres.

Fisheries. The fishing fleet of 4,800 vessels supplies about 62% of fresh marine fish consumed locally. In 1995 the marine fish catch was 203,300 tonnes. Inland freshwater farming and coastal marine farming provided 8,200 tonnes of fish.

457

INDUSTRY

An economic policy based on free enterprise and free trade, a skilled workforce, an efficient commercial infrastructure, the modern and efficient sea-port (including container shipping terminals) and airport facilities; a geographical position relative to markets in North America and traditional trading links with the UK all contributed to Hong Kong's success as a modern industrial territory. Links with China have been growing increasingly strong in recent years and will remain so.

In 1995 there were 31,114 manufacturing firms employing 386,106 persons. Firms by product type (and persons employed): Textiles and clothing, 7,046 (139,931); plastics, 2,250 (15,997); electronics, 1,109 (44,078); watches and clocks, 1,006 (12,119); electrical appliances, 136 (2,589); shipbuilding, 374 (4,510).

Labour. In 1998 the labour force (economically active population aged 15 and over) totalled 3,434,000 (1,356,000 female). The employed population in 1996 included 1,047,000 people in wholesale, retail, restaurants and hotels, 391,000 in finance, insurance, business and real estate, 327,000 in manufacturing, 184,000 in the civil service and 77,000 manual labourers. In 1990, 3,495,000 working days were lost due to strikes and lockouts. Unemployment in June 1998 was running at a 15-year high of 4·5%.

EXTERNAL ECONOMIC RELATIONS

Imports and Exports. Industry is mainly export-oriented. In 1998, the total value of imports (c.i.f.) was HK$1,429·1bn. and exports (f.o.b.) HK$1,347·6bn. The major markets for domestic exports (in HK$1m.), 1996, were: People's Republic of China, 61,600; USA, 53,900; Germany, 11,400; and Japan, 11,300. Totals for the Asia-Pacific Economic Co-operation Group and the EU as a whole (in HK$1m.) were 162,200 and 37,000 respectively. The leading sources of imports (in HK$1m.) in 1996 were: People's Republic of China, 570,400; Japan, 208,220; Taiwan, 123,200; and USA, 121,100. Totals for the Asia-Pacific Economic Co-operation Group and the EU as a whole (in HK$1m.) were 1,287,000 and 170,600 respectively.

In 1996 domestic exports included (in HK$1m.): Clothing and accessories, 69,400; electrical machinery and parts, 30,400; textiles and fabrics, 13,700; watches and clocks, 12,000. The chief import items were consumer goods (573,000), raw materials (540,900), capital goods (324,000) and foodstuffs (65,200).

Visible trade normally carries an adverse balance which is offset by a favourable balance of invisible trade, in particular transactions in connection with air transportation, shipping, tourism and banking services.

Hong Kong has a free exchange market. Foreign merchants may remit profits or repatriate capital. Import and export controls are kept to the minimum, consistent with strategic requirements.

COMMUNICATIONS

Roads. In 1998 there were 1,865 km of roads, more than 900 km of which were in the New Territories. There are 8 major road tunnels, including 2 under Victoria Harbour. In 1998 there were 501,000 licensed motor vehicles, including 318,000 private cars, 115,000 goods vehicles and 23,000 motor cycles. There were 14,790 road accidents in 1995, 259 fatal. A total of 14·8m. tonnes of cargo were transported by road in 1996.

Rail. There is an electric tramway with a total track length of 33 km, and a cable tramway connecting the Peak district with the lower levels in Victoria. The electrified Kowloon-Canton Railway runs for 34 km from the terminus at Hung Hom in Kowloon to the border point at Lo Wu. It carried 232m. passengers in 1995. In 1996, 939,000 tonnes of cargo were transported by rail. A light rail system (32 km) is operated by the Kowloon-Canton Railway Corporation in Tuen Mun, Yuen Long and Tin Shui Wai; it carried 123m. passengers in 1995.

A metro, the Mass Transit Railway system, comprises 43·2 km with 38 stations. It carried 812m. passengers in 1995.

In 1996 a total of 3·9m. passenger journeys were made on public transport (including local railways, buses etc.).

Civil Aviation. The new Chek Lap Kok airport, built on reclaimed land off Lantau Island to the west of Hong Kong, opened in July 1998, replacing Hong Kong International Airport (Kai Tak), which was situated on the north shore of Kowloon Bay. After initial problems following its inauguration, 61 airlines now operate services. British Airways operates 14 flights per week to the UK. Cathay Pacific Airways, one of the 3 Hong Kong-based airlines, operates more than 365 passenger and cargo services weekly to Europe (including 16 passenger and 5 cargo services per week to the UK), the Far and Middle East, South Africa, Australasia and North America. Hong Kong Dragon Airlines Ltd operates scheduled and non-scheduled services to a number of cities in Asia and the People's Republic of China. Air Hong Kong, an all-cargo operator, provides a scheduled service 5 times a week to Manchester, UK, and operates non-scheduled services around the region. In 1995-96, 150,118 aircraft arrived and departed. In 1996, 23·48m. passengers and 1·56m. tonnes of freight were carried on aircraft. Hong Kong International Airport handled more international freight in 1996 than any other airport.

Shipping. The port of Hong Kong handled 12·6m. 20-ft equivalent units in 1995. The Kwai Chung Container Port has 31 berths with 6,059 metres of quay backed by 228 ha of cargo handling area. Merchant shipping in 1995 totalled 8,795,000 GRT. In 1995, more than 41,000 ocean-going vessels, 108,000 river trading vessels and 64,000 international passenger vessels called at Hong Kong. In 1996, 125·4m. tonnes of freight were handled.

Telecommunications. In 1998 there were 3,708,000 telephones (554 per 1,000 population), of which 1,549,000 were for business use and 2,159,000 were residential lines. There were also over 284,000 fax lines. Basic local telephone services are provided by Hong Kong Telecom, which also offers fax services and value-added telephone services. The company also provides international voice, data and video transmission services, telex and telegram services, international private leased circuits, and shore-to-ship and ground-to-air communications. International facilities are provided through submarine cables, microwave and satellite radio systems. There were approximately 850,000 Internet users in April 1998. There were 798,000 cellular phone subscribers (129 per 1,000 persons) in 1995 and 720,000 PCs (116 per 1,000 persons).

Postal Services. There were 126 post offices in March 1996. In 1998 the postal services handled 1,264m. letters and 1,112,000 parcels.

SOCIAL INSTITUTIONS

Justice. The common law of England and the rules of equity were in force so far as they are applicable to the circumstances of Hong Kong. UK Acts of Parliament, however, were only binding if expressly applied to Hong Kong. By 1997 Hong Kong possessed a comprehensive body of law which owed its authority to its own legislature. The Hong Kong Act of 1985 provided for Hong Kong ordinances to replace English laws in specified fields.

The courts of justice comprise the Supreme Court (which includes the Court of Appeal and the High Court), the District Court (which includes the Family Court), the Magistracies, the Coroner's Court, the Juvenile Court and 4 tribunals. The Court of Appeal hears appeals on all matters, civil and criminal, from the lower courts. Pursuant to the Joint Declaration, the powers of final judgement were to be vested in the Court of Final Appeal, inaugurated in the territory in June 1997 to take over the functions of the UK Privy Council. While the High Court has unlimited jurisdiction in both civil and criminal matters, the District Court has limited jurisdiction. The maximum term of imprisonment it may impose is 7 years. Magistracies exercise criminal jurisdiction over a wide range of indictable and summary offences, and the powers of punishment are generally restricted to a maximum of 2 years' imprisonment. The Lands Tribunal determines on statutory claims for compensation over land and certain landlord and tenant matters. The Labour Tribunal provides a quick and inexpensive method of settling disputes between employers and employees. The Small Claims Tribunal deals with monetary claims involving amounts not exceeding HK$15,000.

After being in abeyance for 25 years, the death penalty was abolished in 1992.

71,962 crimes were reported in 1998, of which 14,682 were violent crimes. 40,422 people were arrested in 1998, of whom 9,207 were for violent crimes. The prison population was 13,117 in 1995.

Religion. In 1997 there were 4,790,000 Buddhists and Taoists, 280,000 Protestants, 270,000 Roman Catholics and 1,150,000 people of other beliefs.

Education. Adult literacy was 92·2% in 1995 (96% among males and 88·2% among females). Free and compulsory education is available to all children aged from 6 to 15 years. In 1995–96 there were 180,317 pupils in 731 kindergartens (all private), 467,718 in 860 primary schools (some 10·1% in private schools) and 459,845 in 38 government, 337 aided and 91 private secondary schools.

There are 7 technical institutes with (in 1995–96) 13,972 full-time and 34,409 part-time students; 2 technical colleges with 9,300 students, and 5 teacher training colleges of education with 2,863 full-time students.

The University of Hong Kong (founded 1911) had 10,325 full-time and 2,618 part-time students in the academic year of 1995–96, the Chinese University of Hong Kong (founded 1963), 10,388 full-time and 2,536 part-time students, the Hong Kong University of Science and Technology (founded 1991), 5,792 full-time and 503 part-time students, the Hong Kong Polytechnic University (founded 1972 as the Hong Kong Polytechnic), 11,157 full-time and 9,289 part-time students, the City University of Hong Kong (founded 1984 as the City Polytechnic of Hong Kong), 10,061 full-time and 6,881 part-time students, the Hong Kong Baptist University (founded 1956 as the Hong Kong Baptist College), 4,146 full-time and 600 part-time students and the Lingnan College (founded 1967), 2,059 full-time and 2 part-time students.

Total government expenditure on education in 1995 was HK$31,398m.

Health. In 1996 there were 9,196 doctors, 1,654 dentists, 36,395 nurses, 1,067 pharmacists and 20 midwives; in 1995 there were 88 hospitals and 29,328 hospital beds.

Welfare. The Government co-ordinates and implements expanding programmes in social welfare, which include social security, family services, child care, services for the elderly, youth and community work, probation and corrections and rehabilitation. 170 non-governmental organizations are subsidized by public funds.

The Government gives non-contributory cash assistance to needy families, unemployed able-bodied adults, the severely disabled and the elderly. Caseload as at 31 Dec. 1995 totalled 623,029. Victims of natural disasters, crimes of violence and traffic accidents are financially assisted.

CULTURE

Broadcasting. Broadcasting is regulated by the Broadcasting Authority, a statutory body comprising 3 government officers and 9 non-official members. There is a government broadcasting station, Radio Television Hong Kong, which broadcasts on 7 channels (4 Chinese, 1 English and 1 bi-lingual service, and 1 dedicated to BBC World Service), 6 of which provide a 24-hour service. Hong Kong Commercial Broadcasting Co. Ltd and Metro Broadcast Co. Ltd transmit commercial sound programmes on 6 channels. Television Broadcasts Ltd and Asia Television Ltd transmit commercial television in English and Chinese on 4 channels, in colour (by PAL). Hutchvision Hong Kong broadcasts by satellite to the entire Asian region on 14 TV and 2 radio channels and also carries the BBC World Service. There is also a cable TV network. In 1994 there were some 3·9m. radio receivers; in 1995 there were over 2·3m. TV receivers.

Cinema. In 1995 there were 184 cinemas; attendance was 27·4m. (57m. in 1990). 315 films were made in 1995.

Press. In 1996 there were 52 daily newspapers, and in 1995, 675 periodicals. Circulation of dailies in 1996 was 5,000,000. At 800 newspapers per 1,000 inhabitants, Hong Kong has one of the highest rates of circulation in the world. A number of news agency bulletins are registered as newspapers.

Tourism. There were about 11·7m. visitor arrivals in 1996 (2,380,000 from Japan, 751,000 from the USA). Receipts totalled US$10·84bn.

Libraries. In 1995 there were 2 public libraries and in 1990 there were 17 higher education libraries. These libraries held 8,336,000 volumes for 2,119,383 registered users.

FURTHER READING

Statistical Information: The Census and Statistics Department is responsible for the preparation and collation of Government statistics. These statistics are published mainly in the *Hong Kong Monthly Digest of Statistics.* The Department also publishes monthly trade statistics, economic indicators and an annual review of overseas trade, etc. *Website:* http://www.info.gov.hk/censtatd/

Hong Kong [various years] Hong Kong Government Press
Bonavia, D., *Hong Kong 1997.* London, 1984
Brown, J. M. (ed.) *Hong Kong's Transitions, 1842–1997.* London, 1997
Buckley, R., *Hong Kong: the Road to 1997.* CUP, 1997
Cameron, N., *An Illustrated History of Hong Kong.* OUP, 1991
Chill, H., et al (eds.) *The Future of Hong Kong: Toward 1997 and Beyond.* Westport, 1987
Cottrell, R., *The End of Hong Kong: the Secret Diplomacy of Imperial Retreat.* London, 1993
Courtauld, C. and Holdsworth, M., *The Hong Kong Story.* OUP, 1997
Endacott, G. B., *A History of Hong Kong.* 2nd ed. OUP, 1973.—*Government and People in Hong Kong, 1841–1962: a Constitutional History.* OUP, 1965
Flowerdew, J., *The Final Years of British Hong Kong: the Discourse of Colonial Withdrawal.* Hong Kong, 1997
Keay, J., *Last Post: the End of Empire in the Far East.* London, 1997
Lo, C. P., *Hong Kong.* London, 1992
Lo, S.-H., *The Politics of Democratization in Hong Kong.* London, 1997
Morris, J., *Hong Kong: Epilogue to an Empire.* 2nd ed. [of *Hong Kong: Xianggang*]. London, 1993
Patrikeeff, F., *Mouldering Pearl: Hong Kong at the Crossroads.* London, 1989
Roberti, M., *The Fall of Hong Kong: China's Triumph and Britain's Betrayal.* 2nd ed. Chichester, 1997
Roberts, E. V. et al. *Historical Dictionary of Hong Kong and Macau.* Metuchen (NJ), 1993
Scott, I., *Hong Kong:* [Bibliography]. Oxford and Santa Barbara (CA), 1990
Segal, G., *The Fate of Hong Kong.* London, 1993
Shipp, S., *Hong Kong, China: a Political History of the British Crown Colony's Transfer to Chinese Rule.* Jefferson (NC), 1995
Tsang, S. Y., *Hong Kong: an Appointment with China.* London, 1997
Wang, G. and Wong, S. L. (eds.) *Hong Kong's Transition: a Decade after the Deal.* OUP, 1996
Welsh, F., *A History of Hong Kong.* 3rd ed. London, 1997
Wilson, D., *Hong Kong, Hong Kong.* London, 1991
Yahuda, M., *Hong Kong: China's Challenge.* London, 1996

MACAO

KEY HISTORICAL EVENTS

Macao was visited by Portuguese traders from 1513 and became a Portuguese colony in 1557. It was soon a principal entrepôt for international trade with China and Japan. Initially sovereignty remained vested in China, with the Portuguese paying an annual rent. In 1848-49 the Portuguese declared Macao a free port and established jurisdiction over the territory. A Sino-Portuguese treaty of 1 Dec. 1887 confirmed Portuguese rights to the territory. Diversion of its trade to Hong Kong, and the opening of the treaty ports by China, left Macao handling only local distributive trade, although its entrepôt role was briefly revived during the closure of the Hong Kong/China border in 1939. It was an Overseas Province of Portugal from 1951-74. In 1976 it became a Territory under Portuguese administration. On 6 Jan 1987 Portugal agreed to return Macao to China on 20 Dec. 1999 under a plan in which it would become a special administrative zone of China, with considerable autonomy.

TERRITORY AND POPULATION

The territory, which lies at the mouth of the Pearl River, comprises a peninsula (7·84 sq. km) connected by a narrow isthmus to the People's Republic of China, on which is built the city of Santa Nome de Deus de Macao, and the islands of Taipa (5·79 sq. km), linked to Macao by a 2-km bridge, and Colôane (7·82 sq. km) linked to Taipa by a 2-km causeway. The total area of Macao is 21·45 sq. km. Land is being reclaimed from the sea. The population (1991 census) was 339,464 (174,858 females). Population on 31 Dec. 1997, 415,850 (215,700 females); density, 19,387 people per sq. km. An estimated 98·8% of the population lived in urban areas in 1995. The official language is Portuguese, but Cantonese is used by virtually the entire population.

In Dec. 1993, 19,305 foreigners were legally registered including 12,731 from Hong Kong.

SOCIAL STATISTICS
1997: Births, 5,468 (13·2 per 1,000 population); marriages, 2,106 (5·1); deaths, 1,413 (3·4); divorces, 320 (0·8). Annual growth rate, 1990–95, 4·4%. Infant mortality, 1990–95, 9 per 1,000 live births; fertility rate, 1·6 births per woman.

CLIMATE
Sub-tropical tending towards temperate. The number of rainy days is more than a third of the year. Average annual rainfall varies from 39-79" (1,000-2,000 mm). It is very humid from May to September.

CONSTITUTION AND GOVERNMENT
By agreement with Beijing in 1974, Macao is a Chinese territory under Portuguese administration. An 'organic statute' was published on 17 Feb. 1976. It defined the territory as a collective entity, *pessoa colectiva,* with internal legislative authority which, while remaining subject to Portuguese constitutional laws, would otherwise enjoy administrative, economic and financial autonomy. The Governor is appointed by the Portuguese President, who also appoints up to 7 Under-Secretaries on the Governor's nomination. The Legislative Assembly of 23 deputies, chosen for a 3-year term, comprises 8 members directly elected by universal suffrage, 8 indirectly elected by economic, cultural and social bodies and 7 appointed by the Governor. In April 1990 the Portuguese parliament unanimously approved laws passed by the Legislative Assembly to widen its powers and those of the governor.

RECENT ELECTIONS
At the elections held on 22 Sept. 1996 there were 62 candidates. The business-orientated pro-integration Associação Promotora para a Economia de Macau (Promoting Association for the Economy of Macao) won 2 seats, with 16·6% of the vote, and the pro-Beijing União Promotora para a Progreso (Promoting Union for Progress) also won 2 seats, with 15·2% of the vote. 4 other parties each gained 1 seat. The next elections are due by Sept. 2000.

CURRENT ADMINISTRATION
Governor: Gen. Vasco Rocha Vieira.

ECONOMY
Performance. Real GDP growth was an estimated 3·85% in 1995 and 3·6% in 1996.

Budget. In 1995, revenue was 11,033·8m. patacas and expenditure 10,314·9m. patacas. Provisional figures for 1996 are revenue, 8,569·3m; expenditure, 8,545·1m.

Currency. The unit of currency is the *pataca* (MOP) of 100 *avos* which is tied to the Hong Kong dollar at parity. Inflation was 8·6% in 1995 and an estimated 6·5% in 1996.

Banking and Finance. The bank of issue is the Banco Nacional Ultramarino. The Monetary and Foreign Exchange Authority functions as a central bank (*Director,* António dos Santos Ramos). Commercial business is handled (1993) by 20 banks with 112 branches in Macao, 6 of which are local and 14 foreign (including 4 offshore banking units). Total banks' deposits, 1993, 53,232·6m. patacas (including 4,679·7m. patacas in current and 15,198·3m. patacas in savings accounts).

ENERGY AND NATURAL RESOURCES

Electricity. Installed capacity was 260,000 kW in 1994. Production in 1994 was 1·2bn. kWh. In 1996 the electricity consumption per capita was 3,250 kWh. The net import was 174·0m. kWh.

Fisheries. The catch in 1995 was 1,604 tonnes.

INDUSTRY

The economy is based on gambling and tourism with a light industrial base of textiles and toy-making. In 1996 the number of firms was 1,265 (509 in textiles and clothing). In 1992, output was valued at 14,301,883 patacas. Number of firms (and value of output in 1m. patacas) per sector: textiles, 237 (2,924·40); clothing, 644 (7,316·18); food products, beverages and tobacco, 133 (214·58); paper, paper products, printing and publishing, 137 (306·91); wood and cork, 36 (20·26).

Labour. In 1995 a total of 180,000 people were in employment. In 1996 there was 66·7% employment of which 30·6% were employed in public, social and private services; 27·5%, restaurants and hotels; 20·6%, manufacturing; 7·5%, construction and public works; 6·6%, banks, insurance and services to companies and 7·2% in other employment. Unemployment stood at 4·3%.

INTERNATIONAL TRADE

Imports and Exports. The trade, mostly transit, is handled by Chinese merchants. Imports in 1997 were US$2,079m.; exports, US$2,145m., around 75% of which were textiles and garments.

In 1995, 29% of imports came from Hong Kong and 22% from China. 42% of exports went to USA, 32% to the EU (mainly Germany, France and UK); clothing accounted for 68·2% of exports, textiles for 10·5% and toys 3·6%.

In 1996 exports were valued at 15,898·5m. patacas of which the main products were: textiles and garments, toys, electronics, footwear, cement, travelling articles, ceramic articles and optical products. The main markets were the EU, USA, China, Japan, Hong Kong and Australia. The total imports were 15,930·7m. patacas of which the main products were: foodstuff, beverage and tobacco, other consumer goods, raw materials and semi-manfactured goods, capital goods, fuels and lubricants. The main origins were: EU, USA, China, Japan and Hong Kong.

COMMUNICATIONS

Roads. In 1994 there were 90 km of roads. There were 6,185 traffic accidents in 1993. In 1996 there were 45,206 registered vehicles of which 41,403 were light load and 3,803 heavy load. There were 5,787 vehicles registered during the year. There are 109 cars per 1,000 inhabitants.

Civil Aviation. An international airport opened in Dec. 1995. In 1998 Air Macau flew to Bangkok, Beijing, Chongqing, Fuzhou, Kaohsiung, Manila, Nanjing, Shanghai, Taipei, Wuhan, Xiamen and Zhengzhou. Services were also provided by Air Koryo, China Northern Airlines, China Northwest Airlines, China Southwest, China Yunnan Airlines, EVA Airways, Pacific Airlines, Shanghai Airlines, Singapore Airlines, TAP, Trans Asia Airways, Trans Pacific Air and Xiamen Airways.

Shipping. Macao is served by Portuguese, British and Dutch steamship lines. Regular services connect Macao with Hong Kong, 65 km to the north-east. In 1995 merchant shipping totalled 2,000 GRT.

Telecommunications. There were 206,154 telephones in 1996 and 188 telex instruments. In 1995 there were 37,000 cellular phone subscribers, 40,000 PCs and 7,300 fax machines

SOCIAL INSTITUTIONS

Justice. There is a judicial district court, a criminal court and an administrative court with 13 magistrates in all. Appeals lie to the Court of Appeal and then the Supreme Court, both in Lisbon.

CHINA

In 1996 (1995) there were 8,576 (7,181) cases of crimes known to the police, of which 5,460 (4,618) were against property. There were 625 persons in prison in 1996 (482 in 1995).

Religion. The majority of the Chinese population are Buddhists. About 6% are Roman Catholic.

Education. In 1992–93 there were 108 schools and colleges and 3,536 teachers. Numbers of schools and colleges by category: pre-primary, 16 (7 private); pre-primary and primary, 38 (36); private pre-primary, primary and secondary, 14; primary, 10 (3); primary and secondary, 10 (8); private primary and secondary technical, 2; secondary, 8 (6); secondary and teacher training, 1; secondary and tertiary, 1; private secondary and teacher training, 1; teacher training and tertiary, 1; nurses training, 2 (1); tertiary, 7 (1). There were 9 special schools with 72 teachers and 211 enrolments. The University of East Asia, established in 1981 on Taipa, had 1,647 students and 155 teachers in 1991–92.

	1994–95	1995–96		1994–95	1995–96
Total students	93,587	96,846	teacher training	318	338
pre-primary	20,476	19,770	nurses training	172	177
primary	45,153	46,703	Higher education	5,655	6,418
secondary	20,624	22,277	Special education	349	359
secondary technical	1,189	1,163	Adult education	38,456	38,506

Health. In 1993 there were 2 general hospitals (1 private) and 41 health centres (26 private) with 892 beds. In 1995 there were 467 doctors, 22 dentists, 861 nurses and 41 pharmacists. In 1996 there were 517 inhabitants per doctor and 428 per hospital bed.

CULTURE

Broadcasting. One government and a private commercial radio station are in operation on medium-waves broadcasting in Portuguese and Chinese. Number of receivers (1995), 145,000. Macao receives television broadcasts from Hong Kong and in 1984 a public bilingual TV station began operating. There were (1995) 45,000 receivers (colour by PAL).

Press. In 1993 there were 11 daily newspapers (4 in Portuguese and 7 in Chinese) and 16 periodicals (5 in Portuguese and 11 in Chinese).

Tourism. In 1995 there were 7·8m. visitors, but only 2·2m. spent one night or more. In 1996 there were 8·2m. visitors. Receipts totalled US$3·22bn.

FURTHER READING
Direcção de Serviços de Estatística e Censos. *Anuário Estatístico/Yearbook of Statistics Macau in Figures*. Macao, Annual.
Edmonds, R. L., *Macau*. [Bibliography] Oxford and Santa Barbara (CA), 1989
Porter, J., *Macau, the Imaginary City: Culture and Society, 1557 to the Present*. Oxford, 1996
Roberts, E. V., *Historical Dictionary of Hong Kong and Macau*. Metuchen (NJ), 1993

TAIWAN[1]

KEY HISTORICAL EVENTS

Taiwan, christened Ilha Formosa (beautiful island) by the Portuguese, was ceded to Japan by China by the Treaty of Shimonoseki in 1895. After the Second World War the island was surrendered to Gen. Chiang Kai-shek who made it the headquarters for his crumbling Nationalist Government. Chiang Kai-shek used the ideology of eventual Kuomintang victory as an excuse for authoritarian, military backed rule and the maintenance of a large standing army on the island. On Chiang Kai-shek's death in 1978 he was succeeded by his son, Chiang Ching-Kuo. Until 1970 the US fully supported Taiwan's claims to represent all of China. Only in 1971 did the government of the People's Republic of China manage to replace that of Chiang Kai-shek at the UN. In Jan. 1979 the UN established formal diplomatic relations with the People's Republic of China, breaking off all formal ties with Taiwan.

[1]See note on transcription of names in CHINA: Territory and Population.

Taiwanese fears that USA recognition of China spelt the end of the island's independence were not realized. The US Congress subsequently authorized continuing economic and social ties with Taiwan. Taiwan itself has continued to reject all attempts at reunification, and although there have been frequent threats from mainland China to precipitate direct action (including military manoeuvres off the Taiwanese coast) the prospect of confrontation with the USA supports the status quo.

TERRITORY AND POPULATION

Taiwan lies between the East and South China Seas about 100 miles from the coast of Fujian. The territories currently under the control of the Republic of China include Taiwan, Penghu (the Pescadores), Kinmen (Quemoy), and the Matsu Islands, as well as the archipelagos in the South China Sea. Off the Pacific coast of Taiwan are Green Island and Orchid Island. To the north-east of Taiwan are the Tiaoyutai Islets. The total area of Taiwan Island, the Penghu Archipelago and the Kinmen area (including the fortified offshore islands of Quemoy and Matsu) is 13,970 sq. miles (36,182 sq. km). Population (1997), 21,740,000. The indigenous Han Chinese are of Fujian origin. Of the population 15% is Hakka and 15% mainland Chinese who came with the Nationalist forces. There are also 389,900 aboriginals of Malay origin. Population density: 601 per sq. km.

Taiwan's administrative units comprise (with 1997 populations): 2 special municipalities: Taipei, the capital (2·60m.) and Kaohsiung (1·44m.); 5 cities outside the county structure: Chiayi (262,822), Hsinchu (351,800), Keelung (379,370), Taichung (901,961), Tainan (717,811); 16 counties (*hsien*): Changhwa (1,277,744), Chiayi (567,695), Hsinchu (421,721), Hualien (358,007), Ilan (466,603), Kaohsiung (1,227,160), Miaoli (560,344), Nantou (546,707), Penghu (91,169), Pingtung (913,764), Taichung (1,447,761), Tainan (1,096,251), Taipei (3,420,535), Taitung (253,002), Taoyuan (1,614,471), Yunlin (757,913).

SOCIAL STATISTICS

In 1997 the birth rate was 1·01%; death rate, 1·22%; rate of growth, 0·8% per annum (2000 target: 0·72% per annum). Life expectancy, 1996: Males, 71·89 years; females, 77·77 years. The death rate was 5·71 per 1,000 persons; infant mortality per 1,000 live births, 6·66.

CLIMATE

The climate is subtropical in the north and tropical in the south. The typhoon season extends from July to Sept. The average monthly temperatures of Jan. and July in Taipei are 59·5°F (12·9°C) and 83·3°F (33·8°C) respectively, and average annual rainfall is 83·8" (2,080·4 mm). Kaohsiung's average monthly temperatures of Jan. and July are 65·5°F (15°C) and 83·3°F (31·8°C) respectively, and average annual rainfall is 69" (1,732 mm).

CONSTITUTION AND GOVERNMENT

The ROC Constitution is based on the Principles of Nationalism, Democracy and Social Wellbeing formulated by Dr. Sun Yat-sen, the founding father of the Republic of China. The ROC government is divided into 3 main levels: central, provincial/municipal and county/city each of which has well-defined powers.

The central government consists of the Office of the President, the National Assembly, with 332 seats, and five governing branches called '*yuan*', namely the Executive Yuan, the Legislative Yuan (225 seats, increased from 160 for the 1998 elections), the Judicial Yuan, the Examination Yuan and the Control Yuan.

At the provincial level, the provincial governments exercise administrative responsibility. Since the ROC government administers only Taiwan Province and two counties in Fukien Province, only two provincial governments are currently operational—the Taiwan Provincial Government and the Fukien Provincial Government. Taipei and Kaohsiung are special municipalities which are under the direct jurisdiction of the central government. At the local level, under the Taiwan Provincial Government are five city governments: Keelung, Hsinchu, Taichung, Chiayi and Tainan; and 16 county governments with the governments of their subordinate cities. The Fukien Provincial Government oversees the regional affairs of Kinmen County and Lienchiang County. From 5 May to 23 July 1997 the

Additional Articles of the Constitution of the Republic of China underwent yet another amendment. The roles of the provincial government and the Control Yuan have taken on drastic changes. Under the newest revision:
• The provincial government is to be streamlined and the popular elections of the governor and members of the provincial council are suspended.
• A resolution on the impeachment of the President or Vice President is no longer to be instituted by the Control Yuan but rather by the Legislative Yuan.
• The Legislative Yuan has the power to pass a no-confidence vote against the president of the Executive Yuan, while the president of the Republic has the power to dissolve the Legislative Yuan.
• The president of the Executive Yuan is to be directly appointed by the president of the Republic. Hence the consent of the Legislative Yuan is no longer needed.
• Educational, scientific and cultural budgets, especially the compulsory education budget, will be given priority, but no longer restricted by Article 164 of the Constitution to remain at least 15% of the total national budget.

National Anthem. 'San Min Chu I'; words by Dr Sun Yat-sen, tune by Cheng Mao-yun.

RECENT ELECTIONS
Presidential elections are due in March 2000. Elections to the Legislative Yuan were held on 5 Dec. 1998. The Kuomintang (KMT or Nationalist Party) is in power. It increased its majority in the legislature, winning 124 of the 225 seats. Voter turn-out in the 2 biggest cities, Taipei and Kaohsiung, was over 80%. At the National assembly elections on 23 March 1996 the Kuomintang won 183 of the 332 seats, Min-chu Chin-pu Tang 99, Hsin-Tang 46, Green Party Taiwan 1, and non-partisans and others 3.

CURRENT ADMINISTRATION
President: Lee Teng-hui (b. 1923; sworn in 20 May 1996).
    Vice President: Lien Chan (b. 1936).
    The cabinet comprised the following in March 1999:
    Prime Minister and *President of the Executive Yuan:* Vincent C. Siew. There are 8 ministries under the Executive Yuan: Interior; Foreign Affairs; National Defence; Finance; Education; Justice; Economic Affairs; Transport and Communications.
    Vice-President, Executive Yuan: Liu Chao-shiuan.
    President, Control Yuan: Wang Tso-yung.
    President, Examination Yuan: Hsu Shui-teh.
    President, Judicial Yuan: Weng Yueh-sheng.
    President, Legislative Yuan: Wang Jin-ping.
    Minister of Foreign Affairs: Jason Hu. *National Defence:* Tang Fei. *Interior:* Huang Chu-wen. *Finance:* Paul Chiu. *Education:* Lin Ching-chiang. *Economic Affairs:* Wang Chih-kang. *Justice:* Yeh Chin-fong; *Transport and Communications:* Lin Feng-cheng.
    In addition to the Mongolian and Tibetan Affairs Commission and the Overseas Chinese Affairs Commission, a number of commissions and subordinate organizations have been formed with the resolution of the Executive Yuan Council and the Legislature to meet new demands and handle new affairs. Examples include the Environmental Protection Administration, which was set up in 1987 as public awareness of pollution control rose; the Mainland Affairs Council, which was established in 1990 to handle the thawing of relations between Taiwan and the Chinese mainland; the Fair Trade Commission, which was established in 1992 to promote a fair trade system; and the Consumer Protection Commission, which was set up in July 1994 to study and review basic policies on consumer protection. Since 1995 even more commissions have been set up to provide a wider scope of services: the Public Construction Commission was set up in July 1995, the Council of Aboriginal Affairs in Dec. 1996, and the National Sports Council in July 1997.
    These commissions and councils are headed by:
    Aborigines Commission: Hua Chia-chih. *Agricultural Council:* Peng Tso-kuei. *Atomic Energy Council:* Hu Ching-piao. *Central Election Commission:* Lin Feng-cheng. *Consumers Protection Committee:* Hsu Li-teh. *Cultural Planning and Development Council:* Lin Chung-chih. *Economic Planning and Development*

Council: Chiang Pin-kung. *Fair Trade Commission:* Chao Ching-yang. *Labour Affairs Council:* Hsu Shieh-kwei. *Mainland Affairs Council:* Chang King-yuh. *Mongolian and Tibetan Affairs Commission:* Kao Koong-lian. *National Palace Museum:* Chin Hsiao-yi. *National Research, Development and Evaluation Commission:* Huang Ta-chou. *National Science Council:* Huang Chen-tai. *National Youth Commission:* Lee Chi-chu. *Overseas Chinese Affairs Commission:* Chiao Jen-ho. *Physical Education and Sports Commission:* Nancy Chao Li-yun. *Public Construction Commission:* Ou Chin-teh. *Research, Development and Evaluation Commission:* Yang Chou-hsiang. *Vocational Assistance for Retired Servicemen Commission:* Gen. Yang Ting-yung.

DEFENCE
Conscription is for 2 years. Taiwan has more than 4m. soldiers (mostly reserves).

Defence expenditure in 1997 totalled US$13,657m. (US$634 per capita). In 1997 Taiwan spent US$7·3bn. on defence imports (up from US$1·8bn. in 1996), making it the world's second largest buyer of arms, mainly from the USA and France. Only Saudi Arabia spends more on international arms purchases.

Army. The Army numbered about 230,300 in 1998, including 21,000 military police. In 1997 it consisted of 10 infantry divisions, 2 mechanized infantry divisions, 2 airborne brigades, 6 independent armoured brigades, 1 tank group and 2 surface-to-air missile battalions. The aviation element comprises 6 squadrons with about 100 transport and 65 armed helicopters. The primary weapon systems of the ROC ground forces include M48H and M60A3 tanks; M109 and M110 self-propelled artillery; M113, V150, and CM–21 armoured personnel carriers; UH–1H helicoptors; Kung-feng 6A rocket systems; TOW–type anti-tank guided weapons; chapparal SP, Hawk, Tien-kung (Sky Bow), and Tien-chien (Sky Sword) air defence missile systems; and Hsiung-feng I and Hsiung-feng II anti-ship missile systems.

Navy. Active personnel in 1998 totalled 33,000 in the Navy and 30,000 in the Marine Corps. There are over 67,500 naval and marine reservists. The operational and land-based forces consist of destroyer fleets, a frigate fleet, amphibious landing fleet and amphibious landing vessel fleet, anti-submarine helicopter group etc. The Navy's coastal SAM batteries employ Hsiung-feng missiles which resemble US Harpoon missiles. The Knox-class missile frigates are rented from the US Navy, La Fayette (Kang-ting) frigates are imported from France, and the Cheng-kung frigates are built in Taiwan.

The Naval Air Command operates 31 S-2 Tracker aircraft, 12 small anti-submarine helicopters operated from the destroyers, and 12 SH-2F and 10 S-70 Seahawk helicopters based ashore.

The Customs service operates 12 cutters.

Air Force. Units in the operational system are equipped with aircraft that include locally developed IDF, F–16, Mirage 2000–5 and F–5E fighter-interceptors, C–130H and C–119 transporters, AT–3 trainers, and S–70C helicoptors. The ROC Army will spend over US$385m. to deploy 200 fourth-generation Patriot missiles. Patriot missiles are installed in missile batteries around Taiwan. Total strength in 1996, 68,000 personnel.

INTERNATIONAL RELATIONS
By a treaty of 1 Dec. 1954 the USA was pledged to protect Taiwan, but this treaty lapsed 1 year after the USA established diplomatic relations with the People's Republic of China on 1 Jan. 1979. In April 1979 the Taiwan Relations Act was passed by the US Congress to maintain commercial, cultural and other relations between USA and Taiwan through the American Institute on Taiwan and its Taiwan counterpart, the Taipei Economic and Cultural Representative Office in the USA, which were accorded quasi-diplomatic status in 1980.

The People's Republic took over the China seat in the UN from Taiwan on 25 Oct. 1971.

In May 1991 Taiwan ended its formal state of war with the People's Republic.

As of Dec. 1998 the ROC has formal diplomatic ties with 27 countries and maintains substantive relations with over 100 countries and territories around the globe.

CHINA

In Sept. 1997 at the invitation of the Panamanian government, President Lee participated in the World Congress on the Panama Canal. In the wake of the visit to Panama, President Lee travelled to 3 other nations: Honduras, El Salvador and Paraguay. At a summit meeting with leaders of 6 Latin American nations held in El Salvador, the ROC was invited to join the System of Central American Integration, a regional grouping modelled after the European Union, which is known by its Spanish acronym SICA.

ECONOMY

Policy. As regional economic blocs take shape, Taiwan plans to develop itself into an operations centre for the Asia-Pacific region over the next 10 years. The plan calls for 6 operations centres to handle high value-added manufacturing, air and sea cargo and passenger transportation, and professional services.

Performance. Though Taiwan was less affected by the Asian crisis than many of its neighbours, the forecast for GDP growth in 1999 was just 4·74%, and the government announced that, after the previous year's figure of 4·83%, economic expansion was at its weakest for 16 years. Between 1990 and 1997 growth was around 6% each year.

Budget. There are 2 budgets, the central government's general budget together with some special defence and infrastructure appropriations and the provincial budget for Taiwan proper. For the fiscal year July 1997–June 1998 the central government's general budget was NT$1,253,440m. Expenditure planned: 21·2% on defence; 9·8% on economic development; 12·8% on social security; 15·8% on education, science and culture. Foreign exchange reserves were US$86,558m. in Oct. 1998.

Currency. The unit of currency is the *New Taiwan dollar* (TWD) of 100 *cents*. Gold reserves were 13·57m. oz. in Oct. 1998. Inflation was forecast at 1·65% between Jan. and Nov. 1998.

Banking and Finance. The Central Bank of China (reactivated in 1961) regulates the money supply, manages foreign exchange and issues currency. *Governor:* Perng Fai-nan. The Bank of Taiwan is the largest commercial bank and the fiscal agent of the government. The number of financial institutions totalled 6,257 in Oct. 1998. Banks in Taiwan have the lowest bad-loan ratios in Asia.

There are 2 stock exchanges in Taipei.

ENERGY AND NATURAL RESOURCES

Electricity. Output of electricity in 1997 was 133bn. kWh; total installed capacity was 25,735 MW, comprising 63·4% thermal, 20% nuclear and 16·7% hydro-electric. There are 3 nuclear power stations (capacities 1·72m., 1·97m. and 1·9m. kW) and a fourth is envisaged. Consumption per capita stood at 3,627 litres of oil equivalent in 1997.

Oil and Gas. Refined oil production in 1997 was 37·9m. kilolitres; natural gas, 901m. cu. metres.

Minerals. In 1997 coal production was 0·1m. tonnes.

Agriculture. The cultivated area was 864,817 ha in 1997, of which 364,000 ha were paddy fields. Rice production totalled 1,660,000 tonnes in 1996.

In 1996 livestock production was valued at more than US$3,200m., accounting for 38·18% of Taiwan's total agricultural production value. However, the outbreak of foot and mouth disease in March 1997 posed a major threat to Taiwan's pork industry. A total of 6,147 hog farms in 20 cities and counties along Taiwan's west coast were stricken by the disease. The government soon exterminated all hogs at contaminated farms and imported 21m. doses of vaccine for healthy ones. Pork exports were banned and the outbound shipment of 105 kinds of products from cloven-hoofed animals were also prohibited. The government compensated pig farmers for their slaughtered animals and provided relief to both farmers and pork exporters in the form of US$1,100m. in low-interest loans. The Executive Yuan also allocated a special budget of US$378m. for relevant government agencies to carry forward remedial measures. Accordingly, the disease was soon brought under control and the wholesale price of pork rebounded to the normal level.

Forestry. Forest area, 1996: 2,102,311 ha. Forest reserves: trees, 358,239,000 cu. metres; bamboo, 1,127m. poles. Timber production, 35,603 cu. metres.

Fisheries. By 1997 Taiwan's fishing fleet totalled 28,164 vessels (of which 13,194 were powered craft); the catch was approximately 900,000 tonnes. In 1997 Taiwan produced US$2,800m. worth of fish. Of this, 50% came from deep-sea fishing, 28% from aquaculture, 17% from offshore fishing and 4% from coastal fishing. More than 33% of the catch was exported, with the biggest items being skipjack and eel.

INDUSTRY

Output (in tonnes) in 1997 (and 1996): Steel bars, 7·3m. (6·8m.); sugar, 0·35m. (0·36m.); cement, 21·5m. (21·5m.); pulp, 0·35m. (0·31m.); cotton fabrics, 836,60 sq. metres; computers, 4·6m. portable (3·4m.) and 9·1m. desktop (5·1m.).

Labour. In the third quarter of 1998, the total labour force was 9·6m., of whom 9·3m. were employed. Of the employed population, 8·93% worked in agriculture, forestry and fisheries; 37·63% in industry (including 27·95% in manufacturing and 9·2% in construction); and 53·44% in the service sector (including 21·97% in commerce and 15·83% in social and personal services). The unemployment rate was 2·98%.

INTERNATIONAL TRADE

Restrictions on the repatriation of investment earnings by foreign nationals were removed in 1994.

Taiwan has the world's third-largest foreign reserves and one of the world's lowest foreign debts.

Imports and Exports. Total trade, in US$1m.:

	1992	1993	1994	1995	1996	1997
Imports	72,007	77,061	85,359	103,551	102,371	114,425
Exports	81,470	84,917	93,056	111,659	115,951	122,081

In 1997 the main export markets were the USA (24·2%), Hong Kong (23·5%), Japan (9·6%) and Singapore (4·0%). The main import suppliers were Japan (25·4%), the USA (20·9%), Germany (4·7%) and South Korea (4·4%).

Principal exports in 1997, in US$1bn.: Textiles, 16·66; basic metals and articles, 11·53; machinery, 58·99; plastic and rubber products, 7·71; vehicles and transport equipment, 5·59; footwear, headwear and umbrellas, 1·40; toys, games, sports equipment, 2·38.

Principal imports in 1997, in US$1bn.: Basic metals and articles, 11·67; chemicals, 11·44; machinery, 41·12; minerals, 10·30; vehicles and transport equipment, 5·36; textile products, 3·65; precision instruments, clocks and watches, musical instruments, 6·38.

COMMUNICATIONS

Roads. In 1997 there were 20,144 km of roads. 15·3m. motor vehicles were registered including 4·4m. passenger cars, 22,522 buses, 811,023 trucks and 10m. motor cycles. 1,163m. passengers and 277m. tonnes of freight were transported (including urban buses).

Rail. In Dec. 1997 total route length was 2,363 km. Freight traffic amounted to 16·9m. tonnes and passenger traffic to 165m. in 1997.

Civil Aviation. There are 2 international airports: Chiang Kai-shek at Taoyuan near Taipei, and Kaohsiung in the south. In addition there are several domestic airports: Taipei, Hualien, Taitung, Taichung, Tainan, Chiayi, Pingtung, Makung, Chimei, Orchid Island, Green Island, Wangan, Kinmen and Peikan. In Oct. 1997 there were 17 domestic airlines, of which 4 are international carriers: China Airlines (CAL), EVE Airways Corp. (EVA AIR), Mandarin Airlines (MDA; CAL's subsidiary) and Trans Asia Airways (TNA) operate international services to 42 destinations in 27 countries. 35 foreign airlines also operate services. In 1996, 52m. passengers and 1·2m. tonnes of freight were flown. To accommodate this heavier air passenger and cargo traffic a US$800m. expansion project at Chiang Kai-shek International Airport began in 1989. The project includes a second passenger terminal, aircraft bays, airport connection roads, car parks and the expansion of air freight facilities. It was scheduled for completion in June 1999. The planned facilities are designed to allow the airport to handle an additional 14m. passengers annually by the year 2010.

Shipping. Maritime transportation is vital to the trade-oriented economy of Taiwan. As of Dec. 1996 the ROC's shipping industry had a fleet of 255 vessels over 100 gross tons, for a total of 9·14m. dead weight tons. There are 6 international ports: Kaohsiung, Keelung, Hualien, Taichung, Anping and Suao. The first 2 are container centres. Suao port is an auxiliary port to Keelung.

Telecommunications. In 1997 there were 11m. telephones, 1,253,987 mobile phones and 2,496,090 radio pager subscribers. There were approximately 2·8m. Internet users in Sept. 1998. PCs numbered 1,773,000 in 1995 (83 per 1,000 inhabitants).

SOCIAL INSTITUTIONS

Religion. There were 4·51m. Taoists in 1997 with 8,557 temples and 33,200 priests; 4·86m. Buddhists with 3,938 temples and 9,200 priests; 0·42m. Protestants; and 0·3m. Catholics.

Education. Since 1968 there has been compulsory education for 6–15 year olds with free tuition. The illiteracy rate dropped to 5·99% in 1995 and is still falling. In 1997–98 there were 2,540 elementary schools with 92,104 teachers and 1,905,690 pupils; 1,151 secondary schools with 99,411 teachers and 1,874,747 students; 139 schools of higher education, including 38 universities, 40 colleges and 61 junior colleges, with 38,806 teachers and 856,186 students. More than one-quarter of the total population attended an educational institution.

Health. In 1997 there was 1 physician serving every 844 persons, 1 doctor of Chinese medicine per 6,903 persons and 1 dentist per 2,866 persons. Some 126,162 beds were provided by the 97 public and 653 private hospitals, averaging nearly 56 beds per 10,000 persons. In addition to the 497 public and 19,113 private clinics, there were 368 health stations and 502 health rooms serving residents in the sparsely populated areas. Acute infectious diseases were no longer the number one killer. Malignant neoplasms, cerebrovascular diseases, accidents and adverse effects, and heart diseases were the first 4 leading causes of death.

Welfare. A universal health insurance scheme came into force in March 1995 as an extension to the incorporation of 13 social insurance plans which only cover 59% of Taiwan's population. Premium shares among the government, employer and insured are varied according to the insured statuses. By the end of 1997 about 20·49m. people or 96·27% of the population were covered by the National Health Insurance programme. The 7·99m. new beneficiaries are mainly the elderly, children, students and housewives.

CULTURE

Broadcasting. At Dec. 1998 there were 91 radio stations, 4 commercial TV services and 102 cable systems. June 1997 saw the inauguration of a fourth over-the-air television station—The Kaohsiung-based Formosa Television—which is affiliated with the opposition Democratic Progressive Party and telecasts on VHF low-band. A Public Television Law was promulgated on 18 June 1997.

Cinema. In 1998 cinemas numbered 232. In 1997, 29 full-length films were made.

Press. There were 241 domestic news agencies, 354 newspapers and 5,898 periodicals in 1998.

Tourism. In 1997, 2,372,232 tourists visited Taiwan, and 6,161,932 Taiwanese made visits abroad.

FURTHER READING
Statistical Yearbook of the Republic of China. Taipei, annual. *The Republic of China Yearbook.* Taipei, annual. *Taiwan Statistical Data Book.* Taipei, annual. *Annual Review of Government Administration, Republic of China.* Taipei, annual.

Arrigo, L. G. et al. *The Other Taiwan: 1945 to the Present Day.* New York, 1994
Cooper, J. F., *Historical Dictionary of Taiwan.* Metuchen (NJ), 1993

TAIWAN

Gälli, A., *Taiwan ROC: A Chinese Challenge to the World*. London, 1987

Gold, T. B., *State and Society in the Taiwan Miracle*. Armonk, 1986

Hughes, C., *Taiwan and Chinese Nationalism: National Identity and Status in International Society*. London, 1997

Lee, S.-Y., *Money and Finance in the Economic Development of Taiwan*. London, 1990

Lee, W.-C., *Taiwan* [Bibliography]. Oxford and Santa Barbara (CA), 1990

Liu, A. P. L., *Phoenix and the Lame Lion: Modernization in Taiwan and Mainland China, 1950–1980*. Stanford, 1987

Long, S., *Taiwan: China's Last Frontier*. London, 1991

Moody, P. R., *Political Change in Taiwan: a Study of Ruling Party Adaptability*. New York, 1992

Tsang, S. (ed.) *In the Shadow of China: Political Developments in Taiwan since 1949*. Farnborough, 1994

National library: National Central Library, Taipei (established 1986).

COLOMBIA

República de Colombia

Capital: Bogotá
Population estimate, 2000: 38·9m.
GNP per capita: (PPP$) 6,720
HDI/world rank: 0·850/53

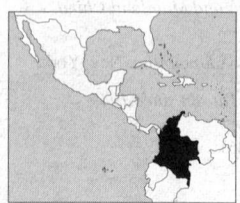

KEY HISTORICAL EVENTS

Columbus sighted what became Colombia in 1499. The conquest of the territory began in 1509; and 30 years later the Spaniards were well established. In 1564 the Spanish Crown appointed a President of New Granada, which included the territories of Colombia, Panama and Venezuela. In 1718 a viceroyalty of New Granada was created. This viceroyalty gained its independence from Spain in 1819, and together with the present territories of Panama, Venezuela and Ecuador was officially constituted on 17 Dec. 1819 as the state of 'Greater Colombia'. This new state lasted only until 1830 when it split up into Venezuela, Ecuador and the republic of New Granada. The constitution of 22 May 1858 changed New Granada into a confederation of eight states, under the name of *Confederación Granadina.* Under the constitution of 8 May 1863 the country was renamed *Estados Unidos de Colombia,* which were nine in number. The revolution of 1885 led the National Council of Bogotá, composed of two delegates from each state, to promulgate the constitution of 5 Aug. 1886, forming the Republic of Colombia. The constitution abolished the sovereignty of the states, converting them into departments with governors appointed by the President of the Republic. The department of Panama, however, became an independent country in 1903.

Conservatives and Liberals have alternated in power. Both have faced unrest, rioting and civil war. Liberal governments were in power 1860–84, Conservatives 1884–1930, Liberals 1930–46 and Conservatives 1946–53. In 1953 Gen. Gustavo Rojas Pinilla established a dictatorship, but he was deposed in 1957. The Conservatives and Liberals fought a civil war from 1948 to 1957 (*La Violencia*) during which some 300,000 people were killed. In a plebiscite in 1957 the two political parties agreed to support a single presidential candidate and to divide government posts equally. This arrangement was modified in 1974 and the growing strength of a third party, ANAPO (the *Allianza Nacional Popular*), led to it being abandoned in 1978. The Liberal, Virgilio Barco Vargas, was elected president in 1986 and although the transfer of power from the Conservatives was successful, powerful drugs lords have made violence endemic. Two Marxist guerrilla forces are active, the Colombian Revolutionary Armed Forces (FARC), and the smaller National Liberation Army (ELN). They are opposed by a well-armed paramilitary organization which emerged after the setting up of rural self-defence groups. The paramilitaries operate independently but are thought to have close links with the state security process. Killings and other abuses by paramilitary squads, guerrillas and the military in 1996 made it the most infamous year in the nation's history for human rights violations, according to a report by the Colombian Commission of Jurists. On average, 10 Colombians were killed every day for political or ideological reasons, while one person disappeared every two days.

There were hopes of a fresh start in 1998 when Andrés Pastrana was elected president, ending 12 years of liberal rule. Offers to talk peace were taken up by the rebels and by their paramilitary enemies. But political differences are wide, with FARC demanding sweeping agrarian reform and a redistribution of wealth. FARC controls around 40% of the country including areas which produce the bulk of illegal drugs. Approximately 80% of the cocaine and 60% of the heroin sold in the USA originates in Colombia.

In Jan. 1999 Colombia suffered its worst earthquake this century.

TERRITORY AND POPULATION

Colombia is bounded in the north by the Caribbean Sea, north-west by Panama, west by the Pacific Ocean, south-west by Ecuador and Peru, north-east by Venezuela and south-east by Brazil. The estimated area is 1,141,748 sq. km (440,829 sq. miles). Population census (1993), 37,127,293; density, 40·2 per sq. km.

COLOMBIA

The UN gives a projected population for 2000 of 38·9m.

In 1995, 72·6% lived in urban areas. Bogotá, the capital (estimate 1997): 6,004,782.

The following table gives population estimates for departments and their capitals for 1997:

Departments	Area (sq. km)	Population	Capital	Population
Antioquia	63,612	5,243,906	Medellín	1,970,691
Atlántico	3,388	1,984,910	Barranquilla	1,157,826
Bogotá[1]	—	6,004,782	—	—
Bolívar	25,978	1,843,630	Cartagena	812,595
Boyacá	23,189	1,351,829	Tunja	118,406
Caldas	7,888	1,084,081	Manizales	358,194
Caquetá	88,965	396,537	Florencia	114,848
Cauca	29,308	1,197,874	Popayán	218,057
César	22,905	873,044	Valledupar	296,624
Chocó	46,530	409,599	Quibdó	123,102
Córdoba	25,020	1,353,922	Montería	327,249
Cundinamarca	22,478	1,975,564	Bogotá[1]	—
Huila	19,890	894,109	Neiva	305,625
La Guajira	20,848	459,326	Riohacha	114,608
Magdalena	23,188	1,218,836	Santa Marta	343,038
Meta	85,635	659,825	Villavicencio	299,296
Nariño	33,268	1,558,045	Pasto	362,227
Norte de Santander	21,658	1,252,867	Cúcuta	589,196
Quindío	1,845	535,711	Armenia	283,842
Risaralda	4,140	905,780	Pereira	434,267
Santander	30,537	1,911,830	Bucaramanga	508,240
San Andrés y Providencia	44	65,700	San Andrés	61,309
Sucre	10,917	749,152	Sincelejo	213,916
Tolima	23,562	1,310,963	Ibagué	419,883
Valle del Cauca	22,140	3,970,302	Cali	1,985,906
Amazonas	109,665	60,251	Leticia	30,450
Arauca	23,818	206,151	Arauca	69,292
Casanare	44,460	226,896	Yopal	68,855
Guainía	72,238	31,148	Puerto Inírida	19,983
Guaviare	42,327	110,631	San José del Guaviare	53,667
Putumayo	24,885	273,981	Mocoa	29,946
Vichada	100,242	66,676	Puerto Carreño	12,063
Vaupés	54,135	26,865	Mitú	14,287

[1]Capital District.

Ethnic divisions (1996): mestizo 58%, white 20%, mulatto 14%, black 4%, mixed black-Indian 3%, Indian 1%.

The official language is Spanish.

SOCIAL STATISTICS

1997 births, 988,000; deaths, 191,000. 1997 birth rate (per 1,000 population) 26·4; death rate, 5·1. Annual growth rate, 1990–95, 1·7%. Life expectancy at birth, 1990–95, was 67·1 years for men and 72·4 years for women. Infant mortality, 1990–95, 28 per 1,000 live births; fertility rate, 2·9 children per woman.

CLIMATE

The climate includes equatorial and tropical conditions, according to situation and altitude. In tropical areas, the wettest months are March to May and Oct. to Nov. Bogotá, Jan. 58°F (14·4°C), July 57°F (13·9°C). Annual rainfall 42" (1,052 mm). Barranquilla, Jan. 80°F (26·7°C), July 82°F (27·8°C). Annual rainfall 32" (799 mm). Cali, Jan. 75°F (23·9°C), July 75°F (23·9°C). Annual rainfall 37" (915 mm). Medellín, Jan. 71°F (21·7°C), July 72°F (22·2°C). Annual rainfall 64" (1,606 mm).

CONSTITUTION AND GOVERNMENT

Simultaneously with the presidential elections of May 1990, a referendum was held in which 7m. votes were cast for the establishment of a special assembly to draft a new constitution. Elections were held on 9 Dec. 1990 for this 74-member 'Constitutional Assembly' which operated from Feb. to July 1991. The electorate was 14·2m.; turn-out was 3·7m. The Liberals gained 24 seats, M19 (a former guerrilla organization), 19. The Assembly produced a new constitution which came into force on 5 July 1991. It stresses the state's obligation to protect human rights, and establishes constitutional rights to healthcare, social security and leisure. Indians are allotted 2 Senate seats. Congress may dismiss ministers, and representatives may be recalled by their electors.

The *President* is elected by direct vote for a term of 4 years, and is not eligible for re-election until 4 years afterwards. A vice-presidency was instituted in July 1991.

The legislative power rests with a *Congress* of 2 houses, the *Senate*, of 102 members, and the *House of Representatives*, of 165 members, both elected for 4 years by proportional representation. Congress meets annually at Bogotá on 20 July.

National Anthem. 'O! Gloria inmarcesible' ('Oh Glory unfading!'); words by R. Núñez, tune by O. Síndici.

RECENT ELECTIONS

In the first round of the presidential election on 31 May 1998, the Liberal Party candidate, Horacio Serpa, won by a mere 25,000 votes from a total of 10·8m, but in the second round on 21 June the Conservative Party candidate, Andrés Pastrana, received approximately 50·5% against 46·5% for Serpa. Congressional elections were held on 8 March 1998, President Samper's Liberal Party beating the Social Conservatives into second place amidst indications of large-scale vote burying. Hundreds of people were arrested with forged identity cards or other evidence of attempted fraud.

CURRENT ADMINISTRATION

President: Andrés Pastrana (b. 1954; sworn in 7 Aug. 1998).

Vice President: Lemas Gustavo Bell.

In March 1999 the government comprised:

Minister of Interior: Nestor Humberto Martinez. *Defence:* Rodrigo Lloreda Caicedo. *Finance:* Juan Camilo Restrepo. *Agriculture and Livestock:* Carlos Murgas Guerrero. *Economic Development:* Fernando Araujo Perdomo. *Labour:* Hernando Yepes Arcila. *Public Health:* Virgilio Galvez. *Mines and Energy:* Luis Carlos Valenzuela Delgado. *Education:* German Bula. *Communications:* Claudia de Francisco de Pardo. *Foreign Trade:* Marta Lucia Ramirez. *Foreign Relations:* Guillermo de Soto Fernandez. *Justice:* Parmenio Cuellar Bastidas. *Environment:* Juan Mayr Maldonaldo. *Transport:* Mauricio Cardenas Santamaria. *Culture:* Elena Bravo. *Planning:* Jaime Ruiz. *Sustainable Development:* Erick Reyes Villa.

Local Government. The country is divided into 32 departments and the Capital District of Bogotá (properly, Santafé de Bogotá), and subdivided into 1,011 municipalities. The governor of each department is elected by universal suffrage, and each has also a directly elected legislature. The departments are subdivided into municipalities. The mayors of these, and the Special District of Bogotá, are elected by direct vote for a 2-year term. Mayoral elections were held on 30 Oct. 1994.

Elections were held in March 1992. The largest number of seats was gained by the Liberal Party, followed by the Conservative Party and M19.

DEFENCE

Selective conscription at 18 years varies from 1 to 2 years of service. Manpower availability (1996): males age 15-49, 10,067,538; males fit for military service, 6,774,105; males reaching military age annually, 346,372.

In 1997 defence expenditure totalled US$3,068m. (US$85 per capita). In 1985 expenditure had been US$604m.

Army. The Army consists of 16 infantry brigades, 2 counter-insurgency brigades, 1 Presidential Guard battalion and 1 air defence artillery battalion. Equipment includes 12 M-3A1 light tanks and 6 light transport aircraft. Personnel (1997) 121,000 (conscripts, 63,800); reserves 54,700. Number of national police (1997) 87,000.

Navy. The Navy has 2 German-built 1,200-tonne diesel powered submarines completed in 1975, 2 Italian-built midget submarines, 4 small German-built missile-armed frigates with helicopter decks, 4 offshore patrol vessels and 11 fast patrol craft. There are 3 river gunboats and 11 riverine patrol craft. Auxiliaries include 2 surveying vessels, 1 small transport and 1 training ship. Naval personnel in 1997 totalled 5,000. There are also 2 brigades of marines numbering 9,000. An air arm operates 7 light reconnaissance aircraft and 4 BO-105 helicopters for ship-borne anti-submarine and rescue duties. There is a shore-based Coastguard integrated with the Navy numbering 4,000.

Air Force. The Air Force has been independent of the Army and Navy since 1943, when its reorganization began with US assistance. It has about 90 combat aircraft, including 2 fighter-bomber squadrons, one with Mirage 5s and one with Kfirs. 2 squadrons of AC-47 armed transports and 1 with A-37B jets for counter-insurgency duties; a transport group equipped with 8 C-130, 8 C-47s, and a small number of Arava and Turbo-Porter light transports; a presidential F-28 Fellowship jet transport; 1 Boeing 707, 2 Bandeirante, UH-1B/H and UH-60 Black Hawk utility helicopters; and a reconnaissance unit with Iroquois, Lama, Hughes OH-6A, 300C and TH-55 helicopters. 10 Aviocars, 2 Boeing 727s, 1 F-28 and 2 HS.748 transports are flown by the Air Force operated airline SATENA. There are several dozen light transports, confiscated from drug smugglers, in use. Cessna T-41D primary trainers, Tucanos, T-34s and 10 T-37C jet advanced trainers are in service. Total strength (1997) 7,300 personnel (3,500 conscripts).

INTERNATIONAL RELATIONS
Colombia is a member of the UN, OAS, the Andean Group and ALADI/LAIA.

ECONOMY

Performance. GDP growth is running at about 3–4% annually. 1998 current account deficit, 7·5% of GDP. Government policy is to reduce this to 2% by 2000. GDP (1996): 88,827,760m. pesos.

Budget. Revenue (1996), US$26bn.; expenditure, US$30bn.

Currency. The unit of currency is the *Colombian peso* (COP) of 100 *centavos*. Inflation was 18% in 1998. In Dec. 1997 gold reserves were 360,000 troy oz. and foreign exchange reserves were US$8,979m. Total money supply was 10,014bn. pesos. in Jan. 1998.

Banking and Finance. In 1923 the Bank of the Republic was inaugurated as a semi-official central bank, with the exclusive privilege of issuing banknotes. Its note issues must be covered by a reserve in gold of foreign exchange of 25% of their value. Its international reserves in May 1992 were US$7,315·2m. Interest rates of 40% plus are imposed.

There are 24 commercial banks, of which 18 are private or mixed, and 6 official. There is also an Agricultural, Industrial and Mining Credit Institute, a Central Mortgage Bank and a Social Savings Bank. Bank deposits totalled 1,446,686 pesos in May 1991.

There are stock exchanges in Bogotá, Medellín and Cali.

Weights and Measures. The metric system was introduced in 1857, but Spanish weights and measures are generally used, *e.g., botella* (750 grammes), *galón* (5 *botellas*), *vara* (70 cm), *arroba* (25 lb., of 500 grammes; 4 *arrobas* = 1 quintal).

ENERGY AND NATURAL RESOURCES

Electricity. Capacity of electric power (1995) was 10,583,700 kW. Electric power produced in 1995, 45·36bn. kWh. Consumption per capita in 1995 was an estimated 963 kWh.

Oil and Gas. Production (1997): crude oil, 216·2m. bbls.; fuel oil, 18·06m. bbls.; diesel oil, 22·1m. bbls.; gasoline 34·4m. bbls.; kerosene, 1·07m. bbls.; propane gas, 7·3ml bbls.

Minerals. Production (1997): gold, 521,797 troy oz.; silver, 109,516 troy oz.; platinum, 13,082 troy oz. Other important minerals include: copper, lead, steel, mercury, manganese and emeralds (of which Colombia accounts for about half of world production).

COLOMBIA

Salt production (1997): 133,293 tonnes. Coal production (1995): 13,471 tonnes; iron ore (1995): 571,607 tonnes.

Agriculture. In 1996 agriculture accounted for 16% of GDP. There is a wide range of climate and, consequently, crops. In 1994 there were 3·92m. ha of arable land, 1·54m. ha of permanent crops and 40·6m. ha of pasture.

Production, 1993 (in 1,000 tonnes): Coffee, 1,080; potatoes, 2,860; rice, 1,650; maize, 1,164; sorghum, 631.

Livestock (1996): 26,088,000 cattle, 2,431,000 pigs, 2,540,000 sheep, 2,450,000 horses, 80m. chickens (1995). Meat production, 1991: Beef and veal, 651,000 tonnes; pork, 134,000 tonnes.

Forestry. In 1995 the area under forests was 52·98m. ha, or 51% of the total land area (down from 52·3% in 1990). Timber production in 1995 was 20·49m. cu. metres.

Fisheries. Total catch (1995), 167,080 tonnes, of which about 70% was from marine waters.

INDUSTRY

Production (1997): Steel ingots, 295,694 tonnes; cement, 8,099,164 tonnes; motor cars, 63,102; industrial vehicles, 11,834; sugar, 1,969,399 tonnes.

Labour. The labour force (1998 estimate) was 7,828,397, of which 6,586,668 were employed and 1,241,729 unemployed; the rate of unemployment was estimated to be 15·8%.

INTERNATIONAL TRADE

Foreign companies are liable for basic income tax of 30% and surtax of 7·5%. Since 1993 tax on profit remittance has started at 12%, reducing (except for oil companies) to 7% after 3 years. Foreign debt was US$28,859m. in 1996.

The Group of Three (G-3) free trade pact with Mexico and Venezuela came into effect on 1 Jan. 1995.

Imports and Exports. In US$1,000:

	1995	1996	1997
Imports	11,806·7	11,754·7	15,378·8
Exports	9,370·6	9,708·5	11,529·4

Main export markets, 1997: USA, EU, Latin America, the Andean Community, Venezuela. Main import suppliers (1997): USA, Venezuela, Japan, Germany.

COMMUNICATIONS

Roads. Total length of highways was estimated to be 106,600 km in 1995. Of the 2,300-mile Simón Bolívar highway, which runs from Caracas in Venezuela to Guayaquil in Ecuador, the Colombian portion is complete. Motor vehicles in 1996 numbered 1,434,000, of which 762,000 were passenger cars and 672,000 vans and trucks.

Rail. The National Railways (2,532 km of route, 914 mm gauge) went into liquidation in 1990 prior to takeover of services and obligations by 3 new public companies in 1992. Freight tonne-km performed in 1995 came to 753m. Total rail track, 3,386 km.

Civil Aviation. There are international airports at Barranquilla, Bogotá (Eldorado), Cali, Cartagena, Medellín and San Andrés. The national carriers are Avianca and ACES. In 1995 Avianca carried 3,861,000 passengers (3,034,000 on domestic flights) and ACES 1,052,000 (987,000 on domestic flights). The busiest airport is Bogotá, which in 1995 handled 7,049,000 passengers and 402,600 tonnes of freight. Services were also provided in 1998 by Aerolíneas Argentinas, Aeroperú, Aerorepublica, Air Aruba, Air France, Aires, Alitalia, American Airlines, British Airways, COPA, Continental Airlines, Cubana, Ecuatoriana, Iberia, LACSA, Lan-Chile, Lloyd Aéreo Boliviano, Lufthansa, Mexicana, Saeta, SAM, SAS, Servivensa and Varig.

Shipping. Vessels entering Colombian ports in 1995 unloaded 13,806,000 tonnes of imports and loaded 26,284,000 tonnes of exports. The merchant marine totalled 0·18m. GRT in 1995, including oil tankers, 9,681 GRT.

The Magdelena River is subject to drought, and navigation is always impeded during the dry season, but it is an important artery of passenger and goods traffic. The river is navigable for 900 miles; steamers ascend to La Dorada, 592 miles from Barranquilla.

Telecommunications. In 1997 there were 5,334,400 telephone main lines in use (147·5 for every 1,000 inhabitants). There were approximately 120,000 Internet users in June 1997. Cellular phone subscribers numbered 275,000 in 1995, and there were 630,000 PCs in use and 100,000 fax machines.

Postal Services. In 1995 there were 1,655 post offices.

SOCIAL INSTITUTIONS

Justice. The July 1991 constitution introduced the offices of public prosecutor and public defence. There is no extradition of Colombians for trial in other countries. The Supreme Court, at Bogotá, of 20 members, is divided into 3 chambers—civil cassation (6), criminal cassation (8), labour cassation (6). Each of the 61 judicial districts has a superior court with various sub-dependent tribunals of lower juridical grade. 257,511 crimes were reported in 1988.

The police force numbered 73,176 in 1989. Colombia abolished the death penalty in 1997.

Religion. The religion is Roman Catholic (33·92m. adherents in 1992), with the Cardinal Archbishop of Bogotá as Primate of Colombia and 9 other archbishoprics. There are also 44 bishops, 8 apostolic vicars, 5 apostolic prefects and 2 prelates. In 1990 there were 1,546 parishes and 4,020 priests. Other forms of religion are permitted so long as their exercise is 'not contrary to Christian morals or the law'.

Education. Primary education is free but not compulsory. Schools are both state and privately controlled. In 1995 there were 19,920 pre-primary schools with 38,915 teachers for 779,923 pupils; 54,180 primary schools with 191,452 teachers for 4,692,614 pupils; and 9,897 secondary schools for 3,080,092 pupils with 157,189 teachers. There were 235 higher education establishments with 562,716 students.

In 1995-96 in the public sector there were 20 universities, 1 open university, 3 technological universities, and universities of education, educational technology and industry. There were also 2 colleges of public administration, 1 school of police studies, 1 institute of fine art, 1 polytechnic and 1 conservatory. In the private sector there were 25 universities, 4 Roman Catholic universities, 1 college of education and 1 school of administration. There were 8 public, and 44 private, other institutions of higher education. In 1994-95 there were 208,394 university students.

Adult literacy, 91·3%; male 91·2%, female 91·4% (1995).

In 1994 total expenditure on education came to 3·7% of GNP and represented 12·9% of total government expenditure.

Health. In 1997 there were 1,657 hospitals with 47,236 beds. Medical personnel was as follows: doctors, 40,355; dentists, 22,121; nurses, 13,558; auxiliaries, 38,723.

CULTURE

Broadcasting. There are 5 radio companies overseen by the Dirección General de Radio-comunicaciones. Instituto Nacional de Radio y Televisión transmits on 3 networks (colour by NTSC) and rents air time to 26 commercial companies. In 1995 there were 20·2m. radio and 4·2m. TV sets. There are 33 television broadcast stations.

Press. There were 34 daily newspapers in 1995, with daily circulation totalling 1·5m.

Tourism. In 1996 there were 1,254,000 foreign tourists, bringing revenue of US$909m.

COLOMBIA

DIPLOMATIC REPRESENTATIVES
Of Colombia in Great Britain (Flat 3a, 3 Hans Cres., London, SW1X 0LN)
Ambassador: Humberto de Calle-Lombana.

Of Great Britain in Colombia (Edificio Ing. Barings, Carrera 9 No 76 - 49, Piso 9, Bogotá)
Ambassador: Leycester Coltman, CMG.

Of Colombia in the USA (2118 Leroy Pl., NW, Washington, D.C., 20008)
Ambassador: Luis Alberto Moreno.

Of the USA in Colombia (Calle 220-BIS, No. 47-51, Apartedo Aereo 3831, Bogotá)
Ambassador: Curtis W. Kamman.

Of Colombia to the United Nations
Ambassador: Alfonso Valdivieso.

Of Colombia to the European Union
Ambassador: José Antonio Vargas Lleras.

FURTHER READING
Departamento Administrativo Nacional de Estadística. *Boletín de Estadística.* Monthly.
Davis, R. H., *Historical Dictionary of Colombia.* 2nd ed. Metuchen (NJ), 1994
Thorp, R., *Economic Management and Economic Development in Peru and Colombia.* London, 1991

National statistical office: Departamento Administrativo Nacional de Estadística (DANE), Avenida Eldorado, Bogotá.
Website: http://www.dane.gov.co/

COMOROS

République Fédérale
Islamique des Comores

Capital: Moroni
Population estimate, 2000: 714,000
GNP per capita: (PPP$) 1,770
HDI/world rank: 0·411/141

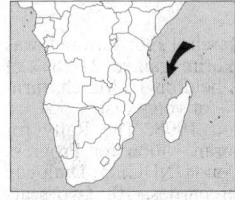

KEY HISTORICAL EVENTS

The 3 islands forming the present state became French protectorates at the end of the 19th century and were proclaimed colonies in 1912. With neighbouring Mayotte they were administratively attached to Madagascar from 1914 until 1947 when the 4 islands became a French Overseas Territory, achieving internal self-government in Dec. 1961. In referendums held on each island on 22 Dec. 1974, the 3 western islands voted overwhelmingly for independence, while Mayotte voted to remain French. The Comorian Chamber of Deputies unilaterally declared the islands' independence on 6 July 1975, but Mayotte remained a French dependency. During a coup by the French mercenary Bob Denard in Sept. 1995, President Djohar was held prisoner by the insurrectionists. The coup was suppressed by French forces, and the President was released but not reinstated. Recent years have been marked by political disruption. In 1997 the islands of Anjouan and Mohéli attempted to secede from the federation.

TERRITORY AND POPULATION

The Comoros consist of 3 islands in the Indian Ocean between the African mainland and Madagascar with a total area of 1,862 sq. km (719 sq. miles). The population at the 1991 census was 446,817; estimate, 1996, 569,200; density, 306 per sq. km.

The UN gives a projected population for 2000 of 714,000.

In 1995, 30·5% of the population were urban.

	Area (sq. km)	Population (1991 census)	Chief town
Njazídja (Grande Comore)	1,148	233,533	Moroni
Nzwani (Anjouan)	424	188,953	Mutsamudu
Mwali (Mohéli)	290	24,331	Fomboni

Estimated population of the chief towns in 1988: Moroni, 22,000; Mutsamudu, 14,000; Fomboni, 7,000.

The indigenous population are a mixture of Malagasy, African, Malay and Arab peoples; the vast majority speak Comorian, an Arabised dialect of Swahili, but a small proportion speak Makua (a Bantu language) or one of the official languages, French and Arabic.

SOCIAL STATISTICS

1996 births, 26,100; deaths, 5,900. Birth rate per 1,000 population, 1996, 45·8; death, 10·3; infant mortality, 75·3 per 1,000 live births; population growth rate, 3·55%. Expectation of life was 58·7 years in 1996. Fertility rate, 1990–95, 6·0 children per woman.

CLIMATE

There is a tropical climate, affected by Indian monsoon winds from the north, which gives a wet season from Nov. to April. Moroni, Jan. 81°F (27·2°C), July 75°F (23·9°C). Annual rainfall, 113" (2,825 mm).

CONSTITUTION AND GOVERNMENT

Under the Constitution approved by referendum on 1 Oct. 1978 (amended 1983), the Comoros were a Federal Islamic Republic. Mayotte had the right to join when it so chose. At a referendum on 7 June 1992, 74·25% of votes cast were in favour of a new constitution. The electorate was 213,000; turn-out was 63·51%.

Under the 1992 constitution the *President* is Head of State, directly elected for a 5-year term (renewable once). He appoints Ministers to form the Council of

Government, on which each island's Governor has a non-voting seat. The 42-member *Legislative Council* is directly elected for 4 years in 2 rounds. There is a 15-member *Senate* (5 members for each island) which is nominated for 6 years by an electoral college.

National Anthem. 'Udzima wa ya Masiwa' ('The union of the islands'); words by S. H. Abderamane, tune by K. Abdallah and S. H. Abderamane.

RECENT ELECTIONS
A first round of Presidential elections took place on 6 March 1996; turn-out was 64%. There were 15 candidates. Mohamed Taki Abdoulkarim gained 21·28% of votes cast, Abbas Djoussouf, 15·71%. A run-off round was held on 16 March, turn-out was 62%. Abdoulkarim was elected *President* by 64·29% of votes cast.

Elections for the Legislative Council were held in Jan. 1998. The Rally for Democracy and Renewal (RDR) won 15 seats; the Comoran Union for Progress (UDZIMA), 8; the Union for Democracy and Decentralization (UNDC), 5; Dialogue Proposition Action (DPA/MWANGAZA), 2; other smaller parties, 10. Two seats remained unfilled.

CURRENT ADMINISTRATION
President (Acting): Tadjiddine Ben Said Massounde (since 6 Nov. 1998).

In March 1999 the government comprised:

Prime Minister: Abbas Djoussouf.

Minister of Finance, Budget, Economy, Commerce and Investments: Said Said Hamadi. *Foreign Affairs and Co-operation:* Salim Hadj Himidi. *Francophony, Culture, Industry and Information:* Issamidine Adaine. *Justice, Public Function, Employment, Professional Training, Administrative Decentralization and Constitutional Reforms:* Mohamed Abdou Mmadi. *National Education, Public Health, Youth and Sports:* Sultan Chouzour. *Production, Fisheries, Environment and Craft:* Mahamoud Ahmed Abdallah. *Regional Planning, Urbanism, Lodging, Transportation, Tourism, Posts and Telecommunications, and Government Spokesman:* Ali Toihir Mohamed. *State Secretary at the Presidency Responsible for Relations with the Arabic and Muslim Countries:* Souef Mohamed El Amine.

DEFENCE
Army. The Army was reorganized after the failed coup of Sept. 1995.

Navy. 1 landing craft with ramps was purchased in 1981. 2 small patrol boats were supplied by Japan in 1982. Personnel in 1996 numbered about 200.

Air Arm. 1 Cessna 402B communications aircraft and 1 Ecureuil helicopter were reported to be in operation.

INTERNATIONAL RELATIONS
Comoros is a member of the UN and Arab League, and an ACP member state of the ACP-EU relationship.

ECONOMY
Performance. Real GDP growth was −2·3% in 1995 (−2·2% in 1994).

Budget. Revenues were an estimated US$55m. and expenditure an estimated US$71m. in 1995.

Currency. The unit of currency is the *Comorian franc* (KMF) of 100 *centimes*. It is within France's Franc Zone (*see* FRANCE: Currency) and was devalued 25% in Jan. 1994. Foreign exchange reserves were US$44m. in Sept. 1997. Total money supply in Sept. 1997 was 11,413m. Comorian francs. The average annual inflation rate during the period 1990–96 was 4·4%.

Banking and Finance. The Central Bank is the bank of issue. The chief commercial banks are the Banque Internationale des Comores and the Banque de Développement des Comores.

Weights and Measures. The metric system is in force.

ENERGY AND NATURAL RESOURCES

Electricity. In 1991 installed capacity was 16,000 kW. Production was 17m. kWh in 1994; consumption per capita was 27 kWh in 1994.

Agriculture. 80% of the economically active population depends upon agriculture, which (including fishing, hunting and forestry) contributes 40% to GDP. The chief product was formerly sugar-cane, but now vanilla, copra, maize and other food crops, cloves and essential oils (citronella, ylang-ylang, lemon grass) are the most important products. Production (1991 in 1,000 tonnes): Cassava, 46; coconuts, 50; bananas, 52; sweet potatoes, 18; rice, 15; maize, 4; and copra, 4.

Livestock (1996): Cattle, 50,000; sheep, 15,000; goats (1995), 128,000; asses, 5,000.

Forestry. In 1995 the area under forest was 9,000 ha, or 4% of the total land area (12,000 ha and 5·4% in 1990). The forested area has been severely reduced because of the shortage of cultivable land and ylang-ylang production.

Fisheries. Fishing is on an individual basis, without modern equipment. The catch was estimated to be 13,200 tonnes in 1995.

INDUSTRY

Branches include perfume distillation, textiles, furniture, jewellery, soft drinks and the processing of vanilla and copra.

Labour. The workforce in 1996 was 286,000 (58% males).

INTERNATIONAL TRADE

Total foreign debt was US$206m. in 1996.

Imports and Exports. In 1995 imports amounted to 25,411m. Comorian francs.; exports to 4,236m. Comorian francs. Main export markets, 1995: France, 36·5%; USA, 28·4%; Germany, 8·0%. Main import suppliers, 1995: France, 32·0%; India, 17·3%; Saudi Arabia, 9·4%. The main exports are vanilla, cloves, ylang-ylang, essences, cocoa, copra and coffee. Rice accounts for 90% of imports.

COMMUNICATIONS

Roads. In 1996 there were estimated to be 900 km of classified roads (440 km highways and main roads, 230 km secondary and 230 km other roads). The number of cars in use has increased dramatically in recent years, from 2,910 in 1992 to 9,100 in 1996.

Civil Aviation. There is an international airport at Moroni (International Prince Said Ibrahim). In 1998 services were provided by Air Austral, Air Madagascar, Air Mauritius, Emirates and Yemenia Yemen Airways. In 1996 International Prince Said Ibrahim handled 92,000 passengers (75,000 on international flights).

Shipping. In 1995 the merchant marine totalled 2,959 GRT.

Telecommunications. There were 5,500 telephone main lines in 1997 (8·4 per 1,000 persons). In 1995 there were 100 fax machines.

Postal Services. In 1993 there were 36 post offices.

SOCIAL INSTITUTIONS

Justice. French and Moslem law is in a new consolidated code. The Supreme Court comprises 7 members, 2 each appointed by the President and the Federal Assembly, and 1 by each island's Legislative Council. The death penalty is authorized for murder. The last execution was in 1996.

Religion. Islam is the official religion: 86% of the population are Sunni Moslems; 14% are Roman Catholics.

Education. After 2 pre-primary years at Koran school, which 50% of children attend, there are 6 years of primary schooling for 7- to 13-year-olds followed by a 4-year secondary stage attended by 25% of children. Some 5% of 17- to 20-year-olds conclude schooling at *lycées*. In 1995–96 there were 327 primary schools with

78,527 pupils. 17,637 pupils attended secondary schools in 1993–94. There were 348 students in higher education in 1995–96.

The adult literacy rate in 1995 was 57·3% (64·2% among males and 50·4% among females).

Health. In 1993 there were 77 doctors; in 1990, 6 dentists, 6 pharmacists, 86 midwives and 155 nursing personnel. In 1980 there were 17 hospitals and clinics with 763 beds.

CULTURE

Broadcasting. The state-controlled Radio Comoro broadcasts in French and Comorian. Number of radios (1995), 84,000; television receivers, 400.

Press. There was (1997) 1 weekly newspaper.

Tourism. In 1996 there were 25,000 foreign tourists (around a third from France), bringing revenue of US$9m.

DIPLOMATIC REPRESENTATIVES
Of Great Britain in the Comoros
Ambassador: Robert S. Dewar (resides in Madagascar).

Of the Comoros in the USA (Temporary: c/o the Permanent Mission of the Federal and Islamic Republic of the Comoros to the United Nations, 336 E 45th Street, 2nd Floor, N.Y. 10017)
Ambassador: Ahmed Djabir.

Of the USA in the Comoros
Ambassador: Harold Geisel (resides in Mauritius).

Of the Comoros to the United Nations
Ambassador: Ahmed Djabir.

Of the Comoros to the European Union
Ambassador: Mahamoud Soilih.

FURTHER READING
Newitt, N., *The Comoro Islands.* London, 1985
Ottenheimer, M. and Ottenheimer, H. J., *Historical Dictionary of the Comoro Islands.* Metuchen (NJ), 1994

CONGO, DEMOCRATIC REPUBLIC OF THE (FORMERLY ZAÏRE)

Capital: Kinshasa
Population estimate, 2000: 51·75m.
GNP per capita: (PPP$) 790
HDI/world rank: 0·383/143

República Démocratique du Congo

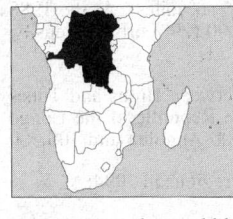

KEY HISTORICAL EVENTS

The area was visited by the Portuguese as early as the 14th century but King Leopold II of the Belgians took the lead in exploring and exploiting the Congo Basin and the Berlin Conference of 1884–85 recognized him as the sovereign head of the Congo Free State. In 1908 the country was annexed to Belgium as the Belgian Congo. After gaining independence in June 1960, the country's name was changed to Zaïre in 1971. Mobutu Sésé Séko came to power in a coup in 1965. At first he was seen as a strongman who could hold together a huge, unstable country comprising hundreds of tribes and language groups. In the 1970s he was feted by the USA which used Zaïre as a springboard for operations into neighbouring Angola where western-backed Unita rebels were locked in civil war with a Cuban- and Soviet-backed government. Because Mobutu was useful in the fight against Communism the brutality and repressiveness of his regime was ignored.

After armed insurrection by Tutsi rebels in the province of Kivu, the government alleged pro-Tutsi intervention by the armies of Burundi and Rwanda and on 25 Oct. 1996 declared a state of emergency. Following attacks on camps for Rwandan refugees, several hundred thousand of the occupants sought safety in flight. By the beginning of Nov. the eastern Zaïrean town of Goma was in the hands of Rwandan and rebel forces. By Dec. the secessionist forces of Laurent-Désiré Kabila, the Alliance of Democratic Forces for the Liberation of Congo-Zaïre (ADFL), had begun to drive the regular Zaïrean army out of Kivu and an attempt was made to establish a rebel administration, 'Democratic Congo'. By the middle of Feb. 1997 large parts of eastern Zaïre were under rebel control, and the government began to mount air attacks. In the face of continuing rebel military successes and the disaffection of the army, the Government accepted a UN resolution demanding the immediate cessation of hostilities. The Security Council asked the rebels also to make a public declaration of their acceptance. However, the latter continued in their victorious advance westwards, capturing Kisangani on 15 March 1997, then Kasai and Shaba, giving Kabila control of eastern Zaïre, and crucially the country's mineral wealth. Mobutu's attempts to cling to power looked hopeless. After another medical visit to France, and a futile attempt to deploy Serbian mercenaries, he succumbed to pressure—particularly from the USA and South Africa—and agreed to meet Kabila in the presence of President Mandela on the South African ship, the *SAS Outeniqua*, offshore from the Republic of the Congo. Little happened but the meeting had all the trappings of a symbolic surrender. Mobutu still hoped for compromise but the final victory of Kabila's troops, east of Kinshasa at Kenge, dashed any remaining illusions and the generals of Mobutu's own shell of an army told him that the situation was lost. In a state of indecision he fled without warning or conditions on the night of 15–16 May 1997. He died of cancer 4 months later. Described as one of the most destructive tyrants of the African independence era, it is said that his personal fortune, if ever recovered, could wipe out his country's national debt. On coming to power Kabila changed the name of the country to the Democratic Republic of the Congo. Hopes for democratic and economic renewal were soon disappointed. The Kabila regime relied too closely on his military backup, mainly Rwandans and eastern Congolese from the Tutsi minority. Those supporters seemed more interested in eliminating tribal enemies in eastern border areas than in establishing democracy. As a result, Rwanda and Uganda switched support to rebel forces. When Zimbabwe and Angola sent in troops to help President Kabila, full-scale civil war threatened. A ceasefire was negotiated at a Franco-African summit in Nov. 1998 but the military build-up continued into the new year and violence intensified.

TERRITORY AND POPULATION
The Democratic Republic of the Congo is bounded in the north by the Central African Republic, north-east by Sudan, east by Uganda, Rwanda, Burundi and Lake Tanganyika, south by Zambia, south-west by Angola and north-west by the Republic of the Congo. There is a 37-km stretch of coastline which gives access to the Atlantic Ocean, with the Angolan exclave of Cabinda to the immediate north, and Angola itself to the south. Area, 2,344,885 sq. km (905,365 sq. miles). At the 1988 census the population was 34·7m. Estimate (1997) 47,440,000 (29% urban); density, 20 per sq. km.

The UN gives a projected population for 2000 of 51·75m.

More than 200,000 refugees who escaped the fighting between Hutus and Tutsis in Rwanda and Burundi in 1994 are still in the Democratic Republic of the Congo (out of 1m. who came originally), and there are also 100,000 Angolan and 100,000 Sudanese refugees in the country.

Area, populations (1994 estimate) and chief towns of the regions in 1994:

Region	Area (sq. km)	Population (in 1,000)	Chief town	Population
Bandundu	295,658	4,907	Bandundu	...
Bas-Zaïre	53,920	2,578	Matadi	172,730
Equateur	403,293	4,789	Mbandaka	169,841
Haut-Zaïre	503,239	5,432	Kisangani	417,517
Kasai Occidental	154,742	3,117	Kananga	393,030
Kasai Oriental	170,302	3,778	Mbuji-Mayi	806,475
Kinshasa City	9,965	4,655	Kinshasa	4,655,313
Maniema[1]	132,250	—	Kindu	—
Nord-Kivu[1]	59,483	—	Goma	109,094
Sud-Kivu[1]	65,130	—	Bukavu	201,569
Shaba	496,965	5,602	Lubumbashi	851,381

[1]Combined population of Maniema, Nord-Kivu and Sud-Kivu, 7,687,000.

Other large cities (with estimated 1994 population): Kolwezi (417,810), Likasi (299,118), Kikwit (182,142), Tshikapa (180,860).

The population is Bantu, with minorities of Sudanese (in the north), Nilotes (north-east), Pygmies and Hamites (in the east). French is the official language, but of more than 200 languages spoken, 4 are recognized as national languages: Kiswahili, Tshiluba, Kikongo and Lingala. Lingala has become the *lingua franca* after French.

SOCIAL STATISTICS
1997 births, 2,263,000; deaths, 788,000. Rates (1997 estimates, per 1,000 population); Birth, 47·7; death, 16·6; growth rate, 2·3%. Infant mortality was 106 per 1,000 live births; expectation of life was 47·0 years (males, 45·2; females, 49·0). Fertility rate, 1990–95, 6·7 children per woman.

CLIMATE
The climate is varied, the central region having an equatorial climate, with year-long high temperatures and rain at all seasons. Elsewhere, depending on position north or south of the Equator, there are well-marked wet and dry seasons. The mountains of the east and south have a temperate mountain climate, with the highest summits having considerable snowfall. Kinshasa, Jan. 79°F (26·1°C), July 73°F (22·8°C). Annual rainfall 45" (1,125 mm). Kananga, Jan. 76°F (24·4°C), July 74°F (23·3°C). Annual rainfall 62" (1,584 mm). Kisangani, Jan. 78°F (25·6°C), July 75°F (23·9°C). Annual rainfall 68" (1,704 mm). Lubumbashi, Jan. 72°F (22·2°C), July 61°F (16·1°C). Annual rainfall 50" (1,237 mm).

CONSTITUTION AND GOVERNMENT

Gen. Laurent-Désiré Kabila seized power on 17 May 1997 after the military defeat of Marshal Mobutu Sésé Séko and his government, and is both chief of state and head of government. Although parties other than the ADFL have been dissolved, a constitutional referendum was due to be held in Dec. 1998, and presidential and parliamentary elections in April 1999.

CURRENT ADMINISTRATION

Laurent Kabila appointed 13 new government ministers in June 1998 after purging his inner circle of 5 cabinet ministers and placing them under arrest. In Aug. 1998, 2 ministers went into exile in South Africa.

In March 1999 the government comprised:

President, Minister of Defence: Gen. Laurent-Désiré Kabila.

Minister of State Attached to the Presidency: Pierre Victor Mpoyo. *Minister of State for Interior:* Gaëtan Kakudji. *Minsiter of State for Planning:* Badimayi Bilembo Mulumba.

Minister of Agriculture and Livestock, Finance and Budget: Mawampanga Mwana Nanga. *Civil Service:* Paul Kapita Shabangi. *Commerce:* Paul Bandoma. *Culture and Arts:* Juliana Lumumba. *Economy:* Henri Nyembo Kabemba. *Education:* Augustin Kamara Rwakaikara. *Energy:* Christian Eleko Botuma. *Environment:* Eddy Angulu Mabengi. *Human Rights:* Leonard Cheik Okitundu. *Industry and Small and Medium-Sized Enterprises:* Richard Babi Mbaye. *Information and Press:* Didier Mumengi. *International Co-operation:* Célestin Lwangi. *Justice:* Mwenze Kongolo. *Labour and Social Affairs:* Thomas Kanza. *Land Affairs:* Anatole Bishikwabo Chubaka. *Mines:* Fréderic Kibassa Maliba. *Development and Strategic Zones:* Gabriel Umba Kyamitala. *Post and Telecommunications:* Jean-Moreno Kinkela Vi Kan'sy. *Public Enterprises:* Prosper Kibwe Molambo. *Public Works:* Bruno Luawulo. *Transport and Communications:* Henri Mova Sakanyi. *Tourism:* Pascaline Birindo Toyi. *Youth and Sports:* Dumba Kimaya.

Local Government. The Democratic Republic of the Congo is composed of Kinshasa (administered by a Governor) and 10 regions, each under a Regional Commissioner and 6 Councillors; all are appointed by the President. The regions are divided into 41 sub-regions.

DEFENCE

Following the overthrow of the Mobutu regime in May 1997, the former Zaïrean armed forces were in disarray. The insurgent Congo Liberation Army has between 20,000 and 40,000 fighters, equipped with small arms and some SA-7 SAMs. Much of this equipment is believed to be non-operational.

Defence expenditure totalled US$308m. in 1997 (US$7 per capita).

INTERNATIONAL RELATIONS

The Democratic Republic of the Congo is a member of the UN, OAU and is an ACP member state of the ACP-EU relationship.

ECONOMY

In Sept. 1998 President Kabila decreed that all purchases of gold and diamonds must be in new Congolese francs and go through a state purchasing company.

Performance. GDP fell 0·7% in 1995 and was reported in Feb. 1998 to be 65% lower than it was in 1960, when the country gained independence.

Budget. Revenues in 1996 were an estimated US$269m. and expenditure US$244m. International economic aid has been made dependent on a coherent plan to revive the economy and progress on democracy and human rights.

Currency. The unit of currency is the *Congo franc* which replaced the former *zaïre* in July 1998. The value of the new currency fell by two-thirds in the six months following its launch. Foreign exchange reserves were US$83m. in Dec. 1996. Inflation was around 14% in Nov. 1997.

Banking and Finance. The central bank is Banque Centrale du Congo. A development bank with state backing is the Société Financière de Développement (SOFIDE). Commercial banks operating in the Democratic Republic of the Congo include Banque de Paris et des Pays-Bas, Banque de Kinshasa, National & Grindlays Bank, Barclays Bank SZPRL, First National City Bank, Banque du Peuple and Caisse Nationale d'Epargne et de Crédit Immobilier.

Since Aug. 1991 commercial banks have been able to trade foreign exchange freely at their own rates.

Weights and Measures. The metric system is in force.

ENERGY AND NATURAL RESOURCES

Electricity. Production (1994), 5,480m. kWh. A dam at Inga, on the River Congo near Matadi, has a potential capacity of 39,600 MW. Installed capacity was 2·83m. kW in 1994. Consumption per capita was estimated to be 87 kWh in 1995.

Oil and Gas. Offshore oil production began in Nov. 1975; estimated crude production (1992) was 1·35m. tonnes. There is an oil refinery at Kinlao-Muanda.

Minerals. Production in 1993 (in 1,000 tonnes): Copper, 48; zinc, 30; cobalt, 2·4; gold, 1,400 kg; diamonds, 15·6m. carats. Coal, tin and silver are also found. The most important mining area is in the region of Shaba (formerly Katanga).

Agriculture. Agriculture accounts for approximately 64% of GDP (the highest proportion anywhere in the world). There were, in 1994, 7·28m. ha of arable land and 15·0m. ha of permanent pasture. The main food crops (1993 production in 1,000 tonnes) are: Cassava, 20,835; plantains, 2,224; sugar-cane, 1,400; maize, 1,201; groundnuts, 604; bananas, 406; yams, 315; rice, 458. Cash crops (1993) include palm oil, 181; coffee, 78; palm kernels, 72; rubber, 5; seed cotton, 77. There are also pineapples, 145; mangoes, 212; oranges, 156; papayas, 210.

Livestock (1996): Cattle, 1,480,000; sheep, 1,043,000; goats, 4,220,000 (1995); pigs, 1,157,000; poultry, 36m. (1995).

Forestry. Equatorial rainforests covered 1,092,000 sq. km in 1995, or 48·2% of the land area, down from 1,129,000 sq. km and 49·8% in 1990. The reduction of 37,000 sq. km in the area under forests between 1990 and 1995 was the biggest in any African country over the same period, and was only exceeded worldwide in Brazil and Indonesia. Timber production in 1995 was 47·19m. cu. metres.

Fisheries. The catch for 1995 was 158,627 tonnes, almost entirely from inland waters.

INDUSTRY

The main manufactures are foodstuffs, beverages, tobacco, textiles, rubber, leather, wood products, cement and building materials, metallurgy and metal extraction, metal items, transport vehicles, electrical equipment and bicycles.

Labour. In 1996 the workforce was 19·62m. (56% males). Agriculture employs around 65% of the total economically active population.

INTERNATIONAL TRADE

With Burundi and Rwanda, the Democratic Republic of the Congo forms part of the Economic Community of the Great Lakes. External debt was more than US$14,000m. in 1997.

Imports and Exports. Exports in 1996 totalled US$592m., imports, US$424m. Main commodities for export are diamonds, copper, coffee, cobalt and crude oil; and for import: consumer goods, foodstuffs, mining and other machinery, transport equipment and fuels. Principal export markets are Belgium, USA, France, Germany, Italy, UK, Japan and South Africa. Principal import suppliers are Belgium, South Africa, USA, France, Germany, Italy, Japan and UK.

COMMUNICATIONS

Roads. In 1996 there were approximately 33,000 km of motorways and main roads, and 40,000 km of secondary roads and 83,000 km of other roads. There were an estimated 787,000 passenger cars in use in 1996 (17 per 1,000 inhabitants) plus 538,000 trucks and vans.

Rail. There was 5,138 km of track on 3 gauges in 1995, of which 858 km was electrified. However, the length of track in use was severely reduced by the civil strife in late 1996 and the early part of 1997.

Civil Aviation. There is an international airport at Kinshasa (Ndjili). Other major airports are at Lubumbashi (Luano), Bukavu, Goma and Kisangani. The national carrier is Congo Airlines. In 1998 services were also provided by Aero-Service, Air Tanzania Corporation, Cameroon Airlines, Compagnie Africaine d'Aviation, Ethiopian Airlines, Nigeria Airways, SABENA, South African Airways, Swissair, TAAG, TAP and Uganda Airlines. In 1996 Kinshasa handled 344,000 passengers (192,000 on domestic flights) and 96,300 tonnes of freight.

Shipping. The River Congo and its tributaries are navigable to 300-tonne vessels for about 14,500 km. Regular traffic has been established between Kinshasa and Kisangani as well as Ilebo, on the Lualaba (*i.e.*, the river above Kisangani), on some tributaries and on the lakes. The Democratic Republic of the Congo has only 37 km of sea coast. In 1995 merchant shipping totalled 15,000 GRT. Matadi, Kinshasa and Kalemie are the main seaports; in 1993 Matadi handled 0·6m. tonnes of freight.

Telecommunications. Telephone main lines numbered 21,000 in 1997, or 0·4 per 1,000 inhabitants—the lowest penetration rate of any country in the world. There is a ground satellite communications station outside Kinshasa. In 1995 there were 10,000 cellular phone subscribers and 5,000 fax machines, and in Jan. 1998 approximately 100 Internet users.

Postal Services. In 1995 there were 304 post offices.

SOCIAL INSTITUTIONS

Justice. There is a Supreme Court at Kinshasa, 11 courts of appeal, 36 courts of first instance and 24 'peace tribunals'.

Religion. In 1996 there were 21·9m. Roman Catholics, 13·1m. Protestants, 7·74m. Kimbanguistes (African Christians) and 0·63m. Moslems. Animist beliefs persist.

Education. In 1994–95 there were 14,885 primary schools with 121,054 teachers for 5·4m. pupils, and in 1993–94, 59,325 secondary teachers for 1·5m. pupils. In 1994–95 there were 93,266 students at university level. In higher education there were 3 universities (Kinshasa, Kisangani and Lubumbashi) in 1994–95, 14 teacher training colleges and 18 technical institutes in the public sector; and 13 university institutes, 4 teacher training colleges and 49 technical institutes in the private sector. There were 20,130 university students and 1,630 academic staff in 1994–95. Adult literacy rate was 77·3% in 1995 (male, 86·6%; female, 67·7%). In 1995 government expenditure on education totalled 27,000m. zaïres.

Health. In 1990 there were 2,469 doctors, 41 dentists and 27,601 nurses. In 1995 government expenditure on health totalled 25,000m. zaïres.

CULTURE

Broadcasting. Broadcasting is provided by government-controlled radio and television stations (colour by SECAM). There is also an educational radio station. In 1995 there were 4·45m. radio and 100,000 TV receivers.

Press. In 1995 there were 9 daily newspapers with a combined circulation of 120,000.

Tourism. In 1996 there were 37,000 foreign tourists, spending US$5m.

DIPLOMATIC REPRESENTATIVES

Of the Democratic Republic of the Congo in Great Britain (26 Chesham Pl., London, SW1X 8HH)
Ambassador: Vacant.

Of Great Britain in the Democratic Republic of the Congo (Ave. de Trois Z, Gombe, Kinshasa)
Ambassador: Mr. D. Scrafton, CMG.

Of the Democratic Republic of the Congo in the USA (1800 New Hampshire Ave., NW, Washington, D.C., 20009)
Chargé d'Affaires a.i.: Faida Mitifu.

Of the USA in the Democratic Republic of the Congo (310 Ave. des Aviateurs, Kinshasa)
Ambassador: Daniel H. Simpson.

Of the Democratic Republic of the Congo to the United Nations
Ambassador: André Mwamba Kapanga.

Of the Democratic Republic of the Congo to the European Union
Ambassador: Justine M'Poyo Kasa-Vubu.

FURTHER READING
Leslie, W. J., *Zaïre: Continuity and Political Change in an Oppressive State.* Boulder (CO), 1993
Williams, D. B. et al. *Zaïre:* [Bibliography] 2nd ed. Oxford and Santa Barbara (CA), 1995

CONGO, REPUBLIC OF THE

République du Congo

Capital: Brazzaville
Population estimate, 2000: 2·98m.
GNP per capita: (PPP$) 1,410
HDI/world rank: 0·519/128

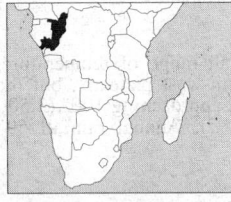

KEY HISTORICAL EVENTS

The Portuguese first reached the mouth of the Congo in the 15th century. Loango, in the Kouilou region, was one of the largest ports connected with slavery in the 18th century. Late in the 19th century Sir Henry Stanley and Savorgnan de Brazza (after whom the capital was named) multiplied the number of explorations and investigations. First occupied by France in 1882, the Congo became a territory of French Equatorial Africa from 1910–58, and then a member state of the French Community. Between 1940 and 1944, thanks to Equatorial Africa's allegiance to General de Gaulle, he named Brazzaville the capital of the Empire and Liberated France. Independence was granted in 1960.

The first President, Fulbert Youlou, was deposed on 15 Aug. 1963 by a coup led by Alphonse Massemba-Débat who became President on 19 Dec. Following a second coup in Aug. 1968, the Army took power under the leadership of Major Marien Ngouabi whose colleague, Major Alfred Raoul, was appointed President from 3 Sept. until 1 Jan. 1969 when Ngouabi himself became President. A Marxist-Leninist state was introduced in 1970. Ngouabi was assassinated on 18 March 1977 and succeeded by Col. Joachim Yhombi-Opango who, in turn, was replaced on 5 Feb. 1979 by Col. Denis Sassou-Nguesso. Free elections were restored in 1992 when the now Gen. Sassou-Nguesso was defeated by Pascal Lissouba but violence erupted when in June 1997 President Lissouba tried to disarm the General's militia ahead of a fresh election. There followed 4 months of civil war with fighting concentrated on Brazzaville which became a ghost town. In Oct. Gen. Sassou-Nguesso proclaimed victory, having relied upon military support from Angola. President Lissouba went into hiding in Burkina Faso.

TERRITORY AND POPULATION

The Republic of the Congo is bounded by Cameroon and the Central African Republic in the north, the Democratic Republic of the Congo to the east and south, Angola and the Atlantic Ocean to the south-west and Gabon to the west, and covers 341,821 sq. km. At the census of 1984 the population was 1,909,248.

Estimated population in 1997, 2,583,000; density, 7·6 per sq. km.

The UN gives a projected population for 2000 of 2·98m.

In 1995 it was estimated that 58·4% of the population were urban. Estimated population of major cities in 1995 were: Brazzaville, the capital, 937,579; Pointe-Noire, 576,206; Loubomo, 83,605; N'Kayi, 42,465; Mossendjo, 16,405; Ouesso, 16,171.

Area, estimated population and county towns of the regions in 1992 were:

Region	Sq. km	Population	County town
Kouilou	13,694	665,502	Pointe-Noire
Niari	25,940	220,087	Loubomo
Lékoumou	20,950	74,420	Sibiti
Bouenza	12,266	219,822	Madingou
Pool	33,955	182,671	Kinkala
Capital District	100	937,579	Brazzaville
Plateaux	38,400	119,722	Djambala
Cuvette	74,850	151,839	Owando
Sangha	55,800	52,132	Ouesso
Likouala	66,044	70,675	Impfondo

Main ethnic groups are: Kongo (48%), Sangha (20%), Teke (17%) and M'Bochi (12%).

French is the official language. Kongo languages are widely spoken. Monokutuba and Lingala serve as lingua francas.

SOCIAL STATISTICS
1997 births, 100,000; deaths, 45,000. Rates, 1997 estimates (per 1,000 population): Births, 38·8; deaths, 17·3. Infant mortality (per 1,000 live births), 106·1. Expectation of life in 1997 was 45·7 years (44·25 for males and 47·3 for females). Growth rate, 2·15% per annum. Fertility rate, 1990–95, 6·3 children per woman.

CLIMATE
An equatorial climate, with moderate rainfall and a small range of temperature. There is a long dry season from May to Oct. in the south-west plateaux, but the Congo Basin in the north-east is more humid, with rainfall approaching 100" (2,500 mm). Brazzaville, Jan. 78°F (25·6°C), July 73°F (22·8°C). Annual rainfall 59" (1,473 mm).

CONSTITUTION AND GOVERNMENT
From Feb. to June 1991 a national conference was held consisting of representatives of 67 political parties, 134 associations and 30 specialists. This abolished the constitution of July 1979, dissolved the National Assembly, Constitutional Council and Economic Council, and adopted a basic law to regulate a period of transition. It established a presidency of the republic with newly defined powers, a 153-member Supreme Council of the Republic and a prime ministership. At a referendum in March 1992 proposing multi-party democracy 96·32% of votes were in favour. Turn-out was 70·93%.

National Anthem. 'La Congolaise; words and tune by Jean Royer and others.

RECENT ELECTIONS
At the elections of 24 June and 19 July 1992 for the new 125-member *National Assembly*, the Pan-African Union for Social Democracy (UPADS) gained 39 seats, the Congolese Movement for Democracy and Integral Development (MCDDI) 29, the Congolese Labour Party 19, the Democratic Rally for Social Progress 9 and the Rally for Democracy and Development 5.

In the 60-member *Senate*, UPADS gained 23 seats, MCDDI 13.

In Nov. 1992 the President dismissed the government of Stéphane Bongho-Nouarra and dissolved the National Assembly. At the first round of elections in May–June 1993 for 114 seats in the National Assembly, the Presidential Movement (PM; a coalition of some 60 parties) gained 62 seats, the Congolese Labour Party–Union for Democratic Renewal Coalition 49 and minor parties 3. At the second round in Oct. for the remaining 11 seats, the PM gained 4 and CLP-UDR 7.

At the 1992 presidential elections, Pascal Lissouba was elected President, defeating Gen. Sassou-Nguesso. In Oct. 1997, following a military-led coup under Gen. Sassou-Nguesso, and 4 months of civil war, Pascal Lissouba went into hiding and Gen. Sassou-Nguesso was sworn in as President.

CURRENT ADMINISTRATION
President: Denis Sassou-Nguesso (sworn in Oct. 1997).

Gen. Sassou-Nguesso subsequently formed a transition government, which in March 1999 comprised:

Minister of the Presidency in Charge of National Defence: Justin Itihi Lekoundzou Ossetoumba. *Minister of the Presidency in Charge of the Presidential Cabinet and State Control:* Gerard Bitsindou. *Agriculture and Livestock:* Célestin Nkoua Gongara. *Communication and Relations with Parliament:* François Ibovi. *Culture and Tourism:* Aimee Mambou Gnali. *Energy and Water Resources:* Jean-Marie Tassoua. *Economy, Finance and Budget:* Mathias Dzon. *Forestry and Fisheries:* Henri Djombo. *Foreign Affairs and Co-operation:* Rodolphe Adada. *Health and National Solidarity:* Leon Alfred Opimbat. *Education and Scientific Research:* Pierre Nzila. *Industry, Mines and Environment:* Michel Mampouya. *Interior:* Pierre Oba. *Justice and Keeper of the Seals:* Jean Martin Mbemba. *Labour and Social Security:* Lambert Ndouane. *Petroleum Affairs:* Jean-Baptiste Taty Loutard. *Posts and Telecommunications:* Jean Delo. *Reconstruction and Urban*

Development: Martin Mberi. *Public Works:* Col. Florent Tsiba. *Technical Education, Professional Training, Youth, Civic Education and Sports:* André Okombi Salissan. *Regional Development:* Pierre Moussa. *Public Service, Administrative Reform and Women's Affairs:* Jeanne Dambenze. *Industrial Development and Private Sector Promotion:* Alphonse Obama. *Commerce and Small and Medium-Sized Enterprises:* Pierre Damien Boussoukou Boumba.

Local Government. In compliance with a law of 18 Sept. 1995, the country was reorganized into 10 regions, which are themselves divided into 76 districts. In addition there are 6 urban councils. The regions are Kouilou, Niari, Lékoumou, Bouenza, Pool, Plateaux, Cuvette, Cuvette Ouest, Sangha and Likouala. Niari's county town, previously Loubomo, became Dolisie. Cuvette Ouest's county town is Ewo. (See also TERRITORY AND POPULATION, above.) The 6 distinct urban councils are Brazzaville, Dolisie, Mossendjo, Nkayi, Owando and Pointe-Noire.

DEFENCE
In 1997 military expenditure totalled US$74m. (US$20 per capita).

Army. The Army consists of 2 infantry battalion groups, 2 armoured and 1 infantry battalion, 1 artillery group, 1 engineer and 1 paracommando battalion. Equipment includes 25 T-54/-55 and 15 T-59 main battle tanks. Total personnel (1997) 8,000. There is a Gendarmerie of 2,000. The 'People's Militia' is being absorbed into the Army.

Navy. The combatant flotilla includes 3 modern Spanish-built and 3 ex-Soviet inshore patrol craft. There is also 1 French-built tug and some river patrol boats. Personnel in 1996 totalled about 600.

Air Force. The Air Force had (1997) about 1,200 personnel, 5 Antonov An-24/26 turboprop transports, 1 Noratlas piston-engined transport and 2 Mi-8 helicopters. Most of these aircraft are in store.

INTERNATIONAL RELATIONS
The Republic of the Congo is a member of the UN, OAU and is an ACP member state of the ACP-EU relationship.

ECONOMY
Policy. An economic and social recovery plan (Paséco) was launched in 1994.

Performance. Real GDP growth was −0·4% in 1995 (−1·5% in 1994).

Budget. Estimated figures for 1997 are: Revenue, US$870m.; expenditure, US$970m. (including capital expenditures).

Currency. The unit of currency is the *franc CFA* with a parity of 100 francs CFA to 1 French franc. Total money supply in Jan. 1998 was 171bn. francs CFA. Foreign exchange reserves were US$53m. in Jan. 1998. Inflation was down to 70% in 1998 with a new currency, the Congolese franc, introduced on 30 June.

Banking and Finance. The *Banque des États de l'Afrique Centrale* (BEAC) is the bank of issue. There are 3 commercial banks and a development bank, in all of which the government has majority stakes.

Weights and Measures. The metric system is in use.

ENERGY AND NATURAL RESOURCES
Electricity. Installed capacity was 165,000 kW in 1995. Total production in 1994 was 440m. kWh. Consumption per capita was an estimated 223 kWh in 1994.

Oil and Gas. Oil was discovered in the mid-1960s when Elf Aquitaine was given exclusive rights to production. Elf still has the lion's share but Agip Congo is also involved in oil exploitation. In 1997 production was averaging 230,000 bbls. a day. Reserves are estimated at 500–1,000m. tonnes, including major off-shore deposits. Oil provides about 90% of government revenue and exports. There is a refinery at Pointe-Noire, the second largest city. Gas reserves are estimated at 71,000m. cu. metres.

Minerals. A government mine produces several metals; gold and diamonds are extracted by individuals. There are reserves of potash (4·5m. tonnes), iron ore (1,000m. tonnes), and also clay, bituminous sand, phosphates, zinc and lead.

Agriculture. In 1996 agriculture produced 10% of GDP. In 1994 there were 145,000 ha of arable land, 25,000 ha of permanent crops and 10m. ha of permanent pasture. Production (1991, in thousand tonnes): Cassava, 780; bananas, 40; plantains, 80; yams, 12; maize, 25; groundnuts, 27; coffee, 1; cocoa, 2; rice, 1.

Livestock (1996): Cattle, 70,000; pigs, 59,000; sheep, 114,000; goats, 305; poultry, 2m. There were some 700 tractors in use in 1994.

Forestry. In 1995 equatorial forests covered 19·54m. ha in (57·2% of the total land area), down from 19·74m. ha in 1990. 3·83m. cu. metres of timber were produced in 1995, mainly okoumé from the south and sapele from the north. Timber companies are required to replant, and to process at least 60% of their production locally. Before the development of the oil industry, forestry was the mainstay of the economy.

Fisheries. The catch for 1995 was 36,824 tonnes, of which 19,824 tonnes were from inland waters.

INDUSTRY
There is a growing manufacturing sector, located mainly in the 4 major towns, producing processed foods, textiles, cement, metal goods and chemicals. Industry produced 37·4% of GDP in 1991, including 7·6% from manufacturing. Production: Printed cloth (1990), 8·79m. metres; cement (1989), 121,000 tonnes; shoes (1989), 14,670 pairs; corrugated iron sheets (1990), 1·68m. tonnes; household goods (1990), 186 tonnes; nails (1990), 377 tonnes.

Labour. In 1996 the labour force was 1,105,000 (57% males). More than 50% of the economically active population were engaged in agriculture.

Trade Unions. In 1964 the existing unions merged into one national body, the Confédération Syndicale Congolaise. The 40,000-strong Confédération Syndicale des Travailleurs Congolais split off from the latter in 1993.

INTERNATIONAL TRADE
Foreign debt was US$5,300m. in 1996.

Imports and Exports. Imports in 1995 totalled US$671m. and exports US$1,176m. Apart from crude oil, other significant commodities for export are lumber, plywood, sugar, cocoa, coffee and diamonds. Principal imported commodities are intermediate manufactures, capital equipment, construction materials, foodstuffs and petroleum products. Main export markets in 1995 were Belgium/Luxembourg, 24·3%, followed by Taiwan, the USA and Italy. Main import suppliers: France, 31·2%, followed by the Netherlands, Italy and the USA.

COMMUNICATIONS
Roads. In 1996 there were 12,800 km of roads, of which 1,240 km were surfaced. Vehicles in use in 1996 numbered 53,000 including approximately 37,000 passenger cars (14 per 1,000 inhabitants).

Rail. A railway (510 km, 1,067 mm gauge) connects Brazzaville with Pointe-Noire via Loubomo and Bilinga, and a 285 km branch links Mont-Belo with Mbinda on the Gabon border. Total length is 795 km. In 1994 railways carried 285m. passenger-km and 223m. tonne-km of freight.

Civil Aviation. The principal airports are at Brazzaville (Maya Maya) and Pointe-Noire. The Republic of the Congo is a member of the multinational Air Afrique, which absorbed the former national carrier Lina-Congo in 1992. Services were also provided in 1998 by Aero-Service, Air France and Cameroon Airlines. In 1996 Brazzaville handled 416,344 passengers (246,000 on domestic flights) and 10,371 tonnes of freight.

Shipping. The only seaport is Pointe-Noire, which handled 2·59m. tonnes of freight in 1990. The merchant marine totalled 11,010 GRT in 1995. There are some 5,000 km of navigable rivers, and river transport is an important service for timber and other freight as well as passengers. There are hydrofoil connections from Brazzaville to Kinshasa.

Telecommunications. There were 22,000 telephone main lines in 1997 (8 per 1,000 persons). In 1995 there were 100 fax machines.

Postal Services. There were 114 post offices in 1995.

SOCIAL INSTITUTIONS

Justice. The Supreme Court, Court of Appeal and a criminal court are situated in Brazzaville, with a network of *tribunaux de grande instance* and *tribunaux d'instance* in the regions.

Religion. In 1990 there were 1·25m. Roman Catholics and 0·5m. Protestants. There are also Moslems, and traditional animist beliefs are still practised.

Education. In 1995–96 there were 1,162 primary schools with 7,060 teachers for 497,305 pupils, 7,173 secondary school teachers for 214,650 pupils; and there were 13,806 students at university level in 1992–93. Adult literacy rate (1995) 74·9% (male, 83·1%; female, 67·2%).

Health. In 1990 there were 613 doctors, 35 dentists, 1,624 nurses and 498 midwives.

CULTURE

Broadcasting. Broadcasting is under the aegis of the government-controlled Radiodiffusion-Télévision Congolaise, which transmits a national and a regional radio programme and a programme in French. In 1993 there were 6 hours of TV broadcasting daily (colour by SECAM). There were 300,000 radio and about 20,000 TV receivers in 1995.

Press. In 1995 there were 6 daily newspapers with a combined circulation of 20,000.

Tourism. There were 27,000 foreign tourists in 1996, bringing revenue of US$4m.

DIPLOMATIC REPRESENTATIVES
Of the Republic of the Congo in Great Britain
Ambassador: Vacant (resides in Paris).

Of Great Britain in the Republic of the Congo
Ambassador: Mr D. Scrafton, CMG (resides in Kinshasa).

Of the Republic of the Congo in the USA (4891 Colorado Ave., NW, Washington, D.C., 20011)
Chargé d'Affaires a.i.: Serge Mombouli.

Of the USA in the Republic of the Congo (PO Box 1015, Brazzaville)
Ambassador: Aubrey Hookes.

Of the Republic of the Congo to the United Nations
Ambassador: Vacant.

Of the Republic of the Congo to the European Union
Ambassador: Vacant.

FURTHER READING
Thompson, V. and Adloff, R., *Historical Dictionary of the People's Republic of the Congo.* 2nd ed. Metuchen (NJ), 1984

COSTA RICA

República de Costa Rica

Capital: San José
Population estimate, 2000: 3·8m.
GNP per capita: (PPP$) 6,470
HDI/world rank: 0·889/34

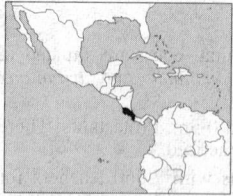

KEY HISTORICAL EVENTS

Discovered by Columbus in 1502 on his last voyage, Costa Rica (Rich Coast) was part of the Spanish viceroyalty of New Spain from 1540 and was thought to be rich in gold. Costa Rica became independent of Spain in 1821. From 1822 to 1823 it was part of Mexico and then part of the Central American Federation until 1838 when it left this confederation and achieved full independence. The first constitution was promulgated on 7 Dec. 1871. Coffee was introduced in 1808 and became a mainstay of the economy, helping to create a peasant land-owning class. Bananas, another important crop, were introduced in 1878. In 1917 Federico Tinoco overthrew the elected president but the USA intervened and Tinoco was deposed in 1919. In 1948 accusations of election fraud led to a 6-week civil war, at the conclusion of which José Figueres Ferrer won power at the head of a revolutionary junta. A new constitution was promulgated with, amongst other changes, the abolition of the army. Ferrer, the founder and leader of the *Partido de Liberación Nacional* (PLN), became the elected president from 1953 to 1958 and again in 1970-74. More conservative governments held office between Ferrer's 2 presidencies and again after Ferrer's PLN successor's single 4-year term. In 1982 the PLN candidate, Luis Alberto Monge, was elected president. In 1986 Oscar Arias Sánchez was elected to succeed Monge. He promised to prevent Nicaraguan anti-Sandinista (*contra*) forces using Costa Rica as a base. In 1987 he received the Nobel Peace Prize as recognition of his Central American peace plan, agreed to by the other Central American states. Costa Rica was beset with economic problems in the early 1990s when several politicians, including President Calderón, were accused of profiting from drug trafficking.

TERRITORY AND POPULATION

Costa Rica is bounded in the north by Nicaragua, east by the Caribbean, south-east by Panama, and south and west by the Pacific. The area is estimated at 51,100 sq. km (19,730 sq. miles). The population at the census of 1 June 1984 was 2,416,809. Estimate (1995) 3,367,400 (49·3% urban); density, 66·2 per sq. km.

The UN gives a projected population for 2000 of 3·8m.

There are 7 provinces (with 1995 population): Alajuela (607,674); Cartago (378,188); Guanacaste (266,198); Heredia (270,096); Limón (255,248); Puntarenas (375,639); San José (1,220,412).

The population is mainly of Spanish (85%) and mixed (8%) descent. About 3% are Afro-Caribbean (including some 70,000 speakers of an English Creole along the Caribbean coast). There is a residual Amerindian population of about 10,000.

Spanish is the official language.

SOCIAL STATISTICS

Statistics for calendar years:

	Marriages	Births	Deaths
1994	21,520	80,391	13,313
1995	24,274	80,306	14,061
1996	23,574	78,203	13,993
1997	24,300	78,018	14,260

1995 rates per 1,000 population: Births, 23·8; deaths, 4·2. Annual growth rate, 1990–95, 3·5%. Life expectancy at birth, 1990–95, was 74·0 years for men and 78·6 years for women. Infant mortality, 1990–95, 14 per 1,000 live births; fertility rate, 3·1 children per woman.

CLIMATE
The climate is tropical, with a small range of temperature and abundant rains. The dry season is from Dec. to April. San José, Jan. 66°F (18·9°C), July 69°F (20·6°C). Annual rainfall 72" (1,793 mm).

CONSTITUTION AND GOVERNMENT
The Constitution was promulgated in Nov. 1949. The legislative power is vested in a single-chamber *Legislative Assembly* of 57 deputies elected for 4 years. The President and 2 Vice-Presidents are elected for 4 years; the candidate receiving the largest vote, provided it is over 40% of the total, is declared elected, but a second ballot is required if no candidate gets 40% of the total. Elections are normally held on the first Sunday in February.

The President may appoint and remove members of the cabinet.

National Anthem. 'Noble patria, tu hermosa bandera' ('Noble fatherland, thy beautiful banner'); words by J. M. Zeledón Brenes, tune by M. M. Gutiérrez.

RECENT ELECTIONS
Presidential elections took place on 1 Feb. 1998. Miguel Angel Rodriguez of the Social Christian Unity Party (PUSC) was elected by 46·9% of votes cast, defeating José Miguel Corrales, of the National Liberation Party (PLN), who obtained 44·4% of the votes, and 4 other candidates.

At the simultaneous parliamentary elections the Social Christian Unity Party won 29 seats (with 41·3% of the votes), the National Liberation Party 22 (with 34·9%) and others 6.

CURRENT ADMINISTRATION
President: Miguel Angel Rodriguez.

In March 1999 the govenment comprised:

First Vice President and Minister of Culture: Astrid Fischel Volio. *Second Vice President and Minister of Environment and Energy:* Elizabeth Odio Benito. *Agriculture and Livestock:* Esteban Brenes Castro. *Economy and Foreign Trade:* Samuel Guzowski Rose. *Finance:* Leonel Baruch Goldberg. *Foreign Relations and Religion:* Roberto Rojas Lopez. *Health:* Rogelio Pardo Evans. *Housing:* Jose Antonio Lobo. *Justice:* Monica Nagel Berger. *Labour and Social Security:* Victor Morales Mora. *Presidency/Planning:* Roberto Tovar Faja. *Public Education:* Claudio Gutierrez Carranza. *Public Security, Government and Police:* Juan Rafael Lizano Saenz. *Public Works and Transportation:* Rodolfo Mendez Maia. *Women's Situation:* Yolanda Ingianna.

DEFENCE
In 1997 defence expenditure totalled US$59m. (US$17 per capita).

Army. The Army was abolished in 1948, and replaced by a Civil Guard, 3,000-strong in 1996.

Navy. The para-military Civil Guard flotilla includes 1 150-tonne ex-US cutter, 1 fast patrol craft, 5 small coastguard cutters and some boats. Personnel (1996), 400.

Air Wing. The Civil Guard operates a small air wing equipped with 10 light planes and helicopters, and 2 Caribou transports.

INTERNATIONAL RELATIONS
Costa Rica is a member of the UN, CACM and OAS.

ECONOMY
Performance. Real GDP growth was 2·5% in 1995 (4·5% in 1994).

Budget. In 1996 revenue was 500·96bn. colones (427·41bn. in 1995) and expenditure 572·97bn. colones (472·25bn. in 1995).

Currency. The unit of currency is the *Costa Rican colón* (CRC) of 100 *céntimos*. The official rate is used for all imports on an essential list and by the Government and autonomous institutions, and a free rate is used for all other transactions. Total money supply was 274m. colones in Dec. 1997. Inflation was 13·0% in Dec. 1998. Foreign exchange reserves were US$1,129m. in Feb. 1998.

Banking and Finance. The bank of issue is the Central Bank (founded 1950) which supervises the national monetary system, foreign exchange dealings and banking operations. The bank has a board of 7 directors appointed by the Government, including *ex officio* the Minister of Finance and the Planning Office Director. The *Governor* is Carlos Manuel Castillo.

There is a stock exchange, which in 1998 was the most successful market in the world, gaining in value by 88% in the course of the year.

Weights and Measures. The metric system is legally established, but in country districts the following old Spanish weights and measures may be found: *Libra* = 1·014 lb. avoirdupois; *arroba* = 25·35 lb. avoirdupois; *quintal* = 101·40 lb. avoirdupois, and *fanega* = 11 Imperial bushels.

ENERGY AND NATURAL RESOURCES

Electricity. Installed capacity was 1,114,400 kW in 1995. Production was 5·14bn. kWh in 1995. Consumption per capita was estimated to be 1,330 kWh in 1995.

Minerals. Gold output is about 3,000 troy oz. per year. Salt production was 50,000 tonnes in 1991.

Agriculture. Agriculture is a key sector: in 1995, 263,000 people were economically active, and in 1996, it accounted for 16% of GDP. The arable area is about 285,000 ha. The principal agricultural products are coffee, bananas, sugar and cattle. Coffee production in 1997 (in tonnes) was 607,831; sugar-cane, 3·15m.; bananas 1·83m.; maize, 30,415; tobacco, 1,089; rice, 218,194; potatoes, 64,597.

Livestock (1996): Cattle, 1·58m.; pigs, 300,000; horses, 115,000; chickens, 15m. (1995).

Forestry. The forest area is being depleted, having been 1·45m. ha and 28·5% of the total land area in 1990, but only 1·25m. ha and 24·4% of the land area in 1995. Timber production in 1995 was 4·81m. cu. metres.

Fisheries. Total catches in 1995 amounted to 27,928 tonnes, mostly from sea fishing.

INDUSTRY

The main manufactured goods are foodstuffs, textiles, fertilizers, pharmaceuticals, furniture, cement, tyres, canning, clothing, plastic goods, plywood and electrical equipment.

Labour. Out of 1,168,000 people in employment in 1995, 287,000 were in community, social and personal services, 263,000 in agriculture and 226,000 in trade, restaurants and hotels. There were 63,500 unemployed persons, or 5·2% of the workforce.

Trade Unions. There are two main trade unions, *Rerum Novarum* (anti-Communist) and *Confederación General de Trabajadores Costarricenses* (Communist).

INTERNATIONAL TRADE

A free trade agreement was signed with Mexico in March 1994. Some 2,300 products were freed from tariffs, with others to follow over 10 years. External debt was US$3,454m. in 1996.

Imports and Exports. The value of imports and exports in US$1m. was:

	1995	1996	1997
Imports	3,274	3,886	3,503
Exports	2,624	2,881	2,995

Chief exports: Manufactured goods and other products, coffee, bananas, sugar, cocoa. Main export markets, 1996: USA, 39·0%; Germany, 7·2%; Italy, 5·2%; Belgium-Luxembourg, 4·4%. Main import suppliers, 1996: USA, 49·9%; Mexico, 6·5%; Venezuela, 6·5%; Guatemala, 3·0%.

COMMUNICATIONS

Roads. In 1996 there were 35,597 km of roads. On the Costa Rica section of the Inter-American Highway it is possible to motor to Panama during the dry season. The Pan-American Highway into Nicaragua is metalled for most of the way and there is now a good highway open almost to Puntarenas. Motor vehicles, 1996, numbered 424,305 (277,888 passenger cars, or 85 per 1,000 inhabitants).

Rail. The nationalized railway system *(Incofer)* was closed in 1995 but was expected to be re-opened by private operators in 1999.

Civil Aviation. There is an international airport at San José. The national carrier is Líneas Aéreas Costarriqunses (LACSA). In 1998 scheduled services were also provided by Aeroperú, American Airlines, Aviateca, British Airways, Continental Airlines, COPA, Cubana, Delta Air Lines, Iberia, Martinair Holland, Mexicana, Nicaraguense de Aviación, SAM, Taca International Airlines, Travelair and United Airlines. In 1996 San José handled 1,761,000 passengers (1,674,000 on international flights) and 69,000 tonnes of freight.

Shipping. The chief ports are Limón on the Atlantic and Caldera on the Pacific. The merchant marine totalled 2,895 GRT in 1995.

Telecommunications. There were 892,200 telephone main lines in 1997. The Government has 202 telegraph offices and 88 official telephone stations. In 1995 cellular phone subscribers numbered 19,000 and there were 2,200 fax machines. There were approximately 50,000 Internet users in June 1997.

SOCIAL INSTITUTIONS

Justice. Justice is administered by the Supreme Court, 5 appeal courts divided into 5 chambers; the Court of Cassation, the Higher and Lower Criminal Courts, and the Higher and Lower Civil Courts. There are also subordinate courts in the separate provinces and local justices throughout the republic. Capital punishment may not be inflicted.

Religion. Roman Catholicism is the state religion; it had 2·55m. adherents in 1991. There is entire religious liberty under the constitution. The Archbishop of Costa Rica has 4 bishops at Alajuela, Limón, San Isidro el General and Tilarán. Protestants number about 40,000.

Education. The adult literacy rate in 1995 was 94·8% (94·7% among males and 95% among females). Primary instruction is compulsory and free from 6 to 15 years; secondary education (since 1949) is also free. Primary schools are provided and maintained by local school councils, while the national government pays the teachers, besides making subventions in aid of local funds. In 1996-97 there were 3,607 public and private primary schools with 17,554 teachers and administrative staff and 208,233 enrolled pupils, and 358 public and private secondary schools with 11,114 teachers and 518,603 pupils. In 1995-96 there was 1 university and 1 technological institute in the public sector, and 8 universities, 1 Adventist university and 1 university of science and technology in the private sector. There were also 4 other institutions of higher education. In 1994-95 there were 48,354 university students and 3,687 academic staff.

In 1994 total expenditure on education came to 4·7% of GNP and represented 19·2% of total government expenditure.

Health. In 1996 there were 4,442 doctors, 1,332 dentists, 2,600 nurses, 1,254 pharmacists and 33 hospitals.

CULTURE

Broadcasting. In 1995 there were 900,000 radio and 490,000 television receivers (colour by NTSC).

Cinema. There were 39 cinemas in 1995, with a total attendance for the year of 1·7m.

Press. There were 5 daily newspapers in 1995 with a combined circulation of 300,000, at a rate of 88 per 1,000 inhabitants.

Tourism. In 1996 there were 781,127 foreign tourists, bringing revenue of US$689m.

National Theatre and Opera. There are 8 national theatres.

Museums and Galleries. Costa Rica has 2 museums.

DIPLOMATIC REPRESENTATIVES

Of Costa Rica in Great Britain (Flat 1, 14 Lancaster Gate, London, W2 3LH)
Ambassador: Rodolfo Gutiérrez.

Of Great Britain in Costa Rica (Edificio Centro Colón, 11th Floor, Apartado 815, San José 1007)
Ambassador and Consul-General: A. S. Green, OBE, MVO.

Of Costa Rica in the USA (2112 Street, NW, Washington, D.C., 20008)
Ambassador: Jaime Daremblum.

Of the USA in Costa Rica (Pavas, Frente Centro Comercial, San José)
Ambassador: Peter J. De Vos.

Of Costa Rica to the United Nations
Ambassador: Bernd Niehaus.

Of Costa Rica to the European Union
Ambassador: Mario Carvajal.

FURTHER READING

Ameringer, C. D., *Democracy in Costa Rica.* New York, 1982
Biesanz, R., et al, *The Costa Ricans.* Hemel Hempstead, 1982
Bird, L., *Costa Rica: Unarmed Democracy.* London, 1984
Creedman, T. S., *Historical Dictionary of Costa Rica.* 2nd ed. Metuchen (N.J.), 1991
Stansifer, C., *Costa Rica.* 2nd ed. [Bibliography] Oxford and Santa Barbara (CA), 1991

National statistical office: Dirección General de Estadística y Censos, San José.

CÔTE D'IVOIRE

République de la
Côte d'Ivoire
(Republic of the Ivory Coast)

Capital: Yamoussoukro
Seat of Government: Abidjan
Population estimate, 2000: 15·14m.
GNP per capita: (PPP$) 1,580
HDI/world rank: 0·368/148

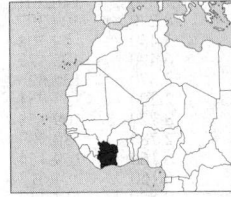

KEY HISTORICAL EVENTS

The Portuguese discovered Côte d'Ivoire (or the Ivory Coast as it was formerly known) in the 15th century but there was little initial interest in the area. The dense forests which covered the southern half of the area that was to become Côte d'Ivoire formed barriers to large-scale socio-political organizations and in the north dissimilar populations did not have the incentive to overcome ethnic differences and so forge a larger state. Even with the development in the 17th and 18th centuries of the Guinea coast gold and slave trades, Côte d'Ivoire generally lay too far to the west to be of significance.

France obtained rights on the coast in 1842 but did not actively and continuously occupy the territory until 1882. In the early 1870s the French ministry responsible for colonies even offered to exchange Côte d'Ivoire with the British for the Gambia, which bisected the French colony of Senegal, but the British refused. Rumours of gold later rekindled French interest and on 10 Jan. 1889 Côte d'Ivoire was declared a French protectorate becoming a colony on 10 March 1893. Over the next 20 years French administrators used the military to subdue African populations which openly resisted French intrusions. In 1904 Côte d'Ivoire became a territory of French West Africa. The French administered Côte d'Ivoire in a direct style, and would routinely dismiss locally selected chiefs. Governors appointed from France administered the colony using a system of centralized rule that allowed little room for participation among the Ivorians. In 1946 Côte d'Ivoire's first political party, the Democratic Party of Côte d'Ivoire, was created under the leadership of Félix Houphouët-Boigny and after confrontations which nearly led to the ruin of the party, he eventually adopted a policy of practical co-operation with the French authorities. By the mid-1950s the country had become the wealthiest in French West Africa and on 4 Dec. 1958 Côte d'Ivoire became an autonomous republic within the French Community.

Côte d'Ivoire achieved full independence on 7 Aug. 1960, with Félix Houphouët-Boigny as its first president. He was authoritarian yet his policies brought two decades of economic growth and political stability. Not until 1990 were opposition parties legalized, 3 years before his death. He was succeeded by Henri Konan Bédié, also of the Democratic Party of Côte d'Ivoire.

TERRITORY AND POPULATION

Côte d'Ivoire is bounded in the west by Liberia and Guinea, north by Mali and Burkina Faso, east by Ghana, and south by the Gulf of Guinea. It has an area of 320,783 sq. km and a population at the 1988 census of 10,812,782 (40% urban; in 1995, 43%). Estimate (1996) 14·76m.; density, 46·0 per sq. km.

The UN gives a projected population for 2000 of 15·14m.

Since 1991, the country has been divided into 10 regions (North-West, North, North-East, West, Centre-West, Centre-North, Centre, Centre-East, South-West, South) comprising 50 departments. Departments are named after their chief towns.

The areas and populations (1988 census) of the departments:

	Area *(in sq. km)*	*Population*		*Area* *(in sq. km)*	*Population*
Abengourou	5,200	214,162	Guiglo	11,220	169,660
Abidjan	8,550	2,492,513	Issia	3,590	194,974
Aboisso	6,250	225,882	Katiola	9,420	131,221
Adzopé	5,230	237,265	Korhogo	12,500	387,947
Agboville	3,850	203,730	Lakota	2,730	115,948
Agnibilekrou[1]	1,700	84,404	Man	4,990	286,860
Bangolo[2]	2,060	80,374	Mankono	10,660	123,723

499

	Area (in sq. km)	Population		Area (in sq. km)	Population
Béoumi[3]	2,860	91,062	M'bahiakro[3]	5,460	102,774
Biankouma	4,950	99,431	Odiénné	20,600	169,433
Bondoukou	10,040	175,632	Oumé	2,400	140,166
Bongouanou	5,570	225,432	Sakassou[3]	1,880	59,494
Bouaflé	3,980	163,917	San Pédro[7]	6,900	168,174
Bouaké	4,700	453,074	Sassandra	5,190	107,616
Bouna	21,470	134,459	Séguéla	11,240	121,120
Boundiali	7,895	127,231	Sinfra[8]	1,690	120,301
Dabakala	9,670	82,094	Soubré	8,270	309,307
Daloa	5,450	361,472	Tabou[7]	5,440	59,708
Danané	4,600	222,045	Tanda[9]	6,490	203,129
Daoukro[4]	3,610	86,425	Tiassalé[6]	3,370	132,626
Dimbokro	4,920	141,934	Tingréla	2,200	55,251
Divo	7,920	389,530	Touba	8,720	109,155
Duékoué[5]	2,930	101,451	Toumodi[3]	2,780	80,909
Ferkessedougou	17,728	172,850	Vavoua[10]	6,160	169,454
Gagnoa	4,500	275,765	Yamoussoukro[3]	6,160	284,613
Grand-Lahou[6]	2,280	52,645	Zuénoula	2,830	114,440

[1]Formerly part of Abengourou. [2]Formerly part of Man. [3]Formerly parts of Bouaké. [4]Formerly part of Dimbokro. [5]Formerly part of Guiglo. [6]Formerly parts of Abidjan. [7]Formerly parts of Sassandra. [8]Formerly part of Bouaflé. [9]Formerly part of Bondoukou. [10]Formerly part of Daloa.

Major towns (with 1988 census population): Abidjan, 1,929,079; Bouaké, 329,850; Daloa, 121,842; Korhogo, 109,445; Yamoussoukro, 106,786.

There are about 60 ethnic groups, the principal being the Baoulé (23%), the Bété (18%) and the Sénoufo (15%).

French is the official language.

SOCIAL STATISTICS
1996 births, 627,000; deaths, 232,000. Rates, 1996 estimates (per 1,000 population): Births, 42·5; deaths, 15·7. Infant mortality (per 1,000 live births), 82·4. Expectation of life in 1996 was 46·7 years (46·2 for males and 47·2 for females). Growth rate, 2·92% per annum. Infant mortality, 1990–95, 91 per 1,000 live births; fertility rate, 5·7 births per woman. 29% of the population are migrants.

CLIMATE
A tropical climate, affected by distance from the sea. In coastal areas, there are wet seasons from May to July and in Oct. and Nov., but in central areas the periods are March to May and July to Nov. In the north, there is one wet season from June to Oct. Abidjan, Jan. 81°F (27·2°C), July 75°F (23·9°C). Annual rainfall 84" (2,100 mm). Bouaké, Jan. 81°F (27·2°C), July 77°F (25°C). Annual rainfall 48" (1,200 mm).

CONSTITUTION AND GOVERNMENT
The 1960 Constitution was amended in 1971, 1975, 1980, 1985 and 1986. The sole legal party was the Democratic Party of Côte d'Ivoire, but opposition parties were legalized in 1990. There is a 175-member *National Assembly* elected by universal suffrage for a 5-year term. The President is also directly elected for a 5-year term (renewable). He and both his parents must be citizens born in Côte d'Ivoire. He appoints and leads a Council of Ministers.

In Nov. 1990 the National Assembly voted that its Speaker should become President in the event of the latter's incapacity, and created the post of Prime Minister to be appointed by the President. Following the death of President Houphouët-Boigny on 7 Dec. 1993, the speaker, Henri Konan Bédié, proclaimed himself head of state till the end of the presidential term in Sept. 1995.

National Anthem. 'L'Abidjanaise'; words by M. Ekra and others, tune by P. M Pango.

CÔTE D'IVOIRE

RECENT ELECTIONS
Presidential elections were held on 22 Oct. 1995; turn-out was 56·03%. President Konan Bédié was re-elected by 96·44% of votes cast against 1 opponent.

At the National Assembly elections of 26 Nov. 1995 the electorate was 3·8m. The Democratic Party won 148 seats; the Republican Rally, 14; the Ivorian Popular Front, 12. There was also 1 vacant seat.

CURRENT ADMINISTRATION
President: Henri Konan Bédié (elected 22 Oct. 1995).

In March 1999 the government comprised:

Prime Minister and Minister of Planning and Industrial Development: Daniel Kablan Duncan.

Minister of Defence: Vincent Bandama N'Gatta. *Justice and Public Freedom, Keeper of the Seals:* Jean Kouakou Brou. *Higher Education and Scientific Research:* Francis Wodie. *Agriculture and Animal Resources:* Lambert Kouassi Konan. *Commodities:* Guy Alain Gauze. *National Education and Basic Training:* Pierre Kipre. *Commerce:* Akon Kouassi. *Mines and Petroleum Resources:* Lamine Mohamed Fadika. *Energy:* Safiatou Ba-N'Daw. *Public Health:* Maurice Kacou Guikahue. *Communications:* Danielle Boni-Claverie. *Housing and Urban Planning:* Albert Kacou Tiapani. *Employment, Civil Service and Social Welfare:* Pierre Achi Atsain. *Security:* Marcel Dibona Kone. *Culture:* Bernard Zadi Zaourou. *Family and Promotion of Women:* Leopoldine Coffie. *Presidential Affairs, Government Spokesman:* Paul Akoto Yau. *Youth and Sports:* Siguide Soumahoro. *Technical Education and Professional Training:* Dossongui Kone. *Economic Infrastructure:* Jean Michel Moulod. *Economy and Finance:* Niamien N'Goran. *Transport:* Adama Coulibaly. *Environment and Forestry:* Jean-Cleaude Kouassi. *Information:* Danielle Boni-Claverie. *Industrial Development and Small- and Medium-Scale Enterprises:* Theophile Ahoua N'Doli. *Internal Trade Promotion:* Adou Kouadio. *Planning and Development Programmes:* Tidrane Thiam. *Tourism and Handicrafts:* Norbert Anney Kablan.

Minister of State in charge of Interior, National Integration and Decentralization: Emile Constant Bombet. *Minister of State in charge of Foreign Affairs:* Amara Essy. *Minister of State in charge of Relations with Institutions:* Timothée Ahoua N'Guetta. *Minister of State in charge of National Solidarity:* Laurent Dona-Fologo. *Minister of State for Religious Affairs and Dialogue with the Opposition:* Leon Konan Koffi.

The *Speaker* is Charles Donwahi.

Local Government. There are 50 departments, each under an appointed Prefect and an elected General Council, sub-divided into 183 sub-prefectures. At the elections of 11 Feb. 1996 turn-out was low. The Democratic Party won control of 156 of the 196 councils contested.

DEFENCE
There is selective conscription for 6 months. Defence expenditure totalled US$101m. in 1997 (US$7 per capita).

Army. There are 4 military regions. The Army consists of 1 armoured battalion, 3 infantry battalions, 1 artillery group and 1 airborne, 1 anti-aircraft and 1 engineer company. Equipment includes 5 AMX-13 light tanks. Total strength (1996), 6,800. Paramilitary forces, 7,800.

Navy. Offshore, riverine and coastal patrol squadrons include 2 fast missile craft, 2 patrol vessels, 1 riverine defence craft, 1 light amphibious transport and 2 minor landing craft. Personnel in 1996 totalled 900 and the force is based at Locodjo (Abidjan).

Air Force. There are 5 Alpha Jet light strike combat aircraft, though only 1 or 2 are operational. Transport aircraft include 5 fixed-wing and 4 rotary-wing aircraft. 4 Bonanzas are used for training and patrol. Personnel (1995) 700.

INTERNATIONAL RELATIONS
Côte d'Ivoire is a member of the UN, OAU, UEMOA, ECOWAS and is an ACP member state of the ACP-EU relationship.

CÔTE D'IVOIRE

ECONOMY

Policy. Austerity measures were introduced in May 1990. A privatization programme, particularly in agro-industrial sectors, was initiated in 1992. 30 companies had been privatized by 1997. The IMF extended a 3-year low-interest loan of US$395m. in March 1998, conditional on continued economic reform, including a reduction in the number of state employees and further liberalization of price controls. Accumulated foreign debt stood at US$16·8bn. in 1998.

Performance. Real GDP growth was 6% in 1997 and around 6·5% in 1998.

Budget. Revenues in 1996 were an estimated US$2·4bn. and expenditure US$2·7bn. VAT is 25%.

Currency. The currency is the *franc CFA* with a parity rate of 100 francs CFA to 1 French franc. In Nov. 1997 gold reserves were 40,000 troy oz.; foreign exchange reserves were US$623m. in Dec. 1997. Total money supply in Dec. 1997 was 1,080bn. francs CFA. Inflation was an annualized 5% in 1996.

Banking and Finance. The regional *Banque Centrale des Etats de l'Afrique de l'Ouest* is the central bank and bank of issue. In 1994 there were 12 commercial banks; 3 other banks maintained representative offices. The African Development Bank is based in Abidjan. There is a stock exchange in Abidjan.

ENERGY AND NATURAL RESOURCES

Electricity. The electricity industry was privatized in 1990. Installed capacity was 1·17m. kW in 1994. Production in 1994 amounted to 1·86bn. kWh, around half of which was from hydro-electric projects. Consumption per capita in 1995 was an estimated 118 kWh.

Oil and Gas. Petroleum has been produced (offshore) since Oct. 1977. Production (1992) 63,000 tonnes. Estimated gas reserves, 1996, 6,516,000m. cu. ft. Daily output, 1997, 75m. cu. ft.

Minerals. Côte d'Ivoire has large deposits of iron ores, bauxite, tantalie, diamonds, gold, nickel and manganese, most of which are untapped. Gold production has steadily increased with around 3 tonnes likely to be produced in 1999.

Agriculture. In 1995 the agricultural population was 14·25m., of whom 2·97m. were economically active. In 1998 agriculture accounted for 33% of GDP and 66% of exports. There were 2·44m. ha of arable land in 1994, 1·27m. ha of permanent cropland and 13m. ha of meadow and pasture. Côte d'Ivoire is the world's largest producer and exporter of cocoa beans, with an annual output of more than 1·1m. tonnes and the fifth largest coffee producer, with around 250,000 tonnes a year. Other main crops are bananas, pineapples, palm oil, palm kernel oil, seed cotton, rubber, yams, cassava, plantains, rice, maize, millet, sugar-cane and groundnuts.

Livestock, 1996: 1·28m. cattle, 1·31m. sheep, 1m. goats (1995), 290,000 pigs and 27m. chickens (1995).

Forestry. In 1995 the rainforest covered 5·47m. ha, or 17·72% of the total land area, down from 5·62m. ha in 1990 and 13m. ha in 1900. Products include teak, mahogany and ebony. In 1995, 14·78m. cu. metres of roundwood were produced. Côte d'Ivoire is the biggest producer of rubber in Africa.

Fisheries. In 1989 the fishing fleet comprised 32 vessels over 100 GRT totalling 9,386 GRT. The catch in 1995 amounted to 70,526 tonnes, of which 58,854 tonnes were from marine waters.

INDUSTRY

Industrialization has developed rapidly since independence, particularly food processing, textiles and sawmills. Output in 1988 (in 1,000 tonnes): Petrol, 311; paraffin, 237; fuel oil, 1,089; cement, 144; sawn timber, 775; veneer wood, 266; centrifugal sugar, 140; palmoil (1989), 190; copra (1989), 75.

Labour. In 1996 the workforce was 5·7m. (67% males).

Trade Unions. The main trade union is the *Union Générale des Travailleurs de Côte d'Ivoire*, with over 100,000 members.

CÔTE D'IVOIRE

INTERNATIONAL TRADE
External debt was US$19,713m. in 1996.

Imports and Exports. Total exports, 1996, US$4,177m; imports, US$3,157m.
Principal exports, 1992 (in 1,000m. francs CFA): Cocoa, 256; petroleum products, 85; timber, 62; coffee, 56; cotton, 29; tinned tuna, 25. Principal imports: Crude oil, 116; machinery and vehicles, 96; pharmaceuticals, 34; fish, 27; plastics, 20. Main export markets, 1994: France, 16·1%; Germany, 9·8%; Netherlands, 8·9%; Italy, 7·1%. Main import suppliers, 1994: France, 28·2%; Nigeria, 26·8%; USA, 5·9%; Germany, 3·3%.

COMMUNICATIONS
Roads. In 1998 roads totalled 70,000 km, of which 6,000 km were paved. There were about 456,000 motor vehicles in 1996 (293,000 cars, or 18 per 1,000 inhabitants, and 163,000 trucks and vans).

Rail. From Abidjan a metre-gauge railway runs to Léraba on the border with Burkina Faso (655 km), and thence through Burkina Faso to Ouagadougou and Kaya. Operation of the railway in both countries is franchised to the mixed public-private company Sitarail. Abidjan is to have an underground railway system.

Civil Aviation. There is an international airport at Abidjan Port-Bouet, which in 1996 handled 809,314 passengers (793,323 on international flights) and 17,189 tonnes of freight. The national carrier is the state-owned Air Ivoire, which provides domestic services and in 1998 operated international flights to Burkina Faso, Ghana, Guinea, Liberia and Mali. Services were also provided in 1998 by Air Afrique, Air Burkina, Air France, Air Gabon, British Airways, Cameroon Airlines, Egyptair, Ethiopian Airlines, Ghana Airways, KLM, Middle East Airlines, Nigeria Airways, Royal Air Maroc, SABENA, South African Airways, Swissair and TAP.

Shipping. The main ports are Abidjan and San Pédro. Abidjan handles around 12m. tonnes of cargo per year and aims to handle 15m. tonnes by 2000. It is the biggest container port in West Africa. In 1995 the merchant marine totalled 76,399 GRT, including oil tankers, 1,170 GRT.

Telecommunications. In 1997 there were 142,300 telephone main lines, or 9·3 per 1,000 inhabitants. In Jan. 1998 there were approximately 1,000 Internet users.

Postal Services. In 1995 there were 364 post offices.

SOCIAL INSTITUTIONS
Justice. There are 28 courts of first instance and 3 assize courts in Abidjan, Bouaké and Daloa, 2 courts of appeal in Abidjan and Bouaké, and a supreme court in Abidjan. The death penalty is authorized, but has not been applied since independence in 1960.

Religion. In 1994 there were 5·2m. Moslems (mainly in the north) and 3·8m. Christians (chiefly Roman Catholics in the south). Traditional animist beliefs are also practised.

Education. The adult literacy rate in 1995 was 40·1% (48·9% among males and 30·0% among females). There were, in 1996–97, 1,734,416 pupils in 7,599 primary schools and, in 1994–95, 474,847 pupils at secondary schools. In 1993–94 there were 51,215 students at higher education institutions. In 1995–96 there was 1 university with 21,000 students and 730 academic staff, and 3 university centres. There were 6 other institutions of higher education.

Health. In 1990 there were 2,020 doctors, 219 dentists, 3,691 nurses, 135 pharmacists and 1,533 midwives. There were 93 hospitals and 669 health centres in 1984. In 1982 there were 10,062 hospital beds.

CULTURE
Broadcasting. The government-controlled Radiodiffusion Télévision Ivoirienne is responsible for broadcasting. In 1995 there were 850,000 television (colour by SECAM) and 2·1m. radio receivers.

Press. In 1995 there was 9 daily newspaper with a combined circulation of 198,000, at a rate of 15 per 1,000 inhabitants.

Tourism. Efforts are being made by the government to revive the tourist industry which has declined over recent years due to the decade-long recession. Tourist development centres in the regions and 11,000 hotel bedrooms are planned. There were 237,000 foreign tourists in 1996, spending US$89m.

DIPLOMATIC REPRESENTATIVES

Of Côte d'Ivoire in Great Britain (2 Upper Belgrave St., London, SW1X 8BJ)
Ambassador: Kouadio Adjoumani.

Of Great Britain in Côte d'Ivoire (3rd Floor, Immeuble 'Les Harmonies', angle Blvd. Carde et Ave. Dr Jamot, Plateau, Abidjan)
Ambassador: H. B. Warren-Gash.

Of Côte d'Ivoire in the USA (2424 Massachusetts Ave., NW, Washington, D.C., 20008)
Ambassador: Koffi Moise Koumoue.

Of the USA in Côte d'Ivoire (5 Rue Jesse Owens, Abidjan)
Ambassador: Lannon Walker.

Of Côte d'Ivoire to the United Nations
Ambassador: Youssoufou Bamba.

Of Côte d'Ivoire to the European Union
Ambassador: Nanan Koliabo N'zi Anet.

FURTHER READING

Direction de la Statistique. *Bulletin Mensuel de Statistique.*
Daniels, M., *Côte d'Ivoire* [Bibliography]. Oxford and Santa Barbara (CA), 1996
Zartman, I. W. and Delgado, C., *The Political Economy of Ivory Coast.* New York, 1984

National statistical office: Direction de la Statistique, Ministère du Plan, Abidjan.

CROATIA

Republika Hrvatska

Capital: Zagreb
Population estimate, 2000: 4·48m.
GNP per capita: (PPP$) 4,290
HDI/world rank: 0·759/76

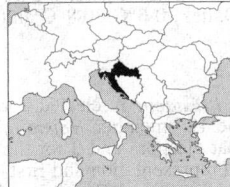

KEY HISTORICAL EVENTS
The original Croats migrated to their present territory in the 6th century and were converted to Roman Catholicism. Croatia was united with Hungary in 1091 and remained under Hungarian administration until the end of the First World War. On 1 Dec. 1918 Croatia became a part of the new Kingdom of Serbs, Croats and Slovenes, which was renamed Yugoslavia in 1929. During the Second World War an independent fascist (Ustaša) state was set up under the aegis of the German occupiers. During the Communist period Croatia became one of the 6 'Socialist Republics' constituting the Yugoslav federation led by Marshal Tito. With the collapse of Communism, an independence movement gained momentum.

In a referendum on 19 May 1991, 94·17% of votes cast were in favour of Croatia becoming an independent sovereign state with the option of joining a future Yugoslav confederation as opposed to remaining in the existing Yugoslav federation. The Krajina and other predominantly Serbian areas of Croatia, wanted union with Serbia and seized power by force of arms. Croatian forces and Serb insurgents backed by federal forces became embroiled in a conflict throughout 1991 until the arrival of a UN peace-keeping mission at the beginning of 1992 and the establishment of 4 UN ('pink zones') peace-keeping zones. Croatia obtained a reduction in the UN peace-keeping forces after 1 April 1995.

In early May 1995 Croatian forces re-took Western Slavonia from the Serbs and opened the Zagreb-Belgrade highway. Serb rockets fell on Zagreb during the campaign and civilians were killed. In a 60-hour operation mounted on 4 Aug. 1995 the former self-declared Serb Republic of Krajina was occupied, provoking an exodus of 0·18m. Serb refugees. Croats who had left the area in 1991 began to return. On 12 Nov. 1995 the Croatian government and Bosnian Serbs reached an agreement to place Eastern Slavonia, the last Croatian territory still under Bosnian Serb control, under UN administration until 15 July 1998.

TERRITORY AND POPULATION
Croatia is bounded in the north by Slovenia and Hungary and in the east by Yugoslavia and Bosnia-Hercegovina. It includes the areas of Dalmatia, Istria and Slavonia which no longer have administrative status. Its area is 56,538 sq. km. Population at the 1991 census was 4,784,265, of whom the predominating ethnic groups were Croats (3,736,356) and Serbs (581,663). Estimate, 1997, 4,664,700; density, 85·5 per sq. km.

The UN gives a projected population for 2000 of 4·48m.

In 1995 an estimated 55·8% of the population lived in urban areas. Principal towns (with 1991 census population): Zagreb (726,770), Split (189,388), Rijeka (167,964), Osijek (104,761).

At the beginning of 1991 there were some 0·6m. resident Serbs. A law of Dec. 1991 guaranteed the autonomy of Serbs in areas where they are in a majority after the establishment of a permanent peace.

The official language is the western variant of Serbo-Croat (in Croatia called Croato-Serb or, familiarly, Croatian).

SOCIAL STATISTICS
1995 births, 50,182; deaths, 50,536; marriages, 24,385; divorces, 4,236. 1995 rates: Birth, 10·5 per 1,000 population; death, 10·6; marriage, 5·1; divorce, 0·89; infant mortality, 10·2 per 1,000 live births. Population growth, 1997, 0·17%. In 1995 the most popular age range for marrying was 25–29 for males and 20–24 for females. Life expectancy at birth, 1990–95, was 67·1 years for males and 75·7 years for females. Fertility rate, 1990–95, 1·7 children per woman.

CLIMATE

Inland Croatia has a Central European type of climate, with cold winters and hot summers, but the Adriatic coastal region experiences a Mediterranean climate with mild, moist winters and hot, brilliantly sunny summers with less than average rainfall. Normal Jan./July temperature and annual rainfall: Dubrovnik, 9·2°C/24·7°C and 1,006 mm. Zadar, 7·2°C/23·5°C and 688 mm. Rijeka, 6·2°C/23°C and 1,251 mm. Zagreb, 0°C/23·5°C and 652 mm. Osijek, 0·6°C/20·8°C and 541 mm.

CONSTITUTION AND GOVERNMENT

A new constitution was adopted on 21 Dec. 1990. The *President* is elected for renewable 5-year terms. Parliament (*Sabor*) consists of the 127-member *House of Representatives*, in which 12 seats are reserved for the Croat diaspora and 3 for the Serb minority. It is elected by a combination of proportional representation and first-past-the-post methods. There is also an upper house, the 68-member *Chamber of Counties*, composed of representatives of counties elected by proportional representation, and 5 members nominated by the President. The role of the Chamber of Counties is primarily consultative.

National Anthem. 'Lijepa nasva domovino' ('Beautiful our homeland'); words by A. Mihanović, tune by J. Runjanin.

RECENT ELECTIONS

Franjo Tudjman was elected President in May 1990, and re-elected on 3 Aug. 1992 against 7 opponents by 56·7% of votes cast. Presidential elections were last held 15 June 1997. There were 3 candidates. Turn-out was 56·2%. President Tudjman was re-elected with 61·41% of votes cast.

At elections to the Sabor on 29 Oct. 1995 the electorate was 3·6m.; turn-out was 66%. The Croatian Democratic Union (HDZ) won 75 seats with 44·82% of votes cast, the Peasant Party coalition 16 with 18·44%, the Croatian Social Liberal Party 12 with 11·62%, the Social Democratic Party 10, the Croat Right-Wing Party 4, the Istrian Democratic Diet 2, and the Independent Democrats 1. At elections to the Chamber of Counties on 17 Apr. 1997 the HDZ gained 41 seats, the Croatian Peasant Party 9, Social Liberals 7 and others 6.

CURRENT ADMINISTRATION

President: Franjo Tudjman, b. 1922 (HDZ; since 1990; re-elected in 1992 and 1997).

The government comprised in March 1999:

Prime Minister: Zlatko Matesa.

Deputy Prime Ministers: Jure Radić (*Development and Reconstruction*); Mate Granić (*Refugee Issues, Foreign Affairs*); Ivica Kostović (*Humanitarian Affairs*); Borislav Skegro (*Economics and Finance*); Ljerka Mintas-Hodak (*Social Affairs*). *Defence:* Pavao Milijavać. *Interior:* Ivan Penić. *Tourism:* Sergej Morsan. *Agriculture and Forestry:* Ivan Djurkić. *Urban Planning, Construction and Housing:* Marko Sirać. *Education and Sport:* Bozidar Pugelnik. *Health:* Zeljko Reiner. *Justice:* Milan Ramljak. *Administration:* Marijan Ramuscak. *Labour and Social Welfare:* Joso Škara. *Maritime Affairs, Transport and Communications:* Zeljko Lužavec. *Economy:* Nenad Porges. *Privatization and State Property Management:* Milan Kovać. *Culture:* Božo Biskupić. *Immigration:* Marijan Petrović. *European Integration:* Ljerka Mintas-Hodak. *Homeland War Defenders and War Veterans:* Jurag Njavro. *Science and Technology:* Milena Zic-Fuchs.

The *Speaker* is Nedjeljko Mihanović.

Local Government. The country is divided into 21 counties (*zvupanija*), 2 districts (Knin and Glina, at present under local Serbian control), 68 towns and 383 municipalities, all administered by elected councils. County councils elect as leader a prefect approved by the President. County councils have broad responsibilities in the spheres of economic development, health and education; town and municipal councils (the latter for areas with fewer than 10,00 population) are concerned with detailed administration. Elections were held in April 1997.

DEFENCE

Conscription is for 10 months. Defence expenditure in 1997 totalled US$1,147m. (US$244 per capita), representing 5·7% of GDP.

Army. The country is divided into 6 operations zones. The Army consists of 10 infantry, 4 air defence, 3 special forces, 1 artillery-multiple rocket launcher, 3 anti-tank, 1 engineer and 1 mechanized brigade, 7 mixed and artillery divisions. Equipment includes 250 T-34, T-55 and M-84 main battle tanks. Personnel, 1997, 50,000 (33,500 conscripts). Paramilitary forces include an armed police of 40,000. There are also 10,000 reserves in 27 Home Defence regiments and 150,000 regular Army reservists.

Navy. In 1996 the fleet comprised 2 inshore submarines for special operations, 1 missile-armed corvette, 4 missile craft, 1 torpedo craft, 3 patrol craft, 2 minelayers and 2 small mine countermeasures vessels. There are 11 small amphibious craft and some 5 support vessels. A Marine service fields 7 independent infantry companies, and the coast defence force mans artillery batteries. Total personnel in 1997 numbered about 3,000 including marines.

Air Force. The Air Force has 7 squadrons, 2 with MiG-21 fighters, 1 with Mi-24 armed helicopters, 1 with Mi-8/17 transport helicopters, 1 with An-2, An-26 and An-32 fixed-wing transports, 1 fixed-wing training squadron with light aircraft and PC-9s and 1 with JetRanger helicopter trainer aircraft. Personnel, 1997, 5,000 (including Air Defence).

INTERNATIONAL RELATIONS

In Jan. 1994 relations with Yugoslavia were established with the opening of mutual representative offices. In late 1997 and early 1998 Croatia signed highway construction agreements with German, Italian and French companies worth US$800m.

Croatia is a member of the UN, the Council of Europe and the Central European Initiative.

ECONOMY

Performance. Real GDP growth was 4·0% in 1996 and 6·0% in 1997.

Budget. Government revenue and expenditure (1m. kuna):

	1995	1996	1997	1998[1]
Revenue	27,385·07	30,812·96	33,702·34	35,214·00
Expenditure	25,969·79	27,125·23	28,839·28	31,771·07

[1]Projected.

Expenditure by function (1997): Education, 3,558·52; health, 7,837·70; social security and welfare, 17,916·79. VAT at 22% was introduced in 1997.

Currency. On 30 May 1994 the *kuna* (HRK; a name used in 1941–45) of 100 *lipa* replaced the Croatian dinar at 1 kuna = 1,000 dinars. Foreign exchange reserves were US$2,800m. in 1996. Inflation was 4·6% in 1997. Total money supply was 12,439m. kuna in Feb. 1998.

Banking and Finance. The National Bank of Croatia (*governor*, Marko Skreb) is the bank of issue. In 1996 there were 57 domestic commercial banks and 1 foreign bank. Total savings deposits on 31 Dec. 1994 were 8,915m. kuna.

There are stock exchanges in Zagreb and Varaždin.

Weights and Measures. The metric system is in use.

ENERGY AND NATURAL RESOURCES

Electricity. Installed capacity in 1994 was 3·59m. kW. Output was 9,146m. kWh in 1995, with consumption per capita in 1995 estimated to be 2,208 kWh.

Oil and Gas. 1·50m. tonnes of crude oil were produced in 1995, and 1,966m. cu. metres of natural gas in 1995.

Minerals. Production, 1994 (in 1,000 tonnes): Coal, 96; brown coal and lignite, 37 (1991); bauxite, 1·3; salt, 21·7.

CROATIA

Agriculture. At the 1993 census 409,647 persons subsisted on agriculture. Agriculture contributes approximately 12% of GDP. Agricultural land totals 2·3m. ha (1·1m. ha arable, 0·77m. ha pasture, 55,000 ha vineyards). The cultivated area is 1·54m. ha. In 1994 approximately 3,000 ha were irrigated. Yields (in 1,000 tonnes, 1994): Wheat, 750; maize, 1,687; potatoes, 563; plums, 36.

Livestock, 1996: Cattle, 462,000; sheep, 427,000; pigs, 1,196,000; chickens, 12m. Animal products, 1994: Meat, 335,000 tonnes; honey, 844 tonnes; milk, 600m. litres; eggs, 0·88m.

Forestry. Forests covered 1,825,000 ha in 1995, or 32·6% of the land area. In 1995, 2·67m. cu. metres of roundwood were produced.

Fisheries. The total catch was 19,160 tonnes in 1995, of which 3,796 tonnes were freshwater fish.

INDUSTRY
Production, 1994 (in 1,000 tonnes): Crude steel, 63; cement, 2,055; cellulose, 127; cotton fabric, 23m. sq. metres; cotton cloth, 10m. sq. metres; woollen yarn, 4 tons; wine, 1·89m. hectolitres; beer, 3·1m. hectolitres.

Labour. The non-agricultural workforce was 1,022,000 in 1994, of whom 368,300 worked in industry (41% female). There were 241,000 registered unemployed in March 1996.

INTERNATIONAL TRADE
Croatia has accepted responsibility for 29·5% of the US$4,400m. commercial bank debt of the former Yugoslavia. Total foreign debt as a percentage of GDP, (1996) 26·6%; (1997) 31·0%.

Imports and Exports. Exports in 1996 were valued at US$4,511m. and in 1997, US$4,800m. Imports for 1996 came to US$7,000m., and for 1997 US$7,540m.

The main exports are machinery and transport equipment, chemicals and foodstuffs. In 1996 the main export markets were Italy, 21·0%; Germany, 18·6%; Slovenia, 13·5%; Austria, 4·4%. Main import suppliers: Germany, 20·6%; Italy, 18·2%; Slovenia, 9·9%; Austria, 7·7%.

COMMUNICATIONS
Roads. There were 27,247 km of roads in 1996 (including 318 km of motorways), of which 81·5% were paved. In 1996 there were 835,714 passenger cars, 4,596 buses and coaches, and 93,769 vans and trucks. 84m. passengers and 5·1m. tonnes of freight were carried by public transport in 1995.

There were 721 deaths in road accidents in 1996, compared to 975 in 1992.

Rail. There are 2,699 km of 1,435 mm gauge (1,213 km electrified). In 1995 railways carried 28·6m. passengers and 10·3m. tonnes of freight.

Civil Aviation. There are international airports at Zagreb (Pleso), Split and Dubrovnik. The national carrier is Croatia Airlines. In 1998 services were also provided by Aeroflot, Air France, Air Urga, Alitalia, Austrian Airlines, British Airways, Czech Airlines, Delta Air Lines, El Al, Iberia, Interimpex-Avioimpex, Lauda Air, LOT, Lufthansa, Malaysia Airlines, SABENA, SAS and Swissair. Croatia Airlines flew 8·1m. km and carried 644,100 passengers in 1995 (317,200 on international flights). In 1996 Zagreb handled 1,004,357 passengers (664,084 on international flights) and 5,188 tonnes of freight, Split handled 503,267 passengers (300,407 on international flights) and Dubrovnik 137,704 passengers (48,826 on international flights).

Shipping. The main port is Rijeka, which handled 3·8m. tonnes of freight in 1995. There were 168 ocean-going vessels in 1995, totalling 3·29m. DWT. 132 of the vessels (94·09% of tonnage) were registered under foreign flags. Total GRT, 0·27m., including oil tankers, 30,549 GRT; and container ships, 46,131 GRT. 5·8m. passengers and 22·39m. tonnes of cargo were transported.

Telecommunications. The repair and expansion of the telecommunications industry has been made a high priority in the development process of the country. The telephone density (the number of lines per 1,000 population) has risen from 17·2% in 1990 to 35% in 1998, with a target of 41% by 2000.

In 1997 there were 1,488,100 telephone main lines in use. Cellular phone subscribers numbered 34,000 in 1995, and there were 100,000 PCs in use, 38,000 fax machines and approximately 24,000 Internet users.

Postal Services. In 1995 there were 1,190 post offices.

SOCIAL INSTITUTIONS

Religion. At the 1991 census there were 76·5% Roman Catholics, 11·1% Orthodox, and 12·4% others (mainly Old Catholics and Moslems).

Education. In 1995–96 there were 902 pre-school institutions with 66,105 children and 5,531 childcare workers; 1,134 primary schools with 207,890 pupils and 10,605 teachers; 482 secondary schools with 417,475 pupils and 29,741 teachers. In 1994–95 there were 64 institutes of higher education with 80,185 students and 5,893 academic staff. In 1995–96 there were 3 universities with 86,357 students and 6,325 academic staff. Adult literacy rate, 1995, 97·6% (male, 98·2%; female, 97·1%).

Health. In 1994 there were 9,138 doctors and 1,798 dentists. There were 84 hospitals with 28,230 beds.

Welfare. The health insurance scheme covered 4,591,341 persons in 1994, of whom 1,354,146 were contributing and 755,644 were receiving retirement pensions.

CULTURE

Broadcasting. Broadcasting is controlled by the state Croatian Radio-Television (colour by PAL). In 1995 there were 1·2m. radio sets and 1·15m. television receivers.

Cinema. There were 150 cinemas with a total of 55,000 seats in 1995. 3 feature films were made in 1995.

Press. In 1995 there were 12 dailies with an annual circulation of 225,000 and 603 other newspapers. There were 64 weeklies and 401 periodicals. An amendment of March 1996 to the criminal code makes it an offence for the press to defame the government.

Tourism. There were 2,649,000 foreign tourists in 1996, spending US$2·1bn. 12·9m. tourist nights were spent in 1995. The tourist industry is now recovering with a 20% rise in receipts since 1995. Night stays were estimated at 21·6m. for 1996.

DIPLOMATIC REPRESENTATIVES
Of Croatia in Great Britain (21 Conway St., London, W1P 5HL)
Ambassador: Andrija Kojaković.

Of Great Britain in Croatia (Vlaška 121/III Floor, POB 454, 10000 Zagreb)
Ambassador: C. Munro.

Of Croatia in the USA (2343 Massachusetts Ave., NW, Washington, D.C., 20008)
Ambassador: Miomir Zuzul.

Of the USA in Croatia (Andrije Hebranga 2, Zagreb)
Ambassador: William D. Montgomery.

Of Croatia to the United Nations
Ambassador: Dr Ivan Šimonović.

Of Croatia to the European Union
Ambassador: Janko Vranyczany-Dobrinović.

FURTHER READING
Central Bureau of Statistics. *Statistical Yearbook.—Monthly Statistical Report.*

Stallaerts, R. and Laurens, J., *Historical Dictionary of the Republic of Croatia.* Metuchen (NJ), 1995
Tanner, M. C., *A Nation Forged in War.* Yale, 1997.

National statistical office: Central Bureau of Statistics, 3 Ilica, Zagreb. *Director:* Ivan Rusan.
Website: http://www.dzs.hr/

CUBA

República de Cuba

Capital: Havana
Population estimate, 2000: 11·2m.
Estimated GDP: $16·2bn.
HDI/world rank: 0·729/85

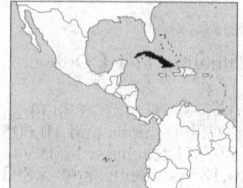

KEY HISTORICAL EVENTS

Cuba was discovered by Columbus in 1492 and, except for the brief British occupancy in 1762-63, remained a Spanish possession until 10 Dec. 1898. Sovereignty was then relinquished under the terms of the Treaty of Paris at the end of the Spanish-American War. Cuba became an independent republic in 1901, although the USA continued to influence Cuban internal affairs and foreign policy until 1934.

In 1933 Fulgencio Batista Zladivar led a successful military revolution. He ruled the country until 1944, as elected president from 1940, and again, after seizing power in a *coup*, from 1952 until 1959. A revolutionary movement against the corrupt Batista dictatorship, led by Dr Fidel Castro from 26 July 1953, was eventually successful and Batista fled the country on 1 Jan. 1959. Under Castro, Cuba's relationship with the USA deteriorated while relations with the USSR became closer. In Jan. 1961 the USA severed diplomatic relations after US business interests in Cuba had been expropriated without compensation for refusing to co-operate with the government's economic plans. On 17 April an invasion force of émigrés and adventurers, encouraged by the USA, landed in Cuba but was defeated at the Bay of Pigs. At the end of 1961 Castro declared Cuba to be a Communist state.

The US Navy imposed a blockade of Cuba from 22 Oct. until 22 Nov. 1962 to force the USSR to withdraw Soviet missile bases. Cuba continued to receive financial aid and technical advice from the USSR until the early 1990s when subsidies of around US$4bn. a year were suspended. This led to a 40% drop in GDP between 1989 and 1993. The USA has maintained an economic embargo against the island, and relations between Cuba and the USA have remained embittered. But in the wake of the Pope's visit to Cuba in Jan. 1998, President Clinton announced a package of measures to alleviate poverty including permission to allow Cuban Americans to send up to US$1,200 per family to relatives on the island.

TERRITORY AND POPULATION

The island of Cuba forms the largest and most westerly of the Greater Antilles group and lies 135 miles south of the tip of Florida, USA. The area is 110,860 sq. km, and comprises the island of Cuba, (104,945 sq. km.); the Isle of Youth (Isla de la Juventud, formerly the Isle of Pines; 2,200 sq. km.); and some 1,600 small isles ('cays'; 3,715 sq. km). Population, census (1981), 9,723,605; estimate, 1996, 10,951,300; density, 99 per sq. km.

The UN gives a projected population for 2000 of 11·2m.

An estimated 75·8% of the population were urban in 1995.

The area, population and density of population of the 14 provinces and the special Municipality of the Isle of Youth (Isla de la Juventud) were as follows (1989 estimate):

	Area sq. km	Population		Area sq. km.	Population
Pinar del Río	10,860	681,500	Camagüey	14,134	727,700
La Habana	5,671	633,400	Las Tunas	6,373	481,500
Ciudad de La Habana	727	2,068,600	Holguín	9,105	927,700
Matanzas	11,669	599,500	Granma	8,452	777,300
Cienfuegos	4,149	356,700	Santiago de Cuba	6,343	974,100
Villa Clara	8,069	788,800	Guantánamo	6,366	487,900
Sancti Spíritus	6,737	422,300			
Ciego de Avila	6,485	355,500	Isla de la Juventud	2,199	70,900

Chief cities (1991 population estimate in 1,000): Havana, the capital (2,124), Santiago de Cuba (418), Camagüey (289), Holguín (206), Guantánamo (206), Santa

CUBA

Clara (200); 1990, Bayamo (125,021), Cienfuegos (123,600), Pinar del Río (121,774), Las Tunas (119,400), Matanzas (113,724) and Manzanillo (107,650).
The official language is Spanish.

SOCIAL STATISTICS
1996 births, 147,000; deaths, 81,000. Rates, 1996 (estimates): Birth, 13·4 per 1,000 population; death, 7·4; infant mortality rate, 9 per 1,000 live births; life expectancy, 75 years (males 73, females 77). Annual growth rate, 1990–95, 0·8%. The fertility rate in 1990–95 was 1·6 births per woman, the lowest in the Americas.

CLIMATE
Situated in the sub-tropical zone, Cuba has a generally rainy climate, affected by the Gulf Stream and the N.E. Trades, though winters are comparatively dry after the heaviest rains in Sept. and Oct. Hurricanes are liable to occur between June and Nov. Havana, Jan. 72°F (22·2°C), July 82°F (27·8°C). Annual rainfall 48" (1,224 mm).

CONSTITUTION AND GOVERNMENT
A Communist Constitution came into force on 24 Feb. 1976. It was amended in July 1992 to permit direct parliamentary elections.

Legislative power is vested in the *National Assembly of People's Power*, which meets twice a year and consists of 601 deputies elected for a 5-year term by universal suffrage. Lists of candidates are drawn up by mass organizations (trade unions, etc.). The National Assembly elects a 31-member *Council of State* as its permanent organ. The Council of State's President, who is head of state and of government, nominates and leads a Council of Ministers approved by the National Assembly.

National Anthem. 'Al combate corred bayameses' ('Run, Bayamans, to the combat'); words and tune by P. Figueredo.

RECENT ELECTIONS
Elections to the National Assembly were held on 11 Jan. 1998. The electorate was 8m.; turn-out was 98·35%. All 601 candidates received the requisite 50% of votes for election.

CURRENT ADMINISTRATION
President: Dr Fidel Castro Ruz (b. 1927) became *President* of the Council of State on 3 Dec. 1976; re-elected for 5 years on 24 Feb. 1998. He is also First Secretary of the Cuban Communist Party and C.-in-C. of the National Defence Council.

In March 1999 the government comprised:
First Vice-President of the Council of State and of the Council of Ministers, Minister of the Revolutionary Armed Forces: Gen. Raúl Castro Ruz. *Vice-Presidents of the Council of Ministers:* Osmani Cienfuegos Gorriarán, José Ramon Fernández Álvarez, Jaime Crombet Hernández-Baquero, Adolfo Díaz Suárez, Pedro Miret Prieto. *Minister of Agriculture:* Alfredo Jordán Morales. *Basic Industries:* Marcos Portal León. *Communications:* Gen. Silvano Colás Sánchez. *Construction:* Juan Junco del Pino. *Construction Materials Industry:* José Cañete Alvárez. *Culture:* Abel Prieto Jiménez. *Domestic Trade:* Barbara Castillo Cuesta. *Economy and Planning:* José Luis Rodríguez García. *Education:* Luís Gómez Gutiérrez. *Finance and Prices:* Manuel Millares Rodríguez. *Fishing Industry:* Orlando Rodríguez Romay. *Food Industry:* Alejandro Roca Iglesias. *Foreign Investment and Economic Co-operation:* Ibrahim Ferradez. *Foreign Relations:* Roberto Robaina Gonzalez. *Foreign Trade:* Ricardo Cabrisas Ruiz. *Higher Education:* Fernando Vecino Alegret. *Interior:* Gen. Abelardo Colomé Ibarra. *Metallurgy and Electronics Industry:* Ignacio González Planas. *Justice:* Roberto Diaz Sotolongo. *Labour and Social Security:* Salvador Valdes Mesa. *Light Industry:* Jesús Pérez Othon. *Public Health:* Carlos Dotres Martínez. *Science, Technology and Environment:* Rosa Simeón Negrín. *Sugar Industry:* Div. Gen. Ulises Rosales del Toro. *Tourism:* Osmany Cienfuegos Gorriarán. *Transport:* Alvaro Perez Morales. *Minister without Portfolio:* Wilfredo López Rodríguez.

The *Speaker* of the National Assembly is Ricardo Alarcón de Quesada.

Various left-wing parties and movements have amalgamated as the Communist Party of Cuba (PCC).

The Congress of the PCC elects a Central Committee of 225 members, which in turn appoints a Political Bureau comprising 26 members.

Local Government. The country is divided into 14 provinces, a special municipality (the Isle of Youth) and 169 municipalities. Elections are held for delegates to the Municipal Assemblies by universal suffrage for 2½ year terms; the municipal assemblies then elect the provincial assemblies for similar terms. Elections for 1,192 representatives to the 14 provincial assemblies were held on 11 Jan. 1998.

DEFENCE
The National Defence Council is headed by the President of the republic. Conscription is for 2 years.

In 1997 defence expenditure totalled US$720m. (US$65 per capita). Defence expenditure in 1985 was US$2,275m.

Army. The strength was 38,000 (including conscripts and Ready Reservists) in 1997. There are 3 regional commands. The Army is organized in 5 armoured, 9 mechanized infantry, 1 airborne, 1 frontier guard, 1 surface-to-air missile and 14 reserve brigades; and 1 air defence regiment. Equipment includes 75 T-34, 1,100 T-54/55 and 400 T-62 main battle tanks. Border Guard and State Security forces total 19,000, and the Territorial Militia, 1·3m. (reservists), all armed.

Navy. Naval combatants, all ex-Soviet, include 2 'Foxtrot' class diesel submarines, 2 'Koni' class frigates, 1 'Pauk' class corvette, 14 fast missile craft, 3 coastal minehunters and 12 inshore minesweepers. There is 1 medium landing ship and 6 craft. The major auxiliaries include 1 tanker and 1 electronic intelligence gatherer. Some 24 minor auxiliaries and service craft complete the total.

Personnel in 1997 totalled about 5,000 conscripts including about 550 marines. Main bases are at Cienfuegos, Havana and Mariel. The USA still occupies the Guantánamo naval base.

There is a coastal defence force equipped with artillery and some anti-ship missiles. A separate coastguard division of the Frontier Guards numbering 4,000 operates about 30 inshore patrol craft.

Air Force. The Air Force has been extensively re-equipped with aircraft supplied by USSR and in 1997 had a strength of some 10,000 and about 130 combat aircraft. About 10 interceptor and 3 ground-attack squadrons fly MiG-29, MiG-23 and MiG-21 jet fighters. There is a squadron of An-26 and An-32 twin-turboprop transports, some An-24 twin-turboprop transports, and about 20 Mi-24 armed helicopters, Mi-8 (some armed), Mi-17 and Mi-2 helicopters, Zlin 326 piston-engined trainers and L-39, MiG-21U, MiG-23U and MiG-29U jet trainers. 10 An-2M biplanes are operated by the Air Force, mainly on agricultural and liaison duties. Soviet-built surface-to-air ('Guideline', 'Goa' and 'Gainful') and coastal defence ('Samlet') missiles are in service.

INTERNATIONAL RELATIONS
Cuba is a member of the UN and SELA (Latin American Economic System).

ECONOMY
Policy. Prices were increased by at least 50% on 1 June 1994. The Central Planning Board was abolished in Jan. 1995. After the economic crisis of the early 1990s, growth has picked up through the legalization of the use of the US dollar, the promotion of dollar-based tourism and of a parallel dollar economy around it. Over 50% of the population now have access to dollars, but there remains 50% who have to survive in the more limited pesos economy.

Performance. A combination of poor commodity export prices and a poor sugar harvest slowed down Cuba's economic growth in 1998 to 1·2%, below the government's original target of 2·5–3·5%.

Budget. The 1995 budget envisaged revenue of 11,680m. pesos and expenditure of 12,680m. pesos. Hard-currency earners and the self-employed became liable to a 10–50% income tax in Nov. 1995.

CUBA

Currency. The unit of currency is the *Cuban peso* (CUP) of 100 *centavos*, which is not convertible, although an official exchange rate is announced daily reflecting any changes in the strength of the US dollar. The US dollar has been legal tender since 1993. 11,750m. pesos were in circulation in 1994. Inflation is expected to be 3·6% in 1999.

Banking and Finance. The Central Bank of Cuba (*Governor*, Francisco Soberón Valdés) replaced the National Bank of Cuba as the central bank in June 1997. On 14 Oct. 1960 all banks were nationalized. Changes to the banking structure beginning in 1996 divested the National Bank of its commercial functions, and created new commercial and investment institutions. There were 7 commercial banks in March 1999 and 9 local non-banking financial institutions. In addition, 17 foreign financial institutions, including 14 foreign banks, had representative offices in 1999; foreign branches are not permitted.

All insurance business was nationalized in Jan. 1964. A National Savings Bank was established in 1983.

Weights and Measures. The metric system is legally compulsory, but the American and old Spanish systems are much used. The sugar industry uses the Spanish long ton (1·03 tonnes) and short ton (0·92 tonne). Cuba sugar sack = 329·59 lb. or 149·49 kg. Land is measured in *caballerías* (of 13·4 ha or 33 acres).

ENERGY AND NATURAL RESOURCES

Electricity. Installed capacity was 4·08m. kW in 1995. Production was 11·19bn. kWh in 1995; consumption per capita in 1995 was estimated to be 822 kWh.

Oil and Gas. Crude oil production (1998), 1,678,000 tonnes. Raw gas production (1998), 120m. cu. metres.

Minerals. Iron ore abounds, with deposits estimated at 3,500m. tonnes. Output of copper concentrate (1989) was 2,800 tonnes; refractory chrome (1987), 52,400 tonnes. Other minerals are nickel (1995, 42,900 tonnes) and cobalt (1989, 46,500 tonnes), silica and barytes. Gold and silver are also worked. Salt output from the solar evaporation of sea water in 1989 was 114,900 tonnes. Sulphuric acid production (1989), 381,500 tonnes.

Agriculture. In 1959 all land over 30 *caballerías* was nationalized and eventually turned into state farms. Under legislation of 1993, state farms are being re-organized as 'units of basic co-operative production'. These units have the use of the land in perpetuity from the state. Unit workers select their own managers, and are paid an advance on earnings. 294,700 persons were employed in these units in 1995. In 1963 private holdings were reduced to a maximum of 5 *caballerías*. In Sept. 1984 there were 1,472 co-operatives comprising 70,000 *caballerías* of land. In 1994 farmers were permitted to trade on free market principles after state delivery quotas had been met.

The most important product is sugar and its by-product, but in 1998 the harvest suffered a series of weather disasters reducing production to 3·2m. tonnes (3·4m. tonnes in 1995–96), the smallest crop for 50 years. Production of other important crops in 1994 was (in 1,000 tonnes): Tobacco (leaves), 44; rice (paddy), 186; coffee, 21; maize, 90.

1994 fruit and vegetable production (in 1,000 tonnes): Oranges, 433; mangoes, 84; bananas, 180; grapefruit and pomelos, 317; and potatoes, 216.

In 1996 livestock included 1·5m. pigs; 580,000 horses; 310,000 sheep; 95,000 goats; 4·5m. cattle; 22m. chickens (1995).

Forestry. Cuba had 1·84m. ha of forests in 1995, representing 16·8% of the land area (1·96m. ha and 17·8% in 1990). These forests contain valuable cabinet woods, such as mahogany and cedar, besides dye-woods, fibres, gums, resins and oils. Cedar is used locally for cigar boxes, and mahogany is exported. In 1995, 3·15m. cu. metres of roundwood were produced.

Fisheries. Fishing is the third most important export industry, after sugar and nickel. The total catch was 94,211 tonnes in 1995, of which 71,678 tonnes were from marine waters.

INDUSTRY
In 1996 manufacturing accounted for 27% of GDP. All industrial enterprises had been state-controlled, but in 1995 the economy was officially stated to comprise state property, commercial property based on activity by state enterprises, joint co-operative and private property. Production in 1989 was: Textiles, 218·6m. sq. metres (cotton fabrics 182·6m. sq. metres); cement, 3,800m. tonnes; wheat flour, 398,000 tonnes; fuel oil, 4,152,800 tonnes; diesel oil, 1,178,500 tonnes; processed crude oil, 7,916,000 tonnes; steel, 314,200 tonnes; steel bars, 367,100 tonnes; nickel and cobalt, 46,500 tonnes; copper, 2,759,100 tonnes; 314,700 tyres; 231,200 inner tubes; leather shoes, 11·0m. pairs; paint, 121,000 hectolitres; soft drinks, 2,396,500 hectolitres; 308m. cigars; 16,519m. cigarettes; fertilizers, 898,600 tonnes; 2,345 buses; 172,700 radios; 70,500 TVs; 9,100 refrigerators.

Labour. In 1996 the labour force was 5,323,000 (62% males). Self-employment was legalized in 1993; there were 0·21m. self-employed persons in 1996. Under legislation of Sept. 1994 employees made redundant must be assigned to other jobs or to strategic social or economic tasks; failing this, they are paid 60% of former salary.

Trade Unions. The Workers' Central Union of Cuba groups 23 unions.

INTERNATIONAL TRADE
Foreign debt to non-communist countries was US$10,400m. in 1997. Since July 1992 foreign investment has been permitted in selected state enterprises, and Cuban companies have been able to import and export without seeking government permission. Foreign ownership is recognized in joint ventures. A free-trade zone opened at Havana in 1993. 3 more were envisaged in legislation of 1996. In 1994 the productive, real estate and service sectors were opened to foreign investment. Legislation of 1995 opened all sectors of the economy to foreign investment except defence, education and health services. 100% foreign-owned investments and investments in property are now permitted.

The Helms-Burton Law of March 1996 gives US nationals the right to sue foreign companies investing in Cuban estate expropriated by the Cuban government.

Imports and Exports. In 1997, exports fell by 11% while imports grew by 6%. In 1998 exports totalled US$1,616m., and imports US$4,084m. The principal exports are sugar, minerals, tobacco, citrus fruit and fish. In 1994-95 sugar exports totalled 2·76m. tonnes (3·19m. tonnes in 1993-94).

COMMUNICATIONS

Roads. In 1996 there were some 26,500 km of roads, of which 14,575 km were paved. Vehicles in use in 1996 included 20,000 passenger cars (2 per 1,000 inhabitants) and 33,000 trucks and vans.

Rail. There were (1992) 4,807 km of public railway (1,435 mm gauge), of which 147 km was electrified. In 1994 it carried 30·5m. passengers and 4·4m. tonnes of freight. In addition, the large sugar estates have 7,773 km of lines on 1,435, 914 and 760 mm gauges.

Civil Aviation. There is an international airport at Havana (Jose Martí). The state airline Cubana operates all services internally, and in 1998 had international flights from Havana to Barcelona, Berlin, Bogotá, Brussels, Buenos Aires, Cancún, Caracas, Cologne, Copenhagen, Curaçao, Fort de France, Frankfurt, Guayaquil, Istanbul, Kingston, Las Palmas, Lima, Lisbon, London, Madrid, Manchester, Maracaibo, Mendoza, Mexico City, Montego Bay, Montreal, Moscow, Paris, Pointe-à-Pitre, Quito, Rio de Janeiro, Rome, St Maarten, San José (Costa Rica), Santa Cruz, Santiago, Santiago de Compostela, Santo Domingo, São Paulo, Toronto and Vitoria. In 1998 scheduled services were also provided by Aeroflot, Aerolíneas Argentinas, Aeropostal Alas de Venezuela, Air Europa, Air Europe, Air France, Air Jamaica, AOM, Aviateca, COPA, Condor Flugdienst, Iberia, LACSA, Mexicana, SAM, Spanair, TAAG and Tame Linea Aerea del Ecuador. In 1996 Havana Jose Martí International handled 1,598,800 passengers (1,077,200 on international flights) and 18,964 tonnes of freight.

Shipping. There are 11 ports, the largest being Havana, Cienfuegos and Mariel. The merchant marine in 1995 totalled 0·54m. GRT, of which 0·1m. GRT were oil tankers.

Telecommunications. There were 370,800 telephone main lines in 1997 (33·6 for every 1,000 persons). In 1995 cellular phone subscribers numbered 1,900 and there were 400 fax machines.

Postal Services. In 1993 there were 1,545 post offices, or 1 for every 7,150 persons.

SOCIAL INSTITUTIONS

Justice. There is a Supreme Court in Havana and 7 regional courts of appeal. The provinces are divided into judicial districts, with courts for civil and criminal actions, and municipal courts for minor offences. The civil code guarantees aliens the same property and personal rights as are enjoyed by nationals.

The 1959 Agrarian Reform Law and the Urban Reform Law passed on 14 Oct. 1960 have placed certain restrictions on both. Revolutionary Summary Tribunals have wide powers.

Stealing from state companies by employees has become an increasing problem during the 1990s.

Religion. Religious liberty was constitutionally guaranteed in July 1992. 60% of the population were estimated to be Roman Catholics in 1996. In 1994 Cardinal Jaime Ortega (b. 1936) was nominated Primate by the Pope. In 1996 there were 260 Roman Catholic priests and monks, nearly half of them foreign nationals. There is a seminary in Havana which had 61 students in 1996. There is a bishop of the American Episcopal Church in Havana; there are congregations of Methodists in Havana and in the provinces as well as Baptists and other denominations. Cults of African origin still persist.

Education. Education is compulsory (between the ages of 6 and 14), free and universal. In 1995 there were 160,283 pre-primary pupils with 6,512 teachers; 9,864 primary schools with 90,565 teachers for 1·07m. pupils; and 704,601 secondary level pupils with 74,139 teachers. There were 122,346 students at university level.

There are 4 universities, and 10 teacher training, 2 agricultural, 4 medical and 10 other higher educational institutions.

The adult literacy rate was 95·7% in 1995 (96·2% among males and 95·3% among females).

Health. In 1992 there were 46,860 doctors, 8,057 dentists, 73,943 nurses and (1993) 244 hospitals. There were 65 beds per 10,000 population in 1993.

Free medical services are provided by the state polyclinics, though a few doctors still have private practices.

CULTURE

Broadcasting. Broadcasting is the responsibility of the state-controlled Instituto Cubano de Radio y Televisión. There are 5 national radio networks, provincial and local stations and an external service, Radio Habana (Spanish, Arabic, Creole, English, Esperanto, French, Guaraní, Portuguese and Quechua). There are 2 TV channels (colour by NTSC). In 1995 there were 3·85m. radio and 2·5m. TV sets.

Cinema. In 1993 there were 461 cinemas with an attendance of 17·6m.

Press. There were (1998) 17 daily newspapers with a combined circulation of 1·3m.

Tourism. Tourism is Cuba's largest foreign exchange earner, and has been growing by nearly 20% per year. There were 1·4m. foreign tourists in 1998 with a projected figure of 1·7m. for 1999, mainly from Canada and Europe. Total gross earnings from tourism in 1998 amounted to US$1·7bn. The age at which Cubans may obtain exit visas was lowered to 20 years in Aug. 1991.

National Theatre and Opera. There were 49 theatres with an attendance of 1,387,700 in 1989.

DIPLOMATIC REPRESENTATIVES
Of Cuba in Great Britain (167 High Holborn, London, WC1 6PA)
Ambassador: Rodney Alejandro López Clemente.

Of Great Britain in Cuba (Calle 34, No. 702/4, entre 7ma Avenida y 17 Miramar, Havana)
Ambassador: Mr D. Ridgway.

Of Cuba to the United Nations
Ambassador: Bruno Rodríguez Parrilla.

Of Cuba to the European Union
Ambassador: René Mujica Cantelar.

The USA broke off diplomatic relations with Cuba on 3 Jan. 1961 but Cuba has an Interests Section in the Swiss Embassy in Washington, D.C., and the USA has an Interests Section in the Swiss Embassy in Havana.

FURTHER READING
Bethell, L., (ed.) *Cuba: a Short History.* CUP, 1993
Bunck, J. M., *Fidel Castro and the Quest for a Revolutionary Culture in Cuba.* Pennsylvania State Univ. Press, 1994
Cabrera Infantye, G., *Mea Cuba*; translated into English from Spanish. London, 1994
Cardoso, E. and Helwege, A., *Cuba after Communism.* Boston (Mass.), 1992
Eckstein, S. E., *Back from the Future: Cuba under Castro.* Princeton Univ. Press, 1994
Fursenko, A., and Naftali, T., *'One Hell of a Gamble': Khrushchev, Castro and Kennedy, 1958-1964.* New York, 1997
May, E. R. and Zelikow, P. D., *The Kennedy Tapes: Inside the White House during the Cuban Missile Crisis.* Belknap Press/Harvard University Press, 1997
Mesa-Lago, C. (ed.) *Cuba: After the Cold War.* Pittsburgh Univ. Press, 1993
Ruttin, P., *Capitalism and Socialism in Cuba: a Study of Dependency, Development and Underdevelopment.* London, 1990
Stubbs, J., et al., *Cuba* [Bibliography]. Oxford and Santa Barbara (CA), 1996
Zimbalist, A. and Brundenius, C., *The Cuban Economy: Measurement and Analysis of Socialist Performance.* Johns Hopkins Univ. Press, 1990

CYPRUS

Kypriaki Dimokratia—
Kibris Çumhuriyeti

(Republic of Cyprus)

Capital: Nicosia
Population estimate, 2000: 793,000
GNP per capita: (PPP$) 20,490
HDI/world rank: 0·913/23

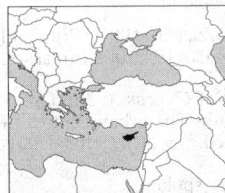

KEY HISTORICAL EVENTS

About the middle of the second millennium BC, Greek colonies were established in Cyprus and later it formed part of the Persian, Roman and Byzantine empires. In 1193 the island became a Frankish kingdom, in 1489 a Venetian dependency, and in 1751 was conquered by the Turks. The Turks retained possession of it until its cession to Britain for administrative purposes under a convention concluded with the Sultan of Constantinople in 1878. In 1914 the island was annexed by Great Britain and on 1 May 1925 it was given the status of a Crown Colony.

In the 1930s the Greek Cypriots began to agitate for ENOSIS (Union with Greece). In 1955 they started a guerrilla movement (EOKA) against the British, with Archbishop Makarios, the head of the Greek Orthodox Church in Cyprus, as leader, and Gen. Grivas in charge of military operations. As the British suspected Makarios of advocating violence he was banished from the island. However, in 1959 the Greek and Turkish Cypriots agreed on a constitution for an independent Cyprus and Makarios returned to be elected President. On 16 June 1960 Cyprus became an independent state. In Dec. 1963 the Turkish Cypriots withdrew from the government. Fighting between Turkish and Greek Cypriots led to a UN peace-keeping force being sent in. On 15 July 1974 a military coup drove out Makarios and appointed as president Nicos Sampson, an EOKA supporter. The coup was short-lived as Sampson resigned on 23 July and Makarios was recalled as President.

Turkey invaded the island on 20 July 1974, eventually occupying the northern part. 0·2m. Greek Cypriots fled to live as refugees in the south. The UN General Assembly unanimously adopted resolutions calling for the withdrawal of all foreign troops from Cyprus and the return of refugees to their homes, but without result. On 13 Feb. 1975 a Turkish Cypriot Federated State was proclaimed. Rauf Denktaş was appointed President. On 15 Nov. 1983 the Turkish state unilaterally proclaimed itself the 'Turkish Republic of Northern Cyprus' (TRNC). In Nov. 1983 and May 1984 the UN Security Council declared all secessionist actions illegal. Several UN-inspired talks were held in 1985–91 without success. In March 1991 the UN Security Council adopted unanimously a resolution rejecting new TRNC demands. In Sept. discussions were held between the UN Secretary-General's representatives, the Greek Cypriot president and Rauf Denktaş. In Oct. the UN Secretary-General rejected Rauf Denktaş' demands for the recognition of separate sovereignty for the TRNC, including a right to secession.

Further talks were held without results in May–Aug. 1992. On 26 Aug. the UN Security Council adopted a resolution endorsing the Secretary-General's ideas and territorial adjustments as the basis for reaching an agreement. Talks were held in Oct. 1992 and in 1993 after the election of President Clerides, without result. Cyprus had accepted confidence-building measures suggested by the UN but these were opposed by the TRNC. In July 1994 the UN Security Council adopted a resolution reaffirming that a settlement must be based on a single sovereignty and exclude any form of partition or succession. In 1998 a proposal by Rauf Denktaş that the Greek and Turkish communities should join in a federation that recognizes 'the equal and sovereign status of Cyprus' Greek and Turkish parts' was rejected by the Greek and Cypriot governments.

TERRITORY AND POPULATION

The island lies in the Mediterranean, about 60 km off the south coast of Turkey and 90 km off the coast of Syria. Area, 3,572 sq. miles (9,251 sq. km). The Turkish-occupied area is 3,335 sq. km. Population by ethnic group:

CYPRUS

Ethnic group	1960	1973	1992	1997
Greek Cypriot	447,901	498,511	599,000	654,900
Turkish Cypriot	103,822	116,000	95,000[1]	88,200
Others	20,984	17,267	20,000	23,000
Total	572,707	631,778	714,000	746,100

[1]Revised to take into account Turkish Cypriots who have emigrated from the Turkish-occupied area since 1974 (estimated at over 41,000).

Estimated population, 1995, 742,000; density, 80 per sq. km.
The UN gives a projected population for 2000 of 793,000.
An estimated 68·9% of the population lived in urban areas in 1997. Principal towns with populations (1997 estimate): Nicosia (the capital), 194,100; Limassol, 152,900; Larnaca, 68,000; Paphos, 38,000.
As a result of the Turkish occupation of the northern part of Cyprus, 0·2m. Greek Cypriots were displaced and forced to find refuge in the south. The urban centres of Famagusta, Kyrenia and Morphou were completely evacuated. *See below* for details of the 'Turkish Republic of Northern Cyprus'.
Greek and Turkish are official languages. English is widely spoken.

SOCIAL STATISTICS
1997 births, 12,500; deaths, 5,500. Rates, 1997 (per 1,000 population): Births, 14·2; deaths, 7·9. Life expectancy at birth, 1996–97, was 75·0 years for males and 80·0 years for females. Infant mortality, 1997, 8 per 1,000 live births; fertility rate, 2·4 children per woman.

CLIMATE
The climate is Mediterranean, with very hot, dry summers and variable winters. Maximum temperatures may reach 112°F (44·5°C) in July and Aug., but minimum figures may fall to 22°F (−5·5°C) in the mountains in winter, when snow is experienced. Rainfall is generally between 10" and 27" (250 and 675 mm) and occurs mainly in the winter months, but it may reach 48" (1,200 mm) in the Troodos mountains. Nicosia, Jan. 50°F (10·0°C), July 83°F (28·3°C). Annual rainfall 15" (371 mm).

CONSTITUTION AND GOVERNMENT
Under the 1960 Constitution executive power is vested in a *President* elected for a 5-year term by universal suffrage, and exercised through a Council of Ministers appointed by him or her. The *House of Representatives* exercises legislative power. It is elected by universal suffrage for 5-year terms, and consists of 80 members, of whom 56 are elected by the Greek Cypriot and 24 by the Turkish Cypriot community. Voting is compulsory, and is by preferential vote in a proportional representation system with reallocation of votes at national level. As from Dec. 1963 the Turkish Cypriot members have ceased to attend.

National Anthem. 'Segnoriso apo tin kopsi' ('Always shall I know you'); words by D. Solomos, tune by N. Mantzaros.

RECENT ELECTIONS
Parliamentary elections were held on 26 May 1996. The Democratic Rally won 20 seats with 34·48% of votes cast, the Communist Progressive Party of the Working People (Akel) 19 with 33·03%, the Democratic Party 10 and the EDEK Party (Socialists) 5.
Presidential elections were held on 8 and 15 Feb. 1998. In the first round Glafcos Clerides won 40·1% of the vote as against 40·6% for his rival George Iakovou, a former foreign minister. The Socialist leader, Vassos Lyssarides, won 10·6%. In the run-off, Glafcos Clerides won 50·8% to 49·2% for George Iakovou. The turn-out was over 90%.
In Jan. 1999, the Socialists withdrew from the governing coalition following the administration's decision to cancel plans to deploy Russian anti-aircraft missiles on the island.

CURRENT ADMINISTRATION
President: Glafcos Clerides, b. 1919 (Democratic Rally; elected 1998).

The Council of Ministers in March 1999 consisted of:

Foreign Affairs: Ioannis Kasoulides. *Interior:* Christodoulos Christodoulou. *Defence:* Yiannakis Chrysostomis. *Agriculture, Natural Resources and Environment:* Costas Themistocleous. *Commerce, Industry and Tourism:* Nicos Rolandis. *Health:* Christos Solomis. *Communications, Public Works and Transport:* Leondios Ierodiaconou. *Finance:* Takis Clerides. *Education and Culture:* Ouranios Ioannides. *Labour:* Andreas Moushouttas. *Justice and Public Order:* Nicos Koshis.

The *Speaker* is Spyros Kypriauou.

Local Government. There are 3 types of local authorities: Municipalities, Improvement Boards and Village Authorities. Municipalities account for about 60% of the population while 85 Improvement Boards and 352 Village authorities cover the rest of the population. The functions of Municipalities are determined by the Municipalities Law of 1985, and their finances derive from municipal taxes, fees and duties as well as state subsidies.

DEFENCE
Conscription is for 26 months. Defence expenditure in 1997 totalled US$505m. (US$594 per capita), representing 5·8% of GDP. At the end of 1998 the President cancelled a US$450m. contract with Russia for the deployment of S-300 anti-aircraft missiles on the island and negotiated to place them on Crete instead.

National Guard. Total strength (1997) 10,000 (8,700 conscripts) organized in 2 light infantry divisions, 2 light infantry and 1 armoured brigade. Equipment includes 62 AMX-30 B-2 main battle tanks, 41 T8OU tanks and 4 Gazelle helicopters with HOT missiles. In Jan. 1997 S-300 ground-to-air missiles were purchased from Russia and the Cypriot government eventually decided that they be installed and deployed on the Greek island of Crete. There is also a para-military force of 3,700 armed police.

There are 2 British bases (Army and Royal Air Force) and some 3,900 personnel. Greek (950) and UN peacekeeping (1,138; UNFICY) forces are also stationed on the island. Plans to install Russian-made air defence missiles have brought Turkish threats of retaliation.

INTERNATIONAL RELATIONS
Cyprus is a member of the UN, Commonwealth and Council of Europe. Since March 1998 Cyprus has entered into accession negotiations with the EU, which are expected to be completed by 2003.

ECONOMY
Performance. Real GDP growth in 1997 was 2·5%.

Budget. Revenues in 1997 (1996) were £C1·37bn. (£C1·32bn.) and expenditure £C1·60bn. (£C1·46bn.). Main sources of revenue in 1997 (in £C1m.) were: Direct taxes, 374·41; indirect taxes, 491·55; social security contributions, 206·41.

Main divisions of expenditure in 1997 (in £C1m.): Wages and salaries, 429·85; pensions and gratuities, 15·56; commodity subsidies, 36·26; expenditures on goods and services, 131·81; social security payments, 234·99; education, 150·50; health, 91·95.

Development expenditure for 1997 (in £C1m.) included 15·6 for water development, 10·4 for agriculture, forests and fisheries, 10·0 for rural development and 28·5 for roads.

The outstanding domestic debt as at 31 Dec. 1997 was £C1,982·26m. and the foreign debt was £C515·32m.

Currency. The *Cyprus pound* (CYP) is divided into 100 *cents*. Inflation was 2·3% in 1998. In Nov. 1997 gold reserves were 460,000 troy oz. and foreign exchange reserves were US$1,484m. In Dec. 1997 total money supply was £C704m.

Banking and Finance. The Central Bank of Cyprus, established in 1963, is the bank of issue; regulates money supply, credit and foreign exchange; and supervises the banking system.

In 1997 there were 9 commercial banks (3 foreign) and 3 specialized banks (co-operative, development and mortgage). At 31 Dec. 1997 total deposits in banks were £C6,483m.

Weights and Measures. The metric (SI) system was introduced in 1986 and is now widely applied.

ENERGY AND NATURAL RESOURCES

Electricity. Installed capacity is 690,000 kW. Production in 1997 was 2,711m. kWh. Consumption was 2,391m. kWh in 1997.

Water. In 1997, £C16·6m. was spent on water dams, water supplies, hydrological research and geophysical surveys. Existing dams had (1997) a capacity of 299m. cu. metres.

Minerals. The principal minerals extracted in 1997 were (in tonnes): Gypsum, 300,000; bentonite, 150,000; umber and other ochres, 8,000; copper, 4,000.

Agriculture. 28% of the government-controlled area is cultivated. About 9·8% (1997) of the economically active population were engaged in agriculture.

Chief agricultural products in 1997 (1,000 tonnes): Grapes, 101·0; potatoes, 81·5; milk, 177·8; cereals (wheat and barley), 47·5; citrus fruit, 142·5; meat, 92·6; carobs, 5·1; fresh fruit, 34·4; olives, 9·0; other vegetables, 88·9; eggs, 12·2m. dozen.

Livestock in 1997: Cattle, 62,400; sheep, 265,000; goats, 275,000; pigs, 414,800; poultry, 3,600,000.

Forestry. Total forest area in 1995 was 1,400 sq. km (15·2% of the land area). In 1997, 30,490 cu. metres of timber were produced.

Fisheries. Total catches in 1997 amounted to 3,377 tonnes.

INDUSTRY

The most important industries in 1997 were: Food, beverages and tobacco, textiles, wearing apparel and leather, chemicals and chemical petroleum, rubber and plastic products, metal products, machinery and equipment, wood and wood products including furniture. Manufacturing industry in 1997 contributed about 11·2% of the GDP.

Labour. Out of 285,000 people in employment in 1995, 75,000 were in trade, restaurants and hotels, 64,000 in community, social and personal services and 44,000 in manufacturing industries. The unemployment rate was 3·4% in 1997.

Trade Unions. About 80% of the workforce is organized and the majority of workers belong either to the Pancyprian Federation of Labour or the Cyprus Workers Confederation.

INTERNATIONAL TRADE

Foreign debt was £C926m. in 1993.

Imports and Exports. Trade figures for calendar years were (in £C1,000):

	1994	1995	1996	1997
Imports[1]	1,417,814	1,616,825	1,754,463	1,803,731
Exports	475,978	555,607	649,027	640,015

[1]Excludes military goods.

Chief civil imports, 1997 (in £C1m.):

Live animals and animal products	28·2	Footwear, headgear, umbrellas, prepared leathers, etc.	22·5
Vegetable products	78·3		
Prepared foodstuffs, beverages and tobacco	398·8	Articles of stone, plaster, cement, etc., ceramic and glass products	41·9
Mineral products	160·8	Machinery, electrical equipment, sound and television recorders	267·3
Products of chemical or allied industries	129·3	Vehicles, aircraft, vessels and equipment	150·4
Plastics and rubber and articles thereof	67·5	Optical, photographic, medical, musical and other instruments, clocks and watches	34·4
Pulp, waste paper and paperboard and articles thereof	66·2		
Textiles and textile articles	128·1		
Base metal and articles of base metal	104·2	Pearls, precious stones and metals, semi-precious stones and articles	23·8
Wood and articles, charcoal, cork and articles, basketware, etc.	26·5		

Chief domestic exports, 1997 (in £C1,000):

Grapes	1,387	Paper products	5,897
Citrus fruit	17,296	Cement	12,482
Potatoes	8,433	Clothing	29,896
Wine	7,890	Footwear	8,049
Fruit, preserved and juices	6,125	Medicinal and pharmaceutical	
Cigarettes	8,922	products	19,648

Main export markets, 1996: Russia, 17·5%; Bulgaria, 15·1%; UK, 10·4%; Greece 5·8%. Main import suppliers, 1996: USA, 16·8%; UK, 11·2%; Italy, 9·2%; Greece, 7·2%.

COMMUNICATIONS

Roads. In 1997 the total length of roads in the government-controlled area was 10,654 km, of which 6,209 km were bituminous and 4,445 km were earth or gravel roads. The asphalted roads maintained by the Ministry of Communications and Works (Public Works Department) by the end of 1997 totalled 2,272 km, of which 264 km were within the municipal areas. Construction of new asphalted roads in 1997 totalled 260 km. In 1997 there were 472,132 motor vehicles including 3,177 buses, 120,000 goods vehicles, 63,264 motor cycles and 12,460 tractors.

The area controlled by the Government of the Republic and that occupied by the TRNC are now served by separate transport systems, and there are no services linking the two areas.

Civil Aviation. Nicosia airport has been closed since Aug. 1974. There are international airports at Larnaca (the main airport) and Paphos. In 1997, 4,799,179 passengers and 63,600 tonnes of commercial freight went through these airports. The national carrier is Cyprus Airways, which is 80·46% state-owned. In 1998 services were also provided by Aeroflot, Aerosweet Airlines, Air 2000, Air Malta, Air Moldova, Air Slovakia, Air Zimbabwe, Alitalia, Austrian Airlines, Balkan, Belavia, British Airways, Czech Airlines, Donavia, Egyptair, El Al, Emirates, Finnair, Gulf Air, Hapag Lloyd, Iberia, Iran Air, JAT, KLM, Korsar, Kuwait Airways, Latvian Airlines, Libyan Airlines, Lithuanian Airlines, LOT, Lufthansa, Malév, Middle East Airlines, Olympic Airways, Royal Jordanian, SAS, Swissair, Syrian Arab Airlines, Tarom and Transaero Airlines. Cyprus Airways flew 20·3m. km in 1995, carrying 1,218,900 passengers (all on international flights). In 1996 Larnaca handled 3,491,153 passengers and 27,418 tonnes of freight.

Shipping. The 2 main ports are Limassol and Larnaca. In 1997, 4,158 ships of 14,243,000 net registered tonnes entered Cyprus ports carrying 5,031,000 tonnes of cargo from, to and via Cyprus. Ships on the Cyprus open registry in 1996 totalled 33,049,967 DWT. Famagusta has been closed to international traffic since Aug. 1974.

Telecommunications. In 1997 there were 385,000 main telephone lines (569·7 for every 1,000 inhabitants). There were 45,000 cellular phone subscribers, 30,000 PCs and 7,000 fax machines in 1995. The Cyprus Telecommunications Authority provides telephone and data transmission services nationally, and to 253 countries automatically.

Postal Services. In 1997 there were 56 post offices and 729 postal agencies.

SOCIAL INSTITUTIONS

Justice. The administration of justice is exercised by a separate and independent judiciary. There is a Supreme Court, Assize Courts and District Courts.

The Supreme Court is composed of 13 judges, one of whom is the President of the Court. There is a continuing Assize Court that holds sessions in every district according to the cases committed for trial before it. The Assize Courts have unlimited criminal jurisdiction, and may order the payment of compensation up to £C3,000. The District Courts exercise original civil and criminal jurisdiction, the extent of which varies with the composition of the Bench.

There is a Supreme Council of Judicature, consisting of the President and Judges of the Supreme Court, entrusted with the appointment, promotion, transfers, termination of appointment and disciplinary control over all judicial officers, other than the Judges of the Supreme Court.

The Attorney-General (Alecos Markides) is head of the independent Law Office and legal advisor to the President and his Ministers.

Religion. The Greek Cypriots are Greek Orthodox Christians, and the Turkish Cypriots are Moslems (mostly Sunnis of the Hanafi sect). There are also small groups of the Armenian Apostolic Church, Roman Catholics (Maronites and Latin Rite) and Protestants (mainly Anglicans). *See also* CYPRUS: Territory and Population.

Education. Greek-Cypriot Education. Elementary education is compulsory and is provided free in 6 grades to children between 5 years 8 months and 11 years 8 months. There are also schools for the deaf and blind, and 10 schools for handicapped children. In 1996–97 the Ministry ran 225 kindergartens for children in the age group 2½–5; there were also 152 communal and 271 private kindergartens. There were 376 primary schools with 64,761 pupils and 4,159 teachers in 1996–97.

Secondary education is also free and attendance for the first cycle is compulsory. The secondary school is 6 years, 3 years at the gymnasium followed by 3 years at the *lykeion* (lyceum) or 3 years at one of the technical schools which provide technical and vocational education for industry. In 1996–97 there were 125 secondary schools with 5,757 teachers and 61,266 pupils.

Post-secondary education is provided at 6 public institutions: The University of Cyprus, which admitted its first students in Sept. 1992 and had 2,097 students by 1996–97; The Higher Technical Institute, which provides 3–4-year courses for technicians in civil, electrical, mechanical and marine engineering; a 2-year Forestry College (administered by the Ministry of Agriculture, Natural Resources and Environment); The Higher Hotel Institute (Ministry of Labour and Social Insurance); the Mediterranean Institute of Management (Ministry of Labour and Social Insurance); the School of Nursing (Ministry of Health) which runs 2–3 year courses; the Cyprus Academy of Public Administration set up to help civil servants improve their management skills.

There are also various public and private institutions which provide courses at various levels. These include the Apprenticeship Training Scheme and Evening Technical Classes, and other vocational and technical courses organized by the Industrial Training Authority.

In 1992 the adult literacy rate was 94·4% (97·8% among males, 90·1% among females).

Health. In 1993 there were 1,455 doctors, 498 dentists, 2,536 nurses, 423 pharmacists and 120 midwives. There were 110 hospitals (excluding psychiatric hospitals) in 1993.

Welfare. The administration of the social security services is in the hands of the Ministry of Labour and Social Insurance, with the Ministry of Health providing medical services through public clinics and hospitals on a means test, except for medical treatment for employment accidents, which is given free to all insured employees and financed by the Social Insurance Scheme.

CULTURE

Broadcasting. Cyprus Broadcasting Corporation has 3 radio channels and broadcasts mainly in Greek, but also in Turkish, English and Armenian. The Corporation also broadcasts on 2 TV channels (colour by PAL). A law of June 1990 permits the operation of commercial radio and TV stations. In 1994 there were 2 independent radio stations broadcasting nationwide and numerous radio stations broadcasting locally. There were also 2 private TV stations operating and 1 private Pay-TV. There are also 2 foreign broadcasting stations. In 1995 there were 230,000 radio and 240,000 TV sets.

Cinema. In the government-controlled area, there were 16 cinemas and 17 screens in 1997.

Press. In 1996 there were 9 daily newspapers with a circulation of 84,000; and 31 other newspapers with a circulation of 185,000.

Tourism. There were 2,069,000 long-stay foreign tourists in 1997, spending £C800m.

Libraries. In 1995 there were 117 public libraries, 1 National library and 1 non-specialized library, holding a combined 454,000 volumes for 30,051 registered users.

Museums and Galleries. In 1993 there were 24 museums which received 515,000 visitors.

DIPLOMATIC REPRESENTATIVES
Of Cyprus in Great Britain (93 Park St., London, W1Y 4ET)
High Commissioner: Michalis Attalides.

Of Great Britain in Cyprus (Alexander Pallis St., Nicosia)
High Commissioner: Vacant.

Of Cyprus in the USA (2211 R. St., NW, Washington, D.C., 20008)
Ambassador: Erato Kozakou Marcoullis.

Of the USA in Cyprus (Metochiou and Ploutarchou Streets, Engomi, Nicosia)
Ambassador: Kenneth Brill.

Of Cyprus to the United Nations
Ambassador: Sotirios Zackheos.

Of Cyprus to the European Union
Ambassador: Michalis Attalides.

FURTHER READING
Calotychos, V., *Cyprus and Its People: Nation, identity and experience in an unimaginable community 1955-1997*, Westview, Oxford, 1999
Christodolou, D., *Inside the Cyprus Miracle: the Labours of an Embattled Mini-Economy.* Univ. of Minnesota Press, 1992
Kitromilides, P. M. and Evriviades, M. L., *Cyprus* [Bibliography]. 2nd ed. Oxford and Santa Barbara (CA), 1995
Salem N. (ed.) *Cyprus: a Regional Conflict and its Resolution.* London, 1992

Statistical Information: Statistics and Research Department, Nicosia.
Website: http://www.pio.gov.cy/dsr/

'TURKISH REPUBLIC OF NORTHERN CYPRUS (TRNC)'

KEY HISTORICAL EVENTS
See CYPRUS: Key Historical Events.

TERRITORY AND POPULATION
The Turkish Republic of Northern Cyprus occupies 3,355 sq. km (about 33% of the island of Cyprus) and its population in 1994 was estimated to be 177,120. Distribution of population by districts (1994): Nicosia, 82,424; Famagusta, 67,167; Kyrenia, 27,529.

CONSTITUTION AND GOVERNMENT
The Turkish Republic of Northern Cyprus was proclaimed on 15 Nov. 1983.

RECENT ELECTIONS
Presidential elections were held in 2 rounds on 15 and 22 April 1995. Rauf Denktaş (b. 1924) failed to gain an outright majority against 6 opponents in the first round but was re-elected at the second round against 1 opponent by 62·48% of the vote.

A 50-seat Legislative Assembly was elected on 6 Dec. 1998. Prime Minister Derviş Eroğlu's National Unity Party (UBP) won 24 seats, Democratic Party (DP) 13, Communal Liberation Party (TKP) 7 and Republican Turkish Party (CTP) 6.

CURRENT ADMINISTRATION
The Council of Ministers consisted in March 1999 of:
Prime Minister: Derviş Eroğlu (UBP).
Minister of State and Deputy Prime Minister: Mustafa Akinci (TKP). *Foreign and Defence:* Tahsin Ertuğruloğlu (UBP). *Interior:* İlkay Kamil (UBP). *Economy and*

CYPRUS

Finance: Mehmet Bayram (UBP). *National Education and Culture:* Mehmet Altınay (TKP). *Agriculture and Forestry:* İrsen Küçük (UBP). *Communications and Works:* Salih Miroğlu (UBP). *Labour and Housing:* Mehmet Albayrak (UBP). *Health and Environment:* Gülsen Bozkurt (TKP). *Youth and Sport:* Tansel Doratlı (UBP).

The *Speaker* of the Legislative Assembly is Ertuğrul Hasipoğlu.

DEFENCE
In 1997, 30,000 members of Turkey's armed forces were stationed in the TRNC with 465 main battle tanks. TRNC forces comprise 7 infantry battalions and 3 patrol boats with a total personnel strength of 4,000. Conscription is for 2 years.

ECONOMY
Budget. Revenue (in 1,000m. Turkish lira) in 1995 was 8,463·4; expenditure, 13,655·4.

Currency. The Turkish lira is used.

Banking and Finance. 50 banks, including offshore banks, were operating in 1995. Control is exercised by the Central Bank of the TRNC.

ENERGY AND NATURAL RESOURCES
Agriculture. Agriculture accounted for 10·9% of GDP in 1994.

INTERNATIONAL TRADE
Exports earned US$67·3m. in 1995. Imports cost US$366·1m. Customs tariffs with Turkey were reduced in July 1990. There is a free port at Famagusta.

COMMUNICATIONS
Civil Aviation. There is an international airport at Ercan. In 1998 there were flights to Istanbul with Turkish Airlines.

SOCIAL INSTITUTIONS
Education. In 1995–96 there were 15,526 pupils and 1,103 teachers in primary schools; 14,816 pupils and 1,107 teachers in secondary and general high schools; 2,477 students and 348 teachers in technical and vocational schools; and 8,932 students in higher education. There are 3 private colleges and 6 universities.

Health. In 1995 there were 353 doctors, 120 dentists, 116 other specialists and 1,214 beds in state hospitals and private clinics.

CULTURE
Broadcasting. The local radio, Radio Bayrak (BRTK), broadcasts in several languages including Greek, Arabic and English. BRT Television broadcasts for an average of 10 hours a day (colour by PAL). In 1994 there were 108,800 TV and radio sets.

Press. In 1995 there were 7 daily and 4 weekly newspapers.

Tourism. There were 385,759 tourists in 1995. Tourist earnings totalled US$388·3m.

FURTHER READING
North Cyprus Almanack, London, 1987
Dodd, C. H. (ed.) *The Political, Social and Economic Development of Northern Cyprus.* Huntingdon, 1993
Hanworth, R., *The Heritage of Northern Cyprus.* Nicosia, 1993
Ioannides, C. P., *In Turkey's Image: the Transformation of Occupied Cyprus into a Turkish Province.* New Rochelle (N.Y.), 1991
Tamkoç, M., *The Turkish Cypriot State.* London, 1988

CZECH REPUBLIC

Ceská Republika

Capital: Prague
Population estimate, 2000: 10·19m.
GNP per capita: (PPP$) 10,870
HDI/world rank: 0·884/39

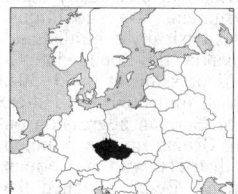

KEY HISTORICAL EVENTS

Although the name Bohemia is Celtic, Slav settlers were well established in the area by the 6th century. The Czech tribe rose to dominance in the 8th century. After the death of Charlemagne a Greater Moravian State emerged before being engulfed by Magyars around 905, though part was recovered by one of the Přemysl ruling family (895-1306).

Dynastic squabbles, exacerbated by German interference, weakened the power of the dukes, but in 1212 Otakar I (1197-1230) received a hereditary kingship from the Holy Roman Emperor. A period of prosperity developed, aided by the immigration of German miners and merchants who were encouraged with special privileges. Bohemia expanded under the last Přemysl kings: Wenceslas I (1230-53) seized Austria in 1251, though it passed to the Hapsburgs when Otakar II was killed at the battle of Marchfeld in 1278; Wenceslas II was elected king of Poland in 1300. Wenceslas was assassinated in 1306 and was succeeded in 1310 by John of Luxemburg. His son, Charles (1346-78), became Holy Roman Emperor as Charles IV in 1355. Bohemia attained a high degree of prosperity and civilization at this time.

The clerical reform movement with which the name of Jan Hus is associated began as a protest against the corruption and venality of the church, but it had undertones of anti-German Czech nationalism and found support amongst the urban middle classes and lesser rural gentry as well as the urban poor and peasantry. Hus was burned at the stake in 1415, but the Hussite movement continued and repelled efforts to enthrone the Hungarian king Sigismund until 1436. There was some post-war recovery under the enlightened Hussite king, George of Poděbrad (1457-71). After his death the Jagiellonian dynasty succeeded, from 1490 ruling Hungary jointly, until the death of Louis against the Turks at Mohács in 1526. During this period the provincial diet of 3 estates (nobility, gentry, burgesses) acted to enhance the power of the nobility and diminish that of the burgesses.

In 1527 the diet elected the Hapsburg Ferdinand as king. The Hapsburgs gradually encroached upon Czech rights and religious freedom. In 1618 Protestants threw 2 Czech Catholic governors out of a window in Prague Castle. This incident sparked off the Thirty Years War. The estates deposed Emperor Ferdinand II in favour of the Calvinist Frederick V but the latter's forces were defeated at the battle of the White Mountain on 8 Nov. 1620, and a period of Hapsburg hegemony ensued: The Czech nobility were replaced by German-speaking adventurers; the burgesses lost their rights; burdens were piled on to the peasantry; and Catholicism was enforced. Risings were savagely repressed. Some relief came with the ideas of the Enlightenment: Amongst other reforms Emperor Joseph II granted the peasantry freedom of movement in 1781, a precondition for the burgeoning industrial revolution of the next century. At first Czech nationalism could find an outlet only in cultural activities. Uprisings in the revolutionary episode of 1848 were ineffective. The increasingly political aspirations of Czech nationalists were not for the resuscitation of the old Bohemia but for the formation of a new Czechoslovakia, an idea fostered by Thomas Masaryk. Manhood suffrage was granted in 1906 but the chamber of deputies was constantly bypassed by the emperor. The First World War brought a complete estrangement between the Czechs and the Germans, the latter supporting the war effort. Masaryk and other leaders went into exile and in 1916 a Czechoslovak National Council was set up under his chairmanship. In 1918 he secured the support of US president Woodrow Wilson for Czech and Slovak unity (*see* Slovakia). On 18 Oct. 1918 the National Council transformed itself into a provisional government and was recognized by the Allies.

Austria accepted President Wilson's terms on 27 Oct. 1918 and the next day a republic was proclaimed with Masaryk as president and Edvard Beneš as foreign minister. On 29 Oct. the Slovak leaders declared Slovakia part of the Czechoslovak nation. In drawing up the frontiers of the new state it was impossible to apply strictly the principles of Wilsonian self-determination because of the ethnic mix; other criteria employed were the partial restoration of the historic provinces and the need to establish an economically viable and defensible state. Amongst the minorities were 3·25m. Sudeten Germans.

The constitution of 1920 provided for a 2-chamber parliament elected by adult suffrage. The electoral system worked so that all governments were coalitions. Slovakia was granted an assembly in 1927 but the state was basically centralist and the Slovaks maintained their own parties. Czechoslovakia developed into a prosperous democracy but was hard hit by the economic depression of the 1930s. Nationalist agitation amongst the Sudeten Germans was fomented by Hitler. Czechoslovakia relied for her defence against the threat of German aggression on her treaty with France of 1925 but France sided with Britain in the Munich agreement of 29 Sept. 1938 which stipulated that all districts with a German population of more than 50% should be ceded to Germany. Beneš resigned the presidency and went into exile. On 14 March 1939 Slovakia declared itself independent under German hegemony, and the next day the German army occupied the rest of the country and proclaimed the 'Protectorate of Bohemia-Moravia'. Czechoslovaks who managed to escape joined Beneš to form a government in exile. In Dec. 1943 Beneš signed a 20-year treaty of alliance with the USSR. In March 1945 he went to Moscow to talk to communists who had spent the war there about the nature of the post-war government which was established in April at Košice in the wake of the Soviet Army. Liberation by the Soviet Army and US Forces was completed by May 1945 and territories taken by Germans, Poles and Hungarians were restored to Czechoslovak sovereignty. Subcarpathian Ruthenia was transferred to the USSR.

Elections were held in May 1946, at which the Communist Party obtained about 38% of the votes. A coalition government under a Communist Prime Minister, Klement Gottwald, remained in power until 20 Feb. 1948, when 12 of the non-Communist ministers resigned in protest against infiltration of Communists into the police. In Feb. a predominantly Communist government was formed by Gottwald. In May elections resulted in an 89% majority for the government, and President Beneš resigned.

In 1968 pressure for liberalization culminated in the overthrow of the Stalinist leader, Antonín Novotný, and his associates. Under Alexander Dubček's leadership the so-called 'Prague Spring' began to take shape, and the outlines of a new political system described as 'socialism with a human face' began to appear as the Communist Party introduced an 'Action Programme' of far-reaching reforms. Soviet pressure to abandon this programme was exerted between May and Aug. 1968, when Warsaw Pact forces occupied Czechoslovakia. The Czechoslovak government was compelled to accept a policy of 'normalization' (*i.e.*, abandonment of most reforms) and the stationing of Soviet forces.

Mass demonstrations demanding political reform began in Nov. 1989. After the authorities' use of violence to break up a demonstration on 17 Nov., the Communist leader resigned. On 30 Nov. the Federal Assembly abolished the Communist Party's sole right to govern and a new Government was formed on 3 Dec. The protest movement continued to grow and on 10 Dec. another government was formed. Gustáv Husák resigned as President and was replaced by Václav Havel on the unanimous vote of 323 members of the Federal Assembly on 29 Dec.

On 25 Nov. 1992 the Federal Assembly voted the dissolution of the Czech and Slovak Federal Republic. This came into effect at midnight on 31 Dec. 1992. Economic property was divided in accordance with a federal law of 13 Nov. 1992. Real estate became the property of the republic in which it was located. Other property was divided by specially constituted commissions in the proportion of 2 (Czech Republic) to 1 (Slovakia) on the basis of population size. Military materiel was divided on the 2:1 principle. Regular military personnel were invited to choose which armed force they would serve in.

TERRITORY AND POPULATION

The Czech Republic is bounded in the west by Germany, north by Poland, east by Slovakia and south by Austria. Minor exchanges of territory to straighten their mutual border were agreed between the Czech Republic and Slovakia on 4 Jan. 1996, but the Czech parliament refused to ratify them on 24 April 1996. Its area is 78,864 sq. km. At the 1991 census the population was 10,302,215. 1996 estimate, 10,331,206 (51·4% female); density, 131 per sq. km.

The UN gives a projected population for 2000 of 10·19m.

In 1995 an estimated 65·4% of the population lived in urban areas.

There are 8 administrative regions *(Kraj)*, one of which is the capital, Prague (Praha).

Region	Chief city	Area in sq. km	Population 1991 census
Prague	—	496	1,212,010
Středočeský	Prague (Praha)	11,038	1,112,374
Jihočeský	České Budějovice	11,345	697,334
Západočeský	Plzeň (Pilsen)	10,873	860,311
Severočeský	Ústí nad Labem	7,777	1,173,681
Východočeský	Hradec Králové	11,240	1,232,646
Jihomoravský	Brno	15,027	2,048,867
Severomoravský	Ostrava	11,068	1,961,508

The estimated population of the principal towns in 1997 (in 1,000):

Prague (Praha)	1,205	Liberec	100	Havířrov	88
Brno	388	Hradec Králové	100	Zlín	83
Ostrava	324	České Budějovice	100	Most	71
Plzeň	170	Ústí nad Labem	97	Karlovy Vary	55
Olomouc	104	Pardubice	93	Jihlava	53

At the 1991 census 81·2% of the population was Czech, 13·2% Moravian and 3·1% Slovak. There were also (in 1,000): Poles, 59; Germans, 48; Silesians, 44; Roma (Gypsies), 34; Hungarians, 21.

The official language is Czech.

SOCIAL STATISTICS
1996 births, 90,000; deaths, 113,000; marriages, 54,000; divorces, 33,000. Rates (per 1,000 population), 1996: Birth, 8·8; death, 10·9; marriage, 5·2; divorce, 3·2; infant mortality, (per 1,000 live births), 6·0. Life expectancy at birth, 1990–95, 68·8 years for males and 75·2 years for females. In 1994 the most popular age range for marrying was 20–24 for both males and females. Annual growth rate, 1990–95, –0·1%. Infant mortality, 1990–95, 9 per 1,000 live births; fertility rate, 1·7 children per woman.

CLIMATE
A humid continental climate, with warm summers and cold winters. Precipitation is generally greater in summer, with thunderstorms. Autumn, with dry clear weather, and spring, which is damp, are each of short duration. Prague, Jan. 29·5°F (–1·5°C), July 67°F (19·4°C). Annual rainfall 19·3" (483 mm). Brno, Jan. 31°F (–0·6°C), July 67°F (19·4°C). Annual rainfall 21" (525 mm).

CONSTITUTION AND GOVERNMENT
The Constitution of 1 Jan. 1993 provides for a parliament comprising a 200-member *Chamber of Deputies*, elected for 4-year terms by proportional representation, and an 81-member *Senate* elected for 6-year terms in single-member districts, 27 senators being elected every 2 years. The main function of the Senate is to scrutinize proposed legislation. Senators must be at least 40 years of age, and are elected on a first-past-the-post basis, with a run-off in constituencies where no candidate wins more than half the votes cast. For the House of Representatives there is a 5% threshold; votes for parties failing to surmount this are redistributed on the basis of results in each of the 8 electoral districts.

There is a *Constitutional Court* at Brno, whose 15 members are nominated by the President and approved by the Senate for 10-year terms.

The *President* of the Republic is elected for a 5-year term by both chambers of parliament. He or she must be at least 40 years of age. The President names the Prime Minister at the suggestion of the Speaker.

CZECH REPUBLIC

RECENT ELECTIONS

The President of the Republic is Václav Havel, elected by parliament on 26 Jan. 1993 against 2 opponents and sworn in on 2 Feb., re-elected 20 Jan. 1998.

Elections for the House of Representatives were held on 21 June 1998. The Social Democratic Party (ČSSD) won 74 seats (61 in 1996) with 32%, ahead of the Civic Democratic Party (63 seats; 38 in 1996) with 28%, the Communists (24 seats; 22 in 1996), Christian Democrats 20 seats (18 in 1996), and the Freedom Union 19 seats (0 in 1996, as only formed in 1998 by rebels from the Civic Democrats and Civic Alliance).

Elections for the Senate were held on 13–14 Nov. and 20–21 Nov. 1998. As a result ODS had 26 seats in the Senate; ČSSD, 23; KDU/ČSL, 17; US/ODA, 11; KSČM, 4.

CURRENT ADMINISTRATION

President: Václav Havel.

Miloš Zeman, the country's first left-wing prime minister since the fall of socialism in 1989, was formally appointed by President Havel on 17 July 1998, and a new minority Social Democratic government was sworn in on 22 July. In March 1999 the government comprised:

Prime Minister: Miloš Zeman (ČSSD).

Deputy Prime Ministers: Pavel Mertlík, Pavel Rychetský, Egon Lánský. *Deputy Prime Minister, Minister of Labour and Social Affairs:* Vladimír Špidla.

Minister of Foreign Affairs: Jan Kavan. *Finance:* Ivo Svoboda. *Agriculture:* Jan Fencl. *Justice:* Otakar Motejl. *Interior:* Václav Grulich. *Environment:* Miloš Kužvart. *Health:* Ivan David. *Culture:* Pavel Dostál. *Education, Youth and Sports:* Eduard Zeman. *Defence:* Vladimír Vetchý. *Transport and Communications:* Antonín Peltrám. *Regional Development:* Jaromír Císař. *Minister without Portfolio:* Jaroslav Bašta.

Local Government. At elections on 18–19 Nov. 1994 turn-out was 60%. The Civic Democratic Party gained 25·4% of votes cast, ind 17%, the Party of Democratic Left 16·6%, the Christian Democratic Party 10·6% and the Social Democratic Party 8·1%. Local authorities have the power to raise local taxes and have responsibility for roads, schools, utilities and public health.

DEFENCE

Conscription is for 12 months. Defence expenditure in 1997 totalled US$987m. (US$96 per capita), representing 2·2% of GDP.

Army. The Army comprises 2 Corps HQ, and 7 mechanized, 2 artillery and 2 engineer brigades. Equipment includes 469 T-54/-55 and 542 T-72M main battle tanks. Strength (1997) 27,000 (15,400 conscripts). There are also paramilitary Border Guards (4,000-strong) and Internal Security Forces (1,600).

Air Force. The Air Force has a strength of some 17,000 (including air defence troops) and operates a regiment of MiG-21s and MiG-23s. The Tactical Air Corps has a regiment of L-39, Su-22 and Su-25 strike aircraft, and a helicopter regiment with Mi-24 armed helicopters.

INTERNATIONAL RELATIONS

In 1974 the German Federal Republic and the then Czechoslovakia annulled the Munich agreement of 1938. On 14 Feb. 1997 the Czech parliament ratified a declaration of German-Czech reconciliation, with particular reference to the Sudeten German problems.

The Czech Republic is a member of the UN, the OECD, CEFTA, the Central European Initiative, NATO, and is an associate member of the EU and an associate partner of the WEU. The Czech Republic became a member of NATO on 12 March 1999. An application to join the EU was made in Jan. 1996.

ECONOMY

Policy. By the end of 1992 assets valued at Kč. 470,000m. had been privatized. 21,400 small businesses were auctioned off in 1992, and some 900 enterprises privatized through the sale of vouchers. A second stage of privatization, affecting

770 enterprises, took place by vouchers on sale to all citizens in Oct.–Nov. 1993. This stage came to an end in Dec. 1994, by which time 80% of the Czech Republic's assets were in private hands. The privatization of shares in 53 large companies was announced in 1995, the state to retain some of these shares. The privatization of the remaining minor state companies was scheduled for completion in 1997.

Performance. In 1997 real GDP growth was 1·0%, compared to 4·5% in 1996. Growth is expected to be negative in 1999, at –2%.

Budget. Revenue and expenditure in Kč. 1m.:

	1994	1995	1996	1997
Revenue	370,503	414,330	460,950	479,209
Expenditure	362,015	410,669	450,938	481,609

Expenditure by category, 1996: Defence, 30,604; education, 64,964; health, 95,416; social security and welfare, 139,433.

The current account deficit was US$–3,271m. in 1997.

Currency. The unit of currency is the *koruna* (CEK) or crown of 100 *haler*, introduced on 8 Feb. 1993 at parity with the former Czechoslovakian koruna. Gold reserves were 2·08m. troy oz. in Feb. 1998. Exchange reserves were US$15,000m. in Dec. 1996. Inflation in Jan. 1999 was 10·7%. The koruna became convertible on 1 Oct. 1995. In May 1997 the koruna was devalued 10% and allowed to float. Total money supply was Kč. 371m. in Feb. 1998.

Banking and Finance. The central bank and bank of issue is the Czech National Bank (*Governor*, Josef Tošovský), which also acts as banking supervisor and regulator. Decentralization of the banking system began in 1991, and private banks began to operate. The Commercial Bank and Investment Bank are privatized nationwide networks with a significant government holding. Specialized banks include the Czech Savings Bank and the Czech Commercial Bank (for foreign trade payments). Private banks tend to be on a regional basis, many of them agricultural banks. There are also subsidiaries of foreign banks, joint ventures with foreign participation, and branches and representative offices of foreign banks. There were 59 banks in 1995. In Nov. 1997 the cabinet agreed to sell off large stakes in 3 of the largest state-held banks to individual foreign investors through tenders, in preparation for European Union entry.

Savings deposits were Kč. 289,163m. in 1993.

A stock exchange was founded in Prague in 1992.

Weights and Measures. The metric system is in force.

ENERGY AND NATURAL RESOURCES

Electricity. Installed capacity was 13·85m. kW in 1994. Production in 1994 was 55·38bn. kWh. In 1993, 76% of electricity was produced by thermal power stations using brown coal, 21% was nuclear (1 station) and the rest was hydro-electric. 29·2% of output was nuclear-generated in 1993. Consumption per capita in 1995 was estimated to be 4,712 kWh.

Minerals. There are hard coal and lignite reserves (chief fields: Most, Chomutov, Kladno, Ostrava and Sokolov). Gold deposits were found near Prague in 1985.

Agriculture. In 1993 there were 4,282,000 ha of agricultural land (3,173,000 ha arable). Approximately 24,000 ha were irrigated in 1994. 31·1% of agricultural land was state-owned, 61% co-operative, 4·4% private and 2·2% public.

A law of May 1991 returned land seized by the Communist regime to its original owners, to a maximum of 150 ha of arable to a single owner.

Selected agricultural production figures, 1995 (1,000 tonnes): Vegetables (including melons), 550; fruits (excluding melons), 443; tree-nuts, 8. The principal crops are wheat and spelt, sugar beet, barley and potatoes

Livestock, 1996: Cattle, 1·99m.; pigs, 4·02m.; sheep, 134,000; chickens (1995), 26m. In 1993 production of meat was 1,140,711 tonnes (live weight); milk, 3,350m. litres; 3,100m. eggs.

Forestry. In 1995 forests covered 2,630,000 ha (34% of the total land area). 12·91m. cu. metres of timber were cut in 1995.

Fisheries. Ponds created for fish-farming number 21,800 and cover about 101,311 acres, the largest of them being 2 lakes in southern Bohemia. Total catches in 1995 amounted to 22,579 tonnes, entirely from inland waters.

INDUSTRY
In 1996 there were 1,123,804 small private businesses (of which 15,072 were incorporated), 117,040 companies (of which 8,002 were joint-stock companies), 6,332 co-operatives and 2,185 state enterprises. Output, 1993, included: Steel, 6·76m. tonnes; cement, 5·4m. tonnes; motor cars, 173,000.

Labour. In 1997 the economically active population numbered 5,215,200. In 1993, 1·71m. persons were employed in mining, manufacture, electricity, gas and water; 609,000 in wholesale and retail trade and repairs; 453,000 in construction; 331,000 in agriculture; 263,000 in health and social work; and 65,000 in financial services. In 1997, unemployment stood at 241,800 (131,400 women). This equated to a rate of 4·7% (3·8% males, 5·8% females). The unemployment forecast for 1999 was 9·5%. The average monthly wage was Kč. 8,500 in 1996. Pay increases are regulated in firms where wages grow faster than production. Fines are levied if wages rise by more than 15% over 4 years. In 1996, 11,500 employees were involved in industrial disputes resulting in a loss of 16,400 working days.

INTERNATIONAL TRADE
A memorandum envisaging a customs union and close economic co-operation was signed with Slovakia in Oct. 1992. An agreement of Dec. 1992 with Hungary, Poland and Slovakia abolished tariffs on raw materials and goods; where exports do not compete directly with locally produced items, and envisaged tariff reductions on agricultural and industrial goods in 1995–97.

Foreign debt was US$16,549m. at the beginning of 1996. There were 10,599 joint ventures in June 1993.

Imports and Exports. Trade, 1997, in US$1m. (1996 in brackets): Imports, 26,986 (28,148); exports, 22,502 (25,761). Main export markets, 1995: Germany, 31·8%; Slovakia, 16·2%; Austria, 6·5%; Poland, 5·4%; Italy, 4%. Main import suppliers: Germany, 25·8%; Slovakia, 13·1%; Russia, 8·9%; Austria, 6·9%; Italy 5·8%.

COMMUNICATIONS

Roads. In 1996 there were 423 km of motorways, 6,410 km of highways and main roads, 14,334 secondary roads and 34,322 other roads, forming a total of network of 55,489 km. Passenger cars in use in 1996 numbered 3,349,008 (324 per 1,000 inhabitants), and there were also 235,114 trucks and vans, 161,120 road tractors and 21,460 buses and coaches. Motor cycles and mopeds numbered 1,105,450. In 1995 passenger transport totalled 16,777m. passenger-km and freight 8,713m. tonne-km.

Rail. In 1994 Czech State Railways had a route length of 9,316 km (1,435 mm gauge), of which 2,640 km were electrified. Passenger-kilometres travelled in 1995 came to 8·02bn. and freight tonne-kilometres to 25·46bn. There is a metro (44 km) and tram/light rail system (496 km) in Prague, and tram/light rail networks in Brno, Liberec, Most, Olomouc, Ostrava, Plzeň and Teplice-Trecianské.

Civil Aviation. There are international airports at Prague (Ruzyné), Ostrava (Mosnov) and Brno (Turany). The national carrier is Czech Airlines, which is 68·1% state-owned. In 1998 services were also provided by Aeroflot, Air Algérie, Air France, Air Lithuania, Air Ostrava, Air Ukraine, Alitalia, Austrian Airlines, Balkan, Belavia, British Airways, British Midland, Canadian Airlines International, Continental Airlines, Croatia Airlines, Crossair, Delta Air Lines, El Al, Finnair, Georgian Airlines, JAT, KLM, LOT, Lufthansa, Malév, Moldavian Airlines, SABENA, SAS, SK Air, Swissair, Tarom, Tatra Air, Thai Airways International, Tunis Air and United Airlines. In 1996 Prague handled 3,700,620 passengers (3,638,047 on international flights) and 19,815 tonnes of freight; Ostrava handled 119,632 passengers, and Brno 110,451 passengers.

Shipping. 4·9m. tonnes of freight were carried by inland waterways in 1993. Merchant shipping totalled 140,000 GRT in 1995.

Telecommunications. In 1997 there were 3,279,800 telephone main lines in use, or 318·4 for every 1,000 inhabitants. Cellular phone subscribers numbered 49,000 in 1995, and there were 550,000 PCs in use (7·1 per 1,000 persons) and 74,000 fax machines. There were approximately 200,000 Internet users in Sept. 1997.

Postal Services. In 1995 there were 3,511 post offices.

SOCIAL INSTITUTIONS

Justice. The post-Communist judicial system was established by a law of July 1991. This provides for a unified system of 4 types of court: civil, criminal, commercial and administrative. Commercial courts arbitrate in disputes arising from business activities. Administrative courts examine the legality of the decisions of state institutions when appealed by citizens. In addition, there are military courts which operate under the jurisdiction of the Ministry of Defence. There is a Supreme Court, and a hierarchy of courts under the Ministry of Justice at republic, region and district level. District courts are courts of first instance. Cases are usually decided by senates comprising a judge and 2 associate judges, though occasionally by a single judge. (Associate judges are citizens in good standing over the age of 25 who are elected for 4-year terms). Regional courts are courts of first instance in more serious cases and also courts of appeal for district courts. Cases are usually decided by a senate of 2 judges and 3 associate judges, although again occasionally by a single judge. There is also a Supreme Administrative Court. The Supreme Court interprets law as a guide to other courts and functions also as a court of appeal. Decisions are made by senates of 3 judges. Judges are appointed for life by the National Council.

There is no death penalty. In 1993, 398,505 crimes were reported, of which 31·7% were solved.

Religion. In 1991, 18 churches were registered. In 1997 church membership was estimated to be: Roman Catholic, 4,020,000; Evangelical Church of the Czech Brethren, 200,000; Hussites, 180,000; Silesian Evangelicals, 30,000; Eastern Orthodox, 20,000. 4,120,000 persons were classified as atheist or non-religious, and there were 1,740,000 adherents of other religions.

Miloslav Vlk (b. 1932) was installed as Archbishop of Prague and Primate of Czechoslovakia in 1991. The national Czech church, created in 1918, took the name 'Hussite' in 1972. In 1991 it had a patriarch, 5 bishops and 300 pastors (40% women). In 1991 there were also around a dozen other Protestant churches, the largest being the Evangelical which unites Calvinists and Lutherans, and numbered about 200,000.

Education. Elementary education up to age 15 is compulsory. 52% of children continue their education in vocational schools and 48% move on to secondary schools.

In 1995-96 there were 9 universities, 4 technical universities, 1 university for economics, 1 for agriculture, 1 for agriculture and forestry, 1 for veterinary and pharmaceutical sciences and 1 for chemical technology. There were also 4 academies (for performing arts, music and dramatic arts, fine arts and arts, architecture and industrial design) and a higher school of teacher training. Together, these 23 higher education institutions had 139,774 students in 1995-96 and 12,890 teaching staff in 1995.

In 1996 total expenditure on education came to Kč. 80,079m., or 5·4% of GNP.

Health. In 1995 there were 32,195 doctors (1 per 321 persons), 6,267 dentists and 4,032 pharmacists. There were 299 hospitals in 1995, with a provision of 89 beds per 10,000 population.

CULTURE

Prague is one of nine European Cities of Culture in the year 2000, along with Avignon (France), Bergen (Norway), Bologna (Italy), Brussels (Belgium), Helsinki (Finland), Kraków (Poland), Reykjavík (Iceland) and Santiago de Compostela (Spain). The title attracts large European Union grants.

Broadcasting. Broadcasting is the responsibility of the independent Board for Radio and Television. Czech Television (CTV, colour by SECAM) and Czech Radio are public corporations. The former Czechoslovakian broadcasting stations in the Czech

Republic have become a second service. There is also a nationwide private TV company and 2 radio companies as well as local private stations. There were 4,950,000 TV receivers and 6,550,000 radio receivers in 1995.

Cinema. In 1995 there were 930 cinemas; attendance for the year was 9·3m. 22 full-length films were made in 1995.

Press. There were 21 daily newspapers in 1996 with a total readership of 2,620,000 (256 per 1,000 inhabitants). There were also 181 non-dailies with total readership 4,200,000 (410 per 1,000 inhabitants).

Tourism. There were 10·9m. foreign tourists in 1996. Foreign currency income from tourism in 1996 was US$4,100m. (6·5% of GDP).

Libraries. In 1995 there were 10 National Libraries and 7,729 public libraries with a combined 54,533,000 volumes and 1,428,317 registered users.

Museums and Galleries. In 1993 there were 254 museums hosting a combined 9,029,000 visitors.

DIPLOMATIC REPRESENTATIVES
Of the Czech Republic in Great Britain (26-30 Kensington Palace Gdns., London, W8 4QY)
Ambassador: Pavel Seifter.

Of Great Britain in the Czech Republic (Thunovská 14, 118 00 Prague 1)
Ambassador: David S. Broucher.

Of the Czech Republic in the USA (3900 Linnean Ave., NW, Washington, D.C., 20008)
Ambassador: Alexandr Vondra.

Of the USA in the Czech Republic (Tržiste 15, 11801, Prague 1)
Ambassador: John Shattuck.

Of the Czech Republic to the United Nations
Ambassador: Vladimir Galuška.

Of the Czech Republic to the European Union
Ambassador: Josef Kreuter.

FURTHER READING
Czech Statistical Office. *Statistical Yearbook of the Czech Republic.*
Havel, V., *Disturbing the Peace.* London, 1990.—*Living in Truth: Twenty-Two Essays.* London, 1990.—*Summer Meditations.* London, 1992
Hermann, A. H., *A History of the Czechs.* London, 1975
Kalvoda, J., *The Genesis of Czechoslovakia.* New York, 1986
Leff, C. S., *National Conflict in Czechoslovakia: The Making and Remaking of a State, 1918–1987.* Princeton, 1988
Short, D., *Czechoslovakia.* [Bibliography] Oxford and Santa Barbara (CA), 1986
Simmons, M., *The Reluctant President: a Political Life of Vaclav Havel.* London, 1992

National statistical office: Czech Statistical Office, Sokolovská 142, 186 04 Prague 8.
Website: http://infox.eunet.cz/csu/csu_e.html

DENMARK

Kongeriget Danmark
(Kingdom of Denmark)

Capital: Copenhagen
Population estimate, 2000: 5·32m.
GNP per capita: (PPP$) 22,120
HDI/world rank: 0·928/18

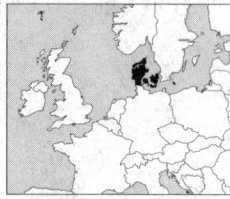

KEY HISTORICAL EVENTS

Denmark was first organized as a unified state in the 10th century with a Christian monarchy. King Canute was also King of England and King of Norway in the 11th century, but the union of the three countries soon dissolved. In 1363 a royal marriage united Denmark and Norway and these two countries joined with Sweden in 1397. Sweden separated herself in 1523 and thereafter was in conflict with Denmark until the Peace with Copenhagen in 1660. Denmark acquired approximately its present boundaries in 1815 at the end of the Napoleonic Wars. Having supported Napoleon, it was forced to cede Norway to Sweden by the Treaty of Kiel (1814); it lost its north-German territory to Prussia 1864-66 and only in 1920 was North Schleswig returned to Denmark.

After 1815 there was much pressure for a more liberal form of government in preference to the traditional absolute monarchy, and on 5 June 1849 the royal assent was given a new constitution. A parliament, the *Rigsdag*, was created, divided into an upper house, the *Landsting*, and a lower house, the *Folketing*. The franchise was granted to men over 30 years old.

During the First World War (1914-18) Denmark remained neutral and in 1939, at the commencement of the Second World War it again declared its neutrality. On this occasion, however, it was soon overwhelmed by the German forces which invaded on 9 April 1940. Throughout the war there was a considerable Danish resistance movement to which the Germans responded by imposing direct rule. Immediately after the Second World War, Denmark recognized the independence of Iceland. Home rule was granted to the Faroes in 1948 and to Greenland in 1979. The constitution was amended in 1953, to allow for a female succession to the throne, the abolition of the *Landsting* (the upper house) and the extension of the franchise to all men and women over 18 years of age. Denmark joined NATO in 1949, took the lead in the formation of the consultative Nordic Council in 1953 and joined the EEC after a referendum held in 1972.

TERRITORY AND POPULATION

Denmark is bounded in the west by the North Sea, north-west and north by the Skagerrak and Kattegat straits (separating it from Norway and Sweden), and south by Germany. A fixed link with Sweden will be created in 2000 when the Öresund motorway and railway bridge between Copenhagen and Malmö is completed.

Administrative divisions		Area (sq. km) 1998	Population Census 1970	Population 1 Jan. 1998	Population per sq. km 1998
København (Copenhagen)	(city)	88	622,773	487,969	5,529·4
Frederiksberg	(borough)	9	101,874	89,507	10,206·0
Københavns	(county)	526	615,343	610,261	1,160·3
Frederiksborg	,,	1,347	259,442	359,839	267·1
Roskilde	,,	891	153,199	228,202	256·0
Vestsjælland	,,	2,984	259,057	292,146	97·9
Storstrøm	,,	3,398	252,363	258,295	76·0
Bornholm	,,	588	47,239	44,786	76·1
Fyn	,,	3,486	432,699	471,873	135·4
Sønderjylland	,,	3,938	238,062	253,836	64·5
Ribe	,,	3,132	197,843	223,818	71·5
Vejle	,,	2,997	306,263	344,507	115·0
Ringkøbing	,,	4,853	241,327	271,978	56·0
Århus	,,	4,561	533,190	631,586	138·5
Viborg	,,	4,122	220,734	233,143	56·6
Nordjylland	,,	6,173	456,171	493,114	79·9
Total		43,094	4,937,579	5,294,860	122·9

DENMARK

The projected population for 2000 is 5·32m.

In 1998 an estimated 85·2% of the population lived in urban areas. In 1998, 94·0% of the inhabitants were born in Denmark, including the Faroe Islands and Greenland.

On 1 Jan. 1997 the population of the capital, Copenhagen (comprising Copenhagen, Frederiksberg and Gentofte municipalities), was 644,878 (including suburbs, 1,379,413); Århus, 215,587; Odense, 145,296; Aalborg, 119,157; Esbjerg, 73,422; Randers, 56,123; Kolding, 53,012; Horsens, 48,410; Vejle, 47,839; Helsingør, 44,860.

The official language is Danish.

SOCIAL STATISTICS

Statistics for calendar years:

	Live births	Still births	Marriages	Divorces	Deaths	Emigration	Immigration
1995	69,771	318	34,736	12,976	63,127	34,630	63,187
1996	67,638	324	35,953	12,776	61,085	37,312	54,445
1997	67,636	…	34,244	12,774	59,925	38,393	50,105

1997 rates per 1,000 population: Birth, 12·8; death, 11·3. Single-parent births: 1994, 46·9%; 1995, 46·5%; 1996, 46·3%; 1997, 45·1%. Annual growth rate, 1990–97, 0·4%. Suicide rate, 1990–96 (per 100,000 population) was 20·6 (men, 27·9; women, 13·6). Life expectancy at birth, 1996–97, was 73·3 years for males and 78·4 years for females. In 1995 the most popular age range for marrying was 25–29 for both males and females. Infant mortality, 1995, 5·3 per 1,000 live births. Fertility rate, 1997, 1·8 births per woman.

CLIMATE

The climate is much modified by marine influences and the effect of the Gulf Stream, to give winters that may be both cold or mild and often cloudy. Summers may be warm and sunny or chilly and rainy. In general, the east is drier than the west. Long periods of calm weather are exceptional and windy conditions are common. Copenhagen, Jan. 33°F (0·5°C), July 63°F (17°C). Annual rainfall 650 mm. Esbjerg, Jan. 33°F (0·5°C), July 61°F (16°C). Annual rainfall 800 mm. 10% of rainfall precipitates as snow.

CONSTITUTION AND GOVERNMENT

The present constitution is founded upon the Basic Law of 5 June 1953. The legislative power lies with the Queen and the *Folketing* (parliament) jointly. The executive power is vested in the monarch, who exercises authority through the ministers.

The reigning Queen is **Margrethe II,** b. 16 April 1940; married 10 June 1967 to Prince Henrik, b. Count de Monpezat. She succeeded to the throne on the death of her father, King Frederik IX, on 14 Jan. 1972. *Offspring:* Crown Prince Frederik, b. 26 May 1968; Prince Joachim, b. 7 June 1969; married 18 Nov. 1995 Alexandra Manley (b. 30 June 1964).

Mother of the Queen; Queen Ingrid, b. Princess of Sweden, 28 March 1910.

Sisters of the Queen; Princess Benedikte, b. 29 April 1944; married 3 Feb. 1968 to Prince Richard of Sayn-Wittgenstein-Berleburg; Princess Anne-Marie, b. 30 Aug. 1946; married 18 Sept. 1964 to King Constantine of Greece.

The crown was elective from the earliest times but became hereditary by right in 1660. The direct male line of the house of Oldenburg became extinct with King Frederik VII on 15 Nov. 1863. In view of the death of the king, without direct heirs, the Great Powers signed a treaty at London on 8 May 1852, by the terms of which the succession to the crown was made over to Prince Christian of Schleswig-Holstein-Sonderburg-Glücksburg, and to the direct male descendants of his union with the Princess Louise of Hesse-Cassel. This became law on 31 July 1853. Linked to the constitution of 5 June 1953, a new law of succession, dated 27 March 1953, has come into force, which restricts the right of succession to the descendants of King Christian X and Queen Alexandrine, and admits the sovereign's daughters to the line of succession, ranking after the sovereign's sons.

The Queen receives a tax-free annual sum of 44·7m. kroner from the state (1998).

The judicial power is with the courts. The monarch must be a member of the Evangelical-Lutheran Church, the official Church of the State, and may not assume major international obligations without the consent of the Folketing. The Folketing consists of one chamber. All men and women of Danish nationality of more than 18 years of age and permanently resident in Denmark possess the franchise, and are eligible for election to the Folketing, which is at present composed of 179 members; 135 members are elected by the method of proportional representation in 17 constituencies. In order to attain an equal representation of the different parties, 40 additional seats are divided among such parties which have not obtained sufficient returns at the constituency elections. 2 members are elected for the Faroe Islands and 2 for Greenland. The term of the legislature is 4 years, but a general election may be called at any time. The Folketing convenes every year on the first Tuesday in October. Besides its legislative functions, every 6 years it appoints judges who, together with the ordinary members of the Supreme Court, form the *Rigsret*, a tribunal which can alone try parliamentary impeachments.

National Anthem. 'Kong Kristian stod ved højen mast' ('King Christian stood by the lofty mast'); words by J. Ewald, tune by J. E. Hartmann.

RECENT ELECTIONS
Parliamentary elections were held on 11 March 1998. The Social Democratic Party won 63 seats, with 35·9% of the votes cast (62 seats with 34·6% in 1994); the Liberal Party 42 with 24% (42 with 23·3%); the Conservative Party 16 with 8·9% (27 with 15%); the Socialist People's Party 13 with 7·6% (13 with 7·3%); and the Danish People's Party 13 with 7·4% (not in 1994 election). The 28 remaining seats went to the Social Liberal Party (7); the Centre Democratic Party (8); the Christian People's Party (4); the Progress Party (4); the Unity List (5). The coalition government led by Poul Nyrup Rasmussen of the Social Democratic Party remained in office.

European Parliament. Denmark has 16 representatives. At the June 1994 elections turn-out was 52·9%. The Liberal Party won 4 seats with 19% of votes cast (group in European Parliament: Liberal, Democratic and Reformist Group); the Conservative Party, 3 with 17·7% (Popular European Party); the SD, 3 with 15·8% (European Socialist Party); the June Movement, 2 with 15·2% (Europe of Nations); the People's Anti-EU Movement, 2 with 10·3% (Europe of Nations); the Socialist People's Party, 1 with 8·6% (Greens); and the Radical Liberal Party, 1 with 8·5% (Liberal, Democratic and Reformist Group).

CURRENT ADMINISTRATION
Following the 1998 elections a coalition government of the Social Democratic (S) and Social Liberal (RV) Parties took office in March 1998. In March 1999 the government comprised:

Prime Minister: Poul Nyrup Rasmussen, b. 1943; (S; elected 11 March 1998).

Minister of Economic Affairs and Minister for Nordic Co-operation: Marianne Jelved (RV). *Trade and Industry:* Pia Gjellerup (S). *Finance:* Mogens Lykketoft (S). *Foreign Affairs:* Niels Helveg Petersen (RV). *Justice:* Frank Jensen (S). *Environment and Energy:* Svend Auken (S). *Education and Ecclesiastical Affairs:* Margrethe Vestager (RV). *Developmental Aid:* Poul Nielson (S). *Interior:* Thorkild Simonsen (S). *Health:* Carsten Koch (S). *Labour:* Ove Hygum (S). *Taxation:* Ole Stavad (S). *Defence:* Hans Haekkerup (S). *Culture:* Elsebeth Gerner Nielsen (RV). *Transport:* Sonja Mikkelsen (S). *Social Affairs:* Karen Jespersen (S). *Housing and Building:* Jytte Andersen (S). *Research:* Jan Trojborg (S). *Food, Agriculture and Fisheries:* Henrik Dam Kristensen (S).

Local Government. For administrative purposes Denmark is divided into 275 communes; each of them has a district council of between 7 and 31 members, headed by an elected mayor. The city of Copenhagen forms a district by itself and is governed by a city council of 55 members, elected every 4 years, and an executive, consisting of the chief burgomaster and 6 burgomasters, appointed by the city council for 4 years. There are 14 counties, each of which is administered by a county council of between 13 and 31 members, headed by an elected mayor. All councils are elected directly by universal suffrage and proportional representation for 4-year terms. There are also about 2,100 parishes. Government at this level is administered by parish councils elected for 4 years.

The counties and Copenhagen are superintended by the Ministry of Interior Affairs. The municipalities are superintended by 14 local supervision committees, headed by a state county prefect, who is a civil servant appointed by the Queen.

County and municipal elections were held on 16 Nov. 1993. The Social Democrats won 34·9% of votes cast, the Liberals 28·8% (county elections).

DEFENCE
The military defence is organized in accordance with the Defence Act of Dec. 1993. The overall organization of the Danish Armed Forces comprises the Headquarter's Chief of Defence, the Army, the Navy, the Air Force and inter-service authorities and institutions; to this should be added the Home Guard, which is an indispensable part of Danish military defence. The Home Guard is based on the Home Guard Act of May 1982 as amended in Dec. 1993.

In accordance with the Defence Act, the Chief of Defence is in full command of the three services: The Army, the Navy and the Air Force. The Chief of Defence and the Defence Staff constitute the Headquarters' Chief of Defence.

The Constitution of 1849 states that it is the duty of every fit man to contribute to the national defence. This provision is still in force. Selection of conscripts takes place at the age of 18–19 years, and the conscripts are normally called up for service ½–1½ years later. Conscripts may subsequently be recalled for refresher training or musters. The initial training period for conscripts is between 4 and 12 months.

In 1997 defence expenditure totalled US$2,816m. (US$538 per capita), representing 1·7% of GDP.

Army. The army is comprised of field army formations and the local defence forces. In 1998 the peacetime strength of the army numbered 19,200 (including about 3,700 civilians and about 6,900 conscripts). The wartime strength was about 58,000. The Army is organized in 1 division; and in brigades and regimental combat groups, headquarter units and support units. There are 4 mechanized infantry brigades including the Danish Reaction Brigade. The field army is equipped with approximately 350 battle tanks, about 530 armoured personnel carriers and 160 specialized light-armoured vehicles as well as artillery including 76 self-propelled howitzers and 1 battery Multiple Launch Rocket System (MRLS). The Army has 12 AS-550 Fennec anti-armour helicopters and 12 Hughes 500 helicopters for observation and liaison. The local defence units are organized in infantry battalions and artillery units as well as a number of support units.

Navy. The Navy was some 6,000-strong (including 1,700 civilians and 500 conscripts) in 1998. The wartime strength was 9,800. The fleet comprises 5 coastal submarines, 3 corvettes, 5 ocean patrol vessels with Lynx helicopters, 14 Standard Flex 300 multi-role ships, 10 fast-missile patrol ships, 3 patrol cutters, 9 patrol boats, 4 coastal minelayers, 2 inshore minelayers and 1 coastal minesweeper. Furthermore, the fleet comprises 2 light auxiliary oilers, the Royal Yacht, and a number of smaller auxiliaries. The Naval Air Arm comprises 8 Lynx helicopters, and the Naval Home Guard operates 35 inshore patrol craft.

Coastal Defence forces comprise 1 permanent fortress armed with 150-mm guns and 2 mobile coastal batteries with Harpoon missiles.

Additionally, the Navy man and control 4 icebreakers, 6 environment control vessels and 6 survey vessels.

The 2 main naval bases are at Frederikshavn and Korsoer.

Air Force. The Air Force comprised some 7,800 in 1998 (including 2,300 civilians and 500 conscripts). The wartime strength force was about 16,800.

The flying squadrons comprise 4 all-weather, air-defence squadrons with a total of 69 F-16s. All squadrons have an air-defence and a fighter-bomber role. One squadron has an additional photo-reconnaissance role. The operational units also comprise 8 HAWK surface-to-air missile squadrons.

In addition, the Air Force has a number of supplementary units, including 1 transport squadron (3 C-130 Hercules, 2 Gulfstream IIIs and 1 Challenger 604), 1 helicopter search and rescue squadron (8 S-61As), and a control and warning system. T-17 Supporter aircraft are used for initial pilot training, and pilots continue training at EURO-NATO Joint Jet Pilot Training in the USA.

Home Guard. The overall Home Guard organization comprises the Home Guard Command, the Army Home Guard, the Navy Home Guard, the Air Force Home Guard, the Service Corps and the Corporation-related Home Guard.

The personnel of the Home Guard is recruited on a voluntary basis. The personnel establishment of the Home Guard was in 1998 about 64,000 persons (48,300 in the Army Home Guard, 4,400 in the Navy Home Guard, 7,800 in the Air Force Home Guard, 1,500 in the Service Corps and 1,800 in the Corporation-related Home Guard).

INTERNATIONAL RELATIONS

In a referendum in June 1992 the electorate voted against ratifying the Maastricht Treaty for closer political union within the EU. Turn-out was 82%. 50·7% of votes were against ratification, 49·3% in favour. However, a second referendum on 18 May 1993 reversed this result, with 56·8% of votes cast in favour of ratification and 43·2% against. Turn-out was 86·2%.

Denmark gave US$1·7bn. in international aid in 1997, which at 0·97% of GDP made it the world's most generous country as a percentage of its gross domestic product.

Denmark is a member of the UN, NATO, OECD, the EU, Council of Europe and the Nordic Council. On 19 Dec. 1996 Denmark acceded to the Schengen Accord of June 1990 which abolishes border controls between Denmark and Austria, Belgium, Finland, France, Germany, Greece, Iceland, Italy, Luxembourg, the Netherlands, Norway, Portugal, Spain and Sweden.

ECONOMY

Policy. The government announced tax reform proposals in June 1998, with the corporate income tax rate being lowered from 34 to 26%. This, plus other changes, would help to trim back GDP growth from 2·7% to 2·5% in 1998, and from a projected 2·9% to 1·7% in 1999.

Performance. Real GDP growth averaged 3% each year between 1992 and 1997 with inflation at less than 2%. The current account has moved into deficit and is unlikely to return to surplus before 2000. As stated in the *OECD's Economic Survey of Denmark (1998–99)*, assessing recent economic performance as a whole, it is evident that fiscal consolidation, monetary policy credibility and the structural reform programme have together been highly successful in creating the conditions for long-term growth.

Budget. The following shows the actual revenue and expenditure as shown in central government accounts for the calendar years 1996 and 1997, the approved budget figures for 1998 and the budget for 1999 (in 1,000 kroner):

	1996	1997	1998	1999
Revenue[1]	363,334,500	394,013,800	411,156,900	394,207,000
Expenditure[1]	379,709,500	380,107,800	383,322,000	388,588,500

[1]Receipts and expenditures of special government funds and expenditures on public works are included.

The 1999 budget envisaged revenue of 122,821m. kroner from income and property taxes and 190,694m. from consumer taxes. The central government debt on 31 Dec. 1997 amounted to 654,130m. kroner.

VAT is 25%.

Currency. The monetary unit is the *Danish krone* (DKK) of 100 øre. Inflation was 2·1% in 1996, 2·2% in 1997 and was forecast to drop to 1·8% in 1998. In Feb. 1998 foreign exchange reserves were US$19,085m. and gold reserves were 1·69m. troy oz. In Feb. 1998 the money supply was 332bn. kroner.

While not participating directly in EMU, the Danish krone is pegged to the new currency in ERM-2, the successor to the exchange rate mechanism.

Banking and Finance. On 31 Dec. 1997 the accounts of the National Bank (*Governor*, Bodil Nyboe) balanced at 209,817m. kroner. The assets included official net foreign reserves of 129,700m. kroner. The liabilities included notes and coins totalling 38,710m. kroner. On 31 Dec. 1997 there were 92 commercial banks and savings banks, with deposits of 670,476m. kroner.

The 2 largest commercial banks are Den Danske Bank and Unibank.

There is a stock exchange in Copenhagen.

ENERGY AND NATURAL RESOURCES

Electricity. Installed capacity is 11·8m. kW. Production (1997), 41,775m. kWh. Consumption per capita in 1997 was 5,541 kWh. In 1997 some 4,784 wind turbines produced 4·6% of output.

Oil and Gas. Oil production was (1997) 11·2m. tonnes. Production of natural gas was (1997) 7·5m. cu. metres.

Agriculture. Agriculture accounts for 2·6% of GDP, 28·1% of exports and 15·8% of imports. Land ownership is widely distributed. In May 1997 there were 63,151 holdings with at least 5 ha of agricultural area (or at least a production equivalent to that from 5 ha of barley). There were 12,549 small holdings (with less than 10 ha), 33,050 medium-sized holdings (10–50 ha) and 17,532 holdings with more than 50 ha. There were 23,257 agricultural workers in 1996.

In 1997 the cultivated area was (in 1,000 ha): Grain, 1,555; pulses, 95; root crops, 146; other crops, 179; green fodder and grass, 554; set aside, 158; total cultivated area, 2,688.

	Area (1,000 ha)				Production (in 1,000 tonnes)			
Chief crops	1994	1995	1996	1997	1994	1995	1996	1997
Wheat	572	607	681	689	3,725	4,599	4,758	4,965
Rye	88	96	72	84	423	500	343	453
Barley	700	714	738	720	3,446	3,898	3,953	3,887
Oats[1]	44	31	32	43	206	158	164	155
Potatoes	39	42	43	39	1,359	1,441	1,617	1,545
Other root crops	126	121	111	106	7,005	6,320	5,656	5,870

[1]Including mixed grain.

Livestock, 1997 (in 1,000): Horses, 39; cattle, 2,004; pigs, 11,383; poultry, 18,994.

Production (in 1,000 tonnes) in 1997: Milk, 4,432; butter, 50; cheese, 291; beef, 195; pork and bacon, 1,639; eggs, 85.

In 1997 tractors numbered 141,293 and combine harvesters 25,418.

Forestry. The area under forests in 1995 was 417,000 ha, or 9·8% of the total land area. 2·29m. cu. metres of roundwood were produced in 1995.

Fisheries. The total value of the fish caught was (in 1m. kroner): 1950, 156; 1955, 252; 1960, 376; 1965, 650; 1970, 854; 1975, 1,442; 1980, 2,888; 1985, 3,542; 1990, 3,439; 1995, 2,939; 1996, 2,960; 1997, 3,344 (provisional figures).

In 1995 total catches were 2,041,133 tonnes (1,916,359 tonnes in 1994), of which 2,005,464 tonnes were from sea fishing.

INDUSTRY

The following table is of gross value added (in 1m. kroner):

	1995[1]	1996[1]	1997[1]
Agriculture, fishing and quarrying	39,978	34,365	45,578
Agriculture, horticulture and forestry	30,075	30,183	29,045
Fishing	2,596	2,660	3,168
Mining and quarrying	7,307	10,521	13,365

[1]Provisional or estimated figures.

In the following table 'number of employees' refers to 23,552 local activity units including single-proprietor units (Nov. 1996):

Branch of industry	Number of employees
Food, beverages and tobacco	91,073
Textiles, wearing apparel, leather	20,067
Wood and wood products	16,912
Paper products	63,993
Refined petroleum products	928
Chemicals and man-made fibres	28,112

Branch of industry	Number of employees
Rubber and plastic products	21,776
Non-metallic mineral products	20,737
Basic metals	56,374
Machinery and equipment	73,206
Electrical and optical equipment	46,442
Transport equipment	21,642
Furniture, other manufactures	35,391
Total manufacturing	496,653

Labour. In 1996 the labour force was 2,935,000. In 1997 5% of the working population lived on agriculture, forestry and fishery, 18% on industries and handicrafts, 6% on construction, 18% on commerce, etc., 7% on transport and communication, and 46% on administration, professional services, etc. In 1997, 476,052 persons were employed in manufacturing. Retirement age is 67. In 1997 the unemployment rate was 7·7%, declining to 6·4% in 1998, and with a forecast of 6·1% for 1999.

INTERNATIONAL TRADE

Imports and Exports. In 1996 imports totalled US$44,495m. (US$45,090m. in 1995) and exports US$50,115m. (US$49,763m. in 1995).

Imports and exports (in 1m. kroner) for calendar years:

	1995[1]		1996[1]	
Leading commodities	Imports	Exports	Imports	Exports
Live animals, meat and meat preparations	2,539	23,662	2,867	24,672
Dairy products, eggs	1,362	9,658	1,602	10,089
Fish, crustaceans, etc. and preparations	6,840	12,239	7,476	13,251
Cereals and cereal preparations	1,962	5,424	1,991	5,673
Sugar, sugar preparations and honey	970	1,748	1,230	1,778
Coffee, tea, cocoa, spices, etc.	2,279	689	2,277	773
Fodder for animals	3,733	3,261	4,483	3,664
Wood and cork	3,826	810	3,817	810
Textile fibres, yarns, fabrics, etc.	6,210	5,311	6,729	727
Mineral fuels, lubricants, etc.	10,468	7,716	9,737	12,889
Medicine and pharmaceutical products	5,009	12,602	5,215	13,930
Fertilizers, etc.	1,983	1,065	1,034	409
Metals, manufacture of metals	21,923	13,547	21,111	14,316
Machinery, electrical, equipment, etc.	55,163	59,139	64,570	67,521
Transport equipment	21,963	11,017	21,306	13,090

[1]Excluding trade not distributed.

Distribution of foreign trade (in 1,000 kroner) according to countries of origin and destination for 1997:

Countries	Imports[1]	Exports[1]
Belgium and Luxembourg	10,502,301	6,395,447
Netherlands	22,832,149	14,168,512
Finland	8,586,193	8,462,902
France	15,656,224	16,964,453
Germany	63,203,278	68,130,739
Italy	12,770,954	11,522,816
Norway	15,657,901	20,064,947
Sweden	37,411,322	36,400,456
Switzerland	3,966,044	4,575,389
UK	21,894,551	31,075,976
Ireland	3,468,023	2,340,011
USA	14,938,934	14,863,095
Greece	498,381	2,549,956
Portugal	3,019,130	1,360,899
Spain	3,951,950	6,229,661
Iceland	787,859	1,458,156
Austria	2,814,652	3,066,052
Faroes	759,249	1,254,039
Lithuania	798,909	1,642,663
Poland	5,022,309	5,936,646

Countries	Imports[1]	Exports[1]
Russia	2,017,513	6,142,507
Saudi Arabia	21,154	1,772,954
India	1,341,172	865,520
Thailand	1,580,504	1,200,825
Singapore	548,104	1,234,971
China	6,004,462	2,425,469
South Korea	1,682,077	2,764,353
Japan	5,887,786	10,776,378
Taiwan	2,243,311	1,146,109
Hong Kong	1,437,697	3,090,792
Australia	559,010	1,924,175

[1]Excluding trade not distributed.

COMMUNICATIONS

Roads. Denmark proper had (1 Jan. 1998) 843 km of motorways, 3,780 km of other state roads, 9,953 km of provincial roads and 59,861 km of commercial roads. Motor vehicles registered at 1 Jan. 1998 comprised 1,782,594 passenger cars, 37,850 trucks, 298,108 vans, 14,375 taxi cabs (including 8,487 for private hire), 13,776 buses and 59,864 cycles.

Rail. In 1997 there were 2,248 km of State railways of 1,435 mm gauge (600 km electrified), which carried 144m. passengers and 8·3m. tonnes of freight. There were also 495 km of private railways.

Civil Aviation. The main international airport is at Copenhagen (Kastrup), and there are also international flights from Aalborg, Århus, Billund and Esbjerg. The Scandinavian Airlines System (SAS) resulted from the 1950 merger of the 3 former Scandinavian airlines. Services were also provided in 1998 by Adria, Aer Lingus, Aeroflot, Air Baltic, Air Canada, Air China, Air France, Air India, Air Lithuania, Air Malta, Alitalia, Atlantic Airways (Faroe Islands), Austrian Airlines, Balkan, Braathens, British Airways, British Midland, Cimber Air, Continental Airlines, Croatia Airlines, Crossair, Czech Airlines, Delta Air Lines, Egyptair, El Al, Estonian Air, Finnair, Go, Greenlandair, Helikopterservice, Iberia, Icelandair, Interimpex-Avioimpex, Iran Air, JAT, KLM, Kenya Airways, Kuwait Airways, Lithuanian Airlines, LOT, Lufthansa, Luxair, Maersk Air, Malév, Muk Air, Olympic Airways, Pakistan International Airlines, Regional Airlines, Royal Air Maroc, SABENA, Singapore Airlines, Skyways, South African Airways, Spanair, Swissair, TAP, Tarom, Thai Airways International, Transeast Airlines, Tunis Air, Turkish Airlines, United Airlines, Varig, Virgin Express and Wideroe's Flyveselskap.

On 1 Jan. 1998 Denmark had 1,091 aircraft with a capacity of 20,535 seats. In 1997 there were 285,020 take-offs and landings to and from abroad, and 406,385 to and from Danish airports, including local flights. Copenhagen (Kastrup) handled 15,591,000 passengers in 1996 (12,696,000 on international flights).

Shipping. On 1 Jan. 1997 the merchant fleet consisted of 794 vessels (above 20 GRT) totalling 5,559,560 GRT. In 1996, 51m. tonnes of cargo were unloaded and 33m. tonnes were loaded in Danish ports; traffic by passenger ships and ferries is not included.

Telecommunications. At 31 Dec. 1996 there were 3·34m. telephone subscribers; 1·44m. mobile telephones were in use. There were 1·1m. Internet users in Nov. 1998. In 1995, 1·42m. PCs were in use (270 per 1,000 persons) and 250,000 fax machines.

Postal Services. In 1997 there were 1,256 post offices.

SOCIAL INSTITUTIONS

Justice. The lowest courts of justice are organized in 82 tribunals *(byretter)*, where minor cases are dealt with by a single judge. The tribunal at Copenhagen has one president and 44 other judges; and Århus one president and 15 other judges; the other tribunals have 1 to 11 judges. Cases of greater consequence are dealt with by the 2 High Courts *(Landsretterne)*; these courts are also courts of appeal for the above-named minor cases. The Eastern High Court in Copenhagen has one president and 61 other judges; and the Western in Viborg one president and 38 other judges. From these an appeal lies to the Supreme Court in Copenhagen, composed of a president and at present 17 other judges. Judges under 65 years of age can be removed only by judicial sentence.

In 1997, 14,754 men and 1,804 women were convicted of violations of the criminal code, fines not included. In 1997 the daily average population in penal institutions was 3,397, of whom 862 men and 55 women were on remand.

Religion. There is complete religious liberty. The state church is the Evangelical-Lutheran to which about 90% of the population belong. It is divided into 10 dioceses each with a Bishop. The Bishop together with the Chief Administrative Officer of the county make up the diocesan-governing body, responsible for all matters of ecclesiastical local finance and general administration. Bishops are appointed by the Crown after an election by the clergy and parish council members. Each diocese is divided into a number of deaneries (107 in the whole country), each with its Dean and Deanery Committee, who have certain financial powers.

Education. Education has been compulsory since 1814. The *folkeskole* (public primary and lower secondary school) comprises a pre-school class *(børne-haveklasse)*, a 9-year basic school corresponding to the period of compulsory education and a 1-year voluntary tenth form. Compulsory education may be fulfilled either through attending the *folkeskole* or private schools or through home instruction, on the condition that the instruction given is comparable to that given in the *folkeskole*. The *folkeskole* is mainly a municipal school and no fees are paid. In the year 1996–97, 2,301 primary and lower secondary schools had 590,792 pupils; they employed 56,323 teachers in 1992–93. 19·6% of the total number of schools were private schools and were attended by 11·6% of the total number of pupils. The 9-year basic school is in practice not streamed. However, a certain differentiation may take place in the eighth and ninth forms.

On completion of the eighth and ninth forms the pupils may sit for the leaving examination of the *folkeskole (folkeskolens afgangsprøve)*. On completion of the tenth form the pupils may sit for either the leaving examination of the *folkeskole (folkeskolens afgangsprøve)* or the advanced leaving examination of the *folkeskole (folkeskolens udvidede afgangsprøve)*.

For 14–18 year olds there is an alternative of completing compulsory education at continuation schools, with the same leaving examinations as in the *folkeskole*. In the year 1996–97 there were 231 continuation schools with 19,749 pupils. Under certain conditions the pupils may continue school either in the 3-year gymnasium (upper secondary school) or 2-year *studenterkursus* (adult upper secondary school), ending with *studentereksamen* (upper secondary school leaving examination); or in the 2-year or 3-year higher preparatory examination course, ending with the *højere forberedelseseksamen*. There were (1996–97) 150 of these upper secondary schools with 73,850 pupils.

Another way of continuing school is to attend HHX (*Højere handelseksamen*) which are diploma courses within the field of trade and commerce (27,000 pupils were enrolled in 1996–97), or HTX (*Højere tekniskeksamen*) which are technical diploma courses (6,304 pupils in 1996–97). Vocational education and training consists of a ½-year or 1-year basic course, followed by a second part of 2–4 years. Vocational education and training cover courses in commerce and trade, iron and metal industry, chemical industry, construction industry, graphic industry, service trades, food industry, agriculture, horticulture, forestry and fishery, transport and communication, and health-related auxiliary programmes. In 1996–97, 40,470 students were enrolled within trade and commerce. 78,890 students were enrolled within technical education.

Tertiary education comprises all education after the 12th year of education, regardless of whether the 3 years after the 9th form of the *folkeskole* have been spent on a course preparing for continued studies *(studentereksamen, højere forberedelseseksamen* or *HHX/HTX)*, or a course preparing for a vocation *(EUD)*. Tertiary education can be divided into 2 main groups; short courses of further education and long courses of higher education. There were a total of 17,872 students at short courses of further education in 1996–97. There were 18 teacher-training colleges with 12,745 students in 1996–97 and 34 colleges for training of personnel for kindergartens, leisure-time and social care institutions with 17,535 students.

Degree courses in engineering: The Technical University of Denmark had 6,199 students in 1996–97. 9 engineering colleges had 6,000 students. Universities, 1996–97: The University of Copenhagen (founded 1479), 27,653 students; the University of Århus (founded in 1928), 17,176 students; the University of Odense (founded in 1964), 9,020 students; the University of Aalborg (founded in 1974), 9,046 students; Roskilde University Centre (founded in 1972), 5,546 students.

Other types of post-secondary education (1996–97): The Royal Veterinary and Agricultural University has 3,006 students; The Danish School of Pharmacy, 1,046 students; 8 colleges of economics, business administration and modern languages, 24,377 students; 2 schools of architecture, 2,066 students; 7 academies of music, 1,219 students; 2 schools of librarianship, 821 students; The Royal Danish School of Educational Studies, 2,787 students; 5 schools of social work, 1,781 students; The Danish School of Journalism, 980 students; 10 colleges of physical therapy, 2,566 students; 2 schools of Midwifery Education, 246 students; 2 colleges of home economics, 488 students; The School of Visual Arts, 192 students; 27 schools of nursing, 9,606 students; 3 military academies, 590 students.

Of adult education institutions, the best-known are *Folkeskolehøjskoler*, folk high schools (with 49,017 students). Adult education includes: single subjects (since 1978, with 94,481 students); labour market training courses for semi-skilled workers and for skilled workers (188,468 students); and courses in single subject education at vocational schools (112,232 students).

In 1995 total expenditure on education came to 8·2% of GNP and represented 13·1% of total government expenditure.

Health. In 1994 there were 14,497 doctors (1 per 358 persons), 5,088 dentists, 63,841 nurses and 1,038 midwives. There were 163 hospitals in 1992, with a provision of 35 beds per 10,000 population.

Welfare. The main body of Danish social welfare legislation is consolidated in 7 acts concerning: (1) public health security, (2) sick-day benefits, (3) social pensions (for early retirement and old age), (4) employment injuries insurance, (5) employment services, unemployment insurance and activation measures, (6) social assistance including assistance to handicapped, rehabilitation, child and juvenile guidance, daycare institutions, care of the aged and sick, and (7) family allowances.

Public health security, covering the entire population, provides free medical care, substantial subsidies for certain essential medicines together with some dental care, and a funeral allowance. Hospitals are primarily municipal and treatment is normally free. All employed workers are granted daily sickness allowances; others can have limited daily sickness allowances. Daily cash benefits are granted in the case of temporary incapacity because of illness, injury or childbirth to all persons in paid employment. The benefit is paid up to the rate of 100% of the average weekly earnings. There is, however, a maximum rate of 2,688 kroner a week.

Social pensions cover the entire population. Entitlement to the old-age pension at the full rate is subject to the condition that the beneficiary has been ordinarily resident in Denmark for 40 years. For a shorter period of residence, the benefits are reduced proportionally. The basic amount of the old-age pension in July 1998 was 134,760 kroner a year to married couples and 93,216 to single persons. Various supplementary allowances, depending on age and income, may be payable with the basic amount. Depending on health and income, persons aged 60–66 may apply for an early retirement pension. Persons over 67 years of age are entitled to the basic amount. The pensions to a married couple are calculated and paid to the husband and the wife separately. Early retirement pension to a disabled person is payable at ages 18–66 years, having regard to the degree of disability (physical as well as otherwise), at a rate of up to 147,420 kroner to a single person. Early retirement pensions may be subject to income regulation. The same applies to the basic amount of the old-age pension to persons aged 67–69.

Employment injuries insurance provides for disability or survivors' pensions and compensations. The scheme covers practically all employees.

Employment services are provided by regional public employment agencies. Insurance against unemployment provides daily allowances and covers about 85% of the unemployed. The unemployment insurance system is based on state subsidized insurance funds linked to the trade unions. The unemployment insurance funds had a membership of 2,199,018 in Aug. 1998.

The *Social Assistance Act* applies to individual benefits in contrast to the other fields of social legislation which apply to fixed benefits. Total social expenditure, including hospital and health services, statutory pensions etc. amounted in the financial year 1997 to 330,125·7m. kroner.

CULTURE

Broadcasting. Danmarks Radio is the government broadcasting station and is financed by household licence fees. Television is broadcast by *Danmarks Radio* and *TV2* with colour programmes by PAL system. Number of licences (1997): TV, 2·12m., including 2·07m. colour sets. There were an estimated 6m. radio receivers in 1996.

Cinema. In 1997 there were 320 auditoria. Total attendance in 1995 was 8·8m.

Press. In 1997 there were 37 daily newspapers with a combined circulation of 1·62m.

Tourism. In 1996, 1,794,000 foreign tourists visited Denmark. In 1997 foreign tourists spent some 21,021m. kroner. Foreigners spent 6,225,000 nights in hotels and 4,246,500 nights at camping sites in 1997.

DIPLOMATIC REPRESENTATIVES

Of Denmark in Great Britain (55 Sloane St., London, SW1X 9SR)
Ambassador: Ole Lønsmann Poulsen.

Of Great Britain in Denmark (Kastelsvej 36/38/40, DK-2100, Copenhagen Ø)
Ambassador: Andrew Bache, CMG.

Of Denmark in the USA (3200 Whitehaven St., NW, Washington, D.C., 20008-3683)
Ambassador: K. Erik Tygesen.

Of the USA in Denmark (Dag Hammarskjölds Allé 24, DK-2100, Copenhagen Ø)
Ambassador: Edward E. Elson.

Of Denmark to the United Nations
Ambassador: Jørgen Bøjer.

FURTHER READING

Statistical Information: Danmarks Statistik (Sejrøgade 11, DK-2100 Copenhagen Ø. *Website:* http://www.dst.dk/) was founded in 1849 and reorganized in 1966 as an independent institution; it is administratively placed under the Minister of Economic Affairs. Its main publications are: *Statistisk Årbog* (Statistical Yearbook). From 1896: *Statistiske Efterretninger* (Statistical News). *Statistiske Månedsoversigt* (Monthly Review of Statistics), *Statistisk tiårsoversigt* (Statistical Ten-Year Review).

Dania polyglotta. Annual Bibliography of Books . . . in Foreign Languages Printed in Denmark. State Library, Copenhagen. Annual
Kongelig Dansk Hof og Statskalender. Copenhagen. Annual
Johansen, H. C., *The Danish Economy in the Twentieth Century.* London, 1987
Miller, K. E., *Denmark.* [Bibliography] Oxford and Santa Barbara (CA), 1987.—*Denmark: a Troubled Welfare State.* Boulder (Colo.), 1991
Petersson, O., *The Government and Politics of the Nordic Countries.* Stockholm, 1994

National library: Det kongelige Bibliotek, P.O.B. 2149, DK-1016 Copenhagen K. *Director:* Erland Kolding Nielsen.

THE FAROE ISLANDS
Føroyar/Færøerne

KEY HISTORICAL EVENTS
A Norwegian province till the peace treaty of 14 January 1814, the islands have been represented by 2 members in the Danish parliament since 1851. In 1852 they obtained an elected parliament of their own which in 1948 secured a certain degree of home-rule. The islands are not included in the EU but left EFTA together with Denmark on 31 Dec. 1972. Recently, negotiations for independence were given a push by the prospect of exploiting offshore oil and gas.

TERRITORY AND POPULATION
The archipelago is situated due north of Scotland, 300 km from the Shetland Islands, 675 km from Norway and 450 km from Iceland, with a total land area of 1,399 sq. km (540 sq. miles). There are 17 inhabited islands (the main ones being Streymoy, Eysturoy, Vágoy, Suðuroy, Sandoy and Borðoy) and numerous islets, all mountainous and of volcanic origin. Population in 1995 was 43,678; density, 31 per sq. km. In 1995 an estimated 67·9% of the population lived in rural areas. The capital is Tórshavn (15,272) on Streymoy.

The official languages are Faroese and Danish.

SOCIAL STATISTICS
Birth rate per 1,000 inhabitants (1996 est.), 13·91; death rate, 8·69. Life expectancy at birth for total population (1996 est.), 77·83.

CONSTITUTION AND GOVERNMENT
The parliament comprises 32 members elected by proportional representation by universal suffrage at age 18. Parliament elects a government of at least 3 members which administers home rule. Denmark is represented in parliament by the chief administrator.

RECENT ELECTIONS
In parliamentary elections held on 30 April 1998 the People's Party (FF) and the Party for People's Government (TF) each won 8 seats, the Equality Party (JF) 7 seats, the Union Party (SF) 6 seats, the Self-Government Party (SSF) 2 seats, and the Centre Party (MF) 1 seat.

CURRENT ADMINISTRATION
Prime Minister: Anfinn Kallsberg (FF).

Following the 1998 elections, a coalition government was formed comprising FF, TF and SSF members.

Local Government. Local government is vested in the 50 *kommunur*, of 29 or more inhabitants, which raise their own income taxes.

ECONOMY
Budget. The 1995 budget balanced at 2,805m. kr. As a result of an economic crash in the early 1990s, Denmark restructured the banks and lent money to the government to meet its international obligations. Since then the economy has improved, but 5·5bn. Danish krone (£480m.) is still owed to the Danish state. Meanwhile, subsidies from Copenhagen are worth at least 1bn. Danish kreone a year.

Currency. Since 1940 the currency has been the Faroese *króna* (kr.) which remains freely interchangeable with the Danish krone.

Banking and Finance. The largest bank is the state-owned Føroya Banki.

ENERGY AND NATURAL RESOURCES
Electricity. Installed capacity is 91,000 kW. Total production in 1995 was 174m. kWh, of which hydro-electric 76m. kWh. There are 5 hydro-electric stations at Vestmanna on Streymoy and one at Eiði on Eysturoy. Consumption per capita was 4,043 kWh in 1995.

Agriculture. Only 2% of the surface is cultivated; it is chiefly used for sheep and cattle grazing. Potatoes are grown for home consumption. Livestock (1996): Sheep, 68,000; cattle, 2,000.

Fisheries. Deep-sea fishing now forms the most important sector (90%) of the economy, primarily in the 200-mile exclusive zone, but also off Greenland, Iceland, Svalbard and Newfoundland and in the Barents Sea. Total catch (1995) 284,971 tonnes, primarily cod, coalfish, redfish, mackerel, blue whiting, capelin, prawns and herring.

INTERNATIONAL TRADE

Imports and Exports. Exports, mainly fresh, frozen, filleted and salted fish, amounted to 2,026m. kr. in 1995; imports to 1,776m. kr. In 1995 Denmark supplied 35% of imports, Norway 16% and UK 8%; exports were mainly to UK (26%), Denmark (22%), Germany (10%), France (8%) and Spain (5%).

COMMUNICATIONS

Roads. In 1995 there were 458 km of highways, 11,528 passenger cars and 2,901 commercial vehicles.

Civil Aviation. The airport is on Vágoy, from which there are regular services to Aberdeen, Billund, Copenhagen, Reykjavík and Glasgow (in summer), with Atlantic Airways (Faroe Islands) and Maersk Air.

Shipping. The chief port is Tórshavn, with smaller ports at Klaksvik, Vestmanna, Skálafjørður, Tvøroyri, Vágur and Fuglafjørður. In 1995 merchant shipping totalled 104,000 GRT, including oil tankers, 230,000 GRT.

Telecommunications. In 1997 there were 23,600 telephone main lines in use (538 for every 1,000 inhabitants).

SOCIAL INSTITUTIONS

Religion. About 80% are Evangelical Lutherans and 20% are Plymouth Brethren, or belong to small communities of Roman Catholics, Pentecostal, Adventists, Jehovah Witnesses and Bahai.

Education. In 1994–95 there were 4,898 primary and 3,041 secondary school pupils with 554 teachers.

Health. In 1994 there were 90 doctors, 38 dentists, 10 pharmacists, 17 midwives and 355 nursing personnel. In 1994 there were 3 hospitals with 297 beds.

CULTURE

Broadcasting. Radio and TV broadcasting (colour by PAL) are provided by Utvarp Føroya and Sjónvarp Føroya respectively. In 1994 there were 24,000 radio and 14,000 TV receivers registered.

FURTHER READING
Árbók fyri Føroyar. Annual.
Rutherford, G. K., (ed.) *The Physical Environment of the Færoe Islands.* The Hague, 1982
West, J. F., *Faroe.* London, 1973
Wylie, J., *The Faroe Islands: Interpretations of History.* Lexington, 1987

GREENLAND
Grønland/Kalaallit Nunaat

KEY HISTORICAL EVENTS
A Danish possession since 1380, Greenland became an integral part of the Danish kingdom on 5 June 1953. Following a referendum in Jan. 1979, home rule was introduced from 1 May 1979.

TERRITORY AND POPULATION

Area, 2,166,086 sq. km (840,000 sq. miles), made up of 1,755,437 sq. km of ice cap and 410,449 sq. km of ice-free land. The population, 1 Jan. 1998, numbered 56,076. In 1998, 45,489 persons were urban (81%); 49,117 were born in Greenland and 6,959 were born outside Greenland. 1998 population of West Greenland, 51,047; East Greenland, 3,499; North Greenland (Thule/Qaanaaq), 875; and 655 not belonging to any specific municipality. The capital is Nuuk (Godthåb), with a population in 1998 of 13,024.

The predominant language is Greenlandic. Danish is widely used in matters relating to teaching, administration and business.

SOCIAL STATISTICS

Registered live births (1996), 1,006. Number of abortions (1997): 865. Death rate per 1,000 population (1996), 7·5. Annual growth rate (1997), 0·2%. Density, 0·03 sq. km.

CONSTITUTION AND GOVERNMENT

There is a 31-member Home Rule Parliament, which is elected for 4-year terms and meets 2 to 3 times a year. The 7-member cabinet is elected by parliament. Ministers need not be members of parliament. In accordance with the Home Rule Act, the Greenland Home Rule Government is constituted by an elected parliament, *Landstinget* (The Greenland Parliament), and an administration headed by a local government, *Landsstyret* (The Cabinet).

RECENT ELECTIONS

At the elections of 16 Feb. 1999 Siumut gained 11 seats and 35·2% of votes cast, Atássut 8 with 25·2%, Inuit Ataqatigiit 7 with 22·1%, Katusseqatigiit 4 with 12·3%, and Per Rosing-Petersen 1 with 5·0%.

CURRENT ADMINISTRATION

In Dec. 1998 the cabinet comprised 5 SDP and 2 LP ministers. Greenland elects 2 representatives to the Danish parliament (*Folketing*). Denmark is represented by an appointed High Commissioner.

The *Prime Minister* is Jonathan Motzfeldt (Siumut).

Local Government. Administratively, Greenland is divided into 3 regions (North, East and West Greenland), and subdivided into 18 municipalities (1 in North, 2 in East and 15 in West Greenland). Town councils are elected for 4-year terms. The last elections were in April 1997.

INTERNATIONAL RELATIONS

Greenland has 2 representatives, appointed by the Greenland Parliament, in the Council for European Politics.

ECONOMY

Policy. (The statistical data is too fragmentary to draw up detailed national accounts showing the flow of money between the individual sectors of Greenland's economy. However, by using the assessment material from the Greenland tax authority, it is possible to compute some crude totals for certain central national account figures.) All figures are in m. kroner.

	1993	1994	1995	1996
GNP at factor cost	5,908	6,270	6,752	6,883
GNP at market prices	6,208	6,563	6,992	7,182
Transfers from the Danish state	2,930	2,920	2,975	3,023
(of which block grants[1])	*2,329*	*2,375*	*2,393*	*2,441*
Gross National Disposable Income at market prices	8,738	9,133	9,692	10,006
Real GNP growth	−3·8	5·2	4·4	1·7
Real GNDI growth	−3·6	4·0	4·0	2·2

[1]Other transfers include (amongst others): defence, fisheries inspection, the judicial system (including the police), which are financed directly by the Danish state.

The figures show that the transfers from the Danish state were 30·2% of gross national disposable income in 1997. There is an ongoing debate regarding the size of the secondary effect of the transfers from the Danish state. According to one estimate, these effects amount to 55% of GNP at market prices.

Performance. Real GNP has been stagnant since 1990.

Budget. The budget (*finanslovsforslag*) for the following year must be approved by the Home Rule Parliament (*Landstinget*) no later than 31 Oct.

The following table shows the actual revenue and expenditure as shown in Home Rule Government accounts for the calendar years 1995-97, and the approved budget figures for 1998. Figures are in 1,000 kroner:

	1995	1996	1997	1998	1999
Revenue[1]	3,953	4,063	4,178	4,204	4,359
Expenditure[1]	3,905	3,562	4,089	4,350	4,359

[1]Receipts and expenditures of special Government funds and expenditures on public works are included.

Currency. The Danish krone is the legal currency.

Banking and Finance. There is 1 private bank, Grønlandsbanken.

Weights and Measures. The metric system in use.

ENERGY AND NATURAL RESOURCES

Electricity. Installed capacity is 92,500 kW. Production in 1997 was 273·5m. GWh. Consumption was 157·7 GWh in 1996-97.

Oil and Gas. Imports of fuel and fuel oil (1997), 192,130 tonnes worth 264m. kroner.

Water. Production of water in tonnes (1997), 5·5m. cu. metres, of which 2·8m. cu. metres was for industry.

Minerals. Exploitation of minerals (1997): number of licences, 59; area, 53,000 sq. km.

Agriculture. Livestock, 1997: Sheep, 21,025; reindeer, 2,800. There are approximately 60 sheep-breeding farms in south-west Greenland. A quota hunt for 2,000 caribous per year has been introduced.

Fisheries. Fishing and product-processing are the principal industry. Total catches in 1995 were 129,018 tonnes. In 1997 shrimps accounted for 64·8% of the country's economic output. Greenland Halibut and other fish made up 20%. In 1997, 169 whales were caught (subject to the International Whaling Commission's regulations) and in 1996, 167,751 seals. Around 76,000 of these were traded, the rest used in domestic households.

INDUSTRY

6 shipyards repair and maintain ships and produce industrial tanks, containers and steel constructions for building. Production of lead and zinc concentrates was, in 1989, about 35,500 tonnes and 130,500 tonnes respectively. The mine closed down in 1990.

Labour. At 1 Jan. 1998 the labour force, born in Greenland, was 30,540.

INTERNATIONAL TRADE

Imports and Exports. Principal commodities (1997 provisional figures, in 1m. kroner):

Imports (c.i.f.), 2,624·8, including: Food and live animals, 318·2 (of which meat and meat preparations 98·2); beverages and tobacco, 105·0 (of which beverages 72·4); minerals, fuels, lubricants, etc., 245·2 (of which petroleum products 242·4); chemicals, 99·9; basic manufactures, 391·8; machinery and transport equipment, 685·4 (of which machinery, 459·2; transport equipment, 226·2); miscellaneous manufactured articles, 298·7.

Exports (f.o.b.), 1,936·6: Prawns, 1,254·7; Greenland halibut, 370·7; cod, 37·8; other fish products, 114·5; other products, 158·9.

Principal trading partners (provisional, 1m. kroner, 1997): Imports (c.i.f.): Denmark, 1,712·1; Norway, 315·4; Japan, 74·5; Others, 522·8. Exports (f.o.b.): Denmark, 1,697·9; UK, 67·7; Japan, 65·5; Others, 105·6.

COMMUNICATIONS

Roads. There are no roads between towns. Registered vehicles (1997): passenger cars, 1,790; lorries and trucks, 1,478; total (including others), 3,646.

Rail. There is no railway system.

Civil Aviation. Number of passengers to/from Greenland (1997): 95,324. Domestic flights—number of passengers (1997): Aeroplanes, 114,312; helicopters, 95,886. Greenland Air operates services to Denmark, Iceland and Frobisher Bay (Canada). Icelandair and SAS also serve Greenland. There are international airports at Kangerlussuaq (Søndre Srømfjord) and Narsarsuaq; and 18 local airports/heliports with scheduled services. There are cargo services to Denmark, Iceland and St John's (Canada).

Shipping. There are no overseas passenger services. In 1996, 88,195 passengers were carried on coastal services. There are cargo services to Denmark, Iceland and St John's (Canada).

Telecommunications. In 1997 there were 23,400 telephone main lines (416 per 1,000 persons) and 1,462 Internet dial-ups.

SOCIAL INSTITUTIONS

Justice. The High Court in Nuuk comprises one professional judge and 2 lay magistrates, while there are 18 district courts under lay assessors.

Religion. About 99% of the population are Evangelical Lutherans. In 1997 there were 17 parishes with 81 churches and chapels, and 22 ministers.

Education. Education is compulsory from 6 to 15 years. A further 3 years of schooling are optional. Pre-primary and primary schools (1997–98): 10,790 pupils; secondary schools: 3 with 502 pupils.

Health. The medical service is free to all citizens. There is a central hospital in Nuuk and 15 smaller district hospitals. In 1997 there were 83 doctors.

Non-natural death occurred in approximately one-fifth of all deaths in 1996. Suicide is the most dominant non-natural cause of death. In 1996 suicide was the cause of death in 10% of all deaths. There were 88 reported cases of tuberculosis in 1997 and 628 cases of venereal disease. In 1996, 3 cases of HIV were reported while a total of 12 new HIV-positive cases were reported in 1997.

Welfare. Old-age pension is granted to persons who are 60 or above. The right to maternity leave has been extended to 2 weeks before the expected birth and up to 19 weeks after birth against a total of 20 weeks in earlier regulations. The father's right to 1 week's maternity leave in connection with the birth has been extended to 2 weeks as from 1 Jan. 1998. Unemployment and illness: Wage earners who are members of SIK (The National Workers' Union) receive financial assistance (unemployment benefit) according to fixed rates, in case of unemployment or illness.

CULTURE

Broadcasting. The government Kalaallit Nunaata Radioa provides broadcasting services, and there are also local services. In 1991 there were estimated to be 25,000 radio and 12,000 TV sets (colour by PAL). Several towns have local television stations.

Cinema. There is 1 cinema in Nuuk at the Cultural Centre Katuaq. Video is widely used.

Press. There are 3 national newspapers.

Tourism. In 1997 there were 181,043 (including 58,792 Danish) visitors.

Libraries. There are 17 municipal libraries and the National Library, Nunatta Atuagaateqarfia, which is administered by the Home Rule authorities.

GREENLAND

Museums and Galleries. There are museums in most towns. Greenland National Museum is in Nuuk. 14,555 persons visited the museum in 1997.

FURTHER READING
Greenland 19xx: Statistical Yearbook has been published annually since 1989 by Statistics Greenland.
Gad, F., *A History of Greenland.* 2 vols. London, 1970–73
Miller, K. E., *Greenland* [Bibliography]. Oxford and Santa Barbara (CA), 1991
Greenland National Library, P.O. Box 1011, DK-3900 Nuuk

National statistical office: Statistics Greenland, PO Box 1025, DK-3900 Nuuk. *Website:* http://www.statgreen.gl/

549

DJIBOUTI

Jumhouriyya Djibouti

(Republic of Djibouti)

Capital: Djibouti
Population estimate, 2000: 687,000
Estimated GDP: $500m.
HDI/world rank: 0·324/162

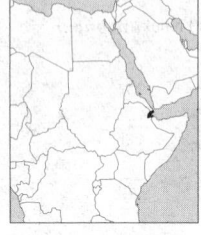

KEY HISTORICAL EVENTS

At a referendum held on 19 March 1967, 60% of the electorate voted for continued association with France rather than independence and the new statute for the territory came into being on 5 July 1967. France affirmed that the Territory of the Afars and the Issas was destined for independence but no date was fixed. Legislative elections were held on 8 May and independence as the Republic of Djibouti was achieved on 27 June 1977.

Afar rebels in the north, belonging to the Front for the Restoration of Unity and Democracy (FRUD), signed a 'Peace and National Reconciliation Agreement' with the government on 26 Dec. 1994, envisaging the formation of a national coalition government, the redrafting of the electoral roll and the integration of FRUD militants into the armed forces and civil service.

TERRITORY AND POPULATION

Djibouti is in effect a city-state surrounded by a semi-desert hinterland. It is bounded in the north-west by Eritrea, north-east by the Gulf of Aden, south-east by Somalia and south-west by Ethiopia. The area is 23,200 sq. km (8,958 sq. miles). The population was estimated in 1995 at 601,000 (82% urban), of whom about half were Somali (Issa, Gadaboursi and Issaq), 35% Afar, and some Europeans (mainly French) and Arabs. 1995 density, 26 per sq. km.

The UN gives a projected population for 2000 of 687,000.

There are 5 administrative districts (areas in sq. km): Ali-Sabieh (2,600); Dikhil (7,800); Djibouti (600); Obock (5,700); Tadjoura (7,300). The capital is Djibouti (1995 population, 383,000).

French and Arabic are official languages; Somali and Afar are also spoken.

SOCIAL STATISTICS

1995 births, 23,500; deaths, 9,500. Birth rate in 1995, 38·8 per 1,000 population; death rate, 15·6; infant mortality, 1996, 108 per 1,000 live births. Growth rate, 1996, 1·5% (estimate). Expectation of life, 1996, 48·2 years or men, 52·1 for women. Fertility rate, 5·8 children per woman.

CLIMATE

Conditions are hot throughout the year, with very little rain. Djibouti, Jan. 78°F (25·6°C), July 96°F (35·6°C). Annual rainfall 5" (130 mm).

CONSTITUTION AND GOVERNMENT

After a referendum at which turn-out was 70%, a new constitution was approved on 4 Sept. 1992 by 96·63% of votes cast, which permits the existence of up to 4 political parties. Parties are required to maintain an ethnic balance in their membership. The *President* is directly elected for a renewable 6-year term. Parliament is a 65-member *Chamber of Deputies* elected for 5-year terms.

National Anthem. 'Hinjinne u sara kaca' ('Arise with strength'); words by A. Elmi, tune by A. Robleh.

RECENT ELECTIONS

At the presidential elections of 7 May 1993 the electorate was 150,487; turn-out was 50·26%. Hassan Gouled Aptidon was elected against 3 opponents by 60·71% of votes cast.

At the parliamentary elections of 19 Dec. 1997 the coalition of RPP and FRUD won 65 seats with 78·6% of votes cast, the Party of Democratic Renewal nil with 19·2%, and the National Democratic Party nil with 2·3%.

CURRENT ADMINISTRATION

President: Hassan Gouled Aptidon, b. 1916 (elected 1977, re-elected 1981, 1987 and 1993).

The Council of Ministers in March 1999 comprised as follows:

Prime Minister, Planning and Territorial Administration: Barkat Gourad Hamadou.

Minister of Interior and Decentralization: Elmi Obsieh Wassi. *Justice, Islamic Affairs and Prisons:* Mohamed Dini Farah. *Foreign Affairs and International Co-operation:* Mohammed Moussa Chehem. *Defence:* Abdullah Chirwa Djibril. *Finance and Economy:* Yacin Elmi Boueh. *Industry, Energy and Mines:* Abdi Farah. *Labour and Training:* Mohamed Ali Mohamed. *Education:* Ahmed Guire Waberi. *Public Works, Urban Affairs and Housing:* Hassan Farah Mighil. *Health and Social Affairs:* Ali Mohammed Daoud. *Transport and Telecommunications:* Abdallah Abdillahi Miguil. *Agriculture and Rural Reform:* Ibrahim Idris Djibril. *Youth, Sport and Culture:* Rifki Abdoulkader Bamakrama. *Civil Service and Administrative Reform:* Ougoureh Kifle Ahmed. *Commerce and Tourism:* Mohamed Abdillahi Barkat. *Environment:* Osman Robleh Daach. *Chief of Staff of the Presidency:* Ismail Omar Guelleh.

DEFENCE

France maintains a naval base and forces numbering 3,900 under an agreement renewed in Feb. 1991. Defence expenditure totalled US$20m. in 1997 (US$30 per capita).

Army. There are 3 Army commands: North, Central and South. The Army comprises 1 infantry battalion, 1 armoured squadron, 1 support battalion, 1 border commando battalion and 1 parachute company, and 1 artillery battery. Equipment includes 31 armoured cars. The strength of the Army was (1996) 8,000. There is also a paramilitary Gendarmerie of some 1,200, and an Interior Ministry National Security Force of 3,000.

Navy. A coastal patrol is maintained consisting of 8 small inshore patrol craft and some boats. Personnel (1996), 200.

Air Force. There is a small air force. There are no combat aircraft. Fixed-wing aircraft comprise 1 An-28 transport and 2 Cessna 206s for liaison. There are also 3 Ecureuil, 3 Mi-8 and 2 Mi-2 helicopters. Personnel (1995), 200.

INTERNATIONAL RELATIONS

Djibouti is a member of the UN, OAU, the Arab League and is an ACP state of the EU.

ECONOMY

Performance. Real GDP growth was 0·2% in 1995 (1·7% in 1994).

Budget. Revenues in 1997 were an estimated US$156m. and expenditure US$175m.

Currency. The currency is the *Djibouti franc* (DJF), notionally of 100 *centimes.* Foreign exchange reserves were US$66m. in Feb. 1998. Total money supply was 26,640m. Djibouti francs in Sept. 1997.

Banking and Finance. The Banque Nationale de Djibouti is the bank of issue (*Governor*, Luc Aden). There are 6 commercial banks.

Weights and Measures. The metric system is in use.

ENERGY AND NATURAL RESOURCES

Electricity. Installed capacity in 1991 was 115,000 kW. Production in 1994 was 185m. kWh; consumption per capita was 327 kWh in 1994.

Agriculture. Approximately 1·3m. ha were permanent pasture in 1994. Production is dependent on irrigation. Tomato production (1992) 1,000 tonnes. Livestock (1996): Cattle, 190,000; sheep, 470,000; goats, 507,000; camels, 62,000.

Forestry. In 1995 the area under forests was 22,000 ha, or 0·9% of the total land area.

Fisheries. In 1995 there were 140 individual fishing boats. The catch was about 350 tonnes, entirely from sea fishing.

INDUSTRY

In 1993 services provided 76% of GDP, industry 21% and agriculture 3%.

Labour. In 1991 the estimated labour force totalled 282,000, with 75% employed in agriculture, 14% in services and 11% in industry. A 40-hour working week is standard. Unemployment in 1994 was estimated at 30%.

INTERNATIONAL TRADE

Foreign debt totalled US$241m. in 1996.

Imports and Exports. The main economic activity is the operation of the port; in 1990 only 36% of imports were destined for Djibouti. Exports are largely re-exports. In 1992 imports totalled US$219m. and exports US$16m. The chief imports are cotton goods, sugar, cement, flour, fuel oil and vehicles; the chief exports are hides, cattle and coffee (transit from Ethiopia).

Main export markets, 1995 (% of total trade): Somalia, 42%; Ethiopia, 35%; Yemen, 7%. Main import suppliers: Thailand, 15%; France, 13%; Ethiopia, 8%; Saudi Arabia, 6%.

COMMUNICATIONS

Roads. In 1996 there were 2,890 km of roads, of which 364 km were hard-surfaced. An estimated 9,200 passenger cars were in use in 1996 (17 per 1,000 inhabitants), plus 2,040 vans and trucks.

Rail. For the line from Djibouti to Addis Ababa, of which 97 km lie within Djibouti, *see* ETHIOPIA: Communications. Traffic carried is mainly in transit to and from Ethiopia.

Civil Aviation. There is an international airport at Djibouti (Ambouli), 5 km south of Djibouti. Services are provided by Air Djibouti, Daallo Airlines and Djibouti Airlines, plus in 1998 Air France, Ethiopian Airlines and Yemenia Yemen Airways. Flights operated in 1998 to Addis Ababa, Aden, Asmara, Assab, Berbera, Borama, Bossaso, Burao, Cairo, Dire Dawa, Dubai, Erigavo, Hargeisa, Jeddah, Johannesburg, Karachi, Khartoum, Mogadishu, Mombasa, Muscat, Paris, Rome, Sana'a, Sharjah and Ta'iz.

Shipping. Djibouti is a free port and container terminal. 950 ships berthed in 1989 (including 177 warships), totalling 3·87m. NRT. 3,211 passengers embarked or disembarked, and 0·87m. tonnes of cargo were handled (1·48m. tonnes in 1992). In 1995 the merchant marine totalled 4,800 GRT.

Telecommunications. There were 8,300 telephone main lines in 1997 (13·1 for every 1,000 inhabitants). In 1995 there were approximatley 1,000 PCs in use and 100 fax machines. In Jan. 1998 there were approximately 400 Internet users.

Postal Services. There were 10 post offices in 1995.

SOCIAL INSTITUTIONS

Justice. There is a Court of First Instance and a Court of Appeal in the capital. The judicial system is based on Islamic law.

Religion. In 1995, 96% of the population were Moslem, with about 12,000 Roman Catholics and 10,000 Protestant and Orthodox.

Education. Adult literacy in 1995 was estimated at 46·2% (60·3% of men; 32·7% of women). In 1994–95 there were 81 primary schools with 35,024 pupils and 881 teachers, and in 1995–96, 11,860 pupils and 628 teachers in secondary schools. In 1995–96 there were 130 students at higher education institutions.

Health. In 1993 there were 2 hospitals, 6 medical centres and 21 dispensaries. There were 97 doctors, 10 dentists and 14 pharmacists in 1989.

CULTURE

Broadcasting. The state-run *Radiodiffusion-Télévision de Djibouti* broadcasts in French, Somali, Afar and Arabic. There is a television transmitter in Djibouti, broadcasting for 35 hours a week. Number of receivers (1995): Radio, 48,000; TV, 26,000 (colour by SECAM).

Tourism. There were 20,000 foreign tourists in 1996, spending US$4m.

DIPLOMATIC REPRESENTATIVES
Of Djibouti in Great Britain
Ambassador: Djama Omar Idleh (resides in Paris).

Of Great Britain in Djibouti
Ambassador: G. G. Wetherell (resides in Addis Ababa).

Of the USA in Djibouti (Plateau du Serpent Blvd., Djibouti)
Ambassador: Lange Schermerhorn.

Of Djibouti to the United Nations and in the USA (1156 15th Street, NW, Suite 515, Washington, D.C., 20005)
Ambassador: Roble Olhaye.

Of Djibouti to the European Union
Ambassador: Vacant.

FURTHER READING
Direction Nationale de la Statistique. *Annuaire Statistique de Djibouti*
Schraeder, P. J., *Djibouti*. [Bibliography] Oxford and Santa Barbara (CA), 1990

National statistical office: Direction Nationale de la Statistique, Ministère du Commerce, des Transports et du Tourisme, BP 1846, Djibouti

DOMINICA

Commonwealth of
Dominica

Capital: Roseau
Population estimate, 2000: 77,000
GNP per capita: (PPP$) 4,390
HDI/world rank: 0·879/41

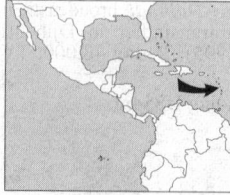

KEY HISTORICAL EVENTS
The earliest-known inhabitants of this island in the Caribbean were two Amerindian tribes: the Arawaks who migrated from South America, and the Caribs who later drove them out. Dominica was discovered by Columbus on Sunday (hence the island's name), 3 Nov. 1493. Neither the Spanish nor the Earl of Carlisle, who was granted the island in 1672 by Charles I, established settlements, and instead it was French settlers who began to create plantations on the island. The island's strategic position, however, later caused it to become the centre of a threefold conflict between the Carib Indians, the British and French. Control of the island was contested between the British and French until it was ultimately awarded to the British in 1783.

Dominica became part of a federation on four occasions: in 1833 with the Leeward Islands, in 1871 in an extended Leeward Islands Colony, in 1940 as part of the Windward Islands group, and in 1958-62 as a member of the Federation of the West Indies.

In March 1967 Dominica became an Associated State of the UK, allowed internal self-government, and became an independent republic as the Commonwealth of Dominica on 3 Nov. 1978.

TERRITORY AND POPULATION
Dominica is an island in the Windward group of the West Indies situated between Martinique and Guadeloupe. It has an area of 748·5 sq. km (289·5 sq. miles) and a population at the 1991 census of 71,794. 1996 estimate, 74,000.

In 2000 the population is projected to be 77,000.

An estimated 69·3% of the population were urban in 1995. The chief town, Roseau, had 15,853 inhabitants in 1991.

The population is mainly of African and mixed origins, with small white and Asian minorities. There is a Carib settlement of about 500, almost entirely of mixed blood.

The official language is English, though 95% of the population speak a French Creole.

SOCIAL STATISTICS
Life expectancy, 1996, 77·4 years; male 74·55, female 80·4. Annual growth rate, 1990–96, 0·3%. Infant mortality rate, 1996, 16 per 1,000 live births.

CLIMATE
A tropical climate, with pleasant conditions between Dec. and March, but there is a rainy season from June to Oct., when hurricanes may occur. Rainfall is heavy, with coastal areas having 70" (1,750 mm) but the mountains may have up to 225" (6,250 mm). Roseau, Jan. 76°F (24·2°C), July 81°F (27·2°C). Annual rainfall 78" (1,956 mm).

CONSTITUTION AND GOVERNMENT
The head of state is the *President*, nominated by the Prime Minister and the Leader of the Opposition, and elected for a 5-year term (renewable once) by the House of Assembly. The *House of Assembly* has 21 elected and 9 members nominated by the President.

National Anthem. 'Isle of beauty, isle of splendour'; words by W. Pond, tune by L. M. Christian.

RECENT ELECTIONS
Elections were held on 12 June 1995. The United Workers Party (UWP) won 11 seats (6 in 1990), the Dominica Labour Party (DLP) 5 (4) and the Dominica Freedom Party 5 (11).

CURRENT ADMINISTRATION
President: Vernon L. Shaw (UWP; elected 6 Oct. 1998).
The Cabinet in March 1999 comprised as follows:
Prime Minister and Minister of External Affairs, Legal Affairs, Trade, Marketing and Labour: Edison James (b. 1944; UWP).
Deputy Prime Minister and Minister of Finance, Industry and Planning: Julius Timothy. *Tourism, Ports and Employment:* Norris Prevost. *Health and Social Security:* Doreen Paul. *Community Development and Women's Affairs:* Gertrude Roberts. *Communications, Works and Housing:* Earl Williams. *Agriculture and the Environment:* Peter Carbon. *Education, Sports and Youth Affairs:* Ronald Green.

Local Government. Roseau and Portsmouth have town councils with powers to raise property taxes. There are 25 rural districts administered by partially elected village councils.

INTERNATIONAL RELATIONS
Dominica is a member of the UN, OAS, CARICOM, the Commonwealth, and is an ACP state of the EU.

ECONOMY
Performance. Real GDP growth was −1·5% in 1995 (1·0% in 1994).

Budget. Revenues for the fiscal year 1995-96 were US$77m. and expenditure US$78m.

Currency. The French *franc,* the £ sterling and the *East Caribbean dollar* are legal tender. Foreign exchange reserves were US$25m. in Feb. 1998.

Banking and Finance. In 1996 there were 4 foreign banks, 1 domestic bank, a development bank and a credit union.

ENERGY AND NATURAL RESOURCES
Electricity. Installed capacity was 13,500 kW in 1995. Production in 1994 was 52m. kWh and consumption per capita in 1994 was 479 kWh. There is a hydro-electric power station.

Agriculture. Agriculture provides approximately 25% of GDP and employs 26% of the labour force. Production (1992): Bananas, 70,000 tonnes; coconuts, 12,000 tonnes. Livestock (1996): Cattle, 13,000; pigs, 5,000; sheep, 8,000; goats, 10,000.

Forestry. In 1995 forests covered 46,000 ha, or 61·3% of the total land area.

Fisheries. In 1996 total catches were 842 tonnes, almost exclusively from sea fishing.

INDUSTRY
Manufactures include clothing, soap, shampoo, cream, footwear, fruit juice, rum, electronic assemblies, candles and paint.

Labour. Around 25% of the economically active population are engaged in agriculture, fishing and forestry. In 1994 the minimum wage was US$0·75 an hour.

INTERNATIONAL TRADE
Imports and Exports. In 1996 imports were worth US$130m. and exports US$51m. Chief products: Bananas, soap, fruit juices, essential oils, coconuts, vegetables, fruit and fruit preparations, and alcoholic drinks. Main export markets, 1996: UK, 35·6%; Jamaica, 20·8%; USA, 7·3%; Antigua and Barbuda, 5·0%. Main import suppliers, 1996: USA, 40·9%; UK, 13·0%; Trinidad and Tobago, 12·5%; Japan, 5·6%.

COMMUNICATIONS

Roads. In 1996 it was estimated there were 780 km of road, of which 393 km were paved. Approximately 7,000 passenger cars and 2,800 commercial vehicles were in use in 1994.

Civil Aviation. There are international airports at Melville Hall and Cane Field. In 1998 there were direct flights to Antigua, Barbados, Guadeloupe, Martinique, Puerto Rico, St Lucia, St Maarten and St Vincent. Services were provided in 1998 by American Airlines, Cardinal Airlines, Helenair, LIAT and Société Nouvelle Air Guadeloupe.

Shipping. There are deep-water harbours at Roseau and Woodbridge Bay. Roseau has a cruise ship berth. In 1995 merchant shipping totalled 2,000 GRT.

Telecommunications. There were 18,700 telephone main lines in 1996, equivalent to 252·3 per 1,000 inhabitants. In 1995 approximately 300 fax machines were in use.

Postal Services. In 1994 there were 131 post offices, or 1 for every 566 persons. Only Nauru, with 1 for every 406 persons in 1995, had an even better provision of post offices.

SOCIAL INSTITUTIONS

Justice. There is a supreme court and 12 magistrates courts. Law is based on UK common law as exercised by the Eastern Caribbean Supreme Court on St Lucia. Final appeal lies to the UK Privy Council.

In 1995 the police force numbered 439; it has a residual responsibility for defence.

Religion. 77% of the population was Roman Catholic in 1995.

Education. In 1994 adult literacy was 90%. In 1993–94 there were 54 private kindergartens. Education is free and compulsory between the ages of 5 and 15 years. In 1994–95 there were 64 primary schools with 641 teachers and 12,627 pupils, and 6,493 pupils in general secondary level education. In 1992–93 there were 484 students and 34 teachers at higher education institutions.

Health. In 1994 there were 54 hospitals and health centres with 312 beds, 23 doctors, 6 dentists, 27 pharmacists and 265 nursing personnel.

CULTURE

Broadcasting. Radio and television broadcasting is provided by the part government-controlled, part-commercial Dominica Broadcasting Corporation. There are also 2 religious radio networks, 2 commercial TV channels (colour by NTSC) and a commercial cable service. In 1995 there were 45,000 radio and 5,200 TV sets.

Cinema. There is 1 cinema with a seating capacity of 1,000.

Press. In 1994 there were 3 newspapers, including 1 government and 1 independent weekly.

Tourism. There were 62,000 foreign tourists in 1996, spending US$30m.

DIPLOMATIC REPRESENTATIVES

Of Dominica in Great Britain (1 Collingham Gdns., South Kensington, London, SW5 0HW)
High Commissioner: George E. Williams.

Of Great Britain in Dominica
High Commissioner: Mr G. M. Baker (resides in Barbados).

Of Dominica in the USA (3216 New Mexico Ave., NW, Washington, D.C., 20016)
Ambassador: Nicholas J. O. Liverpool.

Of the USA in Dominica
Ambassador: Jeanette W. Hyde (resides in Barbados).

Of Dominica to the United Nations
Ambassador: Simon Paul Richards.

Of Dominica to the European Union
Ambassador: Edwin Laurent.

FURTHER READING
Baker, P. L., *Centring the Periphery: Chaos, Order and the Ethnohistory of Dominica:* McGill-
Queen's Univ. Press, 1994
Honychurch, L., *The Dominica Story: a History of the Island.* 2nd ed. London, 1995
Myers, R. A., *Dominica.* [Bibliography] Oxford and Santa Barbara (CA), 1987

National statistical office: Central Statistical Office, Kennedy Avenue, Roseau.

DOMINICAN REPUBLIC

República Dominicana

Capital: Santo Domingo
Population estimate, 2000: 8·49m.
GNP per capita: (PPP$) 4,390
HDI/world rank: 0·720/88

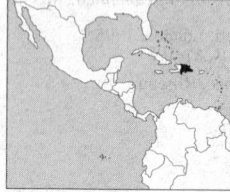

KEY HISTORICAL EVENTS

Columbus discovered the island of Santo Domingo, which he called La Isla Española, and which for a time was also known as Hispaniola. The city of Santo Domingo, founded by his brother, Bartholomew, in 1496, is the oldest city in the Americas. The western third of the island—now the Republic of Haiti—was later occupied and colonized by the French, to whom the Spanish colony of Santo Domingo was also ceded in 1795. In 1808 the Dominican population, under the command of Gen. Juan Sánchez Ramirez, routed an important French military force commanded by Gen. Ferrand at the battle of Palo Hincado. This battle was the beginning of the end for French rule in Santo Domingo and culminated in the successful siege of the capital. Eventually, with the aid of a British naval squadron, the French were forced to capitulate and the colony returned again to Spanish rule, from which it declared its independence in 1821. It was invaded and held by the Haitians from 1822 to 1844, when they were expelled, and the Dominican Republic was founded and a constitution adopted. In 1850 Great Britain was the first country to recognize the Dominican Republic.

Thereafter the rule was dictatorship interspersed with brief democratic interludes. Between 1916 and 1924 the country was under US military occupation. From 1930 until his assassination in 1961, Rafael Trujillo was one of Latin America's legendary dictators. The rise of radicalism following the election of Juan Bosch to the presidency in 1963 led, in 1965, to a further US invasion. The conservative pro-American Joaquin Balaguer was president from 1966 to 1978 when an opposition candidate, Antonio Guzuén, was elected. Resistance to repression of popular movements led to the election of the moderate leftist Salvador Jorge Blanco in 1982. In 1986 Balaguer returned to power at the head of the Socialist Christian Reform Party, leading the way to economic reforms. But there was violent opposition to spending cuts and general austerity. Balaguer was returned to power in 1994 by a narrow margin after accusations of electoral irregularity. The 1996 elections brought in a reforming government pledged to act against corruption.

TERRITORY AND POPULATION

The Dominican Republic occupies the eastern portion (about two-thirds) of the island of Hispaniola, the western division forming the Republic of Haiti. The frontier with Haiti is closed. The area is 48,442 sq. km (18,700 sq. miles). The 1990 area and population of the 29 provinces and National District (Santo Domingo area) was:

	Area (in sq. km)	Popu- lation		Area (in sq. km)	Popu- lation
La Altagracia	3,084	111,241	Monseñor Nouel	1,004	124,794
Azua	2,430	195,420	Monte Cristi	1,989	92,678
Bahoruco	1,376	87,376	Monte Plata	2,179	174,799
Barahona	2,528	152,405	Pedernales	967	18,896
Dajabón	890	64,123	Peravia	1,622	186,810
Distrito Nacional			Puerto Plata	1,881	229,738
(Santo Domingo area)	1,477	2,411,895	La Romana	541	169,223
Duarte	1,292	261,725	Salcedo	533	110,216
Espaillat	1,000	182,248	Samaná	989	73,002
La Estrelleta	1,788	72,651	Sánchez Ramírez	1,174	140,635
Hato Mayor	1,330	77,823	San Cristóbal	1,564	320,921
Independencia	1,861	43,077	San Juan	3,561	266,628
María Trinidad Sánchez	1,310	125,148	San Pedro de Macorís	1,166	197,862

DOMINICAN REPUBLIC

	Area (in sq. km)	Population		Area (in sq. km)	Population
Santiago	3,122	704,835	Valverde	570	111,470
Santiago Rodríguez	1,020	61,570	La Vega	2,373	303,047
El Seíbo	1,659	97,590			

Census population (1981), 5,647,977. Estimate (1996), 8,088,900 (61·9% urban in 1995).

The UN gives a projected population for 2000 of 8·49m.

Population of the main towns (1991 estimate, in 1,000): Santo Domingo, the capital, 2,055; Santiago de los Caballeros, 375; La Vega, 189; San Francisco de Macorís, 162; San Pedro de Macorís, 137; La Romana, 136.

The population is mainly composed of a mixed race of European (Spanish) and African blood. The official language is Spanish; about 0·15m. persons speak a Haitian-French Creole.

SOCIAL STATISTICS
1996 births, 190,000; deaths, 46,000. Rates, 1996: Birth, 23·5 (per 1,000 population); death, 5·7; infant mortality, 47·7 (per 1,000 live births). Annual growth rate, 1990–95, 2·0%. Life expectancy, 1996, 69 years. Fertility rate, 1990–95, 3·1 children per woman.

CLIMATE
A tropical maritime climate with most rain falling in the summer months. The rainy season extends from May to Nov. and amounts are greatest in the north and east. Hurricanes may occur from June to Nov. Santo Domingo, Jan. 75°F (23·9°C), July 81°F (27·2°C). Annual rainfall 56" (1,400 mm).

CONSTITUTION AND GOVERNMENT
The constitution dates from 28 Nov. 1966. The *President* is elected for 4 years, by direct vote, and has executive power. A constitutional amendment of Aug. 1994 prohibits the President from serving consecutive terms. In 1994 the constitution was amended to allow for a second round of voting in a presidential election, when no candidate secures an absolute majority in the first ballot. There is a bicameral legislature, the *Congress*, comprising a 30-member Senate (one member for each province and one for the National District of Santo Domingo) and a 149-member *Chamber of Deputies*, both elected for 4-year terms. Citizens are entitled to vote at the age of 18, or less when married.

National Anthem. 'Quisqueyanos valientes, alcemos' ('Valiant Quisqueyans, Let us raise our voices'); words by E. Prud'homme, tune by J. Reyes.

RECENT ELECTIONS
Presidential elections were held on 16 May 1996 with a run-off on 30 June 1996. Leonel Fernández Reyna was elected at the run-off by 51·25% of votes cast.

Parliamentary elections were held on 16 May 1998. In the election to the Chamber of Deputies, the Dominican Revolutionary Party (PRD) won 83 seats, the Dominican Liberation Party (PLD) 49 and the Social Christian Reformist Party (PRSC) 17. In the Senate elections on the same day, PRD gained 24 seats, PLD 4 and PRSC 2.

CURRENT ADMINISTRATION
President: Leonel Fernández Reyna (b. 1954; Dominican Liberation Party; sworn in 16 Aug. 1996).

Vice-President: Jaime Fernández Mirabal.

In March 1999 the government comprised:

Secretary of State for Agriculture: Amilcar Romero. *Armed Forces:* Maj. Gen. Manuel de Jesus Florentino. *Education, Fine Arts, and Public Worship:* Ligia Amada Melo de Cardona. *Finance:* Daniel Toribio. *Foreign Relations:* Eduardo Latorre Rodriguez. *Industry and Commerce:* Luis Manuel Bonetti. *Interior and Police:* Norge Botello. *Judicial Reform:* Ramon Andres Blanco Fernandez. *Labour:* Rafael Alburquerque de Castro. *Public Health and Social Welfare:* Altagracia

DOMINICAN REPUBLIC

Guzman. *Public Works and Communications:* Diandino Pena. *Sports, Physical Education and Recreation:* Juan Marichal. *Tourism:* Felix Jimenez. *The Presidency:* Danilo Medina. *Without Portfolio:* Lidio Cadet; Rafael Augusto Collado; Julian Serrule.

Local Government. The 29 provinces have a governor appointed by the President. They and the National District are divided into 18 municipal districts and 72 municipalities run by elected councils. Elections for mayors took place simultaneously with the presidential and parliamentary elections of May 1994.

DEFENCE
In 1997 defence expenditure totalled US$120m. (US$15 per capita).

Army. There are 3 defence zones. The Army has a strength (1997) of about 15,000. It is organized in 4 infantry brigades, 1 artillery, 1 engineer, 1 special forces and 1 armoured battalion and a Presidential Guard. Equipment includes 15 light tanks. There is a paramilitary National Police 15,000-strong.

Navy. The Navy is equipped with former US vessels. The combatant force consists of 1 frigate (built 1944) acting as the flagship, 6 offshore, 2 coastal and 8 inshore patrol craft. There is 1 utility landing craft, and support is provided by 1 small oiler, 1 ocean tug and some 12 harbour and service craft. Personnel in 1997 totalled 4,000, based at Santo Domingo and Calderas.

Air Force. The Air Force, with HQ at San Isidoro, has 1 combat squadron with 8 Cessna A-37s; 1 squadron with 6 Bell 205A-1, 1 Dauphin and 1 OH-6A helicopters; 1 transport squadron with 3 C-47s, 5 Cessna 337s and some smaller communications aircraft; and 10 T-34B Mentor and 5 Cessna T-41 trainers. Personnel strength (1997), 5,500.

INTERNATIONAL RELATIONS
The Dominican Republic is a member of the UN and OAS, and an ACP member of the EU.

ECONOMY
Policy. In Jan. 1995 subsidies to the 33 state companies were discontinued. 20 state companies were put up for sale in Nov. 1995.

Performance. Real GDP growth was 4·7% in 1995 (4·3% in 1994).

Budget. Central government budgetary revenue and expenditure in RD$1m. for calendar years:

	1992	1993	1994	1995	1996
Revenue	17,516·4	19,677·8	21,076·4	24,781·7	26,396·4
Expenditure	12,968·2	18,887·0	21,025·4	21,784·8	25,030·2

Tax revenue in 1995 was RD$22,642·7m.; non-tax revenue, RD$2,079·6m.; capital revenue, RD$59·4m.

Currency. The unit of currency is the *peso* (DOP) of 100 *centavos*. Gold reserves were 20,000 troy oz. in Feb. 1998 and foreign exchange reserves were US$335m. Total money supply was RD$22,745m. in Feb. 1998. The average annual inflation rate during the period 1990–96 was 12·3%.

Banking and Finance. In 1947 the Central Bank was established (*Governor*, Hector Váldez Albizú). Its total assets were RD$34,958·7m. in 1993. In 1993 there were 20 commercial banks (2 foreign); total assets, RD$30,765·5m.
    The Santo Domingo Securities Exchange is a member of the Association of Central American Stock Exchanges (Bolcen).

Weights and Measures. The metric system was adopted on 1 Aug. 1913, but English and Spanish units have remained in common use.

ENERGY AND NATURAL RESOURCES
Electricity. Installed capacity was 2,450 MW in 1995. Production was 6·51bn. kWh in 1995; consumption per capita in 1995 was estimated to be 613 kWh.

Minerals. Bauxite output in 1988 was 167,800 tonnes, but had declined to nil by 1992. Output, 1992: Ferro-nickel, 58,313 tonnes; gold, 76,349 troy oz.; silver, 478,320 troy oz.

Agriculture. Agriculture and processing are the chief sources of income, sugar cultivation being the principal industry. In 1996 agriculture accounted for 13% of GDP. In 1994 there were 1·01m. ha of arable land, 0·47m. ha of permanent cropland and 2·1m. ha of pasture.

Production, 1994 (in 1,000 tonnes): Sugar-cane, 7,000 (6,916 in 1992); cocoa beans, 57; coffee, 39; bananas, 550; rice (paddy), 533; tobacco (leaves), 18 (20 in 1992); dry beans, 48; maize, 57; tomatoes, 102.

Livestock in 1996: 2·43m. cattle, 950,000 pigs, 570,000 goats (1995), 34m. chickens (1995). Livestock products, 1994 (in tonnes): Poultry meat, 0·13m.; beef and veal, 90,000; eggs, 43,900; milk, 385,000.

Forestry. Forests and woodlands covered 1·58m. ha in 1995, representing 32·7% of the total land area (down from 1·71m. ha and 35·4% in 1990). In 1995, 982,000 tonnes of timber were cut.

Fisheries. The total catch in 1995 was 20,183 tonnes, of which 16,153 tonnes were from sea fishing.

INDUSTRY
Manufacturing contributed 17% of GDP in 1991. Production, 1992 (in tonnes): Raw sugar, 427,950; refined sugar, 90,021; cement, 1,364,877; paint, 16,328; beer, 195·64m. litres; rum, 43·41m. litres; cigarettes, 220,203 packets (of 20).

Labour. In 1996 the labour force was 3,379,000 (71% males). Average monthly wage, 1992, RD$2,136·98.

INTERNATIONAL TRADE
In 1994 there were 38 industrial free zones (employing 164,296 persons), which enjoy duty-free imports of raw materials and various tax exemptions. Legislation of 1995 allows foreign investments of 100% in all sectors except industries affecting the environment and arms production. Profits may be repatriated. Foreign debt was US$4,310m. in 1996.

Imports and Exports. Total imports and exports in US$1m.:

	1992	1993	1994	1995	1996
Imports	2,501	2,436	2,626	2,976	3,686
Exports	562	511	633	765	815

Main exports, 1993 (in tonnes): Raw sugar, 342,197 (513,920 in 1988); molasses, 176,234; coffee, 18,079; cocoa, 42,077; tobacco, 11,410; ferro-nickel, 67,405; gold, 11,718 troy oz. (139,969 troy oz. in 1990); silver, 53,496 troy oz. (734,987 troy oz. in 1990). Main imports (in US$1m.): Oil and products, 453; coal, 10·3; foodstuffs, 11·6; wheat, 38·1.

Main export markets (% of trade), 1994: USA, 46·6%; Germany, 5·9%; Canada, 4·8%; Belgium, 4·6%. Main import suppliers: USA, 65·2%; Mexico, 7%; Venezuela, 6·8%; Japan, 6·3%.

COMMUNICATIONS
Roads. The road network in 1996 totalled 12,600 km, of which 6,200 km were surfaced. In 1996 there were 224,000 passenger cars (27 per 1,000 inhabitants), 137,000 trucks and vans, and 14,550 buses and coaches.

Rail. In 1995 the total length was 757 km, comprising 375 km of the Central Romana Railroad, 142 km of the Dominican Government Railway between Guayubin and the port of Pepillo, and 240 km operated by the sugar industry.

Civil Aviation. There are international airports at Santo Domingo (Las Americas), Puerto Plata, La Romana and Punta Cana. Dominican Airlines ceased operations in 1995 and was put up for privatization. Aerolíneas Santo Domingo and Air Atlantic Dominicana operate scheduled domestic services, with international services in 1998 also being provided by ACES, Aerolíneas Argentinas, Aeroperú, Aeropostal Alas de Venezuela, Air Europa, Air France, Alitalia, ALM, American Airlines, AOM, APA

International Air, Condor Flugdienst, Continental Airlines, COPA, Cubana, Hapag Lloyd, Iberia, LACSA, Lan-Chile, LTU International Airways, Martinair Holland, SAM, TAP, TCI Skyking and TWA. In 1996 Santo Domingo was the busiest airport, handling 2,190,448 passengers, followed by Puerto Plata (1,423,036 passengers) and Punta Cana (891,385).

Shipping. The main ports are Santo Domingo, Puerto Plata, La Romana and Haina. In 1995 the merchant marine totalled 2,833 GRT. In 1994 vessels totalling 10,821,000 net registered tons entered and vessels totalling 10,683,000 NRT cleared.

Telecommunications. In 1997 there were 709,200 telephone main lines in use (87·6 for every 1,000 inhabitants). Cellular phone subscribers numbered 33,000 in 1995, and there were 2,500 fax machines.

Postal Services. In 1995 there were 215 post offices.

SOCIAL INSTITUTIONS

Justice. The judicial power resides in the Supreme Court of Justice, the courts of appeal, the courts of first instance, the communal courts and other tribunals created by special laws, such as the land courts. The Supreme Court consists of a president and 8 judges chosen by the Senate, and the procurator-general, appointed by the executive; it supervises the lower courts. Each province forms a judicial district, as does the National District, and each has its own procurator fiscal and court of first instance; these districts are subdivided, in all, into 97 municipalities, each with one or more local justices. The death penalty was abolished in 1924.

Religion. The religion of the state is Roman Catholic; there were 6·78m. adherents in 1992.

Education. Primary instruction is free and compulsory for children between 7 and 14 years of age; there are also secondary, normal, vocational and special schools, all of which are either wholly maintained by the State or state-aided. In 1995–96 there were 4,001 primary schools with 42,135 teachers for 1·4m. pupils, and 263,236 pupils at secondary level with 12,054 teachers. There are 4 universities, 3 Roman Catholic universities, 1 Adventist university, 3 technological universities and 1 Roman Catholic university college, and 5 other higher education institutions. Adult literacy was 82·1% in 1995 (male, 82%; female, 82·2%).

In 1994 total expenditure on education came to 1·9% of GNP and represented 12·2% of total government expenditure.

Health. In 1992 there were 11,130 doctors, 1,898 dentists and 6,035 nurses. There were 723 government hospitals in 1992.

CULTURE

Broadcasting. There were (1994) more than 170 broadcasting stations in Santo Domingo and other towns; this includes the 2 government stations. There were 7 television stations (colour by NTSC). In 1995 there were 1·38m. radio and 728,000 television receivers.

Press. In 1995 there were 11 dailies with a combined circulation of 264,000.

Tourism. There were 1,926,000 foreign tourists in 1996, spending US$1·75bn.

DIPLOMATIC REPRESENTATIVES
Of the Dominican Republic in Great Britain (139 Inverness Terrace, London, W2 6JF)
Ambassador: Dr Pedro L. Padilla Tonos.

Of Great Britain in the Dominican Republic (Edificio Corominas Pepin, Ave. 27 de Febrero 233, Santo Domingo)
Ambassador: Vacant.

Of the Dominican Republic in the USA (1715 22nd St., NW, Washington, D.C., 20008)
Ambassador: Bernardo Vega.

Of the USA in the Dominican Republic (Calle Cesar Nicolas Penson, Santo Domingo)
Ambassador: Vacant.

Of the Dominican Republic to the United Nations
Ambassador: Cristina Aguiar.

Of the Dominican Republic to the European Union
Ambassador: Clara Quiñones.

FURTHER READING

Atkins, G. P., *Arms and Politics in the Dominican Republic.* London, 1981

Bell, I., *The Dominican Republic.* London, 1980

Black, J. K., *The Dominican Republic: Politics and Development in an Unsovereign State.* London, 1986

Schoenhals, K., *Dominican Republic* [Bibliography]. London and Santa Barbara (CA), 1990

Wiarda, H. J. and Kryzanek, M. J., *The Dominican Republic: A Caribbean Crucible.* Boulder, 1982

National statistical office: Oficina Nacional de Estadistica, Edificio de Oficinas Gubernamentales 'Juan Pablo Duarte', 8 y 9 piso, Avenida México, Santo Domingo.
Website: http://www.estadistica.gov.do/

ECUADOR

República del Ecuador

Capital: Quito
Population estimate, 2000: 12·65m.
GNP per capita: (PPP$) 4,730
HDI/world rank: 0·767/73

KEY HISTORICAL EVENTS

The Incas of Peru conquered this territory in the 15th century but in 1532 the Spaniards, under Francisco Pizarro, founded a colony in Ecuador, then called Quito. This colony was in turn part of the viceroyalty of Peru and then of New Granada. Spanish rule was first challenged by the rising of Aug. 1809. In 1821 a revolt under Marshal Sucre led to the defeat of the Spaniards at Pichincha in 1821, and thus the winning of independence from Spain. In 1822 Bolivar persuaded the new republic to join the federation of Gran Colombia. However, in 1830 Ecuador left this federation and on 13 March 1830 became the Republic of Ecuador instead of the Presidency of Quito. For 100 years thereafter, considerable difficulty was found in creating a stable régime as presidents and dictators followed one another. Since 1948 first President Galo Plazo Lasso (1948-52) and then President José María Velasco Ibarra (1934-35, 1944-47, 1952-56, 1960-61, 1968-72) gave more continuity to the presidential régimes, although the last named was deposed by military *coups* from four of his five presidencies.

From 1963 to 1966 and from 1976 to 1979 military juntas ruled the country. The second of these juntas produced a new constitution which was accepted by a national referendum in Jan. 1978 and came into force on 10 Aug. 1979. A new Congress was elected, and Jaime Roldós Aguilera was elected president. Since then presidencies have been more stable, although President Roldós Aguilera (1979-81) died in an air crash. A state of emergency was declared in March 1986 when Gen. Frank Vargas Pazos led an anti-government revolt at Quito airbase but this ended quickly.

Civil unrest continued in the wake of economic reforms and attempts to combat political corruption. A serious crisis developed in 1995 when Vice President Alberto Dahik was accused of bribing opposition deputies and was forced to leave the country.

Following his election in July 1996, Congress deposed President Bucarám on 6 Feb. 1997 on the grounds of mental incompetence and elected the Speaker, Fabián Alarcón, as President. The deposition of former President Bucarám and the incumbency of President Alarcón were ratified by referendum on 25 May 1997.

In July 1998 Jamil Mahuad of the centre-right Popular Democracy party won the presidential election amidst allegations of vote rigging and fraud.

TERRITORY AND POPULATION

Ecuador is bounded in the north by Colombia, in the east and south by Peru and in the west by the Pacific ocean. The frontier with Peru has long been a source of dispute. The latest delimitation of it was in the treaty of Rio, 29 Jan. 1942, when, after being invaded by Peru, Ecuador lost over half her Amazonian territories. Ecuador unilaterally denounced this treaty in Sept. 1961. Fighting between Peru and Ecuador began again in Jan. 1981 over this border issue but a ceasefire was agreed in early Feb. Following a confrontation of soldiers in Aug. 1991 the foreign ministers of both countries signed a pact creating a security zone, and took their cases to the UN in Oct. 1991. On 26 Jan. 1995 further armed clashes broke out with Peruvian forces in the undemarcated mutual border area ('Cordillera del Cóndor'). On 2 Feb. talks were held under the auspices of the guarantor nations of the 1942 Protocol of Rio de Janeiro (Argentina, Brazil, Chile and the USA), but fighting continued. Ceasefires were agreed on 17 Feb. which were broken, and on 28 Feb. On 25 July 1995 an agreement between Ecuador and Peru established a demilitarized zone along their joint frontier. The frontier was re-opened on 4 Sept. 1995. Since 23 Feb. 1996 Ecuador and Peru have signed 3 further agreements to regulate the dispute. The dispute was settled in Oct. 1998. Confirming the Peruvian claim that the border lies along the high peaks of the Cóndor, Ecuador gained navigation rights on the Amazon within Peru.

ECUADOR

No definite figure of the area of the country can yet be given. One estimate of the area of Ecuador is 275,830·0 sq. km, excluding the litigation zone between Peru and Ecuador, which is 190,807 sq. km, but including the **Galápagos** Archipelago (8,010 sq. km), situated in the Pacific ocean about 960 km west of Ecuador, and comprising 13 islands and 19 islets. These were discovered in 1535 by Fray Tomás de Berlanga and had a population of 10,207 in 1996. They constitute a national park, and had about 80,000 visitors in 1995.

The population is an amalgam of European, Amerindian and African origins. Some 40% of the population is Amerindian: Quechua, Swiwiar, Achuar and Zaparo. In May 1992 they were granted title to the 1m. ha of land they occupy in Pastaza.

The official language is Spanish. Quechua and other languages are also spoken.

Census population in 1990, 9,648,189. Estimate, 1996, 11,698,400; density, 42 per sq. km.

The UN gives a projected population for 2000 of 12·65m.

In 1995, 58·9% lived in urban areas.

The population was distributed by provinces as follows in 1996:

Province	Sq. km	Population	Capital	Population[1]
Azuay	8,124·7	529,177	Cuenca	194,981
Bolívar	3,939·9	166,957	Guaranda	15,730
Cañar	3,122·1	194,529	Azogues	21,060
Carchi	3,605·1	146,343	Tulcán	37,069
Chimborazo	6,569·3	378,111	Riobamba	94,505
Cotopaxi	6,071·9	289,774	Latacunga	39,882
El Oro	5,850·1	441,025	Machala	144,197
Esmeraldas	15,239·1	327,931	Esmeraldas	98,558
Guayas	20,502·5	2,689,745	Guayaquil	1,508,444
Imbabura	4,559·3	286,155	Ibarra	80,991
Loja	11,026·5	392,877	Loja	94,305
Los Ríos	7,175·0	553,479	Babahoyo	50,285
Manabi	18,878·8	1,076,966	Portoviejo	132,937
Pichincha	12,914·7	1,893,744	Quito	1,100,847
Sucumbíos	18,327·5	90,222	Nueva Loja	13,165
Tungurahua	3,334·8	383,460	Ambato	124,166
Napo	33,930·9	114,380	Tena	7,873
Pastaza	29,773·7	46,095	Puyo	14,438
Morona-Santiago	25,690·0	104,737	Macas	8,246
Zamora-Chinchipe	23,110·8	73,383	Zamora	8,048
Galápagos	8,010·0	10,207	Puerto Baquerizo Moreno	3,023
Non-delimited zones	2,288·8	74,842		

[1]1990 census population.

SOCIAL STATISTICS

1995: Births, 408,983; deaths, 50,867; marriages, 70,480. Rates, 1995 (per 1,000 population): Birth, 35·7; death, 4·4; marriage, 6·2. Life expectancy at birth, 1990–95, was 66·4 years for males and 71·4 years for females. Annual growth rate, 1990–95, 2·2%. Infant mortality, 1990–95, 50 per 1,000 live births; fertility rate, 3·5 children per woman.

CLIMATE

The climate varies from equatorial, through warm temperate to mountain conditions, according to altitude, which affects temperatures and rainfall. In coastal areas, the dry season is from May to Dec., but only from June to Sept. in mountainous parts, where temperatures may be 20°F colder than on the coast. Quito, Jan. 59°F (15°C), July 58°F (14·4°C). Annual rainfall 44″ (1,115 mm). Guayaquil, Jan. 79°F (26·1°C), July 75°F (23·9°C). Annual rainfall 39″ (986 mm).

CONSTITUTION AND GOVERNMENT

A new Constitution came into force on 10 Aug. 1979. It provides for an executive President and a Vice-President to be directly elected for a non-renewable 4-year term by universal suffrage, with a further 'run-off' ballot being held between the two

ECUADOR

leading candidates where no-one has secured an absolute majority of the votes cast. The President appoints and leads a Council of Ministers. A referendum on constitutional reform was held in Nov. 1995. and in the election of Nov. 1997 Ecuador voted in favour of constitutional reform to strengthen the presidency and to limit the participation of the state in the economy.

Legislative power is vested in a 125-member *National Congress*, 105 members in 2- or multi-seat constituencies and 20 members elected at large by proportional representation. Voting is obligatory for all literate citizens of 18–65 years.

National Anthem. 'Salve, Oh Patria, mil veces, Oh Patria' ('Hail, Oh Fatherland, a thousand times, Oh Fatherland'); words by J. L. Mera, music by A. Neumane.

RECENT ELECTIONS
Dissatisfaction with President Fabián Alarcón led to presidential elections in 1998. Jamil Mahuad, candidate of the centre-right Popular Democracy party (DP), won in the second round of the presidential election on 12 July 1998, with 51·3% of the votes, against 48·7% for Alvaro Noboa, a populist businessman. In the first round on 31 May he had defeated 5 other candidates to win 35·3% of the vote.

In *National Congress* elections on 31 May 1998 the People's Democracy–Christian Democrat Union (DP-UDC) won 35 seats, the Social Christian Party (PSC) 26, Ecuadorian Roldosist Party (PRE) 25, the Party of the Democratic Left (ID) 17 and Pluri-National Pachakutik Movement–New Country (MUPP-NP) 6. No other party won more than 3 seats.

Elections to the 70-member *Constitutional Assembly* (members of the *National Congress*) were held on 30 Nov. 1997. The Social Christian Party won 20 seats and the People's Democracy–Christian Democrat Union 10 seats, with the remaining 40 seats going to 15 other parties.

CURRENT ADMINISTRATION
President: Jamil Mahuad, b. 1949 (Popular Democracy Party; elected 12 July 1998).
Vice President: Gustavo Noboa.
In March 1999 the government comprised:
Minister of Agriculture and Livestock: Emilio Gallardo. *Education and Culture:* Rosangela Adoum. *Energy and Mines:* Patricio Rivadeneira. *Environment:* Yolanda Cacabasse. *Finance and Credit:* Ana Lucia Armijos. *Foreign Relations:* José Ayala Lasso. *Government, Police and Municipality:* Vladimiro Alvarez Grau. *Industry and Trade:* Hector Plaza. *Tourism:* Rocio Vasquez. *National Defence:* José Gallardo. *Public Health:* Edgar Rodas. *Public Works:* Raul Samaniego. *Urban Development and Housing:* Teodoro Pena. *Labour:* Angel Chavez. *Social Welfare:* Guillermo Celi.

Local Government. The country is divided administratively into 21 provinces. The provinces are administered by governors, appointed by the Government; their sub-divisions, or cantons, by political chiefs and elected cantonal councillors; and the parishes by political lieutenants. The 21 provinces are made up of 193 cantons, 322 urban parishes and 757 rural parishes. Elections for 54 provincial and 608 municipal councillors were held in June 1994. Elections for all provincial governorships were last held on 19 May 1996.

DEFENCE
Military service is selective, with a 1-year period of conscription. The country is divided into 4 military zones, with headquarters at Quito, Guayaquil, Cuenca and Pastaza.

Defence expenditure totalled US$692m. in 1997 (US$57 per capita).

Army. The Army consists of 1 infantry division, 1 armoured, 2 infantry, 1 special forces and 3 'jungle' brigades, 1 aviation group, 1 air defence artillery group and 3 engineer battalions. Equipment includes 45 American M-3 and 108 French AMX-13 light tanks. The aviation element has about 30 transport and communications aircraft, including 12 helicopters. Strength (1997) 50,000, with about 100,000 reservists.

Navy. Navy combatant forces include 2 German-built diesel submarines, 2 ex-UK missile-armed Leander class frigates, 6 Italian-built missile corvettes (with helicopter deck) and 6 fast-missile craft. Amphibious capability is 1 landing ship and 6 small craft. Auxiliaries consist of 1 ex-German depot ship, 1 small tanker, 1 survey ship, 1 armament carrier, 2 tugs and 1 training ship as well as some 8 harbour and service vessels. The Maritime Air Force has 11 aircraft, including 1 CN-235 transport, 3 Cessna light aircraft, 3 T-34C trainers, and 4 Jet Ranger helicopters. Naval personnel in 1997 totalled 4,100 including some 1,500 marines.

There are 6 inshore Coast Guard cutters and some 20 boats.

Air Force. The Air Force had a 1997 strength of about 3,000 personnel and 60 combat aircraft, and includes a strike squadron equipped with 8 single-seat and 2 two-seat Jaguars; an interceptor squadron of 12 single-seat and 1 two-seat Mirage F.1; an interceptor squadron with 15 Kfirs; 3 counter-insurgency units equipped with 10 Cessna A-37B and 10 Strikemaster light jet attack and training aircraft, 1 squadron with 2 C-130, 1 Buffalo, 1 Twin Otter and 3 HS 748 turboprop transports; Alouette III, Bell 212, UH-1 Iroquois and SA 315B Lama helicopters; and Cessna 150, T-34C-1 and T-41A/D trainers. 1 F.28, 1 Boeing 737 and 3 Boeing 727 transports are operated by the military airline TAME.

INTERNATIONAL RELATIONS

There is a long-standing dispute with Peru over the Cordillera del Cóndor, which was awarded to Peru in 1942. After armed clashes throughout the 1990s, negotiations were under way to find a permanent solution to the border issue. A settlement was reached in Oct. 1998.

Ecuador is a member of the UN, OAS, the Andean Group and LAIA.

ECONOMY

Policy. A reform programme was announced in 1992, including the privatization of 20 state-owned enterprises. Further privatization legislation followed in 1993. A new economic plan was promulgated in Nov. 1996, envisaging privatization of the oil and electricity sectors, but in 1998 privatization was put on hold as the sale of 35% of state telecommunications companies was suspended in April 1998 owing to a lack of serious bidders.

Performance. Real GDP growth was 3·4% in 1997 with a forecast of −1·0% for 1998.

Budget. Total revenue and total expenditure from 1991 to 1995 (in 1bn. sucres) was as follows:

	1991	1992	1993	1994	1995
Revenue	1,907	3,096	4,371	5,374	8,030
Expenditure	1,739	3,145	4,166	5,717	8,451

The budget deficit in 1998 was nearly 6% of GDP.

Currency. The monetary unit is the *sucre* (ECS), of 100 *centavos*. The sucre was devalued by 8% in Aug. 1996. Inflation was 24% in 1996 and had risen to 43% by Dec. 1998. Economic reforms of Nov. 1996 envisaged the convertibility of the currency as from 1 July 1997, with the sucre pegged to the US dollar at US$1 = 4 sucres. Under the reform programme foreign exchange reserves must at least match currency in circulation. In Feb. 1998 foreign exchange reserves were US$1,957m. and gold reserves were 410,000 troy oz. Total money supply was 6,956m. sucres in Dec. 1997.

Banking and Finance. The Central Bank of Ecuador (*Governor*, Fidel Jaramillo), the bank of issue, with a capital and reserves of US$1,557m. at 31 Dec. 1995, is modelled after the Federal Reserve Banks of the USA; through branches opened in 16 towns, it now deals in mortgage bonds. All commercial banks must be affiliated to the Central Bank. Legislation of May 1994 liberalized the financial sector.

There are stock exchanges in Quito and Guayaquil.

Weights and Measures. The metric system is the legal standard but English and old Spanish measures are still in use. A case (*caja*) of bananas = 18·14 kg.

ENERGY AND NATURAL RESOURCES

Electricity. Installed capacity was 2·75m. kW in 1996. Production was 9·27bn. kWh in 1996 and consumption per capita in 1996 was 600 kWh.

Oil and Gas. Production of crude oil in 1995 was 141,151,000 bbls. Estimated reserves, 1997, 2,115m. bbls. In 1995 natural gas production was 102m. cu. metres.

Minerals. Main products are silver, gold, copper and zinc. The country also has some iron, uranium, lead, coal, cobalt, manganese and titanium.

Agriculture. In 1996 agriculture contributed 12% of GDP. In 1995, 28·8% of the economically active population worked in agriculture.

50,000 ha of rich virgin land in the Santo Domingo de los Colorados area has been set aside for settlement by medium and large landowners. A law of 1994 restricts the redistribution of land to small farmers to land which has lain fallow for more than 3 years.

The staple export products are bananas, cacao and coffee. Main crops, in 1,000 tonnes, in 1995: Rice, 1,291; potatoes, 477; maize, 613; barley (1994), 32; cocoa beans, 81; bananas, 5,086; coffee, 187; sugar-cane, 3,635.

Livestock, 1996: Cattle, 5·1m.; sheep, 1·71m.; pigs, 2·6m.; goats, 295,000 (1995); chickens, 62m. (1995).

Forestry. Excepting the agricultural zones and a few arid spots on the Pacific coast, Ecuador is a vast forest. 11·13m. ha, or 40·2% of the land area, was forested in 1995, but much of the forest is not commercially accessible. In 1990, 12·08m. ha and 43·6% of the land area had been under forests. In 1995, 10·36m. cu. metres of roundwood were produced.

Fisheries. In 1993 primary sea export products were valued at US$498·9m. Total catches in 1995 were 591,560 tonnes (about 97% from sea fishing).

INDUSTRY
Production in 1994 included: Residual fuel oils, 3·0m. tonnes; cement, 2·1m. tonnes.

Labour. Out of 2,697,000 people in employment in 1994, 815,000 were in trade, restaurants and hotels, 811,000 in community, social and personal services, and 415,000 in manufacturing industries.

Trade Unions. The main trade union federation is the United Workers' Front.

INTERNATIONAL TRADE
Most restrictions on foreign investment were removed in 1992 and the repatriation of profits was permitted. Foreign debt was US$14,491m. in 1996.

Imports and Exports. Imports and exports for calendar years, in US$1m.:

	1993	1994	1995	1996	1997
Imports	2,562	3,690	4,193	3,935	4,944
Exports	2,904	3,820	4,307	4,900	5,190

Ecuador is a major exporter of shrimps (US$673m. in 1995). Other major exports (1995, in US$1m.): Bananas, 845; coffee beans, 244; cocoa beans and products, 133; cut flowers, 79. Main export markets, 1995 (in US$1m.): USA, 1,847 (42%); Colombia, 246; Chile, 193; Germany, 166; Spain, 149. Main import suppliers: USA, 1,290 (32%); Colombia, 396; Japan, 328; Germany, 192; Brazil, 187.

COMMUNICATIONS
Roads. In 1996 there were estimated to be 43,249 km of roads (5,752 km surfaced). A trunk highway through the coastal plain will link Machala in the extreme south-west with Esmeraldas in the north-west, and with Quito and the northern section of the Pan-American Highway; in 1994, 1,214 km had been built and 273 km were under construction. In 1996 there were 485,000 passenger cars (41 per 1,000 inhabitants) and 44,550 commercial vehicles.

In 1998 storms and floods on the coast, caused by El Niño, resulted in 2,000 km of roads being damaged or destroyed.

Rail. The railway was closed in 1995.

Civil Aviation. There are international airports at Quito (Mariscal Sucre) and Guayaquil (Simon Bolivar). The national carriers are Ecuatoriana, SAETA, SAN and Tame Linea Aerea del Ecuador. In 1998 services were also provided by ACES,

Aeroperú, Air France, American Airlines, Avianca, Continental Airlines, COPA, Cubana, Iberia, KLM, LACSA, Lloyd Aéreo Boliviano, SAM, Servivensa and VASP. In 1995 Quito handled 2,039,000 passengers (1,386,000 on domestic flights) and 59,200 tonnes of freight, and Guayaquil handled 1,305,000 passengers (927,000 on domestic flights) and 44,200 tonnes of freight.

Shipping. Ecuador has 3 major seaports, of which Guayaquil is the most important, and 6 minor ones. In 1995 the merchant navy totalled 0·36m. GRT of ocean-going vessels, including oil tankers, 0·13m. In 1994 vessels totalling 28,976,000 net registered tons entered ports.

Telecommunications. In 1997 there were 898,600 main telephone lines, or 75·3 for every 1,000 persons. Cellular phone subscribers numbered 50,000 in 1995, there were 45,000 PCs in use and 30,000 fax machines. There were approximately 5,000 Internet users in Oct. 1997.

Postal Services. In 1995 there were 267 post offices.

SOCIAL INSTITUTIONS

Justice. The Supreme Court in Quito, consisting of a President and 30 Justices, comprises 6 chambers each of 5 Justices. It is also a Court of Appeal. There is a Superior Court in each province, comprising chambers (as appointed by the Supreme Court) of 3 magistrates each. The Superior Courts are at the apex of a hierarchy of various tribunals. There is no death penalty.

Religion. The state recognizes no religion and grants freedom of worship to all. In 1993 there were 10·21m. Roman Catholics.

Education. In 1995–96 there were 158,679 pre-primary pupils with 9,278 teachers. Primary education is free and compulsory. Private schools, both primary and secondary, are under some state supervision. In 1995 there were 16,868 primary schools and 2,965 secondary schools. In 1995–96 there were 1,793,882 pupils and 70,001 teachers in primary schools. In the public sector in 1995–96 there were: 9 universities, 3 Roman Catholic, 12 technical, 1 agricultural and 2 polytechnical universities, 2 institutes of technology and 1 military polytechnic; and in the private sector: 2 universities, 1 Roman Catholic and 1 technological university. Adult literacy was 90·1% in 1995 (male, 92%; female, 88·2%).

Health. In 1993 there were 12,149 doctors and 433 hospitals, 1,542 dentists and 906 pharmacists.

CULTURE

Broadcasting. There were 3·8m. radios and 1·1m. TV receivers in 1995 (colour by NTSC).

Cinema. In 1991 there were 134 cinemas with an annual attendance of 6·8m.

Press. There were 24 daily newspapers in 1995, with a circulation of 800,000.

Tourism. Foreign tourists numbered 500,000 in 1996, with spending of US$281m.

DIPLOMATIC REPRESENTATIVES

Of Ecuador in Great Britain (Flat 3b, 3 Hans Cres., London, SW1X 0LS)
Ambassador: Oswaldo Ramirez Landazuri.

Of Great Britain in Ecuador (Calle González Suárez 111, Casilla 314, Quito)
Ambassador: John William Forbes-Meyler, OBE.

Of Ecuador in the USA (2535 15th St., NW, Washington, D.C., 20009)
Ambassador: Alberto Maspons.

Of the USA in Ecuador (Avenida 12 de Octubre y Avenida Patria, Quito)
Ambassador: Leslie Alexander.

Of Ecuador to the United Nations
Ambassador: Luis Valencia Rodríguez.

Of Ecuador to the European Union
Ambassador: Alfredo Pinoargote Cevallos.

FURTHER READING

Corkill, D., *Ecuador.* [Bibliography] Oxford and Santa Barbara (CA), 1989
Hidrobo, J. A., *Power and Industrialization in Ecuador.* Boulder (CO), 1993
Martz, J. D., *Ecuador: Conflicting Political Culture and the Quest for Progress.* Boston, 1972.—*Politics and Petroleum in Ecuador.* New Brunswick, 1987

National statistical office: Instituto Nacional de Estadistica y Censos (INEC), Juan Larrea 534 y Riofrío, Quito.
Website: http://www4.inec.gov.ec/

EGYPT

Jumhuriyat Misr al-Arabiya

(Arab Republic of Egypt)

Capital: Cairo
Population estimate, 2000: 68·12m.
GNP per capita: (PPP$) 2,860
HDI/world rank: 0·612/112

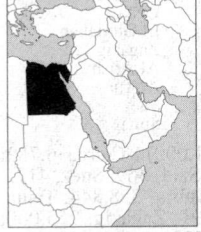

KEY HISTORICAL EVENTS

Egypt was part of the Ottoman Empire from 1517 until 1922 when it achieved independence, albeit qualified, from Britain, which had exercised direct control over Egyptian affairs since occupying the country in 1882. Muhammad Ali (1805–40) succeeded in establishing a hereditary dynasty of Khedives but with the opening of the Suez Canal in 1869 and Britain's purchase of the Khedives' shares, Egypt's strategic importance paved the way for foreign intervention and domination. In 1914 the country became a British protectorate and the Khedive was deposed. On 28 Feb. 1922 Egypt was declared an independent constitutional monarchy.

In the Second World War (1939–45) Egypt supported the Allies. Following a revolution in July 1952 led by Gen. Neguib, King Farouk abdicated in favour of his son but in 1953 the monarchy was abolished. Neguib became president but encountered opposition from the military when he attempted to move towards a parliamentary republic. Col. Gamal Abdel Nasser seized power and Neguib resigned. Nasser became head of state on 14 June 1954 (president from 1956), and remained in office until he died on 28 Sept. 1970. In 1956 Egypt nationalized the Suez Canal, a move which led Britain, France and Israel to mount military attacks against Egypt until forced by the UN and the USA to withdraw.

In 1958 Egypt and Syria united to form the United Arab Republic (UAR), but Syria withdrew in 1961. For ten years Egypt retained the name UAR but a new constitution, approved by a referendum on 11 Sept. 1971, renamed the country the Arab Republic of Egypt.

The 1960s and 1970s saw constant conflict with Israel until President Muhammad Anwar Sadat, who succeeded Nasser, made a dramatic peace treaty with Israel in March 1979. Sadat was assassinated on 6 Oct. 1981, and was succeeded by the vice-president, Lieut.-Gen. Muhammad Hosni Mubarak.

TERRITORY AND POPULATION

Egypt is bounded in the east by Israel and Palestine, the Gulf of Aqaba and the Red Sea, south by Sudan, west by Libya and north by the Mediterranean. The total area is 997,739 sq. km, but the cultivated and settled area, that is, the Nile Valley, Delta and oases, covers only 35,189 sq. km. Population density in this latter, 1992, 1,557·9 per sq. km. In 1995 an estimated 55·4% of the population were rural. In 1997 the population was 61,404,000 (of whom 98% live in the Nile Valley and Delta).

The UN gives a projected population for 2000 of 68·12m.

2·3m. Egyptians were living abroad in 1997.

Area, population and capitals of the governorates (1986 census and 1995 estimate):

Governorate	Area (in sq. km)	Population (1986 census)	1995 estimate (in 1,000)	Capital
Alexandria	2,679·36	2,917,327	3,431	Alexandria
Aswan	678·50	801,408	1,042	Aswan
Asyut	1,553·00	2,223,034	2,843	Asyut
Behera	10,129·49	3,257,168	3,973	Damanhur
Beni Suef	1,321·65	1,442,981	1,836	Beni Suef
Cairo	214·20	6,052,836	6,955	Cairo
Dakahlia	3,470·90	3,500,470	4,226	Mansura
Damietta	589·17	741,264	898	Damietta
Fayum	1,827·15	1,544,047	1,995	Fayum
Gharbia	1,942·21	2,870,960	3,437	Tanta
Giza	1,058·20	3,700,054	4,525	Giza
Ismailia	1,441·59	544,427	681	Ismailia
Kafr El Shaikh	3,437·12	1,800,129	2,266	Kafr El Shaikh

EGYPT

Governorate	Area (in sq. km)	Population (1986 census)	1995 estimate (in 1,000)	Capital
Kalyubia	1,001·09	2,514,244	3,045	Benha
Matruh	212,112·00	160,567	186	Matruh
Menia	2,261·72	2,648,043	3,372	Menia
Menufia	1,532·13	2,227,087	2,672	Shibin Al Kom
New Valley	376,505·00	113,838	136	Al Kharija
Port Said	72·01	399,793	467	Port Said
Qena	1,850·70	2,252,315	2,766	Qena
Red Sea	203,685·00	90,491	115	El Gurdakah
Sharkia	4,179·55	3,420,119	4,220	Zagazig
North Sinai	27,574·00	171,505	219	Al Arish
South Sinai	33,140·00	28,988	35	At Tur
Suez	17,840·42	326,820	411	Suez
Suhag	1,547·21	2,455,134	3,067	Suhag

Principal cities, with estimated 1998 populations (in 1,000): Cairo, 6,789; Alexandria, 3,328; Giza, 4,779; Shubra Al Khayma, 811; Port Said, 469; Suez, 417.

Smaller cities, with 1986 census populations: Mahalla Al Kubra, 358,844; Tanta, 334,505; Hulwan, 328,000; Mansura, 316,870; Asyut, 273,191; Zagazig, 255,000; Kafr Ad Dawwar, 223,000; Ismailia, 212,567; Fayum, 212,523; Aswan, 191,461; Damanhur, 190,840; Menia, 179,136; Beni Suef, 151,813; Uqsur (Luxor), 138,000; Suhag, 132,965; Shibin Al Kom, 132,751; Qena, 119,794; Benha, 115,571; Damietta, 113,000; Kafr Ash Shaikh, 102,910.

The official language is Arabic, although French and English are widely spoken.

SOCIAL STATISTICS
Births, 1995, 1,701,000 (27·4 per 1,000 population); deaths, 472,000 (7·6). Marriages, 1994, 530,000 (rate per 1,000 population, 9·1); divorces, 90,000 (1·5). Annual growth rate, 1990–95, 2·5%. In 1991 the average family size was 4·3 and 40% of the population was under 40 years. Life expectancy at birth, 1990–95, was 62·4 years for males and 64·8 years for females. Infant mortality, 1997, 53 per 1,000 live births; fertility rate, 3·3 births per woman.

CLIMATE
The climate is mainly dry, but there are winter rains along the Mediterranean coast. Elsewhere, rainfall is very low and erratic in its distribution. Winter temperatures are comfortable everywhere, but summer temperatures are very high, especially in the south. Cairo, Jan. 56°F (13·3°C), July 83°F (28·3°C). Annual rainfall 1·2" (28 mm). Alexandria, Jan. 58°F (14·4°C), July 79°F (26·1°C). Annual rainfall 7" (178 mm). Aswan, Jan. 62°F (16·7°C), July 92°F (33·3°C). Annual rainfall trace. Giza, Jan. 55°F (12·8°C), July 78°F (25·6°C). Annual rainfall 16" (389 mm). Ismailia, Jan. 56°F (13·3°C), July 84°F (28·9°C). Annual rainfall 1·5" (37 mm). Luxor, Jan. 59°F (15°C), July 86°F (30°C). Annual rainfall (trace). Port Said, Jan. 58°F (14·4°C), July 78°F (27·2°C). Annual rainfall 3" (76 mm).

CONSTITUTION AND GOVERNMENT
The Constitution was approved by referendum on 11 Sept. 1970. It defines Egypt as 'an Arab Republic with a democratic, socialist system' and the Egyptian people as 'part of the Arab nation'. The *President* is nominated by the People's Assembly and confirmed by plebiscite for a 6-year term. The President may appoint 1 or more *Vice-Presidents*. The *People's Assembly* is a unicameral legislature consisting of 444 members directly elected from 222 constituencies for a 5-year term, and 10 members appointed by the President. There is a *Constitutional Court*.

The President appoints the Prime Minister and a Council of Ministers. It is traditional for 2 ministers to be Coptic Christians.

A 210-member consultative body, the *Shura Council*, was established in 1980. Two-thirds of its members are elected and one-third appointed by the President.

National Anthem. 'Biladi' ('My homeland'); words and tune by S. Darwish.

RECENT ELECTIONS
Elections for the People's Assembly were held in 2 rounds on 29 Nov. and 6 Dec. 1995. The electorate was 21m.; turn-out was 50%. 3,980 candidates representing 14

parties stood. The National Democratic Party (NDP) gained 317 seats; ind (mainly NDP sympathizers), 113; Wafd, 6; Al-Tagamu, 5; Nasserites, 1; Liberal Socialists, 1, Labour Party, 1.

109 results were challenged by the Constitutional Court.

CURRENT ADMINISTRATION

President: Hosni Mubarak, b. 1928 (NDP; sworn in for a third term Oct. 1993).

A new government was formed on 4 Jan. 1996, which comprised in March 1999:

Prime Minister, Minister of Planning and International Co-operation: Dr Kamal El Ganzouri (b. 1934).

Deputy Prime Minister and Minister of Agriculture and Land Reclamation: Dr Youssouf Amin Wali. *Transport and Telecommunication, Maritime Transport, Civil Aviation:* Soliman Metwalli Suliman. *Electricity and Energy:* Mohamed Maher Abaza. *Defence and Military Production:* Fld. Mar. Mohamed Hussein Tantawi. *Information:* Mohamed Safwat El-Sherief. *Foreign Affairs:* Amr Mahmoud Moussa. *Public Enterprises:* Dr Atef Mohammad Ebeid. *Justice:* Counsellor Farouk Seif El-Nasr. *Culture:* Farouk Abdel Aziz Hosni. *Rural Development:* Dr Mahmoud Sayed Ahmed Sherif. *Labour:* Ahmed El-Emawi. *Trade and Supply:* Dr Ahmed Al-Guwaili. *Finance:* Dr Mohidin Abu Bakr El-Ghareeb. *Religious Affairs (Waqfs):* Mahmoud Hamdi Zakzouk. *Industry:* Suliman Reda Ali Soliman. *Health and Population:* Dr Ismail Awad-Allah Sallam. *Economy:* Dr Youssef Boutros Ghali. *Education:* Dr Hussein Kamal Baha'eddin. *Petroleum:* Dr Hamdi Abdel Wahab El-Banbi. *Interior:* Habib Ibrahim Al-Adly. *Tourism:* Mohammad Ahmed Mamdouh El-Beltagi. *Public Works and Water Resources:* Mahmoud Abd Al-Halim Abu-Zeid. *Housing, Utilities, Reconstruction and New Communities:* Dr Mohammad Ibrahim Soliman. *Higher Education and Scientific Research:* Dr Munfid Shinab. *Social Insurance and Social Affairs:* Dr Mervat Mehana Talawi. *People's Assembly and Shura Council Affairs:* Kamal Mohammad El-Shazli. *Administrative Development:* Dr Mohammad Zaki Abu Amer. *Environment:* Dr Nadia Riad Makrum Ebeid. *Local Administration:* Mahmud Sayid Ahmad Sharif. *Cabinet Affairs:* Talaat Hammad.

Local Government. The 26 governorates are divided into districts (*mudiriya*) and communes. Provincial governors are nominated by the President. Municipal elections were held on 3 Nov. 1992.

DEFENCE

Conscription is selective, and for 3 years. Military expenditure totalled US$2,743m. in 1997 (US$45 per capita), representing 4·3% of GDP.

Army. There are 4 military districts and 2 Army headquarters. The Army comprises 1 infantry, 4 armoured and 7 mechanized infantry divisions; 1 Republican Guard, 4 independent armoured, 2 independent infantry, 4 independent mechanized, 1 air mobile, 1 parachute, 15 independent artillery and 2 surface-to-surface missile brigades; and 6 commando groups. Equipment includes 840 T-54/-55, 500 T-62, 1,700 M-60 and 260 Ramses II (modified T-54/55) main battle tanks. Strength (1997) 320,000 (250,000 conscripts).

Navy. 2 of the current submarine force of 6 old ex-Soviet and ex-Chinese 'Romeo' class submarines have been modernized in the USA. Major surface combatants include 1 very old destroyer, 2 Spanish-built, 2 Chinese-built missile-armed frigates and 2 ex-US Knox class. There are also 25 missile craft of mixed British, Soviet and Chinese origin and 18 coastal and inshore patrol craft. A small shore-based naval aviation branch operates 5 Sea King and 9 Gazelle helicopters. Mine warfare forces include 7 coastal minesweepers and 3 inshore minehunters. 3 ex-Soviet medium landing ships provide amphibious lift supported by 11 minor landing craft. There are 6 major auxiliaries and some 14 minor service vessels. There are naval bases at Alexandria, Port Said, Mersa Matruh, Port Tewfik, Hurghada and Safaqa. Naval personnel in 1997 totalled 20,000. An associated para-military coastguard about 2,000 strong operates 33 inshore cutters and numerous boats.

Air Force. Until 1979 the Air Force was equipped largely with aircraft of USSR design, but subsequent re-equipment involves aircraft bought in the West, as well as some supplied by China. Strength (1997) is about 80,000 personnel (50,000 conscripts), over 100 attack helicopters and 420 combat aircraft, of which the interceptors are operated by an independent Air Defence Command, in conjunction with many 'Guideline', 'Goa', 'Gainful', Hawk and Crotale missile batteries. The interceptor/ground attack fighter divisions are equipped with 150 F-16 Fighting Falcons, 50 Mirage 5s, 32 F-4E Phantoms, 19 Mirage 2000s, 70 F-6s (Chinese-built MiG-19s), 14 Alpha Jets and 60 F-7s (Chinese-built MiG-21s). Airborne early warning capability is provided by 5 E-2C Hawkeyes. Transport units have 22 C-130H Hercules turboprop heavy freighters, 5 An-12s, 9 twin-turboprop Buffaloes, 4 Beech 1900s, and over 175 Gazelle, AH-64 Apache, Mi-8, Commando and Agusta-built CH-47C helicopters; some Commando helicopters, Beech 1900s and 2 EC-130H Hercules are equipped for electronic warfare duties. Training units are equipped with Embraer Tucanos, Czech-built L-39 Albatros and French-designed Alpha Jet jet trainers, two-seat FT-6s, Mirage 5s and UH-12E helicopters. Main aircrew training centre is the Air Force Academy at Bilbeis.

INTERNATIONAL RELATIONS
Egypt is a member of the UN, OAU, Arab League and OAPEC (Organization of Arab Petroleum Exporting Countries).

ECONOMY
Policy. A privatization programme which began in 1993 envisaged the sale of 85 out of the 314 public-sector companies by 1998. Foreign investment (US$900m. in 1996) has financed a huge development project in the Sinai Peninsula and Upper Egypt which aims to increase the inhabited area of the country from 6% to 20% in 20 years.

Performance. Real GDP growth was estimated at 5·7% in 1996–97 (2·2% in 1995), with a budget deficit of 0·8% of GDP.

Budget. The financial year runs from 1 July. Revenues in 1995 were £E53,889m. (£E50,483m. in 1994) and expenditure £E49,828m. (£E48,652m. in 1994). Sources of revenue in 1993–94 (in £E1m.) included: Tax, 31,164; customs duties, 6,070; oil industry, 4,610; Suez Canal, 2,610. Items of expenditure included: Salaries, 11,026; pensions, 3,864; subsidies, 3,170; debt service, 16,426; defence, 5,892; public health (1992–93), 6,620.

Currency. The monetary unit is the *Egyptian pound* (EGP) of 100 *piastres*. In Feb. 1991 the official exchange rate was abolished, leaving a free rate and a rate set by a panel of bankers. Annualized inflation was 5·4% in 1997.

Foreign exchange reserves were US$18,541m. in Jan. 1998 and gold reserves were 2·43m. troy oz. Total money supply in Jan. 1998 was £E49,361m.

Banking and Finance. The Central Bank of Egypt (founded 1960) is the central bank and bank of issue. The *Governor* is Ismail Hassan.

In 1994, 4 major public-sector commercial banks accounted for some 70% of all banking assets: the National Bank of Egypt, the Banque Misr, the Bank of Alexandria and the Banque du Caïre. There were 40 other domestic commercial banks, 15 investment banks and 30 regional development banks, as well as foreign banks, branches and joint ventures. Savings and term deposits in 1992 totalled £E83,034m.

There are stock exchanges in Cairo and Alexandria.

Weights and Measures. In 1951 the metric system was made official with the exception of the feddan and its subdivisions. However, other traditional measures are still in use: *Kadah* = 1/96th ardeb = 3·36 pints. *Rob* = 4 kadahs = 1·815 gallons. *Keila* = 8 kadahs = 3·63 gallons. *Ardeb* = 96 kadahs = 43·555 gallons, or 5·44439 bu., or 198 cu. decimetres. *Rotl* = 144 dirhems = 0·9905 lb. *Oke* = 400 dirhems = 2·75137 lb. *Qantar* or 100 rotls or 36 okes = 99·0493 lb. 1 *Qantar* of unginned cotton = 315 lb. 1 *Qantar* of ginned cotton = 99·05 lb.

The approximate weight of the ardeb is as follows: Wheat, 150 kg; beans, 155 kg; barley, 120 kg; maize, 140 kg; cotton seed, 121 kg. *Feddan,* the unit of measure for land = 4,200·8 sq. metres = 7,468·148 sq. pics = 1·03805 acres. 1 sq. pic = 6·0547 sq. ft = 0·5625 sq. metre.

ENERGY AND NATURAL RESOURCES

Electricity. Installed capacity was 13·04m. kW in 1994. Electricity generated in 1996 was 54·4bn. kWh. Power used for domestic and commercial purposes in 1996 was 17·41m. kWh per hour. Consumption per capita was estimated to be 1,500 kWh in 1997. Electricity sector investments reached aproximately £E25bn. (1996–97). The use of solar energy is expanding.

Oil and Gas. Oil was discovered in 1909. Oil policy is controlled by the state-owned Egyptian General Petroleum Corporation, whole or part-owner of the production and refining companies. Production of crude oil (1997–98), 41·5m. tonnes. Gas reserves are estimated to be as high as 21,000,000m. cu. ft. Output was 9·1m. tonnes in 1993–94. By 1995, 75% of power was gas-generated.

Water. The Aswan High Dam, completed in 1970, allows for a perennial irrigation system.
    The world's biggest pumping station is being constructed in Egypt in the Nile Basin. When completed it will pump 5·5bn. cu. metres of water a year into a 67 km canal to irrigate up to 500,000 acres of desert land.

Minerals. Production (1993–94, in tonnes): Phosphate, 0·86m.; iron ore, 2·7m.; salt, 1·12m.; kaolin, 0·2m.; quartz, 84,000; asbestos and fermacolite, 916. Mining for uranium ore began near Aswan in May 1991.

Agriculture. Agriculture accounted for 17% of GDP in 1996. The cultivated area in 1996 was 7·6m. feddans, of which 1·4m. feddans were reclaimed desert. Irrigation is vital to agriculture and is being developed by government programmes; it now reaches most cultivated areas. 6·5% of the land area is arable. The Nile provides 85% of the water used in irrigation, some 55,000m. cu. metres annually.
    In 1994 there were 5,214 agricultural co-operatives. 0·71m. feddan of land had been distributed by 1991 to 0·35m. families under an agrarian reform programme. In 1995, 33·1% of the workforce were engaged in agriculture. Cotton, sugar-cane and rice are subject to government price controls and procurement quotas.
    Output (in 1,000 tonnes), 1994: Barley, 130; broad beans, 357; chickpeas, 11; cotton seed (1993), 652; seed cotton (1993), 1,114; garlic, 150; lentils, 9; flax fibre and tow (1992), 11; maize, 5,550; dry onions, 481; peanuts, 194; potatoes, 1,032; rice, 4,583; sesame, 29; soya beans, 68; sugar-cane, 12,412; sugar-beet, 825; strawberries, 28; wheat, 4,437; sorghum (1992), 736.
    Livestock, 1996: Cattle, 2·7m.; sheep, 3·49m. 1995: buffaloes, 3·25m.; goats, 3·25m.; camels, 1·68m.; chickens, 39m.. Egg production 2,214m., in 1994. 9,000 tonnes of honey were produced in 1994.

Forestry. In 1995, 2·7m. cu. metres of roundwood were produced.

Fisheries. The catch in 1995 was 309,576 tonnes, of which 226,193 tonnes were freshwater fish.

INDUSTRY

Almost all large-scale enterprises are in the public sector, and these account for about two-thirds of total output. The private sector, dominated by food processing and textiles, consists of about 150,000 small and medium businesses, most employing fewer than 50 workers. Industrial production in 1997–98 showed a growth rate of 9% compared to 1996–97. Production during 1995–96 totalled £E74·1bn., compared to £E69·98bn. in 1994–95.
    Production in 1997–98 (in 1,000 tonnes) included: Refined sugar, 1,352·5; tobacco, 595; cotton yarn, 275; paper, 1,399; fertilizers, 4,634. Cars, 36,713 units; refrigerators, 495,000; washing machines, 316,100.

Labour. In 1996–97 the workforce was 17·4m. (from 16·9m. in 1995–96). In 1992, 32·7% of the workforce were employed in agriculture, forestry and fisheries, 29·7% in services, 21·4% in manufacturing, 15·5% in mining, 10·6% in business, 4·5% in transport and communications, and 1·1% in tourism. 2,220 working days were lost through strikes in 1990. Unemployment was 11·8% in 1997.

INTERNATIONAL TRADE

Foreign debt totalled US$33bn. in 1997. Foreign investment in 1996 was £E2·6bn.

Imports and Exports. In 1997 exports were valued at £E13bn. compared to £E16·7bn. in 1995–96. Imports were valued at £E46·6bn. in 1995–96.

Export of principal commodities (in £E1m.) in 1994: Crude oil, 2,684·98; raw cotton, 791·08; cotton yarn, 1,279·54; cotton fabrics, 409·03; clothing, 780; refined petroleum, 742·08; aluminium bars, etc., 405; oranges, 278·4; potatoes, 98·2. Imports (in £E1m.): Wheat, 2,501·17; maize, 892·46; dairy products, 509·4; chemicals, 1,107·3; iron bars, 90·78; motor car parts, 762·05; motor cars, 746·46.

Main export markets, 1996: (percentage share of total trade): Italy, 20·1%; USA, 12·4%; UK, 7·7%; Germany, 5·0%; France, 4·0%. Main import suppliers in 1996: USA, 17·7%; Germany, 9·6%; Italy, 8·1%; France, 8·0%; Japan, 4·5%.

COMMUNICATIONS

Roads. In 1996 there were 26,000 km of highways and main roads, 25,000 km of secondary roads and 13,000 km of other roads. The road link between Sinai and the mainland across the Suez Canal was opened in 1996. Vehicles (in 1,000), 1996: Passenger cars, 1,354 (22 per 1,000 inhabitants); trucks and vans, 397; motor cycles, 418; buses, 38.

Rail. In 1994 there were 5,024 km of state railways (1,435 mm gauge), of which 42 km were electrified. In 1994, 1,030m. passengers and 12·3m. tonnes of freight were carried.

There are tramway networks in Cairo and Alexandria, and a metro (11 km) opened in Cairo in 1996.

Civil Aviation. There are international airports at Cairo, Luxor and Alexandria. The national carrier is Egyptair. In 1998 services were also provided by Aero Lloyd, Aeroflot, Air Algérie, Air Djibouti, Air France, Air Malta, Air Sinai, Air Ukraine, Alitalia, Austrian Airlines, Balkan, British Airways, Cyprus Airways, Czech Airlines, Delta Air Lines, El Al, Emirates, Ethiopian Airlines, Gulf Air, Iberia, JAT, Kenya Airways, KLM, Kuwait Airways, Lufthansa, Malaysia Airlines, Malév, Middle East Airlines, Northwest Airlines, Olympic Airways, Oman Air, Philippine Airlines, Qatar Airways, Royal Air Maroc, Royal Jordanian, SAS, Saudia, Singapore Airlines, Sudan Airways, Swissair, Syrian Arab Airlines, Tarom, Tunis Air, Turkish Airlines, TWA, United Airlines and Yemenia Yemen Airways. In 1996 Cairo handled 7,797,133 passengers (5,828,050 on international flights) and 130,112 tonnes of freight

Shipping. In 1995 the merchant marine totalled 1·9m. GRT, including oil tankers, 0·45m. GRT. Vessels arriving and leaving at major ports in 1995–96: 8,800; tonnes of freight: 427,333m.

Dockyards for containerized shipping were constructed in Alexandria, Dekheila, Damietta and Port Said in 1995–96, with 2 more planned for Adabeya and the Suez Canal.

Suez Canal. The Suez Canal was opened for navigation on 17 Nov. 1869 and nationalized in June 1956. By the convention of Constantinople of 29 Oct. 1888, the canal is open to vessels of all nations and is free from blockade, except in time of war. It is 173 km long (excluding 11 km of approach channels to the harbours), connecting the Mediterranean with the Red Sea. It is being deepened from 16 to 17 metres and widened from 365 to 415 metres to permit the passage of vessels of 180,000 DWT.

In 1994, 16,370 vessels (net tonnage, 364m.; cargo, 290m. tonnes; passengers, 15,800) went through the canal. Toll revenue in 1994 was US$1,897m. Tolls for tankers were reduced by 20% after Jan. 1996.

Telecommunications. Number of telephones main lines in 1997: 3,452,700 (55·7 per 1,000 persons). The internal telecommunications system is owned and operated by the Telecommunications Organization. Cellular phone subscribers numbered 14,000 in 1995, and there were 235,000 PCs in use and 3,500 fax machines. In Jan. 1998 there were approximately 61,000 Internet users.

Postal Services. There were, in 1993–94, 2,035 postal agencies, 1,972 mobile offices, 2,655 government and 2,472 private post offices.

SOCIAL INSTITUTIONS

Justice. The court system comprises: A Court of Cassation with a bench of 5 judges which constitutes the highest court of appeal in both criminal and civil cases; 5 Courts of Appeal with 3 judges; Assize Courts with 3 judges which deal with all cases of serious crime; Central Tribunals with 3 judges which deal with ordinary civil and commercial cases; Summary Tribunals presided over by a single judge which hear minor civil disputes and criminal offences.

The death penalty is in force.

Religion. Islam is constitutionally the state religion. In 1992 there were 50·4m. Moslems, mostly of the Sunni sect. Some 7% of the population are Coptic Christians, the remainder being Roman Catholics, Protestants or Greek Orthodox, with a small number of Jews. A Patriarch heads the Coptic Church, and there are 25 metropolitans and bishops in Egypt; 4 metropolitans for Ethiopia, Jerusalem, Khartoum and Omdurman, and 12 bishops in Ethiopia. The Copts use the Diocletian (or Martyrs') calendar, which begins in AD 284.

Education. The adult literacy rate in 1995 was 51·4% (63·6% among males and 38·8% among females). Free compulsory education is provided in primary schools (8 years). Secondary and technical education is also free. There are no private fee-paying schools except remedial classes, but private coaching is widespread. In 1995–96 there were 2,060 pre-primary schools with 266,502 pupils and 10,913 teachers; 16,188 primary schools with 7,470,437 pupils and 302,916 teachers; 2,753 secondary schools with 6,142,651 pupils and 369,107 teachers

Al Azhar institutes educate students who intend enrolling at Al Azhar University. In 1993–94 in the Al Azhar system there were 1,912 primary schools with 704,446 pupils, 1,030 preparatory schools with 147,762 pupils and 587 secondary schools with 165,829 pupils.

In 1993–94 there were 49,703 students in commerce institutes (24,906 women) and 31,259 in technical institutes (9,401 women). In 1995–96 there were 13 state universities, 1 American university and 1 academy of science and technology. There were 612,844 students (231,065 women) and 33,100 academic staff in 1993–94. 4 private universities opened in 1996.

Education expenditure in 1998 was between 6% and 7% of GDP.

Health. In 1996 there were 129,000 doctors, and in 1992, 15,150 dentists, 34,700 pharmacists and 98,500 other medical personnel. In 1994 there were 6,332 treatment units (including 330 general hospitals) with 113,020 beds.

CULTURE

Broadcasting. Broadcasting is conducted by the government-controlled Egyptian Radio and TV Union. Number of radio receivers in 1995, 19·4m.; TV sets, 6·8m. Colour is by SECAM.

Cinema. In 1994 there were 138 cinemas. 72 films were made in 1995.

Press. In 1995 there were 14 dailies with a total circulation of 2·6m. To set up a newspaper requires permission from the prime minister.

Tourism. There were 3,528,000 foreign tourists in 1996, spending US$3·2bn. Tourism receipts in 1998–99 were forecast at US$3·9bn. Expenditure by Egyptian tourists abroad in 1995 was US$1·28bn., up from US$52m. in 1986. No other country increased its overseas tourist expenditure at such a rate over the same 10-year period.

DIPLOMATIC REPRESENTATIVES

Of Egypt in Great Britain (12 Curzon St., London, W1Y 7FJ)
Ambassador: Adel El-Gazzar.

Of Great Britain in Egypt (Ahmed Ragheb St., Garden City, Cairo)
Ambassador: David E. S. Blatherwick, KCMG, OBE.

Of Egypt in the USA (2310 Decatur Pl., NW, Washington, D.C., 20008)
Ambassador: Ahmed Maher El Sayed.

Of the USA in Egypt (8, Kamal el-Din Salah St., Garden City, Cairo)
Ambassador: Daniel C. Kurtzer.

Of Egypt to the United Nations
Ambassador: Dr Nabil A. Elaraby.

Of Egypt to the European Union
Ambassador: Raouf Saad.

FURTHER READING

CAPMAS, *Statistical Year Book, Arab Republic of Egypt*
Hopwood, D., *Egypt: Politics and Society 1945–1990.* 3rd ed. London, 1992
King, J. W., *Historical Dictionary of Egypt.* 2nd ed. Revised by A. Goldschmidt. Metuchen (NJ), 1995
McDermott, A., *Egypt: From Nasser to Mubarak.* London, 1988
Makar, R. N., *Egypt.* [Bibliography] Oxford and Santa Barbara (CA), 1988
Malek, J. (ed.) *Egypt.* Univ. of Oklahoma Press, 1993
Rodenbeck, M., *Cairo—the City Victorious.* Picador, London, 1998
Vatikiotis, P. J., *History of Modern Egypt: from Muhammad Ali to Mubarak.* London, 1991

National statistical office: Central Agency for Public Mobilization and Statistics (CAPMAS), Nasr City, Cairo.

EL SALVADOR

República de El Salvador

Capital: San Salvador
Population estimate, 2000: 6·32m.
GNP per capita: (PPP$) 2,790
HDI/world rank: 0·604/114

KEY HISTORICAL EVENTS

Conquered by Spain in 1526, El Salvador remained under Spanish rule until freeing itself in 1821. Thereafter, El Salvador was a member of the Central American Federation comprising the states of El Salvador, Guatemala, Honduras, Nicaragua and Costa Rica until this federation was dissolved in 1839. In 1841 El Salvador declared itself an independent republic.

The country's history has been marked by much political violence and a number of enforced changes of rulers. The repressive dictatorship of President Maximiliano Hernandez Martinez lasted from 1931 to 1944 when he was deposed as were his successors in 1948 and 1960. The military junta that followed gave way to more secure presidential succession although there were charges of corruption at the election. Left-wing guerrilla groups became increasingly large and strong and were engaged in constant fighting with government troops in the late 1970s. Many reports circulated of the violation of human rights and in 1980 the Roman Catholic Archbishop of San Salvador, Oscar Romero y Galdames, an acknowledged advocate of human rights by government and army, was assassinated. As the guerrillas grew stronger and gained control over a part of the country, the USA sent economic aid and advisers to El Salvador and assisted in the training of Salvadorean troops. A new constitution was enacted in Dec. 1983 under which Agostín Duarte was elected president in May 1984 but it did nothing to pacify the situation. The presidential election was boycotted as a fraud by the main left-wing organization, the Favabundo Marti National Liberation Front (FMLN).

Talks between the government and the FMLN in April 1991 led to constitutional reforms in May, envisaging the establishment of civilian control over the armed forces and a reduction in their size. In May the UN Security Council sent a mission to observe the government-FMLN negotiations, initially for one year. An agreement reached in Sept. 1991 permitted the FMLN to participate in a newly created police force under civilian authority. On 16 Jan. 1992 the government and the FMLN signed a peace agreement and a ceasefire began on 1 Feb.

TERRITORY AND POPULATION

El Salvador is bounded in the north-east by Guatemala, north-east and east by Honduras and south by the Pacific Ocean. The area (including 247 sq. km of inland lakes) is 21,041 sq. km. Population (1992 census), 5,047,925 (female 52%); 1996 est., 5·79m., giving a population density of 275 per sq. km.

The UN gives a projected population for 2000 of 6·32m.

In 1995 an estimated 54·9% of the population were rural. In 1995, 1m. Salvadoreans were living abroad, mainly in the USA.

El Salvador comprises 14 departments. Areas (sq. km) and 1992 census populations:

Department	Area	Population	Chief town	Population
Ahuachapán	1,240	260,563	Ahuachapán	83,885
Cabañas	1,140	136,293	Sensuntepeque	38,073
Chalatenango	2,017	180,627	Chalatenango	27,600
Cuscatlán	756	167,290	Cojutepeque	43,564
La Libertad	1,653	522,071	Nueva San Salvador	116,575
La Paz	1,224	246,147	Zacatecoluca	57,032
La Unión	2,074	251,143	La Unión	36,927
Morazán	1,447	166,772	San Francisco	20,497
San Miguel	2,077	380,442	San Miguel	182,817
San Salvador	886	1,477,766	San Salvador	422,570[1]
San Vicente	1,184	135,471	San Vicente	45,842
Santa Ana	2,023	451,620	Santa Ana	202,337
Sonsonate	1,226	354,641	Sonsonate	76,200
Usulatán	2,130	317,079	Usulután	62,967

[1]Greater San Salvador conurbation, 1,522,126.

The official language is Spanish.

SOCIAL STATISTICS

1995 births, 164,000; deaths, 35,000. Rates (1995, per 1,000 population): Births, 28·9; deaths, 6·1. Life expectancy at birth over the period 1990–95 was 64·1 years for males and 71·8 years for females. Annual growth rate, 1990–95, 2·2%. Infant mortality, 1990–95, 44 per 1,000 live births; fertility rate, 3·5 births per woman.

CLIMATE

Despite its proximity to the equator, the climate is warm rather than hot, and nights are cool inland. Light rains occur in the dry season from Nov. to April, while the rest of the year has heavy rains, especially on the coastal plain. San Salvador, Jan. 71°F (21·7°C), July 75°F (23·9°C). Annual rainfall 71" (1,775 mm). San Miguel, Jan. 77°F (25°C), July 83°F (28·3°C). Annual rainfall 68" (1,700 mm).

CONSTITUTION AND GOVERNMENT

A new Constitution was enacted in Dec. 1983. Executive power is vested in a *President* and *Vice-President* elected for a non-renewable term of 5 years. There is a *Legislative Assembly* of 84 members elected by universal suffrage and proportional representation: 64 locally and 20 nationally, for a term of 3 years.

National Anthem. 'Saludemos la patria orgullosos' ('We proudly salute the Fatherland'); words by J. J. Cañas, tune by J. Aberle.

RECENT ELECTIONS

Presidential elections were held on 7 March 1999. Francisco Guillermo Flores Perez (Alianza Republicana Nacionalista, ARENA) won with 51·4% against 6 other candidates. He was due to take office on 1 June 1999. In parliamentary elections on 16 March 1997, ARENA gained 28 seats in the Legislative Assembly, the FMLN 27, and 6 other parties 29 seats between them.

CURRENT ADMINISTRATION

President: Dr Armando Calderón Sol (ARENA; sworn in 1 June 1994). He was due to be replaced by Francisco Guillermo Flores on 1 June 1999.

In March 1999 the Cabinet comprised:

Vice-President and Minister of the Presidency: Dr Enrique Borgo Bustamante.

Minister of Agriculture: Ricardo Quiñones Avila. *Economy:* Eduardo Zablah Touche. *Defence:* Gen. Juan Martinez Valera. *Environment and Natural Resources:* Miguel Eduardo Araujo. *Finance:* Manuel Enrique Hinds. *Foreign Affairs:* Ramón González Giner. *Health and Social Assistance:* Dr Eduardo Interiano. *Interior:* Mario Acosta Oertel. *Justice:* Dr Rubén Mejía Peña. *Labour and Social Security:* Dr Eduardo Tomasino. *Public Works:* Roberto Bará Osegueda. *Public Security:* Hugo Cesar Barerra Guerrero.

Local Government. Each of the 14 departments is under an appointed governor. There are 262 municipalities. ARENA has control of 161 municipalities, FMLN 48, the Christian Democratic Party 18.

DEFENCE

There is selective conscription for 2 years. In 1997 defence expenditure totalled US$176m. (US$30 per capita).

Army. There are 3 military zones. The Army comprises 1 special security and 6 infantry brigades, 8 infantry detachments, 1 mechanized cavalry regiment, 1 artillery brigade, 1 engineer command, 2 independent battalions including the Presidential Guard, and 1 special operations group. Equipment includes 68 armoured personnel carriers.

Strength (1997): 25,700 (4,000 conscripts). The National Civilian Police numbers 8,000.

Navy. A small coastguard force based largely at Acajutla, with 1,100 (1997) personnel, operates 5 inshore patrol craft, 2 landing craft and numerous boats. There was also (1996) 1 company of Naval Infantry numbering 150.

Air Force. The Air Force equipment includes 10 A-37B and 5 Magister attack aircraft, 2 Rallye armed trainers, 6 armed C-47 transports, 15 armed Cessna O-2s

EL SALVADOR

and 6 Hughes 500MD helicopters for counter-insurgency operations. Other aircraft include 2 C-47, 3 Arava, 1 DC-6 and 1 C-123 transports, 6 Cessna O-2 patrol aircraft, as well as 60 UH-1H helicopters. Training types include piston-engined Cessna light aircraft and 4 A-37s.

Strength (1997): 1,600 personnel (200 conscripts).

INTERNATIONAL RELATIONS
El Salvador is a member of the UN, CACM, LAIA and OAS.

ECONOMY

Policy. An economic liberalization programme aims at raising exports, foreign investment and domestic savings.

Performance. Real GDP growth was 6·5% in 1995 and 6·0% in 1994.

Budget. Central government budgetary revenue and expenditure in ₡1m. for calendar years:

	1993	1994	1995	1996	1997
Revenue	6,550·4	8,654·4	10,534·7	10,527·9	11,228·0
Expenditure	7,753·0	10,264·3	11,376·3	12,305·6	12,027·3

Currency. The monetary unit is the *colón* (SVC) of 100 *centavos*. Inflation was 7·4% in 1996.

Foreign exchange reserves were US$1,631m. in Feb. 1998 and gold reserves were 470,000 troy oz. Total money supply was ₡9,084m. in Feb. 1998.

Banking and Finance. The bank of issue is the Central Reserve Bank (*Governor*, José Roberto Orellana Milla), formed in 1934 and nationalized in 1961. There are 15 commercial banks (2 foreign). Individual private holdings may not exceed 5% of the total equity.

There is a stock exchange in San Salvador, founded in 1992.

Weights and Measures. The metric system is standard but other units are still commonly in use, of which the principal are as follows: *Libra* = 1·014 lbs; *quintal* = 100 lbs; *arroba* = 25·35 lbs; *fanega* = 1·5745 bushels.

ENERGY AND NATURAL RESOURCES

Electricity. Installed capacity in 1996 was 900,000 kW, around half of it hydro-electric. Production in 1996 was 3,340m. kWh; consumption per capita was an estimated 580 kWh in 1996.

Minerals. El Salvador has few mineral resources. Production (1987, in tonnes): Salt, 3,100; limestone, 1·45m.; gypsum, 4,500.

Agriculture. 27% of the land surface is given over to arable farming. In 1995, 32·4% of the working population was engaged in agriculture, which in 1996 accounted for 13% of GDP. Large landholdings have been progressively expropriated and redistributed in accordance with legislation initiated in 1980. By 1994 some 12,000 individuals had received plots of 4–5 ha.

Since the mid-19th century, El Salvador's economy has been dominated by coffee. Cotton is the second main commercial crop. Production, in 1,000 quintals (1997): Coffee, 3,153; maize, 12,000; (1993): seed cotton, 207; beans, 1,354; rice, 1,564; sorghum, 4,656; sugar cane (in tonnes), 7,994.

Livestock (1996): 1,287,000 cattle, 400,000 pigs, 96,000 horses, 5m. chickens (1995).

Livestock products (1994, in 1,000 tonnes): Beef, 26; pork, 9; poultry, 44; milk, 280; eggs, 52.

Forestry. Forest area was 105,000 ha (5·1% of the land area) in 1995, down from 124,000 ha and 6% in 1990. In the national forests, dye woods are found, and valuable hardwoods including mahogany, cedar and walnut. Balsam trees abound: El Salvador is the world's principal source of this medicinal gum. 6·8m. cu. metres of roundwood were cut in 1995.

Fisheries. In 1989 there were 24 fishing vessels with a tonnage of 3,514 GRT. The catch in 1995 was 15,812 tonnes, of which 11,305 tonnes were from marine waters.

EL SALVADOR

INDUSTRY
Production (1988, in 1,000 tonnes): Petroleum, 136; fuel oil, 208; paper and products, 16. Traditional industries include food processing and textiles.

Labour. Out of 1,973,000 people in employment in 1995, 532,000 were in agriculture, forestry and fishing, 414,000 in community, social and personal services, and 399,000 in trade, restaurants and hotels. There were 163,400 unemployed persons, or 7·7% of the workforce.

INTERNATIONAL TRADE
In May 1992 El Salvador, Guatemala and Honduras agreed to create a free trade zone for almost all goods and capital. External debt was US$2,894m. in 1996.

Imports and Exports. Imports (including parcels' post) and exports in calendar years (in US$1m.):

	1993	1994	1995	1996	1997
Imports	1,912	2,574	2,853	2,671	2,973
Exports	732	844	998	1,024	1,359

In 1991, 139,000 quintals of coffee were exported. Main import suppliers, 1996: USA, 40·0%; Guatemala, 10·5%; Panama, 6·6%; Mexico, 6·5%. Main export markets, 1996: Guatemala, 20·6%; USA, 19·3%; Germany, 15·5%; Honduras, 9·5%.

COMMUNICATIONS

Roads. In 1996 there were 9,977 km of roads, including 1,985 km of paved roads. Vehicles in use in 1996: Passenger cars, 168,234; trucks and vans, 142,016; road tractors, 42,035.

Rail. The railways are run by the National Railways of El Salvador. Route length (1994): 602 km. There is a link to the Guatemalan system. Passenger-kilometres travelled in 1995 came to 5m. and freight tonne-kilometres to 13m.

Civil Aviation. The international airport is at Comalapa, 40 km from San Salvador. The national carrier is Taca International Airlines. It flies to various destinations in the USA, Mexico and all Central American countries. In 1998 international flights were also provided by American Airlines, Aviateca, Canadian Airlines International, Continental Airlines, Delta Air Lines, Iberia, LACSA, Nicaraguense de Aviación, SAM and United Airlines. In 1996 Comalapa International handled 872,685 passengers (all on international flights) and 20,247 tonnes of freight

Shipping. The main ports are Acajutla and Cutuco. Merchant shipping totalled 1,000 GRT in 1995. In 1995 vessels totalling 3,185,000 net registered tons entered ports and vessels totalling 625,000 NRT cleared.

Telecommunications. The telephone and telegraph systems are government-owned; the radio-telephone systems are partly private, partly government-owned. In 1996 there were 325,300 telephone main lines (56·1 per 1,000 inhabitants). There were 14,000 cellular phone subscribers in 1995.

Postal Services. In 1995 there were 297 post offices.

SOCIAL INSTITUTIONS

Justice. Justice is administered by the Supreme Court (6 members appointed for 3-year terms by the Legislative Assembly and 6 by bar associations), courts of first and second instance, and minor tribunals.

Following the disbanding of security forces in Jan. 1992 a new National Civilian Police Force was created which numbered 10,500 by 1997.

Religion. About 90% of the population is Roman Catholic. Under the 1962 Constitution, churches are exempted from the property tax; the Catholic Church is recognized as a legal person, and other churches are entitled to secure similar recognition. There is an archbishop in San Salvador and bishops at Santa Ana, San Miguel, San Vicente, Santiago de María, Usulután, Sonsonate and Zacatecoluca. There are about 200,000 Protestants.

Education. The adult literacy rate in 1995 was 71·5% (73·5% among males and 69·8% among females). Education, run by the state, is free and compulsory. In 1995

there were 134,000 pupils in nursery schools, 1,064,000 in primary and 144,00 in secondary schools. In 1995–96 in the public sector there were 3 universities; in the private sector there were 21 universities and 14 specialized universities (1 American, 3 Evangelical, 1 Roman Catholic, 1 Open and 1 each for business, integrated education, polytechnic, science and development, teaching, science and technology, technical studies and technology). In 1994–95 there were 63,413 university students and 3,983 academic staff.

Health. In 1993 there were 4,525 doctors, 1,182 dentists, 5,094 nurses and 78 hospitals.

Welfare. The Social Security Institute now administers the sickness, old age and death insurance, covering industrial workers and employees earning up to ₡700 a month. Employees in other private institutions with salaries over this amount are included but are excluded from the medical and hospital benefits.

CULTURE

Broadcasting. Broadcasting is under the control of the Administración Nacional de Telecomunicaciones. There are 6 commercial television channels, a government-owned channel and 2 educational channels sponsored by the Ministry of Education. In 1995 there were 23·6m. radio receivers and 3·9m. television sets (colour by NTSC).

Press. In 1995 there were 6 daily newspapers with a combined circulation of 280,000, at a rate of 49 per 1,000 inhabitants.

Tourism. There were 283,000 foreign tourists in 1996, spending US$76m.

DIPLOMATIC REPRESENTATIVES

Of El Salvador in Great Britain (Tennyson House, 159 Great Portland St., London, W1N 5FD)
Ambassador: Vacant.

Of Great Britain in El Salvador (Edificio Inter-Inversiones, Paseo General Escalón 4828, POB 1591, San Salvador)
Ambassador and Consul General: Ian Gerken, LVO.

Of El Salvador in the USA (2308 California St., NW, Washington, D.C., 20008)
Ambassador: Rene A. Leon.

Of the USA in El Salvador (Urbanización Santa Elena, Antiguo Cuscatlán, San Salvador)
Ambassador: Anne W. Patterson.

Of El Salvador to the United Nations
Ambassador: Dr Ricardo G. Castaneda-Cornejo.

Of El Salvador to the European Union
Ambassador: Joaquin Rodezno Munguia.

FURTHER READING

Armstrong, R. and Shenk, J., *El Salvador: the Face of Revolution.* London, 1982
Baloyra, E. A., *El Salvador in Transition.* Univ. of North Carolina Press, 1982
Didion, J., *Salvador.* London, 1983
Kufeld, A., *El Salvador.* NY, 1991
Montgomery, T. S., *Revolution in El Salvador: Origins and Evolution.* Boulder (CO), 1982
North, L., *Bitter Grounds: Roots of Revolt in El Salvador.* London, 1981
Woodward, R. L., *El Salvador.* [Bibliography] Oxford and Santa Barbara (CA), 1988

National statistical office: Dirección General de Estadística y Censos, Calle Arce, San Salvador.

EQUATORIAL GUINEA

República de Guinea
Ecuatorial

Capital: Malabo
Population estimate, 2000: 452,000
GNP per capita: (PPP$) 2,690
HDI/world rank: 0·465/135

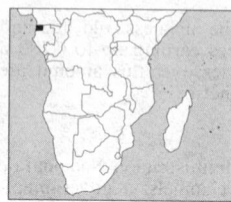

KEY HISTORICAL EVENTS

Equatorial Guinea consists of the island of Bioko, for centuries called Fernando Po; other smaller islands, notably Annobón, formerly Pagalu; and the mainland territory of Rio Muni. The main ethnic group in Rio Muni is the Fang (or Pahouin), members of which also live in neighbouring Gabon; the Bubis, the original inhabitants of Fernando Po, still constitute the majority on Bioko. Fernando Po was called after the Portuguese navigator Fernão do Po, who in 1471-72 became the first European visitor to the island; it was then ruled for 3 centuries by Portugal, but was in 1778 ceded to Spain, along with Annobon and a mainland area, out of which Spain eventually retained a small area, Rio Muni, whose boundaries were recognized by other European countries in 1856.

For some decades after taking possession of Fernando Po, Spain did not effectively occupy it and allowed Britain to establish an important consulate and naval base at Clarence (later Santa Isabel), which dominated the island and were important for the suppression of slave trading over a wide area in the 19th century. Spain asserted its rule from the 1840s. Fernando Po and Rio Muni were together called the Spanish Possessions in the Gulf of Guinea, or simply Spanish Guinea. African resistance to Spanish occupation of the interior of Rio Muni continued for a long time. In Rio Muni timber became the major export; on Fernando Po the Spanish developed cocoa cultivation on European-owned plantations, for which African labour was imported from the early 20th century. This labour traffic led to an international scandal in 1930 when Liberians were found to be sold to virtual slavery. Later many Nigerians were employed, often in poor conditions, and a large Nigerian community came to live on the island.

For much of Spanish rule Africans were kept in a subordinate position under the system called *patronato de indigenas* (patronage over natives). On 30 July 1959 it was announced that Spanish Guinea was to be a part of Spain and its people Spanish citizens. It became 2 provinces, represented in the *Cortes* in Madrid.

African nationalist movements began in the 1950s and 1960s. Internal self-government was granted in 1963, with a joint legislative assembly for the 2 provinces. Bonifacio Ondo Edu, leader of the *Movimiento de Unión Nacional de Guinea Ecuatorial* (MUNGE), became head of government. Other parties included the *Idea Popular de Guinea Ecuatorial* (IPGE), of which Francisco Macías Nguema became the leader. In 1969 Spain briefly suspended the constitution after rivalry among the parties but then, under pressure to grant independence, agreed on condition of its approval by a referendum, which was given on 11 Aug. 1969. The two parts of Equatorial Guinea were united in a state which became independent on 12 Oct. 1968 with Macías Nguema as president.

President Macías established the rule of a single party, the *Partido Unico Nacional de los Trabajadores* (PUNT), in 1970. Under his dictatorship a third of the population was killed or else left the country. He was declared President-for-Life on 14 July 1972 but was overthrown by a military coup on 3 Aug. 1979, led by a relative of his, Col. Teodoro Obiang Nguema. The military régime ended the excesses of the rule of Macías who was executed.

A constitution approved by a referendum on 3 Aug. 1982 restored some political institutions, but left the military régime in power, to stay until economic and social reconstruction was completed. A Supreme Military Council then created was the sole political body until constitutional rule was resumed on 12 Oct. 1982, and opposition parties legalized.

TERRITORY AND POPULATION

The mainland part of Equatorial Guinea is bounded in the north by Cameroon, east and south by Gabon, and west by the Gulf of Guinea, in which lie the islands of Bioko (formerly Macías Nguema, formerly Fernando Póo) and Annobón (called Pagalu from 1973 to 1979). The total area is 28,051 sq. km (10,831 sq. miles) and the population at the 1983 census was 304,000. Estimate (July 1997), 443,000; density, 16 per sq. km. Another 110,000 are estimated to remain in exile abroad.

The UN gives a projected population for 2000 of 452,000.

In 1995 an estimated 57·8% of the population were rural.

The 7 provinces are grouped into 2 regions—Continental (C), chief town Bata; and Insular (I), chief town Malabo—with areas and populations as follows:

	Sq. km	Census 1983	Chief town
Annobón (I)	17	2,006	San Antonio de Palea
Bioko Norte (I)	776	46,221	Malabo
Bioko Sur (I)	1,241	10,969	Luba
Centro Sur (C)	9,931	52,393	Evinayong
Kié-Ntem (C)	3,943	70,202	Ebebiyin
Litoral (C)	6,665[1]	66,370	Bata
Wele-Nzas (C)	5,478	51,839	Mongomo

[1]Including the adjacent islets of Corisco, Elobey Grande and Elobey Chico (17 sq. km).

In 1986 the largest towns were Bata (17,000) and the capital, Malabo (10,000).

The main ethnic group on the mainland is the Fang, which comprises 85% of the total population; there are several minority groups along the coast and adjacent islets. On Bioko the indigenous inhabitants (Bubis) constitute 60% of the population there, the balance being mainly Fang and coast people. On Annobón the indigenous inhabitants are the descendants of Portuguese slaves and still speak a Portuguese patois. The official language is Spanish.

SOCIAL STATISTICS

1997 births, 17,400; deaths, 6,100. Birth rate (per 1,000 population, 1997 estimate): 39·3; death, 13·7. Life expectancy (1997 estimate), 53·5 years (male, 51·2; female, 55·8). Annual growth rate, 1990–95, 2·8%. Infant mortality, 1990–95, 117 per 1,000 live births; fertility rate, 5·9 births per woman.

CLIMATE

The climate is equatorial, with alternate wet and dry seasons. In Rio Muni, the wet season lasts from Dec. to Feb.

CONSTITUTION AND GOVERNMENT

A Constitution was approved in a plebiscite in Aug. 1982 by 95% of the votes cast. It provided for an 11-member Council of State, and for a 41-member House of Representatives of the People, the latter being directly elected on 28 Aug. 1983 for a 5-year term and re-elected on 10 July 1988. The President appointed and leads a Council of Ministers.

On 12 Oct. 1987 a single new political party was formed as the *Partido Democrático de Guinea Ecuatorial*.

A referendum on 17 Nov. 1991 approved the institution of multi-party democracy, and a law to this effect was passed in Jan. 1992. The electorate is restricted to citizens who have resided in Equatorial Guinea for at least 10 years. A parliament created as a result, the *National Assembly*, has 80 seats.

National Anthem. 'Caminemos pisando las sendas' ('Let us journey treading the pathways'); words by A. N. Miyongo, tune anonymous.

RECENT ELECTIONS

At the *National Assembly* elections on 6 March 1999 the main opposition parties called for a boycott. 75 of the 80 seats went to the ruling Democratic Party of Equatorial Guinea, 4 to the Popular Union and 1 to the Convergence for the Social Democracy.

Presidential elections were held on 25 Feb. 1996. It was announced that President Nguema Mbasogo had been re-elected by 99% of votes cast.

CURRENT ADMINISTRATION

President of the Supreme Military Council, Minister of Defence: Brig.-Gen. Teodoro Obiang Nguema Mbasogo, b. 1943 (since 1979; re-elected in 1996).

In March 1999 the government comprised:

Prime Minister and Head of Government: Serafin Seriche Dougan.

First Deputy Prime Minister, Foreign Affairs and Co-operation: Miguel Oyono Ndong. *Deputy Prime Minister, Interior and Local Corporations:* Demetrio Elo Ndong. *Agriculture, Fisheries and Animal Husbandry:* Constantine Eko Nsue. *Culture and Tourism:* Augustin Nse Nfumu. *Education an, Science:* Santiago Ngua Nfumu. *Economy and Finance:* Baltasar Engonga Edjo. *Health and Environment:* Bernabe Ngore. *Industry, Commerce, and Small and Medium Enterprises:* Vidal Djoni Becoba. *Information, Tourism and Culture:* Lucas Nguema Esono. *Justice and Religion:* Ruben Maye Nsue. *Employment and Social Security:* Constantino Congue. *Mines and Energy:* Juan Olo Mba Nseng. *Public Works and Urban Affairs:* Francisco Pascual Obama Asue. *Social Affairs and Women's Development:* Margarita Alene. *Transport and Communication:* Marcelino Oyono Ntutumu. *Territorial Administration and Local Government:* Julio Ndong Ela Mangue. *Youth and Sports:* Ignacio Milam Ntang. *Labour and Social Promotion:* Ernesto Maria Cayetano Toherida. *Forestry and Environment:* Teodoro Nguema Obiang. *Civil Service and Administrative Reforms:* Fernando Mbale Mba. *In Charge of Economy and Commerce:* Dr Marcelino Nguema Onguene. *In Charge of Planning and International Co-operation:* Anatolio Ndong Mba. *At the Presidency in Charge of Relations with Assemblies and Legal Matters, Planning:* Antonio Fernando Nve Ngu. *At the Presidency in Charge of Special Duties, Missions:* Alejandro Evuna Owono Asangono.

Local Government. There are some 600 rural councils.

DEFENCE

In 1997 defence expenditure totalled US$5m. (US$10 per capita).

Army. The Army consists of 3 infantry battalions with (1997) 1,100 personnel. There is also a paramilitary Guardia Civil.

Navy. A small force, numbering 120 in 1997 and based at Malabo, operates 4 inshore patrol craft.

Air Force. There is no formal air service but the National Guard Air Wing has 1 Yak-40 and 2 An-32 transports. Personnel (1997), 100.

INTERNATIONAL RELATIONS

Equatorial Guinea is a member of the UN and OAU, and is an ACP member state of the ACP-EU relationship.

ECONOMY

Policy. Overseas investment, particularly in the oil industry, has transformed the economy.

Performance. The economy grew by more than 40% in 1996 and by 50% in 1997. Between 1990 and 1996 the average annual real growth in GNP per capita was 15·9%—the highest of any country in the world over the same period.

Budget. In 1995 the estimated total revenue was 13,542m. francs CFA and expenditure 13,400m. francs CFA, of which 12,170m. francs CFA were current expenditure.

Currency. On 2 Jan. 1985 the country joined the Franc Zone and the *ekpwele* was replaced by the *franc CFA* which now has a parity value of 50 francs CFA to 1 French franc. Foreign exchange reserves were US$5m. in Jan. 1998. The average annual inflation rate over the period 1990–96 was 3·9%. Total money supply in Jan. 1998 was 13m. francs CFA.

Banking and Finance. The *Banque des Etats de l'Afrique Centrale* became the bank of issue in Jan. 1985. There is 1 commercial bank.

ENERGY AND NATURAL RESOURCES

Electricity. There are 2 hydro-electric plants. Installed capacity was 23,000 kW in 1995. Production was 20m. kWh in 1994; consumption per capita was 51 kWh in 1994.

Oil and Gas. Oil production started in 1992, and in 1997 topped 80,000 bbls. a day. Mobil is the biggest operator in the country but other US-based oil companies are investing heavily. Oil production was estimated to be over 100,000 bbls. a day by 2000.

Minerals. There is some small-scale alluvial gold production.

Agriculture. Agriculture accounted for 34% of GDP in 1996. Subsistence farming predominates, and in 1995 approximately 73% of the economically active population were engaged in agriculture. Production (in 1,000 tonnes, in 1994): Coconuts, 8; palm kernels, 3; bananas, 17; cassava, 48; sweet potatoes, 36. Plantations in the hinterland have been abandoned by their Spanish former owners and except for cocoa and coffee, commercial agriculture is under serious difficulties. Livestock (1996): Cattle, 5,000; goats, 8,000 (1995); pigs, 5,000; sheep, 36,000.

Forestry. In 1995 forests covered 1·78m. ha, or 63·5% of the total land area (down from 65·2% of the land area in 1990). 811,000 cu. metres of roundwood were cut in 1995.

Fisheries. The total catch in 1995 was estimated to be 3,800 tonnes (90% from sea fishing). Tuna and shellfish are caught.

INDUSTRY

The once-flourishing light industry collapsed under the Macías regime. Oil production is now the major activity. Food processing is also being developed.

Labour. In 1996 the labour force was 171,000 (65% males). The wage-earning non-agricultural workforce is small. The average monthly wage was 14,000 francs CFA in 1992.

INTERNATIONAL TRADE

Foreign debt was US$283m. in 1996.

Imports and Exports. In 1995 imports amounted to US$52·3m. and exports to US$83·5m. Main export markets, 1995: USA, 34%; Japan, 16%; China, 12%. Main import suppliers: Spain, 51%; Cameroon, 21%; France, 6%; USA, 4%.

COMMUNICATIONS

Roads. Length of network, 1996, 2,880 km. Most roads are in a state of disrepair. Vehicles in use numbered 2,040 (1,520 passenger cars, or 3 per 1,000 inhabitants, and 540 vans and trucks) in 1996.

Civil Aviation. There is an international airport at Malabo. In 1998 services were provided by Air Afrique, Air Gabon, Cameroon Airlines, Iberia, Spanair and Swissair. There were international flights in 1998 to Abidjan, Brazzaville, Cotonou, Douala, Lagos, Libreville, Madrid, Paris, Pointe Noire, São Tomé, Yaoundé and Zürich. In 1995 Malabo handled 27,000 passengers (14,000 on international flights).

Shipping. Bata is the main port, handling mainly timber. The other ports are Luba, formerly San Carlos (bananas, cocoa), in Bioko, and Malabo, Evinayong and Mbini on the mainland. Ocean-going shipping totalled 3,279 GRT in 1995.

Telecommunications. Telephone services are rudimentary. In 1996 there were 3,700 main telephone lines in use (8·9 for every 1,000 persons) and in 1995 around 100 fax machines. In Jan. 1998 there were approximately 200 Internet users.

Postal Services. There were 23 post offices in 1994.

SOCIAL INSTITUTIONS

Justice. The Constitution guarantees an independent judiciary. The Supreme Tribunal is the highest court of appeal and is located at Malabo. There are Courts of First Instance and Courts of Appeal at Malabo and Bata.

EQUATORIAL GUINEA

Religion. Christianity was proscribed under President Macías but reinstated in 1979. In 1994 there were 0·3m. Roman Catholics and 8,000 Protestants.

Education. In 1994 there were 85 pre-primary schools with 171 teachers for 3,788 pupils; 781 primary schools with 1,381 teachers for 75,751 pupils; and 16,616 secondary pupils with 588 teachers. In 1993 there were 2 teacher training colleges, 2 post-secondary vocational schools and 1 agricultural institute. Adult literacy was 78·5% in 1995 (male, 89·6%; female, 68·1%). The rate for males is second only to Zimbabwe among African countries.

Health. In 1990 there were 99 doctors, 154 nurses and 55 midwives.

CULTURE

Broadcasting. 2 radio programmes are broadcast by the state-controlled Radio Nacional de Guinea Ecuatorial and Televisión Nacional. There is also a commercial radio network, and a cultural programme produced with Spanish collaboration. In 1995 there were 170,000 radio and 4,000 TV receivers (colour by SECAM).

Press. There is one daily newspaper with a circulation of 2,000, at a rate of 5 per 1,000 inhabitants.

Tourism. Foreign tourists brought in revenue of US$2m. in 1996.

DIPLOMATIC REPRESENTATIVES
Of Equatorial Guinea in Great Britain
Ambassador: Lino-Sima Ekua Avomo (resides in Paris).

Of Great Britain in Equatorial Guinea
Ambassador and Consul-General: Mr G. P. R. Boon (resides in Yaoundé).

Of Equatorial Guinea in the USA (Suite 405, 1511 K St., NW, Washington, D.C. 20005)
Ambassador: Pastor Micha Ondo Bile.

Of Equatorial Guinea to the United Nations
Ambassador: Pastor Micha Ondo Bile.

Of Equatorial Guinea to the European Union
Ambassador: Aurelio Mba Olo Andeme.

The USA does not have an embassy in Equatorial Guinea; US relations with Equatorial Guinea are handled through the US Embassy in Yaoundé, Cameroon.

FURTHER READING
Fegley, R., *Equatorial Guinea, an African Tragedy.* New York, 1989.—*Equatorial Guinea:* [Bibliography]. Oxford and Santa Barbara (CA), 1991
Liniger-Goumaz, M., *Guinea Ecuatorial: Bibliografía General.* Geneva, 1974–91.—*Historical Dictionary of Equatorial Guinea.* 2nd ed. Metuchen (NJ), 1988.—*Small Is Not Always Beautiful: the Story of Equatorial Guinea.* London, 1988
Molino, A. M. del, *La Ciudad de Clarence.* Madrid, 1994

ERITREA

Capital: Asmara
Population estimate, 2000: 3·81m.
Estimated GDP: $2bn.
HDI/world rank: 0·275/168

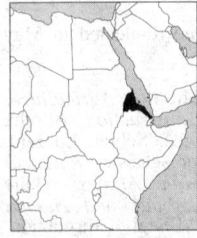

KEY HISTORICAL EVENTS
Italy was the colonial ruler of Eritrea from 1890 until 1941, when it fell to British forces in the Second World War, and a British protectorate was set up. This ended in 1952 when the UN sanctioned its federation with Ethiopia. In 1962 Ethiopia became a unitary state and Eritrea was incorporated as a province.

Eritreans began an armed struggle for independence under the leadership of the Eritrean People's Liberation Front (EPLF) which culminated successfully in the capture of Asmara on 24 May 1991. Thereafter the EPLF maintained a *de facto* independent administration recognized by the Ethiopian government. At a referendum on 23–25 April 1993 there was a 99·8% majority in favour of independence. Sovereignty was proclaimed on 24 May 1993. In 1999 fighting broke out along the border with Ethiopia.

TERRITORY AND POPULATION
Eritrea is bounded in the north-east by the Red Sea, south-east by Djibouti, south by Ethiopia and west by Sudan. Some 300 islands form the Dahlak Archipelago, most of them uninhabited. For the dispute with Yemen over the islands of Greater and Lesser Hanish *see* YEMEN: Territory and Population. Its area is 93,679 sq. km (36,171 sq. miles). Population, 1995 estimate, 3,531,000 (17·1% urban); density, 38 per sq. km.

The UN gives a projected population for 2000 of 3·81m.

1m. Eritreans lived abroad in 1995, 0·5m. as refugees in Sudan. A UN Programme for Refugee Reintegration and Rehabilitation of Resettlement Areas in Eritrea (PROFERI) is in operation.

There are 10 provinces: Akele Guzai, Asmara, Barka, Denkel, Gash-Setir, Hamasien, Sahel, Semhar, Senhit and Seraye. The capital is Asmara (1991 population, 367,300). Other large towns (with 1989 populations) are Assab (39,569), Keren (32,110) and Massawa (19,404). An agreement of July 1993 gives Ethiopia rights to use the ports of Assab and Massawa.

48% of the population speak Tigrinya and 31% Tigré, and there are 7 other indigenous languages. Arabic is spoken on the coast and along the Sudanese border, and English is used in secondary schools. Arabic and Tigrinya are the official languages.

SOCIAL STATISTICS
Births, 1995, 131,000; deaths, 48,000. Rates, 1995 (per 1,000 population): Birth, 41·4; death, 15·2. Annual growth rate, 1990–95, 2·7%. Life expectancy at birth, 1990–95, was 48·0 years for males and 51·2 years for females. Infant mortality, 1990–95, 107 per 1,000 live births; fertility rate, 5·8 births per woman.

CLIMATE
Massawa, Jan. 78°F (25·6°C), July 94°F (34·4°C). Annual rainfall 8" (193 mm).

CONSTITUTION AND GOVERNMENT
A referendum to approve independence was held on 23–25 April 1993. The electorate was 1,173,506. 99·8% of votes cast were in favour.

The transitional government has a 4-year term and consists of the *President* and a 130-member *National Assembly*. The latter consists of the members of the People's Front for Democracy and Justice (PFDJ; until Feb. 1994 EPLF) Central Committee and 60 other deputies (including 11 seats reserved for women). It elects the President, who in turn appoints the *State Council* made up of 14 ministers and the governors of the 10 provinces. The President chairs both the State Council and the National Assembly.

RECENT ELECTIONS
In the presidential and legislative elections in May 1997, President Afewerki was re-elected to office.

CURRENT ADMINISTRATION
President: Issaias Afewerki (b. 1945; elected 22 May 1993 and re-elected in May 1997).

In March 1999 the ministers in the State Council were:

Vice President, Local Government: Mahmud Ahmed Sherifo. *Agriculture:* Arefaine Berhe. *Commerce and Industry:* Ali Said Abdella. *Construction:* Abraha Asfaha. *Culture and Information:* Beraki Gebre Selasie. *Defence:* Sebhat Ephrem. *Education:* Osman Saleh. *Energy and Mining:* Tesfai Ghebreselassie. *Finance:* Gebreselassie Yoseph. *Fisheries:* Petros Solomon. *Foreign Affairs:* Haile Weldensae. *Health:* Saleh Meki. *Justice:* Fozia Hashim. *Labour and Human Welfare:* Ogbe Abraha. *Land, Water and Environment:* Tesfai Ghirmazion. *Tourism:* Ahmed Haj Ali. *Transport and Communications:* Saleh Idris Kekia.

Local Government. There are 10 provinces, each under a governor.

DEFENCE
Conscription for 18 months was introduced in 1994. The total strength of all forces was estimated at 35,000 in 1996.

Defence expenditure totalled US$65m. in 1997 (US$17 per capita).

Navy. Most of the former Ethiopian Navy is now in Eritrean hands. Strength is estimated as 1 small frigate, 1 fast torpedo craft, 6 patrol craft, 2 medium-landing ships and 5 amphibious craft. The main bases and training establishments are at Massawa and Assab.

Air Force. There are 20 aircraft: 3 Y-12 transports, 2 Mi-8 helicopters, 8 L-90TP Redigo liaison/training machines, 1 Astra VIP transport and 6 MB-339 armed trainers.

INTERNATIONAL RELATIONS
A border dispute between Eritrea and Ethiopia broke out in May 1998. Eritrean troops took over the border town of Badame after a skirmish between Ethiopian police units and armed men from Eritrea. Ethiopia maintained that Badame and Sheraro, a nearby town, had always been part of Ethiopia and called Eritrea's action an invasion. Sporadic fighting between Ethiopia and Eritrea continues along the border.

Eritrea is a member of the UN and OAU.

ECONOMY
Eritrea's resources are meagre, the population small and poorly-educated; communications are difficult and there is a shortage of energy.

Performance. Real GDP growth grew by almost 8% a year between 1994 and 1996.

Budget. Revenues in 1996 were US$226m. and expenditure US$453m. Over 40 enterprises are scheduled for privatization.

Currency. A new currency, the *nakfa*, has replaced the Ethiopian currency, the *birr*. Inflation was 9% in 1997.

Banking and Finance. The central bank is the National Bank of Eritrea (*Governor*, Tequie Beyene). All banks and financial institutions are state-run. There is a Commercial Bank of Eritrea with 12 branches, an Agricultural and Industrial Bank, a Housing and Commercial Bank and an Insurance Corporation.

ENERGY AND NATURAL RESOURCES
Electricity. Installed capacity was 73 MW in 1995.

Minerals. There are deposits of gold, silver, copper, zinc, sulphur, nickel, chrome and potash. Basalt, limestone, marble, sand and silicates are extracted. Oil exploration is taking place in the Red Sea.

Agriculture. Agriculture accounted for 10% of GDP in 1996. In 1995 approximately 79% of the economically active population were engaged in agriculture. Several systems of land ownership (state, colonial, traditional) co-exist. In 1994 the PFDJ proclaimed the sole right of the state to own land. Sorghum is cultivated. Livestock, 1995: Cattle, 1·31m.; camels, 69,000; sheep, 1·53m.; goats 1·4m.; chickens, 4m.

Forestry. In 1995 forests covered 282,000 ha, or 2·8% of the total land area.

Fisheries. The total catch in 1996 was 7,900 tonnes, almost exclusively from marine waters, but a joint French-Eritrean project to assess fish stocks in the Red Sea suggests a sustainable yield of up to 70,000 tonnes a year.

INDUSTRY
Light industry was well developed in the colonial period but capability has declined. Processed food, textiles, leatherware, building materials, glassware and oil products are produced.

Labour. In 1996 the labour force was 1,649,000 (53% males).

INTERNATIONAL TRADE
Eritrea is dependent on foreign aid for most of its capital expenditure, but there is no external debt.

Imports and Exports. In 1995 exports were valued at 529·5m. birr and imports at 2,608·5m. birr. The main exports are drinks, leather and products, textiles and oil products. Most exports go to Ethiopia; principal import suppliers: Saudi Arabia, Ethiopia, UAE.

COMMUNICATIONS

Roads. There were some 4,010 km of roads in 1996, around 875 km of which are paved. A tarmac road links the capital Asmara with one of the main ports, Massawa. In 1996 passenger cars in use numbered 5,940 (1·5 per 1,000 inhabitants). About 500 buses operate regular services.

Rail. The 117 km Asmara–Massawa line reopened in Jan. 1997.

Civil Aviation. There are international airports at Asmara and Assab. In 1998 services were provided by Air Djibouti, Daallo Airlines, Egyptair, Lufthansa, Saudia and United Airlines, with flights to Cairo, Djibouti, Dubai, Frankfurt, Jeddah and Riyadh. In 1996 Malabo handled 168,105 passengers (158,294 on international flights) and 2,959 tonnes of freight.

Shipping. Massawa is the main port; Assab is used mainly for imports to Ethiopia. Both are free ports for Ethiopia. Ethiopian Shipping Lines provide services. Merchant shipping totalled 12,000 GRT in 1995.

Telecommunications. International telephone links were restored in 1992. In 1997 there were 21,500 telephone main lines (5·7 for every 1,000 inhabitants), and in 1995, some 800 fax machines. There were approximately 300 Internet users in Jan. 1998.

Postal Services. In 1995 there were 35 post offices, equivalent to 1 for every 95,000 persons.

SOCIAL INSTITUTIONS

Justice. The legal system derives from a decree of May 1993.

Religion. Half the population are Sunni Moslems (along the coast and in the north), and half Coptic Christians (in the south).

Education. Adult literacy was about 25% in 1995. In 1995–96 there were 537 primary schools with 241,725 pupils and 5,828 teachers, and 80,089 pupils at secondary schools with 2,161 teachers. There is 1 university, with 3,200 students and 250 academic staff in 1994–95.

Health. In 1993 there were 10 small regional hospitals, 32 health centres, 65 medical posts, 68 doctors (equivalent to 1 for every 46,200 persons), 488 nurses, 33 midwives and 850 auxiliary medical personnel.

CULTURE

Broadcasting. There is daily radio and TV broadcasting. In 1995 there were 1,000 TV receivers and 310,000 radio receivers.

Press. There is a government daily in Arabic and Tigrinya.

Tourism. There were 417,000 foreign tourists in 1996.

DIPLOMATIC REPRESENTATIVES
Of Eritrea in Great Britain
Ambassador: Andebrhan Weldegiorgis (resides in Brussels).

Of Great Britain in Eritrea
Honorary Consul: Vacant.

Of Eritrea in the USA (1708 New Hampshire Avenue, NW, Washington, D.C., 20009)
Ambassador: Semere Russom.

Of the USA in Eritrea (Franklin D. Roosevelt St., POB 211, Asmara)
Ambassador: Vacant.

Of Eritrea to the United Nations
Ambassador: Haile Menkerios.

Of Eritrea to the European Union
Ambassador: Andebrhan Weldegiorgis.

FURTHER READING
Connel, D., *Against All Odds: a Chronicle of the Eritrean Revolution.* Trenton (NJ), 1993
Fegley, R., *Eritrea* [Bibliography]. Oxford and Santa Barbara (CA), 1995
Lewis, R., *Eritrea: Africa's Newest Country.* London, 1993

ESTONIA

Eesti Vabariik

(Republic of Estonia)

Capital: Tallinn
Population estimate, 2000: 1·42m.
GNP per capita: (PPP$) 4,660
HDI/world rank: 0·758/77

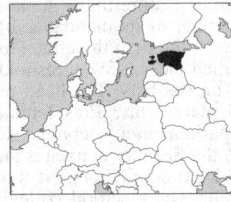

KEY HISTORICAL EVENTS

The disunity of the early Estonians made them subject to Viking incursions. In 1346 the Danes relinquished Estonia to German rule. It became part of the Holy Roman Empire and then a Swedish possession in the middle of the 17th century. On Sweden's defeat by Peter the Great, Estonia passed to the Russian Empire in 1721.

The workers' and soldiers' Soviets in Estonia took over power on 8 Nov. 1917, were overthrown by the German occupying forces in March 1918 and were restored to power as the Germans withdrew in Nov. 1918, establishing the 'Estland Labour Commune'. It was overthrown with the assistance of British naval forces in May 1919 and a democratic republic proclaimed. In March 1934 this régime was, in turn, overthrown by a fascist *coup*.

The secret protocol of the Soviet-German agreement of 23 Aug. 1939 assigned Estonia to the Soviet sphere of interest. An ultimatum (16 June 1940) led to the formation of a government acceptable to the USSR. On 21 July the Estonian parliament proclaimed the establishment of an Estonian Soviet Socialist Republic and applied to join the USSR; on 6 Aug. the Supreme Soviet of the USSR accepted the application.

On 30 March 1990 the Estonian Supreme Soviet proclaimed that the Soviet occupation of Estonia on 17 June 1940 had not disrupted the continuity of the former republic and adopted, by 73 votes to nil with 3 abstentions, a declaration calling for the eventual re-establishment of full sovereignty. At a referendum in March 1991, 77·8% of votes cast were in favour of independence. While an attempted coup was taking place in the USSR, parliament declared independence on 20 Aug. 1991. A fully independent status was conceded by the USSR State Council on 6 Sept. 1991.

TERRITORY AND POPULATION

Estonia is bounded in the west and north by the Baltic Sea, east by Russia and south by Latvia. There are 1,541 offshore islands, of which the largest are Saaremaa and Hiiumaa, but only 14 are permanently inhabited. Area, 45,227 sq. km (17,462 sq. miles); population, 1,462,100 (1997 estimate), giving a density of 32 per sq. km.

The UN gives a projected population for 2000 of 1·42m.

In 1995 an estimated 73·0% of the population lived in urban areas. The 1989 census population was 1,565,662, of whom Estonians accounted for 61·5%, Russians 30·3%, Ukrainians 3·1%, Belorussians 1·8% and Finns 1·1%. A census is scheduled for Jan. 2000. The capital is Tallinn (1997 population, 420,470). Other large towns are Tartu (101,901), Narva (75,211), Kohtla-Järve (53,485) and Pärnu (51,807). There are 15 districts, 33 towns and 26 urban settlements.

The official language is Estonian.

SOCIAL STATISTICS

1996 births, 13,000; deaths, 19,000. Rates (1996, per 1,000 population): Birth, 9·05, death, 12·95; infant mortality (per 1,000 live births), 10·4. There were 19,464 induced abortions in 1996 (25,587 in 1993). Expectation of life was 69·98 years in 1996. Annual growth rate, 1990–95, –0·5%. Fertility rate, 1990–95, 1·6 births per woman.

CLIMATE

Because of its maritime location Estonia has a moderate climate, with cool summers and mild winters. Average daily temperatures in 1996: Jan. –7°C; July 15°C. Rainfall is heavy, 500–700 mm per year, and evaporation low.

CONSTITUTION AND GOVERNMENT

A draft constitution drawn up by a constitutional assembly was approved by 91·1% of votes cast at a referendum on 28 June 1992. Turn-out was 66·6%. The constitution came into effect on 4 July 1992. It defines Estonia as a 'democratic state guided by the rule of law, where universally recognized norms of international law are an inseparable part of the legal system.' It provides for a 101-member national assembly (*Riigikogu*) elected for 4-year terms. There are 11 electoral districts with 8 to 11 mandates each. Candidates may be elected: a) by gaining more than 'quota', i.e. the number of votes cast in a district divided by the number of its mandates; b) by standing for a party which attracts for all of its candidates more than the quota, in order of listing; c) by being listed nationally for parties which clear a 5% threshold and eligible for the seats remaining according to position on the lists. The head of state is the *President*, elected by the Riigikogu for 5-year terms. Presidential candidates must gain the nominations of at least 20% of parliamentary deputies. If no candidate wins a two-thirds majority in any of 3 rounds, the Speaker convenes an electoral college, composed of parliamentary deputies and local councillors. At this stage any 21 electors may nominate an additional candidate. The electoral college elects the President by a simple majority.

Citizenship requirements are 2 years residence and competence in Estonian for existing residents. For residents immigrating after 1 April 1995, 5 years qualifying residence is required.

National Anthem. 'Mu isamaa, mu õnn ja rõõm' ('My native land, my pride and joy'); words by J. V. Jannsen, tune by F. Pacius (same as Finland).

RECENT ELECTIONS

Presidential elections were held in 3 rounds on 26–27 Aug. 1996. There were 2 candidates. No candidate gained sufficient votes to be elected. On 20 Sept. 1996 President Meri was re-elected by an electoral college against 4 opponents.

Parliamentary elections were held on 7 March 1999. The electorate numbered 857,270, turn-out was 57·43%. Of the 101 seats, the Estonian Centre Party (K) won 28 seats (with 23·4% of the total votes); Pro Patria Union (I), 18 seats (16·1%); Estonian Reform Party (RE), 18 seats (15·9%); Mõõdukad (M), 17 seats (15·2%); Estonian Coalition Party (KE), 7 seats (7·6%); the Country People's Party (EME), 7 seats (7·3%); Estonian United People's Party (EÜRP), 6 seats (6·1%).

CURRENT ADMINISTRATION

President: Lennart Meri (b. 1929; first elected 5 Oct. 1992 and sworn in 21 Oct.; re-elected 20 Sept. 1996).

Following the election in March 1999 the Cabinet comprised:

Prime Minister: Mart Laar (I).

Internal Affairs: Jüri Mõis (I). *Economic Affairs:* Mihkel Pärnoja (M). *Finance:* Siim Kallas (RE). *Defence:* Jüri Luik (I). *Foreign Affairs:* Toomas Hendrik Ilves (M). *Social Affairs:* Eiki Nestor (M). *Transport and Communications:* Toivo Jürgenson (I). *Justice:* Märt Rask (RE). *Education:* Tõnis Lukas (I). *Culture:* Signe Kivi (RE). *Agriculture:* Ivari Padar (M). *Environment:* Heiki Kranich (RE). *Minister without Portfolio for Ethnic Affairs:* Katrin Saks (M). *Minister without Portfolio for Regional Affairs:* Toivo Asmer (RE).

The *Speaker* is Toomas Savi.

Local Government. There are 254 local municipalities, of which 207 are rural municipalities, and 47 towns. The electorate consists of citizens and residents of 5 years' standing. Only citizens may stand for office.

Elections were held on 20 Oct. 1996. Turn-out was 52%. Candidates contended for 3,453 seats.

DEFENCE

The President is the head of national defence, advised by the *National Security Council*, comprising the Prime Minister, the Speaker, the Commander of the Estonian Defence Forces, 3 ministers and various military officials. Conscription is 12 months for men and voluntary for women. Conscientious objectors may opt for 15 months civilian service instead.

Defence expenditure in 1997 totalled US$119m. (US$81 per capita), representing 2·5% of GDP.

Army. The Army comprises 3 motorized infantry battalions and 1 signal, 1 logistic and 1 guard battalion. Personnel (1997) 3,742.

Navy. The Navy consists of a Naval base, a Naval Staff and 1 Naval division, and operates 4 minesweepers, 2 patrol craft and 3 support craft. Personnel (1997) 344.

Air Force. The Air Force consists of an Air Force Staff, an airbase at Åmari, and an air defence division, and has 2 Mi-2 helicopters and 2 AN-2 aeroplanes. Personnel (1997) 501.

Supporting units of the Armed Forces include a communications battalion and 1 background battalion. The Border Guards consist of 2,913 personnel (1997), with 10 ships, 25 launches and 37 motorboats. The Estonian Defence League consists of 8,500 volunteers.

INTERNATIONAL RELATIONS
Estonia is a member of the UN, the Council of Europe and the NATO Partnership for Peace, is an associate member of the EU and is an associate partner of the WEU. Estonia applied to join the EU in Nov. 1995.

ECONOMY
Policy. Privatization is being managed by the Estonian Privatization Agency under the jurisdiction of the Ministry of Finance. It has now entered its final phase with only large-scale infrastructure companies left to be sold. By June 1997, 456 enterprises had been privatized, realizing 3,300m. kroons.

Performance. GDP growth rate was 4% for 1996 and 11·4% in 1997. GDP in 1997 was estimated at 65,000m. kroons in current prices.

Budget. Budget estimates for 1998 balanced at 24,693m. kroons. Sources of revenue included sales tax, 6,841m. kroons; and personal and corporate income tax, 3,828m. kroons. Items of expenditure: Education, 2,391m. kroons; health service, 3,736m. kroons; recreational, cultural and religious affairs 1,071m. kroons; and social welfare, 8,975m. kroons. VAT is 18%.

Currency. The unit of currency is the *kroon* (EKR) of 100 *sents*. The kroon is pegged to the German mark within 3% of DM1 = 8 kroons. Foreign exchange reserves were 4,876m. kroons in May 1995. Gold reserves were 34·22m. kroons in Oct. 1998. Total money supply in Feb. 1998 was 12,914m. kroons. Inflation was 11·2% in Jan. 1997.

Banking and Finance. A central bank, the Bank of Estonia, was re-established in 1990 (*Governor:* Vahur Kraft). The Estonian Investment Bank was established in 1992 to provide financing for privatized and private companies. Since 1 Jan. 1996 banks have been required to have an equity of at least 50m. kroons. In 1998 there were 9 commercial banks. As a result of a wave of mergers the two largest groups, Hansabank and the Union Bank of Estonia, control 80% of the market. Total assets and liabilities of commercial banks at 30 Sept. 1997 were 34,093·4m. kroons.

A stock exchange opened in Tallinn in 1996.

Weights and Measures. The metric system is in use.

ENERGY AND NATURAL RESOURCES
Electricity. Most electricity is produced by burning oil shale. Installed capacity was 3·29m. kW in 1994. Production was 8·97bn. kWh in 1996. Consumption per capita in 1995 was estimated to be 4,005 kWh. A pilot wind-turbine project was set up in 1996.

Oil and Gas. There are rich oil-shale deposits estimated at 3,972m. tonnes in 1997. A factory for the production of gas from shale and a 208 km-pipeline from Kohtla-Järve supplies shale gas to Tallinn, and exports to St Petersburg. Natural gas is imported from Russia.

Water. A total of 6 isolated underground water complexes provide 75% of the water consumed.

Minerals. Oil shale is the most valuable mineral resource. Recently, production volume (which was 14·38m. tonnes in 1997) has decreased because of the decrease in oil shale consumption. There are extensive peat deposits, estimated at 1·5bn. tonnes in 1997. Phosphorites and super-phosphates are found and refined, and limestone, dolomite, clay, sand and gravel are mined.

Agriculture. Farming is concentrated on milk and meat production. In 1996 agriculture produced 7% of GDP. Large state and collective farms are being converted into shareholding enterprises. The remainder are being divided into small private holdings for collective farm workers or former owners. Farming employs around 7% of the population. At 1 Jan. 1997 there were 22,722 private farms averaging 22 ha, and 854 co-operatives and state farms. Minimum prices and the quantity of state purchases of agricultural produce were guaranteed by the government for 1997, along with agricultural supports of 332·81m. kroons.

At 1 Jan. 1997 there were 343,000 cattle (171,600 milch cows), 39,200 sheep and goats, 298,400 pigs and 2,324,900 poultry.

Output of main agricultural products (in 1,000 tonnes) in 1996: Wheat, 101·3; rye, 62·1; barley, 317·1; oats, 114·8; potatoes, 500·2; vegetables and greens, 54·7. Livestock products, 1996: Meat, 101,500 tonnes; milk, 674,800 tonnes; eggs, 300·8m.; wool, 159 tonnes.

Forestry. In 1995, 2·01m. ha (47·6% of the land area) were covered by forests, which provide material for sawmills, furniture, match and pulp industries, as well as wood fuel. Private, municipal and state ownership of forests is allowed. In 1996 there were 162,300 ha of privately owned forests out of a total of 2,016,200 ha. In 1995 the annual timber cut was 3·73m. cu. metres, of which 0·8m. cu. metres was from private forests.

Fisheries. Some 12,000 people are employed in the fishing and fish-processing industry. The total catch in 1996 was 108,500 tonnes, with a gross value of US$52m.

INDUSTRY
The main manufacturing industry is food processing which in 1997 accounted for 35·8% of the total manufacturing output. Other important areas are machinery and equipment, wood processing, and the manufacture of textiles, clothes and footwear, which made up 47·0% of the total output in 1997.

Labour. The workforce in 1997 totalled 703,700, of whom 629,800 were employed. There was a monthly minimum wage of 1,100 kroons (1998), and the average monthly wage (1997) was 3,573 kroons.

Retirement age was 63 years for both men and women in 1998.

Trade Unions. The main trade union organization in Estonia is the Estonian Association of Trade Unions, which represents the interests of industrial, service, trade, public and agricultural employees.

INTERNATIONAL TRADE
On 12 April 1990 Estonia, Latvia and Lithuania concluded a Baltic Economic Co-operation Agreement. A free trade agreement came into force on 1 April 1994. Estonia also has free trade agreements with the EU, EFTA, the Czech Republic, Slovakia, Slovenia, Ukraine and Turkey. The signing of the Free Trade and European (associate membership) agreements between Estonia and the European Union has been particularly significant for countries from outside the EU.

Foreign investment by country of origin in 1996 (% of total): Finland, 30%; Sweden, 21%; Russia, 7%; USA, 7%; Denmark, 4%; UK, 4%. Direct foreign investments into the Estonian economy in 1996 totalled 1,800m. kroons. Foreign trade balance in 1997 was US$–1·1bn. External debt was US$405m. in 1996.

Imports and Exports. Exports (in 1m. kroons) in 1995 (and 1996) were valued at 21,048·8 (24,988·3); imports, 29,111·9 (38,552·6). Main export markets, 1996: Finland, 4,583·6 (18·3% of the total); Russia, 4,107·8 (16·4%); Sweden, 2,890·2 (11·6%); Latvia, 2,066·2 (8·3%); Germany, 1,764 (7·1%); Lithuania, 1,434·4 (5·7%); Ukraine, 1,254·7 (5%); Denmark, 885·3 (3·6%); UK, 866·6 (3·5%); Netherlands, 753·3 (3%); USA, 552·4 (2·2%).

Main import suppliers: Finland, 11,257·4 (29·2% of total); Russia, 5,201·6 (13·5%); Germany, 3,843·3 (10%); Sweden, 3,149·8 (8·2%); UK, 1,275·6 (3·3%); Italy, 1,245·6 (3·2%); Netherlands, 1,098·7 (2·9%); Denmark, 1,088 (2·8%); USA, 882 (2·3%); Japan, 781·7 (2%); France, 779·1 (2%).

Around 65% of Estonian trade is with EU member countries and 50% with Finland and Sweden alone.

COMMUNICATIONS

Roads. At 1 Jan. 1997 there were 43,835 km of motor roads (10,080 km paved). The road network is being developed under a 10-year plan inaugurated in 1995.

In 1996 there were 406,598 passenger cars in use (278 per 1,000 inhabitants), plus 71,304 trucks and vans, 6,829 buses and coaches, and 4,680 motor cycles and mopeds.

Rail. Length of railways in 1996 was 1,021 km (1,520 mm gauge), of which 132 km was electrified. In 1996, 6·7m. passengers and 24·8m. tonnes of freight were carried.

Civil Aviation. There is an international airport at Tallinn (Ulemiste). In 1996 it handled 431,212 passengers and 3,997 tonnes of goods. The national carrier is Estonian Air, 34% state-owned. It carried 164,886 passengers in 1996. The smaller Estonian Aviation also provides international services. In 1998 Estonian Air operated services to Amsterdam, Copenhagen, Frankfurt, Hamburg, Helsinki, Kiev, London, Minsk, Moscow, Oslo, Riga, Stockholm and Vilnius, with Estonian Aviation flying to Riga and Turku. In 1998 Estonia was also served by Aeroflot, Air Baltic, Austrian Airlines, Finnair, Icelandair, Lauda Air, Lithuanian Airlines, SAS and Sochi Airlines-Aviaprima.

Shipping. There are 2 major shipping companies, one of which (the Estonian Shipping Company) is state-owned. It had 42 vessels totalling 428,466 DWT at 1 Jan. 1997. There are ice-free, deep-water ports at Tallinn and Muuga (state-owned). Tallinn handled 14m. tonnes of cargo and 4·43m. passengers in 1996. The ex-Soviet naval base at Paldiski is now vacant.

Telecommunications. There were 469,000 telephone main lines in operation in 1997 (321 per 1,000 persons). The total number of mobile phones exceeded 150,000 in Jan. 1998, and there were over 75,000 Internet users. In 1995 there were 10,000 PCs and 13,000 fax machines.

Postal Services. Postal services are run by the state-owned Eesti Post. In 1995 there were 582 post offices.

SOCIAL INSTITUTIONS

Justice. A post-Soviet criminal code was introduced in 1992. There is a 3-tier court system with the State Court at its apex, and there are both city and district courts. The latter act as courts of appeal. The State Court is the final court of appeal, and also functions as a constitutional court. There are also administrative courts for petty offences. Judges are appointed for life. City and district judges are appointed by the President; State Court judges are elected by Parliament.

In 1996, 35,411 crimes were reported (including 268 murders), of which 32·5% were solved. There are 9 prisons; in July 1997, 4,785 persons were in custody.

The death penalty was abolished in 1998.

Religion. There are about 0·35m. Lutherans and a Methodist Church. The Estonian Orthodox Church owed allegiance to Constantinople until it was forcibly brought under Moscow's control in 1940; a synod of the free Estonian Orthodox Church was established in Stockholm. Returning from exile, it registered itself in 1993 as the Estonian Apostolic Orthodox Church. By an agreement in 1996 between the Moscow and Constantinople Orthodox Patriarchates, there are now 2 Orthodox jurisdictions in Estonia. In 1996 there were some 35,000 Orthodox in 84 congregations; 37 congregations had opted for allegiance to Constantinople.

Education. Adult literacy rate in 1995 was over 99%. There are 9 years of comprehensive school starting at age 6, followed by 3 years secondary school. In 1996 pupils in 739 primary, secondary and special schools numbered 222,700; 602 of these general education schools were Estonian-language, 114 Russian-language and 23 mixed-language. In 1996, 59% of children between 1-6 years attended pre-school institutions. In 1996 there were 8 universities and 20 institutes of higher education with a total of 30,072 students, and 91 secondary vocational schools with 31,487 students.

In 1998 central government expenditure on education came to 2,391·1m. kroons.

Health. There were 79 state and 6 private hospitals in 1996, and 76 hospital beds per 10,000 population. In 1996 there were 304 doctors.

Welfare. In 1997 there were 0·37m. pensioners. The average monthly pension was 1,037 kroons in 1997. An official poverty line was introduced in 1993 (then 280 kroons per month). Persons receiving less are entitled to state benefit. Unemployment benefit was 240 kroons a month in 1996.

CULTURE

Broadcasting. Estonian Radio operates under the aegis of the Broadcasting Council. There are also 3 commercial radio networks and the government's foreign service, Radio Estonia (Estonian, English, Esperanto, Finnish, German and Spanish). In 1997 there were 3 TV networks (colour by SECAM): Estonian State Television and 2 commercial channels. Programming ventures must be at least 51% Estonian-owned, and foreign programmes must not exceed 30% of output. In 1995 there were 570,000 TV receivers and 730,000 radio receivers.

Cinema. In 1995 there were 220 cinemas. Attendances were 1m. in 1996.

Press. Most of the dailies and weeklies are in Estonian but there are some Russian papers. The English-language weekly is *The Baltic Times*.

Tourism. There were 2·62m. foreign visitors in 1997 who spent 8,300m. kroons. In 1997 tourism earned around 18% of GDP.

Festivals. Estonia's Song Festival, which was first held in 1869, is held every 5 years and was due to take place on 3–4 July 1999.

Baltoscandal, an international theatre festival which takes place every 2 years, celebrated its 5th anniversary in 1998.

Libraries. The Eesti Rahvusraamatukogu (National Library of Estonia), opened in 1993, hosts exhibitions of local and international art.

National Theatre and Opera. Most performances are in the Estonian language with the exception of the Russian Drama Theatre, and the Estonia Opera and Ballet Theatre which sometimes performs operas in their original language.

DIPLOMATIC REPRESENTATIVES
Of Estonia in Great Britain (16 Hyde Park Gate, London, SW7 5DG)
Ambassador: Raul Mälk.

Of Great Britain in Estonia (Kentmanni 20, Tallinn EE 0100)
Ambassador: Timothy James Craddock.

Of Estonia in the USA (1030 15th Street NW, Washington, D.C., 20005)
Ambassador: Grigore-Kalev Stoicescu.

Of the USA in Estonia (Kentmanni 20, Tallinn EE 0001)
Ambassador: Vacant.

Of Estonia to the United Nations
Ambassador: Sven Jurgenson.

Of Estonia to the European Union
Ambassador: Priit Kolbre.

FURTHER READING
Statistical Office of Estonia. *Statistical Yearbook.*
Ministry of the Economy. *Estonian Economy.* Annual
Hood, N. et al. (eds.) *Transition in the Baltic States.* London, 1997

Lieven, A., *The Baltic Revolution: Estonia, Latvia, Lithuania and the Path to Independence*. 2nd ed. Yale Univ. Press, 1994

Misiunas, R.-J. and Taagepera, R., *The Baltic States: Years of Dependence 1940–1991*. 2nd ed., Farnborough, 1993

Raun, T. U., *Estonia and the Estonians*. Stanford, 1987

Smith, I. A. and Grunts, M. V., *The Baltic States* [Bibliography]. Oxford and Santa Barbara (CA), 1993

Taagepera, R., *Estonia: Return to Independence*. Boulder (CO), 1993

National statistical office: Statistical Office of Estonia, Tallinn.
Website: http://www.stat.ee/

ETHIOPIA

Federal Democratic
Republic of Ethiopia

Capital: Addis Ababa
Population estimate, 2000: 66·18m.
GNP per capita: (PPP$) 500
HDI/world rank: 0·252/169

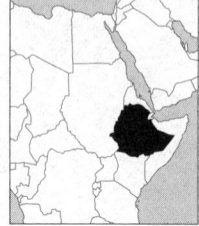

KEY HISTORICAL EVENTS

The ancient empire of Ethiopia has its legendary origin in the meeting of King Solomon and the Queen of Sheba. Historically, the empire developed at Askum in the north in the centuries before and after the birth of Christ as a result of Semitic immigration from South Arabia. The immigrants imposed their language and culture on the indigenous Hamitic people. Ethiopia's subsequent history is one of sporadic expansion southwards and eastwards, checked from the 16th to early 19th centuries by devastating wars with Moslems and Gallas. Modern Ethiopia dates from the reign of the Emperor Theodore (1855-68).

Menelik II (1889-1913) defeated the Italians in 1896 and thereby safeguarded the empire's independence in the scramble for Africa. By successful campaigns in neighbouring kingdoms within Ethiopia (Jimma, Kaffa, Harar, etc.) he united the country under his rule and created the empire as it is today.

In 1923 the heir to the throne, Ras Tafari (crowned Emperor Haile Selassie five years later), succeeded in getting Ethiopia admitted as an independent country to the League of Nations. However, the League was ineffective in preventing a second Italian invasion in 1936. The emperor fled the country, only returning when the Allied forces defeated the Italians in 1941.

In accordance with a resolution of the General Assembly of the UN, dated 2 Dec. 1950, the former Italian colony of Eritrea, from 1941 under British military administration, was handed over to Ethiopia on 15 Sept. 1952. Thereafter, a secessionist movement fought a guerrilla war for independence under the Eritrean Peoples' Liberation Front (EPLF). Another guerrilla campaign was waged in neighbouring Tigray, led by the Tigray Peoples' Liberation Front (TPLF). A provisional military government, known as the Dirgue, assumed power in Ethiopia on 12 Sept. 1974 under the leadership of Lieut. Col. Mengistu Haile Miriam. It deposed the emperor, abolished the monarchy and as a means of abolishing rural feudalism mounted an agricultural collectivization programme.

In 1977 Somalia invaded Ethiopia and took control of the Ogaden region. After an offensive mounted with strong Soviet and Cuban support the area was recaptured and in March 1978 Somalia withdrew all troops from the area. Control was re-established by Ethiopia later in 1978 and nationalist guerrillas were pushed back. Sporadic fighting continued in the Ogaden and along the border. Talks about the normalization of relations between Ethiopia and Somalia commenced in 1986.

The Workers Party of Ethiopia (WPE), set up by the Dirgue in 1984, drew up a constitution for a Peoples' Democratic Republic of Ethiopia which was approved by referendum in 1987. Elections took place in June and all central committee members were returned to office, including Mengistu who was elected President.

Following ever-increasing territorial gains by the insurgent Ethiopian People's Revolutionary Democratic Front (EPRDF) and the Eritrean People's Liberation Front (EPLF), Mengistu stepped down as president and fled the country. An interim EPRDF government led by Meles Zenawi took over after the flight of President Mengistu. In July 1991 a conference of 24 political groups, called to appoint a transitional government, agreed a democratic charter guaranteeing freedom of expression and association and the right to self-determination for ethnic groups. An 87-member Council of Representatives was formed which unanimously elected Meles Zenawi President. Eritrea seceded, and became independent, on 24 May 1993.

In 1999 fighting broke out along Ethiopia's border with Eritrea.

TERRITORY AND POPULATION

Ethiopia is bounded in the north-east by Eritrea, east by Djibouti and Somalia, south by Kenya and west by Sudan. It has a total area of 1,104,300 sq. km. The secession of Eritrea in 1993 left Ethiopia without a coastline. An Eritrean-Ethiopian agreement of July 1993 gives Ethiopia rights to use the Eritrean ports of Assab and Massawa.

The first census was carried out in 1984: Population, 42,019,418 (without Eritrea, 39,570,266). Estimate (1995), 56·68m. (15·4% urban); density, 51 per sq. km.

The UN gives a projected population for 2000 of 66·18m.

The 1994 Constitution provides for a federation of 9 regions: Afar, Amhara, Benshangi, Gambella, Harar, Oromia, The Peoples of the South, Somalia and Tigre.

The population of the capital, Addis Ababa, was estimated at 1·7m. in 1990. Other large towns (population, May 1984): Dire Dawa, in Hararge, 98,104; Nazret, in Shoa, 76,284; Bahr Dar, 54,800; Debre Zeit, 51,143.

There are 6 major ethnic groups (in % of total population in 1996): Oromo, 31%; Amhara, 30%; Tigrinya, 7%; Gurage, 4·7%; Somali, 4·1%; Sidamo, 3·2%. There are also some 60 minor ethnic groups and 286 languages are spoken. The *de facto* official language is Amharic, though Oromo-speakers form the largest group.

SOCIAL STATISTICS
Births, 1995, 2,741,000; deaths, 965,000. Rates per 1,000 population, 1995: Births, 48·6; deaths, 17·1. Expectation of life at birth in the period 1990–95 was 45·9 years for males and 49·1 years for females. The increase compared to the period 1980–85, when life expectancy was 38·4 years for males and 41·6 years for females, was the largest of any country in the world. Infant mortality, 1990–95, 119 per 1,000 live births; fertility rate, 7·0 births per woman.

CLIMATE
The wide range of latitude produces many climatic variations between the high, temperate plateaus and the hot, humid lowlands. The main rainy season lasts from June to Aug., with light rains from Feb. to April, but the country is very vulnerable to drought. Addis Ababa, Jan. 59°F (15°C), July 59°F (15°C). Annual rainfall 50" (1,237 mm). Harar, Jan. 65°F (18·3°C), July 64°F (17·8°C). Annual rainfall 35" (897 mm). Massawa, Jan. 78°F (25·6°C), July 94°F (34·4°C). Annual rainfall 8" (193 mm).

CONSTITUTION AND GOVERNMENT
A 548-member constituent assembly was elected on 5 June 1994; turn-out was 55%. The EPRDF gained 484 seats. On 8 Dec. 1994 it unanimously adopted a new federal Constitution which provides for the creation of a federation of 9 regions based (except the capital and the southern region) on a predominant ethnic group. These regions have the right of secession after a referendum. The *President*, a largely ceremonial post, is elected by parliament, the 548-member *Council of People's Representatives*. There is also an upper house, the 117-member *Federal Council*.

National Anthem. 'Yazegennat keber ba-Ityop yachchen santo' ('In our Ethiopia our civic pride is strong'); words anonymous, tune by S. Lulu.

RECENT ELECTIONS
Parliamentary and regional elections were held in May and June 1995. The electorate was 24m. Candidates from 47 parties stood. The EPRDF won 593 seats.

CURRENT ADMINISTRATION
President: Dr Negasso Gidada, b. 1950 (EPRDF; elected 22 Aug. 1995).

A new government was formed on 24 Aug. 1995 which comprised in March 1999:

Prime Minister: Meles Zenawi, b. 1955 (EPRDF).
Deputy Prime Minister: Kassu Ilala.
Minister of Agriculture: Dr Ketema Seifu. *Defence:* Teferra Walewa. *Economic Planning and Co-operation:* Ghirma Biru. *Education:* Genet Zewdie. *Finance:* Sufyan Ahmad. *Foreign Affairs:* Seyoum Mesfin. *Health:* Adem Ibrahim. *Information and Culture:* Wolde Michael Chamo. *Justice:* Worede-Wold Wolde. *Labour and Social Affairs, State Farms and Coffee and Tea Development:* Hassan Abdella. *Mines and Energy:* Ezaddin Ali. *Construction and Urban Development:* Haile Assegide. *Trade and Industry:* Kasahun Ayele. *Transport and Communications:* Abdulmejid Hussein. *Water Resources:* Shiferaw Jarso.

Speaker of the Council of Peoples' Representatives: Dawit Yohannes. *Speaker of the Federal Council:* Almaz Meko.

Local Government. Local authority elections were held on 21 June 1992. The electorate was about 33m.

DEFENCE
In 1997 defence expenditure totalled US$139m. (US$3 per capita).

Army. Following the overthrow of President Mengistu's government Ethiopian armed forces were constituted from former members of the Tigray Peoples' Liberation Front. Ethiopia auctioned off its naval assets in Sept. 1966. The strength of the armed forces is estimated at 120,000. Equipment includes some 350 T-54/-55 main battle tanks.

Air Force. Most of the Air Force is grounded and in the process of reorganization. Surviving aircraft are reported to include 20 MiG-21 and some MiG-23 fighters, 18 Mi-24 armed helicopters and 25 Mi-8 transport helicopters. There were airfields at Debre Zeit, Asmara, Gode, Dire Dawa and Deke.

INTERNATIONAL RELATIONS
A border dispute between Ethiopia and Eritrea broke out in May 1998. Eritrean troops took over the border town of Badame after a skirmish between Ethiopian police units and armed men from Eritrea. Ethiopia maintained that Badame and Sheraro, a nearby town, had always been part of Ethiopia and called Eritrea's action an invasion. Sporadic fighting between Ethiopia and Eritrea continues along the border.

Ethiopia is a member of the UN, OAU and is an ACP state of the EU.

ECONOMY
Policy. Following a long period of stagnation, the Ethiopian economy came to a turning point in 1991 when peace was restored. An Economic Reform Programme was instituted in 1992 aimed at stabilizing the economy and deregulating economic activities to prepare the ground for a free-market economy. Also in 1992, a government agency, the Ethiopian Investment Authority, was created to promote, facilitate and co-ordinate foreign investment in the country. An Economic Rehabilitation and Reconstruction Programme (ERRP), launched in 1991–92, eased foreign exchange regulations to allow for imports of raw materials and capital equipment.

A privatization programme began in 1995, since when more than 150 companies have been privatized, yielding some US$340m. for the state. Around 300 companies are to be privatized altogether.

Performance. Over the 3-year period from 1992–93 to 1994–95 real overall GDP growth averaged 6·5%. During the same period average growth rates of agricultural and industrial sectors were 2·4% and 14·5% respectively. Similarly, distributive and other services grew by 11·9% and 9·8%.

Budget. The fiscal year ends on 6 July. Revenue, 1996–97, US$1bn.; expenditure, US$1·5bn.

Currency. The *birr* (ETB), of 100 *cents*, is the unit of currency. The birr was devalued in Oct. 1992. Foreign exchange reserves, 1993, US$414·3m. Inflation in March 1998 was running at 5%.

Banking and Finance. The central bank and bank of issue is the National Bank of Ethiopia (founded 1964; *Governor*, Dubale Yale). The country's largest bank is the state-owned Commercial Bank of Ethiopia. The complete monopoly held by the bank ended with deregulation in 1994, but it still commands about 90% of the market share. On 1 Jan. 1975 the Government nationalized all banks, mortgage and insurance companies.

Weights and Measures. The metric system is officially in use. Traditional units include the *frasilla* (= approximately 37½ lb), and the *gasha*, which can vary between 80 and 300 acres. The Julian calendar remains in use; the year has 13 months, and is 7 years behind the Gregorian calendar.

ENERGY AND NATURAL RESOURCES

Electricity. Installed capacity in 1991 was 630,000 kW. Production in 1994 was 1·27bn. kWh. 98% of generation is hydro-electric. Consumption per capita was estimated to be 23 kWh in 1994. Supply: 220 volts; 50 Hz.

Oil and Gas. The Calub gas field in the south-east of Ethiopia has reserves estimated at 2,700bn. cu. ft.

Minerals. Gold, cement and salt are produced. Lege Dembi, an open-pit gold mine in the south of the country, has proven reserves of over 62 tonnes and produces more than 3 tonnes a year.

Agriculture. Agriculture contributes approximately 55% of GDP. Small-scale farmers make up about 85% of Ethiopia's population. There are 85m. ha of arable land, of which 16m. ha were cultivated in 1994. By 1993, 96% of agricultural land was worked by smallholdings averaging 0·5–1·5 ha. Land remains the property of the state, but individuals are granted rights of usage which can be passed to their children, and produce may be sold on the open market instead of compulsorily to the state at low fixed prices.

Coffee is by far the most important source of rural income. Teff (*Eragrastis abyssinica*) is the principal food grain, followed by barley, wheat, maize and durra. Cane sugar is an important crop.

Livestock, 1996: Cattle, 29·9m.; sheep, 21·7m.; goats, 16·7m. (1995); chickens, 54m. (1995).

Forestry. In 1995 forests covered 13·58m. ha, representing 13·6% of the land area (13·89m. ha and 13·9% of the land area in 1990). Timber production in 1995 was 47·34m. cu. metres.

Fisheries. The catch in 1995 was 6,380 tonnes, entirely from inland waters.

INDUSTRY

Most public industrial enterprises are controlled by the state. Industrial activity is centred around Addis Ababa. Processed food, textiles and drinks are the main commodities produced. In 1998 Ethiopia signed a US$500m. deal with the World Bank for power and road development projects.

Labour. The labour force in 1996 was 25,392,000 (59% males); it was estimated by the UN that 30% were unemployed.

INTERNATIONAL TRADE

Foreign debt was US$10,077m. in 1996.

Imports and Exports. Exports, 1994, US$372m.; imports, US$1,033m. Principal exports: Coffee (64%); raw hides and skins (16%). Principal imports: Refined petroleum products (12%); crude petroleum oils (9%); wheat and meslin (8%); motor vehicles for goods transport (7%).

Coffee accounts for about half of the country's export earnings. In 1997, 103,000 tonnes of coffee were exported, earning around US$360m. (£220m.) compared to just US$160m. (£100m.) in 1993. Other important exports include hides and skins, sugar, pulses and cattle.

Main export markets, 1994: Germany, 32%; Japan, 14%; Italy, 8%; Saudi Arabia, 8%. Main import suppliers, 1994: Saudi Arabia, 15%; USA, 12%; Italy, 11%; Germany, 8%.

COMMUNICATIONS

Roads. There were 28,500 km of roads in 1996, only about 4,300 km of which are paved. Passenger cars in use in 1996 numbered 47,715 (less than 1 per 1,000 inhabitants) and there were also 25,432 trucks and vans, and 11,900 buses and coaches.

In 1998 a US$500m. deal was signed with the World Bank for road and power development projects.

Rail. The Ethiopian-Djibouti Railway Corp. (782 km, metre-gauge) in 1993 carried 0·24m. tonnes of freight and 0·71m. passengers.

Civil Aviation. There are international airports at Addis Ababa (Bole) and Dire Dawa. The national carrier is the state-owned Ethiopian Airlines.

In 1998 Ethiopian Airlines served 44 international and 35 domestic destinations. Other scheduled services to Ethiopia were provided in 1998 by Aeroflot, Air Djibouti, Alitalia, Djibouti Airlines, Egyptair, Kenya Airways, Lufthansa, Saudia and Yemenia Yemen Airways. In 1995 Ethiopian Airlines flew 25·1m. km, carrying 749,900 passengers (479,700 on international flights). In 1996 Addis Ababa (Bole) handled 863,448 passengers and 33,476 tonnes of freight.

Shipping. Merchant shipping totalled 80,000 GRT in 1995.

Telecommunications. All the main centres are connected with Addis Ababa by telephone or radio telegraph. In 1998 there were 160,000 telephone main lines (2·6 per 1,000 persons), three-quarters of which are in Addis Adaba. By 2001 Ethiopian Telecommunications Corporation plans to have 550,000 lines installed. In 1995 there were 1,400 fax machines, and in Jan. 1998 approximately 3,000 Internet users.

Postal Services. In 1995 there were 570 post offices, or 1 for every 97,000 persons.

SOCIAL INSTITUTIONS

Justice. The legal system is said to be based on the Justinian Code. A new penal code came into force in 1958 and Special Penal Law in 1974. Codes of criminal procedure, civil, commercial and maritime codes have since been promulgated. Provincial and district courts have been established, and High Court judges visit the provincial courts on circuit. The Supreme Court at Addis Ababa is presided over by the Chief Justice.

Religion. About 53% of the population are Christian, mainly belonging to the Ethiopian Orthodox Church, and 30% Sunni Moslems. Amhara, Tigreans and some Oromos are Christian. Somalis, Afars and some Oromos are Moslems. About 12% of the population follow traditional animist beliefs.

Education. The adult literacy rate in 1995 was 35·5% (45·5% among males and 25·3% among females).

Primary education commences at 7 years and continues with optional secondary education at 13 years. Up to the age of 12, education is in the local language of the federal region. Pupil/teacher ratio: 33. In 1994–95 there were 2,722,192 pupils at 9,276 primary schools with 83,113 teachers, and 756,249 pupils with 23,605 teachers at secondary schools. During the period 1990–95 only 19% of females of primary school age were enrolled in school.

In 1994–95 there was 1 university with 19,200 students and 900 academic staff, and 1 agricultural university with 1,551 students and 324 academic staff. There were 2 institutes of health sciences and water technology; and 2 colleges—1 of teacher training and 1 of town planning.

Health. Population per hospital bed, 1994–95, 293,787; population per health centre, 22,242. In the period 1990–96 only 25% of the population had access to safe drinking water.

CULTURE

Broadcasting. The government-run Voice of Ethiopia broadcasts a national programme and an external service in English. Ethiopian Television (colour by PAL) transmits about 28 hours a week. In 1995 there were 10·9m. radio and 250,000 TV receivers.

Press. There are 4 government-controlled daily newspapers with a combined circulation of about 60,000, and about 50 independent periodicals.

Tourism. In 1997 there were 115,000 foreign visitors. Revenue from tourists in 1996 totalled US$46m.

DIPLOMATIC REPRESENTATIVES
Of Ethiopia in Great Britain (17 Prince's Gate, London, SW7 1PZ)
Ambassador: Dr Beyene Negewo.

ETHIOPIA

Of Great Britain in Ethiopia (Fikre Mariam Abatechan St., Addis Ababa)
Ambassador: G. G. Wetherell.

Of Ethiopia in the USA (2134 Kalorama Rd., NW, Washington, D.C., 20008)
Ambassador: Berhane Gebre-Chirstos.

Of the USA in Ethiopia (Entoto St., Addis Ababa)
Ambassador: David Shinn.

Of Ethiopia to the United Nations
Ambassador: Dr Duri Mohammed.

Of Ethiopia to the European Union
Ambassador: Peter Gabriel Robleh.

FURTHER READING

Alemneh Dejene. *Environment, Famine and Politics in Ethiopia: a View from the Village.* Boulder (Colo.), 1991

Araia, G., *Ethiopia: the Political Economy of Transition.* Univ. Press of America, 1995

Griffin, K. (ed.) *The Economy of Ethiopia.* London, 1992

Keller, E. J. *Revolutionary Ethiopia: From Empire to People's Republic.* Indiana Univ. Press, 1989

Marcus, H.G., *A History of Ethiopia.* California Univ. Press, 1994

Mekonnen, T. (ed.) *The Ethiopian Economy: Structure, Problems and Policy Issues.* Addis Ababa, 1992

Munro-Hay, S. and Pankhurst, R., *Ethiopia* [Bibliography]. Oxford and Santa Barbara (CA), 1991

Tiruneh, A., *The Ethiopian Revolution: a Transformation from an Aristocratic to a Totalitarian Autocracy.* CUP, 1993

National statistical office: Central Statistical Office, Addis Ababa.

FIJI ISLANDS

Capital: Suva
Population estimate, 2000: 848,000
GNP per capita: (PPP$) 4,070
HDI/world rank: 0·869/44

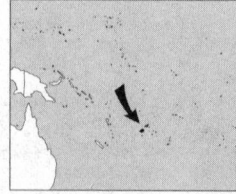

KEY HISTORICAL EVENTS

The Fiji Islands were discovered by Tasman in 1643 and visited by Capt. Cook in 1774, but first recorded in detail by Capt. Bligh after the mutiny of the Bounty (1789). In the 19th century the search for sandalwood, in which enormous profits were made, brought many ships. Deserters and shipwrecked men stayed on; firearms salvaged from wrecks were used in native wars, new diseases swept the islands, and rum and muskets became regular articles of trade. Tribal wars became bloody and general until Fiji was ceded to Britain on 10 Oct. 1874, after a previous offer of cession had been refused. Fiji gained independent status on 10 Oct. 1970.

Fiji remained an independent state within the Commonwealth with a Governor-General appointed by the Queen until 1987. In the general election of 12 April 1987 a left-wing coalition headed by Dr Timoci Bavadra defeated the ruling Alliance Party of Ratu Sir Kamisese Mara. The new government had the support of the Indian population who outnumbered the indigenous Fijians by 50% to 44%. It was, however, overthrown in a military coup on 14 May led by Lieut.-Col. Sitiveni Rabuka.

After a period of uncertainty in which civil government was largely restored, Brigadier Rabuka led a second coup on 25 Sept. On 7 Oct. Fiji declared itself a Republic and Fiji's Commonwealth membership lapsed.

In 1990 a new coalition restored civilian rule but made it impossible for Fijian Indians to hold power. However, a rapprochement with Indian leaders led to an agreement to restore multi-racial government in 1998. Fiji rejoined the Commonwealth in 1997. On 27 July 1998 a new constitution came into effect, whereby the country's name was changed from Fiji to Fiji Islands.

TERRITORY AND POPULATION

The Fiji Islands comprise 332 islands and islets (about one-third are inhabited) lying between 15° and 22° S. lat. and 174° E. and 177° W. long. The largest is Viti Levu, area 10,429 sq. km (4,027 sq. miles); next is Vanua Levu, area 5,556 sq. km (2,145 sq. miles). The island of Rotuma (47 sq. km, 18 sq. miles), about 12° 30' S. lat., 178° E. long., was added to the colony in 1881. Total area, 7,078 sq. miles (18,333 sq. km). Total population (1996), 772,655; density, 42 per sq. km.

The UN gives a projected population for 2000 of 848,000.

Of the Fiji Islands' current population some 60% live in rural areas. Population statistics for urban centres indicate that about 167,421 people live in the two major cities, Suva and Lautoka.

English is the official language; Fijian and Hindustani are also spoken.

SOCIAL STATISTICS

Births, 1995, 18,000; deaths, 3,500. 1994 birth rate per 1,000 population, 23·0; death rate per 1,000 population, 4·6. Annual growth rate, 1990–95, 1·7%. Life expectancy at birth in the period 1990–95 was 73·7 years for males and 69·5 years for females. Infant mortality, 1990–95, 23 per 1,000 live births; fertility rate, 3·0 births per woman.

CLIMATE

A tropical climate, but oceanic influences prevent undue extremes of heat or humidity. The S. E. Trades blow from May to Nov., during which time nights are cool and rainfall amounts least. Suva, Jan. 80°F (26·7°C), July 73°F (22·8°C). Annual rainfall 117" (2,974 mm).

CONSTITUTION AND GOVERNMENT

The executive authority of the State is vested in the President, who is appointed by the Bose Levu Vakaturaga (Great Council of Chiefs). The Prime Minister is appointed by the President. The Prime Minister must establish a multi-party cabinet. The President's term of office is 5 years.

The Upper House or Senate consists of 32 members of whom 14 are appointed by the President on the advice of Bose Levu Vakaturaga. 9 are appointed by the President on the advice of the Leader of the Opposition and 1 appointed by the President on the advice of the Council of Rotuma.

A new Constitution unanimously passed by Parliament and assented to by H.E. the President came into force on 27 July 1998. The country's name was changed from Fiji to Fiji Islands and the people were to be known as Fiji Islanders instead of Fijians. The new Constitution also does away with an indigenous Prime Minister and has a 71-seat *House of Representatives* (Lower House), with 46 elected on a communal role and 25 from an open electoral roll. Of the 46, 23 will be elected on Fijian roll, 19 from Indian roll, 3 from others and 1 from Rotuma.

National Anthem. 'Blessing grant, oh God of Nations, on the isles of Fiji'; words by M. Prescott, tune anonymous.

RECENT ELECTIONS

At elections to the *Vale* or *House of Representatives* on 18 and 25 Feb 1994 the nationalist Fijian Political Party/Soqosoqo ni Vakavulewa ni Taukei (FPP-SVT) won 31 seats of 37 seats from the Fijian roll, the National Federation Party (NFP) 20 of 27 from the Indian roll, the Fiji Labour Party (FLP) the other 7 from the Indian roll, the Fiji Association (FA) 5 from the Fijian roll and the other 7 seats went to smaller parties. Parliamentary elections were scheduled for 2 May 1999.

CURRENT ADMINISTRATION

President: Sir Ratu Kamisese Mara, GCMG, KBE (sworn in 18 Jan. 1994).

In March 1999 the government comprised:

Prime Minister, Minister with Special Responsibility for the Constitution, Multi-Ethnic Affairs, Regional Development: Maj.-Gen. Sitiveni Rabuka, OBE (b. 1948; SVT). *Deputy Prime Minister, Minister for Education and Technology:* Taufa Vakatale OF; *Agriculture, Fisheries and Forests:* Militoni Leveniqila. *Attorney-General:* Ratu Etuate Tavai. *Finance and Economic Development:* James Ah Koy. *Health and Social Welfare:* Leo Smith. *Commerce, Industry, Co-operatives and Public Enterprises:* Isimeli Bose. *Justice and Home Affairs:* Col. Paul Manueli, OBE. *Foreign Affairs and External Trade:* Berenado Vunibobo. *Fijian Affairs and the Agricultural Landlord and Tenant Act (ALTA):* Ratu Finau Mara. *Communications, Information, Public Works and Energy:* Ratu Inoke Kubuabola. *Women and Culture:* Seruwaia Hong Tiy. *National Planning:* Filipe Bole. *Local Government and Environment:* Vilisoni Cagimaivei. *Tourism:* David Pickering. *Labour and Industrial Relations:* Vincent Lobendahn. *Lands and Mineral Resources:* Ratu Timoci Vesikula. *Youth, Employment Opportunities and Sports:* Jonetani Kaukimoce.

Local Government. There are 14 provinces subdivided into 188 *tikinas*, each with its own provincial council. Tikinas are composed of village units headed by a locally elected or appointed chief. The number of tikina councils within a province varies from 4 to 22. Tikina councils have wide powers to make by-laws and levy rates to raise revenue. 50% of the rates collected is credited to the provincial council treasury for the running of the council and 50% is used for the financing of the tikina and village projects.

DEFENCE

In 1997 defence expenditure totalled US$48m. (US$63 per capita).

Army. The Army consists of 7 infantry battalions and 1 engineer battalion. Personnel in (1996) numbered close to 3,796. More than 800 of these are actively involved in peace-keeping duties with the United Nations in the Middle East.

Navy. The naval division of the armed forces consists of 4 Israeli-built fast inshore patrol craft, 5 other patrol craft. Naval personnel in 1997 numbered 275.

Air Force. The Fiji Air Wing operates 1 Dauphin and 1 Ecureuil helicopter, both supplied by France.

INTERNATIONAL RELATIONS

The Fiji Islands is a member of the UN, the Commonwealth, the Colombo Plan, the Pacific Community, the South Pacific Forum, and is an ACP member state of the ACP-EU relationship.

ECONOMY

Operating revenue (1997), $F700·00m. Operating expenditure (1997), $F550·00m.

Performance. The economy contracted in 1998, after the worst drought in a decade reduced sugar production. Economic growth in 1996 was 3·1%.

Budget. The financial year corresponds with the calendar year. Government revenue and expenditure (in $F1m.):

	1992	1993	1994	1995	1996
Revenue	574·37	636·14	689·02	710·18	736·18
Expenditure	646·23	754·40	786·20	801·14	881·44

VAT of 10% was introduced in 1992.

Currency. The unit of currency is the *Fiji dollar* (FJD) of 100 *cents.* Foreign exchange reserves were US$364m. in Jan. 1998. Inflation rate (Oct. 1997) 3%. Total money supply in Jan. 1998 was $F455m. The Fiji dollar was devalued by 20% in Jan. 1998.

Banking and Finance. The central bank and bank of issue is the Reserve Bank of Fiji. Total assets were $F493·07m. in June 1996. The National Bank is a government-owned commercial bank. The Fiji Development Bank has assets totalling $F356·01m. There are 6 foreign banks in the country. Total assets of commercial banks were $F1,797·92m. in June 1996.

ENERGY AND NATURAL RESOURCES

Electricity. The Fiji Electricity Authority is responsible for the generation, transmission and distribution of electricity in the country. It operates six separate supply systems. The largest energy project is one of hydro-electricity generating 95% of the main island's electric needs. Two rural hydro schemes have been completed, one generating 100 kilowatt and the other 800 kilowatt. In 1994 there were 7 thermal and 1 hydro-electric power stations.

Installed capacity in 1993 was 200,000 kW. Production was 510m. kWh in 1994. Consumption per capita in 1995 was an estimated 660 kWh.

Minerals. The main goldmine accounts for almost one tenth of the country's exports and employs about 1,700 people. Since the beginning of 1997 gold prices have been falling. However a total of 2,000 tonnes have been sold since 1991. Net sales in 1996 were 239 tonnes (gross sales were 588 tonnes). Gold is likely to overtake sugar as Fiji Island's main export by 2005. Estimated revenues are 3·5m. ounces.

Agriculture. With a total land area of 1·8m. ha, only 16% is suitable for farming. In 1996 agriculture accounted for 23% of GDP. Arable land: 24% sugar cane, 23% coconut, 53% other crops. In 1997 sugar production was forecast at 460,000 tonnes. Copra production increased to 10,700 tonnes in 1995. Ginger is the most successful diversification crop to date—1995 showed an increase of 1,000 tonnes; total export value for the 1995 crop was $F1,445,000. Rice production increased in 1995 with 18,500 tonnes. Fruits and vegetables were valued at $F1m. for 1,000 tonnes of export.

Livestock (1996): Cattle, 354,000; horses, 44,000; goats (1995), 211,000; pigs, 121,000; poultry (1995), 3m. Products, 1991 (in tonnes): Beef, 2,847; pork, 715; goat meat, 660; chicken meat, 5,888; eggs, 2,191. Total production in tonnes of milk increased in 1994 to 1,621 tonnes.

Forestry. Forests covered 835,000 ha (45·7% of the land area) in 1995, compared to 853,000 ha and 46·7% in 1990. Forestry contributes around 1·5% of GDP. It is the fifth most important export commodity, valued at $F53m. in 1996. Hardwood

FIJI ISLANDS

plantations established 48,270 ha. By 2000 Fiji Pine Ltd aims to establish 16,000 ha of plantation. Log production in 1996 was 556,986 cu. metres.

Fisheries. The catch in 1995 was 34,577 tonnes, of which 30,828 tonnes came from sea fishing. Fisheries accounts for 2% of GDP. Mainstay of export fisheries are the skipjack and albacore tuna for canning. There was an increase in export of fresh and chilled tuna from 53 tonnes (1989) to over 3,000 tonnes (1995).

INDUSTRY
The Tax Free Factory scheme was instituted in 1987 as an encouragement to industry. A total of 133 Tax Free Factories (TFF) were in operation in 1996, a decline from 144 in 1995. Of the total, 68 factories were engaged in garment manufacturing. The garment industry earned $F141m. in 1996.

Output, 1994 (in tonnes): Sugar, 475,000; coconut oil (1991), 8,775; flour, 26,933; butter, 1,477; cigarettes, 585; animal feed, 25,377; cement, 78,800; soap, 7,068; beer, 18·31m. litres.

Labour. Approximately 301,500 persons were in paid employment in 1996. There were 15,400 unemployed persons in 1995, or 5·4% of the workforce.

INTERNATIONAL TRADE
The Tax Free Factory/Tax Free Zone Scheme was introduced in 1987 to stimulate investment and encourage export-oriented businesses.

Foreign debt was US$217m. in 1996.

Imports and Exports. In 1996 total imports were US$990m. and total exports were US$748m. Chief exports are: Sugar, prepared and preserved fish, timber, ginger and molasses. Main export markets, 1996: Australia, 27·9%; UK, 14·4%; New Zealand, 12·4%; USA, 8·5%. Main import suppliers, 1996: Australia, 44·4%; New Zealand, 14·8%; USA, 9·3%; Japan, 5·7%.

COMMUNICATIONS

Roads. Total road length in 1996 was about 5,100 km, of which 1,030 km were sealed. A total of 95,554 vehicles were registered in the Fiji Islands in 1994.

Rail. Fiji Sugar Cane Corporation runs 600 mm gauge railways at four of its mills on Viti Levu and Vanua Levu, totalling 595 km.

Civil Aviation. There are international airports at Nadi and Suva. The national carrier is Air Pacific (78% government-owned). In 1998 it provided services to Australia, Japan, New Zealand, USA and a number of Pacific island nations. Air Fiji only operates on domestic routes. Services were also provided in 1998 by Air Calédonie International, Air Marshall Islands, Air Nauru, Air New Zealand, Air Vanuatu, Canadian Airlines International, Polynesian, Qantas Airways, Royal Tongan Airlines, Solomon Airlines, Sunflower Airlines and United Airlines. In 1996 Nadi handled 940,146 passengers (762,495 on international flights) and 22,203 tonnes of freight.

Shipping. The 3 ports of entry are Suva, Lautoka and Levuka. Ocean-going shipping totalled 27,385 GRT in 1995, including oil tankers, 4,705 GRT. Inter-island shipping fleet is a mix of private and government vessels. A total of 620 foreign vessels called into the Suva port in 1995, 318 and 109 respectively in Lautoka and Levuka. Altogether 7,189 ships including local ships, yachts and foreign vessels called into the three major ports.

Telecommunications. The national telephone service had 71,800 telephone main lines in 1997 (91·9 for every 1,000 population), of which 40% are business customers and 60% residential. There are over 500 cardphones located around the country and approximately 83 in rural areas. In 1995 there were 3,000 fax machines in use and 2,200 cellular phone subscribers.

Postal Services. 19·6m. items were posted in the Fiji Islands for delivery to local addresses in addition to 4·76m. items posted for overseas destinations, making total posting of 24·45m. items in 1995. There are currently 50 major post offices and 108 postal agencies.

SOCIAL INSTITUTIONS

Justice. An independent Judiciary is guaranteed under the constitution. The Constitution allows for a High Court which has unlimited original jurisdiction to hear and determine any civil or criminal proceedings under any law.

The High Court also has jurisdiction to hear and determine constitutional and electoral questions including the membership of members of the House of Representatives.

The Chief Justice of the Fiji Islands is appointed by the President acting after consultation with the Prime Minister.

The Fiji Islands' Court of Appeal, of which the Chief Justice is *ex officio* President, is formed by three specially appointed Justices of Appeal. The Justices of Appeal are appointed by the President acting after consultation with the Judicial and Legal Services Commission. Generally, any person convicted of any offence has a right of appeal from the High Court of Appeal. The final appellant court is the Supreme Court. Most matters coming before the Superior Courts originate in Magistrates' Courts.

Police. The Royal Fiji Police Force had (1997) a total strength of 1,915.

Religion. In 1996 the population consisted of 52% Christians, 39·4% Hindus, 7·8% Muslims, 0·7% Sikhs and 0·1% others.

Education. Adult literacy rate was 91·6% in 1995 (93·8% among males and 89·3% among females). Of the total estimated population of the Fiji Islands in 1996 (mid-year), 26·4% were attending school full-time. The number of registered schools totalled 1,261. Of these there were 391 pre-schools, 16 special schools, 698 primary schools, 151 secondary schools and 5 post secondary schools. The number of primary school teachers was 4,921. The number of civil servant teachers in secondary schools was 2,310.

The University of the South Pacific, which is located in Suva, serves 12 countries in the South Pacific region. The Fiji Islands also has a college of agriculture, school of medicine and nursing, an institute of technology, a primary school teacher training college and an advanced college of education.

Health. There are 409 village clinics, 100 nursing stations, 74 health centres, 3 area hospitals, 3 nursing homes, 16 sub-divisional hospitals, 3 divisional hospitals and 2 speciality hospitals. In 1994 there were 426 doctors, 40 dentists and 1,631 nurses.

Through its national health service system, the government continues to provide the bulk of health services both in the curative and public health programmes.

CULTURE

Broadcasting. There are two major radio stations, Island Network Corporation Ltd and Communications Fiji Ltd. Each has its own unique programmes to suit the culture, age and taste of the nation's radio audience. Fiji Television Company is a commercial network that has 1 free to air and 2 pay channels. In 1995 there were 14,000 TV receivers and 480,000 radio receivers.

Press. There are 2 daily newspapers, *Fiji Times and Herald* and *The Daily Post*. Vernacular newspapers are also published by these two, including *Nai Lalakai, Nai Volasiga* and *Shanti Dut*. Other locally produced periodicals are the *Review, Island's Business, Fiji First, Pacific Islands Monthly* and *Marama Vou.*

Tourism. Visitor arrivals in 1997 totalled 359,441 earning US$460·2m., 20% of GDP. The inauguration of new flight routes and their associated promotions contributed to an increase in visitors.

Festivals. As the focal point of its Millennium celebrations, the Fiji Islands are holding Millennium 2000—Fiji Islands Festival. It will be a two-week global festival of music and arts and will include a dusk-to-dawn New Year's eve concert.

DIPLOMATIC REPRESENTATIVES
Of the Fiji Islands in Great Britain (34 Hyde Park Gate, London, SW7 5DN)
Ambassador: Filimone Jitoko.

FIJI ISLANDS

Of Great Britain in the Fiji Islands (Victoria House, 47 Gladstone Rd., Suva)
High Commissioner: M. A. C. Dibben.

Of the Fiji Islands in the USA (2233 Wisconsin Ave., NW, Washington, D.C., 20007)
Ambassador: Napolioni Masirewa.

Of the USA in the Fiji Islands (31 Loftus St., Suva)
Chargé d'Affaires: Vacant.

Of the Fiji Islands to the United Nations
Ambassador: Poseci Bune.

Of the Fiji Islands to the European Union
Ambassador: Kaliopate Tavola.

FURTHER READING

Bureau of Statistics. *Current Economic Statistics.* Quarterly
Reserve Bank of Fiji. *Quarterly Review*
Bain, K., *Fiji at the Crossroads.* London, 1989
Gorman, G. E. and Mills, J. J., *Fiji* [Bibliography]. Oxford and Santa Barbara (CA), 1994
Howard, M. C., *Fiji: Race and Politics in an Island State.* Univ. of British Columbia Press, 1991
Lal, B. J., *Broken Waves: a History of the Fiji Islands in the Twentieth Century.* Univ. of Hawaii Press, 1992
Lal, V., *Fiji: Coups in Paradise.* London, 1991
Ravuvu, A., *The Façade of Democracy: Fijian Struggles for Political Control.* Suva, 1991
Scarr, D., *Fiji: a Short History.* Sydney, 1984
Sutherland, W., *Beyond the Politics of Race: an Alternative History of Fiji to 1992.* Australian National Univ. Press, 1992
Wright, R., *On Fiji Islands.* London, 1987

National statistical office: Bureau of Statistics, POB 2221, Government Buildings, Suva.

FINLAND

Suomen Tasavalta—
Republiken Finland

Capital: Helsinki
Population estimate, 2000: 5·18m.
GNP per capita: 18,260
HDI/world rank: 0·942/6

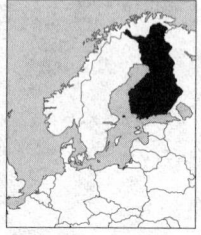

KEY HISTORICAL EVENTS

Finland was part of Sweden until the 18th century when the south-east territory was conquered by Russia. The rest of the country was ceded to Russia by the treaty of Hamina in 1809 when Finland became an autonomous grand-duchy retaining its laws and institutions under a grand duke, the Emperor of Russia. The Diet, elected since 1906 on universal suffrage, produced in 1916 a social democrat majority, the first in Europe. After the Russian revolution Finland declared itself independent but civil war broke out in Jan. 1918 between the 'whites' and 'reds', the latter supported by Russian Bolshevik troops. The defeat of the red guards in May 1918 freed the country from Russian troops. A peace treaty with Soviet Russia was signed in 1920.

On 30 Nov. 1939 Soviet troops invaded in what became known as the Winter War. The subsequent peace treaty of 12 March 1940 compelled Finland to cede 32,806 sq. km including the Carelian Isthmus, Viipuri and the shores of Lake Ladoga.

When the German attack on the USSR was launched in June 1941 Finland again became involved in war against the USSR. On 19 Sept. 1944 an armistice was signed in Moscow. Finland agreed to cede to the USSR the Petsamo area in addition to the cessions made in 1940 (total 42,934 sq. km), to lease to the USSR for 50 years the Porkkala headland as a military base, and to pay 300m. gold dollars in reparations within six years (later extended to eight years). The peace treaty was signed in Paris on 10 Feb. 1947. The payment of reparations was completed on 19 Sept. 1952. The military base at Porkkala was returned to Finland on 26 Jan. 1956. To pacify the USSR, the post-war premier and later president Juho Passikivi pursued a policy of neutralism favourable to the Russians. This policy, known as Finlandization, was continued under Presidents Urho Kekkonen (1956-81) and Mauno Koivisto (1981-94).

With the collapse of the Soviet Union, Finland was able to adopt an independent foreign policy which led to EU admission in 1995.

TERRITORY AND POPULATION

Finland, a country of lakes and forests, is bounded in the north-west and north by Norway, east by Russia, south by the Baltic Sea and west by the Gulf of Bothnia and Sweden. The area and the population of Finland on 31 Dec. 1996 (Swedish names in brackets):

Province	Area (sq. km)[1]	Population	Population per sq. km
Uusimaa (Nyland)	6,366	1,257,702	197·6
Itä–Uusimaa (Östra Nyland)	2,747	87,287	31·8
Varsinais–Suomi (Egentliga Finland)	10,624	439,973	41·4
Satakunta	8,290	242,021	29·2
Kanta–Häme (Egentliga Tavastland)	5,204	165,026	31·7
Pirkanmaa (Birkaland)	12,605	442,053	35·1
Päijät–Häme (Päijänne–Tavastland)	5,133	197,710	38·5
Kymenlaakso (Kymmenedalen)	5,106	190,570	37·3
Etelä–Karjala (Södra Karelen)	5,674	138,852	24·5
Etelä–Savo (Södra Savolax)	14,436	171,827	11·9
Pohjois–Savo (Norra Savolax)	16,510	256,760	15·6
Pohjois–Karjala (Norra Karelen)	17,782	175,137	9·8
Keski-Suomi (Mellersta Finland)	16,248	259,839	16·0

FINLAND

Province	Area (sq. km)[1]	Population	Population per sq. km
Etelä–Pohjanmaa (Södra Österbotten)	13,458	198,641	14·8
Pohjanmaa (Österbotten)	7,675	174,230	22·7
Keski–Pohjanmaa (Mellersta Österbotten)	5,286	72,336	13·7
Pohjois–Pohjanmaa (Norra Österbotten)	35,291	359,724	10·2
Kainuu (Kajanaland)	21,567	93,218	4·3
Lappi (Lappland)	93,003	199,051	2·1
Ahvenanmaa (Åland)	1,527	25,392	16·6
Total	304,529	5,147,349	16·9

[1]Excluding inland water area which totals 33,615 sq. km.

The growth of the population, which was 421,500 in 1750, has been:

End of year	Urban[1]	Semi-urban[2]	Rural	Total	Percentage urban
1800	46,600	. . .	786,100	832,700	5·6
1900	333,300	. . .	2,322,600	2,655,900	12·5
1950	1,302,400	. . .	2,727,400	4,029,800	32·3
1970	2,340,300	. . .	2,258,000	4,598,300	50·9
1980	2,865,100	. . .	1,922,700	4,787,800	59·8
1990	2,846,220	803,224	1,349,034	4,998,500	56·9
1995	2,978,170	896,775	1,241,881	5,116,826	58·2
1996	3,004,850	895,526	1,231,944	5,132,320	58·5
1997	3,077,050	854,015	1,216,284	5,147,349	59·8

The classification urban/rural has been revised as follows:

[1]Urban—at least 90% of the population lives in urban settlements, or in which the population of the largest settlement is at least 15,000.

[2]Semi-urban—at least 60% but less than 90% live in urban settlements, or the population of the largest settlement is more than 4,000 but less than 15,000.

The population on 31 Dec. 1997 by language spoken: Finnish, 4,773,576; Swedish, 293,691; other languages, 78,366; Lappish, 1,716.

The UN gives a projected population for 2000 of 5·18m.

The principal towns with resident population, 31 Dec. 1997, are (Swedish names in brackets):

Helsinki (Helsingfors)—capital	539,363	Rovaniemi	35,718
Espoo (Esbo)	200,834	Kokkola (Karleby)	35,513
Tampere (Tammerfors)	188,726	Järvenpää	34,768
Vantaa (Vanda)	171,297	Lohja (Lojo)	34,172
Turku (Åbo)	168,772	Mikkeli (St Michel)	32,847
Oulu (Uleåborg)	113,567	Kouvola	31,884
Lahti	95,854	Imatra	31,508
Kuopio	85,862	Kerava	29,830
Pori (Björneborg)	76,566	Seinäjoki	29,417
Jyväskylä	76,194	Savonlinna (Nyslott)	28,682
Lappeenranta (Villmanstrand)	57,196	Nokia	26,476
Vaasa (Vasa)	56,277	Riihimäki	25,975
Kotka	55,769	Kemi	24,485
Joensuu	50,980	Varkaus	23,893
Hämeenlinna (Tavastehus)	45,380	Iisalmi	23,772
Porvoo (Borgå)	43,791	Salo	23,561
Hyvinkää (Hyvinge)	41,685	Tornio	23,116
Rauma (Raumo)	37,654	Raisio	22,854
Kajaani	36,541	Kuusankoski	21,713

Nearly 60% of the population live in urban areas. About one-fifth of the total population lives in the Helsinki metropolitan region.

Finnish and Swedish are the official languages. Sami is spoken in Lapland.

SOCIAL STATISTICS
Statistics in calendar years:

	Living births	Of which outside marriage	Still-born	Marriages	Deaths (exclusive of still-born)	Emigration
1991	65,395	17,896	306	24,732	49,294	5,984
1992	66,731	19,257	288	23,560	49,844	6,055
1993	64,826	19,665	271	24,660	50,988	6,405
1994	65,231	20,439	249	24,898	48,000	8,672
1995	63,067	20,886	293	23,737	49,280	8,957
1996	60,723	21,484	231	24,464	49,167	10,587
1997	59,329	21,659	221	23,444	49,108	9,854

In 1997 the rate per 1,000 population was: Births, 12; marriages, 5; deaths, 10; infant deaths (per 1,000 live births), 3·7. Annual growth rate, 1990–95, 0·5%. Over 1990–95, the suicide rate per 100,000 population was 29·8 (men, 48·9; women, 11·7). Life expectancy at birth, 1990–95, 72·0 years for males and 79·6 years for females. In 1995 the most popular age range for marrying was 25–29 for both males and females. Fertility rate, 1990–95, 3·0 births per woman.

CLIMATE
A quarter of Finland lies north of the Arctic Circle. The climate is severe in winter, which lasts about 6 months, but mean temperatures in the south and south-west are less harsh, 21°F (–6°C). In the north, mean temperatures may fall to 8·5°F (–13°C). Snow covers the ground for three months in the south and for over six months in the far north. Summers are short but quite warm, with occasional very hot days. Precipitation is light throughout the country, with one third falling as snow, the remainder mainly as convectional rain in summer and autumn. Helsinki (Helsingfors), Jan. 21°F (–6°C), July 62°F (16·5°C). Annual rainfall 24·7" (618 mm).

CONSTITUTION AND GOVERNMENT
Finland is a republic governed by the Constitution of 17 July 1919.

Parliament consists of one chamber of 200 members chosen by direct and proportional election by all citizens of 18 or over. The country is divided into 15 electoral districts, with a representation proportional to their population. Every citizen over the age of 18 is eligible for Parliament, which is elected for 4 years, but can be dissolved sooner by the President.

The *President* is elected for 6 years by direct popular vote. In the event of no candidate winning an absolute majority, a second round is held between the 2 most successful candidates.

National Anthem. 'Maamme'/'Vårt land' ('Our land'); words by J. L. Runeberg, tune by F. Pacius (same as Estonia).

RECENT ELECTIONS
Presidential elections were held in 2 rounds on 16 Jan. and 6 Feb. 1994. Martti Ahtisaari won the first round against 10 opponents with 25·9% of votes cast, and the second against 1 opponent with 53·9%. Turn-out at the second round was 82·3%. Presidential elections are scheduled for 2000.

At the elections for the 200-member parliament on 21 March 1999, turn-out was 68%. The Social Democratic Party (SDP) won 51 seats with 22·9% of votes cast (63 seats and 28·3% in 1995); Centre Party, 48 with 22·4%; National Coalition Party, 46 with 21·0%; Left Wing League, 20 with 10·9%; Greens, 11 with 7·3%; Swedish People's Party in Finland (SPP), 11 with 5·1%; Finnish Christian League, 10 with 4·2%. 3 other parties each obtained 1 seat.

European Parliament. Finland has 16 representatives. At the Oct. 1996 elections turn-out was 60%. The Centre Party gained 24·4% of votes cast; the SDP, 21·5%; the LWA, 10·5%; the Greens, 7·6%. EU-parliament elections were scheduled for June 1999.

CURRENT ADMINISTRATION
President: Martti Ahtisaari (b. 1937; Social Democrat; sworn in 1 March 1994).

The Council of State (Cabinet) is composed of a 'rainbow' coalition, spanning the former Communist Left Wing Alliance at one end and the conservative National Coalition party at the other. In March 1999 it comprised:

Prime Minister: Paavo Lipponen (b. 1941; SDP).

Minister of Finance: Sauli Niinistö (NCP). *Foreign Affairs:* Tarja Halonen (SDP). *Justice:* Jussi Järventaus (NCP). *Education:* Olli-Pekka Heinonen (NCP). *Culture:* Suvi-Anne Siimes (LWA). *European Affairs:* Ole Norrback (SPP). *Interior (Police Affairs):* Jan-Erik Enestam (SPP). *Trade and Industry:* Antti Kalliomäki (SDP). *Transport and Communications:* Kimmo Sasi. *Social Affairs and Health:* Tertu Huttu-Juntenen (LWA). *Labour:* Liisa Jaakonsaari (SDP). *Defence:* Anneli Taina (NCP). *Environment:* Pekka Haavisto (Greens). *Administrative Affairs:* Jouri Backman (SDP). *Agriculture and Forestry:* Kalevi Hemilä (ind).

The *Speaker* is Riitta Uosukainen.

Local Government. Finland is divided into 6 provinces (*lääni*, Sw.: *län*). The administration of each province is entrusted to a governor (*maaherra*, Sw.: *landshövding*) appointed by the President. The governor directs the activities of the provincial office (*lääninhallitus*, Sw.: *länsstyrelse*) and of local districts (*kihlakunta*, Sw.: *härad*). In 1997 the number of local districts was 88.

The unit of local government is the municipality (*kunta*, Sw.: *kommun*). Main fields of municipal activities are local planning, roads and harbours, sanitary services, education, health services and social aid. The municipalities raise taxes independent from state taxation. Two categories of municipalities are distinguished by names: Towns (*kaupunki*, Sw.: *stad*), and other municipalities. In 1997 there were altogether 452 municipalities of which 107 were towns. In all municipalities, municipal councils are elected for terms of 4 years; all inhabitants (men and women) of the municipality who have reached their 18th year are entitled to vote and eligible. The executive power is in each municipality vested in a board which consists of members elected by the council. Several municipalities regularly form associations for the administration of common institutions, *e.g.*, a hospital or a vocational school, as well as for regional development and planning. Elections were held on 20 Oct. 1996. The SDP gained 24·5% of votes cast, the Centre Party, 21·8%.

The semi-autonomous province of **Åland Islands** occupies a special position as a demilitarized area. **Åland** elects a 30-member Legislature (*Lagting*), which in turn elects the provincial Executive Board. The capital is Mariehamn (Maarianhamina). It is 95% Swedish-speaking. At a referendum on 20 Nov. 1994 Åland voted to join the EU along with the rest of Finland.

DEFENCE

The period of military training is 180, 280 or 362 days with refresher training obligation of 40 to 100 days between conscript service and age 50 (officers and non-commissioned officers age 60). Total strength of trained and equipped reserves is about 500,000.

Defence expenditure in 1997 totalled US$1,956m. (US$381 per capita), representing 1·7% of GDP.

Army. The country is divided into 3 military commands which include 12 military provinces. The Army consists of 1 armoured training brigade, 6 infantry training brigades, 3 infantry regiments, 1 artillery brigade, 3 brigade artillery regiments, 2 coast artillery regiments, 3 independent coast artillery battalions (1 motorized), 4 anti-aircraft regiments, 1 engineer regiment (including ABC school), 3 brigade engineer battalions, 1 signals regiment, 3 brigade signals battalions and a reserve Officer School, making a total strength of 27,300 (21,600 conscripts).

Frontier Guard. This comes under the purview of the Ministry of the Interior, but is militarily organized to participate in the defence of the country. It is in charge of border surveillance and border controls. It is also responsible for conducting maritime search and rescue operations. Personnel, 1998, 3,300 (professional).

Navy. The organization of the Navy was changed on 1 July 1998. The Coastal Defence, comprising the coast artillery and naval infantry, was merged into the navy.

The Navy is divided into 7 units. About 50% of the combatant units are kept manned, with the others on short-notice reserve and re-activated on a regular basis.

The inventory comprises 2 corvettes, 9 missile craft, 4 patrol craft, 10 minelayers and 6 inshore minesweepers. There are 4 landing craft and some 30 auxiliaries and tenders.

Naval bases exist at Upinniemi (near Helsinki), Turku and Kotka. Naval Infantry mobile troops are trained at Tammisaari. Total personnel strength (1998) was 7,750, of whom 5,400 were conscripts.

The National Board of Navigation has 9 civil-manned icebreakers.

Air Force. The Air Force has 3 air commands, 1 support squadron, an Air Force Academy, an aircraft and weapons systems school, a C3 systems school (command, control and communications), 2 depots and an electric support measures group. The air commands have 36 MiG-21-BIS and Saab J35 Draken S and F aircraft, including two-seater trainer models. 7 double-seater and 57 single-seater F-18 Hornets are to replace these by the end of the year 2000. The first were delivered in 1995 and 29 were already in service by the end of Nov. 1998. Other equipment includes 28 Valmet Vinka piston-engine primary trainers of Finnish design, 52 Hawk Mk51/51A advanced jet trainers, 3 Fokker F.27 Friendship transport aircraft, 3 Gates Learjet 35 transport aircraft, 8 Piper Arrow liaison aircraft, 9 locally built Redigo liaison aircraft and 6 Piper Chieftain utility transports. Personnel (1998), 4,300 (1,500 conscripts).

INTERNATIONAL RELATIONS
Finland is a member of the UN, EU, Nordic Council, OECD, the NATO Partnership for Peace and the Council of Europe. Finland has acceded to the Schengen Accord, which abolishes border controls between Finland and Austria, Belgium, Denmark, France, Germany, Greece, Iceland, Italy, Luxembourg, the Netherlands, Norway, Portugal, Spain and Sweden.

ECONOMY
Policy. The Finnish economy not only saw rapid growth in the late 1990s but also redressed a number of imbalances in the economy. Owing to these developments, employment has risen substantially, aided by reductions in taxes and indirect labour costs as well as by structural reforms that have improved the functioning of the labour markets. Finnish public finances have been brought into balance and state debt into decline, as targeted by the government.

Performance. Real GDP growth was 6·0% in 1997 and was forecast to be 5·5% in 1998.

Budget. Revenue and expenditure for the calendar years 1995–99 in 1m. marks:

	1995	1996	1997	1998	1999
Revenue	201,372	198,390	184,668	188,621	187,111
Expenditure	198,332	199,426	187,378	188,619	187,111

Of the total revenue, 1997, 25% derived from value added tax, 27% from income and property tax, 13% from excise duties, 8% from other taxes and similar revenue, 7% from loans and 20% from miscellaneous sources. Reductions in income tax between 1996 and 1999 will reduce the total tax burden from 48·1% of GDP to 45·8%. Of the total expenditure, 1998, 14% went to education and culture, 4% to transport, 23% to health and social security, 6% to agriculture and forestry, 5% to defence and 48% to other expenditure.

VAT is 22% (reduced rates, 12% and 8%).

At the end of Dec. 1997 the central government debt totalled 418,184m. marks. Domestic debt amounted to 262,045m. marks; foreign debt (1996), 175,008m. marks.

Currency. On 1 Jan. 1999 the euro (EUR) became the legal currency in Finland and the *markka* became a subdivision of it; irrevocable conversion rate 5·94573 marks to 1 euro. The euro, which consists of 100 cents, will not be in circulation until 1 Jan. 2002. There will be 7 euro notes in different colours and sizes denominated in 500, 200, 100, 50, 20, 10 and 5 euros, and 8 coins denominated in 2 and 1 euros, then 50, 20, 10, 5, 2 and 1 cents. Even though notes and coins will not be introduced until 1 Jan. 2002 the euro can be used in banking; by means of cheques, travellers' cheques, bank transfers, credit cards and electronic purses. Banking will be possible in both

FINLAND

euros and marks until the markka is withdrawn from circulation—which must be by 1 July 2002.

The *markka* (FIM) or mark consists of 100 *pennis*. The mark was pegged to the ecu in June 1991 with a 3% margin of fluctuation. It was devalued by 12·3% in Nov. 1991, and unpegged from the ecu in Sept. 1992. Inflation in 1997 was running at 1·2%. In Feb. 1998 foreign exchange reserves were US$7,064m. and gold reserves were 1·6m. troy oz. Total money supply in Feb. 1998 was 210,276m. marks. Notes in circulation at the end of 1997 amounted to 17,817m. marks.

Banking and Finance. The central bank is the Bank of Finland (founded in 1811), owned by the State and under the guarantee and supervision of Parliament. Its *Governor* is Matti Vanhala. It is the only bank of issue, and the limit of its right to issue notes is fixed equal to the value of its assets of gold and foreign holdings plus 1,500m. marks.

At the end of 1997 the deposits in banking institutions totalled 303,711m. marks and the loans granted by them 291,989m. marks.

The most important groups of banking institutions in 1997 were:

	Number of institutions	Number of offices	Deposits (1m. marks)	Loans (1m. marks)
Commercial banks	9	930	188,325	190,944
Savings banks	40	233	21,648	15,968
Co-operative banks	294	670	91,727	78,932
Foreign banks	6	12	2,011	6,145

The 3 largest banks are MeritaNordbanken (formed in 1997 when Nordbanken of Sweden merged with Merita of Finland), the state-owned Leonia (formerly Postipankki) and Okobank.

There is a stock exchange in Helsinki.

Weights and Measures. The metric system is in use.

ENERGY AND NATURAL RESOURCES

Electricity. Installed capacity was 15·70m. kW in 1997. Production was (in 1m. kWh) 66,357 in 1996 (17·6% hydro-electric) and 66,149 in 1997 (18·1%). Consumption per capita in 1997 was an estimated 14,338 kWh. In 1998 there were 4 nuclear power stations, which contributed 30·3% of production in 1997. Parliament has rejected the construction of a fifth. Supply: 220 volts; 50 Hz.

Oil and Gas. There is no oil and gas production.

Water. Finland has abundant surface water and groundwater resources relative to its population and level of consumption. The total groundwater yield is estimated to be 10–30bn. cu. metres a day, of which some 6m. is suitable for water supplies. Approximately 15% of this latter figure is made use of at the present time. A total of 2–4% of Finland's exploitable water resources are utilized each year.

Minerals. Notable of the mines are Pyhäsalmi (zinc–copper), Orivesi (gold ore), Vammala (nickel) and Keminmaa (chromium). In 1996 the metal content (in tonnes) of the output of copper ore was 9,261; of zinc ore, 26,924; of nickel ore, 2,136; and of chromium, 228,100.

Agriculture. The cultivated area covers only 7% of the land, and of the economically active population 7% were employed in agriculture and forestry in 1997. The arable area was divided in 1996 into 155,337 farms, and the distribution of this area by the size of the farms was: Less than 5 ha cultivated, 48,484 farms; 5–20 ha, 64,248 farms; 20–50 ha, 35,319 farms; 50–100 ha, 6,355 farms; over 100 ha, 931 farms.

Agriculture accounts for 1·1% of GDP, 7·8% of exports and 8·6% of imports.

The principal crops (area in 1,000 ha, yield in 1,000 tonnes) were in 1997:

Crop	Area	Yield	Crop	Area	Yield
Rye	22·8	47·3	Oats	369·2	1,243·4
Barley	582·8	2,003·5	Potatoes	33·2	754·1
Wheat	124·8	464·1	Hay	219·8	862·5

The total area under cultivation in 1997 was 1,968,100 ha, about three-quarters of the entire country. Production of dairy butter in 1997 was 56,598 tonnes, and of cheese, 82,946 tonnes.

Livestock (1997): Horses, 53,100 (including trotting and riding horses, and ponies); cattle, 1,142,400; pigs, 1,467,000; poultry, 5,439,300; reindeer (1995), 333,000.

Forestry. The total forest land amounts to 23·0m. ha. The productive forest land covered 20·1m. ha in 1995. Timber production in 1995 was 50·22m. cu. metres. Finland is the second largest producer of roundwood in Europe behind Sweden, but in 1995 it was the second largest importer of industrial roundwood in the world after Japan. Finland's per capita consumption of roundwood is the highest in the world, at 11·6m. cu. metres per person in 1995.

Fisheries. The catch in 1995 was 184,829 tonnes, of which 132,971 tonnes came from sea fishing. In 1997 there were 287 food fish production farms in operation, of which 87 were fresh-water farms. Their total production amounted to 16,426 tonnes. In addition there were 134 fry-farms and 322 natural food rearers, most of these in freshwater.

INDUSTRY
Finland originally became industrialized by harnessing its forest resources. Over a century later, forests are still Finland's most crucial raw material resource, although the metal and engineering industry has long been Finland's leading branch of manufacturing, both in terms of value added and as an employer. Today Finland is a typical advanced industrial economy: two-thirds of its total output is generated in the service sector.

In 1996 there were 26,375 establishments in industry (of which 25,095 were manufacturing concerns) with 415,708 personnel (of whom 397,398 were in manufacturing). Gross value of industrial production in 1996 was 436,319m. marks, of which manufacturing accounted for 397,514m. marks

Labour. In 1996 the labour force was 2,603,000 (52% males). In 1995, 32% of the economically active population worked in community, social and personal services, and 21% in manufacturing. In 1998 unemployment was 10·5%, against 3·5% in 1990, but down from 20·0% in 1993.

Trade Unions. According to an incomes policy agreement reached by the central labour market organizations in Dec. 1997, which is in force until Jan. 2000, wages and salaries were raised by 1·6% in Jan. 1998 and by 1·6% in Jan. 1999. The Government has undertaken to cut taxes on wages and salaries to support moderate pay increases.

INTERNATIONAL TRADE
At the start of the 1990s a collapse in trade with Russia led to the worst recession in the country's recent history. Today, exports to Russia are less than 7% of the total.

The product pattern of exports has also changed dramatically over the last 40 years. In 1960 wood and paper industry dominated exports with their 69% contribution. By 1995, the metal and engineering industry was the largest export sector. But as capital goods for the forest industry form a large proportion of machinery exports, 'the forest cluster' can still be considered the dominant exporter.

Region	Exports 1997	Imports 1997
European Union	53%	59%
Other Europe	16%	12%
Developing Countries	13%	7%
EFTA	4%	6%
Other Countries	15%	16%

Industry	Exports 1997
Metal, Engineering, Electronics	51%
Forest Industry	31%
Chemical Industry	10%
Other	8%

Use of Goods	Imports 1997
Raw materials, production necessities	57%
Consumer goods	22%

	Imports 1997
Use of Goods	
Investment goods	15%
Fuels	4%
Other	2%

Imports and Exports. Imports and exports for calendar years, in 1m. marks:

	1996	1997
Imports	140,996	159,192
Exports	185,798	211,695

Trade with principal partners in 1997 was as follows (in 1,000 marks):

	Imports	Exports		Imports	Exports
Australia	1,020,255	2,666,167	Netherlands	6,437,308	8,675,449
Austria	1,702,373	2,002,910	Norway	5,898,532	6,345,361
Belgium-			Poland	1,794,233	3,755,726
Luxembourg	4,048,400	4,889,737	Portugal	1,167,060	1,192,160
Canada	1,033,203	2,047,582	Republic of Korea	701,237	2,455,701
China	2,844,379	3,814,419	Russia	12,521,700	15,462,534
Denmark	5,458,525	6,493,814	Singapore	544,194	2,003,446
Estonia	2,187,842	6,719,499	Spain	2,274,836	4,594,396
France	7,734,021	8,862,287	Sweden	19,088,295	20,830,192
Germany	23,147,212	23,225,939	Switzerland	2,668,542	2,080,337
Hong Kong	633,397	3,944,248	Taiwan	1,298,820	1,057,601
Indonesia	596,569	2,550,801	Thailand	632,130	1,987,607
Ireland	1,241,789	1,681,572	Turkey	389,237	1,672,645
Italy	6,460,827	6,289,541	UK	12,163,669	21,107,835
Japan	8,586,256	4,025,495	USA	11,719,088	14,732,762
Malaysia	594,947	1,462,729			

COMMUNICATIONS

Roads. In Jan. 1998 there were 77,796 km of public roads, of which 49,919 km were paved. At the end of 1997 there were 1,948,126 registered cars, 54,217 lorries, 212,727 vans and pick-ups, 8,450 buses and coaches, and 18,798 special automobiles.

Rail. On 31 Dec. 1997 the total length of the line operated was 5,865 km (2,061 km electrified), of which all was owned by the State. The gauge is 1,524 mm. In 1997, 50m. passengers and 40·3m. tonnes of freight were carried. There is a metro (17 km) and tram/light rail network (75 km) in Helsinki.

In 1995 the Finnish State Railways was transformed into a joint-stock company. Operations continue under the VR Group, the largest transport services group in Finland.

Civil Aviation. The main international airport is at Helsinki (Vantaa), and there are also international airports at Turku, Tampere, Rovaniemi and Oulu. The national carrier is Finnair, which in 1998 operated 4 MD11s, 4 Boeing 757s, 22 MD82/83s and 27 other aircraft. Its scheduled traffic covered 92·0m. km in 1997. The number of passengers was 6·9m. and the number of passenger-km 11,924,000 in 1997; the air transport of freight and mail amounted to 312·6m. tonne-km. In 1998 services were also provided by Aer Lingus, Aeroflot, Air Baltic, Air Botnia, Air Canada, Air China, Air Express, Air France, Alitalia, Austrian Airlines, Balkan, British Airways, Continental Airlines, Czech Airlines, Delta Air Lines, Deutsche BA, El Al, Estonian Air, Iberia, Icelandair, KLM, Lithuanian Airlines, LOT, Lufthansa, Malév, SABENA, SAS, Skyways, Swissair, Thai Airways International, Tyrolean Airways and United Airlines. Helsinki-Vantaa handled 7,689,218 passengers in 1996 (5,423,408 on international flights) and 82,813 tonnes of freight.

Shipping. The total registered mercantile marine on 31 Dec. 1997 was 605 vessels of 1,616,000 GRT. In 1997 the total number of vessels arriving in Finland from abroad was 25,203 and the goods discharged amounted to 39m. tonnes. The goods loaded for export from Finnish ports amounted to 36·1m. tonnes.

The lakes, rivers and canals are navigable for about 6,300 km. Timber floating has some importance, and there are about 9,650 km of floatable inland waterways. In 1997 bundle floating was about 2·4m. tonnes.

FINLAND

Telecommunications. In 1997 there were 2,861,000 telephone main lines in use. 2,162,574 mobile telephones were in use in 1997. The sales of mobile phones are increasing rapidly; according to a survey conducted in May 1998 around 46% of Finns owned a mobile phone—the highest density of users in the world. The rate among 18- and 19-year-olds is almost 100%. The biggest operator is Sonera (formerly Telecom Finland). Approximately 50% of all voice and data traffic streams through the company's networks, and around 70% of all mobile users are Sonera customers. In 1995 there were 930,000 PCs in use (182 per 1,000 persons) and 132,000 fax machines. There were 1·43m. Internet users in Aug. 1998.

Postal Services. In 1997 there were 585 primary post offices and 1,034 agents providing postal services in Finland. Finland Post Group is now exposed to competition in its business operations, with the exception of addressed letter mail for which it holds a licence for nationwide delivery.

SOCIAL INSTITUTIONS

Justice. The lowest court of justice is the District Court. In most civil cases a District Court has a quorum with 3 legally qualified members present. In criminal cases as well as in some cases related to family law the District Court has a quorum with a chair and 3 lay judges present. In the preliminary preparation of a civil case and in a criminal case concerning a minor offence, a District Court is composed of the chair only. From the District Court an appeal lies to the courts of appeal in Turku, Vaasa, Kuopio, Helsinki, Kouvola and Rovaniemi. The Supreme Court sits in Helsinki. Appeals from the decisions of administrative authorities are in the final instance decided by the Supreme Administrative Court, also in Helsinki. Judges can be removed only by judicial sentence.

Two functionaries, the Chancellor of Justice and the Ombudsman or Solicitor-General, exercise control over the administration of justice. The former acts also as counsel and public prosecutor for the Government; the latter is appointed by Parliament.

At the end of 1997 the prison population numbered 2,830 men and 144 women; the number of convictions in 1997 was 307,314, of which 249,460 were for minor offences with a maximum penalty of fines, and 22,448 with penalty of imprisonment. 9,501 of the prison sentences were unconditional.

Religion. Liberty of conscience is guaranteed to members of all religions. National churches are the Lutheran National Church and the Greek Orthodox Church of Finland. The Lutheran Church is divided into 8 bishoprics (Turku being the archiepiscopal see), 80 provostships and 595 parishes. The Greek Orthodox Church is divided into 3 bishoprics (Kuopio being the archiepiscopal see) and 27 parishes, in addition to which there are a monastery and a convent.

Percentage of the total population at the end of 1997: Lutherans, 85·6; Greek Orthodox, 1·1; others, 1·0; not members of any religion, 12·3.

Education. Number of institutions, teachers and pupils (1997).

Primary and Secondary Education:

	Number of institutions	Teachers[1]	Students
First-level Education (Lower sections of the comprehensive schools, grades I–VI)			387,598
Second-level Education General education (Upper sections of the comprehensive schools, grades VII–IX, and senior secondary schools)	4,793	45,732	333,053
Vocational Education	350[2]	15,063[2]	153,656

[1]Data for teachers refers to 1996.
[2]Numbers of institutions and teachers at vocational and professional education institutions refer to second and third level education.

Higher Education. Education at vocational and professional education institutions at third level was provided for 34,232 students in 1997. Education at AMK-institutions (polytechnics) was provided at 16 permanent and 15 experimental AMK institutions with 1,019 teachers and 62,258 students.

University Education. Universities and university-type institutions with the number of teachers and students in 1997:

	Founded[1]	Teachers	Students Total	Students Women
Universities				
Helsinki	1640	1,712	33,452	20,691
Turku (Swedish)	1918	345	5,901	3,514
Turku (Finnish)	1922	758	13,047	8,093
Tampere	1925	577	13,293	8,502
Jyväskylä	1934	575	11,127	7,170
Oulu	1958	840	12,641	6,034
Vaasa	1968	165	3,473	1,902
Joensuu	1969	348	6,127	3,812
Kuopio	1972	310	4,315	2,902
Lapland	1979	177	2,958	1,862
Universities of Technology				
Helsinki	1849	554	13,035	2,481
Tampere	1965	308	8,289	1,466
Lappeenranta	1969	193	3,930	846
Schools of Economics and Business Administration				
Helsinki (Swedish)	1909	111	2,170	881
Helsinki (Finnish)	1911	152	3,789	1,660
Turku (Finnish)	1950	91	1,978	1,021
Universities of Art				
Academy of Fine Arts	1848	19	228	147
University of Art and Design	1871	134	1,465	879
Sibelius Academy	1882	283	1,415	773
Theatre Academy	1943	54	329	179
Total		7,706	142,962	74,815

[1]Year when the institution was founded regardless of university level at the time or not.

There were a total of 2·85m. participants in adult education within the formal education system in 1997 (1,870,800 at general education institutions, 711,800 at vocational and professional education institutions, 158,200 at universities, 71,800 at summer universities and 34,400 at AMK-institutions/polytechnics).

In 1993 total expenditure on education came to 8·4% of GNP and represented 12·8% of total government expenditure.

Health. In 1996 there were 15,192 physicians, 4,839 dentists and (in 1995) 46,362 hospital beds.

Welfare. The Social Insurance Institution administers general systems of old-age pensions (to all persons over 65 years of age and disabled younger persons) and of health insurance. An additional system of compulsory old-age pensions paid for by the employers is in force and works through the Central Pension Security Institute. Systems for other public aid are administered by the communes and supervised by the National Social Board and the Ministry of Social Affairs and Health.

The total cost of social security amounted to 185,385m. marks in 1996. Out of this 38,422m. (20·7%) was spent on health, 25,031m. (13·5%) on unemployment, 80,318m. (43·3%) on old-age and disability, 31,731m. (17·1%) on family allowances and child welfare, and 9,883m. (5·4%) on general welfare purposes and administration. Out of the total expenditure, 28·5% was financed by the State, 16·2% by local authorities, 35·5% by employers, 13% by the insured and 6·7% by property income.

CULTURE

Helsinki is one of nine European Cities of Culture in the year 2000, with the theme of 'Knowledge, Technology and the Future'. 2000 also marks the 450th anniversary of the founding of Helsinki. The other Cities of Culture are Avignon (France), Bergen (Norway), Bologna (Italy), Brussels (Belgium), Kraków (Poland), Prague (Czech Republic), Reykjavík (Iceland) and Santiago de Compostela (Spain). The title attracts large European Union grants.

Broadcasting. The Finnish Broadcasting Company, YLE, is the biggest national radio and television service provider. YLE operates two television channels with full national coverage. The second biggest television broadcaster, the privately owned Commercial MTV3, has one nationwide channel. A new private TV channel, Ruutunelonen, started in 1997. Television programmes from TV Sweden are transmitted over YLE's channel 4. There are some 30 local TV stations that mainly relay foreign and domestic programmes over cable and radio waves, in addition to locally produced material. The only radio broadcaster with full nationwide coverage is YLE. It transmits 3 national channels in Finnish and one in Swedish, as well as various regional channels, including 1 in Sami in Lapland. In 1997 there were 58 local radio stations. Two of them, the news and music stations, Nova and Classic, cover almost 60% of the population. In 1995 there were 2,650,000 TV receivers and 5,150,000 radio receivers. On 31 Dec. 1997 the number of television licences was 1,947,400.

Cinema. In Dec. 1997 there were 321 cinema halls with a seating capacity of 55,532. In 1995 total attendance was 5·3m.

Press. Finland has 56 newspapers that are published 4 to 7 times a week, 9 of which are in Swedish, and 167 with 1 to 3 issues per week. The total circulation of all newspapers is 3·4m. In terms of total circulation of dailies relative to population, Finland ranks second in Europe after Norway. Most newspapers are bought on subscription rather than from newsstands. Only two newspapers depend entirely on newsstand sales. There are 5,015 registered periodicals with a total circulation of over 20m. The five bestselling newspapers in 1997 were: *Helsingin Sanomat* (circulation, 472,056 copies), *Ilta-Sanomat* (218,185), *Aamulehti* (131,444), *Turun Sanomat* (113,284) and *Iltalehti* (110,597). The bestselling newspaper in the Swedish language is *Hufvudstadsbladet*, 59,717.

Tourism. There were 894,000 foreign tourists in 1996. In 1997 the income from tourism was 10,172m. marks and the expenses 11,762m. marks.

Major international tourist attractions include Santa Park on the Polar Circle, the Kemi Snow Castle, and the Bomba House and Carelian Village in Nurmes.

Festivals. Helsinki's Festival of Light will have spectacular displays for 1999 and 2000. Other major festivals include: The Helsinki Festival Week, the Savonlinna Opera Festival, the Kuhmo Chamber Music Festival, Pori Jazz, Kaustinen Folk Music Festival, Tampere Theatre Festival, Kuopio Dance Festival and the Sodankylä Film Festival.

Libraries. The Helsinki University Library doubles as a National Library. The collections of the university libraries and major research libraries include altogether 43·1m. volumes (of which the university libraries have 19·0m.). They issued 8·6m. loans in total (university libraries 7·6m.).

The revised Public Library Act, which came into force on 1 Jan. 1999, requires each municipality to provide basic library services free of charge. The public library network is comprehensive with 992 libraries altogether. These are complemented by 210 mobile units with over 18,000 service stops. The Helsinki City Library doubles as a Central Library in this sector. Additionally the country is divided into 19 regions with a Regional Central Library providing supplementary services. In 1997 there were over 2·5m. registered borrowers, who represent 49·3% of the population. The number of loans issued totalled 102·3m.

National Theatre and Opera. There is (1999) a new Opera House and a new 14,000-seat Arena Show Hall in Helsinki. The city hosts both the National Theatre and the National Opera. All major cities have theatres and showhalls. In the summer season open air theatres are very popular. In 1997 there were 12,690 performances in total with over 2·5m. tickets sold.

Museums and Galleries. The National Museum as well as the National Gallery (the Atheneum) are located in Helsinki. The new Museum of Modern Art (Kiasma) was opened in Helsinki in 1998 and a new Ethnographic Museum opens in 1999. A Media Centre is also scheduled to open. Major cities all host their own art galleries and local museums. The Alvar Aalto Museum is located in Jyväskylä in Central Finland. In 1997 there were 145 museums with full-time personnel. The number of exhibitions was 1,081 in 1997, and there were 4m. visitors.

FINLAND

DIPLOMATIC REPRESENTATIVES
Of Finland in Great Britain (38 Chesham Pl., London, SW1X 8HW)
Ambassador: Pertti Salolainen.

Of Great Britain in Finland (Itäinen Puistotie, 17, 00140 Helsinki)
Ambassador: Gavin Hewitt, CMG.

Of Finland in the USA (3301 Massachusetts Ave., NW, Washington, D.C., 20008)
Ambassador: Jaakko Laajava.

Of the USA in Finland (Itäinen Puistotie 14A, Helsinki 00140)
Ambassador: Eric S. Edelman.

Of Finland to the United Nations
Ambassador: Marjatta Rasi.

FURTHER READING
Statistics Finland. *Statistical Yearbook of Finland* (from 1879).—*Bulletin of Statistics* (monthly, from 1924).
Constitution Act and Parliament Act of Finland. Helsinki, 1984
Suomen valtiokalenteri—Finlands statskalender (State Calendar of Finland). Helsinki. Annual
Facts About Finland. Helsinki. Annual (Union Bank of Finland)
Finland in Figures. Helsinki, Annual
Arter, D., *Politics and Policy-Making in Finland.* Brighton, 1987
Jakobson, M., *Myth and Reality.* Helsinki, 1987
Jutikkala, E. and Pirinen, K., *A History of Finland.* 3rd ed. New York, 1979
Kekkonen, U., *President's View.* London, 1982
Kirby, D. G., *Finland in the Twentieth Century.* 2nd ed. London, 1984
Klinge, M., *A Brief History of Finland.* Helsinki, 1987
Mead, W. R., *Experience of Finland.* Farnborough, 1993
Petersson, O., *The Government and Politics of the Nordic Countries.* Stockholm, 1994
Screen, J. E. O., *Finland.* [Bibliography] Oxford and Santa Barbara (CA), 1998
Singleton, F., *The Economy of Finland in the Twentieth Century.* Univ. of Bradford Press, 1987
Singleton, F., *A Short History of Finland,* 2nd edition. Cambridge University Press, 1998
Tillotson, H. M., *Finland at Peace and War, 1918–1993.* London, 1993

National statistical office: Statistics Finland, Tilastokeskus, FIN-00022.
Website: http://www.stat.fi/

FRANCE

République Française

Capital: Paris
Population estimate, 2000: 59·06m.
GNP per capita: (PPP$) 21,510
HDI/world rank: 0·946/2

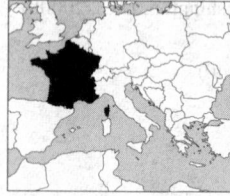

KEY HISTORICAL EVENTS

Gaul, the area that is now France, was conquered by Julius Caesar in the 1st century BC and became a part of the Roman Empire. In the 3rd and 4th centuries it was overrun by Germanic tribes and in the 10th century Norsemen invaded. There was a long period of conflict with England, typified by the Hundred Years' War (1337-1453); and this was followed by rivalry with Spain in the latter part of the 15th and in the 16th century. The Reformation caused a long religious civil war between 1562 and 1598, at the end of which the Huguenot leader Henry of Navarre was converted to Catholicism and reigned as the first Bourbon king, Henry IV. The two powerful ministers of the 17th century, Cardinal Richelieu and Mazarin, successively ensured that France, and not Spain, established itself as the dominant country in Europe. Militarily, this was achieved by the treaties of Westphalia (which ended the Thirty Years' War in 1648) and of the Pyrenees (1659). There followed the brilliant reign of Louis XIV, the 'Sun King' (1643-1715).

The second half of the 18th century saw France defeated by England in the Seven Years' War (1756-63). The French Revolution began in 1789 when the 'Third Estate' assumed power as a National Assembly and overthrew the government. Riots and the storming of the Bastille were followed by the proclamation of a republic (1792) and the execution of the king, Louis XVI (1793). A Reign of Terror followed during which thousands were guillotined. After these excesses the Directory ruled from 1795 until 1799 when it was overthrown by Napoleon Bonaparte, who became First Consul and then Emperor (1804) of the first French Empire. Napoleon went on to gain control of most of Europe until he was finally defeated at the Battle of Waterloo in 1815. The monarchy was restored, with the Bourbon family reigning (officially from 1814). A revolution in 1830 brought Louis Philippe, son of the Duke of Orleans, to the throne as a constitutional monarch. This 'July Monarchy' was overthrown in 1848 and superseded by the Second Republic, with Louis Napoleon (nephew of Napoleon I) elected president. In 1852 he took the title of Emperor Napoleon III, and hence began the Second Empire. However, the early military failures of France in the Franco-Prussian War (1870-71) led to Napoleon being deposed and the proclamation of the Third Republic in 1870. This survived both the First World War, which was fought chiefly on French soil, and also 44 successive governments from the end of the war in 1918 until 1940. In 1940 German troops invaded France, the French government capitulated, and a pro-German government was established at Vichy. Gen. Charles de Gaulle headed a Free French government in London, while in France the Resistance continued to harass the German Army of Occupation and give secret aid to the Allies.

When France was liberated in 1944 a provisional government under de Gaulle ruled the country until the Fourth Republic was established in 1946 and de Gaulle retired. The country now faced problems in Algeria and in Indo-China. There were changes of government up to 1958. In that year de Gaulle was recalled to be prime minister and then president as the Fifth Republic began in 1958. He granted independence to Algeria (1962) and was successful in establishing a firm and stable government until rioting and strikes by students and workers led to his resignation in 1969. He was succeeded by Georges Pompidou, who died in 1974 and was in turn succeeded by Giscard d'Estaing. Both presidents tended to continue Gaullist policies but in 1981 François Mitterrand, a socialist candidate, was elected to the presidency. For a time he had to govern in an uneasy relationship with a right-wing premier, Jacques Chirac. Mitterrand's period of office was clouded by charges of corruption. In 1995 Chirac was elected President in succession to the ailing Mitterrand.

TERRITORY AND POPULATION

France is bounded in the north by the English Channel (*La Manche*), north-east by Belgium and Luxembourg, east by Germany, Switzerland and Italy, south by the Mediterranean (with Monaco as a coastal enclave), south-west by Spain and Andorra, and west by the Atlantic Ocean. The total area is 549,090 sq. km. Paris is the most populous agglomeration in Europe, with a population of over 9·3m. More than 14% of the population of Paris are foreign and 19% are foreign born.

Population (1990 census), 56·6m. Estimate (1996), 58·2m.

The UN gives a projected population for 2000 of 59·06m.; projection (2025), 61·2m. Density (1996), 106 persons per sq. km. In 1995 an estimated 74·7% of the population lived in urban areas.

The growth of the population has been as follows:

Census	Population	Census	Population	Census	Population
1801	27,349,003	1931	41,834,923	1968	49,778,540
1861	37,386,313	1946	40,506,639	1975	52,655,802
1901	38,961,945	1954	42,777,174	1982	54,334,871
1921	39,209,518	1962	46,519,997	1990	56,615,100

According to the 1990 census, there were 3·5m. people of foreign extraction in France (7·4% of the population). The largest groups of foreign residents (1992) were: Portuguese (649,714), Algerians (614,207) and Moroccans (572,652). 92,410 persons were naturalized in 1995 (126,337 in 1994).

Controls on illegal immigration were tightened in July 1991. Automatic right to citizenship for those born on French soil was restored in 1997 by the new left-wing coalition government. New immigration legislation, which was due to come into force in 1998, brought in harsher penalties for organized traffic in illegal immigrants and extended asylum laws to include people whose lives are at risk from non-state as well as state groups. It also extended nationality at the age of 18 to those born in France of non-French parents, provided they have lived a minimum of 5 years in France since the age of 11.

The areas, populations and chief towns of the 22 metropolitan regions at the 1990 census were as follows:

Regions	Area (sq. km)	Population	Chief town
Alsace	8,280	1,624,400	Strasbourg
Aquitaine	41,308	2,795,800	Bordeaux
Auvergne	26,013	1,321,200	Clermont-Ferrand
Basse-Normandie	17,589	1,391,300	Caen
Bourgogne (Burgundy)	31,582	1,609,700	Dijon
Bretagne (Brittany)	27,208	2,795,600	Rennes
Centre	39,151	2,371,000	Orléans
Champagne-Ardenne	25,606	1,347,900	Reims
Corse (Corsica)	8,680	250,400	Ajaccio
Franche-Comté	16,202	1,097,400	Besançon
Haute-Normandie	12,317	1,737,200	Rouen
Île-de-France	12,012	10,660,600	Paris
Languedoc-Roussillon	27,376	2,114,900	Montpellier
Limousin	16,942	722,800	Limoges
Lorraine	23,547	2,305,700	Nancy
Midi-Pyrénées	41,348	2,430,700	Toulouse
Nord-Pas-de-Calais	12,414	3,965,100	Lille
Pays de la Loire	32,082	3,059,200	Nantes
Picardie	19,399	1,810,700	Amiens
Poitou-Charentes	25,810	1,595,100	Poitiers
Provence-Alpes-Côte d'Azur	31,400	4,257,900	Marseilles
Rhône-Alpes	43,698	5,350,800	Lyons

Populations of the principal conurbations (in descending order of size) and towns at the 1990 census:

	Conurbation	Town		Conurbation	Town
Paris	9,318,821[1]	2,152,423	Lille	959,234[4]	172,142
Lyons	1,262,223[2]	415,487	Bordeaux	696,364	210,336
Marseilles-Aix-			Toulouse	650,336	358,688
en-Provence	1,230,936[3]	800,550	Nice	516,740	342,439

	Conurbation	Town		Conurbation	Town
Nantes	496,078	244,995	Nîmes	138,527	128,471
Toulon	437,553	167,619	Thionville	132,413	40,835
Grenoble	404,733	150,758	Saint-Nazaire	131,511	64,812
Strasbourg	388,483	252,338	Annecy	126,729	51,143
Rouen	380,161	102,723	Troyes	122,763	59,271
Valenciennes	338,392	39,276	Besançon	122,623	113,828
Cannes	335,647	68,676	Montbéliard	117,510	30,639
Nancy	329,447	99,351	Lorient	115,488	59,437
Lens	323,174	35,278	Hagondange-Briey	112,061	9,091[5]
Saint-Étienne	313,338	197,536	Valence	107,965	63,437
Tours	282,152	129,509	Melun	107,705	36,489
Béthune	261,535	25,261	Poitiers	107,625	78,894
Clermont-Ferrand	254,416	136,181	Chambéry	103,283	54,120
Le Havre	253,627	195,854	Angoulême	102,908	46,194
Montpellier	248,303	207,996	Maubeuge	102,772	35,225
Rennes	245,065	199,396	Calais	101,768	75,309
Orléans	243,153	105,111	La Rochelle	100,264	71,094
Dijon	230,451	146,703	Forbach	98,758	27,357
Mulhouse	223,856	108,357	Creil	97,119	32,501
Angers	208,282	141,404	Bourges	94,731	75,609
Reims	206,437	180,620	Cherbourg	92,045	28,773
Brest	201,480	147,956	Boulogne-sur-Mer	91,249	44,244
Douai	199,562	44,195	Chartres	85,933	41,850
Metz	193,117	119,594	Saint-Brieuc	83,861	47,370
Caen	191,490	112,846	Colmar	83,816	63,498
Dunkerque	190,879	70,331	Saint-Chamond	81,795	39,262
Le Mans	189,107	145,502	Tarbes	80,680	50,228
Mantes-la-Jolie	189,103	45,254	Arras	79,607	42,715
Avignon	181,136	86,939	Belfort	78,215	50,125
Limoges	170,065	133,464	Chalon-sur-Saône	77,764	54,575
Bayonne	164,378	41,846	Roanne	77,160	42,848
Perpignan	157,873	105,983	Alès	76,856	—
Amiens	156,120	131,872	Béziers	76,304	70,996
Pau	144,674	82,157			

[1]Including Boulogne-Billancourt (101,743), Montreuil (94,754), Argenteuil (93,096), Versailles (87,789), Saint-Denis (89,988), Nanterre (84,565), Vitry-sur-Seine (82,400), Aulnay-sous-Bois (82,314), Créteil (82,088).
[2]Including Villeurbanne (116,872), Vénissieux (60,644).
[3]Including Aix-en-Provence (123,842).
[4]Including Roubaix (97,746), Tourcoing (93,765). [5]1982 census.

Languages. The official language is French. Breton and Basque are spoken in their regions. The *Toubon* legislation of 1994 seeks to restrict the use of foreign words in official communications, broadcasting and advertisements (a previous such decree dated from 1975). The Constitutional Court has since ruled that imposing such restrictions on private citizens would infringe their freedom of expression.
Monnier, A., *La Population de la France*. Paris, 1990

SOCIAL STATISTICS
Statistics for calendar years:

	Marriages	Births	Deaths
1995	254,000	727,800	532,000
1996	279,000	734,000	536,000

Live birth rate (1996) was 12·6 per 1,000 population; death rate, 9·2; marriage rate, 4·8. Divorces, 1995, 117,000; rate, 2·0 per 1,000 population. 38% of births in 1995 were outside marriage. In 1994 the most popular age range for marrying was 25–29 for both males and females. Abortions were legalized in 1975; there were 162,620 in 1990. Life expectancy at birth, 1990–95, 73·8 years for males and 82·4 years for females. Annual growth rate, 1990–95, 0·5%. From 1990–95 the suicide rate per 100,000 population was 20·1 (men, 29·6; women, 11·1). Infant mortality, 1990–95, 7 per 1,000 live births; fertility rate, 1·7 births per woman.

CLIMATE

The north-west has a moderate maritime climate, with small temperature range and abundant rainfall; inland, rainfall becomes more seasonal, with a summer maximum, and the annual range of temperature increases. Southern France has a Mediterranean climate, with mild moist winters and hot dry summers. Eastern France has a continental climate and a rainfall maximum in summer, with thunderstorms prevalent. Paris, Jan. 37°F (3°C), July 64°F (18°C). Annual rainfall 22·9" (573 mm). Bordeaux, Jan. 41°F (5°C), July 68°F (20°C). Annual rainfall 31·4" (786 mm). Lyons, Jan. 37°F (3°C), July 68°F (20°C). Annual rainfall 31·8" (794 mm).

CONSTITUTION AND GOVERNMENT

The Constitution of the Fifth Republic, superseding that of 1946, came into force on 4 Oct. 1958. It consists of a preamble, dealing with the Rights of Man, and 92 articles.

France is a republic, indivisible, secular, democratic and social; all citizens are equal before the law (Art. 1). National sovereignty resides with the people, who exercise it through their representatives and by referendums (Art. 3). Constitutional reforms of July 1995 widened the range of issues on which referendums may be called. Political parties carry out their activities freely, but must respect the principles of national sovereignty and democracy (Art. 4).

A constitutional amendment of 4 Aug. 1995 deleted all references to the 'community' (*communauté*) between France and her overseas possessions, representing an important step towards the constitutional dismantling of the former French colonial empire.

The head of state is the President, who sees that the Constitution is respected; ensures the regular functioning of the public authorities, as well as the continuity of the state; is the protector of national independence and territorial integrity (Art. 5). The President is elected for 7 years by direct universal suffrage (Art. 6). The President appoints (and dismisses) a Prime Minister and, on the latter's advice, appoints and dismisses the other members of the Government (*Council of Ministers*) (Art. 8); presides over the Council of Ministers (Art. 9); may dissolve the National Assembly, after consultation with the Prime Minister and the Presidents of the two Houses (Art. 12); appoints to the civil and military offices of the state (Art. 13). In times of crisis, the President may take such emergency powers as the circumstances demand; the National Assembly cannot be dissolved during such a period (Art. 16).

Parliament consists of the National Assembly and the Senate. The National Assembly is elected by direct suffrage by the second ballot system (by which candidates winning 50% or more of the vote in their constituencies are elected, candidates winning less than 12·5% are eliminated and other candidates go on to a second round of voting); the Senate is elected by indirect suffrage (Art. 24). Since 1996 the National Assembly has convened for an annual 9-month session. It comprises 577 deputies, elected by a two-ballot system for a 5-year term from single-member constituencies (555 in Metropolitan France, 22 in the overseas departments and dependencies); and may be dissolved by the President.

The *Senate* comprises 321 senators elected for 9-year terms (one-third every 3 years) by an electoral college in each Department or overseas dependency, made up of all members of the Departmental Council or its equivalent in overseas dependencies, together with all members of Municipal Councils within that area. The *Speaker* of the Senate deputizes for the President of the Republic in the event of the latter's incapacity. Senate elections were last held on 27 Sept. 1998.

The *Constitutional Council* is composed of 9 members whose term of office is 9 years (non-renewable), one-third every 3 years; 3 are appointed by the President of the Republic, 3 by the President of the National Assembly, 3 by the President of the Senate; in addition, former Presidents of the Republic are, by right, life members of the Constitutional Council (Art. 56). It oversees the fairness of the elections of the President (Art. 58) and Parliament (Art. 59), and of referendums (Art. 60), and acts as a guardian of the Constitution (Art. 61). Its *President* is Roland Dumas (app. 1995).

The *Economic and Social Council* advises on Government and Private Members' Bills (Art. 69). It comprises representatives of employers', workers' and farmers' organizations in each Department and Overseas Territory.

Ameller, M., *L'Assemblée Nationale*. Paris, 1994

FRANCE

Duhamel, O. and Mény, Y., *Dictionnaire Constitutionnel*. Paris, 1992

Elgie, R. (ed.) *Electing the French President: the 1995 Presidential Election*. London, 1996

National Anthem. 'La Marseillaise'; words and tune by C. Rouget de Lisle.

RECENT ELECTIONS

At the first round of presidential elections on 23 April 1995, Lionel Jospin gained the largest number of votes (23·31% of those cast) against 8 opponents. At the second round on 7 May 1995, the electorate was 39,976,944; turn-out was 79·77%. Jacques Chirac was elected President against Jospin by 52·64% of votes cast.

At the elections of 25 May and 1 June 1997 to the National Assembly, there were 6,361 candidates; the electorate was 38,968,660. In the first round, turn-out was 68·93%. The Socialist Party (PS) and allies won 253 seats; the Rassemblement pour la République (RPR; Gaullists), 134; the Union for French Democracy (UDF), 108; the Communist Party (PCF), 38; Greens, 7; other left parties, 21; other right parties, 15; National Front, 1.

Following the election held on 27 Sept. 1998, the Senate was composed of (by group, including affiliates): RPR, 99; PS, 78; Union Centriste (UC), 52; Républicains et Indépendants (RI), 47; Rassemblement Démocratique et Europeén Social (RDES), 22; Républicain, Communiste et Citoyen (RCC), 16; Unattached, 7. In Oct. 1998 Christian Poncelet (RPR) was elected *Speaker* for a 3-year term.

European Parliament. France has 87 representatives. At the June 1994 elections turn-out was 53·5%. The RPR-UDF won 29 seats with 25·5% of votes cast (political affiliation in European Parliament: European Liberal, Democratic and Reformist Group; European People's Party); the PS, 16 with 14·5% (European Socialist Party); the Other Europe group, 13 with 12·3%; the Radical Energy group, 13 with 12%; the National Front, 10 with 10·5% (European Group of Nations); the Communist Party, 6 with 6·9%.

CURRENT ADMINISTRATION

President: Jacques Chirac (RPR; sworn in 17 May 1995).

A new left-wing coalition government (including the anti-Euro Communist group) was formed on 4 June 1997, consisting in March 1999 of:

Prime Minister: Lionel Jospin (PS); *Minister of Justice and Keeper of the Seals:* Elisabeth Guigou (PS). *Foreign Affairs:* Hubert Védrine (PS). *Interior:* Jean-Pierre Chevènement (MDC). *Economy, Finance and Industry:* Dominique Strauss-Kahn (PS). *Defence:* Alain Richard (PS). *Employment and Solidarity:* Martine Aubry (PS). *Education, Research and Technology:* Claude Allègre (PS). *Public Works, Transport and Housing:* Jean-Claude Gayssot (PC). *Relations with the Parliament:* Daniel Vaillant (PS). *Environment and Regional Development:* Dominique Voynet (Green). *Culture and Communication, and Government Spokeswoman:* Catherine Trautmann (PS). *Agriculture, Fisheries and Food:* Jean Glavany (PS). *Civil Service, Administrative Reform and Decentralization:* Emile Zuccarelli (PRS). *Youth and Sport:* Marie-Georges Buffet (PC).

Ministers-Delegate include: *European Affairs:* Pierre Moscovici (PS). *Foreign Trade:* Jacques Dondoux (PRS). *Overseas Territories:* Jean-Jack Queyranne (PS). *Industry:* Christian Pierret (PS). *Tourism:* Michelle Demessine (PC). *Housing:* Louis Besson (PS). *Education:* Ségolène Royal (PS). *Health:* Bernard Kouchner (PRS). *Budget:* Christian Sautter (PS). *Veterans and War Victims:* Jean-Pierre Masseret (PS). *Co-operation:* Charles Josselin. *Small and Medium Business, Commerce and Craft:* Marylise Lebranchu.

Local Government. France is divided into 22 regions for national development, planning and budgetary policy. Many of these regions are broadly comparable with the provinces of pre-revolutionary France, and give a measure of recognition to the distinctive personalities of peripheral areas such as Alsace and Brittany.

By a law of 13 May 1991 Corsica became a territorial collectivity. After the regional elections of March 1992 it had an assembly which elects an executive council. Since Feb. 1995 the Pays Basque, which formed part of the department Pyrénées-Atlantique, has had an elected 65-member council, bringing together parliamentary deputies, regional and general councillors and representatives of mayors.

There are 96 departments within the 22 regions, each governed by a directly elected General Council. In March 1982 state-appointed Regional Prefects were abolished and their executive powers transferred from the state to the presidents of the regional councils. Legislation of 1993 provides for the election every 3 years of half the members of the councils. Elections for 2,009 seats in the General Councils were held in 2 rounds on 20 and 27 March 1994. The electorate was 18,563,056; turn-out was 60·39% at the first round and 58·78% at the second. The PS gained 532 seats, the UDF 446, the RPR 382, various right-wing groups 309, various left-wing groups 171, the Communist Party 145, Greens 7, the National Front 3, others 12.

Elections for the country's 22 regional councils were held on 15 March 1998 and over the next couple of weeks. The vote for the main parties in government (Socialists, Communists and Greens) was 38% and for the moderate right-wing parties (RPR and UDF) 36%. The National Front won 15%. In order to deprive the Left of an overall victory, the Right forged local alliances with the National Front in 5 regions, so as to keep control.

The unit of local government is the *commune*, the size and population of which vary considerably. There were, in 1995, in the 96 metropolitan departments, 36,763 communes (30,919 with fewer than 1,500 inhabitants). The local affairs of the commune are under a Municipal Council, composed of between 9 and 36 members elected by universal suffrage for 6 years. At the last municipal elections in 1995, there were 512,850 municipal councillors. Each municipal council elects a mayor who is both the representative of the commune and agent of the central government. Communes are associated in the *Assemblée des Districts et des Communautés de France*, and also co-operate in inter-commune public enterprise projects, of which there were some 1,200 in 1995.

In Paris the local council *(Conseil de Paris)* is composed of 109 members elected from the 20 *arrondissements.* It combines the functions of departmental General and Municipal Council.

In 1995 the *Pasqua* Law on Guidance for Territorial Management created a new territorial entity, the *pays*. These do not replace administrative divisions, but group regions, departments or communes according to historical, geographical or employment area criteria, with a view to their economic development. Some 200 *pays* had been formed by 1996.

Local revenue is raised from residence, business and property taxes, and amounted to 262,700m. francs in 1995 (250,000m. in 1994).

DEFENCE

The President of the Republic is the supreme head of defence policy and exercises command over the Armed Forces. He is the only person empowered to give the order to use nuclear weapons. He is assisted by the Council of Ministers, which studies defence problems, and by the Defence Council and the Restricted Defence Committee, which formulate directives. The Prime Minister is responsible for national defence, exercising his military responsibilities and co-ordinating inter-ministry defence activities through the General Secretariat of National Defence (SGDN). Under the Prime Minister's authority, the Minister of Defence is responsible for the execution of military policy, in particular the organization and administration of the Armed Forces.

The Ministry of Defence has overall responsibility for defence. The preparation and control of the Armed Forces is exercised by the Chief of Staff of the Armed Forces, the Chiefs of Staff of the 3 services—Army, Navy and Air—and the head of the *Gendarmerie.*

Legislation of 1996 inaugurated a wide-ranging reform of the defence system over 1997–2002, with regard to the professionalization of the armed forces (brought about by the ending of military conscription and consequent switch to an all-volunteer defence force), the modification and modernization of equipment and the restructuring of the defence industry. Defence was reported to be the main casualty of the Jospin administration's first budget. In 1997 defence expenditure totalled US$41,545m. (US$708 per capita). 1998 spending was due to fall by 4·5% in real terms from the 1997 level, with spending on equipment particularly affected. It is estimated under current plans that by 2002 the Army will have been reduced by more than 30% from 1997 levels, the Navy by about 16%, the Air Force by almost

20%. Defence spending as a proportion of GDP has fallen from just below 4% in 1988 to 3% in 1997 (compared with more than 4% of GDP in 1988 to 2·8% in 1997 in the UK).

French forces are not formally under the NATO command structure, although France signed the NATO strategic document on Eastern Europe in Nov. 1991. The Minister of Defence attends informal NATO meetings which have an agenda of French interest, but not the formal twice-yearly meetings. Since Dec. 1995 France has taken a seat on the NATO Military Committee. In 1996, 16,143 service personnel were stationed in Germany, 24,395 in the overseas departments and territories, 7,708 on UN peacekeeping missions and 1,336 constituted the 'French Maritime Presence' abroad.

The General Directorate for Armament (DGA) is responsible for all aspects of the procurement of defence equipment. It employs 48,800 personnel, and co-ordinates another 200,000 others employed in the defence industry. A reform programme for the GDA designed to modernize equipment and reduce costs was initiated in 1996.

Conscription is for 10 months, but as a result of a law of 28 Oct. 1997, males born after 31 Dec. 1978 are no longer compelled to perform national service.

Nuclear weapons. Having carried out its first test in 1961, there have been 210 tests in all. The nuclear arsenal consisted of approximately 450 warheads in Jan. 1998 according to the Stockholm International Peace Research Institute.

Army. The Army comprises the Land Force Command (CFAT) which is a single command over all forces. Actions assets are represented by battalions grouped into brigades built up around a speciality function (armour, mechanized, light armour, infantry airmobility, logisitics). Apart from the Franco-German brigade, there will be 8 brigades, each made up of between 4 and 7 battalions (infantry, MBTS, artillery, engineer), 1 airmobile brigade and 2 logistics brigades.

Specialized combat support or service support battalions are grouped centrally and organized in specialized support brigades: signal, artillery, engineer and intelligence.

In 2002 operational units in the French Army will be fielded with the following major modern equipment: 426 heavy tanks (Leclerc and AMX 30 B2), 350 light tanks (AMX10 RC), 600 armoured combat infantry vehicles, 260 155-mm guns, 48 multiple rocket launchers and 292 helicopters of all types.

The 1997–2002 Programming Act will provide for the following force at the end of the transitional period: 16,000 officers, 50,000 NCOs, 66,500 army enlistees, 5,500 volunteers, 34,000 civilians and 30,000 reservists.

Gendarmerie. The paramilitary police force exists to ensure public security and maintain law and order, as well as participate in the operational defence of French territory as part of the armed forces. It consisted in 1998 of 99,000 personnel including 12,000 conscripts, 2,600 women and 1,500 civilians. It comprises a territorial force of 57,000 personnel in 3,607 brigades throughout the country, a mobile force of 17,000 personnel in 128 squadrons and specialized formations including the Republican Guard, the Air Force and Naval Gendarmeries, and an anti-terrorist unit. It is equipped with 28 VBC-90 armoured gun-carriers, 121 light-armoured cars, 155 armoured vehicles and 3,010 tactical vehicles, as well as 42 helicopters.

Navy. The missions of the Navy are to provide the prime element of the French independent nuclear deterrent through its force of strategic submarines; to assure the security of the French offshore zones; to contribute to NATO's missions; and to provide on-station and deployment forces overseas in support of French territorial interests and UN commitments.

French territorial seas and economic zones are organized into 3 maritime regions, each under the authority of a Maritime Prefect (with headquarters in Cherbourg, Brest and Toulon). Offshore, the seas and oceans are divided into 5 zones: Atlantic, Mediterranean, Indian Ocean, Pacific and Antilles-Guiana. Home-based forces are commanded by Commanders-in-Chief based in Brest and Toulon; those in the Indian Ocean and Pacific by Flag Officers based afloat in the Indian Ocean, and at Nouméa (in New Caledonia). Naval forces in the Caribbean come under a joint force commander based at Cayenne.

FRANCE

Pressures on public expenditure have dictated a phased reduction in fleet strength over 1997–2015, but the following is a summary of the strength of the fleet at the end of selected years:

	1996	1999[1]	2015[1]
Aircraft carriers	2	1	2
Strategic-missile submarines	5	4	4
Other submarines	12	8	6
Transport vessels of landing troops	...	4	4
Frigates	35	39	32

[1]Provisional forecast.

The strategic deterrent force comprises 4 nuclear-powered strategic-missile submarines, including 2 of 4 new-generation ships of a new, much larger, class, *Le Triomphant* and *Le Téméraire*, which entered service in 1997 and 1999, displacing 14,200 tonnes and deploying 16 M-45 missiles. The others comprise *Le Tonnant* and *L'Inflexible*, 9,100 tonnes each, completed in 1980 and 1985, now converted to the same standard, and deploying 16 M-4 missiles. There are also 6 2,700-tonne nuclear-powered submarines.

The principal surface ship is the aircraft carrier *Foch* of 33,000 tonnes, completed in 1963. The operational carrier embarks an air group typically comprising 15 Super-Etendard strike aircraft, 4 Etendard reconnaissance, 8 F-8P Crusader fighters, 8 Alize anti-submarine and warning, and a flight of 4 utility helicopters. *Foch* is to be withdrawn from service in 2000, when the nuclear-powered replacement *Charles de Gaulle*, which was launched at Brest in 1994, is expected to commission. There is 1 cruiser, the helicopter cruiser *Jeanne d'Arc*, of 13,000 tonnes, completed in 1964 and used in peacetime as a training vessel. She could perform amphibious or anti-submarine tasks in war. In these roles she could accommodate up to 8 Lynx helicopters and 700 personnel. Her armament comprises 6 Exocet and 4 100-mm guns.

Other surface combatants include 4 guided-missile destroyers and 35 frigates of which 23 carry helicopters. A modern mine countermeasure force consists of 14 tripartite coastal minehunters and 4 diver support vessels. The amphibious force includes 4 dock-landing ships and 5 medium-landing ships. The Navy deploys a substantial support force which includes 4 large tankers. There are numerous other minor auxiliaries.

A large proportion of warships' weapons are produced by the government armaments service, of which the naval element, *Direction des Constructions Navales* (DCN), operates the shipbuilding yards as well as dockyards. Building takes place at Cherbourg, Brest and Lorient.

The naval air arm, *Aviation Navale*, numbers some 3,500 personnel. Operational aircraft include 52 Super-Etendard nuclear-capable strike aircraft, 5 Etendard reconnaissance aircraft, 10 US-built Crusader F-8P all-weather fighters, 9 Alize turboprop anti-submarine aircraft, 28 Atlantique and 5 Gardian maritime reconnaissance aircraft. The Crusaders' life has been extended to keep a carrier squadron operational until 1999, when the maritime Rafale combat aircraft will enter service on board the *Charles de Gaulle*. Rotary-wing strength includes 16 commando Super Frelon, and 33 anti-submarine and search-and-rescue Lynx helicopters. Other training, utility and transport aircraft bring the total strength to 173 comprising 109 fixed-wing aircraft and 64 helicopters. A small Marine force of 2,900 *Fusiliers Marins* provides 4 assault groups, an attack swimmer section as well as numerous naval base protection units.

Personnel in 1999 numbered 62,600, including 8,158 conscripts and 3,150 women.

Air Force. Created in 1934, the Air Force was reorganized in June 1994. France is divided into 3 air regions corresponding to the 3 military defence regions and 2 air defence zones. There are 2 operational commands (Strategic Air Forces Command—CFAS; Air Defence and Air Operations Command—CDAOA) and 5 organizational commands (Combat Air Force Command—CFAC; Projection Air Force Command—CFAP; Air Observation System, Information and Communication Command—CASSIC; Training Command—CEAA; Air Base

Protection Infantry Command—CFCA). The CFAS is responsible for nuclear weapons; all other combat aircraft are operated by the CFAC which is responsible for maintaining the operational readiness of its units.

The Conventional Forces in Europe (CFE) Agreement imposes a ceiling of 450 combat aircraft. Equipment summary (main types only), Combat: 115 Mirage 2000 B/C, 60 Mirage 2000 N, 43 Mirage 2000 D, 5 Mirage IV P, 35 Mirage F1 B/C, 40 Mirage F1 CT, 40 Mirage F1 CR, 60 Jaguar A/E. Airborne Early Warning: 4 E3F Awacs; Transport: 14 Hercules C 130, 4 DC8, 2 Airbus A 310, 66 C160 Transall, 19 Nord 262. Training: 112 Alphajet; Helicopters: 3 Alouette III, 49 Fennec, 29 Puma, 7 Super Puma and 3 Cougar.

The organization and equipment of the Commands (bases in parentheses) is as follows:

Strategic Air Forces Command (CFAS): Strategic reconnaissance squadron 1/91 (Mont de Marsan) with Mirages IV Ps; fighter squadrons 1/4 and 2/4 with Mirage 2000 Ns (Luxeuil); fighter squadrons 3/4 with Mirage 2000 Ns (Istres); flight refuelling squadron 93 with 12 C 135FRs and 2 KC-135Rs (Istres). 59 Airborne strategic communication squadron (Evreux): 4 C 160 Transall Astarte V/UHF airborne relay posts (flown and maintained by COTAM). Tactical training centre: Falcon 20s, Jaguar Es (Luxeuil).

Combat Air Forces Command (CFAC): (Nancy): 3 squadrons with Mirage 2000Ds (Saint Dizier): 3 squadrons with Jaguar As and Jaguar Es (two-seater) (Colmar): 2 squadrons with Mirage F1 CTs (Reims): Recce squadrons 1/33, 2/33 with Mirage F1 CRs and 1 training squadron with Mirage F1 B/Cs (Djibouti): 1 squadron with 10 Mirage F1Cs (Dijon): 2 squadrons with Mirage 2000 B/Cs (Orange): 2 squadrons with Mirage 2000 B/Cs (Cambrai): 2 squadrons with 30 Mirage 2000 C and Bs. 54 electronic warfare squadrons (Metz): 2 Transall Gabriel for SIGINT operations (flown and maintained by COTAM).

Projection Air Forces Command (CFAP): 3/60 Transport squadron (Creil): DC8s. A 310 (Orléans): transport squadrons 1/61 and 3/61 with C 160F Transall and 2/61 with 11 C130H-30s and 3 C 130Hs. Transport squadrons 1/64 and 2/64 (Evreux): C160 NGs. Transport squadron 1/65 (Villacoublay): 5 N 262s, 8 Mystere 20s, 4 TBM 700s, 2 Falcon 900s, 4 Falcon 50s, 3 Twin Otters. 1/62 Transport squadron (Creil): 10 CASA 235s, 3 Fennecs, 3 Twin Otters. 56 special transport squadron (GAM 56) (Evreux): 3 C160s, 3 Cougar. CIET 340 (Toulouse): C160s, N 262s. CIEH 341 (Toulouse): Alouette IIIs, Fennecs, Pumas. ETE 41 (Metz): N 262s, Paris and TBM 700s. ETE 43 (Bordeaux): 3 N 262s, 2 TBM 700s. ETE 44 (Aix): 4 N 262s and 1 TBM 700. EH 1/67 (Cazaux): Fennecs, Pumas. EH 2/67 (Metz): 3 Alouette IIIs, 5 Fennecs. EH 3/67 (Villacoublay): 3 Alouette IIIs, 3 Super Pumas, 6 Ecureuils, 3 Fennecs. EH 5/67 (Aix): 5 Fennecs, 4 Pumas and 1 Super Puma. EH 6/67 (Solenzara): 2 Pumas. Overseas transport squadron (ETOM 50) (Saint Denis la Réunion): 2 C 160s, 2 Fennecs. ETOM 52 (Nouméa): CN 235s, 2 Fennecs, 5 Pumas. ETOM 55 (Dakar): 1 C 160, 1 Alouette III. ETOM 58 (Martinique): 2 C 160s, 1 Alouette III, 2 Pumas. ETOM 82 (Papeete): 2 CN 235s, 3 Super Pumas. ETOM 88 (Djibouti): 3 Alouette IIIs, 1 C 160.

Air Observation System, Information and Communication Command (CASSIC): 36 AEW squadron (Avord: 2 flights with 4 E3F Awacs).

Air Training Command (CEAA): 1 ETO and 2 ETO Alphajets (Cazaux). GE 312: Training group (Salon de Provence): CAP 20s, CAP 231s, 47 Tucanos. GE 314 (Tours): Alphajets. GE 315 (Cognac): 98 Epsilons. GE 319 (Avord): 25 Xingus.

Personnel (1999) 76,405 (10,998 conscripts; 5,603 civilians).

INTERNATIONAL RELATIONS

France is a member of the UN, the Council of Europe, NATO, WEU, EU, OSCE, OECD and the Pacific Community, and is a signatory to the Schengen Accord (*see* EUROPEAN UNION *under* MAJOR POLICY AREAS).

At a referendum in Sept. 1992 to approve the ratification of the Maastricht treaty on European union of 7 Feb. 1992, 12,967,498 votes (50·81%) were cast for and 12,550,651 (49·18%) against.

France is the focus of the *Communauté Francophone* (French-speaking Community) which formally links France with many of its former colonies in Africa. A wide range of agreements, both with members of the Community and with other French-speaking countries, extend to economic and technical matters, and in particular to the disbursement of overseas aid.

ECONOMY

Performance. Real GDP growth was estimated at 2·3% in 1997 (1·5% in 1996); a rate of 2·7% was forecast for 1998. Contributory factors to economic growth in 1997 were a strong export market and weaker franc. Total GDP (1996, in US$): 1,539,000m. (1997 forecast: 1,358,300m.).

A second phase of privatization (the first being in 1986–87) involving some 20 state enterprises was initiated by legislation of May 1993, by which the state retained the right to acquire a 'golden share' to give itself veto powers in the national interest. In 1997 the sale of state assets included nearly a quarter of France Télécom and a majority stake in the CIC banking network. Other sell-offs in the pipeline (in 1998) included Air France (49%) and a controlling stake in the defence electronics giant Thomson-CSF.

Budget. In 1997 public spending was cut by an extra 10,000m. francs when the new government came to power in June. The budget for 1998 envisaged no further cuts in public spending (but an increase in line with inflation forecast at 1·5%); and a reduction in the public deficit from 3·1% of GDP in 1997 (dramatically reduced in June from an estimated 3·5% and rising by the acquisition of 22,000m. francs in emergency corporate taxes) to 3% of GDP, which is the uppermost limit of the Maastricht criteria on budget deficits.

Receipts and expenditure in 1m. francs:

	1993	1994	1995	1996	1997
Revenue	1,142,698	1,154,165	1,291,700	1,264,162	1,194,700
Expenditure	1,410,129	1,436,333	1,595,700	1,551,969	1,480,800

In Nov. 1997 receipts were up by 18,700m. francs on the previous year; expenditure was up by 16,500m. The budget deficit at 30 Nov. 1997 was some 325,300m. francs (4,100m. francs less than at 31 Dec. 1996).

Breakdown of revenue and expenditure (in 1m. francs):

Receipts	1994	1995	1996
Income tax	296,328	303,525	314,100
Corporation tax	127,857	145,748	143,200
Other direct taxes	111,148	116,820	136,474
Stamp duty	77,758	83,400	81,745
Customs duties	155,080	158,801	158,986
VAT	648,393	673,216	761,627
Other indirect taxes	41,040	44,707	46,083
Non-fiscal receipts	161,661	150,365	115,564

Expenditure			
Public debt	199,834	198,983	226,369
Administration	506,410	524,275	...
Subsidies	406,420	417,531	1,073,496[1]
Civil investments	89,111	86,172	...
Defence	242,558	243,456	241,449

[1]Civil expenditure total.

The standard rate of VAT is 20·6% (reduced rate, 5·5%).

Ministère de l'Economie, des Finances et du Plan. *Le Budget de l'Etat: de la Préparation à l'Exécution*. Paris, 1995

Currency. On 1 Jan. 1999 the euro (EUR) became the legal currency in France and the *franc* became a subdivision of it; irrevocable conversion rate 6·55957 francs to 1 euro. The euro, which consists of 100 cents, will not be in circulation until 1 Jan. 2002. There will be 7 euro notes in different colours and sizes denominated in 500, 200, 100, 50, 20, 10 and 5 euros, and 8 coins denominated in 2 and 1 euros, then 50, 20, 10, 5, 2 and 1 cents. Even though notes and coins will not be introduced until 1 Jan. 2002 the euro can be used in banking; by means of cheques, travellers' cheques, bank transfers, credit cards and electronic purses. Banking will be possible in both euros and francs until the franc is withdrawn from circulation—which must be by 1 July 2002.

The franc (FRF) is made up of 100 centimes. Notes in circulation at 29 Jan. 1998: 261,338m. francs. In Feb. 1998 foreign exchange reserves were US$28,035m. and gold reserves were 81·89m. troy oz. The annualized rate of inflation in 1997 was 1·2% (2% in 1996), with a projected fall to 0·9% in 1998.

Franc Zone. 13 former French colonies (Benin, Burkina Faso, Cameroon, Central African Republic, Chad, Comoros, the Republic of the Congo, Côte d'Ivoire, Gabon, Mali, Niger, Senegal and Togo), the former Spanish colony of Equatorial Guinea and the former Portuguese colony of Guinea-Bissau are members of a Franc Zone, the CFA (*Communauté Financière Africaine*). Comoros uses the Comorian franc. From 1948 to 1994, 1 French franc equalled 50 francs CFA. The franc CFA was devalued by 50% on 11 Jan. 1994 and the Comorian franc by 25%. The franc CFP *(Comptoirs Français du Pacifique)* is the common currency of the French dependencies of French Polynesia, New Caledonia and Wallis and Futuna. It has a parity of CFP francs 18·18 to the French franc.

Banking and Finance. The central bank and bank of issue is the *Banque de France* (*Governor*: Jean-Claude Trichet, appointed 1993), founded in 1800, and nationalized on 2 Dec. 1945. In 1993 it received greater autonomy in line with EU conditions. The Governor is appointed for a 6-year term (renewable once) and heads the 9-member Council of Monetary Policy.

The National Credit Council, formed in 1945 to regulate banking activity and consulted in all political decisions on monetary policy, comprises 45 members nominated by the Government; its president is the Minister for the Economy; its Vice-President is the Governor of the Banque de France.

In 1996 there were 1,445 banks and other credit institutions, including 400 shareholder-owned banks and 342 mutual or savings banks. 4 principal deposit banks were nationalized in 1945, the remainder in 1982; the latter were privatized in 1987. The banking and insurance sectors underwent a flurry of mergers, privatizations, foreign investment, corporate restructuring and consolidation in 1997, in both the national and international fields. Further flotations planned included the sale of the state-owned insurance company GAN (1998) and Crédit Lyonnais (by 2000).

The state savings organization *Caisse Nationale d'Epargne* is administered by the post office on a giro system. There are also commercial savings banks (*caisses d'epargne et de prévoyance*). Deposited funds are centralized by a non-banking body, the *Caisse de Dépôts et Consignations*, which finances a large number of local authorities and state-aided housing projects, and carries an important portfolio of transferable securities.

There is a stock exchange (Bourse) in Paris.

Weights and Measures. The metric system is in general use.

ENERGY AND NATURAL RESOURCES

Electricity. The state-owned monopoly Electricité de France is responsible for power generation and supply under the Ministry of Industry. Installed capacity was 102·94m. kW in 1994. Electricity production (1995, in 1m. kWh): 470,974, of which 358,600 (76·14%) was nuclear. Hydro-electric power contributes about 20% of total electricity output (80,606m. kWh in 1994). Consumption per capita in 1995 was estimated to be 6,278 kWh. In 1997 it was the European Union's biggest exporter of electricity with 71·4bn. kWh.

France, not rich in natural energy resources, is at the centre of Europe's nuclear energy industry. In 1997 there were 56 nuclear reactors in operation, with a capacity of 58·4m. kW, providing some 72·9% of the electricity output. Nuclear reactors accounted for 38% of total energy consumption in 1994. There were 4 new nuclear plants under construction in 1997, one of which (in western France) was cancelled mid-way through the year and Electricité de France announced that it will not be considering any new plants before 2000. Also in 1997, following concern over its safety, it was decided that the 12-year-old Superphénix plant east of Lyons would be shut down.

Oil and Gas. In 1994, 2·8m. tonnes of crude oil were produced. The greater part came from the Parentis oilfield in the Landes. The importation and distribution of natural gas is the responsibility of the government monopoly Gaz de France. Production of natural gas (1994) was 94·4 petajoules. In 1994, 41·2% of total energy consumption came from oil; 13% from gas.

Minerals. France is a significant producer of nickel, uranium, iron ore, bauxite, potash, crude steel, pig iron, aluminium and coal. Société Le Nickel extracts in New Caledonia and is the world's third largest nickel producer; France is the world's seventh largest uranium producer. The mining sector contributed 1% of GDP in 1994, and employed 0·8% of the workforce.

Coal production (1995): 5·1m. tonnes. Coal power generators contributed 6·2% of total energy consumption in 1994. Coal reserves in Jan. 1996: 139m. tonnes. Production of other principal minerals and metals (1994, in 1,000 tonnes): crude steel, 18,242; iron ore (metal content), 708; pig iron, 12,444; aluminium (unwrought, primary), 481·50; potash salts, 936.

Agriculture. France is the world's largest food producer. The agricultural sector contributes about 4·6% of GDP, and employs about 4·5% of the workforce, down from 8·5% in 1980. Agriculture accounts for 14·5% of exports and 11·4% of imports.

In 1998 there were 680,000 holdings, compared to over 1m. in 1988. Co-operatives account for between 30-50% of output. In 1990 crop production accounted for 54·4% of total agricultural output; animal production for 45·6%.

Of the total area of France (54·9m. ha), the utilized agricultural area comprised 29·99m. ha in 1996. 18·29m. ha were arable, 10·53m. ha were under pasture, and 1·16m. ha were under permanent crops including vines (0·91m. ha).

Area under cultivation and yield for principal crops:

	Area (1,000 ha)			Produce (1,000 tonnes)		
	1994	1995	1996	1994	1995	1996
Wheat	4,580	4,744	5,040	30,549	30,879	35,948
Rye	45	46·3	48·6	176	190·7	220·8
Barley	1,405	1,339	1,485	7,646	7,492	9,276
Oats	166	148·8	139·5	685	601·2	621·9
Sugar-beet	437	458·2	456·7	29,037	30,571	30,943
Maize	1,660	1,650	1,733	12,943	12,739	14,529
Sorghum	...	45·6	54·7	...	256·4	343·1

Production of principal fruit crops (in 1,000 tonnes) as follows:

	1994	1995	1996		1994	1995	1996
Apples[1]	2,166	2,078	2,019	Melons	330	329	314
Pears	343	320	353	Nuts	27	38	39
Plums	221	299	364	Table grapes	69	107	95
Peaches	528	526	467	Strawberries	83	81	81·2
Apricots	155	100	174	Clementines	22	27	21

[1]Does not include apples for cider-making.

Total area under cultivation and yield of grapes from the vine (1996): 871,038 ha; 7·57m. tonnes. Estimated wine production (1997–98): 56m. hectolitres.

The area under cultivation (and yield) for vegetables in 1996 was as follows: Leaf and stem, 130,544 ha (2·4m. tonnes); fruit vegetables, 39,882 ha (1·5m. tonnes); roots and bulbs, 44,782 ha (1·33m. tonnes); pods, 86,339 ha (657,461 tonnes); beans, lentils and other dry, 10,213 ha (20,449 tonnes).

Livestock (1996, in 1,000): Horses, 337; asses and mules, 13·7; cattle, 20,655; sheep, 10,457; goats, 1,202; pigs, 14,283; poultry, 231,003 (laying hens, 49,324); rabbits, 14,439. Livestock products (1996, in 1,000 tonnes): beef and veal, 1,470; pork, 2,038; lamb and mutton, 152; poultry, 2,103; rabbit, 90; horse, 14; eggs, 1,026 (1995). Milk production: cows', 243,538,646 hectolitres; sheep's, 2,339,865 hectolitres; goats', 4,574,176 hectolitres.

Forestry. Forestry is France's richest natural resource, with a revenue of about 8,000m. francs a year, and accounts for 0·55m. of the workforce. In 1995 forest covered 15·03m. ha (27·3% of the land area). In 1990 the area under forests had been 14·23m. ha, or 25·9% of the land area. 73·7% of forest is private; 26% state-owned. Timber production in 1995 was 46·34m. cu. metres.

Fisheries. In 1996 there were 6,509 fishing vessels totalling 176,356 GRT, and 17,101 fishermen. Catch (1996, in tonnes): 868,572 (fish, 634,894; shellfish and molluscs, 233,678). Sea fishing accounts for approximately 92% of the total catch.

INDUSTRY

The industrial sector contributes around 28% of GDP and employs about 27% of the workforce. In Nov. 1997 capacity utilization in industry was approaching 85%. Chief industries: steel, chemicals, textiles, aircraft, machinery, electronic equipment, tourism, wine and perfume.

Industrial production (1994, in 1,000 tonnes): sulphuric acid, 2,227; caustic soda, 1,561; cement, 20,184. In 1993 (in 1,000 tonnes): sulphur, 1,106; polystyrene, 481; polyvinyl, 1,176; polyethylene, 1,308; wool, 56; cotton, 152; linen, 6; silk, 71.

Food products (1993, in 1,000 tonnes): chocolate, 547; biscuits, 475; sugar, 4,599; fish preparations, 109; jams and jellies, 161; cheese (1994), 1,562.

Engineering production (1994, in 1,000 units): car tyres, 66,744; motor vehicles, 3,176; television sets, 2,796.

Labour. According to the Employment Survey of March 1994, there was a working population of 25,136,598 (13,898,272 men and 11,238,326 women); out of an economically active population of 22,074,700, 1,127,300 were engaged in agriculture, forestry and fishing, 1,525,600 in building, 1,422,500 in transport and telecommunications, 1,481,100 in manufacturing industries, 608,300 in banking and insurance, 4,278,700 in services, 2,614,100 in commerce. Some 5m. people work in the public sector at national and local level. It was estimated in 1997 that 51% of households have no-one working in the private sector.

A new definition of 'unemployed' was adopted in Aug. 1995, omitting persons who had worked at least 78 hours in the previous month. Unemployment in 1998 was close to 3m. or 11·5% (1997, 12·5%) of the active population. The long-term jobless accounted for almost 40% of those seeking work. Under an 80% state-funded job creation programme announced in 1997, an extra 350,000 public-sector jobs will be created for the young by 2000.

Conciliation boards (*Conseils de Prud'hommes*) mediate in labour disputes. They are elected for 5-year terms by 2 colleges of employers and employees. In Jan. 1998 the minimum wage (SMIC) was 39·29 francs an hour (6,664 francs a month). SMIC affects about 1·5m. wage-earners. The average annual wage was 114,314 francs in 1994. Retirement age is 60. A 5-week annual holiday is statutory.

In May 1998 the national assembly approved a reduction in the working week from 39 to 35 hours. The main provisions obliged all companies employing more than 20 people to introduce the shorter working week from Jan. 2000 and all the rest from 2002. The law offers a sliding scale of incentives to employers provided that they cut working hours and create extra jobs. A second piece of legislation was planned for 1999 to determine how overtime would be paid, the working hours of salaried staff and the number of hours to be worked during the year. The introduction of a 35-hour working week in 1998 is unlikely to create many jobs but may slow wage claims and increase productivity.

Trade Unions. The main trade union confederations in 1997 were as follows: the Communist-led CGT (Confédération Générale du Travail), founded 1895; the CGT-FO (Confédération Générale du Travail–Force Ouvrière) which broke away from the CGT in 1948; the CFTC (Confédération Française des Travailleurs Chrétiens), founded in 1919 and divided in 1964, with a breakaway group retaining the old name and the main body continuing under the new name of CFDT (Confédération Française Démocratique du Travail); and the CGC (Confédération Générale des Cadres) formed in 1944, which represents managerial and supervisory staff. The main haulage confederation is the FNTR; the leading employers' association is the CNPF, often referred to as the *Patronat*. Unions are not required to publish membership figures, but in 1993 the 2 largest federations, the CGT and CFDT, had an estimated 0·63m. and 0·65m. members respectively.

Although France has the lowest rate of trade union membership in Europe, 9% in 1997 (compared to 29% in Germany, 33% in Britain and over 90% in Sweden), its trade unionists have considerable clout: they run France's welfare system; staff the country's dispute-settling industrial tribunals (*conseils de prud'hommes*); and fix national agreements on wages and working conditions. A union call to strike is invariably answered by more than a union's membership. Nearly 6m. working days were lost in French strikes in 1995 compared to 415,000 in Britain and 247,000 in Germany.

INTERNATIONAL TRADE

The trade balance showed a surplus of nearly 200,000m. francs in 1997 due to a strong export market, and a drop in imports owing to sluggish domestic demand. Trade balance (1997 estimate, in US$): 19,900m. (1998 forecast, 24,800m.). Main trading partners: Argentina, USA, Austria, Brazil, Canada, Egypt, Finland, Ghana, Japan, Uruguay, Philippines, Poland, Korea (Rep.) and Singapore.

Privatization legislation of May 1993 gave foreign nationals the right to acquire more than 20% of a firm's capital (the previous limit). In 1997, following intense activity on the equity market, approximately one-third of French equity was owned by foreign investors.

Imports and Exports. Total imports (1997, in US$1): 263,919m.; total exports, 285,084m. Principal imports include: oil, machinery and equipment, chemicals, iron and steel, and foodstuffs. Major exports: metals, chemicals, industrial equipment, consumer goods and agricultural products.

Foreign trade by sector (1992, as % of total trade):

	% Imports	% Exports
Agriculture and agri-food	11·6	16·4
Energy	8·6	2·3
Raw materials and semi-products	24·9	23·7
Capital goods	24·2	27·6
Surface transport equipment	11·1	13·9
Consumer goods	16·9	15·3

In 1997 the chief import sources (as % of total imports) were as follows: Germany, 16·6%; Italy, 9·8%; UK, 8·3%; Belgium-Luxembourg, 8%. The chief export markets (as % of total) were: Germany, 15·9%; UK, 10·1%; Italy, 9·3%; Belgium-Luxembourg, 8·1%. Exports to other European Union members constituted 62·9% of the total, and imports from fellow European Union members accounted for 61·0% of all imports.

COMMUNICATIONS

Roads. In 1997 there were 806,000 km of road, including 7,100 km of motorway. France has the densest road network in the world, and the longest in the EU. Around 90% of all freight is transported by road. In 1996 there were 24·4m. private cars and 4·9m. commercial vehicles (3·62m. trucks, about 42,000 buses and 0·87m. motorcycles and scooters). The average distance travelled by a passenger car in the year 1996 was 14,000 km. In 1996 there were 8,080 road deaths, down from 9,083 in 1992.

Rail. In 1938 all the independent railway companies were merged with the existing state railway system in a Société Nationale des Chemins de Fer Français (SNCF), which became a public industrial and commercial establishment in 1983. Legislation came into effect in 1997 which vested ownership of the railway infrastructure (track and signalling) in a newly established public corporation, the National Railway Network (RFN). The RFN is funded by payments for usage from the SNCF, government and local subventions and authority capital made available by the state derived from the proceeds of privatization. The SNCF remains responsible for maintenance and management of the rail network. The legislation also envisages the establishment of regional railway services which receive funds previously given to the SNCF as well as a state subvention. These regional bodies negotiate with SNCF for the provision of suitable services for their area. SNCF is the most heavily indebted and subsidized (38,000m. francs a year) company in France.

In 1997 SNCF totalled 33,769 km of track (one third of it electrified); it had an annual capacity of 58bn. passenger-km and 45bn. freight tonne-km. High-speed TGV lines link Paris to the south and west of France, and Paris and Lille to the Channel Tunnel (Eurostar). The high-speed TGV line appeared in 1983; it had 1,860 km of track in 1997, and another 4,400 km planned by 2015. Services from London through the Channel Tunnel began operating in 1994.

The Paris transport network consisted in 1993 of 202 km of metro, 352 km of regional express railways, 9·1 km of light rail and 7 km of passenger stock. There are metros in Lille (29 km), Lyons (20·8 km), Toulouse (10 km) and Marseilles (19·5 km), and tram/light railway networks in Grenoble (14·6 km), Lille (23 km), Marseilles (3 km), Nantes (16·5 km), Rouen (17 km), St Étienne (7 km) and Strasbourg (11·4 km).

Civil Aviation. The main international airports are at Paris (Charles de Gaulle), Paris (Orly), Bordeaux (Mérignac), Lyons (Satolas), Marseilles-Provence, Nice-Côte d'Azur, Strasbourg (Entzheim), Toulouse (Blagnac) and Nantes (Atlantique). The following had international flights to only a few destinations in 1998: Brest, Caen, Carcassonne, Clermont-Ferrand, Deauville, Le Havre, Le Touquet, Lille, Pau, Rennes, Rouen and St Étienne. The national airline is Air France. In 1995 it flew 349·9m. km, carrying 49,520,000 passengers (36,840,000 on domestic flights). In 1996 Charles de Gaulle airport handled 31,426,903 passengers (28,665,270 on international flights) and 886,114 tonnes of freight, Orly handled 27,333,472 passengers (16,742,976 on domestic flights) and 246,371 tonnes of freight, and Nice-Côte d'Azur handled 6,543,000 passengers (4,154,000 on domestic flights). Marseilles-Provence was the leading provincial airport in 1996 for freight, with 44,055 tonnes.

Shipping. The merchant fleet of ocean-going steam and motor ships totalling 1,000 gross tonnes or more (excluding special ships such as cable, icebreakers, etc.) comprised 65 vessels of 1,564,000 GRT in Jan. 1996. In 1993 from a total of 215 vessels (all sizes; GRT: 3,928,000), 212m. tonnes of cargo were unloaded, including 130m. tonnes of crude and refined petroleum products, 93m. tonnes were loaded; total passenger traffic was 29·2m. Chief ports: Marseilles, Le Havre, Nantes, Bordeaux and Rouen.

France has extensive inland waterways. Canals are administered by the public authority France Navigable Waterways (FVN). In 1993 there were 8,500 km of navigable rivers, waterways and canals (of which 1,647 km were accessible to vessels over 3,000 tons), with a total traffic of 59·8m. tonnes.

Telecommunications. France Télécom became a limited company on 1 Jan. 1997. In 1997, 33·7m. telephone main lines (575 for every 1,000 inhabitants) and 4·3m. mobile telephones were in use. In 1995 there were 1·7m. fax machines (including 0·4m. in working homes); 7·8m. PCs (equivalent to 134 per 1,000 persons); and 6·5m. Minitel videotext terminals were rented out by France Télécom. There were around 2·5m. Internet users in May 1998—just over 4% of the population.

Postal Services. There were 16,919 post offices in 1994. In 1995 a total of 24,391m. pieces of mail were processed, or 419 items per person. La Poste is a public enterprise under autonomous management responsible for mail delivery and financial services.

SOCIAL INSTITUTIONS

Justice. The system of justice is divided into 2 jurisdictions: the judicial, and the administrative. Within the judicial jurisdiction are common law courts including 473 lower courts (*tribunaux d'instance*, 11 in overseas departments), 186 higher courts (*tribunaux de grande instance*, 5 *tribunaux de première instance* in the overseas territories), and 454 police courts (*tribunaux de police*, 11 in overseas departments).

The *tribunaux d'instance* are presided over by a single judge. The *tribunaux de grande instance* usually have a collegiate composition, but may be presided over by a single judge in some civil cases. The *tribunaux de police*, presided over by a judge on duty in the *tribunal d'instance*, deal with petty offences (*contraventions*); correctional chambers (*chambres correctionelles*, of which there is at least 1 in each *tribunal de grande instance*) deal with graver offences (*délits*), including cases involving imprisonment up to 5 years. Correctional chambers normally consist of 3 judges of a *tribunal de grande instance* (a single judge in some cases). Sometimes in cases of *délit*, and in all cases of more serious *crimes*, a preliminary inquiry is made in secrecy by one of 569 examining magistrates (*juges d'instruction*), who either dismisses the case or sends it for trial before a public prosecutor.

Within the judicial jurisdiction are various specialized courts, including 227 commercial courts (*tribunaux de commerce*), composed of tradesmen and manufacturers elected for 2 years initially, and then for 4 years; 271 conciliation boards (*conseils de prud'hommes*), composed of an equal number of employers and employees elected for 5 years to deal with labour disputes; 437 courts for settling rural landholding disputes (*tribunaux paritaires des baux ruraux*, 11 in overseas departments); and 116 social security courts (*tribunaux des affaires de sécurité sociale*).

When the decisions of any of these courts are susceptible of appeal, the case goes to one of the 35 courts of appeal (*cours d'appel*), composed each of a president and a variable number of members. There are 104 courts of assize (*cours d'assises*), each composed of a president who is a member of the court of appeal, and 2 other magistrates, and assisted by a lay jury of 9 members. These try crimes involving imprisonment of over 5 years. The decisions of the courts of appeal and the courts of assize are final. However, the Court of Cassation (*cour de cassation*) has discretion to verify if the law has been correctly interpreted and if the rules of procedure have been followed exactly. The Court of Cassation may annul any judgment, following which the cases must be retried by a court of appeal or a court of assizes.

The administrative jurisdiction exists to resolve conflicts arising between citizens and central and local government authorities. It consists of 34 administrative courts (*tribunaux administratifs*, 7 in overseas departments and territories) and 5 administrative courts of appeal (*cours administratives d'appel*). The Council of State is the final court of appeal in administrative cases, though it may also act as a court of first instance.

Cases of doubt as to whether the judicial or administrative jurisdiction is competent in any case are resolved by a *Tribunal de conflits* composed in equal measure of members of the Court of Cassation and the Council of State. In 1997 the new government restricted its ability to intervene in individual cases of justice.

Penal code. A revised penal code came into force on 1 March 1994, replacing the *Code Napoléon* of 1810. Penal institutions consist of: (1) *maisons d'arrêt*, where persons awaiting trial as well as those condemned to short periods of imprisonment are kept; (2) punishment institutions – (a) central prisons (*maisons centrales*) for those sentenced to long imprisonment, (b) detention centres for offenders showing promise of rehabilitation, and (c) penitentiary centres, establishments combining (a) and (b); (3) hospitals for the sick. Special attention is being paid to classified treatment and the rehabilitation and vocational re-education of prisoners including work in open-air and semi-free establishments. Juvenile delinquents go before special judges in 138 (11 in overseas departments and territories) juvenile courts (*tribunaux pour enfants*); they are sent to public or private institutions of supervision and re-education.

The first Ombudsman (*Médiateur*) was appointed for a 6-year period in Jan. 1973. The present incumbent is Jacques Pelletier (app. 1992).

Capital punishment was abolished in Aug. 1981. In metropolitan France the detention rate on 1 Jan. 1997 was 88·3 prisoners per 100,000 population, up from 50 per 100,000 in 1975. The average period of detention in 1997 was 8·1 months. The principal offences committed were: theft, 28%; drug-related offences, 18%; rape and other sexual assaults, 18%. The population of the 187 penal establishments (3 for women) in Oct. 1998 was 55,155 men and 2,303 women, giving a total of 57,458.

Weston, M., *English Reader's Guide to the French Legal System.* Oxford, 1991

Religion. A law of 1905 separated church and state. In 1996 there were 95 Roman Catholic dioceses in metropolitan France and 112 bishops. In 1992 there were 43·77m. Roman Catholics (over 75% of the population), 0·8m. Protestants and 1·72m. Moslems.

Education. The primary, secondary and higher state schools constitute the 'Université de France'. Its Supreme Council of 84 members has deliberative, administrative and judiciary functions, and as a consultative committee advises respecting the working of the school system; the inspectors-general are in direct communication with the Minister. For local education administration France is divided into 25 academic areas, each of which has an Academic Council whose members include a certain number elected by the professors or teachers. The Academic Council deals with all grades of education. Each is under a Rector, and each is provided with academy inspectors, 1 for each department.

Compulsory education is provided for children of 6–16. The educational stages are as follows:

1. Non-compulsory pre-school instruction for children aged 2–5, to be given in infant schools or infant classes attached to primary schools.

2. Compulsory elementary instruction for children aged 6–11, to be given in primary schools and certain classes of the *lycées*. It consists of 3 courses: preparatory (1 year), elementary (2 years), intermediary (2 years). Physically or mentally handicapped children are cared for in special institutions or special classes of primary schools.

3. Lower secondary education (*Enseignement du premier cycle du Second Degré*) for pupils aged 11–15, consists of 4 years of study in the *lycées* (grammar schools), *Collèges d'Enseignement Technique* or *Collèges d'Enseignement Général.*

4. Upper secondary education (*Enseignement du second cycle du Second Degré*) for pupils aged 15–18: (1) *Long, général* or *professionel* provided by the *lycées* and leading to the *baccalauréat* or to the *baccalauréat de technicien* after 3 years; and (2) *Court*, professional courses of 3, 2 and 1 year are taught in the *lycées d'enseignement professionel*, or the specialized sections of the *lycées*, CES or CEG.

The following table shows the number of schools in 1994–95 and the numbers of pupils in full-time education:

	State Schools	State Pupils	Private Schools	Private Pupils
Nursery	18,646 ⎫		343 ⎫	
Primary	35,618 ⎬	5,597,600	5,626 ⎬	897,300
Secondary	7,501	4,327,200	3,711	1,142,000

Higher education is provided by the state free of charge in the universities and in special schools, and by private individuals in the free faculties and schools. Legislation of 1968 redefined the activities and working of universities. Bringing several disciplines together, 780 units for teaching and research (*UER–Unités d'Enseignement et de Recherche*) were formed which decided their own teaching activities, research programmes and procedures for checking the level of knowledge gained. They and the other parts of each university must respect the rules designed to maintain the national standard of qualifications. The UERs form the basic units of the 69 state universities and 3 national polytechnic institutes (with university status), which are grouped into 25 *Académies*. There are also 5 Catholic universities in Paris, Angers, Lille, Lyons and Toulouse; and private universities. There were 1,475,181 students at state universities (1993–94); 21,355 at private universities (1991–92).

Outside the university system, higher education (academic, professional and technical) is provided by over 400 schools and institutes, including the 177 *Grandes Écoles*, which are highly selective public or private institutions offering mainly technological or commercial curricula. These have an annual output of about 17,000 graduates, and in 1994–95 there were also 71,271 students in preparatory classes leading to the *Grandes Écoles;* in 1993–94, 232,844 were registered in the Sections de Techniciens Supérieurs, 71,273 in the Écoles d'Ingénieurs.

Adult literacy rate: 99·0%.

In 1993 total expenditure on education came to 5·8% of GNP and represented 10·4% of total government expenditure.

Health. Ordinances of 1996 created a new regional régime of hospital administration and introduced a system of patients' records to prevent abuses of public health benefits. In 1995 there were 160,235 doctors (equivalent to 1 for every 362 persons), 39,284 dentists, 53,085 pharmacists, 330,943 nurses and 11,957 midwives; and 3,810 hospitals, with a provision of 118 beds per 10,000 population.

Welfare. An order of 4 Oct. 1945 laid down the framework of a comprehensive plan of Social Security and created a single organization which superseded the various laws relating to social insurance, workmen's compensation, health insurance, family allowances, etc. All previous matters relating to Social Security are dealt with in the Social Security Code, 1956; this has been revised several times. The Chamber of Deputies and Senate, meeting as Congress on 19 Feb. 1996, adopted an important revision of the Constitution giving parliament powers to review annually the funding of social security (previously managed by the trade unions and employers' associations), and to fix targets for expenditure in the light of anticipated receipts.

In 1997, 6m. people were dependent on the welfare system, which accounted for more than a quarter of GDP (US$333,000m.). The Social Security budget had a deficit of some 17,000m. francs in 1996, and a cumulative debt (1992–96) of 250,000m. francs. A special levy, the new social debt repayment tax (RDS), at 0·5% on all incomes including pensions and unemployment benefit, has been introduced to clear the cumulative debt. A modest reform of the system was announced in June 1997 which will include a review of all welfare benefits.

Contributions. The general social security contribution (CSG) introduced in 1991 was raised by 4% to 7·5% in 1997 by the Jospin administration in an attempt to dramatically reduce the deficit on social security spending, effectively almost doubling the CSG. All wage-earning workers or those of equivalent status are insured regardless of the amount or the nature of the salary or earnings. The funds for the general scheme are raised mainly from professional contributions, these being fixed within the limits of a ceiling and calculated as a percentage of the salaries. The calculation of contributions payable for family allowances, old age and industrial injuries relates only to this amount; on the other hand, the amount payable for sickness, maternity expenses, disability and death is calculated partly within the limit of the 'ceiling' and partly on the whole salary. These contributions are the responsibility of both employer and employee, except in the case of family allowances or industrial injuries, where they are the sole responsibility of the employer.

Self-employed Workers. From 17 Jan. 1948 allowances and old-age pensions were paid to self-employed workers by independent insurance funds set up within their own profession, trade or business. Schemes of compulsory insurance for sickness were instituted in 1961 for farmers, and in 1966, with modifications in 1970, for other non-wage-earning workers.

Social Insurance. The orders laid down in Aug. 1967 ensure that the whole population can benefit from the Social Security Scheme; at present all elderly persons who have been engaged in the professions, as well as the surviving spouse, are entitled to claim an old-age benefit.

Sickness Insurance refunds the costs of treatment required by the insured and the needs of dependants.

Maternity Insurance covers the costs of medical treatment relating to the pregnancy, confinement and lying-in period; the beneficiaries being the insured person or the spouse.

Insurance for Invalids is divided into 3 categories: (1) those who are capable of working; (2) those who cannot work; (3) those who, in addition, are in need of the help of another person. According to the category, the pension rate varies from 30 to 50% of the average salary for the last 10 years, with additional allowance for home help for the third category.

Old-Age Pensions for workers were introduced in 1910 and are now fixed by the Social Security Code of 28 Jan. 1972. Since 1983 people who have paid insurance for at least 37½ years (150 quarters) receive at 60 a pension equal to 60% of basic salary. People who have paid insurance for less than 37½ years but no less than 15 years can expect a pension equal to as many 1/150ths of the full pension as their quarterly payments justify. In the event of death of the insured person, the husband or wife of the deceased person receives half the pension received by the latter. Compulsory supplementary schemes ensure benefits equal to 70% of previous earnings.

Family Allowances. A controversial programme of means-testing for Family Allowance was introduced in 1997 by the new administration. The Family Allowance benefit system comprises: (a) Family allowances proper, equivalent to 25·5% of the basic monthly salary for 2 dependent children, 46% for the third child,

41% for the fourth child, and 39% for the fifth and each subsequent child; a supplement equivalent to 9% of the basic monthly salary for the second and each subsequent dependent child more than 10 years old, and 16% for each dependent child over 15 years. (b) Family supplement for persons with at least 3 children or one child aged less than 3 years. (c) Ante-natal grants. (d) Maternity grant is equal to 260% of basic salary. Increase for multiple births or adoptions, 198%; increase for birth or adoption of third or subsequent child, 457%. (e) Allowance for specialized education of handicapped children. (f) Allowance for orphans. (g) Single parent allowance. (h) Allowance for opening of school term. (i) Allowance for accommodation, under certain circumstances. (j) Minimum family income for those with at least 3 children. Allowances (b), (g), (h) and (j) only apply to those whose annual income falls below a specified level.

Workmen's Compensation. The law passed by the National Assembly on 30 Oct. 1946 forms part of the Social Security Code and is administered by the Social Security Organization. Employers are invited to take preventive measures. The application of these measures is supervised by consulting engineers (assessors) of the local funds dealing with sickness insurance, who may compel employers who do not respect these measures to make additional contributions; they may, in like manner, grant rebates to employers who have in operation suitable preventive measures. The injured person receives free treatment, the insurance fund reimburses the practitioners, hospitals and suppliers chosen freely by the injured. In cases of temporary disablement, the daily payments are equal to half the total daily wage received by the injured. In case of permanent disablement, the injured person receives a pension, the amount of which varies according to the degree of disablement and the salary received during the past 12 months.

Unemployment Benefits vary according to circumstances (full or partial unemployment) which are means-tested.

Ambler, J. S. (ed.) *The French Welfare State: Surviving Social and Ideological Change.* New York Univ. Press, 1992

CULTURE

Avignon is one of nine European Cities of Culture in the year 2000, along with Bergen (Norway), Bologna (Italy), Brussels (Belgium), Helsinki (Finland), Kraków (Poland), Prague (Czech Republic), Reykjavík (Iceland) and Santiago de Compostela (Spain). The title attracts large European Union grants.

Broadcasting. Radio and television broadcasting was reorganized under the Act of 7 Aug. 1974 which replaced the *Office de Radiodiffusion Télévision Française* with 4 broadcasting companies, a production company and an audio-visual institute. The broadcasting authority (an independent regulatory commission) is the *Conseil Supérieur de l'Audiovisuel (CSA)*. Radio programmes are broadcast from 874 VHF transmitters of which 418 belong to 4 stations: *France Info, France Inter, France Musique* and *France Culture.* An external service, *Radio-France Internationale*, was founded in 1931 (as 'Poste Coloniale'), and broadcasts in 20 languages.

There are 2 state-owned TV channels, *Antenne-2* and *FR3*, which are partly financed by advertising, and 5 commercial channels; colour is by SECAM. TV broadcasts must contain at least 60% EU-generated programmes and 50% of these must be French.

There were about 58m. radio receivers in use in 1997; and 34·25m. TV sets (1995).

Cinema. There were 4,365 screens in 1995; attendances totalled 130·1m. (126m. in 1994); 115 full-length films were made in 1994. Around 360 new screens were to be opened between 1998 and 2000.

Press. There were about 80 daily papers (10 nationals, 70 provincials) in 1997. Top dailies: *L'Équipe*; *Le Monde*; *Le Parisien-Aujourd'hui*; *Le Figaro-L'Aurore*; *Libération*; *France-Soir*; *Ouest France*; *Le Progrès*; *Centre France*; *Sud Ouest*; *Voix du Nord*. The *Journal de Dimanche* is the only national Sunday paper. In 1995, total daily press circulation was 13·6m. copies, up from 10·3m. in 1980.

Tourism. There were 62,406,000 foreign tourists in 1996, spending US$28·36bn. France receives more foreign tourists than any other country, and had receipts in

1996 exceeded only in the USA and Italy. Around 11m. foreigners a year visit Paris. Countries of origin (visitors, in 1,000) in 1993: Germany, 12,900; UK, 8,000; Netherlands, 7,100; Italy, 6,300; Spain, 3,000; Belgium, 2,000; USA, 1,900; Switzerland, 1,900; Portugal, 1,700; Sweden, 878; Canada, 694; Denmark, 687; Ireland, 475; Greece, 348; Austria, 329; Japan, 320; Norway, 320. There were 596,670 classified hotel rooms in 1994.

DIPLOMATIC REPRESENTATIVES
Of France in Great Britain (58 Knightsbridge, London, SW1X 7JT)
Ambassador: Daniel Bernard.

Of Great Britain in France (35 rue du Faubourg St Honoré, 75383 Paris Cedex 08)
Ambassador: Sir Michael Jay, KCMG.

Of France in the USA (4101 Reservoir Rd., NW, Washington, D.C., 20007)
Ambassador: François Bujon.

Of the USA in France (2 Ave. Gabriel, Paris)
Ambassador: Felix Rohatyn.

Of France to the United Nations
Ambassador: Alain Dejammet.

FURTHER READING
Institut National de la Statistique et des Études Économiques: *Annuaire statistique de la France* (from 1878); *Bulletin mensuel de statistique* (monthly); *Documentation économique* (bi-monthly); *Economie et Statistique* (monthly); *Tableaux de l'Économie Française* (biennially, from 1956); *Tendances de la Conjoncture* (monthly).

Agulhon, M., *The French Republic, 1879–1992.* Oxford, 1993
Ardant, P., *Les Institutions de la Ve République.* Paris, 1992
Balladur, E., *Deux Ans à Matignon.* Paris, 1995
Braudel, F., *The Identity of France.* 2 vols. London, 1988-90
Caron, F., *An Economic History of Modern France.* London, 1979
Chambers, F. J., *France.* [Bibliography] Oxford and Santa Barbara (CA), (rev. ed.) 1990
Chambers, F. J., *Paris.* [Bibliography] Oxford and Santa Barbara (CA), 1998
Chazal, C., *Balladur.* [in French] Paris, 1993
Cubertafond, A., *Le Pouvoir, la Politique et l'État en France.* Paris, 1993
L'État de la France. Paris, annual
Gildea, R., *France since 1945.* OUP, 1996
Gouze, R., *Mitterrand par Mitterrand.* Paris, 1994
Hollifield, J. F. and Ross, G., *Searching for the New France.* London, 1991
Hudson, G. L., *Corsica.* [World Bibliographical Series, vol. 202] Oxford, 1997
Jones, C., *The Cambridge Illustrated History of France.* CUP, 1994
McMillan, J. F., *Twentieth-Century France: Politics and Society in France, 1898–1991.* 2nd ed. [of *Dreyfus to De Gaulle*]. London, 1992
Mendras, H. and Cole, A., *Social Change in Modern France: towards a Cultural Anthropology of the Fifth Republic.* CUP, 1991
Morris, P., *French Politics Today.* Manchester Univ. Press, 1994
Noin, D. and White, P. *Paris.* Chichester, 1998
Pinchemel, P., *France: A Geographical, Social and Economic Survey.* CUP, 1987
Popkin, J. D., *A History of Modern France.* New York, 1994
Price, R., *Concise History of France.* CUP, 1993
Schmidt, V. A., *Democratizing France: the Political and Administrative History of Decentralization.* CUP, 1991
Stevens, A., *The Government and Politics of France.* London, 1992
Todd, E., *The Making of Modern France: Politics, Ideology and Culture.* Oxford, 1991
Verdié, M. (ed.) *L'État de la France et de ses Habitants.* Paris, 1992
Vesperini, J.-P., *L'Économie de la France sous la Ve République.* Paris, 1993
Who's Who in France [in French]. Paris, annual

(Also see specialized titles listed under relevant selections, above.)

National statistical office: Institut National de la Statistique et des Etudes Économiques (INSEE), 75582 Paris Cedex 12.
Website: http://www.insee.fr/

FRANCE

DEPARTMENTS AND TERRITORIES OVERSEAS

These fall into 3 categories: *Overseas Departments* (French Guiana, Guadeloupe, Martinique, Réunion); *Territorial Collectivities* (Mayotte, St Pierre and Miquelon); and *Overseas Territories* (French Polynesia, New Caledonia, Southern and Antarctic Territories, Wallis and Futuna).

FURTHER READING
Aldrich, R. and Connell, J., *France's Overseas Frontier: Départements et Territoires d'Outre-Mer.* CUP, 1992

OVERSEAS DEPARTMENTS

GUADELOUPE
KEY HISTORICAL EVENTS
The islands were discovered by Columbus in 1493. The Carib inhabitants resisted Spanish attempts to colonize. A French colony was established on 28 June 1635, and apart from short periods of occupancy by British forces, Guadeloupe has since remained a French possession. On 19 March 1946 Guadeloupe became an Overseas Department.

TERRITORY AND POPULATION
Guadeloupe consists of a group of islands in the Lesser Antilles. The two main islands, Basse-Terre (to the west) and Grande-Terre (to the east), are joined by a bridge over a narrow channel. Adjacent to these are the islands of Marie Galante (to the south-east), La Désirade (to the east), and the Îles des Saintes (to the south); the islands of St Martin and St Barthélemy lie 250 km to the north-west.

Island	Area (sq. km)	1990 Census	Chief town
St Martin[1]	54[2]	28,518	Marigot
St Barthélemy	21	5,038	Gustavia
Basse-Terre	848	149,943	Basse-Terre
Grande-Terre	590	177,570	Pointe-à-Pitre
Îles des Saintes	13	2,036	Terre-de-Bas
La Désirade	20	1,610	Grande Anse
Marie-Galante	158	13,463	Grand-Bourg
	1,705	378,178[3]	

[1]Northern part only; the southern third is Dutch.   [2]Includes uninhabited Tintamarre.
[3]Preliminary results.

Population at the last census (1990, final result), 386,987; 1995 estimate, 417,000. The projected population for 2000 is 425,000. An estimated 99·4% of the population were urban in 1995. Population of principal towns: Basse-Terre, 14,082; Pointe-à-Pitre, 26,031; Les Abymes, 62,645. Basse-Terre is the seat of government, while larger Pointe-à-Pitre is the department's main economic centre and port; Les Abymes is a 'suburb' of Pointe-à-Pitre.

French is the official language, but Creole is spoken by the vast majority, except on St Martin.

SOCIAL STATISTICS
1998 estimates (per 1,000 population): birth rate, 16·7; death rate, 5·6. Annual growth rate, 1990–95, 2·1%. Life expectancy at birth, 1990–95, 71·1 years for males and 78·0 years for females.

CLIMATE
Warm and humid. Pointe-à-Pitre, Jan. 74°F (23·4°C), July 80°F (26·7°C). Annual rainfall 71" (1,814 mm).

CONSTITUTION AND GOVERNMENT
Guadeloupe is administered by a General Council of 42 members directly elected for 6-year terms (assisted by an Economic and Social Committee of 40 members) and by a Regional Council of 41 members. It is represented in the National Assembly by 4 deputies; in the Senate by 2 senators; and on the Economic and Social Council by 1 councillor. There are 4 *arrondissements*, sub-divided into 42 cantons and 34 communes, each administered by an elected municipal council. The French government is represented by an appointed Prefect.

CURRENT ADMINISTRATION
Prefect: Michel Diefenbacher.
  President of the General Council: Dominique Larifla (DVG).
  President of the Regional Council: Lucette Michaux-Chevry (RPR).

ECONOMY
Performance. In 1993 the GDP was 18,984m. French francs. GDP per capita (1993) was 46,484 French francs. Real GDP growth was –2·9% in 1995 and 1·9% in 1994.

Currency. The French franc is in use.

Banking and Finance. The Caisse Française de Développement is the official bank of the department, and issues its bank-notes. The main commercial banks in 1995 (with number of branches) were: Banque des Antilles Françaises (6), Banque Régionale d'Escompte et de Depôts (5), Banque Nationale de Paris (8), Crédit Agricole (18), Banque Française Commerciale (8), Société Générale de Banque aux Antilles (5), Credit Lyonnais (6), Credit Martiniquais (3), Banque Inschauspé et Cie (1).

ENERGY AND NATURAL RESOURCES
Electricity. Total production (1994): 1,005m. kWh.

Agriculture. Chief products (1993): bananas, 105,400 tonnes; sugar-cane, 748,000 tonnes; flowers, 8·9m. (1992). Other fruits and vegetables are also grown for both export and domestic consumption.
    Livestock (1996): Cattle, 60,000; goats, 63,000 (1995); sheep, 3,000; pigs, 14,000.

Forestry. In 1995 forests covered 89,000 ha, or 47·3% of the total land area (down from 51·5% in 1990). Timber production in 1995 was 15,000 cu. metres.

Fisheries. Total catches in 1995 were 9,530 tonnes, almost exclusively from sea fishing.

INDUSTRY
The main industries are sugar refining, food processing and rum distilling, carried out by small and medium-sized businesses. Other important industries are cement production and tourism.

Labour. The economically active population in 1997 was approximately 128,000. In 1993 there were 15,020 persons in the trade sector; 6,950 in transport and communications; and 34,223 in services. The minimum wage (SMIC) was 39·29 francs per hour (6,664 a month) in 1997. 46,360 persons were registered unemployed in 1994.

INTERNATIONAL TRADE

Imports and Exports. Total imports (1995): US$1,890m.; total exports: US$159m. Main export products (1993, with % of market share): bananas, 26%; sugar, 26%, rum, 7%. Trade with France (1993): 68% of all imports; 78% of exports.

COMMUNICATIONS

Roads. In 1996 there were 3,200 km of roads. In 1993 there were 101,600 passenger cars and 37,500 commercial vehicles.

Civil Aviation. Air France and a dozen or so other airlines call at Guadeloupe airport. In 1996 there were 38,243 arrivals and departures of aircraft, and 1,688,252 passengers at Le Raizet (Pointe-à-Pitre) airport. There are also airports at Marie-Galante, La Désirade, St Barthélemy and St Martin. Most domestic services are operated by Société Nouvelle Air Guadeloupe.

Shipping. In 1993, 2,812 vessels arrived to disembark 105,217 passengers and 1,933,000 tonnes of freight; and to embark 95,882 passengers and 431,000 tonnes of freight.

Telecommunications. In 1996 there were 170,700 main telephone lines, and in 1995, 3,400 fax machines.

Postal Services. In 1984 there were 47 post offices.

SOCIAL INSTITUTIONS

Justice. There are 4 *tribunaux d'instance* and 2 *tribunaux de grande instance* at Basse-Terre and Pointe-à-Pitre; there is also a court of appeal and a court of assizes.

Religion. The majority of the population are Roman Catholic.

Education. Education is free and compulsory from 6 to 16 years. In 1994 there were 54,493 pupils at 321 pre-elementary and primary schools, and 46,176 at 20 *lycées* and 40 *collèges* at secondary level. In 1993 there were 4,308 students from Guadeloupe at the University of Antilles-Guyana (out of total number of 8,290).

Health. In 1995 there were 13 public hospitals and 16 private clinics. In 1993 there were 590 doctors, 119 dentists, 1,470 nurses, 206 pharmacists and 108 midwives.

CULTURE

Broadcasting. Radiodiffusion Française d'Outre-Mer broadcasts for 17 hours a day in French. There is a local region radio station, and several private stations. There are 2 television channels (1 regional; 1 satellite) broadcasting for 6 hours a day. There were (1995) 98,000 radio and 114,000 TV receivers.

Press. There was (1995) 1 daily newspaper with a circulation of 20,000.

Tourism. Tourism is the chief economic activity. 458,181 tourists visited in 1994, including 313,613 cruise visitors.

FRENCH GUIANA

KEY HISTORICAL EVENTS

A French settlement on the island of Cayenne was established in 1604 and the territory between the Maroni and Oyapock rivers finally became a French possession in 1817. Convict settlements were established from 1852, that on Devil's Island being the most notorious; all were closed by 1945. On 19 March 1946 the status of French Guiana was changed to that of an Overseas Department.

TERRITORY AND POPULATION

French Guiana is situated on the north-east coast of Latin America, and is bounded in the north-east by the Atlantic Ocean, west by Suriname, and south and east by

Brazil. It includes the offshore Devil's Island, Royal Island and St Joseph, and has an area of 85,534 sq. km. Population at the 1990 census: 114,808 (including 34,087 of foreign origin); estimate (1995), 150,000. The projected population for 2000 is 173,000. In 1995, 76·4% lived in urban areas. The chief towns are: the capital, Cayenne (41,600 inhabitants), Kourou (14,000) and Saint-Laurent-du-Maroni (13,900). About 58% of inhabitants are of African descent.

The official language is French.

SOCIAL STATISTICS
1998 estimates (per 1,000 population): Birth rate, 23·7; death rate, 4·5. 49% of the poplation are migrants. Annual growth rate, 1990–95, 4·6%.

CLIMATE
Equatorial type climate with most of the country having a main rainy season between April and July and a fairly dry period between August and Dec. Both temperatures and humidity are high the whole year round. Cayenne, Jan. 26°C, July 29°C. Annual rainfall 3,202 mm.

CONSTITUTION AND GOVERNMENT
French Guiana is administered by a General Council of 19 members directly elected for 5-year terms, and by a Regional Council of 31 members. It is represented in the National Assembly by 2 deputies; in the Senate by 1 senator. The French government is represented by a Prefect. There are 2 *arrondissements* (Cayenne and Saint Laurent-du-Maroni) sub-divided into 22 communes and 19 cantons.

CURRENT ADMINISTRATION
Prefect: Pierre Dartout.
  President of the General Council: Stéphan Phinera (PS).
  President of the Regional Council: Antoine Karam (PS).

ECONOMY
Performance. In 1993 the GDP was 7,989m. French francs. GDP per capita (1993) was 54,516 French francs. Real GDP growth was 20·9% in both 1994 and 1995.

Currency. The French franc is in use.

Banking and Finance. The Caisse Centrale de Coopération Economique is the bank of issue. In 1995 commercial banks included the Banque Nationale de Paris-Guyane, Crédit Populaire Guyanais and Banque Française Commerciale.

ENERGY AND NATURAL RESOURCES
Electricity. Installed capacity was 228,000 kW in 1995. Production in 1994 was 446m. kWh.

Minerals. Placer gold mining is the most important industry in French Guiana. In 1993, 2,795 kg of gold were produced.

Agriculture. Some 21,670 ha are estimated to be under cultivation. Principal crops (1993, in tonnes): rice, 26,962; manioc, 23,350; sugar-cane, 3,200.
  Livestock (1996): 8,000 cattle; 9,000 pigs; 3,000 sheep; 220,000 poultry (1993).

Forestry. The country has immense forests which are rich in many kinds of timber. In 1995 forests covered 79,900 sq. km, or 90·6% of the total land area. 90·7% had been under forests in 1990. Roundwood production (1995) 132,000 cu. metres. The trees also yield oils, essences and gum products.

Fisheries. The catch in 1995 was 7,737 tonnes. Shrimps account for nearly 45% of the total catch.

INDUSTRY
Important products include rum, rosewood essence and beer. The island has sawmills and 1 sugar factory.

Labour. The economically active population (1993) was 46,300. In 1997 the minimum wage (SMIC) was 39·29 francs per hour (6,664 francs a month). 8,324 persons were registered unemployed in 1994.

INTERNATIONAL TRADE

Imports and Exports. Total trade (1995); imports, US$752m.; exports, US$131m.

COMMUNICATIONS

Roads. There were (1996) 356 km of national and 366 km of departmental roads. In 1993 there were 29,100 passenger cars and 10,600 commercial vehicles.

Civil Aviation. In 1996 Rochambeau International Airport (Cayenne) handled 362,756 passengers and 5,460 tonnes of freight. Services were provided in 1998 by Air France, AOM, Société Nouvelle Air Guadeloupe and Surinam Airways. The base of the European Space Agency (ESA) is located near Kourou and has been operational since 1979.

Shipping. 359 vessels arrived and departed in 1993; 249,160 tonnes of petroleum products and 230,179 tonnes of other products were discharged, and 69,185 tonnes of freight loaded. Chief ports: Cayenne, St-Laurent-du-Maroni and Kourou. There are also inland waterways navigable by small craft.

Telecommunications. The number of telephone main lines in 1997 was 46,700 (298·5 per 1,000 population).

SOCIAL INSTITUTIONS

Justice. At Cayenne there is a *tribunal d'instance* and a *tribunal de grande instance*, from which appeal is to the regional *cour d'appel* in Martinique.

Religion. In 1997 approximately 52% of the population was Roman Catholic.

Education. Primary education is free and compulsory. There were 24,000 children at primary schools in 1993; 12,000 at secondary schools; and (1988) a further 2,224 registered at private schools. In 1993, 644 students from French Guiana attended the Henri Visioz Institute, which forms part of the University of Antilles-Guyana (8,290 students in 1993).

Health. In 1995 there were 2 hospitals with 567 beds, 3 private clinics and a care centre. There were (1994) 213 doctors, 38 dentists, 47 pharmacists, 40 midwives and 495 nursing personnel.

CULTURE

Broadcasting. Radiodiffusion Française d'Outre-Mer-Guyane broadcasts for 133 hours each week on medium- and short-waves, and FM in French. Television is broadcast for 60 hours each week on 2 channels. In 1995 there were 95,000 radio and 26,000 TV receivers; colour is by SECAM. Although the number of televisions went up between 1980 and 1995, there were only 181 televisions per 1,000 inhabitants in 1995, down from 191 per 1,000 in 1980. Nowhere else in the world did the rate come down over the same 15-year period—in general access to television has become more widespread.

Press. There was (1996) 1 daily newspaper with a circulation of 1,000, and a second paper published 4 times a week has a circulation of 5,500.

Tourism. Total number of visitors (1993), 54,000.

MARTINIQUE

KEY HISTORICAL EVENTS

Discovered by Columbus in 1502, Martinique became a French colony in 1635, and apart from brief periods of British occupation the island has since remained under French control. On 19 March 1946 its status was altered to that of an Overseas Department.

TERRITORY AND POPULATION
The island, situated in the Lesser Antilles between Dominica and St Lucia, occupies an area of 1,128 sq. km. Population at last census (1990), 359,572; estimate (1995), 383,621; density, 357 per sq. km.

The projected population for 2000 is 416,000.

An estimated 93·3% of the population were urban in 1995. Population of principal towns: the capital and main port Fort-de-France, 101,540; Le Lamentin, 30,026; Schoelcher, 19,825; Sainte-Marie, 19,683; Rivière-Pilote, 11,261; La Trinité, 10,330.

French is the official language but the majority of people speak Creole.

SOCIAL STATISTICS
1998 estimates per 1,000 population: birth rate, 16·5; death rate, 5·9. Annual growth rate, 1990–95, 0·9%. Life expectancy at birth, 1990–95, 73·0 years for males and 79·5 years for females.

CLIMATE
The dry season is from Dec. to May, and the humid season from June to Nov. Fort-de-France, Jan. 74°F (23·5°C), July 78°F (25·6°C). Annual rainfall 72" (1,840 mm).

CONSTITUTION AND GOVERNMENT
The island is administered by a *General Council* of 45 members directly elected for 6-year terms, and by a Regional Council of 42 members. The French government is represented by an appointed Prefect. There are 4 *arrondissements*, sub-divided into 45 cantons and 34 communes, each administered by an elected municipal council. Martinique is represented in the National Assembly by 4 deputies, in the Senate by 2 senators and on the Economic and Social Council by 1 councillor.

CURRENT ADMINISTRATION
Prefect: Jean-François Cordet.
   President of the General Council: Claude Lise (PPM).
   President of the Regional Council: Emile Capgras (PCM).

ECONOMY
Main sectors of activity: tradeable services, distribution, industry, building and public works, transport and telecommunications, agriculture and tourism.

Performance. In 1993 the GDP was FF22,969m. GDP per capita was FF60,861. Real GDP growth was –2·9% in 1995 and 1·9% in 1994.

Banking and Finance. The Institut d'Émission des Départements d'Outre-Mer is the official bank. The Caisse Centrale de Développement is the government's vehicle for the promotion of economic development in the region. There were 5 commercial banks, 4 co-operative banks, 1 savings bank, 5 investment companies and 2 specialized financial institutions in 1999.

ENERGY AND NATURAL RESOURCES

Electricity. A network of 4,084 km of cables supplies 134,331 customers. Electricity is produced by 2 fuel-powered stations. Total production (1994): 903m. kWh.

Agriculture. Chief products: bananas, rum, sugar, pineapples, food and vegetables. In 1993 there were 3,223 ha under sugar-cane, 8,500 ha under bananas and 600 ha under pineapples. Production (1993 in tonnes): sugar, 6,626; sugar-cane, 227,076; bananas (1992), 228,000; pineapples (1992), 28,500.

Livestock (1996): 30,000 cattle, 42,000 sheep, 33,000 pigs, 23,000 goats (1995) and 263,000 poultry (1993).

Forestry. In 1995 there were 38,000 ha of forest, or 35·8% of the total land area (down from 37·7% in 1990). Timber production in 1995 was 12,000 cu. metres.

Fisheries. The catch in 1995 was 5,377 tonnes, almost exclusively from sea fishing.

INDUSTRY

Some food processing and chemical engineering is carried out by small and medium-size businesses. There were 9,443 businesses in 1993 (30% in building). There is an important cement industry; 12 distilleries for rum; and an oil refinery, with an annual treatment capacity of 0·75m. tonnes. Martinique has 5 industrial zones.

Labour. In 1995, 7·6% of the working population were in agriculture; 17·6% in industry; 23·8% in retail; 34·1% in services; 16·9% in distribution. In 1997 the minimum wage (SMIC) was FF6,663 a month (39·43 an hour). The economically active population in 1994 was 164,870. Some 61,100 persons were unemployed in 1995.

INTERNATIONAL TRADE

Imports and Exports. Martinique has a structural trade deficit due to the nature of goods traded. It imports high-value-added goods (foodstuffs, capital goods, consumer goods and motor vehicles) and exports agricultural produce (bananas) and refined oil.

In 1995 imports were valued at US$1,963m.; exports at US$224m. Main trading partners: France, EU, French Guiana and Guadeloupe. Trade with France accounted for 63% of imports and 61% of exports in 1995.

COMMUNICATIONS

Roads. Martinique has 2,176 km of roads. In 1995, FF106m. was spent on improving them. In 1993 there were 108,300 passenger cars and 32,200 commercial vehicles.

Rail. In 1995 there were 1,606 km of roads, of which 1,200 km were surfaced. 252 km were classified as national routes and 862 km as first-class roads. In 1992 there were 12,591 passenger cars and 2,443 commercial vehicles registered.

Civil Aviation. There is an international airport at Fort-de-France (Lamentin). In 1996 it handled 1,611,970 passengers and 13,738 tonnes of freight. 8 scheduled companies use Fort-de-France: Air France, Air Liberté, American Airlines, AOM, Air Calypso, Air Guadeloupe, Corsair and Liat.

Shipping. The island is visited regularly by French, American and other lines. The main sea links to and from Martinique are ensured by CGM Sud. It links Martinique to Europe and some African and American companies. Since 1995 new scheduled links have been introduced between Martinique, French Guiana, Haiti and Panama. These new links will facilitate exchanges between Martinique, Latin America and the Caribbean, especially Cuba. In 1993, 2,856 vessels called at Martinique and discharged 80,605 passengers and 1,612,000 tonnes of freight, and embarked 82,119 passengers and 789,000 tonnes of freight.

Telecommunications. In 1997 there were 169,900 main telephone lines. There were (1995) 12,000 cellular phone subscribers, 20,000 fax machines and 36,000 PCs. The main operator is France Télécom.

SOCIAL INSTITUTIONS

Justice. Justice is administered by 2 lower courts (*tribunaux d'instance*), a higher court (*tribunal de grande instance*), a regional court of appeal, a commercial court and an administrative court.

Religion. In 1997, 95% of the population was Roman Catholic.

Education. Education is compulsory between the ages of 6 and 16 years. In 1994 there were 51,824 pupils in 263 nursery and primary schools, and 43,384 pupils in 61 secondary schools. There were 29 institutes of higher education. In 1993, 3,670 students from Martinique were registered at the University of Antilles-Guyana (out of a total of 8,290).

Health. In 1995 there were 8 hospitals, 3 private clinics and 7 nursing homes. Total number of beds, 2,100. There were 680 doctors, 230 pharmacists, 123 dentists, 1,700 nurses, 147 midwives, 141 physiotherapists and 48 speech therapists.

CULTURE

Broadcasting. Radio Diffusion Française d'Outre-Mer broadcasts on FM wave, and operates 2 channels (1 satellite). There are also 2 commercial TV stations. In 1995 there were 77,000 radio and 55,000 TV receivers (colour by SECAM).

Press. In 1996 there was 1 daily newspaper with a circulation of 30,000.

Tourism. In 1996 there were 477,000 tourist arrivals by air. Receipts totalled US$392m. There are 122 hotels, with 4,460 rooms.

FURTHER READING

Crane, J., *Martinique*. [Bibliography]. Oxford and Santa Barbara (CA), 1995

RÉUNION

KEY HISTORICAL EVENTS

Réunion (formerly Île Bourbon) became a French possession in 1638 and remained so until 19 March 1946, when its status was altered to that of an Overseas Department.

TERRITORY AND POPULATION

The island of Réunion lies in the Indian Ocean, about 880 km east of Madagascar and 210 km south-west of Mauritius. It has an area of 2,504 sq. km. Population at the 1990 census: 597,828; 1996 estimate, 700,000, giving a density of 280 per sq. km; projection (2005), 900,000. An estimated 67·7% of the population were rural in 1995. The capital is Saint-Denis (population, 1995: 207,158); other large towns are Saint-Pierre (192,462), Saint-Paul (113,071) and le Tampon (47,593).

The islands of Juan de Nova, Europa, Bassas da India, Îles Glorieuses and Tromelin, with a combined area of 32 sq. km, are uninhabited and lie in the Indian Ocean adjacent to Madagascar. They remained French after Madagascar's independence in 1960, and are now administered by the Commissioner of Réunion. Both Mauritius and the Seychelles lay claim to Tromelin; and Madagascar claims all 5 islands.

French is the official language, but Creole is also spoken.

SOCIAL STATISTICS

1997: Live births, 13,748; deaths, 3,609; marriages, 3,284. Birth rate per 1,000 population (1994), 20·7; death rate, 5·3. Annual growth rate, 1990–95, 1·7%. Life expectancy at birth, 1990–95, 69·4 years for males and 78·8 years for females. Infant mortality, 1990–95, 8 per 1,000 live births; fertility rate, 2·4 births per woman.

CLIMATE

There is a sub-tropical maritime climate, free from extremes of weather, although the island lies in the cyclone belt of the Indian Ocean. Conditions are generally humid and there is no well-defined dry season. Saint-Denis, Jan. 80°F (26·7°C), July 70°F (21·1°C). Annual rainfall 56" (1,400 mm).

CONSTITUTION AND GOVERNMENT

Réunion is administered by a General Council of 48 members directly elected for 6-year terms, and by a Regional Council of 45 members. Réunion is represented in the National Assembly in Paris by 5 deputies; in the Senate by 3 senators; and in the Economic and Social Council by 1 councillor. There are 4 *arrondissements* sub-divided into 47 cantons and 24 communes, each administered by an elected municipal council. The French government is represented by an appointed Commissioner.

CURRENT ADMINISTRATION

Prefect: Jean Daubigny.
  President of the General Council: Jean-Luc Poudroux.
  President of the Regional Council: Paul Verges.

FRANCE

ECONOMY

Performance. GDP was FF35,266m. in 1994. Real GDP growth was 2·7% in 1995. GDP per capita (1993) was FF52,946s.

Currency. The French franc is in use.

Banking and Finance. The Institut d'Émission des Départements d'Outre-mer has the right to issue bank-notes. Banks operating in Réunion are the Banque de la Réunion (Crédit Lyonnais), the Banque Nationale de Paris Intercontinentale, the Caisse Régionale de Crédit Agricole Mutuel de la Réunion, the Banque Française Commerciale (BFC) CCP, Trésorerie Générale, and the Banque de la Réunion pour l'Économie et la Développement (BRED).

ENERGY AND NATURAL RESOURCES

Electricity. Production (1997), 1,470·8m. kWh. Consumption per capita (1994), 1,670 kWh.

Oil and Gas. Production (1997), 184,035 tonnes.

Water. Production (1997), 100·6m. cu metres.

Agriculture. Production of sugar was 207,110 tonnes in 1997; rum, 71,822 hectolitres (pure alcohol) in 1997. Other important products (1995, in tonnes): tobacco, 37; potatoes, 9; geranium oil, 5·3; onions, 2,415; pineapples (1996), 7·2; vanilla (1997), 48; maize (1992), 13,270.

Livestock (1997): 23,460 cattle, 87,170 pigs, 31,200 sheep, 11,835 poultry and 32,000 goats (1995). Meat production (1993, in tonnes): beef 1,206, pork 9,850 and poultry 14,080. Milk production (1997), 13,986 hectolitres.

Forestry. There were 89,000 ha of forest in 1995, or 35·6% of the total land area. Timber production in 1995 was 36,000 cu. metres.

Fisheries. In 1997 the catch was 5,882 tonnes, almost entirely from marine waters. Deep-sea fishing (1999) is mainly for blue marlin, sail-fish, blue-fin tuna and sea bream.

INDUSTRY

The major industries are electricity and sugar. Food processing, chemical engineering, printing and the production of perfume, textiles, leathers, tobacco, wood and construction materials are carried out by small and medium-sized businesses. At the beginning of 1994 there were 9,465 craft businesses employing about 20,000 persons.

Labour. The workforce was 264,200 in 1993. The minimum wage (SMIC) was 39·29 francs an hour (6,664 a month) in 1997. On 1 Jan. 1997, 96,330 persons were registered unemployed, a rate of 36·7%.

INTERNATIONAL TRADE

Imports and Exports. Trade in 1m. French francs:

	1994	1995	1996	1997
Imports	13,070	13,494	14,214	14,262
Exports	954	1,036	1,071	1,250

The chief export is sugar, accounting for 57% of total exports (1994). In 1994, 67% of imports and 74% of exports were from and to France.

COMMUNICATIONS

Roads. There were, in 1994, 2,724 km of roads. In Jan. 1998 there were 219,456 registered vehicles. In 1999 the County Council was operating bus services to all towns.

Civil Aviation. Réunion is served by Air Austral, Air France, AOM French Airlines, Air Liberté, Air Madagascar, Air Mauritius and Corsair. In 1997, 661,709 passengers and 13,640 tonnes of freight arrived at, and 658,292 passengers and 5,953 tonnes of freight departed from, Roland Garros Saint-Denis airport.

MAYOTTE

Shipping. 604 vessels visited the island in 1997, unloading 2,301,800 tonnes of freight and loading 453,600 tonnes at Port-Réunion.

Telecommunications. The number of telephone main lines in 1997 was 236,500. In 1995 there were 1,900 fax machines.

Postal Services. In 1996 there were 824 post offices.

SOCIAL INSTITUTIONS

Justice. There are 3 lower courts (*tribunaux d'instance*), 2 higher courts (*tribunaux de grande instance*), 1 appeal, 1 administrative court and 1 conciliation board.

Religion. In 1990, 95% of the population was Roman Catholic.

Education. In 1997–98 there were 351 primary schools with 120,190 pupils. Secondary education was provided in 26 *lycées*, 69 colleges, and 16 technical *lycées*, with, together, 94,072 pupils. The *Université Française de l'Océan Indien* (founded 1971) had 12,485 students in 1997–98.

Health. In 1997 there were 19 hospitals with 2,799 beds, 1,268 doctors, 305 dentists, 275 pharmacists, 184 midwives and 2,980 nursing personnel.

CULTURE

Broadcasting. Radiodiffusion Française d'Outre-Mer broadcasts in French on medium- and short-waves for more than 18 hours a day. There are 2 national television channels (*RFD1, Tempo*) and 3 independent channels (*Antenne Réunion, Canal Réunion/Canal +* and *TV Sud*). In 1995 there were 120,000 TV receivers and 165,000 radio receivers.

Cinema. In 1995 there were 17 cinemas.

Press. There were (1998) 3 daily newspapers (*Quotidien, Journal de l'Île, Témoignages*), 2 weekly (*Visu, Télé Magazine*), 3 monthly (*Memento, Via, l'Eco Austral*) and 1 fortnightly magazine (*Leader*), with a combined circulation of 57,000.

Tourism. Tourism is a major resource industry. There were 370,255 visitors in 1997 (82% French). Receipts (1996) totalled US$258m. In 1999 there were 50 hotels, 94 country lodges (*gîtes ruraux*), 204 bed and breakfast houses, 19 stopover lodges (*gîtes d'étape*) and 9 country houses.

Libraries. There were 53 libraries in 1998.

Museums and Galleries. There were 8 national theatres in 1998.

FURTHER READING
Institut National de la Statistique et des Etudes Économiques: *Tableau Économique de la Réunion.* Paris (annual)
Bertile, W., *Atlas Thématique et Régional.* Réunion, 1990

TERRITORIAL COLLECTIVITIES

MAYOTTE

KEY HISTORICAL EVENTS
Mayotte was a French colony from 1843 until 1914 when it was attached, with the other Comoro islands, to the government-general of Madagascar. The Comoro group was granted administrative autonomy within the French Republic and became an Overseas Territory. When the other 3 islands voted to become independent (as the Comoro state) in 1974, Mayotte voted against this and remained a French

dependency. In Dec. 1976 it became (following a further referendum) a Territorial Collectivity.

TERRITORY AND POPULATION

Mayotte, east of the Comoro Islands, consists of a main island (362 sq. km) with (1991 census) 94,385 inhabitants, containing the chief town, Mamoudzou (20,274 inhabitants); and the smaller island of Pamanzi (11 sq. km) lying 2 km to the east (9,775 in 1985) containing the old capital of Dzaoudzi (8,268). The whole territory covers 373 sq. km (144 sq. miles). The projected population for 2000 is 157,000.

The spoken language is Shimaoré (akin to Comorian, an Arabized dialect of Swahili), but French remains the official and commercial language.

CLIMATE

The dry and sunniest season is from May to Oct. The hot but rainy season is from Nov. to April.

CONSTITUTION AND GOVERNMENT

The island is administered by a General Council of 17 members, directly elected for a 6-year term. The French government is represented by an appointed Prefect. Mayotte is represented by 1 deputy in the National Assembly and by 1 member in the Senate. There are 17 communes, including 2 on Pamanzi.

RECENT ELECTIONS

At the General council elections on 23 March 1997 the Mouvement Populaire Mahorais won 8 seats, the Rassemblement Mahorais pour la République 5, the Parti Socialiste 1 and others 5.

CURRENT ADMINISTRATION

Prefect: Philippe Boisadam.

ECONOMY

Currency. Since Feb. 1976 the currency has been the French franc.

Banking and Finance. The Institut d'Emission d'Outre-mer and the Banque Française Commerciale both have branches in Dzaoudzi and Mamoudzou.

ENERGY AND NATURAL RESOURCES

Electricity. Production (1993), 9·64m. kWh.

Agriculture. The area under cultivation in 1998 was 14,400 ha. The chief cash crops (1997) were: ylang-ylang 14,300 kg, vanilla 4,417 kg, cocoa-nut 2,060 kg, cinnamon 27,533 kg. The main food crops (1997) were bananas (30,200 tonnes) and cassava (10,000 tonnes). Livestock (1997): Cattle, 17,000; goats, 25,000; sheep, 2,000.

Forestry. There are some 19,750 ha of forest, of which 1,150 is primary, 15,000 secondary and 3,600 badlands (uncultivable or eroded).

Fisheries. A lobster and shrimp industry has been created. Production (1997): 1,500 tonnes.

INDUSTRY

Labour. In 1994, 18·5% of the active population was engaged in public building and works. In 1997 the minimum monthly wage (SMIC) was 39·29 francs an hour (6,664 a month).

INTERNATIONAL TRADE

Imports and Exports. In 1997 exports of ylang-ylang totalled FF5·5m.; vanilla FF763,023; cocoa-nut FF2,075; cinnamon FF201,319. Imports (1993–94) totalled FF573·6m.

Trade Fairs. There are trade fairs every 2 years.

COMMUNICATIONS

Roads. In 1994 there were 93 km of main roads and 137 km of local roads; and 1,528 motor vehicles.

Civil Aviation. There is an airport at Dzaoudzi, with scheduled services in 1998 provided by Air Austral to the Comoros, Kenya, Madagascar, Réunion and Zimbabwe, by Air Madagascar to Madagascar and Air Mauritius to Mauritius.

Shipping. There are services provided by Tratringa and Ville de Sima to Anjouan (Comores), and by Frégate des Îles to Mohéli, Moroni (Comores) and Majunga (Madagascar).

Telecommunications. In 1995 there were 5,300 telephone main lines.

SOCIAL INSTITUTIONS

Justice. There is a *tribunal de première instance* and a *tribunal supérieur d'appel.*

Religion. The population is 97% Sunni Moslem, with a small Christian (mainly Roman Catholic) minority.

Education. In 1994 there were 25,805 pupils in nursery and primary schools, and 6,190 pupils at 7 *collèges* and 1 *lycée* at secondary level. There were also 1,922 pupils enrolled in pre-professional classes and professional *lycées.* There is a teacher training college.

Health. There were 2 hospitals with 100 beds in 1994. In 1985 there were 9 doctors, 1 dentist, 1 pharmacist, 2 midwives and 51 nursing personnel.

CULTURE

Broadcasting. Broadcasting is conducted by *Radio-Télévision Française d'Outre-Mer* (RFO-Mayotte) with 1 hour a day in Shimaoré. There are 2 private radio stations. In 1994 there were 30,000 radio and 3,500 TV receivers; colour is by SECAM.

Cinema. There is provision for 1 cinema, the Centre Mahoraise d'Animation Culturelle (CMAC), which operates either in Mamoudzou or Dzaoudzi.

Press. There was 1 weekly newspaper in 1997.

Tourism. In 1997 there were 8,545 visitors.

ST PIERRE AND MIQUELON

KEY HISTORICAL EVENTS

The only remaining fragment of the once-extensive French possessions in North America, the archipelago was settled from France in the 17th century. It was a French colony from 1816 until 1976, an overseas department until 1985, and is now a Territorial Collectivity.

TERRITORY AND POPULATION

The archipelago consists of 2 islands off the south coast of Newfoundland, with a total area of 242 sq. km, comprising the Saint-Pierre group (26 sq. km) and the Miquelon-Langlade group (216 sq. km). The population (1990 census) was 6,392, of whom 5,683 were on Saint-Pierre and 709 on Miquelon.The projected population for 2000 is 7,000. The chief town is St Pierre.

The official language is French.

SOCIAL STATISTICS

1997: Births, 92; marriages, 36; divorces, 9; deaths, 51.

CONSTITUTION AND GOVERNMENT

The Territorial Collectivity is administered by a General Council of 19 members directly elected for a 6-year term. It is represented in the National Assembly in Paris by 1 deputy, in the Senate by 1 senator and in the Economic and Social Council by 1 councillor. The French government is represented by a Prefect.

RECENT ELECTIONS
At the General Council elections on 20 March 1994, 12 seats went to Archipel Demain, 3 to Objectifs Miquelonnais, 3 to Saint Pierre et Miquelon 2000 and 1 to Miquelon Avenir.

CURRENT ADMINISTRATION
Prefect: Rémi Thuau.
   President of the General Council: Bernard Le Soavec.

Local Government. There are 2 municipal councils.

ECONOMY
Budget. The budget for 1997 balanced at 245m. francs.

Currency. The French franc is in use. The Euro will be used as in metropolitan France.

Banking and Finance. Banks include the Banque des Îles Saint-Pierre et Miquelon, the Crédit Saint-Pierrais and the Caisse d'Épargne.
   A Development Agency was created in 1996 to help with investment projects.

Weights and Measures. The metric system is in use.

ENERGY AND NATURAL RESOURCES
Electricity. Production (1997): 43m. kWh.; installed capacity, 1995, 23 MW.

Agriculture. The islands, being mostly barren rock, are unsuited for agriculture, but some vegetables are grown and livestock is kept for local consumption.

Fisheries. In June 1992 an international tribunal awarded France a 24-mile fishery and economic zone around the islands and a 10·5-mile-wide corridor extending for 200 miles to the high seas. A Franco-Canadian agreement regulating fishing in the area was signed in Dec. 1994. Catch (1997): 89 tonnes, chiefly cod, lumpfish, snow-crab and shark. In 1986 the total catch had been more than 23,000 tonnes.

INDUSTRY
In 1994 there were 351 businesses (including 144 services, 69 public works, 45 food trade, 8 manufacturing and 2 agriculture). The main industry, fish processing, resumed in 1994 after a temporary cessation due to lack of supplies in 1992. Aquaculture is also of importance.

Labour. The economically active population in 1997 was 3,000. In 1997 the minimum wage (SMIC) was 39·29 francs per hour (6,664 a month). In 1996, 11% of the labour force was registered as unemployed.

INTERNATIONAL TRADE
Imports and Exports.

	1992	1993	1994	1995	1996
Imports	404	344	413	351	363
Exports	199	28	82	55	20

In 1996, 53% of imports came from Canada and 36% from France.

COMMUNICATIONS
Roads. In 1996 there were 117 km of roads, of which 80 km were surfaced. There were 2,508 passenger cars and 1,254 commercial vehicles in 1996.

Civil Aviation. Canadian Airlines International connects St Pierre with Montreal, Halifax, Sydney (Nova Scotia) and St John's (Newfoundland). In addition a new airport capable of receiving medium-haul aeroplanes was due to open in 1999.

Shipping. St Pierre has regular services to Fortune and Halifax in Canada. In 1996, 878 vessels called at St Pierre; 20,195 tonnes of freight were unloaded and 1,873 tonnes were loaded.

Telecommunications. There were 4,165 telephones in 1996.

SOCIAL INSTITUTIONS

Justice. There is a court of first instance and a higher court of appeal at St Pierre.

Religion. The population is chiefly Roman Catholic.

Education. Primary instruction is free. There were, in 1995, 3 nursery and 5 primary schools with 793 pupils; 3 secondary schools with 549 pupils; and 2 technical schools with 152 pupils.

Health. There were (1995) 1 hospital with 44 beds, 1 convalescent home with 20, 1 retirement home with 40; 17 doctors and 1 dentist.

CULTURE

Broadcasting. Radio Télévision Française d'Outre-Mer (RFO) broadcasts in French on medium-wave, and on 2 television channels (1 satellite). In 1997 there were 34 cable TV channels from Canada and the USA; and a private local radio station (*Radio Atlantique*). In 1996 there were about 4,850 radio and 3,350 TV sets in use.

Tourism. There were (1995) 13,760 foreign visitors, including 3,700 cruise visitors.

FURTHER READING
De La Rüe, E. A., *Saint-Pierre et Miquelon*. Paris, 1963
Ribault, J. Y., *Histoire de Saint-Pierre et Miquelon: des Origines à 1814*. St Pierre, 1962

OVERSEAS TERRITORIES

SOUTHERN AND ANTARCTIC TERRITORIES

The Territory of the TAAF was created on 6 Aug. 1955. It comprises the Kerguelen and Crozet archipelagoes, the islands of Saint Paul and Amsterdam (formerly Nouvelle Amsterdam), all in the southern Indian ocean, and Terre Adélie. Since 2 April 1997 the administration has had its seat in Saint-Pierre, Réunion; before that it was in Paris. The Administrator is assisted by a 7-member consultative council which meets twice yearly in Paris; its members are nominated by the Government for 5 years. The 15-member Polar Environment Committee, which in 1993 replaced the former Consultative Committee on the Environment (est. 1982), meets at least once a year to discuss all problems relating to the preservation of the environment.

The French Institute for Polar Research and Technology was set up to organize scientific research and expeditions in Jan. 1992. The staff of the permanent scientific stations of the TAAF (120 in 1998) is renewed every 6 or 12 months and forms the only population.

Administrateur Supérieur: Mme Brigitte Girardin.

Kerguelen Islands Situated 48–50° S. lat., 68–70° E. long.; consists of 1 large and 85 smaller islands, and over 200 islets and rocks, with a total area of 7,215 sq. km (2,786 sq. miles) of which Grande Terre occupies 6,675 sq. km (2,577 sq. miles). It was discovered in 1772 by Yves de Kerguelen, but was effectively occupied by

France only in 1949. Port-aux-Français has several scientific research stations (56 members). Reindeer, trout and sheep have been acclimatized.

Crozet Islands Situated 46° S. lat., 50–52° E. long.; consists of 5 larger and 15 tiny islands, with a total area of 505 sq. km (195 sq. miles). The western group includes Apostles, Pigs and Penguins islands; the eastern group, Possession and Eastern islands. The archipelago was discovered in 1772 by Marion Dufresne, whose mate, Crozet, annexed it for Louis XV. A meteorological and scientific station (17 members) at Base Alfred-Faure on Possession Island was built in 1964.

Amsterdam and **Saint-Paul Islands** Situated 38–39° S. lat., 77° E. long. Amsterdam, with an area of 54 sq. km (21 sq. miles) was discovered in 1522 by Magellan's companions; Saint-Paul, lying about 100 km to the south, with an area of 7 sq. km (2·7 sq. miles), was probably discovered in 1559 by Portuguese sailors. Both were first visited in 1633 by the Dutch explorer, Van Diemen, and were annexed by France in 1843. They are both extinct volcanoes. The only inhabitants are at Base Martin de Vivies (est. 1949 on Amsterdam Island), including several scientific research stations, a hospital, communication and other facilities (20 members). Crayfish are caught commercially on Amsterdam.

Terre Adélie Comprises that section of the Antarctic continent between 136° and 142° E. long., south of 60° S. lat. The ice-covered plateau has an area of about 432,000 sq. km (166,800 sq. miles), and was discovered in 1840 by Dumont d'Urville. A research station (27 members) is situated at Base Dumont d'Urville, which is maintained by the French Institute for Polar Research and Technology.

NEW CALEDONIA

KEY HISTORICAL EVENTS
New Caledonia was discovered by James Cook on 4 Sept. 1774. The first settlers (English Protestants and French Catholics) came in 1840. New Caledonia was annexed by France in 1853 and, together with most of its former dependencies, became an Overseas Territory in 1958.

TERRITORY AND POPULATION
The territory comprises the island of New Caledonia and various outlying islands, all situated in the south-west Pacific with a total land area of 18,576 sq. km (7,172 sq. miles). The population (1996 census) was 196,836, including 67,151 Europeans (majority French), 86,788 Melanesians (Kanaks), 7,825 Vietnamese and Indonesians, 5,171 Polynesians, 17,763 Wallisians, 15,715 others. Density, 10 per sq. km. In 1995 an estimated 62% of the population lived in urban areas. Projected population (2000): 200,000. The capital, Nouméa, had 76,293 inhabitants in 1996.

There are 4 main islands (or groups of):

New Caledonia An area of 16,372 sq. km (about 400 km long, 50 km wide) with a population (1996 census) of 173,365. The east coast is predominantly Melanesian; the Nouméa region predominantly European; and the rest of the west coast is of mixed population.

Loyalty Islands 100 km (60 miles) east of New Caledonia, consisting of 3 large islands: Maré, Lifou and Uvéa, and many small islands. It has a total area of 1,981 sq. km and a population of 20,877, nearly all Melanesians, except on Uvéa which is partly Polynesian. The chief culture in the islands is coconuts; the chief export is copra.

Isle of Pines A tourist and fishing centre 50 km (30 miles) to the south-east of Nouméa, with an area of 152 sq. km and a population of 1,671.

Bélep Archipelago About 50 km north-west of New Caledonia, with an area of 70 sq. km and a population of 923.

The remaining islands are very small and have no permanent inhabitants. The largest are the Chesterfield Islands, a group of 11 well-wooded coral islets with a combined area of 10 sq. km, about 550 km west of the Bélep Archipelago. The Huon Islands, a group of 4 barren coral islets with a combined area of just 65 ha, are 225 km north of the Bélep Archipelago. Walpole, a limestone coral island of 1 sq. km, lies 150 km east of the Isle of Pines; Matthew Island (20 ha) and Hunter Island (2 sq. km), respectively 250 km and 330 km east of Walpole, are spasmodically active volcanic islands; and are also claimed by Vanuatu.

At the 1996 census there were 341 tribes (which have legal status under a high chief) living in 160 reserves, covering a surface area of 392,550 ha (21% of total land), and representing about 28·7 % of the population. 80,443 Melanesians belong to a tribe.

In addition to French, New Caledonia has a remarkable diversity of Melanesian languages (29 vernacular), divided into 4 main groups (Northern, Central, Southern and Loyalty Islands). There were 53,556 speakers (1996). The 3 most spoken forms are Drehu (11,338), Nengone (6,377) and Paicî (5,498). A ministerial decision in 1991 introduced local languages into the baccalauréat system. In 1997-98, 6 Melanesian languages were taught in schools.

SOCIAL STATISTICS
1997: Live births, 4,490; marriages, 1,005; divorces, 179; deaths, 1,016. Growth rate, 17·3 (per 1,000 population). Life expectancy at birth, 1990–95, 69·7 years for males and 74·7 years for females. Infant mortality, 1990–95, 22 per 1,000 live births; fertility rate, 2·7 births per woman.

CLIMATE
Nouméa, Jan. 26·8°C, July 21°C (average temp., 24·1°C; max., 35·8°C; min., 14·5°C). Annual rainfall 1,171 mm.

CONSTITUTION AND GOVERNMENT
Following constitutional changes introduced by the French government in 1985 and 1988, the Territory is administered by a High Commissioner assisted by a 4-member Consultative Committee, consisting of the President of the Territorial Congress (as President) and the Presidents of the 3 Provincial Assemblies. The French government is represented by the appointed High Commissioner.

There is a 54-member Territorial Congress consisting of the complete membership of the 3 Provincial Assemblies.

New Caledonia is represented in the French National Assembly by 2 deputies, in the Senate by 1 senator, in the Economic and Social Council by 1 councillor. The Territory is divided into 3 provinces, Nord, Sud and Îles Loyauté, each under a directly elected Regional Council. They are sub-divided into 32 communes administered by locally elected councils and mayors.

In Sept. 1987 the electorate voted in favour of remaining a French possession. Agreement was reached in June 1988 between the French government and representatives of both the European and Melanesian communities on New Caledonia, and confirmed in Nov. 1988 by plebiscites in both France and New Caledonia, under which the territory has been divided into 3 autonomous provinces.

On 5 May 1998 the Nouméa accords on limited autonomy were signed between the French government, the Rally for Caledonia in the Republic and the Kanak Socialist Front for National Liberation.

RECENT ELECTIONS
On 8 Nov. 1998 there was a referendum for the agreement of the Nouméa accords. The electorate was 106,716; turn-out was 74·2%. Nearly 71·9% of those who voted said 'Yes' to the question 'Do you approve the agreement on New Caledonia, signed in Nouméa on May 5 1998?'. Voting was restricted to those people resident in New Caledonia before 1998.

Elections to the Territorial Congress were held on 9 July 1995. The electorate was 102,487; turn-out was 70·23%. The Rally for Caledonia in the Republic (RPCR) won 22 seats with 36·41% of votes cast; the Kanak Socialist Front for National Liberation, 12 with 19·21%; New Caledonia for All, 9 with 15·27%; the National

Union for Independence, 5 with 9·87%; the National Front, 2 with 3·29%; the Rally for New Caledonia within France, 2 with 3·2%; Socialist Kanak Liberation, 1 with 3·26%; and the Front for the Development of the Loyalty Isles, 1 with 2·12%.

CURRENT ADMINISTRATION
High Commissioner: Dominique Bur.
President of the Territorial Congress: Simon Loueckhote (RPCR).

ECONOMY
Performance. In 1996, the GDP was 335,482m. francs CFP; GDP per capita was 1·7m francs CFP.

Budget. The territorial budget for 1998 balanced at 71,800m. francs CFP.

Currency. The unit of currency is the franc CFP (XPF), with a parity of 18·18 to the French franc. 166,610m. francs CFP were in circulation in Dec. 1996.

Banking and Finance. The banks are: Banque Calédonienne d'Investissement (BCI), the Westpac Banking Corporation (WBC), the Banque Nationale de Paris/Nouvelle-Calédonie (BNP/NC), the Société Générale Calédonienne de Banque (SGCB), the Bank of Hawaii-Nouvelle-Calédonie (BoH-NC) and the Caisse d'Epargne.

ENERGY AND NATURAL RESOURCES
Electricity. Production (1997): 1,524,000 kWh.

Minerals. The mineral resources are extensive: nickel, chrome and iron abound; silver, gold, cobalt, lead, manganese, iron and copper have been mined at different times. The nickel deposits are of special value, being without arsenic, and constitute around 25% of the world's total nickel reserves. Production (1996, in 1,000 tonnes) of nickel ore, 7,266; the furnaces produced 11,239 tonnes of matte nickel and 42,173 tonnes of ferro-nickel.

Agriculture. According to the 1996 Census, 4,663 persons worked in the agricultural sector. The chief products are beef, pork, poultry, coffee, copra, maize, fruit and vegetables. Production (1996, in tonnes): Cereals, 1,730; coffee, 37; copra, 345; potatoes, 2,165; squash, 1,508.
 Livestock (1996): cattle, 113,000; pigs, 39,000; goats (1995), 17,000; poultry (1995), 1m.

Forestry. There were 698,000 ha of forest in 1995, or 38·2% of the total land area (down from 38·3% in 1990). Timber production (1996), 1,244 tonnes.

Fisheries. In 1995 there were 302 fishing boats (1,768 GRT). Catch (1995): 5,292 tonnes. Aquaculture accounts for 25% (964·4 tonnes) of the world prawn market.

INDUSTRY
Local industries include chlorine and oxygen plants, cement, barbed wire, nails, pleasure and fishing boats, clothing, pasta, household cleaners, beer and soft drinks, confectionery and biscuits. The principal resource industries are nickel, fishing and tourism.

Labour. The working population (1996) was 64,377. The guaranteed monthly minimum wage was 76,207 francs CFP in Dec. 1997. In 1996 there were 30 industrial disputes and 13,826 working days were lost. There were 15,018 registered unemployed in 1997 (66% under 30 years of age).

INTERNATIONAL TRADE
Imports and Exports. In 1996 the balance of trade showed a deficit of 42,863m. francs CFP. Imports and exports in 1m. francs CFP:

	1994	1995	1996	1997
Imports	87,305	86,896	93,088	97,700
Exports	41,706	51,235	50,225	55,912

In 1997, 41·9% of imports came from France, 13·3% from Australia; and 28·2% of exports went to France. Refined minerals (mainly ferro-nickel and nickel) accounted for 52% of exports; nickel ore, 26·8%; mattes, 13·1%.

COMMUNICATIONS

Roads. There were (1996) 5,764 km of road, and 70,000 vehicles. In 1996 there were 623 road accidents and 42 fatalities.

Civil Aviation. New Caledonia is connected by air routes with France (by Air France and AOM), Australia (Air Calédonie International, AOM and Qantas Airways), New Zealand (Air Calédonie International and Air New Zealand), Japan (Air France and JAL), Sri Lanka (AOM), Guam (Continental Airlines), the Solomon Islands (Air Calédonie International and Solomon Airlines), the Fiji Islands (Air Calédonie International and Air Pacific), Vanuatu (Air Calédonie International and Air Vanuatu) and Wallis and Futuna (Air Calédonie International). Internal services with Air Calédonie link Nouméa to a number of domestic airfields. In 1996, there were 3,197 international movements via La Tontouta international airport, near Nouméa, carrying 311,538 passengers and 4,462 tonnes of freight.

Shipping. 552 vessels entered Nouméa in 1996, unloading 1,091,400 tonnes of cargo and loading 4,950,700 tonnes.

Telecommunications. In 1997 there were 475,500 telephone main lines, and in 1995, 800 cellular phone subscribers and 2,200 fax machines.

Postal Services. In 1996 there were 42 post offices.

SOCIAL INSTITUTIONS

Justice. There are courts at Nouméa, Koné and Wé (on Lifou Island), a court of appeal, a labour court and a joint commerce tribunal. There were 3,413 cases judged in the magistrates courts in 1996; 207 went before the court of appeal, 41 were sentenced in the court of assizes.

Religion. There were about 0·1m. Roman Catholics in 1994.

Education. In 1996 there were 36,139 pupils and 1,622 teachers in 279 primary schools; 26,276 pupils and 2,201 teachers in 69 secondary schools; and 1,749 students at university with 79 teaching staff; a further 68 were engaged in private further education. The state-funded French University of the Pacific (UFP) was founded in 1987 and comprises 2 campuses: 1 in New Caledonia (1,059 students in 1996); the other in French Polynesia. The South Pacific University Institute for Teacher Training, part of UFP, is based in Nouméa; there are 2 other colleges, in French Polynesia and Wallis and Futuna.

Health. In 1996 there were 362 doctors, 107 dentists, 74 pharmacists, 61 midwives and 1,208 paramedical personnel; there were 26 socio-medical districts, with 4 hospitals, 3 private clinics and 1,173 beds.

Welfare. There are 3 forms of social security cover: Free Medical Aid provides total sickness cover for non-waged persons and low-income earners; the Family Benefit, Workplace Injury and Contingency Fund for Workers (CAFAT); and numerous mutual benefit societies. In 1996 Free Medical Aid paid 53,055 beneficiaries a total of 8,298m. francs CFP; CAFAT paid 147,782 beneficiaries 12,874m. francs CFP in sickness cover.

CULTURE

Broadcasting. Radio Télévision Française d'Outre-Mer broadcasts in French on medium- and short-wave radio, and on 2 television channels; colour is by SECAM. There are also 3 commercial radio stations and 1 commercial TV channel (*Canal Plus*). There were 40,000 TV sets in 1996 and 102,000 radio receivers in 1995.

Cinema. In 1996, in Greater Nouméa, there were 11 cinemas and 1 drive-in.

Press. In 1998 there was 1 daily newspaper.

Tourism. Visitors (1996), 91,121 (30% French, 29% Japanese, 15·8% Australian). Receipts totalled US$109m. There were (1996) 76 hotels providing 2,075 beds.

FURTHER READING

Institut Territorial de la Statistique et des Etudes Économiques: *Journal Officiel de la Nouvelle Calédonie; Tableaux de l'Économie Calédonienne/New Caledonia: Facts & Figures (TEC 97)* (every 3 years)*; Informations Statistiques Rapides de Nouvelle-Calédonie* (monthly).
Dommel, D., *La Crise Calédonienne: Démission ou Guérison?* Paris, 1993

Local statistical office: Institut Territorial de la Statistique et des Études Économiques, BP 823, 98845 Nouméa.

FRENCH POLYNESIA

KEY HISTORICAL EVENTS

French protectorates since 1843, these islands were annexed to France 1880–82 to form 'French Settlements in Oceania', which opted in Nov. 1958 for the status of an overseas territory within the French Community.

TERRITORY AND POPULATION

The total land area of these 5 archipelagoes comprising 130 volcanic islands and coral atolls (76 inhabited) scattered over a wide area in the eastern Pacific, is 4,167 sq. km. The population (1996 census) was 219,521 (105,587 females); density, 53 per sq. km. At Dec.1998 French forces stationed in Polynesia numbered 2,119 (based mostly on Tahiti and the Hao atoll) and employed 1,162 Polynesian citizens. In 1995 an estimated 56·4% of the population lived in urban areas. Projected population (2025), 300,000.

The official languages are French and Tahitian.

The islands are administratively divided into 5 *circonscriptions* as follows:

Windward Islands (Îles du Vent) (162,398 inhabitants, 1996) comprise Tahiti with an area of 1,042 sq. km and 150,707 inhabitants; Mooréa with an area of 132 sq. km and 11,682 inhabitants; Maiao (Tubuai Manu) with an area of 9 sq. km; and the smaller Mehetia and Tetiaroa. The capital is Papeete, Tahiti (79,024 inhabitants, including suburbs).

Leeward Islands (Îles sous le Vent) comprise the 5 volcanic islands of Raiatéa, Tahaa, Huahine, Bora-Bora and Maupiti, together with 4 small atolls (Tupai, Mopelia, Scilly, Bellinghausen), the group having a total land area of 404 sq. km and 26,838 inhabitants in 1996. The chief town is Uturoa on Raiatéa. The Windward and Leeward Islands together are called the Society Archipelago (Archipel de la Société). Tahitian, a Polynesian language, is spoken throughout the archipelago and used as a *lingua franca* in the rest of the territory.

Marquesas Islands 12 islands lying north of the Tuamotu Archipelago, with a total area of 1,049 sq. km and 8,064 inhabitants in 1996. There are 6 inhabited islands: Nuku Hiva, Ua Pou, Ua Uka, Hiva Oa, Tahuata, Fatu Hiva; and 6 smaller (uninhabited) ones; the chief centre is Taiohae on Nukuhiva.

Austral or Tubuai Islands lying south of the Society Archipelago, comprise a 1,300 km chain of volcanic islands and reefs. There are 5 inhabited islands (Rimatara, Rurutu, Tubuai, Raivavae and, 500 km to the south, Rapa), with a combined area of 148 sq. km (6,563 inhabitants in 1996); the chief centre is Mataura on Tubuai.

Tuamotu Archipelago consists of 2 parallel ranges of 76 atolls (53 inhabited) lying north and east of the Society Archipelago, and has a total area of 690 sq. km, with 15,370 inhabitants in 1996. The most populous atolls are Rangiroa (1,913 inhabitants), Hao (1,356) and Manihi (769).

The Mururoa and Fangataufa atolls in the south-east of the group were ceded to France in 1964 by the Territorial Assembly, and were used by France for nuclear tests from 1966-96. The cessation of nuclear testing marked the end of activities of the Pacific Testing Centre (CEP) in French Polynesia. The CEP was entirely dismantled during 1998. A small military presence remains to ensure permanent radiological control.

FRENCH POLYNESIA

The *circonscription* also includes the Gambier Islands further east, with an area of 36 sq. km; the chief centre is Rikitea on the group's only inhabited island, Mangareva.

The uninhabited **Clipperton Island**, 1,000 km off the west coast of Mexico, is a dependency and is administered by the High Commissioner for French Polynesia but does not form part of the Territory; it is an atoll with an area of 5 sq. km.

SOCIAL STATISTICS
Annual population growth rate, 2·2%. Birth rate (1996) was 22·1 per 1,000 inhabitants; death rate, 4·7; marriage rate, 5·5; growth rate, 17·4. Life expectancy at birth, 1990–95, 68·3 years for males and 73·8 years for females. Infant mortality, 1990–95, 11 per 1,000 live births; fertility rate, 3·1 births per woman.

CLIMATE
Papeete. Jan. 81°F (27·1°C), July 75°F (24°C). Annual rainfall 83" (2,106 mm).

CONSTITUTION AND GOVERNMENT
Under the 1984 Constitution, the Territory is administered by a Council of Ministers, whose President is elected by the Territorial Assembly from among its own members; the President appoints a Vice-President and 14 other ministers (16 ministers in total in 1999). There is an advisory Economic and Social Committee. French Polynesia is represented in the French Assembly by 2 deputies, in the Senate by 1 senator, in the Economic and Social Council by 1 councillor. The French government is represented by a High Commissioner. The Territorial Assembly comprises 41 members elected every 5 years from 5 constituencies by universal suffrage, using the same proportional representation system as in metropolitan French regional elections. To be elected a party must gain at least 5% of votes cast. The Assembly elects a head of local government.

A statute drafted at the end of 1995 proposes to create French Polynesia as an Autonomous Overseas Territory in which the President of the Council of Ministers will become the President of the territory.

RECENT ELECTIONS
Elections were held on 12 May 1996. The electorate was 125,000. 412 candidates stood. Rassemblement pour le Peuple (RPP; affiliated to the French Rassemblement pour la République) won 18 seats with 31·41% of votes cast; Polynesian Union, 14 with 23·27%; New Fatherland (NF), 5 with 12·28%; Independent Liberation Front of Polynesia, 4 with 11·43%. An RPR-NF coalition was subsequently formed under Gaston Flosse (RPR).

CURRENT ADMINISTRATION
High Commissioner: Jean Aribaud.
    President of the Council of Ministers: Gaston Flosse (RPR).

ECONOMY
In decline since 1993, it has shown signs of recovery since 1997.

Performance. In 1997 GDP was FF21,600m. (5·5% up on 1996); GDP per capita was FF96,964.

Budget. Total expenditure (1997), FF10,416m., of which FF6,744m. comes directly from France.

Currency. The unit of currency is the franc CFP (XPF). Up to 31 Dec. 1998, its parity was to the French franc: 1F CFP = 0·055 FF; from 1 Jan. 1999 parity was linked to the euro: 1,000 F CFP = 8·38 euros. Since 1 April 1967 currency issue in the three territories (New Caledonia, Wallis and Futuna, French Polynesia) has been the responsibility of the *Institut d'Emission d'Outre-Mer* (IEOM).

Banking and Finance. There are 4 commercial banks: Banque de Tahiti, Banque de Polynésie, Société de Crédit et de Développement de l'Océanie, and the Banque Westpac. There are also 22 credit institutions, including SOFOTOM and the Agence Française de Développement (AFD).

ENERGY AND NATURAL RESOURCES

French Polynesia is heavily dependant on external sources for its energy. Since the early 1980s efforts have been made to reduce this, which have included the development of solar energy. By 1999 it was estimated that production of solar energy was in the region of 2,700 hours a year.

Electricity. Production (1997) was 353m. kWh in 1994, of which 35% was hydroelectric. Consumption per capita (1995) was estimated to be 1,409 kWh. Between 1988 and 1997, 14,212 solar photovoltaic modules were installed in Polynesia.

Oil and Gas. In 1997 over 236,000 tonnes of combustible products were imported (with a value of FF346m.), mainly from Australia and Hawai; 8,600 tonnes of gas was imported.

Agriculture. Agriculture used to be the primary economic sector but now accounts for only a modest 8% (1997) of GDP. An important product is copra (coconut trees cover the coastal plains of the mountainous islands and the greater part of the low-lying islands); production (1997) 9,857 tonnes. A new and increasingly successful crop is the nono fruit, which has medicinal value. Exports of the nono reached FF15m. in 1998. Tropical fruits, such as bananas, pineapples and oranges, are grown for local consumption.

Livestock (1996): Cattle 7,000; pigs 42,000; goats (1995) 27,286; poultry (1995) 297,700.

Forestry. In 1999 there was between 4,000 and 5,000 ha of forest, 2,000 of it exploitable. The industry remains embryonic.

Fisheries. Polynesia has an exclusive zone of 5·2m. sq km, one of the largest in the world. The industry employs some 2,000 people, including 700 traditional fishermen. Catch (1997): 5,600 tonnes, almost exclusively from sea fishing. Subject to annual agreement, a Korean fleet of 70 ships operates in the Polynesian waters; it had a quota of 3,000 tonnes in 1998–99.

INDUSTRY

Some 2,218 industrial enterprises employ 5,800 people. Principal industries include food and drink products, cosmetics, clothing and jewellery, furniture-making, metalwork and shipbuilding. Commerce is an important sector of the economy, employing (1997) some 7,400 persons in 2,448 enterprises across 1,752 retail and 696 manufacturing businesses.

INTERNATIONAL TRADE

Imports and Exports. The trade balance is precarious: Polynesia imports a great deal and exports very little. The trade deficit in 1997 was FF4·15m. Total imports (1997), FF5·46m.; total exports, FF1·31m.

The chief exports are coconut oil, fish, nono juice, mother of pearl and cultured pearls. Pearl production in recent years has doubled, with FF794m. worth of pearls exported in 1998. Representing 27% of the world market, Polynesia is the world's second largest producer of pearls after Australia. It is the second largest industry in Polynesia after tourism, and employs some 4,000 islanders.

Major trading partners: France, Japan (66% of pearl exports), Hong Kong, the USA and the EU, with France accounting for over 38% of total imports and around 25% of exports in 1997, and the EU as a whole 52% of imports.

COMMUNICATIONS

Roads. There were estimated to be 2,590 km of roads in 1999, 67% bitumenized.

Civil Aviation. The main airport is at Papeete (Tahiti-Faa'a). Air France and 8 other international airlines connect Tahiti International Airport with Paris, Auckland, Honolulu, Los Angeles, Santiago, Sydney, Tokyo and many Pacific islands. In 1998 Papeete handled 528,675 passengers (25% with Air France; 19% Air New Zealand; 17% AOM French Airlines). Local companies connect the islands with services from some secondary airports, including those at Bora-Bora, Rangiroa and Raiatea. Internal traffic handled 588,726 passengers and 2,200 tonnes of freight in 1997. Air Tahiti accounted for two-thirds of this; a further 6 local companies provide services from 48 secondary airfields.

Shipping. 10 shipping companies connect France, San Francisco, New Zealand, Japan, Australia, South East Asia and most Pacific locations with Papeete. In 1997 727,000 tonnes of cargo were unloaded and 28,000 tonnes loaded at Papeete's main port. Around 1·4m. people pass through the port each year.

Telecommunications. Number of telephone main lines (1997), 52,300; mobile phones (1998), 11,000. In 1995 there were 900 fax machines.

Postal Services. There are (1999) 56 post offices, handling some 700 tonnes of post a year.

SOCIAL INSTITUTIONS

Justice. There is a *tribunal de première instance* and a *cour d'appel* at Papeete.

Religion. In 1997 there were approximately 114,000 protestants (about 50% of the population) and 90,000 Roman Catholics (25%).

Education. There were (1998–99) 77,300 pupils and 5,200 teachers in 316 schools (46,800 in 255 primary schools; 30,500 in secondary school). The French University of the Pacific (UFP), founded in 1987, has 2 campuses, one in French Polynesia in Tahiti (the other in New Caledonia). The South Pacific University Institute for Teacher Training, founded in 1992 (part of UFP), has 3 colleges: in French Polynesia, Wallis and Futuna, and in Nouméa (New Caledonia), where it is headquartered. In 1997–98, 2,200 students followed university courses.

Health. There were (1999) 1 territorial hospital centre, 4 general hospitals, 1 specialist hospital and 2 private clinics, with a total of 855 beds. Medical personnel numbered 1,590 persons, including 384 doctors (175 per 100,000 inhabitants), 94 dentists and 51 pharmacists. Health spending accounted for 10·2% of GDP in 1997.

Welfare. In 1997, 202,760 people benefitted from social welfare.

CULTURE

Broadcasting. There are 3 TV broadcasters (1 public, 2 independent): *Radio Télévision Française d'Outre-mer* (RFO) which broadcasts on 2 channels in French, Tahitian and English; *Canal + Polynésie*; and *Telefenua* which broadcasts across 16 channels. There are also 11 private radio stations. Number of receivers (1999): radio, 40,350; TV, 40,000.

Cinema. There are 4 cinemas in Papeete.

Press. In 1999 there were 2 daily newspapers.

Tourism. Tourism is the main industry. There were 189,000 tourist arrivals in 1998. Total revenue (1997) FF2m.

FURTHER READING
Bounds, J. H., *Tahiti*. Bend, Oregon, 1978
Luke, Sir Harry, *The Islands of the South Pacific*. London, 1961
O'Reilly, P. and Reitman, E., *Bibliographie de Tahiti et de la Polynésie française*. Paris, 1967
O'Reilly, P. and Teissier, R., *Tahitiens. Répertoire bio-bibliographique de la Polynésie française*. Paris, 1963

Local statistical office: Institut Territorial de la Statistique, Papeete.

WALLIS AND FUTUNA

KEY HISTORICAL EVENTS
French dependencies since 1842, the inhabitants of these islands voted on 22 Dec. 1959 by 4,307 votes out of 4,576 in favour of exchanging their status to that of an overseas territory, which took effect from 29 July 1961.

TERRITORY AND POPULATION
The territory comprises two groups of islands in the central Pacific (total area 240 sq. km, over 14,000 inhabitants in 1996). The projected population for 2000 is

15,000. The Îles de Hoorn lie 255 km north-east of the Fiji Islands and consist of 2 main islands: Futuna (64 sq. km, 5,000 inhabitants) and uninhabited Alofi (51 sq. km). The Wallis Archipelago lies another 160 km further north-east, and has an area of 159 sq. km (9,000 inhabitants). It comprises the main island of Uvéa (60 sq. km; over 1,000 inhabitants) on Uvéa. Wallisian and Futunian are distinct Polynesian languages.

SOCIAL STATISTICS
Estimates per 1,000 population, 1998: birth rate, 23·0; death rate, 4·8.

CONSTITUTION AND GOVERNMENT
A Prefect represents the French government and carries out the duties of head of the territory, assisted by a 20-member Territorial Assembly directly elected for a 5-year term, and a 6-member Territorial Council, comprising the 3 traditional chiefs and 3 nominees of the Prefect agreed by the Territorial Assembly. The territory is represented by 1 deputy in the French National Assembly, by 1 senator in the Senate, and by 1 member on the Economic and Social Council. There are 3 districts: Singave and Alo (both on Futuna), and Wallis; in each, tribal kings exercise customary powers assisted by ministers and district and village chiefs.

RECENT ELECTIONS
Territorial Assembly elections were held in March 1992. The electorate was 6,972; 5,657 votes were cast.

CURRENT ADMINISTRATION
Chief Administrator: Christian Dors.
  President of the Territorial Assembly: Victor Brial (RPR).

ECONOMY
Budget. The budget for 1997 balanced at 120,100m. French francs.

Currency. The unit of currency is the franc CFP (XPF), with a parity of 18·18 to the French franc.

Banking and Finance. There is a branch of Indosuez at Mata-Utu.

ENERGY AND NATURAL RESOURCES
Electricity. There is a thermal power station at Mata-Utu.

Agriculture. The chief products are copra, cassava, yams, taro roots and bananas.
  Livestock (1996): 25,000 pigs; 7,000 goats.

Fisheries. The catch in 1995 was 170 tonnes.

COMMUNICATIONS
Roads. There are about 100 km of roads on Uvéa.

Civil Aviation. There is an airport on Wallis, at Hihifo, and another near Alo on Futuna. 5 flights a week link Wallis and Futuna. Air Calédonie International operates 2 flights a week to Nouméa and 1 a week to French Polynesia.

Shipping. A regular cargo service links Mata-Utu (Wallis) and Singave (Futuna) with Nouméa (New Caledonia).

Telecommunications. There were 340 telephones in 1985.

Postal Services. There were 6 post offices in 1986.

SOCIAL INSTITUTIONS
Justice. There is a court of first instance, from which appeals can be made to the court of appeal in New Caledonia.

Religion. The majority of the population is Roman Catholic.

WALLIS AND FUTUNA

Education. In 1993 there were 3,624 pupils in primary schools and 1,777 in secondary schools. The South Pacific University Institute for Teacher Training, founded in 1992 (part of the French University of the Pacific, UFP) has 3 colleges: in Wallis and Futuna, French Polynesia and Nouméa (New Caledonia), where it is headquartered.

Health. In 1991 there was 1 hospital with 60 beds, and 4 dispensaries.

CULTURE

Broadcasting. There were 2 radio stations in 1986.

GABON

República Gabonaise

Capital: Libreville
Population estimate, 2000: 1·23m.
GNP per capita: (PPP$) 6,300
HDI/world rank: 0·568/120

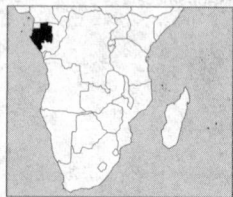

KEY HISTORICAL EVENTS

Between the 16th and 18th centuries, the Fang and other peoples in the region of present-day Gabon were part of a federation of chiefdoms. Some collaborated in the slave-trade, while others suffered from it. The country's capital, Libreville, grew from a settlement of slaves who were rescued from captivity by the French in 1849. Colonized by France around this period, the territory was annexed to French Congo in 1888. There was resistance by the indigenous people between 1905 and 1911 to the depredations of colonial rule, but the country became a separate colony in 1910 as one of the four territories of French Equatorial Africa. Gabon became an autonomous republic within the French Community on 28 Nov. 1958 and achieved independence on 17 Aug. 1960.

TERRITORY AND POPULATION

Gabon is bounded in the west by the Atlantic Ocean, north by Equatorial Guinea and Cameroon and east and south by the Republic of the Congo. The area covers 267,667 sq. km; its population at the 1993 census was 1,014,976; density, 3·8 per sq. km. In 1995 an estimated 50·1% of the population were urban. 1997 estimate, 1,190,000; density, 4·4 per sq. km.

The UN gives a projected population for 2000 of 1·23m.

The capital is Libreville (362,386 inhabitants, 1993 census), other large towns being Port-Gentil (80,841), Franceville (30,246), Oyem (22,669) and Moanda (21,921).

Provincial areas, populations (in 1,000) and capitals:

Province	Area in Sq. km	Population 1993 census	Capital
Estuaire	20,740	463,187	Libreville
Woleu-Ntem	38,465	97,271	Oyem
Ogooué-Ivindo	46,075	48,862	Makokou
Moyen-Ogooué	18,535	42,316	Lambaréné
Ogooué-Maritime	22,890	97,913	Port-Gentil
Nyanga	21,285	39,430	Tchibanga
Ngounié	37,750	77,781	Mouila
Ogooué-Lolo	25,380	43,915	Koulamoutou
Haut-Ogooué	36,547	104,301	Masuku

The largest ethnic groups are the Fang (25%) and Bapounou (24%) in the north. There are some 40 smaller groups. French is the official language.

SOCIAL STATISTICS

1995 births, 39,000; deaths, 16,000. Birth rate (per 1,000 population), 1995: 36·5; death rate, 14·8. Annual growth rate, 1990–95, 2·8%. Expectation of life at birth, 1990–95, 51·9 years for males and 55·2 years for females. Infant mortality, 1990–95, 94 per 1,000 live births; fertility rate, 5·0 births per woman.

CLIMATE

The climate is equatorial, with high temperatures and considerable rainfall. Mid-May to mid-Sept. is the long dry season, followed by a short rainy season, then a dry season again from mid-Dec. to mid-Feb., and finally a long rainy season once more. Libreville, Jan. 80°F (26·7°C), July 75°F (23·9°C). Annual rainfall 99" (2,510 mm).

CONSTITUTION AND GOVERNMENT

On 21 March 1997, the Government presented to the Parliament legislation aimed at reforming the constitution in a numer of key areas: notably, the bill mandated the creation of a Vice-President of the Republic, the extension of the presidential term of office from 5 to 7 years, and the transformation of the Senate into an Upper Chamber of Parliament. The bicameral Chambers of Parliament consist of 120 members of the National Assembly and 91 members of the Senate. At a referendum on electoral reform on 23 July 1995, 96·48% of votes cast were in favour; turn-out was 63·45%. The 1991 Constitution provides for an Executive President directly elected for a 5-year term (renewable once only). The head of government is the Prime Minister who appoints a Council of Ministers. The unicameral *National Assembly* consists of 120 members, directly elected for a 5-year term. There is constitutional provision for the formation of an upper house.

National Anthem. 'Uni dans la concorde' ('United in concord'); words and tune by G. Damas.

RECENT ELECTIONS

Presidential elections were held on 6 Dec. 1998. President Bongo was re-elected against 8 opponents with 66·6% of votes cast.

Elections for the National Assembly were held in 2 rounds on 15 and 22 Dec. 1996. The Gabonese Democratic Party (PDG) gained 85 of the 120 seats, the Gabonese Party of Progress (PGP) 10 and the National Woodcutters' Rally (RNB) 7. Other parties gained either 1 or 2 seats. At the Senate elections on 26 Jan. and 9 Feb. 1997 the PDG won 54 of the 91 seats and the RNB 20.

CURRENT ADMINISTRATION

President: El Hadj Omar Bongo (PDG; succeeded 2 Dec. 1967, re-elected in 1973, 1979, 1986, 1993 and 1998).

Vice President: Didjob Divungi Di Ndinge.

The Council of Ministers in March 1999 comprised:

Prime Minister, Minister of State for Housing, Zoning and Urban Affairs: Jean-Francois Ntoutoume-Emane (since 23 Jan. 1999).

Justice, Keeper of the Seals: Pierre-Louis Okawe. *Foreign Affairs and Co-operation:* Jean Ping. *Defence:* Ali-Ben Bongo. *Equipment and Construction:* Zacharie Myboto. *Labour and Human Resources, National Education, Women's Affairs, Spokesperson for the Government:* Paulette Missambo. *Agriculture, Livestock and Rural Economy:* Emmanuel Ondo Methogo. *Public Health, Population and Social Affairs:* Paulin Obame-Nguema. *National Defence, Transport and Merchant Marine:* Gen. Idriss Ngari. *Interior:* Antoine Mboumbou Miyakou. *Finance:* Emile Doumba. *Civil Service and Administrative Reform:* Patrice Nziengui. *Commerce and Industry:* Martin Fidele Magnaga. *Mining, Energy and Water Resources:* Paul Toungui. *Higher Education and Scientific Research:* Gaston Mozogo Ovono. *Planning:* Casimir Oye-Mba. *Youth and Sports:* Alexandre Sambat. *Social Affairs and National Solidarity:* Zeng Emome. *Tourism and Environment:* Jacques Adiahenot. *Water and Forests:* Andre Berre.

Local Government. The 9 provinces, each administered by a governor appointed by the President, are divided into 37 departments, each under a prefect. Elections were held on 20 Oct. 1996 for departmental assemblies and municipal councils.

DEFENCE

In 1997 military expenditure totalled US$115m. in 1997 (US$83 per capita).

Army. The Army consists of 1 all-arms Presidential Guard battalion group with support units and 8 infantry, 1 airborne commando and 1 engineer company, totalling (1997) 3,200. A referendum of 23 July 1995 favoured the transformation of the Presidential Guard into a republican guard. There is also a paramilitary Gendarmerie of 2,000. France maintains a 600-strong marine infantry battalion.

Navy. The small naval flotilla consists of 1 French-built fast missile craft and 2 coastal patrol craft. The flagship is a French-built medium landing ship, and there are about 3 minor service tenders. A separate Coast Guard operates some 10 small launches. Personnel in 1996 totalled 500.

Air Force. The Air Force has 6 single-seat, 2 two-seat Mirage 5 and 2 Magister ground-attack aircraft, and 1 EMB-111 maritime patrol aircraft. Transport duties are performed primarily by 2 Hercules and 1 EMB-110 Bandeirante turboprop aircraft and 1 CN-235. Single Falcon 900, Gulfstream III and DC-8 aircraft are used for VIP duties. Three T-34C-1 armed turboprop aircraft and a Super Puma are operated for the Presidential Guard. Also in service are 2 Puma, 3 Gazelle, 1 Bell 212, 1 Bell 412 and 2 Alouette III helicopters.

Personnel (1996) 1,000.

INTERNATIONAL RELATIONS
Gabon is a member of the UN, the IMF, the World Bank, the African Development Bank, the OAU, the Islamic Development Bank, the Central African Customs and Economic Union (UDEAC), the Economic Community of the Central African States (CEEAC), the Islamic Conference, the Movement of Non-Aligned Countries and is an ACP member state of the ACP-EU relationship.

ECONOMY

Policy. The *Economic and Social Council* was established in 1993 to advise the Council of Ministers. It comprises representatives of central government, local government, employers' groups, trade unions and other interest groups. 5-year development plans, of which there were 5 after 1966, have been replaced by 3-year rolling investment plans.

Performance. Real GDP growth was 1·0% in 1995 and 0·4% in 1994.

Budget. In 1996 revenues were estimated to be US$1·5bn. and expenditure US$1·3bn.

Currency. The unit of currency is the *franc CFA*, with a parity value of 100 francs CFA to 1 French franc. Foreign exchange reserves were US$404m. in Jan. 1998. Gold reserves were 13,000 troy oz. in March 1992. The average annual inflation rate during the period 1990–96 was 9·8%. Total money supply was 302bn. francs CFA in Jan. 1998.

Banking and Finance. The *Banque des États de l'Afrique Centrale* is the bank of issue. There are 9 commercial banks. The *Banque Gabonaise de Développement* and the *Union Gabonaise de Banque* are Gabonese-controlled.

ENERGY AND NATURAL RESOURCES

Electricity. Installed capacity was 301,000 kW in 1992. The semi-public *Société d'energie et d'eau du Gabon* produced 1,023·9m. kWh in 1995. In 1994, 78% was from hydro-electric stations. Consumption per capita was estimated to be 744 kWh in 1994.

Oil and Gas. Proven crude petroleum reserves (1997) 1,340m. bbls. Production, 1996, 135m. bbls. Natural gas production (1995) was 102m. cu. metres.

Minerals. There are an estimated 200m. tonnes of manganese and 850m. tonnes of iron ore deposits; proven reserves of uranium, 35,000 tonnes. Gold, zinc and phosphates also occur. Output, 1995: Manganese ore, 1·9m. tonnes; uranium, 623 tonnes.

Agriculture. Agriculture accounted for 7% of GDP in 1996. There are 0·46m. ha of cultivable land. The major crops (estimated production, 1995, in 1,000 tonnes) are: plantains, 247; cassava, 215; sugar-cane, 170 (1994); palm products, 73; taro, 56; maize, 28; groundnuts, 16. Other important crops include (1994 estimates in tonnes): soya, 1,792; cocoa, 718; coffee, 260 and rice, 166 (1995).

Livestock (1996): 39,000 cattle, 172,000 sheep, 84,000 goats (1995), 165,000 pigs.

Forestry. Equatorial forests covered 17·86m. ha in 1995, or 69·3% of the total land area (down from 71·1% in 1990). Timber production in 1995 was 4·88m. cu. metres.

Fisheries. In 1992 there were 14 fishing vessels over 100 GRT, totalling 2,141 GRT. Industrial fleets account for about 25% of the catch. The catch in 1995 was 27,978 tonnes, of which 25,478 tonnes were from marine waters.

INDUSTRY

Most manufacturing (5·2% of GDP in 1991) is based on the processing of food (particularly sugar), timber and mineral resources, cement and chemical production and oil refining.

Labour. The workforce in 1996 numbered 519,000 (56% males). Around 60% of the economically active population are engaged in agriculture. In 1993 the legal minimum monthly wage was 1,200 francs CFA. There is a 40-hour working week.

INTERNATIONAL TRADE

Foreign debt was US$4,213m. in 1996. The government retains the right to participate in foreign investment in oil and mineral extraction.

Imports and Exports. In 1995 imports totalled US$881m. and exports US$2,712m. The main exports in 1994 were worth, in millions of francs CFA: crude oil and natural gas, 1,004,387 (accounting for 74% of exports); timber and wood products, 195,677; manganese, 62,434; uranium, 20,069. Imports are mainly industrial goods. Main export markets, 1996: USA, 64·1%; France, 7·6%; China, 4·3%. Main import suppliers, 1996: France, 42·8%; USA, 10·4%; Japan, 6·0%.

COMMUNICATIONS

Roads. There were, in 1996, 7,670 km of roads (629 km asphalted) and some 24,750 passenger cars plus 16,490 trucks and vans. There were 854 road accidents in 1993 with 116 fatalities.

Rail. The 657-km standard gauge Transgabonais railway runs from the port of Owendo to Franceville. Total length of railways, 1994, 639 km. In 1995, 175,000 passengers and 3m. tonnes of freight were transported.

Civil Aviation. There are international airports at Libreville and Port-Gentil; scheduled internal services link these to a number of domestic airfields. The national carrier is Air Gabon (80% state-owned). In 1998 services were also provided by Air Afrique, Air France, Cameroon Airlines, Nigeria Airways, Royal Air Maroc and Swissair. 625,000 passengers and 14·5m. tonnes of freight were carried in and out of Libreville in 1996.

Shipping. In 1995 vessels over 100 GRT totalled 37,000 GRT, including 2 tankers totalling 742 GRT. Owendo (near Libreville), Mayumba and Port-Gentil are the main ports. In 1994, 19·8m. tonnes of cargo were handled at the ports. Rivers are an important means of inland transport.

Telecommunications. In 1997 there were 37,300 telephone main lines, or 32·7 per 1,000 population. There were 4,000 cellular phone subscribers in 1995, 6,000 PCs and 400 fax machines. In Jan. 1998 there were approximately 400 Internet users.

Postal Services. There were 60 post offices in 1995.

SOCIAL INSTITUTIONS

Justice. There are *tribunaux de grande instance* at Libreville, Port-Gentil, Lambaréné, Mouila, Oyem, Masuku and Koulamoutou, from which cases move progressively to a central Criminal Court, Court of Appeal and Supreme Court, all 3 located in Libreville. Civil police number about 900.

Religion. In 1993 there were 0·66m. Roman Catholics, 0·19m. Protestants and 0·12m. followers of African Christian sects. The majority of the remaining population following animist beliefs. There are about 10,000 Moslems.

Education. The adult literacy rate in 1995 was 63·2% (73·7% among males and 53·3% among females).

Education is compulsory between 6–16 years. In 1994–95 there were 247,018 pupils and 4,709 teachers in 1,105 primary schools and 65,718 pupils with 2,382 teachers at secondary schools; in 1993 there were 8,414 students with 421 teachers in 12 technical schools and 780 students with 43 teachers in 8 teacher-training establishments.

In 1994–95 there was 1 university and 1 university of science and technology, with a total of 2,950 students and 410 academic staff.

Health. In 1989 there were 448 doctors, 32 dentists, 71 pharmacists, 240 midwives and 759 nurses. In 1988 there were 27 hospitals and 633 medical centres, with a total of 5,329 beds.

CULTURE

Broadcasting. Broadcasting is the responsibility of the state-controlled Radiodiffusion Télévision Gabonaise which transmits 2 national radio programmes and provincial services. There is also a commercial radio station and 2 TV channels. In 1995 there were 195,000 radio and 51,000 TV sets (colour by SECAM).

Press. There was (1993) a government-run daily, *L'Union*, and 4 independent periodicals.

Tourism. There were 136,000 foreign tourists in 1996, spending US$4m.

DIPLOMATIC REPRESENTATIVES
Of Gabon in Great Britain (27 Elvaston Place, London, SW7 5NL)
Ambassador: Honorine Dossou-Naki.

Of Great Britain in Gabon
Ambassador: Mr. G. P. R. Boon (resides in Yaoundé).

Of Gabon in the USA (2034 20th St., NW, Washington, D.C., 20009)
Ambassador: Paul Bunduku-Latha.

Of the USA in Gabon (Blvd de la Mer, Libreville)
Ambassador: Elizabeth Raspolic.

Of Gabon to the United Nations
Ambassador: Denis Dangue Réwaka.

Of Gabon to the European Union
Ambassador: Jean-Robert Goulongana.

FURTHER READING
Barnes, J. F. G., *Gabon: beyond the Colonial Legacy.* Boulder (Colo.), 1992
Gardiner, D. E. (ed.) *Historical Dictionary of Gabon.* 2nd ed. Metuchen (NJ), 1994
Saint Paul, M. A., *Gabon: the Development of a Nation.* London, 1989

National statistical office: Direction Générale de la Statistique et des Études Économiques, Ministère de la Planification, de l'Économie et de l'Aménagement du Territoire, Libreville.

THE GAMBIA

Republic of The Gambia

Capital: Banjul
Population estimate, 2000: 1·24m.
GNP per capita: (PPP$) 1,280
HDI/world rank: 0·291/165

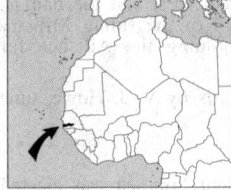

KEY HISTORICAL EVENTS

The Gambia was discovered by the early Portuguese navigators, but they did not settle. During the 17th century various companies of merchants obtained trading charters and established a settlement on the river, which, from 1807, was controlled from Sierra Leone; in 1843 The Gambia became an independent Crown Colony; in 1866 it formed part of the West African Settlements, but in Dec. 1888 it again became a separate Crown Colony. The boundaries were delimited only after 1890. The Gambia achieved full internal self-government on 4 Oct. 1963 and became an independent member of the Commonwealth on 18 Feb. 1965. The Gambia became a republic within the Commonwealth on 24 April 1970. The Gambia with Senegal formed the Senegambia Confederation on 1 Feb. 1982; this was officially dissolved on 21 Sept. 1989.

In a bloodless coup on 22 July 1994 a military junta seized power under the leadership of Lt Yahya Jammeh; President Dawda Jawara left the country.

TERRITORY AND POPULATION

The Gambia takes its name from the River Gambia, and consists of a strip of territory never wider than 10 km on both banks. It is bounded in the west by the Atlantic Ocean and on all other sides by Senegal. The area is 10,689 sq. km, including 2,077 sq. km of inland water. Population (census, 1993), 1,025,867. Estimate, 1995, 1,087,000; density, 102 per sq. km.

The UN gives a projected population for 2000 of 1·24m.

An estimated 71·0% of the population were rural in 1995.

The largest ethnic group is the Mandingo, followed by the Wolofs, Fulas, Jolas and Sarahuley. The country is administratively divided into the capital, Banjul (1993 census, 42,326), and the surrounding urban area, Kombo St Mary (228,214), plus 5 other administrative divisions in the rural areas.

The 5 rural divisions, with their areas, populations and chief towns are (listed west to east, or upriver):

Division	Area in Sq. km	Population 1993 census	Chief town
Western	1,764	234,917	Brikama
North Bank	2,256	156,462	Kerewan/Farafenni
Lower River	1,618	65,146	Soma
Central River	2,894	156,021	Jangjangbureh
Upper River	2,069	155,059	Basse

The official language is English.

SOCIAL STATISTICS

1995 births, 46,000; deaths, 20,000. 1995 birth rate per 1,000 population, 41·6; death rate, 18·3. Annual growth rate, 1990–95, 3·8%. Expectation of life, 1990–95, was 43·4 years for males and 46·6 for females. Infant mortality, 1990–95, 132 per 1,000 live births; fertility rate, 5·6 births per woman.

CLIMATE

The climate is characterized by two very different seasons. The dry season lasts from Nov. to May, when precipitation is very light and humidity moderate. Days are warm but nights quite cool. The SW monsoon is likely to set in with spectacular storms and produces considerable rainfall from July to Oct., with increased humidity. Banjul, Jan. 73°F (22·8°C), July 80°F (26·7°C). Annual rainfall 52" (1,295 mm).

CONSTITUTION AND GOVERNMENT

The 1970 constitution provided for an executive *President* elected directly for renewable 5-year terms. The then President appoints a *Vice-President* who is the government's chief minister. The single-chamber *House of Assembly* has 51 members: 36 elected, 8 nominated (these are from different fields of work and are selected by the Head of State), 5 Head Chief members (nominated by the Head of State), the Attorney-General and the Speaker (both of whom are nominated).

A referendum of 8 Aug. 1996 approved a new Constitution by 70·4% of votes cast. Under this the number of seats in parliament, now the *National Assembly*, is increased to 45 directly elected members and 4 nominated MPs, and the ban on political parties imposed in July 1994 is lifted. Members of the ruling Military Council resigned from their military positions before joining the Alliance for Patriotic Reorientation and Construction (APRC).

National Anthem. 'For The Gambia, our homeland'; words by V. J. Howe, tune traditional.

RECENT ELECTIONS
Presidential elections were held on 26 Sept. 1996. President Jammeh was elected against 3 opponents by 55·76% of votes cast.

Parliamentary elections were held on 2 Jan. 1997. The Alliance for Patriotic Reorientation and Construction (APRC) gained 33 seats and 52·1% of the votes, and the UDR 7 seats with 34·0% of votes cast.

CURRENT ADMINISTRATION
President: Rtd. Col. Yahya Jammeh (APRC; seized power 22 July 1994; elected, 26 Sept. 1996).

In March 1999 the government comprised:

Head of State: Col. Yahya Jammeh.

Vice-President and *Secretary of State for Health and Social Affairs:* Mrs Isatou Njie Saidy.

Secretary of State, Office of the President: Capt. Edward Singhatey. *Local Government and Lands:* Lamine Bajo. *Interior:* Ousman Badjie. *Finance and Economic Affairs:* Famara Jatta. *Foreign Affairs:* Dr Momodou Lamin Sedat Jobe. *Information and Tourism:* Susan Waffa-Ogoo. *Trade, Industry and Employment:* Musa Sillah. *Education:* Ann-Therese Ndong-Jatta. *Justice and Attorney General:* Fatou Bensouda. *Works and Communication:* Momodou Sarjo Jallow. *Agriculture and Natural Resources:* Fa Sainey Dumbuya. *Youth, Sports and Culture:* Yankuba Touray.

Local Government. The Gambia is divided into 35 districts, each traditionally under a Chief, assisted by Village Heads and advisers. These districts are grouped into 7 Area Councils containing a majority of elected members, with the Chiefs of the district as ex-officio members. The city of Banjul is administered by a City Council.

DEFENCE
The Gambia National Army, 800 strong, has 2 infantry battalions and 1 engineer squadron.

The marine unit of the Army consisted in 1996 of 70 personnel operating 2 ex-Chinese and 2 British-built inshore patrol craft and some boats, based at Banjul.

Defence expenditure totalled US$15m. in 1997 (US$13 per capita).

INTERNATIONAL RELATIONS
The Gambia is a member of the UN, OAU, Commonwealth, ECOWAS and is an ACP member state of the ACP-EU relationship.

ECONOMY
Performance. Real GDP growth was 3·0% in 1995 and −5·9% in 1994.

Budget. The fiscal year starts on 1 July. In 1996/97 revenues were estimated to be US$88·6m. and expenditures US$98·2m.

Currency. The unit of currency is the *dalasi* (GMD), of 100 *butut.* Inflation was 5% in 1993. Foreign exchange reserves were US$94·03m. in 1992. Total money supply in Jan. 1998 was 650m. dalasis.

Banking and Finance. The Central Bank of The Gambia (founded 1971) is the bank of issue. There are 5 commercial banks: Standard Chartered, BICI Trust Bank, Western Union Monetary Transfer, Arab Gambian Islamic Bank, Continent Bank.

Weights and Measures. The UK imperial system is in common use, but the metric system is being introduced.

ENERGY AND NATURAL RESOURCES

Electricity. Installed capacity was 30,000 kW in 1995. Production was 75m. kWh in 1994; consumption per capita in 1994 was 69 kWh.

Minerals. Heavy minerals, including ilmenite, zircon and rutile, have been discovered in Sanyang, Batokunku and Kartong areas.

Agriculture. About 75% of the population depend upon agriculture, which in 1996/97 contributed 19·73% of GDP. Almost all commercial activity centres upon the marketing of groundnuts, which is the only export crop of financial significance; in 1996, 46,000 tonnes were produced. Cotton is also exported on a limited scale. Rice is of increasing importance for local consumption; production (1996) 18,185 tonnes.

Livestock (1996): 322,256 cattle, 231,398 goats, 166,170 sheep and 520,657 poultry.

Forestry. In 1995 forests covered 91,000 ha, or 9·1% of the land area. 1·22m. cu. metres of roundwood were cut in 1995.

Fisheries. Total catch (1996) 38,900 tonnes, of which 2,700 tonnes were from inland waters.

INDUSTRY

Labour. The labour force in 1996 totalled 579,000 (55% males). Nearly 80% of the economically active population in 1994 were engaged in agriculture, fisheries and forestry.

INTERNATIONAL TRADE

Foreign debt was US$452m. in 1996.

Imports and Exports. Exports were valued at an estimated US$160m. in 1995 and imports at US$140m. Chief items of export: Groundnuts, groundnut oil, groundnut cake, cotton lint, fish and fish preparations, hides and skins. Chief items of import: Manufactured goods, food and live animals, machinery and transport equipment.

Main export markets, 1994: Belgium-Luxembourg, 50·4%; Japan, 21·5%; Guinea, 6·2%; UK, 3·6%. Main import suppliers, 1994: China, 24·7%; Belgium-Luxembourg, 10·1%; UK, 8·5%; Hong Kong, 7·7%.

COMMUNICATIONS

Roads. There were 2,700 km of roads in 1996, of which 950 km rare paved. Number of vehicles (1996): 8,640 passenger cars; 9,000 buses, trucks and vans.

Civil Aviation. There is an international airport at Banjul (Yundum). The national carrier is Gambia Airways. In 1998 services were also provided by Air Afrique, Air Dabia, Air Mauritanie, Air Sénégal, Condor Flugdienst, Delta Air Lines, Ghana Airways, K.D. Air Corporation, Mahfooz Aviation, Nigeria Airways, SABENA, Swissair and Transportes Aéreos da Cabo Verde. Banjul handled 239,496 passengers in 1996 (all on international flights) and 3,447 tonnes of freight.

Shipping. The chief port is Banjul. Ocean-going vessels can travel up the Gambia River as far as Kuntaur. The merchant marine totalled 2,745 GRT in 1995.

Telecommunications. In 1997 there were 24,800 main telephone lines, or 21·3 per 1,000 population. Cellular phone subscribers numbered 1,400 in 1995 and there were 1,000 fax machines. In Jan. 1998 there were approximately 150 Internet users.

Postal Services. There are several post offices and agencies; postal facilities are also afforded to all towns.

SOCIAL INSTITUTIONS

Justice. Justice is administered by a Supreme Court consisting of a chief justice and puisne judges. The High Court has unlimited original jurisdiction in civil and criminal matters. The Supreme Court is the highest court of appeal and succeeds the judicial committee of the Privy Council in London. There are Magistrates Courts in each of the divisions plus one in Banjul and two in nearby Kombo St Mary's Division—8 in all. There are resident magistrates in provincial areas. There are also Moslem courts, district tribunals dealing with cases concerned with customary law, and 2 juvenile courts.

The death penalty was abolished in 1993 but restored by decree in 1995.

Religion. About 90% of the population is Moslem. Banjul is the seat of an Anglican and a Roman Catholic bishop. There is a Methodist mission. A few sections of the population retain their original animist beliefs.

Education. The adult literacy rate in 1995 was 38·6% (52·8% among males and 24·9% among females). In 1993–94 there were 105,471 pupils at 250 primary schools, 27,120 pupils at 1,126 secondary schools and 1,591 students at 155 institutions of higher education, which comprise The Gambia College, a technical training institute, a management development institute, a multi-media training institute, a hotel training school, and centres for self-development and skills training, and continuing education.

Health. In 1994 there were 2 hospitals, 1 clinic, 10 health centres and some 60 dispensaries.

CULTURE

Broadcasting. Radio Gambia, a government owned station, broadcasts in English and some other local languages. There are 4 private commercial radio stations and 3 community radio stations. Number of radio receivers (1995), 182,000. A television station carries programmes in English and some local languages. TV operations started in 1995 and programmes are transmitted countrywide and beyond. In 1995 there were an estimated 4,000 television receivers.

Cinema. In 1992 there were 15 cinemas.

Press. There is a government-owned daily; an independent newspaper appears 5 times a week, there are two weeklies and several news-sheets and a monthly.

Tourism. Tourism is The Gambia's biggest foreign exchange earner. In 1996/97, 82,207 air chartered tourists visited. Revenue from foreign tourists in 1996 totalled US$22m.

DIPLOMATIC REPRESENTATIVES

Of The Gambia in Great Britain (57 Kensington Ct., London, W8 5DG)
High Commissioner: John P. Bojang.

Of Great Britain in The Gambia (48 Atlantic Rd., Fajara, Banjul)
High Commissioner: T. Millson.

Of The Gambia in USA (1030, 15th St, NW, Washington, D.C., 2005)
Ambassador: Crispin Corey Johnson.

Of the USA in The Gambia (Fajara (East), Kairaba Ave., Banjul)
Ambassador: Gerald W. Scott.

Of The Gambia to the United Nations
Ambassador: Baboucarr-Blaise Ismaila Jagne.

Of The Gambia to the European Union
Ambassador: Ismaila Ceesay.

FURTHER READING

The Gambia since Independence 1965–1980. Banjul, 1980
Gamble, D. P., *The Gambia.* [Bibliography] Oxford and Santa Barbara (CA), 1988
Hughes, A. and Perfect, D., *Political History of The Gambia, 1816–1992.* Farnborough, 1993

GEORGIA

Sakartvelos Respublika

(Republic of Georgia)

Capital: Tbilisi
Population estimate, 2000: 5·42m.
GNP per capita: (PPP$) 1,810
HDI/world rank: 0·633/108

KEY HISTORICAL EVENTS

The independent Georgian Social Democratic Republic was declared on 26 May 1918 and was recognized by the Russian Soviet Federal Socialist Republic on 7 May 1920. A rising in Mingrelia, Abkhazia and Adjaria was put down by Soviet troops. On 25 Feb. 1921 the country was renamed the Georgian Soviet Socialist Republic. On 15 Dec. 1922 Georgia was merged with Armenia and Azerbaijan to form the Transcaucasian Soviet Federal Socialist Republic. In 1936 the Georgian Soviet Socialist Republic became one of the constituent republics of the USSR.

Following nationalist successes at elections in Oct. 1990, the Supreme Soviet resolved in Nov. 1990 to begin a transition to full independence and on 9 April 1991, following a 98·9% popular vote in favour, unanimously declared the republic an independent state based on the treaty of independence of May 1918.

President Zviad Gamsakhurdia was deposed by armed insurrection on 6 Jan. 1992 and a military council took control. After elections in which he gained 95% of votes cast, Eduard Shevardnadze became *de facto* head of state in Oct. 1992. On 22 Oct. 1993 Georgia joined the CIS, a move ratified by parliament on 1 March 1994. Supporters of the deposed president Gamsakhurdia were in intermittent armed conflict with the government, mainly in Mingrelia, but suffered heavy defeats once Russian support became available via the CIS. On 9 Feb. 1998 there was an unsuccessful attempt on the life of Eduard Shevardnadze. Later in the month UN military observers who had been held hostage by opposition forces were released after negotiations with representatives of former president Gamsakhurdia.

TERRITORY AND POPULATION

Georgia is bounded in the west by the Black Sea and south by Turkey, Armenia and Azerbaijan. Area, 69,700 sq. km (26,900 sq. miles). Its population in mid-July 1997 was estimated to be 5,160,000 (2,450,000 male); density, 74 per sq. km.

The UN gives a projected population for 2000 of 5·42m.

In 1995 an estimated 58·3% of the population lived in urban areas. The capital is Tbilisi (1994 population estimate, 1·3m.). Other important towns (with 1991 population estimates) are Kutaisi (235,000), Rustavi (159,000), Batumi (136,000), Sukhumi (121,000), Poti (54,000), Gori (59,000).

Georgians accounted for 70·1% of the 1989 census population of 5,400,841; others included 8·1% Armenians, 6·3% Russians, 5·7% Azerbaijanis, 3% Ossetians, 1·9% Greeks, 1·8% Abkhazians and 1% Ukrainians. Georgia includes the Autonomous Republics of Abkhazia and Adjaria and the former Autonomous Region of South Ossetia.

Georgian is the official language. Armenian, Russian and Azeri are also spoken.

SOCIAL STATISTICS

1997 births, 61,000; deaths, 72,000. Rates, 1997 estimates: Birth, 11·8 per 1,000 population; death, 13·9 per 1,000. Annual growth rate, 1990–95, 0·0. The population has been declining since the mid 1990s. Life expectancy 65·0 years (male, 62·0 years; female, 68·5 years). Infant mortality, 1990–95, 23 per 1,000 live births; fertility rate, 2·1 births per woman.

CLIMATE

The Georgian climate is extremely varied. The relatively small territory covers different climatic zones, ranging from humid sub-tropical zones to permanent snow and glaciers. In Tbilisi summer is hot: 25–35°C. November sees the beginning of the

Georgian winter and the temperature in Tbilisi can drop to –8°C; however, average temperature ranges from 2–6°C.

CONSTITUTION AND GOVERNMENT

A new Constitution of 24 Aug. 1995 defines Georgia as a presidential republic with federal elements. The head of state is the *President*, elected by universal suffrage for not more than two 5-year terms. The 235-member parliament is elected by a system combining 85 single-member districts with proportional representation based on party lists. There is a 5% threshold.

National Anthem. 'Dideba zetsit kurtheuls' ('Praise be to the Heavenly Bestower of Blessings'); words anonymous, tune by K. Potskhverashvili.

RECENT ELECTIONS

Presidential and parliamentary elections were held on 5 Nov. 1995. Turn-out was 69%. Eduard Shevardnadze was re-elected *President* with 74·9% of votes cast against 5 opponents.

54 parties presented parliamentary candidates. The Citizens' Union gained 106 seats; non-partisans, 45; the National Democratic Party, 34; the All-Georgia Revival Union, 29.

CURRENT ADMINISTRATION

President: Eduard Shevardnadze (b. 1928; Citizens' Union of Georgia).

In March 1999 the government comprised:

Minister of State: Vazha Lordkipanidze. *Education:* Aleksandre Kartozia. *Environmental Protection and Natural Resources:* Nino Chkhobadze. *Economy:* Vladimer Papava. *Trade and Foreign Economic Relations:* Tamriko Beruchashvili. *Defence:* David Tevzadze. *Communications:* Sergo Esakia. *Culture:* Valeri Asatiani. *Refugees and Resettlement Issues:* Valerian Vashakidze. *Urban Affairs:* Merab Chkhenkeli. *Foreign Affairs:* Irakli Menagharishvili. *Security:* Vakhtang Kutateladze. *State Property:* Mikheil Ukleba. *Agriculture and Food:* Bakur Gulua. *Social Security and Labour:* Tengiz Gazdeliani. *Finance:* David Onoprishvili. *Internal Affairs:* Kakha Targamadze. *Health:* Avtandil Jorbenadze. *Fuel and Energy:* Temur Giorgadze. *Justice:* Vladimer Chanturia. *Transport:* Merab Adeishvili. *Industry:* Badri Shoshitaishvili.

The *Speaker* is Zurab Zhvania.

Local Government. Georgia consists of the Autonomous Republic of Abkhazia and Adjaria, 9 regions and Tskhinvali Region, the status of which is not yet determined. The capital has special regional status. Sub units are districts, district towns, small towns and villages.

The structure of Georgian Local and Regional administration is on 4 levels. Village councils and district towns are on the first level followed by districts, then regions. At the top level are the autonomous republics.

Administration at all levels is appointed. The heads of regions, districts, capital cities and principal towns are appointed directly by the president.

DEFENCE

The total strength of the Armed Forces consists of 42,678 men. In 1997 some 8,500 Russian troops and 2,100 peace-keeping forces were stationed in 3 military bases. The UN has some 117 observers from 23 countries.

Defence expenditure in 1997 totalled US$109m. (US$20 per capita), representing 2·9% of GDP.

Army. Forces of 24,000 are planned. There are 2 Corps HQ, some 6 infantry brigades, 1 artillery brigade and 1 peace-keeping battalion. Equipment includes 48 T-55 and 31 T-72 main battle tanks.

Navy. Former Soviet facilities at Poti have been taken over. The force comprises 2 small frigates, 4 torpedo boats and some 12 patrol vessels. Personnel, 1997, 2,000.

Air Force. Equipment includes 7 Su-25 fighter-bombers, 3 Mi-24 armed helicopters and 4 Mi-8/17 transport helicopters. Personnel, 1997, 3,000.

INTERNATIONAL RELATIONS

Fighting flared up in Abkhazia between rival militia forces again in May 1998 after Abkhazian forces ejected thousands of ethnic Mingrelian and Georgian refugees who had returned to the southern Abkhazian region of Gali.

A Treaty of Friendship and Co-operation was signed with Russia in Feb. 1994.

Georgia is a member of the UN, CIS and the NATO Partnership for Peace.

ECONOMY

Policy. A privatization programme was inaugurated in 1995.

Performance. Real GDP growth was 14·3% in 1996.

Between 1990 and 1996 the average annual real growth in GNP per capita was −19·3% (the lowest of any country in the world).

Budget. In 1997 revenues were 467·1m. laris and expenditure 662·1m. laris.

Currency. The unit of currency is the *lari* (GEL) of 100 *tetri*, which replaced coupons at 1 lari = 1m. coupons on 25 Sept. 1995. Inflation was an annualized 30% in 1996 (183% in 1995).

Banking and Finance. The *Governor* of the Central Bank is Nodar Javakhishvili. In 1996 there were 65 commercial banks. 1 foreign bank had a representative office.

ENERGY AND NATURAL RESOURCES

Electricity. The many fast-flowing rivers provide an important hydro-electric resource. Installed capacity was 4·56m. kW in 1994. Production in 1996 was 7,100m. kWh. Consumption per capita was estimated in 1995 to be 1,095 kWh.

Oil and Gas. Output (1993) of oil and gas concentrates, 0·1m. tonnes; natural gas (1995 estimate), 3·3m. cu. metres (excluding Abkhazia and South Ossetia). 200,000 tonnes of crude petroleum were produced in 1995. A 920 km long oil pipeline is under construction from an offshore Azerbaijani oil field in the Caspian Sea across Azerbaijan and Georgia to a new oil terminal at Supsa, near Poti, on the Black Sea Coast. The US$570m. pipeline is expected to start pumping oil in 1999 and will have an ultimate capacity of some 15m. tonnes of oil a year.

Minerals. Manganese deposits are calculated at 250m. tonnes. Other important minerals are coal, barytes, clays, gold, diatomite shale, agate, marble, alabaster, iron and other ores, building stone, arsenic, molybdenum, tungsten and mercury. Output of coal in 1995 was estimated to be 42,700 tonnes (excluding Abkhazia and South Ossetia).

Agriculture. In 1994 there were 795,000 ha of arable land, 332,000 ha permanent crops and 1·69m. ha of permanent pasture. Agriculture accounted for 35% of GDP in 1996.

Output of main agricultural products (in 1,000 tonnes) in 1994 (estimates): Watermelons (including melons, pumpkins and squash), 800; grapes, 480; apples, 350; citrus fruits, 260; potatoes, 229; milk, 394 (1993); eggs, 138m. (1993 total).

Livestock, 1996: Cattle, 980,000; sheep, 674,000; pigs, 353,000; chickens, 1995, 17m.

Forestry. There were 2·99m. ha of forest in 1995, or 42·9% of the total land area.

Fisheries. The catch in 1995 was approximately 28,900 tonnes, down from 202,000 tonnes in 1988. Around 90% of fish caught are from marine waters.

INDUSTRY

There is a metallurgical plant and a motor works. There are factories for processing tea, creameries and breweries. There are also textile and silk industries.

Production in 1993 (in tonnes): Rolled steel, 0·1m.; fertilizer, 0·06m.; cement, 0·3m.; processed meat, 0·7m.; textiles, 16·6m. cu. metres; footwear, 1·4m. pairs. Total output was valued at 129,000m. roubles in 1993.

Labour. The total labour force in 1996 was 2·2m. (54% males). The unemployment rate was 21%.

INTERNATIONAL TRADE

In 1997 Georgian exports amounted to US$250,125 and imports US$858,572. Total foreign debt was estimated to be US$1·3bn. The debt was mainly due to the importing of natural gas from Turkmenistan.

Imports and Exports. In 1995 imports were valued at US$250m. and exports at US$140m. Major commodities imported are fuel, grain and other foods, machinery and parts, and transport equipment. Major commodities for export are iron and steel products, food and beverages, machinery, textiles and chemicals. Main export markets, 1994: Azerbaijan, 25·2%; Russia, 22·9%; Armenia, 15·0%; Turkey, 13·1%. Main import suppliers, 1994: Turkmenistan, 65·4%; Turkey, 12·4%; Azerbaijan, 6·8%; Russia, 6·2%. In addition humanitarian food shipments are sent by the EU and the USA.

COMMUNICATIONS

Roads. There were 20,700 km of roads in 1996 (19,355 km hard-surfaced). An estimated 427,000 passenger cars were in use in 1996 (80 per 1,000 inhabitants).

Rail. Total length is 1,583 km of 1,520 mm gauge, (1,483 km electrified). In 1994 railways carried 2·7m. tonnes of freight and 9·8m. passengers.

Civil Aviation. The main airport is at Tbilisi (Novo-Alexeyevka). There are 4 Georgian air carriers—Georgian Airlines, Georgian Airways, Airzena Georgian Airlines and Air Georgia. In 1998 Georgian Airlines operated international flights to Adler/Sochi, Athens, Frankfurt, Kiev, Moscow, Prague, Rostov, St Petersburg, Tel Aviv, Thessaloniki and Volgograd; Georgian Airways had international flights to Atyrau, Delhi, London and Tehran; Airzena Georgian Airlines had flights to Dubai, Tashkent and Vienna; Air Georgia had flights to Frankfurt and Moscow. Services were also provided in 1998 by Aeroflot, Air Enterprise Pulkovo, Air Lines of Kuban, Air Ukraine, Armenian Airlines, Austrian Airlines, Azerbaijan Airlines, British Airways, Samara Airlines, Swissair, Turkish Airlines, Vnukovo Airlines and Volga Aircompany. In 1995 scheduled airline traffic of Georgian carriers flew 4·3m. km, carrying 177,000 passengers (167,000 on international flights).

Shipping. In 1995 sea-going shipping totalled 0·65m. GRT, of which oil tankers accounted for 0·34m. GRT.

Telecommunications. There were 620,400 telephone main lines in 1997, or 114·1 per 1,000 persons. Cellular phone subscribers numbered 200 in 1995 and there were 500 fax machines.

SOCIAL INSTITUTIONS

Religion. The Georgian Orthodox Church has its own organization under Catholicos (patriarch) Ilya II who is resident in Tbilisi.

Education. In 1996 there were 1,332 pre-primary schools with 10,491 teachers for 81,938 pupils and 3,187 primary schools with 17,950 teachers for 288,509 pupils. There were 441,753 pupils at secondary level and 155,033 students at 76 technical colleges and 23 institutions of higher education. There is 1 university and 1 technical university, with a total of 34,590 students and 6,464 academic staff. Adult literacy rate in 1995 was over 99%.

In 1994 total expenditure on education came to 1·9% of GNP and represented 6·9% of total government expenditure.

Health. There were 29,900 doctors and 57,100 hospital beds in 1994.

Welfare. There were 804,000 age and 355,000 other pensioners in 1994.

CULTURE

Broadcasting. The government-controlled Georgian Radio broadcasts 2 national and 3 regional programmes, and a foreign service, Radio Georgia (English, Russian). There are local independent TV stations in 10 towns. In 1995 there were 3m. radio receivers and 2·5m. TV receivers.

Cinema. In 1993 there were 289 cinemas. Total attendance for the year was 30·4m.

Press. In 1995 there were 25 dailies and weeklies.

Tourism. Investment in tourism has increased substantially in recent years. Although numbers are still modest, 200 hotels are to be built in the near future.

DIPLOMATIC REPRESENTATIVES
Of Georgia in Great Britain (3 Hornton Pl., Kensington Place, London, W8 4LZ)
Ambassador: Teimuraz Mamatsashvili.

Of Great Britain in Georgia (Metechi Palace Hotel, 380003 Tbilisi)
Ambassador: R. T. Jenkins, OBE.

Of Georgia in the USA (1511 K Street, NW, Suite 424, Washington, D.C., 20005)
Ambassador: Dr Tedo Japaridze.

Of the USA in Georgia (25, Antoneli Street, 380026 Tbilisi)
Ambassador: Vacant.

Of Georgia to the United Nations
Ambassador: Dr Peter P. Chkheidze.

Of Georgia to the European Union
Ambassador: Zourab Abachidze.

FURTHER READING
Brook, S., *Claws of the Crab: Georgia and Armenia in Crisis.* London, 1992
Gachechiladze, R., *The New Georgia: Space, Society, Politics.* London, 1995
Lang, D. M., *A Modern History of Georgia.* London, 1962.—*The Georgians.* London, 1966
Nasmyth, P., *Georgia: a Rebel in the Caucasus.* London, 1992
Suny, R. G., *The Making of the Georgian Nation.* 2nd ed. Indiana Univ. Press, 1994

ABKHAZIA

Area, 8,600 sq. km (3,320 sq. miles); population (Jan. 1990), 537,500. Capital Sukhumi (1990 population, 121,700). This area, the ancient Colchis, saw the establishment of a West Georgian kingdom in the 4th century and a Russian protectorate in 1810. In March 1921 a congress of local Soviets proclaimed it a Soviet Republic, and its status as an Autonomous Republic, within Georgia, was confirmed on 17 April 1930 and again by the Georgian Constitution of 1995.

Ethnic groups (1989 census) Georgians, 45·7%; Abkhazians, 17·8%; Armenians, 14·6%; and Russians, 14·3%.

In July 1992 the Abkhazian parliament declared sovereignty under the presidency of Vladislav Ardzinba and the restoration of its 1925 constitution. Fighting broke out as Georgian forces moved into Abkhazia. On 3 Sept. and on 19 Nov. ceasefires were agreed, but fighting continued into 1993 and by Sept. Georgian forces were driven out. On 15 May 1994 Georgian and Abkhazian delegates under Russian auspices signed an agreement on a ceasefire and deployment of 2,500 Russian troops as a peace-keeping force. On 26 Nov. 1994 parliament adopted a new Constitution proclaiming Abkhazian sovereignty. CIS economic sanctions were imposed in Jan. 1996. Parliamentary elections were held on 23 Nov. 1996. Neither the constitution nor the elections were recognized by the Georgian government or the international community. Fighting flared up between rival militia forces again in May 1998 after Abkhazian forces ejected thousands of ethnic Mingrelian and Georgian refugees who had returned to the southern Abkhazian region of Gali. After the fighting in 1998, the worst in 5 years, both sides declared a ceasefire. Up to 20,000 Georgians lost their homes.

Head of the Separatist Government: Vladislav Ardzinba (elected by parliament on 26 Nov. 1994).

The republic has coal, electric power, building materials and light industries. In 1985 there were 89 collective farms and 56 state farms; main crops are tobacco, tea, grapes, oranges, tangerines and lemons. Crop area 43,900 ha.

Livestock, 1 Jan. 1987: 147,300 cattle, 127,900 pigs, 28,800 sheep and goats.

In 1990–91 there were 16,700 children attending pre-school institutions. There is a university at Sukhumi with 3,000 students and 270 academic staff in 1995–96. In 1990 there were 2,100 students at colleges and 7,700 students at other institutions of higher education.

In Jan. 1990 there were 2,500 doctors and 6,600 junior medical personnel.

ADJARIA

Area: 2,900 sq. km (1,160 sq. miles); population: 396,400. Capital, Batumi (1990 population, 137,300). Adjaria fell under Turkish rule in the 17th century, and was annexed to Russia (rejoining Georgia) after the Berlin Treaty of 1878. On 16 July 1921 the territory was constituted as an Autonomous Republic within the Georgian SSR, a status confirmed by the Georgian Constitution of 1995.

Ethnic groups (1989 census): Georgians, 82·8%; Russians, 7·7%; and Armenians 4%.

Chairman of the Supreme Council of Adjaria: Aslan Abashidze.

Elections were held in Sept. 1996. A coalition of the Citizens' Union of Georgia and the All-Georgian Union of Revival gained a majority of seats.

Adjaria specializes in sub-tropical agricultural products. These include tea, citruses, bamboo, eucalyptus, tobacco etc. Livestock (Jan. 1990): 112,300 cattle, 6,200 pigs, 7,000 sheep and goats. In 1980 there were 69 collective farms and 21 state farms.

There is a port and a shipyard at Batumi, oil-refining, food-processing and canning factories, clothing, building materials, pharmaceutical factories, etc.

The population is almost exclusively Sunni Moslem.

In 1990–91, 77,239 pupils were engaged in study at all levels.

In Jan. 1990 there were 1,700 doctors and 4,400 junior medical personnel.

SOUTH OSSETIA

Area, 3,900 sq. km (1,505 sq. miles); population (Jan. 1990), 99,800 (ethnic groups at the 1989 census; Ossetians 66·2% and Georgians 29%). Capital, Tskhinvali (34,000). This area was populated by Ossetians from across the Caucasus (North Ossetia), driven out by the Mongols in the 13th century. The region was set up within the Georgian SSR on 20 April 1922. Formerly an Autonomous Region, its administrative autonomy was abolished by the Georgian Supreme Soviet on 11 Dec. 1990, and it has been named the Tskhinvali Region.

Fighting broke out in 1990 between insurgents wishing to unite with North Ossetia (in the Russian Federation) and Georgian forces. By a Russo-Georgian agreement of July 1992 Russian peace-keeping forces moved into a 7-km buffer zone between South Ossetia and Georgia pending negotiations. An OSCE peace-keeping force has been deployed since 1992.

At elections not recognized by the Georgian government on 10 Nov. 1996, Lyudvig Chibirov (b. 1932) was elected *President*.

Though maintaining a commitment to independence, President Chibirov came to a political agreement with the Georgian government in 1996 that neither force nor sanctions should be applied.

Main industries are mining, timber, electrical engineering and building materials. Crop area, chiefly grains, was 21,600 ha in 1985; other pursuits are sheep-farming (128,500 sheep and goats on 1 Jan. 1987) and vine-growing. There were 14 collective farms and 18 state farms.

In 1989–90 there were 21,200 pupils in elementary and secondary schools. There were 6,525 children in pre-school institutions.

In Jan. 1987 there were 511 doctors and 1,400 hospital beds.

GERMANY

Bundesrepublik Deutschland
(Federal Republic of Germany)

Capital: Berlin
Seat of Government: Bonn/Berlin
Population estimate, 2000: 82·69m.
GNP per capita: (PPP$) 21,110
HDI/world rank: 0·925/19

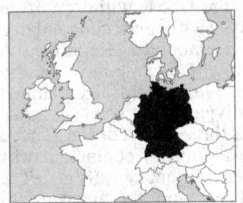

KEY HISTORICAL EVENTS

At the outbreak of the Napoleonic wars Germany consisted of many small states, independent but loosely bound by a common allegiance to the Holy Roman Emperor, a title which for most of its history fell to the Austrian royal house of Hapsburg. In 1806 the Holy Roman Empire was destroyed by Napoleon, who then combined 16 German states as the Confederation of the Rhine.

Following Napoleon's defeat in 1815, a larger Confederation was formed with 38 members (39 after 1817). Austria remained the dominant power with a permanent right to the presidency of the Confederation. Prussia held the vice-presidency. The other important states were: Bavaria, Saxony, Hanover, Württemberg, Baden, Hesse-Kassel, Hesse-Darmstadt, Holstein and Lauenberg, Brunswick, Nassau, Mecklenburg-Schwerin and Mecklenburg-Strelitz.

In 1848–50 attempts were made to draw up a constitution and elect a Confederation parliament. A constitution was published in Dec. 1848 but few states accepted it; a revised version was accepted in May 1849, but not by Austria or Bavaria. The parliament which sat from 20 March to 29 April 1850 was neither recognized by Austria nor powerful enough to control the other dominant state, Prussia. The Federal Diet therefore resumed power and held it until 1866.

In 1866 Prussia defeated Austria and formed the North German Confederation in 1867, under her own control. She had annexed Hanover, Hesse-Kassel and Nassau in 1866 together with the smaller states of Homburg and Frankfurt.

In 1870 Prussia went to war with France, rallied the German states in support and, following German victory, went on to the creation of the German Empire in 1871. The Empire included all German states except Austria and had, therefore, deep North-South, Protestant-Catholic divisions. It was dominated by Prussia, whose king became emperor. Conscious of arriving late on the world scene, Germany acquired colonies in West and South-West Africa in 1884 and at the end of the decade Zanzibar and Tanganyika in the East. The imperial government led Germany into the First World War in 1914 and when defeated, national unity collapsed. The emperor abdicated on 28 Nov. 1918.

After an anarchic period a republican government, with a constitution drawn up at Weimar in 1919, attempted under Chancellor Ebert to restore the economy and political stability. But the scale of reparations demanded by the Treaty of Versailles, the onset of world depression and the loss of resources and territory through warfare were too much for the fledgling government to manage.

In 1933 the National Socialist leader Adolf Hitler was appointed Chancellor. The National Socialist ('Nazi') party appealed to national pride and offered a return to self-respect after humiliation. Hitler became president of the Third Reich in 1934. His policies involved the wide expansion of German power and a theory of Aryan racial supremacy which meant in practice that non-Aryans were persecuted, murdered, and their assets confiscated. Hitler's expansionism led to his annexation of Austria and of German-speaking Czechoslovakia in 1938. In March 1939 he declared all of Czechoslovakia a German protectorate, and in Sept. invaded Poland, attempting to restore the authority exercised there by Prussia before 1918. This precipitated the Second World War.

The War ended in German defeat in 1945. The Allied forces occupied Germany; the UK, the USA and France holding the west and the USSR the east. By the Berlin Declaration of 5 June 1945 these governments assumed authority; each was given a zone of occupation, and the zone commanders-in-chief together made up the Allied

Control Council in Berlin. The area of Greater Berlin was also divided into 4 sectors.

At the Potsdam Conference of 1945 northern East Prussia was transferred to the USSR. It was also agreed that, pending a final peace settlement, Poland should administer the areas east of the rivers Oder and Neisse, with the frontier fixed on the Oder and Western Neisse down to the Czechoslovak frontier.

By 1948 it had become clear that there would be no agreement between the occupying powers as to the future of Germany. Accordingly, the western allies united their zones into one unit in March 1948. In protest, the USSR withdrew from the Allied Control Council, blockaded Berlin until May 1949, and consolidated control of eastern Germany, establishing the German Democratic Republic. A People's Council appointed in 1948 drew up a constitution which came into force in Oct. 1949, providing for a communist state of five Länder with a centrally-planned economy. In 1952 the government made a physical division between its own territory and that of the Federal Republic, in the form of a three-mile cordon fenced and guarded along the frontier. This left Berlin as the only point of contact; it was closed as a migration route by the construction of a concrete boundary wall in 1961. In 1953 there were popular revolts against food shortages and the pressure to collectivize. In 1954 the government eased economic problems, the USSR ceased to collect reparation payments, and sovereignty was granted. The GDR signed the Warsaw Pact in 1955. Socialist policies were stepped up in 1958, leading to flight to the West of skilled workers.

Meanwhile, a constituent assembly met in Bonn in Sept. 1948 and drafted a Basic Law, which came into force in May 1949. In Sept. 1949 the occupation forces limited their own powers and the Federal Republic of Germany came into existence. The occupation forces retained some powers, however, and the Republic did not become a sovereign state until 1955 when the Occupation Statute was revoked. The Republic consisted of the states of Schleswig-Holstein, Hamburg, Lower Saxony, Bremen, North Rhine-Westphalia, Hessen, Rhineland-Palatinate, Baden-Württemberg, Bavaria and Saarland, together with West Berlin.

The first chancellor, Konrad Adenauer (1949–63), was committed to the ultimate reunification of Germany and would not acknowledge the German Democratic Republic as a state. The two German states did not sign an agreement of mutual recognition and intent to co-operate until 1972, under Chancellor Willi Brandt. The most marked feature of the post-war period was rapid population growth and the restoration of industry. Immigration from the German Democratic Republic, about 3m. since 1945, stopped when the Berlin Wall was built in 1961; however there was a strong movement of German-speaking people back into Germany from German settlements in countries of the Soviet bloc. Industrial growth also attracted labour from Turkey, Spain, Italy and the Balkans.

The Paris Treaty, which came into force in 1955, ensured the Republic's contribution to NATO and NATO forces were stationed along the Rhine in large numbers, with consequent dispute about the deployment of nuclear missiles on German soil.

Even before sovereignty the Republic had begun negotiations for a measure of European unity and joined in creating the European Coal and Steel Community in 1951 and the European Economic Community in 1957. In Jan. 1957 the Saarland was returned to full German control. In 1973 the Federal Republic entered the UN.

In the autumn of 1989 movements for political liberalization in the GDR and re-unification with Federal Germany gathered strength. Erich Honecker and other long-serving Communist leaders were replaced in Oct.–Nov. The Berlin Wall was opened on 9 Nov.

Following the reforms in the GDR in Nov. 1989 the Federal Chancellor Helmut Kohl issued a plan for German confederation. The ambassadors of the 4 war-time allies (France, the USSR, the UK and the USA) met in Berlin in Dec. After talks with Chancellor Kohl on 11 Feb. 1990, President Gorbachev made no objection to German re-unification. The allies agreed a formula ('two-plus-four') for re-unification talks to begin after the GDR elections on 18 March. 'Two-plus-four' talks began on 5 May 1990. On 18 May Federal Germany and the GDR signed a treaty extending Federal Germany's currency, its economic, monetary and social legislation, to the GDR as of 1 July. On 23 Aug. the Volkskammer by 294 votes to

62 'declared its accession to the jurisdiction of the Federal Republic as from 3 Oct. according to article 23 of the Basic Law', which provided for the Länder of pre-war Germany to accede to the Federal Republic. On 12 Sept. the Treaty on the Final Settlement with Respect to Germany was signed by Federal Germany, the GDR and the 4 war-time allies.

The Federal Assembly (*Bundestag*) moved from Bonn to the renovated *Reichstag* in Berlin in May 1999.

TERRITORY AND POPULATION

Germany is bounded in the north by Denmark and the North and Baltic Seas, east by Poland, east and south-east by the Czech Republic, south-east and south by Austria, south by Switzerland and west by France, Luxembourg, Belgium and the Netherlands. Area: 357,022 sq. km. Population estimate based on a microcensus of 1995: 81,538,603 (41,893,600 females); density, 228 per sq. km. In 1995 an estimated 86·5% of the population lived in urban areas. June 1997 estimate: 82,061,000, of which 66,652,000 live in the former Federal Republic of Germany and 15,409,000 in the former German Democratic Republic. There were 37·46m. households in April 1997; 13·26m. were single-person, and 11·37m. had a female principal breadwinner. 1996 density, 229 per sq. km.

The UN gives a projected population for 2000 of 82·69m.

On 14 Nov. 1990 Germany and Poland signed a treaty confirming Poland's existing western frontier and renouncing German claims to territory lost as a result of the Second World War.

The capital is Berlin; the Federal German government moved from Bonn to Berlin in 1999.

The Federation comprises 16 Länder (states). Area and population:

Länder	Area in sq. km	Population (in 1,000) 1987 census	Population (in 1,000) 1997 estimate	Density per sq. km (June 1997)
Baden-Württemberg (BW)	35,753	9,286	10,393	291
Bavaria (BY)	70,551	10,903	12,057	171
Berlin (BE)[1]	891	...	3,447	3,869
Brandenburg (BB)[2]	29,479	...	2,562	87
Bremen (HB)	404	660	676	1,673
Hamburg (HH)	755	1,593	1,707	2,261
Hessen (HE)	21,114	5,508	6,031	286
Lower Saxony (NI)	47,611	7,162	7,832	164
Mecklenburg-West Pomerania (MV)[2]	23,170	...	1,816	78
North Rhine-Westphalia (NW)	34,078	16,712	17,962	527
Rhineland-Palatinate (RP)	19,847	3,631	4,010	202
Saarland (SL)	2,570	1,056	1,083	421
Saxony (SN)[2]	18,413	...	4,538	246
Saxony-Anhalt (ST)[2]	20,446	...	2,715	133
Schleswig-Holstein (SH)	15,771	2,554	2,750	174
Thuringia (TH)[2]	16,171	...	2,485	154

[1]1987 census population of West Berlin: 2,013,000.
[2]Reconstituted in 1990 in the Federal Republic.

On 31 Dec. 1997 there were 7,365,800 resident foreigners, including 2,107,400 Turks, 721,000 Yugoslavs, 607,900 Italians and 363,200 Greeks. In 1997, 104,353 foreigners sought asylum (127,937 in 1995; 127,210 in 1994; 322,599 in 1993). Tighter controls on entry from abroad were applied as from 1993. 302,830 persons were naturalized in 1996, of whom 194,849 were from the former USSR. In 1996 there were 677,500 emigrants and 959,700 immigrants.

Populations of the 84 towns of over 100,000 inhabitants in 1996 (in 1,000):

Town (and Land)	Population (in 1,000)	Ranking by population	Town (and Land)	Population (in 1,000)	Ranking by population
Aachen (NW)	247·8	32	Bottrop (NW)	121·5	66
Augsburg (BY)	258·8	28	Braunschweig (NI)	252·3	30
Bergisch Gladbach (NW)	105·7	79	Bremen (HB)	548·9	10
Berlin (BE)	3,467·3	1	Bremerhaven (HB)	129·8	56
Bielefeld (NW)	323·7	18	Chemnitz (SN)	263·3	27
Bochum (NW)	399·3	16	Cologne (NW)	964·4	4
Bonn (NW)	298·6	20	Cottbus (BB)	122·4	63

Town (and Land)	Population (in 1,000)	Ranking by population	Town (and Land)	Population (in 1,000)	Ranking by population
Darmstadt (HE)	138·7	52	Magdeburg (ST)	255·5	29
Dortmund (NW)	597·9	7	Mainz (RP)	183·7	42
Dresden (SN)	466·6	15	Mannheim (BW)	311·7	19
Duisburg (NW)	533·9	11	Moers (NW)	106·9	77
Düsseldorf (NW)	570·8	9	Mönchengladbach (NW)	266·8	25
Erfurt (TH)	210·0	38	Mülheim a. d. Ruhr		
Erlangen (BY)	101·1	83	(NW)	176·1	45
Essen (NW)	612·3	6	Munich (BY)	1,232·8	3
Frankfurt am Main (HE)	648·4	5	Münster (NW)	265·0	26
Freiburg im Breisgau (BW)	199·6	40	Neuss (NW)	148·9	51
Fürth (BY)	108·7	76	Nuremberg (BY)	492·0	13
Gelsenkirchen (NW)	289·8	20	Oberhausen (NW)	224·4	34
Gera (TH)	122·5	62	Offenbach am Main (HE)	116·6	69
Göttingen (NI)	126·3	59	Oldenburg (NI)	152·1	50
Hagen (NW)	211·3	37	Osnabrück (NI)	167·7	46
Halle (ST)	280·1	22	Paderborn (NW)	134·6	55
Hamburg (HH)	1,708·5	2	Pforzheim (BW)	118·8	67
Hamm (NW)	182·8	43	Potsdam (BB)	135·9	54
Hanover (NI)	522·7	12	Recklingshausen (NW)	126·9	58
Heidelberg (BW)	138·7	52	Regensburg (BY)	125·4	61
Heilbronn (BW)	121·6	65	Remscheid (NW)	121·8	64
Herne (NW)	179·2	44	Reutlingen (BW)	108·9	75
Hildesheim (NI)	106·1	78	Rostock (MV)	224·0	35
Ingolstadt (BY)	112·5	72	Saarbrücken (SL)	185·7	41
Jena (TH)	100·9	84	Salzgitter (NI)	117·4	68
Kaiserslautern (RP)	101·9	81	Schwerin (MV)	113·3	71
Karlsruhe (BW)	276·1	23	Siegen (NW)	111·1	73
Kassel (HE)	201·4	39	Solingen (NW)	165·4	48
Kiel (SH)	244·8	33	Stuttgart (BW)	585·4	8
Koblenz (RP)	109·3	74	Ulm (BW)	116·1	70
Krefeld (NW)	248·6	31	Wiesbaden (HE)	267·1	24
Leipzig (SN)	465·2	14	Witten (NW)	104·5	80
Leverkusen (NW)	162·3	49	Wolfsburg (NI)	125·8	60
Lübeck (SH)	216·1	36	Wuppertal (NW)	380·7	17
Ludwigshafen am Rhein			Würzburg (BY)	127·0	57
(RP)	167·0	47	Zwickau	101·9	81

The official language is German. Minor orthographical amendments were agreed in 1995. An agreement between German-speaking countries in Vienna on 1 July 1996 provided for minor orthographical changes and established a Commission for German Orthography in Mannheim. There have been considerable objections within Germany, particularly in the North, and many Länder are to decide their own language programmes for schools. Generally, both old and new spellings are acceptable.

SOCIAL STATISTICS
Calendar years:

	Marriages	Live births	Of these to single parents	Deaths	Divorces
1992	453,428	809,114	120,448	885,443	135,179
1993	442,605	798,447	118,284	897,270	156,646
1994	440,244	769,603	118,460	884,661	166,496
1995	430,534	765,221	122,876	884,588	169,425
1996	427,297	796,013	135,700	882,843	175,550

Of the 427,297 marriages in 1996, 27,907 were between foreign males and German females, and 29,637 vice-versa. The average age of bridegrooms in 1996 was 33·4, and of brides 30·5.

Rates (per 1,000 population), 1996: Birth, 9·7; marriage, 5·2; death, 10·8; infant mortality (per 1,000 live births): 5·0; Stillborn rate, 4·5 per 1,000 births. Expectation of life, 1996: Men, 73·3 years; women, 79·7. Suicide rates over 1990–95, per 100,000 population, 17·5 (men, 24·9; women, 10·7). Fertility rate, 1990–95, 1·3 births per woman.

Legislation of 1995 categorizes abortions as illegal, but stipulates that prosecutions will not be brought if they are performed in the first 3 months of pregnancy after consultation with a doctor.

CLIMATE

Oceanic influences are only found in the north-west where winters are quite mild but stormy. Elsewhere a continental climate is general. To the east and south, winter temperatures are lower, with bright frosty weather and considerable snowfall. Summer temperatures are fairly uniform throughout. Berlin, Jan. 31°F (−0·5°C), July 66°F (19°C). Annual rainfall 22·5" (563 mm). Dresden, Jan. 30°F (−0·1°C), July 65°F (18·5°C). Annual rainfall 27·2" (680 mm). Frankfurt, Jan. 33°F (0·6°C), July 66°F (18·9°C). Annual rainfall 24" (601 mm). Hamburg, Jan. 31°F (−0·6°C), July 63°F (17·2°C). Annual rainfall 29" (726 mm). Hanover, Jan. 33°F (0·6°C), July 64°F (17·8°C). Annual rainfall 24" (604 mm). Köln, Jan. 36°F (2·2°C), July 66°F (18·9°C). Annual rainfall 27" (676 mm). Munich, Jan. 28°F (−2·2°C), July 63°F (17·2°C). Annual rainfall 34" (855 mm). Stuttgart, Jan. 33°F (0·6°C), July 66°F (18·9°C). Annual rainfall 27" (677 mm).

CONSTITUTION AND GOVERNMENT

The Basic Law (*Grundgesetz*) was approved by the parliaments of the participating Länder and came into force on 23 May 1949. It is to remain in force until 'a constitution adopted by a free decision of the German people comes into being'. The Federal Republic is a democratic and social constitutional state on a parliamentary basis. The federation is constituted by the 16 Länder (states). The Basic Law decrees that the general rules of international law form part of the federal law. The constitutions of the Länder must conform to the principles of a republican, democratic and social state based on the rule of law. Executive power is vested in the Länder, unless the Basic Law prescribes or permits otherwise. Federal law takes precedence over state law.

Legislative power is vested in the *Bundestag* (Federal Assembly) and the *Bundesrat* (Federal Council). The Bundestag is currently composed of 669 members and is elected in universal, free, equal and secret elections for a term of 4 years. A party must gain 5% of total votes cast in order to gain representation in the Bundestag, although if a party gets 3 candidates elected directly, they may take their seats even if the party obtains less than 5% of the national vote. The electoral system combines relative-majority and proportional voting; each voter has 2 votes, the first for the direct constituency representative, the second for the competing party lists in the Länder. All directly elected constituency representatives enter parliament, but if a party receives more 'indirect' than 'direct' votes, the first name in order on the party list not to have a seat becomes a member—the number of seats is increased by the difference ('overhang votes'). Thus the number of seats in the Bundestag varies, but is usually around 670. The Bundesrat consists of 69 members appointed by the governments of the Länder in proportions determined by the number of inhabitants. Each *Land* has at least 3 votes.

The Head of State is the Federal *President* who is elected for a 5-year term by a *Federal Convention* specially convened for this purpose. This Convention consists of all the members of the Bundestag and an equal number of members elected by the Länder parliaments in accordance with party strengths, but who need not themselves be members of the parliaments. No president may serve more than 2 terms. Executive power is vested in the Federal Government, which consists of the Federal *Chancellor*, elected by the Bundestag on the proposal of the Federal President, and the Federal Ministers, who are appointed and dismissed by the Federal President upon the proposal of the Federal Chancellor.

The Federal Republic has exclusive legislation on: (1) foreign affairs (2) federal citizenship; (3) freedom of movement, passports, immigration and emigration, and extradition; (4) currency, money and coinage, weights and measures, and regulation of time and calendar; (5) customs, commercial and navigation agreements, traffic in goods and payments with foreign countries, including customs and frontier protection; (6) federal railways and air traffic; (7) post and telecommunications; (8) the legal status of persons in the employment of the Federation and of public law corporations under direct supervision of the Federal Government; (9) trade marks, copyright and publishing rights; (10) co-operation of the Federal Republic and the Länder in the criminal police and in matters concerning the protection of the constitution, the establishment of a Federal Office of Criminal Police, as well as the combating of international crime; (11) federal statistics.

In the field of finance the Federal Republic has exclusive legislation on customs and financial monopolies and concurrent legislation on: (1) excise taxes and taxes on transactions, in particular, taxes on real-estate acquisition, incremented value and on fire protection; (2) taxes on income, property, inheritance and donations; (3) real estate, industrial and trade taxes, with the exception of the determining of the tax rates. The Federal Republic can claim part of the income and corporation taxes to cover its expenditures not covered by other revenues. Financial jurisdiction is uniformly regulated by federal legislation.

Federal laws are passed by the Bundestag and after their adoption submitted to the Bundesrat, which has a limited veto. The Basic Law may be amended only upon the approval of two-thirds of the members of the Bundestag and two-thirds of the votes of the Bundesrat.

Die Bundesrepublik Deutschland: Staatshandbuch. Cologne, annual

Hucko, E. M. (ed.) *The Democratic Tradition* [Texts of German constitutions]. Leamington Spa, 1987

Koch, J. W., *A Constitutional History of Germany in the Nineteenth and Twentieth Centuries.* London, 1984

König, K. *et al.* (eds.) *Public Administration in the Federal Republic of Germany.* Boston (MA), 1983

National Anthem. 'Einigkeit und Recht und Freiheit' ('Unity and right and freedom'); words by H. Hoffmann, tune by J. Haydn.

RECENT ELECTIONS

On 23 May 1994 Roman Herzog was elected President by the Federal Convention against 4 opponents.

Bundestag elections were held on 27 Sept. 1998; the electorate was 60·5m (31·75m women; 28·75m. men) including 3·3m. first-time voters. There were a record 5,062 candidates competing for the 656 seats, 27·3% of them women. The age of the candidates ranged from 18 to 96. Turn-out was 80·2%. The Social Democratic Party (SPD) won 298 seats with 40·9% of votes cast (252 with 36·4% in 1994); the Christian Democratic Union/Christian Social Union (CDU/CSU; the CSU is a Bavarian party where the CDU does not stand) won 245 seats with 35·2% of votes cast (294 with 41·4% in 1994); the Greens, 47 with 6·6% (49 with 7·3%); the Free Democratic Party (FDP), 44 seats with 6·2% (47 with 6·9%); the Party for Democratic Socialism (PDS; former Communists), 35 with 5·2% (30 with 4·4%). With the SPD forming an alliance with the Green party, the new government had a 21-seat majority.

European Parliament. Germany has 99 representatives. At the June 1994 elections turn-out was 60%. The SPD won 40 seats with 32·2% of votes cast (group in European Parliament: European Socialist Party); the CDU, 39 with 32% (Popular European Party); the Greens, 12 with 10·1% (Greens); the CSU, 8 with 6·8% (Popular European Party).

CURRENT ADMINISTRATION

Federal President: Roman Herzog (b. 1934; sworn in 1 July 1994).

Speaker of the Bundestag: Rita Süssmuth (elected Nov. 1988; re-elected Nov. 1994).

In Oct. 1998 an SPD-Green party coalition was formed, the first time that the Green party had entered national government in Germany. The government comprised in March 1999:

Chancellor: Gerhard Schröder (b. 1944; SPD).

Vice-Chancellor and Foreign Minister: Joschka Fischer (Greens). *Without Portfolio and Chief of the Federal Chancellery:* Bodo Hombach (SPD). *Interior:* Otto Schily (SPD). *Justice:* Herta Däubler-Gmelin (SPD). *Finance:* Hans Eichel (SPD). *Economy:* Werner Müller (Ind.). *Food, Agriculture and Forestry:* Karl-Heinz Funke (SPD). *Labour and Social Affairs:* Walter Riester (SPD). *Defence:* Rudolf Scharping (SPD). *Family, Youth, Women and Senior Citizens:* Christine Bergmann (SPD). *Health:* Andrea Fischer (Greens). *Transport and Construction:* Franz

Müntefering (SPD). *Environment, Nature Conservation and Reactor Safety:* Jürgen Trittin (Greens). *Education and Research:* Edelgard Bulmahn (SPD). *Economic Cooperation and Development:* Heidemarie Wieczorek-Zeul (SPD).

Local Government. The 16 Länder are divided into a total of 29 administrative regions (*Regierungsbezirke*). Below Land level local government is carried on by elected councils to 426 rural districts (*Landkreise*) and 117 urban districts (*Kreisfreie Städte*), which form the electoral districts for the *Land* governments, and are subdivided into 16,043 communes (*Gemeinden*).

DEFENCE

Russian (ex-Soviet) forces had withdrawn from the territory of the former GDR by 1994.

Conscription is for 10 months. In July 1994, the Constitutional Court ruled that German armed forces might be sent on peace-keeping missions abroad.

In 1997 defence expenditure totalled US$33,416m. (US$412 per capita), representing 1·6% of GDP.

Army. The Army is organized in the Army Forces Command, comprising 1 airmobile division with 3 airborne brigades, 3 army aviation brigades, 1 signals/electronic intelligence brigade and 1 support brigade; and 8 military district commands grouped in 3 corps—2 with armoured divisions and 1 with an armed infantry division (I Corps: German-Netherlands), 2 with armoured divisions and 1 with a mountain division (II Corps), and 2 with armoured infantry divisions (IV Corps). The 8 military district commands control 6 armoured, 12 armoured infantry and 1 mountain brigade, and the German element of the German-French brigade. 1 armoured division is earmarked for Eurocorps. Corps units comprise 2 armoured reconnaissance battalions, 3 air defence regiments and 3 helicopter regiments. Equipment includes 731 Leopard 1A5 and 1,964 Leopard 2 main battle tanks and 1,511 surface-to-air missiles. The equipment of the former East German army is in store. An air component operates 205 BO 105P anti-armour helicopters, 107 CH-53G and 125 UH-1D Iroquois transport helicopters, as well as 40 Alouette II and 95 BO 105M liaison/observation helicopters. The Territorial Army is organized into 5 Military Districts, under 3 Territorial Commands. Its main task is to defend rear areas and remains under national control even in wartime. Total strength was (1997) 239,950 (conscripts 124,200).

Navy. The Fleet Commander operates from a modern Maritime Headquarters at Glücksburg, close to the Danish border.

The fleet includes 16 diesel coastal submarines, 3 US-built guided-missile destroyers, 10 frigates including 2 new guided-missile ships and 36 fast missile craft. There is a mine-warfare force of 42 vessels, comprising 32 coastal minesweepers and hunters, of which 10 are new combined minelayer/hunters and 6 control ships for TROIKA minesweeping drones, 5 inshore minesweepers and 1 diver support ship. Major auxiliaries include 4 repair ships, 4 transport oilers, 4 minesweeper/patrol craft support and HQ ships, 3 logistic transports, 8 large tugs, 3 intelligence collectors and 2 trial ships. There are several dozen minor auxiliaries and service craft.

The main naval bases are at Wilhelmshaven, Bremerhaven, Kiel, Eckernförde and Warnemünde.

The Naval Air Arm, 4,500 strong, is organized into 3 wings and comprises 54 missile-armed Tornado strike aircraft. 18 Atlantic long range, 20 shore-based Sea King helicopters, 17 Lynx (12 frigate-based) and 2 Do-228 anti-pollution patrol aircraft are also in service.

Procurement of 2 further new mine warfare craft is in hand. Personnel in 1997 numbered 27,760, including 5,460 conscripts.

Air Force. Since 1970 the *Luftwaffe* has comprised the following commands: German Air Force Tactical Command, German Air Force Support Command (including two German Air Force Regional Support Commands—North and South) and General Air Force Office. Personnel in 1995 was 75,300 (18,700 conscripts). Combat units, including 12 heavy fighter-bomber squadrons with Tornados and F-4Fs, 8 surface-to-surface missile squadrons, and an air defence force of 6 interceptor squadrons with F-4Fs and MiG-29s, 24 batteries of *Nike-Hercules* and

GERMANY

36 batteries of *Improved Hawk* surface-to-air missiles, are assigned to NATO. 3 wings operating both Transall C-160 aircraft and UH-1D Iroquois helicopters add to the air mobility of the *Bundeswehr*. There are also VIP, support and light transport aircraft. About 12 L-410 and Tu-154 transports and Mi-8 helicopters from the GDR air force are still in use, the single Tu-154 being assigned to arms control surveillance duties. Guided weapons in service include 8 squadrons of *Pershing* surface-to-surface missiles and 6 battalions of *Nike-Hercules* and 9 battalions of *Improved Hawk* surface-to-air missiles. Personnel in 1997 numbered 76,900, including 22,400 conscripts.

INTERNATIONAL RELATIONS
A treaty of friendship with Poland signed on 17 June 1991 recognized the Oder-Neisse border and guaranteed minorities' rights in both countries.

Germany is a member of the UN, OECD, EU, WEU, NATO and the Council of Europe, and is a signatory to the Schengen Accord which abolishes border controls between Germany, Austria, Belgium, Denmark, Finland, France, Greece, Iceland, Italy, Luxembourg, the Netherlands, Norway, Portugal, Spain and Sweden.

ECONOMY
Performance. Real GDP growth was 1·3% in 1996, 2·2% in 1997, and forecast to rise to 2·7% in 1998. Growth in the Länder of the former German Democratic Republic was estimated to be around 0·6% lower than the overall national average in both 1997 and 1998.

Budget. Tax reforms introduced by the Schröder government in 1998 mean the average working family will be 2,700 DM better off by 2002. The cost is to be borne by industry through the ending or tightening of tax reliefs.

Since 1 Jan. 1979 tax revenues have been distributed as follows: Federal Government. Income tax, 42·5%; capital yield and corporation tax, 50%; turnover tax, 67·5%; trade tax, 15%; capital gains, insurance and accounts taxes, 100%; excise duties (other than on beer), 100%. Länder. Income tax, 42·5%; capital yield and corporation tax, 50%; turnover tax, 32·5%; trade tax, 15%; other taxes, 100%. Local authorities. Income tax, 15%; trade tax, 70%; local taxes, 100%.

VAT is 16% (reduced rate, 7%).

Budget for 1998 (in 1m. DM):

Revenue	All public authorities	Federal portion
	Current	
Taxes	730,176	369,554
Economic activities	17,367	8,937
Interest	5,652	2,242
Current allocations and subsidies	134,354	5,477
Other receipts	31,787	11,209
minus equalising payments	113,740	...
	805,596	397,419
	Capital	
Sale of assets	47,156	36,405
Allocations for investment	27,633	5
Repayment of loans	12,274	4,277
Public sector borrowing	738	...
minus equalising payments	24,544	...
	63,257	40,688
Totals	871,291	438,107
Expenditure	*Current*	
Staff	248,621	52,472
Materials	84,704	39,557
Interest	128,939	56,490
Allocations and subsidies	489,831	287,540
minus equalising payments	113,740	...
	838,355	436,059

Expenditure	All public authorities	Federal portion
	Capital	
Construction	23,516	11,262
Acquisition of property	6,992	2,402
Allocations and subsidies	88,842	34,739
Loans	27,576	9,690
Acquisition of shares	3,071	1,367
Repayments in the public sector	910	. . .
minus equalising payments	24,544	. . .
	126,363	59,460
Totals	960,072	494,593

The current account balance for 1997 was a provisional deficit of DM10·1bn.

Currency. On 1 Jan. 1999 the euro (EUR) became the legal currency in Germany and the *deutsche Mark* became a subdivision of it; irrevocable conversion rate 1·95583 DM to 1 euro. The euro, which consists of 100 cents, will not be in circulation until 1 Jan. 2002. There will be 7 euro notes in different colours and sizes denominated in 500, 200, 100, 50, 20, 10 and 5 euros, and 8 coins denominated in 2 and 1 euros, then 50, 20, 10, 5, 2 and 1 cents. Even though notes and coins will not be introduced until 1 Jan. 2002 the euro can be used in banking; by means of cheques, travellers' cheques, bank transfers, credit cards and electronic purses. Banking will be possible in both euros and deutsche Marks until the deutsche Mark is withdrawn from circulation—which must be by 1 July 2002.

The *deutsche Mark* (DEM) consists of 100 *pfennig* (pf.). In Feb. 1998 gold reserves were 95·18m. troy oz. (only the USA, with 261·7m. troy oz., had more), and foreign exchange reserves were US$69,257m. Inflation was at a record low of 0·9% in 1998, down from 1·8% in 1997. Total money supply in Feb. 1998 was 864bn. DM.

Banking and Finance. The Deutsche Bundesbank (German Federal Bank) is the central bank and bank of issue. Its duty is to protect the stability of the currency. It is independent of the government but obliged to support the government's general policy. Its Governor is appointed by the government for 8 years. The *Governor* is Hans Tietmayer. Its assets were 369,463m. DM in 1997. The largest private banks are the Deutsche Bank, Dresdner Bank and Commerzbank. The former GDR central bank Staatsbank has become a public commercial bank. In 1997 there were 3,414 credit institutes, including 326 banks, 598 savings banks, 35 mortgage lenders and 2,420 credit societies. They are represented in the wholesale market by the 12 public sector Länder banks. Total assets, 1997, 9,109,858m. DM. Savings deposits were 1,204,999m. DM in 1997. A single stock exchange, the Deutsche Börse, was created in 1992, based on the former Frankfurt stock exchange in a union with the smaller exchanges in Berlin, Bremen, Düsseldorf, Hamburg, Hanover, Munich and Stuttgart.

Gull, L. et al., *The Deutsche Bank, 1870–1995*. London, 1996

Marsh, D., *The Bundesbank: the Bank that Rules Europe*. London, 1992

Weights and Measures. The metric system is in force.

ENERGY AND NATURAL RESOURCES

Electricity. Installed capacity in 1994 was 109·73m. kW. In 1994 there were 21 nuclear reactors. Production was 529·1bn. kWh in 1995, of which about a third was nuclear. There is a moratorium on further nuclear plant construction. Consumption per capita was estimated to be 5,727 kWh in 1995.

Oil and Gas. The chief oilfields are in Emsland (Lower Saxony). In 1996, 2·85m. tonnes of crude oil were produced. Gas production was 899,208,000 MWh in 1994, of which 818,034,000 MWh was natural gas.

Minerals. The main production areas are: North Rhine-Westphalia (for coal, iron and metal smelting-works), Central Germany (for lignite), and Lower Saxony (Salzgitter for iron ore; the Harz for metal ore).

Production (in tonnes), 1997: Coal, 46,791,557; lignite, 177,159,708.

Agriculture. Land in agricultural use, 1997 (in 1,000 ha): 17,327·1, including arable, 11,831·6; pasture, 5,268·4. Sown areas included: Wheat, 2,719·7; rye, 843·4;

barley, 2,208·4; oats, 312·4; maize, 368·3; potatoes, 303·6; sugar-beet, 507·7; rape, 914·0; fodder, 1,796·2. Crop production, 1997 (and 1994) (in 1,000 tonnes): Wheat, 19,826·8 (16,480·5); rye, 4,580·1 (3,450·6); barley, 13,398·9 (10,902·5); oats, 1,599·0 (1,663·0); maize, 3,188·4 (2,446·0); potatoes, 11,659·3 (9,668·6); sugar-beet, 25,768·9 (24,211·3); rape, 2,866·9 (2,895·5); fodder, 61,183·8 (52,187·9).

In 1997 there were 525,121 farms, of which 66,737 were under 2 ha and 22,312 over 100 ha. In 1995 there were 561,900 farmers assisted by 586,400 household members and 263,000 hired labourers (84,800 seasonal). In the former GDR in 1990 state farms were leased to farmers until 2004 and will then be sold. Collective farms have continued operating as co-operatives or been turned over to their former members.

In 1997 wine production was 9,249,000 hectolitres.

Livestock, 1997 (in 1,000): Cattle, 15,612·2 (including milch cows, 5,069·3); sheep, 2,884·4; pigs, 24,416·0; horses, 652·4 (1996); poultry, 102,731·3 (1996). Livestock products, 1997 (in 1,000 tonnes): Milk, 28,702; meat, 4,892·4; eggs, 536,931,000 units.

Forestry. Forest area in 1997 was 9,463,300 ha, of which about half was owned by the State. Timber production was 34·0m. cu metres in 1995.

In recent years depredation has occurred through pollution with acid rain.

Fisheries. In 1996 the yield of sea fishing was 113,992 tonnes live weight. The fishing fleet consisted of 49 ocean-going vessels and 2,307 coastal cutters.

INDUSTRY
Public limited companies are managed on the 'co-determination' principle, and have 3 statutory bodies: a board of directors, a works council elected by employees, and a supervisory council which includes employee representatives but has an in-built management majority.

In 1994 there were 67,660 firms (with 20 and more employees) employing 8·9m. persons, made up of 363,000 in energy and water services, 174,000 in mining, 1·3m. in raw materials processing, 3·71m. in the manufacture of producers' goods, 1·28m. in the manufacture of consumer goods, 572,000 in food and tobacco production and 1·50m. in building.

Output of major industrial products, 1996 (in 1,000 tonnes): Cement, 35,845; pig-iron (1994), 29,923; crude steel (1994), 40,837; rolled steel (1994), 26,691; aluminium, 709; copper (1994), 1,926; nitrogenous fertilizers (1994), 1,199; plastics, 10,001; glassware (1994), 4,882; cotton yarn (1994), 108; synthetic fibre (1994), 85; flour, 3,851; paper, 10,636; passenger cars, 4,702,000 (units); refrigerators, 3,102,000; beer, 108·9m. hectolitres.

Labour. Retirement age is 63 years. At April 1997 the workforce was 40·28m. (17·35m. females), of whom 33·40m. (13·50m. females) were working and 3·26m. (1·39m. females) were unemployed. In 1997 there were on average during the year 3·62m. self-employed or helping other family members, 2·48m. officials and 27·78m. employees. 2·69m. foreign workers were employed in 1997. Major categories (1997): Manufacturing industries, 11·52m.; services, 7·99m.; commerce and transport, 6·37m.; agriculture, forestry and fishing, 0·93m. In 1996 there were 327,278 unfilled vacancies. In Dec. 1997 there were 4,500,000 unemployed, a rate of 11·8%. The 1998 seasonally adjusted annual rate was 11·2%, with a forecast of a fall to 10·6% in 1999. In 1996 more than half the unemployed people had not had a job for over 6 months, and 12·4% of people who were unemployed were under 25 years old. Unemployment is highest in eastern Germany, 17·3% at the end of 1998. Of unemployed people in the old Federal Republic of Germany in 1996, 17·3% were foreign nationals.

Trade Unions. The majority of trade unions belong to the *Deutscher Gewerkschaftsbund* (DGB, German Trade Union Federation), which had 8·6m. (2·6m. women) members in 1997, including 5·21m. (1·03m.) manual workers, 2·46m. (1·33m.) white-collar workers and 642,595 (169,770) officials. DGB unions are organized in industrial branches such that only one union operates within each enterprise. Outside the DGB are several smaller unions: The *Deutscher Beamtenbund* (DBB) or public servants' union with 1,116,714 (330,414) members, the *Deutsche Angestellten-Gewerkschaft* (DAG) or union of salaried staff with

GERMANY

489,266 (269,100) members and the *Christlicher Gewerkschaftsbund Deutschlands* (CGD, Christian Trade Union Federation of Germany) with 302,874 (76,222) members. The official GDR trade union organization (FDGB) was merged in the Deutscher Gewerkschaftsbund. Strikes are not legal unless called by a union with the backing of 75% of members. Certain public service employees are contractually not permitted to strike. 98,135 working days were lost through strikes in 1996; 247,460 in 1995.

INTERNATIONAL TRADE
In 1997 Germany had its highest annual trade surplus since unification, at 130·9bn. DM for the year compared to 98·5bn. DM a year earlier.

Imports and Exports. Imports and exports in 1m. DM:

	Imports				Exports		
1994	1995	1996	1997	1994	1995	1996	1997
616,955	634,271	669,060	755,865	690,573	727,732	771,913	886,766

Most important trading partners in 1997 (trade figures in 1m. DM). Imports: France, 79,273; Netherlands, 64,135; Italy, 58,905; USA, 58,551; UK, 52,596; Belgium with Luxembourg, 46,521; Japan, 36,839. Exports: France, 94,431; USA, 76,617; UK, 75,020; Italy, 65,332; Netherlands, 62,022; Belgium with Luxembourg, 51,605; Austria, 45,938; Switzerland, 39,848.

Distribution by commodities in 1997 (in 1m. DM). Imports and exports: Live animals, 592 and 985; foodstuffs, 59,031 and 33,703; drinks and tobacco, 11,910 and 7,251; raw materials, 38,065 and 6,857; semi-finished goods, 71,784 and 42,686; finished goods, 517,480 and 757,055.

COMMUNICATIONS

Roads. In 1996 the total length of classified roads was 231,076 km, including 11,246 km of motorway *(Autobahn)*, 41,487 km of federal highways, 86,789 km of first-class and 91,554 km of second-class country roads. The motorway network is the largest in Europe. On 1 Jan. 1998 there were 49·0m. motor vehicles, including: Passenger cars, 41,326,900 (approximately 1 car for every 2 persons); trucks, 2,344,600; buses, 83,700; motor cycles, 2,759,200. In 1997, 7,838m. passengers were transported by long-distance road traffic. The average distance travelled by a passenger car in the year 1994 was 12,700 km (1995 estimate, 12,400 km).

645,384 motorists were arrested at the scene of an accident for driving offences in 1996, of which 52,185 were alcohol related and 139,117 due to exceeding speed limits.

Road casualties in 1997 (and 1995) totalled 500,707 injured (512,141) and 8,516 killed (9,454).

Rail. Legislation of 1993 provides for the eventual privatization of the railways. On 1 Jan. 1994 West German Bundesbahn and the former GDR Reichsbahn were amalgamated as the Deutsche Bahn, a joint-stock company in which track, long-distance passenger traffic, regional passenger traffic and goods traffic are run as 4 separate administrative entities. These were intended after 3–5 years to become themselves companies, at first under a holding company, and ultimately independent. Initially the government will hold all the shares. Length of railway in 1996 was 46,300 km (1,435 mm gauge) of which 18,866 km were electrified. There were 5,640 stations. 1,735m. passengers were carried in 1997 and 316·0m. tonnes of freight.

There are metros in Berlin (136 km), Hamburg (95 km), Frankfurt am Main (51 km), Munich (63 km) and Nuremberg (23 km), and tram/light rail networks in 56 cities.

Civil Aviation. Lufthansa, the largest carrier, was set up in 1953 and is 36% state-owned. Other airlines include Condor, Deutsche-British Airways, Eurowings and LTU International Airways. In 1997 civil aviation had 476 aircraft over 20 tonnes (441 jets). Lufthansa flew 516·5m. km in 1995, carrying 32,537,700 passengers (19,347,500 on international flights).

In 1997 there were 60·39m. passenger arrivals and 60·76m. departures. Main international airports: Bremen, Cologne-Bonn, Düsseldorf, Frankfurt am Main,

Hamburg (Fuhlsbüttel), Hanover, Leipzig, Munich, Nuremberg, Stuttgart and 3 at
Berlin (Tegel, Tempelhof and Schönefeld). Airports at Dortmund, Dresden,
Mönchengladbach, Paderborn, Rostock and Saarbrücken are used for only a few
scheduled international flights in addition to domestic flights. In 1997 Frankfurt am
Main handled 39,612,000 passengers (30,918,720 on international flights) and
1,367,862 tonnes of freight. It was the busiest airport in Europe in 1996 in terms of
freight handled. Munich was the second busiest German airport in terms of
passenger traffic in 1997 (17,575,000 including 9,590,560 on international flights)
but third for freight. Cologne-Bonn was the second busiest in 1997 for freight, with
375,051 tonnes, but only seventh for passenger traffic.

Shipping. At 31 Dec. 1996 the mercantile marine comprised 1,397 ocean-going
vessels of 6,002,000 GRT. Sea-going ships in 1996 carried 206m. tonnes of cargo.

Navigable rivers have a total length of 4,842 km; canals, 2,087 km. The inland-
waterways fleet on 31 Dec. 1995 included 1,477 motor freight vessels totalling
1·52m. tonnes and 355 tankers of 495,887 tonnes. 227m. tonnes of freight were
transported in 1996.

Telecommunications. Telecommunications were deregulated in 1989. On 1 Jan.
1995, 3 state-owned joint-stock companies were set up: Deutsche Telekom,
Postdienst and Postbank. The partial privatization of Deutsche Telekom began in
Nov. 1996.

In 1997 there were 45·2m. telephone main lines, equivalent to 549·8 per 1,000
population. In 1996 there were 44·2m. private telephones and 164,100 public
telephones. There were 1·45m. fax transmitters in 1995 and 13·5m. PCs (165 per
1,000 persons). 3·71m. mobile telephones were in use in 1996. There were
approximately 7·3m. Internet users in Oct. 1998 (nearly 9% of the population).

Postal Services. In 1996 there were 16,600 post offices and 4,000 affiliated agents.
A total of 19,963m. pieces of mail were processed during the year, or 244 items per
person.

SOCIAL INSTITUTIONS

Justice. Justice is administered by the federal courts and by the courts of the Länder.
In criminal procedures, civil cases and procedures of non-contentious jurisdiction
the courts on the *Land* level are the local courts *(Amtsgerichte)*, the regional courts
(Landgerichte) and the courts of appeal *(Oberlandesgerichte)*. Constitutional federal
disputes are dealt with by the Federal Constitutional Court *(Bundesverfassungs-
gericht)* elected by the Bundestag and Bundesrat. The Länder also have
constitutional courts. In labour law disputes the courts of the first and second
instance are the labour courts and the *Land* labour courts and in the third instance,
the Federal Labour Court *(Bundesarbeitsgericht)*. Disputes about public law in
matters of social security, unemployment insurance, maintenance of war victims and
similar cases are dealt with in the first and second instances by the social courts and
the *Land* social courts and in the third instance by the Federal Social Court
(Bundessozialgericht). In most tax matters the finance courts of the Länder are
competent and in the second instance, the Federal Finance Court *(Bundesfinanzhof)*.
Other controversies of public law in non-constitutional matters are decided in the
first and second instance by the administrative and the higher administrative courts
(Oberverwaltungsgerichte) of the Länder, and in the third instance by the Federal
Administrative Court *(Bundesverwaltungsgericht)*.

For the inquiry into maritime accidents the admiralty courts *(Seeämter)* are
competent on the *Land* level and in the second instance the Federal Admiralty Court
(Bundesoberseeamt) in Hamburg. The death sentence has been abolished.

Religion. In 1996 there were 27,659,000 Protestants in 17,991 parishes, 27,533,000
Roman Catholics in 13,329 parishes, and in 1997, 67,471 Jews with 17 rabbis and
70 synagogues.

There are 5 Roman Catholic archbishoprics (Bamberg, Cologne, Freiburg,
Munich and Freising, Paderborn) and 23 bishoprics. Chairman of the German
Bishops' Conference is Cardinal Joseph Höffner, Archbishop of Cologne. A
concordat between Germany and the Holy See dates from 10 Sept. 1933.

GERMANY

The Evangelical (Protestant) Church (EKD) consists of 24 member-churches including 7 Lutheran Churches, 8 United-Lutheran-Reformed, 2 Reformed Churches and 1 Confederation of United member Churches: 'Church of the Union'. Its organs are the Synod, the Church Conference and the Council under the chairmanship of Bishop Dr Eduard Lohse (Hanover). There are also some 12 Evangelical Free Churches.

Education. Education is compulsory for children aged 6 to 15. After the first 4 (or 6) years at primary school *(Grundschulen)* children attend post-primary *(Hauptschulen)*, secondary modern *(Realschulen)*, grammar *(Gymnasien)*, or comprehensive schools *(Integrierte Gesamtschulen)*. Secondary modern school lasts 6 years and grammar school. Entry to higher education is by the final Grammar School Certificate *(Abitur—Higher School Certificate)*. There are special schools *(Sonderschulen)* for handicapped children and children with special needs.

In 1996–97 there were 4,217 kindergartens with 82,420 pupils and 5,364 teachers; 17,892 primary schools with 3,691,648 pupils and 200,427 teachers; and 8,396 post-primary schools with 1,500,471 pupils and 99,411 teachers. There were also 3,410 special schools with 398,366 pupils and 63,434 teachers; 3,485 secondary modern schools with 1,202,952 pupils and 73,664 teachers; 3,167 grammar schools with 2,181,562 pupils and 153,983 teachers; 965 comprehensive schools with 591,404 pupils and 46,233 teachers.

In the 1996–97 academic year there were 671,733 working teachers, of whom 430,746 were female.

The adult literacy rate is 99·0%.

In 1995 total expenditure on education came to 4·8% of GNP and represented 9·5% of total government expenditure.

Vocational education is provided in part-time, full-time and advanced vocational schools (Berufs-, Berufsaufbau-, Berufsfach- and Fachschulen, including Fachschulen für Technik and Schulen des Gesundheitswesens). Occupation-related, part-time vocational training of 6 to 12 hours per week is compulsory for all (including unemployed) up to the age of 18 years or until the completion of the practical vocational training. Full-time vocational schools comprise courses of at least one year. They prepare for commercial and domestic occupations as well as specialized occupations in the field of handicrafts. Advanced full-time vocational schools are attended by pupils over 18. Courses vary from 6 months to 3 or more years.

In 1996–97 there were 9,300 full- and part-time vocational schools with 2,479,584 students and 108,083 teachers.

Higher Education. In the winter term of the 1997–98 academic year there were 337 institutes of higher education *(Hochschulen)* with 1,832,758 students, including 84 universities (1,199,125 students), 7 polytechnics *(Gesamthochschulen*; 144,976), 6 teacher training colleges (17,738), 16 theological seminaries (2,589), 46 schools of art (29,944), 147 technical colleges (399,817) and 31 management schools (38,569). Only 12·3% of students were in their first year.

Health. In 1997 there were 282,737 doctors (equivalent to 1 for every 290 persons), 62,024 dentists and 52,076 pharmacists. In 1996 there were 2,269 hospitals with 593,743 beds.

Welfare. Social Health Insurance (introduced in 1883). Wage-earners and apprentices, salaried employees with an income below a certain limit and social insurance pensioners are compulsorily insured. Voluntary insurance is also possible.

Benefits: Medical treatment, medicines, hospital and nursing care, maternity benefits, death benefits for the insured and their families, sickness payments and out-patients' allowances. Economy measures of Dec. 1992 introduced prescription charges related to recipients' income.

50·85m. persons were insured in 1997 (29·6m. compulsorily). Number of cases of incapacity for work (1996) totalled 35·99m., and the number of working days lost were 331·8m. (men) and 260·1m. (women). Total disbursements, 234,274m. DM.

Accident Insurance (introduced in 1884). Those insured are all persons in employment or service, apprentices and the majority of the self-employed and the unpaid family workers.

Benefits in the case of industrial injuries and occupational diseases: Medical treatment and nursing care, sickness payments, pensions and other payments in cash and in kind, surviving dependants' pensions.

Number of insured in 1996, 55·42m.; number of current pensions, 1,179,743; total disbursements, 25,734m. DM.

Workers' and Employees' Old-Age Insurance Scheme (introduced in 1889). All wage-earners and salaried employees, the members of certain liberal professions and—subject to certain conditions—self-employed craftsmen are compulsorily insured. The insured may voluntarily continue to insure when no longer liable to do so or increase the insurance.

Benefits: Measures designed to maintain, improve and restore the earning capacity; pensions paid to persons incapable of work, old age and surviving dependants' pensions.

Number of insured in April 1997, 43·75m. (20·46m. women); number of current pensions (in July 1996), 20·30m.; pensions to widows and widowers, 5·06m. Total disbursements in 1995, 398,081m. DM.

There are also special retirement and unemployment pension schemes for miners and farmers, assistance for war victims and compensation payments to members of German minorities in East European countries expelled after the Second World War and persons who suffered damage because of the war or in connection with the currency reform.

Family Allowances. 40,466m. DM were dispensed to 8·56m. recipients (0·95m. foreigners) in 1997 on behalf of 14·33m. children. Paid child care leave is available for 3 years to mothers or fathers.

Unemployment Allowances. In 1996, 1·99m. persons (0·87m. women) were receiving unemployment benefit and 1·10m. (0·47m. women) earnings-related benefit. Total expenditure on these and similar benefits (e.g. short-working supplement, job creation schemes) was 105·59m. DM in 1996.

Public Welfare (introduced in 1962). In 1993, 48·92m. DM were distributed to 5·02m. recipients (2·67m. women).

Public Youth Welfare. For supervision of foster children, official guardianship, assistance with adoptions and affiliations, social assistance in juvenile courts, educational assistance and correctional education under a court order. Total number of recipients in 1996 was 725,468 persons.

CULTURE

Broadcasting. The national public broadcasters Deutschlandfunk, RIAS Berlin and Deutschlandsender Kultur form part of the *Nationaler Hörfunk*. The foreign service, Deutsche Welle, broadcasts in 30 languages, and there is a commercial European service. There are 12 regional radio and TV networks (colour by PAL). The *Arbeitsgemeinschaft der öffentlich-rechtlichen Rundfunkanstalten der Bundesrepublik Deutschland* (ARD) represents public-right broadcasters and organizes co-operation between them and also broadcasts a federal-wide TV programme of its own. There is another public TV channel, ZDF, and 4 commercial TV networks, as well as a sport channel, a pay-TV film channel and Deutsche Telekom's cable network. In 1997 there were 37·5m. radio and 33·5m. TV licences.

Cinema. In 1996 there were 4,035 cinemas with a total seating capacity of 760,282. 64 feature films were made in 1996. Around 400 new screens were scheduled to be opened between 1998 and 2000. A total of 132·9m. visits to the cinema were made in 1996.

Press. 71,515 book titles were published in 1996, of which 53,793 were new works. The daily press is mainly regional. In 1996 the largest dailies with a national circulation were *Das Bild* (Hamburg, 4·5m. copies per day); *Süddeutsche Zeitung* (Munich, 0·4m.); *Frankfurter Allgemeine Zeitung* (0·4m.); *Die Welt* (Berlin, 0·22m.); *Frankfurter Rundschau* (0·2m.). In 1994, 381 newspapers and 9,093 periodicals were published with respective circulations of 30·6m. and 387·8m. The total circulation of daily newspapers in Germany is the highest in Europe.

Tourism. In 1997 there were 53,830 places of accommodation with 2,360,037 beds (including 13,052 hotels with 859,367 beds). 14,891,200 foreign visitors and 77,732,800 tourists resident in Germany spent a total of 287,169,700 nights in holiday accommodation. Berlin is the most visited city with 3,448,996 visitors in 1997, and Bavaria the most visited Land with 19,556,800. More foreign visitors were from the Netherlands (1,806,800) than any other country. In 1996 foreign visitors spent US$16·5bn. in Germany.

Festivals. The first of its kind to be held in Germany, Expo 2000 will take place at the refurbished Hanover Exhibition Grounds and a new development next to it. Even by 1998 the exhibition had broken all records by attracting the support of the largest number of countries and international organizations at the highest level ever. The theme of Expo 2000 is 'Mankind, Nature, Technology' and it runs from 1 June to 31 Oct. 2000.

Libraries. In 1996 there were 1,250 academic and special libraries, and 12,727 public libraries, the latter with 10·26m. active users who borrowed 316·6m. books.

National Theatre and Opera. In 1995–96 there were 154 theatre companies, performing on 655 stages. Audiences totalled 20·6m.

Museums and Galleries. In 1996 there were 4,113 museums which attracted some 90·6m. visitors.

DIPLOMATIC REPRESENTATIVES

Of Germany in Great Britain (23 Belgrave Sq., 1 Chesham Place, London, SW1X 8PZ)
Ambassador: Gebhardt von Moltke.

Of Great Britain in Germany (Friedrich-Ebert-Allee 77, 53113 Bonn)
Ambassador: Sir Paul Lever.

Of Germany in the USA (4645 Reservoir Rd, NW, Washington, D.C., 20007)
Ambassador: Jürgen Chrobog.

Of the USA in Germany (Deichmanns Ave., 53170 Bonn)
Ambassador: John Kornblum.

Of Germany to the United Nations
Ambassador: Dr Dieter Kastrup.

FURTHER READING

Statistisches Bundesamt. *Statistisches Jahrbuch für die Bundesrepublik Deutschland; Wirtschaft und Statistik* (monthly, from 1949); *Das Arbeitsgebiet der Bundesstatistik* (latest issue 1988; Abridged English version: *Survey of German Federal Statistics*).

Ardagh, J., *Germany and the Germans*. 2nd ed. London, 1991
Balfour, M., *Germany: the Tides of Power.* London, 1992
Bark, D. L. and Gress, D. R., *A History of West Germany, 1945–1991.* 2nd ed. 2 vols. Oxford, 1993
Betz, H. G., *Postmodern Politics in Germany.* London, 1991
Blackbourn, D., *Fontana History of Germany, 1780–1918: The long nineteenth century.* London, 1997
Blackbourn, D. and Eley, G., *The Peculiarities of German History.* 1984
Carr, W., *A History of Germany, 1815–1990.* 4th ed. London, 1991
Childs, D., *Germany in the 20th Century.* London, 1991
Dennis, M., *German Democratic Republic.* London, 1987
Detwiler, D. S. and Detwiler, I. E., *West Germany.* [Bibliography] Oxford and Santa Barbara (CA), 1988
Edinger, L. J., *West German Politics.* New York, 1986
Eley, G., *From Unification to Nazism: Reinterpreting the German Past.* London, 1986
Fulbrook, M., *A Concise History of Germany.* CUP, 1991.—*The Divided Nation: a History of Germany, 1918–1990.* CUP, 1992
Glees, A., *Reinventing Germany: German political development since 1945.* Oxford, 1996
Huelshoff, M. G. *et al.* (eds.) *From Bundesrepublik to Deutschland: German Politics after Reunification.* Michigan Univ. Press, 1993
Kielinger, T., *Crossroads and Roundabouts, Junctions in German-British Relations.* Bonn, 1997
Loth, W., *Stalin's Unwanted Child – The Soviet Union, the German Question and the Founding of the GDR.* London, 1998

Maier, C. S., *Dissolution: The Crisis of Communism and the End of East Germany*. Princeton, N.J., 1997

Marsh, D., *The New Germany: at the Crossroads*. London, 1990

Marshall, B., *The Origins of Post-War German Politics*. London, 1988

Nicholls, A. J., *The Bonn Republic: West German Democracy, 1945–1990*. Harlow, 1998

Orlow, D., *The History of Modern Germany, 1871 to the Present*. 3rd ed. New York, 1994

Parkes, S., *Understanding Contemporary Germany*. London, 1996

Pulzer, P., *German Politics, 1945–1995*. OUP, 1995

Schmidt, H., *Handeln für Deutschland*. Berlin, 1993

Schweitzer, D.-C., (ed.) *Politics and Government in the Federal Republic of Germany: Basic Documents*. 2nd ed. Oxford, 1994

Sinn, G. and Sinn, H.-W., *Jumpstart: the Economic Reunification of Germany*. Boston (MA), 1993

Smyser, W.R., *The Economy of United Germany: Colossus at the Crossroads*. New York, 1992

Stürmer, M., *Die Grenzen der Macht*. Berlin, 1992

Taylor, R., *Berlin and its Culture*. Yale University Press, 1997

Thompson, W. C. *et al.*, *Historical Dictionary of Germany*. Metuchen (NJ), 1995

Turner, H. A., *Germany from Partition to Reunification*. 2nd ed. [of *Two Germanies since 1945*]. Yale Univ. Press, 1993

Tusa, A., *The Last Division – A History of Berlin, 1945–1989*. Reading, Mass., 1997

Wallace, I., *East Germany: the German Democratic Republic*. [Bibliography]. Oxford and Santa Barbara (CA), 1987

Watson, A., *The Germans: Who Are They Now?* 2nd ed. London, 1994

Other more specialized titles are listed under CONSTITUTION AND GOVERNMENT *and* BANKING AND FINANCE, *above.*

National statistical office: Statistiches Bundesamt, D-65189 Wiesbaden, Gustav Stresemann Ring 11. *President:* Johann Hahlen. *Website:* http://www.statistik-bund.de

National libraries: Deutsche Bibliothek, Zeppelinallee 4–8; Frankfurt am Main. *Director:* K.-D. Lehmann; (Berliner) Staatsbibliothek Preussischer Kulturbesitz, Potsdamer Str. 33, Postfach 1407, D-10785 Berlin. *Director:* Dr. Richard Landwehrmeyer.

THE LÄNDER

BADEN-WÜRTTEMBERG

KEY HISTORICAL EVENTS

The *Land* is a combination of former states. Baden (the western part of the present *Land*) became a united margravate in 1771, after being divided as Baden-Baden and Baden-Durlach since 1535; Baden-Baden was predominantly Catholic and Baden-Durlach, Protestant.

The margrave became an ally of Napoleon, ceding land west of the Rhine and receiving northern and southern territory as compensation. In 1805 Baden became a grand duchy and in 1806 a member state of the Confederation of the Rhine, extending from the Main to Lake Constance. In 1815 it was a founder-state of the German Confederation. A constitution was granted by the grand duke in 1818, but later rulers were less liberal and there was revolution in 1848, put down with Prussian help. The grand Duchy was abolished and replaced by a *Land* in 1919.

In 1949 Baden was combined with Württemberg to form three states; the three were brought together as 1 in 1952.

Württemberg, having been a duchy since 1495, became a kingdom in 1805 and joined the Confederations as did Baden. A constitution was granted in 1819 and the state remained liberal. In 1866 the king allied himself with Austria against Prussia, but in 1870 joined Prussia in war against France. The liberal monarchy came to an end with the abdication of William II in 1918, and Württemberg became a state of the German Republic. In 1945 the state was divided between different Allied occupation authorities but the divisions ended in 1952.

TERRITORY AND POPULATION

Baden-Württemberg comprises 35,751 sq. km, with a population (at 31 Dec. 1997) of 10,396,610 (5,307,977 females, 5,088,633 males).

The *Land* is divided into 4 administrative regions, 9 urban and 35 rural districts, and numbers 1,111 communes. The capital is Stuttgart.

SOCIAL STATISTICS

Statistics for calendar years:

	Live births	Marriages	Divorces	Deaths
1994	113,398	59,591	19,910	96,638
1995	112,459	58,198	19,921	97,733
1996	114,657	57,898	20,759	98,908
1997	116,419	57,094	21,572	97,167

CONSTITUTION AND GOVERNMENT

The *Land* Baden-Württemberg is a merger of the 3 *Länder*, Baden, Württemberg-Baden and Württemberg-Hohenzollern, which were formed in 1952. The merger was approved by a plebiscite held on 9 Dec. 1951, when 70% of the population voted in its favour. It has 6 votes in the Bundesrat.

RECENT ELECTIONS

At the elections to the 155-member Diet of March 1996, turn-out was 67·6%. The Christian Democrats won 69 seats with 41·3% of the vote, the Social Democrats 39 with 25·1%, the Greens 19 with 12·1%, the Free Democrats 14 with 9·6% and the Republicans 14 with 9·1%.

CURRENT ADMINISTRATION

Erwin Teufel (CDU) is *Prime Minister* (Minister President).

Local Government. Since the creation of the Land in 1952, the CDU has always been the largest party.

ECONOMY

Performance. GDP in 1997 was 523,136m. DM which amounted to 16·2% of Germany's total GDP.

ENERGY AND NATURAL RESOURCES

Electricity. Hydroelectric power is a significant source of electricity in the Land.

Oil and Gas. The amount of oil and gas produced in Baden-Württemberg was insignificant and ceased altogether in Sept. 1997.

Agriculture. Area and yield of the most important crops:

	Area (in 1,000 ha)			Yield (in 1,000 tonnes)		
	1995	1996	1997	1995	1996	1997
Rye	15·5	12·7	11·2	73·0	71·9	60·4
Wheat	214·9	214·7	217·7	1,185·4	1,576·6	1,444·7
Barley	191·1	202·9	211·8	885·7	1,170·0	1,174·1
Oats	55·6	54·8	54·8	254·3	324·5	294·9
Potatoes	9·7	9·7	8·3	274·7	391·7	270·2
Sugar-beet	22·5	22·5	22·0	1,289·8	1,336·2	1,249·1

Livestock in 1,000 (Dec. 1997): Cattle, 1,327·1 (including 465·7 milch cows); pigs, 2,275·8; sheep, 285·3; poultry, 5,490·5 (1996).

INDUSTRY

In 1997, 8,890 establishments (with 20 and more employees) employed 1,225,886 persons; of these, 266,655 were employed in machine construction (excluding office machines, data processing equipment and facilities); 27,486 in the textile industry; 200,813 in electrical engineering; 201,451 in car manufacture.

Labour. Economically active persons totalled 4,769,400 at the 1%-EU-sample survey of April 1997. Of the total 545,700 were self-employed (including family workers). Of 4·22m. employees: 122,600 were engaged in agriculture and forestry; 1,958,600 in power supply, mining, manufacturing and building; 951,700 in commerce and transport; 1,736,600 in other industries and services.

INTERNATIONAL TRADE

Imports and Exports. Total imports (1997): 98,759m. DM. Total exports: 149,664m. DM, of which 70,970m. DM went to the EU.

COMMUNICATIONS

Roads. On 1 Jan. 1998 there were 28,101 km of 'classified' roads, including 1,023 km of Autobahn, 4,972 km of federal roads, 10,030 km of first-class and 12,076 km of second-class highways. Motor vehicles, at 1 Jan. 1998, numbered 6,562,874, including 5,487,322 passenger cars, 9,425 buses, 263,742 trucks, 326,961 tractors and 381,560 motor cycles.

Rail. Railway track operated by Deutsche Bahn AG covered 3,987 km in 1996. In addition, 488 km of track was operated by private railway companies.

Civil Aviation. The largest airport in Baden-Württemberg is at Stuttgart which in 1998 had 6·7m. users. This is expected to rise to over 8m. by 2010. There are another 2 regional airports and 20 airstrips in use in the Land.

Shipping. The harbour in Karlsruhe is the largest in Baden-Württemberg. In 1997 it handled 8·3m. tonnes of freight, compared to 7·9m. tonnes in Mannheim.

SOCIAL INSTITUTIONS

Justice. There are a constitutional court *(Staatsgerichtshof)*, 2 courts of appeal, 17 regional courts, 108 local courts, a *Land* labour court, 9 labour courts, a *Land* social court, 8 social courts, a finance court, a higher administrative court *(Verwaltungsgerichtshof)* and 4 administrative courts.

Religion. On 1 Jan. 1998, 39·0% of the population were Protestants and 43·6% were Roman Catholics.

Education. In 1997–98 there were 2,695 primary schools *(Grund- und Hauptschulen)* with 34,717 teachers and 693,322 pupils; 552 special schools with 9,337 teachers and 50,068 pupils; 452 intermediate schools with 11,512 teachers and 210,949 pupils; 415 high schools with 18,506 teachers and 271,236 pupils; 42 *Freie Waldorf* schools with 1,347 teachers and 19,224 pupils. Other general schools had 584 teachers and 8,507 pupils in total; there were also 739 vocational schools with 364,870 pupils. There were 39 *Fachhochschulen* (colleges of engineering and others) with 57,404 students in winter term 1997–98.

In the winter term 1997–98 there were 9 universities (Freiburg, 20,182 students; Heidelberg, 24,767; Konstanz, 7,953; Tübingen, 21,432; Karlsruhe, 15,868; Stuttgart, 16,770; Hohenheim, 4,745; Mannheim, 10,728; Ulm, 4,802); 6 teacher-training colleges with 17,739 students; 5 colleges of music with 2,680 students and 3 colleges of fine arts with 1,315 students.

CULTURE

National Theatre and Opera. In 1998 the Baden-Baden Festival Hall opened with seating for 2,500 persons.

FURTHER READING

Statistical Information: Statistisches Landesamt Baden-Württemberg (P.O.B. 10 60 33, 70049 Stuttgart) *(President:* Dr Eberhard Leibing), publishes: *'Baden-Württemberg in Wort und Zahl'* (monthly); *Jahrbücher für Statistik und Landeskunde von Baden-Württemberg; Statistik von Baden-Württemberg* (series); *Statistisch-prognostischer Bericht* (latest issue 1998); *Statistisches Taschenbuch* (latest issue 1998).

State libraries: Württembergische Landesbibliothek, Konrad-Adenauer-Str. 8, 70173 Stuttgart. Badische Landesbibliothek Karlsruhe, Lamm-Str. 16, 76133 Karlsruhe.

BAVARIA
Bayern

KEY HISTORICAL EVENTS
Bavaria was ruled by the Wittelsbach family from 1180. The duchy remained Catholic after the Reformation, which made it a natural ally of Austria and the Hapsburg Emperors.

The present boundaries were reached during the Napoleonic wars, and Bavaria became a kingdom in 1805. Despite the granting of a constitution and parliament, radical feeling forced the abdication of King Ludwig I in 1848. Maximilian II was followed by Ludwig II who allied himself with Austria against Prussia in 1866, but was reconciled with Prussia and entered the German Empire in 1871.

In 1918 the King Ludwig III abdicated. The first years of republican government were filled with unrest, attempts at the overthrow of the state by both communist and right-wing groups culminating in an unsuccessful coup by Adolf Hitler in 1923.

The state of Bavaria included the Palatinate from 1214 until 1945, when it was taken from Bavaria and added to the Rhineland. The present *Land* of Bavaria was formed in 1948.

Munich became capital of Bavaria in the reign of Albert IV (1467–1508) and remains capital of the *Land*.

TERRITORY AND POPULATION
Bavaria has an area of 70,548 sq. km. The capital is Munich. There are 7 administrative regions, 25 urban districts, 71 rural districts, 251 unadopted areas and 2,056 communes, 1,004 of which are members of 319 administrative associations. The population (31 Dec. 1997) numbered 12,066,375 (5,884,415 males, 6,181,960 females).

SOCIAL STATISTICS
Statistics for calendar years:

	Live births	*Marriages*	*Divorces*	*Deaths*
1994	127,828	69,401	23,087	121,581
1995	125,995	67,075	23,434	121,992
1996	129,376	66,767	24,259	123,329
1997	130,517	65,419	26,046	121,441

CONSTITUTION AND GOVERNMENT
The Constituent Assembly, elected on 30 June 1946, passed a constitution on the lines of the democratic constitution of 1919, but with greater emphasis on state rights; this was agreed upon by the Christian Social Union (CSU) and the Social Democrats (SPD). Bavaria has 6 seats in the Bundesrat. The CSU replaces the Christian Democratic Party in Bavaria.

RECENT ELECTIONS
At the Diet elections on 13 Sept. 1998 the CSU won 123 seats with 52·9% of votes cast; the SPD, 67 with 28·7%, and Alliance '90/The Greens, 14 with 5·7%. Turnout was 70%.

CURRENT ADMINISTRATION
The *Prime Minister* is Dr Edmund Stoiber (CSU).

Local Government. At the *local government* elections of March 1996 the CSU won 43·1% of votes cast and the SPD 25·7%.

ENERGY AND NATURAL RESOURCES
Agriculture. Area and yield of the most important products:

	Area (in 1,000 ha)			*Yield (in 1,000 tonnes)*		
	1996	*1997*	*1998*	*1996*	*1997*	*1998*
Wheat	446·6	469·1	469·4	3,162·4	3,077·8	3,241·0
Rye	54·0	50·6	58·0	285·4	244·3	319·3

GERMANY

	Area (in 1,000 ha)			Yield (in 1,000 tonnes)		
	1996	1997	1998	1996	1997	1998
Barley	473·4	483·7	460·2	2,511·9	2,575·5	2,574·2
Oats	75·0	76·1	63·6	388·9	385·5	291·6
Potatoes	62·5	55·7	55·1	2,727·2	2,156·4	2,184·7
Sugar-beet	79·0	78·2	79·7	4,804·2	4,601·7	5,024·3

Livestock, 1997: 4,126,000 cattle (including 1,513,000 milch cows); 109,000 horses; 382,000 sheep; 3,651,000 pigs; 9,968,000 poultry.

INDUSTRY
In 1997, 8,013 establishments (with 20 or more employees) employed 1,168,301 persons; of these, 145,483 were employed in the manufacture of motor vehicles, 188,388 in the manufacture of machinery and equipment and 51,970 in the manufacture of textiles and textile products.

Labour. The economically active persons totalled 5,701,000 at the 1% sample survey of the microcensus of 1997. Of the total, 670,000 were self-employed, 119,000 unpaid family workers, 4,913,000 employees; 2,069,000 in power supply, mining, manufacturing and building; 1,277,000 in commerce and transport; 2,134,000 in other industries and services.

COMMUNICATIONS
Roads. There were, on 1 Jan. 1998, 41,671 km of 'classified' roads, including 2,202 km of Autobahn, 6,842 km of federal roads, 13,963 km of first-class and 18,664 km of second-class highways. Number of motor vehicles on 1 Jan. 1998 was 8,177,157, including 6,543,935 passenger cars, 337,384 trucks, 13,935 buses, 588,698 tractors, 577,388 motor cycles.

SOCIAL INSTITUTIONS
Justice. There are a constitutional court *(Verfassungsgerichtshof)*, a supreme *Land* court *(Oberstes Landesgericht)*, 3 courts of appeal, 22 regional courts, 72 local courts, 2 *Land* labour courts, 11 labour courts, a *Land* social court, 7 social courts, 2 finance courts, a higher administrative court *(Verwaltungsgerichtshof)* and 6 administrative courts.

Religion. At the census of 25 May 1987 there were 67·2% Roman Catholics and 23·9% Protestants.

Education. In 1997–98 there were 2,844 primary schools with 47,306 teachers and 858,884 pupils; 374 special schools with 7,322 teachers and 59,680 pupils; 330 intermediate schools with 9,400 teachers and 146,532 pupils; 397 high schools with 21,181 teachers and 305,587 pupils; 236 part-time vocational schools with 7,988 teachers and 283,154 pupils, including 47 special part-time vocational schools with 905 teachers and 12,577 pupils; 604 full-time vocational schools with 4,653 teachers and 61,153 pupils including 268 schools for public health occupations with 1,434 teachers and 18,656 pupils; 373 advanced full-time vocational schools with 2,075 teachers and 24,987 pupils; 118 vocational high schools *(Berufsoberschulen, Fachoberschulen)* with 1,981 teachers and 30,731 pupils.

In 1997–98 there were 11 universities with 177,852 students (Augsburg, 13,154; Bamberg, 7,794; Bayreuth, 7,535; Eichstätt, 4,005; Erlangen-Nürnberg, 22,895; München, 59,804; Passau, 7,532; Regensburg, 15,961; Würzburg, 19,313; the Technical University of München, 17,701; München, University of the Federal Armed Forces *(Universität der Bundeswehr)*, 2,158; plus the college of politics, München, 577; the college of philosophy, München, 383, and 2 philosophical-theological colleges with 268 students in total (Benediktbeuern, 120; Neuendettelsau, 148). There were also 2 colleges of music, 2 colleges of fine arts and 1 college of television and film, with 2,599 students in total; 18 vocational colleges *(Fachhochschulen)* with 56,575 students including one for the civil service *(Bayerische Beamtenfachhochschule)* with 4,003 students.

Welfare. At Dec. 1997 there were 253,000 persons receiving benefits of all kinds.

CULTURE

Tourism. By the end of June 1997 there were 14,152 places of accommodation (with 9 beds or more) providing beds for 549,339 people. In 1997 they received 19,556,751 guests of whom 3,691,548 were foreigners. They stayed an average of 3·4 nights each, totalling 66,752,537 nights (7,551,424 nights stayed by foreign visitors).

Festivals. Oktoberfest, Munich's famous beer festival, takes place each year in late Sept. and early Oct.

National Theatre and Opera. There are 33 theatre companies and opera houses with their own ensembles in Bavaria.

FURTHER READING

Statistical Information: Bayerisches Landesamt für Statistik und Datenverarbeitung, Neuhauser Str. 8, 80331 Munich, was founded in 1833. *President:* Wolfgang Kupfahl. It publishes: *Statistisches Jahrbuch für Bayern.* 1894 ff.—*Bayern in Zahlen.* Monthly (from Jan. 1947).— *Zeitschrift des Bayerischen Statistischen Landesamts.* July 1869–1943; 1948 ff.—*Beiträge zur Statistik Bayerns.* 1850 ff.—*Statistische Berichte.* 1951 ff.—*Kreisdaten.* 1972 ff.— *Gemeindedaten.* 1973 ff.

Nawiasky, H. and Luesser, C., *Die Verfassung des Freistaates Bayern vom 2. Dez. 1946.* Munich, 1948; supplement, by H. Nawiasky and H. Lechner, Munich, 1953

State Library: Bayerische Staatsbibliothek, Munich. *Director:* Dr Hermann Leskin.

BERLIN

KEY HISTORICAL EVENTS

After the end of World War II, Berlin was divided into 4 occupied sectors, each with a military governor from one of the victorious Allied Powers (the USA, the Soviet Union, Britain and France). On 30 Nov. 1948 a seperate municipal government was set up in the Soviet sector which led to the political division of the city. In contravention of the special Allied status agreed for the entire city, East Berlin became 'Capital of the GDR' in 1949 and thus increasingly integrated into the GDR as a whole. In West Berlin, the formal supreme authority of the Western Allies endured until 1990.

On 17 June 1953 the protest by workers in East Berlin against political oppression and economic hardship was supressed by Soviet military forces. To stop refugees, the east German government erected the Berlin Wall to seal off West Berlin's borders on 13 Aug. 1961.

The Berlin Wall unexpectedly collapsed on 9 Nov. 1989 as the regime in the GDR bowed to the internal pressure which had been building for months. East and West Berlin were amalgamated on the re-unification of Germany in Oct. 1990, and Berlin was declared the national capital. With the move of the national government, the parliament (Bundestag), and the federal organ of the Länder (Budesrat) in 1999, Berlin once again fulfils the functions of a capital city.

TERRITORY AND POPULATION

The area is 890·77 sq. km. Population, 31 Dec. 1997, 3,425,759 (51·6% female), including 432,990 foreign nationals; density, 3,846 per sq. km.

SOCIAL STATISTICS

Statistics for calendar years:

	Live births	Marriages	Divorces	Deaths
1994	28,503	17,269	8,108	40,738
1995	28,648	16,383	9,184	39,245
1996	29,905	15,813	9,182	38,099
1997	30,369	15,399	9,782	36,447

GERMANY

CONSTITUTION AND GOVERNMENT
According to the constitutions of Sept. 1950 and Oct. 1995, Berlin is simultaneously a *Land* of the Federal Republic and a city. It is governed by a House of Representatives (of at least 150 members); executive power is vested in a Senate, consisting of the Governing Mayor, the Mayor and not more than 16 senators.

After a proposed merger was rejected by Brandenburg in the 1996 referendum, a Joint Berlin-Brandenburg Co-operation Council was set up.

Berlin has 5 seats in the Bundesrat.

RECENT ELECTIONS
At the elections of 22 Oct. 1995 the Christian Democrats (CDU) won 87 seats in the House of Representatives with 37·4% of votes cast; the Social Democrats (SPD), 55, with 23·6%; the Party of Democratic Socialism (former Communists), 34, with 14·6%; and the Alliance '90/Greens, 30, with 13·2%.

CURRENT ADMINISTRATION
Governing Mayor: Eberhard Diepgen (CDU).

In Jan. 1996 a CPU-SPD coalition government was formed.

INDUSTRY
In 1997 the main industries in terms of percentage of the labour force employed were: Electronics, 28·2%; food and tobacco, 14·0%; machine-building, 11·1%; chemicals, 9·2%; vehicle production, 6·1%; metallurgy, 9·5%; printing, 12·8%.

Labour. In 1997 the workforce was 1,531,300, including 0·24m. craft workers. There were 265,665 persons registered unemployed in 1997 and 5,340 on short time in 1997. 6,714 jobs were available in 1997.

COMMUNICATIONS
Roads. In 1997 there were 252·8 km of roads, made up of 63·6 km of Autobahn and 189·2 km of federal roads. At June 1997, 1,398,734 motor vehicles were registered, including 1,211,348 passenger cars, 86,850 trucks, 2,741 buses, and 72,206 motor cycles. There were 151,588 road accidents in 1997 of which 19,102 involved badly damaged vehicles or injured persons, of whom there were 20,336.

Civil Aviation. 223,880 flights were made from Berlin's 3 airports (Tegel, Tempelhof and Schönefeld) in 1997, carrying a total of 11,564,952 passengers.

SOCIAL INSTITUTIONS
Justice. There are a court of appeal *(Kammergericht)*, a regional court, 9 local courts, a *Land* Labour court, a labour court, a *Land* social court, a social court, a higher administrative court, an administrative court and a finance court.

Religion. In 1997, membership and number of places of worship for major religions was as follows:

Religion	Members	Places of Worship
Protestant	896,353	393
Roman Catholic	344,826	171
Jewish	11,676	6
Moslem	199,259	104

Education. In 1995–96 there were 413,449 pupils attending schools. There were 497 primary schools with 146,622 pupils, 551 post-primary schools with 83,098 pupils, 98 special schools with 13,297 pupils, 87 secondary modern schools with 31,346 pupils, 129 grammar schools with 84,726 pupils and 81 comprehensive schools with 54,360 pupils. In 1994–95 there were 2 universities and 1 technical university, 4 art colleges and 9 technical colleges. There was a total of some 147,000 students in higher education.

FURTHER READING
Statistical Information: The Statistisches Landesamt Berlin was founded in 1862 (Alt-Friedrichsfelde 60, 10315 Berlin (Lichtenberg)). *Director:* Prof. Günther Appel. It publishes:

Statistisches Jahrbuch (from 1867): *Berliner Statistik* (monthly, from 1947).—*100 Jahre Berliner Statistik* (1962).
State Library: Amerika-Gedenkbibliothek-Berliner Zentralbibliothek, Blücherplatz 1, D-10961 Berlin. *Director:* Dr Klaus Bock.

Read, A., and Fisher, D., *Berlin, Biography of a City.* London, 1994
Taylor, R., *Berlin and its Culture.* London, 1997

BRANDENBURG

KEY HISTORICAL EVENTS
For the proposed merger with Berlin *see* BERLIN: Key Historical Events.

TERRITORY AND POPULATION
The area is 29,476 sq. km. Population on 31 Dec. 1997 was 2,573,291 (1,306,095 females). There are 4 urban districts, 14 rural districts and 1,696 communes. The capital is Potsdam.

SOCIAL STATISTICS
Statistics for calendar years:

	Live births	Marriages	Divorces	Deaths
1994	12,443	8,502	3,851	28,490
1995	13,494	8,775	3,949	27,401
1996	15,140	8,756	4,016	27,622
1997	16,370	8,709	5,231	26,756

CONSTITUTION AND GOVERNMENT
The *Land* was reconstituted on former GDR territory on 14 Oct. 1990. Brandenburg has 4 seats in the Bundesrat.

After a proposed merger was rejected by Brandenburg in the 1996 referendum, a Joint Berlin-Brandenburg Co-operation Council was set up.

At a referendum on 14 June 1992, 93·5% of votes cast were in favour of a new constitution guaranteeing direct democracy and the right to work and housing.

RECENT ELECTIONS
At the Diet elections on 11 Sept. 1994 the Social Democrats (SPD) won 52 seats with 54·1% of the vote; the Christian Democrats (CDU), 18, with 18·7%; the Party of Democratic Socialism (PDS, former Communists), 18, with 18·7%.

CURRENT ADMINISTRATION
The *Prime Minister* is Dr Manfred Stolpe (SPD).

Local Government. At the *local government* elections of Sept. 1998 the SPD won 38·97% of votes cast, the PDS 21·62%, the CDU 21·42%, the FDP 4·14% and the Greens, 4·13%.

ECONOMY
Performance. GDP in 1997 was 74,107m. DM.

ENERGY AND NATURAL RESOURCES
Electricity. Power stations in Brandenburg produced 23,851m. kWh in 1997. A minimal amount was produced from hydroelectric power.

Agriculture. Livestock in Dec. 1996: Cattle, 716,436 (including 229,582 milch cows); pigs, 718,415; sheep, 120,617; horses, 21,541; poultry, 6,193,040.
Area and yield of the most important crops:

	Area (in 1,000 ha)			Yield (in 1,000 tonnes)		
	1995	1996	1997	1995	1996	1997
Rye	214·7	220·5	233·4	950·4	883·7	990·0
Wheat	108·0	101·7	109·6	647·5	551·2	578·7

	Area (in 1,000 ha)			Yield (in 1,000 tonnes)		
	1995	1996	1997	1995	1996	1997
Barley	108·4	90·2	102·5	596·4	332·2	484·0
Oats	13·8	18·2	20·0	59·8	76·9	81·6
Potatoes	16·7	17·8	15·4	320·1	542·3	437·9
Sugar-beet	14·7	14·2	12·5	565·3	663·0	515·3

INDUSTRY

In 1997, 1,098 establishments (20 and more employees) employed 95,249 persons; of these, 10,500 were employed in mining and quarrying; 6,815 in machine construction; 12,914 in vehicle construction; 5,202 in chemical industries.

Labour. In April 1997 at the 1%-sample of the microcensus, 1,115,300 persons were economically active, including 88,100 self-employed and family assistants, 456,000 manual and 523,400 white-collar workers, and 47,700 civil servants. In Dec. 1997 there were 456,000 unemployed persons.

INTERNATIONAL TRADE

Imports and Exports. Total imports (1997): 7,723m. DM. Total exports: 5,663m. DM.

COMMUNICATIONS

Roads. In Jan. 1998 there were 1,480,755 registered vehicles including 1,271,356 passenger cars.

SOCIAL INSTITUTIONS

Education. In 1997–98 there were 1,168 schools providing general education (including special schools) with 397,983 pupils, and 43 vocational schools with 74,902 pupils.

In the winter term 1997–98 there were 3 universities and 8 colleges with 25,351 students.

CULTURE

Tourism. In 1997 there were 1,282 places of accommodation (with 9 or more beds), including 449 hotels, providing a total of 67,373 beds. 2,415,306 visitors spent a total of 7,312,522 nights in Brandenburg in 1997.

Libraries. In 1997 there were 279 public libraries with 322,244 active users who borrowed 11,179,020 items.

National Theatre and Opera. There were 34 theatres in 1996 which put on 2,377 performances for audiences totalling 432,418 persons.

BREMEN

Freie Hansestadt Bremen

KEY HISTORICAL EVENTS

The state is dominated by the Free City of Bremen and its port, Bremerhaven. In 1815, when it joined the German Confederation, Bremen was an autonomous city and Hanse port with important Baltic trade. In 1827 the expansion of trade inspired the founding of Bremerhaven on land ceded by Hanover at the confluence of the Geest and Weser rivers. Further expansion followed the founding of the Norddeutscher Lloyd Shipping Company in 1857. Merchant shipping, associated trade and fishing were dominant until 1940 but there was diversification in the post-war years. In 1939 Bremerhaven was absorbed by the Hanoverian town of Wesermünde. The combined port was returned to the jurisdiction of Bremen in 1947.

TERRITORY AND POPULATION
The area of the *Land*, consisting of the 2 urban districts and ports of Bremen and Bremerhaven, is 404 sq. km. Population, 31 Dec. 1996, 677,800 (326,600 males, 351,100 females).

SOCIAL STATISTICS
Statistics for calendar years:

	Live births	Marriages	Divorces	Deaths
1993	6,656	3,969	1,736	8,643
1994	6,288	3,859	1,614	8,123
1995	6,429	3,561	1,799	8,378
1996	6,623	3,509	1,870	8,080

CONSTITUTION AND GOVERNMENT
Political power is vested in the 100-member House of Burgesses *(Bürgerschaft)* which appoints the executive, called the Senate. Bremen has 3 seats in the Bundesrat. At the elections of 14 May 1995 the Social Democratic Party won 37 seats with 33·4% of votes cast (41 with 38·8% in 1991); the Christian Democrats, 37 with 32·6% (32 with 30·7%); the Alliance '90/Greens, 14 with 13·1% (11 with 11·4%) and the AFB, 12 with 10·7%. The Free Democrats gained no seats with 3·4% (10 with 9·5%). The Senate president is Dr Henning Scherf (Social Democrat).

ENERGY AND NATURAL RESOURCES
Agriculture. Agricultural area comprised (1995) 9,400 ha. Livestock (2 Dec. 1996): 12,758 cattle (including 3,746 milch cows); 2,026 pigs; 253 sheep; 1,208 horses; 17,481 poultry.

INDUSTRY
In 1996, 338 establishments (20 and more employees) employed 67,164 persons; of these, 4,241 were employed in shipbuilding (except naval engineering); 5,528 in machine construction; 8,351 in electrical engineering; 1,591 in coffee and tea processing.

Labour. The economically active persons totalled 279,700 at the microcensus of April 1996. Of the total, 25,800 were self-employed, 253,900 employees; 83,200 in production industries, 77,100 in commerce, trade and communications, 117,100 in other industries and services.

COMMUNICATIONS
Roads. On 1 Jan. 1996 there were 112 km of 'classified' roads, including 48 km of Autobahn and 64 km of federal roads. Registered motor vehicles on 1 July 1997 numbered 331,139, including 290,940 passenger cars, 15,800 trucks, 2,766 tractors, 603 buses and 16,074 motor cycles.

Shipping. Vessels entered in 1996, 8,330 of 43,638,905 net tons; cleared, 8,365 of 43,931,175 net tons. Sea traffic, 1996, incoming 19,140,000 tonnes; outgoing, 12,360,000 tonnes.

SOCIAL INSTITUTIONS
Justice. There are a constitutional court *(Staatsgerichtshof)*, a court of appeal, a regional court, 3 local courts, a *Land* labour court, 2 labour courts, a *Land* social court, a finance court, a higher administrative court and an administrative court.

Religion. On 25 May 1987 (census) there were 61% Protestants and 10% Roman Catholics.

Education. In 1996 there were 390 new system schools with 5,026 teachers and 70,521 pupils; 27 special schools with 591 teachers and 2,698 pupils; 26 part-time vocational schools with 17,792 pupils; 25 full-time vocational schools with 4,638 pupils; 8 advanced vocational schools (including institutions for the training of technicians) with 890 pupils; 10 schools for public health occupations with 856 pupils.

In the winter term 1996–97, 17,078 students were enrolled at the university. In addition to the university there were 4 other colleges in 1996–97 with 8,817 students.

FURTHER READING

Statistical Information: Statistisches Landesamt Bremen (An der Weide 14–16, P.B. 101309, D-28195 Bremen), founded in 1850. *Director:* Reg. Dir. Jürgen Dinse. Its current publications include: *Statistisches Jahrbuch Bremen* (from 1992).—*Statistische Mitteilungen* (from 1948).—*Statistische Monatsberichte* (from 1954).—*Statistische Berichte* (from 1956).—*Statistisches Handbuch Bremen (1950–60*, 1961; *1960–64*, 1967; *1965–69*, 1971; *1970–74*, 1975; *1975–80*, 1982; *1981–85*, 1987).—*Bremen im statistischen Zeitvergleich 1950–1976.* 1977.—*Bremen in Zahlen.* 1997.

State and University Library: Bibliotheksstr., D-28359 Bremen. *Director:* Annette Rath-Beckmann.

HAMBURG

Freie und Hansestadt Hamburg

KEY HISTORICAL EVENTS

Hamburg was a free Hanse town owing nominal allegiance to the Holy Roman Emperor until 1806. In 1815 it became part of the German Confederation, sharing a seat in the Federal Diet with Lübeck, Bremen and Frankfurt. During the Empire it retained its autonomy. By 1938 it had become the third largest port in the world and its territory was extended by the cession of land (3 urban and 27 rural districts) from Prussia. In 1945 Hamburg became a *Land* of the Federal Republic with its 1938 boundaries.

TERRITORY AND POPULATION

Total area, 755·3 sq. km (1997), including the islands Neuwerk and Scharhörn (7·6 sq. km). Population (1 Jan. 1998), 1,704,700 (823,200 males, 881,500 females). The *Land* forms a single urban district (*kreisfreie Stadt*) with 7 administrative subdivisions.

SOCIAL STATISTICS

Statistics for calendar years:

	Live births	Marriages	Divorces	Deaths
1994	16,201	8,537	4,545	20,241
1995	15,872	8,242	4,652	20,276
1996	16,594	7,886	4,306	20,196
1997	16,970	7,800	5,092	19,328

CONSTITUTION AND GOVERNMENT

The constitution of 6 June 1952 vests the supreme power in the House of Burgesses (*Bürgerschaft*) of 121 members. The executive is in the hands of the Senate, whose members are elected by the Bürgerschaft. Hamburg has 3 seats in the Bundesrat.

RECENT ELECTIONS

The elections of 21 Sept. 1997 had the following results: Social Democrats, 54 seats with 36·2% of votes cast; Christian Democrats, 46 with 30·7%; Green Alternatives 21, with 13·9%. The First Burgomaster is Ortwin Runde (Social Democrat).

ENERGY AND NATURAL RESOURCES

Agriculture. The agricultural area comprised 13,390 ha in 1997. Yield, 1997, in tonnes, of cereals, 16,700; potatoes, 700.

Livestock (3 Dec. 1996): Cattle, 8,715 (including 1,537 milch cows); pigs, 3,289; horses, 2,847; sheep, 1,634; poultry, 11,764.

INDUSTRY
In June 1997, 624 establishments (with 20 and more employees) employed 107,509 persons; of these, 20,766 were employed in manufacturing transport equipment (including motor vehicles, aircraft and ships), 17,136 in manufacturing machinery, 15,218 in manufacturing electrical and optical equipment, 7,889 in manufacturing chemical products and 6,763 in mineral oil industry.

Labour. The economically active persons totalled 766,300 at the 1%-sample survey of the microcensus of April 1997. Of the total, 92,800 were self-employed or unpaid family workers, and 673,500 were employees; 7,800 were engaged in agriculture and forestry, 169,100 in power supply, mining, manufacturing and building, 224,000 in commerce and transport, 365,400 in other industries and services.

COMMUNICATIONS

Roads. In April 1997 there were 4,369 km of roads, including 82 km of Autobahn, 149 km of federal roads. Number of motor vehicles (1 July 1997), 812,652, including 714,446 passenger cars, 42,687 trucks, 1,446 buses, 5,598 tractors, 34,771 motor cycles and 13,704 other motor vehicles.

Shipping. Hamburg is the largest sea port in Germany.

Vessels	1995	1996	1997
Entered: Number	11,679	11,489	11,749
Tonnage	58,640,110	61,181,978	62,806,340
Cleared: Number	11,798	11,635	11,895
Tonnage	58,898,385	61,045,871	62,617,624

SOCIAL INSTITUTIONS

Justice. There is a constitutional court *(Verfassungsgericht)*, a court of appeal *(Oberlandesgericht)*, a regional court *(Landgericht)*, 6 local courts *(Amtsgerichte)*, a *Land* labour court, a labour court, a *Land* social court, a social court, a finance court, a higher administrative court and an administrative court.

Religion. In 1997, 37·3% of the population went to the Evangelical Church and Free Churches, whilst 10·3% were Roman Catholic.

Education. In 1997 there were 433 schools of general education (not including *Internationale Schule*) with 13,662 teachers and 175,687 pupils; 54 special schools with 7,536 pupils; 43 part-time vocational schools with 33,484 pupils; 42 schools with 3,776 pupils in manual instruction classes; 42 full-time vocational schools with 9,101 pupils; 10 economic secondary schools with 1,842 pupils; 2 technical *Gymnasien* with 357 pupils; 19 advanced vocational schools with 4,235 pupils; 36 schools for public health occupations with 2,508 pupils; 1 vocational introducing school with 54 pupils and 18 technical superior schools with 1,478 pupils; all these vocational and technical schools had a total number of 3,218 teachers.

In the winter term 1997–98 there was 1 university with 41,228 students; 1 technical university with 3,939 students; 1 college of music and 1 college of fine arts with 2,105 students in total; 1 university of the *Bundeswehr* with 1,690 students; 1 university of economics and political sciences with 2,563 students; 3 professional colleges with a total of 14,737 students.

CULTURE
Broadcasting. In the autumn of 1997 there was 1 public broadcasting service as well as 9 private broadcasters.

Cinema. In Dec. 1997 there were 81 cinemas (including 1 drive-in) with a total of 19,327 seats. There were 5,024,360 tickets sold in 1997.

Tourism. At Dec. 1997 there were 249 places of accommodation with 26,067 beds. Of the 2,431,047 visitors in 1997, 20·8% were foreigners.

Libraries. In 1997 there were 123 branches of the Hamburg Public Library which held 1,740,605 books and other forms of media. 9,369,491 items were borrowed in 1997. The city and university library held 2,859,397 books, and lent 939,467 items.

GERMANY

National Theatre and Opera. In the 1996–97 season the 3 national theatre and opera houses put on 1,154 performances, attracting 878,467 visitors. The 2 largest stages in Hamburg, the Neue Flora and Operettenhaus, are both private. The former put on 830 performances during 1996–97 for a total audience of 720,000, whilst Operettenhaus had 412 performances for 440,000 persons.

Museums and Galleries. The 7 national museums were visited by 1,496,199 people in 1997. There are a further 40 or so private and public museums and about 100 art galleries in Hamburg as well as a Planetarium, which received 127,338 visits in 1997.

FURTHER READING

Statistical Information: The Statistisches Landesamt der Freien und Hansestadt Hamburg (Steckelhörn 12, D-20457 Hamburg) publishes: *Hamburg in Zahlen, Statistische Berichte, Statistisches Taschenbuch, Statistik des Hamburgischen Staates, Hamburger Statistische Porträts.*

Hamburgische Gesellschaft für Wirtschaftsförderung mbH, *Hamburg.* Oldenburg, 1993
Klessmann, E., *Geschichte der Stadt Hamburg.* 7th ed. Hamburg, 1994
Kopitzsch, F./ Tilgner, D., *Hamburg Lexicon.* Hamburg, 1998
Möller, I., *Hamburg-Länderprofile.* Hamburg, 1985
Schubert, D. and Harms, H., *Wohnen am Hafen.* Hamburg, 1993
Schütt, E. C., *Die Chronik Hamburgs.* Hamburg, 1991

State Library: Staats- und Universitätsbibliothek, Carl von Ossietzky, Von-Melle-Park 3, D-20146 Hamburg. *Director:* Prof. Dr Horst Gronemeyer.

HESSEN

KEY HISTORICAL EVENTS

The *Land* consists of the former states of Hesse-Darmstadt and Hesse-Kassel, and Nassau. Hesse-Darmstadt was ruled by the Landgrave Louis X from 1790. He became grand duke in 1806 with absolute power, having dismissed the parliament in 1803. However, he granted a constitution and bicameral parliament in 1820. Hesse-Darmstadt lost land to Prussia in the Seven Weeks' War of 1866, but retained its independence, both then and as a state of the German Empire after 1871. In 1918 the grand duke abdicated and the territory became a state of the German Republic. In 1945 areas west of the Rhine were incorporated into the new *Land* of Rhineland-Palatinate, areas east of the Rhine became part of the *Land* of Greater Hesse.

Hesse-Kassel was ruled by the Landgrave William IX from 1785 until he became Elector in 1805. In 1807 the Electorate was absorbed into the Kingdom of Westphalia (a Napoleonic creation), becoming independent again in 1815 as a state of the German Confederation. In 1831 a constitution and parliament were granted but the Electors remained strongly conservative.

In 1866 the Diet approved alliance with Prussia against Austria; the Elector nevertheless supported Austria. He was defeated by the Prussians and exiled and Hesse-Kassel was annexed to Prussia. In 1867 it was combined with Frankfurt and some areas taken from Nassau and Hesse-Darmstadt to form a Prussian province (Hesse-Nassau). In 1801 Nassau west of the Rhine passed to France; Napoleon also took the northern state in 1806. The remnant of the southern states allied in 1803 and three years later they became a duchy. In 1866 the duke supported Austria against Prussia and the duchy was annexed by Prussia as a result. In 1944 the Prussian province of Hesse-Nassau was split in two: Nassau and Electoral Hesse, also called Kurhessen. The following year these were combined with Hesse-Darmstadt as the *Land* of Greater Hesse which became known as Hessen.

TERRITORY AND POPULATION

Area, 21,115 sq. km. Its capital is Wiesbaden. There are 3 administrative regions with 5 urban and 21 rural districts and 426 communes. Population, 31 Dec 1997, was 6,031,705 (2,951,639 males, 3,080,066 females).

SOCIAL STATISTICS
Statistics for calendar years:

	Live births	Marriages	Divorces	Deaths
1994	60,565	35,215	13,697	63,385
1995	59,858	34,517	13,387	63,346
1996	62,391	33,251	13,677	63,387
1997	63,124	32,877	14,830	61,361

CONSTITUTION AND GOVERNMENT
The constitution was put into force by popular referendum on 1 Dec. 1946. Hessen has 5 seats in the Bundesrat.

RECENT ELECTIONS
At the Diet elections on 7 Feb. 1999 the Christian Democrats gained 43·4% of votes cast, the Social Democrats 39·4%, the Greens 7·2% and the Free Democrats 5·1%.

CURRENT ADMINISTRATION
The Social Democrat/Green cabinet is headed by *Prime Minister* Hans Eichel (SPD).

ECONOMY
Performance. The gross domestic product at market prices (GDP) increased by 2·8% at constant prices of 1991 in comparison with the previous year. The total amount was 313·8bn. DM in 1997. The GDP per person engaged in labour productivity was 122,902 DM in 1997 (117,101 DM in 1996).

ENERGY AND NATURAL RESOURCES
Electricity. Electricity production in 1997 was 27,813m. kWh (gross) and 25,156m. kWh (net). Total electricity consumption in 1997 was 31,832m. kWh.

Oil and Gas. Gas consumption in 1997 was 66,270m. kWh. All gas was imported from other parts of Germany.

Water. Public water production in 1995 totalled 600,050,000 cu. metres.

Agriculture. Area and yield of the most important crops:

	Area (in 1,000 ha)			Yield (in 1,000 tonnes)		
	1996	1997	1998	1996	1997	1998
Wheat	140·2	144·9	145·6	1,055·9	1,051·9	1,058·7
Rye	23·7	21·8	25·0	138·7	132·4	146·0
Barley	110·4	116·8	110·1	653·7	684·4	627·4
Oats	25·8	26·1	22·6	150·8	128·1	105·6
Potatoes	6·1	5·7	5·5	245·1	207·9	187·4
Sugar-beet	20·7	20·5	20·7	1,117·4	1,023·7	1,135·8
Rape	48·5	46·6	49·0	96·2	129·7	154·9

Livestock, Dec. 1997: Cattle, 575,153 (including 176,591 milch cows); pigs, 883,541; sheep, 157,799; horses, 46,018 (Dec. 1996); poultry, 2·19m (Dec. 1996).

INDUSTRY
In Sept. 1998, 3,242 establishments (with 20 and more employees) employed 472,469 persons; of these, 67,045 were employed in chemical industry; 64,705 in machine construction; 61,264 in car building; 41,186 in production of metal products.

Labour. The economically active persons totalled 2·7m. at the 1% sample survey of the microcensus of April 1996. Of the total, 276,200 were self-employed, 29,600 unpaid family workers, 2,383,400 employees; 52,900 were engaged in agriculture and forestry, 864,600 in power supply, mining, manufacturing and building, 651,300 in commerce, transport, hotels and restaurants, 1,120,300 in other services.

COMMUNICATIONS
Roads. On 1 Jan. 1998 there were 16,312 km of 'classified' roads, comprising 950 km of Autobahn, 3,111 km of federal highways, 7,181 km of first-class highways and 5,070 km of second-class highways. Motor vehicles licensed on 1 July 1998

totalled 3,894,154, including 3,307,901 passenger cars, 5,975 buses, 160,674 trucks, 135,410 tractors and 203,475 motor cycles.

Civil Aviation. Frankfurt/Main Airport is one of the most important freight airports in the world. In 1997, 392,141 aeroplanes took off and landed, carrying 40,721,919 passengers, 1,400,978 tonnes of air freight and 144,328 tonnes of air mail.

Shipping. Frankfurt/Main Harbour and Hanau Harbour are the two most important harbours. In 1997, 12·8m. tonnes of goods were imported into the Land and 2·6m. tonnes were exported.

SOCIAL INSTITUTIONS

Justice. There are a constitutional court *(Staatsgerichtshof)*, a court of appeal, 9 regional courts, 58 local courts, a *Land* labour court, 12 labour courts, a *Land* social court, 7 social courts, a finance court, a higher administrative court *(Verwaltungsgerichtshof)* and 5 administrative courts.

Religion. In 1987 (census) there were 52·7% Protestants and 30·4% Roman Catholics.

Education. In 1997 there were 1,237 primary schools with 298,859 pupils (including *Förderstufen*); 155 intermediate schools with 49,984 pupils; 18,856 teachers in primary and intermediate schools; 228 special schools with 3,202 teachers and 20,505 pupils; 160 high schools with 8,892 teachers and 131,330 pupils; 216 *Gesamtschulen* (comprehensive schools) with 11,578 teachers and 182,490 pupils; 118 part-time vocational schools with 127,491 pupils; 259 full-time vocational schools with 40,913 pupils; 108 advanced vocational schools with 10,257 pupils; 7,771 teachers in the vocational schools.

In the winter term 1997–98 there were 3 universities (Frankfurt/Main, 35,366 students; Giessen, 20,939; Marburg/Lahn, 17,351); 1 technical university in Darmstadt (15,458); 1 private *Wissenschaftliche Hochschule,* (779); 1 *Gesamthochschule* (17,708); 16 *Fachhochschulen* (41,400); 2 Roman Catholic theological colleges and 1 Protestant theological college with a total of 375; 1 college of music and 2 colleges of fine arts with 1,276 students in total.

CULTURE

Cinema. In 1996 there were 263 cinemas with 48,433 seats in total.

Press. In 1996 there were 86 newspapers published in Hessen with a combined circulation of 2,120,500.

Tourism. In 1997, 8·5m. visitors stayed 22·8m. nights in Hessen.

Libraries. In 1995 there were 1,018 public libraries which lent out 11,267,611 books. There were also 9 academic and scientific libraries.

FURTHER READING
Statistical Information: The Hessisches Statistisches Landesamt (Rheinstr. 35–37, D-65175 Wiesbaden). *President:* Eckart Hohmann. Main publications: *Statistisches Handbuch für das Land Hessen* (zweijährlich).—*Staat und Wirtschaft in Hessen* (monthly).—*Beiträge zur Statistik Hessens.—Statistische Berichte.—Hessische Gemeindestatistik* (annual, 1980 ff.).

State Library: Hessische Landesbibliothek, Rheinstr. 55–57, D-65185 Wiesbaden. *Director:* Dr Dieter Wolf.

LOWER SAXONY

Niedersachsen

KEY HISTORICAL EVENTS
The *Land* consists of the former state of Hanover with Oldenburg, Schaumburg-Lippe and Brunswick. It does not include the cities of Bremen or Bremerhaven.

Oldenburg, Danish from 1667, passed to the bishopric of Lübeck in 1773; the Holy Roman Emperor made it a duchy in 1777. As a small state of the

Confederation after 1815 it supported Prussia, becoming a member of the Prussian Zollverein (1853) and North German Confederation (1867). The grand duke abdicated in 1918 and was replaced by an elected government.

Schaumburg-Lippe was a small sovereign principality. As such it became a member of the Confederation of the Rhine in 1807 and of the German Confederation in 1815. Surrounded by Prussian territory, it also joined the Prussian-led North German Confederation in 1866. Part of the Empire until 1918, it then became a state of the new republic.

Brunswick, a small duchy, was taken into the Kingdom of Westphalia by Napoleon in 1806 but restored to independence in 1814. In 1830 the duke, Charles II, was forced into exile and replaced in 1831 by his more liberal brother, William. The succession passed to a Hanoverian claimant in 913 but the duchy ended in 1918 with the Empire.

As a state of the republican Germany, Brunswick was greatly reduced under the Third Reich. Its boundaries were restored by the British occupation forces in 1945.

Hanover was an autonomous Electorate of the Holy Roman Empire whose rulers were also kings of Great Britain from 1714 to 1837. From 1762 they ruled almost entirely from England. After Napoleonic invasions Hanover was restored in 1815. A constitution of 1819 made no radical change and had to be followed by more liberal versions in 1833 and 1848.

Prussia annexed Hanover, despite its proclaimed neutrality, in 1866; it remained a Prussian province until 1946.

On 1 Nov. 1946 all four states were combined by the British military administration to form the *Land* of Lower Saxony.

TERRITORY AND POPULATION

Lower Saxony has an area of 47,613 sq. km, and is divided into 4 administrative regions, 9 urban districts, 38 rural districts and 1,030 communes; capital, Hanover.

Estimated population, on 31 Dec. 1997, was 7,845,398 (3,831,467 males, 4,013,931 females).

SOCIAL STATISTICS

Statistics for calendar years:

	Live births	Marriages	Divorces	Deaths
1994	81,520	47,349	15,342	85,700
1995	80,994	46,267	15,588	86,827
1996	83,655	46,669	16,761	85,574
1997	85,907	46,490	17,334	83,958

CONSTITUTION AND GOVERNMENT

The *Land* Niedersachsen was formed on 1 Nov. 1946 by merging the former Prussian province of Hanover and the *Länder* Brunswick, Oldenburg and Schaumburg-Lippe. Lower Saxony has 7 seats in the Bundesrat.

RECENT ELECTIONS

At the Diet elections on 1 March 1998 the Social Democratic Party received 47·9% of the votes cast to secure an absolute majority, gaining 83 seats, the Christian Democratic Union 35·9% and the Greens 7·0%.

CURRENT ADMINISTRATION

The cabinet of the Social Democratic Party is headed by *Prime Minister* Gerhard Glogowski (SPD).

ECONOMY

Banking and Finance. 361 credit institutions were operating in 1997. Deposits totalled 99,611m. DM.

ENERGY AND NATURAL RESOURCES

Electricity. Electricity production in 1995 was 54,570m. kWh. Consumption in 1997 was 44,983·7m. kWh.

Agriculture. Area and yield of the most important crops:

	Area (in 1,000 ha)			Yield (in 1,000 tonnes)		
	1995	1996	1997	1995	1996	1997
Wheat	318	336	368	2,537	2,678	3,067
Rye	160	157	168	923	936	1,028
Barley	302	326	330	1,779	1,794	1,985
Oats	38	34	34	174	185	166
Potatoes	125	136	130	4,386	5,230	5,334
Sugar-beet	132	134	130	6,523	6,576	6,575

Livestock, 3 Nov. 1998: Cattle, 2,880,375 (including 802,245 milch cows); pigs, 7,529,489; sheep, 226,237 (1996); horses, 113,479 (1996); poultry, 47,717,770 (1996).

Fisheries. In 1997 the yield of sea and coastal fishing was 31,433·9 tonnes valued at 71·5m. DM.

INDUSTRY
In Sept. 1997, 3,824 establishments employed 545,344 persons; of these 51,544 were employed in machine construction; 55,285 in electrical engineering.

Labour. The economically active persons totalled 3,358,400 in April 1997. Of the total, 330,900 were self-employed, 38,800 unpaid family workers, 2,988,600 employees; 146,300 were engaged in agriculture and forestry, 1,067,100 in power supply, mining, manufacturing and building, 806,700 in commerce and transport, 1,338,300 in other industries and services.

COMMUNICATIONS

Roads. At 1 Jan. 1997 there were 28,278 km of 'classified' roads, including 1,334 km of Autobahn, 4,862 km of federal roads, 8,353 km of first-class and 13,729 km of second-class highways. Number of motor vehicles, 1 Jan. 1998, was 4,906,363 including 4,105,802 passenger cars, 214,630 trucks, 8,286 buses, 233,250 tractors, 277,375 motor cycles.

Rail. In 1997, 25·2m. tonnes of freight came into the Land by rail and 20·3m. tonnes left by rail.

Civil Aviation. 76,500 planes landed at Hanover Airport in 1997, which saw 2,292,853 passenger arrivals and 1,804,374 departures. 4,419 tonnes of freight left by air and 4,781 tonnes came in.

SOCIAL INSTITUTIONS

Justice. There are a constitutional court (*Staatsgerichtshof*), 3 courts of appeal, 11 regional courts, 79 local courts, a *Land* labour court, 15 labour courts, a *Land* social court, 8 social courts, a finance court, a higher administrative court and 4 administrative courts.

Religion. On 25 May 1987 (census) there were 66·12% Protestants and 19·6% Roman Catholics.

Education. In 1997–98 there were 1,875 primary schools with 362,397 pupils; 964 post-primary schools with 224,743 pupils; 289 special schools with 33,307 pupils; 409 secondary modern schools with 106,992 pupils; 234 grammar schools with 144,619 pupils; 30 comprehensive schools with 23,378 pupils. In 1993 there were 1,801 vocational training institutes (full and part-time) with 256,917 pupils and 213 public health schools with 11,952 pupils.

In the winter term 1997–98 there were 6 universities (Göttingen, 27,193 students; Hanover, 31,281; Oldenburg, 11,843; Osnabrück, 12,269; Hildesheim, 3,524; Lüneburg, 6,678); 2 technical universities (Braunschweig, 14,453; Clausthal, 2,810); the medical college of Hanover (3,423); the veterinary college in Hanover (1,822).

Health. At Dec. 1996 there were 23,334 doctors and 211 hospitals with 6·6 beds per 1,000 population.

CULTURE

Broadcasting. Norddeutscher Rundfunk is the public broadcasting service for Lower Saxony.

Tourism. In 1997, 8,832,000 guests spent 31,960,000 nights in Lower Saxony.

Libraries. In 1996 there were 1,269 public libraries and 98 academic libraries.

Museums and Galleries. 6,859,000 people visited 431 museums in 1996.

FURTHER READING

Statistical Information: The Niedersächsisches Landesamt für Statistik, Postfach 4460, D-30044 Hanover. *Head of Division:* President Karl-Ludwig Strelen. Main publications are: *Statistisches Jahrbuch Niedersachsen* (from 1950).—*Statistische Monatshefte Niedersachsen* (from 1947).—*Statistiche Berichte Niedersachsen.*—*Statistisches Taschenbuch Niedersachsen 1998* Biennial.

State Libraries: Niedersächsische Staats- und Universitätsbibliothek, Prinzenstr. 1, D-37073 Göttingen. *Director:* Helmut Vogt; Niedersächsische Landesbibliothek, Waterloostr. 8, D-30169 Hanover. *Director:* Dr W. Dittrich.

MECKLENBURG-WEST POMERANIA

Mecklenburg-Vorpommern

TERRITORY AND POPULATION

The area is 23,170 sq. km. It is divided into 6 urban districts, 12 rural districts and 1,073 communes. Population on 31 Dec. 1997 was 1,807,799 (916,702 females). The capital is Schwerin.

SOCIAL STATISTICS

Statistics for calendar years:

	Live births	Marriages	Divorces	Deaths
1994	8,934	5,626	2,540	19,835
1995	9,878	6,113	3,128	19,290
1996	11,088	6,490	3,595	18,642
1997	12,046	6,299	3,815	17,940

CONSTITUTION AND GOVERNMENT

The *Land* was reconstituted on former GDR territory in 1990. It has 3 seats in the Bundesrat.

RECENT ELECTIONS

At the Diet elections of Sept. 1998, the Christian Democrats (CDU) won 24 seats with 30·2% of the vote; the Social Democrats (SPD), 27, with 34·3%; and the Party of Democratic Socialism (PDS, former Communists), 20, with 24·4%.

CURRENT ADMINISTRATION

The *Prime Minister* is Dr. Harald Ringstorff (SPD).

ENERGY AND NATURAL RESOURCES

Agriculture. Area and yield of the most important crops:

	Area (in 1,000 ha)			Yield (in 1,000 tonnes)		
	1995	1996	1997	1995	1996	1997
Wheat	238·3	236·2	243·2	1,619·1	1,487·5	1,798·2
Rye	100·5	93·8	104·8	544·5	491·8	593·6
Barley	147·8	156·0	158·5	964·6	730·3	1,091·7
Oats	15·5	14·7	16·1	74·8	75·6	85·4
Potatoes	18·3	19·3	16·8	520·9	599·5	507·4
Sugar-beet	34·4	34·7	33·7	1,428·1	1,510·5	1,515·0

Livestock in 1997: Cattle, 611,473 (including 226,013 milch cows); pigs, 601,104; sheep, 70,442; horses, 19,030 (1996); poultry, 7,304,150 (1996).

Fisheries. Sea catch, 1997: 17,891 tonnes (768 tonnes frozen, 17,123 tonnes fresh). Freshwater catch, 1997: 839·5 tonnes (mainly carp, trout and eels). Fish farming, 1997: 457·0 tonnes.

INDUSTRY
In 1997 there were 529 enterprises (with 20 or more employees) employing 45,107 persons.

Labour. 776,600 persons (342,600 females) were employed at the 1%-sample survey of the microcensus of April 1997, including 57,100 self-employed and family assistants, 324,200 manual and 362,500 white-collar workers. 32,900 persons were employed as officials. Employment by sector: Manufacturing and mining, 79,900; agriculture, forestry and fisheries, 49,900; trade and guest business, 134,400; transport and communications, 44,900; construction, 141,100; energy and water resources, 7,600; public administration, 106,000; other services, 212,900.

COMMUNICATIONS

Roads. There were (March 1998) 9,732 km of 'classified' roads, including 262 km of Autobahn, 2,073 km of federal roads, 3,226 km of first-class and 4,171 km of second-class highways. Number of motor vehicles, 1 Jan. 1998, 969,757, including 833,968 passenger cars, 68,888 trucks, 2,019 buses and 28,373 motor cycles.

Shipping. There is a lake district of some 660 lakes. The ports of Rostock, Stralsund and Wismar are important for ship-building and repairs. In 1997 the cargo fleet consisted of 75 vessels (including 2 tankers) of 625,000 GT. Sea traffic, 1997, incoming 13,322,938 tonnes; outgoing 10,280,269 tonnes.

SOCIAL INSTITUTIONS

Justice. There is a court of appeal (*Oberlandesgericht*), 4 regional courts (*Landgerichte*), 31 local courts (*Amtsgerichte*), a *Land* labour court, 4 labour courts, a *Land* social court, 4 social courts, a finance court, a higher administrative court and 2 administrative courts.

Religion. In 1997 the Evangelical Lutheran Church of Mecklenburg had 244,000 adherents, 278 pastors and 342 parishes. Roman Catholics numbered 72,100, with 68 priests and 74 parishes. The Pomeranian Evangelical Church had 138,200 adherents, 167 pastors and 250 parishes in 1997.

Education. In 1997 there were 330 primary schools, 22 comprehensives, 477 secondary schools and 99 special needs schools. There are universities at Rostock and Greifswald with (in 1997–98) 15,492 students and 4,252 academic staff, and 5 institutions of equivalent status with 7,171 students and 1,601 academic staff.

CULTURE

Cinema. 3·4m. cinema goers visited 88 cinemas in 1997.

Tourism. In July 1997 there were 1,868 places of accommodation (with 9 or more beds) providing a total of 107,501 beds. 3,078,170 guests stayed an average of 3·8 nights each.

Libraries. In 1996 there were 237 public libraries with 261,244 active users, who borrowed around 8m. items.

Museums and Galleries. More than 2·5m. visitors saw 283 exhibitions in 114 museums in 1996.

FURTHER READING
Statistical Office: Statistisches Landesamt Mecklenburg-Vorpommern, Postfach 020135, D-19018 Schwerin. Main publications are: *Statistische Monatshefte Mecklenburg-Vorpommern* (since 1991); *Statistische Berichte* (since 1991; various); *Statistisches Jahrbuch Mecklenburg-Vorpommern* (since 1991); *Statistische Sonderhefte* (since 1992; various).

NORTH RHINE-WESTPHALIA

Nordrhein-Westfalen

KEY HISTORICAL EVENTS

Historical Westphalia consisted of many small political units, most of them absorbed by Prussia and Hanover before 1800. In 1807 Napoleon created a Kingdom of Westphalia for his brother Joseph. This included Hesse-Kassel, but was formed mainly from the Prussian and Hanoverian lands between the rivers Elbe and Weser.

In 1815 the kingdom ended with Napoleon's defeat. Most of the area was given to Prussia, with the small principalities of Lippe and Waldeck surviving as independent states. Both joined the North German Confederation in 1867. Lippe remained autonomous after the end of the Empire in 1918; Waldeck was absorbed into Prussia in 1929.

In 1946 the occupying forces combined Lippe with most of the Prussian province of Westphalia to form the *Land* of North Rhine-Westphalia. On 1 March 1947 the allied Control Council formally abolished Prussia.

TERRITORY AND POPULATION

The *Land* comprises 34,079 sq. km. It is divided into 5 administrative regions, 23 urban districts, 31 rural districts and 396 communes. Capital: Düsseldorf. Population, 31 Dec. 1997, 17,974,487 (8,729,381 males, 9,245,106 females).

SOCIAL STATISTICS

Statistics for calendar years:

	Live births	Marriages	Divorces	Deaths
1994	186,079	104,200	40,523	192,669
1995	182,393	100,793	41,476	193,076
1996	188,493	99,922	42,839	194,548
1997	190,386	99,779	44,580	189,946

CONSTITUTION AND GOVERNMENT

Since Oct. 1990 North Rhine-Westphalia has had 6 seats in the Bundesrat.

RECENT ELECTIONS

The Diet, elected on 14 May 1995, consists of 108 Social Democrats (46% of votes cast), 89 Christian Democrats (37·7%) and 24 Greens (10%).

CURRENT ADMINISTRATION

North Rhine-Westphalia is governed by Social Democrats (SPD) and the Greens. *Prime Minister:* Wolfgang Clement (SPD).

ECONOMY

Budget. The predicted total revenue for 1998 was 82,578m. DM. The predicted total expenditure was 88,596m. DM.

ENERGY AND NATURAL RESOURCES

Agriculture. Area and yield of the most important crops:

	Area (in 1,000 ha)			Yield (in 1,000 tonnes)		
	1995	1996	1997	1995	1996	1997
Wheat	250·9	255·5	263·9	2,035·2	2,185·9	2,268·3
Rye	41·0	37·7	37·7	260·2	263·8	256·5
Barley	192·8	195·8	200·0	1,220·9	1,259·9	1,303·6
Oats	30·7	28·2	30·3	134·0	151·4	170·0
Potatoes	29·9	33·4	28·0	1,047·8	1,467·3	1,204·1
Sugar-beet	77·0	78·0	76·8	4,018·0	4,295·7	4,204·5

Livestock, 3 Dec. 1997: Cattle, 1,634,104 (including 451,151 milch cows); pigs, 5,800,743; sheep, 223,560; horses, 116,709 (1996); poultry, 10,859,348 (1996).

INDUSTRY

In Sept. 1997, 10,028 establishments (with 20 and more employees) employed 1,579,842 persons; of these, 104,378 were employed in production of food and tobacco; 237,518 in machine construction; 320,351 in metal production and manufacture of metal goods; 151,588 in the chemical industry; 154,087 in manufacture of office machines, computers, electrical and precision engineering and optics; 104,115 in motor vehicle manufacture.

Output and/or production in 1,000 tonnes, 1997: Hard coal, 39,118; lignite, 99,179; pig-iron, 18,168; raw steel ingots, 23,192; rolled steel, 29,461; castings (iron and steel castings), 932; cement, 11,367; fireproof products, 633; sulphuric acid (including production of cokeries), 1,233; staple fibres and rayon, 260; machine tools, 289 (1,000 pieces); equipment for smelting works and rolling mills, 1,925 (pieces); machines for mining industry, building and building material, 83 (1,000 pieces); cranes and hoisting machinery, 453 (1,000 pieces); electricity distribution and control equipment, 9,374,248 (1,000 pieces); cables and electric lines, 168; springs of all kinds, 174; chains of all kinds, 37; locks and fittings, 256,251 (1,000 pieces); spun yarns, 93. Of the total population, 8·5% were engaged in industry.

Labour. The economically active persons totalled 7,391,000 at the 1%-sample survey of the microcensus of April 1997. Of the total, 677,000 were self-employed, 56,000 unpaid family workers, 6,658,000 employees; 142,000 were engaged in agriculture, forestry and fishing, 2,607,000 in power supply, mining, manufacturing, water supply and building, 1,713,000 in commerce, hotel trade and transport, 2,925,000 in other industries and services.

COMMUNICATIONS

Roads. There were (1 Jan. 1998) 29,686 km of 'classified' roads, including 2,168 km of Autobahn, 5,098 km of federal roads, 12,632 km of first-class and 9,798 km of second-class highways. Number of motor vehicles, 1 July 1998, 10,448,097, including 8,979,844 passenger cars, 450,525 motor trucks/trucks, 17,171 buses, 213,245 tractors and 662,842 motor cycles.

Civil Aviation. In 1997, 86,929 aircraft landed at Düsseldorf, bringing 7,667,735 incoming passengers.

SOCIAL INSTITUTIONS

Justice. There are a constitutional court *(Verfassungsgerichtshof)*, 3 courts of appeal, 19 regional courts, 130 local courts, 3 *Land* labour courts, 30 labour courts, 1 *Land* social court, 8 social courts, 3 finance courts, a higher administrative court and 7 administrative courts.

Religion. On 25 May 1987 (census) there were 35·2% Protestants and 49·4% Roman Catholics.

Education. In 1997 there were 4,205 primary schools with 62,669 teachers and 1,120,532 pupils; 703 special schools with 14,835 teachers and 87,751 pupils; 517 intermediate schools with 15,954 teachers and 294,623 pupils; 252 *Gesamtschulen* (comprehensive schools) with 16,624 teachers and 216,163 pupils; 620 high schools with 34,207 teachers and 519,329 pupils; there were 265 part-time vocational schools with 289,616 pupils; vocational preparatory year 157 schools with 11,392 pupils; 241 full-time vocational schools with 72,310 pupils; 166 full-time vocational schools leading up to vocational colleges with 14,508 pupils; 241 advanced full-time vocational schools with 38,823 pupils; 643 schools for public health occupations with 16,222 teachers and 44,403 pupils; 42 schools within the scope of a pilot system of courses with 83,717 pupils and 3,656 teachers.

In the winter term 1997–98 there were 8 universities (Bielefeld, 20,030 students; Bochum, 35,547; Bonn, 36,598; Cologne (Köln), 57,007; Dortmund, 24,281; Düsseldorf, 22,263; Münster, 44,398; Witten, 763); the Technical University of Aachen (30,960); 3 Roman Catholic and 2 Protestant theological colleges with a total of 682 students. There were also 3 colleges of music, 4 colleges of fine arts and the college for physical education in Cologne with 10,877 students in total; 24 *Fachhochschulen* (vocational colleges) with 97,434 students, and 6 *Universitäten-Gesamthochschulen* with a total of 121,865 students.

Health. In 1996 there were 1,907 hospitals in North Rhine-Westphalia with over 300,000 beds, which had an average occupancy rate of 79·3%.

CULTURE

Tourism. At Dec. 1997 there were 5,666 places of accommodation (9 beds or more) providing 270,797 beds altogether. In 1997, 13,105,046 visitors (2,319,796 foreigners) spent 34,284,304 nights.

Libraries. In 1996 there were 2,599 public libraries lending a total of 67,094,481 items.

Museums and Galleries. In 1996 there were 604 museums which had 11,884,582 visitors.

FURTHER READING

Statistical Information: The Landesamt für Datenverarbeitung und Statistik Nordrhein-Westfalen (Mauerstr. 51, D-40476 Düsseldorf) was founded in 1946, by amalgamating the provincial statistical offices of Rhineland and Westphalia. *President:* Jochen Kehlenbach. The Landesamt publishes: *Statistisches Jahrbuch Nordrhein-Westfalen.* From 1949. More than 550 other publications yearly.

Först, W., *Kleine Geschichte Nordrhein-Westfalens.* Münster, 1986.

Land Library: Universitätsbibliothek, Universitätsstr. 1, D-40225 Düsseldorf. *Director:* Dr Niggemann.

RHINELAND-PALATINATE

Rheinland-Pfalz

KEY HISTORICAL EVENTS

The *Land* was formed from the Rhenisch Palatinate and the Rhine valley areas of Prussia, Hesse-Darmstadt, Hesse-Kassel and Bavaria.

The Palatinate was ruled, from 1214, by the Bavarian house of Wittelsbach; its capital was Heidelberg. In 1797 its land west of the Rhine was taken into France, and Napoleon divided the eastern land between Baden and Hesse. In 1815 the land taken by France was restored to Germany and allotted to Bavaria. The area and its neighbours formed the strategically-important Bavarian Circle of the Rhine.

The rule of the Wittelsbachs ended in 1918 but the Palatinate remained part of Bavaria until the American occupying forces detached it in 1946.

The new *Land*, incorporating the Palatinate and other territory, received its constitution in April 1947.

TERRITORY AND POPULATION

Rhineland-Palatinate has an area of 19,853 sq. km. It comprises 3 administrative regions, 12 urban districts, 24 rural districts and 2,305 communes. The capital is Mainz. Population (at 30 June 1998), 4,018,228 (2,049,559 females).

SOCIAL STATISTICS

Statistics for calendar years:

	Live births	Marriages	Divorces	Deaths
1994	40,539	23,182	9,003	42,857
1995	39,684	22,922	9,040	42,993
1996	40,926	22,741	9,385	43,752
1997	41,677	22,509	10,015	43,211

CONSTITUTION AND GOVERNMENT

The constitution of the *Land* Rheinland-Pfalz was approved by the Consultative Assembly on 25 April 1947 and by referendum on 18 May 1947, when 579,002 voted for and 514,338 against its acceptance. It has 4 seats in the Bundesrat.

RECENT ELECTIONS
At the elections of 24 March 1996 the Social Democratic Party won 43 seats of the 101 in the state parliament with 39·8% of votes cast; the Christian Democrats 41 with 38·7%; the Free Democrats 10 with 8·9%; and the Greens, 7 with 6·9%.

CURRENT ADMINISTRATION
The coalition cabinet is headed by Kurt Beck (b. 1949; Social Democrat).

ENERGY AND NATURAL RESOURCES
Agriculture. Area and yield of the most important products:

	Area (1,000 ha)			Yield (1,000 tonnes)		
	1994	1995	1996	1994	1995	1996
Wheat	77·7	85·3	86·9	484·0	543·2	587·7
Rye	19·0	20·6	15·6	94·3	107·6	93·5
Barley	118·8	113·3	121·1	541·0	542·7	681·7
Oats	22·8	18·3	17·1	87·1	74·0	84·0
Potatoes	10·6	11·1	11·0	329·1	329·7	372·6
Sugar-beet	22·9	23·1	22·6	1,228·1	1,261·5	1,440·0
Wine (1,000 hectolitres)	66·2	65·8	65·3	6,902·2	5,910·9	5,869·8

Livestock (1997, in 1,000): Cattle, 470·3 (including milch cows, 142·0); sheep, 126·7; pigs, 399·7; horses, 29·9 (1996); poultry, 1,874·4 (1996).

Forestry. Total area covered by forests in 1997 was 8,061·8 sq. km or 40·6% of the total area.

INDUSTRY
In 1997, 2,154 establishments (with 20 or more employees) employed 309,286 persons; of these 68,180 were employed in the chemical industry; 19,220 in electrical equipment manufacture; 6,992 in leather goods and footwear; 34,636 in machine construction; 23,493 in processing stones and earthenware.

Labour. The economically active persons totalled 1,709,900 in 1997. Of the total, 166,000 were self-employed, 18,000 were unpaid family workers, 1,525,900 employees; 54,400 were engaged in agriculture and forestry, 625,400 in power supply, mining, manufacturing and building, 371,600 in commerce, transport, hotels and restaurants, 658,500 in other industries and services.

COMMUNICATIONS
Roads. In 1998 there were 18,547 km of 'classified' roads, including 829 km of Autobahn, 3,042 km of federal roads, 7,132 km of first-class and 7,543 km of second-class highways. Number of motor vehicles, 1 July 1998, was 2,630,638, including 2,174,590 passenger cars, 110,373 trucks, 5,423 buses, 137,622 tractors and 170,652 motor cycles.

SOCIAL INSTITUTIONS
Justice. There are a constitutional court (*Verfassungsgerichtshof*), 2 courts of appeal, 8 regional courts, 47 local courts, a *Land* labour court, 5 labour courts, a *Land* social court, 4 social courts, a finance court, a higher administrative court and 4 administrative courts.

Religion. On 25 May 1987 (census) there were 37·7% Protestants and 54·5% Roman Catholics.

Education. In 1997 there were 988 primary schools with 9,246 teachers and 188,700 pupils; 601 secondary schools with 16,461 teachers and 271,349 pupils; 146 special schools with 2,236 teachers and 14,710 pupils; 113 vocational and advanced vocational schools with 4,913 teachers and 118,031 pupils.

In the winter term 1997–98 (provisional) there were the University of Mainz (28,169 students), the University of Kaiserslautern (8,007 students), the University of Trier (10,582 students), the University of Koblenz-Landau (8,565 students), the

Hochschule für Verwaltungswissenschaften in Speyer (565 students), the *Wissenschaftliche Hochschule für Unternehmensführung* (Otto Beisheim Graduate School) in Vallendar (370 students), the Roman Catholic Theological College in Trier (289 students) and the Roman Catholic Theological College in Vallendar (87 students). There were also 9 *Fachhochschulen* with 22,076 students and 4 *Verwaltungsfachhochschulen* with 1,873 students.

FURTHER READING
Statistical Information: The Statistisches Landesamt Rheinland-Pfalz (Mainzer Str., 14–16, D-56130 Bad Ems) was established in 1948. *President:* Klaus Maxeiner. Its publications include: *Statistisches Jahrbuch für Rheinland-Pfalz* (from 1948); *Statistische Monatshefte Rheinland-Pfalz* (from 1958); *Statistik von Rheinland-Pfalz* (from 1949) 367 vols. to date; *Rheinland-Pfalz im Spiegel der Statistik* (from 1968); *Rheinland-Pfalz—seine kreisfreien Städte und Landkreise* (1992); *Rheinland-Pfalz heute* (from 1973); *Benutzerhandbuch des Landesinformationssystems* (1995); *Raumordnungsbericht 1993 der Landesregierung Rheinland-Pfalz* (Mainz, 1993).

SAARLAND

KEY HISTORICAL EVENTS
Long disputed between Germany and France, the area was occupied by France in 1792. Most was allotted to Prussia at the close of the Napoleonic wars in 1815.

In 1870 Prussia defeated France and when, in 1871, the German Empire was founded under Prussian leadership, it was able to incorporate Lorraine. This part of France was the Saar territory's western neighbour so the Saar was no longer a vulnerable boundary state. It began to develop industrially, exploiting Lorraine coal and iron.

In 1919 the League of Nations took control of the Saar until a plebiscite of 1935 favoured return to Germany. In 1945 there was a French occupation, and in 1947 the Saar was made an international area, but in economic union with France. In 1954 France and Germany agreed that the Saar should be a separate and autonomous state, under an independent commissioner. This was rejected by referendum and France agreed to return Saarland to Germany. It became a *Land* of the Federal Republic on 1 Jan. 1957.

TERRITORY AND POPULATION
Saarland has an area of 2,570 sq. km. Population, 31 Dec. 1997, 1,080,790 (524,034 males, 555,756 females). It comprises 6 rural districts and 52 communes. The capital is Saarbrücken.

SOCIAL STATISTICS
Statistics for calendar years:

	Live births	Marriages	Divorces	Deaths
1994	10,028	6,427	3,035	12,711
1995	9,727	6,095	2,785	12,647
1996	9,976	6,181	2,938	12,529
1997	9,987	5,829	3,123	12,455

CONSTITUTION AND GOVERNMENT
Saarland has 3 seats in the Bundesrat.

RECENT ELECTIONS
The Saar Diet, elected on 16 Oct. 1994, is composed as follows: 27 Social Democrats, 21 Christian Democrats, 3 Greens.

CURRENT ADMINISTRATION
Saarland is governed by Social Democrats in Parliament. *Prime Minister:* Reinhard Klimmt (Social Democrat).

ENERGY AND NATURAL RESOURCES

Electricity. In 1997, electricity production was 10,100m kWh. Supply from the electricity grid totalled 7,500m kWh.

Oil and Gas. 8,700m. kWh of gas was used in 1997.

Agriculture. The cultivated area (1997) occupied 115,827 ha or 45·1% of the total area.

Area and yield of the most important crops:

	Area (in 1,000 ha)			Yield (in 1,000 tonnes)		
	1995	1996	1997	1995	1996	1997
Wheat	7·0	7·8	7·6	40·6	46·5	50·8
Rye	5·4	4·9	5·2	29·5	27·5	30·2
Barley	7·6	7·6	8·0	36·6	38·5	42·4
Oats	4·1	3·8	3·9	18·1	16·1	18·6
Potatoes	0·3	0·3	0·3	8·1	8·9	10·1

Livestock, Dec. 1997: Cattle, 62,223 (including 16,522 milch cows); pigs, 24,641; sheep, 15,476; horses, 6,115 (1996); poultry, 193,787 (1996).

Forestry. The forest area comprises nearly 33·4% of the total (257,045 ha).

INDUSTRY

In June 1998, 529 establishments (with 20 or more employees) employed 106,858 persons; of these 12,587 were engaged in coalmining, 18,524 in manufacturing motor vehicles, parts, accessories, 10,721 in iron and steel production, 15,460 in machine construction, 4,788 in electrical engineering, 4,778 in steel construction. In 1997 the coalmines produced 7·4m. tonnes of coal. 4 blast furnaces and 10 steel furnaces produced 3·6m. tonnes of pig-iron and 4·5m. tonnes of crude steel.

Labour. The economically active persons totalled 413,700 at the 1%-sample survey of the microcensus of April 1997. Of the total, 38,500 were self-employed, 373,700 employees; 5,100 were engaged in agriculture and forestry, 128,300 in power supply, mining, manufacturing and building, 101,300 in commerce and transport, 179,000 in other industries and services.

COMMUNICATIONS

Roads. At 1 Jan. 1998 there were 2,031 km of classified roads, including 236 km of Autobahn, 352 km of federal roads, 820 km of first-class and 623 km of second-class highways. Number of motor vehicles, 31 Dec. 1997, 680,975, including 587,283 passenger cars, 28,128 trucks, 1,374 buses, 14,063 tractors and 42,773 motor cycles.

Shipping. During 1997, 1,753 ships docked in Saarland ports, bringing 2·7m. tonnes of freight. In the same period 561 ships left the ports, carrying 768,000 tonnes of freight.

SOCIAL INSTITUTIONS

Justice. There are a constitutional court *(Verfassungsgerichtshof)*, a court of appeal, a regional court, 11 local courts, a *Land* labour court, 3 labour courts, a *Land* social court, a social court, a finance court, a higher administrative court and an administrative court.

Religion. In 1995, 70·5% of the population were Roman Catholics and 20·3% were Protestants.

Education. In 1998–99 there were 293 primary schools with 49,595 pupils; 40 special schools with 3,331 pupils; 100 *Realschulen, Erweiterte Realschulen* and *Sekundarschulen* with 27,632 pupils; 37 high schools with 28,286 pupils; 15 comprehensive high schools with 10,748 pupils; 4 *Freie Waldorfschulen* with 1,072 pupils; 2 evening intermediate schools with 228 pupils; 2 evening high schools and 1 Saarland College with 198 pupils; 39 part-time vocational schools with 21,855 pupils; year of commercial basic training: 52 institutions with 2,274 pupils; 21 advanced full-time vocational schools and schools for technicians with 1,926 pupils; 50 full-time vocational schools with 4,929 pupils; 1 *Berufsaufbauschule* (vocational extension school) with 12 pupils; 29 *Fachoberschulen* (full-time vocational schools leading up to vocational colleges) with 3,873 pupils; 43 schools for public health occupations with 2,268 pupils. The number of pupils visiting the vocational schools amounts to 37,137.

In the winter term 1998–99 (preliminary data) there was the University of the Saarland with 17,444 students; 1 academy of fine art with 328 students; 1 academy of music and theatre with 239 students; 1 vocational college (economics and technics) with 2,576 students; 1 vocational college for social affairs with 262 students; and 1 vocational college for public administration with 219 students.

Health. In 1997 the 28 hospitals in the Saarland contained 8,265 beds and treated 244,652 patients. The average occupancy rate was 83·3%. There were also 22 out-patient and rehabilitation centres which treated 27,376 patients in 1997. On average they were using 69·3% of their capacity.

CULTURE

Tourism. In 1997, 13,966 beds were available in 300 places of accommodation (of 9 or more beds). 568,677 guests spent 1,947,847 nights in the Saarland, staying an average of 3·4 days each.

FURTHER READING

Statistical Information: The Statistisches Landesamt Saarland (Virchowstrasse 7, D-66119 Saarbrücken) was established on 1 April 1938. As from 1 June 1935, it was an independent agency; its predecessor, 1920–35, was the Statistical Office of the Government Commission of the Saar. *Chief:* Direktor Josef Mailänder. The most important publications are: *Statistisches Handbuch für das Saarland,* from 1950.—*Statistisches Taschenbuch für das Saarland,* from 1959.—*Saarland in Zahlen* (special issues).—*Einzelschriften zur Statistik des Saarlandes,* from 1950.—*Statistik-Journal* (monthly), from 1996.

SAXONY

Freistaat Sachsen

TERRITORY AND POPULATION

The area is 18,412 sq. km. It is divided into 3 administrative regions, 7 urban districts, 22 rural districts and 787 communes. Population on 1 Jan. 1998 was 4,522,412 (2,338,244 females, 2,184,168 males); density, 246 per sq. km. The capital is Dresden.

SOCIAL STATISTICS

Statistics for calendar years:

	Live births	Marriages	Divorces	Deaths
1994	22,734	14,795	6,519	58,234
1995	24,004	15,474	7,043	57,550
1996	27,006	15,402	7,754	55,756
1997	29,008	15,287	8,470	53,483

CONSTITUTION AND GOVERNMENT

The *Land* was reconstituted as the Free State of Saxony on former GDR territory in 1990. It has 4 seats in the Bundesrat.

RECENT ELECTIONS

At the Diet elections of Sept. 1994 the Christian Democrats won 77 seats, with 58·1% of the vote; the Social Democrats, 22, with 16·6%; the Party of Democratic Socialism (former Communists), 21, with 16·5%.

CURRENT ADMINISTRATION

The *Prime Minister* is Kurt Biedenkopf (b. 1930; Christian Democrat).

ENERGY AND NATURAL RESOURCES

Agriculture. Area and yield of the most important crops:

	Area (in 1,000 ha)			Yield (in 1,000 tonnes)		
	1996	1997	1998	1996	1997	1998
Wheat	143·1	146·2	151·7	965·0	964·6	1,003·7
Rye	50·2	47·8	50·0	249·1	200·8	269·9
Barley	150·2	156·8	150·3	750·8	928·9	852·2
Maize	86·9	80·7	74·5	3,106·7	3,215·0	3,224·9
Potatoes	9·9	7·9	8·0	375·9	276·4	308·4
Fodder	196·3	195·3	196·6	1,682·1	1,682·7	1,682·0

Livestock in 1997 (in 1,000): Cattle, 618 (including milch cows, 250); pigs, 582; sheep, 116.

INDUSTRY

In Nov. 1998, 2,650 establishments (with 20 or more employees) employed 214,116 persons.

COMMUNICATIONS

Roads. On 1 Jan. 1998 there were 572 km of motorways and 2,474 km of main roads. There were, 1 July 1998, 2,490,049 registered motor vehicles, including 2,160,172 motor cars, 223,629 trucks and tractors, 4,285 buses and 81,476 motor cycles.

SOCIAL INSTITUTIONS

Religion. In 1997, 24·7 of the population belonged to the Evangelical Church and 4·2% were Roman Catholic.

Education. In 1997–98 there were 1,193 primary schools with 200,487 pupils and 11,748 teachers; 651 secondary schools with 221,100 pupils and 14,347 teachers; 190 grammar schools with 145,981 pupils and 9,496 teachers and 205 high schools (*Förderschulen*) with 27,752 pupils and 3,887 teachers. There were 798 professional training schools with 165,945 students and 6,075 teachers. There were 6 universities with 51,266 students, 10 polytechnics with 18,645 students, 6 art schools with 2,292 students and 1 management college with 1,341 students.

CULTURE

Cinema. In 1997 there were 99 cinemas with seating for 41,047 persons. 7m. tickets were sold for performances.

Libraries. In 1996, 869 public libraries with 522,010 active users lent out 20,760,058 items.

National Theatre and Opera. During the 1996–97 season there were 72 stages and seating for 24,431 persons. Audiences totalled 1,900,778.

FURTHER READING

Statistical office: Statistisches Landesamt des Freistaates Sachsen, Postfach 105, D-01911 Kamenz. It publishes *Statistisches Jahrbuch des Freistaates Sachsen* (since 1990).

SAXONY-ANHALT

Sachsen-Anhalt

TERRITORY AND POPULATION

The area is 20,446 sq. km. It is divided into 3 administrative regions, 3 urban districts, 21 rural districts and 1,297 communes. Population in 1997 was 2,701,690 (1,390,490 females). The capital is Magdeburg.

SOCIAL STATISTICS
Statistics for calendar years:

	Live births	Marriages	Divorces	Deaths
1994	14,280	9,415	4,287	33,816
1995	14,568	9,667	3,867	33,519
1996	16,152	9,534	3,432	32,639
1997	17,194	9,285	4,494	30,892

CONSTITUTION AND GOVERNMENT
The *Land* was reconstituted on former GDR territory in 1990. It has 4 seats in the Bundesrat.

RECENT ELECTIONS
At the Diet election on 26 April 1998 the SPD received 35·9% of votes cast giving them 47 seats, the CDU 22·0% (28 seats), the PDS (former Communists) 19·6% (25 seats) and the DVU (extreme right) 12·9% (16 seats). The Free Democratic Party received 4·2% and the Greens 3·2%. Turn-out was 71·7%.

CURRENT ADMINISTRATION
The *Prime Minister* is Dr Manfred Höppner (SPD).

ENERGY AND NATURAL RESOURCES
Agriculture. Area and yield of the most important crops:

	Area (in 1,000 ha)			Yield (in 1,000 tonnes)		
	1995	1996	1997	1995	1996	1997
Cereals	539·7	563·8	602·8	3,607·5	3,473·1	3,860·3
Potatoes	17·5	18·2	15·7	521·8	710·1	561·5
Sugar-beet	61·5	61·4	60·3	2,716·8	2,869·5	2,798·5
Maize	66·3	78·8	70·4	2,299·1	3,420·3	2,459·5

Livestock in 1997 (in 1,000): Cattle, 420·6 (including milch cows, 189·1); pigs, 745·9; sheep, 120·2.

INDUSTRY
In 1997, 1,257 establishments (with 20 or more employees) employed 104,066 persons; of these, 48,420 were employed in basic industry, 30,565 in capital goods industry and 18,292 in food industry. Major sectors are machine and transport equipment, electrical engineering, chemicals and energy and fuel.

Labour. In 1996 there were 1,085,959 economically-active persons. Of these, 469,327 worked in local authorities, social security and services, 187,894 in mining and manufacturing, 198,646 in building, 125,616 in trade, 68,637 in transport and communications and 35,839 in agriculture, forestry and fisheries. Unemployment rate (1996), 18·8%.

COMMUNICATIONS
Roads. In 1997 there were 232 km of motorways, 2,329 km of main and 3,839 km of local roads. In 1997 there were 1,439,439 registered motor vehicles, including 1,247,995 passenger cars, 99,144 trucks, 2,669 buses and 41,927 motor cycles.

SOCIAL INSTITUTIONS
Religion. There are Saxon and Anhalt branches of the Evangelical Church. There were some 0·2m. Roman Catholics in 1990.

Education. In 1997–98 there were 1,521 schools with 374,351 pupils. In 1997 there were 11 universities and institutes of equivalent status with 30,707 students.

FURTHER READING
Statistical office: Statistisches Landesamt Sachsen-Anhalt, Postfach 20 11 56, D-06012 Halle. It publishes *Statistisches Jahrbuch des Landes Sachsen-Anhalt* (since 1991).

SCHLESWIG-HOLSTEIN

KEY HISTORICAL EVENTS

The *Land* is formed from two states formerly contested between Germany and Denmark.

Schleswig was a Danish dependency ruled since 1474 by the King of Denmark as Duke of Schleswig. He also ruled Holstein, its southern neighbour, as Duke of Holstein, but he did so recognizing that it was a fief of the Holy Roman Empire. As such, Holstein joined the German Confederation which replaced the Empire in 1815.

Disputes between Denmark and the powerful German states were accompanied by rising national feeling in the duchies, where the population was part-Danish and part-German. There was war in 1848–50 and in 1864, when Denmark surrendered its claims to Prussia and Austria. Following her defeat of Austria in 1866 Prussia annexed both duchies.

North Schleswig (predominately Danish) was awarded to Denmark in 1920. Prussian Holstein and south Schleswig became the present *Land* in 1946.

TERRITORY AND POPULATION

The area of Schleswig-Holstein in 1996 was 15,771 sq. km. It is divided into 4 urban and 11 rural districts and 1,131 communes. The capital is Kiel. The population (estimate, 31 Dec. 1996) numbered 2,742,293 (1,339,326 males, 1,402,967 females).

SOCIAL STATISTICS

Statistics for calendar years:

	Live births	Marriages	Divorces	Deaths
1993	28,632	18,451	6,250	31,223
1994	27,542	18,295	6,196	30,766
1995	27,430	17,671	6,679	31,288
1996	28,766	17,832	6,822	31,314

CONSTITUTION AND GOVERNMENT

The *Land* has 4 seats in the Bundesrat.

RECENT ELECTIONS

At the elections of 24 March 1996 the Social Democrats won 33 seats with 39·8% of votes cast, the Christian Democrats 30 with 37·2%, the Greens 6 with 8·1%, the Free Democrats 4 with 5·7% and the (Danish) South Schleswig Association 2 with 2·5%.

CURRENT ADMINISTRATION

Prime Minister: Heide Simonis (b. 1943; SPD).

ENERGY AND NATURAL RESOURCES

Agriculture. Area and yield of the most important crops:

	Area (in 1,000 ha)			Yield (in 1,000 tonnes)		
	1994	1995	1996	1994	1995	1996
Wheat	157·2	155·8	166·4	1,223·3	1,333·5	1,433·4
Rye	32·6	35·1	30·5	188·0	207·6	190·9
Barley	67·5	74·8	84·8	430·3	541·4	554·0
Oats	16·9	9·6	8·6	76·4	50·6	50·2
Potatoes	4·8	5·2	5·8	146·3	154·1	192·9
Sugar-beet	15·0	15·3	15·4	699·5	715·3	716·6

Livestock, 3 Dec. 1996: 1,396,970 cattle (including 422,213 milch cows); 1,293,356 pigs; 222,495 sheep; 54,707 horses; 2,885,175 poultry.

Fisheries. In 1996 the yield of small-scale deep-sea and inshore fisheries was 59,306 tonnes valued at 92·6m. DM.

INDUSTRY

In 1996 (average), 1,455 establishments (with 20 and more employees) employed 146,742 persons; of these, 6,976 were employed in shipbuilding (except naval engineering); 25,903 in machine construction; 20,187 in food and kindred industry; 10,368 in electrical engineering.

Labour. The economically active persons totalled 1,250,200 in 1996. Of the total, 128,900 were self-employed, 13,800 unpaid family workers, 1,107,600 employees; 42,800 were engaged in agriculture and forestry, 340,200 in power supply, mining, manufacturing and building, 340,100 in commerce and transport and 527,100 in other industries and services.

COMMUNICATIONS

Roads. There were (1 Jan. 1997) 9,886·1 km of 'classified' roads, including 447·9 km of Autobahn, 1,760·2 km of federal roads, 3,600·8 km of first-class and 4,077·2 km of second-class highways. Number of motor vehicles, 1 July 1997, was 1,706,336, including 1,432,722 passenger cars, 78,012 trucks, 2,940 buses, 69,981 tractors, 94,359 motor cycles.

Shipping. The Kiel Canal (*Nord-Ostsee-Kanal*) is 98·7 km (51 miles) long; in 1996, 37,055 vessels of 32·8m. NRT passed through it.

SOCIAL INSTITUTIONS

Justice. There are a court of appeal, 4 regional courts, 28 local courts, a *Land* labour court, 5 labour courts, a *Land* social court, 4 social courts, a finance court, an upper administrative court and an administrative court.

Religion. On 25 May 1987 (census) there were 73·3% Protestants and 6·2% Roman Catholics.

Education. In 1996–97 there were 624 primary schools with 7,263 teachers and 119,937 pupils; 266 elementary schools with 2,772 teachers and 39,178 pupils; 171 intermediate schools with 2,863 teachers and 52,678 pupils; 102 grammar schools with 5,234 teachers and 63,234 pupils; 23 comprehensive schools with 1,236 teachers and 13,585 pupils; 162 other schools (including special schools) with 2,222 teachers and 16,254 pupils; 353 vocational schools with 4,170 teachers and 86,312 pupils.

In the winter term of the academic year 1997–98 there were 26,059 students at the three universities (Kiel, Flensburg and Lübeck) and 18,419 students at 11 further education colleges.

FURTHER READING

Statistical Information: Statistisches Landesamt Schleswig-Holstein (Fröbel Str. 15–17, D-24113 Kiel). *Director:* Dr Kirschner. Publications: *Statistisches Taschenbuch Schleswig-Holstein,* since 1954.—*Statistisches Jahrbuch Schleswig-Holstein,* since 1951.—*Statistische Monatshefte Schleswig-Holstein,* since 1949.—*Statistische Berichte,* since 1947.—*Beitrage zur historischen Statistik Schleswig-Holstein,* from 1967.—*Lange Reihen,* from 1977.

Baxter, R. R., *The Law of International Waterways.* Harvard Univ. Press, 1964
Brandt, O., *Grundriss der Geschichte Schleswig-Holsteins.* 5th ed. Kiel, 1957
Handbuch für Schleswig-Holstein. 28th ed. Kiel, 1996

State Library: Schleswig-Holsteinische Landesbibliothek, Kiel, Schloss. *Director:* Prof. Dr Dieter Lohmeier.

THURINGIA

Thüringen

TERRITORY AND POPULATION

The area is 16,172 sq. km. Population on 31 Dec. 1997 was 2,478,148 (1,271,481 females); density, 153 per sq. km. It is divided into 6 urban districts, 17 rural districts and 1,053 communes. The capital is Erfurt.

SOCIAL STATISTICS

Statistics for calendar years:

	Live births	Marriages	Divorces	Deaths
1994	12,721	8,581	3,795	28,877
1995	13,788	8,781	3,493	29,027
1996	15,265	8,646	3,955	28,468
1997	16,475	8,619	4,527	27,694

CONSTITUTION AND GOVERNMENT

The *Land* was reconstituted on former GDR territory in 1990. It has 4 seats in the Bundesrat.

RECENT ELECTIONS

At the Diet elections of Oct. 1994 the Christian Democrats (CDU) won 42 seats, with 42·6% of the vote; the Social Democrats (SPD), 29 with 29·6%; the Party of Democratic Socialism (PDS), 17, with 16·6%.

CURRENT ADMINISTRATION

The *Prime Minister* is Dr Bernhard Vogel (CDU).

ENERGY AND NATURAL RESOURCES

Agriculture. Area and yield of the most important crops:

	Area (in 1,000 ha)			Yield (in 1,000 tonnes)		
	1995	1996	1997	1995	1996	1997
Wheat	187·6	185·8	183·3	1,240·5	1,290·9	1,229·2
Rye	27·6	20·9	17·2	170·1	130·5	117·9
Barley	122·7	138·7	146·0	678·9	775·5	814·2
Oats	6·3	6·7	8·2	31·8	33·7	41·6
Potatoes	5·4	5·7	4·3	178·2	235·2	161·6
Sugar-beet	13·5	13·1	13·2	618·9	589·5	619·0

Livestock, 3 Dec. 1997: 445,125 cattle (including 161,658 milch cows); 660,074 pigs; 226,099 sheep; 14,048 horses (1996); 4,065,825 poultry (1996).

INDUSTRY

In 1997, 1,448 establishments (with 20 or more employees) employed 110,091 persons; of these, 48,507 were employed by producers of materials and supplies, 28,360 by producers of investment goods, 9,236 by producers of durables and 23,988 by producers of non-durables.

Labour. The economically active persons totalled 1,082,300 in April 1997, including 494,800 professional workers, 465,900 manual workers and 82,700 self-employed. 39,000 persons were engaged in agriculture and forestry, 373,400 in production industries, 229,800 in commerce, transport and communications and 440,000 in other sectors. There were 232,004 persons registered unemployed in Dec. 1997 (130,478 females) and 5,889 on short time; unemployment rate was 20·4%.

COMMUNICATIONS

Roads. In 1996 there were 7,905·6 km of 'classified' roads (310 km of Autobahn, 1,952·9 km of federal roads, 5,642·7 km of first- and second-class highways). Number of motor vehicles, Jan. 1998, 1,401,902, including 1,204,304 private cars, 97,904 trucks, 2,843 buses, 34,968 tractors and 41,368 motor cycles.

SOCIAL INSTITUTIONS

Religion. In 1997, 216,850 persons were Roman Catholic and 299 were Jewish. In 1996, 740,635 persons were Protestant.

Education. In 1997–98 there were 628 primary schools with 113,935 pupils, 365 core curriculum schools with 121,630 pupils, 113 grammar schools with 86,107 pupils and 101 special schools with 19,102 pupils; there were 86,731 pupils in technical and professional education, and 4,118 in professional training for the disabled.

In the winter term 1997–98 there were 11 universities and colleges with 31,215 students enrolled.

Health. In 1997 there were 57 hospitals with 18,803 beds. There was 1 doctor per 366 population.

Welfare. 1996 expenditure on social welfare was 883·7m. DM.

CULTURE

Tourism. In 1997, 1,435 places of accommodation (with 9 or more beds) received 2,549,800 visitors who stayed 7,327,700 nights.

Libraries. There were 514 public libraries in 1996 with 315,000 active users who borrowed 6,052,000 items.

FURTHER READING

Statistical information: Thüringer Landesamt für Statistik (Postfach 900163, D-99104 Erfurt; Leipziger Str. 71, D-99085 Erfurt). *President:* Gerhard Scheuerer. Publications: *Statistisches Jahrbuch Thüringen,* since 1993. *Kreiszahlen für Thüringen,* since 1995. *Statistische Monatshefte Thüringen,* since 1994. *Statistische Berichte,* since 1991. *Faltblätter,* since 1991.

State library: Thüringer Universitäts- und Landesbibliothek, Jena.

GHANA

Republic of Ghana

Capital: Accra
Population estimate, 2000: 19·93m.
GNP per capita: (PPP$) 1,790
HDI/world rank: 0·473/133

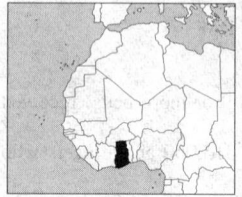

KEY HISTORICAL EVENTS
By the 17th century, several strong chiefdoms and warrior states, notably the powerful Ashanti state, ruled in the area. The Ashanti state was initially strengthened through its collaboration with the slave trade but by 1874 it had been conquered by Britain and made a colony. The hinterland became a protectorate in 1901. A period of indirect British rule began but was challenged after the Second World War by Kwame Nkrumah and the Convention People's Party (CPP), formed in 1949. The state of Ghana came into existence on 6 Mar. 1957 when the former Colony of the Gold Coast and the Trusteeship Territory of Togoland attained Dominion status. In Dec. 1956 the UN General Assembly approved the termination of British administration in Togoland and the eventual union of Togoland with the Gold Coast.

The country was declared a Republic within the Commonwealth on 1 July 1960 with Dr Kwame Nkrumah as the first President. On 24 Feb. 1966 the Nkrumah regime was overthrown in a military coup and Ghana was ruled by the National Liberation Council until 1 Oct. 1969 when the military regime handed over power to a civilian regime under a new constitution. On 13 Jan. 1972 the armed forces regained power.

In Oct. 1975 the National Redemption Council was subordinated to a Supreme Military Council (SMC). In 1979 the SMC was toppled in a coup led by Flight-Lieut. J. J. Rawlings. The new government permitted elections already scheduled and these resulted in a victory for Dr Hilla Limann and his People's National Party. However on 31 Dec. 1981 another coup led by Flight-Lieut. Rawlings dismissed the government and Parliament, suspended the constitution and established a Provisional National Defence Council to exercise all government powers.

A new pluralist democratic constitution was approved by referendum in April 1992. The Fourth Republic was proclaimed on 7 Jan. 1993.

TERRITORY AND POPULATION
Ghana is bounded west by Côte d'Ivoire, north by Burkina Faso, east by Togo and south by the Gulf of Guinea. The area is 238,537 sq. km. Population, 1997 estimate, 18,101,000; density, 76 per sq. km.

The UN gives a projected population for 2000 of 19·93m.

In 1995 an estimated 36% of the population was urban. 1m. Ghanaians lived abroad in 1995.

Ghana is divided into 10 regions:

Regions	Area (sq. km)	Population census 1984	Capital
Eastern	19,977	1,680,890	Koforidua
Western	23,921	1,157,807	Sekondi-Takoradi
Central	9,826	1,142,335	Cape Coast
Ashanti	24,390	2,090,100	Kumasi
Brong-Ahafo	39,557	1,206,608	Sunyani
Northern	70,383	1,164,583	Tamale
Volta	20,572	1,211,907	Ho
Upper East	8,842	772,744	Bolgatanga
Upper West	18,477	438,008	Wa
Greater Accra	2,593	1,431,099	Accra

Chief cities with 1988 estimated populations: Accra, the capital, 949,113; Kumasi, 385,192; Tamale, 151,069; Tema, 109,975; Sekondi-Takoradi, 103,653.

About 44% of the population are Akan. Other tribal groups include Moshi-Dagomba (16%), Ewe (13%) and Ga (8%). About 75 languages are spoken; the official language is English.

SOCIAL STATISTICS
1995 births, 676,000; deaths, 191,000. Birth rate (per 1,000 population), 1995: 39·3; death rate, 11·0. 1997 estimates: Growth rate, 2·21%; infant mortality, 79 per 1,000 live births; life expectancy, 54·5 years for men, 58·6 for women. Fertility rate, 1990–95, 5·7 births per woman.

CLIMATE
The climate ranges from the equatorial type on the coast to savannah in the north and is typified by the existence of well-marked dry and wet seasons. Temperatures are relatively high throughout the year. The amount, duration and seasonal distribution of rain is very marked, from the south, with over 80" (2,000 mm), to the north, with under 50" (1,250 mm). In the extreme north, the wet season is from March to Aug., but further south it lasts until Oct. Near Kumasi, two wet seasons occur, in May and June and again in Oct., and this is repeated, with greater amounts, along the coast of Ghana. Accra, Jan. 80°F (26·7°C), July 77°F (25°C). Annual rainfall 29" (724 mm). Kumasi, Jan. 77°F (25°C), July 76°F (24·4°C). Annual rainfall 58" (1,402 mm). Sekondi-Takoradi, Jan. 77°F (25°C), July 76°F (24·4°C). Annual rainfall 47" (1,181 mm). Tamale, Jan. 82°F (27·8°C), July 78°F (25·6°C). Annual rainfall 41" (1,026 mm).

CONSTITUTION AND GOVERNMENT
After the coup of 31 Dec. 1981, supreme power was vested in the Provisional National Defence Council (PNDC), chaired by Flight-Lieut. Jerry John Rawlings.

A new constitution was approved by 92·6% of votes cast at a referendum on 28 April 1992. The electorate was 8,255,690; turn-out was 43·8%. The constitution sets up a presidential system on the US model, with a multi-party parliament and an independent judiciary. The *President* is elected by universal suffrage for a 4-year term renewable once.

National Anthem. 'God bless our Homeland, Ghana'; words by the government, tune by P. Gbeho.

RECENT ELECTIONS
Presidential and parliamentary elections were held on 7 Dec. 1996. The electorate was 9m.; turn-out was 75%. President Rawlings was re-elected by 57·2% of votes cast against 2 opponents. There were some 700 parliamentary candidates. The National Democratic Congress (NDC) gained 132 seats, ahead of the New Patriotic Party with 60.

CURRENT ADMINISTRATION
In March 1999 the government comprised the following:

President: Jerry John Rawlings, b. 1947 (NDC; sworn in 7 Jan. 1993 and most recently on 7 Jan. 1997).

Vice-President: John Evans Atta Mills.

Secretary of State for Foreign Affairs: James Victor Gbeho. *Justice and Attorney-General:* Dr Obed Y. Asamoah. *Interior:* Nii Okaidja Adamafio. *Defence:* Lt. Col. Enoch Donkoh. *Finance and Economic Planning:* Richard Kwame Peprah. *Trade and Industries:* Dr John Abu. *Communications:* John Mahama. *Food and Agriculture:* J. H. Owusu-Acheampong. *Education:* Ekwow Spio-Garbrah. *Health:* Dr Eunice Brookman-Amissah. *Roads and Transport:* Edward Salia. *Local Government and Rural Development:* Kwamena Ahwoi. *Mines and Energy:* Fred Ohene Kena. *Employment and Social Welfare:* Alhaji Mohammed Mumuni. *Lands and Forestry:* Christine Amoako-Nuamah. *Environment, Science and Technology:* Cletus Apul Avoka. *Parliamentary Affairs:* Dr Kwabena Adjei. *Tourism:* Michael Gizo. *Works and Housing:* Isaac Adjei-Mensah. *Youth and Sports:* Enoch T. Mensah.

The *Speaker* is Daniel Annan.

Local Government. The 10 Regions, each under a Regional Secretary appointed by the PNDC, are divided into 110 districts.

DEFENCE
Defence expenditure totalled US$134m. in 1997 (US$7 per capita).

Army. The Army consists of 2 brigades, 1 reconnaissance regiment, 1 airborne force, 1 field engineer battalion, and 1 mortar battalion, with armoured cars and ancillary units. Total strength (1997) 5,000. There is a paramilitary People's Militia of 5,000, a part-time force with police duties, and a Presidential Guard comprising 1 infantry battalion.

Navy. The Navy, based at Sekondi and Tema, comprises 2 German-built coastal patrol, 2 inshore patrol craft and 2 small service craft. 2 unarmed F-27 aircraft are available for maritime patrol. Naval strength in 1997 was 1,000 including support personnel.

Air Force. The Ghana Air Force has 4 Italian-built Aermacchi M.B.326K light ground attack jets. It also operates, for training, transport, search and rescue, and air survey operations, 4 Fokker Friendship twin-turboprop transports and a twin-turbofan Fokker Fellowship for Presidential use, 4 Islander piston-engined light transports and 4 Shorts Skyvan twin-turboprop short-take-off-and-landing transports; 2 Bell 212 helicopters; 2 Alouette III helicopters, and 8 L-29 Delfin and 2 M.B.339 jet trainers. There are air bases at Takoradi and Tamale. Personnel strength (1997) 1,000.

INTERNATIONAL RELATIONS
In March 1998 the IMF removed barriers to the offer of financial support from aid donors totalling US$1·6bn. in 1998 and 1999.

Ghana is a member of the UN, the Commonwealth, OAU, ECOWAS and is an ACP state of the EU.

ECONOMY

Policy. Ghana is committed to the reform programmes of the IMF and World Bank and is one of Africa's biggest borrowers. In 1996 aid amounted to 11% of GDP, or 4 times the value of Ghana's exports. A privatization programme was inaugurated in 1988. By 1996, 100 of the 260 enterprises in which the government had a majority stake had been sold. Privatization deals raised US$804m. between 1990 and 1996, including the Ashanti Goldfields sell-off worth more than US$300m. Only South Africa among sub-Saharan African nations has raised more from privatization. Building, tourism, technology and financial services account for more than 46% of national income. President Rawlings has set a target date of 2020 for the country to achieve middle income status.

Performance. Real GDP growth was estimated at 2·1% in 1998 (3·0% in 1997).

Budget. The 1996 budget provided for (in ₵1,000m.): Revenue, 2,328·3; expenditure, 2,169·5. VAT was abolished in 1995.

Currency. The monetary unit is the *cedi* (GHC) of 100 *pesewas* (P). In 1996 inflation was an annualized 50%. It had declined to 28·0% in 1997 and was estimated to be 16·0% in 1998. Foreign exchange reserves were US$454m. in Nov. 1997 and gold reserves were 270,000 troy oz. Total money supply in Dec. 1997 was ₵1,724bn.

Banking and Finance. The Bank of Ghana (*Chair,* Godfried K. Agama) was established in 1957 as the central bank and bank of issue. At Dec. 1995 its total assets were ₵3,272,946·6m. There are 3 large commercial banks, 7 secondary banks, 3 merchant banks and 100 rural banks. There are 2 discount houses. Banks are required to have a capital base of at least 6% of net assets. At Dec. 1995 assets of commercial banks totalled ₵1,900,327·1m.

Foreign investment is actively encouraged with the Ghana Free Zone Scheme offering particular incentives such as full exemption of duties and levies on all imports for production and exports from the zones, full exemption on tax on profits for ten years, and no more than 8% after ten years. It is a condition of the scheme that at least 70% of goods made within the zones must be exported. Within 18 months of the scheme being set up in 1995, 50 projects had been registered.

Ghana's stock exchange was one of the world's best performing stock markets in 1998.

ENERGY AND NATURAL RESOURCES
Ghana is facing an energy crisis, with power cuts of up to 12 hours a day because drought has caused the level of Lake Volta to drop to below the danger level.

Electricity. Installed capacity was 1·19m. kW in 1994. Production (1994) 6·1bn. kWh, mainly from 2 hydro-electric stations operated by the Volta River Authority, Akosombo (6 units) and Kpong (4 units). Consumption per capita was estimated to be 304 kWh in 1995. It is planned that electricity production will become less dependent on hydro-electric stations and more so on gas, with the construction of a 600 km pipeline forming part of the proposed West African Gas Pipeline Project.

Oil and Gas. Ghana is pursuing the development of its own gas fields and plans to harness gas at the North and South Tano fields located off the western coast. Estimates put gas reserves at 480bn. cu. feet. Oil reserves are estimated at 129·6m. bbls.

Minerals. In 1994 diamond production was officially estimated at 0·7m. carats; manganese (1993), 362,000 tonnes; bauxite (1994), 396,861 tonnes; gold (1994), 44·5 tonnes; (1993), 41·5 tonnes.

Agriculture. In 1996 agriculture contributed 43% of GDP. Agriculture is the weak spot in Ghana's economy. The rural poor earn little and many small farmers have reverted to subsistence farming. Around 2·5m. households were engaged in the agricultural sector in 1998. In southern and central Ghana main food crops are maize, rice, cassava, plantains, groundnuts, yam and cocoyam, and in northern Ghana groundnuts, rice, maize, sorghum, millet and yam.

Production of main food crops, 1993 (in 1,000 tonnes): Maize, 961; rice, 157; millet, 198; sorghum, 328; cassava, 4,200; cocoyam, 1,236; yam, 1,000; plantains, 1,322.

Cocoa is the main cash crop. Production (1997–98), 395,000 tonnes. Among other cash crops, tobacco and coffee are important, and improved types of palm oil and coconuts are being planted.

Livestock, 1996: Cattle, 1·2m.; sheep, 2·4m.; pigs, 440,000; goats, 1995, 3·34m.; chickens, 1995, 12m.

Forestry. There were 9·02m. ha of forest in 1995, or 39·7% of the total land area (down from 42·2% in 1990). Reserves account for some 30% of the total forest lands. Timber production in 1995 was 26·47m. cu. metres.

Fisheries. In 1995 total catches were 344,460 tonnes, of which 293,910 tonnes came from sea fishing.

INDUSTRY
Production of aluminium (1990) 174,000 tonnes.

Labour. In 1996 the labour force was 8,393,000, of which females constituted 51%. Only Cambodia had a higher percentage of females in its workforce.

In 1994 there were 37,000 persons registered as unemployed.

INTERNATIONAL TRADE
Foreign debt was estimated at US$5·2bn. in 1996.

Imports and Exports. In 1997 estimated exports were US$1·48bn.; imports valued at US$1·75bn. Principal exports, 1995: Gold, 1,539,000m. oz. valued at US$635·90m.; cocoa and products, 236,255 tonnes valued at US$364·63m.; timber valued at US$190m.; plus tuna, bauxite, aluminium, manganese ore and diamonds. Principal imported commodities: capital equipment, petroleum, consumer goods, food. Main export markets, 1996: UK, 16·0%; Togo, 11·0%; USA, 10·0%; Germany, 9·0%. Main import suppliers: UK, 16·0%; Nigeria, 13·0%; USA, 10·0%; Germany, 5·0%.

COMMUNICATIONS

Roads. In 1996 there were 14,700 km of trunk roads and 24,000 km of other roads. About 25% of all roads, including 21 km of expressway, are hard-surfaced. A Road Sector Strategy and Programme to develop the road network is running from 1995 to 2000. There were 90,000 passenger cars in use in 1996, equivalent to 5 per 1,000 inhabitants.

Rail. Total length of railways in 1993 was 953 km of 1,067 mm gauge. In 1994 railways carried 0·7m. tonnes of freight and 2·3m. passengers.

Civil Aviation. There is an international airport at Accra (Kotoka). The national carrier is the state-owned Ghana Airways. In 1998 services were also provided by Aeroflot, Air Afrique, Air Ivoire, Alitalia, Balkan, British Airways, Egyptair, Ethiopian Airlines, KLM, Lufthansa, Nigeria Airways, Sierra National Airlines, South African Airlines and Swissair. In 1995 Ghana Airways flew 4·9m. km and carried 185,900 passengers (all on international flights).

Shipping. The chief ports are Takoradi and Tema. In 1995, 1·2m. tonnes of cargo were unloaded at Takoradi and 3·9m. tonnes at Tema. There is inland water transport on Lake Volta. In 1996 the merchant marine had 4 cargo ships of 1,000 GRT or over, totalling 28,900 GRT. The Volta, Ankobra and Tano rivers provide 168 km of navigable waterways for launches and lighters.

Telecommunications. In 1997 there were 105,500 telephone main lines, or 5·8 for every 1,000 inhabitants. Ghana Telecom expect to install around 200,000 new lines by 2001. There were 6,200 cellular phone subscribers in 1995, 20,000 PCs and 4,500 fax machines. There were approximately 4,500 Internet users in Jan. 1998.

Postal Services. In 1995 there were 1,001 post offices.

SOCIAL INSTITUTIONS

Justice. The Courts are constituted as follows:

Supreme Court. The Supreme Court consists of the Chief Justice who is also the President, and not less than 4 other Justices of the Supreme Court. The Supreme Court is the final court of appeal in Ghana. The final interpretation of the provisions of the constitution has been entrusted to the Supreme Court.

Court of Appeal. The Court of Appeal consists of the Chief Justice together with not less than 5 other Justices of the Appeal court and such other Justices of Superior Courts as the Chief Justice may nominate. The Court of Appeal is duly constituted by 3 Justices. The Court of Appeal is bound by its own previous decisions and all courts inferior to the Court of Appeal are bound to follow the decisions of the Court of Appeal on questions of law. Divisions of the Appeal Court may be created, subject to the discretion of the Chief Justice.

High Court of Justice. The Court has jurisdiction in civil and criminal matters as well as those relating to industrial and labour disputes including administrative complaints. The High Court of Justice has supervisory jurisdiction over all inferior Courts and any adjudicating authority and in exercise of its supervisory jurisdiction has power to issue such directions, orders or writs including writs or orders in the nature of habeas corpus, certiorari, mandamus, prohibition and quo qarrantto. The High Court of Justice has no jurisdiction in cases of treason. The High Court consists of the Chief Justice and not less than 12 other judges and such other Justices of the Superior Court as the Chief Justice may appoint.

The PNDC has established Public Tribunals in addition to the traditional courts of justice.

There is a Public Tribunal Board consisting of not less than 5 members and not more than 15 members of the public appointed by the PNDC, at least one of whom shall be a lawyer of not less than 5 years' standing as a lawyer. The Board is responsible for the administration of all tribunals.

A tribunal consists of at least three persons and not more than five persons, selected by the Board from among persons appointed by the Council as members of public tribunals.

Religion. An estimated 30% of the population are Moslem and 24% Christian, with 38% adherents to indigenous beliefs and 8% other religions.

GHANA

Education. Schooling is free and compulsory, and consists of 6 years of primary, 3 years of junior secondary and 3 years of senior secondary education. In 1990, 75% of eligible children attended primary, and 39% secondary, school. In 1991–92 there were 2·01m. pupils in primary and in 1989–90, 829,518 in secondary schools. University education is free. There are 2 universities, 1 university each for development studies, and science and technology. In 1994–95 there were 11,225 university students and 779 academic staff. There were also 6 polytechnics, 7 colleges and 38 teacher training colleges. Adult literacy in 1995 was 64·5% (75·9% among men and 53·5% among women).

Health. Provision of doctors, 1994: 1 per 22,970 population. Provision of hospital beds, 1994: 1 per 638 population. At the end of 1995 there were 15,890 cases of AIDS, mainly women.

CULTURE

Broadcasting. The Ghana Broadcasting Corporation is an autonomous statutory body. There are 5 national radio programmes. In 1994 there was 1 public national and 1 independent local TV network. In 1995 there were 4m. radio and 1·6m. TV receivers (colour by PAL).

Press. There were (1995) 4 daily newspapers with a combined circulation of 3·1m.

Tourism. There were 298,000 foreign tourists in 1996, spending US$239m. A Ministry of Tourism was established in 1994. A 5-year Tourism Development Plan was instituted in 1996. Many new hotels are planned including two 5-star 400-room hotels.

DIPLOMATIC REPRESENTATIVES
Of Ghana in Great Britain (13 Belgrave Sq., London, SW1X 8PN)
High Commissioner: James E. K. Aggrey-Orleans.

Of Great Britain in Ghana (Osu Link, off Gamel Abdul Nasser Ave., Accra)
High Commissioner: Ian W. Mackley, CMG.

Of Ghana in the USA (3512 International Dr., NW, Washington, D.C., 20008)
Ambassador: Kobina Arthur Koomson.

Of the USA in Ghana (Ring Rd. East, Accra)
Ambassador: Edward Brynn.

Of Ghana to the United Nations
Ambassador: Jacob Botwe Wilmot.

Of Ghana to the European Union
Ambassador: Alex Ntim Abankwa.

FURTHER READING
Carmichael, J., *Profile of Ghana.* London, 1992.—*African Eldorado: Ghana from Gold Coast to Independence.* London, 1993
Davidson, B., *Black Star.* London, 1973
Herbst, J., *The Politics of Reform in Ghana, 1982–1991.* California Univ. Press, 1993
Myers, R. A., *Ghana* [Bibliography]. Oxford and Santa Barbara (CA), 1991
Petchenkine, Y., *Ghana in Search of Stability, 1957–1992.* New York, 1992
Ray, D. I., *Ghana: Politics, Economics and Society.* London, 1986
Rimmer, D., *Staying Poor: Ghana's Political Economy, 1950–1990.* Oxford, 1993
Rothchild., D. (ed.): *Ghana: the Political Economy of Recovery.* Boulder (Colo.), 1991

National statistical office: Statistical Service, Accra.

GREECE

Elliniki Dimokratia

(Hellenic Republic)

Capital: Athens
Population estimate, 2000: 10·6m.
GNP per capita: (PPP$) 12,730
HDI/world rank: 0·924/20

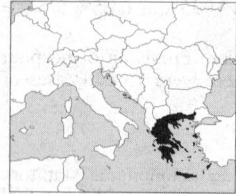

KEY HISTORICAL EVENTS

Greece gained independence from the Ottoman Empire between 1821-29, and by the Protocol of London of 3 Feb. 1830 was declared a kingdom under the protection of Great Britain, France and Russia. Many Greeks were left outside the new state and the cause of the union of all Greeks was championed by Otto I, a Bavarian who was enthroned on 18 Jan. 1833. After his overthrow on 23 Oct. 1862 a Danish prince was elected George I, King of the Hellenes in 1863. The 1844 constitution was replaced by one based on popular sovereignty in 1864. A programme of domestic renewal was launched after 1910, including important land reforms in 1917. In 1864 Great Britain had ceded the Ionian Islands; in 1881 Thessaly and part of Epirus had been taken. Greece's area increased by 70%, the population growing from 2·8m. to 4·8 m. after the Treaty of Bucharest (1913) which recognized Greek sovereignty over Crete.

King Constantine, who succeeded on his father's assassination on 18 March 1913, opted for neutrality in the First World War, while Prime Minister Venezelos favoured the Entente powers. This split or National Schism led to British and French intervention which deposed Constantine on 11 June 1917. When his son Alexander died on 25 Oct. 1920, he returned on 19 Dec. and reigned until 27 Sept. 1922. He was forced to abdicate by a *coup* after defeat by Turkey and the loss of Smyrna. The Treaty of Lausanne (1923) recognized Smyrna as Turkish with Eastern Thrace and the islands of Imvros and Tenedos, all of which had been ceded to Greece by the 1920 Treaty of Sevres.

An exchange of Christian and Moslem populations followed. The presence of over 1m. immigrants brought about social problems, despite an effective peasant settlement in the countryside. The newcomers contributed strongly to the fall of the monarchy in a plebiscite on 13 April 1924. George II was restored after a new plebiscite on 25 Nov. 1935.

The authoritarian Metaxas, premier since 1937, was unable to preserve neutrality after the Italian ultimatum of 28 Oct. 1940. The successful resistance of the Greek army forced the Germans to aid Italy on 6 April 1941. Surrender followed on 20 April and Athens was occupied on 27 April. The harsh occupation lasted until 15 Oct. 1944.

The popular front EAM and its military wing ELAS, both dominated by the communists, took a leading part in resistance to the Germans. The king had moved in April 1941 to Crete, then to Cairo and London. On 30 Dec. 1944 he appointed Archbishop Damaskinos as regent before returning on 28 Sept. 1946 with British backing and the support of a plebiscite. On his death on 1 April 1947 he was succeeded by his brother Paul. A conflict with ELAS developed into a civil war in 1946-47 which made refugees of 10% of the population. Britain handed responsibility to the USA which pledged support against the communists who received only short-lived Yugoslav aid. Peace came after 1949.

The adoption, under US pressure, of a simple majority system rather than proportional representation and the growing industrialization of the economy brought stability, especially after 1955 under the pro-western Konstantinos Karamanlis. The late 1950s saw the emergence of the Left, capitalizing on the movement for union with Cyprus and unease over NATO membership (1952). On 9 Aug. 1954 Greece, Turkey and Yugoslavia signed a 20-year treaty of friendship and mutual aid.

The election of 1963, based on proportional representation, undermined the position of the Right and led to conflict with the new king Constantine, who succeeded his father Paul on 6 March 1964. A military *coup* on 21 April 1967, with fear of communism its stated reason, led to the departure the following year of the king after an unsuccessful counter-*coup*. The authoritarian rule of the 'Colonels' was headed by George Papadopoulos, prime minister, regent (1972) and president after the republic was declared on 29 July 1973. The régime was overthrown in a bloodless *coup* by Gen. Chizikis on 25 Nov. 1973.

Inflation and the failure to defeat President Makarios of Cyprus or to prevent the Turkish invasion of the island led to the collapse of the military dictatorship on 23 July 1974. Karamanlis was recalled from exile to form a civilian government of national unity. On 17 Nov. 1974 he and his New Democracy Party won a large majority. The monarchy was abolished by a referendum on 8 Dec. 1974.

Hostility to the USA grew, especially as it was believed that America favoured Turkey, with whom conflicts persisted. The 1981 election brought Andreas Papandreou to power and the head of a socialist government. Earlier that year Greece had become the tenth member of the EC. Re-elected in 1985, Papandreou imposed economic austerity to combat inflation and soaring budgets but industrial unrest and evidence of widespread corruption led to his fall and a succession of weak governments. Papandreou returned to power in Oct. 1993 but ill-health forced his resignation two years later. His successor Constantinos Simitis took a more pro-European stance instituting economic reforms to prepare the way for entry into EMU.

TERRITORY AND POPULATION

Greece is bounded in the north by Albania, the Former Yugoslav Republic of Macedonia (FYROM) and Bulgaria, east by Turkey and the Aegean Sea, south by the Mediterranean and west by the Ionian Sea. The total area is 131,957 sq. km (50,949 sq. miles), of which the islands account for 25,042 sq. km (9,669 sq. miles).

The population was 10,259,900 (5,204,492 females) according to the census of March 1991. 1997 estimate: 10,511,000; density, 80 per sq. km.

The UN gives a projected population for 2000 of 10·6m.

An estimated 59·2% of the population lived in urban areas in 1995. There were 166,031 resident foreign nationals in 1991. A further 5m. Greeks are estimated to live abroad.

In 1987 the territory of Greece was administratively reorganized into 13 *regions* comprising in all 51 *departments*. Areas and populations according to the 1991 census:

Region/Department	Area in sq. km	Population	Chief town
Attica[1]	*3,808*	*3,523,407*	*Athens*
Aegean North	*3,836*	*199,231*	*Mytilene*
Chios	904	52,184	Chios
Lesbos	2,154	105,082	Mytilene
Samos	778	41,965	Samos
Aegean South	*5,286*	*257,481*	*Hermoupolis*
Cyclades	2,572	94,005	Hermoupolis
Dodecanese	2,714	163,476	Rhodes
Crete	*8,336*	*540,054*	*Heraklion*
Canea	2,376	133,774	Canea
Heraklion	2,641	264,906	Heraklion
Lassithi	1,823	71,279	Aghios Nikolaos
Rethymnon	1,496	70,095	Rethymnon
Epirus	*9,203*	*339,728*	*Ioannina*
Arta	1,662	78,719	Arta
Ioannina	4,990	158,193	Ioannina
Preveza	1,036	58,628	Preveza
Thesprotia	1,515	44,188	Hegoumenitsa
Greece Central[2]	*15,549*	*582,280*	*Lamia*
Boeotia	2,952	134,108	Levadeia
Euboea	4,167	208,408	Chalcis
Evrytania	1,869	24,307	Karpenissi
Phocis	2,120	44,183	Amphissa
Phthiotis	4,441	171,274	Lamia
Greece West	*11,350*	*707,687*	*Patras*
Achaia	3,271	300,078	Patras
Elia	2,618	179,429	Pyrgos

[1]Attica is both region and department. [2]Without Attica.

Region/Department	Area in sq. km	Population	Chief town
Aetolia and Acarnania	5,461	228,180	Messolonghi
Ionian Islands	*2,307*	*193,734*	*Corfu*
Cephalonia	904	32,474	Argostoli
Corfu	641	107,592	Corfu
Leucas	356	21,111	Leucas
Zante	406	32,557	Zante
Macedonia Central	*19,147*	*1,711,513*	*Thessaloniki*
Chalcidice	2,918	92,117	Polygyros
Imathia	1,701	139,934	Veroia
Kilkis	2,519	81,710	Kilkis
Mount Athos	336	1,536	—
Pella	2,506	138,761	Edessa
Pieria	1,516	116,763	Katerini
Serres	3,968	192,828	Serres
Thessaloniki	3,683	946,864	Thessaloniki
Macedonia East and Thrace	*14,157*	*570,496*	*Comotini*
Cavalla	2,111	135,937	Cavalla
Drama	3,468	96,554	Drama
Evros	4,242	143,752	Alexandroupolis
Rhodope	2,543	103,190	Comotini
Xanthi	1,793	91,063	Xanthi
Macedonia West	*9,451*	*293,015*	*Kozani*
Florina	1,924	53,147	Florina
Grevena	2,291	36,797	Grevena
Kastoria	1,720	52,685	Kastoria
Kozani	3,516	150,386	Kozani
Peloponnese	*15,490*	*607,428*	*Tripolis*
Arcadia	4,419	105,309	Tripolis
Argolis	2,154	97,636	Nauplion
Corinth	2,290	141,823	Corinthos
Laconia	3,636	95,696	Sparti
Messenia	2,991	166,964	Calamata
Thessaly	*14,037*	*734,846*	*Larissa*
Karditsa	2,636	126,854	Karditsa
Larissa	5,381	270,612	Larissa
Magnesia	2,636	198,434	Volos
Trikala	3,384	138,946	Trikala

The largest cities (1991 census populations) are Athens (the capital), 772,072 (total conurbation of Greater Athens, 3,072,922); Thessaloniki, 749,048; Piraeus, 182,671; Patras, 170,452; Peristerion, 137,288; Heraklion, 126,907; Larissa, 112,777; Kallithea, 114,233. Greater Athens, composed of the capital city, the port of Priaeus and a number of suburbs, contains about one third of the Greek population. It also contains about 50% of the country's industry and is the principal commercial, financial and diplomatic centre. Efforts have, however, been made to decentralize the economy. The second city, Salonika (Thessaloniki, with 974,000 inhabitants), with its major port, has grown rapidly in population and industrial development. Other important towns are Patras (300,000 inhabitants), Larissa (271,000 inhabitants), Volos and Iraklion on the island of Crete.

The Monastic Republic of **Mount Athos** (or Agion Oros, i.e. 'Holy Mountain'), the easternmost of the three prongs of the peninsula of Chalcidice, is a self-governing community composed of 20 monasteries. The peninsula is administered by a Council of 4 members and an Assembly of 20 members, 1 deputy from each monastery. The Constitution of 1927 gives legal sanction to the Charter of Mount Athos, drawn up by representatives of the 20 monasteries on 20 May 1924, and its status is confirmed by the 1952 and 1975 Constitutions. Women are not permitted to enter. Population, 1997, 4,000.

The modern Greek language had 2 contesting literary standard forms, the archaizing *Katharevousa* ('purist'), and a version based on the spoken vernacular, 'Demotic'. In 1976 Standard Modern Greek was adopted as the official language, with Demotic as its core.

SOCIAL STATISTICS
1996 estimates: 101,495 live births; 100,158 deaths; 63,987 marriages; 9,000 divorces; 599 still births (1994); 2,982 births to unmarried mothers (1994). 1996 rates: Birth (per 1,000 population), 9·7; death, 9·6; marriage, 6·1. Annual growth rate, 1990–95, 0·6%. Over 1990–95, the suicide rate per 100,000 population was 3·5 (men, 5·5; women, 1·5). Expectation of life at birth, 1990–95, 75·0 years for males and 80·1 years for females. In 1995 the most popular age range for marrying was 25–29 for both males and females. Infant mortality, 1990–95, 9 per 1,000 live births; fertility rate, 1·4 births per woman.

CLIMATE
Coastal regions and the islands have typical Mediterranean conditions, with mild, rainy winters and hot, dry, sunny summers. Rainfall comes almost entirely in the winter months, though amounts vary widely according to position and relief. Continental conditions affect the northern mountainous areas, with severe winters, deep snow cover and heavy precipitation, but summers are hot. Athens, Jan. 48°F (8·6°C), July 82·5°F (28·2°C). Annual rainfall 16·6" (414·3 mm).

CONSTITUTION AND GOVERNMENT
Greece is a presidential parliamentary democracy. A new Constitution was introduced in June 1975. The 300-member *Chamber of Deputies* is elected for 4-year terms by proportional representation. There is a 3% threshold. Extra seats are awarded to the party which leads in an election. The Chamber of Deputies elects the head of state, the *President*, for a 5-year term.

National Anthem. 'Imnos eis tin Eleftherian' ('Hymn to Freedom'); words by Dionysios Solomos, tune by N. Mantzaros.

RECENT ELECTIONS
Parliamentary elections were held on 22 Sept. 1996. The electorate was 8,862,014. Seats gained (and % of vote): Pasok (i.e. Panhellenic Socialist Movement), 162 (41·5%); New Democracy, 108 (38·1%); Communist Party, 11 (5·6%); Coalition of Self-Management Left (SYN), 10 (5·1%); Dikki (dissident Pasok), 9 (4%).

European Parliament. Greece has 25 representatives. At the June 1994 elections turn-out was 71·9%. Pasok won 10 seats with 37·6% of votes cast (group in European Parliament: European Socialist Party); New Democracy, 9 with 32·7% (Popular European Party); left-wing coalition, 4 with 12·5%; others, 2 with 8·7%.

CURRENT ADMINISTRATION
President: Constantinos Stephanopoulos (elected 8 March 1995).

A government was formed on 24 Sept. 1996, comprising in March 1999:

Prime Minister: Constantinos Simitis (b. 1937; Pasok).

Minister to the Prime Minister, Interior, Public Administration and Decentralization: Vasso Papandreou. *Defence:* Apostolos-Athanasios Tsohatsopulos. *Foreign Affairs:* Yeoryios Papandreou. *Foreign Affairs (Alternate):* Yiannos Kranidhiotis. *Economy and Finance:* Yiannos Papantoniou. *Agriculture:* George Anomeritis. *Labour and Social Security:* Militiadis Papaioannou. *Health and Welfare:* Lambros Papadimas. *Justice:* Evangelos Yannopoulos. *Education and Religious Affairs:* Gerasimos Arsenis. *Culture:* Elisavet Papazoi. *Merchant Marine:* Stavros Soumakis. *Public Order:* Mikhail Khrisokhoidhis. *Macedonia and Thrace:* Yiannis Magriotis. *The Aegean:* Stavros Benos. *Environment, Town Planning and Public Works:* Costas Laliotis. *Transport and Communications:* Tassos Mantelis. *Press, Mass Media and Media Government Spokesman:* Dimitris Reppas. *Development:* Evangelos Venizelos.

Local Government. Departments are headed by prefects, elected for the first time in Oct. 1994. Mayoral elections were also held in 434 municipalities. Pasok and other socialists gained 213 municipalities and 37 departments with 45% of votes cast; New Democracy, 160 and 13 with 39%. In the mayoral elections of Oct. 1998 Pasok won only half of the 54 regional administrators' posts at stake.

DEFENCE

Conscription is (Army) 19 months, (Navy) 23 months, (Air Force) 21 months.

In 1997 defence expenditure totalled US$5,552m. (US$526 per capita), representing 4·6% of GDP.

Army. The Field Army is organized in 3 military regions, with 1 Army, 5 corps and 4 divisional headquarters. There are 9 infantry divisions, 5 independent armoured, 2 independent mechanized, 2 infantry and 1 marine brigade, 1 commando and 1 raider regiment, 4 reconnaissance, 10 field artillery, 8 air defence artillery, 2 surface-to-air missile and 2 army aviation battalions and 1 independent aviation company. There is also a Territorial Defence Force of 36,000, with 4 military command headquarters, comprising 1 infantry division, 1 parachute regiment and 8 field artillery, 4 air defence artillery and 1 army aviation battalion. Reserves of 35,000 form a National Guard whose role is internal security. Total Army strength (1997) 122,000 (95,000 conscripts, 2,900 women). There is also a paramilitary gendarmerie of 26,500.

Navy. The current strength of the Hellenic Navy includes 8 diesel submarines, 4 ex-US guided-missile destroyers, 11 frigates including 7 helicopter-equipped, 5 corvettes and 19 fast missile craft. Main bases are at Salamis, Patras, and Soudha Bay (Crete). Personnel in 1996 totalled 19,500 (9,800 conscripts, 1,300 women).

The Coastguard and Customs service is 4,000 strong.

Air Force. The Hellenic Air Force (HAF) had a strength (1996) of 26,800 (14,400 conscripts, 1,100 women). There are 3 squadrons of F-4E Phantom and 2 squadrons of Mirage 2000 air-superiority fighters, 2 squadrons of F-16 fighter-bombers, 2 squadrons of Mirage F.1 fighters, 4 squadrons of A-7H Corsair II attack aircraft, 2 squadrons of F-5 fighters, 1 squadron of RF-4E reconnaissance fighters and 1 squadron of P-3–Orion maritime reconnaissance aircraft (under Navy control).

The HAF is organized into Tactical and Air Support Commands.

INTERNATIONAL RELATIONS

Greece is a member of the UN, EU, WEU, Council of Europe and NATO.

ECONOMY

Policy. Greek economic policy is focused on meeting the convergence criteria for joining the European Monetary Union. The aim is to join EMU by 2001 at the latest. In the late 1990s, Greek growth rates have been among the highest in the EU. Besides a restrictive incomes policy, the government has announced a number of structural reforms, including measures to enhance the flexibility of the labour market, improve the social security system, restructure public sector enterprises and speed up privatization.

Performance. Growth rates have averaged 3% of GDP over the past 5 years. Real GDP growth was 3·2% in 1997 (2·4% in 1996), with a forecast of 2·4% for 1998. GDP in US$ was 116·8bn. (1997, provisional) and 122·9bn. (1996).

Budget. Estimated revenue 1999 (in 1,000m. drachmas): 11,090; expenditure: 13,489.

VAT is 18% (reduced rate, 8%).

Currency. The unit of currency is the *drachma* (GRD), notionally divided into 100 *lepta*. In March 1998 the *drachma* was admitted to the Exchange Rate Mechanism, two years' membership of which is one of the conditions for joining the euro. The admission came along with a 14% devaluation. Inflation was 7·5% in Dec. 1996, 5·1% in Nov. 1997 and 5·0% in 1998. Foreign exchange reserves were US$14,189m. and gold reserves 3·62m. troy oz. in Feb. 1998. Total money supply in Oct. 1997 was 4,588bn. drachmas. The Current account (US$1m.) stood at –5,000 in 1997 (provisional) and –4,539 in 1996. Central government debt as percentage of GDP was 109% (provisional) at Dec. 1997 and 111·8% at Dec. 1996.

Banking and Finance. The central bank and bank of issue is the Bank of Greece. Its *Governor* is Loukas Papademos. There were 25 domestic banks in 1994, 8 private and the remainder in 4 state groupings. In 1995 the major banks (with profits in Dr 1,000m.) were: The private Alpha Credit Bank (50·7) and the State-owned National

Bank (41·1), Ergobank (37·4), Commercial Bank (26·2), Mortgage Bank (20·6) and Ionian Bank (13·6). Total assets of all banks were US$15,421,377m. in 1994.

Cretabank, Ionian Bank and Bank of Central Greece, all state banks, were privatized in 1998.

There is a stock exchange in Athens.

Weights and Measures. The metric system was made obligatory in 1959; the use of other systems is prohibited. The Gregorian calendar was adopted in Feb. 1923.

ENERGY AND NATURAL RESOURCES

Electricity. Installed capacity in 1995 was 9·2m. kW. 72% of power is supplied by lignite-fired power stations. A national grid supplies the mainland, and islands near its coast. Power is produced in remoter islands by local generators. Total production in 1995 was 37·55bn. kWh, with consumption per capita in 1995 an estimated 3,466 kWh. Electricity supply is: domestic, 220v, 50 cycles AC; industrial, 280v, AC 3 phase.

Oil and Gas. Output of crude petroleum, 1996, 3m. bbls; proven reserves, 1996, 12m. bbls. The oil sector plays a critical role in the Greek economy, accounting for more than 70% of total energy demand. Supply is mostly imported but oil prospecting is intensifying. Natural gas was introduced in Greece in 1997 through the recently built pipeline from Russia, and an additional source of supply is liquefied natural gas from Algeria. Demand for natural gas is in its infancy. The public monopoly in natural gas, DEPA, has developed only a few sales contracts to some large industrial groups, outside a large contract with DEH.

Minerals. Greece produces a variety of ores and minerals, including (with production, 1995, in tonnes) iron-pyrites (18,737), bauxite (2,200,215), nickel ore (2,069,466), magnesite (565,720), asbestos (4,920,650), chromite (5,650 in 1993), caustic magnesia (206,532), marble (white and coloured) and various other earths. There is little coal, and the lignite is of indifferent quality (56·5m. tonnes, 1995). Salt production (1995) 143,351 tonnes.

Agriculture. Of the total area (131,957 sq. km) 39,435·9 sq. km is arable and fallow. Another 52,101 sq. km is grazing land.

The Greek economy was traditionally based on agriculture, with small-scale farming predominating, except in a few areas in the north. There were 819,000 farms in 1998. However, there has been a steady shift towards industry and although agriculture still employs nearly 19% of the population, it accounts for only 11·6% of GDP. Agriculture accounts for 33·1% of exports (the highest proportion of any EU member country) and 17·9% of imports.

Production (1996, in 1,000 tonnes):

Wheat	2,086	Grapes	917
Rye	33	Wine must	439
Tobacco	155	Citrus fruit	1,525
Seed cotton	1,272	Other fruit	1,695
Sugar-beet	2,395	Milk	1,860
Raisins	69	Meat	505
Olive oil	396		

Olive production in 1996 was 282,000 tonnes. Rice, 1996, 149,478 tonnes. The main kinds of cheese produced are *fetta* (white cheese in brine, 118,225 tonnes in 1993), and hard cheese, 35,989.

Livestock (1996, in 1,000): 580 cattle, 996 pigs, 8,896 sheep, 4,319 goats, 33 horses, 39 mules, 83 asses, 28,025 poultry, 1 buffalo.

Forestry. Area covered by forests in 1995 was 29,400 sq. km. Timber production in 1995 was 2·31m. cu. metres.

Fisheries. In 1996, 12,497 fishermen were active and landed 156,776 tonnes of fish. 11,000 kg of sponges were produced in 1996.

INDUSTRY

Manufacturing contributed an estimated 2,219,730m. drachmas to GDP in 1993. The main products are canned vegetables and fruit, fruit juice, beer, wine, alcoholic beverages, cigarettes, textiles, yarn, leather, shoes, synthetic timber, paper, plastics, rubber products, chemical acids, pigments, pharmaceutical products, cosmetics, soap, disinfectants, fertilizers, glassware, porcelain sanitary items, wire and power coils and household instruments.

Production, 1996 (1,000 tonnes): Textile yarns, 146; cement, 25,355; fertilizers, 1,033; ammonia, 57 (1993); iron (concrete-reinforcing bars), 635; alumina, 620; aluminium, 148; beer, 447,000 litres; bottled wine, 171,821 litres; chemical acids, 1,478; iron wire, 107 (1993); packing materials, 308; cigarettes (1,000 pieces), 38,269; petroleum, 8,090 (1994); detergents, 263.

Though manufacturing accounts for 21·35% of GDP, Greece's performance is hampered by the proliferation of small, traditional, low-tech firms, often run as family businesses. Food, drink and tobacco processing are the most important sectors, but there are also some steel mills and several shipyards. Shipping is of prime importance to the economy. In addition, there are major programmes under way in the fields of power, irrigation and land reclamation.

Labour. Of the total workforce of 4,294,405 in 1997, 3,854,055 persons were employed. 764,984 were engaged in agriculture, 558,658 in manufacturing and 2,530,413 in other employment. Automatic index-linking of wages was abolished at the end of 1990. Wage increases of 6·8% and 5·2% were made in the public sector in 1995 and 1996. In the private sector trade unions agreed to an 8% increase in 1995, 7·6% in 1996 and 7·5% in 1997. Since 1989 a statutory minimum of wage-bills must be spent on training (0·45%). Retirement age is 65 years for men and 60 for women. Unemployment was 10·3% in 1997.

Trade Unions. The status of trade unions is regulated by the Associations Act 1914. Trade union liberties are guaranteed under the Constitution, and a law of June 1982 altered the unions' right to strike.

The national body of trade unions is the Greek General Confederation of Labour.

INTERNATIONAL TRADE

Following the normalization of their relations, Greece lifted its trade embargo (imposed in Feb. 1994) on Macedonia on 13 Oct. 1995. There are quarrels with Turkey over Cyprus, oil rights under the Aegean and ownership of uninhabited islands close to the Turkish coast.

Imports and Exports. In 1996 exports were valued at US$11,302m. and imports at US$26,286m. In 1995 principal exports (in US$1m.) were: Manufactured goods, 3,075; food and beverages, 1,345; petroleum products, 491; raw materials and semi-finished goods, 328; minerals, 212; tobacco, 173. Principal imports were: Manufactured consumer goods, 8,876; capital goods, 5,703; food, 3,219; crude oil, 1,178; chemicals, 1,105; iron and steel, 782.

Exports in 1995 (in 1m. drachmas) were mainly to Germany (561,313), Italy (357,899), France (138,477), UK (154,731) and USA (79,664). Imports were mainly from Germany (993,859), Italy (1,024,901), France (488,019), Japan (158,073), the Netherlands (416,130) and UK (390,071).

COMMUNICATIONS

Roads. There were, in 1996, 117,000 km of roads, including 470 km of motorways, 9,100 km of national roads, 31,300 km of secondary and 75,600 km of other roads. Number of motor vehicles in 1996: 3,797,234, of which 2,339,421 were passenger cars, 914,827 trucks, 517,890 motor cycles and 25,096 buses. There are approximately 226 passenger cars per 1,000 population. Road projects include improved links to Turkey and Bulgaria.

Rail. In 1997 the state network, Hellenic Railways (OSE), totalled 2,503 km including 1,565 km of 1,435 mm gauge, 887 km of 1,000 mm gauge, and 51 km of 750 mm gauge. Railways carried 2·19m. tonnes of freight and 12·4m. passengers in 1997. The Greek Railways Organization is investing US$23bn. in the link from Athens to the northern Bulgarian border.

Civil Aviation. There are international airports at Athens (Hellinikon) and Thessaloniki-Makedonia. The national carrier is the state-owned Olympic Airways, serving some 30 towns and islands. Apart from the international airports, there are a further 25 provincial airports all connected by regular services operated by Olympic Airways. 7·0m. passengers were carried in 1997, of whom 4·1m. were on domestic and 2·9m. on international flights. Olympic Airways operates routes from Athens to all important cities of the country, Europe, the Middle East and USA. Services were also provided in 1998 by Ada Air, Aero Lloyd, Aeroflot, Aerosweet Airlines, Air Canada, Air France, Air Greece, Air Malta, Air Moldova, Air One, Alitalia, Alpi Eagles, Armenian Airlines, Austrian Airlines, Balkan, British Airways, Condor Flugdienst, Cronus Air, Crossair, Cyprus Airways, Czech Airlines, Delta Air Lines, Easyjet, Egyptair, El Al, Emirates, Ethiopian Airlines, Finnair, Georgian Airlines, Gulf Air, Hapag Lloyd, Iberia, JAT, KLM, Kuwait Airways, LOT, LTU International Airways, Lufthansa, Luxair, Malév, Middle East Airlines, Pakistan International Airlines, Royal Air Maroc, Royal Jordanian, SABENA, Singapore Airlines, Swissair, Syrian Arab Airlines, TAP, Tarom, Thai Airways International, Tower Air, Tunis Air, Turkish Airlines, Uzbekiston Airways, VASP and Virgin Atlantic. In 1996 Athens (Hellinikon) handled 10,394,967 passengers (6,628,339 on international flights).

Shipping. In 1997 the merchant navy comprised 1,927 vessels of 25,708,074 GRT. Greek-owned ships under foreign flags numbered 127 of 2,785,865 GRT in 1997. Totalled registered tonnage in 1995, 30·25m. GRT, including 13·45m. GRT of oil tankers and 0·64m. GRT of container ships.

There is a canal (opened 9 Nov. 1893) across the Isthmus of Corinth (about 4 miles). The principal seaports are Piraeus, Thessaloniki, Patras, Volos, Igoumenitsa and Heraklion. Greece has 123 seaports with cargo and passenger handling facilities. Container terminals at the port of Piraeus are to be expanded to 1m. TEUs.

Telecommunications. In 1997 there were 5,430,900 telephone main lines. There were 61·7 telephones per 100 inhabitants in 1996, compared to 14·0 in 1971. Cellular phone subscribers numbered 273,000 in 1995 (26 per 1,000 persons), there were 350,000 PCs (33 per 1,000 persons) and 15,000 fax machines. In Jan. 1998 there were 111,000 Internet users.

Postal Services. In 1996 there were 963 post offices with a staff of 11,520. A total of 465,274,000 letters and 3,186,000 parcels were dispatched worldwide in 1996. Total receipts were valued at 78,550m. drachmas and expenses at GRD92,515m. drachmas

SOCIAL INSTITUTIONS

Justice. Judges are appointed for life by the President after consultation with the judicial council. Judges enjoy personal and functional independence. There are 3 divisions of the courts: Administrative, civil and criminal and they must not give decisions which are contrary to the Constitution. Final jurisdiction lies with a Special Supreme Tribunal.

Religion. The Christian Eastern (Greek) Orthodox Church is the established religion to which 98% of the population belong. It is under an archbishop and 67 metropolitans, 1 archbishop and 7 metropolitans in Crete, and 4 metropolitans in the Dodecanese. Roman Catholics have 3 archbishops (in Naxos and Corfu and, not recognized by the State, in Athens) and 1 bishop (for Syra and Santorin). The Exarchs of the Greek Catholics and the Armenians are not recognized by the State. There were 0·15m. Moslems in 1995.

Complete religious freedom is recognized by the Constitution of 1974, but proselytizing from, and interference with, the Greek Orthodox Church is forbidden.

Education. Public education is provided in nursery, primary and secondary schools, starting at 5½–6½ years of age and free at all levels. Adult literacy rate, 1995, 96·7% (male 98·3%; female 95·3%).

In 1995–96 there were 5,598 nursery schools with 8,370 teachers and 127,089 pupils; 7,075 primary schools with 40,107 teachers and 673,409 pupils; 1,895 high schools with 31,353 teachers and 421,645 pupils; 1,192 lycea with 17,492 teachers and 252,945 pupils; 48 ecclesiastical and technical secondary schools of the first cycle with 291 teachers and 3,554 pupils, and 524 ecclesiastical and technical secondary schools of the second cycle with 10,210 teachers and 131,395 pupils. There was also 1 teacher training school with 5 teachers and 151 students; 12

technical education institutions (TEI) with 5,217 teachers and 51,910 students; 22 vocational and ecclesiastical schools with 432 teachers and 2,762 students and 1 technical teacher training school with 41 teachers (and 102 teachers shared with other institutions) and 2,477 students. In 1995–96 there were 18 universities, 2 technical universities and 3 specialized universities (agriculture; economics and business; economics and political science), 1 institute of home economics and 1 school of fine art. There were 184,516 students and 6,466 academic staff.

Health. Doctor and hospital treatment within the Greek national health system is free, but patients have to pay 25% of prescription charges. Those living in remote areas can reclaim a proportion of private medical expenses. In 1994 there were 362 hospitals and sanatoria with a total of 51,788 beds and 170 health centres. There were 40,487 doctors and 10,865 dentists.

Welfare. The majority of employees are covered by the Social Insurance Institute, financed by employer and employee contributions. Benefits include pensions, medical expenses and long-term disability payments.

CULTURE
Greece will host the Olympic Games in 2004.

Broadcasting. Elliniki Radiophonia Tileorasis (ERT), the Hellenic National Radio and Television Institute, is the government broadcasting station. There are 4 national and regional programmes, and an external service, Voice of Greece (16 languages). ERT broadcasts 2 TV programmes (colour by SECAM). Number of receivers in 1996: Radio, 5m.; television, 2·5m. 97% of households have a radio, 75% have a colour TV set and 33% have a video recorder.

Cinema. There were 322 screens in 1995 and 8·5m. admissions. 17 full-length films were made in 1995.

Press. There were 31 daily newspapers published in Athens, 7 in Piraeus and 119 elsewhere in 1996.

Tourism. Tourism is Greece's biggest industry with an estimated revenue for 1998 of US$7bn. Tourists in 1997 numbered 10·59m. There were 577,259 hotel beds in 1996 (285,956 in 1981). A total of 53,364,507 nights were spent in hotels in 1997, 39,991,655 by foreigners and 13,372,852 by nationals.

Festivals. There are many festivals throughout the year:
    The feast of St. Basil (1 Jan.); Gynaecocracy (8 Jan., female dominion); Carnival Season (mid-Feb. to mid-March); Independence Day (25 March); Feast of St. George (23 April); Anastenaria (21–23 May, firewalking); Navy Week (end of June/beginning of July); Athens Lycabettus Theatre artistic performances (June–Aug.); Athens Festival (June–Sept.); Epidaurus Festival (July–Sept.); Philipi and Thasos Festival (July–Sept.); Dodoni Festival (July–Sept.); Athens Wine Festival and Ithaca Music Festival (end of July); Olympus Festival (Aug.); Epirotika Festival (Aug.); Kos Hippokrateia Festival (Aug.); Thessaloniki Film Festival and Festival of Popular Song (Sept.–Oct.); National Anniversary Procession (28 Oct.).

Libraries. There were 759 libraries in 1996.

National Theatre and Opera. There are 2 National Theatres and 1 Opera House.

Museums and Galleries. Amongst Greece's most important museums are the Acropolis Museum, the Museum of the City of Athens, the National Archaeological Museum and the National Historical Museum. In 1995 there were 85 museums and 182 galleries visited by 2,024,846 guests.

DIPLOMATIC REPRESENTATIVES
Of Greece in Great Britain (1A Holland Park, London, W11 3TP)
Ambassador: Vassilis Zafiropoulos.

Of Great Britain in Greece (1 Ploutarchou St., 106 75 Athens)
Ambassador: Sir Michael Llewellyn Smith, KCVO, CMG.

Of Greece in the USA (2221 Massachusetts Ave., NW, Washington, D.C., 20008)
Ambassador: Alexandre Philon.

Of the USA in Greece (91 Vasilissis Sophias Blvd., 101 60 Athens)
Ambassador: Nicholas Burns.

Of Greece to the United Nations
Ambassador: Christos Zacharakis.

FURTHER READING

Clogg, M. J. and R., *Greece*. [Bibliography] Oxford and Santa Barbara (CA), 1980
Clogg, R., *Greece in the 1980s.* London, 1983.—*A Concise History of Greece.* CUP, 1992
Freris, A. F., *The Greek Economy in the Twentieth Century.* London, 1986
Jougnatos, G. A., *Development of the Greek Economy, 1950–91: an Historical, Empirical and Econometric Analysis.* London, 1992
Legg, K. R. and Roberts, J. M., Modern Greece: A Civilization on the Periphery. Oxford, 1997
Pettifer, J., *The Greeks: the Land and the People since the War.* London, 1994
Sarafis, M. and Eve, M. (eds.) *Background to Contemporary Greece.* London, 1990
Tsakalotos, E., *Alternative Economic Strategies: the Case of Greece.* Aldershot, 1991
Veremis, T., *The Military in Greek Politics: From Independence to Democracy.* C. Hurst and Co, London, 1997
Woodhouse, C. M., *Modern Greece: a Short History.* rev. ed. London, 1991

National statistical office: National Statistical Service; 14–16 Lycourgou St., Athens.

GRENADA

Capital: St George's
Population estimate, 2000: 98,000
GNP per capita: (PPP$) 4,340
HDI/world rank: 0·851/51

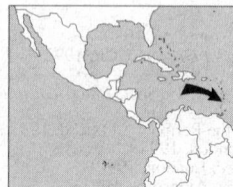

KEY HISTORICAL EVENTS
Grenada became an independent nation within the Commonwealth on 7 Feb. 1974. It was formerly an Associated State under the West Indies Act, 1967. The 1973 Constitution was suspended in 1979 following a revolution.

On 19 Oct. 1983 the army took control after a power struggle led to the killing of Maurice Bishop, the Prime Minister. At the request of a group of Caribbean countries, Grenada was invaded by US-led forces on 25–28 Oct. On 1 Nov. a State of Emergency was imposed which ended on 15 Nov. when an interim government was installed. The 1973 Constitution was restored.

TERRITORY AND POPULATION
Grenada is the most southerly island of the Windward Islands with an area of 133 sq. miles (344 sq. km); the state also includes the Southern Grenadine Islands to the north, chiefly Carriacou (22·5 sq. miles) and Petit Martinique. The total population (Census, 1991) was 95,343 (48,169 females); density, 263 per sq. km. Estimated population (1997) 98,600; density, 287 per sq. km.

In 2000 the population is projected to be 99,400.

An estimated 64·2% of the population were rural in 1995. The Borough of St George's, the capital, had 35,742 inhabitants. 85% of the population is of African descent, 11% of mixed origins, 3% Indian and 1% white.

The official language is English. A French-African patois is also spoken.

SOCIAL STATISTICS
Births, 1996, 2,096; deaths, 782. Rates per 1,000 population, 1996: Birth, 22·8; death, 8·5. Life expectancy, 1994, 72·0 years. Annual growth rate, 1990–95, 0·2%.

CLIMATE
The tropical climate is very agreeable in the dry season, from Jan. to May, when days are warm and nights quite cool, but in the wet season there is very little difference between day and night temperatures. On the coast, annual rainfall is about 60" (1,500 mm) but it is as high as 150–200" (3,750–5,000 mm) in the mountains. Average temperature, 27°C.

CONSTITUTION AND GOVERNMENT
The British sovereign is represented by an appointed Governor-General. There is a bicameral legislature, consisting of a 13-member *Senate,* appointed by the Governor-General, and a 15-member *House of Representatives,* elected by universal suffrage.

National Anthem. 'Hail Grenada, land of ours'; words by I. M. Baptiste, tune by L. A. Masanto.

RECENT ELECTIONS
At the elections of 14 Jan. 1999 for the House of Representatives, the New National Party (NNP) won all 15 seats, with 62·4% of the votes cast.

CURRENT ADMINISTRATION
Governor-General: Sir Daniel Williams.

In March 1999 the government comprised:

Prime Minister, Minister of Information, Finance, Trade and Industry, Foreign Affairs and National Security: Dr Keith Mitchell (NNP).

Minister of Health and the Environment: Clarice Modeste. *Minister of Agriculture, Forestry and Fisheries:* Michael Baptiste. *Education:* Augustine John.

GRENADA

Tourism, Civil Aviation, Co-operatives and Social Security: Joslyn Whiteman. *Social Security, Housing and Women's Affairs:* Laurina Waldron. *Youth, Sports, Culture and Community Development:* Adrian Mitchell. *Communication, Works and Public Utilities:* Gregory Bowen; *Carriacou and Petit Martinique Affairs, Labour, Legal Affairs and Local Government:* Elvin Nimrod.

Local Government. A Commissioner of Local Government was appointed in April 1996 to implement popular participation in local government.

DEFENCE
Royal Grenada Police Force. Modelled on the British system, the 730-strong police force includes an 80-member paramilitary unit and a 30-member coastguard.

INTERNATIONAL RELATIONS
Grenada is a member of the UN, OAS, Caricom, the Commonwealth and is an ACP state of the EU.

ECONOMY
Performance. Real GDP growth was –0·5% in 1995 and 2·3% in 1994.

Budget. In 1996 recurrent revenue was US$74·09m. and recurrent expenditure US$68·8m. Capital expenditure was US$25·7m. Income tax has been abolished. VAT is 25% (reduced rate, 5%).

Currency. The unit of currency is the *Eastern Caribbean dollar* (EC$). Foreign exchange reserves were US$43m. in Jan. 1998. Total money supply in Nov. 1997 was EC$155,000.

Banking and Finance. Grenada is a member of the Eastern Caribbean Central Bank. In 1995 there were 5 commercial banks (2 foreign). The Grenada Agricultural Bank was established in 1965 to encourage agricultural development; in 1975 it became the Grenada Agricultural and Industrial Development Corporation. In 1995 bank deposits were EC$666·8m. (US$249·7m.). Total foreign currency deposits in 1995 amounted to US$11·8m.

ENERGY AND NATURAL RESOURCES
Electricity. Installed capacity in 1995 was 17,300 kW. Production in 1995 was 88m. kWh, with consumption per capita estimated at 794 kWh in 1995.

Agriculture. Agriculture contributed 10·4% of GDP in 1996. Principal crop production (1993): Cocoa, 2,000 tonnes; bananas, 10,000 tonnes and in 1991: nutmegs, 5,800·3 lbs; mace, 451·1 lbs. Corn and pigeon peas, citrus, sugar-cane, root-crops and vegetables are also grown, in addition to small scattered cultivations of cotton, cinnamon, pimento, coffee and fruit trees.

Livestock (1996): Cattle, 4,000; sheep, 13,000; goats, 11,000 (1995); pigs, 5,000.

Forestry. In 1995 the area under forests was 4,000 ha, or 11·8% of the total land area.

Fisheries. The catch in 1995 was 1,486 tonnes, entirely from marine waters.

INDUSTRY
Labour. In 1993 the labour force was estimated at 27,820. Unemployment was 16·7%.

INTERNATIONAL TRADE
Imports and Exports. 1995 exports were valued at EC$57·2m., excluding re-exports, EC$6·0m. Imports, EC$349·7m. The principal exports are nutmeg, cocoa, bananas, mace and textiles. Exports were mainly to the UK, Trinidad and Tobago, the Netherlands and Germany.

COMMUNICATIONS
Roads. In 1996 there were 1,040 km of roads, of which 637 km were hard-surfaced.

GRENADA

Civil Aviation. The main airport is Point Salines International, which was served in 1998 by Air Caribbean, American Airlines, BWIA, British Airways, Helenair Corporation, LIAT and Region Air Caribbean. Union Island and Carriacou have smaller airports. There were direct flights from Point Salines in 1998 to Antigua, Barbados, the British Virgin Islands, London, Miami, the Netherlands Antilles, New York, Puerto Rico, St Lucia, St Vincent, Tobago and Trinidad. In 1996 Point Salines handled 305,000 passengers (292,000 on international flights) and 2,100 tonnes of freight.

Shipping. The main port is at St George's; there are 8 minor ports. Total number of containers handled in 1991 was 5,161; cargo landed, 187,039 tonnes; cargo loaded, 24,786 tonnes. Sea-going shipping totalled 555 GRT in 1995.

Telecommunications. Number of telephone main lines, 1997: 26,500 (261 per 1,000 persons). There were 400 cellular phone subscribers in 1995 and 300 fax machines.

Postal Services. In 1994 there were 58 post offices.

SOCIAL INSTITUTIONS

Justice. The Grenada Supreme Court, situated in St George's, comprises a High Court of Justice, a Court of Magisterial Appeal (which hears appeals from the lower Magistrates' Courts exercising summary jurisdiction) and an Itinerant Court of Appeal (to hear appeals from the High Court). For police *see* DEFENCE, *above*.

Religion. At the 1991 census 53% of the population were Roman Catholic, 14% Anglican, 8·5% Seventh Day Adventists and 7·2% Pentecostal.

Education. Adult literacy was 95% in 1996. In 1992 there were 75 pre-primary schools with 3,916 pupils, 57 primary schools with 22,330 pupils and 18 secondary schools with 6,970 pupils. In 1991 there were 10 schools for special education and 12 day care centres caring for 249 children. The Grenada National College was established in 1988. There is also a branch of the University of the West Indies.

Health. In 1990 there was 1 main hospital with 2 subsidiaries. In 1995 there were 64 doctors, 8 dentists, 28 pharmacists (1990), 36 midwives (1990) and 365 nursing personnel.

CULTURE

Broadcasting. The government-owned Grenada Broadcasting Corporation operates Radio Grenada and Grenada Television. There are also 4 independent radio stations. Grenada Television transmits on 3 channels (colour by NTSC). A private cable TV company provides services on 25 channels, and there is a religious TV service. In 1995 there were 55,000 radio and 32,000 TV sets.

Press. In 1993 there were 5 weekly, 1 monthly and 2 bi-monthly newspapers.

Tourism. In 1996 there were 386,013 visitors, including 266,982 cruise ship passengers. Foreign exchange earnings from the sector were US$62m. in 1996.

DIPLOMATIC REPRESENTATIVES
Of Grenada in Great Britain (1 Collingham Gdns., Earl's Court, London, SW5 0HW)
High Commissioner: F. Marcelle Gairy.

Of Great Britain in Grenada
High Commissioner: Mr. G. M. Baker (resides in Barbados).

Of Grenada in the USA (1701 New Hampshire Ave., NW, Washington, D.C., 20009)
Ambassador: Denis Antoine.

Of the USA in Grenada
Ambassador: Vacant.

Of Grenada to the United Nations
Ambassador: Robert E. Millete.

Of Grenada to the European Union
Ambassador: Vacant.

FURTHER READING

Davidson, J. S., *Grenada: a Study in Politics and the Limits of International Law.* London, 1987

Ferguson, J., *Grenada: Revolution in Reverse.* London, 1991

Gilmore, W. G., *The Grenada Intervention: Analysis and Documentation.* London, 1984

Heine, J. (ed) *A Revolution Aborted: the Lessons of Grenada.* Pittsburgh Univ. Press, 1990

O'Shaughnessy, H., *Grenada: Revolution, Invasion and Aftermath.* London, 1984

Page, A., Sutton, P. and Thorndike, T., *Grenada and Invasion.* London, 1984

Sandford, G. and Vigilante, R., *Grenada: the Untold Story.* London, 1988

Schoenhals, K., *Grenada* [Bibliography]. Oxford and Santa Barbara (CA), 1990

Sinclair, N., *Grenada: Isle of Spice.* London, 1987

Thorndike, T., *Grenada: Politics, Economics and Society.* London, 1985

GUATEMALA

República de Guatemala

Capital: Guatemala City
Population estimate, 2000: 12·22m.
GNP per capita: (PPP$) 3,820
HDI/world rank: 0·615/111

KEY HISTORICAL EVENTS

The Mayan civilisation flourished in the area now known as Guatemala from 2500 BC until 1000 AD. Their descendants were subjugated by the conquistadors from 1523. From 1524 until 1821 Guatemala was part of a Spanish captaincy-general, comprising the whole of Central America. It became independent in 1821 and formed part of the Confederation of Central America from 1823 to 1839 when Rafael Carrera dissolved the Confederation. Since then it has had a turbulent political history with periods of presidential dictatorship, democracy and military dictatorship. Boundary disputes with El Salvador, Honduras and Belize (formerly British Honduras) have caused intermittent fighting.

The economic crisis of the 1930s brought the right-wing dictator Jorge Ubico to power. His overthrow by a revolution in 1944 opened a decade of rising left-wing activity which alarmed the USA. In 1954 the leftist régime of Jacob Arbenz Guzmán was overthrown by a CIA-supported *coup*. A series of right-wing governments failed to produce stability while the toll on human life and the violation of human rights was such as to cause thousands of refugees to flee to Mexico. Over 50,000 people were killed in the 1970s.

On 23 March 1982, ignoring a presidential election of the same month, a junta consisting of Brig.-Gen. Efrain Rios Montt and other army officers took part in a bloodless *coup*. Gen. Rios Montt later became president. A further *coup* on 8 Aug. 1983 removed Montt from the presidency. Maj.-Gen. Oscar Humberto Meijia Victores became head of state. Elections to a National Constituent Assembly were held on 1 July 1984, and a new constitution was promulgated in May 1985. Amidst violence and assassinations, the presidential election was won by Marco Vinicio Cerezo Arévalo. On 14 Jan. 1986 Cerezo's civilian government was installed—the first for 16 years and only the second since 1954. Violence continued, however, and there were frequent reports of torture and killings by right-wing 'death squads' and various attempts to murder the government. Relations with the USA deteriorated and military and economic aid was suspended. By May 1993 President Serranto had imposed martial law, but was then forced into exile. There was a gradual return to constitutional rule and the first genuine efforts to investigate past violations of human rights.

The presidential and legislative elections of Nov. 1995 saw the return of the left-wing to open politics for the first time in over 40 years. Meanwhile the Guatemalan Revolutionary Unit (URNG) declared a ceasefire. On 6 May and 19 Sept. 1996 the government signed agreements with the URNG which envisaged reforms to military, internal security, judicial and agrarian institutions. A ceasefire was concluded in Oslo on 4 Dec. 1996 and a final peace treaty was signed on 29 Dec. 1996 in Guatemala. This final treaty consolidates earlier agreements to reform the electoral system and the economy, especially agriculture, and to guarantee human rights.

The Guatemalan Forensic Anthropology Foundation has been chronicling 36 years of atrocities which took place during the civil war in which it is estimated that 100,000 people were killed and 40,000 more disappeared. In 1998, for the first time interviews were being held with war survivors who were willing to describe the murders and disappearances they witnessed. The war had ended with the signing of the peace agreements in 1996.

TERRITORY AND POPULATION

Guatemala is bounded on the north and west by Mexico, south by the Pacific ocean and east by El Salvador, Honduras and Belize, and the area is 108,889 sq. km (42,042 sq. miles). In March 1936 Guatemala, El Salvador and Honduras agreed to accept the peak of Mount Montecristo as the common boundary point.

GUATEMALA

The population was 11,277,600 in July 1996. Estimate (1997) 11,685,700; density, 107 per sq. km.

The UN gives a projected population for 2000 of 12·22m.

An estimated 61·1% of the population were rural in 1995. In 1996, 44% were Amerindian, of 21 different groups descended from the Maya; 56% Mestizo (mixed Amerindian and Spanish). 60% speak Spanish, with the remainder speaking one or a combination of the 23 Indian dialects.

Guatemala is administratively divided into 22 departments, each with a governor appointed by the President. Population, 1994:

Departments	Area (sq. km)	Population	Departments	Area (sq. km)	Population
Alta Verapaz	8,686	650,120	Petén	35,854	295,169
Baja Verapaz	3,124	200,019	Quezaltenango	1,951	606,556
Chimaltenango	1,979	374,898	Quiché	8,378	631,785
Chiquimula	2,376	268,379	Retalhuleu	1,858	261,136
El Progreso	1,922	115,469	Sacatepéquez	465	196,537
Escuintla	4,384	592,647	San Marcos	3,791	766,950
Guatemala City	2,126	2,188,652	Santa Rosa	2,955	285,456
Huehuetenango	7,403	790,183	Sololá	1,061	265,902
Izabal	9,038	359,056	Suchitepéquez	2,510	392,703
Jalapa	2,063	206,355	Totonicapán	1,061	324,225
Jutiapa	3,219	378,601	Zacapa	2,690	171,146

Populations of main towns, 1993 estimates (in 1,000): Guatemala City, 1,133; Quezaltenango, 98; Escuintla, 66; Mazatenango, 41; Puerto Barrios, 39; Retalhuleu, 38.

SOCIAL STATISTICS
Births, 1996, 382,000; deaths, 62,000. 1996 rates per 1,000 population: Birth, 36·4; death rate, 5·9; life expectancy, 1996 estimate, male 62·6 years, female 68·0. Annual growth rate, 1990–95, 2·9%. Infant mortality, 1990–95, 48 per 1,000 live births; fertility rate, 5·4 births per woman.

CLIMATE
A tropical climate, with little variation in temperature and a well marked wet season from May to Oct. Guatemala City, Jan. 63°F (17·2°C), July 69°F (20·6°C). Annual rainfall 53" (1,316 mm).

CONSTITUTION AND GOVERNMENT
A new Constitution, drawn up by the Constituent Assembly elected on 1 July 1984, was promulgated in June 1985 and came into force on 14 Jan. 1986. In 1993, 43 amendments were adopted, reducing *inter alia* the President's term of office from 5 to 4 years. The President and Vice-President are elected by direct election (with a second round of voting if no candidate secures 50% of the first-round votes) for a non-renewable 4-year term. The unicameral *Congress* comprises 80 members, 64 elected locally and 16 from a national list, for 4-year terms.

A referendum on constitutional reform was held on 30 Jan. 1994. The electorate was 3·4m.; turn-out was 17·5%. The reforms were approved by 83% of votes cast.

National Anthem. 'Guatemala! Feliz' ('Happy Guatemala'); words by J. J. Palma, tune by R. Alvarez.

RECENT ELECTIONS
At the first round of the presidential elections on 12 Nov. 1995 the electorate was 3·7m.; turn-out was 40%. Alvaro Arzú gained 36·56% of votes cast against 18 opponents. At the second round on 7 Jan. 1996 Arzú was elected President against 1 opponent by 51·22% of votes cast.

Congressional elections were held on 12 Nov. 1995. The Party of National Advancement (PNA) won 42 seats, the Guatemalan Republic Front, 21 and the Guatemala New Democratic Front, 5.

The next Presidential and Congressional elections are scheduled to be held in Nov. 2000.

CURRENT ADMINISTRATION

President: Alvaro Arzú Irigoyen (PNA; sworn in 14 Jan. 1996).
 Vice-President: Luis Alberto Flores Asturias.
 In March 1999 the government comprised:
 Minister of Agriculture: Mariano Ventura. *Communications, Transport and Public Works:* Fritz García Gallont. *Defence:* Brig.-Gen. Hector Mario Barrios Celada. *Economy:* Juan José Serra Castillo. *Education:* Arabella Castro. *Energy and Mining:* Julio Campos. *Culture and Sports:* Cuestas Morales. *Finance:* Pedro Miguel Lamport. *Foreign Affairs:* Eduardo Stein Barillas. *Health and Social Welfare:* Marco Tulio Sosa Ramirez. *Government:* Rodolfo Adrian Mendoza Rosales. *Labour and Social Security:* Luis Felipe Linares Lopez.

Local Government. Municipalities are autonomous under elected officials and are funded by 8% of the central government budget.

DEFENCE

There is selective conscription for 30 months. In 1997 defence expenditure totalled US$182m. (US$16 per capita).

Army. The Army numbered (1997) 38,500 (30,000 conscripts) and is organized in 19 military zones. There are 2 strategic reserve brigades, 1 special forces group, 39 infantry, 1 engineer and 2 airborne battalions, 6 armoured squadrons and a Presidential Guard battalion. Equipment includes 10 light tanks and armoured cars. There is a paramilitary national police of 9,800, Treasury police of 2,500 and a territorial militia of about 300,000.

Navy. A naval element of the combined armed forces operates 9 inshore patrol craft, as well as 20 river patrol boats. The force was (1997) 1,500 strong of whom 650 are marines for maintenance of riverine security. Main bases are Puerto Barrios (on the Atlantic Coast), Puerto Quetzal and Puerto San José (Pacific).

Air Force. There is a small Air Force with 8 A-37B light attack aircraft, 1 DC-6, 6 C-47, 3 F.27 and 6 Israeli-built Arava transports, 6 Pilatus PC-7 turboprop trainers, and a number of light aircraft and helicopters, including a few armed UH-1 Iroquois. Strength was (1997) 700.

INTERNATIONAL RELATIONS

Guatemala is a member of the UN and OAS.

ECONOMY

The economy is based on family and corporate agriculture, which accounts for 25% of GDP, employs about 60% of the labour force, and supplies two-thirds of exports.

Policy. Policy targets are set out in the 'Government Programme 1996–2000'. Partial privatization of utilities, telecommunications and railways began in 1997.

Performance. Real GDP growth was 4·9% in 1995 (4·0% in 1994).

Budget. Government revenue and expenditure (in Q.1m.):

	1994	1995	1996	1997
Revenue	5,697·35	7,124·20	8,445·10	9,627·66
Expenditure	6,648·98	7,562·12	8,612·70	10,418·73

VAT is 10%.

Currency. The unit of currency is the *quetzal* (CTQ) of 100 *centavos*, established on 7 May 1925. Foreign exchange reserves were US$1,012m. in Feb. 1998; gold reserves were 210,000 troy oz. Inflation was an annualized 8·7% in 1996. In Jan. 1998 total money supply was Q.11,737m.

Banking and Finance. The Banco de Guatemala is the central bank and bank of issue (*Governor,* Willy Zapata Sagastume). Constitutional amendments of 1993 placed limits on its financing of government spending. In 1996 there were 21 private banks, 3 state banks, 4 international banks and 18 foreign banks, of which latter 2 are authorized to operate as commercial banks.
 There are 2 stock exchanges.

Weights and Measures. The metric system has been officially adopted, but traditional measures are still used locally.

ENERGY AND NATURAL RESOURCES

Electricity. Installed capacity in 1995 was 973,500 kW, of which of which around half was hydro-electric. Production, 1995, 2,262m. kWh; consumption per capita, 1995 estimate, 255 kWh.

Oil and Gas. There are proven reserves of 36·2m. bbls. Production (1992), 0·29m. tonnes.

Minerals. There are deposits of gold, silver and nickel.

Agriculture. Agriculture contributed 24% of GDP in 1996. Production, 1993 (in 1,000 tonnes): Coffee, 177; bananas, 500; cotton lint, 23. Rubber development schemes are under way, assisted by US funds. Guatemala is one of the largest sources of essential oils (citronella and lemon grass). Arable land: 12%, permanent crops: 4%, meadows and pastures: 12%, forest and woodland: 40%, other: 32%.

Livestock (1996): Cattle, 2·29m.; pigs, 950,000; sheep, 551,000; horses, 116,000; chickens (1995), 19m.

Forestry. In 1995 the area under forests was 3·84m ha, or 35·4% of the total land area (4·25m. ha and 39·2% in 1990). Mahogany and cedar are grown, and chick, a chewing gum base, is produced. Timber production in 1995 was 14·12m. cu. metres.

Fisheries. In 1995 the total catch was 11,927 tonnes (6,983 tonnes from sea fishing), up from 2,647 tonnes in 1986. The rate of growth in the annual catch between 1986 and 1995 was exceeded only in the Falkland Islands and Nicaragua.

INDUSTRY

Manufacturing contributed 14·1% of GDP in 1995. The principal industries are food and beverages, tobacco, chemicals, hides and skins, textiles, garments and non-metallic minerals. Raw sugar production in 1992 was 943,000 tonnes. New industries include electrical goods, plastic sheet and metal furniture.

Labour. In 1995 the workforce totalled 3,316,723 including: Agriculture, 1,513,600; commerce, 572,011; services, 439,719; manufacturing, 439,121; building, 214,102; transport and communications, 77,476; finance, 40,474.

The working week is 44 hours, with a 12-day paid holiday annually.

Trade Unions. There are 3 federations for private sector workers.

INTERNATIONAL TRADE

In May 1992 Guatemala, El Salvador and Honduras agreed to create a free trade zone and standardize import duties. External debt was US$2,080m. at 31 Aug. 1996.

Imports and Exports. Values in US$1m. were:

	1992	1993	1994	1995	1996
Imports	2,532	2,599	2,604	3,293	3,146
Exports	1,295	1,340	1,522	2,156	2,031

In 1995 the principal exports were (in US$1m.): Coffee, 550; sugar, 237; bananas, 138; cardamom, 41. Main export markets, 1995: USA, 31%; El Salvador, 13·8%; Honduras, 6·4%; Germany, 5·8%; Costa Rica, 5·2%. Main import suppliers: USA, 43%; Mexico, 9·3%; El Salvador, 5%; Venezuela, 4·6%; Japan, 3·7%.

COMMUNICATIONS

Roads. In 1996 there were 13,100 km of roads, of which 3,615 km were paved. There is a highway from coast to coast via Guatemala City. There are 2 highways from the Mexican to the Salvadorean frontier: the Pacific Highway serving the fertile coastal plain and the Pan-American Highway running through the highlands and Guatemala City. Passenger cars numbered about 102,000 in 1996 (9 per 1,000 inhabitants); vans and trucks, 97,000.

Rail. The state-owned Ferrocarriles de Guatemala operated 953 km of railway in 1996, linking east and west coast seaports to Guatemala City, with branch lines to the north and south borders. Passenger-kilometres travelled in 1995 came to 16·58bn. and freight tonne-kilometres to 85·61bn.

Civil Aviation. There are international airports at Guatemala City (La Aurora) and Flores. The 25%-government-owned airline, Aviateca, furnishes both domestic and international services, as does Mayan World Airlines. In 1998 services were also provided by American Airlines, Canadian Airlines International, Continental Airlines, COPA, Delta Air Lines, Iberia, KLM, LACSA, Mexicana, Nicaraguense de Aviación, SAM, Taca International Airlines and United Airlines. In 1995 scheduled airline traffic of Guatemalan carriers flew 6·2m. km, carrying 300,000 passengers. La Aurora handled 917,000 passengers in 1995.

Shipping. The chief ports on the Atlantic coast are Puerto Barrios and Santo Tomás de Castilla: on the Pacific coast, Puerto Quetzal and Champerico. Merchant shipping totalled 1,000 GRT in 1995.

Telecommunications. The Government own and operate the telecommunications services. In 1997 there were 429,700 telephone main lines, or 40·9 for every 1,000 persons. In 1995 there were 30,000 cellular phone subscribers, 30,000 PCs and 10,000 fax machines.

Postal Services. There were 540 post offices in 1994.

SOCIAL INSTITUTIONS

Justice. Justice is administered in a Constitution Court, a Supreme Court, 6 appeal courts and 28 courts of first instance. Supreme Court and appeal court judges are elected by Congress. Judges of first instance are appointed by the Supreme Court.

The death penalty is authorized for murder and kidnapping. Some executions were carried out in 1996.

There are 3 police forces (strengths in 1996) controlled respectively by the Ministry of the Interior (12,000), the Ministry of Finance (2,100) and the Ministry of Defence (4,000).

Religion. Roman Catholicism is the prevailing faith (7·1m. adherents in 1992) and there is a Roman Catholic archbishopric. Membership of the approximately 100 evangelical Protestant churches was estimated at 30% of the population in 1991 (75% Pentecostalist), with about 14,000 places of worship.

Education. In 1995 there were 1,470,254 pupils at 11,495 primary schools with 43,731 teachers; there were 372,006 pupils at secondary level with 23,807 teachers. 1995 adult literacy rate, 55·6%; male 62·5%, female 48·6%. In 1994–95 there were 5 universities with 70,233 students and 4,450 academic staff.

Health. In 1992 there were 7,601 doctors and 14,401 nurses, and in 1990, 1,065 dentists. There were 60 state hospitals and 100 dispensaries in 1990.

Welfare. A comprehensive system of social security was outlined in a law of 30 Oct. 1946.

CULTURE

Broadcasting. There are 5 government, 6 educational and 84 commercial radio broadcasting services. There are 4 commercial TV stations and 1 government station. There is also reception by US television satellite. In 1995 there were 750,000 radio and 600,000 TV receivers (colour by NTSC).

Press. In 1996 there were 4 independent dailies and 1 evening newspaper, 1 government daily and 2 weeklies.

Tourism. Tourism is an important source of foreign exchange (US$284m. in 1996). There were 520,000 foreign tourists in 1996.

DIPLOMATIC REPRESENTATIVES

Of Guatemala in Great Britain (13 Fawcett St., London, SW10 9HN)
Ambassador: Fernando Andrade Díaz-Durán.

Of Great Britain in Guatemala (Edificio Centro Financiero, 7th Floor, Tower Two, 7a Avenida 5-10, Zona 4, Guatemala City)
Ambassador: Mr. A. J. F. Caie.

Of Guatemala in the USA (2220 R. St., NW, Washington, D.C., 20008)
Ambassador: William Howard Stixrud.

Of the USA in Guatemala (7–01 Avenida de la Reforma, Zone 10, Guatemala City)
Ambassador: Donald J. Planty.

Of Guatemala to the United Nations
Ambassador: Gert Rosenthal.

Of Guatemala to the European Union
Ambassador: Claudio Riedel Telge.

FURTHER READING
Woodward, R. L., *Guatemala.* [Bibliography] Oxford and Santa Barbara (CA), 1992

National library: Biblioteca Nacional, 5a Avenida y 8a Calle, Zona 1, Guatemala City.

GUINEA

République de Guinée

Capital: Conakry
Population estimate, 2000: 7·86m.
GNP per capita: (PPP$) 1,720
HDI/world rank: 0·277/167

KEY HISTORICAL EVENTS

Present-day Guinea was historically a subordinate part of the broader Ghanaian empire in the 10th and 11th centuries and the Malinke empire (Mali-based) until the 16th century. A powerful feudal state of Guinea's Fulani people in the early 18th century resisted intrusions by both the French and the Moslem states to the north-east.

In 1888 Guinea became a French protectorate, in 1893 a colony and in 1904, a constituent territory of French West Africa. Forced labour and other colonial depredations ensued, although a form of representation was introduced in 1946. The independent Republic of Guinea was proclaimed on 2 Oct. 1958, after the territory of French Guinea had decided at the referendum of 28 Sept. to leave the French community rather than being self-governing within it. Ahmed Sékou Touré became the first president of the new republic. Guinea became a single-party state. Ties with France were broken in 1965 and only restored in 1976. For a time Guinea was isolated but in 1975 it joined its African neighbours in the Economic Community of West African States. Touré's strong measures to maintain his rule provoked riots in 1977. In 1977 and 1978, when a more liberal government policy was pursued, Touré spoke of his desire to co-operate with the West.

In 1980 Touré was elected for the fourth time for a 7-year term as president but died in 1984 when the armed forces staged a *coup* and dissolved the National Assembly and the *Parti démocratique de Guinée*. A Military Committee of National Rectification (CMRN) held power until Jan. 1991 when a Transitional Committee for National Rectification (CTRN) took over. Following popular disturbances a multi-party system was introduced in April 1992.

TERRITORY AND POPULATION

Guinea is bounded in the north-west by Guinea-Bissau and Senegal, north-east by Mali, south-east by Côte d'Ivoire, south by Liberia and Sierra Leone, and west by the Atlantic Ocean.

The area is 245,857 sq. km (94,926 sq. miles). Population estimate, 1997, 7,405,400 (3,768,300 female); density, 30 per sq. km. A census of 1992 gave a figure of 5·04m.; it is officially acknowledged that this may be an under-count.

The UN gives a projected population for 2000 of 7·86m.

The capital is Conakry. In 1995, 29·2% of the population were urban.

The areas, populations and chief towns of the major divisions in 1991 were:

	Sq. km	1991 population	Chief town	Population (in year)
Conakry (city)	308	1,320,000	Conakry	950,000 (1992)
Guinée-Maritime	43,980	975,000	Kindia	80,000 (1986)
Moyenne-Guinée	51,710	1,262,000	Labé	110,000 (1986)
Haute-Guinée	92,535	1,147,000	Kankan	70,000 (1992)
Guinée-Forestière	57,324	1,033,000	Nzérékoré	55,356 (1983)

The country has since been divided into 7 administrative regions: Boké, Faranah, Kankan, Kindia, Labé, Mamou and Nzérékoré.

The ethnic composition is Fulani (40·3%, predominant in Moyenne-Guinée), Malinké (or Mandingo, 25·8%, prominent in Haute-Guinée), Susu (11%, prominent in Guinée-Maritime), Kissi (6·5%) and Kpelle (4·8%) in Guinée-Forestière, and Dialonka, Loma and others (11·6%).

The official language is French.

SOCIAL STATISTICS

Births, 1997, 311,000; deaths, 135,000. Rates, 1997: Birth, 42·0 per 1,000 population; death, 18·2; infant mortality, 131·5 per 1,000 live births. Life expectancy, 1997, 45·5 years. Annual growth rate, 1990–95, was 3%. Fertility rate, 1990–95, 7·0 births per woman.

GUINEA

CLIMATE
A tropical climate, with high rainfall near the coast and constant heat, but conditions are a little cooler on the plateau. The wet season on the coast lasts from May to Nov., but only to Oct. inland. Conakry, Jan. 80°F (26·7°C), July 77°F (25°C). Annual rainfall 172" (4,293 mm).

CONSTITUTION AND GOVERNMENT
There is a 114-member *National Assembly*, 38 of whose members are elected on a first-past-the-post system, and the remainder from national lists by proportional representation.

National Anthem. 'Peuple d'Afrique, le passé historique' ('People of Africa, the historic past'); words anonymous, tune by K. Fodeba.

RECENT ELECTIONS
Presidential elections were held on 14 Dec. 1998. President Conté was re-elected against 4 opponents by 54·1% of votes cast.

National assembly elections were held on 11 June 1995. 21 parties or groups stood. The Party of Unity and Progress Party (PUP) gained 71 seats; the Guinean People's Rally, 19; the Renewal and Progress Party, 9; the Union for a New Republic, 9.

CURRENT ADMINISTRATION
President: Gen. Lansana Conté (PUP; seized power 3 April 1984, most recently re-elected 14 Dec. 1998).

On 8 March 1999 the Prime Minister, Sidia Touré, was dismissed and replaced by Lamine Sidime. A cabinet reshuffle was under way as a result.

Local Government. The administrative division comprises the capital Conakry and 33 prefectures grouped into 7 regions: Boké, Faranah, Kankan, Kindia, Labé, Mamou and Nzérékoré.

DEFENCE
Conscription is for 2 years. Defence expenditure totalled US$51m. in 1997 (US$7 per capita).

Army. The Army of 8,500 (1997), comprises 1 armoured, 5 infantry, 1 commando and 1 engineer, 1 artillery, 1 air defence and 1 special forces battalion. Equipment includes 30 T-34 and 8 T-54 main battle tanks. There are also 3 paramilitary forces: People's Militia (7,000), Gendarmerie (1,000) and Republican Guard (1,600).

Navy. A small force of 400 (1997) operate 2 French-built, 1 US-built and 5 Soviet-built inshore patrol craft, and a number of riverine boats from bases at Conakry and Kakanda.

Air Force. The Air Force, formed with Soviet assistance, is reported to be equipped with a few MiG-21 jet fighters, 2 An-2 piston-engined transports and a Yak-40 jet aircraft for VIP duties, all Russian built, and 2 French-supplied helicopters are in service. Personnel (1997) 800.

INTERNATIONAL RELATIONS
Guinea is a member of the UN, OAU and is an ACP member state of the ACP-EU relationship.

ECONOMY
Performance. Real GDP growth in 1995 was officially estimated at 4·6% (4% in 1994).

Budget. Government revenue, 1994 (in 1,000m. Guinean francs): 608, of which taxes, 441·9; grants, 146·6. Expenditure: 730·3, of which current, 342. VAT was applied to non-essential goods in July 1996. In 1995 estimated revenue was US$553m. and expenditure US$652m.

Currency. The monetary unit is the *Guinean franc* (GNF). The average annual inflation rate during the period 1990–96 was 8·8%. In Oct. 1997 foreign exchange reserves were US$70m. Total money supply in Oct. 1997 was 318,491m. Guinean francs.

Banking and Finance. In 1986 the Central Bank (*Governor*, Ibrahim Cherif Bah) and commercial banking were restructured, and commercial banks returned to the private sector. There were 6 commercial banks in 1993.

ENERGY AND NATURAL RESOURCES

Electricity. In 1996 installed capacity was 176 MW. Production was 300m. kWh in 1995. Consumption per capita was 82 kWh in 1994.

Minerals. Mining produced 19·1% of GDP in 1994. Guinea possesses over 25% of the world's bauxite reserves. 1992 output: Bauxite, 16m. tonnes (17,054,000 tonnes in 1991); alumina, 603,000 tonnes (651,000 tonnes in 1991); diamonds, 0·1m. carats; gold, 2,100 kg. There are also deposits of granite, iron ore, chrome, copper, lead, manganese, molybdenum, nickel, platinum, uranium and zinc.

Agriculture. Subsistence agriculture supports about 70% of the population. Agriculture produced 26% of GDP in 1996. Some 25% of potential arable land is cultivated. The chief crops (production, 1993, in 1,000 tonnes) are: Cassava, 781; millet, 10; rice, 733; plantains, 429; sugar-cane, 225; bananas, 115; groundnuts, 105; sweet potatoes, 104; yams, 73; maize, 95; palm-oil, 40; palm kernels, 40; pineapples, 87; pulses, 60; coffee, 29; coconuts, 18.

Livestock (1996): Cattle, 2·21m.; sheep, 618,000; goats (1995), 580,000; pigs, 453,000; chickens (1995), 14m.

Forestry. The area under forests in 1995 was 6·37m. ha, or 25·9% of the total land area (6·74m. ha and 27·4% in 1990). In 1995, 4·79m. cu. metres of roundwood were cut.

Fisheries. In 1995 the total catch was approximately 69,000 tonnes, 94% of which came from sea fishing.

INDUSTRY

Manufacturing accounted for 4·6% of GDP in 1994. Cement, beer, soft drinks and cigarettes are produced.

Labour. In 1996 the labour force was 3,565,000 (53% males). The agricultural sector employs 80% of the workforce.

INTERNATIONAL TRADE

Foreign debt was US$3,000m. in 1996. Imports require authorization and there are restrictions on the export of capital.

Imports and Exports. In 1995 imports totalled US$775m. and exports US$725m. Main exports by value (US$1m.), 1994: Bauxite, 272; alumina, 103; gold, 84; coffee, 58. Main export markets, 1994: Belgium, 26·7%; USA, 15·1%; Ireland, 10%; Spain, 9·6%; Germany, 5·8%; Brazil, 5·4%. Main import suppliers: France, 19·5%; Côte d'Ivoire, 16%; USA, 7·1%; Belgium, 6·9%; Hong Kong, 6·3%.

COMMUNICATIONS

Roads. In 1995 there were about 5,000 km of main and national roads of which 1,200 km were hard-surfaced, and about 9,200 km of other roads. In 1996 there were 14,100 passenger cars, or 2 per 1,000 inhabitants, and 21,000 trucks and vans.

Rail. A railway connects Conakry with Kankan (662 km) and is to be extended to Bougouni in Mali. A line 134 km long linking bauxite deposits at Sangaredi with Port Kamsar was opened in 1973 (carried 12·5m. tonnes in 1993), a third line links Conakry and Fria (144 km; carried 1m. tonnes in 1993) and a fourth, the Kindia Bauxite Railway (102 km) linking Débéle with Conakry, carried 3m. tonnes in 1994.

Civil Aviation. There is an international airport at Conakry (Gbessia). In 1998 services were provided by Aeroflot, Air Afrique, Air Dabia, Air France, Air Gabon, Air Ivoire, Delta Air Lines, Ghana Airways, Royal Air Maroc, SABENA and Transportes Aéreos de Cabo Verde, with scheduled flights to Abidjan, Accra, Bamako, Banjul, Bissau, Brazzaville, Brussels, Casablanca, Dakar, Freetown, Johannesburg, Lagos, Libreville, Monrovia, Moscow, Paris and Praia. In 1996

GUINEA

Conakry handled 222,495 passengers (190,859 on international flights) and 3,289 tonnes of freight.

Shipping. There are ports at Conakry and for bauxite exports at Kamsar (opened 1973). Merchant shipping totalled 7,000 GRT in 1995.

Telecommunications. The Société des Télécommunications de Guinée is 40% state-owned. In 1997 there were 19,800 main telephone lines, equivalent to 2·6 per 1,000 population. There were approximately 100 cellular phone subscribers in 1995, 100 PCs and 200 fax machines. In Jan. 1998 there were an estimated 300 Internet users.

Postal Services. In 1995 there were 83 post offices, or 1 for every 86,000 persons.

SOCIAL INSTITUTIONS

Justice. There are *tribunaux du premier degré* at Conakry and Kankan, and a *juge de paix* at Nzérékoré. The High Court, Court of Appeal and Superior Tribunal of Cassation are at Conakry.

Religion. 85% of the population are Moslem, 5% Christian. Traditional animist beliefs are still found.

Education. In 1995 there were 543,441 pupils (193,140 girls) and 11,352 teachers in 3,118 primary schools, 91,921 pupils (23,874 girls) and 2,791 teachers in 239 secondary schools, 28,311 pupils (6,143 girls) and 1,407 teachers in 61 *lycées* and 8,569 pupils (3,013) and 1,268 teachers in 55 institutions of professional education. In 1996 there were 2 universities with 5,735 students and 525 academic staff.

Besides French, there are 8 official languages taught in schools: Fulani, Malinké, Susu, Kissi, Kpelle, Loma, Basari and Koniagi.

Adult literacy (1995) 35·9% (male, 49·9%; female, 21·9%).

Health. In 1991 there were 375 hospitals and dispensaries. In 1988 there were 3,382 beds; there were also 920 doctors (1991), 22 dentists (1988), 197 pharmacists (1991), 371 midwives (1991) and 1,243 trained nursing personnel (1988).

CULTURE

Broadcasting. Broadcasting is the responsibility of the state-controlled Radiodiffusion Télévision Guinéenne. There were 325,000 radio and 65,000 television receivers in 1995 (colour by PAL).

Cinema. In 1991 there were 79 cinemas.

Press. There is 1 daily newspaper (circulation 20,000).

Tourism. There were 94,000 foreign tourists in 1996.

DIPLOMATIC REPRESENTATIVES
Of Guinea in Great Britain (resides in Paris)
Ambassador: Ibrahima Sylla.

Of Great Britain in Guinea
Ambassador: David R. Snoxell (resides in Dakar).

Of Guinea in the USA (2112 Leroy Pl., NW, Washington, D.C., 20008)
Ambassador: Mohamed Ali Thiam.

Of the USA in Guinea (Rue KA 038, Conakry)
Ambassador: Tibor P. Nagy, Jr.

Of Guinea to the United Nations
Ambassador: Mahawa Bangoura Camara.

Of Guinea to the European Union
Ambassador: Naby Moussa Soumah.

FURTHER READING
Bulletin Statistique et Economique de la Guinée. Monthly. Conakry

Binns, M., *Guinea* [Bibliography]. Oxford and Santa Barbara (CA), 1996

759

GUINEA-BISSAU

Republica da Guiné-Bissau

Capital: Bissau
Population estimate, 2000: 1·18m.
GNP per capita: (PPP$) 1,030
HDI/world rank: 0·295/164

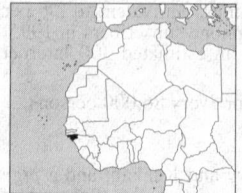

KEY HISTORICAL EVENTS
The area began to be settled with the break up of the ancient Ghanaian and Mali empires. The Portuguese explorer Nuno Tristão visited the coast in 1446. Portugal remained the major influence in the area and in the 19th century established its rule on the coast; however, Portuguese rule was not extended into the interior until later and met African resistance well into the 20th century. Portuguese Guinea came under Cape Verde until 1879 when it became a separate colony. Portuguese Guinea became an Overseas Territory in 1951.

Amilcar Cabral, one of the many Cape Verdians working in government service in Portuguese Guinea, joined other nationalists in 1956 to form the *Partido Africano da Independência da Guiné e Cabo Verde* (PAIGC). From 1963 this party waged a successful guerrilla war against Portuguese rule in Guinea, Guineans and Cape Verdians working together and by 1973 evicting the Portuguese from much of the interior where the PAIGC set up its own administration. On 20 Jan. 1973 Cabral was murdered but elections to a national assembly had already been held in liberated areas and on 23-24 Sept. 1973 the assembly proclaimed the independence of Guinea-Bissau. A Council of State was chosen with Luis Cabral, brother of Amilcar, as chairman.

In 1974, after the Portuguese revolution, Portugal abandoned the struggle to keep Guinea-Bissau and independence was formally recognized on 10 Sept. 1974. In 1975 Cape Verde also became independent under the rule of the PAIGC but the secretary-general of the party, President Pereira of Cape Verde, did not have authority over Guinea-Bissau and the two countries remained separate sovereign states.

On 14 Nov. 1980 Luis Cabral was overthrown in a *coup d'état* in part inspired by resentment in Guinea-Bissau over the privileges enjoyed by Cape Verdians and Guineans obtained a more prominent role under the new government of Major João Bernardo Vieira, previously prime minister.

On 16 May 1984 a new constitution was approved which retained Marxist principles but in Nov. 1986 the PAIGC Congress agreed a return to private enterprise in an attempt to solve critical economic problems and to lift the country out of poverty.

TERRITORY AND POPULATION
Guinea-Bissau is bounded by Senegal in the north, the Atlantic Ocean in the west and by Guinea in the east and south. It includes the adjacent archipelago of Bijagós. Area, 36,125 sq. km (13,948 sq. miles). Population (provisional results of last census, 1991), 983,367, of whom 197,610 resided in the capital, Bissau. In 1995 an estimated 78·3% of the population were rural. Population (estimate, 1997) 1,178,600 (606,800 female); density, 32·6 per sq. km.

The UN gives a projected population for 2000 of 1·18m.

The area population, and chief town of the capital and the 8 regions:

Region	Area in sq. km	Population (1991 census, provisional)	Chief town
Bissau City	78	197,610	—
Bafatá	5,981	143,377	Bafatá
Biombo	838	60,420	Bissau
Bolama	2,624	26,691	Bolama
Cacheu	5,175	146,980	Cacheu
Gabú	9,150	134,971	Gabú
Oio	5,403	156,084	Farim
Quinara	3,138	44,793	Fulacunda
Tombali	3,736	72,441	Catió

The main ethnic groups were (1998) the Balante (30%), Fulani (20%), Manjaco (14%), Mandingo (13%) and Papeis (7%). Portuguese remains the official language, but Crioulo is spoken throughout the country.

SOCIAL STATISTICS
Births, 1997, 46,000; deaths, 19,000. 1997 birth rate, 39·2 per 1,000 population; death rate, 15·9; life expectancy, 48·7 years; growth rate, 2·33%. Infant mortality, 1990–95, 141 per 1,000 live births; fertility rate, 5·8 births per woman.

CLIMATE
The tropical climate has a wet season from June to Nov., when rains are abundant, but the hot, dry Harmattan wind blows from Dec. to May. Bissau, Jan. 76°F (24·4°C), July 80°F (26·7°C). Annual rainfall 78" (1,950 mm).

CONSTITUTION AND GOVERNMENT
A new Constitution was promulgated on 16 May 1984. The Revolutionary Council, established following the 1980 coup, was replaced by a 15-member Council of State, while in April 1984 a new National People's Assembly was elected comprising 150 Representatives elected by and from the directly-elected regional councils for 5-year terms. The sole political movement was the *Partido Africano da Independência da Guiné e Cabo Verde* (PAIGC), but in Dec. 1990 a policy of 'integral multi-partyism' was announced, and in May 1991 the National Assembly voted unanimously to abolish the law making the PAIGC the sole party. The *President* is Head of State and Government and is elected for a 5-year term. The *National Assembly* has 100 members.

National Anthem. 'Sol, suor, o verde e mar' ('Sun, sweat, the green and the sea'); words and tune by A. Lopes Cabral.
  (Same as Cape Verde.)

RECENT ELECTIONS
Presidential elections were held in 2 rounds on 3 July and 7 Aug. 1994. At the first round President Vieira gained 46·18% of votes cast against 7 opponents. At the second round turn-out was 70%. President Vieira was re-elected by 52·02% of votes cast against 1 opponent.
  At the parliamentary elections on 3 July 1994 there were 1,136 candidates. The PAIGC gained 64 seats.

CURRENT ADMINISTRATION
President: João Bernardo Vieira, b. 1939 (seized power 1980; elected 1989; re-elected 1994).
  In March 1999 the government comprised:
  Prime Minister: Francisco Fadul.
  Minister at the Presidency in Charge of Parliamentary Affairs and Information: Malal Sané. *Defence:* Francisco Benante. *Foreign Affairs and Co-operation:* Ilia Barber. *Justice and Labour:* Dr Daniel Ferreira. *Economy and Finance:* Aboubakar Dahaba. *Equipment:* João Gomes Cardoso. *Interior:* Francesca Pereira. *Rural Development, Natural Resources, and Environment:* Jose Avito da Silva. *National Education:* Odette Semedo. *Public Health:* Brandao Gomes Co. *Social Affairs and Advancement of Women:* Nharebat Incaia Intchasso. *Territorial Administration:* Nicandro Barreto Pereira. *Veterans Affairs:* Arafam Mané.

Local Government. The administrative division is in 8 regions (each under a regional council elected for 5 years), in turn subdivided into 37 sectors; and the city of Bissau, an autonomous sector treated as a separate region.

DEFENCE
There is selective conscription. Defence expenditure totalled US$8m. in 1997 (US$7 per capita).

Army. The Army consisted in 1997 of 1 armoured, 1 artillery and 5 infantry battalions and 1 engineer and 1 reconnaissance company. Equipment includes 10

T-34 main battle tanks. Personnel, 6,800. There is a paramilitary Gendarmerie 2,000 strong.

Navy. The naval flotilla, based at Bissau, is equipped with 8 inshore patrol craft of diverse origins and 1 utility landing craft. Personnel in 1997 totalled 350.

Air Force. Formation of a small Air Force began in 1978 with the delivery of a French-built Cessna FTB-337 twin-engined counter-insurgency and general-purpose light transport. It has been followed by 2 Alouette III helicopters and 1 Falcon 20 VIP transport. Personnel (1997) 100.

INTERNATIONAL RELATIONS
Guinea-Bissau is a member of the UN, OAU and is an ACP member state of the ACP-EU relationship.

ECONOMY
Performance. GDP growth was estimated by the IMF at 4·2% in 1995.

Budget. Revenue in 1994 (in 1m. pesos) was 375,778, of which tax revenue, 207,370; expenditure (also in 1m. pesos) totalled 1,045,450.

Currency. On 2 May 1997 Guinea-Bissau joined the French Franc Zone, and the *peso* was replaced by the franc CFA at 65 pesos = 1 franc CFA. The *franc CFA* (XOF) has a parity rate of 100 = 1 French franc. Foreign exchange reserves were US$16m. in March 1997. The average annual inflation rate over the period 1990–96 was 47·8%. Total money supply in Dec. 1996 was 10,913bn. pesos.

Banking and Finance. The Banco da Guiné-Bissau, which replaced the Banco Nacional in 1989, is the central bank and bank of issue (*Governor* Luis Candido Ribeiro). A commercial bank was set up in 1990, with 51% of the capital held by the state and local companies and 49% by Portuguese banks. There is also a commercial bank.

ENERGY AND NATURAL RESOURCES
Electricity. Installed capacity in 1991 was 22,000 kW. Production was 44·9m. kWh in 1994; consumption per capita in 1994 was 43 kWh.

Minerals. Mineral resources are not exploited. There are estimated to be 200m. tonnes of bauxite and 112m. tonnes of phosphate.

Agriculture. Agriculture accounted for 54% of GDP in 1996 and employs 80% of the labour force. Chief crops (production, 1993, in 1,000 tonnes) are: Groundnuts, 18; sugar-cane, 6; plantains, 34; coconuts, 25; rice, 126; palm kernels, 8; millet, 26; palm-oil, 5; sorghum, 14; maize, 13; cashew nuts, 30.

Livestock (1996): Cattle, 475,000; sheep, 255,000; goats (1995), 270,000; pigs, 310,000; chickens (1995), 1m.

Forestry. The area covered by forests in 1995 was 2·31m. ha, or 82·1% of the total land area (2·36m. ha and 84% in 1990). In 1995, 579,000 cu. metres of roundwood were cut.

Fisheries. Total catches in 1995 came to 5,595 tonnes, of which more than 95% was from sea fishing.

INDUSTRY
Labour. The labour force in 1996 was 514,000 (60% males).

INTERNATIONAL TRADE
Foreign debt totalled US$937m. in 1996.

Imports and Exports. Imports in 1996, US$50m.; exports, US$16m. Main exports in 1994 (in US$1m.) were: Cashew nuts, 31; frozen shrimps, 0·1; frozen fish, 0·1; saw timber, 0·3. Imports: Food, 16·4; transport equipment, 14·5; fuel, 6·3; machines, 6·5.

Main export markets, 1994: India, 48·1%; Portugal, 35·7%; China, 8·8%; Cape Verde, 5·5%. Main import suppliers: Portugal, 40·5%; Netherlands, 16·6%; Japan, 14·8%.

COMMUNICATIONS

Roads. In 1995 there were about 4,350 km of roads of which 444 km were paved and, in 1996, 7,120 passenger cars (6 per 1,000 inhabitants) and 5,640 trucks.

Civil Aviation. The national carrier is Transportes Aéreos de Guiné-Bissau. There is an international airport serving Bissau (Osvaldo Vieira). In 1998 services were also provided by Air Afrique, Air Mauritanie, TAP and Transportes Aéreos de Cabo Verde, with scheduled flights to Abidjan, Banjul, Conakry, Dakar, Lisbon, Nouakchott, Praia and Sal. In 1995 scheduled airline traffic flew 500,000 km, carrying 21,000 passengers.

Shipping. The main port is Bissau; minor ports are Bolama, Cacheu and Catió. In 1995 the merchant marine totalled 1,846 GRT.

Telecommunications. Telephone main lines numbered 7,600 in 1997 (6·9 per 1,000 persons). There were 500 fax machines in 1995 and in Jan. 1998 approximately 200 Internet users.

Postal Services. In 1995 there were 26 post offices.

SOCIAL INSTITUTIONS

Religion. In 1998 about 30% of the population were Moslem and about 5% Christian (mainly Roman Catholic). The remainder held traditional animist beliefs.

Education. Adult literacy was 54·9% in 1995 (male, 68%; female, 42·5%). Some 60% of children of primary school age attend school. In 1994–95 there were 100,369 pupils at primary schools.

Health. In 1993 there were 10 private, 2 national and 4 regional hospitals with a total of 1,300 beds. There were 125 dispensaries.

CULTURE

Broadcasting. In 1995 there were 45,000 radio receivers. An experimental TV service started in 1989.

Press. In 1996 there were 3 newspapers, including 1 privately owned.

DIPLOMATIC REPRESENTATIVES
Of Guinea-Bissau in Great Britain
Chargé d'affaires: Maria Filomena Embalo Araujo Vieira (resides in Paris).

Of Great Britain in Guinea-Bissau
Ambassador: David R. Snoxell (resides in Dakar).

Of Guinea-Bissau in the USA (918 16th St., NW, Washington, D.C., 20006)
Ambassador: Mario Lopes da Rosa.

Of the USA in Guinea-Bissau (1 Rua Ulysses S. Grant, 1067 Bissau)
Ambassador: Peggy Blackford.

Of Guinea-Bissau to the United Nations
Ambassador: Alfredo Lopes Cabral.

Of Guinea-Bissau to the European Union
Ambassador: Vacant.

FURTHER READING
Forrest, J. A., *Guinea-Bissau: Power, Conflict and Renewal in a West African Nation.* Boulder (CO), 1992
Galli, R., *Guinea-Bissau* [Bibliography]. Oxford and Santa Barbara (CA), 1991

GUYANA

Co-operative Republic of Guyana

Capital: Georgetown
Population estimate, 2000: 874,000
GNP per capita: (PPP$) 2,280
HDI/world rank: 0·670/100

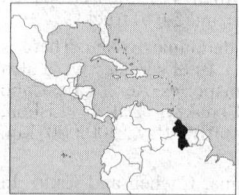

KEY HISTORICAL EVENTS
First settled by the Dutch West Indian Company about 1620, the territory was captured by Britain to whom it was ceded in 1814 and named British Guiana. To work the sugar plantations African slaves were transported here in the 18th century and East Indian and Chinese indentured labourers in the 19th century. From 1950 the anti-colonial struggle was spearheaded by the Peoples Progressive Party (PPP) led by Cheddi Jagan and Forbes Burnham, but after its election with a left-wing programme in the elections of 1953 the British government suspended the constitution. By the time internal autonomy was granted in 1961 Burnham had split with Jagan to form the more moderate People's National Congress (PNC). After much conflict, instigated by Britain and the USA who tried to destabilise Jagan's PPP government of 1961–64, Guyana became an independent member of the Commonwealth in 1966 with Burnham as the first prime minister.

On 3 Feb. 1970 Guyana became the world's first Co-operative Republic, with Arthur Chung as its first non-executive president. In Oct. 1980 the prime minister, Forbes Burnham, declared himself the executive-president. Two months later his party, the PNC, won a large majority of votes at a rigged election for the National Assembly: Burnham was then declared duly elected as president. When he died in Aug. 1985 his prime minister, Desmond Hoyte, succeeded as president. Like his predecessor, Hoyte was declared duly elected when the PNC gained a large majority at another rigged election for the National Assembly in Dec. 1985; but desperate economic straits forced Guyana to seek outside help which came on condition of restoring free elections. Dr Jagan returned to power in 1992. Following his death in March 1997 his wife, Janet Jagan, was sworn in as President on 24 Dec. 1997.

TERRITORY AND POPULATION
Guyana is situated on the north-east coast of Latin America on the Atlantic Ocean, with Suriname on the east, Venezuela on the west and Brazil on the south and west. Area, 83,000 sq. miles (214,969 sq. km). Estimated population (1997), 847,000.

The UN gives a projected population for 2000 of 874,000.

Guyana has the highest proportion of rural population in South America, with only 35·4% living in urban areas in 1995. Ethnic groups by origin: 49% Indian, 36% African, 7% mixed race, 7% Amerindian and 1% others. The capital is Georgetown; other towns are New Amsterdam, Linden, Rose Hall and Corriverton.

Venezuela demanded the return of the Essequibo region in 1963. It was finally agreed in March 1983 that the UN Secretary-General should mediate. There was also an unresolved claim (1984) by Suriname for the return of an area between the New river and the Corentyne river.

The official language is English.

SOCIAL STATISTICS
Births, 1997, 29,000; deaths, 7,000. 1997 birth rate per 1,000 population, 34·7; death rate, 8·6; in 1996 life expectancy was 60·1 years (male 57·5 years and female 62·8 years). Annual growth rate, 1990–95, 1·0%. Infant mortality, 1990–95, 63 per 1,000 live births; fertility rate, 2·6 births per woman.

CLIMATE
A tropical climate, with rainy seasons from April to July and Nov. to Jan. Humidity is high all the year but temperatures are moderated by sea-breezes. Rainfall increases from 90" (2,280 mm) on the coast to 140" (3,560 mm) in the forest zone. Georgetown, Jan. 79°F (26·1°C), July 81°F (27·2°C). Annual rainfall 87" (2,175 mm).

CONSTITUTION AND GOVERNMENT

A new Constitution was promulgated in Oct. 1980. There is an *Executive Presidency*, and a *National Assembly* which consists of 53 elected members and 12 members appointed by the regional authorities. Elections for 5-year terms are held under the single-list system of proportional representation, with the whole of the country forming one electoral area and each voter casting a vote for a party list of candidates.

National Anthem. 'Dear land of Guyana'; words by A. L. Luker, tune by R. Potter.

RECENT ELECTIONS

Janet Jagan and the PPP won the presidential, parliamentary and regional elections of 15 Dec. 1997. The PPP won 220,667 or 55·3% of the national vote (29 seats in the National Assembly), compared to the 161,901 or 40·6% cast for the PNC (22 seats in the National Assembly). In the regional elections the PPP received 219,651 votes, the PNC 160,019 votes. The chief justice rejected the PNC's claims of election rigging. PNC supporters retaliated with looting and rioting in Georgetown.

CURRENT ADMINISTRATION

President: Janet Jagan.

In March 1999 the government comprised:

Prime Minister and Minister of Public Works: Samuel Hinds. *Vice-President, Minister of Agriculture and Parliamentary Affairs:* Reepu Daman Persaud.

Attorney-General and Minister of Legal Affairs: Charles Rishiram Ramson. *Cabinet Secretary:* Roger Luncheon. *Minister of Finance:* Bharrat Jagdeo. *Foreign Affairs:* Clement Rohee. *Health and Labour:* Henry Benfield Jeffrey. *Education:* Dale Bisnauth. *Home Affairs:* Ronald Gajraj. *Trade, Industry and Tourism:* Michael Shree Chan. *Amerindian Affairs:* Vibert D'Souza. *Housing:* Shaik Baksh. *Culture, Youth and Sports:* Gail Teixeira. *Information:* Moses Nagamootoo. *Local Government:* Harripersaud Nokta. *Human Services and Social Security:* Indra Chandrapal. *Marine Resources:* Satyadeow Sawah. *Public Service:* George Fung-On. *Transport and Hydraulics:* Carl Anthony Xavier.

Local Government. There are 10 administrative regions: Barima/Waini, Pomeroon/Supernaam, Essequibo Islands/West Demerara, Demerara/Mahaica, Mahaica/Berbice, East Berbice/Corentyne, Cuyuni/Mazaruni, Potaro/Siparuni, Upper Takutu/Upper Essequibo, Upper Demerara/Berbice.

DEFENCE

Military expenditure totalled US$7m. in 1997 (US$9 per capita).

Army. The Guyana Army had (1997) a strength of 1,400. It comprises 1 infantry battalion and 1 special forces, 1 support weapons and 1 engineer company. There is a paramilitary Guyana People's Militia 1,500 strong.

Navy. The Maritime Corps is an integral part of the Guyana Defence Force. In 1997 it had 17 personnel and 2 armed boats.

Air Force. The Air Command has no combat aircraft. It is equipped with light aircraft and helicopters, including 1 Islander twin-engined short take-off and landing transport, and 1 Bell 206, 1 Bell 212 and 2 Mi-8 helicopters. Personnel (1997) 100.

INTERNATIONAL RELATIONS

Guyana is a member of the UN, Commonwealth, CARICOM, OAS and is an ACP member state of the ACP-EU relationship.

ECONOMY

Policy. State control has been reduced during the 1990s, with some privatization.

Performance. GDP growth in 1997 was estimated at 6·3%. Between 1990 and 1996 the average annual real growth in GNP per capita was 10·4%, a figure only exceeded by Equatorial Guinea and China.

Budget. Current revenue and expenditure for calendar years (in G$1m.):

	1991	1992	1993	1994	1995
Revenue	11,823·5	17,769·5	21,778·0	23,809·1	28,961·4
Expenditure	15,273·4	23,070·7	17,716·8	19,360·8	22,422·3

In 1995 capital account receipts totalled G$3,151·2m.; expenditure, G$12,090·4m. Components of current revenue, 1995 (in G$1m.): Income taxes, 10,865·9; property taxes, 427·8; taxes on production and consumption, 7,351; taxes on international trade, 4,117·4; other taxes, 2,562·5; non-tax revenue, 1,479·5.

Currency. The unit of currency is the *Guyana dollar* (GYD) of 100 *cents*. Inflation was an annualized 4·1% in 1997. Foreign exchange reserves were US$291m. in Feb. 1998. Total money supply in Feb. 1998 was G$16,786.

Banking and Finance. The bank of issue is the Bank of Guyana. Of the 6 commercial banks operating 2 are foreign-owned. At March 1996, the total assets of commercial banks were G$62,587,892,000. Savings deposits were G$26,564·2m.

ENERGY AND NATURAL RESOURCES

Electricity. Capacity in 1995 was estimated at 157,000 kW; in 1997 production was 390·4m. kWh. Consumption per capita was an estimated 301 kWh in 1995.

Minerals. Placer gold mining commenced in 1884, and was followed by diamond mining in 1887. Output of raw gold was 289,514 oz. in 1995. Other minerals include copper, tungsten, iron, nickel, quartz and molybdenum.

Agriculture. Agriculture accounts for approximately 36% of GDP. Production, 1993: Sugar, 243,000 tonnes; rice, 204,511 tonnes. Other products include coffee, cocoa, coconut and edible oils, copra, fruit, vegetables and tobacco.

Livestock (1996): Cattle, 190,000; pigs, 30,000; sheep, 130,000; goats, 79,000; chickens, 11m. Livestock products, 1993 (in 1,000 kg): Beef, 3,840; pork, 1,137; poultry, 4,067. Dairy products, 1995: Eggs, 30·39m.; milk, 797,627 litres.

Forestry. In 1995 the area under forests totalled 18·58m. ha (94·4% of the land area), down from 18·62m. ha and 94·6% in 1990. In terms of percentage coverage, Guyana and Suriname were the world's most heavily forested countries in 1995. 25% of the country's energy needs are met by wood fuel. Production (1996) 580,000 cu. metres of timber.

Fisheries. Total catches in 1995 came to approximately 46,000 tonnes, of which more than 98% was from sea fishing.

INDUSTRY

The main industries are agro-processing (sugar, rice, timber and coconut) and mining (gold and diamonds). There is a light manufacturing sector, and textiles and pharmaceuticals are produced by state and private companies. Production, 1995: Sugar, 253,870 tonnes; rum, 17,926 litres; beer, 8,470 litres; soft drinks, 3,032,130 cases; textiles, 322m. metres; footwear, 54,132 pairs; margarine, 1,262,420 kg; edible oil, 2,388,120 litres; refrigerators, 2,763; paint, 923,847 litres.

Labour. In 1996 the labour force was 353,000 (67% males).

INTERNATIONAL TRADE

Guyana's external debt in early 1998 was US$2·1bn., although the IMF and World Bank were looking to reduce it by US$500m.

Imports and Exports. In 1996 exports were valued at US$574·8m. and imports at US$595·0m. In the budgeted figures for 1998, exports were valued at US$616·0m. and imports at US$652·0m. Principal commodities exported, 1996 (in US$1m.): Sugar, 150·7; gold, 105·9; rice, 93·7; bauxite, 86·0. Other important export commodities included shrimps, timber and rum. Exports by volume, 1995: bauxite, 1,971,063 tonnes; sugar, 225,421 tonnes; rice, 200,544 tonnes; gold, 275,305 oz.; shrimps, 827 tonnes; timber, 35,873 cu. metres.

COMMUNICATIONS

Roads. In 1995 it was estimated there were 7,820 km of roads, of which 571 km were paved. Passenger cars numbered 24,000 in 1993 and commercial vehicles 9,000.

Rail. There is a government-owned railway in the North West District, while the Guyana Mining Enterprise operates a standard gauge railway of 133 km from Linden on the Demerara River to Ituni and Coomacka.

Civil Aviation. There is an international airport at Georgetown (Timehri). The national carrier is the state-owned Guyana Airways Corporation. Services were also provided in 1998 by BWIA, LIAT and Surinam Airways, with direct flights to Antigua, Barbados, Miami, New York, Paramaribo, Port of Spain and Toronto. In 1995 scheduled airline traffic of Guyana-based carriers flew 2·4m. km, carrying 121,000 passengers.

Shipping. The major port is Georgetown; there are 3 other ports. In 1995 sea-going shipping totalled 13,925 GRT. There are 217 nautical miles of river navigation. There are ferry services across the mouths of the Demerara, Berbice and Essequibo rivers.

Telecommunications. The inland public telegraph and radio communication services are operated by the Telecommunication Corporation. In 1997 there were 55,100 telephone main lines, or 65·2 per 1,000 population. Cellular phone subscribers numbered 1,200 in 1995.

Postal Services. In 1995 there were 85 post offices.

SOCIAL INSTITUTIONS

Justice. The law, both civil and criminal, is based on the common and statute law of England, save that the principles of the Roman–Dutch law have been retained in respect of the registration, conveyance and mortgaging of land.

The Supreme Court of Judicature consists of a Court of Appeal, a High Court and a number of courts of summary jurisdiction.

In 1996 there were 4,563 reported serious crimes, including 88 homicides.

Religion. In 1997, 57% of the population were Protestant and Roman Catholic, 33% Hindu, 9% Moslem and 1% other.

Education. In 1995 there were 363 pre-primary schools with 1,545 teachers for 30,004 pupils; 422 primary schools with 3,417 teachers for 99,664 pupils and 1,570 secondary school teachers for 63,838 pupils. There were 6,945 students at university level.

Adult literacy was 98·1% in 1995 (male, 98·6%; female, 97·5%). The rate of 98·1% is the highest in South America.

Health. In 1994 there were 30 hospitals (5 private), 162 health centres and 14 health posts. In 1997 there were 38·8 hospital beds per 10,000 population. There were (1993) 244 doctors, 34 dentists, 22 pharmacists, 172 midwives (1989) and 681 nursing personnel.

CULTURE

Broadcasting. The Guyana Broadcasting Corporation has 2 radio programmes. In 1995 there were 410,000 radio and 40,000 TV receivers (colour by NTSC). The Guyana Television Broadcasting Company (GTV) is state-owned and there are 12 private stations relaying US satellite services.

Cinema. In 1997 there were 18 cinemas.

Press. In 1995 there were 2 daily newspapers with a combined circulation of 39,000.

Tourism. There were 105,000 foreign visitors in 1996. Receipts totalled US$46m.

Festivals. There are a number of Christian, Hindu and Moslem festivals throughout the year.

Libraries. There is a National Library in Georgetown.

Museums and Galleries. The Guyana National Museum contains a broad selection of animal life and Guyanese heritage. Castellani House, the National Gallery, is home to the finest art collection in Guyana.

DIPLOMATIC REPRESENTATIVES

Of Guyana in Great Britain (3 Palace Ct., London, W2 4LP)
High Commissioner: Laleshwar K. N. Singh.

Of Great Britain in Guyana (44 Main St., Georgetown)
High Commissioner: Edmund Glover.

Of Guyana in the USA (2490 Tracy Pl., NW, Washington, D.C., 20008)
Ambassador: Mohammed Ali Odeen Ishmael.

Of the USA in Guyana (99-100 Young and Duke Streets, Kingston, Georgetown)
Ambassador: James F. Mack.

Of Guyana to the United Nations
Ambassador: Samuel Rudolph Insanally.

Of Guyana to the European Union
Ambassador: Havelock Brewster.

FURTHER READING

Baber, C. and Jeffrey, H. B., *Guyana: Politics, Economics and Society.* London, 1986
Braveboy-Wagner, J. A., *The Venezuela-Guyana Border Dispute: Britain's Colonial Legacy in Latin America.* London, 1984
Chambers, F., *Guyana.* [Bibliography] Oxford and Santa Barbara (CA), 1989
Daly, P. H., *From Revolution to Republic.* Georgetown, 1970
Daly, V. T., *A Short History of the Guyanese People.* 3rd. ed. London, 1992
Sanders, A., *The Powerless People.* London, 1987
Spinner, T. J., *A Political and Social History of Guyana, 1945–83.* Epping, 1985
Williams, B. F., *Stains on My Name, War in My Veins: Guyana and the Politics of Cultural Struggle.* Duke Univ. Press, 1992

National statistical office: Bureau of Statistics, Avenue of the Republic and Brickdam, Georgetown

HAITI

République d'Haïti

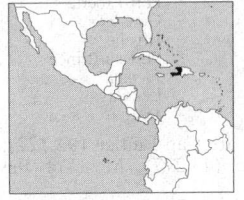

Capital: Port-au-Prince
Population estimate, 2000: 7·82m.
GNP per capita: (PPP$) 1,130
HDI/world rank: 0·340/159

KEY HISTORICAL EVENTS

The island of Hispaniola was discovered by Christopher Columbus in 1492. Haiti occupies the western third. The Spanish colony was ceded to France in 1697. After the extirpation of the Indians by the Spaniards (by 1533) large numbers of African slaves were imported whose descendants now populate the country. The slaves obtained their liberation following the French Revolution but Napoleon restored French authority and imprisoned Toussaint Louverture, the leader of the slaves who had been appointed a French general and governor. Subsequently the French surrendered to a blockading British squadron.

The country declared its independence on 1 Jan. 1804, and Gen. Jean-Jacques Dessalines proclaimed himself Emperor of the newly-named Haiti. After the assassination of Dessalines (1806) a separate régime was set up in the north under Gen. Henri Christophe who in 1811 had himself proclaimed King. In the south and west a republic was constituted, with Alexander Pétion as its first President. Pétion died in 1818 and was succeeded by Jean-Pierre Boyer, under whom the country became re-united after Henri Christophe had committed suicide in 1820. From 1822 to 1844 Haiti and the eastern part of the island (later the Dominican Republic) were united under Haitian rule. After one more monarchical interlude, under the Emperor Faustin (1847–59), Haiti has been a republic. From 1915 to 1934 Haiti was under United States occupation.

Dr François Duvalier was elected President on 22 Sept. 1957 and became president for life in 1964. He died on 21 April 1981 and was succeeded as president for life by his son, Jean-Claude Duvalier who fled the country on 7 Feb. 1986. Gen. Henry Namphy formed a Council of Government. In Jan. 1988 Leslie Manigat was elected president but Namphy again seized power in June 1988. In Sept. 1988 he was deposed and replaced by the military government of Lieut.-Gen. Prosper Avril. In March 1990 Ertha Pascal-Trouillot became head of an interim government. Father Jean-Bertrand Aristide was elected president in Dec. 1990.

On 30 Sept. 1991 President Aristide was deposed by a military junta and went into exile. Under international pressure, parliament again recognized Aristide as president in June 1993. After 2 agreements brokered by the UN and the Organization of American States a new government was formed in Aug. President Aristide was scheduled to return on 30 Oct. However, the military régime prevented UN forces from landing on 11 Oct., and on 13 Oct. the UN Security Council voted to apply new sanctions if the agreements were not adhered to. On 14 Oct. the Minister of Justice was assassinated and the USA and other UN members mounted a naval blockade.

The UN/OAS, Civil Mission (MICIVIH) was expelled by the junta on 11 July 1994. Despite a full embargo under UN Resolution 917, the junta showed no sign of stepping down. Former US President Carter flew to Haiti on 17 Sept. to negotiate their removal. 20,000 US troops moved into Haiti on 19 Sept. in an uncontested occupation. President Aristide returned to office on 15 Oct. 1994 and on 1 April 1995 a UN peacekeeping force (MANUH) took over from the US military mission. All UN contingents were scheduled to leave by 30 Nov. 1996, but a UN Security Council resolution provided for an extension. Aristide was succeeded by René Préval who was generally assumed to be a stand-in for his predecessor. Violence and poverty prevail. An estimated 7% of cocaine sold in the USA passes through Haiti.

TERRITORY AND POPULATION

Haiti is bounded in the east by the Dominican Republic, to the north by the Atlantic and elsewhere by the Caribbean Sea. The area is 27,750 sq. km (10,714 sq. miles). The Île de la Gonave, some 40 miles long, lies in the gulf of the same name. Among other islands is La Tortue, off the north peninsula. Population, (1996 est.) 7·3m.; density, 263 per sq. km. An estimated 68·2% of the population were rural in 1995.

The UN gives a projected population for 2000 of 7·82m.
Areas, populations and chief towns of the 9 departments:

Department	Area (in sq. km)	Population	Chief town
Nord-Ouest	2,094	395,442	Port-de-Paix
Nord	2,175	724,084	Cap Haïtien
Nord-Est	1,698	239,734	Fort-Liberté
L'Artibonite	4,895	961,447	Gonaïves
Centre	3,597	467,514	Hinche
Ouest	4,595	2,285,044	Port-au-Prince
Sud-Est	2,077	444,323	Jacmel
Sud	2,602	630,007	Les Cayes
Grande Anse	3,100	616,151	Jérémie

The capital is Port-au-Prince (1,255,078); other towns are Cap-Haïtien (92,122); Gonaïves (63,291), Les Cayes (45,904) and Jérémie (43,277). Most of the population is of African or mixed origin.

The official languages are French and Créole. Créole is spoken by all Haitians; French by only a small minority.

SOCIAL STATISTICS
1995 births, 247,000; deaths, 92,000. Birth rate (per 1,000 population), 1995, 34·7; death rate, 12·9. Annual growth rate, 1990–95, 2·0%. Expectation of life at birth, 1990–95, 52·7 years for males and 56·1 years for females. Infant mortality, 1990–95, 89 per 1,000 live births; fertility rate, 4·8 births per woman.

CLIMATE
A tropical climate, but the central mountains can cause semi-arid conditions in their lee. There are rainy seasons from April to June and Aug. to Nov. Hurricanes and severe thunderstorms can occur. The annual temperature range is small. Port-au-Prince, Jan. 77°F (25°C), July 84°F (28·9°C). Annual rainfall 53" (1,321 mm).

CONSTITUTION AND GOVERNMENT
The 1987 Constitution, ratified by a referendum, provides for a bicameral legislature (an 83-member *Chamber of Deputies* and a 27-member *Senate*), and an executive *President*, directly elected for a 5-year term. The President can stand for a second term but only after a 5 year interval.

National Anthem. 'La Dessalinienne'; words by J. Lhérisson, tune by N. Geffrard.

RECENT ELECTIONS
At the presidential, parliamentary and local elections of Dec. 1990 the electorate was some 3m.; turn-out was estimated at 55% by international observers. Jean-Bertrand Aristide (b. 1957) was elected President by about 66% of votes cast. He was sworn in on 7 Feb. 1991 but deposed on 30 Sept. 1991 by a military junta. He returned to Haiti in Oct. 1994 to complete his term when the US military intervention forced the junta's departure.

Following the removal of the junta, elections were held in 3 rounds on 25 June, 13 Aug. and 17 Sept. 1995. The electorate was 3·5m. Lavalas gained 17 Senate and 66 Chamber of Deputies seats.

Presidential elections were held on 17 Dec. 1995. There were 14 candidates; turn-out was 28%. Rene Préval was elected with 88% of votes cast. The next presidential elections are to be held in 2000.

CURRENT ADMINISTRATION
President: René Préval, b. 1943 (Lavalas; sworn in 7 Feb. 1996).

From June 1997 until March 1999 government was paralysed, without a Prime Minister, and in July 1998, 6 cabinet seats were vacant.

Prime Minister: Jacques-Edouard Alexis. The government resigned on 9 June 1997 but remained as a caretaker government until Prime Minister Rosny Smarth left office on 20 Oct. 1997. On 3 occasions nominations for Prime Minister (including Hervé Denis twice) were blocked by the largest party in parliament, the Organisation for the People's Struggle. The second attempt to have Denis accepted did succeed in the lower house but was not accepted by the Senate. On 25 March

1999 President René Préval appointed a new government by decree, with Jacques-Edouard Alexis formally becoming Prime Minister.

The *Speaker* of the Senate and National Assembly is Edgard Leblanc, and of the Chamber of Deputies, Kelly Bastien.

Local Government. Elections for 133 mayors and 565 3-member local councils were held on 17 Dec. 1995.

At elections held on 6 Apr. 1997 for 9 senators, 2 deputies and 700 municipal authorities, turn-out was only 10%. The elections were contested and effectively blocked the Senate.

DEFENCE

After the restoration of civilian rule in 1994 the armed forces and police were disbanded and a 3,000-strong Interim Public Security Force formed in 1995. In 1997 defence expenditure totalled US$99m. (US$14 per capita). For Police, *see* JUSTICE, *below.*

Army. The Army has effectively, though not formally, been disbanded.

INTERNATIONAL RELATIONS

Although foreign aid has been promised, political infighting and corruption have held up US$340m. worth of aid. However EU aid continues to arrive.

Haiti is a member of the UN, OAS and is an ACP member state of the ACP-EU relationship. It has not yet formally become a full member of CARICOM.

ECONOMY

Policy. The ongoing political crisis and absence of a Prime Minister since mid-1997 have prevented implementation of economic policy.

Performance. Real GDP growth was 2·8% in 1996, 4·4% in 1995 and –8·3% in 1994.

Budget. In 1996-97 revenues were US$284bn. and expenditure US$308m. No budget was voted for in the fiscal years 1997-98 or 1998-99 because of the absence of a Prime Minister or government.

Currency. The unit of currency is the *gourde* (HTG) of 100 *centimes.* Total money supply in Dec. 1997 was 6,911m. gourdes. Inflation in Sept. 1998 was officially running at 10%. In Feb. 1998 foreign exchange reserves were US$72m.

Banking and Finance. The Banque Nationale de la République d'Haïti is the central bank and bank of issue (*Governor:* Fritz Jean). In 1997 there were 11 commercial banks.

Weights and Measures. The metric system and British imperial and US measures are in use.

ENERGY AND NATURAL RESOURCES

Electricity. Installed capacity was 216,500 kW in 1995. Production in 1995 was 379m. kWh, with consumption per capita in 1995 an estimated 33 kWh.

Oil and Gas. Haiti has no natural oil and gas resources.

Minerals. Until the supply was exhausted in the 1970s, a small quantity of bauxite was mined.

Agriculture. In 1996 agriculture accounted for 42% of GDP. The agricultural area is 1·4m. ha, of which 0·91m. ha are cultivated and 0·49m. ha pasture. 65% of the workforce, mainly smallholders, make a living by agriculture carried on in 7 large plains, from 0·2m. to 25,000 acres, and in 15 smaller plains down to 2,000 acres. Irrigation is used in some areas. The main crops are coffee, sugar, rice, maize, sorghum, millet, beans, cocoa, sweet potatoes, sisal, cotton, bananas and citrus fruits. Livestock (1996): Cattle, 1·25m.; goats 910,000; pigs, 500,000; horses, 490,000; chickens, 6m.

Forestry. The area under forests in 1995 was 21,000 ha, or 0·8% of the total land area (25,000 ha and 0·9% in 1990). In 1995, 6·42m. cu. metres of roundwood were cut.

Fisheries. Total catches in 1995 came to approximately 5,500 tonnes, of which over 90% was from marine waters.

INDUSTRY

Manufacturing is largely based on the assembly of imported components: Toys, sports equipment, clothing, electronic and electrical equipment. Textiles, steel, soap, chemicals, paint and shoes are also produced. Many jobs were lost to other Central American and Caribbean countries during the 1991-94 trade embargo, after President Aristide was deposed. The assembly industries currently employ only 18,500, down from 33,600 in 1991.

Labour. In 1996 the labour force was 3,209,000 (57% males). The unemployment rate in July 1998 was around 60%.

Trade Unions. Whilst at least 6 unions exist, their influence is very limited.

INTERNATIONAL TRADE

Foreign debt was US$1,068·4m. in Aug. 1998.

Imports and Exports. In 1996 exports were US$147m. and imports US$499m. The leading imports are petroleum products, foodstuffs, textiles, machinery, animal and vegetable oils, chemicals, pharmaceuticals, raw materials for transformation industries and vehicles.

COMMUNICATIONS

Roads. Total length of roads was estimated at 4,080 km in 1995, of which 987 km were surfaced. There were 32,000 passenger cars in 1996 (4 per 1,000 inhabitants), plus 21,000 trucks and vans.

Rail. Haiti does not have a rail system.

Civil Aviation. There is an international airport at Port-au-Prince. Services were provided in 1998 by Aerolíneas Santo Domingo, Air Canada, Air France, ALM, American Airlines, COPA, Société Nouvelle Air Guadeloupe and United Airlines, with flights to Aruba, Cayenne, Curaçao, Fort de France, Miami, Montreal, New York, Panama City, Paris, Pointe-à-Pitre, St Maarten, St Martin, San Juan and Santo Domingo. In 1996 Port-au-Prince handled 345,000 passengers and 22,100 tonnes of freight.

Shipping. Port-au-Prince and Cap Haïtien are the principal ports, and there are 12 minor ports. In 1994 vessels entering totalled 347,000 net registered tons.

Telecommunications. The state telecommunications agency is Teleco. Main telephone lines in 1997 numbered 60,000, or 8 for every 1,000 inhabitants. In July 1998 there were approximately 2,000 Internet users.

Postal Services. There were 121 post offices in 1995. The postal service is fairly reliable in the capital and major towns. Many businesses, however, prefer to use express courier services (DHL and Federal Express).

SOCIAL INSTITUTIONS

Justice. The Court of Cassation is the highest court in the judicial system. There are 4 Courts of Appeal and 4 Civil Courts. Judges are appointed by the President. The legal system is basically French. A 5,000-strong police force has been re-recruited from former military personnel and others not implicated in human rights violations.

Religion. Since the Concordat of 1860 Roman Catholicism has been given special recognition, under an archbishop with 9 bishops. The Episcopal Church has one bishop. 90% of the population are nominally Roman Catholic, while other Christian churches number perhaps 10%. Probably two-thirds of the population to some extent adhere to African-derived traditional beliefs ('Voodoo'). A national Voodoo temple began construction in 1995.

Education. The adult literacy rate in 1995 was 45% (48% among males and 42·2% among females). Education is divided into 9 years 'education fondamentale', followed by 4 years to 'Baccalaureate' and university/higher education. The school system is based on the French system and instruction is in French and Créole.

There are 360 primary schools (221 state, 139 religious), 21 public lycées, 123 private secondary schools, 18 vocational training centres and 42 domestic science centres.

There is a state university, several private universities and an Institute of Administration and Management.

Health. In 1994 there were 641 doctors, 95 dentists and 2,725 nurses, and 50 hospitals. There were 10 beds per 10,000 population in 1994. In the period 1990–96 only 28% of the population had access to safe drinking water.

CULTURE

Broadcasting. Under the aegis of the Conseil National des Télécommunications, radio and TV programmes (colour by NTSC) are broadcast by Radio Nationale and Télévision Nationale. There is a privately-owned cable TV company, and several privately-owned radio stations. There were 380,000 radio and 35,000 TV sets in 1995.

Cinema. There are 10 cinemas in Port-au-Prince.

Press. There were 2 daily newspapers in 1998. In 1995 the press had a combined circulation of 45,000, at a rate of 6 per 1,000 inhabitants.

Tourism. In 1996 there were 150,000 foreign tourists, spending US$81m. There are only about 1,000 hotel rooms in the whole country.

Libraries. There is a public library, Bibliothèque Nationale, in Port-au-Prince. A private library open to scholars, Bibliothèque des Frères de l'Instruction Chrétienne, is nearby.

National Theatre and Opera. The Théâtre National is in Port-au-Prince.

Museums and Galleries. The main museums are MUPANAH and the Musée de l'Art Haïtien, both in Port-au-Prince. There are at least 20 private art shops in Port-au-Prince and major towns.

DIPLOMATIC REPRESENTATIVES

Of Haiti in Great Britain. The Embassy closed on 30 March 1987.

Of Great Britain in Haiti
Ambassador: Mr. A. R. Thomas, CMG (resides in Kingston).

Of Haiti in the USA (2311 Massachusetts Ave., NW, Washington, D.C., 20008)
Chargé d'Affaires a.i.: Louis Harold Joseph.

Of the USA in Haiti (Harry Truman Blvd., Port-au-Prince)
Ambassador: Timothy M. Carney.

Of Haiti to the United Nations
Ambassador: Pierre Lelong.

Of Haiti to the European Union
Ambassador: Yolette Azor-Charles.

FURTHER READING

Chambers, F. J., *Haiti*. [Bibliography] 2nd ed. Oxford and Santa Barbara (CA), 1994
Ferguson, J., *Papa Doc, Baby Doc: Haiti and the Duvaliers*. Oxford, 1987
Heinl, Robert & Nancy, revised by Michael Heinl, *Written in Blood*. University Press of America, 1996
Laguerre, M. S., *The Complete Haitiana*. [Bibliography] London and New York, 1982.— *Voodoo and Politics in Haiti*. London, 1989
Lawless, R., *Haiti: a Research Guide*. New York, 1990
Lundahl, M., *The Haitian Economy: Man, Land and Markets*. London, 1983
Nicholls, D., *From Dessalines to Duvalier: Race, Colour and National Independence in Haiti*. 2nd ed. CUP, 1992.—*Haiti in Caribbean Context: Ethnicity, Economy and Revolt*. London, 1985
Thomson, I., *Bonjour Blanc: a Journey through Haiti*. London, 1992
Weinstein, B. and Segal, A., *Haiti: the Failure of Politics*. New York, 1992
Wilentz, A., *The Rainy Season: Haiti since Duvalier*. New York, 1989

National library: Bibliothèque Nationale, Rue du Centre, Port-au-Prince.

HONDURAS

República de Honduras

Capital: Tegucigalpa
Population estimate, 2000: 6·48m.
GNP per capita: (PPP$) 2,130
HDI/world rank: 0·573/119

KEY HISTORICAL EVENTS

In pre-Columbian times the area which is now Honduras was part of the Mayan empire. Discovered by Columbus in 1502, Honduras was ruled by Spain as part of the Captain-Generalcy of Guatemala. In 1821 Honduras gained its independence from Spain and from 1823 was part of the Central American Federation. On 5 Nov. 1838 the country declared itself an independent sovereign state, free from the Federation. Political instability became the rule, punctuated by a period of more serious administration from 1876 to 1891. The instability, with one period of US military occupation, continued until 1933. From 1933 to 1949 Gen. Tiburcio Carias Andino ruled as a dictator. There followed a disturbed period of presidential elections, depositions and military juntas. Dr Ramón Ernesto Cruz Velés was elected president in 1971 but a coup in 1972 led to his being superseded by Gen. López Arellano who ruled by decree until 1975 when he too was ousted by army officers in favour of Col. Melgar Castro. In 1978 a military junta took control, with the commander of the army, Gen. Policarpo Paz Garcia, nominated as head of state.

The end of military rule seemed to come in 1981 when a general election gave victory to the more liberal and non-military party, PLH (Partido Liberal de Honduras). The party's leader, Dr Roberto Svazo Cordova, became president. Considerable power, however, remained with the armed forces, led by their commander-in-chief, Gen. Gustavo Alvarez. While fighting the left-wing guerrillas, the military was also held to be responsible for the disappearance of political opponents.

In 1984 junior army officers forced Gen. Alvarez and other senior officers into exile and Gen. Walter López Reyes took over as commander-in-chief. There followed a period of less friendly relations with the USA and increasingly poor relations with Nicaragua, since the anti Sandinista (contra) rebels maintained bases in Honduras. Internal unrest continued into the 1990s with politicians and military leaders at loggerheads, particularly over attempts to investigate violations of human rights.

In Oct. 1998 much of Central America was devastated by Hurricane Mitch, the worst natural disaster to hit the area in modern times. Honduras and Nicaragua were paralysed by floods and mudslides. In Honduras 7,000 deaths were estimated with twice as many missing. 1m. of the city's inhabitants were left homeless and the country's agriculture was crippled with around a quarter of the coffee plantations destroyed.

TERRITORY AND POPULATION

Honduras is bounded in the north by the Caribbean, east and south-east by Nicaragua, west by Guatemala, south-west by El Salvador and south by the Pacific Ocean. The area is 112,088 sq. km (43,277 sq. miles). The estimated population in 1997 was 5,751,400 (2,870,700 female), giving a density of 51 per sq. km.

The UN gives a projected population for 2000 of 6·47m.

An estimated 56·2% of the population were rural in 1995.

The chief cities (populations in 1,000, 1994) were Tegucigalpa, the capital (775·3), San Pedro Sula (368·5), El Progreso (81·2), Choluteca (72·8), Danlí (43·3) and the Atlantic coast ports of La Ceiba (86·0), Puerto Cortés (33·5) and Tela (24·8); other towns include Olanchito (17·9), Juticalpa (25·6), Comayagua (52·3), Siguatepeque (37·5) and Santa Rosa de Copán (23·4).

Areas and 1988 census populations of the 18 departments and the Central District (Tegucigalpa):

Department	Area (in sq. km)	Population	Department	Area (in sq. km)	Population
Atlántida	4,251	238,742	Colón	8,875	149,677
Choluteca	4,211	295,484	Comayagua	5,196	239,859

Department	Area (in sq. km)	Population	Department	Area (in sq. km)	Population
Copán	3,203	219,455	Lempira	4,290	177,055
Cortés	3,954	662,772	Ocotepeque	1,680	74,276
El Paraíso	7,218	254,295	Olancho	24,350	283,852
Francisco Morazán	6,298	251,613	Santa Bárbara	5,115	278,868
Gracias a Dios	16,630	34,970	Valle	1,565	119,645
Intibucá	3,072	124,681	Yoro	7,939	333,508
Islas de la Bahía	261	22,062	Central District	1,648	576,661
La Paz	2,331	105,927			

The official language is Spanish. The Spanish-speaking population is of mixed Spanish and Amerindian descent (90%), with 7% Amerindians.

SOCIAL STATISTICS
Births, 1997 estimates, 187,000; deaths, 32,000. 1997 birth rate, 32·6 per 1,000 population; death rate 5·6. 1997 life expectancy, 66·4 years for men and 71·4 for women; population growth rate, 2·55%. Infant mortality, 1990–95, 43 per 1,000 live births; fertility rate, 4·9 births per woman.

CLIMATE
The climate is tropical, with a small annual range of temperature but with high rainfall. Upland areas have two wet seasons, from May to July and in Sept. and Oct. The Caribbean Coast has most rain in Dec. and Jan. and temperatures are generally higher than inland. Tegucigalpa, Jan. 66°F (19°C), July 74°F (23·3°C). Annual rainfall 64" (1,621 mm).

CONSTITUTION AND GOVERNMENT
The present Constitution came into force in 1982. The *President* is elected for a 4-year term. Members of the *National Congress* (total 128 seats) and municipal mayors are elected simultaneously on a proportional basis, according to combined votes cast for the Presidential candidate of their party.

National Anthem. 'Tu bandera' ('Thy Banner'); words by A. C. Coello, tune by C. Hartling.

RECENT ELECTIONS
Elections were held on 30 Nov. 1997. The PLH gained 67 seats in Congress (49·7% of votes cast), with the remaining seats apportioned to the following parties: Nacional, 54 seats (41·3%), Inovación y Unidad 5 seats (4·2%), Unificación Democrática 1 seat (2·6%) and Demócrata Cristiano 1 seat (2·2%). The presidential election on the same day was won by Carlos Roberto Flores Facusse (PLH), with 52·8% of the votes cast against 4 other candidates.

CURRENT ADMINISTRATION
President: Carlos Roberto Flores Facusse.
   First Vice President: William Handal. *Second Vice President:* Gladys Caballero de Arevalo. *Third Vice President:* Hector Vidal Cerrato Hernandez.
   In March 1999 the government consisted of:
   Minister of Agriculture and Livestock: Guillermo Alvarado Downing. *Culture, Arts and Sports:* Herman Allan Padgett. *Defence:* Edgardo Dumas Rodriguez. *Education:* Ramon Calix Figueroa. *Finance:* Gabriela Nuñez. *Foreign Relations:* Roberto Flores Bermúdez. *Government and Justice:* Enrique Flores Valeriano. *Industry and Commerce:* Reginaldo Panting Penalba. *Labour:* Rosa America Miranda de Galo. *Natural Resources and Environment:* Silvia Xiomara Gomez de Caballero. *Presidency:* Gustavo Adolfo Alfaro Zelaya. *Public Health:* Plutarco Castellanos. *Public Works, Transportation and Housing:* Tomás Lozano Reyes. *Tourism:* Norman Garcia Paz. *Ministers without Portfolio:* Jorge Arturo Reina, Nahun Valladares, Roberto Leiva.

Local Government. Honduras comprises a Central District (containing the cities of Tegucigalpa and Comayaguela) and 18 departments (each administered by an appointed Governor), sub-divided into 293 municipalities. Mayors are elected simultaneously with Congressional deputies.

DEFENCE
Conscription was abolished in 1995. In 1997 defence expenditure totalled US$101m. (US$16 per capita).

Army. The Army consists of 3 infantry brigades, 1 special tactics group, 1 territorial force, 1 armed cavalry regiment and 1 artillery and 1 engineer battalion. Equipment includes 12 Scorpion light tanks. Strength (1997) 16,000 (12,000 conscripts). There is also a paramilitary Public Security Force of 5,500.

Navy. A small flotilla operates 5 US-built fast inshore patrol craft, some 6 other inshore craft, 4 landing craft and a number of boats. Personnel (1997), 1,000 including 400 marines. Bases are at Puerto Cortés and Amapala.

Air Force. Equipment includes 12 F-5E/F Tiger II fighters, 12 A-37B jet light attack aircraft, 4 Spanish-built CASA C-101BB armed jet trainers, 4 four-engined Lockheed transports, 5 C-47, 1 Israeli-built Arava transport, about 20 helicopters and Tucano and T-41D trainers. Total strength was (1997) about 1,800 personnel (700 conscripts).

INTERNATIONAL RELATIONS
Honduras is a member of the UN and OAS.

ECONOMY
Performance. Real GDP growth was 3·6% in 1995 (−1·5% in 1994). Hurricane Mitch is thought to have set back the economy by 15 to 20 years.

Budget. 1997 estimate: Expenditure was US$850m. (including capital expenditures of US$150m.); revenues totalled US$655m.

Currency. The unit of currency is the *lempira* (HNL) of 100 *centavos*. Foreign exchange reserves were US$672m. in Feb. 1998 and gold reserves were 20,000 troy oz. The average annual inflation rate over the period 1990–96 was 20%. Total money supply in Dec. 1997 was 8,677m. lempiras.

Banking and Finance. The central bank of issue is the Banco Central de Honduras (*President:* Ermin Barjun). There is an agricultural development bank, Banadesa, for small grain producers, a state land bank and a network of rural credit agencies managed by peasant organizations. The Central American Bank for Economic Integration (BCIE) has its head office in Tegucigalpa. In 1993 there were 13 private banks, including 2 foreign.

There are stock exchanges in Tegucigalpa and San Pedro Sula.

Weights and Measures. The metric system has been legal since 1 April 1897, although there are still some minor traces of the Imperial and old Spanish systems.

ENERGY AND NATURAL RESOURCES
Electricity. Installed capacity was 605,900 kW in 1995. Production in 1995 was 2·74bn. kWh (mainly hydro-electric); consumption per capita was an estimated 361 kWh in 1995.

Minerals. Output in 1993 (in 1,000 tonnes): Lead, 4·9; zinc, 26·5. Silver, 24 tonnes. Small quantities of gold are mined, and there are also deposits of tin, iron, copper, coal, antimony and pitchblende.

Agriculture. In 1996 agriculture accounted for 22% of GDP. In 1994, 1·79m. ha were devoted to arable farming and permanent crop land, and 2·5m. ha to permanent pasture. Legislation of 1975 provided for the compulsory redistribution of land, but in 1992 the grounds for this were much reduced, and a 5-ha minimum area for land titles abolished. Members of the 2,800 co-operatives set up in 1975 received individual shareholdings which can be broken up into personal units. Since 1992 women may have tenure in their own right. The state monopoly of the foreign grain trade was abolished in 1992.

Crop production in 1994 (in 1,000 tonnes): Bananas, 411; coffee, 263; maize, 995; dry beans, 120; sorghum, 195.

Livestock (1996): Cattle, 2,127,000; pigs, 600,000; goats, 28,000 (1995); horses, 175,000; poultry, 14m. (1995).

Forestry. In 1995 forests covered 4·11m. ha, or 36·8% of the total land area (down from 41·3% of the land area in 1990). In 1995, 6·46m. cu. metres of roundwood were cut.

Fisheries. Shrimps and lobsters are important catches. Total catch, 1995, 24,333 tonnes, almost entirely from sea fishing.

INDUSTRY
Industry is small-scale and local. 1994 output: Cement, 999·6 tonnes; fabrics, 11,286 yards. 217,835 bottles of beer and 5,300 litres of rum were produced in 1994.

Labour. The workforce was 1·3m. in 1996. In 1995, 37·2% of those in employment were in agriculture, forestry and fishing, 18·0% were in manufacturing industries and 17·0% in community, social and personal services. Unemployment rate (1996 estimate): 15%.

Trade Unions. About 346,000 workers were unionized in 1994.

INTERNATIONAL TRADE
In May 1992 Honduras, El Salvador and Guatemala agreed to create a free trade zone. Import duties are to be standardized. Foreign debt was US$4,453m. in 1996.

Imports and Exports. Imports in 1996 were valued at US$1,840m. and exports at US$1,317m.

Main exports are bananas, coffee, shrimps and lobsters, fruit, lead and zinc, timber, and refrigerated meats. Main imports are machinery and electrical equipment, industrial chemicals and mineral products and lubricants. Principal export markets, 1995: USA, 42·7%; Germany, 19·3%; Japan, 6·7%; Spain, 3·9%. Principal import suppliers, 1995: USA, 46·6%; Netherlands, 7·5%; Guatemala, 6·8%; Mexico, 4·2%.

COMMUNICATIONS

Roads. Honduras is connected with Guatemala, El Salvador and Nicaragua by the Pan-American Highway. Out of a total of 15,100 km of roads (1995), 3,050 km were paved. In 1995 there were 81,439 passenger cars in use, 170,006 commercial vehicles and 22,482 motor cycles and bicycles.

Rail. The small government-run railway was built to serve the banana industry and is confined to the northern coastal region and does not reach Tegucigalpa. In 1995 there were 595 km of track in 3 gauges, which in 1994 carried 1m. passengers and 1·2m. tonnes of freight.

Civil Aviation. There are 4 international airports: San Pedro Sula and Tegucigalpa (Toncontín) are the main ones, plus Roatún and La Ceiba, with over 80 smaller airstrips in various parts of the country. The Honduras-based carriers are Aero Lineas Sosa and Caribbean Air. Services were also provided in 1998 by American Airlines, Aviateca, Continental Airlines, COPA, Iberia, Islena Airlines, LACSA, La Costena, Mayan World Airlines and Taca International Airlines. In addition to domestic flights and services to other parts of central America and the Caribbean, there were flights in 1998 to Barcelona, Dallas/Fort Worth, Houston, Madrid, Miami, New Orleans, New York, Orlando and Quito. In 1996 San Pedro Sula handled 386,327 passengers (291,199 on international flights) and 12,105 tonnes of freight, and Tegucigalpa handled 321,2427 passengers (236,281 on international flights) and 7,526 tonnes of freight.

Shipping. The largest port is Puerto Cortés on the Atlantic coast. There are also ports at Henecán (on the Pacific) and Puerto Castilla and Tela (northern coast). Ships of 1,000 GRT or over in 1996 were estimated at 251, including 153 cargo ships, 24 oil or chemical tankers and 5 container ships. Honduras is a flag of convenience registry.

Telecommunications. In 1997 there were 233,600 telephone main lines, or 36·8 for every 1,000 persons.

Postal Services. There were 435 post offices in 1995.

SOCIAL INSTITUTIONS

Justice. Judicial power is vested in the Supreme Court, with 9 judges elected by the National Congress for 4 years; it appoints the judges of the courts of appeal, and justices of the peace.

Religion. Roman Catholicism is the prevailing religion, but the constitution guarantees freedom to all creeds, and the State does not contribute to the support of any. Evangelical movements from North America are spreading their influence.

Education. Adult literacy was 72·7% in 1995 (male, 72·6%; female, 72·7%). Education is free, compulsory (from 7 to 12 years) and secular. There is a high drop-out rate after the first years in primary education. In 1995 the 8,168 primary schools had 1,008,092 children (28,978 teachers); the 661 secondary, normal and technical schools had 184,589 pupils (12,480 teachers). There were 8 universities or specialized colleges, with a total of 54,293 students and 3,676 academic staff. In addition, 73,491 children attended pre-primary school

In 1994 total expenditure on education came to 4% of GNP and represented 16% of total government expenditure.

Health. In 1993 there were 3,803 doctors, 622 dentists, 6,288 nurses and 975 pharmacists. In 1994 there were 29 public hospitals and 32 private, with 4,737 beds, and 849 health centres.

CULTURE

Broadcasting. There were 6 commercial TV channels in 1993 (colour by NTSC) and various radio stations (mostly local). In 1995 there were 2·3m. radio and 0·5m. TV sets.

Press. Honduras 5 national daily papers in 1995, with a combined circulation of 240,000.

Tourism. In 1996 there were 257,000 foreign tourists, spending US$81m.

DIPLOMATIC REPRESENTATIVES

Of Honduras in Great Britain (115 Gloucester Pl., London, W1H 3PJ)
Ambassador: Roberto Flores Bermúdez.

Of Great Britain in Honduras (Edificio Palmira, 3er Piso, Colonia Palmira, Tegucigalpa)
Ambassador: D. Osborne.

Of Honduras in the USA (3007 Tilden St., NW, Washington, D.C., 20008)
Ambassador: Edgardo Dumas.

Of the USA in Honduras (Av. La Paz, Tegucigalpa)
Ambassador: James Creagan.

Of Honduras to the United Nations
Ambassador: Hugo Noé-Pino.

Of Honduras to the European Union
Ambassador: Alejandro Ulloa de Thuin.

FURTHER READING
Banco Central de Honduras. *Honduras en Cifras 1990–92.* Tegucigalpa, 1993
Howard-Reguindin, P., *Honduras* [Bibliography]. Oxford and Santa Barbara (CA), 1991
Meyer, H. K. and Meyer, J. H., *Historical Dictionary of Honduras.* 2nd ed. Metuchen (NJ), 1994
Sheehan, E. R. F., *Agony in the garden: a Stranger in Central America.* New York, 1989

HUNGARY

Magyar Köztársaság

(Hungarian Republic)

Capital: Budapest
Population estimate, 2000: 9·81m.
GNP per capita: (PPP$) 6,730
HDI/world rank: 0·857/47

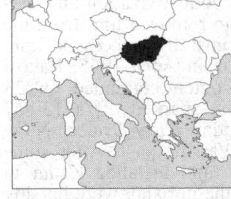

KEY HISTORICAL EVENTS

The Hungarians call themselves "Magyars"; "Hungarian" derives from the Turkic name ("On ogur", i.e, ten arrows) of the tribal federation on the Don which Árpád and his horde left in order to settle the sparsely inhabited middle Danubian basin in 896. The horde spread terror by its forays but was pacified by defeat at the hands of the Germans at Augsburg in 955. In 1000 Stephen adopted Roman Catholicism and received a crown from the Pope. Stephen replaced the tribal structure with a system of counties administered by royal officials. As nomadism gave way to agriculture a feudal society developed led by nobility descended from the original conquerors.

In 1301 Árpád's line died out. Henceforth, with two exceptions, the throne was held by foreigners, sometimes holding other thrones simultaneously. The Angevin king, Lájos the Great (1342-82), was also king of Poland; under him Hungary attained a golden age of prosperity, civilization and international significance.

In the 15th century the expansionist Ottoman empire reached the southern borders of Hungary. This first incursion was repelled by János Hunyádi. His son Matthias Corvinus, elected king in 1458, ruled as an enlightened renaissance despot. In 1526 the Turks again advanced on the Hungarians who were defeated at the battle of Mohács and their king killed. Southern and central Hungary were annexed and turned into a desert. The western rump came under Hapsburg rule which was extended to most of Hungary with the expulsion of the Turks in 1699. A national rising in 1703 under Ferenc Rákoczi forced the crown to come to terms: Emperor Charles IV restored the constitution and the Hungarian assembly recognized the Emperor's claim to the Hungarian throne. The Hapsburgs imposed a centralizing Germanizing régime upon Hungary economically stagnating under protective tariffs designed to restrict industrialization to Austria. Nationalist sentiments led to the radical democracy of Lájos Kossuth who set up a breakaway government in Debrecen in 1848-49. Ruthless repression followed but Austria's military defeats in Italy (1859) and against Prussia (1866) forced the emperor to moderate his absolutism. Under the Compromise (*Ausgleich*) of 1867 a Dual Monarchy was constituted; Hungary gained internal autonomy while foreign affairs and defence became joint Austro-Hungarian responsibilities.

Hungary entered the First World War on Austria's side but as hostilities drew to a close the ideas of Mihaly Károlyi, who stood for peace and independence, grew in popularity. After the armistice of 3 Nov. 1918 a National Council under his chairmanship proclaimed an independent republic. Political and social unrest, however, were compounded by a Romanian invasion. On 21 March 1919 Károlyi was replaced by Béla Kun's Soviet republic and a reign of red terror which antagonized most of the population. Kun fled on 4 Aug. A counter-revolutionary government annulled all his and Károlyi's legislation and appointed Admiral Horthy as regent. Hungary was drastically reduced in size by the Peace Treaty.

The 1920s under the premiership of István Bethlen were a period of consolidation but Bethlen was forced to resign by the collapse of wheat prices in the world depression. Hungary's desire to revise the Versailles peace settlements brought her into alignment with Germany in the 1930s, and this was reinforced by her growing economic dependence on Germany. In 1940 Hungary adhered to the Tripartite pact and in June 1941 sent a force to join the German invaders of the Soviet Union. But pro-German sentiment was never wholehearted until Hitler occupied the country in March 1944. In Oct. Horthy was forced to abdicate in favour of a fascist "Arrow Cross" government but by then Soviet forces were well inside the frontiers.

The four democratic parties permitted by the Soviets formed a provisional government at Debrecen in Dec. 1944 which declared war on Germany and signed an armistice with the Allies. At the elections of Nov. 1945 the Communists polled only 17% of the vote; their way to power was to lie in their leader Rákosi's "salami tactics" of divide and purge, backed up by their acquisition of key ministries under Soviet pressure. In Feb. 1949 Catholic opposition was weakened by the arrest of cardinal Mindszenty, and all political parties were united in a People's Front whose single list of candidates gained 96% of the vote at the May 1949 elections. A Soviet-type constitution was adopted in Aug. Rákosi carried out a drastic purge of "Titoists" and embarked on a programme of such ruthless collectivization and top-heavy industrialization that the post-Stalin Soviet leadership removed him from the premiership. As party leader, however, he intrigued against his successor Imre Nagy's more liberal "new course" and took his place again in April 1955. Rákosi resigned the party leadership in July 1956 but popular discontent continued. On 23 Oct. the attempted suppression of a student demonstration sparked off a 13-day revolution. Nagy became prime minister and János Kádár party leader. Nagy declared Hungary's neutrality and withdrawal from the Warsaw pact. After some hesitation the Soviet army crushed the revolt on 4 Nov. and installed Kádár in power. Nagy was arrested and later executed; the gains of the uprising were harshly suppressed. Cautious economic reforms were introduced in the mid-60s when liberalization brought higher living standards.

A gathering reformist tendency within the Hungarian Socialist Workers' (i.e. Communist) Party led by Imre Pozsgay culminated in its self-dissolution in Oct. 1989 and reconstitution as the Hungarian Socialist Party. The People's Republic was abolished on 23 Oct. 1989.

Nagy was reburied with state honours on 16 Aug. 1989. The following year a multi-party democracy came into being.

TERRITORY AND POPULATION
Hungary is bounded in the north by Slovakia, north-east by Ukraine, east by Romania, south by Croatia and Yugoslavia and west by Austria. The peace treaty of 10 Feb. 1947 restored the frontiers as of 1 Jan. 1938. The area of Hungary is 93,036 sq. km (35,921 sq. miles).

At the census of 1 Jan. 1990 the population was 10,374,823 (5,389,919 females); estimate, 1996, 10,214,000 (5,330,000 females).

The UN gives a projected population for 2000 of 9·81m.

Hungary's population has been falling at such a steady rate since 1980 that its 1996 population was the same as that in the late 1960s.

62·6% of the population was urban (18·7% in Budapest) in 1996; population density, 1996, 109·8 per sq. km. Ethnic minorities, 1995: Germans, 4%; Slovaks, 8%; Romanians, 7%; Gypsies, 4%; Serbs, 2%. A law of 1993 permits ethnic minorities to set up self-governing councils. There is a worldwide Hungarian diaspora, of 1·5m. in 1988 (730,000 in USA; 220,000 in Israel; 140,000 in Canada), and Hungarian minorities (3·5m. in 1992) in Romania (2m.), Slovakia (0·6m.), Yugoslavia (Vojvodina, 0·4m.) and the Ukraine (0·16m.).

Hungary is divided into 19 counties (megyék) and the capital, Budapest, which has county status.

Area (in sq. km) and population (in 1,000) of counties and county towns (estimate, 1 Jan. 1995):

Counties	Area	Population	Chief town	Population
Baranya	4,487	412	Pécs	163
Bács-Kiskun	8,362	541	Kecskemét	105
Békés	5,631	405	Békéscsaba	65
Borsod-Abaúj-Zemplén	7,247	750	Miskolc	182
Csongrád	4,263	429	Szeged	169
Fejér	4,373	426	Székesfehérvár	108
Győr-Moson-Sopron	4,062	426	Győr	127
Hajdú-Bihar	6,211	550	Debrecen	211
Heves	3,637	330	Eger	60
Jász-Nagykún-Szolnok	5,607	423	Szolnok	79
Komárom-Esztergom	2,251	31	Tatabánya	73
Nógrád	2,544	224	Salgótarján	46
Pest	6,394	973	Budapest	1,930
Somogy	6,036	338	Kaposvár	69

HUNGARY

Counties	Area	Population	Chief town	Population
Szabolcs-Szatmár-Bereg	5,937	573	Nyíregyháza	113
Tolna	3,704	250	Szekszárd	36
Vas	3,336	273	Szombathely	84
Veszprém	4,639	379	Veszprém	65
Zala	3,784	302	Zalaegerszeg	62
Budapest	525	4,487	(has county status)	

The official language is Hungarian. 96·6% of the population have Hungarian as their mother tongue. Ethnic minorities have the right to education in their own language.

SOCIAL STATISTICS
Vital statistics, 1995: Births, 112,000; marriages, 54,000 (14,000 remarriages); divorces, 24,000; deaths, 144,000; abortions, 77,000. There were 3,500 suicides. Rates (per 1,000 population), 1995: Birth, 10·9; death, 14·1; marriage, 5·3; divorce, 2·3; infant mortality, 10·7 (per 1,000 live births). Annual growth rate, 1990–95, –0·3%. Over 1990–95, the suicide rate per 100,000 population was 38·6 (men, 58; women, 20·7). In 1995 the most popular age range for marrying was 20–24 for both males and females. Expectation of life at birth, 1990–95, 64·5 years for males and 73·8 years for females. Hungarians have the lowest life expectancy in the OECD and, in contrast with almost all other countries, lifetime prospects for adult males have been falling over the past 20 years. Fertility rate, 1990–95, 1·7 births per woman.

CLIMATE
A humid continental climate, with warm summers and cold winters. Precipitation is generally greater in summer, with thunderstorms. Dry, clear weather is likely in autumn, but spring is damp and both seasons are of short duration. Budapest, Jan. 32°F (0°C), July 71°F (21·5°C). Annual rainfall 25" (625 mm). Pécs, Jan. 30°F (–0·7°C), July 71°F (21·5°C). Annual rainfall 26·4" (661 mm).

CONSTITUTION AND GOVERNMENT
On 18 Oct. 1989 the National Assembly approved by an 88% majority a constitution which abolished the People's Republic, and established Hungary as an independent, democratic, law-based state.

The head of state is the *President*, who is elected for 5-year terms by the National Assembly.

The single-chamber *National Assembly* has 386 members, made up of 176 individual constituency winners, 152 allotted by proportional representation from county party lists and 58 from a national list. It is elected for 4-year terms. A *Constitutional Court* was established in Jan. 1990 to review laws under consideration.

National Anthem. 'Isten áldd meg a magyart' ('God bless the Hungarians'); words by Ferenc Kölcsey, tune by Ferenc Erkel.

RECENT ELECTIONS
On 19 June 1995 Árpád Göncz was re-elected President.

In the Hungarian parliamentary election on 10 and 24 May 1998 the centre-right Fidesz-Hungarian Civic party won 148 seats (20 in 1994) obtaining 28·2% of the votes against 134 seats (209 in 1994) for the ruling Socialist Party. Viktor Orban, the Fidesz leader, became prime minister as a result and formed a coalition government with the support of the right-wing Independent Smallholders' Party and the Hungarian Democratic Forum (MDF). The victory for the centre-right ended 4 years of socialist-led government.

CURRENT ADMINISTRATION
President: Árpád Göncz (b. 1922; AFD; elected 3 Aug. 1990, re-elected 19 June 1995).

An HSP-AFD coalition government was formed, which in March 1999 consisted of:
Prime Minister: Viktor Orban (b. 1963; Fidesz).

781

Interior: Sándor Pintér (Fidesz–MPP). *Environmental Protection:* Pál Pepó (FKgP). *Finance:* Zsigmond Járai (Fidesz–MPP). *Education:* Zoltán Pokorni (Fidesz–MPP). *Economic Affairs:* Atilla Chikán (Fidesz–MPP). *National Cultural Heritage:* József Hámori (Fidesz–MPP). *Social and Family Affairs:* Péter Harrach (Fidesz–MPP). *Defence:* János Szabó (FKgP). *Foreign Affairs:* János Martonyi (Fidesz–MPP). *Health:* Árpád Gógl (Fidesz–MPP). *Transport, Communications and Water Management:* Kálmán Katona (Fidesz–MPP). *Agriculture and Regional Development:* József Torgyán (FKgP). *Justice:* Ibolya Dávid (MDF). *Youth and Sports:* Tamas Deutsch. *Without Portfolio (In charge of Civilian National Security Services):* László Kövér (Fidesz–MPP). *Without Portfolio (For Coordination of EU (PHARE) Programme):* Imre Boros (FKgP). *Without Portfolio (In charge of the Prime Minister's Office):* István Stumpf (Fidesz–MPP).

Local Government. Local elections were held on 18 Oct. 1998. There was a turn-out of 45·57% from almost 8m. eligible voters. Of votes cast for mayors and councillors, independents won 47%, the HSP almost 11%, Fidesz almost 8%, the ISP almost 5%, the AFD 4%, the HFD almost 4%, the CDPP just over 1%, other parties a combined 13% and independent minorities just under 7%. In the ballots for county and assembly lists Fidesz and its allies got almost 40%, the HSP and AFD got over 35%, the right-wing parliamentary Hungarian Justice and Life Party got 5%, and the independents 20%. As a result of the minorities elections, national minorities formed 1,135 self-governing bodies at 930 settlements. All of Hungary's recognized minorities set up self-governments: Gypsies 673, Germans 211, Slovaks 57, Croats 56, Serbs 29, Poles 25, Romanians 24, Armenians 16, Greeks 13, Bulgarians 12, Ruthenes 7, and Slovenes and Ukrainians 6 each.

DEFENCE
The President of the Republic is C.-in-C. of the armed forces.

Men between the ages of 18 and 23 are liable for 9 months' conscription.

Defence expenditure in 1997 totalled US$666m., compared to US$3,380m. in 1985. Per capita spending in 1997 was US$66, down from US$317 in 1985. The 1997 expenditure represented 1·4% of GDP, compared to 7·2% in 1985.

Army. Hungary is divided into 4 army districts: Budapest, Debrecen, Kiskunfélegyháza and Pécs. The strength of the Army was (1997) 31,600 (including 19,000 conscripts). It is organized in 3 tank, 7 mechanized, 3 artillery, 1 engineer, 1 air defence artillery, 1 (Budapest) rivercraft and 1 anti-tank brigade, and 1 multiple rocket launcher, 2 anti-tank, 4 engineer and 2 air defence artillery regiments.

There are also 730 border guards.

Navy. The Danube Flotilla, the maritime wing of the Army, consisted of some 300 personnel in 1996, operating 6 river minesweepers and numerous boats and special-purpose vessels.

Air Force. The Air Force is under the control of the Army General Staff, with a strength (1996) of 17,500 (11,200 conscripts). The combat aircraft strength comprises 1 regiment of MiG-21 and MiG-23 fighters, 1 of MiG-29 interceptors and 1 of MiG-21 and Su-22 fighter-bombers and a regiment of Mi-8 and Mi-24 armed helicopters. Transport units are equipped with An-26 and L-410 aircraft. Other types in service include Mi-8/17 helicopters and L-39 Albatros and Yak-52 trainers.

In addition, 'Guideline' and 'Goa' surface-to-air missiles are operational.

INTERNATIONAL RELATIONS
Hungary is a member of the UN, Council of Europe, OECD, the Central European Initiative, NATO, and is an Associate Member of the EU and an Associate Partner of the WEU. In April 1994 Hungary applied to join the EU and is expected to become a member by 2002. Hungary became a member of NATO on 12 March 1999.

Hungary has had a long-standing dispute with Slovakia over the Gabčíkovo-Nagymaros Project, involving the building of dam structures in both countries for the production of electric power, flood control and improvement of navigation on the Danube as agreed in a treaty signed in 1977 between Hungary and Czechoslovakia. The International Court of Justice delivered judgment on the case

HUNGARY

in Sept. 1997. Since the election of the new Slovak government in 1998 relations are improving and discussions under way.

ECONOMY

Policy. Privatization based on free market principles has been at the centre of economic policy since 1990. In 1995 the State Property Agency and the State Holding Company were merged in a new body charged with extending the private sector's share of former state assets to 80%. Legislation of June 1991 provides for compensating former owners or their descendants for property nationalized after May 1939. A Small Shareholder Programme of Privatization was launched in April 1994. Growing debt and balance of payments gap forced a Stabilization Programme.

The OECD reported in 1998 that 'the extensive macroeconomic package introduced in 1995 (which included the adoption of a crawling-peg exchange rate regime, an impressive programme of privatisation and a substantial fiscal tightening), as well as the deepening of structural reforms implemented earlier, created the conditions for the remarkable progress of the Hungarian economy over the past 2 years'.

Performance. Real GDP growth was 1·3% in 1996, and 4·6% in 1997. For the first 6 months of 1998 growth was measured at 4·8%. Total gross external debt was US$23·7bn. in 1997.

Budget. The budget for calendar years was as follows (in 1m. forints):

	1996	1997
Revenue	2,074,068	2,364,580
Expenditure	2,206,507	2,703,051

Currency. A decree of 26 July 1946 instituted a new monetary unit, the *forint* (HUF) of 100 *fillér*. The forint was made fully convertible in Jan. 1991. In 1996–97 the forint was devalued at a crawling peg exchange rate of 1·2% a month. Inflation was 19·8% in 1996, 18·2% in 1997 and forecast to be 16·0% in 1998 (down from 31% in June 1995). In Feb. 1998 foreign exchange reserves were US$8,601m. and gold reserves were 100,000 troy oz. Total money supply in Sept. 1996 was 1,092bn. forints.

Banking and Finance. In 1987 a two-tier system was established. The National Bank (*Director,* György Surányi) remained the central state financial institution, responsible for the circulation of money and foreign currency exchange, but also became a central clearing bank, with general (but not operational) control over commercial banks and development banks. There are over 40 commercial banks and 20 insurance companies based in Budapest. A law of June 1991 sets capital and reserve requirements, and provides for foreign investment in Hungarian banks. Permission is needed for investments of more than 10%. Privatization of the banking system is well under way.

The Hungarian International Trade Bank opened in London in 1973. In 1980 the Central European International Bank was set up in Budapest with 7 Western banks holding 66% of the shares. The National Savings Bank handles local government as well as personal accounts. Total savings deposits in 1994, 951,900m. forints.

A stock exchange was opened in Budapest in Jan. 1989.

Weights and Measures. The metric system is in use.

ENERGY AND NATURAL RESOURCES

Electricity. Installed capacity in 1994 was 6·98m. kW, about a quarter of which is nuclear. There is an 880-mW nuclear power station at Paks which produced 41% of total output in 1995. 34,037m. kWh were produced in 1995 (14,026m. kWh by nuclear power), and 3,210m. kWh imported. Consumption per capita in 1995 was estimated at 3,200 kWh.

Oil and Gas. Oil and natural gas are found in the Szeged basin and Zala county. Production in 1995: Oil, 1,669,000 tonnes; gas, 5,365m. cu. metres.

Minerals. Production in 1995 (in 1,000 tonnes): Lignite, 7,153; brown coal, 6,458; hard coal (1994), 940; bauxite, 1,015.

Agriculture. Agriculture contributed 7% of GDP in 1996. Agricultural land was collectivized in 1950. It was announced in 1990 that land would be restored to its pre-collectivization owners if they wished to cultivate it. A law of April 1994 restricts the area of land that may be bought by individuals to 300 ha, and prohibits the sale of arable land and land in conservation zones to companies and foreign nationals. Today, although 90% of all cultivated land is in private hands, most farms are little more than smallholdings. Under the 1999 budget, funding for agriculture increased by 40%, with subsidies favouring small family farms. In 1998, agricultural exports totalled $3bn. (an increase of 10% on 1997), including grain exports of more than 4m. tonnes. 20,000 tonnes of sour cherry and 17,000 tonnes of plums were exported in 1998.

In 1996 the agricultural area was (in 1,000 ha) 6,179, of which 4,716 were arable, 1,148 meadows and pastures, 90 market gardens, and 225 orchards and vineyards.

Corn production dropped from 8·6m. tonnes in 1989 to below 6m. tonnes between 1994 and 1996. The annual maize yield has declined from 7m. tonnes to 3·5–4m. tonnes, potatoes from 0·9 to 0·6m. tonnes, and fruit from 1·6 to 1·3m. tonnes.

Livestock has drastically decreased since 1989 from 8·8m. pigs to 5m., from 1·8m. cattle to 1m., and from 1·9m. sheep to 1·5m. Thus the pig stock has declined to the 1938 level, the cattle stock to the 1945 level and the sheep stock to a level of the early 1930s.

The north shore of Lake Balaton and the Tokaj area are important wine-producing districts. Wine production in 1995 was 329m. litres.

Forestry. The forest area in 1995 was 1,719,000 ha, or 18·6% of the land area (up from 1,675,000 ha and 18·1% in 1990). Timber production in 1995 was 4·41m. cu. metres.

Fisheries. There are fisheries in the rivers Danube and Tisza and Lake Balaton. In 1993 there were 27,100 ha of commercial fishponds. In 1995 total catches were 22,866 tonnes, exclusively freshwater fish.

INDUSTRY

In 1995 there were 18,921 limited liability companies, 1,475 co-operative societies and 81,433 individual businesses.

Output growth in 1996 saw highly variable trends among the individual sectors of the manufacturing industry. The most dynamic sector continues to be the engineering industry. Its performance was driven by the 35·6% increase in exports. The manufacturing of non-ferrous mineral products went up by 1·2% (exports rose by 11·1%). With the exception of the engineering industry and manufacturing of non-ferrous mineral products the output of each sector of manufacturing industry declined: the textile and clothing industry by 4·2% and chemical industry by 0·6%. Within this, the domestic sales of the textile and clothing industry dropped by 8·5% and that of the chemical industry by 6·7%, while the exports of both sectors rose (by 3·7% and 35·6%, respectively).

Labour. In 1995 the workforce (in 1,000) was 6,251·4, of whom 6,082 (2,918·5 females) were of working age. The economically active population was 4,564·8 (2,181·4 females) of whom 3,636·4 were active earners. Persons employed, 4,045·2. Employed persons by sector, 1995 (in 1,000, women in parentheses): Mining, manufacturing, electricity, 1,029·4 (453); building, 190·5 (37·8); agriculture and forestry, 348·2 (108·4); transport and telecommunications, 333·2 (113·6); commerce, 550·8 (280); personal and business services, 394·4 (185·3); health, social and cultural services, 810·1 (593·7); public administration, 285 (131·7). Average monthly wages in 1995: 38,900 forints. Minimum monthly wage, 1996, 14,500 forints. The 10·9% unemployment rate in 1995 had dropped to 10·6% by the end of 1996; it was estimated to be 9·9% in 1997 and 9·6% in 1998. In 1996 wage costs remained within originally set limits, resulting in a decrease of 5% in real wages. However, real wages increased 5% in the first half of 1997. Retirement age: Men, 60; women, 55.

Trade Unions. The former official Communist organization (National Council of Trade Unions), renamed the Confederation of Hungarian Trade Unions (MSZOSZ), groups 70 organizations and claimed 1m. members in 1993. A law of 1991 abolished its obligatory levy on pay packets; its assets derived from this period are to be distributed to other unions. Other unions are grouped in 6 federations (with 1993 membership): the Association of Autonomous Trade Unions (ASZOK, 0·3m.); Coalition of Christian Trade Unions (KESZOSZ, 0·15m.); Co-operation Forum of Trade Unions (SZEF, 0·5m.); Council of Intellectual Trade Unions (ÉSZT, 0·1m.); League of Independent Trade Unions (Liga, 0·25m.); Works Councils (60,000).

Social security benefits are administered jointly by elected representatives of trade unions and employers' organizations.

INTERNATIONAL TRADE

Hungary is a member of CEFTA, along with the Czech Republic, Poland, Slovakia and Slovenia. Foreign debt was US$22,900m. in 1998. At the end of 1995, foreign investments totalled US$11,500m. An import surcharge imposed in March 1995 was abolished in July 1997.

Imports and Exports. In 1997 (1996) the value of exports was US$19,637m. (US$14,183m.) and that of imports US$21,371m. (US$16,828m.). The trade deficit, including customs-free zones, totalled US$2·6bn. in 1996. In the first 8 months of 1997 exports totalled US$11·6bn., 16% up on 1996; imports amounted to US$13·3bn. (15·2% up) while the trade balance showed a deficit of US$1·7bn. 80% of exports go to OECD counties with EU members taking a 71% share. The share of CEFTA and CIS countries is around 7% each. In 1996, 29·0% of exports went to Germany and 23·6% of imports came from Germany. Russia was the second biggest supplier of imports in 1996 (12·5% of the total) and Austria the second biggest market for exports (10·6%). In 1996, 5·9% of exports went to Russia, down from 13·1% in 1992. An import surcharge which was imposed in March 1995 was abolished in July 1997.

COMMUNICATIONS

Roads. In 1995 there were 30,023 km of roads, including motorways, 293 km; highways, 85 km and other first class main roads, 2,054 km. Passenger cars numbered (1995) 2,245,000, trucks, vans and special-purpose vehicles, 292,000; buses, 20,000 and motor cycles, 157,327. 40·9m. tonnes of freight and 494·7m. passengers were transported by road in 1994 (excluding intra-urban passengers). In 1995 there were 19,817 road accidents with 589 fatalities.

Rail. Route length of public lines in 1995, 7,610 km, of which 2,283 km were electrified. 46·4m. tonnes of freight and 154·2m. passengers were carried. There is a metro in Budapest (30·1 km), and tram/light rail networks in Budapest (161·2 km), Debrecen, Miskolc and Szeged.

Civil Aviation. Budapest airport (Ferihegy) handled 3,314,020 passengers in 1996 (all on international flights) and 20,185 tonnes of freight. The national carrier is Malév, 65% state-owned, which carried 1·62m. passengers in 1995. In 1998 services were also provided by Aeroflot, Air Engiadina, Air France, Air Kazakhstan, Air Lithuania, Air Malta, Air Ukraine, Alitalia, Austrian Airlines, Balkan, British Airways, Czech Airlines, Delta Air Lines, Dneproavia Joint Stock Aviation Co, Egyptair, El Al, Finnair, KLM, LOT, Lufthansa, Moldavian Airlines, Olympic Airways, SABENA, SAS, Swissair, Syrian Arab Airlines, Tarom, Thai Airways International, Tunis Air, Turkish Airlines and United Airlines.

Shipping. Navigable waterways had (1993) a length of 1,622 km. River craft included: Passenger ships, 63; tugs, 35; self-propelled barges and other ships, 21; barges, 170. In 1995, 3·52m. tonnes of cargo and 2·38m. passengers were carried. Merchant shipping totalled 45,000 GRT in 1995. The Hungarian Shipping Company (MAHART) has agencies at Amsterdam, Alexandria, Algiers, Beirut, Rijeka and Trieste. It has 3 sea-going ships.

Telecommunications. There were 3,095,300 main telephone lines in use in 1997, equivalent to 304·2 per 1,000 population. There were approximately 265,000 cellular phone subscribers in 1995, 400,000 PCs and 45,000 fax machines. In May 1998 there were around 200,000 Internet users.

Postal Services. In 1995 there were 2,599 post offices.

SOCIAL INSTITUTIONS

Justice. The administration of justice is the responsibility of the Procurator-General, elected by Parliament for 6 years. There are 111 local courts, 20 labour law courts, 20 county courts, 6 district courts and a Supreme Court. Criminal proceedings are dealt with by the regional courts through 3-member councils and by the county courts and the Supreme Court in 5-member councils. A new Civil Code was adopted in 1978 and a new Criminal Code in 1979.

Regional courts act as courts of first instance; county courts as either courts of first instance or of appeal. The Supreme Court acts normally as an appeal court, but may act as a court of first instance in cases submitted to it by the Public Prosecutor. All courts, when acting as courts of first instance, consist of 1 professional judge and 2 lay assessors, and, as courts of appeal, of 3 professional judges. Local government Executive Committees may try petty offences.

Regional and county judges and assessors are elected by the appropriate local councils; members of the Supreme Court by Parliament.

The Office of Ombudsman was instituted in 1993. He or she is elected by parliament for a 6-year term, renewable once.

There are also military courts of the first instance. Military cases of the second instance go before the Supreme Court.

The death penalty was abolished in Oct. 1990.

70,787 sentences were imposed on adults in 1994, including 21,404 of imprisonment. There were 14,321 juvenile offenders and 12,455 persons were in prison in 1995.

Religion. Church-state affairs are regulated by a law of Feb. 1990 which guarantees freedom of conscience and religion and separates church and state by prohibiting state interference in church affairs. Religious matters are the concern of the Department for Church Relations, under the auspices of the Prime Minister's Office. State aid to all churches was 2,800m. forints in 1993.

In 1995, 67·5% of the population aged 14 and over were Roman Catholic, 20% Calvinist and 5% Lutheran.

The Primate of Hungary is Archbishop László Paskai, appointed Aug. 1986. There are 11 dioceses, all with bishops or archbishops. There is one Uniate bishopric.

In 1993 there were estimated to be 7m. Roman Catholics, 1·9m. Calvinists and 0·43m. Lutherans. 47 other sects had registered as churches. There were 4 Orthodox denominations with 40,000 members in 1979. The Unitarian Church had 10,000 members, 11 ministers and 6 churches. In 1991 there were 100,000 Jews (444,567 in 1937) with 136 synagogues, 26 rabbis and a rabbinical college which enrols 10 students a year.

Education. Adult literacy rate in 1995 was over 99%. Education is free and compulsory from 6 to 14. Primary schooling ends at 14; thereafter education may be continued at secondary, secondary technical or secondary vocational schools, which offer diplomas entitling students to apply for higher education, or at vocational training schools which offer tradesmen's diplomas. Students at the latter may also take the secondary school diploma examinations after 2 years of evening or correspondence study. Optional religious education was introduced in schools in 1990.

In 1995–96 there were 4,720 kindergartens with 32,320 teachers and 399,300 pupils; 3,809 primary schools with 86,891 teachers and 974,800 pupils; 936 secondary schools with 28,684 teachers and 349,300 pupils; 197 schools for special needs with 41,924 pupils and 6,433 teachers, and 349 trade training schools, with 154,300 apprentices and 5,899 teachers and instructors. In 1994–95 there were 317 vocational training schools with 1,305 teachers and 22,241 trainees. In 1994–95 there were 91 higher education institutions, including 6 universities (Budapest, Pécs, Szeged, Debrecen, Miskolc and Veszprém). At these there were 18,098 teachers and 129,500 full-time students.

Schools for ethnic minorities, 1994–95: Kindergartens, 355, with 19,070 pupils and 882 teachers; primary schools, 397, with 49,679 pupils and 1,210 teachers; secondary schools, 18, with 4,348 pupils and 430 teachers.

HUNGARY

In 1994 total expenditure on education came to 6·7% of GNP and represented 6·9% of total government expenditure.

Health. In 1994 there were 41,562 doctors and dentists, 98,453 hospital beds and 1,479 pharmacies. While there is an excess supply of doctors, there are too few nurses and wages for both groups are exceptionally low.

Welfare. Since 1993 social security and retirement pensions have been administered by the Social Security Administration, composed of members elected from the employers' organizations and trade unions (*see above*). Medical treatment is free. Patients bear 15% of the cost of medicines. Sickness benefit is 75% of wages, old age pensions (at 60 for men, 55 for women) 60–70%. In 1995, 582,200m. forints were paid out in pensions to 2·98m. pensioners (including old age, 1·6m.; disabled, 0·75m.; widows, 0·22m.). In 1995, 100,200m. forints in family allowances were paid to 1·4m. families on behalf of 2·36m. children. Monthly allowances (in forints) are: One child, 2,750; two, 3,250; three and more, 3,750 (more for single parents). Of nearly 2·5m. minors (aged 0–18), 40% live in poverty.

CULTURE

Broadcasting. The government network *Magyar Rádio* broadcasts 4 programmes on medium wave and FM and also regional programmes, including transmissions in German, Romanian and Serbo-Croat. There are 2 other networks, one of them commercial, and 2 further commercial channels were scheduled to start transmitting on 1 Sept. 1997. *Magyar Televizió* operates 2 TV channels (colour by PAL). *Duna Televizió* broadcasts to Hungarians abroad. In 1996 there were 31 independent radio and 26 independent TV stations. There were 7m. radios and 4·4m. TV sets in use in 1996.

Cinema. There were 595 cinemas in 1995; attendance, 14m. 17 full-length feature films were made in 1994.

Press. In 1995 there were 12 national dailies with a combined circulation of 1,023m. copies, and 19 regional dailies (897m.). There were 28 weeklies. 8,749 book titles were published in 1995 in 62·98m. copies.

Tourism. In 1996 there were 20,674,000 foreign tourists. 13·1m. Hungarians travelled abroad in 1995. Revenue from foreign tourists in 1996 was US$2·2bn. 8% of GDP is produced by tourism.

Festivals. The Budapest Spring Festival, comprising music, theatre, dance et cetera, takes place in March. The Szeged Open-Air Theatre Festival is in July–August and the Balaton Festival is in May.

Libraries. In 1996 there were 3,517 Local Authority libraries, 735 work place libraries and 36,388 school libraries.

National Theatre and Opera. Hungary had 47 theatres in 1997.

Museums and Galleries. There were 776 museums and galleries in 1997.

DIPLOMATIC REPRESENTATIVES
Of Hungary in Great Britain (35 Eaton Pl., London, SW1X 8BY)
Ambassador: Gábor Szentiványi.

Of Great Britain in Hungary (Harmincad Utca 6, Budapest 1051)
Ambassador: Nigel Thorpe, CVO.

Of Hungary in the USA (3910 Shoemaker St., NW, Washington, D.C., 20008)
Ambassador: Géza Jeszenszky.

Of the USA in Hungary (Szabadság Tér 12, Budapest V)
Ambassador: Peter Francis Tufo.

Of Hungary to the United Nations
Ambassador: André Erdös.

Of Hungary to the European Union
Ambassador: Endre Juhász.

FURTHER READING

Central Statistical Office. *Statisztikai Évkönyv.* Annual since 1871.—*Magyar Statisztikai Zsebkönyv.* Annual.—*Statistical Yearbook.*—*Statistical Handbook of Hungary.*—*Monthly Bulletin of Statistics.*

Bako, E., *Guide to Hungarian Studies.* 2 vols. Stanford Univ. Press, 1973

Batt, J., *Economic Reform and Political Change in Eastern Europe: a Comparison of the Czechoslovak and Hungarian Experiences.* Basingstoke, 1988

Bölöny, J., *Magyarország Kormányai, 1848–1975.* Budapest, 1978. [Lists governments and politicians]

Bozóki, A., *et al.* (eds.) *Post-Communist Transition: Emerging Pluralism in Hungary.* London, 1992

Brown, D. M., *Towards a Radical Democracy: the Political Economy of the Budapest School.* Cambridge, 1988

Burawoy, M. and Lukács, J., *The Radiant Past: Ideology and Reality in Hungary's Road to Capitalism.* Chicago Univ. Press, 1992

Cox, T. and Furlong, A. (eds.) *Hungary: the Politics of Transition.* London, 1995

Geró, A., *Modern Hungarian Society in the Making: the Unfinished Experience;* translated from Hungarian. Budapest, 1995

Hann, C. M. (ed.), *Market Economy and Civil Society in Hungary.* London, 1990

Kabdebó, T., *Hungary.* [Bibliography] Oxford and Santa Barbara (CA), 1980

Kornai, J., *The Road to a Free Economy: Shifting from a Socialist System—the Example of Hungary.* New York and London, 1990

Lendvai, P., *Hungary: the Art of Survival.* London, 1989

Macartney, C. A., *Hungary: A Short History.* London, 1962

Mitchell, K. D. (ed.) *Political Pluralism in Hungary and Poland: Perspectives on the Reforms.* New York, 1992

Sugar, P. F. (ed.) *A History of Hungary.* London, 1991

Szekely, I. P., *Hungary: an Economy in Transition.* CUP, 1993

National statistical office: Központi Statisztikai Hivatal/Central Statistical Office, Keleti Károly u. 5/7, H-1024 Budapest. *Director:* Dr György Vukovich.

Website: Hungarian Central Statistics Office, http://www.ksh.hu/
National library: Széchenyi Library, Budapest.

ICELAND
Lyðveldið Ísland
(Republic of Iceland)

Capital: Reykjavík
Population estimate, 2000: 282,000
GNP per capita: (PPP$) 21,710
HDI/world rank: 0·942/5

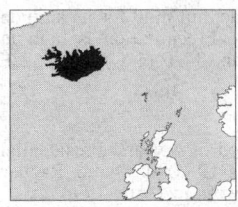

KEY HISTORICAL EVENTS
The first settlers came to Iceland in 874. Between 930 and 1262 Iceland was an independent republic, but by the 'Old Treaty' of 1262 the country recognized the rule of the King of Norway. In 1380 Iceland, together with Norway, came under the rule of the Danish kings, but when Norway was separated from Denmark in 1814, Iceland remained under the rule of Denmark. The invention of motorized fishing boats in the late nineteenth century revolutionized the fishing industry and gave impetus to the campaign for self determination. After 1 Dec. 1918 it was acknowledged as a sovereign state. It was united with Denmark only through the common sovereign until it was proclaimed an independent republic on 17 June 1944 following a referendum favouring severance from the Danish crown.

TERRITORY AND POPULATION
Iceland is an island in the North Atlantic, close to the Arctic Circle. Area, 103,000 sq. km (39,758 sq. miles).
There are 8 regions:

Region	Inhabited land (sq. km)	Mountain pasture (sq. km)	Waste-land (sq. km)	Total area (sq. km)	Popula-tion (1 Dec. 1997)
Capital area } Southwest Peninsula }	1,266	716	–	1,982	{ 164,360 { 15,678
West	5,011	3,415	275	8,711	13,943
Western Peninsula	4,130	3,698	1,652	9,470	8,644
Northland West	4,867	5,278	2,948	13,093	9,796
Northland East	9,890	6,727	5,751	22,368	26,595
East } South }	16,921	17,929	12,555	{ 21,991 { 25,214	12,549 20,504
Iceland	42,085	37,553	23,181	102,819	272,069

The population (1980), according to the National Register of Persons, was 229,187. In 1997 the population was 272,069, of whom 21,529 were domiciled in rural districts and 250,540 (92·1%) in towns and villages (of over 200 inhabitants). Population density (1997), 2·6 per sq. km.
The UN gives a projected population for 2000 of 282,000.
The population is almost entirely Icelandic. In 1997 foreigners numbered 5,635 (918 Danish, 580 US, 332 British, 288 Norwegian, 304 German).
The capital, Reykjavík, had on 1 Dec. 1997, a population of 106,567; other towns were: Akranes, 5,127; Akureyri, 15,041; Bolungarvík, 1,094; Dalvík, 1,505; Eskifjörður, 1,004; Garðabær, 7,840; Grindavík, 2,126; Hafnarfjörður, 18,209; Húsavík, 2,495; Ísafjörður, 2,998; Keflavík, 7,632; Kópavogur, 19,826; Neskaupstaður, 1,562; Njarðvík, 2,641; Ólafsfjörður, 1,099; Sauðárkrókur, 2,674; Selfoss, 4,325; Seltjarnarnes, 4,612; Seyðisfjörður, 799; Siglufjörður, 1,632; Vestmannaeyjar, 4,645.
The official language is Icelandic.

SOCIAL STATISTICS
Statistics for calendar years:

	Living births	Still-born	Marriages	Divorces	Deaths	Infant deaths	Net immigration
1994	4,442	15	1,310	489	1,717	14	760
1995	4,280	8	1,238	472	1,923	26	1,418
1996	4,329	20	1,371 (21 same sex)	530	1,879	16	–444
1997	4,151	13	1,481 (12 same sex)	514	1,844	23	69

1996 rates per 1,000 population: Births, 16·0; deaths, 7·0. Annual growth rate, 1990–95, 1·1%. In 1995 the most popular age range for marrying was 25–29 for both males and females. Life expectancy (1996–97): Males, 76·4 years; females, 81·3. Infant mortality, 1990–95, 5 per 1,000 live births; fertility rate, 2·2 births per woman.

CLIMATE
The climate is cool temperate oceanic and rather changeable, but mild for its latitude because of the Gulf Stream and prevailing S.W. winds. Precipitation is high in upland areas, mainly in the form of snow. Reykjavík, Jan. 34°F (1°C), July 52°F (11°C). Annual rainfall 34" (860 mm).

CONSTITUTION AND GOVERNMENT
The President is elected by direct, popular vote for a period of 4 years. Presidential elections were held on 29 June 1996. The electorate was 195,000. Ólafur Ragnar Grímsson (b. 1943) was elected against 3 opponents and sworn in 1 Aug 1996.

An electoral law of 1984 provides for an *Alþingi* (parliament) of 63 members. Of these, 54 seats are distributed among the 8 constituencies as follows: 14 seats are allotted to Reykjavík, 8 to Reykjanes (i.e. the South-west excluding Reykjavík) and 5 or 6 to each of the remaining 6. From the 9 seats then left, 8 are divided beforehand among the constituencies according to the number of registered voters in the preceding elections. Finally, one seat is given to a constituency after the elections, to compensate the party with the fewest seats as compared to its number of votes.

National Anthem. 'Guð vors lands' ('Oh God of Our Country'); words by M. Jochumsson, tune by S. Sveinbjörnsson.

RECENT ELECTIONS
At the elections on 8 April 1995 the Independence Party (IP) gained 25 seats with 37·1% of votes cast, the Progressive Party (PP) 15 with 23·3%, the People's Alliance 9 with 14·3%, the Social Democratic Party 7 with 11·4%, the People's Movement 4 with 7·2% and the Women's Alliance 3 with 4·9%. Parliamentary elections were scheduled for 8 May 1999.

CURRENT ADMINISTRATION
President: Ólafur Ragnar Grímsson (b. 1943; sworn in 1 Aug 1996.)

An IP-PP coalition government was formed on 22 April 1995 which in March 1999 comprised:

Prime Minister, Minister for Statistics Iceland: Davíð Oddsson (IP).

Foreign Affairs and Foreign Trade: Halldór Ásgrímsson (PP). *Finance:* Gier H. Haarde (IP). *Social Affairs:* Páll Pétursson (PP). *Fisheries, Justice and Church:* Þorsteinn Pálsson (IP). *Agriculture and Environment:* Guðmundur Bjarnason (PP). *Health and Social Security:* Ingibjörg Pálmádottir (PP). *Education and Culture:* Björn Bjarnason (PP). *Trade and Industry:* Finnur Ingólfsson (PP). *Transport and Communications:* Halldór Blöndal (IP).

Local Government. On 1 Dec. 1998 Iceland was divided into 124 communes, of which 31 had the status of a town. The commune councils are elected by universal suffrage, in towns and other urban communes by proportional representation, in rural communes by simple majority. For general co-operation the communes are free to form district councils. All the communes except 10 towns are members in 20 district councils. The communes appoint one or more representatives to the district councils according to their population size. The commune councils are supervised by the Ministry of Social Affairs. In 1992 the government administration and the jurisdictional system at local level were fundamentally reformed, so that the jurisdictional power was totally separated from the executive power, resulting in a new division of responsibilities and functions between the magistrates and the district courts. For national government there are 27 divisions exercised by the magistrates.

Municipal elections were held on 31 May 1998.

DEFENCE

Iceland possesses no armed forces. Under the North Atlantic Treaty, US forces are stationed in Iceland as the Iceland Defence Force. 3 armed offshore patrol craft and 1 smaller vessel for fishery protection are maintained by the National Coastguard, with 1 patrol aircraft and 2 helicopters. Coastguard Service personnel (1998), approximately 125.

INTERNATIONAL RELATIONS

Iceland is a member of the UN, EFTA, OECD, the Council of Europe, NATO and the Nordic Council, and is an Associate Member of the WEU. Iceland has acceded to the Schengen Accord, which abolishes border controls between Iceland and Austria, Belgium, Denmark, Finland, France, Germany, Greece, Italy, Luxembourg, Norway, Portugal, Spain and Sweden.

ECONOMY

Performance. Economic growth in 1997-98 was 5%.

Budget. Total revenue and expenditure for calendar years (in 1m. kr.):

	1991	1992	1993	1994	1995	1996
Revenue	99,953	103,447	103,220	109,602	114,413	127,735
Expenditure	112,487	110,607	112,863	116,986	123,344	139,730

Central government debt was, on 31 Dec. 1997, 241,168m. kr, of which the foreign debt amounted to 126,628m. kr.

Currency. The unit of currency is the *króna* (ISK) of 100 *aurar*, (singular: *eyrir*). Foreign exchange markets were deregulated on 1 Jan. 1992. The krona was devalued 7·5% in June 1993. Inflation was 1·7% in 1998; the average annual rate during the period 1990–96 was 3·1%. Foreign exchange reserves were US$348m. in Feb. 1998 and gold reserves were 50,000 troy oz. Note and coin circulation at 31 Dec. 1997 was 5,752m. kr.

Banking and Finance. The Central Bank of Iceland (founded 1961; *Governor:* Birgir Ísleifur Gunnarsson) is responsible for note issue and carries out the central banking functions which before 1961 were carried out by The National Bank of Iceland (owned entirely by the State), currently the largest commercial bank. There are 2 other commercial banks, 1 state-owned. Banking is being deregulated in stages.

On 31 Dec. 1996 the accounts of the Central Bank balanced at 64,411m. kr. Commercial bank deposits were 151,467m. kr. and deposits in the 27 savings banks, 43,951m. kr.

There is a stock exchange.

Weights and Measures. The metric system is obligatory.

ENERGY AND NATURAL RESOURCES

Electricity. The installed capacity of public electrical power plants at the end of 1997 totalled 1,150,593 kW; installed capacity of hydro-electric plants was 919,478 kW. Total electricity production in public-owned plants in 1997 amounted to 5,581m. kWh; in privately owned plants, 5m. kWh. Consumption per capita was estimated in 1997 to be 20,600 kWh—the second highest in the world after Norway.

Agriculture. Of the total area, about six-sevenths is unproductive, but only about 1·3% is under cultivation, which is largely confined to hay, potatoes and turnips. Arable land totals 138 ha. In 1997 the total hay crop was 2,653,840 cu. metres; the crop of potatoes, 8,557 tonnes, and of turnips, 414 tonnes. Livestock (1997): Horses, 79,804; cattle, 74,791 (milch cows, 29,502); sheep, 477,306; pigs, 3,514; poultry, 154,800. Livestock products (1997, in tonnes): Milk, 105,002; butter and dairy margarines, 1,568; cheese, 3,674; lamb, 7,903.

Forestry. In 1995 forests covered 11,000 ha, or approximately 0·1% of the total land area.

Fisheries. Fishing is of vital importance to the economy. Fishing vessels at the end of 1997 numbered 796 with a gross tonnage of 188,105. Total catch in 1992,

1,567,700 tonnes; 1993, 1,699,300 tonnes; 1994, 1,510,932 tonnes; 1995, 1,605,127 tonnes; 1996, 2,055,244 tonnes; 1997, 2,199,111 tonnes. Virtually all the fish caught is from marine waters.

Fishery limits were extended from 12 to 50 nautical miles in 1972 and to 200 nautical miles in 1975.

INDUSTRY
Production, 1997, in 1,000 tonnes: Aluminium, 122·3; diatomite, 27·5; fertilizer (1995), 50·6; ferro-silicon, 69·9; sales of cement, 108·5.

Labour. In 1997 the economically active population was 147,800, of which 3·9% were unemployed. In April 1998 the unemployment rate among the working population was 3·1%.

Trade Unions. In 1995 trade union membership was 85% of the workforce.

INTERNATIONAL TRADE
The economy is heavily trade-dependent.

Imports and Exports. Total value of imports (c.i.f.) and exports (f.o.b.) in 1,000 kr.:

	1993	1994	1995	1996	1997
Imports	91,306,600	102,571,300	113,613,600	135,994,500	143,226,581
Exports	94,657,600	112,653,800	116,606,700	125,809,800	131,213,200

Main exports, 1997 (in 1m. kr.): Fish, crustaceans, molluscs and preparations thereof, 80,639; non-ferrous metals, 15,211; fodder for animals (excluding unmilled cereals), 11,326; iron and steel, 3,732. Main imports: Road vehicles, 13,241; petroleum and products, 10,186; other transport equipment, 3,736.

Value of trade with principal countries for 3 years (in 1,000 kr.):

	1995		1996		1997	
	Imports (c.i.f.)	Exports (f.o.b.)	Imports (c.i.f.)	Exports (f.o.b.)	Imports (c.i.f.)	Exports (f.o.b.)
Austria	651,400	138,500	836,000	124,700	859,000	130,900
Belgium	2,259,100	2,040,900	2,581,500	1,552,500	2,860,000	1,426,800
Brazil	230,900	467,600	184,900	674,900	175,000	781,900
Canada	1,090,300	1,962,900	1,240,000	1,462,100	1,484,300	1,586,100
China	...	...	1,774,200	69,000	1,959,200	526,200
Czech Republic	402,900	42,900	483,700	74,300	486,800	48,800
Denmark	10,693,000	9,138,800	11,357,800	9,094,100	12,365,800	7,430,700
Faroe Islands	315,400	565,300	191,300	529,400	367,300	1,467,600
Finland	2,092,200	577,700	2,240,700	1,206,700	2,332,800	1,507,900
France	4,823,200	7,915,200	4,457,100	8,442,500	4,741,500	8,317,000
Germany	12,974,400	15,923,300	14,801,500	16,229,200	16,847,400	17,154,800
Greece	101,500	925,200	75,200	840,000	84,700	791,900
Hungary	92,000	2,400	135,400	26,900	127,500	19,800
India	335,500	52,100	375,300	55,000	392,200	46,000
Ireland	1,124,000	193,500	1,383,500	167,700	1,680,500	240,600
Israel	55,400	34,300	102,100	80,400	130,500	131,900
Italy	3,713,100	2,386,200	4,374,000	2,402,700	4,635,500	2,310,600
Japan	4,990,600	13,232,700	5,455,500	12,369,600	7,036,700	8,696,300
Korea, Rep. of	...	...	1,514,100	471,400	1,577,200	253,800
Netherlands	7,770,900	3,445,400	8,116,600	4,522,300	9,262,400	4,392,200
Nigeria	3,400	521,900	5,700	577,600	3,800	904,900
Norway	11,565,000	3,818,500	18,396,300	4,687,000	16,500,600	7,294,900
Poland	1,459,600	112,200	2,660,600	303,400	822,900	319,200
Portugal	990,700	2,119,500	980,200	3,237,600	997,900	3,463,600
Russia	2,653,200	676,800	3,372,700	1,285,200	3,550,000	2,360,500
Spain	1,831,900	4,267,800	2,356,400	4,881,400	2,359,000	5,711,600
Sweden	7,936,300	1,519,600	9,132,100	1,620,600	9,584,200	1,487,500
Switzerland	1,359,200	2,578,900	1,995,900	2,493,300	3,190,200	3,999,500
Taiwan	...	...	1,016,700	1,972,800	1,091,900	2,041,900
UK	10,948,800	22,474,900	13,874,300	23,949,000	14,479,400	24,806,700
USA	9,543,500	14,359,600	12,840,400	14,708,000	13,502,900	18,299,700

COMMUNICATIONS

Roads. On 31 Dec. 1997 the length of the public roads (including roads in towns) was 12,691 km. Of these 8,180 km were national main roads and 4,511 km were provincial roads. Total length of surfaced roads was 3,305 km. A ring road of 1,400 km runs just inland from much of the coast; about 80% of it is smooth-surfaced. Motor vehicles registered at the end of 1997 numbered 149,979, of which 133,951 were passenger cars and 16,208 trucks; there were also 1,457 motor cycles. There were 14 fatal road accidents in 1997 with 15 persons killed.

Civil Aviation. Icelandair is the national carrier. In 1998 it served 12 destinations in western Europe and 6 in north America as well as operating domestic services. In 1996 it carried 958,786 passengers on scheduled foreign flights and 280,922 on domestic routes. The main international airport is at Keflavík (Leifsstöd), with Reykjavík for flights to the Faroe Islands, Greenland and domestic services. Services were also provided in 1998 by Atlantic Airways (Faroe Islands), Islandsflug, Greenlandair and SAS. Keflavík handled 747,692 passengers in 1996 and 21,262 tonnes of freight.

Shipping. Total registered vessels, 977 (244,812 gross tonnage) on 31 Dec. 1997; of these, 796 were sea-going fishing vessels.

Telecommunications. At the end of 1997 the number of telephone and telegraph offices was 127; number of telephone subscribers, 162,310 (596 per 1,000 persons); mobile cellular telephone subscribers, 65,746. In 1995 there were 80,000 fax machines and 55,000 PCs (206 per 1,000 persons). There were 122,000 Internet users in Feb. 1998, or around 44% of the total population.

Postal Services. At the end of 1997 the number of post offices was 87.

SOCIAL INSTITUTIONS

Justice. In 1992 jurisdiction in civil and criminal cases was transferred from the provincial magistrates to 8 new district courts, separating the judiciary from the prosecution. From the district courts there is an appeal to the Supreme Court in Reykjavík, which has 8 judges.

Religion. The national church, the Evangelical Lutheran, is endowed by the state. There is complete religious liberty. The affairs of the national church are under the superintendence of a bishop. At 1 Dec. 1997, 244,684 (89·9%) of the population were members of it (93·2% in 1980). 9,700 persons (3·6%) belonged to Lutheran free churches. 12,098 persons (4·5%) belonged to other religious organizations and 5,582 persons (2·1%) did not belong to any religious community.

Education. Primary education is compulsory and free from 6–15 years of age. Optional secondary education from 16 to 19 is also free. In 1997–98 there were about 42,300 pupils in primary schools, 18,200 in secondary schools and 8,200 tertiary-level students in Iceland. Some 25% of tertiary-level students study abroad.

There are 2 universities, Reykjavík (founded 1911) and Akureyri (1987). Total enrolment was 6,100 students in 1997–98. In Reykjavík there are a teachers' training and a technical college, and various other specialized institutions.

In 1996 public sector spending on education was 5·3% of GNP.

Health. On 31 Dec. 1994 there were 57 hospitals with 3,924 beds, 797 doctors, 273 dentists, 1,952 nurses, and 176 pharmacists.

Welfare. The main body of social welfare legislation is consolidated in 6 acts:

(i) The social security legislation (a) health insurance, including sickness benefits; *(b)* social security pensions, mainly consisting of old age pension, disablement pension and widows' pension, and also children's pension; *(c)* employment injuries insurance.

(ii) The unemployment insurance legislation, where daily allowances are paid to those who have met certain conditions.

(iii) The subsistence legislation. This is controlled by municipal government, and social assistance is granted under special circumstances, when payments from other sources are not sufficient.

(iv) The tax legislation. Prior to 1988 children's support was included in the tax legislation, according to which a certain amount for each child in a family was

subtracted from income taxes or paid out to the family. Since 1988 family allowances are paid directly to all children age 0-15 years. The amount is increased with the second child in the family, and children under the age of 7 get additional benefits. Single parents receive additional allowances. The amounts are linked to income.

(v) The rehabilitation legislation.
(vi) Child and juvenile guidance.

Health insurance covers the entire population. Citizenship is not demanded and there is a 6 month waiting period. Most hospitals are both municipally and state run, a few solely state run and all offer free medical help. Medical treatment out of hospitals is partly paid by the patient; the same applies to medicines, except medicines of lifelong necessary use, which are paid in full by the health insurance. Dental care is partly paid by the state for children under 17 years old and also for old age and disabled pensioners. Sickness benefits are paid to those who lose income because of periodical illness. The daily amount is fixed and paid from the 11th day of illness.

The pension system is composed of the public social security system and some 90 private pension funds. The social security system pays basic old age and disablement pensions of a fixed amount regardless of past or present income, as well as supplementary pensions to individuals with low present income. The pensions are index-linked, i.e. are changed in line with changes in wage and salary rates in the labour market. The private pension funds pay pensions that depend on past payments of premiums that are a fixed proportion of earnings. The payment of pension fund premiums is compulsory for all wage and salary earners. The pensions paid by the funds differ considerably between the individual funds, but are generally index-linked. In the public social security system, entitlement to old age and disablement pensions at the full rates is subject to the condition that the beneficiary has been resident in Iceland for 40 years at the age period of 16–67. For shorter period of residence, the benefits are reduced proportionally. Entitled to old age pension are all those who are 67 years old, and have been residents in Iceland for 3 years of the age period of 16–67. Entitled to disablement pension are those who have lost 75% of their working capacity and have been residents in Iceland for 3 years before application or have had full working capacity at the time when they became residents. Old age and disablement pension are of equally high amount; in the year 1996 the total sum was 160,476 kr. for an individual. Married pensioners are paid 90% of two individuals' pensions. In addition to the basic amount, supplementary allowances are paid according to social circumstances and income possibilities. Widows' pensions are the same amount as old age and disablement pension, provided the applicant is over 60 when she becomes widowed. Women at the age 50–60 get reduced pension. Women under 50 are not entitled to widows' pensions.

The employment injuries insurance covers medical care, daily allowances, disablement pension and survivors' pension and is applicable to practically all employees.

Social assistance is primarily municipal and granted in cases outside the social security legislation. Domestic assistance to old people and disabled is granted within this legislation, besides other services.

Child and juvenile guidance is performed by chosen committees according to special laws, such as home guidance and family assistance. In cases of parents' disablement the committees take over the guidance of the children involved.

CULTURE

Reykjavík is one of nine European Cities of Culture in the year 2000. The city's theme is 'Culture and Nature'. The other Cities of Culture are Avignon (France), Bergen (Norway), Bologna (Italy), Brussels (Belgium), Helsinki (Finland), Kraków (Poland), Prague (Czech Republic) and Santiago de Compostela (Spain). The title attracts large European Union grants.

Broadcasting. The state-owned public service, The Icelandic State Broadcasting Service, broadcasts 2 national and 3 regional radio programmes and 1 national TV channel. 20 privately owned radio stations and 9 private TV stations were in operation in 1998. At 31 Dec. 1997, 95,801 TV sets were licensed (94,702 colour by PAL and 1,099 black and white) and there were 99,793 radio licenses.

ICELAND

Cinema. There were 30 cinemas with 50 screens in 1997 of which the capital had 7 cinemas and 26 screens. Total admissions numbered 1,481,106 in 1997, with the Reykjavík area accounting for 1,333,781.

Press. In 1998 there were 3 daily newspapers with a combined circulation of about 0·1m. There were 26 non-daily newspapers in 1997 (published 1–3 times per week) with a combined circulation of about 0·01m.

Iceland publishes more books per person than any other country in the world. In 1997, 1,039 volumes of books and 613 volumes of booklets were published.

Tourism. There were 200,835 visitors in 1996, bringing revenue of US$154m.

Festivals. The Reykjavík Arts Festival, a biennial programme of international artists and performers, will be staging a special programme in May and June 2000 in conjunction with Reykjavík's status as one of the European Cities of Culture.

Libraries. The National and University Library of Iceland is in Reykjavík and contains some 810,000 volumes. The 5 University libraries contain approximately 110,000 volumes, the 41 special libraries approximately 320,000 volumes and the 104 public libraries approximately 2,080,000 volumes.

National Theatre and Opera. In 1997 there were 8 professional theatres operated on a yearly basis (of which 7 were in the capital region) and 18 professional theatre groups (all in the capital region). In the theatrical season 1997–98 there were 254,357 admissions to performances of the professional theatres, 79,899 admissions the the National Theatre and 70,158 admissions to the City Theatre. Total audience of the Icelandic Opera was 16,775.

There is one symphonic orchestra operated on a regular basis, the Icelandic Symphony Orchestra. In 1997 the orchestra performed 83 times within the country and abroad, with audiences totalling 47,000.

Museums and Galleries. In 1997 there were 96 museums, botanical gardens, aquariums and zoos in operation, with a total of about 0·1m. visitors. There were 27,257 visitors to the National Museum, 28,490 to the National Gallery and 70,000 to the Reykjavík Municipal Art Museum.

DIPLOMATIC REPRESENTATIVES

Of Iceland in Great Britain (1 Eaton Terrace, London, SW1W 8EY)
Ambassador: Benedikt Ásgeirsson.

Of Great Britain in Iceland (Laufásvegur 31, 101 Reykjavík)
Ambassador and Consul-General: James Ray McCulloch.

Of Iceland in the USA (1156 15th Street NW, Suite 1200, Washington, D.C., 20005–1704)
Ambassador: Jón Baldvin Hannibalsson.

Of the USA in Iceland (Laufásvegur 21, 101 Reykjavík)
Ambassador: Day Oline Mount.

Of Iceland to the United Nations
Ambassador: Thorsteinn Ingólfsson.

Of Iceland to the European Union
Ambassador: Gunnar Snorri Gunnarsson.

FURTHER READING

Statistics Iceland, *Landshagir* (Statistical Yearbook of Iceland).—*Hagtíðindi* (Monthly Statistics)
Central Bank of Iceland. *Economic Statistics Quarterly.*—*The Economy of Iceland.* May 1994
Hastrup, K., *A Place Apart:An anthropological study of the Icelandic world.* Clarendon Press, Oxford, 1998
Lacy, T., *Ring of Seasons: Iceland - Its culture and history.* University of Michigan Press, 1998
McBride, *Iceland.* [Bibliography] 2nd ed. Oxford and Santa Barbara (CA), 1996

National statistical office: Statistics Iceland, Skuggasund 3, IS-150 Reykjavík.
Website: http://www.statice.is/
National library: Landsbókasafn Islands.—Háskólabókasafn, Reykjavík, *Librarian:* Einar Sigursson.

INDIA

Bharat

(Republic of India)

Capital: New Delhi
Population estimate, 2000: 1,006·8m.
GNP per capita: (PPP$) 1,580
HDI/world rank: 0·451/139

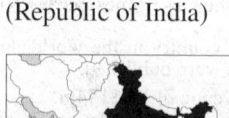

Map. Based upon Survey of India map with the permission of the Surveyor General of India. The responsibility for the correctness of internal details rests with the publisher. The territorial waters of India extend into the sea to a distance of 12 nautical miles measured from the appropriate base line. The external boundaries and coastlines of India agree with the Record/Master Copy certified by the Survey of India.

KEY HISTORICAL EVENTS

The Moghul emperors held power over most of north India and the Deccan (the central plateau of the Indian peninsula) by 1712, when the emperor Bahadur died and his sons weakened the dynasty by disputing the succession.

The power of the states within the empire then revived. The Mahratta rulers of central and western India were led by Shahu; it was he who created the hereditary office of chief minister (*peshwa*) and after his death in 1749 the *peshwas* became the effective rulers of the Mahratta states. In the Deccan, the Moghuls' viceroy of Hyderabad declared himself independent, becoming the founder of the Moslem dynasty of Nizams of Hyderabad. In the north-west in 1739 the Moghuls lost the Punjab to the Persians (who later lost it to the Afghans).

South of Hyderabad were the independent Hindu states of Mysore and Travancore, a number of small principalities and the territory around Madras where the British East India Company was the most powerful force. The Company had maintained a factory at Madras since 1639 and had since established other bases at Bombay (1668) and at Calcutta in Bengal.

In 1740 the Moghul governor (*nawab*) of Bengal rebelled successfully. In 1756, alarmed at the degree to which the Company (anticipating trouble with the French) was arming itself, he attacked and subdued the British base at Calcutta. In 1757 a large British force under Clive retaliated by defeating the Nawab at Plassey. The British were then able to install their own Nawab. Their hold on Bengal and Madras was soon complete and they defeated the French who presented the only serious European challenge. The East India Company thus became the rising power in India at the very time when Moghul power was in decline. Outside the remaining Moghul supremacy the other powers were the Mahrattas, the Punjab Sikhs (nominally under Afghan rule), Hyderabad and Mysore.

Mysore was a Hindu state until 1764 when the Moslem commander Hyder Ali usurped the throne. Having allied themselves to the Nizam of Hyderabad in 1766, the British attached Mysore in 1767; war was intermittent until 1799 when Hyder Ali's successor Tippoo was defeated and the Hindu dynasty restored.

In 1775 a confederacy of Mahratta chiefs, led by the chief of Pune, united against the British power spreading from Bombay and were successful. Mahadaji Sindhia emerged from the war as the leader of a Mahratta empire, to which he added the former Moghul fief of Rajputana.

In 1784 the British government imposed tighter controls on the Company by means of the India Bill.

In 1794 Mahadaji Sindhia died. His successors entered into treaty relations with the British in 1805, by which time the Moghul emperor in Delhi was under Mahratta domination. British-Mahratta relations deteriorated, however, and in 1818 the British annexed the Mahratta states and became the 'protectors' of Rajputana. In 1826 they drove the Burmese out of Assam and in 1830 they occupied Mysore.

In the north-west the Sikh ruler Ranjit Singh had driven the Afghans out of the Punjab and Kashmir by 1819. He died in 1839. Within a short time his strong state and army were highly unstable. Mutual mistrust between Sikhs and British led in 1845-46 to war, ending in British annexation of some Sikh territory. In 1848-49 a second war was fought and the whole Punjab was annexed. Nagpur and Oudh were taken in 1853 and 1856.

INDIA

Since 1818 the East India Company had been the greatest power in India. Within its territory change had been rapid, and the mass of the Hindu population felt threatened by European attitudes, laws and religion. In 1857-58 there was a general rebellion, beginning with a revolt of Indian troops in the Company's army. The excesses of rebels and suppressing forces made the rebellion a national trauma for the British.

The immediate result was the India Act 1858, which transferred the Company's authority and territory to the Crown. The territory (excluding areas now forming Pakistan and Bangladesh) consisted of the Madras and Bombay presidencies; Bengal (which included Assam until 1874 when it became a separate province); the United Provinces and Oudh; the Central Provinces; the Punjab; Ajmere-Merwara; Coorg; and the Andaman Islands. The central government consisted of a viceroy and his executive, and an administrative council in England. This area under direct British rule (British *Raj*) co-existed with the independent states ruled by Indian princes; the viceroy claimed the right to interfere in the latter in emergency, and often did so.

In 1885 the Indian National Congress was founded by A. O. Hume and others, to work for more representative government. In 1892 the first Indian Councils Act added nominated Indian members to the central and provincial legislative councils.

In 1905-11 the experimental partition of Bengal into Hindu and Moslem provinces aroused violent opposition among Hindu Bengalis. This brought to the fore the question of national identity as opposed to religious identity. In 1906 the All-India Moslem League was founded to protect Moslem interests.

From 1909 there were further constitutional reforms, but the Congress thought them insufficient and began, especially after 1917, to work specifically for independence. The India Acts (1919 and 1935) defined and then revised the forms of parliamentary government. After 1930 Mohandas Gandhi led a campaign of civil disobedience for the end of British rule; his attempts at negotiation with Britain were abortive until the Second World War.

The war increased support for the independence movement, Congress being able to claim that Britain had involved India as a combatant state without consultation. In 1940, foreseeing a Hindu-dominated independent India, the Moslem League began to press for a separate Moslem state.

In June 1947 the scheme for partition was announced, after negotiations in which Gandhi had taken part. In Aug. India became independent within the Commonwealth, as a federal union of the former British provinces and the native states. Of the latter, Hyderabad had to be incorporated by force and was later dismembered.

Partition took place (*see* Pakistan), with mass movement of Hindus, Moslems and Sikhs, much violence and many deaths.

In 1950 India became a republic, within the Commonwealth, with Rajendra Prasad as the first president. In 1951 the Congress leader Pandit Nehru became prime minister, establishing a Congress domination which has lasted for all but brief periods. In 1966 his daughter Indira Gandhi became prime minister. She governed by Emergency Rule from 1975 but was defeated in the 1977 election, and re-elected again in 1979. Her son, Rajiv, succeeded her after her assassination by Sikh extremists on 31 Oct. 1984.

In 1956 the States Reorganization Act created a new structure of States and Territories with boundaries based on ethnic and language divisions.

There was an unresolved border war with China in 1962; but the status of Kashmir, disputed with Pakistan, has been the principal difficulty. The war of 1965, mediated at Tashkent (now Toshkent) by the USSR in 1966, left it divided between the two states. War again broke out when in Dec. 1971 India invaded East Pakistan and helped secure the independence of Bangladesh.

The Union was augmented by the annexation of Goa (a surviving Portuguese colony) in 1961 and of Sikkim in 1975.

In 1991 Rajiv Gandhi was assassinated by Tamil extremists after the government had imposed direct rule in Tamil Nadu. Throughout the early 1990s Hindu/Moslem violence was widespread.

India carried out 5 nuclear tests in May 1998. On 11 May 3 devices were exploded followed by 2 more on 13 May, as a result of which US President Bill Clinton imposed wide-ranging economic sanctions, subsequently lifted when India and Pakistan reached an accommodation on nuclear development.

TERRITORY AND POPULATION
India is bounded in the north-west by Pakistan, north by China, Tibet, Nepal and Bhutan, east by Myanmar, and south-east, south and south-west by the Indian Ocean. The far eastern states and territories are almost separated from the rest by Bangladesh. The area (excluding the Pakistan and China-occupied parts of Jammu and Kashmir) is 3,165,596 sq. km. A Sino-Indian agreement of 7 Sept. 1993 settled frontier disputes dating from the war of 1962. Population (excluding occupied Jammu and Kashmir), 1991 census: 846,302,688 (407,072,230 females; 217m. urban). About 24·7% of the population was urban in 1991 (in Maharashtra, 35%; in Arunachal Pradesh, 6·6%). By 1995 this had risen to 26·8%. 1996 estimate: 944m.; density, 299 per sq. km.

The UN gives a projected population for 2000 of 1,006·8m.

By 2050 India is expected to have a population of 1·53bn. and is projected to have overtaken China as the world's most populous country.

Area and population of states and union territories:

	Area in sq. km	1991 census	Population 1994 estimate (in 1,000)	Density per sq. km
States				
Andhra Pradesh (And P)	275,045	66,508,008	71,800	261·0
Arunachal Pradesh (Arun P)	83,743	864,558	965	11·5
Assam (Ass)	78,438	22,414,322	24,200	308·5
Bihar (Bih)	173,877	86,374,465	93,080	535·3
Goa	3,702	1,169,793	1,235	333·5
Gujarat (Guj)	196,024	41,309,582	44,235	225·7
Haryana (Har)	44,212	16,463,648	17,925	405·4
Himachal Pradesh (Him P)	55,673	5,170,877	5,530	99·3
Jammu and Kashmir (J and K)[1]	100,569	7,718,700[2]	8,435	83·9
Karnataka (Kar)	191,791	44,977,201	48,150	251·1
Kerala (Ker)	38,863	29,098,518	30,555	786·3
Madhya Pradesh (MP)	443,446	66,181,170	71,950	162·2
Maharashtra (Mah)	307,713	78,937,187	85,565	278·1
Manipur (Man)	22,327	1,837,149	2,010	90·0
Meghalaya (Meg)	22,429	1,774,778	1,960	87·4
Mizoram (Miz)	21,081	689,756	775	36·7
Nagaland (Nag)	16,579	1,209,546	1,410	85·0
Orissa (Or)	155,707	31,659,736	33,795	217·0
Punjab (Pun)	50,362	20,281,969	21,695	430·8
Rajasthan (Raj)	342,239	44,005,990	48,040	140·4
Sikkim (Sik)	7,096	406,457	444	62·5
Tamil Nadu (TN)	130,058	55,858,946	58,840	452·4
Tripura (Tri)	10,486	2,757,205	3,055	291·4
Uttar Pradesh (UP)	294,411	139,112,287	150,695	511·9
West Bengal (WB)	88,752	68,077,965	73,600	829·3
Union Territories				
Andaman and Nicobar Islands (ANI)	8,249	280,661	322	39·0
Chandigarh (Chan)	114	642,015	725	6,359·7
Dadra and Nagar Haveli (DNH)	491	138,477	153	311·9
Daman and Diu (D and D)	112	101,586	111	990·7
Delhi (Del)	1,483	9,420,644	10,865	7,326·5
Lakshadweep (Lak)	32	51,707	56	1,764·2
Pondicherry (Pon)	492	807,785	894	1,816·3

[1]Excludes the area occupied by Pakistan and China.   [2]Projection.

Urban Agglomerations with populations over 1·6m., together with their core cities at the 1991 census:

	Urban Agglomeration	Core City		Urban Agglomeration	Core City
Bombay	12,596,243	9,925,891	Ahmedabad	3,312,216	2,954,526
Calcutta	11,021,915	4,309,819	Pune (Poona)	2,493,987	1,566,651
Delhi	8,419,084	7,206,704	Kanpur	2,029,889	1,879,420
Madras	5,421,985	3,841,396	Lucknow	1,669,204	1,619,115
Hyderabad	4,253,759	3,145,939	Nagpur	1,664,006	1,624,752
Bangalore	4,130,288	3,302,296			

Smaller Urban Agglomerations and cities with populations over 250,000 (with 1991 census populations, in 1,000):

Agra (UP)	892	Faridabad Complex (Har)	618	Moradabad (UP)	444
Ajmer (Raj)	403	Gaya (Bih)	292	Mysore (Kar)	481
Akola (Mah)	328	Ghaziabad (UP)	454	Nanded (Mah)	275
Aligarh (UP)	481	Gorakhpur (UP)	506	Nashik (Mah)	657
Allahabad (UP)	806	Gulbarga (Kar)	304	Nellore (And P)	316
Amravati (Mah)	422	Guntur (And P)	273	New Bombay (Mah)	308
Amritsar (Pun)	709	Guwahati (Ass)	584	New Delhi (Del)	301
Asansol (WB)	262	Gwalior (MP)	691	Panihati (WB)	276
Aurangabad (Mah)	573	Hubli-Dharwad (Kar)	648	Patna (Bih)	917
Bareilly (UP)	591	Indore (MP)	1,092	Raipur (MP)	439
Belgaum (Mah)	326	Jabalpur (MP)	742	Rajamundry (And P)	325
Bhagalpur (Bih)	253	Jaipur (Raj)	1,458	Rajkot (Raj)	559
Bhavnagar (Guj)	402	Jalandhar (Pun)	510	Ranchi (Bih)	599
Bhilainagar (MP)	386	Jamnagar (Guj)	342	Saharanpur (UP)	375
Bhiwandi (Mah)	379	Jamshedpur (Bih)	461	Salem (TN)	367
Bhopal (MP)	1,063	Jhansi (UP)	313	Sholapur (Mah)	604
Bhubaneswar (Or)	412	Jodhpur (Raj)	668	Srinagar (J and K)	595
Bikaner (Raj)	416	Kakinada (And P)	280	Surat (Guj)	1,499
Bokaro Steel City		Kharagpur (WB)	265	Thiruvananthapuram	
(Bih)	334	Kochi (Ker)	565	(Ker)	524
Chandigarh (Chan)	511	Kolhapur (Mah)	406	Tiruchirapalli (TN)	387
Coimbatore (TN)	816	Kota (Raj)	537	Udaipur (Raj)	309
Cuttack (Or)	403	Kozhikode (Ker)	420	Ujjain (MP)	362
Davangere (Kar)	266	Ludhiana (Pun)	1,043	Vadodara (Guj)	1,031
Dehra Dun (UP)	368	Madurai (TN)	941	Varanasi (UP)	932
Dhanbad (Bih)[1]	815	Malegaon (Mah)	342	Vijayawada (And P)	702
Dhule (Mah)	278	Mangalore (Kar)	273	Visakhapatnam (And P)	752
Durgapur (WB)	426	Meerut (UP)	850	Warangal (And P)	448

[1]Urban Agglomeration.

SOCIAL STATISTICS

Many births and deaths go unregistered. The Registrar General's data suggests a birth rate for 1995–96 of 28·3 per 1,000 population and a death rate of 9·0, which would indicate in a year approximately 26,500,000 births (equivalent to the population of California in the mid 1980s) and 8,500,000 deaths. Expectation of life at birth, 1990–95, 60·3 years for males and 60·6 years for females.

Marriages and divorces are not registered. The minimum age for a civil marriage is 18 for women and 21 for men; for a sacramental marriage, 14 for girls and 18 for youths. Annual growth rate, 1990–95, 2·3%. Infant mortality, 1990–95, 78 per 1,000 live births; fertility rate, 3·4 births per woman.

CLIMATE

India has a variety of climatic sub-divisions. In general, there are four seasons. The cool one lasts from Dec. to March, the hot season is in April and May, the rainy season is June to Sept., followed by a further dry season until Nov. Rainfall, however, varies considerably, from 4" (100 mm) in the N.W. desert to over 400" (10,000 mm) in parts of Assam.

Range of temperature and rainfall: New Delhi, Jan. 57°F (13·9°C), July 88°F (31·1°C). Annual rainfall 26" (640 mm). Bombay, Jan. 75°F (23·9°C), July 81°F (27·2°C). Annual rainfall 72" (1,809 mm). Calcutta, Jan. 67°F (19·4°C), July 84°F (28·9°C). Annual rainfall 64" (1,600 mm). Cherrapunji, Jan. 53°F (11·7°C), July 68°F (20°C). Annual rainfall 432" (10,798 mm). Darjeeling, Jan. 41°F (5°C), July 62°F (16·7°C). Annual rainfall 121" (3,035 mm). Hyderabad, Jan. 72°F (22·2°C), July 80°F (26·7°C). Annual rainfall 30" (752 mm). Kochi, Jan. 80°F (26·7°C), July 79°F (26·1°C). Annual rainfall 117" (2,929 mm). Madras, Jan. 76°F (24·4°C), July 87°F (30·6°C). Annual rainfall 51" (1,270 mm). Patna, Jan. 63°F (17·2°C), July 90°F (32·2°C). Annual rainfall 46" (1,150 mm).

CONSTITUTION AND GOVERNMENT

The Constitution was passed by the Constituent Assembly on 26 Nov. 1949 and came into force on 26 Jan. 1950. It has since been amended 85 times.

INDIA

India is a republic and comprises a Union of 25 States and 7 Union Territories. Each State is administered by a Governor appointed by the President for a term of 5 years while each Union Territory is administered by the President through a Lieut.-Governor or an administrator appointed by him. The head of the Union (head of state) is the *President* in whom all executive power is vested, to be exercised on the advice of ministers responsible to Parliament. The President, who must be an Indian citizen at least 35 years old and eligible for election to the House of the People, is elected by an electoral college of all the elected members of Parliament and of the state legislative assemblies, holds office for 5 years and is eligible for re-election. There is also a *Vice-President* who is *ex-officio* chairman of the Council of States.

There is a *Council of Ministers* to aid and advise the President; this comprises Ministers who are members of the Cabinet and Ministers of State and deputy ministers who are not. A Minister who for any period of 6 consecutive months is not a member of either House of Parliament ceases to be a Minister at the expiration of that period. The *Prime Minister* is appointed by the President; other Ministers are appointed by the President on the Prime Minister's advice. The salary of each Minister is Rs 27,000 per annum.

Parliament consists of the President, the *Council of States* (*Rajya Sabha*) and the *House of the People* (*Lok Sabha*). The Council of States, or the Upper House, consists of not more than 250 members; in Dec. 1996 there were 233 elected members and 5 members nominated by the President. The election to this house is indirect; the representatives of each State are elected by the elected members of the Legislative Assembly of that State. The Council of States is a permanent body not liable to dissolution, but one-third of the members retire every second year. The House of the People, or the Lower House, consists of 545 members, 543 directly elected on the basis of adult suffrage from territorial constituencies in the States, and the Union territories; in Dec. 1997 there were 541 elected members, 2 members nominated by the President to represent the Anglo-Indian community and 2 vacancies. The House of the People unless sooner dissolved continues for a period of 5 years from the date appointed for its first meeting; in emergency, Parliament can extend the term by 1 year.

State Legislatures. For every State there is a legislature which consists of the Governor, and (a) 2 Houses, a Legislative Assembly and a Legislative Council, in the States of Bihar, Jammu and Kashmir, Karnataka, Madhya Pradesh (where it is provided for but not in operation), Maharashtra and Uttar Pradesh, and (b) 1 House, a Legislative Assembly, in the other States. Every Legislative Assembly, unless sooner dissolved, continues for 5 years from the date appointed for its first meeting. In emergency the term can be extended by 1 year. Every State Legislative Council is a permanent body and is not subject to dissolution, but one-third of the members retire every second year. Parliament can, however, abolish an existing Legislative Council or create a new one, if the proposal is supported by a resolution of the Legislative Assembly concerned.

Legislation. The various subjects of legislation are enumerated in three lists in the seventh schedule to the constitution. List I, the Union List, consists of 97 subjects (including defence, foreign affairs, communications, currency and coinage, banking and customs) with respect to which the Union Parliament has exclusive power to make laws. The State legislature has exclusive power to make laws with respect to the 66 subjects in list II, the State List; these include police and public order, agriculture and irrigation, education, public health and local government. The powers to make laws with respect to the 47 subjects (including economic and social planning, legal questions and labour and price control) in list III, the Concurrent List, are held by both Union and State governments, though the former prevails. But Parliament may legislate with respect to any subject in the State List in circumstances when the subject assumes national importance or during emergencies.

Other provisions deal with the administrative relations between the Union and the States, interstate trade and commerce, distribution of revenues between the States and the Union, official language, etc.

Fundamental Rights. Two chapters of the constitution deal with fundamental rights and 'Directive Principles of State Policy'. 'Untouchability' is abolished, and its practice in any form is punishable. The fundamental rights can be enforced through the ordinary courts of law and through the Supreme Court of the Union. The directive principles cannot be enforced through the courts of law; they are nevertheless fundamental in the governance of the country.

Citizenship. Under the Constitution, every person who was on the 26 Jan. 1950, domiciled in India and (a) was born in India or (b) either of whose parents was born in India or (c) who has been ordinarily resident in the territory of India for not less than 5 years immediately preceding that date became a citizen of India. Special provision is made for migrants from Pakistan and for Indians resident abroad. Under the Citizenship Act, 1955, which supplemented the provisions of the Constitution, Indian citizenship is acquired by birth, by descent, by registration and by naturalization. The Act also provides for loss of citizenship by renunciation, termination and deprivation. The right to vote is granted to every person who is a citizen of India and who is not less than 18 years of age on a fixed date and is not otherwise disqualified.

Parliament. Parliament and the state legislatures are organized according to the following schedule (figures show distribution of seats in Dec. 1996):

	House of the People (Lok Sabha)	Parliament Council of States (Rajya Sabha)	State Legislatures Legislative Assemblies (Vidhan Sabhas)	Legislative Councils (Vidhan Parishads)
States:				
Andhra Pradesh	42	18	294	–
Arunachal Pradesh	2	1	60	–
Assam	14	7	126	–
Bihar	54	22	324	96
Goa	2	1	40	–
Gujarat	26	11	182	–
Haryana	10	5	90	–
Himachal Pradesh	4	3	68	–
Jammu and Kashmir	6	4	87[2]	36[3]
Karnataka	28	12	224	75
Kerala	20	9	140	–
Madhya Pradesh	40	16	320	–
Maharashtra	48	19	288	63
Manipur	2	1	60	–
Meghalaya	2	1	60	–
Mizoram	1	1	40	–
Nagaland	1	1	60	–
Orissa	21	10	147	–
Punjab	13	7	117	–
Rajasthan	25	10	200	–
Sikkim	1	1	32	–
Tamil Nadu	39	18	234	–
Tripura	2	1	60	–
Uttar Pradesh	85	34	425	108
West Bengal	42	16	294	–
Union Territories:				
Andaman and Nicobar Islands	1	–	–	–
Chandigarh	1	–	–	–
Dadra and Nagar Haveli	1	–	–	–
Delhi	7	3	70	–
Daman and Diu	1	–	–	–
Lakshadweep	1	–	–	–
Pondicherry	1	1	30	–
Nominated by the President under Article 80 (1) (a) of the Constitution	–	12	–	–
Total	545[1]	245	4,072	378[1]

[1]Includes 2 nominated members to represent Anglo-Indians.
[2]Excludes 24 seats for Pakistan-occupied areas of the State which are in abeyance.
[3]Excludes seats for the Pakistan-occupied areas.

The number of seats allotted to scheduled castes and scheduled tribes in the House of the People is 79 and 41 respectively. Out of the 4,072 seats allotted to the

Legislative Assemblies, 557 are reserved for scheduled castes and 527 for scheduled tribes.

Language. The Constitution provides that the official language of the Union shall be Hindi in the Devanagari script. Hindi is spoken by over 30% of the population. It was originally provided that English should continue to be used for all official purposes until 1965. But the Official Languages Act 1963 provides that, after the expiry of this period of 15 years from the coming into force of the Constitution, English might continue to be used, in addition to Hindi, for all official purposes of the Union for which it was being used immediately before that day, and for the transaction of business in Parliament. According to the Official Languages (Use for official purposes of the Union) Rules 1976, an employee may record in Hindi or in English without being required to furnish a translation thereof in the other language and no employee possessing a working knowledge of Hindi may ask for an English translation of any document in Hindi except in the case of legal or technical documents.

The 58th amendment to the Constitution (26 Nov. 1987) authorized the preparation of a Constitution text in Hindi.

The following 18 languages are included in the Eighth Schedule to the Constitution (with 1994 estimate of speakers where over 5m.): Assamese (14·8m.), Bengali (68·3m.), Gujarati (44m.), Hindi (350·3m.), Kannada (35·7m.), Kashmiri, Konkani, Malayalam (34·4m.), Manipuri, Marathi (65·8m.), Nepali, Oriya (30·3m.), Punjabi (24·7m.), Sanskrit, Sindhi, Tamil (59·3m.), Telugu (71·9m.), Urdu (46·8m.).
Thakur, R., *The Government and Politics of India.* London, 1995

National Anthem. 'Jana-gana-mana' ('Thou art the ruler of the minds of all people'); words and tune by Rabindranath Tagore.

RECENT ELECTIONS

Presidential elections were held on 14 July 1997. Dr Kocheril Raman Narayanan was elected by 94·97% of votes cast against 1 opponent.

Parliamentary elections were held over 7 days from 27 April to 7 May 1996 (23 and 30 May in Jammu and Kashmir). The electorate was 590m. The Bharatiya Janata Party gained 160 seats; the Congress (I), 136. After the elections, a coalition government was formed, led by Bharatiya Janata Party with Atal Behari Vajpayee as Prime Minister. It lasted for 13 days. A 13-party Coalition goverrnment with H. D. Deve Gowda as Prime Minister took office, supported by Congress (I) from outside. When Congress (I) withdrew support in March 1997, Inder Kumar Gujral replaced Deve Gowda and formed the Government. Congress (I) again withdrew support in Nov. 1997 and the Gujral government resigned. The President accepted the resignation and dissolved the House of the People and ordered elections with Gujral heading the caretaker government.

In the parliamentary elections held between 16 Feb. and 7 March 1998 the Bharatiya Janata Party (Hindu Nationalists) won 178 seats, the Indian National Congress 145, the Communist Party of India (Marxist) 32 and Samajwadi Party 21. Other parties won fewer than 20 seats each.

Composition of the Council of States in April 1997: Congress (I) 88; Communist Party of India (Marxist), 15; All-India Anna DMK, 14; Janata Dal, 23; Bharatiya Janata Party, 44; Telugu Desam (Naidu), 8; Samajwadi Party, 7; Communist Party, 6; Independent, 9; Moslem League, 2; Forward Bloc, 2; Shiv Sena, 4; Bahujan Samaj Patry, 3; J & K National Conference, 3; others, 8; nominated, 1; vacant, 8.
Singh, V. B., *Elections in India: Data Handbook on Lok Sabha Elections, 1986–91.* Delhi, 1994

CURRENT ADMINISTRATION

President: Dr Kocheril Raman Narayanan (b. 1920; sworn in 25 July 1997).
Vice-President: Krishan Kant (elected 16 Aug. 1997).
The 13-party coalition government was composed as follows in March 1999:
Prime Minister: Atal Behari Vajpayee (BJP), sworn in 18 March 1998.
Principal Secretary: Brajesh Mishra. *Minister of Home Affairs:* Lal Krishna Advani. *Civil Aviation:* Anant Kumar. *Industry:* Sikander Bakht. *Chemicals and Fertilizers, Food:* Surjit Singh Barnala. *Labour:* Dr. Satyanarain Jatiya. *Human Resources Development, Science and Technology, Ocean Development:* Dr. Murli Manohar Joshi. *Parliamentary Affairs:* Madan Lal Khurana. *Power, Non-*

INDIA

Conventional Energy Resources: P. Rangarajan Kumaramangalam. *Textiles:* Kashi Ram Rana. *Finance:* Yashwant Sinha. *Information and Broadcasting, Food Processing:* Pramod Mahajan. *Defence:* George Fernandes. *Railways:* Nitish Kumar. *Law, Justice and Company Affairs:* M. Thambi Durai. *Urban Development:* Ram Jethmalani. *Communications:* Jagmohan. *Commerce:* Ramakrishna Hegde. *Environment and Forests:* Suresh Prabhakar Prabhu. *Steel and Mines:* Naveen Patnaik. *Petroleum and Natural Gas:* V. K. Ramamurthy. *Animal Husbandry, Atomic Energy:* Atal Behari Vajpayee. *Electronics, External Affairs:* Jaswant Singh. *Water Resources:* Sompal.

Local Government. There were in 1989-90, 72 municipal corporations, 1,770 municipal committees/boards/councils, 663 town area committees and 337 notified area committees. The municipal bodies look after the roads, water supply, drainage, sanitation, medical relief, vaccination, education, street lighting, etc. Their main sources of revenue are taxes on the annual rental value of land and buildings, octroi and terminal, vehicle and other taxes. The municipal councils enact their own bye-laws and frame their budgets, which in the case of municipal bodies other than corporations generally require the sanction of the State government. All municipal councils are elected on the principle of adult franchise.

For rural areas there is a 3-tier system of *panchayati raj* at village, block and district level, although the 3-tier structure may undergo some changes in State legislation to suit local conditions. All *panchayati raj* bodies are organically linked, and representation is given to special interests. Elected directly by and from among villagers, the *panchayats* are responsible for agricultural production, rural industries, medical relief, maternity and child welfare, common grazing grounds, village roads, tanks and wells, and maintenance of sanitation. In some places they also look after primary education, maintenance of village records and collection of land revenue. They have their own powers of taxation. There are judicial *panchayats* or village courts.

Panchayati raj now cover almost all the States and Union Territories with variations in structural pattern. *Panchayati raj* involves a 3-tier arrangement: Village level, block level and district level. Tenure of *Panchayati raj* institutions range from 3–5 years.

The powers and responsibilities of *Panchayati raj* institutions are derived from State Legislatures, and from the executive orders of State governments.

DEFENCE
The Supreme Command of the Armed Forces is vested in the President. Policy is decided at different levels by a number of committees, including the Political Affairs Committee presided over by the Prime Minister and the Defence Minister's Committee. Administrative and operational control rests in the respective Service Headquarters, under the control of the Ministry of Defence. As well as armed forces of 1,145,000 personnel in 1998, there was an active para-military force of 1,088,000, including 185,000 members of the Border Security Force based mainly in the troubled Jammu and Kashmir region. Military service is voluntary but, under the ammended constitution, it is regarded as a fundamental duty of every citizen to perform National Service when called upon. Defence spending for 1998-99 saw an increase of 14% on 1997-98 to US$9·8bn. Defence accounted for 13% of spending in 1998-99.

Nuclear weapons. India's first nuclear test was in 1974. The nuclear arsenal consisted of approximately 65 warheads in early 1998.

Army. The Army Headquarters functioning directly under the Chief of the Army Staff is divided into the following main branches: General Staff Branch; Adjutant General's Branch; Quartermaster-General's Branch; Master-General of Ordnance Branch; Engineer-in-Chief's Branch; Military Secretary's Branch.

The Army is organized into 5 commands each divided into areas, which in turn are subdivided into sub-areas.

The strength of the Army was (1998) 980,000. There are 3 armoured, 17 infantry and 10 mountain divisions and 5 independent armoured, 7 independent infantry, 3 independent artillery, 1 parachute, 1 mountain, 16 air defence and 3 engineer brigades, and 1 surface-to-surface missile regiment. An Aviation Corps operates 150 locally-built Alouette and Lama helicopters.

Equipment includes some 700 T-55, 1,100 T-72/-M1 and 1,700 Vijayanta main battle tanks.

Navy. The Navy has 3 commands; Eastern, Western and Southern, the latter a training and support command. The fleet is divided into 2 elements, Eastern and Western; and well-trained, all-volunteer personnel operate a mix of Soviet and Western vessels.

The principal ship is the light aircraft carrier, *Viraat*, formerly HMS *Hermes*, of 29,000 tonnes, completed in 1959 and transferred to the Indian Navy in 1987. *Viraat* embarks an air group of 12 Sea Harrier fighters and 6 Sea King anti-submarine helicopters. The *Vikrant* was decommissioned on 31 Jan. 1997.

The fleet includes 8 'Kilo' and 1 'Foxtrot' Soviet-built diesel submarines and 4 smaller new German-designed boats. 5 Soviet-built missile-armed destroyers, 3 heavily modified and 6 rather less modified 'Leander' class frigates, all built in India, together with 1 ex-British Batch 3 'Leander' class and 9 other Soviet-type frigates form the main surface force. Coastal forces include 14 Soviet-designed missile and 4 anti-submarine corvettes, 6 fast missile craft, 7 offshore and 10 inshore patrol craft. There are 12 Soviet-built offshore minesweepers, and 8 much smaller inshore vessels. Amphibious lift for the 1,000 strong marine force is provided by 1 tank landing ship and 8 medium landing ships, as well as about 8 craft. Support forces include 1 tanker, 1 submarine depot ship, 1 transport, 10 survey and research ships, 2 tugs and 1 training ship.

The Naval Air force, 5,000 strong, operates 20 Sea Harriers, 5 Il-38 'May', 8 Tu-142M 'Bear-F', 20 Dornier 228 and 13 Britten-Norman Islander maritime patrol aircraft. Armed helicopters include 26 Chetak, 7 Ka-25, 10 Ka-27 and 32 Sea King, and the inventory is completed with some 30 training and communications aircraft.

Main bases are at Bombay (HQ Western Fleet, and main dockyard), Goa, Visakhapatnam (HQ Eastern Fleet) and Calcutta on the sub-continent, Port Blair in the Andaman Islands and Lakhshadweep on the Laccadive Islands. HQ Southern Command is at Kochi.

Naval personnel in 1998 numbered 55,000 including 5,000 Naval Air Arm and 1,000 marines.

The Coast Guard is an independent para-military service 4,000 strong in 1996, which functions under Defence Ministry control, but is funded by the Revenue Department. The force comprises 10 offshore patrol vessels and 40 inshore patrol craft. Its 20 aircraft include Dornier-228, Fokker F-27 and Britten-Norman Islanders, and 13 Chetak helicopters.

Air Force. The Air Headquarters, under the Chief of Air Staff, consists of 4 main branches, viz., Air Staff, Administration, Policy and Plans, and Maintenance. Units of the IAF are organized into 5 operational commands—Western at Delhi, Central at Allahabad, Eastern at Shillong, Southern at Thiruvananthapuram and South-Western at Jodhpur. Training Command HQ is at Bangalore, Maintenance Command at Nagpur. Nominal strength in 1998 was 110,000 personnel, over 600 combat aircraft of all types, in over 40 squadrons of aircraft, 36 armed helicopters and about 30 squadrons of 'Guideline' and 'Goa' surface-to-air missiles, and close-range missiles such as 'Gainful' and Tigercat.

Air defence units include 2 squadrons of MiG-23 variable-geometry interceptors, 3 squadrons of MiG-29s, 16 squadrons of MiG-21s and 2 of Mirage 2000s. Other combat units include 8 squadrons of MiG-27s, 2 of Canberras, 4 of Jaguars, 4 of MiG-23 supersonic fighter-bombers and one of MiG-25 reconnaissance aircraft. Delivery of 40 Su-30 strike aircraft started in 1997.

The large transport force includes An-32s, Il-76s, Do 228s, HS 748s, 2 Boeing 737s, and smaller aircraft and helicopters for VIP and other duties. Helicopter units have Mi-8s and Mi-17s (10 squadrons), Mi-26s, and Mi-25 gunships. Main training types are the Hindustan HPT-32 and Kiran, Polish-built TS-11 Iskra, Hunter T.66, MiG-21UT1 and MiG-23U.

INTERNATIONAL RELATIONS
India is a member of the UN, the Commonwealth and the Colombo Plan.

ECONOMY

Policy. The highest economic decision-making body is the *National Development Council*, of which all state chief ministers are members. There is also a Planning Commission.

The eighth 5-year plan (1992–97) emphasized job creation and increased rural investment, and aimed at an annual growth of 5·6% of GDP, 3% in employment and a domestic savings rate of 21·6% of GDP. Indicative planning, however, is tending to take the place of centralized planning.

As a first step towards partial privatization of the 248 state-owned corporations, selected public sector enterprises are being allowed to raise funds through equity issues.

Requirements for government approval of investment decisions were reduced in 1990. The eighth plan (1992–97) envisaged an outlay of Rs 7,920,000m., with public sector investment of Rs 3,420,000m. Central plan outlay (1997–98), Rs 918,390m.

Performance. Real GDP growth at factor cost in 1996–97 was 6·8% (6·1% in 1995). For 1998 it was forecast to be around 4–5%, indicating that India managed to avoid the worst of the Asian crisis. The current account deficit stood at US$–3,532 in 1997.

Budget. Revenue and expenditure (on revenue account) of the central government for years ending 31 March, in Rs 1m.:

	1995–96	1996–97[1]	1997–98[2]
Revenue	1,685,713	1,983,536	2,310.756
Expenditure	1,983,023	2,265,590	2,613,409

[1]Revised.   [2]Budget estimates.

Important items of revenue and expenditure on the revenue account of the central government for 1997–98 (estimates), in Rs 1m.:

Revenue		Expenditure	
Net tax revenue	1,379,568	General Services	1,167,096
Non-tax revenue	831,188	Defence	276,170
		Major subsidies	182,510

Total capital account receipts (1997–98 budget), Rs 2,774,893m.; capital account disbursements, Rs 2,777,284m. Total (revenue and capital) receipts, Rs 5,085,649m.; disbursements, Rs 5,390,693m.

Under the Constitution (Part XII and 7th Schedule), the power to raise funds has been divided between the central government and the states. Generally, the sources of revenue are mutually exclusive. Certain taxes are levied by the Union for the sake of uniformity and distributed to the states. The Finance Commission (Art. 280 of the Constitution) advises the President on the distribution of the taxes which are distributable between the centre and the states, and on the principles on which grants should be made out of Union revenues to the states. The main sources of central revenue are: customs duties; those excise duties levied by the central government; corporation, income and wealth taxes; estate and succession duties on non-agricultural assets and property; and revenues from the railways and posts and telegraphs. The main heads of revenue in the states are: taxes and duties levied by the state governments (including land revenues and agricultural income tax); civil administration and civil works; state undertakings; taxes shared with the centre; and grants received from the centre.

Currency. A decimal system of coinage was introduced in 1957. The Indian *rupee* (INR) is divided into 100 *paise*. The paper currency consists of Reserve Bank notes and Government of India currency notes.

Foreign exchange reserves in Feb. 1998 were US$24,044m. and gold reserves were 12·74m. troy oz. Inflation was 9·4% in 1997 and forecast to drop to 7·0% in 1998.

The official exchange rate was abolished on 1 March 1993; the rupee now has a single market exchange rate and is convertible. The pound sterling is the currency of intervention. Total money supply in Jan. 1998 was Rs 2,389bn.

Banking and Finance. The Reserve Bank, the central bank for India, was established in 1934 and started functioning on 1 April 1935 as a shareholder's bank;

it became a nationalized institution on 1 Jan. 1949. It has the sole right of issuing currency notes. Its *Governor* is Chakravarty Rangarajan (b. 1932). The Bank acts as adviser to the Government on financial problems and is the banker for central and state governments, commercial banks and some other financial institutions. It manages the rupee public debt of central and state governments and is the custodian of the country's exchange reserve. The Bank has extensive powers of regulation of the banking system, directly under the Banking Regulation Act, 1949, and indirectly by the use of variations in Bank rate, variation in reserve ratios, selective credit controls and open market operations.

The commercial banking system consisted of 300 scheduled banks (*i.e.*, banks which are included in the 2nd schedule to the Reserve Bank Act) and 4 nonscheduled banks in Jan. 1993; scheduled banks included 196 Regional Rural Banks. Total deposits in commercial banks, March 1997, stood at Rs 5,035,960m. The business of non-scheduled banks forms less than 0·1% of commercial bank business. Of the 300 scheduled banks, 35 were foreign banks which specialize in financing foreign trade but also compete for domestic business. The State Bank of India acts as the agent of the Reserve Bank for transacting government business as well as undertaking commercial functions. The 27 public sector banks (which comprise the State Bank of India and its 7 associate banks and 19 nationalized banks) account for about 80·7% of deposits and about 78% of bank credit of all scheduled commercial banks.

There are stock exchanges in Ahmedabad, Bombay, Calcutta, Delhi, Madras and 18 other centres.

Weights and Measures. Uniform standards of weights and measures, based on the metric system, were established for the first time by the Standards of Weights and Measures Act, 1956.

A second Standards of Weights and Measures Act, 1976, recognizes the International System of Units and is in line with the recommendations of the International Organisation of Legal Metrology. This Act also protects consumers through proper indication of weight, quantity, identity, source, date and price on packaged goods.

While the Standards of Weights and Measures are laid down in the Central Act, enforcement of weights and measures laws is entrusted to the state governments; the central Directorate of Weights and Measures is responsible for co-ordinating activities so as to ensure national uniformity.

Calendar. The dates of the Saka era (named after the north Indian dynasty of the first century AD) are used alongside Gregorian dates in issues of the *Gazette* of India, news broadcasts by All-India Radio and government-issued calendars, from 22 March 1957, a date which corresponds with the first day of the year 1879 in the Saka era.

ENERGY AND NATURAL RESOURCES

Electricity. Installed capacity in 1996 was 83·28m. kW. In Nov. 1996, 502,721 villages out of 579,132 had electricity. Production of electricity in 1995–96 was 380,084m. kWh, of which 299,606m. kWh came from thermal stations, 7,965m. kWh from nuclear stations and 72,513m. kWh from hydro-electric stations. 9 nuclear stations supplied 2·1% of output in 1995–96. Consumption per capita in 1995 was 419 kWh.

Oil and Gas. The Oil and Natural Gas Corporation Ltd and Oil India Ltd are the only producers of crude oil. Production 1996–97, 33·43m. tonnes, about 60% of consumption. The main fields are in Assam and Gujarat and offshore in the Gulf of Cambay (the Bombay High field). Natural gas production, 1995–96, 22,308m. cu. metres.

Water. 89·44m. ha (1995–96) irrigation potential had been created of which 79·89m. ha was utilized. Irrigation projects have formed an important part of all the Five-Year Plans. The possibilities of diverting rivers into canals being nearly exhausted, the emphasis is now on damming the monsoon surplus flow and diverting that. Ultimate potential of irrigation is assessed at 107m. ha, total cultivated land being 185m. ha.

A Ganges water-sharing accord was signed with Bangladesh in 1997, ending a 25-year dispute which had hindered and dominated relations between the two countries.

Minerals. The coal industry was nationalized in 1973. Production, including lignite, 1996–97 (provisional), 319m. tonnes; reserves, including lignite, are estimated at (1995–96) 202,000m. tonnes. Production of other minerals, 1996–97 (in 1,000 tonnes): Iron ore, 66,672; bauxite, 5,928; chromite, 1,664 (1995–96); copper ore, 3,900; manganese ore, 1,836; gold, 2,712 kg. Other important minerals are lead, zinc, limestone, apatite and phosphorite, dolomite, magnesite and silver. Value of mineral production, 1996–97, Rs 330,204·3m. of which mineral fuels produced Rs 275,053m., metallic minerals Rs 24,295m. and non-metallic Rs 11,392·4m.

Agriculture. About 70% of the people are dependent on the land for their living. In 1998 agriculture provided about 30% of GDP. The farming year runs from July to June through three crop seasons: Kharif (monsoon); rabi (winter) and summer. In 1994, 166,100,000 ha were used for arable land, 3,550,000 ha for permanent crops and 11,400,000 ha for permanent pasture.

Agricultural production, 1996–97 (in 1,000 tonnes): Rice, 80,530; wheat, 64,660; total foodgrains, 192,120; maize, 9,440; pulses, 14,020; sugar-cane, 267,480; oilseeds, 24,210; cotton, 14·16m. bales (of 170 kg); jute is grown in West Bengal (70% of total yield), Bihar and Assam, total yield, 9·42m. bales (of 170 kg). The coffee industry is growing: The main cash varieties are Arabica and Robusta (main growing areas Karnataka, Kerala and Tamil Nadu).

The tea industry is important, with production concentrated in Assam, West Bengal, Tamil Nadu and Kerala. Total crop in 1997, 810,600 tonnes; exports in 1997, 203,000 tonnes, valued at US$432m.

Livestock (1996): Cattle, 196m.; sheep, 45m.; pigs, 11·9m.; horses, 990,000; asses, 1·6m.; goats, 119·24m. (1995); buffaloes, 79·5m. (1995); chickens, 610m. (1995). There are more cattle and buffaloes in India than in any other country.

Fertilizer consumption in 1996–97 was 14·31m. tonnes.

Land Tenure. There are three main traditional systems of land tenure: *Ryotwari* tenure, where the individual holders, usually peasant proprietors, are responsible for the payment of land revenues; *zamindari* tenure, where one or more persons own large estates and are responsible for payment (in this system there may be a number of intermediary holders); and *mahalwari* tenure, where village communities jointly hold an estate and are jointly and severally responsible for payment.

Agrarian reform, initiated in the first Five-Year Plan, being undertaken by the state governments includes: (1) The abolition of intermediaries under *zamindari* tenure. (2) Tenancy legislation designed to scale down rents to $^1/_4$–$^1/_5$ of the value of the produce, to give permanent rights to tenants (subject to the landlord's right to resume a minimum holding for his personal cultivation), and to enable tenants to acquire ownership of their holdings (subject to the landlord's right of resumption for personal cultivation) on payment of compensation over a number of years. (3) Fixing of ceilings on existing holdings and on future acquisition; the holding of a family is between 4·05 and 7·28 ha if it has assured irrigation to produce two crops a year; 10·93 ha for land with irrigation facilities for only one crop a year; and 21·85 ha for all other categories of land. Tea, coffee, cocoa and cardamom plantations have been exempted. (4) The consolidation of holdings in community project areas and the prevention of fragmentation of holdings by reform of inheritance laws. (5) Promotion of farming by co-operative village management.

The average size of holding for the whole of India is 2·63 ha. Andhra Pradesh, 2·87; Assam, 1·46; Bihar, 1·53; Gujarat, 4·49; Jammu and Kashmir, 1·43; Karnataka, 4·11; Kerala, 0·75; Madhya Pradesh, 3·99; Maharashtra, 4·65; Orissa, 1·98; Punjab, 3·85; Rajasthan, 5·5; Tamil Nadu, 1·49; Uttar Pradesh, 1·78; West Bengal, 1·56.

Of the total 71m. rural households possessing operational holdings, 34% hold on the average less than 0·2 ha of land each.

Opium. By international agreement the poppy is cultivated under licence, and all raw opium is sold to the central government. Opium, other than for wholly medical use, is available only to registered addicts.

Forestry. The lands under the control of the state forest departments are classified as 'reserved forests' (forests intended to be permanently maintained for the supply of timber, etc., or for the protection of water supply, etc.), 'protected forests' and 'unclassed' forest land. In 1995 the total forest area was 650,050 sq. km (21·9% of the land area), up from 649,690 sq. km in 1990. India is one of only two developing countries to have increased its area under forests between 1990 and 1995, the other being Cape Verde. Main types are teak and sal. About 16% of the area is inaccessible, of which about 45% is potentially productive. In 1995, 299·16m. cu. metres of roundwood were produced, making India the third largest producer after the USA and China. India is the world's leading producer of fuelwood and charcoal. Most states have encouraged planting small areas around villages.

Fisheries. Total catch (1995–96) was 4·95m. tonnes, of which Kerala, Tamil Nadu, and Maharashtra produced about half. Of the total catch in 1995–96, 2·71m. tonnes were marine fish. There were 46,918 mechanized boats (1994–95). There were also 31,726 motorized traditional crafts and 159,481 traditional crafts in 1994–95. There were 11,440 fishermen's co-operatives with 1,250,379 members in 1995–96; total sales, Rs 1,495m. (1994–95).

INDUSTRY
In a number of industries new units are set up only by the state. Industries reserved for the public sector are arms and ammunition and allied items of defence equipment, military aircraft and warships, nuclear energy, coal and lignite, mineral oils and minerals specified in nuclear energy and railway transport. In a further group of industries (road transport, manufacture of chemicals such as drugs, dyestuffs, plastics and fertilizers) the state established new undertakings, but private enterprise may develop either on its own or with state backing.

Oil refinery installed capacity, Dec. 1996, was 60·55m. tonnes; production of petroleum refinery products (1995–96), 55·08m. tonnes. The Indian Oil Corporation was established in 1964 and had (1996) the major portion of the market.

There is expansion in petrochemicals, based on the oil and associated gas of the Bombay High field, and gas from Krishna-Godavari Basin, Rajasthan, Tripura, Assam and Bassein field. Small industries numbering 2·72m., (initial outlay on capital equipment of less than Rs 30m.) are important; they employ about 15·26m. and produced (1995–96) goods worth Rs 3,164,210m.

Industrial production, 1995–96 (in 1,000 tonnes): Steel ingots, 12,972; aluminium, 527; 2,588,004 motor cycles, mopeds and scooters; 293,172 commercial vehicles; petroleum products, 55,332; cement, 67,716; board and paper, 3,544; nitrogen fertilizer, 9,768; phosphate fertilizer, 3,792; jute goods, 1,114; man-made fibre and yarn, 468; diesel engines, 1,984,140; electric motors, 6·36m. h.p.; 361,488 passenger cars and jeeps; 19,044 railway wagons; pig-iron (saleable), 2,436; finished steel, 14,533.

Labour. At the 1991 census there were 285·9m. workers, of whom 110·7m. were cultivators, 74·6m. agricultural labourers; 28·7m. in manufacturing, processing, servicing and repairs, 5·5m. in construction and 8·02m. in transport, communications and storage. Workdays lost by industrial disputes, 1995, 14·29m., through strikes and lockouts. An ordinance of 1981 gave the government power to ban strikes in essential services; the ordinance was to remain in force for 6 months and would then be renewable.

The unemployment rate was 5·2% of the workforce in 1997.

Companies. The total number of companies limited by shares at work as on 31 March 1997 was 450,950; aggregate paid-up capital was Rs 1,845,428m. Of these, 64,109 were public limited companies with an aggregate paid-up capital of Rs 1,257,197m., and 386,841 private limited companies (Rs 588,231m.). There were also 419 companies with unlimited liability and 2,578 companies limited by guarantee and associations not for profit.

During 1995–96, 56,433 new limited companies were registered in the Indian Union under the Companies Act 1956 with a total authorized capital of Rs 210,450m.; 11 were government companies (Rs 26,610m.) and 56,422 were non-government companies (Rs 183,840m.). There were 17 private companies with unlimited liability and 90 companies with liability limited by guarantee and association not for profit also registered in 1995–96. During 1995–96, 414 non-government companies with an aggregate paid-up capital of Rs 104m. went into liquidation or were struck off the register.

On 31 March 1996 there were 1,216 government companies at work with a total paid-up capital of Rs 767,665m.; 604 were public limited companies and 611 were private limited companies.

On 31 March 1996, 679 companies incorporated elsewhere were reported to have a place of business in India; 161 were of UK and 150 of US origin.

Co-operative Movement. In 1995–96 there were 411,000 co-operative societies with a total membership of 197·8m. These included Primary Co-operative Marketing Societies, State Co-operative Marketing Federations and the National Agricultural Co-operative Marketing Federation of India. There were also State Co-operative Commodity Marketing Federations, and 29 general purpose and 16 Special Commodities Marketing Federations.

There were, in 1995–96, 28 State Co-operative Banks, 362 District Central Co-operative Banks, 90,783 Primary Agricultural Credit Societies, 20 State Land Development Banks, and 2,970 Primary Land Development Banks which provide long-term credits.

Agricultural credit is provided (31 Dec. 1993) through 32,641 rural and semi-rural branches of commercial banks and 14,543 branches of Regional Rural Banks, and (June 1993) 90,783 Primary Agricultural Credit Societies affiliated to 10,775 branches of District Central Co-operative Banks and 2,970 Primary units of Land Development Banks. Total agricultural credit disbursed by Co-operatives in 1995–96 was Rs 26,450m.

Value of agricultural produce marketed by Co-operatives in 1994–95 was about Rs 95,000m. Commercial and regional rural banks disbursed agricultural credit of Rs 136,840m. in 1995–96.

In 1994–95 there were 2,601 agro-processing units; 245 sugar factories produced 8·66m. tons; 137 spinning mills (capacity 3·2m. spindles) accounted for 12% of total spindleage in the country in 1995–96; there were 129 oilseed processing units; total storage capacity was 13·55m. tons on 31 March 1996.

In 1994–95 there were 76,500 retail depots distributing 4·12m. tons of fertilizers.

Trade Unions. The Indian National Trade Union Conference (INTUC) has 3,796 affiliated unions with a total membership of 5,932,440.

INTERNATIONAL TRADE

Foreign investment is encouraged by a tax holiday on income up to 6% of capital employed for 5 years. There are special depreciation allowances, and customs and excise concessions, for export industries. Proposals for investment ventures involving up to 51% foreign equity require only the Reserve Bank's approval under new liberalized policy. In Feb. 1991 India resumed trans-frontier trade with China, which had ceased in 1962.

Foreign debt was estimated at US$93,843m. in Sept. 1996.

Imports and Exports. The external trade of India (excluding land-borne trade with Tibet and Bhutan) was as follows (in Rs 100,000):

	Imports	Exports and Re-exports
1995–96	12,267,814	10,635,334
1996–97	13,891,968	11,881,708
1997–98	15,417,629	13,010,064

The distribution of commerce by countries was as follows in the year ended 31 March 1998 (in Rs 100,000):

Countries	Exports to	Imports from	Countries	Exports to	Imports from
Argentina	34,455	47,640	Bulgaria	3,361	4,306
Australia	160,079	552,105	Canada	160,658	156,431
Austria	31,652	30,151	China	413,293	266,825
Bahrain	23,966	49,401	Czech Republic	9,426	15,731
Bangladesh	292,276	18,885	Denmark	58,721	33,732
Belgium	449,253	991,587	Egypt	94,172	71,585
Brazil	53,302	74,038	France	281,844	291,737

INDIA

Countries	Exports to	Imports from	Countries	Exports to	Imports from
Germany	714,009	939,638	Poland	32,617	12,152
Hong Kong	715,915	117,537	Qatar	16,734	37,753
Hungary	13,234	4,479	Romania	5,697	22,832
Indonesia	162,502	271,909	Russia	354,167	239,015
Iran	63,765	235,526	Saudi Arabia	256,453	639,299
Israel	131,070	124,737	Senegal	10,765	17,893
Italy	414,004	332,347	Singapore	288,673	372,392
Japan	705,223	797,147	South Africa	146,258	185,120
Jordan	25,732	62,573	Spain	164,383	59,830
Kuwait	69,073	330,689	Sri Lanka	179,090	11,226
North Korea	13,987	21,324	Sweden	61,745	102,010
South Korea	173,613	353,219	Switzerland	133,505	981,404
Malaysia	181,920	438,132	Taiwan	150,032	175,570
Mexico	41,276	29,544	Tanzania	25,606	25,264
Morocco	10,504	171,479	Thailand	127,694	84,204
Myanmar	18,326	83,253	Tunisia	5,510	54,048
Nepal	63,199	35,364	Turkey	90,562	23,906
Netherlands	298,634	165,455	UAE	627,763	548,197
New Zealand	26,743	31,128	UK	793,676	908,043
Nigeria	80,101	414,568	Ukraine	22,554	66,800
Norway	28,767	36,365	USA	2,523,331	1,380,366
Pakistan	53,202	16,519	Vietnam	47,042	3,246
Philippines	88,712	8,570			

The value (in Rs 100,000) of the leading articles of merchandise was as follows in the year ended 31 March 1997:

Exports	Value
Meat and meat preparations	70,888
Marine products	400,763
Processed foods (miscellaneous)	76,408
Rice	317,235
Vegetables and fruits	57,878
Coffee and coffee substitutes	142,654
Tea	103,708
Spices	120,968
Oil meals	349,534
Tobacco unmanufactured and tobacco refuse	66,048
Raw cotton	157,451
Iron ore	170,644
Ores and minerals (excluding iron, mica and coal)	113,266
Cotton yarn, fabrics and made-up articles	1,108,213
Ready-made garments, including clothing accessories of all textile materials	1,332,408
Jute manufactures including twist and yarn	52,237
Leather and leather manufactures	560,850
Natural silk textiles	45,723
Man-made textiles	249,445
Carpets, mill-made	47,886
Plastics and linoleum	191,431
Sports goods	27,709
Gems and jewellery	1,676,990
Handicrafts	168,864
Handmade carpets	154,887
Engineering goods	1,740,887
Petroleum products	171,035
Basic chemicals, pharmaceuticals and cosmetics, chemicals including residual	886,233

Imports	Value
Raw wool	58,146
Pulp and waste paper	82,270
Crude rubber including synthetic and reclaimed	62,958
Fertilizers, crude	47,755
Synthetic and regenerated fibre	42,326
Sulphur and unroasted iron pyrites	32,312
Metalliferous ores and metal scrap	290,960

Imports	Value
Petroleum, petroleum products and related	
materials	3,562,852
Edible oil	292,919
Cashew nuts	76,008
Organic and inorganic chemicals	944,605
Medical and pharmaceutical products	108,918
Fertilizers, manufactured	243,418
Artificial resins, plastic materials etc	282,568
Chemical materials and products	93,570
Paper, paper board and manufactures thereof	67,421
Textile yarn, fabrics and made-up articles	127,214
Pearls, precious and semi-precious stones	1,038,360
Non-metallic mineral manufactures excluding pearls	42,924
Iron and steel	457,893
Non-ferrous metal	392,486
Manufactures of metal	112,308
Machinery other than electric	1,293,739
Electrical machinery	115,496
Transport equipment	526,924
Professional, scientific, controlling instruments,	
photographic, optical goods, watches and clocks	196,177

In 1995–96 the main export markets (percentage of total trade) were: USA, 17·4%; Japan, 6·97%; Germany, 6·22%; UK, 6·3%. Main import suppliers: USA, 10·53%; Belgium, 4·64%; Germany, 8·66%; Saudi Arabia, 5·5%; Japan, 6·73%.

COMMUNICATIONS

Roads. In 1995–96 there were 3·29m. km of roads, of which 1·44m. km were surfaced. Roads are divided into 6 main administrative classes, namely: national highways, state highways, other public works department (PWD) roads, *Panchayati Raj* roads, urban roads and project roads. The national highways (34,298 km in 1996) connect capitals of states, major ports and foreign highways. The national highway system is linked with the UN Economic and Social Commission for Asia and the Pacific international highway system. The state highways are the main trunk roads of the states, while the other PWD roads and *Panchayati Raj* roads connect subsidiary areas of production and markets with distribution centres, and form the main link between headquarters and neighbouring districts.

There were (31 March 1996) 33,558,000 motor vehicles in India, comprising 4·19m. private cars, taxis and jeeps, 23·1m. motor cycles and scooters, 449,000 buses, 1,785,000 goods vehicles and 4,024,000 others.

Rail. The Indian railway system is government-owned (under the control of the Railway Board) and is divided into 9 zones; route-km 1995–96:

Zone	Headquarters	Route-km
Central	Bombay	7,047 km (2,892 km electrified)
Eastern	Calcutta	4,318 km (1,613 km)
Northern	Delhi	11,004 km (1,170 km)
North Eastern	Gorakhpur	5,107 km
North East Frontier	Guwahati	3,816 km
Southern	Madras	7,049 km (1,099 km)
South Central	Secunderabad	7,203 km (1,325 km)
South Eastern	Calcutta	7,351 km (2,905 km)
Western	Bombay	10,020 km (1,791 km)

A further 6 zones were proposed for creation in 1997.

The Konkan Railway (760 km of 1,676 mm gauge) linking Bombay and Mangalore opened in 1996. It is operated as a separate entity.

Principal gauges are 1,676 mm (40,620 km) and 1 metre (18,501 km), with networks also of 762 mm and 610 mm gauge (3,794 km).

Passengers carried in 1996–97 were 4,134m.; freight, 409·2m. tonnes. Revenue (1995–96) from passengers, Rs 61,244·9m.; from goods, Rs 152,904m.

Indian Railways pay to the central government a dividend on capital-at-charge at a rate fixed by the Convention Committee of Parliament. Railway finance in Rs1m.:

INDIA

Financial years	Gross traffic receipts	Gross expenditure	Net revenues (receipts)	Net surplus or deficit (after dividend)
1995–96	224,179	185,249	41,351	+23,180
1996–97 revised	244,500	209,650	37,563	+22,410
1997–98 budget	278,550	251,350	30,037	+13,740

There is a metro (16·4 km) in Calcutta.

Civil Aviation. The main international airports are at Bombay, Calcutta, Delhi (Indira Gandhi), Madras and Thiruvananthapuram, with some international flights from Ahmedabad, Amritsar, Bangalore, Calicut, Goa and Hyderabad. Air transport was nationalized in 1953 with the formation of 2 Air Corporations: Air India for long-distance international air services, and Indian Airlines for air services within India and to adjacent countries. A third airline, Vayudoot, formed in 1981 as an internal feeder, has been merged into Indian Airlines. Domestic air transport has been opened to private companies, and by 1996–97, 7 private airlines had been given scheduled status.

In 1998 Air India operated routes to Africa (Dar-es-Salaam, Lagos and Nairobi); to Mauritius; to Europe (Copenhagen, Frankfurt, London, Manchester, Moscow, Paris, Rome, Vienna and Zürich); to western Asia (Abu Dhabi, Dhahran, Doha, Dubai, Kuwait, Muscat, Jeddah and Riyadh); to east Asia (Bangkok, Hong Kong, Jakarta, Kuala Lumpur, Osaka, Singapore and Tokyo); and to North America (Chicago, New York and Washington). In addition, freight services are operated to Zürich, Brussels, Dubai, Singapore and Luxembourg. Air India carried 2·8m. passengers and made a loss of Rs 2,718·4m. in 1995–96.

Indian Airlines operated international flights in 1998 to Bahrain, Bangkok, Colombo, Dhaka, Doha, Fujairah, Karachi, Káthmandu, Kuala Lumpur, Kuwait, Male, Rangoon (Yangon), Ras-al-Khaimah, Sharjah and Singapore. During 1995–96 the airline carried 7·74m. passengers.

Services were also provided in 1998 by Aeroflot, Air Canada, Air France, Air Lanka, Air Maldives, Air Mauritius, Air Seychelles, Air Ukraine, Alitalia, All Nippon Airways, Archana Airways, Ariana Afghan Airlines, Armenian Airlines, Asiana Airlines, Austrian Airlines, Aviacompany Turkmenistan, Azerbaijan Airlines, Biman Bangladesh Airlines, British Airways, Cathay Pacific, Delta Air Lines, Druk-Air, Egyptair, El Al, Emirates, Ethiopian Airlines, Georgian Airways, Gujarat Airways, Gulf Air, Iran Air, JAL, Jet Airways, K.D. Air Corporation, Kenya Airways, KLM, Korean Air, Kuwait Airways, Kyrgyzstan Airlines, Lufthansa, Malaysia Airlines, Middle East Airlines, Northwest Airlines, Oman Air, Pakistan International Airlines, Qantas Airways, Qatar Airways, Royal Brunei Airlines, Royal Jordanian, Royal Nepal Airlines, Sahara India Airlines, SAS, Saudia, Singapore Airlines, South African Airways, Swissair, Syrian Arab Airlines, Tarom, Thai Airways International, United Airlines, UP Air, Uzbekiston Airways and Yemenia Yemen Airways.

In 1996 Bombay was the busiest airport, handling 10,747,282 passengers (6,363,158 on domestic flights) and 252,580 tonnes of freight, followed by Delhi, with 7,587,382 passengers (4,322,554 on domestic flights) and 201,241 tonnes of freight.

Shipping. In Oct. 1996, 481 ships totalling 7·02m. GRT were on the Indian Register. In Dec. 1995, 219 ships of 0·61m. GRT were engaged in coastal trade, and 251 ships of 6·3m. GRT in overseas trade. Traffic of major ports, 1996–97, was as follows:

Port	Cargo ships cleared	Unloaded (1m. tonnes)	Loaded (1m. tonnes)
Kandla	1,527	27·08	4·48
Bombay	2,583	18·38	15·35
Mormugao	507	4·77	18·41
New Mangalore	644	4·45	7·97
Cochin	787	8·54	2·09
Tuticorin	905	7·61	1·58
Madras	1,660	21·42	9·40
Visakhapatnam	1,437	14·67	13·28
Paradip	556	3·89	7·72
Haldia	946 }	11·99	5·06
Calcutta	822 }		
Jawaharlal Nehru	601	4·68	3·39

There are about 3,700 km of major rivers navigable by motorized craft, of which 2,000 km are used. Canals, 4,300 km, of which 900 km are navigable by motorized craft.

Telecommunications. The telephone system is in the hands of the Telecommunications Department, except in Delhi and Bombay, served by public corporation. Main telephone lines numbered 17,801,700 in 1997, equivalent to 18·6 for every 1,000 persons. There were 136,000 cellular phone subscribers in 1995, 1·2m. PCs and 50,000 fax machines. In April 1996 the Telecommunications Department had 417 telex exchanges. There were approximately 500,000 Internet users in Nov. 1998.

Postal Services. On 31 March 1995 there were 152,792 post offices and 42,766 telegraph offices. India has twice as many post offices as any other country. In 1995 a total of 13,751m. pieces of mail were processed, or 15 items per person.

SOCIAL INSTITUTIONS

Justice. All courts form a single hierarchy, with the Supreme Court at the head, which constitutes the highest court of appeal. Immediately below it are the High Courts and subordinate courts in each state. Every court in this chain administers the whole law of the country, whether made by Parliament or by the state legislatures.

The states of Andhra Pradesh, Assam (in common with Nagaland, Meghalaya, Manipur, Mizoram, Tripura and Arunachal Pradesh), Bihar, Gujarat, Himachal Pradesh, Jammu and Kashmir, Karnataka, Kerala, Madhya Pradesh, Maharashtra (in common with Goa and the Union Territories of Daman and Diu and Dadra and Nagar Haveli), Orissa, Punjab (in common with the state of Haryana and the Union Territory of Chandigarh), Rajasthan, Tamil Nadu (in common with the Union Territory of Pondicherry), Uttar Pradesh, West Bengal and Sikkim each have a High Court. There is a separate High Court for Delhi. For the Andaman and Nicobar Islands the Calcutta High Court, for Pondicherry the High Court of Madras and for Lakshadweep the High Court of Kerala are the highest judicial authorities. The Allahabad High Court has a Bench at Lucknow, the Bombay High Court has Benches at Nagpur, Aurangabad and Panaji, the Gauhati High Court has Benches at Kohima, Aizwal, Imphal and Agartala, the Madhya Pradesh High Court has Benches at Gwalior and Indore, the Patna High Court has a Bench at Ranchi and the Rajasthan High Court has a Bench at Jaipur. Judges and Division Courts of the Guwahati High Court also sit in Meghalaya. Similarly, judges and Division Courts of the Calcutta High Court also sit in the Andaman and Nicobar Islands. Below the High Court each state is divided into a number of districts under the jurisdiction of district judges who preside over civil courts and courts of sessions. There are a number of judicial authorities subordinate to the district civil courts. On the criminal side magistrates of various classes act under the overall supervision of the High Court.

The Code of Criminal Procedure came into force with effect from 1 April 1974. It provides for complete separation of the Judiciary from the Executive throughout India.

In Oct. 1991 the Supreme Court upheld capital punishment by hanging.

Police. The states control their own police forces. The Home Affairs Minister of the central government co-ordinates the work of the states. The Indian Police Service provides senior officers for the state police forces. The Central Bureau of Investigation functions under the control of the Cabinet Secretariat.

The cities of Pune, Ahmedabad, Nagpur, Bangalore, Calcutta, Madras, Bombay, Delhi and Hyderabad have separate police commissionerates.

Religion. India is a secular state; any worship is permitted, but the state itself has no religion. The principal religions in 1997 were: Hindus, 777m.; Sunni Moslems, 80m.; Shiah Moslems, 27m.; Sikhs, 19m.; Protestants, 18m.; Roman Catholics, 16m.; Buddhists, 7m.; Jains, 5m. Zoroastrian (Parsi), 140,000; Other, 19m.

Education. Adult literacy was 52% in 1995 (65·5% among males and 37·7% among females). Of the states and territories, Kerala and Chandigarh have the highest rates.

INDIA

Educational Organization. Education is the concurrent responsibility of state and Union governments. In the Union Territories it is the responsibility of the central government. The Union Government is also directly responsible for the central universities and all institutions declared by parliament to be of national importance; the promotion of Hindi as the federal language and co-ordinating and maintaining standards in higher education, research, science and technology. Professional education rests with the Ministry or Department concerned. There is a Central Advisory Board of Education to advise the Union and the State Governments on any educational question which may be referred to it.

School Education. The school system has 4 stages: Primary, middle, secondary and senior secondary.

Primary education is imparted either at independent primary (or junior basic) schools or primary classes attached to middle or secondary schools. The period of instruction varies from 4 to 5 years and the medium of instruction is in most cases the mother tongue of the child or the regional language. Free primary education is available for all children.

Legislation for compulsory education has been passed by some state governments and Union Territories but it is not practicable to enforce compulsion when the reasons for non-attendance are socio-economic. There are residential schools for country children.

The period for the middle stage varies from 2 to 3 years.

Higher Education. Higher education is given in arts, science or professional colleges, universities and all-India educational or research institutions. In 1995–96 there were 166 universities, 4 institutes established under state legislature act, 11 institutions of national importance and 37 institutions deemed as universities. Of the universities, 13 are central: Aligarh Muslim University; Banaras Hindu University; Delhi University; Hyderabad University; Jamia Millia Islamia, New Delhi; Jawaharlal Nehru University; North Eastern Hill University; Visva Bharati; Pondicherry University; Baba Sahib B. R. Ambedkar University; Assam University; Tezpur University and Nagaland University. The rest are state universities. Total enrolment at universities, 1995–96, 6,425,624, of which 5,667,400 were undergraduates. Women students numbered 2,191,138.

Grants are paid through the University Grants Commission to the central universities and institutions deemed to be universities for their maintenance and development and to state universities for their development projects only; their maintenance is the concern of state governments. During 1995–96 the University Grants Commission sanctioned grants of Rs 6,245·5m.

Technical Education. The number of institutions awarding degrees in engineering and technology in 1996–97 was 418, and those awarding diplomas, 1,029; the former admitted 328,399 students, the latter 357,891 including 58,454 female students.

Adult Education. The Directorate of Adult Education, established in 1971, is the national resource centre.

There is also a National Literacy Mission.

Educational statistics for 1996–97:

Type of recognized institution	No. of institutions	No. of students on rolls	No. of teachers
Primary/junior basic schools	598,354	110,393,406	1,789,733
Middle/senior basic schools	176,772	41,064,849	1,195,845
High/higher secondary schools[1]	102,183	27,036,856	1,542,360
Training schools and colleges	1,931	237,509	—
Arts, Science and Commerce colleges	6,759	6,425,624	239,488

[1]Including Junior Colleges.

Expenditure. Total budgeted central expenditure on revenue account of education and other departments 1997–98 is estimated at Rs 46,383m. Total public expenditure on education, sport, arts and youth welfare during the Eighth (1992–97) Plan, Rs 212,170·2m.; Seventh Plan spending on adult education, Rs 3,007m. in the central and Rs 6,098m. in the state sectors.

Health. Medical services are primarily the responsibility of the states. The Union Government has sponsored major schemes for disease prevention and control which are implemented nationally.

Total central expenditure on health and family welfare in 1997–98 was Rs 14,166·2m. on revenue account. In 1991 there were 15,067 hospitals, and in 1992, 410,875 doctors. In 1993 there were an estimated 1,364 people per hospital bed.

CULTURE

Broadcasting. In March 1997 there were 187 radio stations and 297 transmitters, 19 channels and 41 programme production centres. Television reached 85·8% of the population, through a network of 834 transmitters (colour by PAL). In 1996 there were estimated to be 99m. radio and 57·7m. TV sets.

Cinema. In 1996 there were nearly 13,000 cinemas and 683 feature films were certified. Attendances totalled 90–100m. per week. In 1990, 948 full length films were produced.

Press. There were 41,000 registered newspapers in March 1996, with a total circulation of 72·3m. In 1994 there were 369 dailies in 18 languages with a total circulation of 20m. Hindi papers have the highest number and circulation, followed by English, then Urdu, Bengali and Marathi.

Tourism. In 1996 there were 2,288,000 foreign tourists, spending US$3·03bn. Over 360,000 were from the UK, 229,000 from the USA and 107,000 from Sri Lanka.

DIPLOMATIC REPRESENTATIVES

Of India in Great Britain (India House, Aldwych, London, WC2B 4NA)
High Commissioner: Lalit Mansingh.

Of Great Britain in India (Chanakyapuri, New Delhi 1100021)
High Commissioner: Rob Young, CMG.

Of India in the USA (2107 Massachusetts Ave., NW, Washington, D.C., 20008)
Ambassador: Naresh Chandra.

Of the USA in India (Shanti Path, Chanakyapuri, New Delhi 110021)
Ambassador: Richard F. Celeste.

Of India to the United Nations
Ambassador: Kamalesh Sharma.

Of India to the European Union
Ambassador: Chandrashekhar Dasgupta.

FURTHER READING

Balasubramanyam, V. N., *The Economy of India*. London, 1985
Bardham, P., *The Political Economy of Development in India*. Oxford, 1984
Bhambhri, C. P., *The Political Process in India, 1947–91*. Delhi, 1991
Bose, S. and Jalal, A., (eds.) *Nationalism, Democracy and Development: State and Politics in India*. OUP, 1997
Brown, J., *Modern India: The Origins of an Asian Democracy*. 2nd ed. OUP, 1994
Derbyshire, I. D., *India* [Bibliography]. 2nd ed. Oxford and Santa Barbara (CA), 1995
Gupta, D. C., *Indian Government and Politics*. 3rd ed. London, 1992
Hall, A., *The Emergence of Modern India*. Columbia Univ. Press, 1981
The Indian Annual Register. Calcutta, from 1953
Jaffrelot, C. (ed.) *L'Inde Contemporain de 1950 à nos Jours*. Paris, 1996
Jalan, B., *India's Economic Crisis: the Way Ahead*. OUP, 1991
James, L., *Raj: The making and unmaking of British India*. Little, Brown, 1997
Joshi, V. and Little, I. M. D., *India's Economic Reforms, 1991–2000*. Oxford, 1996
Khilnani, S., *The Idea of India*. London, 1997
King, R., *Nehru and the Language Politics of India*. OUP, 1997
Kulke, H. and Rothermund, D., *A History of India*. rev. ed. London, 1990
Mehra, P., *A Dictionary of Modern Indian History, 1707–1947*. Delhi, 1987
Moon, P., *The British Conquest and Dominion of India*. London and Indiana Univ. Press, 1989
New Cambridge History of India. 2nd ed. 5 vols. CUP, 1994–96

Ray, R. K., *Industrialisation of India*. OUP, 1983
Smith, V. E., *Oxford History of India*. 3rd ed. OUP, 1958
Spear, P., *India: A Modern History*. 2nd ed. Univ. of Michigan Press, 1972
Vohra, R., *The Making of India: A Historical Survey*. Armonk (NY), 1997

Other more specialized titles are listed under CONSTITUTION AND GOVERNMENT and
RECENT ELECTIONS, *above.*

STATES AND TERRITORIES

The Republic of India is composed of the following 25 States and 7 centrally
administered Union Territories:

States	Capital	States	Capital
Andhra Pradesh	Hyderabad	Manipur	Imphal
Arunachal Pradesh	Itanagar	Meghalaya	Shillong
Assam	Dispur	Mizoram	Aizawl
Bihar	Patna	Nagaland	Kohima
Goa	Panaji	Orissa	Bhubaneswar
Gujarat	Gandhinagar	Punjab	Chandigarh
Haryana	Chandigarh	Rajasthan	Jaipur
Himachal Pradesh	Shimla	Sikkim	Gangtok
Jammu and Kashmir	Srinagar	Tamil Nadu	Madras
Karnataka	Bangalore	Tripura	Agartala
Kerala	Thiruvananthapuram	Uttar Pradesh	Lucknow
Madhya Pradesh	Bhopal	West Bengal	Calcutta
Maharashtra	Bombay		

Union Territories

Andaman and Nicobar Islands; Chandigarh; Dadra and Nagar Haveli; Daman and
Diu; Delhi; Lakshadweep; Pondicherry.

ANDHRA PRADESH

KEY HISTORICAL EVENTS

Constituted a separate state on 1 Oct. 1953, Andhra Pradesh was the undisputed
Telugu-speaking area of Madras. To this region was added, on 1 Nov. 1956, the
Telangana area of the former Hyderabad State, comprising the districts of
Hyderabad, Medak, Nizamabad, Karimnagar, Warangal, Khammam, Nalgonda and
Mahbubnagar, parts of the Adilabad district and some taluks of the Raichur,
Gulbarga and Bidar districts and some revenue circles of the Nanded district. On 1
April 1960, 221·4 sq. miles in the Chingleput and Salem districts of Madras were
transferred to Andhra Pradesh in exchange for 410 sq. miles from Chittoor district.
The district of Prakasam was formed on 2 Feb. 1970. Hyderabad was split into 2
districts on 15 Aug. 1978 (Ranga Reddy and Hyderabad). A new district,
Vizianagaram, was formed in 1979.

TERRITORY AND POPULATION

Andhra Pradesh is in south India and is bounded in the south by Tamil Nadu, west
by Karnataka, north and north-west by Maharashtra, north-east by Madhya Pradesh
and Orissa and east by the Bay of Bengal. The state has an area of 275,068 sq. km
and a population (1991 census) of 66·5m. Density, 242 per sq. km. The principal
language is Telugu. Cities with over 250,000 population (1991 census), *see* INDIA:
Territory and Population. Other large cities (1991): Nizamabad (241,034); Kurnool
(236,800); Ramagundam (214,384); Eluru (212,866); Anantapur (174,924); Tirupati
(174,369); Vizianagaram (160,359); Machilipatnam (159,110); Karimnagar
(148,583); Tenali (143,726); Adoni (136,182); Proddutur (133,914); Chittoor
(133,462); Khammam (127,992); Cuddapah (121,463); Bheemavaram (121,314).

SOCIAL STATISTICS

Growth rate 1981–91, 24·2%.

CONSTITUTION AND GOVERNMENT

Andhra Pradesh has a unicameral legislature; the Legislative Council was abolished in June 1985. There are 294 seats in the Legislative Assembly. For administrative purposes there are 23 districts in the state. The capital is Hyderabad.

RECENT ELECTIONS

At the elections of Dec. 1994, the Telugu Desam Party gained 224 seats; Congress (I), 25. Party composition, Feb. 1997: Telugu Desam, 216 seats; Congress (I), 26.

CURRENT ADMINISTRATION

Governor: Chakravarti Rangarajan.
Chief Minister: N. Chandrababu Naidu.

ECONOMY

Budget. Budget estimate, 1996–97: receipts on revenue account, Rs 114,516·3m.; expenditure, Rs 120,561·8m. Annual plan, 1997–98: Rs 35,330m.

ENERGY AND NATURAL RESOURCES

Electricity. There are 13 hydro-electric plants, 9 thermal stations and 2 gas-based units. Installed capacity, 1996–97, 6,800 MW, power generated 27,865m. kWh. In Nov. 1996 all 27,358 villages were electrified and 1·74m. electric pump sets energized.

Oil and Gas. Crude oil is refined at Visakhapatnam in Andhra Pradesh. Oil/gas structures are found in Krishna-Godavari basin which encompasses an area of 20,000 sq. km on land and 21,000 sq. km up to 200 metres isobath off-shore. Reserves of the land basin are estimated at 760 metric tonnes of oil and oil equivalent of gas.

Water. In 1997, 30 major and 75 medium irrigation projects had created irrigation potential of 5·7m. ha. The Telugu Ganga joint project with Tamil Nadu, now in execution, will irrigate about 233,000 ha, besides supplying drinking water to Madras city (Tamil Nadu).

Minerals. The state is an important producer of asbestos and barytes. Other important minerals are copper ore, coal, iron and limestone, steatite, mica and manganese.

Agriculture. There were (1996) about 13·4m. ha of cropped land, of which 8·2m. ha were under foodgrains. Irrigated area, 1996, 5·30m. ha. Production in 1996 (in tonnes): Foodgrains, 11·66m. (rice, 9·01m., wheat, 8,000); pulses, 0·77m.; sugar-cane, 15·16m.; oil seeds, 3·03m.

Livestock (1993): Cattle, 10·95m.; buffaloes, 9·13m.; goats, 4·32m.; sheep, 7·77m.

Forestry. In 1996–97 it was estimated that forests occupy 23·2% of the total area of the state, or 63,813 sq. km; main forest products are teak, eucalyptus, cashew, casuarina, softwoods and bamboo.

Fisheries. Production 1996–97, 152,047 tonnes of marine fish and 207,312 tonnes of inland water fish. The state has a coastline of 974 km.

INDUSTRY

The main industries are textile manufacture, sugar-milling machine tools, pharmaceuticals, electronic equipment, heavy electrical machinery, aircraft parts and paper-making. There is an oil refinery at Visakhapatnam, where India's major shipbuilding yards are situated. A major steel plant at Visakhapatnam and a railway repair shop at Tirupathi are functioning.

At 31 March 1997 there were 1,536 large and medium industries employing 644,480 persons, and 124,209 small-scale industries employing 1m.

There are cottage industries and sericulture. District Industries Centres have been set up to promote small-scale industry.

Tourism is growing; the main centres are Hyderabad, Nagarjunasagar, Warangal, Arakuvalley, Horsley Hills and Tirupathi.

COMMUNICATIONS

Roads. In 1996–97 there were 2,949 km of national highways, 43,763 km of state highways and 103,971 km of major district roads. Number of vehicles as of 31 March 1997 was 2,783,220, including 2,287,029 motor cycles and scooters, 177,516 cars and jeeps and 187,863 goods vehicles.

Rail. There are 5,073 route-km of railway.

Civil Aviation. There are airports at Hyderabad, Tirupathi, Vijayawada and Visakhapatnam, with regular scheduled services to Bombay, Delhi, Calcutta, Bangalore and Chennai (Madras). International flights are operated from Hyderabad to Kuwait, Muscat, Sharjah and Jeddah.

Shipping. The chief port is Visakhapatnam. There are minor ports at Kakinada, Machilipatnam, Bheemunipatnam, Narsapur, Krishnapatnam, Nizampatnam, Vadarevu and Kalingapatnam.

SOCIAL INSTITUTIONS

Justice. The high court of Judicature at Hyderabad has a Chief Justice and 28 puisne judges.

Religion. At the 1991 census Hindus numbered 59,281,950; Moslems, 5,923,954; Christians, 1,216,348; Jains, 26,564; Sikhs, 21,910; Buddhists, 22,153.

Education. In 1991, 44·09% of the population were literate (55·13% of men and 32·72% of women). There were, in 1996–97, 48,899 primary schools (7,898,481 students); 7,733 upper primary (2·30m.); 8,178 high schools (1,055,390). Education is free for children up to 14.

In 1995–96 there were 1,818 junior colleges (676,455 students). In 1996–97 there were 805 degree colleges (427,652 students); 46 oriented colleges and 13 universities: Osmania University, Hyderabad; Andhra University, Waltair; Sri Venkateswara University, Tirupathi; Kakatiya University, Warangal; Nagarjuna University, Guntur; Sri Jawaharlal Nehru Technological University, Hyderabad; Hyderabad University, Hyderabad; N. G. Ranga Agricultural University, Hyderabad; Sri Krishnadevaraya University, Anantapur; Smt. Padmavathi Mahila Vishwavidyalayam (University for Women), Tirupathi; Dr B. R. Ambedkar Open University, Hyderabad; Patti Sriramulu Telugu University, Hyderabad and N. T. R. University of Health Science, Vijayawada.

Health. There were (1996) 1,947 allopathic hospitals and dispensaries, 550 Ayurvedic hospitals and dispensaries, 193 Unani and 283 homeopathy hospitals and dispensaries. There were also 181 nature cure hospitals and (in 1996–97) 1,335 primary health centres. Number of beds in hospitals was 32,116.

ARUNACHAL PRADESH

KEY HISTORICAL EVENTS

Before independence the North East Frontier Agency of Assam was administered for the viceroy by a political agent working through tribal groups. After independence it became the North East Frontier Tract, administered for the central government by the Governor of Assam. In 1972 the area became the Union Territory of Arunachal Pradesh; statehood was achieved in Dec. 1986.

TERRITORY AND POPULATION

The state is in the extreme north-east of India and is bounded in the north by China, east by Myanmar, west by Bhutan and south by Assam and Nagaland. It has 13 districts and comprises the former frontier divisions of Kameng, Tirap, Subansiri, Siang and Lohit; it has an area of 83,743 sq. km and a population (1991 census) of 864,558; density, 10 per sq. km.

The state is mainly tribal; there are 106 tribes using about 50 tribal dialects.

SOCIAL STATISTICS

Growth rate 1981–91, 36·83%.

CONSTITUTION AND GOVERNMENT
There is a Legislative Assembly of 60 members. The capital is Itanagar (population, 1991, 16,545).

CURRENT ADMINISTRATION
Governor: Mata Prasad.
  Chief Minister: Mukut Mithi.

ECONOMY
Budget. Total estimated receipts, 1997–98, Rs 10,581m.; total estimated expenditure, Rs 10,302m. Plan outlay, 1997–98, Rs 6,000m.

ENERGY AND NATURAL RESOURCES
Electricity. Total installed capacity (1995–96), 43·85 MW. Power generated (1995–96): 70·8m. units. 2,188 out of 3,257 villages have electricity.

Oil and Gas. Production, 1995–96, 28,000 tonnes of crude oil and 32m. cu. metres of gas. Crude oil reserves are estimated at 30m. tonnes.

Minerals. Coal reserves are estimated at 90·23m. tonnes; dolomite, 154·13m. tonnes; limestone, 409·35m. tonnes.

Agriculture. Production of foodgrains, 1995–96, 230,200 tonnes.

Forestry. Area under forest, 51,540 sq. km; revenue from forestry (1995–96) Rs 402m.

INDUSTRY
In 1996 there were 18 medium and 3,306 small industries, 80 craft or weaving centres and 225 sericulture centres. Most of the medium industries are forest-based.

COMMUNICATIONS
Total length of roads in the state, 12,250 km of which 9,855 km are surfaced. There were 14,821 vehicles in 1995–96. The state has 330 km of national highway. 4 towns are linked by air services.

SOCIAL INSTITUTIONS
Religion. At the 1991 census Hindus numbered 320,212; Moslems, 11,922; Christians, 89,013; Buddhists, 111,372.

Education. In 1991, 41·59% of the population were literate (51·45% of men and 29·69% of women). There were (1996–97) 1,256 primary schools with 147,676 students, 301 middle schools with 42,197 students, 157 high and higher secondary schools with 24,951 students, 6 colleges and 2 technical schools. Arunachal University, established in 1985, had 4 colleges and 3,240 students in 1994–95.

Health. There are (1996) 13 hospitals, 10 community health centres, 42 primary health centres and 260 sub-centres. There are 2 TB hospitals and 11 leprosy and other hospitals. Total number of beds, 2,539.

ASSAM

KEY HISTORICAL EVENTS
Assam first became a British Protectorate at the close of the first Burmese War in 1826. In 1832 Cachar was annexed; in 1835 the Jaintia Hills were included in the East India Company's dominions, and in 1839 Assam was annexed to Bengal. In 1874 Assam was detached from Bengal and made a separate chief commissionership. On the partition of Bengal in 1905, it was united to the Eastern Districts of Bengal under a Lieut.-Governor. From 1912 the chief commissionership of Assam was revived, and in 1921 a governorship was created. On the partition of

India almost the whole of the predominantly Moslem district of Sylhet was merged with East Bengal (Pakistan). Dewangiri in North Kamrup was ceded to Bhutan in 1951. The Naga Hill district, administered by the Union Government since 1957, became part of Nagaland in 1962. The autonomous state of Meghalaya within Assam, comprising the districts of Garo Hills and Khasi and Jaintia Hills, came into existence on 2 April 1970, and achieved full independent statehood in Jan. 1972, when it was also decided to form a Union Territory, Mizoram (now a state), from the Mizo Hills district.

TERRITORY AND POPULATION

Assam is in north-east India, almost separated from central India by Bangladesh. It is bounded in the west by West Bengal, north by Bhutan and Arunachal Pradesh, east by Nagaland, Manipur and Myanmar, south by Meghalaya, Bangladesh, Mizoram and Tripura. The area of the state is now 78,438 sq. km. Population (census 1991) 22·4m. Density, 286 per sq. km. Principal towns with population (1991) are; Guwahati, 584,342; Dibrugarh, 125,667; Silchar, 115,483; Nagaon, 93,350; Tinsukia, 73,918; Dhubri, 66,216; Jorhat, 58,358; Tezpur, 55,084. The principal language is Assamese.

The central government is surveying the line of a proposed boundary fence to prevent illegal entry from Bangladesh.

SOCIAL STATISTICS

Growth rate 1981–91, 24·24%.

CONSTITUTION AND GOVERNMENT

Assam has a unicameral legislature of 126 members. The temporary capital is Dispur. The state has 23 districts.

RECENT ELECTIONS

In the 1996 elections an Asom Gana Parishad government was returned.

CURRENT ADMINISTRATION

Governor: Lt. Gen. (retd) S. K. Sinha.
   Chief Minister: Prafulla Kumar Mahanta.

ECONOMY

Budget. The budget estimates for 1997–98 showed receipts of Rs 72,312m. and expenditure of Rs 75,064·5m. Plan allocation, 1997–98, Rs 15,000m.

ENERGY AND NATURAL RESOURCES

Electricity. In 1996–97 there was an installed capacity of 597 MW. In March 1996, 21,887 villages (out of 21,995) had electricity. New power stations are under construction at Lakwa, and Karbi-Langpi hydro-electricity project.

Oil and Gas. Assam contains important oilfields and produces about 15% of India's crude oil. Production (1995–96): Crude oil, 5·04m. tonnes (including Nagaland); gas, 1,881m. cu. metres.

Water. Irrigation potential created up to 1994–95 was 0·67m. ha. 2 major and 10 medium projects were in hand.

Minerals. Coal production (1991), 982,000 tonnes. The state also has limestone, refractory clay, dolomite, and corundum.

Agriculture. There are 848 tea plantations, and growing tea is the principal industry. Production in 1990–91, 380m. kg, over 50% of Indian tea. Over 72% of the cultivated area is under food crops, of which the most important is rice. Total foodgrains, 1995–96, 3·56m. tonnes. Main cash crops: Jute, tea, cotton, oilseeds, sugar-cane, fruit and potatoes. Wheat production 95,100 tonnes in 1995–96; rice, 3·39m. tonnes; pulses, 57,100 tonnes. Cattle are important.

Forestry. In 1996 there were 18,242 sq. km of reserved forests under the administration of the Forest Department and 8,530 sq. km of unclassed forests, altogether about 39% of the total area of the state. Revenue from forests, 1993–94, Rs 213·1m.

INDUSTRY

Sericulture and hand-loom weaving, both silk and cotton, are important home industries together with the manufacture of brass, cane and bamboo articles. The main heavy industry is petro-chemicals; there are 3 oil refineries with 1 under construction in 1996. Other industries include manufacturing paper, nylon, electronic goods, cement, fertilizers, sugar, jute and plywood products, rice and oil milling.

There were 17,103 small-scale industries in 1994. The state in 1991 ran 480,622 enterprises employing 1·3m. persons.

COMMUNICATIONS

Roads. In March 1992 there were 65,605 km of road maintained by the Public Works Department. There were 2,033 km of national highway in 1990. There were 358,664 motor vehicles in the state in 1995–96.

Rail. The route km of railways in 1995–96 was 2,441 km.

Civil Aviation. Daily scheduled flights connect the principal towns with the rest of India. There are airports at Guwahati, Tezpur, Jorhat, North Lakhimpur, Silchar and Dibrugarh.

Shipping. Water transport is important in Lower Assam; the main waterway is the Brahmaputra River. Cargo carried in 1988–89 was 109,051 tonnes.

SOCIAL INSTITUTIONS

Justice. The seat of the High Court is Guwahati. It has a Chief Justice and 6 puisne judges.

Religion. At the 1991 census Hindus numbered 15,047,293; Moslems, 6,373,204; Christians, 744,367; Buddhists, 64,008; Jains, 20,645; Sikhs, 21,910.

Education. In 1991, 52·89% of the population were literate (61·87% of men and 43·03% of women). In 1996–97 there were 30,140 primary/junior basic schools with 3,816,603 students; 7,237 middle/senior basic schools with 1,304,504 students; 4,345 high/higher secondary schools with 664,422 students. There were 247 colleges for general education, 7 medical colleges, 3 engineering and 1 agricultural, 22 teacher-training colleges, and a fisheries college at Raha. There were 5 universities: Assam Agricultural University, Jorhat; Dibrugarh University, Dibrugarh with 86 colleges and 55,982 students (1992–93); Gauhati University, Guwahati with 128 colleges and 80,363 students (1992–93); and 2 central universities, at Silchar and Tezpur.

Health. In 1995–96 there were 161 hospitals (12,873 beds), 581 primary health centres and 316 dispensaries.

BIHAR

KEY HISTORICAL EVENTS

Bihar was part of Bengal under British rule until 1912 when it was separated together with Orissa. The two were joined until 1936 when Bihar became a separate province. As a state of the Indian Union it was enlarged in 1956 by the addition of land from West Bengal.

The state contains the ethnic areas of North Bihar, Santhal Pargana and Chota Nagpur. In 1956 certain areas of Purnea and Manbhum districts were transferred to West Bengal.

TERRITORY AND POPULATION

Bihar is in north India and is bounded north by Nepal, east by West Bengal, south by Orissa, south-west by Madhya Pradesh and west by Uttar Pradesh. The area of Bihar is 173,877 sq. km and its population (1991 census), 86,374,465, a density of 497 per sq. km. Population of principal towns, *see* INDIA: Territory and Population. Other large towns (1991): Muzaffarpur, 241,107; Darbhanga, 218,391; Biharsharif, 201,323; Arrah, 157,082; Dhanbad, 151,789; Munger, 150,112; Chapra, 136,877; Katihar, 154,367; Purnea, 114,912.

The state is divided into 14 divisions covering 55 districts. The capital is Patna.

The official language is Hindi (55·8m. speakers at the 1981 census), the second, Urdu (6·9m.), the third, Bengali (2m.).

SOCIAL STATISTICS

Growth rate 1981–91, 23·54%.

CONSTITUTION AND GOVERNMENT

Bihar has a bicameral legislature. The Legislative Assembly consists of 324 elected members, and the Council 96.

RECENT ELECTIONS

After the elections in 1995 the party composition of the Legislative Assembly was: Janata Dal, 31; Rashtriya Janata Dal, 136; Congress (I), 29; Bharatiya Janata Party, 41; Communist Party of India, 26; Jharkhand Mukti Morcha, 19; Communist-Marxist, 6; Samta Party, 6; Independent and others, 21.

CURRENT ADMINISTRATION

Governor: Sunder Singh Bhandari.
  Chief Minister: Rabri Devi.

ECONOMY

Budget. The budget estimates for 1997–98 showed total receipts of Rs 126,770m. and expenditure of Rs 121,216m. Plan allocation, 1997–98, Rs 22,000m.

ENERGY AND NATURAL RESOURCES

Electricity. Installed capacity (1996–97) 4,470 MW. Power generated (1994–95), 2,700m. kWh; there were (March 1996) 47,805 villages with electricity. Hydro-electric projects in hand will add about 149·2 MW capacity.

Minerals. Bihar is very rich in minerals, with about 40% of national production. There are huge deposits of copper, kyanite, coal, mica and china clay. Bihar is a principal producer of iron ore. Other important minerals: Manganese, limestone, graphite, chromite, asbestos, barytes, dolomite, bauxite, uranium ore, feldspar, columbite, pyrites, saltpetre, glass sands, slate, lead, silver, building stones and radioactive minerals. Revenue received from minerals (1994–95) Rs 7,039·3m.

Agriculture. The irrigated area was 4·13m. ha in 1993–94. Cultivable land, 11·6m. ha, of a total area of 17·4m. ha. Total cropped area, 1991–92, 9·79m. ha. Production (1995–96): Rice, 6·91m. tonnes; wheat, 4·18m.; total foodgrains, 13·07m. Other food crops are maize, rabi and pulses. Main cash crops are jute, sugar-cane, oilseeds, tobacco and potato.

Forests in 1995 covered 26,561 sq. km. There are 12 protected forests.

INDUSTRY

There are 28 industrial estates and 33 industrial areas. Iron and steel and aluminium are produced and there is an oil refinery. Other important industries are zinc and copper smelting, machine tools, fertilizers, electrical engineering, sugar-milling, paper-milling, silk-spinning, manufacturing explosives, chemicals and cement. There were 500 large and medium industries and 163,000 small and handicraft units in 1996–97.

COMMUNICATIONS

Roads. In March 1996–97 the state had 87,836 km of roads, including 2,118 km of national highway and 4,192 km of state highway, and 15,526 km of district roads. Passenger transport has been nationalized. There were 1,329,709 motor vehicles registered in March 1996.

Rail. The North Eastern, South Eastern and Eastern railways traverse the state; route-km, 1995–96, 5,283 km.

Civil Aviation. There are airports at Patna, Jamshedpur, Gaya and Ranchi with regular scheduled services to Calcutta and Delhi.

Shipping. The length of waterways open for navigation is 1,300 km.

SOCIAL INSTITUTIONS

Justice. There is a High Court (constituted in 1916) at Patna, and a bench at Ranchi, with a Chief Justice, 25 puisne judges and 4 additional judges.

Police. The police force is under a Director General of Police; in 1990 there were 1,097 police stations.

Religion. At the 1991 census Hindus numbered 71,193,417; Moslems, 12,787,985; Christians, 843,717; Sikhs, 78,212; Jains, 23,049; Buddhists, 3,518.

Education. At the census of 1991 the number of literate people was 26·85m. (38·48%: males, 52·49%; females, 22·89%). There were, 1996–97, 4,149 high and higher secondary schools with 1,080,321 pupils, 13,834 middle schools with 2·42m. pupils and 53,652 primary schools with 9,626,855 pupils. Education is free for children aged 6–11.

There were 14 universities in 1996–97: Patna University (founded 1917) with 14,699 students (1994–95); Bihar University, Muzaffarpur (1952) with 95 colleges, and 84,873 students (1989–90); Bhagalpur University (1960) with 140,718 students (1990–91); Ranchi University (1960) with 106 colleges, 55,731 students (1994–95); Kameswar Singh Darbhanga Sanskrit University (1961); Magadh University, Gaya (1962) with 186 colleges and 122,019 students (1994–95); Lalit Narayan Mithila University (1972), Darbhanga; Bisra Agricultural University, Ranchi (1980); Rajendra Agricultural University, Samastipur (1970); Nalanda Open University, Nalanda and 4 others. There were 742 degree colleges, 11 engineering colleges, 31 medical colleges and 15 teacher training colleges.

Health. In 1986 there were 1,289 hospitals and dispensaries with 28,997 beds in 1992.

CULTURE

Tourism. The main tourist centres are Bodh Gaya, Patna, Nalanda, Jamshedpur, Sasaram, Hazaribagh, Rajgir, Ranchi and Vaishali.

GOA

KEY HISTORICAL EVENTS

The coastal area was captured by the Portuguese in 1510 and the inland area was added in the 18th century. In Dec. 1961 Portuguese rule was ended and Goa incorporated into the Indian Union as a Territory together with Daman and Diu. Goa was granted statehood as a separate unit on 30 May 1987. Daman and Diu remained Union Territories.

TERRITORY AND POPULATION

Goa, bounded on the north by Maharashtra and on the east and south by Karnataka, has a coastline of 105 km. The area is 3,702 sq. km. Population, 1991 census,

INDIA

1,169,793. Density, 316 per sq. km. Mormugao is the largest town; population (urban agglomeration, 1991) 90,429. The capital is Panaji; population (urban agglomeration 1991) 85,515. The state has 2 districts. There are 183 village Panchayats. The languages spoken are Konkani (official language), Marathi, Hindi and English.

CONSTITUTION AND GOVERNMENT
The Indian Parliament passed legislation in March 1962 by which Goa became a Union Territory with retrospective effect from 20 Dec. 1961. On 30 May 1987 Goa attained statehood. It is represented by 3 elected representatives in Parliament. There is a Legislative Assembly of 40 members.

RECENT ELECTIONS
Elections were held in Nov. 1994.

CURRENT ADMINISTRATION
Governor: J. F. R. Jacob.
  Chief Minister: Luizinho Faleiro.

ECONOMY
Budget. The total budget for 1996–97 was Rs 11,756·8m. Annual plan 1997–98, Rs 2,300m.

ENERGY AND NATURAL RESOURCES
Electricity. In 1996 installed capacity was 0·16m. MW, but Goa receives most of its power supply from the states of Maharashtra and Karnataka. In March 1996, 377 out of 386 villages were electrified.

Minerals. Resources include bauxite, ferro-manganese ore and iron ore, all of which are exported. Iron ore production (1992–93) 12,435,334 tonnes. There are also reserves of limestone and clay.

Agriculture. Agriculture is the main occupation, important crops being rice, pulses, ragi, mango, cashew and coconuts. Area under rice (1995–96) 53,500 ha; production, 128,100 tonnes. Area under pulses 9,800 ha, sugar-cane 1,400 ha, groundnut 1,200 ha. Total production of foodgrains, 1995–96, 136,600 tonnes.
  Government poultry and dairy farming schemes produced 94m. eggs and 29,000m. litres of milk in 1992–93.

Forestry. Forests covered 1,250 sq. km in 1995.

Fisheries. Fish is the state's staple food. In 1995–96 the catch of seafish was 84,210 tonnes. There is a coastline of about 104 km and about 2,850 (1994–95) active fishing vessels.

INDUSTRY
In 1992–93 there were 52 large and medium industrial projects and 5,242 small units registered. Production included: Nylon fishing nets, ready made clothing, electronic goods, pesticides, pharmaceuticals, tyres, footwear, fertilizers, automotive components and shipbuilding.
  In 1992–93 the 5,242 small-scale industry units employed 32,597 persons.

COMMUNICATIONS
Roads. There were 7,419 km of roads in 1993–94 (National Highway, 224 km). Motor vehicles numbered 211,756 in March 1996.

Rail. In 1995–96 there were 79 km of route.

Civil Aviation. An airport at Dabolim is connected with Bombay, Delhi and Bangalore.

Shipping. There are seaports at Panaji, Marmugao and Margao.

SOCIAL INSTITUTIONS

Justice. There is a bench of the Bombay High Court at Panaji.

Religion. At the 1991 census Hindus numbered 756,651; Christians, 349,225; Moslems, 61,455; Sikhs, 1,087.

Education. In 1991, 75·51% of the population were literate (83·64% of men and 67·09% of women).

In 1996–97 there were 1,031 primary schools (126,425 students), 97 middle schools (77,275 students) and 445 high and higher secondary schools (73,216 students). There were also 2 engineering colleges, 4 medical colleges, 2 teacher-training colleges, 21 other colleges and 6 polytechnic institutes. Goa University, Taleigao (1985) had 33 colleges and 16,977 students in 1994–95.

Health. There were (1992–93) 129 hospitals (4,232 beds), 256 rural medical dispensaries, health and sub-health centres and 268 family planning units.

FURTHER READING
Hutt, A., *Goa: A Traveller's Historical and Architectural Guide.* Buckhurst Hill, 1988

GUJARAT

KEY HISTORICAL EVENTS
The Gujarati-speaking areas of India were part of the Moghul empire, coming under Mahratta domination in the late 18th century. In 1818 areas of present Gujarat around the Gulf of Cambay were annexed by the British East India Company. The remainder consisted of a group of small principalities, notably Baroda, Rajkot, Bhavnagar and Nawanagar. British areas became part of the Bombay Presidency.

At independence all the area now forming Gujarat became part of Bombay State except for Rajkot and Bhavnagar which formed the state of Saurashtra until incorporated in Bombay in 1956.

In 1960 Bombay State was divided and the Gujarati-speaking areas became Gujarat.

TERRITORY AND POPULATION
Gujarat is in western India and is bounded in the north by Pakistan and Rajasthan, east by Madhya Pradesh, south-east by Maharashtra, south and west by the Indian ocean and Arabian sea. The area of the state is 196,024 sq. km and the population at the 1991 census was 41,309,582; a density of 211 per sq. km. The chief cities, *see* INDIA: Territory and Population. Other important towns (1991) are: Nadiad (167,051), Bharuch (133,102), Junagadh (130,484), Navsari (126,089), Gandhinagar (123,359), Porbandar (116,671), Anand (110,266), Gandhidham (104,585) and Bhuj (102,376). Gujarati and Hindi in the Devanagari script are the official languages.

SOCIAL STATISTICS
Growth rate 1981–91, 21·19%.

CLIMATE
Summers are intensely hot: 31–42°C. Winters: 8–15°C. Monsoon Season: 7–10°C. Annual rainfall: Over 100 cm.

CONSTITUTION AND GOVERNMENT
Gujarat has a unicameral legislature, the *Legislative Assembly*, which has 182 elected members.

The capital is Gandhinagar. There are 25 districts.

RECENT ELECTIONS
After the elections in Feb. 1997 the Bharatiya Janata Party came to power. Party composition of the Legislative Assembly in Dec. 1998: Bharatiya Janata Party, 115 seats; Maha-Gujarat Janata Party, 4; Congress, 53; independents and others, 8; vacant seats, 2.

CURRENT ADMINISTRATION
Governor: Shri Anshuman Singh.
  Chief Minister: Shri Keshubhai S. Patel.

Local Government. At Dec. 1998 there were 13,507 *Gram Panchayats*, 230 *Taluka Panchayats*, 25 District *Panchayats*, 143 Municipalities and 6 Municipal Corporations.

ECONOMY
Budget. The budget estimates for 1998–99 showed revenue receipts of Rs 130,818m. and revenue expenditure of Rs 127,670m. Plan outlay for 1998–99, Rs 54,500m.

Banking and Finance. At June 1997 there were 3,532 commercial banks in the State with combined deposits of Rs 297,620m. Total credit advanced was Rs 140,940m.

ENERGY AND NATURAL RESOURCES
Electricity. In Sept. 1998 total installed capacity was 6,630 MW. In March 1998, 17,885 villages were electrified.

Oil and Gas. There are large crude oil and gas reserves. Production, 1995–96: Crude oil, 5·1m. tonnes; gas, 2,038m. cu. metres.

Water. Water resources are limited. In 1997 irrigation potential was 6·49m. ha.

Minerals. Chief minerals produced in 1996–97 (in tonnes) included limestone (11·8m.), agate stone (388), calcite (110), quartz and silica (252,000), bauxite (744,000), crude china clay (37,397), refined china clays (9,002), dolomite (410,000), crude fluorite (106,000), calcareous and sea sand (92,000) and lignite (5·1m.). Value of production (1996–97) Rs 28,312m. Reserves of coal lie under the Kalol and Mehsana oil and gas fields. The deposit, mixed with crude petroleum, is estimated at 100,000m. tonnes.

Agriculture. 3·7m. ha of the cropped area was irrigated in June 1997.
  Production of principal crops, 1996–97: Rice, 0·95m. tonnes from 642,000 ha; foodgrains, 5·2m. tonnes (wheat, 1·32m. tonnes); pulses (1995–96), 457,000 tonnes; cotton, 2·7m. bales of 170 kg. Tobacco and groundnuts are important cash crops.
  Livestock (1992): Buffaloes, 5·27m.; other cattle, 6·8m.; sheep and goats, 6·27m.; horses and ponies (1988), 16,015.

Forestry. Forests covered 19,393 sq. km in 1999 (9·09% of total area). The State has 4 National Parks and 21 sanctuaries.

Fisheries. There were (1997) 140,208 people engaged in fisheries. In 1996–97 there were 23,522 fishing vessels (14,671 motor vessels). The catch for 1996–97 was 725,000 tonnes.

INDUSTRY
Gujarat is one of the 4 most industrialized states. In 1996 there were 207,946 small-scale units and (1997) 20,050 factories including 1,250 cotton textile factories, 3,000 chemical and chemical products factories, 1,970 non-metallic mineral products factories, 1,825 machinery, machine tools and parts factories and 1,200 rubber, plastic, petroleum and coal products factories. There were 280 industrial estates in 1997. Principal industries are textiles, general and electrical engineering, oil-refining, fertilizers, petrochemicals, machine tools, automobiles, heavy chemicals,

pharmaceuticals, dyes, sugar, soda ash, cement, man-made fibres, salt, sulphuric acid, paper and paperboard.

State production of soda-ash (1997) was 177,000 tonnes. Salt production (1997) 10·07m. tonnes; cement, 6·84m. tonnes.

COMMUNICATIONS

Roads. In 1996–97 there were 72,165 km of roads. Gujarat State Transport Corporation operated 18,152 routes. Number of vehicles, Oct. 1997, 4,018,233.

Rail. In 1996–97 the state had 5,322 route km of railway line.

Civil Aviation. Ahmedabad is the main airport. There are regular services between Ahmedabad and Bombay, Jaipur and Delhi. There are 9 other airports: Bhavnagar, Bhuj, Jamnagar, Kandla, Keshod, Porbandar, Rajkot, Surat and Vadodara.

Shipping. The largest port is Kandla. There are 40 other ports, of which 11 are intermediate and 29 minor.

Telecommunications. There were 1,078,616 telephone connections in the state in 1996–97.

Postal Services. There were (1996–97) 8,962 post offices and 1,770 telegraph offices.

SOCIAL INSTITUTIONS

Justice. The High Court of Judicature at Ahmedabad has a Chief Justice and 30 puisne judges.

Religion. At the 1991 census Hindus numbered 36,964,228; Moslems, 3,606,920; Jains, 491,331, Christians, 181,753; Sikhs, 33,044; Buddhists, 11,615.

Education. In 1991 the number of literate people was 21·28m. (60·91%; male, 72·45%, female 48·5%). Primary and secondary education up to Standard XI are free. Education above Standard XII is free for girls. In 1996–97 there were 33,822 primary schools with 7·34m. students and 5,767 secondary schools with 1,924,000 students.

There are 10 universities in the state. Gujarat University, Ahmedabad, founded in 1950, is teaching and affiliating; it has 157 affiliated colleges. The Maharaja Sayajirao University of Vadodara (1949) is residential and teaching; it has 13 colleges and 26,756 students (1996–97). The Sardar Patel University, Vallabh-Vidyanagar, (1955) has 20 constituent and affiliated colleges; Saurashtra University at Rajkot (1968) has 122 affiliated colleges and 64,754 students (1996–97); South Gujarat University at Surat (1967) has 60 colleges. Bhavnagar University (1978) is residential and teaching with 16 affiliated colleges. North Gujarat University was established at Patan in 1986 and has 68 colleges. Gujarat Vidyapith at Ahmedabad is deemed a university under the University Grants Commission Act. There are also Gujarat Agricultural University, Banaskantha and Gujarat Ayurved University, Jamnagar.

There are 16 engineering and technical colleges, 25 polytechnics, 42 medical colleges and 9 agricultural colleges. There are also 309 arts, science and commerce colleges, 421 teacher-training colleges and 31 law colleges. There were 0·4m. students enrolled in 1993–94 in all colleges.

Health. At March 1998 there were 960 primary health centres and 7,274 sub-centres. There were 25 general hospitals, 23 college hospitals and 21 Taluka-level hospitals. In 1994, 31·37m. patients were treated.

CULTURE

Press. At March 1998 there were 115 dailies, 860 weeklies, 111 biweeklies, 448 monthlies and 29 other periodicals published.

Tourism. There are many sights of religious pilgrimage as well as archaeological sights, attractive beaches, the Lion Sanctuary of Gir Forest and the Wild Ass Sanctuary in Kachchh. Mahatma Ghandi's birthplace at Porbandar is also a popular tourist attraction.

Festivals. Tarnetar Fair (Surendranagar district) is held in Aug./Sept. Madhavraj Fair (Junagadh district) is celebrated in March/April, Ambaji Fair (Banaskantha district) is dedicated to Amba, mother goddess. There are numerous other festivals throughout the region.

FURTHER READING
Desai, I. F., *Untouchability in Rural Gujarat.* Bombay, 1977

HARYANA

KEY HISTORICAL EVENTS
The state of Haryana, created on 1 Nov. 1966 under the Punjab Reorganization Act, 1966, was formed from the Hindi-speaking parts of the state of Punjab (India). It comprises the districts of Hissar, Mahendragarh, Gurgaon, Rohtak, Yamunanagar, Rewari, Kaithal, Karnal; Bhiwani, Faridabad, Jind, Kurukshetra, Sirsa, Sonipat, Ambala.

TERRITORY AND POPULATION
Haryana is in north India and is bounded north by Himachal Pradesh, east by Uttar Pradesh, south and west by Rajasthan and north-west by Punjab. Delhi forms an enclave on its eastern boundary. The state has an area of 44,212 sq. km and a population (1991) of 16,463,648; density, 372 per sq. km. Principal cities, *see* INDIA: Territory and Population. Other large towns (1991) are: Rohtak (216,096), Panipat (191,212), Hisar (181,255), Karnal (173,751), Yamunanagar (144,346), Sonipat (143,922), Ambala (139,889), Gurgaon (135,884), Bhiwani (121,629) and Sirsa (112,841). The principal language is Hindi.

SOCIAL STATISTICS
Growth rate 1981–91, 27·41%.

CONSTITUTION AND GOVERNMENT
The state has a unicameral legislature with 90 members. The capital (shared with Punjab) is Chandigarh. Its transfer to Punjab, intended for 1986, has been postponed. There are 19 districts.

RECENT ELECTIONS
After the 1996 elections Haryana Vikas Party held 32 seats; Samata Party, 24; Bharatiya Janata, 11; Congress (I), 9; independents and others, 13; vacant, 1. The state shares with Punjab (India) a High Court, a university and certain public services.

CURRENT ADMINISTRATION
Governor: Mahabir Prasad.
 Chief Minister: Bansi Lal.

ECONOMY
Budget. Budget estimates for 1997–98 show revenue income of Rs 74,426m. and revenue expenditure of Rs 81,560m. Annual plan 1997–98, Rs 15,750m.

ENERGY AND NATURAL RESOURCES
Electricity. Approximately 1,000 MW are supplied to Haryana, mainly from the Bhakra Nangal system. In 1996–97 installed capacity was 2,382 MW and all the villages had electric power.

Minerals. Minerals include placer gold, barytes and rare earths. Value of production, 1987–88, Rs 40m.

Agriculture. Haryana has sandy soil and erratic rainfall, but the state shares the benefit of the Sutlej-Beas scheme. Agriculture employs over 82% of the working population; in 1981 there were about 0·9m. holdings (average 3·7 ha), and the gross irrigated area was 2·05m. ha in 1993–94. Area under foodgrains, 1995–96, 4·02m. ha. Foodgrain production, 1995–96, 10·21m. tonnes (rice 1·86m. tonnes; wheat 7·35m. tonnes); pulses, 416,400 tonnes; cotton, 1·5m. bales of 170 kg; sugar (gur) and oilseeds are important.

Forestry. Forests covered 603 sq. km in 1995.

INDUSTRY
Haryana has a large market for consumer goods in neighbouring Delhi. In 1996–97 there were 916 large and medium scale industries and 138,759 small units providing employment to about 1m. persons, and 56,012 rural industrial units. The main industries are cotton textiles, agricultural machinery and tractors, woollen textiles, scientific instruments, glass, cement, paper and sugar milling, cars, tyres and tubes, motor cycles, bicycles, steel tubes, engineering goods, electrical and electronic goods. An oil refinery is being set up at Panipat.

COMMUNICATIONS
Roads. There were (1996–97) 22,757 km of metalled roads, linking all villages. Road transport is nationalized. There were 954,563 motor vehicles in 1995–96. Road transport carried 1·65m. passengers daily in 1996–97 with a fleet of 3,818 buses.

Rail. The state is crossed by lines from Delhi to Agra, Ajmer, Ferozepur and Chandigarh. Route km, 1995–96, 1,452 km. The main stations are at Ambala and Kurukshetra.

Civil Aviation. There is no airport within the state but Delhi is on its eastern boundary.

SOCIAL INSTITUTIONS
Justice. Haryana shares the High Court of Punjab and Haryana at Chandigarh.

Religion. At the 1991 census Hindus numbered 14,686,512; Moslems, 763,775; Sikhs, 956,836; Christians, 15,699; Jains, 35,296.

Education. In 1991 the number of literate people was 7·43m. (55·85%); 69·1% of men and 40·47% of women. In 1996–97 there were 5,651 primary schools with 1,981,993 students, 3,233 high and higher secondary schools with 511,377 students, 1,631 middle schools with 832,886 students and 129 colleges of arts, science and commerce, 9 engineering and technical colleges and 10 medical colleges. There are 3 universities: Haryana Agricultural University, Hisar; Kurukshetra University, Kurukshetra with 70 colleges and 70,000 students (1993–94); and Maharshi Dayanand University, Rohtak.

Health. There were (1996–97) 111 hospitals (11,061 beds) and community health centres, 399 primary health centres and 2,416 sub-centres, and 442 Ayurvedic and Unani institutions.

HIMACHAL PRADESH

KEY HISTORICAL EVENTS
Thirty small hill states were merged to form the Territory of Himachal Pradesh in 1948; the state of Bilaspur was added in 1954 and parts of the Punjab in 1966. The whole territory became a state in Jan. 1971. The state is a Himalayan area of hill-tribes, rivers and forests. Its main component areas are Chamba, a former princely state, dominated in turn by Moghuls and Sikhs before coming under British influence in 1848; Bilaspur, an independent Punjab state until it was invaded by Gurkhas in 1814 (the British East India Company forces drove out the Gurkhas in 1815); Simla district around the town built by the Company near Bilaspur on land reclaimed from Gurkha troops (the summer capital of India from 1865 until 1948);

Mandi, a princely state until 1948; Kangra and Kulu districts, originally Rajput areas which had become part of the British-ruled Punjab; they were incorporated into Himachal Pradesh in 1966 when the Punjab was reorganized.

TERRITORY AND POPULATION
Himachal Pradesh is in north India and is bounded north by Kashmir, east by Tibet, south-east by Uttar Pradesh, south by Haryana, south-west and west by Punjab. The area of the state is 55,673 sq. km and it had a population at the 1991 census of 5,170,877. Density, 93 per sq. km. Principal languages are Hindi and Pahari. The capital is Shimla, population (1991 census) of the urban agglomeration, 110,360.

SOCIAL STATISTICS
Growth rate 1981–91, 20·79%.

CONSTITUTION AND GOVERNMENT
Full statehood was attained, as the 18th State of the Union, on 25 Jan. 1971. On 1 Sept. 1972 districts were reorganized and 3 new districts created, Solan, Hamirpur and Una, making a total of 12.

There is a unicameral *Legislative Assembly.*

RECENT ELECTIONS
After the elections in Nov. 1993 a Congress (I) government came to power. Total seats, 68: Congress (I), 52; Bharatiya Janata Party, 8; others, 8. The Legislative Assembly was dissolved on 25 Dec. 1997 and new elections ordered.

CURRENT ADMINISTRATION
Governor: V. S. Rama Devi.
Chief Minister: Prem Kumar Dhumal.

ECONOMY
Budget. Budget estimates for 1997–98 showed receipts of Rs 27,064·2m. and expenditure of Rs 28,905·4m. Annual plan, 1997–98, Rs 10,080m.

ENERGY AND NATURAL RESOURCES
Electricity. All 16,807 villages have electricity. Installed capacity (1995–96), 288·7 MW. Electricity generated (1995–96), 1,286m. kWh.

Water. An artificial confluence of the Sutlej and Beas rivers has been made, directing their united flow into Govind Sagar Lake. Other major rivers are Ravi, Chenab and Yamuna.

Minerals. The state has rock salt, slate, gypsum, limestone, barytes, dolomite and pyrites.

Agriculture. Farming employs 71% of the people. Irrigated area is 17% of the area sown. There are 1,660 tea planters cultivating 2,000 ha. Main crops are seed potatoes, wheat, maize, rice and fruits such as apples, peaches, apricots, nuts and pomegranates; 0·35m. tonnes of fruits were produced in 1996–97.

Production (1994–95): Rice, 112,200 tonnes; wheat, 412,800 tonnes; pulses, 10,300 tonnes. Total foodgrains, 1·21m. tonnes.

Livestock (1992 census): Buffaloes, 701,000; other cattle, 2,152,000; goats and sheep, 2·19m.

Forestry. Himachal Pradesh forests cover 63·8% of the state and supply the largest quantities of coniferous timber in northern India. The forests also ensure the safety of the catchment areas of the Yamuna, Sutlej, Beas, Ravi and Chenab rivers. Commercial felling of green trees has been totally halted and forest working nationalized. Area under forests in 1995–96, 35,318 sq. km, of which 1,896 sq. km are reserved and 31,541 sq. km are protected.

INDUSTRY

The main sources of employment are the forests and their related industries; there are factories making turpentine and rosin. The state also makes fertilizers, cement, electronic items and TV sets. There is a foundry and a brewery. Other industries include salt production and handicrafts, including weaving. The state has 161 large and medium units, 25,000 small scale units, 5 industrial estates, 10 industrial areas and 7 electronic complexes.

COMMUNICATIONS

Roads. The national highway from Chandigarh runs through Shimla; other main highways from Shimla serve Kullu, Manali, Kangra, Chamba and Pathankot. The rest are minor roads. Pathankot is also on national highways from Punjab to Kashmir. Length of roads (March 1996), 24,665 km; number of vehicles (1995–96), 119,037; number of transport buses (1995–96), 1,692.

Rail. There is a line from Chandigarh to Shimla, and the Jammu-Delhi line runs through Pathankot. A Nangal-Talwara rail link has been approved by the central government. There are 2 narrow gauge lines, from Shimla to Kalka (96 km) and Jogindernagar to Pathankot (113 km), and a broad gauge line from Una to Nangal (16 km). Route-km in 1995–96, 266 km.

Civil Aviation. The state has airports at Bhuntar near Kullu, at Jubbarhatti near Shimla and at Gaggal in Kangra district.

SOCIAL INSTITUTIONS

Justice. The state has its own High Court at Shimla.

Religion. At the 1991 census Hindus numbered 4,958,560; Moslems, 89,134; Sikhs, 52,050; Buddhists, 64,081; Christians, 4,435.

Education. In 1991, 63·86% of the population were literate (75·36% of men and 52·32% of women). There were (1996–97) 7,732 primary schools with 728,870 students, 1,037 middle schools with 371,622 students, 1,228 high and higher secondary schools with 271,596 students, 62 (including 18 private) arts, science and commerce colleges, 1 engineering college, 2 medical colleges, 1 teacher training college and 3 universities. The universities are Himachal Pradesh University, Shimla (1970) with 48 affiliated colleges and 32,773 students (1992–93), Himachal Pradesh Agricultural University, Palampur (1978) and Dr Y. S. Parmar University of Horticulture and Forestry, Solan (1985).

Health. There were (Dec. 1996) 80 hospitals (9,525 beds), 286 primary and community health centres and 1,831 sub-health centres, and 838 allopathic and Ayurvedic dispensaries.

JAMMU AND KASHMIR

KEY HISTORICAL EVENTS

The state of Jammu and Kashmir, which had earlier been under Hindu rulers and Moslem sultans, became part of the Mogul Empire under Akbar from 1586. After a period of Afghan rule from 1756, it was annexed by the Sikh rulers of the Punjab in 1819. In 1820 Ranjit Singh made over the territory of Jammu to Gulab Singh. After the decisive battle of Sobraon in 1846 Kashmir also was made over to Gulab Singh under the Treaty of Amritsar. British supremacy was recognized until the Indian Independence Act, 1947, when all states decided on accession to India or Pakistan. Kashmir asked for standstill agreements with both. Pakistan agreed, but India desired further discussion with the Government of Jammu and Kashmir State. In the meantime the state became subject to armed attack from the territory of Pakistan and the Maharajah acceded to India on 26 Oct. 1947 by signing the Instrument of Accession. India approached the UN in Jan. 1948; India-Pakistan conflict ended by ceasefire in Jan. 1949. Further conflict in 1965 was followed by the Tashkent Declaration of Jan. 1966. Following further hostilities between India and Pakistan a ceasefire came into effect on 17 Dec. 1971, followed by the Simla Agreement in July 1972, whereby a new line of control was delineated bilaterally through negotiations between India and Pakistan and came into force on 17 Dec. 1972.

TERRITORY AND POPULATION
The state is in the extreme north and is bounded north by China, east by Tibet, south by Himachal Pradesh and Punjab and west by Pakistan. The area is 222,236 sq. km, of which about 78,932 sq. km is occupied by Pakistan and 42,735 sq. km by China; the population of the territory on the Indian side of the line, 1991 projection, was 7,718,700. Srinagar (population, 1991, 892,506) is the summer and Jammu (1,207,996) the winter capital. The official language is Urdu; other commonly spoken languages are Kashmiri (3·1m. speakers at 1981 census), Hindi (1m.), Dogri, Gujri, Pahari, Ladakhi and Punjabi.

SOCIAL STATISTICS
Growth rate 1981–91, 28·92%.

CONSTITUTION AND GOVERNMENT
The Maharajah's son, Yuvraj Karan Singh, took over as Regent in 1950 and, on the ending of hereditary rule (17 Oct. 1952), was sworn in as Sadar-i-Riyasat. On his father's death (26 April 1961) Yuvraj Karan Singh was recognized as Maharajah by the Indian Government. The permanent Constitution of the state came into force in part on 17 Nov. 1956 and fully on 26 Jan. 1957. There is a bicameral legislature; the Legislative Council has 36 members and the Legislative Assembly has 87. Since the 1967 elections the 6 representatives of Jammu and Kashmir in the central House of the People are directly elected; there are 4 representatives in the Council of States. After a period of President's rule, a National Conference–Indira Congress coalition government was formed in March 1987. The government was dismissed and the state was brought under President's rule on 18 July 1990.

The state has 14 districts.

RECENT ELECTIONS
Elections were held in Sept.-Oct. 1996 and National Conference formed a government. Total seats, 87: National Conference, 57; Bharatiya Janata Party, 8; Congress (I), 7; Janata Dal, 5; Independent and others, 10.

CURRENT ADMINISTRATION
Governor: Girish Chandra Saxena.
Chief Minister: Dr Farooq Abdullah.

ECONOMY
Budget. Budget estimates for 1997–98 show total receipts of Rs 53,628·9m. and total expenditure of Rs 52,748·1m. Annual Plan (1997–98) Rs 15,500m.

ENERGY AND NATURAL RESOURCES
Electricity. Installed capacity (1996–97) 365·8 MW; 6,252 villages had electricity in 1995–96.

Minerals. Minerals include coal, bauxite and gypsum.

Agriculture. About 80% of the population are supported by agriculture. Rice, wheat and maize are the major cereals. The total area under foodgrains (1995–96) was estimated at 887,000 ha. Total foodgrains produced, 1995–96, 1·37m. tonnes (rice, 0·51m. tonnes; wheat, 0·35m. tonnes); pulses, 22,900 tonnes. Fruit is important: Production, 1994–95, 0·9m. tonnes; exports, 0·76m. tonnes.

Irrigated area, 1993–94, 442,000 ha.

Livestock (1982): Cattle, 2,325,200; buffaloes, 5,631,000; goats, 1,003,900; sheep, 1,908,700; horses, 973,000; and poultry, 2,406,760.

Forestry. Forests cover about 20,443 sq. km (1995), forming an important source of revenue, besides providing employment to a large section of the population.

INDUSTRY
There are 2 central public sector industries and 30 medium-scale. There are 35,576 small units (1994–95) employing over 125,000. There are industries based on horticulture; traditional handicrafts are silk spinning, wood-carving, papier mâché and carpet-weaving. 750 tonnes of silk cocoons were produced in 1994–95.

The handicraft sector employed 0·26m. persons and had a production turnover of Rs 2,500m. in 1995–96.

COMMUNICATIONS

Roads. Kashmir is linked with the rest of India by the motorable Jammu-Pathankot road. The Jawahar Tunnel, through the Banihal mountain, connects Srinagar and Jammu, and maintains road communication with the Kashmir Valley during the winter months. In 1994–95 there were 12,252 km of roads.

There were 195,125 motor vehicles in 1995–96.

Rail. Kashmir is linked with the Indian railway system by the line between Jammu and Pathankot; route km of railways in the state, 1995–96, 88 km.

Civil Aviation. Major airports, with daily service from Delhi, are at Srinagar and Jammu. There is a third airport at Leh.

Telecommunications. There were 202 telephone exchanges and 54,644 telephones in 1994–95.

Postal Services. There were 1,583 post offices in 1994.

SOCIAL INSTITUTIONS

Justice. The High Court, at Srinagar and Jammu, has a Chief Justice and 4 puisne judges.

Religion. The majority of the population, except in Jammu, are Moslems. At the 1981 census Moslems numbered 3,843,451; Hindus, 1,930,448; Sikhs, 133,675; Buddhists, 69,706; Christians, 8,481; Jains, 1,576.

Education. The proportion of literate people was 32·68% in 1991 (44·18% of men and 19·55% of women). Education is free. There were (1996–97) 1,351 high and higher secondary schools with 227,699 students, 3,104 middle schools with 405,598 students and 10,483 primary schools with 893,005 students. Jammu University (1969) has 5 constituent and 13 affiliated colleges, with 15,278 students (1992–93); Kashmir University (1948) has 18 colleges (17,000 students, 1992–93); the third university is Sher-E-Kashmir University of Agricultural Sciences and Technology. There are 4 medical colleges, 2 engineering and technology colleges, 4 polytechnics, 8 oriental colleges and an Ayurvedic college, 34 arts, science and commerce colleges and 4 teacher training colleges.

Health. In 1993–94 there were 43 hospitals with 9,256 beds, 264 primary health centres and 1,740 sub-centres, and 35 community health centres. There is a National Institute of Medical Sciences.

FURTHER READING
Lamb, A., *Kashmir: a Disputed Legacy, 1846–1990.* Hertingfordbury, 1991.
Wirsing, R. G., *India, Pakistan and the Kashmir Dispute: on Regional Conflict and its Resolution.* London, 1995

KARNATAKA

KEY HISTORICAL EVENTS
The state of Karnataka, constituted as Mysore under the States Reorganization Act, 1956, brought together the Kannada-speaking people distributed in 5 states, and consisted of the territories of the old states of Mysore and Coorg, the Bijapur,

Kanara and Dharwar districts and the Belgaum district (except one taluk) in former Bombay, the major portions of the Gulbarga, Raichur and Bidar districts in former Hyderabad, the South Kanara district (apart from the Kasaragod taluk) and the Kollegal taluk of the Coimbatore district in Madras. The state was renamed Karnataka in 1973.

TERRITORY AND POPULATION

The state is in south India and is bounded north by Maharashtra, east by Andhra Pradesh, south by Tamil Nadu and Kerala, west by the Indian ocean and north-east by Goa. The area of the state is 191,791 sq. km, and its population (1991 census), 44,977,201, an increase of 21·82% since 1981. Density, 235 per sq. km. Principal cities, *see* INDIA: Territory and Population. The capital is Bangalore. Other large towns (1991) are: Bellary (245,391), Bijapur (186,939), Shimoga (178,882), Raichur (157,551), Timkur (138,903), Gadag-Betigeri (134,051), Mandya (120,265), Hospet (114,154) and Bidar (108,016).

Kannada is the language of administration and is spoken by about 66% of the people. Other languages include Telugu (8·17%), Urdu (9%), Marathi (4·5%), Tamil (3·6%), Tulu and Konkani.

CONSTITUTION AND GOVERNMENT

Karnataka has a bicameral legislature. The Legislative Council has 75 members. The Legislative Assembly consists of 224 elected members.

The state has 20 districts grouped in 4 divisions: Bangalore, Belgaum, Gulbarga and Mysore.

RECENT ELECTIONS

At the elections in Nov. 1994 the Janata Dal gained 116 seats; the Bharatiya Janata Party, 40; Congress (I), 35; the Karnataka Congress Party, 10; independents and others, 23. Janata Dal formed a government.

CURRENT ADMINISTRATION

Governor: Khurshid Alam Khan.
  Chief Minister: J. H. Patel.

ECONOMY

Budget. Budget estimates, 1997–98: Revenue receipts, Rs 117,664·5m.; revenue expenditure, Rs 119,654·5m. Plan allocation 1997–98, Rs 41,300m.

ENERGY AND NATURAL RESOURCES

Electricity. In 1995–96 the state's installed capacity was 3,377·5 MW. Electricity generated, 1994–95, 16,830m. kWh. 26,483 villages had electricity in March 1996.

Water. About 2,327,193 ha were irrigated in 1993–94.

Minerals. Karnataka is an important source of gold and silver. The estimated reserves of high grade iron ore are 8,798m. tonnes. These reserves are found mainly in the Chitradurga belt. The National Mineral Development Corporation of India has indicated total reserves of nearly 332m. tonnes of magnesite and iron ore (with an iron content ranging from 25 to 40) which have been found in Kudremukh Ganga-Mula region in Chickmagalur District. Value of production (1992–93) Rs 2,590m. The estimated reserves of manganese are over 320m. tonnes.

Limestone is found in many regions; deposits (1992–93) are about 5,892m. tonnes.

Karnataka is the largest producer of chromite. It is one of the only two states of India producing magnesite. The other minerals of industrial importance are corundum and garnet.

Agriculture. Agriculture forms the main occupation of more than three-quarters of the population. Physically, Karnataka divides into 4 regions—the coastal region, the southern and northern plains, comprising roughly the districts of Bangalore, Tumkur, Chitradurga, Kolar, Bellary, Mandya and Mysore, and the hill country, comprising the districts of Chickmagalur, Hassan and Shimoga. Rainfall is heavy in the hill country, and there is dense forest. The greater part of the plains are cultivated. Coorg district is essentially agricultural.

The main food crops are rice paddy and jowar, and ragi which is also about 30% of the national crop. Total foodgrains production (1995–96), 8·77m. tonnes (rice 3·02m. tonnes, wheat 150,200 tonnes); pulses 0·72m. tonnes. Sugar, groundnut, castor-seed, safflower, mulberry silk and cotton are important cash crops. The state grows about 70% of the national coffee crop.

Production, 1995–96: Sugar-cane, 24·92m. tonnes; cotton (1993–94), 773,279 bales (each 170 kg).

Livestock (1992–93): Buffaloes, 4·07m.; other cattle, 10·18m.; sheep, 4·73m.; goats, 3·89m.

Forestry. Total forest in the state (1995) is 30,382 sq. km, producing sandalwood, bamboo and other timbers.

Fisheries. Production, 1995–96, 304,870 tonnes.

INDUSTRY
There were 7,765 factories, 125 industrial estates and 5,176 industrial sheds employing 818,000 in March 1994. In 1994–95, 163,524 small industries employed 1,076,312 persons. The Vishveshwaraiah Iron and Steel Works is situated at Bhadravati, while at Bangalore are national undertakings for the manufacture of aircraft, machine tools, telephones, light engineering and electronics goods. The Kudremukh iron ore project is of national importance. An oil refinery is in operation at Mangalore. Other industries include textiles, vehicle manufacture, cement, chemicals, sugar, paper, porcelain and soap. In addition, much of the world's sandalwood is processed, the oil being one of the most valuable productions of the state. Sericulture is a more important cottage industry giving employment, directly or indirectly, to about 2·7m. persons; production of raw silk, 1992–93, 7,147 tonnes, over two-thirds of national production.

COMMUNICATIONS
Roads. In 1993–94 the state had 134,832 km of roads, including 1,997 km of national highway. There were (31 March 1996) 2,249,890 motor vehicles.

Rail. In 1995–96 there were 3,124 km of railway (including 149 km of narrow gauge) in the state.

Civil Aviation. There are airports at Bangalore, Hubli, Mysore, Mangalore, Bellary and Belgaum, with regular scheduled services to Bombay, Calcutta, Delhi and Madras.

Shipping. Mangalore is a deep-water port for the export of mineral ores. Karwar is being developed as an intermediate port.

SOCIAL INSTITUTIONS
Justice. The seat of the High Court is at Bangalore. It has a Chief Justice and 21 puisne judges.

Religion. At the 1991 census there were 38,432,027 Hindus; 5,234,023 Moslems; 859,478 Christians; 326,114 Jains; 73,012 Buddhists; 10,101 Sikhs.

Education. The number of literate people, according to the 1991 census, was 21·08m. (56·04%; 67·26% of men and 44·34% of women). In 1996–97 the state had 22,870 primary schools with 6,507,805 students, 18,485 middle schools with 2,158,487 students, 7,644 high and higher secondary schools with 1,270,794 students, 172 polytechnic and 125 medical colleges, 49 engineering and technology colleges, 761 arts, science and commerce colleges and 12 universities. Education is free up to pre-university level.

Universities: Mysore (1916); Karnataka (1949) at Dharwar; University of Agricultural Sciences (1964) at Hebbal, Bangalore; Gulbarga; Mangalore; University of Agricultural Sciences, Dharwad; Kuvempu University, Shimoga; Kannada University and National Law School of India. Mysore has 6 university and

125 affiliated colleges; Karnataka, 5 and 240; Bangalore, 204 affiliated; Hebbal, 8 constituent colleges.

The Indian Institute of Science, Bangalore, has the status of a university.

Health. There were in 1993–94, 306 hospitals, 208 dispensaries, 1,459 primary health centres and 459 family welfare centres. Total number of beds in 1993–94, 43,308.

KERALA

KEY HISTORICAL EVENTS
The state of Kerala was created in 1956, bringing together the Malayalam-speaking areas. It includes most of the former state of Travancore-Cochin and small areas from the state of Madras. Cochin, an exceptionally safe harbour, was an early site of European trading in India. In 1795 the British took it from the Dutch and British influence remained dominant. Travancore was a Hindu state which became a British protectorate in 1795, having been an ally of the British East India Company for some years. Cochin and Travancore were combined as one state in 1947, reorganized and renamed Kerala in 1956.

TERRITORY AND POPULATION
Kerala is in south India and is bounded north by Karnataka, east and south-east by Tamil Nadu, south-west and west by the Indian ocean. The state has an area of 38,863 sq. km. The 1991 census showed a population of 29,098,518; density of population was 749 per sq. km. Chief cities, *see* INDIA: Territory and Population. Other principal towns (1991): Alappuzha (174,666), Kollam (139,852), Palakkad (123,289) and Thalassery (103,577).

Languages spoken in the state are Malayalam, Tamil and Kannada.

SOCIAL STATISTICS
Growth rate 1981–91, 14·32%.

CONSTITUTION AND GOVERNMENT
The state has a unicameral legislature of 140 elected (and one nominated) members including the Speaker.

The state has 14 districts. The capital is Thiruvananthapuram.

RECENT ELECTIONS
After the elections of April-May 1996 the Left Democratic Front led by CPI (M) and allies held 80 seats, the United Democratic Front led by Congress (I), 59.

CURRENT ADMINISTRATION
Governor: Sukhdev Singh Kang.
  Chief Minister: E. K. Nayanar.

ECONOMY
Budget. Budget estimates for 1997–98 showed revenue receipts of Rs 75,534m.; expenditure Rs 87,957m. Annual Plan expenditure, 1997–98, Rs 28,500m.

ENERGY AND NATURAL RESOURCES
Electricity. Installed capacity (1995–96), 1,505 MW; energy generated in 1995–96 was 6,662m. kWh. The Idukki hydro-electric plant produced 3,064m. kWh and the Sabarigiri scheme 1,674m. kWh. All villages are electrified.

Minerals. The beach sands of Kerala contain monazite, ilmenite, rutile, zircon, sillimanite, etc. There are extensive whiteclay deposits; other minerals of commercial importance include magnesite, china clay, limestone, quartz sand and lignite. Iron ore has been found at Kozhikode (Calicut).

Agriculture. Area under irrigation in 1995–96 was 644,000 ha; 6 irrigation projects were under execution in 1996–97. The chief agricultural products are rice, tapioca, coconut, arecanut, cashewnut, oilseeds, pepper, sugar-cane, rubber, tea, coffee and cardamom. About 98% of Indian black pepper and about 95% of Indian rubber is produced in Kerala. Production of principal crops, 1994–95: Total foodgrains, 1·1m. tonnes (of which rice 953,026 tonnes from 471,000 ha); pulses, 16,800 tonnes; sugar-cane, 464,000 tonnes; rubber, 475,000 tonnes; tea, 64,794 tonnes; coffee, 42,600 tonnes; cashew nuts, 96,780 tonnes.

Livestock (1987); Buffaloes, 329,000; other cattle, 3·4m.; goats, 1·6m. In 1995–96 milk production was 2·24m. tonnes; egg production, 1,991m.

Forestry. Forest occupied 10,336 sq. km in 1995, including teak, sandal wood, ebony and blackwood and varieties of softwood. Net forest revenue, 1995–96, Rs 1,607·7m.

Fisheries. Fishing is a flourishing industry; the total catch in 1995–96 was 582,000 tonnes (of which marine, 532,000 tonnes). Fish exports, 78,896 tonnes in 1995–96.

INDUSTRY

There are numerous cashew and coir factories. Important industries are rubber, tea, coffee, tiles, automotive tyres, watches, electronics, oil, textiles, ceramics, fertilizers and chemicals, pharmaceuticals, zinc-smelting, sugar, cement, rayon, glass, matches, pencils, monazite, ilmenite, titanium oxide, rare earths, aluminium, electrical goods, paper, shark-liver oil, etc. The state has a refinery and a shipyard at Kochi (Cochin).

The number of factories registered under the Factories Act 1948 on 31 Dec. 1995 was 15,965, with daily average employment of 0·41m. There were 143,23 small-scale units employing 0·78m. persons on 31 March 1996.

COMMUNICATIONS

Roads. In 1995–96 there were 144,636 km of roads in the state; national highways, 1,011 km. There were 1·17m. motor vehicles at 31 March 1996.

Rail. There is a coastal line from Mangalore in Karnataka which connects with Tamil Nadu. In 1995–96 there were 1,053 route-km of track.

Civil Aviation. There are airports at Kozhikode, Kochi and Thiruvananthapuram with regular scheduled services to Delhi, Bombay and Madras.

Shipping. Port Kochi, administered by the central government, is one of India's major ports; in 1983 it became the out-port for the Inland Container Depot at Coimbatore in Tamil Nadu. There are 12 other ports and harbours.

SOCIAL INSTITUTIONS

Justice. The High Court at Ernakulam has a Chief Justice and 21 puisne judges.

Religion. At the 1991 census there were 16,668,587 Hindus; 6,788,364 Moslems; 5,621,510 Christians; 3,641 Jains; 2,224 Sikhs.

Education. Kerala is the most literate Indian State with 22·66m. literate people at the 1991 census (89·81%); 93·62% of men and 86·13% of women. Education is free up to the age of 14.

In 1996–97 there were 6,725 primary schools with 2·79m. students, 2,998 middle schools with 1·84m. students and 3,125 high and higher secondary schools with 1·07m. students. There were also 169 junior colleges with 210,074 pupils.

Kerala University (established 1937) at Thiruvananthapuram is affiliating and teaching; in 1995–96 it had 52 affiliated colleges with 113,569 students. The University of Kochi is federal, and for post-graduate studies only. The University of Calicut (established 1968) is teaching and affiliating and has 95 affiliated colleges with 122,343 students (1995–96). Kerala Agricultural University (established 1971) has 7 constituent colleges. Mahatma Gandhi University at Kottayam was established in 1983 and has 64 affiliated colleges with 112,992 students (1995–96). There are 2 other universities, Sree Sankaracharya University and Malabar University. There were also (1995–96) 6 medical colleges, 15 engineering and technology colleges, 19 teacher training colleges and 211 arts and science colleges.

Health. There were 149 allopathic hospitals, 961 primary health centres, 60 community health centres, 53 dispensaries, 21 TB centres/clinics and 15 leprosy control units, with 42,569 beds, in 1995–96. There were also 108 Ayurvedic hospitals with 2,529 beds and 31 homeopathy hospitals with 394 beds.

FURTHER READING
Jeffrey, R., *Politics, Women and Well-Being: How Kerala became a Model.* London, 1992

MADHYA PRADESH

KEY HISTORICAL EVENTS
The state was formed in 1956 to bring together the Hindu-speaking districts of the area including most of the former state of Madhya Bharat, the former states of Bhopal and Vindhya Pradesh and a former Rajput enclave, Sironj. This was an area which the Mahrattas took from the Moghuls between 1712 and 1760. The British overcame Mahratta power in 1818 and established their own Central Provinces. Nagpur became the Provinces capital and was also the capital of Madhya Pradesh until in 1956 boundary changes transferred it to Maharashtra. The present capital, Bhopal, was the centre of a Moslem princely state from 1723. An ally of the British against the Mahrattas, Bhopal (with neighbouring small states) became a British-protected agency in 1818. After independence Bhopal acceded to the Indian Union in 1949. The states of Madhya Bharat and Vindhya Pradesh were then formed as neighbours, and in 1956 were combined with Bhopal and Sironj and renamed Madhya Pradesh.

TERRITORY AND POPULATION
The state is in central India and is bounded north by Uttar Pradesh, east by Bihar and Orissa, south by Andhra Pradesh and Maharashtra, and west by Gujarat and Rajasthan. Madhya Pradesh is the largest Indian state in size, with an area of 443,446 sq. km. In respect of population it ranks fifth. Population (1991 census), 66,181,170, an increase of 26·84% since 1981. Density, 149 per sq. km.

Cities with over 250,000 population, *see* INDIA: Territory and Population. Other large cities (1991): Ratlam, 195,776; Sagar, 195,346; Bilaspur, 192,396; Burhanpur, 172,710; Dewas, 164,364; Murwara, 163,431; Satna, 160,500; Durg, 150,645; Morena, 147,124; Khandwa, 145,133; Rewa, 128,981; Rajnandgaon, 125,371; Korba, 124,501; Bhind, 109,755; Shivpuri, 108,271; Guna, 100,490.

The number of persons speaking each of the more prevalent languages (1981 census) were: Hindi, 43,870,242; Urdu, 1,131,288; Marathi, 1,184,128; Gujarati, 581,084. In April 1990 Hindi became the sole official language.

CONSTITUTION AND GOVERNMENT
Madhya Pradesh is one of the 9 states for which the Constitution provides a bicameral legislature, but the Vidhan Parishad or Upper House (to consist of 90 members) has yet to be formed. The Vidhan Sabha or Lower House has 320 elected members.

For administrative purposes the state has been split into 12 divisions with a Commissioner at the head of each; the headquarters of these are located at Bhopal, Bilaspur, Gwalior, Hoshangabad, Indore, Jabalpur, Jagdalpur, Morena, Raipur, Rewa, Sagar and Ujjain. There are 45 districts.

The seat of government is at Bhopal.

RECENT ELECTIONS
Following the election in Nov. 1998, Congress (I) Party retained power. Congress (I) won 173 seats, Bharatiya Janata Party 120.

MADHYA PRADESH

CURRENT ADMINISTRATION
Governor: Bhai Mahavir.
Chief Minister: Digvijay Singh.

ECONOMY
Budget. Budget estimates for 1996–97 showed revenue receipts of Rs 102,771m. and expenditure of Rs 108,426m. Annual plan, 1997–98, Rs 34,000m.

ENERGY AND NATURAL RESOURCES
Electricity. Madhya Pradesh is rich in low-grade coal suitable for power generation, and also has immense potential hydro-electric energy. Total installed capacity, 1995–96, 3,863·4 MW. Power generated, 17,599m. kWh in 1995–96. There are 6 hydro-electric power station of 848 MW installed capacity. 67,741 out of 71,352 villages were electrified by 1995–96.

Water. Major irrigation projects include the Chambal Valley scheme (started in 1952 with Rajasthan), the Tawa project in Hoshangabad district, the Barna and Hasdeo schemes, the Mahanadi canal system and schemes in the Narmada valley at Bargi and Narmadasagar.

Minerals. The state had (1996) extensive mineral deposits, including 8,001m. tonnes of limestone, 126·8m. tonnes of bauxite, 26,853m. tonnes of coal and 2,186·2m. tonnes of iron ore.

In 1995–96 the output of major minerals was (in tonnes): Limestone, 27·45m.; diamonds, 30,000 carats; iron ore, 17·43m.; manganese ore, 0·4m. Revenue from minerals, 1996–97, Rs 8,500m. Coal output was 79·97m. tonnes in 1995–96.

Agriculture. Agriculture is the mainstay of the state's economy and 76·8% of the people are rural. 43·7% of the land area is cultivable, of which 16·6% is irrigated. Production of principal crops, 1994–95 (in tonnes): Foodgrains, 18·86m. (rice, 6m., wheat, 7·17m.); pulses, 3·4m.; cotton, 0·35m. bales of 170 kg.

Livestock (1992): Buffaloes, 7·97m.; other cattle, 30·34m.; sheep and goats, 7·3m.

Forestry. Forested area total 154,000 sq. km, or about 34·8% of the state. The forests are chiefly of sal, saja and teak species. They are the chief source in India of best-quality teak; they also provide firewood for about 60% of domestic fuel needs, and form valuable watershed protection. Forest revenue, 1995–96, Rs 5,250m.

INDUSTRY
The major industries are steel, aluminium, paper, cement, motor vehicles, ordnance, textiles and heavy electrical equipment. Other industries include sugar, fertilizers, straw board, vegetable oil, refractories, potteries, textile machinery, steel casting and rerolling, industrial gases, synthetic fibres, drugs, biscuit manufacturing, engineering, electronics, optical fibres, plastics, tools, rayon and art silk. The number of heavy and medium industries in the state is 759, with 600 ancillary industries; the number of small-scale establishments in production is 414,000. 39 out of 45 districts in the state are categorized as industrially backward.

There are 23 'growth centres' in operation, and 5 under development.

COMMUNICATIONS
Roads. Total length of roads in 1995–96 was 97,343 km. In 1995–96 there were 2,286,000 motor vehicles.

Rail. Bhopal, Bilaspur, Katni, Khandwa and Ratlam are junctions for the central, south, eastern and western networks. Route length (1995–96), 5,761·5 km.

Civil Aviation. There are airports at Bhopal, Gwalior, Indore, Khajuraho and Raipur with regular scheduled services to Bombay and Delhi, Varanasi, Nagpur, Raipur and Bhubaneswar.

SOCIAL INSTITUTIONS
Justice. The High Court of Judicature at Jabalpur has a Chief Justice and 21 puisne judges. Its benches are located at Gwalior and Indore.

Religion. At the 1991 census Hindus numbered 61,412,898; Moslems, 3,282,800; Christians, 426,598; Buddhists, 216,667; Sikhs, 161,111; Jains, 490,324.

Education. The 1991 census showed 23·49m. people to be literate (44·28%; 58·42% of men and 28·86% of women). Education is free for children aged up to 14.

In 1996 there were 75,000 primary schools with 8·97m. students, 17,800 middle schools with 3·42m. students, 2,582 high schools with 1·1m. students and 3,039 higher secondary schools with 0·61m. students.

There are 14 universities in Madhya Pradesh: Dr. Hari Singh Gour University (established 1946), at Sagar, had 97 affiliated colleges and 74,386 students in 1992–93; Rani Durgavati University at Jabalpur (1957) had 46 affiliated colleges and 45,315 students; Vikram University (1957), at Ujjain, had 83 affiliated colleges and 39,723 students; Indira Kala Sangeet Vishwavidyalaya (1956), at Khairagarh, had 33 affiliated colleges and (1991–92) 6,720 students on roll (this university teaches music and fine arts); Devi Ahilya University at Indore (1964) had 32 affiliated colleges and 28,196 students; Jiwaji University (1963), at Gwalior, had 60 affiliated colleges and (1991–92) 58,825 students; Jawaharlal Nehru Krishi University (1964), at Jabalpur, had 10 constituent colleges and 2,053 students; Ravishankar University (1964), at Raipur, had 89 affiliated colleges; Indira Gandhi Krishi Vishwavidyalaya, Raipur; A. P. Singh University, Rewa had 81 colleges and 24,960 students; Barkatullah Vishwavidyalaya, Bhopal had 44 colleges and 18,817 students; Guru Ghasidas University, Bilaspur had 58 colleges and 34,717 students; Makhanlal Chaturvedi Rashtriya Patrakarita Vishwavidhyalaya Bhopal; Chitrakoot Gramodoya Vishwavidhayalaya Chitrakoot. In 1994–95 there were 448 colleges of arts, science and commerce, 20 teacher-training colleges, and 14 engineering and technology colleges, 7 medical colleges, 41 polytechnics and 69 technical-industrial arts and craft schools.

Health. In March 1996 there were 620 hospitals and dispensaries, and 1,615 primary and mini-primary health centres and 11,936 sub-health centres.

MAHARASHTRA

KEY HISTORICAL EVENTS
The Bombay Presidency of the East India Company began with a trading factory, made over to the Company in 1668. The Presidency expanded, overcoming the surrounding Mahratta chiefs until Mahratta power was finally conquered in 1818. After independence Bombay State succeeded the Presidency; its area was altered in 1956 by adding Kutch and Saurashtra and the Marathi-speaking areas of Hyderabad and Madhya Pradesh, and taking away Kannada-speaking areas (which were added to Mysore). In 1960 the Bombay Reorganization Act divided Bombay State between Gujarati and Marathi areas, the latter becoming Maharashtra. The state of Maharashtra consists of the following districts of the former Bombay State: Ahmednagar, Akola, Amravati, Aurangabad, Bhandara, Bhir, Buldana, Chanda, Dhulia (West Khandesh), Greater Bombay, Jalgaon (East Khandesh), Kolaba, Kolhapur, Nagpur, Nanded, Nasik, Osmanabad, Parbhani, Pune, Ratnagiri, Sangli, Satara, Sholapur, Thane, Wardha, Yeotmal; certain portions of Thane and Dhulia districts have become part of Gujarat.

TERRITORY AND POPULATION
Maharashtra is in central India and is bounded north and east by Madhya Pradesh, south by Andhra Pradesh, Karnataka and Goa, west by the Indian ocean and north-west by Daman and Gujarat. The state has an area of 307,713 sq. km. The population at the 1991 census was 78,937,187 (an increase of 25·73% since 1981), of whom about 30m. were Marathi-speaking (Marathi is the official language). Density, 257 per sq. km. The area of Greater Bombay was 603 sq. km. and its population 9·93m. For other principal cities, *see* INDIA: Territory and Population. Other large towns (1991): Jalgaon (242,193), Chandrapur (226,105), Ichalkaranji (214,950), Latur (197,408), Sangli (193,197), Parbhani (190,255), Ahmadnagar (181,339), Jalna (174,958), Bhusawal (145,143), Miraj (125,407), Bid (112,434), Gondiya (109,470), Yavatmul (108,578) and Wardha (102,985).

MAHARASHTRA

CONSTITUTION AND GOVERNMENT

Maharashtra has a bicameral legislature. The Legislative Council has 78 members. The Legislative Assembly has 288 elected members and 1 member nominated by the Governor to represent the Anglo-Indian community.

The Council of Ministers consists of the Chief Minister, 16 other Ministers, and 19 Ministers of State.

The capital is Bombay. The state has 30 districts.

RECENT ELECTIONS

Following the election of Feb. 1995 Shiv Sena and Bharatiya Janata formed a coalition government. The party composition of the Legislative Council was: Congress (I), 81; Shiv Sena, 73; Bharatiya Janata Party, 65; Janata Dal, 11; People's and Workers' Party, 6; independents and others, 52.

CURRENT ADMINISTRATION

Governor: P. C. Alexander.

Chief Minister: Narayan Rane.

ECONOMY

Budget. Budget estimates, 1995–96: Revenue receipts, Rs 151,802m.; revenue expenditure, Rs 167,657m. Plan outlay, 1997–98, Rs 83,250m.

ENERGY AND NATURAL RESOURCES

Electricity. Installed capacity, 1995–96, 10,039 MW (7,155 MW thermal, 1,602 MW hydro-electric, 1,092 MW gas and 190 MW nuclear). All villages are electrified. Electricity generated, 1996–97, 39,599m. kWh.

Oil and Gas. Bombay High (offshore) produced 22·7m. tonnes of crude oil and 16,579,000 cu. metres of natural gas in 1995–96.

Minerals. The state has coal, silica sand, dolomite, kyanite, chromite, limestone, iron ore, manganese, bauxite. Value of mineral production, 1995, Rs 11,590m.

Agriculture. 3·3m. ha of the cropped area of 21·4m. ha are irrigated. In normal seasons the main food crops are rice, wheat, jowar, bajra and pulses. Main cash crops: Cotton, sugar-cane, groundnuts. Production, 1994–95 (in tonnes): Foodgrains, 11·5m. (rice, 2·4m., wheat, 1·11m.); pulses, 1·7m.; cotton, 401,300; sugar-cane, 42·68m.; groundnuts, 0·63m.

Livestock (1992 census, in 1,000): Buffaloes, 5,447; other cattle, 17,441; sheep and goats, 13,015; poultry, 32,189.

Forestry. Forests occupied 64,300 sq. km in 1995–96. Value of forest products in 1996–97, Rs 2,820m.

Fisheries. In 1995–96 the marine fish catch was estimated at 424,000 tonnes and the inland fish catch at 84,000 tonnes; 18,038 boats, including 8,552 mechanized, were used for marine fishing.

INDUSTRY

Industry is concentrated mainly in Bombay, Nashik, Pune and Thane. The main groups are chemicals and products, textiles, electrical and non-electrical machinery, petroleum and products, aircraft, rubber and plastic products, transport equipment, automobiles, paper, electronic items, engineering goods, pharmaceuticals and food products. The state industrial development corporation invested Rs 77,020m. in 21,452 industrial units in 1994–95. In June 1995 there were 26,642 working factories employing 1·2m. people. In Dec. 1996 there were 203,882 small scale industries employing 1·63m. people.

COMMUNICATIONS

Roads. On 31 March 1996 there were 223,000 km of roads, of which 187,090 km were surfaced. There were 4,359,029 motor vehicles on 1 Jan. 1997, of which 17% were in Greater Bombay. Passenger and freight transport has been nationalized.

Rail. The total length of railway on 31 March 1996 was 5,462 km; 66% was broad gauge, 14% metre gauge and 20% narrow gauge. The main junctions and termini are Bombay, Dadar, Manmad, Akola, Nagpur, Pune and Sholapur.

Civil Aviation. The main airport is Bombay, which has national and international flights. Nagpur airport is on the route from Bombay to Calcutta and there are also airports at Pune and Aurangabad.

Shipping. Maharashtra has a coastline of 720 km. Bombay is the major port, and there are 48 minor ports.

SOCIAL INSTITUTIONS

Justice. The High Court has a Chief Justice and 45 judges. The seat of the High Court is Bombay, but it has benches at Nagpur, Aurangabad and Panaji (Goa).

Religion. At the 1991 census Hindus numbered 64,033,213; Moslems, 7,628,755; Buddhists, 5,040,785; Christians, 885,030; Jains, 965,840; Sikhs, 161,184. Other religions, 99,768; religion not stated, 106,560.

Education. The number of literate people, according to the 1991 census, was 42·8m. (64·87%; men 76·56%, women 52·32%). In 1996–97, there were 13,225 high and higher secondary schools with 2,795,567 pupils; 21,969 middle schools with 4,753,257 pupils; and 41,005 primary schools with 11,685,598 pupils. There are 111 engineering and technology colleges, 156 medical colleges (including dental and Ayurvedic colleges), 244 teacher training colleges, 152 polytechnics and 820 arts, science and commerce colleges.

Bombay University, founded in 1857, is mainly an affiliating university. It has 276 colleges with a total (1993–94) of 234,469 students. Nagpur University (1923) is both teaching and affiliating. It has 258 colleges with 95,664 students. Poona University, founded in 1948, is teaching and affiliating; it has 167 colleges and 151,990 students. The SNDT Women's University had 33 colleges with a total of 33,343 students. Dr B. R. Ambedkar Marathwada University, Aurangabad was founded in 1958 as a teaching and affiliating body to control colleges in the Marathwada or Marathi-speaking area, previously under Osmania University; it has 190 colleges and 195,806 students. Shivaji University, Kolhapur, was established in 1963 to control affiliated colleges previously under Poona University. It has 205 colleges and 115,553 students. Amravati University has 130 colleges and 74,484 students. Other universities are: Marathwada Krishi Vidyapeeth, Parbhani; Y. Chavan Maharashtra Open University, Nashik; North Maharashtra University, Jalgaon, with 101 colleges and 66,092 students; Mahatma Phule Krishi University, Rahuri; Punjabrao Krishi University, Akola; Konkan Krishi University, Dapoli; Dr Babasaheb Ambedkar Technological University; North Maharashtra University and Swami Ramanand Teerth Marathwad University.

Health. In 1995 there were 736 hospitals (124,701 beds), 1,418 dispensaries and 1,695 primary health centres, 161 primary health units and 2,154 TB hospitals and clinics.

MANIPUR

KEY HISTORICAL EVENTS

Formerly a state under the political control of the Government of India, Manipur entered into interim arrangements with the Indian Union on 15 Aug. 1947 and the political agency was abolished. The administration was taken over by the Government of India on 15 Oct. 1949 under a merger agreement, and it was centrally administered by the Government of India through a Chief Commissioner. In 1950–51 an Advisory form of Government was introduced. In 1957 this was replaced by a Territorial Council of 30 elected and 2 nominated members. Later in 1963 a Legislative Assembly of 30 elected and 3 nominated members was established under the Government of Union Territories Act 1963. Because of the

MANIPUR

unstable party position in the Assembly, it had to be dissolved on 16 Oct. 1969 and President's Rule introduced. The status of the administrator was raised from Chief Commissioner to Lieut.-Governor with effect from 19 Dec. 1969. On the 21 Jan. 1972 Manipur became a state and the status of the administrator was changed from Lieut.-Governor to Governor.

TERRITORY AND POPULATION
The state is in north-east India and is bounded north by Nagaland, east by Myanmar, south by Myanmar and Mizoram, and west by Assam. Manipur has an area of 22,327 sq. km and a population (1991) of 1,837,149. Density, 82 per sq. km. The valley, which is about 1,813 sq. km, is 2,600 ft above sea-level. The hills rise in places to nearly 10,000 ft, but are mostly about 5,000–6,000 ft. The average annual rainfall is 65 in. The hill areas are inhabited by various hill tribes who constitute about one-third of the total population of the state. There are about 30 tribes and sub-tribes falling into two main groups of Nagas and Kukis. Manipuri and English are the official languages. A large number of dialects are spoken.

SOCIAL STATISTICS
Growth rate 1981–91, 29·29%.

CONSTITUTION AND GOVERNMENT
With the attainment of statehood, Manipur has a Legislative Assembly of 60 members, of which 19 are from reserved tribal constituencies. There are 9 districts. The capital is Imphal.

RECENT ELECTIONS
Following the elections in Feb. 1995, Congress (I) formed a government with the support of other parties. The party composition of the Legislative Assembly in Dec. 1997 was: Congress (I), 13; Manipur State Congress, 23; Manipur People's Party, 11; Federal Party of Manipur, 2; independents, 2; others, 4; vacant, 5.

CURRENT ADMINISTRATION
Governor: O. N. Srivastava.
   Chief Minister: W. Nipamacha Singh.

ECONOMY
Budget. Budget estimates for 1995–96 show revenue of Rs 6,437·6m. and expenditure of Rs 7,542·4m. Plan allocation 1997–98, Rs 4,100m.

ENERGY AND NATURAL RESOURCES
Electricity. Installed capacity (1995–96) is 12 MW from diesel and hydro-electric generators. This has been augmented since 1981 by the North Eastern Regional Grid. In March 1996 there were 2,015 villages with electricity.

Water. The main power, irrigation and flood-control schemes are the Loktak Lift Irrigation scheme (irrigation potential, 40,000 ha); the Singda scheme (potential 4,000 ha, and improved water supply for Imphal); the Thoubal scheme (potential 34,000 ha), and 4 other large projects. By 1994–95, 59,100 ha had been irrigated.

Agriculture. Rice is the principal crop; with wheat, maize and pulses. Total foodgrains, 1995–96, 0·48m. tonnes (rice, 338,100 tonnes).
   Agricultural work force, 453,040. Only 0·21m. ha are cultivable, of which 134,900 ha are under paddy. Fruit and vegetables are important in the valley, including pineapple, oranges, bananas, mangoes, pears, peaches and plums. Soil erosion, produced by shifting cultivation, is being halted by terracing. Fruit production in 1993–94, 0·11m. tonnes.

Forestry. Forests occupied about 17,588 sq. km in 1995. The main products are teak, jurjan, pine; there are also large areas of bamboo and cane, especially in the Jiri and Barak river drainage areas, yielding about 0·3m. tonnes annually. Total revenue from forests, 1990–91, Rs 9·95m.

Fisheries. Landings in 1995–96, 12,500 tonnes.

INDUSTRY

Handloom weaving is a cottage industry. Larger-scale industries include the manufacture of bicycles and TV sets, sugar, cement, starch, vegetable oil and glucose. Sericulture produces about 45 tonnes of raw silk annually. Estimated non-agricultural work force, 229,408.

COMMUNICATIONS

A national highway from Kaziranga (Assam) runs through Imphal to the border with Myanmar. A railway link was opened in 1990. There is an airport at Imphal with regular scheduled services to Delhi and Calcutta. Length of road (1995), 7,003 km; number of vehicles (1996–97) 65,223.

SOCIAL INSTITUTIONS

Religion. At the 1991 census Hindus numbered 1,059,470; Christians, 626,669; Moslems, 133,535.

Education. The 1991 census gave the number of literate people as 895,223 (59·89%; men 71·63%, women 47·6%). In 1996–97 there were 2,548 primary schools with 230,230 students, 555 middle schools with 106,200 students, 553 high and higher secondary schools with 66,160 students, 50 colleges, 1 medical college, 2 teacher training colleges, 3 polytechnics, Manipur University with 62 colleges and 52,352 students (1997–98), and an agricultural university.

Health. In 1996–97 there were 93 hospitals and public health centres, 52 dispensaries, 16 community health centres, 420 sub-centres and 58 other facilities.

MEGHALAYA

KEY HISTORICAL EVENTS

The state was created under the Assam Reorganization (Meghalaya) Act 1969 and inaugurated on 2 April 1970. Its status was that of a state within the State of Assam until 21 Jan. 1972 when it became a fully-fledged state of the Union. It consists of the former Garo Hills district and United Khasi and Jaintia Hills district of Assam.

TERRITORY AND POPULATION

Meghalaya is bounded in the north and east by Assam, south and west by Bangladesh. In 1991 (census figure) the area was 22,429 sq. km and the population 1,774,778. Density, 79 per sq. km. The people are mainly of the Khasi, Jaintia and Garo tribes. The main languages of the state are Khasi, Jaintia, Garo and English.

SOCIAL STATISTICS

Growth rate 1981–91, 32·86%.

CONSTITUTION AND GOVERNMENT

Meghalaya has a unicameral legislature. The Legislative Assembly has 60 seats.
There are 7 districts. The capital is Shillong (population, 1991, 131,719).

RECENT ELECTIONS

Party position in Feb. 1993: Congress (I), 24; Hill People's Union, 11; Independents, 10; others, 15.

CURRENT ADMINISTRATION

Governor: Madhukar Dighe.
Chief Minister: B. B. Lyngdoh.

ECONOMY

Budget. Budget estimates for 1996–97 showed revenue receipts of Rs 7,758m. and expenditure of Rs 6,502m. Annual Plan outlay, 1997–98, Rs 3,820m.

ENERGY AND NATURAL RESOURCES

Electricity. Total installed capacity (1995–96) was 186·71 MW. 2,408 villages out of 4,902 had electricity in March 1996.

Minerals. The Khasi Hills, Jaintia Hills and Garo Hills districts produce coal, sillimanite (95% of India's total output), limestone, fire clay, dolomite, feldspar, quartz and glass sand. The state also has deposits of coal (estimated reserves 600m. tonnes), limestone (3,000m.), fire clay (6m.) and sandstone which are so far virtually untapped.

Agriculture. About 83% of the people depend on agriculture. Principal crops are rice, maize, potatoes, cotton, oranges, ginger, tezpata, areca nuts, jute, mesta, bananas and pineapples. Production 1995–96 (in tonnes) of principal crops: Rice, 118,900; wheat, 6,400; pulses, 2,400; Potatoes, 146,941; maize, 20,800; jute, 43,444; cotton, 5,432; rape and mustard, 4,200.

Forestry. Forests covered 9,496 sq. km in 1995–6. Forest products are the state's chief resources.

INDUSTRY

Apart from agriculture the main source of employment is the extraction and processing of minerals; there are also important timber processing mills and cement factories. Other industries include electronics, tantalum capacitors, beverages and watches. The state has 5 industrial estates, 2 industrial areas and 1 growth centre. In 1995–96 there were 58 registered factories and 2,533 small-scale industries. There were also, in 1994–95, 1,812 sericultural villages, 6 sericultural farms and 8 silk units and, in 1995–96, 5,400 *khadi* and village industrial units.

COMMUNICATIONS

Roads. Three national highways run through the state for a distance of 460 km. In 1995–96 there were 6,572 km of surfaced and unsurfaced roads. Total number of motor vehicles, 1995–96, 44,715.

Rail. The state has only 1 km of railways.

Civil Aviation. Umroi airport (25 km from Shillong) connects the state with main air services.

SOCIAL INSTITUTIONS

Justice. The Guwahati High Court is common to Assam, Meghalaya, Nagaland, Manipur, Mizoram, Tripura and Arunachal Pradesh. There is a bench of the Guwahati High Court at Shillong.

Religion. At the 1991 census Hindus numbered 260,306; Moslems, 61,462; Christians, 1,146,092; Buddhists, 2,934; Sikhs, 2,612.

Education. In 1991, 50% of the population were literate (55·6% of men and 44·4% of women). In 1996–97 the state had 4,235 primary schools with 299,961 students, 851 middle schools with 78,858 students, 431 high and higher secondary schools with 44,221 students, 10 teacher training schools and 1 college, 1 polytechnic and 28 colleges. The North-eastern Hill University started functioning at Shillong in 1973; in 1993–94 it had 41 colleges and 54,803 students.

Health. In 1995–96 there were 9 government hospitals, 77 primary health centres, 20 government dispensaries and 325 sub-centres. Total beds (hospitals and health centres), 2,352.

MIZORAM

KEY HISTORICAL EVENTS

On 21 Jan. 1972 the former Mizo Hills District of Assam was created a Union Territory. A long dispute between the Mizo National Front (originally Separatist) and the central government was resolved in 1986. Mizoram became a state by the Constitution (53rd Amendment) and the State of Mizoram Acts, July 1986.

TERRITORY AND POPULATION
Mizoram is one of the easternmost Indian states, lying between Bangladesh and Myanmar, and having on its northern boundaries Tripura, Assam and Manipur. The area is 21,081 sq. km and the population (1991 census) 689,756. Density, 33 per sq. km.The main languages spoken are Mizo and English.

SOCIAL STATISTICS
Growth rate 1981–91, 39·7%.

CONSTITUTION AND GOVERNMENT
Mizoram has a unicameral Legislative Assembly with 40 seats. The capital is Aizawl (population, 1991, 155,240).

RECENT ELECTIONS
Following the elections of Nov. 1998, Congress (I) lost to 2 regional parties and won only 6 of a possible 40 seats.

CURRENT ADMINISTRATION
Governor: A. Padmanabhan.
  Chief Minister: Zoramthanga.

ECONOMY
Budget. Budget estimates for 1997–98 show revenue receipts of Rs 6,769·7m. and expenditure of Rs 5,865·9m. Annual plan outlay, 1997–98, Rs 2,900m.

ENERGY AND NATURAL RESOURCES
Electricity. Installed capacity (1993–94), 24·45 MW. 617 out of 721 villages had electricity in March 1996.

Agriculture. About 60% of the people are engaged in agriculture, either on terraced holdings or in shifting cultivation. Total production of foodgrains, 1995–96, 122,700 tonnes (rice, 101,500 tonnes).
  Total forest area, 1995, 18,576 sq. km.

INDUSTRY
Handloom weaving and other cottage industries are important. The state has (1992) 2,300 small scale industrial units, including furniture industries, steel fabrication, TV manufacturing, truck and bus body building.

COMMUNICATIONS
Roads. Aizawl is connected by road with Silchar in Assam. Total length of roads, 31 March 1992, 5,095 km. There were 18,238 motor vehicles in 1995–96.

Civil Aviation. Aizawl is connected by air with Silchar in Assam and with Calcutta.

SOCIAL INSTITUTIONS
Religion. At the 1991 census Christians numbered 591,342; Buddhists, 54,024; Hindus, 34,788; Moslems, 4,538.

Education. The number of literate people in 1991 was 462,246 (82·27%; 85·61% of men and 78·68% of women). In 1996–97 there were 1,263 primary schools with 129,662 students, 702 middle schools with 44,186 students and 346 high and higher secondary schools with 23,140 students; there were 29 colleges, 1 teacher training college, 3 teacher training schools, 1 polytechnic and 29 junior colleges.

Health. In 1993–94 there were 11 hospitals, 38 primary and 22 subsidiary health centres, and 314 health sub-centres. Total beds, 1,444.

NAGALAND

KEY HISTORICAL EVENTS
The state was created in 1961, effective 1963. It consisted of the Naga Hills district of Assam and the Tuensang Frontier Agency. The agency was a British-supervized tribal area on the borders of Myanmar. Its supervision passed to the Government of India at independence, and in 1957 Tuensang and the Naga Hills became a Centrally Administered Area, governed by the central government through the Governor of Assam. A number of Naga leaders fought for independence until a settlement was reached with the Indian Government at the Shillong Peace Agreement of 1975.

TERRITORY AND POPULATION
The state is in the north-east of India and is bounded in the north by Arunachal Pradesh, west by Assam, east by Myanmar and south by Manipur. Nagaland has an area of 16,579 sq. km and a population (1991 census) of 1,209,546. Density, 73 per sq. km. The major towns are the capital, Kohima (1991 population, 51,418) and Dimapur (57,182). Other towns include Wokha, Mon, Zunheboto, Mokokchung and Tuensang. The chief tribes in numerical order are: Angami, Ao, Sumi, Konyak, Chakhesang, Lotha, Phom, Khiamngan, Chang, Yimchunger, Zeliang-Kuki, Rengma, Sangtam and Pochury. The main languages of the state are English, Hindi and Nagamese.

SOCIAL STATISTICS
Growth rate 1981–91, 56·08%.

CONSTITUTION AND GOVERNMENT
An Interim Body (Legislative Assembly) of 42 members elected by the Naga people and an Executive Council (Council of Ministers) of 5 members were formed in 1961, and continued until the State Assembly was elected in Jan. 1964. The Assembly has 60 members. The Governor has extraordinary powers, which include special responsibility for law and order.

The state has 7 districts (Kohima, Mon, Zunheboto, Wokha, Phek, Mokokchung and Tuensang). The capital is Kohima.

RECENT ELECTIONS
After the elections of Feb. 1993 the State Assembly includes: Congress (I), 41; Nagaland People's Council, 10; independents, 7; others, 1; vacant, 1.

CURRENT ADMINISTRATION
Governor: Om Prakash Sharma.
  Chief Minister: S. C. Jamir.

ECONOMY
Budget. Budget estimates for 1996–97 showed total receipts of Rs 9,604·4m. and expenditure of Rs 9,937·8m. Annual Plan, 1997–98, Rs 3,500m.

ENERGY AND NATURAL RESOURCES
Electricity. Installed capacity (1995–96) 6·82 MW; all towns and villages are electrified. In 1995–96, 7 electricity generation schemes were under implementation.

Minerals. Oil has been located in 3 districts. Other minerals include: Coal, limestone, chromite, magnesite, iron ore, copper ore, clay, glass sand and slate.

Agriculture. 90% of the people derive their livelihood from agriculture. The Angamis, in Kohima district, practise a fixed agriculture in the shape of terraced slopes, and wet paddy cultivation in the lowlands. In the other two districts a traditional form of shifting cultivation (*jhumming*) still predominates, but some farmers have begun tea and coffee plantations and horticulture. About 61,000 ha were under terrace cultivation and 74,040 ha under *jhumming* in 1994–95. Production of rice (1995–96) was 0·185m. tonnes, total foodgrains 238,300 tonnes, pulses 12,300 tonnes. Forests covered 8,625 sq. km in 1995–96.

INDUSTRY
There is a forest products factory at Tijit; a paper-mill (100 tonnes daily capacity) at Tuli, a distillery unit and a sugar-mill (1,000 tonnes daily capacity) at Dimapur, and a cement factory (50 tonnes daily capacity) at Wazeho. Bricks and TV sets are also made, and there are 1,850 small units. There is a ceramics plant and sericulture is also important.

COMMUNICATIONS
Roads. There is a national highway from Kaziranga (Assam) to Kohima and on to Manipur. There are state highways connecting Kohima with the district headquarters. Total length of roads in 1992, 14,933 km. There were 95,020 motor vehicles registered in 1994–95.

Rail. Dimapur has a rail-head. Railway route-km in 1995–96, 13 km.

Civil Aviation. Dimapur has a daily air service to Calcutta.

SOCIAL INSTITUTIONS
Justice. A permanent bench of the Guwahati High Court has been established in Kohima.

Religion. At the 1991 census there were 1,057,940 Christians; 122,473 Hindus; 20,642 Moslems; 1,202 Jains; 732 Sikhs.

Education. The 1991 census records 621,048 literate people, or 61·65%: 67·62% of men and 54·75% of women. In 1996–97 there were 1,414 primary schools with 271,932 students, 416 middle schools with 63,437 students, 244 high and higher secondary schools with 24,547 students, 36 colleges, 2 teacher training colleges and 2 polytechnics. The North Eastern Hill University opened at Kohima in 1978. Nagaland University was established in 1994.

Health. In 1995–96 there were 32 hospitals (1,051 beds), 27 primary and 5 community health centres, 65 dispensaries, 243 sub-centres, 5 TB centres and 30 leprosy centres.

FURTHER READING
Aram, M., *Peace in Nagaland,* New Delhi, 1974

ORISSA

KEY HISTORICAL EVENTS
Orissa was divided between Mahratta and Bengal rulers when conquered by the British East India Company, the Bengal area in 1757 and the Mahratta in 1803. The area which now forms the state then consisted of directly controlled British districts and a large number of small princely states with tributary rulers. The British districts were administered as part of Bengal until 1912 when, together with Bihar, they were separated from Bengal to form a single province. Bihar and Orissa were separated from each other in 1936. In 1948 a new state government took control of the whole state, including the former princely states (except Saraikella and Kharswan which were transferred to Bihar, and Mayurbhanj which was not incorporated until 1949).

TERRITORY AND POPULATION
Orissa is in eastern India and is bounded north by Bihar, north-east by West Bengal, east by the Bay of Bengal, south by Andhra Pradesh and west by Madhya Pradesh. The area of the state is 155,707 sq. km, and its population (1991 census), 31,659,736, density 203 per sq. km. Cities with over 250,000 population at 1991 census, *see* INDIA: Territory and Population. Other large cities (1991): Rourkela

(urban agglomeration), 398,864; Brahmapur, 210,418; Sambalpur, 131,138; Puri, 125,199. The principal and official language is Oriya.

SOCIAL STATISTICS
Growth rate 1981–91, 20·06%.

CONSTITUTION AND GOVERNMENT
The Legislative Assembly has 147 members.
The state consists of 30 districts.
The capital is Bhubaneswar (18 miles south of Cuttack).

RECENT ELECTIONS
After the elections in Feb. 1995 Congress (I) formed a government. Parties in the Legislative Assembly: Congress (I), 80 seats; Janata Dal, 17; Niju Janata Dal, 29; Bharatiya Janata Party, 10; Jharkhand Mukti Morcha, 4; independents and others, 7.

CURRENT ADMINISTRATION
Governor: Chakravarti Rangarajan.
Chief Minister: Giridhar Gomango.

ECONOMY
Budget. Budget estimates, 1996–97, showed total receipts of Rs 79,812m. and total expenditure of Rs 84,683m. Annual plan outlay, 1997–98, Rs 25,000m.

ENERGY AND NATURAL RESOURCES
Electricity. The Hirakud Dam Project on the river Mahanadi irrigates 628,000 acres and has an installed capacity of 307·5 MW. There are other projects under construction; hydro-electric power is now serving a large part of the state. Other hydro-power projects are Balimela (360 MW), Upper Kolab (320 MW) and Rengali (250 MW). Total installed capacity (1995–96) 2,152 MW. In 1994–95 the state generated 5,967m. units. In March 1996, 32,068 villages had electricity.

Minerals. Orissa is India's leading producer of chromite (95% of national output), dolomite (50%), manganese ore (25%), graphite (80%), iron ore (16%), fire-clay (34%), limestone (20%), and quartz-quartzite (18%). Production in 1995–96 (1,000 tonnes): Iron ore, 9,330; manganese ore, 630; chromite, 1,650; coal, 32,660; limestone, 2,380; dolomite, 1,350; bauxite, 2,420. Value of production in 1995–96 was Rs 16,340m.

Agriculture. The cultivation of rice is the principal occupation of about 80% of the workforce, and only a very small amount of other cereals is grown. Production of foodgrains (1994–95) totalled 7·2m. tonnes from 7·9m. ha (rice 6·4m. tonnes, wheat 58,000 tonnes); pulses, 0·58m. tonnes; oilseeds, 0·27m. tonnes; sugar-cane, 781,000 tonnes. Turmeric is cultivated in the uplands of the districts of Ganjam, Phulbani and Koraput, and is exported.

Livestock (1993): Buffaloes, 1·04m.; other cattle, 9·2m.; sheep, 1·87m.; goats, 5·4m.; 15·91m. poultry including ducks (1995).

Forestry. Forests occupied 56,059 sq. km in 1995–96. The most important species are sal, teak, kendu, sandal, sisu, bija, kusum, kongada and bamboo.

Fisheries. There were, in March 1996, 603 fishery co-operative societies. Fish production in 1995–96 was 258,040 tonnes. The state has 4 fishing harbours.

INDUSTRY
289 large and medium industries are in operation (1995–96), mostly based on minerals: steel, pig-iron, ferrochrome, ferromanganese, ferrosilicon, aluminium, cement, automotive tyres and synthetic fibres.

Other industries of importance are sugar, glass, paper, fertilizers, caustic soda, salt, industrial explosives, heavy machine tools, a coach-repair factory, a re-rolling mill, textile mills and electronics. An oil refinery is under implementation. Also, there were 49,611 small-scale industries in 1995–96 employing 349,800 persons, and 1,342,561 artisan units providing employment to 2·33m. persons. Handloom weaving and the manufacture of baskets, wooden articles, hats and nets, silver filigree work and hand-woven fabrics are specially well known.

COMMUNICATIONS

Roads. On 31 March 1996 length of roads was: State highway, 4,360 km; national highway, 1,625 km; other roads, 212,490 km. There were 658,401 motor vehicles in 1995–96. A 144-km expressway, part national highway, connects the Daitari mining area with Paradip Port.

Rail. The route-km of railway in 1995–96 was 2,191 km, of which 143 km was narrow gauge.

Civil Aviation. There is an airport at Bhubaneswar with regular scheduled services to New Delhi, Calcutta, Visakhapatnam and Hyderabad.

Shipping. Paradip was declared a 'major' port in 1966; it handled 11·2m. tonnes of traffic in 1995–96. There are minor ports at Bahabalpur and Gopalpur.

SOCIAL INSTITUTIONS

Justice. The High Court of Judicature at Cuttack has a Chief Justice and 13 puisne judges.

Religion. At the 1991 census Hindus numbered 29,971,257; Christians, 666,220; Moslems, 577,775; Sikhs, 17,296; Buddhists, 9,153; Jains, 6,302.

Education. The percentage of literate people in the population in 1991 was 49·09% (males, 63·09%; females, 34·68%).

In 1996–97 there were 42,104 primary schools with 3·95m. students, 12,096 middle schools with 1·3m. students and 6,198 high and higher secondary schools with 945,000 students. There are 10 engineering and technology colleges, 20 medical colleges, 13 teacher training colleges, 15 engineering schools/polytechnics, 497 arts, science and commerce colleges and 440 junior colleges.

Utkal University was established in 1943 at Cuttack and moved to Bhubaneswar in 1962; it is both teaching and affiliating. It has 368 affiliated colleges and 14,000 students (1993–94). Berhampur University has 33 affiliated colleges with 33,755 students, and Orissa University of Agriculture and Technology has 8 constituent colleges with 641 students. Sambalpur University has 97 affiliated colleges and 43,982 students. Sri Jagannath Sanskrit Viswavidyalaya at Puri was established in 1981 for oriental studies.

Health. There were (1995–96) 180 hospitals, 150 dispensaries, 885 primary health centres and 402 health centres/units. There were also 478 homeopathic and 537 Ayurvedic dispensaries.

CULTURE

Tourism. Tourist traffic is concentrated mainly on the 'Golden Triangle' of Konark, Puri, and Bhubaneswar and its temples. Tourists also visit Gopalpur, the Similipal National Park, Nandankanan and Chilka Lake, Bhiar-Kanika and Ushakothi Wildlife Sanctuary.

PUNJAB (INDIA)

KEY HISTORICAL EVENTS

The Punjab was constituted an autonomous province of India in 1937. In 1947 the province was partitioned between India and Pakistan into East and West Punjab respectively. The name of East Punjab was changed to Punjab (India) under the Constitution of India. On 1 Nov. 1956 the erstwhile states of Punjab and Patiala and East Punjab States Union (PEPSU) were integrated to form the state of Punjab. On 1 Nov. 1966, under the Punjab Reorganization Act, 1966, the state was reconstituted as a Punjabi-speaking state comprising the districts of Gurdaspur (excluding Dalhousie), Amritsar, Kapurthala, Jullundur, Ferozepore, Bhatinda, Patiala and Ludhiana; parts of Sangrur, Hoshiarpur and Ambala districts; and part of Kharar tehsil. The remaining area comprising an area of 18,000 sq. miles and an estimated (1967) population of 8·5m. was shared between the new state of Haryana and the Union Territory of Himachal Pradesh. The existing capital of Chandigarh was made joint capital of Punjab and Haryana; its transfer to Punjab alone (due in 1986) has been delayed while the two states seek agreement as to which Hindi-speaking districts shall be transferred to Haryana in exchange.

TERRITORY AND POPULATION
The Punjab is in north India and is bounded at its northernmost point by Kashmir, north-east by Himachal Pradesh, south-east by Haryana, south by Rajasthan, west and north-west by Pakistan. The area of the state is 50,362 sq. km, with census (1991) population of 20,281,969. Density, 403 per sq. km. Cities with over 250,000 population at 1991 census, see INDIA: Territory and Population. Other principal towns (1991): Bathinda (159,042), Pathankot (123,930), Moga (108,304), Abohar (107,163). The official language is Punjabi.

SOCIAL STATISTICS
Growth rate 1981–91, 20·81%.

CONSTITUTION AND GOVERNMENT
Punjab (India) has a unicameral legislature, the Legislative Assembly, of 117 members. Presidential rule was imposed in May 1987 after outbreaks of communal violence. In March 1988 the Assembly was officially dissolved.
    There are 16 districts. The capital is Chandigarh.

RECENT ELECTIONS
Legislative Assembly elections were held in Feb. 1997. The electorate was 15m.; turn-out was 68%. Shiromani Akali Dal (SAD) gained 75 seats; the Bharatiya Janata Party, 18; Congress (I), 14; the Communist Party, 2; independents and others, 8.

CURRENT ADMINISTRATION
Governor: Lieut.-Gen. Bakshi K. N. Chibber.
    Chief Minister: Prakash Singh Badal (SAD).

Local Government. There are 106 municipalities, 118 community development blocks and 9,331 elected village councils (*panchayats*). Elections took place for 95 municipalities on 6 Sept. 1992, and for the 11,500 village councils in Jan. 1993.

ECONOMY
Budget. Budget estimates, 1995–96, showed revenue receipts of Rs 72,634·7m. and revenue expenditure of Rs 75,076·4m. Plan outlay, 1997–98, Rs 21,000m.

ENERGY AND NATURAL RESOURCES
Electricity. Installed capacity, 1996–97, was 3,511 MW; all villages had electricity.

Agriculture. About 75% of the population depends on agriculture which is technically advanced. The irrigated area rose from 2·21m. ha in 1950–51 to 4·2m. ha in 1996–97. In 1994–95 wheat production was 13·6m. tonnes; rice, 7·7m.; 1992–93: maize, 333,000; oilseeds, 90,000; cotton, 2·3m. bales of 170 kg.
    Livestock (1977 census): Buffaloes, 4,110,000; other cattle, 3·31m.; sheep and goats, 1,219,600; horses and ponies, 75,900; poultry, 5·5m.

Forestry. In 1995 there were 1,342 sq. km of forest land.

INDUSTRY
In March 1997 the number of registered industrial units was 194,208, employing about 1·04m. people. In 1996–97 there were 586 large and medium industries. On 31 March 1997 there were 0·19m. small industrial units, investment Rs 25,050m. The chief manufactures are textiles (especially hosiery), sewing machines, sports goods, sugar, bicycles, electronic goods, machine tools, hand tools, automobiles and vehicle

parts, surgical goods, vegetable oils, tractors, chemicals and pharmaceuticals, fertilizers, food processing, electronics, railway coaches, paper and newsprint, cement, engineering goods and telecommunications items. An oil refinery is under construction.

COMMUNICATIONS

Roads. The total length of roads on 31 March 1997 was 47,000 km. State transport services cover 1·9m. effective km daily with a fleet of 3,426 buses carrying a daily average of over 1·2m. passengers. Coverage by private operators is estimated as 40%. There were 1,915,059 vehicles in 1995–96.

Rail. The Punjab possesses an extensive system of railway communications, served by the Northern Railway. Route-km (1995–96), 2,121 km.

Civil Aviation. There is an airport at Amritsar, and Chandigarh airport is on the north-eastern boundary; both have regular scheduled services to Delhi, Jammu, Srinagar and Leh. There are also Vayudoot services to Ludhiana.

SOCIAL INSTITUTIONS

Justice. The Punjab and Haryana High Court exercises jurisdiction over the states of Punjab and Haryana and the territory of Chandigarh. It is located in Chandigarh. It consists (1988) of a Chief Justice and 21 puisne judges.

Religion. At the 1991 census Hindus numbered 6,989,226; Sikhs, 12,767,697; Moslems, 239,401; Christians, 225,163; Jains, 20,763.

Education. Compulsory education was introduced in April 1961; at the same time free education was introduced up to 8th class for boys and 9th class for girls as well as fee concessions. The aim is education for all children of 6–11. In 1991, 58·51% of the population were literate (65·66% of men and 50·41% of women).

In 1996–97 there were 12,590 primary schools with 2,081,965 students, 2,545 middle schools with 968,762 students, 2,159 high schools with 490,888 students and 1,134 higher secondary schools with 259,718 students.

Punjab University was established in 1947 at Chandigarh as an examining, teaching and affiliating body (in 1993–94 it had 94 colleges and 77,868 students). In 1962 Punjabi University was established at Patiala (it had 66 colleges with 40,712 students) and Punjab Agricultural University at Ludhiana. Guru Nanak Dev University has been established at Amritsar to mark the 500th anniversary celebrations for Guru Nanak Dev, first Guru of the Sikhs (it had 85 colleges and 80,330 students, 1992–93). Altogether there are 237 affiliated colleges, 190 for arts, science and commerce, 18 for teacher training, 6 medical and 11 engineering, and 30 polytechnic institutes.

Health. There were (1992–93) 219 hospitals, 2,151 allopathic, homeopathic, Ayurvedic and Unani dispensaries, 446 primary health centres and 38 community health centres. Total number of beds (1991–92), 24,742.

FURTHER READING
Singh, Khushwant, *A History of the Sikhs*. 2 vols. Princeton and OUP, 1964–67
Singh Tatla, D. and Talbot, I., *Punjab*. [Bibliography]. Oxford and Santa Barbara (CA), 1995

RAJASTHAN

KEY HISTORICAL EVENTS
The state is in the largely desert area formerly known as Rajputana. The Rajput princes were tributary to the Moghul emperors when they were conquered by the Mahrattas' leader, Mahadaji Sindhia, in the 1780s. In 1818 Rajputana became a British protectorate and was recognized during British rule as a group of princely states including Jaipur, Jodhpur and Udaipur. After independence the Rajput princes surrendered their powers and in 1950 were replaced by a single state government. In

1956 the state boundaries were altered; small areas of the former Bombay and Madhya Bharat states were added, together with the neighbouring state of Ajmer. Ajmer had been a Moghul power base; it was taken by the Mahrattas in 1770 and annexed by the British in 1818. In 1878 it became Ajmer-Merwara, a British province, and survived as a separate state until until 1956.

TERRITORY AND POPULATION
Rajasthan is in north-west India and is bounded north by Punjab, north-east by Haryana and Uttar Pradesh, east by Madhya Pradesh, south by Gujarat and west by Pakistan. The area of the state is 342,239 sq. km and its population (census 1991), 44,005,990, density 129 per sq. km. For chief cities, *see* INDIA: Territory and Population. Other major towns (1991): Alwar (205,086), Bhilwara (183,965), Ganganagar (161,482), Bharatpur (148,519), Sikar (148,272), Pali (136,842), Beawar (105,363). The main languages spoken are Rajasthani and Hindi.

SOCIAL STATISTICS
Growth rate 1981–91, 28·44%.

CONSTITUTION AND GOVERNMENT
There is a unicameral legislature, the Legislative Assembly, having 200 members. The capital is Jaipur. There are 30 districts.

RECENT ELECTIONS
After the election in Nov. 1998 the Congress Party came to power. Congress (I), 150; Bharatiya Janata Party, 33.

CURRENT ADMINISTRATION
Governor: Anshuman Singh.
   Chief Minister: Ashok Gehlot.

ECONOMY
Budget. Estimates for 1997–98 show total revenue receipts of Rs 89,894·1m., and expenditure of Rs 91,469·2m. Annual plan, 1997–98, Rs 35,000m.

ENERGY AND NATURAL RESOURCES
Electricity. Installed capacity in 1995–96, 1,981 MW; 30,620 villages (March 1996) and 514,758 wells had electric power.

Water. In 1994 the Bhakra Canal irrigated 0·3m. ha, the Chambal Canal 0·2m. ha and the Rajasthan Canal 0·94m. ha. The Indira Gandhi canal is the main canal system, of which (1994) 189 km of main canal, 204 km of feeder and 3,400 km of distributors had been built, creating an irrigation potential of 582,000 ha. There were 36,397 villages with full or partial drinking water facilities in Dec. 1993, out of 37,124.

Minerals. The state is rich in minerals, including silver, tungsten, granite, marble, dolomite, lignite, lead, zinc, emeralds, soapstone, asbestos, feldspar, copper, limestone and salt. Total revenue from minerals in 1995–96, Rs 2,145·2m. 4 blocs are being explored for mineral oils and gas.

Agriculture. The state has suffered drought and encroaching desert for several years. The cultivable area is (1995–96) about 25·6m. ha, of which 4·65m. ha is irrigated. Production of principal crops (in tonnes), 1995–96: Pulses, 1·46m.; total foodgrains, 9·57m. (rice, 117,600; wheat, 5·49m.); cotton, 1m. bales of 170 kg.
   Livestock (1992): Buffaloes, 7·75m.; other cattle, 11·6m.; sheep, 12·17m.; goats, 15·06m.; horses and ponies, 28,000; camels, 731,000.

Forestry. Forests covered 12,320 sq. km in 1995.

INDUSTRY
In 1993–94 there were 167,400 small industrial units with an investment of Rs 13,163·1m. and employment of 0·64m. There were 212 industrial estates. Total capital investment (1993–94) Rs 13,160m. Chief manufactures are textiles, cement, glass, sugar, sodium, oxygen and acetylene units, pesticides, insecticides, dyes, caustic soda, calcium, carbide, synthetic fibres, fertilizers, shaving equipment,

automobiles and automobile components, tyres, watches, nylon tyre cords and refined copper. In 1993–94 there were 583 large and medium industries.

COMMUNICATIONS
Roads. In 1995–96 there were 116,667 km of roads including 61,520 km of good and surfaced roads in Rajasthan; there were 2,846 km of national highway. Motor vehicles numbered 1,768,709 in 1995–96.

Rail. Jodhpur, Marwar, Udaipur, Ajmer, Jaipur, Kota, Bikaner and Sawai Madhopur are important junctions of the north-western network. Route km (1995–96) 5,924.

Civil Aviation. There are airports at Jaipur, Jodhpur, Kota and Udaipur with regular scheduled services by Indian Airlines.

SOCIAL INSTITUTIONS
Justice. The seat of the High Court is at Jodhpur. There is a Chief Justice and 11 puisne judges. There is also a bench of High Court judges at Jaipur.

Religion. At the 1991 census Hindus numbered 39,201,099; Moslems, 3,525,339; Jains, 562,806; Sikhs, 649,174; Christians, 47,989; Buddhists, 4,467.

Education. The proportion of literate people to the total population was 38·55% at the 1991 census; men 54·99% and women 20·44%.

In 1996–97 there were 33,801 primary schools with 6,665,000 students, 12,642 middle schools with 2,091,000 students, 3,439 high schools with 682,600 students and 1,404 higher secondary schools with 500,000 students. Elementary education is free but not compulsory.

In 1996–97 there were 206 colleges. Rajasthan University, established at Jaipur in 1947, is teaching and affiliating; in 1993–94 it had 135 colleges and 160,000 students. There are 5 other universities: Rajasthan Agricultural University, Bikaner; Mohanlal Sukhadia University, Udaipur; Maharishi Dayanand Saraswati University, Ajmer; Jai Narayan Vyas University, Jodhpur; Kota Open University, Kota. There are also 22 medical colleges, 7 engineering colleges, 21,436 adult and other education centres, 32 sanskrit institutions, 39 teacher-training colleges and 27 polytechnics.

Health. In 1995–96 there were 266 hospitals, 283 dispensaries, 1,453 primary health centres, 384 family welfare centres, 1,104 upgraded sub-centres and 118 maternity centres. There were 34,066 beds in hospitals.

SIKKIM
KEY HISTORICAL EVENTS
A small Himalayan kingdom between Nepal and Bhutan, Sikkim was independent in the 1830s although in continual conflict with larger neighbours. In 1839 the British took the Darjeeling district. British political influence increased during the 19th century, as Sikkim was the smallest buffer between India and Tibet. However, Sikkim remained an independent kingdom ruled by the 14th-century Namgyal dynasty. In 1950 a treaty was signed with the Government of India, declaring Sikkim an Indian Protectorate. Indian influence increased from then on. Internal political unrest came to a head in 1973, and led to the granting of constitutional reforms in 1974. Agitation continued until Sikkim became a 'state associated with the Indian Union' later than year. In 1975 the king was deposed and Sikkim became an Indian state, a change approved by referendum.

TERRITORY AND POPULATION
Sikkim is in the Eastern Himalayas and is bounded north by Tibet, east by Tibet and Bhutan, south by West Bengal and west Nepal. Area, 7,096 sq. km. It is inhabited chiefly by the Lepchas, a tribe indigenous to Sikkim, the Bhutias, who originally came from Tibet, and the Nepalis, who entered from Nepal in large numbers in the late 19th and early 20th century. Census population (1991), 406,457, of whom 25,024 lived in the capital, Gangtok. Density, 57 per sq km.

English is the principal language. Lepcha, Bhutia, Nepali and Limboo also have official status.

SOCIAL STATISTICS
Growth rate 1981–91, 28·47%.

CONSTITUTION AND GOVERNMENT
The Assembly has 32 members.

The official language of the Government is English. Lepcha, Bhutia, Nepali and Limboo have also been declared official languages.

Sikkim is divided into 4 districts for administration purposes, Gangtok, Mangan, Namchi and Gyalshing being the headquarters for the Eastern, Northern, Southern and Western districts respectively.

RECENT ELECTIONS
After the election of Nov. 1994 the Sikkim Democratic Front formed a government.

CURRENT ADMINISTRATION
Governor: Chaudhury Randhir Singh.
  Chief Minister: Pawan Kumar Changling.

Local Government. Each of the 4 districts is administered by a District Collector. Within this framework are the Panchayats or Village Councils.

ECONOMY
Budget. Budget estimates for 1996–97 showed a budget of Rs 61,800m. Annual plan outlay for 1997–98 is Rs 2,200m.

ENERGY AND NATURAL RESOURCES
Electricity. Installed capacity (1995–96) 33·6 MW. There are 4 hydro-electric power stations. All villages had electricity in 1991.

Minerals. Copper, zinc and lead are mined.

Agriculture. The economy is mainly agricultural; main food crops are rice, maize, millet, wheat and barley; cash crops are cardamom (a spice), mandarin oranges, apples, potatoes, and buckwheat. Foodgrain production, 1995–96, 104,200 tonnes (rice, 21,900 tonnes; wheat, 15,300 tonnes); pulses, 5,700 tonnes. Tea is grown. Medicinal herbs are exported.

Forestry. Forests occupied about 3,127 sq. km. in 1995 and the potential for a timber and wood-pulp industry is being explored.

INDUSTRY
Small-scale industries include cigarettes, distilling, tanning, fruit preservation, carpets and watchmaking. Local crafts include carpet weaving, making handmade paper, wood carving and silverwork. The State Trading Corporation of Sikkim stimulates trade in indigenous products.

COMMUNICATIONS
Roads. There are 1,615 km of roads, all on mountainous terrain, and 18 major bridges under the Public Works Department. Public transport and road haulage is nationalized. There were 8,997 motor vehicles in 1995–96.

Rail. The nearest railhead is at Siliguri (115 km from Gangtok).

Civil Aviation. The nearest airport is at Bagdogra (128 km from Gangtok), linked to Gangtok by helicopter service.

Telecommunications. There are 1,445 telephones (1987) and 37 wireless stations.

SOCIAL INSTITUTIONS
Religion. At the 1991 census there were 277,881 Hindus; 3,849 Moslems; 13,413 Christians; 110,371 Buddhists; 375 Sikhs; 40 Jains.

Education. At the 1991 census there were 186,789 literate people (56·94%; men 65·74% and women 46·69%). Sikkim had (1996–97) 723 pre-primary schools with 19,946 students, 341 primary schools with 83,410 students, 117 middle schools with 21,955 students, 72 high schools with 8,295 students and 27 higher secondary schools with 3,368 students. Education is free up to class XII; text books are free up to class V. There are 500 adult education centres. There is also a training institute for primary teachers, 2 degree colleges and a teacher training college.

CULTURE

Broadcasting. A radio broadcasting station, Akashvani Gangtok, was built in 1982, and a permanent station in 1983. Gangtok also has a low-power TV transmitter.

Tourism. There is great potential for the tourist industry, which has been stimulated by the opening of new roads.

TAMIL NADU

KEY HISTORICAL EVENTS

The first trading establishment made by the British in the Madras State was at Peddapali (now Nizampatnam) in 1611 and then at Masulipatnam. In 1639 the English were permitted to make a settlement at the place which is now Madras, and Fort St George was founded. By 1801 the whole of the country from the Northern Circars to Cape Comorin (with the exception of certain French and Danish settlements) had been brought under British rule.

Under the provisions of the States Reorganization Act, 1956, the Malabar district (excluding the islands of Laccadive and Minicoy) and the Kasaragod district taluk of South Kanara were transferred to the new state of Kerala; the South Kanara district (excluding Kasaragod taluk and the Amindivi Islands) and the Kollegal taluk of the Coimbatore district were transferred to the new state of Mysore; and the Laccadive, Amindivi and Minicoy Islands were constituted a separate Territory. Four taluks of the Trivandrum district and the Shencottah taluk of Quilon district were transferred from Travancore-Cochin to the new Madras State. On 1 April 1960, 405 sq. miles from the Chittoor district of Andhra Pradesh were transferred to Madras in exchange for 326 sq. miles from the Chingleput and Salem districts. In Aug. 1968 the state was renamed Tamil Nadu.

TERRITORY AND POPULATION

Tamil Nadu is in south India and is bounded north by Karnataka and Andhra Pradesh, east and south by the Indian Ocean and west by Kerala. Area, 130,058 sq. km. Population (1991 census), 55,858,946, density of 429 per sq. km. Tamil is the principal language and has been adopted as the state language with effect from 14 Jan. 1958. For the principal towns, *see* INDIA: Territory and Population. Other large towns (1991): Ambattur (215,424), Thanjavur City (202,013), Tuticorin (199,854), Nagercoil City (190,084), Avadi (183,215), Dindigul City (182,477), Vellore (175,061), Thiruvottir (168,642), Erode (159,232), Kanchipuram (144,955), Cuddalore City (144,561), Tirunelveli (135,825), Alandur (125,244), Neyveli (118,080), Rajapalaiyam City (114,202), Pallavaram (111,866), Tambaran (107,187). There are 21 districts. The capital is Madras.

SOCIAL STATISTICS

Growth rate 1981–91, 15·39%.

CONSTITUTION AND GOVERNMENT

There is a unicameral legislature; the Legislative Assembly has 235 members:

RECENT ELECTIONS

Following elections in 1996 the representation in the Legislative Assembly is: Dravida Munnetra Kazagam (DMK), 172 seats; Tamil Maanila Congress, 39; Communist Party, 8; others, 16.

CURRENT ADMINISTRATION
Governor: Meera Sahib Fathima Beevi.
Chief Minister: K. Muthuvel Karunanidhi.

ECONOMY
Budget. Budget estimates for 1997–98, revenue receipts, Rs 126,410·5m., revenue expenditure, Rs 143,776·2m. Annual plan, 1997–98, Rs 40,000m.

ENERGY AND NATURAL RESOURCES
Electricity. Installed capacity in 1995–96 was 5,067 MW, of which 1,948 MW was hydro-electricity and 2,970 MW thermal. All villages were supplied with electricity. The Kalpakkam nuclear power plant became operational in 1983; capacity, 330 MW.

Water. A joint project with Andhra Pradesh was agreed in 1983, to supply Madras with water from the Krishna river, also providing irrigation, *en route,* for Andhra Pradesh. In 1993–94, 3·54m. ha were irrigated.

Minerals. Value of mineral production, 1987, Rs 1,760m. The state has magnesite, salt, coal, lignite, chromite, bauxite, limestone, manganese, mica, quartz, gypsum and feldspar.

Agriculture. The land is a fertile plain watered by rivers flowing east from the Western Ghats, particularly the Cauvery and the Tambaraparani. Temperature ranges between 6°C and 40°C, rainfall between 442 mm and 934 mm. Of the total land area (13m. ha), 7,158,464 ha were cropped and 298,659 ha of waste were cultivable in 1996. The staple food crops grown are paddy, maize, jawar, bajra, pulses and millets. Important commercial crops are sugar-cane, oilseeds, cashew-nuts, cotton, tobacco, coffee, tea, rubber and pepper. Production, 1995–96 (in tonnes): Total foodgrains, 9·16m. (rice, 7·56m.); pulses, 359,700.

Livestock (1993): Buffaloes, 3,116,647; other cattle, 9,318,666; sheep, 5,865,989; goats, 5,938,475; poultry, 21,454,890.

Forestry. Forest area, 1993–94, 2·14m. ha, of which 1,948,627 ha were reserved forest. Forests cover about 17·21% of land area. Main products are teak, soft wood, wattle, sandalwood, pulp wood, cashew and cinchona bark.

Fisheries. In 1995–96, 448,000 tonnes of fish were produced; marine, 340,000 tonnes.

INDUSTRY
The number of working factories was 18,480 in 1994, employing 1m. workers. In 1993–94 there were 178,114 small industries employing over 1·6m. persons. The biggest central sector project is Salem steel plant. Cotton textiles is one of the major industries. There were 449 cotton textile mills in 1991–92 and many spinning mills supplying yarn to the decentralized handloom industry. Other important industries are cement, sugar, manufacture of textile machinery, power-driven pumps, bicycles, electrical machinery, tractors, motor-cars, rubber tyres and tubes, bricks and tiles and silk.

Main exports: Cotton goods, tea, coffee, spices, engineering goods, motor-car ancillaries, leather and granite.

Trade Unions. In 1994 there were 5,981 registered trade unions. Work-days lost by strikes and lockouts in 1994, 1,668,484.

COMMUNICATIONS
Roads. On 31 March 1992 the state had 172,936 km of national and state highways, major and other district roads. In 1995–96 there were 2,771,845 registered motor vehicles.

Rail. On 31 March 1996 there were 4,005 route km. Madras and Madurai are the main centres.

Civil Aviation. There are airports at Madras, Tiruchirapalli and Madurai, with regular scheduled services to Bombay, Calcutta and Delhi. Madras is an international airport and the main centre of airline routes in South India.

Shipping. Madras and Tuticorin are the chief ports. Important minor ports are Cuddalore and Nagapattinam. Madras handled 26·5m. tonnes of cargo in 1993–94, Tuticorin, 6·7m. The Inland Container Depot at Coimbatore has a capacity of 50,000 tonnes of export traffic; it is linked to Cochin (Kerala).

SOCIAL INSTITUTIONS

Justice. There is a High Court at Madras with a Chief Justice and 26 judges. *Police:* Strength of police force, 1 Jan. 1995, 76,447.

Religion. At the 1991 census Hindus numbered 49,532,052 (88·67%), Christians, 3,179,410 (5·69%); Moslems, 3,052,717 (5·47%).

Education. At the 1991 census 30·38m. people were literate (62·66%; men 73·75% and women 51·33%).

Education is free up to pre-university level. In 1996–97 there were 30,619 primary schools with 6·8m. students, 5,503 middle schools with 3·51m. students, 3,574 high schools with 1,465,631 students and 2,734 higher secondary schools with 0·69m. students. There are also 78 medical colleges, 74 engineering and technology colleges, 22 teacher training colleges and 280 general education colleges.

There are 13 universities. Madras University (founded in 1857) is affiliating and teaching (it had 119 colleges and 125,082 students in 1993–94); Annamalai University, Annamalainagar (founded 1929) is residential; Madurai Kamaraj University (founded 1966) is an affiliating and teaching university; 10 others include one agricultural university, Mother Theresa Women's University, and Tamil University, Tanjavur. There are 4 institutions which are deemed to be universities.

Health. There were (1993–94) 427 hospitals, 484 dispensaries (of which 56 were Indian medicine and homoeopathy), 1,683 primary health centres and 8,681 health sub-centres; total number of beds, 48,128.

CULTURE

Tourism. In 1992, 203,985 foreign tourists visited the state.

FURTHER READING

Statistical Information: The Department of Statistics (Fort St George, Madras) was established in 1948 and reorganized in 1953. *Director:* C. Sethu. Main publications:
Annual Statistical Abstract; Decennial Statistical Atlas; Season and Crop Report; Quinquennial Wages Census; Quarterly Abstract of Statistics.

TRIPURA

KEY HISTORICAL EVENTS

Tripura is a Hindu state of great antiquity having been ruled by the Maharajahs for 1,300 years before its accession to the Indian Union on 15 Oct. 1949. With the reorganization of states on 1 Sept. 1956 Tripura became a Union Territory, and was so declared on 1 Nov. 1957. The Territory was made a State on 21 Jan. 1972.

TERRITORY AND POPULATION

Tripura is bounded by Bangladesh, except in the north-east where it joins Assam and Mizoram. The major portion of the state is hilly and mainly jungle. It has an area of 10,486 sq. km and a population of 2,757,205 (1991 census); Density, 263 per sq. km.

The official languages are Bengali and Kokbarak. Manipuri is also spoken.

SOCIAL STATISTICS

Growth rate 1981–91, 34·3%.

CONSTITUTION AND GOVERNMENT

The territory has 4 districts, divided into 14 administrative subdivisions, namely: Sadar, Khowai, Kailasahar, Dharmanagar, Sonamura, Udaipur, Gandachhara,

TRIPURA

Belonia, Kamalpur, Sabroom, Bishalgarh, Longthorai Velly, Kanchanpur and Amarpur. The capital is Agartala (population, 1991, 157,358).

RECENT ELECTIONS
The Communist Party won the elections of 6 April 1993.

CURRENT ADMINISTRATION
Governor: Siddheshwar Prasad.
  Chief Minister: Manik Sarkar.

ECONOMY
Budget. Budget estimates, 1994–95, show an expenditure of Rs 3,605m. Annual plan outlay for 1997–98 is Rs 4,370m.

ENERGY AND NATURAL RESOURCES
Electricity. Installed capacity (1995–96), 69·36 MW; there were (March 1996) 3,640 villages with electricity out of a total of 4,856.

Agriculture. About 24% of the land area is cultivable. The tribes practise shifting cultivation, but this is being replaced by modern methods. The main crops are rice, wheat, jute, mesta, potatoes, oilseeds and sugar-cane. Foodgrain production (1995–96), 477,100 tonnes. There are 55 registered tea gardens producing 5,432,000 kg per year, and employing 14,170 in 1994–95.

Forestry. Forests covered 5,538 sq. km in 1995, about 53% of the land area. They have been much depleted by clearance for shifting cultivation and, recently, for refugee settlements of Bangladeshis. About 8% of the forest area still consists of dense natural forest; losses elsewhere are being replaced by plantation. Commercial rubber plantation has also been encouraged. In 1994–95, 30,328 ha were under new rubber plantations.

INDUSTRY
Tea is the main industry. There is also a jute mill producing about 15 tonnes per day and employing about 2,000. Main small industries: Aluminium utensils, rubber, saw-milling, soap, piping, fruit canning, handloom weaving and sericulture. There were 1,174 registered factories which employed 31,912 persons, and 700 notified factories with 3,000 workers in 1995–96. 330,980 persons were employed in handloom, handicrafts and sericulture industries in 1995–96.

COMMUNICATIONS
Roads. Total length of roads (1995–96) 5,760 km, of which 2,258 km were surfaced. Vehicles registered, 31 March 1996, 34,683 of which 4,701 were trucks.

Rail. There is a railway between Kumarghat and Kalkalighat (Assam). Route-km in 1995–96, 45 km.

Civil Aviation. There is 1 airport and 3 airstrips. The airport (Agartala) has regular scheduled services to Calcutta.

SOCIAL INSTITUTIONS
Religion. At the 1991 census Hindus numbered 2,384,934; Moslems, 196,495; Christians, 46,472; Buddhists, 128,260; Sikhs, 740; Jains, 301.

Education. In 1991, 60·44% of the population were literate (70·58% of men and 49·65% of women).

   In 1996–97 there were 2,045 primary schools (434,143 pupils); 411 middle schools (126,129); 558 high and higher secondary schools (82,273). There were 14 colleges of general education, 1 engineering college, 1 teacher training college and 1 polytechnic. Tripura University, established in 1987, has 20 affiliated colleges with 20,000 students.

Health. There were (1995–96) 27 hospitals, with 2,171 beds, 548 dispensaries, 818 doctors and 729 nurses. There were 53 primary health centres and 67 family planning centres.

UTTAR PRADESH

KEY HISTORICAL EVENTS
In 1833 the then Bengal Presidency was divided into two parts, one of which became the Presidency of Agra. In 1836 the Agra area was styled the NorthWest Province and placed under a Lieut.-Governor. In 1877 the two provinces of Agra and Oudh were placed under one administrator, styled Lieut.-Governor of the North-West Province and Chief Commissioner of Oudh. In 1902 the name was changed to 'United Provinces of Agra and Oudh', under a Lieut.-Governor, and the Lieut.-Governorship was altered to a Governorship in 1921. In 1935 the name was shortened to 'United Provinces'. On Independence, the states of Rampur, Banaras and Tehri-Garwhal were merged with United Provinces. In 1950 the name of the United Provinces was changed to Uttar Pradesh.

TERRITORY AND POPULATION
Uttar Pradesh is in north India and is bounded north by Himachal Pradesh, Tibet and Nepal, east by Bihar, south by Madhya Pradesh and west by Rajasthan, Haryana and Delhi. The area of the state is 294,411 sq. km. Population (1991 census), 139,112,287, a density of 473 per sq. km. Cities with more than 250,000 population, *see* INDIA: Territory and Population. Other important towns (1991): Rampur (243,742), Muzaffarnagar (240,609), Shahjahanpur (237,717), Mathura (226,691), Firozabad (215,128), Farrukhabad-Cum-Fatehgarh (194,567), Mirzapur-Cum-Vindhyachal (169,336), Sambhal (150,819), Hardwar (147,305), Noida (146,514), Hapur (146,262), Amroha (137,061), Maunath Bhanjan (136,697), Jaunpur (136,062), Bahraich (135,400), Rae Bareli (129,904), Bulandshahr (127,201), Faizabad (124,437), Etawah (124,072), Sitapur (121,842), Fatehpur (117,675), Budaun (116,695), Hathras (113,285), Unnao (107,425), Pilibhit (106,605), Haldwani-Cum-Kathgodam (104,195), Modinagar (101,660). The sole official language has been Hindi since April 1990.

SOCIAL STATISTICS
Growth rate 1981–91, 25·48%.

CONSTITUTION AND GOVERNMENT
Uttar Pradesh has had an autonomous system of government since 1937. There is a bicameral legislature. The Legislative Council has 108 members; the Legislative Assembly has 426, of which 425 are elected. The state was brought under presidential rule on 18 Oct. 1995 and the Legislative Assembly dissolved on 27 Oct. 1995.

There are 14 administrative divisions, each under a Commissioner, and 68 districts.

The capital is Lucknow.

RECENT ELECTIONS
Elections were held in Oct. 1996. Bharatiya Janata Party, 174; Samajwadi Party, 110; Bahujan Samaj Party, 67; Congress (I), 33; Janata Dal, 7; independent and others, 34. As no party was in a position to form a stable government, presidential rule was reimposed.

CURRENT ADMINISTRATION
Governor: Suraj Bhan.
Chief Minister: Kalyan Singh.

ECONOMY

Budget. Budget estimates for 1996–97 showed revenue receipts of Rs 155,963·2m.; expenditure, Rs 194,039·9m. Annual plan outlay, 1997–98, Rs 70,800m.

ENERGY AND NATURAL RESOURCES

Electricity. The state had, 1995–96, an installed capacity of 6,049 MW. There were 85,657 villages with electricity in March 1996, out of a total 112,804.

Minerals. The state has magnesite, china-clay, coal, granite, sandstone, copper-lead-zinc, dolomite, limestone, soapstone, bauxite, diaspore, ochre, phosphorite, pyrophyllite, silica sand and steatite among others. In 1995–96 about 13m. tonnes of minerals were produced.

Agriculture. Agriculture occupies 78% of the workforce. 10·13m. ha are irrigated. The state is India's largest producer of foodgrains; production (1995–96), 38·94m. tonnes (rice 10·4m. tonnes, wheat 22·2m. tonnes); pulses, 2·25m. tonnes. The state is one of India's main producers of sugar; production of sugar-cane (1995–96), 119·9m. tonnes. There were (1995–96) 1,965 veterinary centres for cattle.

Forestry. In 1995 forests covered about 51,663 sq. km.

INDUSTRY

Sugar production is important; other industries include oil refining, aluminium smelting edible oils, textiles, distilleries, brewing, leather working, agricultural engineering, paper, automobile tyres, fertilizers, cement, jute, glass, heavy electricals, chemicals, automobiles and synthetic fibres. Large public-sector enterprises have been set up in electrical engineering, pharmaceuticals, locomotive building, general engineering, electronics and aeronautics. Village and small-scale industries are important; there were 0·64m. small units in 1995–96 providing employment to 1·19m. people. The state had 1,661 large and medium industries with an investment of Rs 223,002m. and employing 0·57m. persons in 1995–96.

COMMUNICATIONS

Roads. There were, 31 March 1995, 185,575 km of roads. In 1995–96 there were 2,977,275 motor vehicles of which 2,057,408 were two-wheelers.

Rail. Lucknow is the main junction of the northern network; other important junctions are Agra, Kanpur, Allahabad, Mughal Sarai, Dehra Dun and Varanasi. Route-km in 1995–96, 8,934 km.

Civil Aviation. There are airports at Lucknow, Kanpur, Varanasi, Allahabad, Agra, Gorakhpur and 7 other places.

SOCIAL INSTITUTIONS

Justice. The High Court of Judicature at Allahabad (with a bench at Lucknow) has a Chief Justice and 63 puisne judges including additional judges. There are 63 sessions divisions in the state.

Religion. At the 1991 census Hindus numbered 113,712,829; Moslems, 24,109,684; Sikhs, 675,775; Christians, 383,477; Jains, 176,259; Buddhists, 221,443.

Education. At the 1991 census 46·87m. people were literate (41·6%; 55·73% of men and 25·31% of women). In 1996–97 there were 91,093 primary schools with 16·26m. students, 19,917 middle schools with 5·63m. students, 2,628 high schools with 2,329,904 students and 4,375 higher secondary schools with 1,167,552 students.

Uttar Pradesh has 20 universities including: Allahabad University (founded 1887); Agra University (1927); the Banaras Hindu University, Varanasi (1916); Lucknow University (1921); Aligarh Muslim University (1920) with 4 colleges and 13,437 students in 1993–94; Roorkee University (1949), formerly Thomason College of Civil Engineering (established in 1847); Gorakhpur University (1957) with 33 colleges and 96,504 students; Sampurnanand Sanskrit Vishwavidyalaya, Varanasi (1958); Kanpur University (1966); Ch. Charan Singh University (1966), with 82 colleges and 96,004 students in 1993–94; Govind Ballabh Pant University of

Agriculture and Technology, Pantnagar (1960); H. N. Bahuguna Garhwal University, Srinagar, (1973). C. S. Azad University of Agriculture and Technology, Kanpur, Narendra Deva University of Agriculture and Technology, Faizabad, and Dr Ram Manohar Lohia Awadh (32 colleges and 64,142 students), Kumaon, Rohilkhand (32 colleges and 86,996 students) and Bundelkhand Universities were founded in 1975. Jaunpur University (Purvanchal Vishwavidyalaya) was founded in 1987.

There are also 6 institutions with university status: Gurukul Kangri Vishwavidyalaya, Hardwar; Indian Veterinary Research Institute; Central Institute of Higher Tibetan Studies; Forest Research Institute; Sanjay Gandhi Post-Graduate Institute of Medical Sciences; and Dayal Bagh Educational Institute. There are 35 medical colleges, 18 engineering colleges, 62 teacher training colleges and 550 arts, science and commerce colleges.

Health. In 1994–95 there were 5,011 allopathic, 2,690 Ayurvedic and Unani and 1,149 homoeopathic hospitals and dispensaries. There were also 3,766 primary health centres and 20,153 sub-centres, and TB hospitals and clinics.

WEST BENGAL

KEY HISTORICAL EVENTS
Bengal was under the overlordship of the Moghul emperor and ruled by a Moghul governor (*nawab*) who declared himself independent in 1740. The British East India Company based at Calcutta was in conflict with the *nawab* from 1756 until 1757 when British forces defeated him at Plassey and installed their own *nawab* in 1760. The French were also in Bengal; the British captured their trading settlement at Chandernagore in 1757 and in 1794, restoring it to France in 1815.

The area of British Bengal included modern Orissa and Bihar, Bangladesh and (until 1833) Uttar Pradesh. Calcutta was the capital of British India from 1772 until 1912.

The first division into East and West took place in 1905-11 and was not popular. However, at Partition in 1947 the East (Moslem) chose to join what was then East Pakistan (now Bangladesh), leaving West Bengal as an Indian frontier state and promoting a steady flow of non-Moslem Bengali immigrants from the East. In 1950 West Bengal received the former princely state of Cooch Behar and, in 1954, Chandernagore. Small areas were transferred from Bihar in 1956.

TERRITORY AND POPULATION
West Bengal is in north-east India and is bounded north by Sikkim and Bhutan, east by Assam and Bangladesh, south by the Bay of Bengal, south-west by Orissa, west by Bihar and north-west by Nepal. The total area of West Bengal is 88,752 sq. km. At the 1991 census its population was 68,077,965, an increase of 24·73% since 1981; density of population, 767 per sq. km. The capital is Calcutta. Population of chief cities, *see* INDIA: Territory and Population. Other major towns (1991): Barddhaman (245,079), South Dum Dum (232,811), Baranagar (224,821), Siliguri (216,950), Bally (181,978), Burnpur (174,933), Uluberia (155,172), Hugli-Chinsura (151,806), Raiganj (151,045), North Dum Dum (149,965), Dabgram (147,217), English Bazar (139,204), Serampur (137,028), Barrackpur (133,265), Naihati (132,701), Medinipur (125,498), Nabadwip (125,037), Krishnanagar (121,110), Chandannagar (120,378), Balurghat (119,796), Baharampur (115,144), Bankura (114,876), Titagarh (114,085), Halisahar (114,028), Santipur (109,956), Kulti-Barakar (108,518), Basirhat (101,409), Haldia (100,347), Habra (100,223), Kanchrapara (100,194). The principal language is Bengali.

CONSTITUTION AND GOVERNMENT
The state of West Bengal came into existence as a result of the Indian Independence Act, 1947. The territory of Cooch-Behar State was merged with West Bengal on 1 Jan. 1950, and the former French possession of Chandernagore became part of the

state on 2 Oct. 1954. Under the States Reorganization Act, 1956, certain portions of Bihar State (an area of 3,157 sq. miles with a population of 1,446,385) were transferred to West Bengal.

The Legislative Assembly has 295 seats (294 elected and 1 nominated).

For administrative purposes there are 3 divisions (Jalpaiguri, Burdwan and Presidency), under which there are 18 districts, including Calcutta. The Calcutta Metropolitan Development Authority has been set up to co-ordinate development in the metropolitan area (1,350 sq. km). For the purposes of local self-government there are 16 *zila parishads* (district boards) excluding Darjeeling, 328 *panchayat samities* (regional boards), and 3,222 *gram* (village) *panchayats*. There are 113 municipalities, 3 Corporations and 11 Notified Areas. The Calcutta Municipal Corporation is headed by a mayor in council.

RECENT ELECTIONS

Distribution of seats after the Legislative Assembly elections, Dec. 1996: Communist Party of India (Marxist), 150; Indian National Congress, 82; All India Forward Bloc, 21; Revolutionary Socialist Party, 18; Communist Party of India, 6; Independents and others, 17.

CURRENT ADMINISTRATION

Governor: Akhlay ar-Rahman Kidwai.
  Chief Minister: Jyoti Basu.

ECONOMY

Budget. Budget estimates for 1997–98, revenue receipts Rs 102,582·9m. and expenditure Rs 120,329·1m. Plan outlay for 1997–98 was Rs 29,456m.

ENERGY AND NATURAL RESOURCES

Electricity. Installed capacity, 1995–96, 5,481·5 MW; 29,237 villages had electricity in Nov. 1996.

Water. The largest irrigation and power scheme under construction is the Teesta Barrage (irrigation potential, 533,520 ha). Other major irrigation schemes are the Mayurakshi Reservoir, Kangsabati Reservoir, Mahananda Barrage and Aqueduct and Damodar Valley. In 1995–96 there were 9,171 tubewells, 7,170 open dugwells and 3,170 riverlift irrigation schemes.

Minerals. Value of production, 1995, Rs 10,094m. The state has coal (the Raniganj field is one of the 3 biggest in India) including coking coal. Coal production (1995) 17·56m. tonnes.

Agriculture. About 5·95m. ha were under rice-paddy in 1995–96. Total foodgrain production, 1995–96, 12·99m. tonnes (rice 11·89m. tonnes, wheat 850,000 tonnes); pulses, 125,900 tonnes; oilseeds, 415,500 tonnes; jute, 5·7m. bales of 180 kg; tea (1995), 160·3m. kg. The state produces 63·4% of the national output of jute and *mesta* (1994–95).

  Livestock (1989 census): 16,509,487 cattle; 965,517 buffaloes; 1,459,771 sheep; 11,890,278 goats and 35,542,444 poultry.

  The recorded forest area (1995–96) was 11,879 sq. km.

Fisheries. Landings, 1995–96, 0·89m. tonnes, of which inland 740,000 tonnes. During 1996–97 Rs 407·1m. was invested in fishery schemes. The state is the largest inland fish producer in the country.

INDUSTRY

The total number of registered factories, 1995, was 10,236 (excluding defence factories); average daily employment, 1995, 920,763. The coalmining industry, 1993, had 110 units with average daily employment of 107,000.

  There is a large automobile factory at Uttarpara, and an aluminium rolling-mill at Belur. There is a steel plant at Burnpur (Asansol) and a spun pipe factory at Kulti. Durgapur has a large steel plant and other industries under the state sector—a thermal power plant, coke oven plant, fertilizer factory, alloy steel plant and ophthalmic glass plant. There is a locomotive factory at Chittaranjan and a cable factory at Rupnarayanpur. A refinery and fertilizer factory are operating at Haldia. Other industries include chemicals, engineering goods, electronics, textiles, automobile tyres, paper, cigarettes, distillery, aluminium foil, tea, pharmaceuticals, carbon black, graphite, iron foundry, silk and explosives.

Small industries are important; 453,831 units were registered at 31 March 1996, employing 3m. persons. The silk industry is also important; 376,000 persons were employed in the handloom industry in the organized sector in 1995–96.

COMMUNICATIONS

Roads. In 1995 the total length of roads was 68,375 km. On 31 March 1996 the state had 1,198,733 motor vehicles.

Rail. The route-km of railways within the state (1995–96) is 3,817 km. The main centres are Asansol, New Jalpaiguri and Kharagpur. There is a metro in Calcutta (16·4 km).

Civil Aviation. The main airport is Calcutta which has national and international flights. The second airport is at Bagdogra in the extreme north, which has regular scheduled services to Calcutta and Delhi.

Shipping. Calcutta is the chief port: A barrage has been built at Farakka to control the flow of the Ganges and to provide a rail and road link between North and South Bengal. A second port has been developed at Haldia, between the present port and the sea, which is intended mainly for bulk cargoes. West Bengal possesses 779 km of navigable canals.

SOCIAL INSTITUTIONS

Justice. The High Court of Judicature at Calcutta has a Chief Justice and 45 puisne judges. The Andaman and Nicobar Islands come under its jurisdiction.

Police. In March 1995 the police force numbered about 56,550, under a director-general and an inspector-general. Calcutta has a separate force under a commissioner directly responsible to the Government; its strength was about 22,000 in March 1995.

Religion. At the 1991 census Hindus numbered 50,866,624; Moslems, 16,075,836; Christians, 383,477; Buddhists, 203,578; Sikhs, 55,392; Jains, 34,355.

Education. In 1996, 70·64% of the total population were literate (men, 78·62%; women, 61·67%).

In 1996–97 there were 51,021 primary schools with 10,117,000 students, 3,156 junior high schools with 4,603,000 students and 6,728 high and higher secondary schools with 1,881,226 students. Education is free up to higher secondary stage. There are 10 universities.

The University of Calcutta (founded in 1857) is affiliating and teaching; in 1993–94 it had 212 colleges and 150,000 students. Visva Bharati, Santiniketan, was established in 1951 and is residential and teaching; it had 5,226 students in 1993–94. The University of Jadavpur, Calcutta (1955), had 7,087 students in 1992–93. Burdwan University was established in 1960; in 1992–93 there were 91,379 students. Kalyani University was established in 1960 (2,520 students in 1993–94). The University of North Bengal (1962) had 34,000 students in 1993–94. Rabindra Bharati University had 8,309 students in 1992–93. Bidhan Chandra Krishi Viswavidyalaya (1974) had 389 students in 1992–93. There is also Vidyasagar University, Medinipur. Bengal Engineering College has university status. There are 12 engineering and technology colleges, 19 medical colleges, 24 teacher training colleges, 41 polytechnics and 308 arts, science and commerce colleges.

Health. As at 31 March 1996 there were 402 hospitals, 1,352 clinics, 1,266 health centres and 8,126 sub-centres with a total of 68,901 beds, and 566 dispensaries.

FURTHER READING
Chatterjee, P., *The Present History of West Bengal: Essays in Political Criticism.* OUP, 1997

UNION TERRITORIES

ANDAMAN AND NICOBAR ISLANDS

The Andaman and Nicobar Islands are administered by the President of the Republic of India acting through a Lieut.-Governor. There is a 30-member Pradesh Council, 5 members of which are selected by the Administrator as advisory counsellors. The seat of administration is at Port Blair, which is connected with Calcutta (1,255 km away) and Madras (1,190 km) by steamer service which calls about every 10 days; there are air services from Calcutta and Madras. Roads in the islands, 733 km black-topped and 48 km others. There are 2 districts.

The population (1991 census) was 280,661; Area, 8,249 sq. km; density 34 per sq. km. Growth rate 1981–91, 48·7%. Port Blair (1991), 74,955.

The climate is tropical, with little variation in temperature. Heavy rain (125" annually) is mainly brought by the south-west monsoon. Humidity is high.

Budget figures for 1997–98 show total revenue receipts of Rs 819m., and total expenditure on revenue account of Rs 3,027m. Plan outlay, 1997–98, Rs 2,550m.

In 1996–97 there were 188 primary schools with 41,976 students, 45 middle schools with 22,862 students, 38 high schools with 11,151 students and 42 higher secondary schools with 3,858 students. There is a teachers' training college, 2 polytechnics and 2 colleges. Literacy (1991 census), 73·02% (78·99% of men and 65·46% of women).

Lieut.-Governor: Rajendra Kumari Bajpai.

The **Andaman Islands** lie in the Bay of Bengal, 193 km from Cape Negrais in Myanmar, 1,255 from Calcutta and 1,190 from Madras. Five large islands grouped together are called the Great Andamans, and to the south is the island of Little Andaman. There are some 204 islets, the two principal groups being the Ritchie Archipelago and the Labyrinth Islands. The Great Andaman group is about 467 km long and, at the widest, 51 km broad.

The original inhabitants live in the forests by hunting and fishing. The total population of the Andaman Islands (including about 430 aboriginals) was 240,089 in 1991. Main aboriginal tribes: Andamanese, Onges, Jarawas and Sentinelese.

The Great Andaman group, densely wooded (forests covered 7,615 sq. km in 1995), contains hardwood and softwood and supplies the match and plywood industries. Annually the Forest Department export about 25,000 tons of timber to the mainland. Coconut, coffee and rubber are cultivated. The islands are slowly being made self-sufficient in paddy and rice, and now grow approximately half their annual requirements. Livestock (1982): 27,400 cattle, 9,720 buffaloes, 17,600 goats and 21,220 pigs. Fishing is important. There is a sawmill at Port Blair and a coconut-oil mill. Little Andaman has a palm-oil mill.

The islands possess a number of harbours and safe anchorages, notably Port Blair in the south, Port Cornwallis in the north and Elphinstone and Mayabandar in the middle.

The **Nicobar Islands** are situated to the south of the Andamans, 121 km from Little Andaman. The British were in possession 1869–1947. There are 19 islands, 7 uninhabited; total area, 1,841 sq. km. The islands are usually divided into 3 sub-groups (southern, central and northern), the chief islands in each being respectively Great Nicobar, Camotra with Nancowrie and Car Nicobar. There is a harbour between the islands of Camotra and Nancowrie, Nancowrie Harbour.

The population numbered, in 1991, 39,208, including about 22,200 of Nicobarese and Shompen tribes. The coconut and areca nut are the main items of trade, and coconuts are a major item in the people's diet.

CHANDIGARH

On 1 Nov. 1966 the city of Chandigarh and the area surrounding it was constituted a Union Territory. Population (1991), 642,015; density, 5,632 per sq. km.; growth rate, 1981–91, 42·16%. Area, 114 sq. km. It serves as the joint capital of both Punjab (India) and the state of Haryana, and is the seat of a High Court. The city will ultimately be the capital of just the Punjab; joint status is to last while a new capital is built for Haryana.

Budget for 1997–98 showed revenue of Rs 3,412m. and expenditure of Rs 3,989m.

There is some cultivated land and some forest (27·5% of the territory).

In 1992 there were 15 large and medium scale industries and about 2,800 small scale industries.

In 1996–97 there were 44 primary schools (60,012 students), 33 middle schools (34,095 students), 50 high schools (18,510 students) and 47 higher secondary schools (16,710 students). There were also 2 engineering and technology colleges, 12 arts, science and commerce colleges, 2 polytechnic institutes and a university.

In 1991, 77·81% of the population were literate (82·04% of men and 72·34% of women).

Administrator: Lieut.-Gen. Bakshi K. N. Chibber.

DADRA AND NAGAR HAVELI

GENERAL DETAILS
Formerly Portuguese, the territories of Dadra and Nagar Haveli were occupied in July 1954 by nationalists, and a pro-India administration was formed; this body made a request for incorporation into the Union on 1 June 1961. By the 10th amendment to the constitution the territories became a centrally administered Union Territory with effect from 11 Aug. 1961, forming an enclave at the southernmost point of the border between Gujarat and Maharashtra. Area 491 sq. km.; population (census 1991), 138,477; density 282 per sq. km; growth rate, 1981–91, 33·57%. There is an Administrator appointed by the Government of India. The day-to-day business is done by specialized departments, co-ordinated by the Resident Deputy Collector, Collector or Assistant Secretary. Headquarters are at Silvassa. 78·82% of the population is tribal and organized in 72 villages. Languages used are Bhilli, Gujarati, Bhilodi (91·1%), Marathi and Hindi.

CURRENT ADMINISTRATION
Administrator: Ramesh Negi.
  Collector: S. P. Marwah.

ECONOMY
Budget. The budget for 1997–98 shows revenue receipts of Rs 377m. and revenue expenditure of Rs 1,154·5m. For 1998–99, revenue receipt target is RS 344m.; budget estimate is RS 415·8m. under Plan Sector and RS 1,318·8m. under Non-Plan sector.

ENERGY AND NATURAL RESOURCES
Electricity. Electricity is supplied by Gujarat, and all villages have been electrified.

Oil and Gas. There are no oil and gas resources in the Union Territory.

Water. As the result of a joint project with the governments of Gujarat, Goa and Daman and Diu there is a reservoir at Damanganga with irrigation potential of 7,044 ha.

Minerals. There are few natural mineral resources though there is some ordinary sand and quarry stone.

Agriculture. Farming is the chief occupation, and 22,697 ha were under crops in 1996–97. Much of the land is terraced and there is a 100% subsidy for soil conservation. The major food crops are rice and ragi; wheat, small millets and pulses are also grown. There is little irrigation (6,841 ha). There are 9 veterinary aid centres, a veterinary hospital, an agricultural research centre and breeding centres to improve strains of cattle and poultry. During 1997–98 the Administration distributed 168 tonnes of high-yielding paddy and wheat seed and 1,439 tonnes of fertilizer.

Forestry. 19,967 ha or 40·8% of the total area is forest, mainly of teak, sadad and khair. There was (1985) a moratorium on commercial felling, to preserve the environmental function of the forests and ensure local supplies of firewood, timber and fodder. The moratorium still continued in 1998. The tribals have been given exclusive right to collect minor forest produce from the reserved forest area for domestic use.

Fisheries. There is little inland fishing in water reservoir project area and individual ponds, and no marine fishing. During 1997–98 fish production was 15·31 tonnes.

INDUSTRY

There is no heavy industry, and the Territory is a 'No Industry District'. Industrial estates for small and medium units have been set up at Piparia, Masat and Khadoli. There were (1998) 618 small units, 253 medium scale and 15 large scale units employing 18,400. Concessions (15 years' sales tax holiday) are available for small units. Income tax benefit has been extended up to March 2000 by the Indian Government.

Labour. The Labour Enforcement Office ensure the application of the Monitoring of Minimum Wages Act (1948), the Industrial Disputes Act (1947), the Contract Labour (Regulation and Abolition) Act (1970) and the Workmens' Compensation Act (1923).

Trade Unions. There are no registered trade unions at present.

COMMUNICATIONS

Roads. There were (1998) 533·74 km of roads of which 467 km was surfaced. Out of 72 villages, 68 are connected by all-weather road. There were 13,739 motor vehicles in 1997–98. The National Highway no. 8 passes through Vapi, 18 km away from Silvassa.

Rail. There is no railway passing through the territory. The railway line from Bombay to Ahmedabad runs through Vapi, 18 km from Silvassa.

Civil Aviation. The nearest airport is at Mumbai (formerly called Bombay), 180 km from Silvassa.

Telecommunications. There are 5 telephone exchanges, 1 telex exchange and 1 wireless station in the region. In addition, the Telephone Department provided 1,200 extra connections in Silvassa and 150 lines at Dadra, and also opened a new telephone exchange at Silli during 1997–98.

Postal Services. There is currently 1 post and telegraph office with 1 sub-post office and 25 branch post offices covering 66 villages.

SOCIAL INSTITUTIONS

Justice. The territory is under the jurisdiction of the Bombay (Maharashtra) High Court. There is a District and Sessions Court and one Junior Division Civil Court at Silvassa.

Religion. Numbers of religious followers (1991 census): Hindu, 132,213 (95·48%); Moslems, 3,341 (2·41%); Christians, 2,092 (1·51%); Jains, 529 (0·38%); Buddhists, 200 (0·14%). There are also, amongst others, Sikh and Zoroastrian populations.

Education. Literacy was 40·71% of the population at the 1991 census (53·56% of men and 26·98% of women). In 1997–98 there were 150 adult education centres (4,500 students); there were 193 primary and middle schools and 15 high and higher secondary schools. Total primary and middle school enrolment was 29,707; high-school and higher secondary, 5,114.

Health. The territory had (1997–98) 1 cottage hospital, 6 primary health centres and 4 dispensaries; there is also a mobile dispensary. A Community Health Centre has been established at Khanvel, 20 km from Silvassa.

Welfare. The Social Welfare Department implements the welfare schemes for poor Scheduled castes, Scheduled tribes, women and physically handicapped persons etc.

CULTURE

Broadcasting. There is a low power TV transmission centre.

Cinema. There is 1 cinema at Silvassa.

Press. There are no newspapers or magazines published in the territory.

Tourism. The territory is a rural area between the industrial centres of Bombay and Surat-Vapi. The Tourism Department is developing areas of natural beauty to promote acceptable tourism. About 500,000 visitors came to the region during 1998. The government is constructing a tourist accommodation complex at Silvassa.

Festivals. Normally all Hindu, Moslem and Christian festivals are celebrated in the territory while tribals celebrate their own festivals. Diwaso is celebrated by Dhodia and Varli tribes and Rakhsabandhan is celebrated by Dhodias. The Varli and Koli tribes celebrate Bhavada, and Khali pooja is celebrated by all tribes after the harvesting of the crops.

Libraries. There are 10 libraries, 1 in each of 10 Gram Panchayat HQs.

Museums and Galleries. There are no major museums or galleries in the territory, though there is a tribal museum at Silvassa with presentations of the lifestyle and culture of tribals.

DAMAN AND DIU

GENERAL DETAILS

Daman (Damão) on the Gujarat coast, 100 miles (160 km) north of Bombay, was seized by the Portuguese in 1531 and ceded to them (1539) by the Shar of Gujarat. The island of Diu, captured in 1534, lies off the south-east coast of Kathiawar (Gujarat); there is a small coastal area. Former Portuguese forts on either side of the entrance to the Gulf of Cambay, in Dec. 1961 the territories were occupied by India and incorporated into the Indian Union; they were administered as one unit together with Goa, to which they were attached until 30 May 1987, when Goa was separated from them and became a state.

TERRITORY AND POPULATION

Daman, 72 sq. km, population (1991) 62,101; Diu, 40 sq. km, population 39,485. Density, 907 per sq. km. The main language spoken is Gujarati.

The chief towns are Daman (population, 1991, 26,905) and Diu (20,643).

Daman and Diu have been governed as parts of a Union Territory since Dec. 1961, becoming the whole of that Territory on 30 May 1987.

The main activities are tourism, fishing and tapping the toddy palm. In Daman there is rice-growing, some wheat and dairying. Diu has fine tourist beaches, grows coconuts and pearl millet, and processes salt.

SOCIAL STATISTICS

Growth rate 1981–91, 28·62%.

CURRENT ADMINISTRATION

Administrator: S. P. Aggarwal.

ECONOMY

Budget. The budget for 1997–98 shows revenue receipts of Rs 397·7m. and revenue expenditure of Rs 312·2m. Plan outlay, 1995–96, Rs 230m.

SOCIAL INSTITUTIONS

Education. In 1991, 71·2% of the population were literate (82·66% of men and 59·4% of women). In 1996–97 there were 53 primary schools with 14,531 students, 20 middle schools with 6,834 students, 20 high schools with 3,220 students and 3 higher secondary schools with 1,202 students. There is a degree college and a polytechnic.

DELHI

GENERAL DETAILS

Delhi became a Union Territory on 1 Nov. 1956 and was designated the National Capital Territory in 1995.

TERRITORY AND POPULATION

The territory forms an enclave near the eastern frontier of Haryana and the western frontier of Uttar Pradesh in north India. Delhi has an area of 1,483 sq. km. At the 1991 census its population was 9,420,644 (density per sq. km, 6,352). Growth rate, 1981–91, 51·45%. In the rural area of Delhi there are 231 villages and 27 census towns. They are distributed in 5 community development blocks.

CONSTITUTION AND GOVERNMENT

The Lieut-Governor is the Administrator. Under the New Delhi Municipal Act 1994 New Delhi Municipal Council is nominated by central government and replaces the former New Delhi Municipal Committee.

RECENT ELECTIONS

Elections for the 70-member Legislative Assembly were held in Nov. 1998 and the Congress Party formed the government. Congress (I) won 51 seats; Bharatiya Janata Party, 15; others, 3.

CURRENT ADMINISTRATION

Lieut.-Governor: Tejendra Khanna.
  Chief Minister: Sheila Dikshit.

ECONOMY

Budget. Estimates for 1996–97 show revenue receipts of Rs 25,911·2m. and expenditure of Rs 37,624·7m. Plan outlay (1997–98) Rs 23,250m.

ENERGY AND NATURAL RESOURCES

Agriculture. The contribution to the economy is not significant. In 1995–96 about 53,900 ha were cropped (of which 36,000 ha were irrigated). Animal husbandry is increasing and mixed farms are common. Chief crops are wheat, bajra, paddy, sugar-cane and vegetables.

INDUSTRY

The modern city is the largest commercial centre in northern India and an important industrial centre. Since 1947 a large number of industrial units have been established; these include factories for the manufacture of razor blades, sports goods, electronic goods, bicycles and parts, plastic and PVC goods including footwear, textiles, chemicals, fertilizers, medicines, hosiery, leather goods, soft drinks and hand tools. There are also metal forging, casting, galvanising, electro-plating and printing enterprises. The number of industrial units functioning was about 126,218 in 1996–97; average number of workers employed was 1·14m. Production was worth Rs 63,100m. and investment was about Rs 25,240m. in 1996–97.

Some traditional handicrafts, for which Delhi was formerly famous, still flourish; among them are ivory carving, miniature painting, gold and silver jewellery and papier mâché work. The handwoven textiles of Delhi are particularly fine; this craft is being successfully revived.

COMMUNICATIONS

Roads. 5 national highways pass through the city. There were (1995–96) 2,629,545 registered motor vehicles. The Transport Corporation had 3,206 buses in 1995–96.

Rail. Delhi is an important rail junction with 3 main stations. There is an electric ring railway for commuters (route-km in 1995–96, 214).

Civil Aviation. Indira Gandhi International Airport operates international flights; Palam airport operates internal flights.

SOCIAL INSTITUTIONS

Religion. At the 1991 census Hindus numbered 7,882,164; Sikhs, 455,657; Moslems, 889,641; Jains, 94,672; Christians, 83,152; Buddhists, 13,906; others, 1,452.

Education. The proportion of literate people to the total population was 75·29% at the 1991 census (82·01% of males and 66·99% of females). In 1996–97 there were 2,184 primary schools with 1,146,691 students, 559 middle schools with 535,511 students, 324 high schools with 676,209 students and 994 higher secondary schools with 460,334 students. There are 9 engineering and technology colleges, 9 medical colleges and 25 polytechnics.

The University of Delhi was founded in 1922; it had 66 affiliated colleges and 189,332 students in 1994–95. There are also Jawahar Lal Nehru University, Indira Gandhi National Open University and the Jamia Millia Islamia University; the Indian Institute of Technology at Hauz Khas; the Indian Agricultural Research Institute at Pusa; the All India Institute of Medical Science at Ansari Nagar and the Indian Institute of Public Administration are the other important institutions.

Health. In 1992 there were 82 hospitals including 46 general, 27 special, 6 Ayurvedic, 1 Unani, 2 Homoeopathic. There were 656 dispensaries.

CULTURE

Press. Delhi publishes major daily newspapers, including the *Times of India, Hindustan Times, The Hindu, Indian Express, National Herald, Patriot, Economic Times, The Pioneer, The Observer of Business and Politics, Financial Express, Statesman, Asian Age* and *Business Standard* (all in English); *Nav Bharat Times, Rashtriya Sahara, Jansatta* and *Hindustan* (in Hindi); and 3 Urdu dailies.

LAKSHADWEEP

The territory consists of an archipelago of 36 islands (10 inhabited), about 300 km off the west coast of Kerala. It was constituted a Union Territory in 1956 as the Laccadive, Minicoy and Amindivi Islands, and renamed in Nov. 1973. The total area of the islands is 32 sq. km. The northern portion is called the Amindivis. The remaining islands are called the Laccadives (except Minicoy Island). The inhabited islands are: Androth (the largest), Amini, Agatti, Bitra, Chetlat, Kadmat, Kalpeni,

Kavaratti, Kiltan and Minicoy. Androth is 4·8 sq. km, and is nearest to Kerala. An Advisory Committee associated with the Union Home Minister and an Advisory Council to the Administrator assist in the administration of the islands; these are constituted annually. Population (1991 census), 51,707, nearly all Moslems. Density, 1,616 per sq. km.; growth rate, 1981–91, 28·4%. The language is Malayalam, but the language in Minicoy is Mahl. Budget for 1997–98 showed revenue of Rs 73·1m. and expenditure of Rs 1,255·7m. In 1991, 81·78% of the population were literate (90·18% of men and 72·89% of women). There were, in 1996–97, 9 high schools (2,043 students) and 9 nursery schools (1,197 students), 19 junior basic schools (9,015 students), 4 senior basic schools (4,797 students) and 2 junior colleges. There are 2 hospitals and 7 primary health centres. The staple products are copra and fish; coconut is the only major crop. There is a tourist resort at Bangarem, an uninhabited island with an extensive lagoon. Headquarters of administration, Kavaratti Island. An airport, with Vayudoot services, opened on Agatti island in April 1988. The islands are also served by ship from the mainland and have helicopter inter-island services.

Administrator: Rajeev Talwar.

PONDICHERRY

GENERAL DETAILS
Formerly the chief French settlement in India, Pondicherry was founded by the French in 1673, taken by the Dutch in 1693 and restored to the French in 1699. The English took it in 1761, restored it in 1765, re-took it in 1778, restored it a second time in 1785, re-took it a third time in 1793 and finally restored it to the French in 1816. Administration was transferred to India on 1 Nov. 1954. A Treaty of Cession (together with Karaikal, Mahé and Yanam) was signed on 28 May 1956; instruments of ratification were signed on 16 Aug. 1962 from which date (by the 14th amendment to the Indian Constitution) Pondicherry, comprising the 4 territories, became a Union Territory.

TERRITORY AND POPULATION
The territory is composed of enclaves on the Coromandel Coast of Tamil Nadu and Andhra Pradesh, with Mahé forming an enclave on the coast of Kerala. The total area of Pondicherry is 492 sq. km, divided into 4 Districts. On Tamil Nadu coast: Pondicherry (293 sq. km; population, 1991 census, 607,600), Karaikal (160; 145,723). On Kerala coast: Mahé (9; 33,425). On Andhra Pradesh coast: Yanam (30; 20,297). Total population (1991 census), 807,785; density, 1,642 per sq. km. Pondicherry Municipality had (1991) 203,065 inhabitants. The principal languages spoken are Tamil, Telugu, Malayalam, French and English.

SOCIAL STATISTICS
Growth rate 1981–91, 33·64%. In 1990 family schemes had reduced the birth rate to 19·9 per 1,000 and the infant mortality rate to 34·79 per 1,000 live births.

CONSTITUTION AND GOVERNMENT
By the Government of Union Territories Act 1963 Pondicherry is governed by a Lieut.-Governor, appointed by the President, and a Council of Ministers responsible to a Legislative Assembly.

RECENT ELECTIONS
A DMK led government was formed after the election in June 1996. Total seats, 30: Congress (I), 9; DMK, 7; Ramil Maanila Congress, 6; All India Anna DMK, 3; CPI, 2; Independents and others, 3.

INDIA

CURRENT ADMINISTRATION
Governor: Rajendra Kumari Bajpai.
  Chief Minister: R. V. Janakiraman.

ECONOMY
Budget. Budget estimates for 1996–97 showed expenditure of Rs 5,354·8m. Plan outlay, 1996–97, Rs 2,000m.

ENERGY AND NATURAL RESOURCES
Electricity. Power is bought from neighbouring states. All 292 villages have electricity. Consumption, 1991–92, 747 units per head. Peak demand, 130 MW; total consumption, 607·73m. units.

Agriculture. Nearly 45% of the population is engaged in agriculture and allied pursuits; 90% of the cultivated area is irrigated. The main food crop is rice. Foodgrain production, 71,600 tonnes in 1995–96. Rice production, 67,100 tonnes from 26,600 ha in 1995–96; principal cash crops are cotton (10,934 bales of 180 kg), sugar-cane (258,400 tonnes) and groundnuts; minor food crops include ragi, bajra and pulses.

INDUSTRY
There were, 1994–95, 23 large and 73 medium-scale enterprises manufacturing items such as textiles, sugar, cotton yarn, spirits and beer, potassium chlorate, rice bran oil, vehicle parts, soap, amino acids, paper, plastics, steel ingots, washing machines, glass and tin containers and bio polymers. There were also 5,197 small industrial units engaged in varied manufacturing.

COMMUNICATIONS
Roads. There were (1992–93) 3,282 km of roads of which 1,248 km were surfaced. Motor vehicles (March 1996) 119,290.

Rail. Pondicherry is connected to Villupuram Junction. Route-km in 1995–96, 11 km.

Civil Aviation. The nearest main airport is Madras. Vayudoot domestic airline connects Pondicherry with Madras.

SOCIAL INSTITUTIONS
Education. In 1991, 74·74% of the population were literate (83·68% of men and 65·63% of women). There were, in 1996–97, 178 pre-primary schools (15,107 pupils), 350 primary schools (103,201), 120 middle schools (64,617), 89 high schools (28,731) and 52 higher secondary schools (11,168). There were (1996–97) 7 general education colleges, 2 medical colleges, a law college, an engineering college, an agricultural college and a dental college, and 4 polytechnics. Pondicherry University had, in 1994–95, 19 colleges and 9,910 students.

Health. In 1995–96 there were 9 hospitals, 55 health centres and dispensaries and 79 sub-centres.

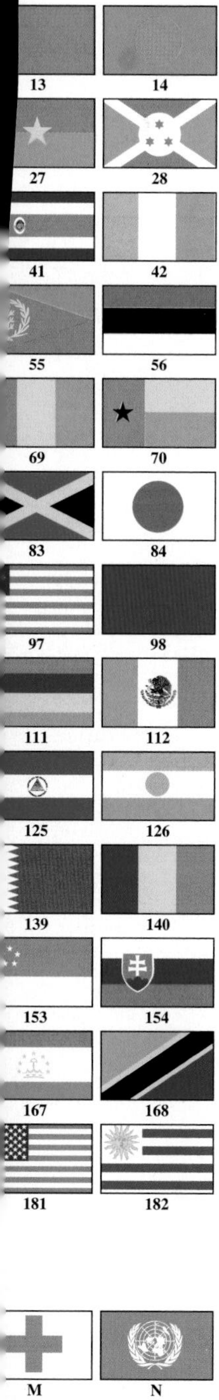

KEY

Flag panel labels:

13 14
27 28
41 42
55 56
69 70
83 84
97 98
111 112
125 126
139 140
153 154
167 168
181 182
M N

1. Afghanistan
2. Albania
3. Algeria
4. Andorra
5. Angola
6. Antigua and Barbuda
7. Argentina
8. Armenia
9. Australia
10. Austria
11. Azerbaijan
12. Bahamas
13. Bahrein
14. Bangladesh
15. Barbados
16. Belarus
17. Belgium
18. Belize
19. Benin
20. Bhutan
21. Bolivia
22. Bosnia-Hercegovina
23. Botswana
24. Brazil
25. Brunei
26. Bulgaria
27. Burkina Faso
28. Burundi
29. Cambodia
30. Cameroon
31. Canada
32. Cape Verde
33. Central African Republic
34. Chad
35. Chile
36. China, People's Republic of
37. Colombia
38. Comoros
39. Congo, Democratic Republic of (former Zaïre)
40. Congo, Republic of
41. Costa Rica
42. Côte d'Ivoire
43. Croatia
44. Cuba
45. Cyprus
46. Czech Republic
47. Denmark
48. Djibouti
49. Dominica
50. Dominican Republic
51. Ecuador
52. Egypt
53. El Salvador
54. Equatorial Guinea
55. Eritrea
56. Estonia
57. Ethiopia
58. Fiji Islands
59. Finland
60. France
61. Gabon
62. The Gambia
63. Georgia
64. Germany
65. Ghana
66. Greece
67. Grenada
68. Guatemala
69. Guinea
70. Guinea-Bissau
71. Guyana
72. Haiti

73. Honduras
74. Hungary
75. Iceland
76. India
77. Indonesia
78. Iran
79. Iraq
80. Ireland
81. Israel
82. Italy
83. Jamaica
84. Japan
85. Jordan
86. Kazakhstan
87. Kenya
88. Kiribati
89. Korea (South)
90. Korea (North)
91. Kuwait
92. Kyrgyzstan
93. Laos
94. Latvia
95. Lebanon
96. Lesotho
97. Liberia
98. Libya
99. Liechtenstein
100. Lithuania
101. Luxembourg
102. Macedonia
103. Madagascar
104. Malawi
105. Malaysia
106. Maldives
107. Mali
108. Malta
109. Marshall Islands
110. Mauritania
111. Mauritius
112. Mexico
113. Micronesia
114. Moldova
115. Monaco
116. Mongolia
117. Morocco
118. Mozambique
119. Myanmar
120. Namibia
121. Nauru
122. Nepal
123. Netherlands
124. New Zealand
125. Nicaragua
126. Niger
127. Nigeria
128. Norway
129. Oman
130. Pakistan
131. Palau
132. Panama
133. Papua New Guinea
134. Paraguay
135. Peru
136. Philippines
137. Poland
138. Portugal
139. Qatar
140. Romania
141. Russia
142. Rwanda
143. St Kitts and Nevis
144. St Lucia
145. St Vincent & the Grenadines

146. Samoa
147. San Marino
148. São Tomé and Príncipe
149. Saudi Arabia
150. Senegal
151. Seychelles
152. Sierra Leone
153. Singapore
154. Slovakia
155. Slovenia
156. Solomon Islands
157. Somalia
158. South Africa
159. Spain
160. Sri Lanka
161. Sudan
162. Suriname
163. Swaziland
164. Sweden
165. Switzerland
166. Syria
167. Tajikistan
168. Tanzania
169. Thailand
170. Togo
171. Tonga
172. Trinidad and Tobago
173. Tunisia
174. Turkey
175. Turkmenistan
176. Tuvalu
177. Uganda
178. Ukraine
179. United Arab Emirates
180. United Kingdom
181. United States of America
182. Uruguay
183. Uzbekistan
184. Vanuatu
185. Vatican City
186. Venezuela
187. Vietnam
188. Yemen
189. Yugoslavia
190. Zambia
191. Zimbabwe

FLAGS OF INTERNATIONAL ORGANISATIONS

A. Arab League
B. Association of South East Asian Nations (ASEAN)
C. Caricom
D. Commonwealth of Independent States (CIS)
E. Commonwealth
F. Danube Commission
G. Europe
H. North Atlantic Treaty Organisation (NATO)
I. Organisation of American States (OAS)
J. Organisation of African Unity (OAU)
K. Organisation of Oil Exporting Countries (OPEC)
L. Red Crescent
M. Red Cross
N. United Nations Organisation (UNO)

Key

— International border
▫ Capital city

Arctic Circle
ALASKA (USA)
CANADA
Ottawa
UNITED STATES OF AMERICA
Washington, DC
THE BAHAMAS
Tropic of Cancer
Havana
MEXICO
CUBA
Mexico City
JAMAICA
DOMINICAN R
HAITI
DOMINI
BELIZE
BARBA
GUATEMALA
HONDURAS
EL SALVADOR
NICARAGUA
Caracas
TRINIDA
COSTA RICA
VENEZUELA
GUYAN
PANAMA
SUR
Bogotá
COLOMBIA
Quito
Equator
Galapagos Is (Ecu.)
ECUADOR
Hawaii (USA)
PACIFIC OCEAN
BRA
PERU
Lima
La Paz
BOLIVIA
French Polynesia (Fr.)
Tropic of Capricorn
PARA
CHILE
Santiago
Buenos Aires
ARGENTI
Antarctic Circle
ANTARCTICA

The Political World

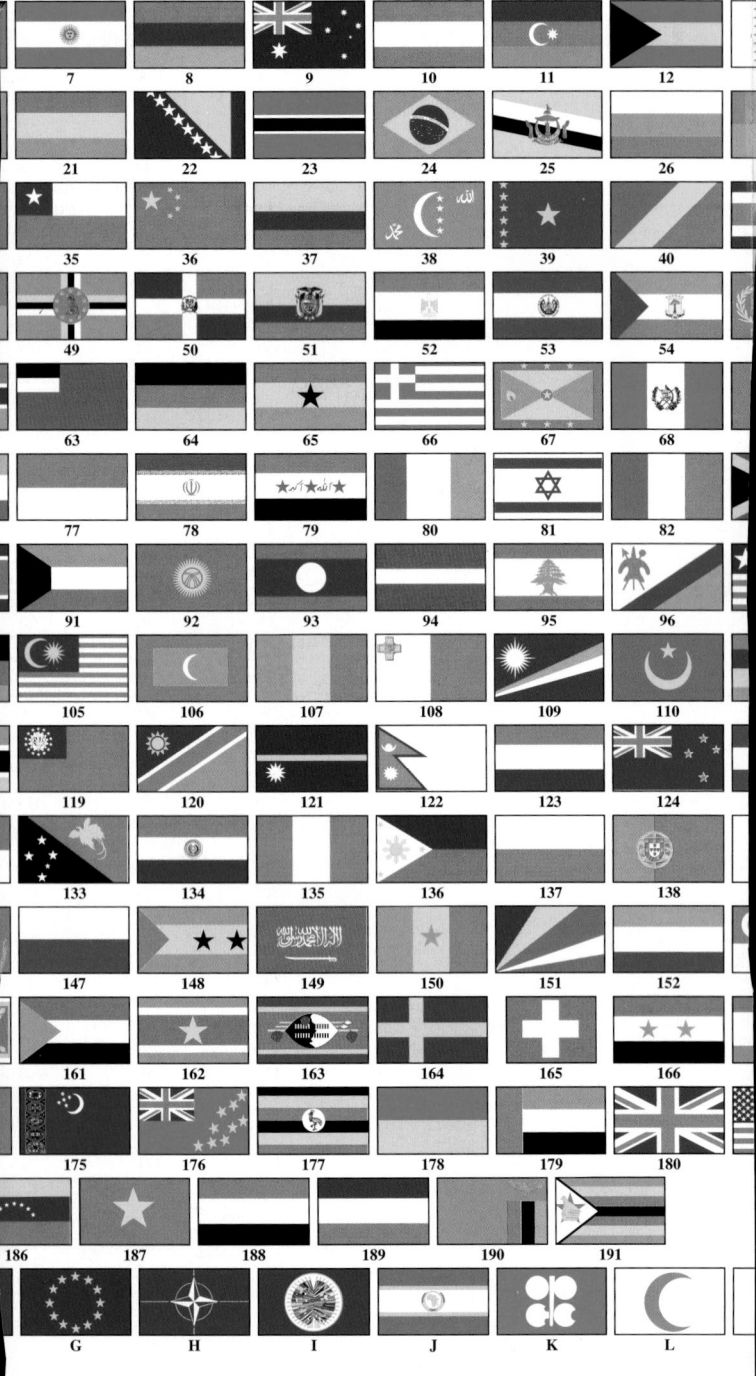

N
W · E
S

150°
180°
Arctic Circle
60°
A
Jlan Bator
MONGOLIA
Beijing
NORTH KOREA
Seoul
SOUTH
KOREA
Tokyo
JAPAN
CHINA
BHUTAN
ESH
Tai-pei
30°
MYANMAR
Hanoi
TAIWAN
Tropic of Cancer
LAOS
Yangon
THAILAND
VIETNAM
Manila
PACIFIC OCEAN
Bangkok
CAMBODIA
ANKA
Phnom Penh
PHILIPPINES
MARSHALL
ISLANDS
Kuala Lumpur
BRUNEI
PALAU
MICRONESIA
KIRIBATI
MALAYSIA
SINGAPORE
Equator
0°
INDONESIA
NAURU
Jakarta
PAPUA
NEW GUINEA
SOLOMON ISLANDS
TUVALU
Port
Moresby
SAMOA
VANUATU
FIJI
ISLANDS
TONGA
Tropic of Capricorn
AUSTRALIA
30°
Canberra
NEW
ZEALAND
Wellington
60°
Antarctic Circle
150°
180°

0   2000 miles
0   4000 km

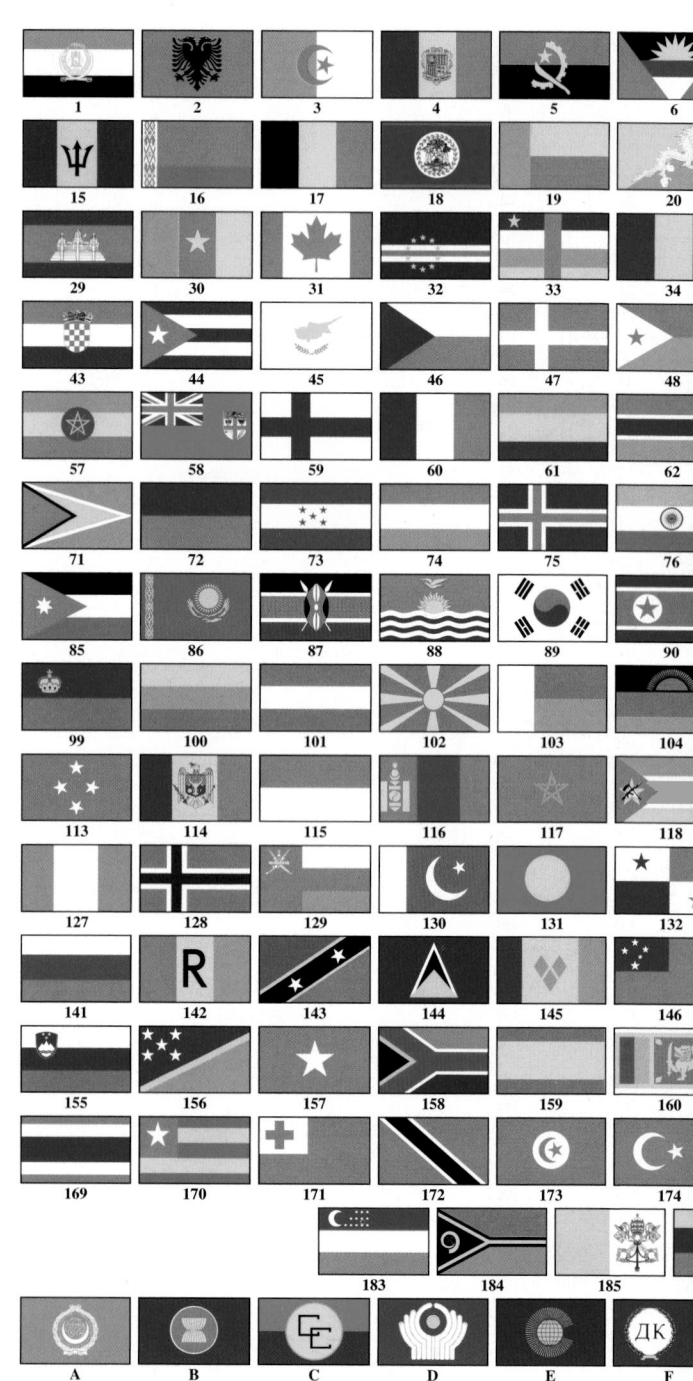

INDONESIA

Republik Indonesia

Capital: Jakarta
Population estimate, 2000: 212·56m.
GNP per capita: (PPP$) 3,310
HDI/world rank: 0·679/96

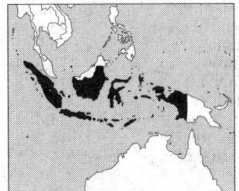

KEY HISTORICAL EVENTS
In the 16th century Portuguese traders settled in some of the islands which now comprise Indonesia, but were ejected by the British, who in turn were ousted by the Dutch in 1595. From 1602 the Netherlands East India Company conquered the area and ruled until the dissolution of the Company in 1798. The Netherlands government then ruled the colony from 1816 until 1941, when it was occupied by the Japanese until 1945. On 17 Aug. 1945 an independent republic was proclaimed by Dr Sukarno and Dr Hatta, the nationalist leaders. The republic was not, however, recognized by the Netherlands with whom negotiations and fighting continued until 1949. On 27 Dec. 1949 complete and unconditional sovereignty was transferred to the Republic of the United States of Indonesia.

A settlement of the New Guinea (Irian Jaya) question was, however, delayed until 15 Aug. 1962, when through the offices of the UN, an agreement was concluded for the transfer of the territory to Indonesia on 1 May 1963.

In 1950 the federal form of government which had sprung up in 1946–48 was abolished, and Indonesia was again made a unitary state. On 5 July 1959, by presidential decree, the constitution of 1945 was reinstated.

On 12 Jan. 1960 President Sukarno issued a decree enabling him to control and dissolve the political parties. He also set up a mass organization, the National Front, and a supreme state body called the Provisional People's Consultative Assembly. On 6 March 1960 he prorogued parliament to be reorganized on the basis of the 1945 constitution with the local administrations nominating members to the new 'Mutual Co-operation House of Representatives'.

On 11–12 March 1966 the military commanders under the leadership of Lieut.-Gen. Suharto took over executive power while leaving President Sukarno as the head of state. The Communist party, which had twice attempted to overthrow the government and had killed six generals in 1965, was at once outlawed; the National Front was dissolved in Oct. 1966. On 22 Feb. 1967 Sukarno handed over all his powers to Gen. Suharto. Re-elected president at five-year intervals, most recently on 10 March 1998, Suharto presided over a booming economy but one which was characterized by corruption and croneyism. The weaknesses became apparent when, in 1997, a failure of economic confidence spread from Japan across Asia. By May 1998 Indonesia had regressed to the verge of civil war. As food prices doubled, then trebled, riots broke out in Jakarta destroying homes and shops. The risk of society fragmenting along ethnic and religious lines was emphasized by the particular sufferings of the Chinese community. President Suharto was forced to stand down on 21 May 1998 and was succeeded by his Vice-President, Bacharuddin Jusuf Habibie, who promised political and economic reforms. Continuing protest centred on the Suharto family which continues to exercise control over large part of the Indonesian economy. Several of the country's discontented regions are wanting to break free. The government has said that it may grant independence to East Timor, the former Portuguese colony it invaded in 1975.

TERRITORY AND POPULATION
Indonesia, with a land area of 741,098 sq. miles (1,919,443 sq. km), consists of 17,508 islands (6,000 of which are inhabited) extending about 3,200 miles east to west through three time-zones (East, Central and West Indonesian Standard time) and 1,250 miles north to south. The largest islands are Sumatra, Java, Kalimantan (Indonesian Borneo), Sulawesi (Celebes) and Irian Jaya (the western part of New Guinea). Most of the smaller islands except Madura and Bali are grouped together. The two largest groups of islands are Maluku (the Moluccas) and Nusa Tenggara (the Lesser Sundas).

INDONESIA

Population at the 1990 census was 179,378,946. Estimate, 1995, 195·28m. (35·4% urban); density, 102 per sq. km.

The UN gives a projected population for 2000 of 212·56m.

Area, population and chief towns of the provinces, autonomous districts and major islands at the 1990 census:

	Area (in sq. km)	Population	Chief town	Population
Aceh[1]	55,392	3,416,156	Banda Aceh	143,409
Sumatera Utara	70,787	10,256,027	Medan	1,685,972
Sumatera Barat	49,778	4,000,207	Padang	477,344
Riau	94,561	3,303,976	Pakanbaru	341,328
Jambi	44,800	2,020,568	Jambi[2]	301,359
Sumatera Selatan	103,688	6,313,074	Palembang	1,084,483
Bengkulu	21,168	1,179,122	Bengkulu	146,439
Lampung	33,307	6,016,573	Tanjungkarang	284,275[3]
Sumatra	473,481	36,505,703		
Jakarta Raya[1]	590	8,259,266	Jakarta	8,259,266
Jawa Barat	46,300	35,384,352	Bandung	2,026,893
Jawa Tengah	34,206	28,520,643	Semarang	1,005,316
Yogyakarta[1]	3,169	2,913,054	Yogyakarta	412,392
Jawa Timur	47,921	32,503,991	Surabaya	2,421,016
Java and Madura	132,186	107,581,306		
Kalimantan Barat	146,760	3,229,153	Pontianak	387,112
Kalimantan Tengah	152,600	1,396,486	Palangkaraya	60,447[3]
Kalimantan Selatan	37,660	2,597,572	Banjarmasin	443,738
Kalimantan Timur	202,440	1,876,663	Samarinda	335,016
Kalimantan	539,460	9,099,874		
Sulawesi Utara	19,023	2,478,119	Menado	275,374
Sulawesi Tengah	69,726	1,711,327	Palu	298,584[3]
Sulawesi Selatan	72,781	6,981,646	Ujung Padang	913,196
Sulawesi Tenggara	27,686	1,349,619	Kendari	41,021[3]
Sulawesi	189,216	12,520,711		
Bali	5,561	2,777,811	Denpasar	261,263[3]
Nusa Tenggara Barat	20,177	3,369,649	Mataram	141,387[3]
Nusa Tenggara Timur	47,876	3,268,644	Kupang	403,110[3]
Timor Timur[4]	14,874	747,750	Dili	60,150[3]
Maluku	74,505	1,857,790	Amboina	206,260
Irian Jaya	421,981	1,648,708	Jayapura	149,618[3]
Pulau—Pulau Lain	584,974	13,670,352		

[1]Autonomous District [2]Formerly Telanaipura. [3]1980 census. [4]See section below.

The capital, Jakarta, had a population of 9m. in 1993. Other major cities (census 1990 in 1m.): Surabaya, 2·5; Bandung, 2; Medan, 1·7; Semarang, 1·3; Palembang, 1·1.

The principal ethnic groups are the Acehnese, Bataks and Minangkabaus in Sumatra, the Javanese and Sundanese in Java, the Madurese in Madura, the Balinese in Bali, the Sasaks in Lombok, the Menadonese, Minahasans, Torajas and Buginese in Sulawesi, the Dayaks in Kalimantan, Irianese in Irian Jaya, the Ambonese in the Moluccas and Timorese in Timor Timur. There were some 6m. Chinese resident in 1991.

Bahasa Indonesia is the official language; Dutch is spoken as a colonial inheritance.

East Timor. Portugal abandoned its former colony, whose population is largely Roman Catholic, in 1975, when it was occupied by Indonesia and claimed as the province of Timor Timur. The UN does not recognize Indonesian sovereignty over the territory. An independence movement, FRETILIN, has maintained a guerilla resistance to the Indonesian government which has resulted in large-scale casualties and alleged atrocities. On 24 July 1998 Indonesia announced a withdrawal of troops from East Timor and an amnesty for some political prisoners, although no indication was given of how many of the estimated 12,000 troops and police would pull out. On 5 Aug. Indonesia and Portugal reached agreement on the outlines of an autonomy plan which would give the Timorese the right to self-government except in foreign affairs and defence.

Carey, P. and Bentley, G. C. (eds.) *East Timor at the Crossroads: the Forging of a Nation.* London, 1995

SOCIAL STATISTICS

Births, 1995, 4,719,000; deaths, 1,580,000. 1995 birth rate, 23·9 per 1,000 population; death rate, 8·0. Life expectancy in 1996 was 63 years. Annual growth rate, 1990–95, 1·5%. Infant mortality, 1990–95, 58 per 1,000 live births; fertility rate, 2·9 births per woman.

CLIMATE

Conditions vary greatly over this spread of islands, but generally the climate is tropical monsoon, with a dry season from June to Sept. and a wet one from Oct. to April. Temperatures are high all the year and rainfall varies according to situation on lee or windward shores. Jakarta, Jan. 78°F (25·6°C), July 78°F (25·6°C). Annual rainfall 71" (1,775 mm). Padang, Jan. 79°F (26·1°C), July 79°F (26·1°C). Annual rainfall 177" (4,427 mm). Surabaya, Jan. 79°F (26·1°C), July 78°F (25·6°C). Annual rainfall 51" (1,285 mm).

CONSTITUTION AND GOVERNMENT

The political system is based on *pancasila*, in which deliberations lead to a consensus. 425 members of the *House of People's Representatives* are elected every 5 years, and the remaining 75 are appointed from the armed forces. Together with 500 government appointees they make up the *People's Consultative Assembly* which meets every 5 years to choose a president. There is no limit to the number of presidential terms. The military perform a dual function enshrined in law, combining conventional defence duties with participation in all areas of political and social life. Golkar is a 'functional group'. There are 2 officially-sanctioned parties also in the House of People's Representatives: the United Development Party (UDP, largely Moslem), and the Indonesian Democratic Party (IDP nationalist Christian).

National Anthem. 'Indonesia, tanah jang mulia' ('Indonesia, our native land'); words and tune by W. R. Supratman.

RECENT ELECTIONS

General elections to the 425 elected seats in the House of Representatives were held on 29 May 1997. The electorate was 124·7m.; turn-out was 93%. Golkar won 425 seats with 74% of votes cast (68% in 1992), UDP received 22·5% of the votes (17·5% in 1992) and IDP 3% (15% in 1992). A general election was due to be held on 7 June 1999.

CURRENT ADMINISTRATION

The Cabinet was as follows in March 1999:
President: Bacharuddin Jusuf Habibie (since 21 May 1998).
Co-ordinating Ministers: (Political *Affairs and Security*) Feisal Tanjung; (*Economy, Finance and Industry*) Ginanjar Kartasasmita; (*Welfare*) Haryono Suyono; (*Development Supervisions and Administrative Reform*) Hartarto Sastrosunarto.
Minister of Home Affairs: Lt. Gen. Syarwan Hamid. *Foreign Affairs:* Ali Abdullah Alatas. *Defence and Security:* Gen. Wiranto. *Justice:* Dr H. Muladi. *Information:* Lt. Gen. Yunus Yosfiah. *Finance:* Bambang Subianto. *Trade and Industry:* Rahardi Ramelan. *Agriculture:* Soleh Solahuddin. *Mines and Energy:* Kuntoro Mangkusubroto. *Public Works:* Rachmadi Bambang Sumadio. *Co-operatives and Small Business:* Adi Sasono. *Manpower:* Fahmi Idris. *Transmigration:* Lt. Gen. Hendro Priyono. *Tourism, Arts and Culture:* Marzuki Usman. *Communications:* Giri Hadiharjono Suseno. *Education:* Juwono Sudarsono. *Health:* Dr Farid Antara Muluk. *Religious Affairs:* Malik Fajar. *Social Affairs:*

Yustika Sjarifudin Baharsjah. *Forestry and Plantations:* Muslimin Nasution. *Secretary of State:* Akbar Tanjung.

Local Government. There are 27 provinces, 3 of which are special territories (the capital city of Jakarta, Yogyakarta and Aceh), each administered by a Governor appointed by the President; they are divided into 246 districts (*kabupatens*), each under a district head (*bupati*), and 55 municipalities (*kotamadya*), each under a mayor (*wali kota*). The districts are divided into 3,592 sub-districts (*kecamtans*), each headed by a *camat*.

DEFENCE
There is selective conscription for 2 years. Defence expenditure in 1997 totalled US$4,812m. (US$24 per capita).

Army. The Army is organized in a strategic reserve, with 2 infantry divisional headquarters, 3 infantry and 3 airborne brigades, 2 field artillery and 1 air defence artillery regiment and 2 engineer battalions; and 10 military area commands, with 62 infantry, 8 cavalry, 11 field artillery, 10 air defence and 8 engineer battalions, and 1 composite aviation and 1 helicopter squadron. Equipment includes 275 AMX-13, 30 PT-76 and 26 Scorpion light tanks. The Army has about 100 aircraft, including 1 Islander, 4 Aviocars and 12 other fixed-wing types, 30 Bell 205, 12 BO 105, 9 Hughes 300, 24 locally-built Bell 412 helicopters. There is a paramilitary police some 177,000 strong, and 2 part-time local auxiliary forces: KAMRA (People's Security) and WANRA (People's Resistance). Army personnel in 1997 numbered 220,000.

Navy. The Navy in 1996 numbered about 43,000, including 12,000 in the Commando Corps, and 1,000 in the Naval Air Arm. Combatant strength includes 2 German-built diesel submarines (1 in long refit) and 13 frigates of which 6 are former Dutch Van Speijk class, and 3 former British Ashanti class each equipped with 1 helicopter. Delivery of 16 ex-East German Parchim class anti-submarine corvettes completed in 1996. There are also 4 fast missile craft, 2 torpedo-armed craft and 35 miscellaneous patrol craft as well as 2 Dutch-built tripartite coastal minehunters and 11 other minesweepers. Amphibious lift is provided by 14 tank landing ships (4 with helicopter facilities), 14 smaller ex-East German units and 50 craft. The auxiliary force includes 2 replenishment tankers, 2 transport tankers, 6 surveying vessels, 1 command and submarine support ship, 1 repair ship, 3 training ships and some dozens of minor auxiliaries and service craft.

The Naval Air Arm operates 60 aircraft, including 15 Searchmaster maritime reconnaissance and 8 NC-212 Aviocar transport aircraft, and 10 anti-submarine helicopters as well as miscellaneous communications and utility aircraft.

The Marine Commando Force of 12,000 comprises 2 brigades and is equipped with some 100 light tanks and 48 artillery pieces.

A separate Military Sealift Command operates about 25 inter-island transport ships (which number includes 3 of the tank landing ships in the navy listing) totalling approximately 30,000 tonnes. The Maritime Security Agency operates 10 cutters, the Customs about 70 and the armed Marine Police 60 craft.

Air Force. Operational combat units comprise 3 squadrons of British Aerospace Hawk and 1 of A-4E Skyhawk attack aircraft, and single squadrons of F-5E Tiger II and of F-16 fighters. There are 5 transport squadrons, equipped with turboprop C-130 Hercules, Nurtanio/CASA NC-212 Aviocar and CN-235 and F27 Friendship aircraft, as well as 3 specially-equipped Boeing 737 dual-purpose maritime surveillance/transports; and an assortment of other aircraft in transport, helicopter and training units including 15 Hawks, 15 T-34C-1 armed turboprop trainers, and 36 Swiss-built AS 202 Bravo piston-engined primary trainers. Personnel (1996) approximately 21,000.

INTERNATIONAL RELATIONS
Indonesia is in dispute with Malaysia over sovereignty of 2 islands in the Celebes Sea. Both countries have agreed to accept the Judgment of the International Court of Justice.

Indonesia is a member of the UN, OPEC and ASEAN.

ECONOMY

Policy. The Government's plan for growth has been hit by financial instability in the Asian money markets and international concern about corruption, a shaky banking system and the slow pace of deregulation and privatization; but this is not to deny the economic successes which were achieved by the Suharto administration. Since 1970 the economy has grown, on average, by more than 6% a year.

Performance. Economic growth was 7·5% in 1994, 8·1% in 1995, 8% in 1996 and an estimated 5% in 1997, but was forecast to decline dramatically to an estimated −17% in 1998. The Asian crisis and the economic collapse affected Indonesia more than any other country.

Budget. By law the budget must balance. The fiscal year starts 1 April. Revenue and expenditure for 1995–96 were 78,000,000m. rupiahs. Current revenue (in 1,000m. rupiahs), 1993–94, 52,280; current expenditure, 38,799; capital revenue, 10,372; capital expenditure, 25,661.

Currency. The monetary unit is the *rupiah* (IDR) notionally of 100 *sen*. Annual inflation was running at about 52% in mid-1998. In March 1998 Indonesia's official hard currency reserves were US$16·33bn., although usable reserves were just under US$10bn. Gold reserves were 3·1m. troy oz. in Feb. 1998. Total money supply in Nov. 1997 was 61,563bn. rupiahs.

Banking and Finance. The Bank Indonesia, successor to De Javasche Bank established by the Dutch in 1828, was made the central bank of Indonesia on 1 July 1953. Its *Governor* is Sudradjat Djiwandono. It had an original capital of 25m. rupiahs; a reserve fund of 18m. rupiahs and a special reserve of 84m. rupiahs. Total assets and liabilities as at Dec. 1992, 123,689,000m. rupiahs. Total savings deposits at July 1996 were 41,858,000m. rupiahs.

There are 117 commercial banks, 28 development banks and other financial institutions, 8 development finance companies and 9 joint venture merchant banks. Commercial banking is dominated by 7 state-owned banks: Bank Rakyat Indonesia provides services to smallholder agriculture and rural development; Bank Bumi Daya, estate agriculture and forestry; Bank Negara Indonesia 1946, industry; Bank Dagang Negara, mining; and Bank Expor-Impor Indonesia, export commodity sector. All state banks are authorized to deal in foreign exchange.

There are 70 private commercial banks owned and operated by Indonesians. The 11 foreign banks specialize in foreign exchange transactions and direct lending operations to foreign joint ventures. The government owns 1 Savings Bank, Bank Tabungan Negara, and 1,000 Post Office Savings Banks. There are also over 3,500 rural and village savings bank and credit co-operatives. At least 16 banks closed in the wake of the 1997 financial crisis.

The World Bank board agreed to resume lending in Indonesia in June 1998 by approving a US$225m. loan to reduce poverty. Also in June 1998 Indonesia reached agreement with foreign banks on a comprehensive private-sector debt restructuring programme, involving the rescheduling of some US$60bn. of Indonesian corporate debt over 8 years and the extension by up to 4 years of Indonesian bank liabilities totalling US$9·2bn. The most important element of the deal was the creation of the Indonesian Debt Restructuring Agency which provided protection against foreign exchange risk covering up to US$60bn. in corporate debt.

There is a stock exchange in Jakarta.

Weights and Measures. The metric system is in use.

The following are the old weights and measures: *Pikol* = 136·16 lb. avoirdupois; *Katti* = 1·36 lb. avoirdupois; *Bau* = 1·7536 acres; *Square Pal* = 227 hectares = 561·16 acres; *Jengkal* = 4 yd; *Pal* (Java) = 1,506 metres; *Pal* (Sumatra) = 1,852 metres.

ENERGY AND NATURAL RESOURCES

Electricity. Installed capacity in 1994 was 16·27m. kW. There were 7 hydro-electric plants in 1989; 19,044 out of 66,594 villages are supplied with electricity in Java and Sumatra. Production was 61·37bn. kWh in 1994. Consumption per capita was estimated at 276 kWh in 1995.

Oil and Gas. The importance of oil in the economy is declining. The 1995 output of crude oil was 1,476,000 bbls. Natural gas production, 1994, was 2,949,635m. cu. ft.

Minerals. The high cost of extraction means that little of the large mineral resources outside Java is exploited; however, there is copper mining in Irian Jaya, nickel mining and processing on Sulawesi, aluminium smelting in northern Sumatra. Open-cast coal mining has been conducted since the 1890s, but since the 1970s coal production has been developed as an alternative to oil. Reserves are estimated at 28,000m. tonnes. Coal production (1994, in tonnes) 28·6m. tonnes; bauxite, 1,342,400 tonnes; iron ore, 334·9; copper, 1,065·5; silver, 105,961 kg; gold, 44,843 kg; nickel ore, 2,302; tin, 30·6.

Agriculture. Agriculture contributed 16% of GDP in 1996. Production (1994, in 1,000 tonnes): Rice, 46,641; cassava, 15,729; maize, 6,869; sweet potatoes, 1,845; sugar-cane (1993), 32,400; coconuts (1993), 14m.; copra (1993), 1,100; palm oil, 1,930; palm kernels, 472; soybeans, 1,565; rubber (1993), 1,370; coffee, 43·7; groundnuts, 632; vegetables (1993), 4,912; fruits (1993), 7,341; tea, 97·4; tobacco (1993), 85. In 1991, 6,750 tonnes of nutmeg were produced, about 75% of world production.

Livestock (1996): Cattle, 11·93m.; buffaloes, 3·56m. (1995); horses, 727,000; sheep, 7·68m.; goats, 12·53m. (1995); pigs, 7·82m.; chickens, 650m. (1995).

Forestry. In 1995 the area under forests was 109·79m. ha, or 60·6% of the total land area (115·21m. ha and 63·6% in 1990). Approximately 46% of the forested area is scheduled for selective logging, 33% for preservation for national parks and watersheds and 21% for removal for agriculture, industry and settlement. The loss of 5·42m. ha between 1990 and 1995 was exceeded during the same period only in Brazil. In 1995, 185·89m. cu. metres of roundwood were cut, most of it fuelwood and charcoal.

Fisheries. In 1995 total catches were 4,118,000 tonnes, of which 3,296,310 tonnes were sea fish. In 1991 there were 130,712 motorized and 373,086 other fishing vessels.

INDUSTRY
Manufacturing contributed 14·9% of GDP in 1990. There are shipyards at Jakarta Raya, Surabaya, Semarang and Amboina. There were (1985) more than 2,000 textile factories (total production in 1987–88, 2,925·6m. metres), large paper factories (817,200 tonnes, 1986–87), match factories, automobile and bicycle assembly works, large construction works, tyre factories, glass factories, a caustic soda and other chemical factories. Production (1987–88): Cement, 22,419,000 tonnes; fertilizers, 5,811,000 tonnes; 160,372 motor vehicles and 249,573 motor cycles; 2·36m. boxes of matches; glasses and bottles, 126,060 tonnes; steel ingots, 1,337,000 tonnes; 640 TV sets and 159,020 refrigerators.

Labour. Reforms announced in Nov. 1994 included an annual review of regional minimum wages, enhanced enforcement of salary, safety and health regulations, and an improved dispute resolution process. In 1996 the labour force was 93,618,000. National daily average wage, 1996, 4,073 rupiahs. Unemployment in 1998 reached 15·4m., or about 17% of the total workforce of 90m.

Trade Unions. Workers have a constitutional right to organize. Unions are expected to affiliate to the Indonesian Welfare Labour Union (SBSI) which enjoys government approval, but in Nov. 1990 an independent union, Setia Kawan (Solidarity) was set up. About 40% of the labour force belong to unions. In 1993 (and 1992) there were 169 (197) strikes involving 97,807 (98,764) workers and resulting in the loss of 857,845 (1,044,519) working hours. Strikes are forbidden by law. President Habibie lifted the ban on labour unions on 26 May 1998, and shortly afterwards an Indonesian Workers' Party was launched to challenge Golkar, the ruling party.

INTERNATIONAL TRADE
Since 1992 foreigners have been permitted to hold 100% of the equity of new companies in Indonesia with more than US$50m. part capital, or situated in remote

provinces. Foreign investment in 1994 totalled US$23,724·3m. (including from Hong Kong, US$6,041·7m.; UK, US$2,957·1m.; Taiwan, US$2,487·5m.). Foreign debt was US$129,033m. in 1996.

Pressure on Indonesia's currency and stock market led to an appeal to the IMF and World Bank for long-term support funds in Oct. 1997. A bail-out package worth US$38,000m. was eventually agreed on condition that Indonesia tightened financial controls and instituted reforms, including the establishment of an independent privatization board, liberalizing foreign investment, cutting import tariffs and phasing out export levies.

Imports and Exports. In June 1994 import duties were cut on 739 commodities, surcharges on 108 imports were removed and non-tariff barriers on 27 items abolished. Imports and exports (including oil and gas) in US$1m.:

	1993	1994	1995	1996
Imports	28,328	31,983	40,630	42,929
Exports	36,823	40,055	45,417	49,814

Main export items: Gas and oil, forestry products, manufactured goods, rubber, coffee, fishery products, coal, copper, tin, pepper, palm products and tea. Main export markets, 1996: Japan, 25·9%; USA, 13·6%; Singapore, 9·2%; South Korea, 6·6%. Main import suppliers, 1996: Japan, 19·8%; USA, 11·8%; Germany, 7·0%; Singapore, 6·7%.

COMMUNICATIONS

Roads. In 1996 there were 393,000 km of roads (31,000 km of highways or main roads), of which 179,000 km were surfaced. Motor vehicles, 1996: Passenger cars, 2,204,000, equivalent to 11 per 1,000 inhabitants; buses and coaches, 771,000; trucks and vans, 1,391,000; motor cycles, 9,382,000.

Rail. In 1992 the national railways totalled 6,458 km of 1,067 mm gauge, comprising 4,967 km on Java (of which 125 km electrified) and 1,491 km on Sumatra. Passenger-kilometres travelled in 1995 came to 15·52bn. and freight tonne-kilometres to 45·17bn.

Civil Aviation. Garuda Indonesia is the state-owned national flag carrier. Merpati Nusantara Airlines is their domestic subsidiary. Domestic services are also provided by Bouraq Indonesia. There are international airports at Jakarta (Sukarno-Hatta), Denpasar (on Bali), Medan (Sumatra), Pekanbaru (Sumatra), Ujung Pandang (Sulawesi), Solo (Java) and Manado. Jakarta is the busiest airport, in 1996 handling 13,420,761 passengers (8,420,867 on domestic flights) and 316,415 tonnes of freight. In 1995 Garuda Indonesia flew 107·7m. km and carried 5,490,000 passengers. In 1998 services were also provided by Aeroflot, Air France, Air India, All Nippon Airways, Ansett Australia, British Airways, Cathay Pacific Airways, China Airlines, China Southern Airlines, Continental Airlines, Emirates, Eva Airways, Gulf Air, JAL, Japan Asia Airways, KLM, Korean Air, Kuwait Airways, Lauda Air, Lufthansa, Malaysia Airlines, Pakistan International Airlines, Pelangi Air, Philippine Airlines, Qantas Airways, Royal Brunei Airlines, Royal Jordanian, Saudia, Silk Air, Singapore Airlines, Swissair and Thai Airways International.

Shipping. There are 16 ports for ocean-going ships, the largest of which is Tanjung Priok, which serves the Jakarta area and has a container terminal. The national shipping company Pelajaran Nasional Indonesia (PELNI) maintains inter-island communications. Jakarta Lloyd maintains regular services between Jakarta, Amsterdam, Hamburg and London. In 1995 the merchant marine comprised 535 ocean-going ships totalling 4·13m. DWT. 95 vessels (36·22% of total tonnage) were registered under foreign flags. Total tonnage registered, 2·69m. GRT, including oil tankers, 0·65m. GRT, and container ships, 154,518 GRT. In 1995 vessels totalling 155,869,000 net registered tons entered ports and vessels totalling 48,857,000 NRT cleared.

Telecommunications. There were 4,982,500 main telephone lines (equivalent to 24·7 per 1,000 population) in 1997. In 1996 there were 0·2m. mobile phones, and in 1995, 730,000 PCs and 85,000 fax machines. There were approximately 80,000 Internet users in May 1998.

The telephone utility Telekomunikasi Indonesia (Telkom) is the largest of a number of companies up for sale, but an unresolved dispute with foreign telecommunication companies led to a delay in its privatization.

Postal Services. In 1995 there were 8,146 post offices.

SOCIAL INSTITUTIONS

Justice. There are courts of first instance, high courts of appeal in every provincial capital and a Supreme Court of Justice for the whole of Indonesia in Jakarta.

In civil law the population is divided into three main groups: Indonesians, Europeans and foreign Orientals, to whom different law systems are applicable. When, however, people from different groups are involved, a system of so-called 'inter-gentile' law is applied.

The present criminal law, which has been in force since 1918, is codified and is based on European penal law. This law is equally applicable to all groups of the population.

Religion. Religious liberty is granted to all denominations. In 1992 there were 160·62m. Moslems, 11·94m. Protestants and 5·78m. Roman Catholics. There were also 1·81m. Buddhists, probably for the greater part Chinese, and 3·59m. Hindus, of whom 2·5m. were on Bali.

Education. Adult literacy was 83·8% in 1995 (89·6% among males and 78% among females). In 1994–95 there were 29,721,859 pupils and 1,311,571 teachers at 173,696 primary schools, and 12,223,753 pupils and 864,587 teachers at secondary schools. Number of students in higher education (1995–96) 2,303,469. In 1994–95 in the state sector there were 31 universities and 1 open university, and 13 institutes of higher education, including 10 teacher training colleges. In the private sector there were 66 universities and the following specialized universities: Adventist, 1; Christian, 7; Islamic, 10; Methodist, 1; Roman Catholic, 5; Veterans', 1. There were 19 institutes of higher education in the private sector, including 12 teacher training colleges. In 1994–95 there were 694,152 university students and 44,014 academic staff.

In 1994 total expenditure on education came to 1·3% of GNP.

Health. In 1994 there were 28,989 doctors, 138,816 nurses and midwives and 3,988 pharmacies. There were 1,039 hospitals in 1994, with a provision of 6 beds per 10,000 population.

CULTURE

Broadcasting. Radio Republik Indonesia, under the Department of Information, operates 49 stations. In 1995 there were 29·5m. radio receivers and 13m. television receivers

Cinema. There were 2,173 cinemas in 1990.

Press. In 1995 there were 77 daily newspapers (combined circulation of 5,144,000 at a rate of 24 per 1,000 inhabitants). 1,396 book titles were published in 1989.

Tourism. In 1996 there were 5,034,000 foreign tourists, spending US$6·09bn.

DIPLOMATIC REPRESENTATIVES
Of Indonesia in Great Britain (38 Grosvenor Sq., London, W1X 9AD)
Ambassador: Vacant.

Of Great Britain in Indonesia (Jalan M.H. Thamrin 75, Jakarta 10310)
Ambassador: D. R. C. Christopher, CMG.

Of Indonesia in the USA (2020 Massachusetts Ave., NW, Washington, D.C., 20036)
Ambassador: Dorodjatun Kuntjuro Jakti.

Of the USA in Indonesia (Medan Merdeka Selatan 5, Jakarta)
Ambassador: J. Stapleton Roy.

Of Indonesia to the United Nations
Ambassador: Dr Makarim Wibisono.

Of Indonesia to the European Union
Ambassador: Poedji Koentarso.

FURTHER READING
Central Bureau of Statistics. *Statistical Yearbook of Indonesia.—Monthly Statistical Bulletin: Economic Indicator.*
Cribb, R., *Historical Dictionary of Indonesia.* Metuchen (NJ), 1993.—and Brown, C., *Modern Indonesia: a History since 1945.* Harlow, 1995
International Commission of Jurists, *Indonesia and the Rule of Law.* London, 1987
Kim, T. J. *et al.*, *Spatial Development in Indonesia.* Aldershot, 1992
Krausse, G. H. and Krausse, S. C. E., *Indonesia* [Bibliography]. Oxford and Santa Barbara (CA), 1994
Palmier, L., *Understanding Indonesia.* London, 1986
Ricklefs, M. C., *A History of Modern Indonesia since 1300.* 2nd ed. London, 1993
Schwartz, A., *A Nation in Waiting: Indonesia in the 1990s.* London, 1994
Thoolen, H., *Indonesia and the R.ule of Law.* London, 1987
Vatikiotis, M.R.J., *Indonesian Politics under Suharto: Order, Development and Pressure for Change.* 2nd ed. London, 1994

See also **East Timor**, *above.*

National statistical office: Central Bureau of Statistics, POB 1003, Jakarta, 10010.
Website: http://www.bps.go.id/

IRAN

Jomhuri-e-Eslami-e-Iran

(Islamic Republic of Iran)

Capital: Tehran
Population estimate, 2000: 76·43m.
GNP per capita: (PPP$) 5,360
HDI/world rank: 0·758/78

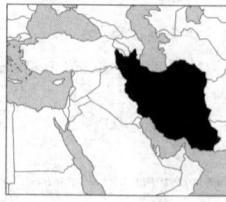

KEY HISTORICAL EVENTS

Persia was ruled by the Shahs as an absolute monarchy from the 16th century until 30 Dec. 1906, when the first constitution was granted and a national assembly established. After a coup in 1921, Reza Khan began his rise to power which culminated in his deposing the last Shah of the Qajar Dynasty on 31 Oct. 1925. He was declared Shah as Reza Shah Pahlavi on 12 Dec. 1925 and the country's name was changed to Iran on 21 March 1935. When in the Second World War Iran supported Germany, the Allies occupied the country and forced Reza Shah to abdicate on 16 Sept. 1941 in favour of his son, Muhammad Reza Pahlavi.

Iran's oil industry was nationalized in March 1951. This was an important part of the policy of the National Front Party, whose leader, Dr Muhammad Mussadeq, became prime minister in April 1951. He was opposed by the Shah, but although ousted in 1952, quickly regained power. The Shah fled the country temporarily until Aug. 1953 when the monarchists staged a coup which led to Mussadeq finally being deposed.

The Shah's policy, which included the redistribution of land to small farmers and the enfranchisement of women, was opposed by the Shia religious scholars who considered it to be contrary to Islamic teaching. This group was considered responsible for the assassination of the prime minister, Hassan Ali Mansur, in 1965.

Despite economic growth, the country suffered considerable unrest because of opposition to the Shah's harsh repressive measures and his extensive use of the Savak, the secret police. The opposition was widespread and that led by Ayatollah Ruhollah Khomeini, the Shia Moslem spiritual leader who had been exiled in 1965, was particularly successful. Following intense civil unrest in Tehran, the Shah left Iran with his family on 17 Jan. 1979 (and died in Egypt on 27 July 1980). The Ayatollah Khomeini returned from exile on 1 Feb. 1979 and appointed a provisional government on 5 Feb. The Shah's government resigned and parliament dissolved itself on 11 Feb. Following a referendum in March, an Islamic Republic was proclaimed on 1 April 1979. The constitution of the Islamic Republic, approved by a national referendum in Dec. 1979, gave supreme authority to a religious leader (*wali faqih*), a position to be held by Ayatollah Khomeini for the rest of his life. In Sept. 1980 war began with Iraq with destruction of some Iranian towns and damage to the oil installations at Abadan. A UN-arranged ceasefire took place on 20 Aug. 1988, and UN-sponsored peace talks continued in 1989. On 15 Aug. 1990, following Iraq's invasion of Kuwait, the Iraqi President Saddam Hussein offered peace terms and began the withdrawal of troops from Iranian soil.

In 1997 the election of Mohammad Khatami as president signalled a shift away from Islamic extremism. A clampdown on Islamic vigilantes who wage a violent campaign against western 'decadence' is the latest sign of a cautiously liberal integration of the constitution. But the conservative faction led by the spiritual leader Ayatollah Ali Khamenei retains huge power including the final say on defence and foreign policy. In Oct. 1998 elections to the Assembly of Experts, the country's supreme constitutional authority, returned conservatives in 63 of the 86 seats. Turn-out was low. Apathy was blamed on the clergy-inspired screening process which resulted in two-thirds of the aspiring candidates, including all women, being rejected in advance. However, subsequent local government elections signalled a liberal reaction which encouraged President Mohammad Khatami to stamp down on abuse of power and violence against secular critics.

TERRITORY AND POPULATION

Iran is bounded in the north by Armenia, Azerbaijan, the Caspian Sea and Turkmenistan, east by Afghanistan and Pakistan, south by the Gulf of Oman and the

Persian Gulf, and west by Iraq and Turkey. It has an area of 1,648,000 sq. km (634,293 sq. miles), but a vast portion is desert. Population (1996 census): 60·1m. (1995, 59% urban). Population density: 36 per sq. km.

The UN gives a projected population for 2000 of 76·43m.

By 1992 there were 2m. refugees from Afghanistan in Iran; repatriation began in 1993, but in 1996 Iran still had 13·9% of the world's refugees and asylum-seekers.

The areas, populations and capitals of the 26 provinces *(ostan)* were:

Province	Area (sq. km)	Census 1991	Census 1996	Capital
Ardebil[1]	17,881	...	1,168,011	Ardebil
Azarbayejan, East	47,830	3,278,718	3,325,540	Tabriz
Azarbayejan, West	39,487	2,284,208	2,496,320	Orumiyeh
Bushehr	23,191	694,252	743,675	Bushehr
Chahar Mahal and Bakhtyari	16,201	747,297	761,168	Shahr-e-Kord
Esfahan	107,027	3,682,444	3,923,255	Esfahan
Fars	122,416	3,543,828	3,817,036	Shiraz
Gilan	14,106	2,204,047	2,241,896	Rasht
Hamadan	19,547	1,651,320	1,677,957	Hamadan
Hormozgan	71,193	924,433	1,062,155	Bandar-e-Abbas
Ilam	20,151	440,693	487,886	Ilam
Kerman	181,814	1,862,542	2,004,328	Kerman
Kermanshah	24,741	1,622,159	1,778,596	Kermanshah
Khorasan	302,766	6,013,200	6,047,661	Mashhad
Khuzestan	63,238	3,175,852	3,746,772	Ahvaz
Kohgiluyeh and Boyer Ahmad	15,563	496,739	544,356	Yasuj
Kordestan	29,151	1,233,480	1,346,383	Sanandaj
Lorestan	28,392	1,501,778	1,584,434	Khorramabad
Markazi	29,406	1,182,611	1,228,812	Arak
Mazandaran	43,525	3,793,149	4,028,296	Sari
Semnan	96,816	458,125	501,447	Semnan
Sistan and Baluchestan	178,431	1,455,102	1,722,579	Zahedan
Tehran	31,952	9,982,309	11,176,239	Tehran
Yazd	73,467	691,119	750,769	Yazd
Zanjan	24,312	1,776,133	1,936,873	Zanjan
Qom[1]	11,237	...	853,044	Qom

[1]In 1991, Qom and Ardebil were not separate provinces.

At the 1996 census the populations of the principal cities were:

Population		Population	
Tehran	6,758,845	Arak	380,755
Mashhad	1,887,405	Ardabil	340,386
Esfahan	1,266,072	Yazd	326,776
Tabriz	1,191,043	Qazvin	291,117
Shiraz	1,053,025	Zanjan	286,295
Karaj	940,968	Sanandaj	277,808
Ahvaz	804,980	Bandar-e-Abbas	273,578
Qom	777,677	Khorramabad	272,815
Kermanshah	692,986	Eslamshahr	265,450
Orumiyeh	435,200	Borujerd	217,804
Zahedan	419,518	Abadan	206,073
Rasht	417,748	Dezful	202,639
Hamadan	401,281	Khorramshahr	105,636
Kerman	384,991		

The national language is Farsi or Persian, spoken by 45% of the population in 1986. 28% spoke related languages, including Kurdish (9%) and Luri in the west, Gilaki and Mazandarami in the north, and Baluchi in the south-east; 22% speak Turkic languages, primarily in the north-west.

SOCIAL STATISTICS

1995 births, 2,454,000; deaths, 438,000. Birth rate (1995, per 1,000 population), 35·9; death rate, 6·4. Abortion is illegal, but a family planning scheme was inaugurated in 1988. Expectation of life at birth, 1990–95, 67·0 years for males and 68·0 years for females. Infant mortality, 1990–95, 43 per 1,000 live births; fertility rate, 5·3 births per woman.

CLIMATE
Mainly a desert climate, but with more temperate conditions on the shores of the Caspian Sea. Seasonal range of temperature is considerable, as is rain (ranging from 2" in the south-east to 78" in the Caspian region). Winter is normally the rainy season for the whole country. Abadan, Jan. 54°F (12·2°C), July 97°F (36·1°C). Annual rainfall 8" (204 mm). Tehran, Jan. 36°F (2·2°C), July 85°F (29·4°C). Annual rainfall 10" (246 mm).

CONSTITUTION AND GOVERNMENT
The Constitution of the Islamic Republic was approved by a national referendum in Dec. 1979. It gives supreme authority to the *Spiritual Leader (wali faqih)*, which position was held by Ayatollah Khomeini until his death on 3 June 1989. Ayatollah Seyed Ali Khamenei was elected to succeed him on 4 June 1989. Following the death of the previous incumbent, Ayatollah Ali Khamenei was proclaimed the *Source of Knowledge (Marja e Taghlid)* at the head of all Shi'ite Moslems in Dec. 1994.

The 83-member *Assembly of Experts* was established in 1982. It is popularly elected every 8 years. Its mandate is to interpret the constitution and select the Spiritual Leader. Candidates for election are examined by the *Council of Guardians.*

The *Islamic Consultative Assembly* has 270 members, elected for a 4-year term in single-seat constituencies. All candidates have to be approved by the *Council of Guardians.*

The *President* of the Republic is popularly elected for not more than two 4-year terms and is head of the executive; he appoints Ministers subject to approval by the *Islamic Consultative Assembly (Majlis).*

Legislative power is held by the 270-member Islamic Consultative Assembly, directly elected on a non-party basis for a 4-year term by all citizens aged 15 or over. The voting age of 15 in Iran is lower than in any other country. Two-thirds of the electorate is under 30. Voting is secret but ballot papers are not printed; electors must write the name of their preferred candidate themselves. 5 seats are reserved for religious minorities. All legislation is subject to approval by a 12-member *Council of Guardians* who ensure it is in accordance with the Islamic code and with the Constitution. The Spiritual Leader appoints 6 members, as does the judiciary.

National Anthem. 'Sar zad az ofogh mehr-e khavaran' ('Rose from the horizon the affectionate sun of the East'); words by a group of poets; tune by Dr Riahi.

RECENT ELECTIONS
Presidential elections held on 23 May 1997 produced a landslide vote for Mohammad Khatami, who favours greater freedom and adherence to the rule of law. There were 4 candidates. Turn-out was 14m. Mohammad Khatami was elected with 69% of votes cast.

At the Islamic Consultative Assembly elections on 8 March 1996, with a run-off on 19 April, the Jameh-ye Ruhaniyat Mobarez (Combatant Clergy Association) won 110 seats, the Servants of Iran's Construction won 80 and others 58, with 22 vacant. The Council of Guardians annulled 13 results which were subsequently filled through by-elections. The electorate was 32m.; 3,231 candidates stood.

Elections to the Assembly of Experts were held on 23 Oct. 1998; turn-out was 46%. Conservative candidates won 54 seats, 13 went to moderates and the remaining 21 went to conservative-allied independents.

CURRENT ADMINISTRATION
The Cabinet included the following in March 1999:

President: Ali Mohammad Khatami-Ardakani.

Vice President: Hasan Ebrahim Habibi.

Vice President for Atomic Energy: Gholamreza Aghazedeh-Khoi. *Vice President for Executive Affairs:* Mohammad Hashemi-Rafsanjani. *Vice President for Environmental Protection:* Mrs Masoomeh Ebtekar. *Vice President For Civil Service:* Mohammad Baqerian. *Vice President for Development and Social Affairs:* Abdollah Nuri-Hoseiniabadi. *Vice President for Legal and Parliamentary Affairs:* Mohammad Ali Saduqi. *Vice President for Physical Training:* Mostafa Hashemi-Taba. *Vice President for Plan and Budget:* Mohammad Ali Najafi. *Minister of*

IRAN

Foreign Affairs: Kamal Kharrazi. *Oil:* Bijan Namdar Zanganeh. *Interior:* Abdol Vahed Musavi-Lari. *Economic Affairs and Finance:* Hossein Namazi. *Agriculture:* Issa Kalantari. *Commerce:* Mohammad Shariatmadar. *Energy:* Habibollah Bitaraf. *Roads and Transport:* Mahmoud Hojjati-Najafabadi. *Construction Jihad:* Mohammad Saidi Kya. *Industry:* Gholamreza Shafei. *Housing and Urban Development:* Ali Abdolalizadeh. *Labour and Social Affairs:* Hossein Kamali. *Posts, Telephones and Telegraphs:* Mohammad Reza Aref-Yazdi. *Health, Treatment and Medical Education:* Mohammad Farhadi. *Education and Training:* Hossein Mozaffar. *Higher Education and Culture:* Mostafa Moin-Najafabadi. *Justice:* Mohammad Esmael Shoushtari. *Defence and Armed Forces Logistics:* Ali Shamkhani. *Islamic Culture and Guidance:* Ataollah Mohajerani. *Mines and Metals:* Eshaq Jahangiri. *Co-operatives:* Morteza Haji-Qaem.

Local Government. The country is divided into 26 provinces (*ostan*). These are sub-divided into 195 counties, each under a governor, and thence into 500 districts, each under a district head. The districts are subdivided into *dehistan* (groups of villages), each under a *dehdar*, each village having its elected headman.

In March 1999, the first municipal and village elections since 1979 returned moderate candidates for most of the 200,000 contested council seats.

DEFENCE

Two years' military service is compulsory. Military expenditure totalled US$4,695m. in 1997, down from US$20,258m. in 1985. The 1997 spending represented 6·6% of GDP, compared to 36·0% in 1985. The expenditure in 1997 was equivalent to US$68 per capita.

Nuclear weapons. Although Iran is a member of the Non-Proliferation Treaty (NPT), it may be developing weapons using its nuclear power programme.

Army. The Army is organized in 4 armoured, 2 special force and 7 infantry divisions, 1 airborne brigade, some independent armoured, infantry and commando brigades, and 5 artillery groups. Equipment includes some 110 T-54/-55, 220 Chinese T-59, 150 T-62, 200 T-72, 250 Chieftain Mk 3/5, 150 M-47/-48, 160 M-60A1 and 200 Chinese T-69 main battle tanks and 664 multiple rocket launchers. The Army is estimated to have an inventory of 50 fixed-wing aircraft and over 200 helicopters but the effective strength is not known. There are reports of Iran developing non-conventional long-range missiles.

Strength (1997): 350,000 (about 250,000 conscripts). There is also a paramilitary gendarmerie of 120,000, including border guards.

Revolutionary Guard. The ground forces are loosely organized in battalions of no fixed size, and are grouped into 13 infantry and 2 armoured divisions plus other independent units. It controls the *Basij*, a volunteer 'popular mobilization army' of about 0·2m., which may reach 1m. strong in wartime.

Strength (1996): 100,000 ground forces and 20,000 naval.

Navy. The Navy received the first 2 of 3 Soviet-built 'Kilo' class submarines in late 1993, but these suffered battery problems and the third was not delivered until the end of 1996. The remainder of the fleet comprises 2 ex-US 'Sumner' class destroyers, 3 UK-built frigates, 2 very old ex-US patrol frigates, and 10 French-built and 10 new Chinese-built missile craft. Other units include 35 inshore patrol craft (some of them hovercraft), 3 small minesweepers, 7 tank landing ships and 3 tank landing craft. Auxiliaries include 3 replenishment tankers, 1 repair ship, 4 water tankers and 2 accommodation ships.

Naval Aviation comprises 1 anti-submarine helicopter squadron with 9 Sea King and AB-212 helicopters, a mine counter-measures squadron with 2 RH-53D helicopters, a transport squadron with about a dozen various aircraft and about 20 AB-205 and AB-206 transport and liaison helicopters. The main naval bases are at Bandar-e-Abbas, Bushehr and Chah Bahar.

Strength (1996): 18,000, including naval air and 3 battalions of Marines.

Air Force. Combat aircraft include some Chinese-built F-6 fighter-bombers and F-7 interceptors, surviving US fighters that include F-14 Tomcat, F-5E Tiger II and F-4D/E Phantom II fighter-bombers, as well as a few RF-4E reconnaissance-fighters, and a number of MiG-29 interceptors and Su-24 strike aircraft purchased from

Russia. Transport aircraft include F27s, C-130 Hercules, PC-6 Turbo-Porters, Boeing 707s and 747s, some equipped as flight refuelling tankers. The status of the large fleet of CH-47C Chinook, Bell Model 214 and other helicopters is not known; but two P-3F Orion maritime patrol aircraft remain operational. Training aircraft include Pakistani-built Mushshak and Bonanza basic trainers and French-built Socata light aircraft, 30 PC-7 Turbo-Trainers and 15 Tucanos for advanced training.

Strength (1996): 30,000 personnel (about 12,000 air defence).

INTERNATIONAL RELATIONS

Relations between Iran and Afghanistan have deteriorated as Taliban militants gain ground against government forces supported by Iran. Threats of war were provoked in Oct. 1998 after the Taliban, the militant Islamic movement in Afghanistan, allegedly killed 6 Iranian diplomats and a journalist during the capture of Mazar i Sharif, Afghanistan's 4th largest city, and Bamiyan, one of the last strongholds of the Iranian-backed Shia Muslims. Border clashes were reported on 8 Oct. near the north-eastern city of Torbat-e-Jam; 1·5m. Afghan refugees, mostly from the Shia minority, fled to Iran.

Iran is a member of the UN, OPEC, ECO and the Colombo Plan.

ECONOMY

Policy. A 5-year plan, the Second Five-Year Development Plan (SFYDP), is running from March 1995. At the beginning of 1991 about 70% of industry was state-owned, much of it nationalized after the 1979 revolution, but the government is now committed to partial privatization. Strategic heavy industry will remain in the public sector.

Performance. Real GDP growth was 4·2% in 1995 (0·7% in 1994).

Budget. Total revenue and expenditure for 1998–99 (in 1,000m. rials) is put at 231,200, an increase of 20% over the 1997–98 budget. The accuracy of budget figures is questionable given the policy of dividing the budget into 2 parts: the first covering ministerial expenditure, the second dealing with state banks and industries, which receive allocations by the expediency of printing money.

Currency. The unit of currency is the *rial* (IRR) of which 10 = 1 *toman*. The value of the rial has fallen from IRR 70 to the US\$ in 1979 to a low of IRR 4,630 in 1997. Gold reserves were 5·42m. troy oz. in March 1996. Inflation in Aug. 1998 was running at 20%. Total money supply in Oct. 1997 was 60,706m. rials.

Banking and Finance. The Central Bank is the note-issuing authority and government bank. Its *Governor* is Moshen Nurbakhach. All other banks and insurance companies were nationalized in 1979, and re-organized into new state banking corporations, of which there were 5 in 1994. Private banks were permitted to operate from 1994; their initial capital must be at least 5,000m. rials. The 'Law for Usury-Free Banking' dates from 1983. In 1985 interest on accounts was abolished.

A stock exchange re-opened in Tehran in 1992.

Weights and Measures. The metric system is in force.

Calendar. The Iranian year is a solar year running from 21 March to 20 March. The current solar year is 1378 (21 March 1999 to 20 March 2000). The Islamic *hegira* (622 AD, when Mohammed left Mecca for Medina) year 1420 corresponds to 17 April 1999–10 April 2000, and is the current lunar year.

ENERGY AND NATURAL RESOURCES

Electricity. Total installed capacity in 1996: 22,420,000 kW.; production, 85,825m. kWh (62,364m. steam, 15,475m. gas and combined, 7,376m. hydro-electric, 610m. diesel). Consumption per capita in 1995 was estimated to be 1,137 kWh.

Oil and Gas. Iran has 8·9% of proven global oil reserves. Oil is its chief source of revenue. The main oilfields are in the Zagros Mountains where oil was first discovered in 1908. Oil companies were nationalized in 1979 and operations of crude oil and natural gas exploitation are now run by the National Iranian Oil Company. Refining operations of crude oil are run by the National Company for

Refining and Distribution of Oil Products. Iran produced 5·5% of the world total oil output in 1996, and had reserves amounting to 93·0bn. bbls. in 1996.

Crude oil production (1995): 3,625,000 bbls. a day. Refining capacity (1990): 766·9 bbls. a day. Petroleum production (1996): 3,595,000 bbls. a day.

Iran has nearly one fifth of proven global gas reserves. A deal reached in Nov. 1997 between Gazprom, the Russian gas company, and Total, the French energy group, involves the investment of US$2,000m. into the development of a gas field.

In Dec. 1997 the first national gas pipeline linking Iran with the Caspian Sea via Turkmenistan was opened. The 200-km line links gas fields in western Turkmenistan to industrial markets in northern Iran.

Natural gas production (1994): 95,691m. cu. metres.

Minerals. Output (1996, in tonnes): Iron ore, 5,236,259; coal, 1,211,403; zinc and lead, 321,766; copper, 370,234; manganese, 82,694; chromite, 322,367; salt, 1,410,644; bauxite, 230,420; decorative stone, 6,120,071.

Agriculture. Agriculture accounts for approximately 25% of GDP. In 1998 cultivable land totalled 14,001,279 ha: 12,001,514 ha were under annual crops (of which 5,789,530 ha were irrigated). In 1998 there were 1,879,128 ha and 120,637 ha of productive and non-productive orchards and nurseries respectively.

Crop production (1993, in tonnes): Wheat, 10,869,560; barley, 3,044,695; rice (paddy), 2,258,969; sugar beet, 5,294,729; tobacco, 9,887. Wool (1991): 32,000 tonnes greasy; 17,600 tonnes scoured.

Livestock (1996): 51·5m. sheep, 25·7m. goats (1995), 8·49m. cattle, 440,000 buffaloes (1995), 1·4m. asses, 186m. chickens (1995).

Forestry. Approximately 11% of Iran is forested, much of it in the Caspian region. Timber production in 1995 was 7·46m. cu. metres.

Fisheries. In 1995 total catches were 368,300 tonnes (251,000 tonnes from sea fishing).

INDUSTRY

Major industries: petrochemical, automotive, food, beverages and tobacco, textiles, clothing and leather, wood and fibre, paper and cardboard, chemical products, non-metal mining products, basic materials, machinery and equipment, copper, steel and aluminium. The textile industry uses local cotton and silk; carpet manufacture is an important industry. The country's steel industry is the largest in the Middle East.

Production of selected commodities in large-scale manufacturing establishments with 50 workers and more (1996): Sugar, 636,616 tonnes; stockings, 8·3m. pairs; machine-made bricks, 2,984m.; cement, 16,441,701 tonnes. In 1995 there were 2,433 large-scale manufacturing establishments and the number of workers was 647,661.

Labour. The economically active population numbered 16m. in 1996-97, of which 14·6m. were employed. In Aug. 1998 unemployment was 11%.

INTERNATIONAL TRADE

There had been a limit on foreign investment, but legislation of 1995 permits foreign nationals to hold more than 50% of the equity of joint ventures with the consent of the Foreign Investment Board. Foreign debt was US$21,183m. in 1996.

Imports and Exports. Iran's main trading partners are Germany, Japan and Italy for imports; and Japan, the UK and USA for exports. Exports (1996, in US$1m.) totalled 22,496; imports 14,973. Main imports: machinery and motor vehicles, iron and steel, chemicals, pharmaceuticals, food. Main exports: oil, carpets, pistachios, leather and caviar. Petroleum and crude oil exports (1996): 2,620,000 bbls. a day. Crude oil exports account for 85% of hard currency earnings. Carpet exports are the second-largest hard currency earner.

COMMUNICATIONS

Roads. In 1997 the total length of roads was 165,724 km, of which 712 km were freeways, 24,662 km main roads, 40,437 km by-roads, 86,209 km rural roads and 14,597 km other roads. In 1996–97 registered motor vehicles numbered 370,067.

There were 246,318 passenger cars; 2,059 buses; 2,297 minibuses; 37,501 vans and trucks; 10,923 lorries; 2,792 articulated lorries; 68,175 motor cycles.

Rail. The State Railways totalled 5,995 km of main lines in 1997, of which 149 km were electrified. In 1997 the railways carried 9·45m. passengers and 24·4m. tonnes of freight. An isolated 1,676 mm gauge line (96 km) in the south-east provides a link with Pakistan Railways. A rail link to Turkmenistan was opened in May 1996.

Civil Aviation. There are international airports at Tehran (Mehrabad), Shiraz and Bandar Abbas. Tehran is the busiest airport, in 1996 handling 9·1m. passengers and 42,949 tonnes of freight. The state-owned Iran Air carried 5·3m. passengers and 33,857 tonnes of freight (1996). In 1998 services were also provided by Aeroflot, Alitalia, Armenian Airlines, Austrian Airlines, Azerbaijan Airlines, Balkan, British Airways, Emirates, Georgian Airlines, Georgian Airways, Gulf Air, KLM, Kuwait Airways, Lufthansa, Malaysia Airlines, Miravia Romanian Airlines, Pakistan International Airlines, Royal Jordanian, SAS, Swissair, Syrian Arab Airlines and Turkish Airlines.

Shipping. In 1995 the merchant fleet comprised 146 vessels totalling 6·71m. DWT, representing 1·01% of the world's total fleet tonnage. Total tonnage registered: 3·8m. GRT, including oil tankers: 2·14m. GRT, and container ships: 1,593 GRT. In 1997, 3,722 ships with a capacity of 27·8m. tonnes entered commercial ports, loading and unloading 5·7m. and 36·5m. tonnes of goods respectively (excluding oil products).

Telecommunications. In 1997 there were 6·5m. telephones, 107·3 per 1,000 population. Cellular phone subscribers numbered 9,200 in 1995 and there were 30,000 fax machines.

Postal Services. In 1995 there were 10,539 post offices. 223m. pieces of mail were processed during the year, or 3 items per person.

SOCIAL INSTITUTIONS

Justice. A legal system based on Islamic law (*Sharia*) was introduced by the 1979 constitution. A new criminal code on similar principles was introduced in Nov. 1995. The President of the Supreme Court and the public Prosecutor-General are appointed by the Spiritual Leader. The Supreme Court has 16 branches and 109 offences carry the death penalty. To these were added economic crimes in 1990. There were 110 executions in 1996.

Religion. The official religion is the Shi'a branch of Islam. Adherents numbered 93·8% of the population in 1990; 6% were Sunni Moslems.

Education. Adult literacy was 72·1% in 1995 (78·4% among males and 65·8% among females). Most primary and secondary schools are state schools. Elementary education in state schools and university education is free; small fees are charged for state-run secondary schools. In 1994–95 there were 9,745,600 pupils and 1,740,436 teachers at 61,889 primary schools, 7,652,829 pupils and 249,307 teachers at secondary schools, and 1,048,093 pupils and 52,812 teachers at institutions of higher education.

In 1994–95 there were 30 universities, 30 medical universities, 12 specialized universities (1 agriculture, 1 art, 1 oil engineering, 4 teacher training, 5 technology) and 2 open (distance-learning) universities. There were 289,392 students and 10,745 academic staff.

In 1994 total expenditure on education came to 5·9% of GNP and represented 18·1% of total government expenditure.

Health. There were 653 hospitals in 1992, and a provision of 15 beds per 10,000 population in 1995. Medical personnel included 37,000 physicians (1994), 6,080 dentists and 4,185 pharmacists (1993), and 48,639 nurses and midwives (1991).

CULTURE

Broadcasting. Broadcasting is controlled by the government agency, Islamic Republic of Iran Broadcasting (IRIB). Both television and radio operate under a single organization, the National Iranian Radio and Television Organization (NIRT) established by an Act of Parliament in 1967, which in 1990 employed some 11,620 people. There are 2 national radio stations (Radio One and Radio Two) and 27 regional radio stations, including a Koran service and an external service (Voice of the Islamic Republic of Iran, which publishes in 20 languages). There are no commercial radio stations; radio broadcasting is a state monopoly. There were (1997) 138 radio transmitters in operation. There are 4 television networks (colour by SECAM). A 3-year ban on TV satellite receiver dishes was imposed in Jan. 1995. There were 16·6m. radio receivers and 4·5m. television receivers in 1996.

Cinema. There were 294 cinemas with 176,396 seats in 1995.

Press. In 1996 there were 38 daily and 162 weekly newspapers. Approximately 80% of the Iranian press is printed in Farsi; much of the remaining 20% is in English or Arabic.

Tourism. There were 465,000 foreign tourists in 1996, spending US$165m.

Libraries. In 1996 there were 1,047 libraries affiliated to the Ministry of Culture and Islamic Guidance.

DIPLOMATIC REPRESENTATIVES
Of Iran in Great Britain (16 Prince's Gate, London, SW7 1PT)
Chargé d'Affaires: Gholamreza Ansari.

Of Great Britain in Iran (143 Ferdowsi Ave., Tehran 11344)
Chargé d'Affaires: N. W. Browne.

Of Iran to the United Nations
Ambassador: Seyed Mohammed Hadi Nejad Hosseinian

Of Iran to the European Union
Ambassador: Hamid Aboutalebi.

FURTHER READING
Abrahamian, E., *Khomeinism: Essays on the Islamic Republic.* Univ. of California Press, 1993
Amuzegar, J., *Iran's Economy under the Islamic Republic.* London, 1992
Bina, C. and Zanganeh, H. (eds.), *Modern Capitalism and Islamic Ideology in Iran.* London, 1991
Cambridge History of Iran. 7 vols. CUP, 1968–91
Daneshvar, P., *Revolution in Iran.* London, 1996
Ehtesami, A., *After Khomeini: the Iranian Second Republic.* London, 1994
Foran, J., *Fragile Resistance: Social Transformation in Iran from 1500 to the Revolution.* Boulder (Colo.), 1993
Fuller, G. E., *Centre of the Universe: Geopolitics of Iran.* Boulder (Colo.), 1992
Hunter, S. T., *Iran after Khomeini.* New York, 1992
Hussain, A., *Islamic Iran: Revolution and Counter-Revolution.* London, 1985
Kamrava, M., *Political History of Modern Iran: from Tribalism to Theocracy.* London, 1993
Karshenas, M., *Oil, State and Industry in Iran.* CUP, 1990
Katouzian, H., *The Political Economy of Iran.* London, 1981
Lahsaelzadeh, A., *Contemporary Rural Iran.* London, 1993
Modaddel, M., *Class, Politics and Ideology in the Iranian Revolution.* Columbia Univ. Press, 1992
Navabpour, A. R., *Iran.* [Bibliography] Oxford and Santa Barbara (CA), 1988
Omid, H., *Islam and the Post-Revolutionary State in Iran.* London, 1994
Rahnema, A. and Nomani, F., *The Secular Miracle: Religion, Politics and Economic Activity.* London, 1990.—and Behdad, S. (eds.) *Iran after the Revolution: the crisis of an Islamic State.* London, 1995

National statistical office. Statistical Centre of Iran, Dr Fatemi Avenue, Tehran 14144, Iran.

IRAQ

Jumhouriya al 'Iraqia

(Republic of Iraq)

Capital: Baghdad
Population estimate, 2000: 23·11m.
Estimated GDP: $42bn.
HDI/world rank: 0·538/127

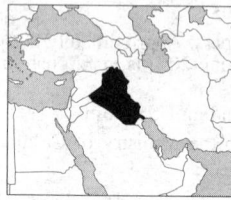

KEY HISTORICAL EVENTS

Iraq, formerly Mesopotamia, was part of the Ottoman Empire from 1534 until it was captured by British forces in 1916. Under a League of Nations mandate, administered by Britain, Amir Faisal Ibn Hussain was crowned king in 1921. On 3 Oct. 1932 Britain's mandate expired, and Iraq became an independent country. The pro-British policy was continued, and in Jan. 1943 Iraq declared war on the Axis powers.

The ruling Hashemite dynasty was overthrown by an armed coup led by a group of army officers on 14 July 1958. King Faisal II and his uncle, the ex-Regent the Emir Abdul Ilah, and Nuri al Said, the prime minister, were killed. A republic was established, controlled by a military-led Council of Sovereignty under Gen. Qassim. The republican regime terminated the adherence of Iraq to the Arab Federation, which Iraq and Jordan had formed in Feb. 1958.

In 1963 Qassim was overthrown, and Gen. Abdul Salam Aref became president, with a partial return to a civilian government. In 1966 Abdul Rahman Aref succeeded his brother as president, but on 17 July 1968 a successful coup was mounted by the Ba'ath Party and Gen. Ahmed Al Bakr became president, prime minister, and chairman of a newly established ruling 9-member Revolutionary Command Council. In July 1979 Saddam Hussein, the vice-president, became president in a peaceful transfer of power.

In Sept. 1980 Iraq invaded Iran in a dispute over territorial rights in the Shatt-al-Arab waterway which developed into a full-scale war. A UN-arranged ceasefire took place on 20 Aug. 1988 and UN-sponsored peace talks continued in 1989. On 15 Aug. 1990 Iraq offered peace terms and began the withdrawal of troops from Iranian soil.

Early on 2 Aug. 1990 Iraqi forces invaded and rapidly overran Kuwait, meeting little resistance. The Amir escaped to Saudi Arabia. President Saddam declared the annexation of Kuwait on 8 Aug.

On 6 Aug. the UN Security Council voted by 13 to nil with 2 abstentions (Cuba and Yemen) to impose total economic sanctions on Iraq until it withdrew from Kuwait. On 7 Aug. the USA announced it was sending a large military force to Saudi Arabia at the latter's request to prevent a further Iraqi invasion of the area, and the UK made a similar commitment the following day. Various other countries announced the despatch of forces and equipment to this coalition force, including 12 Arab League countries on 10 Aug.

Measures to secure Iraq's withdrawal from Kuwait were given international legal sanction by a UN Security Council Resolution of 25 Aug. (by 13 votes to nil), authorizing a naval blockade of Iraq under UN auspices. Further Security Council resolutions included (25 Sept., by 14 votes to 1) an air embargo of Iraq and (29 Oct., 13–nil), a call for compensation to be paid by Iraq to states for losses resulting from the invasion of Kuwait. A 12th resolution of 29 Nov. (12 in favour, Cuba and Yemen against, China abstaining) authorized the use of military force if Iraq did not withdraw by 15 Jan. 1991.

On the night of 16–17 Jan. coalition forces began an air attack on strategic targets in Iraq. A land offensive followed on 24 Feb. The Iraqi army was routed and sustained massive destruction. Kuwait City was liberated on 27 Feb. and on 28 Feb. Iraq agreed to the conditions of a provisional cease-fire, including withdrawal from Kuwait.

On 3 April 1991 the UN Security Council adopted a permanent cease-fire resolution by 12 votes to 1 (Cuba) with 2 abstentions (Ecuador, Yemen). This provided for Iraq and Kuwait to respect the disputed border, the UN to demarcate it, and the Security Council to guarantee it. A UN observer force was to monitor a demilitarized zone extending 10 km into Iraq and 5 km into Kuwait. Iraq accepted the destruction of all chemical and biological weapons and nuclear weapons-usable material, under international supervision, and liability for damages arising from its invasion of Kuwait.

Insurrections amongst Shi'ites in the south and Kurds in the north were put down by government forces. A massive exodus of Kurdish refugees to the borders of Iran and Turkey followed. International relief operations were succeeded in April by the establishment of 'safe havens' for refugees within Iraqi borders policed by US and other coalition troops. Kurdish opposition leaders began talks with the Iraqi government at the end of April, and refugees began to move from the border areas into camps in north Iraq under the supervision of US, UK and other coalition forces. In May 1991 a UN Security Council resolution adopted by 14 votes to 1 (Cuba) provided for a fund to compensate victims for damage caused during the Iraqi invasion of Kuwait. The fund is based at Geneva, administered by a council of representatives of all the Security Council members, and supplied from not more than 30% of Iraqi oil-export earnings. Iraq denounced the resolution as illegal, but said it would comply with it as it had no choice. Following a UN-Iraqi agreement, about 500 UN security guards were brought in to protect Kurds in the north in June 1991. Coalition forces in Iraq withdrew in 1991, leaving only air forces based in Turkey.

In Sept. a UN Security Council resolution adopted by 13 votes to 1 (Cuba) with 1 abstention (Yemen) permitted Iraq to sell oil worth US$1,600m. to pay for food and medical supplies and start a reparations fund. In Oct. the Security Council voted unanimously to prohibit Iraq from all nuclear activities except medical. Imports of materials used in the manufacture of nuclear, biological or chemical weapons are banned, and UN inspectors have received wide powers to examine and retain data throughout Iraq.

In Aug. 1992 the USA, UK and France began to enforce an air exclusion zone over southern Iraq in response to the government's persecution of Shi'ite Moslems. Following Iraqi violations of this zone, and incursions over the Kuwaiti border, US, British and French forces made air and missile attacks on Iraqi military targets in Jan. 1993. On 27 June 1993 US forces made a missile attack on an intelligence centre in Baghdad in retaliation for an attempt on former US President Bush's life while he was visiting Kuwait in April. On 10 Nov. 1994 Iraq recognized the independence and boundaries of Kuwait. In the first half of 1995 UN weapons inspectors secured information on an extensive biological weapons programme.

An agreement between the UN and Iraq of 20 May 1996 (renewed in June 1997) permitted Iraq to export crude oil worth US$2,000m. in order to purchase foodstuffs and medicine.

At the beginning of Sept. 1996 Iraqi troops occupied the town of Arbol in a Kurdish safe haven in support of the Kurdish Democratic Party faction which was at odds with another Kurdish faction, the Patriotic Union of Kurdistan. On 3 Sept. 1996 US forces fired missiles at targets in southern Iraq and extended the no-fly area northwards to the southern suburbs of Baghdad (33rd parallel).

Relations with the USA deteriorated still further in 1997 when Iraq refused co-operation with UN weapons inspectors. On 29 Oct. the Iraqi Revolutionary Command Council announced that it had 'postponed' a decision to stop working with UNSCOM, the UN commission responsible for the destruction of Iraq's ballistic, chemical and biological weapons programmes, but it went on to demand that there should be no American nationals among the UN inspectors. The UN team suspended its operations in Iraq and the Security Council warned Saddam Hussein of 'serious consequences' if he carried out his threat to expel the Americans.

While the USA and the UK threatened retaliatory action, the larger Arab countries with Russia, China and France urged compromise. However, a renewal of hostilities looked probable until late Feb. 1998 when Kofi Annan, the UN Secretary General, forged an agreement in Baghdad allowing for 'immediate, unconditional and unrestricted access' to all suspected weapons sites. Then, in Aug. 1998, Saddam Hussein engineered another stand-off with the UN arms inspectors, demanding a declaration that Iraq had rid itself of all weapons of mass destruction. This the UN chief inspector refused to do. Co-operation was suspended, an act that was condemned by the UN Security Council. In Nov., all UN personnel left Iraq as the USA threatened air strikes unless Iraq complied with UN resolutions. Russia and France urged further diplomatic efforts, but on 16 Dec. the USA and Britain launched air and missile attacks aimed at destroying Sadaam Hussein's arsenal of nuclear, chemical and biological weapons. In all, 97 targets were destroyed. In the aftermath, the USA and Britain continued attacks on selected military and communication targets while encouraging the Iraqi opposition and tightening the trade embargo.

TERRITORY AND POPULATION
Iraq is bounded in the north by Turkey, east by Iran, south-east by the Persian (Arabian) Gulf, south by Kuwait and Saudi Arabia, and west by Jordan and Syria. In April 1992 the UN Boundary Commission redefined Iraq's border with Kuwait, moving it slightly northwards in line with an agreement of 1932. Area, 438,317 sq. km. Population, 1987 census, 16,335,198; 1997 estimate, 22·22m.; density, 50·7 per sq. km.

The UN gives a projected population for 2000 of 23·11m.

In 1995 an estimated 74·5% of the population lived in urban areas.

The areas, populations and capitals of the governorates:

Governorate	sq. km	Population (1987 census)	Capital	Population (1987 census)
Al-Anbar	138,501	820,690	Ar-Ramadi	192,556
Babil (Babylon)	6,468	1,109,574	Al-Hillah	268,834
Baghdad	734	3,841,268	Baghdad	3,841,268
Al-Basrah	19,070	872,176	Al-Basrah	406,296
Dahuk	6,553	293,304	Dahuk	19,736[2]
Dhi Qar	12,900	921,066	An-Nasiriyah	265,937
Diyala	19,076	961,073	Ba'qubah	114,516[3]
Irbil	14,471	770,439	Irbil	485,968
Karbala	5,034	469,282	Karbala	296,705
Maysan	16,072	487,448	Al-Amarah	208,797
Al-Muthanna	51,740	315,815	As-Samawah	33,473[1]
An-Najaf	28,824	590,078	An-Najaf	309,010
Ninawa (Nineveh)	37,323	1,479,430	Mosul	664,221
Al-Qadisiyah	8,153	559,805	Ad-Diwaniyah	196,519
Salah ad-Din	24,751	726,138	Samarra	62,008[2]
As-Sulaymaniyah	17,023	951,723	As-Sulaymaniyah	364,096
Ta'mim	10,282	601,219	Kirkuk	418,624
Wasit	17,153	564,670	Al-Kut	183,183

[1]Census 1965. [2]Estimate 1970. [3]Estimate 1985.

In 1993 there were 3,688,000 Kurds and 270,000 Turkmens.

The national language is Arabic.

SOCIAL STATISTICS
Births, 1997, 944,000; deaths, 140,000. 1997 rates (per 1,000 population). Births, 42·5; deaths, 6·3. Expectation of life in 1997 was 67·4 years (66·3 for males and 65·8 for females). Growth rate, 3·62% per annum. Infant mortality, 1990–95, 127 per 1,000 live births, up from 78 per 1,000 live births in the period 1980–85, the largest increase anywhere in the world over the same period. Fertility rate, 1990–95, 5·7 births per woman.

CLIMATE
The climate is mainly arid, with small and unreliable rainfall and a large annual range of temperature. Summers are very hot and winters cold. Al-Basrah, Jan. 55°F (12·8°C), July 92°F (33·3°C). Annual rainfall 7" (175 mm). Baghdad, Jan. 50°F (10°C), July 95°F (35°C). Annual rainfall 6" (140 mm). Mosul, Jan. 44°F (6·7°C), July 90°F (32·2°C). Annual rainfall 15" (384 mm).

CONSTITUTION AND GOVERNMENT
The Provisional Constitution was promulgated on 16 July 1970. The highest state authority is the Revolutionary Command Council (RCC) but some legislative power has now been given to the 220-member *National Assembly*. National Assembly elections were held on 24 March 1996. There were 689 candidates. The Ba'ath Party gained a majority of seats.

The only legal political grouping was the National Progressive Front (founded 1973) comprising the Arab Socialist Renaissance (Ba'ath) Party and various Kurdish groups, but a law of Aug. 1991 legalized political parties provided they are not based on religion, racism or ethnicity.

The President and Vice-President are elected by the RCC; the President appoints and leads a Council of Ministers responsible for administration.

National Anthem. 'Watanum Mede, al alufqi janalia' ('A homeland which extended its wings over the horizon'); words by S. Jabar Al Kamali, tune by W. G. Gholmieh.

RECENT ELECTIONS
On 15 Sept. 1995 a referendum was held to determine whether President Saddam Hussein should remain in office for a further 7 years. The electorate was 8·4m. It was announced that turn-out was 99·47% and 99·96% of votes cast were in favour.

CURRENT ADMINISTRATION
President: Saddam Hussein at-Takriti, b. 1937 (assumed office 17 July 1979; re-investiture, 17 Oct. 1995).

Vice-Presidents: Taha Yassin Ramadhan; Taha Muhyi al-Din Maruf.

In Nov. 1996 the RCC comprised: President Saddam Hussein(*Chairman*); Ezzat Ibrahim (*Vice-Chairman*); Ahmed Hussein Al Khodair (*Head of the President's Office*); Mohieddin Masarouf; Tariq Aziz; Taha Yassin Ramadhan; Mohammed Hamza Al Zubaidi; Gen. Ali Hassan Al Majid; Mizban Khider Hadi.

In March 1999 the Cabinet comprised:

Prime Minister: President Saddam Hussein.

Deputy Prime Ministers: Tariq Aziz; Taha Yassin Ramadhan; Mohammed Hamza Al Zubaidi.

Minister of Trade: Mohamed Mehdi Saleh. *Oil:* Lieut.-Gen. Amir Rashid Mohammed al-Ubaydi. *Culture and Information:* Humam Abd Al Khaliq Abd Al Ghafur. *Defence:* Lieut.-Gen. Sultan Hashim Ahmed Al Jabburi Tai. *Higher Education and Scientific Research:* Abduljabbar Tawfiq Mohammed. *Industry and Minerals:* Adnan Abdul-Majid Jassim Al Ani. *Justice:* Shabib Lazim Al Malki. *Education:* Fahd Salim Shaqrah. *Labour and Social Affairs:* Sadi Tumah Abbas. *Awqaf (Religious Endowments) and Religious Affairs:* Abdul-Muneim Ahmed Saleh. *Finance:* Aikmet Mezban Ibrahim Al Azzawi. *Interior:* Mohammed Zammam Abdel-Razzak. *Foreign Affairs:* Mohammed Said Kazim Al Sahhaf. *Health:* Umeed Madhat Mubarak. *Housing and Reconstruction:* Maan Abdullah Al Sarsam. *Transport and Communications:* Ahmed Murtada Ahmed Khalil. *Agriculture:* Abdullah Hamid Mahmoud Al Saleh. *Irrigation:* Mahmoud Diyab Al Ahmed.

Local Government. Iraq is divided into 18 governorates (*liwa*), each administered by an appointed Governor; three of the governorates form a (Kurdish) Autonomous Region, with an elected 57-member Kurdish Legislative Council. Each governorate is divided into qadhas (under *Qaimaqams*) and *nahiyahs* (under Mudirs).

DEFENCE
Conscription is 18-24 months. Military service is waived on payment of the equivalent of US$800.

Military expenditure totalled US$1,250m. in 1997, compared to US$18,328m. in 1985. The 1997 expenditure represented 7·4% of GDP, down from 25·9% in 1985. The expenditure in 1997 was equivalent to US$56 per capita.

Nuclear weapons. Although Iraq is suspected of having a secret programme, UN inspections seem to have halted progress in nuclear weapons' development.

Army. The Army is organized into 19 armoured/mechanized/infantry divisions, 7 Republican Guard divisions and 10 special forces brigades. Equipment includes 2,700 main battle tanks, including T-54/-55/M-77, Chinese T-59/-69, T-62, T-72 and Chieftain. Strength (1997 estimate) 350,000, including 100,000 active reserves.

Navy. The Iraqi Navy continues to lack operational capability. Current strength is believed to comprise 1 training frigate (currently non-operational), 1 missile craft, 7 small patrol craft and 4 inshore minesweepers.

In 1997 naval personnel were estimated at about 2,500. Bases exist at Basra and Az Zubayr (exit controlled by Kuwait).

Air Force. The Iraqi Air Force suffered heavy losses during the Gulf War; over 60 aircraft were destroyed by the opposing Allied forces, many more were damaged beyond repair on the ground in Iraq and at least 100 aircraft were impounded in Iran. Reliable data on the status of the service are not available and the following are estimates. The combat aircraft are mostly of Soviet manufacture (MiG-21/23/29, Su-22/25), although there are French-supplied Mirage F1-E/B fighters, Alouette, Super Frelon and Super Puma helicopters, F-6 and F-7 fighters from China, Bell 214ST helicopters from the USA, Czech-built L-39 light attack/trainer aircraft, and BO 105 and BK-117 helicopters from Germany.

The combat helicopter inventory comprises anti-armour Gazelles, Mi-24s and BO 105s, and Super Pumas equipped for anti-shipping duties. Transports include fixed-wing An-12s, An-26s and Il-76s, and Puma, Bell 214ST, BO 105, BK-117, Mil, Mi-6, Mi-8/17, AB.212 and AS-61 transport and liaison helicopters. Training aircraft comprise AS.202 Bravo primary trainers, Tucano, PC-7 and PC-9 basic trainers and two-seat models of most combat types. Personnel (1997), about 35,000 (including 17,000 air defence).

INTERNATIONAL RELATIONS
Iraq is a member of the UN and Arab League.

ECONOMY
Performance. Real GDP growth was –4·0% in 1995 (–23·0% in 1994 and –26·2% in 1993).

Budget. Before UN sanctions were applied, oil revenues accounted for nearly 50% and customs and excise for about 26% of the total revenue.

Currency. The monetary unit is the *Iraqi dinar* (IQD) of 1,000 *fils.*

Banking and Finance. All banks were nationalized on 14 July 1964. The Central Bank of Iraq is the sole bank of issue. In 1941 the Rafidain Bank, financed by the Iraqi Government, was instituted to carry out normal banking transactions. Its head office is in Baghdad and it has 239 branches, 11 abroad, including London. Its assets were US$47,000m. in Sept. 1990. In addition, there are 4 government banks which are authorized to issue loans to companies and individuals: the Industrial Bank, the Agricultural Bank, the Estate Bank, and the Mortgage Bank.

There is a stock exchange in Baghdad.

Weights and Measures. The metric system is in general use.

ENERGY AND NATURAL RESOURCES
Electricity. Installed capacity was 6·83m. kW in 1996. Production in 1996 was 31,800m. kWh, with consumption per capita in 1996 estimated at 1,362 kWh.

Oil and Gas. Crude oil production was 3·6m. tonnes in 1995. Natural gas, 123 petajoules. Since 1991 sanctions against Iraq have held back oil sales of some US$100,000m.

Agriculture. There are 5·45m. ha of arable land and 4m. ha of permanent cropland. Production (1994 estimates, in 1,000 tonnes): Wheat, 1,008; barley, 1,002; tomatoes, 750; dates, 600; watermelons, 460.

Livestock (1996): Cattle, 1·0m.; sheep, 5·0m.; goats, 1·1m. (1995); asses, 145,000; chickens, 45m. (1995).

Forestry. In 1995 forests covered 83,000 ha, representing 0·2% of the land area. 161,000 cu. metres of roundwood were cut in 1995.

Fisheries. Catches in 1995 totalled approximately 22,550 tonnes, of which 82% were freshwater fish.

INDUSTRY

Iraq is still relatively under-developed industrially but work has begun on new industrial plants.

Labour. In 1996 the labour force was 5,573,000 (75% males).

INTERNATIONAL TRADE

Imports and Exports. Imports and exports (in US$1m.):

	1988	1989	1990	1991
Imports	9,311	10,170	6,605	International embargo
Exports	9,613	12,408	10,353	International embargo

Crude oil is the main export commodity, with Jordan and Turkey being significant export partners in 1996. Manufactures and food are the main import commodities, with major partners in 1996 being France, Turkey, Jordan, Vietnam and Australia.

COMMUNICATIONS

Roads. In 1995 there were 46,500 km of roads, of which 39,990 km were paved. Vehicles in use in 1995 totalled 680,000 passenger cars and 320,000 commercial vehicles.

Rail. In 1993 railways comprised 2,032 km of 1,435 mm gauge route. Passenger-kilometres travelled in 1995 came to 2·2bn. and freight tonne-kilometres to 1·12bn.

Civil Aviation. There are no scheduled flights to or from Iraq.

Shipping. The merchant fleet in 1995 had a total tonnage of 1·55m. GRT, of which oil tankers account for more than 80%. A 565-km canal was opened in 1992 between Baghdad and the Persian (Arabian) Gulf for shipping, irrigation, the drainage of saline water and the reclamation of marsh land.

Telecommunications. Number of main telephone lines, 1997: 675,000 (31·9 per 1,000 population).

SOCIAL INSTITUTIONS

Justice. For civil matters: The court of cassation in Baghdad; 6 courts of appeal at Baghdad (2), Basra, Babylon, Mosul and Kirkuk; 18 courts of first instance with unlimited powers and 150 courts of first instance with limited powers, all being courts of single judges. In addition, 6 peace courts have peace court jurisdiction only. 'Revolutionary courts' deal with cases affecting state security.

For religious matters: The Sharia courts at all places where there are civil courts, constituted in some places of specially appointed Qadhis (religious judges) and in other places of the judges of the civil courts. For criminal matters: The court of cassation; 6 sessions courts (2 being presided over by the judge of the local court of first instance and 4 being identical with the courts of appeal). Magistrates' courts at all places where there are civil courts, constituted of civil judges exercising magisterial powers of the first and second class. There are also a number of third-class magistrates' courts, powers for this purpose being granted to municipal councils and a number of administrative officials.

The death penalty was introduced for serious theft in 1992; amputation of a hand for theft in 1994.

Religion. The constitution proclaims Islam the state religion, but also stipulates freedom of religious belief and expression. In 1993 there were 11·9m. Shi'ite Moslems and 6·6m. Sunni Moslems (including 3·5m. Kurds). There were 0·72m. Christians in 14 sects, including: 0·48m. Chaldean (Eastern rite Roman Catholic) Church, with some 100 priests in 9 dioceses; 0·15m. Apostolic Assyrian (Nestorian) Church, with 29 priests in 3 dioceses and 80,000 Syriac Orthodox in 2 dioceses. There were some 10,000 in various Protestant sects.

Education. Primary and secondary education is free and primary education became compulsory in 1976. Primary school age is 6–12. Secondary education is for 6 years, of which the first 3 are termed intermediate. The medium of instruction is Arabic; Kurdish is used in primary schools in northern districts.

There were, in 1995, 576 pre-primary schools with 4,972 teachers for 93,028 pupils. In 1993 there were 8,003 primary schools with 131,271 teachers for

2,857,467 pupils and 59,117 secondary level teachers for 1·14m. pupils. Adult literacy rate was 58·0% in 1995 (male, 70·7%; female, 45·0%). In 1994–95 there were 10 universities and 1 technological university, 1 institute of administration, 1 institute of applied arts, 1 technical teacher training institute and 22 technical institutes.

Health. In 1993 there were 8,787 doctors, 1,656 dentists, 1,561 pharmacists and 13,206 nurses (1991). There were 185 hospitals in 1993, with a provision of 14 beds per 10,000 population.

CULTURE

Broadcasting. Broadcasting is controlled by the government Broadcasting Service, and Baghdad Television. In 1995 there were 4·5m. radio and 1·6m. TV receivers (colour by SECAM).

Press. In 1995 there were 4 main daily newspapers (one of which is in English) with a combined circulation of 530,000.

Tourism. In 1996 there were 345,000 foreign tourists, bringing revenue of US$13m.

DIPLOMATIC REPRESENTATIVES
On 6 Feb. 1991 Iraq broke off diplomatic relations with Great Britain and the USA.

Of Iraq to the United Nations
Ambassador: Nizar Hamdoon.

FURTHER READING
Abdulrahman, A. J., *Iraq* [Bibliography]. Oxford and Santa Barbara (CA), 1984
Al-Khalil, S., *Republic of Fear: the Politics of Modern Iraq.* Univ. of California Press, 1989
Baram, A., *Cultural History and Ideology in the Formation of Ba'athist Iraq, 1968–89.* London, 1991
Bleaney, C. H., *Iraq* [Bibliography]. 2nd ed. Oxford and Santa Barbara (CA), 1995
Bulloch, J. and Morris, H., *Saddam's War: the Origins of the Kuwait Conflict and the International Response.* London, 1991
Chubin, S. and Tripp, C., *Iran and Iraq at War.* London, 1988
Farouk-Sluglett, M., and Sluglett, P., *Iraq since 1958: from Revolution to Dictatorship.* London, 1991

National statistical office: Central Statistical Organization, Ministry of Planning, Baghdad.

IRELAND

Republic of Ireland—
Poblacht na hÉireann

Capital: Dublin
Population estimate, 2000: 3·71m.
GNP per capita: (PPP$) 16,750
HDI/world rank: 0·930/17

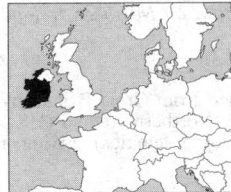

KEY HISTORICAL EVENTS

With the collapse of the Roman empire, Ireland developed its own Gaelic culture and language. But from the 12th century, the English dominated. Vast tracts of land were granted to English settlers and English law was introduced. In 1541, Henry VIII was recognized as King of Ireland. Most Irish remained Roman Catholic and in the reign of Elizabeth insurrection broke out against the Protestant overlords. In the early 17th century Scottish settlers in the north of Ireland established a strong Protestant enclave which led to rebellion in 1640. After 1649 Cromwell restored English domination. Irish resistance was brought to a bloody conclusion by the Battle of the Boyne (1690).

For over a century, the Roman Catholic majority had no share in government. The 1801 Act of Union gave Ireland representation at Westminster but opposition to British rule was reinforced in 1846 when the failure of the potato harvest and the apparent unwillingness of Britain to provide aid led to widespread famine. The subsequent mass emigration, chiefly to the United States, further damaged the Irish economy and intensified demands for Home Rule. In the north, however, Home Rule was bitterly opposed by the Protestant interest. In 1898 the Ulster Unionist party was set up to campaign for the right to remain part of the UK.

In April 1916 an insurrection against British rule took place and a republic was proclaimed. The armed struggle was renewed in 1919 and continued until 1921. The independence of Ireland was reaffirmed in Jan. 1919 by the Irish Parliament (*Dáil Éireann*), elected in Dec. 1918.

In 1920 an Act was passed by the British Parliament, under which separate Parliaments were set up for 'Southern Ireland' (26 counties) and 'Northern Ireland' (6 counties). The Unionists of the 6 counties accepted this scheme, and a Northern Parliament was duly elected on 24 May 1921. The rest of Ireland, however, ignored the Act.

On 6 Dec. 1921 a treaty was signed between Great Britain and Ireland by which Ireland accepted dominion status subject to the right of Northern Ireland to opt out. This right was exercised, and the border between the Irish Free State (26 counties) and Northern Ireland (6 counties) was fixed in Dec. 1925 as the outcome of an agreement between Great Britain, Ireland and Northern Ireland.

Subsequently the constitutional links between Ireland and the UK were gradually removed by the *Dáil*. The remaining formal association with the British Commonwealth by virtue of the External Relations Act, 1936 was severed when the Republic of Ireland Act, 1948 came into operation on 18 April 1949.

Ireland joined the European Economic Community in 1973 and has since benefitted enormously from inward investment leading to strong economic growth.

In the mid-1950s, the Irish Republican Army, which had led a violent campaign for Irish unity in the 1920s, re-emerged as a fighting force with a bombing campaign in Northern Ireland. Differences between the two religious communities intensified to the point, in 1969, when British troops had to be deployed to keep the peace. In 1972, the Unionist government in Belfast resigned and direct rule from London was imposed. By 1984 sectarian violence had accounted for the deaths of 2,400 civilians and 700 members of the security forces.

On 22 Feb. 1995 the Irish and British Prime Ministers (John Bruton and John Major) announced joint proposals for a settlement in Northern Ireland which envisaged: An elected single-chamber 90-member Northern Ireland Assembly; a north-south body comprising members of the assembly and representatives of the Irish government; and changes to the Irish constitution to withdraw the Republic's territorial claim to Northern Ireland if it were contrary to the will of a majority of its people. Under the chairmanship of former US Senator George Mitchell, a marathon negotiating struggle on 9–10 April 1998 led to a framework for sharing power designed to satisfy Protestant demands for a reaffirmation of their national identity as British, Catholic desires for a closer relationship with the predominantly Catholic Republic of Ireland and Britain's wish to return to Northern Ireland the powers London assumed in 1972 when the local Stormont legislature was disbanded.

In the referendum on 22 May 1998, 94·4% of votes in the Republic and 71·12% in Northern Ireland were cast in favour of the Good Friday peace agreement.

For details of recent peace negotiations turn to the section on Northern Ireland on page 1655.

TERRITORY AND POPULATION

The Republic of Ireland lies in the Atlantic Ocean, separated from Great Britain by the Irish Sea to the east, and bounded in the north-east by Northern Ireland (UK). The population at the 1996 census was 3,626,087 (1,825,855 females), giving a density of 52 persons per sq. km.

The projected population for 2000 is 3·71m.

In 1995 an estimated 57·5% of the population lived in urban areas.

The capital is Dublin (Baile Átha Cliath). Town populations, 1996: Greater Dublin, 952,692; Cork, 179,954; Limerick, 75,729; Galway, 57,363; Waterford, 44,155.

Counties and county boroughs	Area in ha[1]	Population, 1996[2]		
		Males	Females	Totals
Province of Leinster				
Carlow	89,655	21,086	20,530	41,616
Dublin County Borough	11,758	228,401	253,453	481,854
Dun Laoghaire-Rathdown	12,638	90,435	99,564	189,999
Fingal	45,467	82,720	84,963	167,683
South Dublin	22,364	107,410	111,318	218,728
Kildare	169,540	68,007	66,985	134,992
Kilkenny	207,289	38,144	37,192	75,336
Laoighis	171,990	27,160	25,785	52,945
Longford	109,116	15,468	14,698	30,166
Louth	82,613	45,641	46,525	92,166
Meath	234,207	55,340	54,392	109,732
Offaly	200,117	30,003	29,114	59,117
Westmeath	183,965	31,599	31,715	63,314
Wexford	236,685	52,432	51,939	104,371
Wicklow	202,662	50,823	51,860	102,683
Total of Leinster	1,980,066	944,669	980,033	1,924,702
Province of Munster				
Clare	345,004	47,789	46,217	94,006
Cork County Borough	3,953	61,254	65,933	127,187
Cork	746,042	147,923	145,400	293,323
Kerry	480,689	63,801	62,329	126,130
Limerick County Borough	2,087	25,092	26,947	52,039
Limerick	273,504	57,454	55,549	113,003
Tipperary, N. R.	204,627	29,290	28,731	58,021
Tipperary, S. R.	225,845	38,312	37,202	75,514
Waterford County Borough	4,103	20,790	21,750	42,540
Waterford	181,556	26,512	25,628	52,140
Total of Munster	2,467,410	518,217	515,686	1,033,903
Province of Connacht				
Galway County Borough	5,057	26,973	30,268	57,241
Galway	609,820	67,556	64,057	131,613
Leitrim	159,003	13,044	12,013	25,057
Mayo	558,605	56,371	55,153	111,524
Roscommon	254,819	26,695	25,280	51,975

IRELAND

Counties and county boroughs	Area in ha[1]	Males	Population, 1996[2] Females	Totals
Sligo	183,752	27,748	28,073	55,821
Total of Connacht	1,771,056	218,387	214,844	433,231
Province of Ulster (part of)				
Cavan	193,177	27,263	25,633	52,944
Donegal	486,091	65,520	64,474	129,944
Monaghan	129,508	26,158	25,155	51,313
Total of Ulster (part of)	808,776	118,959	115,292	234,251
Total	7,027,308	1,800,232	1,825,855	3,626,087

[1]Area Details Provided by Ordnance Survey.
[2]Revised Based on 1996 Census of Population.

Population density in 1996 was 51·6 per sq. km.

The official languages are Irish (the national language) and English; according to the National Survey of Languages of 1994, Irish is spoken as a mother tongue only by 2% of the population, in certain western areas (Gaeltacht), and is no longer a compulsory subject at school.

SOCIAL STATISTICS
Statistics for 6 calendar years:

	Births	Marriages	Deaths		Births	Marriages	Deaths
1992	51,089	16,636	30,931	1995	48,787	15,604	32,259
1993	49,404	16,824	32,148	1996[1]	50,390	16,255	31,786
1994	48,255	16,621	30,948	1997[1]	52,311	15,631	31,605

[1]Provisional figures—based on year of registration.

1997 rates (provisional): Birth, 14·3; death, 8·6; marriage, 4·3. Annual growth rate, 1990–95, 0·4%. Expectation of life at birth, 1990–95, 73·2 years for males and 78·6 years for females.

In 1997 the suicide rate per 100,000 population (provisional) was 11·8 (men, 19·5; women, 4·2). Infant mortality in 1997, 6·2 per 1,000 live births; fertility rate, 1·9 births per woman.

At a referendum on 24 Nov. 1995 on the legalization of civil divorce the electorate was 1,628,580; 818,852 votes were in favour, 809,728 against.

CLIMATE
Influenced by the Gulf Stream, there is an equable climate with mild south-west winds, making temperatures almost uniform over the whole country. The coldest months are Jan. and Feb. (39–45°F, 4–7°C) and the warmest July and Aug. (57–61°F, 14–16°C). May and June are the sunniest months, averaging 5·5 to 6·5 hours each day, but over 7 hours in the extreme S.E. Rainfall is lowest along the eastern coastal strip. The central parts vary between 30–44" (750–1,125 mm), and up to 60" (1,500 mm) may be experienced in low-lying areas in the west. Dublin, Jan. 40°F (4°C), July 59°F (15°C). Annual rainfall 30" (750 mm). Cork, Jan. 42°F (5°C), July 61°F (16°C). Annual rainfall 41" (1,025 mm).

CONSTITUTION AND GOVERNMENT
Ireland is a sovereign independent, democratic republic. Its parliament exercises jurisdiction in 26 of the 32 counties of the island of Ireland. The first Constitution of the Irish Free State came into operation on 6 Dec. 1922. Certain provisions which were regarded as contrary to the national sentiments were gradually removed by successive amendments, with the result that at the end of 1936 the text differed considerably from the original document. On 14 June 1937 a new Constitution was approved by Parliament and enacted by a plebiscite on 1 July 1937. This Constitution came into operation on 29 Dec. 1937. Under it the name Ireland (Éire) was restored. It states that the whole island of Ireland is the national territory, but that, pending its reintegration, laws enacted by Parliament have the same area and extent of application as those of the former Irish Free State.

The head of state is the *President*, whose role is largely ceremonial, but who has the power to refer proposed legislation which might infringe the Constitution to the Supreme Court.

The *Oireachtas* or National Parliament consists of the President, a House of Representatives (*Dáil Éireann*) and a Senate (*Seanad Éireann*). The *Dáil*, consisting of 166 members, is elected by adult suffrage on the Single Transferable Vote system in constituencies of 3, 4 or 5 members. Of the 60 members of the Senate, 11 are nominated by the *Taoiseach* (Prime Minister), 6 are elected by the universities and the remaining 43 are elected from 5 panels of candidates established on a vocational basis, representing the following public services and interests: (1) national language and culture, literature, art, education and such professional interests as may be defined by law for the purpose of this panel; (2) agricultural and allied interests, and fisheries; (3) labour, whether organized or unorganized; (4) industry and commerce, including banking, finance, accountancy, engineering and architecture; (5) public administration and social services, including voluntary social activities. The electing body comprises members of the *Dáil*, Senate, county boroughs and county councils.

A maximum period of 90 days is afforded to the Senate for the consideration or amendment of Bills sent to that House by the *Dáil*, but the Senate has no power to veto legislative proposals.

No amendment of the Constitution can be effected except with the approval of the people given at a referendum.

National Anthem. 'Amhrán na bhFiann' ('The Soldier's Song'); words by P. Kearney, tune by P. Heeney.

RECENT ELECTIONS

A general election was held on 6 June 1997: Fianna Fáil (FF) gained 76 seats with 39·33% of votes cast (in 1992, 68 seats); Fine Gael (FG), 54 with 27·95% (45); Labour Party (L), 17 with 10·4% (33); Progressive Democrats (PD), 4 with 4·68% (10); Democratic Left (DL), 4 with 2·51%; Green Party (G), 2 with 2·76%; Socialist Party, 1 with 0·7%; Sinn Féin, 1 with 2·55%; others, 6 with 6·88%.

European Parliament. Ireland has 15 representatives. At the June 1994 election turn-out was 44%. Fianna Fáil gained 7 seats (group in European Parliament: Union for Europe); Fine Gael, 4 (European People's Party); Greens, 2 (Green Group); Labour, 1 (European Socialist Party); independent, 1 (Liberal/ELDR).

CURRENT ADMINISTRATION

President: Mary McAleese (b. 1951), elected out of 5 candidates on 30 Oct. 1997 and inaugurated 11 Nov. 1997.

A new coalition Government was formed on 26 June 1997 between Fianna Fáil (FF) and The Progressive Democrats (PD). In March 1999 it comprised:

Taoiseach (Prime Minister): Bertie Ahern (b. 1951; FF). *Tánaiste (Deputy Prime Minister), Minister for Enterprise and Employment:* Mary Harney (b. 1953; PD). *Finance:* Charlie McCreevy (b. 1949; FF). *Social, Community and Family Affairs:* Dermot Ahern (b. 1955; FF). *Justice, Equality and Law Reform:* John O'Donoghue (b. 1956; FF). *Environment and Rural Development:* Noel Dempsey (b. 1953; FF). *Defence:* Michael Smith (b. 1940; FF). *Agriculture, Forestry and Food:* Joe Walsh (b. 1943; FF). *Tourism and Trade:* Dr. Jim McDaid (b. 1949; FF). *Transport, Energy and Communications:* Mary O'Rourke (b. 1937; FF). *Arts, Culture, Gaeltacht and the Islands:* Síle de Valera (b. 1954; FF). *Health and Children:* Brian Cowen (b. 1960; FF). *Education, Science and Technology:* Micheál Martin (b. 1960; FF). *Marine and Natural Resources:* Michael Woods (b. 1935; FF). *Foreign Affairs:* David Andrews (b. 1935; FF).

There are 17 Ministers of State.

Attorney-General: David Byrne, SC.

Local Government. The elected local authorities comprise 29 county councils, 5 county borough corporations, 5 borough corporations, 49 urban district councils and 26 Boards of Town Commissioners. All the members of these authorities are elected under a system of proportional representation, normally every 5 years. All residents of an area who have reached the age of 18 and whose names appear on the register of electors are entitled to vote in the local election for their area. Elected members are not paid, but provision is made for the payment of travelling expenses and subsistence allowances.

The range of services for which local authorities are responsible is broken down into 8 main programme groups as follows: Housing and Building; Road Transportation and Safety; Water Supply and Sewerage; Development Incentives and Controls; Environmental Protection; Recreation and Amenity; Agriculture, Education, Health and Welfare; Miscellaneous Services. Because of the small size of their administrative areas the functions carried out by town commissioners and some of the smaller urban district councils have tended to become increasingly limited, and the more important tasks of local government have tended to become the responsibility of the county councils.

The local authorities have a system of government which combines an elected council and a whole-time manager. The elected members have specific functions reserved to them which include the striking of rates (local tax), the borrowing of money, the adoption of development plans, the making, amending or revoking of bye-laws and the nomination of persons to other bodies. The managers, who are paid officers of their authorities, are responsible for the performance of all functions which are not reserved to the elected members, including the employment of staff, making of contracts, management of local authority property, collection of rates and rents and the day-to-day administration of local authority affairs. The manager for a county council is manager also for every borough corporation, urban district council and board town commissioners whose functional area is wholly within the county.

At the elections of June 1991 at city and county council level, 883 seats were contested. Fianna Fáil won 357 seats with 38% of votes cast, Fine Gael 270 with 26%, Labour 90 with 11%, the Progressive Democrats 37 with 5%, the Workers' Party 24 with 4%, the Greens 13 with 2%, and Sinn Féin 7 with 2%. Independents gained 85 seats.

DEFENCE

Supreme command of the Defence Forces is vested in the President. Exercise of the supreme command is regulated by law (Defence Act 1954). Military Command is exercised by the government through the Minister for Defence who is the overall commander of the Defence Forces.

The Defence Forces comprise the Permanent Defence Force (the regular Army, the Air Corps and the Naval Service) and the Reserve Defence Force (comprising a First Line Reserve of members who have served in the Permanent Defence Force, a second-line Territorial Army Reserve and a second-line Naval Reserve). A review of the Reserve Forces is currently being carried out. The total strength of the Permanent Defence Force in 1997 averaged 11,750. The total strength of the Reserve in 1998 averaged 14,000. The Defence Forces supplied an average of 750 personnel to 14 peace-support missions throughout the world in 1998.

Defence expenditure in 1997 totalled US$767m. (US$210 per capita), representing 1·0% of GDP.

Army. The Army is organized in 3 brigades, each with a territorial responsibility. The brigades are identical in organization and include 3 infantry battalions, a field artillery regiment, a cavalry squadron, a field engineer company, a field communications company, a military police company and a logistics support battallion which provides transport, medical, ordnance, catering and administrative services. A Training Centre at the Curragh, Co. Kildare provides military training and education for personnel of the Defence Forces. A Logistics Base, with elements located at the Curragh and Dublin provides force level logistical support. The average army strength in 1998 was 9,600 personnel.

Navy. The Naval Service, based at Haulbowline in Co. Cork, comprises 6 offshore patrol vessels and 1 helicopter patrol vessel. Two Dauphin helicopters (operated by the Air Corps) for use from the helicopter patrol vessel and 2 maritime reconnaissance aircraft are deployed for fishery protection and other duties. A contract for an additional Fishery Protection Vessel was placed in Dec. 1997, and delivery is expected in late 1999. The average Naval Service strength in 1998 was 1,000 personnel.

Air Corps. The Air Corps has its headquarters in Dublin and has 2 other bases. Most of the Corps' technical and administrative services are located at Casement

Aerodrome, Baldonnel, Co. Dublin which is the main centre for flying and technical training. Fixed-wing aircraft types in service include 4 Fouga Magister armed jet trainers, 7 SIAI Marchetti SF 260W armed piston-engined trainers, 7 Cessna F 172 reconnaissance aircraft, 2 CASA CN 235 maritime patrol aircraft and 1 Beech Super Kingair and 1 Gulfstream G IV aircraft for VIP transport. The Corps also has 7 Alouette III, 5 Dauphin and 2 Gazelle helicopters in use. The Air Corps currently operates 1 PBN Defender 4000 and 1 Squirrel SA 355N on behalf of the Gardai Siochana. A review of the Naval Service and Air Corps was completed in mid-1998 and Implementation Plans for the re-organization of both are being drawn up. The average Air Corps strength in 1998 was 1,000 personnel.

INTERNATIONAL RELATIONS
Ireland is a member of the UN, OECD, the Council of Europe and the EU.

ECONOMY
Performance. GDP growth was 7·4% in 1996, rising to 9·8% in 1997. For 1998 it was forecast to be 8·3%, making it the fastest-growing economy in the European Union.

Budget. Current revenue and expenditure (in IR£1m.):

Current Revenue	1997[1]	1998[2]
Customs duties	180	176
Excise duties	2,507	2,659
Capital taxes	225	198
Stamp duties	429	467
Income tax	5,218	5,522
Income levy	1	–
Corporation tax	1,699	1,926
Value-added tax	3,718	4,017
Agricultural levies (EU)	9	9
Motor vehicle duties	100[3]	–
Employment and training levy	189	193
Tax Amnesty proceeds	–	–
Non-Tax Revenue	345	330
Total	14,619	15,497

Current expenditure		
Debt service	2,755	2,625
Industry and Labour	572	632
Agriculture	624	589
Fisheries, Forestry, Tourism	91	101
Health	2,678	2,943
Education	2,361	2,351
Social Welfare	4,568	4,866
Other (excl. Balances)	3,317	3,392
Less: Receipts, e.g. social security	(–)2,939	(–)3,091
Total (including other items)	14,027	14,408

[1]Provisional outturn. [2]Budget targets. [3]Now retained by Local Authorities.

VAT is 21% (reduced rate 12·5%).

Total Public Capital Programme Expenditure amounted to IR£3,640m. in 1997, with provision for IR£4,324m. in 1998. On 31 Dec. 1996 the National Debt amounted to IR£29,912m. of which IR£21,193m. was denominated in Irish pounds and IR£8,718m. in foreign currencies. The official external reserves of the Central Bank of Ireland amounted to IR£5,092m. at the end June of 1997. Ireland is the largest recipient of EU aid per head of population.

Currency. On 1 Jan. 1999 the euro (EUR) became the legal currency in Ireland and the *Irish pound* became a subdivision of it; irrevocable conversion rate 0·787564 Irish pounds to 1 euro. The euro, which consists of 100 cents, will not be in circulation until 1 Jan. 2002. There will be 7 euro notes in different colours and sizes denominated in 500, 200, 100, 50, 20, 10 and 5 euros, and 8 coins denominated in 2 and 1 euros, then 50, 20, 10, 5, 2 and 1 cents. Even though notes and coins will not be introduced until 1 Jan. 2002 the euro can be used in banking, by means of cheques, travellers' cheques, bank transfers, credit cards and electronic purses. Banking will be possible in both euros and Irish pounds until the Irish pound is withdrawn from circulation—which must be by 1 July 2002.

The *Irish pound* (IEP) or *punt Éireannach* consists of 100 *pence*. From 10 Sept. 1928 when the first Irish legal-tender notes were issued, the Irish currency was linked to Sterling on a one-for-one basis. This relationship was discontinued on 30 March 1979 when, following Ireland's adherence to the EMS (which it had joined on its inception on 13 March 1979), it became inconsistent with Ireland's obligations. The Central Bank has the sole right of issuing legal tender notes; token coinage is issued by the Minister for Finance through the Bank. The volume of legal-tender notes outstanding on 30 June 1997 was IR£2,213m. The Irish pound was realigned within the ERM on 30 Jan. 1993 with bilateral central rates of the IR£ against other ERM currencies being reduced by 10% effective 1 Feb. Inflation was forecast to be 2·6% in 1998 (1·4% in 1997). Gold reserves were 360,000 troy oz. in Feb. 1998 and foreign exchange reserves were US$6,019m.

Banking and Finance. The Central Bank (founded in 1943), replaced the Currency Commission as the note-issuing authority. The Central Bank has the power of receiving deposits from banks and public authorities, of rediscounting Exchequer bills and bills of exchange, of making advances to banks against such bills or against Government securities, of fixing and publishing rates of interest for rediscounting bills, or buying and selling certain Government securities and securities of any international bank or financial institution formed wholly or mainly by governments. The Bank also collects and publishes information relating to monetary and credit matters. The Central Bank Acts, 1971, 1989 and 1997, together with the Building Societies Act, 1989, the Investment Intermediaries Act, 1995 and the Stock Exchange Act, 1995, give further powers to the Central Bank in the regulation and supervision of financial institutions and payment systems. The capital of the Bank is IR£40,000, of which IR£24,000 has been paid up and is held by the Minister for Finance.

The Board of Directors of the Central Bank consists of a Governor, appointed for a 7-year term by the President on the advice of the Government, and 9 directors, all appointed by the Minister for Finance. The Governor is Maurice O'Connell (b. 1937; appointed 1994).

At 31 Dec. 1996 there were 42 credit institutions authorized to carry on banking business in the State; 5 building societies and 3 State banks, ICC Bank, ACC Bank and the Trustee Savings Bank. In addition there were 13 credit institutions authorized in another Member State of the European Union operating in Ireland.

At 31 Dec. 1996 total assets of within-the-State offices of all credit institutions amounted to IR£67bn.

The Dublin stock exchange has been affiliated to the London exchange since 1973.

Weights and Measures. Conversion to the metric system is in progress; with some exceptions which are confined to the domestic market, all imperial units of measurement ceased to be legal, for general use, after 31 Dec. 1994.

ENERGY AND NATURAL RESOURCES

Electricity. The total generating capacity was (1997) 4,297 MW. In 1996 the total sales of electricity amounted to 16,726m. units supplied to 1,483,740 customers. Production in 1995 totalled 17·9bn. kWh; consumption per capita in 1995 was an estimated 4,343 kWh.

Oil and Gas. Over 0·6m. sq. km of the Irish continental shelf has been designated an exploration area for oil and gas; at the furthest point the limit of jurisdiction is 520 nautical miles from the coast. It has been established that there is potential for discoveries both offshore and onshore. In the offshore there is a vast Continental Shelf in which 13 major basins and troughs have been identified. Much of the shelf remains unexplored but from 1971 to date 129 exploration wells have been drilled, and since 1965 a total of 348 separate surveys have been carried out from which approximately 316,000 line kilometres of seismic data has been produced since 1985.

A number of encouraging oil and gas flows have been recorded, including the Corrib North Prospect in the Slyne/Erris Trough and '7 Heads' and 'Helvick' fields which are located in the Celtic Sea. In Nov. 1992 revised licensing terms were issued which allowed for a range of generous allowances against tax. In 1994 a Frontier Licensing Round in the Erris and Slyne Troughs resulted in the award of five licences over 28 blocks. A further 8 licences over 32 blocks were awarded under the Porcupine Basin Frontier Licensing Round in 1995.

Eleven licences were awarded over 58 full and part blocks under the Petroleum Exploration round in the Rockall Trough in June 1997. The area in the Round covered 615 full and 35 part blocks in an area of almost 150,000 sq. km. The Rockall Trough lies some 100 to 650 km west of Ireland with water depths ranging from 500 metres to 2,500 metres.

Comprehensive work programmes will be undertaken that will ensure licensed areas are fully explored. Up to 18,000 km of new 2D seismic, and up to 2,000 sq. km of 3D seismic data will be acquired and assessed by the end of the first four years of the licences.

An invitation was issued to interested petroleum companies to apply for a Lease Undertaking over the 'Seven Heads' oil and gas accumulation in the Celtic Sea. The area which covers almost 520 sq. km has been closed to the granting of authorizations since March 1997.

At the same time details of a Petroleum Licensing Round in the South Porcupine Basin were also announced. The acreage on offer covers 156 blocks in the Irish offshore—an area of over 5,000 sq. km. Due to the special difficulties created by the physical environment of the area, it has been designated as a Frontier Area. Long term licences for a period of 15 years will be granted.

The South Porcupine Basin lies off the south-west coast of Ireland. Water depths vary from 200 metres in the east to over 2,500 metres in the south-west.

An Onshore Petroleum Prospecting Licence was issued for a three year period from 1 Dec. 1997 covering 1,960 km of the Northwest Carboniferous Basin in counties Sligo, Leitrim, Roscommon, Cavan and Monaghan.

These steps in conjunction with the maintenance of Ireland's 'open door' approach to licensing, its favourable environment and existing tax regime achieves a risk/reward balance which reflects Ireland's circumstances and acknowledges the realities of competition for internationally mobile exploration and production investment.

In 1997 consumption of natural gas was 3,400m. cu. metres, of which 70% came from the Kinsale Head gas field, 50 km off the south coast, and the smaller Ballycotton field about 16 km north-west of Kinsale Head field, which was discovered in 1989 and which went into production in July 1991. These gas reserves are expected to be exhausted by the year 2003. Gas transmission and distribution is carried out by Bord Gais Eireann (Irish Gas Board). A gas pipeline from County Dublin to south-west Scotland was completed in 1994. 30% of gas used in 1997 was imported via the Interconnector. At Dec. 1997 there were 290,000 gas consumers in Ireland.

Peat. The country has very little indigenous coal, but possesses large reserves of peat, the development of which is handled largely by Bord na Mona (Peat Board). To date, the Board has acquired and developed 85,000 ha of bog and has 20 locations around the country. In the year ending 31 March 1998, the Board sold 67,000 tonnes of sod peat and 3,005,000 tonnes of milled peat for use in 5 milled peat electricity generating stations. 263,000 tonnes of briquettes were produced for sale to the domestic heating market. The Board also sold 1·5m. cu. metres of horticultural peat.

Minerals. Lead and zinc concentrates are important. In 1997 mineable resources stood at over 6m. tonnes of zinc and over 1m. tonnes of lead. Metal content of concentrates production, 1996: Zinc, 164,500 tonnes; lead, 45,300 tonnes. Gypsum, limestone and aggregates are important, and there is some production of silver (contained in lead) and dolomite. About 50 companies are involved in exploration, which is centred on base metals, but with interest also in gold, gem minerals, industrial minerals and coal. There is a thriving sand, gravel and aggregate extraction industry, employing some 7,500 people.

Agriculture. The CSO's Labour Force Survey shows in 1997, 134,000 people whose primary source of income was from agriculture. A total of 301,000 people worked on farms on a regular basis, working the equivalent of 223,400 full-time jobs. There were 149,500 farm holdings in Ireland, almost all of which were family farms. Average farm size was 29·2 ha. 48% of farms were under 20 ha. 12% of farmers were under 35 and 45% were over 55.

Agriculture represented 6·3% of GDP in 1997. The total area used for agricultural and forestry purposes is almost 5m. ha. Over 90% of the agricultural area is devoted to grass, and beef and milk production currently account for two-thirds of gross agricultural output.

At June 1997 the total area used for crops was 308,800 ha, of which wheat accounted (in ha.) for 91,300; oats, 21,300; barley, 190,000; other cereals, 6,100; potatoes, 20,400.

Gross agricultural output (including changes in stock) for the year 1997 was estimated at IR£3·3bn.; aggregate income from agriculture is IR£2bn. Direct income payments, financed or co-financed by the EU, amounted to IR£941m. or 47% of aggregate income. Livestock (June 1998): Cattle, 7,794,500; sheep, 8,373,400; pigs, 1,818,600; poultry,13,146,900.

Forestry. Current forest area cover (570,000 ha in 1995, up from 500,000 ha in 1990) amounts to 11% of the agricultural and forestry area, or about 8% of total land area. Timber production in 1995 was 2·2m. cu. metres.

Fisheries. In 1992 approximately 16,000 people were engaged full- or part-time in the sea fishing industry. In 1997 the fishing fleet consisted of 1,185 vessels. The quantities and values of fish landed during 1997 were: Wetfish, 261,400·8 tonnes, value IR£98,242,610·17; Shellfish, 46,538·5 tonnes, value IR£46,534,492·70. Total quantity: 307,939·30 tonnes; total value, IR£144,777,102·87. The main types of fish caught were horse mackerel (75,002·2 tonnes), herring (57,154·9 tonnes), mackerel (53,093·5 tonnes) and blue whiting (25,986·9 tonnes).

INDUSTRY

Enterprise Ireland. Enterprise Ireland is the organization established by the Government to help increase the sales, exports and employment of Irish companies. A key part of the Enterprise Ireland mission is to bring science, technology and innovation, marketing, enterprise development and business training into the mainstream of economic development in Ireland.

IDA Ireland. The IDA was established by the Irish Government in 1969 but its remit was altered in 1993 when responsibility for development of indigenous industry was moved to Enterprise Ireland. The objective of IDA Ireland is to create employment in Ireland by attracting and developing overseas industry.

Today, Ireland is recognised as a base for a wide range of activities, from software development and information technology to international services and pharmaceuticals. Over 1,250 foreign-owned enterprises have established businesses in Ireland.

Forfás. Forfás is the policy advisory and coordination board for industrial development and science and technology. It is the statutory agency through which powers are delegated to Enterprise Ireland for the promotion of indigenous enterprise and to IDA Ireland for the promotion of inward investment. It also aims to encourage the development of industry, technology, marketing and human resources.

The census of industrial production for 1995 gives the following details of the values (in IR£1m.) of gross and net output for the principal manufacturing industries. The figures for net output are those of gross output minus cost of materials, including fuel, light and power, repairs to plant and machinery and amounts paid to others in connection with products made.

	Gross output	Net output
Slaughtering, preparing and preserving meat	1,994·4	251·2
Manufacture of dairy products	2,257·6	405·2
Bread, biscuit and flour confectionery	320·5	143·1

	Gross output	Net output
Cocoa, chocolate and sugar confectionery	421·6	148·7
Animal and poultry foods	495·4	123·7
Brewing and malting	582·5	435·5
Spirit distilling and compounding	545·1	299·6
Paper and paper products	467·3	222·3
Printing and publishing	2,573·0	1,960·4
Manufacture of metal articles	993·2	389·3
Manufacture of non-metallic mineral products	716·5	402·2
Chemicals, including manmade fibres	5,446·2	3,857·4
Manufacture of machinery and equipment	1,072·3	518·7
General mechanical engineering	11·2	6·0
Office machinery and data-processing machinery	5,993·8	2,162·8
Electrical engineering	2,160·6	865·0
Manufacture and assembly of motor vehicles, parts and accessories	280·0	116·1
Manufacture of other means of transport	245·2	133·4
Instrument engineering	1,004·9	618·1
Textiles	442·3	189·3
Manufacture of footwear and clothing	352·3	168·5
Timber and wooden furniture	321·9	115·1
Processing rubber and plastics	734·2	348·8
Gas, water and electricity	1,471·7	835·6
All other industries	4,760·3	2,727·6
Total (all industries)	35,566·0	17,443·6

By 1996, gross output was IR£38,456m. and net, IR£19,483m. Annual volume of production was up 15·3% in 1997. In 1998 foreign companies in Ireland generated three-quarters of the country's manufacturing exports, over half of manufacturing output and more than two-thirds of manufacturing employment. Companies are attracted by 10% corporation tax.

Labour. The total labour force for 1998 was estimated to be 1,621,100, of which 127,000 were out of work. The unemployment rate in 1998 was an estimated 7·8%. Of those at work, 136,000 were employed in the Agricultural sector in 1998, 437,600 in the Industrial sector and 921,000 in the Services sector. The retirement age is 65 years.

Trade Unions. The number of trade unions in Dec. 1997 was 50; total membership, 502,962. The 6 largest unions accounted for 70% of total membership. There were 11 employers' associations holding negotiation licences, with membership of 10,320. A series of three year social pacts, which, in addition to covering a range of economic and social policy measures, include provision for pay increases, have been negotiated between the Government, trade unions and employers' organizations since 1987. The fourth such agreement concluded in Jan. 1997, Partnership 2000, provides pay increases of 7·25% of basic pay in the public and private sectors of the economy over the period of the agreement, 1997–99. In addition, employers and unions may engage in local level bargaining for a further increase, which must not exceed 2% of the basic pay cost of the particular group of employees.

INTERNATIONAL TRADE
The trade balance in 1998 was an estimated US$21·2bn.

Imports and Exports. Value of imports and exports of merchandise for calendar years (in IR£1m.):

	1994	1995	1996	1997
Imports	17,283·4	20,619·1	22,429·4	25,901·7
Exports	22,753·4	27,824·7	30,407·0	35,231·5

The values of the chief imports and total exports are shown below (in IR£1m.):

	Imports		Exports	
	1996	1997	1996	1997
Live animals and food	1,545·8	1,655·8	4,143·2	3,612·7
Raw materials	407·3	448·1	556·7	600·2
Mineral fuels and lubricants	823·7	896·8	116·6	147·3
Chemicals	2,762·1	3,211·7	6,724·3	8,855·6
Manufactured goods	2,442·8	2,696·8	1,358·4	1,376·1

IRELAND

	Imports		Exports	
	1996	1997	1996	1997
Machinery and transport equipment	9,468·2	11,741·3	10,627·7	13,327·7
Manufactured articles	2,862·2	3,122·2	4,601·9	4,750·2
Beverages and tobacco	233·4	275·8	517·8	549·6

Ireland is one of the most trade-dependent countries in the world. Exports constitute an increasing share of the economy's output of goods and services. In 1997, the total value of merchandise exports amounted to just over IR£35bn. and generated a trade surplus of IR£9·2bn. In employment terms, taking the economy as a whole, one job in four is directly dependent on exports. When indirect influences are taken into account, almost one job in two depends on exports. Exports of goods and services in 1996 contributed over 80% of GDP. In 1997, 67·5% of exports went to other European Union countries and 56·2% of imports were from within the EU. Information technology has become increasingly important, and by 1998 Ireland had become the second biggest exporter of software after the USA.

Exports, in IR£1m., for 1997 (and 1996): UK, 8,644 (7,477); Germany, 4,413 (3,987); France, 2,836 (2,503); USA, 3,996 (2,814); Netherlands, 2,460 (2,043); Belgium and Luxembourg, 1,770 (1,443); Italy, 1,155 (1,090); Japan, 1,117 (860); Spain, 908 (701); Sweden, 563 (549); Switzerland, 601 (561); Denmark, 397 (388); Norway, 384 (336); Canada, 230 (247).

Imports: UK, 8,964 (7,798); USA, 3,876 (3,462); Germany, 1,555 (1,528); Japan, 1,785 (1,207); Singapore, 1,416 (989); France, 1,251 (878); Netherlands, 849 (672); Italy, 500 (462); Norway, 380 (276); Taiwan, 357 (270); Belgium and Luxembourg, 305 (292); Sweden, 296 (303); China, 322 (253).

COMMUNICATIONS

Roads. At 31 Oct. 1997 there were 94,900 km of public roads, consisting of 2,739 km of National Primary Roads (including 90 km of motorway), 2,686 km of National Secondary Roads, 11,607 km of Regional Roads and 77,868 km of Local Roads.

Number of licensed motor vehicles at 31 Dec. 1997: Private cars, 1,134,429; Public-Service Vehicles, 16,185; Goods Vehicles, 158,158; Agricultural Vehicles, 74,106; Motor Cycles, 24,424; Other Vehicles, 25,028.

Rail. The total length of railway open for traffic at 31 Dec. 1997 was 1,872 km (38 km electrified), all 1,600 mm gauge.

Railway statistics for years ending 31 Dec.	1996	1997
Passengers (journeys)	27,930,000	29,413,000
Km run by passenger train	11,052,000	11,128,000
Freight (tonne-km)	569,885,000	522,376,930
Km run by freight trains	4,335,000	3,806,285
Receipts (IR£)	89,451,000	95,942,000
Expenditure (IR£)	*223,116,000	*190,497,000

*Expenditure figures include exceptional restructuring costs of IR£37·1m. (1996) and IR£0·501m. (1997).

Civil Aviation. Aer Lingus was incorporated in 1936 as a State-owned enterprise. Its principal business is the provision of passenger and cargo services to a range of points in the UK, Europe and the USA. In 1993, the company was restructured into the present Aer Lingus Group plc. Within the Group there are three airline operating companies: Aer Lingus which operates services to London and Europe; Aer Lingus Shannon, which operates services to the United States; Aer Lingus Commuter, which operates domestic services within Ireland and to UK provincial points.

During the year ended 31 March 1998 Aer Lingus carried almost 6m. passengers and 37,000 tonnes of cargo.

In addition to Aer Lingus, there were in 1998, 18 independent air transport operators, most notably Ryanair, TransAer and Cityjet, which operate scheduled and/or charter services to and from Ireland. In 1998 services were also provided by Aer Arran, Aeroflot, AB Airlines, Air Engiadina, Air France, Air Liberté, Air Malta, Air Ukraine, Alitalia, Austrian Airlines, Belavia, British Airways, British Midland, Condor Flugdienst, Continental Airlines, Crossair, Delta Air Lines, Finnair, Iberia,

Icelandair, Jersey European Airways, KLM, KLM-UK, Lufthansa, Malaysia Airlines, Manx Airlines, SABENA, Saudia, SAS, TAP, Tarom, Tyrolean Airways and Virgin Atlantic.

The principal airports are at Dublin, Shannon and Cork; there are also 6 privately-owned airports. In 1996 Dublin handled 9,021,000 passengers (8,556,000 on international flights) and 67,300 tonnes of freight.

Shipping. The merchant fleet totalled 193,934 GRT in 1996, including oil tankers, 191 GRT and container ships, 17,276 GRT. Total cargo traffic passing through the country's ports amounted to 33,918,000 tonnes in 1996.

Inland Waterways. The principal inland waterways open to navigation are the Shannon Navigation (270 km), which includes the Shannon-Erne Waterway (Ballinamore/Ballyconnell Canal), and the Grand Canal and Barrow Navigation (249 km). The Waterways Service of the Department of Arts, Culture and the Gaeltacht is responsible for the waterways system as a public amenity. Merchandise traffic has now ceased and navigation is confined to pleasure craft operated either privately or commercially. The Royal Canal (146 km) from Dublin to Mullingar (53 km) was reopened for navigation in 1995.

Telecommunications. Ireland's telecommunications sector has been fully liberalized with effect from 1 Dec. 1998 when the last remaining elements of Telecom Éireann's exclusive privilege were removed. All elements of the market are now open to competition from other licensed operators. There are 2 licensed mobile telephone operators, Eircell (a subsidiary of Telecom Éireann) with both TACS and GSM networks, and Esat Digifone, operating a GSM network. A competition for the award of a combined GSM and DCS 1800 licence to a third operator was held in 1998.

The Minister for Public Enterprise, a member of the Government, has overall policy responsibility for the development of the sector. Among the key elements of the Government's policy is the objective of creating a fully open and competitive telecommunications market that will stimulate investment in advanced information infrastructure and services in Ireland and develop Ireland as a global leader in the growth of internet-based industries and electronic commerce.

The Director of Telecommunications Regulation, established by legislation as an independent officer with a separate office and staff in June 1997, is responsible for licensing of operators, allocation of numbers and radio frequency spectrum, supervision of network interconnection arrangements and other regulatory functions.

Telecom Éireann—Operational Information. The dominant operator in the telecommunications sector remains Telecom Éireann, a statutory body set up under the Postal and Telecommunications Services Act, 1983. In 1996, 20% of the State's holding was sold to KPN/Telia, a Dutch-Swedish consortium, and they have an option of a further 15%. The government recently concluded an Employee Share Ownership Scheme under which 14·9% of the company is being made available to employees and has indicated its intention to have an Initial Public Offer (IPO) of shares in the company in mid-1999.

Number of working lines (April 1998), 1·5m; data lines, 31,609; Eircell (mobile telephone network), 415,000 customers approx.. Number of telex lines, 2,000 customers approx.; Eirpac (public packet-switched network), 2,500 customers approx.; Eirpage (radio paging network), customer base 40,175 (Oct. 1997). There were 520,000 PCs in use in 1995 and 300,000 Internet users in Oct. 1998.

Postal Services. Postal services are provided by An Post, a statutory body established under the Postal and Telecommunications Services Act, 1983. Number of Post Offices as of 31 Dec. 1996, 1,921; delivery points, 1,261,000. Number of items delivered in the year ended 31 Dec. 1996, 578·0m. An Post also offers a range of services to the business community through a dedicated unit, Special Delivery Services, subsidiaries PostGEM, Printpost and Precision Marketing Information. A range of services are provided through the Post Office network including Savings and Investments, passport applications, bill payments, National Lottery products and the payment of Social Welfare benefits on an agency basis for the State.

SOCIAL INSTITUTIONS

Justice. The Constitution provides that justice shall be administered in public in Courts established by law by Judges appointed by the President on the advice of the Government. The jurisdiction and organization of the Courts are dealt with in the Courts (Establishment and Constitution) Act, 1961 and the Courts (Supplemental Provisions) Acts, 1961–91. These Courts consist of Courts of First Instance and a Court of Final Appeal, called the Supreme Court. The Courts of First Instance are the High Court with full original jurisdiction and the Circuit and the District Courts with local and limited jurisdictions. A judge may not be removed from office except for stated misbehaviour or incapacity and then only on resolutions passed by both Houses of the Oireachtas. Judges of the Supreme and High Courts are appointed from among practising barristers or serving Circuit Court judges. Judges of the Circuit and District Courts may be appointed from among practising barristers or practising solicitors.

The Supreme Court, which consists of the Chief Justice (who is ex officio an additional judge of the High Court) and 7 ordinary judges, may sit in two Divisions and has appellate jurisdiction from all decisions of the High Court. The President may, after consultation with the Council of State, refer a Bill, which has been passed by both Houses of the Oireachtas (other than a money bill and certain other bills), to the Supreme Court for a decision on the question as to whether such Bill or any provision thereof is repugnant to the Constitution.

The High Court, which consists of a President (who is ex officio an additional Judge of the Supreme Court) and 23 ordinary judges, has full original jurisdiction in and power to determine all matters and questions, whether of law or fact, civil or criminal. In all cases in which questions arise concerning the validity of any law having regard to the provisions of the Constitution, the High Court alone exercises original jurisdiction. The High Court on Circuit acts as an appeal court from the Circuit Court.

The Court of Criminal Appeal consists of the Chief Justice or an ordinary Judge of the Supreme Court, together with either 2 ordinary judges of the High Court or the President and one ordinary judge of the High Court. It deals with appeals by persons convicted on indictment where the appellant obtains a certificate from the trial judge that the case is a fit one for appeal, or, in case such certificate is refused, where the court itself, on appeal from such refusal, grants leave to appeal. The decision of the Court of Criminal Appeal is final, unless that court, the Attorney-General or the Director of Public Prosecutions certifies that the decision involves a point of law of exceptional public importance, in which case an appeal is taken to the Supreme Court.

The Offences against the State Act, 1939 provides in Part V for the establishment of Special Criminal Courts. A Special Criminal Court sits without a jury. The rules of evidence that apply in proceedings before a Special Criminal Court are the same as those applicable in trials in the Central Criminal Court. A Special Criminal Court is authorized by the 1939 Act to make rules governing its own practice and procedure. An appeal against conviction or sentence by a Special Criminal Court may be taken to the Court of Criminal Appeal. On 30 May 1972 Orders were made establishing a Special Criminal Court and declaring that offences of a particular class or kind (as set out) were to be scheduled offences for the purposes of Part V of the Act, the effect of which was to give the Special Criminal Court jurisdiction to try persons charged with those offences.

The High Court exercising criminal jurisdiction is known as the Central Criminal Court. It consists of a judge or judges of the High Court, nominated by the President of the High Court. The Court sits in Dublin and tries criminal cases which are outside the jurisdiction of the Circuit Court.

The Circuit Court consists of a President (who is ex officio an additional judge of the High Court) and 25 ordinary judges. The country is divided into 8 circuits. The jurisdiction of the court in civil proceedings is subject to a financial ceiling, save by consent of the parties, in which event the jurisdiction is unlimited. In criminal matters it has jurisdiction in all cases except murder, treason, piracy, rape, serious and aggravated sexual assault and allied offences. The Circuit Court acts as an appeal court from the District Court.

The District Court, which consists of a President and 50 ordinary judges, has summary jurisdiction in a large number of criminal cases where the offence is not of a serious nature. In civil matters the Court has jurisdiction in contract and tort (except slander, libel, seduction, slander of title and false imprisonment) where the claim does not exceed IR£5,000; in proceedings founded on hire-purchase and credit-sale agreements, the jurisdiction is IR£5,000.

All criminal cases, except those of a minor nature, and those tried in the Special Criminal Court, are tried by a judge and a jury of 12. Generally, a verdict need not be unanimous in a case where there are not fewer than 11 jurors if 10 of them agree on the verdict.

At 31 Dec. 1996 the police force, the Garda, had a total staff of 10,817. There were 100,785 indictable crimes reported, of which 41,056 were solved, and 451,267 non-indictable crimes resulted in proceedings. 241,095 persons were convicted in total. There were 1·19 murders per 100,000 population and 4·595 juvenile offenders cautioned per 1,000 population.

Religion. In 1997 there were an estimated 3·34m. Roman Catholics and 300,000 members of other religions. According to the census of population taken in 1991 the principal religious professions were as follows:

	Leinster	Munster	Connacht	Ulster (part of)	Total
Roman Catholics	1,685,334	941,675	397,848	203,470	3,228,327
Church of Ireland (Anglican)	50,912	15,758	5,321	10,849	82,840
Protestants	3,391	1,385	516	1,055	6,347
Presbyterians	3,799	548	333	8,519	13,199
Methodists	2,815	1,185	286	751	5,037
Jewish	1,439	111	21	10	1,581
Other religious denominations	24,829	9,192	3,208	1,514	38,743
Not stated or no religion	88,430	39,679	15,498	6,038	149,645

Sean Brady (b. 1939) is the Roman Catholic Cardinal of Armagh and Primate of All Ireland.

In May 1990 the General Synod of the Church of Ireland voted to ordain women.

Education. In 1997 total expenditure on education came to 5·9% of GNP.

Elementary. Elementary education is free and was given in about 3,329 national schools (including 119 special schools) in 1997–98. The total number of pupils on rolls in 1997–98 was 460,000, including pupils in special schools and classes; the number of teachers of all classes was about 21,100 in 1997–98, including remedial teachers and teachers of special classes. The total salaries for teachers for 1998, including superannuation etc., was IR£599,774,000.

Special. Special provision is made for handicapped and deprived children in special schools which are recognized on the same basis as primary schools, in special classes attached to ordinary schools and in certain voluntary centres where educational services appropriate to the needs of the children are provided. Integration of handicapped children in ordinary schools and classes is encouraged wherever possible, if necessary with special additional support. There are also part-time teaching facilities in hospitals, child guidance clinics, rehabilitation workshops, special 'Saturday-morning' centres and home teaching schemes. Special schools (1996–97) numbered 119 with approximately 7,438 pupils. There were also some 5,998 pupils enrolled in about 476 special classes, and 1,302 (Sept. 1998) remedial teachers were employed for pupils in ordinary national schools. There is a National Education Officer for travelling children.

Secondary. Voluntary secondary schools are under private control and are conducted in most cases by religious orders. These schools receive grants from the State and are open to inspection by the Department of Education. The number of recognized secondary schools during the school year 1998–99 was 432, and the number of pupils in attendance was 211,365.

Vocational Education Committee schools provide courses of general and technical education. Pupils are prepared for State examinations and for entrance to universities and institutes of further education. The number of vocational schools during the school year 1998–99 was 245, and the number of full-time students in attendance was 98,685. These schools are controlled by the local Vocational Education Committees; they are financed mainly by State grants and also by contributions from local rating authorities and Vocational Education Committee receipts. These schools also provide adult education facilities for their own areas.

Comprehensive and Community Schools. Comprehensive schools which are financed by the State combine academic and technical subjects in one broad curriculum so that each pupil may be offered educational options suited to his needs, abilities and interests. Pupils are prepared for State examinations and for entrance to universities and institutes of further education. The number of comprehensive and community schools during the school year 1998–99 was 82 and the number of students in attendance was 52,675. These schools also provide adult education facilities for their own areas and make facilities available to voluntary organizations and to the adult community generally.

The net non capital State expenditure for second level and further education for 1997 was IR£807,274,000.

Education Third-Level. Traditionally, the third-level education system in Ireland has comprised the university sector, the technical and technological colleges and the colleges of education, all of which are substantially funded by the State and are autonomous. In recent years, a number of independent private colleges have developed, offering a range of mainly business-related courses conferring professional qualifications and, in some instances, recognized diplomas and certificates.

University education is provided by the National University of Ireland, founded in Dublin in 1908, by the University of Dublin (Trinity College), founded in 1592, and by the Dublin City University and the University of Limerick established in 1989. The National University comprises 4 constituent universities, NUI Dublin, NUI Cork, NUI Galway and NUI Maynooth.

St Patrick's College, Maynooth, Co. Kildare, is a national seminary for Catholic priests and a pontifical university with the power to confer degrees up to doctoral level in philosophy, theology and canon law.

Besides the University medical schools, the Royal College of Surgeons in Ireland (a long-established independent medical school) provides medical qualifications which are internationally recognized. Courses to degree level are available at the National College of Art and Design, Dublin.

Institutes of Technology in 12 centres (Athlone, Carlow, Cork, Dundalk, Dun Laoghaire, Limerick, Tallaght, Galway, Letterkenny, Sligo, Tralee and Waterford) provide vocational and technical education and training for trade and industry from craft to professional level through certificate, diploma and some degree courses. These colleges (with the exception of Dun Laoghaire) were established on a statutory basis on 1 Jan. 1993. Prior to this they operated under the aegis of the Vocational Education Committees (VECs) for their areas. Dun Laoghaire College of Art and Design was designated under the RTC Act 1992, from 1 April 1997. The Dublin Institute of Technology (DIT) was also established on a statutory basis on 1 Jan. 1993. Prior to this it operated under the aegis of City of Dublin VEC. The DIT provides certificate, degree and diploma level courses in engineering, architecture, business studies, catering, music, etc. The Hotel and Catering College in Killybegs continues to operate under the aegis of Co. Donegal VEC.

Total full-time enrolments in the 1997–98 academic year were approximately 42,000.

There are 5 Colleges of Education for training primary school teachers. For degree awarding purposes, 3 of these colleges are associated with Trinity College, 1 with Dublin City University and 1 with The University of Limerick. There are also 2 Home Economics Colleges for teacher training, 1 associated with Trinity College and the other with The National University of Ireland, Galway.

The total full-time enrolment at third-level in institutions aided by the Department of Education and Science in 1996–97 was 100,204. The total current expenditure from public funds on third level education during the financial year ended 31 Dec. 1996 was approximately IR£497,900,000. The National Council for Educational Awards, established on a statutory basis in 1979, is the validating and awarding authority for courses in the third-level sector outside the universities.

Agricultural. Teagasc, the Agriculture and Food Development Authority, is the State agency responsible for providing advisory, training, research and development services for the agriculture and food industries. Full-time instruction in agriculture is provided for all sections of the farming community. There are 4 agricultural colleges, administered by Teagasc, and 7 private Teagasc-aided agricultural colleges. Courses in commercial horticulture are also offered, and short courses for adults already farming.

Coolahan, J., *Irish Education: its History and Structure.* Dublin, 1981

Health. Everybody ordinarily resident in Ireland has either full or limited eligibility for the public health services.

(i) A person who satisfies the criteria of a means test receives a medical card which confers Category 1 or full eligibility on them and their dependants. This entitles the holder to the full range of public health and hospital services, free of charge, i.e. family doctor, drugs and medicines, hospital and specialist services as well as dental, aural and optical services. Maternity care and infant welfare services are also provided.

(ii) The remainder of the population have Category 2 or limited eligibility. Category 2 patients receive public consultant and public hospital services subject to certain charges. They are not entitled to free drugs or medicines but receive reimbursement of their drug expenditure in excess of IR£90 in any quarter commencing Jan., April, July and Oct. or a refund of all drug expenditure over IR£32 per month if they suffer from a long term medical condition requiring ongoing medication.

Persons in Category 2 are liable for a hospital in-patient charge of IR£25 per night up to a maximum of IR£250 in any 12 consecutive months (with effect from 1 Jan. 1998). There is no charge for out-patient services. However persons in Category 2 are liable for a charge of IR£12 if they attend the Accident and Emergency Department of a hospital without a letter of referral from a General Practitioner.

The Long Term Illness Scheme entitles persons to free drugs and medicines which are prescribed in respect of 15 specific illnesses. The needs of individuals with significant or ongoing medical expenses are met by a range of other schemes which provide assistance towards the cost of prescribed drugs and medicines. The *Drug Cost Subsidization Scheme* caters for people who do not have a medical card or a long term illness book and are certified as having a medical condition with a regular and ongoing requirement for prescribed drugs and medicines. Persons who qualify for inclusion in this scheme will not have to spend more than IR£32 in any month on prescribed medication. Under the *Drugs Refund Scheme* which covers expenditure by the whole family, any expenditure on prescribed medication above IR£90 in a calendar quarter is refunded by the Health Board.

Where an individual or a family is subjected to a significant level of ongoing expenditure on medical expenses, such as general practitioner fees or prescribed drugs due to a long term medical condition, these expenses may be reckoned in determining eligibility for a medical card. Eligibility for a medical card is solely a matter for the Chief Executive Officer of the relevant health board to decide.

Services for Children: Health Boards provide, with the co-operation of a wide range of voluntary organizations, comprehensive child welfare and protection services including adoption, fostering, residential care, day care, social work and family support services.

Welfare Services: There are various services provided for the elderly, the chronically sick, the disabled and families in stress, such as social support services, day care services for children, home helps, home nursing, meals-on-wheels, day centres, cheap fuel, etc. Health Boards also provide disabled persons, without charge, with training for employment and place them in jobs.

Grants and Allowances: The Department of Health and Children provide, through the Health Boards, a wide range of services for people with disabilities. These include day care, therapy services, training, employment, sheltered work and residential services as well as transport to and from these services.

Blind welfare allowance—provides a means-tested supplementary weekly allowance to unemployed recipients of the following allowances from the Department of Social, Community and Family Affairs, Disability Allowance, Blind Allowance or Old Age Pension.

Motorized Transport Grant—a grant of up to IR£2,884 is payable, subject to a means test, to disabled persons towards the purchase of a car, in order that they might obtain or retain employment; in some cases the grant is paid to those living in very isolated areas.

Health Contributions—A health contribution of 2% of income is payable by those with Category 2 eligibility. Employers meet the levy in respect of those employees who have a medical card.

In 1996 there were 62 general government hospitals with a total of 11,937 beds with an 82·2% occupancy rate. In Health Board hospitals, voluntary/Joint Board hospitals and homes for the mentally handicapped there was a total staff of 65,755. Of these 4,684 were medical/dental staff, 5,576 were para-medics and 27,264 were nurses.

Welfare. Social Welfare Services (SWS) is the executive arm of the Department of Social, Community and Family Affairs and is responsible for the day to day administration and management of social welfare schemes and services through a network of local, regional and decentralized offices. The Department's local delivery of services is structured on a regional basis. There are a total of 10 regions, with offices in Waterford, Cork, Limerick, Galway, Longford, Sligo, Dundalk and three in Dublin.

The Social Welfare Appeals Office (SWAO) is an independent office responsible for determining appeals against decisions on social welfare entitlements.

There are, in addition, three statutory agencies under the aegis of the Department:
—*the Combat Poverty Agency* which has responsibilities in the areas of advice to the Minister, research, action programmes and public information in relation to poverty;
—*the Pensions Board* which has the function of promoting the security of occupational pensions, their development and the general issue of pensions coverage;
—*the National Social Service Board* which has the function of ensuring that all citizens have easy access to the highest quality of information, advice and advocacy on social services.

Social Welfare Schemes. The social welfare supports can be divided into three categories:
Social Insurance (Contributory) payments made on the basis of a Pay Related Social Insurance (PRSI) record. Such payments are funded by employers, employees and the self-employed. Any deficit in the fund is met by Exchequer subvention.
Social Assistance (Non Contributory) payments made on the basis of satisfying a means test. These payments are financed entirely by the Exchequer.
Universal services such as Child Benefit or Free Travel which do not depend on PRSI or a means test.

CULTURE

Broadcasting. Public service broadcasting is provided by Radio Telefis Éireann (RTÉ), a statutory body established under the Broadcasting Authority Acts 1960–93. RTÉ is financed principally by TV licence and advertising. In 1996 a total of 972,069 TV licences were issued. Legislation enacted in 1988 provided for the establishment of the Independent Radio and Television Commission to arrange provision of independent commercial radio stations and an independent TV service. There were (1996) 21 local commercial radio stations, 10 community radio stations, 2 special interest Irish language radio stations, 1 independent national radio station and 4 hospital radio stations. There were 2·5m. radio receivers in 1996 and 1·46m. TV receivers. The IRTC have recently awarded the contract for the first independent TV service which was due to come on air in Sept. 1998. An Irish-language TV channel, Teilifis na Gaeilge, began broadcasting for 4 hours a day in 1996.

Cinema. In 1995 Ireland made 17 films and there were 197 cinema screens.

Press. In 1997 there were 8 weekday newspapers and 5 Sunday newspapers (all in English) with a combined circulation of 1,310,411 for Jan. to June 1997.

Tourism. Total number of overseas tourists in 1997 was 5,007,000. These, together with cross-border visitors, spent IR£2,105m.

Festivals. St. Patrick's Day is celebrated annually, but the 1999 festival was earmarked as a 'homecoming festival' when the entire Irish diaspora could come together from around the world and mark the millennium.

Libraries. In 1995 there were 2 National Libraries, 516 public libraries, 33 Higher Education libraries and 4 non-specialized. They held a total of 17,750,000 volumes and had a combined 863,918 registered users.

DIPLOMATIC REPRESENTATIVES
Of Ireland in Great Britain (17 Grosvenor Pl., London, SW1X 7HR)
Ambassador: Edward Barrington.

Of Great Britain in Ireland (29 Merrion Rd., Ballsbridge, Dublin, 4)
Ambassador: Ivor Anthony Roberts, CMG.

Of Ireland in the USA (2234 Massachusetts Ave., NW, Washington, D.C., 20008)
Ambassador: Seán O'Huiginn.

Of the USA in Ireland (42 Elgin Rd., Ballsbridge, Dublin)
Ambassador: Michael J. Sullivan.

Of Ireland to the United Nations
Ambassador: Richard Ryan.

FURTHER READING

Central Statistics Office. *National Income and Expenditure* (annual), *Statistical Abstract* (annual), *Census of Population Reports* (quinquennial), *Census of Industrial Production Reports* (annual), *Trade and Shipping Statistics* (annual and monthly), *Trend of Employment and Unemployment, Reports on Vital Statistics* (annual and quarterly), *Statistical Bulletin* (quarterly), *Labour Force Surveys* (annual), *Trade Statistics* (monthly), *Economic Series* (monthly).

Ardagh, J., *Ireland and the Irish: a Portrait of a Changing Society.* London, 1994
Chubb, B., *Government and Politics in Ireland.* 3rd ed. London, 1992
Collins, N. (ed.), *Political Issues in Ireland Today.* Manchester, Univ. Press, 1994
Eager, A. R., *A Guide to Irish Bibliographical Material.* 2nd ed. London, 1980
Delanty, G. and O'Mahony, P., *Rethinking Irish History: Nationalism, Identity and Ideology.* London, 1997
Encyclopaedia of Ireland. Dublin, 1968
Fitzgerald, G., *All in a Life: an Autobiography.* London, 1991
Foster, R. F., *Modern Ireland 1600–1972.* London, 1988.—(ed.) *The Oxford Illustrated History of Ireland.* OUP, 1991
Garvin, T., *1922 The Birth of Irish Democracy.* Dublin, 1997
Harkness, D., *Ireland in the Twentieth Century: a Divided Island.* London, 1995
Hickey, D. J. and Doherty, J. E., *A Dictionary of Irish History since 1800.* Dublin, 1980
Hussey, G., *Ireland Today: Anatomy of a Changing State.* Dublin, 1993
Institute of Public Administration, *Ireland: a Directory.* Dublin, annual
Kostick, C., *Revolution in Ireland – Popular Militancy 1917-1923.* London, 1997
Lee, J. J., *Ireland 1912-1985: Politics and Society.* CUP, 1989
Munck, R., *The Irish Economy: Results and Prospects.* London, 1993
A New History of Ireland. 6 vols. Oxford, 1996
O'Beirne Ranelagh, J., *A Short History of Ireland.* 2nd ed. CUP, 1994
O'Hagan, J. W. (ed.) *The Economy of Ireland: Policy and Performance of a Small European Country.* London, 1995
Shannon, M. O., *Irish Republic.* [Bibliography] Oxford and Santa Barbara (CA), 1986
Vaughan, W. E. (ed.), *A New History of Ireland,* 6 vols. Oxford, 1997
Wiles, J. L. and Finnegan, R. B., *Aspirations and Realities: a Documentary History of Economic Development Policy in Ireland since 1922.* London, 1992.

A more specialized title is listed under EDUCATION, *above*

National statistical office: Central Statistics Office, Skehard Road, Cork. *Director-General:* Donal Murphy, M.Sc., M.Econ.Sc., M.Sc.(Mgt).
Website: http://www.cso.ie/

ISRAEL

Medinat Israel

(State of Israel)

Capital: Jerusalem
Population estimate, 2000: 6·08m.
GNP per capita: (PPP$) 18,100
HDI/world rank: 0·913/22

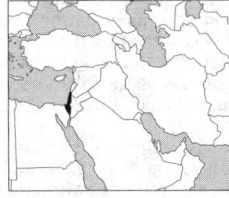

KEY HISTORICAL EVENTS

The area once designated as Palestine, of which Israel forms part, was formerly part of Turkey's Ottoman Empire. During the First World War, when Turkey was allied with Germany, the Arabs under Ottoman rule rebelled and Palestine was occupied by British forces. In 1917 the British Government issued the Balfour Declaration, stating that it viewed 'with favour the establishment in Palestine of a national home for the Jewish people'. In 1922 the League of Nations recognized 'the historical connection of the Jewish people with Palestine' and 'the grounds for reconstituting their national home in that country,' and Britain assumed a mandate over Palestine, pending the establishment there of such a national home. In accordance with the mandate, Jewish settlers were admitted to Palestine, under the direction of Zionist settlement agencies, where the population had remained almost entirely Arab. There were anti-Zionist riots in 1921 and 1929. In the 1930s the Nazi persecution of the Jews led to escalated immigration into Palestine.

In Nov. 1947 the UN General Assembly passed a resolution calling for the establishment of a Jewish and an Arab state in Palestine. On 14 May 1948 the British Government terminated its mandate, and the Jewish leaders proclaimed the State of Israel. No independent Arab state was established in Palestine. Instead the neighbouring Arab states invaded the new Israel on 15 May 1948. The Jewish state defended itself successfully, and the cease-fire in Jan. 1949 left Israel with one-third more land than had been originally assigned by the UN. The Suez crisis of 1956 saw Israel joined with Britain and France in a tripartite attack on Egypt in an effort to topple Nasser's regime which they each regarded as inimical to their own interests in the region.

In 1967, following some years of uneasy peace, local clashes on the Israeli–Syrian border were followed by Egyptian mass concentration of forces on the borders of Israel. The UN emergency force in Gaza was expelled and a blockade of shipping to and from Israel was imposed by Egypt in the Red Sea. Israel struck out at Egypt on land and in the air on 5–9 June 1967. Jordan joined in the conflict which spread to the Syrian borders. By 11 June the Israelis had occupied the Gaza Strip and the Sinai peninsula as far as the Suez Canal in Egypt, West Jordan as far as the Jordan valley and the heights east of the Sea of Galilee, including Quneitra in Syria.

A further war broke out on 6 Oct. 1973 when Egyptian and Syrian offensives were launched. Following UN Security Council resolutions a cease-fire finally came into being on 24 Oct. In Dec. Egypt and Israel signed a dis-engagement agreement; as did Israel and Syria on 31 May 1974. A further dis-engagement agreement was signed between Israel and Egypt in Sept. 1975.

Developments in 1977 included President Sadat of Egypt's visit to Israel and peace initiative. In March 1978 Israeli troops entered southern Lebanon but later withdrew after the arrival of a UN peace-keeping force. In Sept. 1978 US President Carter convened the Camp David conference at which Egypt and Israel agreed on frameworks for peace in the Middle East with treaties to be negotiated between Israel and her neighbours. Negotiations began in the USA between Egypt and Israel in Oct. 1978 and a treaty was signed in Washington on 26 March 1979. Under this treaty Israel withdrew from the Sinai Desert in two phases; part was achieved on 26 Jan. 1980 and the final withdrawal by 26 April 1982.

In June 1982 Israeli forces once again invaded the Lebanon, this time in massive strength, and swept through the country, laying siege to and bombing Beirut. On 16 Feb. 1985 the Israeli forces started a complete withdrawal, leaving behind an Israeli trained and equipped Christian Lebanese force to act as a control over and buffer against Moslem Shi'a or Palestinian guerrilla attacks.

In 1993 following declarations by the Prime Minister, Yitzhak Rabin, recognizing the Palestine Liberation Organization (PLO) as representative of the Palestinian people, and by Yasser Arafat, leader of the PLO, renouncing terrorism and recognizing the State of Israel, an agreement was signed in Washington providing for limited Palestinian self-rule in the Gaza Strip and Jericho. A further agreement, signed by the Foreign Minister, Shimon Peres, and Yasser Arafat on 9 Feb. 1994 dealt with control over the Egypt–Gaza Strip and Jericho–Jordan border crossings, and security arrangements for Jewish settlers in Gaza which would divide the strip into 3 zones. On 4 May 1994 in Cairo an Israeli–Palestinian agreement on the first phase of Palestinian self-rule in the Gaza Strip and Jericho was signed by the Israeli Prime Minister Yitzhak Rabin and Yasser Arafat. An Israeli–Palestinian agreement was signed in Washington on 28 Sept. 1995. (For details *see* PALESTINIAN-ADMINISTERED TERRITORIES: Key Historical Events). Negotiations on the permanent status of the West Bank and Gaza began in 1996.

On 4 Nov. 1995 Yitzhak Rabin was assassinated by a Jewish religious extremist. In the subsequent election, a right wing coalition led by Binyamin Netanyahu took office. Peace talks with the Palestinians then stalled, partly as a result of Palestinian terrorism but also because it became clear that Israel balked at the basic conditions for a settlement. In Feb. 1998 plans were announced to construct a new Jewish settlement in East Jerusalem, a move which Palestinians said could kill the peace progress.

Following a visit to the Middle East by UK Prime Minister Tony Blair, representing the EU, the two sides agreed to meet in London. No agreement was reached on an American proposal that Israel should withdraw from 13·1% of the West Bank. But a further meeting was agreed, for Oct. 1998. It took place at the Wye Plantation in Maryland, USA where Israel accepted partial withdrawal on condition that the Palestinians cracked down on terrorism. The following month, 2% of the West Bank was handed over to Palestinian control and 250 Palestinian prisoners were released. Further moves were put on hold after the collapse of the Netanyahu coalition and the announcement of early elections.

TERRITORY AND POPULATION

The area of Israel, including the Golan Heights (1,150 sq. km) and East Jerusalem (70 sq. km), is 21,946 sq. km (8,473 sq. miles), with a population estimated in 1997 to be 5·53m., including East Jerusalem, the Golan Heights and Israeli settlers in the occupied territories.

The UN gives a projected population for 2000 of 6·08m.

In 1995 an estimated 90·7% of the population lived in urban areas. Population density, 252 per sq. km.

Population by place of origin as of 1995: Europe and America, 1·8m.; former USSR, 0·66m.; Morocco, 0·5m.; Poland, 0·25m.; Romania, 0·25m.; Iraq, 0·25m.; Yemen, 0·15m.; Iran, 0·13m.; Algeria and Tunisia, 0·12m.

The Jewish Agency, which, in accordance with Article IV of the Palestine Mandate, played a leading role in establishing the State of Israel, continues to organize immigration.

Israel is administratively divided into 6 districts:

District	Area (sq. km)	Population[1]	Chief town
Northern	4,501	952,100	Nazareth
Haifa	854	740,300	Haifa
Central	1,242	1,213,200	Ramla
Tel Aviv	170	1,141,900	Tel Aviv
Jerusalem[2]	627	662,700	Jerusalem
Southern	14,107	770,200	Beersheba

[1]31 Dec. 1995. [2]Includes East Jerusalem.

On 23 Jan. 1950 the Knesset proclaimed Jerusalem the capital of the State and on 14 Dec. 1981 extended Israeli law into the Golan Heights. Population of the main towns (1995): Jerusalem, 591,400; Tel Aviv/Jaffa, 355,900; Haifa, 252,300; Holon, 163,900; Petach Tikva, 153,100; Bat Yam, 142,300; Rishon le-Ziyyon, 165,300; Netanya, 148,400; Beersheba, 152,600; Ramat Gan, 121,700; Bene Berak, 128,600.

The official languages are Hebrew and Arabic.

ISRAEL

SOCIAL STATISTICS
Crude birth rate per 1,000 population of Jewish population (1995), 18·1; non-Jewish: Moslems, 37·9; (1994): Christians, 18·7; Druzes, 29·2. Crude death rate (1994), Jewish, 6·9; non-Jewish: Moslems, 3; Christians, 4·3; Druzes, 3·2. Infant mortality rate per 1,000 live births (1995), Jewish, 6·3; non-Jewish: Moslems, 13; (1994): Christians, 10·4; Druzes, 8·7. Life expectancy (1997), 78·2 years (males, 76·3; females, 80·2). Average annual population growth rate, 1990–95, 3·5%. Growth rate in 1997 was estimated to be 2·0%. Fertility rate, 1990–95, 2·9 births per woman.

Immigration. The following table shows the numbers of Jewish immigrants entering Palestine/Israel.

| 1990 | 199,516 | 1992 | 77,057 | 1994 | 79,844 |
| 1991 | 176,100 | 1993 | 76,805 | 1995 | 76,361 |

CLIMATE
From April to Oct., the summers are long and hot, and almost rainless. From Nov. to March, the weather is generally mild, though colder in hilly areas, and this is the wet season. Jerusalem, Jan. 12·8°C, July 28·9°C. Annual rainfall, 657 mm. Tel Aviv, Jan. 17·2°C, July 30·2°C. Annual rainfall, 803 mm.

CONSTITUTION AND GOVERNMENT
Israel is an independent sovereign republic, established by proclamation on 14 May 1948.

In 1950 the Knesset (*Parliament*), which in 1949 had passed the Transition Law dealing in general terms with the powers of the Knesset, President and Cabinet, resolved to enact from time to time fundamental laws, which eventually, taken together, would form the Constitution. The 9 fundamental laws that have been passed: The Knesset (1958), Israel Lands (1960), the President (1964), the Government (1968), the State Economy (1975), the Army (1976), Jerusalem, capital of Israel (1980), the Judicature (1984) and the Electoral System (1996).

The *President* (head of state) is elected by the Knesset by secret ballot by a simple majority; his term of office is 5 years. He may be re-elected once.

The Knesset, a one-chamber Parliament, consists of 120 members. It is elected for a 4-year term by secret ballot and universal direct suffrage. Under the system of election introduced in 1996, electors vote once for a party and once for a candidate for Prime Minister. To be elected Prime Minister, a candidate must gain more than half the votes cast, and be elected to the Knesset. If there are more than 2 candidates and none gain half the vote, a second round is held 15 days later. The Prime Minister forms a cabinet (no fewer than 8 members and no more than 18) with the approval of the Knesset.

Sayer, S., *The Parliamentary System of Israel.* Syracuse Univ. Press, 1986

National Anthem. 'Hatikvah' ('The Hope'); words by N. H. Imber.

RECENT ELECTIONS
At the parliamentary elections of 29 May 1996, 20 parties put up candidates. Binyamin Netanyahu (Likud) was elected Prime Minister against 1 opponent by 50·4% of votes cast. Labour gained 34 seats (44 in 1992); Likud-Tsomet-Gesher (L), 32 (Likud alone, 32); Shas (Oriental Religious Jews), 10 (6); Meretz, 9 (12); National Religious Party (NRP), 9 (6); Yisrael ba-Aliyah, 7; Hadash, 5 (2); Third Way, 4; United Torah-Jewry, 4 (4); United Arab List, 4; Moledet, 2 (3).

CURRENT ADMINISTRATION
President: Ezer Weizman (b. 1924; elected 24 March 1993 and sworn in 13 May 1993, re-elected in 1998).

Following the elections of May 1996 a Likud-led coalition government was formed in June. In March 1999 the government comprised:

Prime Minister, Minister of Housing and Construction: Binyamin Netanyahu (b. 1940; L).

Deputy Prime Minister, Minister of Agriculture and the Environment: Rafael Eitan (Tsomet). *Deputy Prime Minister, Minister of Tourism:* Moshe Katzav (L). *Defence:* Moshe Arens. *Finance:* Meir Sheetrit. *Foreign Affairs, Infrastructure:*

Ariel Sharon (L). *Justice:* Tzahi Hanegbi (L). *Internal Security:* Avigdor Kahalani (Third Way). *Labour, Social and Religious Affairs:* Eliyahu Yishai (Shas). *Interior:* Eli Suissa (Shas). *Transport:* Shaul Yahalom (NRP). *Trade and Industry:* Natan Sharansky (Israel with Immigration). *Immigrant Absorption:* Yuli Edelstein (Israel with Immigration). *Communications:* Limor Livnat (L). *Health:* Yehoshua Matza (L). *Education and Culture:* Yitzhak Levi (NRP). *Science and Technology:* Silvan Shalom. *Without Portfolio:* Sha'ul 'Amor.

Local Government. In 1995 there were 57 municipalities (5 Arab), 138 local councils (66 Arab or Druze) and 78 regional councils. Regional councils are local authorities set up in agricultural areas and include all the agricultural settlements in the area under their jurisdiction. All local authorities exercise their authority mainly by means of bye-laws approved by the Minister of the Interior. Their revenue is derived from rates and a surcharge on income tax. Local authorities are elected for a 4-year term. Elections were held for 158 municipal councils in Nov. 1993. The electorate was 3·3m.; turn-out was 36%.

DEFENCE
Conscription (for Jews and Druze only) is 3 years (usually 4 years for officers; 2 years for women).

The Israel Defence Force is a unified force, in which army, navy and air force are subordinate to a single chief-of-staff. The Minister of Defence is *de facto* C.-in-C. The cabinet usually forms a defence committee with authority to make decisions on military operations.

Defence expenditure in 1997 totalled US$11,143m., representing 11·5% of GDP. Expenditure per capita in 1997 was US$1,917, a figure exceeded only by Qatar.

Nuclear weapons. Israel has an undeclared nuclear weapons capability. Although known to have a nuclear bomb, it pledges not to introduce nuclear testing to the Middle East.

Army. The Army is organized in 3 territorial and 1 home front command, and has 3 corps headquarters, 2 divisional headquarters, 3 armoured divisions, 3 regional infantry divisions, 4 mechanized infantry brigades and 3 artillery battalions. The Reserves are organized in 9 armoured divisions, 1 mechanized (air mobile) division, 10 regional infantry and 4 artillery brigades. Equipment includes 1,080 Centurion, 325 M-48A5, 400 M-60, 600 M-60A1, 200 M-60A3, 150 Magach 7, 300 T-54/-55, 110 T-62 and 930 Merkava main battle tanks. Strength (1997) 134,000 (conscripts 114,700). There are also 430,000 reservists available on mobilization.

Navy. The Navy, tasked primarily for coastal protection and based at Haifa, Ashdod and Eilat, includes 3 small diesel submarines, 3 well-armed Sa'aR-5 corvettes of 1,200 tonnes, 22 missile craft of the smaller evolving Sa'aR types, from 250 to 500 tonnes, 40 fast inshore patrol craft, 1 tank landing ship, 4 amphibious craft and a few minor auxiliaries. The first of 3 new German-built diesel submarines commenced sea trials in 1996.

Naval personnel in 1997 totalled 9,000 including a Naval Commando of 300, of whom 3,000 are conscripts. There are also 10,000 naval reservists available on mobilization.

Air Force. The Air Force (including air defence) has a personnel strength (1997) of 32,000 (21,800 conscripts), with about 600 first-line aircraft, all jets, of Israeli and US manufacture. There are 4 squadrons with about 70 F-15s, and 8 squadrons with 240 F-16s in an interceptor role; 3 squadrons with 80 F-4E Phantoms, supported by 4 Boeing 707 airborne early warning and control aircraft, RC-12 electronic intelligence aircraft. There are transport squadrons of turboprop C-130/KC-130 Hercules, C-47, Arava, Islander, and Boeing 707 (some equipped for tanker duties) aircraft, helicopter squadrons of UH-60 Black Hawk, CH-53, AH-64A Apache, AH-1Huey-Cobra, JetRanger, Agusta-Bell 205, 206 and 212 aircraft, SOCATA Trinidad and DO-28 communications aircraft and training units with locally-built Magister jet trainers, which can be used also in a light ground attack role. Missiles in service include surface-to-air Hawks and surface-to-surface Lances.

INTERNATIONAL RELATIONS

A 46-year old formal state of hostilities with Jordan was brought to an end by a peace agreement on 26 Oct. 1994.

Israel is a member of the UN.

ECONOMY

Policy. 30 to 40 of some 150 state-owned companies are scheduled for privatization under a scaled-down programme of 1991. During the period 1986–95, the proceeds of privatization totalled US$2,000m. (target, US$5,000m.). In 1996, the Prime Minister inaugurated an acceleration of the privatization process, and took over privatization powers from the Ministry of Finance. Efforts to generate some 0·5m. jobs are being made to cope with the influx of Soviet immigrants.

Performance. The economy was estimated to be growing by 1·5% in 1998, compared to 1·9% in 1997, and down from an average of 6% between 1991 and 1995. The current account deficit in 1997 stood at US$–5,014m.

Budget. The budget year runs from 1 Jan to 31 Dec. beginning with 1992. (Previously it ran from 1 April to 31 March).

Budget revenue and expenditure (in 1m. shekels):

	1992	1993	1994	1995	1996[1]
Revenue:	58,994	68,457	82,515	95,489	108,701
Expenditure:	68,094	74,232	87,016	102,311	121,471

[1]Provisional

Currency. The unit of currency is the *shekel* (ILS) of 100 *agorot*. Foreign exchange reserves were US$21,530m. and gold reserves 10,000 troy oz. in Feb. 1998. Inflation in 1997 was 7% (10·6% in 1996). By Sept. 1998 it had come down to 4·5%, the lowest rate in 30 years. Total money supply in Sept. 1996 was 17,280m. shekels.

Banking and Finance. The Bank of Israel was established by law in 1954 as Israel's central bank. Its *Governor* is appointed by the President on the recommendation of the Cabinet for a 5-year term. He acts as economic adviser to the Government and has ministerial status. The *Governor* is Jacob Frenkel. There are 26 commercial banks headed by Bank Leumi Le Israel, Bank Hapoalim and Israel Discount Bank, 2 merchant banks, 1 foreign bank, 15 mortgage banks and 9 lending institutions specifically set up to aid industry and agriculture. The government holds a majority stake in the 4 largest banks, but these are now (1997) in process of privatization.

There is a stock exchange in Tel Aviv.

Weights and Measures. The metric system is in general use. The (metrical) *dunam* = 1,000 sq. metres (about 0·25 acre).

Jewish Year. The Jewish year 5759 corresponds to 21 Sept. 1998–10 Sept. 1999; 5760 to 11 Sept. 1999–29 Sept. 2000.

ENERGY AND NATURAL RESOURCES

Electricity. Installed capacity in 1997 was an estimated 7·804m. kW. Electric-power production amounted during 1997 to 35,098m. kWh; consumption per capita in 1995 was estimated to be 4,738 kWh.

Oil and Gas. The only significant hydrocarbon is oil shale.

Water. In the northern Negev farming has been aided by the Yarkon–Negev water pipeline. This has become part of the overall project of the 'National Water Carrier', which is to take water from the Sea of Galilee (Lake Kinnereth) to the south. The plan includes a number of regional projects such as the Lake Kinnereth–Negev pipeline which came into operation in 1964; it has an annual capacity of 320m. cu. metres. Total water production in 1997 amounted to 2,188m. cu. metres of which 1,959m. cu. metres was consumed.

Minerals. The most valuable natural resources are the potash, bromine and other salt deposits of the Dead Sea. Potash production in 1995 was 2,214,000 tonnes.

Agriculture. In the coastal plain mixed farming, poultry raising, citriculture and vineyards are the main agricultural activities. The Emek (the Valley of Jezreel) is the main agricultural centre of Israel. Mixed farming is to be found throughout the valleys; the sub-tropical Beisan and Jordan plainlands are also centres of banana plantations and fish breeding. In Galilee mixed farming, olive and tobacco plantations prevail. The Hills of Ephraim are a vineyard centre; many parts of the hill country are under afforestation.

The area under cultivation (in 1,000 dunams) in 1994 was 4,344, of which 1,930 were under irrigation. Of the total cultivated area (1994) 2,129 dunams were under field crops, 550 under vegetables, potatoes, pumpkins and melons, 830 under citrus and plantations, 32 under fish ponds and the rest under miscellaneous crops. Production, 1995 (in 1,000 tonnes): Wheat, 242; barley, 7·2; maize grain, 2·5; potatoes, 281; melons, 79·4; tomatoes, 503·7; citrus fruit, 942·3; grapefruit, 404·4; cotton, 42·8.

Livestock (1997) 375,000 cattle, 350,000 sheep, 105,000 pigs (1996), 70,000 goats, 28,120,000 poultry.

Types of rural settlement: (1) The *Kibbutz* and *Kvutza* (communal collective settlement), where all property and earnings are collectively owned and work is collectively organized. (124,600 people lived in 269 *Kibbutzim* in 1995.) (2) The *Moshav* (workers' co-operative smallholders' settlement) which is founded on the principles of mutual aid and equality of opportunity between the members, all farms being equal in size (160,000 in 411). (3) The *Moshav Shitufi* (co-operative settlement), which is based on collective ownership and economy as in the *Kibbutz,* but with each family having its own house and being responsible for its own domestic services (13,100 in 43). (4) Other rural settlements in which land and property are privately owned and every resident is responsible for his own well-being. In 1996 there were 233 villages with a population of 141,500.

Forestry. In 1995 forests covered 102,000 ha or 4·9% of the total land area. Timber production was 113,000 cu. metres in 1995.

Fisheries. Catches in 1995 totalled 20,564 tonnes, of which 17,410 tonnes were freshwater fish.

INDUSTRY
Products include chemicals, metal products, textiles, tyres, diamonds, paper, plastics, leather goods, glass and ceramics, building materials, precision instruments, tobacco, foodstuffs, electrical and electronic equipment.

Labour. The workforce was 2,040,200 in 1997 (884,800 females). A 'social-economic pact' between government, employers and trade unions in May 1991 aimed to create some 32,000 new jobs to lessen the impact of increased immigration. Unemployment was 9·3% in May 1998, up from 6·4% in 1996.

Trade Unions. The General Federation of Labour (Histadrut) founded in 1920, had, in 1987, 1·6m. members (including 0·17m. Arab and Druze members); including workers' families, this membership represents 71·5% of the population covering 87% of all wage-earners. Several trades unions also exist representing other political and religious groups.

INTERNATIONAL TRADE
Total foreign debt amounted to US$34,000m. in July 1996.

Imports and Exports. External trade, in US$1m., for calendar years:

	1991	1992	1993	1994	1995	1996
Imports	18,621	20,523	22,624	25,237	29,579	31,694
Exports	11,911	13,075	14,781	16,881	19,046	20,510

The main exportable commodities are citrus fruit and by-products, fruit-juices, flowers, wines and liquor, sweets, polished diamonds, chemicals, tyres, textiles, metal products, machinery, electronic and transportation equipment. The main exports were, in 1995 (US$1m.): Diamonds, 4,921·6; chemicals and chemical products, 2,369·7; agricultural products including citrus fruit, 740·5; machinery and equipment, 958·9. Of exports in 1995, US$6,529·8m. went to EU and EFTA countries and US$5,735·9m. to USA. In 1995 the main export markets were: USA, 30·1%; UK, 6·1%; Germany, 5·5%; Belgium, 5·4%. Main import suppliers: USA, 18·6%; Belgium, 12·1%; Germany, 9·7%; UK, 8·3%.

COMMUNICATIONS

Roads. There were 15,464 km of paved roads in 1997. Registered motor vehicles in 1997 totalled 1,617,000, including 10,794 buses (1995), 274,000 trucks and 1,229,000 private cars. There were 25,491 road accidents in 1997 resulting in 47,451 casualties of which 530 were fatal.

Rail. There were 609 km of standard gauge line in 1997. In 1997, 5,919,000 passengers and 8,639,000 tonnes of freight were carried.

Civil Aviation. There are international airports at Tel Aviv (Ben Gurion), Eilat and Haifa. In 1997 there were 26,778 aircraft landings. 3,841,000 passengers arrived and 3,833,000 departed. 117,767 tonnes of freight were unloaded and 153,004 loaded. El Al is the state-owned airline. In 1995 it flew 65·7m. km and carried 2,786,700 passengers. In 1998 services were also provided by anotther Israeli airline, Arkia, and by Adria Airways, Aerosweet Airlines, Air Canada, Air Enterprise Pulkovo, Air France, Air Malta, Air Sinai, Air Slovakia, Alitalia, Austrian Airlines, Azerbaijan Airlines, Balkan, Belavia, British Airways, Croatia Airlines, Cyprus Airways, Czech Airlines, Donavia, El Al, Ethiopian Airlines, Finnair, Georgian Airlines, Iberia, JAT, KLM, Latpass Airlines, LOT, Lufthansa, Malév, Olympic Airways, Royal Jordanian, SABENA, SAS, South African Airways, Swissair, Tarom, Tie Aviation, Tower Air, Transaero Airlines, Turkish Airlines, TWA and Uzbekiston Airways.

Shipping. Israel has 3 commercial ports—Haifa, Ashdod and Eilat. In 1997, 6,230 ships departed from Israeli ports; 41,490,000 tons of freight and 1,082,000 passengers were handled. The merchant fleet consisted in 1995 of 65 vessels, totalling 1·5m. GRT.

Telecommunications. A public company responsible to the Ministry of Communications administers the telecommunications service. There were 2,656,000 main telephone lines (equivalent to 449·8 per 1,000 population) in 1997. In 1995 there were 300,000 cellular phone subscribers, 540,000 PCs and 140,000 fax machines. There were approximately 500,000 Internet users in July 1998.

Postal Services. The Ministry of Communications supervises the postal service. In 1995 there were 662 post offices and postal agencies, and 48 mobile post offices.

SOCIAL INSTITUTIONS

Justice. Law. Under the Law and Administration Ordinance, 5708/1948, the first law passed by the Provisional Council of State, the law of Israel is the law which was obtaining in Palestine on 14 May 1948 in so far as it is not in conflict with that Ordinance or any other law passed by the Israel legislature and with such modifications as result from the establishment of the State and its authorities.

Capital punishment was abolished in 1954, except for support given to the Nazis and for high treason.

The law of Palestine was derived from Ottoman law, English law (Common Law and Equity) and the law enacted by the Palestine legislature, which to a great extent was modelled on English law.

Civil Courts. Municipal courts, established in certain municipal areas, have criminal jurisdiction over offences against municipal regulations and bye-laws and certain specified offences committed within a municipal area. Magistrates courts, established in each district and sub-district, have limited jurisdiction in both civil and criminal matters. District courts, sitting at Jerusalem, Tel Aviv and Haifa, have jurisdiction, as courts of first instance, in all civil matters not within the jurisdiction of magistrates courts, and in all criminal matters, and as appellate courts from magistrates courts and municipal courts. The 14-member Supreme Court has jurisdiction as a court of first instance (sitting as a High Court of Justice dealing mainly with administrative matters) and as an appellate court from the district courts (sitting as a Court of Civil or of Criminal Appeal).

In addition, there are various tribunals for special classes of cases. Settlement Officers deal with disputes with regard to the ownership or possession of land in settlement areas constituted under the Land (Settlement of Title) Ordinance.

Religious Courts. The rabbinical courts of the Jewish community have exclusive jurisdiction in matters of marriage and divorce, alimony and confirmation of wills of members of their community and concurrent jurisdiction with the civil courts in all other matters of personal status of all members of their community with the consent of all parties to the action.

The courts of the several recognized Christian communities have a similar jurisdiction over members of their respective communities.

The Moslem religious courts have exclusive jurisdiction in all matters of personal status over Moslems who are not foreigners, and over Moslems who are foreigners, if under the law of their nationality they are subject in such matters to the jurisdiction of Moslem religious courts.

Where any action of personal status involves persons of different religious communities, the President of the Supreme Court will decide which court shall have jurisdiction, and whenever a question arises as to whether or not a case is one of personal status within the exclusive jurisdiction of a religious court, the matter must be referred to a special tribunal composed of 2 judges of the Supreme Court and the president of the highest court of the religious community concerned in Israel.

In 1996 government expenditure on public order and safety totalled 4,481m. shekels.

Religion. Religious affairs are under the supervision of a special Ministry, with departments for the Christian and Moslem communities. The religious affairs of each community remain under the full control of the ecclesiastical authorities concerned: in the case of the Jews, the Sephardi and Ashkenazi Chief Rabbis, in the case of the Christians, the heads of the various communities, and in the case of the Moslems, the Qadis. The Druze were officially recognized in 1957 as an autonomous religious community.

In 1997 there were: Jews, 4,701,600; Moslems, 867,900; Christians, 126,100; Druze, 96,700.

The Chief Rabbi is Israel Meir Lau.

Education. The adult literacy rate in 1995 was 95·6% (male, 97·7%; female, 93·6%). There is free and compulsory education from 5 to 16 years and optional free education until 18. There is a unified state-controlled elementary school system with a provision for special religious schools. The standard curriculum for all elementary schools is issued by the Ministry with a possibility of adding supplementary subjects comprising not more than 25% of the total syllabus. Most schools in towns are maintained by municipalities, a number are private and some are administered by teachers' co-operatives or trustees.

Statistics relating to schools under government supervision, 1995–96:

Type of School[1]	School	Teachers	Pupils
Hebrew Education			
Primary schools	1,365	42,946	528,429
Schools for handicapped children	203	5,276	12,392
Schools of intermediate division	371	19,945	150,804
Secondary schools	621	⎫	240,990
Vocational schools	313	⎬ 31,803	102,716
Agricultural schools	23	⎭	6,513
Arab Education			
Primary schools	326	8,802	150,083
Schools for handicapped children	43	549	2,461
Schools of intermediate division	104	3,828	44,984
Secondary schools	101	⎫	43,510
Vocational schools	62	⎬ 3,543	12,765
Agricultural schools	2	⎭	621

[1]Schools providing more than one type of education are included more than once.

There are also a number of private schools maintained by religious foundations—Jewish, Christian and Moslem—and also by private societies.

The Hebrew University of Jerusalem, founded in 1925, comprises faculties of the humanities, social sciences, law, science, medicine and agriculture. In 1995–96 it had 20,290 students. The Technion in Haifa had 10,370 students. The Weizmann Institute of Science in Rehovoth, founded in 1949, had 760 students.

Tel Aviv University had 26,100 students. The religious Bar-Ilan University at Ramat Gan, opened in 1965, had 19,110 students. The Haifa University had 12,820 students. The Ben Gurion University had 12,250 students.

ISRAEL

In 1996 government expenditure on education totalled 20,630m. shekels.

Health. In 1995 there were 259 hospitals with 33,159 beds and (1993) 24,344 doctors (provision of 1 for every 214 persons). In 1996 government expenditure on health totalled 15,052m. shekels.

Welfare. The National Insurance Law of 1954 provides for old-age pensions, survivors' insurance, work-injury insurance, maternity insurance, family allowances and unemployment benefits. In 1996 government expenditure on social security and welfare totalled 38,082m. shekels.

CULTURE

Broadcasting. Television and the state radio station, Kol Israel (Voice of Israel), are controlled by the Israel Broadcasting Authority. There is a national programme, 2 commercial programmes, a music programme and a service in Arabic. In 1995 there were 2·7m. radio and 1·6m. TV sets (colour by PAL).

Cinema. There were 266 screens in 1994; attendances totalled 10·0m.

Press. In 1996 there were 34 daily newspapers. Combined circulation was 1,650,000, at a rate of 291 per 1,000 inhabitants.

Tourism. In 1997 there were 2,010,400 foreign tourists, bringing revenue of US$2·8bn.

Libraries. In 1995 there was 1 National Library with 3,000,000 volumes and 2,176 registered users. In 1993 there were 1,180 public libraries with 11,242,000 volumes and 737,565 registered users.

Museums and Galleries. In 1993 there were 111 museums playing host to 6,029,000 visitors.

DIPLOMATIC REPRESENTATIVES
Of Israel in Great Britain (2 Palace Green, Kensington, London, W8 4QB)
Ambassador: Dror Zeigerman.

Of Great Britain in Israel (192 Hayarkon St., Tel Aviv 63405)
Ambassador: Mr. F. Cornish, CMG, LVO.

Of Israel in the USA (3514 International Dr., NW, Washington, D.C., 20008)
Ambassador: Zalman Shoval.

Of the USA in Israel (71 Hayarkon St., Tel Aviv)
Ambassador: Edward S. Walker, Jr.

Of Israel to the UN
Ambassador: Dr Dore Gold.

Of Israel to the European Union
Ambassador: Efraïm Halevy.

FURTHER READING
Central Bureau of Statistics. *Statistical Abstract of Israel.* (Annual).—*Statistical Bulletin of Israel.* (Monthly).
Atlas of Israel. 3rd ed. 1985
Aharoni, Y., *The Israeli Economy: the Dreams and Realities.* London, 1991
Ben-Gurion, D., *Ben-Gurion Looks Back.* London, 1965.—*The Jews in Their Land.* London, 1966.—*Israel: A Personal History.* New York, 1971
Beitlin, Y., *Israel: a Concise History.* London, 1992
Bleaney, C. H., *Israel* [Bibliography]. 2nd ed. Oxford and Santa Barbara (CA), 1994
Freedman, R. (ed.) *Israel under Rabin.* Boulder (CO), 1995
Garfinkle, A., *Politics and Society in Modern Israel: Myths and Realities.* Armonk (NY), 1997
Gilbert, Martin, *Israel: A History.* New York, 1998
Harkabi, Y., *Israel's Fateful Decisions.* London, 1989
Louis, W. R. and Stookey, R. W., *The End of the Palestine Mandate.* London, 1986
Peres, S., *Battling for Peace: Memoirs.* London and New York, 1995
Reich, B., *Israel: Land of Tradition and Conflict.* London, 1986.— and Kieval (eds.) *Israeli Politics in the 1990s: Key Domestic and Foreign Policy Factors.* London, 1991
Sachar, H. M., *A History of Israel.* 2 vols. OUP, 1976–87
Segev, T., *1949: The First Israelis.* New York, 1986

Sharkansky, I., *The Political Economy of Israel*. Oxford and Santa Barbara (CA), 1986

Other more specialized titles are entered under CONSTITUTION AND GOVERNMENT, *above,* and PALESTINIAN-ADMINISTERED TERRITORIES.

National statistical office: Central Bureau of Statistics, Prime Minister's Office, POB 13015, Jerusalem 91130. *Website:* http://www.cbs.gov.il/
National library: The Jewish National and University Library, Jerusalem.

PALESTINIAN-ADMINISTERED TERRITORIES

KEY HISTORICAL EVENTS

Under the Israeli–Palestinian agreement of 28 Sept. 1995 the Israeli army redeployed from 6 of the 7 of the largest Palestinian towns in the West Bank and from 460 smaller towns and villages. Following this in April 1996 an 82-member *Palestinian Council* was elected and also a head (*Rais*) of the executive authority of the Council. The rest of the West Bank stayed under Israeli army control with some progressive redeployments at 6-month intervals, although Palestinian civil affairs here too were administered by the Palestinian Council. Negotiations on the permanent status of the West Bank and Gaza began in May 1996. Issues to be resolved include the position of 0·17m. Israelis in the West Bank and 0·18m. in East Jerusalem, the status of Jerusalem, military locations and water supplies.

Following the opening of an archaeological tunnel in Jerusalem, armed clashes broke out at the end of Sept. 1996 between demonstrators and Palestinian police on the one hand and Israeli troops. On 18 Nov. 1996 the Israeli Minister of Defence approved plans for an expansion of Jewish settlement in the West Bank. Under an agreement brokered by King Hussein of Jordan and signed by the Prime Minister of Israel and the President of the Palestinian Authority on 15 Jan. 1997 Israeli troop withdrawals from 80% of Hebron and all rural areas of the West Bank were scheduled to take place in 3 phases between 28 Feb. 1996 and 31 Aug. 1998.

The Israeli decision in Feb. 1997 to continue to promote Jewish settlement in the Jerusalem suburb of Har Homa was perceived by the Palestinian authorities as a hostile move and caused a setback to peace negotiations. In 1998, an American proposal that Israel should withdraw from 13·1% of the West Bank was not agreed on, but at a meeting in the USA in Oct. Israel accepted partial withdrawal on condition that the Palestinians cracked down on terrorism.

CONSTITUTION AND GOVERNMENT

In April 1996 the Palestinian Council removed from its Charter all clauses contrary to its recognition by Israel, including references to armed struggle as the only means of liberating Palestine, and the elimination of Zionism from Palestine. The *President* is directly elected and heads the executive organ, the Palestinian National Authority, one fifth of whose members he appoints, while four fifths are elected by the *National Council*. The latter comprises 88 members and is directly elected by the first-past-the-post system from 16 electoral districts.

Following an Israeli–Palestinian agreement on customs duties and VAT in Aug. 1994 the Palestinians set up their own customs and immigration points into Gaza and Jericho. Israel collects customs dues on Palestinian imports through Israeli entry points and transfers these to the Palestinian treasury.

Israeli currency is in use. Banking is regulated by the Palestinian Monetary Authority.

There is a Palestinian *Council for Reconstruction and Development.*

The Palestinian police consists of some 15,000; they are not empowered to arrest Israelis, but may detain them and hand them over to the Israeli authorities. A securities exchange opened in Nablus in Feb. 1997.

The **West Bank** (preferred Palestinian term, Northern District) has an area of 5,879 sq. km (2,270 sq. miles) and a projected population for 2000 of 1,662,000.

97% of the population in 1988 were Palestinian Arabs of whom some 85% were Moslems, 7·4% Jewish and 8% Christian. In 1995 there was a Palestinian diaspora of 3·3m. The birth rate in 1997 was estimated at 37·7 per 1,000 population and the death rate 4·5 per 1,000. In 1994, there were 77,604 private cars and 21,714 commercial vehicles and trucks registered. There were (1993) 225,595 pupils in primary schools and 125,305 in secondary schools, plus 21,399 students in institutions of higher education. In 1993 there were 17 hospitals and clinics with 1,418 beds.

The **Gaza Strip** (preferred Palestinian term, Gaza District) has an area of 363 sq. km (140 sq. miles) and a population of 792,000 in 1995. The population doubled between 1975 and 1995. The projected population for 2000 is 1,163,000. The fertility rate in the period 1990–95, of 8·8 births per woman, was the highest anywhere in the world. Infant mortality, 1990–95, 44 per 1,000 live births.

The chief town is Gaza itself. In 1984, over 98% of the population were Arabic-speaking Moslems. In 1995 an estimated 94·2% of the population lived in urban areas. Citrus fruits, wheat and olives are grown, with farm land covering 193 sq. km (1980) and occupying most of the active workforce. In 1993 there were 20,434 private cars and 4,518 commercial vehicles and trucks registered. Gaza International Airport, at the southern edge of the Gaza Strip, opened in Nov. 1998. There were (1993) 141,902 pupils in primary schools and 75,494 in secondary schools, plus (1994) 12,473 students in higher education, up from 4,701 in 1991. In 1993 there were 6 hospitals and clinics with 957 beds.

RECENT ELECTIONS

Elections for *President* and *National Council* were held on 20 Jan. 1996. The electorate was 1,013,200; turn-out was 84%. 672 candidates stood for the Council. Yasser Arafat was elected *President* against 1 opponent by 88·1% of votes cast, and was sworn in on 12 Feb. 1996. In the *National Council* elections, 55 seats went to the Liberation Movement of Palestine, 15 to independents, 7 to Independent Fatah, 4 to Independent Islamists, 3 to Independent Christians, 1 to Samaritans and 1 other, with 2 vacant.

CURRENT ADMINISTRATION

President: Yasser Arafat.
  Governor: Fouad Hamdi.

FURTHER READING

Kimmerling, B. and Migdal J. S., *Palestinians: the Making of a People.* Harvard Univ. Press, 1994
Robinson, G. E., *Building a Palestinian State: the Incomplete Revolution.* Indiana Univ. Press, 1997
Rubin, B., *Revolution until Victory? The Politics and History of the PLO.* Harvard Univ. Press, 1994
Stendel, O., *The Arabs in Israel.* Brighton, 1996
Tessler, M., *A History of the Israeli-Palestinian Conflict.* Indiana Univ. Press, 1994

ITALY

Repubblica Italiana

Capital: Rome
Population estimate, 2000: 57·46m.
GNP per capita: (PPP$) 19,890
HDI/world rank: 0·922/21

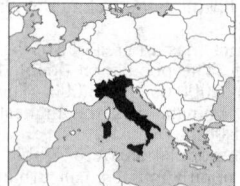

KEY HISTORICAL EVENTS

A part of the Roman Empire and the Holy Roman Empire that succeeded it, Italy was divided into several states including a number of city states such as Venice, Florence and Genoa. Much of the territory was under the rule of the Pope while France, Spain and Austria had possessions at various times.

From 1815 a strong movement grew throughout the Italian states for *risorgimento* (unification) and for independence from Austrian control. Victor Emmanuel II, King of Sardinia-Piedmont from 1849, his prime minister from 1852, Count Cavour, and Giuseppe Garibaldi, an Italian soldier, together achieved success for the movement. The first Italian parliament assembled in Feb. 1861, and on 17 March declared Victor Emmanuel King of Italy. During the remaining years of the 19th century, Italy acquired an African colonial empire composed of Eritrea, Somaliland and Libya. For her support of the allies in the First World War (1914-18) Italy gained the Trentino and the Istrian peninsula on the North Adriatic.

Fascism spread rapidly after the war and in 1922 Benito Mussolini, leader of the Fascist Party, was appointed prime minister. In 1924 he established himself as dictator with the title *Duce.* His internal policy, with a programme of public works, greater efficiency and better law and order, was successful. In 1929 the Lateran Treaties with the Papacy ended over a century of tension between Church and State. However, his aggressive foreign policy as evinced by the invasion of Ethiopia in 1935 and his alliance with Nazi Germany in 1936 was eventually to lead to his downfall. During the Second World War (1939-45) British forces captured much of Italy's colonial empire, and in 1942 occupied Libya. The allies conquered Sicily and Mussolini was compelled to resign in July 1943. In 1945 he was captured and killed by Italian partisans.

June 1946 saw the end of the reign of the House of Savoy, whose kings had ruled over Piedmont for nine centuries and as Kings of Italy since 1861. The Crown Prince Umberto, son of King Victor Emmanuel III, had become Lieut.-Gen. (i.e. Regent) of the kingdom on 5 June 1944. Following the abdication and retirement to Egypt of his father on 9 May 1946, Umberto was declared King Umberto II, but his reign only lasted until 13 June when he left the country. Three days before, on 10 June 1946, Italy had become a republic, following a referendum.

In the post war years the ruling Christian Democrat Party resisted the challenge of the Communists to pursue a strongly pro-West and European policy. But no single government was able to reform an ailing economy or face up to lawlessness and corruption. Changes of administration were frequent. From 1947 to the early 1990s, Italy had no less than 57 governments. In 1992, in the wake of Italy's humiliating exit from Europe's Exchange Rate Mechanism (ERM), the old political establishment was driven out of office. Several prominent politicians were accused of links to organized crime and some went to prison. A new era for Italian politics opened the way for a radical modernization of the country's economic and social structure.

On 9 Oct. 1998 prime minister Romano Prodi resigned after losing a vote of confidence following his refusal to bow to demands made by his Communist allies. He was asked to try and form a new government but he was unable to do so and was replaced by Massimo D'Alema, the first former Italian Communist to become prime minister.

TERRITORY AND POPULATION

Italy is bounded in the north by Switzerland and Austria, east by Slovenia and the Adriatic Sea, south-east by the Ionian Sea, south by the Mediterranean Sea, south-west by the Tyrrhenian Sea and Ligurian Sea and west by France.

ITALY

The area is 301,308 sq. km. Populations at successive censuses were as follows:

10 Feb. 1901	33,370,138	4 Nov. 1951	47,158,738
10 June 1911	35,694,582	15 Oct. 1961	49,903,878
1 Dec. 1921	37,403,956	24 Oct. 1971	53,744,737
21 April 1931	40,582,043	25 Oct. 1981	56,335,678
21 April 1936	42,302,680	20 Oct. 1991	56,764,854

Population estimate, 1 Jan. 1998: 57,563,354 (29,612,762 females). Density: 191 per sq. km.

The projected population for 2000 is 57·46m.

In 1995 an estimated 66·6% of the population lived in urban areas, down slightly from 66·7% in 1990. Italy and Austria are the only European countries to have had a decline in the proportion of the population living in urban areas in the period 1990-95.

The following table gives area and population of the Autonomous Regions (census 1991 and estimate 1996):

Regions	Area in sq. km (1996)	Resident pop. census, 1991	Resident pop. 1997	Density per sq. km
Piedmont	25,399	4,302,565	4,291,441	169
Valle d'Aosta[1]	3,263	115,938	119,610	37
Lombardy	23,861	8,856,074	8,988,951	375
Trentino-Alto Adige[1]	13,607	90,360	924,281	68
Bolzano-Bozen	7,404	440,508	457,370	61
Trento	6,207	449,852	466,911	75
Veneto	18,379	4,380,797	4,469,156	242
Friuli-Venezia Giulia[1]	7,844	1,197,666	1,184,654	151
Liguria	5,421	1,676,282	1,641,835	305
Emilia Romagna	22,124	3,909,512	3,947,102	178
Tuscany	22,997	3,529,946	3,527,303	153
Umbria	8,456	811,831	831,714	98
Marche	9,693	1,429,205	1,450,879	149
Lazio	17,208	5,140,371	5,242,709	303
Abruzzi	10,799	1,249,054	1,276,040	118
Molise	4,438	330,90	329,894	75
Campania	13,595	5,630,280	5,796,899	426
Puglia	19,363	4,031,885	4,090,068	211
Basilicata	9,992	610,528	610,330	61
Calabria	15,080	2,070,203	2,070,992	138
Sicily[1]	25,707	4,966,386	5,108,067	198
Sardinia[1]	24,090	1,648,248	1,661,429	69

[1]With special statute.

Communes of more than 100,000 inhabitants, with population resident at the census of 20 Oct. 1991 and on 31 Dec.1996:

	1991	1996		1991	1996
Rome	2,775,250	2,645,322	Foggia	156,268	156,301
Milan	1,369,231	1,303,925	Salerno	148,932	143,751
Naples	1,067,365	1,045,874	Perugia	144,732	151,118
Turin	962,507	919,612	Ferrara	138,015	135,326
Palermo	698,556	687,855	Ravenna	135,844	134,297
Genoa	678,771	653,529	Reggio nell'Emilia	132,030	137,337
Bologna	404,376	385,136	Rimini	127,960	129,596
Florence	403,294	380,058	Syracuse	125,941	127,224
Bari	342,309	335,410	Sassari	122,339	121,412
Catania	333,075	341,455	Pescara	122,236	117,957
Venice	309,422	296,422	Monza	120,651	119,197
Verona	255,824	254,520	Bergamo	114,936	117,193
Taranto	232,334	211,660	Forli	109,541	107,827
Messina	231,693	262,224	Terni	108,248	108,432
Trieste	213,100	221,551	Vicenza	107,454	108,281
Padua	215,137	212,542	Latina	106,203	111,679
Cagliari	204,237	174,175	Piacenza	102,268	99,665
Brescia	194,502	189,767	Trento	101,545	103,474
Reggio di Calabria	177,580	180,034	La Spezia	101,442	97,712
Modena	176,990	175,124	Torre del Greco	101,361	97,438
Parma	170,520	167,504	Ancona	101,285	99,453
Livorno	167,512	163,950	Novara	101,112	102,408
Prato	165,707	168,892	Lecce	100,884	99,763

The official language is Italian, spoken by 94·1% of the population in 1991. There are 0·3m. German-speakers in Bolzano and 30,000 French-speakers in Valle d'Aosta.

In addition to Sicily and Sardinia, there are a number of other Italian islands, the largest being Elba (363 sq. km), and the most distant Lampedusa, which is 205 km from Sicily but only 113 km from Tunisia.

SOCIAL STATISTICS

Vital statistics (and rates per 1,000 population), 1997: Births, 528,901 (9·2); deaths, 533,078 (9·6); marriages, 273,111 (4·7); natural increase, –24,177 (–0·4); infant deaths, (up to 1 year of age) 3,436 (6·5 per 1,000 live births). Expectation of life: females, 81·3 years; males, 74·9.

Fertility rate, 1990–95, 1·2 births per woman.

In 1997 there were 3,459 suicides; 75·6% were men.

In 1997 there were 1m. legal immigrants living in Italy, plus an estimated 250,000 illegal immigrants. In 1995, 96,710 people emigrated from Italy and there were 99,105 immigrants into the country in 1994.

CLIMATE

The climate varies considerably with latitude. In the south, it is warm temperate, with little rain in the summer months, but the north is cool temperate with rainfall more evenly distributed over the year. Florence, Jan. 46·8°F (8·2°C), July 74·3°F (23·5°C). Annual rainfall 38" (974 mm). Milan, Jan. 37·9°F (3·3°C), July 68·3°F (20·2°C). Annual rainfall 32" (819 mm). Naples, Jan. 52·5°F (11·4°C), July 76·1°F (24·5°C). Annual rainfall 45" (1,143 mm). Palermo, Jan. 56·8°F (13·8°C), July 78·2°F (25·7°C). Annual rainfall 35" (897 mm). Rome, Jan. 48·4°F (9·1°C), July 74·3°F (23·5°C). Annual rainfall 30" (751 mm). Venice, Jan. 41·2°F (5·1°C), July 72·0°F (22·2°C). Annual rainfall 36" (926 mm).

CONSTITUTION AND GOVERNMENT

The Constitution dates from 1948. Italy is 'a democratic republic founded on work'. Parliament consists of the *Chamber of Deputies* and the *Senate*. The Chamber is elected for 5 years by universal and direct suffrage and consists of 630 deputies. The Senate is elected for 5 years on a regional basis by electors over the age of 25; each Region having at least 7 senators, consisting of 315 elected senators; the Valle d'Aosta is represented by 1 senator only, the Molise by 2. The President of the Republic can nominate 11 senators for life from eminent persons in the social, scientific, artistic and literary spheres. The President may become a senator for life. The *President* is elected in a joint session of Chamber and Senate, to which are added 3 delegates from each Regional Council (1 from the Valle d'Aosta). A two-thirds majority is required for the election, but after a third indecisive scrutiny the absolute majority of votes is sufficient. The President must be 50 years or over; term of office, 7 years. The Speaker of the Senate acts as the deputy President. The President can dissolve the chambers of parliament, except during the last 6 months of the presidential term. An attempt to create a new constitution, which had been under consideration for 18 months, collapsed in June 1998.

A *Constitutional Court*, consisting of 15 judges who are appointed, 5 each by the President, Parliament (in joint session) and the highest law and administrative courts, can decide on the constitutionality of laws and decrees, define the powers of the State and Regions, judge conflicts between the State and Regions and between the Regions, and try the President and Ministers.

The reorganization of the Fascist Party is forbidden. Direct male descendants of King Victor Emmanuel are excluded from all public offices, have no right to vote or to be elected, and are banned from Italian territory; their estates are forfeit to the State. Titles of nobility are no longer recognized, but those existing before 28 Oct. 1922 are retained as part of the name.

A referendum was held in June 1991 to decide whether the system of preferential voting by indicating 4 candidates by their listed number should be changed to a simpler system, less open to abuse, of indicating a single candidate by name. The electorate was 46m. Turn-out was 62·5% (there was a 50% quorum). 95·6% of votes cast were in favour of the change. As a result, an electoral reform of 1993 provides for the replacement of proportional representation by a system in which 475 seats in the Chamber of Deputies are elected by a first-past-the-post single-round vote and 155 seats by proportional representation in a separate single-round vote on the same day. There are 27 electoral regions. There is a 4% threshold for entry to the Chamber of Deputies.

At a further referendum in April 1993, turn-out was 77%. Votes favoured the 8 reforms proposed, including a new system of election to the Senate and the abolition of some ministries. 75% of the Senate is now elected by a first-past-the-post system, the remainder by proportional representation; no party may present more than 1 candidate in each constituency. In July 1997 an all-party parliamentary commission on constitutional reform proposed a directly elected president with responsibility for defence and foreign policy, the devolving of powers to the regions, a reduction in the number of seats in the Senate and in the lower house and the creation of a third chamber to speak on behalf of the regions.

National Anthem. 'Fratelli d'Italia' ('Brothers of Italy'; words by G. Mameli; tune by M. Novaro, 1847).

RECENT ELECTIONS
Parliamentary elections were held on 21 April 1996. There were 1,574 candidates. The Olive Tree Alliance gained 284 seats in the Chamber of Deputies and 157 in the Senate with 41·2% of the national vote, the Freedom Alliance 246 and 116 with 37·3%, the Northern League 59 and 27 with 37·3%, the Refounded Communists 35 and 10 with 8·6%. In the Chamber of Deputies minor parties won 6 seats. In the Senate the Pannella List won 27 seats and minor parties won 4.

European Parliament. Italy has 87 representatives. At the June 1994 elections turn-out was 74·8%. Forza Italia gained 27 seats with 30·6% of votes cast; the Party of the Democratic Left (former Communists), 16 with 19·1% (group in European Parliament: European Socialist Party); the National Alliance, 11 with 12·5%; the Popular Party (former Christian Democrats), 8 with 10% (Popular European Party); the Northern League, 6 with 6·6%; the Reformed Communists, 5 with 6·1%; the Greens, 3 with 3·2% (Greens); Segni, 3 with 3·2%; the Pannella Reformers, 2 with 2·1%; the Socialist Party, 2 with 1·8% (European Socialist Party); Rete, 1 with 1·1%; the Republican Party, 1 with 0·7% (Liberals, Democrats, Reformers); the Social Democratic Party, 1 with 0·7% (European Socialist Party); the South Tyrol People's Party, 1 with 0·6% (Popular European Party).

CURRENT ADMINISTRATION
President: Oscar Luigi Scalfaro, b. 1919 (DC; sworn in 28 May 1992).

A government was formed on 17 May 1996 which in March 1999 comprised (PDS = Democratic Party of the Left; PPI = Popular Party; RI = Italian Renewal):

Prime Minister: Massimo D'Alema, b. 1949 (Demcorats of the Left; sworn in 21 Oct. 1998).

Deputy Prime Minister: Sergio Mattarella (PPI). *Foreign Affairs:* Lamberto Dini (RI). *Finance:* Vincenzo Visco (PDS). *Interior:* Rosa Russo Jervolino (PPI). *Agriculture:* Paulo de Castro (Ind). *Education:* Luigi Berlinguer (PDS). *Environment:* Edo Ronchi (Greens). *Foreign Trade:* Piero Fassino (PDS). *Health:* Rosaria Bindi (PPI). *Industry:* Pierluigi Bersani (PDS). *Justice:* Oliviero Diliberto (PCDI). *Labour and Southern Affairs:* Antonio Bassolino (DS). *Communications:* Salvatore Cardinale (UDR). *Public Works:* Enrico Micheli (Ind). *Transport:* Tiziano Treu (RI). *Treasury and Budget:* Carlo Azeglio Ciampi (Technocrats). *Family and Social Affairs:* Livia Turco (PDS). *Equal Opportunities:* Laura Balbo (Greens). *Regional Affairs:* Katia Bellillo (PCDI). *Public Administration:* Angelo Piazza (SDI). *University and Scientific Research:* Ortensio Zecchino (PPI). *European Union Affairs:* Enrico Letta (PPI). *Relations with Parliament:* Gian Guido Folloni (UDR). *Culture:* Giovanna Mallandri (PDS). *Defence:* Carlo Scognamiglio (UDR). *Institutional Reforms:* Giuliano Amato (Ind.).

The *Speaker* is Luciano Voilante (PDS). The *Speaker of the Senate* is Nicola Mancini (PPI).

Local Government. Italy is administratively divided into 15 autonomous regions and 5 autonomous regions with a special constitutional status; these are subdivided

ITALY

into 102 provinces and 1,230 municipalities. The regions have their own councils and governments with certain legislative and administrative functions adapted to the circumstances of each region. A government commissioner co-ordinates regional and national activities. Since 1993 mayors have been directly elected for 4-year terms in towns of more than 15,000 inhabitants and allot 60% of seats on municipal councils, the remainder being apportioned according to party vote.

Measures for the autonomy of the largely German-speaking **Alto Adige** (South Tyrol) were granted in Jan. 1992 and accepted by Austria in June 1992.

A powerful separatist movement, the Northern League, campaigns for autonomy for the regions around the Po Valley. Local government elections were held on 27 April 1997 and 11 May 1997, involving 11 provinces and 1,192 communes. The electorate was 14·4m. Regional elections held in Nov. 1997 resulted in landslide victories for the ruling centre-left coalition. In mayoral elections on 7 June 1998 the ruling centre-left coalition gained only 5 out of 16 seats in provincial capitals, with the centre-right Freedom Alliance winning 10 seats. The centrist former Christian Democrats took one seat.

DEFENCE

Head of the armed forces is the Defence Chief of Staff. There is conscription for 12 months. In Aug. 1998 the government voted to allow women into the armed forces.

In 1997 defence expenditure totalled US$21,837m. (US$377 per capita), representing 1·9% of GDP.

Army. The Field Army is organized into 3 corps headquarters (1 mountain), consisting of 3 mechanized, 2 armoured and 4 mountain brigades, 2 armoured cavalry, 2 heavy artillery and 2 amphibious battalions, 3 aviation groups, 3 artillery regiments and 2 anti-aircraft regiments; an air defence command with surface-to-air missiles; and an aviation group. There is a territorial defence force of 8 independent mechanized brigades deployed in 7 military regions, and a rapid intervention force and a support brigade with missiles. Equipment includes 167 M-60A1, 910 Leopard and 242 Centauro main battle tanks. The Army air corps operates 8 DO228 transports, over 40 light aircraft and 360 helicopters. Strength (1998) 165,600 (99,100 conscripts). The paramilitary Carabinieri number 113,200.

Navy. The principal ships of the Navy are the light aircraft carrier *Giuseppe Garibaldi* and the helicopter-carrying cruiser *Vittorio Veneto*. The *Giuseppe Garibaldi*, 13,450 tonnes, was completed in 1985 and operates an air group of 10 SH-3D Sea King anti-submarine helicopters and 5 AV8-B Harrier aircraft. She is also armed with 4 Teseo anti-ship missiles. The *Vittorio Veneto*, completed in 1969, is of 9,650 tonnes, and operates a squadron of 6 AB-212 anti-submarine helicopters as well as a twin launcher for anti-submarine rockets and US Standard SM-1 surface-to-air missiles, and Teseo anti-ship missiles.

The combatant forces also include 8 diesel submarines, 4 guided-missile destroyers armed with Standard SM-I, 26 frigates, of which 18 carry one or more AB-212 helicopters and 6 missile-armed patrol hydrofoils. Mine countermeasure forces comprise 12 coastal minehunters. There are 4 new helicopter-carrying offshore patrol vessels for the protection of economic resources. Amphibious lift for the San Marco commando group (1,000 men) is provided by 3 dock landing ships and 35 craft. Auxiliaries include 2 replenishment oilers, 4 water carriers, 3 survey ships, 4 trial vessels, 2 training ships and 8 large tugs.

The Naval Air Arm, 1,600 strong, operates 75 anti-submarine and training helicopters and has acquired the first 8 operational and 2 training Harrier-type TAV-8B short take off/vertical landing aircraft for the carrier squadron.

There is a Special Forces commando of some 600 assault swimmers.

Main naval bases are at Spezia, Naples, Taranto and Ancona, with minor bases at Brindisi and Venice. The personnel of the Navy in 1998 numbered 40,000 (16,000 conscripts), including the naval air arm and the marine battalion.

Paramilitary maritime tasks are carried out by the Financial Guards fleet of some 70 patrol craft and a harbour control force with 12 inshore patrol craft and numerous boats.

Air Force. Control is exercised through 2 regional headquarters near Taranto and Milan. Units assigned to NATO comprise the 1st air brigade of Nike-Hercules surface-to-air missiles, 9 fighter-bomber, 7 interceptor and 1 tactical reconnaissance

ITALY

squadron, with supporting transport, search and rescue, and training units. 4 of the fighter-bomber squadrons have Tornados, and 5 squadrons operate AM-X Centauros. F-104S Starfighters have been standardized throughout the 7 interceptor squadrons.

One transport squadron has turboprop C-130H Hercules aircraft; 2 others have turboprop Aeritalia G222s, Piaggio PD-808s and Boeing 707s. There is a VIP and personnel transport squadron, equipped with AS-61, DC-9, Gulfstream III and Falcon 50 aircraft.

Electronic warfare duties are performed by specially equipped G222s, PD-808s and MB 339s. Two land-based anti-submarine squadrons operate Breguet Atlantics. Search and rescue are performed by 30 Agusta-Sikorsky HH-3F helicopters and smaller types. There are also strong support and training elements; some MB 339 jet trainers have armament provisions for secondary close air support and anti-helicopter roles.

Air Force strength in 1998 was about 60,000 (18,000 conscripts).

INTERNATIONAL RELATIONS
Italy is a member of the UN, NATO, EU, WEU and the Central European Initiative. Italy is a signatory to the Schengen Accord of June 1990 which abolishes border controls between Italy and Austria, Belgium, Denmark, Finland, France, Germany, Greece, Iceland, Luxembourg, the Netherlands, Norway, Portugal, Spain and Sweden.

ECONOMY

Policy. The government is committed to a reduction in borrowing, a strong currency and low inflation. It has embarked on an ambitious privatization programme to reduce radically its presence in industry and banking. In 1997 the government completed its biggest privatization to date with the 26,000bn. lire flotation of Telecom Italia. It also sold a third tranche in the Eni oil and gas group, privatized the Banca di Roma, Italy's second largest banking group, and pursued this programme with further sell-offs in 1998.

In May 1998 Italy became one of the 11 founder members of the EMU. The OECD reports that with this primary political objective achieved, the tasks of economic policy are to consolidate the progress made on the macroeconomic front, and implement the structural reforms needed for faster employment growth.

Performance. GDP growth at current market prices was 5·7% in 1996 and 4·2% in 1997. Total GDP in 1997 was 1,939,875bn. lire and 2,024,105bn. lire in 1998. Real GDP growth in 1998 was 1·4%, and forecast to be 1·5% in 1999, although the rate of growth was likely to remain weaker than in most European countries. With the terms of trade improving and import growth decelerating, the trade surplus is expected to grow despite the adverse affects of currency depreciation in Asian countries. The OECD commented that this, together with the projected disappearance of the deficit on the invisible account, may keep the current account surplus close to 3·5% in 1999, reinforcing Italy's newly-achieved position as a net creditor *vis-à-vis* the rest of the world.

Budget. Total revenue and expenditure for fiscal years, in 1,000bn. lire:

	Revenue	Expenditure		Revenue	Expenditure
1991	456,995	579,966	1994	504,320	641,910
1992	512,718	627,579	1995	557,657	699,534
1993	516,655	663,237	1996	591,991	727,402

Budgets for 1998 (and 1997) in 1,000,000m. lire: revenue, 581,188 (591,161) of which tax 546,188 (554,194); expenditure, 673,182 (690,737) of which capital expenditure 68,598 (67,070) and interest payments 181,121 (193,002).

The 1998 budget provided for an increase in value-added tax. Some reforms due to take place in 1998 were meant to reallocate the existing tax burden in a more business-friendly way. The rate of corporation tax was to come down from 53·2% to 37%. Other measure include reducing social security contributions, and a new two-tier income tax, brought in to encourage entrepreneurs to reinvest in profits and issue equity. Accompanying the tax reform was the devolution of substantial taxing powers from the central government to the regions.

VAT is 20% (reduced rate, 10%).

The public debt at 31 Dec. 1997 totalled 2,100,686,000m. lire. Between 1992 and 1997 the public deficit came down from more than 10% to 3%, or possibly less, of gross domestic product. Interest rates have also declined significantly.

Currency. On 1 Jan. 1999 the euro (EUR) became the legal currency in Italy and the *lira* became a subdivision of it; irrevocable conversion rate 1,936·27 lira to 1 euro. The euro, which consists of 100 cents, will not be in circulation until 1 Jan. 2002. There will be 7 euro notes in different colours and sizes denominated in 500, 200, 100, 50, 20, 10 and 5 euros, and 8 coins denominated in 2 and 1 euros, then 50, 20, 10, 5, 2 and 1 cents. Even though notes and coins will not be introduced until 1 Jan. 2002 the euro can be used in banking; by means of cheques, travellers' cheques, bank transfers, credit cards and electronic purses. Banking will be possible in both euros and lire until the lira is withdrawn from circulation—which must be by 1 July 2002.

The *lira* (ITL) notionally consists of 100 *centesimi*. Inflation was 1·7% in 1997 (the lowest rate in 30 years) and 1·8% in 1998. The Economic Bulletin reported that "professional forecasters expect inflation to decline to just above 1% in line with the forecast for the euro area as a whole". The lira left the ERM in Sept. 1993 and rejoined in Nov. 1996. Gold reserves were 66·67m. troy oz. in Feb. 1998 and foreign exchange reserves were US$51,542m. Total money supply in Dec. 1997 was 646,000bn. lire.

Banking and Finance. The bank of issue is the Bank of Italy (founded 1893). It is owned by public-sector banks. Its *governor* (Antonio Fazio, b. 1936) is selected without fixed term by the 13 directors of the Bank's non-executive board. In 1991 it received increased responsibility for the supervision of banking and stock exchange affairs, and in 1993 greater independence from the government. Its gold reserve amounted to 40,929bn. lire in Dec. 1998; the foreign credit reserves of the Exchange Bureau (*Ufficio Italiano Cambi*) amounted to 88,611bn. lire.

Credit institutions are under the control of the state's 'Inspectorate of Credit'. Other credit institutions are classified as: (1) 176 commercial banks including 80 banche popolari and 51 branches of foreign banks; (2) 591 co-operative banks; (3) 700 rural and artisans' banks; (4) 6 Istituti di Categoria.

The 'Amato' law of July 1990 gave public sector banks the right to become joint stock companies and permitted the placing of up to 49% of their equity with private shareholders.

On 31 Dec. 1997 the post office savings banks had deposits and current accounts of 307,481,000m. lire. On 31 Dec. 1998 credit institutions had deposits of 892,091bn. lire.

Legislation reforming stock markets came into effect in Dec. 1990. In 1996 local stock exchanges, relics of pre-unification Italy, were closed, and stock exchange activities concentrated in Milan.

Weights and Measures. The metric system is in use. 1 quintal = 100 kg.

ENERGY AND NATURAL RESOURCES

Electricity. Installed capacity was 57·19m. kW in 1994. In 1997 the total power generated was 251,462m. kWh, of which 46,676m. kWh were generated by hydro-electric plants. Consumption in 1997 was 253,673m. kWh, of which 58,507m. kWh was for domestic use. Consumption per capita was an estimated 4,238 kWh in 1995.

Oil and Gas. Oil production, 1997, 5,892,055 tonnes. In 1997, natural gas production in 1,000 cu. metres was 19,123,396.

Minerals. Fuel and mineral resources are inadequate to needs. Only sulphur and mercury yield a substantial surplus for exports.

Production of metals and minerals (in tonnes) was as follows:

	1993	1994	1995	1996	1997
Bentonite	150,503	326,992	590,845	471,535	511,760
Cement	13,902,392	12,285,703	11,733,556	12,480,388	12,166,878
Zinc	62,558	7,379	43,669	20,137	15,416

	1993	1994	1995	1996	1997
Sulphur	3,503,891	3,021,427	3,430,374	3,528,120	. . .
Lead	27,475	8,011	22,658	20,260	17,630
Feldspar	1,387,968	1,534,421	2,199,315	2,287,086	2,118,117

Agriculture. In 1997, 1,872,000 persons were dependent on agriculture, of whom 1,370,000 were economically active. In 1993 there were 205,819 sq. km of agricultural and forest lands, distributed as follows (in 1,000 ha): Forage and pasture, 6,746; woods, 5,874; cereals, 4,214; olive trees, 1,106; vines, 899; garden produce, 597; leguminous plants, 97.

At the 1991 census agricultural holdings numbered 3,023,344 and covered 22,702,356 ha. 2,893,145 owners (95·7%) farmed directly 15,961,093 ha (70·3%); 118,020 owners (3·9%) worked with hired labour on 6,603,522 ha (29·1%); 95,045 share-croppers (3·1%) tilled 1,208,337 ha (5·3%); the remaining 12,179 holdings (0·4%) of 137,740 ha (0·6%) were operated in other ways. By 1997, agricultural and forest lands covered 20,445,268 ha, of which 14,753,107 ha was in active agricultural use. There were 2·5m. farms in 1998. Agriculture accounts for 2·7% of GDP, 7·1% of exports and 15·3% of imports.

In 1994, 1,470,000 tractors were in use.

The production of the principal crops (in 1,000 metric quintals) in 1997: Sugar beet, 135,794; maize, 99,926; wheat, 68,156; tomatoes, 55,340; potatoes, 20,088; oranges, 18,092; barley, 11,491; rice, 14,240; olives, 35,274; lemons, 6,062; tangerines, mandarins and clementines, 5,131; oats, 2,761; grapes for wine, 67,543; tobacco (in tonnes), 1,325 (1996).

Livestock, 1996: Cattle, 7,173,932; sheep, 1,094,245; pigs, 8,171,092; goats, 1,098,543; horses, 315 (1995); donkeys, 26 (1995); mules, 12 (1995); chickens for meat, 115,359,613; poultry farming, 191,549,016.

Livestock products, 1996 (in 1,000 quintals): Milk, 118,184; meat, 37,451; cheese, 9,845; wool, 117; eggs, 6,971 (1,000 pieces).

Forestry. In 1995 forests covered 6·77m. ha or 22·5% of the total land area. Timber production was 9·8m. cu. metres in 1995.

Fisheries. The fishing fleet comprised, in 1994, 15,798 motor boats of 245,637 gross tonnes. The catch in 1996 was 3,325,990 quintals, of which 3,258,346 quintals were from marine waters.

INDUSTRY

Industry accounted for 25·6% of GDP in 1997. The main branches of industry are: (% of industrial value added at factor cost in 1996) Textiles, clothing, leather and footwear (11·2%), food, beverages and tobacco (8·0%), energy products (11·8%), agricultural and industrial machines (9·2%), metal products except machines and means of transport (8·9%), mineral and non-metallic mineral products (5·8%), timber and wooden furniture (4·5%), electric plants and equipment (6·7%), chemicals and pharmaceuticals (8·2%), means of transport (5·4%).

Production, 1997: Motor vehicles, 199,251; artificial and synthetic fibres (including staple fibre and waste), 690,494 tonnes; cement, 33,718,169 tonnes; polyethylene resins, 1,065,115 tonnes; steel, 24,284,985 tonnes (1996).

Labour. In 1997 the workforce was 22,892,000 (8,685,000 females) of whom 20,087,000 were employed. 2,805,000 (1,457,000 females) were unemployed and looking for work—a rate of 12·2%—although only 1,031,000 (424,000) were actually registered. In 1996, 60·9% of the workforce were in services, 32·1% in industry and 7% in agriculture. There are strong indications of labour markets having become less rigid, especially in the north. In the centre and north unemployment was 6·9% in July 1998; in the relatively poor south, it was 22·5%. In 1995 the difference in the unemployment rates in the north and in the south was 14%, compared to a difference of just 2% in the 1960s. Over 50% of Italy's jobless have been out of work for more than a year. Pensionable retirement age was 60 for men and 55 for women in 1991, but this is being progressively raised to 65 for both sexes. Agreements between the government, employers and trade unions in 1992 and 1993 ended automatic wage indexation and regulated labour relations and wage increases. There are plans to introduce a 35-hour week in 2001.

In 1997 parliament approved the so-called 'Trev Package', which involves a large number of institutional changes regarding working hours and apprenticeships, mainly for young people from the south, and the introduction of employment agencies.

Trade Unions. There are 3 main groups: the Confederazione Generale Italiana del Lavoro (CGIL; no longer Communist-dominated), the Confederazione Italiana Sindacati Lavoratori (CISL; Catholic), and the Unione Italiana del Lavoro (UIL). Membership in 1994: CGIL, 5·2m. (2·7m. retired); CISL, 3·7m. (1·5m. retired); UIL, 1·7m. (0·5m. retired). In referendums held in June 1995 the electorate voted to remove some restrictions on trade union representation, end government involvement in public sector trade unions and end the automatic deduction of trade union dues from wage packets.

INTERNATIONAL TRADE
Foreign debt in Dec. 1996 was 68,013bn. lire.

Imports and Exports. The territory covered by foreign trade statistics includes Italy and San Marino, but excludes the municipalities of Livigno and Campione.

The following table shows the value of Italy's foreign trade (in 1,000m. lire):

	1993	1994	1995	1996	1997
Imports	232,991	272,382	335,661	321,286	354,456
Exports	266,214	308,046	381,175	388,885	405,732

Percentage of trade with EU countries in 1997: Exports, 54·6%; imports, 60·6%. Principal export markets, 1996 (% of total trade): Germany, 16·4%; France, 12·2%; USA, 7·9%; UK, 7·1%; Spain, 5·2%. Principal import suppliers: Germany, 18·0%; France, 13·2%; UK, 6·7%; Netherlands, 6·2%; USA, 5·0%; Belgium and Luxembourg, 4·7%.

Exports/imports by category, 1997 (in 1,000m. lire):

	Exports	Imports
Metal products and machinery	145,295	84,249
Textiles and leather goods	67,157	26,992
Wood, paper and rubber goods	52,101	29,237
Transport equipment	39,863	42,974
Chemical products	34,946	49,872
Foodstuffs, beverages and tobacco	16,841	24,831
Metallic minerals	16,439	32,422
Non-metallic minerals and products	15,866	6,094
Agricultural, forestry and fish products	10,430	20,455
Energy	6,800	37,330

The OECD reports that Italy's competitiveness in some important export sectors was affected by the devaluations in 1998 in Asia, but export performance is sound and export-market growth remains quite buoyant.

COMMUNICATIONS

Roads. Roads totalled 316,400 km in 1996, of which 9,500 km were motorway, 46,900 km were highways and main roads, 118,000 km were secondary roads and 142,000 km other roads. In 1996 there were 38,586,000 motor vehicles, made up of: Passenger cars, 32,789,000 (568 per 1,000 inhabitants); buses and coaches, 78,000; vans and trucks, 5,719,000. There were 6,512 fatalities in traffic accidents in 1995 (6,578 in 1994).

Rail. Total of railways (1995), 19,485 km. The state-run railway (*Ferrovie dello Stato*) was 15,955 km (10,202 km electrified). In 1997 the state railways carried 461,000,000 passengers and 82,744,000 tonnes of freight. There are metros in Milan (68 km) and Rome (33·5 km), and tram/light rail networks in Genoa (2·3 km), Milan (240 km), Naples (23 km), Trieste and Turin (119 km).

Civil Aviation. There are major international airports at Bologna (G. Marconi), Genoa (Cristoforo Colombo), Milan (Linate and Malpensa), Naples (Capodichino), Pisa (Galileo Galilei), Rome (Leonardo da Vinci), Turin and Venice (Marco Polo). A number of other airports have a small selection of international flights. The national carrier, Alitalia, is 89·3% owned by the state. In 1995 it flew 238·6m. km and carried 20,873,500 passengers. There are a number of other Italian airlines, most notably Meridiana, which flew 21·2m. km and carried 2,522,100 passengers in 1995. The busiest airport is Rome, which in 1996 handled 22,762,967 passengers (12,230,672 on international flights) and 256,300 tonnes of freight. In 1996 Milan Linate was the second busiest for passengers, handling 12,556,207 (6,776,782 on international flights), and Milan Malpensa the second busiest for freight, with 98,000 tonnes.

Shipping. The mercantile marine in 1995 consisted of 614 vessels of 11·88m. DWT, representing 1·79% of the world's tonnage. 112 vessels (26·42% of tonnage) were registered under foreign flags. Total tonnage registered was 6·82m. GRT, including oil tankers, 2·18m. GRT and container ships, 0·14m. GRT. In 1995, 234,115,000 tonnes of cargo were unloaded, and 48,254,000 were loaded. 2,039,697 passengers embarked and 2,185,645 departed in 1995.

Telecommunications. There were 25,698,000 main telephone lines in 1997, or 446·8 per 1,000 persons. In 1997 cellular phone subscribers numbered 5,266,094; in 1995 there were 4·8m. PCs and 202,000 fax machines. There were approximately 2·6m. Internet users in May 1998.

Postal Services. In 1995 there were 14,142 post offices, or 1 for every 4,050 persons.

SOCIAL INSTITUTIONS

Justice. Italy has 1 court of cassation, in Rome, and is divided for the administration of justice into 28 appeal court districts, subdivided into 164 tribunal *circondari* (districts), and these again into about 617 districts each with its own magistracy (*Pretura*). There are also 90 first degree assize courts and 28 assize courts of appeal. For civil business, besides the magistracy above mentioned, *Conciliatori* have jurisdiction in petty plaints (those to a maximum of 1m. lire).

2,840,077 crimes were reported in 1997; 552,787 persons were indicted. In 1997 there were 88,024 persons in prison (6,588 females).

Religion. The treaty between the Holy See and Italy of 11 Feb. 1929, confirmed by article 7 of the Constitution of the republic, lays down that the Catholic Apostolic Roman Religion is the only religion of the State. Other creeds are permitted, provided they do not profess principles, or follow rites, contrary to public order or moral behaviour.

The appointment of archbishops and of bishops is made by the Holy See; but the Holy See submits to the Italian Government the name of the person to be appointed in order to obtain an assurance that the latter will not raise objections of a political nature.

Catholic religious teaching is given in elementary and intermediate schools. Marriages celebrated before a Catholic priest are automatically transferred to the civil register. Marriages celebrated by clergy of other denominations must be made valid before a registrar.

There were 47,000,000 Roman Catholics in 1997, 700,000 Moslems and 9,800,000 other (mostly non-religious and atheist).

Education. 5 years of primary and 3 years of secondary education are compulsory from the age of 6. In 1997–98 there were 26,122 pre-school institutions with 1,594,062 pupils (including 13,624 state-run institutions with 917,881 pupils); 19,418 primary schools with 2,816,161 pupils (including 17,544 state schools with 2,618,077 pupils); 8,829 compulsory secondary schools (*scuole medie*) with 1,806,613 pupils (including 8,049 state schools with 1,740,355 pupils); and 7,848 higher secondary schools with 2,628,377 pupils (including 5,967 state-run with 2,449,347 pupils). Numbers of teachers: Pre-primary institutions, 1996–97, 121,062; primary schools, 1996–97, 281,326; compulsory secondary schools, 1996–97, 230,945; higher secondary schools, 1996–97, 315,920.

Higher secondary education is subdivided into classical (*ginnasio* and classical *liceo*), scientific (scientific *liceo*), language lyceum, professional institutes and technical education: agricultural, industrial, commercial, technical, nautical institutes, institutes for surveyors, institutes for girls (5-year course) and teacher-training institutes (4-year course).

In 1995–96 there were 47 universities, 2 universities of Italian studies for foreigners and 3 specialized universities (commerce; education; Roman Catholic), 3 polytechnical university institutes and 7 other specialized university institutes: (architecture; bio-medicine; modern languages; naval studies; oriental studies; social studies; teacher training). In 1996–97 there were 1,672,330 university students and 58,111 academic staff.

Adult literacy rate, 1995, 98·1% (male 98·6%; female 97·6%).

In 1993 total expenditure on education came to 5·2% of GNP and represented 9·0% of total government expenditure.

Health. The provision of health services is a regional responsibility, but they are funded by central government. Medical consultations are free, but a portion of prescription costs are payable. In 1996 there were 1,005 public hospitals with 274,282 beds and 782 private hospitals with 81,457 beds. In 1996 there were 110,261 doctors in public hospitals and 264,774 auxiliary medical personnel.

Welfare. Social expenditure is made up of transfers which the central public departments, local departments and social security departments make to families. Payment is principally for pensions, family allowances and health services. Expenditure on subsidies, public assistance to various classes of people and people injured by political events or national disasters are also included.

Public pensions are indexed to prices; 21,551,751 pensions were paid in 1996 (18,423,597 private sector, 3,128,154 public sector). Current social security expenditure in 1996 was 316,842,000m. lire, of which 301,451,000m. lire were paid out in benefits. Social contributions totalled 227,991,000m. lire. In 1997 pension expenditure, which was 15% of GDP, was one of the highest in Europe.

CULTURE

Bologna is one of nine European Cities of Culture in the year 2000, and has as its theme 'Information and Communication'. The other Cities of Culture are Avignon (France), Bergen (Norway), Brussels (Belgium), Helsinki (Finland), Kraków (Poland), Prague (Czech Republic), Reykjavík (Iceland) and Santiago de Compostela (Spain). The title attracts large European Union grants.

Estimates vary of how many pilgrims will go to Rome for Millennium celebrations, but city authorities have predicted more than 40m.

Broadcasting. Broadcasting is regulated by the Public Radio-Television Administration Council. This consists of 8 members elected by parliament who choose a ninth member as chair for 3-year terms. *Radiotelevisione Italiana* broadcasts 3 radio programmes and additional regional programmes. It also broadcasts 2 TV programmes. There are 12 national and about 820 local independent TV networks. In 1995 there were 47m. sets (colour by PAL). In 1996, 16,114,572 television licences were bought.

Cinema. In 1996 there were 4,004 screens (1,200 full-time) and 96,512,000 admissions.

Press. There were (1996) 115 dailies (84 are general information) and 569 weeklies. The combined circulation of the dailies (including unsold copies) is 2,177,409 every day, and of the weeklies 907,091.

Tourism. In 1997, 56,370,381 foreigners visited Italy; they included Swiss, 8,164,696; Germans, 8,441,385; French, 9,726,229; Austrians, 5,872,836. Foreign tourist revenue was 50,847,000m. lire in 1997.

Libraries. There were 2 National libraries and 35 non-specialized libraries (1995), 10 higher education libraries (1993) and 2,366 public libraries (1990). They held a combined 112,492,000 volumes and were utilized by 9,261,185 registered users.

Museums and Galleries. In 1992 there were 3,442 museums visited by 87,092,000 visitors.

DIPLOMATIC REPRESENTATIVES

Of Italy in Great Britain (14 Three Kings Yard, Davies Street, London, W1Y 2EH)
Ambassador: Dr Paolo Galli.

Of Great Britain in Italy (Via XX Settembre 80A, 00187, Rome)
Ambassador: Tom Richardson, CMG.

ITALY

Of Italy in the USA (1601 Fuller St., NW, Washington, D.C., 20009)
Ambassador: Ferdinando Salleo.

Of the USA in Italy (Via Veneto 119/A, Rome)
Ambassador: Thomas M. Foglietta.

Of Italy to the United Nations
Ambassador: Francesco Paolo Fulci.

FURTHER READING

Istituto Nazionale di Statistica. *Annuario Statistico Italiano.—Compendio Statistico Italiano.* (Annual).—*Italian Statistical Abstract* (Annual).—*Bollettino Mensile di Statistica* (Monthly).

Absalom, R., *Italy since 1880: a Nation in the Balance?* Harlow, 1995
Baldassarri, M. (ed.) *The Italian Economy: Heaven or Hell?* London, 1993
Clark, M., *Modern Italy 1871–1982.* London, 1984
Di Scala, S. M., *Italy from Revolution to Republic: 1700 to the Present.* Boulder (CO), 1995
Duggan, C., *A Concise History of Italy.* CUP, 1994
Frei, M., *Italy: the Unfinished Revolution.* London, 1996
Furlong, P., *Modern Italy: Representation and Reform.* London, 1994
Gilbert, M. *Italian Revolution: the Ignominious End of Politics, Italian Style.* Boulder (CO), 1995
Ginsborg, P., *A History of Contemporary Italy: Society and Politics, 1943–1988.* London, 1990
Gundie, S. and Parker, S. (eds.) *The New Italian Republic: from the Fall of the Berlin Wall to Berlusconi.* London, 1995
Hearder, H., *Italy: a Short History.* CUP, 1991
McCarthy, P., *The Crisis of the Italian State: from the Origins of the Cold War to the Fall of Berlusconi.* London, 1996
OECD, *OECD Economic Surveys 1998–99: Italy.* Paris, 1998
Putnam, R. *et al., Making Democracy Work: Civic Traditions in Modern Italy.* Princeton Univ. Press, 1993
Richards, C., *The New Italians.* London, 1994
Smith, D. M., *Modern Italy: A Political History.* Yale University Press, 1997
Sponza, L. and Zancani, D., *Italy.* [Bibliography]. Oxford and Santa Barbara (CA), 1995

National statistical office: Istituto Nazionale di Statistica (ISTAT), 16 Via Cesare Balbo, 00184 Rome. *Website:* http://www.istat.it/
National library: Biblioteca Nazionale Centrale, Vittorio Emanuele II, Viale Castro Pretorio, Rome.

JAMAICA

Capital: Kingston
Population estimate, 2000: 2·59m.
GNP per capita: (PPP$) 3,450
HDI/world rank: 0·735/84

KEY HISTORICAL EVENTS

Jamaica was discovered by Columbus in 1494 and was occupied by the Spaniards from 1509 until 1655 when the island was captured by the English. Their possession was confirmed by the Treaty of Madrid of 1670. In 1661, a representative constitution was established consisting of a governor, privy council, legislative council and legislative assembly. The slavery introduced by the Spanish was augmented as sugar production increased in value and extent in the 18th century. The plantation economy collapsed with the abolition of the slave trade in the late 1830s. The 1866 Crown Colony government was introduced, with a legislative council consisting of official and unofficial members. In 1884 a partially elective legislative council was instituted. Women were enfranchised in 1919. By the late 1930s, demands for self-government increased and the constitution of Nov. 1944 stated that the governor was to be assisted by a house of representatives of 32 elected members, a legislative council (the upper house) of 15 members, and an executive council. Every person over 21 years of age was granted the right to vote.

In 1958 Jamaica joined with Trinidad, Barbados, the Leeward Islands and the Windward Islands to create the West Indies Federation; but Jamaica withdrew in 1961. In 1959 internal self-government was achieved and in 1962 Jamaica became an independent state within the British Commonwealth.

TERRITORY AND POPULATION

Jamaica is an island which lies in the Caribbean Sea about 150 km south of Cuba. The area is 4,411 sq. miles (11,425 sq. km). The population at the census of 7 April 1991 was 2,374,193. Estimated population in 1995 was 2,500,025, distributed on the basis of the 13 parishes of the island as follows: Kingston and St Andrew, 683,700; St Thomas, 88,600; Portland, 78,300; St Mary, 111,200; St Ann, 155,800; Trelawny, 72,100; St James, 167,100; Hanover, 67,600; Westmoreland, 133,800; St Elizabeth, 148,200; Manchester, 173,500; St Catherine, 398,600; Clarendon, 221,500. 1995 density; 219 per sq. km.

The UN gives a projected population for 2000 of 2·59m.

An estimated 53·7% of the population were urban in 1995.

Chief towns (population, 1995): Kingston and St Andrew, 538,100, metropolitan area; Spanish Town, 110,400; Portmore, 93,800; Montego Bay, 82,000; May Pen, 45,900; Mandeville, 39,900.

The population is about 75% of African ethnic origin.

SOCIAL STATISTICS

Vital statistics (1995): Births, 57,607 (23·0 per 1,000 population); deaths, 12,776 (5·1); marriages, 16,515 (6·6); divorces, 1,332 (0·5). There were 17,669 emigrants in 1995, mainly to the USA. Expectation of life at birth, 1990–95, 71·4 years for males and 75·8 years for females. Infant mortality, 1990–95, 14 per 1,000 live births; fertility rate, 2·6 births per woman.

CLIMATE

A tropical climate but with considerable variation. High temperatures on the coast are usually mitigated by sea breezes, while upland areas enjoy cooler and less humid conditions. Rainfall is plentiful over most of Jamaica, being heaviest in May and from Aug. to Nov. The island lies in the hurricane zone. Kingston, Jan. 76°F (24·4°C), July 81°F (27·2°C). Annual rainfall 32" (800 mm).

CONSTITUTION AND GOVERNMENT

Under the Constitution of Aug. 1962 the Crown is represented by a Governor-General appointed by the Crown on the advice of the Prime Minister. The Governor-General is assisted by a Privy Council of 6 appointed members. The Legislature comprises the *House of Representatives* and the *Senate*. The Senate consists of 21 senators appointed by the Governor-General, 13 on the advice of the Prime Minister, 8 on the advice of the Leader of the Opposition. The House of Representatives (60 members) is elected by universal adult suffrage for a period not exceeding 5 years. Electors and elected must be Jamaican or Commonwealth citizens resident in Jamaica for at least 12 months before registration. It is likely that Jamaica will become a republic in the early part of the 21st century, with Queen Elizabeth II being replaced as head of state by a ceremonial president.

National Anthem. 'Eternal Father, bless our land' (words by H. Sherlock, tune by R. Lightbourne).

RECENT ELECTIONS
At the elections of Dec. 1997 the People's National Party (PNP) gained 60 seats and the Jamaica Labour Party, 8.

CURRENT ADMINISTRATION
Governor-General: Sir Howard Felix Cooke.

The Cabinet comprised in March 1999:

Prime Minister and Minister of Defence and Information: Percival Patterson, QC (b. 1935; PNP).

Deputy Prime Minister and Minister of Foreign Affairs and Trade: Seymour Mullings. *National Security and Justice:* Keith Knight. *Education, Youth and Culture:* Burchell Whiteman. *Health:* John Junor. *Labour, Social Security and Sport:* Portia Simpson-Miller. *Mining and Energy:* Robert Pickersgill. *Local Government and Community Development:* Arnold Bertram. *Industry and Investment:* Dr Paul Robertson. *Transportation and Works:* Peter Phillips. *Commerce and Technology;* Phillip Paulwell. *Housing and the Environment:* Easton Douglas. *Agriculture:* Roger Clarke. *Water:* Karl Blythe. *Finance and Planning:* Omar Davies. *Tourism:* Francis Tulloch. *Without Portfolio:* Maxine Henry-Wilson.

DEFENCE
In 1997 defence expenditure totalled US$29m. (US$11 per capita).

Army. The Jamaica Defence Force consists of a Regular and a Reserve Force. The Regular Force is comprised of the 1st battalion, Jamaica Regiment and Support Services which include the Air Wing and Coast Guard. The Coast Guard, numbering 150 in 1995, operates 5 inshore patrol craft based at Port Royal. The Reserve Force consists of the 3rd battalion, Jamaica Regiment. Total strength (army, 1996), 3,000. Reserves, 800.

Navy. The Coast Guard, numbering 150 in 1996, operates 5 inshore patrol craft based at Port Royal.

Air Force. The Air Wing of the Jamaica Defence Force was formed in July 1963 and has since been expanded and trained successively by the British Army Air Corps and Canadian Air Force personnel. There are no combat aircraft. Equipment for army liaison, search and rescue, police co-operation, survey and transport duties includes 2 Defender armed STOL transports; 1 Beech King Air and 1 Cessna 210 light transports; 4 JetRanger, 4 Bell 205 and 2 Bell 212 helicopters. Personnel (1997), 170.

INTERNATIONAL RELATIONS
Jamaica is a member of the UN, the Commonwealth, OAS, CARICOM and is an ACP member state of the ACP-EU relationship.

ECONOMY
Performance. Real GDP growth was 0·5% in 1995 (0·7% in 1994).

Budget. Revenue and expenditure for fiscal years ending 31 March (in J$1m.):

	1992–93	1993–94	1994–95	1995–96
Revenue	21,029	34,243	43,636	59,438
Expenditure	26,871	41,256	68,384	73,869

The chief items of current revenue are income tax; consumption, customs and stamp duties. The other major share of current resources is generated by the Bauxite

Production Levy. The chief items of current expenditure are public debt, education and health.

Currency. The unit of currency is the *Jamaican dollar* (JMD) of 100 *cents*. The Jamaican dollar was floated in Sept. 1990. The average annual inflation rate during the period 1990–96 was 36·1%. Foreign exchange reserves were US$723m. in May 1997. Total money supply in Nov. 1997 was J$31,850m.

Banking and Finance. The central bank and bank of issue is the Bank of Jamaica.

In 1997 there were 9 commercial banks with 208 branches and agencies in operation. 5 of these banks are subsidiaries of major British and North American banks, of which 4 are incorporated locally. Total assets of commercial banks in 1995 were J$121,324·9m.; deposits were J$89,135·4m.

There is a stock exchange in Kingston, which participates in the regional Caribbean exchange.

ENERGY AND NATURAL RESOURCES

Electricity. The Jamaica Public Service Co. is the public supplier. Total installed capacity, 1995, 624·9 MW. Production (1995) 2,417m. kWh. Consumption per capita in 1995 was an estimated 2,014 kWh.

Minerals. Jamaica is the third largest producer of bauxite, behind Australia and Guinea. Ceramic clays, marble, silica sand and gypsum are also commercially viable. Production in 1996 (in tonnes): Bauxite ore, 10·8m. (12·1m. in 1997); gypsum, 208,017; marble, 2,800; sand and gravel, 1·8m.; industrial lime, 3·4m.

Agriculture. In 1996 agriculture accounted for 8% of GDP. 1995 production (in tonnes): Sugar-cane, 2,295,000; bananas for export, 85,303; citrus fruit, 27,693; cocoa, 6,186; coconuts, 18,135.

Livestock (1996): Cattle, 420,000; goats, 440,000 (1995); pigs, 180,000; poultry, 7m. (1995). Slaughtered livestock in 1994: Cattle, 72,717 head; goats, 41,240; pigs, 111,297; poultry, 44,900 tonnes.

Forestry. Forests covered 175,000 ha in 1995 or 16·2% of the total land area (down from 254,000 ha and 23·5% in 1990). Jamaica's annual deforestation rate in the years from 1990–95 was 7·2%, the second highest in the world behind Lebanon over the same period. Timber production was 577,000 cu. metres in 1995.

Fisheries. Catches in 1995 totalled approximately 13,600 tonnes, of which 72% were sea fish.

INDUSTRY

Alumina production, 1995, 3m. tonnes. Output of other products, 1995 (in tonnes): Sugar, 207,000; molasses, 95,900; cornmeal, 13,400; flour, 146,000; edible oils, 6m. litres; condensed milk, 15,800; fertilizer, 57,500; petrol, 852·8m. litres; glass bottles, 20,588; cement, 523,000; cigarettes, 989·8m. units. There is an oil refinery in Kingston. In 1995, manufacturing contributed J$28,775m. to the total GDP at current prices.

Labour. Average total labour force (1995), 1·15m., of whom 963,300 were employed. 551,400 were employed in services (including 201,400 in trade and catering, 51,600 in business), 223,200 in agriculture, forestry and fisheries, 104,700 in manufacturing, 76,000 in building and 7,000 in mining.

INTERNATIONAL TRADE
Foreign debt was US$4,041m. in 1996.

Imports and Exports. Value of imports and domestic exports for calendar years (in US$1m.):

	1992	1993	1994	1995	1996
Imports	1,675	2,097	2,161	2,756	2,915
Exports	1,048	1,069	1,191	1,380	1,357

Principal imports in 1995 (in US$1m.): Consumer goods, 686 (24·7%), of which food including beverages, 197 (7·1%); raw materials, 1,548 (55·8%); capital goods, 539 (19·4%), of which construction materials, 144 (5·2%) and machinery and equipment, 284 (10·3%).

Principal domestic exports in 1995 (in US$1m.): Traditional exports, 916 (64%), of which bauxite, 72 (5%), alumina, 632 (44·2%), gypsum, 1 (0·1%), sugar, 96 (6·7%) and bananas, 48 (3·4%); non-traditional exports, 464 (32·5%), of which food, 77 (5·4%), beverages and tobacco, 22 (1·5%), mineral fuels, lubricants and related materials, 7 (0·5%), crude materials, 7 (0·5%), chemicals, 36 (2·5%), manufactured goods, 16 (1·1%), machinery and transport equipment, 4 (0·3%) and miscellaneous manufactures, 294 (20·5%).

Main import suppliers, 1996: USA, 52·3%; Trinidad and Tobago, 8·3%; Japan, 5·6%; UK, 4·0%. Main export markets, 1996: USA, 37·1%; UK, 13·2%; Canada, 11·8%; Netherlands, 8·9%.

COMMUNICATIONS

Roads. In 1996 the island had 19,000 km of roads (13,400 km surfaced). In 1995 there were 135,059 licensed vehicles (including 86,791 passenger cars). There were 7,379 traffic accidents in 1995 with 367 fatalities.

Civil Aviation. International airlines operate through the Norman Manley and Sangster airports at Palisadoes and Montego Bay. In 1996 Norman Manley airport had 18,620 aircraft movements and handled 1,354,788 passengers and 29,892 tonnes of freight. Sangster had 23,085 aircraft movements, with 2,125,689 passengers and 10,270 tonnes of freight. Air Jamaica, originally set up in conjunction with BOAC and BWIA in 1966, became a new company, Air Jamaica (1968) Ltd. In 1969 it began operations as Jamaica's national airline. In 1995 Air Jamaica flew 11·8m. km and carried 1,060,400 passengers.

In 1998 services were also provided by Air Canada, Air Negril, ALM, American Airlines, British Airways, BWIA, Cayman Airways, COPA, Cubana, Delta Air Lines, LTU International Airways, Martinair Holland, Northwest Airlines, TWA and US Airways.

Shipping. In 1995 the merchant marine totalled 10,545 GRT, including oil tankers, 3,292 GRT. In 1995 there were 3,275 visits to all ports; 13·9m. tonnes of cargo were handled. Kingston had 2,120 visits and handled 4·4m. tonnes.

Telecommunications. In 1996 there were 353,000 main telephone lines (140·3 per 1,000 population). Cellular phone subscribers numbered 45,000 in 1995 and there were 600 fax machines.

Postal Services. In 1995 there were 316 post offices and 477 postal agencies.

SOCIAL INSTITUTIONS

Justice. The Judicature comprises a Supreme Court, a court of appeal, resident magistrates' courts, petty sessional courts, coroners' courts, a traffic court and a family court which was instituted in 1975. The Chief Justice is head of the judiciary. 54,595 crimes were reported in 1995, of which 33,889 were cleared up. The daily average prison population, 1995, was 3,289.

Police. The Constabulary Force in 1995 stood at approximately 5,861 officers, subofficers and constables (men and women).

Religion. Freedom of worship is guaranteed under the Constitution. The main Christian denominations are Anglican, Baptist, Roman Catholic, Methodist, Church of God, United Church of Jamaica and Grand Cayman (Presbyterian–Congregational–Disciples of Christ), Moravian, Seventh-Day Adventist, Pentecostal, Salvation Army and Quaker. Pocomania is a mixture of Christianity and African survivals. Non-Christians include Hindus, Jews, Moslems, Bahai followers and Rastafarians.

Education. Adult literacy was 85% in 1995 (89·1% among females but only 80·8% among males). Jamaica has the biggest difference in literacy rates between the sexes in favour of females of any country in the world.

Education is free in government-operated schools. Schools and colleges in 1994–95 (government-operated and grant-aided): Basic, 1,694; infant, 29; primary, 792; primary with infant department, 83; all-age, 430; primary and junior high, 20; new secondary, 47; secondary high, 56; comprehensive high, 23; technical high, 12; agricultural/vocational, 6; special, 11; (independent): Kindergarten/preparatory, 126;

secondary high with preparatory department, 28; high/vocational, 5; business education, 29; (tertiary): Teacher-training, 13.

Numbers of pupils and students, 1994–95: Basic schools, 116,390; infant, 9,710; infant departments in primary schools, 6,737; primary, 172,510; all-age and primary and junior high (grades 1 to 6), 132,728; all-age and primary and junior high (grades 7 to 9), 54,371; new secondary, 30,797; secondary high, 70,613; technical high, 14,199; comprehensive high, 45,332; agricultural/vocational, 1,699. Numbers of teachers, 1994–95: Infant schools, 299; primary, 5,399; all-age and primary and junior high (grades 1 to 9), 6,424; new secondary, 1,852; secondary high, 4,132; technical high, 831; comprehensive high, 2,393; agricultural/vocational, 119.

The University of the West Indies is at Kingston. In 1994–95 it had 12,630 students, 800 external students and about 900 academic staff. The University of Technology in Kingston had 6,374 students, and the College of Agriculture, Science and Education in Portland, 533 students.

In 1994 total expenditure on education came to 4·7% of GNP.

Health. In 1995 the public health service had 4,058 staff in medicine, nursing and pharmacology; 326 in dentistry; 260 public health inspectors; 70 in nutrition. In 1995 there were 371 primary health centres, 5,021 public hospital beds and 305 private beds.

CULTURE

Broadcasting. There were (1995) 7 commercial and 1 publicly owned broadcasting stations; the latter also operates a television service (colour by NTSC), and there was 1 commercial television station. In 1995 there were 1,080,000 radio and 400,000 TV sets.

Cinema. In 1993 there were 35 cinemas and 2 drive-in cinemas.

Tourism. In 1996 there were 1,162,000 foreign tourists, bringing revenue of US$1·09bn.

DIPLOMATIC REPRESENTATIVES

Of Jamaica in Great Britain (1-2 Prince Consort Rd., London, SW7 2BZ)
High Commissioner: Derick R. Heaven.

Of Great Britain in Jamaica (Trafalgar Rd., Kingston 10)
High Commissioner: Richard Thomas, CMG.

Of Jamaica in the USA (1850 K. St., NW, Washington, D.C., 20006)
Ambassador: Richard Leighton Bernal.

Of the USA in Jamaica (2 Oxford Rd., Kingston 5)
Ambassador: Stanley L. McLelland.

Of Jamaica to the United Nations
Ambassador: M. Patricia Durrant, CD.

Of Jamaica to the European Union
Ambassador: Douglas A. C. Saunders.

FURTHER READING
Planning Institute of Jamaica. *Economic and Social Survey, Jamaica.* Annual.—*Survey of Living Conditions.* Annual
  Statistical Institute of Jamaica. *Statistical Abstract.* Annual.—*Demographic Statistics.* Annual.—*Production Statistics.* Annual.

Bakan, A. B. *Ideology and Class Conflict in Jamaica: the Politics of Rebellion.* Montreal, 1990
Goulbourne, H., *Teachers, Education and Politics in Jamaica, 1892–1972.* London, 1988
Ingram, K. E., *Jamaica.* [Bibliography] Oxford and Santa Barbara (CA), 1997
Manley, M., *A Voice at the Workplace.* London, 1975.—*Jamaica: Struggle in the Periphery.* London, 1983
Payne, A. J., *Politics in Jamaica.* London and New York, 1988

National library: National Library of Jamaica, Kingston.
National statistical office: Statistical Institute of Jamaica (STATIN), POB 643, Kingston 5.
Director General, Vernon James.

JAPAN

Nihon (or Nippon[1]) Koku

(Land of the Rising Sun)

Capital: Tokyo
Population estimate, 2000: 126·43m.
GNP per capita: (PPP$) 23,420
HDI/world rank: 0·940/8

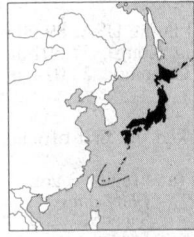

KEY HISTORICAL EVENTS

The house of Yamato united the nation in about 200 AD. The present imperial family are their direct descendants. From 1186 until 1867 successive families of the military Shoguns exercised the temporal power. For centuries Japan followed a policy of national isolation. The 16th century marked the beginning of foreign trade but in the 17th century all exchange with Europeans and all trade, except with the Dutch, was proscribed. Not until 1859 was the country opened to foreign trade and residence. In 1867 the Emperor Meiji recovered the imperial power after the abdication on 14 Oct. 1867 of the fifteenth and last Tokugawa Shogun Keiko. In 1871 the feudal system (*Hōken Seido*) was abolished and in the early 1890s constitutional government was introduced by the Emperor.

Japan's victory over Russia in the war of 1904 prevented Russian expansion into Korea and consolidated Japan's position as the strongest military power in Asia. Japan used the pretext of the Anglo-Japanese alliance to attack Chinese territory during the First World War. Bad feelings over the terms of the subsequent peace treaty led to continuing hostility between the two countries.

Economic distress, population growth (from 30m. in 1868 to 65m. in 1930) and a sense of dissatisfaction with the 'unjapanese' system of constitutional government led to the emergence between the wars of extremist nationalist and militarist movements in Japan. Plots among the young army officers, a revolt in Manchuria and the assassination of two prime ministers (a third only escaped when his brother-in-law was shot by mistake) highlighted the weaknesses of central government. In 1936 a military revolt in Tokyo gave the premiership to Konoe Fumimaro, a popular but ineffective figure, who failed to prevent further militarization of the country. In 1938 a national mobilization law was passed and in 1940 all political parties merged into the Imperial Rule Assistance Association.

On 27 Sept. 1940 Germany, Italy and Japan signed a 10 year pact to assure their mutual co-operation in the establishment of a 'new world order', with Japanese leadership recognized in Asia. In 1940 Japan invaded North Indochina and on 7 Dec. 1941 attacked the United States (principally at Pearl Harbour) and British bases in the Pacific, and then declared war on these two countries. Japanese forces eventually surrendered in Aug. 1945 after the dropping of atomic bombs on Hiroshima and Nagasaki. The country was placed under US military occupation, and in a new constitution in 1947 the Japanese people renounced the war and pledged themselves to uphold democracy and peace. The Emperor became a constitutional monarch instead of a divine ruler.

At San Francisco on 8 Sept. 1951 a Treaty of Peace was signed by Japan and representatives of 48 countries. A security treaty with the USA provided for the stationing of American troops in Japan until the latter was able to undertake its own defence. The peace treaty came into force on 28 April 1952, when Japan regained her sovereignty. Of the islands under US administration since 1945, the Bonin (Ogasawara), Volcano, and Daito groups and Marcus Island were returned to Japan in 1968, and the southern Ryukyu Islands (Okinawa) in 1972.

Confidence in what had been a world beating economy fell drastically after 1997 causing the government to cut taxes, provide financial support for small companies and to begin the reform of the heavily indebted banking system.

TERRITORY AND POPULATION

Japan consists of 4 major islands, Honshu, Hokkaido, Kyushu and Shikoku, and many small islands, with an area of 377,819 sq. km. Census population (1 Oct. 1995) 125,568,504 (males 61,575,570, females 63,992,934); density, 337 per sq. km. Population estimate, 1997, 126·17m.

[1]Both forms are valid, and derive from different pronunciations of a Chinese character.

943

The UN gives a projected population for 2000 of 126·43m.

In 1995 an estimated 78·1% of the population lived in urban areas. Foreigners registered on 31 Dec. 1997 were 1,482,707 of whom 645,373 were Koreans, 252,164 were Chinese, 233,254 were Brazilians, 93,265 were Filipinos, 43,690 were Americans, 40,394 were Peruvians, 20,669 were Thais, 14,438 were British, 11,936 were Indonesians, 11,897 were Vietnamese, 8,841 were Canadians, 7,946 were Iranians, 7,478 were Indians, 6,940 were Australians, and 2,194 were stateless persons.

Japanese overseas, Oct. 1997, 782,568; of these 284,006 lived in the USA, 89,906 in Brazil, 54,649 in the UK, 46,821 in China (26,600 in Hong Kong), 27,601 in Canada, 26,631 in Australia, 26,684 in Singapore, 22,318 in Germany, 23,014 in Thailand, 20,167 in France.

The official language is Japanese.

A law of May 1997 'on the promotion of Ainu culture' marked the first official recognition of the existence of an ethnic minority in Japan.

The areas, populations and chief cities of the principal islands (and regions) are:

Island/Region	Sq. km	Popn. estimate 1997	Chief cities
Hokkaido	83,452	5,702,000	Sapporo
Honshu/Tohoku	66,947	8,844,000	Sendai
Honshu/Kanto	32,419	39,839,000	Tokyo
Honshu/Chubu	66,781	21,538,000	Nagoya
Honshu/Kinki	33,098	22,554,000	Osaka
Honshu/Chugoku	31,910	7,768,000	Hiroshima
Shikoku	18,799	4,177,000	Matsuyama
Kyushu	42,157	13,452,000	Fukuoka
Okinawa	2,267	1,291,000	Naha

The leading cities, with population, 31 March 1997 (in 1,000), are:

City	Pop.	City	Pop.	City	Pop.
Akashi	288	Kasugai	277	Okazaki	323
Akita	309	Kawagoe	320	Omiya	435
Amagasaki	474	Kawaguchi	449	Osaka	2,479
Aomori	297	Kawasaki	1,186	Otsu	279
Asahikawa	363	Kitakyushu	1,012	Sagamihara	576
Chiba	846	Kobe	1,442	Sakai	791
Fujisawa	367	Kochi	322	Sapporo	1,768
Fukui	251	Koriyama	323	Sasebo	245
Fukuoka	1,248	Koshigaya	298	Sendai	957
Fukushima	286	Kumamoto	638	Shimonoseki	252
Fukuyama	376	Kurashiki	426	Shizuoka	471
Funabashi	538	Kyoto	1,390	Suita	334
Gifu	403	Machida	359	Takamatsu	331
Hachioji	492	Maebashi	283	Takatsuki	360
Hakodate	294	Matsudo	455	Tokorozawa	321
Hamamatsu	558	Matsuyama	465	Tokushima	263
Higashiosaka	497	Miyazaki	300	Tokyo	7,830
Himeji	470	Morioka	282	Toyama	322
Hirakata	399	Nagano	356	Toyohashi	349
Hiroshima	1,093	Nagasaki	430	Toyonaka	390
Ibaraki	254	Nagoya	2,085	Toyota	335
Ichihara	278	Naha	300	Urawa	460
Ichinomiya	270	Nara	361	Utsunomiya	435
Ichikawa	428	Neyagawa	256	Wakayama	397
Iwaki	365	Niigata	484	Yao	269
Kagoshima	541	Nishinomiya	396	Yokkaichi	285
Kanazawa	436	Oita	427	Yokohama	3,301
Kashiwa	319	Okayama	608	Yokosuka	434

SOCIAL STATISTICS

Statistics (in 1,000) for calendar years:

	1991	1992	1993	1994	1995	1996	1997
Births	1,224	1,228	1,204	1,229	1,221	1,203	1,209
Deaths	830	854	882	877	924	896	921

Crude birth rate of Japanese nationals in present area, 1996, was 9·7 per 1,000 population (1947: 34·3); crude death rate, 7·2; crude marriage rate, 6·4. In 1995 the most popular age range for marrying was 25–29 for both males and females. The infant mortality rate per 1,000 live births, 3·8 in 1996, is the lowest in the world. Expectation of life was 77·01 years for men and 83·59 years for women in 1996, up from 76·36 and 82·84 years respectively in 1995. Annual growth rate, 1990–95, 0·3%.

In 1997 the average number of children a Japanese woman bears in her life reached a record low of 1·39.

The suicide rate per 100,000 population in 1997 was 18·8 (men, 25·7; women, 11·8).

CLIMATE

The islands of Japan lie in the temperate zone, north-east of the main monsoon region of South-East Asia. The climate is temperate with warm, humid summers and relatively mild winters except in the island of Hokkaido and northern parts of Honshu facing the Japan Sea. There is a month's rainy season in June-July, but the best seasons are spring and autumn, though Sept. may bring typhoons. There is a summer rainfall maximum. Tokyo, Jan. 5·2°C, July 25·2°C. Annual rainfall 1,405 mm. Hiroshima, Jan. 4°C, July 25·7°C. Annual rainfall 1,555 mm. Nagasaki, Jan. 6·4°C, July 26·6°C. Annual rainfall 1,945 mm. Osaka, Jan. 5·5°C, July 27°C. Annual rainfall 1,318 mm. Sapporo, Jan. –4·6°C, July 20·2°C. Annual rainfall 1,130 mm.

CONSTITUTION AND GOVERNMENT

The Emperor is Akihito (b. 23 Dec. 1933), who succeeded his father, Hirohito on 7 Jan. 1989 (enthroned, 12 Nov. 1990); married 10 April 1959, to Michiko Shoda (b. 20 Oct. 1934). *Offspring:* Crown Prince Naruhito (Hironomiya; b. 23 Feb. 1960), married Masako Owada (b. 9 Dec. 1963) 9 June 1993; Prince Fumihito (Akishinomiya; b. 30 Nov. 1965); Princess Sayako (Norinomiya; b. 18 April 1969). The succession to the throne is fixed upon the male descendants. The 1947 constitution supersedes the Meiji constitution of 1889. In it the Japanese people pledge themselves to uphold the ideas of democracy and peace. The Emperor is the symbol of the States and of the unity of the people. Sovereign power rests with the people. The Emperor has no powers related to government. Fundamental human rights are guaranteed.

Legislative power rests with the *Diet*, which consists of the *House of Representatives*, elected by men and women over 20 years of age for a 4-year term, and an upper house, the *House of Councillors* of 252 members (100 elected by party list system with proportional representation according to the d'Hondt method and 152 from prefectural districts), one-half of its members being elected every 3 years.

In Nov. 1994 the Diet adopted electoral reforms changing the number of members in the House of Representatives from 511 to 500, of whom 300 are to be elected from single-seat constituencies, and 200 by proportional representation on a base of 11 regions. There is a 2% threshold to gain one of the latter seats. Donations to individual politicians are to be supplanted over 5 years by state subsidies to parties.

National Anthem. 'Kimi ga yo' ('The Reign of Our Emperor'); words 9th century, tune by Hiromori Hayashi.

RECENT ELECTIONS

Elections to 126 seats of the House of Councillors (upper house) were held on 12 July 1998; turn-out was 58·8%. The Liberal Democratic Party (LDP) gained 42 seats, the Democratic Party (DP) 25, Komei 9, the Social Democratic Party (SDP) 4, the Communists 14, the Liberal Party (LP) 5, and others 27.

Elections to the House of Representatives (lower house) were held on 30 July 1998. Turn-out was 59·6%. The Liberal Democratic Party (LDP) gained 239 seats; New Frontier Party, 156; Democratic Party of Japan, 52; Japan Communist Party (JCP), 26; Social Democratic Party (SDP), 15; New Harbinger Party, 2; minor parties and ind, 10.

In Sept. 1998 party strength in the House of Representatives was as follows: LDP 264, DP 93, Peace and Reform Network 47, LP 40, JCP 26, SDP 14, and others 16.

The largest opposition party, Shinshinto, was dissolved in Dec. 1997, and at the beginning of Jan. 1998, 6 new parties emerged.

CURRENT ADMINISTRATION
A new government was formed on 30 July 1998 and on 15 Jan. 1999 a coalition government between the Liberal Democratic Party and the Liberal Party was established. In March 1999 it comprised:

Prime Minister: Keizo Obuchi (b. 1927; LDP).

Minister of Justice: Shozaburo Nakamura. *Foreign Affairs:* Masahiko Komura. *Finance:* Kiichi Miyazawa. *Education:* Akito Arima. *Health and Welfare:* Sohei Miyashita. *Agriculture, Forestry and Fisheries:* Soichi Nakagawa. *International Trade and Industry:* Kaoru Yosano. *Transport:* Jiro Kawasaki. *Posts and Telecommunications:* Seiko Noda. *Labour:* Akira Amari. *Construction:* Katsutsugu Sekiya. *Home Affairs:* Takeshi Noda. *Chief Cabinet Secretary:* Hiromu Nonaka. *Director General, National Land Agency:* Hakuo Yanagisawa. *Director General, Management and Co-ordination Agency:* Seiichi Ota. *Director General, Defence Agency:* Fukushiro Nukaga. *Director General, Economic Planning Agency:* Taichi Sakaiya. *Director General, Environment Agency:* Kenji Manabe. *Director General, Science and Technology Agency:* Yutaka Takeyama. *Director General, Hokkaido and Okinawa Development Agency:* Kichio Inoue.

Local Government. The country is divided into 47 prefectures, each with an elected governor. Each prefecture, city, town and village has a representative elected assembly. There were 3,233 local authorities at 31 March 1997. Elections were held on 9 and 22 April 1995 for 13 prefectural governorships, 43 prefectural assemblies and 86 mayorships. Turn-out was 60%. 60% of prefectural assembly seats were won by independents.

DEFENCE
Japan has renounced war as a sovereign right and the threat or the use of force as a means of settling disputes with other nations. Its troops had not been able to serve abroad, but in 1992 the House of Representatives voted to allow up to 2,000 troops to take part in UN peacekeeping missions. A law of Nov. 1994 authorizes the Self-Defence Force to send aircraft abroad in rescue operations where Japanese citizens are involved.

In Jan. 1991 Japan and the USA signed a renewal agreement under which Japan pays 40% of the costs of stationing US forces and 100% of the associated labour costs. US forces in Japan totalled 47,000 in 1997, of whom 28,000 were on Okinawa. A US-Japanese agreement of Dec. 1996 stipulates that one fifth of the territory on Okinawa occupied by the US military is to be returned to local landowners by 2008.

Defence expenditure in 1997 totalled US$40,891m. (US$325 per capita).

Army. The 'Ground Self-Defence Force' is organized in 5 regional commands and in 1997 had an authorized strength of 148,000 (5,200 women) and a reserve of 46,000 men. The Army is organized in 12 infantry divisions, 1 armoured division, 1 airborne brigade, 2 air defence brigades, 1 artillery, 2 combined, 5 engineer and 1 helicopter brigade in addition to 4 training brigades. Equipment includes 190 T-61, 870 T-74 and 100 T-90 main battle tanks, approximately 90 AH-1S attack helicopters, as well as some 200 transport helicopters and 16 MU-2H fixed-wing aircraft.

Navy. The 'Maritime Self-Defence Force' is tasked with coastal protection and defence of the sea lanes to 1,000 nautical miles range from Japan. The modern and well-equipped combatant forces are mainly fitted with American weapon systems, which in many cases have been re-engineered and improved in Japan.

The combatant fleet, all home-built, includes 17 diesel submarines and 1 trials and training boat. There are 3 Aegis-equipped guided-missile destroyers, 5 other guided-missile destroyers armed with US Standard SM-1 surface-to-air missiles, 25 helicopter-carrying frigates and 27 other frigates, of which 2 are employed on non-military tasks. Light forces comprise 3 missile hydrofoils and 3 small inshore patrol craft. There are 39 mine warfare vessels: 1 minelayer, 1 layer/command ship, 3 1,200-tonne offshore mine countermeasure vessels, 27 coastal minesweepers and 2 smaller vessels. A substantial amphibious capability is provided by 6 tank landing ships supported by some 40 smaller craft. Major auxiliaries include 4 combined oiler/ammunition ships, 8 survey vessels and 5 training support vessels, and there are several hundred minor auxiliaries and service craft.

JAPAN

The Air Arm, organized into 7 operational Air Groups, includes 88 Orion anti-submarine patrol aircraft, 7 US-1A rescue flying boats, 60 Sea King anti-submarine helicopters, 10 mine countermeasures helicopters as well as about 100 transport, training and utility aircraft.

The main elements of the fleet are organized into 4 escort flotillas based at Yokosuka (2), Sasebo and Maizuru. The submarines are based at Sasebo and Kure.

Personnel in 1996 numbered 43,000 including about 12,000 in the Naval Air Arm.

Coastguard. This is administered by the Ministry of Transport. For details *see* under COMMUNICATIONS *below.*

Air Force. An 'Air Self-Defence Force' was inaugurated on 1 July 1954. Its equipment includes 7 interceptor squadrons of F-15J/DJ Eagles and 3 of F-4EJ Phantoms; 3 squadrons of Mitsubishi F-1 close-support fighters; 1 squadron of RF-4E reconnaissance fighters; 13 E-2C Hawkeye AWACS aircraft; ECM flight with 2 YS-11Es; 2 squadrons of turbofan Kawasaki C-1 and 1 with turboprop C-130H Hercules and NAMC YS-11 transports. About 90 KV-107, CH-47 Chinook and Black Hawk helicopters, and MU-2 twin-turboprop aircraft perform search, rescue and general duties. Training units use piston-engined Fuji T-3 basic trainers, Fuji T-1 jet intermediate trainers, Kawasaki T-4 jet trainers and supersonic Mitsubishi T-2 jet advanced trainers. 6 surface-to-air missile groups (19 squadrons) are in service. Strength (1996) 44,500.

INTERNATIONAL RELATIONS

In terms of total aid given, Japan was the most generous country in the world in 1997, donating US$9·4bn. in international aid in the course of the year. This represented 0·22% of its GDP.

Japan is a member of the UN, Colombo Plan, APEC and OECD.

ECONOMY

Policy. The head of the Economic Planning Agency (Taichi Sakaiya) has cabinet rank. In Dec. 1996 the Government adopted a 5-year economic and financial reform plan centred on the relaxing of state controls and the creation of jobs. Its implementation is co-ordinated by the Ministry of International Trade and Industry. In late 1997 the economy was thrown off course by the collapse of three leading financial institutions which had been saddled with bad debts following the stock market and property crash in 1990. Following a period of recession, this raised fears of another but more severe downturn.

A series of packages of measures aimed at reviving the Japanese economy were introduced in late 1997 and early 1998. Key measures included proposals to stabilize the financial sector, deregulate share buy-backs, promote discussion of US-style pension plans and allow companies to change the way they value land assets. However, the ruling Liberal Democratic Party remained strictly opposed to income tax cuts, which many of Japan's trading partners wanted to see introduced to boost domestic demand.

Performance. The real growth rate for 1998 was estimated at –2·2%, the first negative economic growth rate since the oil crisis of 1974 savaged the economy. Bankruptcies have been running at record levels. Yet, for all the financial blues, Japan remains one of the world's strongest economies with a highly trained workforce and the talent to exploit profitable export markets.

Budget. Ordinary revenue and expenditure for fiscal year ending 31 March 1999 balanced at 77,669,200m. yen.

Of the proposed revenue (in yen) in 1998, 58,522,000m. was to come from taxes and stamps, 15,557,000m. from public bonds. Main items of expenditure: Social security, 14,843,100m.; public works, 8,985,300m.; local government, 15,870,000m.; education, 6,345,700m.; defence, 4,939,700m.

The outstanding national debt incurred by public bonds was estimated in March 1997 to be 247,462,000m. yen.

The estimated 1998 budgets of the prefectures and other local authorities forecast a total revenue of 87,096,000m. yen, to be made up partly by local taxes and partly by government grants and local loans.

Currency. The unit of currency is the *yen* (JPY). Inflation in 1997 was 1·8%, with a forecast of 0·3% in 1998. Japan's foreign exchange reserves totalled US$209,778m. in Feb. 1998 (the highest of any country). Gold reserves in Feb. 1998 were 24·23m. troy oz. In Dec. 1997 the currency in circulation consisted of 54,670,000m. yen Bank of Japan notes and 4,046,000m. yen subsidiary coins.

Banking and Finance. The Nippon Ginko (Bank of Japan), founded 1882, finances the government and the banks, its function being similar to that of a central bank in other countries. The Bank undertakes the management of Treasury funds and foreign exchange control. Its *Governor* is Masaru Hayami (b. 1925; appointed March 1998 for a 5-year term). Its gold bullion and cash holdings at 31 Dec. 1997 stood at 517,000m. yen.

There were on 31 Dec. 1997, 10 city banks, 64 regional banks, 33 trust banks, 3 long-term credit banks, 64 member banks of the second association of regional banks, 405 Shinkin banks (credit associations), 352 credit co-operatives, and 93 foreign banks. There are also various governmental financial institutions, including postal savings which amounted to 247,114,700m. yen in Sept. 1998. Total savings by individuals, including insurance and securities, stood at 1,182,335,600m. yen on 30 Sept. 1998, and about 58% of these savings were deposited in banks and the post-office.

1997 saw the disappearance of Yamaichi Securities, Japan's fourth largest stockholder; also Sanyo Securities and the Hokkaido Takushoku bank.

Japan's banks are in a situation where many of them would be insolvent if they admitted the market value of the loans, shares and property they hold. As at 30 Sept. 1998 it was estimated that the banking system's bad loans amounted to 21,230bn. yen (US$179bn.).

There are 8 stock exchanges, the largest being in Tokyo, Osaka and Nagoya.

Weights and Measures. The metric system is obligatory.

ENERGY AND NATURAL RESOURCES

Electricity. Japan is poor in energy resources, and nuclear power generation is important in reducing dependence on foreign supplies. In 1996 generating facilities were capable of an output of 233·7m. kW; electricity produced was 1,009,349m. kWh. There were 51 nuclear reactors in 19 power plants, producing 33·4% of electricity, and 6 more were under construction in 1996. 10 regional publicly-held supply companies produce 74·4% of output. Consumption per capita in 1995 was an estimated 6,895 kWh.

Oil and Gas. Output of crude petroleum, 1996, was 837,000 kilolitres, almost entirely from oilfields on the island of Honshu, but 263·4m. kilolitres of crude oil had to be imported. Output of natural gas, 1996, 2,230m. cu. metres.

Minerals. Ore production in tonnes, 1996, of coal, 6,166,000; iron, 3,563; zinc, 79,709; copper, 1,145; lead, 7,753; tungsten, 66 (1993); silver, 85,115 kg; gold, 8,627 kg.

Agriculture. Agricultural workers in 1997 on farms with 0·3 ha or more of cultivated land or 0·5m. yen annual sales were 3·9m. (including 0·3m. subsidiary and seasonal workers), representing 5·1% (1995) of the labour force as opposed to 24·7% in 1962. The arable land area in 1997 was 4,949,000 ha. Rice is the staple food, but its consumption is declining. Rice cultivation accounted for 1,953,000 ha in 1997. The area planted with industrial crops such as rapeseed, tobacco, tea, rush, etc., was 202,000 ha in 1996.

Average farm size was 1·5 ha in 1997.

In 1995 there were 3,467,000 power cultivators and tractors and 1,650,000 rice power planters. (1990): 1,871,000 power sprayers and dusters.

Output of rice (in 1,000 tonnes), was 10,748 in 1995, 10,344 in 1996 and 10,025 in 1997.

Production in 1997 (in 1,000 tonnes) of barley was 194; wheat, 573; soybeans, 145. Sweet potatoes, which in the past mitigated the effects of rice famines, have, in view of rice over-production, decreased from 4,955,000 tonnes in 1965 to 1,130,000 tonnes in 1997. Domestic sugar-beet and sugar-cane production accounted for only

35% of requirement in 1995. In 1997, 1·71m. tonnes were imported, 38·8% of this being imported from Australia, 37·8% from Thailand, 13·4% from Cuba and 8·2% from South Africa.

Fruit production, 1996 (in 1,000 tonnes): Mandarins, 1,153; apples, 899; pears, 397; grapes, 244; persimmons, 241; and peaches, 169.

Livestock (1997): 4·75m. cattle (including about 1·90m. milch cows), 9·8m. pigs, 16,000 sheep, 27,000 horses, 29,000 goats, 307m. chickens. Milk (1996), 8·66m. tonnes.

Forestry. Forests covered 25·15m. ha in 1995, or 66·8% of the land area. There was an estimated timber stand of 3,483m. cu. metres in 1995. Timber production was 29·29m. cu. metres in 1995. Japan is the world s leading importer of roundwood, accounting for 34% of all imports in 1995. Consumption of roundwood in 1995 was 72·01m. cu. metres.

Fisheries. The catch in 1996 was 7·42m. tonnes, excluding whaling. More than 97% of fish caught are from marine waters. Japan is the leading importer of fishery commodities in the world, with imports in 1995 totalling US$17·85bn. The value of Japan's imports exceed the combined totals of the next four largest importers—the USA, with US$7·14bn. in 1995, France (US$3·22bn.), Spain (US$3·11bn.) and Germany (US$2·48bn.).

INDUSTRY
The industrial structure is dominated by corporate groups (*keiretsu*) either linking companies in different branches or linking individual companies with their suppliers and distributors.

Japan's industrial equipment, 1995, numbered 654,436 plants of all sizes, employing 10·88m. production workers.

Output in 1997 includes: Television sets 7·56m., radio sets 2·8m., cameras 12·28m., computers 10·4m. The chemical industry ranks fourth in shipment value after machinery, metals and food products. Production, 1997, included (in tonnes): Sulphuric acid, 6·8m.; caustic soda, 4·26m.; ammonium sulphate, 1·83m.; calcium superphosphate, 0·33m.

Output (1997), in 1,000 tonnes, of pig iron was 78,519; crude steel, 104,545; ordinary rolled steel, 82,201.

In 1997 paper production was 18,268,000 tonnes; paperboard, 12·75m. tonnes.

Output of cotton yarn, 1997, 184,000 tonnes, and of cotton cloth, 917m. sq. metres. Output, 1997, 62,000 tonnes of woollen yarns and 247m. sq. metres of woollen fabrics. Output, 1997, of rayon woven fabrics, 415m. sq. metres; synthetic woven fabrics, 2,041m. sq. metres; silk fabrics, 55m. sq. metres.

In 1997 Japan was the largest shipbuilder in the world, with orders totalling 12,990,000 GRT. In 1996, 9,270,000 GRT were launched, of which 2,937,000 GRT were tankers.

Labour. Total labour force, 1997, was 65·6m., of which 3·24m. were in agriculture and forestry, 0·26m. in fishing, 70,000 in mining, 6·85m. in construction, 14·42m. in manufacturing, 17·28m. in commerce and finance, 4·48m. in transport and other public utilities, 16·48m. in services (including the professions) and 2·15m. in government work. Retirement age is being raised progressively from 60 years to reach 65 by 2013.

In Feb. 1999 unemployment stood at 4·6%, with the number out of work being 3·31m.—the highest since records began in 1953. In 1997, 110,000 working days were lost in industrial stoppages. In 1997 the average working week was 39·58 hours.

Trade Unions. In 1997 there were 12,285,000 workers organized in 70,821 unions. In Nov. 1989, the 'Japanese Private Sector Trade Union Confederation' (Rengo), which was organized in 1987, was reorganized into the 'Japan Trade Union Confederation' (Rengo) with the former 'General Council of Japanese Trade Unions' (Sohyo) and other unions, and was the largest federation with 7,573,000 members in 1997. The 'National Confederation of Trade Unions' (Zenroren) had 844,000 members in 1997 and the 'National Trade Union Council' (Zenrokyo) 275,000 members in 1997.

INTERNATIONAL TRADE

Imports and Exports. Trade (in US$1m.):

	1992	1993	1994	1995	1996	1997
Imports	233,021	240,670	274,742	336,094	333,832	338,705
Exports	339,650	360,911	395,600	442,937	393,035	420,896

Distribution of trade by countries (customs clearance basis) (US$1m.):

	Exports		Imports	
	1996	1997	1996	1997
Africa	5,874	5,520	5,062	4,905
Australia	7,082	7,958	13,604	14,586
Canada	4,898	6,089	9,670	9,813
China	20,933	21,689	38,658	41,846
Germany	17,405	17,982	13,539	12,441
Hong Kong	24,251	27,241	2,461	2,252
Latin America	17,919	21,149	11,487	11,520
ASEAN[1]	73,096	69,938	52,388	50,201
Korea, Republic of	28,050	26,086	15,248	14,590
Taiwan	24,823	27,552	14,302	12,506
UK	11,933	13,706	6,853	7,183
USA	106,995	117,092	75,837	75,693

[1]Data of Asia and ASEAN have been published instead of those of south-east Asia since 1995.

Principal items in 1997, with value in 1m. yen were:

Imports, c.i.f.		Exports, f.o.b.	
Mineral fuels	7,542,000	Machinery and transport	
Foodstuffs	5,579,000	equipment	37,567,000
Metal ores and scrap	1,040,000	Metals and metal products	3,246,000
Machinery and transport		Textile products	1,003,000
equipment	10,476,000	Chemicals	3,623,000

The importation of rice used to be prohibited, but in 1993–94 there was an emergency importation of 1m. tonnes from Australia, China, Thailand and the USA to offset a poor domestic harvest. The prohibition was lifted in line with WTO agreements. Until 2000 rice imports will have limited access; thereafter the market will be fully open.

COMMUNICATIONS

Roads. The total length of roads (including urban and other local roads) was 1,147,532 km at 1 April 1996. There were 53,278 km of national roads, of which 52,539 km were paved. Motor vehicles, at 31 Dec. 1997, numbered 68,503,000, including 48,611,000 passenger cars and 19,652,000 commercial vehicles. In 1994 there were 10,649 road deaths (10,942 in 1993 and 11,457 in 1992).

The world's longest undersea road tunnel, spanning Tokyo Bay, was opened in Dec. 1997. The Tokyo Bay Aqualine, built at a cost of 1·44 trillion yen (US$11·3bn.), consists of a 4·4 km (2·7 mile) bridge and a 9·4 km tunnel that allows commuters to cross the bay in about 15 minutes.

Rail. The first railway was completed in 1872, between Tokyo and Yokohama (29 km). Most railways are of 1,067 mm gauge, but the high-speed 'Shinkansen' lines are standard 1,435 mm gauge. In April 1987 the Japanese National Railways was reorganized into 7 private companies, the Japanese Railways (JR) Group—6 passenger companies and 1 freight company. Total length of railways in March 1997, was 27,397 km, of which the JR had 20,059 km and other private railways, 7,339 km. In 1996 the JR carried 8,997m. passengers (other private, 13,596m.) and 49m. tons of freight (other private, 24m.). An undersea tunnel linking Honshu with Hokkaido was opened to rail services in 1988.

There are metros in Tokyo (2 systems, total 237 km in 1996), Fukuoka (18 km), Kobe (2 systems total 30 km), Kyoto (11 km), Nagoya (77 km), Osaka (106 km), Sapporo (45 km), Sendai (15 km) and Yokohama (33 km), and tram/light rail networks in 19 cities.

Civil Aviation. There are international airports at Tokyo (Narita), Fukuoka, Kagoshima, Nagoya Komaki, Sapporo and Osaka (Kansai International). The principal airlines are Japan Airlines (JAL), Japan Air System and All Nippon Airways. In the financial year 1996 Japanese companies carried 82·13m. passengers on domestic services and 15·54m. passengers on international services. JAL flew 312·3m. km in 1995 and carried 28,845,900 passengers, All Nippon Airways flew 212·6m. km and carried 37,821,600 passengers, and Japan Air System flew 86·3m. km and carried 16,787,800 passengers. In 1996 Tokyo handled 23,456,952 passengers (22,665,870 on international flights) and 1,574,381 tonnes of freight. Tokyo Narita was the busiest airport in the world for freight outside of the USA in 1996. Kansai International handled 18,351,000 passengers (10,126,000 on international flights) and 565,700 tonnes of freight in 1996. Built on a reclaimed offshore island, it was only opened in Sept. 1994 but in 1996 was the 25th busiest airport in the world for international traffic, with Tokyo Narita ranked 7th. Tokyo Haneda is only used for domestic flights, but handled 46,599,000 passengers in 1996, making it the 6th busiest airport in the world for overall traffic volume.

Shipping. On 1 July 1997 the merchant fleet consisted of 6,756 vessels of 100 GRT and over; total tonnage 18m. GRT; there were 202 ships for passenger transport (239,000 GRT), 2,100 cargo ships (1,122,000 GRT) and 1,048 oil tankers (5·7m. GRT). In 1995 vessels totalling 412,163,000 net registered tons entered ports.

Coastguard. The 'Maritime Safety Agency' (Coastguard) consists of 1 headquarters, 11 regional headquarters, 66 offices, 1 maritime guard and rescue office, 51 stations, 14 air stations, 1 special security station, 1 special rescue station, 11 district communications centres, 6 traffic advisory service centres, 4 hydrographic observatories, 1 Loran navigation system centre, and 84 navigation aids offices (with 5,497 navigation aids facilities) and controls 48 large patrol vessels, 47 medium patrol vessels, 19 small patrol vessels, 225 patrol craft, 12 hydrographic service vessels, 5 large firefighting boats, 10 medium firefighting boats and 77 guard and rescue boats, and 1 aids-to-navigation evaluation vessel, 4 buoy tenders, 64 aids-to-navigation tenders (as of 1 April 1998). Personnel in the financial year ending March 1999 numbered 12,224.

The Coastguard aviation service includes 26 fixed-wing aircraft and 44 helicopters.

Telecommunications. Telephone services have been operated by private companies (NTT and others) since 1985. There were 60,380,900 main telephone lines (equivalent to 478·6 per 1,000 population) in 1997. In 1996 there were 27m. cellular phone subscribers, and in 1995, 19·1m. PCs (153 per 1,000 persons) and 8m. fax machines. There were approximately 14m. Internet users in Oct. 1998 (11% of the population).

Postal Services. There were 24,638 post offices in 1996, handling a total of 24,971m. items of domestic mail, and foreign items of mails numbering 120m. out of and 294m. into Japan.

SOCIAL INSTITUTIONS

Justice. The Supreme Court is composed of the Chief Justice and 14 other judges. The Chief Justice is appointed by the Emperor, the other judges by the Cabinet. Every 10 years a justice must submit himself to the electorate. All justices and judges of the lower courts serve until they are 70 years of age.

Below the Supreme Court are 8 regional higher courts, district courts in each prefecture (4 in Hokkaido) and the local courts.

The Supreme Court is authorized to declare unconstitutional any act of the Legislature or the Executive which violates the Constitution.

The police are under central government control.

Religion. State subsidies have ceased for all religions, and all religious teachings are forbidden in public schools. In Dec. 1996 Shintoism claimed 102·0m. adherents, Buddhism 91·58m.; these figures obviously overlap. Christians numbered 3·17m.

Education. Education is compulsory and free between the ages of 6 and 15. Almost all national and municipal institutions are co-educational. On 1 May 1997 there were 14,624 kindergartens with 103,839 teachers and 1,789,523 pupils; 23,775 elementary schools with 420,901 teachers and 7,855,387 pupils; 11,185 junior high schools with 270,299 teachers and 4,481,480 pupils; 5,353 senior high schools with 276,108 teachers and 4,371,360 pupils; 595 junior colleges with 19,885 teachers and 446,750 pupils.

There were also 899 special schools for handicapped children (53,991 teachers, 86,544 pupils).

Japan has 7 main state universities: Tokyo University (1877); Kyoto University (1897); Tohoku University, Sendai (1907); Kyushu University, Fukuoka (1910); Hokkaido University, Sapporo (1918); Osaka University (1931); and Nagoya University (1939). In addition, there are various other state and municipal as well as private universities. There are 586 colleges and universities altogether with (1 May 1997) 2,633,790 students and 141,782 teachers.

Health. Hospitals on 1 Oct. 1996 numbered 9,490 with 1,664,629 beds. The hospital bed provision of 135 per 10,000 population was one of the highest in the world. Physicians at the end of 1996 numbered 240,908 (provision of 1 for every 542 persons); dentists, 85,518.

Welfare. There are in force various types of social security schemes, such as health insurance, unemployment insurance and age pensions. Citizens over 60 receive pensions of 70% of the average wage. In 1995 the basic retirement pension was 214,300 yen per month, funded by contributions of 17·35% of salary. There was a total of 34m. pensioners in 1996.

In 1995, 10,586,753 persons and 7,223,101 households received some form of regular public assistance, the total of which came to 1,540,465m. yen.

14 weeks maternity leave is statutory.

CULTURE

Broadcasting. Broadcasting is under the aegis of the public Japan Broadcasting Corporation (Nippon Hoso Kyokai) and the National Association of Commercial Broadcasters (Minporen). The former transmits 2 national networks and an external service, Radio Japan (22 languages). There is also a university station and a religious broadcasting station. Nippon Hoso Kyokai transmits a general and an educational TV programme, and there are 5 commercial networks. In 1996 there were 120m. radio and 85·7m. TV sets (colour by NTSC).

Cinema. In 1997 cinemas numbered 1,884 with an annual attendance of 141m. (1960: 1,014m.).

Press. In 1996 daily newspapers numbered 122 with aggregate circulation of 72·71m., including 4 major English-language newspapers. Japan has the highest circulation of daily newspapers in the world, with 72m. a day in 1996, up from 66m. a day in 1980.

Tourism. In 1997, 4,669,514 foreigners visited Japan, 642,933 of whom came from the USA and 401,850 from UK. Receipts totalled US$4·08bn. Japanese travelling abroad totalled 16,818,399 in 1997.

Libraries. In 1996 libraries numbered 2,397 including 1 National Diet Library, holding 249m. books.

National Theatre and Opera. In 1998 there were 4 National Theatres: National Theatre (traditional Japanese performances); Nogakudo (Noh Theatre); Bunraku Theatre (Japanese puppet show); and the New National Theatre (Opera House).

Museums and Galleries. In 1996 there were 985 museums, including 29 nationals. These included 332 historical, 325 fine arts and 118 general museums.

DIPLOMATIC REPRESENTATIVES
Of Japan in Great Britain (101-104 Piccadilly, London, W1V 9FN)
Ambassador: Sadayuki Hayashi.

Of Great Britain in Japan (1 Ichiban-cho, Chiyoda-ku, Tokyo 102-8381)
Ambassador: Sir David Wright, KCMG, LVO.

Of Japan in the USA (2520 Massachusetts Ave., NW, Washington, D.C., 20008)
Ambassador: Kunihiko Saito.

Of the USA in Japan (10–5, Akasaka 1-chome, Minato-ku, Tokyo)
Ambassador: Thomas S. Folley.

Of Japan to the United Nations
Ambassador: Yukio Satoh.

Of Japan to the European Union
Ambassador: Atsushi Tokinoya.

FURTHER READING

Statistics Bureau of the Prime Minister's Office: *Statistical Year-Book* (from 1949).—*Statistical Abstract* (from 1950).—*Monthly Bulletin* (from April 1950)

Economic Planning Agency: *Economic Survey* (annual), *Economic Statistics* (monthly), *Economic Indicators* (monthly)

Ministry of International Trade: *Foreign Trade of Japan* (annual)

Allinson, G. D., *Japan's Postwar History*. London, 1997

Argy, V. and Stein, L., *The Japanese Economy*. London, 1996

Bailey, P. J., *Post-war Japan: 1945 to the Present*. Oxford, 1996

Beasley, W. G., *The Rise of Modern Japan: Political, Economic and Social Change since 1850*. 2nd ed. London, 1995

The Cambridge Encyclopedia of Japan. CUP, 1993

Cambridge History of Japan. vols. 1-5. CUP, 1990–93

Campbell, A. (ed.) *Japan: an Illustrated Encyclopedia*. Tokyo, 1994

Clesse, A. *et al*, (eds.) *The Vitality of Japan: Sources of National Strength and Weakness*. London, 1997

Cortazzi, H., *The Japanese Achievement*. London, 1990

Francks, P., *Japanese Economic Development: Theory and Practice*. London, 1991

Gordon, A., *Postwar Japan as History*. Univ. of California Press, 1993

Horsley, W. and Buckky, R., *Nippon, New Superpower: Japan since 1945*. London, 1990

Ito, T., *The Japanese Economy*. Boston (Mass.), 1992

Jain, P. and Inoguchi, T., *Japanese Politics Today*. London, 1997

Japan: an Illustrated Encyclopedia. London, 1993

Japan Times Year Book. Tokyo, first issue 1933

Johnson, C., *Japan: Who Governs? The Rise of the Developmental State*. New York, 1995

Martineau, L., *Caught in a Mirror: Reflections on Japan*. London, 1993

Nakano, M., *The Policy-making Process in Contemporary Japan*. London, 1996

Okabe, M., (ed.) *The Structure of the Japanese Economy: Changes on the Domestic and International Fronts*. London, 1994

Perren, R., *Japanese Studies From Pre-History to 1990*. Manchester Univ. Press, 1992

Reischauer, E. O., *The Japanese Today: Change and Continuity*. Harvard Univ. Press, 1991

Schirokauer, C., *Brief History of Japanese Civilization*. New York, 1993

Shulman, F. J., *Japan*. [Bibliography] Oxford and Santa Barbara (CA), 1990

Woronoff, J., *The Japanese Economic Crisis*. 2nd ed. London, 1996

National statistical office: Statistics Bureau, Prime Minister's Office, Tokyo.
Website: http://www.stat.go.jp/

JORDAN

Al-Mamlaka Al-Urduniya
Al-Hashemiyah

(Hashemite[1] Kingdom
of Jordan)

Capital: Amman
Population estimate, 2000: 6·33m.
GNP per capita: (PPP$) 3,570
HDI/world rank: 0·729/87

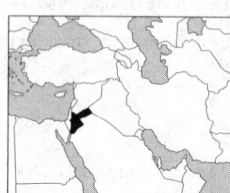

KEY HISTORICAL EVENTS

During the first World War (1914–18) the Arabs of Transjordan and Palestine rebelled against the suzerainty of Turkey, which had become an ally of Germany. Britain supported the rebellion, occupied the areas and in 1920 was given a League of Nations mandate for Transjordan and Palestine. In April 1921 the Amir Abdullah Ibn Hussein (brother of King Feisal of Iraq) became the ruler of Transjordan, which was officially separated from Palestine in 1923. On 20 Feb. 1928 an agreement was signed between Transjordan and Britain whereby the latter (with the approval of the League of Nations) recognized the existence of an independent government in Transjordan under the rule of the Amir Abdullah.

By a treaty signed in London on 22 March 1946 Britain recognized Transjordan as a sovereign independent state. On 25 May 1946 the Amir Abdullah assumed the title of king; and when the treaty was ratified on 17 June 1949 the name of the territory was changed to that of the Hashemite Kingdom of Jordan. On 13 March 1957 the Anglo-Transjordan treaty of March 1948 was terminated by mutual consent, and all British troops were withdrawn.

The part of Palestine remaining to the Arabs under the armistice with Israel on 3 April 1949, with the exception of the Gaza Strip on the Mediterranean coast, was in Dec. 1949 placed under Jordanian rule and formally incorporated in Jordan on 24 April 1950. In June 1967 this territory ('the West Bank') was occupied by Israel. On 31 July 1988 King Hussein announced the dissolution of Jordan's legal and administrative ties with the West Bank.

King Hussein, who became king in 1953 at the age of 17 after his father was declared mentally unfit to rule, remained in executive control in the face of attempted assassinations and frequent changes of prime ministers for 35 years until his death on 7 Feb. 1999.

TERRITORY AND POPULATION

Jordan is bounded in the north by Syria, east by Iraq, south-east and south by Saudi Arabia and west by Israel. It has an outlet to an arm of the Red Sea at Aqaba. Its area is 91,860 sq. km. 1995 population estimate, 5,373,000.

The UN gives a projected population for 2000 of 6·33m.

In 1995 an estimated 71·4% of the population lived in urban areas. Population of the 12 governorates:

Governorate	1995	Governorate	1995
Ajloun	98,600	Jerash	128,700
Amman	1,613,000	Ma'an	85,800
Aqaba	85,800	Madaba	111,400
Balqa	287,400	Mafraq	184,500
Irbid	776,600	Tafilah	64,300
Karak	175,900	Zarqa	661,000

The largest towns with suburbs, with estimated population, 1994: Amman, the capital, 1,300,042; Irbid, 379,844; Zarqa, 608,626.

The official language is Arabic.

[1]'Hashemite' denotes a descendant of the prophet Mohammed.

JORDAN

SOCIAL STATISTICS
Births, 1997 estimates, 156,000; deaths, 16,000. Rates, 1997 estimates per 1,000 population: Birth, 36; death rate, 3·8. 1997 population growth, 2·6%; life expectancy, 72·7 years (70·8 for men, 74·7 for women). Jordan has a young population: 1997 estimates showed 44% aged under 15, 53% aged 15–64 and 3% aged 65 and over. Infant mortality, 1990–95, 36 per 1,000 live births; fertility rate, 5·6 births per woman.

CLIMATE
Predominantly a Mediterranean climate, with hot dry summers and cool wet winters, but in hilly parts summers are cooler and winters colder. Those areas below sea-level are very hot in summer and warm in winter. Eastern parts have a desert climate. Amman, Jan. 46°F (7·5°C), July 77°F (24·9°C). Annual rainfall 12" (290 mm). Aqaba, Jan. 61°F (16°C), July 89°F (31·5°C). Annual rainfall 1·5" (35 mm).

CONSTITUTION AND GOVERNMENT
The Kingdom is a constitutional monarchy headed by H.M. King **Abdullah Bin Al Hussein** II, born 30 Jan. 1962, married to Princess Rania. *Offspring:* Hussein. *Crown Prince:* Prince Hamzah (younger brother of the King). In Jan. 1999, the late King Hussein had confirmed by royal decree that his eldest son, Prince Abdullah, was his heir in place of the King's brother Prince Hassan Bin Talal who had held the position of Crown Prince for 34 years. King Hussein died on 7 Feb. 1999.

The Constitution ratified on 8 Dec. 1952 provides that the Cabinet is responsible to Parliament. The legislature consists of a *Senate* of 40 members appointed by the King and a *Chamber of Deputies* of 80 members elected by universal suffrage. 9 seats are reserved for Christians, 6 for Bedouin and 3 for Circassians. A law of 1993 restricts each elector to a single vote, replacing a system in which electors had several votes depending on the number of seats in the constituency.

The lower house was dissolved in 1976 and elections postponed because no elections could be held in the West Bank under Israeli occupation. Parliament was reconvened on 9 Jan. 1984. By-elections were held in March 1984 and 6 members were nominated for the West Bank, bringing Parliament to 60 members. Women voted for the first time in 1984. On 9 June 1991 the King and the main political movements endorsed a national charter which legalized political parties in return for the acceptance of the constitution and monarchy. Movements linked to, or financed by, non-Jordanian bodies are not allowed.

National Anthem. 'Asha al Malik' ('Long Live the King'); words by A. Al Rifai, tune by A. Al Tanir.

RECENT ELECTIONS
Elections were held on 4 Nov. 1997. Of the 80 seats, 76 went to non-partisans of various orientations, 3 to the National Constitutional Party and 1 to the Ba'ath Party.

CURRENT ADMINISTRATION
In March 1999 the government consisted of:
Prime Minister, Minister of Defence: Abd al-Rauf al-Rawabidah (since 4 March 1999).
First Deputy Prime Minister: Marwan al-Hmoud.
Second Deputy Prime Ministers: Ayman Majali; Rima Khalaf.
Minister of Education: Izzat Jaradat. *Interior:* Nayef al-Qadi. *Public Works, Housing and Transport:* Husni Abu Ghida. *Justice:* Hamzeh Haddad. *Water and Irrigation:* Kamal Mahadin. *Industry and Trade:* Mohammad Asfour. *Tourism:* Aqel Biltaji. *Municipal and Rural Affairs:* Tawfiq Khreishan. *Health:* Ishaq Maraqa. *Awqaf (Religious Endowments), Islamic and Religious Affairs:* Abd al-Salam al-Abbadi. *Energy and Mineral Resources:* Suleiman Abu-Alam. *Labour:* Aid el-Fayez. *Information and Culture:* Nasser Lawzi. *Agriculture:* Hashem Shboul. *Finance:* Michel Marto. *Administrative Development and Social Development:* Faisal al-Rufua. *Foreign Affairs:* Abdul Ilah al-Khatib. *Post and Telecommunications:* Jamal al-Sarayirah. *Youth and Sports:* Mamser Mohammad Kheir.

Local Government. The 12 governorates are divided into cities, towns, districts and sub-districts. Municipal elections were held in July 1995; turn-out was low.

DEFENCE
Defence expenditure in 1997 totalled US$496m. (US$105 per capita), representing 6·4% of GDP.

Army. The Army is organized in 2 armoured and 2 mechanized infantry divisions, 1 Royal Guard, 1 special force, and 1 field artillery brigade. Equipment includes 270 M-47/-48A5, 218 M-60A1/3, 360 Khalid Chieftain and 293 Tariq (Centurion) main battle tanks. Total strength (1997) 90,000.

Navy. The Royal Jordanian Naval Force numbered 650 in 1997 and operates 3 fast inshore patrol boats, 2 ex-East German patrol craft and some boats all based at Aqaba.

Air Force. The Air Force has 1 interceptor and 4 ground attack squadrons equipped with Mirage F1 and F-5E Tiger II fighters, and 2-seat F-5Fs. Two anti-armour squadrons have Bell AH-1S Huey Cobra helicopters. There are 4 C-130H Hercules and 2 CASA Aviocar turboprop transports, S-70 Blackhawk, Gazelle, and Hughes 500D helicopters, piston-engined Bulldog basic trainers and CASA Aviojet jet trainers. Hawk surface-to-air missiles equip 14 batteries. Strength (1998) 13,500 personnel, 93 combat aircraft and 16 armed helicopters.

INTERNATIONAL RELATIONS
A 46-year-old formal state of hostilities with Israel was brought to an end by a peace agreement on 26 Oct. 1994.

Jordan is a member of the UN and the Arab League.

ECONOMY
Performance. Nominal total GDP was JD.5,120m. in 1996. Real GDP growth was 4·1% in 1996 (6·4% in 1995).

Budget. Revenue and expenditure over a 5-year period (in millions of dinar):

	1992	1993	1994	1995	1996
Revenue	1,109·4	1,119·6	1,162·4	1,332·6	1,366·9
Expenditure	1,081·2	1,235·1	1,312·8	1,471·5	1,666·9

Estimated total revenue (in US$1) in 1997 was 2·7bn.; expenditure 2·8bn.

Currency. The unit of currency is the *Jordan dinar* (JD.) of 1,000 *fils*. The average annual inflation rate during the period 1990–96 was 4·0%. Foreign exchange controls were abolished in July 1997. Foreign exchange reserves were US$2,065m. and gold reserves 820,000 troy oz. in Feb. 1998. Total money supply in Nov. 1997 was JD.1,613m.

Banking and Finance. The Central Bank of Jordan was established in 1964 (*Governor*, Dr Ziad Fariz). In 1993 there were 28 licensed banks with a total of 410 branches and 95 offices. Assets and liabilities of the banking system (including the Central Bank, commercial banks, the Housing Bank and investment banks) totalled JD.10,641·5m. in 1994.

There is a stock exchange in Amman (Amman Financial Market).

Weights and Measures. The metric system is in force. Land area is measured in *dunums* (1 dunum = 0·1 ha).

ENERGY AND NATURAL RESOURCES
Electricity. Installed capacity was 1·07m. kW in 1994. Production (1994) 4·76bn. kWh. Consumption per capita in 1995 was estimated to be 1,173 kWh.

Minerals. Phosphates production in 1994 was 4·08m. tonnes; potash, 1·55m. tonnes.

Agriculture. In 1996 agriculture produced 5% of GDP. The country east of the Hejaz Railway line is largely desert; northwestern Jordan is potentially of agricultural value and an integrated Jordan Valley project began in 1973. In 1993 about 15% of land was given over to agricultural use (including 9% permanent pasture and 4% arable crops). In 1994 it was estimated that there was 640 sq. km of irrigated land. The agricultural cropping pattern for irrigated vegetable cultivation was introduced in 1984 to regulate production and diversify the crops being cultivated. In 1986 the government began to lease state-owned land in the semi-arid southern regions for agricultural development by private investors, mostly for wheat and barley.

Production in 1994 (in tonnes): wheat, 50,000; barley, 65,000; tomatoes, 550,000; potatoes, 70,000; olives, 70,000; citrus fruits, 187,000; grapes, 50,000; aubergines, 50,000; watermelons, melons and squashes, 105,000.

Livestock (1996): 2·1m. sheep; 555,000 goats; 43,000 cattle; 19,000 asses; 18,000 camels; 78m. chickens (1995). Total meat production was 102,000 tonnes in 1993; milk, 96,000 tonnes.

There were 7,634 tractors in 1994.

Forestry. Forests covered 45,000 ha in 1995, or 0·5% of the land area. In 1995, 11,000 cu. metres of roundwood was cut.

Fisheries. Catches in 1995 totalled 172 tonnes, almost entirely from inland waters.

INDUSTRY

In 1995 service industries accounted for 66% of GDP and industry 28%. The number of industrial units in 1994 was 18,980, employing more than 0·1m. persons. The principal industrial concerns are the production or processing of phosphates, potash, fertilizers, cement and oil.

Production (1994, in 1,000 tonnes): Phosphate, 4,215; petroleum products, 2,815; cement, 3,437; potash, 1,370; chemical acids, 846; fertilizers, 470.

Labour. The workforce in 1996 was 935,000. In 1993, 434,806 persons worked in social and public administration, 91,087 in mining and manufacturing, 129,754 in commerce, 57,573 in transport and communications and 54,995 in agriculture. Unemployment was 16% in 1994.

INTERNATIONAL TRADE

Foreign debt was US$7,006m. in 1996. Legislation of 1995 eases restrictions on foreign investment and makes some reductions in taxes and customs duties.

Imports and Exports. Imports in 1996 totalled US$4,293m. and exports US$1,817m. Major exports are phosphate, potash, fertilizers, foodstuffs, pharmaceuticals, fruit and vegetables, textiles, cement, plastics, detergent and soap.

Exports in 1994 (in JD.1m.) were mainly to India, 88; Saudi Arabia, 72; Iraq, 78; Indonesia, 28; United Arab Emirates, 39. Imports were mainly from USA, 232; Germany, 184; Japan, 94; Italy, 139; UK, 120; Turkey, 62.

COMMUNICATIONS

Roads. Total length of roads, 1995 estimate, 6,750 km, of which 2,820 km were main roads. In 1996 there were 213,874 passenger cars (48 per 1,000 inhabitants), 369 motor cycles, 10,309 coaches and buses, and 68,844 trucks and vans. There were 552 deaths in road accidents in 1996 (388 in 1992).

Rail. The 1,050 mm gauge Hejaz Jordan and Aqaba Railway runs from the Syrian border at Nassib to Ma'an and Naqb Ishtar and Aqaba Port (total, 618 km). The state railway is only minimally operational. Passenger-kilometres travelled in 1995 came to 1m. and freight tonne-kilometres to 698m.

Civil Aviation. The Queen Alia International airport is at Zizya, 30 km south of Amman. There are also international airports at Amman and Aqaba. Queen Alia International handled 1,361,991 passengers in 1996 (1,327,388 on international flights) and 68,343 tonnes of freight. The national carrier is the state-owned Royal Jordanian, which flew 38·4m. km and carried 1·27m. passengers in 1995.

In 1998 services were also provided by Aeroflot, Air Algérie, Air France, Air Lanka, Alitalia, Austrian Airlines, British Airways, Cyprus Airways, Delta Air Lines, Egyptair, El Al, Emirates, Gulf Air, Iberia, JAT, KLM, Kuwait Airways, Lufthansa, Malaysia Airlines, Middle East Airlines, Olympic Airways, Pakistan International Airlines, Qatar Airways, Saudia, Sudan Airways, Swissair, Tarom, Tunis Air, Turkish Airlines and Yemenia Yemen Airways.

Shipping. In 1995 sea-going shipping totalled 0·11m. GRT, including oil tankers, 97,286 GRT. In 1994 vessels totalling 1,910,000 NRT entered ports and vessels totalling 576,000 NRT cleared.

Telecommunications. There were 402,600 main telephone lines in 1997, or 69·7 per 1,000 persons. Cellular phone subscribers numbered 12,000 in 1995, there were 35,000 PCs and 32,000 fax machines. There were approximately 20,000 Internet users in Jan. 1998.

Postal Services. In 1996 there were 836 post offices and agencies.

SOCIAL INSTITUTIONS

Religion. About 96% of the population are Sunni Moslems.

Education. Adult literacy in 1995 was 86·6% (93·4% of men and 79·4% of women). Basic primary and secondary education is free and compulsory. In 1994 there were 664 kindergartens (662 private) with 2,422 teachers and 55,996 pupils; 2,482 basic schools (322 private) with 48,158 teachers and 1,036,079 pupils; 741 secondary schools (77 private) with 4,572 teachers and 93,773 pupils and 54 vocational schools with 2,519 teachers and 30,052 pupils. In 1996–97 there were 6 state and 11 private universities. 22,500 Jordanians were studying abroad in 1994.

In 1994 total expenditure on education came to 3·8% of GNP and represented 10·5% of total government expenditure.

Health. In 1996 there were 7,322 doctors, 2,180 dentists and 4,304 nurses (1994). In 1995 there were a total of 6,800 hospital beds in 63 hospitals.

CULTURE

Broadcasting. Broadcasting is the responsibility of the Jordan Radio and Television Corporation, which transmits 2 national radio services (1 in English), a Koran service and an external service, Radio Jordan. There are 2 television services (colour by PAL). In 1995, 430,000 radio and 2·2m. TV sets were in use.

Cinema. In 1993 there were 35 cinemas with an annual attendance of 0·2m.

Press. In 1996 there were 4 daily (including 1 in English) and 22 weekly papers. Newspapers were denationalized in 1990, though government institutions still hold majority ownership.

Tourism. Tourism accounts for nearly 13% of GDP. In 1996 there were 1,103,000 foreign tourists, bringing revenue of US$744m.

DIPLOMATIC REPRESENTATIVES

Of Jordan in Great Britain (6 Upper Phillimore Gdns., Kensington, London, W8 7HB)
Ambassador: Fouad Ayoub.

Of Great Britain in Jordan (PO Box 87, Abdoun, Amman)
Ambassador: Christopher Battiscombe, CMG.

Of Jordan in the USA (3504 International Dr., NW, Washington, D.C., 20008)
Ambassador: Marwan Jamil Muasher.

Of the USA in Jordan (Abdoun, Amman)
Ambassador: Wesley W. Egan.

Of Jordan to the United Nations
Ambassador: Hasan Abu-Nimah.

Of Jordan to the European Union
Ambassador: Umayya Toukan.

FURTHER READING

Department of Statistics. *Statistical Yearbook*
Central Bank of Jordan. *Monthly Statistical Bulletin*
Dallas R., *King Hussein, The Great Survivor.* Profile Books, London, 1998
Gubser, P., *Jordan.* Boulder (CO), 1982
Rogan, E. and Tell, T. (eds.) *Village, Steppe and State: the Social Origins of Modern Jordan.* London, 1994
Salibi, K., *A Modern History of Jordan.* London, 1992
Satloff, R. B., *From Abdullah to Hussein: Jordan in Transition.* OUP, 1994
Seccombe, I., *Jordan.* [Bibliography] Oxford and Santa Barbara (CA), 1984
Wilson, M. C., *King Abdullah, Britain and the making of Jordan.* CUP, 1987

National statistical office: Department of Statistics, Amman

KAZAKHSTAN

Kazak Respublikasy

Capital: Astana
Population estimate, 2000: 16·93m.
GNP per capita: (PPP$) 3,230
HDI/world rank: 0·695/93

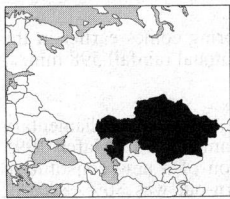

KEY HISTORICAL EVENTS

What was formerly known as Soviet Central Asia embraced the Kazakh Soviet Socialist Republic, the Uzbek Soviet Socialist Republic and the Kirghiz Soviet Socialist Republic.

Turkestan (by which name part of this territory was then known) was conquered by the Russians in the 1860s. In 1866 Tashkent (now Toshkent) was occupied and in 1868 Samarkand (now Samarqand), and subsequently further territory was conquered and united with Russian Turkestan. In the 1870s Bokhara was subjugated, the emir, by an agreement of 1873, recognizing the suzerainty of Russia. In the same year Khiva became a vassal state to Russia. Until 1917 Russian Central Asia was divided politically into the Khanate of Khiva, the Emirate of Bokhara and the Governor-Generalship of Turkestan.

In the summer of 1919 the authority of the Soviet Government was established in these regions. The Khan of Khiva was deposed in Feb. 1920, and a People's Soviet Republic was set up, the medieval name of Khorezm being revived. In Aug. 1920 the Emir of Bokhara suffered the same fate, and a similar régime was set up in Bokhara. The former Governor-Generalship of Turkestan was constituted an Autonomous Soviet Socialist Republic within the RSFSR on 11 April 1921.

In the autumn of 1924 the Soviets of the Turkestan, Bokhara and Khiva Republics decided to redistribute the territories of these republics on a nationality basis; at the same time Bokhara and Khiva became Socialist Republics. The redistribution was completed in May 1925, when the new states of Uzbekistan (now Uzbekiston), Turkmenistan and Tajikistan were accepted into the USSR as Union Republics. The remaining districts of Turkestan populated by Kazakhs were united with Kazakhstan which was established as an Autonomous Soviet Republic in 1925 and became a constituent republic in 1936.

Independence was declared on 16 Dec. 1991 when Kazakhstan joined the CIS.

TERRITORY AND POPULATION

Kazakhstan is bounded in the west by the Caspian Sea and Russia, in the north by Russia, in the east by China and in the south by Uzbekiston (formerly Uzbekistan) and Kyrgyzstan. The area is 2,717,300 sq. km (1,049,155 sq. miles). The 1989 census population was 16,464,464, of whom Kazakhs accounted for 39·7%, Russians 37·8%, Germans 5·8%, Ukrainians 5·4%, Uzbeks and Tatars 2% each. In 1997 there were 0·5m. Germans. Since 1992 a further 0·5m. have emigrated to Germany. Estimate, Jan. 1996, 16·5m. (51·4% female; 59·6% urban) with a population density of 6·1 per sq. km.

The UN gives a projected population for 2000 of 16·93m.

Kazakhstan consists of 19 provinces as follows, with area and population:

	Area (sq. km)	Population (1996)		Area (sq. km)	Population (1996)
Astana[1]	92,000	808,600	Kzyl-Orda	226,000	679,000
Aktube	300,600	750,400	Mangyshlak	165,600	340,100
Almaty[2]	105,700	2,141,100	North Kazakhstan	45,000	575,600
Atyrau[3]	118,600	463,200	Pavlodar	124,800	921,000
East Kazakhstan	97,500	918,800	South Kazakhstan	117,300	2,029,100
Jeskazgan	312,600	479,600	West Kazakhstan	151,300	668,500
Karaganda	115,400	1,234,100	Zhambyl[4]	144,300	1,037,000
Kostanay	113,900	1,022,800			

[1]Formerly Tselinograd and then Akmola. [2]Formerly Alma-Ata. [3]Formerly Gurev.
[4]Formerly Dzhambul.

In Dec. 1997 the capital was moved from Almaty to Akmola, which was renamed Astana in May 1998. In all there are 82 towns, 197 urban settlements and 221 rural districts.

The official language is Kazakh.

SOCIAL STATISTICS
1998 estimates: Births, 290,000; deaths, 171,000. Rates, 1998 (per 1,000 population): Births, 17·2; deaths, 10·1. Expectation of life at birth, 1990–95, 62·8 years for males and 72·5 years for females. Infant mortality, 1990–95, 34 per 1,000 live births; fertility rate, 2·5 births per woman.

CLIMATE
The climate is generally fairly dry. Winters are cold but spring comes earlier in the south than in the far north. Almaty, Jan. –4°C, July 24°C. Annual rainfall 598 mm.

CONSTITUTION AND GOVERNMENT
Relying on a judgement of the Constitutional Court that the 1994 parliamentary elections were invalid, President Nazarbaev dissolved parliament on 11 March 1995 and began to rule by decree. A referendum on the adoption of a new constitution was held on 30 Aug. 1995. The electorate was 8·8m.; turn-out was 80%. 89% of votes cast were in favour. The Constitution thus adopted allows the President to rule by decree and to dissolve parliament if it holds a no-confidence vote or twice rejects his nominee for Prime Minister. It establishes a parliament consisting of a 47-member Senate, 40 senators being elected by some 4,000 representatives of local authorities and 7 appointed by the President; and a lower house of 67, directly elected, though heads of families may cast votes for all of their family members. Candidates must gain an absolute majority of votes to be elected, and are not permitted to disclose their political affiliation.

A Constitutional Court was set up in Dec. 1991 and a new Constitution adopted on 28 Jan. 1993, but President Nazarbaev abolished the Constitutional Court in 1995.

National Anthem. A competition for a new anthem had no result, and the old Soviet anthem is retained.

RECENT ELECTIONS
At the presidential elections of 10 Jan. 1999 Nursultan Nazarbaev was re-elected with 79·8% of votes cast against 3 other candidates.

At the elections of 9 Dec. 1995 turn-out was 78%. 43 candidates were elected. A second round of voting was held on 31 Jan. 1996.

CURRENT ADMINISTRATION
President: Nursultan Nazarbaev (b. 1940; elected in 1991 and re-elected in 1999).

In March 1999 the government comprised:

Prime Minister: Nurlan Balgimbayev.

First Deputy Premier, Minister of Finance: Uraz Zhandosov. *Deputy Premiers:* Zhanybek Karibzhanov (also *Minister of Agriculture*), Aleksandr Pavlov. *Defence:* Lt.-Gen. Mukhtar Altynbayev. *Ecology and Natural Resources:* Serikbek Daukeyev. *Education and Health:* Krimbek Kysherbayev. *Power, Industry and Trade:* Mukhtar Ablyazov. *Foreign Affairs:* Kasymzhomart Tokaev. *Internal Affairs:* Lt.-Gen. Kairbek Suleymenov. *Justice:* Bayurzhan Mukhamedzhanov. *Labour and Social Security:* Natalya Korzhova. *Science, President of the Academy of Sciences:* Vladimir Shkolnik. *Transport and Communications:* Serit Burkitbayev. *Culture and Information:* Altynbek Sarsenbayev. *Revenues:* Zianulla Kaimzhanov. *Minister and Chairman of Presidential Agency for Strategic Planning and Reform:* Yerzhan Utembayev.

Chairman, Senate (Upper House): Umirbek Baygeldiyev.
Chairman, Majlis (Lower House): Murat Ospanov.

Local Government. Elections were held in Dec. 1989. Local government was directly subordinated to the President in Jan. 1992.

DEFENCE
In 1991 the former Soviet Union transferred some 2,680 T-64/-720, 2,428 ACVs and 6,900 artillery to storage bases in Kazakhstan. The equipment is deteriorating. A US funded programme for nuclear dismantlement and demilitarization continues.

Defence expenditure in 1997 totalled US$503m. (US$31 per capita).

Army. The Army is organized in 1 tank and 2 motor rifle divisions; 1 independent motor rifle, 1 artillery, 1 multiple rocket launcher and 1 surface-to-surface missile regiment; and 1 artillery and 1 airborne brigade. Equipment includes 624 T-62 and T-72 main battle tanks. Personnel, 1996, 25,000. Paramilitary units: Republican Guard (2,500), Ministry of the Interior Security Troops (20,000), Frontier Guards (12,000).

Navy. Formally constituted in Aug. 1996, a force of 9 inshore patrol craft with further craft on order from Germany operates on the Caspian Sea. Personnel, 250.

Air Force. In 1995 there was an Air Force division with about 15,000 personnel with some 150 combat aircraft, including MiG-29 and Su-27 interceptors and MiG-27 and Su-24 strike aircraft.

INTERNATIONAL RELATIONS
In Jan. 1995 agreements were reached for closer integration with Russia, including the combining of military forces, currency convertibility and a customs union.

Kazakhstan is a member of the UN, CIS and the NATO Partnership for Peace. Sandwiched between Russia and China, in 1998 President Nazarbaev signed major treaties with both countries in the hope of improving relations with both.

ECONOMY
Policy. A National Council for Economic Reform was instituted in Jan. 1993. A privatization programme for 1993–95 envisaged the sale of most state enterprises with more than 200 employees by a combination of cash and vouchers. Enterprises of national importance remain controlled by the government through holding companies. President Nazarbaev is overseeing a process of wholesale privatization, the reform of financial and credit systems, the liberalization of prices for goods and services, the adoption of a system of free trade and the attraction of foreign investment. A privatization programme started in April 1994 involving the auctioning of 3,500 medium-size enterprises. Coupons are issued to citizens to be exchanged for shares in investment funds. Foreign nationals may participate in trading after the auctions. Large (i.e. with over 2,000 employees) and small (i.e. with fewer than 500) enterprises are being sold for cash.

Performance. The break-up of the Soviet Union triggered an economic collapse, as orders from Russian factories for Kazakhstan's metals and phosphates, 2 mainstays of the economy, dried up. Low oil and commodity prices cut revenues by a third in 1998. Real GDP growth was 1·1% in 1997 and forecast to be 1·8% in 1998, having been –8·9% in 1995.

Budget. The government was forced to withdraw the 1999 budget in order to recalculate the effect of lower commodity prices on GDP. Budgetary income in 1996 (1997 in brackets) was 218,278m. tenge (278,737m. tenge); expenditure was 259,564m. tenge (300,945m. tenge).

Currency. The unit of currency is the *tenge* of 100 *tiyn*, which was introduced on 15 Nov. 1993 at 1 tenge = 500 roubles. It became the sole legal tender on 25 Nov. 1993. Inflation was running at 1,250% in 1994, but had dropped to 130% in 1997, and it was hoped that it would be around 17% by the end of 1998. In Jan. 1997 foreign exchange reserves were US$2,700m. Total money supply in Sept. 1997 was 102,541m. tenge.

Banking and Finance. The central bank and bank of issue is the National Bank (*Governor,* Uraz Djandosov). In 1998 there were 90 banks, compared to 240 in 1993.

ENERGY AND NATURAL RESOURCES
Electricity. Installed capacity is 17m. kW. Output in 1996 was 58,600m. kWh. (1997 estimate, 61,000m. kWh). There is 1 nuclear power station. Consumption per capita was an estimated 3,800 kWh in 1996.

Oil and Gas. By 2010 Kazakhstan aims to have become the world's sixth largest oil producer.

KAZAKHSTAN

Proven oil reserves in 1996 were 2,000m. tonnes. The Tengiz field has estimated oil reserves between 6,000m. and 9,000m. bbls.; the Karachaganak field has oil reserves of 2,000m. bbls., and gas reserves of 20,000,000m. cu. feet. Output of crude oil (including gas concentrates), 1996, 22·9m. tonnes (1997 estimate, 26·2m. tonnes); natural gas, 6,396m. cu. metres (1997 estimate, 7,300m. cu. metres). In Sept. 1997 Kazakhstan signed oil agreements with China worth US$9·5bn.; these include a 3,000 km pipeline to Xinjiang province in western China. Oil and gas investment by foreign companies is now driving the economy. In 1997 oil production sharing deals were concluded with 2 international consortia to explore the North Caspian basin and to develop the Karachaganak gas field.

It is hoped that by 2003 exploitation of the oil reserves of the Caspian shelf will start. Initially production is expected to amount to 100,000 bbls. per day, possibly rising to as much as 1·2m. bbls. per day by 2013. It is believed that there may be as much as 14bn. tonnes of oil and gas reserves under Kazakhstan's portion of the Caspian Sea. In early 1998 the Tengiz field was yielding 170,000 bbls. per day, which should rise to 250,000 per day by 2000.

Minerals. Kazakstan is extremely rich in mineral resources, including coal, bauxite, cobalt, vanadium, iron ores, chromium, phosphates, borates and other salts, copper, lead, manganese, molybdenum, nickel, tin, gold, silver tungsten and zinc. Coal production (1996 estimate), 76·6m. tonnes; iron ore (1996), 12·6m. tonnes; gold (1993), 14·6 tonnes; steel (1996), 3·22m. tonnes; refined copper (1997 estimate), 0·30m. tonnes.

Agriculture. Kazakh agriculture has changed from primarily nomad cattle breeding to production of grain, cotton and other industrial crops. In 1996 agriculture accounted for 13% of GDP. In 1993, 181·3m. ha were under cultivation, of which private subsidiary agriculture accounted for 0·3m. ha and commercial farming 6·3m. ha in 16,300 farms. Private and commercial agriculture accounted for 35% of output by value in 1992; agricultural output was valued at 13,700m. roubles (in constant 1983 prices) in 1993, 97% of the 1992 figure. In 1993 agriculture contributed 37% of GNP. Around 60,000 private farms have emerged since independence.

Tobacco, rubber plants and mustard are also cultivated. Kazakhstan has rich orchards and vineyards, which accounted for 95,000 ha of cultivated land in 1985. Kazakhstan is noted for its livestock, particularly its sheep, from which excellent quality wool is obtained. Livestock (1996): 6·86m. cattle (down from 9·57m. in 1993), 18·72m. sheep (down from 33·63m. in 1993), 1·7m. horses and (1995) 50m. chickens.

Output of main agricultural products (in 1m. tonnes) in 1997 (estimate): Grain, 14·2; sugar-beet, 0·4; cotton, 0·2; vegetables, 0·8; meat (cattle and poultry), 1·4 (1996); milk, 3·7; and 1,400m. eggs. About half of the grain is exported, mainly to Russia (around 5·5m. tonnes annually), Ukraine and Turkmenistan.

Forestry. Forests covered 10·50m. ha in 1995, or 3·9% of the land area (up from 9·54m. ha and 3·6% in 1990). Only the USA and Uzbekiston exceeded the 0·96m. ha afforested in Kazakhstan between 1990 and 1995. In 1997, 290,000 cu. metres of timber were cut.

Fisheries. Catches in 1995 totalled 49,602 tonnes, exclusively freshwater fish.

INDUSTRY

Kazakhstan was heavily industrialized in the Soviet period, with non-ferrous metallurgy, heavy engineering and the chemical industries prominent. Output was valued at 30,000m. tenge in current prices in 1996 and 35,000m. tenge in 1997. Production (1997 estimate, in tonnes) included ferroalloy, 680,000; mineral fertilizer, 200,000; chemical fibre, 1,900 (1993); cardboard, 7,400 (1996); lead, 85,000; fabrics, 24·6m. sq. metres; leather footwear, 0·8m. pairs; forge-press machines, 180; tractors, 3,100; radio sets, 600; refrigerators and freezers, 12,900 (1993); washing machines, 23,200.

Labour. In 1996 the population of working age was estimated as 7·4m. In Jan. 1997, 3% of the labour force were registered unemployed, of whom 15,400 were receiving benefits. Average monthly salaries in 1993 were 134·9 tenge.

INTERNATIONAL TRADE

In Jan. 1994 an agreement to create a single economic zone was signed with Kyrgyzstan and Uzbekistan (now Uzbekiston). Since Jan. 1992 individuals and enterprises have been able to engage in foreign trade without needing government permission, except for goods 'of national interest' (fuel, minerals, mineral fertilizers, grain, cotton, wool, caviar and pharmaceutical products) which may be exported only by state organizations. Foreign nationals may be licensed to purchase Kazakh assets for privatization. Foreign debt was US$4,500m. in 1997.

Imports and Exports. In 1997 imports were valued at US$6,656m. and exports at US$6,015m. Main export markets (% of trade in 1996): CIS countries, 55·7%; Europe, 26·4%; Asia, 16·2%; America, 1·5%. Main import suppliers: CIS, 69·6%; Europe, 18·3%; Asia, 9·4%; America, 2·5%. Main imports: machinery and parts, industrial materials. Main exports: oil, ferrous and non-ferrous metals, and cotton.

COMMUNICATIONS

Roads. In 1997 there were estimated to be 115,400 km of motor roads with hard cover. In 1997 an estimated 1bn. passengers used public transport and 1bn. tonnes of freight were carried. Passenger cars in use in 1996 numbered 997,544 (961 per 1,000 inhabitants), and there were also 295,378 trucks and vans, 54,310 road tractors and 49,310 buses and coaches.

Rail. In 1997 there were estimated to be 14,400 km of 1,520 mm gauge railways (3,528 km electrified 1994). In 1997 about 37·5m. passengers and 150m. tonnes of freight were carried.

Civil Aviation. The national carrier is Air Kazakhstan. There is an international airport at Almaty, which in 1996 handled 1,745,000 passengers and 20,800 tones of freight. In 1998 services were also provided by Aeroflot, Aerosweet Airlines, Air Enterprise Pulkovo, Asiana Airlines, Austrian Airlines, Aviacompany Turkmenistan, British Airways, Iran Air, Kaliningrad Air Enterprise, KLM, Kyrgyzstan Airlines, Lufthansa, Pakistan International Airlines, Sakha Avia, Samara Airlines, SAN Air Company, SAS, Siberia Airlines, Swissair, Transaero Airlines, Turkestan Airlines, Turkish Airlines, Uzbekiston Airways, VIP Air and Xinjiang Airlines.

Shipping. There is 1 large port, Aktau. In 1993, 1·2m. passengers and 4m. tonnes of freight were carried on inland waterways. Merchant shipping totalled 12,000 GRT in 1995.

Telecommunications. Main telephone lines numbered 1,818,200 in 1997, or 108 per 1,000 persons. There were 4,600 cellular phone subscribers and 2,900 fax machines in 1995.

Postal Services. In 1995 there were 4,355 post offices.

SOCIAL INSTITUTIONS

Justice. In 1994, 201,796 crimes were reported, including 2,549 murders or attempted murders.

Religion. There were some 4,000 mosques in 1996 (63 in 1990). An Islamic Institute opened in 1991 to train imams. A Roman Catholic diocese was established in 1991. In 1995 the Union of Evangelical Baptist Churches had 140 communities, the Russian Orthodox Church 177, and the Evangelical Lutheran Church 112.

Education. In Jan. 1994, 0·7m. children (39% of those eligible) were attending pre-school institutions. In 1995–96 there were 1,372,600 pupils at 8,611 primary schools, 1,670,200 pupils at secondary schools and 419,460 students at higher education institutions. Adult literacy rate is more than 99%.

Health. In 1995 there were 62,290 doctors, and in Jan. 1994, 187,000 junior medical personnel and 1,899 hospitals with 225,000 beds.

Welfare. In Jan. 1994 there were 2·1m. age and 0·9m. other pensioners. Pension contributions are 20% of salary and are payable to the State Pension Fund. The Fund was scheduled for privatization in 1998, with half the mandatory 20% contribution from salary going into private pension schemes.

CULTURE

Broadcasting. Broadcasting is the responsibility of the Kazakh State Radio and Television Co. There are 3 national and 13 regional radio programmes, a Radio Moscow relay and a foreign service, Radio Alma-Ata (Kazakh, English). There is 1 TV channel (colour by SECAM). There were 6·46m. radio receivers and 3·87m. television receivers in 1996.

Cinema. In 1995 there were 1,580 cinemas.

Press. In 1995 there were 472 periodicals in Kazakh, 511 in Russian and 60 in both languages.

DIPLOMATIC REPRESENTATIVES

Of Kazakhstan in Great Britain (33 Thurlowe Sq., London, SW7 2DS)
Ambassador: Kanat B. Saudabaev.

Of Great Britain in Kazakhstan (Ul. Furmanova 173, Almaty)
Ambassador: Douglas B. McAdam.

Of Kazakhstan in the USA (1401 16th Street, NW, Washington, D.C., 20036)
Ambassador: Bolat K. Nurgaliyev.

Of the USA in Kazakhstan (Ul. Furmanova 99/97a, Almaty 480091)
Ambassador: A. Elizabeth Jones.

Of Kazakhstan to the United Nations
Ambassador: Akmaral Arystanbekova.

Of Kazakhstan to the European Union
Ambassador: Aoueskhan Kyrbassov.

FURTHER READING

Olcott, M. B., *The Kazakhs.* Stanford, 1987

KENYA

Jamhuri ya Kenya

(Republic of Kenya)

Capital: Nairobi
Population estimate, 2000: 30·34m.
GNP per capita: (PPP$) 1,130
HDI/world rank: 0·463/137

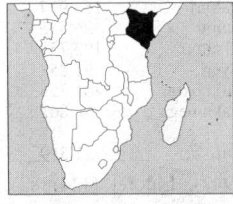

KEY HISTORICAL EVENTS

Prior to colonialism, the area covered by Kenya comprised African farming communities, notably the Kikuyu and the Masai. From the 16th century through to the 19th, they were loosely controlled by the Arabic rulers of Oman (whose base moved to Zanzibar in the early 19th century). In 1895, the British declared part of the region the East Africa Protectorate, including the mainland dominions of the Sultan of Zanzibar as well as Mau, Kipini, the island of Lamu and all adjacent islands between the rivers Umba and Tana. In 1905 the colony and the protectorate, formerly known as the East African Protectorate, was transferred from the Foreign Office to the Colonial Office. In Nov. 1906 the protectorate, excluding the Sultan of Zanzibar's dominions, was placed under the control of a governor and annexed to the Crown, and known from 1920 as the Colony of Kenya. It was only in Dec. 1963 that the Sultan ceded his coastal strip to Kenya.

In the First World War the Germans in East Africa invaded the south of Kenya but the British army, under Gen. Smuts, counter-attacked and captured much of German East Africa.

The influx of European settlers was resented by Africans not only for the whites' land holdings, but also for their exclusive political representation in the colonial Legislative Council. A state of emergency existed between Oct. 1952 and Jan. 1960 during the period of the Mau Mau uprising caused by discontent, particularly among the Kikuyu people, over colonial rule and land policy. Over 13,000 Africans and 100 Europeans were killed. The Kenya African Union was banned and its president, Jomo Kenyatta, imprisoned. When the state of emergency ended in 1960 political activity resumed, to pave the way to independence, and two political parties emerged.

On his release from imprisonment Jomo Kenyatta became president of the Kenya Africa National Union, while the Kenya African Democratic Union, which favoured a regional form of government, was led by Ronald Ngala and Daniel T. arap Moi.

Full internal self-government was achieved in 1962 and in Dec. 1963 Kenya became an independent member of the Commonwealth.

Before independence the East African High Commission had been administering services of an inter-territorial nature for Kenya, Tanzania and Uganda and this continued after independence. The arrangement was changed to the East African Community in 1967. The Community practically ceased to function after 30 June 1977, chiefly because of the failure to agree a budget and the refusal of President Nyerere of Tanzania to negotiate with President Amin of Uganda.

In 1964 and 1965 constitutional amendments provided for Kenya to become a republic with a president as head of state, and a further change in 1966 required members who changed their parties to seek re-election. Later that year another amendment amalgamated the Senate and the House of Representatives to form a unicameral National Assembly.

In 1982 Kenya became a one-party state and in 1986 party preliminary elections were instituted to reduce the number of parliamentary candidates at general elections. Only those candidates obtaining over 30% of the preliminary vote were eligible to stand.

On the death of Kenyatta in Aug. 1978 Daniel T. arap Moi, the vice-president, became acting president and was elected in 1979, and then re-elected in 1983, 1988, 1992 and 1997. An attempted coup in 1982 was unsuccessful. A multi-party election was permitted in 1992 and again in 1997, the first genuinely competitive elections since 1963.

TERRITORY AND POPULATION

Kenya is bounded by Sudan and Ethiopia in the north, Uganda in the west, Tanzania in the south and Somalia and the Indian Ocean in the east. The total area is 582,646 sq. km, of which 571,416 sq. km is land area. In the 1989 census, the population was 21,443,636 (19% urban).

The UN gives a projected population for 2000 of 30·34m.

The land areas, populations and capitals of the provinces are:

Province	Sq. km	Census 1989	Estimate 1993	Capital	Census 1989
Rift Valley	182,413	4,981,613	6,107,900	Nakuru	163,927
Eastern	154,354	3,768,677	4,940,900	Embu	26,525
Nyanza	12,507	3,507,162	4,804,500	Kisumu	192,733
Central	13,236	3,116,703	4,152,600	Nyeri	91,258
Coast	84,113	1,829,191	2,430,700	Mombasa	461,753
Western	8,285	2,544,329	3,176,000	Kakamega	58,862
Nairobi	693	1,324,570	1,758,900		
North-Eastern	126,186	371,391	741,400	Garissa	31,319

Other towns (1989): Machakos (116,293), Meru (94,947), Eldoret (111,882), Thika (57,603).

Most of Kenya's 26·44m. people belong to 13 tribes, the main ones including Kikuyu (about 22% of the population), Luhya (14%), Luo (13%), Kalenjin (12%), Kamba (11%), Gusii (6%), Meru (5%) and Mijikenda (5%).

Swahili is the official language, but people belonging to the different tribes have their own language as their mother tongue. English is spoken in commercial centres.

SOCIAL STATISTICS

1995 births, 1,013,000; deaths, 312,000. Birth rate (per 1,000 population), 1995, 37·3; death rate, 11·5. Growth rate: 1996 and 1997, 2·7%; 1995, 2·8%. Expectation of life at birth, 1990–95, 52·7 years for males and 55·4 years for females. Infant mortality, 1990–95, 71 per 1,000 live births. Fertility rate, 1997, 4·5 births per woman.

CLIMATE

The climate is tropical, with wet and dry seasons, but considerable differences in altitude make for varied conditions between the hot, coastal lowlands and the plateau, where temperatures are very much cooler. Heaviest rains occur in April and May, but in some parts there is a second wet season in Nov. and Dec. Nairobi, Jan. 65°F (18·3°C), July 60°F (15·6°C). Annual rainfall 39" (958 mm). Mombasa, Jan. 81°F (27·2°C), July 76°F (24·4°C). Annual rainfall 47" (1,201 mm).

CONSTITUTION AND GOVERNMENT

There is a unicameral *National Assembly*, which until the Dec. 1997 elections had 200 members, comprising 188 elected by universal suffrage for a 5-year term, 10 members appointed by the President, and the Speaker and Attorney-General ex-officio. Following a review of constituency boundaries, the National Assembly now has 210 elected members, 12 members appointed and the two ex-officio members, making 224 in total. The President is also directly elected for 5 years; he appoints a Vice-President and other Ministers to a Cabinet over which he presides. A constitutional amendment of Aug. 1992 stipulates that the winning presidential candidate must receive a nationwide majority and also the vote of 25% of electors in at least 5 of the 8 provinces. The sole legal political party had been the Kenya African National Union (KANU), but after demonstrations by the pro-reform lobby which led to extreme violence, KANU agreed to legalize opposition parties.

National Anthem. 'Ee Mungu nguvu yetu' ('Oh God of all creation'); words by a collective, tune traditional.

RECENT ELECTIONS

The most recent presidential and parliamentary elections were held on 29 Dec. 1997. In the presidential election Daniel T. arap Moi was opposed by 14 candidates including Charity Ngilu for the Social Democratic Party (SDP), who was aiming to become Africa's first elected female head of state. In the event, Daniel T. arap Moi

KENYA

benefited from an opposition split along tribal lines and won comfortably, with a 40·4% show of the vote, passing the 25% threshold in 5 out of 8 provinces. Mwai Kibaki (Democratic Party) came next with 30·9% and Raila Odinga (National Development Party) third, with 10·8%.

At the National Assembly elections of 29 Dec. 1997, KANU gained 107 seats, the Democratic Party (DP) 39, the National Development Party 21, the Forum for the Restoration of Democracy (FORD)-Kenya 17, the Social Democratic Party 15; and 5 other parties won 11 seats between them. Of the 12 members appointed by the president, 6 were from KANU and 2 from DP, plus 1 each from 4 other parties.

CURRENT ADMINISTRATION

President: Daniel T. arap Moi (b. 1924).

In March 1999 the government comprised:

Minister of Finance: Yekoyada Francis Omoto Masakhalia. *Planning and National Development*: George Saitoti. *East African Affairs:* Nicholas Biwott. *Education and Human Resource Development:* Stephen Kalonzo Musyoka. *Agriculture, Livestock and Marketing:* Musalia Mudavadi. *Foreign Affairs:* Bonaya Godana. *Water Resources:* Kipng'eno arap Ngeny. *Energy:* Chrisanthus Okemo. *Natural Resources:* Francis Lotodo. *Transport and Communications:* William Ole Ntimama. *Tourism and Wildlife:* Kipkalia Kosgey. *Health:* Jackson Kalweo. *Local Authorities:* Sam Ongeri. *Lands and Settlement:* Gideon Ndambuki. *Labour and Manpower Development:* Philip J. W. Masinde. *Information and Broadcasting:* Joseph Nyagah. *Co-operatives Development:* Andrew Kiptoon. *Public Works and Housing:* Katana Ngala. *Environment and Conservation:* Francis Nyenze. *Home Affairs, Culture and Social Services:* Shariff Nassir. *Research and Technology:* Andrew Kones. *Trade:* Joseph Kamotho. *Commerce:* Joseph Mulanda Angatia. *Rural Development:* Hussein Maalim Mohamed. *Attorney-General:* Amos Wako.

Local Government. The country is divided into the Nairobi Municipality and 7 provinces and there are 53 districts.

DEFENCE

In 1997 defence expenditure totalled US$235m. (US$8 per capita).

Army. The Army consists of 1 armoured, 1 engineer, 1 artillery and 2 infantry brigades and 1 air defence, 1 airborne, 1 independent air cavalry and 2 engineer battalions. Equipment includes 80 Vickers Mk3 main battle tanks. Total strength (1997) 20,500.

Navy. The Navy, based in Mombasa, consisted in 1996 of two 56-metre fast missile craft, 4 smaller missile craft, and 1 inshore patrol craft, all built in Britain, plus 1 tug. Personnel in 1997 totalled 1,200.

The Marine police and Customs operate an additional 15 patrol boats.

Air Force. An air force, formed on 1 June 1964, was built up with RAF assistance. Equipment includes 8 F-5E/F-5F supersonic combat aircraft/trainers, 12 Hawk light jet attack/trainers, 11 twin-turboprop Buffaloes and Dash-8s for transport, air ambulance, anti-locust spraying and security duties, 6 Skyservant light twins, 10 Bulldog piston-engined primary trainers, 12 Tucano turbo-prop basic trainers and Puma, Gazelle and Hughes 500 helicopters. Personnel (1997) 2,500, with 18 combat aircraft and 20 armed helicopters.

INTERNATIONAL RELATIONS

Kenya is a member of the UN, Commonwealth, OAU and is an ACP member state of the ACP-EU relationship.

ECONOMY

Policy. Since a privatization programme was launched in 1992, the government has completed the sale of the vast majority of the 207 enterprises originally targeted. In 1996 a Presidential Economic Commission was set up to implement reforms to public companies over 1996–98. A US$215m. IMF loan agreement signed in April 1995 has been suspended while the government considers measures against corruption.

967

KENYA

Performance. Real GDP growth was 2·9% in 1997 compared to 4·7% in 1996, and was estimated to be between 1 and 2% in 1998.

Budget. The fiscal year ends on 30 June. Government revenue, 1995–96, 143,088m. shillings; expenditure, 152,832m. shillings.

Currency. The monetary unit is the *Kenya shilling* (KES) of 100 *cents.* The currency became convertible in May 1994. The shilling was devalued by 23% in April 1993. Inflation was 11·2% in 1997 (9% in 1996 and 1·6% in 1995). Foreign exchange reserves were US$580m. in Feb. 1998 and gold reserves were 80,000 troy oz. In Feb. 1998 total money supply was 90,490m. shillings.

Banking and Finance. The central bank and bank of issue is the Central Bank of Kenya (*Governor*, Micah Cheserem). There are 50 banks, 40 non-banking financial institutions and a couple of building societies. In March 1995 their combined assets totalled KSh.£268,811m. On 15 Oct. 1997 the government announced its decision to offload a further 25% of its stake in the Kenya Commercial Bank, which lowers its shareholding to 35%. Savings deposits totalled KSh.£724m. in March 1990.

There is a stock exchange in Nairobi.

ENERGY AND NATURAL RESOURCES

Electricity. Installed generating capacity was 807 MW in 1994; mostly provided by hydropower from power stations on the Tana river, with some from oil-fired power stations and by geothermal power. Production (1994) 3,538m. kWh. Consumption per capita in 1995 was 125 kWh.

Oil and Gas. Kenya signed an oil and gas exploration deal in 1997 with Canada's Tornado Resources Ltd, who pledged to commit a minimum of US$7m. over a 3-year period.

Minerals. In 1989 there were 49 mines and quarries. Production, 1994 (in 1,000 tonnes): Soda ash, 224; fluorspar, 89; salt, 75·8. Other minerals included gold, raw soda, lime and limestone, diatomite, garnets and vermiculite.

Agriculture. As agriculture is possible from sea-level to altitudes of over 9,000 ft, tropical, sub-tropical and temperate crops can be grown and mixed farming is pursued. Agriculture produced 29% of GDP in 1996. In 1994 there were 4m. ha of arable land, 520,000 ha of permanent crop land and 21·3m. ha of pasture. Four-fifths of the country is range-land which produces mainly livestock products and the wild game which is a major tourist attraction.

Tea and coffee are the two big foreign exchange earners, ahead of tourism. Horticultural products, particularly flowers, are in fourth position.

Kenya has about 110,000 ha under tea production, and is the world's largest exporter of tea. The production is high quality tea, raised in near-perfect agronomic conditions. It is plucked the whole year round, and almost exclusively by hand. In 1996 production reached a record 257m. kg (244·5m. in 1995) and earned about US$350m. in exports.

Coffee production in 1996–97 is estimated at between 75,000 and 78,000 tonnes (97,500 tonnes in 1995–96 and 96,000 tonnes in 1994–95). Arabica coffee covers 176,500 ha of land under coffee in Kenya. Some 70% of the total hectarage under coffee is cultivated by 335,000 smallholders, although their production has been in decline in recent years.

Fresh horticultural exports were 84,824 tonnes in 1996, up 18% on the 71,758 tonnes in 1995, earning about US$340m. By the year 2000 Kenyan horticultural exports are expected to pass the 100,000 tonnes mark, with increases in pre-packed vegetables, salads, cut flowers, avocados, passion fruit and mangoes. The biggest growth has been in cut flowers, up 20% from 29,374 tonnes in 1995 to 35,212 tonnes in 1996. Around two-thirds of the flowers are destined for the Netherlands, largely for re-export. 1996 vegetable exports totalled 32,742 tonnes and fruit 16,869 tonnes, both up on 1995.

Maize is Kenya's most important food crop with about 1·4m. ha under cultivation and annual production in excess of 2m. tonnes. Sisal, pyrethrum, maize and wheat are crops of major importance in the Highlands, while coconuts, cashew nuts, cotton, sugar, sisal and maize are the principal crops grown at the lower altitudes.

Livestock (1996): Cattle, 13·84m.; sheep, 5·6m.; goats, 7·4m. (1995); camels, 810,000 (1995); chickens, 25m. (1995).

More than half the agricultural labour force is employed in the livestock sector, accounting for 10% of GDP.

Forestry. Forests covered 1·29m. ha in 1995 (2·3% of the land area), mainly between 6,000 and 11,000 ft above sea-level. There are coniferous, broad-leaved, hardwood and bamboo forests. Timber production was 41·7m. cu. metres in 1995.

Fisheries. Catches in 1995 totalled 193,790 tonnes, of which 188,324 tonnes were freshwater fish. While the aggregate landings from Kenya's inland waters (more than 90% from Lake Victoria) have grown over the past 20 years, marine fishing has not reached its full potential, despite a coastline of 680 km. Fish landed from the sea totals between 5,000 and 7,000 tonnes annually, but there is an estimated potential of 200,000 tonnes in tuna and similar species.

INDUSTRY

In 1994 there were 648 manufacturing firms employing more than 50 persons. The main products are textiles, chemicals, vehicle assembly and transport equipment, leather and footwear, printing and publishing, food and tobacco processing and oil refining. Production in 1994 included (in tonnes): Sugar, 303,000; maize meal, 233,200; wheat flour, 191,400; animal feed (1988), 184,266; cotton yarn, 4,767; cotton fabrics, 45·69m. sq. metres.

Labour. The labour force in 1996 was 13,953,000 (54% males). In 1997 the unemployment level was close to 3m.

INTERNATIONAL TRADE

Foreign debt was US$6,893m. in 1996. Foreign investment on the stock exchange has been permitted since 1 Jan. 1995. Export Processing Zones were introduced in 1990, offering foreign companies exemption from taxes and duties for 10 years.

Imports and Exports. Exports were valued at US$2,852m. in 1996; imports, US$2,067m. Exports are estimated to have increased by 13·7% in 1995 and by 21·4% in 1996. The estimated growth for 1997 was 25%.

Principal exports (in 1,000m. shillings) 1994: Tea, 16·9; coffee, 13; horticultural produce, 8·3. Imports: Petroleum, 18·6; machinery and transport equipment, 31·8; chemicals (1993), 19·9; manufactures, 14·7.

Main import suppliers, 1996: UK, 13·2%; United Arab Emirates, 8·2%; Japan, 7·4%; Germany, 6·1%. Main export markets, 1996: Uganda, 15·4%; Tanzania, 12·0%; UK, 10·8%; Germany, 7·7%.

The UK is the largest foreign investor in Kenya with over US$1,500m. in more than 60 enterprises.

COMMUNICATIONS

Roads. Of some 63,800 km of roads in 1996, only about 8,900 km, or 14%, have been surfaced. More than 80,000 km of roads are unclassified. The network has seriously deteriorated since the mid 1980s through poor maintenance. Urban roads comprise around 7,000 km, or about 5% of the total road network, but less than half of them are classified as 'good' or in 'fair' condition. Yet more than 70% of all vehicles in the country use urban roads because of the heavy concentration of economic activities in urban areas. Overall, more than 80% of passengers and freight are carried on the roads. There were, in 1996, 278,000 passenger cars, 32,000 motor cycles, 62,000 vans and trucks and 19,200 buses and coaches, plus 28,420 road tractors. There were 11,785 road accidents in 1994 (2,424 fatal).

Rail. In 1994 route length was 2,506 km of metre-gauge. In 1994–95, 1·6m. passengers and 2·1m. tonnes of freight were carried.

Civil Aviation. There are international airports at Mombasa (Moi International) and Nairobi (Jomo Kenyatta International). The national carrier is the now privatized Kenya Airways. KLM has a 26% share of Kenya Airways. In 1998 services were also provided by Aero Zambia, Aeroflot, Air Austral, Air Djibouti, Air France, Air Gabon, Air India, Air Madagascar, Air Malaŵi, Air Mauritius, Air Seychelles, Air Tanzania Corporation, Air Zimbabwe, Airkenya Aviation, Alitalia, Alliance Air,

British Airways, Cameroon Airlines, Delta Air Lines, Eagle Aviation, Egyptair, El Al, Emirates, Ethiopian Airlines, Gulf Air, Iran Air, K.D. Air Corporation, KLM, Lufthansa, Olympic Airways, Pakistan International Airlines, Royal Swazi National Airways Corporation, SABENA, SAS, Saudia, South African Airways, Swissair, Uganda Airlines, United Airlines and Yemenia Yemen Airways. In 1995 Kenya Airways flew 16·1m. km and carried 740,400 passengers. In 1996 Jomo Kenyatta International handled 2,061,000 passengers and 73,500 tonnes of freight, and Moi International 890,000 passengers and 2,500 tonnes of freight.

Shipping. The main port is Mombasa, which averages 7·8m. tonnes of cargo a year. Container traffic has nearly doubled since 1990 to 217,028 TEUs (twenty-foot equivalent units) in 1996. The merchant marine totalled 15,579 GRT in 1995, including oil tankers, 6,412 GRT.

Telecommunications. Kenya had 269,800 main telephone lines in 1997, or 8·1 per 1,000 persons. The government aims to improve telephone availability in rural areas from 0·16 lines per 100 persons in 1997 to 1 line per 100 by 2015, and in urban areas from 4 lines to 20 lines per 100 persons. Cellular phone subscribers numbered 2,300 in 1995, there were 18,000 PCs and 3,800 fax machines. In Jan. 1998 there were approximately 5,000 Internet users.

Postal Services. In 1995 there were 1,061 post offices, or 1 for every 26,000 persons.

SOCIAL INSTITUTIONS

Justice. The courts of Justice comprises the court of Appeal, the High Court and a large number of subsidiary courts. The court of Appeal is the final Apellant court in the country and is based in Nairobi. It comprises 7 Judges of Appeal. In the course of its Appellate duties the court of Appeal visits Mombasa, Kisumu, Nakuru and Nyeri. The High court with full jurisdiction in both civil and criminal matters comprises a total of 28 puisne Judges. Puisne Judges sit in Nairobi (16), Mombasa (2), Nakuru, Kisumu, Nyeri, Eldoret Meru and Kisii (1 each).

The Magistracy consists of approximately 300 magistrates of various cadres based in all provincial, district and some divisional centres. In addition to the above there are the Kadhi courts established in areas of concentrated Moslem populations: Mombasa, Nairobi, Malindi, Lamu, Garissa, Kisumu and Marsabit. They exercise limited jurisdiction in matters governed by Islamic Law.

There were 17,589 criminal convictions in 1993; the prison population was 130,393 in 1994.

Religion. In 1992 there were 7·12m. Roman Catholics, 1·94m. Protestants and 1·62m. Moslems. Traditional beliefs persist.

Education. The adult literacy rate in 1995 was 78·1% (86·3% among males and 70·0% among females). In 1994 there were 19,083 pre-primary schools with 27,829 teachers and 951,997 pupils; 15,906 primary schools with 5,544,998 pupils and 181,975 teachers; 2,834 secondary schools with 619,839 pupils and 38,307 teachers; 20 teacher training schools with 16,461 students; 20 technical training institutes with 8,148 students. There were 3 polytechnics with 10,836 students, and 5 universities (Nairobi, Moi, Kenyatta, Egerton and Jomo Kenyatta University College of Agriculture and Technology) with 39,340 students.

Health. In 1994 there were 4,558 doctors and 630 dentists. There were 324 hospitals (with 37,271 beds), 522 health centres and 2,868 sub-centres and dispensaries. Free medical service for all children and adult out-patients was launched in 1965.

CULTURE

Broadcasting. Broadcasting is the responsibility of KBC, which transmits the following services: National (in Swahili), General (English), Central (4 languages), Western (6 languages), North-Eastern and Coastal (4 languages). KBC also provides television programmes, mainly in English and Swahili. There are several private broadcasting stations, including Kenya Television Network (which broadcasts CNN), Stellavision (which broadcasts Sky News), Capital Radio and Metro FM. The

KENYA

BBC has been awarded a licence to broadcast on the FM frequency. In 1995, 2·6m. radio and 500,000 TV sets were in use.

Cinema. In 1993 there were 17 cinemas.

Press. In 1995 there were 5 daily papers with a total circulation of 450,000.

Tourism. In 1996 there were 670,000 holiday visitors. Once Kenya's fastest growing source of foreign exchange, receipts from tourism had dropped from US$500m. a year to US$300m. a year by 1998.

DIPLOMATIC REPRESENTATIVES
Of Kenya in Great Britain (45 Portland Pl., London, W1N 4AS)
High Commissioner: Mwanyengela Ngali.

Of Great Britain in Kenya (Upper Hill Road, Nairobi)
High Commissioner: Jeffrey R. James, CMG.

Of Kenya in the USA (2249 R. St., NW, Washington, D.C., 20008)
Ambassador: Samson Kipkoech Chemai.

Of the USA in Kenya (Moi/Haile Selassie Ave., Nairobi)
Ambassador: Prudence Bushnell.

Of Kenya to the United Nations
Ambassador: Njuguna M. Mahugu, OGW.

Of Kenya to the European Union
Ambassador: Philip Mwanzia.

FURTHER READING
Coger, D., *Kenya*. [Bibliography] 2nd ed. London and Santa Barbara (CA), 1996
Haugerud, A., *The Culture of Politics in Modern Kenya*. CUP, 1995
Miller, N. N., *Kenya: the Quest for Prosperity*. 2nd ed. Boulder (CO), 1994
Ochieng, W. R., (ed.) *Themes in Kenyan History*. Nairobi and Ohio Univ. Press, 1990
Ogot, B. A. and Ochieng, W. R. (eds.) *Decolonization and Independence in Kenya, 1940–93*. London, 1995
Widner, J. A., *The Rise of a Party State in Kenya: from 'Harambee' to 'Nayayo'*. Univ. of California Press, 1993

National statistical office: Central Bureau of Statistics, Ministry of Planning and National Development, POB 30266, Nairobi

KIRIBATI

Ribaberikin Kiribati

(Republic of Kiribati)

Capital: Bairiki (Tarawa)
Population estimate, 2000: 87,000
Estimated GDP: $62m.

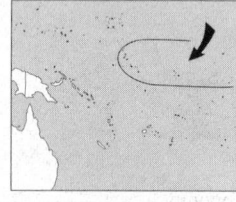

KEY HISTORICAL EVENTS
The islands that now constitute Kiribati were first settled by early Austronesian-speaking peoples long before the 1st century AD. Fijians and Tongans arrived about the 14th century and subsequently merged with the older groups to form the traditional I-Kiribati Micronesian society and culture. The Gilbert and Ellice Islands were proclaimed a British protectorate in 1892 and annexed at the request of the native governments as the Gilbert and Ellice Islands Colony on 10 Nov. 1915 (effective on 12 Jan. 1916). Formally part of the British Colony of Gilbert and Ellice Islands, which separated into two parts in 1976, the Gilberts achieved full independence as Kiribati in 1979. Internal self-government was obtained on 1 Nov. 1976 and independence achieved on 12 July 1979 as the Republic of Kiribati. On 1 Oct. 1975 the former Ellice Islands severed constitutional links with the Gilbert Islands and took on a new name, Tuvalu.

TERRITORY AND POPULATION
Kiribati (pronounced Kiribahss) consists of 3 groups of coral atolls and one isolated volcanic island, spread over a large expanse of the Central Pacific with a total land area of 717·1 sq. km (276·9 sq. miles). It comprises **Banaba** or Ocean Island (5 sq. km), the 16 **Gilbert Islands** (295 sq. km), the 8 **Phoenix Islands** (55 sq. km), and 8 of the 11 **Line Islands** (329 sq. km), the other 3 Line Islands (Jarvis, Palmyra and Kingman Reef) being uninhabited dependencies of the USA. The capital is the island of Bairiki in Tarawa.

Population, 1990 census, 72,298. 1997 estimate, 82,400; density, 115 per sq. km. In 2000 the population is projected to be 87,000.

In 1995 an estimated 64·3% of the population lived in rural areas. Between 1988 and 1993, 4,700 people were resettled on Teraina and Tabuaeran atolls because the main island group was overcrowded. Banaba, all 16 Gilbert Islands, Kanton (or Abariringa) in the Phoenix Islands and 3 atolls in the Line Islands (Teraina, Tabuaeran and Kiritimati—formerly Washington, Fanning and Christmas Islands respectively) are inhabited; their populations in 1990 (census) were as follows:

Banaba (Ocean Is.)	284	Abemama	3,218	Onotoa	2,112
Makin	1,762	Kuria	985	Tamana	1,396
Butaritari	3,786	Aranuka	1,002	Arorae	1,440
Marakei	2,863	Nonouti	2,766	Kanton	45
Abaiang	5,314	North Tabiteuea	3,275	Teraina	936
North Tarawa	3,648	South Tabiteuea	1,325	Tabuaeran	1,309
South Tarawa	25,154	Beru	2,909	Kiritimati	2,537
Maiana	2,184	Nikunau	2,048		

The remaining 11 atolls have no permanent population; the 7 Phoenix Islands comprise Birnie, Rawaki (formerly Phoenix), Enderbury, Manra (formerly Sydney), Orona (formerly Hull), McKean and Nikumaroro (formerly Gardner), while the others are Malden and Starbuck in the Central Line Islands, and Caroline, Flint and Vostok in the Southern Line Islands. The population is almost entirely Micronesian.

English is the official language; Gilbertese is also spoken.

SOCIAL STATISTICS
1997 births (estimate), 2,200; deaths, 600. 1997 estimated birth rate, 26·8 per 1,000 population; death rate, 7·7 per 1,000; infant mortality rate, 51·5 per 1,000 live births; life expectancy, 62·3 years. Annual growth rate, 1990–95, 1·9%.

CLIMATE
The Line Islands, Phoenix Islands and Banaba have a maritime equatorial climate, but the islands further north and south are tropical. Annual and daily ranges of temperature are small; mean annual rainfall ranges from 50" (1,250 mm) near the

equator to 120" (3,000 mm) in the north. Typhoons are prevalent (Nov.–March) and there are occasional tornadoes. Tarawa, Jan. 83°F (28·3°C), July 82°F (27·8°C). Annual rainfall 79" (1,977 mm).

CONSTITUTION AND GOVERNMENT
Under the constitution founded 12 July 1979 the republic has a unicameral legislature, the *House of Assembly* (Maneaba ni Maungatabu), comprising 41 members, 39 of whom are elected by popular vote, and 2 (the Attorney-General *ex-officio* and a representative from the Banaban community) appointed for a 4-year term. The *President* is directly elected and is both Head of State and Government.

National Anthem. 'Teirake kain Kiribati' ('Stand up, Kiribatians'); words and tune by U. Ioteba.

RECENT ELECTIONS
The last House of Assembly election, on 23 and 30 Sept. 1998, was won by the Mwaneaaban te Mauri Party, with 14 seats. 11 seats went to the Boutokanto Koaua Party and 15 to others. At the presidential election of 27 Nov. 1998 Tebururo Tito was re-elected against 2 opponents with 52·3% of votes cast.

CURRENT ADMINISTRATION
In March 1999 the government comprised:

President, Minister of Foreign Affairs and *International Trade:* Teburoro Tito (since 1 Oct. 1994, re-elected in 1998).

Vice-President, Minister of Home Affairs and *Rural Development:* Tewareka Tentoa. *Minister of Education, Science and Technology:* Willie Tokataake. *Finance and Economic Planning:* Beniamina Tinga. *Environment and Natural Resource Development:* Anote Tong. *Health, Family Planning and Social Welfare:* Kataotika Tekee. *Transport, Communications and Tourism:* Manraoi Kaiea. *Commerce, Industry and Employment:* Tanieru Awerika. *Works and Energy:* Emile Schutz. *Line and Phoenix Islands Development:* Teiraoi Tatabea.

INTERNATIONAL RELATIONS
Kiribati is a member of the Commonwealth, South Pacific Forum and the Pacific Community (formerly the South Pacific Commission), and is an ACP member state of the ACP-EU relationship.

ECONOMY
Performance. Real GDP growth was 2·5% in 1995 (1·8% in 1994).

Budget. Foreign financial aid, mainly from the UK and Japan, has amounted to 25–50% of GDP in recent years. Budget estimates for 1996 showed revenue at US$33·3m.; expenditure at US$47·7m.

Currency. The currency in use is the Australian *dollar*. The average annual inflation rate during the period 1990–96 was 6·4%.

ENERGY AND NATURAL RESOURCES
Electricity. Capacity (1994), 5,000 kW; production (1994), 10m. kWh.

Agriculture. Copra and fish represent the bulk of production and exports. The principal tree is the coconut; other food-bearing trees are the pandanus palm and the breadfruit. The only vegetable which grows in any quantity is a coarse calladium (alocasia) with the local name 'bwabwai', which is cultivated in pits; taro and sweet potatoes are also grown. Copra production (1994), 12,216 tonnes; coconuts, 65,000 tonnes. Principal livestock: pigs (10,000 in 1996) and fowl.

Fisheries. Tuna fishing is an important industry; licenses are held by the USA, Japan and the Republic of Korea. Catches in 1995 totalled approximately 24,700 tonnes, almost exclusively sea fish.

INDUSTRY
Mostly fishing and handicrafts.

Labour. The economically active population in paid employment (not including subsistence farmers) totalled 11,167 in 1990. In 1994 11% were employed in agriculture, 4% in industry, 85% in services. Some 70% of the labour force are underemployed; 2% unemployed.

INTERNATIONAL TRADE

Imports and Exports. Total exports (1995 est.), US$6·3m.; imports, US$38·6m. Main trading partners: the Fiji Islands, USA, Australia, Japan and New Zealand. Principal exports: copra, seaweed, fish; imports: foodstuffs, machinery and equipment, manufactured goods and fuel.

COMMUNICATIONS

Roads. There were (1995) 655 km of roads, of which 483 km were suitable for vehicles.

Civil Aviation. There were (1996) 20 airports (9 paved). In 1998 Air Marshall Islands operated scheduled services from Tarawa (Bonriki) to Tuvalu, the Marshall Islands and to the Fiji Islands, and Air Nauru had services to Nauru and also to the Fiji Islands.

Shipping. The main port is at Betio (Tarawa). Other ports of entry are Banaba, English Harbor and Kanton. There is also a small network of canals in the Line Islands. The merchant marine fleet (1996) had 2 vessels totalling 3,248 GRT.

Telecommunications. Main telephone lines numbered 2,500 in 1997, or 30·6 per 1,000 popualtion. There were 200 fax machines in 1995.

SOCIAL INSTITUTIONS

Justice. In 1989 Kiribati had a police force of 232 under the command of a Commissioner of Police. The Commissioner of Police is also responsible for prisons, immigration, fire service (both domestic and airport) and firearms licensing. There is a Court of Appeal and High Court, with judges at all levels appointed by the President.

Religion. In 1990, 53% of the population were Roman Catholic, 39% Protestant (Congregational); there are also small numbers of Seventh-Day Adventists, Latter-day Saints (Mormons) (6%), Baha'i and Church of God.

Education. In 1995 there were 17,017 pupils and 624 teachers at 85 primary schools and 3,532 pupils in general secondary education with (1992) 237 teachers. There is also a teachers' training college with 110 students (1995) and a marine training centre offering training for about 100 merchant seamen a year. The Tarawa Technical Institute at Betio (389 students in 1986) offers part-time technical and commercial courses.

In 1992 total expenditure on education came to 7·4% of GNP.

Health. In 1993 there were 10 doctors and 147 nurses. There was 1 hospital in 1990.

Welfare. The government maintains free medical and other services. In 1990 there were 16 doctors and 1 hospital on Tarawa with 283 beds, and dispensaries on other islands.

CULTURE

Broadcasting. Radio Kiribati, a division of the Broadcasting and Publications Authority, transmits daily in English and I-Kiribati from Tarawa. A satellite link to Australia was established in 1985. There were 17,000 radio receivers and 700 TV receivers in 1995.

Cinema. There are no cinemas. There is a private-owned projector with film shows once a week in every village on South Tarawa.

Press. There was (1991) 1 bilingual weekly newspaper.

Tourism. Tourism is in the early stages of development. In 1996 there were 3,000 foreign tourists.

DIPLOMATIC REPRESENTATIVES

Of Great Britain in Kiribati
High Commissioner: Mr M. A. C. Dibben (resides in Suva).

Of the USA in Kiribati (assigned from Majuro in the Marshall Islands)
Ambassador: Joan M. Plaisted.

FURTHER READING

Bailey, E., *The Christmas Island Story.* London, 1977
Kiribati: Aspects of History. University of South Pacific, 1979
Sabatier, E., *Astride the Equator.* Melbourne, 1978
Tearo, T., *Coming of Age.* Tarawa, 1989
Whincup, T., *Nareau's Nation.* London, 1979

KOREA

Daehan Min-kuk

(Republic of Korea)

Capital: Seoul
Population estimate, 2000: 46·88m.
GNP per capita: (PPP$) 13,080
HDI/world rank: 0·894/30

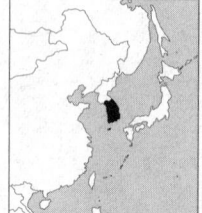

KEY HISTORICAL EVENTS

Korea was united in a single kingdom under the Silla dynasty from 668. China, which claimed a vague suzerainty over Korea, recognized the latter's independence in 1895. Korea concluded trade agreements with the USA in 1882 and with Great Britain and Germany in 1883. After the Russo-Japanese war of 1904–05, Korea was virtually a Japanese protectorate. On 29 Aug. 1910 it was formally annexed by Japan, thus ending 600 years of Confucian rule under the Yi dynasty.

Following the collapse of Japan in 1945, American and Soviet forces entered Korea to enforce the surrender of the Japanese troops, dividing the country into portions separated by the 38th parallel of latitude. Negotiations between the Americans and the Russians regarding the future of Korea broke down in May 1946. In 1948 two separate states were proclaimed. In the south, Syngman Rhee, former president of the Korean government in exile, was elected president of the Republic of Korea, which was recognized by the UN as the only legal government of Korea. In the north, Kim Il-sung, a major in the Red Army who had marched back into Korea with the Soviet forces, was proclaimed premier of the Democratic Peoples' Republic of Korea—which was recognized by the USSR as the only legal government of Korea.

The US occupation forces withdrew from South Korea in June 1949. Military equipment promised by the USA as part of their aid programme was still on its way to Korea when the North Koreans launched, in June 1950, a full-scale invasion across the 38th parallel. The next day the Security Council of the UN approved a resolution condemning the invasion and asking all member-states to assist in the restoration of peace.

The war, in which North Korea received support from the Chinese army and South Korea from the UN forces and the USA, lasted for three years, killed some 5m. people and destroyed an estimated 43% of Korea's industrial plant and 33% of her homes. It was concluded by an armistice signed on 27 July 1953 which implicitly recognized the 38th parallel and the *de facto* boundary between North and South Korea.

Twelve years of Syngman Rhee's authoritarian rule collapsed after student demonstrations brought the country to the brink of civil war in April 1960. There followed nine months of multi-party parliamentary government. A military coup in May 1961 led to the dissolution of the National Assembly, the introduction of martial law and the establishment of Gen. Park Chung Hee as president for the next 17 years. Park's assassination in Oct. 1979 threw the country again into a state of crisis. The prime minister, Choi Kyu Hah, became President until Aug. 1980. He was succeeded by Gen. Chun Doo Hwan who was re-elected under a revised constitution in March 1981 and retained his majority again in Feb. 1985. A new, more democratic, constitution, approved by both ruling and opposition parties, came into force in 1988.

On 13 Dec. 1991 the prime ministers of North and South Korea signed a declaration of non-aggression and reconciliation, agreeing to respect each other's political systems, and not to interfere in each other's internal affairs or slander each other.

The Four-Party Meeting to Promote Peace on the Korean Peninsula (South Korea, North Korea, USA and China) held the first plenary session in Geneva, Switzerland in Dec. 1997.

Security worries in the region were stirred up again on 31 Aug. 1998 when North Korea launched what was first thought to be a new medium-range ballistic missile, but was later believed to be a satellite, across Japan into the Pacific Ocean.

KOREA

After many months of little progress, there was a significant development in The Four-Party Meeting to Promote Peace on the Korean Peninsula at a further session in Geneva in Oct. 1998, with the establishment of sub-committees to look into the most important issues in detail.

TERRITORY AND POPULATION
South Korea is bounded in the north by the demilitarized zone (separating it from North Korea), east by the East Sea (Sea of Japan), south by the Korea Strait (separating it from Japan) and west by the Yellow Sea. The area is 99,392 sq. km. The population (census, 1 Nov. 1990) was 43,412,000 (urban, 74·4%). Results of an official survey in Nov. 1995, 44,608,726 (22,219,402 females) (84% urban); density, 454·3 per sq. km. Population estimate, July 1998, 46·43m; density, 467·2 per sq. km.

The UN gives a projected population for 2000 of 46·88m.

The official language is Korean.

There are 9 provinces (*do*) and 7 cities with provincial status. Area and population in 1998:

Province	Area (in sq. km)	Population (in 1,000)	Province	Area (in sq. km)	Population (in 1,000)
Seoul (city)	606	10,289	Kangwon	16,814	1,548
Pusan (city)	751	3,865	North Chungchong	7,433	1,521
Taegu (city)	886	2,490	South Chungchong	8,590	1,909
Inchon (city)	958	2,470	North Cholla	8,047	2,006
Kwangju (city)	501	1,334	South Cholla	11,956	2,166
Taejon (city)	540	1,323	North Kyongsang	19,021	2,806
Ulsan (city)	1,056	1,013	South Kyongsang	11,511	3,061
Kyonggi	10,190	8,514	Cheju	1,846	528

Cities with over 500,000 inhabitants (census 1995):

Seoul	10,231,217	Ulsan	967,429	Chonchu	563,153
Pusan	3,814,325	Seongnam	869,094	Chongchu	531,376
Taegu	2,449,420	Puchon	779,412	Ko-yank	518,282
Inchon	2,308,188	Suwon	755,550	Ansan	510,314
Taejon	1,272,121	Anyang	591,106	Pohang	508,899
Kwangchu	1,257,636				

SOCIAL STATISTICS
1996 births, 725,000; deaths, 272,000. Rates per 1,000 population in 1997: Birth, 14·6; death, 5·3; growth, 0·98%. Expectation of life, 77·4 years for females and 69·5 for males. In 1955 life expectancy had been 47. Infant mortality, 1990–95, 11 per 1,000 live births; fertility rate, 1·7 births per woman. There were 12·96m. households in 1995, with on average 3·3 members per household. In 1998, 13,974 South Koreans emigrated. Between 1962 and 1998 a total of 847,714 Koreans emigrated, 77·8% of them to the USA.

5·5m. Koreans lived abroad in 1997.

CLIMATE
The country experiences continental temperate conditions. Rainfall is concentrated in the period April to Sept. and ranges from 40" (1,020 mm) to 60" (1,520 mm). Pusan, Jan. 36°F (2·2°C), July 76°F (24·4°C). Annual rainfall 56" (1,407 mm). Seoul, Jan. 23°F (–5°C), July 77°F (25°C). Annual rainfall 50" (1,250 mm).

CONSTITUTION AND GOVERNMENT
The 1988 Constitution provides for a *President*, directly elected for a single 5-year term, who appoints the members of the *State Council* and heads it, and for a *National Assembly* (299 members) directly elected for 4 years (253 from constituencies and 46 from party lists in proportion to the overall vote).

The minimum voting age is 20.

National Anthem. 'Aegukka' ('A Song of Love for the Country'); words anonymous, tune by Ahm Eaktay.

RECENT ELECTIONS

Presidential elections were held on 18 Dec. 1997. In the closest political contest in Korea's history, Kim Dae-jung, the standard-bearer of a generation of pro-democracy campaigners, was elected with 40·4% of votes against 38·6% for Lee Hoi-chang, the candidate of the governing party. The next presidential election is due on 19 Dec. 2002.

Elections to the National Assembly were held on 11 April 1996. 1,389 candidates stood. The electorate was 31,488,294; turn-out was 63·9%. The New Korea Party (since renamed the Grand National Party) won 139 seats with 34·5% of votes cast; the National Congress for New Politics, 79 with 25·3%; the United Liberal Democrats, 50 with 16·2%; the Democratic Party, 15 with 11·2%; ind, 16 with 11·9%. Following defections from the opposition to the ruling parties, in Jan. 1999 the ruling coalition made up of the National Congress for New Politics (the party of President Kim Dae-jung) and the United Liberal Democrats gained a majority in the National Assembly with 158 seats against 136 for the opposition and 4 ind.

CURRENT ADMINISTRATION

President: Kim Dae-jung, b. 1925 (National Congress for New Politics; sworn in 25 Feb. 1998).

On 23 Feb. 1998 Kim Dae-jung nominated his former political rival Kim Jong-pil (United Liberal Democrats) as his *Prime Minister*. His nomination was finally approved on 17 Aug.

The cabinet in March 1999 comprised:

Prime Minister: Kim Jong-pil.

Minister of Agriculture and Forestry: Kim Sung-hoon. *Commerce, Industry and Energy:* Park Tae-young. *Construction and Transportation:* Lee Yung Moo. *Culture and Tourism:* Shin Nakyun. *Education:* Lee Hai Chan. *Environment:* Choi Jae-wook. *Finance and Economy:* Lee Kyu-sung. *Foreign Affairs and Trade:* Hong Soon-young. *Government Administration and Home Affairs:* Kim Ki-chae. *Health and Welfare:* Kim Mo Im. *Information and Communication:* Namgoong Suek. *Justice:* Pak Sang-cheon. *Labour Affairs:* Lee Ki-ho. *Maritime Affairs and Fisheries:* Chong Wa Dae. *National Defence:* Chun Yong Taek. *Science and Technology:* Seo Jung-uck. *Unification:* Kang In Duk.

Speaker: Park Jyun-kyu.

Local Government. The 16 provinces are divided into 91 districts (*Gun*) and 72 cities (*Shi*). Elections were held on 4 June 1998 for the 9 provinces and 7 cities of provincial status and 4,338 other local government posts. The NCNP gained 6 governorships, the GNP 6, and the ULD 4.

DEFENCE

Peacetime operational control, which had been transferred to the United Nations Command (UNC) under a US general in July 1950 after the outbreak of the Korean War, was restored to South Korea on 1 Dec. 1994. In the event of a new crisis, operational control over the Korean armed forces will revert to CFC. Conscription is 26 months in the Army, 28 months in the Navy and 30 months in the Air Force. Conscripts may choose or be required to exchange military service for civilian work.

Defence expenditure in 1997 totalled US$14,732m. (US$320 per capita).

Army. The Army is organized in 19 infantry and 3 mechanized infantry divisions, 2 independent infantry brigades, 7 special forces brigades, 3 air defence artillery brigades, 3 counter-infiltration brigades, 1 army aviation command, 5 surface-to-air and 3 surface-to-surface missile battalions. Equipment includes 800 Type 88, 400 M-47 and 850 M-48A5 main battle tanks. Army aviation equipment includes 250 Hughes 500 and McDonnell Douglas 530 and 60 AH-1F helicopters for anti-armour operations, observation and liaison, and 18 CH-47D transport helicopters and 70 Bell UH-1 utility helicopters. Delivery of 150 UH-60 Black Hawk transport helicopters began in 1991 and continued through to 1998. Strength (1997) 548,000 (140,000 conscripts). Paramilitary Civilian Defence Corps, 3·5m.

Navy. A substantial force of 60,000 (19,000 conscripts), including 25,000 marines (1996), continues its steady modernization programme. Current strength includes 4 German-designed ocean-going diesel submarines, 3 midget submarines (175 tonnes), 7 aged (1943–46) ex-US destroyers, and 33 locally-built frigates with modern US and European weapons, 4 corvettes, 11 fast missile craft, together with a patrol force of 100 inshore craft. There are 14 coastal mine counter-measure vessels and an amphibious force of 8 tank landing ships and 7 medium landing ships, together with 35 amphibious craft. Major auxiliaries include 2 replenishment and 2 transport tankers, 2 large tugs, 4 survey vessels and 35 service craft. The Navy aviation element operates 8 P-3-C Orion, 15 shore-based S-2E Tracker anti-submarine aircraft and 25 Hughes 500MD, 12 Super-Lynx and 10 Alouette helicopters, some of which embark in frigates and destroyers.

The main bases are at Chinhae, Inchon and Pusan.

The Coastguard numbering some 5,000 (mostly shore-based) operates 10 offshore, 26 coastal and 38 inshore patrol craft as well as 9 light helicopters.

Air Force. In 1996 the Air Force had a strength of 52,000 men and 450 combat aircraft. Its combat aircraft include 100 F-16C/D Fighting Falcons, about 180 F-4D/E Phantoms, 200 F-5E/F tactical fighters, 15 RF-4E Phantom reconnaissance fighters, 10 O-2A and 10 OV-1 forward air control aircraft and 10 Hughes 500 Defender helicopters. There are also 12 CN-235, 10 C-130 Hercules turboprop-engined transports, 2 HS.748s, 1 Boeing 737 for VIP transport; UH-1, Bell 212 and Bell 412 transport helicopters, and Hawk T-41, T-33, T-37C and T-38 trainers.

INTERNATIONAL RELATIONS

Defections to South Korea from North Korea totalled 86 in 1997, up from 40 in 1995 and 8 in 1993.

South Korea is a member of the UN and OECD.

The aim of Korea's foreign policy is to secure international support for peace and stability in Northeast Asia, including a means to reunify the Korean Peninsula without confrontation.

ECONOMY

Policy. The seventh 5-year social and economic plan (1993–97) aimed at controlling growth and strengthening national competitiveness. Part of the plan ('the core industrial sector system') was to make the powerful family-owned conglomerates (*chaebol*) more competitive by restricting the industrial areas in which they may engage. Results so far have been mixed. Samsung and the SK Group have restructured but others in the top 5 are resisting change.

After thirty years of impressive economic growth, South Korea was hit by financial crisis in 1997 when it became clear that the *chaebol* had been allowed to borrow too heavily against inadequate returns. In Dec. 1997, Korea's international debts were estimated at US$200,000m. An IMF and World Bank rescue was tied to undertakings to transform the economy into one based on market principles instead of state directives. Korea's lack of foreign reserves was also identified as a major problem, thus assistance was secured from the IMF and other global financial institutions totalling US$58·3bn. Reforms so far approved by the National Assembly include greater monetary policy independence for the central bank, a new structure for financial negotiations and the lifting of the 50% ceiling on foreign ownership of listed Korean companies. During 1998 the government tightened accounting rules to make business more open, gave minority shareholders and institutional investors more say in corporate affairs and opened South Korea's capital markets. A genuine attempt is also being made to welcome foreign investors; foreign investment, which stood at US$8·9bn. in 1998, is expected almost to double in 1999.

A schedule for privatization was announced in July 1998, whereby out of 24 non-financial state owned enterprises (parent companies), 11 would be privatized in stages by 2002. In addition, the 61 subsidiaries of these 24 parent companies would also be privatized immediately or in stages. It was hoped this scheme would raise US$10bn. from foreign investors by 2002.

Performance. GDP growth rate was 5·0% in 1997 (6·8% in 1996 and 8·9% in 1995), but fell to –5·8% for 1998. In 1999 the rate was expected to be 3·8%. Between 1990 and 1996 the average annual real growth in GNP per capita was 6·2%.

It is unlikely that South Korea would be strong enough to face unification unaided. In Dec. 1997 South Korea turned to the IMF for a US$58bn. bail-out. External liabilities by Nov. 1998 were estimated to be US$152·5bn.

Budget. Revenue and expenditure (in 1,000,000m. won), including bond insurance, at the 1999 budget: 84·9 and 84·9. Sources of revenue: National tax, 61·9; non-tax, 18·2. Expenditure includes: defence, 13·7; infrastructure, 12·2; education, 17·4; agriculture and fisheries, 8·1; technology, 3·8; environment, 1·8.

Currency. The unit of currency is the *won* (KRW). Inflation was 8·5% in 1998. Usable foreign exchange reserves were US$48·51bn. in Jan. 1999, up from US$8·9bn. in 1997. Gold reserves were 330,000 troy oz. in Feb. 1998. Total money supply in Jan. 1998 was 34,891bn. won.

Banking and Finance. The central bank and bank of issue is the Bank of Korea (*Governor*, Chol-hwan Chon). In Sept. 1998 bank deposits totalled 462,000,000m. won, of which 199,000,000m. won were savings and time deposits.

There are 22 national and provincial commercial banks. The largest bank is Hanvit Bank, formed in Feb. 1999 through the merger of Commercial Bank of Korea and Hanil Bank, their combined assets totalling 102,000,000m. won (US$82bn.). There were 73 foreign banks in Dec. 1998. These are granted parity of treatment with domestic banks.

In addition, there are non-bank financial institutions including 45 insurance companies such as the Land Bank of Korea, the Credit Guarantee Fund, and 14 merchant banks. The use of real names in financial dealings has been required since 1994.

There is a stock exchange in Seoul.

Weights and Measures. The metric system is in use alongside traditional measures. 1 *sok* = 144 kg. 1 *pyong* = 3·3 sq. metres.

ENERGY AND NATURAL RESOURCES

Electricity. Installed capacity in 1997 was 41·04m. kW. Electricity generated (1997) was 224,440m. kWh. Sources of power in 1997: Nuclear, 34·4%; oil, 19·1%; coal, 29·9%; liquefied natural gas, 14·2%; hydro-electric, 2·4%. Consumption per capita in 1997 was estimated to be 4,366 kWh.

Oil and Gas. In 1997 the imports of petroleum products reached 1,032m. bbls., of which crude oil was 873·4m. bbls. The output of petroleum products was 878·1m. bbls., consumption 748·5m. bbls. and the volume of exports 230·1m. bbls. Crude oil imports in 1997 reached 873·4m. bbls.

In 1997 the imports of natural gas totalled 11·6m. tonnes, consumption 11·4m. tonnes; inventory 605,000 tonnes. The cost of import was US$2,295m. The total output of city gas in 1997 reached 7,764m. cu. metres and consumption 7,897m. cu. metres of which 5,046m. cu. metres was used for household purposes, 1,428m. cu. metres for commercial use, and 1,423m. cu. metres for industrial use.

Water. Water consumption in 1994 was 23,670m. cu. metres, of which 6,210m. cu. metres was supplied to households, 2,580m. cu. metres for industrial use, and 14,880m. cu. metres for agricultural purposes. Of the total population, 83·6% had tap water in 1996 and per capita supply was 409 litres per day. As of 1997, there were 732 dams with walls higher than 15 metres and containing a total of 16,681m. cu. metres of water.

Minerals. In 1997, 1,606 mining companies employed 15,735 people. Output, 1997, included (in tonnes): Anthracite coal, 4·51m.; iron ore, 0·3m.; limestone, 92m.; graphite, 59,100 (1993); lead ore, 7,264; zinc ore, 17,984.

Agriculture. Agriculture accounted for 6% of GDP in 1996. Cultivated land was 1·92m. ha in 1997, of which 1·16m. ha were rice paddies. In 1997, the farming population was 4·47m. and in 1997 there were 1·44m. farms. The agricultural workforce was 2·2m. in 1996.

In 1997, 1·05m. ha were sown to rice. Production (1997, in tonnes): Rice, 5,450,000; barley, 258,680; wheat, 7,433; potatoes, 637,621; beans, 181,738. There were 131,358 tractors in 1997.

Livestock in 1997 (in 1,000): Cows, 3,396; pigs, 7,096; sheep, 605; chickens, 88,251.

Forestry. Forest area was 6·44m. ha in 1997 (77·2% of the land area). Total stock (1997) was 341·0m. cu. metres. In 1997, 71% of the total forest area was privately owned. Timber production was 0·84m. cu. metres in 1997.

Fisheries. In 1997, there were a total of 81,000 boats (971,808 gross tonnes). 637 deep-sea fishing vessels were operating overseas in 1997. The fish catch (inland and marine) was 3·24m. tonnes in 1997.

INDUSTRY

Manufacturing industry is concentrated primarily on oil, petro-chemicals, chemical fibres, construction, iron and steel, cement, machinery, chips, shipbuilding, automobiles and electronics. Tobacco manufacture is a government monopoly. Industry is dominated by giant conglomerates (*chaebol*). There were 2·77m. businesses in 1995, of which 224,654 were incorporated. 521,496 businesses were in catering, 314,283 in manufacturing, 298,136 in services and 211,425 in transport and communications. In Sept. 1998 the five leading *chaebol* launched a series of industrial mergers in response to demands by the government to consolidate their weakest businesses.

Production in 1997: Petrol products, 878·1m. bbls.; cars, 2·3m. units; microwave ovens, 12m; (in 1,000 sq. metres): Cotton fabrics, 461,011; silk fabrics, 32,702; synthetic fabrics, 7,720; (in 1,000 tonnes): Paper and products, 8,365; artificial fertilizers, 3,983; plastic products, 4,076; pig-iron, 22,712; steel bars, 1,747; steel sections, 4,037.

South Korea is the world's largest producer of memory chips, second to Japan for shipbuilding, and the fifth largest car maker.

Industry and mining accounted for 25·9% of GDP in 1997.

Labour. At June 1998 the population of working age (15 to 59 years) was 35·23m. The economically-active population was 21·71m.; 1·52m. were registered unemployed. In June 1998, 3·79m. persons were employed in manufacturing, 10·2m. in services, 1·61m. in building, 19,000 in mining and 2·76m. in agriculture, fisheries and forestry. 5·82m. persons were self-employed in June 1998. Unemployment, which was 2·6% in 1997, had soared to 8·7% by Feb. 1999. An annual legal minimum wage is set by the *Minimum Wage Council* each Sept. applicable to firms with more than 10 employees; in 1998 it was 12,200 won per day. In June 1998 the average monthly wage was 1·5m. The working week averaged 45·5 hours in 1998.

Legislation abolishing security of job tenure and giving employers powers to introduce flexible working hours and use substitute labour in the event of strikes was passed in March 1997. In addition, in the wake of the financial crisis, labour reforms were carried out including revision of the labour law aimed at, among other things, legalizing dismissals of workers for managerial reasons.

Trade Unions. In 1997 there were 5,733 unions with a total membership of 1,484,194. The government-recognized Federation of Korean Trade Unions groups 0·93m. of these. Since 1997 unions have been permitted to engage in political activities, and the ban on more than one union in a work place was abolished in 1998.

INTERNATIONAL TRADE

Foreign debt was US$152,448m. at Nov. 1998. In May 1998, the Government removed restrictions on foreign investment in the Korean stock market. It also began to allow foreign businesses to engage in mergers and acquisitions. From July 1998, foreigners were allowed to buy plots of land for both business and non-business purposes. Since Aug. 1990 South Korean businesses and individuals have been permitted to make investments and set up branch offices in North Korea, on an approval basis. South Korea donated 0·15m. tonnes of rice to North Korea in 1995 and in the period 1995–98 provided US$273m. of financial assistance as well.

Imports and Exports. At Dec. 1998 exports were US$133,223m.; imports, US$93,344m. Main import suppliers (in US$1m.): USA, 19,768; Japan, 16,278;

China, 6,274. Main export markets: USA, 21,781; Japan, 11,866; Germany, 3,922; China, 11,450.

Major exports in 1998 (provisional figures) included (in US$1m.): Transistors and chips, 16,246; textiles, 8,488; clothing, 5,320; ships, 7,095; motor cars, 9,239; iron and steel, 7,678; electrical appliances, 5,057; office machines, 5,090; chemicals, 9,298. Major imports included: Machinery and transport equipment, 13,509; minerals, 20,001; chemicals, 16,252; semi-conductors, 11,871; agricultural produce, 6,562. Rice imports were prohibited until 1994, but following the GATT Uruguay Round the rice market opened to foreign imports in 1995.

Trade Fairs. In 1998 there were 122 trade fairs, and 1,402 Korean companies participated in trade fairs held in 70 other countries.

COMMUNICATIONS

Roads. In 1997 there were 84,968 km of roads. 28·3m. passengers and 1,979·5m. tonnes of freight were carried in 1996. In 1997 motor vehicles registered totalled 9,964,000 including 2,072,256 trucks, 719,127 buses and 7,586,474 passenger cars. There were 11,603 road deaths in 1997, the highest total in a year since 1991.

Rail. In 1997 the National Railroad totalled 3,098 km of 1,435 mm gauge (661·3 km electrified) and 20 km of 762 mm gauge. In 1997 railways carried 832m. passengers and 53·8m. tonnes of freight.

There are metros in Seoul (218·4 km) and Pusan (35·2 km).

Civil Aviation. There are international airports at Seoul (Kimpo), Pusan (Kimhae), Taegu and Cheju. The national carrier is Korean Air. Another Korean carrier, Asiana Airlines, also provides services, as did in 1998 the foreign airlines Aeroflot, Air Canada, Air China, Air France, Alitalia, All Nippon Airways, American Airlines, Cathay Pacific Airways, China Eastern Airlines, China Northern Airlines, China Southern Airlines, Delta Air Lines, Garuda Indonesia, JAL, Japan Air System, KLM, Lufthansa, Malaysia Airlines, MIAT-Mongolian Airlines, Northwest Airlines, Philippine Airlines, Qantas Airways, Singapore Airlines, Thai Airways International, United Airlines, Uzbekiston Airways, VASP, Vietnam Airlines and Vladivostok Air. In 1998, 19·5m.passengers and 0·3m. tonnes of cargo were carried on domestic routes and 14·1m. passengers and 1·5m. tonnes of cargo on international routes.

Shipping. In 1998 there were 50 ports, including 28 for international trade. In 1997 the merchant marine comprised 562 vessels totalling 25·15m. DWT, representing 3·4% of the world's tonnage. 298 vessels (66·87% of gross tonnage) were registered under foreign flags. Total GRT, 7·42m., including oil tankers, 0·38m. GRT and container ships, 1·42m. GRT. 9·89m. passengers and 144m. tonnes of freight were carried on domestic routes in 1997, and 0·56m. passengers and 485·03m. tonnes of cargo on international routes.

Telecommunications. There were 20,421,900 main telephone lines in 1997 (444 per 1,000 persons). In Feb. 1999 the Minstry of Information and Communication announced plans to digitize the country's entire phone switching system by 2001. In 1997 public telephones totalled 423,502, and 7·04m. cellular phones were in use. In 1995 there were 5,420,000 PCs (121 per 1,000 persons) and 375,000 fax machines. There were approximately 3·1m. Internet users in Jan. 1999.

Postal Services. Post offices totalled 3,596 in 1997.

SOCIAL INSTITUTIONS

Justice. Judicial power is vested in the Supreme Court, High Courts, District Courts and Family Court, as well as the Administrative Court and Patent Court. The single 6-year term Chief Justice is appointed by the President with the consent of the National Assembly. The other 13 Justices of the Supreme Court are appointed by the President with the consent of the National Assembly, upon the recommendation of the Chief Justice, for renewable 6-year terms; the Chief Justice appoints other judges. The President appoints the Prosecutor-General. The death penalty is authorized.

Religion. The main religions have been Shamanism, Buddhism (introduced AD 372) and Confucianism, which was the official faith from 1392 to 1910. Catholic converts from China introduced Christianity in the 18th century, but a ban on Roman Catholicism was not lifted until 1882. The Anglican Church was introduced in 1890 and became an independent jurisdiction in 1993 under the Archbishop of Korea. In 1998 it had 110 churches, 175 priests and some 65,000 faithful. Religious affiliations of the population in 1995 (and 1985): Buddhism, 23·2% (27·7%); Protestantism, 19·7% (18·6%); Roman Catholicism, 6·6% (5·7%); Confucianism, 0·5% (1%); others, 0·7% (1%); no religion, 49·3% (46%).

Education. After 1 or 2 years of kindergarten, education is compulsory from 6 to 12, followed by the options of middle school until 15 and general or vocational high school to 18.

In 1997–98 there were 8,973 kindergartens with 533,912 pupils and 26,721 teachers; 5,688 elementary schools with 3,834,561 pupils and 140,121 teachers; and 4,388,348 pupils and 201,961 teachers at secondary schools. In 1997–98 there were 158 junior colleges with 804,335 students and 10,966 teachers; 11 Universities of Education with 20,969 students and 693 teachers; 156 colleges and universities with 1,477,715 students and 40,345 teachers; 18 open colleges with 146,563 students and 2,019 teachers; and 280 other institutions with 394,430 students and 5,809 teachers.

The adult literacy was 98% in 1995 (99·3% among males and 96·7% among females).

Around 133,000 South Koreans were studying abroad in 1997.

Health. In 1997 there were 262 general hospitals (with 101,615 beds), 16,381 other hospitals and clinics (112,293 beds), 6,446 oriental medical hospitals and clinics (5,702 beds) and 9,243 dental hospitals and clinics. In 1997 there were 62,609 physicians (735 people per doctor), 9,289 oriental medical doctors, 15,383 dentists, 8,516 midwives (1992), 133,920 nurses and 45,820 pharmacists.

Welfare. In 1997, 7·84m. persons were covered by the National Pension System introduced in 1988. Employers and employees make equal contributions; persons joining by choice or in rural areas pay their own contributions. The System covers age pensions, disability payments and survivors' pensions. Recipients of benefit in 1997 included: Public livelihood aid, 1·41m.; veterans, 197,349.

Under a system of unemployment insurance introduced in March 1998, workers laid off after working at least 6 months for a member employer are entitled to benefits averaging 50% of their previous wage for a period of 60 to 210 days.

CULTURE

Broadcasting. The Korean Broadcasting System (KBS) is a public corporation which broadcasts 6 radio channels, 2 terrestrial TV channels, 2 satellite TV channels and 1 special broadcasting channel for the disabled. KBS maintains a nationwide network that connects the key station in Seoul with 25 local stations. It also maintains 9 bureaux overseas. In addition to KBS, there is another public TV broadcaster (MBC) and 1 commercial TV network (SBS). The first 4 local commercial TV stations based in major cities began in 1994, and the second group of 4 began in 1997. Cable TV was inaugurated in March 1995 and had 825,000 paying subscribers in 1998. There were 46m. radio receivers in 1995 and 16m. television receivers in 1997.

Cinema. In 1997 there were 497 cinemas with a seating capacity of 181,742. 59 full-length films were produced in 1997.

Press. There were 387 dailies in 1998 and 6,783 periodicals.

Tourism. In 1998, approximately 3,061,000 Koreans travelled abroad and 4,257,000 foreign nationals visited South Korea (4,542,159 in 1997). In 1998 tourist revenues from foreign visitors totalled US$5·76bn.; overseas travel expenditure by Koreans going abroad totalled US$2·09bn. On 18 Nov. 1998 the first South Korean tourists to visit North Korea set sail on a cruise and tour organized by the South Korean firm Hyundai.

Festivals. As of Nov. 1996 there were 412 regional festivals, 66 of which were centred on traditional religious rituals, arts or folk games. The rest included exhibitions of modern art and handicrafts, athletic events and entertainment programmes.

South and North Korean musicians gave a joint concert at the 'Yun Isang Unification Music Festival' in Pyongyang, North Korea on 4 Nov. 1998.

Libraries. There were 9,854 libraries in 1997, including 1 national library, 1 congressional, 370 public, 388 university and 8,651 libraries at primary, middle and high schools. There were also 443 specialized and professional libraries.

National Theatre and Opera. There are 142 national or public theatres and 200 private theatres. The Seoul Arts Centre has an opera house.

Museums and Galleries. At 1997 there were 233 museums, including 25 national museums, 33 public museums, 94 private museums and 81 university museums. As of 1997 there were an estimated 500 art galleries.

DIPLOMATIC REPRESENTATIVES

Of the Republic of Korea in Great Britain (60 Buckingham Gate, London, SW1E 6AJ)
Ambassador: Choi Dong-Jin.

Of Great Britain in the Republic of Korea (4 Chung-Dong, Chung-Ku, Seoul 100-120)
Ambassador: Stephen D. R. Brown.

Of the Republic of Korea in the USA (2370 Massachusetts Ave., NW, Washington, D.C., 20008)
Ambassador: Hong-Koo Lee.

Of the USA in the Republic of Korea (82 Sejong-Ro, Chongro-ku, Seoul)
Ambassador: Stephen W. Bosworth.

Of the Republic of Korea to the United Nations
Ambassador: Lee See-Young.

Of the Republic of Korea to the European Union
Ambassador: Jai-Chun Lee.

FURTHER READING
National Bureau of Statistics. *Korea Statistical Yearbook*
Bank of Korea. *Economic Statistics Yearbook*
Castley, R., *Korea's Economic Miracle*. London, 1997
Cumings, B., *Korea's Place in the Sun: A Modern History*. New York, 1997
Das, D. K., *Korean Economic Dynamism*. London, 1991
Eckert, C. J. *et al., Korea Old and New: a History*. Harvard Univ. Press, 1991
Gibney, F., *Korea's Quiet Revolution: from Garrison State to Democracy*. New York, 1992
Hoare, James E., *Korea* [Bibliography]. Oxford and Santa Barbara (CA), 1997
Kang, M.-H. *The Korean Business Conglomerate: Chaebol Then and Now*. Univ. of California Press, 1996
Kim, D.-H. and Tat, Y.-K. (*eds.*) *The Korean Peninsula in Transition*. London, 1997
Simons, G., *Korea: the Search for Sovereignty*. London, 1995
Song, P.-N., *The Rise of the Korean Economy*. 2nd ed. OUP, 1994
Tennant, R., *A History of Korea*. London, 1996

National statistical office: National Bureau of Statistics, Ministry of Finance and Economy, Seoul

NORTH KOREA

Chosun Minchu-chui Inmin Konghwa-guk
(People's Democratic Republic of Korea)

Capital: Pyongyang
Population estimate, 2000: 23·91m.
Estimated GDP: \$20·9m.
HDI/world rank: 0·766/75

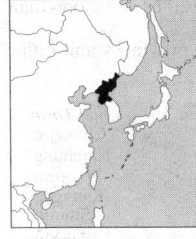

KEY HISTORICAL EVENTS

Following the collapse of Japan in 1945 Soviet forces arrived in North Korea, one month ahead of the Americans, and established a Communist-led provisional government. The newly created Korean Workers' (i.e. Communist) Party, with other pro-Communist groups and individuals, formed the United Democratic front. On 25 Aug. 1948 the Communists organized elections for a Supreme People's Assembly, both in the Soviet-occupied north and the American-occupied south; some southern deputies went to the north and took their seats. A People's Democratic Republic was proclaimed on 9 Sept. 1948 and Kim Il-sung became premier, purging all rivals.

On 25 June 1950 North Korea invaded the south; its advance was stopped with the aid of UN forces. Chinese Communist 'volunteers' joined the war in Oct. 1950. Truce negotiations were begun in 1951 and concluded on 27 July 1953. A demilitarized zone was set up along the final battle line between North and South Korea.

On 13 Dec. 1991 the prime ministers of North and South Korea signed a declaration of non-aggression, agreeing not to interfere in each other's internal affairs. 3 agreements were reached between the North and South Korean prime ministers in 1992 on proposals for military, economic, political and social co-operation.

Kim Il-sung, head of state, Communist Party and the military since 1948, died on 8 July 1994, and was succeeded by his son, Kim Jong Il, who was formally elected general-secretary of the ruling North Korean Workers' Party in Oct. 1997.

In June 1993, after negotiations with the USA, North Korea reversed its decision to withdraw from the Nuclear Non-Proliferation Treaty. On 21 Oct. 1994 an agreement to restrict nuclear power to peaceful purposes in Korea was signed by North Korea and the USA. Talks on setting up a four-way peace conference involving the USA, China and North and South Korea broke down in Sept. 1997 on the question of food aid as a precondition of negotiations. Initial problems were subsequently resolved and the Four-Party Meeting to Promote Peace on the Korean Peninsula, with representatives from the four countries, held the first plenary session at Geneva, Switzerland in Dec. 1997.

Although food aid has been stepped up, the UN World Food Programme estimated in 1997 that 2m. North Koreans face starvation. An American congressional delegation estimated in 1998 that famine has killed between 300,000 and 800,000 North Koreans in each of the previous 3 years.

Celebrating its 50th anniversary in 1998, North Korea confirmed Kim Jong II as paramount leader and military supreme commander.

Security worries in the region were stirred up again on 31 Aug. 1998 when North Korea launched what was first thought to be a new medium-range ballistic missile, but was later believed to be a satellite, across Japan into the Pacific Ocean.

After many months of little progress, there was a significant development in The Four-Party Meeting to Promote Peace on the Korean Peninsula at a further session in Geneva in Oct. 1998, with the establishment of sub-committees to look into the most important issues in detail. Since then, North Korea has called on the USA to pay US\$300m. to inspect an underground site which the Americans suspect is part of a revived programme to develop nuclear weapons.

TERRITORY AND POPULATION

North Korea is bounded in the north by China, east by the sea of Japan, west by the Yellow Sea and south by South Korea, from which it is separated by a demilitarized zone of 1,262 sq. km. Its area is 122,762 sq. km. Official population estimate in 1995, 23,261,000 (64% urban); density, 187·6 per sq. km.

The UN gives a projected population for 2000 of 23·91m.

In the elections to the Supreme People's Assembly held on 26 July 1998, 687 deputies were elected, as was the case in 1990. The South Korean weekly NEWSREVIEW states that North Korea has made it a rule that there should be one deputy per 30,000 people, suggesting that the population has remained stable since 1990. 30,000 multiplied by 687 would give a population of 20·61m., more than 2·5m. less than official estimates.

The area, 1987 population (in 1,000) and chief towns of the provinces and cities with provincial status:

	Area in sq. km	Population	Chief Town
North Hamgyong	17,570	2,003	Chongjin
South Hamgyong	18,970	2,547	Hamhung
Yanggang	14,317	628	Hyesan
Chagang	16,968	1,156	Kanggye
North Pyongan	12,191	2,408	Sinuiju
South Pyongan	11,577	2,653	Pyongsan
Pyongyang (city)	2,000	2,355	
Nampo (city)	753	715	
Kangwon	11,152	1,227	Wonsan
North Hwanghae	8,007	1,409	Sariwon
Kaesong (city)	1,255	331	
South Hwanghae	8,002	1,914	Haeju

Large towns (estimate, 1984): Pyongyang, the capital (2,639,448); Chongjin (754,128); Nampo (691,284); Sinuiju (500,000); Wonsan (350,000); Kaesong (345,642); Kimchaek (281,000); Haeju (131,000); Sariwon (130,000); Hamhung (775,000 in 1981).

The official language is Korean.

SOCIAL STATISTICS

1995 births, 477,000; deaths, 122,000. 1995 birth rate, 21·6 per 1,000 population; death rate, 5·5. Annual growth rate, 1990–95, 1·9%. Marriage is discouraged before the age of 32 for men and 29 for women. Life expectancy at birth, 1990–95, was 67·7 years for males and 73·9 years for females. Infant mortality, 1990–95, 24 per 1,000 live births; fertility rate, 2·1 births per woman.

CLIMATE

There is a warm temperate climate, though winters can be very cold in the north. Rainfall is concentrated in the summer months. Pyongyang, Jan. 18°F (–7·8°C), July 75°F (23·9°C). Annual rainfall 37" (916 mm).

CONSTITUTION AND GOVERNMENT

The political structure is based upon the Constitution of 27 Dec. 1972. Constitutional amendments of April 1992 delete references to Marxism-Leninism but retain the Communist Party's monopoly of rule. The Constitution provides for a *Supreme People's Assembly* elected every 5 years by universal suffrage. Citizens of 17 years and over can vote and be elected. The government consists of the *Administration Council* directed by the Central People's Committee (*Secretary,* Chi Chang Ik).

The head of state is the *President,* elected for 4-year terms. On the death of Kim Il-sung on 8 July 1994 his son and designated successor, Kim Jong Il (b. 1942), assumed all his father's posts. On 5 Sept. 1998 he took over as President and 'Supreme Leader'.

Party membership was 2m. in 1995. There are also the puppet religious Chongu and Korean Social Democratic Parties and various organizations combined in a Fatherland Front.

NORTH KOREA

National Anthem. 'A chi mun bin na ra i gang san' ('Shine bright, o dawn, on this land so fair'); words by Pak Se Yong, tune by Kim Won Gyun.

RECENT ELECTIONS
Elections to the Supreme People's Assembly were held on 26 July 1998, the first ones since 1990. Only the list of the Democratic Front for the Reunification of the Fatherland was allowed to participate. 687 deputies were elected. 443 out of the 687, or 64%, were elected to the Assembly for the first time. In 1990 only 31·4% of the deputies were elected for the first time.

CURRENT ADMINISTRATION
President: Kim Jong Il. He also holds the posts of *Supreme Commander of the Korean People's Army* and *Chairman of the National Defence Commission.*

In Feb. 1997 Hong Song Nam became *Prime Minister.* In March 1999 the government also included:

Vice Prime Ministers: Cho Ch'ang-tok, Kwak Pom-ki. *Agriculture:* Yi Ha-sop. *Chemical Industry:* Pak Pong-chu. *City Management and Land and Environment Protection:* Ch'oe Chong-kon. *Commerce:* Yi Yong-son. *Construction and Building Materials Industry:* Cho Yun-hui. *Culture:* Ch'oe Chae-hyon. *Education:* Ch'oe Ki-yong. *Extractive Industries:* Kil Song-nam. *Finance:* Yim Kyong-suk. *Fisheries:* Yi Song-un. *Foreign Affairs:* Paek Nam-sun. *Foreign Trade:* Kang Chong-mo. *Forestry:* Yi Sang-mu. *Labour:* Yi Won-il. *Land and Marine Transport:* Kim Yong-il. *Light Industry:* Yi Yon-su. *Metal and Machine-Building Industries:* Chong Sung-hun. *Physical Culture and Sports:* Pak Myong-ch'ol. *Post and Telecommunications:* Yi Kum-pom. *Power and Coal Industries:* Sin T'ae-nok. *Procurement and Food Administration:* Paek Ch'ang-yong. *Public Health:* Kim Su-hak. *Public Security:* V. Mar. Paek Hak-nim. *Railways:* Kim Yong-sam. *State Construction Control:* Pae Tal-chun. *State Inspection:* Kim Ui-sun.

President, Supreme People's Assembly Praesidium: Kim Yong-nam. *Vice Presidents:* Yang Hyong-sop, Kim Yong-t'ae.

In practice the country is ruled by the Korean Workers' (*i.e.*, Communist) Party which elects a Central Committee which in turn appoints a Politburo.

Local Government. The country is divided into 12 administrative units: 3 cities (Pyongyang, Nampo and Kaesong) and 9 provinces. These are sub-divided into 152 counties. There are 26,539 deputies in People's Assemblies at city/province, county and commune level. Elections were held in Nov. 1991. Turn-out was said to be 99·5%.

DEFENCE
The Supreme Commander of the Armed Forces is Kim Jong Il. Military service is compulsory at the age of 16 for periods of 5–8 years in the Army, 5–10 years in the Navy and 3–4 years in the Air Force, followed by obligatory part-time service in the Pacification Corps to age 40.

Defence expenditure in 1997 totalled US$5,409m. (US$246 per capita), and represented 27·2% of GDP, the highest percentage of any country in the world.

Nuclear wweapons. North Korea is suspected of having a secret nuclear-weapons programme, and perhaps has enough material to build 2 warheads.

Army. One of the world's biggest, the Army is organized in 26 infantry divisions (some motorized); 14 armoured, 23 motorized infantry and 5 independent infantry brigades; 1 special purpose corps numbering 88,000; 6 heavy artillery brigades with multiple rocket launchers, 1 independent surface-to-surface missile brigade and 1 regiment. Equipment includes some 3,400 T-34, T-54/55, T-62 and Type-59 main battle tanks, chemical weapons and possibly nuclear warheads. Strength (1996) 1m., with 0·75m. reserves. There is also a paramilitary worker-peasant Red Guard of some 3·8m. and a Ministry of Public Security force of 115,000 including border guards.

Navy. The Navy, principally tasked to coastal patrol and defence, comprises 24 diesel submarines (20 of Chinese design and 4 ex-Soviet) and 12 small coastal submarines. Surface forces include 3 small missile-armed frigates, 4 corvettes, 42 missile craft, 200 fast torpedo craft, 18 anti-submarine patrol craft and some 180 inshore patrol craft. Amphibious forces consist of some 130 small craft. Support is provided by 2 ex-Soviet ocean tugs and 100 service craft. There is a coastal defence element equipped with 6 missile batteries and old 122 mm, 130 mm and 152 mm guns. Personnel in 1996 totalled about 46,000 with 40,000 reserves.

Air Force. The Air Force had a total of 700 combat aircraft and 80 armed helicopters and 82,000 personnel in 1995. Combat aircraft include 60 MiG-23 and 30 MiG-29 interceptors, 40 Su-25 fighter-bombers and more than 100 F-6s (Chinese-built MiG-19s) for ground attack and reconnaissance, as well as 40 Chinese-built A5 fighter-bombers. There are 200 An-2 light transport aircraft, about 20 larger fixed-wing transports, 50 Mi-8 transport helicopters and 80 US Hughes 300 and 500 helicopters.

INTERNATIONAL RELATIONS
North Korea is a member of the UN.

ECONOMY
Policy. In Dec. 1993 it was officially admitted that the third 7-year plan had failed to achieve its industrial targets owing to the disappearance of Communist markets and aid. Policy now concentrates on the development of agriculture, light industry and foreign trade.

Performance. GDP growth rate was negative in 1996 at –4·6%.

Budget. Estimated revenue, 1992, US$19·3bn.; expenditure, US$19·3bn.

Currency. The monetary unit is the *won* (KPW) of 100 *chon*. Banknotes were replaced by a new issue in July 1992. Exchanges of new for old notes were limited to 500 won.

Banking and Finance. The bank of issue is the Central Bank of Korea (*governor*, Chong Song Taek).

Weights and Measures. While the metric system is in force traditional measures are in frequent use. The *jungbo* = 1 ha; the *ri* = 3,927 metres. A new yearly calendar was announced on 9 July 1997 based on Kim Il-sung's birthday on 15 April 1912. Thus 15 April 1999–14 April 2000 is Year 88.

ENERGY AND NATURAL RESOURCES
Electricity. There are 3 thermal power stations and 4 hydro-electric plants. A nuclear power plant is being built. Installed capacity was 9·5m. kW in 1994. Production in 1994 was 35·96bn. kWh. Consumption per capita was an estimated 1,394 kWh in 1995. Hydro-electric potential exceeds 8m. kW. A hydro-electric plant and dam under construction on the Pukhan near Mount Kumgang has been denounced as a flood threat by the South Koreans, who constructed a defensive 'Peace Dam' in retaliation. American aid to increase energy supply slowed after evidence that North Korea had broken its promise to freeze its nuclear weapons programme. But in Oct. 1998 Japan agreed to contribute US$1bn. towards building 2 nuclear power stations and the US Congress agreed to funds to supply fuel oil on condition that North Korea abandons its nuclear ambitions.

Oil and Gas. Oilwells went into production in 1957. An oil pipeline from China came on stream in 1976. Crude oil refining capacity was 70,000 bbls. a day in 1990.

Minerals. North Korea is rich in minerals. Estimated reserves in tonnes: Iron ore, 3,300m.; copper, 2·15m.; lead, 6m.; zinc, 12m.; coal, 11,990m.; uranium, 26m.; manganese, 6,500m. 98m. tonnes of coal and lignite were mined in 1994, 11m. tonnes of iron ore in 1996 and 16,000 tonnes of copper ore in 1994. 1994 production of gold was 5,000 kg; silver, 50 tonnes; salt, 600,000 tonnes.

Agriculture. In 1994 there were 1·7m. ha of arable land, 300,000 ha of permanent crop land and 50,000 ha of pasture. In 1995 there were 0·65m. ha of paddy fields. In 1995, 4·09m. persons were economically active in agriculture.

Collectivization took place between 1954 and 1958. 90% of the cultivated land is farmed by co-operatives. Land belongs either to the State or to co-operatives, and it is intended gradually to transform the latter into the former, but small individually-tended plots producing for 'farmers' markets' are tolerated as a 'transition measure'. Livestock farming is mainly carried on by large state farms.

There is a large-scale tideland reclamation project. In 1994, 1·46m. ha were under irrigation, making possible 2 rice harvests a year. There were 75,000 tractors in 1994. The technical revolution in agriculture (nearly 95% of ploughing, etc., is mechanized) has considerably increased the yield of wheat (sown on 90,000 ha). Production (1993, in 1,000 tonnes): Wheat, 100; rice, 2,940; maize, 1,960; potatoes, 1,750; soya beans, 380. Total grain production was 2·52m. tonnes in 1996.

Livestock, 1996: Cattle, 1·35m.; pigs, 3·35m.; sheep, 395,000; goats, 305,000 (1995); 23m. chickens (1995).

A chronic food shortage has led to repeated efforts by UN agencies to stave off famine. In Jan. 1998, the UN launched an appeal for US$378m. for food for North Korea, the largest ever relief effort mounted by its World Fund Programme.

Forestry. Forest area in 1995 was 6·17m. ha (51·2% of the land area). Timber production was 4·92m. cu. metres in 1995.

Fisheries. In 1995 total catches were approximately 1,850,000 tonnes, of which 94% were sea fish. There is a fishing fleet of 30,600 vessels including 20,000 motor vessels.

INDUSTRY
Industries were intensively developed by the Japanese occupiers, notably cotton spinning, hydro-electric power, cotton, silk and rayon weaving, and chemical fertilizers. Production in 1986: Cement, 9m. tonnes; textiles, 600m. metres; motorcars (1993), 10,000; TV sets, 240,000; ships, 50,000 GRT. Annual steel production capacity was 4·3m. tonnes in 1987.

Labour. The labour force totalled 11,881,000 (55% males) in 1996. Nearly 35% of the economically active population in 1995 were engaged in agriculture, fisheries and forestry.

INTERNATIONAL TRADE
Joint ventures with foreign firms have been permitted since 1984. A law of Oct. 1992 revised the 1984 rules: Foreign investors may now set up wholly-owned facilities in special economic zones, repatriate part of profits and enjoy tax concessions. Economic zones have been set up at the ports of Sonbong and Najin. In 1996 foreign debt was estimated at US$11,830m. The USA imposed sanctions in Jan. 1988 for alleged terrorist activities. Since June 1995 South Korean businesses and individuals have been permitted to make investments and set up branch offices in North Korea. South Korea donated 0·15m. tonnes of rice to North Korea in 1995 and a further 50,000 tonnes in 1997.

Imports and Exports. Exports in 1997 were US$904m.; imports, US$1,270m. In 1992 China was the biggest trade partner (total trade US$620m.), followed by Japan, CIS and Iran. The chief exports are metal ores and products, the chief imports machinery and petroleum products.

COMMUNICATIONS
Roads. There were 31,200 km of road in 1996, of which 2,000 km were paved. There were 248,000 motor cars in 1990.

Rail. The railway network totalled 8,533 km in 1990, of which 3,250 km were electrified. In 1990, 38·5m. tonnes of freight and 35m. passengers were carried.

There is a metro and tramway in Pyongyang.

Civil Aviation. There is an international airport at Pyongyang (Sunan). The national carrier, Air Koryo, had flights in 1998 to Bangkok, Beijing, Berlin, Macao, Moscow, Sofia and Vladivostok, and China Northern Airlines flew to Beijing and Dalian.

Shipping. The leading ports are Chongjin, Wonsan and Hungnam. Pyongyang is connected to the port of Nampo by railway and river. In 1995 the ocean-going merchant fleet totalled 1·08m. GRT, including oil tankers, 0·23m. GRT.

The biggest navigable river is the Yalu, 698 km up to the Hyesan district.

Telecommunications. An agreement to share in Japan's telecommunications satellites was reached in Sept. 1990. There were 1,100,000 main telephone lines in 1997, or 48·2 per 1,000 population. In 1995 there were 3,000 fax machines.

SOCIAL INSTITUTIONS

Justice. The judiciary consists of the Supreme Court, whose judges are elected by the Assembly for 3 years; provincial courts; and city or county people's courts. The procurator-general, appointed by the Assembly, has supervisory powers over the judiciary and the administration; the Supreme Court controls the judicial administration.

In Jan. 1999 approximately 200,000 political prisoners were being held at 10 detention camps in the country.

Religion. The Constitution provides for 'freedom of religion as well as the freedom of anti-religious propaganda'. In 1986 there were 3m. Chondoists, 400,000 Buddhists and 200,000 Christians. Another 3m. followed traditional beliefs.

Education. Free compulsory universal technical education lasts 11 years: 1 pre-school year, 4 years primary education starting at the age of 6, followed by 6 years secondary. In 1994-95 there were 37 universities, 31 specialized universities (agriculture, 2; chemical industry; cinema; coal mining; construction; economics, 2; education, 5; fine arts; foreign studies; geology; hydraulics and dynamics; light industry; mechanical engineering; medicine; mining and metallurgy; music and dance; pharmacy; physical education; printing; railways; science; sea transport; technology, 2; veterinary science) and 108 specialized colleges.

The adult literacy rate is 95%.

Health. Medical treatment is free. In 1993 there were 61,200 doctors, giving a doctor/inhabitant ratio of 1:370. The hospital bed provision in 1989 of 135 per 10,000 population was one of the highest in the world.

CULTURE

Broadcasting. The government-controlled Korean Central Broadcasting Station and Korean Central Television Station are responsible for radio and TV broadcasting. In 1991 there were 34 radio and 11 TV stations (colour by PAL). There were 3·3m. radio and 1·1m. TV sets in 1996.

Cinema. There were 1,778 cinemas in 1985 and 3,515 mobile cinemas.

Press. There were 3 national and 12 local newspapers in 1994. The party newspaper is *Nodong* (or *Rodong*) *Sinmun* (Workers' Daily News). Circulation about 600,000.

Tourism. A 40-year ban on non-Communist tourists was lifted in 1986. In 1996 there were 127,000 foreign tourists. On 19 Nov. 1998 North Korea received its first tourists from South Korea, on a cruise and tour organized by the South Korean firm Hyundai.

Festivals. North and South Korean musicians gave a joint concert at the 'Yun Isang Unification Music Festival' in Pyongyang on 4 Nov. 1998.

DIPLOMATIC REPRESENTATIVES
Of North Korea to the United Nations
Ambassador: Li Hyong Chol.

FURTHER READING
North Korea Directory. Tokyo, annual since 1988
Kihl, Y. W., *Politics and Policies in Divided Korea.* Boulder, 1984
Park, J. K. and Kim, J.-G., *The Politics of North Korea.* Boulder (CO), 1979
Scalapino, R. A. and Lee, C.-S., *Communism in Korea.* Univ. of California Press, 1972—and Kim, J-Y. (eds.), *North Korea Today: Strategic and Domestic Issues.* Univ. of California Press, 1983
Smith, H. *et al.* (eds.) *North Korea in the New World Order.* London, 1996
Suh, D.-S., *Korean Communism, 1945–1980: A Reference Guide to the Political System.* Honolulu, 1981

National statistical office: Central Statistics Bureau, Pyongyang.

KUWAIT

Dowlat al Kuwait

(State of Kuwait)

Capital: Kuwait
Population estimate, 2000: 1·97m.
Estimated GDP: $32·5bn.
HDI/world rank: 0·848/54

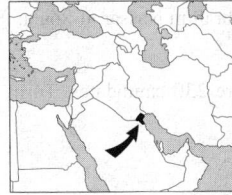

KEY HISTORICAL EVENTS
The ruling dynasty was founded by Shaikh Sabah al-Awwal, who ruled from 1756 to 1772. In 1899 the then ruler, Shaikh Mubarak, concluded a treaty with Great Britain wherein, in return for the assurance of British protection, he undertook to support British interests. In 1914 the British Government recognized Kuwait as an independent government under British protection. On 19 June 1961 an agreement reaffirmed the independence and sovereignty of Kuwait and recognized the Government of Kuwait's responsibility for the conduct of internal and external affairs; the agreement of 1899 was terminated.

On 2 Aug. 1990 Iraqi forces invaded the country, meeting little resistance, and President Saddam of Iraq declared the annexation of Kuwait on 8 Aug. Following the expiry of the date required by the UN for the withdrawal of Iraqi forces on 15 Jan. 1991, an air offensive was launched by coalition forces against targets in Kuwait, followed by a land attack on 24 Feb. Iraqi forces were routed, and Kuwait City was liberated on 26 Feb. Iraq withdrew all its forces from Kuwait. On 10 Nov. 1994 Iraq recognized the independence and boundaries of Kuwait.

TERRITORY AND POPULATION
Kuwait is bounded in the east by the Arabian (Persian) Gulf, north and west by Iraq and south and south-west by Saudi Arabia, with an area of 17,818 sq. km. In 1992-93 the UN Boundary Commission redefined Kuwait's border with Iraq, moving it slightly northwards in conformity with an agreement of 1932. The population at the census of 1995 was 1,590,013 (96% urban), of whom about 56% were non-Kuwaitis. Population density, 89 per sq. km.

The UN gives a projected population for 2000 of 1·97m.

Following the Iraqi occupation of 1990-91, the government announced plans to reduce its population to about 1m. to ensure that Kuwaitis formed a majority at about 0·55m.

The country is divided into 5 governorates: The capital (comprising Kuwait City, Kuwait's 9 islands and territorial and shared territorial waters) (population 305,964, 1998 estimate); Hawalli (496,245); Ahmadi (313,424); Jahra (252,157) and Farwaniya (498,584).

The chief cities are (1993 population estimate) Kuwait, the capital (31,241), and its suburbs Hawalli (84,478), as-Salimiya (116,104), Jahra (139,476) and Farwaniya (47,106).

The Neutral Zone (Kuwait's share, 2,590 sq. km), jointly owned and administered by Kuwait and Saudi Arabia from 1922 to 1966, was partitioned between the two countries in May 1966, but the exploitation of the oil and other natural resources continues to be shared.

Over 78% speak Arabic, the official language. English is also used as a second language.

SOCIAL STATISTICS
Births, 1996, 44,620; deaths, 3,812. In 1996 the birth rate was 25·4 per 1,000 population. Kuwait's 1996 death rate, at 2·2 per 1,000 population, was the lowest in the world. Expectation of life at birth, 1990–95, 73·3 years for males and 77·2 years for females. Infant mortality, 1990–95, 18 per 1,000 live births; fertility rate, 3·1 births per woman.

CLIMATE
Kuwait has a dry, desert climate which is cool in winter but very hot and humid in summer. Rainfall is extremely light. Kuwait, Jan. 56°F (13·5°C), July 99°F (36·6°C). Annual rainfall 5" (125 mm).

CONSTITUTION AND GOVERNMENT

The ruler is HH Shaikh Jaber al-Ahmed al-Jaber al-Sabah, the 13th Amir of Kuwait, who succeeded on 31 Dec. 1977.

In 1990 the *National Council* was established, consisting of 50 elected members and 25 appointed by the Amir. The franchise is limited to men over 21 whose families have been of Kuwaiti nationality since before 1920 and the sons of persons naturalized since 1992.

National Anthem. Words by Moshari al-Adwani; tune by Ibrahim Nassar al-Soula.

RECENT ELECTIONS

At the National Council elections of 7 Oct. 1996 there were 230 candidates. Turnout was 80% from an electorate of 107,169.

CURRENT ADMINISTRATION

Executive authority is vested in the *Council of Ministers.*

On 15 March 1998 the cabinet resigned to avoid a showdown in parliament in a no-confidence vote against Shaikh Soud Nasser al-Sabah, the Information and Health Minister and a member of the ruling family. On 16 March the Amir accepted the resignation but reappointed the Prime Minister and asked him to form a new cabinet, which in March 1999 comprised:

Prime Minister: HRH Crown Prince Shaikh Saad al-Abdullah al-Salim al-Sabah.

First Deputy Prime Minister and Foreign Minister: Shaikh Sabah al-Ahmed al-Jaber al-Sabah. *Deputy Prime Minister and Defence Minister:* Shaikh Salem al-Sabah al-Salem al-Sabah. *Deputy Prime Minister and State Minister for Cabinet Affairs:* Abd al-Aziz Dakhil al-Dakhil. *Social Affairs, Labour and Housing:* Jasim Mohammed al-Awn. *Commerce and Industry:* Hisham Sulayman al-Utaybi. *Finance and Communications:* Ali Salim al-Sabah. *Interior:* Shaikh Mohammed al-Khalid al-Hamad al-Sabah. *Justice, Religious Endowments (Awqaf) and Islamic Affairs:* Ahmed Khalid al-Kulaib. *Public Works, Electricity and Water:* Hamud Abdallah al-Ruqba. *Education and Higher Education:* Abd al-Aziz al-Ghanim. *Planning:* Ali Musa Musa. *National Assembly Affairs:* Mohammed Dhaifallah al-Sharar. *Oil:* Shaikh Soud Nasser al-Sabah. *Public Health:* Dr. Adil Khalid al-Sabih. *Information:* Yusif Mohammed Sumait.

Speaker: Ahmad Abd al-Aziz al-Sadun.

DEFENCE

In Sept. 1991 the USA signed a 10-year agreement with Kuwait to store equipment, use ports and carry out joint training exercises. In Feb. 1992 the UK signed an agreement with Kuwait to provide advisers and equipment. Conscription is for 2 years.

Defence expenditure in 1997 totalled US$3,618m. (US$1,681 per capita), representing 11·4% of GDP.

Army. The army consists of 2 mechanized, 2 armoured, 1 reserve; 1 engineer and 1 artillery brigade, 1 commando battalion and the Amiri Guard brigade. Equipment includes 150 M-84, 50 M-1A2 and 20 Chieftain main battle tanks. Strength (1997) about 11,000.

Navy. The navy operates 2 German-built fast missile craft, 4 Australian-built inshore patrol craft together with 1 logistic support craft. Some 50 boats are operated by the Coast Guard. Personnel in 1997 numbered 1,800, including 400 Coast Guard personnel.

Air Force. From a small initial combat force the Air Force has grown rapidly, although it suffered heavy losses after the Iraqi invasion of 1990–91. It has 2 squadrons with 40 F/A-18 Hornet strike aircraft. Other equipment includes 1 DC-9 and 1 MD-83 jet transport, 3 L-100-30 Hercules turboprop transports and 12 Hawk jet trainers, 9 Puma, 3 Exocet missile-armed Super Puma and 16 missile-armed Gazelle helicopters. 16 Tucano aircraft are in use. Hawk surface-to-air missiles are in service. Personnel strength (1996) 2,500, with 40 Combat aircraft and 16 armed helicopters.

KUWAIT

INTERNATIONAL RELATIONS

Kuwait is a member of the UN, Arab League, Gulf Co-operation Council and OPEC.

ECONOMY

Policy. The 4-year reconstruction and development plan covers 1995-2000.

Performance. GDP growth in 1996 was 1·6%. In 1997 there was a current account surplus of US$7,816m.

Budget. The fiscal year begins on 1 July. Revenue and expenditure over a 5-year span (in millions of dinar):

	1993	1994	1995	1996	1997
Revenue	2,285	2,545	2,987	3,306	4,250
Expenditure	3,610	3,847	3,790	3,845	3,453

Expenditure by function (in 1996): defence, 1,163; public order and safety, 331; education, 476; health, 247; social security and welfare, 656.

Currency. The unit of currency is the *Kuwaiti dinar* (KD) of 1,000 *fils*. Inflation in 1996 was 1·8%. Foreign exchange reserves were US$3,193m. in Feb. 1998 and gold reserves 2·54m. troy oz. Total money supply in Feb. 1998 was KD 1,222m.

Banking and Finance. The *Governor* of the Central Bank is Shaikh Salem Abdel-Aziz al-Sabah. There is also the Kuwait Finance House. In 1995 there were 8 local banks. Total assets of commercial banks as at 31 Dec. 1994 were KD 8,671·9m.; private deposits were KD 5,562m., of which KD 582m. were in savings accounts.

There is a stock exchange, linked with those of Bahrain and Oman.

Weights and Measures. The metric system is in force.

ENERGY AND NATURAL RESOURCES

Electricity. There are 4 power stations with a total installed capacity of 6,898 MW in 1994. 21·76 bn. kWh were produced in 1994. Consumption per capita was an estimated 12,793 kWh in 1995.

Oil and Gas. Estimated crude oil production in 1997, 2·5m bbls. a day. Kuwait produced 3·2% of the world total oil output in 1996, and had reserves amounting to 96·5bn. bbls. in 1996. Gas production was 5,170m. cu. metres in 1993.

Water. The country depends upon desalination plants. In 1993 there were 4 plants with a daily total capacity of 216m. gallons. Fresh mineral water is pumped and bottled at Rawdhatain. Underground brackish water is used for irrigation, street cleaning and livestock. Production, 1996, 89,684m. gallons (67,674m. gallons fresh, 22,010m. gallons brackish). Consumption, 1996, 80,298m. gallons (62,423m. gallons fresh, 17,875m. gallons brackish).

Agriculture. In 1994 there were 5,000 ha of arable land and 137,000 ha of permanent pasture. Production of main crops, 1995 (in tonnes): Melons, 5,000; tomatoes, 12,000; onions, 16,000; dates, 1,000.

Livestock (1996): Cattle, 19,476; sheep, 394,896; goats 95,946; camels (1995), 8,000; poultry, 25,974,899. Milk production (1993) 30,000 tonnes.

Forestry. Forests covered 5,000 ha in 1995, or 0·3% of the land area.

Fisheries. Total catch in 1996, 13,011 tonnes (wholesale value, KD 15,368,100), entirely from sea fishing. Shrimp fishing was important, but has declined since the 1990-91 war through oil pollution of coastal waters. Pearl fishing is now on a small scale.

INDUSTRY

Industries, apart from oil, include boat building, fishing, food production, petrochemicals, gases and construction.

Labour. In 1994 the labour force totalled 990,518 (including 824,658 non-Kuwaitis) distributed by sector as follows: Social services, 469,645 (non-Kuwaitis, 333,743); commerce and catering, 184,284 (181,371); building, 128,813 (128,171); industry, 70,659 (64,979); transport and communications, 38,706 (33,939); finance and business, 35,341 (30,297); agriculture and fishing, 15,985 (15,939); mining, 7,017 (3,615); public utilities, 7,017 (3,383); others, 33,051 (29,221). Registered unemployment was 1·4% in 1996.

Trade Unions. In 1986 there were 16 trade unions and 17 labour federations.

INTERNATIONAL TRADE
Imports and Exports. Imports were valued at US$7,541m. in 1996 and exports at US$14,803m. Oil accounts for 93% of revenue from exports. The main non-oil export is chemical fertilizer.

Main export markets, 1994 (in KD 1m.): France, 36; Saudi Arabia, 33·31; UAE, 31·64; India, 30·93. Main import suppliers: USA, 289·1; Japan, 233·1; Germany, 163·5; UK, 138; France, 126·2.

COMMUNICATIONS
Roads. There were 4,450 km of roads in 1996. Number of vehicles in 1996 was 693,000 (538,000 passenger cars, or 358 per 1,000 inhabitants, and 155,000 trucks and vans). There were 15,921 road accidents in 1993 with 290 fatalities.

Civil Aviation. There is an international airport (Kuwait International). The national carrier is the state-owned Kuwait Airways. In 1998 services were also provided by Aeroflot, Air China, Air India, Air Lanka, Air Slovakia, Alitalia, Balkan, Biman Bangladesh Airlines, British Airways, Czech Airlines, Egyptair, Emirates, Ethiopian Airlines, Gulf Air, Indian Airlines, Iran Air, JAT, KLM, Lufthansa, Middle East Airlines, Olympic Airways, Oman Air, Pakistan International Airlines, Qatar Airways, Royal Jordanian, SAS, Saudia, Syrian Arab Airlines, Tarom, Turkish Airlines and United Airlines. In 1995 Kuwait Airways flew 38·3m. km and carried 1,950,800 passengers (all on international flights). Kuwait International airport handled 3,607,222 passengers in 1996 and 132,877 tonnes of freight.

Shipping. The port of Kuwait formerly served mainly as an entrepôt, but this function is declining in importance with the development of the oil industry. The largest oil terminal is at Mina Ahmadi. 3 small oil ports lie to the south of Mina Ahmadi: Mina Shuaiba, Mina Abdullah and Mina Al-Zor. The main ports for other traffic are at Shuwaikh, Shuiaba and Doha. The merchant fleet totalled 2,057,000 GRT in 1995, of which 1,343,000 GRT were tankers.

Telecommunications. Kuwait had 411,600 main telephone lines in 1997, or 227·4 per 1,000 population. Cellular phone subscribers numbered 118,000 in 1995, and there were 95,000 PCs and 35,000 fax machines. There were approximately 42,000 Internet users in Jan. 1998.

Postal Services. In 1996 there were 86,618 post office boxes. There were 179,126 outgoing telegrams and 114,763 incoming in 1996.

SOCIAL INSTITUTIONS
Justice. In 1960 Kuwait adopted a unified judicial system covering all levels of courts. These are: Courts of Summary Justice, Courts of the First Instance, Supreme Court of Appeal, Court of Cassation, Constitutional Court and State Security Court. Islamic Sharia is a major source of legislation. The death penalty was imposed for drug smuggling in April 1995.

Religion. In 1996, 810,000 people were Sunni Moslems, 540,000 Shiah Moslems, 180,000 other Moslems, and 270,000 other (mostly Christian and Hindu).

Education. Education is free and compulsory from 6 to 14 years. In 1996 there were 201 pre-primary schools with 3,145 teachers for 49,393 pupils; 266 primary schools with 9,747 teachers for 141,841 pupils and 19,087 teachers in secondary schools for 206,934 pupils. There were 28,705 students in higher education, of which 14,884 were at university. Adult literacy rate in 1995 was 78·6% (82·2% men, 74·9% women). Total expenditure on education in 1995: KD 490,000,000 or 5·7% of GDP.

Health. Medical services are free to all residents. In 1995 there were 16 hospitals and sanatoria, with a provision of 4,425 beds (25·25 per 10,000 population); there were 2,938 doctors (16·75 per 10,000 population), 437 dentists, 8,337 nurses and 19

KUWAIT

midwives. There were 70 clinics and other health centres and 1,295,132 people were admitted to public hospitals during the year.

CULTURE

Broadcasting. The government-controlled Radio Kuwait and Kuwait Television broadcast a main and a second radio programme, a Koran programme and a service in English and 2 TV programmes (colour by PAL). In 1995 there were 860,000 TV receivers and 1,160,000 radios.

Cinema. In 1996 there were 6 cinemas, with a total annual attendance of 800,000.

Press. In 1995 there were 7 daily newspapers in Arabic and 2 in English, with a combined circulation of about 655,000. Formal press censorship was lifted in Jan. 1992.

Tourism. There were 37,000 foreign tourists in 1996, bringing revenue of US$109m. There were 21 hotels providing 3,473 beds.

Libraries. In 1992 there were 11 non-specialized and 18 public libraries, stocking 407,000 books for 12,500 registered users.

Museums and Galleries. There were 6 museums attracting 36,000 visitors in 1995.

DIPLOMATIC REPRESENTATIVES
Of Kuwait in Great Britain (2 Albert Gate, Kensington, London, SW1X 7JU)
Ambassador: Khaled al-Duwaisan, GCVO.

Of Great Britain in Kuwait (Arabian Gulf St., Kuwait)
Ambassador: Richard Muir.

Of Kuwait in the USA (2940 Tilden St., NW, Washington, D.C., 20008)
Ambassador: Dr Mohammed Sabah Al-Salim Al-Sabah.

Of the USA in Kuwait (PO Box 77, Safat, Kuwait)
Ambassador: James A. Larocco.

Of Kuwait to the United Nations
Ambassador: Mohammad A. Abulhasan.

Of Kuwait to the European Union
Ambassador: Ahmad Al-Ebrahim.

FURTHER READING
Al-Yahya, M.A., *Kuwait: Fall and Rebirth.* London, 1993
Clements, F. A., *Kuwait.* [Bibliography] 2nd ed. Oxford and Santa Barbara (CA), 1996
Crystal, J., *Kuwait: the Transformation of an Oil State.* Boulder (Colo.), 1992
Finnie, D. H., *Shifting Lines in the Sand: Kuwait's Elusive Frontier with Iraq.* London, 1992

KYRGYZSTAN

Kyrgyz Respublikasy

Capital: Bishkek
Population estimate, 2000: 4·54m.
GNP per capita: (PPP$) 1,970
HDI/world rank: 0·633/109

KEY HISTORICAL EVENTS
After the establishment of the Soviet regime in Russia, Kyrgyzstan became part of Soviet Turkestan, which itself became an Autonomous Soviet Socialist Republic within the Russian Soviet Federal Socialist Republic (RSFSR) in April 1921. In 1924, when Central Asia was reorganized territorially on a national basis, Kyrgyzstan was separated from Turkestan and formed into an autonomous region within the RSFSR. On 1 Feb. 1926 the Government of the RSFSR transformed Kyrgyzstan into an Autonomous Soviet Socialist Republic within the RSFSR, and finally in Dec. 1936 Kyrgyzstan was proclaimed one of the constituent Soviet Socialist Republics of the USSR. With the collapse of the Soviet Empire, the republic asserted its claim to sovereignty in 1990 and declared independence in Sept. 1991.

Kyrgyzstan became a member of the CIS in Dec. 1991.

TERRITORY AND POPULATION
Kyrgyzstan is situated on the Tien-Shan mountains and bordered in the east by China, west by Kazakhstan and Uzbekiston (formerly Uzbekistan), north by Kazakhstan and south by Tajikistan. Area, 199,900 sq. km (77,180 sq. miles). Population (estimate, July 1997), 4,512,800; density, 23 per sq. km.

The UN gives a projected population for 2000 of 4·54m.

An estimated 61·2% of the population lived in rural areas in 1995.

The republic comprises 6 provinces: Djalal-Abad, Issyk-Kul, Naryn, Osh, Talas and Chu. There are 18 towns, 31 urban settlements and 40 rural districts. Its capital is Bishkek (formerly Frunze; 1991 population estimate, 641,400). Other large towns are Osh (238,200), Djalal-Abad (74,200), Tokmak (71,200), Przhevalsk (64,300) and Kyzyl-Kiya.

The Kyrgyz are of Turkic origin and formed 52·4% of the 1989 census population of 4,257,755; the rest include Russians (21·5%), Uzbeks (12·9%), Ukrainians (2·5%), Germans (2·4%), and Tatars (1·6%).

The official language is Kyrgyz, and also Russian in provinces where Russians are in a majority. The Roman alphabet (in use 1928–40) was re-introduced in 1992.

SOCIAL STATISTICS
1997 births, estimate, 101,000; deaths, 39,000; 1995 marriages, 28,866. Rates, 1997 estimate (per 1,000 population): Birth, 22·3; death, 8·6; infant mortality (per 1,000 live births), 73·6. Life expectancy, 1997 estimate, 64 years. In 1995 the most popular age range for marrying was 20–24 for both males and females. Fertility rate, 1990–95, 3·6 births per woman.

CLIMATE
The climate varies from dry continental to polar in the high Tien-Shan, to sub-tropical in the south-west (Fergana Valley) and temperate in the northern foothills. Bishkek, Jan. 9°F (–13°C), July 70°F (21°C). Annual rainfall 14·8" (375 mm).

CONSTITUTION AND GOVERNMENT
A new Constitution was adopted on 5 May 1993. The Presidency is executive, and directly elected for renewable 5-year terms. At a referendum on 30 Jan. 1994, 96% of votes cast favoured President Akaev's serving out the rest of his term of office; turn-out was 95%. At a referendum on 22–23 Oct. 1994 turn-out was 87%. 75% of votes cast were in favour of instituting referendums as a constitutional mechanism, and 73% were in favour of establishing a new bicameral parliament (*Jogorku Kenesh*), with a 35-member directly-elected legislature, and a 70-member upper house elected on a regional basis and meeting twice a year. 94·5% of votes cast at a

referendum on 10 Feb. 1996 were in favour of giving the President the right to appoint all ministers except the Prime Minister without reference to parliament.

RECENT ELECTIONS
Elections were held in 2 rounds on 5 and 19 Feb. 1995. 90 of the 105 seats went to independents, with only 15 going to members of parties (including 4 to the Party of Kyrgyz Communists). Parliamentary elections are due to take place in Oct. 1999.

Presidential elections were held on 24 Dec. 1995. President Akaev was re-elected by 71·6% of votes cast against 2 opponents. Turn-out was 82%.

CURRENT ADMINISTRATION
President: Askar Akaev (b. 1945).

A new government was appointed in March 1996 which in March 1999 comprised:

Prime Minister: Zhumabek Ibraimov.

First Deputy Prime Minister: Boris Silayev. *Agriculture and Water Resources:* Emilbek Uzakbayev. *Foreign Affairs:* Muratbek Imanaliyev. *Internal Affairs:* Maj. Gen. Omurbek Kutuyev. *Finance:* Marat Sultanov. *Defence:* Col. Gen. Myrzakan Subanov. *National Security (KNB):* Misir Ashirkulov. *Emergency Situations and Civil Defence:* Sultan Urmanayev. *Industry and Foreign Trade:* Esengul Omuraliyev. *Justice:* Neliya Beyshenaliyeva. *Labour and Social Welfare:* Mira Dzhangarachev. *Health:* Naken Kasiev. *Education, Science and Culture:* Svotbek Toktomyshev. *Environmental Protection:* Tynybek Alykulov. *Transportation and Communications:* Jantoro Satybaldiyev.

Local Government. Elections were held on 25 Feb. 1990. The appointment of leaders of local councils is approved or vetoed by the President of the Republic.

DEFENCE
Conscription is for 18 months. Defence expenditure in 1997 totalled US$45m. (US$10 per capita).

Army. The Army consists of 1 motor rifle division and 1 mountain brigade. Equipment includes 204 T-72 main battle tanks. Personnel, 1997, 9,800.

Air Force. There is an aviation element with MiG-21 fighters and a variety of other ex-Soviet equipment, including L-29 and L-39 trainers. The Government is selling aircraft to other countries to finance the operation of its remaining equipment. Personnel, 1997, 2,400.

INTERNATIONAL RELATIONS
Kyrgyzstan is a member of the UN, CIS and the NATO Partnership for Peace.

ECONOMY
Performance. Real GDP growth was –6·2% in 1995 (–20·1% in 1994).

Budget. In 1996 revenues were an estimated US$225m. and expenditure US$308m.

Currency. On 10 May 1993 Kyrgyzstan introduced its own currency unit, the *som* (KGS), of 100 *tyiyn*, at a rate of 1 som = 200 roubles. The average annual inflation rate during the period 1990–96 was 256·2%.

Banking and Finance. The central bank and bank of issue is the National Bank (*Chairman:* Narat Sultanov). There were 13 commercial banks and 1 German-Kyrgyz industrial bank in 1996.

ENERGY AND NATURAL RESOURCES
Electricity. Installed capacity was 3·63m. kW in 1994. Production in 1996 was estimated at 13·7bn. kWh, around 90% hydro-electric. Consumption per capita in 1995 was an estimated 1,912 kWh.

Oil and Gas. Output of oil (including gas concentrate), 1995, 1·79m. tonnes; natural gas, 36m. cu. metres.

Water. Kyrgyzstan's most valuable natural resource is water.

Minerals. In 1995, 474,000 tonnes of coal were produced. Some gold is mined.

Agriculture. In 1996 agriculture accounted for 52% of GDP. Kyrgyzstan is famed for its livestock breeding. In 1996 there were 869,000 cattle, 250,000 horses, 4,075,000 sheep, 219,000 goats and 12m. chickens. Yaks are bred as meat and dairy cattle, and graze on high altitudes unsuitable for other cattle. Crossed with domestic cattle, hybrids give twice the yield of milk. The small Kyrgyz horse is famed.

Area under cultivation (1993), 16m. ha, of which private subsidiary agriculture accounted for 0·15m. ha and commercial farming 3·3m. ha in 12,800 farms. Private and commercial agriculture accounted for 46% of output by value in 1993. Total output was valued at 2,400m. roubles (in constant 1983 prices) in 1993.

Principal crops include wheat, barley, corn and vegetables. Kyrgyzstan raises wheat sufficient for its own use and other grains and fodder, particularly lucerne; also sugar-beet, hemp, kenaf, kendyr, tobacco, medicinal plants and rice. Sericulture, fruit, grapes and vegetables and bee-keeping are major branches.

Output of main agricultural products (in 1,000 tonnes) in 1995: Grain, 776; cottonseed, 40; sugar-beet, 110; potatoes, 431; tomatoes, 159; apples, 65; tobacco (leaves), 58; beef and veal, 68; mutton and lamb, 50; milk, 864; and 83m. eggs.

Forestry. In 1995 forests covered 730,000 ha, or 3·8% of the land area.

Fisheries. The catch in 1995 was 364 tonnes, entirely freshwater fish.

INDUSTRY
Industrial enterprises include sugar refineries, tanneries, cotton and wool-cleansing works, flour-mills, a tobacco factory, food, timber, textile, engineering, metallurgical, oil and mining enterprises. Output was valued at 3,300m. som in current prices in 1993, 75·8% of the 1992 figure.

Production, 1995: Cement, 0·31m. tonnes; textile fabrics, 23,208,000 sq. metres; carpets, 0·98m. sq. metres; footwear, 728,000 pairs; 4,000 washing machines.

Labour. Out of 1,641,000 people in employment in 1995, 689,000 were engaged in agriculture and forestry, 240,000 in industry, 170,000 in education and 112,000 in trade and catering. In Jan. 1994 there were 2,900 registered unemployed (0·2% of the labour force), of whom 1,700 were receiving benefits. Average monthly salaries in 1993 were 85·90 som.

INTERNATIONAL TRADE
In Jan. 1994 an agreement to create a single economic zone was signed with Kazakhstan and Uzbekistan (now Uzbekiston). In March 1996 Kyrgyzstan joined a customs union with Russia, Kazakhstan and Belarus.

Imports and Exports. In 1995 imports were valued at US$610m. and exports at US$412m.

Principal imports in 1995 (in US$1m.): Petroleum and gas, 162·4; machinery and metalworking, 103·6; food and beverages, 96·7. Principal exports: Food and beverages, 82·8; light industry, 82·6; non-ferrous metallurgy, 62·7.

Main import suppliers in 1995 (in US$1m.): Russia, 114·3; Kazakhstan, 112·5; Uzbekiston (formerly Uzbekistan), 88·9; Turkey, 38·3; Cuba, 22·7. Main export markets: Russia, 104·8; Uzbekiston (formerly Uzbekistan), 70; People's Republic of China, 68·5; Kazakhstan, 66·8; UK, 27·4.

COMMUNICATIONS
Roads. There were 18,560 km of roads (16,890 km paved) in 1997. Passenger cars in use in 1996 numbered 146,000 (32 per 1,000 inhabitants), and there were also 18,430 road tractors and 4,200 motor cycles and mopeds.

Rail. In the north a railway runs from Lugovaya through Bishkek to Rybachi on Lake Issyk-Kul. Towns in the southern valleys are linked by short lines with the Ursatyevskaya–Andizhan railway in Uzbekiston (formerly Uzbekistan). Total length of railway, 1994, 318 km. In 1994, 1·1m. passengers and 1·1m. tonnes of freight were carried.

Civil Aviation. There is an international airport at Bishkek (Manas). The national carrier is Kyrgyzstan Airlines. In 1998 services were also provided by Aeroflot, Air

Enterprise Pulkovo, Austrian Airlines, British Airways, Kaliningrad Air Enterprise, Siberia Airlines and Turkish Airlines. In 1996 Bishkek handled 786,290 passengers (674,065 on domestic flights) and 3,055 tonnes of freight.

Shipping. The total length of inland waterways was 600 km in 1990. In 1993, 0·1m. tonnes of freight were carried.

Telecommunications. Telephone main lines numbered 350,900 in 1997, equivalent to 75·6 for every 1,000 persons.

Postal Services. In 1995 there were 918 post offices.

SOCIAL INSTITUTIONS

Justice. In 1994, 41,155 crimes were reported, including 546 murders or attempted murders.

Religion. In 1996, 70% of the population was Sunni Moslem. There were some 1,000 mosques, 30 Russian Orthodox, 17 Evangelical, 9 Seventh Day Adventist and 8 Lutheran churches.

Education. In 1996 there were 453 pre-primary schools with 4,013 teachers for 35,254 pupils; 1,885 primary schools with 24,086 teachers for 473,077 pupils; 42,286 secondary teachers for 530,854 pupils, and 3,691 university level teachers for 49,744 students. There are 21 higher educational institutions and 51 technical and teachers' training colleges, as well as music and art schools. Kyrgyz University had 7,300 students in 1994–95. Adult literacy is over 99%.

In 1994 total expenditure on education came to 6·8% of GNP and represented 25·6% of total government expenditure.

Health. In 1995 there were 15,000 doctors, 42,300 nurses and 1,100 dentists; in 1994 there were 348 hospitals with 48,900 beds.

Welfare. In Jan. 1994 there were 443,000 age and 196,000 other pensioners.

CULTURE

Broadcasting. Kyrgyz Radio and Kyrgyz Television are state-controlled. There are 2 national radio programmes, with some broadcasting in English and German. There is 1 commercial radio station. In 1993 there were 3 hours of TV broadcasting a day (colour by SECAM). In 1995 there were 510,000 radio and 150,000 television receivers.

Cinema. In 1995 there were 343 cinemas with an annual attendance of 0·6m.

Press. There were 3 daily newspapers in 1995, with a combined circulation of 53,000.

Tourism. In 1996 there were 13,000 foreign tourists, bringing revenue of US$5m.

DIPLOMATIC REPRESENTATIVES

Of Kyrgyzstan in Great Britain (Ascot House, 119 Crawford St., London, W1H 1AF)
Ambassador: Roza I. Otunbaeva.

Of Great Britain in Kyrgyzstan
Ambassador: Douglas B. McAdam (resides in Almaty).

Of Kyrgyzstan in the USA (1732 Wisconsin Ave., NW, Washington, D.C., 20007)
Ambassador: Baktybek Abdrissaev.

Of the USA in Kyrgyzstan (66 Erkindik Prospekt, Bishkek 720002)
Ambassador: Anne M. Sigmund.

Of Kyrgyzstan to the United Nations
Ambassador: Zamira B. Eshmambetova.

Of Kyrgyzstan to the European Union
Ambassador: Tchinguiz Aitmatov.

LAOS

Sathalanalath Pasathipatai
Pasasonlao

(Lao People's Democratic
Republic)

Capital: Vientiane
Population estimate, 2000: 5·69m.
GNP per capita: (PPP$) 1,250
HDI/world rank: 0·465/136

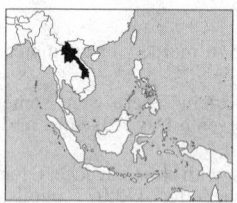

KEY HISTORICAL EVENTS

The Kingdom of Laos, once called Lanxang (the Land of a Million Elephants), was founded in the 14th century. The kingdom has always depended on the maintenance of good relations with its more powerful neighbours, Thailand, Myanmar and Vietnam.

In 1893 Laos became a French protectorate and in 1907 acquired its present frontiers. In 1945, after French authority had been suppressed by the Japanese, an independence movement known as Lao Issara (Free Laos) set up a government under Prince Phetzarath, the viceroy of Luang Prabang. This government collapsed with the return of the French in 1946, its leaders fleeing to Thailand.

Under a new constitution of 1947 Laos became a constitutional monarchy under the Luang Prabang dynasty, and in 1949 became an independent sovereign state within the French Union. A few Lao Issara leaders remained in dissidence under Prince Souphanouvong who allied himself with the Vietminh and subsequently formed the 'Pathet Lao' (Lao state) rebel movement.

An almost continuous state of war began in 1953 between the Royal Lao Government, supported by American bombing and Thai mercenaries, and the Patriotic Front Pathet Lao, supported by North Vietnamese troops. Peace talks from 1972 resulted in an agreement on 21 Feb. 1973 providing for the formation of a provisional government of national union, and the withdrawal of foreign troops. A provisional coalition government was duly formed in 1974. However, after the Communist victories in neighbouring Vietnam and Cambodia in April 1975, the Pathet Lao took over the running of the whole country, maintaining only a façade of a coalition. On 29 Nov. 1975 HM King Savang Vatthana abdicated and the People's Congress proclaimed a People's Democratic Republic of Laos on 2 Dec. 1975.

TERRITORY AND POPULATION

Laos is a landlocked country of about 91,400 sq. miles (236,800 sq. km) bordered on the north by China, the east by Vietnam, the south by Cambodia and the west by Thailand and Myanmar. Apart from the Mekong River plains along the border of Thailand, the country is mountainous, particularly in the north, and in places densely forested.

The population (census, 1996) was 4,581,258 (2,315,931 females); density, 19 per sq. km. Population, 1997 estimate; 5,117,000. Density, 19·4 per sq. km.

The UN gives a projected population for 2000 of 5·69m.

An estimated 79·3% of the population lived in rural areas in 1995.

There are 17 provinces divided into 133 districts and 1 special region. Area, population and administrative centres in 1996:

Province	Sq. km	Population (in 1,000)	Administrative centre
Vientiane (town)	3,920	531·8	...
Vientiane	19,990	286·8	Phonehong
Phongsaly	16,270	153·4	Phongsaly
Luang Nam Tha	9,325	115·2	Luang Nam Tha
Oudomsai	21,190	211·3	Ban Nahin
Bokeo	4,970	114·9	Ban Honei Sai
Luang Prabang	16,875	367·2	Luang Prabang
Houaphan	16,500	247·3	Sam Neua
Sayaboury	11,795	293·3	Sayaboury

Province	Sq. km	Population (in 1,000)	Administrative centre
Xiang Khouang	17,315	201·2	Xiang Khouang
Bolikhamsai	16,470	164·9	Paksane
Khammouane	16,315	275·4	Thakhek
Savannakhet	22,080	674·9	Savannakhet
Saravane	10,385	258·3	Saravane
Sekong	7,665	64·2	Sekong
Champassak	15,415	503·3	Pakse
Attopei	10,320	87·7	Attopei

The Special Region had a population of 54,200 in 1995.

The capital and largest town is Vientiane, with a population of (census 1985) 377,409. Other important towns are Savannakhet, 96,652; Luang Prabang, 68,399; Pakse, 47,323.

The population is divided into 3 groups: about 67% Lao-Lum (Valley-Lao); 17% Lao-Theung (Lao of the mountain sides); and 5% Lao-Soung (Lao of the mountain tops), who comprise the Meo and Yao. Lao is the official language. French and English are spoken.

SOCIAL STATISTICS
Estimated 1997 births, 211,000; deaths, 69,000. 1997 rates per 1,000 population, estimate: Birth, 41·2 per 1,000 population; death, 13·4; infant mortality, 94·3 per 1,000 live births; life expectancy, 53·6 years. Annual growth rate, 1990–95, 3·0%. Fertility rate, 1990–95, 6·7 births per woman.

CLIMATE
A tropical monsoon climate, with high temperatures throughout the year and very heavy rains from May to Oct. Vientiane, Jan. 70°F (21·1°C), July 81°F (27·2°C). Annual rainfall 69" (1,715 mm).

CONSTITUTION AND GOVERNMENT
On 15 Aug. 1991 the National Assembly adopted a new constitution. The head of state is the President, elected by the National Assembly.

Under the constitution the Lao People's Revolutionary Party (LPRP) remains the 'central nucleus' of the 'people's democracy'; other parties are not permitted. The LPRP's Politburo comprises 9 members, including Khamtay Siphandone (LPRP, *President*).

National Anthem. 'Xatlao tangtae dayma lao thookthuana nentxoo sootchay' ('For the whole of time the Lao people have glorified their Fatherland'); words by Sisana Sisane, tune by Thongdy Sounthonevichit.

RECENT ELECTIONS
The National Assembly (Fourth Legislature) elected Khamtay Siphandone as President at the first session of the Fourth National Assembly held on 23–26 Feb. 1998.

CURRENT ADMINISTRATION
President: Gen. Khamtay Siphandone (elected 24 Feb. 1998).
   Vice President: Oudom Khattigna.
   In March 1999 the government consisted of:
   Prime Minister: Gen. Sisavath Keobounphanh.
   Deputy Prime Ministers: Boungnang Volachit, Choummali Saignason (also *Defence*), Somsavat Lengsavat (also *Foreign Affairs*), Khamphoui Keoboualapha (also *Finance*). *Commerce and Tourism:* Phoumy Thipphavone. *Communications, Transport, Posts, and Construction:* Col. Phao Bounnaphon. *Education:* Phimmasone Leuangkhamma. *Interior:* Maj. Gen. Asang Laoli. *Information and Culture:* Sileua Bounkham. *Industry and Handicrafts:* Soulivong Daravong. *Labour and Social Welfare:* Somphanh Phengkhammi. *Justice:* Kham Ouane Boupha. *Public Health:* Ponemek Dalaloi. *Agriculture and Forestry:* Sian Saphangthong.

Governor of the State Bank, Minister: Cheuang Somboukhan. *Head of the Prime Minister's Office, Minister:* Saisomphon Phomvihan.

Local Government. Each province is headed by a governor.

DEFENCE

Military service is compulsory for a minimum of 18 months. Defence expenditure in 1997 totalled US$63m. (US$12 per capita).

Army. There are 4 military regions. The Army is organized in 5 infantry divisions; 3 engineering regiments, 7 independent infantry regiments and 65 independent infantry companies; and 5 artillery and 9 anti-aircraft battalions. Equipment includes 30 T-54/-55 main battle tanks. Strength (1997) about 25,000.

Navy. There is a riverine force of about 500 personnel (1997) organized into 4 squadrons running some 12 patrol craft, 4 landing craft and 40 smaller river patrol for operations on the Mekong.

Air Force. The Air Force has about 50 aircraft, including 20 MiG-21 fighters, 6 An-2, 6 An-24, 3 An-26, 2 Y-12 and 2 Yak-40 transports and 10 Mi-8 helicopters. Personnel strength, about 3,500 in 1997.

INTERNATIONAL RELATIONS

Laos is a member of the UN and ASEAN.

ECONOMY

Policy. The fourth 5-year plan (1996–2000) aims at an annual growth of 8%.

Performance. Real GDP growth over 1990–94 averaged 6%. Estimates for 1995 and 1996, between 7% and 7.5%.

Budget. Revenues in 1996 were an estimated US$230·2m. and expenditure US$365·9m.

Currency. The unit of currency is the *kip* (LAK). Inflation was 12% in 1996 (21·4% in 1995). Foreign exchange reserves were US$150m. in Sept. 1997; gold reserves were 20,000 troy oz. in Feb. 1998. Total money supply in Sept. 1997 was 73,495m. kip.

Banking and Finance. The central bank and bank of issue is the State Bank (*Governor*, Cheuang Somboukhanh). There were 12 commercial banks in 1995 (6 foreign). Total savings and time deposits in 1991 amounted to 4,075m. kip.

Weights and Measures. The metric system is in force.

ENERGY AND NATURAL RESOURCES

Electricity. Total installed capacity in 1996 was 217,000 kW, of which 93% was hydro-electric. Production (1994) 890m. kWh, around 95% hydro-electric. Consumption per capita was estimated to be 48 kWh in 1995. In 1996, 16% of households had electricity, mainly in Vientiane.

Minerals. 1991 output (in tonnes): Coal, 1,250; baryte, 4,500; 1995: Tin, 687; gypsum, 0·11m.

Agriculture. Agriculture accounted for 54·6% of GDP in 1996. In 1994 there were 875,000 ha of arable land, 25,000 ha of permanent crop land and 800,000 ha of permanent pasture. The chief products (1995 output in 1,000 tonnes) are rice 1,423 (1,600 in 1997); tobacco, 62; coffee, 10; and sweet potatoes and cassava, 164; maize, 79; seed-cotton, 84; sugar-cane, 123; soya beans, 72; tea 17. Opium is produced but its manufacture is controlled by the state.

Livestock (1996): Cattle, 1·2m.; buffaloes (1995), 1·3m.; pigs, 1·68m.; goats (1995), 162,000; poultry (1995), 9m.

Forestry. Forests covered 12·44m. ha in 1995, or 53·9% of the land area, down from 13·18m. ha in 1990. They produce valuable woods such as teak. Timber production, 1995, 5·51m. cu. metres.

Fisheries. The catch in 1995 was 40,250 tonnes, entirely from inland waters.

LAOS

INDUSTRY

Industry accounted for 16% of GDP in 1995. Production in 1995: Corrugated iron, 1m. sheets; nails, 58 tonnes; oxygen, 13,000 cylinders; detergent, 800 tonnes; cigarettes, 40m. packets; beer, 126,000 hectolitres; soft drinks, 108,000 hectolitres; reinforced concrete, 24,000 cu. metres; plastic, 500 tonnes; salt, 12,000 tonnes.

Labour. The working age is 16–55 for females and 16–60 for males. At the 1995 census there were 1,086,172 females and 1,051,112 males within those age groups. Over 75% of the economically active population in 1995 were engaged in agriculture, fishing and forestry.

INTERNATIONAL TRADE

Since 1988 foreign companies have been permitted to participate in Lao enterprises. In 1990 foreign investments amounted to US$189m., mainly in hotels and textiles. Total foreign debt was US$2,263m. in 1996.

Imports and Exports. In 1996 imports amounted to US$690m. and exports to US$323m. The main imports in 1995 were: Electricity, 43·1m. kWh; lorries, 105; motor cars, 1,390; motor cycles, 4,288; bicycles, 17,501; (in tonnes) fuel, 43,200; cement, 4,400; iron, 4,900; paper, 617; fabrics, 2,098; medicines, 3,621; sugar, 2,433; rice, 1,172. Main exports: Electricity, 705·2m. kWh; timber, 86,100 cu. metres; lumber, 88,200 cu. metres; plywood, 1,512,000 sheets; coffee, 2,830 tonnes; gypsum, 110,000 tonnes; tin, 653 tonnes. Main import suppliers, 1994: Thailand, 48·4%; Japan, 11·8%; Vietnam, 4·1%, Singapore, 4·0%. Main export markets, 1995 (US$1,000): Thailand, 142,300; Vietnam, 87,700; France, 23,600; USA, 11,200; Russia, 11,200; China, 9,500; Germany, 5,000.

COMMUNICATIONS

Roads. In 1996 there were 16,760 km of roads (14% hard-surfaced) classified as: National highways, 4,460 km (38% hard-surfaced); provincial roads, 6,380 km (9% hard-surfaced); district roads, 5,920 km. 955,000 tonnes of freight were transported by road in 1995. In 1996 there were 16,320 passenger cars (3 per 1,000 inhabitants), 4,200 trucks and vans and 231,000 motor cycles. There were 1,820 traffic accidents with 600 fatalities in 1992. A bridge over the River Mekong, providing an important north-south link, was opened in 1994.

Rail. The Thai railway system extends to Nongkhai, on the Thai bank of the Mekong River.

Civil Aviation. There is an international airport at Vientiane (Wattay). The national carrier is Lao Aviation, which in 1998 operated domestic services and international flights to Bangkok, Chiang Mai, Hanoi, Ho Chi Minh City, Kunming and Phnom Penh. Services were also provided in 1998 by Royal Air Cambodge, Vietnam Airlines and Thai Airways International. In 1995 scheduled airline traffic of Laos-based carriers flew 1·5m. km, carrying 125,000 passengers (31,000 on international flights).

Shipping. The River Mekong and its tributaries are an important means of transport. 898,000 tonnes of freight were carried on inland waterways in 1995. Merchant shipping totalled 3,000 GRT in 1995.

Telecommunications. Laos had 24,600 main telephone lines in 1997, or 5·1 per 1,000 persons. There were 1,500 cellular phone subscribers and 500 fax machines in 1995.

Postal Services. There were 417 post offices in 1995.

SOCIAL INSTITUTIONS

Justice. Criminal legislation of 1990 established a system of courts and a prosecutor's office. Polygamy became an offence.

Religion. In 1992 some 2·55m. were Buddhists (Hinayana), but about a third of the population follow tribal religions.

Education. In 1995–96 there were 685 kindergartens with 33,500 pupils and 1,900 teachers, 8,425 primary schools with 724,100 pupils and 24,600 teachers, 705

LAOS

secondary schools with 117,900 pupils and 7,700 teachers and 129 higher secondary schools with 44,600 pupils and 2,800 teachers. There is 1 teachers' training college, 1 college of education, 1 school of medicine, 1 agricultural college and an advanced school of Pali.

In 1994–95 there was 1 university of medical science, 1 institute of pedagogy and 1 national polytechnic institute, and 8 other institutes of higher education. There were 4,507 university students and 494 academic staff.

Adult literacy (1995) 56·6% (male, 69·4%; female, 44·4%).

Health. In 1995 there were 25 hospitals, 131 health centres, 542 dispensaries and 3,100 doctors.

CULTURE

Broadcasting. The government-controlled National Radio of Laos broadcasts a national and 6 regional programmes and an external service (6 languages). Lao National TV transmits for 3 hours daily. There were 630,000 radio and 45,000 television receivers in 1995.

Cinema. In 1993 there were 5 cinemas with an annual attendance of 10,000.

Press. In 1996 there were 3 dailies (1 in English).

Tourism. There were 470,000 foreign visitors in 1997, and an expected 1m. in 1998.

DIPLOMATIC REPRESENTATIVES
Of Laos in Great Britain (resides in Paris)
Ambassador: Khamphan Simmalavong.

Of Great Britain in Laos
Ambassador: Sir James W. Hodge, KCVO, CMG (resides in Bangkok).

Of Laos in the USA (2222 S. St., NW, Washington, D.C., 20008)
Ambassador: Vang Rattanavong.

Of the USA in Laos (Rue Bartholonie, Vientiane)
Ambassador: Wendy Jean Chamberlin.

Of Laos to the United Nations
Ambassador: Alounkeo Kittikhoun.

Of Laos to the European Union
Ambassador: Khamphan Simmalavong.

FURTHER READING
National Statistical Centre. *Basic Statistics about the Socio-Economic Development in the Lao P.D.R.* Annual.

Cordell, H., *Laos.* [Bibliography] Oxford and Santa Barbara (CA), 1990
Stuart-Fox, M., *Laos: Politics, Economics and Society.* London, 1986—*History of Laos.* Cambridge University Press, 1998
Zasloff, J. J., and Unger, L. (eds.) *Laos: Beyond the Revolution.* London, 1991

National statistical office: National Statistical Centre, Vientiane.

LATVIA

Latvijas Republika

Capital: Riga
Population estimate, 2000: 2·4m.
GNP per capita: (PPP$) 3,650
HDI/world rank: 0·704/92

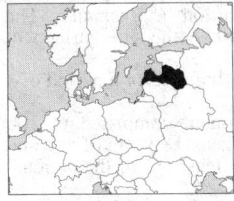

KEY HISTORICAL EVENTS
The territory that is now Latvia was controlled by crusaders, primarily the German Order of Livonian Knights, until 1561, when Latvia fell into Polish and Swedish hands. Between 1721 and 1795 Latvia was absorbed into the Russian empire. In the part of Latvia unoccupied by the Germans during the First World War, the Bolsheviks won 72% of the votes in the Constituent Assembly elections (Nov. 1917). Soviet power was proclaimed in Dec. 1917, but was overthrown when the Germans occupied all Latvia (Feb. 1918). Restored when they withdrew (Dec. 1918), it was overthrown once more by combined British naval and German military forces (May–Dec. 1919), and a democratic government set up. This régime was in turn replaced when a coup took place in May 1934.

The secret protocol of the Soviet–German agreement of 23 Aug. 1939 assigned Latvia to the Soviet sphere of interest. An ultimatum (16 June 1940) led to the formation of a government acceptable to the USSR. On 21 July a People's Diet proclaimed the establishment of the Latvian Soviet Socialist Republic and applied to join the USSR, whose Supreme Soviet accepted the application on 5 Aug.

On 4 May 1990 the Latvian Supreme Soviet declared, by 138 votes to nil with 58 abstentions, that the Soviet occupation of Latvia on 17 June 1940 was illegal, and resolved to re-establish the authority of the Constitution of 1922. A transition period was set for the restoration of independence. In a referendum in March 1991 the principle of independence was supported by 73·6% of votes cast. A fully independent status was conceded by the USSR State Council in Sept. 1991.

TERRITORY AND POPULATION
Latvia is situated in north-eastern Europe. It is bordered by Estonia on the north and by Lithuania on the south-west, while on the east there is a frontier with the Russian Federation and to the south-east with Belarus. Territory, 64,600 sq. km (larger than Denmark, the Netherlands, Belgium and Switzerland). Population (1996), 2,479,870; density, 38 per sq. km.

The UN gives a projected population for 2000 of 2·4m.

In 1995 an estimated 72·8% of the population were urban. Nationalities: Latvians 55·3%, Russians 32·5%, Belarussians 4%, Ukrainians 2·9%, Poles 2·2%, Lithuanians 1·3%, Jews 0·4%, Gypsies 0·3%, Estonians 0·1%, Germans 0·1%.

In 1998, 72·72% of the population were Latvian citizens. There was a population of over 700,000 ethnic Russians in 1998.

There are 26 districts, 56 towns and 37 urban settlements. The capital is Riga (820,577 in 1996); other principal towns are Daugavpils (117,835), Liepāja (97,917), Jelgava (70,943), Jurmala (58,959) and Ventspils (46,567).

The official language is Latvian.

SOCIAL STATISTICS
1997: Births, 18,830 (rate of 7·6 per 1,000 population); deaths, 33,503 (13·6 per 1,000 population). 1996: Marriages, 9,634 (3·9 per 1,000 population); divorce, 6,051 (2·4 per 1,000 population); infant mortality, 15·8 per 1,000 live births. In 1996 life expectancy was 63·9 years for males but 75·6 years for females. In 1994 the most popular age range for marrying was 20–24 for both males and females. Fertility rate, 1990–95, 1·6 births per woman. In 1995 there were 2,799 immigrants and 13,346 emigrants.

CLIMATE
Owing to the influence of maritime factors, the climate is relatively temperate but changeable. Average temperatures in January range from –2·8°C in the western

coastal town of Liepāja to –6·6°C in the inland town of Daugavpils. The average summer temperature is 20°C.

CONSTITUTION AND GOVERNMENT
The Declaration of the Renewal of the Independence of the Republic of Latvia dated 4 May 1990, and the 21 Aug. 1991 declaration re-establishing de facto independence, proclaimed the authority of the Constitution *(Satversme)*. The Constitution was fully re-instituted as of 6 July 1993, when the 5th Parliament *(Saeima)* was elected.

The head of state in Latvia is the *President*, elected by parliament for a period of 3 years, set to rise to 4 years.

The highest legislative body is the one-chamber parliament comprised of 100 deputies and elected in direct, proportional elections by citizens 18 years of age and over. Deputies serve for 4 years and parties must receive at least 5% of the national vote to gain seats in parliament.

In a referendum on 3 Oct. 1998, 53% of votes cast were in favour of liberalizing laws on citizenship, which would simplify the naturalization of the Russian-speakers who make up nearly a third of the total population and who were not granted automatic citizenship when Latvia regained its independence from the former Soviet Union in 1991.

Executive power is held by the *Cabinet of Ministers*.

National Anthem. 'Dievs, svēti Latviju' ('God bless Latvia'); words and tune by Kārlis Baumanis.

RECENT ELECTIONS
Guntis Ulmanis (LZS) was elected President of the Republic of Latvia on 7 July 1993 and re-elected for a second term on 18 June 1996.

At the parliamentary elections of 3 Oct. 1998, the number of seats won, with percentages, party and chair were as follows: People Party *(Tautas Partija)*, 24 with 21·2%, Andris Skēle; Latvia's Way (LC) *(Latvijas Ceļš)*, 21 with 18·1%, Andrejs Pantelējevs; Fatherland and Freedom Union-LNCP(TB) *(Tēvzemei un Brīvībai/LNNK)*, 17 with 14·1%, Jānis Straume; People Unity Party *(Tautas Saskaņas Partija)*, 16 with 14·6%, Jānis Jurkāns; Latvian Social Democratic Union *(Latvijas Sociāldemokrātu apvienība)*, 14 with 12·8%, Juris Bojars; New Party *(Jaunā Partija)*, 8 with 7·3%), Raimunds Pauls.

A 7-member *Constitutional Court* was established in 1996 with powers to invalidate legislation not in conformity with the constitution. Its members are appointed by parliament for 10-year terms.

CURRENT ADMINISTRATION
President: Guntis Ulmanis (LZS).

The government comprised at March 1999:

Prime Minister: Vilis Krištopans (LC).

Deputy Prime Minister for European Integration: Guntars Krasts (TB/LNNK). *Deputy Prime Minister and Minister of Transport:* Anatolijs Gorbunovs (LC).

Minister of Education and Science: Jānis Gaigals (LC). *Defence:* Girts Valdis Kristovskis. *Agriculture:* Peteris Salkazanovs (LSDA). *Environmental and Regional Development:* Vents Balodis (TB/LNNK). *Foreign Affairs:* Valdis Birkavs (LC). *Economy:* Ainars Slesers (JP). *Finance:* Ivars Godmanis (LC). *Interior:* Roberts Jurdzs (TB/LNNK). *Welfare:* Vladimirs Makārovs (TB/LNNK). *Justice:* Ingrida Labucka (JP). *Culture:* Karina Petersone (LC). *Minister of Special Tasks for co-operation with with International Financial Institutions:* Roberts Zile (TB/LNNK). *State Minister for the Environment:* Inese Vaidere (TB/LNNK). *State Minister for State Revenues:* Alja Poca (LC),

N.B. State Ministers cannot be regarded as fully fledged cabinet members, but have voting rights in the issues concerning their field.

Local Government. There are 2 tiers of local authorities: Regional, which are appointed, and county, which are elected for 4-year terms. Citizens of 21 years or over who have resided in a locality for 12 months may stand for election. Elections took place on 9 March 1997 for 77 city and 489 town councils. There were 11,942 candidates from 1,454 registers of candidates which represented 29 political parties. The next elections will be held in March 2001.

DEFENCE

Since Latvia gained its independence in Aug. 1991, a renewal process for Latvia's armed forces, including the National Armed forces, the Home Guard and Border Guard, has been under way. Military service is compulsory for male citizens from the age of 19 (women and men 18 years and older can join the national defence forces voluntarily) and the duration of military service is 18 months. Conscientious objectors have the option of serving in non-military service. Latvia has signed a defence co-operation treaty with Lithuania and Estonia to co-ordinate Baltic States' defence and security activities. A joint Baltic peace-keeping force has been established (BALTBAT) as well as a joint navy fleet (BALTRON), and a joint air control system (BALNET) was introduced in 1998. A sub-unit of Latvia's National Armed Forces is participating in the NATO led IFOR operations in the former Yugoslavia as a part of a joint Latvian-Danish military battalion.

In 1997 military expenditure totalled US$156m. (US$63 per capita), representing 4·6% of GDP.

Army. The Army is organized in 1 infantry, 1 reconnaissance and 1 engineer battalion, and was 2,350 strong in 1998. There is a Home Guard reserve of 5 brigades, and a paramilitary Frontier Guard of 3,500.

Navy. A small coastal protection force numbered 880 in 1998 and operates 12 patrol vessels of Swedish, German and Soviet origins based at Riga and Liepāja. There is a coastal defence battalion numbering 220, and a coastguard operates 9 small craft.

Air Force. Personnel numbered 130 in 1998. There are 1 L-410 and 2 An-2 transports and 6 Mi-2 helicopters.

INTERNATIONAL RELATIONS

Latvia is a member of the UN, OSCE, the Council of Europe and the NATO Partnership for Peace (and is looking for full NATO membership), an Associate Partner in WEU, and an Associate Member of the EU. It has also been a member of WTO since Oct. 1998.

ECONOMY

The Latvian Privatization Agency, established in 1994 to oversee the entire privatization process, has adopted a case-by-case approach in determining the privatization method for each entity earmarked for privatization. Only 37 state-owned companies remain at various stages of privatization, of which only 9 employ more than 50 people. Latvian citizens, local and state authorities and legal entities which are either majority owned by Latvian citizens or foreign nationals from countries with which Latvia has mutual investment protection agreements can freely purchase both industrial and agricultural land that has been entered in the Land Book.

Policy. By 1994, 70% of industrial capacity was still in state ownership, and a Privatization Agency was set up to accelerate the transfer to private hands. By Jan. 1995, 86·9% of residents had taken out privatization vouchers. 230 state enterprises were privatized in 1995, realising 37·3m. lats, of which 21·8m. lats were provided by vouchers. The private sector accounted for some 65% of GDP in 1998.

Performance. GDP growth of 5-6% was expected in 1998 after 6·5% growth in 1997. Services contribute 54% of GDP. Some 300 companies were privatized in 1997.

Budget. The financial year is the calendar year. The 1997 budget balanced at US$993,211m. Main items of expenditure, 1995 (in 1m. lats): Social and cultural, 226; economic development, 47; administration, 36; defence, 23.

Budgets for 1997 and 1998 have been adopted by the parliament as non-deficit budgets. Revenues of the general government budget exceeded expenditure by 7·3m. lats in the first quarter of 1997.

Currency. The unit of currency is the *lats* (LVL) of 100 *santims*. The lats has been pledged to the SDR basket. Inflation was 4·8% in 1998, down from 8·4% in 1997, 17·6% in 1996 and 23·1% in 1995. Total money supply in Feb. 1998 was 550m. lats.

Banking and Finance. The Bank of Latvia both legally and practically is a completely independent institution. Governor of the Bank and Council members are appointed by Parliament for office for 6 years (*present governor*, Einārs Repše). In 1997 there were 35 licensed banks, 4 savings and loan associations, a Riga branch of Société Générale and Vereinsbank, and a representative office of Dresdner Bank. A law on credit institutions stipulates a gradual increase of minimal foundation capital up to 5m. ECU. The only bank fully owned by the state is Latvijas Hipoteku un Zemes Banka.

There is a stock exchange in Riga.

ENERGY AND NATURAL RESOURCES

Electricity. Installed capacity was 2·02m. kW in 1993. Electricity supply for 1996 was 6·56bn. kWh, of which 3·12bn. kWh was produced domestically and 3·44bn. kWh imported. Total electricity power supply in 1997 was forecast at 6·2–6·4bn. kWh. Output of electrical power as follows (in 1bn. kWh): hydro-electric, 2-2·4; thermoelectric, 1·3-1·5; block stations, 0·1; small hydro-electric, 0·005; wind generators, 0·001. Consumption per capita in 1995 was estimated at 2,197 kWh.

Oil and Gas. Of the total amount of energy resources in 1998, natural and liquefied gas constituted 25-27% and oil products 35-40%.

Minerals. Peat deposits extend over 645,000 ha or about 10% of the total area, and it is estimated that total deposits are 3,000-4,000m. tons. The average annual output of peat at the moment reaches 450,000-550,000 tonnes.

Resources:

	deposits (in m.)	production (in 1,000) 1995	1996
Dolomite (metres³)	661·3	379·7	429·4
Clay for bricks (metres³)	218·5	70·5	72·9
Clay for cement (tonnes)	416·6	85·8	120·0
Sand and gravel mix (metres³)	413·2	534·5	775·4
Sand (metres³)	72·8	184·3	153·5
Limestone for cement (tonnes)	477·5	324·0	367·0

Agriculture. Area under cultivation was 3·9m. ha in 1990. In 1996 agriculture accounted for 9% of GDP. Cattle and dairy farming are the chief agricultural occupations. Oats, barley, rye, potatoes and flax are the main crops.

On 1 Jan. 1989 there were 248 state farms and 331 (including 11 fishery) collective farms. There were 55,600 tractors and 39,300 harvester-threshers in 1994. Large state and collective farms are being converted into shareholding enterprises; the remainder are being divided into small private holdings for collective farm workers or former owners. There were 52,000 such farms in 1993 averaging 16 ha and 99,000 smallholdings averaging 4·4 ha.

Persons employed in agriculture, 1996, 13·6%.

In 1996 there were 24% state farms, collective farms and statutory companies, 35% peasant farms, 41% household plots and private subsidiary farms. The total area of agricultural land was 2·52 m. ha.

Output of crops (in 1,000 tonnes) 1996: Grain 969 (made up of: wheat, 279·7; rye, 112·9; barley, 366·6; oats, 101·4); flax 0·8; sugar beet 257·8; potatoes 1,082; vegetables 179·5.

Livestock (in 1,000) 1996: Cattle, 509·4 (of which cows, 277·4); sheep, 55·5; pigs, 459·6; poultry, 3,790·7. Livestock products (1,000 tonnes): Meat, 75·7; milk, 922·7; eggs, 470·8; wool, 134.

Forestry. In 1995, forest covered 2·88m. ha (46·4% of the land area), with wood resources of 426m. cu. metres. 6·9m. cu. metres were removed in 1995. In 1996 the total forested area was 2·86m. ha (44·3% of the total territory of Latvia) of which 0·377m. ha were privately owned.

To provide the protection of forests there are three forest categories: protected forests, 11%; restricted management forests, 18·6%; commercial forests, 70·4%.

LATVIA

Fisheries. There are 7 fishing ports in Latvia. In 1996 the total catch (in 1,000 tonnes) was 135·7, comprised of: freshwater fish 0·9; and marine fish 134·8. Fish catch by fishing ground (1,000 tonnes): inland waters, 0·9; northwest Atlantic, 1; northeast Atlantic 71 of which Baltic Sea, 69·7; East central Atlantic, 63·7; southwest Atlantic, 4·1.

INDUSTRY
In 1996 the decline of production in manufacturing was stopped for the first time since the beginning of economic reforms. Structure of sectors of industry by outputs, current prices in %, 1996: Food products and beverages, 44·3%; textile, 8·2%; wood products, 8·2%; chemicals, 7·6%; motor vehicles, 0·9%; publishing, 2·5%; radio and communication equipment, 1·2%; building materials, 2·5%.

Labour. In June 1996, 1,170,000 persons were employed. In 1995 there was a monthly minimum wage of 50-60 lats. Average monthly salary was 120 lats in 1995. Retirement age was fixed at 60 years for men and 55 for women, but flexible retirement ages have become possible under a new contributory pension scheme introduced in 1995. There were 89,345 registered unemployed in Sept. 1996.

Registered unemployed at May 1998 was 7%. The average monthly wage in the public sector was 135·64 lats.

Trade Unions. The Latvian Free Trade Union has Juris Radzevičs as chairman.

INTERNATIONAL TRADE
External debt of Latvia at the end of 1996 was 227·3m. lats, 8·2% of GDP. The free trade agreements on industrial and agricultural goods are in force among the Baltic states; the Baltic Customs Union will be the next step to be implemented. In 1996 Latvia established free trade regimes with the EU and EFTA. In June 1997 the Competition Act was adopted on the EU directives. In Oct. 1998 Latvia became a member of the WTO. Direct foreign investments in 1996 was US$65 per capita; total amount was 369·2m. lats.

Imports and Exports. The main exports are wood and products, textiles and foodstuffs. Main import suppliers, 1997: Germany, 16·0%; Russia, 15·6%; Finland, 9·7%; Lithuania, 6·4%; Estonia, 6·0%. Main export markets, 1997: Russia, 21·0%; UK, 14·3%; Germany, 13·8%; Sweden, 8·3%. In 1997, 48·9% of exports went to the EU and 53·2% of imports were from the EU.

Total imports and exports (in 1,000 lats).

	Imports	Exports
1995	959,636	688,413
1996	1,278,169	795,172

The main export markets in 1996 were: EU, 355,457; CIS, 326,279.

COMMUNICATIONS
Roads. In 1995 there were estimated to be 60,046 km of roads. In 1995, 4,926,700 tonnes of freight were carried by road. In 1995 there were 4,056 traffic accidents with 611 fatalities. In 1996 the number of road accidents with casualties decreased by 8·5% with 3,711 accidents and 550 deaths. In 1996, 213·5 km of road was repaired and 13·1 km of new road built. Passenger cars in 1996 numbered 379,875 (153 per 1,000 inhabitants), in addition to which there were 45,918 road tractors, 18,772 motor cycles and mopeds and 17,275 buses and coaches.

Rail. In 1996 there were 2,413 km of 1,520 mm gauge route (271 km electrified). In 1995, 44·53m. passengers and 28·8m. tonnes of freight were carried. In 1996 freight turnover was 35·26m. tonnes.

Civil Aviation. There is an international airport at Riga. A new national carrier, Air Baltic, assumed control of Latavio and Baltic International Airlines in 1995 and began flying in Oct. 1995. In 1998 it operated scheduled services to Copenhagen, Frankfurt, Hamburg, Helsinki, Kyiv, London, Minsk, Munich, Stockholm, Tallinn, Vilnius, Zürich and Warsaw. It is 51% state-owned, with SAS owning the remainder. In 1998 services were also provided by Aeroflot, Aerosweet, Air Baltic,

Air Express, Austrian Airlines, British Airways, Czech Airlines, Delta Air Lines, Dneproavia Joint Stock Aviation Co, Estonian Air, Estonian Aviation, Eurowings, Finnair, Latpass Airlines, Lauda Air, LOT, Lufthansa, Riga Airlines, SAS, Swissair, Transaero Airlines and Transeast Airlines. In 1997, 531,000 passengers arrived and departed and 4,261 tonnes of freight (including mail) were handled.

Shipping. There are 3 large ports (with 54m. tonnes of cargo handled, 1998): Riga (12m.), Ventspils (35m.) and Liepāja (7m.). 4,600 ships in all docked at Riga and Ventspils in 1997. In 1995, 10·59m. tonnes of cargo were transported. In 1995 the merchant marine totalled 1·18m. GRT, including oil tankers, 0·73m. GRT.

Ventspils can handle up to 100,000 containers a year and it is estimated that it will be able to handle 250,000 a year when the second stage of a US$70m. development project is completed early in the next century. This project will change Ventspils from a port principally designed for the export of oil and other products from Russia to one which is also a major import centre.

Telecommunications. Telecommunications are conducted by companies in which the government has a 51% stake, under the aegis of the state-controlled Lattelekom. Main telephone lines numbered 772,000 in 1997 (301·6 per 1,000 inhabitants). There were 12,206 mobile telephones in 1997, 20,000 PCs and 900 fax machines.

Postal Services. In 1997 there were 993 post offices.

SOCIAL INSTITUTIONS

Justice. The new criminal code came into force in 1998. Judges are appointed for life. There are a Supreme Court, regional and district courts and administrative courts. The death penalty is retained, but has been subject to a moratorium since Oct. 1996. 36,865 crimes were reported in 1997 (38,205 in 1996), 51·4% of which were solved.

Religion. In order to practise in public, religious organizations must be licensed by the Department of Religious Affairs attached to the Ministry of Justice. New sects are required to demonstrate loyalty to the state and its traditional religions over a 3-year period. Traditionally Lutherans constitute the largest church, with 304,000 members in 1997. Congregations in Jan. 1997: Lutherans, 304; Roman Catholics, 231; Russian Orthodox, 112; Old Believers, 62; Baptists, 78; Adventists, 44; Jews, 5; others, 43.

Education. Adult literacy rate in 1995 was over 99%. The Soviet education system has been restructured on the UNESCO model. Education may begin in kindergarten. From the age of 6 or 7 education is compulsory for 9 years in comprehensive schools. This may be followed by 3 years in special secondary school or 1 to 6 years in art, technical or vocational schools. In 1995–96 there were 716 comprehensive schools with 0·35m. pupils and 52 special secondary schools with 17,200 pupils, with a combined total of 34,700 teachers. 188,700 pupils were attending Latvian-language schools, 108,000 Russian and 41,300 mixed. 25,000 pupils were attending vocational schools. Schools for ethnic minorities were established in 1990: there were 8 in 1994–95.

In 1997 in the whole field of higher education there were 33 institutions with 64,900 students.

Total expenditure on education in 1994 came to 6·5% of GNP and represented 16·1% of total government expenditure.

Health. In 1995 there were 8,400 doctors, 18,300 paramedics and 166 hospitals with 27,800 beds.

Welfare. Benefits are paid from the State Social Insurance Fund and the government budget. It is a statutory requirement that the rate of pensions be reviewed twice a year, taking inflation into account. A compulsory contributory health insurance scheme was inaugurated on 1 Jan. 1997. In 1995 there were 666,000 pensioners, including retirement, 497,000; disability, 103,400; survivors, 38,400; social, 19,600. The average monthly pension was 36 lats in 1996. Legislation of 1995 provides for the phasing in of a new retirement pension scheme which links benefits to contributions made during working years and average life expectancy.

LATVIA

CULTURE

Broadcasting. Broadcasting is overseen by the 9-member National Radio and Television Council appointed by parliament for 4-year terms. There are 26 TV broadcasting companies and 23 radio broadcasting companies. Latvijas Radio broadcasts 3 programmes and an external service (English, German, Swedish). Latvijas Televizija transmits on 2 networks (colour by PAL). There were 1·72m. radio receivers and 1·2m. television receivers in 1995.

Cinema. In 1997 there were 35 cinemas; attendances totalled 1·27m.

Press. Latvia had 229 newspapers and periodicals in 1997, including 22 dailies, 38 published 2–4 times a week and 1 English-language weekly. 2,320 book titles were published.

Tourism. In 1997 there were 63,167 foreign tourists. In 1996, foreign tourists brought in revenue of US$182m. 98,002 Latvian nationals travelled abroad in 1997. At the end of 1997 there were 220 hotels and other accommodation facilities.

Festivals. The National Song Festival is scheduled for 2001, and there is an annual Riga Opera Festival.

Libraries. In 1997 there were 998 public libraries with 15·1m. volumes and 514,000 members.

National Theatre and Opera. There are a National Opera and Ballet and 9 professional theatres.

Museums and Galleries. There are 96 museums.

DIPLOMATIC REPRESENTATIVES

Of Latvia in Great Britain (45 Nottingham Place, London, W1M 3FE)
Ambassador: Normans Penke.

Of Great Britain in Latvia (5 Alunana ielā Street, Riga, LV 1010)
Ambassador: Nicholas Jarrold.

Of Latvia in the USA (4325 17th St., NW, Washington, D.C., 20011)
Ambassador: Ojars Eriks Kalnins.

Of the USA in Latvia (7 Raina Boulevard, Riga, LV 1510)
Ambassador: James Holmes.

Of Latvia to the United Nations
Ambassador: Dr. Jānis Priedkalns.

Of Latvia to the European Union
Ambassador: Andris Piebalgs.

FURTHER READING

Central Statistical Bureau. *Statistical Yearbook of Latvia.—Latvia in Figures.* Annual.
Bilmanis, A., *A History of Latvia.* Princeton Univ. Press, 1951
Dreifeld, J., *Latvia in Transition.* Riga, 1997
Lieven, A., *The Baltic Revolution: Estonia, Latvia, Lithuania and the Path to Independence.* 2nd ed. Yale UP, 1994
Misiunas, R. J. and Taagepera, R., *The Baltic States: the Years of Dependence, 1940–91.* 2nd ed. Farnborough, 1993
Smith, I. A. and Grunts, M. V., *The Baltic States* [Bibliography]. Oxford and Santa Barbara (CA), 1993
Spekke, A., *History of Latvia.* Stockholm, 1951
Who Is Who in Latvia. Riga, 1996

National statistical office: Central Statistical Bureau, Lācplēša ielā 1, 1301 Riga.
Website: http://www.csb.lv/

LEBANON

Jumhouriya al-Lubnaniya

(Republic of Lebanon)

Capital: Beirut
Population estimate, 2000: 3·29m.
GNP per capita: (PPP$) 6,060
HDI/world rank: 0·796/66

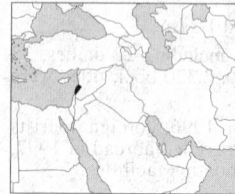

KEY HISTORICAL EVENTS

The Ottomans invaded Lebanon, then part of Syria, in 1516-17 and held nominal control until 1918. After 20 years' French mandatory regime, Lebanon was proclaimed independent on 26 Nov. 1941. On 27 Dec. 1943 an agreement was signed between representatives of the French National Committee of Liberation and of Lebanon by which most of the powers and capacities exercised hitherto by France were transferred as from 1 Jan. 1944 to the Lebanese Government. The evacuation of foreign troops was completed in Dec. 1946.

In early May 1958 the Moslem opposition to President Chamoun rose in insurrection and for 5 months the Moslem quarters of Beirut, Tripoli, Sidon and the northern Bekaa were in insurgent hands. On 15 July the US Government acceded to President Chamoun's request and landed a force of army and marines who re-established Government authority.

Internal problems were exacerbated by the politically active Palestine population and by the deeply divisive question of the Palestinian problem itself. An attempt to regulate the activities of Palestinian fighters through the secret Cairo agreement of 1969 was frustrated both by the inability of the Government to enforce its provisions, and by an influx of battle-hardened fighters expelled from Jordan in Sept. 1970. A further attempt to control the guerrillas in 1973 also failed. From March 1975, Lebanon was beset by civil disorder by which the economy was brought to a virtual standstill.

By Nov. 1976 large-scale fighting had been brought to an end by the intervention of the Syrian-dominated Arab Deterrent Force which ensured sufficient security to permit Lebanon to establish quasi-normal conditions under President Sarkis. Large areas of the country, however, remained outside governmental control, including West Beirut, which was the scene of frequent conflict between opposing militia groups. The south, where the Arab Deterrent Force could not deploy, remained unsettled and subject to frequent Israeli attacks. In March 1978 there was an Israeli invasion following a Palestinian attack inside Israel. Israeli troops eventually withdrew in June, but instead of handing over all their positions to UN Peacekeeping Forces, they installed Israeli-controlled Christian Lebanese militia forces in border areas. Severe disruption continued in the south. In June 1982 Israeli forces once again invaded, this time in massive strength, and swept through the country, eventually laying siege to and bombing Beirut. In Sept. Palestinian forces, together with the PLO leadership, evacuated Beirut. On 23 Aug. 1982 Bachir Gemayel was elected President of Lebanon. On 14 Sept. he was assassinated. There followed a period of 'no peace, no war' with intermittent clashes between various *de facto* forces on the ground. Israeli forces started a complete withdrawal on 16 Feb. 1985. Western forces pulled out after a peace agreement was signed by the leaders of the Druze, Amal and (Christian) Lebanese Forces to end the civil war on 28 Dec. 1985 but it was not until the end of 1990 that the various militias which had held sway in Beirut withdrew. A new Government of National Reconciliation was announced on 24 Dec. 1990. The dissolution of all militias was decreed by the National Assembly in April 1991, but the Shi'ite Moslem militia Hizbollah was allowed to remain active and deploy heavy weapons. In July the army defeated the Palestine Liberation Organization at Sidon, depriving the latter of their territorial base in South Lebanon, and bringing the army up to the Israeli-occupied southern strip ('security zone').

Following a 17-day Israeli bombardment of Hizbollah positions and South Lebanon generally in April 1996, a US-brokered unsigned 'understanding' of 26 April 1996 guaranteed that Hizbollah guerrillas and Palestinian radical groups would cease attacks on civilians in northern Israel and granted Israel the right to self-defence and return of fire. Hizbollah maintained the right to resist Israel's occupation of Lebanese soil.

LEBANON

TERRITORY AND POPULATION

Lebanon is mountainous, bounded on the north and east by Syria, on the west by the Mediterranean and on the south by Israel. The area is 10,452 sq. km (4,036 sq. miles). Population (1991 estimate), 2·84m.; density, 265 per sq. km. In 1995, 69·4% of the population were urban.

The UN gives a projected population for 2000 of 3·29m.

The principal towns, with estimated population (1998), are: Beirut (the capital), 1·5m.; Tripoli, 160,000; Zahlé, 45,000; Saida (Sidon), 38,000.

The official language is Arabic. French and, increasingly, English are widely spoken in official and commercial circles. Armenian is spoken by a minority group.

SOCIAL STATISTICS

1995 births, 77,000; deaths, 20,000. Birth rate per 1,000 population, 1995, 25·6; death rate, 6·8. Infant mortality was 29 per 1,000 live births in 1997; expectation of life, 69·9 years. Annual growth rate, 1990–95, 3·3%. Fertility rate, 1990–95, 3·1 births per woman.

CLIMATE

A Mediterranean climate with short, warm winters and long, hot and rainless summers, with high humidity in coastal areas. Rainfall is largely confined to the winter months and can be torrential, with snow on high ground. Beirut, Jan. 55°F (13°C), July 81°F (27°C). Annual rainfall 35·7" (893 mm).

CONSTITUTION AND GOVERNMENT

The first Constitution was established under the French Mandate on 23 May 1926. It has since been amended in 1927, 1929, 1943 (twice), 1947 and 1990. It is based on a separation of powers, with a President, a single-chamber *National Assembly* elected by universal suffrage at age 21 in 12 electoral constituencies, and an independent judiciary. In Oct. 1995 the National Assembly extended the President's term of office from 6 to 9 years. The executive consists of the President and a Prime Minister and Cabinet appointed after consultation between the President and the National Assembly. The system is adapted to the communal balance on which Lebanese political life depends by an electoral law which allocates deputies according to the religious distribution of the population, and by a series of constitutional conventions whereby, *e.g.,* the President is always a Maronite Christian, the Prime Minister a Sunni Moslem and the Speaker of the Assembly a Shia Moslem. There is no party system. In Aug. 1990, and again in July 1992, the National Assembly voted to increase its membership, and now has 128 deputies with equal numbers of Christians and Moslems.

On 21 Sept. 1990 President Hrawi established the Second Republic by signing constitutional amendments which had been negotiated at Taif (Saudi Arabia) in Oct. 1989. These institute an executive collegium between the President, Prime Minister and Speaker, and remove from the President the right to recall the Prime Minister, dissolve the Assembly and vote in the Council of Ministers.

National Anthem. 'Kulluna lil watan lil 'ula lil 'alam' ('All of us for our country, flag and glory'); words by Rashid Nachleh, tune by W. Sabra.

RECENT ELECTIONS

5-stage elections were held in Aug.–Sept. 1996; turn-out averaged 45%. 34 seats went to Maronites, 27 to Sunnis, 27 to Shi'ites, 14 to Greek Orthodox, 8 to Greek Catholics, 8 to Druze, 5 to Armenian Orthodox, 2 to Alaoui, 1 to Armenian Catholics, 1 to Protestants and 1 to the Christian Minority.

CURRENT ADMINISTRATION

President: Emile Lahoud.

In Nov. 1996 a new government was formed, comprising in March 1999:

Prime Minister, Minister of Foreign Affairs: Selim al-Hoss.

Deputy Prime Minister, Minister of Interior, Minister of Municipal and Rural Affairs: Michel al-Murr. *Agriculture:* Sulaymah Franjiya. *Cultural and Higher Education Affairs, Vocational and Technical Education, National Education, Youth and Sports:* Mohammed Yousef Beydoun. *Displaced Persons:* Khalil al-Anwar.

Environment and Tourism: Artur Nazarian. *Finance:* George Corm. *Housing and Co-operatives:* Mahmud Abu Hamdan. *Industry and Oil:* Sulayman Trablousi. *Information:* Anwar al-Khalil. *Justice:* Joseph Shaoul. *Labour and Social Affairs:* Michel Moussa. *National Defence:* Ghazi Zaytar. *National Economy and Trade:* Nasser Saidi. *Post and Telecommunications:* Issam Naaman. *Public Health:* Karam Karam. *Public Works and Transportation:* Najib Mikati. *Minister of State for Administrative Reform Affairs:* Hassan Shalaq.

Local Government. The 6 governorates (including the city of Beirut) are subdivided into 26 districts.

In municipal elections held in May and June 1998 Hizbollah, the Shia group opposed to the government, won a landslide victory in Mount Lebanon in the first local poll in 35 years.

DEFENCE

There were 30,000 Syrian troops in the country in 1995. In the Israeli-occupied southern strip the pro-Israeli South Lebanese Army is estimated to number 2,500 and has 30 main battle tanks.

Conscription is for 12 months.

Defence expenditure in 1997 totalled US$676m. (US$163 per capita), representing 4·5% of GDP.

Army. The strength of the Army was 53,300 in 1997. It is organized into a Presidential Guard, 11 infantry brigades, 2 artillery and 3 special forces regiments, and 1 ranger and 1 air assault regiment. Its equipment includes 100 M48A1/A5 and 200 T-54/-55 main battle tanks. There is an internal security force, run by the Ministry of the Interior, some 13,000 strong.

Navy. The flotilla consists of 14 inshore patrol craft, 2 tank landing craft and some armed boats, manned and supported by about 1,000 personnel (1997).

Air Force. The Air Force had (1997) about 800 personnel. About 30 Alouette, Gazelle, Puma and AB.212 helicopters survived the civil war, while the US government supplied 16 UH-1H Iroquois helicopters in 1994. No combat aircraft are operated.

INTERNATIONAL RELATIONS

A Treaty of Brotherhood, Co-operation and Co-ordination with Syria of May 1991 provides for close relations in the fields of foreign policy, the economy, military affairs and security. The treaty stipulates that Lebanese government decisions are subject to review by 6 joint Syrian-Lebanese bodies.

Lebanon is a member of the UN and Arab League.

ECONOMY

Policy. The semi-autonomous Council of Development and Reconstruction, originally set up in 1977, was revived in 1991 to oversee a post-civil war rehabilitation programme 'Horizon 2000'. In 1995 this programme was revised and extended up to 2007.

Performance. Total GDP was US$14·8bn. in 1997, up from US$9·5bn. in 1995. Real GDP growth was 3·5% in 1997 and forecast to be 3·2% in 1998.

Budget. The fiscal year is the calendar year. Budget for 1997: Revenue, £Leb.4,100,000m.; expenditure, £Leb.6,433,000m.

Currency. The unit of currency is the *Lebanese pound* (LBP) of 100 *piastres.* Inflation was an annualized 15% in 1995, but had declined to 5·2% in 1997, with a forecast of a further drop to 4·8% for 1998. Foreign exchange reserves were US$3,100m. in June 1998; gold reserves were 9·22m. troy oz. in Feb. 1998. Total money supply in Feb. 1998 was £Leb.1,857m. There is a fluctuating official rate of exchange, fixed monthly; in practice it is used only for the calculation of *ad-valorem* customs duties on Lebanese imports and for import statistics. For other purposes the free market is used.

Banking and Finance. The Bank of Lebanon (*Governor,* Riad Salameh) is the bank of issue. In 1994 there were 52 domestic banks, 14 subsidiaries and 12 foreign banks, with 590 branches in all. Commercial bank deposits in June 1998 totalled £Leb.41,836,800m. There is a stock exchange in Beirut (closed 1983-95).

Weights and Measures. The use of the metric system is legal.

ENERGY AND NATURAL RESOURCES

Electricity. Installed capacity in 1994 was 1·22m. kW. Production was 4·75bn. kWh in 1994. Consumption per capita in 1995 was 1,285 kWh.

Minerals. There are no commercially viable deposits.

Agriculture. In 1996 agriculture accounted for 12% of GDP. In 1994 there were 216,000 ha of arable land, 90,000 ha of permanent crop land and 10,000 ha of pasture. Crop production (in 1,000 tonnes), 1993: Total fruits excluding melons, 1,332; apples, 160; grapes, 365; potatoes, 280; sugar-beet, 190; wheat, 55; bananas, 62; olives, 103.

Livestock (1996): Sheep, 246,000; cattle, 80,000; pigs, 55,000; goats, 480,000 (1995); chickens, 18m. (1995).

Forestry. The forests of the past have been denuded by exploitation and in 1995 covered 52,000 ha (78,000 ha in 1990). The annual deforestation rate during the years from 1990 to 1995, at 7·8%, was the highest anywhere in the world over the same period. Timber production was 515,000 cu. metres in 1995.

Fisheries. The catch in 1995 was 4,385 tonnes, of which 4,065 tonnes were sea fish.

INDUSTRY

In 1994 there were 23,518 factories operating.

Labour. The workforce was some 650,000 in 1995, of whom 72,000 worked in agriculture. Following considerable labour unrest, an agreement on wage increases and social benefits was concluded between the government and the GCLW in Dec. 1993.

Trade Unions. The main unions are the General Confederation of Lebanese Workers (GCLW) and the General Confederation of Sectoral Unions.

INTERNATIONAL TRADE

Foreign and domestic trade is the principal source of income. Foreign debt was US$2,500m. in 1996.

Imports and Exports. Imports, 1997: US$7,456m.; exports, US$642m.

In 1997 the main export markets (in % of total trade) were: Saudi Arabia, 15·1; UAE, 9·1; USA, 6·1; France, 5·0. Main import suppliers: Italy, 13·2; France, 9·5; USA, 9·2.

COMMUNICATIONS

Roads. There were 7,370 km of roads in 1997, of which 6,265 km were paved. Passenger cars in 1996 numbered 1,217,000 (731 per 1,000 inhabitants), and there were also 81,000 trucks and vans, 54,450 motor cycles and mopeds and 5,640 buses and coaches.

Rail. Railways are state-owned. There is 222 km of standard gauge track.

Civil Aviation. Beirut International Airport was served in 1998 by Aeroflot, Air France, Alitalia, Armenian Airlines, Austrian Airlines, Balkan, British Airways, Cyprus Airways, Czech Airlines, Egyptair, Emirates, Gulf Air, JAT, KLM, Kuwait Airways, Lufthansa, Malaysia Airlines, Malév, Middle East Airlines, Olympic Airways, Qatar Airways, Royal Jordanian, SABENA, Saudia, Swissair, Syrian Arab Airlines, Tarom, Turkish Airlines and Yemenia Yemen Airways. Beirut International handled 1,645,479 passengers in 1996 and 46,505 tonnes of freight. The national airline is the state-owned Middle East Airlines, which in 1995 flew 16·3m. km, carrying 769,800 passengers (all on international flights).

Shipping. Beirut is the largest port, followed by Tripoli, Jounieh and Sidon. Total GRT, 1995, 0·41m., including oil tankers 2,431 GRT and container ships, 1,162 GRT. There are 58 ships in total (1,000 GRT or over).

Telecommunications. In 1997 telephone main lines numbered 561,700, or 178·6 per 1,000 persons. 2 companies are operating a mobile telephone network with 100,000 subscribers in 1996. There were 50,000 PCs and 3,000 fax machines in 1995, and approximately 44,000 Internet users in Jan. 1998.

SOCIAL INSTITUTIONS

Religion. In 1994 it was estimated that the population was 55·3% Moslem (34% Shi'ite and 21·3% Sunni), 37·6% Christian (mainly Maronite) and 7·1% Druze. In 1996 there were 119 Roman Catholic bishops.

Education. There are state and private primary and secondary schools. In 1995–96 there were 367,862 pupils at primary schools and 289,024 in general secondary education plus 47,946 in vocational education. There are 13 universities, including 2 American and 1 French, and 10 other institutions of higher education. In 1995–96 there were 81,588 students in higher education and 10,444 academic staff. Adult literacy was 92·4% in 1995 (94·7% among males and 90·3% among females). In 1994 total expenditure on education came to 2% of GNP.

There is an Academy of Fine Arts.

Health. There were 153 hospitals in 1995 (provision of 22 beds per 10,000 population), and 6,987 doctors, 3,100 dentists, 3,500 nurses and 2,369 pharmacists.

CULTURE

Broadcasting. The government-controlled Radio Lebanon transmits in Arabic, French, English and Armenian. Télé-Liban, which is government-owned, transmits programmes from 13 stations. Colour is by SECAM. There were 1·1m. TV sets in 1995 and 2·68m. radios.

Cinema. In 1993 there were 76 cinemas.

Press. There were about 30 daily newspapers in 1994 in Arabic, 2 in French, 1 in English and 4 in Armenian, and 60 weekly periodicals. A second English language newspaper began publication in 1997.

Tourism. In 1996 there were 420,000 foreign tourists, spending US$715m.

DIPLOMATIC REPRESENTATIVES

Of Lebanon in Great Britain (21 Kensington Palace Gdns., London, W8 4QM)
Ambassador: Dr Mahmoud Hammoud.

Of Great Britain in Lebanon (8th St., Rabieh, Beirut)
Ambassador: David R. MacLennan.

Of Lebanon in the USA (2560 28th St., NW, Washington, D.C., 20008)
Ambassador: Mohamad Bahaa Chatah.

Of the USA in Lebanon (POB 70-840, Antelias, Beirut)
Ambassador: Richard H. Jones.

Of Lebanon to the United Nations
Ambassador: Samir Moubarak.

Of Lebanon to the European Union
Ambassdor: Jihad Mortada.

FURTHER READING
Bleaney, C. H., *Lebanon* [Bibliography]. 2nd ed. Oxford and Santa Barbara (CA), 1991
Choueiri, Y. M., *State and Society in Syria and Lebanon.* Exeter Univ. Press, 1994
Cobban, H., *The Making of Modern Lebanon.* London, 1985
Fisk, R., *Pity the Nation: Lebanon at War.* 2nd ed. OUP, 1992
Gemayel, A., *Rebuilding Lebanon.* New York, 1992
Hiro, D., *Lebanon Fire and Embers: a History of the Lebanese Civil War.* New York, 1993
Shehadi, N. and Mills, D.H., *Lebanon: A History of Conflict and Consensus.* London, 1988
Weinberger, N. J., *Syrian Intervention in Lebanon.* New York, 1986

National library: Dar el Kutub, Parliament Sq., Beirut.
National statistical office: Service de Statistique Générale, Beirut.

LESOTHO

Kingdom of Lesotho

Capital: Maseru
Population estimate, 2000: 2·29m.
GNP per capita: (PPP$) 2,380
HDI/world rank: 0·469/134

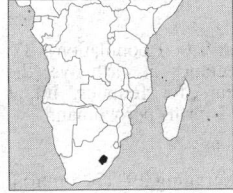

KEY HISTORICAL EVENTS

The Basotho nation was constituted in the 19th century under the leadership of Moshoeshoe I, bringing together refugees from disparate tribes scattered by Zulu expansionism in southern Africa. War with land-hungry Boer settlers in 1856 (and again in 1886) cost the Basotho significant territory, and Moshoeshoe appealed for British protection. This was granted in 1868, and in 1871 the territory was annexed to the Cape Colony (now Republic of South Africa), but in 1883 it was restored to the direct control of the British government through the High Commissioner for South Africa.

In 1955 the Basutoland Council, which had been established in 1903, sought and obtained the right to pass its own laws for its internal affairs. In 1965 full internal self-government was achieved and the paramount chief became King Moshoeshoe II. On 4 Oct. 1966 Basutoland became an independent and sovereign member of the British Commonwealth as the Kingdom of Lesotho. Chief Leabua Jonathan, leader of the Basotho National Party and prime minister from 1965, forced the king to refrain from trying to gain some executive power in 1967, and suspended the constitution when the elections of 1970 were declared invalid. Parliamentary rule, with a national assembly of nominated members, was reintroduced in April 1973; although there was subsequent talk of elections, these were constantly postponed.

On 20 Jan. 1986, after a border blockade by the Republic of South Africa, Chief Jonathan was deposed in a bloodless military *coup* led by Maj.-Gen. Justin Lekhanya who became the chairman of a newly formed military council, banned political parties and granted significant powers to the king. South Africa embarked on a major scheme to develop Lesotho's water resources.

King Moeshoeshoe II was deposed by the Military Council in Nov. 1990 and replaced by King Letsie III. Maj.-Gen. Lekhanya was deposed from the chairmanship of the Military Council in a bloodless coup on 30 April 1991. The Military Council was dissolved and a democratic constitution promulgated in April 1993.

The elections in May 1998 were won by the ruling Lesotho Congress for Democracy, but its opponents said that the poll was rigged. In Sept. 1998 an army mutiny prompted intervention from South Africa to support the government. An agreement was reached allowing the LCD to stay in power for up to 18 months pending new elections, but also foreign troops would remain in Lesotho until its own security forces were ready to maintain law and order.

TERRITORY AND POPULATION

Lesotho is an enclave within South Africa. The area is 11,720 sq. miles (30,355 sq. km). The census in 1986 showed a total population of 1,577,536 persons. Estimate (1996) 2,110,000 (24·0% urban in 1995); density, 69·5 per sq. km.

The UN gives a projected population for 2000 of 2·29m.

There are 10 districts, all named after their chief towns, except Berea (chief town, Teyateyaneng). Area and population:

Region	Area (in sq. km.)	Population (1986 census, in 1,000)	Population (1995 estimate, in 1,000)
Berea	2,222	194·6	206·2
Butha-Buthe	1,767	100·6	135·4
Leribe	2,828	258·0	349·5
Mafeteng	2,119	195·6	259·0
Maseru	4,279	311·1	400·2
Mohale's Hoek	3,530	164·4	231·3
Mokhotlong	4,075	74·7	100·3
Qacha's Nek	2,349	64·0	86·8
Quthing	2,916	110·4	151·9
Thaba-Tseka	4,270	104·1	136·2

LESOTHO

The chief towns (with 1986 census population) are: Maseru, 109,382; Qacha's Nek, 10,000 (1992 estimate); Teyateyaneng, 14,251; Mafeteng, 12,667; Hlotse, 9,595.

The official languages are Sesotho and English.

The population is more than 98% Basotho. The rest is made up of Xhosas, approximately 3,000 expatriate Europeans and several hundred Asians.

SOCIAL STATISTICS

1995 births, 76,000; deaths, 21,000. Rates, 1995: Birth (per 1,000 population), 37; death, 10. Annual growth rate, 1990–95, 2·7%. Life expectancy at birth over the period 1990–95 was 56·4 years for males and 59·0 years for females. Infant mortality, 1990–95, 81 per 1,000 live births; fertility rate, 5·2 births per woman.

CLIMATE

A healthy and pleasant climate, with variable rainfall, but averaging 29" (725 mm) a year over most of the country. The rain falls mainly in the summer months of Oct. to April, while the winters are dry and may produce heavy frosts in lowland areas and frequent snow in the highlands. Temperatures in the lowlands range from a maximum of 90°F (32·2°C) in summer to a minimum of 20°F (–6·7°C) in winter.

CONSTITUTION AND GOVERNMENT

Lesotho is a constitutional monarchy with the King as Head of State. Following the death of his father, Moeshoeshoe II, **Letsie III** succeeded to the throne in Jan. 1996.

The 1993 constitution provides for a *National Assembly* comprising an elected 80-member lower house and a *Senate* of 22 principal chiefs and 11 members nominated by the King.

National Anthem. 'Lesotho fatsela bontat'a rona' ('Lesotho, land of our fathers'); words by F. Coillard, tune by L. Laur.

RECENT ELECTIONS

Parliamentary elections were held on 23 May 1998 for the *National Assembly*. The Lesotho Congress for Democracy won 78 out of the 80 seats with 60·7% of the votes cast.

Following the elections the King swore allegiance to a new constitution and the Military Council was dissolved.

CURRENT ADMINISTRATION

In March 1999 the Council of Ministers comprised:

Prime Minister, Minister of Public Service, Minister of Defence: Bethuel Pakalitha Mosisili (sworn in May 1998).

Deputy Prime Minister, Minister of Agriculture: Kelebone Maope. *Finance and Development Planning:* Leketekete Victor Ketso. *Foreign Affairs:* Motsoahae Thomas Thabane. *Education:* Archibald Lesao Lehohla. *Justice, Human Rights, Law and Constitutional Affairs:* Sephiri Enoch Motanyane. *Employment and Labour:* Notsi Victor Molopo. *Local Government and Home Affairs:* Mopshatla Mabitle. *Environment, Women and Youth Affairs:* Mamoshebi Kabi. *Industry, Trade and Marketing:* Mpho Meli Malie. *Health and Social Welfare:* Vova Bulane. *Tourism, Sport and Culture:* Hlalele Motaung. *Communication (Broadcasting, Posts and Telecommunications):* Nyane Mphafi. *Natural Resources:* Monyane Moleleki. *Works and Transport:* Shakhane Mokhehle.

The *College of Chiefs* settles the recognition and succession of Chiefs and adjudicates cases of inefficiency, criminality and absenteeism among them.

Local Government. The country is divided into 10 districts, subdivided into 22 wards. Most of the wards are presided over by hereditary chiefs.

DEFENCE

The Royal Lesotho Defence Force has 2,000 personnel and is organized in 7 infantry and 1 support company and 1 air squadron with 2 Aviocar transports, 1 Bell 47, 1 Bell 412 and 2 BO-105 helicopters and 1 Cessna 182 light aircraft.

Defence expenditure totalled US$32m. in 1997 (US$15 per capita).

LESOTHO

INTERNATIONAL RELATIONS
Lesotho is a member of the UN, OAU, the Commonwealth, the SADC and is an ACP member state of the ACP-EU relationship.

ECONOMY
Policy. The Lesotho National Development Corporation promotes industrial and tourist trade development.

Performance. Real GDP growth was 7·4% in 1995 (13·5% in 1994).

Budget. In 1m. maloti:

	1992–93	1993–94	1994–95	1995–96	1996–97
Revenue	1,003·1	1,269·4	1,438·5	1,685·3	2,034·6
Expenditure	1,050·9	1,169·4	1,356·0	1,675·9	2,041·7

Currency. The unit of currency is the *loti* (plural *maloti*) (LSL) of 100 *lisente*, at par with the South African rand, which is legal tender. Total money supply in Sept. 1997 was 720m. maloti. The average annual inflation rate during the period 1990–96 was 8·8%. Foreign exchange reserves were US$569m. in Sept. 1997.

Banking and Finance. The Central Bank of Lesotho is the bank of issue, founded in 1982 to succeed the Lesotho Monetary Authority. There are 3 commercial banks. Savings deposits totalled 342·8m. maloti in 1993.

Weights and Measures. The metric system is in use.

ENERGY AND NATURAL RESOURCES
Electricity. Capacity (1993) 13,400 kW (98% supplied by South Africa).

Minerals. Diamonds are the main product. 1990 output was 11,400 carats.

Agriculture. Agriculture contributed 11% of GDP in 1996, and employs two-thirds of the workforce. The chief crops were (1993 production in 1,000 tonnes): Wheat, 9; maize, 92; sorghum, 52; beans, 2; peas and other vegetables are also grown. Soil conservation and the improvement of crops and pasture are matters of vital importance. Area sown to crops, 1993, 264,000 ha.

Livestock (1996): Cattle, 590,000; horses, 120,000; asses, 152,000; sheep, 1·2m.; goats, 670,000 (1995); chickens, 1m.

Forestry. Timber production was 709,000 cu. metres in 1995.

Fisheries. The catch in 1995 was approximately 32 tonnes, exclusively from inland waters.

INDUSTRY
Manufacturing contributed 15·1% of GDP in 1991.

Labour. The labour force in 1996 was 847,000 (63% males). In 1993, 117,600 were working in mines in South Africa.

INTERNATIONAL TRADE
Lesotho, Botswana and Swaziland are members of the South African Customs Union, by agreement dated 29 June 1910. Foreign debt was US$654m. in 1996.

Imports and Exports. In 1995 (in 1,000 maloti) imports were 3,576,000; and exports 581,000.

Principal exports in 1993 (in 1,000 maloti): Cattle, 8,409; wheat flour, 1,717; canned vegetables, 2,275; wool, 16,853; mohair, 5,131; manufactures, 13,426; machinery and transport equipment, 25,540.

The bulk of international trade is with South Africa.

COMMUNICATIONS
Roads. The road network in 1996 totalled 4,955 km, of which 887 km were paved. In 1996 there were 12,610 passenger cars (6 per 1,000 inhabitants) plus 25,000 trucks and vans. In 1993 there were 1,650 traffic accidents with 286 fatalities.

Rail. A branch line built by the South African Railways, 1 mile long, connects Maseru with the Bloemfontein–Natal line at Marseilles for transport of cargo.

Civil Aviation. The national carrier is Air Lesotho, which in 1998 operated services from Maseru Moshoeshoe I International to Cape Town and Johannesburg. South African Airways has flights from Maseru to Johannesburg. Air Lesotho also has regular internal flights to remote districts of Lesotho. In 1996 Maseru handled 31,379 passengers (23,912 on international flights).

Telecommunications. Lesotho had 20,400 main telephone lines in 1997, or 9·6 for every 1,000 persons. There were 600 fax machines in 1995, and approximately 100 Internet users in Jan. 1998. Mobile phones have been available since 1996.

Postal Services. In 1995 there were 155 post offices.

SOCIAL INSTITUTIONS

Justice. The legal system is based on Roman-Dutch law. The Lesotho High Court and the Court of Appeal are situated in Maseru, and there are Magistrates' Courts in the districts. 5,888 criminal offences were reported in 1993.

Religion. In 1995 there were 0·88m. Roman Catholics, 0·6m. Evangelical Protestants, 0·44m. other Christians and 0·14m. of other faiths.

Education. Education levels: Pre-school, 3 to 5 years; first level (elementary), 6 to 12; second level (secondary or teacher training or technical training), 7 to 13; third level (university or teacher training college). Lesotho has the highest proportion of female pupils at primary schools in Africa, with 53% in 1994, and the highest proportion of female teachers at primary schools in mainland Africa, with 79% in 1994. It also has the highest proportion of female pupils in Africa at secondary level education, with 60% in 1994. In 1994–95 there were 366,935 pupils in 1,234 primary schools with 7,433 teachers and 62,399 pupils in 187 secondary schools with 2,655 teachers; in 1993–94 there were 751 students in the National Teacher-Training College with 117 teachers and 1,575 students in 8 technical schools with 108 teachers. The National University of Lesotho was established in 1975 at Roma; enrolment in 1992–93, 1,612 students and 190 teaching staff. The adult literacy rate in 1995 was 71·3% (81·1% among males and 62·3% among females).

Health. There were 136 doctors in 1993, equivalent to 1 for every 14,306 persons. In 1990 there were 874 nurses and 60 pharmacists.

CULTURE

Broadcasting. Radio Lesotho transmits daily in English and Sesotho. The broadcasting authority is the Lesotho National Broadcasting Service. In 1995 there were 75,000 radio and 25,000 TV sets (colour by PAL).

Press. There were 10 weekly and 2 daily newspapers in 1995. Combined circulation of the daily papers was 14,000, at a rate of 7 per 1,000 inhabitants.

Tourism. In 1996 there were 108,000 foreign tourists, spending US$19m.

DIPLOMATIC REPRESENTATIVES
Of Lesotho in Great Britain (7 Chesham Pl., Belgravia, London, SW1 8HN)
High Commissioner: Benjamin M. Masilo.

Of Great Britain in Lesotho (PO Box Ms 521, Maseru 100)
High Commissioner: Kaye Oliver, OBE.

Of Lesotho in the USA (2511 Massachusetts Ave., NW, Washington, D.C., 20008)
Ambassador: Eunice Bulane.

Of the USA in Lesotho (PO Box 333, Maseru 100)
Ambassador: Bismarck Myrick.

Of Lesotho to the United Nations
Ambassador: Percy Metsing Mangoaela.

Of Lesotho to the European Union
Ambassador: R. V. Lechesa.

FURTHER READING
Bureau of Statistics. *Statistical Reports.* Occasional
Bardill, J. E. and Cobbe, J. H., *Lesotho: Dilemmas of Dependence in South Africa.* London, 1986
Johnston, D., *Lesotho* [Bibliography]. 2nd ed. Oxford and Santa Barbara (CA), 1997
Murray, C., *Families Divided: The Impact of Migrant Labour in Lesotho.* OUP, 1981
Willet, S. M. and Ambrose, D. P., *Lesotho.* [Bibliography] Oxford and Santa Barbara (CA), 1981

National statistical office: Bureau of Statistics, PO Box 455, Maseru.

LIBERIA

Republic of Liberia

Capital: Monrovia
Population estimate, 2000: 3·26m.
Estimated GDP: $2·4bn.

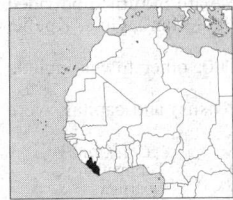

KEY HISTORICAL EVENTS

The Republic of Liberia had its origin in the efforts of several American philanthropic societies to establish freed American slaves in a colony on the West African coast. In 1822 a settlement was formed near the spot where Monrovia now stands. On 26 July 1847 the State was constituted as the Free and Independent Republic of Liberia.

On 12 April 1980, President Tolbert was assassinated and his government overthrown in a coup led by Master-Sergeant Samuel Doe, who was later installed as Head of State and Commander-in-Chief of the army. At the beginning of 1990 rebel forces entered Liberia from the north and fought their way successfully southwards to confront President Doe's forces in Monrovia. The rebels comprised the National Patriotic Front of Liberia (NPFL) led by Charles Taylor, and the hostile breakaway Independent National Patriotic Front led by Prince Johnson. A peacekeeping force dispatched by the Economic Community of West African States (ECOWAS) disembarked at Monrovia on 25 Aug. 1990, and attempts to form a new provisional government were made.

On 9 Sept. 1990 President Doe was assassinated by Prince Johnson's rebels. At an ECOWAS summit at Bamako (Mali) on 28 Nov., government forces and the two rebel factions signed a ceasefire. ECOWAS installed a provisional government led by Amos Sawyer. Charles Taylor also declared himself president, as did the former vice-president, Harry Moniba. On 13 Feb. 1991 Taylor, Johnson and the commander of the Liberian armed forces signed a second ceasefire. After a West African 12-nation summit meeting from July to Oct. 1991 Taylor signed an agreement to allow ECOWAS to disarm his troops and organize elections. However, fighting continued. A UN Security Council resolution in Nov. 1992 imposed an arms embargo and expressed support for ECOWAS's action.

Peace negotiations opened in Geneva in July 1993 between the interim government, the armed forces, the NPFL and the United Liberation Movement (ULIMO) under OAU auspices. A peace agreement was signed on 25 July. On 12 Sept. 1994 the leaders of the 3 military factions, Charles Taylor (NPFL), Alhaji Kromah (ULIMO) and Gen. Hezekiah Bowen, commander of the Armed Forces, met in Ghana and agreed to form a new Council of State, but other warring factions and civilian forces in Monrovia repudiated this. On 21 Dec. 1994 at Accra under Ghanaian auspices the factions concluded an agreement providing for a cease-fire on 28 Dec. 1994, the establishment of safe zones and buffer zones under ECOWAS control, elections on 14 Nov. 1995 and a new 5-member transitional executive. However, factional fighting continued into 1995. On 19 Aug. 1995 an eleventh peace agreement was signed in Abuja by Taylor, Kromah and George Boley (Council for Peace in Liberia, CPL). Fighting broke out in April 1996 between the Krahn and Mandingo branches of ULIMO. It was terminated on 31 July 1996 by an unconditional ceasefire between all factions.

A peace agreement was signed on 17 Aug. 1996 under the auspices of ECOWAS in Abuja which provided for the disarmament of all factions by the end of Jan. 1997 and the election of a president on 31 May 1997. ECOWAS's peacekeeping force, ECOMOG, was increased from 8,500 to 18,000 troops. By the end of Jan. 1997 some 20,000 out of perhaps 60,000 insurgents had surrendered their arms. Possession of arms after that date became a criminal offence. The civil war is reckoned to have killed up to 200,000 people, and made 1m. homeless. A presidential election was held in July 1997. Charles Taylor was elected by an overwhelming majority.

TERRITORY AND POPULATION

Liberia is bounded in the north-west by Sierra Leone, north by Guinea, east by Côte d'Ivoire and south-west by the Atlantic ocean. The total area is 99,067 sq. km. At

LIBERIA

the census (1984) the population was 2,101,628. Estimate (1997) 2,602,100, of whom some 25% were refugees abroad. Density, 26 per sq. km.

The UN gives a projected population for 2000 of 3·26m.

In 1995 an estimated 55% of the population were rural. English is the official language spoken by 15% of the population. The rest belong in the main to 3 linguistic groups: Mande, West Atlantic, and the Kwa. These are in turn subdivided into 16 ethnic groups: Bassa, Bella, Gbandi, Mende, Gio, Dey, Mano, Gola, Kpelle, Kissi, Krahn, Kru, Lorma, Mandingo, Vai and Grebo.

Monrovia, the capital, had (1984) a population of 425,000; other towns include Buchanan (24,000).

There are 13 counties, whose areas, populations (1984 census) and capitals were as follows:

County	Sq. km	1984	Chief town
Bomi	1,955	66,420	Tubmanburg
Bong	8,099	255,813	Gbarnga
Grand Bassa	8,759	159,648	Buchanan
Grand Cape Mount	5,827	79,322	Robertsport
Grand Gedeh	17,029	102,810	Zwedru
Lofa	19,360	247,641	Voinjama
Margibi	3,263	97,992	Kakata
Maryland	5,351	132,058	Harper
Montserrado	2,740	544,878	Bensonville
Nimba	12,043	313,050	Saniquillie
Rivercess	4,385	37,849	Rivercess
Sinoe	10,254	64,147	Greenville

The county of Grand Kru (chief town, Barclayville) was created in 1985 from the former territories of Kru Coast and Sasstown.

SOCIAL STATISTICS
1997 births, estimate, 110,000; deaths, 30,000. 1997 rates (per 1,000 population), estimate: Birth, 42·3; death, 11·5. Annual growth rate, 1990–95, 2·7%. Life expectancy at birth (1997 estimate): Male, 56·4 years; female, 61·7 years. Infant mortality in the period 1990–95 was the highest in the world, at 200 per 1,000 live births, up from 153 per 1,000 live births over the period 1980–85. Fertility rate, 1990–95, 6·8 births per woman.

CLIMATE
An equatorial climate, with constant high temperatures and plentiful rainfall, although Jan. to May is drier than the rest of the year. Monrovia, Jan. 79°F (26·1°C), July 76°F (24·4°C). Annual rainfall 206" (5,138 mm).

CONSTITUTION AND GOVERNMENT
A Constitution was approved by referendum in July 1984 and came into force on 6 Jan. 1986. Under it the National Assembly consisted of a 26-member Senate and a 64-member House of Representatives.

National Anthem. 'All hail, Liberia, hail!'; words by President Daniel Warner, tune by O. Lucas.

RECENT ELECTIONS
Presidential and parliamentary elections were held on 20 July 1997. The electorate was 700,000; turn-out was 85%. Charles Taylor was elected President with 75·3% of the vote. His closest rival, Ellen Johnson-Sirleaf, won 9·6% of the vote. In the elections to the House of Representatives the National Patriotic Party (NPP) won 49 of the 64 seats and in the Senate 21 of the 26 seats.

CURRENT ADMINISTRATION
President: Charles Taylor (NPP).

In March 1999 the Liberian government comprised:

Minister of Agriculture: Roland Massaquoi. *Commerce and Industry:* Brahima Kaba. *Defence:* Daniel Chea. *Education:* Evelyne Kandakai. *Finance:* John Bestman. *Foreign Affairs:* Monie Captan. *Health and Social Welfare:* Peter Coleman. *Information, Culture and Tourism:* Joe W. Mulbah. *Internal Affairs:* Edward Komo Sackor. *Justice:* Eddington Varmah. *Employment:* Thomas

Woewiyu. *Land, Mines and Energy:* Pwandell Faya. *National Security:* Philip Kammah. *Planning and Economic Affairs:* J. Wessah McClaim. *Posts and Telecommunications:* Maxwell Kaba. *Public Works:* Irwin Coleman. *Rural Development:* Hezekiah Bowen. *Transport:* Lamine Kawa. *Youth and Sports:* François Massaquoi. *Minister of State for Presidential Affairs and Chief of Office Staff:* Jonathan Taylor. *Minister of State for Economic Affairs:* Amelia Ward.

DEFENCE
The Armed Forces of Liberia are confined to the capital, Monrovia, and number about 2,000. ULIMO, NPFL and CPL forces control most of the country with combat strengths of 7,000, 12,000 and 2,000 respectively.

An ECOWAS peacekeeping force (ECOMOG, with forces from Ghana, Guinea, Nigeria and Sierra Leone) of some 8,600 is deployed. There is also a 70-strong UN Observer Mission (UNOMIL).

Defence expenditure totalled US$45m. in 1997 (US$14 per capita).

INTERNATIONAL RELATIONS
Liberia is a member of the UN, OAU, ECOWAS and is an ACP member state of the ACP-EU relationship.

ECONOMY
Performance. Real GDP growth was 2·7% in 1995 (2·2% in 1994).

Currency. US currency is legal tender. There is a *Liberian dollar* (LRD), in theory at parity with the US dollar. Since 1993 different notes have been in use in government-held Monrovia and the rebel-held country areas.

Banking and Finance. The National Bank of Liberia opened on 22 July 1974 to act as a central bank. The Governor of the bank is Charles Bright.

Weights and Measures. Weights and measures are the same as in UK and USA.

ENERGY AND NATURAL RESOURCES
Electricity. Installed capacity in 1991 was 430,000 kW. Production, 1994, 485m. kWh. Consumption per capita in 1994 was 179 kWh.

Minerals. Iron ore production was 1·1m. tonnes in 1992. Gold production (1991) 600 kg and diamond production (1992) 150,000 carats.

Agriculture. In 1995 more than 70% of the labour force were engaged in agriculture. The soil is productive, but due to excessive rainfall there are large swamp areas. Principal crops (1995) in 1,000 metric tonnes: Cassava, 450; rice, 50; sugar cane, 234; bananas, 82; vegetables and melons, 76. Coffee, cocoa and palm-kernels are produced mainly by the traditional agricultural sector. Livestock (1996): Cattle, 36,000; pigs, 120,000; sheep, 210,000; goats, 220,000; chickens, 4m.

Forestry. Forest area was 4·51m. ha (46·8% of the land area) in 1995, down from 4·64m. ha and 48·2% in 1990. In 1995, 6·27m. cu. metres of roundwood were cut. There are rubber plantations.

Fisheries. The catch in 1995 was estimated to be 7,700 tonnes, of which approximately 52% were from sea fishing.

INDUSTRY
There are a number of small factories.

Labour. In 1996 the labour force was 977,000 (61% males). In 1995 around 70% of the population were engaged in agriculture, fisheries and forestry.

INTERNATIONAL TRADE
Foreign debt was US$2,107m. in 1996.

Imports and Exports. Imports in 1995 were estimated at US$5·8bn. and exports at US$667m. Liberia's main trading partners are the USA and European Union member countries.

In 1987 iron ore accounted for about 70% of total export earnings, rubber 15% and sawn timber over 5%. Other exports were coffee, cocoa, palm-kernel oil, diamonds and gold.

LIBERIA

COMMUNICATIONS

Roads. There were 10,600 km of roads in 1996 (660 km paved). In 1995 there were 10,300 cars and 28,300 goods vehicles.

Rail. There is a total of 490 km single track. A 148-km freight line connects iron mines to Monrovia. There is a line from Bong to Monrovia (78 km). All railways were out of use in 1997 because of the civil war.

Civil Aviation. There are 2 international airports (Roberts International and Sprigg Payne), both near Monrovia. In 1998 there were services to Abidjan (with Ghana Airways and Air Ivoire), Accra (Ghana Airways), Banjul (Air Afrique), Conakry (Air Ivoire), Dakar (Air Afrique) and Freetown (Ghana Airways).

Shipping. There are ports at Buchanan, Greenville, Harper and Monrovia. Over 2,000 vessels enter Monrovia each year. The Liberian Government requires only a modest registration fee and an almost nominal annual charge and maintains no control over the operation of ships flying the Liberian flag. In 1995 shipping registered totalled 91·76m. DWT, all foreign-owned.

Telecommunications. Telephone main lines numbered 6,400 in 1997, or 2·2 per 1,000 persons.

SOCIAL INSTITUTIONS

Religion. There were (1993) about 0·85m. Sunni Moslems, and some 125,000 Roman Catholics, 50,000 Methodists, 40,000 Baptists, 32,000 Lutherans and 25,000 Anglicans.

Education. Schools are classified as: (1) Public schools, maintained and run by the Government; (2) Mission schools, supported by foreign Missions and subsidized by the Government, and operated by qualified Missionaries and Liberian teachers; (3) Private schools, maintained by endowments and sometimes subsidized by the Government. There are no up-to-date figures for schools, teachers or pupils. Adult literacy (1995) is 38·3%; 53·9% among males, 22·4% among females.

Health. There were 82 hospitals in 1988.

CULTURE

Broadcasting. In 1995 there were 675,000 radio and 56,000 television receivers.

Press. There were 8 daily newspapers in 1995 with a combined circulation of 35,000.

DIPLOMATIC REPRESENTATIVES

Of Liberia in Great Britain (2 Pembridge Pl., London, W2 4XB)
Ambassador: William V. S. Bull.

Of Great Britain in Liberia
Ambassador: H. B. Warren-Gash (resides in Abidjan).

Of Liberia in the USA (5201 16th St., NW, Washington, D.C., 20011)
Ambassador: Rachel Diggs.

Of the USA in Liberia (111 United Nations Drive, Mamba Point, Monrovia)
Ambassador: William B. Milam.

Of Liberia to the United Nations
Ambassador: Vacant.

Of Liberia to the European Union
Ambassador: Vacant.

FURTHER READING
Daniels, A., *Monrovia Mon Amour: a Visit to Liberia*. London, 1992
Elwood Dunn, D., *Liberia*. [Bibliography]. Oxford and Santa Barbara (CA), 1995
Sawyer, A., *The Emergence of Autocracy in Liberia: Tragedy and Challenge*. San Francisco, 1992

LIBYA

Jamahiriya Al-Arabiya
Al-Libiya Al-Shabiya
Al-Ishtirakiya Al-Uzma
(Great Socialist People's
Libyan Arab Republic)

Capital: Tripoli
Population estimate, 2000: 6·39m.
Estimated GDP: $34·5bn.
HDI/world rank: 0·806/64

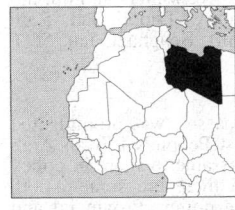

KEY HISTORICAL EVENTS

Tripoli fell under Ottoman domination in the 16th century, and although in 1711 the Arab population secured some measure of independence, the country came under the direct rule of Turkey in 1835. In 1911, Italy occupied Tripoli and in 1912, by the Treaty of Ouchy, Turkey recognized the sovereignty of Italy in Tripoli.

During the Second World War, the British army expelled the Italians and their German allies, and Tripolitania and Cyrenaica were placed under British, and Fezzan under French, military administration. This continued until 1950 under a UN directive. Libya became an independent, sovereign kingdom with the former Amir of Cyrenaica, Muhammad Idris al Senussi, as king on 24 Dec. 1951.

King Idris was deposed in Sept. 1969 by a group of army officers, 12 of whom formed the Revolutionary Command Council which, chaired by Col. Muammar Qadhafi, proclaimed the Libyan Arab Republic. Qadhafi favoured Arab unity, but his efforts in that direction have been abortive. The Federation of the Arab Republics formed in 1972 with Libya, Egypt and Syria as members, an agreement to merge Libya and Egypt in 1973, a proposed union with Tunisia in 1974, and a union with Syria in 1980 have all proved unsuccessful.

In 1977 the country's name was changed to Great Socialist People's Libyan Arab Jamahiriya. At the same time the Revolutionary Command Council was superceded by a more democratic system of People's Congress and Popular Committees. Qadhafi remained head of state. Throughout the 1980s Libya had constant disagreements with its neighbours and its relations with the USA and other Western countries deteriorated, culminating in the US bombing of the capital in April 1987, in an attempt to punish Qadhafi for his alleged support of international terrorism.

A US trade embargo was enforced in 1986. In 1992 the UN imposed sanctions and the USA banned international flights and the sale of defence equipment to Libya because it refused to surrender suspects in the 1988 bombing of a Pan Am flight over Lockerbie in Scotland. In 1996 US sanctions were widened to penalize any foreign company that invested more than US$40m. in Libya's oil industry. In April 1999, Libya handed over 2 men suspected of planting the bomb on the Pan Am airliner to be tried in the Netherlands but under Scottish law. The UN responded to Libya's disavowal of terrorism with a promise to lift sanctions but the US trade embargo remains in place.

TERRITORY AND POPULATION

Libya is bounded in the north by the Mediterranean Sea, east by Egypt and Sudan, south by Chad and Niger and west by Algeria and Tunisia. The area is estimated at 1,775,500 sq. km. The population at the census on 31 July 1984 was 3,637,488. Estimate (1996), 5·59m. (86% urban; 47·9% female); density, 3·18 per sq. km.

The UN gives a projected population for 2000 of 6·39m.

The country was formerly divided into 13 administrative regions, but as of 1998 there are 26 administrative regions (*Shabiyat*). They are Shabiya Al-Batan, Shabiya Jabal Al-Akhdar, Shabiya Al-Wahad, Shabiya Al-Jofra, Shabiya Wadi Al-Hait, Shabiya Al-Morqib, Shabiya Tripoli, Shabiya Sabrata/Sorman, Shabiya Yefrin, Shabiya Derna, Shabiya Al-Marj, Shabiya Al-Kofra, Shabiya Murzaq, Shabiya Wadi Al-Shaati, Shabiya Ben Walid, Shabiya Al-Jafarah, Shabiya Nikat Al-Khams,

Shabiya Nalout, Shabiya Al-Qoba, Shabiya Benghazi, Shabiya Sirte, Shabiya Sabah, Shabiya Musrata, Shabiya Tarhouna/Msallata, Shabiya Zawiyah and Shabiya Gharyan.

The official language is Arabic.

SOCIAL STATISTICS
1997 births, 255,000; deaths, 43,000. Birth rate, 1997 (per 1,000 population), 43·9; death rate, 7·5. Life expectancy (1997 estimate), 65·0 years; growth rate, 3·64%. Infant mortality, 1990–95, 68 per 1,000 live births; fertility rate, 6·4 births per woman.

CLIMATE
The coastal region has a warm temperate climate, with mild wet winters and hot dry summers, although most of the country suffers from aridity. Tripoli, Jan. 52°F (11·1°C), July 81°F (27·2°C). Annual rainfall 16" (400 mm). Benghazi, Jan. 56°F (13·3°C), July 77°F (25°C). Annual rainfall 11" (267 mm).

CONSTITUTION AND GOVERNMENT
In 1977 a new form of direct democracy, the state of the masses, was promulgated and the name of the country was changed to Great Socialist People's Libyan Arab Jamahiriya. Under this system, every adult is supposed to be able to share in policy making through the Basic People's Congresses of which there are some 2,000. These Congresses appoint People's Committees to execute policy. Provincial and urban affairs are handled by People's Committees responsible to Municipality People's Congresses, of which there are 26, now called *Shabiyat*. Officials of these Congresses and Committees form at national level the 3,000-member General People's Congress which normally meets for about a week early each year (usually in March). This is the highest policy-making body in the country. The General People's Congress appoints its own General Secretariat and the General People's Committee, whose members (the equivalents of ministers elsewhere) head the government departments which execute policy at national level.

Until 1977 Libya was ruled by a Revolutionary Command Council (RCC) headed by Col. Muammar Qadhafi. Upon its abolition in that year the 5 surviving members of the RCC became the General Secretariat of the General People's Congress, still under Qadhafi's direction. In 1979 they stood down to be replaced by officials elected by the Congress. Since then, Col. Qadhafi has retained his position as Leader of the Revolution. Neither he nor his former RCC colleagues have any formal posts in the present administration, although they continue to wield considerable authority.

National Anthem. 'Allah Akbar' ('God is Great'); words by Abdullah Al-Din, tune by Mahmoud Al-Sharif.

CURRENT ADMINISTRATION
Leader: Col. Muammar Abu Minyar al-Qadhafi.

In March 1999 the General People's Congress comprised:

Secretary: Muhammad al-Zanati. *Assistant:* Ali Mursi al-Shairi.

In March 1999 the General People's Committee comprised:

Secretary: Muhammad Ahmad al-Manqush. *Secretary of Agriculture:* Ali Yusuf Juma. *Animal Wealth:* Masud Abu-Suwa. *Culture:* Juma Fazani. *Communications and Transport:* Izz al-Din al-Muhammad al-Hinshiri. *Economy and Trade:* Abd al-Hafidh Mahmud Zalitni. *Education and Vocational Training:* Matuq Muhammad Matuq. *Energy:* Abdallah Salim al-Badri. *Finance:* Muhammad Bayt al-Mal. *Health and Social Security:* Dr. Hutaywish Faraj Hutaywish. *Housing and Utilities:* Mubarak al-Shamikh. *Industry and Mines:* Muftah Azzouz. *Information, Culture and Mass Mobilization:* Fawziyah al-Shalabi. *Justice and Public Security:* Muhammad Abu al-Qasim al-Zuwayy. *Marine Resources:* Bashir Ramadan Abu-Jinah. *People's Control and Follow-Up:* Mahmud Badi. *People's External Liaison and International Co-operation Bureau:* Omar Mustafa al-Montassir. *Planning:* Jadallah Azzouz al-Talhi. *Tourism:* Al-Bukhair Salem Huda. *Youth and Sport:* Muhhamad Mahmud al-Hijazi.

The *Speaker* of the Congress is Abd Al-Raziq Sawsa.

Local Government. An administrative decentralizing reform of 1992 divided the country into some 1,500 self-managing communes, each with an elected 13-member

LIBYA

People's Committee, grouped into 13 administrative regions (*Baladiyat*). This system was replaced in 1998 by a new one, known as *Shabiyat*, with the country being divided into 26 *Shabiyat*.

DEFENCE
There is selective conscription for 1–2 years. Defence expenditure in 1997 totalled US$1,250m. (US$215 per capita), representing 4·7% of GDP.

Nuclear weapons. It is still thought that Libya is interested in acquiring nuclear weapons, but a UN embargo has hampered progress.

Army. There are 7 military districts. The Army is organized into 5 elite and 5 surface-to-surface missile brigades and 21 infantry, 8 mechanized infantry, 22 artillery, 8 air defence, 10 tank and 15 parachute commando battalions. Equipment includes 1,600 T-54/-55, 350 T-62 and 260 T-72 main battle tanks. Strength (1997) 35,000 (25,000 conscripts).

Navy. The fleet, a mixture of Soviet and West European-built ships, comprises 4 old Soviet-built diesel submarines, 2 missile-armed frigates, 4 missile-armed corvettes, 24 fast missile craft, 8 inshore patrol craft and 8 offshore minesweepers. There are 2 tank landing ships and 3 medium landing ships as well as 3 landing craft. Auxiliaries include 1 logistic support ship, 1 salvage ship, 6 transports and 1 diving support ship.
  There is a small Naval Aviation wing operating 25 Mi-14 Haze and 5 Super-Frelon helicopters from shore bases.
  Personnel in 1997 totalled 8,000, including coastguard. The forces are based at Tripoli, Benghazi, Derna, Tobruk, Sidi Bilal and Al Khums.

Air Force. The Air Force has over 300 combat aircraft but most are in storage. About 100 MiG-23, MiG-25 and Su-22 aircraft can be flown and there are also some armed Gazelle and Mi-24 helicopters. Other equipment includes 10 C-130/L-100 Hercules, 10 An-26, 12 Il-76 and 20 Aeritalia G222T transports, 8 Super Frelon and 6 Agusta-built CH-47C Chinook heavy-lift helicopters, and a total of 16 Bell 212, Bell 47, Alouette III and Mi-8 helicopters. Training is performed on piston-engined SF.260Ms (some of which are armed for light attack duties) from Italy; L-39 Albatros, Galeb and Magister jet aircraft; and twin-engined L-410s built in the former Czechoslovakia. Personnel total (1997) about 22,000, with some of the combat aircraft operated by Syrian aircrew.

INTERNATIONAL RELATIONS
Libya is a member of the UN, OAU, OPEC and the Arab League.

ECONOMY

Policy. An enactment of the People's General Congress in Sept. 1992 authorizes the privatization of enterprises.

Performance. Real GDP growth was 1·2% in 1995 (1·3% in 1994).

Budget. In 1995 revenues were estimated to be US$10·4bn. and expenditures US$10·3bn.

Currency. The unit of currency is the *Libyan dinar* (LYD) of 1,000 *millemes*. The dinar was devalued 15% in Nov. 1994, and alongside the official exchange rate a new rate was applied to private sector imports. Total money supply in June 1997 was 6,627m. dinars.

Banking and Finance. A National Bank of Libya was established in 1955; it was renamed the Central Bank of Libya in 1972. The *Governor* is Tahir al-Jihimi. All foreign banks were nationalized by Dec. 1970. In 1972 the government set up the Libyan Arab Foreign Bank whose function is overseas investment and to participate in multinational banking corporations. The National Agricultural Bank has been set up to give loans and subsidies to farmers to develop their land and to assist them in marketing their crops.

Weights and Measures. Although the metric system has been officially adopted and is obligatory for all contracts, the following weights and measures are still used: *oke* = 1·282 kg; *kantar* = 51·28 kg; *draa* = 46 cm; *handaza* = 68 cm.

ENERGY AND NATURAL RESOURCES

Electricity. Installed capacity in 1996 was 4·2m. kW. Production was 11·91bn. kWh in 1996. Consumption per capita was estimated to be 3,012 kWh in 1995.

Oil and Gas. As a total GDP of US$32,280·8m. in 1996, the oil sector accounted for US$7,731·5m. Crude oil production (1996) 1,410,000 bbls. a day. Reserves 23,000m. bbls. The Libyan National Oil Corporation (NOC) is the state's organization for the exploitation of oil resources. Since US oil companies withdrew due to sanctions, European rivals have been quick to move in.

Gas reserves 620,000m. cu. metres. Agip, the Italian oil company, is investing US$3bn. in a project to export natural gas to Europe. Production (1995) 246 petajoules.

Water. Since 1984 a major project has been under way to bring water from wells in southern Libya to the coast. This scheme, called the 'Great Man-Made River', is planned, on completion, to irrigate some 185,000 acres of land with water brought along some 4,000 km of pipes. Phase I was completed in Aug. 1991 at a cost of US$3,300m.; Phase II of the project (covering the west of Libya) was announced in Sept. 1989.

Minerals. Cement production (1994 estimate) 2·3m. tonnes. Iron ore deposits have been found in the south.

Agriculture. Only the coastal zone, which covers an area of about 17,000 sq. miles, is really suitable for agriculture. Of some 25m. acres of productive land, nearly 20m. are used for grazing and about 1m. for static farming. The sub-desert zone produces the alfalfa plant. The desert zone and the Fezzan contain some fertile oases.

Cyrenaica has about 10m. acres of potentially productive land and is suitable for grazing. Certain areas are suitable for dry farming; in addition, grapes, olives and dates are grown. About 143,000 acres are used for settled farming; about 272,000 acres are covered by natural forests. The Agricultural Development Authority plans to reclaim 6,000 ha each year for agriculture. In the Fezzan there are about 6,700 acres of irrigated gardens and about 297,000 acres are planted with date palms.

Production (1995, in tonnes): Wheat, 167,000; barley, 148,000; olives, 62,000; dates, 68,000.

Livestock (1996): 4·4m. sheep, 800,000 goats (1995), 100,000 cattle, 130,000 camels (1995), 17m. chickens. (1995).

Forestry. Forest area in 1995 was 6,000 ha (0·2% of the land area). In 1995, 651,000 cu. metres of roundwood were cut.

Fisheries. The catch in 1995 was approximately 34,500 tonnes, almost entirely from marine waters.

INDUSTRY

Industry is nationalized. Small scale private sector industrialization in the form of partnerships is permitted. Output (1994) per 1,000 metric tonnes: Residual fuel oils, 4,900; distillate fuel oils, 4,100.

Labour. The labour force in 1996 was 1,601,000 (79% males).

INTERNATIONAL TRADE

Since 1986 the USA has applied a trade embargo on the grounds of Libya's alleged complicity in terrorism. In 1992 UN sanctions were imposed for Libya's refusal to deliver suspected terrorists for trial in the UK or USA. In Feb. 1989 Libya signed a treaty of economic co-operation with the 4 other Maghreb countries; Algeria, Mauritania, Morocco and Tunisia.

Imports and Exports. Some 80% of GDP derives from trade. Oil accounts for over 95% of exports worth 1,914·5m. dinars and exports at 3,578·8m. dinars. Main export markets in 1995 were Italy, Germany, Spain, France, UK and Turkey; main import suppliers were Italy, Germany, UK, France, Spain and Turkey.

COMMUNICATIONS

Roads. There were 83,200 km of roads in 1996, of which 47,600 km were surfaced. Passenger cars numbered 448,000 in 1996 (81 per 1,000 inhabitants), in addition to which there were 332,000 trucks and vans.

LIBYA

Civil Aviation. The UN ban on air traffic to and from Libya enforced since April 1992 now seems likely to be lifted following the handing over for trial of 2 suspected Lockerbie bombers. Libyan Arab Airlines provides domestic services, and flew 3·5m. km in 1995, carrying 623,200 passengers.

Shipping. Sea-going vessels totalled 1·22m. GRT in 1995, including oil tankers, 1·09m. GRT.

Telecommunications. In 1996 main telephone lines numbered 380,000 (67·9 per 1,000 population).

Postal Services. In 1994 there were 383 post offices, or 1 for every 13,700 persons.

SOCIAL INSTITUTIONS

Justice. The Civil, Commercial and Criminal codes are based mainly on the Egyptian model. Matters of personal status of family or succession matters affecting Moslems are dealt with in special courts according to the Moslem law. All other matters, civil, commercial and criminal, are tried in the ordinary courts, which have jurisdiction over everyone.

There are civil and penal courts in Tripoli and Benghazi, with subsidiary courts at Misurata and Derna; courts of assize in Tripoli and Benghazi, and courts of appeal in Tripoli and Benghazi.

Religion. Islam is declared the State religion, but the right of others to practise their religions is provided for. In 1990, 97% were Sunni Moslems.

Education. In 1995–96 there were 1,460,433 primary and preparatory (called basic education) school pupils, and in 1992–93 there were 310,556 secondary level pupils. In 1994–95 there were 3 universities and 1 medical and 1 technological university. There were 3 other institutes of higher education. In 1994–95 there were 31,140 university students and 1,710 academic staff. Adult literacy (1995) 76·2%; male 87·9%, female 63%.

Health. In 1990 there were 4,749 physicians, 686 dentists and 13,849 nurses. Provision of hospital beds in 1990 was 41 per 10,000 population.

CULTURE

Broadcasting. Broadcasting is controlled by the government Libyan Jamihiriya Broadcasting and People's Revolution Broadcasting-Television. Radio has a home service, external services in English, French and Arabic and a Holy Koran programme. In 1995 there were estimated to be 1·25m. radio and 550,000 TV receivers (colour by PAL).

Press. In 1995 there were 4 daily newspapers with a combined circulation of 71,000.

Tourism. In 1996 there were 88,000 foreign tourists, spending US$6m.

DIPLOMATIC REPRESENTATIVES

UK broke off diplomatic relations with Libya on 22 April 1984. Saudi Arabia looks after Libyan interests in UK and Italy looks after the UK's interests in Libya.

USA suspended all embassy activities in Tripoli on 2 May 1980.

Of Libya to the United Nations
Ambassador: Abuzed Omar Dorda.

Of Libya to the European Union
Ambassador: Hamed Elhouderi.

FURTHER READING
Bearman, J., *Qadhafi's Libya*. London, 1986
Blundy, D. and Lycett, A., *Qadhafi and the Libyan Revolution*. London, 1987
Davis, J., *Libyan Politics: Tribe and Revolution*. London, 1988
Harris, L. C., *Libya: Qadhafi's Revolution and the Modern State*. Boulder (CO) and London, 1986
Lawless, R. I., *Libya*. [Bibliography] Oxford and Santa Barbara (CA), 1987
Pazzanita, A. G., *The Maghreb*. [Bibliography] Oxford and Santa Barbara (CA), 1998
Simons, G., *Libya: the Struggle for Survival*. London, 1993
Vandewalle, D. (ed.) *Qadhafi's Libya, 1969-1994*. London, 1995
Wright, J., *Libya: a Modern History*. London, 1982

LIECHTENSTEIN

Fürstentum Liechtenstein

(Principality of Liechtenstein)

Capital: Vaduz
Population estimate 2000: 33,000
Estimated GDP: $713m.

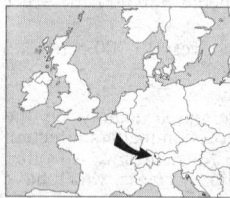

KEY HISTORICAL EVENTS

Liechtenstein is a sovereign state whose history dates back to 3 May 1342 when Count Hartmann III became ruler of the county of Vaduz. Additions were later made to the count's domains and by 1434 the territory reached its present boundaries. It consists of the two former counties of Schellenberg and Vaduz (until 1806 immediate fiefs of the Holy Roman Empire). The former in 1699 and the latter in 1712 came into the possession of the house of Liechtenstein. On 23 Jan. 1719 the Emperor Charles VI constituted the two counties as the Principality of Liechtenstein. In 1862 the constitution established an elected diet which was to participate in the legislative process. After the First World War, Liechtenstein severed its treaties with Austria in 1919 and turned towards Switzerland, adopting Swiss currency in 1921. Liechtenstein has been represented abroad by Switzerland since 1919. On 5 Oct. 1921 a new constitution based on that of Switzerland extended democratic rights. It also stated that the head of government must be a Liechtenstein citizen.

TERRITORY AND POPULATION

Liechtenstein is bounded on the east by Austria and the west by Switzerland. Total area 160 sq. km (61·8 sq. miles). The population was 31,320 (census 1997) (16,113 females), including 10,730 resident foreigners, giving a density of 195 per sq. km.

In 2000 the population is projected to be 33,000.

The population of Liechtenstein is predominantly rural. Population of Vaduz (1997) 4,975. The language is German.

SOCIAL STATISTICS

In 1997 there were 435 births and 230 deaths (rates of 13·9 per 1,000 population and 7·3 respectively). The annual growth rate was 1·3% over the period 1990–95.

CLIMATE

There is a distinct difference in climate between the higher mountains and the valleys. In summer the peaks can often be foggy while the valleys remain sunny and warm, while in winter the valleys can often be foggy and cold whilst the peaks remain sunny and comparatively warm. Vaduz, Jan. 0°C, July 20°C. Annual rainfall 1,090 mm.

CONSTITUTION AND GOVERNMENT

Liechtenstein is a constitutional monarchy ruled by the princes of the House of Liechtenstein.

The reigning Prince is **Hans-Adam II,** b. 14 Feb. 1945; he succeeded his father Prince Francis-Joseph, 13 Nov. 1989 (he exercised the prerogatives to which the Sovereign is entitled from 26 Aug. 1984); married on 30 July 1967 to Countess Marie Kinsky. *Offspring:* Hereditary Prince Alois (b. 11 June 1968), married Duchess Sophie of Bavaria on 3 July 1993 (*Offspring:* Prince Joseph Wenzel, b. 16 May 1995; Marie Caroline, b. 17 Oct. 1996); Prince Maximilian (b. 16 May 1969); Prince Constantin (b. 15 March 1972); Princess Tatjana (b. 10 April 1973). The monarchy is hereditary in the male line.

The present constitution of 5 Oct. 1921 provided for a unicameral parliament (*Landtag*) of 15 members elected for 4 years, but this was amended to 25 members in 1988. Election is on the basis of proportional representation. The prince can call and dismiss the parliament. On parliamentary recommendation, he appoints the prime minister and the 4 councillors for a 4-year term. Any group of 1,000 persons or any 3 communes may propose legislation (initiative). Bills passed by the parliament may be submitted to popular referendum. A law is valid when it receives a majority approval by the parliament and the prince's signed concurrence. The capital is Vaduz.

National Anthem. 'Oben am jungen Rhein' ('Up above the young Rhine'); words by H. H. Jauch; tune, 'God save the Queen'.

RECENT ELECTIONS
At the elections on 2 Feb. 1997 the Fatherland Union (VU) gained 13 seats; the Progressive Citizens' Party, 10; Free List, 2.

CURRENT ADMINISTRATION
Head of Government, Minister for Finance and Construction: Dr Mario Frick (b. 1965; VU; sworn in 14 April 1997). On becoming prime minister following the election of 24 Oct. 1993, he became the world's youngest prime minister, at the age of 28.

Deputy Head of Government, Minister for the Economy, the Interior, Health and Social Services: Michael Ritter. *Culture and Sport, Family Affairs and Equal Rights and Foreign Relations:* Andrea Willi. *Education, Environment, Agriculture and Forestry and Transportation:* Norbert Marxer. *Justice:* Heinz Frommelt.

Local Government. There are 11 communes, fully independent administrative bodies within the laws of the principality. They levy additional taxes to the state taxes.

INTERNATIONAL RELATIONS
Liechtenstein is a member of the UN, EFTA, EEA and the Council of Europe.

ECONOMY
Liechtenstein is one of the world's richest countries with a well diversified economy. Low taxes and strict bank secrecy laws have made Liechtenstein a successful offshore financial centre.

Performance. Real GDP growth was 0·7% in 1995 and 1·2% in 1994.

Budget. Budget (in Swiss francs), 1998: Revenue, 591,317,000; expenditure, 557,492,000. There is no public debt.

Currency. Swiss currency has been in use since 1921.

Banking and Finance. There are 8 banks (1998). Combined total assets were 29,076m. Swiss francs in 1997.

Weights and Measures. The metric system is in force.

ENERGY AND NATURAL RESOURCES
Electricity. In 1997 imported capacity was 1,171,569 MW; electricity produced was 77,816 MWh.

Agriculture. In 1990 there were 3,890 ha of cultivated land and 2,510 ha of Alpine pasture. The rearing of cattle on the Alpine pastures is highly developed. In 1997 there were 5,489 cattle (including 2,614 milch cows), 342 horses, 3,608 sheep, 287 goats, 2,056 pigs. Total production of dairy produce in 1997 was 13,079 tonnes.

Forestry. In 1995 there were 5,560 ha of forest (34·7% of the land area). 19,527 cu. metres of timber were cut in 1997.

INDUSTRY
The country is highly industrialized, and has a great variety of light industries (textiles, ceramics, steel screws, precision instruments, canned food, pharmaceutical products, heating appliances, etc.).

Labour. The farming population has gone down from 70% in 1930 to 1·3% in 1997. The rapid change-over has led to the immigration of foreign workers (Austrians, Germans, Italians, Spaniards). The workforce was 15,922 in 1997, excluding employees commuting from abroad (8,743 in 1997). Industrial undertakings affiliated to the Liechtenstein Chamber of Commerce in 1996 employed 6,825 workers earning 469·83m. Swiss francs.

INTERNATIONAL TRADE

Liechtenstein has been in a customs union with Switzerland since 1923.

Imports and Exports. Exports of home produce in 1996 (in Swiss francs), for member companies affiliated to the Chamber of Industry and Commerce, amounted to 3,510m. Swiss francs: 458m. (13%) went to Switzerland, 1,584m. (45·2%) went to EEA countries and 1,468m. (41·8%) went to other countries. Imports in 1997 amounted to 1,179·32m. Swiss francs.

COMMUNICATIONS

Roads. There are 250 km of roads. Postal buses are the chief means of public transportation within the country and to Austria and Switzerland. There were 19,926 cars in 1997. There were 367 road accidents in 1997 (6 fatal).

Rail. The 18·5 km of main railway passing through the country is operated by Austrian Federal Railways.

Telecommunications. In 1996 there were 19,916 telephones and 129 telex.

Postal Services. Post and telegraphs are administered by Switzerland.

SOCIAL INSTITUTIONS

Justice. The principality has its own civil and penal codes. The lowest court is the county court, *Landgericht*, presided over by one judge, which decides minor civil cases and summary criminal offences. The criminal court, *Kriminalgericht*, with a bench of 5 judges is for major crimes. Another court of mixed jurisdiction is the court of assizes (with 3 judges) for misdemeanours. Juvenile cases are treated in the Juvenile Court (with a bench of 3 judges). The superior court, *Obergericht*, and Supreme Court, *Oberster Gerichtshof*, are courts of appeal for civil and criminal cases (both with benches of 5 judges). An administrative court of appeal from government actions and the State Court determines the constitutionality of laws.
　　The death penalty was abolished in 1989.

Police. The principality has no army. 1998: Police force 62, auxiliary police 14.

Religion. In 1997 there were 24,962 Roman Catholics and 2,279 Protestants.

Education. In 1997 there were 14 primary, 3 upper, 5 secondary and 1 grammar schools, with 3,955 pupils and 367 teachers. There is also an evening technical school, a music school and a children's pedagogic-welfare day school.

Health. There is an obligatory sickness insurance scheme. In 1989 there was 1 hospital, but Liechtenstein has an agreement with the Swiss cantons of St Gallen and Graubünden and the Austrian Federal State of Vorarlberg that her citizens may use certain hospitals. In 1995 there were 32 doctors, 12 dentists and 2 pharmacists.

CULTURE

Broadcasting. In 1996 there were 12,382 radios and 11,979 TV sets.

Cinema. There were 2 cinemas in 1998.

Press. In 1998 there were 2 daily newspapers with a total circulation of 17,900, and 1 weekly with a circulation of 13,900.

Tourism. In 1997, 58,197 visitors arrived in Liechtenstein.

DIPLOMATIC REPRESENTATIVES

In 1919 Switzerland agreed to represent the interests of Liechtenstein in countries where it has diplomatic missions and where Liechtenstein is not represented in its own right. In so doing Switzerland always acts only on the basis of mandates of a general or specific nature, which it may either accept or refuse, while Liechtenstein is free to enter into direct relations with foreign states or to set up its own additional diplomatic missions.

LIECHTENSTEIN

Of Great Britain in Liechtenstein
Ambassador: Mr C. Hulse (resides in Berne).

Of Liechtenstein to the United Nations
Ambassador: Claudia Fritsche.

Of Liechtenstein to the European Union
Ambassador: Prince Nicolas of Liechtenstein.

FURTHER READING

Amt für Volkswirtschaft. *Statistisches Jahrbuch.* Vaduz

Rechenschaftsbericht der Fürstlichen Regierung. Vaduz. Annual, from 1922
Jahrbuch des Historischen Vereins. Vaduz. Annual since 1901
National library: Landesbibliothek, Vaduz

National statistical office: Amt für Volkswirtschaft, Vaduz

LITHUANIA

Lietuvos Respublika

Capital: Vilnius
Population estimate, 2000: 3·69m.
GNP per capita: (PPP$) 4,390
HDI/world rank: 0·750/79

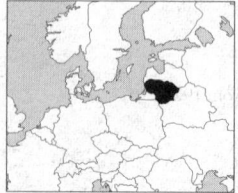

KEY HISTORICAL EVENTS

Lithuanian tribes which were organized into state units in the 9th century unified in the face of encroachment by the German order of Teutonic Knights. At the time of Tatar-Mongol domination of Russia, Lithuania annexed Russian lands until by the middle of the 15th century Belorussia, parts of Russia and Ukraine as far as the Black Sea were under its rule. Lithuania united with Poland dynastically in 1385 and politically in 1569. During the partitions of the Polish-Lithuanian Commonwealth by Russia, Prussia and Austria in the 18th century, Lithuania yielded its Russian territories and was absorbed into the Russian empire in 1795.

Following the German occupation during the First World War and the Russian revolution on 16 Feb. 1918, the Lithuanian Council proclaimed the restoration of the Lithuanian state. The Soviets attempted re-capturing the lost lands and heavy fighting occurred between the Soviet, German, Polish and Lithuanian forces. In April 1919, the Soviets withdrew and the re-formed Lithuanian government established a democratic republic. Lithuanian independence was recognized by the Treaty of Versailles. The peace treaty between Lithuania and the Soviet Union was signed in July 1920. In Oct. 1919, Poland occupied Vilnius, the capital of the historic Lithuanian state, and incorporated it into Poland in 1923 (this was acknowledged by Lithuania only in 1938). In Dec. 1926, the democratic régime was overthrown by a coup.

The secret protocol of the Soviet-German frontier treaty of 23 Sept. 1939 assigned the greater part of Lithuania to the Soviet sphere of influence. In Oct. 1939, the province and city of Vilnius (in Polish occupation 1920-39) were ceded by the USSR. An ultimatum (14 June 1940) led to the formation of a government acceptable to the USSR. Lithuania became a Soviet Socialist Republic of the USSR on 3 Aug. 1940.

On 11 March 1990 the newly-elected Lithuanian Supreme Soviet, by 120 votes to nil, proclaimed independence based on the continuing validity of the act of independence of 16 Feb. 1918. This decision was not accepted by the USSR government.

Massive price rises in Jan. 1991 triggered demonstrations from ethnic Russians and led the Prime Minister, Kazimiera Prunskiene, to resign. Initially dispatched to Vilnius to enforce conscription, Soviet army units occupied key buildings in the face of mounting popular unrest. On 13 Jan. the army fired on demonstrators and there were fatal casualties. A referendum on independence was held in Feb. 1991 at which 90·5% voted in favour. A fully independent status was conceded by the USSR State Council on 6 Sept. 1991.

TERRITORY AND POPULATION

Lithuania is bounded in the north by Latvia, east and south by Belarus, and west by Poland, the Russian enclave of Kaliningrad and the Baltic Sea. The total area is 65,300 sq. km (25,170 sq. miles) and the population (Aug. 1997) 3,707,200 (1,958,200 females; 2,534,500, or 68·3%, urban); density, 56·8 per sq. km.

The UN gives a projected population for 2000 of 3·69m.

The 1989 census population was 3,674,802, of whom Lithuanians accounted for 79·6%, Russians 9·4%, Poles 7%, Belorussians 1·7% and Ukrainians 1·2%. In 1997 there were the following ethnic groups (in 1,000): Russians, 324·9; Poles, 256·6; Belorussians, 54·4; Ukrainians, 36·9; Jews, 5·2; others, 24·9.

There are 10 provinces (with capitals of the same name): Alytus; Kaunas; Klaipėda; Marijampolė; Panevėžys; Šiauliai; Tauragė; Telšiai; Utena; Vilnius.

The capital is Vilnius (1997 population, 580,100). Other large towns are Kaunas (1997 population, 418,700), Klaipėda (203,300), Šiauliai (147,000) and Panevėžys (133,300).

LITHUANIA

The official language is Lithuanian, but ethnic minorities have the right to official use of their language where they form a substantial part of the population. All residents who applied by 3 Nov. 1991 received Lithuanian citizenship, requirements for which now are 10 years' residence and competence in Lithuanian.

SOCIAL STATISTICS

1996: Births, 39,169; deaths, 42,896; marriages, 20,433; divorces, 11,311; infant deaths (1994), 603. Rates (per 1,000 population): Birth, 10·6; death, 11·6; marriage, 5·5; divorce, 3·05; infant mortality, 1994 (per 1,000 live births), 13·9. The population started to decline in 1994, a trend which is set to continue. 4,607 births were registered to unmarried mothers in 1994. There were 1,703 suicides in 1994 (262 women). In 1994 there were 30,326 legally induced abortions. Life expectancy at birth over the period 1990–95 was 64·9 years for males and 76·0 years for females. In 1994 the most popular age range for marrying was 20–24 for both males and females. Infant mortality, 1990–95, 15 per 1,000 live births; fertility rate, 1·8 births per woman. In 1994 there were 4,246 emigrants and 1,664 immigrants.

Lithuania has the world's highest suicide rate, at 46 per 100,000 inhabitants.

CLIMATE

Vilnius, Jan. –2°C, July 15·6°C. Annual rainfall 826 mm. Klaipėda, Jan. 0·9°C, July 16·5°C. Annual rainfall 685 mm.

CONSTITUTION AND GOVERNMENT

A referendum to approve a new constitution was held on 25 Oct. 1992. Parliament is the 141-member *Seimas*. It is elected by a system partly proportional and partly constituency-based. 70 seats are allocated to parties according to their share of the vote (with a 5% threshold). The 71 constituency seats require candidates to poll more than 50% of the vote, otherwise there are run-offs.

The *Constitutional Court* is empowered to rule on whether proposed laws conflict with the constitution or existing legislation. It comprises 9 judges who serve 9-year terms, one third rotating every 3 years.

National Anthem. 'Lietuva tėvynė mūsu' ('Lithuania land of heroes'); words and tune by V. Kurdirka.

RECENT ELECTIONS

Presidential elections were held in two rounds, 21 Dec. 1997 and 4 Feb. 1998. In the run-off vote Valdas Adamkus defeated Arjuras Pauluska by 11,000 votes, 49·9% against 49·29%. President Adamkus lived in the USA for 50 years, having fled Lithuania as a teenager in 1944 when Soviet troops occupied its Baltic states.

Parliamentary elections were held in 2 rounds on 20 Oct. and 10 Nov. 1996. 28 parties stood. The electorate was 2,501,886; turn-out in the first round was 54%, in the second, 40%. The Homeland Union (HU) gained 70 seats, the Christian Democrats (CD) 16, the Lithuanian Centre Union (LCU) 13, the Lithuanian Social Democratic Party 12, the Lithuanian Democratic Labour Party 12, the Lithuanian Democratic Party 2; 7 other parties gained 1 seat each, independents gained 4.

CURRENT ADMINISTRATION

President: Valdas Adamkus (sworn in on 25 Feb. 1998).

Gediminas Vagnorius (HU) was appointed *Prime Minister* by the President with the approval of the parliament on 26 Nov. 1996 and formed an HU-CD coalition government in Dec. which in March 1999 comprised:

Minister of Finance: Algirdas Gediminas Semeta. *Economy:* Vincas Kestutis Babilius. *Social Security and Labour:* Irena Degutiene. *Internal Affairs:* Mecys Laurinkus. *Health:* Laurynas Mindaugas Stankevicius. *Justice:* Vytautas Pakalniskis. *Agriculture and Forestry:* Edvardas Makelis. *Foreign Affairs:* Algirdas Saudargas. *Defence:* Ceslovas Vytautas Stankevicius. *Environmental Protection:* Algis Ciaplikas. *Transport:* Didziokas Rimantas. *Administration Reform and Municipal Affairs:* Kestutis Skrebys. *Culture:* Saulius Saltenis. *Education and Science:* Kornelijus Platelis.

The *Speaker* is Vytautas Landsbergis (HU).

Local Government. There are 10 provinces administered by governors comprising 92 towns, 19 urban districts, 44 regions and 427 rural districts, each with an appropriate authority. Elections were held 23 March 1997 for 1,484 seats in 56 districts. Turn-out was 39·92%. 24 parties stood for about 1,000 council seats. HU won 34% of votes cast, the Lithuanian Democratic Labour Party 16% and the Christian Democrats 13%.

DEFENCE
Conscription is for 12 months.

In 1997 military expenditure totalled US$135m. (US$36 per capita), representing 4·4% of GDP.

Army. The Army consists of 1 motorized infantry brigade with separate battalion and 1 peacekeeping company, and in 1997 numbered 4,300. There is a 12,000-strong volunteer Home Guard reserve.

Navy. A small coastal defence flotilla numbering some 350 in 1996 mans 2 ex-Soviet light frigates, 1 ex-Norwegian fast patrol boat, 1 auxiliary vessel and several harbour patrol craft. It is based at Klaipėda.

Air Force. A combat squadron has L-39 unarmed trainers, while 2 transport squadrons operate Antonov aircraft, Mi-8 helicopters and a few L-410s. Personnel (1997), 250.

INTERNATIONAL RELATIONS
Lithuania is a member of the UN, Council of Europe, OSCE, EBRD, IMF, UNESCO, FAO, IMO, the NATO Partnership for Peace and EAPC, is an Associate Member of the EU and Associate Partner of the WEU. In Dec. 1995 Lithuania applied to join the EU.

ECONOMY
Policy. Privatization in Lithuania is close to completion since currently as much as 70% of GDP in Lithuania is generated by the private entities. The restructuring of priority sectors of the Lithuanian economy is presently facilitated by the second stage of privatization: privatization for cash, giving equal rights to local and foreign investors. The Ministry of European Affairs of the Republic of Lithuania co-ordinates the privatization process in Lithuania and directly organizes privatization of the largest state-controlled entities in industry and infrastructure. Privatization of these enterprises is carried out by a competitive procedure of international tenders, prepared and executed by internationally renowned advisors.

Performance. Among the wealthiest province of the former Soviet Union, Lithuania has weathered the economic crisis overspilling from Russia. 30% of exports go to the EU compared to 20% to Russia. The growth forecast for 1998 has been cut from 7% to 5·5%.

Budget. The 1997 budget envisaged revenue of 7,600m. litas and expenditure of 6,400m. litas. Revenue in 1996 included (in 1m. litas): VAT, 2,280; personal income tax, 2,087; tax on corporate profit, 587. Expenditure in 1996 included: General public services, 553; defence, 178; public order, 830; education, 1,713; health, 1,703; social welfare, 746; housing and community amenities, 353; recreational, cultural and religious affairs, 290; fuel and energy, 297; agriculture, forestry and fishing, 632; transport and communications, 168.

VAT is 18%.

Currency. The unit of currency is the *litas* of 100 *cents*, which was introduced on 25 June 1993 and became the sole legal tender on 1 Aug. The litas was pegged to the US dollar on 1 April 1994 at US$1 = 4 litas. Inflation was 25% in 1996. Consumer Price index was 6·9% in Oct. 1997. 2,395·5m. litas were in circulation in Sept. 1997.

Standard & Poor's assigned Lithuania an investment grade rating of BBB+ for local currency and BBB– for foreign currency in July 1997.

Banking and Finance. The central bank and bank of issue is the Bank of Lithuania (*Governor*, Reinoldijas Šarkinas). There are three state banks—the Savings Bank,

LITHUANIA

the Agricultural Bank and the State Commercial Bank. State banks have been partially privatized. A programme to restructure and privatize 3 state banks was started in 1996. There were 8 commercial banks in Sept. 1997. Lithuanian Development Bank, jointly owned by the government and the EBRB in the proportions 2:1, was founded in 1994. Four representatives offices of the foreign banks are registered in Lithuania.

A stock exchange opened in Vilnius in 1993. In Oct. 1997 its capitalization was US$2·5bn. and it had 541 companies listed.

ENERGY AND NATURAL RESOURCES

Electricity. Installed capacity was 5·46m. kW in 1994. Production was 17·1bn. kWh in 1996. A nuclear power station in Ignalina is responsible for 80% of total output, and there are also 2 hydro-electric and 5 thermal plants. Consumption per capita in 1995 was estimated at 2,151 kWh.

Oil and Gas. Oil production started from a small field at Kretinga in 1990. In 1996 recoverable reserves were estimated at 4·7m. tonnes.

Minerals. Peat reserves total 127·7m. tonnes. Output, 1996, 233,000 tonnes.

Agriculture. In 1996, agriculture contributed 10·4% of GDP and employed about 24% of the workforce. The average farm size is 11·9 ha, one of the lowest in eastern Europe. As of 1 Jan. 1997 the agricultural land area was 3,513,000 ha, of which 2,958,000 ha were arable, 495,900 ha pasture and 58,800 ha orchards. 390,100 persons were employed in agriculture and forestry in 1994. Output of main agricultural products (in 1,000 tonnes) in 1996: grain, 2,702·5; potatoes, 2,044·3; sugar-beet, 795·5; vegetables, 432·6; meat, 198·6; milk, 1,831·5; eggs, 750·9m. units; flax fibre, 6·2. Value of agricultural production, 1996 (in 1m. litas), reached 6,963·5, of which from agricultural partnerships and enterprises, 2,237·5; and from individual farm holdings, 4,726·0.

Livestock, 1996 (in 1,000): Cattle, 1,054·1 (of which milch cows, 589·9); pigs, 1,127·6; sheep and goats, 45·1; horses, 81·4; poultry, 7,775·4. 91,261 tractors were in use in 1996.

Forestry. In 1995 forests covered 1·98m. ha, or 30·5% of Lithuania's territory, and consist of conifers, mostly pine. Output of timber, 1996, 4·77m. cu. metres.

Fisheries. In 1996 the fishing fleet comprised 167 vessels totalling 230,610 GRT. Total catches in 1995 amounted to 49,510 tonnes (46,536 tonnes from sea fishing), compared to more than 475,000 tonnes in 1991.

INDUSTRY

Industry accounted for 28·3% of GDP in 1996. Industrial output included, in 1996 (in 1,000 tonnes): extraction of peat, 233; quarrying of stone, clay and sand, 1·2m. cu. metres; sulphuric acid, 424; mineral fertilizers, 459; paper, 16·8; petrol, 3,748; television picture tubes, 1,695,000; silk, 7·8m. sq. metres; linen, 13·5m. sq. metres; woollen fabrics, 12·6m. sq. metres; cotton fabrics, 39·9m. cu. metres; TV sets, 54,600; bicycles, 142,900; refrigerators, 143,800.

Labour. Total population in 1996 was 3·7m., of which the workforce was 1·8m., employed were 1·7m. (66·6% in private enterprises and 34·4% in the public sector). Employed population by activity (in per cent): Manufacturing, 17·4; construction, 7·2; education, 8·9; transport and communications, 5·7; wholesale and retail trade, 12·7; health and social work, 6·2; real estate, 2·4. Employment skills, 17·9% with higher degrees, 44·1% with a specialized education. In July 1997 average monthly wage was US$215·36. Legal minimum wage was 400 litas (= US$100).

Up to 1995, old age pension for men and women started at 55. Starting with 1995, this age has been increased by 2 months per year for men and 4 months for women until it reaches 62 years 6 months for men and 60 years for women. Average number of persons entitled to pensions in 1996 was 879,800. Unemployment rate as of July 1997 was 5·3%.

Trade Unions. In 1996 there were 44 unions grouped in 4 federations: Trade Union Centre; Workers' Union; Trade Unions' Association; Trade Union Society.

LITHUANIA

INTERNATIONAL TRADE

In order to foster export growth, Lithuania maintains rather a liberal foreign trade régime. There is no quantitative import restriction and the import duties are one of the lowest throughout central Europe. By the end of 1996 free trade agreements with the European Union, European Free Trade Association (EFTA) countries, neighbouring Latvia and Estonia, as well as with a number of Central European Free Trade Agreement countries (CEFTA) and Ukraine were signed. Meanwhile, most favoured-nation status is applied to trade with Russia.

Foreign investors may purchase up to 100% of the equity companies in Lithuania. By mid-1997, US$762m. of foreign capital has been invested.

Total foreign debt was US$1,203m. in 1996.

Individual laws on 3 free economic zones (namely the laws on Šiauliai, Klaipėda and Kaunas) have been cleared by Lithuania's Parliament, the Seimas. All referred zones are presently in different stages of development.

Imports and Exports. In 1996, exports were valued at US$3,356·4m. and imports at US$4,558·6m. Main export markets, 1996 (% of trade): Russia, 24·0%; Germany, 12·8%; Latvia, 9·2%. Main import suppliers: Russia, 25·5%; Germany, 15·8%; Ukraine, 3·3%. Main exports are meat, dairy produce, spirits, electricity, wood and wooden articles, iron and steel and TV sets.

COMMUNICATIONS

Roads. In 1996 there were 45,340 km of surfaced roads. The Via Baltica, the US$180m. project, will upgrade a 1,000 km (620 mile) international highway linking Finland, Estonia, Latvia, Lithuania and Poland, and there are plans to continue the link to Western and Southern Europe.

The number of passenger cars in 1996 was 785,088 (doubled since 1987), and there were also 16,026 buses and trolley buses, 81,291 goods vehicles and 19,402 motor cycles. In 1996, road transport carried 593·1m. passengers and 123·1m. tonnes of freight. There were 4,579 traffic accidents in 1996, with 667 fatalities.

Rail. There are 2,898 km of railway track in Lithuania. Lithuania's railroads are used considerably for both passenger and freight traffic. The majority of rail traffic is diesel propelled, though 350 km of track are electrified. In 1996, 13·2m. passengers and 29·14m. tonnes of freight were carried.

Civil Aviation. The main international terminal is based in the capital, Vilnius. The largest airline, a state-owned joint stock company, Lithuanian Airlines (on the list of privatization), has regular scheduled flights to most of Europe's main transit hubs, and in 1998 a number of other international airlines (Aeroflot, Air Baltic, Austrian Airlines, British Airways, Estonian Air, Finnair, LOT, Lufthansa, SAS, Swissair and United Airlines) ran regular scheduled flights into the country as well. Other international airports are at Kaunas and Palanga, which are served primarily by Air Lithuania. In 1996 Vilnius was the busiest airport for passenger traffic, handling 370,537 passengers (all on international flights), but Kaunas was the busiest for freight, with 7,600 tonnes.

Shipping. The ice-free port of Klaipėda plays a dominant role in sea traffic. It has the second largest tonnage in the Baltic region. A 1,028 ha site has been set aside as a *Free Economic Zone,* which will offer a number of attractive conditions to foreign investors, including a five year exemption from profit taxes.

In 1996 the merchant fleet numbered 96 ships totalling 372,967 GRT and 6 tankers totalling 7,036 GRT. The port has a cargo capacity of 20m. tonnes; the turnover of the port in 1996 was almost 15m. tonnes (up from almost 13m. in 1995).

The port's planned annual capacity will increase to 30m. tonnes by the year 2000 after the completion of several modernization projects. In 1994 there were 788 km of navigable inland waterways. The inland fleet comprised 94 vessels.

Telecommunications. Main telephone lines numbered 1,048,200 in 1997. Telephone provision in 1996 was 26·1 per 100 inhabitants (31·4 urban, 16·8 rural). A majority stake in Lithuanian Telecom was to be be privatized in an inernational tender in 1998. By 2000 it is expected that 130,000 subscribers will be using the services of mobile digital connection (GSM).

LITHUANIA

On average, there are three computers per 100 inhabitants; about 20% of these are connected to the telecommunications network. In 1995 there were 3,800 fax machines.

Postal Services. In 1995 there were 1,009 post offices.

SOCIAL INSTITUTIONS

Justice. The Supreme Court is at the apex of the court system. In 1996 there were 54 local courts, 5 district courts and the Court of Appeal. Trial by jury has been introduced for capital offences. The death penalty is retained for premeditated murder but there is a moratorium on it. 68,053 crimes were reported in 1996, of which 41·3% were solved. In 1996 there were 366 murders and 39 attempted murders. 16,983 persons were convicted. 10 prisons hold 9,742 inmates (502 women).

Religion. Under the Constitution, the state supports religious groups which have been active in Lithuania for 400 years, i.e., the Roman Catholic, Evangelical Lutheran, Evangelical Reformats and Orthodox Churches. 90% of the population are Roman Catholic. As of 1 Jan. 1997, there were 691 Roman Catholic churches with 743 priests, and 44 Orthodox churches with 31 priests. There is an archbishopric of Vilnius and 10 bishops. In 1997 the Lutheran Church had 41 churches, 54 parishes, 17 pastors headed by a bishop.

Education. Education is compulsory from 7 to 16. In 1996-97, there were 729 pre-school establishments with 93,800 pupils and 2,561 schools (including 36 private) with 67,324 teachers and 688,000 pupils, in the following categories:

Type of School	No. of Schools	No. of Pupils
Nursery	151	16,500
Primary	828	37,000
Junior	21	2,100
Elementary	597	59,200
Special	53	7,500
Secondary	698	418,400
College type	68	26,500
Vocational	105	51,700
Adult	25	10,500

58,800 students (33,100 females) attended 15 institutions of higher education in 1996-97, including 8 universities. The adult literacy rate in 1995 was over 99%.

In 1994 total expenditure on education came to 4·5% of GNP and represented 21·8% of total government expenditure.

Health. In 1996 there were 14,763 physicians, 1,709 dentists and 39,585 para-medical personnel. There were 197 hospitals with 39,182 beds, and 643 pharmacies.

Welfare. The social security system is financed by the State Social Insurance Fund. As of 31 Dec. 1996, 879,800 persons were eligible for pensions, including (in 1,000): retirement, 655·3; disability, 147·0; loss of breadwinner, 47·8; widow's/widower's and orphan's, 27·3. Average monthly pensions (in litas in 1996) was 180·10.

CULTURE

Broadcasting. There are 12 commercial and 10 TV companies. There were 1·5m. radio receivers and 1·4m. television receivers in 1995. There were 77 radio and 78 TV sets per 100 households in 1996. Approaching 120,000 households have cable television. This comprises 13% of the total number of households in Lithuania.

Cinema. There were 93 cinemas in 1996; attendance, 470,200.

Press. In 1996 there were 443 (including 6 dailies) newspapers (389 in Lithuanian, 37 in Russian, 8 in Polish, 5 in English, 3 in German, 1 in Yiddish) and 351 periodicals. 3,645 book titles were published.

Tourism. There were 211,000 foreign tourists in 1995, spending US$124m.

DIPLOMATIC REPRESENTATIVES

Of Lithuania in Great Britain (84 Gloucester Place, London, W1H 3HN)
Ambassador: Justas V. Paleckis.

Of Great Britain in Lithuania (2 Antakalnio, 2055 Vilnius)
Ambassador: C. Robbins.

Of Lithuania in the USA (2622 16th St., NW, Washington, D.C., 20009)
Ambassador: Stasys Sakalauskas.

Of the USA in Lithuania (Ak Menu 6, 2600 Vilnius)
Ambassador: Keith C. Smith.

Of Lithuania to the United Nations
Ambassador: Oskaras Jusys.

Of Lithuania to the European Union
Ambassador: Romualdas Kalonaitis.

FURTHER READING

Department of Statistics to the Government. *Statistical Yearbook of Lithuania – Economic and Social Development in Lithuania.* Monthly.

Hood, N. et al (eds.), *Transition in the Baltic States.* 1997

Jurgéla, C. R., *History of the Lithuanian Nation.* New York, 1948

Kantantas, A. and F., *A Lithuanian Bibliography.* Univ. of Alberta Press, 1975

Lieven, A., *The Baltic Revolution: Estonia, Latvia, Lithuania and the Path to Independence.* 2nd ed. Yale UP, 1994

Misiunas, R. J. and Taagepera, R., *The Baltic States: the Years of Dependence, 1940–91.* 2nd ed. Farnborough, 1993

Smith, I. A. and Grunts, M. V., *The Baltic States.* [Bibliography] Oxford and Santa Barbara (CA), 1993

Vardys, V. S. and Sedaitis, J. B., *Lithuania: the Rebel Nation.* Boulder (CO), 1997

National statistical office: Department of Statistics to the Government, Gedimino Pr. 29, 2746 Vilnius. *Director:* Kestutis Zaborskas.
Website: http://www.std.lt/

LUXEMBOURG

Grand-Duché de
Luxembourg

Capital: Luxembourg
Population estimate, 2000: 430,000
GNP per capita: (PPP$) 34,480
HDI/world rank: 0·900/26

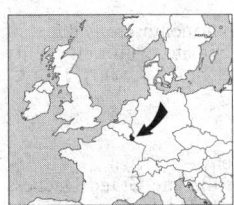

KEY HISTORICAL EVENTS

Lying at the heart of Western Europe between Belgium, France and Germany, the Grand-Duchy of Luxembourg has been an independent State ever since the Treaty of London of 19 April 1839, concluded between the major powers of that time—the United Kingdom, Austria, France, Prussia and Russia—and Belgium and the Netherlands.

The origins of Luxembourg stretch back as far as 963 AD when Count Sigfried founded the castle of Lutzilinburhurch, which rapidly developed into an important fortress. The House of Luxembourg was most prominent on the European scene during the 14th and 15th centuries, when four Counts of the House of Luxembourg became Emperors of the Holy Roman Empire and Kings of Bohemia (e.g. Wenceslas, who founded the University of Prague and built the Wenceslas Bridge in the Golden City). The House of Luxembourg went into decline after this bright period and was successively occupied by Burgundy, Spain, Austria (under Empress Marie-Theresa and Emperor Joseph II) and finally by revolutionary France.

In 1815 the Vienna Treaty decided that the Grand Duchy of Luxembourg would come under the house of Orange-Nassau, also sovereigns of the Netherlands. This meant that the King of the Netherlands was at the same time Grand-Duke of Luxembourg with the country as his personal property (personal union). In 1839 the Walloon-speaking area was joined to Belgium.

In 1890 the personal union with the Netherlands ended with the accession of a member of another branch of the house of Nassau, Grand-Duke Adolphe of Weilburg. In both world wars (1914–18 and 1939–45) Luxembourg, a neutral country, was invaded and occupied by German forces. From May 1940 until Sept. 1944 the government carried on an independent administration in London. In June 1942, Luxembourg became the only nazi-occupied country to stage a general strike against the occupation. Harsh repression of the population (deportations, executions) followed.

In 1948 a Benelux customs union formed by Belgium, the Netherlands and Luxembourg allowed for standardization of prices, taxes and wages and the free movement of labour among the three countries. Luxembourg was a founder member of the European Union.

TERRITORY AND POPULATION

Luxembourg has an area of 2,586 sq. km (999 sq. miles) and is bounded on the west by Belgium, south by France, east by Germany. The population (1998) was 423,700 (including 147,700 foreigners); density, 164 per sq. km.

The UN gives a projected population for 2000 of 430,000.

In 1998 an estimated 89·2% of the population were urban. The capital, Luxembourg, had (1998) 79,500 inhabitants; Esch-sur-Alzette, the centre of the mining district, 24,600; Differdange, 16,800; Dudelange, 16,400, and Pétange, 13,300.

Letzebuergesch is spoken by most of the population, and since 1985 has been an official language with French and German.

SOCIAL STATISTICS

Statistics (figures in parentheses indicate births and deaths of resident foreigners):

	Births	Deaths	Marriages	Divorces
1996	5,689 (2,401)	3,895 (516)	2,105	817
1997	5,503 (2,419)	3,937 (524)	2,007	1,001

1997 rates per 1,000 population; Birth, 13·1; death, 9·4; marriage, 4·8; divorce, 2·4. In 1994 the most popular age range for marrying was 25–29 for both males and females. Life expectancy at birth over the period 1995–97 was 73·5 years for males and 79·6 years for females. Annual growth rate, 1990–97, was 1·6%. Infant mortality, 1990–97, 4·2 per 1,000 live births; fertility rate, 1·7 births per woman.

CLIMATE
Cold, raw winters with snow covering the ground for up to a month are features of the upland areas. The remainder resembles Belgium in its climate, with rain evenly distributed throughout the year. Average temperatures are Jan. 0·8°C, July 17·5°C. Annual rainfall 30·8" (782·2 mm).

CONSTITUTION AND GOVERNMENT
The Grand Duchy of Luxembourg is a constitutional monarchy.

The reigning Grand Duke is **Jean**, b. 5 Jan. 1921, son of the late Grand Duchess Charlotte and the late Prince Felix of Bourbon-Parma; succeeded 12 Nov. 1964 on the abdication of his mother; married to Princess Joséphine-Charlotte of Belgium, 9 April 1953. *Offspring:* Princess Marie-Astrid, b. 17 Feb. 1954, married Christian of Habsbourg-Lorraine 6 Feb. 1982 (*Offspring:* Marie Christine, b. 31 July 1983; Imre, b. 8 Dec. 1985; Christophe, b. 2 Feb. 1988; Alexander, b. 26 Sept. 1990; Gabriella, b. 26 March 1994); Prince Henri, hereditary Grand-Duke appointed Lieutenant of the Grand-Duke in March 1998, b. 16 April 1955, married Maria Teresa Mestre 14 Feb. 1981 (*Offspring:* Prince Guillaume, b. 11 Nov. 1981, Prince Felix, b. 3 June 1984, Prince Louis, b. 3 Aug. 1986, Princess Alexandra, b. 16 Feb. 1991, Prince Sebastian, b. 16 April 1992); Prince Jean, b. 15 May 1957, married Hélène Vestur (*Offspring:* Marie-Gabrielle, b. 18 Dec. 1986, Constantin, b. 22 July 1988, Wenceslas, b. 17 Nov. 1990, Carl-Johann, b. 15 Aug. 1992); Princess Margaretha, b. 15 May 1957, married Prince Nicolas of Liechtenstein 20 March 1982 (*Offspring:* Marie-Annunciata, b. 12 May 1985, Marie-Astrid, b. 26 June 1987, Joseph-Emmanuel, b. 7 May 1989); Prince Guillaume, b. 1 May 1963, married Sibilla Weiller 24 Sept. 1994 (*Offspring:* Paul-Louis, b. 4 March 1998).

The constitution of 17 Oct. 1868 was revised in 1919, 1948, 1956, 1972, 1983, 1988, 1989, 1994, 1996 and 1998. In March 1998 Grand-Duke Jean designated his eldest son, Henri, the heir to the throne, his 'Lieutenant-Representant' according to article 42 of the Luxembourg Constitution. The oath was sworn in the presence of the Grand-Duke and Grand-Duchess, the Prime Minister, the Government Ministers and the members of Parliament. The Lieutenant-Representant has the same prerogatives as the Sovereign himself.

The separation of powers is not clearly defined between the legislature and the executive, resulting in much interaction between the two bodies. Only the judiciary is completely independent.

The 12 cantons are divided into 4 electoral districts: the South, the East, the Centre and the North. Voters choose between party lists of candidates in multi-member constituencies. The parliament is the *Chamber of Deputies*, which consists of a maximum of 60 members elected for 5 years. Voting is compulsory and there is universal suffrage. Seats are allocated according to the rules of proportional representation and the principle of the smallest electoral quote. There is a *Council of State* of 21 members appointed by the Sovereign for life. It advises on proposed laws and any other question referred to it.

The head of state takes part in the legislative power, exercises executive power and has a part in the judicial power. The constitution leaves to the sovereign the right to organize the Government, which consists of a Minister of State, who is Prime Minister, and of at least 3 Ministers. Direct consultation by referendum is provided for in the Constitution.

National Anthem. 'Ons Hemecht' ('Our Homeland'); words by M. Lentz, tune by J. A. Zinnen.

RECENT ELECTIONS
At the elections of 12 June 1994 the electorate was 217,131; turn-out was 82·5%. The Christian Social Party (CS) gained 21 seats, the Socialist Workers' Party (S) 17,

the Democratic Party 12, the Action Committee for Democracy 5 and Déi Gréng GLEI-GAP 5. General elections were scheduled for 13 June 1999.

European Parliament. Luxembourg has 6 representatives. At the June 1994 elections, turn-out was 90%. CS won 2 seats with 31·4% of votes cast (group in European Parliament: Popular European Party); S, 2 with 24·8% (European Socialist Party); the Democratic Party, 1 with 18·8% (Liberal, Democratic and Reformist Group); the Greens, 1 with 10·9% (Greens). Elections for representatives to the European Parliament were scheduled for 13 June 1999.

CURRENT ADMINISTRATION
In March 1999 the Christian Social-Socialist coalition comprised:

Prime Minister, Minister of State, Labour and Employment, Finance and the Exchequer: Jean-Claude Juncker, b. 1945 (CS; sworn in 20 Jan. 1995).

Deputy Prime Minister, Minister of Foreign Affairs, Trade and Co-operation: Jacques Poos (S). *Agriculture, Viticulture, Rural Development, Middle Class, Housing and Tourism:* Fernand Boden (CS). *European Economic and Monetary Union, Justice, Budget and Relations with Parliament:* Luc Frieden (CS). *The Family, Women and the Disabled:* Marie-Josée Jacobs (CS). *Education, Vocational Training, Cultural and Religious Affairs:* Erna Hennicot-Schoepges (CS). *The Interior, Civil Service and Administrative Reforms:* Michel Wolter (CS). *Economy, Public Works and Energy:* Robert Goebbels (S). *Health, Physical Education and Sport:* Georges Wohlfahrt (S). *Youth, Environment, Land Management and Defence:* Alex Bodry (S). *Social Security, Transport, Post and Communications:* Mady Delvaux-Stehres (S).

The *Speaker* is Jean Spautz.

Local Government. In Luxembourg, where there are neither provinces nor departments (as in France), the commune is the only application of the principle of territorial decentralization. The commune forms an autonomous authority, from the administrative point of view, on a territorial basis. It administers its patrimony and its interests through local representatives, under the control of the central authority.

Each commune has its own commune council directly elected by the inhabitants. Communal elections are held automatically on the 2nd Sunday of Oct. preceding the expiration of the mandate of the communal council (6 years). Elections are held under the absolute majority system, except in larger communes (at least 3,500 inhabitants) where elections are held on the party-list system, with proportional representation as for the legislative elections.

Communal authority is exercised by the communal council and by the corporate body of burgomasters and aldermen (SYVICOL). Burgomasters are appointed and dismissed by the Grand-Duke. Town aldermen are appointed by the Grand-Duke, and those of other communes by the Minister of the Interior.

DEFENCE
There is a volunteer light infantry battalion of (1996) 800, of which only the career officers are professionals. In recent years Luxembourg soldiers and officers have been actively participating in peace-keeping missions, mainly in the former Yugoslavia. There is also a Gendarmerie of 560.

In 1997 military expenditure totalled US$129m. (US$313 per capita), representing 0·8% of GDP.

INTERNATIONAL RELATIONS
Luxembourg is a member of the UN, Benelux, the EU, OECD, the Council of Europe, NATO and WEU. The Schengen Accord of June 1990 abolished border controls between Luxembourg, Belgium, Denmark, Finland, France, Germany, Greece, Iceland, Italy, the Netherlands, Norway, Portugal, Spain and Sweden.

ECONOMY
Policy. The world economic crisis of 1973–74 hit the then monolithic Luxembourg economy very hard. The previously strong steel sector had to be thoroughly restructured and this, along with industrial diversification and the emergence of the new service sector, helped to consolidate Luxembourg's economic indicators. The

service sector employs the most people, including 21,500 employees in more than 200 banks (1997). Companies dealing with insurance, reinsurance and pension funds are the next biggest employers. Other prospering sectors of the Luxembourg economy include telecommunications, audio-visual and multimedia, and industrial plastics.

Performance. In terms of GDP per head, Luxembourg is the richest sovereign country in the world, with 31,531 PPS (purchasing power standards) in 1997.

Real GDP growth was 4·0% in 1998 (4·8% in 1997) against a European average of 2·7%. Real GDP is projected to grow at around 3·5% in 1999 and 2000. Total GDP in 1998 was LUF595·4bn.

The OECD Economic Survey of 1999 reports: 'The Luxembourg economy has continued to perform well... Exports have been a major driving force, underpinned by buoyant export markets and a strong export performance of the financial and communication sectors. Private consumption has strengthened due to higher wage increases and robust employment growth. Investment has also been buoyant, partly due to special factors such as the purchase of some aircraft.'

Budget. Revenue and expenditure (including extraordinary) for years ending 30 April (in 1m. francs):

	1995	1996	1997	1998
Revenue	149·8	164·3	163·9	170·3
Expenditure	148·8	161·4	163·15	170·4

Central government spending was expected to rise by almost 5·9% in nominal terms in 1999. Public debt in June 1998 was LUF28·8bn., of which LUF27·0bn. was domestic.

VAT is 15%, with reduced rates of 6% and 3% (for books).

According to government projections, the general government surplus was expected to be 1·4% of GDP in 1998 (down from 2·9% in 1997). Income taxes and business taxes have been reduced to preserve competitiveness in the international environment. The normal tax rate for companies came down to 37·45% in 1998, compared with 40·3% in 1996.

Currency. On 1 Jan. 1999 the euro (EUR) became the legal currency in Luxembourg and the *Luxembourg franc* became a subdivision of it; irrevocable conversion rate 40·3399 Luxembourg francs to 1 euro. The euro, which consists of 100 cents, will not be in circulation until 1 Jan. 2002. There will be 7 euro notes in different colours and sizes denominated in 500, 200, 100, 50, 20, 10 and 5 euros, and 8 coins denominated in 2 and 1 euros, then 50, 20, 10, 5, 2 and 1 cents. Even though notes and coins will not be introduced until 1 Jan. 2002, the euro can be used in banking, by means of cheques, travellers' cheques, bank transfers, credit cards and electronic purses. Banking will be possible in both euros and Luxembourg francs until the Luxembourg franc is withdrawn from circulation—which must be by 1 July 2002. As a result of the adoption of the euro, monetary union with Belgium has been terminated.

The *Luxembourg franc* (LUF) notionally consists of 100 *centimes*, and is at parity with the Belgian franc. Inflation in 1999 was an estimated 1·7%. Foreign exchange reserves (excluding gold) were US\$75,000m. in 1995. Gold reserves were 310,000 troy oz. in Feb. 1998.

Banking and Finance. Luxembourg's Central Bank (formerly the Monetary Institute) was established in July 1998 (*Director-General*, Yves Mersch). In 1997 there were 215 banks and 75 other credit institutions established in Luxembourg, which has become an international financial centre. German banks make up nearly a third of all the banks. Total deposits in 1997 were LUF7,834·0bn.; net assets in unit trusts, LUF7,560·7bn.; net assets in investment companies, LUF4,754·9bn. There is a stock exchange.

The financial sector accounted for 18·9% of GDP in 1997 and the banks showed a net profit of LUF76·5bn. The total number of approved insurance companies in 1996 was 89, with reinsurance companies numbering 244; the amount of premiums due was LUF121,408·0m.

According to the OECD Economic Survey of 1999: 'Tax advantages in comparison with neighbouring countries, strict bank secrecy rules, a liberal

LUXEMBOURG

regulatory environment and the rapid implementation of EU directives in Luxembourg law, combined with a favourable geographical location at the heart of Europe and a qualified and multilingual labour force, have been central in creating competitive advantages in financial services.'

Weights and Measures. The metric system is in force.

ENERGY AND NATURAL RESOURCES

Electricity. Apart from hydroelectricity and electricity generated from fossil fuels, Luxembourg has no national energy resources. Installed capacity in 1997 was 1·2m. kW. Power production was 1,145m. kWh in 1997. Consumption per capita in 1997 was estimated to be 15,053 kWh.

Minerals. The national steel industry mainly relies on imported ore. In 1997 production (in tonnes) of pig-iron, 1,438,030; of steel, 2,580,219.

Agriculture. The contribution of agriculture, viticulture and forestry to the economy has been gradually declining over the years, accounting for only 1·5% of GDP in 1994. However, the actual output of this sector has nearly tripled during the past 30 years, a trend common to many EU countries. Agriculture accounts for 11·9% of exports and 12·9% of imports. There were 6,039 workers engaged in agricultural work (including wine-growing and forestry) in 1997 (1,703 wage-earners), and 2,976 farms with an average area of 48·98 ha; 126,629 ha were under cultivation in 1997.

Production, 1997 (in tonnes) of main crops: Maize, 496,100; roots and tubers, 31,275; bread crops, 59,789; forage crops, 145,498; pulses, 1,530; grassland, 223,732. Production, 1997 (in 1,000 tonnes) of meat, 27·4; milk, 264·0; butter, 3·1 (1996); cheese, 3·0 (1996). In 1997, 174,708 hectolitres of wine were produced. In 1997 there were 7,659 tractors, 882 harvester-threshers, 1,818 manure spreaders and 1,971 gatherer-presses.

Livestock (1997): 2,295 horses, 212,335 cattle, 77,149 pigs, 8,009 sheep.

Forestry. In 1995 there were 88,620 ha of forests, which in 1994 produced 166,018 cu. metres of broadleaved and 245,582 cu. metres of coniferous wood.

INDUSTRY

In 1996 there were 2,501 industrial enterprises, of which 1,546 were in the building industry. Production, 1997 (in 1,000 tonnes): Steel, 2,580; rolled steel products, 3,887.

Labour. In 1997 the estimated total workforce was 226,500, of which 118,500 worked in the service industries. The government fixes a legal minimum wage. Retirement is at 65. Employment creation averaged 3·3% every year between 1985 and 1997, with a total increase in jobs of 47·8% over the period. In 1997 the unemployment rate was 3·6%, but by Sept. 1998 it had dropped to 3·0%. This is the lowest rate of unemployment for any EU nation.

The OECD reports that Luxembourg has one of the lowest unemployment rates among OECD members, but 'a broader concept of labour under-utilization ("broad unemployment"), which adds people of working age in benefit schemes and labour market programmes to registered unemployment, shows a less favourable development, with broad unemployment exceeding 13% of the broad labour force in 1997, compared with less than 12% in 1995.'

Trade Unions. The main trade unions are the O–GBL (Socialist) and the LCGB (Christian–Social). Other sectorial unions include ALEBA (the banking sector), FNCTLL (railworkers), and FEP (private employers). In Oct. 1998, union representatives were elected in both the private and public sectors.

INTERNATIONAL TRADE

Luxembourg is in the process of turning itself into a centre for electronic commerce, the world's fastest-growing industry.

Imports and Exports. Exports in 1997 (provisional figures) totalled LUF249,765m., and imports LUF335,109m. Luxembourg exports 90% of GDP, of which 75% goes to Germany, Belgium and France.

Principal imports and exports by type of goods:

	Exports		Imports	
	1996	1997	1996	1997
Food, beverages, tobacco	5,643	6,339	17,810	20,057
Minerals	2,250	2,211	28,946	30,445
Chemicals	8,844	9,508	24,110	26,219
Plastics/rubber goods	31,318	32,261	17,832	19,409
Textiles, clothing	14,332	16,775	15,143	16,655
Iron, steel	71,251	83,252	49,533	55,033
Mechanical/electrical equipment	43,651	47,866	53,152	60,847
Transport equipment	11,999	12,076	36,861	47,561

Trade with selected countries (in LUF1m.)

	Exports		Imports	
	1996	1997	1996	1997
Austria	3,249	3,460	2,401	1,969
Belgium	30,141	33,271	116,617	127,091
France	45,328	48,953	35,276	39,772
Germany	63,044	66,317	86,195	94,235
Italy	11,358	13,675	7,119	8,018
Netherlands	11,833	12,360	15,303	15,107
Spain	4,554	5,800	1,711	1,683
UK	14,582	16,827	4,970	5,532
Total EU	193,113	210,484	272,740	297,434
Japan	1,016	1,745	3,694	4,573
USA	6,181	8,762	9,316	19,516

Trade Fairs. The *Foires Internationales de Luxembourg* occurs twice a year, and there are a growing number of specialized fairs.

COMMUNICATIONS

Roads. In 1998 there were 2,863 km of roads of which 115 km were motorways. Motor vehicles registered in 1997 included 244,130 passenger cars, 17,240 trucks, 944 coaches, 9,297 motor cycles, 23,842 tractors and special vehicles.

Rail. In 1997 there were 274 km of railway (standard gauge) of which 261 km were electrified. Railways carried (1997) 17·7m. passengers.

Civil Aviation. Findel is the airport for Luxembourg. 1,413,000 passengers and 339,573 tonnes of freight were handled in 1997. The national carrier is Luxair, 23·1% state-owned. In 1998 services were also provided by Aeroflot, Air France, Austrian Airlines, British Airways, Condor Flugdienst, Delta Air Lines, Hapag Lloyd, Icelandair, KLM, Lufthansa, Malév, SABENA, SAS, Swissair, TAP, Tunis Air and Tyrolean Airways. Cargolux has developed into one of the major international freight carriers.

Shipping. A shipping register was set up in 1990. In 1995 merchant shipping totalled 881,000 GRT. 76 vessels were registered at 1 Jan. 1998.

Telecommunications. Luxembourg had 279,736 main telephone lines in 1997 (660·5 for every 1,000 population). There were also 67,208 mobile telephones. In 1995 there were some 6,500 Internet users.

Postal Services. In 1997 there were 106 post offices. In 1995 a total of 155m. items of mail were processed (378 items per person).

SOCIAL INSTITUTIONS

Justice. The Constitution makes the Courts of Law independent in performing their functions, restricting their sphere of activity, defining their limit of jurisdiction and providing a number of procedural guarantees. The Constitution has additionally laid down a number of provisions designed to ensure judges remain independent of persons under their jurisdiction, and to ensure no interference from the executive and legislative organs. All judges are appointed by Grand-Ducal order and are irremovable.

LUXEMBOURG

The judicial organization comprises 3 Justices of the Peace (conciliation and police courts). The country is, in addition, divided into 2 judicial districts, i.e. Luxembourg and Diekirck. District courts deal with matters such as civic and commercial cases. Offences which are punishable under the Penal Code or by specific laws with imprisonment or hard labour fall within the jurisdiction of the criminal chambers of District Courts, as the Assize Court was repealed by law in 1987. The High Court of Justice consists of a Supreme Court of Appeal and a Court of Appeal.

The judicial organization of the Grand-Duchy does not include the jury system. A division of votes between the judges on the issue of guilt/innocence may lead to acquittal. Society before the Courts of Law is represented by the Public Prosecutor Department, composed of members of the judiciary directly answerable to the government.

Religion. The population is mostly Roman Catholic, although perhaps only 30% are practising Catholics. There are small Protestant, Jewish, Greek Orthodox and Moslem communities as well.

Education. Adult literacy rate, 1995, 97·4% (male, 98·0%; female, 96·8%). Education is compulsory for all children between the ages of 6 and 15. In 1996–97 there were 9,932 children in pre-primary school with 584 teachers; 28,232 pupils in primary schools; 28,483 pupils in secondary schools (including vocational training). In higher education (1996–97) the Higher Institute of Technology had 298 students. In 1996–97 there were 326 students in teacher training. In 1996–97 the University Centre of Luxembourg had 1,606 students and around 200 academic staff. Luxembourg does not have a full-time university, so many students have to go abroad, predominantly to France, Germany and Belgium. In 1996–97, 984 students pursued university studies.

In 1995 total expenditure on education came to LUF22m. (3·9% of GNP).

Health. In 1997 there were 1,030 doctors (344 GPs and 686 specialists) and 247 dentists. There were 34 hospitals in 1994 and 4,438 hospital beds in 1992. Total health spending accounted for 7% of GDP in 1997.

Welfare. In Luxembourg the social security system was built in several stages. It has been extended with regard to both the socio-professional categories and the risk groups covered. The law of 26 July 1986 introduced the minimum wage, a mechanism to guarantee private means. It consists of a supplementary benefit paid up to a set threshold determined according to the composition of the household. This benefit is awarded irrespective of the causes of the need.

Public contributions play a growing role in financing the system. In 1995 they accounted for 40% of the resources, with employees' and employers' contributions forming just over half. Around 50% of social security benefits goes towards pension schemes, and around 25% goes to health insurance. Nearly half the ordinary budget is absorbed by social security.

CULTURE

Broadcasting. The major broadcaster of TV and radio programmes is CLT (*Compagnie Luxembourgeoise de Télédiffusion*), along with local and regional radio stations that have emerged since the 1991 Law on Electronic Media. CLT was set up in 1929 and started broadcasting in 1932. In the same year Radio Luxembourg started broadcasting its multilingual programmes. In 1954, CLT received an exclusive licence for broadcasting radio and TV in the Grand-Duchy, which was extended until the end of 2010 in 1995.

In 1995, 12 TV channels and 12 radio stations belonged to the CLT group. It also broadcast 4 TV channels and 3 radio stations via the ASTRA satellite system. The 1991 Law on Electronic Media allowed the creation of 4 new radio networks and 15 local radio stations, and thus ended the CLT monopoly.

The commercial *Radio-Télé-Luxembourg* broadcasts 1 programme in Letzebuergesch on FM. There are commercial and religious programmes in French, German, English and Italian. 10 TV programmes are broadcast. Colour transmission is by the SECAM system. In 1995 there were 155,000 TV sets in use and 260,000 radio receivers. Satellite and cable TV is widespread.

LUXEMBOURG

Cinema. In 1997 there were 26 cinemas.

Press. There were 5 daily newspapers in 1997 with a circulation of 156,000, equivalent to 368 per 1,000 inhabitants. 4 of these papers are published in the Grand-Duchy, and 1 in neighbouring France. There are a number of weekly titles with a circulation of 77,800. LUF65m. of direct government aid is granted to the Luxembourg press.

Tourism. In 1997 there were 711,000 tourists, 7,638 hotel rooms and 1,109,000 overnight stays. Tourists spent US$295m. in 1996. Camping is widespread, and weekend and short-stay tourism accounts for many tourists.

Festivals. Every year there is Echternach–Luxembourg (May–June) and Wiltz (June–July). Both feature a variety of classical music, jazz, theatre and recitals.

Libraries. The National Library is in Luxembourg City, and there are smaller municipal libraries in most towns.

National Theatre and Opera. There are several theatres in Luxembourg City, including *Théâtre Municipal*, *Théâtre des Capucins* and *Théâtre du Centaure*. There are also a number of theatres in Esch/Alzette.

Museums and Galleries. The main museums are the *Musée d'Histoire de la Ville*, the *Villa Vauban*, the *Musée National d'Histoire Naturelle*, the *Cercle Municipal* and the *Musée National d'Histoire et d'Art*.

DIPLOMATIC REPRESENTATIVES
Of Luxembourg in Great Britain (27 Wilton Crescent, London, SWIX 8SD)
Ambassador: Joseph Weyland.

Of Great Britain in Luxembourg (14 Blvd Roosevelt, L-2450 Luxembourg)
Ambassador and Consul-General: William Ehrman.

Of Luxembourg in the USA (2200 Massachusetts Ave., NW, Washington, D.C., 20008)
Ambassador: Arlette Conzemius.

Of the USA in Luxembourg (22 Blvd. Emmanuel Servais, Luxembourg)
Ambassador: Clay Constantinou.

Of Luxembourg to the United Nations
Ambassador: Hubert Wurth.

FURTHER READING
STATEC. *Annuaire Statistique.*

The Institutions of the Grand Duchy of Luxembourg. Information and Press Service, Luxembourg, 1989
Calmes, C., *The Making of a Nation from 1815 up to our Days.* Luxembourg, 1989
Hury, C. and Christophory, J., *Luxembourg.* [Bibliography] Oxford and Santa Barbara (CA), 1981
Newcomer, J., *The Grand Duchy of Luxembourg: the Evolution of Nationhood, 963 A.D. to 1983.* Washington, 1983
Trausch, G., *The Significance of the Historical Date of 1839.* Luxembourg, 1989

National Library: 37 Boulevard Roosevelt, Luxembourg City.
National statistical office: Service Central de la Statistique et des Etudes Economiques (STATEC), CP 304, Luxembourg City
Website: http://statec.gouvernement.lu/

MACEDONIA

Republika Makedonija

The Republic of Macedonia
(Former Yugoslav Republic of
Macedonia)

Capital: Skopje
Population estimate, 2000: 2·23m.
Estimated GDP: $2·0bn.
HDI/world rank: 0·749/80

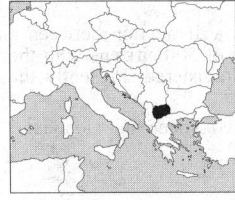

KEY HISTORICAL EVENTS
The history of Macedonia can be traced to the reign of
King Karan (808–778 BC), but the country was at its
most powerful at the time of Philip II (359–336 BC) and
Alexander the Great (336–323 BC). At the end of the 6th
century AD, Slavs began to settle in Macedonia. There
followed a long period of internal fighting but the spread
of Christianity led to consolidation and the creation of
the first Macedonian Slav state, the Kingdom of
Samuel, 976–1018. In the 14th century it fell to Serbia,
and in 1355 to the Turks.

After the Balkan wars of 1912–13 Turkey was ousted and Serbia received part of
the territory, the rest going to Bulgaria and Greece. In 1918 Yugoslav Macedonia
was incorporated into Serbia as South Serbia, becoming a republic in the Socialist
Federal Republic of Yugoslavia. Claims to the historical Macedonian territory have
long been a source of contention with Bulgaria and Greece. Macedonia declared its
independence on 18 Sept. 1991 and was admitted to the UN on 8 April 1993. In
April 1999 the Kosovo crisis which led to NATO air attacks on Yugoslavian
military targets set off a flood of refugees into Macedonia.

TERRITORY AND POPULATION
Macedonia is bounded in the north by Yugoslavia, in the east by Bulgaria, in the
south by Greece and in the west by Albania. Its area is 25,713 sq. km. According to
the 1994 census final results, the population on 20 June 1994 was 1,945,932. The
ethnic groups were Macedonians (1,295,964), Albanians (441,104), Turks (78,019),
Rhomas (43,707), Serbs (40,228), Vlachs (8,601). There were 36,427 others and
1,882 not stated. Ethnic Albanians predominate on the western side of Macedonia.
Minorities are represented in the Council for Inter-Ethnic Relations. 1996 population
estimate, 1·98m.; density, 77 per sq. km.

The UN gives a projected population for 2000 of 2·23m.

In 1995 an estimated 59·9% of the population lived in urban areas.

The major cities (with 1994 census population) are: Skopje, the capital, 444,299;
Bitola, 77,464; Prilep, 68,148; Kumanovo, 71,853; Tetovo, 50,344.

The official language is Macedonian, which uses the Cyrillic alphabet.

SOCIAL STATISTICS
Statistics, 1996: Births, 31,403; deaths, 16,063; marriages, 14,089; divorces, 705;
infant deaths, 515. Rates (per 1,000 population): Birth, 15·8; death, 8·1; marriage,
7·1; divorce, 0·3; infant mortality (per 1,000 live births), 16·4. Expectation of life at
birth over the period 1990–95 was 69·3 years for males and 73·6 years for females.
Annual growth rate, 1990–95, 1·3%. In 1995 the most popular age range for
marrying was 20–24 for both males and females. Fertility rate, 1990–95, 2·1 births
per woman.

Migration within the Republic of Macedonia, 1996: Emigrated persons, 11,653;
immigrated persons, 12,283; net migration 630. International (external) migration:
Emigrated persons, 220; immigrated persons 850.

CLIMATE
Macedonia has a mixed Mediterranean-continental type climate, with cold moist
winters and hot dry summers. Skopje, Jan. –0·4°C, July 23·1°C.

MACEDONIA

CONSTITUTION AND GOVERNMENT

At a referendum held on 8 Sept. 1991 turn-out was 74%; 99% of votes cast were in favour of a sovereign Macedonia. On 17 Nov. 1991 parliament promulgated a new constitution which officially proclaimed Macedonia's independence.

The *President* is directly elected for 5-year terms. Candidates must be citizens aged at least 40 years. The parliament is a 120-member single-chamber *Assembly* (*Sobranie*), elected by universal suffrage for 4-year terms. There is a *Constitutional Court* whose members are elected by the assembly for non-renewable 8-year terms, and a *National Security Council* chaired by the President. Laws passed by the Assembly must be countersigned by the President, who may return them for reconsideration, but cannot veto them if they gain a two-thirds majority.

Political Parties. The new Law on Political Parties makes a distinction between a political party and an association of citizens. The signatures of 500 citizens with the right to vote must be produced for a party to be legally registered. Presently the country has 34 legally registered parties.

National Anthem. 'Denes nad Makedonija se radja novo sonce na slobodata' ('Today a new sun of liberty appears over Macedonia').

RECENT ELECTIONS

In the presidential election held on 14 Oct. 1994 Kiro Gligorov (Social Democratic League of Macedonia) gained 78·4% of votes cast, against 21·6% for Ljupco Georgievski (Internal Macedonian Revolutionary Organization).

In the run-off vote in a 2-round general election on 1 Nov. 1998 the ruling Social Democrats were beaten by the Internal Macedonian Revolutionary Organization (VMRO), which formed a coalition government with the new pro-business Democratic Alternative party (DA). Between them they won 59 of the 120 seats, against 29 for the Social Democrats. VMRO won 28·1% of the votes, and the Social Democrats 25·1%.

CURRENT ADMINISTRATION

President: Kiro Gligorov (b. 1917; elected in 1990 and re-elected in 1994).

In March 1999 the government comprised :

Prime Minister: Ljupco Georgievski (VMRO).

Deputy Prime Ministers: Dosta Dimovska, Bedredin Ibrahimi (also *Minister of Labour and Social Affairs*), Radmila Kiprijanova.

Minister of Defence: Nikola Kijusev. *Internal Affairs:* Pavle Trajanov. *Foreign Affairs:* Aleksandar Dimitrov. *Justice and Administration:* Vlado Kambovski. *Finance:* Boris Stojmenov. *Economy:* Zanko Cado. *Development:* Milijana Danevska. *Urban and City Development, Communications and Ecology:* Dusko Kadijevski. *Transport and Communications:* Bobi Spirkovski. *Agriculture, Forestry and Water Resources:* Vladimir Dzabirski. *Education and Physical Culture:* Nenad Novkovski. *Science:* Merie Rushani. *Culture:* Dimitar Dimitrov. *Health:* Stojan Bogdanov. *Youth and Sports:* Georgi Boev. *Trade:* Nikola Gruevski. *Local Self-Government:* Dzevdet Nasufi. *Information:* Rexhep Zlatku. *Environment and Ecology:* Toni Popovski. *Emigration:* Martin Trenevski. *Ministers without Portfolio:* Ernad Fejzulahu, Adnan Kahil, Gjorgji Naumov.

Local Government. Macedonia is administratively divided into 125 communes.

DEFENCE

The President is the C.-in-C. of the armed forces. There is conscription for 9 months. The Army numbered 15,400 (8,000 conscripts) in 1997, and was operating at least 4 Mi-8 transport helicopters, 3 Zlin 242 trainers and some light communications aircraft. There is a paramilitary police force of 7,500.

Defence expenditure in 1997 totalled US$132m. (US$58 per capita), representing 10·2% of GDP.

INTERNATIONAL RELATIONS

On 13 Sept. 1995 under the auspices of the UN, Macedonia and Greece agreed to normalize their relations.

MACEDONIA

Macedonia is a member of the UN, the Council of Europe and the Central European Initiative.

ECONOMY

Policy. According to the Privatization Agency, 914 firms had been privatized by the end of 1996, 257 were in the process of transformation, and 45 were awaiting privatization.

At the same time, a number of firms which had been experiencing heavy losses were obliged by law to embark on a re-structuring programme. Comprehensive measures were taken for a well-planned financial and ownership re-structuring of 25 large firms which had experienced extremely heavy losses.

88·2% of companies are privately owned, 8·5% are publicly owned, 1·6% have mixed ownership, 1·5% are co-operatives and 0·2% are state owned.

By the end of Nov. 1998, 107,978 legal commercial entities were registered in the Institute of Statistics.

Performance. Real GDP growth was 1·5% in 1997 (0·6% in 1996).

Budget. In 1997 revenue and expenditure balanced at 41,564m. denars.

Currency. The national currency of Macedonia is the denar (MKD), of 100 deni.

As of 31 Oct. 1997, gold reserves were US$25·1m. Inflation was 3·0% for 1996, and 3·6% in 1997.

Banking and Finance. The central bank and bank of issue is the National Bank of Macedonia. Its *Governor* is Dr Ljube Trpeski. As of 30 Sept. 1997, commercial banks' total non-government deposits were 17,774m. denars, and non-government savings deposits were 11,959m. denars.

A stock exchange opened in Skopje in 1996.

Weights and Measures. The metric system is in use.

ENERGY AND NATURAL RESOURCES

Electricity. Installed capacity in 1996 was 1·38m. kW. Output in 1997: 6,732,806 MWh, of which 1,277,039 MWh were hydro-electric. Consumption per capita was an estimated 3,372 kWh in 1997.

Minerals. Macedonia is relatively rich in minerals, including lead, zinc, copper, iron, chromium, nickel, antimony, manganese, silver and gold. Output in 1997 (in tonnes): Lead-zinc ore 838,856; lead-zinc concentrates 50,650; copper ore 4,138,000; copper concentrate 46,809; chromium concentrate 1,535; refined silver 28.

Agriculture. At the 1994 census the active agricultural population was 91,354. In 1997 there were 647,445 ha of arable land and 636,027 ha of pasture. 139,851 ha of arable land were owned by agricultural organizations, and 457,899 ha by individual farmers.

Crop production, 1997 (in 1,000 tonnes): Wheat, 294; barley, 120; maize, 157; rice, 25; sugar-beet, 72; sunflower, 15; tobacco, 25; lucerne, 100; potatoes, 158; beans, 13; tomatoes, 117; peppers, 100; apples, 77; pears, 8; plums, 18; grapes, 258.

Livestock, 1997 (in 1,000): Cattle, 289; horses, 66; sheep, 1,631; pigs, 184; chickens, 3,275. Livestock products, 1997 (in 1,000 tonnes): Beef, 8; pork, 9; mutton, 7; poultry, 3; wool, 3; honey, 1; cow's milk, 133m. litres; sheep's milk, 49m. litres; eggs (total), 426m.

There were 53,384 tractors in use in 1997.

Forestry. Forests covered 1,023,145 ha in 1997, chiefly oak and beech. In 1997, 1,000,000 cu. metres of timber were cut.

Fisheries. Total catch of freshwater fish in 1997 was 1,009 tonnes.

INDUSTRY

In 1997 there were 94,404 enterprises (90,426 private, 1,112 public, 1,257 co-operative, 1,577 mixed and 32 state-owned). Production (in tonnes): Ferro-alloys, 85,908; steel ingots, 596; buses, 718 (units); refrigerators, 11,974 (units); sulphuric acid, 105,039; medicines, 501; detergents, 22,885; cotton yarn, 3,971.

Labour. At the 1994 census the population of working age was 1,247,481. The economically active population in 1998 was 823,826 and the number of unemployed persons 284,064.

INTERNATIONAL TRADE

The foreign debt of Macedonia, including debt taken over from the former Yugoslavia, was US$1,172·4m. on 31 Dec. 1996.

Imports and Exports. Imports and exports (in US$1,000)

	1994	1995	1996	1997
Imports	1,484,092	1,718,904	1,626,917	1,754,448
Exports	1,086,343	1,204,048	1,147,440	1,180,133

Main export markets, 1997: Germany, Yugoslavia, Slovenia, Greece, Italy, Russia, Bulgaria, USA, Croatia, Ukraine.

COMMUNICATIONS

Roads. In 1997 there were 909 km of main roads, 3,404 km of regional roads and 6,152 km of local roads: 1,093 km of roads were macadamized and 5,984 km asphalted. 20m. passengers and 2·4m. tonnes of freight were transported. There were 289,204 cars and 19,815 lorries in 1997.

Rail. In 1997 there were 699 km of railways (233 km electrified). 1·7m. passengers and 2·1m. tonnes of freight were transported.

Civil Aviation. There are international airports at Skopje and Ohrid. There are 2 Macedonia-based carriers—Interimpex-Avioimpex and the smaller Macedonian Airlines. In 1998 services were also provided by Ada Air, Adria Airways, Aeroflot, Austrian Airlines, Balkan, Croatia Airlines, Hemus Air, JAT and Swissair. In 1996 Skopje handled 419,978 passengers (all on international flights) and 2,716 tonnes of freight, and Ohrid handled 101,191 passengers and 736 tonnes of freight.

Telecommunications. There were 592,733 telephones in 1997. In 1995 there were 1,800 fax machines.

Postal Services. In 1997 there were 295 post offices.

SOCIAL INSTITUTIONS

Justice. Courts are autonomous and independent. Judges are tenured and elected for life on the proposal of the *Judicial Council*, whose members are themselves elected for renewable 6-year terms. The highest court is the Supreme Court. There are 28 courts of first instance and 3 higher courts.

Religion. Macedonia is traditionally Orthodox but the church is not established and there is freedom of religion. At the 1994 census 66·3% of the population were Orthodox, 30% Moslem and 0·4% Roman Catholic. In 1967 an autocephalous Orthodox church split off from the Serbian. Its head is the Archbishop of Ohrid and Macedonia whose seat is at Skopje. It has 5 bishoprics in Macedonia and representatives in USA, Canada and Australia. It has some 300 priests.

The Moslem Religious Union has a superiorate at Skopje. The Roman Catholic Church has a seat at Skopje.

Education. Education is free and compulsory for 8 years. In 1996, 37,506 children attended 52 pre-school institutions and 365 infant schools of elementary education. In 1996 there were 259,594 pupils enrolled in 1,044 primary, 83,402 in 91 secondary and (in 1995-96) 1,237 in higher schools, and 29,517 students in higher education. There are universities at Skopje (Cyril and Methodius, founded in 1949; 25,593 students and 1,177 academic staff in 1996-97) and Bitola (founded 1979; 5,161 students and 164 academic staff in 1996-97).

In 1996 total expenditure on education came to 5·6% of GNP and represented 20·0% of total government expenditure.

Health. There were 4,464 doctors in 1996, and 58 hospitals with 10,311 beds.

Welfare. In 1997 there were 227,477 pensioners (118,148 old age). 75,227 adults and 66,522 children received social benefits in 1993.

MACEDONIA

CULTURE

Broadcasting. The national Macedonian Radio and Television is government-funded. It broadcasts on 3 TV channels. There are also state-owned and private local TV stations. There were 89 local radio stations (56 private) in 1996, and 306,159 TV subscribers (colour by PAL). There were 395,000 radio receivers in 1995.

Cinema. There were 40 cinemas and 278,197 admissions in 1996.

Press. There were 4 national newspapers in 1996, 2 in Macedonian, 1 in Albanian and 1 in Turkish, and 142 other newspapers and periodicals.

Tourism. In 1997, 451,871 tourists spent 1·587m. nights in Macedonia.

DIPLOMATIC REPRESENTATIVES

Of Macedonia in Great Britain (10 Harcourt House, 19A Cavendish Sq., London, W1M 9AD)
Ambassador: Stevo Crvenkovski.

Of Great Britain in Macedonia (Veljko Vlahovic 26, 4th Floor, Skopje 9100)
Ambassador: Mark Dickinson.

Of Macedonia in the USA (3050 K Street, NW, Suite 210, Washington, D.C., 20007)
Ambassador: Lubica Acevska.

Of the USA in Macedonia (Bd. Linden, 91000 Skopje)
Ambassador: Christopher R. Hill.

Of Macedonia to the United Nations
Ambassador: Naste Calovski.

Of Macedonia to the European Union
Ambassador: Jovan Tegovski.

FURTHER READING

Danforth, L. M., *The Macedonian Conflict: Ethnic Nationalism in a Transnational World.* Princeton Univ. Press, 1996
Poulton, H., *Who Are the Macedonians?* Farnborough, 1996

National statistical office: Republic of Macedonia Statisitical Office, Dame Gruev 4, Skopje.

MADAGASCAR

Repoblikan'i

Madagasikara

Capital: Antananarivo
Population estimate, 2000: 17·39m.
GNP per capita: (PPP$) 900
HDI/world rank: 0·348/153

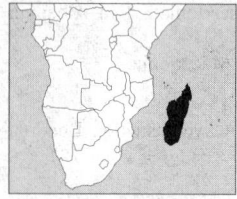

KEY HISTORICAL EVENTS

Evidence of human inhabitants on Madagascar dates back 2,000 years, and the island was settled by people of African and Indonesian origin when it was visited by the Portuguese explorer, Diego Diaz, in 1500. The island was unified under the Imérina monarchy between 1797 and 1861, but French claims to a protectorate led to hostilities culminating in the establishment of a French protectorate on 30 Sept. 1895. The monarchy was abolished and Madagascar became a French colony on 6 Aug. 1896.

Madagascar became an Overseas Territory of France in 1946, and on 14 Oct. 1958, following a referendum, was proclaimed the autonomous Malagasy Republic within the French community, achieving full independence on 26 June 1960.

In Feb. 1975 Col. Richard Ratsimandrava, Head of State, was assassinated. A National Military Directorate was established on 12 Feb. On 15 June it handed over power to a Supreme Revolutionary Council under Didier Ratsiraka. The 1975 Constitution instituted a 'Democratic Republic' in which only a single political party was permitted.

After 6 months of anti-government unrest, during which the opposition formed an alternative 'government', in Oct. 1991 the government and the Committee of Living Forces, a coalition of 16 opposition parties led by Albert Zafy, agreed to form an 18-month transitional administration. However, Zafy refused to join a government formed on 13 Nov., and was instead appointed chairman of the High State Authority for a Provisional Government formed on 23 Nov.

A new Constitution instituted the Third Republic in Sept. 1992.

TERRITORY AND POPULATION

Madagascar is situated off the south-east coast of Africa, from which it is separated by the Mozambique channel. Its area is 587,041 sq. km (226,658 sq. miles). At the 1993 census the population was 12,092,157 (50·45% female); density, 20·6 per sq. km. Estimate (1997), 14,062,000 (26·4% urban in 1995). Population density, 24·0 per sq. km.

The UN gives a projected population for 2000 of 17·39m.

Province	Area in Sq. km	Population (1993 census)	Chief town	Population (1993 census)
Antsiranana	43,046	942,410	Antsiranana	54,418[1]
Mahajanga	150,023	1,330,612	Mahajanga	100,807
Toamasina	71,911	1,935,330	Toamasina	127,441
Antananarivo	58,283	3,483,236	Antananarivo	1,052,835
Fianarantsoa	102,373	2,671,150	Fianarantsoa	99,005
Toliary	161,405	1,729,419	Toliary	61,460[1]

[1]1990 estimate.

The indigenous population is of Malayo–Polynesian stock, divided into 18 ethnic groups of which the principal are Merina (26%) of the central plateau, the Betsimisaraka (15%) of the east coast, and the Betsileo (12%) of the southern plateau. Foreign communities include Europeans, mainly French (30,000), Indians (15,000), Chinese (9,000), Comorians and Arabs.

The official language is Malagasy. French is the language of international communication.

SOCIAL STATISTICS

1997, estimated births, 595,000; deaths, 198,000. Rates, 1997 estimates (per 1,000 population): Births, 42·3; deaths, 14·1. Infant mortality (per 1,000 live births), 92.

Expectation of life in 1997 was 52·5 years (51·4 for males and 53·7 for females). Growth rate, 2·82% per annum. Fertility rate, 1990–95, 6·1 births per woman.

CLIMATE
A tropical climate, but the mountains cause big variations in rainfall, which is very heavy in the east and very light in the west. Antananarivo, Jan. 70°F (21·1°C), July 59°F (15°C). Annual rainfall 54" (1,350 mm). Toamasina, Jan. 80°F (26·7°C), July 70°F (21·1°C). Annual rainfall 128" (3,256 mm).

CONSTITUTION AND GOVERNMENT
Following a referendum, a Constitution came into force on 30 Dec. 1975 establishing a Democratic Republic. It provided for a National People's Assembly elected by universal suffrage from the single list of the *Front National pour la Défense de la Révolution Socialiste Malgache*. Executive power was vested in the President with the guidance of a Supreme Revolutionary Council.

Under a convention of 31 Oct. 1991 the powers of the National People's Assembly and the Supreme Revolutionary Council were delegated to a High State Authority for a Provisional Government. Following a referendum on 19 Aug. 1992 at which turn-out was 77·68% and 75·44% of votes cast were in favour, a new Constitution was adopted on 21 Sept. 1992 establishing the Third Republic. Under this the *National Assembly* has 138 seats.

A referendum on 17 Sept. 1995 was in favour of the President appointing and dismissing the Prime Minister, hitherto elected by parliament. The electorate was 6m.; turn-out was 50%.

National Anthem. 'Ry tanindrazanay malala ô!' ('O our beloved Fatherland'); words by Pastor Rahajason, tune by N. Raharisoa.

RECENT ELECTIONS
National assembly elections were held on 17 May 1998. The Pillar and Structure for the Salvation of Madagascar (AREMA) gained 63 seats; Fanilo (Torch) gained 16 seats; Ny Asa Vita no Ifampitsanara (AVI) gained 14 seats and Rally for Socialism and Democracy gained 11 seats. The remaining seats went to other parties and independents.

At the first round of presidential elections on 3 Nov. 1996 there were 15 candidates. The electorate was 6,453,612; turn-out was 58·41%. President Albert Zafy gained 36·61% of votes cast. At the second round on 29 Dec. 1996 turn-out was 49·66%. Didier Ratsiraka was elected by 50·71% of votes cast.

CURRENT ADMINISTRATION
President: Didier Ratsiraka (b. 1935; sworn in 9 Feb. 1997).

In March 1999 the government comprised:

Prime Minister in charge of the Economy and Finance: Tantely Adrianarivo.

Deputy Prime Minister in charge of Development of Autonomous Provinces and Budget: Pierrot Jocelyn Rajaonarivelo. *Foreign Affairs:* Lila Ratsifandrihamanana. *Minister of Agriculture:* Marcel Theophile Raveloarijaona. *Armed Forces:* Brig. Gen. Marcel Ranjeva. *Civil Service, Labour and Social Laws:* Alice Razafinakanga. *Environment, Commerce and Consumer Affairs:* Alphonse Randrianambinina. *Energy and Mines:* Charles Rasoza. *Fisheries and Ocean Resources:* Houssen Abdallah. *Health:* Henriette Rahantalalao. *Higher Education:* Joseph Sydson. *Industry and Crafts:* Mamy Ratovomalala. *Information, Culture and Communication:* Fredo Betsimifira. *Interior:* Col. Jean-Jacques Rasolondraibe. *Justice:* Anaclet Imbiky. *Livestock:* Rakotondrasoa. *Population, Women's Issues and Childhood:* Noeline Jaotody. *Posts and Telecommunications:* Ny Hasina Andriamanjato. *Public Works:* Col. Jean Emile Tsaranazy. *Private Sector and Privatization:* Horace Constant. *Scientific Research:* Georges Solay Rakotonirainy. *Secondary and Primary Education:* Simon Jacquit. *Technical and Professional Education:* Boniface Levelo. *Tourism:* Blandin Razafimanjato. *Transport and Meteorology:* Charles Rasolonay. *Urban and Territorial Management:* Herivelona Ramanantsoa. *Water Resources and Forests:* Rija Rajohnson. *Youth and Sports:* Ndrianasolo.

Local Government. The 6 provinces (*faritany*) are sub-divided into 113 *fivondronana*, which in turn are divided into 13,476 *fokontany* (the traditional communal divisions). Each level is governed by an elected council.

DEFENCE
There is conscription (including civilian labour service) for 18 months. Defence expenditure totalled US$37m. in 1997 (US$3 per capita).

Army. The Army is organized in 2 battalion groups, and 1 engineer regiment. Equipment includes 12 PT-76 light tanks. Strength (1997) 20,000 and gendarmerie, 7,500.

Navy. In 1997 the maritime force had a strength of 500 (including 100 marines), and was equipped with one 250-tonne patrol craft, 1 medium landing ship and 4 landing craft, together with a 1,200-tonne former trawler used for transport and training.

Air Force. Equipment includes 1 Britten-Norman Defender armed transport, 2 C-47s, and 1 Yak-40 for VIP use, 1 Aztec, 2 Cessna Skymasters, 4 Cessna 172Ms and 4 Mi-8 helicopters. Personnel (1997), 500. The 12 MiG-17 and MiG-21 combat aircraft are grounded.

INTERNATIONAL RELATIONS
Madagascar is a member of the UN, OAU and is an ACP member state of the ACP-EU relationship.

ECONOMY
Performance. Real GDP growth was 1·8% in 1995 (0·0% in 1994).

Budget. Budget revenue and expenditure (in MGFr1,000m.):

	1992	1993	1994	1995	1996
Revenue:	503·6	556·0	748·5	1,148·7	1,404·6
Expenditure:	817·3	996·4	1,379·7	1,921·0	2,177·5

Currency. The unit of currency is the *Malagasy franc* (MGFr). 1 *ariary* = MGFr5. In Feb. 1998 foreign exchange reserves were US$274m. Inflation in 1996 was 19·8%. Total money supply in Dec. 1997 was MGFr2,664bn.

Banking and Finance. A Central Bank was formed in 1973, replacing the former *Institut d'Emission Malgache* as the central bank of issue. All commercial banking and insurance was nationalized in 1975 and privatized in 1988. Industrial development is financed through the *Bankin'ny Indostria.* Other commercial banking is undertaken by the *Bankin'ny Tantsaha Mpamokatra,* the *Banky Fampandrosoana ny Varotra.* The Malagasy Bank of the Indian Ocean was set up in Sept. 1990 as part of a bank privatization programme.

Weights and Measures. The metric system is in use.

ENERGY AND NATURAL RESOURCES
Electricity. Installed capacity was 208,000 kW in 1991. Production in 1994 was 605m. kWh, with consumption per capita in 1994 estimated at 42 kWh.

Oil and Gas. Annual crude oil production is 37,000 tonnes. Natural gas production is 2,500 tonnes per annum.

Minerals. Mining production in 1995 (provisional figures) included: Salt, 80,000 tonnes; chromite, 74,000 tonnes; graphite, 13,900 tonnes.

Agriculture. 80–85% of the workforce is employed in agriculture, which in 1996 produced 35% of GDP. The principal agricultural products in 1995 were (estimates in 1,000 tonnes): Rice, 2,596; cassava, 2,420; sugar-cane, 1,980; sweet potatoes, 560; vegetables and melons, 333; potatoes, 270; bananas, 210; mangoes, 200.

Cattle breeding and agriculture are the chief occupations. There were, in 1996, 10,320,000 cattle, 1,629,000 pigs, 1,300,000 goats (1995), 756,000 sheep and 23m. chickens (1995).

Forestry. In 1995 the area under forests was 15·11m. ha, or 26% of the total land area (27·1% in 1990).The forests contain many valuable woods, while gum, resins and plants for tanning, dyeing and medicinal purposes abound. Timber production was 10·89m. cu. metres in 1995.

Fisheries. In 1989 the fishing fleet numbered 44 vessels over 100 GRT totalling 6,852 GRT. The catch of fish in 1995 was 120,140 tonnes, of which 86,963 tonnes were from marine waters.

INDUSTRY
Industry, hitherto confined mainly to the processing of agricultural products, is now extending to cover other fields.

Labour. In 1996 the workforce was 7,199,000 (55% males). In 1995 approximately 75% of the economically active population were engaged in agriculture, fisheries and forestry.

INTERNATIONAL TRADE
Foreign debt was US$4,175m. in 1996.

Imports and Exports. Exports, 1996, US$299m.; imports, US$508m. Chief exports (1995) were coffee (45%), vanilla (20%), plus cloves, shellfish (especially prawns), sugar and petroleum products. Principal imports in 1995 were intermediate manufactures (30%), capital goods (28%), plus petroleum products, consumer goods and foodstuffs. Main import suppliers, 1995: France, 29·7%; Germany, 10·1%; Iran, 10·1%; Southern African Customs Union, 6·3%. Main export markets, 1995: France, 28·4%; Germany, 8·3%; USA, 6·6%; Japan, 6·2%.

COMMUNICATIONS
Roads. In 1995 there were 49,837 km of roads (5,731 km paved). There were 58,100 passenger cars in 1996, 11,000 trucks and vans and 4,340 buses and coaches.

Rail. In 1994 there were 883 km of railways, all metre gauge. In 1994, 0·6m. passengers and 0·3m. tonnes of freight were transported.

Civil Aviation. There are international airports at Antananarivo (Ivato) and Mahajanga (Amborovy). The national carrier is Air Madagascar, which is 89·5% state-owned. In 1998 services were also provided by Air Austral, Air France, Air Mauritius, Inter Air and Travaux Aeriens de Madagascar. In 1996 Antananarivo handled 506,947 passengers (293,982 on domestic flights) and 10,042 tonnes of freight. Air Madagascar flew 8·2m. km in 1995, carrying 15,417,800 passsengers (8,332,400 on domestic flights).

Shipping. In 1989, 760,100 tonnes were loaded and 1,062,900 tonnes unloaded at Toamasina, Mahajanga, Antsiranana and Nosy-Be. In 1995 registered merchant marine totalled 37,721 GRT, including oil tankers, 13,859 GRT.

Telecommunications. Madagascar had 43,200 main telephone lines in 1997, equivalent to 2·7 per 1,000 persons. There were around 700 Internet users in Jan. 1998.

Postal Services. There are 724 post offices and agencies.

SOCIAL INSTITUTIONS
Justice. The Supreme Court and the Court of Appeal are in Antananarivo. In most towns there are Courts of First Instance for civil and commercial cases. For criminal cases there are ordinary criminal courts in most towns. In 1996 government expenditure on public order and safety totalled MGFr59,200m.

Religion. About 50% of the population practise the traditional religion, 43% are Christians (of whom approximately half are Roman Catholic and half are Protestant, mainly belonging to the Fiangonan'i Jesosy Kristy eto Madagasikara) and 7% Moslem.

Education. Education is compulsory from 6 to 14 years of age. In 1994 there were 13,624 primary schools with 37,676 teachers for 1·5m. pupils, 298,241 pupils at secondary level with 15,118 teachers and (1993) 42,681 students at university level. In 1994–95 there were 6 universities. In 1996 government expenditure on education totalled MGFr255,500m. Adult literacy rate (1995) was 45·7% (male, 59·8%; female, 32%).

Health. In 1990 there were 1,392 doctors, 89 dentists, 3,124 nurses, 19 pharmacists and 1,703 midwives; provision of hospital beds was 9 per 10,000 population. In 1996 government expenditure on health totalled MGFr191,300m.

Welfare. In 1996 government expenditure on social security and welfare totalled MGFr26,000m.

CULTURE

Broadcasting. The government-controlled Radio-Television Malagasy is responsible for broadcasting. There are radio programmes in Malagasy and French, and 3–4 hours TV transmission a day (colour by SECAM). In 1995 there were 2·8m. radio and 0·29m. TV sets.

Cinema. In 1991 there were 11 cinemas with an annual attendance of 0·4m.

Press. In 1995 there were 6 daily newspapers with a total circulation of 59,000.

Tourism. There were an estimated 78,800 tourists in 1995.

DIPLOMATIC REPRESENTATIVES
Of Madagascar in Great Britain
Ambassador: Vacant (resides in Paris).

Of Great Britain in Madagascar (First Floor, Immeuble 'Ny Havana', Cite de 67 Ha, BP167, Antananarivo)
Ambassador: Robert S. Dewar.

Of Madagascar in the USA (2374 Massachusetts Ave., NW, Washington, D.C., 20008)
Chargé d'Affaires a.i.: Biclair H. G. Andrianantoandro.

Of the USA in Madagascar (14-16 rue Rainitovo, Antsahavola, Antananarivo)
Ambassador: Vacant.

Of Madagascar to the United Nations
Ambassador: Jean Delacroix Bakoniarivo.

Of Madagascar to the European Union
Ambassador: Jean Beriziky.

FURTHER READING
Banque des Données de l'Etat. *Bulletin Mensuel de Statistique*
Allen, P. M., *Madagascar.* Boulder (CO), 1995
Brandt, H., *Guide to Madagascar.* Chalfont St Peter, 1988
Brandt, H. and Brown, M., *Madagascar.* [Bibliography] Oxford and Santa Barbara (CA), 1993
Deschamps, H., *Histoire de Madagascar.* Paris, 4th ed. 1972
Rabetafika, R., *Réforme Fiscal et Révolution Socialiste à Madagascar.* Paris, 1990
Rajoelina, P. and Ramelet, A., *Madagascar, la Grande Ile.* Paris, 1989
Ramahatra, O., *Madagascar: une Economie en Phase d'Ajustement.* Paris, 1989

National statistical office: Banque des Données de l'Etat, Antananarivo.

MALAŴI

Dziko la Malaŵi

(Republic of Malaŵi)

Capital: Lilongwe
Population estimate, 2000: 10·98m.
GNP per capita: (PPP$) 690
HDI/world rank: 0·334/161

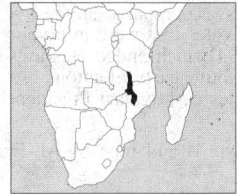

KEY HISTORICAL EVENTS

A powerful kingdom dominated much of Malaŵi and the surrounding area from the 15th to the 18th centuries, based on the Bantu-speaking people who began settling there 200 years earlier. However, by the beginning of the 19th century, this had disintegrated into many small entities, and occupation by Ngoni people from the south facilitated European control. The explorer David Livingstone reached Lake Nyasa, now Lake Malaŵi, in 1859 and it was the land along the lake's western shore that became, in 1891, the British Protectorate of Nyasaland. The name was changed to British Central Africa Protectorate in 1893 but reverted to Nyasaland in 1907.

In 1884 the British South Africa Company applied for a charter to trade. Within a few years the slavery and the slave trade had been suppressed. Pressure on land, the colour bar and other grievances about colonial rule generated Malaŵian resistance which was only checked by 1915. After the Second World War, the Nyasaland African Congress was formed to lead a new wave of resistance, particularly against the impending federation of the country to two neighbouring British colonies.

In 1953 Nyasaland was joined with Southern Rhodesia (Zimbabwe) and Northern Rhodesia (Zambia) to form the Federation of Rhodesia and Nyasaland, under British control. This union was dissolved in 1963 when Nyasaland was for a year self-governing, until on 6 July 1964 it became independent, adopting the name of Malaŵi. In 1966 Malaŵi was declared a republic and Dr Hastings Banda became the first president. Jailed in 1959–60 for his activities in the resistance, Banda had led the Malaŵi Congress Party to victory in elections in 1961 and established a one party dictatorship which lasted for 30 years. In 1994, with the election of Bakili Muluzi, Malaŵi returned to multi-party democracy.

TERRITORY AND POPULATION

Malaŵi lies along the southern and western shores of Lake Malaŵi (the third largest lake in Africa), and is otherwise bounded in the north by Tanzania, south by Mozambique and west by Zambia. Area (including the inland water areas of Lake Malombe, Chilwa, Chiuta and the Malaŵi portion of Lake Malaŵi, which total 24,208 sq. km), 118,484 sq. km (45,747 sq. miles).

Population at census 1987, 7,982,607. Estimate (1998), 10·70m. (13·8% urban), density; 94 per sq. km.

The UN gives a projected population for 2000 of 10·98m.

Population of main towns (estimated 1998): Blantyre, 2m.; Lilongwe, 1m.; Mzuzu, 100,000; Zomba, 70,000. Population of the regions (estimated 1998): Northern, 1·2m.; Central, 4·3m.; Southern, 5·2m.

The official languages are Chichewa, spoken by over 50% of the population, and English.

SOCIAL STATISTICS

1995 births, 476,000; deaths, 217,000. The birth rate in 1998 was 50·2 per 1,000 population and the death rate 22·7. Annual growth rate, 1990–95, 3·3%. Expectation of life at birth in 1998 was 41 years, down from a high of 45 between 1985 and 1990. It had last been 41 in the mid 1970s. The sharp decline is largely attributed to the huge number of people in the country with HIV. Infant mortality, 1990–95, 148 per 1,000 live births; fertility rate, 7·2 births per woman.

CLIMATE

The tropical climate is marked by a dry season from May to Oct. and a wet season for the remaining months. Rainfall amounts are variable, within the range of 29–

100" (725–2,500 mm), and maximum temperatures average 75–89°F (24–32°C), and minimum temperatures 58–67°F (14·4–19·4°C). Lilongwe, Jan. 73°F (22·8°C), July 60°F (15·6°C). Annual rainfall 36" (900 mm). Blantyre, Jan. 75°F (23·9°C), July 63°F (17·2°C). Annual rainfall 45" (1,125 mm). Zomba, Jan. 73°F (22·8°C), July 63°F (17·2°C). Annual rainfall 54" (1,344 mm).

CONSTITUTION AND GOVERNMENT

The *President* is also head of Government. Malaŵi was a one-party state, but following a referendum on 14 June 1993, in which 63% of votes cast were in favour of reform, a new Constitution was adopted on 17 May 1994 which ended Hastings Banda's life presidency and provided for the holding of multi-party elections. At these Bakili Muluzi was elected President by 47·16% of votes cast against President Banda and 2 other opponents.

National Anthem. 'O God Bless our Land of Malaŵi'; words and tune by M.-F. Sauka.

RECENT ELECTIONS

Parliament is composed of 177 members. At the elections of 17 May 1994 the United Democratic Front (UDF) won 84 seats; the Malaŵi Congress Party (the former single party), 55; and the Alliance for Democracy (AFORD), 36. Results in the remaining 2 seats were nullified. Presidential and parliamentary elections were scheduled for May 1999.

CURRENT ADMINISTRATION

President and Minister for Home Affairs: Dr Bakili Muluzi, b. 1943 (UDF; sworn in 21 May 1994).

In March 1999 the government comprised:

Vice-President and Minister responsible for Privatization: Justin Malewezi.

Minister of Agriculture and Irrigation: Aleka Banda. *Commerce and Industry:* Matembo Mzunda. *Defence:* Joseph Kubwalo. *Education, Sports and Culture:* Brown James Mpinganjira. *Energy and Mining:* Rev. Dumbo Lemani. *Finance:* Cassim Chilumpha. *Foreign Affairs:* Mapopa Chipeta. *Forestry, Fisheries and Environmental Affairs:* Mayinga Mkandawire. *Health and Population:* Harry Thompson. *Information, Broadcasting, Post and Telecommunications:* Sam Mpasu. *Justice and Attorney-General:* Peter Fachi. *Labour and Vocational Training:* Dr Kaliyoma Phumisa. *National Heritage, Lands, Housing, Physical Planning and Surveys:* Richard Sembereka. *Local Government and Sports:* Chakakal Chaziya. *Tourism, Parks and Wildlife:* Patrick Mbewe. *Transport and Civil Aviation:* Kamangadazi Chambalo. *Water and Irrigation:* Melvin Moyo. *Women, Youth, and Community Services:* Lillian Patel. *Works and Supplies:* Peter Chupa.

Local Government. There are 3 regions and 26 districts, each administered by a district commissioner.

DEFENCE

All services form part of the Army. Defence expenditure totalled US$23m. in 1997 (US$2 per capita).

Army. The army is organized into 3 infantry battalions, 1 support battalion and 1 commando battalion. Personnel (1997) 5,000.

Navy. 3 patrol craft, 2 landing craft and some boats are operated by about (1997) 220 personnel based at Chilumba on Lake Nyasa.

Air Wing. To support the infantry battalion, the Air Wing has 2 C-47 and 4 Do 228 light transports, and 2 Ecureuil helicopters. An HS 125 jet is used for VIP transport. Personnel (1997), 80. There is also a paramilitary police force numbering 1,000.

INTERNATIONAL RELATIONS

Malaŵi is a member of the UN, the Commonwealth, COMESA (the Common Market for Eastern and Southern Africa), OAU and SADC and is an ACP member state of the ACP-EU relationship.

ECONOMY

Policy. The government operates a 3-year 'rolling' public-sector investment programme, revised annually to take into account changing needs and the expected level of resources available. The greatest part of the development programme is annually financed from external aid. Some 200 state enterprises are marked down for privatization.

Performance. Real GDP growth was 4·6% in 1995 (15·7% in 1994 and 9·6% in 1993).

Budget. Revenue Account receipts and expenditure (in K.1,000) for years ending 31 March:

	1993–94	1994–95	1995–96	1996–97
Revenue	1,569,270	2,194,590	4,355,830	5,728,170
Expenditure	3,263,930	4,286,030	7,101,930	8,877,000

Currency. The unit of currency is the *kwacha* (MWK) of 100 *tambala*. Foreign exchange reserves were US$128m. and gold reserves 10,000 troy oz. in Feb. 1998. Foreign exchange controls were abolished in Feb. 1994. The average annual inflation rate over the period 1990–96 was 33·2%. Inflation has fallen from 98·2% in 1994 to 11% in 1998 and interest rates have come down from 37% to 24%. Total money supply in Oct. 1997 was K.3,322m.

Banking and Finance. The central bank and bank of issue is the Reserve Bank of Malaŵi (founded 1964). There are 4 commercial banks and an Investment Development Bank.

Weights and Measures. The metric system is in use.

ENERGY AND NATURAL RESOURCES

Electricity. The Electricity Supply Commission of Malaŵi is the sole supplier. Capacity is 220 MW with demand at 180 MW. Production was 857·5m. kWh in 1995. Consumption per capita in 1994 was an estimated 74 kWh.

Oil and Gas. In 1997 Malaŵi and Mozambique came to an agreement on the construction of an oil pipeline between the two countries.

Minerals. The main product in 1976 was marble (149,254 tonnes) for the manufacture of cement. Coal mining began in 1985.

Agriculture. Malaŵi is predominantly an agricultural country. In 1997 agriculture accounted for about 40% of GDP, and agricultural produce contributed 90% of export earnings. Maize is the main subsistence crop and is grown by over 95% of all smallholders; production, 1995, 2,033m. tonnes. Tobacco is the chief cash crop, providing 70% of export earnings. Also important are groundnuts, cassava, millet and rice. There are large plantations which produce sugar, tea and coffee. Production (1995): Tobacco, 129,630 tonnes; sugar-cane, 1,980,000 tonnes; tea, 34,160 tonnes.

Livestock in 1996: Cattle, 700,000; sheep, 101,000; goats, 890,000 (1995); pigs, 220,000; chickens, 9m.

Forestry. In 1995 the area under forests was 3·34m. ha, or 35·5% of the total land area (down from 38·4% in 1990). Production, 1997, 10·2m. cu. metres.

Fisheries. Landings in 1995 were 45,427 tonnes, entirely from inland waters.

INDUSTRY

Index of manufacturing output in 1995 (1984 = 100): manufacturing for domestic consumption, excluding mining and quarrying, 114·9; of this consumer goods were at 127 and intermediate goods for building and construction were at 85·2. Manufacturing for export, 116·7.

Labour. The labour force in 1996 was 4,807,000 (51% males). Approximately 85% of the economically active population in 1995 were engaged in agriculture, fisheries and forestry.

INTERNATIONAL TRADE

External debt was US$2,312m. in 1996.

Imports and Exports. Major exports 1995 (in K.1m.): Tobacco, 4,051; tea, 427·8; sugar, 481·7; cotton, 57·7; groundnuts, 4·0. Major imports: Petroleum products, 214,820 cu. metres.

Trade statistics for calendar years are (in US$1m.):

	1993	1994	1995	1996
Imports	545	495	475	624
Exports	319	325	405	481

Trade Fairs. The Malaŵi International Trade Fair takes place in June.

COMMUNICATIONS

Roads. The road network consisted of 28,400 km 1996, of which 3,360 km were highways and main roads, 2,850 km were secondary roads and 22,200 km were other roads. Approximately 5,250 km of roads are paved. A major repair programme is under way. There were 27,000 passenger cars and 29,700 trucks and vans in 1996.

Rail. Malaŵi Railways operate 797 km on 1,067 mm gauge, providing links to the Mozambican ports of Beira and Nacala. In 1995 railways carried 0·4m. passengers and 0·3m. tonnes of freight.

Civil Aviation. The national carrier is the state-owned Air Malaŵi (soon to be privatized). Air Malaŵi flies to a number of regional centres in Mozambique, Zambia, Zimbabwe, South Africa, Tanzania and Kenya and in 1998 operated a service to London. There are international airports at Lilongwe (Kamuzu International Airport) and Blantyre (Chileka). In 1998 services were also provided by Air Tanzania Corporation, Air Zimbabwe, British Airways, Ethiopian Airlines, Kenya Airways, KLM, South African Airways and Zambian Express. In 1996 Lilongwe handled 181,587 passengers (108,932 on international flights) and 3,228 tonnes of freight, and Blantyre had 113,617 passengers (65,980 on domestic flights) and 1,240 tonnes of freight.

Shipping. In 1995 lake ships carried 169,000 passengers and 6,000 tonnes of freight.

Telecommunications. In 1996 there were 35,500 main telephone lines, or 3·5 for every 1,000 population. Cellular phone subscribers numbered 400 in 1995, and there were 1,100 fax machines. In 1998 there were around 400 Internet users.

Postal Services. In 1995 there were 307 post offices.

SOCIAL INSTITUTIONS

Justice. Justice is administered in the High Court and in the magistrates' courts. Traditional courts were abolished in 1994. Appeals from magistrates' courts lie to the High Court, and appeals from the High Court to Malaŵi's Supreme Court of Appeal.

Religion. 1997 estimates: 1,970,000 Protestant (mostly Presbyterian); 1,920,000 Muslim; 1,730,000 Roman Catholic; 960,000 traditional beliefs; 950,000 African Christian; 2,080,000 other.

Education. The adult literacy rate in 1995 was 56·4% (71·9% among males and 41·8% among females). Fees for primary education were abolished in 1994. In 1995–96 the number of pupils in primary schools was 3m. The primary school course is of 8 years' duration, followed by a 4-year secondary course. In 1994–95 there were 49,412 pupils in secondary schools. English is taught from the 1st year and becomes the general medium of instruction from the 4th year.

The University of Malaŵi had 3,657 students and 366 academic staff in 1994–95. There were also 4 colleges and 1 polytechnic.

Health. In 1989 there were 189 doctors, giving a provision of 1 doctor for every 49,118 persons—the lowest ratio in the world. At the other extreme, Monaco had 1 doctor for every 164 persons in 1996. There are 3 central hospitals, 1 mental hospital, 2 leprosaria and 45 hospitals of which 21 are government district hospitals.

In the period 1990–96 only 37% of the population had access to safe drinking water.

CULTURE
The dances of the Malaŵi are a strong part of their culture. The National Dance Troupe (formerly the Kwacha Cultural Troupe) formed in Nov. 1987 as a part of the Department of Arts and Crafts of the Ministry of Education.

Broadcasting. The Malaŵi Broadcasting Corporation, a statutory body, broadcasts in English and Chichewa. There were 3·2m. radio sets in 1998, up from 260,000 in 1980. No other country had such a large percentage increase in the number of radio receivers in use over the same period. There is a national radio station in Blantyre providing 2 channels and 5 private radio stations have been operating since 1997. Television is in the early stages of development.

Press. There are more than 16 newspapers in circulation, the main 4 are: *The Daily Times* (English, Monday to Friday); 17,000 copies daily. *The Nation* (English, Monday to Friday); 16,000 copies daily. *Malaŵi News* (English and Chichewa, Saturdays); 23,000 copies weekly and *Weekend Nation* (English and Chichewa, Saturdays); 16,000 copies weekly. In addition there is *Odini* (English and Chichewa); 8,500 copies fortnightly. *Boma Lathu* (Chichewa); 150,000 copies monthly. *Za Alimi* (English and Chichewa); 10,000 copies monthly.

Tourism. There were 230,000 tourists in 1997.

Museums and Galleries. The main attraction is the Museum of Malaŵi.

DIPLOMATIC REPRESENTATIVES
Of Malaŵi in Great Britain (33 Grosvenor St., London, W1X 0DE)
High Commissioner: Bright McBin Msaka.

Of Great Britain in Malaŵi (PO Box 30042, Lilongwe, 3)
High Commissioner: Mr. G. Finlayson.

Of Malaŵi in the USA (2408 Massachusetts Ave., NW, Washington, D.C., 20008)
Ambassador: Willie Chokani.

Of the USA in Malaŵi (PO Box 30016, Lilongwe 3)
Ambassador: A. Ellen Shippy.

Of Malaŵi to the United Nations
Ambassador: David Rubadiri.

Of Malaŵi to the European Union
Ambassador: Julie Mphande.

FURTHER READING
National Statistical Office. *Monthly Statistical Bulletin*
Ministry of Economic Planning and Development. *Economic Report*. Annual
Decalo, S., *Malaŵi* [Bibliography]. 2nd ed. Oxford and Santa Barbara (CA), 1995

National statistical office: National Statistical Office, POB 333, Zomba.

MALAYSIA

Persekutuan Tanah Malaysia
(Federation of Malaysia)

Capital: Kuala Lumpur
Population estimate, 2000: 22·3m.
GNP per capita: (PPP$) 10,390
HDI/world rank: 0·834/60

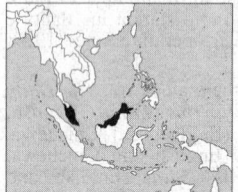

KEY HISTORICAL EVENTS

Malaysia is a federation consisting of the eleven States of Peninsular Malaysia and the two states of Sabah and Sarawak.

The Portuguese were the first Europeans to settle in the area and Malacca became a Portuguese possession in 1541. The Dutch took Malacca in 1641 and held it until 1794 when it was occupied by the British who had established three trading posts at the end of the 18th century. Although Malacca was returned to the Dutch in 1814, it was finally ceded to Britain in 1824. At the same time (1814-24) Stamford Raffles established a settlement and Singapore became British territory.

In 1826 Singapore and Malacca were incorporated with Penang to form the Straits Settlements. In 1896 Negri Sembilan, Penang, Perak and Selangor became the Federated Malay States; these were 'protected' states and were not part of the Straits Settlements. The remaining five Malay states became known as the Unfederated Malay States.

Singapore and what is now Malaysia were occupied by the Japanese from 1941 to 1945. Soon thereafter, in Jan. 1946, plans were published to create a Malaysian Union excluding Singapore but including the four Federated and the five Unfederated Malay States and the Settlements of Penang and Malacca. The Union came into being in April 1946 but was soon abandoned in the face of opposition. However, in Jan. 1948 the Union was reconstituted as the Federation of Malaya.

From 1948 to 1960 a State of Emergency existed in order to counter revolt by Malayan Communists aimed at the disruption of the country's economy. Commonwealth forces supported the Federation's own armed forces.

Following lengthy negotiations independence was granted to the Federation of Malaya on 31 Aug. 1957.

On 31 Aug. 1963 Malaysia was created from the Federation of Malaya, Singapore, North Borneo (renamed Sabah) and Sarawak. Brunei was also invited to join but no agreement could be reached. The UK relinquished sovereignty over Singapore, North Borneo and Sarawak from independence day and extended the 1957 defence agreement with Malaya to apply to Malaysia. Malaysia became a member of the Commonwealth. Singapore left Malaysia on 9 Aug. 1965 to become an independent sovereign state.

Under the leadership of Mahathir Mohamad, south-east Asia's longest-serving leader, Malaysia entered on a period of economic prosperity, broken eventually by the 1997-98 recession. Economic turbulence caused political dissent within the government. In Sept. 1998 Anwar Ibrahim was sacked from his job as finance minister and deputy prime minister and expelled from the dominant UMNO party. His support for continuing economic reform was in conflict with Dr Mahathir's policy of introducing capital controls to insulate the economy. Facing allegations of corruption and sexual promiscuity, Mr Anwar was subsequently arrested and jailed for 6 years.

TERRITORY AND POPULATION

The federal state of Malaysia comprises the 11 states and 1 federal territory of Peninsular Malaysia, bounded in the north by Thailand, and with the island of Singapore as an enclave on its southern tip; and, on the island of Borneo to the east, the state of Sabah (which includes the federal territory of the island of Labuan), and the state of Sarawak, with Brunei as an enclave, both bounded in the south by Indonesia and in the north-west and north-east by the South China and Sulu Seas.

The area of Malaysia is 329,758 sq. km (127,317 sq. miles) and the population (1997 estimate) is 21·7m.; density, 62 per sq. km. Malaysia's national waters cover 515,256 sq. km.

MALAYSIA

The UN gives a projected population for 2000 of 22·3m.
An estimated 53·6% of the population lived in urban areas in 1995. The growth of the population has been:

Year	Peninsular Malaysia	Sarawak	Sabah/Labuan	Total Malaysia
1980	11,426,613	1,307,582	1,011,046	13,745,241
1990	14,127,556	1,648,217	1,791,209	17,566,982
1997	17,047,300	1,954,300	2,663,800	21,665,400

The areas, populations and chief towns of the states and federal territories are:

Peninsular States	Area (in sq. km)	Population (1997 estimate)	Chief Town	Population (1996 census)
Johor	18,986	2,554,100	Johor Baharu	328,436
Kedah	9,426	1,530,100	Alor Setar	124,412
Kelantan	14,920	1,447,000	Kota Baharu	219,582
Kuala Lumpur[1]	243	1,374,700	Kuala Lumpur	1,145,342
Malacca	1,650	582,000	Malacca	75,909
Negeri Sembilan	6,643	810,500	Seremban	182,869
Pahang	35,965	1,239,000	Kuantan	199,484
Penang	1,031	1,222,100	Penang (Georgetown)	219,603
Perak	21,005	2,094,800	Ipoh	382,853
Perlis	795	217,400	Kangar	14,247
Selangor	7,956	2,999,800	Shah Alam	102,019
Terengganu	12,955	975,800	Kuala Terengganu	228,119
Other states				
Labuan[1]	91	70,400	Victoria	. . .
Sabah	73,619	2,663,800	Kota Kinabalu	76,120
Sarawak	124,449	1,954,300	Kuching	148,059

[1]Federal territory.

Other large cities (1997 estimate): Petaling Jaya (254,350), Kelang (243,355), Taiping (183,261), Sibu (126,381), Sandakan (125,841) and Miri (87,167).

Malay is the national language of the country. The government promotes the use of the national language to foster national unity. However, the people are free to use their mother tongue and other languages. English as the second language is widely used in business. In Peninsular Malaysia Chinese dialects and Tamil are also spoken. In Sabah there are numerous tribal dialects and Chinese (Mandarin and Hakka dialects predominate). In Sarawak Mandarin and numerous tribal languages are spoken.

SOCIAL STATISTICS
1997 births, 558,100; deaths, 98,000. 1997 rates (per 1,000 population): Birth, 25·8 (26·1 in 1996); death, 4·5 (4·4 in 1996); infant mortality rate 8·8 per 1,000 live births (9·1 in 1996); natural increase, 21·4 per 1,000 (21·7 in 1996). Life expectancy: Males, 69·5 years (1997), 69·3 (1996); females, 74·3 (1997), 74·1 (1996). Infant mortality, 1990–95, 13 per 1,000 live births; fertility rate, 3·6 births per woman.

CLIMATE
Malaysia lies near the Equator between latitudes 1° and 7° North and longitudes 100° and 119° East. Malaysia is subject to maritime influence and the interplay of wind systems which originate in the Indian Ocean and the South China Sea. The year is generally divided into the South-East and the North-East Monsoon seasons. The average daily temperature throughout Malaysia varies from 21°C to 32°C. Humidity is high.

CONSTITUTION AND GOVERNMENT
The Constitution of Malaysia is based on the Constitution of the former Federation of Malaya, but includes safeguards for the special interests of Sabah and Sarawak. It was amended in 1983.
    The Constitution provides for one of the Rulers of the Malay States to be elected from among themselves to be the *Yang di-Pertuan Agong* (Supreme Head of the

Federation). He holds office for a period of 5 years. The Rulers also elect from among themselves a Deputy Supreme Head of State, also for a period of 5 years.

In Feb. 1993 the Rulers accepted constitutional amendments abolishing their legal immunity.

Supreme Head of State (Yang di-Pertuan Agong): HM Tuanku Ja'afar ibni Al-Marhum Tuanku Abdul Rahman, D.K., D.K.M., D.M.N., D.K.M.B., elected as 10th *Yang di-Pertuan Agong* on 4 Feb. 1994, crowned 26 April 1994.

Deputy Supreme Head of State, Sultan of Selangor: HRH Sultan Tunku Salahuddin Abdul Aziz Shah ibni Al-Marhum Sultan Hisamuddin 'Alam Shah Al-Haj, D.K., D.M.N., S.P.M.S., S.S.S.A., D.K.M.B., S.P.D.K., D.P., D.U.N.M., P.J.K., acceded 3 Sept. 1960.

Raja of Perlis: HRH Tuanku Syed Putra ibni Al-Marhum Syed Hassan Jamalullail, D.K., D.K.M., D.M.N., S.M.N., S.P.M.P., S.P.D.K., D.K.M.B., acceded 12 March 1949.

Sultan of Kedah: HRH Tuanku Haji Abdul Halim Mu'adzam Shah ibni Al-Marhum Sultan Badlishah, D.K., D.K.H., D.K.M., D.M.N., D.U.K., S.P.M.K., S.S.D.K., D.P., D.U.N.M., D.H.M.S., acceded 20 Feb. 1959.

Sultan of Johor: HRH Sultan Mahmood Iskandar ibni Al-Marhum Sultan Ismail, D.K., S.P.M.J., S.P.D.K., D.K. (Brunei), S.S.I.J., P.I.S., B.S.I., acceded 11 May 1981 (Supreme Head of State from 26 April 1984 to 25 April 1989), returned as Sultan of Johor 26 April 1989.

Sultan of Perak: HRH Sultan Azlan Shah Muhibbuddin Shah ibni Al-Marhum Sultan Yussuf Izzuddin Ghafarullahu-lahu Shah, D.K., D.M.N., P.M.N., S.P.C.M., S.P.M.P., D.K.M., D.K.M.B., S.S.M., P.S.M., S.P.T.S., S.I.M.P.

Regent of Negeri Sembilan: HRH Tengku Naquiyuddin, D.K.Y.R., S.P.N.S., P.P.T., appointed 26 April 1994.

Sultan of Kelantan: HRH Sultan Ismail Petra ibni Al-Marhum Sultan Yahya Petra, D.K., S.P.M.K., S.J.M.K., S.P.S.M., D.M.N., D.K.M.B., D.P.S.S., S.P.K.K., S.P.S.K., D.P., appointed 29 March 1979.

Sultan of Terengganu: HRH Sultan Mahmud Tuanku Mizan Zainal Abidin ibni al-Mahrum, appointed 15 May 1998.

Sultan of Pahang: Sultan Haji Ahmad Shah Al-Musta'in Billah ibni Al-Marhum Sultan Abu Bakar Ri'Ayatuddin Al-Mu'Adzam Shah, D.K.M., D.K.P., D.K., S.S.A.P., S.P.C.M., S.P.M.J., S.I.M.P., D.M.N.

Yang di-Pertua Negeri Pulau Pinang: HE Tun Haji Hamdan Sheikh Tahir, S.M.N., P.S.M., D.U.P.N., D.P., D.M.P.N., appointed 2 May 1989.

Yang di-Pertua Negeri Melaka: HE Tun Datuk Seri Utama Syed Ahmad Al-Haj bin Syed Mahmud Shahabudin, S.S.M., P.S.M., D.U.N.M., S.P.M.K., S.S.D.K., P.G.D.K., P.N.B.S., J.M.N., J.P., S.M.N., S.P.M.S., D.P., appointed 4 Dec. 1984.

Yang di-Pertua Negeri Sarawak: HE Datuk Patinggi Haji Ahmad Zaidi Adruce bin Muhammad Noor, S.S.M., D.P., D.U.N.M., P.N.B.S., B.M. Adipradana (Indonesia), S.M.N., D.U.P.N., appointed 2 April 1985.

Yang di-Pertua Negeri Sabah: HE Tan Sri Sakaran Dandai, P.M.N., S.P.D.K., D.S.M., S.S.A.P., P.G.D.K., A.D.K., J.P., appointed 31 Dec. 1994.

The federal parliament consists of the *Yang di-Pertuan Agong* and two *Majlis* (Houses of Parliament) known as the *Dewan Negara* (Senate) of 69 members (26 elected, 2 by each state legislature; and 43 appointed by the Yang di-Pertuan Agong) and *Dewan Rakyat* (House of Representatives) of 192 members (BN 168, DAP 9, PAS 7, PBS 7, STAR 1). Appointment to the Senate is for 3 years. The maximum life of the House of Representatives is 5 years, subject to its dissolution at any time by the *Yang di-Pertuan Agong* on the advice of his Ministers.

National Anthem. 'Negara-Ku' ('My Country'); words collective, tune by Pierre de Béranger.

RECENT ELECTIONS

Parliamentary and 11 state assembly elections were held on 24–25 April 1995. The 14-party National Front Coalition, in which the United Malays National Organization was the predominant partner, gained 162 seats with 63% of votes cast. The Democratic Action Party gained 9 seats. The National Front Coalition also gained a majority in every state assembly except Kelantan, which was won by the Islamic Party of Malaysia.

MALAYSIA

Although the next election is not due until 2000 an early election is likely to be called before then, so as to strengthen the government's mandate to deal with the economic crisis.

CURRENT ADMINISTRATION
In March 1999 the government comprised:

Prime Minister: Datuk Seri Dr Mahathir Mohamad (b. 1926).
Deputy Prime Minister and Minister for Home Affairs: Datuk Seri Abdullah Ahmad Badawi. *Transport:* Dato Seri Dr Ling Liong Sik. *Energy, Communications and Multimedia:* Datuk Seri Leo Moggie Anak Irok. *Finance:* Tun Daim Zainuddin. *Second Finance Minister and Entrepreneur Development:* Datuk Mustapha Mohamed. *Primary Industries:* Dato Seri Dr Lim Keng Yaik. *Works:* Datuk Seri S. Samy Vellu. *International Trade and Industry:* Dato Seri Rafidah Aziz. *Education:* Datuk Seri Najib Tun Razak. *Rural Development:* Datuk Annuar Musa. *Agriculture:* Datuk Amar Dr Sulaiman Daud. *Domestic Trade and Consumer Affairs:* Dato Seri Megat Junid Megat Ayob. *Health:* Dato Chua Jui Meng. *Foreign Affairs:* Datuk Seri Syed Hamid Albar. *Defence:* Datuk Abang Abu Baker bin Datu Bandar Abang Haji Mustapha. *Information:* Dato Seri Muhammad Rahmat. *Culture, Arts and Tourism:* Dato Seri Sabbaruddin Chik. *National Unity and Social Development:* Datin Paduka Zaleha Ismail. *Human Resources:* Dato Lim Ah Lek. *Science, Technology and Environment:* Datuk Law Hieng Ding. *Housing and Local Government:* Dato Dr Ting Chew Peh. *Land and Co-operative Development:* Tank Sri Kasitah Gadam. *Youth and Sports:* Tan Sri Muhyiddin Yassin. *Minister of Special Functions in the Prime Minister's Department:* Daim Zainuddin.

Local Government. States have elected single-chamber legislative assemblies. The ruler appoints an executive council on the advice of the chief minister. In Peninsular Malaysia each state is divided into districts under a district officer. Each district is divided into *mukims* under a chief, and each village in the *mukim* has a headman.

DEFENCE
The Constitution provides for the Head of State to be the Supreme Commander of the Armed Forces who exercises his powers in accordance with the advice of the Cabinet. Under their authority the Armed Forces Council is responsible for all matters relating to the Armed Forces, other than those relating to their operational use. The Council is chaired by the Minister of Defence and its membership consists of the chief of the Defence Forces, the 3 Service Chiefs and 2 other senior military officers, the Secretary-General of the Ministry of Defence, a representative of State Rulers and an appointed member.

The chief of the Armed Forces Staff is the professional head of the Armed Forces and the senior military member in the Armed Forces Council. He chairs the Armed Forces Staff's committee, the highest level at which joint planning and co-ordination with the Armed Forces are carried out.

The Ministry of Defence has established bilateral defence relations with countries within as well as outside the region. The bilateral activities are mainly in the areas of training, joint exercises, military operations, exchange of information and co-operation in logisitics, defence industry and defence science. Malaysia is a member of the Five Powers Defence Arrangement with Australia, New Zealand, Singapore and the UK.

The Malaysian Armed Forces (MAF) are currently undergoing restructuring (1999). The MAF has participated in 16 UN Peace-Keeping missions in Africa, the Middle East, Indo-China and Europe. 5 of the operations are military contingents, the remainder are Observer Groups.

In 1997 defence expenditure totalled US$3,777m. (US$157 per capita).

Army. The Army is organized into 2 military regions, 1 corps and 5 divisional headquarters. There are 10 infantry brigades made up of 35 infantry battalions, 4 armoured, 5 field artillery, 1 air defence artillery, 1 special forces and 5 engineer regiments, and 1 Rapid Deployment Force. Equipment includes 26 Scorpion light tanks. Strength (1996) about 85,000. There is a paramilitary Police Field Force of 18,000.

Navy. The Royal Malaysian Navy is commanded by the Chief of the Navy from the integrated Ministry of Defence in Kuala Lumpur. There are 4 operational areas: No. 1, covering the eastern peninsular coast (headquarters Kuantan); No. 2, Sabah (headquarters Labuan); No. 3, the western peninsular coast (headquarters Lumut); and No. 4, Sarawak (headquarters Kuching). The peace-time tasks include fishery protection and anti-piracy patrols.

The combatants include 2 German-built and 2 British-built frigates all with helicopter platforms, 8 fast missile craft and 2 offshore and 27 inshore patrol craft. There are also 4 Italian-type offshore mine countermeasure vessels and 4 tank landing ships normally employed in support of patrol and missile craft. Auxiliaries include 2 multi-purpose support ships, 1 survey ship, 1 diving support ship and 33 amphibious craft. The first of 2 new well-equipped British-built frigates were expected to be delivered in 1996.

A Naval aviation squadron operates 12 ex-British Wasp helicopters. Navy personnel in 1995 totalled 12,000 and 2,700 reserves.

Paramilitary maritime forces include 50 armed patrol launches, 48 operated by the Royal Malaysian Police and 2 by the Government of Sabah which also operates 4 other patrol boats, 1 landing craft and a yacht.

Air Force. Formed on 1 June 1958, the Royal Malaysian Air Force is equipped primarily to provide air defence and air support for the Army, Navy and Police. Its secondary role is to render assistance to Government departments and civilian organizations. There are 16 squadrons, of which 9 operate transport aircraft and helicopters. Some 18 MiG-29s equip 2 squadrons. Other equipment includes 25 Hawk strike/trainer aircraft, 10 F-5E Tiger II jet fighterbombers, 2 RF-5E reconnaissance-fighters, and 3 F-5F trainers, 1 F.28 Fellowship and 1 Falcon 900 VIP transports, 14 C-130 Hercules four-engined transport and patrol aircraft, 12 Caribou twin-engined short-take-off-and-landing transports, 2 HU-16 amphibians, 31 Sikorsky S-61A-4 Nuri heavy troop and cargo transport helicopters, 20 Alouette III, and 6 Bell 47 helicopters, 9 Cessna 402Bs for twin-engine training and liaison, 39 PC-7 Turbo-Trainers, 11 MB.339 jet trainers, 2 H.S. 125 Merpati twin-jet executive transports, 2 AS-61 VIP transport helicopters, and 20 MD30160 primary trainers. Personnel (1995) totalled about 12,500, with 120 combat aircraft.

INTERNATIONAL RELATIONS
Malaysia is in dispute with Indonesia over sovereignty of 2 islands in the Celebes Sea. Both countries have agreed to accept the Judgment of the International Court of Justice.

Malaysia is a member of the UN, the Commonwealth, the Colombo Plan, Organization of Islamic Conference and ASEAN.

ECONOMY

Policy. Malaysia's response to the economic crisis that swept Asia in 1997-98 was to put much of the blame on foreign speculators. After a fall in the value of of the *ringgit* by 48% between July 1997 and July 1998, Dr Mahathir announced tough restrictions on currency transactions. The aim was to meet head on the problem of bank debt. Interest rates could be lowered without leading to a run on the ringgit. But short-term stability may not be enough to restore Malaysia to economic prosperity. In 1998 the economy shrank by over 5% and bank debt remains one of the highest in south-east Asia.

Performance. During the sixth 5-year plan (1991–95) economic growth averaged 8·7% a year (target, 8·1%). Between 1990 and 1996 the average annual real growth in GNP per capita was 6·1%. In 1997 growth was an estimated 8% but was estimated to be –6% for 1998.

Budget. 1997 budget: Revenue, RM60,780m.; expenditure, RM59,980m. Revenue and expenditure for calendar years, in RM1m.:

	1993	1994	1995	1996	1997[1]
Revenue	41,231	44,730	50,953	56,549	60,947
Operating expenditure	32,315	32,285	36,573	43,268	43,304

[1]Forecast

Sources of revenue in 1996: Direct taxes, 45·6% (45·8%—1997 est.); indirect taxes, 36% (36·2%—1997 est.); non-tax revenue, 18·4 % (18·0%—1997 est.).

Federal government net development (in addition to operating) expenditure in 1996: RM11,156m. (RM 12,525m. 1997), of which economic services 49·9% (47·4%—1997 est.), social services, 25·3% (30%—1997 est.), security, 19·0% (16·6%—1997 est.) and general administration, 5·8% (6·0%—1997 est.).

Currency. The unit of currency is the Malaysian *ringgit* (MYR) of 100 *sen*. Foreign exchange reserves were US$20,984m. in Nov. 1997 and gold reserves 2·35m. troy oz. The average annual inflation rate during the period 1990–96 was 4·4%. Total money supply in Nov. 1997 was RM79,553m.

Banking and Finance. The central bank and bank of issue is the Bank Negara Malaysia (*Governor*, Ahmad Mohamad Don). 37 commercial banks were operating at 31 Dec. 1996 (including 16 foreign) with a total of 1,433 branches. Number of employees 69,154. Total deposits with commercial banks at 31 Dec. 1996 were RM194,974m. There were 12 merchant banks at 31 Dec. 1996. Number of employees 2,592. Their total assets were RM34m. The Islamic Bank of Malaysia began operations in July 1983. There were 40 finance companies in 1996 with 1,096 offices. Number of employees 26,728.

There is a stock exchange at Kuala Lumpur.

The economy suffered from the financial crisis that hit south-east Asia in Nov. 1997, but while the *ringgit* lost nearly 30% of its value in the second half of 1997, the underlying strength of the economy (a modest foreign debt and few non-performing loans) is expected to lead to an early recovery.

Weights and Measures. The metric system is standard, but British imperial units are still in residual use.

ENERGY AND NATURAL RESOURCES

Electricity. Installed capacity in 1995, 11,427 MW. In 1995, 41,961m. kWh were generated. Electricity consumption in 1997 was 50,703m. kWh.

Oil and Gas. Estimated oil production (1995) 706,000 bbls. a day. Natural gas reserves, 1987, 1,400,000m. cu. metres. Production of liquefied natural gas in 1995 was an estimated 11·68m. tonnes. In April 1998 Malaysia and Thailand agreed to share equally the natural gas jointly produced in an offshore area which both countries claim as their own territory. It is expected that from 2001 around 640m. cu. ft of natural gas will be produced in the area every day.

Minerals. In 1992 mining contributed 8·6% of GDP. Tin production was an estimated 5,000 tonnes in 1996.

Agriculture. In 1996 agriculture contributed 13% of GDP. In 1994 approximately 340,000 ha were irrigated. Production (1996 estimates): Rubber, 1,082,500 tonnes; palm oil, 8,385,900 tonnes. Livestock (1996): Pigs, 3·23m.; cattle, 720,000; sheep, 269,000; goats 312,000 (1995); chickens, 100m. (1995).

Forestry. In 1997 there were 13·2m. ha of forests, down from 17·47m. ha in 1990. In 1995, 45·57m. cu. metres of roundwood were cut.

Fisheries. Total catches in 1995 amounted to 1,239,755 tonnes (1,220,298 tonnes from sea fishing). In 1997, 1,158,900 tonnes came from the sea.

INDUSTRY

In 1995 manufacturing contributed 33·1% of GDP.

Labour. In 1997 the workforce was 8·4m. (47·2% female), of whom 8,606,400 were employed (27·7% in manufacturing, 15·2% in agriculture and 9·1% in construction). Unemployment was 2·7%.

Trade Unions. Membership was 737,484 at 30 Sept. 1997, of which the Malaysian Trades Union Congress, an umbrella organization of 158 unions, accounted for 0·4m. Number of unions was 536.

INTERNATIONAL TRADE

Privatization policy permits foreign investment of 25–30% generally; total foreign ownership is permitted of export-oriented projects. External debt was US$39,777m. in 1996.

Imports and Exports. In 1996 exports totalled RM197,707m. with an estimated rise to RM221,550 in 1997, and imports RM198,580m. (RM219,394 in 1997 est.).

In 1996 imports of consumer goods totalled RM27,801m.; intermediate goods, RM89,361m.; capital goods, RM80,425m.

Chief exports, 1997 (in RM1m.): Rubber, 2,971; palm oil, 10,809; saw logs and sawn timber, 5,127; crude oil, 7,069; liquified natural gas, 6,752; plain plywood, 1,071.

In 1997 imports (in RM1m.) came chiefly from Japan (48,509), USA (37,053) and Singapore (29,004). Exports went chiefly to USA (41,126), Singapore (44,356) and Japan (27,800).

COMMUNICATIONS

Roads. Total road length in 1997 was 67,608 km (estimate), of which 51,700 km were paved and 15,908 km were unpaved. In 1997 there were 8,550,469 motor vehicles.

Rail. In 1997 there were 2,227 km of railway tracks. It was estimated about 33·7m. passenger journeys were made in the year and 4·9m. tonnes of freight were carried.

Civil Aviation. There are a total of 19 airports of which 5 are international airports and 14 are domestic airports at which regular public air transport is operated. *International airports;* Kuala Lumpur, Penang, Kota Kinabalu, Kuching and Langkawi. *Domestic airports;* Johor Bahru, Alor Setar, Ipoh, Kota Bharu, Kuala Terengganu, Kuantan, Melaka, Sandakan, Lahat Datu, Tawau, Labuan, Bintulu, Sibu and Miri. There are 39 Malaysian airstrips of which 10 are in Sabah, 15 in Sarawak and 14 in peninsular Malaysia.

33 international airlines operate through Kuala Lumpur (Subang). Malaysia Airlines, the national airline, is 39% state-owned, and operates domestic flights within Peninsular Malaysia as well as between Kuala Lumpur and Sabah and Sarawak. In 1998 it flew to nearly 40 different countries. Services were also provided in 1998 by Aeroflot, Aerolíneas Argentinas, Air India, Air Lanka, Air Mauritius, Airasia, All Nippon Airways, Ansett Australia, Berjaya Air, Biman Bangaldesh Airlines, British Airways, Canadian Airlines International, Cathay Pacific Airways, China Airlines, China Southern Airlines, China Yunnan Airlines, Emirates, Eva Airways, Garuda Indonesia, Gulf Air, Indian Airlines, Iran Air, JAL, KLM, Korean Air, Lauda Air, Lufthansa, Mafira Air Charter, Merpati Nusantara Airlines, Myanma Airways International, Pakistan International Airlines, Pelangi Air, Philippine Airlines, Qantas Airways, Royal Air Cambodge, Royal Brunei Airlines, Royal Jordanian, Saudia, Singapore Airlines, Swissair, Thai Airways International, Trans Pacific Air, Uzbekiston Airways, Vietnam Airlines and Virgin Atlantic. In 1996 Kuala Lumpur handled 14,314,547 passengers (8,456,166 on international flights) and 372,338 tonnes of freight. Penang was the second busiest airport, with 2,849,399 passengers (1,686,184 on domestic flights) and 101,716 tonnes of freight.

Shipping. The major ports are Port Kelang, Penang, Johor, Tg. Bruas, Miri, Rajang, Pel Pel Sabah, Port Dickson Kemaman, Teluk Ewa, Kuantan, Kuching and Bintulu. In 1996 there were 2,429 marine vessels including 118 oil tankers (0·73m. GRT), 198 passenger carriers (0·03m. GRT) and 426 general cargo ships (0·76m. GRT), with a total GRT of 4·27m. In 1996, 167·9m. tonnes of cargo were loaded and unloaded. The figure in 1997 is estimated to be 185·6m. tonnes.

Telecommunications. In 1997 there were 4·13m. telephones. There were 755,000 mobile telephones and 6,578 telex in 1995, and (1994) 58,090 fax subscribers. There were approximately 800,000 PCs in 1995 and 600,000 Internet users in Jan. 1998.

Postal Services. Postal services are the responsibility of the Ministry of Energy, Communications and Multimedia. At the end of Oct. 1997, there were 6,036 postal services networks established in Malaysia, including 620 post offices, 290 mini posts and 493 post representatives.

SOCIAL INSTITUTIONS

Justice. The judicial power is vested in the Federal Court, the High Court of Malaya, the High Court of Borneo and subordinate courts: Sessions Courts, Magistrates' Courts and *Mukim* chiefs' Courts.

The head of the Judiciary is the Lord President of the Federal Court which consists of himself, the Chief Justices of the High Courts and Judges of the Federal Court. The Federal Court has jurisdiction to determine the validity of any law made by Parliament or by a State legislature and disputes between States or between the Federation and any State. It also has jurisdiction to hear and determine appeals from the High Courts.

Religion. One of the unique features of Malaysia is its multi-racial population divided between Islam, Buddhism, Taoism, Hinduism and Christianity. Under the Federal constitution, Islam is the official religion of Malaysia but there is freedom of worship. In 1992 there were 9·86m. Moslems, 3·22m. Buddhists, 2·16m. adherents of Chinese traditional religions and 1·3m. Hindus.

Education. School education is free; tertiary education is provided at a nominal fee. There are 6 years of primary schooling starting at age 6, 3 years of universal lower secondary, 2 years of selective upper secondary and 2 years of pre-university education. During the Seventh Plan period, a number of major changes will be introduced to the education and training system with a view to strengthening and improving the system. These efforts are expected to improve the quality and increase the quantity of output to meet the manpower needs of the nation, particularly in the fields of science and technology. In addition, continued emphasis will be given to expand educational opportunities for those in the rural and remote areas. Under the Seventh Plan, the Education Ministry allocated RM8,437,200 on this education programme and RM1,661,600 for training purposes.

In 1998 there were 2,872,427 pupils at 7,124 primary schools with 154,829 teachers, 1,889,592 pupils at secondary schools and, in 1997, 229,814 students and 16,175 teachers at higher education institutions.

Adult literacy was 83·5% in 1995 (89·1% among males and 78·1% among females).

In 1996 total expenditure on education came to 5·2% of GNP.

Health. In 1997 medical professionals numbered 32,181 of which 14,248 were doctors, 1,865 dentists and 16,068 nurses. In 1995 there were 42,878 allied health professionals. These were divided into dental, paramedics and auxiliary (2,720), medical assistants and laboratory technologists (5,392), nurses (32,401), occupational therapists and physiotherapists (410), public health inspectors (1,418) and radiographers (537). At the end of 1995 the Ministry of Health ran a total of 1,375 dental clinics. In the same year there were 39,738 beds in hospitals, clinics and other medical institutions.

Welfare. The Employment Injury Insurance Scheme provides medical and cash benefits and the Invalidity Pension Scheme provides protection to employees against invalidity due to disease or injury from any cause. Other supplementary measures are the Employees' Provident Fund, the pension scheme for government employees, free medical benefits for all who are unable to pay and the provision of medical benefits particularly for workers under the Labour Code. In 1997 there are 48 welfare service institutions with capacity for 7,020.

CULTURE

Broadcasting. The Government-controlled Radio Television Malaysia broadcasts radio and TV programmes nationally. The Voice of Malaysia (broadcasting in 8 languages) is beamed internationally. System TV Malaysia Berhad transmits from Kuala Lumpur and is also beamed throughout the country. There were 8·9m. radio receivers and 3·5m. television receivers in 1996.

Cinema. In 1993 there were 258 cinemas with a total attendance of 39·4m. English, Malay, Chinese, Hindi and Indonesian films are shown.

Press. The Malaysian Media Agencies are comprised of the press, magazine and press agencies/local media, which are further divided into home and foreign news. In 1996 there were a total of 143 press and liaison divisions.

Tourism. In 1996 there were 7,138,000 foreign tourists, spending US$3·93bn.

Festivals. National Day (31 Aug.) is celebrated in Kuala Lumpur at the Dataran Merdeka and marks Malaysia's independence.

Libraries. The National Library of Malaysia is strong on information technology. The 14 state public libraries and 31 ministry and government department libraries are linked in a Common User Scheme called *Jaringan Ilmu* (Knowledge Network).

National Theatre and Opera. Highlights include Premiere Theatre Staging, Dance Drama, National Choir Concerts, National Symphony Orchestra, Chamber Music; Traditional and Folk music are performances by the National Budaya Group. Local theatre groups regularly stage contemporary Asian and Western dramas, dance dramas and the *bangsawan* (traditional Malay opera).

Museums and Galleries. There is a National Museum for preserving, restoring and imparting knowledge on the historical and cultural heritage of Malaysia. The National Art Gallery promotes Malaysisan visual arts through exhibitions, competitions and support programmes which are held locally and abroad.

DIPLOMATIC REPRESENTATIVES
Of Malaysia in Great Britain (45 Belgrave Sq., London, SW1X 8QT)
High Commissioner: Dato Mohamed Amir Bin Jaafar.

Of Great Britain in Malaysia (185 Jalan Ampang, 50450 Kuala Lumpur)
High Commissioner: Mr. G. H. Fry.

Of Malaysia in the USA (2401 Massachusetts Ave., NW, Washington, D.C., 20008)
Ambassador: Dato Dali Mahmud Hashim.

Of the USA in Malaysia (376 Jalan Tun Razak, Kuala Lumpur)
Ambassador: John R. Malott.

Of Malaysia to the United Nations
Ambassador: Datuk Hasmy Agam.

Of Malaysia to the European Union
Ambassador: Dato M. M. Sathiah.

FURTHER READING
Department of Statistics. *Yearbook of Statistics.*

Prime Minister's Department. Economic Planning Unit. *Malaysian Economy in Figures.* Annual

Brown, I. and Ampalavanar, R., *Malaysia.* [Bibliography] Oxford and Santa Barbara (CA), 1986

Gullick, J., *Malaysia: Economic Expansion and National Unity.* Boulder and London, 1982

Information Malaysia Yearbook. Kuala Lumpur

Jomo, K. S., *Growth and Structural Change in the Malaysian Economy.* London, 1990

Kahn, J. S. and Wah, F. L. K., *Fragmented Vision: Culture and Politics in Contemporary Malaysia.* Sydney, 1992

King, V. T. and Parnwell, M. J. (eds), *Margins and Minorities: the Peripheral Areas and People of Malaysia.* Hull Univ. Press, 1990

Means, G. P., *Malaysian Politics: the Second Generation.* OUP, 1991

Zakaria, A., *Government and Politics in Malaysia.* OUP, 1987

National statistical office: Department of Statistics, Wisma Statistik, Jalan Cenderasari, 50514 Kuala Lumpur.
Website: http://www.statistics.gov.my/

MALDIVES

Divehi Raajjeyge
Jumhooriyyaa

(Republic of the Maldives)

Capital: Malé
Population estimate, 2000: 302,000
GNP per capita: (PPP$) 3,140
HDI/world rank: 0·683/95

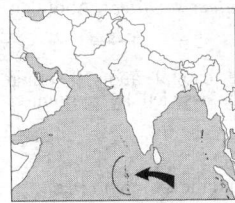

KEY HISTORICAL EVENTS
The islands were under British protection from 1887 until complete independence was achieved on 26 July 1965. The Maldives became a republic on 11 Nov. 1968.

TERRITORY AND POPULATION
The republic, some 400 miles to the south-west of Sri Lanka, consists of 1,200 low-lying (the highest point is 6 feet above sea-level) coral islands, grouped into 26 atolls. 199 are inhabited. Area 115 sq. miles (298 sq. km). At the 1995 census, the population was 244,644 (119,592 females). Estimate (1996), 253,300; density, 850 per sq. km.

The UN gives a projected population for 2000 of 302,000.

An estimated 73·1% of the population lived in rural areas in 1995. Capital, Malé (1995 population, 62,973).

The official and spoken language is Divehi.

SOCIAL STATISTICS
1995 births, 10,500; deaths, 2,000. Birth rate, 1995, per 1,000 population, 41·7; death rate, 8·0. Annual growth rate, 1990–95, 3·3%. Life expectancy at birth over the period 1990–95 was 60·8 years for females but 63·4 years for males. With a difference of 2·6 years, no other country has a life expectancy for males so high compared to that for females. Infant mortality, 1990–95, 60 per 1,000 live births; fertility rate, 6·8 births per woman.

In the Human Development Index, or HDI (measuring progress in countries in longevity, knowledge and standard of living), Maldives achieved the second biggest rise in 1995 compared to 1994 (after Oman), with a jump of 16 places from 111th in the world to 95th.

CLIMATE
The islands are hot and humid, and affected by monsoons. Malé: Average temperature 81°F (27°C), annual rainfall 59" (1,500 mm).

CONSTITUTION AND GOVERNMENT
There is a Citizens' *Majlis* (Parliament) which consists of 48 members, 8 of whom are nominated by the President and 40 directly elected (2 each from Malé and the 19 administrative districts) for a term of 5 years. There are no political parties. The President of the Republic is elected by the Citizens' Majlis.

National Anthem. 'Gavmii mi ekuverikan matii tibegen kuriime salaam' ('In national unity we salute our nation'); words by M. J. Didi, tune by W. Amaradeva.

RECENT ELECTIONS
President Maumoon Abdul Gayoom was re-elected in a referendum held on 16 Oct. 1998. As sole candidate, he won 91% of the 95,168 votes cast. Turn-out was 75%. At the last elections to the Majlis on 2 Dec. 1994 only non-partisans were elected.

CURRENT ADMINISTRATION
In March 1999 the Government consisted of:

President, Minister of Defence and National Security, Minister of Finance and Treasury: Maumoon Abdul Gayoom (b. 1937; re-elected unopposed for a fifth 5-year term in Oct. 1998).

Atolls Administration, Agriculture, Fisheries and Marine Resources: Abdul Rasheed Hussain. *Foreign Affairs:* Fathullah Jameel. *Youth, Sports and Women's Affairs:* Rashida Yoosuf. *Minister of Home Affairs, Housing and Environment:* Ismail Shafeen. *Construction and Public Works:* Umar Zahir. *Justice and Islamic Affairs:* Mohamed Rasheed Ibrahim. *Transport and Civil Aviation:* Alyas Ibrahim. *Planning and National Development:* Ibrahim Hussain Zaki. *Human Resources, Employment and Labour:* Abdulla Kamaluddeen. *Tourism:* Hassan Sobir. *Education:* Dr Mohamed Latheef. *Information, Arts and Culture:* Ibrahim Manik. *Trade and Industries:* Abdullah Yameen. *Minister, President's Office:* Abdullah Jameel. *Attorney General:* Dr Mohamed Mumawar.

Speaker of Citizens' Majlis: Abdulla Hameed.

Local Government. The Maldives is divided into the capital and 19 other administrative districts, each under an appointed governor assisted by appointed local chiefs.

INTERNATIONAL RELATIONS

The Maldives is a member of the UN, the Commonwealth and the Colombo Plan.

ECONOMY

Performance. Real GDP growth was 7·2% in 1995 (6·6% in 1994).

Budget. 1997 provisional estimates: Revenue, 1,581·1m. Rufiyaa; expenditure 1,935·9m. Rufiyaa (capital expenditure, 790·8m. Rufiyaa).

Currency. The unit of currency is the *rufiyaa* (MVR) of 100 *laari*. The average annual inflation rate over the period 1990–96 was 9·9%. Total money supply in Feb. 1998 was 1,191m. Rufiyaa.

ENERGY AND NATURAL RESOURCES

Electricity. Installed capacity was 18,000 kW in 1994. Production in 1996 was 68·33m. kWh. Consumption per capita in 1994 was estimated to be 163 kWh.

Minerals. Inshore coral mining has been banned as a measure against the encroachment of the sea.

Agriculture. In 1994 approximately 3,000 ha were arable land. Principal crops in 1993 (in 1,000 tonnes): Coconuts (number of nuts), 15,324,732; maize, 9; cassava, 8; sweet potatoes, 44; onions, 0·1; chillies, 40·3.

Fisheries. Catch, 1996, 105,500 tonnes. The Maldives has the highest consumption of fish and fishery products of any country in the world. In the period 1991–93 the average person consumed over 125 kg (276 lbs) a year, or more than 9 times the average for the world as a whole.

INDUSTRY

The main industries are fishing, tourism, shipping, lacquerwork and garment manufacturing.

Labour. In 1996 the workforce was 107,000 (58% males).

INTERNATIONAL TRADE

Imports and Exports. In 1996 imports amounted to 3,551,289,000 Rufiyaa and exports to 699,191,000 Rufiyaa. Bonito ('Maldive fish') is the main export commodity. It is exported principally to Thailand, Singapore, Sri Lanka, Japan, and some European markets.

COMMUNICATIONS

Roads. In 1996 there were 787 cars, 5,319 motorbikes/auto cycles, 377 lorries/trucks/tractors, 209 vans/buses, 658 jeeps/land rovers/pickups, 271 taxis and 274 other vehicles.

Civil Aviation. Air Maldives operates domestic and international flights. In 1998 there were direct flights from Abu Dhabi, Bahrain, Berlin, Cologne, Colombo,

Dubai, Düsseldorf, Frankfurt, Hamburg, Hanover, Karachi, Kuala Lumpur, Kuwait, Moscow, Munich, Singapore, Sofia, Stuttgart, Thiruvananthapuram, Vienna and Zürich. Services were also operated in 1998 by Aeroflot, Air Lanka, Austrian Airlines, Balkan, Condor Flugdienst, Emirates, Indian Airlines, Lauda Air, LTU International Airways, Malaysia Airlines, Pakistan International Airlines and Singapore Airlines. In 1996, 7,710 aircraft, 1,153,750 passengers and 13,370,436 kg of mail and air freight were handled at Malé International Airport. There are 4 domestic airports.

Shipping. The Maldives Shipping Line operated (1992) 10 vessels. In 1995 merchant shipping totalled 85,000 GRT.

Telecommunications. There were 18,000 telephone main lines in 1997, equivalent to 65·8 per 1,000 inhabitants. In 1995 there were 3,500 fax machines and 3,000 PCs.

Postal Services. In 1995 there were 362 post offices, or 1 for every 700 persons.

SOCIAL INSTITUTIONS

Justice. Justice is based on the Islamic Shari'ah.

Religion. The State religion is Islam.

Education. Adult literacy was 93·2% in 1995 (93·3% among males and 93·0% among females). Education is not compulsory. In 1996 there were 60 government schools (40,935 pupils) and 32 private schools (40,153 pupils) and 171 community schools (9,509 pupils) with a total of 3,278 teachers.

Health. In 1996 there were 193 beds at the Indira Gandhi Memorial Hospital in Malé, 4 regional hospitals (125 beds) and 27 health centres. In 1996 there were 99 doctors and 303 nurses.

CULTURE

Broadcasting. Voice of Maldives and Television Maldives are government-controlled. There were (1995) 29,484 radio receivers and (1995) 9,879 television sets (colour by PAL).

Press. There were (1996) 3 daily newspapers, 2 weekly, 2 fortnightly and a number of monthly periodicals.

Tourism. Tourism is the major foreign currency earner. There were 338,733 visitors in 1996, spending US$265m.

DIPLOMATIC REPRESENTATIVES

Of the Maldives in Great Britain (22 Nottingham Pl., London W1M 3FB)
High Commissioner: Vacant.

Of Great Britain in the Maldives
High Commissioner: David Tatham, CMG (resides in Colombo).

Of the USA in the Maldives
Ambassador: Vacant.

Permanent Representative of the Maldives to the United Nations
Ambassador: Hussain Shihab.

FURTHER READING

Reynolds, C. H. B., *Maldives*. [Bibliography] Oxford and Santa Barbara (CA), 1993

MALI

République du Mali

Capital: Bamako
Population estimate, 2000: 12·56m.
GNP per capita: (PPP$) 710
HDI/world rank: 0·236/171

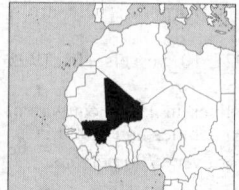

KEY HISTORICAL EVENTS

Mali's political organization and power reached their peak between the 11th and 13th centuries when its gold-based empire controlled much of the surrounding area. It declined thereafter and the French began invading from Senegal in the mid-19th century, fully annexing the country by 1904. The region became the territory of French Sudan as part of French West Africa. The Sudanese Union, led by Modibo Keita, gained strength in the 1950s and took over the internal running of the country after winning elections in 1957. The country became an autonomous state within the French Community on 24 Nov. 1958, and on 4 April 1959 joined with Senegal to form the Federation of Mali. The Federation achieved independence on 20 June 1960, but Senegal seceded on 22 Aug. and Mali proclaimed itself an independent republic on 22 Sept., with Keita as president. Much later, in March 1982, Guinea and Mali were to agree to pursue gradual unification. The National Assembly was dissolved on 17 Jan. 1968 by President Modibo Keita, whose government was then overthrown by an army coup on 19 Nov. 1968; power was assumed by a Military Committee for National Liberation led by Lieut. Moussa Traoré, who became president on 19 Sept. 1969. He ruled on the basis of tight control during the severe drought of the 1970s. Traoré formed a political party in 1976, the *Union démocratique du peuple malien* (UDPM), and was confirmed as president in elections in June 1979. He was deposed on 26 March 1991 in a military coup. Lieut.-Col. Amadou Touré was named head of a Transitional Committee of Public Safety.

In Jan. 1991 a cease-fire was signed with Tuareg insurgents in the north, but sporadic skirmishing continued. A further agreement was reached at a Special Conference on the North held in Dec. 1991, and in April 1992 a national pact was concluded providing for a special administration for the Tuareg north. A further accord with Tuareg insurgents under which their northern bases would be dismantled was signed in May 1994.

Under its current president, Alpha Oumar Konaré, 2 elections for the National Assembly have been held, but the first (April 1997) was cancelled by the Constitutional Court and the second, in July 1997, was boycotted by opposition parties which are weakened by internal fighting.

TERRITORY AND POPULATION

Mali is bounded in the west by Senegal, north-west by Mauritania, north-east by Algeria, east by Niger and south by Burkina Faso, Côte d'Ivoire and Guinea. Its area is 1,248,574 sq. km (482,077 sq. miles) and had a population of 7,696,348 at the 1987 census (20·3% urban; 1995, 26·8%). Estimate, 1997, 9,789,000; density, 7·8 per sq. km.

The UN gives a projected population for 2000 of 12·56m.

The areas, populations and chief towns of the regions are:

Region	Sq. km	Census 1987	Chief town
Kayes	197,760	1,058,575	Kayes
Koulikoro	89,833	1,180,260	Koulikoro
Capital District	267	646,153	Bamako
Sikasso	76,480	1,308,828	Sikasso
Ségou	56,127	1,328,250	Ségou
Mopti	88,752	1,261,383	Mopti
Tombouctou	408,977	453,032	Tombouctou
Gao	321,996	383,734	Gao

An 8th region, Kidal (chief town, Kidal), was instituted in the north in 1991.

In 1996 the principal ethnic groups numbered (in 1,000): Bambara, 2,930; Fulani, 1,290; Senufo, 1,100; Soninke, 800; Tuareg, 675; Songhai, 660; Malinke, 610; Dogon, 370. The official language is French; Bambara is spoken by about 60% of the population.

SOCIAL STATISTICS
1997 births, estimate, 492,000; deaths, 191,000. Vital statistics rates, 1997 estimates (per 1,000 population). Births, 50·3; deaths, 19·5. Infant mortality (per 1,000 live births), 124. Expectation of life in 1997 was 46·6 years (45·25 for males and 47·9 for females); growth rate, 3·18% per annum; fertility rate, 6·7 children per woman.

CLIMATE
A tropical climate, with adequate rain in the south and west, but conditions become increasingly arid towards the north and east. Bamako, Jan. 76°F (24·4°C), July 80°F (26·7°C). Annual rainfall 45" (1,120 mm). Kayes, Jan. 76°F (24·4°C), July 93°F (33·9°C). Annual rainfall 29" (725 mm). Tombouctou, Jan. 71°F (21·7°C), July 90°F (32·2°C). Annual rainfall 9" (231 mm).

CONSTITUTION AND GOVERNMENT
A constitution was approved by a national referendum in 1974; it was amended by the National Assembly on 2 Sept. 1981. The sole legal party was the *Union démocratique du peuple malien* (UDPM).

A national conference of 1,800 delegates agreed a draft constitution enshrining multi-party democracy in Aug. 1991, and this was approved by 99·76% of votes cast at a referendum in Jan. 1992. Turn-out was 43%.

The *President* is elected for not more than 2 terms of 5 years.

A *Constitutional Court* was established in 1994.

National Anthem. 'A ton appel, Mali' ('At your call, Mali'); words by S. Kouyate, tune by B. Sissoko.

RECENT ELECTIONS
Elections were held in on 20 July and 3 Aug. 1997 for the 160-member National Assembly. The Alliance for Democracy in Mali (ADEMA) won 128 seats.

In the presidential elections on 11 May 1997 Alpha Oumar Konaré was re-elected against a single opponent. As with the elections to the National Assembly, many parties boycotted the elections.

CURRENT ADMINISTRATION
President: Alpha Oumar Konaré (b. 1946; sworn in on 8 June 1997).

In March 1999 the government comprised:

Prime Minister: Ibrahim Boubacar Keita (b. 1945; ADEMA).

Minister of Foreign Affairs and Malians Abroad: Modibo Sidibe. *Culture and Tourism:* Aminata Drame Traoré. *Industry, Artisanry and Trade:* Fatou Haidara. *Communications:* Ascofare Ouleymatou Tamboura. *Finance:* Soumeyla Cissé. *Economic Affairs, Planning and Integration:* Ahmed el Madani Diallo. *Youth:* Boubacar Karamoko Coulibaly. *Sports:* Adama Kone. *Health, Solidarity and the Elderly:* Diakite Fatoumata Ndiaye. *Mines and Energy:* Yoro Diakite. *Rural Development and Water Resources:* Modibo Traoré. *Environment:* Mohamed Ag Erlaf. *Employment, Civil Service and Labour:* Ousmane Oumarou Sidibe. *Primary Education and Government Spokesman:* Adama Sammassekou. *Secondary Education, Higher Education and Scientific Research:* Younouss Hamaye Dicko. *Promotion of Women, Children and Family Affairs:* Diarra Hafsatou Thierro. *Justice and Keeper of the Seals:* Hamidou Diabate. *Territorial Administration and Security:* Lieut.-Col. Sada Samake. *Public Works and Transportation:* Ibrehima Siby. *Relations with Institutions and Political Parties:* Hassane Diallo. *Defence, Armed Forces and Veterans:* Mohammed Salia Sokona. *Urban Development and Housing:* Sy Kadiatou Sow.

Local Government. Mali is divided into the Capital District of Bamako and 8 regions, sub-divided into 46 *cercles* and then into 279 *arrondissements*.

At the elections of Jan. 1992 turn-out was 35%. The Alliance for Democracy in Mali (ADEMA) gained 214 of the 751 seats contested, the Sudanese Union-RDA (US-RDA) 130, and the National Committee for Democratic Initiative (CNID) 96.

DEFENCE
There is a selective system of 2 years' conscription, for civilian or military service. Defence expenditure totalled US$43m. in 1997 (US$4 per capita).

Army. The Army consists of 4 infantry, 2 tank, 1 engineer, 1 parachute, 1 special force, 2 artillery battalions and 2 air defence and 1 surface-to-air missile battery. Equipment includes 21 T-34 main battle tanks. Strength (1997) 7,000. There are also paramilitary forces of 4,800.

Air Force. The Air Force MiG fighters are withdrawn from use. There are 2 An-24, 2 An-26 and 1 Mi-8 helicopter. A twin-turbofan Corvette is used for VIP transport. Personnel (1997) total about 400.

INTERNATIONAL RELATIONS
Mali is a member of the UN, OAU and is an ACP member state of the ACP-EU relationship.

ECONOMY
Performance. The economy was virtually ruined by the Traoré regime, but with IMF and World Bank help has recovered rapidly. Real GDP growth was 6% in 1996.

Budget. Revenues for 1997 were estimated to be US$730m. and expenditures US$770m.

Currency. The unit of currency is the *franc CFA*, which replaced the Mali franc in 1984. Total money supply in Dec. 1997 was 256bn. francs CFA. Foreign exchange reserves were US$403m. in Feb. 1998; gold reserves were 20,000 troy oz. Annualized inflation was 3% in 1996.

Banking and Finance. There are 4 domestic and 2 French-owned banks.

ENERGY AND NATURAL RESOURCES
Electricity. Installed capacity in 1990 was 84,100 kW. Production in 1995 totalled 235m. kWh, much of it hydro-electric. Consumption per capita was an estimated 28 kWh in 1994.

Minerals. There are deposits of iron ore, uranium, diamonds, bauxite, manganese, copper and lithium. 7·8 tonnes of gold were extracted in 1994.

Agriculture. About 80% of the population depends on agriculture, mainly carried on by small peasant holdings. It contributed 48% of GDP in 1996. Mali is second only to Egypt among African cotton producers. In 1994 there were 2·5m. ha of arable land, 3,000 ha of permanent cropland and 30m. ha of permanent pasture. Production in 1995 included (estimates, in 1,000 tonnes): Millet, sorghum and fonio, 1,604; rice, 469; maize, 322; vegetables, 267; sugar cane, 262; groundnuts, 215; cottonseed, 150; cotton (lint), 110.

Livestock, 1996: Cattle, 5·71m.; asses, 611,000; sheep, 5·43m.; goats, 7,380,000 (1995); camels, 260,000 (1995); chickens, 23m. (1995).

0·21m. ha were irrigated in 1992.

Forestry. In 1995 forests covered 11·58m. ha, or 9·5% of the total land area (down from 12·15m. ha in 1990). 6·54m. cu. metres of roundwood were cut in 1995.

Fisheries. In 1995, 133,000 tonnes of fish were caught in the rivers.

INDUSTRY
Manufacturing accounted for 11% of GDP in 1991. The main branch is food processing, followed by cotton processing, textiles and clothes. Cement and pharmaceuticals are also produced.

MALI

Labour. In 1996 the workforce was estimated to be 5,472,000 (54% males). In 1995 over 80% of the economically active population were engaged in agriculture, fisheries and forestry. Large numbers of Malians emigrate temporarily to work abroad, principally in Côte d'Ivoire.

INTERNATIONAL TRADE
Foreign debt was US$3,020m. in 1996.

Imports and Exports. Exports in 1996 totalled US$1,331m.; imports, US$2,085m. Principal export commodities are cotton, livestock and gold. The main export markets are the franc zone, western Europe and the People's Republic of China. Principal import commodities are machinery and equipment, foodstuffs, construction materials, petroleum and textiles. Main import suppliers are also the franc zone (in particular Côte d'Ivoire and France), western Europe and the People's Republic of China.

COMMUNICATIONS
Roads. There were (1995 estimate) 14,776 km of classified roads, of which 1,773 km were paved. In 1996 there were 26,190 passenger cars (3 per 1,000 inhabitants) and 18,240 trucks and vans.

Rail. Mali has a railway from Kayes to Koulikoro by way of Bamako, a continuation of the Dakar–Kayes line in Senegal. Total length 642 km (metre-gauge) and in 1990 carried 184m. passenger-km and 273m. tonne-km of freight.

Civil Aviation. There is an international airport at Bamako (Senou). Air Mali operates domestic services to 8 other airports. In 1998 there were international flights to Abidjan, Accra, Addis Ababa, Algiers, Banjul, Bobo-Dioulasso, Bouaké, Brazzaville, Brussels, Casablanca, Conakry, Cotonou, Dakar, Douala, Johannesburg, Libreville, N'Djaména, Néma, Niamey, Nouakchott, Ouagadougou, Paris and Zürich, with services operated by Air Afrique, Air Algérie, Air Burkina, Air Dabia, Air France, Air Gabon, Air Ivoire, Air Mauritanie, Ethiopian Airlines, Ghana Airways, Royal Air Maroc, SABENA and Swissair.

Shipping. For about 7 months in the year small steamboats operate a service from Koulikoro to Tombouctou and Gao, and from Bamako to Kouroussa.

Telecommunications. Mali had 23,500 main telephone lines in 1997, or 2 per 1,000 population. There were around 400 Internet users in Jan. 1998.

Postal Services. In 1995 there were 124 post offices.

SOCIAL INSTITUTIONS
Justice. The Supreme Court was established at Bamako in 1969 with both judicial and administrative powers. The Court of Appeal is also at Bamako, at the apex of a system of regional tribunals and local *juges de paix*.

Religion. The state is secular, but predominantly Sunni Moslem. About 15% of the population follow traditional animist beliefs and there is a small Christian minority.

Education. The adult literacy rate in 1995 was 31% (39·4% among males and 23·1% among females). In 1994 there were 151 pre-primary schools with 503 teachers for 15,908 pupils. In 1995 there were 1,996 primary schools with 8,738 teachers for 608,444 pupils. During the period 1990–95 only 19% of females of primary school age were enrolled in school. In 1993 there were 111,568 secondary level pupils, and in 1990 there were 6,703 students at university level.

Health. In 1993 there were 483 doctors and 1,674 nurses.

CULTURE
Broadcasting. Broadcasting is the responsibility of the autonomous Radiodiffusion Télévision du Mali. In 1993 there were 7 independent radio networks, 6 private and 1 public. In 1995 there were 500,000 radio and 20,000 TV sets (colour by SECAM).

Press. In 1995 there were 2 daily newspapers with a combined circulation of 41,000.

Tourism. There were 50,000 foreign tourists in 1996, bringing in revenue of US$20m.

DIPLOMATIC REPRESENTATIVES
Of Mali in Great Britain (resides in Brussels)
Ambassador: N'Tji Laico Traoré.

Of Great Britain in Mali (resides in Dakar)
Ambassador: David R. Snoxell.

Of Mali in the USA (2130 R. St., NW, Washington, D.C., 20008)
Ambassador: Cheick Oumar Diarrah.

Of the USA in Mali (Rue Rochester NY and Rue Mohamed V, Bamako)
Ambassador: David P. Rawson.

Of Mali to the United Nations
Ambassador: Moctar Ouane.

Of Mali to the European Union
Ambassador: N'Tji Laïco Traoré.

MALTA

Repubblika ta' Malta

Capital: Valletta
Population estimate, 2000: 378,000
GNP per capita: (PPP$) 13,870
HDI/world rank: 0·899/27

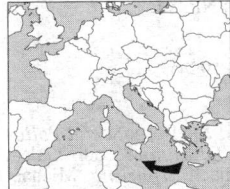

KEY HISTORICAL EVENTS
Malta was held in turn by Phoenicians, Carthaginians and Romans, and was conquered by Arabs in 870. From 1090 it was subject to the same rulers as Sicily until 1530, when it was handed over to the Knights of St John, who ruled until dispersed by Napoleon in 1798. The Maltese rose in rebellion against the French and the island was subsequently blockaded by the British aided by the Maltese from 1798 to 1800. The Maltese people requested the protection of the British Crown in 1802 on condition that their rights and privileges be preserved. The islands were finally annexed to the British Crown by the Treaty of Paris in 1814. On 15 April 1942, in recognition of the fortitude of the people of Malta during the Second World War, King George VI awarded the George Cross to the island. Malta became independent on 21 Sept. 1964 and a republic within the Commonwealth on 13 Dec. 1974. On 16 July 1990 Malta applied for full membership of the European Union.

TERRITORY AND POPULATION
The 3 Maltese islands and minor islets lie in the Mediterranean 93 km (at the nearest point) south of Sicily and 288 km east of Tunisia. The area of Malta is 246 sq. km (94·9 sq. miles); Gozo, 67 sq. km (25·9 sq. miles) and the virtually uninhabited Comino, 3 sq. km (1·1 sq. miles); total area, 316 sq. km (121·9 sq. miles). Population, 31 Dec. 1997, 376,513 (Malta island, 347,625; Gozo and Comino, 28,888). Density 1,189 per sq. km.

The UN gives a projected population for 2000 of 378,000.

In 1995 an estimated 89·3% of the population were urban. Chief town and port, Valletta, population 7,146 (1997) but the inner harbour area, 87,407. Other towns: Birkirkara, 21, 255; Qormi, 17,848; Mosta, 16,869; Sliema, 12,352; Zabbar, 14,324.

The constitution provides that the national language and language of the courts is Maltese, but both Maltese and English are official languages. Italian is also spoken.

SOCIAL STATISTICS
1997: Births, 4,835; deaths, 2,888; marriages, 2,414; emigrants (1998), 57; returned emigrants (1995), 622. 1997 rates per 1,000 population: Birth, 12·8; death, 7·7; marriage, 6·4. In 1995 the most popular age range for marrying was 25–29 for males and 20–24 for females. Life expectancy at birth in 1997: 74·9 years for males and 81·0 years for females. Annual growth, 1996–97: 0·7%. Infant mortality in 1997: 6·4 per 1,000 live births; fertility rate, 1·9 births per woman.

CLIMATE
The climate is Mediterranean, with hot, dry and sunny conditions in summer and very little rain from May to Aug. Rainfall is not excessive and falls mainly between Oct. and March. Average daily sunshine in winter is 6 hours and in summer over 10 hours. Valletta, Jan. 12·8°C (55°F), July 25·6°C (78°F). Annual rainfall 578 mm (23").

CONSTITUTION AND GOVERNMENT
Malta is a parliamentary democracy. The Constitution of 1964 provides for a *President*, a *House of Representatives* of members elected by universal suffrage and a Cabinet consisting of the Prime Minister and such number of Ministers as may be appointed. The Constitution makes provision for the protection of fundamental rights and freedom of the individual, and for freedom of conscience and religious worship, and guarantees the separation of executive, judicial and legislative powers. In 1999 the House of Representatives had 65 members directly elected on a plurality basis.

National Anthem. 'Lil din l'art helwa, l'omm li tatna isimha' ('Guard her, O Lord, as ever Thou hast guarded'); words by Dun Karm Psaila, tune by Dr Robert Samut.

RECENT ELECTIONS
At the elections of 5 Sept. 1998 the electorate was 0·28m. Turn-out was 95·40%. The Nationalist Party (NP) gained 35 seats with 51·81% of votes cast; the Labour Party (MLP), 30 seats with 46·97%. A constitutional amendment of March 1996 rules that where more than 2 parties stand, but only 2 parties gain seats, the party with the most votes is allocated extra seats. Thus, in Nov. 1996 the party composition of the House of Representatives was: MLP, 35; NP, 34.

CURRENT ADMINISTRATION
President: Dr Ugo Mifsud Bonnici (b. 1932; sworn in April 1994).
  The MLP Cabinet in March 1999 comprised:
  Prime Minister: Eddie Fenech Adami (Nationalist Party).
  Deputy Prime Minister: Guido de Marco. *Foreign Affairs:* Joe Borg. *Social Policy and Leader of House of Representatives:* Lawrence Gonzi. *Education:* Louis Galea. *Finance:* John Dalli. *Environment:* Francis Zammit Dimech. *Tourism:* Michael Refalo. *Justice and Local Councils:* Charles Mangion. *Economic Services:* Josef Bonnici. *Home Affairs:* Tonio Borg. *Transport and Communications:* Censu Galea. *Without portfolio in the Office of the Prime Minister:* Joseph Mizzi. *Public Works and Construction:* Charles Buhagiar. *Health:* Louis Deguara. *Social Welfare:* Edwin Grech. *Housing:* Freddie Portelli. *Agriculture and Fisheries:* Ninu Zammit. *Minister for Gozo:* Giovanna Debono.
  Speaker: Anton Tabone.

Local Government. Legislation of 1993 provides for the election of 67 local councils on Malta and Gozo.

DEFENCE
In 1998 the Armed Forces of Malta (AFM) had a strength of about 2,000 and consisted of the Headquarters and 3 Regiments. 1st Regiment AFM is an Infantry Battalion, 2nd Regiment AFM comprises an Air Defence Battery, an Air Squadron and the Maritime Squadron. 3rd Regiment AFM consists of the logistics and support element and a Revenue Security Corps. An Emergency Volunteer Reserve Force was introduced in 1998; initial intake, 60.
  In addition to infantry and low-level air defence artillery weapons, AFM are equipped with helicopters (Alouette IIIs and NH500s), fixed-wing aircraft (PBN Islander and Cessna Birdogs), and a number of patrol craft for inshore and offshore duties, including 3 Kondor Class 52 metre patrol boats.
  Apart from normal military duties, AFM are also responsible for Search and Rescue, airport security, surveillance of Malta's territorial and fishing zones, harbour traffic control and anti-pollution duties.
  In 1997 military expenditure totalled US$31m. (US$82 per capita), representing 0·9% of GDP.

INTERNATIONAL RELATIONS
Malta is a member of the UN, the Commonwealth, the Council of Europe, the Organization for Security and Co-operation in Europe, the International Atomic Energy Agency, the Organization for the Prohibition of Chemical Weapons, the Comprehensive Test-Ban Treaty Organization and the Inter-Parliamentary Union.
  Malta's application to join the EU made in July 1990 by the Nationalist government was on hold during the 2 years in which the Labour Party was in power, but following the Nationalist Party's victory in the 1998 general election the bid for membership was renewed, with the hope of being in the first group of applicants.

ECONOMY
The Maltese economy has developed and expanded significantly over the past decade. The manufacturing and tourism industries have become the pillars of the domestic economy. Malta's economic strategy aims to consolidate these two industries and to strengthen and expand other service-related sectors. The national industrial strategy encourages the need for technologies that promote high quality manufactured products and increased value-added output. Direct investment by both local and foreign entrepreneurs is actively promoted and supported, with various incentives available, while particular importance is attached to the development of small- and medium-sized companies. The national tourism strategy focuses on the

promotion of Malta as an upmarket tourist destination. Importance is also attached to the development of niche tourism, including conference travel, education and cultural tourism. The cruise-liner business is also being developed and the island is currently serving as a hub port for Mediterranean cruises.

The contribution of manufacturing and tourism to domestic economic growth is complemented by financial and freeport services. Malta is now established as an international financial centre. The container transhipment and feeder sector is also becoming a growth area for the Maltese economy. The Malta Freeport plays an important role in this activity as it is effectively positioned to act as a distribution centre in the Mediterranean. Apart from providing efficient transhipment operations to the major shipping lines, the Freeport offers warehouse facilities and other related services.

Since 1971, Malta has had an Association Agreement with the European Union which enables market access to mainland Europe. An application to join the European Union is currently under discussion.

Performance. The average annual GDP growth in 1994–98 was 5·5%.

Budget. Revenue and expenditure (in Lm1m.):

	1993	1994	1995	1996	1997
Revenue	396·6	429·0	487·3	468·3	514·2
Expenditure	410·9	450·9	498·1	548·9	600·6

The most important sources of revenue are VAT, customs and excise duties, income tax, social security and receipts from the Central Bank of Malta.

Currency. The unit of currency is the *Maltese lira* (formerly *pound*) (MTL) of 100 *cents*. Total notes and coins in circulation at end of Sept. 1998, Lm387·6m. (Lm372m. notes, Lm15·6m. coins). Annualized inflation was 2·85% as at Oct. 1998. Gold reserves were 10,000 troy oz. in Jan. 1998 and foreign exchange reserves US$1,443m. in Oct. 1997.

Banking and Finance. The Central Bank of Malta (*Governor*, Emanuel Ellul) was founded in 1968. In 1998 there were 5 domestic and 1 foreign bank undertaking business in the local market. 11 local financial institutions, licensed in terms of the Financial Institutions Act 1994, also provided services that ranged from exchange bureau-related business to merchant banking. There are also 12 international banks.

During 1998 Malta continued to establish itself as a financial international business centre. The Malta Financial Services Centre is the autonomous government authority set up in 1994 as the primary regulator of financial services.

Weights and Measures. The metric system is used.

ENERGY AND NATURAL RESOURCES

Electricity. Electricity is generated at 2 interconnected power stations located at Marsa (272 MW) and Delimara (195 MW). The primary transmission voltages are 132,000, 33,000 and 11,000 volts while the low-voltage system is 415/240V, 50Hz with neutral point earthed. Installed capacity was 405,000 kW in 1994. Production in 1994 was 1·41bn. kWh.

Oil and Gas. Intensive negotiations with AGIP led to the successful conclusion of an oil exploration agreement in an offshore area of approximately 9,000 sq. km. Onshore exploration was revived and a deep stratigraphic well is currently being drilled onshore at Gozo (1998–99). In 1998, 2 consortia received Exploration Study Agreements from Malta to investigate the possibility of offshore drilling.

Water. The Water Services Corporation manages water supply to the Maltese Islands. 1996–97: demand for water, 46·5m. cu. metres. Ground water provided 47·3% of the total water delivered to the distribution system. Desalination (Reverse Osmosis Plants) provided 52·7% of the total potable water requirements.

Agriculture. Despite the dry climate and the lack of fertile land, a wide-range of fruits and vegetables are cultivated. The two main crops are potatoes and tomatoes. The former is the country's primary export crop whilst the latter are the main input for the local canning industry. Peaches, plums, nectarines and apricots are Malta's main fruits. Sugar-melons, water-melons and strawberries are grown intensively and have significant export potential. Cereals and sulla are mainly grown for hay and straw for livestock feeding.

Malta is self-sufficient in chicken, eggs, pork and fresh milk. During 1997 export of pork was initated and it appears that there is a significant potential in such a venture. Livestock in 1996: Cattle, 21,000; sheep, 16,000; pigs, 69,000; chickens, 1m. Livestock produce accounted for 68·5% of the total value of agricultural production during 1998.

During 1998 the contribution of agriculture to GDP was estimated at Lm35·2m. or 3%. There are about 2,582 full-time farmers (1·9% of the economically active workforce).

Fisheries. In Dec. 1997 the fishing industry employed 1,699 power-propelled and 9 other fishing boats, engaging some 374 full-time and 1,442 part-time fishermen. The catch for 1997 was 887 tonnes, valued at Lm1,549,693. Production from fish farms was 1,800 tonnes. It is estimated that during 1998 the local aquaculture industry produced a total of about 2,000 tonnes of sea bass and sea bream valued at Lm4·4m. 95% of local production was harvested for export, mainly to Italy. The production forecast for the marine hatchery at the National Aquaculture Centre in 1998 is 1·1m. It is estimated that all the aquaculture industry employs about 120 full-timers and around 60 part-timers.

INDUSTRY
Besides manufacturing (food, clothing, chemicals, electrical machinery parts and electronic components and products), the mainstays of the economy are ship repair and shipbuilding, agriculture, small crafts units, tourism and the provision of other services such as the freeport facilities. The majority of state-aided manufacturing enterprises operating in Malta are foreign-owned or with foreign interests. The Malta Development Corporation is the Government agency responsible for promoting investment, while the Malta Export Trade Corporation serves as a catalyst to the export of local products.

Labour. The labour supply in Oct. 1998 was 144,583 (females, 39,847), including 37,373 in private direct production (agriculture and fisheries, 2,559; manufacturing, 29,320; oil drilling, construction and quarrying, 5,494), 45,339 in private market services, 49,745 in the public sector (including government departments, armed forces, revenue security corps, airport company, independent statutory bodies and companies with public sector majority shareholding), and 4,838 in temporary employment. Registered unemployed were 7,288 in Oct. 1998 (5·0% of labour supply).

Trade Unions. There were 34 trade unions registered 1997–98, with a total membership of 81,703, and 21 employers' associations with a total membership of 8,819.

INTERNATIONAL TRADE
Imports are being liberalized. Marsaxlokk is an all-weather freeport zone for transhipment activities. External debt was US$953m. in 1996.

Imports and Exports. Imports and exports including bullion and specie (in Lm1,000):

	1992	1993	1994	1995	1996	1997
Imports	747,770	830,920	918,766	1,037,657	1,007,616	984,238
Exports	490,903	518,325	592,422	674,947	624,154	628,925

In 1997 the principal items of imports were: Semi-manufactures, Lm140·8m.; machinery and transport equipment, Lm459·6m.; foodstuffs, Lm94·8m.; fuels, Lm51·8m.; manufactures, Lm113·2m.; chemicals, Lm78·9m. Of domestic exports: Manufactures, Lm145·7m.; machinery and transport equipment, Lm342·6m.; semi-manufactures, Lm42·7m.; beverages and tobacco, Lm2·1m.; foodstuffs, Lm13·7m.; chemicals, Lm14·7m.

In 1997 imports valued at Lm199·1m. came from Italy, Lm163m. from France, Lm145·1m. from UK, Lm98·3m. from Germany, Lm78m. from USA. Main export markets: France, Lm120·6m.; Germany, Lm80·4m.; USA, Lm88·5m.; Singapore Lm61·1m.; Italy, Lm31·8m.; UK, Lm43·8m.

Trade Fairs. Organized by Malta Trade Fairs Corporation: International Fair of Malta (29 June–14 July); Food & Drink (Feb.); Furniture & Interiors, The Boat

MALTA

Show (March); Green Week, The Motor Fair (April); Finance & Business
Exhibition and Conference (Sept.); Information Technology & Telecommunications,
Machinery & Tools (Oct.); Fashion & Beauty Care/Health Care, The Book Fair
(Nov.).

COMMUNICATIONS

Roads. In 1997 there were 1,961 km of roads, including 157 km arterial roads, 1,167
km urban roads, and 647 km non-urban roads. About 94% of roads are paved. Motor
vehicles registered at 30 June 1998: Private cars, 180,832; commercial vehicles,
47,331; cars for hire, 6,466; buses and minibuses, 1,099; motor cycles, 14,169.

Civil Aviation. The national carrier is Air Malta, which is 96·4% state-owned. In
1998 services were also provided by Aeroflot, Aerosweet Airlines, Alitalia, Balkan,
British Airways, Condor Flugdienst, Corsair, Egyptair, Emirates, Gulf Air, JAT,
LTU International Airways, Lufthansa, Romavia, Swissair, Transavia Airlines and
United Airlines. There were scheduled services in 1998 to over 30 different
countries. In 1997 there were 27,150 commercial aircraft movements at Malta
International Airport. 2,781,031 passengers and 11,530 tonnes of freight and 950
tonnes of mail were handled. In 1995 Air Malta flew 20·5m. km and carried
1,065,900 passengers.

Shipping. There is a car ferry between Malta and Gozo. The number of vessels
registered on 31 Dec. 1998 was 3,120 totalling 24,921,216 GT. Ships entering
harbour, excluding yachts and fishing vessels, during 1996, 4,600. 150 cruise vessels
put in during 1996.

Telecommunications. Telecommunications are operated by MaltaCom plc. There
are 15 telephone exchanges and 7 remote switching exchanges with a total installed
capacity of 213,000 lines. There is a digital data transmission network. In 1997 main
telephone lines in use numbered 187,000, or 497·6 per 1,000 inhabitants. There were
30,000 PCs in 1995, 11,000 cellular phone subscribers and 3,200 fax machines.
Malta Com also owns Terranet, one of the largest internet service providers in
Malta.

Postal Services. In 1994 there were 50 post offices operated by Maltapost plc.

SOCIAL INSTITUTIONS

Justice. The number of persons convicted of crimes in 1995 was 1,743; those
convicted for contraventions against various laws and regulations numbered 5,761.
133 persons were committed to prison and 7,371 awarded fines and other
punishments.

On 31 Dec. 1997, police numbered 90 officers (5 women) and 1,710 other ranks
(190 women).

Religion. 98% of the population belong to the Roman Catholic Church, which is
established by law as the religion of the country, though full liberty of conscience
and freedom of worship are guaranteed.

Education. Adult literacy rate, 1995, 91·3% (male, 90·6%; female, 91·9%).
Education is compulsory between the ages of 5 and 16 and free in government
schools from kindergarten to university. Kindergarten education is provided for 3-
and 4-year old children. The primary school course lasts 6 years. In Oct. 1998, there
were 9,600 children in state kindergartens and 23,000 (12,000 boys and 11,000 girls)
in 80 state primary schools. There are education centres for children with special
needs, but these are taught in ordinary schools if possible.

Secondary schools, trade schools and junior lyceums provide secondary education
in the state sector. At the end of their primary education, pupils sit for the 11+
examination to start a secondary education course. Pupils who qualify are admitted
in the junior lyceum, while the others attend secondary schools. In 1998, 11 junior
lyceums had a total of 9,400 students (5,800 girls and 3,600 boys), 17 Secondary
schools had a total population of 8,100 (4,100 girls, 4,000 boys), and 5 centres cater
for 1,300 children (400 girls and 900 boys) at secondary level whose cultural capital
is low or negligible. Secondary schools and junior lyceums offer a 5-year course
leading to the Secondary Education Certificate and the General Certificate of

Education, Ordinary Level. At the end of the third year of secondary education, students may opt for a course with a technology bias in a trade school, where the full course may last 6 years. Trade School students generally come from the secondary schools. Courses run by Trade Schools lead to a Journeyman's Certificate and/or a City and Guilds of London Institute certificate. In Oct. 1998, there were 2,200 students (100 girls) enrolled in trade schools. At the end of the 5-year secondary course, students may opt to follow a higher academic or technical or vocational course of from 1 to 4 years. The academic courses generally lead to Intermediate and Advanced Level examinations set by the British universities. The junior college, administered by the University, prepares students specifically for a university course. The Matriculation Certificate, which qualifies students for admission to university, is a broad-based holistic qualification covering the humanities, sciences and operacy subjects, together with systems of knowledge. About 4,500 students (2,150 females) attend state higher secondary educational institutions; 2,200 students (1,300 females) attend the junior college (1998). Students following higher secondary courses who qualify for the Extended Skill Training Scheme or Technician Apprenticeship Scheme or the Sixth Form Students' Scheme receive an allowance.

About 30% of the student population attend non-state schools, from kindergarten to higher secondary level. In Oct. 1998 there were about 26,000 pupils attending non-state schools, 17,600 of whom were in schools run by the Roman Catholic Church, while 8,400 students were attending private schools. Under an agreement between the Government and the Church, the Government subsidizes Church schools and students attending these schools do not pay any fees.

Nearly 7,500 students (3,800 females) were following courses at the University in 1997. University students receive a stipend.

In Oct. 1998 about 5,700 students were attending adult or evening courses covering a very wide spectrum of studies at different levels. Many of these courses lead to a recognized certification.

In 1995 total expenditure on education came to 5·2% of GNP and represented 11·4% of total government expenditure.

Health. In 1996 there were 925 doctors, 122 dentists, 648 pharmacists, 200 midwives and 4,000 nursing personnel. There were 7 hospitals (2 private) with 2,140 beds and 8 health centres.

Welfare. Legislation provides a national contributory insurance scheme and also for the payment of non-contributory allowances, assistances and pensions. It covers the payment of marriage grants, maternity benefits, child allowances, parental allowances, handicapped child allowance, family bonus, sickness benefit, injury benefits, disablement benefits, unemployment benefit, contributory pensions in respect of retirement, invalidity and widowhood, and non-contributory medical assistance, free medical aids, social assistance, a carers' pension and pensions for the handicapped, the blind and the aged.

CULTURE

Broadcasting. Radio and TV services are under the control of the Broadcasting Authority, an independent statutory body. The government-owned Public Broadcasting Services Ltd was set up in 1991 and operates 2 radio stations and a TV station (colour by PAL). Legislation of 1991 introduced private commercial broadcasting. In 1998 there were 12 radio and 3 TV services and a cable TV network. On 31 Dec. 1995 there were some 160,000 licensed television sets. There were 200,000 radio receivers in 1995.

Cinema. In 1996 there were 22 cinemas with a seating capacity of 4,237.

Press. 1998: 3 English and 2 Maltese dailies, 5 Maltese and 3 English weeklies, 1 financial weekly in English.

Tourism. Tourism is the major foreign currency earner. 941,288 tourists visited Malta, generating earnings of Lm193·2m. (Jan.–Sept 1998). Cruise passenger visits totalled 109,283 in 1998. A Lm10m. Valletta Cruise Terminal is being built at the Malta Grand Harbour (1998–99). Employment in hotel and catering establishments was 9,296 in 1997.

Festivals. Carnival Festivals at Valletta (Feb.); History and Elegance Festival at Valletta and Mdina (April); National Folk Singing (May); Malta International Arts Festival, Malta Jazz Festival, International Food and Beer Festival (June/July); Festa Season (June–Sept.); Malta International Choir Festival, Amateur Film and Video Festival (Nov.).

Libraries. The National Library, housed in one of Valletta's finest 18th Century buildings, is Malta's foremost research Library, founded in 1763. There is a Central Public Library in Floriana, Branch Libraries in Government Schools in most towns and villages, and the University of Malta Library. *Specialized libraries:* Central Bank of Malta, Central Office of Statistics, Foundation for International Studies, Franco-Maltese Documentation and Research Centre, Malta External Trade Corporation.

National Theatre and Opera. The Manoel Theatre (built 1731) is Malta's National Theatre. There is also the Mediterranean Conference Centre in Valletta, and the Astra Theatre in Victoria, Gozo.

Museums and Galleries. In Valletta: National Museum of Archaeology, National Museum of Fine Arts, Palace Armoury, war Museum (Fort St. Elmo). Mdian and Rabat: National Museum of Natural History, Museum of Roman antiquities, St. Paul's Catacombs, the Cathedral Museum. Paula: Hal Saflieni Hypoguem. Qrendi: Hagar Qim and Mnajra Megalithic Temples. Birzebbuga: Ghar Dalam Cave and Museum. Vittoriosa: Maritime Museum. Gozo (Victoria): Museum of Archaeology, Natural Science Museum, Folklore Museum. Xaghra: Ggantija Megalithic Temples.

DIPLOMATIC REPRESENTATIVES
Of Malta in Great Britain (36-38 Piccadilly, London, W1V 0PQ)
High Commissioner: Vacant.

Of Great Britain in Malta (7 St Anne St., Floriana)
High Commissioner: Graham Archer.

Of Malta in the USA (2017 Connecticut Ave., NW, Washington, D.C., 20008)
Charge d'Affaires a.i.: Mark Anthony Micallef.

Of the USA in Malta (Development Hse., St Anne St., Floriana)
Ambassador: Kathryn H. Proffitt.

Of Malta to the United Nations
Ambassador: George Saliba.

Of Malta to the European Union
Ambassador: Victor Camilleri.

FURTHER READING
Central Office of Statistics. *Statistical Abstracts of the Maltese Islands*, a quarterly digest of statistics, quarterly and annual trade returns, annual vital statistics and annual publications on shipping and aviation, education, agriculture, industry, National Accounts and Balance of Payments.
Department of Information (3 Castille Place, Valletta). *The Malta Government Gazette, Malta Information, Economic Survey [year], Reports on the Working of Government Departments, The Maltese Economy in Figures, 1986–1995, Business Opportunities on Malta, Acts of Parliament and Subsidiary Legislation, Laws of Malta, Constitution of Malta 1992.*

Berg, W. G., *Historical Dictionary of Malta*. Metuchen (NJ), 1995
Central Bank of Malta. *Annual Reports.*
Chamber of Commerce (annual). *Trade Directory.*
Blouet, B., *The Story of Malta*. London, Rev. ed. 1981
Boswell, D. and Beeley, B., *Malta* [Bibliography]. 2nd ed. Oxford and Santa Barbara (CA), 1998.
Cremona, J. J., *The Constitutional Developments of Malta under British Rule*. Malta Univ. Press, 1963.—*Human Rights Documentation in Malta*. Malta Univ. Press, 1966
Gerada, E. and Zuber, C., *Malta: an Island Republic*. Paris, 1979
The Malta Yearbook. Valletta
Thackrah, J. R., *Malta* [Bibliography]. Oxford and Santa Barbara (CA), 1985

National statistical office: Central Office of Statistics, Auberge d'Italie, Valletta.
Website: http://www.magnet.mt/home/cos/

MARSHALL ISLANDS

Republic of the
Marshall Islands

Capital: Majuro Atoll
Population estimate, 2000: 68,000
Estimated GDP: $94m.

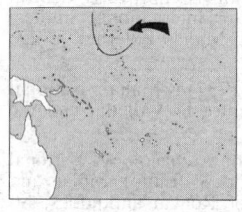

KEY HISTORICAL EVENTS

A German protectorate was formed in 1886 which was occupied at the beginning of the First World War by Japan. Japan was awarded a mandate by the League of Nations in 1919. During the Second World War the Islands were occupied by Allied forces in 1944, and became part of the UN Trust Territory of the Pacific Islands created on 18 July 1947 and administered by the USA. On 21 Oct. 1986 the islands gained independence and a Compact of Free Association with the USA came into force. The UN recognized the termination of the US Trusteeship on 22 Dec. 1990, and the Islands became a full UN member state on 17 Sept. 1991.

TERRITORY AND POPULATION

The Marshall Islands lie in the North Pacific Ocean north of Kiribati and east of Micronesia, and consist of an archipelago of 31 coral atolls, 5 single islands and 1,152 islets strung out in 2 chains, eastern and western. The land area is 181 sq. km (70 sq. miles). The capital is Majuro Atoll in the eastern chain (population, 1997 estimate, 28,000). The principal atoll in the western chain is Kwajalein containing the only other town, Ebeye (population estimate, 1997, 15,000). The two archipelagic island chains of Bikini and Enewetak are former US nuclear test sites; Kwajalein is now used as a US missile test range. The islands lay claim to the US territory of Wake Island. At the census of 1988 the population was 43,380 (48% urban); 1997 estimate, 60,652; density, 335 per sq. km.

In 2000 the population is projected to be 68,000.

In 1995 some 69% of the population lived in urban areas. About 97% of the population are Marshallese, a Micronesian people.

English is universally spoken and is the official language. Two major Marshallese dialects from the Malayo-Polynesian family, and Japanese, are also spoken.

SOCIAL STATISTICS

1997 births, estimate, 2,800; deaths, 400. 1997 rates per 1,000 population, estimates: Birth rate, 45·5; death rate, 7·0; infant mortality rate, 45·7 per 1,000 live births; life expectancy, 64·1 years. Annual growth rate, 1990–95, 3·7%.

CLIMATE

Hot and humid, with wet season from May to Nov. The islands border the typhoon belt. Jaluit, Jan. 81°F (27·2°C), July 82°F (27·8°C). Annual rainfall 161" (4,034 mm).

CONSTITUTION AND GOVERNMENT

Under the constitution which came into force on 1 May 1979, the Marshall Islands form a republic with a *President* as head of state and government, who is elected for 4-year terms by the parliament. The parliament consists of a 33-member *House of Assembly* (Nitijela), directly elected by popular vote for 4-year terms. There is also a 12-member appointed *Council of Chiefs* (Iroij) which has a consultative and advisory capacity on matters affecting customary law and practice.

RECENT ELECTIONS

The last presidential election was held on 14 Jan. 1997. At the House of Assembly elections in Nov. 1995 only non-partsians were elected.

CURRENT ADMINISTRATION
President: Imata Kabua (since 14 Jan. 1997).

In March 1999 the government comprised:

Minister of Finance: Tony de Brum. *Foreign Affairs:* Phillip Muller. *Transport and Telecommunications:* Kunio D. Lemari. *Resources, Development and Public Works:* Wilfred J. Kendall. *Education:* Justin de Brum. *Internal Affairs and Social Welfare:* Hiroshi Yamamura. *Health and Environment:* Thomas D. Kijiner. *Justice:* Hemos Jack. *Assistance to the President:* Johnsay Riklon. *Chief Secretary:* Philip Kabua. *Attorney General:* Gerald Zackhras.

DEFENCE
The Compact of Free Association gave the USA responsibility for defence in return for US assistance. There is a police force, and a coast guard may be established.

INTERNATIONAL RELATIONS
The Marshall Islands are a member of the UN, Pacific Community (formerly the South Pacific Commission) and the South Pacific Forum.

ECONOMY
Policy. Fisheries and tourism offer the best potentials for economic growth and development and the government plans to devote increased resources into developing these activities.

Performance. Real GDP growth was –2·0% in 1995 (2·0% in 1994).

Budget. 1994/95 estimate: revenue, US$67·2m.; expenditure: US$79·6m. Under the terms of the Compact of Free Association, the USA provides approximately US$4m. a year in aid.

Currency. US currency is used. The average annual inflation rate during the period 1990–96 was 6·4%.

Banking and Finance. There are 3 Banks: The Bank of Marshall Islands, The Bank of Hawaii and The Bank of Guam.

ENERGY AND NATURAL RESOURCES
Electricity. Total installed capacity (1997), 20,200 kW. Production (1994), 57m. kWh.

Minerals. High-grade phosphate deposits are mined on Ailinglaplap Atoll. Deep-seabed minerals are an important natural resource.

Agriculture. A small amount of agricultural produce is exported: coconuts, tomatoes, melons and breadfruit. Other important crops include copra, taro, cassava and sweet potatoes. Pigs and chicken constitute the main livestock.

Fisheries. There is a commercial tuna-fishing industry with a canning factory on Majuro. Seaweed is cultivated. Total catches in 1995 amounted to approximately 260 tonnes.

INDUSTRY
The main industries are copra, fish, tourism, handicrafts (items made from shell, wood and pearl), mining, manufacturing, construction and power.

Labour. The total labour force numbered 11,488 in 1988. An estimated 16% were unemployed in 1991. In 1994, agriculture accounted for 16% of the working population; industry, 14%; services, 70%.

INTERNATIONAL TRADE
The Compact of Free Association with the USA is the major source of income for the Marshall Islands, and accounts for about 70% of total GDP.

Imports and Exports. Imports (mainly oil) were estimated at US$69·9m. in 1995; exports, US$21·3m. Main trading partners: USA and Japan. There is also increasing trade with Australia, New Zealand, the Fiji Islands and Taiwan, and in 1998 trade agreements were initiated with China and Indonesia.

Main exports: coconut oil, copra cake, chilled and frozen fish, pet fish, shells and handicrafts. Imports exceed exports, resulting in a trade deficit of approaching US$50m. per year.

COMMUNICATIONS

Roads. There are paved roads on major islands (Majuro, Kwajalein); roads are otherwise stone-, coral- or laterite-surfaced.

Civil Aviation. There are 9 paved and 7 unpaved airports (1996). The main airport is Majuro International. Air Marshall Islands operates flights to the Fiji Islands, Kiribati, Micronesia and Tuvalu as well as domestic services. In 1998 Continental Airlines also operated services to Guam, Honolulu and Johnston Island. Air Marshall Islands carried 46,000 passengers in 1995.

Shipping. Majuro is the main port. There were 94 ships in 1996, totalling over 4m. GRT.

Telecommunications. In 1997 there were nearly 3,500 telephones in use. There is a US satellite communications system on Kwajalein and 2 Intelsat satellite earth stations (Pacific Ocean). The National Telecommunications Authority provides domestic and international services.

Postal Services. Postal services are available on the main island of Majuro and also in Ebeye.

SOCIAL INSTITUTIONS

Justice. The Supreme Court is situated on Majuro. There is also a High Court, a District Court and 23 Community Courts. A Traditional Court deals with disputes involving land properties and customs.

Religion. The population is mainly Protestant, with Roman Catholics next. Other Churches and denominations include Mormons, Jehovah's Witnesses, Baptists, Baha'i, Seventh Day Adventists and Assembly of God.

Education. In 1994 there were 13,565 pupils in 104 primary schools, and 2,483 pupils in 11 secondary schools. There is a College of the Marshall Islands, and a subsidiary of the University of the South Pacific, on Majuro.

Health. There were 2 hospitals in 1997, with a total of 129 beds. There are 34 doctors, 141 nurses and health assistants, and 4 dentists.

CULTURE

Broadcasting. There is 1 TV and 3 radio stations.

Press. There is a publication called Micronitor (The Marshall Islands Journal).

Tourism. In 1996 there were 6,000 foreign tourists, spending US$2m.

Festivals. Custom Day and the Annual Canoe Race are the main festivals.

Libraries. There is 1 public library.

DIPLOMATIC REPRESENTATIVES
Of Great Britain in the Marshall Islands (resides in the Fiji Islands)
Ambassador: Vernon M. Scarborough.

Of the Marshall Islands in the USA (2433 Massachusetts Ave., NW, Washington, D.C., 20008)
Ambassador: Banny de Brum.

Of the USA in the Marshall Islands (Oceanside Mejen Weto, Long Island, Majuro)
Ambassador: Joan M. Plaisted.

Of the Marshall Islands to the United Nations
Chargé d'Affaires a.i.: Jackeo A. Relang.

MAURITANIA

République Islamique Arabe
et Africaine de Mauritanie

Capital: Nouakchott
Population estimate, 2000: 2·58m.
GNP per capita: (PPP$) 1,810
HDI/world rank: 0·361/149

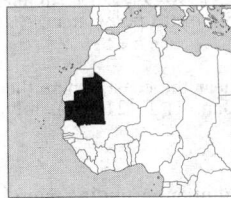

KEY HISTORICAL EVENTS

Mauritania became a French protectorate in 1903, a colony in 1920 and an autonomous republic within the French Community on 28 Nov. 1958. It achieved full independence on 28 Nov. 1960. Under its first President, Moktar Ould Daddah, Mauritania became a one-party state in 1964.

Following a coup on 10 July 1978, power was placed in the hands of a Military Committee for National Recovery (CMRN); the constitution was suspended and the 70-member National Assembly dissolved. On 6 April 1979 the CMRN was renamed the Military Committee for National Salvation (CMSN). A coup in Jan. 1980 installed Lieut.-Col. Mohammed Haidalla in power, and under his rule slavery was finally abolished in Mauritania. In Feb. 1984 he recognized Polisario's declaration of a Sahrawi Arab Democratic Republic. He was overthrown in Dec. 1984 when his prime minister, Lieut.-Col. Maaouiya Ould Sidi Ahmed Taya, seized power.

The 1980s were characterized by territorial disputes with Morocco and Senegal. In April 1991 Taya announced a new constitution allowing for a multi-party political system, but which also gave extensive powers to the president. The proposed constitution was approved by referendum in July 1991. Taya was re-elected in Jan. 1992 but legislative elections in March were boycotted by opposition parties who accused the government of electoral fraud. Subsequent elections were dominated by President Taya and his Democratic and Socialist Republican Party.

TERRITORY AND POPULATION

Mauritania is bounded west by the Atlantic Ocean, north by Western Sahara, north-east by Algeria, east and south-east by Mali, and south by Senegal. The total area is 1,030,700 sq. km (398,000 sq. miles) of which 47% is desert, and the population at the census of 1988 was 1,864,236. Estimate, 1996, 2,332,000 (52·8% urban); density, 2·26 per sq. km.

The UN gives a projected population for 2000 of 2·58m.

Area, population and chief towns of the Nouakchott Capital District and 12 regions at the 1988 census:

Region	Area (sq. km)	Population (1992 estimate)	Chief town
Nouakchott District	1,000	324,037	Nouakchott
Hodh ech-Chargui	182,700	234,011	Néma
Hodh el-Gharbi	53,400	175,089	Aïoun el Atrouss
Açâba	36,600	185,574	Kiffa
Gorgol	13,600	201,301	Kaédi
Brakna	37,100	207,590	Aleg
Trarza	67,800	217,867	Rosso
Adrar	215,300	62,906	Atâr
Dakhlet Nouâdhibou	22,300	83,246	Nouâdhibou
Tagant	95,200	67,939	Tidjikdja
Guidimaka	10,300	129,797	Sélibaby
Tiris Zemmour	252,900	37,534	Zouérate
Inchiri	46,800	13,630	Akjoujt

Principal towns (1992 population): Nouakchott, 480,408 including suburbs; Nouâdhibou, 72,305; Kaédi, 35,241.

In 1987 there were also 0·43m. nomads.

The major ethnic groups are (with numbers in 1993): Moors (of mixed Arab, Berber and African origin), 1,513,400; Wolof, 147,000; Tukulor, 114,600; Soninke, 60,000.

MAURITANIA

Arabic is the official language. French no longer has official status. Pulaar, Soninke and Wolof are national languages.

SOCIAL STATISTICS
1996 births, estimate, 109,000; deaths, 35,000. 1996 rates, estimate (per 1,000 population): Births, 46·9; deaths, 15·2. Expectation of life in 1996 was 49·0 years (46·1 for males and 52·1 for females). Annual growth rate, 1990–95, 2·6%. Infant mortality, 1990–95, 101 per 1,000 live births; fertility rate, 5·4 births per woman.

CLIMATE
A tropical climate, but conditions are generally arid, even near the coast, where the only appreciable rains come in July to Sept. Nouakchott, Jan. 71°F (21·7°C), July 82°F (27·8°C). Annual rainfall 6" (158 mm).

CONSTITUTION AND GOVERNMENT
A referendum was held in July 1991 to approve a new constitution instituting multi-party politics. Turn-out was 85·34%; 97·94% of votes cast were in favour.

The new constitution envisages that the President is elected by universal suffrage for renewable 6-year terms. There is a *Senate* and a 72-member *National Assembly.* Parties specifically Islamic are not permitted.

National Anthem. No words, tune by T. Nikiprowetzky.

RECENT ELECTIONS
Presidential elections were held on 12 Dec. 1997. There were 5 candidates. Col. Maaouiya Ould Sidi Ahmed Taya was re-elected with 90·2% of votes cast, compared to 62·8% in the elections of 24 Jan. 1992.

Elections for the National Assembly were held on 19 Oct. 1996. 21 parties stood. The Democratic and Socialist Republican Party (PRDS) gained 72 seats. In the Senate elections of 17 April 1998 the PRDS obtained 54 of the 56 seats.

CURRENT ADMINISTRATION
President: Maaouiya Ould Sidi Ahmed Taya (assumed office 12 Dec. 1984; re-elected 1992 and 1997).

In March 1999 the government comprised:
Prime Minister: Cheikel Afia Ould Mohamed Khouna.

Minister of National Defence: Kaba Ould Elewa. *Interior, Posts and Telecommunications:* Dahould Abdel Jelil. *Foreign Affairs and Co-operation:* Ahmed Ould Sid Ahmed. *Justice:* Mohamed Ould Ahmed Lemine. *Planning:* Mohamedou Ould Michel. *Finance:* Camara Aly Gueladio. *Fisheries and Maritime Economy:* Mohamed El Moctar Ould Zamel. *Trade, Handicrafts and Tourism:* Ehemdi Ould Hamadi. *Mines and Industry:* Ishagh Ould Rajel. *Health and Social Affairs:* Diye Ba. *Culture and Islamic Orientation:* Moustaph Ould sid 'El Isselmou. *Civil Service, Labour, Youth and Sports:* Baba Ould Sidi. *Equipment and Transportation:* Ngalde Lamine Kayo. *Education:* Sghair Ould M'Bareck. *Rural Development and the Environment:* Col. Mohamed Ould Sid' Ahmed Lekhal. *Hydraulics and Energy:* Mohamed Salem Ould Merzoug. *Communications and Relations with Parliament:* Rachid Ould Saleh. *Women's Affairs:* Mintata Mint Hiddeid.

Local Government. Mauritania is divided into a capital district and 12 regions. These are sub-divided into 49 departments and 208 communes. At the municipal elections of Jan.–Feb. 1994 the PRDS won a majority in 172 communes.

DEFENCE
Conscription is authorized for 2 years. Defence expenditure in 1997 totalled US$24m. (US$10 per capita), representing 2·2% of GDP.

Army. There are 6 military regions. The Army consists of 7 motorized infantry, 1 parachute, 1 Presidential security, 3 artillery, 8 infantry and 2 Camel Corps battalions, 1 armoured car squadron, 4 air defence artillery batteries and 1 engineer company. Equipment includes 35 T-54/-55 main battle tanks. Strength 15,000 in 1997.

Navy. The Navy, some 500 strong in 1997, is based at Nouâdhibou and consists of 2 offshore patrol craft for fishery protection, 9 inshore patrol craft and a few boats.

Air Force. The Air Force has 5 Britten-Norman Defender armed light transports, 2 Maritime Surveillance Cheyennes for coastal patrol, 1 Buffalo transport, 2 Y-12 transports, 4 Reims-Cessna 337 Milirole twin-engined counter-insurgency, forward air control and training aircraft and 2 Hughes 500 helicopters for communications. Personnel (1997), 150 with 7 combat aircraft.

INTERNATIONAL RELATIONS
Mauritania is a member of the UN, OAU, the Arab League and is an ACP member state of the ACP-EU relationship.

ECONOMY
Performance. A once highly centralized economy has gone though 8 years of structural change to produce a 5% economic growth for 1998 and an average 4% over the past 4 years.

Budget. Revenues were an estimated US$329m. in 1996 and expenditures US$265m.

Currency. The monetary unit is the *ouguiya* (MRO) which is divided into 5 *khoums*. In Oct. 1992 the ouguiya was devalued 28%. Foreign exchange reserves were US$202m. in Feb. 1998. Inflation was 3·5% in 1995, but had grown to an estimated 16·6% in 1998. Total money supply in Feb. 1998 was 18,040m. ouguiya.

Banking and Finance. The Central Bank (created 1973) is the bank of issue, and there are 4 commercial banks. Bank deposits totalled 12,304m. ouguiya in 1992.

Weights and Measures. The metric system is in use.

ENERGY AND NATURAL RESOURCES
Electricity. Installed capacity was 105,000 kW in 1991. Production in 1994 was 148m. kWh. Consumption per capita was 67 kWh in 1994.

Minerals. There are reserves of copper, gold, phosphate and gypsum. Iron ore production (1993) was 9·20m. tonnes. Iron ore, 11·4m. tonnes of which were mined in 1996, accounts for about 11% of GNP and 40% of exports. Prospecting licences have also been issued for diamonds.

Agriculture. Only 1% of the country receives enough rain to grow crops, so agriculture is mainly confined to the south, in the Senegal river valley. In 1996 agriculture accounted for 25% of GDP. Production in tonnes (1995) of millet and sorghum, 165,000; rice, 79,000; dates, 25,000; pulses, 17,000; watermelons, 6,000; yams, 3,000; groundnuts, 2,000; sweet potatoes, 2,000.

Herding is the main occupation of the rural population and accounted for 16% of GDP in 1992. In 1996 there were 6·2m. sheep, 3·53m. goats (1995), 1·31m. cattle, 1·09m. camels, 4m. chickens (1995).

Forestry. There were 556,000 ha of forests in 1995 covering 0·5% of the land area, chiefly in the southern regions, where wild acacias yield the main product, gum arabic. In 1995, 14,000 cu. metres of roundwood were cut.

Fisheries. Total catches in 1995 were approximately 90,000 tonnes, 94% from sea fishing and the rest from inland waters.

INDUSTRY
Output, 1988 (in tonnes): Fish products, 352,200; cheese, 1,754; butter, 647.

Labour. In 1996 the workforce was 1,072,000 (56% males). In 1994, 430,000 people worked in agriculture, forestry and fishing, 177,000 in services and 80,000 in industry.

INTERNATIONAL TRADE
Total foreign debt was US$2,363m. in 1996. In Feb. 1989 Mauritania signed a treaty of economic co-operation with the 4 other Maghreb countries—Algeria, Libya, Morocco and Tunisia.

MAURITANIA

Imports and Exports. In 1994 imports (in US$1) totalled 390m. and exports 355m. Main exports are fish and fish products (57% of total exports) and iron ore (40%). Main imports are foodstuffs, consumer goods, petroleum products and capital goods. Principal export markets in 1994 were Japan (27%), followed by Italy and Belgium. Main import suppliers were Algeria (15%), followed by China and the USA.

COMMUNICATIONS

Roads. There were 7,660 km of roads in 1996, of which 865 km were asphalted. In 1995 there were 17,300 passenger cars and 9,200 commercial vehicles.

Rail. A 704-km railway links Zouérate with the port of Point-Central, 10 km south of Nouâdhibou, and is used primarily for iron ore exports. In 1995 it carried 11·3m. tonnes of freight.

Civil Aviation. There are international airports at Nouakchott, Nouâdhibou and Némy. Air Mauritanie provides domestic services, and in 1998 operated international services to Banjul, Bissau, Casablanca, Dakar, Las Palmas and Niamey. In 1998 there were also international flights to Algiers, Bamako, Paris and Tunis. Flights were also operated in 1998 by Air Afrique, Air France, Air Algérie, Air Senegal, Royal Air Maroc and Tunis Air. In 1995 scheduled airline traffic of Mauritania-based carriers flew 4·1m. km, carrying 228,000 passengers (130,000 on domestic flights).

Shipping. In 1995 the merchant fleet totalled 20,311 GRT. The major ports are at Point-Central (for mineral exports), Nouakchott and Nouâdhibou.

Telecommunications. Mauritania had 13,100 main telephone lines in 1997 (5·5 per 1,000 persons). There were 300 fax machines in 1995 and around 100 Internet users in Jan. 1998.

Postal Services. In 1995 there were 60 post offices.

SOCIAL INSTITUTIONS

Justice. There are courts of first instance at Nouakchott, Atâr, Kaédi, Aïoun el Atrouss and Kiffa. The Appeal Court and Supreme Court are situated in Nouakchott. Islamic jurisprudence was adopted in 1980.

Religion. Over 99% of Mauritanians are Sunni Moslem, mainly of the Qadiriyah sect.

Education. In 1992–93 there were 36 pre-primary schools with 108 teachers for 800 pupils; in 1995 there were 1,854 primary schools with 5,648 teachers for 289,945 pupils. In 1994 there were 45,810 secondary level pupils with 1,038 teachers, and 7,501 students at university level. The University of Nouakchott had 2,850 students and 70 academic staff in 1994–95. Adult literacy rate (1995), 37·7% (male, 49·6%; female, 26·3%).

Health. There were about 200 doctors in 1994.

CULTURE

Broadcasting. The government-controlled Office de Radiodiffusion-Télévision de Mauritanie is responsible for broadcasting. There are 2 radio and 1 TV networks. In 1995 there were estimated to be 340,000 radio and 57,000 TV sets (colour by SECAM).

Press. In 1995 there was 1 daily newspaper with a circulation of 1,000.

Tourism. In 1996 revenue from foreign tourists totalled US$11m.

DIPLOMATIC REPRESENTATIVES
Of Mauritania in Great Britain
Ambassador: Dah Ould Abdi (resides in Paris).

Of Great Britain in Mauritania
Ambassador: William H. Fullerton, CMG (resides in Morocco).

MAURITANIA

Of Mauritania in the USA (2129 Leroy Pl., NW, Washington, D.C., 20008)
Ambassador: Ahmed Ould Sid Ahmed.

Of the USA in Mauritania (PO Box 222, Nouakchott)
Ambassador: Timberlake Foster.

Of Mauritania to the United Nations
Ambassador: Mahfoudh Ould Deddach.

Of Mauritania to the European Union
Ambassador: Boullah Ould Mogueye.

FURTHER READING
Belvaud, C., *La Mauritanie*. Paris, 1992
Calderini, S. *et al., Mauritania*. [Bibliography] Oxford and Santa Barbara (CA), 1992
Pazzanita, A. G., *The Maghreb*. [Bibliography] Oxford and Santa Barbara (CA), 1998

MAURITIUS

Republic of Mauritius

Capital: Port Louis
Population estimate, 2000: 1·18m.
GNP per capita: (PPP$) 9,000
HDI/world rank: 0·833/61

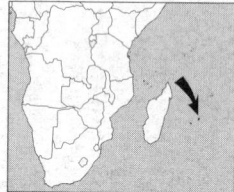

KEY HISTORICAL EVENTS
Mauritius was known to Arab navigators probably not later than the 10th century. Malays almost certainly visited in the 15th century and it was discovered by the Portuguese between 1507 and 1512. But the Dutch were the first settlers in 1598 who named it after their stadtholder, Count Maurice. In 1710 they abandoned the island which was occupied by the French under the name of Ile de France in 1715. The British occupied the island in 1810 and it was formally ceded to Great Britain by the Treaty of Paris, 1814. The majority of the population were descendants of slaves brought by the French from Madagascar and East Africa, and indentured Indian labourers brought by Britain. European settlers unsuccessfully opposed calls for independence, and the elections in August 1967 provided an overwhelming mandate; independence was attained within the Commonwealth on 12 March 1968. Mauritius became a republic on 12 March 1992.

TERRITORY AND POPULATION
Mauritius, the main island, lies 500 miles (800 km) east of Madagascar. Rodrigues is 350 miles (560 km) east. The outer islands are Agalega and the St Brandon Group. Area and population:

Island	Area in sq. km	Census 1990	Estimate 1 July 1997
Mauritius	1,865	1,024,571	1,112,636
Rodrigues	104	34,204	35,070
Outer Islands	71	167	170
Total	2,040	1,058,942	1,147,876

Port Louis is the capital (146,322). Other towns: Beau Bassin-Rose Hill: 99,069, Quatre Bornes: 75,554, Curepipe: 78,516 and Vacoas-Phoenix: 96,928.

The UN gives a projected population for 2000 of 1·18m.

In 1995 an estimated 59·5% of the population were rural.

Ethnic composition, 1996: Hindus, 52% 'General Population' (i.e. European, African, Creole), 33%; Moslems, 10%; Chinese, 5%.

The official language is English, although French is widely used. Creole and Bhojpuri are vernacular languages.

SOCIAL STATISTICS
1996: Births, 20,763 (rate of 18·3 per 1,000 population); deaths, 7,670 (6·8 per 1,000); marriages, 10,697 (18·9 per 1,000). The population growth rate in 1996 was 1·2%. In 1996 the most popular age range for marrying was 25–29 for males and 20–24 for females. The life expectancy at birth for the period 1990–95 was 66·9 years for males and 73·8 for females. Infant mortality, 1990–95, 18 per 1,000 live births; fertility rate, 2·4 births per woman.

CLIMATE
The sub-tropical climate is humid. Most rain falls in the summer. Rainfall varies between 40" (1,000 mm) on the coast to 200" (5,000 mm) on the central plateau, though the west coast only has 35" (875 mm). Mauritius lies in the cyclone belt, whose season runs from Nov. to April, but is seldom affected by intense storms. Port Louis, Jan. 73°F (22·8°C), July 81°F (27·2°C). Annual rainfall 40" (1,000 mm).

CONSTITUTION AND GOVERNMENT
The head of state is the *President*, elected by a simple majority of members of the National Assembly.

MAURITIUS

The *National Assembly* consists of 62 elected members (3 each for the 20 constituencies of Mauritius and 2 for Rodrigues) and 8 additional seats in order to ensure a fair and adequate representation of each community within the Assembly. Elections are held every 5 years on the basis of universal adult suffrage.

National Anthem. 'Glory to thee, Motherland'; words by J. G. Prosper, tune by P. Gentille.

RECENT ELECTIONS
Parliamentary elections were held on 20 Dec. 1995. 481 candidates representing 42 parties stood. The electorate was 567,810; turn-out was 79·39%. All 62 elected seats were won by a coalition of the Labour Party (Parti Travailliste; LP) and the Mauritian Militant Movement, with 65·2% of votes cast. The coalition split in mid-1997 and the Mauritian Militant Movement is now in opposition.

CURRENT ADMINISTRATION
President: Sir Cassam Uteem.
   Vice President: Angidi Chettiar.
   The Cabinet was composed as follows in March 1999:
   Prime Minister, Minister of Defence and Home Affairs, Civil Service Affairs, Urban and Rural Development: Dr Navinchandra Ramgoolam (b. 1947; LP).
   Deputy Prime Minister, Minister of Foreign Affairs, and International Trade: Rajkeswur Purryag. *Minister of Housing and Land Development:* Clarel Désiré Malherbe. *Attorney-General and Minister of Justice, Human Rights and Corporate Affairs, Labour and Industrial Relations:* Abdool Razack Mohamed Ameen Peeroo. *Minister of Land Transport, Shipping and Public Safety:* Dr Ahmed Rashid Beebeejaun. *Minister of Finance:* Dr Vasant Kumar Bunwaree. *Minister of Local Government and Environment:* James Burty David. *Minister of Education and Human Resource Development:* Ramsamy Chedumbarum Kadress Pillay. *Minister of Agriculture, Fisheries and Co-operatives:* Dr Arvin Boolell. *Minister of Economic Development and Regional Co-operation:* Rundheersing Bheenick. *Minister of Arts and Culture:* Tsang Fan Hin Tsang Mang Kin. *Minister of Public Infrastructure:* Dr Mohummud Siddick Chady. *Minister of Public Utilities:* Devanand Virahswamy. *Minister of Women, Family Welfare and Child Development:* Indira Savitree Thacoor-Sidaya. *Minister of Youth and Sports:* Sachindev Mahess Kumar Soonarane. *Minister of Tourism and Leisure:* Marie Joseph Jacques Chasteau de Balyon. *Minister of Health and Quality of Life:* Dr Nankeswarsingh Deerpalsingh. *Minister of Industry and Commerce:* Sathiamoorthy Sunassee. *Minister of Telecommunications and Information Technology:* Sarat Dutt Lallah. *Minister for Rodrigues:* Benoit Jolicoeur.

Local Government. The Island of Mauritius (only) is divided into 5 municipalities and 4 district councils.

DEFENCE
The Police Department, which is responsible for defence, is equipped with arms, 1 offshore patrol vessel, 4 inshore patrol craft, 1 Dornier and 1 Defender aircraft, 4 helicopters and 32 boats; its strength was (1997) 8,500.
   Defence expenditure totalled US$87m. in 1997 (US$75 per capita).

INTERNATIONAL RELATIONS
Mauritius is a member of the UN, Commonwealth, OAU, La Francophonie, SADC and is an ACP member state of the ACP-EU relationship. Mauritius is also a founder member of the Indian Ocean Rim Association for Regional Co-operation.

ECONOMY
Performance. Real GDP growth was 4·1% in 1995 (4·8% in 1994).

Budget. Revenue and expenditure (in Rs 1m.) for years ending 30 June:

	1994–95	1995–96	1996–97	1997–98 (estimate)
Revenue	12,862	12,612	16,410	18,375
Expenditure	15,559	17,208	19,150	20,500

MAURITIUS

Principal sources of revenue, 1997–98 (Estimate): Direct taxes, Rs 3,662m.; indirect taxes, Rs 12,453m.; receipts from public utilities, Rs 277m.; receipts from public services, Rs 516,842m.; rental of government property, Rs 44m.; interest and royalties, Rs 1,248·7m.; reimbursement, Rs 173·6m. On 30 June 1997, the public debt of Mauritius was Rs 4,505m.

Currency. The unit of currency is the *Mauritius rupee* (MUR) of 100 *cents*. There are Bank of Mauritius notes, cupro-nickel coins, nickel-plated steel coins and copper-plated steel coins. The average annual inflation rate during the period 1990–96 was 6·5%. Foreign exchange reserves were US$604m. in Feb. 1998 and gold reserves were 60,000 troy oz. In Feb. 1998 total money supply was Rs 9,582m.

Banking and Finance. The Bank of Mauritius (founded 1967) is the central bank. The *Governor* is Mitrajeet Dhaneswar Maraye. There are 10 commercial banks. Non-bank financial intermediaries are the Post Office Savings Bank, the State Investment Corporation Ltd, the Mauritius Leasing Company, the National Mutual Fund, the National Investment Trust and the National Pension Fund. Other financial institutions are the Mauritius Housing Company and the Development Bank of Mauritius. There is also a stock exchange.

ENERGY AND NATURAL RESOURCES

Electricity. Installed capacity was 235,000 kW in 1991. Production (1996) was 2,173m. kWh. Consumption per capita in 1994 was 906 kWh.

Agriculture. In 1996 agriculture accounted for 10% of GDP. 75,000 ha were planted with sugar cane in 1998. There were 16 sugar mills, and sugar production (1998, in tonnes) was 640,000. Main secondary crops (1996, in tonnes): tea (1,109 ha) from which 2,497 were produced, tobacco 878, potatoes 10,639, and maize 438.

Livestock 1996: cattle, 12,525; goats, 12,955; and pigs, 15,925.

Livestock products (1996) in tonnes: beef, 2,321; pork, 1,112; goat meat and mutton, 140.

Forestry. The total forest area was 12,000 ha in 1995 (5·9% of the land area). In 1995 production totalled 21,000 cu. metres of timber, poles and fuel wood.

Fisheries. The catch in 1996 totalled 11,010 tonnes, almost exclusively sea fish.

INDUSTRY

Manufacturing includes: textile products, footwear and other leather products, diamond cutting, jewellery, furniture, watches and watchstraps, sunglasses, plastic ware, chemical products, electronic products, pharmaceutical products, electrical appliances, ship models and canned food.

Labour. In 1996, the labour force was estimated at 492,800. Manufacturing employed the largest proportion, with 27·9% of total employment; community, social and personal services, 26%; agriculture and fishing, 13·6%; trade, restaurants and hotels, 15·6%. The unemployment rate was estimated at 5·5% (provisional).

Trade Unions. In 1996 there were 330 registered trade unions with a total membership of about 110,000.

INTERNATIONAL TRADE
External debt was US$1,818m. in 1996.

Imports and Exports. Total trade (in Rs 1m.) for calendar years:

	1994	1995	1996 (provisional)
Imports c.i.f	34,548	34,363	40,892
Exports f.o.b.	24,097	27,326	31,991

In 1996, Rs 4,554m. of the imports came from France, Rs 4,893m. from the Republic of South Africa, Rs 2,648m. from the UK, and Rs 1,1811m. from Australia. In 1996, Rs 10,799m. of the exports went to the UK, Rs 6,109m. to France, Rs 4,092m. to the USA, and Rs 1,748m. to Germany.

Sugar exports in 1996 were 612,000 tonnes, Rs 8,024m. Other major exports (1996) included articles of apparel and clothing, Rs 270m.; chemicals and related

MAURITIUS

products, Rs 159m.; cut flowers and foliage, Rs 126m. Major imports included (1996) manufactured goods (paper, textiles, iron and steel), Rs 13,715m.; machinery and transport equipment, Rs 8,917m.; food and live animals, Rs 5,922m.

COMMUNICATIONS

Roads. In 1996 there were 31 km of motorway, 902 km of main roads, 966 km of secondary and other roads. At 31 Dec. 1996, there were 45,563 cars, 2,348 buses, 22,229 motor cycles, 79,524 auto cycles, and 20,482 trucks and vans.

Civil Aviation. In 1996, 630,240 passengers arrived at Sir Seewoosagur Ramgoolam International Airport and 16,856 tonnes of freight were unloaded. The national carrier is Air Mauritius, which is partly state-owned. In 1998 services were also provided by Aeroflot, Air Austral, Air Europe, Air France, Air India, Air Madagascar, Air Mauritius, Air Seychelles, Air Zimbabwe, Alitalia, Austrian Airlines, British Airways, Condor Flugdienst, Singapore Airlines and South African Airways.

Shipping. A free port was established at Port Louis in September 1991. In 1995 merchant shipping totalled 238,000 GRT. In 1996, 1,300 vessels entered Port Louis with a total gross registered tonnage of 5m tonnes.

Telecommunications. In 1997 there were 222,700 main telephone lines, equivalent to 195·2 per 1,000 population. Mauritius Telecom, formed in 1992, provided telephone services to 183,902 subscribers in 1996 through 58 exchanges. There were 23,000 cellular telephone subscribers in 1996. Communication with other parts of the world is by satellite and microwave links. In 1995 there were 36,000 PCs and 20,000 fax machines. There were around 1,000 Internet users in Jan. 1998.

Postal Services. In 1995 there were 103 post offices.

SOCIAL INSTITUTIONS

Justice. There is an Ombudsman. The death penalty was abolished in 1995.

Religion. At the 1990 Census (excluding Rodrigues) there were 287,726 Roman Catholics, 4,399 Protestants, 530,456 Hindus and 172,047 Moslems.

Education. The adult literacy rate in 1995 was 82·9% (87·1% among males and 78·8% among females). Primary and secondary education is free, primary education being compulsory. About 91% of children aged 5-11 years attend schools. In 1996 there were 119,655 pupils in 269 primary schools and 90,120 pupils in 127 secondary schools in the island of Mauritius, and 4,934 pupils in 12 primary schools and 2,917 in 3 secondary schools in Rodrigues. In 1996, 3,061 teachers were enrolled for training at the Mauritius Institute of Education.

In 1997-98 there were 3,462 students and 193 academic staff at the University of Mauritius.

Health. In 1996 (provisional) there were 1,008 doctors, 15 hospitals with 3,420 beds, 156 health centres and 12 private clinics with about 300 beds.

CULTURE

Broadcasting. Broadcasting is run by the commercial Mauritius Broadcasting Corporation. At 31 Dec 1996 there were 172,080 television sets (colour by SECAM) and 300,000 radio sets.

Cinema. In 1997 there were 25 cinemas, with a seating capacity of about 25,000.

Press. There are (1997) 7 daily papers in French (with occasional articles in English) with a combined circulation of about 100,000.

Tourism. In 1998 there were 500,000 who contributed 5% of GDP.

DIPLOMATIC REPRESENTATIVES
Of Mauritius in Great Britain (32/33 Elvaston Pl., London, SW7 5NW)
High Commissioner: Sir Satcam Boolell, QC.

Of Great Britain in Mauritius (Les Cascades Bldg., Edith Cavell St., Port Louis)
High Commissioner: James Daly, CVO.

Of Mauritius in the USA (4301 Connecticut Ave., NW, Washington, D.C., 20008)
Ambassador: Chitmansing Jesseramsing.

Of the USA in Mauritius (Rogers Hse., John Kennedy St., Port Louis)
Ambassador: H. W. Geisel.

Of Mauritius to the United Nations
Ambassador: Taye Wah Michel Wan Chat Kwong.

Of Mauritius to the European Union
Ambassador: Parrwiz Hossen.

FURTHER READING

Central Statistical Information Office. *Bi-annual Digest of Statistics.*
Bennett, P. R., *Mauritius.* [Bibliography] Oxford and Santa Barbara (CA), 1992
Bowman, L. W., *Mauritius: Democracy and Development in the Indian Ocean.* Aldershot, 1991
Mathur, H., *Parliament in Mauritius.* Rose Hill, 1991

National statistical office: Central Statistical Information Office, Rose Hill.

MEXICO

Estados Unidos Mexicanos
(United States of Mexico)

Capital: Mexico City
Population estimate, 2000: 98·88m.
GNP per capita: (PPP$) 7,660
HDI/world rank: 0·855/49

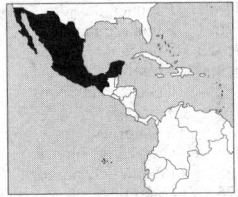

KEY HISTORICAL EVENTS

Mexico's history falls into four epochs: the era of the Indian empires (before 1521), the Spanish colonial phase (1521–1810), the period of national formation (1810–1910), which includes the war of independence (1810–21) and the long presidency of Porfirio Díaz (1876–80, 1884–1911), and the present period which began with the social revolution of 1910–21.

Mexico was conquered for Spain by Cortés in 1521 and became part of the viceroyalty of New Spain. The fight for independence starting in 1810 was eventually achieved in 1821. A substantial part of Mexico's territory (including the present state of California) was lost to the USA by the Mexican War of 1846–48. In the 1860s France, Britain and the USA declared war on Mexico; France invaded the country and declared Maximilian, Archduke of Austria, to be Emperor. When the French withdrew in 1867, Maximilian was executed by the Mexicans. The leader of the opposition to the French, Benito Juárez, again became president. In 1876 began the long presidency of Porfirio Diaz (1876–80, 1884–1911) who established himself as a dictator.

The latest period of Mexican history—regarded as one of social and national consolidation—began with the social revolution of 1910-21 led by Francisco Madero. The constitution of 1917 established a representative, democratic and federal republic, comprising 31 states and a federal district. There is a complete separation of legislative, executive and judicial powers. The president, who is the supreme executive authority, is directly elected for a single 6-year term. Women were enfranchised in 1958.

Despite democratic elections, the PRI (Partido Revolucionario Institucional) has been in power for 60 years; in 1982 the PRI won all 64 seats in the Senate, and in 1985, 289 of the 300 single-member seats in the Chamber of Deputies. The chief opposition party, PAN (Partido de Acción Nacional), has caused civil disturbances, claiming illegalities in the elections.

In recent years Mexico has been beset by financial crises which have taken the shine off an otherwise booming economy. In 1994–95 the government stepped in to save the banking system by buying in bad loans of up to 552bn. pesos. It is estimated that no more than 30% of the debt is ever likely to be recovered.

TERRITORY AND POPULATION

Mexico is bounded in the north by the USA, west and south by the Pacific Ocean, south-east by Guatemala, Belize and the Caribbean Sea, and north-east by the Gulf of Mexico. It comprises 1,967,183 sq. km (759,529 sq. miles), including uninhabited islands (5,073 sq. km) offshore.

Population at recent censuses: 1970, 48,225,288; 1980, 66,846,833; 1990, 81,249,645. Estimate, 1995, 91,158,290; 46,257,791 (females). 1997 est., 95·5m.; density, 49 per sq. km.

The UN gives a projected population for 2000 of 98·88m.

An estimated 73·4% of the population were urban in 1995.

Area, population and capitals of the Federal District and 31 states:

	Area (Sq. km)	Population (1990 census)	Population (1995 counting)	Capital
Federal District	1,499	8,235,744	8,489,007	Mexico City
Aguascalientes	5,589	719,659	862,720	Aguascalientes
Baja California	70,113	1,660,855	2,112,140	Mexicali
Baja California Sur	73,677	317,764	375,494	La Paz
Campeche	51,833	535,185	642,516	Campeche
Coahuila	151,571	1,972,340	2,173,775	Saltillo
Colima	5,455	428,510	488,028	Colima

	Area (Sq. km)	Population (1990 census)	Population (1995 counting)	Capital
Chiapas	73,887	3,210,496	3,584,786	Tuxtla Gutiérrez
Chihuahua	247,087	2,441,873	2,793,537	Chihuahua
Durango	119,648	1,349,378	1,431,748	Victoria de Durango
Guanajuato	30,589	3,982,593	4,406,568	Guanajuato
Guerrero	63,794	2,620,637	2,916,567	Chilpancingo
Hidalgo	20,987	1,888,366	2,112,473	Pachuca de Soto
Jalisco	80,137	5,302,689	5,991,176	Guadalajara
México	21,461	9,815,795	11,707,964	Toluca de Lerdo
Michoacán	59,864	3,548,199	3,870,604	Morelia
Morelos	4,941	1,195,059	1,442,662	Cuernavaca
Nayarit	27,621	824,643	896,702	Tepic
Nuevo Léon	64,555	3,098,736	3,550,114	Monterrey
Oaxaca	95,364	3,019,560	3,228,895	Oaxaca de Juárez
Puebla	33,919	4,126,101	4,624,365	Puebla de Zaragoza
Querétaro	11,769	1,051,235	1,250,476	Querétaro
Quintana Roo	50,350	493,277	703,536	Chetumal
San Luis Potosí	62,848	2,003,187	2,200,763	San Luis Potosí
Sinaloa	58,092	2,204,054	2,425,675	Culiacán Rosales
Sonora	184,934	1,823,606	2,085,536	Hermosillo
Tabasco	24,661	1,501,744	1,748,769	Villahermosa
Tamaulipas	79,829	2,249,581	2,527,328	Ciudad Victoria
Tlaxcala	3,914	761,277	883,924	Tlaxcala
Veracruz	72,815	6,228,239	6,737,324	Jalapa Enríquez
Yucatán	39,340	1,362,940	1,556,622	Mérida
Zacatecas	75,040	1,276,323	1,336,496	Zacatecas

At the 1980 census 33,039,307 were males, 33,807,526 females. The official language is Spanish, the mother tongue of over 92% of the population, but there are some indigenous language groups (of which Náhuatl, Maya, Zapotec, Otomi and Mixtec are the most important) spoken by 5,282,347 persons over 5 years of age (1990 census).

The populations (1995 Census) of the largest cities (150,000 and more) were:

Mexico City[1]	16,674,160	Morelia[1]	578,061	Poza Rica[1]	273,148
Guadalajara[1]	3,461,819	Orizaba[1]	567,185	Monclova[1]	253,585
Monterrey[1]	3,022,268	Veracruz[1]	560,200	Uruapán	250,794
Puebla[1]	1,561,558	Hermosillo	559,154	Pachuca[1]	249,036
Léon[1]	1,174,180	Villahermosa[1]	533,598	Tapachula	244,855
Toluca de Lerdo[1]	1,080,081	Durango	464,566	Victoria	243,960
Ciudad Juárez[1]	1,011,786	Irapuato	412,639	Carmen	233,423
Tijuana	991,592	Oaxaca[1]	394,068	La Piedad[1]	229,716
Torreón[1]	870,651	Tuxtla Gutierrez	386,135	Zacatecas	226,265
San Luis Potosí[1]	781,964	Xalapa[1]	370,430	Salamanca	221,125
Mérida[1]	779,648	Matamoros	363,487	Zamora[1]	214,938
Tampico-Cd. Madera[1]	718,906	Mazatlan	357,619	Cuautla[1]	207,267
Culiacán Rosales	696,262	Celaya	354,473	Campeche	204,533
Mexicali	696,034	Cajeme	345,222	Chetumal	202,046
Acapulco de Juárez	687,292	Reynosa	337,053	Tehuacan	190,468
Querétaro[1]	679,757	Tlaxcala[1]	336,637	Colima[1]	187,081
Cuernavaca[1]	672,307	Ensenada	315,289	La Paz	182,418
Aguascalientes[1]	637,303	Cancun	311,696	Fresnillo	176,885
Chihuahua[1]	627,662	Cardenas	302,508	Chilpancingo	170,368
Ahome[1]	604,679	Tepic	292,780	Lazaro Cardenas	155,366
Coatzacoalcos[1]	593,888	Nuevo Laredo	275,060	San Juan del Rio	154,922
Saltillo[1]	583,326				

[1]Metropolitan Area.

SOCIAL STATISTICS
Statistics for calendar years:

	Births	Deaths	Marriages	Divorces
1993	2,839,686	416,335	659,567	32,483
1994	2,904,389	419,074	671,640	35,029
1995	2,750,444	430,278	658,114	37,455

Rates per 1,000 population, 1995: Births, 30·2; deaths, 4·7. In 1996 the most popular age range for marrying was 20–24 for both males and females. Infant mortality was 36 per 1,000 live births in 1996. Life expectancy at birth over the period 1990–95 was 68·5 years for males and 74·5 years for females. Annual growth rate, 1990–95, 1·8%. Fertility rate, 1990–95, 3·1 births per woman.

CLIMATE
Latitude and relief produce a variety of climates. Arid and semi-arid conditions are found in the north, with extreme temperatures, whereas in the south there is a humid tropical climate, with temperatures varying with altitude. Conditions on the shores of the Gulf of Mexico are very warm and humid. In general, the rainy season lasts from May to Nov. Mexico City, Jan. 55°F (12·6°C), July 61°F (16·1°C). Annual rainfall 30" (747 mm). Guadalajara, Jan. 59°F (15·2°C), July 69°F (20·5°C). Annual rainfall 36" (902 mm). La Paz, Jan. 64°F (17·8°C), July 85°F (29·4°C). Annual rainfall 6" (145 mm). Mazatlán, Jan. 66°F (18·9°C), July 82°F (27·8°C). Annual rainfall 33" (828 mm). Mérida, Jan. 72°F (22·2°C), July 83°F (28·3°C). Annual rainfall 38" (957 mm). Monterrey, Jan. 58°F (14·4°C), July 81°F (27·2°C). Annual rainfall 23" (588 mm). Puebla de Zaragoza, Jan. 54°F (12·2°C), July 63°F (17·2°C). Annual rainfall 34" (850 mm).

CONSTITUTION AND GOVERNMENT
A new Constitution was promulgated on 5 Feb. 1917 and has been amended from time to time. Mexico is a representative, democratic and federal republic, comprising 31 states and a federal district, each state being free and sovereign in all internal affairs, but united in a federation established according to the principles of the Fundamental Law. The head of state and supreme executive authority is the *President*, directly elected for a non-renewable 6-year term.

There is complete separation of legislative, executive and judicial powers (Art. 49). Legislative power is vested in a General Congress of 2 chambers, a *Chamber of Deputies* and a *Senate*. The Chamber of Deputies consists of 500 members directly elected for 3 years, 300 of them from single-member constituencies and 200 chosen under a system of proportional representation. In 1990 Congress voted a new Electoral Code. This establishes a body to organize elections (IFE), an electoral court (TFE) to resolve disputes, new electoral rolls and introduce a voter's registration card. Priests were enfranchised in 1991.

The Senate comprises 128 members, 4 from each state and 4 from the federal district, directly elected for 6 years. Members of both chambers are not immediately re-eligible for election. Congress sits from 1 Sept. to 31 Dec. each year; during the recess there is a permanent committee of 15 deputies and 14 senators appointed by the respective chambers.

National Anthem. 'Mexicanos, al grito de guerra' ('Mexicans, at the war-cry'); words by F. González Bocanegra, tune by Jaime Nunó.

RECENT ELECTIONS
At the presidential and parliamentary elections of Aug. 1994 the electorate was 45·7m. Ernesto Zedillo was elected President by 48·77% of votes cast against 2 opponents. In the Chamber of Deputies 277 of the single-member seats were won by the Institutional Revolutionary Party (PRI) and 27 by proportional representation (PR); 18 by the Party of National Action (PAN) and 101 by PR; 5 by the Revolutionary Democratic Party (PRD) and 66 by PR; and 10 by the Workers' Party (PT), all by PR. At the mid-term elections of Aug. 1991 for 300 electoral districts, 32 Senate seats and 6 governorships, the PRI gained 61·4% of votes cast and won 290 Congress seats, 31 Senate seats and all 6 governorships. PAN gained 17·7% of votes cast, and the Party of Democratic Revolution, 8·3%.

Elections were held on 6 July 1997 for the Chamber of Deputies, 32 members of the Senate, 6 State Governors and the Mayor of Mexico City. In the Chamber of Deputies PRI gained 239 seats, PRD 125, PAN 122, the Ecology Party 8 and the Labour Party 6. Following the election the composition of the Senate was: PRI, 77 seats; PAN, 33; PRD, 13. The PRI gained 4 State Governorships and the PAN 2. This was the first time the PRI had lost its overall majority in the lower house.

After the elections of Aug. 1994, the party composition of the Senate was: PRI, 95; PAN, 25; PRD, 8. The PRI won 60 seats and the FDN 4 seats.

CURRENT ADMINISTRATION

President: Ernesto Zedillo Ponce de León (b. 1952; PRI; sworn in 1 Dec. 1994).

In March 1999 the government comprised:

Minister of Government: Francisco Labastida Ochoa. *Foreign Affairs:* Rosario Green. *Defence:* Gen. Enrique Cervantes Aguirre. *Naval Affairs:* Adm. José Ramón Lorenzo Franco. *Finance and Public Credit:* José Angel Gurría Treviño. *Social Development:* Esteban Moctezuma Barragan. *Comptroller-General:* Arsenio Farell Cubillas. *Energy:* Luis Téllez Kuenzler. *Trade and Industry:* Herminio Blanco Mendoza. *Agriculture, Rural Development and Livestock:* Romarico Arroyo Marroquin. *Communication and Transport:* Carlos Ruiz Sacristán. *Education:* Miguel Limón Rojas. *Health:* Dr. Juan Ramón de la Fuente Ramírez. *Labour and Social Welfare:* José Antonio González Fernandez. *Agrarian Reform:* Arturo Warman Gryj. *Tourism:* Oscar Espinosa Villarreal. *Fishing, Environment and Natural Resources:* Julia Caravias Lillo. *Attorney-General:* Jorge Madrazo Cuéllar. *Federal District Attorney of Justice:* Samuel del Villar Kretchmar. *Mexico City Mayor:* Cuauhtémoc Cárdenas Solórzano. *Private Secretary to the President:* David Melo Alvarado. *Head of the Co-ordination Office of the Presidency:* Roger Iván Recio. *Social Communication of the Presidency:* Fernando Lerdo de Tejada. *Presidential Chief of Staff:* Gen. Roberto Miranda. *Director of PEMEX:* Adrian Lajous. *Director of Federal Electricity Commission:* Rogelio Gasca Neri. *Director of Mexican Social Security Institute:* Genaro Borrego Estrada. *Director of the Institute of Security and Social Services for the State Workers:* Manuel Aguilera Gómez.

Local Government. Mexico is divided into 31 states and a Federal District. The latter is co-extensive with Mexico City and is administered by a Governor directly elected for a 6 year term. Each state has its own constitution, with the right to legislate and to levy taxes (but not inter-state customs duties); its Governor is directly elected for 6 years and its unicameral legislature for 3 years; judicial officers are appointed by the state governments. Mexico City is sub-divided into 16 districts and the 31 states into 2,428 municipalities.

DEFENCE

In 1997 defence expenditure totalled US$3,664m. (US$39 per capita).

Army. Enlistment into the regular army is voluntary, but there is also one year of conscription (4 hours per week) by lottery. The army consists of 36 zonal garrisons, 1 armoured, 1 motorized infantry, 2 infantry, 2 airborne and 1 Presidential Guard brigade, and air defence, engineer and support units. Equipment includes 50 M-8 light tanks and 110 armoured cars. Strength of the regular army (1996) 130,000 (60,000 conscripts).

Navy. The Navy is primarily equipped and organized for offshore and coastal patrol duties. It comprises 3 old ex-US destroyers, 2 modern and 2 old ex-US frigates, 10 modern offshore patrol vessels with small helicopter decks and hangars, and 29 older offshore ships, mostly ex-US. There are also 44 inshore patrol vessels and 20 small riverine patrol craft. There are 2 ex-US landing ships, and auxiliaries include 3 support tankers, 3 survey ships, 1 repair ship, 4 logistic support ships, 2 training ships, 6 tugs and 24 service craft.

The naval air force, 1,100 strong, operates 9 Aviocars for maritime patrol, 12 Bo-105 helicopters for service afloat, and 20 fixed wing and 12 helicopters for transport, training and liaison duties.

Naval personnel in 1997 totalled 37,000, including the naval air force and 8,500 marines comprising 1 airborne brigade and 21 regionally-based battalions.

Air Force. The Air Force had (1997) a strength of about 8,000 with over 90 combat aircraft and 25 armed helicopters, and has 4 operational groups, each with 1 or 2 squadrons. No. 1 Group comprises No. 209 Squadron with Bell 205A, 206B JetRanger, 212 and MD-530 helicopters as well as PC-6 Turbo-Porter transports, and No. 216 Squadron with MD-530 and S-70 helicopters. No. 2 Group has 2 Squadrons (Nos. 206 and 207) of Swiss-built Pilatus PC-7 Turbo-Trainers for light attack duty. No. 3 Group (203 and 204 Squadrons) also operates PC-7s; No. 4 Group (201 and 205 Squadrons) is equipped with PC-7s. No. 5 Group consists of No. 101 communications Squadron and a photo-reconnaissance unit, both equipped with Aero Commander 500S piston-engined light twins. Nos. 301 and 302 Squadrons, in No. 6 Group, operate a total of 9 turboprop-powered Lockheed C-130 Hercules and 6 C-118A piston-engined transports. The main combat Group, No. 7, comprises No. 401 Squadron with 11 F-5E Tiger II and F-5F 2-seat fighters, and No. 202 Squadron with AT-33A jet trainer/fighter-bombers. No. 8 Group has a variety of VIP transports and 2 S-70 helicopters. No. 9 Group operates the Air Force's remaining 10 C-47s in Nos. 311 and 312 transport Squadrons, and No. 208 Squadron with Arava transports. No. 10 Group comprises 3 squadrons (Nos. 210, 211 and 212) of T-33 trainers. No. 11 Group has 1 squadron (No. 214) with Bell 212 and MD-530 helicopters, and PC-6 Turbo-Porter transports. The Aviation College has Maute Mx-7 and Beech Bonanza trainers.

INTERNATIONAL RELATIONS
Mexico is a member of the UN (and most UN System organizations), OAS, APEC, WTO, NAFTA and OECD.

ECONOMY
Policy. An economic programme for 1995 aimed to reduce inflation and provided tax concessions to stimulate investment. After the peso was devalued in Dec. 1994 an emergency economic plan was introduced to include an agreement between labour and employers to contain inflation, a fiscal adjustment to reduce the current account deficit, further privatization of infrastructural enterprises and the establishment of an international assistance fund. In 1997 the economy grew by 7% and 800,000 new jobs were created. An economic programme to attack 'the roots of poverty' was announced.

Performance. Real GDP declined by 5·1% in 1996 (1995 showed a rate of –6·2%) but grew by 7% in 1997. An increase of around 5% was expected for 1998.

Budget. In 1996 revenue was 392,566m. new pesos; expenditure, 372,874m. new pesos.

Currency. The unit of currency is the *Mexican peso* (MXP) of 100 *centavos*. A new peso was introduced on 1 Jan. 1993: 1 new peso = 1,000 old pesos. The peso was devalued by 13·94% in Dec. 1994. Foreign exchange reserves were US$28,469m. in Feb. 1998 and gold reserves were 170,000 troy oz. The annual inflation rate for 1998 was 18·6%. Total money supply in Jan. 1998 was 261,132m. new pesos.

Banking and Finance. The Bank of Mexico, established 1 Sept. 1925, is the central bank of issue (*Governor*, Guillermo Ortiz). It gained autonomy over monetary policy in 1993. Exchange rate policy is determined jointly by the bank and the Finance Ministry. Banks were nationalized in 1982, but in May 1990 the government approved their reprivatization. The state continues to have a majority holding in foreign trade and rural development banks. Foreign holdings are limited to 30%. There were 23 banks in 1993; deposits were 4,500,000m. old pesos in 1992.

There is a stock exchange in Mexico City.

Weights and Measures. The metric system is legal.

ENERGY AND NATURAL RESOURCES
Electricity. Installed capacity, 1995, 32,737 MW. Output in 1996 was 145·7bn. kWh. Consumption per capita in 1995 was estimated to be 1,206 kWh.

Oil and Gas. Crude petroleum output was 2,858,000 bbls. a day in 1996. Mexico produced 4·9% of the world total oil output in 1996, and had reserves amounting to 48·8bn. bbls. in 1996. Natural gas, 1996, 4,195m. cu. ft.

Minerals. Output, (in 1,000 tonnes) 1996: Lead, 167·1; copper, 328·0; zinc, 348·3; gypsum, 3,758·9; silica, 1,424·8; fluorite, 524·66; iron, 6,109·5; sulphur, 921·3; manganese, 173·4; barite, 470·0; graphite, 40·4; silver, 2,536·1; gold, 24,083 kg; coal, 8,779·5; feldspar, 140·0.

Agriculture. In 1994 Mexico had 23·15m. ha of arable land, 1·58m. ha of permanent cropland and 74·5m. ha of permanent pasture. Agriculture provided 5% of GDP in 1996. Some 60% of agricultural land belongs to about 30,000 *ejidos* (with 15m. members), communal lands with each member farming his plot independently. *Ejidos* can now be inherited, sold or rented. A land-titling programme (PROCEDE) is establishing the boundaries of 4·6m. plots of land totalling 102m. ha. Other private farmers may not own more than 100 ha of irrigated land or an equivalent in unirrigated land. There is a theoretical legal minimum of 10 ha for holdings, but some 60% of private farms were less than 5 ha in 1990. Laws abolishing the *ejido* system were passed in 1992.

Sown areas, 1995 (in 1,000 ha) included: Maize, 9,082; beans, 2,367; sorghum, 1,592; wheat, 964; cotton-seed, 297; barley, 272; soya, 151; safflower, 107; rice, 90.

Production in 1995 (in 1,000 tonnes): Wheat, 3,468; rice (washed), 367; beans, 1,271; soya, 190; barley, 487; maize, 18,353; sorghum, 4,170; cotton-seed, 369; grapes, 550; apples, 427; oranges, 3,922; lemons, 961; mangoes, 1,088; pineapples, 229 (1994); bananas, 2,069; melons, 404; watermelons, 402; avocado pears, 787.

Livestock (1996): Cattle, 28·14m.; sheep, 5·9m.; pigs, 18m.; goats (1995), 10·5m.; horses, 6·25m.; mules, 3·28m.; assess, 3·25m.; chickens (1995), 288m. Meat production, 1994 (in 1,000 tonnes): Beef, 1,364·7; pork, 807·5; goat meat, 40·1; sheep meat, 31·4. Dairy production, 1995 (in tonnes): Milk, 7,537,647; eggs, 1,241,987; honey, 49,228; wool, 4,045.

Forestry. Forests extended over 55·39m. ha in 1995, representing 29% of the land area (down from 57·93m. ha in 1990), containing pine, spruce, cedar, mahogany, logwood and rosewood. There are 14 forest reserves (nearly 0·8m. ha) and 47 national park forests of 0·75m. ha. Timber production was 22·47m. cu. metres in 1995.

Fisheries. Total catch, 1996, 1,379,219 tonnes (approximately 89% sea fish).

INDUSTRY
In 1996 the manufacturing industry provided 18·7% of GDP. Output in 1996 (in 1,000 tonnes): Petrol, 16,975; cement, 28,168; crude iron, 6,109; crude steel, 5,867; aluminium, 95·8; copper, 328; lead, 167·1; zinc, 348·3; wheat flour, 1,835; butter, 34; passenger cars (units), 782,743; lorries, 429,843.

Labour. In 1996 the workforce was 24,063,283 (5,644,588 female). The daily minimum wage at the end of 1998 was 40 new pesos. Registered unemployment rate, 1998, 3·2% (1997, 4·3%).

Trade Unions. The Mexican Labour Congress (CTM) is incorporated into the Institutional Revolutionary Party, and is an umbrella organization numbering some 5m. An agreement, 'Alliance for Economic Recovery', was reached in Nov. 1995 between the government, trade unions and business, providing for an increase in the minimum wage of 10·1%, increased unemployment benefits, tax incentives, the staggering of price increases, and a commitment to reduce public spending. A breakaway from CTM took place in 1997 when rebel labour leaders set up the National Union of Workers (UNT) to combat what they saw as a sharp drop in real wages.

INTERNATIONAL TRADE
In Sept. 1991 Mexico signed the free trade Treaty of Santiago with Chile, envisaging an annual 10% tariffs reduction from Jan. 1992. The North American Free Trade Agreement (NAFTA), between Canada, Mexico and the USA, was signed on 7 Oct. 1992. A free trade agreement was signed with Costa Rica in March 1994. Some 8,300 products were freed from tariffs, with others to follow over 10 years. The Group of Three (G3) free trade pact with Colombia and Venezuela, came into effect 1 Jan. 1995. Total foreign debt was US$157,125m. in 1996—a figure exceeded only by Brazil.

Imports and Exports. Trade for calendar years in US$1m.:

	1994	1995	1996	1997	1998
Imports	79,346	72,453	89,469	78,814	91,852
Exports	60,882	79,542	96,030	80,716	86,671

Of total imports in 1996, 75·4% came from USA, 4·4% from Japan, 3·5% from Germany and 0·8% from UK.

Of total exports in 1997, 85% went to USA, 4·8% to Latin America, 2% to Canada, 1·1% to Japan, 1·0% to Spain, 0·6% to UK.

The in-bond (*maquiladora*) assembly plants along the US border generate the largest flow of foreign exchange with oil (11·2% of exports in 1996) and tourism.

COMMUNICATIONS

Roads. Total length, 1994, 307,142 km, of which 48,960 km were main roads, 57,364 km were secondary roads and 200,818 km by-roads. In 1994, 8,433,709 motor vehicles (8,080,419 private), 3,839,369 trucks, 105,390 buses and 264,650 motor cycles were registered.

Rail. The National Railway, *Ferrocarriles Nacionales de Mexico*, was split into 5 companies in 1996 as a preliminary to privatization. It comprises 20,445 km of 1,435 mm gauge (246 km electrified). In 1996 it carried 59·1m. tonnes of freight and 6m. passengers. There is a 178 km metro in Mexico City. There are light rail lines in Guadalajara (48 km) and Monterrey (35 km).

Civil Aviation. There is an international airport at Mexico City (Benito Juárez) and 49 other international and 33 national airports. Each of the larger states has a local airline which links it with main airports. The national carriers are Aeromexico, Mexicana, Taesa, Aerocalifornia and Aerolíneas Internacionales. In 1998 services were also provided by Aeroejecutivo, Aeroflot, Aerolíneas Argentinas, Aeroperú, Air France, Alitalia, America West Airlines, American Airlines, Austrian Airlines, Aviacsa, Avianca, Aviateca, British Airways, Canadian Airlines International, City Bird, Condor Flugdienst, Continental Airlines, COPA, Cubana, Delta Air Lines, Ecuatoriana, Iberia, JAL, KLM, LACSA, Lan-Chile, Lloyd Aéreo Boliviano, LTU International Airways, Lufthansa, Northwest Airlines, SAS, Servivensa, Swissair, Taca International Airlines, TAESA, Transportes Aeromar, United Airlines and Varig. In 1996 Mexico City handled 16,265,384 passengers (10,955,196 on domestic flights) and 114,080 tonnes of freight. Cancun was the second busiest airport for passengers in 1996, with 5,095,589 (3,718,318 on international flights) and Guadalajara the second busiest for freight, with 18,210 tonnes.

Shipping. Mexico has 49 ocean ports, of which, on the Gulf coast, the most important include Coatzacoalcos, Ciudad del Carmen (Campeche), Tampico, Veracruz and Tuxpan. On the Pacific Coast are Salina Cruz, Isla de Cedros, Guaymas, Santa Rosalia, Manzanillo, Lázaro Cárdenas and Mazatlán. It was announced in 1992 that ports would be privatized.

Merchant shipping loaded 139·5m. tonnes and unloaded 62m. tonnes of cargo in 1996. In 1995, the merchant marine had a total tonnage of 1·55m. GRT, including oil tankers, 0·71m. GRT, and container ships, 0·14m. GRT.

Telecommunications. Telmex, previously a state-controlled company, was privatized in 1991. It controls about 98% of all the telephone service. There were 9,253,700 telephone main lines in 1997, or 96 for every 1,000 persons. Cellular phone subscribers numbered 642,000 in 1995, and there were 2,400,000 PCs (26 per 1,000 population) and 180,000 fax machines. In Nov. 1997 there were approximately 370,000 Internet users.

Postal Services. There were 7,382 post offices in 1995, equivalent to 1 for every 12,300 persons.

SOCIAL INSTITUTIONS

Justice. Magistrates of the Supreme Court are appointed for 6 years by the President and confirmed by the Senate; they can be removed only on impeachment. The courts include the Supreme Court with 21 magistrates, 12 collegiate circuit courts with 3 judges each and 9 unitary circuit courts with 1 judge each, and 68 district courts with 1 judge each.

The penal code of 1 Jan. 1930 abolished the death penalty, except for the armed forces.

Religion. 93·5% of the population was Roman Catholic in 1992, with (1983) 3 cardinals, 12 archbishops and 87 bishops. The Church is separated from the State, and the constitution of 1917 provided strict regulation of this and all other religions. In Nov. 1991 Congress approved an amendment to the 1917 constitution permitting the recognition of churches by the state, the possession of property by churches and the enfranchisement of priests. Church buildings remain state property. Diplomatic relations with the Vatican were established in Sept. 1992. At the 1990 census there were also 4·9% Protestants, and 5·4% members of other religions. There were 783,000 Latter-day Saints (Mormons) in 1997.

Education. Adult literacy was 89·6% in 1995 (male, 91·8%; female, 87·4%). Primary and secondary education is free and compulsory, and secular, although religious instruction is permitted in private schools.

In 1996–97 there were:

	Establishments	Teachers	Students (in 1,000)
Pre-school	63,319	146,247	3,238·3
Primary	95,855	524,922	14,650·5
Secondary	24,402	275,331	4,809·3
Vocational training	4,710	27,543	498·8
Professional	1,900	36,131	383·8
Higher education	1,786	142,952	1,329·7
Postgraduate education	860	12,674	94·3

In 1994–95 in the public sector there were 36 universities, 1 technical institute and 3 specialized universities (1 agricultural; 2 pedagogical). In the private sector there were 48 universities, 1 institute of technical and higher educational studies, 1 women's university and 1 technical university.

In 1994 total expenditure on education came to 5·8% of GNP.

Health. In 1993 there were 1,539 hospitals, with a provision of 10 beds per 10,000 population. In 1994 there were 146,021 doctors, 5,612 government-employed dentists and 166,644 government-employed nurses.

Welfare. In 1997 there were 11·28m. workers insured as permanent beneficiaries with the Social Security Institute.

CULTURE

Broadcasting. There are over 1,500 stations licensed by the Dirección General de Concesiones y Permisos de Telecomunicaciones. Most carry the 'National Hour' programme. Television services are provided by the recently privatized Televisión Azteca and Azteca Televisa. In 1995 there were 24m. radio and 20m. TV sets (colour by NTSC).

Cinema. In 1995 there were 1,495 cinemas and 63m. admissions.

Press. In 1995 there were 310 daily newspapers with a circulation of 10,500,000, equivalent to 115 per 1,000 inhabitants.

Tourism. There were 19·3m. tourists in 1997, putting Mexico 8th in the world list; gross revenue, including border visitors, amounted to US$7,593m.

DIPLOMATIC REPRESENTATIVES
Of Mexico in Great Britain (42 Hertford Street, London, W1Y 7TF)
Ambassador: Santiago Oñate Laborde.

Of Great Britain in Mexico (Rio Lerma 71, Col. Cuauhtémoc, 06500 Mexico City, D.F.)
Ambassador: A. C. Thorpe, CMG.

Of Mexico in the USA (1911 Pennsylvania Ave., NW, Washington, D.C., 20006)
Ambassador: Jesús Reyes Heroles.

Of the USA in Mexico (Paseo de la Reforma 305, México City 5, D.F.)
Ambassador: Jeffrey Davidow.

Of Mexico to the United Nations
Ambassador: Manuel Tello.

Of Mexico to the European Union
Ambassador: Armendariz Etchegaray.

FURTHER READING

Instituto Nacional de Estadística, Geografía e Informática. *Anuario Estadístico de los Estados Unidos Mexicanos. Mexican Bulletin of Statistical Information.* Quarterly.

Aspe, P., *Economic Transformation: the Mexican Way.* Cambridge (MA), 1993
Bailey, J. J., *Governing Mexico: The Statecraft of Crisis Management.* London and New York, 1988
Bartra, R., *Agrarian Structure and Political Power in Mexico.* Johns Hopkins Univ. Press, 1993
Bazant, J., *A Concise History of Mexico.* CUP, 1977
Bethell, L. (ed.) *Mexico since Independence.* CUP, 1992
Camp, R. A., *Politics in Mexico.* 2nd ed. OUP, 1996
Grayson, G. W., *Oil and Mexican Foreign Policy.* Univ. of Pittsburgh Press, 1988
Hamilton, N. and Harding, T. F., (eds.) *Mexico: State, Economy and Social Conflict.* London, 1986
Krauze, E., *Mexico, Biography of Power: A History of Modern Mexico, 1810-1996.* London, 1997
Philip, G., (ed.) *Politics in Mexico.* London, 1985.—*The Presidency in Mexican Politics.* London, 1991.—*Mexico* [Bibliography]. 2nd ed. Oxford and Santa Barbara (CA), 1993
Riding, A., *Distant Neighbours.* London, 1985.—*Mexico: Inside the Volcano.* London, 1987
Robbins, N. C., *Mexico.* [Bibliography] Oxford and Santa Barbara (CA), 1984
Rodríguez, J. E., *The Evolution of the Mexican Political System.* New York, 1993
Ruíz, R. E., *Triumphs and Tragedy: a History of the Mexican People.* New York, 1992
Whiting, V. R., *The Political Economy of Foreign Investment in Mexico: Nationalism, Liberalism, Constraints on Choice.* Johns Hopkins Univ. Press, 1992

National statistical office: Instituto Nacional de Estadística, Geografía e Informática (INEGI), Aguascalientes.
Website: http://www.inegi.gob.mx/

MICRONESIA

Federated States of Micronesia

Capital: Palikir
Population estimate, 2000: 122,000
Estimated GDP: $205m.

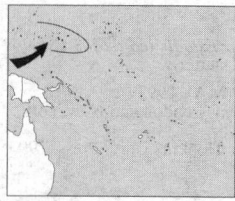

KEY HISTORICAL EVENTS

Spain acquired sovereignty over the Caroline Islands in 1886, but sold the archipelago to Germany in 1899. Japan occupied the Islands at the beginning of the First World War, and in 1921 they were mandated to Japan by the League of Nations. Captured by Allied Forces in the Second World War in 1944, the Islands became part of the UN Trust Territory of the Pacific Islands created on 18 July 1947 and administered by the USA. The Federated States of Micronesia came into being on 10 May 1979 comprising all of the Caroline Islands except the Belau (Palau) group. Its trusteeship was terminated on 3 Nov. 1986 by the UN Security Council and on the same day it entered into a 15-year Free Association with the USA. The UN recognized the termination of the Trusteeship Agreement on 22 Dec. 1990, and Micronesia became a full UN member state on 17 Sept. 1991.

TERRITORY AND POPULATION

The Federated States lie in the North Pacific Ocean between 137° and 163° E, comprising 607 islands with a total land area of 702 sq. km (271 sq. miles). The population (1994 census) was 104,724; 1997 estimate, 127,600; density, 181 per sq. km.

In 2000 the population is projected to be 122,000.

In 1995 an estimated 72·3% of the population lived in rural areas.

The areas and populations of the 4 major groups of island states (east to west) are as follows:

State	Area (sq. km)	Population (1994 census)	Headquarters
Kosrae	109	7,354	Tofol
Pohnpei	344	33,372	Kolonia
Chuuk	127	52,870	Weno
Yap	119	11,128	Colonia

Kosrae
consists of a single island. Its main town is Lelu (2,422 inhabitants in 1989).
Pohnpei
comprises a single island (covering 334 sq. km with 30,000 inhabitants in 1994) and 8 scattered coral atolls. Kolonia (6,169 inhabitants in 1989) was the national capital of the Federated States. The new capital, Palikir, lies approximately 10 km southwest in the Palikir valley.
Chuuk
consists of a group of 14 islands within a large reef-fringed lagoon (44,000 inhabitants in 1994); the state also includes 12 coral atolls (8,000 inhabitants), the most important being the Mortlock Islands. The chief town is Weno (15,253 inhabitants in 1989).
Yap
comprises a main group of 4 islands (covering 100 sq. km with 7,000 inhabitants in 1994) and 13 coral atolls (4,000 inhabitants), the main ones being Ulithi and Woleai. Colonia is its chief town (3,456 inhabitants in 1989).

English is used in schools and is the official language. Trukese, Pohnpeian, Yapese and Kosrean are also spoken.

SOCIAL STATISTICS

1997 births, estimate, 3,500; deaths, 800. 1997 rates, estimate: Birth rate, 27·7 per 1,000 population; death rate, 6·1 per 1,000; infant mortality rate, 35·1 per 1,000 live births. 1997 life expectancy, 68·2 years. Annual growth rate, 1990–95, 1·0%.

CLIMATE
Tropical, with heavy year-round rainfall, especially in the eastern islands, and occasional typhoons (June-Dec.). Kolonia, Jan. 80°F (26·7°C), July 79°F (26·1°C). Annual rainfall 194" (4,859 mm).

CONSTITUTION AND GOVERNMENT
Under the Constitution founded on 10 May 1979, there is an executive presidency and a 14-member National Congress, comprising 10 members elected for 2-year terms from single-member constituencies of similar electorates, and 4 members elected one from each State for a 4-year term. The Federal President and Vice-President first run for the Congress before they are elected by members of Congress for a 4-year term.

RECENT ELECTIONS
The last election was held on 11 May 1995.

CURRENT ADMINISTRATION
President: Jacob Nena (app. May 1997).
Vice-President: Leo A. Falcam.
In March 1999 the government comprised:
Minister of Foreign Affairs: Epel K. Ilon. *Finance and Administration:* John Ehsa. *Health, Education and Social Affairs:* Dr Eliuel K. Pretrick. *Economic Affairs:* Sebastian Anefal. *Justice:* Emilio Musrasrik. *Transportation, Communications and Infrastructure:* Lukner Weilbacher. *Public Defender:* Joseph Phillip. *Postmaster-General:* Bethwell Henry.
Speaker of the Congress: Jack Fritz.

Local Government. Each State has an executive branch headed by a Governor and a unicameral State Legislature (except Chuuk which has a bicameral legislature), all directly elected for a 4-year term.

INTERNATIONAL RELATIONS
Micronesia is a member of the UN, Pacific Community (formerly the South Pacific Commission) and the South Pacific Forum.

ECONOMY
Policy. The modern sector of the economy consists of a small private sector supported by public service incomes and demand. The traditional sector is based on subsistence farming and fishing.

Performance. Real GDP growth was 2·8% in 1995 (–0·4% in 1994).

Budget. US compact funds are an annual US$100m. Revenue (1995/96 estimate), US$58m.; expenditure, US$52m.

Currency. US currency is used.

Banking and Finance. 3 commercial banks; Bank of Guam, Bank of Hawaii and Bank of the Federated States of Micronesia. There is also a Federated States of Micronesia Development Bank.

ENERGY AND NATURAL RESOURCES
Electricity. Capacity (1995), 38,500 kW.

Minerals. The islands have few mineral deposits except for high-grade phosphates.

Agriculture. Agriculture consists mainly of subsistence farming: coconuts, breadfruit, bananas, sweet potatoes and cassava. A small amount of crops are produced for export, including copra, tropical fruits, peppers and taro. Pigs and chickens constitute the main livestock.

Fisheries. In 1995 the catch amounted to approximately 21,150 tonnes, almost entirely from marine waters. Fishing licence fees were US$20m. in 1993 and are a primary revenue source.

INDUSTRY

The chief industries are construction, fish processing, tourism and handicrafts (items from shell, wood and pearl).

Labour. Two-thirds of the labour force are government employees. In 1990, 12,720 people worked in agriculture, fisheries and forestry out of a total labour force of 30,640. Unemployment was 13·5%.

INTERNATIONAL TRADE

Imports and Exports. Total exports (1994 est.), US$29·1m.; imports, US$141·1m. Main import suppliers, 1994: USA, 32·9%; Japan, 32·0%; Guam, 23·2%. Main export markets, 1994: Japan, 72·7%; Guam, 5·1%; USA, 3·5%. The main exports are copra, bananas, black pepper, fish and garments. Main imports: foodstuffs and beverages, manufactured goods, machinery and equipment.

COMMUNICATIONS

Roads. In 1995 there were 235 km of roads (41 km paved).

Civil Aviation. There are international airports on Pohnpei, Chuuk, Yap and Kosrae. Services are provided by Air Nauru and Continental Airlines. In 1998 there were international flights to Guam, Honolulu, Johnston Island, Manila and the Marshall Islands in addition to domestic services. There were 5 airports in 1996 (4 paved).

Shipping. The main ports are Kolonia (Pohnpei), Colonia (Yap), Lepukos (Chuuk), Okat and Lelu (Kosrae).

Telecommunications. Micronesia had 8,400 main telephone lines in 1997, or 75·8 per 1,000 population. There were 300 fax machines in 1995. The islands are interconnected by shortwave radiotelephone. There are 4 earth stations linked to the Intelsat satellite system.

Postal Services. All 4 states have postal services.

SOCIAL INSTITUTIONS

Justice. There is a Supreme Court headed by the Chief Justice with 2 other judges, and a State Court in each of the 4 states with 13 judges in total.

Religion. Predominantly Christian. Yap is mainly Roman Catholic; Protestantism is prevalent elsewhere.

Education. In 1987 there were 25,139 pupils in 177 primary schools, with 1,051 teachers; 5,385 pupils in 17 high schools, with 314 teachers; and 861 students (1986) at the College of Micronesia in Pohnpei. The Micronesia Maritime and Fisheries Academy in Yap (est. 1990) provides education and training in fisheries technology at secondary and tertiary levels.

Health. In 1994 there were 45 doctors, and in 1993, 7 dentists, 7 pharmacists, 230 nurses and 4 hospitals with 325 beds.

CULTURE

Broadcasting. There were 5 radio and 6 TV stations, and 22,000 radio and 19,800 TV sets in 1996.

Tourism. In 1990 there were 20,475 visitors.

DIPLOMATIC REPRESENTATIVES

Of Great Britain in Micronesia (resides in the Fiji Islands)
Ambassador: Vernon M. Scarborough.

Of Micronesia in the USA (1725 N St., NW, Washington, D.C., 20036)
Ambassador: Jesse B. Marehalau.

Of the USA in Micronesia (POB 1286, Kolonia, Pohnpei)
Chargé d'Affaires: Ann Wright.

Of Micronesia to the United Nations
Ambassador: Masao Nakayama.

FURTHER READING

Kluge, P. F., *The Edge of Paradise: America in Micronesia.* New York, 1991
Wuerch, W. L. and Ballendorf, D. A., *Historical Dictionary of Guam and Micronesia.* Metuchen (NJ), 1995

MOLDOVA

Republica Moldova

Capital: Chişinău
Population estimate, 2000: 4·46m.
GNP per capita: (PPP$) 1,440
HDI/world rank: 0·610/113

KEY HISTORICAL EVENTS

The Moldavian SSR (in 1990 renamed Moldova) was formed by the union of part of the former Moldavian ASSR (organized 12 Oct. 1924), formerly included in the Ukrainian SSR, and the areas of Bessarabia (ceded by Romania to the USSR, 28 June 1940) with a mainly Moldovan population. As from 2 Aug. 1940 the Moldavian SSR included the following regions of the former Moldavian ASSR: Grigoriopol, Dubasari, Camenca, Rybnitsa, Slobozia and Tiraspol, and the following districts of Bessarabia: Beltsi, Bender (Tighina), Chişinău (*then* Kishinev), Cahul, Orhey and Soroca. In Dec. 1991 Moldova became a member of the CIS, a decision ratified by parliament in April 1994. Fighting took place in 1992 between government forces and separatists in the (largely Russian and Ukrainian) area east of the River Nistru (Transnistria).

An agreement signed by the presidents of Moldova and Russia on 21 July 1992 brought to an end the armed conflict and established a 'security zone' controlled by the 'peace-keeping forces' formed by military from Russia, Moldova and Transnistria. On 21 Oct. 1994, a Moldo-Russian agreement was signed in compliance with which the Russian Federation was obliged to withdraw its troops (former 14th Soviet army) from the territory of Moldova over 3 years but the agreement was not ratified by the State Russian Duma. On 8 May 1997, an agreement between Transnistria and the Moldovan government to end the separatist conflict was signed in Moscow, brokered by the presidents of Russia and Ukraine, and stipulated that Transnistria would remain part of Moldova as it was territorially constituted in Jan. 1990. In 1997 some 7,000 Russian troops were stationed in Transnistria.

TERRITORY AND POPULATION

Moldova is bounded in the east and south by Ukraine and on the west by Romania. The area is 33,700 sq. km (13,000 sq. miles). In Jan. 1994 the population was 4,353,000 (52·3% female).

The UN gives a projected population for 2000 of 4·46m.

In 1995 an estimated 51·6% of the population lived in urban areas. The 1989 census population was 4,335,360, of whom Moldovans accounted for 64·5%, Ukrainians 13·9%, Russians 13%, Gagauzi 3·5%, Bulgarians 2% and Jews 1·5%.

Apart from Chişinău, the capital (0·7m. population in 1994), larger towns are Tiraspol (186,000), Beltsy (161,000) and Bender (133,000). The official Moldovan language (i.e. Romanian) was written in Cyrillic prior to the restoration of the Roman alphabet in 1989. It is spoken by 75% of the population; the use of other languages (Russian, Gagauz) is safeguarded by the Constitution.

SOCIAL STATISTICS

1998 estimates: Births, 64,000; deaths, 55,000. Rates, 1998 estimates (per 1,000 population): Births, 14·3; deaths, 12·4. In 1994 the most popular age range for marrying was 20–24 for both males and females. Life expectancy at birth over the period 1990–95 was 63·5 years for males and 71·5 years for females. Infant mortality, 1990–95, 26 per 1,000 live births; fertility rate, 2·2 births per woman.

CLIMATE

The climate is temperate, with warm summers, crisp, sunny autumns and cold winters with snow. Chişinău, Jan. –7°C, Jul. 20°C. Annual rainfall 677 mm.

CONSTITUTION AND GOVERNMENT

A declaration of republican sovereignty was adopted in June 1990 and in Aug. 1991 the republic declared itself independent. A new Constitution came into effect on 27

MOLDOVA

Aug. 1994, which defines Moldova as an 'independent, democratic and unitary state'. At a referendum on 6 March 1994 turn-out was 75·1%; 95·4% of votes cast favoured 'an independent Moldova within its 1990 borders'. The referendum (and the Feb. parliamentary elections) were not held by the authorities in Transnistria.

Parliament has 104 seats and is elected for 4-year terms. There is a 4% threshold for election; votes falling below this are re-distributed to successful parties. The *President* is elected for 4-year terms.

The 1994 Constitution makes provision for the autonomy of Transnistria and the Gagauz (Gagauzi Yeri) region.

Transnistria. In the predominantly Russian-speaking areas of Transnistria a self-styled republic was established in Sept. 1991, and approved by a local referendum in Dec. 1991. A Russo-Moldovan agreement of 21 July 1992 provided for a special statute for Transnistria and a guarantee of self-determination should Moldova unite with Romania. The population in 1995 was 0·72m. Romanian here is still written in the Cyrillic alphabet. At a referendum on 24 Dec. 1995, 81% of votes cast were in favour of adopting a new constitution proclaiming independence.

On 17 June 1996 the Moldovan government granted Transnistria a special status as 'a state-territorial formation in the form of a republic within Moldova's internationally recognized border'.

Elections for chief regional executive were held on 22 Dec. 1996. The electorate was 428,000; turn-out was 57·3%. Igor Smirnov (b. 1941) was re-elected for a further 5-year term against 1 opponent by 71·9% of votes cast.

Gagauz Yeri. This was created an autonomous territorial unit by Moldovan legislation of 13 Jan. 1995. In 1995 the population was 153,000. There is a 35-member *Popular Assembly* directly elected for 4-year terms and headed by a *Governor*, who is a member of the Moldovan cabinet. At the elections of 28 May and 11 June 1995 turn-out was 68%.

Governor: Gheorghi Tabunshchik (b. 1939).

National Anthem. The Romanian anthem was replaced in Aug. 1994 by a traditional tune, 'Lîmbă noastră' ('Our Language').

RECENT ELECTIONS

At the parliamentary elections held on 22 March 1998 the PCM (Communists) won 40 seats with 30·1% of the votes and the CDM (nationalists) 26 with 19·2%. 24 seats went to the PMDP and 11 to the PFD.

Presidential elections were held on 17 Nov. 1996. President Snegur won the first round with 38·24% of votes cast. A run-off round was held on 1 Dec. 1996 between President Snegur and the Speaker, Petru Lucinschi. Turn-out was 72%. Lucinschi was elected by 54% of votes cast.

CURRENT ADMINISTRATION

President: Petru Lucinschi (ind; elected 1 Dec. 1996).

In March 1999 the government comprised:

Prime Minister: Ion Sturza.

Deputy First Prime Minister: Nicolae Andronic. *Deputy Prime Ministers:* Valentin Dolganiuc, Alexander Muravschi (also *Economy and Reform*), Oleg Stratulat. *Minister of Agriculture, Food Industry and Forestry:* Bulgari Valeriu. *Culture:* Ghenadie Ciobanu. *Defence:* Valeriu Pasat. *Education and Sciences:* Anatol Grimalschi. *Finance:* Anatol Arapu. *Foreign Affairs:* Nicolae Tabacaru. *Health:* Eugen Gladun. *Industry and Trade:* Georgi Cucu. *Internal Affairs:* Victor Catan. *Justice:* Ion Paduraru. *Labour, Social Protection and Family:* Vladimir Guritenco. *National Security:* Tudor Botnaru. *Environment Protection:* Arcadie Capcelea. *Territory Development, Construction and Communal Services:* Mihai Severovan.

Local Government. There are local authorities at district, municipality and town/village level. Prefects and mayors of districts and municipalities are appointed by the President on the nomination of the local councils; mayors of towns and villages are elected. Local elections were held on 16 April 1995. The Agrarian Democratic Party gained most seats.

DEFENCE

Conscription is up to 18 months. In 1997 military expenditure totalled US$53m. (US$122 per capita), representing 4·4% of GDP.

Army. The Army is organized in 3 motor rifle and 1 artillery brigade and 1 reconnaissance battalion. Personnel, 1997, 9,300 (5,200 conscripts). There is also a paramilitary Interior Ministry force of 2,500 and riot police numbering 900.

Air Force. The Air Force has a small number of MiG-29 fighters, Antonov transport and Ilyushin aircraft and Mi-8 transport helicopters. Personnel (including air defence), 1997, 1,730.

INTERNATIONAL RELATIONS
Moldova is a member of the UN, OCSE, CIS, the Council of Europe and the NATO Partnership for Peace.

ECONOMY
Policy. Starting in April 1993, 33% of state property, mainly small and medium-sized firms in construction, light industry, commerce and services, were being privatized through the distribution of vouchers to citizens. This phase was completed in Nov. 1995 with the sale of 657 state-owned enterprises. The second phase aims to attract foreign investment for the sale of two thirds of state property.

Performance. There was no economic growth in 1997, following a fall of 9% in 1996.

Between 1990 and 1996 the average annual real growth in GNP per capita was – 16·8%.

Budget. In 1997 revenues were estimated to be US$570m. and expenditure US$641m.

Currency. A new unit of currency, the *leu* (MDL), replaced the rouble in Nov. 1993. Inflation was 11·2% in 1997, compared to 16% in 1996. Total money supply in Dec. 1997 was 1,229,000 lei.

Banking and Finance. The central bank and bank of issue is the National Bank (*Governor*, Leonid Talmaci). In 1996 there were 26 commercial banks and 1 foreign branch office (Romanian).

ENERGY AND NATURAL RESOURCES
Electricity. Installed capacity in 1995 was 3·22m. kW. Production was 8·58bn. kWh in 1994; consumption per capita was 1,941 kWh in 1994.

Minerals. There are deposits of lignite, phosphorites, gypsum and building materials.

Agriculture. Agriculture contributed 43% of GDP in 1996 and employs about 700,000. Land under cultivation in 1997 was 2·5m. ha, of which 0·3m. ha was accounted for by private subsidiary agriculture and 6,700 ha (in 1993) by commercial agriculture in 3,100 farms. Private and commercial agriculture accounted for 31% of the value of all output in 1993. The free sale of land is not permitted.

Output of main agricultural products (in 1,000 tonnes) in 1994: Grain, 2,900; sugar-beet, 2,400; sunflower seeds 210; potatoes, 300; vegetables, 900; fruit and berries (1992), 511; processed meat, 178; milk, 896; and 540m. eggs. Livestock (1995): 832,000 cattle, 1·06m. pigs, 1·43m. sheep and 14m. chickens.

Forestry. In 1995 forests covered 357,000 ha, or 10·8% of the total land area.

Fisheries. The south is rich in sturgeon, mackerel and brill. The catch in 1996 was approximately 4,900 tonnes, entirely from inland waters.

INDUSTRY
There are canning plants, wine-making plants, woodworking and metallurgical factories, a factory of ferro-concrete building materials, footwear, dairy products and textile plants. Output was valued at 1,200m. lei in 1993. Production, 1993 (in tonnes): Rolled ferrous metals (1992), 0·5m.; cement, 0·6m.; processed meat, 56,100; fabrics, 31·1m. sq. metres; footwear, 11·9m. pairs; 4,200 tractors; 167,000 TV sets; 57,600 refrigerators and freezers; 123,000 washing machines.

Labour. In 1996 the labour force totalled 2,181,000 (51% males). Approximately 45% of the economically active population in 1994 were engaged in agriculture, fisheries and forestry. In 1995 there were 24,500 registered unemployed (1·0% of the workforce). Average monthly salaries in 1993 were 21,582 roubles.

INTERNATIONAL TRADE
Foreign debt was US$834m. in 1996.

Imports and Exports. In 1997 imports were valued at US$1,148m. (US$1,079m. in 1996) and exports at US$843m. (US$802m. in 1996). Chief export markets are CIS countries—68·1% (of which Russia takes 53·7%, Ukraine 6·0%, Belarus 4·3% and Kazakhstan 1·0%). Central and eastern European countries take 16·5% (of which Romania 9·3%, Lithuania 1·9%, Latvia 1·8%, Bulgaria 1·6% and Hungary 0·4%).

Trade with the EU amounts to 9·8% (of which Germany 3·7%, Italy 2·6%, Netherlands 1·1%, Austria 0·5%). 61·5% of imports come from CIS countries with central and eastern Europe's share at 16·6% and that of EU countries at 15·1%.

Basic exports are alimentation industry products, beverages and tobacco, vegetative origin products, livestock and cattle farming products, textile and textile based articles, machines, electrical equipment, articles made from stone, gypsum, cement and glass.

Basic imports are power resources, industrial equipment, fortified alcoholic beverages and wines, plastics and articles made from plastics, natural cork, furniture, rolled metal, steel pipes and motor transport.

COMMUNICATIONS

Roads. There were 12,300 km of roads (10,700 km paved) in 1996. Passenger cars in use in 1996 numbered 166,757 (46 per 1,000 inhabitants), and there were also 109,822 motor cycles and mopeds, 58,418 trucks and vans and 9,220 buses and coaches.

Rail. Total length in 1996 was 1,318 km of 1,520 mm gauge. Passenger-kilometres travelled in 1995 came to 1·02bn. and freight tonne-kilometres to 3·13bn.

Civil Aviation. The national carriers are Air Moldova, Air Moldova International and Moldavian Airlines. Air Moldova had flights in 1998 to Athens, Bucharest, Ekaterinburg, Istanbul, Larnaca, London, Moscow, Paris, St Petersburg, Varna and Vienna. In 1998 Air Moldova International flew to Amsterdam, Berlin, Chernovtsy, Dnipropetrovsk, Donetsk, Frankfurt, Iasi, Kharkiv, Kyiv, Mineralnye Vody, Munich, Odesa, Volgograd and Warsaw. Moldavian Airlines flew to Bologna, Budapest, Moscow, Prague, Rostov and Verona. Services were also provided by Balkan, Belavia, Minskavia, Tarom, Transaero Airlines, Tyrolean Airways and Volga Aircompany. In 1995 scheduled airline traffic of Moldova-based carriers flew 4·2m. km, carrying 170,000 passengers (all on international flights).

Shipping. In 1993, 0·3m. passengers and 0·3m. tonnes of freight were carried on inland waterways.

Telecommunications. In 1997 there were 627,100 telephone main lines (145·4 per 1,000 persons). There were 9,000 PCs in 1995 and 600 fax machines.

Postal Services. In 1995 there were 1,307 post offices.

SOCIAL INSTITUTIONS

Justice. 47,515 crimes were reported in 1994.

Education. In 1996 there were 1,880 pre-schools, 736,000 pupils in 1,698 primary, secondary and special schools, 43,000 students in 97 vocational secondary schools and 54 technical colleges and 47,000 students in 9 higher educational institutions including the state university. In Jan. 1994, 0·2m. children (52% of those eligible) attended pre-school institutions. Adult literacy rate, 1995, 98·9% (male, 98·4%; female, 99·5%).

In 1994 total expenditure on education came to 5·5% of GNP and represented 28·9% of total government expenditure.

Health. In Jan. 1996 there were 17,400 doctors, 48,400 junior medical personnel and 312 hospitals with 54,300 beds.

Welfare. There were 649,000 age pensioners and 267,000 other pensioners in Jan. 1994.

CULTURE

Broadcasting. The government authority Radioteleviziunea Nationala is responsible for broadcasting. There are 2 national radio programmes, a Radio Moscow relay, and a foreign service, Radio Moldova International. There is a national state TV service and a private TV network. Romanian and Russian channels are also broadcast. There were 3·2m. radio receivers and 1·25m. television receivers in 1996.

Cinema. There were 49 cinemas in 1995, with an a total attendance for the year of 1·4m.

Press. Moldova has 567 newspapers and magazines. Of these 323 are published in Moldovan, 4 in English and the rest in Russian.

Tourism. In 1996 there were 33,000 foreign tourists, spending US$59m.

DIPLOMATIC REPRESENTATIVES
Of Moldova in Great Britain (resides in Brussels)
Ambassador: Tudor Botnaru.

Of Great Britain in Moldova (resides in Moscow)
Ambassador: Sir Andrew Wood, KCMG.

Of Moldova in the USA (2101 S St., NW, Washington, D.C., 20008)
Chargé d'Affaires a.i.: Vlad Spanu.

Of the USA in Moldova (103 strada Alexei Matveevici, Chişinau)
Ambassador: John T. Stewart.

Of Moldova to the United Nations
Ambassador: Dr Ion Botnaru.

Of Moldova to the European Union
Ambassador: Anatol Arapu.

MONACO

Principauté de Monaco

Capital: Monaco
Population estimate, 2000: 32,000
Estimated GDP: $800m.

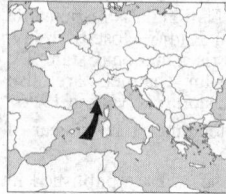

KEY HISTORICAL EVENTS

From 1297 Monaco belonged to the house of Grimaldi. In 1731 it passed into the female line, Louise Hippolyte, daughter of Antoine I, heiress of Monaco, marrying Jacques de Goyon Matignon, Count of Torigni, who took the name and arms of Grimaldi. The Principality was placed under the protection of the Kingdom of Sardinia by the Treaty of Vienna, 1815, and under that of France in 1861. Prince Albert I (reigned 1889–1922) acquired fame as an oceanographer; and his son Louis II (1922–49) was instrumental in establishing the International Hydrographic Bureau.

TERRITORY AND POPULATION

Monaco is bounded in the south by the Mediterranean and elsewhere by France (Department of Alpes Maritimes). The area is 195 ha. The Principality is divided into 4 districts: Monaco-Ville, la Condamine, Monte-Carlo and Fontvieille. Population (1990 census), 29,972 (15,735 females), of whom 5,070 were Monegasques (16·92%), 12,047 were French (40·19%) and 5,000 were Italian (16·68%); (1995 estimate) 31,515.

In 2000 the population is projected to be 32,000.

The official language is French.

SOCIAL STATISTICS

1997: Births, 713; deaths, 485; marriages, 208; divorces, 66. Rates per 1,000 population: Birth, 26·3; death, 17·8; marriage, 6·0; divorce, 2·5. Annual growth rate, 1990–95, was 1·3%.

CLIMATE

A Mediterranean climate, with mild moist winters and hot dry summers. Monaco, Jan. 50°F (10°C), July 74°F (23·3°C). Annual rainfall 30" (758 mm).

CONSTITUTION AND GOVERNMENT

On 17 Dec. 1962 a new constitution was promulgated which maintains the hereditary monarchy.

The reigning Prince is **Rainier III**, b. 31 May 1923, son of Princess Charlotte, Duchess of Valentinois, daughter of Prince Louis II, 1898–1977 (married 19 March 1920 to Prince Pierre, Comte de Polignac, who had taken the name Grimaldi, from whom she was divorced 18 Feb. 1933). Prince Rainier succeeded his grandfather Louis II, who died on 9 May 1949. He married on 19 April 1956 Miss Grace Kelly, a citizen of the USA (died 14 Sept. 1982). *Offspring:* Princess Caroline Louise Marguerite, b. 23 Jan. 1957; married Philippe Junot on 28 June 1978, divorced 9 Oct. 1980; married Stefano Casiraghi on 29 Dec. 1983 (died 3 Oct. 1990). *Offspring:* Andrea, b. 8 June 1984; Charlotte, b. 3 Aug. 1986; Pierre, b. 7 Sept. 1987. Prince Albert Alexandre Louis Pierre, b. 14 March 1958 *(heir apparent)*. Princess Stéphanie Marie Elisabeth, b. 1 Feb. 1965, married Daniel Ducruet on 1 July 1995, divorced 4 Oct. 1996. *Offspring:* Louis, b. 27 Nov. 1992; Pauline, b. 4 May 1994.

Prince Rainier renounces the principle of divine right. Executive power is exercised jointly by the Prince and a 4-member *Council of Government*, headed by a Minister of State (Michel Leveque). An 18-member *National Council* is elected for 5-year terms.

The constitution can be modified only with the approval of the National Council. A law of 1992 permits Monegasque women to give their nationality to their children.

MONACO

National Anthem. 'Principauté Monaco ma patrie' ('Principality of Monaco my fatherland'); words by T. Bellando de Castro, tune by C. Albrecht.

RECENT ELECTIONS

At the election held on 2 Feb. 1998 all 18 seats were won by the National and Democratic Union (UND).

CURRENT ADMINISTRATION

Chief of State: Prince Rainier III.

The government comprised at March 1999:

Minister of State: Michel Leveque.

Finance and Economics: Henri Fissore. *Public Works and Social Affairs:* Michel Sosso. *President of the National Council:* Jean-Charles Rey.

Local Government. The 15-member *Conseil Communal* is elected for 4 years.

INTERNATIONAL RELATIONS

Monegasque relations with France are based on conventions of 1963. French citizens are treated as if in France. Monaco is a member of the UN.

ECONOMY

Policy. A 22-ha site reclaimed from the sea at Fontvieille has been earmarked for office and residential development. The present industrial zone is to be reorganized and developed with a view to attracting new light industry.

Performance. Real GDP growth was 2·2% in 1995 (2·7% in 1994).

Budget. The budget (in 1,000 francs) was as follows:

	1995	1996	1997
Revenue	2,851,699	3,205,310	3,225,658
Expenditure	2,973,434	3,258,380	3,139,854

Currency. Monaco is a member of the French Franc Zone.

Banking and Finance. There were 41 banks and 7 *sociétés financières* in 1998.

Weights and Measures. The metric system is in use.

ENERGY AND NATURAL RESOURCES

Electricity. Electricity is imported from France. 403 GWh were supplied to 23,757 customers in 1997. Output capacity (1997), 71 MW. Installed capacity on standby, 10,000 kW.

Oil and Gas. In 1997, 49 GWh were supplied to 4,990 customers. Output capacity (1997) was 18 MW.

Water. Total consumption (1997), 5·64m. cu. metres.

INDUSTRY

Light industry made up 9·9% of economic activity in 1995. There were some 700 small businesses, including chemicals, plastics, electronics, engineering and paper in 1993.

Labour. There were 32,691 persons employed at 1 Jan. 1998. 29,311 worked in the private sector; 3,380 in the public sector. On 1 July 1997 the minimum wage (SMIC) was 39·43 francs an hour (4% up on 1996).

Trade Unions. Membership of trade unions was estimated at 2,000 out of a workforce of 25,600 in 1989.

INTERNATIONAL TRADE

Imports and Exports. There is a customs union with France. Exports for 1997 totalled FF2,284m.; imports, FF2,284m. Main imports (and exports): pharmaceuticals, perfumes, clothing, paper, synthetic and non-metallic products, and building materials.

MONACO

COMMUNICATIONS

Roads. There were estimated to be 50 km of roads in 1997 and 29,0580 vehicles. In 1997 4,105,239 people travelled by bus.

Rail. The 1·7 km of main line passing through the country are operated by the French National Railways (SNCF). In 1997, 2,171,099 people arrived at or departed from Monaco railway station, while 3,357 tonnes of freight left and 3,363 tonnes arrived there.

Civil Aviation. There are helicopter flights to Nice with Heli Air Monaco and Heli Inter. Helicopter movements (1997) at the Heliport of Monaco (Fontvieille), 52,333; the number of passengers carried was 131,038. The nearest airport is at Nice in France.

Shipping. In 1997 there were 994 vessels registered, of which 9 were over 100 tonnes (down by 10·93% on 1983). 1,679 yachts put in to the port of Monaco and 659 at Fontvieille in 1997. 88 liners put in to port in Monaco in 1997; 2,515 people embarked, 2,332 disembarked and 16,703 were in transit.

Telecommunications. In 1997 there were 30,435 land-based telephone lines and 7,957 mobile phones.

Postal Services. 15m. items were posted and 18·07m. items were delivered by the Post Office in 1997.

SOCIAL INSTITUTIONS

Justice. There are the following courts: *Tribunal Supreme*, *Cour de Révision*, *Cour d'Appel*, a Correctional Tribunal, a Work Tribunal, a Tribunal of the First Instance, 2 Arbitration Commissions for Rents (1 commercial, 1 domestic), courts for Work-related Accidents, and Supervision, a *Juge de Paix*, and a Police Tribunal. There is no death penalty.

Police: In 1993 the police force (*Sûreté Publique*) comprised 500 personnel.

Religion. 90% of the resident population are Roman Catholic. There is a Roman Catholic archbishop.

Education. In 1996–97, in the public sector, there were 7 pre-school institutions with 737 pupils; 4 primary schools with 1,292 pupils and 127 teachers; 3 secondary schools with 1,713 pupils and 4 technical schools with 532 pupils; total secondary school teachers, 267. In the private sector there were 4 pre-school and 4 primary schools with 259 and 625 pupils respectively; and 3 secondary schools with 703 pupils.

The University of Southern Europe in Monaco had 112 students in 1996–97.

Health. In 1997 there were 555 hospital beds and 188 doctors, 22 dentists and 19 nurses. The provision of 1 doctor for every 170 persons is the highest ratio in the world. At the other extreme, Malawi had 1 doctor for every 49,118 persons in 1989. Monaco also has the highest provision of hospital beds of any country, with 173 per 10,000 population in 1997.

CULTURE

Broadcasting. Radio Monte Carlo broadcasts FM commercial programmes in French (long- and medium-waves). Radio Monte Carlo owns 55% of *Radio Monte Carlo* Relay Station on Cyprus. The foreign service is dedicated exclusively to religious broadcasts and is maintained by voluntary contributions. It operates in 36 languages under the name 'Trans World Radio' and has relay facilities on Bonaire, West Indies; it is planning to build relay facilities in the southern parts of Africa. *Télé Monte-Carlo* broadcasts TV programmes in French, Italian and English. There is a 30-channel cable service. In 1995 there were 33,000 radio receivers and 24,000 television receivers.

Cinema. In 1996 there were 2 cinemas.

Press. Monaco had 1 newspaper in 1995 with a circulation of 8,000, equivalent to 250 per 1,000 inhabitants.

Tourism. In 1997, 258,604 foreign visitors, including 68,920 from Italy, 38,339 from the USA and 39,478 from France, spent a total of 781,907 nights (21·69% up on 1996). 84,846 people attended 759 congresses in 1997. There are 3 casinos run by the state, including the one at Monte Carlo attracting 0·4m. visitors a year.

DIPLOMATIC REPRESENTATIVES
British Consul-General (resident in Marseilles)*:* I. Davies.

British Honorary Consul: Eric G. Blair.

Consul-General for Monaco in London: I. B. Ivanovic.

Of Monaco to the United Nations
Ambassador: Jacques Louis Boisson.

FURTHER READING
Journal de Monaco. Bulletin Officiel. 1858 ff.

Hudson, G. L. *Monaco* [Bibliography]. Oxford and Santa Barbara (CA), 1990

MONGOLIA

Mongol Uls

Capital: Ulan Bator
Population estimate, 2000: 2·74m.
GNP per capita: (PPP$) 1,820
HDI/world rank: 0·669/101

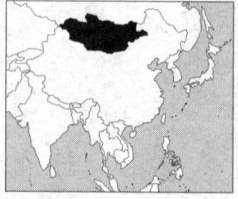

KEY HISTORICAL EVENTS

Temujin became khan of Hamag Mongolia in 1190. Having united by conquest various Tatar and Mongolian tribes he was confirmed as 'Universal' ('Genghis', 'Chingiz') khan in 1206. The expansionist impulse of his nomadic empire (Beijing captured in 1215; Samarkand in 1220) continued after his death in 1227, although the empire was by then administratively divided among his sons. Tamurlaine (died 1405) was the last of the conquering khans. In 1368 the Chinese drove the Mongols from Beijing, and for the next 2 centuries Sino-Mongolian relations alternated between war and trade. Lamaism spread from Tibet in the 16th century. The last Mongol khan, Ligden (1604-34), failed to stem the tide of Manchu expansion; southern (Inner) Mongolia was conquered in 1636 and Beijing in 1644. In 1691 Outer Mongolia accepted Manchu rule. The head of the Lamaist faith became the symbol of national identity, and his seat ('Urga', now Ulan Bator) was made the Mongolian capital.

When the Manchu dynasty was overthrown in 1911 Outer Mongolia declared its independence under its spiritual ruler and turned to Russia for support against China. 'Autonomy' (not independence) was agreed by the Sino-Russo-Mongolian agreement of May 1915. In 1919 China re-established central rule, but Soviet and Mongolian revolutionary forces set up a provisional government in March 1921. On the death of the spiritual ruler (the 'Urga Living Buddha') a people's republic and new constitution were proclaimed in May 1924.

With Soviet help Japanese invaders were fended off during the Second World War. The Mongols then took part in the successful Soviet campaign against Inner Mongolia and Manchuria. On 5 Jan. 1946 China recognized the independence of Outer Mongolia after a plebiscite in Mongolia (20 Oct. 1945) had resulted in an overwhelming vote for independence. A Sino-Soviet treaty of 14 Feb. 1950 guaranteed this independence. In Aug. 1986 a consular agreement, in June 1987 a boundary agreement, and in Nov. 1988 a border treaty, were signed with China.

Until 1990 sole power was in the hands of the Mongolian People's Revolutionary (Communist) Party (MPRP), but an opposition Mongolian Democratic Party, founded in Dec. 1989, achieved tacit recognition and held its first congress in Feb. 1990. Following demonstrations and hunger-strikes, on 12 March the entire MPRP Politburo resigned and political opposition was legalized. On 24 July 1998 parliament voted to oust the three-month-old government of Tsakhiagiin Elbegdorj in a row over bank privatization.

TERRITORY AND POPULATION

Mongolia is bounded in the north by the Russian Federation, and in the east and south and west by China. Area, 1,565,008 sq. km (604,250 sq. miles). Population (1989 census), 2,095,600; 1997 estimate, 2,356,000 (61% urban; 49·7% male). Density, 1·5 per sq. km.

The UN gives a projected population for 2000 of 2·74m.

The population is predominantly made up of Mongolian peoples (78·8% Halh). There is a Turkic Kazakh minority (5·9% of the population) and 20 Mongol minorities. The official language is Halh Mongol.

The republic is administratively divided into 3 cities: Ulan Bator, the capital, (1996 population, 619,200), Darhan, (89,900) and Erdenet (65,600), and 18 provinces *(aimag)*. The provinces are sub-divided into 334 districts or counties *(suums)*.

SOCIAL STATISTICS

Births, 1995, 52,000; deaths, 16,000. Birth rate (1995), 23·7 per 1,000 population; death rate, 7·3 per 1,000; marriage rate, 12 per 1,000; divorce rate, 0·7 per 1,000. Rate of increase, 16·4 per 1,000. Infant mortality rate, 1997, 46·8 per 1,000 live births. Expectation of life in 1997 was 63·7 years. Fertility rate, 1990–95, 3·6 births per woman.

CLIMATE
A very extreme climate, with six months of mean temperatures below freezing, but much higher temperatures occur for a month or two in summer. Rainfall is very low and limited to the months mid-May to mid-Sept. Ulan Bator, Jan. −14°F (−25·6°C), July 61°F (16·1°C). Annual rainfall 8" (208 mm).

CONSTITUTION AND GOVERNMENT
The Constitution of 12 Feb. 1992 abolished the 'People's Democracy', introduced democratic institutions and a market economy and guarantees freedom of speech.

The *President* is directly elected for renewable 4-year terms.

Since June 1992 the legislature has consisted of a single-chamber 76-seat parliament, *the Great Hural*, which elects the Prime Minister.

National Anthem. 'Darkhan manai khuvsgalt uls' ('Our sacred revolutionary republic'); words by Tsendiyn Damdinsüren, tune by Bilegin Damdinsüren and Luvsanjamts Murjorj.

RECENT ELECTIONS
At the parliamentary election of 30 June 1996 the electorate was 1·2m.; turn-out was 90%. The Democratic Coalition (DC, consisting of the National Democratic Party and the Social Democratic Party) gained 50 seats; the Mongolian People's Revolutionary Party (former Communists), 25 (70 in 1992); ind, 1.

At the presidential election on 18 May 1997 Natsagiin Bagabandi obtained 60·8% of the votes cast, against 29·8% for President Punsalmaagiyn Ochirbat.

CURRENT ADMINISTRATION
President: Natsagiin Bagabandi (b. 1940; Mongolian People's Revolutionary Party, elected May 1997).

A Democratic Coalition government was formed in July 1996 which comprised in March 1999:

Prime Minister: Janlaviin Narantsatsralt.

External Relations: Nyam-Osorin Tuyaa. *Environment:* Sangajavin Sonomtserengiin. *Defence:* Sharavdoriyn Tuvdendorj. *Finance:* Yansanjaviyn Ochirsuh. *Infrastructure and Development:* G. Bathuu. *Justice:* L. Tsog. *Health and Welfare:* S. Sonin. *Education:* A. Battur. *Agriculture and Industry:* Ch. Sodnomtseren.

Local Government. Local government is carried out by 380 local authorities. Some 13,000 deputies were elected in July 1990.

DEFENCE
Conscription is for 1 year for males aged 18-28 years. Defence expenditure in 1997 totalled US$18m. (US$8 per capita).

Army. The Army comprises 4 motorized infantry divisions (3 under strength), 1 artillery and 1 air defence brigade and 1 airborne and 2 independent infantry battalions. Equipment includes 650 T-54/-55/-62 main battle tanks. Strength (1997) 15,500 (11,000 conscripts). There is a border guard of 5,000 and some 1,000 internal security troops.

Air Force. The Air Force had a strength of 2,000 in 1996 (500 conscripts). There are 24 Antonov An-24 and An-26 transports used mainly on civil air services, 10 Mi-8 helicopters and a few Yak-18 trainers.

INTERNATIONAL RELATIONS
Mongolia is a member of the UN.

ECONOMY
Policy. Mongolia has for centuries had a traditional nomadic pastoral economy, which the Government aims to transform into a market economy. An Agency for National Development, whose head has cabinet rank, co-ordinates economic policy. A law of May 1991 envisages privatization by the issue of vouchers worth 10,000 tugriks to all citizens to acquire holdings in large privatizations or to buy small business or livestock.

Performance. Real GDP growth was 6·3% in 1995 (2·3% in 1994).

Budget. (in 1m. tugriks):

	1991	1992	1993	1994	1995	1996
Revenue	6,497	8,378	44,310	57,797	94,811	112,983
Expenditure	8,929	7,111	34,850	45,230	66,834	88,470

Sources of revenue, 1995 (in 1m. tugriks): Taxes, 109,269·5 (comprising: Income, Profits and Capital Gains Tax, 49,999·4; social security contributions, 18,906·1; payroll taxes, 43·5; taxes on goods and services, 27,364·7; taxes on foreign trade, 9,630·5; other, 3,325·3); non-tax revenue, 18,243·2; capital revenue, 3,751·2; grants, 5,010·5. Items of expenditure: Current, 105,536·2 (comprising: Goods and services, 75,083·5; wages, 25,542·5; employer contributions, 7,161·1; other purchases, 42,379·9); interest payments, 1,794·4; subsidies, 28,658·5; capital, 22,559·3; foreign amortization, 16,836.

Currency. The unit of currency is the *tugrik* (MNT) of 100 *möngö*. The tugrik was made convertible in 1993. Foreign exchange reserves were US$123m. in Feb. 1998 and gold reserves were 70,000 troy oz. The average annual inflation rate over the period 1990–96 was 106·2%. Total money supply was 70,435m. tugriks in Feb. 1998.

Banking and Finance. The Mongolian Bank (established 1924) is the bank of issue, being also a commercial, savings and development bank: the *Governor* is J. Unenbat. It has 21 main branches. There are also a Trade and Industry Bank, an Insurance Bank and a Co-operative Bank.

A stock exchange opened in Ulan Bator in 1992.

Weights and Measures. The metric system is in use.

ENERGY AND NATURAL RESOURCES

Electricity. Installed capacity was 900,000 kW in 1995. There are 6 thermal electric power stations. Production, 1996, 2,047m. kWh. Consumption per capita was 1,215 kWh in 1995.

Minerals. There are large deposits of copper, nickel, zinc, molybdenum, phosphorites, tin, wolfram and fluorspar; production of the latter in 1995, 526,900 tonnes. There are major coalmines near Ulan Bator and Darhan. Coal (mainly lignite) production in 1995 was 5m. tonnes. Copper production, 0·35m. tonnes.

Agriculture. Agriculture accounted for 31% of GDP in 1996. The prevailing Mongolian style of life is pastoral nomadism. 73% of agricultural production derives from cattle-raising. In 1996 there were 2·15m. horses, 3·48m. cattle, 13·61m. sheep, 390,000 camels and 99,300 poultry. The number of goats in 1998 has doubled to 11m. since 1992 as production of cashmere has increased along with the market economy.

Production 1995 (in 1,000 tonnes): Meat, 216 (249 in 1990); cow's milk, 343; fermented mare's milk (1992), 25m. litres.

The total agricultural area in 1995 was 118·5m. ha. 96% was sown to cereals, 1·6% to fodder and 0·9% to vegetables. In 1995 there was 1·3m. ha of arable land, 1,000 ha of permanent crop land and 117·1m. ha of pasture. The 1995 crop was 256,700 tonnes of wheat; 52,000 tonnes of potatoes; (1993) 10,000 tonnes of oats; 18,000 tonnes of barley. In 1994 there were 11,700 tractors and 2,600 harvester-threshers.

Collectivized farms, set up in the 1950s under Stalin, have been broken up and the land redistributed.

Forestry. Forests, chiefly larch, cedar, fir and birch, occupied 9·41m. ha in 1995 (6% of the land area). Timber production was 541,000 cu. metres in 1995.

Fisheries. The catch in 1996 was approximately 130 tonnes, entirely from inland waters.

INDUSTRY

Industry is still small in scale and local in character. The food industry accounts for 25% of industrial production. The main industrial centre is Ulan Bator; others are at Erdenet and Baga-Nur, and a northern territorial industrial complex is being developed based on Darhan and Erdenet to produce copper and molybdenum concentrates, lime, cement, machinery and wood- and metal-worked products.

Production figures (1995): Scoured wool, 1,200 tonnes; cement, 108,800 tonnes; leather footwear, 0·25m. pairs; meat, 11,300 tonnes; soap, 600 tonnes.

Labour. The labour force was 1,103,100 in 1995, including 108,100 in industry, 354,300 in agriculture, 29,500 in building, 31,600 in transport and communications and 64,800 in trade. Average wage was 16,000 tugriks per month in 1995. As of 1 Feb. 1997, 57,900 people were officially registered as unemployed.

Trade Unions. The Confederation of Mongolian Trade Unions had 450,000 members in 1994.

INTERNATIONAL TRADE
Mongolia is dependent on foreign aid. The largest donor in 1992 was Japan. Foreign debt was US$524m. in 1996.

Joint ventures with foreign firms are permitted. Foreign investors may acquire up to 49% of the equity in Mongolian companies. Foreign companies (except in precious metal mining) have a 5-year tax holiday and a further 5 years at 50% of the tax rate.

Imports and Exports. Value of exports, 1996: US$423m.; imports, US$439m. Main exports (in tonnes): Copper concentrate, 435,000; molybdenum concentrate, 3,438; wheat, 8,300; sawn wood, 37,200 cu. metres; 62,000 horse skins; 1,818,500 sheepskins; 314,600 goatskins; 20,600 woollen blankets.

Main export markets, 1995 (trade in US$1m.): Japan, 95·6; Kazakhstan, 77·7; China, 73·2; Switzerland, 67·6; Russia, 66·9; USA, 29·9; South Korea, 25·5; UK, 19·4. Main import suppliers: Russia, 202; Japan, 44·5; China, 39·4; South Korea, 20·3; USA, 14·1.

COMMUNICATIONS
Roads. The total road network covered approximately 42,000 km in 1996. There are 1,185 km of surfaced roads running around Ulan Bator, from Ulan Bator to Darhan, at points on the frontier with the Russian Federation and towards the south. Truck services run where there are no surfaced roads. Vehicles in use in 1996 included more than 31,000 trucks and vans and 30,000 passenger cars. 1·6m. tonnes of freight were carried in 1995, and 107·2m. passengers.

Rail. The Trans-Mongolian Railway (1,928 km of 1,524 mm gauge in 1992) connects Ulan Bator with the Russian Federation and China. There are spur lines to Erdenet and to the coalmines at Nalayh and Sharyn Gol. A separate line connects Choybalsan in the east with Borzaya on the Trans-Siberian Railway. 2·8m. passengers and 7·3m. tonnes of freight were carried in 1995.

Civil Aviation. MIAT-Mongolian Airlines operates internal services, and in 1998 flew from Ulan Bator to Beijing, Berlin, Frankfurt, Hohhot, Irkutsk, Istanbul, Moscow, Osaka and Seoul. Aeroflot and Air China also provided international services in 1998. In 1995 scheduled airline traffic of Mongolia-based carriers flew 12·6m. km, carrying 662,000 passengers (617,000 on domestic flights). Ulan Bator airport (Buyant Uhaa) was modernized and expanded in 1985.

Shipping. There is a steamer service on the Selenge River and a tug and barge service on Hövsgöl Lake. 70,000 tonnes of freight were carried in 1990.

Telecommunications. Mongolia had 87,300 main telephone lines in 1997, or 36·6 for every 1,000 persons. There were 2,200 fax machines in 1995.

Postal Services. There were, in 1995, 391 post offices.

SOCIAL INSTITUTIONS
Justice. The Procurator-General is appointed, and the Supreme Court elected, by parliament for 5 years. There are also courts at province, town and district level. Lay assessors sit with professional judges.

Religion. Tibetan Buddhist Lamaism is the prevalent religion; the Dalai Lama is its spiritual head. In 1995 there were about 100 monasteries and 2,500 monks.

Education. Adult literacy was 82·9% in 1995 (88·6% among males and 77·2% among females). In 1995 there were 711 nurseries with 68,100 children. Schooling begins at the age of 7. In 1995 there were 664 general education schools with 403,800 pupils and 19,400 teachers. In 1990–91 there were 31 specialized secondary schools with 18,500 students and 1,300 teachers and 44 vocational technical schools with 29,100 pupils.

In 1994–95 there were 1 university and 4 specialized universities (agricultural; medical; pedagogical; technical). There were also colleges of commerce and business, economics, and railway engineering, and an institute of culture and art.

In 1994 total expenditure on education came to 5·2% of GNP.

Health. In 1995 there were 250 doctors and 96 hospital beds per 10,000 population. Annual average per capita consumption (in kg) of foodstuffs in 1995: Meat, 97; milk and products, 126; sugar, 8·7; flour, 94; potatoes, 11; fresh vegetables, 8.

Welfare. In 1995, 102·8m. tugriks were spent on maternity benefits.

CULTURE

Broadcasting. The government-controlled Ulan Bator Radio broadcasts 2 national programmes and an external service (English, Chinese, Japanese, Russian). Mongol Televiz transmits a daily programme and a Moscow relay (colour by SECAM). In 1995, 153,442 radio and 142,800 TV sets were in use.

Cinema. In 1990 there were 30 cinemas, 522 mobile cinemas and 30 theatres.

Press. In 1995 there was 1 government daily with a circulation of 50,000, and a police-run weekly. About 300 other titles were registered, but few were actually publishing. 717 book titles were published in 1990 in 6·4m. copies.

Tourism. In 1996 there were 153,000 foreign tourists, spending US$21m.

DIPLOMATIC REPRESENTATIVES
Of Mongolia in Great Britain (7 Kensington Ct., London, W8 5DL)
Ambassador: Tsedenjavyn Suhbaatar.

Of Great Britain in Mongolia (30 Enkh Taivny Gudamzh, Ulan Bator 13)
Ambassador: John Durham.

Of Mongolia in the USA (2833 M Street, NW, Washington, D.C., 20007)
Ambassador: Jalbuu Choinhor.

Of the USA in Mongolia (Micro Region 11, Big Ring Road, Ulan Bator)
Ambassador: Alphonse F. La Porta.

Of Mongolia to the United Nations
Ambassador: Jargalsaikhany Enkhsaikhan.

Of Mongolia to the European Union
Ambassador: Jagvaralin Hanibal.

FURTHER READING
State Statistical Office: *Mongolian Economy and Society in [year]: Statistical Yearbook.*— *National Economy of the MPR, 1924–1984: Anniversary Statistical Collection.* Ulan Bator, 1984

Akiner. S. (ed.) *Mongolia Today.* London, 1992
Bawden, C. R., *The Modern History of Mongolia.* London, 1968
Becker, J., *The Lost Country.* London, 1992
Bruun, O. and Odgaard, O. (eds.) *Mongolia in Transition.* Richmond, 1996
Griffin, K. (ed.) *Poverty and the Transition to a Market Economy in Mongolia.* London, 1995
Jagchid, S. and Hyer, P., *Mongolia's Culture and Society.* Folkestone, 1979
Lattimore, O., *Nationalism and Revolution in Mongolia.* Leiden, 1955.—*Nomads and Commissars.* OUP, 1963
Nordby, J., *Mongolia in the Twentieth Century.* Farnborough, 1993
Sanders, A. J. K., *Mongolia: Politics, Economics and Society.* London, 1987
Shirendev, B. and Sanjdorj, M. (eds.) *History of the Mongolian People's Republic.* Vol. 3 (vols. 1 and 2 not translated). Harvard Univ. Press, 1976

National Statistical Office: State Statistical Office, Ulan Bator

MOROCCO

Mamlaka al-Maghrebia

(Kingdom of Morocco)

Capital: Rabat
Population estimate, 2000: 28·98m.
GNP per capita: (PPP$) 3,320
HDI/world rank: 0·567/125

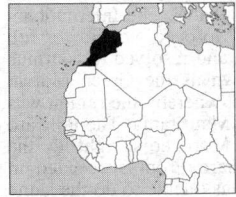

KEY HISTORICAL EVENTS

The native people of Morocco are the Berbers, an ancient race who have seen their country invaded by a succession of foreign powers. In the 12th century BC the first of these invaders were the Phoenicians who established trading posts at several points along the North African coast. The Carthaginians later took over these Phoenician colonies and expanded them as part of the mighty Carthaginian Empire. When the city of Carthage fell to Rome in the second century BC, the African Mediterranean coast was under Roman dominance for almost six hundred years. When the Roman Empire in turn fell into decline, the area was invaded first by the Vandals in AD 429 and later by Byzantium in AD 533. An Arab invasion of Morocco in AD 682 marked the end of Byzantium dominance and the first Arab rulers, the Idrisid dynasty, ruled for 150 years.

Arab and Berber dynasties succeeded the Idrisids; notably the Almoravids (1062–1147) and the Almohads (1147–1258). The Almohad Empire declined after the defeat of the Moroccans by the Spanish at the Battle of Las Navas de Tolosa in 1212. By 1250 its power had completely collapsed and the country was plunged into bitter civil war between Arab and Berber factions. The reign of Ahmed I al-Man-sur in the first Sharifian dynasty stabilized and unified the country between 1579 and 1603. Moors and Jews expelled from Spain settled in Morocco during this time and the country flourished and prospered. It became a centre for the arts and this period was known as Morocco's golden age.

Portuguese and Spanish power had been growing in the Mediterranean region since the beginning of the 15th century and in 1415 the Moroccan port of Ceuta was captured by Portugal. Moroccan forces defeated the Portuguese in 1578 and by 1700 had regained control of many coastal towns which had previously been in Portuguese hands. During the 18th and early 19th centuries the Barbary Coast became the scene of widespread piracy. Ships which traded in the Mediterranean were plundered and protection money was extorted from several sea-going nations.

Morocco shared possession of the Straits of Gibraltar with Spain, resulting in a focus of attention from the maritime powers in Europe, particularly France and Britain. By the beginning of the 20th century Britain had recognized Morocco as a French sphere of influence and in 1904 Morocco was divided between France and Spain, with the former receiving the larger area. These arrangements were regarded as spurious by Imperial Germany and, despite the Act of Algeciras (an agreement signed by the major powers in 1906, which guaranteed equal economic rights in Morocco), Germany was still dissatisfied.

In 1911, a German gunboat was dispatched to the Moroccan port of Agadir, in an attempt to excite further nationalist unrest against the French. From 1912 to 1956 Morocco was divided into three areas: a French protectorate, established by the Treaty of Fez of 1912 concluded between France and the Sultan; a Spanish protectorate, established by the Franco-Spanish Convention of 1912; and the international zone of Tangier which was established by France, Great Britain and Spain in 1923. Gen. Lyautey, the first French resident-general, was responsible for much modernization and by 1934 had pacified the country. However, as tribesmen were defeated so nationalism in various forms developed. On 2 March 1956 France and the Sultan terminated the Treaty of Fez and on 7 April 1956 Spain relinquished her protectorate. On 29 Oct. 1956 the international status of the Tangier Zone was abolished by common consent and Morocco became a kingdom on 18 Aug. 1957, with the Sultan taking the title Mohammed V. The country became territorially complete when the northern strip of Spanish Sahara was ceded by Spain on 10 April 1958 and the former Spanish province of Ifni was returned to Morocco on 30 June 1969.

MOROCCO

Crown Prince Moulay Hassan succeeded his father on 3 March 1961 as Hassan II. King Hassan tried to combine the various parties in government and established an elected House of Representatives but political unrest led him to discard any attempt at a parliamentary government and to rule autocratically from 1965 to 1977. In 1977 a new Chamber of Representatives was elected and under the constitution Morocco became a constitutional monarchy with a single elected chamber.

In 1974 Morocco embarked on a campaign aimed at forcing Spain to withdraw from the Western region of the Sahara, an area rich in phosphates. The International Court of Justice, meeting in The Hague in 1975, rejected Morocco's claim for full sovereignty over the region. Morocco ignored this decision and resolved to continue the fight alone, organizing a massive demonstration known as the Green March. Spain entered into secret negotiations and a deal was struck, whereby the region was divided into three and administered by Morocco, Spain and Mauritania. The Polisaro front, a Saharan nationalist movement, hotly disputed Morocco's right to the territory and guerrilla fighting ensued. In 1978 the Polisaro Front succeeded in forcing Mauritania to relinquish its Saharan interests, but was unable to do the same with Morocco. The United Nations has continued to mediate in this dispute but the proposed referendum on independence has been repeatedly delayed. Currently the dispute is over voting rights.

TERRITORY AND POPULATION

Morocco is bounded by Algeria to the east and south-east, Mauritania to the south, the Atlantic Ocean to the north-west and the Mediterranean to the north. Excluding the Western Saharan territory claimed and retrieved since 1976 by Morocco, the area is 458,730 sq. km and population at the 1982 census was 20,255,687. Western Sahara had an area of 252,120 sq. km and 163,868 population. The Moroccan superficie is 710,850 sq. km. Population estimate, 1995, 28·3m (51·9% urban); density, 61·7 per sq. km.

The UN gives a projected population for 2000 of 28·98m.

There was a census in Sept. 1994. The 49 provinces and 22 prefectures are grouped into 7 economic regions (in parentheses). Area and population in 1994:

Province	Area in sq. km	Population in 1,000	Province	Area in sq. km	Population in 1,000
(South)			Settat	9,750	847
Agadir	5,910	921			
Boujdour	100,120	22	(North-West)		
Es-Semara	61,760	40	Chefchaouen	4,350	439
Guelmim	28,750	147	Kénitra	4,745	979
El-Aaiún	39,360	154	Khémisset	8,305	486
Ouarzazate	41,550	695	Rabat		623
Oued Eddahab	50,880	37	Salé	1,275	632
Tan-Tan	17,295	58	Skhirate-Témara		245
Taroudannt	16,460	694	Sidi Kacem	4,060	646
Tata	25,925	119	Tangiers	1,195	628
Tiznit	6,960	348	Tétouan	6,025	537
			Larache		
(Tensift)					
El Kelâa Srahna	10,070	682	(Centre-North)		
Essaouira	6,335	434	Al Hoceima	3,550	383
Marrakesh	14,755	1,608	Boulemane	14,395	162
Safi	7,285	823	Fes	5,400	1,161
			Taounate	5,585	629
(Centre)			Taza	15,020	708
Azilal	10,050	455			
Béni Mellal	7,075	870	(Eastern)		
Ben Slimane	2,760	213	Figuig	55,990	117
Aïn Chok-Hay Hassani		516	Nador	6,130	684
Aïn Sebaâ-Hay			Oujda	20,700	968
Mohammadi		521			
Ben Msik-Sidi Othmane	1,615	704	(Centre-South)		
Casablanca-Anfa		523	Errachidia	59,585	522
Mohammadia-Znata		170	Ifrane	3,310	128
El Jadida	6,000	971	Khenifra	12,320	465
Khouribga	4,250	481	Meknès	3,995	789

The chief cities (with estimated populations in 1,000, 1993) are as follows:

Casablanca	3,200	Oujda	331	Mohammedia	156
Rabat	1,220	Tangiers	307	Béni Mellal	139
Marrakesh	602	Safi	278	Agadir	137
Fez	564	Tétouan	272	El Jadida	125
Salé	521	Kénitra	234		
Meknès	401	Khouribga	190		

The official language is Arabic, spoken by 75% of the population; the remainder speak Berber. French and Spanish are considered subsidiary languages and, more recently, English.

SOCIAL STATISTICS
1995 births, 719,000; deaths, 191,000. Rates, 1995 (per 1,000 population): Birth, 27·1; death, 7·2. Annual growth rate, 1990–95, 2·0%. Life expectancy at birth over the period 1990–95 was 62·8 years for males and 66·2 years for females. Infant mortality, 1990–95, 62 per 1,000 live births; fertility rate, 3·8 births per woman.

CLIMATE
Morocco is dominated by the Mediterranean climate which is made temperate by the influence of the Atlantic Ocean in the northern and southern parts of the country. Central Morocco is continental while the south is desert. Rabat, Jan. 55°F (12·9°C), July 72°F (22·2°C). Annual rainfall 23" (564 mm). Agadir, Jan. 57°F (13·9°C), July 72°F (22·2°C). Annual rainfall 9" (224 mm). Casablanca, Jan. 54°F (12·2°C), July 72°F (22·2°C). Annual rainfall 16" (404 mm). Marrakesh, Jan. 52°F (11·1°C), July 84°F (28·9°C). Annual rainfall 10" (239 mm). Tangiers, Jan. 53°F (11·7°C), July 72°F (22·2°C). Annual rainfall 36" (897 mm).

CONSTITUTION AND GOVERNMENT
The ruling King is **Hassan II,** born on 9 July 1929, succeeded on 3 March 1961, on the death of his father Mohammed V, who reigned 1927–61. The royal style was changed from 'His Sherifian Majesty the Sultan' to 'His Majesty the King' on 18 Aug. 1957. *Heir apparent:* Crown Prince Sidi Mohammed, born 21 Aug. 1963. The King holds supreme civil and religious authority, the latter in his capacity of Emir-el-Muminin or Commander of the Faithful. He resides usually at Rabat, but occasionally in one of the other traditional capitals, Fez (founded in 808), Marrakesh (founded in 1062), or at Skhirat.

A new Constitution was approved by referendum in March 1972 and amendments were approved by referendum in May 1980 and Sept. 1992. The Kingdom of Morocco is a constitutional monarchy. Parliament consists of a *Chamber of Representatives* composed of 325 deputies directly elected for 6-year terms. A referendum on 13 Sept. 1996 established a second *Chamber of Counsellors,* of whom 60% are elected for 9-year terms in tranches of one-third of the members by local councils, 20% by employers' associations and 20% by trade unions. The Chamber of Counsellors has power to initiate legislation, issue warnings of censure to the government and ultimately to force the government's resignation by a two-thirds majority vote. The electorate was 12·3m. and turn-out was 82·95%. The King, as sovereign head of State, appoints the Prime Minister and other Ministers, has the right to dissolve Parliament and approves legislation.

A new electoral code of March 1997 fixed voting at 20 and made enrolment on the electoral roll compulsory.

National Anthem. 'Manbit al Ahrah, mashriq al anwar' ('Fountain of freedom, source of light'); words by Ali Squalli Houssaini, tune by Leo Morgan.

RECENT ELECTIONS
The new Chamber of Representatives was elected on 14 Nov. 1997 during the General Elections. At this election, the USFP (Socialist Opposition) won 57 seats, UC (Constitutional Union) won 50 and PI (Istiqlal; Independence Party) won 32. These general elections demonstrated that no party is able to constitute a government without the support of the other parties. The opposition parties won 102

seats, the coalition of ruling parties won 100, and the centre won 91. The opposition and the centre were expected to make an arrangement to constitute the next government. In elections to the Chamber of Counsellors on 5 Dec. 1997, the centre National Rally of Independents gained 42 seats, ahead of a second centre party, the Democratic and Social Movement, with 33 seats.

CURRENT ADMINISTRATION
Prime Minister: Abderrahmane Youssoufi.

A new cabinet was formed in March 1998, which in March 1999 comprised:
Minister of State for Foreign Affairs and Co-operation: Abdellatif Filali. *Minister of State for the Interior:* Driss Basri. *Minister of Agriculture, Rural Development and Fisheries:* Habib Maliki. *Civil Service and Administrative Reform:* Aziz Houcine. *Communication:* Mohamed Larbi Messari. *Cultural Affairs:* Mohamed Achari. *Development Planning, Environment, Urban Development and Housing:* Mohamed Yazghi. *Economy and Finance:* Fathallah Oualalou. *Endowment and Religious Affairs:* Abdelkebir Alaoui M'Daghri. *Energy and Mines:* Youssef Tahiri. *Equipment:* Bouamour Taghouane. *Health:* Abdelouhad Fassi. *Higher Education, Executive Training and Scientific Research:* Najib Zerouali. *Human Rights:* Mohamed Oujar. *Industry, Commerce and Handicrafts:* Alami Tazi. *Justice:* Omar Azziman. *National Education:* Ismail Alaoui. *Public Sector and Privatization:* Rachid Filali. *Parliamentary Relations:* Mohamed Bouzouba. *Social Development, Solidarity, Employment, Vocational Training and Government Spokesman:* Khalid Alioua. *Tourism:* Hassan Sabbar. *Transport and Merchant Marine:* Mustapha Mansouri. *Youth and Sports:* Ahmed Moussaoui. *Minister Delegate to the Prime Minister for Administration of National Defence:* Abderrahmane Sbai.

Local Government. The country is administratively divided into 49 provinces and 22 prefectures divided into 159 circles, which are subdivided into 248 urban and 1,297 rural communes.

Elections were held on 13 June 1997. The Democratic Bloc (Koutla) gained 102 seats, the Right Bloc 100 and the Rassemblement National des Indépendants 97 seats. There were 3,000 candidates and turn-out was 58·3%. Two women were elected.

DEFENCE
Conscription is authorized for 18 months. Defence expenditure in 1997 totalled US$1,386m. (US$48 per capita), representing 4·2% of GDP.

Army. The Army is deployed in 2 commands: Northern Zone and Southern Zone. It comprises 3 mechanized infantry, 1 light security and 2 parachute brigades; 8 mechanized infantry regiments; 1 air defence group; 37 infantry, 3 camel corps, 2 cavalry, 1 mountain, 10 armoured, 12 artillery, 7 engineer and 2 airborne battalions and 4 commando units. There is also a Royal guard of 1,500. Equipment includes 224 M-48A5 and 300 M-60 main battle tanks. Strength (1998), 175,000 (100,000 conscripts). There is also a Royal Gendarmerie of 12,000 and an Auxiliary Force of 30,000.

Navy. The Navy includes 1 missile-armed Spanish-built frigate, 2 Italian-built missile-armed corvettes, 4 fast missile craft, 14 coastal patrol craft and 6 inshore patrol craft. There are additionally 1 ex-US tank landing ship, 3 medium landing ships of French origin, 2 transports and 1 Ro-Ro ferry in naval use. Personnel in 1998 numbered 7,800, including a 1,500 strong brigade of Naval Infantry. Bases are located at Casablanca, Agadir, Al-Hoceima and Dakhla.

The Coast Guard wing of the Royal Gendarmerie operates 12 patrol craft.

Air Force. Equipment in current use includes 32 Mirage F1s, a total of 32 F-5A/B/E/F fighter-bombers and RF-5A reconnaissance-fighters, 3 OV-10 Bronco counter-insurgency aircraft, 2 Falcon 20s for electronic warfare, and 18 Gazelle armed helicopters, 20 Alpha Jet advanced trainers, 20 Magister armed jet basic trainers, 10 T-34C-1 turboprop basic trainers, 10 Swiss-built Bravo primary trainers, 2 Mudry CAP 10B and 4 CAP 230 aerobatic trainers, 70 Agusta-Bell 205 and 212, Puma and JetRanger helicopters, 2 Do 28D Skyservants for coastal patrol, 9 CH-47C heavy-lift helicopters, 15 C-130H turboprop transport aircraft, 2 KC-130H tanker/transports, 2 Citation V, a Falcon 50 and a Gulfstream III VIP transport, 2

Boeing 707s (1 modified as a tanker), 7 CN-235s, 10 turboprop King Air light transports and 14 T-37 trainers. Personnel strength (1998) about 13,500, with 89 combat aircraft and 24 armed helicopters.

INTERNATIONAL RELATIONS
Morocco is a member of the UN and the Arab League.

ECONOMY
Policy. There is a programme of privatization involving 112 companies. 30 had been privatized by mid-1995.

Performance. Economic growth was 11·8% in 1996.

Budget. Revenues in 1995 were DH82,018m. (DH81,442m. in 1994) and expenditure DH93,889m. (DH90,072m. in 1994). VAT is 20%.

Currency. The unit of currency is the *dirham* (MAD) of 100 *centimes*, introduced in 1959. Foreign exchange reserves were US$3,971m. and gold reserves 700,000 troy oz. in Feb. 1998. Since 1993 the dirham has been convertible for current account operations. Inflation was 3% in 1996. Total money supply in Jan. 1998 was DH152,845m.

Banking and Finance. The central bank is the Bank Al Maghrib, which had assets of DH60,968m. on 31 Dec. 1993. There are 14 commercial banks (11 foreign). There are also 3 development banks, specializing respectively in industry, housing and agriculture.

There is a stock exchange at Casablanca. The global volume, in 1989, was DH672m.; in 1996, it was DH23·9bn.

Weights and Measures. The metric system is legal.

ENERGY AND NATURAL RESOURCES
Electricity. Installed capacity was 3·79m. kW in 1994. Production was 9,276·6m. kWh. (855·1m. hydro-electric) in 1994. Consumption per capita was an estimated 385 kWh in 1995.

Minerals. The principal mineral exploited is phosphate, the output of which was 20·68m. tonnes in 1995. Other minerals (in tonnes, 1995) are: Lead (101,545), zinc (150,160), silver (259·1), copper (33,685), iron ore (33,500), manganese (22,000), barytine (273,809) and salt (182,000).

Agriculture. In 1996 agriculture contributed 20% of GDP. Agricultural production is subject to drought; about 1·25m. ha are irrigated. 85% of farmland is individually owned. Only 1% of farms are over 50 ha; most are under 3 ha. Land suitable for cultivation, 1993, 9·26m. ha, of which (in 1,000 ha): Cereals, 6,074; leguminous vegetables, 347; market gardening, 204; oil-producing, 98, industrial crops, 151; fodder, 168; dense fruit plantations, 664; fallow, 2,687.

Production in 1995/96 (in 1,000 tonnes): Wheat, 22,697; barley, 38,311; maize, 2,350; fruit, 2,890 (of which citrus fruits, 1,324); pulses, 276·7; sunflower seeds, 60·8; groundnuts, 30; sugar beets, 3,144; sugar-cane, 925; cotton, 31·2.

Dairy production in 1994 included: Milk, 490m. litres; butter, 5,600 tonnes. Meat production, 454,000 tonnes.

Livestock, 1996: Cattle, 2·42m.; sheep, 16·27m.; goats, 4·42m. (1995); asses, 954,000; chickens, 157m. (1995).

Forestry. Forests covered 3·84m. ha in 1995, or 8·6% of the total land area (down from 3·89m. ha in 1990). Produce includes firewood, building and industrial timber and some cork and charcoal. Timber production was 2·35m. cu. metres in 1995.

Fisheries. The fishing fleet numbered 2,564 coastal vessels in 1993 and 462 deep-sea vessels, the latter totalling 152,417 GRT. Total catch in 1995 was 846,201 tonnes (sea fish, 844,001 tonnes). Morocco's annual catch is the highest of any African country. Total catch value in 1994 was DH3,195m.

INDUSTRY
In 1992 there were 5,855 industrial firms employing 351,149 persons. 1,785 of these employed fewer than 10 persons; 80, more than 500. 1,434 firms were engaged in food production, 789 in clothing, 723 in textiles and 397 in paper- and board-making and printing. Production, 1993 (in tonnes): Sugar, 497,767; olive oil, 38,000; cement, 6,175,000. In 1995, the industrial investment was DH14·2bn. of which 92% came from the private sector.

Labour. In 1996 the labour force totalled 10,448,000 (65% males). Approximately 40% of the economically active population in 1994 were engaged in agriculture, fisheries and forestry. In 1993 the monthly non-agricultural minimum wage was DH1,510. The agricultural minimum was DH37·60 per day in 1994.

Trade Unions. In 1996 there were 6 trade unions: UMT (Union Marocaine de Travail), CDT (Confédération Démocratique du Travail), UGTM (Union Générale des Travailleurs Marocaine), UNTM (National Union of Moroccan Workers), USP (Union of Popular Workers) and the SNP (National Popular Union).

INTERNATIONAL TRADE
In 1989 Morocco signed a treaty of economic co-operation with the 4 other Maghreb countries: Algeria, Libya, Mauritania and Tunisia. In 1995, Morocco signed an association agreement with the EU to create a free trade zone in 12 years. Foreign debt was US$21,767m. in 1996.

Imports and Exports. In 1996 imports were US$7,999m. and exports US$4,628m. Imports in 1994 included (in 1,000 tonnes): Crude oil, 6,855; grain, 1,191; sulphur, 2,653; chemicals, 588; sawn wood, 663. Exports included: Foodstuffs and tobacco, 1,310; phosphates, 9,527; other mineral products (1993), 2,063; natural and artificial fertilizers, 1,674.

Main export markets in 1995 (in DH1m.): France, 11,940; Spain, 3,779; India, 2,640; Italy, 2,291; Japan, 3,085. Main import suppliers: France, 15,915; Spain, 6,215; Italy, 4,470; Germany, 4,563; USA, 4,770.

COMMUNICATIONS

Roads. In 1996 there were 60,626 km of classified roads, of which 30,556 km were surfaced and including 10,913 km of main roads. A motorway links Rabat to Casablanca. 3·4m. passengers and 16·1m. tonnes of freight were carried in 1993. In 1996 there were 1,071,000 passenger cars, 72,000 trucks and vans and 20,160 motor cycles and mopeds. There were 38,646 road accidents in 1996 (2,807 fatalities).

Rail. In 1995 there were 1,907 km of railways, of which 1,003 km were electrified. In 1995 the railways carried 1·64bn. passenger-km and 4·62bn. tonne-km of freight.

Civil Aviation. The national carrier is Royal Air Maroc. In 1998 services were also provided by Aeroflot, Air Afrique, Air Algérie, Air France, Air Malta, Air Mauritanie, Air Toulouse, Alitalia, Balkan, British Airways, Condor Flugdienst, Egyptair, Gulf Air, Hapag Lloyd, Iberia, KLM, Kuwait Airways, Lauda Air, LTU International Airways, Lufthansa, Regional Air Lines, Romavia, Royal Jordanian, SABENA, Saudia, Swissair, Transavia Airlines and Tunis Air. The major international airport is Mohammed V at Casablanca; there are 8 other airports. Casablanca handled 2,483,694 passengers in 1996 (1,887,598 on international flights) and 38,475 tonnes of freight. Agadir (Al Massira) is the second busiest airport, with 820,288 passengers (577,335 on international flights) and 3,041 tonnes of freight in 1996. In July 1997 Morocco launched its first private air company 'Regional Air Lines' to serve the major regions of the kingdom, in addition to southern Spain and the Canary Islands.

Shipping. There are 12 ports, the largest being Casablanca, Tangiers and Jorf Lasfar. 1·56m. passengers and 40·6m. tonnes of freight were handled in 1994. In 1995 sea-going shipping totalled 0·39m. GRT, including oil tankers, 25,092 GRT, and container ships, 10,071 GRT. The Fleet: No. of boats; 3,200 units. Inshore fishing, 2,921 (70,000 tonnes per day), offshore fishing, 470 (150,000 tonnes per day).

Telecommunications. In 1997 there were 1,375,000 main telephone lines, equivalent to 50 per 1,000 population. There were 45,000 PCs in 1995, 7,500 fax machines and 1,600 cellular phone subscribers. In Jan. 1998 Morocco had around 6,000 Internet users.

Postal Services. In 1994 there were 621 main post offices.

SOCIAL INSTITUTIONS

Justice. The legal system is based on French and Islamic law codes. There are a Supreme Court, 21 courts of appeal, 65 courts of first instance, 196 centres with resident judges and 706 communal jurisdictions for petty offences.

Religion. Islam is the established state religion. 98% of the population are Sunni Moslems of the Malekite school and 0·16% are Christians, mainly Roman Catholic, and there is a small Jewish community (0·05%).

Education. The adult literacy rate in 1995 was 44·7% (56·6% among males and 31% among females). Education in Berber languages has been permitted since 1994. Education is compulsory from the age of 7 to 13. In 1993–94 there were 28,335 Koranic schools (33,721 in 1990) with 30,367 teachers and 611,729 pupils; 3,563 modern pre-primary schools (343 in 1990) with 5,836 teachers and 171,727 pupils; 4,349 primary schools (392 private) with 91,487 teachers and 2,769,323 pupils; 1,168 secondary schools with (in the public sector) 75,407 teachers and 1,226,194 pupils (38,692 private). There were 13 universities with 7,566 teachers and 218,516 students (89,223 women), 8,390 students (1,761 women) in teacher training and (1992–93) 8,967 students and 1,145 teachers in other higher education institutions. An English-language university was opened at Ifrane in Jan. 1995, initially with a staff of 35 and 300 students (scheduled to rise to 3,500).

Health. In the public sector in 1994 there were 4,422 doctors, and 72 dentists; in the private sector there were 4,416 doctors and 1,132 dentists. In 1994 there were 2,470 pharmacists. In 1993 in the public sector there were 98 hospitals with 24,725 beds, 103 health centres with 1,548 beds and 1,220 dispensaries.

CULTURE

Broadcasting. The government-controlled Radiodiffusion Télévision Marocaine broadcasts 3 national (1 in French, English and Spanish) and 8 regional radio programmes and 1 TV channel (colour by SECAM). Broadcasting in Berber languages commenced in 1994. There is also a government commercial radio service and an independent TV channel. In 1995 there were 6m. radio and 2·5m. TV sets in use.

Cinema. There were 218 cinemas in 1995 and a total attendance of 22·01m. 5 full-length films were made.

Press. In 1995 the number of newspapers was 475, including dailies, weeklies and periodicals, of which 314 come out in Arabic, 160 in French and 1 in English.

Tourism. There were 2,693,000 foreign tourists in 1996, spending US$1·38bn.

DIPLOMATIC REPRESENTATIVES
Of Morocco in Great Britain (49 Queen's Gate Gdns., London, SW7 5NE)
Ambassador: Khalil Haddaoui.

Of Great Britain in Morocco (17 Blvd de la Tour Hassan, Rabat)
Ambassador: Anthony Layden.

Of Morocco in the USA (1601 21st St., NW, Washington, D.C., 20009)
Ambassador: Mohamed Benaissa.

Of the USA in Morocco (2 Ave. de Marrakech, Rabat)
Ambassador: Edward M. Gabriel.

Of Morocco to the United Nations

Ambassador: Ahmed Snoussi.

Of Morocco to the European Union
Ambassador: Rachad Bouhlal.

FURTHER READING
Direction de la Statistique. *Annuaire Statistique du Maroc.—Conjoncture Économique.*
 Quarterly *Bulletin Official.* Rabat. Weekly
Findlay, A. M., *Morocco* [Bibliography]. 2nd ed. Oxford and Santa Barbara (CA), 1995
Pazzanita, A. G., *The Maghreb.* [Bibliography]. Oxford and Santa Barbara (CA), 1998

National library: Bibliothèque Générale et Archives, Rabat.
National statistical office: Direction de la Statistique, BP178, Rabat.

WESTERN SAHARA

The Western Sahara was designated by The United Nations in 1975, its borders
having been marked as a result of agreements made between France, Spain and
Morocco in 1900, 1904 and 1912. Sovereignty of the territory is in dispute between
Morocco and the Polisario Front (Popular Front for the Liberation of the Saguia el
Hamra and Rio de Oro), which formally proclaimed a government-in-exile of the
Sahrawi Arab Democratic Republic (SADR) in Feb. 1976.
  Area 266,769 sq. km (102,680 sq. miles). Around 230,000 inhabitants (estimate
July1997) are within Moroccan jurisdiction. Another estimated 196,000 Saharawis
live in refugee camps around Tindouf in south-west Algeria. The main towns (1982
census) are El-Aaiún, the capital (96,784), Dakhla (17,822) and Es-Semara (17,753).
  Life expectancy at birth (1997 est.) male, 46·7 years; female, 50·0 years. Birth rate
(1997 est.) per 1,000 population: 46·1; death rate: 17·5. The projected population for
2000 is 245,000.
  The population is Arabic-speaking, and almost entirely Sunni Moslem.

President: Mohammed Abdelaziz.
Prime Minister: Mahfoud Ali Larous Beiba.

  Rich phosphate deposits were discovered in 1963 at Bu Craa. Morocco holds 65%
of the shares of the former Spanish state-controlled company. Production reached
5·6m. tonnes in 1975, but exploitation has been severely reduced by guerrilla
activity. After a nearly complete collapse, production and transportation of
phosphate resumed in 1978, ceased again, and then resumed in 1982. Installed
electrical capacity was 56,000 kW in 1995, with production of 85m. kWh in 1995.
There are about 6,100 km of motorable tracks, but only about 500 km of paved
roads. There are airports at El-Aaiún and Dakhla. As most of the land is desert, less
than 19% is in agricultural use, with about 2,000 tonnes of grain produced annually.
In 1989 there were 27 primary schools with 14,794 pupils and 18 secondary schools
with 9,218 pupils.

FURTHER READING
Damis, J., *Conflict in Northwest Africa: The Western Sahara Dispute.* Stanford, 1983
Hodges, T., *Western Sahara: The Roots of a Desert War.* London and Westport, 1984
Pazzanita, A. G., *Western Sahara* [Bibliography]. Oxford and Santa Barbara (CA), 1996
Sipe, L. F., *Western Sahara: A Comprehensive Bibliography.* New York, 1984
Thompson, V. and Adloff, R., *The Western Saharans: Background to Conflict.* London, 1980
Zoubir, Y. H. and Volman, D. (eds.) *The International Dimensions of the Western Sahara
 Conflict.* New York, 1993

MOZAMBIQUE

República de Moçambique

Capital: Maputo
Population estimate, 2000: 19·56m.
GNP per capita: (PPP$) 500
HDI/world rank: 0·281/166

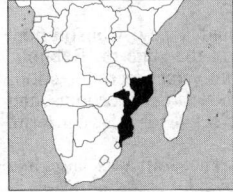

KEY HISTORICAL EVENTS

In 1506 Sofala was occupied by the Portuguese. Mozambique was at first ruled as part of Portuguese India but a separate administration was created in 1752. In 1951 Mozambique became an Overseas Province of Portugal. Following a decade of guerrilla activity, Portugal and the nationalists jointly established a transitional government on 20 Sept. 1974. Independence was achieved on 25 June 1975. A one-party state dominated by the Mozambique Liberation Front (FRELIMO) was set up but armed insurgency led by the Mozambique National Resistance (RENAMO) continued until on 4 Oct. 1992 President Chissano and Afonso Dhlakama, leader of RENAMO, signed a treaty in Rome ending the civil war. The treaty provided for all weapons to be handed over to the UN and all armed groups to be disbanded within 6 months. In 1994 the country held its first multi-party elections won by the Frelimo Party and a new Parliament was inaugurated with 250 seats. The UN presence ended in Jan. 1995.

TERRITORY AND POPULATION

Mozambique is bounded east by the Indian ocean, south by South Africa, south-west by Swaziland, west by South Africa and Zimbabwe and north by Zambia, Malaŵi and Tanzania. It has an area of 799,380 sq. km (308,642 sq. miles) and a population, according to the 1997 census, of 15·7m, giving a density of 20 per sq. km. Up to 1·5m. refugees abroad and 5m. internally displaced persons during the Civil War have begun to return home.

The UN gives a projected population for 2000 of 19·56m.

In 1995 an estimated 66·2% of the population were rural, but urbanization is increasing rapidly. In the period 1990-95 the annual growth in the urban population was 8·7%, a rate only exceeded by Botswana.The areas, populations and capitals of the provinces are:

Province	Sq. km	1 Jan 1987	Estimate 1991	Capital
Cabo Delgado	82,625	1,109,921	1,202,200	Pemba
Niassa	129,056	607,670	686,700	Lichinga
Nampula	81,606	2,837,856	2,841,400	Nampula
Zambézia	105,008	2,952,251	2,619,300	Quelimane
Tete	100,724	981,319	734,600	Tete
Manica	61,661	756,886	609,500	Chimoio
Sofala	68,018	1,257,710	1,427,500	Beira
Inhambane	68,615	1,167,022	1,157,000	Inhambane
Gaza	75,709	1,138,724	1,401,500	Xai-Xai
Province of Maputo	25,756	544,692	840,800	Maputo
City of Maputo	602	1,006,765	931,600	

The capital is Maputo (estimated population, 1997, 1,095,000). Other large cities are Beira (1991 population, 294,197), Nampula (232,670) and Nacala (125,208).

The main ethnolinguistic groups are the Makua/Lomwe (52% of the population), the Nyanja and Sena (12%), Shona (6%) and Tsonga (24%).

Portuguese remains the official language, but vernaculars are widely spoken throughout the country. English is also widely spoken.

SOCIAL STATISTICS

1995 births, 758,000; deaths, 312,000. Birth rate per 1,000 population, 1995, 43·9; death rate, 18·1. Infant mortality per 1,000 live births, 1995, 147. Life expectancy at birth, 1990–95, was 44·4 years for males and 47·5 years for females. Annual growth rate, 1997, 6%. Fertility rate, 1990–95, 6·5 births per woman.

CLIMATE
A humid tropical climate, with a dry season from June to Sept. In general, temperatures and rainfall decrease from north to south. Maputo, Jan. 78°F (25·6°C), July 65°F (18·3°C). Annual rainfall 30" (760 mm). Beira, Jan. 82°F (27·8°C), July 69°F (20·6°C). Annual rainfall 60" (1,522 mm).

CONSTITUTION AND GOVERNMENT
On 2 Nov. 1990 the People's Assembly unanimously voted a new Constitution, which came into force on 30 Nov. This changed the name of the state to 'Republic of Mozambique', legalized opposition parties, provided for universal secret elections and introduced a bill of rights including the right to strike, press freedoms and habeas corpus. The head of state is the *President*, directly elected for a 5-year term. Parliament is a 250-member *National Assembly*.

The 1990 Constitution was under review in early 1999. The draft was launched for public debate before being tabled to parliament for approval.

National Anthem. 'Viva, viva a Frelimo' ('Long live Frelimo'); words and tune by J. Sigaulane Chemane. A parliamentary ad-hoc committee has been established to produce a new national anthem to reflect the multiparty democracy prevailing in the country.

RECENT ELECTIONS
Presidential and parliamentary elections were held on 27-29 Oct. 1994. The electorate was 6·5m.; turn-out was 90%. President Chissano was re-elected by 53·3% of votes cast against 1 opponent. FRELIMO gained 44·3% of votes cast for the National Assembly, and RENAMO 37·7%.

The next presidential and parliamentary elections are expected in Oct. 1999.

CURRENT ADMINISTRATION
President: Joaquim A. Chissano (FRELIMO; sworn in 9 Dec. 1994).

A new government was formed on 16 Dec. 1994 which in March 1999 comprised: *Prime Minister:* Dr Pascoal M. Mocumbi. *Economic and Social Affairs (President's Office):* Dr Eneas C. Comiche. *Parliamentary Affairs (President's Office):* Francisco C. J. Madeira. *Defence and Security Affairs (President's Office) and Home Affairs:* Almerinho Manhenje. *Foreign Affairs and Co-operation:* Dr Leonardo S. Simão. *National Defence:* Aguiar J. R. Mazula. *Justice:* Jose I. Abudo. *Finance:* Tomas A. Salomão. *Education:* Arnaldo V. Nhavotso. *Health:* Aurelio A. Zilhao. *Culture, Youth and Sports:* Jose Mateus Muaria Katupha. *Industry, Trade and Tourism:* Oldemiro J. Baloi. *Mineral Resources and Energy:* John W. Katchamila. *Labour:* Guilherme L. Mavila. *Environmental Action Co-ordinator:* Bernardo P. Ferraz. *State Administration:* Alfredo M. S. C. Gamito. *Agriculture and Fisheries:* Carlos A. Rosario. *Public Construction and Housing:* Roberto C. White. *Transport and Communication:* Paulo Muxanga. *Social Action:* Alcinda Albreu. *Social Welfare:* Acucena Xavier Duarte. *Interior:* Almerinho Menhenje.

Local Government. The capital of Maputo and 10 provinces, each under a Governor, are sub-divided into 112 districts.

DEFENCE
The President of the Republic is C.-in-C. of the armed forces. Defence expenditure totalled US$72m. in 1997 (US$5 per capita).

Army. Equipment includes about 80 T-54/-55 main battle tanks. Personnel 4–5,000.

Navy. A small flotilla based principally at Maputo, with subsidiary bases at Beira, Nacala, Pemba and Inhambane, comprises 3 ex-Soviet inshore patrol craft, 2 ex-Soviet inshore minesweepers and 2 landing craft, but none is believed operational. Some boats are based at Metangula on Lake Nyasa. Naval personnel in 1997 were believed to total 100.

Air Force. The Air Force was reported to have about 40 MiG-21 fighters and 5 An-26 turboprop transports. About 4 Mi-24 armed helicopters and 5 Mi-8 transport helicopters, 4 Cherokee primary trainers and 4 Cessna light aircraft. Personnel

(1997) 1,000 (including air defence units), with 40 combat aircraft and 5 armed helicopters.

INTERNATIONAL RELATIONS
Mozambique is a member of the UN, Commonwealth, OAU, SADC, Non-Aligned Movement, Organization of the Islamic Conference, Indian Ocean Rim, Organization of the Portuguese Language Countries and is an ACP member state of the ACP-EU relationship.

ECONOMY
Policy. In 1990 the government abandoned economic planning in favour of a market economy. In Dec. 1993 the National Reconstruction Plan was launched to repair the rural economic and social infrastructure. Its implementation is dependent upon foreign aid.

Performance. Real GDP growth was 3% in 1995 and 6% in 1996.

Budget. In 1996 revenues were an estimated US$324m. and expenditure US$600m.

Currency. The unit of currency is the *metical* (MZM) of 100 *centavos*. Inflation was an estimated 40% in 1995, but declined to 18% in 1996. Foreign exchange reserves were US$493m. in Feb. 1998. Total money supply in Feb. 1998 was 6,734m. meticais.

Banking and Finance. Most banks had been nationalized by 1979. The central bank and bank of issue is the Bank of Mozambique, which hived off its commercial functions in 1992 to the newly-founded Commercial Bank of Mozambique. There is a state Development Bank.

Weights and Measures. The metric system is in force.

ENERGY AND NATURAL RESOURCES
Electricity. Installed capacity was 2·36m. kW in 1994. Production in 1994 was 490m. kWh. Consumption per capita in 1993 was 45 kWh.

Oil and Gas. Natural gas finds are being explored for potential exploitation, and both onshore and offshore foreign companies are prospecting for oil.

Water. Although the country is rich in water resources, the provision of drinking water to rural areas remains a major concern. Some river basins, especially the Rovuma, Zambezi and Lumpopo, are of interest to oil prospectors.

Minerals. There are deposits of pegamite, tantalite, graphite, apatite, tin, iron ore and bauxite. Other known reserves are: nepheline syenite magnelite, copper, garnet, kaolin, asbestos, bentonite, limestone, gold, titanium and tin.

Output (in 1,000 tonnes), 1991: Coking coal, 584; lignite, 167; charcoal, 572; salt, 3,839; marble, 118; gold, 5,773 kg.

Agriculture. Agriculture accounted for 37% of GDP in 1996. All land is owned by the state but concessions are given. In 1996 there were 3m. ha of arable land. Production in tonnes (1994): Cereals, 819,000; maize, 526,000; bananas (1992), 80,000; rice, 98,000; groundnuts, 74,000; copra (1992), 72,000; vegetables (1992), 115,000; potatoes (1992), 72,000; cashews, 54,000; sunflower seed, 10,000; cotton (lint) (1992), 13,000; sugar cane (1994) 234,000; raw cotton (1994) 29,400.

Livestock 1996: 1·29m. cattle, 385,000 goats (1995), 122,000 sheep, 175,000 pigs, 23m. chickens (1995).

Forestry. In 1995 there were 16·86m. ha of forests, or 21·5% of the land area (down from 17·44m. ha in 1990), including eucalyptus, pine and rare hardwoods. In 1995 timber production was 18·39m. cu. metres.

Fisheries. The catch in 1995 was 26,870 tonnes, of which 21,740 tonnes were from sea fishing. Prawns and shrimps are the major export at 14,000 tonnes per year. The potential sustainable annual catch is estimated at 500,000 tonnes of fish (anchovies 300,000 tonnes, the rest mainly mackerel).

INDUSTRY

Although the country is overwhelmingly rural, there is some substantial industry in and around Maputo (steel, engineering, textiles, processing, docks and railways).

Labour. The labour force in 1996 totalled 9,221,000 (52% males). In 1998, 83% of the economically active population were engaged in agriculture, 8% in industry and 9% in services. Women represent 48% of the total labour force.

Trade Unions. The main trade union confederation is the Organização dos Trabalhadores de Moçambique, but several unions have broken away.

INTERNATIONAL TRADE

Foreign debt was US$5,842m. in 1996.

Imports and Exports. Imports in 1995 totalled US$784m. and exports US$168m. Principal exports, 1995 (in US$1m.): Prawns, 70; cashew nuts, 3; cotton, 19; sugar, 11. Main export markets, 1994: Spain, 22·7%; South Africa, 17%; USA, 10%; Japan, 16%; Portugal, 14·7%. Main import suppliers: South Africa, 42·8%; Portugal, 4·6%; Zimbabwe, 6·7%; France, 2·6%.

In 1996 exports rose 33% to US$226m., whilst imports rose only 10%.

Trade Fairs. There is an annual trade fair, FACIM, which takes place in Aug. and Sept.

COMMUNICATIONS

Roads. In 1996 there were 5,700 km of paved and 24,700 km of unpaved roads, but most were in bad condition or mined. Passenger cars numbered 30,977 in 1994 (2 per 1,000 inhabitants).

Rail. The state railway consists of 5 separate networks, with principal routes on 1,067 mm gauge radiating from the ports of Maputo (950 km), Beira (994 km) and Nacala (914 km). Total length in 1995 was 2,983 km of 1,067 mm gauge and 140 km of 762 mm gauge. In 1995, 5·4m. passengers and 3·1m. tonnes of freight were carried.

Civil Aviation. There are international airports at Maputo and Beira. The national carrier is the state-owned Linhas Aéreas de Moçambique (LAM). It provides domestic services and in 1998 operated international routes to Harare, Johannesburg and Lisbon. In 1998 services were also provided by Air France, Air Malawi, Air Zimbabwe, Metavia Airlines, Royal Swazi National Airways Corporation, South African Airways and TAP. In 1996 Maputo handled 263,117 passengers (153,032 on international flights) and Beira 53,997 (49,820 on domestic flights).

Shipping. The principal ports are Maputo, Beira, Nacala and Quelimane. In 1995 sea-going shipping totalled 26,080 GRT.

Telecommunications. Main telephone lines numbered 66,100 in 1997 (3·6 per 1,000 persons). In 1995 there were 7,200 fax machines and in Jan. 1998 approximately 3,500 Internet users.

Postal Services. In 1995 there were 425 post offices. Postal services in Mozambique are provided by a public company, Correios de Moçambique, EP (CDM).

SOCIAL INSTITUTIONS

Justice. The 1990 Constitution provides for an independent judiciary, habeas corpus, and an entitlement to legal advice on arrest. The death penalty was abolished in Nov. 1990.

Religion. About 40% of the population follow traditional animist religions. In 1992 there were 4·72m. Christians (mainly Roman Catholic) and 1·95m. Moslems.

Education. The adult literacy rate in 1995 was 41·1% (57·7% among males but only 23·3% among females). Only Yemen has a bigger difference in literacy rates between the sexes.

In 1997 there were 1,750,000 pupils in 5,600 primary schools and (1995) 185,181 with 5,615 at 216 secondary schools. Private schools and universities were permitted to function in 1990. Eduardo Mondlane University had 3,470 students and 390 academic staff in 1995–96. In the last couple of years 4 more institutions of higher education have been opened, namely: The Higher Institute of International Relations (ISRI), the Pedagogical University (UP), the University and Polytechnic Higher Institute (ISPU) and the Catholic University (UC).

Health. There were (1997) 10 hospitals, 418 health centres and 996 medical posts. There were 2 psychiatric hospitals. In 1990 there were 387 doctors (equivalent to 1 for every 36,320 persons), 1,139 midwives, 3,533 nursing personnel, 108 dentists and 353 pharmacists. Private health care was introduced alongside the national health service in 1992.

CULTURE

Broadcasting. Radio Moçambique is part state-owned and part commercial. There are 3 national programmes in Tsonga and Portuguese and an external service in English. Television is at a trial stage (colour by PAL). In 1995 there were about 660,000 radio and 60,000 TV receivers.

TVM is the national television station and RTK, Klint Radio and Television, is privately owned.

Press. There are 2 well-established daily newspapers (Noticias and Diário in Maputo and Beira respectively). 5 additional newspapers were registered in 1998: Savana, Mediacoop, Demos, Metical and Domingo.

Tourism. Tourism is a potential growth area for the country. There are 2,500 km of Indian Ocean beaches, coral reefs, diving, deep-sea fishing, wildlife, game parks, highlands and plains.

Festivals. There are annual culture festivals throughout the country.

Libraries. As well as libraries at the higher education institutes, there is an independent public library in Maputo.

National Theatre and Opera. In addition to state-owned theatres and opera houses, Avenida and Matchedge are privately owned.

DIPLOMATIC REPRESENTATIVES
Of Mozambique in Great Britain (21 Fitzroy Sq., London, W1P 5HJ)
High Commissioner: Dr Eduardo Jose Baciao Koloma.

Of Great Britain in Mozambique (Ave. Vladimir I. Lenine 310, Maputo)
High Commissioner: Bernard Everett.

Of Mozambique in the USA (1990 M. St., NW, Washington, D.C., 20036)
Ambassador: Geraldo Namashulua.

Of the USA in Mozambique (Ave Kenneth Kaunda 193, Maputo)
Ambassador: Brian D. Curran.

Of Mozambique to the United Nations
Ambassador: Carlos Dos Santos.

Of Mozambique to the European Union
Ambassador: Trindade O Da Silva.

FURTHER READING
Andersson, H., *Mozambique: a War against the People.* London, 1993
Darch, C., *Mozambique.* [Bibliography] Oxford and Santa Barbara (CA), 1987
Finnegan, W., *A Complicated War: the Harrowing of Mozambique.* California Univ. Press, 1992
Newitt, M., *A History of Mozambique.* Farnborough, 1996

MYANMAR

Myanmar Naingngandaw
(Union of Myanmar)

Capital: Yangon (Rangoon)
Population estimate, 2000: 49·34m.
Estimated GDP: $51·5bn.
HDI/world rank: 0·481/131

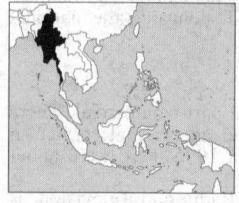

KEY HISTORICAL EVENTS

In 1785 the Alaugpaya dynasty of Burma conquered Arakan in the south-west. Arakanese refugees fled into India in large numbers and turned Chittagong into a base for guerrilla raids on Burma, thus provoking reprisal raids into India by Burmese forces.

This was followed by Burma's invasions of the kingdom of Assam. The British East India Company then took action in defence of its Indian interests and in 1826 finally drove the Burmese out of India and annexed territory in south Burma. The kingdom of Upper Burma, ruled from Mandalay in the north, remained independent. A second war with Britain in 1852 ended with the British annexation of the Irrawaddy Delta.

In 1862 and 1867 trade treaties were concluded with Upper Burma. However, in 1885 the British invaded, deposed the king and occupied Upper Burma. In 1886 all Burma became a province of the Indian empire. The Chin tribes of the Burmese-Indian borderlands were subdued in 1889-90. The Indian system of administration was not suitable for the country and exacerbated resentment at imperial economic policies and Britain's refusal to support Buddhism as the state religion. There were violent uprisings in the 1930s and in 1937 Burma was separated from India and some degree of self-government was introduced.

Following the Japanese invasion and occupation of 1942-45, Britain and Burma began to negotiate the establishment of independence, which was achieved in 1948 with the creation of the Union of Burma, an independent republic outside the Commonwealth. The president was Sao Shwe Thaike.

In 1958 there was an army *coup*, and another in 1962 led by Gen. Ne Win, who installed a Revolutionary Council and dissolved parliament. The Council lasted until March 1974 when the country become a one-party socialist republic, a new constitution having been approved by referendum in Dec. 1973. The name was changed to Socialist Republic of the Union of Burma. U Ne Win became president, serving until 1982, when he was succeeded by U San Yu. On 18 Sept. 1988, the Armed Forces seized power and set up the State Law and Order Restoration Council (SLORC). On 19 June 1989 the government changed the official name of the country in English to the Union of Myanmar.

The military junta did not accept the outcome of the 1990 general election, and the leader of the party which won the elections, Aung San Suu Kyi, was under house arrest from July 1989 to July 1995. She is still under restraint, and many of her followers, friends and relations have been arrested. She was awarded the Nobel Peace Prize in 1991.

In Aug. 1998 the National League for Democracy under Aung San Suu Kyi's leadership declared that it would convene a 'people's parliament' of all representatives who were elected at the 1990 election. The opposition maintains a high profile with mainly student-led anti-government demonstrations.

TERRITORY AND POPULATION

Myanmar is bounded in the east by China, Laos and Thailand, and west by the Indian Ocean, Bangladesh and India. Three parallel mountain ranges run from north to south; the Western Yama or Rakhine Yama, the Bagu Yama and the Shaun Plateau. The total area of the Union is 261,228 sq. miles (676,577 sq. km). The population in 1983 (census) was 35,313,905. Estimate (1996) 45·92m. (23·05m. female); density, 68 per sq. km.

The UN gives a projected population for 2000 of 49·34m.

An estimated 74·1% of the population lived in rural areas in 1995.

The leading towns are: Rangoon (Yangon), the capital (1983), 2,458,712; other towns, Mandalay, 532,985; Moulmein, 219,991; Pegu, 150,447; Bassein, 144,092; Sittwe (Akyab), 107,907; Taunggye, 107,607; Monywa, 106,873.

MYANMAR

The population of the 7 states and 7 administrative divisions at the 1983 census:
Kachin State, 903,982; Kayah State, 168,355; Karen State, 1,057,505; Chin State,
368,985; Sagaing Division, 3,855,991; Tenasserim Division, 917,628; Pegu
Division, 3,800,240; Magwe Division, 3,241,103; Mandalay Division, 4,580,923;
Mon State, 1,682,041; Rakhine State, 2,045,891; Rangoon Division, 3,973,782;
Shan State, 3,718,706; Irrawaddy Division, 4,991,057. Myanmar is inhabited by
many ethnic nationalities. There are as many as 135 national groups with the
Bamars, comprising about 68·96% of the population, forming the largest group.

The official language is Burmese; English is also in use.

SOCIAL STATISTICS
1995 births, 1,263,000; deaths, 465,000. Birth rate (1995), 28·0 per 1,000
population; death rate, 10·3. Growth rate in 1996, 1·87%. Life expectancy at birth,
1990–95, was 56·0 years for males and 59·3 years for females. Infant mortality,
1990–95, 90 per 1,000 live births; fertility rate, 3·6 births per woman.

CLIMATE
The climate is equatorial in coastal areas, changing to tropical monsoon over most of
the interior, but humid temperate in the extreme north, where there is a more
significant range of temperature and a dry season lasting from Nov. to April. In
coastal parts, the dry season is shorter. Very heavy rains occur in the monsoon
months May to Sept. Rangoon, Jan. 77°F (25°C), July 80°F (26·7°C). Annual
rainfall 104" (2,616 mm). Akyab, Jan. 70°F (21·1°C), July 81°F (27·2°C). Annual
rainfall 206" (5,154 mm). Mandalay, Jan. 68°F (20°C), July 85°F (29·4°C). Annual
rainfall 33" (828 mm).

CONSTITUTION AND GOVERNMENT
Following elections in May 1990, the ruling State Law and Order Restoration
Council (SLORC) said it would hand over power after the People's Assembly had
agreed on a new constitution, but in July 1990 it stipulated that any such constitution
must conform to guidelines which it would itself prescribe.

In May 1991, 48 members of the National League for Democracy (NLD) were
given prison sentences on charges of treason. In July 1991 opposition members of
the People's Assembly were unseated for alleged offences ranging from treason to
illicit foreign exchange dealing. Such members, and unsuccessful candidates in the
May 1990 elections, are forbidden to stand in future elections.

On 28 Nov. 1995 the government re-opened a 706-member Constitutional
Convention in which the NLD was given 107 places. The NLD withdrew on 29
Nov.

In Nov. 1997 the country's ruling generals changed the name of the government
to the State Peace and Development Council (SPDC), and reshuffled the cabinet. In
Dec. 1997, following a period when the national currency fell to a record low, there
were further changes to the cabinet, while corruption investigations were begun
against some former ministers.

National Anthem. 'Gba majay Bma' ('We shall love Burma for ever'); words and
tune by Saya Tin.

RECENT ELECTIONS
In elections in May 1990 the opposition National League for Democracy (NLD), led
by Aung San Suu Kyi (b. 1945), won 392 of the 485 People's Assembly seats
contested with some 60% of the valid vote. Turn-out was 72%, but 12·4% of ballots
cast were declared invalid. The military ignored the result and refused to hand over
power.

CURRENT ADMINISTRATION
In March 1999 the government comprised:
Prime Minister and Minister of Defence: Senior Gen. Than Shwe.
Deputy Ministers: Vice-Admiral Maung Maung Khin; Lieut.-Gen. Tin Tun;
Lieut.-Gen. Tin Hla.
Minister of Agriculture and Irrigation: Maj. Gen. Nyunt Tin. *Industry:* Aung
Thaung; Maj.-Gen. Saw Lwin. *Foreign Affairs:* Win Aung. *National Planning and
Economic Development:* Soe Tha. *Transport:* Maj. Gen. Hla Myint Swe. *Labour:*

MYANMAR

Vice-Adm. Tin Aye. *Co-operatives:* Col. Aung San. *Rail Transportation:* Pan Aung. *Energy:* Brig.-Gen. Lun Thi. *Education:* Than Aung. *Health:* Maj.-Gen. Ket Sein. *Commerce:* Maj.-Gen. Kyaw Than. *Hotels and Tourism:* Lt. Gen. Saw Lwin. *Communications, Posts and Telegraphs:* Brig.-Gen. Win Tin. *Finance and Revenue:* Khin Maung Thein. *Religious Affairs:* Maj.-Gen. Sein Htwa. *Construction:* Maj.-Gen. Saw Tun. *Science and Technology:* U Thaung. *Culture:* Win Sein. *Immigration and Population:* Saw Tun. *Information:* Maj.-Gen. Kyi Aung. *Progress of Border Areas, National Races and Development Affairs:* Col. Thein Nyunt. *Electric Power:* Maj.-Gen. Tin Htut. *Sports:* Brig.-Gen. Sein Win. *Forestry:* Aung Phone. *Home Affairs:* Col. Tin Hlaing. *Mines:* Brig.-Gen. Ohn Myint. *Social Welfare, Relief and Resettlement:* Brig.-Gen. Pyei Son. *Livestock and Fisheries:* Brig.-Gen. Maung Maung Thein. *Military Affairs:* Lt. Gen. Tin Hla. *Office of the Chairman of the State Peace and Development Council:* Lieut.-Gen. Min Thein; Brig.-Gen. Maung Maung; Brig.-Gen. David Oliver Abel. *Office of the Prime Minister:* Brig.-Gen. Lun Maung; Than Shwe; Maj.-Gen. Tin Ngwe; Lt. Gen. Tim Ngwe.

Local Government. Myanmar is divided into 7 states and 7 administrative divisions; these are sub-divided into 314 townships and then into villages and wards.

DEFENCE
Military expenditure in 1997 totalled US$2,167m. (US$45 per capita).

Army. The strength of the Army was reported to be about 300,000 in 1997. The Army is organized into 10 regional commands comprising 10 light infantry divisions. Combat units comprise 3 armoured, 245 infantry and 7 artillery battalions, and 1 anti-aircraft artillery battalion. Equipment includes 26 Comet and 36 Ch T-69II main battle tanks. There are 2 paramilitary units: People's Police Force (50,000) and People's Militia (35,000).

Navy. The fleet includes 2 old escort patrol vessels (ex-USA PCE and MSF types) and about 50 patrol craft, half sea-going and half riverine. Auxiliaries include 1 patrol craft support ship, 2 survey ships and 15 small landing craft. Personnel in 1996 totalled about 14,000 including 800 naval infantry.

The Fishery Protection Service (under the Pearl and Fishery Department) operates 3 coastal and 8 inshore patrol craft.

Air Force. The Air Force is intended primarily for internal security duties. Its combat force comprises 10 G-4 Super Galeb supplied by Yugoslavia, 30 F-7 fighters and 24 A-5 fighter-bombers received from China, 18 turboprop Pilatus PC-7s and PC-9s. Transport and second-line units are equipped with 10 Mi-17 helicopters, 4 FH-227, 1 Turbo-Porter, 2 Chinese-built Y-8s, 1 Citation and 6 Cessna 180 aircraft, 10 Polish-built W-3 Sokol, 12 Bell UH-1, and 10 Alouette III helicopters. Personnel (1996) 9,000.

INTERNATIONAL RELATIONS
Myanmar is a member of the UN, Colombo Plan and ASEAN.

ECONOMY

Policy. A short-term plan ran from 1992–93 to 1995–96. There were within it annual plans with targets. Liberalization measures to promote a market economy were introduced in 1990.

Performance. Real GDP growth was 7·1% in 1995 (7·5% in 1994).

Budget. The fiscal year ends 31 March. Estimates for 1995–96: Revenue, K.129,507m.; current expenditure, K.122,904m., capital expenditure, K.39,620m.

State budget estimates are classified into 3 parts, *viz.* State Administrative Organizations, State Economic Enterprises and Town and City Development Committees.

Receipts in 1995–96 included: Tax revenue, K.19,945m.; receipts from state economic enterprises, K.92,899·6m.

Currency. The unit of currency is the *kyat* (MMK) of 100 *pyas*. In 1995 K.110,866m. were in circulation. Foreign exchange reserves were US$250m. and gold reserves 230,000 troy oz. in Dec. 1997. The average annual inflation rate over the period 1990–96 was 21·9%. Since 1 June 1996 import duties have been calculated at a rate US$1 = K.100.

Banking and Finance. The Central Bank of Myanmar was established in 1990. Its *Governor* is Kyi Aye. In 1995 there were 15 private domestic banks. Since 1996 foreign banks with representative offices (there were 31 in 1996) have been permitted to set up joint ventures with Burmese banks. The foreign partner must provide at least 35% of the capital. The state insurance company is the Myanmar Insurance Corporation. Deposits in savings banks were K.30,963m. in 1994.

A stock exchange opened in Rangoon in 1996.

Weights and Measures. The British system of weights and measures is generally used. The metric system has also been introduced in many areas. But in the markets the use of Myanmar weights and measures, as outlined below, is common:

viss (peit-tha)	= 3·6 lbs	= 1·633 kilograms
tical (kyat-tha)	= 0·576 oz	= 16·33 grams
622·22 *viss*	= 1 long ton (2,240 lbs)	= 1·016 metric ton
612·39 *viss*	= 2,204·62 lbs	= 1 metric ton

ENERGY AND NATURAL RESOURCES

Electricity. In 1995–96 the installed capacity of Myanma Electric Power was 1,000 MW, of which 328 MW was hydro-electric, 62 MW thermal, 530 MW natural gas and 80 MW diesel. Capacity of other networks was 344 MW. Total generated, 3,922m. kWh. Consumption per capita in 1995 was an estimated 73 kWh.

Oil and Gas. Production (1995–96) of crude oil was 6·9m. bbls.; natural gas, 69,540m. cu. feet.

Minerals. Production in 1995–96 (in tonnes): Zinc concentrates, 6,070; nickel speiss, 60; antimonial lead, 210; refined lead, 4,250; tin concentrates, 492; tungsten concentrates, 95; tin, tungsten and scheelite mixed, 1,400; refined silver, 260,000 fine oz.; gold, 22,496 troy oz.; refined tin metal, 310; copper concentrates, 42,500; coal, 49.

Agriculture. In 1995–96, 4·5m. peasant families cultivated 24·9m. acres. Agriculture accounted for 60% of GDP in 1996. Only in the Democratic Republic of the Congo did agriculture contribute a higher percentage.

Liberalization measures of 1990 permit farmers to grow crops of their choice. The total sown area in 1995–96 was 22·5m. acres. 4·76m. acres were irrigated. In 1995–96, 429,864 tonnes of fertilizer were distributed. Production (1995–96, in 1,000 tonnes): Paddy, 19,568; sugar-cane, 3,060; maize, 212; jute, 43; cotton, 214; wheat, 109; butter beans, 29; soya beans, 64; rubber, 28; groundnuts, 569.

Livestock (1995–96): Cattle, 12m.; buffaloes, 2·3m.; pigs, 3·2m.; sheep and goats, 1·5m.; poultry, 31·9m. In 1995–96 there were 6·8m. draught cattle and about 8,000 tractors.

Net output of agriculture for 1993–94 was valued at K.23,595m.

Forestry. Forest area in 1995 was 27·15m. ha, covering 41·3% of the total land area (29·09m. ha in 1990). Teak resources cover about 6m. hectares (15m. acres). Teak extracted in 1995–96, 256,000 cu. tons; hardwood, 1,109,000 cu. tons.

Fisheries. In 1995–96 sea fishing produced 371·4m. *viss* (606,476 tonnes) and freshwater fisheries 138·4m. *viss* (226,000 tonnes). Aquacultural fish production was 48·9m. *viss* (79,851 tonnes). Cultured pearls and oyster shells are produced.

INDUSTRY

Of the 48,601 industrial enterprises in 1995–96, 1,607 were state-owned, 636 were co-operatives and 46,358 were private. Production (1995–96) in 1,000 tonnes: Cement, 524; fertilizers, 300; sugar, 67·6; paper, 15·5; 1,429 motor cars, 597 tractors; (1994–95) cotton yarn, 16·8; 35,042 bicycles were produced. In 1995–96 manufacturing output was valued at K.6,556m.

Labour. The population of working age (15 to 59) in 1995–96 was 26·34m. Economically active persons in 1995–96: 17·59m., of whom 11·27m. were employed in agriculture, 1·34m. in services, 1·48m. in manufacturing and 1·72m. in trade. In 1994 there were 541,500 persons registered as unemployed.

INTERNATIONAL TRADE

In Aug. 1991 the USA imposed trade sanctions in response to alleged civil rights violations. Foreign debt was US$5,184m. in 1996. A law of 1989 permitted joint ventures, with foreign companies or individuals able to hold 100% of the shares.

Imports and Exports. Since 1990 in line with market-oriented measures firms have been able to participate directly in trade.

Imports in 1996 totalled US$1,355m. and exports US$745m. Main imports (in K.1m.), 1994–95: Raw materials, 1,854·3; transport equipment, 1,251; tools and spares, 303·5; machinery, 1,099·9; construction materials, 472. Main exports: Teak, 953·1; pulses and beans, 799·4; rubber, 443·1; hardwood, 107·8; rice, 1,165·8. Main export markets: India, 695·4; Singapore, 883·5; Thailand, 542·7; China, 277·5; Hong Kong, 269·1.

COMMUNICATIONS

There were 16,770 miles of road in 1993–94, of which 2,452 miles were union highway. In 1995–96 the state service ran 951 buses, 197 taxis and 1,969 lorries. There were also 155,107 buses and 29,694 lorries in private co-operative ownership. In 1995–96, 121·28m. passengers and 1·19m. tonnes of freight were carried by road.

Roads. There were 28,200 km of roads in 1996, of which 3,440 km were surfaced. An estimated 27,000 passenger cars were in use in 1996 (less than 1 per 1,000 inhabitants) and 42,000 vans and trucks.

Rail. In 1995 there were 3,955 km of route on metre gauge. In 1995–96 Myanma Railways carried 3·28m. tonnes of freight and 53·4m. passengers.

Civil Aviation. Myanma Airways International operates domestic services and in 1998 had international services to Bangkok, Hong Kong and Singapore. In 1998 services were also provided by Air China, Air Mandalay, All Nippon Airways, Biman Bangladesh Airlines, China Airlines, Druk-Air, Indian Airlines, Lufthansa, Malaysia Airlines, Pakistan International Airlines, Silk Air and Thai Airways International. There were, in 1995, 43 civil airfields. In 1995–96, 0·72m. passengers were carried on domestic and 138,000 on international flights (121,000 in 1994–95).

Shipping. There are nearly 100 km of navigable canals. The Irrawaddy is navigable up to Myitkyina, 1,450 km from the sea, and its tributary, the Chindwin, is navigable for 630 km. The Irrawaddy delta has approximately 3,000 km of navigable water. The Salween, the Attaran and the G'yne provide about 400 km of navigable waters around Moulmein. In 1995 merchant shipping totalled 523,000 GRT. Vessels totalling 2,338,000 net registered tons entered ports and vessels totalling 1,624,000 NRT cleared in 1995.

In 1995–96, 24·5m. passengers and 1·03m. tonnes of freight were carried on inland waterways. The ocean-going fleet of the state-owned Myanma Five Star Line in 1995 comprised 11 liners, 4 short-haul vessels and 3 coastal passenger/cargo vessels. In 1995–96, 60,000 passengers and 1,030,000 tonnes of freight were transported coastally and overseas. The port is Rangoon.

Telecommunications. Myanmar had 213,500 main telephone lines in 1997, or 4·6 per 1,000 persons—the lowest penetration rate of any country outside Africa. Cellular phone subscribers numbered 2,100 in 1995 and there were 1,400 fax machines.

Postal Services. In 1995–96 there were 1,205 post offices.

SOCIAL INSTITUTIONS

Justice. The highest judicial authority is the Chief Judge, appointed by the government.

Religion. About 89·4% of the population—mainly Bamars, Shans, Mons, Rakhines and some Kayins—are Buddhists, while the rest are Christians, Moslems, Hindus and Animists. The Christian population is composed mainly of Kayins, Kachins and Chins. Islam and Hinduism are practised mainly by people of Indian origin.

Education. Education is free in primary, middle and vocational schools; fees are charged in senior secondary schools and universities. In 1995–96 there were 36,499 primary schools with 187,344 teachers and 5,995,015 pupils; 1,578 monastic primary schools (permitted since 1992) with 80,863 pupils; 2,112 middle schools with 60,759 teachers and 1,417,189 pupils and 927 high schools with 19,120 teachers and 402,411 pupils.

In higher education in 1995–96 there were 12 teacher training schools with 315 teachers and 2,067 students, 5 teacher training institutes with 304 teachers and 2,170 students, 17 technical high schools with 498 teachers and 7,145 students, 11 technical institutes with 668 teachers and 12,080 students, 10 agricultural high schools with 100 teachers and 1,053 students, 7 agricultural institutes with 162 teachers and 1,844 students, 41 vocational schools with 369 teachers and 6,532 students, 6 universities with 3,050 teachers and 154,680 students, 6 degree colleges with 705 teachers and 53,362 students and 10 colleges with 629 teachers and 40,327 students.

There was also a University for the Development of the National Races of the Union and institutes of medicine (3), dentistry, paramedical science, pharmacy, nursing, veterinary science, economics, technology (2), agriculture, education (2), foreign languages, computer science and forestry. An institute of remote education maintains a correspondence course at university level.

The adult literacy was 83·1% in 1995 (88·7% among males and 77·7% among females).

Expenditure on education in 1994 represented 14·4% of total government expenditure.

Health. In 1995–96 there were 12,950 doctors, 860 dentists, 9,851 nurses, 8,143 midwives and 737 hospitals with 28,372 beds.

Welfare. In 1995–96 contributions to social security totalled (K.1m.) 117·5 (from employers, 73·2; from employees, 43·9). Benefits paid totalled 82·6, and included: Sickness, 12·9; maternity, 3·9; disability, 3·7; survivors' pensions, 1·3.

CULTURE

Broadcasting. The government runs a TV and a radio station. In 1995 there were 3·2m. radio and 1m. television receivers (colour by NTSC).

Press. There are 4 daily newspapers, one of which is in English.

Tourism. In 1996 there were 165,000 foreign tourists, spending US$90m.

DIPLOMATIC REPRESENTATIVES

Of Myanmar in Great Britain (19A Charles St., London, W1X 8ER)
Ambassador: Vacant.

Of Great Britain in Myanmar (80 Strand Rd., Rangoon)
Ambassador: Robert A. Gordon, OBE.

Of Myanmar in the USA (2300 S. St., NW, Washington, D.C., 20008)
Ambassador: Tin Winn.

Of the USA in Myanmar (581 Merchant St., Rangoon)
Ambassador: Kent Wiedemann.

Of Myanmar to the United Nations
Ambassador: Win Mra.

Of Myanmar to the European Union
Ambassador: Vacant.

FURTHER READING
Carey, P. (ed.): *Burma: The Challenge of Change in a Divided Society.* London, 1997
Herbert, P., *Burma* [Bibliography]. Santa Barbara and Oxford, 1991
Lintner, B., *Outrage: Burma's Struggle for Democracy.* 2nd ed. London, 1990
O'Brien, H., *Forgotten Land: a Rediscovery of Burma.* London, 1991
Silverstein, Josef: *Burma, Military Rule and the Politics of Stagnation.* Cornell, 1977
Smith, M., *Burma: Insurgency and the Politics of Ethnicity.* London, 1991
Suu Kyi, Aung San, *Freedom from Fear and Other Writings.* London, 1991
Taylor, R. H., *The State in Burma.* London, 1987

National statistical office: Ministry of National Planning and Economic Development, Rangoon.

NAMIBIA

Republic of Namibia

Capital: Windhoek
Population estimate, 2000: 1·73m.
GNP per capita: (PPP$) 5,390
HDI/world rank: 0·644/107

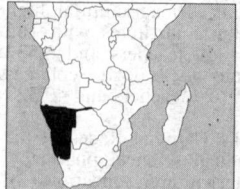

KEY HISTORICAL EVENTS

Namibia's first inhabitants were the Bushmen (Sands). Around 1300 the Namas and the Damaras came from the north pushing the Bushmen towards the Kalahari Desert. Around 1500 the Owambos settled on the high plateau and in the Okavongo delta. Around 1600 Herero herdsmen arrived from the north.

German migration accelerated from 1850 onwards. In 1884 South West Africa was declared a German protectorate. Germany then introduced racial segregation and the exploitation of the diamond mines began. In 1915 the Union of South Africa occupied German South West Africa at the request of the Allied powers. On 17 Dec. 1920 the League of Nations entrusted South West Africa as a Mandate to the Union of South Africa, to be administered under the laws of the mandatory power. After World War II South Africa refused to place the territory under the UN Trusteeship system, and formally applied for its annexation to the Union. In Oct. 1966 the General Assembly of the UN terminated South Africa's mandate and established a UN Council for South West Africa in May 1967. However, South Africa continued to administer the territory in defiance of various UN resolutions. In June 1968 the UN changed the name of the territory to Namibia. In 1971 the International Court of Justice ruled in an advisory opinion that South Africa's presence in Namibia was illegal. In Dec. 1973 the UN appointed a UN Commissioner for Namibia.

After negotiations between South Africa and the UN, a multi-racial Advisory Council was appointed in 1973. Representatives of all the population groups assembled in Windhoek for the Constitutional Conference which in Aug. 1976 resolved that a multi-racial interim government be formed by early 1977 and that the country should become independent by 31 Dec. 1978. This resolution was rejected by the UK, the USA, the Federal Republic of Germany, France and Canada, after which South Africa agreed to universal suffrage elections. The Administrator-General appointed in Sept. 1977 to govern the territory until independence, moved to abolish all laws based on racial discrimination—a precondition for elections. In April 1978 South Africa accepted a plan for UN-supervised elections leading to independence which was endorsed in UN Security Council Resolution 435 of 27 July 1978. After the final plans for the UN-supervised elections were published, South Africa announced on 20 Sept. 1978 that it was going ahead with internally sponsored elections for a Constituent Assembly. In the elections held on 4–8 Dec. 1978 the Democratic Turnhalle Alliance (DTA) gained 41 of the 50 seats in a percentage poll of 82%, in spite of the fact that the South West Africa People's Organization (SWAPO) instructed its members not to take part in the elections.

A 12-member Ministers' Council was instituted and in Sept. 1981 it was enlarged to 15 members and given executive authority on all matters except constitutional issues, security and foreign affairs. On 11-13 Nov. 1980 elections were held for the second-tier Representative Authorities, each controlling certain administrative functions for a specific ethnic group but not for any particular geographical area. In Jan. 1983 the Ministers' Council and the National Assembly were dissolved and executive and legislative powers reverted to the Administrator-General.

In Sept. 1983 the Multi-Party Conference (MPC) of internal parties was formed. In May 1984 talks were held in Lusaka between the MPC and SWAPO. SWAPO refused to take part in further constitutional talks with the MPC. The MPC then petitioned South Africa for a form of self-government for Namibia, and on 17 June 1985 the Transitional Government of National Unit was installed. Negotiations began again in May and July 1988 between Angola, Cuba and South Africa. A peaceful settlement was agreed and the Geneva Protocol was signed on 5 Aug. 1988. In Dec. it was agreed that Cuban troops should withdraw from Angola and South African troops from Namibia by 1 April 1989. The Transitional Government of

National Unity resigned on 28 Feb. 1988 to make provision for the implementation of UN Security Council Resolution 435. The UN Transition Assistance Group (UNTAG) supervised elections for the constituent assembly in Nov. 1989. Independence was achieved on 21 March 1990. In 1998, around a quarter of the Namibian army was sent to support the beleaguered government of the Democratic Republic of Congo. A secessionist plot in Caprivi was uncovered in 1998 and, as a result, over 700 people fled into neighbouring Botswana.

TERRITORY AND POPULATION

Namibia is bounded in the north by Angola and Zambia, west by the Atlantic Ocean, south and south-east by South Africa and east by Botswana. The Caprivi Strip (Caprivi Region), about 300 km long, extends eastwards up to the Zambezi river, projecting into Zambia and Botswana and touching Zimbabwe. The area, including the Caprivi Strip and Walvis Bay, is 824,269 sq. km. South Africa transferred Walvis Bay to Namibian jurisdiction on 1 March 1994. Census population, 1991, 1,401,711 (720,784 females; urban, 32·76%). Estimate, 1996, 1,677,200; density, 2 per sq. km.

The UN gives a projected population for 2000 of 1·73m.

An estimated 64% of the population were rural in 1995.

Population by ethnic group at the censuses of 1970 and 1981 and estimates for 1991:

	1970	1981	1991
Ovambos	342,455	506,114	665,000
Whites	90,658	76,430	85,000
Damaras	64,973	76,179	100,000
Hereros	55,670	76,296	100,000
Namas	32,853	48,541	64,000
Kavangos	49,577	95,055	124,000
Caprivians	25,009	38,594	50,000
Coloureds	28,275	42,254	...
Basters	16,474	25,181	...
Bushmen	21,909	29,443	...
Tswanas	4,407	6,706	...
Other	...	12,403	...
	732,260	1,033,196	1,401,711

Namibia is administratively divided into 13 regions. Area, estimated population and chief towns in 1997:

Region	Area (in sq. km)	Population	Chief town
Caprivi	19,532	92,000	Katima Mulilo
Okavango	43,417	136,000	Rundu
Otjozondjupa	105,327	85,000	Grootfontein
Oshikoto	26,607	176,000	Tsumeb
Omusati	13,637	158,000	Outapi
Oshana	5,290	159,000	Oshakati
Ohangwena	10,582	178,000	Oshikango
Kunene	144,254	58,500	Opuwo
Erongo	63,719	98,500	Swakopmund
Khomas	36,804	174,000	Windhoek
Omaheke	84,731	55,600	Gobabis
Hardap	109,888	80,000	Mariental
Karas	161,324	73,000	Keetmanshoop

Towns with populations over 5,000 (1997): Windhoek, 169,000; Walvis Bay, 50,000; Oshakati, 37,000; Ondangwa, 33,000; Rehoboth, 21,000; Swakopmund, 18,000; Rundu, 18,000; Keetmanshoop, 16,000; Otjiwarongo, 16,000; Tsumeb, 15,000; Okahandja, 11,000; Grootfontein, 11,000; Mariental, 8,000; Gobabis, 7,000; Khorixas, 7,000; Lüderitz, 7,000.

English is the official language. Afrikaans and German are also spoken.

SOCIAL STATISTICS
1996 births, estimate, 63,000; deaths, 13,000. Rates (1996 estimate) per 1,000 population: Birth, 37·3; death, 8·0. Expectation of life, 1996 estimate: Males, 62·8 years; females, 66·2. Infant mortality, 1990–95, 64 per 1,000 live births; fertility rate, 5·3 births per woman.

In the Human Development Index, or HDI (measuring progress in countries in longevity, knowledge and standard of living), Namibia and Cambodia were the countries which made the most progress in 1995 compared to 1994—both recording increases of 0·074. Namibia's HDI value was 0·644 out of a maximum of 1·0 in 1995, up from 0·570 in 1994, resulting in a rise from 118th in the world to 107th.

CLIMATE
The rainfall increases steadily from less than 50 mm in the west and south-west up to 600 mm in the Caprivi Strip. The main rainy season is from Jan. to March, with lesser showers from Sept. to Dec. Namibia is the driest African country south of the Sahara.

CONSTITUTION AND GOVERNMENT
On 9 Feb. 1990 with a unanimous vote the Constituent Assembly approved the Constitution which stipulated a multi-party republic, an independent judiciary and an executive *President* who may serve a maximum of two 5-year terms. The bicameral legislature consists of a 78-seat *National Assembly*, 72 members of which are elected for 5-year terms by proportional representation and up to 6 appointed by the president by virtue of position or special expertise, and a *National Council* consisting of 2 members from each Regional Council elected for 6-year terms.

National Anthem. 'Namibia, land of the brave'; words and tune by Axali Doeseb.

RECENT ELECTIONS
Presidential and parliamentary elections were held on 7-8 Dec. 1994. The electorate was 0·65m.; turn-out was 76%. Sam Nujoma was re-elected President by 76·3% of votes cast against 1 opponent. The South West Africa People's Organization (SWAPO) won 53 of the electable National Assembly seats; the Democratic Turnhalle Alliance, 15; the United Democratic Front, 2; others, 2.

CURRENT ADMINISTRATION
President: Sam Nujoma, b. 1928 (SWAPO, elected Feb. 1990; re-elected Dec. 1994; sworn in 21 March 1995).

In March 1999 the government comprised:
Prime Minister: Hage Geingob.
Deputy Prime Minister: Hendrik Witbooi.
Minister of Home Affairs: Jerry Ekandjo. *Foreign Affairs:* Theo-Ben Gurirab. *Defence:* Erikki Nghimtina. *Finance:* Nangolo Mbumba. *Tertiary Education and Vocational Training:* Nahas Angula. *Information and Broadcasting:* Ben Amathila. *Health and Social Services:* Dr Libertine Amathila. *Mines and Energy:* Andimba Toiva Ya Toiva. *Justice:* Ngarikutuke Tjiriange. *Regional and Local Government and Housing:* Nicky Iyambo. *Agriculture, Water and Rural Development:* Helmut Angula. *Trade and Industry:* Hidipo Hamutenya. *Environment and Tourism:* Philemon Malima. *Works, Transport and Communications:* Hampie Plichta. *Lands, Resettlement and Rehabilitation:* Pendukeni Iithana. *Youth and Sport:* Richard Kapelwa-Kabajani. *Fisheries and Marine Resources:* Abraham Iyambo. *Prisons and Correctional Services:* Marco Hausiku. *Basic Education and Culture:* John Mutorwa. *Without Portfolio:* Hifikepunye Pohamba.

Local Government. There are 13 elected regional and 93 local authority councils. Elections to regional councils and local authorities took place in Dec. 1992. SWAPO gained 70 regional seats with 67·3% of votes cast; DTA, 20 with 27·1%.

A *Council of Traditional Chiefs* advises the President on the utilization and control of communal land.

DEFENCE
In 1997 defence expenditure totalled US$89m. (US$51 per capita).

NAMIBIA

Army. The army consists of 1 Presidential Guard, 4 motorized infantry, 1 artillery, 1 air defence artillery and 1 anti-tank battalion. An Air Wing has 6 Cessna 337 patrol aircraft, along with 2 Alouette and 2 Lama helicopters. Personnel (1997), 5,700.

Coastguard. A force of 100 (1996) operates 2 offshore and 1 inshore patrol craft based at Walvis Bay. There is 1 Cessna Caravan II maritime patrol aircraft.

INTERNATIONAL RELATIONS
Namibia is a member of the UN, Commonwealth, SADC and OAU.

ECONOMY
The Namibian economy is heavily dependent on mining and fisheries.

Policy. The National Development Plan aims for annual average growth of 5% up to 2000.

Performance. Real GDP growth was 3% in 1996 and was expected to be around 2% in 1998.

Budget. The financial year runs from 1 April. In 1996-97 revenue was N$4,489m. and expenditure, N$5,073m. Tax revenue totalled N$3,988m.; re-current expenditure was N$4,099m.

Currency. The unit of currency is the *Namibia dollar* (NAD) of 100 *cents*, introduced on 14 Sept. 1993 and pegged to the South African rand. The rand is also legal tender at parity. The average annual inflation rate over the period 1990–96 was 9·6%. In Feb. 1998 foreign exchange reserves were US$285m. Total money supply in Feb. 1998 was N$3,053m.

Banking and Finance. The Bank of Namibia is the central bank. Its *Governor* is Tom Alweendo. Commercial banks include First National Bank of Namibia, Namibia Banking Corporation, Standard Bank Namibia, Commercial Bank of Namibia, Bank Windhoek (the only locally-owned bank) and City Savings and Investment Bank. There is a state-owned Agricultural Bank. Total assets of commercial banks were R2,383·2m. at 31 Dec. 1991.

There are 2 building societies with total assets (31 March 1990) R424·9m. A Post Office Savings Bank was established in 1916. In March 1991 its total assets were R21·8m. A stock exchange (NSE) is in operation.

ENERGY AND NATURAL RESOURCES

Electricity. Namibia imports electricity from South Africa. Consumption per capita in 1995 was 584 kWh.

Water. The 12 most important dams have a total capacity of 589·2m. cu. metres. The Kunene, the Okavango, the Zambezi, the Kwando or Mashi and the Orange River are the only permanently running rivers but water can generally be obtained by sinking shallow wells. Except for a few springs, mostly hot, there is no surface water.

Minerals. There are diamond deposits off the coast, which produce a third of diamond production. Namibia produces 1·3m. carats per year, accounting for around 8% of world diamond production. 1996 output (in tonnes): Uranium oxide, 2,886; copper, 25,000; lead, 67,760; zinc, 64,600; silver, 69,200 kg; gold, 2,205 kg; diamonds, 1,420,000 carats.

Agriculture. Agriculture accounted for 14% of GDP in 1996. Namibia is essentially a stock-raising country, the scarcity of water and poor rainfall rendering crop-farming, except in the northern and north-eastern parts, almost impossible. Generally speaking, the southern half is suited for the raising of small stock, while the central and northern parts are more suited for cattle. In 1994 there were 660,000 ha of arable land, 2,000 ha of permanent cropland and 38m. ha of pasture. Guano is harvested from the coast, converted into fertilizer in South Africa and most of it exported to Europe. In 1995, 45% of the active labour force worked in the agricultural sector, and 45% of the population was dependent on agriculture.

Livestock (1996): 2·2m. cattle, 3·3m. sheep, 2m. goats.

In 1996, 13m. litres of milk were produced. Principal crops (1994 in tonnes): Wheat, 6,400; maize, 38,500; sunflower seed, 845; sorghum (1990), 8,000; vegetables (1990), 32,000.

Forestry. Forests covered 12·37m. ha in 1995, or 15% of the land area, down from 12·58m. ha in 1990.

Fisheries. Pilchards, mackerel and hake are the principal fish caught. Since 1993 there has been a dearth of fish. The catch in 1995 was 285,980 tonnes (330,026 tonnes in 1993), almost entirely from marine waters. Conservation policies are in place. The policy aims at ensuring that the country's fisheries resources are utilized on a sustainable basis and also aims to ensure their lasting contribution to the country's economy.

INDUSTRY
Manufacturing contributed 12% of GDP in 1996. Of the estimated total of 400 undertakings, the most important branches are food production (accounting for 29·3% of total output), metals (12·7%) and wooden products (7%). The supply of specialized equipment to the mining industry, the assembly of goods from predominantly imported materials and the manufacture of metal products and construction material play an important part. Small industries, including home industries, textile mills, leather and steel goods, have expanded. Products manufactured locally include chocolates, beer, cement, leather shoes and delicatessen meats and game meat products.

Labour. In 1996 the labour force totalled 650,000 (59% males). Nearly half the economically active population in 1991 were engaged in agriculture, fisheries and forestry. Around 20% of the workforce was unemployed in 1991. The main employers were government services, agriculture and mining.

INTERNATIONAL TRADE
Total foreign debt was US$140m. in 1996. Export Processing Zones were established in 1995 to grant companies with EPZ status some tax exemptions and other incentives. The Offshore Development Company (ODC) is the flagship of the Export Processing Zone regime. The EPZ regime does not restrict; any investor (local or foreign) enjoys the same or equal advantages in engaging themselves in any choice of business (allowed by law).

Imports and Exports. Trade in 1996 (in US$1m.): Imports, 1,374; exports, 1,349, including cattle (58·1), karakul pelts (2·08), small stock (42), fish (289), diamonds (542), uranium and other minerals (237) and meat products (82). The largest import supplier in 1996 was South Africa with 87%; largest export markets: UK, 34%; South Africa, 27%.

COMMUNICATIONS

Roads. In 1996 the total national road network was 65,220 km, including 5,000 km of tarred roads. In 1996 there were 132,000 registered motor vehicles, including 64,000 passenger cars and 63,000 trucks and vans.

Rail. The Namibia system connects with the main system of the South African railways at Ariamsvlei. The total length of the line inside Namibia was 2,382 km of 1,065 mm gauge in 1996. In 1995–96 railways carried 124,000 passengers and 1·7m. tonnes of freight.

Civil Aviation. The national carrier is the state-owned Air Namibia. In 1998 Windhoek was also served by Air Botswana, British Airways, LTU International Airways, Lufthansa, South African Airways and TAAG. In 1996 the major airport, Windhoek International, handled 392,3865 passengers (349,529 on international flights). Eros is used mainly for domestic flights.

Shipping. The main port is Walvis Bay. During 1991–92, 820 ships called and 1m. tonnes of cargo were unloaded. There is a harbour at Lüderitz which handles mainly fishing vessels. In 1995 merchant shipping totalled 52,000 GRT.

Telecommunications. Telecom Namibia is the responsible corporation. In 1997 main telephone lines numbered 92,800 (57·6 per 1,000 inhabitants). Cellular phone subscribers numbered 3,500 in 1995, and there were 466 telex users in 1996. There were around 2,000 Internet users in Jan. 1998.

Postal Services. Namibia Post is the responsible corporation. In 1996 there were 76 post offices and 15 postal agencies which served 74,400 private box renters and 961 private bag services distributed by rail or road transport.

SOCIAL INSTITUTIONS

Justice. There is a Supreme Court, a High Court and a number of magistrates' and lower courts. An Ombudsman is appointed. Judges are appointed by the president on the recommendation of the Judicial Service Commission.

Religion. About 90% of the population is Christian.

Education. Literacy was 60% in 1997. Primary education is free and compulsory. In 1995 there were 368,222 pupils at primary schools, 103,308 at secondary schools and 11,344 at institutions of higher education. The University of Namibia had 2,240 students and 160 academic staff in 1994–95. Namibia has the highest proportion of female students in higher education of any African country, with 61% in 1994.

In 1994 total expenditure on education came to 8·7% of GNP.

Health. In 1992 there were 47 hospitals (4 private) and 238 clinics and health centres. There were 324 doctors, 51 dentists and 4,471 nursing staff.

CULTURE

Broadcasting. The Namibian Broadcasting Corporation operates a national radio service from 3 stations and vernacular services. It also operates 10 TV stations (colour by PAL). In 1995 there were 39,000 TV sets and 215,000 radios in use. One privately-owned television channel and two privately-owned radio stations operate from Windhoek.

Press. There were 4 daily and 3 weekly newspapers in 1997.

Tourism. In 1996 there were 560,202 visitors who spent R45,000,000.

DIPLOMATIC REPRESENTATIVES

Of Namibia in Great Britain (6 Chandos St., London, W1M 0LQ)
High Commissioner: Vacant.

Of Great Britain in Namibia (116 Robert Mugabe Ave., 9000 Windhoek)
High Commissioner: Glyn Davis.

Of Namibia in the USA (1605 New Hampshire Ave., NW, Washington D.C., 20009)
Ambassador: Veiccoh K. Nghiwete.

Of the USA in Namibia (14 Lossen St., Private Bag 12029, Windhoek)
Ambassador: George F. Ward.

Of Namibia to the United Nations
Ambassador: Martin Andjaba.

Of Namibia to the European Union
Ambassador: Zedekia Ngavirue.

FURTHER READING
Gupta, V., *Independent Namibia: Problems and Prospects.* Delhi, 1990
Herbstein, D. and Evenston, J., *The Devils are Among Us: the War for Namibia.* London, 1989
Kaela, L. C. W., *The Question of Namibia.* London, 1996
Katjavivi, P.H., *A History of Resistance in Namibia.* London, 1988
Schoeman, Elna and Stanley, *Namibia.* [Bibliography] Oxford and Santa Barbara (CA), 1997
Sparks, D.L. and Green, D., *Namibia: the Nation after Independence.* Boulder, (CO), 1992

National statistical office: Central Statistics Office, Windhoek.

NAURU

Republic of Nauru

Population estimate, 2000: 11,000
Estimated GDP: $100m.

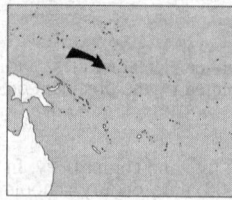

KEY HISTORICAL EVENTS
The island was discovered by Capt. Fearn in 1798, annexed by Germany in Oct. 1888 and surrendered to Australian forces in 1914. It was administered by the UK under a League of Nations mandate from 1920 until 1947 when the UN approved a trusteeship agreement with Australia, New Zealand and the UK as joint administering authorities. Independence was gained on 31 Jan. 1968.

TERRITORY AND POPULATION
Nauru is a coral island surrounded by a reef situated 0° 32' S. lat. and 166° 56' E. long. Area, 21·3 sq. km. At the 1983 census the population totalled 8,100, of whom 5,285 were Nauruans. Estimated population in July 1997: 10,390; density, 488 per sq. km.

In 2000 the population is projected to be 11,000.

Nauruan is the official language, although English is widely used for government purposes.

SOCIAL STATISTICS
1995 births, estimate, 180; deaths, 50. Rates, 1995 estimate (per 1,000 population): Births, 18; deaths, 5; infant mortality, 41 (per 1,000 live births). Annual growth rate, 1990–95, 1·5%.

CLIMATE
A tropical climate, tempered by sea breezes, but with a high and irregular rainfall, averaging 82" (2,060 mm). Average temperature, Jan. 81°F (27·2°C), July 82°F (27·8°C). Annual rainfall 75" (1,862 mm).

CONSTITUTION AND GOVERNMENT
A Legislative Council was inaugurated on 31 Jan. 1966. An 18-member Parliament is elected on a 3-yearly basis.

National Anthem. 'Nauru bwiema, ngabena ma auwe' ('Nauru our homeland, the country we love'); words by a collective, tune by L. H. Hicks.

RECENT ELECTIONS
No political parties exist in Nauru. At the last elections on 8 Feb. 1997 only non-partisans were elected.

CURRENT ADMINISTRATION
President: Bernard Dowiyogo (b. 1946; serving a 4th term since 17 June 1998).

The government in March 1999 comprised:

Minister of Public Service, External Affairs: Kinza Clodumar. *Finance and Budgetary Reforms, Island Development and Industry, Civil Aviation and Education:* Bernard Dowiyogo. *Internal Affairs and Sports:* Vinson F. Detenamo. *Health and Youth Affairs:* Ludwig Scotty. *Justice:* Vassal Gadoengin. *Works and Community Services:* Derog Gioura. *Assistant to the President:* Reubun Kun.

INTERNATIONAL RELATIONS
Nauru is a member of the Pacific Community, the South Pacific Forum and has a special relationship with the Commonwealth. It was scheduled to become a full member of the Commonwealth in May 1999.

ECONOMY
Performance. Real GDP growth was 7·0% in 1995 (4·5% in 1994).

Budget. Revenues in 1995/96 were estimated to be US$23·4m. and expenditure US$64·8m.

Currency. The Australian dollar is in use.

ENERGY AND NATURAL RESOURCES

Electricity. Installed capacity in 1995 was 13,250 kW; production was 48m. kWh in 1995.

Minerals. A central plateau contained high-grade phosphate deposits. The interests in the phosphate deposits were purchased in 1919 from the Pacific Phosphate Company by the UK, Australia and New Zealand. In 1967 the British Phosphate Corporation agreed to hand over the phosphate industry to Nauru for approximately $A20m. over 3 years. Nauru took over the industry in July 1969. It is estimated that the deposits will be exhausted by 2008. In May 1989 Nauru filed a claim against Australia for environmental damage caused by the mining. In Aug. 1993 Australia agreed to pay compensation of $A73m. In March 1994 New Zealand and the UK each agreed to pay compensation of $A12m.

Agriculture. Livestock (1996): Pigs, 3,000.

Fisheries. The catch in 1996 was approximately 450 tonnes.

INTERNATIONAL TRADE

Imports and Exports. The export trade consists almost entirely of phosphate shipped to Australia, New Zealand, the Philippines and Japan. Imports: food, building construction materials, machinery for the phosphate industry and medical supplies. Exports, 1991 estimate, US$25m; imports, US$21m.

COMMUNICATIONS

Roads. In 1996 there were 24 km of paved and 6 km of unpaved roads.

Civil Aviation. There is an airfield on the island capable of accepting medium size jet aircraft. The national carrier, Air Nauru, is a wholly owned government subsidiary. In 1998 it flew to Brisbane, Guam, Manila, Melbourne, Pohnpei and Tarawa. In 1995 Air Nauru flew 2·7m. km, carrying 123,000 passengers.

Shipping. Deep offshore moorings can accommodate medium-size vessels. Shipping coming to the island consists of vessels under charter to the phosphate industry or general purpose vessels bringing cargo by way of imports.

Telecommunications. There were 1,000 telephones in 1992. International telephone, telex and fax communications are maintained by satellite. A satellite earth station was commissioned in 1990.

Postal Services. In 1995 there were 25 post offices, equivalent to approximately 1 for every 400 persons (the highest ratio of post offices per person of any country in the world).

SOCIAL INSTITUTIONS

Justice. The highest Court is the Supreme Court of Nauru. It is the Superior Court of record and has the jurisdiction to deal with constitutional matters in addition to its other jurisdiction. There is also a District Court which is presided over by the Resident Magistrate who is also the Chairman of the Family Court and the Registrar of Supreme Court. The laws applicable in Nauru are its own Acts of Parliament. A large number of British statutes and much common law has been adopted insofar as is compatible with Nauruan custom.

Religion. The population is mainly Roman Catholic or Protestant.

Education. Attendance at school is compulsory between the ages of 6 and 17. In 1989 there were 10 infant and primary schools and 2 secondary schools with a total of 165 teachers and 2,707 pupils. There is also a trade school with 4 instructors and an enrolment of 88 trainees. Scholarships are available for Nauruan children to receive secondary and higher education and vocational training in Australia and New Zealand.

CULTURE

Broadcasting. The government-controlled Nauru Broadcasting Service broadcasts a home service in Nauruan and English for 3 hours daily. There were 6,000 radio sets in use in 1995. New Zealand television programmes are received.

Cinema. In 1989 there were 3 cinemas with seating capacity of 500.

DIPLOMATIC REPRESENTATIVES
Of Great Britain in Nauru
High Commissioner: M. A. C. Dibben (resides in the Fiji Islands).

Of the USA in Nauru
Ambassador: Don Lee Gevirtz (resides in the Fiji Islands).

FURTHER READING
Macdonald, B., *Trusteeship and Independence in Nauru.* Wellington, 1988
Weeremantry, C., *Nauru: Environmental Damage under International Trusteeship.* OUP, 1992
Williams, M. and Macdonald, B., *The Phosphateers.* Melbourne Univ. Press, 1985

NEPAL

Nepal Adhirajya
(Kingdom of Nepal)

Capital: Káthmandu
Population estimate, 2000: 24·35m.
GNP per capita: (PPP$) 1,090
HDI/world rank: 0·351/152

KEY HISTORICAL EVENTS

Nepal is an independent Himalayan Kingdom located between India and the Tibetan region of China. For centuries, the history of Nepal was the struggle of rival chiefs for the consolidation of the surrounding area into a unified kingdom and its role as an asylum for refugees from the plains of India. Buddhism was introduced in about 639 AD.

From the 8th to the 11th centuries, many Buddhists fled to Nepal from India, which had been invaded by Muslims. In the 18th century Nepal was a collection of small principalities (many of Rajput origin) and the three kingdoms of the Malla dynasty: Káthmandu, Pátan and Bhádgaon. In central Nepal lay the principality of Gurkha (or Gorkha); its ruler after 1742 was Prithvi Náráyan Sháh, who conquered the small states which were his neighbours. Fearing his ambitions, in 1767 the Mallas brought in forces lent by the British East India Company to keep him in check. In 1769, these forces were withdrawn and Gurkha was then able to conquer the Malla kingdoms and unite Nepal as one state with its capital at Káthmandu. Prithvi Náráyan also enlarged Nepal by annexing Sikkim and the Tarai, Kumáon, Garhwál and Simla areas of India. He died in 1775 and his successors were beset by internal rivalry. Most of the Indian annexations were lost to the British.

In 1846, the Ráná family became the effective rulers of Nepal, establishing the office of prime minister as hereditary. In 1860, Nepal reached agreement with the British in India whereby Nepali independence was preserved and the recruitment of Gurkhas to the British army was sanctioned.

In 1950, the Sháh royal family allied itself with Nepalis abroad to end the power of the Ránás. The last Ráná prime minister resigned in Nov. 1951, the king having proclaimed a constitutional monarchy in Feb. 1951. A new constitution, approved in 1959, led to confrontation between the king and his ministers; it was replaced by one less liberal in 1962. King Mahendra died in Jan. 1972 and was succeeded by his son Birendra Bir Bikram Sháh Dev. Following pro-democracy demonstrations, on 16 April 1990 when 45 people died, King Birendra dismissed the government and proclaimed the abolition of the *panchayat* system of nominated councils but continuing pressure from pro-democracy activists persuaded the King to concede a new constitution. In Nov. 1990 he relinquished his absolute power. A general election held the following year was won by the Nepali Congress Party. The present government is a coalition led by the United Marxist-Leninist Party. Nepal remains one of the poorest countries but a five-year plan encompasses economic reform with the hope of ending illiteracy among the young by 2005.

TERRITORY AND POPULATION

Nepal is bounded in the north by China (Tibet) and the east, south and west by India. Area 140,800 sq. km; population (estimate, July 1997), 23,107,000, giving a density of 164 per sq. km; (census, 1991) 18,462,081 (9,241,167 females; 9·6% urban). By 1995 the urban population had risen to 10·3%.

The UN gives a projected population for 2000 of 24·35m.

The country is divided into 5 regions and subdivided into 14 zones. Area, population and administrative centres in 1990:

Zone/Region	Sq. km	Population (in 1,000)	Administrative centre
Mechi	8,196	1,268	Ilam
Koshi	9,669	1,885	Biratnagar (Morang)
Sagarmatha	10,591	1,597	Rajbiraj
East Region	28,456	4,750	Dhankuta
Janakpur	9,669	2,052	Jaleswar
Narayani	8,313	1,923	Birganj

Zone/Region	Sq. km	Population (in 1,000)	Administrative centre
Bagmati	9,428	2,093	Káthmandu
Central Region	27,410	6,068	Káthmandu
Gandaki	12,275	1,320	Pokhara
Lumbini	8,975	2,056	Butwal
Dhanlagiri	8,148	508	Baglung
West Region	29,398	3,884	Pokhara
Rapti	10,482	1,035	Tulsipur
Bheri	10,545	1,153	Nepalganj
Karuali	21,351	281	Jumla
Mid-West Region	42,378	2,469	Surkhet
Seti	12,550	724	Dhangarhi
Mahakali	6,989	1,022	Mahendra Nagar
Far West Region	19,539	1,746	Dipayal

Capital, Káthmandu; population (census 1991) 419,073. Other towns include Patan (Lalitpur), 117,203; Biratnagar (Morang), 130,129; Bhadgaon (Bhaktapur), 61,122.

The indigenous people are of Tibetan origin with a considerable Hindu admixture. The Gurkha clan became predominant in 1559 and has given its name to men from all parts of Nepal. There are 18 ethnic groups, the largest being: Newars, Indians, Tibetans, Gurungs, Mogars, Tamangs, Bhotias, Rais, Limbus and Sherpas. The official language is Nepalese but there are 20 new languages divided into numerous dialects.

SOCIAL STATISTICS
Births, 1995, 815,000; deaths, 257,000. 1995 birth rate per 1,000 population, 38·0; death rate, 12·0. Growth rate, 1997 estimate, 2·5%. Expectation of life was 57·6 years for males and 57·1 years for females in 1997. Only in the Maldives is the margin by which males are expected to outlive females greater. Infant mortality, 1990–95, 96 per 1,000 live births; fertility rate, 5·4 births per woman.

CLIMATE
Varies from cool summers and severe winters in the north to sub-tropical summers and mild winters in the south. The rainfall is high, with maximum amounts from June to Sept., but conditions are very dry from Nov. to Jan. Káthmandu, Jan. 10°C, July, 25°C. Average annual rainfall, 1,424 mm.

CONSTITUTION AND GOVERNMENT
The sovereign is HM Maharajadhiraja **Birendra Bir Bikram Sháh Dev** (b. 1946), who succeeded his father Mahendra Bir Bikram Sháh Dev on 31 Jan. 1972.

Under the constitution of 9 Nov. 1990 Nepal became a constitutional monarchy based on multi-party democracy. *Parliament* has 2 chambers: a 205-member House of Representatives (*Pratinidhi Sabha*) elected for 5-year terms, and a 60-member National Council (*Rastriya Sabha*), of which 10 members are nominated by the king.

National Anthem. 'Sri man gumbhira nepali prachanda pratapi bhupati' ('May glory crown our illustrious sovereign, the gallant Nepalese'); words by C. Chalise, tune by B. Budhapirthi.

RECENT ELECTIONS
Elections were held on 15 Nov. 1994. The electorate was 12·3m.; turn-out was 58%. 24 parties stood. The Communist Party of Nepal-United Marxist-Leninist Party (CPN-UML) won 88 seats, the Nepali Congress, 75, and the National Democratic Party, 20. Parliamentary elections were scheduled for May 1999.

CURRENT ADMINISTRATION
A Nepali Congress-Rastriya Prajatantra-Nepal Sadhavana coalition government was formed on 11 Sept. 1995. In Dec. 1998 the Prime Minister, Girija Prasad Koirala, resigned, but was reappointed to the prime ministership and put together a new coalition. However, a parliamentary election was scheduled to take place on 20 May 1999. In March 1999 the Cabinet comprised:

Prime Minister: Girija Prasad Koirala.

NEPAL

Deputy Prime Minister: Sailja Acharya.

Minister of Industry: Gajendra Narayan Singh. *Information and Communications:* Jaya Prakash Gupa. *Education, Women and Social Welfare:* Kul Bahadur Gurung. *Water Resources and Health:* Pradip Nepal. *Science and Technology, Tourism and Civil Aviation:* Bhim Bahadur Rawal. *Finance, Law and Justice:* Bharat Mohan Adhikari. *Commerce, Youth, Sports and Culture:* Purna Bahadur Khadka. *Local Development:* Amrit Bohara. *Population and Environment:* Ramesh Nath Pandey. *Parliamentary Affairs:* Jaya Prakash Gupta. *General Administration and Home Affairs:* Govinda Raj Joshi.

Local Government. The country is administratively divided into 14 zones, subdivided into 75 districts and over 3,500 villages. Elections were held in May 1992. The Nepali Congress gained a majority of seats.

DEFENCE
The King is commander-in-chief of the armed forces, but shares supreme military authority with the National Defence Council, of which the Prime Minister is chairman.

Defence expenditure in 1997 totalled US$42m. (US$2 per capita).

Army. The Army consists of 1 Royal Guard brigade and 5 infantry and 1 support brigade. Strength (1997) 46,000, and there is also a 40,000-strong paramilitary police force.

Air Force. Independent of the army since 1979, the Air Force has 1 Twin Otter and 2 Skyvan transport aircraft, 1 Puma helicopter and 3 Chetak helicopters. An H.S. 748 turboprop transport and 1 Super Puma and 1 Puma helicopter are operated by the Royal Flight. There are no combat aircraft. Personnel, 1997, 215.

INTERNATIONAL RELATIONS
Nepal is a member of the UN and the Colombo Plan.

ECONOMY
Policy. Since May 1991 the government has been moving forward with economic reforms, particularly those that encourage trade and foreign investment, e.g., by eliminating business licenses and registration requirements in order to simplify investment procedures. The government has also been cutting public expenditures by reducing subsidies, privatizing state industries, and laying off civil servants. Prospects for foreign trade and investment, particularly in areas other than power development and tourism, are limited by the small size of the economy, its remoteness and its susceptibility to natural disaster. The international community provides funding for 62% of Nepal's developmental budget and for 34% of total budgetary expenditures. Industrial activity is limited, mainly involving the processing of agricultural produce (jute, sugarcane, tobacco, and grain). Production of textiles and carpets has expanded recently and accounts for 85% of foreign exchange earnings. Apart from agricultural land and forests, exploitable natural resources are mica, hydropower and tourism. Agricultural production in the late 1980s grew by about 5%, compared to annual population growth of 2·6%.

Performance. Real GDP growth was 5·8% in 1995 (7·1% in 1994).

Budget. Revenues and expenditures in NRs 1m. for fiscal years:

	1993–94	1994–95	1995–96	1996–97[1]
Revenue	18,862	23,206	26,641	30,019
Expenditure	29,309	36,242	43,519	47,573

[1]Provisional.

Currency. The unit of currency is the *Nepalese rupee* (NPR) of 100 *paisas.* 50 *paisas* = 1 *mohur.* The average annual inflation rate over the period 1990–96 was 10·1%. In Nov. 1997 foreign exchange reserves were US$624m. and in Dec. 1997 gold reserves totalled 150,000 troy oz. Total money supply in Oct. 1997 was NRs 38,927m.

Banking and Finance. The Central Bank is the bank of issue. There were 438 commercial bank branches in 1994 with total deposits of NRs 52,327·7m.

ENERGY AND NATURAL RESOURCES

Electricity. Installed capacity is 280,000 kW. Production in 1994 was 940m. kWh, almost entirely hydro-electric. Consumption per capita was estimated in 1996 to be 48 kWh.

Minerals. Production (in tonnes), 1994: Lignite, 290; talcum, 1,363; magnesite (1990), 25,000; limestone, 295,000.

Agriculture. Agriculture is the mainstay of the economy, providing a livelihood for over 80% of the population. Arable land accounts for 17% of land use; forest and woodland 42%. In 1996 agriculture accounted for 42% of GDP. Crop production (1994 in 1,000 tonnes): Rice, 2,928; maize, 1,273; wheat, 914; sugar-cane, 1,500; potatoes, 840; millet, 268.

Livestock (1996); Cattle, 7m.; buffaloes, 3·28m.; sheep, 859,000; goats, 5·65m. (1995); pigs, 670,000; chickens, 10m. (1995).

Forestry. In 1995 the area under forests was 4·82m. ha, or 35·2% of the total land area (5·1m. ha and 37·3% in 1990). There are 8 national parks, covering 1m. ha, 5 wildlife reserves (170,490 ha) and 2 conservation areas (349,000 ha). Timber production was 20·82m. cu. metres in 1995, of which 20·2m. cu. metres were fuelwood and charcoal. Expansion of agricultural land has led to widespread deforestation.

Fisheries. The catch in 1996 was 21,148 tonnes, entirely from inland waters.

INDUSTRY

In 1992 there were 4,271 firms employing 10 or more persons in which 223,463 persons were working. Production, 1994: Cement, 326,839 tonnes; electrical cable, 9·3m. metres; soap, 18,600 tonnes; paper, 8,863 tonnes; leather, 1,369,750 sq. metres; shoes, 0·69m. pairs; jute goods, 20,187 tonnes; cotton fabrics, 5·1m. metres; synthetic textiles, 14·7m. metres; sugar, 49,227 tonnes; tea, 2,351 tonnes; beer, 16,776 litres; animal feed, 19,500 tonnes.

Labour. The labour force in 1996 totalled 10,179,000 (60% males). In 1992, 84% of the economically active population were engaged in agriculture, forestry or fisheries.

INTERNATIONAL TRADE

External debt was an estimated US$2,414m. in 1996.

Imports and Exports. Principal exports are food grains, jute, timber, oilseeds, ghee (clarified butter), potatoes, medicinal herbs, hides and skins, cattle.

Exports: US$430m. (1995 est.) but does not include unrecorded border trade with India. *Commodities:* carpets, clothing, leather goods, jute goods, grain. *Main partners:* India, USA, Germany, UK.

Imports: US$1·4bn. (1995 est.). *Commodities:* petroleum products 20%, fertilizer 11%, machinery 10%. *Main partners:* India, Singapore, Japan, Germany.

COMMUNICATIONS

Roads. In 1995 there were 9,933 km of roads, of which 3,421 km were macadamized and 6,512 km unpaved.

Rail. 101 km (762 mm gauge) connect Jayanagar on the North Eastern Indian Railway with Janakpur and thence with Bizalpura (54 km). 653,000 passengers and 9,151 tonnes of freight were carried in 1994.

Civil Aviation. There is an international airport (Tribhuvan) at Káthmandu. The national carrier is the state-owned Royal Nepal Airlines. It operates domestic services and in 1998 flew to Bangkok, Bombay, Calcutta, Delhi, Dubai, Frankfurt, Hong Kong, London, Osaka, Paris, Shanghai and Singapore. Services were also provided in 1998 by Aeroflot, Austrian Airlines, Biman Bangladesh Airlines, China Southwest Airlines, Condor Flugdienst, Druk-Air, Everest Air, Gulf Air, Indian Airlines, Lufthansa, Necon Air, Pakistan International Airlines, Qatar Airways, Singapore Airlines, Thai Airways International and Transavia Airlines. In 1995 Káthmandu handled 1,357,000 passengers (868,000 on international flights) and 13·9m. tonnes of freight.

Telecommunications. In 1997 Nepal had 160,200 main telephone lines, equivalent to 7·7 per 1,000 persons. There were 600 fax machines in 1995.

Postal Services. In 1994 there were 2,493 post offices.

SOCIAL INSTITUTIONS

Justice. The Supreme Court Act established a uniform judicial system, culminating in a supreme court of a Chief Justice and no more than 6 judges. Special courts to deal with minor offences may be established at the discretion of the Government. The Chief Justice is appointed by the king on recommendation of the Constitutional Council. Other judges are appointed by the king on the recommendation of the Judicial Council.

Religion. Nepal is a Hindu state. Hinduism was the religion of 90% of the people in 1992. Buddhists comprise 5% and Moslems 3%. Christian missions are permitted, but conversion is forbidden.

Education. The adult literacy rate in 1995 was 27·5% (40·9% among males and 14·0% among females). The overall rate and those both for males and for females is the lowest outside Africa. In 1994–95 there were 21,102 primary schools with 3,191,000 pupils and 81,544 teachers (33,536 trained); 4,739 lower secondary schools, with 0·67m. pupils and 15,358 teachers (4,820 trained); and 2,482 secondary schools, with 274,000 pupils and 13,820 teachers (5,865 trained). The Tribhuvan University had 93,800 students and 4,300 academic staff in 1995–96. There is also a Sanskrit University.

Health. There were 872 doctors and 4,606 nurses in 1996. There were 82 hospitals with 3,604 beds, 17 health centres and 775 medical posts. More than 40% of the population is undernourished. In 1995 hospital bed provision was just 2 for every 10,000 persons.

CULTURE

Broadcasting. Radio Nepal is part government-owned and part commercial. It broadcasts in Nepali and English from 3 stations. The government-owned Nepal Television Corporate transmits from 1 station (colour by PAL). In 1995 there were 780,000 radio and 110,000 TV sets.

Press. In 1997 there were 59 daily newspapers, including the official English-language *Rising Nepal*, 3 bi-weeklies, 454 weeklies and 48 fortnightlies. Press censorship was relaxed in June 1991.

Tourism. In 1996 there were 404,000 foreign tourists, spending US$130m.

DIPLOMATIC REPRESENTATIVES
Of Nepal in Great Britain (12A Kensington Palace Gdns., London, W8 4QU)
Ambassador: Dr Singha B. Basnyat.

Of Great Britain in Nepal (Lainchaur, Káthmandu, POB 106)
Ambassador: Lloyd B. Smith.

Of Nepal in the USA (2131 Leroy Pl., NW, Washington, D.C., 20008)
Ambassador: Damodar Gautam.

Of the USA in Nepal (Pani Pokhari, Káthmandu)
Ambassador: Ralph Frank.

Of Nepal to the United Nations
Ambassador: Narendra Bikram Shah.

Of Nepal to the European Union
Ambassador: Kedar Bhakta Shrestha.

FURTHER READING
Central Bureau of Statistics. *Statistical Pocket Book.* [Various years]

Borre, O. et al., *Nepalese Political Behaviour.* Aarhus Univ. Press, 1994
Ghimire, K., *Forest or Farm? The Politics of Poverty and Land Hunger in Nepal.* OUP, 1993
Pant, Y. P., *Trade and Co-operation in South Asia: a Nepalese Perspective.* Delhi, 1991
Sanwal, D. B., *Social and Political History of Nepal.* London, 1993
Wadwha, D.N., *Nepal* [Bibliography]. Oxford and Santa Barbara (CA), 1986

National statistical office: Central Bureau of Statistics, National Planning Commission Secretariat, Káthmandu

THE NETHERLANDS

Koninkrijk der Nederlanden
(Kingdom of the Netherlands)

Capital: Amsterdam
Seat of Government: The Hague
Population estimate, 2000: 15·87m.
GNP per capita: (PPP$) 20,850
HDI/world rank: 0·941/7

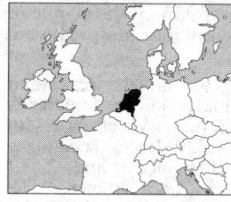

KEY HISTORICAL EVENTS

As the German Count of Nassau, William of Orange (1533–84) inherited vast possessions in the Netherlands and the Princedom of Orange in France. He was the initiator of the struggle for independence from Spain. The Revolt of the Netherlands began in 1568, and by the Union of Utrecht the more easily defensible seven provinces of the North—Holland, Zeeland, Utrecht, Overijssel, Groningen, Drenthe and Friesland—declared themselves independent. At the end of the Thirty Years War , by the Treaty of Westphalia (1648), Spain recognized the Republic of the United Netherlands. Members of the Orange-Nassau family became in succession the 'first servant of the Republic' with the title of 'Stadhouder' (governor). In 1689 Willem III acceded to the throne of England, becoming joint sovereign with his wife Mary. Willem III died in 1702 without issue, and there was no stadhouder until a member of the Frisian branch of Orange–Nassau was nominated hereditary stadhouder in 1747. However, his successor, Willem V, had to take refuge in England in 1795 when the French Army invaded. The country was freed from French domination in Nov. 1813.

The Congress of Vienna (1815) joined the Belgian provinces, called the 'Spanish' or the 'Austrian Netherlands' before the French Revolution, to the Northern Netherlands. The son of the former stadhouder, Willem V, was proclaimed King of the Netherlands as King Willem I on 16 March 1815. The union was dissolved by the Belgian revolution of 1830, and in 1839 Belgium and the Netherlands were recognized as two separate independent kingdoms.

In 1840 Willem I abdicated in favour of his son, Willem II, who was liberal in his outlook and who moved the Netherlands towards a constitutional monarchy, developing ministerial responsibility and electoral equality among direct tax payers. Willem II was succeeded by Willem III in 1849 under whom the liberal development continued. In 1890 Wilhelmina, the first of three successive queens, ascended the throne (the Netherlands is a hereditary monarchy with the succession in the direct male or female line in the order of primogeniture).

The Netherlands followed a policy of non-participation in the European conflicts of the early 20th century and during the First World War remained neutral. In the Second World War, however, the Netherlands was occupied by Germany from 1940 until 1945. After liberation in 1945, the country abandoned its traditional policy of neutrality. In 1948 the Netherlands joined with Belgium and Luxembourg to form the Benelux economic union; in 1957 it was a founder member of the EEC, and in 1949 joined NATO.

Since the Second World War the Netherlands has granted independence to her overseas possessions of Indonesia (in 1949 after much fighting) and Suriname (in 1975), leaving the Netherlands Antilles and Aruba as the only remaining Dutch dependencies.

In April 1980 Queen Juliana, who had reigned since 1948, abdicated in favour of her daughter Beatrix.

TERRITORY AND POPULATION

The Netherlands is bounded in the north and west by the North Sea, south by Belgium and east by Germany. The area (1997) is 41,526 sq. km, of which 33,889 sq. km is land. Projects of sea-flood control and land reclamation (polders) by the construction of dams and drainage schemes have continued since 1920.

The population was 13,060,115 at the census of 1971 and estimated to be 15·6m. in 1997. Population growth in 1996, 0·45%.

THE NETHERLANDS

The UN gives a projected population for 2000 of 15·87m.
On-going 'rolling' censuses have replaced the former decennial counts.
Area, estimated population and density, and chief towns of the 12 provinces on 1 Jan. 1996:

	Area 1995 (in sq. km)	Population 1996	Density 1996 per sq. km land area	Provincial Capital
Groningen	2,967·10	558,100	238	Groningen
Friesland	5,740·75	612,000	182	Leeuwarden
Drenthe	2,680·49	457,300	172	Assen
Overijssel	3,420·06	1,054,000	316	Zwolle
Flevoland	2,412·29	272,800	191	Lelijstad
Gelderland	5,143·36	1,876,300	376	Arnhem
Utrecht	1,434·24	1,070,600	789	Utrecht
Noord-Holland	4,059·09	2,468,400	928	Haarlem
Zuid-Holland[1]	3,445·75	3,332,900	1,166	The Hague
Zeeland	2,931·91	367,400	205	Middelburg
Noord-Brabant	5,016·11	2,290,400	464	's-Hertogenbosch
Limburg	2,195·98	1,133,700	523	Maastricht
Total	41,447·18	15,493,900[2]	457	

[1]Since 29 Sept. 1994 includes inhabitants of the municipality of The Hague formerly registered in the abolished Central Population Register.
[2]7,662,300 males; 7,831,600 females.

In 1995 an estimated 89% of the population lived in urban areas.
Population of municipalities with over 50,000 inhabitants on 1 Jan. 1996:

Alkmaar	93,052	Gouda	70,935	Oosterhout	51,046
Almelo	65,211	Groningen	169,627	Oss	63,199
Almere	112,704	Haarlem	147,617	Purmerend	65,604
Alphen a/d Rijn	67,583	Haarlemmermeer	106,095	Roosendaal en	
Amersfoort	114,884	The Hague	442,503	Nispen	63,854
Amstelveen	75,869	Heerlen	96,015	Rotterdam	592,745
Amsterdam	718,119	Den Helder	60,573	Schiedam	74,162
Apeldoorn	150,915	Helmond	74,918	Smallingerland	50,199
Arnhem	135,026	Hengelo	77,440	Spijkenisse	70,515
Assen	53,480	's-Hertogenbosch	125,044	Tilburg	164,380
Breda	130,033	Hilversum	83,272	Utrecht	234,254
Capelle a/d Ijssel	61,421	Hoorn	61,800	Veenendaal	55,325
Delft	93,229	Kerkrade	52,617	Velsen	65,509
Deventer	69,023	Leeuwarden	88,239	Venlo	64,781
Dordrecht	116,196	Leiden	116,224	Vlaardingen	74,271
Ede	99,927	Lelystad	60,707	Zaanstad	133,817
Eindhoven	197,374	Maastricht	118,518	Zeist	59,188
Emmen	94,114	Nieuwegein	59,214	Zoetermeer	106,581
Enschede	147,832	Nijmegen	147,600	Zwolle	100,835

Urban agglomerations as at 1 Jan. 1996: Amsterdam, 1,101,850; Rotterdam, 1,076,878; The Hague, 694,895; Utrecht, 548,464; Eindhoven, 398,359; Arnhem, 315,321; Heerlen-Kerkrade, 271,134; Enschede-Hengelo, 254,414; Nijmegen, 250,891; Tilburg, 238,643; Dordrecht/Zwijndrecht, 216,007; Haarlem, 211,139; Groningen, 209,494; 's-Hertogenbosch, 202,173; Leiden, 196,066; Geleen-Sittard, 186,695; Breda, 166,899; Maastricht, 164,813; Zaanstreek, 148,301; Velsen-Beverwijk, 136,297; Hilversum, 101,633.

The first national language is Dutch and the second is Friesian.

SOCIAL STATISTICS

Vital statistics for calendar years:

	Live births		Marriages	Divorces	Deaths	Net migration
	Total	Outside marriage				
1993	195,748	25,648	88,273	30,496	137,795	+59,932
1994	195,611	27,899	82,982	36,182	133,471	+37,156
1995	190,513	29,561	81,469	34,170	135,675	+32,800
1996	189,000	...	84,000	35,100	138,000	...

THE NETHERLANDS

1996 rates per 1,000 population; Birth, 12·2; death, 8·9. Annual growth rate, 1990–95, was 0·7%. Over 1990–95 the suicide rate per 100,000 population was 9·7 (men, 12·3; women, 7·2). In 1994 the most popular age range for marrying was 25–29 for both males and females. Expectation of life, 1997, was 74·7 years for males and 80·4 for females. Infant mortality, 1990–95, 6 per 1,000 live births; fertility rate, 1·6 births per woman. Percentage of population by age in 1997: 0–19 years, 24·3%; 20–39, 31·9%; 40–64, 30·5%; 65 and over, 13·3%.

CLIMATE
A cool temperate maritime climate, marked by mild winters and cool summers, but with occasional continental influences. Coastal temperatures vary from 37°F (3°C) in winter to 61°F (16°C) in summer, but inland the winters are slightly colder and the summers slightly warmer. Rainfall is least in the months Feb. to May, but inland there is a well-defined summer maximum in July and Aug. The Hague, Jan. 37°F (2·7°C), July 61°F (16·3°C). Annual rainfall 32·8" (820 mm). Amsterdam, Jan. 36°F (2·3°C), July 62°F (16·5°C). Annual rainfall 34" (850 mm). Rotterdam, Jan. 36·5°F (2·6°C), July 62°F (16·6°C). Annual rainfall 32" (800 mm).

CONSTITUTION AND GOVERNMENT
According to the Constitution (promulgated 1814; last revision, 1983), the Kingdom consists of the Netherlands, Aruba and the Netherlands Antilles. Their relations are regulated by the 'Statute' for the Kingdom, which came into force on 29 Dec. 1954. Each part enjoys full autonomy; they are united, on a footing of equality, for mutual assistance and the protection of their common interests.

The Netherlands is a constitutional and hereditary monarchy.

The reigning Queen is **Beatrix Wilhelmina Armgard,** born 31 Jan. 1938, daughter of Queen Juliana and Prince Bernhard; married to Claus von Amsberg on 10 March 1966; succeeded to the crown on 1 May 1980, on the abdication of her mother. *Offspring:* Prince Willem-Alexander, born 27 April 1967; Prince Johan Friso, born 25 Sept. 1968; Prince Constantijn, born 11 Oct. 1969.

The Queen receives an allowance from the civil list. This was 6·3m. guilders in 1992; that of Prince Claus was 1·2m. guilders and that of Crown Prince Willem Alexander, 1·5m. guilders.

Mother of the Queen: Queen Juliana Louise Emma Marie Wilhelmina, born 30 April 1909, daughter of Queen Wilhelmina (born 31 Aug. 1880, died 28 Nov. 1962) and Prince Henry of Mecklenburg-Schwerin (born 19 April 1876, died 3 July 1934); married to Prince Bernhard Leopold Frederik Everhard Julius Coert Karel Godfried Pieter of Lippe-Biesterfeld (born 29 June 1911) on 7 Jan. 1937. Abdicated in favour of her daughter, the Reigning Queen, on 30 April 1980.

Sisters of the Queen: Princess Irene Emma Elisabeth, born 5 Aug. 1939, married to Prince Charles Hugues de Bourbon-Parma on 29 April 1964, divorced 1981 (*sons:* Prince Carlos Javier Bernardo, born 27 Jan. 1970; Prince Jaime Bernardo, born 13 Oct. 1972; *daughters:* Princess Margarita Maria Beatriz, born 13 Oct. 1972; Princess Maria Carolina Christina, born 23 June 1974); Princess Margriet Francisca, born in Ottawa, 19 Jan. 1943, married to Pieter van Vollenhoven on 10 Jan. 1967 (*sons:* Prince Maurits, born 17 April 1968; Prince Bernhard, born 25 Dec. 1969; Prince Pieter-Christiaan, born 22 March 1972; Prince Floris, born 10 April 1975); Princess Maria Christina, born 18 Feb. 1947, married to Jorge Guillermo on 28 June 1975 (*sons:* Bernardo, born 17 June 1977; Nicolas, born 6 July 1979; *daughter:* Juliana, born 8 Oct. 1981).

The royal succession is in the direct female or male line in order of birth.

The central executive power of the State rests with the Crown, while the central legislative power is vested in the Crown and Parliament (the *States-General*), consisting of 2 Chambers. The upper *First Chamber* is composed of 75 members, elected by the members of the Provincial States (*see* Local Government, *below*). The 150-member *Second Chamber* is directly elected by proportional representation for 4-year terms. Members of the States-General must be Netherlands subjects of 18 years of age or over.

The *Council of State*, appointed by the Crown, is composed of a vice-president and not more than 28 members. The monarch is president, but the day-to-day

THE NETHERLANDS

running of the Council is in the hands of the vice-president. The Council has to be consulted on all legislative matters.

The Hague is the seat of the Court, Government and Parliament; Amsterdam is the capital.

The Sovereign has the power to dissolve either Chambers, subject to the condition that new elections take place within 40 days, and the new Chamber be convoked within 3 months.

Both the Government and the Second Chamber may propose Bills; the First Chamber can only approve or reject them without inserting amendments. The meetings of both Chambers are public, though each of them may by a majority vote decide on a secret session. A Minister or Secretary of State cannot be a member of Parliament at the same time.

The Constitution can be revised only by a Bill declaring that there is reason for introducing such revision and containing the proposed alterations. The passing of this Bill is followed by a dissolution of both Chambers and a second confirmation by the new States-General by two-thirds of the votes. Unless it is expressly stated, all laws concern only the realm in Europe, and not the overseas part of the kingdom, Aruba and the Netherlands Antilles.

National Anthem. 'Wilhelmus van Nassaue'; words by Philip Marnix van St Aldegonde, tune anonymous.

RECENT ELECTIONS

Party affiliation in the First Chamber as elected on 29 May 1995: Liberals (VVD), 23 seats; Christian Democrats (CDA), 19; Democrats (PvdA), 14; Democrats '66 (D66), 7; Green Left, 4; Party for the Elderly (AOV), 2; Political Calvinists (SGP), 2; Reformed Political Association (GPV), 1; Calvinist Evangelical Party (RPF), 1; Socialist Party (SP), 1; List Kuperus (regional parties and Green Party), 1.

Elections to the Second Chamber were held on 6 May 1998, with the ruling coalition gaining a substantial victory. The PvdA, party of Prime Minister Wim Kok, won 45 seats with 29% of the votes cast (37 seats and 24% of the votes in 1994), the VVD 38 with 24·7% (31 and 20%), the CDA 29 with 18·4% (34 and 22·2%), D66 14 with 9% (24 and 15·5%) and Green Left 11 with 7·2% (5 and 3·5%). The remaining 13 seats were won by 4 other parties. Following several weeks of talks a new cabinet consisting of Labour, Liberals and centrist parties was formed in Aug. 1998.

European Parliament. The Netherlands has 31 representatives. At the June 1994 elections turn-out was 35·6%. The CDA won 10 seats with 30·8% of votes cast (group in European Parliament: Popular European Party); the PvdA, 8 with 22·9% (European Socialist Party); the VVD, 6 with 17·9% (Liberal, Democratic and Reformist Group); D66, 4 with 11·7% (Liberal Democratic and Reformist Group); GPV/RPF/SGP, 2 with 7·8%; Greens, 1 with 3·7% (Greens).

CURRENT ADMINISTRATION

A new coalition government of PvdA-VVD-D66 was sworn in on 3 Aug. 1998.

In March 1999 the cabinet comprised:

Prime Minister: Wim Kok, b. 1938 (PvdA; Prime Minister since 22 Aug. 1994).

Deputy Prime Minister, Minister for Economic Affairs: Annemarie Jorritsma *née* Lebbink (VVD). *Deputy Prime Minister, Minister of Health, Welfare and Sport:* Dr Els Borst *née* Eilers (D66). *Minister for Major Cities and Integration:* Roger van Boxtel (VVD). *Minister of Home Affairs:* Dr Bram Peper (PvdA). *Minister for Foreign Affairs:* Jozias van Aartsen (VVD). *Minister for Development Co-operation:* Eveline Herfkens (PvdA). *Minister of Agriculture, Nature, Management and Fisheries:* Haijo Apotheker (D66). *Minister of Defence:* Frank de Grave (VVD). *Minister of Education, Culture and Science:* Loek Hermans (VVD). *Minister of Finance:* Gerrit Zalm (VVD). *Minister of Housing, Physical Planning and the Environment:* Jan Pronk (PvdA). *Minister of Justice:* Benk Korthals (VVD). *Minister of Social Affairs and Employment:* Klaas de Vries (PvdA). *Minister of Transport, Public Works and Water Management:* Tineke Netelenbos (PvdA).

Local Government. The kingdom is divided into 12 provinces and 636 municipalities.

Each province has its own representative body, the Provincial States. The members must be 21 years of age or over; they are directly elected for 4 years. The electoral register is the same as for the Second Chamber. Membership varies according to the population of the province. The Provincial States are entitled to issue ordinances concerning the welfare of the province, and to raise taxes pursuant to legal provisions. The provincial budgets and the provincial ordinances and resolutions relating to provincial property, loans, taxes, etc., must be approved by the Crown. The members of the Provincial States elect the First Chamber of the States-General. They meet twice a year, as a rule in public. A permanent commission composed of 6 of their members, called the 'Deputy States', is charged with the executive power and, if required, with the enforcement of the law in the province. Deputy as well as Provincial States are presided over by a Commissioner of the Queen, appointed by the Crown, who in the former assembly has a deciding vote, but attends the latter in only a deliberative capacity. He is the chief magistrate in the province. Elections to the Provincial States were held in March 1995; turn-out was 50%. VVD gained 27·2% of all votes cast; CDA, 22·9%; PvdA, 17%; D66, 9·2%.

Each municipality is governed by a Municipal Council, directly elected by residents who are 18 years of age or over, for 4 years. All Netherlands inhabitants and non-Netherlands inhabitants aged 21 or over who meet certain requirements are eligible to stand, the number of members varying according to the population. The Municipal Council may issue by-laws and levy taxes pursuant to legal provisions; these must be approved by the Crown. The Municipal Budget and resolutions to alienate municipal property require the approbation of the Deputy States of the province. The Council meets in public as often as may be necessary, and is presided over by a Burgomaster, appointed by the Crown. The day-to-day administration is carried out by the Burgomaster and Aldermen, elected by and from the Council; this body is also charged with the enforcement of the law. In maintaining public order, the Burgomaster acts as the chief of police. Municipal Council elections were held on 2 March 1994; turn-out was 64%. CDA gained 21·6% of all votes cast; PvdA, 16·9%; local independent parties, 16·4%; VVD, 15·5%.

DEFENCE
Conscription ended on 30 Aug. 1996.

The total strength of the armed forces in 1998 was 57,180, including 2,600 women. In 1997 defence expenditure totalled US$6,888m. (US$442 per capita), representing 1·9% of GDP.

Army. The 1st Netherlands Army Corps is assigned to NATO. It consists of 10 brigades and Corps troops. The active part of the Corps comprises 2 armoured brigades and 4 armoured infantry brigades, grouped in 2 divisions and 40% of the Corps troops.

The mobilizable part of the Corps comprises 1 armoured brigade, 2 armoured infantry brigades, 1 infantry brigade and the remaining Corps troops.

The mechanized brigades comprise tank battalions (Leopard I improved and Leopard 2), armoured infantry battalions (YPR-765), medium artillery battalions (155 mm self-propelled), armoured engineer units and armoured anti-armour units. Equipment includes 298 Leopard 1A4 and 445 Leopard 2 main battle tanks. Personnel in 1998 numbered 27,000.

The National Territorial Command forces consist of territorial brigades, security forces, some logistical units and staffs. Some units in the Netherlands may be assigned to the UN as peace-keeping forces. The army is responsible for the training of these units.

There is a paramilitary Royal Military Constabulary, 3,600 strong.

Navy. The principal headquarters and main base of the Royal Netherlands Navy is at Den Helder, with minor bases at Vlissingen (Flushing), Curaçao (Netherlands Antilles) and Oranjestad (Aruba). Command and control in home waters is exercised jointly with the Belgian Navy (submarines excepted).

The combatant fleet includes 4 diesel submarines of the new Zeeleeuw class, 4 guided-missile destroyers armed with US Standard SM1-MR surface-to-air missiles, 12 frigates each with 1 or 2 Lynx anti-submarine helicopters, 10 coastal minehunters and 2 coastal minesweepers.

In 1998 personnel totalled 13,800 (1,200 women), including 950 in the Naval Air Service and 2,800 in the Royal Netherlands Marine Corps.

Air Force. The Royal Netherlands Air Force (RNLAF) had 11,980 personnel in 1998 (720 women). It has a first-line combat force of 7 squadrons of aircraft and 2 groups of surface-to-air missiles in Germany. All squadrons are operated by Tactical Air Command.

INTERNATIONAL RELATIONS

The Netherlands is a member of the UN, EU, OECD, Council of Europe, WEU and NATO, and is a signatory of the Schengen Accord which abolishes border controls between the Netherlands and Austria, Belgium, Denmark, Finland, France, Germany, Greece, Iceland, Italy, Luxembourg, Norway, Portugal, Spain and Sweden.

In 1899 the first International Peace Conference was held in The Hague with the aim of developing mechanisms of interventional law to contribute to disarmament, the prevention of war, and the peaceful settlement of disputes. In 1999 The Hague Appeal for Peace 1999 Conference was scheduled to bring together a wide variety of organizations, activists, citizens and world leaders to discuss new projects and initiatives for the promotion of peace in the 21st century from 11–16 May 1999.

The Hague is the seat of several international organizations, including the International Court of Justice.

ECONOMY

Performance. Real GDP growth was 3·3% in both 1996 and 1997, and was forecast to grow to 3·7% in 1998. The 1998 World Competitiveness Yearbook put the Netherlands fourth behind the USA, Singapore and Hong Kong, thus ranking it as Europe's most competitive economy.

Budget. The revenue and expenditure of the central government (ordinary and extraordinary) were, in 1m. guilders, for calendar years:

	1991	1992	1993	1994	1995	1996
Revenue	171,639	171,528	180,824	170,955	168,474	181,600
Expenditure	189,932	195,398	196,924	190,441	225,262	202,200

VAT is 17·5% (reduced rate, 6%).

Currency. On 1 Jan. 1999 the euro (EUR) became the legal currency in the Netherlands and the *gulden* became a subdivision of it; irrevocable conversion rate 2·20371 guilders to 1 euro. The euro, which consists of 100 cents, will not be in circulation until 1 Jan. 2002. There will be 7 euro notes in different colours and sizes denominated in 500, 200, 100, 50, 20, 10 and 5 euros, and 8 coins denominated in 2 and 1 euros, then 50, 20, 10, 5, 2 and 1 cents. Even though notes and coins will not be introduced until 1 Jan. 2002 the euro can be used in banking; by means of cheques, travellers' cheques, bank transfers, credit cards and electronic purses. Banking will be possible in both euros and guilders until the guilder is withdrawn from circulation—which must be by 1 July 2002.

The *gulden* (NLG; written as fl[orin]; in English, 'guilder') consists of 100 *cents*. It is tied to the German Deutschmark. Gold reserves were 27·07m. troy oz. in Feb. 1998 and foreign exchange reserves US$21,236m. Inflation was 2·1% in 1996, rising to 2·2% in 1997, but then dropped back to 2·0% in 1998. Total money supply in Dec. 1997 was 209bn. guilders.

Banking and Finance. The central bank and bank of issue is the Netherlands Bank (*President*, Dr N. Welling), founded in 1814 and nationalized in 1948. Its Governor is appointed by the government for 7-year terms. The capital amounts to 75m. guilders.

There is a stock exchange in Amsterdam.

Weights and Measures. The metric system is in use.

ENERGY AND NATURAL RESOURCES

Electricity. Installed capacity is 18·65m. kW. Production of electrical energy in 1996, 88,503m. kWh (6% nuclear). Consumption per capita was an estimated 5,140 kWh in 1995. 790 windmills were installed in 1994 to produce 238m. kWh.

Oil and Gas. Production of natural gas in 1996, 90,630m. cu. metres.

Agriculture. The Netherlands is one of the world's largest exporters of agricultural produce. There were 120,000 farms in 1998. Agriculture accounts for 2·9% of GDP, 22·8% of exports and 15·1% of imports. The agricultural sector employs 2·7% of the workforce. The total area of cultivated land in 1997 was 1,965,100 ha: Grassland, 1,030,500 ha; arable crops, 808,800 ha; horticultural crops, 111,800 ha, of which 101,700 ha was in the open and 10,100 ha was under glass; fallow land, 14,000 ha. In 1997, 282,480 people were employed in agriculture (93,798 women).

The yield of the more important arable crops, in 1,000 tonnes, was as follows:

Crop	1994	1995	1996
Wheat	981·0	1,166·7	1,268·9
Rye	26·5	42·5	38·2
Barley	227·6	202·5	234·8
Oats	27·9	15·5	10·7
Kidney beans	4·8	5·4	7·8
Peas	9·4	4·6	7·6
Colza	4·2	4·5	3·1
Flax	32·9	34·4	...
Potatoes	7,088·4	7,340·4	8,055·9
Sugar-beet	6,149·4	6,499·4	6,415·7
Sown onions	464·7	479·1	623·2
Fodder maize	2,728·1	2,527·4	2,694·6

Livestock, 1997 (in 1,000) included: 4,411 cattle; 9,240 fattening pigs and breeding sows; 113 horses and ponies; 717 lambs; 94,463 turkeys and chickens.

Animal products in 1996 (in 1,000 tonnes) included: Butter, 127; cheese, 704; hens' eggs, 593; beef, 389; horsemeat, 1.

Forestry. Forests covered 334,000 ha in 1995, or 9·8% of the land area. In 1995, 1·1m. cu. metres of roundwood were cut.

Fisheries. Marine catch in 1996: 541,396 tonnes; chiefly scad, herring and mackerel. Fish caught from inland waters in 1995 totalled 6,711 tonnes. There were 1,004 fishing vessels in 1996.

INDUSTRY

The three largest industrial sectors are chemicals, food processing and metal, mechanical and electrical engineering.

At 31 Dec. 1995 there were 6,672 enterprises in the manufacturing industry (excepting construction), of which 3,269 had 20–49 employees and 198 had 500 employees or more; total annual sales for 1995 were 280,571m. guilders.

In 1994 there were 6,710 enterprises with 20 or more employees. The food products and beverages industry employed 114,185 people at 30 Sept. 1994 (annual sales for 1994 in 1m. guilders, 71,040); tobacco products, 5,524 (4,673); chemicals and chemical products, 76,260 (48,486); electrical machinery and apparatus, 82,450 (18,663); transport equipment, 45,928 (18,006); machinery and equipment, 67,793 (17,711); publishing, printing and reproduction of recorded media, 61,058 (17,501); other fabricated metal products, 65,789 (17,028).

In 1994 total annual sales for mining and quarrying were 17,748m. guilders and for public utilities, 24,434m. guilders.

Labour. The total labour force in 1996 was 6,681,000 persons (2,586,000 women) of whom 494,000 (271,000) were unemployed, with 440,000 (201,000) registered unemployed. By education level, the 1996 labour force included (in 1,000): Primary education, 562; junior general secondary, 459; pre-vocational secondary, 990; senior general secondary, 365; senior vocational secondary, 2,600; vocational colleges, 1,152; university, 541.

The unemployment rate of 6·9% in 1995 had dropped to 5·3% in 1998.

In 1995 the weekly working hours (excluding overtime) of employees were 36·0 for men and 26·1 for women. In 1995, full-time employees' working hours (excluding overtime) totalled 1,735; part-time, 926 and flexible, 862. Employees in the private sector worked a total of 1,455 hours, those in the public sector 1,455 hours and those in the subsidized sector 1,269 hours (all excluding overtime). The working hours of employees ranged from a total of 1,701 in mining and quarrying, 1,659 in public utilities, 1,644 in construction and 1,625 in manufacturing to 1,193 in health and social work and 1,050 in hotels and restaurants (all excluding overtime). Average annual gross earnings of employees in 1995 were 56,000 guilders for men and 30,100 guilders for women. In 1996, gross hourly wage earnings (in guilders) by type of employment ranged from 44·63 in mining and quarrying, 38·00 in education and 37·23 in public utilities to 20·60 in hotels and restaurants and 15·81 for domestic personnel in private households.

Trade Unions. Trade unions are grouped in 4 central federations. Total membership was 1,894,700 in 1997, approximately 28% of waged employees. In Nov. 1993 an agreement on wage restraint was concluded between the trade unions and the employers' federations, in return for an enhancement of the roles of works committees and professional training for employees.

INTERNATIONAL TRADE

On 5 Sept. 1944 and 14 March 1947 the Netherlands signed agreements with Belgium and Luxembourg for the establishment of a customs union. On 1 Jan. 1948 this union came into force and the existing customs tariffs of the Belgium–Luxembourg Economic Union and of the Netherlands were superseded by the joint Benelux Customs Union Tariff. It applied to imports into the 3 countries from outside sources, and exempted from customs duties all imports into each of the 3 countries from the other 2.

Imports and Exports. Imports and exports for calendar years (in 1m. guilders):

	Imports	Exports		Imports	Exports
1969	39,955	36,205	1994	256,439	287,452
1979	134,885	127,689	1995	285,140	316,161
1989	221,412	229,409	1996	304,557	332,916

Value of trade with major partners (in 1m. guilders):

Country	Imports 1996	Exports 1996	Imports (% change on 1995)	Exports (% change on 1995)
Belgium–Luxembourg	34,249	44,057	+2	+8
France	22,499	37,028	+7	+5
Germany	68,140	95,698	+2	+6
Italy	10,840	19,723	+6	+12
Japan	10,780	3,440	+7	+3
Spain	6,303	9,679	+14	+6
Sweden	8,395	7,805	+9	+18
Switzerland	3,487	4,607	0	+10
UK	30,506	31,973	+6	+4
USA	24,718	10,683	+9	+3

The main imports in 1996 (in 1m. guilders) included machines (including electrical machines), 69,244; road vehicles, 21,945; crude petroleum, 15,809; clothing, 9,171; organic chemicals, 8,853; iron and steel, 7,132; oil products, 5,122; paper and paperboard, 4,733; non-ferrous metals, 4,081. Main exports included machines (including electrical machines), 69,391; oil products, 15,791; organic chemicals, 14,344; road vehicles, 14,071; fruit and vegetables, 11,474; crude vegetable materials, 8,529; beverages and tobacco, 8,282; natural and manufactured gas, 8,158; meat, 7,401; iron and steel, 6,304.

COMMUNICATIONS

Roads. In 1996 the length of the Netherlands network of surfaced inter-urban roads was 58,133 km, of which 2,207 km were motorways. Number of private cars (1996), 5·74m.; trucks and vans, 597,000; motor cycles, 335,000.

Rail. All railways are run by the mixed company 'N.V. Nederlandse Spoorwegen'. Route length in 1996 was 2,739 km, of which 1,991 km were electrified. Passengers carried (1996), 306m.; goods transported, 20·8m. tonnes. There is a metro (23 km) and tram/light rail network (153 km) in Amsterdam and in Rotterdam (28 km and 141 km). Tram/light rail networks operate in The Hague (122 km) and Utrecht (28 km).

Civil Aviation. There are international airports at Amsterdam (Schiphol), Rotterdam, Maastricht and Eindhoven. The Royal Dutch Airlines (KLM) was founded on 7 Oct. 1919. Revenue traffic, 1995–96: Passengers, 12·34m.; freight and mail, 598m. kg. Services were provided in 1998 by around 90 foreign airlines. In 1996 Amsterdam handled 27,259,781 passengers (27,085,359 on international flights) and 1,082,845 tonnes of freight. It was the second busiest airport in Europe in 1996 for freight handled, after Frankfurt am Main.

Sea-going Shipping. Survey of the Netherlands mercantile marine as at 1 Jan. (capacity in 1,000 GRT):

Ships under Netherlands flag	1995		1996	
	Number	Capacity	Number	Capacity
Passenger ships[1]	6	147	6	147
Freighters (100 GRT and over)	326	2,140	322	2,056
Tankers	53	616	51	592
	385	2,903	379	2,795

[1]With accommodation for 13 or more cabin passengers.

In 1995, 43,556 sea-going ships of 486·64m. gross tons entered Netherlands ports. Total goods traffic by sea-going ships in 1994 (with 1993 figures in brackets), in 1m. tonnes, amounted to 287 (277) unloaded, of which 129 (130) tankshipping, and 88 (88) loaded, of which 24 (24) tankshipping; total seaborne goods traffic in 1995 (and 1994) at Rotterdam was 291·2 (293·4) and at Amsterdam 31·4 (29·3).

The number of containers (including flats) at Rotterdam in 1995 (and 1994) was: Unloaded from ships, 1·56m. (1,516,000) and 1,535,000 (1·48m.) loaded into ships.

Inland Shipping. The total length of navigable rivers and canals is 5,046 km, of which 2,398 km is for ships with a capacity of 1,000 and more tonnes. On 1 Jan. 1996 the inland fleet used for transport (with carrying capacity in 1,000 tonnes) was composed as follows:

	Number	Capacity
Self-propelled barges	4,439	4,159
Dumb barges	377	263
Pushed barges	743	1,675
	5,559	6,097

In 1995, 208·4m. tonnes of goods were transported on rivers and canals, of which 131·6m. tonnes was by international shipping. Goods transport on the Rhine across the Dutch-German frontier near Lobith amounted to 139·5m. tonnes.

Telecommunications. There were 8,860,000 telephone main lines in 1997, equivalent to 564·3 per 1,000 population. Cellular phone subscribers numbered 513,000 in 1995 (33 per 1,000 population), and there were 3·1m. PCs and 500,000 fax machines. There were 1·5m. Internet users in Nov. 1998.

Postal Services. In 1995 there were 2,009 post offices, equivalent to 1 for every 7,675 persons.

SOCIAL INSTITUTIONS

Justice. Justice is administered by the High Court (Court of Cassation), by 5 courts of justice (Courts of Appeal), by 19 district courts and by 63 cantonal courts. The Cantonal Court, which deals with minor offences, comprises a single judge; more serious cases are tried by the district courts, comprising as a rule 3 judges (in some cases one judge is sufficient); the courts of appeal are constituted of 3 and the High Court of 5 judges. All judges are appointed for life by the Sovereign (the judges of the High Court from a list prepared by the Second Chamber of the States-General). They can be removed only by a decision of the High Court.

At the district court the juvenile judge is specially appointed to try children's civil cases and at the same time charged with administration of justice for criminal actions committed by young persons between 12 and 18 years old, unless imprisonment of more than 6 months ought to be inflicted; such cases are tried by 3 judges.

Number of sentences, and cases in which prosecution was evaded by paying a fine to the public prosecutor (excluding violation of economic and tax laws):

Major offences   *Minor offences*[1]

1992	112,815	1992	582,799
1993	132,432	1993	351,484
1994	136,943	1994	248,568

[1]Excluding an estimated 2m. minor traffic violations.

The population in penal institutions at 31 Dec. 1996 was 11,931, of which 6,404 were convicted. The total number of inmates during the year was 38,756 (37,264 men). 1,183,200 crimes were reported and there were 1·15 murders per 100,000 population.

Police. In 1994 the police force was divided into 25 regions. There is also a National Police Service which includes the Central Criminal Investigation Office, which deals with serious crimes throughout the country, and the International Criminal Investigation Office, which informs foreign countries of international crimes.

Religion. Entire liberty of conscience is granted to the members of all denominations. The royal family belong to the Dutch Reformed Church.

According to survey estimates of 1995, the distribution of the population aged 18 years and over was: Roman Catholics, 33%; Dutch Reformed Church, 14%; Calvinist, 7%; other creeds, 7%; no religion, 40%. The government of the Reformed Church is Presbyterian. On 1 July 1992 the Dutch Reformed Church had 1 synod, 9 provincial districts, 75 classes, about 160 districts and about 2,000 parishes. Their clergy numbered 1,735. The Roman Catholic Church had, Jan. 1992, 1 archbishop (of Utrecht), 6 bishops, 4 assistant bishops and about 1,750 parishes and rectorships. The Old Catholics had (1 July 1992) 1 archbishop (Utrecht), 1 bishop and 28 parishes. The Jews had, in 1992, 40 communities. At 1 Jan. 1997 there were an estimated 667,900 Moslems (4·3% of the population) and 79,100 Hindus (0·5%).

Education. Statistics for the scholastic year 1996–97:

	Schools	Full-time Pupils/Students (in 1,000) Total
Primary education	7,287	1,502
Special education	967	120
General secondary education	656	656
Pre-vocational education	419	202
Senior vocational secondary education	112	285
Vocational colleges	70	233
University education	19	166

| | | Academic Year 1994–95 | | | |
| | | Full-time Students | | Part-time Students | |
	Schools	Total	Female	Total	Female
University education:					
Agriculture		5,253	2,226	30	8
Science		13,449	4,375	278	52
Engineering		26,346	4,138	65	5
Health	20	17,424	10,201	643	409
Economics		27,995	7,074	657	131
Law		24,716	12,569	3,490	1,586
Behaviour and Society		30,625	19,426	4,113	2,679
Language and Culture		27,139	17,993	2,244	1,241
Education		681	370	67	23

In 1995, there were 125,428 participants in adult basic education, and 25,051 Open University students (40% women). In 1995, 176,943 people participated in private correspondence courses, with subjects including the humanities (23,415 people), commerce (21,683), business administration (18,701), service trades (15,384), retail trade (15,178), technical (13,116) and public order and security (10,128).

In 1995 total expenditure on education came to 5·2% of GNP and represented 8·7% of total government expenditure.

Health. On 1 Jan. 1996 there were 7,170 general practitioners, 13,917 specialists, 7,258 dentists, 1,332 midwives, 11,701 physiotherapists (1995) and 2,556 pharmacists; there were 59,461 licensed hospital beds (excluding mental hospitals). Provision of hospital beds in 1996 was 38 per 10,000 population.

Welfare. The General Old Age Pension Act (AOW) entitles everyone to draw an old age pension from the age of 65. At 31 Dec. 1995 there were 2,186,200 persons entitled to receive an old age pension, and 195,700 a pension under the General Widows and Orphans Act; 1,814,000 parents were receiving benefits under the General Family Allowances Act; 326,800 persons were receiving assistance under the State Group Regulations for the Unemployed; there were 860,700 persons claiming disablement insurance under the General and Industrial Disablement Acts.

CULTURE

Broadcasting. Public broadcasting programmes are provided by broadcasting associations representing clearly identifiable social or religious ideals or groupings. The 6 associations, currently holding licences until 2000, work together in the Netherlands Broadcasting Corporation, *Nederlandse Omroepprogramma Stichting* (NOS). There are 3 national television channels (colour by PAL) and 5 radio stations. In addition, there are regional radio stations in every province, a limited number of regional television stations and 400 local radio stations. Commercial broadcasting was introduced in 1992. Dutch-language commercial companies include RTL 4 and 5 which broadcast in Dutch from Luxembourg, Veronica, SBS6, TV10 and the Music Factory. Public broadcasting revenue is obtained from radio and television licences and from advertising.

At 31 Dec. 1995 there were 5,837,000 registered owners of television and radio sets and 123,000 of radio only.

Cinema. In 1996 there were 573 cinemas and film houses with a seating capacity of 100,000. Total attendance was 17·7m.

Press. In 1995 there were 46 daily newspapers with a combined circulation of 5·1m., equivalent to 329 per 1,000 inhabitants.

Tourism. Tourism is a major sector of the economy earning 35bn. guilders in revenue each year. There were 6,043,000 foreign visitors in 1993-94, of whom 4,045,000 spent 8,555,000 nights in hotels.

Festivals. An international music festival, the Holland Festival, is held in Amsterdam throughout June each year and the Early Music Festival is held in Utrecht. The North Sea Jazz Festival, the largest in Europe, takes place in The Hague. Each year, the most important Dutch and Flemish theatre productions of the previous season are performed at the Theatre Festival in Amsterdam and Antwerp (Belgium). The Holland Dance Festival is held every other year in The Hague and the Springdance Festival in Utrecht annually. Film festivals include the Rotterdam Film Festival in Feb., the World Wide Video Festival in April, the Dutch Film Festival in Sept. and the International Documentary Film Festival of Amsterdam in Dec.

Libraries. In 1995 there were 605 public libraries with 44,320,000 books and records and 4,549,000 registered users (2,152,000 children). There are 5 special libraries for the blind to which over 40,000 people subscribe.

National Theatre and Opera. In 1995–96 there were 55,230 music and theatre performances (including rock concerts) of which 15,410 were plays, 7,670 concerts, 2,340 opera and operetta and 2,680 ballet and dance, with a total attendance of 15,100,000.

Museums and Galleries. In 1995 there were 744 museums open to the public, to which visits totalled 21,921,000. The Rijksmuseum and Vincent Van Gogh Museums in Amsterdam and the Kröller-Müller Museum in Otterlo attract the most visitors.

DIPLOMATIC REPRESENTATIVES

Of the Netherlands in Great Britain (38 Hyde Park Gate, London, SW7 5DP)
Ambassador: Jan Hermann R. D. van Roijen.

Of Great Britain in the Netherlands (Lange Voorhout 10, 2514 ED The Hague)
Ambassador: Rosemary J. Spencer, CMG.

Of the Netherlands in the USA (4200 Linnean Ave., NW, Washington, D.C., 20008)
Ambassador: Joris Vos.

Of the USA in the Netherlands (Lange Voorhout 102, The Hague)
Ambassador: Cynthia P. Schneider.

Of the Netherlands to the United Nations
Ambassador: Jaap P. Ramaker.

FURTHER READING
Centraal Bureau voor de Statistiek. *Statistical Yearbook of the Netherlands.* From 1923/24.—
  Statistisch Jaarboek. From 1899/1924.—*CBS Select (Statistical Essays).* From 1980.—
  Statistisch Bulletin. From 1945; weekly.—*Maandschrift.* From 1944; monthly bulletin.—*90
  Jaren Statistiek in Tijdreeksen* (historical series of the Netherlands 1899–1989)
Nationale Rekeningen (National Accounts). From 1948–50.—*Statistische onderzoekingen.*
  From 1977.—*Regionaal Statistisch Zakboek* (Regional Pocket Yearbook). From 1972.—
  Environmental Statistics of the Netherlands, 1987
Staatsalmanak voor het Koninkrijk der Nederlanden. Annual. The Hague, from 1814
Staatsblad van het Koninkrijk der Nederlanden. The Hague, from 1814
Staatscourant (State Gazette). The Hague, from 1813
Anderweg, R. B. and Irwin, G. A., *Dutch Government and Politics.* London, 1993
Cox, R. H., *The Development of the Dutch Welfare State: from Workers' Insurance to
  Universal Entitlement.* Pittsburgh Univ. Press, 1994
Gladdish, K., *Governing from the Centre: Politics and Policy-Making in the Netherlands.*
  London, 1991
King, P. K. and Wintle, M., *The Netherlands.* [Bibliography] Oxford and Santa Barbara (CA),
  1988

National library: De Koninklijke Bibliotheek, Prinz Willem Alexanderhof 5, The Hague.
National statistical office: Centraal Bureau voor de Statistiek, Netherlands Central Bureau of
Statistics, POB 959, 2270 AZ Voorburg.
Website: *Statistics Netherlands* http://www.cbs.nl

ARUBA

KEY HISTORICAL EVENTS
Discovered by Alonzo de Ojeda in 1499, the island of Aruba was claimed for Spain
but not settled. It was acquired by the Dutch in 1634, but apart from garrisons was
left to the indigenous Caiquetios (Arawak) Indians until the 19th century. From 1828
it formed part of the Dutch West Indies and, from 1845, part of the Netherlands
Antilles, with which on 29 Dec. 1954 it achieved internal self-government.

Following a referendum in March 1977, the Dutch government announced on 28
Oct. 1981 that Aruba would proceed to independence separately from the other
islands. Aruba was constitutionally separated from the Netherlands Antilles from 1
Jan. 1986, and full independence had been promised by the Netherlands after a 10-
year period. However, an agreement with the Netherlands government in June 1990
deletes, at Aruba's request, references to eventual independence.

TERRITORY AND POPULATION
The island, which lies in the southern Caribbean 32 km north of the Venezuelan
coast and 68 km west of Curaçao, has an area of 180 sq. km (75 sq. miles) and a
population at the 1995 census of 65,974; density, 369 per sq. km. Population in
1997, 91,364; density, 508 per sq. km. The chief towns are Oranjestad, the capital
(1996 population estimate, 21,000) and Sint Nicolaas. Dutch is the official language,
but the language usually spoken is Papiamento, a creole language. Over half the
population is of Indian stock, with the balance of Dutch, Spanish and mestizo origin.

SOCIAL STATISTICS
Annual growth rate, 1997, 3·9%. Life expectancy (1991 census), 74 years. Birth rate
per 1,000 population (1997), 16·3; death rate, 5·6; infant mortality (1994), 3·0.

THE NETHERLANDS

CLIMATE
Aruba has a tropical marine climate, with a brief rainy season from Oct. to Dec. Oranjestad, Jan. 79°F (26·4°C), July 84°F (28·7°C). Annual rainfall 17" (432 mm).

CONSTITUTION AND GOVERNMENT
Under the separate constitution inaugurated on 1 Jan. 1986, Aruba is an autonomous part of the Kingdom of the Netherlands with its own legislature, government, judiciary, civil service and police force. The Netherlands is represented by a Governor appointed by the monarch (in 1997, Governor General Olindo Koolman). The unicameral legislature *(Staten)* consists of 21 members elected for a 4-year term of office.

RECENT ELECTIONS
Elections were held on 12 Dec. 1997. The electorate was 52,166; turn-out was 86%. Arubaanse Volkspartij (AVP) won 10 seats (41·3% of votes cast), the Movimento Electoral di Pueblo, 9 (38·8%), and the Organización Liberal Arubianco (OLA), 2 (8·9%).

CURRENT ADMINISTRATION
An AVP-OLA coalition government was formed as a result of the election. In March 1999 it comprised:
Prime Minister and Minister of General Affairs: Jan H. Eman (AVP).
Deputy Prime Minister: Glenbert F. Croes.
Minister of Economy: Lilia G. Beke-Martínez. *Education and Labour:* Mary Wever-Lacle. *Finance:* Robertico R. Croes. *Health, Social Affairs, Culture and Sport:* Israel Posner. *Justice and Public Works:* Edgar. J. Vos. *Transport and Communications:* Gilbert F. Croes.
Representative in the Netherlands: Gilbert F. Croes.

ECONOMY
Performance. Annual economic growth was 3% in 1997. GDP per capita (1997) was 32,626 Aflorins.

Budget. The 1997 budget totalled 621m. Aflorins tax revenue.

Currency. Since 1 Jan. 1986 the currency has been the *Aruban florin*, at par with the Netherlands Antilles guilder. Total money supply in Feb. 1998 was 495m. Aruban florins. Inflation was 6·9% in 1994. Foreign exchange reserves in Feb. 1998 were US$181m.; gold reserves were 10,000 troy oz. Inflation was around 3% in 1998. Net foreign assets (including gold and revaluation of gold) in 1997 were 427·7m. Aflorins.

Banking and Finance. There were 6 domestic and Dutch banks, and 1 foreign bank in 1997. There is a special tax regime for offshore banks. The *President* of the Central Bank of Aruba is J. H. du Marchie Sarvaas.

ENERGY AND NATURAL RESOURCES
Electricity. Generating capacity totalled 675,210 MWh in 1997.

Water. There is a desalination plant with an annual capacity of 22,000 tonnes. Water production in 1997 was 11,766,420 cu. metres.

Fisheries. In 1995 the catch totalled approximately 130 tonnes.

INDUSTRY
The government has established 6 industrial sites at Oranjestad harbour. An oil refinery closed in 1985 was re-opened in 1991 with a capacity in 1997 of 0·14m. bbls. a day.

EXTERNAL ECONOMIC RELATIONS
There are 2 Free Zones at Oranjestad.

Imports and Exports. Exports, 43m. Aflorins (1997); imports, 1,102m. Aflorins.

COMMUNICATIONS

Roads. In 1984 there were 380 km of surfaced highways. In 1997 there were 36,112 passenger cars and 5,952 commercial vehicles.

Civil Aviation. There is an international airport (Aeropuerto Internacional Reina Beatrix). Air Aruba had flights in 1998 to Amsterdam (jointly with KLM), Bogotá, Bonaire, Caracas, Curaçao, Medellin, Miami, New York and Tampa. In 1998 services were also provided by Aeropostal Alas de Venezuela, Aeroservicios Carababo, ALM, American Airlines, Avianca, Continental Airlines, KLM, SAM, Servivensa, Sun Country Airlines, Surinam Airways, United Airlines and VASP. In 1996 Aruba handled 122,203 passengers and 2,406 tonnes of freight.

Shipping. Oranjestad has a container terminal and cruise ship port. The port at Barcadera services the offshore and energy sector and a deep-water port at Sint Nicolaas services the oil refinery.

Telecommunications. Aruba had 33,924 main telephone lines in 1997, or 366·9 per 1,000 inhabitants. There were 1,700 cellular phone subscribers and 500 fax machines in 1995.

Postal Services. In 1995 there were 4 post offices.

SOCIAL INSTITUTIONS

Justice. There is a Common Court of Justice with the Netherlands Antilles. Final Appeal is to the Supreme Court in the Netherlands.

Religion. In 1997, 88% of the population were Roman Catholic.

Education. There are 23 pre-primary, 36 primary, 12 secondary and 4 middle-level schools, also a teacher training college and law school. Literacy rate (1991 census), 97·0%. The share of education in the 1994 budget was 16·9%.

Health. In 1997 there were 103 doctors, 21 dentists, 15 pharmacists and 1 hospital with 307 beds.

Welfare. All citizens are entitled to an old age pension at the age of 60.

CULTURE

Broadcasting. In 1997 there were 16 radio stations and 3 commercial television station (colour by NTSC). In 1995 there were 41,000 radio and 19,000 TV sets.

Press. In 1997, there were 8 daily newspapers with a combined circulation of 52,000. At more than 700 newspapers per 1,000 inhabitants, Aruba has one of the highest rates of circulation in the world.

Tourism. In 1997 there were 649,893 staying tourists and 297,650 cruise-ship visitors. In 1997 tourist receipts were 1,192·3m. Aflorins. The majority of tourists are from the USA (56·1%); Venezuela (13·6%) and the Netherlands (5·1%).

FURTHER READING
Schoenhals, K., *Netherlands Antilles and Aruba*. [Bibliography] Oxford and Santa Barbara (CA), 1993

THE NETHERLANDS ANTILLES

KEY HISTORICAL EVENTS
Bonaire and Curaçao islands, originally populated by Arawak Indians, were discovered in 1499 by Alonso de Ojeda, and claimed for Spain. They were settled in 1527, and the indigenous population exterminated and replaced by a slave-worked plantation economy. The 3 Windward Islands, inhabited by Caribs, were discovered by Columbus in 1493. They were taken by the Dutch in 1632 (Saba and Sint Eustatius), 1634 (Curaçao and Bonaire) and 1648 (the southern part of Sint Maarten,

with France acquiring the northern part). With Aruba, the islands formed part of the Dutch West Indies from 1828, and the Netherlands Antilles from 1845, with internal self-government being granted on 29 Dec. 1954. Aruba was separated from 1 Jan. 1986. At a referendum in Nov. 1993 Curaçao voted to remain part of the Netherlands Antilles.

TERRITORY AND POPULATION

The Netherlands Antilles comprise two groups of islands, the Leeward group (Curaçao and Bonaire) being situated 100 km north of the Venezuelan coast and the Windward group (Saba, Sint Eustatius and the southern portion of Sint Maarten) situated 800 km away to the north-east, at the northern end of the Lesser Antilles. The total area is 800 sq. km (308 sq. miles) and the census population in 1995 was 207,333. The projected population for 2000 is 210,000. An estimated 69·2% of the population were urban in 1995. Willemstad is the capital.

The areas, populations and chief towns of the islands are:

Island	Sq. km	1995 Census	Chief town
Bonaire	288	14,218	Kralendijk
Curaçao	444	151,448	Willemstad
Saba	13	1,200	The Bottom
Sint Eustatius	21	1,900	Oranjestad
Sint Maarten[1]	43	38,567	Philipsburg

[1]The northern portion (St Martin) belongs to France.

Dutch is the official language, but the languages usually spoken are Papiamento (derived from Dutch, Spanish and Portuguese) on Curaçao and Bonaire, and English in the Windward Islands.

SOCIAL STATISTICS

1995, Live births, 3,753; marriages, 1,056; divorces, 521; deaths, 1,363. Annual growth rate, 1990–95, 1·2%. Expectation of life, 1990–95, was 72·4 years for males and 78·5 for females. Infant mortality, 1990–95, 13 per 1,000 live births; fertility rate, 2·2 births per woman.

CLIMATE

All the islands have a tropical marine climate, with very little difference in temperatures over the year. There is a short rainy season from Oct. to Jan. Willemstad. Feb. 27·7°C, Aug. 29°C. Annual rainfall 499 mm.

CONSTITUTION AND GOVERNMENT

On 29 Dec. 1954, the Netherlands Antilles became an integral part of the Kingdom of the Netherlands but are fully autonomous in internal affairs, and constitutionally equal with the Netherlands and Aruba. The Sovereign of the Kingdom of the Netherlands is Head of State and Government, and is represented by a Governor.

The executive power in internal affairs rests with the Governor and the Council of Ministers, who together form the Government. The Ministers are responsible to a unicameral legislature *(States)* consisting of 22 members, elected for a 4-year term in 3 multi-seat constituencies and 2 single-seat constituencies.

The executive power in external affairs is vested in the Council of Ministers of the Kingdom, in which the Antilles is represented by a Minister Plenipotentiary with full voting powers. On each of the insular communities, local autonomous power is divided between an Island Council (elected by universal suffrage), the Executive Council and the Lieut.-Governor, responsible for law and order.

At a referendum in Curaçao on 19 Nov. 1993, 73% of votes cast favoured maintaining the status quo of Curaçao as part of the Netherlands Antilles. The other options were: Autonomy (18%), unification with the Netherlands (8%) or complete independence (1%). At a referendum in Oct. 1994 Sint Maarten, Sint Eustatius and Saba voted to remain part of the Netherlands Antilles.

RECENT ELECTIONS

In elections held for the States on 30 Jan. 1998 the Party for the Restructured Antilles gained 4 seats, National People's Party 3, Labour Party People's Crusade 3, Social Independence-Workers' Liberation Front 2, New Antilles Movement 2,

THE NETHERLANDS ANTILLES

Democratic Party Sint Maarten 2, Bonaire Democratic Party 2, with 1 seat each going to Sint Maarten Patriotic Alliance, Bonaire Patriotic Union, Sint Eustatius Alliance and Windward Islands Patriotic Movement.

CURRENT ADMINISTRATION
Governor: Dr Jaime M. Saleh.

The Cabinet included the following in March 1999:

Prime Minister: Susanne Camelia-Römer (PNP; currently serving a second term).

Deputy Prime Minister and Minister for Education, Sport, Culture and Youth Affairs: Philip A. E. Nieuw. *Transport:* Leo A. I. Chance. *Justice:* Rutsel S. J. Martha. *Finance:* Frank E. Mingo. *Economic Affairs, Labour and Social Affairs:* E. M. Goeloe. *Traffic and Communications:* Maurice Adriaans.

ECONOMY
Performance. Real GDP growth was 1·3% in 1995 and 1·7% in 1994.

Budget. The central government budget for 1995 envisaged 470·5m. NA guilders revenue and 565·5m. NA guilders expenditure.

Currency. The unit of currency is the *Netherlands Antilles guilder, gulden* (ANG) or *florin* (NAfl.) divided into 100 *cents.* The NA guilder has been pegged to the US dollar at US$1 = 1·79 NA guilder since 12 Dec. 1971. In Jan. 1998 gold reserves were 550,000 troy oz. and foreign exchange reserves US$199m. Total money supply in Nov. 1997 was 902m. NA guilders.

Banking and Finance. At 31 Dec. 1994 the Bank of Netherlands Antilles had total assets and liabilities of 514·4m. NA guilders; commercial banks, 3,913m. NA guilders.

ENERGY AND NATURAL RESOURCES
Electricity. Installed capacity in 1995 was 307,000 kW; production in 1995 totalled 1,000m. kWh. Consumption per capita in 1994 was estimated at 4,580 kWh.

Oil and Gas. The economy was formerly based largely on oil refining at the Shell refinery on Curaçao, but following an announcement by Shell that closure was imminent, this was sold to the Netherlands Antilles government in Sept. 1985, and leased to Petróleos de Venezuela to operate on a reduced scale. The refinery has a capacity of 470,000 bbls. a day, but output has not reached this for several years.

Minerals. Calcium carbonate (limestone) has been mined since 1980; production (1991), 0·32m. tonnes. Production of limestone, 1990 (estimate), 0·36m. tonnes.

Agriculture. Livestock (1996): Cattle, 1,000; goats, 13,000 (1995); pigs, 2,000; sheep, 7,000; asses, 3,000.

Fisheries. Catch (1995), 1,010 tonnes.

INDUSTRY
Curaçao has an oil refinery and a large ship-repair dry docks. Bonaire has a textile factory and a modern equipped salt plant. Sint Maarten's industrial activities are primarily based on a rum factory and a fishing factory.

Labour. In 1992 (census) the economically active population numbered 87,756; unemployment rate 15·3% (Curaçao, 1995: 62,236; unemployment rate 13·1%).

INTERNATIONAL TRADE
Imports and Exports. There is a Free Zone on Curaçao. Total imports (1994) amounted to 2,462m. (crude and petroleum products, 1,301m.) NA guilders, total exports to 1,730m. (crude and petroleum products, 1,484m.) NA guilders.

COMMUNICATIONS
Roads. In 1989 the Netherlands Antilles had 845 km of surfaced highway distributed as follows: Curaçao, 590; Bonaire, 226; Sint Maarten, 19. Number of motor vehicles registered in 1994, 166,392.

Civil Aviation. There are international airports on Curaçao (Curaçao International Airport), Bonaire (Flamingo Airport) and Sint Maarten (Princess Juliana Airport). The local carrier, AirALM, had 7 aircraft in 1998. In addition to operating on domestic routes, in 1998 it also served Amsterdam (jointly with KLM), Aruba, Atlanta, Caracas, Kingston, Miami, Paramaribo, Port au Prince, Port of Spain, Puerto Rico, Santo Domingo and Valencia (Venezuela). Services were also provided in 1998 by Aeropostal Alas de Venezuela, Air Aruba, Air France, Air St Barthélemy, American Airlines, AOM French Airlines, Avianca, BWIA International, Cardinal Airlines, Continental Airlines, Cubana, KLM, LIAT, Servivensa, Société Nouvelle Air Guadeloupe, Surinam Airways, TAP, United Airlines, US Airways and Windward Islands Airways. In 1995 Curaçao handled 1,196,935 passengers, Bonaire 286,117, Sint Maarten 1,497,359, Sint Eustatius 49,369 and Saba (1994) 45,457.

Shipping. 5,152 ships (totalling 31,785,000 GRT) entered the port of Curaçao in 1995; 1,011 ships (15,911,000 GRT) entered the port of Bonaire; 1,400 ships entered the port of Sint Maarten. In 1995 Curaçao handled 171,854 passengers; in 1994 Bonaire handled 12,736 and Sint Maarten 718,550. Merchant shipping in 1995 totalled 1,197,000 GRT.

Telecommunications. Number of telephones in 1995 was 75,868 (365·9 per 1,000 population). There were 12,000 cellular phone subscribers in 1995.

SOCIAL INSTITUTIONS

Justice. There is a Court of First Instance, which sits in each island, and a Court of Appeal in Willemstad.

Religion. In 1992, 73% of the population were Roman Catholics, 10% were Protestants (Sint Maarten and Sint Eustatius being primarily Protestant).

Education. In 1994–95 there were 23,007 pupils in primary schools, 1,859 pupils in special schools, 8,678 pupils in general secondary schools, 6,685 pupils in junior and senior secondary vocational schools, and 848 students in vocational colleges and universities.

Health. In 1996 there were 314 doctors, 67 dentists, 11 hospitals with 1,466 beds and 1,498 nursing personnel.

CULTURE

Broadcasting. In 1995 there were 32 radio transmitters (8 on Bonaire, 17 on Curaçao, 2 on Saba, 1 on Sint Eustatius and 4 on Sint Maarten) and each island had 1 cable television station. These stations broadcast in Papiamento, Dutch, English and Spanish and are mainly financed by income from advertisements. Broadcasting is administered by Landsradio, Telecommunication Administration and Tele Curaçao. In 1995 there were 212,000 radio and 67,000 TV sets (colour by NTSC) in use. In addition, Radio Nederland and Trans World Radio have powerful relay stations operating on medium- and short-waves from Bonaire.

Press. In 1995 there were 9 daily and 2 weekly newspapers.

Tourism. In 1995, 752,000 tourists visited the islands (Sint Maarten, Curaçao and Bonaire) and there were 757,000 cruise passengers.

DIPLOMATIC REPRESENTATIVES
US Consul-General: James L. Williams (J. B. Gorsiraweg 1, Curaçao).

FURTHER READING
Central Bureau of Statistics. *Statistical Yearbook of the Netherlands Antilles*

Bank of the Netherlands Antilles. *Annual Report.*
Schoenhals, K., *Netherlands Antilles and Aruba.* [Bibliography] Oxford and Santa Barbara (CA), 1993

NEW ZEALAND

Capital: Wellington
Population estimate, 2000: 3·8m.
GNP per capita: (PPP$) 16,500
HDI/world rank: 0·939/9

KEY HISTORICAL EVENTS

New Zealand was first called *Aotearoa* by the Maori who migrated from other northern islands in Polynesia, sometime around the AD 1400. The first European to discover New Zealand was Abel Tasman in 1642. He named the south island after the Dutch province of Zeeland. The coast was explored by Capt. Cook in 1769. From about 1800 onwards, New Zealand became a resort for whalers and traders, chiefly from Australia. New Zealand's European constitutional history can be traced back to 1840 when the Maori entered into an agreement with the Crown under the Treaty of Waitangi and New Zealand became a British colony with the Maori retaining full rights of self-governance. However, the effective administration of the country was soon taken over by European settlers although there were movements for Maori self-government. These movements declined in the early 1900s but the struggle for self-determination has re-emerged in recent years which have also seen a relative decline in the number of immigrants from England, Scotland and Ireland. New Zealand had its first elected House of Representatives in 1852 along with a nominated legislative Council and a Governor. Sheep farming came to dominate the economy and in 1882 the first refrigerated meat was sent to Britain.

In the last years of the 19th century, New Zealand adopted a succession of radical social reforms. New Zealand women gained the vote in 1893, the first in the world to be enfranchised.

TERRITORY AND POPULATION

New Zealand lies south-east of Australia in the south Pacific, Wellington being 1,983 km from Sydney. There are two principal islands, the North and South Islands, besides Stewart Island, Chatham Islands and small outlying islands, as well as the territories overseas.

New Zealand (*i.e.*, North, South and Stewart Islands) extends over 1,750 km from north to south. Area, excluding territories overseas, 270,534 sq. km comprising North Island, 115,777 sq. km; South Island, 151,215 sq. km; Stewart Island, 1,746 sq. km; Chatham Islands, 963 sq. km. The minor islands (total area, 320 sq. miles or 829 sq. km) included within the geographical boundaries of New Zealand (but not within any local government area) are the following: Kermadec Islands (34 sq. km), Three Kings Islands (8 sq. km), Auckland Islands (606 sq. km), Campbell Island (114 sq. km), Antipodes Islands (62 sq. km), Bounty Islands (1 sq. km), Snares Islands (3 sq. km), Solander Island (1 sq. km). With the exception of meteorological station staff on Raoul Island in the Kermadec Group and Campbell Island there are no inhabitants.

The Kermadec Islands were annexed to New Zealand in 1887, have no separate administration and all New Zealand laws apply to them. Situation, 29° 10' to 31° 30' S. lat., 177° 45' to 179° W. long., 1,000 miles NNE of New Zealand. The largest of the group is Raoul or Sunday Island, 29 sq. km, smaller islands being Macaulay and Curtis, while Macaulay Island is 3 miles in circuit.

Growth in census population, exclusive of territories overseas:

	Total population	Average annual increase %		Total population	Average annual increase %
1858	115,462	—	1911	1,058,308	2·52
1878	458,007	7·33	1916[1]	1,149,225	1·50
1881	534,030	5·10	1921	1,271,644	2·27
1886	620,451	3·05	1926	1,408,139	2·06
1891	668,632	1·50	1936[2]	1,573,810	1·13
1896	743,207	2·13	1945[1,2]	1,702,298	0·83
1901[1]	815,853	1·89	1951[1]	1,939,472	2·37
1906	936,304	2·75	1956[1]	2,174,062	2·31

NEW ZEALAND

	Total population	Average annual increase %		Total population	Average annual increase %
1961[1]	2,414,984	2·12	1981[1]	3,175,737	0·20
1966[1]	2,676,919	2·10	1986[1]	3,307,084	0·82
1971[1]	2,862,631	1·34	1991[1]	3,434,950	0·77
1976[1]	3,129,383	1·71	1996[1]	3,681,546	1·40

[1]Excluding members of the Armed Forces overseas.

[2]The census of New Zealand is quinquennial, but the census falling in 1931 was abandoned as an act of national economy, and owing to war conditions the census due in 1941 was not taken until 25 Sept. 1945.

In 1995, 85·9% of the population lived in urban areas.

The populations of regional councils (all data conforms with boundaries redrawn after the 1989 re-organization of local government) at the 1996 census:

Local Government Region	Total Population 1991 census	1996 census	Percentage change 1991-96 (%)
Northland	131,620	141,865	7·8
Auckland	953,980	1,077,205	12·9
Waikato	338,959	357,294	5·4
Bay of Plenty	208,163	230,465	10·7
Gisborne	44,387	46,089	3·8
Hawke's Bay	139,479	144,292	3·4
Taranaki	107,222	106,570	−0·6
Manuwatu-Wanganui	226,616	229,989	1·5
Wellington	402,892	416,019	3·3
Total North Island	2,553,413	2,749,788	7·7
Tasman	34,416	40,036	9·9
Nelson	38,003	42,073	10·7
Marlborough	36,765	40,242	9·4
West Coast	33,961	35,671	5·0
Canterbury	446,114	478,912	7·4
Otago	186,067	193,132	3·8
Southland	103,442	100,758	−2·6
Total South Island	881,537	930,824	5·7
Remainder New Zealand[1]	864	934	8·1
Total New Zealand	3,435,814	3,681,546	7·2

[1]Includes Kermadec, Campbell and Chatham Islands and oil rigs.

1997 population estimate, 3·77m.; density, 14 per sq. km.

The projected population for 2000 is 3·8m.

Between 1986 and 1996, the number of people who identified themselves as being of European ethnicity dropped from 81·2% to 71·7%. Pacific Island people made up 4·8% of the population in 1996 (3·7% in 1986); Asian ethnic groups went from 1·5% to 4·4% in 1996.

Maori population: 1896, 42,113; 1936, 82,326; 1945, 98,744; 1951, 115,676; 1961, 171,553; 1971, 227,414; 1981, 279,255; 1986, 294,201; 1991, 324,000; 1996, 523,374. This is an increase of 20·4% since 1991. In addition, 579,714 people said they have Maori ancestry, up 13·4% on 1991. There were estimated in 1995 to be 10,123 fully fluent speakers of Maori and a further 12,153 who were at the medium to high fluency level. In the 1996 Census, 153,669 New Zealanders said they could hold a conversation about everyday matters in Maori.

From the 1970s organizations were formed to pursue Maori grievances over loss of land and resources. The Waitangi Tribunal was set up in 1975 as a forum for complaints about breaches of the Treaty of Waitangi, and in 1984 empowered to hear claims against Crown actions since 1840. Direct negotiations with the Crown have been offered to claimants and a range of proposals to resolve historical grievances launched for public discussion in Dec. 1994. These proposals specify that all claims are to be met over 10 years with treaty rights being converted to economic assets. There have been four recent major treaty settlements: NZ$170m. each for Tainui and Ngai Tahu, the NZ$150m. Sealord fishing agreement and NZ$40m. for Whakatohea in the Bay of Plenty. The Maori Land Court has jurisdiction over Maori freehold land and some general land owned by Maoris under the Te Ture Whenue Maori Act 1993.

Populations of main urban areas as at the 1996 census were as follows:

Auckland	997,940	Invercargill	49,306
Christchurch	331,443	Nelson	52,348
Dunedin	112,279	New Plymouth	49,079
Hamilton	159,234	Rotorua	56,928
Hastings and		Tauranga	82,832
Napier	113,719	Wanganui	41,320
Palmerston North	73,862	Wellington	335,468
Gisborne	32,653	Whangarei	45,785

English is the official language; Maori is also spoken.

SOCIAL STATISTICS
Statistics for calendar years:

	Total live births	Single-parent births	Deaths	Marriages	Divorces (decrees absolute)
1993	58,867	22,355	27,248	22,056	9,193
1994	57,435	22,180	27,092	21,858	9,213
1995	57,791	23,499	27,960	21,579	9,574
1996	57,434	23,722	28,375	21,506	10,009
1997	57,734	24,127	27,599	21,038	—

Birth rate, 1997, 15·3 per 1,000 population; death rate, 7·3; marriage rate, 5·6; infant mortality, 1996, 6·68 per 1,000 live births. Population increase 1996, 1·5%. Expectation of life, 1996: males, 73·7 years; females, 79·1.

In 1996 there were 80,288 immigrants (77,563 in 1995) and 54,212 emigrants (49,077 in 1995). Fertility rate, 1990–95, 2·1 births per woman.

CLIMATE
Lying in the cool temperate zone, New Zealand enjoys very mild winters for its latitude owing to its oceanic situation, and only the extreme south has cold winters. The situation of the mountain chain produces much sharper climatic contrasts between east and west than in a north-south direction. Observations for mid-summer and mid-winter daily averages in 1990:

	Jan (°C)	July (°C)	Annual rainfall (mm) in 1996
Auckland	23·4	7·8	1,105
Christchurch	21·7	1·5	645
Dunedin	19·1	3·1	800
Hokitika	19·3	2·8	2,810
New Plymouth	21·5	5·4	1,455
Wellington	20·1	5·6	1,270

Although cool overall, the highest extreme temperature recorded in 1997 was 34·1°C at Timaru Airport on 15 Dec. The lowest temperature was –8·8°C, recorded at Lauder, Central Otago on the morning of 16 July 1997.

CONSTITUTION AND GOVERNMENT
Definition was given to the status of New Zealand by the (Imperial) Statute of Westminster of Dec. 1931, which had received the antecedent approval of the New Zealand Parliament in July 1931. The Governor-General's assent was given to the Statute of Westminster Adoption Bill on 25 Nov. 1947.

The powers, duties and responsibilities of the Governor-General and the Executive Council are set out in Royal Letters Patent and Instructions thereunder of 11 May 1917. In the execution of the powers vested in him the Governor-General must be guided by the advice of the Executive Council.

At a referendum on 6 Nov. 1993 a change from a first-past-the-post to a proportional representation electoral system was favoured by 53·9% of votes cast.

Parliament is the *House of Representatives*, since 1996 consisting of 120 members: 60 for general seats, 55 for party list seats and 5 for Maori seats, elected by universal adult suffrage on the mixed-member-proportional system (MMP) for 3-year terms. The 5 Maori electoral districts cover the whole country. Maori and people of Maori descent are entitled to register either for a general or a Maori electoral district. As at Sept. 1997, there were 163,310 persons on the Maori electoral roll. At the next general election there will be six Maori seats.

Joseph, P. A., *Constitutional Law in New Zealand.* Sydney, 1993.—(ed.) *Essays on the Constitution.* Sydney, 1995
McGee, D. G., *Parliamentary Practice in New Zealand.* 2nd ed. Wellington, 1994
Ringer, J. B., *An Introduction to New Zealand Government.* Christchurch, 1992
Vowles, J. and Aimer, P. (eds.) *Double Decision: the 1993 Election and Referendum in New Zealand.* Victoria (Wellington) Univ. Press, 1994

National Anthem. 'God Defend New Zealand'; words by T. Bracken, tune by J. J. Woods. There is a Maori version, Aotearoa, words by T. H. Smith. The UK national anthem has equal status.

RECENT ELECTIONS
At the elections on 12 Oct. 1996 the electorate was 2,418,587; turn-out was 88%. 27 parties stood. The National Party (NP) gained 44 seats with 34·13% of votes cast (83·31% in 1993), the Labour Party 37 with 28·27% (34·68%), New Zealand First (NZF) 17 with 13·13% (8·4%), the Alliance coalition 13 with 10·12% (18·21%), Association of Consumers and Tax Payers (ACT) 8 with 6·17%, United Party 1 with 0·91%. In Dec. 1997, Prime Minister Jim Bolger was ousted as leader of the National Party. He was replaced by Jenny Shipley who became the country's first woman prime minister.

Parliamentary elections are due to take place no later than Oct. 1999.

CURRENT ADMINISTRATION
Governor-General: Sir Michael Hardie Boys, GCMG, GNZM (b. 1931; sworn in March 1996).

An NP-NZF coalition government was formed on 16 Dec. 1996. On 13 Aug. 1998 the coalition collapsed after 4 ministers from the junior coalition partner, New Zealand First, left the cabinet. After a week of turmoil 6 MPs defected from NZF to give a working majority of 1 seat in parliament.

In March 1999 the government consisted of:
Prime Minister: Jenny Shipley (b. 1952; NP).
Deputy Prime Minister, Minister of Health: Wyatt Creech (NP). *Minister of Foreign Affairs and Trade, War Pensions, Disarmament and Arms Controls:* Don McKinnon (NP). *Finance, Revenue:* Bill English (NP). *Defence, Tertiary Education, Enterprise and Commerce:* Max Bradford (NP). *Local Government, Communications, Information Technology, Research, Science and Technology, Statistics and Transport:* Maurice Williamson (NP). *State-owned Enterprises, Justice, Housing New Zealand, Youth Affairs and Radio NZ:* Tony Ryall (NP). *Attorney General, Treaty of Waitangi Negotiations:* Doug Graham (NP). *Education and Conservation:* Dr Nick Smith (NP). *Courts, Women's Affairs:* Georgina te Heu Heu (NP). *Police, Racing and Corrections:* Clem Simich (NP). *Maori Affairs:* Tau Henare (NZF). *International Trade:* Lockwood Smith (NP). *Pacific Island Affairs and Immigration:* Tuariki John Delamere (ind). *Environment, State Services and Crown Research Institutes:* Simon Upton (NP). *Food, Fibre, Biosecurity and Border Security:* John Luxton (NP). *Tourism, Sport, Fitness and Leisure, Accident Rehabilitation and Compensation Insurance:* Murray McCully (NP). *Social Services, Work, Income and Housing Corporation of New Zealand:* Roger Sowry (NP).

There are also 5 ministers outside the cabinet.

Local Government. Since the reform of local government in Nov. 1989 it comprises 12 regional councils, 74 territorial authorities (15 city councils, 58 district councils and the Chatham Islands council), 155 community boards and 6 special authorities. Territorial authorities and regional councils are directly elected. A city must have a minimum of 50,000 persons, be predominantly urban in character, be a distinct entity and a major centre of activity within the region. A district, on the other hand, serves a combination of rural and urban communities. There is no distinction in structural status or responsibility between a city council and a district council. There are a few other local authorities created for specific functions.

Local elections were held on 14 Oct. 1995.

Bush, G., *Local Government and Politics in New Zealand.* Auckland, 1995

DEFENCE
The control and co-ordination of defence activities is obtained through the Ministry of Defence. New Zealand forces serve abroad in Australia and Singapore, and with UN peacekeeping missions.

Defence expenditure in 1997 totalled US$901m. (US$251 per capita), representing 1·6% of GDP.

Rolfe, J., *Defending New Zealand.* Wellington, 1993

Army. The Army is organized into Land Command, 2 Land Force Groups, 1 armoured regiment, 2 infantry battalions, 1 artillery, 1 engineer regiment and 2 special forces squadrons. Major equipment of the NZ Army includes: 8 Scorpion armoured reconnaissance vehicles, 78 armoured personnel carriers, 491 Land-Rover 4x4, 351 Unimog 4 tonne trucks and 18 105-mm Howitzer guns; 5 very low-level air-defence ground-to-air missile systems will be introduced.

Personnel total: regular force 4,400 (400 women), territorial force 3,539 and civilian employees 832.

Navy. On 1 Jan. 1998, the Navy comprised 1 Anzac class frigate (Te Kaha) with a second (Te Mana) to enter service in 1999, 2 Leander frigates (Canterbury and Wellington), one 12,400-tonne fleet replenishment tanker (Endeavour), 1 naval sea-lift vessel (Charles Upham), 1 diving support vessel (Manawanui), 1 oceanographic survey and 2 inshore survey vessels plus 4 inshore patrol craft. Wasp helicopters were being replaced by 4 Kaman SH 2G helicopters during 1998, which in turn will be replaced by 5 Kaman SH 2F helicopters in 2000. The main base and Fleet headquarters is at Auckland.

At 1 Jan. 1998 the Royal New Zealand Navy personnel totalled 2,080 uniformed plus 405 Reserve personnel and 562 civilians.

Air Force. Maritime (P-3K Orion), long and medium-range transport (Boeing 727 and C-130H Hercules), and helicopter (UH-1H Iroquois and HAS1 Wasp) squadrons are based at RNZAF Base Auckland, and air-attack force (A-4) Skyhawk at RNZAF Base Ohakea and RANAS Nowra (Australia). Flying training is conducted at Ohakea, (CT/4B) Airtrainer and (MB 339CB) Macchi, and Auckland (Andover and Sioux). Ground training is carried out at RNZAF Base Woodbourne.

The uniform strength in 1997 was 3,235 (560 women), and 480 civilian personnel, with 38 combat aircraft.

INTERNATIONAL RELATIONS
New Zealand is a member of the UN, the Commonwealth, OECD, the Pacific Community, South Pacific Forum and the Colombo Plan.

ECONOMY

Performance. GDP at current prices grew 4·4% to NZ$95,816m. in the year ended March 1997, an increase of 2·4% in constant prices. The previous year's growth was respectively 3·1% and 6·9%. It was forecast that the economy would contract in 1998. The current account deficit was 8% of GDP in 1997.

Budget. The following tables of revenue and expenditure relate to the Consolidated Account, which covers the ordinary revenue and expenditure of the government—*i.e.*, apart from capital items, commercial and special undertakings, advances, etc. Total revenue and expenditure of the Consolidated Account, in NZ$1m., year ended 30 June:

	1993	1994	1995	1996	1997
Revenue	29,835	30,183	33,648	35,059	34,778
Expenditure	31,429	29,639	30,400	31,743	32,953

1997 tax revenue included (in NZ$1m.): Income tax, NZ$15,324; company tax, NZ$3,233; withholding taxes, NZ$1,932; domestic goods and services, NZ$7,725. Non-tax revenue was NZ$2,862m.

The gross public debt at June 1997 was NZ$35,972m., of which NZ$29,625m. was held in New Zealand currency and NZ$6,347m. in foreign currency. The gross annual interest charge on the public debt at June 1997 was NZ$3,072m. (1996 NZ$3,703m.).

New Zealand System of National Accounts. National Accounts aggregates for 6 years are given in the following table (in NZ$1m.):

Year ended 31 March	Gross domestic product	Gross national product	National income
1992	73,213	69,700	62,839
1993	77,067	74,281	67,090
1994	80,864	77,644	70,506
1995	86,304	82,145	73,865
1996	91,045	85,561	77,072
1997	95,206	87,139	77,987

Currency. The monetary unit is the *New Zealand dollar* (NZD), of 100 *cents*. The total value of notes and coins on issue from the Reserve Bank in Dec. 1997 was NZ$2,033m. Inflation was 1·1% at 30 June 1997. In Feb. 1998 foreign exchange reserves were US$4,190m. Total money supply in Feb. 1998 was NZ$34,211m.

Banking and Finance. The central bank and bank of issue is the Reserve Bank (*Governor*, Dr. Don Brash).

The financial system comprises a central bank (the Reserve Bank of New Zealand), registered banks, and other financial institutions. Registered banks include banks from abroad, which have to satisfy capital adequacy and managerial quality requirements. Other financial institutions include the regional trustee banks, now grouped under Trust Bank, building societies, finance companies, merchant banks and stock and station agents. The number of registered banks was 18 in 1997. Around 99% of the assets of the New Zealand banking system were under the ownership of a foreign bank parent.

The primary functions of the Reserve Bank are the formulation and implementation of monetary policy to achieve the economic objectives set by the government, and the promotion of the efficiency and soundness of the financial system, through the registration of banks, and supervision of financial institutions. Since 1996 supervision has been conducted on a basis of public disclosure by banks of their activities every quarter.

On 30 June 1996 the funding (financial liabilities including deposits) and claims (financial assets including loans) for all registered banks and other financial institutions were: funding, NZ$119,028m. (foreign currency, NZ$11,800m.); claims, NZ$104,053m. (foreign currency, NZ$3,690m.).

The stock exchange in Wellington conducts on-screen trading, unifying the 3 former trading floors in Auckland, Christchurch and Wellington.

Weights and Measures. The metric system of weights and measures operates.

ENERGY AND NATURAL RESOURCES

Electricity. On 1 April 1987 the former Electricity Division of the Ministry of Energy became a state-owned enterprise, the Electricity Corporation of N.Z. Ltd. In 1995 it had 40 power stations (31 hydro-electric and 9 thermal, with a total nominal capacity of 7,268 MW) producing almost 100% of the country's electricity. The remainder is generated by the Electrical Supply Authorities from 23 small plants. Consumption per capita was an estimated 9,400 kWh in 1997.

A wind farm was opened in 1996.

Statistics for 6 years ended 31 March are:

	1991	1992	1993	1994	1995	1996
Total sales revenue (NZ$1m.)	1,580	1,589	1,543	1,700	1,520	1,383
Total sales volume (gWh)	27,892	28,660	27,753	29,228	29,780	...
Generation (gWh) (nett)	29,556	30,339	29,569	32,453	33,415	32,653
Number of employees	3,974	3,096	2,861	2,835	...	...
Production/total staff employed (gWh/person)	7·46	8·89	9·93	10·95	...	...

With privatization much of this material is no longer attainable.

Oil and Gas. Crude oil and condensate production was 90·68 petajoules in 1996.

In 1996 there were 7 gasfields in production, with an output of 180 petajoules.

Agriculture. Two-thirds of the land area is suitable for agriculture and grazing. The total area of farmland in use at 30 June 1996 was 16,547,113 ha. There were

13,265,431 ha of grazing, arable, fodder and fallow land, 122,988 ha of land for horticulture and 1,683,216 ha of plantations of exotic timber.

The largest freehold estates are held in the South Island. The number of occupied holdings as at 30 June 1995 were as follows:

Regional Council	No. of farms	Total area of farms (1,000 ha)	Regional Council	No. of farms	Total area of farms (1,000 ha)
Northland	5,770	862	Marlborough	1,413	702
Auckland	5,298	310	Nelson	132	15
Waikato	11,954	1,734	West Coast	890	407
Bay of Plenty	5,511	628	Canterbury	9,381	3,408
Gisborne	1,394	699	Otago	3,895	2,507
Hawke's Bay	3,860	1,086	Southland	4,575	1,257
Taranaki	3,963	497	Tasman	1,919	272
Wanganui and Manawatu	6,612	1,611	*Total South Island*	*22,165*	*8,638*
Wellington	2,249	512			
Total North Island	*46,611*	*7,940*	*Total New Zealand*	*68,776*	*16,578*

The area and yield for each of the principal crops are given as follows (area and yield for threshing only, not including that grown for chaff, hay, silage, etc.):

	Wheat		Maize		Barley	
Crop years	Area (1,000 ha)	Yield (1,000 tonnes)	Area (1,000 ha)	Yield (1,000 tonnes)	Area (1,000 ha)	Yield (1,000 tonnes)
1992	37·8	191·0	18·0	163·8	67·4	318·8
1993	40·9	219·4	15·9	133·1	79·8	389·5
1994	44·7	241·9	14·7	142·8	76·9	395·5
1995	52·4	245·2	16·5	160·8	68·2	302·8

In 1996, a total of 2,205,568 (provisional) tonnes of fertilizer were sold.

Livestock 1996: deer, 1·2m.; goats, 228,000; pigs, 424,000. In 1997 there were: dairy cattle, 3·6m.; beef cattle, 4·7m.; sheep, 47·2m. Total meat produced in the year ended 30 Sept. 1997 was estimated at 1·4m. tonnes (including 646,000 tonnes of beef and veal, and 542,000 tonnes of lamb).

Production of wool for the year ended Sept. 1997 was 203,300 tonnes. Milk production for the year ended May 1998 was expected to reach a new record level of 900m. kg of milk solids.

Forestry. Forests covered 7·88m. ha in 1995 (29·4% of New Zealand's land area), up from 7·67m. ha in 1990. Of this, about 6·4m. ha are indigenous forest and 1·5m. ha planted productive forest. New planting has increased from 15,000 ha in 1991 to 66,000 ha in 1997. Introduced pines form the bulk of the large exotic forest estate and among these radiata pine is the best multi-purpose tree, reaching log size in 25–30 years. Other species planted are Douglas fir and Eucalyptus species. Total roundwood production in 1996–97 was 16m. cu. metres. The table below shows production of rough sawn timber in 1,000 cu. metres for years ending 31 March:

	Indigenous			Exotic			All Species
	Rimu and Miro	Beech	Total	Pines	Douglas Fir	Total	Total
1991–92	51	4	63	1,935	221	2,238	2,301
1992–93	55	4	67	2,281	160	2,567	2,634
1993–94	66	4	79	2,497	123	2,736	2,810
1994–95	66	7	79	2,591	128	2,870	2,949
1995–96	44	4	55	2,631	104	2,849	2,904

In 1996–97 forest industries consisted of 440 sawmills, 6 plywood and 8 veneer plants, 4 particle board mills, 8 pulp and paper mills and 4 fibreboard mills.

The basic products of the pulp and paper mills are mechanical and chemical pulp which are converted into newsprint, kraft and other papers, paperboard and fibreboard. Production of woodpulp in the year ending 31 March 1997 amounted to 1·37m. tonnes and of paper (including newsprint paper and paperboard) to 877,152 tonnes.

Fisheries. In 1995 the total catch (including shellfish) was 654,654 tonnes. The total value of New Zealand Fisheries exports during the year ended 30 June 1995 was NZ$1,105·5m. Exports: Fish, 175,400 tonnes, value NZ$705·6m.; crustaceans, 3,157 tonnes, value NZ$131·5m.

INDUSTRY

Statistics of manufacturing industries:

Production year	Hours worked	Salaries and wages paid (NZ$1m.)	Stocks (NZ$1m.)		Sales and other income (NZ$1m.)	Ratio of total stocks to sales
			Materials	Finished goods		
1995–96	498·2m.	8,083	10,864	15,342	51,341	...

The following is a statement of the value of the products (including repairs) of the principal industries for the year 1994–95 (in NZ$1m.):

Industry group	Purchases and operating expenses	Sales and other income	Additions to fixed tangible assets
Primary food	9,495	10,791	467
Textiles, apparel and leathergoods	2,298	3,171	88
Wood and wood products (including furniture)	2,884	4,056	186
Paper and paper products, printing and publishing	3,217	4,886	346
Chemicals and chemical, petroleum, coal, rubber and plastic products	4,313	6,103	463
Non-metallic mineral products	908	1,344	61
Basic metal industries	1,503	1,849	105
Fabricated metal products, machinery and equipment	7,642	10,477	338
Other manufacturing industries	296	418	15
Total	37,865	49,954	2,373

Labour. There were 1,707,400 persons employed in the quarter ending Dec. 1997, 753,200 females. Unemployment was 6·6% of the workforce in the same quarter, declining slightly to 6·5% by April 1998. Unemployment figures for the quarter ending Dec. 1997 were 121,400. Women made up 44·6% of the workforce in 1997.

In the year ending March 1997, 37,100 had been unemployed for longer than 6 months. The weekly average wage in the Aug. quarter 1997 was NZ$736·82 for men, NZ$547·18 for women. A minimum wage is set by the government annually. In 1997 it was NZ$7 an hour. In 1997 a minimum wage was fixed for 16 to 19-year-old workers, NZ$4·20 an hour. In the year to Aug. 1997 there were 62 industrial stoppages (73 in 1996) with 47,719 working days lost (42,690 in 1996).

Trade Unions. In 1997, 22 industrial unions of workers (representing 80% of all union members) were affiliated to the council of Trade Unions (*President*, Ken Douglas).

Compulsory trade union membership was made illegal in 1991, and the national wage award system was replaced by local wage agreements under the Employment Contracts Act 1991. In Dec. 1996, 339,327 persons (19·9% of the workforce) belonged to trade unions (409,112 in Dec. 1993, 603,118 in May 1991).

INTERNATIONAL TRADE

Total overseas debt was NZ$7,550m. in March 1997. In 1990 New Zealand and Australia completed the Closer Economic Relations Agreement (initiated in 1983), which provides for mutual free trade in goods.

Imports and Exports. Trade (excluding specie and bullion) in NZ$1m. for 12 months ended 30 June:

	Total merchandise imported (v.f.d.)[1]	Exports of domestic produce	Re-exports	Total merchandise exported (f.o.b.)
1992–93	15,979·4	18,240·4	730·3	18,970·8
1993–94	17,019·3	19,166·4	660·7	19,827·1
1994–95	19,746·4	20,199·8	725·1	20,924·9
1995–96	21,352·5	19,958·8	586·9	20,545·7
1996–97	19,784·8	20,045·1	628·1	21,033·2

[1]Value for duty.

NEW ZEALAND

The principal imports for the 12 months ended 30 June 1997:

Commodity	Value (NZ$1m. v.f.d.)
Fruit	132·5
Sugar and sugar confectionery	139·3
Beer, wine and spirits	152·9
Crude petroleum oil	754·2
Inorganic chemicals (excluding aluminium oxide)	160·8
Aluminium oxide	190·2
Knitted or crocheted fabrics and articles	283·5
Glass and glassware	127·8
Iron and steel	346·3
Articles of iron and steel	320·7
Copper and articles of copper	101·8
Aluminium and articles of aluminium	202·3
Tools, implements and articles of base metals	206·6
Machinery and mechanical appliances	3,102·5
Organic chemicals	254·8
Pharmaceutical products	531·3
Plastics and articles of plastic	829·3
Rubber and articles of rubber	248·8
Paper, paperboard and articles thereof	568·8
Printed books, newspapers etc.	314·4
Cotton yarn and fabrics	88·1
Man-made filaments and fibres	177·8
Electrical machinery and equipment	2,124·2
Motor cars, station wagons, utilities	1,647·9
Trucks, buses and vans	374·3
Aircraft	303·4
Ships and boats	298·2
Optical, photographic, technical and surgical equipment	649·8

The principal exports of New Zealand produce for the 12 months ended 30 June 1997 were:

Commodity	Value (NZ$1m. f.o.b.)	Commodity	Value (NZ$1m. f.o.b.)
Live animals	125·3	Fish, fresh, chilled or frozen	688·6
Meat, fresh, chilled or frozen		Vegetables	270·9
Beef and veal	992·7	Fresh kiwifruit	376·8
Lamb and mutton	1,502·5	Fresh apples	342·0
Dairy products		Forest products	
Milk, cream and yoghurt	1,738·1	Sawn timber and logs	1,140·4
Butter	917·4	Paper and paper products	365·4
Cheese	838·4	Wood pulp	356·7
Raw hides, skins and leather	662·2	Iron and steel and	
Wool	946·3	articles thereof	416·7
Aluminium and		Machinery and	
articles thereof	810·9	mechanical appliances	759·1
Casein and caseinates	569·4	Electrical machinery and	
Plastic materials and		equipment	575·6
articles thereof	261·1		
Sausage casings	127·6		

The following table shows the trade with different countries for the year ended 30 June (in NZ$1m.):

Countries	Imports v.f.d. from 1995	1996	Exports and re-exports f.o.b. to 1994	1995	1996
Total EU countries	3,555·0	4,265·4	3,058·2	3,263·1	3,423·3
Australia	4,146·4	4,648·7	4,162·2	4,342·4	4,275·7
Belgium	135·5	151·0	239·1	224·1	307·3
Canada	280·9	382·6	361·9	334·6	313·1
China	644·2	712·8	528·6	544·7	559·7
Fiji Islands	—	—	215·7	193·3	188·1
France	331·6	499·2	211·6	232·1	191·2
Germany	910·6	979·7	490·8	507·8	512·1

Countries	Imports v.f.d. from		Exports and re-exports f.o.b. to		
	1995	1996	1994	1995	1996
Hong Kong	213·1	193·1	481·9	595·6	574·9
Iran	—	—	72·8	68·1	67·1
Italy	427·8	503·4	265·3	290·4	300·9
Japan	2,916·1	2,628·0	2,886·8	3,416·6	3,137·7
Korea, Republic of	308·7	350·0	928·6	398·5	978·3
Malaysia	257·2	406·3	392·8	120·6	491·6
Netherlands	214·5	221·3	123·1	89·3	114·8
Peru	—	—	88·4	194·7	80·5
Philippines	—	—	202·1	168·6	293·6
Saudi Arabia	254·9	302·3	215·9	281·3	192·2
Singapore	377·5	385·8	269·6	—	283·0
Sweden	340·1	326·2	—	—	—
Switzerland	187·9	203·7	—	623·3	—
Taiwan	536·6	498·0	507·3	260·6	552·9
Thailand	142·3	150·7	192·2	192·2	282·4
UK	1,233·2	1,076·9	1,182·3	1,290·5	1,358·8
USA	4,022·4	3413·9	2,228·7	2,168·3	2,085·7

COMMUNICATIONS

Roads. Total length of maintained roads at 30 June 1997 was 91,996·4 km (56,338·4 km sealed and 35,628 km gravel) with 15,800 bridges. There were 74 national and provincial state highways comprising 10,486·4 km of roadway, including the principal arterial traffic routes.

In Feb. 1997 there were 9,080 full-time equivalent persons employed in the provision of road passenger transport and 21,660 persons providing road freight transport.

Total expenditure on roads (including state highways), streets and bridges—by the central government and local authorities combined—amounted to NZ$1·1bn. in 1997.

At 31 March 1997 motor vehicles licensed numbered 2,457,116; of which 1,675,301 were cars, 16,139 omnibuses/public taxis, and 38,288 motor cycles. Included in the remaining numbers were 8,425 power cycles, 346,489 trucks and 303,371 trailers and caravans.

In 1997 there were 539 deaths in road accidents (513 in 1996).

Rail. New Zealand Rail was privatized in 1993 and is now known as Tranz Rail. In 1994 a 24-hour freight link was introduced between Auckland and Christchurch. There were, in 1996, 4,439 km of 1,067 mm gauge railway open for traffic (524 km electrified). In 1997 Tranz Rail carried 11·5m. tonnes of freight and 11·57m. passengers. Operating profit in 1997 was NZ$86·1m.

At 30 June 1997 Tranz Rail track and rolling stock included 357 diesel, electric and shunting locomotives, 6,728 freight wagons, 301 passenger carriages and commuter units, 3 rail/road ferries (linking the North and South Islands) and plant and support equipment.

Civil Aviation. There are international airports at Wellington, Auckland and Christchurch, with Auckland International being the main airport. The national carrier is Air New Zealand. Ansett New Zealand provides some domestic services. In 1998 services were also provided by Aerolíneas Argentinas, Air Calédonie International, Air Chathams, Air Pacific, Air Vanuatu, American Airlines, Ansett Australia, Associated Airlines, British Airways, Canadian Airlines International, Cathay Pacific Airways, Chathams Airlink, EVA Airways, Evergreen International, Garuda Indonesia, JAL, Korean Air, Lan-Chile, Lufthansa, Malaysia Airlines, Mandarin Airlines, Polynesian Airlines, Qantas Airways, Royal Tongan Airlines, Singapore Airlines, Solomon Airlines, Thai Airways International and United Airlines. Trans-Tasman air travel is subject to agreement between Air New Zealand and Qantas.

Shipping. In 1995 sea-going shipping totalled 260,000 GRT, including oil tankers, 94,169 GRT. In 1994 vessels totalling 39,700,000 GRT entered ports and vessels totalling 37,421,000 GRT cleared. As at 31 Dec. 1997 there were 3,135 ships on the New Zealand Register of Ships.

NEW ZEALAND

Telecommunications. The provision of telecommunication services is the responsibility of the Telecom Corporation of New Zealand, formed in 1987 and privatized in 1990; and CLEAR Communications, which began operations in Dec. 1990. In 1996-97 there were 1,719,000 main lines, or 477 for every 1,000 persons. Cellular phone subscribers numbered 388,000 (108 per 1,000 persons) in 1995, and there were 800,000 PCs (223 per 1,000 persons) and 65,000 fax machines. There were approximately 561,000 Internet users in Nov. 1998.

Postal Services. The provision of postal services is the responsibility of the state-owned New Zealand Post, which began operations on 1 April 1987. New Zealand Post ran the only telegram service in 1996. In 1997 there were 297 post shops, 705 post centre franchises and 3,663 stamp resellers.

SOCIAL INSTITUTIONS

Justice. The judiciary consists of the Court of Appeal, the High Court and District Courts. All exercise both civil and criminal jurisdiction. Final appeal lies to the Privy Council in London. Special courts include the Maori Land Court, the Maori Appellate Court, Family Courts, the Youth Court, Environment Court and the Employment Court. During 1996 prisons contained an average 4,216 prisoners. Some 526,372 offences, including 165 homicides were reported in the year ending June 1997. The death penalty for murder was replaced by life imprisonment in 1961.

The Criminal Injuries Compensation Act, 1963, which came into force on 1 Jan. 1964, provided for compensation of persons injured by certain criminal acts and the dependants of persons killed by such acts. However, this has now been phased out in favour of the Accident Compensation Act, 1982, except in the residual area of property damage caused by escapees. The Offenders Legal Aid Act 1954 provides that any person charged or convicted of any offence may apply for legal aid which may be granted depending on the person's means and the gravity of the offence etc. Since 1970 legal aid in civil proceedings (except divorce) has been available for persons of small or moderate means. The Legal Services Act 1991 now brings together in one statute the civil and criminal legal aid schemes.

Police. The police are a national body maintained by the central government. Legislation of 1994 permits the private management of prisons and prisoner escort services. For operational purposes New Zealand was divided into 4 police regions in July 1997, each controlled by an assistant commissioner.

The total cost of law and order for the year 1995–96 was NZ$1,237m. (NZ$581m. for the police). In 1991, 1,100 traffic officers merged with the police, who previously did not control traffic. In June 1996 there were 6,492 full-time equivalent sworn officers and 1,909 non-sworn full-time equivalent positions.

Ombudsmen. The office of Ombudsman was created in 1962. From 1975 additional Ombudsmen have been authorized. There are currently two. Ombudsmen's functions are to investigate complaints under the Ombudsman Act, the Official Information Act and the Local Government Official Information and Meetings Act from members of the public relating to administrative decisions of central, regional and local government.

During the year ended 30 June 1996, a total of 5,167 complaints were received, 49 of which were sustained and 593 were still under investigation.

Religion. No direct state aid is given to any form of religion. For the Church of England the country is divided into 7 dioceses, with a separate bishopric (Aotearoa) for the Maori. The Presbyterian Church is divided into 23 presbyteries and the Maori Synod. The Moderator is elected annually. The Methodist Church is divided into 10 districts; the President is elected annually. The Roman Catholic Church is divided into 4 dioceses, with the Archbishop of Wellington as Metropolitan Archbishop.

Religious denomination	Number of adherents	
	1991 census	1996 census
Church of England	732,048	631,764
Presbyterian	541,050	458,289
Roman Catholic (including 'Catholic' undefined)	498,612	473,112
Methodist	139,494	121,650
Baptist	70,155	53,613
Brethren	20,337	19,950

Religious denomination	Number of adherents	
	1991 census	*1996 census*
Ratana	47,592	36,450
Buddhist	12,765	28,131
Salvation Army	19,992	14,625
Latter-day Saints (Mormons)	48,009	41,166
Pentecostal	25,368	39,228
Seventh-day Adventist	13,005	12,324
Hindu	17,661	25,293
Jehovah's Witnesses	19,182	19,524
Assemblies of God	17,226	17,520
All other religious affiliations	164,687	273,732
No religion	672,654	893,910
Not specified	56,286	187,881
Object to state	251,709	256,593
Total	3,373,926	3,618,303

Education. New Zealand has 7 universities—the University of Auckland, University of Waikato (at Hamilton), Victoria University of Wellington, Massey University (at Palmerston North), the University of Canterbury (at Christchurch), the University of Otago (at Dunedin) and Lincoln University (near Christchurch). The number of students attending universities in 1997 was 106,486. There were 4 teachers' training colleges with 12,453 students in 1997.

In 1996 there were 320 state secondary schools with 14,119 full-time teachers and 206,153 pupils. There were also 51 state composite area schools with 4,509 scholars in the secondary division. 95,346 students were enrolled in polytechnic courses in 1996; of these 51,568 were part-time. In 1996, 3,364 pupils received tuition from the secondary department of the correspondence school. There were 19 registered private secondary schools with 553 teachers and 11,249 pupils.

In 1996, there were 2,240 state primary schools (including intermediate and state contributing schools), with 422,596 pupils; the number of teachers was 21,177. A correspondence school for children in remote areas and those otherwise unable to attend school had 4,629 primary and secondary pupils. There were 61 registered private primary and intermediate schools with 446 teachers and 12,765 pupils.

Education is compulsory between the ages of 6 and 15. Children aged 3 and 4 years may enrol at the 594 free kindergartens maintained by Free Kindergarten Associations, which receive government assistance. There are also 557 play centres which also receive government subsidy. In 1996 there were 46,960 and 17,596 children on the rolls respectively. There are also 1,213 childcare centres with 57,582 children, 767 *kohanga reo* (providing early childhood education in the Maori language) with 14,302 children, and a number of other smaller providers of early childhood care and education.

Total budgeted expenditure in 1996–97 on education was NZ$5,353m. In 1995 total expenditure on education came to 7·3% of GNP.

The universities are autonomous bodies. All state-funded primary and secondary schools are controlled by boards of trustees. Education in state schools is free for children under 19 years of age. All educational institutions are reviewed every 3 years by teams of educational reviewers.

A series of reforms is being implemented by the government following reports of 18 working groups on tertiary education. These include a new funding system, begun in 1991 and based solely on student numbers.

Health. At 30 June 1996 there were 11,557 doctors on the medical register. In 1996 there were 15,270 public hospital beds. There are 4 regional health authorities, but these are being amalgamated into one transitional health authority. Total expenditure on health in 1995–96 was NZ$5,163m.

Welfare. Non-contributory old-age pensions were introduced in 1898. Large reductions in welfare expenditure were introduced by the government in Dec. 1990.

At 1 April 1997 Family Support for families on the lowest incomes was NZ$44·50 for the first child aged under 16, NZ$37·50 for subsequent children aged 13–15, and NZ$29·50 under 13. Child allowance for single persons with one child was NZ$209·30 per week; with 2 or more children, NZ$244·12 per week.

The weekly unemployment benefit in April 1997 for a single person aged 25 and over was NZ$146·13, aged 16–17 NZ$97·97 and aged 18–24 NZ$121·77. Persons made redundant become eligible for benefit after 26 weeks. In 1991 subsidized housing was replaced by cash subsidies.

In 1993 earners of NZ$17,500 a year and less received subsidized healthcare; a lesser subsidy applied up to NZ$27,000; over that healthcare was paid for by patients.

In the budget of July 1991 it was announced that current rates of Guaranteed Retirement Income Scheme (GRI) payment would be frozen until 1 April 1993, thereafter to be on the previous year's consumer price index. On 1 April 1992 GRI was replaced by the national superannuation scheme which is income-tested. Eligibility will be gradually increased to 65 years by 2001. Universal eligibility is available at 70 years. At 1 April 1997 a married couple received NZ$379·04 per week, a single person NZ$252·82 per week.

Social Welfare Benefits and War Pensions:

Benefits	Number in force at 30 June 1995	Total payments 1995–96 (NZ$1,000)
SOCIAL WELFARE:		
Monetary—		
National Superannuation	459,901	5,170,506
Widows	9,047	85,008
Invalids	42,450	494,849
Miners	n/a	n/a
Orphans	4,662	22,929
Domestic purposes	108,789	1,440,122
Unemployment	134,133	1,276,540
Sickness	33,386	378,850
War pensions	6,559	60,612
Training	11,389	96,973
Total	810,316	9,026,389

Health benefits in 1996: Payments for primary services, NZ$322·2m.; pharmaceutical, NZ$695·93m.

Reciprocity with Other Countries. There are reciprocal arrangements between New Zealand and Australia in respect of age, invalids', widows', family, unemployment and sickness benefits, and between New Zealand and the UK in respect of family, age, superannuation, widows', orphans', invalids', sickness and unemployment benefits. Some of these payments are also available to former New Zealand residents living in Canada (effective 1 May 1997) and New Zealand pays people eligible for New Zealand Superannuation or veterans' pensions who live in the Cook Islands, Niue or Tokelau.

CULTURE

Some 800 km east of Christchurch, the Chatham Islands lie 250 km from the dateline and seem to have the best claim to be the first inhabited landmass to witness the millennium dawn. According to their calculations, the sun will rise over the summit of Mt Hakepa on Pitt Island, the most easterly inhabited island in the group, at 3.59 a.m. (15.59 GMT on 31 Dec 1999) on the morning of 1 Jan 2000.

Broadcasting. Legislation of 1995 split the state-owned Radio New Zealand into a government-owned public radio broadcasting company and some 40 commercial stations. As at 1 July 1998 there were 47 AM and 17 FM stations broadcasting, 30 of which were privately owned.

Television New Zealand operates 2 channels. 2 other channels, TV3 and TV4, are commercial. There are also regional TV networks. Pay television was introduced in May 1990—Sky Entertainment operates on 5 channels. The New Zealand Public Radio Service also includes the Radio New Zealand International, a short-wave which broadcasts to the South Pole. In Nov. 1996, there were over 180 radio stations including 21 regional Maori stations for the promotion of Maori culture and 10 community access radio stations. Number of TV receiving licences (1996) was approximately 1,126,000. In 1995 there were 3,550,000 radio receivers.

Cinema. There were 255 cinemas in 1995; attendances totalled 14m. in that year.

Press. In 1997 there were 28 daily newspapers, of which 20 were evening papers. The *New Zealand Herald,* published in Auckland, had the largest daily circulation of 226,702. Other dailies ranged from 2,200–100,000 copies.

Tourism. There were 1,551,341 tourists in the year to March 1997 (including 433,010 from Australia, 143,574 from the USA, 161,046 from Japan and 148,182 from the UK). International tourism (including revenue from airfares) generated NZ$4·8bn. in 1996. International visitor expenditure for the year ending June 1997 was NZ$3,232m.

DIPLOMATIC REPRESENTATIVES
Of New Zealand in Great Britain (New Zealand Hse., Haymarket, London, SW1Y 4TQ)
High Commissioner: Dr. Richard Sturge Grant.

Of Great Britain in New Zealand (44 Hill St., Wellington, 1)
High Commissioner: M. Williams, CVO, OBE.

Of New Zealand in the USA (37 Observatory Cir., NW, Washington, D.C., 20008)
Ambassador: James Bolger.

Of the USA in New Zealand (29 Fitzherbert Terr., Wellington)
Ambassador: Josiah Beeman.

Of New Zealand to the United Nations
Ambassador: Michael John Powles.

Of New Zealand to the European Union
Ambassador: Derek Leask.

FURTHER READING
Statistics New Zealand. *New Zealand Official Yearbook.—Key Statistics: a monthly Abstract of Statistics.—New Zealand in Profile: annual publication.*
Dictionary of New Zealand Biography. vol. 1 (to 1868). Wellington, 1990
Encyclopaedia of New Zealand. 3 vols. Wellington, 1966
Alley, R., *New Zealand and the Pacific.* Boulder (CO), 1984
Belich, J., *Making peoples: a History of the new Zealanders from Polynesian Settlement to the end of the Nineteenth century.* London, 1997
Grover, R. R., *New Zealand* [Bibliography]. Oxford and Santa Barbara (CA), 1981
Harland, B., *On Our Own: New Zealand in a Tripolar World.* Victoria Univ. Press, 1992
Harris, P. and Levine, S. (eds.) *The New Zealand politics source book.* 2nd ed. Palmerston North, 1994
Hawke, G. R., *The Making of New Zealand: an Economic History.* CUP, 1985
Massey, P., *New Zealand: Market Liberalization in a Developed Economy.* London, 1995
Oliver, W. H. (ed.), *The Oxford History of New Zealand.* OUP, 1981
Patterson, B. and K., *New Zealand* [Bibliography]. 2nd ed. Oxford and Santa Barbara (CA), 1998
Sinclair, K., *A History of New Zealand.* 2nd ed. London, 1980.— (ed.) *The Oxford Illustrated History of New Zealand. 2nd ed.* OUP, 1994

For other more specialized titles see under CONSTITUTION AND GOVERNMENT, LOCAL GOVERNMENT *and* DEFENCE, *above.*

National statistical office: Statistics New Zealand, POB 2922, Wellington, 1.
Website: http://www.stats.govt.nz/statsweb.nsf

TERRITORIES OVERSEAS

Territories Overseas coming within the jurisdiction of New Zealand consist of Tokelau and the Ross Dependency.

Tokelau
Situated some 500 km to Samoa's north and comprises three dispersed atolls—Atafu, Fakaofo and Nukunonu. The land area is 12 sq. km. and the population at the 1996 census was 1,487, giving a density of 124 per sq. km.

The British Government transferred administrative control of Tokelau to New Zealand in 1925. Formal sovereignty was transferred to New Zealand in 1948 by act of the New Zealand Parliament. New Zealand statue law, however, does not apply to Tokelau unless it is expressly extended to Tokelau. In practice New Zealand legislation is extended to Tokelau only with its consent.

Tokelau's three villages are its foundation, and have remained largely autonomous. There has never been any resident New Zealand administration. At the national level Tokelau's needs remain formally the responsibility of the New Zealand Government, and in particular, the Administration of Tokelau.

Under a programme agreed in 1992, the role of Tokelau's political institutions is being better defined and expanded. The process under way enables the base of Tokelau government to be located within Tokelau's national level institutions rather than as before, within a public service located largely in Samoa. In 1994, the Administrator's powers were delegated to the *General Fono* (the national representative body), and when the *General Fono* is not in session, to the *Council of Faipule*. The Tokelau Amendment Act 1996 conferred on the *General Fono* a power to make rules for Tokelau, including the power to impose taxes.

Coconuts (the source of copra) are the only cash crop. Pulaka, breadfruit, papayas, the screw-pine and bananas are cultivated as food crops. Livestock comprises pigs, poultry and goats.

Development prospects are restricted by the small land area and population, geographic isolation, and the relatively high cost of providing education, health and other services including telecommunications and shipping, to three widely separated communities. For these reasons Tokelau relies substantially on external financial support, particularly from New Zealand. Nonetheless the development of government structures at the national level has promoted a wish for Tokelau to be self-reliant to the greatest extent possible.

Tokelau affirmed to the United Nations in 1994 that it had under active consideration both the Constitution of a self-governing Tokelau and an act of self-determination. It also expressed a strong preference for a future status of free association with New Zealand.

Ross Dependency
By Imperial Order in Council, dated 30 July 1923, the territories between 160° E. long. and 150° W. long. and south of 60° S. lat. were brought within the jurisdiction of the New Zealand Government. The region was named the Ross Dependency. From time to time laws for the Dependency have been made by regulations promulgated by the Governor-General of New Zealand.

The mainland area is estimated at 400,000–450,000 sq. km and is mostly ice-covered. In Jan. 1957 a New Zealand expedition under Sir Edmund Hillary established a base in the Dependency. In Jan. 1958 Sir Edmund Hillary and 4 other New Zealanders reached the South Pole.

The main base—Scott Base, at Pram Point, Ross Island—is manned throughout the year, about 12 people being present during winter. Temporary accommodation facilities provide support for specific activities in the Dry Valleys and elsewhere in the Ross Sea Region. The annual activities of 200–300 scientists and support staff are managed by a crown agency, Antarctica New Zealand, based in Christchurch.

SELF-GOVERNING TERRITORIES OVERSEAS

THE COOK ISLANDS

KEY HISTORICAL EVENTS
The Cook Islands, which lie between 8° and 23° S. lat., and 156° and 167° W. long., were made a British protectorate in 1888, and on 11 June 1901 were annexed as part of New Zealand. In 1965 the Cook Islands became a self-governing territory in 'free association' with New Zealand.

TERRITORY AND POPULATION

The islands fall roughly into two groups—the scattered islands towards the north (Northern group) and the islands towards the south (Southern group). The islands with their populations at the census of 1996:

Lower Group—	Area sq. km	Population	Northern Group—	Area sq. km	Population
Rarotonga	67·1	11,225	Nassau	1·3	99
Mangaia	51·8	1,081	Palmerston (Avarua)	2·1	49
Atiu	26·9	956	Penrhyn (Tongareva)	9·8	606
Aitutaki	18·3	2,389	Manihiki (Humphrey)	5·4	668
Mauke (Parry Is.)	18·4	652	Rakahanga (Reirson)	4·1	249
Mitiaro	22·3	319	Pukapuka (Danger)	1·3	779
Manuae and Te au-o-tu	6·2	—	Suwarrow (Anchorage)	0·4	4
			Total	235·4	19,103

Population density in 1996 was 76 per sq. km. In 1996 an estimated 58·8% of the population lived in urban areas. The projected population for 2000 is 20,000.

SOCIAL STATISTICS

Birth rate (1998 estimate, per 1,000 population), 22·5; death rate, 5·2. The estimated annual growth rate is 1·6%. Life expectancy was estimated (1998) at: males, 62·2 years; females 73·1.

CLIMATE

Oceanic climate where rainfall is moderate to heavy throughout the year, with Nov. to March being particularly wet. Weather can be changeable from day to day and can end in rainfall after an otherwise sunny day. Rarotonga, Jan. 26°C, July 20°C. Annual rainfall 2,060 mm.

CONSTITUTION AND GOVERNMENT

The Cook Islands Constitution of 1965 provides for internal self-government but linked to New Zealand by a common Head of State and a common citizenship, that of New Zealand. It provides for a ministerial system of government with a Cabinet consisting of a Prime Minister and not more than 8 nor fewer than 6 other Ministers. There is also an advisory council composed of hereditary chiefs, the 15-member House of Ariki, without legislative powers. The New Zealand Government is represented by a New Zealand Representative and the Queen, as head of state, by the Queen's Representative. The capital is Avarua on Rarotonga.

The unicameral *Parliament* comprises 25 members elected for a term of 5 years.

RECENT ELECTIONS

In March 1994 the Cook Islands Party (CIP) gained 20 seats, the Democratic Coalition Party 3 and the Alliance Party, 2. Subsequently the Democratic and Alliance Parties merged to form the Democratic-Alliance Party (DAP). DAP won two by-elections—one for the seat of Nikao on Rarotonga held on 2 July 1996 and another for the seat of Ivirua on Mangaia held on 2 Dec. 1997. DAP now holds 7 seats and the CIP 18. However, in 1998, 3 members of the DAP broke away to form a second opposition party—the New Alliance Party.

Elections were due to take place between March and June 1999.

CURRENT ADMINISTRATION

Prime Minister: Sir Geoffrey A. Henry (CIP; re-elected March 1994).
Deputy Prime Minister: Inatio Akaruru.

Local Government. Each inhabited island except Nassau has an island council which is charged with the general administration of the affairs of that island. Rarotonga, the largest and most populated island, has 3 *vaka* or local councils.

ECONOMY

Policy. A package of economic reforms including privatization and deregulation was initiated in July 1996 to deal with a national debt of US$141m., 120% of GDP.

THE COOK ISLANDS

Performance. Real GDP growth was 1·3% in 1995 (1·5% in 1994).

Budget. Revenue, 1996–97, NZ$45·8m.; expenditure, NZ$44·8m. Revenue is derived chiefly from customs duties which follow the New Zealand customs tariff, income tax and stamp sales.

Grants from New Zealand, mainly for medical, educational and general administrative purposes, totalled NZ$11·3m. in 1996–97.

Currency. The Cook Island *dollar* was at par with the New Zealand *dollar*, but was replaced in 1995 by New Zealand currency.

Banking and Finance. There are 4 banks in the Cook Islands. The Cook Islands Savings Bank is state owned and deposit services throughout the islands. The Cook Islands Development Bank is a state-owned corporation funded in part by loans from the Asian Development Bank. The 2 remaining banks are subsidiaries of the Australia and New Zealand Banking Group Limited and the Westpac Bank, which are both Australian-owned and major banks in Australasia.

Weights and Measures. The metric system is in operation.

ENERGY AND NATURAL RESOURCES

Electricity. 4,867,000 kWh were generated in 1997; 4,173,000 on the island of Rarotonga.

Oil and Gas. The Cook Islands has no domestic resources of oil or gas.

Water. There are 12 intakes on the island of Rarotonga. The other inhabited islands obtain their water from either artesian or roof catchment or a combination of the two. The consumption of water in Rarotonga averages 260 litres per person per day. There are periodic water shortages, particularly in the northern group of islands.

Minerals. The islands of the Cook group have no significant mineral resources. However, the seabed which forms part of the exclusive economic zone has some of the highest concentrations of manganese nodules in the world. Manganese nodules are rich in cobalt and nickel.

Agriculture. In 1994 there were approximately 2,000 ha of arable land and 3,000 ha of permanent crops. Livestock (1996): 21,988 pigs, 3,697 goats.

Forestry. Timber production was 5,000 cu. metres in 1995.

Fisheries. In 1995 the total catch was estimated 1,124 tonnes, almost entirely from sea fishing.

INDUSTRY

Labour. In 1996 there were 5,230 persons actively employed in the Cook Islands and 764 unemployed. Of those employed, 3,072 were men and 2,158 were women.

Trade Unions. There are no trade unions although there are a number of worker collectives. These include the Public Service Association, Cook Islands Workers Association, Nurses Association and Teachers Association.

INTERNATIONAL TRADE

Imports and Exports. Exports, mainly to New Zealand, were valued at NZ$4·27m. in 1997. Main items exported were fresh fruit and vegetables and black pearls. Imports totalled NZ$72·33m.

COMMUNICATIONS

Roads. In 1992 there were 320 km of roads and, in 1991, 5,015 vehicles.

Rail. There are no railways in the Cook Islands.

Civil Aviation. New Zealand has financed the construction of an international airport at Rarotonga which became operational for jet services in 1973. There are 9 useable airports. Domestic services are provided by Air Rarotonga, and in 1998 there were also services to Auckland, Honolulu, Los Angeles, the Fiji Islands and French Polynesia, with Air New Zealand and United Airlines.

Shipping. A fortnightly cargo shipping service is provided between New Zealand, Niue and Rarotonga. In 1995 merchant shipping totalled 4,000 GRT.

Telecommunications. Eight Satellite Earth Stations are located at 8 of the most populated islands with HF Radio provided as backup. In the remaining islands HF radio is the only means of communication. In March 1997 there were 5,141 telephone lines in service.

Postal Services. A full range of postal services are offered and there are post agents in all inhabited islands.

SOCIAL INSTITUTIONS

Justice. There is a High Court and a Court of Appeal, from which further appeal is to the Privy Council in the UK.

Religion. From the census of 1996, 58% of the population belong to the Cook Islands Christian Church; about 17% are Roman Catholics, and the rest are Latter-day Saints and Seventh-Day Adventists and other religions.

Education. In March 1998 there were 28 primary schools with 140 teachers and 2,711 pupils, 23 secondary schools with 129 teachers and 1,779 pupils, and 26 pre-schools with 30 teachers and 460 pupils.

Health. A user pay scheme was introduced in July 1996 where all Cook Islanders pay a fee of NZ$5·00 for any medical or surgical treatment including consultation. Those under the age of 16 years or over the age of 60 years are exempted from payment of this charge. The dental department is privatized except for the school dental health provision. This service continues to be free to all schools.

The Rarotonga Hospital, which is the referral hospital for the outer islands, consists of 80 beds. The hospital has 8 doctors, 33 registered nurses and 11 hospital aides.

CULTURE

Broadcasting. There are 2 radio stations (AM and FM) operating in the Cook Islands with 3,693 radio receivers (Dec. 1996) of which 2,525 are located on Rarotonga. In 1995 there were an estimated 4,000 TV receivers.

Cinema. There is 1 cinema, located on the island of Rarotonga.

Press. The *Cook Islands News* (circulation 1,800 in 1996) is the sole daily newspaper. The *Cook Islands Star*, which is published fortnightly, is sold in the Cook Islands and in New Zealand.

Tourism. In 1996 there were 48,500 tourists arrivals by air.

Libraries. There are 3 libraries. The Parliamentary Library is available for use by members of the public on written request to the Clerk of the House. The National Library and the Library and Museum Library are both on Rarotonga and are lending libraries open to the public.

National Theatre and Opera. All significant cultural events in Rarotonga are held at the Auditorium, also known as the Cultural Centre.

Museums and Galleries. There are 2 small museums on Rarotonga.

FURTHER READING
Local statistical office: Ministry of Finance and Economic Management, P.O. Box 41, Rarotonga, Cook Islands.

NIUE

KEY HISTORICAL EVENTS
Captain James Cook sighted Niue in 1774 and called it Savage Island. Christian missionaries arrived in 1846. Niue became a British Protectorate in 1900 and was annexed to New Zealand in 1901. Internal self-government was achieved in free

NIUE

association with New Zealand on 19 Oct. 1974, New Zealand taking responsibility for external affairs and defence. Niue is a member of the South Pacific Forum.

TERRITORY AND POPULATION
Niue is the largest uplifted coral island in the world. Distance from Auckland, New Zealand, 1,343 miles; from Rarotonga, 580 miles. Area, 258 sq. km; height above sea level, 220 ft. Population (census, 1991) 2,239 (1,134 males, 1,105 females); (July 1997 estimate) 1,708, giving a density of 7 per sq. km. In 1995 an estimated 70·6% of the population lived in urban areas. Migration to New Zealand is the main factor in population change. The capital is Alofi (682 inhabitants in census, 1991).

SOCIAL STATISTICS
During 1992 births registered numbered 31, deaths 12.

CLIMATE
Oceanic, warm and humid, tempered by trade winds. May to Oct. are cooler months. Temperatures range from 20° to 28°C.

CONSTITUTION AND GOVERNMENT
There is a Legislative Assembly (*Fono*) of 20 members, 14 elected from 14 constituencies and 6 elected by all constituencies.

RECENT ELECTIONS
In elections held on 19 March 1999 only non-partisans were elected.

CURRENT ADMINISTRATION
High Commissioner: Mike Pointer.
   Prime Minister and Minister of Finance: Frank Lui (re-elected 16 Feb. 1996).

ECONOMY
Budget. Financial aid from New Zealand, 1995–96, totalled NZ$8·4m.

ENERGY AND NATURAL RESOURCES
Electricity. Production in 1995 was 3m. kWh.

Agriculture. In 1994 there were approximately 5,000 ha of arable land, 2,000 ha of permanent crops and 1,000 ha of permanent pasture. The main commercial crops of the island are coconuts, taros and yams.
   In 1996 there were 2,000 pigs.

Fisheries. In 1995 the total catch was 115 tonnes, exclusively from marine waters.

INTERNATIONAL TRADE
Imports and Exports. Exports, 1993, NZ$0·42m.; imports, NZ$3·52m.

COMMUNICATIONS
Civil Aviation. A weekly commercial air service links Niue with New Zealand and there are also flights to Tonga.

Telecommunications. There is a wireless station at Alofi, the port of the island. Telephones (1992) 276.

SOCIAL INSTITUTIONS
Justice. There is a High Court under a Chief Justice, with a right of appeal to the New Zealand Supreme Court.

Religion. (1991 census). 1,487 belong to the Congregational (Ekalesia Niue); Latter-day Saints (213), Roman Catholics (90), Jehovah's Witness (47), Seventh Day Adventists (27), other (63), No religion (34), not stated (1).

Education. In 1991 there was 1 primary school with 22 teachers and 337 pupils, and 1 secondary school with 27 teachers and 304 pupils.

Health. In 1992 there were 4 doctors, 1 dentist, 6 midwives and 19 nursing personnel. There is a 24-bed hospital at Alofi.

CULTURE

Broadcasting. Cable television is available.

Press. A weekly newspaper is published in English and Niuean; circulation about 400.

Tourism. In 1992 there were 2,329 visitors (1,668 tourists).

NICARAGUA

República de Nicaragua

Capital: Managua
Population estimate, 2000: 4·69m.
GNP per capita: (PPP$) 1,760
HDI/world rank: 0·547/126

KEY HISTORICAL EVENTS

Colonization of the Nicaraguan Pacific coast was undertaken by Spaniards from Panama, beginning in 1523. France and Britain, however, and later the USA, have all tried to play a colonial or semi-colonial role in Nicaragua. Between 1740 and 1786 Britain attempted to organize a colony on the Miskito Coast and from 1848 to 1860 the British occupied the port of San Juan de Norte. After links with other Central American territories and with Mexico, Nicaragua became an independent republic in 1838. Its independence was often threatened by US intervention. William Wolber, the filibuster from Tennessee, conquered the country and declared himself President in 1856-57. Between 1910 and 1930 the country was under almost continuous US military occupation.

In 1914 the Bryan-Chamarro Treaty between Nicaragua and the USA was signed under which the USA, in return for US$3m., acquired a permanent option for a canal route through Nicaragua, a 99-year option for a naval base in the Bay of Fonseca on the Pacific coast, and the Corn Islands on the Atlantic coast. The Bryan-Chamarro Treaty was ratified in 1916 and was not abrogated until 14 July 1970 when the Corn Islands returned to Nicaragua.

The Samoza family held political domination of Nicaragua from 1933 to 1979. Through a brutal dictatorship imposed through the National Guard, they secured for themselves a large share of the national wealth. In 1962 the radical Sandanista National Liberation Front was formed with the object of overthrowing the Samozas. After 17 years of civil war the Sandanistas triumphed. On 17 July 1979 President Samoza was overthrown and fled into exile. A Government Junta of National Reconstruction was established by the revolutionary government on 20 July, and a 51-member Council of State was later created.

The USA made efforts to unseat the revolutionary government by supporting the Contras (counter-revolutionary forces). In March 1984 the Nicaraguan government filed a case against the USA in the International Court of Justice; the court's subsequent ruling was, however, ignored by the USA.

The elections that were expected after the 1979 revolution did not take place until Nov. 1984. The Government Junta of National Reconstruction and the Council of State were dissolved on 10 Jan. 1985 following the presidential and legislative elections; the Constituent Assembly which replaced them drew up a constitution within two years as instructed. On 9 Jan. 1987 the Sandanista president, Daniel Ortega, signed the new constitution but immediately reimposed a state of emergency, suspending many of the liberties granted under the constitution. The state of emergency was lifted early in 1988 as part of the Central American peace process. Rebel anti-Sandinista activities had ceased by 1990; the last organized insurgent group negotiated an agreement with the government in April 1994.

In Oct. 1998 Hurricane Mitch devastated the country causing 3,800 deaths. The country's agriculture was crippled with around 20% of the coffee plantations destroyed.

TERRITORY AND POPULATION

Nicaragua is bounded in the north by Honduras, east by the Caribbean, south by Costa Rica and west by the Pacific. Area, 130,671 sq. km (121,428 sq. km dry land). The coastline runs 450 km on the Atlantic and 305 km on the Pacific. Population: July 1996, 4,272,400 (1997 estimate, 4,386,400; density, 34 per sq. km).

The UN gives a projected population for 2000 of 4·69m.

An estimated 62·1% of the population were urban in 1995.

16 administrative departments are grouped in 3 zones. Areas (in sq. km), populations (in 1,000) and chief towns in 1993:

	Area	Population	Chief town
Pacific Zone	18,429	2,622·5	
Chinandega	4,926	357·7	Chinandega
León	5,107	373·4	León
Managua	3,672	1,188·1	Managua
Masaya	590	225·1	Masaya
Granada	929	165·2	Granada
Carazo	1,050	165·2	Jinotepe
Rivas	2,155	147·8	Rivas
Central-North Zone	35,960	1,417·0	
Chontales	6,378	276·6	Juigalpa
Boaco	4,244	129·0	Boaco
Matagalpa	8,523	403·7	Matagalpa
Jinotega	9,755	190·1	Jinotega
Estelí	2,335	181·2	Estelí
Madriz	1,602	104·4	Somoto
Nueva Segovia	3,123	132·0	Ocotal
Atlantic Zone	67,039	225·3	
Rio San Juan	7,473	37·6	San Carlos
Zelaya	59,566	187·7	Bluefields

The capital is Managua with (1955 estimate) 1,200,000 inhabitants. Other cities: León, 100,982; Granada, 88,636; Masaya, 74,946; Chinandega, 67,792; Matagalpa, 36,983; Estelí, 30,635; Tipitapa, 30,078; Chichigalpa, 28,889; Juigalpa, 25,625; Corinto, 24,250; Jinotepe, 23,538.

The population is of Spanish and Amerindian origins with an admixture of Afro-Americans on the Caribbean coast. Ethnic groups in 1997: Mestizo (mixed Amerindian and white), 69%; white, 17%; black, 9%; Amerindian, 5%. The official language is Spanish.

SOCIAL STATISTICS
1996 births, estimate, 150,000; deaths, 26,000. Birth rate 35 (per 1,000 population), death rate 6. Annual growth rate, 1990–95, 3·2%. 1996 life expectancy 65·7 years; male 63·4, female 68·1. Infant mortality, 1990–95, 52 per 1,000 live births; fertility rate, 4·4 births per woman.

CLIMATE
The climate is tropical, with a wet season from May to Jan. Temperatures vary with altitude. Managua, Jan. 81°F (27°C), July 81°F (27°C). Annual rainfall 38" (976 mm).

CONSTITUTION AND GOVERNMENT
A new Constitution was promulgated on 9 Jan. 1987. It provides for a unicameral *National Assembly* comprising 90 members directly elected by proportional representation, together with unsuccessful presidential election candidates obtaining a minimum level of votes.

The *President* and *Vice-President* are directly elected for a 5-year term commencing on the 10 Jan. following their date of election. The President may stand for a second term, but not consecutively.

National Anthem. 'Salve a ti Nicaragua' ('Hail to thee, Nicaragua'); words by S. Ibarra Mayorga, tune by L. A. Delgadillo.

RECENT ELECTIONS
Presidential and parliamentary elections were held on 20 Oct. 1996. The electorate was 2·4m. There were 23 presidential candidates. Arnoldo Alemán was elected by 49·34% of votes cast. At the parliamentary elections the Liberal Alliance gained 42 seats; the Sandinista National Liberation Front, 36; the Christian Way Party, 4; 8 minor parties, 11.

CURRENT ADMINISTRATION

President: Arnoldo Alemán Lacayo (Liberal Alliance; sworn in on 10 Jan. 1997).
Vice President: Enrique Bolanos Geyer.
In March 1999 the government included:
Minister of Agriculture and Livestock: Mario de Franco. *Infrastructure and Transportation:* Jaime Bonilla. *Education, Sports and Culture:* Jose Antonio Alvarado. *Defence:* Pedro Joaquin Chamorro Barrios. *Development, Industry and Commerce:* Noel Sacasa. *Environment and Natural Resources:* Roberto Stadhagen. *Finance:* Esteban Duque Estrada. *Foreign Affairs:* Eduardo Montealegre. *Foreign Co-operation:* David Robleto Lang. *Health:* Lombardo Martinez Cabezas. *Labour:* Wilfredo Navarro Moreira. *Government:* Jaime Cuadra Somarriba. *Family:* Humberto Belli.

Local Government. There are 16 departments and 143 municipalities.

DEFENCE

In 1997 defence expenditure totalled US$36m. (US$8 per capita).

Army. The Army is being reorganized. There are 5 regional commands, and in 1996 the Army comprised 2 military detachments, 1 light mechanized and 1 special forces brigade, 1 infantry, 1 security and 3 special forces battalions. Equipment included 130 T-54/-55 main battle tanks. Strength (1997) 15,000.

Navy. The Nicaraguan Navy was some 800 strong in 1997 and operates 12 inshore patrol craft of mixed Soviet and North Korean origins and 2 small inshore minesweepers.

Air Force. The Air Force has been semi-independent since 1947. Personnel (1997) 1,200, with no combat aircraft and 16 armed helicopters. There are 10 transport and trainer aircraft.

INTERNATIONAL RELATIONS

Nicaragua is a member of the UN, OAS, SELA and the Central American Common Market.

ECONOMY

Performance. Real GDP growth was 4·2% in 1995 (3·3% in 1994).

Budget. (Millions of córdobas)

	1992	1993	1994	1995
Revenue	1,893·92	2,162·38	2,476·72	3,136·35
Expenditure	2,497·27	2,982·56	3,514·57	4,176·86

Expenditure by function (1994): Defence 231·56, public order 316·29, education 615·86, health 531·36, social security 584·43.

Currency. The monetary unit is the *córdoba* (NIO), of 100 *centavos*, which replaced the córdoba oro in 1991 at par. The average annual inflation rate during the period 1990–96 was 70·9%. In Feb. 1998 total money supply was 2,205m. córdobas.

Banking and Finance. The Central Bank of Nicaragua came into operation on 1 Jan. 1961 as an autonomous bank of issue, absorbing the issue department of the National Bank. Its *Governor* is José Evenor Taboada. There were 9 private commercial banks in 1994.

Weights and Measures. The metric system is recommended.

ENERGY AND NATURAL RESOURCES

Electricity. Installed capacity in 1995 was 417,700 kW. In 1995 it was estimated that 1·713bn. kWh were produced, and that consumption per capita was 279 kWh.

Minerals. Production of gold in 1993 was 39,900 troy oz.; silver, 71,900 troy oz.; limestone, 12,000 cu. metres.

Agriculture. Agriculture produced 34% of GDP in 1996. In 1994 there were 1·1m. ha arable land, 170,000 ha permanent cropland and 5·55m. ha pasture. 88,000 ha were irrigated in 1994. Production (in 1,000 tonnes) in 1993-94: Rice, 106; maize,

254; sorghum, 105; dry beans, 73; soya beans, 13; sesame seed, 8; cotton seed, 2; raw sugar, 173; bananas, 68; green coffee, 49; green tobacco, 1; raw cotton, 4.

In 1996 there were 1·81m. cattle, 410,000 pigs, 246,000 horses and (1995) 7m. chickens. Animal products (in 1,000 tonnes), 1993: Beef, 49; pork, 4; poultry, 23; milk, 47m. gallons; eggs, 34.

Forestry. The forest area in 1995 was 5·56m. ha, or 45·8% of the land area, compared to 6·31m. ha and 52% in 1990. Timber production was 3·81m. cu. metres in 1995.

Fisheries. In 1995 the catch was 13,503 tonnes (12,960 tonnes from sea fishing), up from 2,501 tonnes in 1986. The rate of growth in the annual catch between 1986 and 1995 was exceeded only in the Falkland Islands.

INDUSTRY

Production in 1993 (in 1,000 tonnes): Vegetable oil, 27; wheat flour, 48; main chemical products, 13; cement, 258; metallic products, 2,483; rum, 9,868 litres; processed leather, 309 sq. yards.

Labour. The workforce in 1996 was 1,642,000 (64% males). In 1994, 37% of the economically active population were engaged in agriculture, fisheries and forestry, and 17% in trade, restaurants and hotels. There were 0·32m. unemployed in 1993.

INTERNATIONAL TRADE

Foreign debt was US$5,929m. in 1996.

Imports and Exports. Foreign trade in US$1m. (1997): Exports, 678, consisting of cotton, coffee, chemical products, meat, sugar; imports, 1,335.

Main import suppliers, 1996: USA, 33·9%; Costa Rica, 8·4%; Guatemala, 8·4%; Japan, 7·7%. Main export markets, 1996: USA, 44·9%; Spain, 11·1%; Germany, 9·2%; El Salvador, 8·8%.

Nicaragua signed a letter of intent with the IMF for an enhanced structural adjustment facility up to 2000 and hoped to secure assistance of up to US$1·5bn. from a meeting in April 1998 of a consultative group of donor countries.

COMMUNICATIONS

Roads. Road length in 1995 was estimated at 17,146 km, of which 1,715 km were asphalted. In 1996 there were 73,000 passenger cars (18 per 1,000 inhabitants), 5,200 buses and coaches, 56,430 trucks and vans and 22,770 motor cycles and mopeds.

Civil Aviation. The national carrier is Nicaraguense de Aviación. In 1998 services were also provided by American Airlines, Aviateca, Canadian Airlines International, Continental Airlines, COPA, Iberia, Islena Airlines, LACSA, La Costena, Mayan World Airlines and Taca International Airlines. In 1995 Nicaraguense de Aviación flew 1·0m. km, carrying 38,400 passengers (all on international flights). The Augusto Sandino international airport at Managua handled 374,000 passengers in 1996 (300,000 on international flights).

Shipping. The merchant marine totalled 1,483 GRT in 1995. The Pacific ports are Corinto (the largest), San Juan del Sur and Puerto Sandino through which pass most of the external trade. The chief eastern ports are El Bluff (for Bluefields) and Puerto Cabezas. In 1993, 0·2m. tonnes of cargo were loaded, and 1·07m. tonnes discharged.

Telecommunications. There were 127,800 main telephone lines in 1997, or 29·4 per 1,000 population. Cellular phone subscribers numbered 4,400 in 1995.

Postal Services. In 1994 there were 202 post offices.

SOCIAL INSTITUTIONS

Justice. The judicial power is vested in a Supreme Court of Justice at Managua, 5 chambers of second instance and 153 judges of lower courts.

Religion. The prevailing form of religion is Roman Catholic (3·75m. adherents in 1992), but religious liberty is guaranteed by the Constitution. There is 1 arch-bishopric and 7 bishoprics.

Education. Adult literacy rate (1995) 65·7%; male 64·6%, female 66·6%. In 1995 there were 5,251 primary schools with 20,116 teachers for 764,587 pupils. In 1993 there were 203,962 pupils at secondary level and 32,464 students at university level.

In 1994–95 there were 2 universities and 3 specialized universities (agriculture; engineering; polytechnic) with 1,260 academic staff.

In 1994 total expenditure on education came to 3·8% of GNP and represented 12·2% of total government expenditure.

Health. In 1994 there were 56 hospitals, with a provision of 11 beds per 20,000 population. There were 2,577 doctors, 321 dentists and 2,144 nurses.

CULTURE

Broadcasting. Broadcasting is administered by the Instituto Nicaragüense de Telecomunicaciones y Correos (Telcor). Number of radio sets in 1995 was 1·15m. and television sets 300,000. There were 7 television stations at Managua (colour by NTSC) in 1994.

Press. In 1995 there were 4 daily newspapers in Managua, with a total circulation of 130,000.

Tourism. In 1996 there were 303,000 foreign tourists, spending US$54m.

DIPLOMATIC REPRESENTATIVES

Of Nicaragua in Great Britain (Suite 12, Vicarage House, 58–60 Kensington Church St., London, W8 4DP)
Ambassador: Nora Campos de Lankes.

Of Great Britain in Nicaragua (Plaza Churchill Reparto 'Los Robles', Apartado 1-169, Managua)
Ambassador: Roy Osborne.

Of Nicaragua in the USA (1627 New Hampshire Ave., NW, Washington, D.C., 20009)
Ambassador: Francisco Javier Aguirre Sacasa.

Of the USA in Nicaragua (Km. 4½ Carretera Sur., Managua)
Ambassador: Lino Gutiérrez.

Of Nicaragua to the United Nations
Ambassador: Alfonso Ortega Urbina.

Of Nicaragua to the European Union
Ambassador: Roger Guevara Mena.

FURTHER READING
Dematteis, L. and Vail, C., *Nicaragua: a Decade of Revolution.* New York, 1991
Dijkstra, G., *Industrialization in Sandinista Nicaragua: Policy and Party in a Mixed Economy.* Boulder (CO), 1992
Walker, T. W., *Nicaragua: the Land of Sandino.* 2nd ed. Boulder (Colo.), 1991
Woodward, R. L., *Nicaragua.* [Bibliography] Oxford and Santa Barbara (CA), 1983

National statistical office: Dirección General de Estadística y Censos, Managua

NIGER

République du Niger

Capital: Niamey
Population estimate, 2000: 10·8m.
GNP per capita: (PPP$) 920
HDI/world rank: 0·207/173

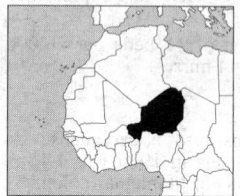

KEY HISTORICAL EVENTS
Niger was occupied by France between 1883 and 1899. It was constituted a military territory in 1901 and became a part of French West Africa in 1904. It became an autonomous republic within the French Community on 18 Dec. 1958 and achieved full independence on 3 Aug. 1960.

Guerilla activity by Tuaregs of the Armed Resistance Organization (ORA) seeking local autonomy in the north continued into 1995. On 15 April a peace agreement between the Government and the ORA was initialled under the auspices of Algeria, Burkina Faso and France but the ORA suspended the agreement on 27 Nov. 1995.

On 27 Jan. 1996 in a bloodless coup the army chief of staff Gen. (then Col.) Barré Maïnassara deposed President Ousmane Mahamane, dissolved parliament and began to rule through a National Security Council which he headed. In April 1999, President Maïnassara was assassinated by bodyguards at Niamey airport, prompting troops and tanks onto the streets of the capital. Prime Minister Ibrahim Assane Mayaki suspended all political activity. Opposition forces had called earlier for Maïnassara to resign following the Supreme Court's annulment of some local poll results. A week after the President's assassination, Daouda Mallam Wanké, leader of the presidential guard and the officer widely suspected of being behind the killing, was named as Maïnassara's successor.

TERRITORY AND POPULATION
Niger is bounded in the north by Algeria and Libya, east by Chad, south by Nigeria, south-west by Benin and Burkina Faso, and west by Mali. Area, 1,186,408 sq. km, with a population at the 1988 census of 7,250,383. Estimate (1997), 9,388,900; density, 8 per sq. km.

The UN gives a projected population for 2000 of 10·8m.

In 1995 an estimated 81·8% of the population were rural.

The country is divided into the capital, Niamey, an autonomous district, and 7 departments. Area, population and chief towns at the 1988 census:

Department	Sq. km	Population	Chief town	Population
Niamey	670	398,265	Niamey	392,169
Agadez	634,209	203,959	Agadez	49,361
Diffa	140,216	189,316	Diffa	–
Dosso	31,002	1,019,997	Dosso	–
Maradi	38,581	1,388,999	Maradi	109,386
Tahoua	106,677	1,306,652	Tahoua	49,941
Tillabéry	89,623	1,332,398	Tillabéry	–
Zinder	145,430	1,410,797	Zinder	119,838

The population is composed chiefly of Hausa (53%), Songhai and Djerma (21%), Tuareg (10·5%), Fulani (10%) and Kanuri-Manga (4·5%). The official language is French. Hausa, Djerma and Fulani are national languages.

SOCIAL STATISTICS
1997 births, estimate, 504,000; deaths, 225,000. Rates, 1997 estimates, per 1,000 population: Birth rate, 53·7 (the highest birth rate in the world); death rate, 24·0; infant mortality, 116 per 1,000 live births; expectation of life, 41·1 years; growth rate, 2·98%. Fertility rate, 1997, 7·4 children per woman, the highest rate in Africa.

CLIMATE
Precipitation determines the geographical division into a southern zone of agriculture, a central zone of pasturage and a desert-like northern zone. The country lacks water, with the exception of the south-western districts, which are watered by the Niger and its tributaries, and the southern zone, where there are a number of wells. Niamey, 95°F (35°C). Annual rainfall varies from 22" (560 mm) in the south

to 7" (180 mm) in the Sahara zone. The rainy season lasts from May until Sept., but there are periodic droughts.

CONSTITUTION AND GOVERNMENT

Theoretically, Niger is a unitary multi-party democracy. The *President* is directly elected for a 5-year term renewable once. There is an 83-member *National Assembly* elected for a 5-year term by proportional representation.

At a referendum on 12 May 1996, 90% of votes cast were in favour of a new constitution; turn-out was 33%. The ban on political parties which had been in force since 27 Jan. was lifted on 20 May 1996.

National Anthem. 'Auprès du grand Niger puissant' ('By the banks of the mighty great Niger'); words by M. Thiriet, tune by R. Jacquet and N. Frionnet.

RECENT ELECTIONS

Presidential elections were held on 7–8 July 1996. Before they ended the National Security Council dissolved the Independent National Electoral Commission and replaced it with a body of its own nomination. Turn-out was 70%. Gen. Maïnassara was elected *President* by 52·22% of votes cast against 4 opponents, one of whom was the deposed president, Ousmane Mahamane, who polled 19·75% of votes cast. Parliamentary elections were held on 23 Nov. 1996. The electorate was 3·8m.; turn-out was 27%. The pro-presidential National Union of Independents for Democratic Renewal gained a majority of seats.

CURRENT ADMINISTRATION

President: Daouda Mallam Wanké.

In March 1999 the government comprised:

Prime Minister: Ibrahim Assane Mayaki.

Minister of Agriculture and Livestock: Idi Ango Omar. *Civil Service, Labour, and Employment:* Moussa Oumarou. *Commerce and Industry:* Ibrahim Koussou. *Communication and Culture:* Issa Moussa. *Foreign Affairs and African Integration:* Mamane Sambo Sidikou. *Economic Reform, Finance, and Privatization:* Ide Niandou. *Education:* Aissata Moumouni. *Equipment and Infrastructure:* Cherif Chako. *Higher Education, Research and Technology:* Oumarou Boube. *Interior and Territorial Administration:* Abdoulaye Souley. *Justice, Human Rights, and Keeper of the Seals:* Issoufou Aba Moussa. *Mines and Energy:* Mai Manga Boukar. *National Defence:* Yahaya Tounkara. *Planning:* Yacouba Nabassoua. *Public Health:* Illo Almoustapha. *Social Development, Population, and Promotion of Women and Children:* Mariama Sambo Abdoulaye. *Tourism and Crafts:* Aissa Abdoulaye Diallo. *Transportation:* Oubandawaki Issofou Ousmane. *Water Resources and Environment:* Harouna Niandou. *Youth, Sports, National Solidarity and Government Spokesman:* Abdourauhamane Saidou.

Local Government. The 8 departments are each under a prefect, sub-divided into 32 *arrondissements*, each under a sub-prefect, and some 150 communes.

DEFENCE

Selective conscription for 2 years operates. Defence expenditure totalled US$22m. in 1997 (US$2 per capita).

Army. There are 3 military districts. The Army consists of 4 armoured reconnaissance squadrons, 7 infantry, 1 engineer and 2 parachute companies. Equipment includes 90 AML-90 armoured cars. Strength (1997) 5,200. There are additional paramilitary forces of some 5,400.

Air Force. The Air Force had (1997) 100 personnel, 1 C-130H transport, 1 Boeing 737 VIP transport, 2 Cessna Skymasters and 2 Do 28D Skyservants and 1 Do 228 for communications duties. There are no combat aircraft.

INTERNATIONAL RELATIONS

Niger is a member of the UN, OAU and is an ACP member state of the ACP-EU relationship.

ECONOMY

Performance. Real GDP growth was 3·8% in 1995 (2·6% in 1994).

Budget. In 1995 (estimates) revenue (in 1,000m. francs CFA) was 115·7 and expenditure, 143·6. Revenue included: Tax revenue, 63·9; grants, 45·4. Current expenditure, 102·7; capital expenditure, 44·1.

Currency. The unit of currency is the *franc CFA* (XAF), with a parity rate of 100 francs CFA to 1 French franc. In Dec. 1997 total money supply was 73bn. francs CFA. Foreign exchange reserves were US$42m. in Dec. 1997. The average annual inflation rate during the period 1990–96 was 7·4%.

Banking and Finance. The regional Central Bank of West African States (BCEAO) functions as the bank of issue, and there were 6 commercial banks in 1994.

Weights and Measures. The metric system is legal, but traditional units are still in use.

ENERGY AND NATURAL RESOURCES

Electricity. Installed capacity was 105,000 kW in 1991. Production in 1994 amounted to 178m. kWh. Consumption per capita in 1991 was an estimated 53 kWh.

Minerals. Large uranium deposits are mined at Arlit and Akouta. Concentrate production (1992), 2,504 tonnes. Phosphates are mined in the Niger valley, and coal reserves are being exploited by open-cast mining (production of hard coal in 1994 was an estimated 172,000 tonnes). Tin ore production in 1994 was 20 tonnes; salt, 3,000 tonnes.

Agriculture. In 1996 agriculture accounted for 39% of GDP. Production is dependent upon adequate rainfall. In 1994 there were 3·61m. ha of arable land and 10·44m. ha of permanent pasture. 66,000 ha were irrigated in 1994. Production in 1993 (in 1,000 tonnes): Millet, 1,430; maize, 1,000; sorghum, 305; groundnuts, 60; cassava, 220; sugar-cane, 140; sweet potatoes, 35·0; cotton, 3·0.

Livestock (1996): Cattle, 1·99m.; asses, 450,000; sheep, 3·85m.; goats, 5·72m. in 1995; camels, 380,000 in 1995; chickens, 20m. in 1995.

Livestock products (in 1,000 tonnes), 1993: Butter, 4·4; cheese, 12.

There were 180 tractors in 1994.

Forestry. There is a government programme of afforestation as a protection from desert encroachment. There were 2·56m. ha of forests in 1995 (2% of the land area). Production in 1995 was 5·87m. cu. metres, mainly for fuel.

Fisheries. There are fisheries on the River Niger and along the shores of Lake Chad. In 1995 the catch was 3,586 tonnes, exclusively freshwater fish.

INDUSTRY

Some small manufacturing industries, mainly in Niamey, produce textiles, food products, furniture and chemicals. Output of cement in 1994, 29,000 tonnes.

Labour. The labour force in 1996 totalled 4,497,000 (56% males). Nearly 90% of the economically active population in 1994 were engaged in agriculture, fisheries and forestry.

Trade Unions. The national confederation is the *Union Syndicale des Travailleurs du Niger,* which has 15,000 members in 31 unions.

INTERNATIONAL TRADE
Foreign debt was US$1,557m. in 1996.

Imports and Exports. In 1996 imports were valued at US$329m. and exports at US$281m. Uranium and livestock are the principal exports. Major trading partners are France and Nigeria.

COMMUNICATIONS

Roads. In 1995 there were 9,863 km of all-weather roads and 779 km of paved roads. Niamey and Zinder are the termini of two trans-Sahara motor routes; the Hoggar–Aïr–Zinder road extends to Kano and the Tanezrouft–Gao–Niamey road to Benin. A 648-km 'uranium road' runs from Arlit to Tahoua. There were, in 1996, 38,220 passenger cars (4 per 1,000 inhabitants) and 15,200 trucks and vans.

Civil Aviation. There are international airports at Niamey and Agadez. Niger is a member of Air Afrique, and in 1998 there were also services by Air Algérie, Air France, Ethiopian Airlines and Royal Air Maroc, with international flights to Abidjan, Abu Dhabi, Addis Adaba, Agades, Algiers, Bamako, Casablanca, Cotonou, Dakar, Jeddah, Lagos, N'Djaména, Nouakchott, Ouagadougou, Paris and Tamanrasset.

Shipping. Sea-going vessels can reach Niamey (300 km inside the country) between Sept. and March.

Telecommunications. Niger had 16,400 main telephone lines in 1997 (1·7 per 1,000 population). There were around 200 Internet users in Jan. 1998.

Postal Services. In 1995 there were 66 post offices, or 1 for every 134,000 persons.

SOCIAL INSTITUTIONS

Justice. There are Magistrates' and Assize Courts at Niamey, Zinder and Maradi, and justices of the peace in smaller centres. The Court of Appeal is at Niamey.

Religion. In 1997 there were 9·34m. Sunni Moslems. There are some Roman Catholics, and traditional animist beliefs survive.

Education. In 1996 there were 105 pre-primary schools with 417 teachers for 9,013 pupils and 2,908 primary schools with 11,978 teachers for 440,586 pupils. During the period 1990–95 only 18% of females of primary school age were enrolled in school. In 1992 there were 80,009 pupils in secondary schools. In 1988–89 there were 5 teacher training colleges with 1,578 students, and in 1989–90 there were 2 professional training colleges with 859 students (61 women) and 69 teachers. There is a university and an Islamic university, with a total in 1994–95 of 3,980 students and 281 academic staff.

Adult literacy (1995) 13·6% (male, 20·9%; female, 6·6%). The overall rate and the rates for both males and females are the lowest in the world.

Health. In 1993 there were 237 doctors and 2,213 nurses, and in 1990, 5 dentists, 29 pharmacists and 457 midwives.

CULTURE

Broadcasting. La Voix du Sahel and Télé-Sahel under the government's Office de Radiodiffusion Télévision du Niger are responsible for radio and TV broadcasting (colour by SECAM). In 1995 there were estimated to be 620,000 radio and 105,000 TV sets.

Press. In 1998 there were 2 daily newspapers with a combined circulation of 4,000.

Tourism. In 1996 there were 17,000 foreign tourists, bringing revenue of US$17m.

DIPLOMATIC REPRESENTATIVES
Of Niger in Great Britain (resides in Paris)
Ambassador: Vacant.

Of Great Britain in Niger
Ambassador: H. B. Warren-Gash (resides in Côte d'Ivoire).

Of Niger in the USA (2204 R. St., NW, Washington, D.C., 20008)
Ambassador: Joseph Diatta.

Of the USA in Niger (PO Box 11201, Niamey)
Ambassador: Charles O. Cecil.

Of Niger to the United Nations
Ambassador: Joseph Diatta.

Of Niger to the European Union
Ambassador: Houseini Abdou Saleye.

FURTHER READING
Fugelstad, F., *A History of Niger, 1850–1960*. OUP, 1984
Zamponi, L. F., *Niger* [Bibliography]. Oxford and Santa Barbara (CA), 1994

National statistical office: Direction de la Statistique et de l'Informatique, Ministère du Plan, Niamey.

NIGERIA

Federal Republic of Nigeria

Capital: Abuja
Population estimate, 2000: 128·79m.
GNP per capita: (PPP$) 870
HDI/world rank: 0·391/142

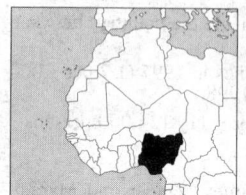

KEY HISTORICAL EVENTS

Farming communities settled in the area 4,000 years ago, displacing the hunter-gatherers. They developed the large centralized state of Kanem-Bornu in the 8th century based on control of trans-Saharan trade. Adjacent states notably the Hausa, Oyo and Benin empires arose later and became caught up in the slave trade by the 18th century. British occupation aimed at enforcing the abolition of the trade.

The port of Lagos was captured by Britain in 1851 and annexed in Aug. 1861, administered first from Sierra Leone and then from the Gold Coast. Growing British involvement in the Lagos hinterland and in the Niger Delta led to the establishment of protectorates in the former in Jan. 1886 with Lagos itself becoming a separate colony and in the latter, known as the Oil Rivers Protectorate, in June 1885. British commercial interests among the Moslem emirates of the north led in July 1886 to the chartering of the Royal Niger Company which established its own political administration over a wide territory.

In 1893 the Oil Rivers Protectorate was expanded and renamed the Niger Coast Protectorate. On 1 Jan. 1900 the Royal Niger Company transferred its territory to the British Crown. The southern sector was amalgamated with the Niger Coast Protectorate to form the Protectorate of Southern Nigeria (to which the colony and protectorate of Lagos was added in Feb. 1906), while the remainder was constituted as the Protectorate of Northern Nigeria. On 1 Jan. 1914 the two territories were merged to form the 'colony and protectorate of Nigeria'.

Through the system of indirect rule Africans were excluded from political power until the end of the Second World War. A constitution was promulgated in 1947, and on 1 Oct. 1954 Nigeria adopted a federal system of government comprising Eastern, Western and Northern Regions; the first two of these secured internal self-government in 1956 and the Northern Region in 1959. Full independence was achieved by the Federation of Nigeria on 1 Oct. 1960 and it became a republic on 1 Oct. 1963.

The republic was overthrown by a military coup on 15 Jan. 1966, and a military government established. In May 1967 a decree replaced the existing regions by 12 new states. Ethnic and regional conflict ensued with Hausa northerners fearing domination by the Igbo people from the east of the country. The Chairman of the Supreme Military Council, Johnson Aguiyi-Ironsi, was killed in an army mutiny and replaced by Lieut.-Col. Yakubu Gowon. He restored the federal system but the Eastern Region decided to secede as the Republic of Biafra in May 1967. This set off a bloody civil war, prolonged by international involvement, and a severe famine. Federal forces re-established control in Jan. 1970. Besides the political problems, Gowon also faced economic problems related to Nigeria's new oil wealth and he was ousted in a coup on 27 July 1975. He was succeeded by Brig. Murtala Muhammed who was assassinated the following year. Lieut.-Gen. Olusegun Obasanjo replaced him, returning the country (by now 19 states) to civilian rule in Oct. 1979 when Shehu Shagari was elected president. Shagari was re-elected in Sept. 1983, but overthrown by the military later that year. In Aug. 1985 Maj.-Gen. Ibrahim Babangida replaced Maj.-Gen. Muhammadu Buhari as head of the Armed Forces Ruling Council. This was dissolved in Jan. 1993 and replaced by a transitional civilian council. Presidential elections held in June 1993 were annulled. President Babangida stepped down from office on 26 Aug., nominating Chief Ernest Shonekan as interim head of state.

On 17 Nov. 1993 Gen. Sani Abacha having forced Shonekan to resign, assumed the function of head of state. Moshood Abiola, who claimed to have won the annulled 1993 presidential election, declared himself head of state in June 1994 and was arrested for treason.

NIGERIA

Following the execution of Ogoni separatist Ken Saro-wiwa and 8 other civil rights activists in Nov. 1995, Nigeria was suspended from the Commonwealth. Gen. Abacha promised to restore constitutional government by Oct. 1998 but died on 8 June 1998, reportedly of a heart attack. He was replaced as president by Gen. Abdulsalam Abubakar who scrapped election plans designed to retain power for Abacha and released political detainees. Chief Moshood Abiola, the imprisoned undeclared winner of the 1993 presidential election, died on 7 July 1998 the day before his expected release from prison.

Gen. Abubakar launched a corruption probe, announced a cabinet with civilians occupying most of the key posts and promised to give up power in May 1999 to allow for a return to civilian rule. Presidential elections were held on 27 Feb. 1999. The victor was Olusegun Obasanjo, a 62-year-old retired general who once led his country as part of a military junta.

TERRITORY AND POPULATION

Nigeria is bounded in the north by Niger, east by Chad and Cameroon, south by the Gulf of Guinea and west by Benin. It has an area of 356,669 sq. miles (923,773 sq. km). For sovereignty over the Bakassi Peninsula *see* CAMEROON: Territory and Population. Census population, 1991, 88,514,501 (43,969,970 females, urban, 36%); population density, 95·8 per sq. km. Official estimate, 1997, 107,115,000. Density, 116 per sq. km.

The UN gives a projected population for 2000 of 128·79m.

In 1995 an estimated 60·4% of the population were rural.

There were 30 states and a Federal Capital Territory (Abuja) in 1991.

Area, population and capitals of these states:

State	Area (in sq. km)	Population (1991 census)	Capital
Sokoto	65,735	4,392,391	Sokoto
Kebbi	36,800	2,124,093	Birnin-Kebbi
Niger	76,363	2,482,367	Minna
Kwara	36,825	1,566,469	Ilorin
Kogi	29,833	2,099,046	Lokoja
Benue	34,059	2,780,398	Makurdi
Plateau	58,030	3,283,704	Jos
Taraba	54,473	1,480,590	Jalingo
Adamawa	36,917	2,124,049	Yola
Borno	70,898	2,596,589	Maiduguri
Yobe	45,502	1,411,481	Damaturu
Bauchi	64,605	4,294,413	Bauchi
Jigawa	23,154	2,829,929	Dutse
Kano	20,131	5,632,040	Kano
Katsina	24,192	3,878,344	Katsina
Kaduna	46,053	3,969,252	Kaduna
Federal Capital Territory	7,315	378,671	Abuja
Total North	730,885	47,261,959	

State	Area (in sq. km)	Population (1991 census)	Capital
Oyo	28,454	3,488,789	Ibadan
Osun	9,251	2,203,016	Oshogbo
Ogun	16,762	2,338,570	Abeokuta
Lagos	3,345	5,685,781	Ikeja
Ondo	20,959	3,884,485	Akure
Edo	17,802	2,159,848	Benin City
Delta	17,698	2,570,181	Asaba
Rivers	21,850	3,983,857	Port-Harcourt
Abia	6,320	2,297,978	Umuahia
Imo	5,530	2,485,499	Owerri
Anambra	4,844	2,767,903	Awka
Enugu	12,831	3,161,295	Enugu
Cross River	20,156	1,865,604	Calabar
Akwa Ibom	7,081	2,359,736	Uyo
Total South	192,883	41,252,542	

6 new states were created in 1996, 3 in the north and 3 in the south. In the north, Zamfara State was created from Sokoto, with its headquarters at Gusau; Nassarawa State was created from Plateau, with its headquarters at Lafia; and Gombe State was created from Bauchi, with its headquarters at Gombe. In the south, Ekiti State was created from Ondo, with its capital at Ado-Ekiti; Bayelsa State was created from Rivers, with its headquarters at Yenagoa; and Ebonyi State was created by merging Abia and Enugu, with its headquarters at Abakaliki.

Abuja replaced Lagos as the federal capital and seat of government in Dec. 1991.

Estimated population of the largest cities, 1995:

City	Population	City	Population	City	Population
Lagos	1,484,000	Ila	257,400	Kumo	144,400
Ibadan	1,365,000	Oyo	250,100	Shomolu	144,100
Ogbomosho	711,900	Ikerre	238,500	Oka	139,600
Kano	657,300	Benin City	223,900	Ikare	137,300
Oshogbo	465,000	Iseyin	211,800	Sapele	135,800
Ilorin	464,000	Katsina	201,500	Deba Habe	135,400
Abeokuta	416,800	Jos	201,200	Minna	133,600
Port Harcourt	399,700	Sokoto	199,900	Warri	122,900
Zaria	369,800	Ilobu	194,400	Bida	122,500
Ilesha	369,000	Offa	192,300	Ikire	120,200
Onitsha	362,700	Ikorodu	180,300	Makurdi	120,110
Iwo	353,000	Ilawe-Ekiti	179,900	Lafia	119,500
Ado-Ekiti	350,500	Owo	178,900	Inisa	116,800
Abuja (capital)	339,100	Ikirun	177,000	Shagamu	114,300
Kaduna	333,600	Calabar	170,000	Awka	108,400
Mushin	324,900	Shaki	169,700	Gombe	105,200
Maiduguri	312,100	Ondo	165,400	Igboho	103,300
Enugu	308,200	Akure	158,200	Ejigbo	103,300
Ede	299,500	Gusau	154,000	Agege	100,300
Aba	291,600	Ijebu-Ode	152,500	Ugep	100,000
Ife	289,500	Effon-Alaiye	149,300		

There are about 250 ethnic groups. The largest linguistic groups are the Hausa (21·4% of the total) and the Yoruba (also 21·4%), followed by Igbo (18%), Fulani (11·3%), Ibibio (5·6%), Kanuri (4·1%), Edo (3·4%), Tiv (2·2%), Ijaw (1·8%), Bura (1·5%) and Nupe (1·3%). The official languages are English and (since 1997) French, but 50% of the population speak Hausa as a lingua franca.

SOCIAL STATISTICS
1995 births, estimate, 4,760,000; deaths, 1,360,000. Rates, 1995: Birth, 49 (per 1,000 population); death, 14. Infant mortality, 195 (per 1,000 live births). Annual growth rate, 1990–95, 3·0%. Life expectancy at birth, 1990–95, was 48·8 years for males and 52·0 years for females. Fertility rate, 1997, 6·5 children per woman.

CLIMATE
Lying wholly within the tropics, temperatures everywhere are high. Rainfall varies greatly, but decreases from the coast to the interior. The main rains occur from April to Oct. Lagos, Jan. 81°F (27·2°C), July 78°F (25·6°C). Annual rainfall 72" (1,836 mm). Ibadan, Jan. 80°F (26·7°C), July 76°F (24·4°C). Annual rainfall 45" (1,120 mm). Kano, Jan. 70°F (21·1°C), July 79°F (26·1°C). Annual rainfall 35" (869 mm). Port Harcourt, Jan. 79°F (26·1°C), July 77°F (25°C). Annual rainfall 100" (2,497 mm).

CONSTITUTION AND GOVERNMENT
Under the 1978 Constitution, Nigeria is a sovereign, federal republic comprising states and a federal capital district. As part of the process of demilitarization and democratization, in 1993 the government created 2 parties, the Social Democratic Party (SDP) and the National Republican Convention (NRC).Voting has not been secret since March 1991; voters indicate a poster of the candidate of their choice.

On stepping down from all his offices on 26 Aug. 1993 President Babangida nominated an interim government of national unity headed by Ernest Shonekan (ING).

On 17 Nov. 1993 the Minister of Defence, Gen. Sani Abacha, assumed the functions of head of state and set up an 11-member Provisional Ruling Council headed by himself. Parliament, the 30 state Executive Councils and the 2 political parties were dissolved. A 33-member cabinet, the Federal Executive Council, was appointed, chaired by Gen. Abacha. In June 1994 a Constitutional Conference opened with 360 participants, 90 of whom were appointed by the government. In Oct. 1994 the Conference recommended the introduction of a plurality of political parties, and the rotation of the presidency between North and South to overcome the bitter hostility between the two regions. In June 1995 the Conference submitted a proposal for a new constitution to the head of state, and the latter lifted the ban on political parties. 5 parties gained government recognition in Oct. 1996. However, by March 1998 the proposed new constitution was still on the drawing board.

Parliament consists of a 360-member *House of Representatives* and a 109-member *Senate*.

National Anthem. 'Arise, O compatriots, Nigeria's call obey'; words by a collective, tune by B. Odiase.

RECENT ELECTIONS

Presidential elections were held on 27 Feb. 1999. Former military ruler Olusegun Obasanjo (People's Democratic Party) won against 1 opponent with 62·8% of the votes cast and was scheduled to take office on 29 May.

At the elections to the House of Representatives on 20 Feb. 1999 the People's Democratic Party won 206 seats, the All People's Party 74 and the Alliance for Democracy 68, with 12 vacant. In the Senate elections on the same day 59 seats went to the PDP, 29 to the APP and 20 to the AD, with 1 vacant.

CURRENT ADMINISTRATION

President: Gen. Abdulsalam Abubakar.

In March 1999 the Federal Executive Council comprised:

Minister of Agriculture: Alfa Wali. *Minister of State for Agriculture:* Dr Johan Madugu. *Aviation:* Capt. Benoni Briggs. *Commerce and Tourism:* Maj. Gen. Patrick Aziza. *Communications:* Avm Canice Umenwaliri. *Education:* Samuel Olaiya Oni. *Minister of State for Education:* Saka Sa'adu. *Employment, Labour and Productivity:* Dr Emmanuel Udogu. *Federal Capital Territory:* M. T. Kotangora. *Minister of State for Federal Capital Territory:* Princess Oguneye. *Finance:* Ismaila Usman. *Minister of State for Finance:* Akpan Wilson Etuk-Udo. *Foreign Affairs:* Ignatius Olisiemeka. *Minister of State for Foreign Affairs:* Buhari Bala. *Health:* Debo Adeyemi. *Minister of State for Health:* Dr. Abubakar Ali. *Industry:* Onikepo Akande. *Information:* John Nwodo. *Internal Affairs:* Musa Yakubu. *Justice and Attorney General:* Abdullahi Ibrahim. *National Planning:* Rasheed Gbadamosi. *Power and Steel:* Bello Suleiman. *Minister of State for Power and Steel:* Godwin Ogbaga. *Science and Technology:* Maj.-Gen. Samuel Momah. *Solid Minerals:* Patrick Yakowa. *Transport:* Rear Adm. Festus Porbeni. *Water Resources:* Hamza Sakwa. *Works and Housing:* Maj. Gen. Garba Ali Mohammed. *Minister of State for Works and Housing:* Ambrose Fesse. *Women's Affairs:* Dr Laraba Gambo Abdullahi. *Youth and Sports:* Air Commodore Samson Omeruah.

Local Government. Each state is administered by a directly-elected governor, who appoints and presides over a State Executive Council. The states are subdivided into local government areas, and there is a Federal Capital Territory, Abuja. Elections were held in Jan. 1999 resulting in a landslide victory for a coalition of centrist politicians. The People's Democratic Party (PDP) won control of about 60% of 774 councils. The All People's Party (APP) won control of about a quarter of contested seats.

DEFENCE

In 1997 defence expenditure totalled US$1,965m. (US$18 per capita).

Army. The Army consists of 1 armoured division, 2 mechanized divisions, 1 air defence brigade and 1 composite division (motorized infantry, airborne amphibious), each with supporting artillery and engineer and reconnaissance units. Equipment includes 60 T-55 and 150 Vickers Mk 3 main battle tanks. Strength (1997) 62,000.

Navy. The Navy comprises 1 German-built MEKO-type frigate with a helicopter and 1 frigate-type training ship (both beyond economic repair), 1 British-built corvette, 2 fast missile craft, 2 minehunters, and some 45 inshore patrol craft. There are also 2 German-built tank landing ships, 1 survey ship and some 15 service craft. The Navy has a small aviation element equipped with 2 Lynx anti-submarine helicopters. Naval personnel in 1997 totalled 5,500, including Coastguard. The main bases are at Apapa (Lagos) and Calabar.

The Coastguard operate 10 patrol craft launches, and the police numerous boats.

Air Force. The Air Force has been built up with the aid of a German mission; much first-line equipment was received from the former Soviet Union. It has 12 MiG-21 supersonic jetfighters and MiG-21U fighter-trainers, and 22 Alpha Jet light attack/trainers. About 15 BO 105 twin-turbine helicopters serve for search and rescue, while 1 F.27MPA is used for maritime patrol. Transport units operate 7 C-130H-30 and C-130H Hercules 4-turboprop heavy transports, 5 twin-turboprop Aeritalia G222s, 4 Super Puma helicopters, 18 Dornier 128-6 twin-turboprop and 18 DO 28D twin-piston utility aircraft, 2 Navajos and a Navajo Chieftain. Training types include 20 Bulldog primary trainers, 12 MB 339 jets for instrument training, 12 Hughes 300 helicopters and 30 L-39 Albatros advanced trainers. Personnel (1997) total about 9,500, with 62 combat aircraft.

INTERNATIONAL RELATIONS
Involvement in Sierra Leone where Nigeria supported the exiled government of President Ahmed Tejan Kabbah led to a full-scale attack in Feb. 1998 and the routing of the Sierra Leone military junta. Nigeria is in dispute with Cameroon over both its land and its maritime boundary. The two countries are in conflict on the question of sovereignty over the Bakassi Peninsula and also territory which Cameroon claims in the area of Lake Chad.

Nigeria is a member of the UN, ECOWAS, OAU, OPEC and is an ACP member state of the ACP-EU relationship. Membership of the Commonwealth was suspended in Nov. 1995.

ECONOMY
Policy. With the change of leadership, the long promised privatization programme is under way. Money owed to oil companies has been paid. Sanctions, except for the ban on arms sales, have been lifted. A 10-year rift with the IMF ended with an agreement (Jan. 1999) on a Fund-monitored economic reform programme. Promised reforms included abolishing the dual exchange rate, ending the subsidy of local fuel and increasing the pace of privatization. If the incoming government does stick to this programme, expected benefits include a rescheduling of foreign debt and a further IMF agreement on a US$1bn. loan. The new legislation is also committed to implementing the Vision 2010 programme drawn up in the mid 1990s, although many observers doubt whether its goals are realistically attainable.

Performance. Real GDP growth in 1998 was 2·3% (3·25% in 1996). The projected growth for 1999, according to the IMF, is 1·6%. Before the discovery of oil in the early 1970s Nigeria's GDP per head was around US$200. By the early 1980s it had reached around US$800, but has now declined to some US$300.

Budget. The financial year is the calendar year. 1995 revenue, N350,700m. (of which N150,000m. from oil); expenditure, N204,200m. (of which N44,500m. capital expenditure, N57,000m. debt service).

Currency. The unit of currency is the *naira* (NGN) of 100 *kobo*. Foreign exchange reserves were US$4,100m. in Dec. 1996, but a dual exchange rate allows the government to purchase US dollars for 25% of the market price; gold reserves were 690,000 troy oz. in June 1992. Government figures showed inflation at 28% at the end of 1996. In Nov. 1997 total money supply was N268,746m.

Banking and Finance. The Central Bank of Nigeria is the bank of issue (*Governor*, Paul Ogwuma). There were 65 commercial banks (with 2,403 branches) and 51 merchant banks in 1995 (with 144 branches), in 20 of which central or state governments held a controlling interest. Total assets of commercial banks, 1995, N463,671m.; merchant banks, N91,803m. Total saving deposits, Dec. 1995, N121,026m.

A subsequent banking crisis resulted in a decline in the number of banks to 74 at March 1999. Of these, 17 had missed the deadline for increasing their capital to

US$5·75m. by the end of 1998 and faced closure if they did not recapitalise, merge or get taken over by the end of the first quarter of 1999. In banking surveys for 1998, 26 banks were classed as 'distressed' and only 25 as 'acceptable risks or better'. It was predicted that there would be further bank closures as the industry becomes more competitive.

There is a stock exchange.

Weights and Measures. The metric system is in force.

ENERGY AND NATURAL RESOURCES

Electricity. Installed capacity, 1994, 5·88m. kW. Production, 1995, 14,482·6m. kWh (5,500·2m. kWh hydro-electric). Consumption per capita in 1995 was estimated to be 141 kWh.

Oil and Gas. Nigeria depends on oil for more than 90% of its overseas earnings. The cumulative income from oil over 25 years exceeds US$220,000m. With the collapse in the world oil price to around US$10 a barrel (down from US$40 in 1980), it was forecast that there would be a 54% drop in revenue for 1999. Nigeria's oil production amounted to 2·1m. bbls. a day in 1998, up from 1·5m. bbls. per day in 1986. There are 4 refineries. Oil income in 1998 was around US$1bn. a month, representing more than 75% of government revenue, but unrest which threatened to escalate into civil war caused production to be cut by around a third.

Natural gas reserves, 1995, were estimated at 3,114,870m. cu. metres. Production, 1995, 4,131m. cu. metres.

Water. 11 River Basin Development Authorities have been established for water resources development.

Minerals. Production, 1995 (in tonnes): Columbite, 37; coal, 20,000; limestone, 3·66m.; marble, 22,460; cassiterite, 203. There are large deposits of iron ore, coal (reserves estimate 245m. tonnes), lead and zinc. There are small quantities of gold and uranium. Lead production was 3,000 tonnes in 1990; tin, 149 tonnes in 1992.

Agriculture. Agriculture accounted for 43% of GDP in 1996. Of the total land mass, 75% is suitable for agriculture, including arable farming, forestry, livestock husbandry and fisheries. In 1994, 30·16m. ha were arable, 2·54m. ha permanent cropland and 40m. ha permanent pasture. 0·23m. ha were irrigated in 1994. 90% of production was by smallholders with less than 3 ha in 1998, and less than 1% of farmers had access to mechanised tractors. Main food crops are millet and sorghum in the north, plantains and oil palms in the south, and maize, yams, cassava and rice in much of the country, the north being, however, the main food producing area. Output, 1995 (in 1,000 tonnes): Millet, 4,900; sorghum, 6,377; plantains, 1,604; maize, 7,240; yams, 24,370; groundnuts, 1,523; cotton seed, 308; palm kernel, 543,000; palm oil, 871,000; cassava, 31,404; rice, 2,920; cocoa, 331.

Livestock, 1996: Cattle, 18·11m.; sheep, 14m.; goats, 24·5m.; pigs, 6·93m.; 124m. chickens (1995). Products (in 1,000 tonnes), 1995: Beef and veal, 192; pork, 31; mutton and lamb, 94; goat meat, 88; poultry meat, 73; milk, 961; eggs, 399.

Forestry. There were 13·78m. ha of forests in 1995, or 15·1% of the land area (14·39m. ha and 15·8% in 1990). The most important timber species include mahogany, iroko, obeche, abwa, ebony and camwood. Nigeria is Africa's leading roundwood producer, with removals totalling 111·05m. cu. metres in 1995.

Fisheries. The total catch (1995) was (in 1,000 tonnes): Coastal fishing, 142; deep-sea, 11; fish farms, 21; other freshwater, 127.

INDUSTRY

Manufacturing contributes about 9% of GDP. 1994 production (in 1,000 tonnes) included: Sugar, 55; paper and products, 43; cement, 3,086; cigarettes, 9,228. Also plywood, 72,000 cu. metres.

Labour. The labour force in 1996 totalled 45,565,000 (64% males). There were 196 work stoppages in 1995 with 235·1m. working days lost. Unemployment was 1·8% in 1995.

Trade Unions. All trade unions are affiliated to the Nigerian Labour Congress.

INTERNATIONAL TRADE

Nigeria's estimated debt (1997) exceeded US$34,000m. Rescheduling the debt depends on an IMF agreement which requires the ending of a two-tier exchange rate.

Imports and Exports. Exports in 1996 were valued at US$18,614m.; imports at US$7,997m. Principal exports, 1992 (in ₦1m.): Oil, 201,349; cocoa, 1,345; rubber, 766; urea and ammonia, 447; fish, 400. Principal imports: Machinery and transport equipment, 61,841; other manufactures, 35,072; chemicals, 22,904; foodstuffs, 12,597.

In 1993 the main export markets were: USA, 44·1%; Germany, 6·8%; Spain, 6%; India, 5·9%; France, 5·9%. Main import suppliers: UK, 14%; USA, 13·1%; Germany, 10·1%; France, 8·3%; Japan, 7·3%.

COMMUNICATIONS

Roads. The road network covered 193,198 km in 1996, of which 3,600 km were surfaced, including 2,044 km of motorways. Nigeria has the longest motorway network in Africa. In 1995 there were 663,000 motor cars and 68,000 trucks and vans. There were 12,212 road accidents with 4,908 fatalities in 1995.

Rail. There are 3,505 route-km of line 1,067 mm gauge, which in 1995 carried 108m. tonne-kilometres of freight and 1,729,000 passengers.

Civil Aviation. Lagos (Murtala Muhammed) is the major airport, and there are also international airports at Port Harcourt and Kano. The national carrier is the state-owned Nigeria Airways. In 1998 services were also provided by Aeroflot, Air Afrique, Air Gabon, Air India, Alitalia, Balkan, British Airways, Cameroon Airlines, Egyptair, Ethiopian Airlines, Ghana Airways, K.D. Air Corporation, Kenya Airways, KLM, Lufthansa, Middle East Airlines, SABENA, Sierra National Airlines and Swissair. In 1996 Lagos handled 2,409,000 passengers (1,694,000 on domestic flights) and 19,500 tonnes of freight. Nigeria Airways flew 6·2m. km in 1995, carrying 547,900 passengers (355,500 on domestic flights).

Shipping. In 1995 the merchant marine totalled 0·7m. GRT, including oil tankers, 0·47m. GRT. The principal ports are Lagos, Port Harcourt, Warri and Calabar. There is an extensive network of inland waterways.

Telecommunications. There were 412,800 main telephone lines in 1996 (3·6 per 1,000 persons). Cellular phone subscribers numbered 13,000 in 1995, there were 440,000 PCs and 6,767 telex machines. Nigeria had around 1,000 Internet users in Jan. 1998.

Postal Services. In 1995 there were 3,651 post offices. A total of 812m. pieces of mail were processed in 1995.

SOCIAL INSTITUTIONS

Justice. The highest court is the Federal Supreme Court, which consists of the Chief Justice of the Republic, and up to 15 Justices appointed by the government. It has original jurisdiction in any dispute between the Federal Republic and any State or between States; and to hear and determine appeals from the Federal Court of Appeal, which acts as an intermediate appellate Court to consider appeals from the High Court.

High Courts, presided over by a Chief Justice, are established in each state. All judges are appointed by the government. Magistrates' courts are established throughout the Republic, and customary law courts in southern Nigeria. In each of the northern States of Nigeria there are the Sharia Court of Appeal and the Court of Resolution. Moslem Law has been codified in a Penal Code and is applied through Alkali courts.

Religion. Moslems, 48%; Christians, 34% (17% Protestants and 17% Roman Catholic); others, 18%. Northern Nigeria is mainly Moslem; Southern Nigeria is predominantly Christian and Western Nigeria is evenly divided between Christians, Moslems and animists.

Education. The adult literacy rate was 57·1% in 1995 (67·3% among males and 47·3% among females). In 1994 there were 38,649 primary schools with 16·19m.

pupils and 435,210 teachers, and 6,987 secondary and tertiary schools with 4·64m. students and 162,242 teachers.

In 1995 there were 13 universities, 2 agricultural and 5 technological universities, 21 polytechnics, 7 colleges and 2 institutes. There were 150,072 university students and 10,742 academic staff.

Health. Health provision, 1995: 1 doctor per 3,707 population; 1 nurse per 605; 1 hospital bed per 1,477.

CULTURE

Broadcasting. The Federal Radio Corporation of Nigeria, a statutory body, broadcasts 3 national radio programmes in English, Yoruba, Hausa and Igbo, and an international service, Voice of Nigeria (5 languages). The government Nigerian Television Authority transmits a national service (colour by PAL), and 10 states have services. In 1995 there were an estimated 22m. radio and 6·1m. TV sets.

Press. In 1995 there were 27 daily newspapers with a combined circulation of 1,950,000.

Tourism. Annual tourist arrivals are about 200,000, mostly from other African countries.

DIPLOMATIC REPRESENTATIVES

Of Nigeria in Great Britain (Nigeria Hse., 9 Northumberland Ave., London, WC2N 5BX)
Acting High Commissioner: Uche O. Okeke.

Of Great Britain in Nigeria (Shehu Shangari Way North, Maitama, Abuja).
High Commissioner: Mr G. S. Burton, CMG.

Of Nigeria in the USA (1333 16th St., NW, Washington, D.C., 20036)
Ambassador: Wakili Hassan Adamu.

Of the USA in Nigeria (2 Eleke Cres., Lagos)
Ambassador: William Twaddell.

Of Nigeria to the United Nations
Ambassador: Ibrahim A. Gambari.

Of Nigeria to the European Union
Ambassador: Vacant.

FURTHER READING

Achebe, C., *The Trouble with Nigeria*. Heinemann, 1983
Adamolekun, L., *Politics and Administration in Nigeria*. Ibadan, 1986
Burns, A., *History of Nigeria*. 8th ed. London, 1978
Crowder, M. and Abdullahi, G., *Nigeria: an Introduction to its History*. London, 1979
Forrest, T., *Politics and Economic Development in Nigeria*. Boulder (CO), 1993
Myers, R. A., *Nigeria*. [Bibliography] Oxford and Santa Barbara (CA), 1989
Oyovbaine, S. E., *Federalism in Nigeria: A Study in the Development of the Nigerian State*. London, 1985

Further information
Nigeria High Commission Library, London WC2, UK
National statistical office: Federal Office of Statistics.

NORWAY

Kongeriket Norge

(Kingdom of Norway)

Capital: Oslo
Population estimate, 2000: 4·41m.
GNP per capita: (PPP$) 23,220
HDI/world rank: 0·943/3

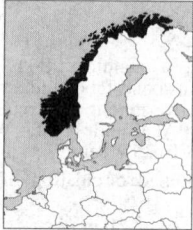

KEY HISTORICAL EVENTS

Norway was under Danish domination from the 14th century. By a Treaty of 14 Jan. 1814, the King of Denmark ceded Norway to the King of Sweden but the Norwegian people declared themselves independent and elected Prince Christian Frederik of Denmark as their king. The foreign Powers refused to recognize this election, and on 14 Aug. a convention proclaimed the independence of Norway in a personal union with Sweden. This was followed on 4 Nov. by the election of Karl XIII (II) as King of Norway. Norway declared this union dissolved on 7 June 1905 and Sweden agreed to the repeal of the union on 26 Oct. 1905. The throne was offered to a prince of the reigning house of Sweden who declined. After a plebiscite, Prince Carl of Denmark was formally elected King on 18 Nov. 1905, taking the name of Haakon VII. He reigned for 52 years, after which he was succeeded by his son.

From 1940 to 1944, during the Second World War, the Germans occupied Norway and set up a widely resented pro-German government under Vidkun Quisling.

Apart from this wartime episode, the Labour Party held office, and the majority in the Storting (parliament), from 1935 to 1965. From 1965 coalitions or minority governments have held power with Labour remaining the largest single party. The discovery of extensive off shore oil reserves in the 1960s transformed the Norwegian economy, making it one of the world's richest.

TERRITORY AND POPULATION

Norway is bounded in the north by the Arctic Ocean, east by Russia, Finland and Sweden, south by the Skagerrak Straits and west by the North Sea. The total area of mainland Norway is 323,758 sq. km, including 17,506 sq. km of fresh water.

Population (1990 census) was 4,247,546 (2,099,881 males; 2,147,655 females); population density per sq. km, 13·8. Estimated population in 1998, 4,417,599; population density, 14.

The UN gives a projected population for 2000 of 4·41m.

There are 19 counties (*folk*). Land area, population and densities:

	Land area (sq. km)	Population (1990 census)	Population (1998 estimate)	Density per sq. km 1998
Oslo (City)	427	461,190	499,693	1,170
Akershus	4,587	417,653	453,490	99
Østfold	3,889	238,296	243,585	63
Hedmark	26,120	187,276	186,118	7
Oppland	23,827	182,578	182,162	8
Buskerud	13,856	225,172	232,967	17
Vestfold	2,140	198,399	208,687	98
Telemark	14,186	162,907	163,857	12
Aust-Agder	8,485	97,333	101,152	12
Vest-Agder	6,817	144,917	152,553	22
Rogaland	8,553	337,504	364,341	43
Hordaland	14,962	410,567	428,823	29
Sogn og Fjordane	17,864	106,659	107,790	6
Møre og Romsdal	14,596	238,409	241,972	17
Sør-Trøndelag	17,839	250,978	259,177	15
Nord-Trøndelag	20,777	127,157	126,785	6
Nordland	36,302	239,311	239,280	7
Troms	25,147	146,716	150,288	6
Finnmark	45,879	74,524	74,879	2
Mainland total	306,253[1]	4,247,546	4,417,599	14

Svalbard and Jan Mayen have an area of 61,606 sq. km. Persons staying on Svalbard and Jan Mayen are registered as residents of their home Norwegian municipality.
[1]118,244 sq. miles.

NORWAY

In 1995 an estimated 73·2% of the population lived in urban areas.
Population of the principal urban settlements on 1 Jan. 1997:

Oslo	741,621	Tønsberg	41,345	Moss	30,359
Bergen	198,627	Sarpsborg	39,747	Hamar	28,600
Trondheim	137,123	Sandnes	36,999	Arendal	25,411
Stavanger	107,570	Porsgrunn	35,906	Ålesund	24,574
Drammen	60,384	Haugesund	34,790	Larvik	21,140
Kristiansand	57,826	Sandefjord	34,283	Halden	20,694
Frederikstad	51,550	Bodø	33,453	Mo i Rana	19,821
Tromsø	47,847	Skien	30,618	Lillehammer	18,664

The official language is Norwegian, which has 2 versions: Bokmål (or Riksmål) and Nynorsk (or Landsmål).

The Sami, the indigenous people of the far north, number some 30,000 and form a distinct ethnic minority with their own culture and language.

SOCIAL STATISTICS
Statistics for calendar years:

	Marriages	Divorces	Births	Still-born	Outside marriage[1]	Deaths
1994	20,605	10,934	60,092	276	27,581	44,071
1995	21,677	10,360	60,292	236	28,680	45,190
1996	...	...	60,927	276	29,435	43,860
1997	...	...	59,801	230	29,133	44,595

[1]Excluding still-born.

Rates per 1,000 population, 1995, birth, 13·8; death, 10·4; marriage, 5·0; divorce, 2·4. Annual growth rate, 1990–95, was 0·6%. Over 1990–95, the suicide rate per 100,000 population was 15·5 (men, 23·3; women, 8).

Expectation of life at birth, 1997, was 75·45 years for males and 80·97 years for females. Infant mortality, 1997, 4·1 per 1,000 live births; fertility rate, 1·86 births per woman.

At 1 Jan. 1997 the immigrant population totalled 232,192, of whom 39% held Norwegian citizenship.

CLIMATE
There is considerable variation in the climate because of the extent of latitude, the topography and the varying effectiveness of prevailing westerly winds and the Gulf Stream. Winters along the whole west coast are exceptionally mild but precipitation is considerable. Oslo, Jan. 24°F (−4·7°C), July 63°F (17·3°C). Annual rainfall 29·1" (740 mm). Bergen, Jan. 35°F (1·4°C), July 60°F (15·3°C). Annual rainfall 83" (2,108 mm). Trondheim, Jan. 26°F (−3·5°C), July 57°F (14°C). Annual rainfall 32·1" (870 mm).

CONSTITUTION AND GOVERNMENT
Norway is a constitutional and hereditary monarchy.

The reigning King is Harald V, born 21 Feb. 1937, married on 29 Aug. 1968 to Sonja Haraldsen. He succeeded on the death of his father, King Olav V, on 21 Jan. 1991. *Offspring:* Princess Märtha Louise, born 22 Sept. 1971; Crown Prince Haakon Magnus, born 20 July 1973. The king receives a tax-free annual allowance of 19·8m. kroner from the civil list. Women have been eligible to succeed to the throne since 1990. There is no coronation ceremony. The royal succession is in direct male line in the order of primogeniture. In default of male heirs the King may propose a successor to the Storting, but this assembly has the right to nominate another, if it does not agree with the proposal.

The Constitution, voted by a constituent assembly on 17 May 1814 and modified at various times, vests the legislative power of the realm in the *Storting* (Parliament). The royal veto may be exercised; but if the same Bill passes two Stortings formed by separate and subsequent elections it becomes the law of the land without the assent of the sovereign. The King has the command of the land, sea and air forces, and makes all appointments.

The 165-member Storting is directly elected by proportional representation. The country is divided into 19 districts, each electing from 4 to 15 representatives.

The Storting, when assembled, divides itself by election into the *Lagting* and the *Odelsting*. The former is composed of one-fourth of the members of the Storting, and the other of the remaining three-fourths. Each Ting (the Storting, the Odelsting and the Lagting) nominates its own president. Most questions are decided by the Storting, but questions relating to legislation must be considered and decided by the Odelsting and the Lagting separately. Only when the Odelsting and the Lagting disagree, the Bill has to be considered by the Storting in plenary sitting, and a new law can then only be decided by a majority of two-thirds of the voters. The same majority is required for alterations of the Constitution, which can only be decided by the Storting in plenary sitting. The Storting elects 5 delegates, whose duty it is to revise the public accounts. The Lagting and the ordinary members of the Supreme Court of Justice (the *Høyesterett*) form a High Court of the Realm (the *Riksrett*) for the trial of ministers, members of the *Høyesterett* and members of the Storting. The impeachment before the *Riksrett* can only be decided by the Odelsting.

The executive is represented by the King, who exercises his authority through the Cabinet. Cabinet ministers are entitled to be present in the Storting and to take part in the discussions, but without a vote.

National Anthem. 'Ja, vi elsker dette landet' ('Yes, we love this land'); words by B. Bjørnson, tune by R. Nordraak.

RECENT ELECTIONS

At the elections for the Storting held on 16 Sept. 1997 the following parties were elected: Labour Party, 65 (with 35% of the vote); Christian Democratic Party, 25; Progress Party 25; Conservative Party, 23; Centre Party, 11; Socialist Left Party, 9; Liberal Party, 6; Coastal Party, 1.

During the election campaign, Prime Minister Thorbjørn Jagland announced his decision to resign if the Labour Party failed to attract at least 36·9% of the vote, the same share that the party received in 1993. He resigned on 14 Oct. 1997 and on 17 Oct. Kjell Magne Bondevik formed a coalition government of the 3 centrist parties (Christian Democratic, Centre and Liberal) with a combined 26·1% of the vote.

CURRENT ADMINISTRATION

In March 1999 the minority Coalition government comprised:

Prime Minister: Kjell Magne Bondevik (b. 1947).

Minister of Culture: Anne Enger Lahnstein. *Children and Family Affairs:* Valgerd Svarstad Haugland. *Industry and Trade:* Lars Sponheim. *Foreign Affairs:* Knut Vollebæk. *Fisheries:* Peter Angelsen. *Finance:* Gudmund Restad. *Local Government, Labour, Nordic Co-operation:* Ragnhild Queseth Haarstad. *Agriculture:* Kåre Gjønnes. *Justice and Police:* Aud Inger Aure. *National Planning and Co-ordination:* Eldbjørg Løwer. *Transport:* Odd Einar Dørum. *Education, Research and Church Affairs:* Jon Lilletun. *Defence:* Dag Jostein Fjærvoll. *Social Affairs:* Magnhild Meltveit Kleppa. *Health:* Dagfinn Høybråten. *Oil and Energy:* Marit Arnstad. *Environment:* Guro Fjellanger. *International Development Aid and Human Rights:* Hilde Frafjord Johnson.

Local Government. There are 18 counties and the urban district of Oslo, in each of which the central government is represented by a county governor. The counties are divided into 435 municipalities, each of which usually corresponds in size to a parish. The municipalities are administered by municipal councils, whose membership may vary between 25 and 85 directly-elected councillors. Elections were held in Sept. 1995; turn-out was 62·8%. The Labour Party gained 30·5% of all votes cast; the Conservative Party, 20·2%; the Centre Party, 11·6%; the Progress Party, 10·5%.

DEFENCE

Conscription is for 12 months, with 4 to 5 refresher training periods.

In 1997 defence spending totalled US$3,336m. (US$760 per capita), representing 2·3% of GDP. Expenditure per capita was the highest of any European country in 1997.

Army. There are a Northern and a Southern command, and within these the Army is organized in 4 district commands, 1 divisional headquarters and 14 territorial commands. North Command consists of 1 brigade group. South Command consists of 2 infantry battalions, including the Royal Guard. Equipment includes 170 Leopard main battle tanks. Strength (1997) 14,700 (including 9,200 conscripts). The fast mobilization reserve numbers 255,000.

Navy. The Royal Norwegian Navy has 3 components: The Navy, Coast Guard and Coastal Artillery. Main Naval combatants include 12 coastal submarines (including 6 new German-built Ula class), 4 frigates, 28 missile craft, 3 coastal minesweepers, 6 minehunters and 2 minelayers. Auxiliaries comprise 1 submarine/missile craft support ship, 1 Royal Yacht and some 10 small general-purpose tenders. The Coastal Artillery man 26 coastal batteries and other static defence systems.

The personnel of the navy totalled 6,400 in 1996, of whom 3,600 were conscripts. 1,000 served in Coastal Artillery and 700 in the Coast Guard. The main naval base is at Bergen (Håkonsvern), with subsidiary bases at Horten, Ramsund and Tromsø.

The naval elements of the Home Guard on mobilization can muster some 6,000 personnel, and man 2 tank landing craft, 7 torpedo craft and about 400 requisitioned fishing vessels.

The 12 Coast Guard offshore patrol vessels (of which 3 are armed, and of frigate capability) are Navy-subordinated, and assist other government agencies in rescue service, environmental patrols, surveillance and police duties.

Air Force. The Royal Norwegian Air Force comprises the Air Force and the Anti-air Artillery. The Air Force consists of 4 squadrons of F-16 Fighting Falcons, 1 squadron of F-5 fighter-bombers, 1 maritime patrol squadron of P-3N and P-3C Orions, 1 squadron of C-130 Hercules transports, 1 squadron of Falcon 20s equipped for EW duties, 1 squadron with DHC-6 Twin Otter light transports and 2 squadrons of Bell 412SP helicopters. The Anti-air Artillery deploy 4 Nike surface-to-air missile batteries and several light anti-aircraft artillery units. 6 NOAH (Norwegian adapted Hawk missiles) batteries provide area and airfield defence co-ordinated with 10 SAM batteries with the mobile missile system RBS-70; finally 27 batteries with 40 mm Bofors AA-guns and 12·7 mm machine guns. 12 Westland Sea King helicopters are used for search and rescue duties; 5 Lynx helicopters are operated for the Coast Guard; 17 Saab Safaris are used for primary training; pilots then go to the USA for advanced training.

Total strength (1996) is about 7,900 personnel, including 4,100 conscripts.

Home Guard. The Home Guard is organized in small units equipped and trained for special tasks. Service after basic training is 1 week a year. The Home Guard consists of the Land Home Guard (strength, 1996, 71,000), Sea Home Guard and Anti-Air Home Guard organized in 18 districts. *See also under* NAVY, *above.*

INTERNATIONAL RELATIONS

Norway is a member of the UN, NATO, EFTA, OECD, the Council of Europe and the Nordic Council, and an Associate Member of the WEU. Norway has acceded to the Schengen Accord abolishing border controls between Norway and Austria, Belgium, Denmark, Finland, France, Germany, Greece, Iceland, Italy, Luxembourg, Netherlands, Portugal, Spain and Sweden.

In a referendum on 27–28 Nov. 1994, 52·2% of votes cast were against joining the EU. The electorate was 3,266,182; turn-out was 88·88%.

ECONOMY

Performance. Major oil discoveries on the Norwegian continental shelf coincided with the 1974 and 1979 oil shocks, resulting in a pronounced upswing in mainland economy which lasted until the 1986 oil price collapse. Norway only began to recover from the subsequent slump in the economy in 1993. The strong performance of the Norwegian economy in 1993–98 lifted mainland GDP by 20%, but a significant slowdown now seems to be under way. As in 1986, the oil price collapse of 1998 occurred at a critical time when the labour market was overheated. As a result, economic developments have been marked by several adverse shocks, such as deteriorating terms of trade, coupled with increased wages and high interest rates.

Real GDP growth was estimated at 3·4% in 1998 (3·7% in 1997).

Budget. Central government revenue and expenditure (in 1m. kroner) for years ending 31 Dec.:

	1994	1995	1996	1997
Revenue	347,260	381,849	423,676	429,000
Expenditure	345,046	350,667	365,247	374,600

The 1999 budget, presented in Oct. 1998, projected the central government surplus to rebound by 23·5bn. kroner to over 52bn. kroner—almost 50% of the increase is due to a narrowing of the non-oil budget deficit. As in 1998 the entire budget surplus will be allocated to the Government Petroleum Fund.

Currency. The unit of currency is the *Norwegian krone* (NOK) of 100 *øre*. After Oct. 1990 the krone was fixed to the ecu in the EMS of the EU in the narrow band of 2·25%, but it was freed in Dec. 1992. Annualized inflation was 1·3% in 1996 and 2·6% in 1997, with a forecast of 2·4% in 1998. In Feb. 1998 foreign exchange reserves were US$22,884m. and gold reserves were 1·18m. troy oz. In Jan. 1998 total money supply was 421bn. kroner.

Banking and Finance. Norges Bank is the central bank and bank of issue. Supreme authority is vested in the Executive Board consisting of 7 members appointed by the King and the Supervisory Council consisting of 15 members elected by the Storting. The *Governor* is Svein Gjedrem.

There are 3 major commercial banks: Den Norske Bank, Christiana and Fokus. Total assets and liabilities of the 20 commercial banks at 31 Dec. 1996 were 552,348m. kroner.

At the end of 1992 there were 23 private joint-stock banks. Their total amount of capital and funds was 21,284m. kroner (capital 12,029m., funds 9,255m.). Deposits at the end of 1995 amounted to 248,187m. kroner.

The number of savings banks at 31 Dec. 1996 was 132; ordinary deposits totalled 247,678m. kroner.

There is a stock exchange in Oslo.

Weights and Measures. The metric system is obligatory.

ENERGY AND NATURAL RESOURCES

Electricity. Norway is a large producer of hydro-electric energy. The potential total hydro-electric power was estimated at 178,335m. kWh in 1997. Installed capacity in 1994 was 26·43m. kW, more than 95% of it hydro-electric. Production, 1997 estimate, was 111,636m. kWh (104,712m. kWh in 1996, of which 104,148m. kWh was hydro-electric). Consumption per capita in 1995, estimated at 24,586 kWh, was the highest in the world.

Oil and Gas. There are enormous oil reserves in the Norwegian continental shelf. In 1966 the first exploration well was drilled. Production of crude oil, 1997 (provisional), 156,215,000 tonnes. Norway is the world's second biggest oil exporter after Saudi Arabia, producing around 3·5m. bbls. a day in 1996. It had proven reserves of 11·2bn. bbls. in Sept. 1997. In March 1998 Norway announced that it would reduce its output for the year by 100,000 bbls. per day as part of a plan to cut global crude production.

Output of natural gas, 1997 (provisional), 47,053m. cu. metres.

Minerals. Production, 1996 (in tonnes): iron ore, 1,554,599; ferrotitanium ore, 758,711; copper concentrates, 31,736; lead ore (1995), 3,721; zinc ore, 8,619.

Agriculture. Norway is barren and mountainous. The arable area is in strips in valleys and around fiords and lakes.

In 1996 the agricultural area[1] was 1,031,200 ha, of which 609,300 ha were meadow and pasture, 174,600 ha were sown to barley, 97,000 ha to oats, 58,800 ha to wheat and 18,100 ha to potatoes. Production (in 1,000 tonnes) in 1995: Barley, 547; oats, 354; wheat, 312; potatoes, 400; hay, 3,274; vegetables, 132; meat, 240.

Livestock, 1996[1], 1,005,800 cattle (342,700 milch cows), 1,032,300 sheep, 57,900 goats, 1,328,500 pigs, 3,460,600 hens. 1995: 0·1m. silver and platinum fox, 0·52m. blue fox, 0·33m. mink, 203,900 reindeer.

[1]Holdings with at least 50 ha agricultural area in use.

Forestry. In 1995 the total area under forests was 8·07m. ha, or 26·3% of the total land area (7·94m. ha and 25·9% in 1990). Productive forest area, 1997, approximately 67,375 sq. km. About 80% of the productive forest area consists of conifers and 20% of broadleaves. The annual increment (in 1993) was 20,332,000 cu. metres with bark. In 1995–96, 7·8m. cu. metres of roundwood were cut: 37m. cu. metres were special and saw timber and 36m. cu. metres pulpwood.

Fisheries. The total number of fishermen in 1996 was 23,397, of whom 6,310 had another chief occupation. In 1996, the number of registered fishing vessels (all with motor) was 13,944, and of these 5,290 were open boats.

The catch in 1996 totalled 2,632,867 tonnes, almost entirely from sea fishing. Norway has the highest annual catch in Europe. Total salmon catch in 1997 was 708 tonnes (405 tonnes sea fishing, 303 tonnes river fishing). 10,114 seals were caught in 1997 (including 234 harp seal and 67 hodded seal for research purposes). Commercial whaling was prohibited in 1988, but recommenced in 1993: 503 whales were caught in 1997.

Environment. In 1997 there were 18 national parks (total area, 1,378,840 ha), 1,318 nature reserves (242,906 ha), 86 landscape protected areas (506,303 ha) and 76 other areas with protected flora and fauna (11,052 ha).

INDUSTRY

Industry is chiefly based on raw materials. Paper and paper products, industrial chemicals and basic metals are important export manufactures. In the following table figures are given for industrial establishments in 1995. The values are given in 1m. kroner.

Industries	Establish- ments	Number of Employees	Gross value of produc- tion	Value added
Coal and peat	12	325	165	32
Metal ores	8	1,161	1,118	348
Other mining and quarrying	333	2,868	3,336	1,464
Food products	1,712	45,503	79,500	13,481
Beverages and tobacco	56	5,942	12,705	9,460
Textiles	307	4,777	3,520	1,298
Clothing, etc.	154	2,465	1,431	514
Leather and leather products	45	776	527	179
Wood and wood products	959	14,469	14,737	4,173
Pulp, paper and paper products	115	10,869	22,230	7,236
Printing and publishing	1,785	36,033	25,927	11,616
Basic chemicals	65	8,439	20,785	7,251
Other chemical products	97	5,422	8,748	3,492
Coal and refined petroleum products	78	1,636	13,425	870
Rubber and plastic products	337	6,312	6,507	2,294
Other non-metallic mineral products	500	8,349	9,906	3,840
Basic metals	116	15,107	37,113	9,867
Metal products, except machinery/equipment	1,150	16,891	13,793	5,564
Machinery and equipment	1,123	21,972	23,812	8,084
Office machinery and computers	21	889	1,292	352
Electrical machinery and apparatus	304	9,325	10,673	3,828
Radio, television, communication equipment	66	4,171	5,672	1,976
Medical, precision and optical instruments	285	5,155	5,859	2,187
Oil platforms	99	18,006	16,486	6,728
Motor vehicles and trailers	91	4,553	4,404	1,464
Other transport equipment	483	17,827	19,611	5,381
Other manufacturing industries	720	12,428	9,296	3,441
Total (all industries)	11,021	281,490	372,578	116,419

Income at factor cost (in 1m. kroner):

	1990	1991	1992
Net domestic product	561,727	584,224	598,762
Less Indirect taxes	111,089	115,617	121,441
Add Subsidies	39,992	42,770	44,395
	490,630	511,377	521,718

Labour. Norway has a tradition of centralized wage bargaining. Since the early 1960s the contract period has been for 2 years with intermediate bargaining after 12 months, to take into consideration such changes as the rate of inflation.

The labour force (i.e. employed persons plus non-employed persons seeking work aged 16–74) averaged 2,285,000 in 1997 (1,053,000 females); the total number of employed persons averaged 2,192,000 (1,009,000 females). Of a total workforce of 2,137,000, in 1996, 1,952,000 were salaried employees and wage earners, 165,000 self-employed and 19,000 family workers.

Distribution of employed persons by occupation in 1995 showed 560,000 in technical, physical science, humanistic and artistic work; 146,000 administrative executive work; 197,000 clerical; 222,000 sales; 105,000 agriculture, forestry, fishing etc.; 8,000 mining and quarrying; 131,000 transport and communication; 385,000 manufacturing; 285,000 service; and 39,000 military and occupation not specified.

There were 93,000 registered unemployed in 1997 (44,000 females).

There were 6 work stoppages in 1997: 6,972 working days were lost.

Trade Unions. There were 1,426,837 union members in 1996.

INTERNATIONAL TRADE

Imports and Exports. Total imports and exports in calendar years (in 1m. kroner):

	1993	1994	1995	1996	1997[1]
Imports	170,991	192,963	208,626	229,720	371,024
Exports	226,626	244,475	265,883	320,128	447,582

[1]Estimate

Major import suppliers in 1996 (value in 1m. kroner): Sweden, 37,857·4; Germany, 30,106·7; UK, 22,630·6; Denmark, 17,136·4; USA, 15,376·2; Japan, 10,512·6; Netherlands, 9,877·7; France, 9,424·1; Italy, 9,265·7; Finland, 7,945·7. Imports from economic areas: EU, 160,759·5; Nordic countries, 63,599·3; EFTA, 3,641·6.

Major export markets in 1996: UK, 62,885·1; Netherlands, 36,432·6; Germany, 35,596·5; Sweden, 29,176·9; France, 27,753·9; USA, 22,670·1; Denmark, 14,514·7; Canada, 12,917·7; Belgium, 10,219·2; Italy, 8,490·8; Finland, 7,171·1. Exports to economic areas: EU, 245,387·2; Nordic countries, 52,968·1; EFTA, 3,115·9.

Principal imports in 1996 (in 1m. kroner): machinery, 24,263·3; motor vehicles, 23,010·2; electrical machinery, 12,121·4; iron and steel, 10,169; office machines and computers, 10,096·8; metalliferous ores and metal scrap, 9,319·1; clothing and accessories, 8,903·8; telecommunications and sound apparatus and equipment, 7,351·1; ships over 100 tonnes, 6,091·5; paper, paperboard and products, 6,054·6; petroleum and products, 5,532·9. Principal exports in 1996 (in 1m. kroner): crude petroleum, 135,729·5; fish, crustaceans and molluscs, and preparations thereof, 21,383·4; natural gas, 20,959·5; non-ferrous metals, 20,554·1; paper, paperboard and products, 9,490·3; iron and steel, 9,311·9; ships over 100 tonnes, 7,512·9.

COMMUNICATIONS

Roads. In 1997 the length of public roads (including roads in towns) totalled 91,346 km. In 1996 there were 65,750 km of paved roads. Total road length included: National roads, 26,535 km; provincial roads, 27,127 km; local roads, 37,684 km. Number of registered motor vehicles, 1996: 1,661,247 passenger cars (including station wagons and ambulances), 33,959 buses, 186,523 vans, 102,233 combined vehicles, 69,372 goods vehicles, 218,552 tractors, 39,809 snow scooters, 50,661 motor cycles and 114,114 mopeds. In 1996 there were 8,779 road accidents with 255 fatalities.

Rail. The length of state railways in 1996 was 4,021 km (2,420 km electrified); of private companies in 1995, 16 km (electrified). Total receipts of the state railways in 1995 were 5,560m. kroner; total expenses, 5,328m. kroner. The state railways carried 14,559,000 tonnes of freight and 40,701,000 passengers in 1996.

There is a metro (98 km) and tram/light rail line (54 km) in Oslo.

Civil Aviation. The main international airports are at Oslo (Fornebu), Bergen (Flesland) and Stavanger (Sola). Kristiansand and Trondheim also have a few international flights. Denmark and Norway each hold two-sevenths and Sweden three-sevenths of the capital of SAS (Scandinavian Airlines System), but they have joint responsibility towards third parties. At 31 Dec. 1996 there were 864 registered aircraft. 23,744,601 passengers, 87,489 tonnes of freight and 50,154 tonnes of mail were carried on all domestic and international flights in 1996. Braathens is the major airline after SAS, carrying 4,725,900 passengers in 1995 (268,400 on international flights).

In 1998 services were also provided by Aeroflot, Air Canada, Air France, Air Lithuania, Air Malta, Air Stord, Air Team, Aviosarda, British Airways, British Midland, Coast Air, Continental Airlines, Czech Airlines, Delta Air Lines, Finnair, Golden Air Flyg, Hemus Air, Iberia, Icelandair, Interimpex-Avioimpex, KLM, KLM UK, LOT, Lufthansa, Maersk Air, Muk Air, Ryanair, SABENA, Skyways, Swissair, TAP, Teddy Air, Thai Airways International, Tyrolean Airways, United Airlines and Wideroe's Flyveselskap. In 1996 Oslo (Fornebu) handled 10,845,000 passengers (6,514,000 on domestic flights) and 50,600 tonnes of freight. Bergen was the second busiest in 1996 for passenger traffic, with 3,064,000 (2,573,000 on domestic flights), and Stavanger second busiest for freight, with 7,100 tonnes.

Shipping. The Norwegian International Ship Register was set up in 1987. At 31 Dec. 1996, 664 ships were registered (438 Norwegian) totalling 18,886,000 GRT. There were also 923 ships totalling 2,385,000 GRT on the Norwegian Ordinary Register. These figures do not include fishing boats, tugs, salvage vessels, icebreakers and similar special types of vessels.

Goods (in 1,000 tonnes) in 1993 discharged, 18,929; loaded, 108,268.

In 1995, 43,213,000 passengers were carried by coastwise shipping on long distance, local and ferry services, and in 1993 (excluding long distance except Bergen–Stavanger), 34·6m. tonnes of cargo.

Telecommunications. Number of telephone connections on 31 Dec. 1996 was 2,440,185. In 1996 there were 1,261,445 mobile telephones in use. In 1995 there were 1,193,000 PCs (273 for every 1,000 persons) and 130,000 fax machines. There were around 601,000 Internet users in Jan. 1998.

Postal Services. There were 2,091 post offices in 1996. In 1995 a total of 2,176m. items of mail were processed, or 499 per person.

SOCIAL INSTITUTIONS

Justice. The judicature is common to civil and criminal cases; the same professional judges preside over both. These judges are state officials. The participation of lay judges and jurors, both summoned for the individual case, varies according to the kind of court and kind of case.

The 96 city or district courts of first instance are in criminal cases composed of one professional judge and 2 lay judges, chosen by ballot from a panel elected by the local authority. In civil cases 2 lay judges may participate. These courts are competent in all cases except criminal cases where the maximum penalty exceeds 6 years imprisonment.

In every community there is a Conciliation Board composed of 3 lay persons elected by the district council. A civil lawsuit usually begins with mediation by the Board which can pronounce judgement in certain cases.

The 5 high courts, or courts of second instance, are composed of 3 professional judges. Additionally, in civil cases 2 or 4 lay judges may be summoned. In serious criminal cases, which are brought before high courts in the first instance, a jury of 10 lay persons is summoned to determine whether the defendant is guilty according to the charge. In less serious criminal cases the court is composed of 2 professional and 3 lay judges. In civil cases, the court of second instance is an ordinary court of appeal. In criminal cases in which the lower court does not have judicial authority, it is itself the court of first instance. In other criminal cases it is an appeal court as far as the appeal is based on an attack against the lower court's assessment of the facts when determining the guilt of the defendant. An appeal based on any other alleged mistakes is brought directly before the Supreme Court.

The Supreme Court *(Høyesterett)* is the court of last resort. There are 18 Supreme Court judges. Each individual case is heard by 5 judges. Some major cases are determined in plenary session. The Supreme Court may in general examine every aspect of the case and the handling of it by the lower courts. However, in criminal cases the Court may not overrule the lower court's assessment of the facts as far as the guilt of the defendant is concerned.

The Court of Impeachment *(Riksretten)* is composed of 5 judges of the Supreme Court and 10 members of Parliament.

All serious offences are prosecuted by the State. The Public Prosecution Authority consists of the Attorney General, 18 district attorneys and legally qualified officers of the ordinary police force. Counsel for the defence is in general provided for by the State.

Religion. There is freedom of religion, the Church of Norway (Evangelical Lutheran), however, being the national church, endowed by the State. Its clergy are nominated by the King. Ecclesiastically Norway is divided into 11 bishoprics, 96 archdeaconries and 626 clerical districts. There were 237,733 members of registered and unregistered religious communities outside the Evangelical Lutheran Church, subsidized by central government and local authorities in 1996. At 1 Jan. 1997 there were 59 Moslem congregations with 46,500 members. The Roman Catholics are under a Bishop at Oslo, a Vicar Apostolic at Trondheim and a Vicar Apostolic at Tromsø.

Education. Free compulsory schooling in primary and lower secondary schools was extended to 10 years from 9, and the starting age lowered to 6 from 7, in July 1997. All young people between the ages of 16 and 19 have the statutory right to 3 years of upper secondary education. In 1996 there were 6,409 kindergartens (children up to 6 years old) with 192,446 children (not including 33,082 children aged 5 to 7 who attended educational programmes for 6-year-olds) and 52,084 staff. In 1995–96 there were 3,285 primary and lower secondary schools with 477,236 pupils and 37,966 teachers; (1991–92) 75 special schools with 1,980 pupils and (1990–91) 1,099 teachers; 730 upper secondary schools with 216,126 pupils and 20,849 teachers; and 74 colleges, with 93,788 students and 5,116 teachers.

There are 4 universities: Bergen, founded 1946; Oslo, 1811; Tromsø, 1968; and the Norwegian University of Science and Technology, 1996 (formerly the University of Trondheim and the Norwegian Institute of Technology); and 10 specialized institutions of equivalent status. In 1995–96 these had 82,957 students and 6,031 academic staff. The University of Tromsø is responsible for Sami language and studies.

In 1996 total expenditure on education came to 7·5% of GNP.

Health. The health care system, which is predominantly publicly financed (mainly by a national insurance tax), is run on both county and municipal levels. Persons who fall ill are guaranteed medical treatment, and health services are distributed according to need. In 1996 there were 15,368 doctors (equivalent to 1 for every 284 persons), 5,222 dentists and 65,232 nurses. In 1994 provision of hospital beds was 51 per 10,000 population.

Welfare. In 1996 there were 625,940 old age pensioners who received a total of 50,426m. kroner, 239,429 disability pensioners who received 23,473·7m. kroner, 30,895 widows and widowers who received 1,774·8m. kroner and 45,529 single parents who received 2,425·4m. kroner. In 1996, 910,009 children received family allowances.

Maternity leave is for 1 year on 80% of previous salary; unused portions may pass to a husband. In 1996 sickness benefits totalling 24,784·9m. kroner were paid: 13,220·5m. kroner in sickness allowances and 11,564·4m. kroner in medical benefits. Expenditure on benefits at childbirth and adoption totalled 6,262·5m. kroner to 87,714 cases in 1996.

CULTURE

Bergen is one of nine European Cities of Culture in the year 2000. Its theme will be 'Art, Work and Leisure', part of which will coincide with the Bergen International Festival held in May 2000. The other Cities of Culture are Avignon (France), Bologna (Italy), Brussels (Belgium), Helsinki (Finland), Kraków (Poland), Prague

(Czech Republic), Reykjavík (Iceland) and Santiago de Compostela (Spain). The title attracts large European Union grants.

Broadcasting. The Norwegian Broadcasting Corporation is a non-commercial enterprise operated by an independent state organization and broadcasts 1 programme (P1) on long-, medium-, and short-waves and on FM and 1 programme (P2) on FM. Local programmes are also broadcast. It broadcasts 1 TV programme from 2,259 transmitters. Colour programmes are broadcast by PAL system. Number of television licences, 1997, 1,678,140. In 1996 there were 4m. radio receivers.

Cinema. There were 395 cinemas in 1996, with a seating capacity of 90,290 (in 1995). In 1996 attendances totalled 11·5m.

Press. There were 64 daily newspapers with a combined average net circulation of 2·22m. in 1997, and 90 weeklies and semi-weeklies with 709,000. Norway has the highest circulation rate of daily newspapers in Europe, at 596 per 1,000 inhabitants in 1995.

Tourism. In 1996 there were 2,476,000 foreign tourists, who spent 5·05m. nights in the 1,186 hotels and 1,936,000 nights in the 744 camping sites. Receipts from foreign tourism totalled US$2·4bn.

Libraries. In 1996 there were 1,136 public libraries, 3,689 school libraries, and 374 special and research libraries (9 national).

National Theatre and Opera. There were 6,639 theatre and opera performances attended by 1,287,026 people at 20 theatres in 1995.

Museums and Galleries. There were 552 museums in 1996 (38 art, 455 social history, 14 natural history and 45 mixed social and natural history), with 8,838,608 visitors.

DIPLOMATIC REPRESENTATIVES
Of Norway in Great Britain (25 Belgrave Sq., London, SW1X 8QD)
Ambassador: Kjell Colding, CMG.

Of Great Britain in Norway (Thomas Heftyesgate 8, 0244 Oslo, 2)
Ambassador: R. Dales, CMG.

Of Norway in the USA (2720 34th St., NW, Washington, D.C., 20008)
Ambassador: Tom Eric Vraalsen, GCVO.

Of the USA in Norway (Drammensveien 18, 0244 Oslo, 2)
Ambassador: David B. Hermelin.

Of Norway to the United Nations
Ambassador: Ole Peter Kolby.

Of Norway to the European Union
Ambassador: Einar Bull.

FURTHER READING
Central Bureau of Statistics. *Statistisk Årbok; Statistical Yearbook of Norway.—Economic survey* (annual, from 1935; with English summary from 1952, now published in *Økonomiske Analyser*, annual).—*Historisk Statistikk; Historical Statistics.—Statistisk Månedshefte* (with English index)
Norges Statskalender. From 1816; annual from 1877
Arntzen, J. G. and Knudsen, B. B., *Political Life and Institutions in Norway.* Oslo, 1981
Derry, T. K., *A History of Modern Norway, 1814–1972.* OUP, 1973.—*A History of Scandinavia.* London, 1979
Petersson, O., *The Government and Politics of the Nordic Countries.* Stockholm, 1994
Sather, L. B., *Norway.* [Bibliography] Oxford and Santa Barbara (CA), 1986
Selbyg, A., *Norway Today: An Introduction to Modern Norwegian Society.* Oslo, 1986

National library: The University Library, Drammensvein 42b, 0255 Oslo.
National statistical office: Central Bureau of Statistics, PB 8131 Dep., N-0033 Oslo.
Website: http://www.ssb.no/

SVALBARD

An archipelago situated between 10° and 35° E. long. and between 74° and 81° N. lat. Total area, 61,229 sq. km (23,640 sq. miles). The main islands are Spitsbergen, Nordaustlandet, Edgeøya, Barentsøya, Prins Karls Forland, Bjørnøya, Hopen, Kong Karls Land and Kvitøya. The Arctic climate is tempered by mild winds from the Atlantic.

The archipelago was probably discovered by Norsemen in 1194 and rediscovered by the Dutch navigator Barents in 1596. In the 17th century whale-hunting gave rise to rival Dutch, British and Danish–Norwegian claims to sovereignty; but when in the 18th century the whale-hunting ended, the question of the sovereignty of Svalbard lost its significance. It was again raised in the 20th century, owing to the discovery and exploitation of coalfields. By a treaty, signed on 9 Feb. 1920 in Paris, Norway's sovereignty over the archipelago was recognized. On 14 Aug. 1925 the archipelago was officially incorporated in Norway.

Total population on 1 Jan. 1997 was an estimated 3,231, of whom 1,739 were Norwegians, 1,482 Russians, and 10 Poles. Coal is the principal product. There are 2 Norwegian and 2 Russian mining camps. 292,094 tonnes of coal were produced from Norwegian mines in 1995 valued at 73,275,000 kroner.

There were 2,104 motor vehicles and trailers registered at 31 Dec. 1996, including 1,168 snow scooters.

There are research and radio stations, and an airport near Longyearbyen (Svalbard Lufthavn) opened in 1975.

Greve, T., *Svalbard: Norway in the Arctic*. Oslo, 1975
Hisdal, V., *Geography of Svalbard*. Norsk Polarinstitutt, Oslo, rev. ed., 1984

JAN MAYEN

This bleak, desolate and mountainous island of volcanic origin and partly covered by glaciers, is situated at 71° N. lat. and 8° 30' W. long., 300 miles north-northeast of Iceland. The total area is 377 sq. km (146 sq. miles). Beerenberg, its highest peak, reaches a height of 2,277 metres. Volcanic activity, which had been dormant, was reactivated in Sept. 1970.

The island was possibly discovered by Henry Hudson in 1608, and it was first named Hudson's Tutches (Touches). It was again and again rediscovered and renamed. Its present name derives from the Dutch whaling captain Jan Jacobsz May, who indisputably discovered the island in 1614. It was uninhabited, but occasionally visited by seal hunters and trappers, until 1921 when Norway established a radio and meteorological station. On 8 May 1929 Jan Mayen was officially proclaimed as incorporated in the Kingdom of Norway. Its relation to Norway was finally settled by law of 27 Feb. 1930. A LORAN station (1959) and a CONSOL station (1968) have been established.

BOUVET ISLAND

This uninhabited volcanic island, mostly covered by glaciers and situated at 54° 25' S. lat. and 3° 21' E. long., was discovered in 1739 by a French naval officer, Jean Baptiste Loziert Bouvet, but no flag was hoisted till, in 1825, Capt. Norris raised the Union Jack. In 1928 Great Britain waived its claim to the island in favour of Norway, which in Dec. 1927 had occupied it. A law of 27 Feb. 1930 declared Bouvetøya a Norwegian dependency. The area is 59 sq. km (23 sq. miles). Since 1977 Norway has had an automatic meteorological station on the island.

PETER I ISLAND

This uninhabited island, situated at 68° 48' S. lat. and 90° 35' W. long., was sighted in 1821 by the Russian explorer, Admiral von Bellingshausen. The first landing was made in 1929 by a Norwegian expedition which hoisted the Norwegian flag. On 1 May 1931 Peter I Island was placed under Norwegian sovereignty, and on 24 March 1933 it was incorporated in Norway as a dependency. The area is 249 sq. km (96 sq. miles).

QUEEN MAUD LAND

On 14 Jan. 1939 the Norwegian Cabinet placed that part of the Antarctic Continent from the border of Falkland Islands dependencies in the west to the border of the Australian Antarctic Dependency in the east (between 20° W. and 45° E.) under Norwegian sovereignty. The territory had been explored only by Norwegians and hitherto been ownerless. In 1957 it was given the status of a dependency.

OMAN

Saltanat 'Uman

(Sultanate of Oman)

Capital: Muscat
Population estimate, 2000: 2·72m.
GNP per capita: (PPP$) 8,660
HDI/world rank: 0·771/71

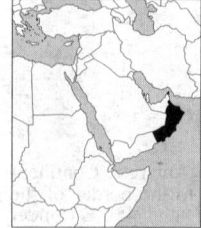

KEY HISTORICAL EVENTS

Little is known about Oman's pre-Islamic past though it is clear from recent archaeological discoveries that early civilizations existed at least 5,000 years ago. The ancestors of present day Oman are believed to have arrived in two waves of migration over a number of years, the first from the Yemen and the second from northern Arabia at a time when various parts of the country were occupied by the Persians. In the 9th century maritime trade flourished and Sohar became the greatest sea port in the Islamic world. In the early 16th century after the Portuguese under Vasco de Gama had discovered the sea route round the Cape of Good Hope to India, they occupied Muscat and its trade until they were expelled in 1650. The Ya'aruba dynasty introduced a period of renaissance in Omani fortunes both at home and abroad, uniting the country and bringing prosperity; but, on the death in 1718 of Sultan bin Saif II, civil war broke out over the election of his successor. Persian troops occupied Muttrah and Muscat but failed to take Sohar which was defended by Ahmad bin Said who continued to fight the Persians and drive them from Oman after the civil war had ended.

In 1744, the Al bu Said family assumed power and has ruled to the present day. The early part of this century saw a period of decline and, at the time of the First World War, Oman's share of international commercial activities was very limited. Indeed, Oman remained largely isolated from the rest of the world until 1970 when Said bin Taimur was deposed by his son Qaboos in a bloodless *coup*. Sultan Qaboos bin Said introduced reforms including the setting up of an advisory council of regional representatives.

TERRITORY AND POPULATION

Situated at the south-east corner of the Arabian peninsular, Oman is bounded in the north-east by the Gulf of Oman and south-east by the Arabian Sea, south-west by Yemen and north-west by Saudi Arabia and the United Arab Emirates. There is an enclave at the northern tip of the Musandam Peninsula between the United Arab Emirates of Ras al-Khaimah in the west and Fujairah in the south-east. An agreement of June 1995 completed the demarcation of the border with Yemen, and an agreement with Saudi Arabia of July 1995 permits the demarcation of their mutual border.

With a coastline of 1,700 sq. km. from the Strait of Hormuz in the north to the borders of the Republic of Yemen, the Sultanate is strategically located overlooking ancient maritime trade routes linking the Far East and Africa with the Mediterranean.

The Sultanate of Oman occupies a total area of 309,500 sq. km and includes different terrains that vary from plain to highlands and mountains. The coastal plain overlooking the Gulf of Oman and the Arabian Sea forms the most important and fertile plain in Oman.

The **Kuria Muria** islands were ceded to the UK in 1854 by the Sultan of Muscat and Oman. On 30 Nov. 1967 the islands were retroceded to the Sultan of Muscat and Oman, in accordance with the wishes of the population.

Estimated population (1995), 2,139,000, chiefly Arabs, and including 0·58m. foreign workers; density 7 per sq. km. In 2000 the population is projected to be 2·72m., and is expected to have doubled by 2020.

An estimated 75·6% of the population lived in urban areas in 1995. In the period 1990-95 the annual growth in the urban population was 8·2%, a rate only exceeded by Botswana and Mozambique.

The official language is Arabic; English is in commercial use.

OMAN

SOCIAL STATISTICS

1997 births, estimate, 66,000; deaths, 10,000. Birth rate, 1997 est. (per 1,000 population), 29·0; death rate, 4·4; infant mortality rate (1998), 18 per 1,000 live births. Expectation of life at birth, 1990–95, was 67·7 years for males and 71·8 years for females. Oman has achieved some of the most rapid advances ever recorded. Infant mortality declined from 200 per 1,000 live births in 1960 to 30 per 1,000 in the early 1990s, and as recently as 1970 life expectancy was just 40. Infant mortality, 1990–95, 14 per 1,000 live births; fertility rate, 7·2 births per woman.

In the Human Development Index, or HDI (measuring progress in countries in longevity, knowledge and standard of living), Oman achieved the biggest rise of any country in 1995 compared to 1994, with a jump of 17 places from 88th in the world to 71st.

CLIMATE

Oman has a desert climate, with exceptionally hot and humid months from April to Oct., when temperatures may reach 47°C. Light monsoon rains fall in the south from June to Sept., with highest amounts in the western highland region. Muscat, Jan. 28°C, July 46°C. Annual rainfall 101 mm. Salalah, Jan. 29°C, July 32°C. Annual rainfall 98 mm.

CONSTITUTION AND GOVERNMENT

Oman is a hereditary absolute monarchy. The Sultan legislates by decree and appoints a Cabinet to assist him.

The present Sultan is **Qaboos bin Said Al Said** (born Nov. 1940).

In 1991 a new consultative assembly, the *Majlis al Shura*, replaced the former State Consultative Chamber. The Majlis consists of a president and 59 representatives (including 2 women) who are nominated one from each governorate, and ultimately approved by the Sultan. It debates domestic issues, but has no legislative or veto powers.

National Anthem. 'Ya Rabbana elifidh lana jalalat al Saltan' ('O Lord, protect for us his majesty the Sultan'); words and tune anonymous.

CURRENT ADMINISTRATION

The Sultan is nominally Prime Minister and Minister of Foreign Affairs, Defence and Finance.

The other Ministers were in March 1999:

Special Representative of the Sultan: Thuwayni bin Shihab Al Said.

Deputy Prime Minister for Cabinet Affairs: Fahd bin Mahmud Al Said. *Defence Affairs:* Badr bin Saud bin Harib Al Busaidi. *Foreign Affairs:* Yusuf bin Alawi bin Abdallah. *Agriculture and Fisheries:* Ahmad bin Khalfan bin Muhammad al-Rawahi. *Civil Service:* Abd al-Aziz bin Matar al-Azizi. *Commerce, Industry and Minerals:* Maqbul bin Ali bin Sultan. *Transportation:* Salim bin Abdallah al-Ghazali. *Education:* Saud bin Ibrahim bin Saud Al Busaidi. *Electricity and Water:* Muhammad bin Ali al-Qutaybi. *Regional Municipalities and Environment:* Khamis bin Mubarak bin Isa al-Alawi. *National Economy:* Ahmad bin Abd al-Nabi al-Makki. *Health:* Ali bin Muhammad bin Musa. *Housing:* Malik bin Sulayman al-Mamari. *Information:* Abd al-Aziz bin Muhammad al-Ruwas. *Interior:* Ali bin Hamud bin Ali Al Busaidi. *Justice:* Muhammad bin Abdallah bin Zahir al-Hinai. *National Heritage and Culture:* Faysal bin Ali Al Said. *Oil and Gas:* Muhammad bin Hamad bin Sayf al-Rumhi. *Posts, Telegraphs and Telephones:* Ahmad bin Suwaydan al-Baluchi. *Social Affairs, Labour and Vocational Training:* Amir bin Shuwayn al-Husni. *Awqaf and Religious Affairs:* Abdallah bin Muhammad bin Abdallah al-Salimi. *Diwan of the Royal Court:* Sayf bin Hamad bin Busaidi. *Palace Office Affairs:* Gen. Ali bin Majid al-Mamari. *Water Resources:* Lt.-Gen. Hamid bin Said al-Aufi. *Higher Education:* Yahya bin Mahfudh al-Manthiri. *Legal Affairs:* Muhammad bin Ali bin Nasir al-Alawi. *Development Affairs:* Mohammed bin Moosa al-Yousef. *Minister of State and Governor of the Capital:* Mutasim bin Hamud bin Nasir Al Busaidi. *Minister of State and Governor of Dhofar:* Musalam bin Ali AlBusaidi.

Local Government. Oman is divided into 8 regions and 59 governorates *(wilayats)*.

DEFENCE
Military expenditure in 1997 totalled US$1,815m. (US$887 per capita), representing 10·9% of GDP.

Army. The Army consists of 1 divisional and 2 brigade headquarters, 2 armoured, 1 armoured reconnaissance, 4 artillery, 1 air defence, 8 infantry, 1 infantry reconnaissance, 1 field engineer and 1 airborne regiment and a security force. Equipment includes 6 M-60A1, 43 M-60A3, 24 Chieftain and 18 Challenger 2 main battle tanks. Strength (1997) about 25,000. (Regiments are of battalion size). The armed forces include 6,500 Royal Household troops, and the Musandam Security Force, an independent rifle company. A paramilitary tribal home guard numbers 4,000.

Navy. The Navy, which is based principally at Seeb (HQ) and Wudam, includes 2 new British-built missile corvettes, 4 fast missile craft, 3 coastal and 6 inshore patrol craft. Naval personnel in 1996 totalled 4,200.

The marine police coastguard, 400 strong in 1996, operates 10 coastal patrol craft.

The wholly separate Royal Yacht Squadron consists of a 3,800-tonne yacht and an 11,000-tonne support ship with helicopter and troop-carrying capability.

Air Force. The Air Force, formed in 1959, has 46 combat aircraft including in 1996 two strike/interceptor squadrons of Jaguars, a ground attack squadron of Hawk 200s and a squadron of Strikemaster light jet training/attack aircraft. The defence force has batteries of Rapier low-level surface-to-air missiles. Personnel (1996) about 4,100.

INTERNATIONAL RELATIONS
A 1982 Memorandum of Understanding with the UK provided for regular consultations on international and bilateral issues.

Oman is a member of the UN, the Arab League, the Organization of the Islamic Conference and the Gulf Co-operation Council.

ECONOMY
Policy. The fifth 5-year development plan (1996–2000) projects that total public expenditure during the period will reach RO 10,630 m. The deficit will be reduced to RO 538m., compared with the RO 2,355m. deficit of the fourth 5-year development plan. The non-oil revenue is estimated at RO 2,639m. of total revenue compared with the RO 2,095m. non-oil revenue of the previous plan. The current plan is based on an estimated oil production average of 880,000 bbls. a day valued at US$15 per barrel. If oil revenues exceed the projected barrel price of US$15–17, the surplus will be placed in the State General Reserve Fund. Total revenues are expected to increase by 17·4% from RO 8,595m. to RO 10,092m. Oil revenues are expected to constitute 73·9% of total revenues.

Operating expenditure will amount to RO 8,696m. (81·8% of total Government expenditure) and capital expenditure will amount to RO 1,854m. (17·4%). Contributions and loans to the private sector will amount to about RO 80m.

The public debt will be maintained at RO 1,500m. over the period of the plan. It is expected to range between 20–22% of GDP as the latter expands. The aim is to attain a GDP annual average growth rate of 4·6% at current prices and to increase the GDP share of the non-oil sectors to 69% by the year 2000.

Privatization of water and electricity is under way.

Performance. GDP, 1998: RO 5,890·3m.

Budget. Revenue (1996) RO 1,990·2m. of which RO 1,473m. from oil; expenditure, RO 2,253·7m.

Currency. The unit of currency is the *Rial Omani* (OMR). It is divided into 1,000 *baiza*. The rial is pegged to the US dollar. Foreign exchange reserves were US$1,334m. and gold reserves 290,000 troy oz. in Feb. 1998. Total money supply in Jan. 1998 was RO 566m.

Banking and Finance. The bank of issue is the Central Bank of Oman, which commenced operations in 1975 (*President*, Hamood Sangur Hashim). All banks must comply with BIS capital adequacy ratios and have a minimum capital of OR

10m. In 1998 there were 17 commercial banks. There are 3 specialized banks: The Oman Housing Bank, The Oman Development Bank (which merged with the Oman Agriculture and Fisheries Bank) and the Alliance Housing Bank.

There is a stock exchange in Muscat, which is linked with those in Bahrain and Kuwait.

Weights and Measures. The metric system is in operation.

ENERGY AND NATURAL RESOURCES

Electricity. Installed capacity was 1·74m. kW in 1994. Production in 1995 was 6,500m. kWh. Consumption per capita was estimated to be 3,412 kWh in 1995.

Oil and Gas. The economy is dominated by the oil industry, which provided 83% of Government revenue in 1990 and 49·2% of GDP. Oil in commercial quantities was discovered in 1964 and production began in 1967. Production in 1996 was 853,000 bbls. a day. Total proven reserves were estimated in 1991 to be 5·2m. bbls.

Gas is likely to become the second major source of income for the country. Oman's estimated gas reserves are 25 trillion cu. ft, of which 16 trillion cu. ft are proven, with exploration continuing.

Water. Oman relies on a combination of aquifers and desalination plants for its water, augmented by a construction programme of some 60 recharge dams. Desalination plants at Ghubriah and Wadi Adai provide most of the water needs of the capital area. In 1995 water production was 16,755m. gallons.

Minerals. Production of refined copper at the smelter at Sohar was 12,015 tonnes in 1990. The mountains of the Sultanate of Oman are rich in mineral deposits; these include copper ore, chromite, coal, asbestos, manganese, gypsum, limestone and marble. The government is studying the exploitation of gold, platinum and sulphide.

Agriculture. Agriculture and fisheries are the traditional occupations of Omanis and remain important to the people and economy of Oman to this day. The country now produces a wide variety of fresh fruit, vegetables and field crops. The country is rapidly moving towards its goal of self-sufficiency in agriculture with the total area under cultivation standing at over 70,000 hectares and total output more than 1m. tonnes. This effort has not been achieved without effort. In a country where water is a scarce commodity it has meant educating farmers on efficient methods of irrigation and building recharge dams to make the most of infrequent rainfall.

The coastal plain (Batinah) north-west of Muscat is fertile, as are the Dhofar highlands in the south. In the valleys of the interior, as well as on the Batinah coastal plain, date cultivation has reached a high level, and there are possibilities of agricultural development. The crop of dates was 625,000 tonnes in 1995. Vegetable and fruit production are also important, and livestock are raised in the south where there are monsoon rains. Camels (94,000 in 1995) are bred by the inland tribes. Other livestock, 1996: Sheep, 148,000; cattle, 142,000; goats (1995), 735,000; chickens (1995), 3m. Live animals and meat constitute more than 25% of the country's non-oil exports.

Fisheries. The catch, which is the largest in the Arabian Gulf, was 139,864 tonnes in 1995, exclusively sea fish. More than 80% is taken by some 85,000 self-employed fishermen. Agriculture and fisheries now contribute more than 5% to Oman's GDP.

INDUSTRY

In 1990 manufacturing accounted for only 3·7% of GDP. Apart from oil production, copper mining and smelting and cement production, there are light industries, mainly food processing and chemical products. The government gives priority to import substitute industries.

Labour. Males constituted 85% of the labour force in 1996. In 1995 there were 619,351 employees in the private sector and 110,529 persons in government service. The employment of foreign labour is being discouraged following 'Omanization' regulations of 1994.

INTERNATIONAL TRADE

Total foreign debt was US$3,415m. in 1996. A royal decree of 1994 permits up to 65% foreign ownership of Omani companies with a 5-year tax and customs duties exemption.

OMAN

Imports and Exports. Total imports, 1995: RO 1,683·6m.; exports, RO 2,333·2m. (of which oil: RO 1,829·3m.). Principal non-oil exports are metal, metal goods, animals and products and textiles. Main export markets (% of total trade), 1995: Japan, 28·5; South Korea, 15·8; United Arab Emirates, 10·2; China, 9·7. Main import suppliers: United Arab Emirates, 23·8; Japan, 15·8; UK, 10·5; USA, 6·5.

COMMUNICATIONS

Roads. A network of adequate graded roads links all the main sectors of population, and only a few mountain villages are not accessible by motor vehicles. In 1995 there were 6,257 km of asphalt roads and 24,276 km of graded roads. In Dec. 1995 there were 299,749 cars registered. The average distance travelled by a passenger car in the year 1995 was 37,615 km.

Civil Aviation. Oman has a 25% share in Gulf Air with Bahrain, Qatar and the UAE. For details *see* BAHRAIN: Civil Aviation. In 1998 Gulf Air ran services in and out of Seeb international airport (20 miles from Muscat) to Abu Dhabi, Al Ain, Amman, Amsterdam, Athens, Bahrain, Bangkok, Beirut, Bombay, Cairo, Casablanca, Colombo, Dar es Salaam, Delhi, Dhaka, Doha, Dubai, Entebbe, Hong Kong, Jeddah, Karachi, Khartoum, Kuwait, London, Madras, Manila, Nairobi, Ras Al Khaima, Riyadh, Sharjah, Thiruvananthapuram and Zanzibar. Oman Air also flies on some international routes. Other airlines serving Muscat in 1998 were Air Djibouti, Air India, Air Lanka, Air Tanzania Corporation, American Airlines, Biman Bangladesh Airlines, British Airways, Delta Air Lines, Egyptair, Emirates, Ethiopian Airlines, Indian Airlines, KLM, Kuwait Airways, Pakistan International Airlines, Royal Jordanian, Saudia, Sudan Airways, Swissair, Syrian Arab Airlines and Thai Airways International. In 1996 Muscat handled 2,115,561 passengers and 43,426 tonnes of freight.

Shipping. In Mutrah a deep-water port (named Mina Qaboos) was completed in 1974. The annual handling capacity is 1·5m. tonnes. Mina Salalah, the port of Salalah, has a capacity of 1m. tonnes per year. Sea-going shipping totalled 10,604 GRT in 1995.

Telecommunications. The General Telecommunications Organization maintains a telegraph office at Muscat and an automatic telephone exchange. In 1997 there were 200,600 main telephone lines (86·6 per 1,000 persons). Cellular phone subscribers numbered 8,100 in 1995, and there were 28,000 PCs and 1,600 fax machines. Oman joined the Internet at the end of 1996 and in Jan. 1998 there were approximately 21,000 users.

Postal Services. In 1995 there were 90 post offices.

SOCIAL INSTITUTIONS

Religion. In 1995, 87·7% of the population were Moslem.

Education. Adult literacy was 59% in 1994. In 1995–96 there were 965 schools with 490,482 pupils and 22,506 teachers. Plans have been implemented for the development of technical and agricultural training and craft training at intermediate and secondary level. Oman's first university, the Sultan Qaboos University, opened in 1986 and in 1994–95 there were 4,331 students and 483 academic staff.

In 1994 total expenditure on education came to 4·5% of GNP and represented 15·5% of total government expenditure.

Health. In 1995 there were 53 hospitals with 4,411 beds, 121 health centres, 2,476 doctors, 152 dentists (1993), 370 pharmacists and 6,036 nursing staff.

CULTURE

Broadcasting. The government-owned Radio Oman broadcasts in Arabic and English. A colour (PAL) television service, the government-owned Oman Television, covering Muscat and the surrounding area, started transmission in 1974. A television service for Dhofar opened in 1975. In 1991 there were 7 television stations. Total number of radios, 1·28m., and televisions, 1·45m. (657 per 1,000 inhabitants) in 1995. Television usage has increased dramatically since 1980, when there were just 35,000 TV receivers in Oman (31 per 1,000 inhabitants). Oman had

OMAN

both the greatest percentage increase in the number of TV receivers of any country in the world between 1980 and 1995 and the greatest numerical increase in the number of receivers per 1,000 inhabitants.

Cinema. Oman has 5 cinemas.

Press. There are 3 Arabic-language and 2 English-language daily newspapers.

Tourism. Foreign visitors increased by nearly 50%, from 256,000 in 1993 to 375,000 in 1997. Tourism revenue over this period increased from RO 31m. to RO 48m.

Festivals. National Day (18 Nov.); Spring Festival in Salalah (July–Aug.); Ramadham (Dec.).

Libraries. 3 public libraries are run by the Royal Court of Diwan, the Islamic Institute and the Ministry of National Heritage.

National Theatre and Opera. There is 1 national theatre.

Museums and Galleries. The main attractions are The Omani Museum (est. 1974) at Medinat al-Alam; the Omani-French Museum, Children's Museum, and Bait al-Zubair (a historic house) at Muscat; the Natural History Museum at the Ministry of National Heritage and Culture; The Sultan's Armed Forces museum at Bait al-Falaj; The Oil & Gas Exhibition at Mina al-Fahal. There is also a museum in the historic fort at Sohar.

DIPLOMATIC REPRESENTATIVES
Of Oman in Great Britain (167 Queen's Gate, London, SW7 5HE)
Ambassador: Hussain bin Ali bin Abdullatif.

Of Great Britain in Oman (PO Box 300, Muscat)
Ambassador: R. J. S. Muir, CMG.

Of Oman in the USA (2342 Massachusetts Ave., NW, Washington, D.C., 20008)
Ambassador: Abdulla Moh'd Aqeel Al Dhahab.

Of the USA in Oman (PO Box 202, Medinat Qaboos, Muscat)
Ambassador: John Craig.

Of Oman to the United Nations
Ambassador: Fuad Mubarak Al-Hinai.

FURTHER READING
Carter, J. R. L., *Tribes of Oman.* London, 1981
Clements, F. A., *Oman: The Reborn Land.* London and New York, 1980.—*Oman.* [Bibliography] 2nd ed. Oxford and Santa Barbara (CA), 1994
Hawley, D., *Oman and its Renaissance.* London, 1977
Peterson, J. E., *Oman in the Twentieth Century.* London and New York, 1978
Peyton, W. D., *Oman before 1970: The End of an Era.* London, 1985
Pridham, B. R., (ed.) *Oman: Economic, Social and Strategic Developments.* London, 1987
Shannon, M. O., *Oman and South-Eastern Arabia: A Bibliographic Survey.* Boston, 1978
Skeet, I., *Muscat and Oman: The End of an Era.* London, 1974.—*Oman: Politics and Development.* London, 1992
Wilkinson, J. C., *The Imamate Tradition of Oman.* CUP, 1987

National statistical office: Directorate General of National Statistics, POB 881, Muscat 113.

PAKISTAN

Islami Jamhuriya e Pakistan

(Islamic Republic of
Pakistan)

Capital: Islamabad
Population estimate, 2000: 156·01m.
GNP per capita: (PPP$) 1,600
HDI/world rank: 0·453/138

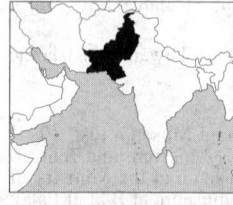

KEY HISTORICAL EVENTS

The State of Pakistan was created on 14 Aug. 1947 by the Partition of India and consisted of the former East Bengal (with a district of Assam), the North West Frontier, Sind, the West Punjab and Balochistan. Kashmir was disputed between Pakistan and India. Pakistan was formed to provide Indian Moslems with their own state. This aim had been expressed by the All-India Moslem League since 1940 and was successfully pressed by Mohammad Ali Jinnah (1876–1948) despite initial strong opposition from the predominantly Hindu Indian National Congress.

East Bengal acceded to Pakistan in 1947 and seceded after civil war in Dec. 1971 when it became the independent republic of Bangladesh.

The North West Frontier was created by the government of British India as a military buffer zone to protect its Indian empire from Tsarist Russian expansion through central Asia; it was administered as a tribal agency, and included parts of the Punjab across the Indus River, the Peshawar valley and the mountain areas between Chitrál and the Vihowa River. The people were Moslem Pathan hill tribes; government contact with them was often difficult but essential to protect the vital routes across the province through the Khyber, Kuram, Tochi and Gomal passes. The centre was Peshawar, an ancient city on a caravan route.

Sind was a tributary state of the Mughal empire from 1592, its people having previously come under Persian and Arabian influence. The British took Sind in 1843 and governed it as part of the Bombay Presidency, developing Karachi as a supply port.

The western Punjab was part of the Sikh homeland annexed by the British in 1849 (*see* India).

Balochistan was an independent state which entered into treaty relations with British India in 1854 and 1876. The British then obtained a small area around Quetta, British Balochistan. They also received the right to fortify and administer Quetta and Bolan and to bring troops into the territory of the paramount Baloch chief, the Khan of Kalat, who in return received a subsidy. Outside Quetta, Bolan and British Balochistan there was Kalat as an independent state and an independent northern area which was not ruled by the khan and was mainly Pathan. In 1887 British Balochistan was incorporated into British India.

In 1947 Pakistan came into being with Jinnah as its first governor-general. The state incorporated the whole of Balochistan, an action which is still the cause of unrest. Pakistan's status was that of a Dominion within the Commonwealth; it became a republic in 1956 and left the Commonwealth in 1972. Efforts to rejoin were opposed by India until 1989 when Pakistan once more became a full member of the Commonwealth.

The first of several periods of martial law began in 1958, followed by the rule of Field Marshal Mohammad Ayub Khan (until 1969) and Maj.-Gen. Agha Mohammad Yahya Khan (until 1971). During the latter's term, differences between East and West Pakistan came to a head. The East Pakistan Awami League won the majority of seats in the general election of 7 Dec. 1970, pressing for autonomy. Martial law continued while attempts were made to negotiate but civil war broke out in March 1971 and ended in Dec. 1971 with the creation of Bangladesh. President Yahya Khan resigned and was succeeded by Zulfiquar Ali Bhutto.

A new constitution came into force on 14 Aug. 1973, providing a federal parliamentary government with a president as head of state and a prime minister as head of the government. Mr Bhutto became prime minister, relinquishing the post of president. His government was thought by traditionalists to be too Western and not sufficiently Islamic. There was an army *coup* led by Gen. Mohammad Zia ul-Haq in July 1977. The prime minister, Zulfiquar Ali Bhutto was hanged for conspiring to murder. Gen. Zia ul-Haq became president in 1978. The constitution of 1973 was held in abeyance and national elections were not held until Feb. 1985. The president set up a National Security Council to control the elected government in March 1985; in April 1985 this was replaced by a Federal Cabinet. Martial law ended on 30 Dec. 1985. The Constitution (Ninth Amendment) Bill, 1986, confirmed Islamic teaching as the basis of national law.

On 6 Aug. 1990 the President, accusing the government of corruption and undermining the constitution, dismissed the Prime Minister, Benazir Bhutto, and all her cabinet, dissolved the National Assembly and declared a state of emergency. New governors were appointed for all 4 provinces. On 18 April 1993 President Ghulam Ishaq Khan dismissed the next Prime Minister, Nawaz Sharif, but he was reinstated by the Constitutional Court. Both President and Prime Minister resigned on 18 July 1993, and new elections took place. On 5 Nov. 1996 the President, Farooq Leghari, accusing the government of corruption and mismanaging the economy, again dismissed the Prime Minister, Benazir Bhutto, and all her cabinet, and dissolved the National Assembly, paving the way for Nawaz Sharif's re-election on 3 Feb. 1997.

Relations between Pakistan and India have foundered on the issue of Kashmir, a disputed territory divided by a cease-fire line negotiated by the UN in 1949. In March 1997 the two countries held talks for the first time in three years.

The invasion of neighbouring Afghanistan by Soviet forces in 1979 caused a flow of Afghan refugees into Pakistan, chiefly into the North West Frontier Province which still functions as a military buffer zone.

On 28 May 1998 Pakistan carried out five nuclear tests in the deserts of Balochistan in response to India's tests earlier in the month. US President Bill Clinton invoked sanctions but Pakistan subsequently carried out a sixth test. With first steps towards a nuclear agreement, the USA lifted most sanctions. On 11 June, following India's example, Pakistan announced a unilateral moratorium on nuclear tests.

TERRITORY AND POPULATION
Pakistan is bounded in the west by Iran, north-west by Afghanistan, north by China, east by India and south by the Arabian Sea. The area (excluding the disputed area of Kashmir) is 307,293 sq. miles (796,095 sq. km); population (1998 census, excluding Azad, Kashmir, Baltistan, Diamir and Gilgit), 130,579,571 (females, 62,739,434).

The UN gives a projected population for 2000 of 156·01m.

In 1995, 65·7% lived in rural areas.

The population of the principal cities is as follows:

1998 census

Karachi	9,269,265	Rawalpindi	1,406,214	Peshawar	988,005
Lahore	5,063,499	Hyderabad	1,151,274	Quetta	560,307
Faisalabad	1,977,246	Gujranwala	1,124,799	Islamabad	524,500

Population of the provinces (census of 1998) in 1,000:

	Area (sq. km)	1998 census population			Urban	1998 density per sq. km (number)
		Total	Male	Female		
North-West Frontier Province	74,521	17,555	8,963	8,592	2,973	236
Federally administered Tribal Areas	27,219	3,138	1,635	1,503	83	115
Federal Capital Territory Islamabad	907	799	430	369	524	881
Punjab	205,344	72,585	37,509	35,076	22,699	353
Sind	140,914	29,991	15,823	14,168	14,662	213
Balochistan	347,190	6,511	3,481	3,030	1,516	19

Urdu is the national language, though only spoken by 7·6% of the population at the 1981 census; English is used in business, higher education and in central government. In 1981, 48% of the population spoke Punjabi.

SOCIAL STATISTICS
1997 births, estimate, 4,950,000; deaths, 1,240,000. Rates, 1997 (per 1,000 population): Birth, 36; death, 9; infant mortality (per 1,000 live births), 90. Formal registration of marriages and divorces has not been required since 1992. Expectation of life was 63·7 years in 1997. Annual growth rate, 1998, 2·3%. Fertility rate, 1990–95, 5·5 births per woman.

CLIMATE
A weak form of tropical monsoon climate occurs over much of the country, with arid conditions in the north and west, where the wet season is only from Dec. to March. Elsewhere, rain comes mainly in the summer. Summer temperatures are high everywhere, but winters can be cold in the mountainous north. Islamabad, Jan. 50°F (10°C), July 90°F (32·2°C). Annual rainfall 36" (900 mm). Karachi, Jan. 61°F (16·1°C), July 86°F (30°C). Annual rainfall 8" (196 mm). Lahore, Jan. 53°F (11·7°C), July 89°F (31·7°C). Annual rainfall 18" (452 mm). Multan, Jan. 51°F (10·6°C), July 93°F (33·9°C). Annual rainfall 7" (170 mm). Quetta, Jan. 38°F (3·3°C), July 80°F (26·7°C). Annual rainfall 10" (239 mm).

CONSTITUTION AND GOVERNMENT
Under the 1973 Constitution, the *President* is elected for a 5-year term by a college of parliamentary deputies, senators and members of the Provincial Assemblies. Parliament is bi-cameral, comprising a *Senate* of 87 members and a *National Assembly* of 217. The 4 Provincial Assemblies each elect 19 senators, the tribal areas are represented by 8 senators elected by the National Assembly and the Federal Capital has 3 representatives. About half the senators are elected for 6-year terms every 3 years. The National Assembly is directly elected with 10 religious minority representatives.

During the period of martial law (1977–85) the Constitution was in abeyance, but not abrogated. In 1985 it was amended to extend the powers of the President, including those of appointing and dismissing ministers and vetoing new legislation until 1990. Legislation of 1 April 1997 abolished the President's right to dissolve parliament, appoint provincial governors and nominate the heads of the armed services.

The Constitution obliges the Government to enable the people to order their lives in accordance with Islam.

National Anthem. 'Pak sarzamin shadbad' ('Blessed be the sacred land'); words by Abul Asr Hafeez Jaulandhari, tune by Abdul Karim Chaagla.

RECENT ELECTIONS
Following the President's dismissal of Benazir Bhutto's government in Nov. 1996, elections were held on 3 Feb. 1997 for the 217 contestable seats in the National Assembly. The electorate was 54m.; turn-out was 38%. The Moslem League (N) gained 142 seats; the Pakistan People's Party, 18. 6 women were elected to the National Assembly. The *Speaker* of the Assembly is Illahi Bukhsh Soomro.

Elections to 46 of the 87 seats of the Senate were held on 21 March 1997. The Moslem League and its sympathizers held 30 seats, the Pakistan People's Party, 19 seats. The Senate has 2 women members. Wasim Sajjad is Chairman of the Senate for the fourth consecutive period.

CURRENT ADMINISTRATION
President: Rafiq Tarar, b. 2 Nov. 1929 (Moslem League; sworn in 1 Jan. 1998).

A Moslem League government was formed on 26 Feb. 1997 which in March 1999 included:

Prime Minister and Minister of Defence: Nawaz Sharif (b. 1949; sworn in 17 Feb. 1997). *Finance and Commerce:* Ishaq Dar. *Foreign Affairs:* Sartaj Aziz. *Kashmir, Northern Areas, State and Frontier Regions:* Majid Malik. *Interior:* Chaudhry

PAKISTAN

Shujaat Hussain. *Water and Power:* Gohar Ayub Khan. *Petroleum and Natural Resources:* Chaudhary Nisar Ali Khan. *Population Welfare:* Syeda Abida Hussain. *Education:* Syed Ghaus Ali Shah. *Communications:* Raja Nadir Pervez. *Food and Agriculture;* Abdul Sattar Laleka. *Health:* Makhdoom Javed Hashmi. *Production and Industries:* Nishat Malik. *Labour, Manpower and Overseas Pakistanis:* Ahmed Rashid. *Law:* Khalid Anwar. *Parliamentary Affairs:* Yasin Wattoo. *Religious Affairs:* Raja Zafarul Haq.

Local Government. Pakistan comprises the Federal Capital Territory (Islamabad), the provinces of the Punjab, the North-West Frontier (NWFP), Sind and Balochistan, and the tribal areas of the north-west. The provincial capitals are Peshawar (NWFP), Lahore (Punjab), Karachi (Sind) and Quetta (Balochistan). Provincial governors are appointed by the President and are assisted by elected provincial assemblies. That of Punjab has 248 seats (8 reserved for non-Moslems); Sind, 99; Balochistan, 40; NWFP, 80. Elections were held on 8 Oct. 1993. Seats gained in the Punjab assembly: PML 106, PPP 94, PML-Junejo 18, ind 17, minor parties 5; Sind: PPP 56, Mohajir 27, PML 8, ind 5, minor parties 3; Balochistan: minor parties 21, ind 9, PML 6, PPP 3, Awami 1; NWFP: PPP 22, Awami 20, PML 15, ind 11, minor parties 7, PML-Junejo 4. Municipal elections were held in the Punjab in Dec. 1991. Direct rule was imposed in Punjab in Sept. 1995.

Within the provinces there are divisions administered by Commissioners appointed by the President; the divisions are divided into districts and agencies administered by Deputy Commissioners or Political Agents who are responsible to the Provincial Governments.

The tribal areas (Khyber, Kurram, Malakand, Mohmand, North Waziristan, South Waziristan) are administered by political agents responsible to the federal government.

DEFENCE

A *Council for Defence and National Security* was set up in Jan. 1997, comprising the President, the Prime Minister, the Ministers of Defence, Foreign Affairs, Interior, Finance and the military chiefs of staff. The Council advises the Government on the determination of national strategy and security priorities.

Defence expenditure in 1997 totalled US$3,503m. (US$26 per capita).

Nuclear weapons. Pakistan began a secret weapons programme in 1972 to reach parity with India, but was restricted for some years by US sanctions. In May 1998 it carried out five nuclear tests in response to India's tests earlier in the month.

Army. The Army is organized into 9 corps headquarters and 1 area command, and consists of 2 armoured and 19 infantry divisions; 7 independent armoured, 9 independent infantry, 9 artillery and 7 engineer brigades; 3 armoured reconnaissance regiments, 1 air defence command and 1 Special Services Group. Equipment includes 120 M–47, 50 T–54/–55, 280 M–48, 1,200 Chinese Type–59, 200 Chinese Type–69 and 200 Chinese Type–85 main battle tanks, 850 surface-to-air and 18 surface-to-surface missiles. The Army has an air component with about 140 fixed-wing aircraft for transport, reconnaissance and observation duties and 150 helicopters for anti-armour operations, transport, liaison and training. Strength (1997) 520,000. There are also 257,000 personnel in paramilitary units: National Guard, Frontier Corps and Pakistan Rangers.

Navy. The combatant fleet comprises 6 French-built diesel submarines, 3 midget submarines for swimmer delivery, 3 ex-US Second World War vintage destroyers and 6 ex-British Amazon and 2 Leander class frigates, 8 fast missile craft, 1 coastal and 4 inshore patrol craft, 3 French-built tripartite minehunters and 2 coastal mine-sweepers. Auxiliaries include 2 fleet replenishment tankers, 1 survey ship and 1 salvage tug. There are about a dozen minor auxiliaries.

The Air Force operates the first of 3 P–3C Orion and 4 Atlantic aircraft under naval control for maritime patrol duties and 3 F–27 patrol aircraft, whilst the Navy operates 6 Sea King helicopters, 2 Lynx and 4 Alouette III anti-submarine and liaison helicopters.

The principal naval base and dockyard are at Karachi. Naval personnel in 1996 totalled 22,000. There is a marine force of 1,200.

A navy-subordinated Maritime Safety Agency, 2,000 strong (1996), operates 1 ex-naval destroyer and 6 fast coastal patrol craft on economic exclusion zone protection duties.

Air Force. The Pakistan Air Force came into being on 14 Aug. 1947. It has its headquarters at Peshawar and is organized within 3 air defence sectors, in the northern, central and southern areas of the country. Air defence units include 3 squadrons of F–16 Fighting Falcons, 5 squadrons of F–7P Skybolts and 3 squadrons of Chinese-built F–6s (MiG–19). Tactical units include 2 squadrons of Mirage 5 supersonic fighters and 3 with A–5 fighter-bombers, 1 squadron equipped with Mirage III strike and reconnaissance aircraft, and 1 with C–130 Hercules turboprop transports. Flying training schools are equipped with Mashshaq (Saab Supporter) armed piston-engined primary trainers, T–33 and T–37B/C jet trainers supplied by the USA, Mirage III–DPs and Chinese-built FT–5s (two-seat MiG–17s) and FT–6s (two-seat MiG–19s). A VIP transport squadron operates the Presidential F27 turboprop aircraft and Boeing 737 jet, 3 four-jet Boeing 707s, 3 twin-jet Falcon 20s and a Puma helicopter. There is a flying college at Risalpur and an aeronautical engineering college at Korangi Creek. Total strength in 1996 was 430 combat aircraft and 45,000 personnel.

INTERNATIONAL RELATIONS

Pakistan is a member of the UN, the Commonwealth (not 1972–89), Organisation of Islamic Conference (OIC), Non-Aligned Movement (NAM), South Asian Association for Regional Cooperation (SAARC), Economic Cooperation Organisation (ECO), Inter-Parliamentary Union (IPU), IMCO, International Atomic Energy Agency (IAEA), D-8, Conference on Disarmament, United Nations Commission on Human Rights, International Narcotics Control Board, United Nations Environment Programme and the Colombo Plan.

ECONOMY

Policy. The 8th Five-Year Plan ran from 1993 to 1998. Growth targets: GDP, 7%; agriculture, 4·9%; manufacturing, 9·9%; services, 6·7%. The 9th Five-Year Plan is currently being formulated by the government and is due to be launched shortly. There is also a Perspective Plan for 1993–2008. There is a Privatization Commission. In Jan. 1999, the IMF approved a loan of US$575m. to Pakistan.

Performance. The pace of economic growth maintained during the 1980s of around 6% accelerated sharply to 7·7% in 1991–92. However it then declined in 1992–93 when the agriculture sector sank to a negative growth of 5·3% whilst the manufacturing sector came down to 5·4%. The downward drift was checked in 1993–94 but in 1996–97 real GDP growth had plummeted to as low as 1·3%. The sharp deceleration in economic activity was mainly due to the poor performance of agriculture and manufacturing which grew by 0·06% and 1·2% respectively. The performances of all other components of national accounts were also far from satisfactory. In 1997–98 both agriculture and manufacturing experienced growth of 6·0%, and real GDP growth for the fiscal year 1997–98 rose to 5·4%, but the economy remains vulnerable with low reserves of foreign exchange and sluggish industrial growth.

Budget. The financial year ends on 30 June. The consolidated federal and provincial revenue collection for 1996–97 was Rs388,248m. (Rs326,508m. from taxes and Rs61,740m. from non-taxes) and expenditure was Rs543,106m. (current expenditure, Rs457,596m.; development, Rs85,150m.). Defence spending, Rs127,441m. Pakistan's foreign debt in 1998 amounted to US$32bn.

Currency. The monetary unit is the *Pakistan rupee* (PKR) of 100 *paisas*. Gold reserves in Feb. 1998 were 2·07m. troy oz.; approved foreign exchange reserves, US$1,144m. Inflation was 11·8% during 1996–97, but had declined to 7·8% by 1997–98. The rupee was devalued by 3·65% in Sept. 1996 and 8% in Oct. 1997, and by 4·2% in June 1998 in response to the financial problems in Asia. In Jan. 1998 total money supply was Rs660,756m.

Banking and Finance. The State Bank of Pakistan is the central bank (*Governor*, Mohammad Yaqub); it came into operation as the Central Bank on 1 July 1948 and was nationalized in 1974 with other banks.

The State Bank of Pakistan is the issuing authority of domestic currency, custodian of foreign exchange reserves and bankers for the federal and provincial governments and for scheduled banks. It also manages the rupee public debt of the federal and provincial governments. The National Bank of Pakistan acts as an agent of the State Bank where the State Bank has no offices of its own.

The State Bank of Pakistan was granted more autonomy in Feb. 1994 to regulate the monetary sector of the economy.

In Jan. 1985 banks and financial institutions abandoned, in conformity with Islamic doctrine, the payment of interest on new transactions. This does not apply to international business, but does apply to the domestic business of foreign banks operating in Pakistan.

Banks were nationalized in 1974, but a federal government decision of Dec. 1990 again allows banks in the private sector. It was announced in Nov. 1990 that 51% of the equity of state-owned banks was to be privatized in 2 phases.

In June 1995 total assets of the issue department of the State Bank of Pakistan amounted to Rs230,613m. and those of the banking department Rs241,329m.; total deposits, Rs135,593m.

In June 1995 there were 40 banks (21 foreign) with total assets of Rs1,654,094m.

There are stock exchanges at Islamabad, Karachi and Lahore.

Weights and Measures. The metric system is in general use.

ENERGY AND NATURAL RESOURCES

Electricity. Installed capacity of the State Power System in 1997–98 was 15·3m. kW, of which 4·82m kW was hydro-electric, 10·34 kW was thermal and 0·14 kW was nuclear. Production in 1997–98 was 58·014bn. kWh, of which 65% was hydro-electric and 35% was thermal. Around 19% was from private power generation. Consumption per capita in 1995 was an estimated 403 kWh. By 1998, 65,473 villages (of a total of 125,083) had access to electric power.

Oil and Gas. Oil production in 1997–98 was 20,543,000 bbls. Exploitation is mainly through government incentives and concessions to foreign private sector companies. Gas production in 1997–98 was 699,709m. cu. ft.

Water. Pakistan's Indus Basin irrigation system is the largest and oldest in the world. It includes a network of 43 independent canal systems and 2 storage reservoirs. Total length of main canals is 58,000 km which serve 35m. acres of cultivatable land.

Currently 3 major surface water projects are under way, as are flood control schemes and programmes to check the problems of waterlogging and salinity.

Minerals. Production (tonnes, 1997–98): Coal, 3·50m.; chromite, 30,000; limestone, 9·94m.; gypsum, 310,000; rock salt, 960,000; fire clay, 93,000; bauxite, 26·9m.; barytes, 30,000; china clay, 66,000; dolomite, 146,046; fullers earth, 15,154. Other minerals of which useful deposits have been found are magnesite, sulphur, marble, antimony ore, bentonite, celestite, fluorite, phosphate rock, silica sand and soapstone.

Agriculture. The north and west are covered by mountain ranges. The rest of the country consists of a fertile plain watered by 5 big rivers and their tributaries. Agriculture is dependent almost entirely on the irrigation system based on these rivers. Area irrigated, 1996–97, 17·85m. ha. Agriculture employs around half of the workforce and in 1997–98 contributed 24·6% of GDP.

Pakistan is self-sufficient in wheat, rice and sugar. Areas harvested, 1997–98: Wheat, 8·4m. ha; rice, 2·3m. ha; sugar-cane, 1·1m. ha; cotton, 2·69m. ha; maize, 0·87m. ha. Production, 1997–98 (1,000 tonnes): Rice, 4,333; wheat, 18,894; sugar-cane, 53,104; cotton, 1,562; maize, 1,251; dates, 537·5; sorghum, 219; millet, 211·3.

A Land Reforms Act of 1977 reduced the upper limit of land holding to 100 irrigated or 200 non-irrigated acres. A new agricultural income tax was introduced in 1995, from which holders of up to 25 irrigated or 50 unirrigated acres are exempt.

Of about 5m. farms, 12% are of less than 10 ha. In 1997–98, 31·87m. ha were arable land; 22·73m. ha were cropland; 3·58m. ha were forest.

Livestock, 1997–98 (in 1m.): Cattle, 21·4; buffaloes, 20·2; sheep, 23·8; goats, 44·2; camels, 0·8; poultry, 276.

Dairy products, 1997–98 (in 1,000 tonnes): Mutton and lamb, 1,075; beef and buffalo, 1,082; wool, 57·2; milk, 22,039; eggs, 57·37m. units.

Forestry. The area under forests in 1997–98 was 3·58m. ha, some 4·5% of the total land area. The government considers a 20–25% coverage desirable for economic growth and environmental stability. 0·13m. cu. metres of timber and 0·22m. cu. metres of firewood were produced by state-owned forests in 1996–97.

Fisheries. In 1997–98 the catch totalled 590,000 tonnes, approximately 75% from marine waters and the rest from inland waters.

INDUSTRY
Industry is based largely on agricultural processing, with engineering and electronics. Government policy is to encourage private industry, particularly small industry. The public sector, however, is still dominant in large industries. Steel, cement, fertilizer and vegetable ghee are the most valuable public sector industries.

Production in tonnes in 1997–98: Cement, 9,400,000; sugar, 3,554,774; cotton yarn, 1,533,000; pig-iron, 1,015,827; vegetable products, 678,050; hot-rolled steel sheets and coils, 422,193; cold-rolled, 220,003; steel billets, 348,145; soda ash, 239,315; caustic soda, 115,675; paper and board, 344,792; tea, 58,704; jute textiles, 91,971; sulphuric acid, 27,610; coke, 662,121 (1996–97); cotton cloth, 339·9m. sq. metres.; jeeps and cars, 35,687 items; tractors, 14,012 items; bicycles, 952,124 items.

Labour. Out of 33·05m. people in employment in 1995, 4·81m. were females. In 1994, 50·04% of the economically active workforce were engaged in agriculture, forestry and fishing, 10·3% in manufacturing; the textile industry was the largest single manufacturing employer. Services employed 13·2%; commerce, 12·78%; construction, 6·5%; transport, storage and communication, 4·95%. 1·6m. were unemployed (0·52m. females) in 1992. At the end of 1993, 183,801 job seekers were registered at labour exchanges.

In 1994 there were 25 industrial disputes and 341,196 working days were lost.

Trade Unions. In 1997 there were 7,355 trades unions with a membership of 1,022,275.

INTERNATIONAL TRADE
Foreign debt was US$28,600m. in 1996. Most foreign exchange controls were removed in Feb. 1991. Foreign investors may repatriate both capital and profits, and tax exemptions are available for companies set up before 30 June 1995.

Imports and Exports. In 1996–97 imports were valued at Rs465,001m., exports at Rs325,313m., and re-exports at Rs2,662m. Major exports in 1996–97 (in Rs1m.): cotton yarns, 55,239; cotton cloth, 49,354; rice, 18,453; leather, 9,322; carpets, 7,820; raw cotton, 1,239. Major imports in 1996–97 (in Rs1m.): machinery, 128,849; minerals and fuels, 93,389; chemicals, 77,020; manufactures, 43,391; food and animals, 42,884; oils and fats, 25,981.

Major export markets in 1996–97 (in Rs1m.): USA, 57,629; Hong Kong, 30,462; Germany, 24,408; UK, 23,282; Japan, 18,700. Major import suppliers in 1996–97 (in Rs1m.): USA, 55,966; Japan, 40,137; Kuwait, 32,243; Saudi Arabia, 27,793; Germany, 26,209.

COMMUNICATIONS

Roads. According to officially revised figures, in 1997–98 there were 240,885 km of roads, of which 133,462 km were 'high type' roads. In 1997 there were 141,283 trucks, 133,783 buses, 83,142 taxis, 1,048,906 motor cars, jeeps and station wagons, 1,969,162 motor cycles (2 wheels) and 75,131 motor cycles (3 wheels), and 669,603 other vehicles, totalling 4,121,010. There were 10,916 road accidents in 1993–94, with 4,511 fatalities.

PAKISTAN

A US$1bn. 333-km motorway linking Islamabad and Lahore was opened in 1998, and a new Karachi to Peshawar highway is under construction.

All traffic in Pakistan drives on the left. All cars must be insured and registered. Minimum age for driving: 18 years.

Rail. Pakistan Railways had (1997–98) a route length of 8,775 km (of which 293 km electrified) mainly on 1,676 mm gauge, with some metre gauge line. In 1997–98, 64·9m. passengers and 5·98m. tonnes of freight were carried.

Civil Aviation. There are international airports at Karachi, Islamabad, Lahore, Peshawar and Quetta.

The national carrier is Pakistan International Airlines, or PIA (founded 1955; 56% of shares are held by the Government). It covers 55 international and 37 domestic stations. In 1998 services were also provided by Aero Asia, Aeroflot, Air China, Air Djibouti, Air Lanka, Aviacompany Turkmenistan, Bhoja Air, Biman Bangladesh Airlines, British Airways, Delta Air Lines, Egyptair, Emirates, Ethiopian Airlines, Gulf Air, Indian Airlines, Iran Air, Kenya Airways, KLM, Kuwait Airways, Kyrgyzstan Airlines, Lufthansa, Malaysia Airlines, Oman Air, Qatar Airways, Royal Jordanian, Saudia, Shaheen Air International, Singapore Airlines, Swissair, Syrian Arab Airlines, Thai Airways International, Turkish Airlines, United Airlines, Uzbekiston Airways, Xinjiang Airlines and Yemenia Yemen Airways. During 1997–98, 73,663,000 revenue km were flown, compared with 78,796,000 during 1996–97. The revenue passengers carried were 5,531m. and revenue tonne km were 1,425m. during 1997–98. Operating revenues of the corporation stood at Rs16,745bn. and operating expenditure at Rs19,603bn. during 1997–98.

Shipping. In 1996–97 ocean-going shipping totalled 0·58m. tonnes, including oil tankers, 90,821 GRT. There are ports at Karachi and Port Qasim. Cargo handled at Karachi 1997–98 (tonnes): imports, 12,796,000; exports, 4,224,000. Port Qasim: imports, 10,821,000; exports, 200,000. In 1995–96, 2,093 international vessels entered, and 2,087 cleared, these ports.

Telecommunications. The telegraph and telephone system is government-owned. Main telephone lines numbered 2,750,000 in June 1998 (2·2 per 100 population). There were 448 telegraph offices working in the country and 50,000 internet users. In 1995 there were 159,000 fax machines, 155,000 PCs and 43,000 cellular phone subscribers.

Postal Services. In 1997–98 there were 13,216 post offices.

SOCIAL INSTITUTIONS

Justice. The Federal Judiciary consists of the Supreme Court of Pakistan, which is a court of record and has three-fold jurisdiction; original, appellate and advisory. There are 4 High Courts in Lahore, Peshawar, Quetta and Karachi. Under the Constitution, each has power to issue directions of writs of *Habeas Corpus, Mandamus, Certiorari* and others. Under them are district and sessions courts of first instance in each district; they have also some appellate jurisdiction. Criminal cases not being sessions cases are tried by judicial magistrates. There are subordinate civil courts also.

The Constitution provides for an independent judiciary, as the greatest safeguard of citizens' rights. There is an Attorney-General, appointed by the President, who has right of audience in all courts and the Parliament, and a Federal Ombudsman.

A Federal Shariat Court at the High Court level has been established to decide whether any law is wholly or partially un-Islamic. In Aug. 1990 a presidential ordinance decreed that the criminal code must conform to Islamic law (Shariah), and in May 1991 parliament passed a law incorporating it into the legal system.

320,807 crimes were reported in 1994 (290,255 in 1993). Execution of the death penalty for murder, in abeyance since 1986, was resumed in 1992. There were 8,303 murders in 1994 (7,258 in 1993).

Religion. Pakistan was created as a Moslem state. The Moslems are mainly Sunni, with an admixture of 15–20% Shi'ite. Religious groups: Moslems, 97%; Christians, 2%; Hindus, Parsees, Buddhists, and others. There is a Minorities Wing at the Religious Affairs Ministry to safeguard the constitutional rights of religious minorities.

Education. The National Education Policy (1998–2010) was launched in March 1998. The major aim was the eradication of illiteracy and the spread of a basic education. The policy stresses vocational and technical education, disseminating a common culture based on Islamic ideology. The principle of free and compulsory primary education has been accepted as the responsibility of the state; duration has been fixed provisionally at 5 years. The adult literacy rate in 1997–98 was 40·0%. Adult literacy programmes are being strengthened.

About 76% of children aged 5–9 are enrolled at school. Figures for 1997–98:

	Students (in 1,000)	Teachers (in 1,000)	Institutions
Primary	15,050	346·0	150,000
Middle	4,790	100·8	15,900
Secondary	2,050	160·7	11,000
Secondary vocational	34	3·5	435
Colleges	360	20·9	535
Universities	73	6·9	42

Health. In 1997 there were 865 hospitals and 4,253 dispensaries (with a total of 89,929 beds) and 853 maternity and child welfare centres. There were 78,470 doctors, 3,159 dentists and 28,661 nurses.

CULTURE

The Government of Pakistan established the Pakistan National Council of the Arts, a cultural organization to promote art and culture in Pakistan and abroad.

Broadcasting. The Pakistan Broadcasting Corporation is an autonomous body operating 24 stations for 19 regional languages. 5 of its major stations have 3 channels (2 AM and 1 FM). The second AM is generally reserved for sports, educational and entertainment broadcasting whilst FM channels cater mostly for music lovers. A school channel has recently been started on FM.

The network of PBC transmitters consists of 28 medium wave transmitters with a radiating power of 2,261 kW, 13 short wave transmitters of 1,131 kW and 5 FM transmitters of 12 kW. It covers 95% of the population and 75% of the total area of the country. A separate government authority, Azad Kashmir Radio, broadcasts in Kashmir.

The commercial Pakistan Television Corporation transmits on 13 VHF/UHF channels (colour by PAL). PTV's signal is also uplinked through Asiasat Transponder. There are 6 PTV centres in the major cities—Islamabad, Lahore, Karachi, Peshawar and Quetta. Its HQ is in Islamabad. Its transmissions reach 89% of the population. In 1996, 10m. radio and 2·7m. TV sets were in use.

Cinema. There were 650 screens in 1997. 66 full-length films were made in 1997 in Urdu, Punjabi, Pushto and Sindhi. There were 7 film studios.

Press. In 1995 there were 370 dailies, 506 weeklies, 62 fortnightlies and 373 periodicals of lesser frequencies. Average circulation of all dailies in 1995 was 3,580,934.

Tourism. In 1997 there were 351,000 foreign tourists, of whom 21·5% came from the UK. More than half of foreign tourist arrivals in 1997 were for the purpose of visiting friends and relatives, followed by business (18·3%), holidays and recreation (13·4%) and religion (2·5%). Tourist revenue in 1996 was US$146m.

Festivals. Pakistan is rich in culture. Famous festivals include the Eid Festival, Eid-e-Milad un Nabi (Birthday of Prophet Muhammad P.B.U.H.), the Basnat Festival, Shah-e-Baraat Festival, and the Independence Day Festival. There are also regional folk festivals that take place throughout the year, such as Mela Cheraghan, Urs Data Ganj Baksh and Bri Imam.

Libraries. The Liaqat National Library is in Karachi, and the library of the National Archives is in Islamabad. Baitul Quran at Lahore is exclusively devoted to the manuscripts of the Holy Quran. The libraries of the Punjab University, Karachi University and the Quaid-i-Azam library in Lahore hold a combined 700,000 volumes.

National Theatre and Opera. There are regular theatrical productions throughout the country. There are 15 fully equipped Theatre Halls in Rawalpindi, Lahore, Karachi and Peshawar, and traditional street theatre is still prominent.

Museums and Galleries. There are dozens of galleries and museums in Islamabad, Lahore, Karachi, Peshawar and Quetta. Amongst the most famous are the National Art Gallery, Shakir Ali Museum, Choukandi Art Gallery, Karachi Art Council, Tasneen Art Gallery, the Lahore Art Museum, the National Heritage Museum and the National Archives. There are also dozens of archaeological sites in Pakistan dating back to 3,000 BC.

DIPLOMATIC REPRESENTATIVES
Of Pakistan in Great Britain (35–36 Lowndes Sq., London, SW1X 9JN)
High Commissioner: Mian Riaz Samee.

Of Great Britain in Pakistan (Diplomatic Enclave, Ramna 5, Islamabad)
High Commissioner: Sir David Dain, KCVO, CMG.

Of Pakistan in the USA (2315 Massachusetts Ave., NW, Washington, D.C., 20008)
Ambassador: Riaz Khokhar.

Of the USA in Pakistan (Diplomatic Enclave, Ramna, 5, Islamabad)
Ambassador: Thomas W. Simons.

Of Pakistan to the United Nations
Ambassador: Ahmad Kamal.

Of Pakistan to the European Union
Ambassador: Riaz M. Khan.

FURTHER READING
Government Planning Commission. *Eighth Five Year Plan, 1993–1998.* Karachi, 1994
Federal Bureau of Statistics.—*Pakistan Statistical Yearbook.—Statistical Pocket Book of Pakistan.* (annual)
Ahmed, A. S., *Jinnah, Pakistan and Islamic Identity: The Search for Saladin.* London, 1997
Ahsan, A., *The Indus Saga and the Making of Pakistan.* Oxford, 1997
Akhtar, R., *Pakistan Year Book.* Karachi/Lahore
Bhutto, B., *Daughter of the East.* London, 1988
Burki, S. J., *Historical Dictionary of Pakistan.* Metuchen (NJ), 1991.—*Pakistan: the Continuing Search for Nationhood.* 2nd ed. Boulder (Colo.), 1992
Choudhury, G. W., *Pakistan: Transition from Military to Civilian Rule.* London, 1988
Gilmartin, D., *Empire and Islam: Punjab and the making of Pakistan.* London, 1988
Hyman, A. *et al., Pakistan: Zia and After.* London, 1989
James, W. E. and Roy, S. (eds.) *The Foundations of Pakistan's Political Economy: towards an Agenda for the 1990s.* London, 1992
Joshi, V. T., *Pakistan: Zia to Benazir.* Delhi, 1995
Kapur, A., *Pakistan in Crisis.* London, 1991
Lamb, C., *Waiting for Allah: Pakistan's Struggle for Democracy.* London, 1991
Low, D. A. (ed.), *The Political Inheritance of Pakistan.* London, 1991
Malik, I. H., *State and Civil Society in Pakistan: the Politics of Authority, Ideology and Ethnicity.* London, 1996
Taylor, D., *Pakistan.* [Bibliography] Oxford and Santa Barbara, 1989

National library: National Library of Pakistan, Islamabad.
National statistical office: Federal Bureau of Statistics, Statistics Division, Karachi.

PALAU

Republic of Palau

Capital: Koror
Population estimate, 2000: 18,000
Estimated GDP: $81·8m.

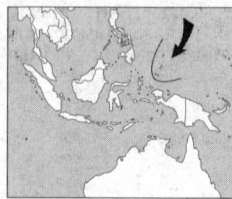

KEY HISTORICAL EVENTS

The actual origin of the first Palauans is uncertain but archaeological and linguistic studies have shown that Malays from Indonesia, Melanesians from New Guinea and some Polynesians formed the basic genetic stock, resulting in a diversity of facial types. Palauan money consisting of orange and yellow glass beads, similar to money found in Indonesia, helps in tracing the origins of Palauans to the Malay region. Ancient village sites on one of the islands which make up Palau have been carbon-dated to 1000 BC.

The most noteworthy first foreign contact occurred in 1783 when the vessel *Antelope*, under the command of its English captain Henry Wilson, was shipwrecked. With the assistance of the local High Chief, he and his men were able to stay for three months to rebuild the ship.

Spain acquired sovereignty over the Palau Islands in 1886 but sold the archipelago to Germany in 1899. Japan occupied the islands in 1914, and in 1921 they were mandated to Japan by the League of Nations. Captured by Allied Forces in 1944, the islands became part of the UN Trust Territory of the Pacific Islands created on 18 July 1947 and administered by the USA. Following a referendum in July 1978 in which Palauans voted against joining the new Federated States of Micronesia, the islands became an autonomous republic from 1 Jan. 1981, but acquisition of a free-association status with the USA was delayed by disputes over US intentions to base nuclear weapons on the islands. At a referendum in Nov. 1993 (the ninth of a series) 68% of votes cast favoured a Compact of Free Association with the USA, which provides US$450m. over 15 years in return for military facilities.

Palau became an independent republic on 1 Oct. 1994.

TERRITORY AND POPULATION

The archipelago lies in the Western Pacific and has a total area of 1,632 sq. km (630 sq. miles); water covers 1,124 sq. km (434 sq. miles). It comprises 26 islands and over 300 islets. Only 8 of the islands are inhabited, the largest being Babelthuap (368 sq. km), but most inhabitants live on the small island of Koror (8 sq. km) to the south, containing the present headquarters (a new capital is being built in eastern Babelthuap). Koror had an estimated population of 11,500 in 1995. The total population at the time of the 1990 census was 15,122; 1996 estimate, 17,000, giving a density of 33 per sq. km.

In 2000 the population is projected to be 18,000.

In 1995 an estimated 71·2% of the population lived in urban areas. Some 6,000 Palauans live abroad. The local language is Palauan; both Palauan and English are official.

SOCIAL STATISTICS

1996 approx. births, 370; deaths, 110. Rates, 1996 (per 1,000 population): Births, 21·6; deaths, 6·6; infant mortality (per 1,000 live births), 25·1. Expectation of life: Males, 69 years; females, 73.

CLIMATE

Palau has a pleasantly warm climate throughout the year with temperatures averaging 81°F (27°C). The heaviest rainfall is between July and Oct.

CONSTITUTION AND GOVERNMENT

The Constitution was adopted on 2 April 1979 and took effect from 1 Jan. 1981. The Republic has a bicameral legislature, the *Olbiil era Kelulau* (National Congress), comprising a 16-member *Senate* (one from each of the Republic's 16 component

PALAU

states) and an 18-member *House of Delegates*, both elected for a term of 4 years as are the *President* and *Vice-President*. Customary social roles and land and sea rights are allocated by a matriarchal 16-clan system.

RECENT ELECTIONS
At the elections on 12 Nov. 1992, Kuniwo Nakamura was elected President by 4,841 votes to 4,707 against a single opponent. He was re-elected in 1996, defeating two other candidates and gaining 62% of the votes cast in the second round on 5 Nov. At the National Congress elections which were also held on 5 Nov. 1996 only non-partisans were elected.

CURRENT ADMINISTRATION
President: Kuniwo Nakamura.
  Vice-President: Tommy Remengesau.

INTERNATIONAL RELATIONS
Palau is a member of the UN, the South Pacific Forum and the Pacific Community.

ECONOMY
Performance. Real GDP growth was 2·5% in 1995 (1·8% in 1994).

Budget. Revenues for 1997 are estimated at US$52·9m. and expenditures at US$59·9m.

Currency. US currency is used.

Banking and Finance. The National Development Bank of Palau is situated in Koror.

ENERGY AND NATURAL RESOURCES
Agriculture. The main agricultural products are bananas, coconuts, copra, cassava and sweet potatoes.

Fisheries. In 1995 the catch totalled approximately 1,450 tonnes, mainly tuna.

INDUSTRY
There is little industry, but the principal activities are food-processing and boat-building.

Labour. The economically active population totalled 10,686 in 1995, of whom 2,630 worked in government services, 1,896 in agriculture and 1,005 in tourism.

INTERNATIONAL TRADE
Imports and Exports. Imports (1989) US$24·6m. Exports (1989) US$600,000. The main trading partners are the USA and Japan for exports and the USA for imports.

COMMUNICATIONS
Roads. There were 61 km of roads in 1996 of which 36 km are paved.

Civil Aviation. The main airport is on Koror (Airai). In 1998 Continental Airlines flew daily to Guam and there were also scheduled services to Manila and Yap (Micronesia). Far Eastern Air Transport had flights twice a week in 1998 to Kaohsiung (Taiwan).

Shipping. In 1985, 56,000 tonnes of cargo were discharged and 2,000 tonnes were loaded.

Telecommunications. In 1988 there were 1,500 telephones.

SOCIAL INSTITUTIONS
Justice. There is a Supreme Court and various subsidiary courts.

Religion. The majority of the population are Roman Catholic.

Education. In 1987 there were 2,784 pupils in 26 primary schools, 1,009 pupils in 6 secondary schools and 382 students (1984) in a technical school. The adult literacy rate is 92%.

Health. In 1990 there were 10 doctors and 84 nurses, and in 1986, 1 hospital with 70 beds.

CULTURE

Broadcasting. There is a radio station (WSZB) which broadcasts daily on AM and FM, and ICTV Cable TV presents 12 channels with CNN. In 1993 there were an estimated 1,600 televisions and 9,000 radios.

Press. The local newspaper *Tia Belau* is published bi-weekly.

Tourism. Tourism is a major industry, particularly marine-based. There were 44,000 foreign tourists in 1996.

DIPLOMATIC REPRESENTATIVES
Of Great Britain in Palau
Ambassador: Vernon M. Scarborough (resides in the Fiji Islands).

Of Palau in the USA (1150 18th Street, NW, Suite 750, Washington D.C., 20036)
Ambassador: Hersey Kyota.

Of the USA in Palau
Ambassador: Thomas C. Hubbard (resides in The Philippines).

Of Palau at the United Nations
Ambassador: Vacant.

PANAMA

República de Panamá

Capital: Panama City
Population estimate, 2000: 2·86m.
GNP per capita: (PPP$) 7,060
HDI/world rank: 0·868/45

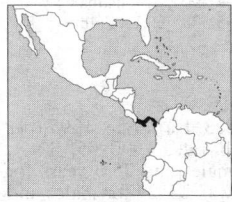

KEY HISTORICAL EVENTS

A revolution, inspired by the USA, led to the separation of Panama from the United States of Colombia and the declaration of its independence on 3 Nov. 1903. The *de facto* government was recognized by the USA on 5 Nov., and soon afterwards by the other major powers. Diplomatic relations between Colombia and Panama were finally established on 8 May 1924.

On 18 Nov. 1903 a treaty between the USA and the Republic of Panama was signed making it possible for the USA to build and operate a canal connecting the Atlantic and Pacific oceans through the Isthmus of Panama. The treaty granted the USA in perpetuity the use, occupation and control of a Canal Zone, in which the USA would possess full sovereign rights. In return the USA guaranteed the independence of the republic and agreed to pay the republic US$10m. and an annuity of US$250,000. The USA purchased the French rights and properties—the French had been labouring from 1879 to 1899 in an effort to build the canal—for US$40m. and in addition paid private landholders within what would be the Canal Zone a mutually agreeable price for their properties. The Canal was opened on 15 Aug. 1914.

The US domination of Panama has provoked frequent anti-American political actions. In 1968 a more independently minded president, Col. Omar Torryas Herrera, took power in a *coup* and attempted to negotiate a more advantageous treaty with the USA. Two new treaties between Panama and the USA were agreed on 10 Aug. and signed on 7 Sept. 1977. One deals with the operation and defence of the Canal until the end of 1999 and the other guarantees permanent neutrality.

The USA maintains operational control over all lands, waters and installations, including military bases, necessary to manage, operate and defend the Canal until 31 Dec. 1999. Six months after the exchange of instruments of ratification Panama assumed general territorial jurisdiction over the former Canal Zone and became able to use portions of the area not needed for the operation and defence of the Canal.

Torryas vacated the presidency in 1978 but maintained his power as head of the National Guard until his death in an air crash in 1981. Subsequently Gen. Manuel Noriega, Torryas' successor as head of the National Guard, became the strong man of the régime. His position was threatened by some internal political opposition and economic pressure applied by the USA but in Oct. 1989 a US-backed coup attempt failed. On 15 Dec. Gen. Noriega declared a 'state of war' with the USA. On 20 Dec. the USA invaded Panama to remove Gen. Noriega from power and he surrendered on 3 Jan. 1990. Accused as a drug dealer he was convicted by a court in Miami and is now serving a 40-year jail sentence. Currently Panama is preparing for life without America. By 31 Dec. 1999 all American troops—10,000 a few years ago—will have left.

TERRITORY AND POPULATION

Panama is bounded in the north by the Caribbean Sea, east by Colombia, south by the Pacific Ocean and west by Costa Rica. The area is 75,517 sq. km. Population at the census of 1990 was 2,329,329 (49% urban; estimate, 56% in 1996). July 1997 estimate, 2·7m.; density, 36 per sq. km.

The UN gives a projected population for 2000 of 2·86m.

The largest towns (1995) are Panama City, the capital, on the Pacific coast (658,102); its suburb San Miguelito (290,919); Colón, the port on the Atlantic coast (156,289); and David (113,527).

The areas and populations of the 9 provinces and the Special Territory were:

Province	Sq. km	Census 1980	1995 (est.)	Capital
Bocas del Toro	9,506	53,579	119,336	Bocas del Toro
Chiriquí	8,924	287,801	407,849	David
Veraguas	11,226	173,195	219,049	Santiago

PANAMA

Province	Sq. km	Census 1980	1995 (est.)	Capital
Herrera	2,185	81,866	101,198	Chitré
Los Santos	4,587	70,200	79,935	Las Tablas
Coclé	4,981	140,320	189,579	Penonomé
Colón	7,205 }	166,439	226,139	Colón
San Blas (Special Territory)	3,206 }			El Porvenir
Panama	11,400	830,278	1,232,390	Panama City
Darién	15,458	26,497	55,538	La Palma

The official language is Spanish.

SOCIAL STATISTICS
1995 births, 62,000; deaths, 14,000; marriages (1994), 13,523. Birth rate, 1995 (per 1,000 population): 23·7; death rate: 5·2. Annual growth rate, 1990–95, 1·9%. Expectation of life at birth, 1990–95, was 70·9 years for males and 75·0 years for females. In 1994 the most popular age range for marrying was 25–29 for males and 20–24 for females. Infant mortality, 1990–95, 25 per 1,000 live births; fertility rate, 2·9 births per woman.

CLIMATE
A tropical climate, unvaryingly with high temperatures and only a short dry season from Jan. to April. Rainfall amounts are much higher on the north side of the isthmus. Panama City, Jan. 79°F (26·1°C), July 81°F (27·2°C). Annual rainfall 70" (1,770 mm). Colón, Jan. 80°F (26·7°C), July 80°F (26·7°C). Annual rainfall 127" (3,175 mm). Balboa Heights, Jan. 80°F (26·7°C), July 81°F (27·2°C). Annual rainfall 70" (1,759 mm). Cristóbal, Jan. 80°F (26·7°C), July 81°F (27·2°C). Annual rainfall 130" (3,255 mm).

CONSTITUTION AND GOVERNMENT
The 1972 Constitution, as amended in 1978 and 1983, provides for a *President*, elected for 5 years, 2 *Vice-Presidents* and a 72-seat *Legislative Assembly* to be elected for 5-year terms by a direct vote. To remain registered, parties must have attained at least 50,000 votes at the last election. A referendum held on 15 Nov. 1992 rejected constitutional reforms by 64% of votes cast. Turn-out was 40%. In a referendum on 30 Aug. 1998 voters rejected proposed changes to the constitution which would allow for a President to serve a second consecutive term.

National Anthem. 'Alcanzamos por fin la victoria' ('We achieve victory in the end'); words by J. de la Ossa, tune by Santos Jorge.

RECENT ELECTIONS
Presidential and parliamentary elections were held on 8 May 1994. The electorate was 1,499,848; turn-out was 73·7%. Ernesto Pérez Balladares was elected President by 33·3% of votes cast against 6 opponents. Representatives of 16 parties stood for election to the Legislative Assembly, 13 grouped in alliances. The Revolutionary Democratic Party (RDP) gained 31 seats in the 'United People' alliance with the Liberal Republican Party (LRP; 1) and the Labour Party (1); the Arnulfist Party (AP) gained 15 in the 'Democratic Alliance' with the Authentic Liberal Party (4), the National Liberal Party (1) and the Democratic Independent Union (1); the Papá Egoró Movement gained 6; the Liberal Republican Nationalist Movement (MORILENA) gained 5 in the 'Change 94' alliance with the Civil Renovation Party (3) and the National Renovation Party (1); the Solidarity Party gained 2; the Christian Democrat Party gained 1.
Presidential and parliamentary elections were scheduled for May 1999.

CURRENT ADMINISTRATION
President: Ernesto Pérez Balladares (RDP; sworn in 1 Sept. 1994).
First Vice-President: Tomas Altamirano Duque; *Second Vice-President:* Felipe Virzi.
In March 1999 the government comprised:
Minister of Government and Justice: Mariela Sagela. *Foreign Relations and Canal Affairs:* Jorge Eduardo Ritter. *Public Works:* Luis Blanco. *Economy and*

Finance: Fernando Aramburu Porras. *Agricultural Development:* Manuel Miranda. *Commerce and Industry:* Raúl Hernandez. *Health:* Aida de Rivera. *Labour and Social Welfare:* Reynaldo Rivera. *Education:* Pablo Thalassinos. *Housing:* Roosevelt Thayer. *Women, Youth, Family and Childhood:* Leonor Calderon. *Minister of the Presidency:* Olmedo Miranda.

Local Government. The 9 provinces and a Special Territory are divided into 67 municipal districts and sub-divided into 511 local authorities.

DEFENCE
The armed forces were disbanded in 1990 and constitutionally abolished in 1994. Divided between both coasts, the National Maritime Service, a coast guard rather than a navy, comprises 5 inshore patrol craft and 1 LCM amphibious craft. In 1996 personnel totalled 400. In 1997 defence expenditure totalled US$114m. (US$41 per capita). For Police *see* JUSTICE, *below.*

INTERNATIONAL RELATIONS
Panama is a member of the UN, OAS Non-aligned Movement, WTO.

ECONOMY
Policy. A 5-year programme of trade liberalization aims to attract foreign investment. Hopes of diversifying an economy heavily dependent on the Canal rest largely on shipping services, mining and tourism.

Performance. Real GDP growth was 3·0% in 1995 (3·7% in 1994).

Budget. Revenues in 1996 were 2,140·3m. balboas (2,065·1m. balboas in 1995); expenditures were 2,255·3m. balboas in 1996 (1,953·3m. balboas in 1995).

Currency. The monetary unit is the *balboa* (PAB) of 100 *centésimos*, at parity with the US dollar. The only paper currency used is that of the USA. US coinage is also legal tender. The average annual inflation rate over the period 1990–96 was 2·7%. In Feb. 1998 foreign exchange reserves were US$1,103m. In Dec. 1997 total money supply was 996m. balboas.

Banking and Finance. There is no statutory central bank. Banking is supervised and promoted by the National Banking Commission. Government accounts are handled through the state-owned *Banco Nacional de Panama.* There are 2 other state banks. The number of commercial banks was 108 in 1996. Total assets, June 1996, US$33,400m., total deposits, US$25,000m. (including offshore, US$15,900m.).

Weights and Measures. US Customary weights and measures are in general use; the metric system is the official system.

ENERGY AND NATURAL RESOURCES
Electricity. In 1995 capacity was 921 MW. Output, 1995, 551 MWh. Production was 3·52bn. kWh in 1995, with consumption per capita in 1995 estimated at 1,069 kWh.

Minerals. Limestone, clay and salt are produced. There are known to be copper deposits.

Agriculture. In 1994 there were 500,000 ha of arable land, 165,000 ha of permanent crops and 1·47m. ha of permanent pasture. Agriculture accounted for 8% of GDP in 1996. Production in 1995 (in 1,000 quintales; 1 quintal = 46 kg): Rice, 4,935; maize, 2,335; dry beans, 138; raw sugar, 1,516; coffee, 244; tobacco, 244. Livestock (1996): 1,456,000 cattle, 261,000 pigs, 165,000 horses and 11m. chickens (1995).

Forestry. Forests covered 2·8m. ha in 1995 (37·6% of the land area), compared to 3·12m. ha in 1990. There are great timber resources, notably mahogany.

Fisheries. In 1995 the catch totalled 181,781 tonnes, almost entirely from sea fishing. Shrimps are the principal species caught.

INDUSTRY
The main industry is agricultural produce processing. Other areas include oil refining, chemicals and paper-making.

PANAMA

Labour. In 1996 the workforce (persons 15 years and over) numbered 1,001,439, of whom 870,622 were employed.

Trade Unions. 77,500 workers belonged to trade unions in 1994, of whom 27,000 were members of the Confederación de Trabajadores de la República de Panamá.

INTERNATIONAL TRADE
The Colón Free Zone is an autonomous institution set up in 1953. 1,556 companies were operating there in 1997. Factories in export zones are granted tax exemption on profits for 10–20 years and exemption from the provisions of the labour code. Foreign debt was US$6,990m. in 1996.

Imports and Exports. Trade in 1996: Exports, US$620m.; imports, US$2,780m. Main exports: Bananas, shellfish, sugar.

Chief export markets: USA, 37·5%; Germany, 12·2%; Sweden, 9%; Costa Rica, 7·1%; Belgium, 7%. Chief import suppliers: USA, 38%; Japan, 7·1%; Ecuador, 4%; Costa Rica, 3%.

COMMUNICATIONS

Roads. In 1995 there were 10,792 km of roads, about one-third paved or tarred. The road from Panama City westward to the cities of David and Concepción and to the Costa Rican frontier, with several branches, is part of the Pan-American Highway. The Trans-Isthmian Highway connects Panama City and Colón. In 1995 there were 250,319 registered motor vehicles.

Rail. The 1,524 mm gauge *Ferrocarril de Panama*, which connects Ancón on the Pacific with Cristóbal on the Atlantic along the bank of the Panama Canal, is the principal railway. 43,000 tonnes of freight were carried in 1994. The United Brands Company runs 376 km of railway, and the Chiriquí National Railroad 171 km.

Civil Aviation. There is an international airport at Panama City (Tocumén International). The national carrier is COPA. In 1996 COPA flew to 22 destinations in 16 countries and carried 0·7m. passengers. In 1998 services were also provided by ACES, Aeroperlas, Aeroperú, Aeropostal Alas de Venezuela, American Airlines, Avianca, Aviateca, Continental Airlines, Delta Air Lines, Ecuatoriana, EVA Airways, Iberia, LACSA, Lloyd Aéreo Boliviano, Mexicana, Nicaraguense de Aviación, SAM, Servivensa and Taca International Airlines. In 1996 Tocumén International handled 1,084,000 passengers and 67,700 tonnes of freight.

Shipping. Ships under Panamanian registry in 1995 totalled 86·46m. DWT, all foreign-owned. As at Sept. 1996, 13,618 vessels were registered. Most of these ships elect Panamanian registry because fees are low and labour laws lenient. Revenue from the registry was US$44m. in 1996. All the international maritime traffic for Colón and Panama runs through the Canal ports of Cristóbal, Balboa and Bahia Las Minas (Colón); Almirante is used for both the provincial and international trade. There is an oil transfer terminal at Puerto Armuelles on the Pacific coast. In 1995 vessels totalling 2,168,000 net registered tons entered ports and vessels totalling 1,645,000 NRT cleared.

Panama Canal. The Panama Canal Commission is concerned primarily with the operation of the Canal. Since 1 Oct. 1995, tolls assessment has been based on the Panama Canal/Universal Measurement System (PC/UMS), which incorporates the principles of the 1969 International Convention on Tonnage Measurement of Ships. Toll rates are US$2·21 a PC/UMS ton for vessels carrying passengers or cargo and US$1·90 per ton for vessels in transit in ballast. The toll rate for warships, hospital ships and supply ships, which pay on a displacement basis, is US$1·33 a ton.

The rates are set to continue the approximately break-even financial operating results after paying its own expenses.

Administrator of the Panama Canal Commission: Alberto Alemán Zubieta.

US military personnel: Army, 4,090; Navy, 700; Marines, 120; Air Force, 2,050.

PANAMA

Particulars of the ocean-going commercial traffic through the canal are given as follows (vessels of 300 PC/UMS tons net and 500 displacement tons and over; cargo in long tons):

Fiscal year ending 30 Sept.	No. of vessels transiting	PC/UMS net tonnage	Cargo in long tons	Tolls levied (in US$1)
1995	13,459[1]	215,355,914	190,303,065	460,043,676
1996	13,700	228,000,000	198,000,000	486,000,000

[1]6,933 Atlantic to Pacific; 6,526 Pacific to Atlantic.

In the fiscal year ending 30 Sept. 1996, 15,187 ships of all sizes passed through the Canal. Most numerous transits by flag: Panama, 2,560; Liberia, 1,663; Bahamas, 1,242; Greece, 999; Cyprus, 956; Norway, 393.

Statistical Information: The Panama Canal Commission Office of Public Affairs.
Annual Reports on the Panama Canal, by the Administrator of the Panama Canal Commission.
Rules and Regulations Governing Navigation of the Panama Canal. The Panama Canal Commission, Miami, Florida *or* Washington, D.C.
Cameron, I., *The Impossible Dream.* London, 1972
Le Feber, W., *The Panama Canal: The Crisis in Historical Perspective.* OUP, 1978
McCullough, D., *The Path Between the Seas.* New York and London, 1978
Major, J., *Prize Possession: the United States and the Panama Canal, 1903–1979.* CUP, 1994

Telecommunications. Panama had 365,700 main telephone lines in 1997, or 134·4 per 1,000 persons.

Postal Services. In 1995 there were 343 post offices.

SOCIAL INSTITUTIONS

Justice. The Supreme Court consists of 9 justices appointed by the executive. There is no death penalty. The police force numbered 11,000 in 1996, and includes a Presidential Guard.

Religion. 85% of the population is Roman Catholic, 5% Protestant, 4·5% Moslem. There is freedom of religious worship and separation of Church and State. Clergymen may teach in the schools but may not hold public office.

Education. Adult literacy was 90·8% in 1995 (male, 91·4%; female, 90·2%). Elementary education is compulsory for all children from 7 to 15 years of age. In 1994 there were 365,286 pupils at 3,019 primary schools and 208,775 pupils at 11,440 secondary schools. In 1995 there were 3 universities and 1 technological university with a total of 75,951 students and 4,106 academic staff. There were also a nautical school, a business school and institutes of teacher training and tourism.

In 1994 total expenditure on education came to 4·6% of GNP and represented 20·9% of total government expenditure.

Health. In 1995 there were 3,074 doctors, 656 dentists and 2,823 nursing personnel. There were 59 hospitals, 174 health centres and 443 health sub-centres with a total of 7,138 beds.

CULTURE

Broadcasting. There are about 60 broadcasting stations, mostly commercial, grouped in the Asociación Panameña de Radiodifusión. There are 4 television channels (colour by NTSC), an educational channel, and a radio and TV network for US forces. In 1995 there were 600,000 radio and 460,000 TV sets in use.

Press. In 1995 there were 7 dailies with a combined circulation of 160,000, equivalent to 61 per 1,000 inhabitants.

Tourism. In 1996 there were 362,000 foreign tourists, bringing revenue of US$343m.

DIPLOMATIC REPRESENTATIVES

Of Panama in Great Britain (Ground Floor and Basement, 48 Park St., London, W1Y 3PD)
Ambassador: Vacant.

Of Great Britain in Panama (Torre Swiss Bank, Calle 53, Apartado 889, Panama City 1)
Ambassador and Consul-General: William Sinton.

Of Panama in the USA (2862 McGill Terr., NW, Washington, D.C., 20008)
Ambassador: Eloy Alfaro.

Of the USA in Panama (Apartado 6959, Panama City 5)
Ambassador: William J. Hughes.

Of Panama to the United Nations
Ambassador: Aquilino E. Boyd.

Of Panama to the European Union
Ambassador: Vilma Ramírez.

FURTHER READING

Statistical Information: The Comptroller-General of the Republic (Contraloria General de la República, Calle 35 y Avenida 6, Panama City) publishes an annual report and other statistical publications.

Jorden, W. J., *Panama Odyssey.* Univ. of Texas Press, 1984
Langstaff, E. DeS., *Panama.* [Bibliography] Oxford and Santa Barbara (CA), 1982
Ropp, S. C., *Panamanian Politics.* New York, 1982
Sahota, G. S., *Poverty Theory and Policy: a Study of Panama.* Johns Hopkins Univ. Press, 1990

Other titles are listed under PANAMA CANAL, *above.*

National library: Biblioteca Nacional, Departamento de Información, Calle 22, Panama.

PAPUA NEW GUINEA

Capital: Port Moresby
Population estimate, 2000: 4·81m.
GNP per capita: (PPP$) 2,820
HDI/world rank: 0·507/129

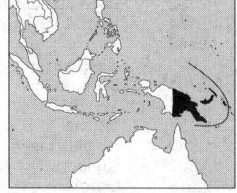

KEY HISTORICAL EVENTS

New Guinea, especially the eastern half (Irian Jaya), was known to Indonesian and Asian seafarers centuries before it was known to the Europeans. In 1512 the Portuguese sighted the New Guinea coast but made no landing until 1527. The Spanish first claimed the island in 1545 but the first attempt at colonization was made in 1793 by the British. The Dutch, however, claimed the west half of the island as part of the Dutch East Indies in 1828.

In order to prevent that portion of the island of New Guinea not claimed by the Netherlands or Germany from passing into the hands of another foreign power, the government of Queensland annexed Papua in 1883. This step was not sanctioned by the Imperial Government but on 6 Nov. 1884 a British Protectorate was proclaimed over the southern portion of the eastern half of New Guinea and in 1887 Queensland, New South Wales and Victoria undertook to defray the cost of administration. The territory was annexed to the Crown the following year. By 1884 the south-east of New Guinea had been annexed to Britain and the German New Guinea Company took over the north-east of the country. The Australian federal government took over control in 1901; the political transfer was completed by the Papua Act of the federal parliament in Nov. 1905. On 1 Sept. 1906 the Governor-General of Australia declared that British New Guinea was to be known henceforth as the Territory of Papua. The northern portion of New Guinea was a German colony until 1914 when Australian armed forces occupied it and it remained under their administration for the next seven years. It became a League of Nations mandated territory in 1921, administered by Australia, and later a UN Trust Territory (of New Guinea).

The Papua New Guinea Act 1949–72 provided for the administration of the UN Australian Trust Territory of New Guinea in an administrative union with the Territory of Papua, under the title of Papua New Guinea. Australia granted Papua New Guinea self-government on 1 Dec. 1973, and on 16 Sept. 1975 Papua New Guinea became a fully independent state.

What began in 1988 as an armed campaign by tribes claiming traditional land rights against the Australian owner of the massive Panguna copper field soon escalated into a civil war for the secession of the island of Bougainville. Fighting between the government and the secessionist Bougainville Revolutionary Army (BRA) continued until 3 Sept. 1994 when a peace agreement was signed. This provides for 4 neutral zones to be occupied by a Pacific peacekeeping force drawn from the Fiji Islands, Tonga and Vanuatu with logistic support from Australia and New Zealand. The agreement also set up a provisional Bougainville government. The ceasefire was broken by the rebels in mid-1995 and the provisional government leader was assassinated in Oct. 1996. In March 1997 the Government began to employ foreign mercenaries in the campaign against secessionist rebels. This caused public disturbances and led to the resignation of the Prime Minister, Sir Julius Chan. Nevertheless, the use of mercenaries went ahead. In April 1998 the government of Papua New Guinea signed a 'permanent' truce with the secessionists. The 9-year rebellion had claimed 20,000 lives.

Northern Papua New Guinea was struck by 3 tidal waves in July 1998, resulting in some 3,000 deaths.

TERRITORY AND POPULATION

Papua New Guinea extends from the equator to Cape Baganowa in the Louisiade Archipelago to 11° 40' S. lat. and from the border of West Irian to 160° E. long. with a total area of 462,840 sq. km. According to the census the 1990 population was 3,529,538 (excluding North Solomons, estimated 1990 population 159,500). Estimate, 1994, 4·07m.; density, 9 per sq. km.

The UN gives a projected population for 2000 of 4·81m.

In 1995 an estimated 83·9% of the population lived in rural areas. Population of main towns (1990 census): Port Moresby (National Capital District), 193,242; Lae, 80,655; Rabaul, 17,022; Madang, 27,057; Wewak, 23,224; Goroka, 17,855; Mount Hagen, 17,392. Area and population of the provinces:

Provinces	Sq.km	Census 1980	Census 1990	Capital
Milne Bay	14,000	127,975	157,288	Alotau
Northern	22,800	77,442	96,762	Popondetta
Central	29,500	116,964	140,584	Port Moresby
National Capital District	240	123,624	193,242	—
Gulf	34,500	64,120	68,060	Kerema
Western	99,300	78,575	108,705[1]	Daru
Southern Highlands	23,800	236,052	302,724	Mendi
Enga	12,800	164,534	238,357	Wabag
Western Highlands	8,500	265,656	291,090	Mount Hagen
Chimbu	6,100	178,290	183,801	Kundiawa
Eastern Highlands	11,200	276,726	299,619	Goroka
Morobe	34,500	310,622	363,535	Lae
Madang	29,000	211,069	270,299	Madang
East Sepik	42,800	221,890	248,308	Wewak
West Sepik	36,300	114,192	135,185[2]	Vanimo
Manus	2,100	26,036	32,830	Lorengau
West New Britain	21,000	88,941	127,547	Kimbe
East New Britain	15,500	133,197	184,408	Rabaul
New Ireland	9,600	66,028	87,194	Kavieng
North Solomons	9,300	128,794	. . .	Arawa

[1]Excludes 3 census divisions, estimated total 1,500.
[2]Excludes 2 census divisions, estimated total 3,000.

The principal local languages are Neo-Melanesian (or Pidgin, a creole of English) and Hiri Motu. English is in official use.

SOCIAL STATISTICS
1995 births, 142,000; deaths, 44,000. 1995 birth rate, 32·9 per 1,000 population; death rate, 10·3. Expectation of life at birth, 1990–95, was 55·2 years for males and 56·7 years for females. Infant mortality, 1990–95, 68 per 1,000 live births; fertility rate, 5·1 births per woman.

CLIMATE
There is a monsoon climate, with high temperatures and humidity the year round. Port Moresby is in a rain shadow and is not typical of the rest of Papua New Guinea, Jan. 82°F (27·8°C), July 78°F (25·6°C). Annual rainfall 40" (1,011 mm).

CONSTITUTION AND GOVERNMENT
A single legislative house, known as the *National Parliament*, is made up of 109 members from all parts of the country. The members are elected by universal suffrage; elections are held every 5 years. All citizens over the age of 18 are eligible to vote and stand for election. Voting is by secret ballot and follows the preferential system. The Governor-General is nominated by parliament for 6-year terms.

National Anthem. 'Arise, all you sons of this land'; words and tune by T. Shacklady.

RECENT ELECTIONS
At the elections of June 1997 no party held a majority. The People's Progress Party won 16 seats, the Papua New Guinea United Party 13, People's Democratic Movement 10 and other parties 6 or fewer. Following coalition negotiations, William Skate of the People's National Congress was elected prime minister, heading a government composed of representatives from the five main parties (People's National Congress, People's Progress Party, Pangu Pati, People's Democratic Movement and People's Resource Party).

CURRENT ADMINISTRATION
Governor-General: Sir Silas Atopare.

In March 1999 the government comprised:

Prime Minister and Minister for Public Service: William Skate (elected 22 July 1997).

Deputy Prime Minister and Minister for Treasury and Planning: Iairo Lasaro. *Senior Minister for State:* Sir Rabbie Namaliu. *Minister of Agriculture and Livestock:* Tukape Masani. *Defence:* Peter Waieng. *Commerce and Industry:* Ian Ling-Stuckey. *Foreign Affairs and Trade:* Roy Yaki. *Petroleum and Gas:* Sir Rabbie Namaliu. *Mining and Energy:* Masket Iangalio. *Forests:* Peter Arul. *Provincial and Local Level Government Affairs:* Simon Kaumi. *Transport:* Vincent Auali. *Justice:* Jacob Wama. *Public Enterprise, Communications, Infrastructure and Public Investment:* Fabian Pok. *Fisheries:* Sir Mekere Morauta. *Environment:* Herowa Agiwa. *Education, Culture and Science:* Muki Taranupi. *Lands:* Viviso Seravo. *Health:* Ludger Mondo. *Police:* Thomas Pelika. *Youth and Employment:* Mathias Karani. *Family and Church Affairs:* Andrew Kumbakor. *Works and Implementation:* Yauwe Riyong. *Housing and Resettlement:* Mao Zeming. *Finance and Internal Affairs:* Digbara Yagabo. *Rural Development:* Jimson Sauk. *Tourism and Civil Aviation:* Kala Swokin. *Bougainville Affairs:* Sam Akoitai.

Local Government. In 1950 the first village council was formed which established the basis of an extensive local government system. A system of provincial government was introduced in 1976 and the importance of lower-level local government diminished. However, lower-level community government had replaced local government councils in some provinces by 1991. Each of the 19 provinces has its own government which may levy taxes to supplement grants received from the national government.

DEFENCE
The Papua New Guinea Defence Force has a total strength of 3,800 (1996) consisting of land, maritime and air elements. The Army is organized in 2 infantry and 1 engineer battalion. The Navy, based at Port Moresby and Manus, is all of Australian build and comprises 4 inshore patrol craft, 2 tank landing craft and some boats. Personnel numbered 400 in 1996. The Defence Force has an Air Transport Squadron, grounded through shortage of funds in 1996. Current equipment comprises 2 CN-235 transports and 3 Arava, 1 Australian-built N22B Nomad and 4 Iroquois helicopters.

Defence expenditure in 1997 totalled US$63m. (US$14 per capita).

INTERNATIONAL RELATIONS
Papua New Guinea is a member of the UN, the Commonwealth, the Colombo Plan, the South Pacific Commission and the Pacific Community and is an observer at ASEAN and an ACP member state of the ACP-EU relationship.

ECONOMY

Performance. Real GDP growth was –4·8% in 1995 (3·5% in 1994).

Budget. Budgetary income (in K1m.) for calendar years was:

Source	1996	1997[1]
Tax revenue	1,526·3	1,555·7
Non-tax revenue	201·2	200·8
Foreign grants	170·1	125·5
Total	1,897·7	1,882·0
Expenditure:		
National departmental	720·6	742·8
Provincial governments	521·8	568·3
Interest	257·1	328·6
Other grants and expenditure	112·2	120·3
Net lending and investment	–4·0	–5·1
Development	252·8	246·2
Total	1,860·7	2,001·1

[1]Estimates.

PAPUA NEW GUINEA

Currency. The unit of currency is the *kina* (PGK) of 100 *toea*. The kina was floated in Oct. 1994. Foreign exchange reserves were US$313m. and gold reserves 60,000 troy oz. in Feb. 1998. The average annual inflation rate over the period 1990–96 was 6·6%. In Sept. 1997 total money supply was K1,014m.

Banking and Finance. The Bank of Papua New Guinea assumed the central banking functions formerly undertaken by the Reserve Bank of Australia on 1 Nov. 1973. A national banking institution, the Papua New Guinea Banking Corporation, has been established. This bank has assumed the Papua New Guinea business of the Commonwealth Trading Bank of Australia.

There are 5 commercial banks; 3 Australian and 2 with 51% Papuan ownership. Total deposits, 1992, K1318·2m. Total savings account deposits, 1992, K226·8m.

In addition, the Agriculture Bank of Papua New Guinea had assets of K82·6m. in 1992, and finance companies and merchant banks had total assets of K198·4m.

Weights and Measures. The metric system is in force.

ENERGY AND NATURAL RESOURCES

Electricity. Installed capacity was 252,000 kW in 1992. Production in 1994 was 1·71bn. kWh, around a third of it hydro-electric. Consumption per capita in 1995 was estimated to be 382 kWh.

Oil and Gas. The Iagifu field in the Southern Highlands had (1988) potential recoverable reserves of 500m. bbls. Crude oil production (1992), 2·12m. tonnes.

Minerals. In 1991 mining produced 15% of GDP. Copper is the main mineral product. Gold, copper and silver are the only minerals produced in quantity. The Misima open-pit gold mine was opened in 1989. Production was forecast at 0·21m. oz. a year with a life of 10 years. The Porgera gold mine opened in 1990 with an expected life of 20 years; in the first quarter of 1997 it produced 121,000 oz. Major copper deposits in Bougainville have proven reserves of about 800m. tonnes; mining was halted by secessionist rebel activity. Copper and gold deposits in the Star Mountains of the Western Province are being developed by Ok Tedi Mining Ltd at the M. Fubilan mine. Production of gold commenced in 1984 and of copper concentrates in 1987. In 1996 Ok Tedi Mining Ltd produced 47 tons of gold, 127,700 tons of copper and 39m. barrels of crude oil. Figures for 1997 point to a 50% increase in copper and 10% increase in gold. Gold mining also began at Lihir in 1997. Total yields for export in 1996 were: gold, 47 tonnes; copper, 127,700 tonnes; crude petroleum, 39·3m. bbls.

Agriculture. Agriculture accounted for 26% of GDP in 1996. In 1995 it employed nearly 78% of the workforce. In 1994 there were 40,000 ha of arable land, 0·37m. ha of permanent cropland and 90,000 ha of permanent pasture. Minor commercial crops include pyrethrum, tea, peanuts and spices. Locally consumed food crops include sweet potatoes, maize, taro, bananas, rice and sago. Tropical fruits grow abundantly. There is extensive grassland. The sugar industry has made the country self-sufficient in this commodity while a beef-cattle industry is being developed.

Production for export (1996, in tonnes): coffee, 62,300; copra, 99,200; copra oil, 49,600; cocoa, 41,000.

Livestock (1996): Cattle, 110,000; pigs, 1·03m.; chickens (1995), 3m.

Forestry. The forest area totalled 36·94m. ha in 1995 (81·6% of the land area), of which about 15m. ha of high quality tropical hardwoods are considered suitable for development. In 1990 the area under forests had been 37·6m. ha (83% of the land area). Timber production is important for both local consumption and export. Timber production was 8·77m. cu. metres in 1995. In 1997, 577,300 cu. metres of logs were exported.

Fisheries. Tuna is the major resource. In 1995 the fish catch was an estimated 26,000 tonnes (52% freshwater fish and 48% sea fish), of which approximately 2,800 tonnes were exported.

INDUSTRY

Secondary and service industries are expanding for the local market. The main industries were (1988) food processing, beverages, tobacco, timber products, wood, and fabricated metal products. In 1988 there were 692 factories employing 30,503 persons. Value of output K768m.

Labour. The labour force in 1996 totalled 2,160,000 (58% males). In 1996 formal employment in the building and construction industries rose by 27·5%, but around 85% of the population is dependent on non-monetarized agriculture.

INTERNATIONAL TRADE
Australian aid amounts to an annual $A300m. The 'Pactra II' agreement of 1991 establishes a free trade zone with Australia and protects Australian investments. Foreign debt was US$2,359m. in 1996.

Imports and Exports. Exports in 1996 were US$2,515m.; imports, US$1,741m. Imports (in K1,000) for calendar years:

	1988	1989	1990
Food and live animals	181,789	190,853	194,624
Beverages and tobacco	15,456	14,957	14,764
Crude materials, inedible, except fuels	8,577	7,769	8,712
Mineral fuels, lubricants and related materials	98,175	63,704	80,132
Oils and fats (animal and vegetable)	3,350	3,387	4,793
Chemicals	84,403	78,588	81,563
Manufactured goods, chiefly by material	205,654	253,251	223,045
Machinery and transport equipment	424,587	524,966	423,019
Miscellaneous manufactured articles	99,113	109,776	97,560
Commodities and transactions of merchandise trade, not elsewhere specified	12,356	12,877	13,711
Total imports	1,133,459	1,260,128	1,141,922

Exports (in K1,000) for calendar years:

	1995	1996
Cocoa	47,700	66,200
Coffee beans	214,500	190,300
Tea	5,400	12,700
Copra and copra oil	57,100	100,400
Palm oil	142,200	182,400
Logs	436,700	464,800
Crude petroleum	827,700	1,073,900
Gold	840,100	773,600
Copper	754,500	387,000
Fish	12,300	10,400

Papua New Guinea's main export markets are Australia, Germany, Japan, South Korea and UK. The main import suppliers are Australia, Japan, Singapore, UK and USA.

COMMUNICATIONS

Roads. In 1996 there were 19,600 km of roads, only about 700 km of which were paved. Motor vehicles numbered 116,000 in 1996 (31,000 passenger cars and 85,000 trucks and vans).

Civil Aviation. Jacksons International Airport is at Port Moresby. The state-owned national carrier is Air Niugini. In 1998 services were also provided by Islands Nationair, MBA Pty Ltd, Missionary Aviation Fellowship, North Coast Aviation, Philippine Airlines, Qantas Airways and Solomon Airlines, with international flights to Brisbane, Cairns, Honiara, Manila, Singapore, Sydney and Townsville. There are a total of 177 airports and airstrips with scheduled services.

Shipping. There are 12 entry and 4 other main ports served by 5 major shipping lines; the Papua New Guinea Shipping Corporation is state-owned. Sea-going shipping totalled 51,051 GRT in 1995, including oil tankers, 5,044 GRT.

Telecommunications. In 1996 there were 47,000 main telephone lines in 1997, or 10·7 for every 1,000 inhabitants. There were 800 fax machines in 1995.

PAPUA NEW GUINEA

SOCIAL INSTITUTIONS

Justice. In 1983, over 1,500 criminal and civil cases were heard in the National Court and an estimated 120,000 cases in district and local courts. The discretionary use of the death penalty for murder and rape was introduced in 1991.

Religion. In 1992 there were 2·24m. Protestants and 1·26m. Roman Catholics.

Education. Obligatory universal primary education is a government objective. In 1990 about two-thirds of eligible children were attending school. In 1994 there were 2,864 primary schools with 505,153 pupils and 15,298 teachers, and in 1995 there were 78,759 pupils in secondary schools and 13,663 students in institutes of higher education. There are 2 universities (the University of Papua New Guinea and the Papua New Guinea University of Technology). Adult literacy rate was 72·2% in 1995 (81·0% among males and 62·7% among females).

Health. In 1993 there were 736 doctors and 2,614 nurses. Provision of hospital beds in 1993 was 34 per 10,000 persons.

In the period 1990–96 only 28% of the population had access to safe drinking water.

CULTURE

Broadcasting. The National Broadcasting Commission operates 3 networks: national, provincial and commercial. A national service is relayed throughout the country. Each province has a broadcasting service, while the larger urban centres are also covered by a commercial network relayed from Port Moresby. 2 commercial television stations broadcast from Port Moresby (colour by PAL). In 1995 there were 15,000 television and 330,000 radio receivers.

Press. In 1995 there was 2 daily newspapers with a combined circulation of 49,000, equivalent to 15 per 1,000 inhabitants, and a number of weeklies and monthlies.

Tourism. In 1996 there were 56,000 foreign tourists, bringing revenue of US$68m.

DIPLOMATIC REPRESENTATIVES
Of Papua New Guinea in Great Britain (3rd Floor, 14 Waterloo Pl., London, SW1R 4AR)
High Commissioner: Sir Kina Bona, KBE.

Of Great Britain in Papua New Guinea (PO Box 212, Waigani NCD 131)
High Commissioner: C. D. S. Drace-Francis, CMG.

Of Papua New Guinea in the USA (1615 New Hampshire Ave., NW, Washington D.C., 20036)
Ambassador: Sir Nagora Bogan, KBE.

Of the USA in Papua New Guinea (Douglas St., Port Moresby)
Ambassador: Arma Jane Karaer.

Of Papua New Guinea to the United Nations
Ambassador: Vacant.

Of Papua New Guinea to the European Union
Ambassador: Gabriel Pepson.

FURTHER READING
National Statistical Office. *Summary of Statistics.* Annual.—*Abstract of Statistics.* Quarterly.— *Economic Indicators.*
Monthly Bank of Papua New Guinea. *Quarterly Economic Bulletin.*
McConnell, F., *Papua New Guinea.* [Bibliography] Oxford and Santa Barbara (CA), 1988
Ryan, P. (ed.) *Encyclopaedia of Papua and New Guinea.* Melbourne Univ. Press, 1972
Turner, A., *Historical Dictionary of Papua New Guinea.* Metuchen (NJ), 1995
Waiko, J. D., *Short History of Papua New Guinea.* OUP, 1993

National statistical office: National Statistical Office, PO Wards Strip.

PARAGUAY

República del Paraguay

Capital: Asunción
Population estimate, 2000: 5·5m.
GNP per capita: (PPP$) 3,480
HDI/world rank: 0·707/91

KEY HISTORICAL EVENTS

A landlocked territory bordered by Brazil, Argentina and Bolivia, Paraguay was occupied by the Spanish in 1537 and became a Spanish colony as part of the viceroyalty of Peru. The Guaraní-speaking population gained some protection from the powerful Jesuit mission stations until the expulsion of the Jesuits in 1767. In 1776 the area became part of the vice-royalty of Rio de la Plata, gaining its independence from Spain, as the Republic of Paraguay, on 14 May 1811. Paraguay was then ruled by a succession of dictators, the first being Dr José Gaspar Rodriguez de Francia, who was elected dictator in 1814 by the national assembly and became perpetual dictator in 1816; he died in 1840. In 1844 a new constitution was adopted under which Carlos Antonio López (nephew of Dr Francia) and his son, Francisco López, ruled until 1870.

During a devastating war fought from 1865 to 1870 between Paraguay and a coalition of Argentina, Brazil and Uruguay, Paraguay's population was reduced from about 600,000 to 233,000. Further severe losses were incurred during the war with Bolivia (1932-35) over territorial claims in the Chaco inspired by the unfounded belief that minerals existed in the territory. A peace treaty by which Paraguay obtained most of the area her troops had conquered was signed in July 1938.

The dictatorship of Gen. Higinio Moringo was ended following a civil war in which the right-wing party (*Partido Colorado*) defeated the Liberals. A period of unrest ensued until Gen. Alfredo Stroessner Mattiauda, the C.-in-C. of the Army, assumed power in a military *coup* in 1954. He was deposed in a further coup in Feb. 1989.

A new constitution took effect in Feb. 1968 under which executive power is discharged by an executive president. In 1977 the constitution was amended to enable the president to stand for more than two consecutive terms of office. Gen. Stroessner was re-elected 7 times between 1958 and 1988. Since then, Paraguay has been under more or less democratic government. The third consecutive general democratic elections held in May 1998 were won by the ruling Colorado Party. Raúl Cubas Grau became president. In Aug. 1998 Paraguay faced another crisis when the new president was threatened with impeachment after issuing a presidential decree to free his former running-mate, Gen. Lino Oviedo who had been imprisoned in 1996 for attempting a coup against the previous president, Juan Carlos Wasmosy. On 23 March 1999, Paraguay's vice-president Luis Maria Argaña was assassinated. The following day, Congress voted to impeach President Cubas who then resigned.

TERRITORY AND POPULATION

Paraguay is bounded in the north-west by Bolivia, north-east and east by Brazil and south-east, south and south-west by Argentina. The area is 406,752 sq. km (157,042 sq. miles).

The population (census 1992) was 4·12m.; estimate (July 1998) 5·29m.; density, 13·0 per sq. km.

The UN gives a projected population for 2000 of 5·5m.

In 1995, 52·4% lived in urban areas.

At the 1992 census the capital, Asunción (and metropolitan area), had 637,737 inhabitants and Ciudad del Este (formerly Presidente Stroessner), 133,893.

There are 17 departments and the capital city. Area and population at the 1992 census:

Department	Area in sq. km	Population	Department	Area in sq. km	Population
Asunción (city)	117	502,426	Caaguazú	11,474	383,319
Central	2,465	864,540	Itapúa	16,525	375,748
Alto Paraná	14,895	403,858	San Pedro	20,002	277,110

Department	Area in sq. km	Population	Department	Area in sq. km	Population
Cordillera	4,948	206,097	Misiones	9,556	88,624
Paraguari	8,705	203,012	Neembucú	12,147	69,884
Concepción	18,051	166,946	*Oriental*	*159,827*	*4,026,342*
Guairá	3,846	162,244	Presidente Hayes	72,907	59,100
Caazapá	9,496	128,550	Boquerón[1]	91,669	26,292
Amambay	12,933	97,158	Alto Paraguay[2]	83,349	11,816
Canendiyú	14,667	96,826	*Occidental*	*246,925*	*97,208*

[1]Incorporates former department of Nueva Asunción.
[2]Incorporates former department of Chaco.

The population is mixed Spanish and Guaraní Indian. There are some 46,700 unassimilated Indians of other tribal origin, in the Chaco and the forests of eastern Paraguay. 40·1% of the population speak only Guaraní; 48·2% are bilingual (Spanish/Guaraní); and 6·4% speak only Spanish.

Mennonites, who arrived in 3 groups (1927, 1930 and 1947), are settled in the Chaco and eastern Paraguay. There are also Korean and Japanese settlers.

SOCIAL STATISTICS
1997 births, estimate, 172,000; deaths, 24,000. Rates, 1997 estimates (per 1,000 population): Birth, 30·5; death, 4·2. 1997 growth, 2·62%; expectation of life, 74·1 years. Infant mortality, 1990–95, 43 per 1,000 live births; fertility rate, 4·6 births per woman.

CLIMATE
A tropical climate, with abundant rainfall and only a short dry season from July to Sept., when temperatures are lowest. Asunción, Jan. 81°F (27°C), July 64°F (17·8°C). Annual rainfall 53" (1,316 mm).

CONSTITUTION AND GOVERNMENT
On 18 June 1992 a Constituent Assembly approved a new constitution. The head of state is the *President,* elected for a non-renewable 5-year term. Parliament consists of an 80-member *Chamber of Deputies,* elected from departmental constituencies, and a 45-member *Senate,* elected from a single national constituency.

National Anthem. 'Paraguayos, república o muerte!' ('Paraguayans, republic or death!'); words by F. Acuña de Figueroa, tune by F. Dupuy.

RECENT ELECTIONS
Parliamentary and presidential elections were held on 10 May 1998. Raúl Cubas Grau of the authoritarian Republican National Alliance/Colorado Party was elected President against 1 opponent with 55·4% of votes cast. At the parliamentary elections the Colorado Party gained 45 seats in the Chamber of Deputies with 53·8% of votes cast (and 24 in the Senate), the Authentic Radical Liberal Party 27 (and 13) and National Encounter 8 (and 7). The alliance of the liberal Authentic Radical Liberal Party and the centrist National Encounter received 42·7% of the votes.

CURRENT ADMINISTRATION
President: Luis González Macchi, b. 1947 (sworn in 28 March 1999).

At the end of March 1999 a new cabinet was in the process of being formed.

Local Government. There are 17 departments with directly-elected councils and governors, and 212 municipalities.

DEFENCE
The army, navy and air forces are separate services under a single command. The President of the Republic is the active C.-in-C. Conscription is for 12 months (2 years in the navy).

Defence expenditure totalled US$134m. in 1997 (US$26 per capita).

Army. The Army is organized into 3 corps and 9 divisional headquarters and consists of 1 armoured, 2 mechanized and 4 horsed cavalry regiments, 7 infantry regiments (of battalion strength), 6 artillery groups (of battalion strength), 1 air defence and 4 engineer battalions and 20 frontier detachments. Equipment includes 5 M-4A3 main battle tanks. Strength (1997) 14,900 (10,400 conscripts).

Navy. The flotilla includes 7 armed river defence gunboats (the average age of which exceeds 50 years), 7 river patrol boats, and about 12 service craft. Personnel in 1996 totalled 3,600 including 900 marines.

Air Force. The Air Force has 3 combat units, 1 with Xavante light jet strike/training aircraft, 1 with armed T-33 trainers and the other with armed Tucano turboprop trainers. HQ and flying school are at Campo Grande, Asunción. Personnel (1996) 1,700 (600 conscripts).

INTERNATIONAL RELATIONS
Paraguay is a member of the UN, OAS, Mercosur and LAIA.

ECONOMY
Policy. There is a privatization programme for large state enterprises.

Performance. Real GDP growth was 4·6% in 1995 (3·1% in 1994).

Budget. In 1995 (in 1m. guaranís) revenue was 2,078,993 and expenditure 2,971,354; in 1994 revenue was 2,253,138 and expenditure 2,038,193.

Revenue items, 1995: Import duties, 369,650; domestic taxes, 587,572; income tax, 308,584. Items of expenditure: Public debt service, 293,632; public works, 445,570; education, 579,754; defence, 267,373; agriculture, 283,794; health, 192,151.

Currency. The unit of currency is the *guaraní* (PYG), notionally divided into 100 *céntimos.* In Nov. 1997 total money supply was 1,607m. guaranís. In Feb. 1998 foreign exchange reserves were US$486m. and gold reserves were 30,000 troy oz. Inflation was 8·2% in 1996.

Banking and Finance. The Central Bank is a state-owned autonomous agency with the sole right of note issue, control over foreign exchange and the supervision of commercial banks (*Governor*, Hermes Gomez). In 1994 there were 28 commercial banks (mostly foreign), 2 other banking institutions, 1 investment bank, 1 development bank and 6 building societies.

There is a stock exchange in Asunción.

Weights and Measures. The metric system was officially adopted in 1901, but some traditional measures continue in use.

ENERGY AND NATURAL RESOURCES
Electricity. There is a vast hydro-electric potential; only 2% of output is thermal. Installed capacity was 6,927,500 kW in 1995. Output (1995), 41·63bn. kWh. Consumption per capita was estimated at 616 kWh in 1995.

Minerals. The country is poor in minerals. Limestone, gypsum, kaolin and salt are extracted. Deposits of bauxite, iron ore, copper, manganese and uranium exist.

Agriculture. In 1996 agriculture produced 24% of GDP and in 1995 it employed 35% of the workforce. In 1994 there were approximately 2·19m. ha of arable land, 80,000 ha of permanent crops and 21·7m. ha of permanent pasture.

At the agrarian census of 1991 there were 307,221 farms working 23,799,737 ha. 122,750 farms had fewer than 5 ha; 884 had over 5,000 ha.

Output (in 1,000 tonnes), 1995: Soybeans, 2,200; maize, 816; wheat, 250; cotton, 438; sugar-cane, 2,000; 1993: Cassava, 2,680; rice, 50; tobacco, 11. *Yerba maté,* or strongly flavoured Paraguayan tea, continues to be produced but is declining in importance.

Livestock (1996); 9·79m. cattle, 370,000 horses, 2·53m. pigs, 390,000 sheep and 13m. chickens 1995.

Forestry. The area under forests in 1995 was 11·53m. ha, or 29% of the total land area (13·16m. ha and 33·1% in 1990). Palm and tung oil are produced. Timber production was 10·4m. cu. metres in 1995.

Fisheries. In 1995 the catch totalled approximately 14,500 tonnes, exclusively from inland waters.

INDUSTRY
In 1994 industry produced 15·1% of GDP. Production, 1994 (1,000 tons): Frozen meat, 45·8; cotton fibre, 136·8; sugar, 110·8; rice, 81·9; wheat flour, 47·8; edible oil, 78·9; industrial oil, 10·0; tung oil, 6·8; cement, 528·8; soybean, peanut and coconut flour, 468; cigarettes (1988) (1m. packets), 46,598; matches (1,000 boxes), 8,979.

Labour. The labour force in 1996 totalled 1,831,000 (71% males). Over 40% of the economically active population in 1993 were engaged in agriculture, fisheries and forestry. In 1993 there was a monthly minimum wage of 269,445 guaranís.

Trade Unions. Trade unionists number about 30,000 (*Confederación Paraguaya de Trabajadores* and *Confederación Cristiana de Trabajadores*).

INTERNATIONAL TRADE
Foreign debt was US$2,141m. in 1996. In 1992 direct foreign investment totalled US$117m. (40% from Brazil, 19% from France, 12% from USA).

Imports and Exports. Imports and exports (in US$1m.):

	1991	1992	1993	1994	1995
Imports	1,460	1,422	1,689	2,370	3,144
Exports	737	657	725	817	919

Main exports in 1994 (in US$1m.): Cotton fibre, 170·9; soya, 222·3; timber, 78·6; hides, 63; meat, 55·4. Main imports: Machinery, 476·2; vehicles, 276·8; fuel and lubricants, 159·4; beverages and tobacco, 179; chemicals, 145; foodstuffs, 99·1.

Main export markets in 1994 (in US$1m.): Brazil, 323·7; Netherlands, 160; Argentina, 90·7; USA, 56·9; Italy, 24·2; Germany, 13·2. Main import suppliers: Brazil, 555; Argentina, 308·1; USA, 243·3; Japan, 193·3; UK, 58·2.

COMMUNICATIONS

Roads. In 1996 there were 29,500 km of roads, of which 2,802 km were paved. Passenger cars numbered 71,000 in 1996 (14 per 1,000 inhabitants), and there were 50,000 trucks and vans.

Rail. The President Carlos Antonio López (formerly Paraguay Central) Railway runs from Asunción to Encarnación, on the Río Alto Paraná, with a length of 441 km (1,435 mm gauge), and connects with Argentine Railways over the Encarnación-Posadas bridge opened in 1989. In 1994 traffic amounted to 182,000 tonnes and 24,000 passengers.

Civil Aviation. There is an international airport at Asunción (Silvio Pettirossi). The main Paraguay-based carrier is Transportes Aereos del Mercosur. In 1998 services were also provided by Aerolíneas Argentinas, Aeroperú, ALTA, American Airlines, Brasil Central, Iberia, Lan-Chile, Lloyd Aérea Boliviano, National Airlines, Pluna and Varig. In 1996 Asunción handled 537,478 passengers (475,683 on international flights) and 6,267 tonnes of freight.

Shipping. Asunción, the chief port, is 950 miles from the sea. In 1995, ocean-going shipping totalled 32,226 GRT, including oil tankers, 2,850 GRT.

Telecommunications. Telephone main lines numbered 218,000 in 1997 (42·9 per 1,000 population). In 1995 there were 16,000 cellular phone subscribers and 1,700 fax machines. There were approximately 1,000 Internet users in Oct. 1997.

Postal Services. In 1995 there were 321 post offices.

SOCIAL INSTITUTIONS
Justice. The 1992 constitution confers a large measure of judicial autonomy. The highest court is the Supreme Court with 9 members. Nominations for membership must be backed by 6 of the 8 members of the Magistracy Council, which appoints all judges, magistrates and the electoral tribunal. The Council comprises elected representatives of the Presidency, Congress and the bar. There are special Chambers

of Appeal for civil and commercial cases, and criminal cases. Judges of first instance deal with civil, commercial and criminal cases in 6 departments. Minor cases are dealt with by Justices of the Peace.

The Attorney-General represents the State in all jurisdictions, with representatives in each judicial department and in every jurisdiction.

Religion. Religious liberty was guaranteed by the 1967 constitution. Article 6 recognized Roman Catholicism as the official religion of the country. It had 4·34m. adherents in 1992. There are Mennonite, Anglican and other communities.

Education. Adult literacy was 92·1% in 1995 (male, 93·5%; female, 90·6%). Education is free and nominally compulsory. In 1994 there were 5,318 primary schools (public and private) with 835,089 pupils and 34,580 teachers, and 214,272 pupils and 20,793 teachers at secondary schools. There were 11 universities (1 Roman Catholic) in 1994–95 and 1 institute of education catering for 43,000 students.

In 1994 total expenditure on education came to 2·9% of GNP.

Health. In 1993 there were 3,341 doctors, and in 1992, 1,160 dentists and 4,558 nurses. Provision of hospital beds in 1993 was 12 per 10,000 population.

CULTURE

Broadcasting. In 1993 there were 30 commercial radio stations and 2 TV stations. In 1995 there were 450,000 television and 870,000 radio receivers.

Cinema. There are 6 cinemas in Asunción.

Press. Paraguay has 5 daily and 6 weekly newspapers.

Tourism. In 1996 there were 425,000 foreign tourists, bringing revenue of US$236m.

DIPLOMATIC REPRESENTATIVES

Of Paraguay in Great Britain (Braemar Lodge, Cornwall Gdns, London, SW7 4AQ)
Ambassador: Raul Dos Santos.

Of Great Britain in Paraguay (Calle Presidente Franco, 706, Asunción)
Ambassador and Consul-General: A. N. George.

Of Paraguay in the USA (2400 Massachusetts Ave., NW, Washington, D.C., 20008)
Chargé d'Affaires a.i.: Elianne Cibils.

Of the USA in Paraguay (1776 Mariscal López Ave., Asunción)
Ambassador: Maura Harty.

Of Paraguay to the United Nations
Ambassador: Hugo Saguier Caballero.

Of Paraguay to the European Union
Ambassador: Manuel María Cáceres Cardozo.

FURTHER READING

Gaceta Official, published by Imprenta Nacional, Estrella y Estero Bellaco, Asunción
Anuario Daumas. Asunción
Anuario Estadístico de la República del Paraguay. Asunción. Annual
Lewis, P. H., *Paraguay under Stroessner.* Univ. of North Carolina Press, 1980
Nickson, R. A., *Paraguay.* [Bibliography] Oxford and Santa Barbara (CA), 1987

National Library: Biblioteca Nacional, De la Rosidenta, Asunción.

PERU

República del Perú

Capital: Lima
Population estimate, 2000: 25·66m.
GNP per capita: (PPP$) 4,410
HDI/world rank: 0·729/86

KEY HISTORICAL EVENTS

The Incas of Peru were conquered by the Spanish in the 16th century, and subsequent Spanish colonial settlement made Peru the most important of the Spanish viceroyalties in South America. On 28 July 1821 Peru declared its independence, but it was not until after a war which ended in 1824 that the country gained its freedom. The two presidential terms served by Gen. Ramón Castilla (1845–51 and 1855–62) were prosperous ones for Peru, but in a disastrous war with Chile (1879–83) Peru's capital, Lima, was captured and she lost some of her southern territory to Chile under the peace treaty. Tacna, in the far south of the country, remained in Chilean control from 1880 until 1929.

In 1924 Dr Victor Raúl Haya de la Torre founded the *Alianza Popular Revolucionaria Americana* to oppose the dictatorial government then in power. The party was banned between 1931 and 1945 and between 1948 and 1956 its leader failed regularly in the presidential elections but it was at times the largest party in Congress.

In Oct. 1948 Gen. Manuel Odria deposed President José Luis Bustamante y Rivera and became president in 1950. He was succeeded by an elected president, Dr Manuel Prado y Ugarteche in 1956, but the closeness of the 1962 elections led Gen. Ricardo Pérez Godoy, Chairman of the Joint Chiefs-of-Staff, to seize power. A *coup* led by Gen. Nicolás Lindley López deposed him in 1963. There followed, after elections, a period of civilian rule under President Fernando Belaúnde Terry, who enacted important legislation and measures to promote agrarian reforms. The military staged yet another *coup* in 1968, and the Army Chief-of-staff, Gen. Juan Valasco Alvarado, usurped the presidency and dissolved Congress. He in turn was overthrown and superseded by Gen. Francisco Morales Bermudez in 1975. In 1978–79 a constituent assembly drew up a new constitution, after which a civilian government was installed and President Fernando Belaúnde Terry again took office on 28 July 1980. He was succeeded in a constitutional process of election by President Alan Garcia Pérez in July 1985.

On 6 April 1992 the President suspended the constitution and dissolved the parliament. A new constitution was promulgated on 29 Dec. 1993.

On 17 Dec. 1996 Tupac Amaru Revolutionary Movement guerrillas seized the residence of the Japanese ambassador, holding 72 hostages in a demand for the release of guerrilla prisoners. The stand-off continued until the following April when the Peruvian army launched an assault to liberate the hostages.

TERRITORY AND POPULATION

Peru is bounded in the north by Ecuador and Colombia, east by Brazil and Bolivia, south by Chile and west by the Pacific Ocean. Area, 1,285,216 sq. km.

For an account of the border dispute with Ecuador *see* ECUADOR: Territory and Population.

Census population, 1993, 22,639,443. Urban 17,732,549 (71·5%); rural 7,068,219; 1998 estimate, 24,800,768. Density, 19 per sq. km.

The UN gives a projected population for 2000 of 25·66m.

Area and 1998 population estimate of the 24 departments and the constitutional province of Callao, together with their capitals:

Department	Area (in sq. km)	Population	Capital	Population
Amazonas	39,249	391,078	Chachapoyas	17,527
Ancash	35,826	1,045,921	Huaraz	79,012
Apurímac	15,666	418,775	Abancay	49,513
Arequipa	63,345	1,035,773	Arequipa	710,103
Ayacucho	43,814	525,601	Ayacucho	118,960
Cajamarca	33,247	1,377,297	Cajamarca	108,009

Department	Area (in sq. km)	Population	Capital	Population
Callao[1]	147	736,243	Callao	424,294
Cusco	71,892	1,131,061	Cusco	278,590
Huancavelica	22,131	423,041	Huancavelica	35,123
Huánuco	36,938	747,263	Huánuco	129,688
Ica	21,328	628,684	Ica	194,820
Junín	44,410	1,161,581	Huancayo	305,039
La Libertad	25,570	1,415,512	Trujillo	603,657
Lambayeque	14,231	1,050,280	Chiclayo	375,058
Lima	34,802	7,194,816	Lima	6,464,693
Loreto	368,852	839,748	Iquitos	334,013
Madre de Dios	85,183	79,172	Puerto Maldonado	27,407
Moquegua	15,734	142,475	Moquegua	44,824
Pasco	25,320	245,651	Cerro de Pasco	70,058
Piura	35,892	1,506,716	Piura	308,155
Puno	71,999	1,171,838	Puno	101,578
San Martín	51,253	692,408	Moyobamba	31,256
Tacna	16,076	261,336	Tacna	215,683
Tumbes	4,669	183,609	Tumbes	87,557
Ucayali	102,411	394,889	Pucallpa	220,866

[1]Constitutional province.

In 1991 there were some 100,000 Peruvians of Japanese origin.

The official languages are Spanish (spoken by 80·3% of the population in 1993), Quechua (16·5%) and Aymara (3%).

SOCIAL STATISTICS
1996 births, 615,300; deaths, 156,800; infant deaths (under 1 year), 58,300. Rates per 1,000 population (1998 estimate): Birth, 25·7; death, 6·5. Annual growth rate, 1990–95, 2%; infant mortality, 1996, 43 per 1,000 live births. Life expectancy, 1996: males, 65·5 years; females, 70·4. Fertility rate, 1996: 3·5 births per woman.

CLIMATE
There is a very wide variety of climate, ranging from equatorial to desert (or perpetual snow on the high mountains). In coastal areas, temperatures vary very little, either daily or annually, though humidity and cloudiness show considerable variation, with highest humidity from May to Sept. Little rain is experienced in that period. In the Sierra, temperatures remain fairly constant over the year, but the daily range is considerable. There the dry season is from April to Nov. Desert conditions occur in the extreme south, where the climate is uniformly dry, with a few heavy showers falling between Jan. and March. Lima, Jan. 74°F (23·3°C), July 62°F (16·7°C). Annual rainfall 2" (48 mm). Cuzco, Jan. 56°F (13·3°C), July 50°F (10°C). Annual rainfall 32" (804 mm). El Niño is the annual warm Pacific current which moves to the coasts of Peru and Ecuador. El Niño in 1982–83 resulted in agricultural production down by 8·5% and fishing output down by 40%. El Niño in 1991–94 was unusually long. El Niño in 1997–98 resulted in a sudden rise in the surface temperature of the Pacific by 9°F (5°C) and caused widespread damage and loss of life.

CONSTITUTION AND GOVERNMENT
The 1980 Constitution provided for a legislative *Congress* consisting of a *Senate* (60 members) and a *Chamber of Deputies* (180 members) and an Executive formed of the President and a Council of Ministers appointed by him. Elections were to be every 5 years with the President and Congress elected, at the same time, by separate ballots.

On 5 April 1992 President Fujimori suspended the 1980 constitution and dissolved Congress.

A referendum was held on 31 Oct. 1993 to approve the twelfth constitution, including a provision for the president to serve a consecutive second term. 52·24% of votes cast were in favour. The constitution was promulgated on 29 Dec. 1993. In Aug. 1996 Congress voted for the eligibility of the President to serve a third consecutive term of office. All citizens over the age of 18 are eligible to vote. Voting is compulsory.

President Fujimori estimates that El Niño caused US$12m. worth of infrastructure damage, killed over 100 people and resulted in tens of thousands becoming homeless. The government declared a state of emergency in 9 out of the country's 24 regions. A programme to rebuild the infrastructure, namely communication lines (bridges, roads, railway lines and canals) and healthcare facilities, to prevent the spread of epidemics, has been initiated. President Fujimori regained popularity owing to his efforts to combat the effects of El Niño.

National Anthem. 'Somos libres, seámoslo siempre' ('We are free, let us always be so'); words by J. De La Torre Ugarte, tune by J. B. Alcedo.

RECENT ELECTIONS
Elections were held on 9 April 1995 for President and a new 120-member, single-chamber Congress, to replace the former 80-member Constituent Assembly. The electorate was 12m. President Fujimori was re-elected by 64·42% of votes cast. In the Congressional elections, Change 90-New Mayoralty won 67 seats with 52·1% of votes cast, Pérez de Cuellar's movement gained 17 seats, APRA 8, Popular Action 4 and the United Left 2.

CURRENT ADMINISTRATION
President: Alberto Kenyo Fujimori, b. 1938 (Change 90 Movement; sworn in 28 July 1990).

The President formed a new government in July 1995, which in March 1999 comprised:

President of the Council of Ministers, Prime Minister and Minister of Economy and Finance: Victor Joy Way Rojas.

Minister of Fisheries: Gustavo Caillaux Zazzali. *Foreign Affairs:* Fernando De Trazegnies Granda. *Interior:* Gen. José Villanueva Ruesta. *Justice:* Maria Carlota Valenzuela De Puelles. *Defence:* Gen. Julio Salazar Monroe. *Public Health:* Carlos Augusto de Romana y Garcia. *Labour and Social Promotion:* Jorge Jamil Mufarech Nemi. *Agriculture:* Belisario De Las Casas Piedras. *Energy and Mines:* Daniel Hokama Tokashiki. *Industry, Tourism, Commerce, Integration and International Trade Affairs:* Cesar Luna Victoria Leon. *Transport, Communications, Housing and Construction:* Alberto Pandolfi Arbulu. *Education:* Felipe Ignacio Garcia Escudero. *Minister of the Presidency:* Maria Cristina Rizo Patron Velarde. *Minister for the Promotion of Women and Human Development:* Luisa Maria Cuculiza Torre.

Local Government. There are 24 departments and 1 constitutional province divided into 192 provinces and 1,812 districts. There are also 14 administrative regions with their own authorities. Municipal elections were last held in 1998.

DEFENCE
There is selective conscription for 2 years. Defence expenditure totalled US$1,276m. in 1997 (US$52 per capita).

Army. There are 6 military regions. The Army comprises (1997) approximately 85,000 personnel (60,000 conscripts) and 188,000 reserves. There are 3 armoured, 1 cavalry, 7 infantry, 1 airborne and 1 jungle division with supporting artillery, engineer and helicopter battalions, 1 Presidential Escort regiment and 1 air defence artillery group. There is an air element of 50 Mil Mi-8 and Mi-17 and 25 other helicopters, as well as about 14 fixed-wing transport and liaison aircraft. Equipment includes 300 T-54/-55 main battle tanks (perhaps 50 operational).

There is a paramilitary national police force of 60,000 personnel.

Navy. The principal ships of the Navy are the former Netherlands cruisers *Almirante Grau* and *Aguirre* built in 1953. *Almirante Grau*'s main armament is 8 152-mm guns and 8 Otomat surface-to-surface missiles. *Aguirre* has been converted to a helicopter cruiser and mounts only 4 152-mm guns, the two after-turrets having been removed in favour of a hangar and flight deck capable of supporting 4 SH-3D Sea King helicopters. There are 6 diesel submarines built in what was then West Germany (1974–82). Other combatants include 1 modernized former British Daring class destroyer, 4 Italian Lupo class frigates, 6 French-built fast missile craft and 3 tank landing ships. Major auxiliaries include 1 transport, 1 Antarctic patrol ship, 2 replenishment and 1 freighting tankers, 1 survey ship and 1 ocean tug, and 30 minor auxiliaries and service craft. A river flotilla of 9 patrol craft police the Upper Amazon, based at Puerto Maldonado and Iquitos.

The Naval Aviation branch comprises 6 S-2 Trackers and 3 EMB-111 anti-submarine aircraft based ashore, 8 Sea King and 6 AB-212 anti-submarine helicopters for service afloat, and over 30 miscellaneous transport and utility aircraft.

Callao is the main base, where the dockyard is located and most training takes place. Smaller ocean bases exist at Paita and Talara.

Naval personnel in 1997 totalled 25,000 (12,500 conscripts) including 700 Naval Air Arm and 3,000 Marines. There are 3 batteries of coastal defence artillery.

The Coast Guard, 600 strong in 1996, includes 5 coastal patrol craft, 3 inshore and 8 river patrol craft.

Air Force. The operational force consists of 5 combat groups. No. 6 Group has 1 squadron of Mirage 5 jet fighters; No. 9 Group has 1 squadron of Canberra jet bombers; No. 7 Group has 2 squadrons of A-37B light attack aircraft; No. 11 Group has Soviet-built Su-22 variable-geometry fighter bombers in 1 operational squadron; No. 4 Group has one squadron of Su-22s and one with Mirage 2000s. MiG-29 interceptors were bought from Belarus in 1997. Other aircraft in service include medium transports (1 F.28 Fellowship, 20 An-32, 10 C-130/L-100 Hercules), light transports (16 Twin Otter, 5 Y-12, 1 twin-jet Falcon and 12 Turbo-Porter), helicopters (40 Mi-8/17, 25 Mi-24 gunships, Bell 206, 212, 214ST, 412 and UH-1, BO 105 and Ecureuil), 60 training aircraft (including Aermacchi MB 339, Tucano and T-41D) and a small number of miscellaneous types for photographic and communications duties. There are military airfields at Talara, Chiclayo, Piura, Pisco, Lima (2), Iquitos and La Joya, and a floatplane base at Iquitos. In 1997 there were some 15,000 personnel (2,000 conscripts) and 90 combat aircraft and 20 armed helicopters.

INTERNATIONAL RELATIONS
Peru is a member of the UN, OAS, the Andean Group and LAIA.

ECONOMY

Policy. Privatization began in 1991 under the aegis of the Privatization Commission (COPRI). By early 1995, 95 state companies had been sold bringing in revenue of US$4,400m. In 1996, 31 state companies were sold, bringing in US$871m. In 1994 a 'citizen participation' scheme was initiated to increase the extent of private shareholding in state enterprises; retirement pensions may also be taken as shares.

Performance. Forecasts for GDP growth for 1998 ranged from 2·5% to 6%. In 1997 the GDP growth (Jan. to Aug.) was 7·2%.

Budget. At US$10·2bn., the 1998 budget is 10% higher in real terms than in 1997. There was a trade deficit of US$1·7bn. in 1997. In 1997 the World Bank approved a US$150m. loan to help Peru overcome expected problems associated with El Niño.

Currency. The monetary unit is the *nuevo sol* (PES), of 100 *céntimos*, which replaced the inti in 1990 at a rate of 1m. intis = 1 nuevo sol. Inflation was 5·7% in 1997 and was forecast to rise to 8% in 1998. Foreign exchange reserves were US$10,954m. in Jan. 1998 and gold reserves 1·11m. troy oz. in Feb. 1998. In Dec. 1997 total money supply was 14,825m. sols.

Banking and Finance. The bank of issue is the Banco Central de Reserva (*Governor*, Germán Suárez Chávez), which was established in 1922. The government's fiscal agent is the Banco de la Nación. In 1995 there were additionally 17 domestic commercial, 1 foreign and 4 multinational banks. Legislation of April 1991 permitted financial institutions to fix their own interest rates and reopened the country to foreign banks. The Central Reserve Banks sets the upper limit.

There are stock exchanges in Lima and Arequipa.

Weights and Measures. The metric system is in use.

ENERGY AND NATURAL RESOURCES
Peru lays claim to 84 of the world's 114 ecosystems; 28 of its climate types; 19% of all bird species; 20% of all plant species; and 25 conservation areas (7 national parks, 8 national reserves, 7 national sanctuaries and 3 historic sanctuaries.)

PERU

Electricity. In 1996 output was 16,541·6m. kWh (13,222·7m. kWh hydro-electric). Total generating capacity was 4,771·7 MW. 66·1% of the population were supplied with electricity in 1996. Consumption per capita in 1995 was an estimated 519 kWh. Peru's reliance on hydro-generated electricity means that electricity production was affected by the drought brought on by the 1997–98 El Niño.

Oil and Gas. Proven oil reserves in 1996 amounted to 340·3m. bbls. Output, 1996, 43·91m. bbls. Development of the huge Camisea gas field, Peru's largest commercial project, is on hold while negotiations continue with the Shell-Mobil consortium.

Minerals. Mining accounts for some 8·4% of GDP (1996). Lead, copper, iron, silver, zinc and petroleum are the chief minerals exploited. Mineral production, 1996 (in 1,000 tonnes): Iron, 2,875·6; zinc, 760·6; copper, 484·2; lead, 248·8; silver, 1,970·2; gold, 64·8. Early in 1998 Southern Peru Copper, the country's largest mining company, estimated that 3,000 tonnes of copper production had been lost due to flooding caused by El Niño.

Agriculture. Agriculture produced 7% of GDP in 1996. There are 4 natural zones: The Coast strip, with an average width of 80 km; the Sierra or Uplands, formed by the coast range of mountains and the Andes proper; the Montaña or high wooded region which lies on the eastern slopes of the Andes; and the jungle in the Amazon Basin, known as the Selva. Legislation of 1991 permits the unrestricted sale of agricultural land. Workers in co-operatives may elect to form limited liability companies and become shareholders.

Production in 1996 (in 1,000 tonnes): Potatoes, 2,327·3; wheat, 130; seed cotton, 268·6; coffee, 106·5; rice, 1,203; maize, 559·4; beans, 68·9; sugar-cane 6,119.

Livestock, 1996: Alpacas, 2·6m.; cattle, 4·6m.; pigs, 2·5m.; sheep, 12·7m.; poultry, 77·2m. Livestock products (in 1,000 tonnes), 1996: Poultry meat, 310·5; mutton and lamb, 20·3; pork, 83; beef, 110·1.

Arable land (in 1,000 ha), 1996: 35,381·8, of which 5,477 was given over to agricultural production: 4,314·4 was cultivated, 892·3 was permanent crops and 270·3 was permanent pasture. 29,904·8 ha of arable land was not used for agricultural production, with 16,906·4 natural pasture, 9,053·7 left wild and 3,944·7 was other types of earth. In Nov. 1997 more than 3,000 ha of farmlands were washed away in floods caused by El Niño.

Forestry. In 1995 the area covered by forests was 67·56m. ha, or 52·8% of the total land area (68·65m. ha and 53·6% in 1990). The forests contain valuable hardwoods; oak and cedar account for about 40%. In 1995 roundwood removals totalled 12·58m. cu. metres.

Fisheries. Sardines and anchovies are caught offshore to be processed into fishmeal, of which Peru is a major producer. Fishing in deeper waters is being developed, subject to government conservation by the imposition of quotas and fishing bans. Total catches in 1995 were 8·99m. tonnes, almost entirely from sea fishing, with a value of US$936·7m. (1994, 11·58m. tonnes, US$901·5m.). In 1993, 1994 and 1995 Peru's annual catch was the second largest in the world after that of China. In the first 9 months of 1997, 1·3m tonnes of fishmeal was produced, up 3·4% over the same period for 1996. The central bank forecasts that El Niño will shrink the fishing industry by 14% in 1998–99.

INDUSTRY
About 70% of industries are located in the Lima/Callao metropolitan area. Products include pig-iron, blooms, billets, largets, round and round-deformed bars, wire rod, black and galvanized sheets and galvanized roofing sheets.

Labour. The labour force in 1996 totalled 8,652,000 (71% males). In 1993, 1,852,800 people worked in agriculture, 72,200 in mining, 783,900 in manufacturing, 18,700 in electricity production, 255,000 in building, 1,167,000 in commerce, 347,500 in transport and 599,700 in services. In Dec. 1994 the minimum monthly wage was 132 sols.

Trade Unions. Trade unions have about 2m. members (approximately 1·5m. in peasant organizations and 500,000 in industrial). The major trade union organization is the *Confederación de Trabajadores del Perú*, which was reconstituted in 1959 after being in abeyance for some years. The other labour organizations recognized by the Government are the *Confederación General de Trabajadores del Perú*, the *Confederación Nacional de Trabajadores* and the *Central de Trabajadores de la Revolución Peruana.*

INTERNATIONAL TRADE
An agreement of 1992 gives Bolivia duty-free transit for imports and exports through a corridor leading to the Peruvian Pacific port of Ilo from the Bolivian frontier town of Desaguadero, in return for Peruvian access to the Atlantic via Bolivia's roads and railways. Foreign debt was US$26,890m. in June 1997.

Imports and Exports. The value of trade has been as follows (in US$1m.):

	1990	1991	1992	1993	1994	1995	1996
Imports	2,930	3,630	4,090	4,123	5,596	7,761	7,897
Exports	3,323	3,391	3,594	3,536	4,598	5,591	5,897

In 1996 the main export markets (in US$1m.) were: USA, 1,154·4; UK, 424·2; Japan, 388; China, 419·4; Germany, 300·7. Main import suppliers: USA, 1,858·4; Japan, 317·8; Brazil, 328·6; Colombia, 633·2, Venezuela, 528·7. Main exports, 1996 (in US$1m.): Fishmeal, 834·9; gold, 579·3; refined copper, 715·6, zinc, 273·3.

The central bank predicts that the combined effects of the Asian economic crisis of 1997 and El Niño will result in lower export earnings and increased food imports to compensate for lost agricultural production.

COMMUNICATIONS
Roads. In 1996 there were 73,766 km of roads, of which 8,565 km were paved, 13,280 km were gravel, 16,876 were without a surface and 35,045 were narrow roads. By the end of March 1998, 700 km of road had been affected by El Niño. In 1996 there were 936,501 registered motor vehicles, including 483,413 cars, 73,629 station wagons, 233,166 vans, 43,154 buses and 83,084 trucks.

Rail. Total length (1996), 1,992 km on 1,435- and 914-mm gauges. In 1996 railways carried 6·1m. tonnes of freight and 1·2m. passengers.

Civil Aviation. There is an international airport at Lima (Jorge Chávez International). The national carrier is Aeroperú. In 1996 there were 32 airports. 180 civil aircraft were registered in 1996, of which 87 were in commercial use, 13 were in tourist use and 80 were for private use. In 1998 services were also provided by the domestic airlines Aero Continente and Trans Perú, and by Aeroflot, Aerolíneas Argentinas, Aeromexico, Alitalia, American Airlines, Canadian Airlines International, Continental Airlines, COPA, Cubana, Delta Air Lines, Ecuatoriana, Iberia, KLM, LACSA, Lan-Chile, Lloyd Aéreo Boliviano, Lufthansa, Mexicana, SAETA, SAS, Servivensa, United Airlines and Varig. In 1995 Jorge Chávez International handled 3,793,000 passengers (2,239,000 on domestic flights) and 79,700 tonnes of freight.

Shipping. In 1994 there were 30 sea-going vessels and 519 lake and river craft. In 1995, sea-going shipping totalled 0·32m. GRT, including oil tankers, 0·13m. GRT. In 1995 vessels totalling 7,757,000 net registered tons entered ports and vessels totalling 5,177,000 NRT cleared.

Telecommunications. Peru had 1,645,900 main telephone lines in 1997, or 67·5 per 1,000 population. There were 74,000 cellular phone subscribers, 140,000 PCs and 15,000 fax machines in 1995, and 48,000 Internet users in July 1997.

Postal Services. In 1994 there were 836 post offices.

SOCIAL INSTITUTIONS
Justice. The judicial system is a pyramid at the base of which are the justices of the peace who decide minor criminal cases and civil cases involving small sums of money. The apex is the Supreme Court with a President and 12 members; in between are the judges of first instance, who usually sit in the provincial capitals, and the superior courts.

The police had some 85,000 personnel in 1991.

Religion. Religious liberty exists, but the Roman Catholic religion is protected by the State, and since 1929 only Roman Catholic religious instruction is permitted in schools, state or private. There were 21·56m. adherents in 1992.

Education. Adult literacy was 88·7% in 1995 (male, 94·5%; female, 83%). Elementary education is compulsory and free between the ages of 7 and 16; secondary education is also free. In 1994–95 there were 597,800 children in pre-school education, 4,085,000 pupils in primary and 1,996,200 in secondary schools. In 1993 the number of students at the 28 state and 23 private universities was 727,200. There were 251,700 students in other forms of further education.

Health. There were 455 hospitals and 1,083 health centres, 23,771 doctors, 7,945 dentists, 15,026 nurses, 5,940 pharmacists and 3,520 midwives in 1992.

Welfare. An option to transfer from state social security (IPSS) to privately-managed funds was introduced in 1993.

CULTURE

Broadcasting. Radio broadcasting is conducted by hundreds of national, provincial and local stations grouped in the Asociación de Radiodifusores del Perú and the Unión de Radioemisores de Provincias del Perú. There are 59 TV companies (colour by NTSC). In 1995 there were 6·1m. radio and 2·5m. TV sets in use.

Press. There were 48 dailies in 1995 with a combined circulation of 2m.

Tourism. There were 635,000 foreign visitors in 1996 (485,169 in 1995), bringing foreign exchange earnings of US$631m.

DIPLOMATIC REPRESENTATIVES

Of Peru in Great Britain (52 Sloane St., London, SW1X 9SP)
Ambassador: J. Eduardo Ponce-Vivanco.

Of Great Britain in Peru (Edificio El Pacifico Washington ASO 12, Ave. Arequipa, Lima 100)
Ambassador: John Illman.

Of Peru in the USA (1700 Massachusetts Ave., NW, Washington, D.C., 20036)
Ambassador: Ricardo V. Luna.

Of the USA in Peru (PO Box 1995, Lima)
Ambassador: Dennis C. Jett.

Of Peru to the United Nations
Ambassador: Dr Fernando Guillén Salas.

Of Peru to the European Union
Ambassador: José Antonio Arrospide-del Busto.

FURTHER READING

Instituto Nacional de Estadística e Informática.—*Anuario Estadistico del Perú.—Perú: Compendio Estadístico*. Annual.—*Boletin de Estadistica Peruana*. Quarterly
Banco Central de Reserva. Monthly Bulletin.—*Renta Nacional del Perú*. Annual, Lima

Cameron, M. A., *Democracy and Authoritarianism in Peru: Political Coalitions and Social Change*. London, 1995
Daeschner, J., *The War of the End of Democracy: Mario Vargas Llosa vs. Alberto Fujimori*. Lima, 1993
Figueroa, A., *Capitalist Development and the Peasant Economy of Peru*. CUP, 1984
Fisher, J., *Peru* [Bibliography]. Oxford and Santa Barbara (CA), 1989
Stokes, S. C., *Cultures in Conflict: Social Movements and the State in Peru*. California Univ. Press, 1995
Strong, S., *Shining Path*. London, 1993
Thorp, R., *Economic Management and Economic Development in Peru and Colombia*. London, 1991
Vargas Llosa, A., *The Madness of Things Peruvian: Democracy under Siege*. Brunswick (NJ), 1994

National statistical office: Instituto Nacional de Estadística e Informática, Avenida 28 de Julio, 1056 Lima
Website: http://www.inei.gob.pe/

PHILIPPINES

Republika ng Pilipinas

Capital: Manila
Population estimate, 2000: 75·04m.
GNP per capita: (PPP$) 3,550
HDI/world rank: 0·677/98

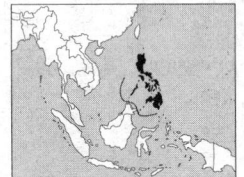

KEY HISTORICAL EVENTS

Discovered by Magellan in 1521, the Philippine islands were conquered by Spain in 1565 and named after the Spanish king, Philip. The independence of the Philippines was declared in June 1898 but in Dec. 1898 at the signing of the Treaty of Paris, following the Spanish-American War, the Philippines were ceded to the USA. A four-year war followed with considerable loss of life of Filipinos.

The Philippines acquired self-government as a Commonwealth of the USA in March 1934. This Act provided for complete independence after a ten-year transitional period. The islands were occupied by the Japanese from 1942 to 1945. Independence was achieved in July 1946. From independence until 1972, the Philippines were governed under a constitution based largely on the US pattern, consisting of a president with a fixed four-year term of office, a bicameral legislature and an independent judiciary. Two political parties dominated the political scene during this period, the Liberals and the Nationalists.

In 1971 changes were planned for the constitution. However, in Sept. 1972 before the constitution could be ratified, President Ferdinand Marcos declared martial law. Following the death sentence on Benigno Aquino, Jr (the main opposition leader, in Nov. 1977) criticism of Marcos increased. A stay of execution was allowed, and in May 1980 Aquino was released from prison to go to the USA for medical treatment. Jan. 1981 saw the lifting of martial law and in Aug. 1983 Aquino returned to the Philippines after three years' in exile and was shot dead on arrival at Manila airport. This action united the opposition parties against Marcos.

At the presidential elections of Feb. 1986 Ferdinand Marcos was opposed by Corazón Aquino, widow of Benigno Aquino. Though Marcos was proclaimed president by parliament, the elections proved to be fraudulent and Aquino became president. Marcos fled the country and a new constitution limiting the president to a single, six-year term in office was ratified in Feb. 1987.

Insurgent activities carried out since 1972 by the Moro National Liberation Front (Moslems) were ended by a peace agreement of 2 Sept. 1996. The agreement provides for the establishment of a Moslem autonomous region covering 14 provinces and 9 cities in Mindanao, Palawan, Sulu and Basilan under the administrative council; but Moslem rebels continue their guerrilla war against the state.

TERRITORY AND POPULATION

The Philippines is situated between 21° 25' and 4° 23' N. lat. and between 116° and 127° E. long. It is composed of 7,100 islands and islets, 2,773 of which are named. Approximate land area, 300,000 sq. km (115,830 sq. miles). The largest islands (in sq. km) are Luzon (104,688), Mindanao (94,630), Samar (13,080), Negros (12,710), Palawan (11,785), Panay (11,515), Mindoro (9,735), Leyte (7,214), Cebu (4,422), Bohol (3,865), Masbate (3,269).

Census population (1995) was 68,614,536. Estimate, 1997, 73·53m.; density, 244·5 per sq. km.

The UN gives a projected population for 2000 of 75·04m.

In 1995, 54·0% of the population lived in urban areas.

The area (in 1,000) and population of the 16 regions (from north to south):

Region	Sq. km	1995	Region	Sq. km	1995
Ilocos	12,840	3,803,890	Bicol	17,633	4,325,307
Cordillera[1]	18,294	1,254,838	Western Visayas	20,223	5,776,938
Cagayan Valley	26,838	2,536,035	Central Visayas	14,952	5,014,588
Central Luzon	18,231	6,932,570	Eastern Visayas	21,432	3,366,917
National Capital	636	9,454,040	Northern Mindanao	14,033	2,483,272
Southern Tagalog	46,924	9,940,722	Southern Mindanao	27,141	4,604,158

Region	Sq. km	1995	Region	Sq. km	1995
Central Mindanao	14,373	2,359,880	Moslem Mindanao[2]	11,638	2,020,903
Western Mindanao	16,042	2,794,659	Caraga	18,847	1,942,687

[1]Administrative region.   [2]Autonomous region.

City populations (1995 census, in 1,000) are as follows; all on Luzon unless indicated in parenthesis.

Quezon City[1]	1,989	Malabon[2]	347
Manila (the capital)[1]	1,655	Iloilo (Panay)	335
Caloocan[1]	1,023	General Santos (Mindanao)	327
Davao (Mindanao)	1,007	Mandaluyong[1]	287
Cebu (Cebu)	662	Iligan (Mindanao)	273
Zamboanga (Mindanao)	511	Butuan (Mindanao)	247
Makati[1]	484	Angeles	234
Pasig[1]	471	Navotas[2]	229
Valenzuela[2]	437	Baguio[1]	227
Cagayan de Oro (Mindanao)	428	Batangas[1]	212
Las Piñas[2]	413	Cabanatuan	201
Pasay[1]	409	Mandaue (Cebu)	195
Bacolod (Negros)	402	San Pablo	184
Muntilupa[1]	400	Olongapo[1]	180
Parañaque[2]	391	Lipa	178
Taguig[2]	381	Lucena	178
Marikina[2]	357		

[1]City within Metropolitan Manila   [2]Municipality within Metropolitan Manila

Filipino (based on Tagalog) is spoken by 55% of the population, but as a mother tongue by only 27·9%; among the 76 other indigenous languages spoken, Cebuano is spoken as a mother tongue by 24·3% and Ilocano by 9·8%. English is widely spoken.

SOCIAL STATISTICS
Births, 1995, 2,022,000; deaths, 414,000. 1995 birth rate per 1,000 population, 29·8; death rate, 6·1. Expectation of life at birth, 1990–95, was 64·5 years for males and 68·2 years for females. Annual growth rate, 1990–95, 2·7%. Infant mortality, 1990–95, 40 per 1,000 live births; fertility rate, 4·0 births per woman.

CLIMATE
Some areas have an equatorial climate while others experience tropical monsoon conditions, with a wet season extending from June to Nov. Mean temperatures are high all year, with very little variation. Manila. Jan. 77°F (25°C), July 82°F (27·8°C). Annual rainfall 83·3" (2,115·9 mm).

CONSTITUTION AND GOVERNMENT
A new Constitution was ratified by referendum in 1987 with the approval of 78·5% of voters. The head of state is the executive *President*, directly elected for a non-renewable 6-year term.

Congress consists of a 24-member upper house, the *Senate* (elected for a 6-year term by proportional representation, half of them renewed every 3 years), and a *House of Representatives* of 250 members.

A campaign led by President Ramos to amend the constitution to allow him to stand for a second term was voted down by the Senate by 23 to one in Dec. 1996.

National Anthem. 'Land of the Morning', lyric in English by M. A. Sane and C. Osias, tune by Julian Felipe; 'Bayang Magiliw'; Tagalog lyric by the Institute of National Language.

RECENT ELECTIONS
At the presidential elections on 11 May 1998, Joseph Estrada received 46·4% of the votes cast against 7 opponents. The electorate was 32,674,959. Elections to the House of Representatives were also held on 11 May 1998. 110 out of a total of 221 seats went to Laban ng Masang Pilipino (Party of the Philippine Masses), 50 to Lakas ng Edsa (National Union of Christian Democrats and United Moslem Democratic Party alliance), 15 to the Nationalist People's Coalition, 14 to the

Partido Liberal and 7 to Laban ng Demokratikong Pilipino (Philippine Democratic Party). The other 26 seats were shared among party list representatives, non-partisans and others or were vacant. Senate elections were also most recently held on 11 May 1998, following which Laban ng Masang Pilipino had 10 seats, Lakas ng Edsa 7, non-partisans and others 6 with 1 vacant.

CURRENT ADMINISTRATION

President (and Minister of the Interior and Local Governments): Joseph Estrada (sworn in 30 June 1998).

In March 1999 the government comprised:

Vice-President: Gloria Macapagal-Arroyo.

Secretary for Foreign Affairs: Domingo Siazon. *Justice:* Serafin Cuevas. *National Defence:* Orlando Mercado. *Trade and Industry:* José Pardo. *Finance:* Edgardo Espiritu. *Agriculture:* William Dar. *Public Works and Highways:* Gregorio Vigilar. *Energy:* Mario Tiaoqui. *Education, Culture and Sports:* Brother Andrew Gonzales. *Labour and Employment:* Bienvenido Laguesma. *Health:* Dr Alberto Romualdez. *Social Welfare and Development:* Gloria Macapagal-Arroyo. *Agrarian Reform:* Horacio Morales. *Tourism:* Gemma Cruz Araneta. *Budget and Management:* Benjamin Diokno. *Transport and Communications:* Vicente Rivera Jr. *Science and Technology:* William Padolina. *Environment and Natural Resources:* Antonio Cerilles. *Socio-Economic Planning:* Felipe Medalla.

Executive Secretary: Ronaldo Zamora.

Local Government. The country is divided administratively into 16 regions, 77 provinces, 67 cities, 1,540 municipalities and 42,985 *barangays* (units of no fewer than 1,000 inhabitants administered by elected officials). Local government authorities are directly elected for 3-year terms. A reform of Oct. 1991 devolved more power to local authorities, giving them 40% of local tax revenues to deliver local services. Elections were held simultaneously with the national elections on 8 May 1995 for provincial governors, city and municipal mayors and councillors.

DEFENCE

An extension of the 1947 agreement granting the USA the use of several army, navy and air force bases was rejected by the Senate in Sept. 1991. An agreement of Dec. 1994 authorizes US naval vessels to be revictualled and repaired in Philippine ports. The Philippines is a signatory of the South-East Asia Collective Defence Treaty.

Defence expenditure in 1997 totalled US$1,422m. (US$20 per capita).

Army. The Army is organized into 5 area joint-service commands, and comprises 8 infantry divisions, 3 engineer brigades, 1 special services regiment, 1 light armoured brigade, 1 scout ranger regiment, the Presidential Security Group and 8 artillery battalions. Equipment includes 41 Scorpion light tanks.

Strength (1997) 20,000, with reserves totalling 100,000.

Navy. The Navy consists principally of ex-US ships completed in 1944 and 1945, and serviceability and spares are a problem. The modernization programme in progress has been revised and delayed, but the first 30 inshore patrol craft of US and Korean design have been delivered.

The present fleet includes 1 ex-US frigate, 9 offshore patrol vessels (ex-US minesweepers and escorts) and about 50 inshore patrol craft. There are 5 tank landing ships and 2 medium landing ships, and some 30 landing craft. Auxiliaries include 1 repair ship, 2 small oilers, 3 survey ships and 2 water tankers, as well as some 20 minor auxiliaries. 8 BN Defender maritime patrol aircraft and 10 BO-105 helicopters are in use.

Navy personnel in 1997 totalled 24,000 including 9,500 marines.

Coastguard. The Coastguard is no longer part of the Navy. In 1996 there were some 60 patrol and search-and-rescue craft. Personnel, 2,000.

Air Force. The Air Force had (1997) a strength of 16,500, with 40 combat aircraft and 104 armed helicopters, but serviceability is impaired due to shortage of funds. Its fighter-bomber wing is equipped with 1 squadron of F-5As (only 3 or 4 operational). A strike wing includes 1 squadron having OV-10 Broncos and 1 squadron, T-28s. There are 7 transport and counter-insurgency squadrons (1 with C-

130/L-100 Hercules, 1 with F27s, 1 with Nomads, 1 with C-47s, 2 with UH-1 Iroquois helicopters, 1 with MD-500 helicopters and 1 with S-76 helicopters). Training aircraft include SF.260TPs, T-41s, T-34s, S.211 and T-33 jets. 2 Pumas and 1 S-70 helicopter are used as VIP transports.

INTERNATIONAL RELATIONS
The Philippines is a member of the UN, ASEAN and the Colombo Plan.

ECONOMY
Policy. In 1992–95 most state industrial assets were privatized. In 1996, a 'third wave' of privatization was initiated involving state pensions and social security funds. Monopolies have been dismantled in telecommunication, oil, civil aviation, shipping, water and power industries. In Dec. 1997 a comprehensive tax reform was approved, setting an exemption level of 98,400 pesos for a family of six.

Performance. Real GDP growth was 4·9% in 1995, 6·8% in 1996 and an estimated 5% in 1997. In 1998 it was forecast to grow 2%.

Budget. Government revenue and expenditure (in 1m. pesos):

	1992	1993	1994	1995	1996	1997
Revenue	223,300	260,300	335,300	370,000	417,200	485,110
Expenditure	286,603	313,752	327,768	392,450	415,557	476,170

Expenditure (1997) included (in 1,000m. pesos): Defence, 37·1; economic services, 125; social services, 156·4; general public administration, 82·4.
Total internal public debt was 721,335·2m. pesos in 1996.

Currency. The unit of currency is the *peso* (PHP) of 100 *centavos*. Inflation was 6·5% in 1997. Foreign exchange reserves were US$7,147m. and gold reserves 4·99m. troy oz. in Dec. 1997. Total money supply in Dec. 1997 was 266m. pesos.

Banking and Finance. The Central Bank (*Chairman*, Gabriel Singson) issues the currency, manages foreign exchange reserves and supervises the banking system. In 1995 there were 28 domestic commercial and 14 foreign banks. A law of May 1994 allows the entry of up to 10 foreign banks with 6 branches each in the subsequent 5 years, after which banking will be closed to further foreign participation. 70% of total bank resources must remain in Filipino hands. In 1993 there were also 653 thrift banks (for savings and mortgages) with total deposits of 33,303m. pesos, and 1,045 rural banks (for savings and agricultural loans) with deposits of 13,422m. pesos. In June 1995 the total number of banking institutions was 5,269, with total assets of 1,509,600m. pesos and total deposits of 860,900m. pesos.
There is a stock exchange in Manila.
The financial crisis that struck south-east Asia in 1997 led to the floating of the piso in July. It subsequently lost 36% of its value against the dollar.

Weights and Measures. The metric system was established by law in 1869 and since 1916 has come into general use, but there are local units including the picul (63·25 kg) for sugar and fibres, and the cavan (16·5 gallons) for cereals.

ENERGY AND NATURAL RESOURCES
Electricity. Total Installed capacity was 11,636 MW in 1997. Production was 25·22bn. kWh in 1994. Consumption per capita was 326 kWh in 1995.

Oil and Gas. The recent discovery of a gas field off the island of Palawan is expected to yield up to 2·6 trillion cu. feet of natural gas. It is estimated that reserves of up to 34 trillion cu. feet are waiting to be discovered.

Water. Water production in 1997 was 997m. cu. metres while water consumption was 230m. cu. metres. Breakdown of water consumption: industrial, 89m. cu. metres; residential, 82m. cu. metres and commercial, 59m. cu. metres.

Minerals. Mineral production in 1994 (in tonnes): Copper, 547,400; coal, 1,458,100; gold, 27,100 kg; silver, 29,600 kg; chromite refractory ore, 64,100; 1992: Nickel metal, 14,000; salt, 495,800; silica sand, 500,300. Other minerals include cement, rock asphalt, sand and gravel. Total value of mineral production, 1994, 18,773m. pesos.

PHILIPPINES

Agriculture. Agriculture accounted for 21% of GDP in 1996. In 1994 there were approximately 5·52m. ha of arable land, 3·67m. ha of permanent crops and 1·28m. ha of permanent pasture. In Oct. 1995, 12,465,340 persons were employed in agriculture (44·5% of the working population).

Output (in 1,000 tonnes) in 1996: Rough rice, 11,284; coconuts, 11,935; sugarcane, 23,640; bananas, 3,071; corn, 4,151; pineapple, 1,405. Minor crops are fruits, nuts, vegetables, coffee, cacao, peanuts, ramie, rubber, maguey, kapok, abaca and tobacco.

Livestock, 1997 : water buffaloes (carabao), 2·99m.; cattle, 2·26m.; pigs, 9·75m.; goats, 3·01m. and poultry, 149·5m.

Forestry. Forests covered 6·7m. ha (22·7% of the land area) in 1995, compared to 8·08m. ha and 27·1% in 1990. Approximately two-thirds of the total forest area is timberland. Timber production was 39·86m. cu. metres in 1995.

Fisheries. The catch in 1995 was 2,269,234 tonnes, of which 1,732,890 tonnes were sea fish.

INDUSTRY
Leading sectors are foodstuffs, oil refining and chemicals. In June 1993 there were about 11,000 large manufacturing establishments employing 908,700 persons.

Labour. In Oct. 1998 the total workforce was 31,278,000, of whom 28,262,000 were employed (16,981,000 in non-agricultural work). Employees by sector, 1998: 11·2m. in agriculture, forestry and fisheries, 5·6m. in services, 2·68m. in manufacturing, 1·88m. in transport and communications and 1·51m. in building work. 3·01m. persons were registered unemployed in Oct. 1998. 636,832 persons worked overseas in 1997.

The 1998 unemployment rate was 9·6% (7·9% in 1997).

Trade Unions. In 1997 there were 8,822 trade unions with a total membership of 3,587,934.

INTERNATIONAL TRADE
Foreign debt was 51·8% of GDP in 1997 (51·0% in 1996). In 1996 it totalled US$41,214m. A law of June 1991 gave foreign nationals the right to full ownership of export and other firms, considered strategic for the economy.

Imports and Exports. Values of imports and exports (f.o.b.) in US$1m.:

	1993	1994	1995	1996	1997
Imports	17,597	21,333	26,538	32,427	35,936
Exports	11,375	13,483	17,447	20,543	25,228

Principal exports: electronics, garments, coconut oil, woodcraft and furniture, ignition wiring sets.

Main imports: electronics and components, mineral fuels, lubricants and related materials, industrial machinery and equipment, telecommunications equipment, transport equipment.

Main export markets, 1997: USA, 34·9%; Japan, 16·6%; Singapore, 6·4%. Main sources of import: Japan, 20·6%; USA, 19·9%; Singapore, 6·0%.

COMMUNICATIONS
Roads. In 1995 roads totalled 187,608 km; of these, 21,019 km were concrete, 19,492 km asphalt, 8,716 km earth and 138,380 km gravel. In 1993 there were 26,594 km of national highway. In 1995, 2,581,300 motor vehicles were registered, including 626,600 passenger cars, 192,800 trucks, 28,200 buses and 708,000 motor cycles. In 1993 there were 13,292 road accidents, with 581 fatalities.

Rail. In 1995 the National Railways totalled 429 km (1,067 mm gauge). In 1995, 4·6m. passengers and 14,000 tonnes of freight were carried. There is a light railway in Manila.

Civil Aviation. There are international airports at Manila (Ninoy Aquino) and Cebu (Mactan International). In Sept. 1998, the Asian economic crisis forced the closure of the national carrier, Philippine Airlines, after it had suffered huge losses. Services were provided in 1998 by Air France, Air Macau, Air Nauru, Air Niugini, Alitalia, Asiana Airlines, British Airways, Canadian Airlines International, Cathay Pacific Airways, Cebu Pacific Air, China Airlines, China Southern Airlines, Continental Airlines, Egyptair, Emirates, EVA Airways, Garuda Indonesia, Grandair, Gulf Air, JAL, KLM, Korean Air, Kuwait Airways, Lufthansa, Malaysia Airlines, Northwest Airlines, Pacific Air, Pakistan International Airlines, Qantas Airways, Royal Brunei Airlines, Saudia, Silk Air, Singapore Airlines, Swissair, Thai Airways International, Trans Pacific Air and Vietnam Airlines. In 1996 Manila handled 12,235,000 passengers (7,342,000 on international flights) and 354,000 tonnes of freight.

Shipping. In 1995 there were 415 ports; the main ones are Manila, Cebu, Iloilo and Zamboanga. In 1995 merchant shipping totalled 8,744,000 GRT, including oil tankers, 147,000 GRT. In 1991, 139,969 vessels on domestic routes totalling 71,819 NRT, and in 1993, 10,714 vessels on international routes totalling 61,426 NRT, entered and cleared all ports.

Telecommunications. Main telephone lines numbered 2,078,000 in 1997, or 29 per 1,000 inhabitants. There were 770,000 PCs in 1995, 493,000 cellular phone subscribers and 35,000 fax machines. In Jan. 1998 there were approximately 320,000 Internet users.

Postal Services. In 1995 there were 1,948 post offices.

SOCIAL INSTITUTIONS

Justice. There is a Supreme Court which is composed of a chief justice and 14 associate justices; it can declare a law or treaty unconstitutional by the concurrent votes of the majority sitting. There is a Court of Appeals, which consists of a presiding justice and 50 associate justices. There are 15 regional trial courts, one for each judicial region, with a presiding regional trial judge in its 720 branches. There is a metropolitan trial court in the Metropolitan Manila Area, a municipal trial court in each of the other cities or municipalities and a municipal circuit trial court in each area defined as a municipal circuit comprising one or more cities and/or one or more municipalities.

The Supreme Court may designate certain branches of the regional trial courts to handle exclusively criminal cases, juvenile and domestic relations cases, agrarian cases, urban land reform cases which do not fall under the jurisdiction of quasijudicial bodies and agencies and/or such other special cases as the Supreme Court may determine. The death penalty, abolished in 1987, was restored in 1993 for 13 offences. No-one can be executed until a year after final appeal. In Feb. 1999 a rapist was executed, ending the *de facto* ban on capital punishment which had been in place since 1976.

In 1994 there were 96,365 police. Local police forces are supplemented by the Philippine Constabulary, which is part of the armed forces.

In 1995 the prison population was 17,850.

Constabulary. Public order is maintained partly through the Philippine Constabulary and partly through the local police forces. The Constabulary is part of the armed forces and has some 45,000 personnel.

Religion. In 1990 there were 50,217,801 Roman Catholics, 3,287,355 Protestants, 2,769,643 Moslems, 1,590,208 Aglipayans, 1,414,393 Iglesia ni Kristo, 323,789 Born Again Christians and 736,239 members of other religions. There were 386,000 Latter-day Saints (Mormons) in 1997.

The Roman Catholics are organized with 2 cardinals, 23 archbishoprics, 91 bishoprics, 79 diocese, 2,328 parishes and some 20,873 chapels or missions.

Education. Public elementary education is free and schools are established almost everywhere. The majority of secondary and post-secondary schools are private. Formal education consists of an optional 1 to 2 years of pre-school education; 6 years of elementary education; 4 years of secondary education; and 4 to 5 years of tertiary or college education leading to academic degrees. 3-year post-secondary non-degree technical/vocational education is also considered formal education. In 1994–95 there were 6,362 pre-school institutions (1,892 private) with, in 1990–91,

9,644 teachers; 35,671 elementary schools (2,052 private) with 10·9m. pupils and 6,055 secondary schools (2,294 private) with 4·8m. pupils; and 2,563 tertiary schools with 2·2m. students. In 1993–94 there were 10,731,453 pupils in elementary schools, 4,590,037 in secondary schools and 1,564,763 students in tertiary education.

Non-formal education consists of adult literacy classes, agricultural and farming training programmes, occupation skills training, youth clubs, and community programmes of instructions in health, nutrition, family planning and co-operatives.

In 1994–95 in the public sector there were 20 universities, 1 technological university, 1 polytechnic and 1 technological institute, and 123 other institutions of higher education. In the private sector there were 49 universities, 4 specialized universities (1 Christian; 1 Roman Catholic; 1 medical; 1 for women) and 405 other institutions of higher education.

The adult literacy rate in 1995 was 94·6% (95·0% among males and 94·3% among females).

Health. In 1993 there were 1,723 hospitals (1,095 private) with 77,434 beds. There were 1,895 dentists, 8,849 nurses and 10,831 midwives. In 1993 there were 76,913 doctors.

Welfare. The Social Security System (SSS) is a contributory scheme for employees. Disbursements in 1994 (in 1m. pesos): SSS (sickness, maternity, disability, survivors'; benefits), 14,861; medicare (hospitalization), 1,754; employees' compensation (occupational accidents or sickness), 596.

CULTURE

Broadcasting. In 1995 there were 370 AM and FM radio stations and 120 television stations. In 1995 there were 3·3m. TV and 10m. Radio receivers in use.

Press. There were 42 daily newspapers in 1995, with a combined circulation of 4,200,000, equivalent to 62 per 1,000 inhabitants.

Tourism. In 1997, 2,300,000 foreign visitors brought foreign exchange receipts of US$2,300m. (1,900m. in 1996).

DIPLOMATIC REPRESENTATIVES

Of the Philippines in Great Britain (9A Palace Green, London, W8 4QE)
Ambassador: César Bautista.

Of Great Britain in the Philippines (Floors 15-17, LV Locsin Building, 6752 Ayala Avenue, Makati, Metro Manila)
Ambassador: A. Collins, CMG.

Of the Philippines in the USA (1617 Massachusetts Ave., NW, Washington, D.C., 20036)
Ambassador: Raul Chaves Rabe.

Of the USA in the Philippines (1201 Roxas Blvd., Manila)
Ambassador: Thomas C. Hubbard.

Of the Philippines to the United Nations
Ambassador: Felipe H. Mabilangan.

Of the Philippines to the European Union
Ambassador: Pacifico A. Castro.

FURTHER READING

National Statistics Office. *Philippine Statistical Yearbook.*
Boyce, J. K., *The Political Economy of Growth and Impoverishment in the Marcos Era.* London, 1993
Bresnan, J., (ed.) *Crisis in the Philippines: The Marcos Era and Beyond.* Princeton Univ. Press, 1986
Hamilton-Paterson, J., *America's Boy: The Marcoses and the Philippines.*Granta, London, 1998
Karnow, S., *In Our Image: America's Empire in the Philippines.* New York, 1989

PHILIPPINES

Kerkvliet, B. J. and Mojares, R. B. (eds.), *From Marcos to Aquino: Local Perspectives on Political Transition in the Philippines.* Hawaii Univ. Press, 1992

Larkin, J. A., *Sugar and the Origins of Modern Philippine Society.* California Univ. Press, 1993

Richardson, J. A., *Philippines.* [Bibliography] Oxford and Santa Barbara (CA), 1989

Vob, R. and Yap, J. T., *The Philippine Economy: East Asia's Stray Cat? Structure, Finance and Adjustment.* London and The Hague, 1996

National statistical office: National Statistics Office, POB 779, Manila
Website: http://www.census.gov.ph/

POLAND

Rzeczpospolita Polska

(Polish Republic)

Capital: Warsaw
Population estimate, 2000: 38·73m.
GNP per capita: (PPP$) 6,000
HDI/world rank: 0·851/52

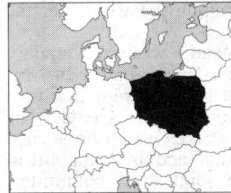

KEY HISTORICAL EVENTS

Poland takes its name from the Polanie ('plain dwellers'), whose ruler Mieszko I had achieved a federation by 966, a date taken as that of the foundation of the Polish state. He placed Poland under the Roman Holy See around 990. His son Bolesław I (992–1025) continued his father's territorial expansionism until by the time of his coronation in 1024 Poland's boundaries were much as they are today. The tendency of this state to fragment under German pressure was formalized by Bolesław III (1102–38), whose sons divided the kingdom into 3 duchies. In the 13th century Poland was laid waste by incursions from the pagan proto-Russians and Mongols. In 1320 Władysław of Kraków succeeded in being crowned king of Poland. The work of unification was consolidated by his son, Kazimierz III (1333–70), whose reign brought prosperity and administrative efficiency. A descendant of his married the pagan duke of Lithuania, Jagiełło, who was converted to Catholicism and became king of Poland in 1386, uniting Poland and Lithuania in a vast multi-ethnic empire which was able to break the power of the Teutonic Knights at Tannenberg in 1410.

The Jagiełłonian period to 1572 is regarded as an economic and cultural 'golden age'. In 1648 a Cossack revolt in Ukraine resulted in a Russian victory and acquisition of territory; immediately afterwards Sweden occupied and devastated the whole country. Turkish inroads were only finally quelled by King Jan Sobieski's victory at Vienna in 1683. Poland's involvement in the Russo-Swedish wars of 1700–09 brought not only further economic ruin but also the political dependence of the Polish king on the might of Peter the Great. In 1701 the Hohenzollern prince Frederick assumed the title of King of Prussia; his descendant, Frederick the Great, brought Prussia to the position of European power. In the 'First Partition' of 1772 Russia and Prussia in conjunction with Austria took over a third of Poland's territory on the pretext of a Polish uprising at Bar (1768). Poland was wiped off the map by the Second and Third partitions (1793, 1795), except for a brief independent interlude under Napoleon.

Risings in 1830, 1846, 1848 and 1863 were unsuccessful. Thereafter nationalist efforts were channelled more into cultural and economic development. Political parties were formed: the National Democrats under Roman Dmowski campaigned for autonomy; the Socialists under Józef Piłsudski joined the 1905 uprising in search of independence. With the impending collapse of the partitioning powers in the First World War, a Polish National Committee was formed in Paris in 1917 and recognized by the Allies. The thirteenth of President Woodrow Wilson's 'Fourteen Points' guaranteed Poland's independence and access to the sea. A Polish army was organized in France in 1918. Inside Poland Piłsudski had formed a fighting force of his own, the 'Polish legions', and he set up a rival government. The breach was healed by the appointment to the premiership of the neutral Jan Paderewski, with Piłsudski remaining chief of state.

A constitution was voted in March 1921. Poland's frontiers were not established until 1923 after plebiscites in Silesia and East Prussia and a war with Soviet Russia in 1920 which Poland nearly lost. Piłsudski took power in a coup in May 1926. His dictatorship endured until 1935. In foreign affairs Poland attempted to maintain a balance between Germany and the USSR, but after Munich it accepted a British guarantee of its independence in April 1939. In Aug. Hitler signed a non-aggression pact with Stalin which provided for a partition of Poland; this took place a few days after the outbreak of war.

Poland was rapidly overrun, but Polish forces were able to reform on Allied soil under a government-in-exile. Moscow broke off relations with the 'London' Poles in 1943 and recognized the Polish Committee of National Liberation (the 'Lublin committee') which proclaimed itself the sole legal government when Lublin was liberated in July 1944. In Aug. and Sept. the Soviet army stopped short of the city while the resistance forces were destroyed in the Warsaw uprising. At the Yalta conference Stalin agreed that the Lublin government should be extended to include non-Communists and the 'London' Polish leader Mikolajczyk with 3 colleagues joined the cabinet in July 1945.

Elections were held on 19 Jan. 1947. Of the 12·7m. votes cast, 9m. were given for the Communist-dominated 'Democratic Bloc'. After riots in Poznań in June 1956 nationalist anti-Stalinist elements gained control of the Communist Party under the leadership of Władysław Gomułka.

In 1970 the Federal Republic of Germany recognized Poland's western boundary as laid down by the Potsdam Conference of 1945 (the 'Oder-Neisse line'). In Dec. 1970 strikes and riots in Gdańsk, Szczecin and Gdynia led to the resignation of a number of leaders including Gomułka. He was replaced by Edward Gierek. The raising of meat prices on 1 July 1980 resulted in a wave of strikes which broadened into generalized wage demands and eventually by mid-Aug. acquired a political character. Workers in Gdańsk, Gdynia and Sopot elected a joint strike committee, led by Lech Wałęsa to demand the right to strike and to form independent trade unions, the abolition of censorship, access to the media and the release of political prisoners.

On 31. Aug. the government and Wałęsa signed the 'Gdańsk Agreements' permitting the formation of independent trade unions. On 5 Sept. Gierek suffered a heart attack and retired from the party leadership. On 17 Sept. various trade unions decided to form a national confederation ('Solidarity') and applied for legal status, which was granted on 24 Oct. after some government resistance. On 9 Feb. 1981 the Defence Minister, Gen. Wojciech Jaruzelski, became Prime Minister. On 13 Dec. 1981 the Government imposed martial law and set up a Military Council of National Salvation. Solidarity was proscribed.

Following strikes and demands for the reinstatement of Solidarity, the government resigned in Sept. 1988. After the parliamentary elections of June 1989 the Communists were unable to form a government against the opposition of Solidarity and Tadeusz Mazowiecki, a Solidarity member, was elected Prime Minister by the Sejm on 24 Aug. Unconditionally free parliamentary elections were held in Oct. 1991.

TERRITORY AND POPULATION
Poland is bounded in the north by the Baltic Sea and Russia, east by Lithuania, Belarus and Ukraine, south by the Czech Republic and Slovakia and west by Germany. Poland comprises an area of 312,685 sq. km (120,628 sq. miles).

At the census of 7 Dec. 1988 the population was 37,879,000 (18·47m. males; 63·7% urban). Population in 1997, 38,660,000 (51·3% female; 61·9% urban), density, 125 per sq. km.

The UN gives a projected population for 2000 of 38·73m.

The country is divided into 16 regions or voivodships (*wojewodztwo*), created from the previous 49 on 1 Jan. 1999 following administrative reform. Area (in sq. km) and population (in 1,000) in 1997 (% urban in brackets).

Voivodship	Area	Population	
Dolnoslaskie	19,948	2,985	(71·7)
Kujawsko-Pomorskie	17,970	2,098	(62·1)
Lubelskie	25,115	2,242	(46·4)
Lubuskie	13,984	1,020	(64·8)
Łódzkie	18,219	2,673	(64·9)
Malopolskie	15,144	3,207	(50·6)
Mazowieckie	35,597	5,065	(64·2)
Opolskie	9,412	1,091	(52·5)
Podkarpackie	17,926	2,117	(41·0)
Podlaskie	20,180	1,224	(57·8)
Pomorskie	18,293	2,179	(68·8)
Slaskie	12,294	4,894	(79·8)
Swietokrzyskie	11,672	1,328	(45·7)
Warminsko-Mazurskie	24,203	1,460	(59·6)
Wielkopolskie	29,826	3,346	(57·6)
Zachodniopomorskie	22,902	1,730	(69·8)

POLAND

Population (in 1,000) of the largest towns and cities (1997):

Warsaw	1,632·5	Lublin	356·0	Gliwice	212·8
Łódź	812·3	Katowice	349·0	Kielce	212·6
Kraków (Cracow)	740·5	Białystok	282·5	Toruń	205·8
Wrocław (Breslau)	639·4	Częstochowa	258·1	Zabrze	201·0
Poznań	580·0	Gdynia	251·6	Bielsko-Biała	179·8
Gdańsk	461·3	Sosnowiec	244·0	Olsztyn	169·9
Szczecin (Stettin)	419·0	Radom	232·6	Ruda Śląska	165·0
Bydgoszcz	386·3	Bytom	225·8	Rzeszów	161·3

The 6 largest towns and cities all saw a decline in population in 1997, and in 15 out of the 20 largest the population went down during 1997.

Ethnic minorities are not identified. There were estimated to be 1·2m. Germans in 1984, and there are Ukrainians, Belorussians and Lithuanians. A movement for Silesian autonomy has attracted sufficient support to suggest that further moves towards decentralization may soon be considered. A Council of National Minorities was set up in March 1991. There is a large Polish diaspora, some 65% in USA.

The national language is Polish.

SOCIAL STATISTICS

1997 (in 1,000): Marriages, 204·85; births, 412·7; deaths, 380·2; infant deaths, 2·2. Rates (per 1,000 population), 1997: Marriage, 5·3; birth, 10·7; death, 9·8; infant mortality (per 1,000 live births), 10·2. A law prohibiting abortion was passed in 1993, but an amendment of Aug. 1996 permits it in cases of hardship or difficult personal situation. In 1994 the most popular age range for marrying was 20–24 for both males and females. Expectation of life at birth, 1997, was 68·5 years for males and 77·0 years for females. In 1997 there were 20,222 emigrants and 8,426 immigrants. Number of suicides, 1997, 4,936. Over the period 1990–95 the suicide rate per 100,000 population was 23·9 among males and 4·4 among females. Fertility rate, 1997, 1·5 births per woman.

CLIMATE

Climate is continental, marked by long and severe winters. Rainfall amounts are moderate, with a marked summer maximum. Warsaw, Jan. 24°F (−4·3°C), July 64°F (17·9°C). Annual rainfall 18·3" (465 mm). Gdańsk, Jan. 29°F (−1·7°C), July 63°F (17·2°C). Annual rainfall 22·0" (559 mm). Kraków, Jan. 27°F (−2·8°C), July 67°F (19·4°C). Annual rainfall 28·7" (729 mm). Poznań, Jan. 26°F (−3·3°C), July 64°F (17·9°C). Annual rainfall 21·0" (534 mm). Szczecin, Jan. 27°F (−3·0°C), July 64°F (17·7°C). Annual rainfall 18·4" (467 mm). Wrocław, Jan. 24°F (−4·3°C), July 64°F (17·9°C). Annual rainfall 20·7" (525 mm).

CONSTITUTION AND GOVERNMENT

The present Constitution was adopted on 2 April 1997. The head of state is the *President*, who is directly elected for a 5-year term (renewable once). The President may appoint, but may not dismiss, cabinets.

The authority of the republic is vested in the *Sejm* (Parliament of 460 members), elected by proportional representation for 4 years by all citizens over 18. There is a 5% threshold for parties and 8% for coalitions, but seats are reserved for representatives of ethnic minorities even if their vote falls below 5%. 69 of the Sejm seats are awarded from the national lists of parties polling more than 7% of the vote. The Sejm elects a *Council of State* and a *Council of Ministers*. There is also an elected 100-member upper house, the *Senate*. The President and the Senate each has a power of veto which only a two-thirds majority of the Sejm can override. The President does not, however, have a veto over the annual budget. The Prime Minister is chosen by the President with the approval of the Sejm.

A Political Council consultative to the presidency consisting of representatives of all the major political tendencies was set up in Jan. 1991.

National Anthem. 'Jeszcze Polska nie zginęła' ('Poland has not yet perished'); words by J. Wybicki; tune by M. Ogiński.

RECENT ELECTIONS

At the first round of the presidential elections on 5 Nov. 1995, 13 candidates stood; turn-out was 64·7%. Aleksander Kwaśniewski gained 35·11% of votes cast,

President Lech Wałęsa, 33·11%. At the run-off round on 19 Nov. 1995 Kwaśniewski was elected by 51·72% of votes cast; turn-out was 68%.

Parliamentary elections were held on 19 Sept. 1997; turn-out was 64·7%. These resulted in the defeat of the reformed communist government and the return of a coalition led by Solidarity Electoral Action (AWS) and the Federal Union (UW). The AWS won 201 seats with 33·83% of the votes and the Federal Union 60 with 13·37% against the Communist Democratic Left Alliance (SLD) 164 seats with 27·13%. The Peasant Party won 27 seats, the Movement for the Reconstruction of Poland 6 and 2 went to German ethnic committees. 51 seats in the Senate went to AWS, 28 to SLD and 8 to UW, with the other 13 going to other parties. On 15 Oct. Jerzy Buzek was nominated by AWS to be prime minister. In Dec. Józef Oleksy, leader of the former communists, was replaced by Leszek Miller.

CURRENT ADMINISTRATION
President: Aleksander Kwaśniewski, b. 1954 (SLD; elected Nov. 1995).

In March 1999 the government was:

Prime Minister: Jerzy Buzek (AWS).

Deputy Prime Minister and Minister of Finance: Leszek Balcerowicz (UW). *Deputy Prime Minister and Minister of Internal Affairs and Administration:* Janusz Tomaszewski (AWS). *Foreign Affairs:* Bronislaw Geremek (UW). *Defence:* Janusz Onyszkiewicz (UW). *Treasury:* Emil Wąsacz (AWS). *Economy:* Janusz Steinhoff (AWS). *Justice:* Hanna Suchocka (UW). *Labour and Social Policy:* Longin Komolowski (AWS). *Education:* Miroslaw Handke (AWS). *Culture and Arts:* Joanna Wnuk-Nazarowa (UW). *Agriculture and Food Economy:* Jacek Janiszewski (AWS). *Health:* Wieslaw Maksymowicz (AWS). *Transport and Maritime Economy:* Tadeusz Syryjczyk (UW). *Environmental Protection:* Andrzej Szyszko (AWS). *Communications:* Marek Zdrojewski (AWS).

Speaker of the Sejm: Maciej Płażyński (AWS).

Local Government. The 16 voivodships (regions) are administratively divided into 308 districts (*powiat*) and subdivided into 2,483 wards *(gmina)*. Local government is carried out by councils elected every 4 years at every level. Local government is financed partly by local taxes and partly by central government taxes. There are also district agencies which form a link between local and central government. Communities of fewer than 40,000 inhabitants elect councils on a first-past-the-post system; larger communities have a proportional party-list system. Elections were held on 19 June 1994 for 52,173 seats on 2,465 councils; turn-out was 35·8%. Administrative reforms introduced as from 1993 devolve responsibility for education and health from voivodships to wards. The 1998 administrative reform decentralizes government. Governors act as 'supervisors' of regional government but real power belongs to elected assemblies and to their chairmen who are the new regions' chief executives. They control 30% of income tax and 15% of VAT raised within their regions. A new level of government, 320 elected counties (*powiaty*), administers much state welfare including health and education beyond primary level.

DEFENCE
Poland is divided into 4 military districts: Warsaw, Pomerania, Kraków and Silesia. In 1997 military expenditure totalled US$3,073m. (US$79 per capita), representing 2·3% of GDP.

3-year civilian duty as a conscientious alternative to conscription was introduced in 1988.

Army. The basic combat composition of the Army comprises 8 mechanized divisions and 1 air assault brigade, plus 4 engineer, 4 rocket-artillery and 1 highland infantry brigade, signal, reconnaissance and electronic warfare (ECM), anti-tank, mixed artillery regiments, and chemical and logistics units. A body responsible for the peace-time training and combat command of the Army is the Army Command, founded in 1996.

Personnel for the land forces are educated in the National Defence Academy, 3 Officers' Training Schools (Poznań, Toruń and Wrocław) and specialized training centres.

The Army has 1,727 tanks, predominantly PT-91s, T-72 Ms and T-55 AMs.

The land component is equipped with 1,405 Armoured Infantry Fighting Vehicles and 1,580 artillery pieces (with a calibre of 100 mm or more).

The support element of the land forces are aeromobile forces, which possess 76 combat helicopters. The main types used by the army are Mi-24s (W/D), Mi-17s, Mi-2s and W-3-W Sokół helicopters. Strength (1998) 142,500 (including 101,670 conscripts). In accordance with a programme of modernization of the armed forces, the land component of the Army is expected to reach a final number of around 108,000 soldiers.

Navy. The fleet comprises 3 ex-Soviet diesel submarines, 1 ex-Soviet guided missile destroyer armed with SA-N-1 Goa surface-to-air and SS-N-2C Styx anti-ship missiles, 1 small frigate, 4 missile corvettes, 7 smaller fast missile craft, 3 coastal and 19 inshore patrol craft, 6 coastal and 18 inshore minesweepers, 5 medium landing ships and about 3 landing craft. Auxiliaries include 1 command ship, 4 support tankers, 2 intelligence vessels, 2 survey vessels, and 3 training ships together with about 60 minor auxiliaries.

The Fleet Air Arm comprises 2 regiments, one with 12 Iskra patrol aircraft and the other with 20 Mig-21 fighter bombers, 1 squadron with 3 Mi-14 Haze and 7W-3 Sokół helicopters, and 1 squadron with 7 An-2 and An-28 transports. Naval-manned coast defences provide 6 artillery battalions and 3 missile batteries.

Personnel in 1997 totalled 17,080 including 10,680 conscripts. Bases are at Gdynia, Hel, Swinoujście and Kołobrzeg.

A para-military border guard service operates 28 inshore patrol craft and some 30 boats.

Air Force. The Air Force had a strength (1997) of 56,100 (27,800 conscripts). There are 7 air defence regiments (16 squadrons) with 210 MiG-21, MiG-23 and MiG-29 supersonic interceptors, and 4 tactical regiments (11 squadrons) operating variable-geometry Su-22 close-support fighters. There are also reconnaissance, ECM, transport, helicopter (including Mi-2s for observation and Mi-24 gunships) and training units. Soviet 'Guideline' 'Goa', 'Ganef', 'Gainful' and 'Gaskin' surface-to-air missiles are operational.

INTERNATIONAL RELATIONS
A treaty of friendship with Germany signed on 17 June 1991 renounced the use of force, recognized Poland's western border as laid down at the Potsdam conference of 1945 (the 'Oder-Neisse line') and guaranteed minority rights in both countries.

Poland is a member of the UN, the Council of Europe, NATO, OECD, CEFTA, the Central European Initiative, an associate partner of the WEU and an associate member of the EU. Poland become a member of NATO on 12 March 1999, and full membership of the EU is likely by 2002.

ECONOMY
Policy. The Central Planning Office was absorbed by the newly created Economies Ministry in Jan. 1997. An economic plan ran from 1994 to 1997. In 1995, 15 National Investment Funds were set up to oversee the privatization of 444 state enterprises. All citizens may purchase titles to participate in these funds for 10% of their annual salary, which will enable them to buy shares in the enterprises when privatized (Mass Privatization Scheme). By May 1997, 25·9m. persons had purchased titles to participate. As of Jan. 1997, 4,107 enterprises had been privatized and 1,900 wound up.

Performance. Real GDP growth was 4·8% in 1998 (6·8% in 1997 and 6·0% in 1996). Poland's economy is one of the fastest growing of the ex-communist countries in Europe. The private sector accounts for more than 60% of GDP.

Budget. Figures for recent years (in 1m. złotys)

	1995	1996	1997
Revenue	81,240	96,048	119,772
Expenditure	65,813	80,521	125,675

Currency. The currency unit is the *złoty* (PLZ) of 100 *groszy*. A new złoty was introduced on 1 Jan. 1995 at 1 new złoty = 10,000 old złotys. Inflation dropped from 249% in 1990 to 14·5% in 1997, and further to 9·8% in 1998. The złoty became convertible on 1 Jan. 1990. In 1995 the złoty was subject to a creeping devaluation of 1·2% per month; it was allowed to float in a 14% (+/–7%) band from 16 May 1995. Foreign exchange reserves were US$27·5bn. in Dec. 1998 and gold reserves were 900,000 troy oz. in Feb. 1998. In Dec. 1996 total money supply was 49,338bn. złotys.

Banking and Finance. The National Bank of Poland (established 1945) is the central bank and bank of issue. Its Governor is nominated by the President and approved by the Sejm (*Governor*, Hanna Gronkiewicz-Waltz). 81 commercial banks were operating in 1996. About 50% of the sector was still state-owned. The 5 largest banks—Pekao, Bank Handlowy, PKO BP, Bank Gospodarki Zywnosciowej and Powszechny Bank Gospodarczy—have between them an 80% share of assets. The General Savings Bank (Powszechna Kasa Oszczędności) exercises central control over savings activities.

There is a stock exchange in Warsaw.

Weights and Measures. The metric system is in general use.

ENERGY AND NATURAL RESOURCES

Electricity. Installed capacity was 29·64m. kW in 1994. Production (1997) 143bn. kWh; consumption per capita was 3,124 kWh in 1995.

Oil and Gas. Total oil reserves amount to some 100m. tonnes. Crude oil production was 289,000 tonnes in 1997; natural gas, 4,836 cu. metres. *Petrochemia Płock*, the country's largest oil refinery, and CPN, the petrol distribution network, are to be privatized.

Minerals. Poland is a major producer of coal (reserves of some 120,000m. tonnes), copper (56m. tonnes) and sulphur. Production in 1997 (in tonnes): Coal, 113m.; brown coal, 63·2m.

Agriculture. Poland's agriculture sector is the largest in central Europe, employing 25% of the working population. In 1997 there were 18·66m. ha of agricultural land, comprising: Arable, 14·29m. ha; meadows, 2·42m. ha; pasture, 1·63m. ha; orchards, 0·29m. ha. In 1997, 15·17m. ha were owned by private farmers, 1·37m. ha by state farms and 0·54m. ha by co-operatives. 6·68m. ha were irrigated in 1997. There were 2m. farms in 1997.

Some government subsidies and guaranteed prices were restored in 1992.

Output in 1997 (in 1,000 tonnes): Wheat, 8,193; rye, 5,299; barley, 3,866; oats, 1,630; potatoes, 20,776; sugar-beet, 15,886; apples, 2,036.

Livestock, 1997 (in 1m.): Cattle, 6·78 (including cows, 3·3); pigs, 15·82; sheep, 0·39; horses, 0·54; chickens, 45·18. Milk production was 11,770m. litres; meat, 2·48m. tonnes; eggs, 7,661m.

Tractors in use in 1997: 1,311,000 (in 15-h.p. units).

Forestry. In 1997 forest area was 8·80m. ha (predominantly coniferous), or 28·1% of the land area. The area under forests in 1990 had been 8·67m. ha. In 1997, 7·3m. ha were in the public domain and 1·5m. in the private. In 1995, 77,800 ha were afforested. Timber production, 1997, 23·5m. cu. metres.

Fisheries. The catch was 372,700 tonnes in 1997, of which 334,700 tonnes were sea fish.

INDUSTRY

In March 1996 there were 4,197 state firms, 101,687 limited liability companies, 220,234 other companies and 19,834 co-operatives. Production in 1997 (in 1,000 tonnes): Steel, 11,589; cement, 15,000; cellulose, 707; electrolytic copper, 441; fertilizers, 7,893; paper, 1,473; sulphur, 2,419; refined petroleum products (1995), 13,444; petrol, 5,213; cleaning agents, 319; plastics, 860; metal-working machines, 17,200 units; cars, 520,000 units; lorries and tractor trailers, 57,300 units; buses, 2,000 units; bricks, 1,156m. units; washing machines, 412,000 units; refrigerators, 705,000 units; telephone sets, 654,000 units; television receivers, 3·02m. units.

Output of light industry in 1997: Cotton fabrics, 229m. cu. metres; woollen fabrics, 31·8m. metres; synthetic fibres, 46·2m. metres; silk fabrics, 75,400 tonnes; shoes, 71·8m. pairs.

Restructuring plans were announced in June 1998 aimed at halving within 5 years the 330,000 workforce employed in the coal and steel industries, with 24 out of 65 coal-mines due to be closed. The steel plan contained a commitment to privatize the industry by the end of 2001.

Labour. In Dec. 1998 the population of working age was 28·38m. (14·92m. females). In 1997 the economically active population was 17,052,000 (7,788,000 females). Unemployment rates in 1996, 1997 and Dec. 1998 were 14·3%, 11·5% and 10·4% respectively; in 1994 the rate had been nearly 17%. In Dec. 1998 there were 1·83m. registered unemployed and 33,000 job vacancies. In Oct. 1997, 2,395,400 persons worked in industry, 1,979,600 in trade, 0·83m. in building, 0·83m. in transport and communications (March 1996), 0·91m. in education (March 1996), 0·29m. in financial services (March 1996) and 1m. in health and social services (March 1996). Workers made redundant are entitled to one month's wages after one year's service, 2 months after 2 years' service and 3 months after 3 or more years' service. Retirement age is 60 for women and 65 for men.

Trade Unions. In 1980 under Lech Wałęsa, Solidarity was an engine of political reform. Dissolved in 1982 it was re-legalized in 1989 and successfully contested the parliamentary elections, but was defeated in 1993. It had 2·3m. members in 1991 and 1·2m. in 1998. The official union in the 1980s, OPZZ, had 5m. members in 1990; there were also about 4,000 small unions not affiliated to it. In 1998 OPZZ had 3m. members, and there were some 340 registered unions nationwide. As 22% of members of parliament belong to the 2 leading unions, they constitute a significant political influence.

INTERNATIONAL TRADE
Since Jan. 1989 foreign investors have been allowed to own 100% of companies on Polish soil. There were over 30,000 joint ventures in Dec. 1998. Legislation of 1991 removed limits on the repatriation of profits, reduced the number of cases needing licences and ended a 10% ceiling on share purchases. Licenses are required for investment in ports, airports, arms manufacture, estate agency and legal services. In Dec. 1998 foreign investments totalled US$29bn.

Foreign debt was US$39bn. in Dec. 1998.

An agreement of Dec. 1992 with the Czech Republic, Hungary and Slovakia abolished tariffs on raw materials and goods where exports do not compete directly with locally-produced items, and envisaged tariff reductions on agricultural and industrial goods in 1995–97.

Imports and Exports. Exports (in US$1m.), 1997: 25,751; imports, 42,307.

Imports in 1996 included (in tonnes): Crude oil, 21·53m.; iron ore, 9·80m.; fertilizers, 1·11m.; wheat, 2·19m.; machinery and transport equipment, 14,966. Exports (in tonnes): Coal, 28·92m.; coke, 2·21m.; copper, 267,000; sulphur, 1·30m.; cement, 3·48m.; paper and products, 0·21m.

Main export markets, 1996: Germany, 32·9%; Russia, 8·4%; Italy, 5·9%; Netherlands, 4·7%; Ukraine, 4·7%. Main import suppliers: Germany, 24·1%; Italy, 9·9%; Russia, 6·3%; France, 5·9%; UK, 5·5%. By 1998 west-bound exports were accounting for 60% of the total, compared with 8% to Russia and 7% to the rest of the CIS.

Trade Fairs. Oveer 400 trade fairs took place in Poland in 1998. The majority of firms organizing fairs are associated in *Polska Korporacja Targowa*. The leader of fair organizers is the International Poznań Fairs with 454,353 sq. metres of exhibition area.

COMMUNICATIONS

Roads. In 1997 there were 242,000 km of hard-surfaced roads. In 1995 there were 257 km of motorways. There were 8·05m. passenger cars, 1·37m. trucks, 85,325 buses and 0·87m. motor cycles in 1996. Public road transport carried 1,065m. passengers and 1,110·76m. tonnes of freight in 1997. There were 66,586 road accidents in 1997, with 7,310 fatalities (6,359 fatalities in 1996).

Rail. In 1997 railways comprised 23,328 km of 1,435 mm gauge (11,626 km electrified, 13,397 km single-track) and 1,039 km of narrow gauge. In 1996 railways carried 417·35m. passengers and 226·96m. tonnes of freight. Some regional railways are operated by local authorities. A 12 km metro opened in Warsaw in 1995, and there are tram/light rail networks in 13 cities.

POLAND

Civil Aviation. The main international airport is at Warsaw (Okęcie), with some international flights from Kraków (John Paul II Balice International), Gdańsk, Katowice, Poznań, Szczecin and Wrocław. The national carrier is LOT-Polish Airlines, state-owned but with 49% of its equity scheduled for privatization. 2,287,000 passengers and 36,000 tonnes of freight were flown in 1997. In 1998 services were also provided by Aeroflot, Air Algérie, France, Air Moldova International, Air Ukraine, Alitalia, American Airlines, Austrian Airlines, Balkan, Belavia, British Airways, British Midland, Czech Airlines, Delta Air Lines, El Al, Eurowings, Finnair, JAT, KLM, Lithuanian Airlines, Lufthansa, Malév, SABENA, SAS, Swissair, Tarom, Thai Airways International, Tunis Air and United Airlines. In 1996 Warsaw handled 3,090,000 passengers (2,720,000 on international flights) and 37,500 tonnes of freight.

Shipping. The principal ports are Gdynia, Gdańsk and Szczecin. 49·18m. tonnes of cargo were handled in 1995. Ocean-going services are grouped into Polish Ocean Lines based on Gdynia and operating regular liner services, and the Polish Shipping Company based on Szczecin and operating cargo services. Poland also has a share in the Gdynia America Line. In 1997, 25·48m. tonnes of freight and 583,000 passengers were carried. In 1997 the merchant marine comprised 154 ships totalling 3·37m. GRT. 524,000 GRT of shipping completed building in 1995.

In 1995 there were 3,980 km of navigable inland waterways. 9·34m. tonnes of freight were carried in 1997 (including coastal traffic).

Telecommunications. There were 8m. telephone subscribers in 1998, but the queue for telephones stood at around 2m. There were an estimated 812,000 cellular phone subscribers in 1997 (penetration rate of 2·22% of the population), compared to 82,000 in 1995. By 2000 the figure is expected to rise above 3m. The privatization of *Telekomunikacja Polska* (TP SA), the state telecom operator, was inaugurated in Nov. 1998, when 15% of its shares were distributed free among its employees.

In 1995 there were 1·1m. PCs (29 per 1,000 persons) and 55,000 fax machines. There were around 700,000 Internet users in Nov. 1997.

Postal Services. In 1995 there were 8,011 post offices. A total of 1,217m. pieces of mail were handled during the year, or 32 items per person.

SOCIAL INSTITUTIONS

Justice. The penal code was adopted in 1969. Espionage and treason carry the severest penalties. For minor crimes there is provision for probation sentences and fines. In 1995 the death penalty was suspended for 5 years; it had not been applied since 1988. A new penal code abolishing the death penalty was adopted in June 1997.

There exist the following courts: 1 Supreme Court, 1 high administrative court, 10 appeal courts, 44 voivodship courts, 288 district courts, 66 family consultative centres and 34 juvenile courts. Judges and lay assessors are appointed. Judges for higher courts are appointed by the President of the Republic from candidatures proposed by the National Council of the Judiciary. Assessors are nominated by the Minister of Justice. Judges have life tenure. An ombudsman's office was established in 1987.

Family consultative centres were established in 1977 for cases involving divorce and domestic relations, but divorce suits were transferred to ordinary courts in 1990. 238,391 criminal sentences were passed in 1997. There were 1,093 convictions for murder in 1997. 57,382 persons were in 86 prisons as at 31 Dec. 1997.

Religion. Church–State relations are regulated by laws of 1989 which guarantee religious freedom, grant the Church radio and TV programmes and permit it to run schools, hospitals and old age homes. The Church has a university (Lublin), an Academy of Catholic Theology and seminaries. On 28 July 1993 the government signed a Concordat with the Vatican regulating mutual relations. The archbishop of Warsaw is the primate of Poland (since 1981, Cardinal Józef Glemp). The religious capital is Gniezno, whose archbishop will be the future primate. In Oct. 1978 Cardinal Karol Wojtyla, archbishop of Cracow, was elected Pope as John Paul II.

Statistics of major churches as at Dec. 1997:

Church	Congregations	Places of Worship[1]	Clergy	Adherents
Roman Catholic	9,941	17,188	26,911	34,841,893
Uniate	63	101	72	110,380
Old Catholics	149	148	145	50,918
Polish Orthodox	249	3250	292	555,765
Protestant (30 sects)	1,189	865	1,882	159,906
Moslem	10	12	10	5,227
Jewish	24	17	3	1,402
Jehovah's Witnesses	1,692	–	–	122,982

[1]Dec. 1994

Education. Basic education from 7 to 16 is free and compulsory. Free secondary education is then optional in general or vocational schools. Primary schools are organized in complexes based on wards under one director ('ward collective schools'). In 1997–98 there were: Nursery schools, 20,576 with 979,500 pupils and 74,400 teachers; primary schools, 19,299 with 4,896,400 pupils and 308,400 teachers; secondary schools, 1,847 with 757,700 pupils and 38,100 teachers; vocational schools, 7,455 with 1,568,258 pupils and 83,918 teachers, 1,831 tertiary (post-lycée) schools with 190,800 students and 246 institutions of higher education (including 13 universities, 30 polytechnics, 10 agricultural schools, 93 schools of economics, 19 teachers' training colleges, 16 theological colleges and 11 medical schools) with 1,091,800 students and 73,041 teaching staff.

The adult literacy rate is 99%.

Religious (Catholic) instruction was introduced in all schools in 1990; for children of dissenting parents there are classes in ethics.

In 1997 total expenditure on education came to 5·2% of total government expenditure.

Health. Medical treatment is free and funded from the state budget. Medical care is also available in private clinics. In Dec. 1997 there were 717 hospitals and 48 psychiatric hospitals with 209,961 beds. In 1997 there were 91,121 doctors, 17,869 dentists, 20,139 pharmacists and 215,295 nurses. In Jan. 1999 reform of the health care system was inaugurated. All citizens can now choose their own doctor, who is paid by one of the health-maintenance organizations which are financed directly from the state budget. The share of income tax paid by employers, equalling 7·5% of the amount earned by them, is assigned for the financing of the health care system.

Welfare. Social security benefits are administered by the State Insurance Office and funded 45% by a payroll tax and 55% from the state budget. Pensions, disability payments, child allowances, survivor benefits, maternity benefits, funeral subsidies, sickness compensation and alimony supplements are provided. In Sept. 1997 old-age, disability and survivors' pensions were paid to 7m. recipients; these are index-linked to the average wage. Unemployment benefits are paid from a fund financed by a 3% payroll tax. It is indexed in various categories to the average wage and payable for 12 months. Social assistance is administered and partly-funded by local government. It provides last-resort benefits in cash and kind. A special social security system for independent farmers is administered by the Agricultural Social Security Fund.

CULTURE

Kraków is one of nine European Cities of Culture in the year 2000, along with Avignon (France), Bergen (Norway), Bologna (Italy), Brussels (Belgium), Helsinki (Finland), Prague (Czech Republic), Reykjavík (Iceland) and Santiago de Compostela (Spain). The title attracts large European Union grants.

Broadcasting. The public *Polskie Radio i Telewizja* broadcasts 3 radio programmes and 2 TV programmes. There are also 4 commercial TV channels, *Polsat*, *TVN*, *RTL7* and *Nazsa TV*. Colour programmes are transmitted by the PAL system. A direct-to-home satellite pay television service was launched in 1998. A digital TV platform *Wizja TV* started broadcasting in Sept. 1998, followed by *Canal Plus'* digital platform. Links with the West are provided through the Eutelstat satellite. Some cable programmes are broadcast in Polish from abroad. In 1992 independent radio and TV broadcasting were introduced under the aegis of a 9-member National Council of Broadcasting and Television. Radio licences in 1995, 10·9m.; TV licences, 10·11m.

Cinema. In Dec. 1997 there were 686 cinemas; admissions, 24·33m. 20 full-length films were made in 1997.

Press. In 1996 there were 87 newspapers with an overall daily circulation of 3·87m. and 5,260 periodicals. 14,104 book titles were published in 1996. The most popular newspapers are *Gazeta Wyborcza* and *Rzeczpospolita*, plus the tabloid *Super Express*.

Tourism. There were 87·44m. foreign visitors in 1996.

Festivals. The Kraków 2000 Festival has four main themes—Images of God, Sounds of Eternity, Places of Mystery and Magical Words. Over Easter of 2000 Kraków will also host the fourth annual Beethoven Festival.

Libraries. In 1997 the 9,230 libraries housed 135·87m. books.

National Theatre and Opera. The audience in 127 theatres in 1997 was 5·63m. and the 21 opera houses had a total audience for the year of 1·49m.

Museums and Galleries. There were 608 museums and 218 art galleries in 1998, with 17·69m. and 2·26m. visitors respectively.

DIPLOMATIC REPRESENTATIVES
Of Poland in Great Britain (47 Portland Pl., London, W1N 3AG)
Ambassador: Ryszard Stemplowski.

Of Great Britain in Poland (Aleja Róż 1, 00-556 Warsaw)
Ambassador: John M. Macgregor, CVO.

Of Poland in the USA (2640 16th St., NW, Washington, D.C., 20009)
Ambassador: Jerzy Koźmiński.

Of the USA in Poland (Aleje Ujazdowskie 29/31, Warsaw)
Ambassador: Daniel Fried.

Of Poland to the United Nations
Ambassador: Eugeniusz Wyzner.

Of Poland to the European Union
Ambassador: Jan Truszczynski.

FURTHER READING
Central Statistical Office, *Rocznik Statystyczny*. Annual.—*Concise Statistical Yearbook of Poland.—Statistical Bulletin*. Monthly.

Bromke, A., *The Meaning and Uses of Polish History*. New York, 1987
Davies, N., *Poland, Past and Present: a Select Bibliography of Works in English*. Newtonville, 1977.—*God's Playground: a History of Poland*. 2 vols. OUP, 1981.—*Heart of Europe: a Short History of Poland*. OUP, 1984
Halecki, O., *A History of Poland*. 4th ed. London, 1983
Kaminski, B., *The Collapse of the State of Socialism: the Case of Poland*. Princeton Univ. Press, 1991
Kanka, A. G., *Poland: an Annotated Bibliography of Books in English*. New York, 1988
Kurski, J., *Lech Wałęsa: Democrat or Dictator?* Boulder (CO), 1993
Leslie, R. F., (ed.) *The History of Poland since 1863*. CUP, 1980
Mitchell, K. D. (ed.) *Political Pluralism in Hungary and Poland: Perspectives on the Reforms*. New York, 1992
Sanford, G. and Gozdecka-Sanford, A., *Poland* [Bibliography]. Oxford and Santa Barbara (CA), 1993
Sikorski, R., *The Polish House: An Intimate History of Poland*. London, 1997; US title: *Full Circle*. New York, 1997
Slay, B., *The Polish Economy: Crisis, Reform and Transformation*. Princeton Univ. Press, 1994
Staar, R. F., (ed.) *Transition to Democracy in Poland*. New York, 1993
Staniszkis, J., *The Dynamics of the Breakthrough in Eastern Europe: the Polish Experience*. California Univ. Press, 1991
Wałęsa, L., *A Path of Hope*. London, 1989
Wedel, J., *The Unplanned Society: Poland during and after Communism*. Columbia Univ. Press, 1992

National library: Biblioteka Narodowa, Rakowiecka 6, Warsaw.
National statistical office: Central Statistical Office, Aleje Niepodległości 208, 00-925 Warsaw.
Website: http://www.stat.gov.pl/

PORTUGAL

República Portuguesa

Capital: Lisbon
Population estimate, 2000: 9·79m.
GNP per capita: (PPP$) 13,450
HDI/world rank: 0·892/33

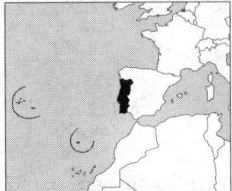

KEY HISTORICAL EVENTS

Portugal has been an independent state since the 12th century apart from one period of Spanish rule (1580-1640). It became a kingdom in 1139 under Alfonso I. During the 15th century Portugal played a leading role in oceanic exploration, opening up new trade routes and establishing colonies. Portuguese influence spread in Guinea, Brazil, the Indies and on the African coast.

In 1807, during the Napoleonic wars, the Spaniards again invaded Portugal, but were driven out by the Duke of Wellington and Portuguese guerrillas during the peninsula war. Brazil, where the king had fled during the French invasion, became independent in 1822.

During much of the 19th century liberal governments, led by financial and agrarian oligarchs and chosen by an electorate composed of fewer than one per cent of the population, were in office. The excluded nationalistic republicans finally deposed King Manual II on 5 Oct. 1910. Another *coup* on 28 May 1926 removed the unstable parliamentary republic which had fought from 1916 on the Allied side in the First World War. The military government established on 1 June 1926 was succeeded in 1932 when Dr Antonio de Oliveira Salzaar became Prime Minister. The corporalist constitution of the New State was adopted on 19 March 1933 under which a civil dictatorship governed in a one-party state. The Iberian Pact with Spain was signed on 17 March 1939.

In the 1960s Portugal faced economic stagnation at home and rebellion in her colonies. Goa was seized by India in 1961. War raged in the African colonies. In Sept. 1968 Salzaar was succeeded by Dr Caetano, but the government party, from 1970 called the *Acção Nacional Popoular*, remained in power.

There was a fresh *coup* on 25 April 1974, establishing a junta of National Salvation. Gen. Antonio Ribeiro de Spinola became president. When he resigned in Sept. he was succeeded by Gen. Francisco de Costa Gomes. During 1974-75 most of the Portuguese overseas possessions, notably the African colonies, gained independence.

Following an attempted revolt on 11 March 1975, the junta was dissolved and a Supreme Revolutionary Council formed which ruled until 25 April 1976 when constitutional government was resumed. The Supreme Revolutionary Council was renamed the Council of the Revolution, becoming a consultative body chaired by the president. The transit to full civilian government was completed in 1982 when the constitution of 1976 was revised to abolish the Council of the Revolution and to reduce the powers of the president.

TERRITORY AND POPULATION

Mainland Portugal is bounded in the north and east by Spain and south and west by the Atlantic Ocean. The Atlantic archipelagoes of the Azores and of Madeira form autonomous but integral parts of the republic, which has a total area of 91,905 sq. km. Population (1991 census), 9,862,700 (5,107,500 females).

In 1996 mainland Portugal was divided into 5 regions, with estimated population: North (3,544,780); Central (1,710,070); Lisbon and Tagus Valley (3,313,450); Alentejo (519,040); Algarve (346,110). Density (1996 estimate), 108 per sq. km. (North, 167; Central, 72; Lisbon and Tagus Valley, 278; Alentejo, 19; Algarve, 69; Azores, 104; Madeira, 331).

The UN gives a projected population for 2000 of 9·79m.

In 1995 an estimated 64·4% of the population lived in rural areas. The areas and populations (in 1,000) of the districts and Autonomous Regions (1996):

Areas	Resident Population	Areas	Resident Population
North		**North**–contd.	
Minho-Lima	249,650	Ave	477,210
Cávado	371,000	Grande Porto	1,191,740

North–contd.		Central–contd.	
Tâmega	531,540	Beira Interior Sul	78,180
Entre Douro e Vouga	263,080	Cova da Beira	89,770
Douro	234,670	*Lisbon and Tagus Valley*	
Alto Trás os Montes	225,890	Oeste	362,710
Central		Grande Lisboa	1,833,140
Baixo Vouga	360,200	Península de Setúbal	662,380
Baixo Mondego	326,710	Médio Tejo	224,850
Pinhal Litoral	228,700	Lezíria do Tejo	230,370
Pinhal Interior Norte	133,520	*Alentejo*	
Dâo Lafões	281,450	Alentejo Litoral	94,270
Pinhal Interior Sul	46,150	Alto Alentejo	122,220
Serra da Estrela	52,340	Alentejo Cental	168,370
Beira Interior Norte	113,050	Baixo Alentejo	134,180

In 1996, 172,912 foreigners were legally registered: 81,176 African; 20,082 Brazilian; 11,939 British; 9,314 Spanish; 8,503 USA. In 1996 there were 3,637 immigrants in total.

Origin	Immigrants	Origin	Immigrants	Origin	Immigrants
Europe	*2,149*	United Kingdom	456	Guinea-Bissau	89
EU	1,946	*North America*	*263*	Mozambique	15
Germany	485	USA	227	São Tomé e Príncipe	24
Spain	276	*Africa*	*593*	*Central South America*	*468*
France	239	Angola	123	Brazil	339
Netherlands	143	Cape Verde	260	*Asia*	*164*

The total number of emigrants was 7,286 comprised as follows:

Destination	Emigrants
Europe	*6,682*
EU	4,849
Germany	1,425
Spain	498
France	2,063
United Kingdom	436
Africa	*604*

The chief cities are Lisbon (the capital), Oporto, Amadora, Setúbal and Coimbra. The national language is Portuguese.

The Azores islands lie in the mid-Atlantic Ocean, between 1,200 and 1,600 km west of Lisbon. They are divided into 3 widely separated groups with clear channels between, São Miguel (759 sq. km) together with Santa Maria (97 sq. km) being the most easterly; about 100 miles north-west of them lies the central cluster of Terceira (382 sq. km), Graciosa (62 sq. km), São Jorge (246 sq. km), Pico (446 sq. km) and Faial (173 sq. km); still another 150 miles to the north-west are Flores (143 sq. km) and Corvo (17 sq. km), the latter being the most isolated and undeveloped of the islands. São Miguel contains over half the total population of the archipelago.

Madeira comprises the island of Madeira (745 sq. km), containing the capital, Funchal; the smaller island of Porto Santo (40 sq. km), lying 46 km to the north-east of Madeira; and two groups of uninhabited islets, Ilhas Desertas (15 sq. km), being 20 km south-east of Funchal and Ilhas Selvagens (4 sq. km), near the Canaries.

SOCIAL STATISTICS
Statistics for calendar years:

	Marriages	Live births	Still births	Deaths	Separations	Dissolutions
1992	69,887	115,018	909	101,161	192	58,181
1993	68,176	114,030	887	106,384	229	59,670
1994	66,003	109,287	825	99,621	292	58,443
1995	65,776	107,184	747	103,939	360	59,140
1996	63,672	110,363	759	107,259	—	—

Vital statistics rates, 1996 (per 1,000 population): birth, 11·1; death, 10·8. Annual growth rate, 1990–95, 1·7%. In 1995 the most popular age range for marrying was 25–29 for males and 20–24 for females. Expectation of life at birth, 1990–95, was 70·8 years for males and 78·1 years for females. Infant mortality in 1996 was 6·9 per 1,000 live births, down from 77 per 1,000 live births in 1960, representing the greatest reduction in infant mortality rates in Europe over the past 40 years. Fertility rate, 1990–95, 1·5 births per woman.

In 1996 the births comprised 57,374 boys and 52,989 girls; deaths, 56,444 males and 50,815 females.

CLIMATE

Because of westerly winds and the effect of the Gulf Stream, the climate ranges from the cool, damp Atlantic type in the north to a warmer and drier Mediterranean type in the south. July and Aug. are virtually rainless everywhere. Inland areas in the north have greater temperature variation, with continental winds blowing from the interior. Lisbon, Jan. 52°F (11°C), July 72°F (22°C). Annual rainfall 27·4" (686 mm). Porto, Jan. 48°F (8·9°C), July 67°F (19·4°C). Annual rainfall 46" (1,151 mm).

CONSTITUTION AND GOVERNMENT

A new Constitution, replacing that of 1976, was approved by the Assembly of the Republic (by 197 votes to 40) on 12 Aug. 1982 and promulgated in Sept. It abolished the (military) Council of the Revolution and reduced the role of the President under it. Portugal is a sovereign, unitary republic. Executive power is vested in the *President*, directly elected for a 5-year term (for a maximum of 2 consecutive terms). The President appoints a Prime Minister and, upon the latter's nomination, other members of the Council of Ministers.

The 230-member *National Assembly* is a unicameral legislature elected for 4-year terms by universal adult suffrage under a system of proportional representation.

National Anthem. 'Herois do mar, nobre povo' ('Heroes of the sea, noble breed'); words by Lopes de Mendonça, tune by Alfredo Keil.

RECENT ELECTIONS

At the presidential elections of 14 Jan. 1996, Jorge Sampãio was elected President by 53·8% of votes cast against former prime minister Anibal Cavaco Silva (Social Democrat).

At the parliamentary elections of 1 Oct. 1995, turn-out was 68%. The Socialist Party won 112 seats with 43·9% of votes cast (72 with 29·1% in 1991); the Social Democratic Party, 88 with 34% (135 with 50%); the Christian Democratic Party, 15 with 9·1% (5 with 4·4%); and the Communist Alliance, 15 with 8·6% (17 with 8·8%). The next election is due to take place by 1 Oct. 1999.

European Parliament. Portugal has 25 representatives. At the June 1994 elections turn-out was 35·7%. The Socialist Party won 10 seats with 34·7% of votes cast (Group in European Parliament: European Socialist Party); the Social Democratic Party, 9 with 34·3% (Popular European Party; Liberal, Democratic and Reformist Group); the Social Democratic Centre, 3 with 12·4% (European Democrats' Rally); the United Democratic Alliance, 3 with 11·2%.

The next elections for the European Parliament were scheduled to take place in June 1999.

CURRENT ADMINISTRATION

President: Jorge Sampãio (Socialist; sworn in 9 March 1996).

The Socialist government was composed in March 1999 of:

Prime Minister: António Guterres. *Adjunct Secretary of State to the Prime Minister:* Antonio José Seguro. *Minister of Agriculture and Fisheries:* Luis Manuel Capoulas Santos. *Culture:* Manuel Maria Carrilho. *Defence:* José Veiga Simão. *Economy:* Joaquím Pina Moura. *Education:* Eduardo Marçal Grilo. *Environment:* Elisa Ferreira. *Finance:* António Sousa Franco. *Foreign Affairs:* Jaime Gama. *Health:* Maria de Belém Roseira. *Parliamentary Affairs:* Antonio Costa. *Justice:* José Vera Jardím. *Science and Technology:* José Mariano Gago. *Solidarity, Social Security and Employment:* Eduardo Ferro Rodrigues. *Planning, Public Works and Territorial Administration:* João Cravinho. *Youth, Drug Addiction, Sports:* José Socrates. *Internal Administration:* Jorge Coelho.

The *Speaker* is António Almedia Santos (Socialist).

Local Government. Since 1976, the archipelagoes of the Azores and of Madeira have been Autonomous Regions with their own legislatures and governments.

Elections were held in Oct. 1992. The Social Democrats gained 28 seats out of 51 in the Azores and 39 out of 55 in Madeira. Pending the formation of other regional governments, Continental Portugal is divided into 18 districts. Regions and districts are divided into 305 municipal councils and sub-divided into 4,209 parishes. Each level is governed by an assembly elected by direct universal suffrage under a system of proportional representation, with an executive body responsible to the assembly. Elections for municipal 305 councils were held on 14 Dec. 1997. The Socialist Party achieved victories in Lisbon, Oporto and other big cities, with 39·9% of votes cast (up from 36·1% in 1993), and the opposition Social Democrats 32·9% (33·7%). In Lisbon the Socialist candidate won just over 50% of the vote, while in Oporto, the party had around 60%.

DEFENCE
Conscription is 4–18 months.

In 1997 defence expenditure totalled US$2,559m. (US$259 per capita), representing 2·6% of GDP.

Army. There are 5 territorial commands. The Army consists of 1 composite and 1 airborne brigade and 2 armoured cavalry, 11 infantry, 2 field, 1 military police, 1 tank and 2 engineer regiments. Equipment includes 24 M-47, 86 M-48A5 and 88 M-60A3 main battle tanks. Strength (1997) 32,100 (11,800 conscripts). Paramilitary forces are the National Republican Guard (20,900), Public Security Police (20,000), and the Border Guard (8,900).

Navy. The combatant fleet comprises 3 French-built Daphne class diesel submarines, 3 missile-armed frigates of the Vasco da Gama class of West German MEKO design which can embark 2 Lynx helicopters, 8 other small frigates, 6 offshore, 10 coastal and 12 inshore patrol vessels. Auxiliaries include 1 tanker, 2 survey ships, 1 sail training ship and 1 ocean tug. There are 10 small amphibious craft and some 20 service vessels. Naval personnel in 1997 totalled 14,800 (900 conscripts) including 1,700 marines.

Air Force. The Air Force in 1997 had a strength of about 7,700 (14,800 conscripts). Equipment comprises 1 interceptor unit with 20 F16s, 2 strike squadrons with 30 A-7P Corsair IIs; 1 squadron of P-3P Orion maritime patrol aircraft; 1 squadron of C-130H Hercules and 3 squadrons of CASA 212 Aviocars for transport and search and rescue operations; 12 Cessna 337 Skymasters and a force of Puma and Alouette III helicopters. Other aircraft in service include 1 Falcon 20 and 3 Falcon 50 VIP transports, 16 Epsilon piston-engined trainers and 40 AlphaJet advanced trainers.

INTERNATIONAL RELATIONS
Portugal is a member of the UN, EU, OECD, NATO, WEU and the Council of Europe. Portugal is a signatory to the Schengen Accord abolishing border controls between Belgium, Denmark, Finland, France, Germany, Iceland, Italy, Norway, Portugal, Spain and Sweden.

The Community of Portuguese-speaking Countries (CPLP, comprising Angola, Brazil, Cape Verde, Guinea-Bissau, Mozambique, Portugal and São Tomé e Príncipe) was founded in July 1996 with headquarters in Lisbon, primarily as a cultural and linguistic organization.

ECONOMY
Policy. Large-scale privatization has been under way since 1989. 22 companies were offered for privatization in 1996–97.

Portugal has introduced a wide range of structural reform to deregulate and liberalize the economy starting with a programme of privatization. Transactions associated with more than 43 companies during the period 1989–95 has reached 1·243m. contos (1 conto = 1,000 escudos). The Government intends to accelerate the privatization programme. The Privatization Programme for 1998–99 focuses on 7 major companies: ANA (Airports and Air Navigation), BRISA (Motorways), CIMPOR (Cements—3rd phase), PETROGAL (Oil—last phase), PORTUCEL (Wood-Pulp), TABAQUEIRA (Tobaccos—2nd/3rd phase), Comanhia das Lez'rias (Agriculture). US$2·2bn. was raised in June 1998 from the third-stage privatization of Électricidade de Portugal (EDP).

Performance. Real GDP growth was 1·9% in 1995 (0·7% in 1994). Total GDP was US$100,800m.

	1997 Estimates	1998 Forecasts
Total GDP, nominal (US$1bn.)	104·6	108·0
Real GDP growth (annual % change)	3·3	4·0
Inflation (annual % change in CPI)	2·2	2·4
Wage Rates (annual % change)	4·5	4·5
Industrial Production (annual % change)	3·5	3·5
Unemployment Rate (% workforce)	7·1	7·0
Government Deficit (% GDP)	2·9	2·5
Gross External Debt (% GDP)	15·7	14·9
Current Account Balance (US$1bn.)	−1·6	−1·9

Budget. 1998 budget (in 1m. escudos): total income, 10,147,350·1; current income, 4,653,511·0; capital income, 5,270,150·4.

Currency. On 1 Jan. 1999 the euro (EUR) became the legal currency in Portugal and the *escudo* became a subdivision of it; irrevocable conversion rate 200·482 escudos to 1 euro. The euro, which consists of 100 cents, will not be in circulation until 1 Jan. 2002. There will be 7 euro notes in different colours and sizes denominated in 500, 200, 100, 50, 20, 10 and 5 euros, and 8 coins denominated in 2 and 1 euros, then 50, 20, 10, 5, 2 and 1 cents. Even though notes and coins will not be introduced until 1 Jan. 2002 the euro can be used in banking; by means of cheques, travellers' cheques, bank transfers, credit cards and electronic purses. Banking will be possible in both euros and escudos until the escudo is withdrawn from circulation—which must be by 1 July 2002.

The *escudo* (PTE) consists of 100 *centavos*. Inflation in 1997 was 2·4%; in 1998 it was forecast to be 2·6%, declining to 2% in 1999. Gold reserves were 16·07m. troy oz. in Feb. 1998 and foreign exchange reserves were US$14,894m. Total money supply in Jan. 1998 was 5,275bn. escudos.

Banking and Finance. The central bank and bank of issue is the Bank of Portugal, founded in 1846 and nationalized in 1974. Its *Governor* is António de Sousa. In 1991 there were 26 commercial banks (9 foreign), 4 investment banks and 3 savings banks.

Since the privatization of the Bank sector in 1984–85 and the entry of Portugal into the European Union, the financial system registered significant structural alterations. The Finance Authorities (Bank of Portugal and The Finance Ministry) are creating a less restrictive and more transparent legal system through the creation of new institutions and financial instruments.

On 31 Dec. 1995 there were 46 banks. The major ones are: Caixa Geral de Depósitos, Banco Comercial Português do Atlântico. Total assets: 40,437,218m. contos, credits: 16,787,999m. contos, resources: 72,747,082m. contos, capital surplus: 1,912,602m. contos and gross proceeds 833,177m. contos.

There are stock exchanges in Lisbon and Oporto.

Weights and Measures. The metric system is the legal standard.

ENERGY AND NATURAL RESOURCES

Electricity. Installed capacity was 8·83m. kW in 1994. Production in 1995 was 33·1bn. kWh; consumption per capita was estimated to be 2,863 kWh in 1995.

Minerals. Portugal possesses considerable mineral wealth. Production in tonnes (1987): gold (refined) 0·320; uranium, 167; wolframite, 2,011; coal, 228,648; tin ore, 90; kaolin, 66,736. (1992): tungsten, 1,870; (1993): non-crystalline limestone, 32,176,852; granite, 17,771,910; (1995): copper, 536,724; tin, 8,466; marble (and similar rocks), 940,756.

Agriculture. There were 489,000 farms in 1998. Agriculture accounts for 2% of GDP, 8·3% of exports and 16·5% of imports. The agricultural sector employs 11·5% of the workforce.

The following figures show the production (in 1,000 tonnes) of the chief crops on the mainland:

Crop	1990/1994 Average	1995	1996	Crop	1990/1994 Average	1995	1996
Wheat	431·9	359·8	406·1	Rye	75·4	36·3	53·9
Maize	655·0	759·6	854·4	Rice	127·4	124·6	172·3

PORTUGAL

Crop	1990/1994 Average	1995	1996	Crop	1990/1994 Average	1995	1996
Oats	69·8	57·6	60·5	pears	99·8	73·1	100·9
Barley	92·1	53·1	69·9	oranges	168·2	199·9	169·9
Potatoes	1,323·1	1,378·3	1,325·9	peaches	94·3	89·6	75·7
Wine[1]	7,784·1	7,000·0	9,479·5	Tomatoes	672·4	838·9	914·3
Olive Oil[1]	370·7	427·1	452·0	Sunflower	46·2	26·1	—
Fruits				Tobacco	4·2	4·8	6·2
apples	257·1	231·4	253·2				

[1]In hectolitres.

Livestock (1,000 head):

	1994	1995	1996
Cattle	1,329	1,324	1,311
Pigs	2,416	2,402	2,344
Sheep	3,416	3,428	3,380
Goats	819	799	781

Animal products (mainland) in 1996 (1,000 tonnes): meat, 668·5; milk, 1,437·9; eggs, 87·1; cheese, 51·1. Estimated gross income from farming (1997), 331,854m. escudos.

Forestry. Forests covered 2·87m. ha (31·3% of the land area) in 1995, compared to 2·75m. ha and 30% in 1990. Portugal is a major producer of cork. Estimated production, 1996, 147,000 tonnes. Production of resin was 20,000 tonnes in 1993. Timber production was 9·45m. cu. metres in 1995.

Fisheries. The fishing industry is important, and the Portuguese eat more fish per person than in any other European Union member country. In 1995 there were 12,162 registered fishing vessels (9,402 with motors) and (in 1996) 29,453 registered fishermen. Registered catches of fish, 1996, 217,039 tonnes (almost exclusively from marine waters), down from 410,000 tonnes in 1986.

Species	1995 tonnes	escudos	1996 tonnes	escudos
Total	244,447	61,528,225	217,039	56,161,445
Tuna	22,429	3,569,163	17,005	3,360,505
Codfish	4,494	1,486,011	3,974	876,861
Mackerel	20,525	3,650,813	16,776	2,951,689
Swordfish	16,743	4,668,062	15,335	4,299,267
Sardine	87,711	5,345,050	83,006	6,844,126
Shellfish	22,108	12,341,204	24,428	13,704,722

INDUSTRY

Output of major industrial products: (in tonnes unless otherwise specified):

Product	1994	1995
Rice	145,253	142,285
Refined sugar	294,126	295,633
Compound feedstuff	3,755,207	3,628,435
Beer (hectolitres)	6,901,582	7,219,698
Discontinuous synthetic fibre fabric[1]	57,055	56,436
Knitted fabrics	73,716	108,970
Footwear with leather vamp (1,000 pairs)	66,104	62,800
Wood pulp	1,334,634	1,635,524
Paper and cardboard	854,740	907,409
Petrol	3,532,413	3,600,887
Diesel fuel	4,199,222	4,051,969
Fuel oil	4,694,797	4,172,576
Glass bottles (1,000)	2,290,310	2,486,732
Ready-mix concrete	7,540,566	8,350,529

[1]In 1,000 sq. metres.

Ammonia, raw steel, tin, plate and matches are also produced.

Labour. The maximum working week was reduced to 40 hours in 1997. A minimum wage is fixed by the government. Retirement is at 65 years for men and 62 for women. In 1995, out of a working population of 4,754,300 (2,141,100 female), 4,415,900 (1,960,400 female) were employed. Unemployment was 7·1% (8·1%

female). In 1997 the rate was down to 6·7% and was forecast to drop further to 5·2% in 1998. Employment (in 1,000) by sector, 1995 (females in parentheses): agriculture, forestry and fishing, 508·9 (248·0); industry, construction, energy and water, 1,415·3 (446·2); services, 2,491·7 (1,274·2).

Employment by sector (in 1,000):

Sector	4th quarter 1995		4th quarter 1996	
(Mainland)	Total	Men	Total	Men
Total	4,228·8	2,329·0	4,248·9	2,341·1
Agriculture, forestry, hunting and fishing	476·0	238·9	526·3	255·9
Mining and quarrying	17·4	15·8	15·2	14·3
Manufacturing	962·4	562·1	920·0	530·8
Electricity, gas and water	32·0	25·9	31·6	28·0
Construction	337·0	326·2	358·3	341·9
Retail and wholesale trade, repairs, hotels and restaurants	821·4	461·0	831·1	476·8
Transport, storage and communication	171·6	132·5	168·1	132·4
Financial intermediation	332·0	196·8	339·8	203·6
Public administration	312·2	181·0	288·4	171·9
Education	306·9	74·6	284·5	65·6
Health and social work	194·1	53·9	198·6	48·5
Other service activities	265·8	60·3	286·7	71·1

Trade Unions. In 1996 there were 383 unions. An agreement between trade unions, employers and the government for 1997 involved employment, social security, investment, tax reform and education.

INTERNATIONAL TRADE

As at 31 Dec. 1995 the foreign debt was 1,887,300m. escudos and the total debt was 9,223,000m. escudos.

Imports and Exports. In 1996 exports totalled $23,845m. and imports $34,114m.

Imports, in 1997, included (in 1m. escudos): plastics, 162,239; iron and steel, 135,028; cotton, 122,685; fish and crustaceans, 115,533; pharmaceutical products, 96,216; cereals, 90,528; articles of iron or steel, 80,082; rubber, 75,584; raw hides, skins (other than fur skins) and leather, 74,874; clothing accessories, 65,214; meat and edible meat offal, 56,099.

Exports, 1997 (in 1m. escudos): vehicles, parts and accessories, 555,520; electrical machinery and parts, 438,730; articles of apparel and clothing accessories, 302,290; footwear, 286,963; nuclear reactors, boilers, machinery and mechanical appliances, 169,662; cork and articles of cork, 108,545.

Imports and exports to main trade partners, 1996-97 (in 1m. escudos):

	Imports		Exports	
From or to	1996	1997[1]	1996	1997[1]
EU	4,140,460	4,442,646	3,056,168	3,249,150
Belgium/Luxembourg	180,791	183,288	157,309	181,043
France	606,736	632,857	544,887	570,432
Germany	841,262	882,703	800,071	810,708
Italy	458,287	473,477	141,744	157,033
Japan	117,291	146,850	27,706	26,491
Netherlands	242,116	264,352	186,332	193,717
Spain	1,233,403	1,349,071	554,067	571,409
EFTA	142,770	125,058	104,109	99,564
OPEC	257,000[2]	258,000[3]	25,000[2]	23,000[3]
UK	364,778	413,109	410,678	491,285
USA	170,395	192,530	167,236	196,097

[1]Provisional   [2]1994 data   [3]1995 data

In 1997 fellow European Union members accounted for 80·2% of exports and 75·3% of imports.

Trade Fairs. It was estimated that Expo '98 in Lisbon generated 1·2% of GDP in 1998.

COMMUNICATIONS

Roads. In 1996 there were 9,742 km of national roads on the mainland, including 710 km of motorways. On 31 Dec. 1996 the number of light and heavy motor vehicles registered was 5,308,542; motor cycles, 243,877; tractors, 242,672. In 1996 there were 51,156 road accidents with 2,153 deaths (2,104 in 1995).

The 11-mile Vasco da Gama bridge across the River Tagus north of Lisbon is the longest in Europe. It opened in March 1998.

Rail. In 1994 total railway length was 3,072 km (1,668 mm and metre gauges), of which 461 km of broad-gauge was electrified. Passenger-kilometres travelled in 1996 came to 4·5bn. and freight tonne-kilometres to 2·2bn. There is a metro (19 km) and tramway (94 km) in Lisbon.

Civil Aviation. There are international airports at Portela (Lisbon), Pedras Rubras (Porto), Faro (Algarve) and Funchal (Madeira). The national carrier is the state-owned TAP-Air Portugal, with some domestic and international flights being provided by Portugália. In 1998 services were also provided by AB Airlines, Aerocondor, Aeroflot, Air Afrique, Air France, Air Malta, Air Namibia, Air Toulouse, Alitalia, British Airways, British Midland, Condor Flugdienst, Continental Airlines, Crossair, Cubana, Debonair, Delta Air Lines, El Al, Finnair, Go, Hapag Lloyd, Iberia, KLM, LAM, Lauda Air, LTU International Airways, Lufthansa, Luxair, Regional Airlines, Royal Air Maroc, SABENA, SAS, Swissair, TAAG, Thai Airways International, Transavia Airlines, Transbrasil, Transportes Aéreos de Cabo Verde, Transportes Aéreos de Guiné-Bissau, Tunis Air and Varig. In 1996 Lisbon handled 6,189,947 passengers (4,912,579 on international flights) and 89,992 tonnes of freight. Faro was the second busiest in terms of passenger traffic in 1996 (3,511,884, of which 3,379,657 were on international flights) and Porto was the second busiest in 1996 for freight, with 24,243 tonnes.

Shipping. In 1996, 14,873 vessels of 85·44m. tonnes entered the ports; 181,545 passengers embarked and 180,745 disembarked. 15·3m. tonnes of cargo were loaded and 40·6m. tonnes unloaded. In 1995 merchant shipping totalled 897,000 GRT.

Telecommunications. Portugal Telecom (PT) was formed from a merger of 3 state-owned utilities in 1994. It is 51% state-owned. Main telephone lines numbered 4,002,500 in 1997 (402·5 per 1,000 population). In 1995 there were 341,000 cellular phone subscribers, 600,000 PCs (61 per 1,000 persons) and 35,000 fax machines. There were around 188,000 Internet users in Jan. 1998.

Postal Services. The number of post offices was 1,045 in 1996.

SOCIAL INSTITUTIONS

Justice. There are 4 judicial districts (Lisbon, Porto, Coimbra and Evora) divided into 47 circuits. In 1994 there were 370 common courts, including 324 of the first instance (71 specialized). There are also 29 administration and fiscal courts.

There are 4 courts of appeal in each district, and a Supreme Court in Lisbon.

Capital punishment was abolished completely in the Constitution of 1976.

In 1996 there were 54 prisons. The prison population as at 31 Dec. 1996 was 14,236 including 12,955 men and 828 inmates aged under 21 years.

Religion. There is freedom of worship, both in public and private, with the exception of creeds incompatible with morals and the life and physical integrity of the people. There were 9·86m. Roman Catholics in 1992.

Education. Adult literacy rate, which was 80% in 1990, was 89·6% in 1995 (male 92·5%; female 87·0%). Portugal has the lowest literacy rate in the European Union. Compulsory education has been in force since 1911.

In 1993–94 there were 5,388 pre-school establishments (3–6 years) with 183,298 pupils (190,435 in 1995–96). There were 10,308 basic primary establishments (6–10 years) with 586,034 pupils and 43,070 teachers (669 private with 44,647 pupils and 2,257 teachers). There were 1,758 preparatory establishments (6–8 years) with 343,437 pupils. The total number of pupils in basic education (including private) was 1,408,449 in 1994–95.

In 1993–94, secondary education: General Unified schools, 446,676 pupils aged 11–14 years, complementary secondary, 171,409 pupils aged 14–16 years and

PORTUGAL

104,555 pupils aged 17–18 years; 1,860 *lycées* with 99,842 pupils aged 14–17 years; 31,975 pupils aged 14–16 years in technical schools (in 1992–93); 22,339 pupils aged 15 onwards in professional schools. There are also establishments for students aged 17–20 years for teaching kindergarten and basic primary pupils. In 1994–95 there were 4,571,194 pupils in secondary schools.

In 1994–95 there were in the public sector 12 universities, an open university, a technical university, an institute of dentistry and an institute of industrial and business studies. In the private sector there were 4 universities and 1 Roman Catholic university. There were 125,483 students and 10,066 academic staff (not including the open university).

In 1994–95 there were 62 other higher education establishments with 300,573 registered students distributed as follows: university institutions, 139,027; polytechnics, 49,048; nursing schools, 4,787; military and police institutions, 1,190; other institutions, 1,353; universities, 46,066; other establishments, 59,102.

In 1995 total expenditure on education came to 5·5% of GNP.

Health. In 1995 there were 200 hospitals (4·1 hospital beds per 1,000 inhabitants), 383 clinics and 463 medical centres. In 1996 there were 29,902 doctors, 1,653 dentists, 337 dental surgeons and 6,781 pharmacists.

Welfare. In 1996, 3,237,238m. escudos were paid in social security benefits. Cash payments in escudos (and types) included: 1,068,165m. (sickness), 376,143m. (disability), 1,165,865m. (old age), 237,291m. (widows), 181,676m. (family), 187,147m. (unemployment), 747m. (housing), 20,205m. (social exclusion).

CULTURE

Broadcasting. Radiodifusão Portuguesa broadcasts 3 programmes on medium-waves and on FM as well as 3 regional services and an external service, Radio Portugal (English, French, Italian). There are 2 state-owned TV channels (Canal 1 and Radiotelevisão Portuguesa 2) and 2 independent channels, including 1 religious (colour by PAL). Radio Trans Europe is a high-powered short-wave station, retransmitting programmes of different broadcasting organizations. Number of receivers (1995): Radio, 2·4m.; TV, 3·2m.

Cinema. In 1996 there were 270 cinemas with a seating capacity of 76,756; admissions totalled 9·4m.

Press. In 1996 there were 27 daily newspapers (23 in 1994) with a combined circulation (1994) of 137,301,000 including 6 in the Azores and 2 on Madeira. There were 988 other periodicals, in 1994, with a combined circulation of 311,545,000.

Tourism. In 1997 tourist revenue increased to 667bn. escudos. Number of visitors, 9·9m. In 1995 there were (in 1,000) 22,875 foreign visitors (21,759 in 1994), including from Spain, 17,141; UK, 1,574; Germany, 1,072; the Netherlands, 407; Italy, 319. There were 1,733 hotel establishments with 204,051 accommodation capacity in 1995.

Libraries. There were, in 1996, 1,621 libraries with 4,368,771 registered users.

Museums and Galleries. In 1996, 8,395,333 persons visited the 309 museums, and there were 2,466 exhibitions held at the 306 art galleries and other spaces.

DIPLOMATIC REPRESENTATIVES
Of Portugal in Great Britain (11 Belgrave Sq., London, SW1X 8PP)
Ambassador: José Gregóro Faria.

Of Great Britain in Portugal (Rua de São Bernardo 33, 1200 Lisbon)
Ambassador: Roger Westbrook, CMG.

Of Portugal in the USA (2125 Kalorama Rd., NW, Washington, D.C., 20008)
Ambassador: Fernando Andresen Guimarães.

Of the USA in Portugal (Ave. das Forcas Armadas, 1600 Lisbon)
Ambassador: Gerald S. McGowan.

Of Portugal to the United Nations
Ambassador: António Monteiro.

FURTHER READING

Instituto Nacional de Estatística. *Anuário Estatístico de Portugal/Statistics Year-Book.—Estatísticas do Comércio Externo.* 2 vols. Annual from 1967

Birmingham, D., *A Concise History of Portugal.* CUP, 1993
Corkill, D., *The Portuguese Economy since 1974.* Edinburgh UP, 1993
Laidlar, J., *Lisbon.* [Bibliography] Oxford and Santa Barbara (CA), 1997
Maxwell, K., *The Making of Portuguese Democracy.* CUP, 1995
Opello, W., *Portugal: from Monarchy to Pluralist Democracy.* Boulder (Colo.), 1991
Saraiva, J. H., *Portugal: A Companion History.* Manchester, 1997
Unwin, P. T. H., *Portugal.* [Bibliography] Oxford and Santa Barbara (CA), 1987
Wheeler, D. L., *Historical Dictionary of Portugal.* Metuchen (NJ), 1994

National library: Biblioteca Nacional de Lisboa, Campo Grande, Lisbon.
National statistical office: Instituto Nacional de Estatística (INE), Avenida António José de Almeida, 1000 Lisbon.
Website: http://infoline.ine.pt/si/index.html

MACAO

KEY HISTORICAL EVENTS

On 6 Jan 1987 Portugal agreed to return Macao to China on 20 Dec. 1999 under a plan in which it would become a special administrative zone of China, with considerable autonomy.

For detailed information see entry on Macao under China, p. 461.

QATAR

Dawlat Qatar

(State of Qatar)

Capital: Doha
Population estimate, 2000: 599,000
GNP per capita: (PPP$) 16,330
HDI/world rank: 0·840/57

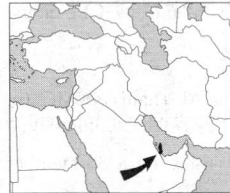

KEY HISTORICAL EVENTS

There is evidence of human habitation in Qatar dating as far back as the 5th or 6th centuries BC. The Greek historian, Herodotus, refers to the seafaring Canaanites as being the original inhabitants of the country. Qatar embraced Islam in the 7th century AD, and since then it has been noted regularly in the accounts of Arab historians and writers.

Like all of the countries in the area, it eventually came under Turkish rule and control for several centuries. Ottoman power was in fact mostly nominal, with real power being in the hands of local sheikhs and tribal leaders. In 1915 the Turks withdrew, and on 3 Nov. 1916 Qatar signed a protection treaty with Britain. However, British influence was restricted to the supervision of administrative matters.

The dominant economic activity had traditionally been pearl diving, but around 1930 the pearl market collapsed, affecting the whole economy of the country. It was at this time that initial suggestions were being made that oil might be found, and in 1939 oil was discovered in commercial quantities. Although the Second World War delayed progress, exporting began in 1949. This was to change Qatar dramatically. Qatar declared its independence from Britain on 3 Sept. 1971, ending the Treaty of 1916 which was replaced by a Treaty of friendship between the 2 countries. In 1974 the Qatar General Petroleum Corporation was set up, resulting in petroleum extraction coming under national control.

The ruling family, the Al-Thani, arrived in Qatar in the early 18th century and in the mid-19th century moved to the capital, Doha. The family's ancestor, Thani bin Mohammed, was the father of the first Al-Thani sheikh to rule over the entire Qatari peninsula, in the mid-19th century. On 27 June 1995 the Heir Apparent, Sheikh Hamad, deposed his father, the Amir Sheikh Khalifa bin Hamad Al-Thani, while Khalifa was travelling abroad.

TERRITORY AND POPULATION

Qatar is a peninsula running north into the Arabian Gulf. It is bounded in the south by the United Arab Emirates. An agreement of 26 Oct. 1996 with Saudi Arabia provided for a definitive delimitation of the common frontier by 1998. The territory includes a number of islands in the coastal waters of the peninsula, the most important of which is Halul, the storage and export terminal for the offshore oilfields. Area, 11,437 sq. km; population census (1986) 369,079; estimate, 1998, 580,000; density 47·1 per sq. km.

The UN gives a projected population for 2000 of 599,000.

In 1995, 91·4% of the population lived in urban areas.

Area and estimated population of municipalities, 1993:

Municipality	Area (in sq. km)	Population	Municipality	Area (in sq. km)	Population
Doha	131·8	339,471	Al Shamal	901·3	5,347
Al Rayyan	889·2	143,046	Al Ghwayriyah	622·3	2,517
Al Wakra	1,114·0	30,976	Al Jumayliyah	2,564·8	8,674
Umm Salal	492·6	16,785	Jarian Al Batnah	3,714·7	2,518
Al Khour	996·3	10,234			

The capital is Doha, which is the main port. Other towns are Dukhan (the centre of oil production), Umm Said (the oil-terminal of Qatar), Ruwais, Wakra, Al-Khour, Umm Salal Mohammad and Umm-Bab.

About 40% of the population are Arabs, 18% Indian, 18% Pakistani and 10% Iranian. Other nationalities make up the remaining 14%.

The official language is Arabic.

QATAR

SOCIAL STATISTICS
Births, 1996 estimates, 11,500; deaths, 2,000. Rates, 1996 estimates (per 1,000 population). Births, 21·0; deaths, 3·6. Infant mortality (per 1,000 live births), 19·6. Expectation of life in 1996 was 73·3 years (70·75 for males and 75·8 for females). Growth rate, 2·39% per annum. Fertility rate, 1990–95, 4·1 births per woman.

CLIMATE
The climate is hot and humid. Doha, Jan. 62°F (16·7°C), July 98°F (36·7°C). Annual rainfall 2·5" (62 mm).

CONSTITUTION AND GOVERNMENT
Qatar is ruled by an *Amir*. HH Sheikh Hamad bin Khalifa Al Thani, KCMG (b. 1950) assumed power after deposing his father on 27 June 1995. The heir apparent is Sheikh Hamad's son, Jasim bin Hamad Al Thani (b. 1978).

There is no Parliament, but a *Council of Ministers* is assisted by a 30-member nominated Advisory Council.

RECENT ELECTIONS
It was decided in 1998 that the Central Municipal Council should be an elected Assembly.

CURRENT ADMINISTRATION
In March 1999 the government comprised:

Amir, Minister of Defence and C.-in-C. of the Armed Forces: HH Sheikh Hamad bin Khalifa Al Thani.

Prime Minister, Minister of the Interior: Sheikh Abdallah bin Khalifa Al Thani. *Deputy Prime Minister:* Muhammad bin Khalifa Al Thani. *Finance, Economy and Trade:* Yusif Husayn al-Kamal. *Foreign Affairs:* Sheikh Hamad bin Jasim bin Jabir Al Thani. *Education and Higher Education:* Muhammad Abd al-Rahim al-Kafud. *Justice:* Hasan bin Abdallah al-Ghanim. *Endowments and Islamic Affairs:* Ahmad Abdallah al-Marri. *Municipal Affairs and Agriculture:* Ali bin Said al-Khayarin. *Communications and Transport:* Sheikh Ahmad bin Nasir Al Thani. *Public Health:* Dr Hajar bin Ahmad al-Hajar. *Housing and Civil Service Affairs:* Sheikh Falah bin Jasim bin Jabir Al Thani. *Energy and Industry, Electricity and Water:* Abdallah bin Hamad al-Attiyah.

Local Government. Qatar is divided into 9 municipalities.

DEFENCE
Defence expenditure in 1997 totalled US$1,346m. (US$2,380 per capita), representing 13·7% of GDP. The expenditure per capita in 1997 was the highest of any country in the world and the expenditure as a percentage of GDP was the second highest behind North Korea.

Army. The Army consists of 1 Royal Guard regiment, 1 tank and 4 mechanized infantry battalions, 1 special forces company and 1 field artillery regiment. Equipment includes 24 AMX-30 main battle tanks. Personnel (1996) 8,500.

Navy. The navy operates 4 new British-built 380-tonne and 3 390-tonne French-built fast missile craft. There is 1 tank landing craft and some 30 boats. There are also 4 quadruple shore-based Exocet missile batteries. Personnel in 1996 totalled 1,800; the base is at Doha.

Air Force. The Air Force has 6 Mirage F1 fighters and 12 Commando and 14 Gazelle helicopters and 6 Alpha Jet armed trainers and Tigercat surface-to-air missile systems. Personnel (1996) 800 with 11 combat aircraft and 20 armed helicopters.

INTERNATIONAL RELATIONS
Qatar is a member of the UN, the Arab League and the Gulf Co-operation Council.

ECONOMY
Performance. Real GDP growth was 1·1% in 1995 (2·3% in 1994).

Budget. Revenue (1995–96) US$2,500bn.; expenditure US$3,500bn.

Currency. The unit of currency is the *Qatari riyal* (QAR) of 100 *dirhams*, introduced in 1973. The inflation rate in 1993 was 3%. In Sept. 1995 foreign exchange reserves were US$618m. Gold reserves were 50,000 troy oz. in Nov. 1997. Total money supply in Dec. 1997 was 4,131m. riyals.

Banking and Finance. The Qatar Monetary Agency, which functioned as a bank of issue, became the Central Bank in 1995. In 1993 there were 6 domestic and 8 foreign banks with total deposits of 18,870·7bn. riyals.

A stock exchange was established in Doha by the Amir's decree in 1995, initially to trade only in Qatari stocks.

Heavy investment in energy development has increased foreign debt from US$1,300bn. in 1991 to US$10,400bn. in 1997.

Weights and Measures. The metric system is in general use.

ENERGY AND NATURAL RESOURCES

Electricity. Installed capacity was 1·3m. kW in 1994. Production was 5·5bn. kWh in 1994. Consumption per capita was an estimated 10,095 kWh in 1995.

Oil and Gas. Proven reserves (1995) 3,700m. bbls. Output, 1997, 600,000 bbls. a day. Production is likely to increase to 700,000 bbls. a day by 2000.

The North Field, the world's biggest single reservoir of gas and containing 12% of the known world gas reserves, is half the size of Qatar itself. Development cost is estimated at US$25bn.

Water. 2 main desalination stations have a daily capacity of 167·6m. gallons of drinkable water. A third station is planned, with a capacity of 40m. gallons a day. Total water production in 1993 (well field and distillate) was 20,136·1m. gallons.

Agriculture. 10% of the working population is engaged in agriculture. Percentage of total agricultural area under various crops in 1993: Vegetables, 28%; green fodder, 23%; cereals, 22%; palm dates, 20%; and fruits, 7%. Government policy aims at ensuring self-sufficiency in agricultural products. In 1994, 8,000 ha were irrigated. Production (1993) in tons: Cereals, 5,368; dates, 10,723; fruits, 1,038; vegetables, 36,851; meat, 2,595; poultry meat, 3,672; milk and dairy products, 29,917; eggs, 3,303.

Livestock (1996): Cattle, 13,000; camels, 45,000 (1995); sheep, 187,000; goats, 160,000 (1995); chickens, 3·0m. (1995).

Fisheries. The catch in 1995 totalled 4,271 tonnes, entirely from sea fishing. The state-owned Qatar National Fishing Company has 3 trawlers and its refrigeration unit processes 10 tonnes of shrimps a day.

INDUSTRY

1993 output (in 1,000 tonnes): Ammonia, 763·0; urea, 825·0; reinforcing steel bars, 608·6; ethylene, 351·6; polyethylene, 181·5; sulphur, 68·2; flour, 33·0; bran, 11·5; butane, 454·7; propane, 646·1. There is an industrial zone at Umm Said.

Labour. In 1996 the labour force totalled 308,000. Males constituted 87% of the labour force in 1996—the highest proportion of men in the workforce anywhere in the world.

INTERNATIONAL TRADE

Imports and Exports. Imports in 1995, US$2,900bn.; exports, US$2,000bn. The main exports are petroleum products (75%), steel and fertilizers. Main imports are machinery and equipment, consumer goods, food and chemicals. The principal partners for exports in 1994 were Japan (61%), Australia (5%), followed by the United Arab Emirates and Singapore; and for imports, Germany (14%), Japan (12%), UK (11%), USA (9%) and Italy (5%).

COMMUNICATIONS

Roads. In 1995 there were about 1,210 km of roads, of which 1,089 km were paved. Passenger cars in 1996 numbered 126,000 (218 per 1,000 inhabitants) and there were 64,000 trucks and vans. In 1993 there were 76 fatal accidents with 84 deaths.

Civil Aviation. Gulf Air is owned equally by Qatar, Bahrain, Oman and the UAE. For details *see* BAHRAIN: Civil Aviation. In 1998 it operated services from Doha International to Abu Dhabi, Al Ain, Amsterdam, Bahrain, Beirut, Bombay, Cairo, Damascus, Delhi, Dhahran, Dhaka, Dubai, Frankfurt, Fujairah, Jeddah, Karachi, Khartoum, Kuwait, London, Madras, Manila, Muscat, Paris, Riyadh, Sana'a, Sharjah, Shiraz, Tehran and Thiruvananthapuram. A Qatari airline, Qatar Airways, operates on some of the same routes, and in 1998 additionally flew to Colombo, Káthmandu and Peshawar. In 1998 services were also provided by Air India, Air Lanka, American Airlines, Biman Bangladesh Airlines, British Airways, Egyptair, Emirates, Indian Airlines, Iran Air, Kuwait Airways, Lufthansa, Oman Air, Pakistan International Airlines, Royal Jordanian, Saudia, Sudan Airways, Syrian Arab Airlines and Yemenia Yemen Airways.

Shipping. In 1995, sea-going vessels totalled 0·92m. GRT, including oil tankers, 0·33m. GRT, and container ships, 91,536 GRT. In 1993, 1,383 vessels with a total tonnage of 66,255,841 GRT and 2,697,629 tonnage of cargo was discharged.

Telecommunications. Qatar had 141,900 main telephone lines in 1997, or 249·4 per 1,000 persons. In 1995 there were 30,000 PCs, 19,000 cellular phone subscribers and 9,400 fax machines. There were approximately 17,000 Internet users in Jan. 1998.

Postal Services. There were 30 post offices in 1995.

SOCIAL INSTITUTIONS

Justice. The Judiciary System is administered by the Ministry of Justice which comprises three main departments: Legal affairs, courts of justice and land and real estate register. There are 5 Courts of Justice proclaiming sentences in the name of H. H. the Amir: The Court of Appeal, the Labour Court, the Higher Criminal Court, the Civil Court and the Lower Criminal Court. The death penalty is in force.

All issues related to personal affairs of Moslems under Islamic Law embodied in the Holy Quran and Sunna are decided by Sharia Courts.

Religion. The population is almost entirely Moslem.

Education. Adult literacy rate was 79·4% in 1995 (79·2% among males and 79·9% among females). There were, in 1994–95, 52,130 pupils and 5,853 teachers at 169 primary schools, 37,635 pupils and 3,858 teachers at secondary schools and, in 1995–96, 8,271 students and 645 teachers at higher education institutions. There were 48 Arab and foreign private schools with 27,895 pupils and 1,692 teachers in 1992–93. The University of Qatar had 7,294 students and 881 academic staff in 1993–94.

Students abroad (1993–94) numbered 1,262. In 1992–93, 3,567 men and 2,639 women attended night schools and literacy centres.

Health. There were 4 hospitals in 1995, with a provision of 18 beds for every 10,000 persons. In 1995 there were 715 government-employed doctors, 88 government-employed dentists, 187 government-employed pharmacists and 1,834 government-employed nurses.

CULTURE

Broadcasting. Broadcasting is the responsibility of the state-run Qatar Broadcasting Service and Qatar Television Service. There were 240,000 radios in 1995 and 220,000 television receivers (colour by PAL).

Cinema. In 1993 there were 3 cinemas with a total attendance of 281,128.

Press. In 1993 there were 4 daily, 1 weekly newspaper and 9 magazines.

Tourism. In 1996 there were 263,000 foreign tourists.

DIPLOMATIC REPRESENTATIVES

Of Qatar in Great Britain (1 South Audley St., London, WIY 5DQ)
Ambassador: Ali M. Jaidah.

Of Great Britain in Qatar (POB 3, Doha, Qatar)
Ambassador: David A. Wright.

Of Qatar in the USA (600 New Hampshire Ave., NW, Washington, D.C., 20037)
Ambassador: Saad Mohamed Al Kobaisi.

Of the USA in Qatar (149 Ahmed bin Ali St., Fariq Bin Omran, Doha)
Ambassador: Elizabeth McKune.

Of Qatar to the United Nations
Ambassador: Nassir Abdulaziz Al-Nasser.

Of Qatar to the European Union
Ambassador: Vacant.

FURTHER READING

Central Statistical Organization. *Annual Statistical Abstract.*
Unwin, P. T. H., *Qatar.* [Bibliography] Oxford and Santa Barbara (CA), 1982

National statistical office: Central Statistical Organization, Presidency of the Council of Ministers, Doha.

ROMANIA

România

Capital: Bucharest
Population estimate, 2000: 22·5m.
GNP per capita: (PPP$) 4,580
HDI/world rank: 0·767/74

KEY HISTORICAL EVENTS

The Romanians cherish their Latin origins and language, which date from Trajan's occupation of Dacia. The foundation of the feudal 'Danubian Principalities' of Wallachia and Moldavia in the late 13th and early 14th centuries marks the beginning of an era. (Transylvania, also part of the modern Romania by this time, was in the hands of the Magyars). The Orthodox church and quarrelsome nobility were nearly as powerful as the princes, a balance of power which the expansionist Turks were able to manipulate after the 14th century. Wallachia and Moldavia became tribute-paying vassals without ever being formally incorporated into the Ottoman Empire. The nobility acted as the Turks' agents until 1711 when, suspected of pro-Russian sentiments (Peter the Great was on their northern doorstep), they were replaced by Greek merchant adventurers, the Phanariots.

The Phanariot period of ruthless extortion and corruption was ameliorated by Russian interference. Bessarabia was annexed and Russian support after the rebellion of Tudor Vladimirescu in 1821 brought about the restoration of Romanian princes. Between 1829 and 1834 the foundations of the modern state were laid under a Russian protectorate, but in the revolutionary episode of 1848 Russian interference became repressive. After the Crimean War, Bessarabia was restored to Moldavia, and under the auspices of the great powers elections were held in both principalities which resulted in the election of Alexandru Cuza to both thrones in Jan. 1859; the Moldavian and Wallachian assemblies were fused in 1862. Cuza's reforms brought him into conflict with the nobility, who deposed him in 1866. Carol of Hohenzollern was brought to the throne, and a constitution adopted based on that of Belgium of 1831. Romania was formally declared independent by the Treaty of Berlin of 1878, and became a kingdom (the 'Old Kingdom') in 1881. Romania regained Bessarabia by the Treaty, and gained Dobrudja from Bulgaria in the Balkan wars of 1913.

This was a period of expansion for an economy firmly in the hands of the land-owners (represented by the Conservative party) and nascent industrialists (of the Liberal party). The condition of the peasantry remained miserable, and the rebellion of 1907 was an expression of their discontent. Romania joined the First World War on the allied side in 1916. The spoils of victory brought Transylvania (with large Hungarian and German populations), Bessarabia, Bukovina and Dobrudja into the union with the 'Old Kingdom'. The centralizing constitution of 1923 reduced the autonomy of the Transylvanian Romanians; the National Peasant party of Iuliu Maniu was formed in 1926 in protest. The Liberals had broken the power of the Conservatives by the land reform of 1920, and continued in office until the (relatively fair) elections of 1928, at which the Peasants gained 330 seats to the Liberals' 13. Carol II's advent to the throne was delayed by a sexual scandal; when he acceded in 1930 Maniu resigned. Hit by the world recession, Romania was increasingly drawn into Germany's economic orbit. Against this background the fascist Iron Guard assassinated the Liberal leader in 1934. Carol himself adopted increasingly totalitarian modes of rule, banning political parties by his constitution of 1938. Following Nazi and Soviet annexations of Romanian territory in 1940, he abdicated in favour of his son Michael. The government of the fascist Ion Antonescu declared war on the USSR on 22 June 1941. On 23 Aug. 1944, Michael with the backing of a bloc of opposition parties deposed Antonescu and switched sides.

The armistice of Sept. 1944 gave the Soviet army control of Romania's territory. This, and the 'spheres of influence' diplomacy of the Allies, predetermined the establishment of communism in Romania. A government under the pro-communist peasant leader Petru Groza was installed in March 1945. Transylvania was restored to Romania (though it lost Bessarabia and Southern Dobrudja), and large estates were broken up for the benefit of the peasantry. Elections in Nov. 1946 were held in an atmosphere of intimidation and fraudulence; the communist bloc received 376

ROMANIA

seats, the Peasants 33, the Liberals 3. In 1947, the latter parties were abolished, Michael was forced to abdicate and a people's republic was proclaimed. The communist leader, Gheorghe Gheorghiu-Dej purged himself of his fellow leaders in the early 1950s. Under his successor, Nicolae Ceauşescu, Romania took a relatively independent stand in foreign affairs while becoming increasingly repressive and impoverished domestically.

An attempt by the authorities on 16 Dec. 1989 to evict a Protestant pastor, László Tökés, from his home in Timişoara, provoked a popular protest which escalated into a mass demonstration against the government. Despite the use of armed force against the demonstrators, the uprising spread to other areas. On 21 Dec. the government called for an official rally in Bucharest, but this turned against the régime. A state of emergency was declared but the Army went over to the rebels and Nicolae and Elena Ceauşescu fled the capital. A dissident group which had been active before the uprising, the National Salvation Front (NSF), proclaimed itself the provisional government.

The Ceauşescus were captured and after a secret two hour trial by military tribunal, summarily executed on 25 Dec. on four charges of genocide, undermining the power of the state, undermining the economy and embezzlement. Fighting by pro-Ceauşescu 'Securitate' forces continued until 27 Dec. It is estimated that 7,689 people were killed in the uprising.

On 26 Dec. 1989 Ion Iliescu, leader of the National Salvation Front, and Petre Román, were sworn in as President and Prime Minister respectively. But the Iliescu-led administration, while committed to reform, was inhibited by its communist origins. The economy stalled and the debts piled up. After seven years, Iliescu was voted out of office and his government replaced by a four party coalition led by President Emil Constantinescu and Prime Minister Victor Ciorbea. On 30 March 1998 Victor Ciorbea and his Cabinet resigned in the face of concerted pressure from coalition partners, after the passing of the budget had been delayed for over 5 months as a result of a series of disagreements.

TERRITORY AND POPULATION
Romania is bounded in the north by Ukraine, in the east by Moldova, Ukraine and the Black Sea, south by Bulgaria, south-west by Yugoslavia and north-west by Hungary. The area is 236,391 sq. km. Population (1998), 22,520,000; density, 95·3 per sq. km.

The UN gives a projected population for 2000 of 22·5m.

In 1995 an estimated 55·9% of the population lived in urban areas.

Romania is divided into 41 counties (judeţ), of which the capital, Bucharest (Bucuresti), is one.

County	Area in sq. km	Population (1994)	Capital	Population (1994)
Bucharest	1,820	2,339,156		
Alba	6,231	408,457	Alba Iulia	72,962
Arad	7,652	482,144	Arad	187,876
Argeş	6,801	679,868	Piteşti	184,171
Bacău	6,606	742,901	Bacău	207,730
Bihor	7,535	633,629	Oradea	221,885
Bistriţa-Năsăud	5,305	328,786	Bistriţa	87,646
Botoşani	4,965	462,370	Botoşani	128,322
Braşov	5,351	642,764	Braşov	324,210
Brăila	4,724	391,923	Brăila	235,763
Buzău	6,072	515,202	Buzău	149,610
Caraş-Severin	8,503	370,058	Reşiţa	96,197
Călăraşi	5,074	336,657	Călărasi	78,874
Cluj	6,650	727,033	Cluj-Napoca	326,017
Constanţa	7,055	747,441	Constanţa	348,575
Covasna	3,705	232,951	Sf. Gheorghe	68,073
Dîmboviţa	4,036	558,518	Tîrgovişte	99,235
Dolj	7,413	758,895	Craiova	306,825
Galaţi	4,425	642,983	Galaţi	326,728
Giurgiu	3,511	305,661	Giurgiu	73,997
Gorj	5,641	397,927	Tîrgu Jiu	98,050
Harghita	6,610	347,145	Miercurea-Ciuc	46,854

County	Area in sq. km	Population (1994)	Capital	Population (1994)
Hunedoara	7,016	547,180	Deva	77,218
Ialomiţa	4,449	305,454	Slobozia	56,719
Iaşi	5,469	815,368	Iaşi	339,889
Maramureş	6,215	539,718	Baia Mare	149,975
Mehedinţi	4,900	330,017	Drobeta-Turnu Severin	118,383
Mureş	6,696	607,355	Tîrgu Mureş	166,315
Neamţ	5,890	584,364	Piatra-Neamţ	125,622
Olt	5,507	520,871	Slatina	87,012
Prahova	4,694	874,219	Ploieşti	254,136
Satu Mare	4,405	398,401	Satu Mare	131,431
Sălaj	3,850	264,448	Zalău	70,358
Sibiu	5,422	448,474	Sibiu	170,528
Suceava	8,555	708,571	Suceava	117,314
Teleorman	5,760	477,527	Alexandria	59,414
Timiş	8,692	691,797	Timişoara	327,830
Tulcea	8,430	269,311	Tulcea	97,616
Vaslui	5,297	463,832	Vaslui	80,316
Vâlcea	5,705	436,989	Râmnicu Vâlcea	114,286
Vrancea	4,863	394,257	Focşani	100,900

At the 1992 census the following ethnic minorities numbered over 100,000: Hungarians, 1,624,959 (mainly in Transylvania); Gipsies, 401,087; Germans, 119,462. A *Council of National Minorities* made up of representatives of the government and ethnic groups was set up in 1993.

The official language is Romanian.

SOCIAL STATISTICS
1997: Births, 238,000; deaths, 281,000; marriages, 147,000. 1994: Divorces, 39,663; stillborn, 1,623; infant deaths, 5,894. 1997 rates (per 1,000 population): Live births, 10·5; deaths, 12·4; marriages, 6·5. 1994 rates (per 1,000 population); divorces, 1·7; stillborn (per 1,000 live births), 6·5; infant mortality (per 1,000 live births), 23·9. Expectation of life at birth, 1990–95, was 66·0 years for males and 73·2 years for females. In 1995 the most popular age range for marrying was 20–24 for both males and females. Measures designed to raise the birth rate were abolished in 1990, and abortion and contraception legalized. Fertility rate, 1990–95, 1·5 births per woman.

CLIMATE
A continental climate with an annual average temperature varying between 8°C in the north and 11°C in the south. Bucharest, Jan. 27°F (–2·7°C), July 74°F (23·5°C). Annual rainfall 23·1" (579 mm). Constanţa, Jan. 31°F (–0·6°C), July 71°F (21·7°C). Annual rainfall 15" (371 mm).

CONSTITUTION AND GOVERNMENT
A new Constitution was approved by a referendum on 8 Dec. 1991. Turn-out was 66%, and 77·3% of votes cast were in favour. The Constitution defines Romania as a republic where the rule of law prevails in a social and democratic state. Private property rights and a market economy are guaranteed.

The head of state is the *President*, who must not be a member of a political party, elected by direct vote for a maximum of two 4-year terms. The President is empowered to veto legislation unless it is upheld by a two-thirds parliamentary majority. The National Assembly consists of a 343-member *Chamber of Deputies* and a 143-member *Senate*; both are elected for 4-year terms from 41 constituencies by modified proportional representation, the number of seats won in each constituency being determined by the proportion of the total vote. 15 seats in the Chamber of Deputies are reserved for ethnic minorities. There is a 3% threshold for admission to either house. Votes for parties not reaching this threshold are redistributed.

There is a *Constitutional Court.*

National Anthem. 'Deşteaptă, Române, din somnul cel de moarte' ('Wake up, Romanians, from your deadly slumber'); words by A. Muresianu, tune by A. Pann.

ROMANIA

RECENT ELECTIONS
The first rounds of the presidential and parliamentary elections were held on 3 Nov. 1996. Turn-out was 77%. There were 7 presidential candidates. President Iliescu won with 32·3% of votes cast. At the second run-off round of the presidential elections on 17 Nov. turn-out was 75·9%. Emil Constantinescu was elected with 54·41% of votes cast.

At the parliamentary elections, 6 parties passed the 3% threshold. The Democratic Convention of Romania (CDR) bloc won 31% of votes cast; the Party of Social Democracy in Romania, 22%; the Social Democratic Union bloc (USD), 13%; the Hungarian Democratic Union of Romania (UDMR), 6·7%; the Greater Romania Party, 4·5%; the Romanian National Unity Party, 4·2%. Seats gained:

Party	Chamber of Deputies seats	Senate seats
Democratic Convention of Romania		
Christian Democratic National Peasants Party (PNTCD)	88	31
National Liberal Party (PNL)	25	17
Romanian Ecological Party	5	1
Romania's Alternative (PAR)	3	1
Romanian Ecological Federation	1	1
Party of Social Democracy of Romania (PDSR)	91	41
Social Democratic Union		
Democratic Party (PD)	43	22
Romanian Social Democratic Party	10	1
Hungarian Democratic Union of Romania (UDMR)	25	11
Greater Romania Party	19	8
Romanian National Unity Party	18	7

CURRENT ADMINISTRATION
President: Emil Constantinescu, b. 1939 (CDR; sworn in 29 Nov. 1996).

In March 1999 the government was:

Prime Minister: Radu Vasile.

Minister of Defence: Victor Babiuc. *Justice:* Valeriu Stoica. *Foreign Affairs:* Andrei Gabriel Pleşu. *Interior:* Constantin Dudu Ionescu. *Finance:* Traian Decebal Remes. *Industry and Trade:* Radu Mircea Berceanu. *Labour and Social Protection:* Alexandru Athanasiu. *Food and Agriculture:* Ioan Avram Muresan. *Transport:* Traian Basescu. *Public Works and Territorial Planning:* Nicolae Stefan Noica. *Water, Forests and Environmental Protection:* Romica Tomescu. *Education:* Andrei Marga. *Health:* Gabor Hajdu. *Culture:* Ion Caramitru. *Sports:* Crin Antonescu. *Minister-Delegate for European Integration:* Alexandru Herlea. *Minister-Delegate for Ethnic Minorities:* Peter Eckstein-Kovacs.

Local Government. Councils are elected at county (*judeţ*) level (on a proportional representation system) and municipal level (on a first-past-the-post system), and mayors are also elected. Elections were held in June 1996; turn-out was 56·4%. The PDSR won 26·49% of the mayoral vote, the CDR 26·45%, but the latter gained more county council seats.

DEFENCE
Military service is compulsory for 12 months in the Army and Air Force and 18 months in the Navy.

In 1997 military expenditure totalled US$793m. (US$35 per capita), representing 2·3% of GDP.

Army. The 4 Army Areas consist of 2 tank and 8 motor rifle divisions; 4 mountain, 2 artillery, 3 anti-aircraft and 2 surface-to-surface missile brigades; and 4 artillery, 3 anti-tank and 4 airborne regiments. Equipment includes 146 T-34, 822 T-55, 30 T-72, 620 TR-85 and 225 TR-580 main battle tanks. Strength (1997) 129,350 (90,000 conscripts), and 400,000 reservists. The Ministry of the Interior operates a paramilitary Frontier Guard (22,300 strong), a Gendarmerie (10,000) and a Security Guard (46,800).

Navy. The fleet comprises 1 ex-Soviet diesel submarine, 1 Romanian-built missile-armed destroyer with a hangar for 2 helicopters, 5 frigates, 3 missile-armed corvettes, 6 fast missile craft, 32 fast torpedo craft, 4 offshore, and 8 inshore patrol vessels, 2 minelayer/mine countermeasure support ships and 35 small minesweepers. The Danube flotilla counts 4 river monitors (100-mm guns) and some 20 river patrol craft. Auxiliaries include 2 logistic ships, 3 small tankers, 2 oceanographic ships, 1 training ship and 2 tugs. A force of naval infantry some 8,000 strong in 1996 is equipped with 120 tanks and some 120 artillery pieces, but lacks amphibious transport.

There is a coastal defence force numbering 800 (1996) organized into 4 main batteries of artillery with 32 130-mm guns and 10 anti-aircraft batteries.

Headquarters of the Navy is at Mangalia with the main base at Constanţa, and of the Danube flotilla at Braila. Personnel in 1997 totalled 17,500 (9,500 conscripts).

Air Force. The Air Force numbered some 47,600, with 300 combat aircraft and 80 armed helicopters in 1997. These were organized into 12 interceptor squadrons with MiG-21, MiG-23 and MiG-29 fighters, 3 ground-attack and close-support squadrons with IAR-93 fighter-bombers, and 1 reconnaissance squadron of L-39s. There were also more than 150 training aircraft, 28 An-24/26/30 transports and about 200 helicopters (Mi-8, Alouette and Puma), some armed. 'Guideline' and 'Gainful' surface-to-air missiles were operational, and short-range surface-to-surface missiles have been displayed.

INTERNATIONAL RELATIONS
Romania is a member of the UN, the Council of Europe, the Central European Initiative, the NATO Partnership for Peace and is an Associate Partner of the WEU and an Associate Member of the EU.

ECONOMY
Policy. With the change of government, the pace of reform has accelerated. There are more than 80 economic reform laws in the planning stage. Privatization of the banks has begun with the Romanian Development Bank. Foreign investment is actively encouraged. Legislation of 1995 offered 60% of shares in state companies to citizens in exchange for privatization coupons, and 40% to foreign investors.

In 1997 over 1,850 state companies were privatized. Most of the companies still in state hands were to be privatized by the end of 1998. The liquidation of bankrupt state enterprises is proceeding slowly. Even so, the freeing of prices and ending of many subsidies has pushed up inflation to 20% plus. Also, there is the risk of a political breakdown which could damage the fragile economy.

Legislation of Nov. 1995 compensates former owners of 0·2m. nationalized properties. Compensation is limited to the ownership of 1 home if lived in or 50m. lei.

Performance. Real GDP growth was –7·0% in 1997 (4% in 1996), but was forecast to rise to –4·0% in 1998. Services contribute around 47% of GDP and industry 38%.

Budget. Revenue and expenditure (in 1bn. lei) for calendar years:

	1993	1994	1995	1996
Revenue	3,792	8,858	12,886	18,367
Expenditure	4,201	10,696	14,869	21,634

The current account deficit was expected to reach US$3bn., or 7% of GDP, in 1998.

VAT was introduced in July 1993.

Currency. The monetary unit is the *leu*, pl. *lei* (ROL) notionally of 100 *bani*. Foreign exchange reserves were US$3,503m. and gold reserves 3·07m. troy oz. in Feb. 1998. Inflation was 151% in 1997 having been 57% in 1996, but was forecast to be 40% in 1998. Total money supply was 14,912bn. lei in Feb. 1998.

Banking and Finance. The National Bank of Romania (founded 1880, nationalized 1946; *governor*, Mugur Isarescu) is the central bank and bank of issue under the Minister of Finance. It manages monetary policy. In May 1996 total assets of commercial banks were 37,000,000m. lei, 67% of which were controlled by 4 state-owned banks: Bancorex (for foreign trade), Banca Agricola, Romanian Commercial Bank and Romanian Development Bank. Total assets, 1994, 20,415,121m. lei. Savings were 617,692m. lei in 1993.

A stock exchange re-opened in Bucharest in 1995.

Weights and Measures. The Gregorian calendar was adopted in 1919. The metric system is in use.

ENERGY AND NATURAL RESOURCES

Electricity. Installed electric power 1998: 19,400,000 kW; output, 1994, 55,136m. kWh (13,046m. kWh hydro-electric). Consumption per capita was estimated to be 2,245 kWh in 1995. A nuclear power plant at Cernavoda began working in April 1996.

Oil and Gas. Oil production in 1994 was 6·7m. tonnes.

Minerals. The principal minerals are oil and natural gas, salt, brown coal, lignite, iron and copper ores, bauxite, chromium, manganese and uranium. Output, 1994 (in 1,000 tonnes): Iron ore, 951; coal, 6,307; lignite, 36,385; methane gas (cu. metres, 1991), 17,252m.

Agriculture. Romania has the biggest agricultural area in Eastern Europe after Poland. In 1997, 30% of the workforce was employed in agriculture, which contributed 22% of GDP. There were 14,797,500 ha of agricultural land in 1994, including (in 1,000 ha): Arable, 9,338; meadows, 1,494; pasture, 3,378; vineyards, 2,398 and orchards and nurseries, 289. There were 3,205,200 ha of irrigated land. In 1997 private households had on average 2·53 ha per family.

Production (in 1,000 tonnes): Wheat and rye, 7,000; barley, 2,134; oats, 497; maize, 9,343; potatoes, 2,947; sunflower seeds, 764; sugar-beet, 2,764.

Livestock, 1995 (in 1,000): Cattle, 3,481 (including milch cows, 1,963); pigs, 7,758; sheep, 10,897; goats, 745; horses, 784; poultry, 70,157. There were 161,223 tractors in 1994.

A law of Feb. 1991 provided for the restitution of collectivized land to its former owners or their heirs up to a limit of 10 ha. Land may be resold, but there is a limit of 100 ha on total holdings. Landless peasants received a distribution from the residue. There are 74 state farms; peasants receive shares in their equity worth up to 10 ha. Collective farms may become private co-operative associations. By 1997, 72% of farmed land was in private hands. The government has pledged an end to state ownership of farms.

Forestry. Total forest area was 6·25m. ha in 1995 (27·1% of the land area) including 1·91m. ha coniferous, 1·9m. ha beech and 1·14m. ha oak. 14,744 ha were afforested in 1994. Timber production in 1995 was 12·86m. cu. metres.

Fisheries. The catch in 1995 totalled 69,105 tonnes (271,126 tonnes in 1986), of which 40,227 tonnes were from sea fishing.

INDUSTRY

In 1994 there were 33,824 industrial enterprises, of which 2,182 were state-controlled, 374 local government-controlled and 554 co-operatives. 50 enterprises employed more than 5,000 persons; 31,043 fewer than 100.

Output of main products in 1994 (in tonnes): Pig-iron, 3,496; steel, 5,800; steel tubes, 472; rolled steel, 4,510; chemical fertilizers, 1,163; sulphuric acid, 491; caustic soda, 291; paper, 288; cement, 5,998; sugar, 231; edible oils, 194; plastics, 304; chemical fibres, 83. In 1,000 units: Tractors, 14; TV sets, 452; washing machines, 109.

Industry contributes some 38% of GDP.

Labour. The labour force in 1996 totalled 10·67m. The employed population in 1994 was 10·01m., of whom 3·6m. worked in agriculture and 3·4m. in industry and building. In 1994, 46% of the total workforce, and 39·4% of the industrial workforce, were women. Men retire at 62, women at 57. A law of 1991 established an unemployment fund and provides for retraining unemployed persons. A minimum monthly wage was set in 1993; it was 45,000 lei in 1994. The average monthly wage was 141,951 lei in 1994. Unemployment was 8·9% in Dec. 1996.

Trade Unions. In 1994 the National Confederation of Free Trade Unions-Fratia had 65 branch federations and 3·7m. members. The other major confederations were Alfa Cartel and the National Trade Union Bloc.

INTERNATIONAL TRADE

Foreign debt was US$8,291m. in 1996. In Nov. 1993 the USA granted Romania most-favoured-nation status.

Foreign investors may establish joint ventures or 100%-owned domestic companies in all but a few strategic industries. After an initial 2-year exemption, profits are taxed at 30%, dividends at 10%. Foreign investors register with the Romanian Development Agency. The 1991 constitution prohibits foreign nationals from owning real estate.

Imports and Exports. In 1996 exports totalled US$7,200m. and imports US$9,000m. In 1997, exports totalled US$8,000m. and imports US$9,200m.

In 1996 Romania's main export markets were: Germany (18·7%); Netherlands (4·2%); Italy (16·7%); France (5·6%); Turkey (5·0%); Eastern Europe (7·4%). Romania's main import markets were: Germany (17·1%); Italy (15·6%); France (5%); Russia (12·6%); Eastern Europe (6·8%).

COMMUNICATIONS

Roads. There were 153,358 km of roads in 1996 (113 km of motorways, 14,570 km of main roads). At least two-thirds of the main roads are in urgent need of repair. Passenger cars in 1996 numbered 2,408,000 (106 per 1,000 inhabitants).

Rail. Length of standard-gauge route in 1994 was 10,887 km, of which 3,866 km were electrified; there were 427 km of narrow-gauge lines and 60 km of 1,524 mm gauge. Freight carried in 1995, 105·1m. tonnes; passengers, 211m. There is a metro (57 km) and tram/light rail network (353 km) in Bucharest, and tramways in 13 other cities.

Civil Aviation. Tarom (*Transporturi Aeriene Române*) is the 70%-state-owned airline. In 1998 it provided domestic services and international flights to Abu Dhabi, Amman, Amsterdam, Athens, Barcelona, Beijing, Beirut, Belgrade, Berlin, Brussels, Budapest, Cairo, Chicago, Chişinău, Copenhagen, Damascus, Delhi, Dubai, Düsseldorf, Frankfurt, Istanbul, Kiev, Kuwait, Larnaca, London, Madrid, Milan, Moscow, New York, Paris, Prague, Rome, Shannon, Sofia, Tel Aviv, Vienna, Warsaw and Zürich. Miravia Romanian Airlines and Romavia had some international flights flights in 1998. Services were also provided by Acvila Air, Aeroflot, Air France, Air Moldova, Air Moldova International, Alitalia, Austrian Airlines, British Airways, Czech Airlines, El Al, Hemus Air, Iberia, JAT, KLM, Lufthansa, Malév, Odessa Airlines, Olympic Airways, Royal Jordanian, Swissair, Syrian Arab Airlines and Turkish Airlines.

Bucharest's airports are at Baneasa (mainly internal flights) and Otopeni (international flights). Constanţa, Iaşi and Timişoara also have some international flights. In 1996 Otopeni handled 1,407,355 passengers (all on international flights) and 18,396 tonnes of freight. Banaesa was the second busiest airport in 1996 for passengers, with 248,850 (201,784 on domestic flights), and Timişoara the second busiest for freight, with 3,660 tonnes.

Shipping. In 1995 the merchant marine comprised 297 vessels totalling 4·81m. DWT, of which 30 (20·78% of tonnage) were registered under foreign flags. Total GRT was 2·69m., including oil tankers, 0·44m. GRT, and container ships, 15,160 GRT. The main ports are Constanţa and Agigea on the Black Sea and Galaţi and Braila on the Danube. In 1994 sea-going transport carried 30·2m. tonnes of freight; river transport, 7·99m. tonnes and 0·99m. passengers.

Telecommunications. Main telephone lines numbered 3,161,200 in 1996, or 139·8 per 1,000 population. Mobile phones were introduced in 1997, with 2 private operators. A law of June 1994 puts broadcasting under parliamentary control through the supervision of the National Audiovisual Council. In 1995 there were 120,000 PCs, 21,000 fax machines and some 16,000 Internet users.

Postal Services. There were 5,243 post offices in 1995.

SOCIAL INSTITUTIONS

Justice. Justice is administered by the Supreme Court, the 41 county courts, 81 courts of first instance and 15 courts of appeal. Lay assessors (elected for 4 years) participate in most court trials, collaborating with the judges. In 1994 there were 2,471 judges. The *Procurator-General* exercises 'supreme supervisory power to ensure the observance of the law'. The Procurator's Office and its organs are independent of any organs of justice or administration, and only responsible to the Grand National Assembly, which appoints the Procurator-General for 4 years. The death penalty was abolished in Jan. 1990 and is forbidden by the 1991 constitution. In 1994 criminal sentences were awarded to 95,795 persons (11,710 females, 9,121 juveniles) and 31,190 persons were imprisoned.

Religion. The State Secretariat for Religious Denominations oversees religious affairs. Churches' expenses and salaries are paid by the State. There are 14 Churches, the largest being the Romanian Orthodox Church. It is autocephalous, but retains dogmatic unity with the Eastern Orthodox Church. It is organized into 12 dioceses grouped into 5 metropolitan bishoprics and headed by Patriarch Teoctist Arapasu. There are some 11,800 churches, 2 theological colleges and 6 'schools of cantors', as well as seminaries. The Uniate (Greek Catholic) Church (which severed its connection with the Vatican in 1698) was suppressed in 1948 but in 1990 was re-legalized. Property seized by the state in 1948 was restored to it, but not property which had passed to the Orthodox Church.

Religious affiliation at the 1992 census: Romanian Orthodox, 19,762,135; Roman Catholic, 1,144,820; Protestant, 801,577; Uniate, 228,377; Pentecostal, 220,051; Baptist, 109,677; Seventh Day Adventist, 78,658; Unitarian, 76,333; Moslem, 55,988.

Education. Education is free and compulsory from 6 to 16, consisting of 8 years of primary school and 2 years of secondary (*gymnasium*). Further secondary education is available at *lycées*, professional schools or advanced technical schools.

In 1994–95 there were 12,665 kindergartens with 37,603 teachers and 715,514 children; 13,963 primary and secondary schools with 168,702 teachers and 2,532,169 pupils; 1,276 *lycées* with 60,514 teachers and 757,673 pupils; 761 professional schools with 7,313 teachers and 288,221 pupils; and 596 advanced technical institutes with 1,728 teachers and 45,321 students. In 1994–95 primary and secondary education in Hungarian was given to 154,222 pupils by 11,555 teachers and in German to 13,586 pupils by 808 teachers. In the 1996–97 school years there were 796 school units in vocational and apprentice education, with 262,057 pupils and 7,627 teachers.

In 1994–95 there were 19 universities, 16 specialized universities (agriculture, 4; medicine and pharmacy, 5; petroleum and gas, 1; technical, 6), a polytechnic institute, a merchant navy institute, a school of political and administrative studies and 9 specialized academies (architecture; dramatic art; economics; fine arts; 2 music; physical education and sport; theatre and film; visual arts). Adult literacy rate, 1995, 97·9% (male 98·9%; female 96·9%).

In 1994 total expenditure on education came to 3·1% of GNP and represented 13·6% of total government expenditure.

Health. In 1994 there were 174,900 hospital beds and 47,990 doctors (including 6,163 dentists).

Welfare. In 1994 pensioners comprised 3·44m. old age and retirement, 374,000 disability, 585,000 successor allowance, 58,000 war invalidity and dependants, 20,000 social assistance and 1,478,000 retired farmers. These drew average monthly pensions ranging from 12,254 to 77,960 lei. In 1997 social security spending was raised by more than 2% of GDP to 10·4%.

CULTURE

Broadcasting. Radio-televiziunea Româna broadcasts 3 radio programmes on medium-waves and FM. In March 1995, 436 cable TV stations, 66 local TV stations and 135 local radio stations were registered. There is also radio and TV transmission in Hungarian and German. There are 2 independent TV channels. Radio receivers, 1995, 4·8m.; TV (colour by PAL), 5·0m.

Cinema. There were, in 1994, 713 cinemas, of which 394 were for standard-sized films. These latter had 162,442 seats; admissions were 24·72m. 18 full-length films were made in 1994 (4 in 1990).

Press. There were, in 1994, 97 daily papers and 870 periodicals, including 13 dailies and 92 periodicals in minority languages. 4,074 book titles were published in 1994 in 50·2m. copies (33 titles in minority languages).

Tourism. In 1995 there were 2,608,000 foreign tourists, bringing revenue of US$574m. In 1994, 5·9m. foreign nationals visited Romania.

DIPLOMATIC REPRESENTATIVES
Of Romania in Great Britain (Arundel House, 4 Palace Green, London, W8 4QD)
Ambassador: Radu Onofrei.

Of Great Britain in Romania (24 Strada Jules Michelet, 70154 Bucharest)
Ambassador: Christopher D. Crabbe, CMG.

Of Romania in the USA (1607 23rd St., NW, Washington, D.C., 20008)
Ambassador: Mircea Dan Geoana.

Of the USA in Romania (7–9 Strada Tudor Arghezi, Bucharest)
Ambassador: James C. Rosapepe.

Of Romania to the United Nations
Ambassador: Ion Goriţa.

Of Romania to the European Union
Ambassador: Constantin Ene.

FURTHER READING
Comisia Nationala pentru Statistica. *Anuarul Statistic al României/Romanian Statistical Yearbook.* Bucharest, annual.—*Revista de Statistica.* Monthly

Deletant, A. and D., *Romania* [Bibliography]. Oxford and Santa Barbara (CA), 1985
Gallagher, T., *Romania after Ceauşescu; the Politics of Intolerance.* Edinburgh Univ. Press, 1995
Rady, M., *Romania in Turmoil: a Contemporary History.* London, 1992
Ratesh, N., *Romania: the Entangled Revolution.* New York, 1991
Siani-Davies, M. and P., *Romania* [Bibliography]. 2nd ed. Oxford and Santa Barbara (CA), (rev. ed.) 1998

National statistical office: Comisia Nationala pentru Statistica, 16 Libertatii Ave., sector 5, Bucharest
Website: http://cns.kappa.ro/

RUSSIA

Rossiiskaya Federatsiya

Capital: Moscow
Population estimate, 2000: 146·2m.
GNP per capita: (PPP$) 4,190
HDI/world rank: 0·769/72

KEY HISTORICAL EVENTS

At the end of the 17th century the Russian Empire embraced much of eastern Europe and northern and central Asia. The Empire was governed as an autocracy under the Romanovs who had ruled since 1613.

On 8 March 1917 a revolution broke out. The Duma parties set up a Provisional Committee of the State Duma on 12 March, while the factory workmen and the insurgent garrison of Petrograd elected a Council (Soviet) of Workers' and Soldiers' Deputies. Soviets were also elected by the workmen in other towns, in the Army and Navy and, as time went on, by the peasantry. On 15 March 1917 Tsar Nicholas II abdicated, and the Provisional Committee, by agreement with the Petrograd Soviet, appointed a Provisional Government and, on 14 Sept., proclaimed a republic. However, a political struggle went on between the supporters of the Provisional Government—the Mensheviks and the Socialist Revolutionaries—and the Bolsheviks who advocated the assumption of power by the Soviets. When they had won majorities in the Soviets of the principal cities and of the armed forces on several fronts, the Bolsheviks organized an insurrection through a Military-Revolutionary Committee of the Petrograd Soviet. On 7 Nov. 1917 the Committee arrested the Provisional Government and transferred power to the second All-Russian Congress of Soviets. This elected a new government, the Council of People's Commissars, headed by Lenin.

On 25 Jan. 1918 the third All-Russian Congress of Soviets issued a Declaration of Rights of the Toiling and Exploited People, which proclaimed Russia a Republic of Soviets of Workers', Soldiers' and Peasants' Deputies; and on 10 July 1918 the fifth Congress adopted a constitution for the Russian Soviet Federal Socialist Republic (RSFSR). In the course of the following civil war other Soviet republics were set up in the Ukraine, Belorussia and Transcaucasia. These first entered into treaty relations with the RSFSR and then, in 1922, joined with it in a closely integrated Union.

The Union of Soviet Socialist Republics (USSR) was formed by the union of the RSFSR, the Ukrainian Soviet Socialist Republic, the Belorussian Soviet Socialist Republic and the Transcaucasian Soviet Socialist Republic; the Treaty of Union was adopted by the first Soviet Congress of the USSR on 30 Dec. 1922. In Oct. 1924 the Uzbek and Turkmen Autonomous Soviet Socialist Republics and in Dec. 1929 the Tadzhik Autonomous Soviet Socialist Republic were declared constituent members of the USSR, becoming Union Republics.

From about 1929 Stalin's authority was supreme. Resistance to agricultural collectivization was ruthlessly suppressed. A series of Five-Year Plans (1928, 1933, 1937, 1946 and 1951) transformed the USSR into a powerful industrial state. Opposition in party and government was crushed by the purges of 1933 and 1936-38.

At the eighth Congress of the Soviets on 5 Dec. 1936, a new constitution of the USSR was adopted. The Transcaucasian Republic was split up into the Armenian Soviet Socialist Republic, the Azerbaijan Soviet Socialist Republic and the Georgian Soviet Socialist Republic, each of which became constituent republics of the Union. At the same time the Kazakh Soviet Socialist Republic and the Kirghiz Soviet Socialist Republic, previously autonomous republics within the RSFSR, were proclaimed constituent republics of the USSR.

In Sept. 1939 (under a secret clause of the 10-year non-aggression signed with Nazi Germany on 23 Aug. 1939) Soviet troops occupied eastern Poland as far as the 'Curzon line', which in 1919 had been drawn on ethnographical grounds as the eastern frontier of Poland, and incorporated it into the Ukrainian and Belorussian

Soviet Socialist Republics. In Feb. 1951 some districts of the Drogobych Region of the Ukraine and the Lublin Voivodship of Poland were exchanged.

On 31 March 1940 territory ceded by Finland was joined to that of the Autonomous Soviet Socialist Republic of Karelia to form the Karelo-Finnish Soviet Socialist Republic, which was admitted into the Union as the 12th Union Republic. On 16 July 1956 the Supreme Soviet of the USSR altered the status of the Karelo-Finnish Republic from that of a Union Republic of the USSR to that of an Autonomous (Karelian) Republic within the RSFSR.

On 2 Aug. 1940 the Moldavian Soviet Socialist Republic was constituted as the 13th Union Republic. It comprised the former Moldavian Autonomous Soviet Socialist Republic and Bessarabia (44,290 sq. km, ceded by Romania on 28 June 1940), except for the districts of Khotin, Akerman and Izmail, which together with Northern Bukovina (10,440 sq. km) were incorporated in the Ukrainian Soviet Socialist Republic. The Soviet-Romanian frontier thus constituted was confirmed by the peace treaty with Romania, signed on 10 Feb. 1947. On 29 June 1945 Ruthenia (Sub-Carpathian Russia, 12,742 sq. km) was by treaty with Czechoslovakia incorporated into the Ukrainian Soviet Socialist Republic.

On 3, 5 and 6 Aug. 1940 Lithuania, Latvia and Estonia were incorporated in the Soviet Union as the 14th, 15th and 16th Union Republics respectively. The change in the status of the Karelo-Finnish Republic reduced the number of Union Republics to 15.

After the defeat of Nazi Germany it was agreed by the governments of the UK, the USA and the USSR that part of East Prussia should be embodied in the USSR. The area (11,655 sq. km), which includes the towns of Königsberg (renamed Kaliningrad), Tilsit (renamed Sovyetsk) and Insterburg (renamed Chernyakhovsk), was joined to the RSFSR by decree of 7 April 1946.

By the peace treaty with Finland, signed on 10 Feb. 1947, the province of Petsamo (Pechenga), ceded to Finland on 14 Oct. 1920 and 12 March 1946, was returned to the Soviet Union. On 19 Sept. 1955 the Soviet Union renounced its treaty rights to the naval base of Porkkala-Udd and on 26 Jan. 1956 completed the withdrawal of its forces from Finnish territory.

In 1945, after the defeat of Japan, the southern half of Sakhalin (36,000 sq. km) and the Kurile Islands (10,200 sq. km) were, by agreement with the Allies, incorporated in the USSR. However, Japan has since asked for the return of the Etorofu and Kunashiri Islands as not belonging to the Kurile Islands proper. The Soviet government informed Japan on 27 Jan. 1960 that the Habomai Islands and Shikotan would be handed back to Japan on the withdrawal of American troops from Japan.

Nikita Khruschev, Secretary-General of the Party, criticized the regime of Stalin who died in 1953 at the Twentieth Party Congress in 1956. This encouraged a liberalizing of the Russian-backed communist regimes of Hungary and Poland, and later Czechoslovakia (1968) which the USSR crushed with its forces and those of the Warsaw Pact (established 1955). A policy of 'peaceful co-existence' with the West, especially after the war scare with the USA in 1962 over Cuban missiles, led to years of strained relations with China. After 1985, with Mikhail Gorbachev as Secretary-General of the Communist Party, a new period of *glasnost* (openness) and *perestroika* (reconstruction) was inaugurated; but desperate economic problems helped to accelerate liberalization and in 1991 the Soviet Union broke up into its constituent parts.

After the dissolution of the USSR in Dec. 1991, Russia became one of the founding members of the Commonwealth of Independent States. Boris Yeltsin was elected President in June 1991. A period of confrontation in 1992-93 between President Yeltsin and parliament culminated on 21 Sept. in a presidential decree on 'gradual constitutional reform' which suspended the operations of parliament, called new parliamentary elections for Dec. and assumed emergency executive powers. Parliament and the Constitutional Court rejected this action, and parliament proclaimed Vice-President Rutskoi acting president. The USA, the EC and other countries expressed support for President Yeltsin, as did Ukraine and Belarus. Many deputies refused to leave the parliament building and mounted an armed guard which was cordoned off by pro-Yeltsin forces. Public demonstrations and counter-demonstrations began on 26 Sept. After a week in which deputies remained in the parliament building, some thousands of armed anti-Yeltsin demonstrators assembled on 3 Oct. and were urged to seize the Kremlin and television centre. Shots were fired and there were fatal casualties. On 4 Oct. troops took the parliament building by storm after a 10-hour assault in which 140 people died. Vice-President Rutskoi and Speaker Khasbulatov were stripped of their offices and arrested.

In Feb. 1994 parliament amnestied not only those arrested after the occupation of the parliament building in Sept.-Oct. 1993, but also the instigators of the failed *coup* against the Soviet government in Aug. 1991.

Boris Yeltsin was re-elected president in 1996. Many took this as a signal of confidence in the new, democratic Russia. But the reality was a state in which democratic institutions were weakened to the point of impotence by cynicism, racketeering and bureaucratic dead-weight. In March 1998, President Yeltsin dismissed his prime minister, Victor Chernomyrdin. His successor, the 35-year-old Sergei Kiriyenko lasted barely six months before President Yeltsin recalled Mr Chernomyrdin, a decision the Duma refused to ratify. Meanwhile, Russia defaulted on its debt, the rouble halved in value, imports fell by 45% and oil revenues slumped. On 17 Aug. the government freed the rouble, in effect devaluing it, imposed currency controls and froze the domestic debt market. In Sept. 1998, Yevgeniy Primakov, formerly head of the secret service and latterly foreign minister, took over as prime minister with Communist support. His reconstituted government gave the dominant voice to anti-reformers. In Oct. the Kremlin signalled that President Yeltsin, known to be in failing health, had withdrawn from day-to-day politics.

TERRITORY AND POPULATION

Russia is bounded in the north by various seas (Barents, Kara, Laptev, East Siberian) which join the Arctic Ocean, and in which is a fringe of islands, some of them large. In the east Russia is separated from the USA (Alaska) by the Bering Strait; the Kamchatka peninsula separates the coastal Bering and Okhotsk Seas. Sakhalin Island, north of Japan, is Russian territory. Russia is bounded in the south by North Korea, China, Mongolia, Kazakhstan, the Caspian Sea, Georgia, the Black Sea and Ukraine, and in the west by Belarus, Latvia, Estonia, the Baltic Sea and Finland. Kaliningrad (the former East Prussia) is an exclave on the Baltic Sea between Lithuania and Poland in the west. Russia's area is 17,075,400 sq. km and has 11 time zones. Its 1989 census population was 147,021,869 (53·3% female), of whom 81·5% were Russians, 3·8% Tatars, 3% Ukrainians, 1·2% Chuvash, 0·9% Bashkir, 0·8% Belorussians, and 0·7% Mordovians. Chechens, Germans, Udmurts, Mari, Kazakhs, Avars, Jews and Armenians all numbered 0·5m. or more. Population estimate, 1998, 147,100,000 (female, 53%; urban, 73%); density, 9 per sq. km.

The UN gives a projected population for 2000 of 146·2m.

In 1995 an estimated 75·9% of the population lived in urban areas. Age structure: 16–29 years, 34%; 30–44, 42%; 45+, 24%.

There were 915,000 immigrants in 1995, mainly from the former Soviet republics. In Jan. 1995 there were 702,451 refugees, mostly from Tajikistan, Georgia, Azerbaijan, Chechnya and Ingushetia.

The 2 principal cities are Moscow, the capital, with a population of 8·6m. and St Petersburg (formerly Leningrad), 4·8m. Administrative breakdown of the Russian Federation, population and territory, 1 Jan. 1997:

	Popu-lation (in 1,000)	Territory (in 1,000 sq. km)		Popu-lation (in 1,000)	Territory (in 1,000 sq. km)
North	5,833	1,466	Pskov Oblast	827	55
Arkhangelsk Oblast	1,506	587	Central	29,751	485
Nenets Autonomous			Bryansk Oblast	1,473	35
Okrug	55	178	Ivanovo Oblast	1,256	24
Republic of Karelia	780	172	Kaluga Oblast	1,096	30
Republic of Komi	1,172	416	Kostroma Oblast	801	60
Murmansk Oblast	1,030	145	Moscow Oblast	6,573	47
Vologda Oblast	1,344	146	Moscow City	8,637	n/a
North-west	8,017	197	Orel Oblast	910	25
St Petersburg City	4,774	n/a	Ryazan Oblast	1,316	40
Leningrad Oblast	1,677	86	Smolensk Oblast	1,166	50
Novgorod Oblast	738	55	Tver Oblast	1,642	84

	Popu- lation (in 1,000)	Territory (in 1,000 sq. km)		Popu- lation (in 1,000)	Territory (in 1,000 sq. km)
Tula Oblast	1,800	26	Sverdlovsk Oblast	4,668	195
Vladimir Oblast	1,637	29	Udmurt Republic	1,636	42
Yaroslavl Oblast	1,443	36	*Western Siberia*	*15,087*	*2,427*
Volgo-Vyatka	*8,404*	*263*	Altai Krai	2,675	169
Republic of Chuvash	1,359	18	Republic of Altai	202	93
Kirov Oblast	1,623	121	Kemerovo Oblast	3,042	96
Republic of Mary-El	764	23	Novosibirsk Oblast	2,745	178
Mordovian Republic	950	26	Omsk Oblast	2,174	140
Nizhy Novgorod Oblast	3,710	75	omsk Oblast	1,072	317
Central Black Earth	*7,863*	*168*	Tyumen Oblast	3,177	1,435
Belgorod Oblast	1,477	27	Khanty-Mansy		
Kirsk Oblast	1,341	30	Autonomous Okrug	1,314	523
Lipetsk Oblast	1,248	24	Yamal-Nenets		
Tambov Oblast	1,301	34	Autonomous Okrug	493	750
Voronezh Oblast	2,495	52	*Eastern Siberia*	*9,407*	*4,123*
Volga	*16,890*	*536*	Republic of Buryatia	1,050	351
Astrakhan Oblast	1,029	44	Chita Oblast	1,288	432
Republic of Kalmykia	317	76	Aginskoe Buryat		
Penza Oblast	1,555	43	Autonomous Okrug	78	19
Samara Oblast	3,763	54	Irkutsk Oblast	2,785	768
Saratov Oblast	2,726	100	Ust-Orda Buryat		
Republic of Tatarstan	3,763	68	Autonomous Okrug	138	22
Ulianovsk Oblast	1,490	37	Krasnoyarsk Krai	3,095	2,340
Volgograd Oblast	2,702	114	Taimyr (Dolgano-Nenets)		
North Caucasus	*17,778*	*355*	Autonomous Okrug	54	862
Republic of Dagestan	2,121	50	Evenk Autonomous		
Chechen Republic	862	19	Okrug	25	768
Ingush Republic	303	n/a	Republic of Khakasia	584	62
Kabaardino-Balkar			Republic of Tuva	310	171
Republic	789	13	*Far East*	*7,421*	*6,216*
Krasnodarsk Krai	5,066	76	Amur Oblast	1,016	364
Republic of Adygeya	449	8	Kamchatka Oblast	402	472
North-Osetian Republic	664	8	Koriak Autonomous		
Rostov Oblast	4,415	101	Okrug	40	302
Stavropol Krai	2,672	67	Khabarovsk Krai	1,555	825
Karachevo-Cherkess			Jewish Autonomous		
Republic	436	14	Area	207	36
Urals	*20,410*	*824*	Magadan Oblast	251	1,199
Republic of			Chukchi Autonomous		
Bashkortostan	4,134	144	Okrug	87	738
Chelyabinsk Oblast	3,675	88	Primorskii Krai	2,239	166
Kurgan Oblast	1,105	71	Sakhalin Oblast	632	87
Orenburg Oblast	2,226	124	Republic of Sakha		
Perm Oblast	2,997	161	(Yakutia)	1,032	3,103
Komi-Permyatsk			Kaliningrad Oblast	935	15
Autonomous Okrug	160	33	Russian Federation	147,501	17,075

The national language is Russian.

SOCIAL STATISTICS
1996 births, 1,313,000; deaths, 2,316,000; 1995 marriages, 1,075,219. Rates, 1996 (per 1,000 population): Birth, 8·9; death, 15·7. 1995: marriage, 7·3; divorce, 4·5; infant mortality, 18·1 (per 1,000 live births). There were 3·1m. induced abortions in 1994. There were 61·9 divorces per 100 marriages in 1995. The most popular age range for marrying in 1995 was 20–24 for both males and females. Expectation of life at birth, 1990–95, was 60·4 years for males and 72·7 years for females. With a difference of 11·8 years, no other country has a life expectancy for females so high compared to that for males. Fertility rate, 1990–95, 1·5 births per woman.

CLIMATE
Moscow, Jan. –9·4°C, July 18·3°C. Annual rainfall 630 mm. Arkhangelsk, Jan. –15°C, July 13·9°C. Annual rainfall 503 mm. St Petersburg, Jan. –8·3°C, July 17·8°C. Annual rainfall 488 mm. Vladivostok, Jan. –14·4°C, July 18·3°C. Annual rainfall 599 mm.

RUSSIA

CONSTITUTION AND GOVERNMENT

The Russian Soviet Federative Socialist Republic (RSFSR) adopted a constitution in April 1978. In June 1990, pending the promulgation of a new constitution, it adopted a declaration of republican sovereignty by 544 votes to 271. It became a founding member of the CIS in Dec. 1991, and adopted the name 'Russian Federation'. A law of Nov. 1991 extended citizenship to all who lived in Russia at the time of its adoption and to those in other Soviet republics who requested it.

There is a 19-member *Constitutional Court*, whose functions under the 1993 Constitution include making decisions on the constitutionality of federal laws, presidential and government decrees, and the constitutions and laws of the subjects of the Federation. It is governed by a Law on the Constitutional Court, adopted in July 1994. Judges are elected for non-renewable 12-year terms.

At a referendum on 25 April 1993 the electorate was 107·3m.; turn-out was 69·2m. 4 questions were put: Confidence in President Yeltsin (58·7% of votes cast); approval of economic reforms (53% of votes cast); early presidential elections (31·7% of the electorate); early parliamentary elections (43·1% of the electorate). This referendum had no constitutional effect, however.

Voting was held on 12 Dec. 1993 on the adoption of a new constitution and the election of a new parliament for a 2-year term. The electorate was 106,170,335; turn-out was 54·8%. The constitution was approved by 58·4% of votes cast, and came into effect on 24 Dec. 1993.

According to the 1993 Constitution the Russian Federation is a 'democratic federal legally-based state with a republican form of government'. The state is a secular one, and religious organizations are independent of state control. Individuals have freedom of movement within or across the boundaries of the Federation; there is freedom of assembly and association, and freedom to engage in any entrepreneurial activity not forbidden by law. All citizens have a right to housing, to free medical care, and to a free education. The state itself is based upon a separation of powers and upon federal principles, including a Constitutional Court. The most important matters of state are reserved for the federal government, including socio-economic policy, the budget, taxation, energy, foreign affairs and defence. Other matters, including the use of land and water, education and culture, health and social security, are for the joint management of the federal and local governments, which also have the right to legislate within their spheres of competence. A central role is accorded to the *President*, who defines the 'basic directions of domestic and foreign policy' and represents the state internationally. The President is directly elected for a 4-year term, and for not more than 2 consecutive terms; he or she must be at least 35 years old, a Russian citizen, and a resident in Russia for at least the previous 10 years. 1m. signatures are needed to validate a presidential candidate, no more than 7% of which may come from any one region or republic. The President has the right to appoint the prime minister, and (on his nomination) to appoint and dismiss deputy prime ministers and ministers, and may dismiss the government as a whole. In the event of the death or incapacity of the President, the Prime Minister becomes head of state.

Parliament is known as the *Federal Assembly*. The 'representative and legislative organ of the Russian Federation', it consists of 2 chambers: the *Council of the Federation* and the *State Duma*. The Council of the Federation, or upper house, consists of 178 deputies, 2 from each of the 89 subjects of the Federation. The Federation is made up of 21 republics, 1 autonomous region, 10 autonomous areas, 6 territories, 49 regions and 2 federal cities. The State Duma, or lower house, consists of 450 deputies chosen for a 4-year term. 225 of these are elected from single-member constituencies on the first-past-the-post system, the remainder from party lists by proportional representation. To qualify for candidacy an individual must obtain signatures from at least 1% of voters in the constituency; a party or electoral alliance must obtain a minimum of 100,000 supporting signatures from at least 7 regions, but not more than 15% from any one region. There is a 5% threshold for the party-list seats. Parties which gain at least 35 seats may register as a faction, which gives them the right to join the Duma Council and chair committees. Any citizen aged over 21 may be elected to the State Duma, but may not at the same time be a member of the upper house or of other representative bodies, and all deputies work on a 'permanent professional basis'. Both houses elect a chair, committees and commissions. The Council of the Federation considers all matters that apply to the

Federation as a whole, including state boundaries, martial law, and the deployment of Russian forces elsewhere. The Duma approves nominations for Prime Minister, and adopts federal laws (they are also considered by the Council of the Federation, but any objection may be overridden by a two-thirds majority; objections on the part of the President may be overridden by both houses on the same basis). The Duma for its part can reject nominations for Prime Minister, but after the third such rejection it is automatically dissolved. It is also dissolved if it twice votes a lack of confidence in the government as a whole, or if it refuses to express confidence in the government when the matter is raised by the Prime Minister.

National Anthem. 'Patriotic Song'; no words, tune from an opera by Mikhail Glinka, arranged by Andrei Petrov.

RECENT ELECTIONS

Boris Yeltsin became President for a 5-year term at the elections of 12 June 1991, gaining 57·3% of the votes cast against 5 opponents. Presidential elections took place in 2 rounds in 1996. In the first round on 16 June, 11 candidates stood. The electorate was 104m.; turn-out was 69·8%. President Yeltsin won 35·28% of votes cast, Gennadi Zyuganov (Communist) 32·08% and Aleksandr Lebed, 14·52%. In the second run-off round on 3 July turn-out was 68·8%. Yeltsin was re-elected with 53·8% of votes cast.

Elections for the State Duma were held on 17 Dec. 1995. The electorate was 107·5m.; turn out was 64·4%. 2,687 candidates stood representing 43 parties or groups. 4 parties exceeded the 5% threshold for party-list seats: Communist Party, 99 seats; Liberal Democratic Party (of Vladimir Zhirinovsky), 50; Our Home is Russia, 45; Yabloko, 31. Total seats gained: Communist Party, 157 with 22·3% of votes cast (48 with 12·4% in 1993); Our Home is Russia, 55 with 10·13%; Liberal Democratic Party, 51 with 11·18% (64 with 22·92% in 1993); Yabloko, 45 with 6·89% (23 with 7·86% in 1993); Agrarian Party, 20 with 3·78% (33 with 7·99% in 1993); Power to the People, 9 with 1·61%, Russia's Democratic Choice, 9 with 3·86% (70 with 15·51% in 1993); Congress of Russian Communities, 5 with 4·31%; Women of Russia, 3 with 4·61% (23 with 8·13% in 1993); Forward Russia, 3 with 1·94%; Ivan Rybkin's Bloc, 3 with 1·11%; Pamfilova-Gurev-Lysenko, 2 with 1·6%. 78 seats went to independents (141 in 1993) and 10 to minor parties. The Communist Party delegated some seats to the Agrarian Party to enable it to register as a faction. Registered factions (with seats held) in Jan. 1996: Communist Party (149), Our Home is Russia (55), Liberal Democratic Party (51), Yabloko (46), Russian Regions (42), Power to the People (37), Agrarian Party (35).

CURRENT ADMINISTRATION

President: Boris Yeltsin (b. 1931; sworn in 9 Aug. 1996).

In March 1999 the government comprised:

Prime Minister: Yevgeniy Primakov.

First Deputy Prime Ministers: Vadim Gustov; Yuriy Maslyukov. *Deputy Prime Ministers:* Vladimir Bulgak; Gennadiy Kulik; Valentina Matviyenko. *Minister of Agriculture and Food:* Viktor Semenov. *Anti-Monopoly Policy and Enterprise Support:* Gennadiy Khodyrev. *Atomic Energy:* Yevgeniy Adamov. *Civil Defence, Emergencies and Natural Disasters:* Sergey Shoygu. *CIS Affairs:* Boris Pastukhov. *Culture:* Vladimir Yegorov. *Defence:* Marshal Igor Sergeyev. *Economics:* Andrey Shapovalyants. *Finance:* Mikhail Zadornov. *Foreign Affairs:* Igor Ivanov. *Fuel and Energy:* Sergey Generalov. *General and Vocational Education:* Vladimir Filippov. *Health:* Vladimir Starodubov. *Internal Affairs (MVD):* Sergey Stepashin. *Justice:* Pavel Krasheninnikov. *Labour and Social Development:* Sergey Kalashnikov. *Nationalities:* Ramazan Abdulatipov. *Natural Resources:* Viktor Orlov. *Railways:* Nikolay Aksenenko. *Regional Policy:* Valeriy Kirpichnikov. *Science and Technology:* Mikhail Kirpichnikov. *State Property:* Farit Gazizullin. *Tax and Levies:* Georgiy Boos. *Trade:* Georgiy Gabuniya. *Transportation:* Sergey Frank.

Local Government. There are 49 provinces, 6 territories, 21 republics (including Chechnya) and 10 autonomous areas. The republics are homelands of non-Russian minorities and as such enjoy a high degree of autonomy including the right to elect a president. Provinces (*oblasts*) and territories (*krais*) are led by governors, formerly presidential appointments but now elected. Local councils include 24,230 rural settlements, 2,048 urban settlements, 318 urban districts, 1,086 towns and 1,863 sub-regions.

A presidential decree of Oct. 1993 established a new regime for local authorities. Their membership is limited to 50. During 1996, 47 of the 89 federal units held elections for presidents or governors, these being areas where regional heads had been appointed before elections were instituted in 1995.

DEFENCE

The President of the Republic is C.-in-C. of the armed forces. Conscription was raised from 18 months to 2 years in April 1995. There are plans to end conscription by 2005. The START 2 nuclear arms cutting treaty has been held up by the Duma. A presidential decree of Feb. 1997 ordered a cut in the armed forces of 200,000 men, reducing them to an authorized strength of 1·2m. by the end of 1997. This figure included 200,000 staff at the Ministry of Defence and 583,000 paramilitary troops (including 220,000 border troops).

Military expenditure totalled US$64,000m. in 1997 (US$435 per capita), representing 5·8% of GDP. Only the USA spent more on defence in 1997.

Nuclear weapons. Once a major player in the nuclear race, Russia's warhead count is now shrinking and stood at 6,210 in Jan. 1998 according to the Stockholm International Peace Research Institute.

Army. A Russian Army was created by presidential decree in March 1992. In 1997 forces numbered 420,000 (170,000 conscripts). The Army is deployed in 8 military districts and 1 Group of Forces, and comprises: 14 Army and 8 Corps headquarters, 12 tank, 28 motor rifle, 5 airborne, 4 machine gun/artillery and 4 artillery divisions, and some 47 artillery, 4 heavy artillery, 7 airborne, 8 special forces, 23 surface-to-surface missile, 2 independent tank, and 17 independent motor rifle brigades, and 19 anti-tank and 28 surface-to-air missile regiments. Equipment includes some 16,800 main battle tanks, including T-54/-55, T-62, T-64A/-B, T-72L/-M and T-80/-M9, 200 PT-76 light tanks, 1,962 multiple rocket launchers, 144 surface-to-surface nuclear-capable missile launchers and 2,300 surface-to-air missiles.

The Army air element has some 2,450 helicopters in the inventory, including 2,000 Mi-8/17 transport, assault and battlefield electronic countermeasures and electronic intelligence machines and 950 armed Mi-24s. There are a small number of Mi-6 and Mi-26 heavy-lift helicopters as well as a small number of fixed-wing transport and communications aircraft. Funding shortages have reduced serviceability drastically.

Strategic Nuclear Ground Forces. In 1995 there were 5 rocket armies, each with launcher groups, 10 silos and 1 control centre. Inter-continental ballistic missiles numbered 928. Personnel, 100,000 (50,000 conscripts).

Navy. The Russian Navy continues to reduce steadily and levels of sea-going activity remain very low with activity concentrated on a few operational units in each fleet. The safe deployment and protection of the reduced force of strategic missile-firing submarines remains its first priority; and the defence of the Russian homeland its second. The strategic missile submarine force operates under command of the Strategic Nuclear Force commander whilst the remainder come under the Main Naval Staff in Moscow, through the Commanders of the fleets.

The Northern and Pacific fleets count the entirety of the ballistic missile submarine force, all nuclear-powered submarines, the sole operational aircraft carrier and most major surface warships. The Baltic Fleet organization is based in the St Petersburg area and in the Kaliningrad exclave. Some minor war vessels have been ceded to the Baltic republics. The Black Sea Fleet continues to be the object of wrangling between Russia and Ukraine, and remains operationally paralyzed by the dispute. While a political decision has been made to divide the fleet between the nations, the practical and personnel issues remain unresolved. The small Caspian Sea flotilla, formerly a sub-unit of the Black Sea Fleet, has been divided between Azerbaijan (25%), and Russia, Kazakhstan and Turkmenistan, the littoral republics (75%).

The material state of all the fleets is suffering from continued inactivity and lack of spares and fuel. The nuclear submarine refitting and refuelling operations in the Northern and Pacific Fleets remain in disarray, given the large numbers of nuclear submarines awaiting defuelling and disposal. The strength of the submarine force has now essentially stabilized, but there are still large numbers of decommissioned vessels awaiting their turn for scrapping in a steadily deteriorating state.

The aircraft carrier *Admiral Kuznetsov* is now operational, albeit with a limited aviation capability, and she deployed to the Mediterranean in Dec. 1995.

The overall strength of the Navy at the end of the indicated year was as follows:

Category	1991	1992	1993	1994	1995	1996
Strategic Submarines	59	55	50	46	38	34
Nuclear Attack Submarines	100	95	80	63	66	62
Diesel Submarines	80	75	70	62	55	26
Aircraft Carriers	5	4	3	1	1	1
Cruisers	38	33	31	25	26	24
Destroyers	29	26	22	22	21	20
Frigates	146	129	114	112	101	101

The strength of the disputed Black Sea Fleet at the end of 1996 was 12 diesel-powered submarines, 4 cruisers, 3 destroyers and 22 frigates, as well as some 30 mine warfare amphibious ships and 100 support units. The force of Strategic Submarines is constituted as follows:

Class	No.	Tonnage	Speed	Missiles	Other Weapons
Typhoon	6	27,000	27	20 SS-N-20	Torpedoes
Delta-IV	7	12,350	24	16 SS-N-23	Torpedoes
Delta-III	13	11,900	24	16 SS-N-18	Torpedoes
Delta-II	4	11,500	24	16 SS-N-8	Torpedoes
Delta-I	8	11,000	25	12 SS-N-8	Torpedoes

Some other non-operational strategic submarines continue to be counted to START totals.

The SS-N-20 'Sturgeon' missile carried by the Typhoon carries 6 warheads to a maximum range of 4,500 nautical miles, while the SS-N-23 'Skiff' in the other modern class, the 'Delta-IV', carries 10 warheads over the same range. The other older missiles carry 1 to 3 warheads over ranges varying between 1,300 and 4,000 nautical miles.

The attack submarine fleet comprises a wide range of classes, from the enormous 16,250 tonne 'Oscar' nuclear-powered missile submarine to diesel boats of around 2,000 tonnes. The inventory of anti-ship missile-firing submarines comprises 13 'Oscar I' and 'II' built 1982–1994, 24 SS-N-19 'Shipwreck' missiles, 2 'Charlie-II', 1972–75, 8 SS-N-7 'Starbright'; and 1 'Echo-II', 1961–67, 8 SS-N-3 'Shaddock' or SS-N-12 'Sandbox', all nuclear-propelled. Finally, there are 3 former strategic 'Yankee'-class submarines converted to fire the SS-N-21 'Sampson' land-attack cruise missile, which has a range of 1,600 nautical miles. Torpedo-firing boats currently building are the 'Akula' class, nuclear-powered and of 8,100 tonnes, of which there are 13, and the 'Sierra' class, nuclear-powered, 7,700 tonnes now numbering 4. The 'Victor-III' class, nuclear-powered, 6,400 tonnes, totals 26 units. The diesel-powered 'Kilo' class, of which the Navy operates 17, is still building at a reduced rate mostly for export. There are a further 9 diesel submarines nominally on the active list.

Cruisers (7,500–8,000 tonnes full load and upwards) are divided into 2 categories; those optimized for anti-submarine warfare (ASW) are classified as 'Large Anti-Submarine Ships' and those primarily configured for anti-surface ship operations are classified 'Rocket Cruisers'. The principal surface ships of the Russian Navy include the following classes:

Aircraft Carrier. The *Admiral Kuznetsov* of 65,000 tonnes was completed in 1989, is capable of 30 knots, and armed with 12 SS-N-19 'Shipwreck' anti-ship missiles and SA-N-9 anti-air missiles; it is capable of embarking 25–30 aircraft and 8–10 helicopters. All other aircraft carriers have been decommissioned or scrapped.

Anti-Shipping Rocket Cruisers. The ships of this classification are headed by the 4 ships of the Admiral Ushakov (formerly Kirov) class, the largest combatant warships, apart from aircraft carriers, to be built since the Second World War. *Admiral Ushakov* (1980), *Admiral Lazarev* (1984), *Admiral Nakhimov* (1988) and *Petr Velikii* (1995). They displace 28,400 tonnes and are capable under combined

RUSSIA

nuclear and oil-fired steam propulsion of 33 knots and are armed with 20 SS-N-19 anti-ship missiles, 12 batteries of SA-N-6 anti-air missiles, 3 helicopters and a wide range of lesser armaments. There are 4 Slava class: *Slava* (1982), *Marshal Ustinov* (1986), *Chervona Ukraina* (1988) and *Admiral Lobov* (1995), each of 12,700 tonnes capable of 34 knots, and armed with 16 SS-N-12 anti-ship missiles, 8 batteries of SA-N-6 anti-air missiles, 8 torpedo tubes and a single helicopter.

Anti-Submarine Cruisers. There are 4 ships of the Nikolaev ('Kara') class, displacing 9,800 tonnes, capable of 34 knots, completed 1973–79, and armed with SS-N-14 anti-submarine missiles with a secondary anti-ship role, SA-N-3 anti-air missiles, torpedo-tubes and a single helicopter and 12 newer Udaloy class, the first of which entered service in 1981. These displace 8,600 tonnes, are capable of 30 knots and are armed with SS-N-14 missiles, torpedo tubes and 100-mm guns, and carry 2 helicopters.

Smaller ships include the 17 Sovremenny class guided missile destroyers and the single remaining 'modified Kashin' class. There are a further 2 'Kashin', 26 large frigates including the first of a new class, the *Neustrashimy*, and 75 smaller frigates.

The coastal defence force includes 80 missile corvettes, 16 fast missile craft, 25 hydrofoil fast torpedo craft and 15 patrol craft (many more are laid up). Mine warfare forces include 3 minelayers and 33 offshore, 80 coastal and about 65 inshore mine countermeasure vessels.

Amphibious ships include 3 large dock landing ships of the Ivan Rogov class, 22 Ropucha and 7 Alligator class tank landing ships, 20 medium landing ships, and some 80 minor craft. Amphibious landing forces are found from the Naval Infantry, 14,000 strong, units of which are assigned to all fleets. Organized into a single division, 7,000 strong, and 3 active independent brigades, its principal equipment includes 240 main battle tanks, 100 amphibious light tanks, 300 artillery pieces and about 900 armoured personnel carriers. A separate force of 6,000 Coastal Defence troops mans artillery and missile batteries as well as conventional mechanized units positioned to defend the main naval bases and ports.

There is 1 multi-purpose underway replenishment ship, the *Berezina*, an additional 6 dual-purpose stores and fuel replenishment ships, 6 purpose-built tankers, and 18 other tankers converted from a commercial design with limited underway replenishment capability. Second line support is provided by 12 tankers, and about 230 maintenance and logistic ships, 60 electronic intelligence gatherers, 70 other special-purpose auxiliaries, and 210 survey, research and space support ships.

The Russian Naval Air Force includes some 100 bombers, 170 maritime patrol and anti-submarine aircraft, 175 fighter/ground attack aircraft and 280 helicopters. Maritime reconnaissance and anti-submarine tasks are performed by 65 Tu-95 and Tu-142 'Bear' with numerous shorter range aircraft tasked to anti-submarine operations, electronic countermeasures, intelligence gathering, and tankers. The helicopter force includes 200 anti-submarine, 25 combat assault, and 15 mine countermeasures aircraft.

Personnel in 1997 numbered 220,000, of whom 142,000 were conscripts. Some 13,000 serve in the strategic submarine force, 40,000 in naval aviation, 14,000 marines or naval infantry, and 6,000 in coastal artillery and coastal defence troops.

Coastguard, customs and border patrol duties are performed by the substantial maritime element of the Committee for the Protection of State Borders, which operates some 7 large helicopter-carrying frigates of a modified naval 'Krivak' class, 18 small frigates, 40 coastal and 150 inshore patrol craft divided among all the Russian coastal areas.

Air Force. Russia has both Air Force (1997: 130,000 personnel) and Air Defence Forces (170,000). Under the terms of the Conventional Forces in Europe (CFE) treaty, Russia is allowed to have up to 3,450 combat aircraft, 890 helicopters and 300 naval combat aircraft.

The Air Force is organized into 4 main Commands: Long-Range Aviation, Frontal Aviation, Military Transport Aviation and Reserve and Training Command.

Long-Range Aviation is reported to have 10 Tu-160, 100 Tu-22M, 120 Tu-95 bombers, some equipped to carry nuclear weapons. There are 150 MiG-25s and Su-24s equipped for electronic countermeasures and electronic intelligence missions and 30 Il-78 tanker aircraft. Frontal Aviation has over 3,500 combat and 1,800 support aircraft and is divided into 8 Air Armies, 7 in Russia and 1 in Trans-Caucasia. The main bomber type is the Su-24 of which 500 are available. The MiG-23/27, Su-17/20 and Su-25 serve for fighter and attack missions. There are also MiG-29s for air defence duties. The MiG-21 and most older combat aircraft have been withdrawn from service. Military Transport Aviation has over 300 Il-76s, which are replacing An-12s for heavy-lift operations. The other main transport type is the An-2, of which 300 are available, although there are about 100 An-24/26/32 medium transports and 15 An-124 and 30 An-22 very heavy-lift aircraft. 30-plus Il-62, Tu-134, Tu-154 and Yak-40 aircraft are assigned to VIP transport. Reserve and Training Command uses Yak-18 and Yak-52 primary trainers and L-29s and L-39s for jet conversion, plus two-seat models of many front-line types, such as the MiG-23, MiG-29, Su-17/20 and Su-25. It is being reorganized and slimmed down. Strength (1997), 130,000.

The Border Guards have their own aviation component to patrol Russia's borders. It has An-24 fixed-wing aircraft, now being succeeded by armed An-72Ps and Mi-8 and armed Mi-24 helicopters.

INTERNATIONAL RELATIONS
Russia is a member of the UN (Security Council), CIS, the Council of Europe and the NATO Partnership for Peace. On 16 May 1997 NATO ratified a 'Fundamental Act on Relations, Co-operation and Mutual Security' with Russia.

ECONOMY
In Oct. 1991 the President announced an economic programme whose aim was the establishment of a 'healthy mixed economy with a powerful private sector'. As part of this programme the prices of most commodities were freed on 2 Jan. 1992.

A bankruptcy law of Nov. 1992 permits the winding-up of indebted enterprises; further legislation came into force in April 1993. Centralized distribution of resources to enterprises was abolished from 1993.

Privatization is overseen by the State Committee on the Management of State Property, and began with small and medium-sized enterprises. A state programme of privatization of state and municipal enterprises was approved by parliament in June 1992, and vouchers worth 10,000 roubles each began to be distributed to all citizens in Oct. 1992. These may be sold or exchanged for shares. Employees have the right to purchase 51% of the equity of their enterprises. 25 categories of industry (including raw materials and arms) remain in state ownership. The voucher phase of privatization ended on 30 June 1994. A post-voucher stage authorized by presidential decree of 22 July 1994 provides for firms to be auctioned for cash following the completion of the sale of up to 70% of manufacturing industry for vouchers. By Dec. 1997 a total of 127,000 enterprises had been privatized; 59% in trade, public catering and personal services, 33% of which were in manufacturing, construction, transport and communications and 2·4% in agriculture.

Performance. GDP grew by at least 0·4% in 1997, the first expansion since the Soviet Union's collapse in 1991; but many economists believe that the booming informal economy adds over 25% to the value of GDP. Even so, 1998 was a disastrous year for the economy. With oil revenues well down and a collapse of the rouble, Russia defaulted on its debt. For 1998 real GDP growth was estimatd to be 1·0%.

Budget. Budgetary incomes were valued at 459,224bn. roubles in 1996. The main sources of revenue (in roubles) were: taxes on profits (82,365bn.), value added tax (116,222bn.), income tax (49,185bn.), income from foreign trade (37,016bn.) and excise duties (41,281bn.). Budgetary expenditures were valued at 542,060bn. roubles. Items of expenditure (in roubles) included: National economy, 136,500bn.; socio-cultural (including education, health and social security), 121,335bn.; defence, 53,170bn.; foreign trade 18,315bn. In 1997 the budget deficit was 6·1% of GDP. The current account surplus was US$3,336m.

Currency. The unit of currency is the *rouble* (RUR), of 100 *kopeks*. In Jan. 1998 the rouble was redenominated by a factor of a thousand. In 1994 foreign exchange reserves were US$3,976m. Gold reserves were 16·07m. troy oz. in Feb. 1998. In

1997 the rouble was tied to the US dollar on a sliding scale ranging from US$1 = 5,500–6,100 roubles on 1 Jan. 1997 to 6 roubles on 31 Jan. 1998. Inflation was 15% in 1997 and 22% in 1996. It was an annualized 197·4% in 1995 and in that year the total external debt was US$120,461m., most of it inherited from the Soviet Union. Total money supply in Dec. 1997 was 269,363m. roubles.

Banking and Finance. The central bank and bank of issue is the State Bank of Russia (*Governor*, Viktor Gerashchenko). The Russian Bank for Reconstruction and Development and the State Investment Company were created in 1993 to channel foreign and domestic investment. Foreign bank branches have been operating since Nov. 1992.

By 1995 the number of registered commercial banks had increased to around 5,000 but following the Aug. 1997 liquidity crisis, due to the ensuing bankruptcies, mergers and the Central Bank's revoking of licences, the number fell to 2,500. Approximately 80% of the commercial banks in 1997 were state-owned through ministries or state enterprises.

In 1997, the top 6 banks in terms of assets (in US$1m.) were: Sberbank, 29·1; Vneshtorgbank, 3·9; Uneximbank, 3·6; Inkombank, 3·4; National Reserve Bank, 2·0. Sberbank is the only Russian bank to appear in the world top 20.

By Jan. 1995, 166 exchanges were in operation, and 28,700 firms of brokers.

In 1994 all forms of investment were valued at 108,809,000m. roubles, of which 30·3% was invested in industry, 25·5% in housing and 10·9% in transport; 64·2% was provided by enterprises themselves, 13·4% by the federal budget and 10·6% by regional budgets.

In the wake of one of the worst financial crises which Russia's market economy had experienced, the central bank tripled interest rates to 150% in May 1998 in an effort to restore stability to the financial system.

There are stock exchanges in St Petersburg and Vladivostok.

Weights and Measures. The metric system is in use. The Gregorian Calendar was adopted as from 14 Feb. 1918.

ENERGY AND NATURAL RESOURCES

Electricity. Installed capacity was 214·69m. kW in 1994. Production in 1996 was 867·49bn. kWh. Consumption per capita in 1995 was estimated to be 5,114 kWh. There were 9 nuclear plants in 1997.

Oil and Gas. In 1997 there were proven crude petroleum reserves of 155,146m. bbls., enough to last another 71 years. Production in 1996 of crude petroleum was 2,183m. bbls., consumption (1994) was 1,375m. bbls. and refining capacity (1997) was 6,733,000 bbls. per day. There were 63,000 km of pipeline for crude petroleum. Output of natural gas in 1996 was 590,000m. cu. metres. Consumption (1994) was 327,275m. cu. metres. In 1997 the Russian Federation had proven gas reserves of 48,334,000m. cu. metres.

Minerals. Russia contains great mineral resources: Iron ore, coal, gold, platinum, copper, zinc, lead, tin and rare metals. Output (in tonnes), 1995: Coal, 262m.; iron ore (1996), 69·6m.; gold ores and concentrates, 131·9.

Agriculture. Agriculture accounted for 7% of GDP in 1996. A presidential decree of Dec. 1991 authorized the private ownership of land on a general basis; a further decree of March 1996 authorized its free sale. Collective and state farms which wish to start private farming are required to re-register as co-operatives or share companies. Members of collectives may withdraw with a certificate of land ownership and a share of the collective's equipment or compensation in lieu; members may also elect to remain in co-operatives voluntarily. The decree permits foreign nationals to own land through joint ventures.

In Jan. 1995 there were 26,900 agricultural enterprises including 6,000 collective farms, 3,600 state farms and 17,300 commercial farms; 6·4m. were employed in agriculture, and output was valued at 38,491,000m. roubles. In 1995, 220·8m. ha were in cultivation, of which 105·1m. ha were in the hands of companies and co-operatives, 32·2m. ha in collective farms, 18·5m. ha in state farms, 10·1m. ha in commercial farms and 5·7m. ha in individual private plots.

RUSSIA

Output in 1996 (in tonnes) included: Grain, 6·9m.; sunflower seeds, 2·8m.; potatoes, 38·5m.; other vegetables, 10·7m.; Sugarbeet, 16·1m.; fruit and berries (1995), 2·5m.

Livestock, Jan. 1997: Cattle, 35·8m.; sheep and goats, 23·6m.; pigs, 19·6m. Livestock products in 1996 (in tonnes): Meat, 5·3m.; milk, 35·8m.; (in units) eggs, 31,902m.; wool (1995), 98,000.

Forestry. Russia has the largest area covered by forests of any country in the world, with 7,635,000 sq. km in 1995 (45·2% of the land area). 109·55m. cu. metres of timber were produced in 1995, down from 228·52m. in 1992.

Fisheries. Total catch in 1995 was 4,373,827 tonnes (up from 3,780,538 tonnes in 1994, but down from 8,337,704 tonnes in 1988). Approximately 94% of the fish caught are from marine waters.

INDUSTRY

Output in 1994 (in tonnes) included: Cast-iron, 36·5m.; steel, 48·8m.; rolled iron, 35·9m.; steel pipe, 3·6m.; caustic soda, 1·1m.; synthetic fibre, 198,000; soap, 56,300; cellulose, 3·3m.; paper, 2·2m.; cement, 37·2m.; confectionery, 1·5m.; (in sq. metres) glass, 58·6m.; (in units) bricks, 14,700m.; tractors, 28,700; combine harvesters, 12,100; bulldozers, 2,200; tins of food, 2,817m.; personal computers, 82,100; watches, 25·9m.; televisions, 2·2m. (colour, 1·2m.); refrigerators, 2·7m.; motor cars, 798,000; cigarettes, 94,300m.; liquor, 125m. decalitres. Total output in physical terms was 79% of the 1993 total, and 51% of 1990.

Labour. In 1997 the subsistence minimum was estimated at 393,600 roubles; 22% of the population fell below it. In Jan. 1997 the official monthly minimum wage was 83,490 roubles; the average monthly wage was 870,000 roubles. The state Federal Employment Service was set up in 1992. Unemployment benefits are paid for 15 months: 3 months at full salary, 3 months at 75% and a final 9 months at a progressively reducing rate. Annual paid leave is 24 working days. The workforce was 73·1m. on 31 March 1996. In 1994, 30·6m. were in the state or municipal and 22·6m. in the private sector; 27·1% were employed in industry, 15·4% in agriculture and 10·8% in education and culture. In the third quarter of 1997, 6·6m. persons (9·2% of the workforce) were unemployed, of whom 3·4% were registered with the Federal Employment Service. In 1996, 4,007 man-days were lost through strikes. In 1996, 84·3m. people were of working age and 30·5m. people were above working age. Retirement age is 55 years for women, 60 for men.

Trade Unions. The Federation of Independent Trade Unions (founded 1990) is the successor to the former Communist official union organization. In 1993 it comprised 77 regional and 46 sectoral trade unions, with a total membership of 60m. There are also free trade unions.

INTERNATIONAL TRADE

Foreign debt was US$124,785m. in 1996. Most CIS republics have given up claims on Soviet assets in return for Russia assuming their portion of foreign debt. A Foreign Investment Agency was set up in Dec. 1992. In Jan. 1994 there were 6,359 joint enterprises in operation, employing 304,000 and accounting for 8% of foreign trade.

Imports and Exports. In 1996 exports were valued at US$87,008·1m. (to other CIS states, US$15,617·3m.), and imports at US$45,438·7m. (from other CIS states, US$14,090·6m.). In 1996 the CIS accounted for 20·5% of exports, Ukraine 9·0%, Germany 8·0% and the USA 6·0%. The CIS provided 29·9% of imports in 1996, Ukraine 14·0%, Germany 11·0% and the USA 6·0%. In 1995, of exports, 26·4% by value were minerals and 29·8% metals and precious stones. Of imports, 38·9% by value was machinery, 29·2% foodstuffs and 11·5% chemical products.

COMMUNICATIONS

Roads. In 1995 there were 945,000 km of roads, of which 80% were hard surfaced; 22,817m. passengers were carried by bus services, 8,547m. by trolley buses and 7,564m. by trams. 40% of villages cannot be reached by road. There were

13,550,000 passenger cars in 1996 (90 per 1,000 inhabitants) and 9,860,000 trucks and vans.

Rail. Length of railways in 1996 was 87,000 km of 1,520 mm gauge (of which 44% were electrified). 908·3m. tonnes of freight were carried. There are metro services in 6 cities. It is estimated that 10% of all railways are in some way defective.

Civil Aviation. The main international airports at Moscow (Sheremetevo) and St Petersburg (Pulkovo). The national carrier is Aeroflot International Russian Airlines, which is 51% state- and 49% employee-owned. Services were also provided in 1998 by Adria Airways, Aerolíneas Argentinas, Aerosweet Airlines, Air Algérie, Air China, Air Enterprise Pulkovo, Air France, Air India, Air Kazakhstan, Air Koryo, Air Lines of Kuban, Air Moldova, Air Ukraine, Alaska Airlines, Alitalia, All Nippon Airways, Arax Airways, Armenian Airlines, Austrian Airlines, Azerbaijan Airlines, Baikal Airlines, Balkan, Bashkir Airlines, Belavia, British Airways, Croatia Airlines, Cubana, Cyprus Airways, Czech Airlines, Delta Air Lines, Donavia, Egyptair, El Al, Estonian Air, Estonian Aviation, Finnair, Gomelavia, Iberia, Intourtrans, Iran Air, JAL, JAT, Kaliningrad Air Enterprise Pulkovo, Kavminvodyavia, Khabarovsk Aviation, KLM, Korean Air, Korsar, Krasnoyarsk Airlines, Kyrgyzstan Airlines, Lithuanian Airlines, LOT, Lufthansa, Magadan Airlines, Malév, MDA Airlines, MIAT-Mongolian Airlines, Minskavia, Moldavian Airlines, Novosibirsk Airlines, Odesa Airlines, Olympic Airways, Royal Jordanian, SABENA, Sakha Avia, Samara Airlines, SAS, Siberia Airlines, Slovak Airlines, State Orenburg Avia, Swissair, Syrian Arab Airlines, Tarom, Transaero Airlines, Turan Air, Turkish Airlines, Ukraine International Airlines, Uzbekiston Airways, Vietnam Airlines, Vladivostok Air, Volga Air Company and Xinjiang Airlines.

In 1995 Aeroflot flew 143·1m. km, carrying 3,200,800 passengers (3,199,100 on international flights). Air Enterprise Pulkovo flew 31·2m. km in 1995, carrying 1,551,800 passengers (365,300 on international flights). Moscow Sheremetevo handled 8,408,642 passengers in 1996 (6,578,151 on international flights) and 74,130 tonnes of freight. The second busiest airport in 1996 was Moscow Vnukovo, which is mainly used for internal flights. It handled 4,334,721 passengers in 1996 (3,262,560 on domestic flights) and 39,986 tonnes of freight. St Petersburg was the third busiest in 1996 for both passengers (2,703,262) and freight (18,345 tonnes).

Shipping. In 1996 the merchant fleet comprised 4,866 vessels totalling 13,755,400 GRT. In 1995, 236 vessels (24% of tonnage) were registered under foreign flags. Total GRT, 16·54m., including oil tankers, 2·38m. GRT, and container ships, 0·46m. GRT. In 1994, 155m. tonnes of freight (about two-thirds was building materials) and 40m. passengers were carried on the 94,000 km of inland waterways. Kaliningrad was opened to shipping in May 1991. In 1996, 14,120,000 tonnes of freight were loaded and 1,423,000 tonnes were unloaded at Russian docks.

Telecommunications. Russia had 26,874,600 main telephone lines in 1997, or 182·7 for every 1,000 persons. Telephone density, 1996: Moscow, 50%; St Petersburg, 39%; Nizhni Novgorod, 18%. In 1995 there were 89,000 cellular phone subscribers, 2,600,000 PCs (18 per 1,000 persons) and 70,200 fax machines. There were 1m. Internet users in July 1998.

Postal Services. In mid-1995 there were 51,800 post offices (35,400 in rural areas).

SOCIAL INSTITUTIONS

Justice. The Supreme Court is the highest judicial body on civil, criminal and administrative law. The Supreme Arbitration Court deals with economic cases. The KGB, and the Federal Security Bureau which succeeded it, were replaced in Dec. 1992 by the Federal Counter-Intelligence Service.

A new civil code was introduced in 1993 to replace the former Soviet code. It guarantees the inviolability of private property and includes provisions for the freedom of movement of capital and goods.

12-member juries were introduced in a number of courts after Nov. 1993. A new criminal code came into force on 1 Jan. 1997, based on respect for the rights and freedoms of the individual and the sanctity of private property. The death penalty is retained for 5 crimes against the person. It is not applied to minors, women or men over 65.

In 1996, 2,625,000 crimes were reported; 29,400 were cases of murder or attempted murder; 53,400 were cases of GBH and 10,900 were cases of rape. In 1994, 924,600 sentences were passed, of which 36% involved imprisonment. In 1996 there were 56 executions (86 in 1995; 1 in 1992). Organized crime groups control up to 40,000 commercial organizations. In 1996 there were 1,047,000 prisoners, or 710 prisoners per 100,000 population (the highest rate in the world).

Religion. The Russian Orthodox Church, represented by the Patriarchate of Moscow, had, in 1997, an estimated 24m. adherents. In 1996, there were over 14,000 parishes, 136 monasteries, and 26 secondary and higher educational institutions. There are still many Old Believers, whose schism from the Orthodox Church dates from the 17th century. The Russian Church is headed by the Patriarch of Moscow and All Russia (Metropolitan Aleksei II of St Petersburg and Novgorod, b. 1929; elected June 1990), assisted by the Holy Synod, which has 7 members—the Patriarch himself and the Metropolitans of Krutitsy and Kolomna (Moscow), St Petersburg and Kiev *ex officio*, and 3 bishops alternating for 6 months in order of seniority from the 3 regions forming the Moscow Patriarchate. The Patriarchate of Moscow maintains jurisdiction over 119 eparchies, of which 59 are in Russia; there are parishes of Russian Orthodox abroad, in Belarus, Ukraine, Kazakhstan, Moldova, Uzbekiston, the Baltic states, and in Damascus, Geneva, Prague, New York and Japan. There is a spiritual mission in Jerusalem, and a monastery at Mt Athos in Greece. There are Jewish communities, primarily in Moscow and St Petersburg, that numbered 600,000 in 1997; there were also 14,720,000 Moslems and 1,340,000 Protestants.

Education. Adult literacy rate in 1995 was over 99%. In 1995 there were 21·5m. pupils in 68,400 primary and secondary day schools; 2·7m. students in 559 higher educational establishments (including 746,800 correspondence students), 3·6m. students in 6,800 technical colleges of all kinds (including correspondence students); and 5·6m. children in 68,600 pre-school institutions. In 1994–95 there were 822 grammar schools and 505 *lycées* with a combined total of 1m. students. In addition there were 447 private schools with 40,000 pupils.

In 1957 a Siberian branch of the Academy of Sciences was organized. Pre-dating the foundation of a Russian Academy of Sciences, St Petersburg and Urals branches were founded in 1990 and 1991 respectively. The Soviet became the Russian Academy of Sciences in Dec. 1991. There were 3,968 scientific institutes, of which 2,166 are independent research institutes.

In 1993 total expenditure on education came to 4·4% of GNP and represented 9·6% of total government expenditure.

Health. Doctors in Jan. 1995 numbered 663,100 (1996, 650,000), and hospital beds 1·9m. In 1995 the doctor/inhabitant ratio was 1:235 and in 1994 hospital bed provision was 119 for every 10,000 persons. There were 12,300 hospitals. In Jan. 1995 there were 863 recorded cases of HIV (156 of whom had AIDS). Respiratory diseases are the chief killer.

Welfare. Vouchers are issued to cover basic health care and pensions contributions. These may be topped up to buy better services. A transition from state-financed to insurance-based health care is taking place.

There were 37·1m. pensioners in 1996. A lump sum of 2,700 roubles was payable in 1992 to parents on the birth of a child. From Dec. 1996 the minimum pension was 75,900 roubles a month. The average monthly pension in June 1995 was 201,874 roubles.

Personal pensions conferred by the former Communist régime conferring special benefits on party or state personnel or awarded for services rendered were abolished in 1992.

There are an estimated 52·1m. private households (based on 1994 micro-census). In 1995 the percentage of households which had various facilities was as follows: Running water, 71; sewerage, 66; central heating, 68; bathroom, 61; gas, 69; hot running water, 54; electric cooker, 15.

Consumer expenditure in 1995 (%): Household services, 19·3; public transport, 28; communications, 7·6; housing services, 19·4; childcare, 2·5; culture, 1·1; tourism/excursions, 1·3; sport, 0·3; healthcare, 2·6; sanatoriums, 3·4; legal services, 8·1; other, 6·4.

Over 80m. Russians live in areas where concentrations of air pollutants are well in excess of permissible levels. 30–40% of children's diseases are caused by air pollution; respiratory diseases such as asthma have increased sixfold since the early 1990s.

CULTURE

Broadcasting. In 1997, 56m. households had TVs. Television broadcasting is still largely state-controlled, although an independent service began in 1993. There are 2 major channels, Ostankino and Russian Television (colour by SECAM). In 1994, 98·8% of the population could receive TV broadcasts. There are also local city channels (e.g. 6 in Moscow in 1993). Access to cable TV varies with locality; satellite TV reached about 5% of the population in 1993. As well as state radio, 24% of the population in 1995 could receive commercial broadcasts. In 1995 there were 50·5m. radio receivers.

Cinema. There were 2,016 cinemas in 1995; attendances in the year totalled 140·1m. 46 long films were made.

Press. In 1996 there were 285 daily newspapers with a combined circulation of 15,517,000 (105 per 1,000 population). In the same year there were 4,596 non-daily newspapers with a combined circulation of 98,558,000 (665 per 1,000 population). A presidential decree of 22 Dec. 1993 brought the press agencies ITAR-TASS and RIA-Novosti under state control. In 1996, 30,200 titles (books and brochures) were published.

Tourism. There were 5,311,000 foreign visitors in 1995 (including 2·2m. on business and 1·8m. tourists).

Libraries. In 1995 there were 2 National libraries and 96,177 public libraries, which held 983,356,000 volumes for 54,201,300 registered users.

National Theatre and Opera. In 1995 there were 470,000 theatres.

Museums and Galleries. Russia had 1,725,000 museums in 1995.

DIPLOMATIC REPRESENTATIVES

Of Russia in Great Britain (13 Kensington Palace Gdns., London, W8 4QX)
Ambassador: Yuri E. Fokine.

Of Great Britain in Russia (Sofiiskaya Naberezhnaya 14, 109072 Moscow)
Ambassador: Sir Andrew Wood, KCMG.

Of Russia in the USA (1125 16th St., NW, Washington, D.C., 20036)
Ambassador: Yuli Vorontsov.

Of the USA in Russia (Novinski Bul'var 19/23, Moscow)
Ambassador: James F. Collins.

Of Russia to the United Nations
Ambassador: Sergey V. Lavrov.

Of Russia to the European Union
Ambassador: Vacant.

FURTHER READING
Rossiiskii Statisticheskii Ezhegodnik. Moscow, annual (title varies)

Acton, E. *et al. Critical Companion to the Russian Revolution.* Indiana University Press, 1997
Aslund, A. (ed.) *Economic Transformation in Russia.* New York, 1994
Cambridge Encyclopedia of Russia and the Former Soviet Union. CUP, 1995
Dukes, P., *A History of Russia: Medieval, Modern, Contemporary.* 2nd ed. London, 1990
Dunlop, J., *Russia Confronts Chechnya: Roots of a Separatist Conflict, Vol. 1.* CUP, 1998
Fowkes, B. (ed), *Russia and Chechnia: The Permanent Crisis, Essays on Russo-Chechen Relations.* St Martin's Press, New York, 1998
Freeze, G. (ed), *Russia: A History.* OUP, 1997
Gall, C. and de Waal, T., *Chechnya: Calamity in the Caucasus.* New York, 1998

Kochan, L., *The Making of Modern Russia.* 2nd ed, revised by R. Abraham. London, 1994
Lieven, A., *Chechnya:Tombstone of Russian Power.* Yale University Press, 1998
Lloyd, J., *Rebirth of a Nation.* London, 1998
McCauley, M., *Who's Who in Russia since 1900.* London 1991
Paxton, J., *Encyclopedia of Russian History.* Denver (CO), 1993
Pitman, L., *Russia/USSR* [Bibliography]. 2nd ed. Oxford and Santa Barbara (CA), 1994
Remnick, D., *Resurrection: The Struggle for a New Russia.* Picador, London, 1998
Riasanovsky, N. V., *A History of Russia.* 5th ed. OUP, 1993
Sakwa, R., *Russian Politics and Society.* 2nd ed. London, 1996
Service, R., *A History of Twentieth-Century Russia.* Harvard University Press, 1997
Treadgold, D. W., *Twentieth Century Russia.* 6th ed. Boston, 1987
Westwood, J.N., *Endurance and Endeavour: Russian History, 1812–1992.* 4th ed. OUP, 1993
White, S. *et al. How Russia Votes.* Chatham House (NJ), 1997.—(eds.) *Developments in Russian Politics.* London, 1997
Yeltsin, B., *The View from the Kremlin* (in USA *The Struggle for Russia*). London and New York, 1994

National statistical office: Gosudarstvennyi Komitet po Statistike (*Goskomstat*), Moscow.

THE REPUBLICS

Status
The 21 republics that with Russia itself constitute the Russian Federation were part of the RSFSR in the Soviet period. On 31 March 1992 the federal government concluded treaties with the then 20 republics, except Checheno-Ingushetia and Tatarstan, defining their mutual responsibilities. The *Council of the Heads of the Republics* is chaired by the Russian President and includes the Russian Prime Minister. Its function is to provide an interaction between the federal government and the republican authorities.

ADYGEYA

Part of Krasnodar Territory. Area, 7,600 sq. km (2,934 sq. miles); population (1996), 450,000. Capital, Maikop (149,000). Established 27 July 1922; granted republican status in 1991.

President: Aslan Dzharimov.

Chief industries are timber, woodworking, food processing and there is some engineering and gas production. Agriculture consists primarily of crops (beets, wheat, maize), on partly irrigated land. Industrial output was valued in 1993 at 112,000m. roubles, agricultural output at 68,000m. roubles.

In 1994–95 there were 174 schools with 67,000 pupils, 3 technical colleges with 5,200 students and 2 higher educational institutions with 6,200 students.

In 1995 the rates of doctors and hospital beds per 10,000 population were 32·7 and 113 respectively.

ALTAI

Part of Altai Territory. Area, 92,600 sq. km (35,740 sq. miles); population (1996), 202,000. Capital, Gorno-Altaisk (39,000). Established 1 June 1922 as Oirot Autonomous Region; renamed 7 Jan. 1948; granted republican status in 1991 and renamed in 1992.

BURYATIA

Chairman of the State Assembly (El-Kurultai): Daniil Ivanovich Tabayev.
Chairman of the Government: Seymon Ivanovich Zubakin.

Chief industries are clothing and footwear, foodstuffs, gold mining, timber, chemicals and dairying. Cattle breeding predominates; pasturages and hay meadows cover over 1m. ha, but 142,000 ha are under crops. Industrial output was valued at 19,900m. roubles in 1993, agricultural output at 43,000m. roubles.

In 1994–95 there were 39,000 pupils in 194 schools; 4 technical colleges had 3,100 students and 3,700 students were attending a pedagogical institute.

The rates of doctors and hospital beds per 10,000 population in 1995 were 32·7 and 153 respectively.

BASHKORTOSTAN

Area 143,600 sq. km (55,430 sq. miles), population (1998), 4,096,000. Capital, Ufa (1989 census population 1·1m.). Bashkiria was annexed to Russia in 1557. It was constituted as an Autonomous Soviet Republic on 23 March 1919. A declaration of republican sovereignty was adopted in 1990, and a declaration of independence on 28 March 1992. A treaty of Aug. 1994 with Russia preserves the common legislative framework of the Russian Federation while defining mutual areas of competence. The population, census 1989, was 39·3% Russian, 28·4% Tatar, 21·9% Bashkir, 3% Chuvash and 2·7% Mari.

A constitution was adopted on 24 Dec. 1993. It states that Bashkiria conducts its own domestic and foreign policy, that its laws take precedence in Bashkiria, and that it forms part of the Russian Federation on a voluntary and equal basis.

President: Murtaza Gubaidullovich Rakhimov. *Chairman of the State Assembly:* Mikhail Alexeyevich Zaitsev. *Prime Minister:* Rim Sagitovich Bakiev.

Industrial production was valued at 4,188,000m. roubles in 1993, agricultural output at 617,000m. roubles. The most important industries are oil and oil products; there are also engineering, glass and building materials enterprises. Agriculture specializes in wheat, barley, oats and livestock.

In 1994–95 there were 658,000 pupils in 3,317 schools. There is a state university and a branch of the Academy of Sciences with 8 learned institutions (511 research workers). There were 59,800 students in 75 technical colleges and 49,800 in 11 higher educational establishments.

In 1995 the rates of doctors and hospital beds per 10,000 population were 40·1 and 131 respectively.

BURYATIA

Area is 351,300 sq. km (135,650 sq. miles). The Buryat Republic, situated to the south of Sakha, adopted the Soviet system on 1 March 1920. This area was penetrated by the Russians in the 17th century and finally annexed from China by the treaties of Nerchinsk (1689) and Kyakhta (1727). The population (1996) was 1,050,000. Capital, Ulan-Ude (1989 census population, 353,000). The population (1989 census) was 69·9% Russian, 24% Buryat, 2·2% Ukrainian, 1% Tatar and 0·5% Belorussian.

There is a 65-member parliament, the *People's Hural.*

President: Leonid Potapov

The main industries are engineering, brown coal and graphite, timber, building materials, sheep and cattle farming. Industrial production was valued at 384,000m. roubles in 1993, agricultural output at 181,000m. roubles.

In 1994–95 there were 615 schools with 196,000 pupils, 20 technical colleges with 13,400 students and 4 higher educational institutions with 19,300 students. A branch of the Siberian Department of the Academy of Sciences had 4 institutions with 281 research workers.

In 1995 the rates of doctors and hospital beds per 10,000 population were 37·4 and 114 respectively.

CHECHNYA

The area of the former Checheno-Ingush Republic was 19,300 sq. km (7,350 sq. miles); population (1997), around 500,000. Capital, Dzhohar (since March 1998; previously Grozny). The Chechens and Ingushes were conquered by Russia in the late 1850s. In 1918 each nationality separately established its 'National Soviet' within the Terek Autonomous Republic, and in 1920 (after the Civil War) were constituted areas within the Mountain Republic. The Chechens separated out as an Autonomous Region on 30 Nov. 1922 and the Ingushes on 7 July 1924. In Jan. 1934 the two regions were united, and on 5 Dec. 1936 constituted as an Autonomous Republic. This was dissolved in 1944 and the population was deported en masse, allegedly for collaboration with the German occupation forces. It was reconstituted on 9 Jan. 1957: 232,000 Chechens and Ingushes returned to their homes in the next 2 years. The population (1989 census) included 70·7% Chechens and Ingushes, 23·1% Russians, 1·2% Armenians and 1% Ukrainians.

A Chechen Republic declared its independence in Nov. 1991. (A separate Ingush Republic was declared in June 1993).

In April 1993 President Dudaev dissolved parliament. Hostilities continued throughout 1994 between the government and forces loosely grouped under the 'Provisional Chechen Council'. The Russian government, which had never recognized the Chechen declaration of independence of Nov. 1991, moved troops and armour into Chechnya on 11 Dec. 1994 'to re-establish constitutional order'. Grozny was bombed and attacked by Russian ground forces at the end of Dec. 1994 and the presidential palace was captured on 19 Jan. 1995, but fighting continued. On 30 July 1995 the Russian and Chechen authorities signed a ceasefire. On 8 Dec. 1995 an agreement between the Russian and Chechen prime ministers amnestied insurgents who laid down their arms. However, hostilities, raids and hostage-taking continued. The Chechen President was killed during fighting in April 1996. A further ceasefire was concluded on 30 Aug. 1996, and it was agreed that the status of Chechnya would be determined by a referendum in 2001. On 23 Nov. 1996 the Russian President decreed the withdrawal of all Russian troops by the end of 1996.

Presidential and a first round of parliamentary elections were held on 27 Jan. 1997. The electorate was 513,000. There were 14 presidential candidates. There were some 150 foreign observers, including 72 from OSCE. The second round of parliamentary elections was declared invalid because turn-out failed to reach the necessary 50%. A third round was held in May 1997.

President: Aslan Maskhadov. *Vice-President:* Vakha Arsanov. *Prime Minister:* Shamil Basayev. *Minister of Information:* Movladi Udugov. *Finance:* Taimaz Abubakarov.

Ingush desire to separate from Chechnya led to fighting along the Chechen-Ingush border and a deployment of Russian troops. An agreement to withdraw was reached between Russia and Chechnya on 15 Nov. 1992. The separation of Chechnya and Ingushetia was formalized by an amendment of Dec. 1992 to the Russian Constitution.

Checheno-Ingushetia had a major oilfield, and a number of engineering works, chemical factories, building materials works and food canneries. There was a timber, woodworking and furniture industry. Industrial output in the two republics was valued at 213,000m. roubles in 1993, agricultural output at 79,000m. roubles.

There were, in the Chechen and Ingush republics in 1993–94, 548 schools with 251,000 pupils, 12 technical colleges with 8,700 students and 3 places of higher education with 13,100 students.

In 1992 it was decided to revert to the Roman alphabet (which had replaced Arabic script in 1927 and been itself replaced by Cyrillic in 1938).

In 1995 the rates of doctors and hospital beds in the Chechen and Ingush republics per 10,000 population were 21·1 and 91 respectively.

CHUVASHIA

Area, 18,300 sq. km (7,064 sq. miles); population (1996), 1,360,800. Capital, Cheboksary (1989 census population, 0·42m.). The territory was annexed by Russia in the middle of the 16th century. On 24 June 1920 it was constituted as an Autonomous Region, and on 21 April 1925 as an Autonomous Republic. The population (1989 census) was 67·8% Chuvash, 26·7% Russian, 2·7% Tatar and 1·4% Mordovian. Republican sovereignty was declared in Sept. 1990.

President: Nikolai Fedorov

The timber industry antedates the Soviet period. Other industries include railway repair works, electrical and other engineering industries, building materials, chemicals, textiles and food industries. Grain crops account for nearly two-thirds of all sowings and fodder crops for nearly a quarter. Industrial output was valued at 641,000m. roubles in 1993, agricultural output at 224,000m. roubles.

In 1994–95 there were 218,000 pupils at 719 schools, 20,000 students at 27 technical colleges and 18,900 students at 3 higher educational establishments.

In 1995 the rates of doctors and hospital beds per 10,000 population were 37·9 and 124 respectively.

DAGESTAN

Area, 50,300 sq. km (19,416 sq. miles); population (1998), 2,060,000. Capital, Makhachkala (1989 census population, 315,000). Over 30 nationalities inhabit this republic apart from Russians (9·2% at 1989 census); the most numerous are Dagestani nationalities (80·2%), Azerbaijanis (4·2%), Chechens (3·22%) and Jews (0·5%). Annexed from Persia in 1723, Dagestan was constituted an Autonomous Republic on 20 Jan. 1921. In 1991 the Supreme Soviet declared the area of republican, rather than autonomous republican, status.

Chairman of the State Council, Head of the Republic: Magomedali Magomedovich Magomedov. *Chairman of the People's Assembly:* Mukhu Gimbatovich Aliyev.

There are engineering, oil, chemical, woodworking, textile, food and other light industries. Agriculture is varied, ranging from wheat to grapes, with sheep farming and cattle breeding. Industrial output was valued at 136,000m. roubles in 1993, agricultural output at 155,000m. roubles.

In 1994–95 there were 1,609 schools with 413,000 pupils, 17,700 students at 27 technical colleges and 6 higher education establishments with 28,400 students.

In 1995 the rates of doctors and hospital beds per 10,000 population were 36·5 and 88 respectively.

INGUSHETIA

The history of Ingushetia is interwoven with that of Chechnya (*see above*). Ingush desire to separate from Chechnya led to fighting along the Chechen-Ingush border and a deployment of Russian troops. The separation of Ingushetia from Chechnya was formalized by an amendment of Dec. 1992 to the Russian Constitution. On 15 May 1993 an extraordinary congress of the peoples of Ingushetia adopted a declaration of state sovereignty within the Russian Federation.

The capital is Nazran.

Area, 3,600 sq. km (1,390 sq. miles) (to be confirmed); estimated population, 1997, 301,900.

There is a 27-member parliament. On 27 Feb. 1994 presidential elections and a constitutional referendum were held. Turn-out was 70%. At the referendum 97% of votes cast approved a new constitution stating that Ingushetia is a democratic law-based secular republic forming part of the Russian Federation on a treaty basis.

President: Ruslan Sultanovich Aushev. *Vice President:* Boris Nikolaevich Agapov. *Chairman of the People's Assembly (of the Parliament):* Arsamak Arsamakovich Malsagov. *Prime Minister:* Belan Bagaudinovich Khamchiyev.

A special economic zone for Russian residents was set up in 1994, and an 'offshore' banking tax haven in 1996.

In 1995 the rates of doctors and hospital beds per 10,000 population were 19·6 and 59 respectively.

KABARDINO-BALKARIA

Area, 12,500 sq. km (4,825 sq. miles); population (1997), 800,000. Capital, Nalchik (1989 census population, 235,000). Kabarda was annexed to Russia in 1557. The republic was constituted on 5 Dec. 1936. Population (1989 census) included Kabardinians (48·2%), Balkars (9·4%), Russians (31·9%), Ukrainians (1·7%), Ossetians (1·3%) and Germans (1·1%).

A treaty with Russia of 1 July 1994 defines their mutual areas of competence within the legislative framework of the Russian Federation.

President: Valeri Kokov.

Main industries are ore-mining, timber, engineering, coal, food processing, timber and light industries, building materials. Grain, livestock breeding, dairy farming and wine-growing are the principal branches of agriculture. Industrial output was valued at 176,000m. roubles in 1993, agricultural output at 113,000m. roubles.

In 1994–95 there were 252 schools with 139,000 pupils, 6,900 students in 8 technical colleges and 12,900 students at 3 higher educational establishments.

In 1995 the rates of doctors and hospital beds per 10,000 population were 44·8 and 120 respectively.

KALMYKIA

Area, 76,100 sq. km (29,382 sq. miles); population (1997), 320,000. Capital, Elista (85,000). The population (1989 census) was 45·4% Kalmyk, 37·7% Russian, 2·6% Chechen, 1·9% Kazakh and 1·7% German.

The Kalmyks migrated from western China to Russia (Nogai Steppe) in the early 17th century. The territory was constituted an Autonomous Region on 4 Nov. 1920, and an Autonomous Republic on 22 Oct. 1935; this was dissolved in 1943. On 9 Jan. 1957 it was reconstituted as an Autonomous Region and on 29 July 1958 as an Autonomous Republic once more. In Oct. 1990 the republic was renamed the Kalmyk Soviet Socialist Republic; it was given its present name in Feb. 1992.

President: Kirsan Nikolaevich Ilyumzhinov.

In April 1993 the Supreme Soviet was dissolved and replaced by a professional parliament consisting of 25 of the former deputies. On 5 April 1994 a specially-constituted 300-member constituent assembly adopted a 'Steppe Code' as Kalmykia's basic law. This is not a constitution and renounces the declaration of republican sovereignty of 18 Oct. 1990. It provides for a *President* elected for 5-year terms with the power to dissolve parliament, and a 27-member parliament, the *People's Hural*, elected every 4 years. It stipulates that Kalmykia is an equal member and integral part of the Russian Federation, functioning in accordance with the Russian constitution.

Main industries are fishing, canning and building materials. Cattle breeding and irrigated farming (mainly fodder crops) are the principal branches of agriculture. Industrial output was valued at 35,600m. roubles in 1993, agricultural output at 89,000m. roubles.

In 1994–95 there were 59,000 pupils in 252 schools, 4,200 students in 6 technical colleges and 5,100 in higher education.

In 1995 the rates of doctors and hospital beds per 10,000 population were 48·8 and 151 respectively.

KARACHAI-CHERKESSIA

Area, 14,300 sq. km (5,521 sq. miles); population (1997), 440,000. Capital, Cherkessk (113,000). A Karachai Autonomous Region was established on 26 April 1926 (out of a previously united Karachaevo-Cherkess Autonomous Region created in 1922), and dissolved in 1943. A Cherkess Autonomous Region was established on 30 April 1928. The present Autonomous Region was re-established on 9 Jan. 1957. The Region declared itself a Soviet Socialist Republic in Dec. 1990.

Head of the Republic: Vladimir Islamovich Khubiev. *Chairman of the People's Assembly:* Igor Vladimirovich Ivanov. *Chairman of the Government:* Anatoly Galimzhanovich Ozov.

There are ore-mining, engineering, chemical and woodworking industries. The Kuban-Kalaussi irrigation scheme irrigates 200,000 ha. Livestock breeding and grain growing predominate in agriculture. Industrial output was valued at 114,000m. roubles in 1993, agricultural output at 92,000m. roubles.

In 1994–95 there were 74,000 pupils in 188 secondary schools, 6 technical colleges with 4,800 students and 2 institutes with 6,200 students.

In 1995 the rates of doctors and hospital beds per 10,000 population were 29 and 102 respectively.

KARELIA

The Karelian Republic, capital Petrozavodsk (1989 census population, 0·27m.), covers an area of 172,400 sq. km, with a population of 800,000 (1997). Karelians represent 10% of the population, Russians 73·6%, Belorussians 7% and Ukrainians 3·6% (1989 census).

Karelia (formerly Olonets Province) became part of the RSFSR after 1917. In June 1920 a Karelian Labour Commune was formed and in July 1923 this was transformed into the Karelian Autonomous Soviet Socialist Republic (one of the autonomous republics of the RSFSR). On 31 March 1940, after the Soviet–Finnish war, practically all the territory (with the exception of a small section in the neighbourhood of the Leningrad area) which had been ceded by Finland to the USSR was added to Karelia, and the Karelian Autonomous Republic was transformed into the Karelo-Finnish Soviet Socialist Republic as the 12th republic of the USSR. In 1946, however, the southern part of the republic, including its whole seaboard and the towns of Viipuri (Vyborg) and Keksholm, was attached to the

RSFSR, reverting in 1956 to autonomous republican status within the RSFSR. In Nov. 1991 it declared itself the 'Republic of Karelia'.

Chairman of the Government: Sergei Leonidovich Katanandov. *Chairman of the Chamber of the Republic of the Legislative Assembly:* Ivan Petrovich Alexandrov. *Chairman of the Chamber of Representatives of the Legislative Assembly:* Valentina Nikolaevna Pivmenko.

Karelia has a wealth of timber, some 70% of its territory being forest land. It is also rich in other natural resources, having large deposits of mica, diabase, spar, quartz, marble, granite, zinc, lead, silver, copper, molybdenum, tin, baryta and iron ore. Its lakes and rivers are rich in fish.

There are timber mills, paper-cellulose works, mica, chemical plants, power stations and furniture factories. Industrial output was valued at 520,000m. roubles in 1993, agricultural output at 97,000m. roubles.

In 1994–95 there were 0·12m. pupils in 341 schools. There were 9,700 students in 3 institutions of higher education and 11,300 in 16 technical colleges.

In 1995 the rates of doctors and hospital beds per 10,000 population were 47·2 and 135 respectively.

KHAKASSIA

Area, 61,900 sq. km (23,855 sq. miles); population (1997), 585,000. Capital, Abakan (1989 census, 154,000). Established 20 Oct. 1930; granted republican status in 1991.

Chairman of the Government: Alexei Ivanovich Lebed.

There are coal- and ore-mining, timber and woodworking industries. The region is linked by rail with the Trans-Siberian line. Industrial output was valued at 545,000m. roubles in 1993, agricultural output at 83,000m. roubles.

In 1994–95 there were 97,000 pupils in 282 secondary schools, 6,200 students in 7 technical colleges and 5,600 students at a higher education institution.

In 1995 the rates of doctors and hospital beds per 10,000 population were 36 and 132 respectively.

KOMI

Area, 415,900 sq. km (160,540 sq. miles); population (1997), 1,200,000. Capital, Syktyvkar (1989 census population, 233,000). Annexed by the princes of Moscow in the 14th century, the territory was constituted as an Autonomous Region on 22 Aug. 1921 and as an Autonomous Republic on 5 Dec. 1936. The population (1989 census) was 57·7% Russian, 23·3% Komi, 8·3% Ukrainian and 2·1% Belorussian.

A declaration of sovereignty was adopted by the republican parliament in Sept. 1990, and the designation 'Autonomous' dropped from the republic's official name.

Head of the Republic, Chairman of the Government: Yury Alexeyevich Spiridonov. *Chairman of the State Council:* Vladimir Alexandrovich Torlopov.

There are coal, oil, timber, gas, asphalt and building materials industries, and light industry is expanding. Livestock breeding (including dairy farming) is the main branch of agriculture. Crop area, 92,000 ha. Industrial output was valued at 1,038,000m. roubles in 1993, agricultural output at 134,000m. roubles.

In 1994–95 there were 196,000 pupils in 595 schools, 11,300 students in 3 higher educational establishments, 14,200 students in 20 technical colleges; and a branch of the Academy of Sciences with 4 institutions (297 research workers).

In 1995 the rates of doctors and hospital beds per 10,000 population were 39·6 and 134 respectively.

MARI EL

Area, 23,200 sq. km (8,955 sq. miles); population (1998), 760,000. Capital, Yoshkar-Ola (1989 census population, 242,000). The Mari people were annexed to Russia, with other peoples of the Kazan Tatar Khanate, when the latter was overthrown in 1552. On 4 Nov. 1920 the territory was constituted as an Autonomous Region, and on 5 Dec. 1936 as an Autonomous Republic. The republic renamed itself the Mari Soviet Socialist Republic in Oct. 1990, and adopted a new constitution in June 1995. In Dec. 1991 Vladislav Zotin was elected the first president. The population (1989 census) was 47·5% Russian, 43·3% Mari, and 5·9% Tatar.

President, Head of the Government: Vyacheslav Alexandrovich Kislitsyn. *First Deputy Head of the Government:* Nikolai Nikandrovich Gavrilov. *Chairman of the State Assembly:* Mikhail Mikhailovich Zhukov.

Coal is mined. The main industries are metalworking, timber, paper, woodworking and food processing. Crops include grain, flax, potatoes, fruit and vegetables. Industrial output was valued at 257,000m. roubles in 1993, agricultural output at 153,000m. roubles.

In 1994–95 there were 432 schools with 128,000 pupils; 14 technical colleges and 3 higher education establishments had 8,900 and 13,100 students respectively.

In 1995 the rates of doctors and hospital beds per 10,000 population were 38 and 126 respectively.

MORDOVIA

Area, 26,200 sq. km (10,110 sq. miles); population (1997), 956,000. Capital, Saransk (1989 census population, 312,000). By the 13th century the Mordovian tribes had been subjugated by Russian princes. In 1928 the territory was constituted as a Mordovian Area within the Middle-Volga Territory, on 10 Jan. 1930 as an Autonomous Region and on 20 Dec. 1934 as an Autonomous Republic. The population (1989 census) was 60·8% Russian, 32·5% Mordovian and 4·9% Tatar.

President: Nikolai Merkushkin. *Chairman of the State Assembly:* Valery Alexeyevich Kechkin. *Chairmen of the Government of the Republic:* Vladimir Dmitrievich Volkov.

Industries include wood-processing and the production of building materials, furniture, textiles and leather goods. Agriculture is devoted chiefly to grain, sugar-beet, sheep and dairy farming. Industrial output was valued at 457,000m. roubles in 1993, agricultural output at 185,000m. roubles.

In 1994–95 there were 139,000 pupils in 828 schools, 12,600 students in 21 technical colleges and 22,900 attending 2 higher educational institutions.

In 1995 the rates of doctors and hospital beds per 10,000 population were 45·2 and 155 respectively.

NORTH OSSETIA (ALANIA)

Area, 8,000 sq. km (3,088 sq. miles); population (1997), around 700,000. Capital, Vladikavkaz (1989 census population, 0·3m.). North Ossetia was annexed by Russia from Turkey and named the Terek region in 1861. On 4 March 1918 it was proclaimed an Autonomous Soviet Republic, and on 20 Jan. 1921 set up with others as the Mountain Autonomous Republic, with North Ossetia as the Ossetian (Vladikavkaz) Area within it. On 7 July 1924 the latter was constituted as an Autonomous Region and on 5 Dec. 1936 as an Autonomous Republic. A new

Constitution was adopted on 12 Nov. 1994 under which the republic reverted to its former name, Alania. The population (1989 census) was 53% Ossetian, 29% Russian, 5·2% Chechen, 1·9% Armenian and 1·6% Ukrainian.

President: Aleksandr Dzasokhov. *Chairman of the Parliament:* Vyacheslav Parinov. *Chair of the Government:* Taimuraz Dzambekovich.

The main industries are non-ferrous metals (mining and metallurgy), maize processing, timber and woodworking, textiles, building materials, distilleries and food processing. There is also a varied agriculture. Industrial output was valued at 167,000m. roubles in 1993, agricultural output at 175,000m. roubles.

There were, in 1994–95, 104,000 children in 214 schools, 10,800 students in 14 technical colleges and 18,100 students in 5 higher educational establishments.

In 1995 the rates of doctors and hospital beds per 10,000 population were 68·3 and 127 respectively.

SAKHA

The area is 3,103,200 sq. km (1,197,760 sq. miles); population (1997), 1,028,400. Capital, Yakutsk (187,000). The Yakuts were subjugated by the Russians in the 17th century. The territory was constituted an Autonomous Republic on 27 April 1922. The population (1989 census) was 50·3% Russian, 33·4% Yakut, 7% Ukrainian and 1·6% Tatar.

President: Mikhail Nikolaev. *Vice-President:* Spartak Stepanovich Borisov.

The principal industries are mining (gold, tin, mica, coal) and livestock-breeding. Silver- and lead-bearing ores and coal are worked. Large diamond fields have been opened up; Sakha produces most of the Russian Federation's output. Timber and food industries are developing. Trapping and breeding of fur-bearing animals (sable, squirrel, silver fox) are an important source of income. Industrial production was valued at 1,771,000m. roubles in 1993, agricultural output at 373,000m. roubles.

In 1994–95 there were 193,000 pupils in 715 secondary schools, 10,400 students at 19 technical colleges and 9,700 attending 3 higher education institutions.

In 1995 the rates of doctors and hospital beds per 10,000 population were 41·3 and 156 respectively.

TATARSTAN

Area, 68,000 sq. km (26,250 sq. miles); population (1997), 3,766,500. Capital, Kazan (1989 census population 1·1m.). From the 10th to the 13th centuries this was the territory of the Volga-Kama Bulgar State; conquered by the Mongols, it became the seat of the Kazan (Tatar) Khans when the Mongol Empire broke up in the 15th century, and in 1552 was conquered again by Russia. On 27 May 1920 it was constituted as an Autonomous Republic. The population (1989 census) was 48·5% Tatar, 43·3% Russian, 3·7% Chuvash, 0·9% Ukrainian and 0·8% Mordovian.

In Oct. 1991 the Supreme Soviet adopted a declaration of independence. At a referendum in March 1992, 61·4% of votes cast were in favour of increased autonomy. A Constitution was adopted in April 1992, which proclaims Tatarstan a sovereign state which conducts its relations with the Russian Federation on an equal basis. On 15 Feb. 1994 the Russian and Tatar presidents signed a treaty defining Tatarstan as a state united with Russia on the basis of the constitutions of both, but the Russian parliament has not ratified it.

President: Mintimer Sharipovich Shaimiyev. *Chairman of the State Council:* Vassily Nikolayevich Likhachev. *Prime Minister:* Farid Khairullovich Mukhametshin.

The republic has engineering, oil and chemical, timber, building materials, textiles, clothing and food industries. Industrial production was valued at 2,955,000m. roubles in 1993, agricultural output at 532,000m. roubles.

In 1994–95 there were 2,463 schools with 0·56m. pupils, 65 technical colleges with 52,500 students and 16 higher educational establishments with 63,000 students (including a state university). There is a branch of the USSR Academy of Sciences with 5 institutions (512 research workers).

In 1995 the rates of doctors and hospital beds per 10,000 population were 42·3 and 124 respectively.

TUVA

Area, 170,500 sq. km (65,810 sq. miles); population (1998), 310,000. Capital, Kyzyl (80,000). Tuva was incorporated in the USSR as an autonomous region on 11 Oct. 1944 and elevated to an Autonomous Republic on 10 Oct. 1961. The population (1989 census) was 64·3% Tuvans and 32% Russian. Tuva renamed itself the 'Republic of Tuva' in Oct. 1991.

A new constitution was promulgated on 22 Oct. 1993 which adopts the name 'Tyva' for the republic. This constitution provides for a 32-member parliament (*Supreme Hural*), and a *Grand Hural* alone empowered to change the constitution, asserts the precedence of Tuvan law and adopts powers to conduct foreign policy. It was approved by 62·2% of votes cast at a referendum on 12 Dec. 1993.

President: Sherig-ool Dizizhikovich Oorzhhak. *Vice President:* Alexei Alexandrovich Melnikov.

Tuva is well-watered and hydro-electric resources are important. The Tuvans are mainly herdsmen and cattle farmers and there is much good pastoral land. There are deposits of gold, cobalt and asbestos. The main exports are hair, hides and wool. There are mining, woodworking, garment, leather, food and other industries. Industrial production was valued at 25,800m. roubles in 1993, agricultural output at 44,000m. roubles.

In 1994–95 there were 167 schools with 62,000 pupils; 6 technical colleges with 3,800 students, and 1 higher education institution with 2,800 students.

In 1995 the rates of doctors and hospital beds per 10,000 population were 36·7 and 187 respectively.

UDMURTIA

Area, 42,100 sq. km (16,250 sq. miles); population (1998), 1,639,000. Capital, Izhevsk (1989 census population 635,109). The Udmurts (formerly known as 'Votyaks') were annexed by the Russians in the 15th and 16th centuries. On 4 Nov. 1920 the Votyak Autonomous Region was constituted (the name was changed to Udmurt in 1932), and on 28 Dec. 1934 was raised to the status of an Autonomous Republic. The population (1989 census) was 58·9% Russian, 30·9% Udmurt, 6·9% Tatar, 0·9% Ukrainian and 0·6% Mari. A declaration of sovereignty and the present state title were adopted in Sept. 1990.

A new parliament was established in Dec. 1993 consisting of a 50-member upper house, the *Council of Representatives*, and a full-time 35-member lower house.

Chairman of the State Council: Alexander Alexandrovich Volkov. *Chairman of the Council of Ministers:* Pavel Nikolayevich Vershinin.

Heavy industry includes the manufacture of locomotives, machine tools and other engineering products, most of them for the defence industries, as well as timber and building materials. There are also light industries: Clothing, leather, furniture and food. Industrial production was valued at 958,000m. roubles in 1993, agricultural output at 368,000m. roubles.

In 1994–95 there were 902 schools with 263,000 pupils; there were 19,900 students at 30 technical colleges and 24,800 at 5 higher educational institutions.

In 1995 the rates of doctors and hospital beds per 10,000 population were 48·1 and 129 respectively.

JEWISH AUTONOMOUS REGION (BIROBIJAN)

Part of Khabarovsk Territory. Area, 36,000 sq. km (13,895 sq. miles); population (1997), 208,000 (1989 census, Russians, 83·2%; Ukrainians, 7·4%; Jews, 4·2%). Capital, Birobijan (82,000). Established as Jewish National District in 1928, became an Autonomous Region 7 May 1934. In Oct. 1991 the region declared itself an Autonomous Republic.

Governor, Chairman of the Government: Nikolai Volkov.

Chief industries are non-ferrous metallurgy, building materials, timber, engineering, textiles, paper and food processing. There were 161,000 ha under cultivation in 1983; main crops are wheat, soya, oats, barley. Industrial production was valued at 74,500m. roubles in 1993, agricultural output at 73,000m. roubles.

In 1991–92 there were 35,000 pupils in 111 schools; students in 6 technical colleges numbered 4,900. There are a Yiddish national theatre, newspaper and broadcasting service.

In 1995 the rates of doctors and hospital beds per 10,000 population were 38·3 and 175 respectively.

AUTONOMOUS AREAS

Agin-Buryat
Situated in Chita region (Eastern Siberia); area, 19,000 sq. km, population (1997), 78,400. Capital, Aginskoe. Formed 1937, its economy is basically pastoral.

Chukot
Situated in Magadan region (Far East); area, 737,700 sq. km. Population (1997), 90,000. Capital, Anadyr. Formed 1930. Population chiefly Russian, also Chukchi, Koryak, Yakut, Even. Minerals are extracted in the north, including gold, tin, mercury and tungsten.

Evenki
Situated in Krasnoyarsk territory (Eastern Siberia); area, 767,600 sq. km, population, (1997) 20,000, chiefly Evenks. Capital, Tura. Formed 1930.

Khanty-Mansi
Situated in Tyumen region (Western Siberia); area, 523,100 sq. km, population (1997), 1,336,000, chiefly Russians but also Khants and Mansi. Capital, Khanty-Mansiisk. Formed 1930.

Komi-Permyak
Situated in Perm region (Northern Russia); area, 32,900 sq. km, population (1997), 160,000, chiefly Komi-Permyaks. Formed 1925. Capital, Kudymkar. Forestry is the main occupation.

Koryak
Situated in Kamchatka; area, 301,500 sq. km, population (1997), 32,000. Capital, Palana. Formed 1930.

Nenets
Situated in Archangel region (Northern Russia); area, 176,700 sq. km, population (1997), 46,600. Capital, Naryan-Mar. Formed 1929.

Taimyr
Situated in Krasnoyarsk territory, this most northerly part of Siberia comprises the Taimyr peninsula and the Arctic islands of Severnaya Zemlya. Area, 862,100 sq. km, population (1997), 46,300, excluding the mining city of Norilsk which is separately administered. Capital, Dudinka. Formed 1930.

Ust-Ordyn-Buryat
Situated in Irkutsk region (Eastern Siberia); area, 22,400 sq. km, population (1996), 145,000. Capital, Ust-Ordynsk. Formed 1937.

Yamalo-Nenets
Situated in Tyumen region (Western Siberia); area, 750,300 sq. km, population (1997), 600,000. Capital, Salekhard. Formed 1930.

RWANDA

Republika y'u Rwanda

Capital: Kigali
Population estimate, 2000: 7·67m.
GNP per capita: (PPP$) 630

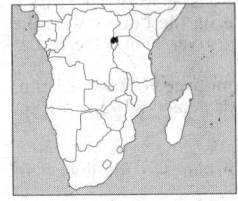

KEY HISTORICAL EVENTS

From the 16th century to 1959 the Tutsi kingdom of Rwanda shared the history of Burundi. In 1959 an uprising of the Hutu destroyed the Tutsi feudal hierarchy and overthrew the monarchy. Elections and a referendum under the auspices of the UN in Sept. 1961 resulted in an overwhelming majority for the republican party, the Parmehutu (*Parti du Mouvement de l'Emancipation du Bahutu*), and the rejection of the monarchy. The republic proclaimed by the Parmehutu on 28 Jan. 1961 was recognized by the Belgian administration (but not by the UN) in Oct. 1961. Internal self-government was granted on 1 Jan. 1962, and by decision of the General Assembly of the UN the Republic of Rwanda became independent on 1 July 1962.

Conflict between the Hutu and Tutsi in 1963 was renewed and again trouble broke out, with much bloodshed, in 1972–73. A coup on 5 July 1973 deposed the first president, Gregoire Kayibanda, and a military government was established. The military leader of this coup, Gen. Juvénal Habyarimana, became president. There was gradual return to civilian rule. In 1978 a new constitution was accepted by a national referendum. President Habyarimana was confirmed in office in elections in 1978 and again in 1983, when candidates from the country's sole political party, the National Revolutionary Democratic Movement, were also returned. However, for much of the time since then the country has contended with the problem of refugees fleeing repression and war in neighbouring Uganda.

In Oct. 1990 rebel Tutsi forces of the Rwandan Patriotic Front (RPF) invaded from Uganda. An agreement was signed on 14 Aug. 1992 to end the civil war, but fighting continued. Rebels and government agreed to merge their forces at peace talks in March 1993. A peace agreement was signed on 4 Aug. 1993 at Arusha (Tanzania). On 5 Oct. the UN Security Council unanimously decided to send a peacekeeping force to oversee the establishment of transitional organs in line with the Aug. agreement. However, President Habyarimana was killed, possibly assassinated, on 6 April 1994. Fatalities in the fighting which broke out included the Prime Minister and UN personnel. Rebel Tutsi forces of the RPF began an attack from the north of the country.

An interim government was formed on 10 April with the Speaker Théodore Sindikubwabo (National Republican Movement for Development; MRND) as President and Jean Kambanda (Democratic Republican Movement; MDR) as Prime Minister.

Most UN forces were withdrawn during the fighting and massacres of April 1994 but following a UN Security Council resolution of 17 May 1994 a new force of 5,500 was sent in. On 22 June 1994 the UN Security Council approved France's dispatch of 2,000 troops on a humanitarian mission. The RPF, however, said it would treat the force as invaders. The French forces maintained a 'safe zone' for refugees in the south-west of Rwanda until their withdrawal on 21 Aug. 1994. Under the aegis of the OAU at Tunis representatives of the Rwandan interim government and the RPF agreed a ceasefire. At the request of the RPF on 6 July 1994 in Brussels Faustin Twagiramungu agreed to form a 22-member government of national unity in which 8 posts were held by the RPF.

It is estimated that more than 1m. Rwandans were killed in 1994 through genocide and the civil war, and that more than 2m. were forced to flee to neighbouring countries.

On 8 Nov. 1994 the UN Security Council resolved by 13 votes (China abstaining and Rwanda opposing) to set up an international tribunal to try crimes of genocide in Rwanda. It was inaugurated on 27 June 1995 and subsequently merged with that for Yugoslavia. UN forces (UNAMIR) left Rwanda on 8 March 1996, and although progress has been made since then, the civil strife between the two factions continues, particularly in the north-west of the country. In Dec. 1997 over 300 Tutsis were killed at a large refugee camp. In Sept. 1998 Jean Kambanda, the former Prime Minister, was sentenced to life imprisonment for his part in the 1994 genocide.

TERRITORY AND POPULATION
Rwanda is bounded south by Burundi, west by the Democratic Republic of the Congo, north by Uganda and east by Tanzania. A mountainous state of 26,338 sq. km (10,169 sq. miles), its western third drains to Lake Kivu on the border with the Democratic Republic of the Congo and thence to the Congo river, while the rest is drained by the Kagera river into the Nile system.

The population was 7,164,994 at the 1991 census, of whom over 90% were Hutu, 9% Tutsi and 1% Twa (pygmy); estimate (1996) 5,100,000; density, 193·6 per sq. km.

The UN gives a projected population for 2000 of 7·67m.

In 1995 the percentage of the population considered as urban was the lowest of any country in the world, at 5·7%.

The areas and populations of the 10 prefectures are:

Prefecture	Area (in sq. km)	Population (1991 census)	Prefecture	Area (in sq. km)	Population (1991 census)
Cyangugu	1,845	515,129	Kigali	3,118	1,156,651
Kibuye	1,705	470,747	Kibungo	4,046	655,368
Gisenyi	2,050	734,697	Gitarama	2,189	851,516
Ruhengeri	1,663	766,112	Gikongoro	2,057	464,585
Byumba	4,761	783,350	Butare	1,837	766,839

Kigali, the capital, had 234,500 inhabitants in 1993; other towns are Butare, Ruhengeri and Gisenyi.

Kinyarwanda, the language of the entire population, French and English (since 1996) are the official languages. Swahili is spoken in the commercial centres.

SOCIAL STATISTICS
1998 estimates: Births, 260,000; deaths, 127,000. Estimated birth rate (per 1,000 population, 1998), 39; estimated death rate (per 1,000 population, 1998), 19. Annual growth rate, 1990–95, 2·0%.

Life expectancy at birth over the period 1990–95 was the lowest in the world, at 22·1 years for males and 23·1 years for females. No other country saw such a great reduction in life expectancy compared to the period 1980–85, when the figures were 44·6 for males and 48·1 for females. Infant mortality, 1990–95, 139 per 1,000 live births; fertility rate, 6·6 births per woman.

CLIMATE
Despite the equatorial situation, there is a highland tropical climate. The wet seasons are from Oct. to Dec. and March to May. Highest rainfall occurs in the west, at around 70" (1,770 mm), decreasing to 40–55" (1,020–1,400 mm) in the central uplands and to 30" (760 mm) in the north and east. Kigali, Jan. 67°F (19·4°C), July 70°F (21·1°C). Annual rainfall 40" (1,000 mm).

CONSTITUTION AND GOVERNMENT
Under the 1978 Constitution the MRND was the sole political organization.

A new Constitution was promulgated in June 1991 which permits multi-party democracy.

The Arusha Agreement of Aug. 1994 provided for a transitional 70-member National Assembly, which began functioning in Nov. 1994. The seats won by the MRNDD (formerly MRND) were taken over by other parties on the grounds that the MRNDD was culpable of genocide.

National Anthem. 'Rwanda rwacu, Rwanda gihugu cyambyage' ('My Rwanda, Rwanda who gave me birth'); words by a collective, tune traditional.

CURRENT ADMINISTRATION
President: Pasteur Bizimungu (b. 1950; RPF; installed 19 July 1994).

In March 1999 the government comprised:

Vice-President and Minister of Defence: Paul Kagame (RPF).

RWANDA

Prime Minister: Pierre-Célestin Rwigema (MDR).

Minister of Agriculture: Augustin Iyamuremye. *Civil Service and Labour:* Joseph Nsengimana. *Commerce, Industry and Co-operatives:* Bonaventure Niyibizi. *Communications and Transportation:* Charles Ntakirutinka. *Crafts, Mines and Tourism:* Marc Rugenera. *Education:* Joseph Karemera. *Gender, Family and Social Affairs:* Aloysia Inyumba. *Finance and Planning:* Donat Kaberuka. *Foreign Affairs:* Amri Sued. *Health:* Vincent Biruta. *Information:* Jean Nepomcene Nayinzira. *Interior and Communal Development:* Sheik Abdelkarim Harelimana. *Justice:* Faustin Nteziryayo. *Public Works and Energy:* Laurien Ngirabanzi. *Youth:* Jacques Bihozagara. *Minister to the President's Office:* Patrick Mazimhaka.

Local Government. The 10 prefectures, each under an appointed Prefect, are divided into 143 communes, each with an appointed Burgomaster and an elected Council. On 29 March 1999 Rwanda held local elections—the first elections of any sort since the genocide of 1994.

DEFENCE
In 1997 defence expenditure totalled US$103m. (US$13 per capita).

Army. The Army consisted of 1 commando battalion, 1 reconnaissance, 8 infantry and 1 engineer company. Equipment included 12 AML-60 armoured cars. Strength (1997) about 55,000. There was a paramilitary gendarmerie of some 7,000.

INTERNATIONAL RELATIONS
Rwanda is a member of the UN, OAU and is an ACP member state of the ACP-EU relationship.

ECONOMY

Performance. Real GDP growth was 60·7% in 1995, following 5 years of negative growth peaking in a rate of −51·8% in 1994 at the height of the the civil war.

Budget. In 1996 revenues were estimated to be US$231m. and expenditures US$319m.

Currency. The unit of currency is the *Rwanda franc* (RWF) notionally of 100 *centimes*. On 3 Jan. 1995, 500-, 1,000- and 5,000-Rwanda franc notes were replaced by new issues, demonetarizing the currency taken abroad by exiles. The currency is not convertible. Foreign exchange reserves were US$123m. in Feb. 1998. There are no gold reserves. The average annual inflation rate over the period 1990–96 was 19·5%. Total money supply in Feb. 1998 was 53,850m. Rwanda francs.

Banking and Finance. The central bank is the National Bank of Rwanda (founded 1960; *Governor* Augustin Ruzidana) which became the bank of issue in 1964. There are 4 commercial banks (independent with state equity participation, the Economic Community of the Great Lakes Bank, and a state-run savings bank and development bank).

ENERGY AND NATURAL RESOURCES

Electricity. Installed capacity is 60,000 kW. Production was 177m. kWh in 1994 and consumption per capita 23 kWh in 1994.

Minerals. Production (1991): Cassiterite, 871 tonnes; wolfram, 212 tonnes. About 1m. cu. metres of natural gas are obtained from under the lake each year.

Agriculture. Agriculture accounted for 40% of GDP in 1996. Staple food crops (production 1995, in 1,000 tonnes) are plantains (2,600), sweet potatoes (1,100), cassava (250), potatoes (150), dry beans (118), sorghum (72), maize (71), taro (30), dry peas (12) and groundnuts (8). The main cash crops are coffee (22), tea (5) and pyrethrum. There is a pilot rice-growing project.

Long-horned Ankole cattle play an important traditional role. Efforts are being made to improve their present negligible economic value. There were, in 1995, 465,000 cattle, 920,000 goats, 250,000 sheep, 80,000 pigs and 1m. chickens.

Forestry. Forests covered 250,000 ha (10·1% of the land area) in 1995. 5·6m. cu. metres of roundwood were cut in 1995.

Fisheries. The catch in 1995 totalled approximately 3,350 tonnes, entirely from inland waters.

INDUSTRY

There are about 100 small-sized modern manufacturing enterprises in the country. Food manufacturing is the dominant industrial activity (64%) followed by construction (15·3%) and mining (9%). There is a large modern brewery.

Labour. The labour force in 1996 totalled 3,021,000 (51% males). Over 90% of the economically active population in 1995 were engaged in agriculture, fisheries and forestry.

INTERNATIONAL TRADE

With Burundi and the Democratic Republic of the Congo, Rwanda forms part of the Economic Community of the Great Lakes. Foreign debt was US$1,034m. in 1996.

Imports and Exports. In 1996 exports amounted to US$60m. and imports US$257m. Major exports are coffee, tea and tin. Main export markets, 1991: Germany, 21·3%; Netherlands, 18·8%; Belgium, 11·8%; UK, 6·4%. Main import suppliers: Belgium, 17·1%; Kenya, 13·4%; South Africa, 10·4%; France, 6·8%.

COMMUNICATIONS

Roads. There were 14,900 km of roads in 1996, of which 1,350 km were surfaced. There are road links with Burundi, Uganda, Tanzania and the Democratic Republic of the Congo. In 1996 there were 13,000 passenger cars and 17,100 trucks and vans.

Civil Aviation. There is an international airport at Kigali (Gregoire Kayibanda). In 1998 there were flights to Addis Ababa, Brussels, Dar es Salaam, Douala, Entebbe, Johannesburg, Luanda, Mwanza and Nairobi. Rwanda does not have a national airline, but services were provided in 1998 by Air Tanzania Corporation, Alliance Air, Cameroon Airlines, Delta Air Lines, Ethiopian Airlines, Kenya Airways, SABENA and Uganda Airlines.

Telecommunications. Rwanda had 15,000 telephone main lines in 1996, or 2·8 per 1,000 persons. In 1995 there were 500 fax machines, and in Jan. 1998 around 100 Internet users.

Postal Services. In 1994 there was just 1 post office serving the entire population.

SOCIAL INSTITUTIONS

Justice. A system of Courts of First Instance and provincial courts refer appeals to Courts of Appeal and a Court of Cassation situated in Kigali.

In 1998 a number of people were executed who had been found guilty of genocide during the civil war in 1994, including 22 at 5 different locations throughout the country on 24 Apr. 1998.

Religion. In 1997 approximately 65% of the population were Roman Catholics, 9% Protestants and 1% Moslems. Some of the population follow traditional animist religions. Before the civil war there were 9 Roman Catholic bishops and 370 priests. By the end of 1994, 3 bishops had been killed and 3 reached retiring age; 106 priests had been killed and 130 had sought refuge abroad.

Education. In 1992 there were 1,710 primary schools with 18,937 teachers for 1·1m. pupils; 94,586 secondary pupils with 3,413 teachers; and 3,389 students at university level. Adult literacy rate, 1995, 60·5% (male, 69·8%; female, 51·6%).

Health. In 1989 there were 272 doctors, 7 dentists, 25 pharmacists and 835 nursing personnel. Hospital bed provision in 1989 was 8 per 10,000 population.

There were 10,706 reported cases of AIDS by Dec. 1996, and 1·38m. reported of malaria in 1992.

CULTURE

Broadcasting. The state-controlled *Radiodiffusion de la République Rwandaise* is responsible for broadcasting. There is no television. There were about 525,000 radio sets in 1995.

Press. In 1995 there was 1 daily newspaper with a circulation of 500, equivalent to a rate of 1 per 10,000 population.

DIPLOMATIC REPRESENTATIVES
Of Rwanda in Great Britain (Uganda Hse., 58-59 Trafalgar Sq., London, WC2N 5DX)
Ambassador: Dr Zac Nsenga.

Of Great Britain in Rwanda (Parcelle No. 1131, Blvd. De l'Umuganda, Kacyira-Sud, POB 576, Kigali)
Ambassador: G. N. Loten.

Of Rwanda in the USA (1714 New Hampshire Ave., NW, Washington, D.C., 20009)
Ambassador: Theogene Rudasingwa.

Of the USA in Rwanda (Blvd. de la Révolution, Kigali, POB 28)
Ambassador: Robert Gribbin III.

Of Rwanda to the United Nations
Ambassador: Gideon Kayinamura.

Of Rwanda to the European Union
Ambassador: Manzi Bakuramutsa.

FURTHER READING
Braeckman, C., *Rwanda: Histoire d'un Génocide.* Paris, 1994
Dorsey, L., *Historical Dictionary of Rwanda.* Metuchen (NJ), 1995
Gourevitch, P., *We Wish to Inform You That Tomorrow we Will be Killed With Our Families.* Picador, London, 1998
Prunier, G., *The Rwanda Crisis: History of a Genocide.* Farnborough, 1995

ST KITTS AND NEVIS

Federation of St Kitts
and Nevis

Capital: Basseterre
Population estimate, 2000: 45,000
GNP per capita: (PPP$) 7,310
HDI/world rank: 0·854/50

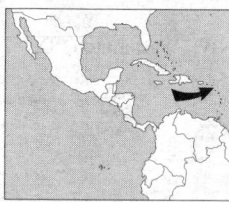

KEY HISTORICAL EVENTS

The islands of St Kitts (formerly St Christopher) and Nevis were discovered and named by Columbus in 1493. They were settled by Britain in 1623 and 1628 respectively, but ownership was disputed with France until 1783. They formed part of the Leeward Islands Federation from 1871 to 1956, and part of the Federation of the West Indies from 1958 to 1962. In Feb. 1967 the colonial status was replaced by an 'association' with Britain, giving the islands full internal self-government. St Kitts and Nevis became fully independent on 19 Sept. 1983.

In Oct. 1997 the 5-person Nevis legislature voted to end the federation with St Kitts. However, in a referendum held on 10 Aug. 1998 voters rejected independence, only 62% voting for secession when a two-thirds vote in favour was needed.

In Sept. 1998 Hurricane Georges caused devastation, leaving 25,000 people homeless, with some 80% of the houses in the islands damaged.

TERRITORY AND POPULATION

The 2 islands of St Kitts and Nevis are situated at the northern end of the Leeward Islands in the Eastern Caribbean. Nevis lies 3 km to the south-east of St Kitts. Population, census (1991) 40,618. Estimate, 1997, 44,000 (9,000 on Nevis).

In 2000 the population is projected to be 45,000.

An estimated 66% of the population were rural in 1995.

	sq. km	Census 1980	Census 1991	Chief town	1994 estimate
St Kitts	168·4	33,881	31,824	Basseterre	12,605
Nevis	93·2	9,428	8,794	Charlestown	1,411
	261·6	43,309	40,618		

In 1991, 94·9% of the population were Black. English is the official and spoken language.

SOCIAL STATISTICS

Births, 1997 estimate, 1,000; deaths, 400. Rates, 1997 estimates (per 1,000 population). Births, 23·1; deaths, 8·9. Infant mortality (per 1,000 live births), 18·4. Expectation of life in 1997 was 67·2 years (64·2 for males and 70·4 for females). Growth rate, 1·1% per annum.

CLIMATE

Temperature varies between 17–33°C, with a sea breeze throughout the year, low humidity. Average annual rainfall is 1,300 mm.

CONSTITUTION AND GOVERNMENT

The 1983 Constitution described the country as 'a sovereign democratic federal state'. The Queen of the UK is the head of state, represented by a Governor-General. It allowed for a unicameral Parliament consisting of 11 elected Members (8 from St Kitts and 3 from Nevis) and 3 appointed Senators. Nevis was given its own Island Assembly and the right to secession from St Kitts.

National Anthem. 'O Land of beauty! Our country where peace abounds'; words and tune by K. A. Georges.

RECENT ELECTIONS
At the elections on 3 July 1995, the Labour Party gained 7 seats, the People's Action Movement 1, the Concerned Citizens Movement 2, and the Nevis Reformation Party 1.

CURRENT ADMINISTRATION
Governor-General: Sir Cuthbert Montraville Sebastian, GCMG, OBE.

In March 1999 the government comprised:

Prime Minister, Minister of Finance, Minister of Foreign Affairs, National Security, Planning and Information: Dr Denzil L. Douglas. *Deputy Prime Minister, Minister of Trade and Industry, Minister of Youth, Sports, Community Affairs and CARICOM Affairs:* Sam Condor.

Minister of Agriculture, Lands and Housing: Timothy Harris. *Communications, Works, Public Utilities and Ports:* Cedric Liburd. *Education, Labour and Social Security:* Rupert Herbert. *Tourism, Culture and Environment:* G. A. Dwyer Astaphan. *Women's Affairs and Health:* Dr Earl Asim Martin.

The *Speaker* is Walford Gumbs.

The *Nevis Island* legislature comprises an Assembly of 3 nominated members and elected members from each electoral district on the Island, and an Administration consisting of the Premier and 2 other persons appointed by the Deputy Governor-General.

The Premier of *Nevis* is Vance Amory.

Local Government. There are 14 parishes.

INTERNATIONAL RELATIONS
St Kitts and Nevis is a member of the UN, the OAS, the Commonwealth and is an ACP member state of the ACP-EU relationship.

ECONOMY
Performance. Real GDP growth in 1996 was estimated to be 4%.

Budget. In 1996 revenues were estimated to be US$100·2m. and expenditures US$100·1m.

Currency. The East Caribbean *dollar* (XCD) (of 100 *cents*) is in use. Inflation was 3% in 1995. In Feb. 1998 foreign exchange reserves were US$38m.

Banking and Finance. The East Caribbean Central Bank (*Governor,* K. Dwight Venner) is the bank of issue. It operates 4 branches in St Kitts and Nevis. The main office is located in Basseterre. There are 7 commercial banks, including 3 foreign. Commercial banks' assets (Dec. 1992) EC$646·47m.; deposits EC$481·28m. Nevis has some 9,000 offshore businesses registered.

ENERGY AND NATURAL RESOURCES
Electricity. Installed capacity was 15,000 kW in 1995. Production in 1995 was 42m. kWh. Consumption per capita was estimated at 2,098 kWh in 1994.

Agriculture. Agriculture accounted for 6% of GDP in 1996. The main crops are sugar, coconut, copra and cotton. In 1995, 3,327 ha were sown to sugar-cane. Most of the farms are small-holdings and there are a number of coconut estates amounting to some 400 ha under public and private ownership. Production, 1995 (in tonnes): Sugar, 20,760; sugar-cane, 19,960; coconuts, 2,000; fruit and vegetables, 3,000; cotton (1994), 4,783 lbs of clean lint; copra (1990), 12 tonnes.

Livestock (1996): Sheep, 17,000; goats, 11,000 (1995); pigs, 3,000; cattle, 2,000.

Forestry. The area under forests in 1995 was 11,000 ha, or 30·6% of the total land area.

Fisheries. The catch in 1995 was approximately 220 tonnes.

INDUSTRY
In 1996 industry accounted for 22% of GDP. There are 3 industrial estates on St Kitts and 1 on Nevis. Export products include electronics and data processing equipment, and garments for the US market. Other small enterprises include food

and drink processing, particularly sugar and cane spirit, and construction. 180,285 tonnes of sugar were produced in 1995.

INTERNATIONAL TRADE

Imports and Exports. Exports, 1995, EC$76m.; imports, EC$359·2m. Main trading partners are the USA, the UK and other CARICOM members. The chief export is sugar. Other significant exports are machinery, food, electronics, beverages and tobacco. Main imports include machinery, manufactures, food and fuels.

COMMUNICATIONS

Roads. There were (1996) about 250 km of roads, of which 200 km were surfaced (124 km paved), and (1995) 5,200 passenger cars and 2,300 commercial vehicles.

Rail. There are 58 km of railway operated by the sugar industry.

Civil Aviation. The main airport is the Robert Llewelyn Bradshaw International Airport (just over 3 km from Basseterre). In 1998 there were flights to Anguilla, Antigua, Barbados, British Virgin Islands, Netherlands Antilles, Nevis (Newcastle), Puerto Rico and the US Virgin Islands, with services provided by American Airlines, LIAT and Windward Islands Airways International.

Shipping. There is a deep-water port at Bird Rock (Basseterre). 169,042 tons of cargo were unloaded in 1995 and 30,832 tons loaded. The government maintains a commercial motor boat service between the islands.

Telecommunications. In 1997 there were 17,200 telephone main lines, or 418·3 per 1,000 population.

Postal Services. There are 2 post offices with 7 branches.

SOCIAL INSTITUTIONS

Justice. Justice is administered by the Supreme Court and by Magistrates' Courts. They have both civil and criminal jurisdiction.

Religion. In 1994, 27·5% of the population were Anglican, 25·3% Methodist, 6·9% Roman Catholic, 5·5% Pentecostal, 3·9% Baptist and 3·9% Church of God.

Education. Adult literacy was 95% in 1996. Primary education is compulsory between the ages of 5 and 17. In 1993–94 there were 2,203 pupils and 156 teachers in 45 pre-primary schools. In 1994–95 there were 5,802 pupils and 290 teachers in 23 primary schools, 4,541 pupils and 326 teachers in 7 secondary schools, and (1993) 1,299 pupils and 76 teachers in 8 private schools. There is an Extra-Mural Department of the University of the West Indies, a Technical College and a Teachers' Training College.

Health. In 1992 there were 39 doctors, 8 dentists, 260 nurses and 14 pharmacists; and 4 hospitals, with a provision of 67 beds per 10,000 population.

CULTURE

Broadcasting. There are 3 AM radio stations and 2 TV stations. Cable television is also available. In 1995 there were 10,000 television (colour by NTSC) and 27,000 radio receivers.

Press. In 1996 there were 2 weekly and 1 twice weekly newspapers.

Tourism. In 1996 there were 238,000 foreign tourists, bringing revenue of US$297m. There were 31 hotels in 1995 with 1,593 rooms.

DIPLOMATIC REPRESENTATIVES

Of St Kitts and Nevis in Great Britain (10 Kensington Ct., London, W8 5DL)
High Commissioner: Aubrey E. Hart.

Of Great Britain in St Kitts and Nevis
High Commissioner: G. M. Baker (resides in Barbados).

Of St Kitts and Nevis in the USA (OECS Building, 3216 New Mexico Ave., NW, 3rd Floor, Washington, D.C., 20016)
Ambassador: Dr Osbert Liburd.

Of the USA in St Kitts and Nevis
Ambassador: Jeanette Hyde (resides in Barbados).

Of St Kitts and Nevis to the United Nations
Ambassador: Lee L. Moore, QC.

Of St Kitts and Nevis to the European Union
Ambassador: Edwin Laurent.

FURTHER READING

Statistics Division. *National Accounts.* Annual.—*St Kitts and Nevis Quarterly.*
Gordon, J., *Nevis: Queen of the Caribees.* London, 1985
Moll, V. P., *St Kitts and Nevis* [Bibliography]. Oxford and Santa Barbara (CA), 1995

National library: Public Library, Basseterre.
National statistical office: Statistics Division, Ministry of Development, Basseterre.

ST LUCIA

Capital: Castries
Population estimate, 2000: 161,000
GNP per capita: (PPP$) 4,920
HDI/world rank: 0·839/58

KEY HISTORICAL EVENTS

An island state of the lesser Antilles in the eastern Caribbean, St Lucia is believed to have been settled by the Arawaks, Amerindians who were subsequently driven out by the warlike Caribs. The island was probably discovered by Columbus in 1502. An unsuccessful attempt to colonize by the British took place in 1605, and again in 1638 when settlers were soon murdered by the Caribs who inhabited the island. France claimed the right of sovereignty, and ceded it to the French West India Company in 1642. The French settlers fought constant battles with the Caribs until peace was established in 1660. St Lucia regularly and constantly changed hands between Britain and France, until it was finally ceded to Britain in 1814 by the Treaty of Paris.

Since 1924 the island has had representative government. It was a part of the federal government of the Windward Islands until, in Jan. 1960, along with the colonies in the group, it was given its own administrator. In March 1967 St Lucia gained full control of its internal affairs while Britain remained responsible for foreign affairs and defence; the Administrator became the Governor, and a House of Assembly replaced the Legislative Council. On 22 Feb. 1979 St Lucia achieved independence, opting to remain in the British Commonwealth.

TERRITORY AND POPULATION

St Lucia is an island of the Lesser Antilles in the Eastern Caribbean between Martinique and St Vincent, with an area of 238 sq. miles (617 sq. km). Population (census, 1991) 133,308. Estimate, 1997, 150,600 (37·2% urban in 1995); density, 244·1 per sq. km.

In 2000 the population is projected to be 161,000.

Area and estimated population of the 10 administrative districts in 1992 were:

Districts	Sq. km	Population estimate	Districts	Sq. km	Population estimate
Ane-la-Raye	} 47	{ 5,218	Gros Inlet	101	13,996
Canaries	}	{ 1,864	Laborie	38	7,763
Castries	79	53,883	Micoud	78	15,636
Choiseul	31	6,638	Soufrière	51	7,962
Dennery	70	11,574	Vieux Fort	44	13,617

The official language is English, but 80% of the population speak a French creole.

In 1990 over 90% of the population was Black, 6% were of mixed race and 3% of south Asian ethnic origin.

The capital is Castries (population, 1991, 2,063).

SOCIAL STATISTICS

1997 births, 3,500; deaths, 850. Rates, 1997 estimates (per 1,000 population): Births, 23·3; deaths, 5·7. Infant mortality (per 1,000 live births), 17·3. Expectation of life in 1997 was 71·3 years (67·7 for males and 75·2 for females). Growth rate, 1·14% per annum.

CLIMATE

The climate is tropical, with a dry season from Jan. to April. Most rain falls in Nov.–Dec.; annual amount varies from 60" (1,500 mm) to 138" (3,450 mm). Temperature is about 80°F (26·7°C).

CONSTITUTION AND GOVERNMENT

There is a 17-seat *House of Assembly* elected for 5 years and an 11-seat *Senate* appointed by the Governor-General.

ST LUCIA

National Anthem. 'Sons and daughters of St Lucia'; words by C. Jesse, tune by L. F. Thomas.

RECENT ELECTIONS
At the elections of 23 May 1997, the St Lucia Labour Party gained 16 seats and the United Workers' Party 1.

CURRENT ADMINISTRATION
Governor-General: Dr Perlette Louisy.
   In March 1999 the government comprised:
   Prime Minister and Minister of Finance, Planning and Development: Dr Kenny Anthony. *Deputy Prime Minister and Minister of Education, Human Resource Development, Youth and Sports:* Mario Michel.
   Minister of Agriculture, Fisheries and the Environment: Cassius Elias. *Commerce, Industry and Consumer Affairs:* Walter François. *Communications, Works, Transport and Public Utilities:* George Calixte. *Community Development, Culture, Local Government and Co-operatives:* Damian Greaves. *Foreign Affairs and International Trade:* George Odlum. *Health, Family Affairs, Human Services and Women:* Sarah Flood. *Legal Affairs, Home Affairs and Labour:* Velon John. *Tourism and Civil Aviation:* Phillip Pierre.

Local Government. There are 10 administrative districts.

INTERNATIONAL RELATIONS
St Lucia is a member of the UN, OAS, CARICOM, the Commonwealth and is an ACP member state of the ACP-EU relationship.

ECONOMY
Performance. Real GDP growth was 3·0% in 1995 (2·8% in 1994).

Budget. Revenues were an estimated US$155m. in the fiscal year 1996–97, and expenditures US$169m.

Currency. The East Caribbean *dollar* (XCD) (of 100 *cents*) is in use. US dollars are also normally accepted. Foreign exchange reserves were US$61m. in Feb. 1998.

Banking and Finance. There are 3 domestic and 4 foreign banks. Inflation in 1996 was 3%.

ENERGY AND NATURAL RESOURCES
Electricity. Installed capacity in 1995 was 34,000 kW. Production in 1994 was 112m. kWh. Consumption per capita in 1995 was estimated at 801 kWh.

Agriculture. In 1996 agriculture contributed 11% of GDP. Bananas, cocoa, breadfruit and mango are the principal crops, but changes in the world's trading rules and changes in taste are combining to depress the banana trade. Farmers are experimenting with okra, tomatoes and avocados to help make up for the loss.
   Livestock (1996): Cattle, 12,000; pigs, 15,000; sheep, 12,000; goats (1995), 12,000.

Forestry. In 1995 the area under forests was 5,000 ha (8·2% of the total land area).

Fisheries. In 1995 the total catch was 1,023 tonnes, almost entirely from sea fishing.

INDUSTRY
The main products are clothing, assembly of electronic components, beverages, corrugated cardboard boxes, tourism, lime processing and coconut processing.

Labour. In 1993 the economically active population totalled 81,000, around a quarter of whom were engaged in agriculture, fisheries and forestry.

INTERNATIONAL TRADE
Imports and Exports. Value of imports (1995), US$270·5m.; of exports, US$104·1m. Bananas accounted for 60% of exports. The main export markets in 1991 were the UK (56%), followed by the USA (22%) and CARICOM countries

(19%). In 1995 manufactured goods accounted for 21% of imports, as did machinery and transportation equipment. Main import suppliers, 1995: USA, 38·1%; Trinidad and Tobago, 12·4%; UK, 11·1%; Japan, 4·6%. Main export markets, 1995: UK, 53·1%; USA, 26·0%; Dominica, 5·4%; Trinidad and Tobago, 3·0%.

COMMUNICATIONS

Roads. The island had 1,210 km of roads in 1996, of which 150 km were main roads and a further 150 km secondary roads. Passenger cars numbered 14,550 in 1996.

Civil Aviation. There are international airports at Hewanorra (near Vieux-Fort) and Vigie (near Castries). In 1998 the island was served by Air Canada, Air Jamaica, Air Liberté, American Airlines, British Airways, BWIA, Condor Flugdienst, Delta Air Lines, Helenair Corporation and Virgin Atlantic. In 1996 Hewanorra handled 320,000 passengers (314,000 on international flights) and Vigie 294,000 (291,000 on international flights).

Shipping. There are 2 ports; Castries and Vieux Fort. Merchant shipping in 1995 totalled 1,000 GRT. In 1995 vessels totalling 2,077,000 net registered tons entered the ports.

Telecommunications. Main telephone lines numbered 37,000 in 1997 (247·2 per 1,000 persons). In 1994 there were 68 telex and 560 fax machines.

SOCIAL INSTITUTIONS

Justice. The island is divided into 2 judicial districts, and there are 9 magistrates' courts. Appeals lie to the Eastern Caribbean Supreme Court of Appeal.

Religion. In 1997 over 80% of the population was Roman Catholic.

Education. Primary education is free and compulsory. In 1993 there were 88 primary schools with 1,204 teachers for 32,545 pupils, and 14 secondary schools with 10,356 pupils and 558 teachers. There is a community college. Adult literacy rate is 82%.

Health. In 1992 there were 64 doctors, 6 dentists and 256 nursing personnel employed by the government, 4 hospitals with 435 beds and 34 health centres.

CULTURE

Broadcasting. In 1993 there were 2 private radio stations, 2 privately-owned local TV stations and a cable TV service. There were 30,000 TV and 108,000 radio receivers in 1995.

Press. In 1993 there were 3 newspapers with a nationwide circulation.

Tourism. The total number of visitors during 1994 was 394,000 (219,000 stop-over visitors and 175,000 cruise-ship passenger arrivals). Receipts totalled US$224m.

DIPLOMATIC REPRESENTATIVES
Of St Lucia in Great Britain (10 Kensington Ct., London, W8 5DL)
High Commissioner: Emmanuel H. Cotter.

Of Great Britain in St Lucia (NIS Waterfront Building, 2nd Floor, Castries)
High Commissioner: G. M. Baker (resides in Barbados).

Of St Lucia in the USA (3216 New Mexico Ave., NW, Washington, D.C., 20016)
Ambassador: Sonia Merlyn Johnny.

Of the USA in St Lucia
Ambassador: Jeanette Hyde (resides in Barbados).

Of St Lucia to the United Nations
Ambassador: Julian Robert Hunte.

Of St Lucia to the European Union
Ambassador: Edwin Laurent.

FURTHER READING
Mommsen, J. H., *St Lucia* [Bibliography]. Oxford and Santa Barbara (CA), 1996

ST VINCENT AND THE GRENADINES

Capital: Kingstown
Population estimate, 2000: 118,000
GNP per capita: (PPP$) 4,160
HDI/world rank: 0·845/55

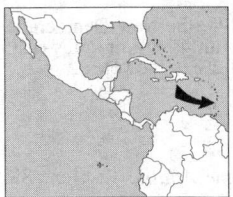

KEY HISTORICAL EVENTS
These islands in the eastern Caribbean were originally inhabited by the Carib tribes. St Vincent was discovered by Columbus on 22 Jan. (St Vincent's Day) 1498. British and French settlers occupied parts of the islands after 1627.

In 1773 the Caribs recognized British sovereignty and agreed to a division of territory between themselves and the British. Resentful of British rule, the Caribs rebelled in 1795, aided by the French, but the revolt was subdued within a year. Most of the Carib population was deported to islands in the Gulf of Honduras and the surviving population was further reduced by eruptions of the volcano Santiere in 1812 and 1902.

The islands were part of the federal government of the Windward Islands until, in Jan. 1960, along with other colonies in the group, they were given their own Administrator. Universal adult suffrage had been in existence on the islands since 1951. On 27 Oct. 1969 St Vincent became an Associated State with the UK responsible only for foreign policy and defence, while the islands were given full internal self-government. The Administrator became the Governor-General, and a House of Assembly replaced the Legislative Council. On 27 Oct. 1979 the colony acquired full independence as St Vincent and the Grenadines.

TERRITORY AND POPULATION
St Vincent is an island of the Lesser Antilles, situated in the Eastern Caribbean between St Lucia and Grenada, from which latter it is separated by a chain of small islands known as the Grenadines. The total area of 389 sq. km (150 sq. miles) comprises the island of St Vincent itself (345 sq. km) and those of the Grenadines attached to it, of which the largest are Bequia, Mustique, Canouan, Mayreau and Union.

The population at the 1991 Census was 106,499, of whom 8,367 lived in the St Vincent Grenadines. 1996 estimate, 115,000 (24·6% urban in 1994); density 296 per sq. km.

In 2000 the population is projected to be 118,000.

An estimated 51·9% of the population were rural in 1995. The capital, Kingstown, had 26,223 inhabitants in 1991 (including suburbs). The population is mainly of black (82%) and mixed (13·9%) origin, with small white, Asian and American minorities.

English and French patois are spoken.

SOCIAL STATISTICS
Births, 1996, 2,300; deaths, 600. 1996 birth rate, 19·4 per 1,000 population; death rate, 5·4; infant mortality, 16·8 per 1,000 live births; life expectancy, 73 years. Annual growth rate, 1990–95, 0·7%.

CLIMATE
The climate is tropical marine, with north-east Trades predominating and rainfall ranging from 150" (3,750 mm) a year in the mountains to 60" (1,500 mm) on the south-east coast. The rainy season is from June to Dec., and temperatures are equable throughout the year.

CONSTITUTION AND GOVERNMENT
The head of state is Queen Elizabeth II, represented by a *Governor*. Parliament is unicameral and consists of a 21-member *House of Assembly,* 15 of which are directly elected for a 5-year term from single-member constituencies. The remaining

6 are senators appointed by the Governor (4 on the advice of the Prime Minister and 2 on the advice of the Leader of the Opposition).

National Anthem. 'St Vincent, land so beautiful'; words by Phyllis Punnett, tune by J. B. Miguel.

RECENT ELECTIONS
At the elections to the House of Assembly on 15 June 1998, the New Democratic Party (NDP, conservative) won 8 of the 15 elected seats, with 45·8% of votes cast; the Unity Labour Party (ULP, social-democratic) won 7 (54·2% of the votes).

CURRENT ADMINISTRATION
Governor-General: Charles Antrobus (1996).
    In March 1999 the government comprised:
    Prime Minister, Minister of National Security and Home Affairs: Rt Hon. Sir James F. Mitchell, KCMG.
    Minister of Agriculture and Labour: Jeremiah C. Scott. *Communications and Works:* Glenford Stewart. *Education, Ecclesiastical Affairs, Culture and Women:* Alpian Allen. *Finance and Public Service:* Arnhim Eustace. *Foreign Affairs, Tourism, and Information:* Allan Cruickshank. *Health and Environment:* Dr St. Clair Thomas. *Housing, Local Government, Youth and Sports, and Community Development:* Monty Roberts. *Justice:* Carl Joseph. *Trade, Industry and Commerce:* John Horne.

INTERNATIONAL RELATIONS
St Vincent and the Grenadines is a member of UN, OAS, CARICOM, the Commonwealth and is an ACP member state of the ACP-EU relationship.

ECONOMY
Performance. Real GDP growth was 4·4% in 1995 (0·4% in 1994).

Budget. Central government consolidated revenue and expenditure in US$1m. for calendar years:

	1993	1994	1995	1996	1997[1]
Revenue	185·1	195·6	204·1	220·1	230·6
Expenditure	208·3	204·4	207·8	236·9	316·7

[1]Provisional.

    Expenditure by function in 1996 (and 1997) in US$1m.: Education, 387 (434); health, 317 (333); social security and welfare, 196 (139); public order and safety, 187 (198); housing and community amenities, 5 (5).

Currency. The currency in use is the *East Caribbean dollar* (XCD). Foreign exchange reserves were US$29m. in Feb. 1998.

Banking and Finance. The East Caribbean Central Bank is the bank of issue. There are branches of Barclays Bank PLC, the Caribbean Banking Corporation, the Canadian Imperial Bank of Commerce, the Bank of Nova Scotia. Locally-owned banks: First St Vincent Bank, the National Commercial Bank and St Vincent Co-operative Bank.

ENERGY AND NATURAL RESOURCES
Electricity. Installed capacity was 20,000 kW in 1993. Production in 1995 was 73m. kWh. Consumption per capita in 1994 was estimated to be 577 kWh.

Agriculture. Agriculture accounts for approximately 13% of GDP. According to the 1985–86 census of agriculture, 29,649 acres of the total acreage of 85,120 were classified as agricultural lands; 5,500 acres were under forest and woodland and all other lands accounted for 1,030 acres. The total arable land was about 8,932 acres, of which 4,016 acres were under temporary crops, 2,256 acres under temporary pasture, 2,289 acres under temporary fallow and other arable land covering 371 acres. 16,062 acres were under permanent crops, of which approximately 5,500 acres were under coconuts and 7,224 acres under bananas; the remainder produce cocoa, citrus, mangoes, avocado pears, guavas and miscellaneous crops. In 1994 there were an estimated 9,900 acres of arable land, 17,300 acres of permanent cropland and 5,000 acres of pasture. The sugar industry was closed down in 1985 although some sugar-cane is grown for rum production. Production (1995, in 1,000 tonnes): Bananas, 55; sugar-cane, 44; coconuts, 23. Production (1990, in tonnes): Nutmeg and mace, 111; arrowroot starch, 56; ginger, 834; taro, 5,240.

Livestock (1995, in 1,000): Cattle, 6; pigs, 9; sheep, 13; goats, 6.

Forestry. Forests covered 11,000 ha in 1995, or 28·2% of the land area.

Fisheries. Total catch, 1995, 1,480 tonnes.

INDUSTRY
Industries include assembly of electronic equipment, manufacture of garments, electrical products, animal feeds and flour, corrugated galvanized sheets, exhaust systems, industrial gases, concrete blocks, plastics, soft drinks, beer and rum, wood products and furniture, and processing of milk, fruit juices and food items. Rum production, 1994, 0·4m. litres.

Labour. The Department of Labour is charged with looking after the interest and welfare of all categories of workers, including providing advice and guidance to employers and employees and their organizations and enforcing the labour laws. In 1991 the total labour force was 41,682, of whom 33,355 (11,699 females) were employed.

INTERNATIONAL TRADE
Foreign debt was US$213m. in 1996.

Imports and Exports. In 1996 imports totalled EC$323·6m.; exports, EC$125·2m.

Principal exports, 1995 (in US$1m., preliminary): Dasheen, 15; bananas, 219; manufactured goods, 232 (flour, 87; rice, 64). Principal imports: Manufactured goods, 448; food, 24; machinery and transport equipment, 21; chemicals, 165.

Main export markets, 1995 (in US$1m., preliminary): UK, 9; St Lucia, 71; USA, 54; Trinidad and Tobago, 5. Main import suppliers: USA, 436; Trinidad and Tobago, 203; UK, 154.

COMMUNICATIONS

Roads. In 1996 there were 1,040 km of roads, of which 320 km were paved. Vehicles in use (1995): 5,300 passenger cars; 3,700 commercial vehicles.

Civil Aviation. There is an airport (E. T. Joshua) on mainland St Vincent at Arnos Vale. Scheduled services were operated in 1998 by Air Mustique, American Airlines, Helenair Corporation, LIAT, Société Nouvelle Air Guadeloupe. An airport on Union also has regular scheduled services. In 1995 E. T. Joshua handled 185,000 passengers and 1,200 tonnes of freight.

Shipping. In 1994 there were some 200 ships in the Vincentian open register. Merchant shipping in 1995 totalled 6,165,000 GRT. In 1995 vessels totalling 932,000 net registered tons entered.

Telecommunications. There is a fully digital automatic telephone system with 20,500 main telephone lines in 1997, equivalent to 179·3 for every 1,000 inhabitants; 17,500 stations and digital radio provide links to Bequia, Mustique, Union, Petit St Vincent and Palm Island. The telephone network has almost 100% geographical coverage.

Postal Services. There is a General Post Office at Kingstown and 56 district post offices.

SOCIAL INSTITUTIONS

Justice. Law is based on UK common law as exercised by the Eastern Caribbean Supreme Court on St Lucia. Final appeal lies to the UK Privy Council. In 1995 there were 4,700 criminal matters disposed of in the 3 magisterial districts which comprise 11 courts. 62 cases were dealt with in the Criminal Assizes in the High Court. Strength of police force (1995), 663 (including 19 gazetted officers).

ST VINCENT AND THE GRENADINES

Religion. In 1997 there were estimated to be 47,000 Anglicans, 23,000 Methodists, 13,000 Roman Catholics and 29,000 followers of other religions.

Education. In 1994 there were 97 pre-primary schools with 175 teachers for 2,500 pupils and 65 primary schools with 1,080 teachers for 21,386 pupils. In 1991 there were 10,719 secondary pupils with 431 teachers and, in 1989, 677 students at university level. Adult literacy (1994) 82%.

Health. In 1992 there was a general hospital in Kingstown with 207 beds, 6 rural hospitals, 2 private hospitals and 38 clinics. There were 40 doctors, 6 dentists, 224 registered nurses, 144 nursing assistants and 39 community health aides.

CULTURE

Broadcasting. The National Broadcasting Corporation is part government-owned and part commercial. In 1995 there were 75,000 radio and 18,000 TV sets (colour by NTSC).

Tourism. There were 218,014 visitors (85,258 cruise-ship passengers) in 1995. Receipts totalled US$57m.

Libraries. There is a St Vincent Public Library at Kingstown. The librarian is Mrs Pearl Herbert.

DIPLOMATIC REPRESENTATIVES
Of St Vincent and the Grenadines in Great Britain (10 Kensington Ct, London, W8 5DL)
High Commissioner: Carlyle Dennis Dougan.

Of Great Britain in St Vincent and the Grenadines (POB 132, Granby St., Kingstown)
High Commissioner: G. M. Baker (resides in Barbados).

Of St Vincent and the Grenadines in the USA (3216 New Mexico Ave., NW, Washington, D.C., 20016)
Ambassador: Kingsley C. A. Layne.

Of the USA in St Vincent and the Grenadines
Ambassador: Jeanette Hyde (resides in Barbados).

Of St Vincent and the Grenadines to the United Nations
Ambassador: Herbert G. V. Young.

Of St Vincent and the Grenadines to the European Union
Ambassador: Edwin Laurent.

FURTHER READING
Jenkins, D. and Bobrow, J., *St Vincent and the Grenadines: a Plural Country.* St Vincent, 1985
Potter, R. B., *St Vincent and the Grenadines* [Bibliography]. Oxford and Santa Barbara (CA), 1992
Price, N., *Behind the Planter's Back.* London, 1988
Sutty, L., *St Vincent and the Grenadines.* London, 1993

SAMOA

O le Malo Tutoatasi o Samoa—

Independent State of Samoa

Capital: Apia
Population estimate, 2000: 174,000
Estimated GDP: $415m.
HDI/world rank: 0·694/94

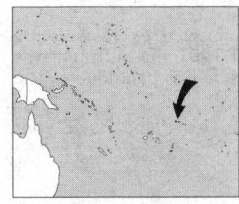

KEY HISTORICAL EVENTS

Polynesians settled in the Samoan group of islands in the southern Pacific from about 1000 BC. Shortly before the European arrival, stratified society with paramount chiefs and fortified settlements developed. Although probably sighted by the Dutch in 1722, the first European visitor was French in 1768. Treaties were signed between the Chiefs and European nations in 1838–39. Continuing strife among the chiefs was compounded by British, German and US rivalry for influence. In the Treaty of Berlin 1889 the three powers agreed to Western Samoa's independence and neutrality. When strife continued, the treaty was annulled and the Samoan group was annexed.

Western Samoa became a German protectorate until in 1914 it was occupied by a New Zealand expeditionary force. The island was administered by New Zealand from 1920 to 1961, at first under a League of Nations Mandate and from 1946 under a United Nations Trusteeship Agreement. In May 1961 a plebiscite held under the supervision of the UN on the basis of universal adult suffrage voted overwhelmingly in favour of independence. In Oct. 1961 the General Assembly of the United Nations passed a resolution to terminate the trusteeship agreement as from 1 Jan. 1962, on which date Western Samoa became an independent sovereign state. In July 1997 the country renamed itself the Independent State of Samoa.

TERRITORY AND POPULATION

Samoa lies between 13° and 15° S. lat. and 171° and 173° W. long. It comprises the two large islands of Savai'i and Upolu, the small islands of Manono and Apolima, and several uninhabited islets lying off the coast. The total land area is 1,093 sq. miles (2,830·8 sq. km), of which 659·4 sq. miles (1,707·8 sq. km) are in Savai'i, and 431·5 sq. miles (1,117·6 sq. km) in Upolu; other islands, 2·1 sq. miles (5·4 sq. km). The islands are of volcanic origin, and the coasts are surrounded by coral reefs. Rugged mountain ranges form the core of both main islands. The large area laid waste by lava-flows in Savai'i is a primary cause of that island supporting less than one-third of the population of the islands despite its greater size than Upolu.

Population at the 1991 census, 161,298.

The UN gives a projected population for 2000 of 174,000.

In 1995, 79% of the population lived in rural areas. The population at the 1986 census was 112,228 in Upolu (including Manono and Apolima) and 44,930 in Savai'i. The capital and chief port is Apia in Upolu (population 32,196 in 1986).

The official languages are Samoan and English.

SOCIAL STATISTICS

Births, 1995, 4,400; deaths, 1,000. 1995 birth rate per 1,000 population, 25·8; death rate, 6·1. Expectation of life was 69·1 years in 1997. Annual growth rate, 1990–95, was 0·9%. Infant mortality, 1990–95, 64 per 1,000 live births; fertility rate, 4·2 births per woman.

CLIMATE

A tropical marine climate, with cooler conditions from May to Nov. and a rainy season from Dec. to April. The rainfall is unevenly distributed, with south and east coasts having the greater quantities. Average annual rainfall is about 100" (2,500 mm) in the drier areas. Apia, Jan. 80°F (26·7°C), July 78°F (25·6°C). Annual rainfall 112" (2,800 mm).

CONSTITUTION AND GOVERNMENT

HH Malietoa Tanumafili II is the sole Head of State for life. Future Heads of State will be elected by the Legislative Assembly and hold office for 5-year terms.

The executive power is vested in the *Head of State*, who swears in the *Prime Minister* (who is elected by the Legislative Assembly) and, on the Prime Minister's advice, the Ministers to form the Cabinet. The Constitution also provides for a *Council of Deputies* of 3 members, of whom the chairman is the Deputy Head of State.

Before 1991 the 49-member *Legislative Assembly* was elected exclusively by *matai* (customary family heads). At the elections of April 1991 the suffrage was universal, but only the approximately 20,000 *matai* could stand as candidates. The electorate was 56,000.

National Anthem. 'Samoa, tula'i ma sisi ia laufu'a/Samoa, Arise and Raise your Banner'; words and tune by S. I. Kuresa.

RECENT ELECTIONS

At the most recent elections, on 26 April 1996, the Human Rights Protection Party won 24 seats; the Samoan National Development Party, 11; Non-partisans, 13; and others, 1.

CURRENT ADMINISTRATION

Head of State: HH Malietoa Tanumafili II, GCMG, CBE.

The cabinet in March 1999 was composed as follows:

Prime Minister, Minister of Finance, Minister of Foreign Affairs, Minister of Commerce, Trade and Industry, Minister of Treasury, Inland Revenue and Customs: Tuilaepa Sailele Malielegaoi. *Agriculture, Forestry, Fisheries and Meteorological Services:* Molioo Teofilo. *Education:* Fiame Naomi Mataafa. *Health:* Misa Telefoni Retzlaff. *Immigration, Internal Affairs, Police and Prisons, and Public Service:* Tofilau Eti Alesana. *Public Works:* Luagalau Levaula Kamu. *Lands, Survey and Environment:* Tuala Sale Tagaloa Kerslake. *Justice:* Solia Papu Vaai. *Women's Affairs:* Leniu Tofaeono Avamagalo. *Labour:* Polataivao Fosi. *Transportation and Civil Aviation:* Hans Joachim Keil.

INTERNATIONAL RELATIONS

Samoa, as an independent state, deals directly with other governments and international organizations. It has diplomatic relations with a number of countries.

Samoa is a member of the UN, the Commonwealth, the South Pacific Forum and is an ACP member state of the ACP-EU relationship.

ECONOMY

Performance. Real GDP growth was 12·6% in 1995 (−5·5% in 1994).

Budget. For 1996–97 revenue was WS$288·4m.; expenditure, WS$312·7m. For 1997–98 budgeted revenue was WS$292·6m. and expenditure WS$306·6m.

Currency. The unit of currency is the *tala* (WST) of 100 *sene*. The average annual inflation rate during the years 1990–96 was 2·2%.

Banking and Finance. The Central Bank of Samoa (founded 1984) is the bank of issue.

ENERGY AND NATURAL RESOURCES

Electricity. Installed capacity in 1990 was 29,000 kW. Production was 69m. kWh. in 1995; consumption per capita in 1995 was estimated at 287 kWh.

Agriculture. In 1994 there were 55,000 ha of arable land, 67,000 ha of permanent cropland and approximately 1,000 ha of pasture. The main products (1993, in 1,000 tonnes) are coconuts (130), taro (37), copra (11), bananas (10), papayas (10), mangoes (5), pineapples (6) and cocoa beans (1, in 1991).

Livestock (1996): Cattle, 26,000; pigs, 179,000; asses, 7,000.

Forestry. Forests covered 136,000 ha (48·1% of the land area) in 1995, compared to 144,000 ha and 50·9% in 1990. Timber production was 131,000 cu. metres in 1995.

SAMOA

Fisheries. Total catches in 1995 were estimated to be 1,400 tonnes.

INDUSTRY
Some industrial activity is being developed associated with agricultural products and forestry.

Labour. In 1991 the total labour force numbered 57,142 (39,839 males).

INTERNATIONAL TRADE
Imports and Exports. In 1997 exports were valued at US$15m and imports at US$97m. Principal exports are coconuts, palm oil, taro and taamu, coffee and beer. Main imports are machinery and transport equipment, foodstuffs and basic manufactures. New Zealand is the principal trading partner.

COMMUNICATIONS
Roads. In 1996 the road network covered 790 km, of which 240 km were highways and main roads. In 1993 there were 1,269 private cars, 1,936 pick-up trucks, 472 trucks, 334 buses, 936 taxis and 67 motor cycles.

Civil Aviation. There is an international airport at Apia (Faleolo). The national carrier is Polynesian Airlines. In 1998 it operated domestic services and international flights to American Samoa, Auckland, the Fiji Islands, Honolulu, Los Angeles, Melbourne, Sydney, Tonga and Wellington. Services were also provided by Air New Zealand, Air Pacific and Royal Tongan Airlines. Samoa Aviation provides international services between Samoa and American Samoa (a US Trust Territory).

Shipping. Sea-going shipping totalled 6,501 GRT in 1995. Samoa is linked to Japan, USA, Europe, the Fiji Islands, Australia and New Zealand by regular shipping services.

Telecommunications. There are 3 radio communication stations at Apia. Radio telephone service connects Samoa with American Samoa, the Fiji Islands, New Zealand, Australia, Canada, USA and UK. Main telephone lines numbered 8,500 in 1997 (50·6 per 1,000 population). In 1995 there were 400 fax machines.

Postal Services. In 1995 there were 38 post offices.

SOCIAL INSTITUTIONS
Religion. At the 1991 census, 43% of the population were Congregationalist, 21% Roman Catholic, 17% Methodist, 10% Latter-day Saints (Mormons) and 3% Seventh Day Adventist.

Education. In 1995 there were 35,811 pupils at 155 primary schools with 1,475 teachers, and 13,241 pupils and 715 teachers at secondary schools. The University of the South Pacific has a School of Agriculture in Samoa, at Apia. A National University was established in 1984. In 1994–95 it had 614 students and 30 academic staff. There is also a Polytechnic Institute which provides mainly vocational and training courses.

The adult literacy rate is 98·0%.

Health. In 1994 there were 2 national hospitals, 14 district hospitals, 9 health centres and 22 subcentres. There were 44 doctors in 1990.

CULTURE
Broadcasting. Broadcasting is the responsibility of the government-run commercial Western Samoa Broadcasting Department, which transmits radio programmes in Samoan and English. In 1995 there were 80,000 radio receivers and about 7,000 television sets.

Cinema. In 1995 there were 3 cinemas.

Press. There are 4 weeklies (circulation 12,000) and 2 monthlies (8,000); all are in Samoan and English.

Tourism. In 1996 there were 73,000 foreign tourists, bringing revenue of US$39m.

DIPLOMATIC REPRESENTATIVES

Of Samoa in Great Britain and to the European Union
High Commissioner: Tauiliili Uili Meredith (resides in Brussels).

Of Great Britain in Samoa
High Commissioner: J. M. Williams, CVO, OBE (resides in Wellington).

Of the USA in Samoa
Ambassador: Josiah H. Beeman (resides in Wellington).

Of Samoa in the USA and to the United Nations (1115 15th St., NW, Washington, D.C., 20005)
Ambassador: Tauiliili Uili Meredith.

FURTHER READING

Hughes, H. G. A. *American Samoa, Western Samoa, Samoans Abroad* [Bibliography]. Oxford and Santa Barbara (CA), 1997

SAN MARINO

Repubblica di San Marino

Capital: San Marino
Population estimate, 2000: 26,800
Estimated GDP: $408m.

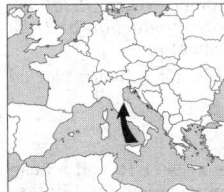

KEY HISTORICAL EVENTS
San Marino is a small republic situated on the Adriatic side of central Italy. According to tradition, St Marinus and a group of Christians settled there to escape persecution. By the 12th century San Marino had developed into a commune ruled by its own statutes and consul. Unsuccessful attempts were made to annex the republic to the papal states in the 18th century and when Napoleon invaded Italy in 1797 he respected the rights of the republic and even offered to extend its territories.

In 1815 the Congress of Vienna recognized the independence of the republic. On 22 March 1862 San Marino concluded a treaty of friendship and co-operation, including a *de facto* customs union, with the Kingdom of Italy, thus preserving its ancient independence although completely surrounded by Italian territory. This treaty was renewed in 1872, 1879, 1939 and, with several amendments, between 1942 and 1987.

TERRITORY AND POPULATION
San Marino is a land-locked state in central Italy, 20 km from the Adriatic. Area is 61·19 sq. km (23·6 sq. miles) and the population (1998), 26,207; at Dec. 1997 some 13,360 citizens lived abroad.

The projected population for 2000 is 26,800.

In 1997 an estimated 90% of the population were urban. Population density, 422·8 per sq. km. The capital, San Marino, has 4,407 inhabitants (1997); the largest town is Serravalle (8,051 in 1997), an industrial centre in the north.

SOCIAL STATISTICS
Annual growth rate, 1994–98, 1·2%.

CLIMATE
Temperate climate with cold, dry winters and warm summers.

CONSTITUTION AND GOVERNMENT
The legislative power is vested in the *Great and General Council* of 60 members elected every 5 years by popular vote, 2 of whom are appointed every 6 months to act as *Captains Regent*, who are the heads of state.

Executive power is exercised by the 10-member *Congress of State*, presided over by the Captains Regent. The *Council of Twelve*, also presided over by the Captains Regent, is appointed by the Great and General Council to perform administrative functions and is a court of third instance.

National Anthem. No words, tune monastic, transcribed by F. Consolo.

RECENT ELECTIONS
At the elections of 31 May 1998 the Christian Democrats gained 40·85% of votes cast and the Socialist Party 23·23%, forming a coalition government with 39 seats in the Great and General Council. The Progressive Democrats (former Communists) gained 18·64% of votes cast and 11 seats, the Popular Democratic Alliance gained 9·81% of votes cast and 6 seats, the Refounded Communists gained 3·27% of votes cast and 2 seats, and the Socialists for Reforms gained 4·19% of votes cast and 2 seats.

CURRENT ADMINISTRATION
In March 1999 the Congress of State comprised:

Minister of Foreign and Political Affairs: Gabriele Gatti. *Finance, Budget, Planning and Relations with the Autonomous Philatelic and Numismatic State*

Company: Clelio Galassi. *Home Affairs and Civil Defence:* Antonio Lazzaro Volpinari. *Industry, Handicraft, Economic Co-operation, Post and Telecommunications:* Fiorenzo Stolfi. *Territory, Environment and Agriculture:* Augusto Casali. *Tourism, Commerce and Sport:* Claudio Podeschi. *Health and Social Security:* Luciano Ciavatta. *Education, Social Affairs, Cultural Institutions and Justice:* Sante Canducci. *Labour and Co-operation:* Romeo Morri. *Relations with Township Councils, the Autonomous State Company for Production and the Autonomous State Company for Services:* Cesare Antonio Gasperoni.

Local Government. There are 9 districts (*castelli*), each run by a board elected every 5 years.

DEFENCE
Military service is not obligatory, but all citizens between the ages of 16 and 55 can be called upon to defend the State. They may also serve as volunteers in the Military Corps. There is a military Gendarmerie.

INTERNATIONAL RELATIONS
San Marino maintains a traditional neutrality, and remained so in the First and Second World Wars. It has diplomatic and consular relations with over 70 countries.

San Marino is a member of the UN, the Council of Europe, the OSCE and various UN specialized agencies.

ECONOMY
Performance. Real GDP growth was 5·0% in 1996.

Budget. The budget (ordinary and extraordinary) for the financial year ending 31 Dec. 1998 balanced at 856,525,618,310bn. lire.

Currency. Italian currency is in use, but the republic issues its own coins.

ENERGY AND NATURAL RESOURCES
Agriculture. 3,940 ha of land area are arable. Wheat, barley, maize and vines are grown.

INDUSTRY
Labour. Out of 17,900 people in employment in 1998, 5,787 worked in manufacturing and 3,342 in wholesale and retail trade. In Sept. 1998 there were 540 registered unemployed persons.

Trade Unions. There are 2 Confederations of Trade Unions: the Democratic Confederation of Sammarinese Workers and the Sammarinese Confederation of Labour.

INTERNATIONAL TRADE
Imports and Exports. Export commodities are building stone, lime, wine, baked goods, textiles, varnishes and ceramics. Import commodities are a wide range of consumer manufactures and foodstuffs. San Marino maintains a customs union with Italy.

COMMUNICATIONS
Roads. A bus service connects San Marino with Rimini. There are 252 km of public roads and 40 km of private roads, and (1998) 25,571 passenger cars and 2,636 commercial vehicles.

Civil Aviation. The nearest airport is Rimini, 10 km to the east, which had flights in 1998 to Baku, London, Moscow and Rome.

Telecommunications. San Marino had 18,050 telephones in 1998.

Postal Services. In 1998 there were 10 post offices.

SOCIAL INSTITUTIONS

Justice. Judges are appointed permanently by the Great and General Council; they may not be San Marino citizens. Petty civil cases are dealt with by a justice of the peace; legal commissioners deal with more serious civil cases and all criminal cases and appeals lie to them from the justice of the peace. Appeals against the legal commissioners lie to an appeals judge, and the Council of the Twelve functions as a court of third instance.

Religion. The great majority of the population are Roman Catholic.

Education. Education is compulsory up to 16 years of age. In 1998 there were 15 nursery schools with 934 pupils and 120 teachers, 14 elementary schools with 1,227 pupils and 196 teachers, 3 junior high schools with 703 pupils and 102 teachers, and 1 high school with 380 pupils and 49 teachers. The University of San Marino began operating in 1988.

Health. In 1998 there were 152 hospital beds and 84 doctors.

CULTURE

Broadcasting. There were 15,000 radio receivers and 9,055 television receivers in 1998. San Marino RTV is the state broadcasting company.

Cinema. In 1998 there were 4 cinemas with a seating capacity of 1,800.

Press. San Marino had 3 daily newspapers in 1998.

Tourism. In 1998, 3·5m. tourists visited San Marino.

DIPLOMATIC REPRESENTATIVES
British Consul-General (resides at Florence)
R. J. Griffiths, OBE.

Of San Marino to the United Nations
Ambassador: Gian Nicola Filippi Balestra.

Of San Marino to the European Union
Ambassador: Savina Zafferani.

FURTHER READING
Edwards, A. and Michaelides, C., *San Marino* [Bibliography]. Oxford and Santa Barbara (CA), 1996
Matteini, N., *The Republic of San Marino*. San Marino, 1981

Information: Office of Cultural Affairs and Information of the Department of Foreign Affairs.

SÃO TOMÉ E PRÍNCIPE

República Democrática de São Tomé
e Príncipe

Capital: São Tomé
Population estimate, 2000: 149,000
Estimated GDP: $149m.
HDI/world rank: 0·563/121

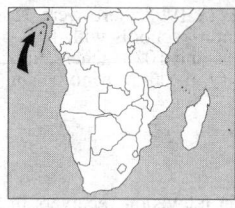

KEY HISTORICAL EVENTS

The islands of São Tomé and Príncipe off the west coast of Africa were colonized by Portugal for 5 centuries after being first visited by Portuguese navigators on 21 Dec. 1470. There may have been a few African inhabitants or visitors earlier but most of the population arrived during the centuries when the islands served as an important slave-trading depot for South America and some slaves were kept on the islands to work on the sugar plantations. In the 19th century the islands became the first parts of Africa to grow cocoa. Although in 1876 Portugal abolished slavery in name, in practice it continued thereafter with many Angolans, Mozambicans and Cape Verdians being transported to work on the cocoa plantations. Because the slave-descended population was cut off from African culture, São Tomé had a higher proportion than other Portuguese colonies of *assimilados* (Africans acquiring full Portuguese culture and certain rights).

After becoming an Overseas Province of Portugal in 1951, São Tomé saw serious riots against Portuguese rule in 1953. From 1960 a Committee for the Liberation of São Tomé e Príncipe operated from neighbouring African territories. There was, however, no armed resistance on the islands, where in 1970 Portugal introduced some reforms and formed a 16-member legislative council and a provincial consultative council. Following the Portuguese revolution of 1974, the Movement for the Liberation of São Tomé e Príncipe, headed by Manoel Pinto da Costa, held talks with Portugal. A transitional government was formed later that year and, after a period of tension due to landowners' resistance to decolonization and the temporary retention of Portuguese troops, independence came on 12 July 1975. Pinto da Costa became the first president and was re-elected for a further 5 years in 1985.

Independent São Tomé e Príncipe officially proclaimed Marxist-Leninist policies, but maintained a non-aligned foreign policy and has received aid from Portugal.

TERRITORY AND POPULATION

The republic, which lies about 200 km off the west coast of Gabon, in the Gulf of Guinea, comprises the main islands of São Tomé (845 sq. km) and Príncipe and several smaller islets including Pedras Tinhosas and Rolas. It has a total area of 1,001 sq. km (387 sq. miles). Population (census, 1991) 120,146. Estimate (1997), 147,900; density, 148 per sq. km.

In 2000 the population is projected to be 149,000.

An estimated 57·1% of the population were rural in 1995.

The areas and populations of the 2 provinces:

Province	Sq. km	Census 1991	Estimate 1995	Chief town	Census 1991
São Tomé	859	114,507	125,200	São Tomé	43,420
Príncipe	142	5,639	5,900	São António	1,000

The official language is Portuguese. Lungwa São Tomé, a Portuguese creole, and Fang, a Bantu language, are the spoken languages.

SOCIAL STATISTICS

1997 births, estimate, 5,000; deaths, 1,200. Rates (1997 estimate): Birth rate per 1,000 population, 33·8; death rate, 8·4; infant mortality (per 1,000 live births), 60·2. Expectation of life, 64·1 years. Annual growth rate, 1990–95, 2·0%.

CLIMATE

The tropical climate is modified by altitude and the effect of the cool Benguela current. The wet season is generally from Oct. to May, but rainfall varies considerably, from 40" (1,000 mm) in the hot and humid north-east to 150–200" (3,800–5,000 mm) on the plateau. São Tomé, Jan. 79°F (26·1°C), July 75°F (23·9°C). Annual rainfall 38" (951 mm).

CONSTITUTION AND GOVERNMENT

The 1990 constitution was approved by 72% of votes at a referendum of Aug. 1990. It abolished the monopoly of the Movement for the Liberation of São Tomé e Príncipe (MLSTP). The *President* must be over 34 years old, and is elected by universal suffrage for one or two (only) 5-year terms. He or she is also head of government and appoints a Council of Ministers. The 55-member *National Assembly* is elected for 4 years.

Since April 1995 **Príncipe** has enjoyed internal self-government, with a 5-member regional government and an elected assembly.

National Anthem. 'Independência total, glorioso canto do povo' ('Total independence, glorious song of the people'); words by A. N. do Espírito Santo, tune by M. de Sousa e Almeida.

RECENT ELECTIONS

At the presidential elections on 21 July 1996, President Trovoada was re-elected by 52·2% of votes cast against 1 opponent.

At the National Assembly elections on 8 Nov. 1998 the Liberation Movement of São Tomé e Príncipe (MLSTP) won 31 seats, Independent Democratic Action (IDA) 16 and the Democratic Convergence Party (DCP) 8.

CURRENT ADMINISTRATION

President, C.-in-C.: Miguel Trovoada, b. 1946 (IDA; re-elected 21 July 1996).

The government comprised in March 1999:

Prime Minister: Guilherme Posser da Costa. *Deputy Secretary of State to the Prime Minister:* Emilio Guadalupe Fernandes Lima.

Minister of Agriculture and Fisheries: Hermenilgido de Assunção Sousa Santos. *Commerce, Industry and Tourism:* Cosme Afonso da Trindade Rita. *Defence and Internal Order:* Col. João Quaresma Viegas Bexigas. *Economics:* Maria das Neves Ceita Batista de Sousa. *Education and Culture:* Peregrino do Sacramento da Costa. *Equipment and Environment:* Arlindo Afonso Carvalho. *Foreign Affairs and São Toméan Communities Overseas:* Alberto Paulino. *Health:* Antonio Soares Marqués de Lima. *Infrastructure and Natural Resources:* Luis Alberto Carneiro dos Prazeres. *Internal and Territorial Administration:* Manuel da Cruz Margal Lima. *Justice and Parliamentary Affairs:* Paulo Jorge Rodrigues do Espirito Santo. *Planning, Finance and Co-operation:* Adelino Castelo David.

Local Government. São Tomé province comprises 6 districts. Districts have assemblies elected universally for 3-year terms. In elections in Dec. 1992 the MLSTP won 38 of the 59 district assembly seats with 70% of votes cast, the DCP won 15 seats, IDA 6.

INTERNATIONAL RELATIONS

São Tomé e Príncipe is a member of the UN, OAU and is an ACP member state of the ACP-EU relationship.

ECONOMY

Policy. Most branches of the economy were nationalized after independence, but economic liberalization began in 1985 and was increased in 1991.

Performance. Real GDP growth was 2·6% in 1995 (2·4% in 1994).

Budget. The 1995 budget set revenue at 11,000m. dobras and expenditure at 50,000m. dobras.

Currency. The unit of currency is the *dobra* (STD) of 100 *centimos*. The average annual inflation rate over the period 1990–96 was 52·5%. In Dec. 1997 foreign exchange reserves were US$12m. Total money supply in Dec. 1997 was 49,202m. dobras (up from 23,683m. in Dec. 1996).

Banking and Finance. In 1991 the Banco Central de São Tomé e Príncipe replaced the Banco Nacional as the central bank and bank of issue. A private commercial bank, the Banco Internacional de São Tomé e Príncipe, began operations in 1993.

Weights and Measures. The metric system is in use.

ENERGY AND NATURAL RESOURCES

Electricity. Installed capacity, 1992, 7,200 kW. Production was 16m. kWh in 1994, with consumption per capita in 1994 of 123 kWh.

Agriculture. Agriculture accounted for 20% of GDP in 1996. After independence all landholdings over 200 ha were nationalized into 15 state farms. These were partially privatized in 1985 by granting management contracts to foreign companies, and distributing some state land as small private plots. Production (1995 in tonnes): Coconuts, 22,000; cocoa, 4,500; copra, 500; bananas, 3,000; palm oil, 250. Food crops include cassava, sweet potatoes and yams. There were 4,000 cattle, 2,000 sheep and 2,000 pigs in 1996 and 5,000 goats in 1995.

Forestry. In 1995 forests covered 56,000 ha, or 76% of the land area. In 1995, 9,000 cu. metres of timber were cut.

Fisheries. There are rich tuna shoals. Estimated total catches in 1995 were 2,800 tonnes.

INDUSTRY

Manufacturing contributes less than 10% of GDP. There are a few small factories in agricultural and timber processing, bricks, ceramics, printing, textiles and soap-making.

Labour. In 1994 the economically active population was 54,000. There were 15,000 registered unemployed.

INTERNATIONAL TRADE

Foreign debt was US$261m. in 1996.

Imports and Exports. Trade figures for 1996 (estimates): Imports, US$26m.; exports, US$8m. The main exports are cocoa (92% in 1995), copra, coffee, bananas and palm-oil.

Main export markets, 1995: Netherlands, US$3·6m.; Portugal, US$0·1m. Main import suppliers, 1995: Portugal, US$11·2m.; France, US$4·9m.; Japan, US$4·2m.

COMMUNICATIONS

Roads. There were 320 km of roads in 1996, 218 km of which were asphalted. Approximately 4,000 passenger cars were in use in 1996 (30 per 1,000 inhabitants), plus 1,540 trucks and vans.

Civil Aviation. São Tomé airport had flights in 1998 to Abidjan, Cabinda, Libreville, Lisbon, Luanda, Malabo and Port Gentil, with services provided by Air Gabon, TAAG and TAP. In 1996 São Tomé handled 25,686 passengers and 1,114 tonnes of freight. There is a light aircraft service to Príncipe.

Shipping. São Tomé is the main port, but it lacks a deep water harbour. Neves handles oil imports and is the main fishing port. Portuguese shipping lines run routes to Lisbon, Oporto, Rotterdam and Antwerp. In 1995 merchant shipping totalled 3,000 GRT.

Telecommunications. There were 2,900 main telephone lines in 1997, or 20·5 per 1,000 population. In 1995 there were 200 fax machines.

Postal Services. In 1994 there were 10 post offices.

SOCIAL INSTITUTIONS

Justice. Members of the Supreme Court are appointed by the National Assembly. There is no death penalty.

SÃO TOMÉ E PRÍNCIPE

Religion. About 90% of the population are Roman Catholic. There is a small Protestant church and a Seventh Day Adventist school.

Education. Adult literacy was 67·1% in 1994. Education is free and compulsory. In 1993 there were 85 primary and 5 secondary schools; 90% of primary age children were attending school. There is a vocational centre, a school of agriculture and a pre-university *lycée*.

Health. In 1989 there were 61 doctors, 5 dentists, 223 nurses, 1 pharmacists and 54 midwives.

CULTURE

Broadcasting. Radio broadcasting is conducted by the government-controlled Rádio Nacional. There is a Voice of America radio station, a religious station and a private German station. There were about 36,000 radio receivers and 21,000 TV receivers in 1995.

Press. There are 4 weekly newspapers.

Tourism. In 1996 there were 2,000 foreign tourists, bringing revenue of US$2m.

DIPLOMATIC REPRESENTATIVES

São Tomé e Príncipe in Great Britain (resides in Brussels)
Ambassador: Vacant.

Of Great Britain in São Tomé e Príncipe
Ambassador: Miss Catherine Elmes (resides in Angola).

Of São Tomé e Príncipe in the USA
Ambassador: Vacant.

Of the USA in São Tomé e Príncipe
Ambassador: Elizabeth Raspolic.

Of São Tomé e Príncipe to the United Nations
Ambassador: Vacant.

Of São Tomé e Príncipe to the European Union
Ambassador: Vacant.

FURTHER READING

Shaw, C. S., *São Tomé e Príncipe.* [Bibliography] Oxford and Santa Barbara (CA), 1994

SAUDI ARABIA

Mamlaka al-Arabiya as-Saudiya

(Kingdom of Saudi Arabia)

Capital: Riyadh
Population estimate, 2000: 21·66m.
GNP per capita: (PPP$) 9,700
HDI/world rank: 0·778/70

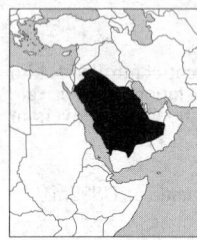

KEY HISTORICAL EVENTS

In the 6th century AD Makkah, now in western Saudi Arabia, was a thriving commercial centre. Around 610 the Prophet Mohammed began to attract a following. In 622, learning of an assassination plot against him, he led his followers to the town of Yathrib (now Madinah). This was the *Hijrah*, or migration, which marks the beginning of the Islamic calendar. Battles ensued between Mohammed's followers and the pagans of Makkah but by 628 Mohammed had united the tribes so successfully he and his followers entered Makkah without bloodshed. Less than 100 years from the advent of Islam, its empire extended from Spain to areas of India and China. Islamic rule thrived well into the 17th century.

Today the Kingdom of Saudi Arabia is a union of two regions, Nejd and Hejaz. In the 18th century, Nejd was an autonomous region governed from Diriya, the stronghold of the Wahhabis, a puritanical Islamic sect. It subsequently fell under Turkish rule but in 1913 Abdulaziz Ibn Abdul Rahman Al-Saud defeated the Turks and also captured the Turkish province of al Hasa. In 1920 he captured the Asir and in 1921 he added the Jebel Shammar territory of the Rashid family. In 1925 he completed the conquest of the Hejaz.

Great Britain recognized Abdulaziz as an independent ruler, King of the Hejaz and of Nejd and its dependencies, by the Treaty of Jiddah on 20 May 1927. The name was changed to the Kingdom of Saudi Arabia in Sept. 1932. King Abdulaziz ruled until his death in Nov. 1953. During his time there was development of the country's oil resources. Although begun before the Second World War, oil exploitation grew greatly with the support of the USA after 1945.

King Abdulaziz was succeeded by his sons, Saud, Faisal, Khalid and Fahd. Saud succeeded to the throne in 1953 but in March 1964 abdicated in favour of Faisal Ibn Abdulaziz who had carried considerable power during the older brother's reign, being for a time prime minister with control over foreign and economic policy. Faisal was assassinated in 1975 and was succeeded by his brother, Khalid Ibn Abdulaziz. On Khalid's death in 1982, Fahd Ibn Abdulaziz became king. In 1995, after King Kahd suffered a stroke, he appointed his half-brother Crown Prince Abdullah Ibn Abdulaziz to act on his behalf.

TERRITORY AND POPULATION

Saudi Arabia, which occupies nearly 80% of the Arabian peninsula, is bounded in the west by the Red Sea, east by the Arabian/Persian Gulf and the United Arab Emirates, north by Jordan, Iraq and Kuwait and south by Yemen and Oman. An agreement with Qatar of 26 Oct. 1996 provided for the definitive delimitation of their common frontier by 1998. For the border dispute with Yemen *see* YEMEN: Territory and Population. The total area is estimated to be 849,400 sq. miles (2·2m. sq. km). Riyadh is the political, and Makkah the religious, capital.

The total population was (1974 census) 7,012,642, of which 5,128,655 were categorized as settled and 1,883,987 as nomadic. Estimate (1992), 16,929,294 (7,462,753 females), of whom 12,304,835 were Saudi Arabians. 1995 estimate, 17·88m.; density, 8 per sq. km. In 1995, 82·8% of the population lived in urban areas.

The UN gives a projected population for 2000 of 21·66m.

Principal cities with 1991 population estimates (in 1m.): Riyadh, 1·8; Jiddah, 1·5; Makkah, 0·63; Taif, 0·41; Madinah, 0·4; Dammam, 0·35.

The Neutral Zone (3,560 sq. miles, 5,700 sq. km), jointly owned and administered by Kuwait and Saudi Arabia from 1922 to 1966, was partitioned between the two countries in 1966, but the exploitation of the oil and other natural resources continues to be shared.

The official language is Arabic.

SOCIAL STATISTICS
Births, 1995, 633,000; deaths, 80,000. Birth rate (1995) was 34·7 per 1,000 population; death rate, 4·4. 75% of the population is under the age of 30. Expectation of life at birth, 1990–95, was 68·4 years for males and 71·4 years for females, up from 61·4 for males and 64·1 for females in 1980–85. Only Ethiopia had a greater increase in its life expectancy over the same period. Infant mortality, 1990–95, was 29 per 1,000 live births, down from 58 in the years 1980–85. Fertility rate, 1990–95, 6·4 births per woman.

CLIMATE
A desert climate, with very little rain and none at all from June to Dec. The months May to Sept. are very hot and humid, but winter temperatures are quite pleasant. Riyadh, Jan. 58°F (14·4°C), July 108°F (42°C). Annual rainfall 4" (100 mm). Jiddah, Jan. 73°F (22·8°C), July 87°F (30·6°C). Annual rainfall 3" (81 mm).

CONSTITUTION AND GOVERNMENT
The reigning King, **Fahd Ibn Abdulaziz Al-Saud** (b. 1923), Custodian of the two Holy Mosques, succeeded in May 1982, after King Khalid's death. *Crown Prince:* Prince Abdullah Ibn Abdulaziz Al-Saud, half-brother of the King.

Constitutional practice derives from Sharia law. There is no formal Constitution, but 3 royal decrees of 1 March 1992 established a Basic Law which defines the systems of central and municipal government, and set up a 60-man Consultative Council (*Majlis Al-Shura*) of royal nominees in Aug. 1993. *Chairman* is Mohammed Ibn Uthman Ibn Jubair.

In July 1997 the King decreed an increase of the Consultative Council to chairman plus 90 members, selected from men of science and experience.

Saudi Arabia is an absolute monarchy; executive power is discharged through a *Council of Ministers,* consisting of the King, Deputy Prime Minister, Second Deputy Prime Minister and Cabinet Ministers.

The King has the post of *Prime Minister* and can veto any decision of the Council of Ministers within 30 days.

National Anthem. 'Sarei lil majd walaya' ('Onward towards the glory and the heights'); words by Ibrahim Khafaji, tune by Abdul Rahman al Katib.

CURRENT ADMINISTRATION
In March 1999 the Council of Ministers comprised:

Prime Minister: Fahd Ibn Abdulaziz Al-Saud.

First Deputy Prime Minister and Commander of the National Guard: Crown Prince Abdullah Ibn Abdulaziz Al-Saud. *Second Deputy Prime Minister and Minister of Defence and Aviation:* Prince Sultan Ibn Abdulaziz Al-Saud. *Housing and Public Works:* Prince Met'eb Ibn Abdulaziz Al-Saud. *Interior:* Prince Naif Ibn Abdulaziz Al-Saud. *Foreign Affairs:* Prince Saud Al-Faisal Ibn Abdulaziz Al-Saud. *Labour and Social Affairs:* Musaid Ibn Mohammed Al-Sanani. *Communications:* Dr Nasir Ibn Mohammed Al-Salloum. *Finance and National Economy:* Dr Ibrahim Ibn Abdulaziz Al-Assaf. *Information:* Dr Fouad Ibn Abdul Salaam Farsi. *Industry and Electricity:* Dr Hashim Ibn Abdullah Ibn Hashim Al-Yamani. *Commerce:* Osama Ibn Jafar Faqih. *Justice:* Dr Abdullah Ibn Mohammed Ibn Ibrahim Al-Shaik. *Education:* Dr Mohammed Ibn Ahmed Al-Rasheed. *Higher Education:* Dr Khalid Ibn Mohammed Al-Angary. *Petroleum and Mineral Resources:* Ali Ibn Ibrahim Al-Naimi. *Islamic Guidance:* Dr Abdullah Ibn Abdulmohsen Al-Turki. *Pilgrimage Affairs and Religious Trusts:* Dr Mahmoud Ibn Mohammed Safar. *Municipal and Rural Affairs:* Dr Mohammed Ibn Ibrahim Al-Jarallah. *Planning:* Dr Abdul Al-Wahab Ibn Abdul Al-Salam Al-Attar. *Agriculture and Water:* Dr Abdullah Ibn Abdulaziz Ibn Mu'amar. *Health:* Dr Osama Ibn Abdul Majeed Shobokshi. *Posts, Telegraphs and Telephones:* Dr Ali Ibn Talal Al-Jahani.

Local Government. 13 provinces were designated in 1993, each governed by an emir with ministerial rank appointed by the King. Each province has a consultative council which meets every 3 months and consists of provincial government officials ex officio and at least 10 Saudi citizens recommended by the emir for the King's appointment. Council members serve 4 years and meet once every 2 weeks.

DEFENCE
In 1997 Saudi Arabia spent US$11·0bn. on defence imports (US$9·4bn. in 1996), making it the world's largest buyer of arms, mainly from the USA and the UK. Defence expenditure in 1997 totalled US$18,151m. (US$1,071 per capita), representing 12·4% of GDP.

The USA stations Air Force units on rotational detachment. The Peninsular Shield Force of about 7,000 comprises units from all Gulf Co-operation Council countries.

Army. The Army comprises 3 armoured brigades, 5 mechanized brigades, 1 airborne brigade, 1 Royal Guard regiment and 8 artillery battalions. Equipment includes 315 M-1A2, 290 AMX-30, 450 M-60A3 main battle tanks and 10 surface-to-surface missiles. The Army Aviation Command disposes of nearly 50 Blackhawk, Dauphin and armed AH-64A Apache and Bell 406 helicopters. Strength (1997) was approximately 70,000. There is a para-military Frontier Force (approximately 10,500).

Navy. The Royal Saudi Naval Forces comprise 4 French-built 2,900-tonnes frigates armed with Otomat anti-ship missiles, 4 smaller US-built missile frigates, 9 US-built fast missile craft, 3 German-built torpedo craft, 4 US-built coastal minesweepers and the first 3 of 6 UK-built Sandown class minehunters. Auxiliaries include 2 French-built replenishment tankers each embarking 2 helicopters, 3 ocean tugs and a Royal Yacht. There are numerous minor auxiliaries and boats.

Naval Aviation forces operate 6 Super Puma armed with Exocet missiles, 6 for search and rescue and 21 Dauphin helicopters, both ship and shore based.

The main naval bases are at Jiddah (Red Sea) and Jubail (The Gulf). Naval personnel in 1997 totalled 13,500, including 3,000 marines.

The Coast Guard operates some 35 inshore patrol craft, 24 hovercraft and over 300 boats of various types.

Air Force. Current combat units include 4 squadrons of F-15 Eagle interceptors, 4 squadrons of F-5E Tiger II supersonic fighter-bombers and RF-5E Tigereye reconnaissance aircraft, supported by a conversion unit with F-5B/F combat trainers. 2 squadrons operate Tornado strike aircraft and another 2 have Tornado interceptors. There is a squadron with Boeing E-3 Sentry airborne early-warning aircraft and KE-3 flight refuelling tankers. 1 squadron of Hawk light jet attack/trainers is based at the Al Kharj and a second at King Faisal Air Academy, Riyadh, together with 12 Reims/Cessna FR172 piston-engined primary trainers, PC-9 basic trainers and Jetstream navigation trainers. Other types in current service include 60 C-130E/H and KC-130H Hercules transports and tankers, 1 Boeing 747 SP, 1 Boeing 747-200, 1 Boeing 737, 3 Boeing 707, 4 CN-235s, 12 BAe-125s, 3 Learjets and 2 JetStar VIP jet transports, more than 80 Agusta-Bell 205, 212 and JetRanger and KV-107 helicopters, 2 Agusta AS-61A-4 VIP transport helicopters and communications aircraft. Personnel (1998), about 18,000 with 432 combat aircraft.

Air Defence Force. This separate Command was formerly part of the Army, which retains a point air defence capability. In 1998 it had 33 surface-to-air missile batteries and a strength of 4,000.

National Guard. The National Guard comprises 2 mechanized and 6 infantry brigades and 1 ceremonial cavalry squadron. Additionally there are a number of regular and irregular units, the total strength of the National Guard amounting to approximately 77,000 (57,000 active, 20,000 tribal levies). The National Guard's primary role is the protection of the Royal Family and vital points in the Kingdom. It is directly under royal command. The UK provides small advisory teams to the National Guard in the fields of general training and communications.

INTERNATIONAL RELATIONS
Saudi Arabia is a member of the UN, the Arab League, the Gulf Co-operation Council and OPEC.

ECONOMY

Policy. The sixth 5-year development plan (1995–99) continues the emphasis on developing the private sector, and aims to increase and indigenize the workforce, enhance defence capacity, achieve a balanced economic development and protect the environment. The 1998 budget emphasised expenditure and capital projects such as roads and schools. 80% of the budget goes on public sector salaries.

Performance. Real GDP growth was 1·0% in 1997. The current account surplus stood at US$254m. in 1997.

Budget. In 1986 the financial year became the calendar year. Estimated revenue, 1996: SAR177bn. 1997 budget: Revenue, SAR164bn.; expenditure, SAR181bn. Revenues for 1998 were forecast at SAR178bn., and expenditure at SAR196bn.

Oil sales account for 80% of state income. Estimated 1993 expenditure (in 1m. rials): Defence and security, 61·6; education, 34·1; health and social welfare, 14·1; economic and social subsidies, 9·2; transport and communications, 9·1.

Currency. The unit of currency is the *rial* (SAR) of 100 *halalah*. In Feb. 1998 foreign exchange reserves totalled US$6,656m. and gold reserves were 4·6m. troy oz. Inflation was 2·6% in 1997 (0·9% in 1996). Total money supply in Feb. 1998 was SAR144bn.

Banking and Finance. The Saudi Arabian Monetary Agency (*governor*, Hamad Saud al Sayari), established in 1953, functions as the central bank and the government's fiscal agent. There were 12 commercial banks with 1,160 branches, 5 special credit institutions and a variety of other financial institutions in 1995. Sharia (the religious law of Islam) forbids the charging of interest; Islamic banking is based on sharing clients' profits and losses and imposing service charges. The Saudi Arabian Agricultural Bank, with 70 branches and offices, extended 755m. rials in credit services to farmers during 1989. At 30 Sept. 1995 total assets of commercial banks were 323,900m. rials.

There is a stock exchange.

ENERGY AND NATURAL RESOURCES

Electricity. By 1995 the over 100 electricity producers had been amalgamated into 4 companies. Installed capacity was 21,901 MW in 1994. All electricity is thermally generated. Production was 62·75bn. kWh in 1994. Consumption per capita was estimated at 3,228 kWh in 1995.

Oil and Gas. Proven reserves (1996) 260,100m. bbls. (26% of world resources). Oil production began in 1938 by Aramco, which is now 100% state-owned and accounts for about 97% of total crude oil production.

Saudi Arabia's 1997 OPEC quota was 8·76m. bbls. a day. In 1996 it produced 12·8% of the world total oil output.

Production comes from 14 major oilfields, mostly in the Eastern Province and offshore, and including production from the Neutral Zone.

Saudi Arabia is dependent on oil earnings for over 70% of budget revenues. In 1996 oil export revenues were SAR130bn. compared to a planned SAR85bn., in 1997 they were SAR155bn. compared to a planned SAR115bn. but in 1998 they were forecast to be only SAR105bn. compared to a planned SAR125bn. In Oct. 1998 US oil companies were invited back to help develop Saudi Arabia's energy resources, nearly 20 years after they had been expelled. In 1998, revenue fell by a third following the collapse of the price of oil.

In 1996, gas reserves were estimated at 190,100,000m. cu. ft.

Water. Efforts are under way to provide adequate supplies of water for urban, industrial, rural and agricultural use. Most investment has gone into sea-water desalination. In 1996, 33 plants produced 1·9m. cu. metres a day, meeting 70% of drinking water needs. Total annual consumption was 18,200m. cu. metres in 1995. Irrigation for agriculture consumes the largest amount, from fossil reserves (the country's principal water source), and from surface water collected during seasonal floods. In 1996 there were 183 dams with a holding capacity of 450m. cu. metres. Treated urban waste water is an increasing resource for domestic purposes; in 1996 there were 2 recycling plants in operation.

Minerals. Production began in 1988 at Mahd Al-Dahab gold mine, the largest in the country, which produces 170,000 oz of gold a year. In 1993, 189,353 tonnes of ore were extracted. In July 1998 plans were announced for the investment of US$98m. to double gold production by 2001. 1997 production totalled 7 tonnes. Deposits of iron, phosphate, bauxite, uranium, silver, tin, tungsten, nickel, chrome, zinc, lead, potassium ore and copper have also been found.

Agriculture. Since 1970 the Government has spent substantially on desert reclamation, irrigation schemes, drainage and control of surface water and of moving sands. Undeveloped land has been distributed to farmers and there are research and extension programmes. Large scale private investment has concentrated on wheat, poultry and dairy production.

In 1994 there were 3·7m. ha of arable land, 100,000 ha of permanent cropland and 120m. ha of permanent pasture. In 1995, 13·9% of the economically active population were engaged in agriculture.

Date production in 1995 was 600,000 tonnes; wheat, 3·0m. tonnes. About 2m. tonnes of barley are produced annually as animal fodder. Estimated production of other crops, 1995 (in 1,000 tonnes): Vegetables, 2,280; fruit, 237. Livestock products: Milk, 587; poultry and red meat, 453; eggs, 126.

Livestock (1996): 225,000 cattle, 7,800,000 sheep, 418,000 camels (1995), 4,200,000 goats (1995) and 83m. chickens (1995).

Forestry. The area under forests was 222,000 ha (0·1% of the land area) in 1995.

Fisheries. In 1995 the total catch was 54,486 tonnes, of which 52,051 tonnes were sea fish.

INDUSTRY

The Government encourages the establishment of manufacturing industries. Its policy focuses on establishing industries that use petroleum products, petrochemicals and minerals. Petrochemical and oil-based industries have been concentrated at 8 new industrial cities, with the 2 principal cities at Jubail and Yanbu. In 1996, there were 15 major plants and other industrial facilities, a dedicated desalination plant, a vocational training institute and a college at Jubail, and 3 major refineries, a petrochemical complex and many manufacturing and support enterprises at Yanbu. Products include chemical, plastics, industrial gases, steel and other metals. In 1995 there were 2,234 factories employing 196,000 workers.

Labour. The labour force in 1996 totalled 6,187,000 (86% males). In 1995, 32·3% of the economically active population were engaged in community and personal services, 15·5% in construction and 15·1% in trade. Less than 1% worked in the oil sector. There were 4m. foreign workers in 1995.

INTERNATIONAL TRADE

In 1992, foreign debt totalled US$17,089m.

Imports and Exports. In 1995 imports totalled US$28,091m. and exports US$50,040m. (90% oil and products). The principal export is crude oil; refined oil, petro-chemicals and wheat are other major exports. Share of exports, 1994: USA, 18·5%; Japan, 16·0%; South Korea, 8·1%; France, 5·3%. Imports: USA, 21·3%; Japan, 11·7%; UK, 8·5%; Germany, 8·3%.

COMMUNICATIONS

Roads. In 1996 there were 43,200 km of primary roads and 96,000 km of secondary roads. A causeway links Saudi Arabia with Bahrain. Passenger cars in use in 1996 numbered 1,744,000 (99 per 1,000 inhabitants) and there were 1,169,000 trucks and vans. The average distance travelled by a passenger car in the year 1994 was 30,794 km. Women are not allowed to drive.

Rail. 1,435 mm gauge lines link Riyadh and Dammam with stops at Hofuf and Abqaiq. This line is being extended to Jubail. In 1994–95 railways carried 453,000 passengers and 1·9m. tonnes of freight.

Civil Aviation. The national carrier is the state-owned Saudia. In 1995 it flew 115·1m. km and carried 11,525,000 passengers (3,809,900 on international flights).

In 1998 services were also provided by Air Afrique, Air Djibouti, Air France, Air India, Air Lanka, Air Tanzania Corporation, Alitalia, Ariana Afghan Airlines, Biman Bangladesh Airlines, British Airways, Cameroon Airlines, Cyprus Airways, Daallo Airlines, Delta Air Lines, Djibouti Airlines, Egyptair, Emirates, Ethiopian Airlines, Garuda Indonesia, Gulf Air, Iran Air, KLM, Kuwait Airways, Lufthansa, Malaysia Airlines, Middle East Airlines, Nigeria Airways, Olympic Airways, Pakistan International Airlines, Philippine Airlines, Qatar Airways, Royal Air Maroc, Royal Brunei Airlines, Royal Jordanian, SAS, Singapore Airlines, Sudan Airways, Swissair, Syrian Arab Airlines, Tunis Air, Turkish Airlines, TWA, United Airlines and Yemenia Yemen Airways. There are 3 major international airports at Jiddah (King Abdulaziz), Dhahran and Riyadh (King Khaled) and 22 domestic airports. King Fahd International Airport in Eastern Province is under construction. In 1995 Saudia flew 115·1m. km, carrying 11,525,000 passengers (3,809,900 on international flights). In 1996 Jiddah handled 9,297,788 passengers (4,915,837 on international flights) and 175,579 tonnes of freight. Riyadh was the second busiest airport in 1996, handling 7,745,377 passengers (5,004,453 on domestic flights) and 137,216 tonnes of freight.

Shipping. The ports of Dammam and Jubail are on the Arabian/Persian Gulf and Jiddah, Yanbu and Jizan on the Red Sea. There is a deepwater oil terminal at Ras Tanura, and 16 minor ports. In 1994 the ports handled 86·8m. tonnes of cargo. In 1995 the merchant marine comprised 110 vessels totalling 8·2m. DWT, representing 1·24% of the world's total fleet tonnage. 49 vessels (89·13% of tonnage) were registered under foreign flags. GRT totalled 1·08m; including oil tankers, 210,370 GRT, and container ships, 67,599 GRT.

Telecommunications. Saudi Arabia had 2,285,400 main telephone lines in 1997, or 117·2 per 1,000 persons. In 1995 there were 15,590 cellular phone subscribers, 600,000 PCs (35 per 1,000 population), 75,000 fax machines and 10,100 telex machines.

Postal Services. Number of post offices in 1995 was 1,282.

SOCIAL INSTITUTIONS

Justice. The religious law of Islam (Sharia) is the common law of the land, and is administered by religious courts, at the head of which is a chief judge, who is responsible for the Department of Sharia Affairs. Sharia courts are concerned primarily with family inheritance and property matters. The Committee for the Settlement of Commercial Disputes is the commercial court. Other specialized courts or committees include one dealing exclusively with labour and employment matters; the Negotiable Instruments Committee, which deals with cases relating to cheques, bills of exchange and promissory notes, and the Board of Grievances, whose preserve is disputes with the government or its agencies and which also has jurisdiction in trademark-infringement cases and is the authority for enforcing foreign court judgements.

The death penalty is in force for murder, rape, sodomy, armed robbery, sabotage, drug trafficking, adultery and apostasy; executions may be held in public. There were 58 executions in 1994.

Religion. In 1997, 18,210,000 persons were Sunni Moslems and 640,000 Shiites. There were 230,000 with other beliefs. The *Grand Mufti*, Abdul Aziz ben Baz, has cabinet rank. A special police force, the Mutaween, exists to enforce religious norms.

Education. The educational system provides students with free education, books and health services. General education consists of kindergarten, 6 years of primary school and 3 years each of intermediate and high school. In 1996–97, there were 893 pre-primary schools with 7,703 teachers and 85,484 pupils, 11,506 primary schools with 175,458 teachers and 2,256,185 pupils, and there were 115,907 high school teachers teaching 1,500,072 students. At teacher training colleges there were 1,438 teachers and 21,366 students and at vocational schools 2,536 teachers and 21,551 students. Students can attend either high schools offering programmes in arts and sciences, or vocational schools. Girls' education is administered separately. In 1996 there were over 30 special schools for the handicapped with about 4,550 students. The adult literacy rate in 1995 was 62·8% (71·5% among males and 50·2% among females).

In 1996 there were 2,343 adult education centres. In 1995-96 there were 4 universities, 2 Islamic universities and 1 university of petroleum and minerals. In tertiary education as a whole there were 15,868 teachers and 273,992 students. Education expenditure in 1996 was SAR27,205m. or around 6% of all government expenditure.

Health. In 1995 there were 3,254 primary health care centres and clinics and 279 hospitals with 41,923 beds. 29,227 doctors, 61,627 nursing and 32,167 technical staff were employed at these facilities. At Jiddah there is a quarantine centre for pilgrims.

CULTURE

Broadcasting. The government-controlled Broadcasting Service of the Kingdom of Saudi Arabia and Saudi Arabian Television are responsible for broadcasting. Radio programmes include 2 home services, 2 religious services, services in English and French and an external service. Aramco Oil have a private station. There are TV programmes in Arabic and English; Channel 3 TV is a non-commercial independent. Colour is by SECAM and PAL. In 1995 there were estimated to be 5·32m. radio and 4·7m. TV sets.

Press. In 1996 there were 13 daily newspapers with a combined circulation of 1,105,000, equivalent to 59 per 1,000 inhabitants. In 1995 there were 168 non-daily newspapers with a combined circulation of 2,150,000 or 117 per 1,000.

Tourism. There were 3,458,000 foreign tourists in 1996, bringing revenue of US$1·31bn.

Libraries. There was 1 National library in 1995 and in 1993 there were 21 higher education libraries, holding a combined 4,904,000 volumes for 490,111 registered users.

Museums and Galleries. In 1993 there were 12 museums, receiving a total of 44,147 visitors.

DIPLOMATIC REPRESENTATIVES
Of Saudi Arabia in Great Britain (30 Charles St., London, W1X 7PM)
Ambassador: Dr Ghazi A. Algosaibi.

Of Great Britain in Saudi Arabia (PO Box 94351, Riyadh 11693)
Ambassador: Andrew F. Green, KCMG.

Of Saudi Arabia in the USA (601 New Hampshire Ave., NW, Washington, D.C., 20037)
Ambassador: HRH Prince Bandar bin Sultan.

Of the USA in Saudi Arabia (PO Box 94309, Riyadh)
Ambassador: Wyche Fowler.

Of Saudi Arabia to the United Nations
Ambassador: Vacant.

Of Saudi Arabia to the European Union
Ambassador: Nassir Alassaf.

FURTHER READING
Azzam, H., *Saudi Arabia: Economic Trends, Business Environment and Investment Opportunities.* London, 1993
Clements, F. A., *Saudi Arabia.* [Bibliography] Oxford and Santa Barbara (CA), 1988
Holden, D. and Johns, R., *The House of Saud.* London and New York, 1981
Kostiner, J., *The Making of Saudi Arabia: from Chieftaincy to Monarchical State.* OUP, 1994
Peterson, J. E., *Historical Dictionary of Saudi Arabia.* Metuchen (NJ), 1994
Wright, J. W. (ed.) *Business and Economic Development in Saudi Arabia: Essays with Saudi Scholars.* London, 1996

National statistical office: Ministry of Finance and National Economy, Department of Statistics, Riyadh.
Website: http://www.saudinf.com

SENEGAL

République du Sénégal

Capital: Dakar
Population estimate, 2000: 9·49m.
GNP per capita: (PPP$) 1,650
HDI/world rank: 0·342/158

KEY HISTORICAL EVENTS

The major ethnic groups of Senegal are the Wolof, Serer, Tukulor (or Toucouleur), Soninke (or Sarakole), Mandinka and Diola peoples. Some of them had important traditional kingdoms. In Fouta Toro in the east there was the state of Tekrur and then an Islamic state founded in 1776 by Muslim Tukulors. Islam reached the Senegal river valley by the 11th century, and later the Fulanis (whose migration all over West Africa began from Senegal) and the related Tukolors helped spread Islam over a large area.

For several centuries, starting in the 14th, the Wolofs had a supreme ruler, the Bourba Jolof, and several important kingdoms under him, notably the kingdom of Kayor (Kajoor) ruled by 30 kings or *damels* from the 16th century to 1886. The last *damel*, the Muslim Lat Dior, was famous for his resistance to French rule.

While in the mid-1400s the Portuguese were the first Europeans to reach the area around the Senegal river estuary; in succeeding centuries the French became the dominant Europeans on the coast in that area, except for the Gambia, where the British were installed. The French founded Saint-Louis in 1659 and also occupied the island of Goree, an important slave-trading depot. By the 18th century Saint-Louis had an important small elite community, partly African, called the *habitants*. In the 19th century French rule, interrupted earlier by occasional British occupation, was confirmed over Saint-Louis and Goree. Free Africans received the vote in 1833, and the franchise was further extended in 1848 when slavery was abolished in all French colonies. The Africans in Saint-Louis and Goree, and also in Dakar and Rufisque, were in the 19th century called the *originaires* and had the rights of French citizens. They elected a deputy to the French national Assembly and voted for local government councils (or *communes*).

From the late 1870s France began a sustained push up the river and into the interior. Here, groundnuts were already being grown for export to France, but African monarchs still ruled, including the new Islamic conqueror, El Hadj Umar and, after his death in 1864, his son Ahmadu. There was strong resistance to the French, notably that led by Lat Dior from 1882 until his death in action in 1886. French rule was established by the mid-1890s, while the British then consolidated their rule inland in The Gambia; French efforts to obtain cession of that territory, entirely surrounded by Senegal, did not succeed.

The normal French colonial system prevailed, one of its features being the breaking up of traditional kingdoms (completed in Senegal by the 1920s). Senegal was part of French West Africa *(Afrique Occidentale Française)* from 1902 and became an autonomous state within the French Community on 25 Nov. 1958. On 4 April 1959 Senegal joined with French Sudan to form the Federation of Mali, which achieved independence on 20 June 1960, but on 22 Aug. Senegal withdrew from the Federation and became a separate independent republic. Senegal was a one-Party state from 1966 until 1974, when a pluralist system was re-established.

TERRITORY AND POPULATION

Senegal is bounded by Mauritania to the north and north-east, Mali to the east, Guinea and Guinea-Bissau to the south and the Atlantic to the west with The Gambia forming an enclave along that shore. Area, 196,190 sq. km; population (census, 1988), 6,982,084; (estimate, 1996) 9·09m. (44% urban). Population density, 40·5 per sq. km. Age structure: 1–14 years, 48%; 15–64, 49%; 65 and over, 3%.

The UN gives a projected population for 2000 of 9·49m.

The areas, populations and capitals of the 10 regions:

Region	Area (in sq. km)	1988 Census	Capital
Dakar	550	1,571,614	Dakar
Diourbel	4,359	620,197	Diourbel

Region	Area (in sq. km)	1988 Census	Capital
Fatick	7,935	507,651	Fatick
Kaolack	16,010	805,859	Kaolack
Kolda	21,011	593,199	Kolda
Louga	29,188	507,572	Louga
Saint-Louis	44,127	656,941	Saint-Louis
Tambacounda	57,602	383,572	Tambacounda
Thiès	6,601	937,412	Thiès
Ziguinchor	7,339	398,067	Ziguinchor

The largest cities (with 1992 estimated population) are: Dakar, the capital (1,729,823), Kaolack (179,894), Saint-Louis (125,717), Thiès (201,350) and Ziguinchor (148,831).

Ethnic groups are the Wolof (36% of the population), Serer (16%), Fulani (16%), Tukulor (9%), Diola (9%), Malinké (6%), Bambara (6%) and Sarakole (2%).

The official language is French; Wolof is widely spoken.

SOCIAL STATISTICS
Births, 1995, 349,000; deaths, 126,000. Birth rate (1995) per 1,000 population, 42·0; death rate (1997), 18. Annual growth rate, 1990–95, 2·0%; infant mortality (1997), 68 per 1,000 live births. Life expectancy in 1996 was 53·75 years for men and 59·3 for women. Fertility rate, 1997, 5·7 births per woman (down from 6·6 in 1988).

CLIMATE
A tropical climate with wet and dry seasons. The rains fall almost exclusively in the hot season, from June to Oct., with high humidity. Dakar, Jan. 72°F (22·2°C), July 82°F (27·8°C). Annual rainfall 22" (541 mm).

CONSTITUTION AND GOVERNMENT
The 1963 constitution was revised in 1991. The head of state is the *President*, elected by universal suffrage for not more than two 7-year terms. For the unicameral, 140-member National Assembly, 70 members are elected in multi-seat and single-seat constituencies and 70 by proportional representation, all for a 5-year term. In Dec. 1995 it was decided that a Senate would be established to represent territorial collectives in parliament. The Senate has 60 members, 45 elected by legislators and local, municipal and regional councillors; 12 appointed by the President; and 3 by Senegalese people living abroad.

In Sept. 1998 parliament passed a law allowing Abdou Diouf, Senegal's president since 1981, to become president-for-life.

National Anthem. 'Pincez tous vos koras, frappez les balafos' ('All pluck the koras, strike the balafos'); words by Léopold Sédar Senghor, tune by Herbert Pepper.

RECENT ELECTIONS
At the presidential elections of 21 Feb. 1993, there were 8 candidates; turn-out was 51·46%. Abdou Diouf was re-elected with 58·4% of votes cast.

At the parliamentary elections of 25 May 1998, candidates from 11 parties stood. The Senegalese Socialist Party (PSS) gained 93 seats (50·2% of votes cast); the Senegalese Democratic Party (PDS) 23 (19·1%); Alliance Jëf-Jël-USD (JJ, centrist) 11 (13·2%); African Party for Democracy and Socialism (AJ, socialist) 4 (5%); Democratic League (LD, communist) 3; Convent of Democrats and Patriots (CDP, socialist) 1; Front for Socialism and Democracy (FSD, social-democratic) 1; Senegalese Democratic Party-Renewal (PDS-R, centrist) 1; Party of Independence and Work (PIT, communist) 1; National Democratic Rally (RND, extreme left) 1; Bloc of Centrists (BC) 1.

Fraud and the electoral system tend to favour the ruling party. The ruling Socialist Party split in March 1998, leading to the creation of the new Democratic Party for Renewal.

The Senate was elected on 24 Jan. 1999. All 45 elected members are members of the PSS.

SENEGAL

CURRENT ADMINISTRATION
President: Abdou Diouf (PSS), took office in Jan. 1981, re-elected 1983, 1988 and 1993.

The Cabinet was composed as follows in March 1999:

Prime Minister: Mamadou Lamine Loum (PSS).

Deputy Prime Minister and Minister of State for Presidential Services: Ousmane Tanor Dieng.

Minister of Foreign Affairs and Expatriates: Jacques Baudin. *Interior:* Lamine Cissé. *Minister of the Armed Forces:* Cheikh Hamidou Kane. *Communications:* Aissata Tall Sall. *Culture:* Abdoulaye Elimane Kane. *Economic Affairs, Finance and Planning:* Mouhamed El Moustapha Diagne. *Employment and Labour:* Marie Louise Corréa. *Education:* André Sonko. *Energy, Mining and Industry:* Magued Diouf. *Environment and Conservation of Nature:* Souty Toure. *Equipment and Land Transport:* Landing Sané. *Fisheries and Marine Transport:* Alassane Ndiaye. *Justice and Keeper of the Seals:* Serigne Diop. *State Modernization:* Abdoulaye Makhtar Diop. *Tourism and Civil Aviation:* Tijane Sylla. *Housing and Town Planning:* Abdourahmane Sow. *Commerce and Crafts:* Khalifa Sall. *Water Resources:* Moustapha Faye. *Family, Social Welfare and National Solidarity:* Aminata Ndiaye. *Youth and Sport:* Iba Gueye. *Health:* Assane Diop. *Scientific Research and Technology:* Balla Moussa Daffé; *Stockbreeding:* Sanghe Mballo.

The *Speaker* is Sheikh Abdul Khadre Cissokho (PSS).

Local Government. Senegal is divided into 10 regions, each with an appointed governor and an elected regional assembly. They are divided into 30 departments, each under an appointed prefect, and thence into 99 *arrondissements.* Legislation of 1996 increased the powers of local authorities. Local elections were held on 1 Dec. 1996; SP gained a large majority of seats.

DEFENCE
There is selective conscription for 2 years. Defence expenditure totalled US$71m. in 1997 (US$8 per capita).

Army. There are 4 military zones. The Army had a strength of 12,000 (mostly conscripts) in 1996, organized in 6 infantry battalions, 1 engineer, 1 armoured, 1 airborne, 1 commando and 1 artillery battalion, 1 horsed Presidential Guard and 3 construction companies. Equipment includes 67 armoured cars. There is also a paramilitary force of gendarmerie and customs.

Navy. The flotilla includes 2 coastal patrol craft, 8 inshore patrol craft, 1 tank landing craft, 2 smaller amphibious craft, and about 6 service craft. Personnel (1996) totalled 700, and bases are at Dakar and Casamance.

Air Force. The Air Force, formed with French assistance, has 3 Rallye Guerrier and 5 Magister armed trainers, 5 F.27 twin-turboprop transports, 2 Puma, 1 Gazelle and 2 Alouette II helicopters, plus 2 Rallye trainers, but serviceability is low. Personnel (1995) 650, with 8 combat aircraft.

INTERNATIONAL RELATIONS
Senegal is a member of the UN, OAU and is an ACP member state of the ACP-EU relationship.

A short section of the boundary with The Gambia is indefinite; the boundary with Mauritania is in dispute.

ECONOMY
Policy. Privatization began in 1987 and by 1996 a total of 20 companies had been sold off. An austerity programme was adopted in 1993 and the following year Senegal embarked on a structural adjustment aimed to exploit a 50% devaluation of the currency in the 14 francophone African countries. A start has been made on liberalizing labour laws, closing tax loopholes and ending monopolies. With IMF targets met, the second part of a loan facility was approved in 1995.

Performance. Real GDP growth was 5·7% in 1998 (4·5% in 1996).

Budget. The 1998 budget is estimated to have produced revenues of US$733m. and an expenditure of US$801m.

SENEGAL

Currency. Senegal is a member of the Union Economique et Monétaire Ouest-Africaine (UEMOA). The currency is the *franc CFA* (XOF) at a parity of 100 *francs CFA* to 1 French *franc*. In Nov. 1997 gold reserves were 30,000 troy oz., and in Dec. 1997 foreign exchange reserves totalled US$384m. The average annual inflation rate over the period 1990–96 was 8·4%. Total money supply in Dec. 1997 was 342bn. francs CFA.

Banking and Finance. The Banque Centrale des États de l'Afrique de l'Ouest is the bank of issue of the franc CFA for all the countries of the West African Economic and Monetary Union (Benin, Burkina Faso, Côte d'Ivoire, Mali, Niger, Senegal and Togo) but has had its headquarters in Dakar, the Senegalese capital, since 1973. Its *governor* is Charles Konan Banny. There are few major banks, the largest including the Banque Internationale pour le Commerce et l'Industrie and Banque de l'Habitat (9% state-owned).

ENERGY AND NATURAL RESOURCES

Electricity. In 1996 installed capacity was 230 MW. Production in 1997 was estimated to be 1·03bn. kWh and consumption per capita in 1997 was estimated at 109 kWh.

Minerals. 1,128,000 tonnes of calcium phosphate were produced in 1992 and 93,000 tonnes of aluminium phosphate in 1989. There are gold deposits and exploration was under way by 1996.

Agriculture. Because of erratic rainfall 25% of agricultural land needs irrigation. Agriculture accounted for 18% of GDP in 1996. Most land is owned under customary rights and holdings tend to be small. In 1994, 2·33m. ha were used as arable land, 20,00 ha for permanent crops and 5·7m. ha for permanent pasture. Production, 1997–98 (in tonnes): Cereals, 781,217; groundnuts, 505,594; cotton, 20,626; potatoes, 219,540; water melon, 2,498.

Livestock (1997): 4·19m. sheep, 3·57m. goats, 2·89m. cattle, 191,000 pigs, 375,000 asses, 444,000 horses and 4,000 camels. Animal products (1997, in 1,000 tonnes): Beef and veal, 49; pork, 6; horseflesh, 24; mutton and lamb, 28; milk, 104,000.

Forestry. Forests covered 7·63m. ha in 1990 and 7·38m. ha (38·3% of the land area) in 1995. Roundwood production in 1995 amounted to 5·22m. cu. metres.

Fisheries. The fishing fleet comprises 167 vessels totalling 40,600 GRT. In 1995 the total catch was 348,288 tonnes (318,228 tonnes from sea fishing).

INDUSTRY

Predominantly agricultural and fish processing, phosphate mining, petroleum refining and contruction materials.

Labour. The workforce (10 years and over) in 1996 was 2,509,000, of whom 77% were engaged in subsistence farming; 60% of the workforce is in the public sector.

Trade Unions. There are two major unions, the *Union Nationale des Travailleurs Sénégalais* (government-controlled) and the *Confédération Nationale des Travailleurs Sénégalais* (independent) which broke away from the former in 1969 and in 1994 comprised 75% of salaried workers.

INTERNATIONAL TRADE

Foreign debt was US$3,663m. in 1996.

Imports and Exports. In 1996 imports totalled US$1,383m. and exports US$871m. Chief exports: fish, groundnuts, petroleum products, phosphates and cotton. Chief imports: food and beverages, capital goods. Main import suppliers, 1995: France, 31·6%; Nigeria, 6·4%; USA, 5·7%; Japan, 3·7%. Main export markets, 1995: India, 25·7%; France, 11·1%; Mali, 8·5%; Italy, 7·2%.

COMMUNICATIONS

Roads. The length of roads in 1996 was 14,576 km, of which 4,265 km were bitumenized. There were 85,488 passenger cars (9 per 1,000 inhabitants), 24,040 trucks and vans and 10,359 buses and coaches in 1996.

SENEGAL

Rail. There are 4 railway lines: Dakar-Kidira (continuing in Mali), Thiès-Saint-Louis (193 km), Guinguinéo-Kaolack (22 km), and Diourbel-Touba (46 km). Total length (1996), 905 km (metre gauge). In 1996 railways carried 6·38m. passengers and 429,332 tonnes of freight, of which 331,850 were for export.

Civil Aviation. The international airport is Léopold Sédar Senghor. Air Sénégal is 50% state-owned, and in 1998 flew to Banjul, Nouakchott and Praia in addition to operating on domestic routes. Senegal is also a member of the multinational Air Afrique. In 1998 other airlines flying to Senegal were Aeroflot, Air Algérie, Air Dabia, Air France, Air Gabon, Air Mauritanie, Air Toulouse, Alitalia, Condor Flugdienst, Ethiopian Airlines, Ghana Airways, Iberia, Mahfooz Aviation, Royal Air Maroc, SABENA, Saudia, South African Airways, Swissair, TAP, Transportes Aéreos de Cabo Verde and Tunis Air. In 1995 scheduled airline traffic of Senegal-based carriers flew 3·4m. km. In 1997, 470,264 passengers left, and 469,713 arrived, at Léopold Sédar Senghor airport.

Shipping. In 1995 the merchant marine totalled 27,640 GRT. 5·5m. tonnes of freight were handled in the port of Dakar in 1995. There is a river service on the Senegal from Saint-Louis to Podor (363 km) open throughout the year, and to Kayes (924 km) open from July to Oct. The Senegal River is closed to foreign flags. The Saloum River is navigable as far as Kaolack, the Casamance River as far as Ziguinchor.

Telecommunications. In 1997 main telephone lines numbered 115,900 (13·2 for every 1,000 persons). There were 60,000 PCs in 1995 and around 100 cellular phone subscribers. In Jan. 1998 Senegal had approximately 2,500 Internet users.

Postal Services. There were, in 1995, 131 post offices.

SOCIAL INSTITUTIONS

Justice. There are *juges de paix* in each *département* and a court of first instance in each region. Assize courts are situated in Dakar, Kaolack, Saint-Louis and Ziguinchor, while the Court of Appeal resides in Dakar. The death penalty is authorized.

Religion. The population is 90% Sunni Moslem, the remainder being Christian (mainly Roman Catholic) or animist.

Education. The adult literacy rate in 1995 was 33·1% (43% among males and 23·2% among females). In 1996-97 there were 954,758 pupils and 15,503 teachers in 3,530 primary schools; 151,735 pupils in 334 junior schools; 55,199 pupils in 79 secondary schools; and 26,616 students at 3 universities (Cheikh Anta Diop; Gaston Berger; Dakar Bourguiba). In 1995-96 there were a further 19 institutions of higher education.

Health. In 1996 there were 17 government hospitals, 646 maternity homes, 53 health centres, 768 clinics. There were 649 doctors (266 in government service), 93 dentists, 588 midwives (547 government) and 1,876 other medical personnel (1,630 government). There were 322 pharmacists (16 in government service).

CULTURE

Broadcasting. The government-owned *Office de Radio-Télévision du Sénégal* broadcasts a national and an international radio service from 10 main transmitters. There are also regional services. There is also a TV service (colour by SECAM). In 1995 there were 1m. radio receivers (120 per 1,000 inhabitants) and 320,000 TV receivers (38 per 1,000 inhabitants). As recently as 1980 there had been just 8,000 TV receivers, or only 1·4 per 1,000. The percentage rise in the proportion of the population having TV receivers, at more than 2,600%, was the highest anywhere in the world over the same 15-year period.

Press. In 1995 there were 3 daily newspapers with a combined circulation of 48,000, equivalent to 6 per 1,000 inhabitants.

Tourism. 406,300 foreign tourists visited in 1997. Revenue in 1996 amounted to US$147m.

DIPLOMATIC REPRESENTATIVES
Of Senegal in Great Britain (39 Marloes Rd, London, W8 6LA)
Ambassador: Gabriel Alexandre Sar.

Of Great Britain in Senegal (20 Rue du Docteur Guillet, Dakar)
Ambassador: David R. Snoxell.

Of Senegal in the USA (2112 Wyoming Ave., NW, Washington, D.C., 20008)
Ambassador: Mamadou Mansour Seck.

Of the USA in Senegal (Ave. Jean XXIII, Dakar)
Ambassador: Dane F. Smith, Jr.

Of Senegal to the United Nations
Ambassador: Ibra Deguène Ka.

Of Senegal to the European Union
Ambassador: Saloum Kande.

FURTHER READING
Centre Français du Commerce Extérieur. *Sénégal: un Marché.* Paris, 1993

Adams, A. and So, J., *A Claim in Senegal, 1720–1994.* Paris, 1996
Delgado, C. L. and Jammeh, S., *The Political Economy of Senegal under Structural Adjustment.* New York, 1991
Dilley, R. M. and Eades, J. S., *Senegal.* [Bibliography] Oxford and Santa Barbara (CA), 1994
Gellar, S., *Senegal.* Boulder (Colo.), 1982.—*Senegal: an African Nation between Islam and the West.* Aldershot, 1983
Phillips, L. C., *Historical Dictionary of Senegal.* 2nd ed, revised by A. F. Clark. Metuchen (NJ), 1995

National statistical office: Direction de la Statistique, BP 116, Dakar.

SEYCHELLES

Republic of Seychelles

Capital: Victoria
Population estimate, 2000: 80,000
Estimated GDP: $450m.
HDI/world rank: 0·845/56

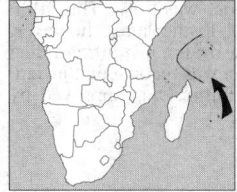

KEY HISTORICAL EVENTS

The Seychelles were first colonized by the French in 1756 in order to establish plantations for growing spices to compete with the Dutch monopoly. The islands were captured by the English in 1794. During discussions before the Treaty of Paris was signed, Britain offered to return Mauritius and its dependencies which included the Seychelles to France if that country would renounce all claims to her possessions in India. France refused and the Seychelles were formally ceded to Britain as a dependency of Mauritius. In Nov. 1903 the Seychelles archipelago became a separate British Crown Colony. Internal self-government was achieved on 1 Oct. 1975 and independence as a republic within the British Commonwealth on 29 June 1976.

The first president, James Mancham, was deposed in a *coup* on 5 June 1977 and replaced by his prime minister, Albert René. The National Assembly was dissolved and the constitution suspended. A new constitution came into force on 5 June 1979, under which the Seychelles People's Progressive Front became the sole legal party and nominates all candidates for election. There were several attempts to overthrow the regime, but in 1979 and 1984 Albert René was the only candidate in the presidential elections. Under the new constitution approved in June 1993, President René was re-elected against two opponents with 59·5% of the vote.

TERRITORY AND POPULATION

The Seychelles consists of 115 islands in the Indian Ocean, north of Madagascar, with a combined area of 175 sq. miles (455 sq. km) in two distinct groups. The Granitic group of 32 islands cover 92 sq. miles (239 sq. km); the principal island is Mahé, with 59 sq. miles (153 sq. km) and 59,500 inhabitants at the 1987 census, the other inhabited islands of the group being Praslin, La Digue, Silhouette, Fregate and North, which together had 7,100 inhabitants.

The Outer or Coralline group comprises 83 islands spread over a wide area of ocean between the Mahé group and Madagascar, with a total land area of 83 sq. miles (214 sq. km) and a population of about 400. The main islands are the Amirante Isles (including Desroches, Poivre, Daros and Alphonse), Coetivy Island and Platte Island, all lying south of the Mahé group; the Farquhar, St Pierre and Providence Islands, north of Madagascar; and Aldabra, Astove, Assumption and the Cosmoledo Islands, about 1,000 km south-west of the Mahé group. Aldabra (whose lagoon covers 55 sq. miles), Farquhar and Desroches were transferred to the new British Indian Ocean Territory in 1965, but were returned by Britain to the Seychelles on the latter's independence in 1976. Population, 76,400 (1996); 54·4% urban (1995).

In 2000 the population is projected to be 80,000.

The official languages are Creole, English and French but 95% of the population speak Creole.

SOCIAL STATISTICS

(1996). Births, 1,611; deaths, 566; infant mortality, 9·3 per 1,000 births. 1996 rates per 1,000 population, birth, 21·1; death, 7·4. Annual growth rate, 1990–95, 1·6%. Life expectancy at birth in 1997 was estimated to be was 70 years (65 for males and 74 for females).

CLIMATE

Though close to the equator, the climate is tropical. The hot, wet season is from Dec. to May, when conditions are humid, but south-east trades bring cooler conditions from June to Nov. Temperatures are high throughout the year, but the islands lie outside the cyclone belt. Victoria, Jan. 80°F (26·7°C), July 78°F (25·6°C). Annual rainfall 95" (2,287 mm).

CONSTITUTION AND GOVERNMENT
Under the 1979 Constitution the Seychelles People's Progressive Front (SPPF) was the sole legal Party. There is a unicameral People's Assembly consisting of 33 seats, of which 22 are directly elected and 11 are allocated on a proportional basis, and an executive president directly elected for a 5-year term. A constitutional amendment of Dec. 1991 legalized other parties. A commission was elected in July 1992 to draft a new constitution. The electorate was some 50,000; turn-out was 90%. The SPPF gained 14 seats on the commission, the Democratic Party, 8; the latter, however, eventually withdrew. At a referendum in Nov. 1992 the new draft constitution failed to obtain the necessary 60% approval votes. The commission was reconvened in Jan. 1993. At a further referendum on 18 June 1993 the constitution was approved by 73·6% of votes cast.

National Anthem. 'Koste Seselwa' ('Seychellois, Unite').

RECENT ELECTIONS
Both presidential and parliamentary elections were held on 22 March 1998. In the presidential election France Albert René was re-elected for a 5th term, obtaining 66·7% of the votes, with his nearest rival, Wavel Ramkalawan of the United Opposition, polling 19·5%. In the parliamentary elections the ruling SPPF gained 30 seats (28 in 1993), the UO gained 3 (1 in 1993) and the Democratic party gained 1 (4 in 1993).

CURRENT ADMINISTRATION
President: France Albert René, b. 1935 (SPPF; president since 1977 and re-elected for a 5th term in 1998). The President is *Minister of Internal Affairs, Defence and Legal Affairs.*

    Vice-President: James Michel.

    The Government in March 1999 comprised:

    Minister of Administration: Noellie Alexander. *Agriculture and Marine Resources:* Ronny Jumeau. *Education:* Danny Faure. *Foreign Affairs, Planning and Environment:* Jeremie Bonnelame. *Health:* Jacqueline Dugasse. *Industry and International Business:* Joseph Belmont. *Land Use and Habitat:* Dolor Ernesta. *Local Government and Sports:* Sylvette Pool. *Youth and Culture:* Patrick Pillay. *Social Affairs and Manpower Development:* William Herminie. *Tourism and Civil Aviation:* Simone de Comarmond.

DEFENCE
The Defence Force comprises all services. Personnel (1996) Army, 200; Paramilitary, 250; Coast Guard, 200; Air Wing, 20; 1 infantry battalion and 2 artillery troops. The Coast Guard, based at Port Victoria, operates 4 fast inshore patrol craft, 1 tank landing craft and 1 Defender patrol craft.

    Defence expenditure totalled US$10m. in 1997 (US$141 per capita).

INTERNATIONAL RELATIONS
Seychelles is a member of the UN, Commonwealth and OAU and is an ACP member state of the ACP-EU relationship.

ECONOMY
Policy. A gradual move from socialism to a free market economy anticipates Seychelles becoming an international offshore financial centre.

Performance. Real GDP growth was 2·3% in 1995 having been 0·0% in 1994.

Budget. Budget in 1m. rupees, for calendar years:

	1991	1992	1993	1994	1995
Recurrent revenue	961·5	1,097·6	1,209·5	1,319·5	1,158·4
Recurrent expenditure	870·5	1,014·7	1,122·2	1,126·7	1,276·5

Currency. The unit of currency is the *Seychelles rupee* (SCR) divided into 100 *cents.* In Feb. 1998 foreign exchange reserves were US$37m. In Dec. 1997 total money supply was 649m. rupees.

Banking and Finance. Central Bank of Seychelles (the bank of issue), Development Bank of Seychelles, Seychelles Savings Bank and Seychelles International Mercantile Banking Co-operation have head offices and Barclays Bank, Banque Française Commerciale, Habib Bank and Bank of Baroda, have branches in Victoria and Mahé. Inflation in 1996 was 0·0%.

ENERGY AND NATURAL RESOURCES

Electricity. Installed capacity was 33,000 kW in 1995. Production in 1996 was 135·2m. kWh. Consumption per capita in 1994 was 1,726 kWh.

Agriculture. Coconuts are the main cash crop (production, 1995, 3,000 tonnes). Other main crops produced for export are cinnamon bark (1996, 318 tonnes) and copra (1995, 353 tonnes). Tea production, 1995, 226 tonnes (green leaf). Crops grown for local consumption include cassava, sweet potatoes, yams, sugar-cane, bananas and vegetables. The staple food crop, rice, is imported. Livestock, 1996: 18,000 pigs; 5,000 goats (1995); 2,000 cattle; 1m. chickens (1995).

Forestry. In 1995 forests covered 4,000 ha, or 8·9% of the total land area.

Fisheries. Seychelles is located in abundant tuna fishing grounds. Catch (1996) 4,508 tonnes.

INDUSTRY

Local industry is expanding, the largest development in recent years being the brewery (output, 1996, 6,365,000 litres of beer and stout and 7,852,000 litres of soft drinks). Other main activities include production of cigarettes (62m. in 1996), tuna canning (12,708 tonnes in 1996) and paints, dairy, processing of cinnamon and coconuts.

Labour. Some 70% of the workforce is employed in services, including tourism.

INTERNATIONAL TRADE

Imports and Exports. Total trade, in 1m. rupees, for calendar years:

	1991	1992	1993	1994	1995
Imports (less re-exports)	910·4	980·9	1,234·9	1,042·4	1,319·4
Domestic exports	87·6	93·2	78·8	114·3	113·7

Principal imports (1996): Manufactured goods, Rs 277·7m.; food, beverages and tobacco, Rs 330·7m.; petroleum products, Rs 143·6m., machinery and transport equipment, Rs 327·2m., mainly from UK (13·3%), Singapore (13·1%), South Africa (12·8%), USA (7·7%) and France (6·2%). Principal exports (1996): Fresh and frozen fish, Rs 11·0m.; canned tuna, Rs 170·0m.; frozen prawns, Rs 11·0m.; cinnamon bark, Rs 4·7m. Main export markets, 1995, China (15·0%), UK (12·4%), Thailand (11·5%) and India (3·5%).

COMMUNICATIONS

Roads. In 1996 there were 277 km of surfaced roads and 68 km of earth roads. There were 8,460 vehicles registered in 1996.

Civil Aviation. Seychelles International airport is on Mahé. In 1998 Air Seychelles flew on domestic routes and to Bombay, Dubai, Frankfurt, Johannesburg, London, Mauritius, Paris, Rome, Singapore and Zürich. Services were also provided in 1998 by Aeroflot, Air Austral, Air France, Air India, Air Madagascar, Air Mauritius, Alitalia, British Airways, Condor Flugdienst and Kenya Airways. In 1996 Seychelles International handled 552,156 passengers (291,498 on international flights) and 4,331 tonnes of freight.

Shipping. The main port is Victoria, which is also a tuna-fishing and fuel and services supply centre. In 1995 merchant shipping totalled 5,000 GRT. In 1994 vessels totalling 764,000 net registered tons entered. Sea freight (1996), 363,000 tonnes.

Telecommunications. Services operated by Cable & Wireless Ltd provide telegraphic communications with all parts of the world by satellite. Main telephone lines numbered 15,712 in 1996, or 206 per 1,000 population. In 1995 there were approximately 300 cellular phone subscribers and 600 fax machines.

Postal Services. In 1995 there were 5 post offices.

SOCIAL INSTITUTIONS

Justice. In 1996, 3,710 criminal and other offences were recorded by the police.

Religion. 92% of the inhabitants are Roman Catholic and 8% Anglican.

Education. Adult literacy was 84% in 1996. Education is free from 5 to 15 years in primary schools, 16 to 18 in secondary schools and 18 to 21 in polytechnics. In 1996 there were 9,588 pupils and 562 teachers in primary schools, 6,192 pupils and 412 teachers in secondary schools and 1,437 students and 145 teachers at polytechnic level.

In 1994 total expenditure on education came to 7·4% of GNP.

Health. In 1996 there were 84 doctors, 9 dentists, 346 nurses and 414 hospital beds. The health service is free.

CULTURE

Broadcasting. Broadcasting is under the auspices of the Seychelles Broadcasting Corporation, an independent body. There is a radio programme in English, French and Creole. There is also a religious station. TV colour is by PAL. In 1995 there were 40,000 radio and 10,000 TV sets.

Press. There is 1 daily and 2 weekly newspapers.

Tourism. Tourism is the main foreign exchange earner. Visitor numbers were 131,000 in 1996, with receipts totalling US$147m.

DIPLOMATIC REPRESENTATIVES

Of Seychelles in Great Britain (Box 4PE, 2nd Floor, Eros House, 111 Baker Street, London, W1M 1FE)
High Commissioner: Callixte D'Offay (resides in Paris).

Of Great Britain in Seychelles (Victoria Hse., 3rd Floor, PO Box 161, Victoria, Mahé)
High Commissioner: J. W. Yapp.

Of Seychelles in the USA (800 2nd Avenue, Suite 400C, New York, NY 10017)
Ambassador: Claude Sylvestre Anthony Morel.

Of the USA in Seychelles
Ambassador: Harold Geisel (resides in Comoros).

Of Seychelles to the United Nations
Ambassador: Claude Morel.

Of Seychelles to the European Union
Ambassador: Claude Morel.

FURTHER READING
Statistical Information: Information Office, 52 Kingsgate House, Victoria, Mahé.
Seychelles in Figures. Statistics Division, Mahé, 1989

Benedict, M. and Benedict, B., *Men, Women and Money in Seychelles.* Univ. of California Press, 1983
Bennett, G. and Bennett, P. R., *Seychelles.* [Bibliography] Oxford and Santa Barbara (CA), 1993
Franda, M., *The Seychelles: Unquiet Islands.* Boulder (CO), 1982
Lionnet, G., *The Seychelles.* Newton Abbot, 1972
Mancham, J. R., *Paradise Raped: Life, Love and Power in the Seychelles.* London, 1983

SIERRA LEONE

Republic of Sierra Leone

Capital: Freetown
Population estimate, 2000: 4·87m.
GNP per capita: (PPP$) 510
HDI/world rank: 0·185/174

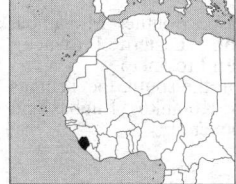

KEY HISTORICAL EVENTS

The Colony of Sierra Leone originated in 1787, when English settlers bought a piece of land intended as a home for natives of Africa who were waifs in London. The land was later used as a settlement for Africans rescued from slave-ships. The hinterland was declared a British protectorate on 21 Aug. 1896.

The first constitution was introduced in 1951 and this removed the political component from the privileged status of the Creoles of the colony by giving power to the majority. Sierra Leone became independent as a member state of the British Commonwealth on 27 April 1961. In a general election in March 1967, Dr Siaka Stevens' All People's Congress came to power and was installed despite a military coup to prevent his taking office. Sierra Leone became a republic on 19 April 1971, with Dr Siaka Stevens as executive president.

Following a referendum in June 1978, a new constitution was instituted under which the ruling All People's Congress became the sole legal party.

Stevens remained president until 1985 when he handed over to Maj.-Gen. Dr Joseph Saidu Momoh, the army C.-in-C., who was the only candidate in the presidential election that year and received 99% of the votes cast.

A military coup on 29 April 1992 deposed the president and set up a National Provisional Ruling Council. The chairman of this, Captain Valentine Strasser, was in turn deposed in a bloodless military coup on 16 Jan. 1996, and Gen. Julius Maada Bio assumed power. Presidential and parliamentary elections in Feb.–March 1996 resulted in a new government led by President Ahmed Tejan Kabbah. In May 1997 a group of junior officers led by Maj. Johnny Paul Koroma mounted a successful coup and ousted President Kabbah. The group, calling themselves the Armed Forces Ruling council (AFRC), in alliance with the Revolutionary United Front (RUF), a rebel gang that had terrorized the south-east of the country in the early 1990s, maintained the Kabbah had lost all credibility by encouraging tribalism and sectionalism. In Feb. 1998 a Nigerian-led intervention force launched an air and artillery offensive against the military junta. For the first time a group of African states were joining together to eject a regime and try to restore a democratically-elected president. On 10 March President Kabbah returned from exile in Guinea, promising a 'new beginning'. But in Jan. 1999, the country again erupted into civil war. On 6 Jan. the rebels entered Freetown setting fire to many buildings. Nigeria sent troops to support President Kabbah but having lost control of the diamond fields and with no other resources, the government was powerless. The war, which has been on and off for nearly 10 years, has reduced Sierra Leone to one of the poorest countries in the world.

"One of the war's worst aspects is that many of these locally recruited fighters, on both sides, are children. Some are "voluntary" recruits. Others are seduced by promises of wealth if they win, or are straightforwardly forced into service. To cut them off from their roots, they may be told to kill their parents or the local chieftain. Some are inducted into the secret societies common in Sierra Leone, many of which involve cannibalism. Outcast, illiterate and brainwashed, they become dependent solely on their guns." (*The Economist*, 9 Jan. 1999)

TERRITORY AND POPULATION

Sierra Leone is bounded on the north-west, north and north-east by Guinea, on the south-east by Liberia and on the south-west by the Atlantic Ocean. The area is 27,925 sq. miles (73,326 sq. km). Population (census 1985), 3,517,530, of whom about 2,000 were Europeans, 3,500 Asiatics and 30,000 non-native Africans. Estimate (1995), 4,509,000 (33·3% urban); density, 61·5 per sq. km.

The UN gives a projected population for 2000 of 4·87m.

The capital is Freetown, with 469,776 inhabitants in 1985.

Sierra Leone is divided into 4 provinces:

	Sq. km	Census 1985	Capital	Estimate 1988
Western Province	557	554,243	Freetown	469,776
Southern Province	19,694	740,510	Bo	26,000
Eastern Province	15,553	960,551	Kenema	13,000
Northern Province	35,936	1,262,226	Makeni	12,000

The provinces are divided into districts as follows: Bo, Bonthe, Moyamba, Pujehun (Southern Province); Kailahun, Kenema, Kono (Eastern Province); Bombali, Kambia, Koinaduga, Port Loko, Toukolili (Northern Province).

The principal peoples are the Mendes (34% of the total) in the south, the Temnes (31%) in the north and centre, the Konos, Fulanis, Bulloms, Korankos, Limbas and Kissis. English is the official language; a Creole (Krio) is spoken.

SOCIAL STATISTICS

Births, 1995, 201,000; deaths, 116,000. Rates (1995, per 1,000 population); Birth, 47·8; death, 27·7. Annual growth rate, 1990–95, 2·4%. Expectation of life at birth, 1990–95, was 32·9 years for males and 35·9 years for females. Only Rwanda had a lower life expectancy in the same period. Infant mortality was 195 per 1,000 live births in 1990–95, the second highest behind Liberia. Fertility rate, 1990–95, 6·5 births per woman.

CLIMATE

A tropical climate, with marked wet and dry seasons and high temperatures throughout the year. The rainy season lasts from about April to Nov., when humidity can be very high. Thunderstorms are common from April to June and in Sept. and Oct. Rainfall is particularly heavy at Freetown because of the effect of neighbouring relief. Freetown, Jan. 80°F (26·7°C), July 78°F (25·6°C). Annual rainfall 135" (3,434 mm).

CONSTITUTION AND GOVERNMENT

In a referendum in Sept. 1991 some 60% of the 2·5m. electorate voted for the introduction of a new constitution instituting multi-party democracy. There is a 68-member *National Assembly.*

There is a *Supreme Council of State (SCS)*, and a *Council of State Secretaries.*

National Anthem. 'High We Exalt Thee, Realm of the Free'; words by C. Nelson Fyle, tune by J. J. Akar.

RECENT ELECTIONS

Presidential and National Assembly elections were held on 26–27 Feb. 1996. 13 parties stood. Turn-out was 60%. Ahmed Tejan Kabbah gained 35·8% of votes cast for the presidency in a first round. There was a qualifying threshold of 55% of votes for outright election in this round. At the second round on 17 March 1996 Kabbah was elected by 59·49% of votes cast against 1 opponent.

At the National Assembly elections the Sierra Leone People's Party (SLPP) won 36·1% of votes cast, the United People's Party 21·6% and the People's Democratic Party 15·3%.

CURRENT ADMINISTRATION

President and Minister of Defence: Ahmed Tejan Kabbah (b. 1931; SLPP; elected 17 March 1996).

Vice-President: Albert Joe Demby.

In March 1999 the government comprised:

Minister of Agriculture, Forestry and Environment: Dr Harry Will. *Education, Youth and Sports:* Dr Alpha Wurie. *Energy and Works:* Thaimu Bangura. *Finance and Economic Planning:* Dr James Jonah. *Fisheries and Marine Resources:* Lawrence Kamara. *Foreign Affairs and International Co-operation:* Dr Sama Banya. *Health and Sanitation:* Sulaiman Tejan-Jalloh. *Information, Communication, Tourism and Culture:* Dr Julius Spencer. *Internal Affairs and Local Administration:* Charles Margai. *Justice and Attorney General:* Solomon Berewa. *Lands, Housing and Country Planning:* Hafsatu Kabba. *Mineral Resources:* Mohammed Deen;

SIERRA LEONE

Political and Parliamentary Affairs: Abu Aya Koroma. *Social Welfare, Gender and Children's Affairs:* Shirley Gbujama. *Trade, Industry and Transportation:* Allie Bangura.

Local Government. The provinces are administered through the Ministry of Internal Affairs and divided into 148 Chiefdoms, each under the control of a Paramount Chief and Council of Elders known as the Tribal Authorities, who are responsible for the maintenance of law and order and for the administration of justice (except for serious crimes). All of these Chiefdoms have been organized into local government units, empowered to raise and disburse funds for the development of the Chiefdom concerned.

DEFENCE
In 1997 military expenditure totalled US$52m. (US$10 per capita).

Army. Following the civil war, the army has disbanded and a new National Army is expected to form with a strength of some 5,000.

INTERNATIONAL RELATIONS
Sierra Leone is a member of the UN, OAU, ECOWAS and the Commonwealth and is an ACP member state of the ACP-EU relationship.

ECONOMY
Performance. GNP per capita was US$200 in 1996 compared to US$390 in 1982. Real GDP growth was −2·8% in 1995 (2·6% in 1994).

Budget. The fiscal year is from 1 July to 30 June. Revenue and expenditures in 1m. leones:

	1993-94	1994-95	1995-96	1996-97
Revenue	67,414	61,743	69,713	85,498
Expenditure	104,654	107,312	128,167	143,293

Currency. The unit of currency is the *leone* (SLL) of 100 *cents*. Foreign exchange reserves were US$27m. in Dec. 1998. Inflation was running at 23·1% in 1996. Exchange controls were liberalized in 1993. Total money supply in March 1997 was 56,989m. leones.

Banking and Finance. The bank of issue is the Bank of Sierra Leone (established 1964). There are 4 commercial banks (2 foreign).

Weights and Measures. The metric system is in use.

ENERGY AND NATURAL RESOURCES
Electricity. Installed capacity was 126 MW in 1991. Production in 1994 was 237m. kWh; consumption per capita in 1994 was 54 kWh.

Minerals. The chief minerals mined are gold (12,900 troy oz, 1994), diamonds (197,000 metric carats), bauxite (729,000 tonnes), and rutile (144,000 tonnes). The presence of rich diamond deposits partly explains the close interest of neighbouring countries in the politics of Sierra Leone.

Agriculture. Agriculture contributed 44% of GDP in 1996, and engaged nearly 67% of the workforce in 1995, mainly in small-scale peasant production. Cattle production is important in the north. Production (1995, in 1,000 tonnes): Rice, 284; cassava, 219; palm oil, 45·2; palm kernels, 29·2; coffee, 25; cocoa, 10.

Livestock (1995): Cattle, 360,000; goats, 166,000; sheep, 302,000; pigs, 50,000; chickens, 6m.

Forestry. In 1995 forests covered 1,309,000 ha, or 18·3% of the total land area (down from 1,522,000 ha in 1990). Timber production in 1995 was 3·33m. cu. metres.

Fisheries. In 1995, 62,313 tonnes of fish were caught (47,313 tonnes from marine waters).

INDUSTRY
Manufacturing contributed 6% of GDP in 1990. There are palm-oil and rice mills; sawn timber, joinery products and furniture are produced.

Labour. The workforce was 1,610,000 in 1996 (64% males). In 1995 around two-thirds of the economically active population were engaged in agriculture, fisheries and forestry. 14,800 persons were registered unemployed in 1992.

INTERNATIONAL TRADE
Foreign debt was US$1,167m. in 1996.

Imports and Exports. Total trade for 1996: Imports, US$212m.; exports, US$47m.
Main exports are bauxite, diamonds, gold, coffee and cocoa.
The main import suppliers in 1994-95 were USA (42·7%), Netherlands (14·2%), UK (5·7%) and Indonesia (3·7%). Principal export markets in 1994-95 were USA (44·8%), UK (17·3%), Belgium (16·8%) and Netherlands (4·1%).

COMMUNICATIONS

Roads. There were 11,700 km of roads in 1996, of which 1,290 km were surfaced. In 1995 there were 20,860 passenger cars and 11,014 commercial vehicles.

Civil Aviation. Freetown Airport (Lungi) is the international airport. In 1998 Sierra National Airlines flew to Accra and Lagos, and other services were provided by Air Dabia, Ghana Airways and Mahfooz Aviation. In 1995 scheduled airline traffic of Sierra Leone-based carriers flew 0·2m. km, carrying 15,000 passengers (all on international flights).

Shipping. The port of Freetown has a very large natural harbour. Iron ore is exported through Pepel, and there are small ports at Bonthe and Sulima. In 1995 the merchant fleet totalled 15,100 GRT, including oil tankers, 1,835 GRT. 1·8m. tonnes of cargo were loaded in 1990 and 0·53m. tonnes discharged.

Telecommunications. Telephone provision in 1997 was 17,400 main lines (3·9 per 1,000 population). There were around 100 fax machines in 1995 and 50 Internet users in Jan. 1998.

Postal Services. In 1995 there were 54 post offices.

SOCIAL INSTITUTIONS

Justice. The High Court has jurisdiction in civil and criminal matters. Subordinate courts are held by magistrates in the various districts. Native Courts, headed by court Chairmen, apply native law and custom under a criminal and civil jurisdiction. Appeals from the decisions of magistrates' courts are heard by the High Court. Appeals from the decisions of the High Court are heard by the Sierra Leone Court of Appeal. Appeal lies from the Sierra Leone Court of Appeal to the Supreme Court which is the highest court.
The death penalty is in force, and 24 soldiers were executed on 19 Oct. 1998 for their part in the May 1997 coup.

Religion. There were 1·72m. Moslems in 1992. Traditional animist beliefs persist.

Education. The adult literacy rate in 1995 was 31·4% (45·4% among males and 18·2% among females). Primary education is partially free but not compulsory. In 1990–91 there were 2,072 primary schools with 414,200 pupils and 14,972 teachers, 227 secondary schools with 116,648 pupils and 5,610 teachers, 19 vocational training colleges with 4,530 students and 326 staff, and 6 teacher training schools. There were 5 institutes of higher education with 4,742 students and 600 teachers. Fourah Bay College and Njala University College are the 2 constituent colleges of the University of Sierra Leone. They had 2,571 students and 257 academic staff in 1990–91.

Health. In 1992 there were 404 doctors, and in 1998, 4,025 hospital beds. In the period 1990–96 only 34% of the population had access to safe drinking water.

CULTURE

Broadcasting. Broadcasting is under the auspices of the government-controlled Sierra Leone Broadcasting Service and Sierra Leone Television, which is part commercial. In 1995 there were 1,050,000 radio and 49,000 TV sets (colour by PAL).

Press. In 1995 there was one daily newspaper with a circulation of 20,000.

Tourism. In 1996 there were 46,000 foreign tourists, bringing revenue of US$10m.

DIPLOMATIC REPRESENTATIVES
Of Sierra Leone in Great Britain (33 Portland Pl., London, W1N 3AG)
High Commissioner: Prof. Cyril Patrick Foray.

Of Great Britain in Sierra Leone (Spur Rd., Freetown)
High Commissioner: Peter A. Penfold, CMG, OBE.

Of Sierra Leone in the USA (1701 19th St., NW, Washington, D.C., 20009)
Ambassador: John E. Leigh.

Of the USA in Sierra Leone (Corner Walpole and Siaka Stevens St., Freetown)
Ambassador: John L. Hirsch.

Of Sierra Leone to the United Nations
Ambassador: Vacant.

Of Sierra Leone to the European Union
Ambassador: Peter J. Kuyembeh.

FURTHER READING
Binns, M. and Binns, T., *Sierra Leone* [Bibliography]. Oxford and Santa Barbara (CA), 1992
Fyfe, C., *A History of Sierra Leone*. OUP, 1962

SINGAPORE

Republic of Singapore

Population estimate, 2000: 3·95m.
GNP per capita: (PPP$) 26,910
HDI/world rank: 0·896/28

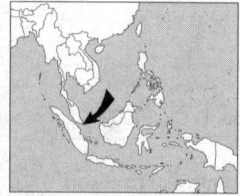

KEY HISTORICAL EVENTS

Singapore Island became part of the Javanese Majapahit Empire in the 14th century. The Portuguese established hegemony in the area in the 16th century, followed by the Dutch a hundred years later. In 1819 Sir Thomas Stamford Raffles, the British East India Administrator, established a trading settlement there. The original lease of the site of a factory to the British East India Company by the Sultan of Johore was followed by the treaty of 2 Aug. 1824 ceding the entire island in perpetuity to the company. In 1826 Penang, Malacca and Singapore were combined as the Straits Settlements in an Indian presidency. On 1 April 1867 the settlements were transferred from the control of the Indian government to that of the British Secretary of State for the Colonies. With the opening of the Suez Canal in 1869 and the advent of the steamship, an era of prosperity began for Singapore. Growth continued with the export of tin and rubber from the Malay peninsula.

Thought to be impregnable by land, Singapore fell to the Japanese in 1942 whose occupation continued until the end of the Second World War. In 1945 Singapore became a Crown Colony, being separated from Penang and Malacca. In June 1959 the state was granted complete internal self-government. When the Federation of Malaysia was formed in Sept. 1963, Singapore became one of the 14 states of the newly created country.

On 7 Aug. 1965, by agreement with the Malaysian government, Singapore left the Federation of Malaysia and became an independent sovereign state. The name of the state was changed to 'Republic of Singapore' with a president as its head. Singapore and Malaysia agreed to enter into a treaty for external defence and mutual assistance. The British military presence was withdrawn from Singapore in 1971. Continuing economic prosperity has made Singapore a powerful influence in ASEAN.

TERRITORY AND POPULATION

The Republic of Singapore consists of Singapore Island and some 63 smaller islands. Singapore Island is situated off the southern extremity of the Malay peninsula, to which it is joined by a 1·1 km causeway carrying a road, railway and water pipeline across the Strait of Johor and by a 1·9 km bridge at Tuas, opened on 2 Jan. 1998. The Straits of Johore between the island and the mainland are 914 metres wide. The island is 647·8 sq. km in area, including the offshore islands.

Census of population (1990): 2,089,400 Chinese, 380,600 Malays, 191,000 Indians and 29,200 others; total 2,690,200. In June 1997 Chinese residents numbered 2,394,200 (77·2%), Malays 437,900 (14·1%), Indians 230,600 (7·4%) and others 40,800 (1·3%); total 3,103,500. 1997 estimate, 3,736,700; density, 5,768 per sq. km.

The projected population for 2000 is 3·95m.

Malay, Chinese (Mandarin), Tamil and English are the official languages; Malay is the national language and English is the language of administration.

SOCIAL STATISTICS

1995 births, 57,000; deaths, 17,000. Birth rate per 1,000 population, 1995, 17·0; death rate, 5·0. Resident growth rate, 1·9%; infant mortality, 1997, 3·3 per 1,000 live births; life expectancy, 1997, 75·0 years for males and 79·2 years for females. Fertility rate, 1990–95, 1·8 births per woman.

CLIMATE

The climate is equatorial, with relatively uniform temperature, abundant rainfall and high humidity. Rain falls throughout the year but tends to be heaviest from Nov. to Jan. Average daily temperature in 1997 was a maximum of 32·4°C and a minimum of 25·3°C. Total rainfall in 1997 was 1,119 mm.

SINGAPORE

CONSTITUTION AND GOVERNMENT

Singapore is a republic with a parliamentary system of government. The organs of state—the executive, the legislature and the judiciary—are provided for by a written constitution. The Constitution is the supreme law of Singapore and any law enacted after the date of its commencement, which is inconsistent with its provisions, is automatically void.

The Head of State is the President. The administration of the Government is vested in the Cabinet headed by the Prime Minister. The Prime Minister and the other Cabinet Members are appointed by the President from among the Members of Parliament (MPs). The Cabinet is collectively responsible to Parliament.

Parliament is unicameral consisting of 83 elected members, elected by secret ballot from single-member and group representation constituencies. With the customary exception of those serving criminal sentences, all citizens over 21 are eligible to vote. Voting in an election is compulsory. Group representation constituencies may return up to 6 Members of Parliament (4 before 1996), one of whom must be from the Malay community, the Indian or other minority communities. To ensure representation of parties not in the government, provision is made for the appointment of 3 (or up to a maximum of 6) Non-Constituency Members of Parliament (NCMPs). The number of NCMPs is reduced by one for each opposition candidate returned.

A Presidential Council to consider and report on minorities' rights was established in 1970. The particular function of this council is to draw attention to any Bill or to any subsidiary legislation which, in its opinion, discriminates against any racial or religious community.

National Anthem. 'Majulah Singapura' ('Onward Singapore'); words and tune by Zubir Said.

RECENT ELECTIONS

At the elections of 2 Jan. 1997 opposition parties contested only 36 seats. The People's Action Party (PAP) won 81 seats with 65% of votes cast (77 and 61% in 1991); the Singapore People's Party gained 1 seat and the Workers' Party 1 seat. As 2 members from opposition parties were returned, a further non-constituency seat was awarded to the Workers' Party.

At the presidential elections of 28 Aug. 1993 there were 2 PAP candidates. Ong Teng Cheong was elected by 58·7% of votes cast.

CURRENT ADMINISTRATION

President: Ong Teng Cheong (sworn in 1 Sept. 1993).

In March 1999 the Cabinet comprised as follows:

Prime Minister: Goh Chok Tong (b. 1941; PAP).

Senior Minister, Prime Minister's Office: Lee Kuan Yew, GCMG, CH. *Deputy Prime Ministers:* Lee Hsien Loong; Dr Tony Tan Keng Yam (*Minister of Defence*). *Health and Environment:* Yeo Cheow Tong. *Finance:* Dr Richard Hu Tsu Tau. *Education:* Teo Chee Hean. *Law and Foreign Affairs:* Prof. Shunmugam Jayakumar. *Labour:* Dr Lee Boon Yang. *Home Affairs:* Wong Kan Seng. *Information and the Arts:* George Yeo Yong-Boon. *Community Development and Moslem Affairs:* Abdullah Tarmugi. *Communications:* Mah Bow Tan. *National Development:* Lim Hng Kiang. *Trade and Industry:* Lee Yock Suan.

DEFENCE

The Ministry of Defence is organized into the Defence Administration Group, which oversees the manpower, financial and administrative aspects of defence, the Defence Technology Group, which provides the material, technology and infrastructural support for the Singapore Armed Forces (SAF), and the Defence Policy Group, which is responsible for formulating and coordinating defence relations, information and security policies. Compulsory military service in peace-time for all male citizens and permanent residents was introduced in 1967. The period of service for officers and non-commissioned officers is 30 months, other ranks 24 months. Reserve liability continues to age 40 for other ranks, 50 for officers. Today the SAF comprises 250,000 NSmen and 50,000 regulars and full-time National Servicemen.

An agreement with the USA in Nov. 1990 provided for an increase in US use of naval and air force facilities.

Singapore is a member of the Five Powers Defence Arrangement, with Australia, New Zealand, Malaysia and the UK.

In 1997 defence expenditure totalled US$4,122m. (US$1,360 per capita), representing 4·3% of GDP.

Army. The Army consists of 3 Combined Arms Divisions, 2 People's Defence Force (PDF) Commands and some other non-divisional units. Strength (1997) 55,000 (including 35,000 conscripts) and 250,000 reserves.

The Combined Arms Divisions are 3rd, 6th and 9th Divisions. Each Division consists of units such as the Infantry/Mechanised Brigades, the Division Reconnaisance Battalion, the 155-mm Gun Howitzer Battalions, the Field Artillery Target Acquisition Battery, the Division Field Engineer Battalion, the Division Signals Battalion, the Air Defence Artillery Battalion and the Division Support Command.

The non-divisional units include the People's Defence Force (comprising 1st PDF and 2nd PDF), an Armour Brigade, the 155-mm Gun Howitzer Battalions, the 105-mm Light Gun Battalions, the 160-mm Mortar Battalions, Combat Engineer units, the Signals Battalion and the Commando Battalions.

Navy. The Republic of Singapore Navy comprises 4 commands: Fleet, Coastal Command (COSCOM), Naval Logistics Command and Training Command. The Fleet comprises the 1st and 3rd Flotillas. The 1st Flotilla comprises 3 squadrons of Missile Corvettes, Missile Gun Boats and Anti-submarine capable Patrol Vessels. The 3rd Flotilla comprises 3 squadrons of Landing Ship Tank, fast craft and civil resource vessels. COSCOM maintains security in the Singapore Straits through Patrol Vessels and Mine Counter-Measure Vessels. The Navy also acquired 4 second-hand Sjöormen-class submarines for training as well as 4 new vessels to replace the existing fleet of County-class Landing Ship Tanks (LSTs). The Republic of Singapore Navy has approximately 4,500 officers, specialists and ratings and there are 2 naval bases: Brani Naval Base and Tuas Naval Base. A new naval base is being built at Changi to replace the one at Brani which has to make way for port expansion.

The Marine Police operates 4 inshore patrol craft and some 80 patrol boats, some armed.

Air Force. The Republic of Singapore Air Force (RSAF) has fighter squadrons comprising the F16 Falcon and the F5E Tiger. It also has a multi-layered air defence system consisting of surface-to-air missiles such as the Improved Hawk, Rapier, Mistral and RBS–70 and anti-aircraft guns. It also employs the sophisticated E2C Hawkeye for airborne early warning.

For tactical and maritime air operations, the RSAF has the A4 squadrons comprising the A4SU Super Skyhawk. In addition, it operates the C130 and Fokker 50 for tactical and utility transport. The Fokker 50s are also used for maritime air surveillance. The RSAF has a fleet of helicopters comprising the Super Puma, UH1H, Fennec and the CH–47D Chinook.

Recent acquisitions by RSAF include the Portable Search and Target Acquisition Radar (P–STAR) system and the IGLA short range surface-to-air defence missile system to complement the Short Range Air Defence (SHORAD) system. The air force also purchased a squadron of 18 F–16C/D Fighting Falcons. 4 refurbished KC–135 air-to-air refuelling aircraft were procured to support overseas training and F–16 C/Ds on training and exercises overseas. The RSAF F–5 fighters are being upgraded and will be fitted with a new radar and avionics.

Personnel strength (1997) about 6,000 (3,000 conscripts), with 155 combat aircraft and 20 armed helicopters.

INTERNATIONAL RELATIONS

Singapore is a member of the UN, the Commonwealth, the Colombo Plan, and ASEAN and has ratified the Convention on the Prohibition of the Development, Production, Stockpiling and Use of Chemical Weapons and on their Destruction (CWC), and the UN Framework Convention on Climate Change (UNFCCC).

ECONOMY

After slowing in 1996 on the back of the Asian Economic downturn, the Singapore economy grew by 7·8% in 1997.

Policy. The central objective is to build up a strong science and technology base to support high-tech industries and to innovate new products and processes. The Government recognizes the need for Singapore to be early adopters of information technology (IT) and innovators of IT applications for the economy to remain competitive.

The Economic Development Board (EDB) is the lead government agency responsible for the formulation and implementation of economic and industrial development strategies. Its purpose is to develop Singapore into a global city with total business capabilities by attracting foreign investments and developing local enterprise as well as promoting outward investments into the region.

Performance. Real GDP growth was 7·8% in 1997 and 6·9% in 1996, but was forecast to be –1% in 1998. Singapore was top of the World Economic Forum's Global Competitiveness Report, which assesses countries on their potential for economic growth and their income levels, in both 1997 and 1998.

Budget. The fiscal year begins on 1 April. Budgetary central government revenue and expenditure for financial years (in S$1m.):

	1994	1995	1996	1997
Revenue	23,280·3	24,781·6	28,038·3	30,612·7
Expenditure	14,118·1	15,555·0	19,174·3	25,864·9

Currency. The unit of currency is the *Singapore dollar* (SGD) of 100 *cents*. Gross circulation at Dec. 1997 was S$11,732·7m. Inflation was 2% in 1997. Total foreign reserves at Dec. 1997 were S$119,616·8m.

Banking and Finance. The Monetary Authority of Singapore performs the functions of a central bank, except the issuing of currency which is the responsibility of the Board of the Commissioners of Currency.

The Development Bank of Singapore and the Post Office savings Bank were merged in 1998 to become the largest bank in South-East Asia and one of the leading banks in Asia, with a customer base of more that 3·3m. and a total deposit base of about S$71bn. Together, their total asset value is approximately S$99bn.

At the end of 1997, there were 149 commercial banks in Singapore, of which 12 were local. The total assets/liabilities amounted to S$289,722·3m. in 1997. Total deposits of non-bank customers amounted to S$124,134·8m. and advances including bills financing, totalled S$143,243·8m. in 1997. There were 81 merchant banks as at 31 Dec. 1997.

There is a stock exchange.

Weights and Measures. The metric system is in use.

ENERGY AND NATURAL RESOURCES

Electricity. In 1995 Singapore Power Pte. Ltd. took over from the Public Utilities Board the responsibility for the provision of electricity and gas. Electrical power is generated by 4 oil-fired power stations, with a total generating capacity of more than 5,641 MW. Production (1997) 26,188·1m. kWh. Consumption per capita (1995) 7,002 kWh.

Oil and Gas. Replacing the Kallang Gasworks, the Senoko Gasworks started operations in Oct. 1996. It had a total gas production capacity of 1·6m. cu. metres per day.

Water. Singapore uses an average of 1·21m. cu. metres of water per day. Singapore's water supply comes from local sources and sources in Johor, Malaysia. The total water supply system comprises 19 raw water reservoirs, 9 treatment works, 14 storage or service reservoirs and 4,760 km of pipelines.

Agriculture. Only about 1·43% of the total area is used for farming. Local farms provide only 31·8% of hen eggs, 1·6% of chickens and 2·4% of ducks. 16,281 tonnes of vegetables were produced for domestic consumption in 1997. In 1997 alone,

Singapore imported 44m. chickens, 7·5m. ducks, 719m. hen eggs, 112,000 tonnes of meat and meat products, 254,000 tonnes of fish and fish products, 363,000 tonnes of vegetables and 376,000 tonnes of fruits for local consumption.

Agro-technology parks house large-scale intensive farms to improve production of fresh food. As of the end of 1997, a total of 1,465 ha of land in Murai, Sungei Tengah, Nee Soon, Loyang, Mandai and Lim Chu Kang have been developed into Agro-technology Parks. Through open tenders, auctions and direct allocations, 273 farms have been allocated land for the production of livestock, eggs, milk, aquarium fish, food fish (fish for consumption), fruits, vegetables, orchids and ornamental and aquatic plants, as well as for the breeding of birds and dogs. In 1997, the local farms produced some S$221m. worth of primary produce. When the Agro-technology Parks are fully developed, their output is expected to reach S$450m.

Forestry. In 1995 forests covered 4,000 ha, or 6·6% of the total land area. Timber production was 120,000 cu. metres in 1995.

Fisheries. The total local supply of fish in 1997 was 13,049 tonnes. Singapore imported 254,000 tonnes of fish and fish products.

The Punggol Fishing Port was closed in Aug. 1997 to make way for public housing development. To provide a home base for the local fishing fleet, the Primary Production Department built a new fishing port at Senoko. The new Senoko Fishing Port has an area of 3·24 ha and is equipped with a wholesale market for the auctioning of fresh fish, a 180-metre long jetty, a water batching system and office units for the fish merchants.

INDUSTRY

The largest industrial area is at Jurong, with 35 modern industrial estates housing over 6,500 companies in 1996, and 333,099 workers in 1994.

Production, 1997 (in S$1m.), totalled 125,536·6, including electronic products, machinery and appliances, 66,521·2; petroleum, 14,502·5; chemicals and chemical products, 9,197·5; transport equipment, 5,025·9; fabricated metal products, 6,323·0; food, beverages and tobacco, 3,475·9; paper products and printing, 3,764·9.

Labour. In June 1997, Singapore's labour force comprised 1,876,000 people, of whom 45,5000 were unemployed. The majority were employed in manufacturing, 414,100; commerce, 398,200; financial and business services, 273,500; transport and communications, 210,000; construction, 126,100.

Legislation regulates the principal terms and conditions of employment such as hours of work, sick leave and other fringe benefits. Youths of 14–16 years may work in industrial establishments, and children of 12–14 years may be employed in approved apprenticeship schemes. A trade dispute may be referred to the Industrial Arbitration Court.

The Ministry of Manpower operates an employment service and provides the handicapped with specialized on-the-job training. The Central Provident Fund was established in 1955 to make provision for employees in their old age. At the end of 1995 there were 2,683,525 members with S$66,035·4m. standing to their credit in the fund.

Trade Unions. In 1997, there were 82 registered employee trade unions, 3 employer unions and 1 federation of trade unions—the Nation Trades Union Congress (NTUC). The total membership of the trade unions increased from 256,357 in 1996 to 261,652 in 1997. The vast majority (98·6%) of the total union membership belonged to the 74 NTUC-affiliated unions.

INTERNATIONAL TRADE

Foreign investment in up to 40% of the equity of domestic banks is permitted. Net foreign investment commitments in the manufacturing sector totalled S$5,908·1m. in 1997 (S$5,716·2m. in 1996). Total external trade in 1997 was S$382,217·7m.

In Jan. 1998 Singapore's Trade Development Board projected that trade growth in 1998 would be between 3·5% and 5·5% but warned there could be a revision because of 'volatility of development in the region'. The Board said Singapore's full-year, non-oil domestic exports increased 5·3% to S$91·6bn. in 1997, with growth already slowed by the regional economic turmoil.

Imports and Exports. Imports and exports (in S$1m.), by country, 1997:

	Imports (c.i.f.)	Exports (f.o.b.)
Australia	2,668	4,328
China	8,447	6,038
France	5,431	3,648
Germany	6,723	5,278
Hong Kong	5,780	17,848
Italy	2,903	771
Japan	34,564	13,125
Korea (South)	6,056	5,483
Malaysia	29,548	32,405
Saudi Arabia	7,974	555
Taiwan	8,208	8,367
Thailand	10,080	8,532
UK	5,513	6,190
USA	33,017	34,117

The major export markets for 1997 were USA (18·4%), Malaysia (17·5%), Europe (15·4%), Hong Kong (9·6%) and Japan (7·1%). Total imports increased to S$196,605·2m. in 1997 from S$185,183·4m. in 1996. Exports increased to S$185,612·5m. in 1997 from S$176,271·9m. in 1996.

Exports (1997, in S$1m.): Machinery and transport equipment, 122,474 (of which electrical machinery, 56,008; transport equipment, 3,874; non-electrical machinery, 62,592); mineral fuels, 16,219; raw materials, 1,797 (including rubber, 568); chemicals, 11,136; food, beverages and tobacco, 5,986; clothing, 2,215; animal and vegetable oils, 509; textiles, 1,844; scientific and optical instruments, 4,165; metal goods, 1,982; iron and steel, 1,230.

Imports (1997, in S$1m.): Machinery and transport equipment, 113,163 (of which electrical machinery, 55,975; transport equipment, 11,652; non-electrical machinery, 45,536); mineral fuels, 18,635; food, beverages and tobacco, 7,864; chemicals, 11,268; crude materials, 1,787 (of which rubber, 455); textiles, 2,556; iron and steel, 4,254; animal and vegetable oils, 514; metal goods, 3,549; scientific and optical instruments, 6,461; non-metal mineral goods, 3,025; paper, paperboard and related articles, 1,376.

Trade Fairs. Singapore ranks as the world's 7th major convention city by the Union des Associations Internationales (UAI). In 1997, 18 out of 46 Asia Pacific events recognized by Union des Foires Internationales (UFI) were held in Singapore. These Exhibitions included Asia Telecom '97, ASEANPLAS, MDEX Asia '97, COMDEX Asia '97 and Global Franchising and Hospimedica, featuring medical equipment and supplies.

COMMUNICATIONS

Roads. There were (1997) 3,101 km of public roads, of which 3,017 km are asphalt-paved. In 1997 motor vehicles numbered 638,204, of which 379,497 were private cars, 11,240 buses, 132,629 motor cycles and scooters, 16,933 taxis and 142,905 goods and other vehicles.

Rail. A 25·8-km main line runs through Singapore, connecting with the States of Malaysia and as far as Bangkok. Branch lines serve the port of Singapore and the industrial estates at Jurong. The Mass Rapid Transit metro extended to 83 km in 1997.

Civil Aviation. In 1997 the SIA Group (Singapore Airlines and Silk Air Services) (54% state-owned) flew to 98 destinations in 46 countries. 68 international airlines operated more than 3,300 scheduled flights a week, totalling 172,672 commercial aircraft movements at Singapore International Airport in Changi ('Airtropolis') in 1997, from which routes were flown to 133 destinations in 53 countries. In 1998 services were provided by Aeroflot, Air China, Air France, Air India, Air Lanka, Air Mauritius, Air New Zealand, Air Niugini, Air Seychelles, Alitalia, All Nippon Airways, American Airlines, Asiana, Austrian Airlines, Biman Bangladesh Airlines, Bouraq Indonesia, British Airways, Cathay Pacific Airways, China Airlines, China Eastern Airlines, China Southern Airlines, China Southwest, China Yunnan Airlines,

Delta Air Lines, Egyptair, Emirates, EVA Airways, Finnair, Garuda Indonesia, Gulf Air, Indian Airlines, JAL, KLM, Korean Air, Kuwait Airways, Lufthansa, Malaysia Airlines, Middle East Airlines, Myanma Airways International, Northwest Airlines, Pakistan International Airlines, Philippine Airlines, Qantas Airways, Royal Air Cambodge, Royal Brunei Airlines, Royal Nepal Airlines, SAS, Saudia, Silk Air, Swissair, Thai Airways International, Turkish Airlines, United Airlines, Vietnam Airlines and Yunnan Airlines. In 1997, 25,174,344 passengers and 1,336,348 tonnes of freight were handled.

Shipping. Singapore is a large container port. The economy is dependent on shipping and entrepôt trade. An estimated total of 130,333 vessels of 808,305,000 gross tonnes (GT) entered Singapore during 1997. In 1997, 3,380 vessels with a total of 20,774,000 GT were registered in Singapore. The fleet ranks 10th among the principle merchant fleets of the world. In 1995, 202 vessels (31·88% of total tonnage) were registered under foreign flags. Total cargo was 327,507,000 tonnes, and total container throughput was 14,136,000 twenty-foot equivalent units (TEUs).

Telecommunications. In 1997, there were 1,656,000 telephone subscribers, 743,000 cellular phone subscribers, 1,073,000 pager subscribers and 267,000 dial-up Internet subscribers. In 1997 Singapore Telecom, one of the largest companies in Asia, lost its monopoly with the entry of a new cellular phone operator and 3 new paging operators. Singapore has 2 cellular mobile phone operators, 3 Internet service providers, and 4 paging operators. The Telecommunication Authority of Singapore (TAS), is the national regulator and promoter of the telecommunication and postal industries.

Postal Services. In 1997, there were 1,575 postal outlets in operation, comprising 64 main branches, 83 smaller branches, 1,283 stamp vendors, 48 postage label vending machines, 17 self-service Postal Automated Machines and 80 Overseas Chinese Banking Corporation (OCBC) Automated Teller Machines dispensing postage stamps. 1,453,700,000 postal articles were handled in 1997.

SOCIAL INSTITUTIONS

Justice. There is a Supreme Court in Singapore which consists of the High Court and the Court of Appeal. The Supreme Court is composed of a Chief Justice and 13 Judges. The High Court has unlimited original jurisdiction in both civil and criminal cases. The Court of Appeal is the final appellate court. It hears appeals from any judgement or order of the High Court in any civil matter. The Subordinate Courts consist of 30 district courts, 7 magistrates' courts, 1 juvenile and 1 coroner's court and a small claims tribunal. The right of appeal to the UK Privy Council was abolished in 1994.

Penalties for drug trafficking and abuse are severe, including a mandatory death penalty. In 1994 there were 76 executions, and since then there have been approximately 40 a year.

Religion. In 1995, 53·9% of the population aged 10 years and above were Buddhists and Taoists, 12·9% Christians, 14·9% Muslims and 3·3% Hindus.

Education. The general literacy rate rose from 84% in 1980 to 92·8% in 1997. Kindergartens are private and fee-paying. Compulsory primary state education starts at 6 years and culminates at 11 or 12 years with an examination which influences choice of secondary schooling. There are 18 autonomous and 8 private fee-paying secondary schools. Tertiary education at 16 years is divided into 3 branches: Junior colleges leading to university; 4 polytechnics with 53,553 students at 30 June 1997; and 10 technical institutes with 9,906 students in 1997.

Statistics of schools in Dec. 1997:

	Schools	Pupils	Teachers
Primary schools	196	280,108	11,189
Secondary schools	147	187,415	9,049
Junior colleges and Centralised institutes	18	22,419	1,624

There are 2 universities: the National University of Singapore (established 1905) with 24,012 students in 1997–98, and the Nanyang Technological University (established 1991) with 16,280 in 1997–98.

In 1994 total expenditure on education came to 3·3% of GNP and represented 24·2% of total government expenditure.

Health. There were 23 hospitals (2 government, 8 government-structured and 13 private) with 11,030 beds in 1997. There were 4,912 doctors, 877 dentists and 14,075 registered nurses and midwives.

Welfare. The Central Provident Fund (CPF) was set up in 1955 to provide financial security for workers upon retirement or when they are no longer able to work. In 1997 there were 2,782,000 members with S$79,657·4m. standing to their credit in the Fund.

CULTURE
The National Arts Council (NAC) was established in 1991 to spearhead the development of the arts.

Broadcasting. The Television Corporation of Singapore broadcasts mainly English and Chinese programmes. Singapore Television 12 broadcasts Malay and Tamil programmes as well as sports, documentaries and arts programmes. In 1994 there were 210,370 radio and (1997) 600,382 TV licences (colour by PAL).

Cinema. In 1997 there were 135 cinemas with a total seating capacity of 53,000.

Press. In 1997 there were 8 daily newspapers, in 4 languages, with a total daily circulation of 1,024,532.

Tourism. There were 7,198,000 visitors in 1997. Most came from the Association of South East Asian Nations, Japan, Taiwan, Australia, United Kingdom and the USA. The total tourism receipts for 1997 came to S$10·2bn. The total number of gazetted hotels increased from 90 in 1996 to 94 in 1997, providing 27,915 rooms. By the end of 1998, the number of gazetted hotels was expected to reach 108 with close to 32,000 rooms.

Festivals. Every Jan. or Feb. the Lunar New Year is celebrated. Other Chinese festivals include Qing Ming (a time for the remembrance of ancestors), Yu Lan Jie (Feast of the Hungry Ghosts) and the Mid-Autumn Festival (Mooncake or Lantern festival).

Moslems in Singapore celebrate Hari Raya Puasa (to celebrate the end of a month long fast) and Hari Raya Haji (a festival of prayer and remembrance). There are also Muharram (a New Year celebration) and Maulud (Prophet Muhammad's birthday).

Hindus celebrate the Tamil New Year in mid-April. Thaipusam is a penetential Hindu festival popular with Tamils; and Deepavali, the Festival of Lights, is celebrated by Hindus and Sikhs. Other festivals include Thimithi (a fire-walking ceremony) and Navarathiri (9 nights' prayer).

Bhuddists observe Vesak Day, which commemorates the birth, enlightenment and Nirvana of the Buddha, and falls on the full moon day in April.

Christmas, Good Friday and Easter Sunday are also recognized.

Libraries. The National Library Board (NLB) was inaugurated on 3 July 1996, having become a statutory board in Sept. 1995. The Board's main aim is to implement the recommendations set down in the Library 2000 Report on how libraries can meet the needs of the 21st century.

The NLB has 1 regional library, 15 community libraries and 38 community children's libraries. It aims to have 4 regional, 18 community and 100 children's libraries by 2003.

NLB's membership numbers 1,318,800 and its service outlets hold 4,840,000 books, 386,618 serials and 125,102 audio-visual items in 4 languages. In 1997, library loans numbered 22,500,100.

National Theatre and Opera. Some of the main theatre companies in Singapore, performing mainly in English, include TheatreWorks, The Necessary Stage and the Singapore Repertory Theatre. Other language companies include Teater Kami (Malay), The Theatre Practice (Chinese) and Ravindran Drama Group (Tamil).

Museums and Galleries. The National Heritage Board was formed on 1 Aug. 1993 through the amalgamation of the National Archives, the National Museum and the Oral History Department. The Board's National Museum arm comprises the Singapore History Museum, the Singapore Art Museum and the first wing of the Asian Civilisations Museum.

DIPLOMATIC REPRESENTATIVES

Of Singapore in Great Britain (9 Wilton Crescent, London, SW1X 8RW)
High Commissioner: J. Y. Pillay.

Of Great Britain in Singapore (Tanglin Rd, Singapore 247919)
High Commissioner: Alan Hunt, CMG.

Of Singapore in the USA (3501 International Pl., NW, Washington, D.C., 20008)
Ambassador: Heng-Chee Chan.

Of the USA in Singapore (27 Napier Rd, Singapore 258508)
Ambassador: Steven Green.

Of Singapore to the United Nations
Ambassador: Kishore Mahbubani.

Of Singapore to the European Union
Ambassador: Eng Fong Pang.

FURTHER READING

Department of Statistics. *Monthly Digest of Statistics.—Yearbook of Statistics.*
The Constitution of Singapore. Singapore, 1992
Information Division, Ministry of Information and the Arts. *Singapore* [*year*]: a Review of [*the previous year*].
Ministry of Trade and Industry, *Economic Survey of Singapore.* (Quarterly and Annual)

Chew, E. C. T., *A History of Singapore.* Singapore, 1992
Clammer, J. R., *Singapore: Ideology, Society, Culture.* Singapore, 1985
Huff, W. G., *Economic Growth of Singapore: Trade and Development in the Twentieth Century.* CUP, 1994
Myint, S., *The Principles of Singapore Law.* 2nd ed. Singapore, 1992
National Library. *Books about Singapore.* Singapore, irregular
Quah, J. S. T., *Government and Politics of Singapore.* OUP, 1985
Quah, S. R. and Quah, J. S. T., *Singapore* [Bibliography]. Oxford and Santa Barbara (CA), 1988
Tan, C. H., *Financial Markets and Institutions in Singapore.* 7th ed. Singapore, 1992
Turnbull, C. M., *A History of Singapore, 1819–1988.* 2nd ed. OUP, 1989
Vasil, R. K., *Governing Singapore.* Singapore, 1992

National library: National Library, Stamford Rd, Singapore, 178896.
National statistical office: Department of Statistics, Minister of Trade and Industry, Singapore 068811.
Website: http://www.singstat.gov.sg/

SLOVAKIA

Slovenská Republika

Capital: Bratislava
Population estimate, 2000: 5·37m.
GNP per capita: (PPP$) 7,460
HDI/world rank: 0·875/42

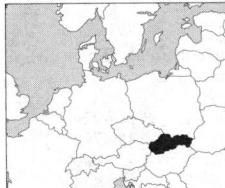

KEY HISTORICAL EVENTS

The Czechoslovak State came into existence on 28 Oct. 1918, when the Czech *Národni Výbor* (National Committee) took over the government of the Czech lands upon the dissolution of Austria-Hungary. Two days later the Slovak National Council manifested its desire to unite politically with the Czechs. On 14 Nov. 1918 the first Czechoslovak National Assembly declared the Czechoslovak State to be a republic with T. G. Masaryk as President (1918-35). The Treaty of St Germain-en-Laye (1919) recognized the Czechoslovak Republic, consisting of the Czech lands (Bohemia, Moravia, part of Silesia) and Slovakia. To these lands were added, as a trust, the autonomous province of Subcarpathian Ruthenia. This territory was broken up for the benefit of Germany, Poland and Hungary by the Munich agreement (29 Sept. 1938) between UK, France, Germany and Italy.

In March 1939 the German-sponsored Slovak government proclaimed Slovakia independent and Germany incorporated the Czech lands into the Reich as the 'Protectorate of Bohemia and Moravia'. A government-in-exile, headed by Dr Beneš, was set up in London in July 1940. Liberation by the Soviet Army and US Forces was completed by May 1945. Territories taken by the Germans, Poles and Hungarians were restored to Czechoslovak sovereignty. Subcarpathian Ruthenia was transferred to the USSR. Elections were held in May 1946 at which the Communist Party obtained about 38% of the votes. A coalition government under a Communist Prime Minister, Klement Gottwald, remained in power until 20 Feb. 1948, when 12 of the non-Communist ministers resigned in protest against infiltration of Communists into the police. In Feb. a predominantly Communist government was formed by Gottwald. In May elections resulted in an 89% majority for the government and President Beneš resigned.

In 1968 pressure for liberalization culminated in the overthrow of the Stalinist leader, Antonín Novotný, and his associates. Under Alexander Dubček's leadership the so-called 'Prague Spring' began to take shape, and the outlines of a new political system described as 'socialism with a human face' began to appear as the Communist Party introduced an 'Action Programme' of far-reaching reforms. Soviet pressure to abandon this programme was exerted between May and Aug. 1968 and finally Warsaw Pact forces occupied Czechoslovakia on 21 Aug. The Czechoslovak government was compelled to accept a policy of 'normalization' (*i.e.*, abandonment of most reforms) and the stationing of Soviet forces.

Mass demonstrations demanding political reform began in Nov. 1989. After the authorities' use of violence to break up a demonstration on 17 Nov. , the Communist leader resigned. On 30 Nov. the Federal Assembly abolished the Communist Party's sole right to govern, and a new Government was formed on 3 Dec. The protest movement continued to grow and on 10 Dec. another Government was formed. Gustáv Husák resigned as President, and was replaced by Václav Havel on the unanimous vote of 323 members of the Federal Assembly on 29 Dec.

At the June 1992 elections the Movement for Democratic Slovakia led by Vladimír Meciar campaigned on the issue of Slovak independence, and on 17 July the Slovak National Council adopted a declaration of sovereignty by 113 to 24 votes. President Havel resigned as Federal president on 20 July. On 1 Sept. 1992 the Slovak National Council adopted, by 114 votes to 16 with 4 abstentions (and a boycott by the Hungarian deputies), a Constitution for an independent Slovakia to come into being on 1 Jan. 1993. Economic property was divided between Slovakia and the Czech Republic in accordance with a Czechoslovakian law of 13 Nov. 1992. Real estate became the property of the republic in which it was located. Other property was divided by specially-constituted commissions in the proportion of 2 (Czech Republic) to 1 (Slovakia) on the basis of population size. Military materiel was divided on the 2:1 principle. Regular military personnel were invited to choose which armed force they would serve in.

TERRITORY AND POPULATION
Slovakia is bounded in the north-west by the Czech Republic, north by Poland, east by Ukraine, south by Hungary and south-west by Austria. Estimated population in 1995, 5,368,000; density, 109 per sq. km.

The UN gives a projected population for 2000 of 5·37m.

In 1995 an estimated 58·8% of the population lived in urban areas. There are 4 administrative regions *(Kraj)*, one of which is the capital, Bratislava.

Region	Chief city	Area in sq. km	Population
Bratislava	—	368	450,776
Západoslovenský	Bratislava	14,492	1,727,800
Stredoslovenský	Banská Bystrica	17,982	1,615,438
Východoslovenský	Košice	16,193	1,503,421

The population of the principal towns in 1993 (in 1,000): Bratislava, 448; Banská Bystrica, 85; Zilina, 86; Trnava, 72; Košice, 239; Nitra, 87; Prešov, 91; Martin, 60.

There was a Hungarian minority of 567,000 in 1996.

A law of Nov. 1995 makes Slovak the sole official language.

SOCIAL STATISTICS
Births, 1995, 60,000; deaths, 54,000. Rates (per 1,000 population), 1995: Birth, 11·2; death, 10; marriage, 5·4; divorce, 1; infant mortality (per 1,000 live births), 13·6. Expectation of life, 1990–95, was 66·5 years for males and 75·4 for females. In 1995 the most popular age range for marrying was 20–24 for both males and females. Annual growth rate, 1990–95, 0·2%. Fertility rate, 1990–95, 1·9 births per woman.

CLIMATE
A humid continental climate, with warm summers and cold winters. Precipitation is generally greater in summer, with thunderstorms. Autumn, with dry, clear weather and spring, which is damp, are each of short duration. Bratislava, Jan. –0·7°C. June 19·1°C. Annual rainfall 649 mm.

CONSTITUTION AND GOVERNMENT
Parliament is the *National Council*. It has 150 members elected by proportional representation.

There is a *Constitutional Court* whose judges are normally nominated by the President.

Citizenship belongs to all citizens of the former federal Slovak Republic; other residents of 5 years standing may apply for citizenship. Slovakia grants dual citizenship.

National Anthem. 'Nad Tatrou sa blýska' ('Over Tatra it lightens'); words by J. Matuška, tune anonymous.

RECENT ELECTIONS
Elections to the National Council were held on 25 and 26 Sept. 1998. Vladimír Meciar's coalition was defeated. The electorate was 3,389,346; turn-out was 84%. The Movement for a Democratic Slovakia (HZDS) gained 43 seats with 27% of votes cast; the Slovak Democratic Coalition (SDK) 42 with 26·3%; the Slovak National Party (SNS), 14 with 9·1%.

CURRENT ADMINISTRATION
President: Position vacant.

A coalition government was appointed on 30 Oct. 1998 composed of members of the Slovak Democratic Coalition (SDK), the Party of the Democratic Left (SDL), the Party of Civic Understanding (SOP) and the Hungarian Coalition Party (SMK). It comprised in March 1999:

Prime Minister: Mikuláš Dzurinda (SDK).

SLOVAKIA

Deputy Prime Minister for Legislature: Lubomír Fogaš (SDL). *Deputy Prime Minister for the Economy:* Ivan Mikloš (SDK). *Deputy Prime Minister for Human Rights and Regional Development:* Pál Csáky (SMK). *Deputy Prime Minister for European Integration:* Pavol Hamžík (SOP).

Minister of Foreign Affairs: Eduard Kukan (SDK). *Finance:* Brigita Schmögnerová (SDL). *Defence:* Pavol Kanis (SDL). *Economy:* Ludovit Černák (SDK). *Privatization:* Mária Machová (SOP). *Interior:* Ladislav Pittner (SDK). *Labour, Social Affairs and the Family:* Peter Magvaši (SDL). *Culture:* Milan Kňažko (SDK). *Justice:* Ján Čarnogurský (SDK). *Education:* Milan Ftáčnik (SDL). *Health:* Tibor Šagát (SDK). *Agriculture:* Pavel Koncoš (SDL). *Transport, Posts and Telecommunications:* Gabriel Palacka (SDK). *Environment:* László Miklós (SMK). *Construction and Public Works:* Istvá Harna (SMK).

The *Speaker* is Ivan Gáspárovič.

Local Government. The local authorities are the district bureaux with the power to raise local taxes and with responsibility for roads, schools, utilities and public health. Elections for 2,853 mayors and 35,524 municipal councillors were held on 18–19 Nov. 1994. Turn-out was 52%. Independents gained 28·5% of the mayoralties, the Democratic Left 17·9%; HZDS 15·9%; Christian Democrats 14·8%. HZDS gained 22·8% of the councillor posts; Christian Democrats 19·7%; Party of the Democratic Left 15·7%. Local Government elections were scheduled for 18–19 Dec. 1998.

DEFENCE
Conscription is for 12 months. In 1997 military expenditure totalled US$414m. (US$77 per capita), representing 2·1% of GDP.

Army. There are 3 tank and 3 mechanized infantry brigades. Equipment includes 478 T-72M and T-54/-55 main battle tanks. Personnel (1997), 23,800 (including 15,000 conscripts).

Air Force. There are 72 combat aircraft, including 20 Su-22 and 12 Su-25, 16 MiG-21 and 24 MiG-29 fighters and 19 attack helicopters. Transport equipment includes 13 fixed-wing aircraft and 30 Mi-8/17 helicopters, while 18 Mi-2s are used for liaison duties. Personnel (1997), 12,000.

INTERNATIONAL RELATIONS
Slovakia is a member of the UN, CEFTA, the Central European Initiative, the NATO Partnership for Peace and is an associate member of the EU and an associate partner of the WEU. An application to join the EU was made in June 1995. A referendum on whether Slovakia should apply to join NATO took place on 23–24 May 1997. Turn-out was 9·8% and the results were declared invalid. 55% of votes cast were against participation.

Slovakia has had a long-standing dispute with Hungary over the Gabčíkovo-Nagymaros Project, involving the building of dam structures in both countries for the production of electric power, flood control and improvement of navigation on the Danube as agreed in a treaty signed in 1977 between Czechoslovakia and Hungary. The International Court of Justice delivered judgment on the case in Sept. 1997.

ECONOMY
Policy. By the end of 1992, 503 large joint stock companies had been privatized by the voucher scheme, and 330 large firms and 9,676 small businesses had been sold off. 3·2m. persons had invested in privatization vouchers by the end of 1994. Legislation of July 1995 ended privatization by vouchers, which became exchangeable instead against state securities. At the end of 1995 the private sector share of total GDP reached 64·9%.

New economic policy in 1998 had the key aims of the substantial reduction of the fiscal deficit, an increase in regulated prices towards international levels and the acceleration of the restructuring of state-owned banks and enterprises.

Performance. Real GDP growth was 6·9% in 1996 and 6% in 1997 (estimate). Preliminary data for 1998 suggests this rate was being sustained, making Slovakia's one of the fastest growing economies in Europe. At May 1998 the current account balance stood at US$–1·3bn.

Budget. In 1997, revenue was Ks. 180,825m. and expenditure, Ks. 192,847m.

VAT, personal and company income tax, real estate taxes and inheritance taxes came into force in Jan. 1993.

Currency. The unit of currency is the *Slovak koruna* or crown (SKK) of 100 *haliers*, introduced on 8 Feb. 1993. The koruna was revalued 4% in May 1995. Foreign exchange reserves were US$7,469m. in May 1998. Inflation was 5·8% in 1996–97. Total money supply in Nov. 1997 was Ks. 159,376m.

Banking and Finance. The central bank and bank of issue is the Slovak National Bank, founded in 1993 (*Governor,* Vladímir Masár). It has an autonomous statute modelled on the German Bundesbank, with the duties of maintaining control over monetary policy and inflation, ensuring the stability of the currency, and supervising commercial banks. However, it is now proposed to amend the central bank law to allow the government to appoint half the members of the board and force the bank to increase its financing of the budget deficit.

In Oct. 1998 the Slovak National Bank abandoned its fixed exchange rate system, whereby the crown's value was fixed within a fluctuation band against a number of currencies, and chose to float the currency.

Decentralization of the banking system began in 1991, and private banks began to operate. Foreign investors may acquire up to 25% of major banks' assets (100% of small banks), but no single investor may acquire more than 10%. There were 26 commercial banks in 1993, and 9 foreign bank branches. Total subscribed bank capital was Ks. 11,800m. in 1993. Savings accounts totalled Ks. 94,859m. in 1992.

There is a stock exchange in Bratislava.

Weights and Measures. The metric system is in force.

ENERGY AND NATURAL RESOURCES

Electricity. Installed capacity in 1994 was 7·12m. kW. Production in 1994 was 23·6bn. kWh. Consumption per capita in 1995 was estimated at 4,400 kWh. There is a nuclear power station at Bohunice, and a hydro-electric dam at Gabčíkovo on the Danube, from which Hungary has withdrawn. In 1995 about 55% of electricity was nuclear-generated.

Minerals. In 1993, 2·81m. tonnes of brown coal were produced; and in 1991, 1·34m. tonnes of lignite. 1·09m. tonnes of iron ore were extracted in 1993.

Agriculture. In 1994 there were 1·48m. ha of arable land. In 1996 agriculture produced 5% of GDP.

A federal law of May 1991 returned land seized by the Communist regime to its original owners, to a maximum of 150 ha of arable to a single owner.

Livestock, 1997: Cattle, 800,000; pigs, 1·81m.; sheep, 420,000; chickens, 14·22m. Livestock products, 1993: Meat, 410,540 tonnes; eggs, 1,000,220; milk, 944,382 litres.

Forestry. The area under forests in 1995 was 1·99m. ha, or 41·4% of the total land area. In 1995 timber production was 5·32m. cu. metres.

Fisheries. In 1995 the total catch was 3,565 tonnes, exclusively freshwater fish.

INDUSTRY

In Czechoslovakia Slovakia was less industrialized than the Czech Republic, though there are concentrations of heavy engineering and munitions plants. Consumer industries include textiles and footwear. 1993 output included (in 1m. tonnes): Pig iron, 3·21; crude steel, 3·92; iron and steel plates, 2·86; zinc (1991), 0·81; plastics, 0·37; TV receivers (1991), 201,851.

Labour. Out of 2,147,000 people in employment in 1995, 575,000 were in manufacturing, 222,000 in wholesale and retail trade and 197,000 in agriculture, fishing and forestry. The average monthly salary in 1997 was Ks. 9,555. Unemployment was 13·2% in April 1998.

INTERNATIONAL TRADE

A memorandum envisaging a customs union and close economic co-operation was signed with the Czech Republic in Oct. 1992. An agreement of Dec. 1992 with the Czech Republic, Hungary and Poland abolishes tariffs on raw materials and goods where exports do not compete directly with locally-produced items, and envisaged tariff reductions on agricultural and industrial goods in 1995–97.

Tax holidays of up to 7 years are available to foreign investors.

Foreign debt was US$12bn. gross (62% of GDP) in Dec. 1998. The net figure amounted to just under 30%. By Sept. 1994 total foreign investments since 1990 amounted to US$416m.

Imports and Exports. While keen to join the EU, Slovakia is currently excluded from Brussels' list of east European countries scheduled for early negotiations because of 'shortcomings' in the functioning of its democracy.

1996 imports, US$11,107m.; exports, US$8,823m. By 1997, the major foreign trade partner, the Czech Republic, accounted for 26·7% of all exports from Slovakia and 23·0% of all imports into the country. The EU accounted for 45·0% of exports and 39·5% of imports; OECD for 85·5% of exports and 75·3% of imports. Russia provided 15·6% of imports (mainly crude oil, gas and other raw materials) and took 3·7% of exports.

Basic figures in Ks. 1m. (1997):

Foreign trade turnover	Slovak exports	Slovak imports	Foreign trade balance (deficit)
640,623	295,574	345,049	–49,475

Leading foreign trade partners as of March 1997:

Country	% of total exports	% of total imports
Czech Republic	28·2	23·2
Germany	24·5	17·1
Austria	6·2	14·9
Poland	5·7	5·4
Italy	5·3	4·6
UK	1·7	2·4

COMMUNICATIONS

Roads. In 1995 there were 198 km of motorways and 17,869 km of main roads. In 1995 there were 1,015,794 passenger cars, 16,930 vans, 85,704 trucks, 11,812 buses and 229,119 motor cycles.

Rail. In 1995 the length of railway routes was 3,665 km of 1,435 mm gauge (1,473 km electrified) with short sections on 3 other gauges. In 1995 railways carried 89·5m. passengers and 60·8m. tonnes of freight. There are tram/light rail networks in Bratislava and Košice.

Civil Aviation. The main international airport is at Bratislava (M. R. Stefánik), with some international flights from Košice. There are 3 Slovakia-based airlines. In 1998 Air Slovakia had flights to Kuwait and Tel Aviv, Slovak Airlines operated domestic services and flew to Moscow and Tatra Air operated domestic services and had flights to Zürich. Services were also provided in 1998 by Aeroflot, Austrian Airlines, Air Ostrava, Air Ukraine, Continental Airlines, Czech Airlines, Hemus, Swissair, Tunis Air and Tyrolean Airways. In 1996 Bratislava handled 249,569 passengers (227,307 on international flights) and 2,128 tonnes of freight.

Shipping. Merchant shipping in 1995 totalled 19,000 GRT.

Telecommunications. There were 1,391,900 telephone main lines in 1997, or 258·6 per 1,000 persons. In 1995 there were 12,000 cellular phone subscribers, 220,000 PCs and 45,000 fax machines. Slovakia had around 190,000 Internet users in Nov. 1997.

Postal Services. In 1995 there were 1,617 post offices.

SOCIAL INSTITUTIONS

Justice. The post-Communist judicial system was established by a federal law of July 1991. This provided for a unified system of 4 types of court: civil, criminal, commercial and administrative. Commercial courts arbitrate in disputes arising from business activities. Administrative courts examine the legality of the decisions of state institutions when appealed by citizens. In addition, there are military courts which operate under the jurisdiction of the Ministry of Defence. There is a Supreme Court, and a hierarchy of courts under the Ministry of Justice at republic, region and district level. District courts are courts of first instance. Cases are usually decided by senates comprising a judge and 2 associate judges, though occasionally by a single judge. (Associate judges are citizens in good standing over the age of 25 who are elected for 4-year terms). Regional courts are courts of first instance in more serious cases and also courts of appeal for district courts. Cases are usually decided by a senate of 2 judges and 3 associate judges, although again occasionally by a single judge. The Supreme Court interprets law as a guide to other courts and functions also as a court of appeal. Decisions are made by senates of 3 judges. The judges of the Supreme Court are nominated by the President; other judges are appointed by the National Council.

Religion. A federal Czechoslovakian law of July 1991 provides the basis for church-state relations and guarantees the religious and civic rights of citizens and churches. Churches must register to become legal entities but operate independently of the state. A law of 1993 restored confiscated property to churches and religious communities unless it had passed into private hands, co-operative farms or trading companies. An official poll of Oct. 1995 showed that 73% of the population were religious. Of these, 75% were Roman Catholic, 12% Protestant and 7% Uniate.

Education. In 1995 there were 3,322 pre-school institutions with 161,697 children and 14,933 teachers and 2,485 primary schools with 661,082 pupils and 39,224 teachers. There were 190 grammar schools with 76,380 students and 5,457 teachers and 364 vocational schools with 119,853 pupils and 9,558 teachers. There were 357 secondary vocational apprentice training centres with 139,688 pupils and 6,056 teachers and 400 special schools with 29,914 children and 3,862 teachers. 14 universities or university-type institutions with 74,322 students.

In 1994 total expenditure on education came to 4·9% of GNP.

Health. In 1995 there were 14,447 doctors. Population per doctor: 371. There were 62,634 beds in health establishments in total, out of which 41,727 were in hospitals.

CULTURE

Broadcasting. Broadcasting is the responsibility of the government-controlled Slovak Broadcasting Council. The state-run Slovak Radio broadcasts on 4 wavelengths, and there are 12 private regional stations. Slovak Television is a public corporation. It transmits on 2 channels (colour by SECAM), the second being shared with a commercial station. There are several independent local TV stations, and 2 cable networks. In 1995 there were 3·04m. radio and 2·54m. TV receivers in use.

Cinema. There were 472 cinemas in 1995. 57 films were completed in 1995, out of which 4 were full-length feature films.

Press. Slovakia had 20 daily newspapers in 1996 with 989,000 readers.

Tourism. In 1996 there were 951,000 foreign tourists, spending US$673m.

Festivals. The Bratislava Rock Festival takes place in June and the Bratislava Music Festival and Interpodium is in October. The Myjava Folklore Festival is held each June, the Zvolen Castle Games run June–July, Theatrical Nitra is in Sept., and there is an annual Spring Music Festival in Košice.

Libraries. In 1995 there were 3,005 public libraries, 1 National library, 546 Higher Education and 5 non-specialized libraries. They held a combined 33,811,000 volumes for 922,955 registered users.

Museums and Galleries. The Slovak National Museum and the Slovak National Gallery are both in Bratislava. In 1993 there were a total of 70 museums with 2,825,000 visitors.

DIPLOMATIC REPRESENTATIVES
Of Slovakia in Great Britain (25 Kensington Palace Gdns., London, W8 4QY)
Ambassador: Igor Slobodnik.

SLOVAKIA

Of Great Britain in Slovakia (Panska 16, 81101 Bratislava)
Ambassador: D. Lyscom.

Of Slovakia in the USA (2201 Wisconsin Ave., NW, Washington, D.C., 20007)
Chargé d'Affaires a.i.: Jan Gabor.

Of the USA in Slovakia (4 Hviezdoslavovo Namestie, 81102 Bratislava)
Ambassador: Ralph R. Johnson.

Of Slovakia to the United Nations
Ambassador: Vacant.

Of Slovakia to the European Union
Ambassador: Emil Kuchár.

FURTHER READING

Kirschbaum, S. J., *A History of Slovakia: the Struggle for Survival.* London and New York, 1995
Krejcí, J., *Czechoslovakia at the Crossroads of History.* London, 1990
Leff, C. S., *National Conflict in Czechoslovakia: The Making and Remaking of a State, 1918–1987.* Princeton Univ. Press, 1988
Short, D., *Czechoslovakia.* [Bibliography] Oxford and Santa Barbara (CA), 1986
Stone, N. and Strouhal, E., (eds.) *Czechoslovakia: Crossroads and Crises, 1918-88.* London, 1989
Wheaton, B. and Kavan, Z., *Velvet Revolution: Czechoslovakia 1988-91.* Boulder (CO), 1992

National statistical office: Statistical Office of the Slovak Republic, Miletičova 3, 82467 Bratislava.
Website: http://www.statistics.sk/

SLOVENIA

Republika Slovenija

Capital: Ljubljana
Population estimate, 2000: 1·99m.
GNP per capita: (PPP$) 12,110
HDI/world rank: 0·887/37

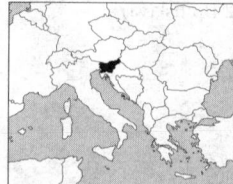

KEY HISTORICAL EVENTS
The lands originally settled by Slovenes in the 6th century were steadily encroached upon by Germans. Slovenia developed as part of Austria-Hungary, after the defeat of the latter in the First World War becoming part of the Kingdom of the Serbs, Croats and Slovenes (Yugoslavia) on 1 Dec. 1918.

In Oct. 1989 the Slovene Assembly voted a constitutional amendment giving it the right to secede from Yugoslavia. On 2 July 1990 the Assembly adopted a 'declaration of sovereignty' by 187 votes to 3, and in Sept. proclaimed its control over the territorial defence force on its soil. At a referendum on 23 Dec., 88·5% of participants voted for independence. On 25 June 1991 Slovenia declared independence, but agreed to suspend this for 3 months at peace talks sponsored by the EU. Federal troops moved into Slovenia on 27 June to secure Yugoslavia's external borders, but after some fighting withdrew by the end of July. After the agreed 3-month moratorium Slovenia (and Croatia) declared their independence from the Yugoslav Federation on 8 Oct. 1991.

TERRITORY AND POPULATION
Slovenia is bounded in the north by Austria, in the north-east by Hungary, in the south-east by Croatia and in the west by Italy. There is a small strip of coast south of Trieste. Its area is 20,273 sq. km. The capital is Ljubljana (1997 population), 330,000. Population (30 June 1995), 1,987,505 (females, 1,021,855), density per sq. km, 98·1. 1998 estimate, 1,987,000.

The projected population for 2000 is 1·99m.

In 1995 an estimated 51·3% of the population lived in urban areas.

The population is predominantly Slovene. The official language is Slovene.

SOCIAL STATISTICS
Statistics for calendar years:

	Live births	Marriages	Deaths	Growth rate per 1,000
1990	22,368	8,517	18,555	1·9
1993	19,793	9,022	20,012	−0·1
1994	19,463	8,314	19,359	0·1
1995	18,980	8,245	18,968	0·0
1996	18,788	7,555	18,620	0·1

Rates 1996 (per 1,000 population): birth, 9·5; death, 9·4; marriage, 3·8; divorce, 1·0; infant mortality, 4·7 (per 1,000 live births).

In 1995 the most popular age range for marrying was 25–29 years for males and 20–24 for females. Expectation of life, 1990–95, was 68·2 years for males and 77·3 for females. Annual growth rate, 1990–95, –0·1%.

CLIMATE
Summers are warm, winters are cold with frequent snow. Ljubljana, Jan. –4°C, July 22°C. Annual rainfall 1,383 mm.

CONSTITUTION AND GOVERNMENT
There is a bicameral parliament consisting of a 90-member *National Assembly*, elected for 4-year terms by proportional representation with a 3% threshold; and a 40-member *State Council*, elected for 5-year terms by interest groups. It has veto powers over the National Assembly.

National Anthem. 'Prijateli obrodile so trte vince nam sladko' ('Friends, the vines have produced wine sweet to us'); words by France Prešeren, tune by S. Premrl.

RECENT ELECTIONS

Presidential elections were held on 23 Nov. 1997. The electorate was 1·6m; turn-out was 68%. Milan Kučan was re-elected President against 7 opponents by 56% of votes cast.

Elections were held for the National Assembly on 10 Nov. 1996. The electorate was 1·53m.; turn-out was 74%. The Liberal Democratic Party (LDS) won 25 seats with 27·05% of votes cast; the Slovenian People's Party (SLS), 19 with 19·6%; the Social Democratic Party, 16 with 16%; the Christian Democratic Party, 10 with 9·5%; the United List of Social Democrats (former Communists) gained 9 seats; the Pensioners Democratic Party (DeSUS), 5; the National Party, 4. According to the constitution the Hungarian and Italian authorities are entitled to 1 seat each.

CURRENT ADMINISTRATION

President: Milan Kučan (b. 1941; elected 6 Dec. 1992; re-elected 23 Nov. 1997).

In Feb. 1997 an LDS-SLS-DeSUS coalition government was formed which in March 1999 comprised:

Prime Minister: Janez Drnovšek (b. 1950; LDP).

Deputy Prime Minister: Marjan Podobnik (SLS). *Minister of Agriculture, Food and Forestry:* Ciril Smrkolj (SLS). *Culture:* Jozef Školć (LDS). *Defence (Acting):* Lojze Marinček (SLS). *Economic Affairs:* Metod Dragonja (LDS). *Economic Relations and Development:* Marjan Senjur (SLS). *Education and Sport:* Slavko Gaber (LDS). *Environment:* Pavel Gantar (LDS). *European Affairs:* Igor Bavčar (LDS). *Finance:* Mitja Gaspari (ind). *Foreign Affairs:* Dr Boris Frlec (LDS). *Health:* Marjan Jereb (SLS). *Interior:* Borut Suklje (LDS). *Justice:* Tomaž Marušič (SLS). *Labour, Family and Social Affairs:* Anton Rop (LDS). *Science and Technology:* Lojze Marinček. *Transport and Communications:* Anton Bergauer (SLS). *Small Business and Tourism:* Janko Razgorsek (SLS).

Local Government. There are 62 administrative districts. Municipal elections were held in 2 rounds on 4 and 18 Dec. 1994 for 147 mayoralties. Turn-out was 50%.

DEFENCE

There is military service for 7 months with between 10,000–12,000 conscripts annually.

In 1997 military expenditure totalled US$310m. (US$154 per capita), representing 1·7% of GDP.

Army. There are 6 military districts. The Army is organized in 7 infantry and 1 surface-to-air missile brigades and 2 independent mechanized battalions. Equipment includes some 42 M-84 and 40 T-55 main battle tanks. Personnel (1998), 9,500 (5,500 conscripts). There is a paramilitary police force of 4,500 with 5,000 reserves.

INTERNATIONAL RELATIONS

Slovenia is a member of the UN, CEFTA, the Central European Initiative and the NATO Partnership for Peace, and is an Associate Partner of the WEU and an Associate Member of the EU. Intensive negotiations regarding Slovenia's accession to full membership of the EU begin in April 1998. Slovenia hopes to become a full member of the Union by 2002.

ECONOMY

Policy. Privatization is being carried out in 2 stages, beginning with small businesses, by transferring the capital to an investment fund to act as intermediary. 20% of the capital is to be transferred to savings banks, 10–20% to commercial banks, 20% to wage-earners and 10% to former owners.

Performance. GDP growth rate was 3·25% in 1997 (3·1% in 1996). In 1997, preliminary figures indicate that real exports and imports of goods will have increased by around 7·8% and 7·6% respectively. The trade deficit is estimated to be US$940m.

Budget. The 1997 Budget was adopted by the Parliament in the beginning of Dec. 1997. It sets expenditure at 743·6bn. tolars. Due to this delay, the government proposed to extend the budgetary year until the end of Jan. 1998. In view of this budgetary expenditure, public finance expenditure would amount to 46·5% of GDP. Revenue in 1997 was 1,295,107m. tolars; expenditure, 1,335,442m. tolars. Items of revenue (in 1m. tolars) comprised: Tax revenues, 726,327 (corporate income tax, 32,906; personal income tax, 193,540; taxes on goods and services, 394,013; custom duties and import taxes, 59,350; other income taxes, 1,216); social security contributions, 452,299 (contributions for unemployment, 2,428; health care, 190,524; pension fund, 259,347); non-tax revenues, 101,781; proceeds of privatization, 14,700. Items of expenditure: Central government, 483,575; local government, 137,964; pensions, 387,447; health care, 195,583; privatization expenditure, 14,800.

Currency. The unit of currency is the *tolar* (SLT) of 100 *stotinas*, which replaced the Yugoslav dinar. It is based on the ecu according to a floating exchange rate, and became convertible on 1 Sept. 1995. Inflation was 9·5% in 1997 and was expected to drop in 1998 to around 8%. Foreign exchange reserves were US$4,467m. in Oct. 1997. Total money supply in Feb. 1998 was 215m. tolars.

Banking and Finance. A central bank and bank of issue, the Bank of Slovenia, was founded in June 1991. Its *Governor* is Franc Arhar. In 1996 there were 31 commercial banks (3 foreign) and 7 savings banks.

There is a stock exchange in Ljubljana (LSE).

ENERGY AND NATURAL RESOURCES

Electricity. Installed capacity was 2·36m. kW in 1994. There is 1 nuclear power station. In the first ten months of 1997, 3,886m. kWh were nuclear-produced, 3,465m. kWh thermal and 2,297m. kWh hydro-electric. The total amount of electricity produced in 1997 was 13,094m. kWh.

Consumption per capita in 1995 was estimated to be 5,362 kWh.

Minerals. Brown coal production was 812,000 tonnes in 1997.

Agriculture. Agriculture contributed 4·5% (estimate) of GDP in 1997 (4·6% in 1996). In 1994 agricultural land totalled 791,000 ha (640,000 ha arable, 148,000 ha pasture, 22,000 ha vineyards). The cultivated area was 649,285 ha. Yields (in tonnes) in 1997: Wheat, 138,900; maize, 355,000; sugar-beet, 284,000; potatoes, 177,900; grapes, 127,700.

Livestock in 1997 (in 1,000): Cattle, 484; sheep, 28; pigs, 559; poultry, 5,573. Livestock products, 1996: Meat, 123,000 tonnes; milk, 590m. litres.

Forestry. In 1995 the area under forests was 1·08m. ha, or 53·5% of the total land area. 1·94m. cu. metres of timber were cut in 1995.

Fisheries. There were 46 sea fishing vessels in 1989. Total catches in 1995 amounted to 2,929 tonnes (1,911 tonnes from sea fishing).

INDUSTRY

There were 51,647 enterprises and companies at March 1996, of which 55 were public, 955 social, 185 private, 84 financial and 1 co-operative. Industry contributed 32·8% of GDP in 1996. Traditional industries are metallurgy, furniture-making and sports equipment. The manufacture of electric goods and transport equipment is being developed.

Production (in tonnes) in 1997: cement, 1,113; paper, 476; macaroni, 12,894; soaps and detergents, 31.

Labour. Registered labour force was 870,600 in Sept. 1997. In 1995, 370,000 people worked in manufacturing, 102,000 in wholesale and retail trade and 96,000 in agriculture, forestry and fishing. There were 125,400 registered unemployed in Sept. 1997, which is fractionally higher than in 1996. However, using international standards the level of unemployment was 7·1% in the second quarter of 1997, which is slightly less than a year earlier (7·3%). In Sept. 1997 the average monthly gross wage per employee was 145,362 tolars.

INTERNATIONAL TRADE

Foreign debt amounted to US$4,117m. in Sept. 1997. Slovenia accepted 18% of the US$4,400m. commercial bank debt of the former Yugoslavia.

Imports and Exports. Exports of goods and services in 1996 were worth US$10,497m. and imports, US$10,675m. Major exports in 1998 included: road vehicles, petroleum and petroleum products, clothing, general industrial machinery and textiles. Major imports (1998): food and livestock, machinery and transport equipment, chemical products and mineral fuels. Share of exports to principal markets in 1996: Germany, 30·6%; Italy, 13·3%; Croatia, 10·3%; France, 7·2%; Austria, 6·6%. Imports: Germany, 21·7%; Italy, 16·9%; France, 9·8%; Croatia, 6·3%.

COMMUNICATIONS

Roads. In 1997 there were 14,851 km of road; in 1995, 293 km of motorways.

There were (in 1997) 767,534 passenger cars; 2,372 buses; 42,538 trucks; and 8,342 motor cycles. 110m. passengers and 4·5m. tonnes of freight were carried by road in 1997.

There were 6,951 traffic accidents in 1997 in which 358 persons were killed.

Rail. In 1997 there were 1,201 km of 1,435 mm gauge, of which 499 km were electrified. In 1997, 13·6m. passengers and 14·4m. tonnes of freight were carried.

Civil Aviation. There is an international airport at Ljubljana (Brnik). The national carrier, Adria Airways, has flights to most major European cities and Tel Aviv. In 1998 services were also provided by Aeroflot, Air Ostrava, Austrian Airlines, British Airways, Czech Airlines, Delta Air Lines, Interimpex-Avioimpex, Lufthansa, SABENA and Swissair. In 1997, 629,000 passengers and 3,745 tonnes of freight were flown.

Shipping. There is a port at Koper. Sea-going shipping totalled 9,061 GRT in 1995.

Telecommunications. Slovenia had 722,500 main telephone lines in 1997, equivalent to 364 per 1,000 population. There were 157,000 cellular phone subscribers, 95,000 PCs and 80,000 fax machines in 1995.

Postal Services. In 1995 there were 515 post offices.

SOCIAL INSTITUTIONS

Justice. There are 8 courts of first instance, 4 higher courts and a supreme court.

Religion. 75% of the population were Roman Catholic in 1996.

Education. Adult literacy rate in 1995 was over 99%. In 1995–96 there were 823 primary schools with 207,975 pupils and 15,364 teachers and 151 secondary schools with 104,827 pupils and 8,053 teachers. In 1995–96 there were 37 institutions of higher education with 45,951 students and 2,102 academic staff. There were 2 universities with 54,582 students and approximately 2,422 academic staff in 1997–98.

In 1994 total expenditure on education came to 6·2% of GNP and represented 12·8% of total government expenditure.

Health. In 1995 there were 4,183 doctors and 11,607 hospital beds.

Welfare. There were 462,895 people receiving pensions in 1997, of which 266,854 were old-age pensioners. Benefits totalled 625,353m. tolars in the first 10 months of 1997.

CULTURE

Broadcasting. The government-controlled Radiotelevizija Slovenija broadcasts 1 national and local radio programme, and also programmes in German and Italian. In 1995 there were in all 6 nationwide radio networks as well as regional and local stations. Public television transmission is carried out by the 2 stations of Televizija Slovenija (colour by PAL). There are also a national independent TV network, a network serving Ljubljana and district and several local stations. In 1995 there were 740,000 radio and 630,000 television receivers.

Cinema. There were 98 cinemas with a total of 29,000 seats in 1995, and an annual attendance of 2·9m.

Press. In 1997 there were 6 national dailies, 1 national evening and 20 weekly newspapers.

Tourism. 2,551,000 nights were spent by 832,000 foreign visitors in 1996. Receipts totalled US$1·21bn.

Libraries. As well as the National Library there was a total of 954 public libraries in 1995.

Museums and Galleries. Museums totalled 78 in 1994, with 1·8m. visitors that year.

DIPLOMATIC REPRESENTATIVES
Of Slovenia in Great Britain (Cavendish Crt, 11-15 Wigmore St., London, W1H 9LA)
Ambassador: Marjan Setinc.

Of Great Britain in Slovenia (4th Floor, 3 Trg Republike, 61000 Ljubljana)
Ambassador: David Lloyd, OBE.

Of Slovenia in the USA (1525 New Hampshire Ave., NW, Washington, D.C., 20036)
Ambassador: Dr Dimitrij Rupel.

Of the USA in Slovenia (4 Prazakova, 1000 Ljubljana)
Ambassador: Vacant.

Of Slovenia to the United Nations
Ambassador: Danilo Türk.

Of Slovenia to the European Union
Ambassador: Boris Cizelj.

FURTHER READING
Benderly, J. and Kraft, E. (eds.) *Independent Slovenia: Origins, Movements, Prospects.* London, 1995
Carmichael, C., *Slovenia* [Bibliography]. Oxford and Santa Barbara (CA), 1996

National statistical office: National Statistical Office, Vožarski Pot 12, 1000 Ljubljana.
Website: http://www.sigov.si/zrs/index_e.html

SOLOMON ISLANDS

Capital: Honiara
Population estimate, 2000: 444,000
GNP per capita: (PPP$) 2,250
HDI/world rank: 0·560/123

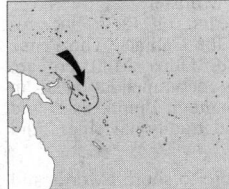

KEY HISTORICAL EVENTS
The Solomon Islands were discovered by Europeans in 1568; 200 years passed before contact was made again. The southern Solomon Islands were placed under British protection in 1893; the eastern and southern outliers were added in 1898 and 1899. Santa Isabel and the other islands to the north were ceded by Germany in 1900. Full internal self-government was achieved on 2 Jan. 1976 and independence on 7 July 1978.

TERRITORY AND POPULATION
The Solomon Islands lie within the area 5° to 12° 30' S. lat. and 155° 30' to 169° 45' E. long. The group includes the main islands of Guadalcanal, Malaita, New Georgia, San Cristobal (now Makira), Santa Isabel and Choiseul; the smaller Florida and Russell groups; the Shortland, Mono (or Treasury), Vella La Vella, Kolombangara, Ranongga, Gizo and Rendova Islands; to the east, Santa Cruz, Tikopia, the Reef and Duff groups; Rennell and Bellona in the south; Ontong Java or Lord Howe to the north; and many smaller islands. The land area is estimated at 10,954 sq. miles (28,370 sq. km). The larger islands are mountainous and forest clad, with flood-prone rivers of considerable energy potential. Guadalcanal has the largest land area and the greatest amount of flat coastal plain. Population (1997 estimate), 426,900; density per sq. km, 15·0.

The UN gives a projected population for 2000 of 444,000.

In 1995, 83% of the population lived in rural areas.

The islands are administratively divided into a Capital Territory and 9 provinces. Area and population:

Province	Sq.km	Census 1986	Estimate 1991	Capital
Western	5,475 ⎱	55,250	91,321 ⎰	Gizo
Choiseul	3,837 ⎰			Taro
Isabel	4,136	14,616	21,795	Buala
Central Islands	615 ⎱	18,457	28,968 ⎰	Tulagi
Renell and Bellona	671 ⎰			Tigoa
Capital Territory	22	30,413	43,643	. . .
Guadalcanal	5,336	49,831	59,064	Honiara
Malaita	4,225	80,032	102,719	Auki
Makira and Ulawa	3,188	21,796	28,064	Kirakira
Temotu	895	14,781	20,472	Lata (Santa Cruz)

The capital, Honiara, on Guadalcanal, is the largest urban area, with an estimated population in 1989 of 33,749. 93% of the population are Melanesian; other ethnic groups include Polynesian, Micronesian, European and Chinese.

English is the official language, and is spoken by 1–2% of the population. In all 120 indigenous languages are spoken; Melanesian languages are spoken by 85% of the population.

SOCIAL STATISTICS
Births, 1997, 15,900; deaths, 1,800. 1997 birth rate (per 1,000 population), 37·3; death rate, 4·3. Life expectancy, 1997, 71·5 years. Population growth rate is estimated at 3·3% (1997). Infant mortality, 1990–95, 27 per 1,000 live births; fertility rate, 5·4 births per woman.

CLIMATE
An equatorial climate with only small seasonal variations. South-east winds cause cooler conditions from April to Nov., but north-west winds for the rest of the year bring higher temperatures and greater rainfall, with annual totals ranging between 80" (2,000 mm) and 120" (3,000 mm).

CONSTITUTION AND GOVERNMENT

The Solomon Islands is a constitutional monarchy with the British Sovereign (represented locally by a Governor-General, who must be a Solomon Island citizen) as Head of State. Legislative power is vested in the single-chamber *National Parliament* composed of 50 members, elected by universal adult suffrage for 5 years. Parliamentary democracy is based on a multi-party system. Executive authority is effectively held by the Cabinet, led by the Prime Minister.

The Governor-General is appointed for up to five years, on the advice of Parliament, and acts in almost all matters on the advice of the Cabinet. The Prime Minister is elected by and from members of Parliament. Other Ministers are appointed by the Governor-General on the Prime Minister's recommendation, from members of Parliament. The Cabinet is responsible to Parliament. Emphasis is laid on the devolution of power to provincial governments, and traditional chiefs and leaders have a special role within the arrangement.

National Anthem. 'God save our Solomon Islands from shore to shore'; words and tune by P. Balekana.

RECENT ELECTIONS

National elections were held on 6 Aug. 1997. The electorate was 143,275; 333 candidates stood. Though the National Unity Party won up to 15 seats in Parliament, smaller parties including the People's Alliance, National, Labour and Liberal Parties decided to form a coalition government now called the Solomon Islands Alliance for Change (SIAC).

CURRENT ADMINISTRATION

Governor-General: Sir Moses Puibangara. (His term ends in 1999 when Parliament will elect a successor.)

In March 1999 the government comprised:

Prime Minister and Acting Minister for Finance: Bartholomew Ulufa'alu.

Deputy Prime Minister and Minister for Transport, Works and Utilities, and Minister of Communications: Sir Baddeley Devesi.

Minister of Agriculture and Fisheries: Stephen S. Aumanu. *Commerce, Employment and Tourism:* Enele Kwanairara. *Education and Training:* Ronnie Mani. *Foreign Affairs and Trade:* Patteson J. Oti. *Forests, Environment and Conservation:* Hilda Kari. *Health and Medical Services:* Dick Warakohia. *Home and Cultural Affairs:* Rev. Leslie Boseto. *Lands and Housing:* Jackson Piasi. *Mines and Energy:* Walton Naeson. *Planning and Development:* Fred Fono. *Police and National Security:* Rev. Rueben Mesepitu. *Provincial Governments:* Japhet Waipora. *Youth, Sports and Women:* Gordon Mara. *Justice and Legal Affairs:* Edmond Andresen Karaer. *Indigenous Business Development:* David Holosivi.

Provincial and Local Governments. There are 9 Provincial Governments established under the Provincial Government Act of 1981. Certain responsibilities are further delegated to Area Councils. Honiara Municipal Authority comprises elected members who at the discretion of the Minister responsible for the Local Governments Ordinance can be replaced by appointed councillors.

DEFENCE

The marine wing of the Royal Solomon Islands Police operates 3 patrol boats and a number of fast crafts for surveillance of fisheries and maritime boundaries. There is also an RSI Police Field Force stationed at the border with Papua New Guinea.

INTERNATIONAL RELATIONS

The Solomon Islands is a member of the UN, the Commonwealth, the Pacific Community, South Pacific Forum and is an ACP member state of the ACP-EU relationship. The Solomon Islands is also a member of the World Trade Organization and other organizations for regional technical co-operation. It maintains bilateral relations with 46 countries in the international community.

ECONOMY

Policy. When the Solomon Islands Alliance for Change (SIAC) coalition assumed office in Aug. 1997, the government had SI$200m. in debts despite a 6% growth rate of the economy during the previous year. The debt was reduced to SI$147m. by Sept. 1998 in a debt-servicing programme established jointly with the Central Bank of the Solomon Islands. The SIAC coalition embarked on a reform programme to encourage private enterprise which included a reduction of the civil service and a tightening of government revenue collection. The 1998 and 1999 Government estimates are based on balanced budgeting. In Dec. 1997 the Solomon Islands dollar was devalued by 20%.

Performance. Real GDP growth was 7·0% in 1995 (4·5% in 1994).

Budget. The budget estimate for 1998 was for expenditure of SI$631·8m.; total revenue forecast, SI$482m. plus SI$149m. to be secured through concessionary loans.

Currency. The *Solomon Island dollar* (SBD) of 100 *cents* was introduced in 1977. The average annual inflation rate over the period 1990–96 was 11·3%. In Dec. 1997 foreign exchange reserves were US$31m. Total money supply was SI$210m. in Nov. 1997.

Banking and Finance. The Central Bank of Solomon Islands is the bank of issue. There are 3 commercial banks.

Weights and Measures. The metric system is in force.

ENERGY AND NATURAL RESOURCES

Electricity. Installed capacity in 1994 was 20,000 kW. Production in 1994 was 55m. kWh and consumption per capita in 1994 was an estimated 149 kWh. The Solomon Islands Electricity Authority is undertaking projects to increase power generation capacity including the construction of a major hydro-electricity power plant.

Oil and Gas. The potential for oil, petroleum and gas production has yet to be tapped.

Water. Supply of clean drinking water is abundant in most of the large islands, though smaller and outlying islands have to rely on underground table water.

Minerals. Gold earned SI$1·3m. in 1991, decreasing to SI$0·3m. for 8 kg in 1994. The 3 Gold Ridge mines opened in July/Aug. 1998, one of them owned by an Australian firm, Ross Mining. There is the prospect of nickel mining on San George Island and other mineral deposits are known to exist.

Agriculture. Land is held either as customary land (88% of holdings) or registered land. Customary land rights depend on clan membership or kinship. Only Solomon Islanders own customary land; only Islanders or government members may hold perpetual estates of registered land. Coconuts, cocoa, rice and other minor crops are grown. Main food crops: coconut, cassava, sweet potato, yam, taro and banana. Production value of copra (in SI$), 29m.; palm products, SI$62·9m.; cocoa, SI$12·8m., earning SI$104·7m. in exports in 1997.

Livestock (1996): Cattle, 10,000; pigs, 55,000.

Forestry. Forests covered 2·39m. ha in 1995 (85·4% of the land area). Earnings from forest resources increased from SI$266·6m. in 1994 to SI$309·9m. in 1995 and SI$349·3m. in 1996 but then slumped in 1997 to SI$309·4m. due to a fall in prices and a government moratorium on the issue of new logging licences.

Fisheries. Solomon Islands' waters are among the richest in tuna. Catches have remained well below the maximum sustainable catch limits. Previously closed areas within its territorial waters have been opened to American fishing interests but sustainable harvest rates will not be at risk. Total catch, 1995, 46,462 tonnes.

INDUSTRY

Industries include palm oil milling, rice milling, fish canning, fish freezing, saw milling, food, tobacco and soft drinks. Other products include wood and rattan furniture, fibreglass articles, boats, clothing and spices.

Labour. The Labour Division of the Ministry of Commerce, Employment and Tourism monitors and regulates the domestic labour market. The labour force in 1996 totalled 202,000 (54% males). Around 38% of the economically active population in 1993 were engaged in community, social and personal services and 27% in agriculture, fisheries and forestry.

SOLOMON ISLANDS

Trade Unions. Trade Unions exist by virtue of the Trade Unions Act of 1976. The Solomon Islands Council of Trade Unions (SICTU) is the central body. Affiliated members of the SICTU are Solomon Islands National Union of Workers and the Solomon Islands Public Employees Union (SIPEU). SIPEU, which represents employees of the public sector, is the largest single trade union.

INTERNATIONAL TRADE

The Solomon Islands is a member of the World Trade Organization. The Government recognizes the private sector as an engine for growth. Through encouraging the private sector the Government hopes that the base for a broad diversification of tradeable goods and services can be established.

Imports and Exports. Imports 1997 (1996), SI$616·9m. (SI$538·6m.); exports, SI$648·7m. (SI$575·5m.). Value of main imports, 1996 (in SI$1,000): Food, SI$81·3m.; fuels and lubricants, SI$60·8m.; machinery and transport equipment, SI$162·8m.; manufactured goods, SI$119·1m.; chemicals, SI$23·8m.; drinks and tobacco, SI$12·0m. and others, SI$77·0m. Main exports: Timber, SI$309·4m.; fish, SI$182·4m.; cocoa, SI$44·5m.; palm products, SI$57·4m.; coconut products, SI$17·7m.; and others, SI$37·3m. In 1997 the principal suppliers were Australia (37·2%), Japan (17·1%), New Zealand (9·6%) and Singapore (8·4%); the principal export markets were Japan (41·1%), South Korea (14·1%) and UK (13·1%).

Trade Fairs. An annual National Cultural and Trade Show/Fair is held in July to coincide with the anniversary of independence.

COMMUNICATIONS

Roads. In 1995 there was estimated to be a total of 2,100 km of roads, of which 32 km were paved. The unpaved roads included 800 km of private plantation roads.

Civil Aviation. A new terminal has been opened at Henderson International Airport in Honiara. The airport is served by the national carrier, Solomon Airlines and also Air Niugini, Air Vanuatu and joint services by Solomon Airlines with Qantas and Air Pacific. Local routes are serviced by Solomon Airlines and Western Pacific Air Services. Air Transport Limited runs helicopter services in Solomon Islands and Pacific Air Express runs cargo services to Australia on a regular basis. In 1995 Solomon Airlines carried 89,500 passengers (27,000 on international flights).

Shipping. There are international ports at Honiara, Yandina in the Russell Islands and Noro in New Georgia, Western Province. In 1995 the merchant marine totalled 5,746 GRT.

Telecommunications. Telecommunications are operated by Solomon Telekom, a joint venture between the Government of Solomon Islands and Cable & Wireless (UK). Telecommunications between Honiara and provincial centres are facilitated by modern satellite communication systems. Main telephone lines numbered 7,800 in 1997 (19·3 per 1,000 inhabitants). There were approximately 200 cellular phone subscribers and 800 fax machines in 1995.

Postal Services. The Solomon Islands Postal Corporation, a statutory company established in 1996, administers postal services. In 1995 there were 140 post offices.

SOCIAL INSTITUTIONS

Justice. Civil and criminal jurisdiction is exercised by the High Court of Solomon Islands, constituted 1975. A Solomon Islands Court of Appeal was established in 1982. Jurisdiction is based on the principles of English law (as applying on 1 Jan. 1981). Magistrates' courts can try civil cases on claims not exceeding SI$2,000, and criminal cases with penalties not exceeding 14 years' imprisonment. Certain crimes, such as burglary and arson, where the maximum sentence is for life, may also be tried by magistrates. There are also local courts, which decide matters concerning customary titles to land; decisions may be put to the Customary Land Appeal Court. There is no capital punishment.

Religion. 95% of the population are Christians.

Education. In 1994 there were 12,627 pre-primary pupils, and 65,493 primary pupils, with 2,514 teachers. There were 7,811 pupils at secondary level. Adult literacy (1994) is 62·0%.

Training of teachers and trade and vocational training is carried out at the college of Higher Education. The University of the South Pacific Centre is at Honiara. Other rural training centres run by churches are also involved in vocational training.

Health. A free medical service is supplemented by the private sector. An international standard immunization programme is conducted in conjunction with the WHO for infants. Tuberculosis has been eradicated but malaria remains a problem. In 1997 there were 11 hospitals, 31 doctors and 464 registered nurses and 283 nursing aides.

CULTURE

Broadcasting. The Solomon Islands Broadcasting Corporation (SIBC) operates a national service and an FM service for Honiara. The other FM station—FM100—is privately operated and broadcasts news and entertainment on a 24-hour basis. In 1995 there were 46,000 radio receivers and 2,000 TV receivers.

Cinema. Private interests operate 3 cinemas in the capital. There are small cinemas in the provincial centres.

Press. There are 2 main newspapers in circulation. *The Solomon Star* which used to produce 4 issues during the week is now daily. *Solomon Voice* is a weekly which publishes on Fridays. The Government Information Service publishes a monthly issue of the *Solomon Nius* which exclusively disseminates news of government activities. Non-government organizations such as the Solomon Islands Development Trust (SIDT) also publish monthly papers on environmental issues.

Tourism. Tourism in Solomon Islands is still in a development stage. The emphasis is on establishing major hotels in the capital and provincial centres, to be supplemented by satellite Eco-tourism projects in the rural areas. The Solomon Islands Visitors Bureau is the statutory institution for domestic co-ordination and international marketing. In 1996 there were 11,000 foreign tourists, bringing revenue of US$13m.

Festivals. Festivities and parades in the capital and provincial centres normally mark the National Day of Independence. The highlight is the annual National Trade and Cultural Show.

Libraries. There is a National Library operated by Government in Honiara. The other library facilities are those of the Solomon Islands College of Higher Education and the University of the South Pacific (SI) Centre.

Museums and Galleries. There is a National Museum which has a display of traditional artefacts. Early government and public records are kept at the National Archives and a National Art Gallery displays a number of fine arts and works by Solomon Islands artists.

DIPLOMATIC REPRESENTATIVES
Of the Solomon Islands in Great Britain (resides in Brussels).
High Commissioner: Robert Sisilo.

Of Great Britain in the Solomon Islands (Telekom House, Mendana Ave., Honiara)
High Commissioner: Allan Waters.

Of the USA in the Solomon Islands
Ambassador: Richard W. Teare (resides in Papua New Guinea).

Of the Solomon Islands in the USA and to the United Nations (800 2nd. Ave. Suite 400L, New York, NY 10017)
Ambassador: Rex Stephen Horoi.

Of the Solomon Islands to the European Union
Ambassador: Robert Sisilo.

FURTHER READING
Bennett, J. A., *Wealth of the Solomons: A History of a Pacific Archipelago, 1800–1978.* Univ. of Hawaii Press, 1987
Kent, J., *The Solomon Islands.* Newton Abbot, 1972

SOMALIA

Jamhuriyadda Dimugradiga
ee Soomaaliya

(Somali Democratic Republic)

Capital: Mogadishu
Population estimate, 2000: 11·53m.
Estimated GDP: $3·6bn.

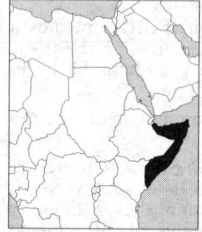

KEY HISTORICAL EVENTS

The origins of the Somali people can be traced back 2,000 years when they migrated to the region, displacing and absorbing an earlier Arabic people. They converted to Islam in the 10th century and were organized in loose Islamic states by the 19th century. The northern part of Somaliland was created a British protectorate in 1884. The southern part belonged to two local rulers who, in 1889, accepted Italian protection for their lands. The Italian invasion of Ethiopia in 1935 was launched from Somaliland and in 1936 Somaliland was incorporated with Eritrea and Ethiopia to become Italian East Africa. In 1940 Italian forces invaded British Somaliland but in 1941 the British, with South African and Indian troops, recaptured this territory as well as occupying Italian Somaliland. After the Second World War British Somaliland reverted to its colonial status and ex-Italian Somaliland became the UN Trust Territory of Somaliland, administered by Italy.

The independent Somali Republic came into being on 1 July 1960 as a result of the merger of the British Somaliland Protectorate, which first became independent on 26 June 1960, and the Italian Trusteeship Territory of Somaliland. Aden Abdullah Osman was elected president of the new republic, and the legislatures of the two territories were merged to create a single national assembly.

On 21 Oct. 1969 Maj.-Gen. Mohammed Siyad Barre, the C.-in-C. of the armed forces, took power in a *coup.* He suspended the constitution and formed a Supreme Revolutionary Council to administer the country, which was renamed the Somali Democratic Republic.

Various insurgent forces combined to oppose the Barre regime in a bloody civil war. Barre fled on 27 Jan. 1991. Ali Mahdi Muhammad, of the United Somali Congress, became president in Aug. 1991, but interfactional fighting continued. In Aug. 1992 a new coalition government agreed a UN military presence to back up relief efforts to help the estimated 1·5–2m. victims of famine. In accordance with a unanimous UN Security Council resolution of 3 Nov. 1992, troops from the USA and other countries mounted a mission to ensure the supply of aid to victims of the civil war and drought. On 11 Dec. 1992 the leaders of the two most prominent of the warring factions, Ali Mahdi Muhammad and Muhammad Farah Aidid, agreed to a peace plan under the aegis of the UN, and a pact was signed on 15 Jan. 1993. At the end of March, the warring factions agreed to disarm and form a 74-member National Transitional Council.

Following the killing of 24 Pakistani soldiers of the UN 29-nation peacekeeping force on 17 June 1993, UN troops attacked and seized the stronghold of Muhammad Aidid and sought his arrest. After an escalation of violence in which hundreds of Somalis were killed, an envoy from the US President negotiated the release of hostages from Gen. Aidid and it was agreed to set up an independent commission of enquiry. After Dec. 1993 various national contingents began to leave the peace-keeping force, including US forces in March 1994. A unanimous UN National Security Council resolution of 4 Feb. 1994 laid stress on the need for reconciliation and the promotion of democratic government, and scaled down the number of UN forces in the country. On 4 Nov. 1994 the UN Security Council unanimously decided to withdraw UN forces; the last of these left on 2 March 1995.

The principal insurgent group in the north of the country, the Somali National Movement, declared the secession of an independent **'Somaliland Republic'** on 17 May 1991, based on the territory of the former British protectorate, with a capital at Hargeisa and a port at Berbera. Its president is Muhammad Ibrahim Egal. The

Somalian government rejected the secession. Clan warfare broke out in Hargeisa in Nov. 1994, and Muhammad Aidid's forces launched a campaign to reoccupy the 'Republic' in Jan. 1996.

Muhammad Farah Aidid was assassinated in July 1996 and succeeded by his son Hussein Aidid (b. 1965). Fighting between the Ali Mahdi Muhammad and the Hussein Aidid factions broke out in Dec. 1996 in Mogadishu, but on 20 Jan. 1997 the factions agreed to unify the city.

TERRITORY AND POPULATION

Somalia is bounded north by the Gulf of Aden, east and south by the Indian ocean, and west by Kenya, Ethiopia and Djibouti. Total area 637,657 sq. km (246,201 sq. miles). Estimated population: 10,070,000 (1997); density, 15·8 per sq. km. Population counting is complicated due to large number of nomads and refugee movements due to famine and clan warfare.

The UN gives a projected population for 2000 of 11·53m.

In 1995 an estimated 74·4% of the population were rural.

The country is administratively divided into 18 regions (with chief cities): Awdal (Saylac), Bakol (Xuddur), Bay (Baydhabo), Benadir (Mogadishu), East (Boosaso), Galgudug (Duusa Marreeb), Gedo (Garbahaarrey), Hiran (Beledweyne), Central Juba (Jilib), Lower Juba (Kismaayo), Mudug (Gaalkacyo), Nogal (Gaarowe), North-West (Hargeysa), Sanaag (Ceerigabo), Central Shabele (Jawhar), Lower Shabele (Marka), Sol (Las Anod), Togder (Burao). The capital is Mogadishu (1987 population, 1m.). Other large towns are Hargeysa (0·4m.), Kismaayo (0·2m.), Marka (0·1m.) and Berbera.

The national language is Somali. Arabic is also an official language and English and Italian are spoken extensively.

SOCIAL STATISTICS

Births, 1997 estimate, 300,000; deaths, 121,000. Rates, 1997 estimate (per 1,000 population): Birth, 45·5; death, 18·3. Infant mortality, 1997, 126 per 1,000 live births; growth, 3·03%. Life expectancy in 1997, 46·2 years. Fertility rate, 1990–95, 7·0 births per woman.

CLIMATE

Much of the country is arid, though rainfall is more adequate towards the south. Temperatures are very high on the northern coasts. Mogadishu, Jan. 79°F (26·1°C), July 78°F (25·6°C). Annual rainfall 17" (429 mm). Berbera, Jan. 76°F (24·4°C), July 97°F (36·1°C). Annual rainfall 2" (51 mm).

CONSTITUTION AND GOVERNMENT

The Constitution of 1984 authorized a sole legal party, the Somali Revolutionary Socialist Party. There was an elected President and People's Assembly.

A conference of national reconciliation in July 1991 and again in March 1993 allowed for the setting up of a transitional government charged with reorganizing free elections, but inter-factional fighting and anarchy have replaced settled government.

CURRENT ADMINISTRATION

Somalia has no functioning government as such.

Local Government. The 18 regions are sub-divided into 84 districts.

DEFENCE

With the breakdown of government following the 1991 revolution armed forces broke up into clan groupings, four of those in the north and six in the south.

Defence expenditure totalled US$40m. in 1997 (US$7 per capita).

INTERNATIONAL RELATIONS

Somalia is a member of the UN, OAU and the Arab League and is an ACP member state of the ACP-EU relationship.

ECONOMY

Performance. Real GDP growth was 0·0% in 1995 (−21·0% in 1994).

Budget. Budget for 1990: Revenue, Som.Sh. 49,264m.; expenditure, Som.Sh. 68,970m.

Currency. The unit of currency is the *Somali shilling* (SOS) of 100 *cents*.

Banking and Finance. The bank of issue is the Central Bank of Somalia (founded in 1960 as the Somali National Bank). All banks were nationalized in 1970. The Somali Development Bank (founded 1983) and the Commercial Bank of Somalia are the only banks.

Weights and Measures. The metric system is in use.

ENERGY AND NATURAL RESOURCES

Electricity. Capacity: 144,000 kW prior to the civil war, now largely shut down; some localities operate their own generating plants. Production (1994 estimate): 259m. kWh.

Minerals. There are deposits of chromium, coal, copper, gold, gypsum, lead, limestone, manganese, nickel, silver, titanium, tungsten, uranium and zinc.

Agriculture. Somalia is essentially a pastoral country, and about 80% of the inhabitants depend on livestock-rearing (cattle, sheep, goats and camels). Half the population is nomadic. In 1994 there were 1·0m. ha of arable land, 20,000 ha of permanent cropland and 43m. ha of permanent pasture. Estimated production, 1995 (in 1,000 tonnes): Sugar-cane, 200; bananas, 45; maize, 146; sorghum, 136; grapefruit, 19.

Livestock (1995): 13·5m. sheep; 12·5m. goats; 6·2m. camels; 5·2m. cattle. Somalia has the greatest number of camels of any country in the world.

Forestry. In 1995 the area under forests was 754,000 ha, or 1·2% of the total land area. In 1995, 8·79m. cu. metres of roundwood were cut. Wood and charcoal are the main energy sources. Frankincense and myrrh are produced.

Fisheries. In 1988 the fishing fleet comprised 28 vessels totalling 5,188 DWT. 15,500 tonnes were caught in 1995, of which 15,200 tonnes were sea fish.

INDUSTRY

A few small industries existed in 1986 including sugar refining, food processing, textiles and petroleum refining.

Labour. The labour force totalled 4,291,000 in 1996 (57% males). Approximately 74% of the economically active population in 1995 were engaged in agriculture, fisheries and forestry.

INTERNATIONAL TRADE

Foreign debt was US$2,643m. in 1996.

Imports and Exports. Exports in 1994 were estimated at US$130m. and imports at US$269m.

Principal exports: Livestock, hides and skins, bananas. Main export markets in 1992 (trade in US$1m.): Saudi Arabia, 24·9; Italy, 11. Main import suppliers: Saudi Arabia, 12·9; USA, 10·9; Italy, 10·6.

COMMUNICATIONS

Roads. In 1996 there were 22,100 km of roads, of which 2,600 km were paved. Passenger cars numbered 1,020 in 1996, and there were 6,440 trucks and vans.

Civil Aviation. There are international airports at Mogadishu, Berbera and Erigavo. In 1998 internal services and flights to Djibouti were provided by Air Djibouti, Daallo Airlines and Djibouti Airlines.

Shipping. There are deep-water harbours at Kismayo, Berbera, Marka and Mogadishu. The merchant fleet (1995) totalled 17,288 GRT.

Telecommunications. Somalia had 15,000 main telephone lines in 1997, equivalent to 1·5 for every 1,000 persons.

SOCIAL INSTITUTIONS

Justice. There are 84 district courts, each with a civil and a criminal section. There are 8 regional courts and 2 Courts of Appeal (at Mogadishu and Hargeysa), each with a general section and an assize section. The Supreme Court is in Mogadishu.

Religion. The population is almost entirely Sunni Moslems.

Education. The nomadic life of a large percentage of the population inhibits education progress. In 1990 adult literacy was estimated at 24%. In 1985 there were 194,335 pupils and 9,676 teachers in primary schools, there were 37,181 pupils and 2,320 teachers in secondary schools, and in 1984, 613 students with 30 teachers at teacher-training establishments. The National University of Somalia in Mogadishu (founded 1959) had 4,650 students and 550 academic staff in 1994–95.

Health. In 1986 there were 88 hospitals, 358 doctors, 113 pharmacists, 2 dentists, 556 midwives and 1,834 nursing personnel.

CULTURE

Broadcasting. The state radio stations transmit in Somali, Arabic, English and Italian from Mogadishu and Hargeysa. The television station was destroyed in fighting in 1991; in 1995 there were estimated to be 400,000 radio and 124,000 TV receivers.

Press. In 1995 there was one daily newspaper, with a circulation of 10,000.

Tourism. In 1996 there were 10,000 foreign tourists.

DIPLOMATIC REPRESENTATIVES
The Embassy of Somalia in Great Britain closed on 2 Jan. 1992.

Of Great Britain in Somalia (Waddada Xasan Geedd Abtoow 7/8, Mogadishu) Staff temporarily withdrawn.

The Embassy of Somalia in the USA closed on 8 May 1991. A liaison office opened in March 1994, and withdrew to Nairobi in Sept. 1994.

Of Somalia to the United Nations
Ambassador: Vacant.

Of Somalia to the European Union
Ambassador: Vacant.

FURTHER READING
Abdisalam, M. I.-S., *The Collapse of the Somali State*. London, 1995
DeLancey, M. W., *et al. Somalia*. [Bibliography] Oxford and Santa Barbara (CA), 1988
Ghalib, J. M., *The Cost of Dictatorship: the Somali Experience*. New York, 1995
Lewis, I. M., *Blood and Bone: the Call of Kinship in Somali Society*. Lawrenceville (NJ), 1995.—*Understanding Somalia: a Guide to Culture, History and Social Institutions*. 2nd ed. London 1995
Omar, M. O., *The Road to Zero: Somalia's Self-Destruction*. London, 1995
Samatar, A. I. (ed.) *The Somali Challenge: from Catastrophe to Renewal?* Boulder (CO), 1994

National statistical office: Central Statistical Department, State Planning Commission, Mogadishu.

SOUTH AFRICA

Republic of South Africa

Capitals: Pretoria (Administrative),
Cape Town (Legislative), Bloem-
fontein (Judicial)
Seats of Parliament: Cape Town
Seats of Government: Cape Town,
Pretoria
Population estimate, 2000: 46·26m.
GNP per capita: (PPP$) 7,450
HDI/world rank: 0·717/89

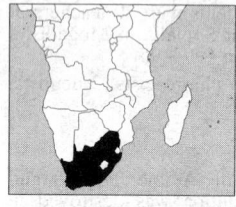

KEY HISTORICAL EVENTS

The Dutch first established a trading post at the Cape in 1652. The hinterland was then inhabited by the Khoisan peoples and, further east and north, by Bantu-speaking peoples. There was some white settlement over the next century. During the Napoleonic Wars, Britain took possession of the Cape and later many Boer (Dutch) settlers migrated north-east in the Great Trek. In the mid-19th century Britain ruled the Cape Colony and Natal along the coast of southern Africa, while in the interior the Afrikaners or Boers, descendants of Dutch settlers, established their own independent republics in the Transvaal and the Orange Free State. Some Bantu African peoples remained unconquered, notably the Xhosas east of the Cape Colony and, north of Natal, the Zulus, whose leader Shaka (died 1828) had formed a powerful kingdom in a great political and demographic upheaval called the *Mfecane*. The Sothos, who formed another new state under Moshoeshoe, resisted the Boers' encroachment on their land, until in 1868 Britain granted Moshoeshoe's request for a protectorate over Basutoland. Meanwhile, British settlers emigrated to Cape Colony and Natal in the 19th century, and from the 1860s many Indians were brought to Natal as indentured labourers on the sugar plantations. The population of the Cape Colony included many Afrikaners as well as the 'Coloured' community, descendants of Dutch settlers and indigenous Khoisan women and of Malay slaves. Most coloureds spoke Afrikaans, the offshoot of Dutch spoken by the Boers.

Britain annexed the Transvaal in 1877, and fought in 1879 with the Zulus who, under King Ketshwayo, won a victory at Isandhlwana, but were then defeated at Ulundi. Britain restored independence to the Transvaal (South African Republic) in 1884 and annexed Zululand in 1887. Both the British and the Boers fought African resistance for many years, the last major rising being in Natal in 1906. However, the British and Boers were also rivals for supremacy, especially after the discovery of diamonds at Kimberley in 1867 and of gold in the Transvaal in 1884. This led to an economic boom and wealth for many, of whom Cecil Rhodes, for a time prime minister of the Cape, was the dominant entrepreneurial figure.

In the South African War of 1899–1902 the British defeated and annexed the Boer republics. The Boer republics were given self-government again in 1907, and on 31 May 1910 Cape Colony, Natal, the Transvaal and the Orange Free State combined to form the Union of South Africa, a self-governing dominion under the British Crown. The Union was ruled by the white minority; the franchise accorded to some non-whites in Cape Colony was kept, but not extended to the other three provinces.

The Union's economy was based on gold and diamond mining, for which there was organized recruitment of migrant African labourers from Union territory and other parts of Africa. Pass Laws were in operation, controlling Africans' movements in the towns and industrial areas, where they were regarded officially as temporary residents and segregated in 'townships'. By an Act of 1913, 87% of the land was reserved for white ownership only, much of it being owned by white farmers, while Africans farmed as tenants or squatters.

African protests at segregation and lack of political rights were led by the African National Congress (ANC). From 1918 there were also many African labour protests. African rights were further suppressed after the coming to power in 1924 of the Afrikaner Nationalist Party, led by J. B. Hertzog. Hertzog's government secured recognition of full independence for South Africa by the Statute of Westminster on

1416

11 Dec. 1931. It also promoted the status of the Afrikaans language and introduced new segregation measures. From 1948 the National Party government reinforced the segregation system, developing it into the system of Apartheid, enforced under prime ministers Malan (1948–54), Strijdom (1954–58), Verwoerd (1958–66) and Voerster (1966–78). The shooting by police of protesters against the Pass Laws at Sharpeville on 21 March 1960 led to a major crisis from which, however, the government emerged only stronger. The ANC and the Pan African Congress were banned, and the leaders forced to operate from exile after internal ANC leaders, including Nelson Mandela, were jailed in 1964.

On 31 May 1961 South Africa became a Republic outside the Commonwealth.

When P. W. Botha became prime minister in 1978, elements of the Apartheid system were modified. Africans were allowed to form legal trade unions, creation of Black local government authorities in cities was enacted, and the Acts banning marriage and sexual relations between people of different races were repealed.

A new constitution, approved in a referendum of white voters on 2 Nov. 1983 and in force from 3 Sept. 1984, created a new three-part parliament, with a House of Assembly for the Whites, a House of Representatives for the Coloureds, and a House of Delegates for the Indians; Africans remained without representation. At the same time an executive presidency was created, to which Botha was elected. Boycotts ensured low polls in the elections for the Coloured and Indian houses held on 22 and 28 Aug. 1984 respectively. The Whites retained their House of Assembly as elected in 1981 with its massive National Party majority.

From late 1984 Blacks in the cities and industrial areas staged large-scale protests, including strikes. Largely spontaneous—though the jailed ANC leader Mandela was seen as the Africans' hero—the protests involved large-scale violence. In June 1986 a state of emergency was imposed. Foreign condemnation of this led to the first economic sanctions against South Africa, imposed by a number of countries including the USA.

By 1989 the restrictions of Apartheid began to be removed, and the government announced its willingness to consider the extension of Black South Africans' political rights. In Feb. 1990 a 30-year ban on the African National Congress (ANC) was lifted and its leader, Nelson Mandela, released from prison.

At the Whites-only referendum on 17 March 1992, on the granting of constitutional equality to all races, turn-out was 85·6%. 1,924,186 (68·7%) votes were in favour; 875,619 against.

On 22 Dec. 1993 parliament approved (by 237 votes to 45) a Transitional Constitution paving the way for a new multi-racial parliament which was elected on 26–29 April 1994, and South Africa rejoined the Commonwealth. On 9 May 1994 Nelson Mandela was elected President and sworn in the following day. A new Constitution was signed into law in Dec. 1996. Also in Dec. 1996, South Africa set up the Truth and Reconciliation Commission which reported in Oct. 1998, concluding that most gross human rights violations committed by the former state had been through its security forces.

TERRITORY AND POPULATION

South Africa is bounded in the north by Namibia, Botswana and Zimbabwe, north-east by Mozambique and Swaziland, east by the Indian Ocean, and south and west by the South Atlantic, with Lesotho forming an enclave. Area: 1,224,691 sq. km. This area includes the uninhabited Prince Edward Island (41 sq. km) and Marion Island (388 sq. km), lying 1,900 km south-east of Cape Town and taken possession of in Dec. 1947. In 1994 Walvis Bay was ceded to Namibia, and Transkei, Bophuthatswana, Venda and Ciskei were re-integrated into South Africa.

At the census of 1996 the population was 40,583,573 (21,062,685 females), consisting of: African/Black, 31,127,631 (76·7% of total population); White, 4,434,697 (10·9%); Coloured, 3,600,446 (8·9%); Indian/Asian, 1,045 (2·6%).

The UN gives a projected population for 2000 of 46·26m.

Urban population (Oct. 1996 census) was 21,781,807.

Of the 5,407 immigrants in 1996, 2,315 were from Europe (of whom 1,052, UK); 1,020 from Asia (of whom 244, Taiwan); 1,549 from Africa, 257 from the Americas and 86 from Oceania. Of the 9,708 emigrants in 1996, 3,198 went to Europe (of

SOUTH AFRICA

whom 2,243 to UK); 3,035 to Oceania (of whom 1,767, Australia); 1,786 to the Americas; 1,151 to Africa and 136 to Asia.

Population by province, according to the 1996 census:

Province	Total	African/ Black	White	Coloured	Indian/ Asian
Eastern Cape	6,302,525	5,448,495	330,294	468,532	19,356
Free State	2,633,504	1,223,940	316,459	79,038	2,805
Gauteng	7,348,423	5,147,444	1,702,343	278,692	161,289
Kwazulu-Natal	8,417,021	6,880,652	558,182	117,951	790,813
Mpumalanga	2,800,711	2,497,834	253,392	20,283	13,083
Northern Cape	840,321	278,633	111,844	435,368	2,268
Northern Province	4,929,368	4,765,255	117,878	7,821	5,510
North West	3,354,825	3,058,686	222,755	46,652	10,097
Western Cape	3,956,875	826,691	821,551	2,146,109	40,376

There are 11 official languages. Numbers of home speakers at the 1996 census: IsiZulu, 9,200,144 (22·9% of population); IsiXhosa, 7,196,118 (17·9%); Afrikaans, 5,811,547 (14·4%); Sepedi, 3,695,846 (9·2%); English, 3,457,467 (8·6%); Setswana, 3,301,774 (8·2%); Sesotho, 3,104,197 (7·7%); Xitsonga, 1,756,105 (4·4%); Siswati, 1,013,193 (2·5%); Tshivenda, 876,409 (2·2%); IsiNdebele, 586,961 (1·5%). The use of any of these is a constitutional right 'wherever practicable'. Each province may adopt any of these as its official language. English is the sole language of command and instruction in the armed forces.

SOCIAL STATISTICS
Statistics for calendar years:

	Births	Still Births	Deaths	Marriages	Immigrants	Emigrants
1994	677,107	6,968	213,279	133,309	6,398	10,235
1995	809,439	8,946	268,028	148,148	5,064	8,725
1996	...	...	...	146,732	5,407	9,708
1997	...	...	...	...	4,103	8,946

Due to under-registration and the high percentage of late registration, the collection of Black birth information was discontinued in 1981–89. As from 1991 no distinction between racial groups was made. The 1995 live birth figure includes 548,559 late registrations of births which actually took place between 1989–94. Infant mortality, 1990–95, 53 per 1,000 live births; fertility rate, 4·1 births per woman. Divorces in 1996: White, 15,831; African/Black, 7,243; Coloured, 4,190; Indian/Asian, 1,489. Expectation of life, 1990–95, was 60·0 years for males and 66·0 for females.

CLIMATE
There is abundant sunshine and relatively low rainfall. The south-west has a Mediterranean climate, with rain mainly in winter, but most of the country has a summer maximum, though quantities show a decrease from east to west. Pretoria, Jan. 72·5°F (22·5°C), July 52·3°F (11·3°C). Annual rainfall 29·5" (750 mm). Bloemfontein, Jan. 73°F (22·8°C), July 47°F (8·3°C). Annual rainfall 23" (564 mm). Cape Town, Jan. 69°F (20·6°C), July 54°F (12·2°C). Annual rainfall 20" (508 mm). Johannesburg, Jan. 68°F (20°C), July 51°F (10·6°C). Annual rainfall 28" (709 mm).

CONSTITUTION AND GOVERNMENT
A Transitional Constitution came into effect on 27 April 1994 and was in force until 3 Feb. 1997. Under it, the National Assembly and Senate formed a Constitutional Assembly (chaired by Mr Cyril Ramaphosa of the African National Congress [ANC]) which had the task of adopting a definitive Constitution by a two-thirds majority. This was adopted on 9 May 1996 and signed into law in Dec. 1996. The 1993 Constitution provided for an executive President, elected by Parliament; Deputy Presidents, nominated one each by parties gaining at least 20% of electoral votes; and a Parliament of 2 houses: a *National Assembly* and a *Senate*. The 1996 Constitution defines the powers of the President, Parliament (consisting of the National Assembly and the new National Council of Provinces), the national executive, the judiciary, public administration, the security services and the relationship between the 3 spheres of government. It incorporates a Bill of Rights

pertaining to, *inter alia*, education, housing, food and water supply, security as well as political rights.

A *Constitutional Court*, consisting of a president, a deputy president and 9 other judges, was inaugurated in Feb. 1995. The Court's judges are appointed by the President of the Republic from a list provided by the Judicial Service Commission, after consulting the President of the Constitutional Court and the leaders of parties represented in the National Assembly. A Constitutional Court judge is appointed for a non-renewable term of 12 years but must retire at the age of 70. The Court reviews the actions of the legislature, executive and judiciary in the light of the Bill of Rights, and the Constitution and can overturn legislation. The Court had to certify that the new Constitution conforms with the constitutional principles contained in the 1993 Constitution before it could become law.

The *National Assembly* is a legislature consisting of no fewer than 350 and more than 400 members directly elected for 5 years, 200 from a national list and 200 from provincial lists in the following proportions: Eastern Cape, 28; Free State, 14; Gauteng, 44; KwaZulu-Natal, 42; Mpumalanga, 11; Northern Cape, 4; Northern Province, 25; North-West, 12; Western Cape, 20. Parties gaining at least 5% of votes are entitled to Cabinet representation. In terms of the 1993 Constitution, which still regulates the 1999 elections, the 9 provincial legislatures are elected at the same time and candidates may stand for both. If elected to both, they have to choose between sitting in the national or provincial assembly. In the former case, the runner-up is elected to the Provincial Assembly. The National Council of Provinces (NCOP) consists of 90 members (10 from each province) indirectly elected by the provincial legislatures by proportional representation.

Bills (except money bills) may be introduced in either house but must be passed by both. A money bill may only be introduced in the National Assembly. If a bill is rejected by one house it is referred back to both after consideration by a joint National Asssembly-NCOP committee called the Mediation Committee. Bills relating to the provinces must be passed by the NCOP.

National Anthem. A combination of shortened forms of 'Die Stem van Suid-Afrika'/'The Call of South Africa' (words by C. J. Langenhoven; tune by M. L. de Villiers) and the ANC anthem 'Nkosi sikelel' iAfrika'/'God bless Africa'.

RECENT ELECTIONS

Parliamentary elections were held on 26–28 April 1994 (extended to 29 April in some areas). The electorate was 22·7m.; turn-out was 86%. 19 parties stood. The African National Congress (ANC) gained 252 seats with 62·7% of votes cast, the National Party (NP) 82 with 20·4%, the Inkatha Freedom Party (IFP) 43 with 10·5%, the Freedom Front (FF) 9 with 2·2%, the Democratic Party (DP) 7 with 1·7%, the Pan-Africanist Congress (PAC) 5 with 1·2% and the African Christian Democratic Party (ACDP) 2 with 0·5%. The second all-race elections were to be held on 2 June 1999.

The current state of parties in the National Assembly is as follows: ANC, 252; NP, 82; IFP, 43; FF, 9; DP, 7; PAC, 5; ACDP, 2. The 90 seats in the NCOP are divided as follows: ANC, 60; NP, 17; IFP, 5; FF, 5; DP, 3.

CURRENT ADMINISTRATION

President: Nelson Mandela, b. 1918 (ANC; elected 9 May 1994, sworn in 10 May; due to retire on 2 June 1999.

A Government of National Unity took office on 6 May 1994 which, after the withdrawal of NP members in March 1998, comprised:

Executive Deputy President: Thabo Mbeki (ANC). *Minister of Agriculture and Land Affairs:* Derek Hanekom (ANC). *Arts, Culture, Science and Technology:* Baldwin (Ben) Nugubane (IFP). *Correctional Services:* Ben Skosana (IFA). *Defence:* Joe Modise (ANC). *Education:* Prof. Sibusiso Bengu (ANC). *Environmental Affairs and Tourism:* Dr Z. Pallo Jordan (ANC). *Finance:* Trevor Manuel (ANC). *Foreign Affairs:* Alfred Nzo (ANC). *Health:* Dr Nkosazana Dlamini-Zuma (ANC). *Home Affairs:* Dr Mangosuthu Buthelezi (IFP). *Housing:* Sankie Mthembi-Mahanyele (ANC). *Justice:* Dullah Omar (ANC). *Labour:* Shepard Mdladlana (ANC). *Mineral and Energy Affairs:* Penuell Maduna (ANC). *Posts, Telecommunications and Broadcasting:* Jay Naidoo (ANC). *Provincial Affairs and*

Constitutional Development: Mohammed Valli Moosa (ANC). *Public Enterprises:* Stella Sigcau (ANC). *Public Service and Administration:* Dr Zola Skweyiya (ANC). *Public Works:* Jeff Radebe (ANC). *Safety and Security:* Sidney Mufamadi (ANC). *Sport and Recreation:* Steve Tshwete (ANC). *Trade and Industry:* Alec Erwin (ANC). *Transport:* Mac Maharaj (ANC). *Water Affairs and Forestry:* Prof. Kadar Asmal (ANC). *Welfare and Population Development:* Geraldine Fraser-Moleketi (ANC).

The *Speaker* is Dr Frene Ginwala.

Provincial Government. The 1993 Transitional Constitution provided for 9 provinces, which may with a two-thirds majority adopt a constitution for the province in question. A provincial constitution may not be inconsistent with the provisions of the transitional Constitution except that different legislative and executive structures may be provided for. A provincial constitution only becomes effective after the Constitutional Court has certified that it is in accordance with the provisions of the Constitution. Each province has a provincial legislature in which the legislative authority of that province rests and which accordingly has the power to make laws for the province. A provincial legislature consists of a minimum of 30 and a maximum of 80 members elected by proportional representation. A provincial legislature is elected for 5 years or less in certain circumstances. If a legislature adopts a motion of no-confidence in the executive council of the province, including the Premier, the Premier must resign or dissolve the legislature for an election.

The executive council of a province consists of the Premier as chairperson and a maximum of 10 members who are appointed by the Premier from among the members of the provincial legislature.

Parliament and the provincial legislatures have concurrent legislative competence with regard to, *inter alia*, the following functional area or topics: agriculture, education (excluding tertiary education), health services, welfare services, housing, police, cultural matters, nature conservation (excluding national parks), soil conservation, the environment, animal control and diseases, casinos, racing and gambling, language policy, media services, airports, public transport, road traffic regulation, regional planning and development, tourism, trade and industrial promotion, consumer protection, indigenous law and customary law, traditional leadership, and urban and rural development. A provincial legislature has exclusive legislative competence regarding the following areas: abattoirs, ambulance services, archives (other than national archives), libraries (other than national libraries), liquor licences, museums (other than national museums), provincial planning, provincial cultural matters, provincial recreation and amenities, provincial sport, provincial roads and traffic, and veterinary services (excluding regulation of the profession).

Local Government. The 1996 Constitution envisages a transformation of the local government system, to give it a major role in building democracy and promoting socio-economic development.

The Local Government: Municipal Demarcation Act, 1998 provides for the establishment of an independent Municipal Demarcation Board. The Local Government Structures Act, 1998 makes provision for the division of powers and functions between the different categories of municipalities, and a system for the election of municipal councillors.

The Local Government: Systems Bill, which will provide for issues such as integrated development planning, performance management and credit control, was due to be finalized in 1999. The drafting process for the Local Government: Property Rates Bill, which will provide for a uniform system for the rating of all property in South Africa, has already commenced.

DEFENCE

A Defence Review has been approved by Parliament and the provision of new equipment for the Navy and Air Force is moving ahead. The cost is R29·7bn., against which the countertrade offers amount to R110bn. A Chief of Joint Operations is now responsible for the employment of all forces. There are 4 arms of the Service: the Army, Air Force, Navy and the newly styled Military Health Service. The final strength of the Department of Defence (DoD) is still under discussion. What is certain is that there will be a marked improvement in the ratio of combat troops to support troops, and a substantial reduction in the total force strength. Part of the downsizing will be accomplished through natural attrition, voluntary severance and the non-renewal of expired contracts. Throughout 1998 the DoD continued to provide support to the SA Police Service in the fight against crime and violence. Defence expenditure totalled US$2,326m. in 1997 (US$60 per capita) and represented 1·8% of GDP.

Army. The Army numbered 54,300 in 1998. There is a paramilitary South African Police Service 140,000 strong.

Navy. Navy personnel in 1998 totalled 8,000.

INTERNATIONAL RELATIONS

South Africa was chairman of the Southern African Development Community and the Non-Aligned Movement in 1999 and is also a member of the UN, the Commonwealth (except during 1961–94) and the OAU.

In Sept. 1998 the Lesotho Prime Minister appealed to the Southern African Development Community for military intervention to restore normality. The SADC instructed South Africa and Botswana to plan for military intervention. All military objectives were achieved, albeit after a fierce firefight at the Makoanyane Base. Some of the forces originally committed have been withdrawn. The remainder are continuing with stabilization operations.

ECONOMY

Policy. A Reconstruction and Development Programme (RDP) was instituted under a government minister in 1994 (since 1996 the Minister of Finance) to run until 1999. Its policy aims are to meet basic needs, develop human resources, build the economy and democratize the state and society, and include as targets: Redistributing 30% of agricultural land; raising the annual number of houses built from 50,000 to 0·3m.; providing safe drinking water for 12m. persons; providing sanitation for 21m.; creating 0·3m. non-agricultural jobs; reversing privatization 'contrary to the public interest'; introducing anti-trust legislation; 'de-racializing' business ownership; improving industrial relations. In 1996 a decision was taken to integrate the RDP Fund into the budgets of the various delivery departments.

In spite of the reversing of privatization 'contrary to the public interest', privatization deals between 1990 and 1996 raised some US$1·2bn., more than in any other African country.

Performance. On account of the international financial crisis the economy slowed down significantly in 1998. After 6 years of growth, output and national income fell in the second half of the year. GDP growth was estimated to be 0·1% in 1998, well below what was expected.

The impact of instability in the global financial markets in 1998 is registered through the balance of payments and the present crisis was initially felt through the capital account. From 1994 to mid-1998, a net surplus, peaking at R34·6bn., was recorded on the capital account. However, from May 1998 investor sentiment changed, leading to an outflow of R5·4bn. in the third quarter. The current account of the balance of payments was expected to register a deficit of 2% in 1998, compared to 1·5% in 1997.

Gross foreign reserves increased in the first half of 1998 as a result of capital inflows. After falling from June to Nov., gross official reserves at the end of Jan. 1999 were R32·6bn., enough to cover 2·4 months' worth of imports. Net official reserves were US$2·4bn. at the end of Jan. 1999.

The economy is projected to grow by 1·8% in the 1999 fiscal year and by 3·2% and 3·8% in 2000 and 2001 respectively. Interest rates are expected to come down further during 1999.

Budget. Total revenue and expenditure of the central government's State Revenue Account in R1bn.:

	1995–96	1996–97	1997–98	1998–99
Revenue	127,269	144,857	161,976	179,000
Expenditure	157,360	173,659	186,747	204,300

The 1999 budget provides for expenditure of R216·8bn. or 30·6% of GDP; revenue, R191·7bn. National government gets R87·7bn. (47% of the total);

provincial governments get R86·3bn. (52%); local government gets R1·7bn. The national share includes R8·8bn. in conditional grants for provinces and local government, mainly in support of health services. R1bn. has been allocated for targeted poverty relief programmes in 1999, giving effect to several Jobs Summit commitments. This rises to R1·2bn. and R1·5bn. in 2000 and 2001.

From Sept. 1991 VAT at 10% replaced the 13% general sales tax. From 7 April 1993 the rate was increased from 10% to 14%. Corporate tax was reduced from 50% to 48% in April 1991, and in March 1993 was lowered from 48% to 40% of taxable income, but an additional tax of 15% on distributed profits was introduced.

Currency. The unit of currency is the *rand* (ZAR) of 100 *cents*. A single free-floating exchange rate replaced the former 2-tier system on 13 March 1995. Inflation fell to 6·9% in 1998, its lowest level in 25 years. In Jan. 1998 foreign exchange reserves were US$4,519m. and in Feb. 1998 gold reserves were 4·04m. troy oz.

Banking and Finance. The central bank and bank of issue is the South African Reserve Bank (established 1920), which functions independently. Its *Governor* is Mr Tito Mboweni. Total deposits, 31 Dec. 1998, R8,955m.; assets, R58,838m.

In 1997, 50 banks, including 9 branches of foreign banks and 4 mutual banks, were registered with the Office of the Registrar of Banks. 60 foreign banks have authorized representative offices in South Africa.

At 31 Dec. 1997, the 54 registered banking institutions collectively employed around 123,000 workers and had combined assets amounting to R550bn. Their offices (including both branches and agencies) totalled 3,272. If the 2,464 post offices through which the Postbank's services are rendered are included, banking services are provided at some 5,736 offices throughout the country. The Postbank receives deposits from but does not provide credit to the public.

The Banks Act, 1990 (Act No. 94 of 1990) governs the operations and prudential requirements of banks. As at 31 Oct. 1997 the minimum capital adequacy requirement was 8%.

There is a stock exchange at Johannesburg (JSE). Foreign nationals have been eligible for membership since March 1996.

Weights and Measures. The metric system is in use.

ENERGY AND NATURAL RESOURCES

Electricity. The total power station nominal capacity was 39,154 MW in 1997. There were 23 coal-fired power stations, 1 nuclear, 1 bagasse, 10 hydro-electric, 3 pumped storage and 11 gas turbine in service in 1996. Production in 1997 was 187,458m. kWh. Consumption per capita was 3,686 kWh in 1997. Eskom, a public utility, generates and sells 98·3% of all the electricity consumed in southern Africa.

In 1997, 63% of households had electricity.

Oil and Gas. With the development of the EM gas field, there are sufficient resources of off-shore natural gas to yield 30,000 bbls. a day as petroleum products until 2006. During 1998, 1,236,259 tonnes of gas and 249,812 tonnes of condensate were brought ashore.

Water. South Africa's average annual rainfall of about 497 mm is well below the world average. The unevenly distributed rainfall and high evaporation rate greatly affects the reliability and variability of river flow. Only about 62% or 33,000m. cu. metres of the mean annual run-off can be exploited economically. In addition about 5,400m. cu. metres may be obtainable from underground sources. Government activities are governed by the Water Act of 1998. They are administered by the Department of Water Affairs and Forestry which manages water quantity and quality as well as the demand for the resource.

A Water Research Commission was established in 1971 to co-ordinate and promote water research. Water availability is distributed poorly in relation to regions of economic growth, and major inter-basin water transfer schemes are therefore a feature of the South African infrastructure. The latest such scheme, the first of which has just been completed, is the Lesotho Highlands Water Project which diverts the Orange River headwaters within Lesotho through tunnels into the Vaal River System, which serves an area where about 60% of the gross domestic product of the country is generated. Lesotho receives royalties in exchange.

SOUTH AFRICA

Minerals. Value of the main mineral production sales (in R1,000):

	1994	1995	1996	1997
Asbestos	140,238	119,711	100,418	71,988
Chrome ore	400,056	606,826	811,221	952,141
Coal	10,352,607	12,817,789	14,909,980	16,093,907
Copper	1,253,874	1,673,145	1,488,737	1,681,548
Gold	24,953,110	23,333,195	26,482,352	24,904,737
Iron ore	1,400,258	1,657,887	1,691,683	2,085,980
Lime and limestone	604,767	693,440	692,484	703,117
Manganese ore	644,921	692,094	783,874	887,130
Silver	78,127	68,640	83,013	102,261
Nickel	547,662	851,519	983,480	1,003,850
Platinum-group metals	5,809,613	6,572,506	7,637,913	8,510,766

Total value of all minerals sold, 1996: R65,109m.; 1997: R65,825m.

Mineral production (tonnes) 1997: Coal, 248·6m.; iron ore, 32·7m.; manganese, 3·1m.; chrome ore, 5·7m.; copper, 153,058; limestone, 21·2m.; gold, 492; silver, 144; nickel, 34,830; platinum-group metals, 196; diamonds, 10,041,380 carats.

South Africa is a major producer of gold. Reserves were estimated at 401·54 tonnes in 1997. The value of gold production was R24·9bn. In 1996 the number of persons engaged in the mining industry was 551,677, of which 343,922 were involved in underground gold-mining operations.

Agriculture. The redistribution of 30% of land, expropriated since 1913, is envisaged by the Reconstruction and Development Programme. By 1998, 35,528 households had been reached and 377,347 ha of land had been designated. Dispossessed landowners are entitled to restitution from the state, though the rights of present landowners must be respected and compensation paid.

Much of the land suitable for mechanized farming has unreliable rainfall. Of the total farming area, natural pasture occupies 81% (69·6m. ha) and planted pasture 2·3% (2m. ha). About 13% of South Africa's surface area can be used for crop production. High potential arable land comprises only 22% of the total arable land. Annual crops and orchards are cultivated on 9·9m. ha of dry land and 1·2m. ha under irrigation.

There were some 57,000 commercial farming units in 1996. The following data exist on Black farmers: Smallholders who produce at or near to subsistence level, 1·03m. households; progressive small-scale farmers who consistently market agricultural products but for whom agriculture is not the sole or main source of income, 238,000 households; market-orientated commercial farmers for whom agriculture is the sole or main source of income, 3,100 households.

In 1997 agriculture, forestry and fisheries contributed 4·5% of GDP.

Production (1997, in 1,000 tonnes): Maize, 10,136; sorghum, 433; wheat, 2,478; groundnuts, 106; sunflower seed, 463; sugar cane, 22,155; oranges, 962; potatoes, 1,581; other vegetables, 2,058; grapes, 154; apples, 519.

Livestock, in 1,000 (1997): 13,667 cattle, 29,187 sheep, 6,644 goats, 1,617 pigs.

The 1997 production of red meat was 705,000 tonnes; poultry meat, 922,000 tonnes; wool, 57,268 tonnes; eggs, 282,000 tonnes; milk, 2·7m. tonnes.

Cotton-growing is undertaken by some farmers, the plant being better drought-resistant than either tobacco or maize. Viticulture and fruit-growing are important, and were valued at R5,106m. in 1996.

In 1997 the gross value of agricultural production was R41,745m. (field crops, R13,900m.; livestock products, R18,370m.; horticultural products, R9,475m.).

Forestry. The commercial forest plantations cover about 1·52m. ha, and indigenous high forests about 400,000 ha. At 31 March 1997 there were 797,610 ha of pine plantations, 597,964 ha of eucalyptus, 112,029 ha of wattle and 10,535 ha of other species. Total roundwood sales from the plantations were 18,641 cu. metres valued at R1,746m. Saw logs and veneer contributed 6,122 cu. metres (value R415·1m.) to these amounts; pulpwood, 8,788 cu. metres (R1,187·2m.); mining timber, 2,206 cu. metres (R89·1m.); and others—poles, matchwood, etc.—1,525 cu. metres (R54·5m.).

Fisheries. In 1995 fisheries landed 575,177 tonnes of fish, shellfish, seaweed and guano (almost exclusively from marine waters). Total output, wholesale value, 1995, R1,730m. The fishing fleet consisted of 3,974 vessels in 1995.

INDUSTRY
Net value of sales of the principal groups of industries (in R1m.) in 1997: food and food products, 54,843; beverages, 18,318; vehicles and vehicle parts, 33,829; basic iron and steel products, 24,710; basic precious and non-ferrous metal products, 11,995; petroleum products, 20,392; chemicals and products, 38,486; non-electrical machinery, 18,337; electrical machinery, 11,081; fabricated metal products except machinery, 22,327; printing and publishing, 10,264; wood and wood products, 6,073; clothing, 9,875; paper and products, 17,420; textiles, 10,138; plastic products, 9,128. Total net value including other groups, R360,764m. Manufacturing industry contributed R126,669m. (23·9%) of GDP which totalled R529,557m. in 1997.

Labour. According to the South African Reserve Bank, productivity increased from 107·2 in 1994 to 126·4 in June 1998. In Oct. 1996 the population of economically active age (15–65 years) in employment numbered 9,113,847 (3,631,944 females). Number of unemployed, Oct. 1996, 4,671,647 (2,631,730 females), comprising African/Black, 4,205,992 (2,395,421); Coloured, 299,231 (157,676); White, 89,066 (43,127); Indian/Asian, 50,379 (21,068). Unemployment rate, 1996, 33·9%. Unemployment is getting worse. Each day, some 1,000 people enter the labour market, while the formal sector of the economy sheds 200 jobs.

Of the economically active population, only 3m. are skilled or highly skilled (some 20%) while 7m. are employed in semi-skilled or unskilled jobs (together some 80% of the economically active population). The Skills Development Act, aspects of which came into effect on 2 Feb. 1999, aims to address the shortage of skills. South African professionals constitute fewer than 4% of the labour force; in craft and related trade, the percentage is 12%.

Industrial employment (except mining) at Sept. 1998: Manufacturing employed 1,375,072 workers; construction, 378,018; trade and accommodation services, 680,267. The Employment Standards Act, 1997, shortened the working week to 40 hours.

The Labour Relations Act, 1996 has had a significant impact on South Africa's workplaces and in laying the basis for a more stable and peaceful labour relations environment. It encourages the establishment of workplace forums and imposes collective bargaining in manufacturing industries. The Act set up the *Commission for Conciliation and Arbitration.*

The Government has set 3 broad representation targets for departments and provinces. Two of the targets, to be achieved by 1999, were an increase in black management to 50%, and more than doubling the number of women in middle and senior management from 11% to 30%. By 2005, at least 2% of public servants must be disabled people.

Trade Unions. The number of unionized workers has increased from 2·4m. in 1994 to 3·8m. in 1998. This constitutes almost 77% of workers in registered non-agricultural employment, and approximately 26% of the estimated 14,356,000 economically active population. The Congress of South African Trade Unions (COSATU; *General Secretary*, Sam Shilowa) has formed links with the ANC. It had 1·3m. members in 1994.

INTERNATIONAL TRADE
International sanctions on trade with South Africa were lifted in 1993.

Imports and Exports. South Africa, Botswana, Lesotho, Namibia and Swaziland are members of a customs union and the foreign trade statistics shown below represent the combined imports and exports of these countries. The total value of the imports and exports was as follows (in R1bn.):

Imports		Exports	
1995	98·5	1995	101·5
1996	115·5	1996	123·2
1997	129·8	1997	142·4
1998	144·1	1998	141·9

The main exports (in R1m.) in 1998 were: Natural or cultured pearls, 32·6; base metals and articles thereof, 22·0; mineral products, 18·9; chemical and allied products, 8·9; machinery and mechanical appliances, 9·5.

SOUTH AFRICA

In Oct. 1998 a transshipment facility for containers opened at Kidatu, south-west of Dar es Salaam, Tanzania, providing a link between the 1,067 mm gauge railways of the southern part of Africa and the 1,000 mm gauge lines of the north. With the opening up of new markets for South Africa elsewhere in the continent, it will help to boost trade and facilitate the shipment of cargo to countries to the north.

COMMUNICATIONS
In 1990 Transnet, a public company comprising railways, harbours, pipelines and road transport, was set up, with the government as sole shareholder, as a first step to possible privatization.

Roads. In 1997 there were 361,145 km of non-urban roads (72·2% of these were paved). Of the total road network length, 6,592 km were national roads (5,512 km paved) and 354,553 km were provincial roads (55,710 km paved). In 1996 private firms and local authorities transported 474,409 passengers; Transnet carried 1·8m. tonnes of freight; and private firms, 407,905 tonnes. Motor vehicles in use as at Nov. 1998 included 3,788,847 passenger cars, 1,218,829 light commercial vehicles, 249,659 minibuses, 29,429 buses, 227,976 trucks and 161,976 motor cycles. In 1995 there were 500,233 road accidents with 10,256 fatalities.

Rail. In 1995 there were 20,005 km of 1,065 mm gauge (9,078 km electrified) and 314 km of 762 mm gauge. In 1995 railways carried 6m. long-distance passengers and 175m. tonnes of freight. In 1990 the South African Rail Commuter Corporation was set up to run commuter trains in major cities; it carried 458m. passengers in 1996–97.

Civil Aviation. Responsibility for civil aviation safety and security matters lies with the South African Civil Aviation Authority (CAA) which was established on 1 Oct. 1998. There are 3 international airports—at Cape Town, Durban and Johannesburg, and 6 major domestic passenger airports—at Bloemfontein, East London, George, Kimberley, Port Elizabeth and Upington. These airports are administered by the Airports Company of South Africa (ACSA) which was partially privatized in 1998.

South African Airways (SAA), Sun Air and Nationwide Air operate scheduled international air services within Africa and to Europe, Latin America and the Middle and Far East. Alliance Airlines was founded in Dec. 1994 as a joint venture between SAA and the governments and national carriers of Tanzania and Uganda. In 1995 SAA flew 77·9m. km and carried 4,907,700 passengers (1,402,600 on international flights). In 1998 services were also provided by Aero Zambia, Aeroflot, Aerolíneas Argentinas, Air Afrique, Air Austral, Air Botswana, Air Djibouti, Air France, Air Gabon, Air Madagascar, Air Malaŵi, Air Mauritius, Air Namibia, Air Seychelles, Air Tanzania Corporation, Air Zimbabwe, Alitalia, Alliance Air, American Airlines, Austrian Airlines, Balkan, British Airways, Cameroon Airlines, Cathay Pacific Airways, Congo Airlines, Delta Air Lines, Egyptair, El Al, Emirates, Ethiopian Airlines, Expedition Airways, Ghana Airways, Iberia, Intensive Air, Inter Air, JAL, Kenya Airways, KLM, LAM, Lesotho Airways, Lufthansa, Malaysia Airlines, Metavia Airlines, National Airlines, Olympic Airways, Qantas Airways, Royal Air Maroc, Royal Swazi National Airways Corporation, SABENA, SAS, Saudia, Singapore Airlines, Swissair, TAAG, TAP, Thai Airways International, Turkish Airlines, Uganda Airlines, United Airlines, Varig, Virgin Atlantic, Zambian Express and Zimbabwe Express Airlines.

South Africa has 34 registered carriers (passenger and freight)—14 international and 20 domestic. In 1998 the total number of passengers from South African airports was 8,810,873 (domestic, 6,199,214; international, 2,389,513; regional, 189,994; non-scheduled, 32,152).

Shipping. The South African Maritime Safety Authority (SAMSA) was established on 1 April 1998 as the authority responsible for ensuring the safety of life and property at sea and the prevention of pollution of the marine environment from ships. In 1998, the merchant fleet totalled 321,173 GRT. There are 7 major ports of which 2—Durban and Cape Town—are considered to be major hub ports offering a wide range of terminals and facilities. The 2 deep-water bulk ports are Saldanha and Richards Bay. The latter is situated on the east coast north of Durban and is the world's largest bulk coal terminal. Saldanha, which is situated on the west coast north of Cape Town, handles both bulk oil and ore. The other major ports—at Mossel Bay, Port Elizabeth and East London—are multi-purpose ports. During 1998 the major ports handled a total of 186,500,391 tonnes of cargo, and a total of 13,559 ships calls were registered.

Telecommunications. Telkom SA Ltd officially came into being on 1 Oct. 1991. It is the second largest listed industrial company in South Africa and accounts for 2·2% of GDP. Some 96·5% of the network is digital. In 1997, there were 5·3m. installed telephones and 4·3m. installed exchange lines. In 1998, 35% of homes had telephones. In 1995 there were 535,000 cellular phone subscribers (13 per 1,000 persons), 1,100,000 PCs (27 per 1,000 population) and 75,000 fax machines, and in 1994, 7,300 telex subscribers. There were 1·04m. Internet users in Nov. 1998, around 2·3% of the population.

Postal Services. In 1997 there were 2,469 post offices and postal agencies, with plans to increase the network to 2,761. In 1997 around 8m. postal items were handled by the Post Office each working day, in excess of 2,400m. a year. South Africa has joined the Pan African Postal Union, a specialized agency of the OAU.

SOCIAL INSTITUTIONS

Justice. The common law of the republic is the Roman–Dutch law—that is, the uncodified law of Holland as it was at the date of the cession of the Cape in 1806. The law of England as such is not recognized as authoritative, though by statute the principles of English law relating to evidence and to mercantile matters, e.g., companies, patents, trademarks, insolvency and the like, have been introduced. In shipping and insurance, English law is followed in the former Cape Province, and it has also largely influenced civil and criminal procedure throughout the republic. In all other matters, family relations, property, succession, contract, etc., Roman–Dutch law rules, English decisions being valued only so far as they agree therewith.

The Judicial system in South Africa is constituted as follows: (a) the Constitutional Court, consisting of a President, Deputy President and 9 other judges; (b) the Supreme Court of Appeal, consisting of a Chief Justice, a Deputy Chief Justice and the number of judges of appeal determined by an Act of Parliament. It is the highest court of appeal, except in constitutional matters; (c) the High Courts, including any high court of appeal that may be established by an Act of Parliament to hear appeals from the High Courts. The High Courts may decide any constitutional matter, except a matter that only the Constitutional Court may decide, or a matter which is assigned to another court of a status similar to a High Court by an Act of Parliament. The Judge President of a provincial division may divide the area under his jurisdiction into circuit districts. In each such district there shall be held at least twice in every year and at such times and places determined by the Judge President, a court which shall be presided over by a judge of the division in which that district is situated. Such a court is known as the circuit local division for the district in question and is deemed to be a local division. The judges hold office till they attain the age of 70 years. A judge is expected to be available to perform service for an aggregate of 3 months a year until the age of 75. No judge can be removed from office except by the President after the National Assembly (at least two-thirds support from its members) has called for such judge to be removed on the grounds of incapacity, incompetence or gross misconduct. (d) Magistrates' Courts; and (e) any other court established or recognized in terms of an Act of Parliament, including any court of a status similar to either the High Courts or the Magistrates' Courts. The Magistrates' Court and all other courts may decide any matter determined by an Act of Parliament but a court of a status lower than a High Court may not enquire into or rule on the constitutionality of any legislation or any conduct of the President.

The 9 provinces are further divided into 435 magisterial districts each with a magistrates' court having a prescribed civil and criminal jurisdiction. In 1998, 1,566 were magistrates appointed. From this court there is an appeal to the provincial division of the High Court and then to the Court of Appeal. Magistrates' convictions carrying above a prescribed limit are subject to automatic review by a judge.

Magisterial districts have been grouped into 14 clusters headed by Chief Magistrates and in a few cases by Senior Magistrates. This system streamlined, simplified and provided uniform court management systems applicable throughout South Africa.

All criminal and civil cases are dealt with by judges (in the High Court) and magistrates (in the low court). Judges and magistrates are entitled to take judicial cognizance of customary (indigenous) laws and must, where relevant, apply them. A limited civil and criminal jurisdiction is conferred upon the courts of traditional leaders over his own tribe.

In 1998 there were 121 small claims courts, which have been introduced in a number of areas since 1984. These courts (where Commissioners preside) have jurisdiction only, limited by the quantum of damages and the nature of the claim.

The death penalty was abolished in June 1995. No executions have taken place since 1989.

The *Land Claims Court*, established under the Restitution of Land Rights Act of 1994 have jurisdiction throughout the Republic and have all such powers in relation to matters falling within its jurisdiction as are possessed by a High Court having jurisdiction in civil proceedings at the place where the land in question is situated, including the powers of a High Court, in relation to any contempt of court; and all the ancillary powers necessary or reasonably incidental to the performance of its functions, including the power to grant interlocutory orders and interdicts. The Courts have the power: to determine a right to restitution of any right in land accordance with this Act; to determine or approve compensation payable in respect of land owned by or in possession of a private person upon expropriation or acquisition of such land; to determine the person entitled to title to land; at the instance of any interested person and in its discretion, to grant a declaratory order on a question of law relating to matters in respect of which the Court has jurisdiction, notwithstanding that such person might not be able to claim any relief consequential upon the granting of such order; to determine whether compensation or any other consideration received by any person at the time of any dispossession of a right in land was just and equitable; to determine any matter involving the interpretation or application of this Act or the Land Reform (Labour Tenants) Act, 1996; to decide any constitutional matter in relation to this Act or the Land Reform (Labour Tenants) Acts, 1996; and to determine all other matters which require to be determined in terms of this Act.

The Labour Court established under the Labour Relations Act, 1995 is a superior court that has authority, inherent powers and standing, in relation to matters under its jurisdiction, equal to that which a court of a provincial division of the High Court has in relation to matters under its jurisdiction.

Spending on police, prisons and justice services will amount to R23·5bn. in 1999.

Religion. Almost 80% of the population in South Africa professes the Christian faith. Other major religious groups are the Hindus, Muslims and Jews. A sizeable minority of the population does not belong to any of the major religions but regard themselves as traditionalists or of no specific religious affiliation. Freedom of worship is guaranteed by the Constitution and official policy is one of non-interference in religious practices. In 1992 the Anglican Church of Southern Africa voted by 79% of votes cast for the ordination of women.

Education. The South African Schools Act, 1996 became effective on 1 Jan. 1997 and provides for: compulsory education for learners between the ages of 7 and 15 years of age, or learners reaching the ninth grade, whichever occurs first; two categories of schools, namely public schools and independent schools and the establishment and maintenance of public schools on private property; conditions of admission of learners to public schools; governance and management of public schools, the election of governing bodies and their functions; funding of public schools.

The process of review and renewal in South African education began in Aug. 1995 in response to the need to normalize and transform teaching and learning in a new democratic South Africa. From the outset, emphasis was placed on a shift from the traditional content-driven approach to outcomes-based education. It was announced that a new curriculum would be phased in—Curriculum 2005.

SOUTH AFRICA

The R40bn. education budget accounted for 21·3% of the Government's total 1997-98 expenditure. This equals 6·5% of GDP. Tertiary education was allocated R5,431bn., with R4,934bn. going directly to universities and technikons. An amount of R300m. was set aside for the National Student Financial Aid Scheme, of which R200m. came from the Government and the rest from donors. The Government increased its spending on adult education from R6·5m. to R131·1m.

South Africa has 21 fully fledged universities, 2 of which are mainly non-residential institutions offering distance tuition. At present, only 1 of the 129 technical colleges in South Africa offers distance education.

The adult literacy rate in 1995 was 81·8% (81·9% among males and 81·7% among females). The female literacy rate is the highest in Africa.

Health. In 1998 the Interim South African Medical and Dental Council had registered the following personnel: 29,020 medical practitioners of whom 8,568 had specialist qualifications, 4,298 dentists, 365 dental specialists, 9,774 pharmacists and 87,783 nurses and midwives. In 1998 there were 596 hospitals with 140,218 beds, of which 27% were provided by private medical care.

Treatment in the public health service covers 75–80% of the population and is free of charge for the indigent, children under 6 years and pregnant mothers. Other patients are charged on a sliding scale based on their means. 60% of private health care is funded by medical insurance schemes and the remainder by privately paying patients. The free medical treatment scheme amounts to about R500m.

South Africa's first-of-its-kind telemedicine site has been launched to improve primary health care. Telemedicine, a stated Government priority for 1999, enables the remote diagnosis of patients at a distance through the transmission of the patient's medical data via telephone lines, microwave or satellite.

Welfare. The Government's most effective poverty alleviation programme is the payment of grants and pensions to about 2·9m. South Africans every month. Funded entirely by the state, this programme of social assistance amounted to R16·7bn. in the 1998-99 financial year. R50m. was allocated to 1,133 poverty alleviation projects in 1997-98. Child-support grants to care-givers of more than 23,823 children are paid out every month.

This welfare programme includes the payment of old age pensions, disability grants and foster care grants. In April 1998 a new grant—the child support grant—was introduced to assist poor households in caring for young children under the age of 7. It is envisaged that this grant will reach about 3m. children within 5 years.

The social assistance programme also includes social relief to applicants of a pension or grant as an interim measure.

South Africa's re-admission to world bodies has meant the ratification of international instruments such as the Convention on the Rights of the Child and reporting under the Convention on the Elimination of Discrimination Against Women.

The provision of welfare service—including care and protection services—is based on a partnership between government and private welfare organizations. These organizations receive financial support from Government.

Legislation was passed to amend the Child Care Act so as to promote the best interests of the child and to provide for the registration of shelters for street children, and the establishment of a Child Protection Register. A national protocol on the abuse and neglect of children has been finalized in all 9 provinces.

The rights of fathers of children born out of wedlock has also been upgraded in legislation to provide them with an opportunity to participate in adoption proceedings. The law provides for their consent to be given or for them to withhold such consent.

A Drug Master Plan has been finalized which will assist in curbing substance abuse, the trafficking in illegal drugs and will establish a Central Drug Authority.

Several pilot projects to test aspects of a new child and youth care system were completed and are being expanded in line with the policy guidelines which were developed. These aspects include youth justice services, professional foster care, residential care and wilderness outreach programmes for young people.

Pilot projects to test community-based models of care for older persons were also completed. This is in line with the new approach to ageing. Legislation has also been passed which makes abuse of the elderly a criminal offence and which seeks to ensure that there is no racial discrimination in the admission of persons to old-age homes.

Welfare is responsible for the Victim Empowerment Programme (VEP) which seeks to offer support services to victims of crime and violence and ensure that victims' rights are enshrined in a victim's charter.

As part of the Department of Welfare, the National Population Unit (NPU) is tasked with ensuring that population concerns are integrated into the development planning of government.

CULTURE

Broadcasting. Broadcasting is supervized by the Independent Broadcasting Authority (IBA), set up in 1994 to establish a system free from political control. The IBA has granted licences to 76 community radio broadcasters and 12 private radio stations. The South African Broadcasting Corporation (SABC) as the public broadcaster has 16 radio services and 16m. listeners. The SABC offers 3 television channels in 11 languages, namely SABC1, SABC2 and SABC3. Midi Television with its E-TV channel was awarded the first private free-to-air television licence on 30 March 1998. M-Net (Electronic Media Network Limited), South Africa's first private subscription television service, was launched in 1986. Today, it is the premier pay-TV service with almost 1·2m. subscribers in 37 countries across the African continent.

In 1998, 85% of the population was able to receive a television signal.

Cinema. In 1990 there were approximately 1,200 cinemas.

Press. Initiated by the political and cultural changes, black empowerment of the media was assisted by the largely white ownership of the bigger media groups. Of the more important ones were control over *Sowetan* (circulation, 1997, 225,987), the largest daily of the former Argus Newspapers, by New Africa Investments Limited (Nail) of the Prosper Africa Group (1994); and *CityPress* (circulation, 258,3350) of Nasionale Pers through Ukhozi Media of the Ukhozi Investments Group (1996). Since 1996, local newspapers, 'freebies' and corporate newspapers have ventured into reporting in black languages.

There are 17 dailies and 12 weeklies. More than 100 provincial or country newspapers, most of which are weekly tabloids, serve particular towns or districts. Most are bilingual (English and Afrikaans).

Tourism. South Africa has moved up from the 55th most popular tourist destination in the world in 1990 to the 25th in 1998. There has been a 10% growth in the number of tourists over the last 3 years. The travel and tourism industry represents 7% of total employment with more than 730,000 South Africans directly involved in tourism. In 1997, 5,189,430 foreign tourists visited South Africa, of whom 3,724,940 were from African countries and 916,400 from Europe (332,790 from the UK and 192,280 from Germany), and contributed 4·6% to GDP.

Festivals. Best-known arts festivals: the Grahamstown Arts Festival in Eastern Cape province, is held in June/July; the Kleinkaroo Festival (Oudtshoorn, Western Cape), which has a strong Afrikaans component, is held in April; the Potchefstroom Arts Festival, in North-West province, is held in October; and the Manguang African Cultural Festival (Macufe) is held in September in Bloemfontein.

Libraries. There are 2 national libraries and hundreds of public (municipal) libraries, special libraries, government libraries, and university and college libraries.

There are 5 legal deposit libraries—the State Library, the South African Library, the Library of Parliament, the Bloemfontein Public Library and the Natal Society Library in Pietermaritzburg. South Africa's previous 2 national libraries—the South African Library in Cape Town and the State Library in Pretoria—have been amalgamated into the National Library of South Africa.

National Theatre and Opera. The 4 regional councils are the Performing Arts Council of the Transvaal (Pact), the Cape Performing Arts Board (Capab), the Performing Arts Council of the Orange Free State (Pacofs) and the KwaZulu-Natal Playhouse Company. Each of these councils operates from its own theatre complex—Pact from the State Theatre in Pretoria; Pacofs from the Sand du Plessis Theatre complex in Bloemfontein; Capab from the Nico Malan Theatre centre in Cape Town; and the KwaZulu-Natal Playhouse Company from the Natal Playhouse, Durban.

Museums and Galleries. Almost half of the approximately 1m. museums in Africa are situated in South Africa. The biggest museums are situated in Johannesburg, Pretoria, Cape Town, Durban, Pietermaritzburg and Bloemfontein. Art galleries include: South African National Gallery, Cape Town; Johannesburg Art Gallery; Pretoria Art Museum; William Humphreys Art Gallery, Kimberley.

DIPLOMATIC REPRESENTATIVES
Of South Africa in Great Britain (South Africa Hse., Trafalgar Sq., London, WC2N 5DP)
High Commissioner: Cheryll Ann Carolus.

Of Great Britain in South Africa (91 Parliament St., Cape Town, 8001)
High Commissioner: HE Dame Maeve G. Fort, DCMG.

Of South Africa in the USA (3051 Massachusetts Ave., NW, Washington, D.C., 20008)
Ambassador: S. V. M. Sisulu.

Of the USA in South Africa (877 Pretorius St., Arcadia 0083, Pretoria)
Ambassador: James A. Joseph.

Of South Africa to the United Nations
Ambassador: Khiphusizi Jele.

Of South Africa to the European Union
Ambassador: Dr Elias Links.

FURTHER READING
Government Communication and Information System (GCIS), including extracts from the *South Africa Yearbook 1998*, compiled and published by GCIS.
SA Government website: http://www.gov.za
SA Reserve Bank website: http://www.resbank.co.za

Beinart, W., *Twentieth Century South Africa.* OUP, 1994
Brewer, J., (ed.) *Restructuring South Africa.* London, 1994
Davenport, T. R. H., *South Africa: a Modern History.* 4th ed. CUP, 1991
Davies, G. V., *South Africa* [Bibliography]. 2nd ed. Oxford and Santa Barbara (CA), 1994
De Klerk, F. W., *The Last Trek—A New Beginning,* Macmillan, London, 1999
Fine, B and Rustomjee Z., *The Political Economy of South Africa,* 1997
Hough, M. and Du Plessis, A. (eds.) *Selected Documents and Commentaries on Negotiations and Constitutional Development in the RSA, 1989–1994.* Pretoria Univ., 1994
Johnson, R. W. and Schlemmer, L. (eds.) *Launching Democracy in South Africa: the First Open Election, 1994.* Yale Univ. Press, 1996
Mandela, N., *Long Walk to Freedom: the Autobiography of Nelson Mandela.* London, 1994
Meredith, M., *South Africa's New Era: the 1994 Election.* London, 1994
Mostert, N., *Frontiers: the Epic of South Africa's Creation and the Tragedy of the Xhosa People.* London, 1992
Nattrass, N. and Ardington, E. (eds.) *The Political Economy of South Africa.* Cape Town and OUP, 1990
Oxford History of South Africa. OUP, 1969
Thompson, L., *A History of South Africa.* 2nd ed. Yale Univ. Press, 1996
The Truth and Reconciliation Commission of South Africa Report, 5 vols. Macmillan, London 1999
Waldmeir, P., *Anatomy of a Miracle: the End of Apartheid and the Birth of the New South Africa,* London, 1997
Who's Who in South African Politics. 5th ed. London, 1995

National statistical office: Statistics South Africa, Private Bag X44, Pretoria 0001.
Website: http://www.statssa.gov.za/

SOUTH AFRICAN PROVINCES

In 1994 the former provinces of the Cape of Good Hope, Natal, the Orange Free State and the Transvaal, together with the former 'homelands' or 'TBVC countries' of Transkei, Bophuthatswana, Venda and Ciskei, were replaced by 9 new provinces. Transkei and Ciskei were integrated into Eastern Cape, Venda into Northern Province, and Bophuthatswana into Free State, Mpumalanga and North-West.

The administrative powers of the provincial governments in relation to the central government are set out in the 1999 Constitution after a revision of the original text demanded by the Constitutional Court in 1996.

EASTERN CAPE

TERRITORY AND POPULATION
The area is 169,600 sq. km and the population at the Oct. 1996 census was 6,302,525, the third largest population in South Africa. Of that number: female, 3,394,469; African/Black, 5,448,495 (86% of the population); White, 330,294 (5%); Coloured, 468,532 (7%); Indian/Asian, 19,356 (0·3%). 37% of the population lived in urban areas. At the 1996 census, 83·8% spoke IsiXhosa as their home language, 9·6% Afrikaans, 3·7% English and 2·2% Sesotho.

Eastern Cape comprises 77 administrative districts (including Umzimkulu district, an enclave within KwaZulu-Natal).

CONSTITUTION AND GOVERNMENT
The provincial capital is Bisho. There is a 56-seat provincial legislature.

RECENT ELECTIONS
At the provincial elections held 27–29 April 1994, 48 seats were won by the ANC (with 84·6% of votes cast), 6 by the NP (with 9·9%), 1 by the DP (with 2·1%) and 1 by the PAC (with 2·0%).

CURRENT ADMINISTRATION
In Jan. 1999 the Executive Council comprised:
Premier: Rev. M. A. Stofile (ANC).
Minister of Agriculture and Land Affairs: M. Mamase (ANC). *Education and Training:* Prof. S. Mayatula (ANC). *Finance, Economic Affairs, Environment and Tourism:* E. Godongwana (ANC). *Health:* Dr Trudie Thomas (ANC). *Housing and Local Government:* S. Mazosiwe (ANC). *Public Works and Transport:* T. Mhahlo (ANC). *Safety and Security:* Denis Neer (ANC). *Sports, Arts and Culture:* S. Mancotywa (ANC). *Welfare:* N. L. Jajula (ANC).

ENERGY AND NATURAL RESOURCES
Electricity. In 1996, 6,027m. kWh of electricity were consumed.

Minerals. There were 50 mines in 1993, employing 1,044 paid workers.

Agriculture. In 1993 (excluding the former Ciskei and Transkei now within the province) there were 6,106 farms with 104,583 agricultural workers; gross farming income amounted to R1,203·9m.

INDUSTRY
The number of manufacturing establishments (according to the Census of Manufacturing 1993) numbered 2,114, with 150,075 employees.

Labour. As at Oct. 1996 the economically active population numbered 1,529,000, of whom 786,818 were unemployed. Of those employed, 217,469 were in elementary occupations; 96,195 professionals; 88,833 craft and related trades;

66,686 service, shop and market sales workers; 52,655 clerks; 47,329 technicians and associate professionals; 42,546 plant and machine operators and assemblers; 34,422 skilled agricultural and fishery workers.

COMMUNICATIONS

Roads. Motor vehicles registered (1991, excluding Ciskei and Transkei) totalled 341,759, including 197,151 passenger cars and 71,985 commercial vehicles. In 1995 there were 31,750 road accidents with 724 fatalities.

SOCIAL INSTITUTIONS

Education. In 1993 there were 16,336 pupils in pre-primary schools, 4,289 pupils in special schools, 1,602,255 pupils in primary schools and 694,688 in secondary schools, with altogether 56,462 teachers; there were also 574 lecturers and 7,630 students in technical colleges, and 1,175 lecturers and 14,373 students in teachers training establishments.

At Oct. 1996 more than 20% of people aged 20 years and above had no schooling at all, while 21% had some primary schooling and 33% had some secondary education.

Health. In 1996 there were 106 hospitals (including 10 private hospitals) and 16,444 hospital beds.

CULTURE

Broadcasting. In 1996 there were 243,662 TV licence holders.

FREE STATE

TERRITORY AND POPULATION

The Free State lies in the centre of South Africa and is situated between the Vaal River in the north and the Orange River in the south. It borders on the Northern Cape, Eastern Cape, North-West, Mpumalanga, KwaZulu-Natal and Gauteng Province and shares a border with Lesotho. The area is 129,480 sq. km, 10·62% of South Africa's total surface area. The province is the third largest in South Africa but has the second smallest population and the second lowest population density (22 persons per sq. km). The population at the Oct. 1996 census was 2,633,504. Of that number: female, 1,335,156; African/Black, 2,223,940; White, 316,459; Coloured, 79,038; Indian/Asian, 2,805. The population is 52% male, the main reason being the large number of male migrants from outside the province who work in the mines. 63% of the population are between 15 and 64. At least 69% of the population lived in urban areas (in 1911, 80% lived in rural areas). Annual population growth rate: 1–2%. At the 1996 census, 62·1% of the population spoke Sesotho as their home language, 14·5% Afrikaans, 9·4% IsiXhosa, 6·5% Setswana, 4·8% IsiZulu and 1·3% English.

Free State comprises 52 administrative districts. The provincial capital is Bloemfontein (meaning 'fountain of flowers'). Bloemfontein's indigenous name is Mangaung, which means 'place of the big cats'.

SOCIAL STATISTICS

The racial structure (1996 census) was 84% African/Black; 12% White; 3% Coloured; 0·1% Indian/Asian.

CLIMATE

Temperatures are mild with averages ranging from 19·5°C in the west to 15°C in the east. Maximum temperatures in the west can reach 36°C in summer. Winter temperatures in the high-lying areas of the eastern Free State can drop as low as −15°C. The western and southern areas are semi-desert.

CONSTITUTION AND GOVERNMENT

There is a 30-seat provincial legislature. The Free State Executive Council, headed by the *Premier*, administers the province through 10 Departments.

The Free State of Traditional Leaders advises the Legislature on matters pertaining to traditional authorities and tribal matters.

RECENT ELECTIONS

In the first democratic election held on 27 April 1994, turnout was 83%. The following political parties obtained seats in the Provincial Legislature: African National Congress (ANC), 24 (with 77·5% of votes cast), National Party (NP), 4 (12·7%) and Freedom Front (FF), 2 (6·1%).

Next elections were to be held in May 1999.

CURRENT ADMINISTRATION

In Jan. 1999 the government comprised:
Premier: Dr Ivy F. Matsepe-Casaburri (ANC).

Minister of Finance and Economic Affairs: Z. A. Dingani (ANC). *Education:* D. A. Kganare (ANC). *Public Works, Roads and Transport:* S. M. A. Malebo (ANC). *Health:* S. N. Ntlabathi (ANC). *Agriculture:* C. H. Human (ANC). *Environmental Affairs and Tourism:* P. H. I. Makgoe (ANC). *Local Government and Housing:* B. Kotsoane (ANC). *Social Welfare:* M. A. Motsumi-Tsopo (ANC). *Safety and Security:* A. Buthelezi-Phori. *Sport, Arts, Culture, Science and Technology:* M. W. Mfebe.

Local Government. The Free State has been demarcated into 4 District Councils with the function of assisting local authorities in the development and maintenance of infrastructural services.

Turn-out at the local government elections held on 1 Nov. 1995 was 53%. Of the combined seats (wards and proportional representation), the ANC won 661 (57%) of the 1,150 seats; Independents, 146 (13%), NP, 116 (10%), Rate Payers, 59 (3%), FF, 13 (1%), and others, 155. In 74 of the 80 towns the ANC obtained a majority. In 11 of the 15 Rural Councils the Rural Development Forum has the majority, compared to 3 for the ANC.

ECONOMY

Policy. Economic policy for the province is in line with the South African Government's Macro-Economic Policy. It is aimed at obtaining higher levels of growth, development and employment through accelerated growth of non-gold exports, a brisk expansion in private-sector capital formation, growth of public-sector investment, an improvement in the employment intensity of investment and output growth, and an increase in infrastructural development and service delivery making intensive use of labour-based techniques. The central thrust of trade and industry development is the expansion of the manufacturing industry and the promotion of value-added exports.

ENERGY AND NATURAL RESOURCES

Electricity. In the Free State, Eskom distributes electricity through 3,000 km of distribution lines, 9,000 km of reticulation (network) lines; and has an installed capacity of 1,200,740 MVA. Mining (60% of sales) and local governments (30% of sales) are Eskom's biggest Free State's customers.

In 1996, 10,803m. kWh of electricity were consumed.

Water. The Free State is susceptible to drought. The Orange River includes the Gariep and Vanderkloof dams, the largest in the country, and the Lesotho Highlands Water Project has an important impact on the Free State as water from the Katse Dam in Lesotho reaches the Vaal Dam via rivers running through the Free State. Large wetland areas in the north-eastern part of the province are an important source of groundwater for the agricultural industry in the area.

In 1996 piped water was available in the homes of 40% of the population.

Minerals. Apart from rich gold and diamond deposits, the Free State is the source of numerous other minerals and is the founding home of South Africa's famous oil-from-coal industry centred on Sasolburg. Bentonite clays, gypsum, salt and phosphates are to be found while large concentrates of thorium-ilminite-zircon also occur. In 1993 there were 82 mines with 121,352 employees.

Agriculture. Good agricultural conditions allow for a wide variety of farming industries. Of the total 12·7m. ha., 90% (11·5m. ha) is utilized as farmland. Of this, 63·9% is natural grazing; 2·1% is for nature conservation; and 1·1% is used for other purposes. Dryland cultivation is practised on 97% of the arable land, while the remaining 3% is under irrigation.

In 1998 there were a total of 11,647 commercial farmers working 48,420 farming units in the province. The eastern region is the major producer of small grains; the northern region, maize and beef; and the southern region, mutton and wool. The province produces about 40% of total maize and 50% of total wheat production in South Africa.

INDUSTRY

The number of manufacturing establishments (according to the Census of Manufacturing 1993) numbered 926, with 49,395 employees.

Labour. As at Oct. 1996 the economically active population numbered 1,001,122, of whom 701,175 were employed—an unemployment rate of 26·1%. Of those employed, 251,245 were in elementary occupations; 49,539 professionals; 92,949 craft and related trades; 54,491 service, shop and market sales workers; 40,005 clerks; 26,188 technicians and associate professionals; 65,161 plant and machine operators and assemblers; 39,906 skilled agricultural and fishery workers.

COMMUNICATIONS

Roads. The Free State Department of Public Works, Roads and Transport is responsible for maintenance of a rural network, which consists of 20,452 km tertiary gravel roads, 21,470 km secondary gravel roads, 6,965 km primary paved roads, and 910 km national roads, of which 25 km are not tarred. In 1995 there were 26,163 road accidents with 997 fatalities.

Rail. Spoornet is one of the biggest companies in the Free State with 4,217 employees. Spoornet transports most of the province's maize, wheat, gold ore, petroleum and fertilizer. The Spoornet infrastructure consists of approximately 4,000 km of tracks, of which 1,300 km are electrified.

Telecommunications. The main service providers are Telkom, Vodacom and MTN (Mobile Telephone Network).

Postal Services. In 1998 there were 330 post offices, 29 part-time post offices, 7 Postpoints (situated in locations such as chainstores, etc.) and 144 retail postal agencies.

SOCIAL INSTITUTIONS

Justice. Small claims courts operate in 11 centres, providing informal forums where citizens appear in person before a commissioner. The decision of the commissioner is final and the parties cannot appeal to a higher court. Civil claims can be instituted in the magistrates' court, there being 67 magistrate's offices in the province. The Free State provincial division of the Supreme Court is in Bloemfontein. The Circuit Court is a local division of the provincial division of the Supreme Court which visits certain areas. The Circuit Court tries criminal cases only. In 1998, 523 attorneys and 42 advocates practised in the province.

Education. Twelve education districts were established in 1994 to deal with the administration of the province's schools (over 3,000), 787,000 pupils and 23,000 teachers. The total enrolment of pupils, 1995–98, showed a 10·74% growth. More than 2,000 farm schools cater for 95,000 pupils. 9 technical colleges provide vocational training for school leavers. Technikon Free State has 8,000 students on the main campus in Bloemfontein and 4 campuses for distance education situated in Welkom, Kimberley, Kroonstad and Qwaqwa. There are 8 teacher training colleges with 4,600 students. The University of the Orange Free State is the only fully fledged residential university, and had a student population (in 1996) of 10,000.

1998 literacy rate: 84·42%. In 1996, 16% of those aged 20 and over had no schooling; 33% had some secondary education.

Health. In 1996 there were 48 hospitals (including 14 private hospitals) and 9,072 hospital beds.

CULTURE

Broadcasting. Apart from the national broadcaster, SABC, several private and community radio stations exist, catering for the 3 primary language groups in the province. In 1996 there were 164,092 TV licence holders.

Press. There is 1 daily newspaper, *Di Volksblad*, which is published in Afrikaans. Several 'knock-and drop-type' weekly newspapers are produced on a regional basis.

Festivals. A Water and Wine Festival is held annually in Feb./March at Jacobsdal; the Witblitz Festival in Philippolis is held annually at the end of March/beginning of April; the Ficksburg Cherry Festival is held annually during the cherry season in November; and the Bloemfontein Show, the largest agricultural show in the province, is held each March.

Libraries. There are 128 community and public libraries and 15 library depots.

National Theatre and Opera. The Performing Arts Council of the Free State (PACOFS) operates from the Sand du Plessis Theatre complex in Bloemfontein, one of the most modern theatre complexes in South Africa. The Andre Huguenet Theatre is housed in the same complex. The Observatory Theatre is based in a former observatory in Bloemfontein. The Bloemfontein Civic, the Ernest Oppenheimer, in Welkom, and the Kroonstad Civic are all municipal theatres managed by PACOFS.

Museums and Galleries. There are over 30 museums in the province covering a broad cultural medium.

FURTHER READING

Free State: The Winning Province. Chris van Rensburg Publications, Johannesburg, 1997.
South African Yearbook 1998. Government Communication and Information System, ABC, Cape Town, 1997.

GAUTENG

TERRITORY AND POPULATION

The area is 18,810 sq. km and the population at the Oct. 1996 census was 7,348,423. Of that number: female, 3,597,578; African/Black, 5,147,444 (70%); White, 1,702,343 (23%); Coloured, 278,692 (3·8%); Indian/Asian, 161,289 (2·2%). 97% of the population lived in urban areas. At the 1996 census, 21·5% spoke IsiZulu as their home language, 16·7% Afrikaans, 13·1% Sesotho, 13·0% English, 9·5% Sepedi, 7·9% Setswana, 7·5% IsiXhosa, 5·3% Xitsonga, 1·6% IsiNdebele, 1·4% Tshivenda and 1·3% SiSwati.

The province of Gauteng, at first called Pretoria-Witwatersrand-Vereeniging (PWV), comprises 23 administrative districts. The provincial capital is Johannesburg.

CONSTITUTION AND GOVERNMENT

There is an 86-seat provincial legislature.

RECENT ELECTIONS

At the provincial elections held on 27–29 April 1994, 50 seats were won by the ANC (with 58·4% of the 4,143,901 votes cast), 21 by the NP (24·2%), 5 by the FF (6·2%), 5 by the DP (5·4%), 3 by the IFP (3·7%), and 1 each by the PAC (1·5%) and ACDP (0·6%).

CURRENT ADMINISTRATION

In Jan. 1999 the government comprised:

Premier: Dr M. S. Motshekga (ANC).

Minister of Agriculture, Conservation and Environment: Nomvula P. Mokonyane (ANC). *Development Planning and Local Government:* Sicelo S. Shiceka (ANC). *Education:* Mary Metcalfe (ANC). *Economic Affairs and Finance:* P. Jabu Moleketi (ANC). *Health:* M. Gungubele (ANC). *Housing and Land Affairs:* Daniel Mofokeng (ANC). *Safety and Security:* S. P. Mashatile (ANC). *Sport, Recreation, Arts and Culture:* Peter V. Skosana (ANC). *Welfare and Population Development:* Ignatius P. Jacobs (ANC). *Transport and Public Works:* J. Kgoali (ANC).

ENERGY AND NATURAL RESOURCES

Electricity. In 1996, 54,150m. kWh of electricity were consumed.

Minerals. There were 133 mines with 162,531 employees in 1993.

Agriculture. In 1993 there were 2,500 farms with 34,302 agricultural workers; gross farming income amounted to R1,386·7m.

INDUSTRY

The number of manufacturing establishments (according to the Census of Manufacturing 1993) numbered 9,652, with 508,189 employees.

Labour. As at Oct. 1996 the economically active population numbered 3,572,009, of whom 1,007,766 were unemployed. Of those employed, 498,279 were in elementary occupations; 250,676 professionals; 410,630 craft and related trades; 258,104 service, shop and market sales workers; 256,633 clerks; 192,410 technicians and associate professionals; 175,937 plant and machine operators and assemblers; 52,972 skilled agricultural and fishery workers.

COMMUNICATIONS

Roads. Motor vehicles registered (1991) totalled 2,328,273 including 1,479,537 passenger cars and 404,468 commercial vehicles. In 1995 there were 202,583 road accidents with 2,318 fatalities.

Telecommunications. In 1996 at least 45% of the population had telephones or cellular phones; 4% had no access at all to a telephone.

SOCIAL INSTITUTIONS

Education. In 1993 there were 45,522 pupils in pre-primary schools, 15,296 pupils in special schools, 903,157 pupils in primary schools and 692,783 in secondary schools, with altogether 59,804 teachers; there were also 1,196 lecturers and 21,639 students in technical colleges, and 1,094 lecturers and 12,361 students in teacher training establishments.

In 1996, 40% of the population had some secondary education—the highest rate in any of South Africa's provinces.

Health. In 1996 there were 115 hospitals (including 78 private hospitals) and 29,860 hospital beds.

CULTURE

Broadcasting. There were 978,762 TV licence holders in 1996.

KWAZULU-NATAL

TERRITORY AND POPULATION

The area is 92,180 sq. km and the population at the Oct. 1996 census was 8,417,021. Of that number: female, 4,466,493; African/Black, 6,880,652 (82·0% of the population); Indian/Asian, 790,813 (9·4%); White, 558,182 (6·6); Coloured, 117,951 (1·4%). 43% lived in urban areas. At the 1996 census, 79·8% spoke IsiZulu as their home language, 15·8% English, 1·6% Afrikaans and 1·6% IsiXhosa.

KwaZulu-Natal comprises 66 administrative districts. The provincial capital is Pietermaritzburg, chosen by referendum in 1995.

CONSTITUTION AND GOVERNMENT
There is an 81-seat provincial legislature.

RECENT ELECTIONS
At the provincial elections held on 27–29 April 1994, 41 seats were won by the Inkatha Freedom Party (52·2% of votes cast), 26 by the ANC (33·4%), 9 by the NP (11·6%), 2 by the DP (2·2%) and 1 each by the PAC (0·8%), the African Christian Democratic Party (0·7%) and Minority Front (1·4%).

CURRENT ADMINISTRATION
In Jan. 1999 the government comprised:
Premier: L. P. H. M. Mtshali (IFP).
Minister of Agriculture and Housing: N. Singh (IFP). *Economic Affairs and Tourism:* Jacob G. Zuma (ANC). *Education and Culture:* E. E. N. kaNkosi-Shandu (IFP). *Finance (Gaming and Betting), Local Government and Planning:* P. M. Miller (IFP). *Health:* Dr Z. L. Mkhize (ANC). *Public Works:* Rev. C. J. Mtetwa (IFP). *Traditional and Environmental Affairs, Safety and Security:* Nyanga J. Ngubane (IFP). *Transport:* J. S. Ndebele (ANC). *Welfare and Population Development:* Prince Gideon L. Zulu (IFP).

Local Government. There are 2 tiers of local authority: 7 regional councils and 13 town or rural councils. Elections were held on 26 June 1996 (postponed for a second time from 1 Nov. 1995 and 29 May 1996 because of civil violence). Electors voted first for directly elected ward candidates and second for a party, seats being allotted by proportional representation. Turn-out was 44%. Inkatha won 44·4% of votes cast; ANC, 33%; NP, 12·7%; Democratic Party, 3%; ind, 6%. ANC won control of all town councils.

ENERGY AND NATURAL RESOURCES
Electricity. 35,235m. kWh of electricity were consumed in 1996.

Water. In 1996 piped water was available in the homes of 39% of the population.

Minerals. There were 74 mines with 14,139 employees in 1993.

Agriculture. In 1993 there were 6,080 farms with 165,505 agricultural workers; gross farming income amounted to R3,163·0m.

INDUSTRY
The number of manufacturing establishments (according to the Census of Manufacturing 1993) numbered 4,383, with 317,593 employees.

Labour. As at Oct. 1996 the economically active population numbered 2,579,517, of whom 1,008,944 were unemployed. Of those employed, 377,072 were in elementary occupations; 144,273 professionals; 186,319 craft and related trades; 126,425 service, shop and market sales workers; 109,067 clerks; 89,794 technicians and associate professionals; 118,776 plant and machine operators and assemblers; 51,696 skilled agricultural and fishery workers.

COMMUNICATIONS
Roads. Motor vehicles registered (1991) totalled 964,917, including 550,380 passenger cars and 200,317 commercial vehicles. In 1995 there were 93,309 road accidents with 2,097 fatalities.

SOCIAL INSTITUTIONS
Education. In 1993 there were 38,127 pupils in pre-primary schools, 2,465 pupils in special schools, 1,481,712 pupils in primary schools and 818,976 in secondary

schools, with altogether 63,921 teachers; there were also 717 lecturers and 9,188 students in technical colleges, and 1,062 lecturers and 12,147 students in teacher training establishments.

In 1996, 23% of the population aged 20 and above had no schooling; 32% had some secondary education.

Since 1995 education has been provided by a unified KwaZulu-Natal Education Department (KZNED).

Health. In 1996 there were 101 hospitals (including 31 private hospitals) and 26,152 hospital beds.

CULTURE
Broadcasting. There were 392,573 TV licence holders in 1996.

MPUMALANGA

TERRITORY AND POPULATION
The area is 78,370 sq. km and the population at the Oct. 1996 census was 2,800,711. Of that number: female, 1,438,683; African/Black, 2,497,834 (89% of the population); White, 253,392 (9%); Coloured, 20,283 (0·7%); Indian/Asian, 13,083 (0·5%). 39·1% lived in urban areas. At the 1996 census, 30·0% spoke SiSwati as their home language, 25·4% IsiZulu, 12·5% IsiNdebele, 10·5% Sepedi, 8·3% Afrikaans, 3·5% Xitsonga, 3·2% Sesotho, 2·7% Setswana, 2·0% English and 1·4% IsiXhosa.

Mpumalanga comprises 28 administrative districts. The provincial capital is Nelspruit.

CONSTITUTION AND GOVERNMENT
There is a 30-seat provincial legislature.

RECENT ELECTIONS
At the provincial elections held on 27–29 April 1994, 25 seats were won by the ANC (with 81·5% of votes cast), 3 by the NP (with 9·1%) and 2 by the FF (with 5·7%).

CURRENT ADMINISTRATION
In Jan. 1999 the government comprised:
Premier: N. M. Phosa (ANC).
Minister of Agriculture: J. B. Masilela (ANC). *Economic Affairs and Gaming:* Jacob L. Mabena (ANC). *Education and Training:* David D. Mabuza (ANC). *Environmental Affairs and Tourism:* N. L. Mathebula (ANC). *Finance and Central Services:* L. L. L. Chiwayo (ANC). *Health and Welfare:* K. C. Mashego (ANC). *Local Government, Housing and Land Administration:* Craig N. M. Padayachee (ANC). *Public Works, Roads and Transport:* J. M. Mthembu (ANC). *Safety and Security:* B. J. Modipane (ANC). *Sports, Arts, Culture and Recreation:* F. Mahlalela (ANC).

Local Government. Local elections were held in Oct. 1996.

ENERGY AND NATURAL RESOURCES
Electricity. In 1996, 24,619m. kWh of electricity were consumed.

Water. In 1996 piped water was available in the homes of more than 36% of the population, with 20% relying on public taps.

Minerals. There were 117 mines with 73,916 employees in 1993.

Agriculture. In 1993 (excluding that part of the former Bophuthatswana now within the province) there were 5,406 farms with 144,474 agricultural workers; gross farming income amounted to R2,765·6m.

INDUSTRY
The number of manufacturing establishments (according to the Census of Manufacturing 1993) numbered 763, with 70,957 employees.

Labour. As at Oct. 1996 the economically active population numbered 903,215 of whom 297,290 were unemployed. Of those employed, 179,233 were in elementary occupations; 42,114 professionals; 98,941 craft and related trades; 52,669 service, shop and market sales workers; 33,235 clerks; 22,108 technicians and associate professionals; 56,150 plant and machine operators and assemblers; 40,916 skilled agricultural and fishery workers.

COMMUNICATIONS
Roads. Motor vehicles registered (mid-1991, excluding Bophuthatswana) totalled 381,346 including 158,587 passenger cars and 100,546 commercial vehicles; new vehicle registrations in the year to mid-1992 totalled 15,307 including 6,893 passenger cars and 4,184 commercial vehicles. In 1995 there were 22,744 road accidents with 1,191 fatalities.

SOCIAL INSTITUTIONS
Education. In 1993 there were 6,731 pupils in pre-primary schools, 2,006 pupils in special schools, 471,079 pupils in primary schools and 285,345 in secondary schools, with altogether 21,952 teachers; there were also 250 lecturers and 3,884 students in technical colleges, and 302 lecturers and 3,628 students in teacher training establishments.

In 1996, 28% of those aged 20 years and over had no schooling; 38% had some secondary education.

Health. In 1996 there were 48 hospitals (including 19 private hospitals) and 5,553 hospital beds.

CULTURE
Broadcasting. There were 138,085 TV licence holders in 1996.

NORTHERN CAPE

TERRITORY AND POPULATION
The area is 361,800 sq. km. and the population at the Oct. 1996 census was 840,321. Of that number: female, 427,639; Coloured, 435,368 (52% of the population); African/Black, 278,633 (33%); White, 111,878 (13%); Indian/Asian, 2,268 (0·3%). At least 70% lived in urban areas. At the 1996 census, 69·3% spoke Afrikaans as their home language, 19·9% Setswana, 6·3% IsiXhosa and 2·4% English.

Northern Cape comprises 6 administrative districts: Diamond Fields with Kimberley as the provincial and economic capital; Kalahari, which is the second richest and densely populated area in the province and includes the magisterial districts of Kuruman and Postmasburg; Hantam (North-West) with the towns of Calvinia, Sutherland, Williston, Fraserburg and Carnavon; Benede-Orange with Upington as the agricultural, economic and cultural capital of the region; Bo-Karoo with De Aar as the capital of the area; and Namaqualand which is strong in mining.

CONSTITUTION AND GOVERNMENT
There is a 30-seat provincial legislature.

RECENT ELECTIONS
At the provincial elections held on 27–29 April 1994, 15 seats were won by the ANC (50·0% of votes cast), 12 by the NP (40·7%), 2 by the FF (6·0%) and 1 by the DP (1·9%). An ANC-NP coalition government was formed.

SOUTH AFRICA

CURRENT ADMINISTRATION
In Jan. 1999 the government comprised:

Premier: Manne E. Dipico (ANC).

Minister of Agriculture, Nature Conservation and Land Reform: T. Makweya (ANC). *Education, Arts and Culture:* Tina M. Joemat (ANC). *Finance, Economic Affairs, and Tourism, Trade and Industry:* Goolam H. Akharwaray (ANC). *Health, Welfare and Environment Affairs:* Dr Modise F. Matlaopane (ANC). *Local Government and Housing:* Ouneas P. Dikgetsi (ANC). *Safety, Security and Public Works:* Eunice V. Komane (ANC). *Sport, Recreation, Science, Technology and Transport:* Prof. Jozef J. Henning (FF).

ENERGY AND NATURAL RESOURCES
Electricity. In 1996, 3,613m. kWh of electricity were consumed.

Water. The province's only perennial rivers which supply the drinking and irrigation needs are the Orange, Vaal Harts and Riet River. In 1996 piped water was available in the homes of almost 50% of the population.

Minerals. The province is well endowed with a variety of mineral deposits. Diamonds are found in shallow water at Port Nolloth, Hondeklipbaai and Lamberts Bay, and also mined inland along the entire coastal strip from the Orange river mouth in the north to Lamberts Bay in the south. Copper is mined in Namaqualand. Iron and manganese occur in two parallel north-south belts from Postmasburg in the south to Sishen/Kathu/Hotazel in the north. Limestone, asbestos and gypsum salt are also mined. There are small mining operations for specialized stones or gems such as tiger's-eye, jasper, pegmatite, dimension stone and verdite.

Agriculture. Intensive irrigation takes place along the Orange River which supports vineyards and agribusiness. Stock farming predominates in the Bo-Karoo and Hantam areas. In 1993 there were 6,593 farms with 75,969 agricultural workers; gross farming income amounted to R103·9m.

INDUSTRY
The number of manufacturing establishments (according to the Census of Manufacturing 1993) numbered 266, with 8,505 employees.

Labour. As at Oct. 1996 the economically active population numbered 301,583, of whom 86,060 were unemployed. Of those employed, 82,686 were in elementary occupations; 14,382 professionals; 23,136 craft and related trades; 16,844 service, shop and market sales workers; 13,974 clerks; 9,152 technicians and associate professionals; 8,946 plant and machine operators and assemblers; 17,365 skilled agricultural and fishery workers.

COMMUNICATIONS
Roads. Motor vehicles registered (1991) totalled 143,315, including 63,504 passenger cars and 44,042 commercial vehicles. In 1995 there were 7,273 road accidents with 326 fatalities.

Rail. The main rail link is between Cape Town and Johannesburg, via Kimberley. Other main lines link the Northern Cape with Port Elizabeth via De Aar while another links Upington with Namibia.

Civil Aviation. Five airports are used for scheduled flights in Kimberley, Upington, Aggeneys, Springbok and Alexander Bay.

SOCIAL INSTITUTIONS
Education. In 1993 there were 1,666 pupils in pre-primary schools, 1,801 pupils in special schools, 118,851 pupils in primary schools and 69,470 in secondary schools, with altogether 7,677 teachers; there were also 103 lecturers and 1,599 students in technical colleges, and 83 lecturers and 763 students in teacher training establishments.

In 1996 almost 21% of those aged 20 years and over had no schooling; 31% had some secondary education.

Health. In 1996 there were 46 hospitals (including 14 private hospitals) and 3,020 hospital beds.

CULTURE

Broadcasting. There were 85,140 TV licence holders in 1996.

Tourism. Parks are a major tourism asset, with the total area under protection being 1,080,200 ha. Provincial nature reserves occupy 50,240 ha. Hunting is a growing activity in the province.

FURTHER READING
Website: http://www.ncwebpage.ncape.gov.za

NORTHERN PROVINCE

TERRITORY AND POPULATION
The area is 123,280 sq. km and the population at the Oct. 1996 census was 4,929,368. Of that number: female, 2,676,296; African/Black, 4,765,255 (96% of the population); White, 117,878 (2·4%); Coloured, 7,821 (0·2%); Indian/Asian, 5,510 (0·1%). 11·9% lived in urban areas. At the 1996 census 52·7% spoke Sepedi as their home language, 22·6% Xitsonga, 15·5% Tshivenda, 2·2% Afrikaans and 1·5% IsiNdebele.

Northern Province comprises 32 administrative districts. The provincial capital is Pietersburg.

CONSTITUTION AND GOVERNMENT
There is a 40-seat provincial legislature.

RECENT ELECTIONS
At the provincial elections held on 27–29 April 1994, 38 seats were won by the ANC (with 92·3% of votes cast) and 1 each by the NP (3·3%) and the FF (2·2%).

CURRENT ADMINISTRATION
In Jan. 1999 the government comprised:
Premier: Ngoako A. Ramathlodi (ANC).
Minister of Agriculture, Land and Environmental Affairs: Dr R. S. Farisani (ANC). *Education:* Dr M. J. Phaala (ANC). *Finance, Trade, Industry and Tourism:* Thaba A. Mufamadi (ANC). *Health and Welfare:* Dr H. E. Mateme (ANC). *Housing and Water Affairs:* C. E. Mushwana (ANC). *Local Government and Traditional Affairs:* N. M. Mashabane (ANC). *Public Works:* C. O. Chabane (ANC). *Safety and Security:* Seth A. Nthai (ANC). *Sports, Arts and Culture:* K. E. Nong (ANC). *Transport:* Dr A. Motsoaledi (ANC).

ENERGY AND NATURAL RESOURCES

Electricity. In 1996, 7,315m. kWh of electricity were consumed.

Water. In 1996 piped water was available in the homes of 17% of the population, with 40% relying on public taps.

Minerals. There were 59 mines with 37,814 employees in 1993.

Agriculture. In 1993 (excluding the former Venda now within the province) there were 5,053 farms with 123,116 agricultural workers; gross farming income amounted to R1,284·9m.

INDUSTRY
The number of manufacturing establishments (according to the Census of Manufacturing 1993) numbered 768, with 29,225 employees.

Labour. As at Oct. 1996 the economically active population numbered 1,056,683, of whom 486,554 were unemployed. Of those employed, 164,692 were in elementary occupations; 73,320 professionals; 79,517 craft and related trades; 50,008 service, shop and market sales workers; 25,260 clerks; 20,135 technicians and associate professionals; 26,835 plant and machine operators and assemblers; 45,455 skilled agricultural and fishery workers.

COMMUNICATIONS

Roads. Motor vehicles registered (1991, excluding Venda) totalled 240,801, including 95,627 passenger cars and 81,237 commercial vehicles. In 1995 there were 15,841 road accidents with 693 fatalities.

SOCIAL INSTITUTIONS

Education. In 1993 there were 72,805 pupils in pre-primary schools, 1,185 pupils in special schools, 1,043,566 pupils in primary schools and 757,058 in secondary schools, with altogether 53,026 teachers; there were also 387 lecturers and 3,123 students in technical colleges, and 1,532 lecturers and 20,085 students in teacher training establishments.

In 1996, almost 37% of the population aged 20 years and over had no schooling.

Health. In 1996 there were 47 hospitals (including 4 private hospitals) and 15,765 hospital beds.

CULTURE

Broadcasting. There were 99,362 TV licence holders in 1996.

NORTH-WEST

TERRITORY AND POPULATION

The area is 116,190 sq. km and the population at the Oct. 1996 census was 3,354,825. Of that number: female, 1,704,990; African/Black, 3,058,686 (91·0% of the total population); White, 222,755 (6·6%); Coloured, 46,652 (1·4%); Indian/Asian, 10,097 (0·3%). At the 1996 census (including the former Bophuthatswana), 67·2% spoke Setswana as their home language, 7·5% Afrikaans, 5·4% IsiXhosa, 5·1% Sesotho, 4·7% Xitsonga, 4·0% Sepedi, 2·5% IsiZulu, 1·3% IsiNdebele, 1·0% English and 0·5% SiSwati.

North-West Province comprises 32 administrative districts. The provincial capital is Mmabatho.

CONSTITUTION AND GOVERNMENT

There is a 30-seat provincial legislature.

RECENT ELECTIONS

At the provincial elections held on 27–29 April 1994, 26 seats were won by the ANC (83·5% of the 1,568,574 votes cast), 3 by the NP (8·9%) and 1 by the FF (4·6%).

CURRENT ADMINISTRATION

In Jan. 1999 the government comprised:

Premier: Popo S. Molefe (ANC).

Minister of Agriculture: O. J. Tselapedi (ANC). *Education:* Z. P. Tolo (ANC). *Finance and Economic Affairs:* Martin J. Kuscus (ANC). *Health, Social Welfare and Public Media:* Dr Molefi Paul Sefularo (ANC). *Local Government, Housing and Development:* D. E. Africa (ANC). *Public Works and Roads:* R. Motsepe (ANC). *Safety and Security:* Satish Roopa (ANC). *Sport, Arts, Culture and*

Recreation: Z. Tumagole. *Tourism and Conservation:* B. E. E. Molewa (ANC). *Transport and Aviation:* Frans P. Vilakazi (ANC).

ENERGY AND NATURAL RESOURCES

Electricity. In 1996, 21,654m. kWh of electricity were consumed.

Water. In 1996 piped water was available in the homes of almost 30% of the population. The most-used source of water was the public tap, used by more than 31% of the population.

Minerals. There were 87 mines in 1993 with 100,027 employees.

Agriculture. In 1993 (excluding the TBVC countries of Transkei, Bophuthatswana, Venda and Ciskei now within the province) there were 7,638 farms with 126,530 agricultural workers; gross farming income amounted to R1,909·8m.

INDUSTRY

The number of manufacturing establishments (according to the Census of Manufacturing, 1993) numbered 983, with 57,049 employees.

Labour. As at Oct. 1996 the economically active population numbered 1,168,833, of whom 443,546 were unemployed. Of those employed, 200,910 were in elementary occupations; 57,539 professionals; 143,011 craft and related trades; 64,105 service, shop and market sales workers; 42,478 clerks; 29,277 technicians and associate professionals; 57,015 plant and machine operators and assemblers; 33,428 skilled agricultural and fishery workers.

COMMUNICATIONS

Roads. Motor vehicles registered (1991, excluding Bophuthatswana) totalled 319,805 including 140,802 passenger cars and 71,237 commercial vehicles. In 1995 there were 13,453 road accidents with 624 fatalities.

Telecommunications. Around 17% of the population had telephones or cellular phones in 1996; 19% had no access at all to a telephone.

SOCIAL INSTITUTIONS

Education. In 1993 there were 22,261 pupils in pre-primary schools, 2,708 pupils in special schools, 400,436 pupils in primary schools and 233,436 in secondary schools, with altogether 21,750 teachers; there were also 110 lecturers and 1,684 students in technical colleges, and 274 lecturers and 3,275 students in teacher training establishments.

In 1996 almost 22% of those aged 20 or over had no schooling.

Health. There were 54 hospitals in 1996 (including 17 private hospitals), and 9,806 hospital beds.

CULTURE

Broadcasting. In 1996 there were 116,680 TV licence holders.

WESTERN CAPE

TERRITORY AND POPULATION

The area is 129,370 sq. km. Population, 1996 census, 3,956,875. Of that number: females, 2,021,381; urban, 3·5m. (88·9% of total population); Coloured, 2,146,109 (54·2%); African/Black, 826,691 (20·9%); White, 821,551 (20·8%); Indian/Asian, 40,376 (1·0%). At the 1996 census, 59·2% spoke Afrikaans as their home language, 20·3% English and 19·1% IsiXhosa.

There are 41 administrative districts. The capital is Cape Town.

CONSTITUTION AND GOVERNMENT
There is a 42-seat provincial legislature.

RECENT ELECTIONS
At the provincial elections held on 27–29 April 1994, 23 seats were won by the NP (54·2% of votes cast), 14 by the ANC (33·6%), 3 by the DP (6·8%), and 1 each by the FF (2·1%) and African Christian Democratic Party (1·2%).

CURRENT ADMINISTRATION
In Jan. 1999 the government comprised:
Premier: G. N. Morkel (NP).
Minister of Agriculture and Property Management: L. H. Fick (NP). *Business Promotion and Tourism:* H. J. Bester (NP). *Community Safety:* M. G. E. Wiley (NP). *Development Planning:* M. Louis (ACDP). *Education:* N. J. J. Koornhof (NP). *Environmental and Cultural Affairs and Sport:* J. W. H. Meiring (NP). *Health and Social Services:* P. J. Marais (NP). *Housing:* C. B. Herandien (NP). *Local Government:* P. C. McKenzie (NP). *Transport and Public Works:* P. Meyer (NP).

Local Government. Elections for some areas were held on 29 May 1996 (postponed from 1 Nov. 1995 while boundaries were finalized). The NP gained control of all 3 district councils comprising 11 regional councils.

ENERGY AND NATURAL RESOURCES
Electricity. In 1996, 15,520m. kWh of electricity were consumed.

Minerals. In 1993 there were 120 mines with 4,165 employees.

Agriculture. There were 8,747 farms with 288,438 agricultural workers in 1996; gross farming income amounted to R6,760·5m.

INDUSTRY
The number of manufacturing establishments (according to the Census of Manufacturing 1993) numbered 4,146, with 236,109 employees.

Labour. As at Oct. 1996 the economically active population numbered 1,673,288, of whom 299,114 were unemployed. Of those employed, 403,862 were in elementary occupations; 124,540 professionals; 156,551 craft and related trades; 121,471 service, shop and market sales workers; 133,725 clerks; 97,776 technicians and associate professionals; 88,668 plant and machine operators and assemblers; 39,466 skilled agricultural and fishery workers.

COMMUNICATIONS
Roads. Motor vehicles registered (1996) totalled 1,102,226, including 679,977 passenger cars, 238,087 light commercial vehicles, 35,478 heavy commercial vehicles and 28,153 motor cycles. In 1995 there were 87,117 road accidents with 1,286 fatalities.

Telecommunications. In 1996, 55·2% of the population had a telephone or cellular phone; 3% having no access at all to a telephone.

SOCIAL INSTITUTIONS
Education. In 1996 there were 886 pupils in pre-primary schools, 13,627 pupils in special schools, 517,057 pupils in primary schools, 74,408 in intermediate schools, 255,042 in secondary schools and 22,800 in combined schools, with altogether 32,272 teachers; there were also 794 lecturers and 14,637 students in technical colleges, and 410 lecturers and 6,790 students in teacher training establishments.
10·6% of people aged 20 years and over had higher education qualifications.

Health. In 1996 there were 1,822 medical practitioners, 13,864 nurses, 93 hospitals (including 30 private hospitals) and 16,444 hospital beds.

CULTURE
Broadcasting. There were 681,644 TV licence holders in 1996.

SPAIN

Reino de España

(Kingdom of Spain)

Capital: Madrid
Population estimate, 2000: 39·8m.
GNP per capita: (PPP$) 15,290
HDI/world rank: 0·935/11

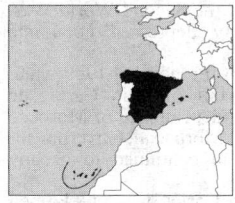

KEY HISTORICAL EVENTS

The modern Spanish state was founded with the marriage in 1469 of the heirs of the crowns of Castile and Aragón, respectively Isabel I and Fernando V. Under their joint reign Spain recovered Granada, the last Islamic territory in the Iberian peninsula and sponsored the modern discovery of America, both events in 1492. This dynasty ended in 1700 and subsequently the French Bourbon dynasty was enthroned, with Felipe V as its first king; the present monarch, Juan Carlos I, installed in 1975, is his direct descendant.

Queen Isabel II, who came to the throne in 1833, was deposed and exiled in 1868 by a liberal revolution. A provisional government, headed by the Duke de la Torre, established universal male suffrage and convened a constituent election for Jan. 1869. The Cortes (Parliament) approved a new constitution and the deputies chose as the new king Amadeo I of the then reigning Italian dynasty of Savoy. Unable to adapt to Spanish politics, he abdicated on 11 Feb. 1873. The Cortes immediately proclaimed a republic.

The first brief republican experience saw great instability. On 29 Dec. 1874, in Sagunto, Gen. Martínez Campos led a *coup* and restored the Bourbon monarchy, with Alfonso XII, the son of the exiled Queen Isabel II, as king. A general election took place early in 1876 and the new Cortes approved a constitution which was effective until 1923. This period, known as the Restoration, saw the reimposition of a restricted suffrage (universal suffrage was not re-established until 1890), and was dominated by two parties, Conservative and Liberal, led respectively by A. Cánovas del Castillo and P. M. Sagasta, both of whom served as prime minister several times in the last quarter of the 19th century. Alfonso XII died in 1885. His wife María Cristina of Hapsburg was regent till their son, Alfonso XIII, reached his majority in 1902.

During the period of the Restoration, Spain still had a very backward economy and very low standards of living. At the same time Spain was embroiled in external conflicts, with wars in northern Morocco and in the remaining colonies of Cuba and the Philippines. The US intervention led to the cession of Philippines, Puerto Rico and Guam, and also of Cuba which formally became independent in 1901.

Spain was neutral in the First World War, leading to a boom in industry and trade. A new industrial working class was then emerging, amidst a climate of industrial unrest which also showed itself in opposition to conscription for the war in the north of Morocco. In Sept. 1923 Gen. Primo de Rivera led a *coup* and abolished the 1876 constitution, closed down the Cortes and governed by decree until his resignation in Jan. 1930. During his dictatorship the war in the Spanish Protectorate in Morocco came to an end.

An interim period followed until the municipal elections of 12 April 1931, which were won by a republican-socialist coalition in Madrid, provincial capitals and other urban areas. Two days later Alfonso XIII exiled himself and the republic was proclaimed a second time. In June a new Cortes was elected; it drafted a new constitution, which was in force by Dec. 1931. Complete religious freedom and an agrarian reform were the significant landmarks of this period. An election in 1932, for the first time with female suffrage, established a very conservative coalition government, which resulted in serious rioting in Oct. 1934. An election in Feb. 1936 gave power to the Popular Front, a coalition of all left parties, including the then tiny Communist party.

On 18 July 1936 the colonial army in northern Morocco, led by Gen. Francisco Franco, and some other military units rebelled against the government. The rebellion was crushed in a few days in Madrid, Barcelona, Valencia and almost all industrial and mining areas. But the rural regions were easily controlled by the rebels who received substantial help in men, tanks and aircraft from Germany, Italy and Portugal. The government, however, suffered from the 'non-intervention' policy declared by the democracies, notably Britain and France. The International Brigades, a volunteer force, and conditional aid from the USSR were the only significant foreign support received by the Spanish republic. Franco's forces finally overcame all resistance and the war ended on 1 April 1939. Gen. Franco was chief of state till his death on 20 Nov. 1975. His brutal régime was modelled on those of the Axis countries. Nevertheless, Franco's Spain did not take part in the Second World War. The 15 years following the Civil War saw extremely depressed economic conditions.

A nominal monarchy existed from 1947 but with a vacant throne until 1969 when the francoist state accepted the future succession in favour of Juan Carlos de Borbón, grandson of Alfonso XIII. Franco recognized the independence of Morocco in 1956 and ceded the small Spanish protectorate to the Moroccan Government. Spain also withdrew from Equatorial Guinea in 1968 but continued to occupy Western Sahara until 1976.

On 22 Nov. 1975, following Gen. Franco's death, Juan Carlos was proclaimed king. A gradual return to democracy began. A referendum held in Dec. 1976 endorsed some key reforms making possible a free election on 15 June 1977. The elected bicameral Cortes drafted a new constitution which came into force on 29 Dec. 1978.

In the Basque region terrorist activity by the separatist organisation ETA has brought a reaction from the local population in the form of a strong peace movement. In 1994 it was believed that 10 ETA units were operational in Spain. ETA announced an indefinite ceasefire in Sept. 1998.

TERRITORY AND POPULATION
Spain is bounded in the north by the Bay of Biscay, France and Andorra, east and south by the Mediterranean and the Straits of Gibraltar, south-west by the Atlantic and west by Portugal and the Atlantic. Continental Spain has an area of 492,592 sq. km, and including the Balearic and Canary Islands and the towns of Ceuta and Melilla on the northern coast of Morocco, 504,750 sq. km (194,884 sq. miles). Population (last census, 1991), 38,872,268 (19,835,822 female). In 1995 an estimated 76·5% of the population lived in urban areas; population density was 80 per sq. km. Latest provisional figures for population (1996), 39,669,394 (20,269,845 females).

The UN gives a projected population for 2000 of 39·8m.

The growth of the population has been as follows:

Census year	Population	Rate of annual increase	Census year	Population	Rate of annual increase
1860	15,655,467	0·34	1950	27,976,755	0·81
1910	19,927,150	0·72	1960	30,903,137	0·88
1920	21,303,162	0·69	1970	33,823,918	0·94
1930	23,563,867	1·06	1981	37,746,260	1·15
1940	25,877,971	0·98	1991	38,872,268	0·29

In 1996 the number of foreigners legally registered was 526,014 (largest foreign communities: Moroccan, 78,045; British, 66,620).

Area and population of the autonomous communities and provinces in 1995:

Autonomous community/ Province	Area (sq. km)	Population	Per sq. km	Autonomous community/ Province	Area (sq. km)	Population	Per sq. km
Andalusia	87,268	7,314,644	83	Teruel	14,804	143,055	9
Almería	8,774	493,126	56	Zaragoza	17,194	852,332	49
Cádiz	7,385	1,127,622	152	Asturias	10,565	1,117,370	105
Córdoba	13,718	782,221	57	Baleares	5,014	787,984	157
Granada	12,531	841,829	67	Basque			
Huelva	10,085	458,674	45	Country	7,261	2,130,783	293
Jaén	13,498	666,767	49	Álava	3,047	282,944	92
Málaga	7,276	1,224,959	168	Guipúzcoa	1,997	684,113	342
Sevilla	14,001	1,719,446	122	Vizcaya	2,217	1,163,726	524
Aragón	47,669	1,205,663	25	Canary Islands	7,273	1,631,498	224
Huesca	15,671	210,276	13	Palmas, Las	4,065	844,140	207

SPAIN

Autonomous community/ Province	Area (sq. km)	Population	Per sq. km
Santa Cruz de Tenerife	3,208	787,358	245
Cantabria	5,289	541,885	102
Castilla-La Mancha	79,226	1,730,717	21
Albacete	14,858	361,327	24
Ciudad Real	19,749	490,573	24
Cuenca	17,061	207,499	12
Guadalajara	12,190	155,884	12
Toledo	15,368	515,434	33
Castilla y León	94,147	2,584,407	27
Ávila	8,048	176,791	21
Burgos	14,269	360,677	24
León	15,468	532,706	34
Palencia	8,029	186,035	23
Salamanca	12,336	365,293	29
Segovia	6,949	149,653	21
Soria	10,287	94,396	9
Valladolid	8,202	504,583	61
Zamora	10,559	214,273	20
Catalonia	31,930	6,226,869	195
Barcelona	7,773	4,748,236	610
Gerona	5,886	541,995	92
Lérida	12,028	360,407	29
Tarragona	6,283	576,231	91
Extremadura	41,602	1,100,538	26
Badajoz	21,657	675,592	31
Cáceres	19,945	424,946	21
Galicia	29,434	2,825,020	95
Coruña, La	7,876	1,136,283	144
Lugo	9,803	386,405	39
Orense	7,278	364,521	50
Pontevedra	4,477	937,811	209
Madrid	7,995	5,181,659	648
Murcia	11,317	1,109,977	98
Navarra	10,421	536,192	51
Rioja, La	5,034	268,206	53
Valencian Community	23,305	4,028,774	172
Alicante	5,863	1,363,785	232
Castellón	6,679	464,670	69
Valencia	10,763	2,200,319	204
Ceuta[1]	18	73,142	4,063
Melilla[1]	14	64,727	4,623
Total	504,750	40,460,055	80

[1]Ceuta and Melilla gained limited autonomous status in 1994.

The capitals of the autonomous communities are: *Andalusia*: Seville; *Aragón*: Zaragoza (Saragossa); *Asturias*: Oviedo; *Baleares*: Palma de Mallorca; *Basque Country*: Vitoria; *Canary Islands*, dual and alternative capital, Las Palmas and Santa Cruz de Tenerife; *Cantabria*: Santander; *Castilla-La Mancha*: Toledo; *Castilla y León*: Valladolid; *Catalonia*: Barcelona; *Extremadura:* Mérida; *Galicia*: Santiago de Compostela; *Madrid*: Madrid; *Murcia*: Murcia (but regional parliament in Cartagena); *Navarra*: Pamplona; *La Rioja*: Logroño; *Valencian Community*: Valencia.

The capitals of the provinces are the towns from which they take the name, except in the cases of Álava (capital, Vitoria), Asturias (Oviedo), Baleares (Palma de Mallorca), Cantabria (Santander), Guipúzcoa (San Sebastián), La Rioja (Logroño), Navarra (Pamplona) and Vizcaya (Bilbao).

The islands which form the Balearics include Majorca, Minorca, Ibiza and Formentera. Those which form the Canary Archipelago are divided into 2 provinces, under the name of their respective capitals: Santa Cruz de Tenerife and Las Palmas de Gran Canaria. The province of Santa Cruz de Tenerife is constituted by the islands of Tenerife, La Palma, Gomera and Hierro; that of Las Palmas by Gran Canaria, Lanzarote and Fuerteventura, with the small barren islands of Alegranza, Roque del Este, Roque del Oeste, Graciosa, Montaña Clara and Lobos.

Places under Spanish sovereignty in Morocco (Alhucemas, Ceuta, Chafarinas, Melilla and Peñón de Vélez) constitute the 2 provinces of Ceuta and Melilla.

Estimated populations of principal towns in 1996:

Town	Population	Town	Population	Town	Population
Albacete	143,779	Burgos	163,156	Fuenlabrada	163,567
Alcalá de Henares	163,386	Cáceres	77,768	Getafe	143,153
Alcobendas	83,031	Cádiz	145,595	Gijón	264,381
Alcorcón	141,465	Cartagena	170,483	Granada	245,640
Algeciras	101,907	Castellón de		Guecho	82,196
Alicante	274,577	la Plana	135,729	Hermanas, Dos	91,138
Almería	170,503	Córdoba	306,248	Hospitalet	255,050
Avilés	85,696	Cornellá de		Huelva	140,675
Badajoz	122,510	Llobregat	82,490	Jaén	104,776
Badalona	210,987	Coruña, La	243,785	Jerez de la Frontera	182,269
Baracaldo	100,474	Coslada	76,001	Laguna, La	121,769
Barcelona	1,508,805	Elche	191,660	Leganés	174,593
Bilbao	358,875	Ferrol, El	83,048	León	145,242

Town	Population	Town	Population	Town	Population
Lérida	112,035	Palmas, Las	355,563	Santander	185,410
Logroño	123,841	Pamplona	166,279	Santiago de	
Lugo	85,174	Reus	90,993	Compostela	93,672
Madrid	2,866,850	Sabadell	185,798	Sevilla	697,487
Málaga	549,135	Salamanca	159,225	Tarragona	112,176
Marbella	98,823	San Baudilio del		Tarrasa	163,862
Mataró	102,018	Llobregat	78,005	Telde	84,389
Móstoles	196,173	San Fernando	85,882	Torrejón de Ardoz	88,821
Murcia	345,759	San Sebastián	176,908	Valencia	746,683
Orense	107,060	Santa Coloma de		Valladolid	319,805
Oviedo	200,049	Grammanet	123,175	Vigo	286,774
Palencia	78,831	Santa Cruz de		Vitoria	214,234
Palma de Mallorca	304,250	Tenerife	203,787	Zaragoza	601,674

Languages. The Constitution states that 'Castilian is the Spanish official language of the State', but also that 'All other Spanish languages will also be official in the corresponding Autonomous Communities'. At the last census (1991) Catalan (an official EU language since 1990) was spoken in Catalonia by 68% of people, Baleares (66·9%), Valencian Community (51%, where it is frequently called Valencian), and in Aragón, a narrow strip close to the Catalonian and Valencian Community boundaries. Galician, a language very close to Portuguese, was spoken by a majority of people in Galicia (91%); Basque by a significant and increasing minority in the Basque Country (26·3%), and by a small minority in north-west Navarra (12%). It is estimated that one-third of all Spaniards speaks one of the other 3 official languages as well as standard Castilian. In bilingual communities, both Castilian and the regional language are taught in schools and universities.

SOCIAL STATISTICS
Statistics for calendar years:

	Marriages	Births	Deaths
1993	201,463	385,786	339,661
1994	199,731	370,148	338,242
1995	200,688	363,469	346,227
1996[1]	190,780	358,879	349,347
1997[1]	192,627	361,811	348,084

[1]Provisional.

Rate per 1,000 population, 1995: Births, 9·2; deaths, 8·7; marriages, 5·0. In 1994 the most popular age range for marrying was 25–29 for both males and females. Annual growth rate, 1990–95, 0·1%. Suicide rates (per 100,000 population), 1990–95: 7·7 (males, 11·6; females, 3·9). Expectation of life, 1990–95, was 73·7 years for males and 81·0 for females. Infant mortality, 1990–95, 8 per 1,000 live births; fertility rate, 1·3 births per woman.

CLIMATE
Most of Spain has a form of Mediterranean climate with mild, moist winters and hot, dry summers, but the northern coastal region has a moist, equable climate, with rainfall well distributed throughout the year, mild winters and warm summers, and less sunshine than the rest of Spain. The south, in particular Andalusia, is dry and prone to drought. At the Earth Summit in New York in 1997, the President of the Spanish Government, José María Aznar, highlighted the problem of desertification in Spain and the need to combat it.

Madrid, Jan. 41°F (5°C), July 77°F (25°C). Annual rainfall 16·8" (419 mm). Barcelona, Jan. 46°F (8°C), July 74°F (23·5°C). Annual rainfall 21" (525 mm). Cartagena, Jan. 51°F (10·5°C), July 75°F (24°C). Annual rainfall 14·9" (373 mm). La Coruña, Jan. 51°F (10·5°C), July 66°F (19°C). Annual rainfall 32" (800 mm). Sevilla, Jan. 51°F (10·5°C), July 85°F (29·5°C). Annual rainfall 19·5" (486 mm). Palma de Mallorca, Jan. 51°F (11°C), July 77°F (25°C). Annual rainfall 13·6" (347 mm). Santa Cruz de Tenerife, Jan. 64°F (17·9°C), July 76°F (24·4°C). Annual rainfall 7·72" (196 mm).

CONSTITUTION AND GOVERNMENT

Following the death of General Franco in 1975 and the transition to a democracy, the first democratic elections were held on 15 June 1977. A new Constitution was approved by referendum on 6 Dec. 1978, and came into force 29 Dec. 1978. It established a parliamentary monarchy.

The reigning king is **Juan Carlos I**, born 5 Jan. 1938. The eldest son of Don Juan, Conde de Barcelona, Juan Carlos was given precedence over his father as pretender to the Spanish throne in an agreement in 1954 between Don Juan and General Franco. Don Juan, who resigned his claims to the throne in May 1977, died on 1 April 1993. King (then Prince) Juan Carlos married, in 1962, Princess Sophia of Greece, daughter of the late King Paul of the Hellenes and Queen Frederika. *Offspring:* Elena, born 20 Dec. 1963, married 18 March 1995 Jaime de Marichalar; Cristina, born 13 June 1965, married 4 Oct. 1997 Iñaki Urdangarín; Felipe, Prince of Asturias, Heir to the throne, born 30 Jan. 1968.

The King receives an allowance, part of which is taxable, approved by parliament each year. In 1997 it was 990m. pesetas. There is no formal court; the (private) *Diputación de la Grandeza* represents the interests of the aristocracy.

Legislative power is vested in the *Cortes Generales*, a bicameral parliament composed of the Congress of Deputies (lower house) and the Senate (upper house). The *Congress of Deputies* has not less than 300 nor more than 400 members (350 in the general election of 1996) elected in a proportional system under which electors choose between party lists of candidates in multi-member constituencies.

The *Senate* has 257 members of whom 208 are elected by a majority system: the 47 mainland provinces elect 4 senators each, regardless of population; the island provinces 5 (Baleares, Las Palmas) or 6 (Santa Cruz de Tenerife); and Ceuta and Melilla, 2 senators each. To these are added 49 senators elected by the parliaments of the autonomous communities as regional representatives. Deputies and senators are elected by universal secret suffrage for 4-year terms. The Prime Minister is elected by the Congress of Deputies.

The *Constitutional Court* is empowered to solve conflicts between the State and the Autonomous Communities; to determine if legislation passed by the Cortes is contrary to the Constitution; and to protect the constitutional rights of individuals violated by any authority. Its 12 members are appointed by the monarch: 4 on the proposal of the Congress of Deputies; 4 on the proposal of the Senate; 2 on the proposal of the General Council of the Judicial Power (*see under* JUSTICE, *below*); and 2 on the proposal of the cabinet. It has a 9-year term, with a third of the membership being renewed every 3 years.

European Parliament. Spain has 64 representatives. At the June 1994 elections turn-out was 59·1%. The PP won 28 seats with 40·2% of votes cast (political affiliation in European Parliament: European People's Party); the PSOE, 22 with 30·6% (European Socialist Party); the IU, 9 with 13·4% (European United Left); the CiU, 3 with 4·6% (European People's Party; European Liberal Democratic and Reformist Group); the Nationalist Coalition, 2 with 2·8% (European People's Party).

National Anthem. 'Marcha Real' ('Royal March'); no words, tune anonymous.

RECENT ELECTIONS

The last general election took place on 3 March 1996; 67 parties presented candidates. The electorate was 24,985,343; turn-out was 78·06%. In the *Congress of Deputies* the Popular Party (PP) won 156 seats with 38·2% of votes cast; the Spanish Workers' Socialist Party (PSOE), 141 with 37·4%; the Communist-led United Left Coalition (IU), 21 with 10·5%; Convergence and Union (CiU; Catalan nationalists), 16 with 4·6%; Basque Nationalist Party (PNV), 5 with 1·2%; Canarian Coalition (CC), 4 with 0·8%; Galician Nationalist Bloc (BNG), 2 with 0·8% (first time in Parliament); the Basque separatist Herri Batasuna Party (HB), 2 with 0·7%; the Catalan separatist Esquerra Republicana de Catalunya (ERC), 1 with 0·6%; the non-radical Basque separatist Eusko Alkartasuna Party (EA), 1 with 0·4%; Valencian Union (UV), 1 with 0·3%. In the *Senate*, the Popular Party won 112 seats; PSOE, 81; CiU, 8; PNV, 4; CC, 1; others, 1 each.

Parliamentary elections are due to take place no later than March 2000.

CURRENT ADMINISTRATION

A government was formed in May 1996. José María Aznar, leader of the democratic right-wing Popular Party, was appointed President of the *Council of Ministers* at the head of a minority PP government supported by 3 regionalist parties, from Catalonia, the Basque Country and Canary Islands, of which the most decisive is the Catalan nationalist coalition, the CiU. In March 1999 the government comprised:

President of the Council and Prime Minister: José María Aznar López (b. 1953; PP; elected 3 March 1996; sworn in 5 May 1996).

Deputy Vice-President and Minister of the Prime Minister's Office: Francisco Álvarez Cascos Fernandez (PP). *Deputy Vice-President and Minister of Economy and Finance:* Rodrigo Rato Figaredo (PP). *Foreign Affairs:* Abel Juan Matutes (PP). *Justice:* Margarita Mariscal de Gante y Mirón (ind). *Defence:* Eduardo Serra i Rexach (ind). *Interior:* Jaime Mayor Oreja (PP). *Development, Public Works:* Rafael Arias-Salgado y Montalvo (PP). *Education and Culture:* Esperanza Aguirre y Gil de Biedma (PP). *Labour and Social Affairs:* Javier Arenas Bocanegra (PP). *Industry, Energy and Tourism:* Josep Piqué i Camps (ind). *Agriculture, Fisheries and Food:* Loyola de Palacio del Valle-Lersundi (PP). *Public Administration:* Mariano Rajoy Brey (PP). *Health and Consumer Affairs:* José Manuel Romay Beccaría (PP). *Environment:* Isabel Tocino Biscarolasaga (PP).

The *Speaker* (and President) of the Congress of Deputies is Federico Trillo (PP); the *Speaker* (and President) of the Senate is José Ignacio Barrero (PP).

The IU (United Left Coalition) adopted 6 resolutions in Sept. 1997 which effectively provoked the break-up of the coalition and the distancing from it of its former regionalist elements, among them the Catalan Left.

Local Government. The Constitution of 1978 establishes a semi-federal system of regional administration, with the Autonomous Community (*Comunidad Autónoma*) as its basic element. There are 17 autonomous communities, each of them having a Parliament elected by universal vote, and a regional government; all possess exclusive legislative and executive power in many matters, as listed in the national Constitution and in their own fundamental law (*estatuto de autonomía*). The 17 communities comprise 50 provinces (established by the administrative division of 1833): 7 communities (Asturias, Baleares, Cantabria, La Rioja, Madrid, Murcia and Navarra) are composed of 1 province only; the other 10 are formed by 2 or more.

In Sept. 1994 Ceuta and Melilla gained limited autonomous status, with legislative assemblies replacing their municipal councils. In 1997, 10 Communities (Aragón, Asturias, Baleares, Cantabria, Castilla-La Mancha, Castilla y León, Extremadura, Madrid, Murcia, La Rioja) gained authority (not previously held) over matters such as health and education, under new statutes (Art 143 of the Constitution); and an all-party initiative to re-examine the constitutional status of the Basque Country and neighbouring part-Basque province of Navarra was mooted. This was following a year during which the government consolidated a tough approach to Basque separatist terrorism after national outrage in July over ETA's assassination of a young local councillor.

Date of last elections and party composition of the autonomous communities: *Andalusia* (March 1996), PSOE 52, PP 40, IU, 13, Andalusian Party 4. *Aragón* (May 1995), PP 27, PSOE 19, Aragonese Regionalist Party 14, IU 5, others 2. *Asturias* (May 1995), PP 21, PSOE 17, IU 6, others 1. *Baleares* (May 1995), PP 30, PSOE 16, nationalists 6, IU 3, others 4. *Basque Country* (Oct. 1998), PNV 21, PSE-Euskadiko Ezquerra/PSOE 14, HB 14, PP 16, EA 6, IU-EB (United Left-Ezker Batua) 2, UAL 2. *Canary Islands* (May 1995), PP 18, PSOE 16, CC 22, others 4. *Cantabria* (May 1995), PP 13, PSOE 10, regionalists 6, IU 3, others 7. *Castilla-La Mancha* (May 1995), PSOE 24, PP 22, IU 1. *Castilla y León* (May 1995), PP 50, PSOE 27, IU 5, others 2. *Catalonia* (Nov. 1995), CiU 60, PSOE 34, PP 17, ERC 13, Iniciativa per Catalunya 11. *Extremadura* (May 1995), PSOE 31, PP 27, IU 6, others 1. *Galicia* (Oct. 1997), PP 42, PSdG/EG/OV 15, BNG 18. *La Rioja* (May 1995), PP 17, PSOE 12, regionalists 2, IU 2. *Madrid* (May 1995), PP 54, PSOE 32, IU 17. *Murcia* (May 1995), PP 26, PSOE 15, IU 4. *Navarra* (May 1995), PP 17, PSOE 11, regionalists 10, HB 5, EA 2, IU 5. *Valencian Community* (May 1995), PP 42, PSOE 32, UV 5, IU 10.

The Provincial Council (*Diputación Provincial*) is the administrative organ of the province, except in the 7 autonomous communities composed of only one province, where there are only the regional legislative and executive powers. The provincial council is indirectly elected, except in the 3 Basque provinces where they are elected by universal suffrage every 4 years. Each of the 7 main islands of the Canaries has a directly elected corporation, the *Cabildo Insular*, to rule its special interests; in the main islands of the Balearics there is an elected *Consell Insular*.

The provinces are constituted by the association of municipalities (8,095 in 1997). Municipalities are autonomous in their own sphere. At their head stands the Municipal Council *(ayuntamiento)*, members of which are elected in a universal ballot every 4 years, and they, in turn, elect one amongst them as Mayor *(alcalde)*. In 1997, 6,462 municipalities had fewer than 3,000 inhabitants (3,713 less than 500). Resource-poor municipalities may form associations *(mancomunidades)* to share services. Elections were held in May 1995 for 65,732 municipal councillors. The electorate was 32,019,932. Turn-out was 69·79%. The Popular Party won 35·2% of votes cast (25·1% in 1991), the PSOE 30·8% (38·5%), the IU coalition 11·6% (8·5%).

DEFENCE
Conscription is for 9 months. Civilian service may be offered as an alternative. Recruits to the national police are exempt from conscription. Since 1989 women have been accepted in all sections of the armed forces. In 1996 the government began the phased abolition of conscription (starting with males born in 1984).

In 1997 defence expenditure totalled US$7,671m. (US$196 per capita), representing 1·4% of GDP.

Army. The Army is divided into 8 Regional Operation Commands (including 2 overseas) and consists of 1 mechanized division, 2 armoured cavalry, 1 mountain, 3 light infantry, 1 airborne, 1 artillery, 1 engineer and 1 air-portable brigade; 3 island garrisons, 3 special operations battalions and the Spanish Legion. A Rapid Reaction Force is formed from the Spanish Legion and the airborne and air-portable brigades. There is also an Army Aviation brigade. Equipment includes 210 AMX-30, 164 M-48A5E and 294 M-60 main battle tanks. The Aviation Brigade consists of 170 helicopters (40 attack).

Strength (1997) 128,500 (including 81,500 conscripts). Of these 2,500 are stationed on the Balearic Islands, 6,500 on the Canary Islands and 10,000 in Ceuta and Melilla.

Guardia Civil. The paramilitary *Guardia Civil* numbers 75,000 (2,200 conscripts).

Navy. The principal ship of the Navy is the 17,000-tonne *Príncipe de Asturias*, a light vertical/short take-off and landing aircraft carrier. Her air group comprises 8 AV-8S Matador, 8 Sea King anti-submarine helicopters, 2 Sea King early warning helicopters and about 4 AB-212 light helicopters. There are also 8 French-designed submarines (4 Daphne class, 4 Agosta class), 6 US-design Santa María guided missile frigates with Standard SM-1 surface-to-air missiles, 5 other guided missile frigates, and 6 smaller frigates, 5 offshore patrol vessels, 10 coastal and 16 inshore patrol craft, 4 ocean minesweepers, 8 coastal minesweepers, 2 amphibious troop transports, 2 tank landing ships and 13 landing craft. Major auxiliaries include 3 tankers, 2 transports, 5 ocean tugs, 1 training ship, 4 water carriers and 6 survey ships. There are about 80 minor auxiliaries and service craft.

The Naval Air Service operates 20 AV-8S Matador and EAV-8B Harrier-II attack aircraft, 34 S-70B Seahawk, Sea King, SH 60B, AB-212 and Hughes 500 anti-submarine helicopters, 3 radar early warning Sea Kings and a few additional training and utility aircraft. The Air Force operates 7 Orion maritime patrol aircraft on anti-submarine tasks.

There are 8,000 marines, who provide 1 amphibious regiment and garrison regiments at the main bases. Main naval bases are at Ferrol, Rota, Cádiz, Cartagena, Palma de Mallorca, Mahón and Las Palmas (Canary Islands).

In 1997 personnel totalled 39,000 (13,500 conscripts) including the marines and 1,000 naval air arm.

Air Force. The Air Force is organized as an independent service, dating from 1939. It is administered through 4 operational commands. These are geographically oriented following a reorganization in 1991 and comprise Central Air Command, Straits Air Command, Eastern Air Command and Air Command of the Canaries.

The Tactical Air Command has 2 fighter-bomber squadrons of Spanish-built Northrop SF-5s and 1 aero-naval co-operation squadron with P-3 Orion anti-submarine aircraft. Air Combat Command has 1 squadron of RF-4C Phantom IIs, 4 squadrons of F-18 Hornets and 3 squadrons of Mirage F-1s. 2 Boeing 707 and 5 KC-130H tankers support the fighter squadrons. 3 wings of Air Transport Command operate C-130 Hercules, CN-235s and Spanish-built CASA Aviocars. Air Command of the Canaries has 3 squadrons, equipped with Aviocar transports, Mirage F1 fighter-bombers, F27 Maritime aircraft and Super Puma helicopters for search and rescue. Other equipment includes 3 Boeing 707s, 8 Falcons and helicopters for VIP transport; and aircraft for photographic, firefighting, target towing and research duties. Air-sea rescue units have Aviocars and Super Puma helicopters.

American-built F33 Bonanza and Chilean-built Pillan piston-engined aircraft are used for basic training, after which pupil pilots progress to CASA C-101 jet aircraft. Two-seat versions of operational types are used as advanced trainers. Other training types include Hughes 300 and S-76 helicopters.

Strength (1997) 30,000 (13,000 conscripts).

INTERNATIONAL RELATIONS
Spain is a member of the UN, the Council of Europe, NATO, WEU, the EU, OSCE and OECD, and is a signatory to the Schengen Accord (*see* EUROPEAN UNION *under* MAJOR POLICY AREAS, *above*).

ECONOMY
Performance. Spain's current account on its balance of payments came out of deficit in 1995 for the first time since the mid-1980s. The balance showed a surplus of 586,500m. pesetas for the first 9 months of 1997. Real GDP growth (forecast 1998), 3·7%; (estimate, 1997), 3%—up from 2·1% in 1996. Total GDP (estimate 1997, in US$1): 604,400m. Government debt (1996, % of GDP): 69·5%. Foreign debt (1995, in US$1): 277,500m.

A privatization programme has led to the selling of profitable state concerns but loss makers such as the Iberian airline absorb a disproportionate amount of public money.

Budget. A Convergence Plan covering 1997-2000 envisages an annual GDP growth of 3·2%, a reduction of public debt to 1·6% of GDP, the limitation of inflation to below 2·5%, and the creation of 1m. jobs by deregulating and increasing the flexibility of the economy and redistributing taxes. Government expenditure (1996, % of GDP): 43·1% (1997 estimate: 41·6%).

Revenue and expenditure in 1m. pesetas:

	1995	1996	1997	1998
Revenue	19,402,252	18,448,253	16,209,545	17,351,000
Expenditure	19,402,252	19,448,253	23,882,592	24,111,000

The budget for 1998 was made up as follows (in 1m. pesetas):

Revenue		Expenditure	
Direct taxes	7,950,000	Staff costs	3,071,000
Indirect taxes	6,901,000	Current goods	
Levies and various revenues	355,000	and services	316,000
Current transfers	742,000	Financial costs	3,190,000
Income on assets	979,000	Current transfers	10,369,000
Sale on real investments	23,000	Real investment	873,000
Capital transfers	293,000	Capital transfers	911,000
Financial assets	109,000	Financial investments	1,048,000

VAT is normally 16%, with a rate of 7% on certain services (catering and hospitality), and 4% on basic foodstuffs.

Currency. On 1 Jan. 1999 the euro (EUR) became the legal currency in Spain and the *peseta* became a subdivision of it; irrevocable conversion rate 166·386 pesetas to 1 euro. The euro, which consists of 100 cents, will not be in circulation until 1 Jan. 2002. There will be 7 euro notes in different colours and sizes denominated in 500, 200, 100, 50, 20, 10 and 5 euros, and 8 coins denominated in 2 and 1 euros, then 50, 20, 10, 5, 2 and 1 cents. Even though notes and coins will not be introduced until 1 Jan. 2002 the euro can be used in banking; by means of cheques, travellers' cheques, bank transfers, credit cards and electronic purses. Banking will be possible in both euros and pesetas until the peseta is withdrawn from circulation—which must be by 1 July 2002.

The *peseta* is notionally divided into 100 *céntimos*, though they have not been in use since 1984. In Feb. 1998 foreign exchange reserves were US$65,773m. and gold reserves were 15·63m. troy oz. Inflation in 1997 was 2% (3·2% in Dec. 1996), with a forecast of 2% for 1998. Total money supply in Feb. 1998 was 23,491bn. pesetas.

Banking and Finance. The central bank is the Bank of Spain (*Governor*: Luis Ángel Rojo) which gained autonomy under an ordinance of 1994. Its governor is appointed for a 6-year term. The Banking Corporation of Spain, *Argentaria*, groups together the shares of all state-owned banks, and competes in the financial market with private banks. In 1993 the government sold 49·9% of the capital of Argentaria; the remainder in 2 flotations ending on 13 Feb. 1998.

In terms of assets held in Nov. 1997 (in 1m. pesetas), the main banks were: Grupo Santander, 12,277,367; Banco Bilbao Vizcaya, 13,077,448; Banco Central Hispano, 10,444,037; Banco Popular, 2,433,008; Banesto, 5,305,252; Argentaria (no consolidated balance). On 31 Oct. 1997 Spanish banks deposits (in 1,000m. pesetas) amounted to 17,721 (private banks, 10,178; government banks, 7,543); foreign banks, 1,667; savings banks, 24,525; rural (farmers) savings banks, 3,235.

There are stock exchanges in Madrid, Barcelona, Bilbao and Valencia. The flotation in 1997 of public-sector holdings brought some 2m. new domestic investors into the Spanish equity market; privatization receipts in 1997 were expected to total 1,600,000m. pesetas.

Weights and Measures. The metric system was introduced in 1859.

ENERGY AND NATURAL RESOURCES

Electricity. Installed capacity was 39·58m. kW in 1995. Nuclear and hydro-electric power stations provided just over half of Spain's electricity in 1990. The government announced in 1991 that no new nuclear power stations (there were 9 in 1997) would commence operating before 2000. The total electricity output in 1996 amounted to 175,604m. kWh, of which 41,619m. was hydro-electric, 56,204m. nuclear, and 77,781m. other (carbon, natural gas, petroleum). Consumption per capita in 1995 was an estimated 3,752 kWh.

In Feb. 1997 the government disposed of a 25% stake in Endesa, the country's main electricity generator and distributor, reducing its shareholding in the group to 41%; full privatization was due for completion in 1999. The Electrical Protocol drawn up between the government and electricity utilities to meet EU requirements is to be completed over a 10-year period, and will largely dismantle the highly regulated, interventionist structure which preceded it. This should provide for a more open market; construction of new generators will be liberalized and prices are expected to fall in real terms by 25-30% over 5 years. Industry analysts forecast a market which will favour hydro- and gas-powered generators.

Oil and Gas. Spain is heavily dependent on imported oil; Mexico is its largest supplier. Crude oil production (1996), 554,000 tonnes.

The government sold its remaining stake in the oil, gas and chemicals group Repsol in 1997. Natural gas production (1996) totalled 596m. cu. metres. Efforts are being made to increase consumption; on 1 Nov. 1996 Spain opened the Algerian gas link (Maghreb-Europe Pipeline), which is expected to supply 6,200m. cu. metres by 2000.

Minerals. Spain has a relatively wide range of minerals; the mining sector accounted for 1% of GDP in 1994. Coal production (1995), 13m. tonnes; other principal minerals (1992, in 1,000 tonnes): anthracite, 6,177; lignite, 18,689; iron, 1,334; pyrites, 406; copper, 9; lead, 30; zinc, 205; fluorspar, 97; potassium salts, 594; (1992, in tonnes) uranium, 862; tin, 7. In 1995 a large mercury deposit was found in southern Spain which could raise mercury levels to within a quarter of proven world reserves. A modern gold mine in Asturias (opened Oct. 1996) is expected to produce about 1,000 troy oz a year.

Agriculture. There were 1,384,000 farms in Spain in 1998. Agriculture contributed about 3% of GDP and employed about 9·3% of the workforce in 1998. It accounts for 15·8% of exports and 15·6% of imports. Crop production accounted for 62·2% of total agricultural production in 1990; animal production for 37·8%.

19,354,700 ha were under cultivation in 1995, including 4,372,600 ha under irrigation and 6,434,000 ha under pasture. There were (1994) 789,747 tractors, 280,989 motor ploughs (1992) and 49,080 harvesters in use.

Principal crops	Area (in 1,000 ha)				Yield (in 1,000 tonnes)			
	1993	1994	1995	1996	1993	1994	1995	1996
Wheat	2,025	1,994	2,093	2,022	4,989	4,311	2,957	6,169
Barley	3,499	3,602	3,573	3,529	9,532	7,596	5,194	10,636
Oats	326	346	364	410	400	402	216	653
Rye	170	155	159	170	300	220	173	295
Rice	50	63	54	106	315	394	327	761
Maize	284	342	346	454	1,673	2,266	2,539	3,834
Potatoes	213	207	211	208	3,922	4,074	4,195	4,174
Sugar-beet	181	175	173	160	8,226	8,004	7,612	7,686
Sunflower	2,264	1,349	1,005	1,158	1,214	984	574	1,137

Spain has more land dedicated to the grape than any other country in the world and is ranked third among wine producers (behind Italy and France). Wine exports increased in value by nearly 600% from 1991-97. Total export receipts in 1996 totalled some £600m. A large part of Spain's output goes to Italy for bottling. In 1992, 1,333,000 ha were under vines. Production of wine (1996), 32,720,000 hectolitres; of grapes, 3.3m. tonnes.

The area under onions in 1996 was 28,200 ha, yielding 1,018,100 tonnes; of tomatoes, 58,400 ha, 3,224,800 tonnes (21% of EU production).

In fruit, Spain contributes a fifth of EU total harvest, and more than half of all citrus fruits. Fruit production (1996, in tonnes; ha, 1992): Oranges and mandarins, 3·5m. (201,282 ha); lemons, 433,100 (45,022 ha); apples, 893,600; peaches, 892,300.

Production of olive oil (1996), 670,000 tonnes. EU policy to reform the complex aid system for olive oil (based on hand-outs per tree rather than oil production) is strongly opposed in all 5 EU olive oil-producing countries, nowhere more than Spain which, in Andalusia, has the world's largest producing zone. In 1997 Spain's olive growers marched on Madrid in protest over the reforms, which have provoked fear of plantation neglect and loss of employment.

Other important products are esparto, flax, tobacco, hemp and pulse; raw cotton production (1995): 88,000 tonnes.

Livestock (1995): Cattle, 5·51m.; sheep, 21·32m.; goats, 2·60m.; pigs, 18·16m.; laying hens, 45·72m.; horses, 0·24m.; asses and mules (1992), 0·25m. Livestock density per 100 ha is among the lowest in the EU. Livestock products (1995 in 1,000 tonnes): Pork, 2,174; beef, 508·49; mutton, 227·12; poultry meat, 924·31; goat, 14·93; rabbit, 110·88; milk, 6,580; honey, 28; eggs, 6,940.

Forestry. In 1995 the area under forests was 8·39m. ha, or 16·8% of the total land area. In 1995 timber production was 15·12m. cu. metres. Other forest products (1992, in tonnes): Resins, 1,771; cork, 72,090; esparto, 792. Total value of forest products (1992): 127,815m. pesetas.

Fisheries. Spain is the second largest fishing country in the EU after Denmark. Its annual catch is around 1·3m. tonnes and accounts for a fifth of the EU's annual catch. Fish-farming output (1991), 222,427 tonnes, of which 200,922 were molluscs and shellfish, 21,505 fish; Spain supplies around half of total EU mussel production. Fishing vessels had a total tonnage of 524,602 tonnes in 1995 (596,441 GRT in 1994); fleets have been gradually reduced from 20,558 boats in 1991 to 18,091 in 1996. Total catch in 1995 amounted to 1,320,000 tonnes, of which more than 97% were sea fish.

INDUSTRY

The industrial sector represented 28·1% of GNP in 1995. In 1996-97 industrial production was up by 3·3% on the previous 12 months, and industry accounted for 22·9% of the labour force (29·7% in 1994).

Principal textile production (1993, in 1,000 tonnes): Yarn, 227; cotton cloth, 64; synthetic and artificial fabrics, 62; knitwear, 23. Industrial products (1993, in tonnes): Sulphuric acid, 1,161,000; nitrogenous fertilizers, 642,000; plastics, 2·7m.; pulp and paper, 6·06m.; cement (1995), 24·47m.; crude oil refined (1995, in the 9 oil refineries), 55·2m. tonnes; steel production (1996), 12·3m.

The number of vehicles manufactured in 1995 was 2,333,785 of which 1,958,789 were passenger cars and 374,998 commercial. In 1996, 1·39m. refrigerators and freezers, 2·6m. cookers, hotplates and microwaves, and 1·53m. washing machines, dishwashers and clothes driers were manufactured; number of TV sets (1993), 3·8m. There are also important toy and shoe industries.

Labour. The economically active population numbered 16·12m. in 1997 (16·03m. in 1996). Of these, 12·76m. were employed: 1·07m. in agriculture and fishing, 2·58m. in industry, 1·27m. in construction and 7·87m. in trade, transport and other public and personal services. Post-Franco legislation brought radical changes to the labour market, including the legalization in 1984 of fixed-term contracts. A third of Spain's wage earners were on temporary contracts by 1998. The monthly minimum wage for adults (1998) was 68,040 pesetas; the average monthly wage for workers in industry and services was 190,500 pesetas (1,331 pesetas an hour); average hourly earnings increased by 4% in 1997. The retirement age is 65 years.

In terms of unemployment, Spain has the highest rate among developed countries. 18·7% of the active population was unemployed at the end of 1998. On 17 Sept. 1997, the Council of Ministers passed the Multi-Year Employment Plan co-ordinating the actions of 9 ministries with the aim of creating 1m. jobs to bring unemployment down to 17% by the year 2000. The scheme represents a 20% increase in budget spending for job creation.

Trade Unions. The Constitution guarantees the establishment and activities of trade unions provided they have a democratic structure.

The most important trade unions are *Unión General de Trabajadores* (UGT) and *Comisiones Obreras* (CO). In Jan. 1997 the UGT and CO and employers' associations signed an agreement to be in force until 2000 providing for compulsory mediation before strike action; in April, employers' associations and trade unions reached an agreement covering 1997-2000 to combat job insecurity and reform collective bargaining. A National Employment Committee was subsequently set up to oversee the workings of the agreement.

INTERNATIONAL TRADE
In the first quarter of 1997 exports were up by 15%, imports by 8%. The economy recorded a foreign trade surplus of 302,000m. pesetas and a 32% reduction in the trade deficit (1997 estimate in US$1: 16,000m.).

Total foreign investments (Jan-July 1997), 535,202,000m. pesetas, representing a 16% increase on 1996: 21% to EU countries; and 61% to Latin America (forged mainly by Tisa, the international arm of Telefonica, which operates 10m. lines and services 1m. cable TV and cellular phone subscribers in the region, with assets of US$ 5,000m.).

Imports and Exports. Foreign trade of Spain (including Baleares, Canaries, Ceuta, Melilla, in 1m. pesetas):

	1993	1994	1995	1996
Imports	10,482,688	12,348,734	14,318,133	11,290,380
Exports	7,982,704	9,796,340	11,423,085	9,253,281

Merchandise imports (1997 estimate in US$1): 126,100m.; exports, 110,100m.

Breakdown of imports in 1996 (in 1m. pesetas): Semi-finished products, 2,440,658 (21·6%); capital goods, 2,765,974 (24·5%); vehicles and other transport equipment, 1,648,229 (14·6%); consumer manufactures, 283,549 (2·5%); food products, 1,409,992 (12·5%); energy products, 1,034,706 (9·2%); raw materials, 542,249 (4·6%); durable consumer goods, 1,148,525 (10·2%); other goods, 34,498 (0·3%).

Breakdown of exports in 1996 (in 1m. pesetas): Vehicles and other transport equipment, 2,134,154 (23·1%); semi-finished products, 2,048,939 (22·1%); capital goods, 1,843,791 (19·9%); food products, 1,416,740 (15·3%); consumer manufactures, 1,083,544 (11·7%); raw materials, 204,392 (2·2%); energy products, 230,700 (2·5%); durable consumer goods, 219,680 (2·4%); other goods, 71,342 (0·8%).

SPAIN

Distribution of trade (in 1m. pesetas) by origin and destination:

	Imports		Exports	
	1995	1996	1995	1996
EU	9,362,806	7,410,808	8,264,560	6,674,299
France	2,454,944	2,019,464	2,345,844	1,926,507
Germany	2,189,575	1,653,814	1,760,143	1,344,502
Italy	1,310,004	1,078,200	1,045,250	818,109
UK	1,120,096	897,271	915,922	772,864
Netherlands	619,751	433,494	420,386	326,771
Belgium–Luxembourg	492,853	388,777	350,753	278,625
Portugal	421,658	329,891	951,129	792,512
USA	919,164	749,027	472,214	384,317
Japan	472,716	323,759	157,060	114,885
Latin America	558,963	431,169	522,523	430,742
Mexico	124,699	97,093	69,555	47,663
Brazil	141,483	114,736	107,411	83,842
Switzerland	212,175	143,842	127,927	105,725
Eastern Europe	370,940	269,393	196,064	194,502
Nigeria	141,979	137,337	9,989	15,316
Libya	148,740	102,156	21,133	17,661
Saudi Arabia	160,483	117,176	60,005	43,492
Iran	94,700	87,909	20,933	26,052
Algeria	121,705	103,427	126,833	63,948

COMMUNICATIONS

Roads. In 1996 the total length of highways and roads was 344,847 km; the main network comprised 7,747 km of motorways, 23,131 km of highways/national roads and 138,969 km of secondary roads. 90% of all roads in Spain were paved in 1996. Travel by road accounted for 90·6% of internal passenger traffic in 1995; and for 77·24% of freight. Number of cars (1996), 14,754,000; trucks and vans, 3,057,000; buses, 48,000; motor cycles, 1,308,000. In 1996, 3,998 persons were killed in road accidents.

Rail. The total length of the state railways in 1995 was 13,060 km, mostly broad (1,668-mm) gauge (6,736 km electrified). State railways are run by the National Spanish Railway Network (RENFE). There is a high-speed standard-gauge (1,435-mm) railway from Madrid to Seville. In 1995 freight carried was 26m. tonnes (4·2% of total freight) and 464·8m. passengers (5·9% of internal passenger traffic). There are metros in Madrid (112 km), Barcelona (72 km) and Bilbao (26 km), and a light railway in Valencia.

Civil Aviation. There are international airports at Madrid (Barajas), Barcelona (Prat del Llobregat), Alicante, Almería, Bilbao, Gerona, Gran Canaria, Ibiza, Lanzarote, Málaga, Palma de Mallorca, Santiago de Compostela, Seville, Tenerife (Los Rodeos and Reina Sofía), Valladolid, Valencia and Zaragoza. There are 43 airports open to civil traffic. A small airport in Seo de Urgel operates in Andorra. The national carrier is Iberia Airlines (99·8% state-owned but scheduled for privatization in 1999). There are 2 other regular carriers: Air Europa and Spanair. Services are also provided by about 70 foreign airlines.

In 1995 Iberia flew 179·8m. km, carrying 14,228,300 passengers (6,240,500 on international flights). Aircraft movements in 1996, 1,027,920: 449,943 internal and 577,977 international. In 1996, 79,945,244 passengers (32·64m. internal and 47·3m. international) and 451,663 tonnes of freight were carried. Madrid was the busiest airport in 1996, handling 21,269,637 passengers (10,172,246 on international flights) and 237,337 tonnes of freight. Palma de Mallorca was the second busiest in 1996 for passenger traffic, with 15,266,958 (11,338,114 on international flights) and Barcelona the second busiest for freight, with 76,623 tonnes.

Shipping. The merchant navy in 1995 had 1,101 vessels with a gross tonnage of 637,000; shipyards launched 219,673 GRT in 1996. In 1994, 107,595 ships entered Spanish ports; 7·08m. passengers disembarked and 7·24m. embarked; total cargo discharged and loaded, 248m. tonnes.

Telecommunications. In 1997 Telefonica was operating 15,854,400 main telephone lines (403·2 per 1,000 persons). The government disposed of its remaining 21% stake in Telefonica in Feb. 1997, bringing 1·4m. shareholders into the company's equity base. A second operator, Rétévision, is expected to account for 10% of the domestic market, which was scheduled to be wholly deregulated by the end of 1998. The cellular phone business was deregulated in 1995; the market is shared by Telefonica and Airtel.

Spain had 966,000 cellular phone subscribers in 1995 (25 for every 1,000 persons), 3,200,000 PCs (82 per 1,000 persons) and 215,000 fax machines. There were 2,247,000 Internet users in Oct. 1998.

Postal Services. There were 4,527 post offices in 1995. Receipts (1994) totalled 137,626m. pesetas; expenses, 201,581m. pesetas. In 1995 a total of 4,295m. pieces of mail were processed, or 110 items per person.

SOCIAL INSTITUTIONS

Justice. Justice is administered by Tribunals and Courts, which jointly form the Judicial Power. Judges and magistrates cannot be removed, suspended or transferred except as set forth by law. The Constitution of 1978 established the *General Council of the Judicial Power*, consisting of a President and 20 magistrates, judges, attorneys and lawyers, governing the Judicial Power in full independence from the state's legislative and executive organs. Its members are appointed by the *Cortes Generales*. Its President is that of the Supreme Court (*Tribunal Supremo*), who is appointed by the monarch on the proposal of the General Council of the Judicial.

The Judicature is composed of the Supreme Court; 17 Higher Courts of Justice, 1 for each autonomous community; 52 Provincial High Courts; Courts of First Instance; Courts of Judicial Proceedings, not passing sentences; and Penal Courts, passing sentences.

The Supreme Court consists of a President, and various judges distributed among 7 chambers: 1 for civil matters, 3 for administrative purposes, 1 for criminal trials, 1 for social matters and 1 for military cases. The Supreme Court has disciplinary faculties; is court of appeal in all criminal trials; for administrative purposes decides in first and second instance disputes arising between private individuals and the State; and in social matters makes final decisions.

A new penal code came into force in May 1996, replacing the code of 1848. It provides for a maximum of 30 years imprisonment in specified exceptional cases, with a normal maximum of 20 years. Sanctions with a rehabilitative intent include fines adjusted to means, community service and weekend imprisonment. The death penalty was abolished by the 1978 Constitution. The prison population in 1996 was 43,033 (39,051 men, 3,982 women); 901,696 criminal offences were reported in 1994.

A juvenile criminal law of 1995 lays emphasis on rehabilitation. It raised the age of responsibility from 12 to 14 years. Criminal conduct on the part of children under 14 is a matter for legal protection and custody. 14- and 15-year-olds are classified as 'minors'; 16- and 17-year-olds as 'young persons'; and the legal majority for criminal offences is set at 18 years. Persons up to the age of 21 may, at the courts' discretion, be dealt with as juveniles.

A jury system commenced operating in Nov. 1995 in criminal cases (first trials in May 1996). Juries consist of 9 members. In Sept. 1997 at the opening ceremony of the Judicial Year, presided over by the king, the President of the General Council of the Judicial Power called for a general agreement from Parliament and the government on legal reform for solving the problems in the administration of justice, namely its slowness and esoteric nature.

The *Audiencia Nacional* deals with terrorism, monetary offences and drug-trafficking where more than 1 province is involved. Its president is appointed by the General Council of the Judicial Power.

There is an Ombudsman (*Defensor del Pueblo*), who in 1994 received 18,594 complaints.

Religion. There is no official religion. Roman Catholicism is the religion of the majority. There are 11 metropolitan sees and 52 suffragan sees, the chief being Toledo, where the Primate resides. The archdioceses of Madrid-Alcalá and Barcelona depend directly from the Vatican. There are about 0·25m. other Christians, including several Protestant denominations, about 60,000 Jehovah's Witnesses and 29,000 Latter-day Saints (Mormons), and 0·45m. Moslems, including Spanish Moslems in

Morocco. The first synagogue since the expulsion of the Jews in 1492 was opened in Madrid in 1959. The number of people of Judaist faith is estimated at about 15,000.

Education. In 1991 the General Regulation of the Educational System Act came into force. This Act gradually extends the school-leaving age to 16 years and determines the following levels of education: Infants (3–5 years of age), primary (6–11), secondary (12–15) and baccalaureate or vocational and technical (16–17). Primary and secondary levels of education are now compulsory and free. Religious instruction is optional.

In Sept. 1997 a joint declaration with trade unions, parents' and schools' associations was signed in support of a new finance law guaranteeing that spending on education will reach 6% of GDP within 5 years, thus protecting it from changes in the political sphere. In 1993 total expenditure on education came to 4·7% of GNP.

A new compulsory secondary education programme has replaced the Basic General Education programme which was in force since 1970. In addition, university entrance exams underwent reform in 1997, resulting in greater emphasis now being placed on the teaching of Humanities at secondary level.

In 1997–98 pre-primary education (under 6 years) was undertaken by 2,522 schools, with 1,123,003 pupils; primary or basic education (6–14 years): 13,037 schools, with 2,607,602 pupils. There were 215,584 teachers in pre-primary and primary schools. Secondary education (14–17 years), including high schools and technical schools, was conducted at 5,449 schools, with 3,492,726 pupils and 150,220 teachers.

In 1997–98 there were 60 universities: 40 public state universities, 3 polytechnic universities, 13 private universities (including 3 Catholic); plus 4 Open universities. In 1997–98 there were 1,571,300 students at state universities; 64,423 at private universities.

Adult literacy rate, 1995, 97·1% (male 98·2%; female 96·1%).

Health. In 1995 there were 162,089 doctors (3·8 per 1,000 inhabitants), 13,242 dentists, 40,323 pharmacists and 167,957 nurses (including 6,105 midwives). Number of hospitals (1992), 801, with 161,537 beds.

Welfare. The social security budget was 12,134,637m. pesetas in 1997. The budget for 1998 was: for pensions, 8,356,100m. pesetas; health, 3,822,000m.; social benefits and incapacity, 1,554,000m.; unemployment, 1,495,400m. The minimum monthly pension in 1996 was 53,435 pesetas.

In 1997 the system of contributions to the social security and employment scheme was: For pensions, sickness, invalidity, maternity and children, a contribution of 28·3% of the basic wage (23·6% paid by the employer, 4·7% by the employee); for unemployment benefit, a contribution of 7·8% (6·2% paid by the employer, 1·6% by the employee). There are also minor contributions for a Fund of Guaranteed Salaries, working accidents and professional sicknesses, and for vocational training.

CULTURE

Santiago de Compostela is one of nine European Cities of Culture in the year 2000, along with Avignon (France), Bergen (Norway), Bologna (Italy), Brussels (Belgium), Helsinki (Finland), Kraków (Poland), Prague (Czech Republic) and Reykjavík (Iceland). The title attracts large European Union grants.

Broadcasting. Radio Nacional de España broadcasts 5 programmes on medium-wave and FM, as well as many regional programmes; it has one commercial programme. The most successful domestic network is that of an independent, Cadena SER (*Sociedad Española de Radiodifusión*); *Cadena de Ondas Populares Españolas* (COPE) is owned by the Roman Catholic church. Two independent radio networks cover the whole of Spain. They are *Antena 3* and *Radio 80* (taken over by SER in 1992). *Radio Exterior* broadcasts abroad, and *Antena 3* has been broadcasting to 400,000 subscribers in Miami since Sept. 1997.

Televisión Española broadcasts 2 channels (TVE1 and TVE2) and has an international channel also. There are 3 nationwide commercial TV networks: *Antena 3*, *Tele 5* and the pay-TV channel *Canal Plus*, which had 1·4m. subscribers in 1997. There were in 1994 the following regional TV networks: *TV3* (launched in 1983) and *Canal 33* (1989), both broadcasting in Catalan; *ETB1* (1983) and *ETB2* (1987), both Basque, the first one broadcasting in Basque; *Televisión de Galicia* (1985), in

Galician; *TM3* (1989), in Castilian, for the area of Madrid; *Canal 9* (1989), mostly in Valencian (Catalan); and *Tele-Sur* (1989), in Castilian, for Andalusia. There are 2 digital TV channels, Vía Digital and Canal Satelite Digital, both launched in 1997. Colour transmissions are carried by PAL.

Number of receivers (1995): radios, 12·45m. (314 per 1,000 population); TV sets, 16m. (404 per 1,000 population).

Cinema. There were (1996) 1,934 cinemas with an audience of 47·17m. In Nov. 1997 the Madrid School of Cinema was established. It has an annual budget of 225m. pesetas from the Community of Madrid, and is backed by the Spanish Academy and Ministry of Education and Culture.

Press. In 1996 there were about 90 daily newspapers with a total daily circulation of 3·93m. copies (valued at 262·3m. pesetas). 8 publishing groups controlled around 80% of the daily press, with another 100 or so independents accounting for the other 20%. Prisa, the biggest conglomerate, had a daily readership of 541,691 in 1996 (13·7% of the sector). The main titles are: *El País, ABC, El Mundo* and *Marca*.

In 1995, 51,934 book titles were published, including some 7,000 translations. 41,301 titles were in Castilian, 5,793 in Catalan, 968 in Basque and 1,148 in Galician.

Tourism. In 1996 Spain was behind only France and the USA in the number of foreign visitor arrivals. In 1997 tourism accounted for 10·4% of GDP with net receipts up by 15% at 2,535,000m. pesetas (an expected revenue of £15,000m.). In 1996, 62m. tourists visited Spain (41·4m. staying overnight). Hotel beds (1996), 914,338.

Festivals. As a predominantly Catholic country Spain is celebrating the Millennium in churches and cathedrals nationwide. In particular, magnificent processions will be held during Semana Santa (Easter week) and Corpus Christi (June).

Libraries. In 1996 there were 4,466 libraries (including national and public); 7·66m. books were lent out.

Museums and Galleries. Spain had 1,054 museums in 1994, including 332 for art and 200 for archaeology and history.

DIPLOMATIC REPRESENTATIVES
Of Spain in Great Britain (39 Chesham Pl., London, SW1X 8SB)
Ambassador: Alberto Aza Arias.

Of Great Britain in Spain (Calle de Fernando el Santo, 16, 28010 Madrid)
Ambassador: P. J. Torry.

Of Spain in the USA (2700 15th St., NW, Washington, D.C., 20009)
Ambassador: Antonio Oyarzabal.

Of the USA in Spain (Serrano 75, 28006 Madrid)
Ambassador: Vacant.

Of Spain to the United Nations
Ambassador: Inocencio F. Arias.

FURTHER READING
Conversi, D., *The Basques, The Catalans and Spain.* Hurst, London, 1997
Donaghy, P. J. and Newton, M. T., *Spain: A Guide to Political and Economic Institutions.* CUP, 1987
Heywood, P., *The Government and Politics of Spain.* London, 1995
Hooper, J., *The New Spaniards.* 2nd ed. [of *The Spaniards*] London, 1995
Péréz-Díaz, V. M., *The Return of Civil Society: the Emergence of Democratic Spain.* Harvard Univ. Press, 1993
Powell, C., *Juan Carlos of Spain: Self-Made Monarch.* London and New York, 1996
Preston, P., *The Triumph of Democracy in Spain.* London and New York, 1986
Shields, G. J., *Spain.* [Bibliography] 2nd ed. Oxford and Santa Barbara (CA), 1994
Shubert, A., *A Social History of Modern Spain.* London, 1990

National library: Biblioteca Nacional, Madrid.
National statistical office: Instituto Nacional de Estadística (INE), Paseo de la Castellana, 183, Madrid.
Website: http://www.ine.es

SRI LANKA

Sri Lanka Prajathanthrika
Samajavadi Janarajaya

(Democratic Socialist
Republic of Sri Lanka)

Capital: Colombo
Population estimate, 2000: 18·82m.
GNP per capita: (PPP$) 2,290
HDI/world rank: 0·716/90

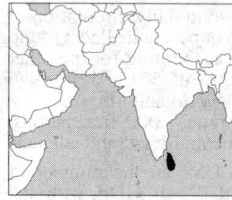

KEY HISTORICAL EVENTS

In the 18th century the central kingdom, Kandy, was the only surviving independent state on the island of Ceylon. The Dutch, who had obtained their first coastal possessions in 1636, had driven out the preceding Portuguese interests to become the dominant power in most of the island. The Dutch attacked Kandy but were unable to hold it. The interior terrain was mountainous and thickly forested and the king of Kandy's forces were well trained to make use of it as guerrillas.

The king attracted British attention by asking for help against the Dutch. In 1796 the British East India Company sent a naval force to Ceylon (as the British then called it). The Dutch surrendered their possessions, which left the British in control of the maritime areas surrounding Kandy. These areas were at first attached to the Madras Presidency of India, whence the naval force had come, but in 1802 they were constituted a separate colony under the Crown.

Once the British began to develop their new territory they came to see Kandy as a threat. An attack in 1803 failed, but by 1815 the chiefs of Kandy were discontented with their king who was of alien (south Indian) stock and a despot. The chiefs approached the British, who invaded Kandy with their help. The king was deposed and the British crown succeeded him as sovereign.

The Kandyan Convention of 1815 annexed Kandy to British Ceylon while recognizing most of the traditional rights of the chiefs. However, in 1817, dissatisfied with the terms, the chiefs rebelled. The rebellion was suppressed and the rights established by the Convention were abolished.

Ceylon was then united for the first time since the 12th century. The British (like the preceding Dutch and Portuguese) built up a plantation economy. Coffee was dominant until an outbreak of *Hoemilia vastatrix* fungus destroyed the plants in 1870. Spices, cocoa and rice all followed but tea became the main cash crop after successful experiments in the 1880s.

Foreign rule served to subdue the traditional hostility between northern Tamils and southern Sinhalese, providing as it did a new frame of reference to an alien culture. The Ceylon National Congress, formed in 1919, contained both Sinhalese and Ceylon Tamil groups. (The Indian Tamils brought in as a labour force for the tea estates were a separate community.) Tamil national feeling, however, was expressed over the issue of the use of Tamil languages in schools.

On 4 Feb. 1948 the Ceylon Independence Act took effect, and Ceylon became a Dominion of the Commonwealth. UK defence forces were to be allowed to remain as mutually agreeable, although it was later decided that all UK bases should be transferred or withdrawn by 1962.

In 1956 Solomon Bandaranaike became prime minister at the head of the People's United Front, advocating neutral foreign policy and the promotion of Sinhalese national culture at home. In Sept. 1959 he was murdered; his widow Sirimavo Bandaranaike succeeded him in July 1960 at the head of an increasingly socialist government. Agreements were made with India (in 1964 and 1974) for the repatriation of Indian nationals. In May 1972 Ceylon became a republic and adopted the name Sri Lanka.

In July 1977 Mrs Bandaranaike's government fell, mainly because of economic failures and the repression of non-Sinhalese elements. The United National Party (dominant until 1956) returned to power and in 1978 a new constitution provided a presidential system with the United National Party leader Junius Jayawardene as the first executive president. Economic problems were approached through large-scale investment of foreign capital.

SRI LANKA

The problem of communal unrest remained unsolved and Tamil separatists were active. In 1983 the Tamil United Liberation Front members of parliament were asked to renounce their objective for a separate Tamil state. They refused and withdrew from parliament. Militant Tamils then began armed action which developed into civil war.

A state of emergency ended on 11 Jan. 1989, but violence continued. President Ranasinghe Premadasa was assassinated on 1 May 1993. A ceasefire was signed on 3 Jan. 1995, but fighting broke out again in April. The 'Liberation Tigers of the Tamil Eelam' stronghold of Jaffna was captured by government forces in Dec. 1995 and by mid-1997 was under government control; but the army has still not opened a safe route to Jaffna from the south of the island. 1998 saw some of the fiercest fighting in the 15-year civil war which has claimed up to 50,000 lives.

TERRITORY AND POPULATION
Sri Lanka is an island in the Indian Ocean, south of the Indian peninsula from which it is separated by the Palk Strait. On 28 June 1974 the frontier between India and Sri Lanka in the Palk Strait was redefined, giving to Sri Lanka the island of Kachchativu.

Area (in sq. km.) and census population on 17 March 1981:

Provinces	Area	Population	Provinces	Area	Population
Western	3,708·61	3,919,807	North-Central	10,723·59	849,492
Central	5,583·50	2,009,248	Uva	8,487·91	914,522
Southern	5,559·15	1,882,661	Sabaragamuwa	4,901·55	1,482,031
Northern	8,882·11	1,109,404			
Eastern	9,951·26	975,251	Total	65,609·86	14,846,750
North-Western	7,812·18	1,704,334			

Population (in 1,000) according to ethnic group and nationality at the 1981 census: 10,980 Sinhalese, 1,887 Sri Lanka Tamils, 1,047 Sri Lanka Moors, 39 Burghers, 47 Malays, 819 Indian Tamils, 28 others. Non-nationals of Sri Lanka totalled 635,150. Population, 1997 (estimate), 18,721,200 (9,437,500 females); density, 285 per sq. km. Ethnic mix, 74% Sinhalese, 18% Tamil.

In 1995, 77·9% of the population lived in rural areas.

The UN gives a projected population for 2000 of 18·82m.

By 1997, approximately 0·3m. Tamils had left the country since the mid-1980s, one-third as refugees to India and two-thirds to seek political asylum in the West.

Principal towns and their population according to the census of 1981 are: Colombo (the capital), 587,647; Dehiwela-Mt. Lavinia, 173,529; Moratuwa, 134,826; Jaffna, 118,224; Kotte, 101,039; Kandy, 97,872; Galle, 76,863; Negombo, 60,762; Trincomalee, 44,313; Batticaloa, 42,963; Matara, 38,843; Ratnapura, 37,497; Anuradhapura, 35,981; Badulla, 33,068; Kalutara, 31,503. Population of the Greater Colombo area, 1980, about 1m.

Sinhala and Tamil are the official languages; English is in use.

SOCIAL STATISTICS
Births, 1997, 348,000; deaths, 110,000. 1997 birth rate (per 1,000 population), 18·6; death rate, 5·9; infant mortality rate (per 1,000 live births), 16·5; life expectancy, 72·4 years. Annual growth rate, 1990–95, 1·5%. Infant mortality, 1990–95, 18 per 1,000 live births; fertility rate, 2·2 births per woman.

CLIMATE
Sri Lanka, which has an equatorial climate, is affected by the North-east Monsoon (Dec. to Feb.), the South-west Monsoon (May to July) and 2 inter-monsoons (March to April and Aug. to Nov.). Rainfall is heaviest in the south-west highlands while the north-east and south-east are relatively dry. Colombo, Jan. 79·9°F (26·6°C), July 81·7°F (27·6°C). Annual rainfall 95·4" (2,424 mm). Trincomalee, Jan. 78·8°F (26°C), July 86·2°F (30·1°C). Annual rainfall 62·2" (1,580 mm). Kandy, Jan. 73·9°F (23·3°C), July 76·1°F (24·5°C). Annual rainfall 72·4" (1,840 mm). Nuwara Eliya, Jan. 58·5°F (14·7°C), July 60·3°F (15·7°C). Annual rainfall 75" (1,905 mm).

CONSTITUTION AND GOVERNMENT
A new constitution for the Democratic Socialist Republic of Sri Lanka was promulgated in Sept. 1978. An amended constitution allowing for more devolved powers to the regions was under consideration in 1998.

The Executive *President* is directly elected for a 6-year term renewable once.

Parliament consists of one chamber, composed of 225 members (196 elected and 29 from the National List). Election is by proportional representation by universal suffrage at 18 years. The term of Parliament is 6 years. The Prime Minister and other Ministers, who must be members of Parliament, are appointed by the President.

National Anthem. 'Sri Lanka Matha, Apa Sri Lanka' ('Mother Sri Lanka, thee Sri Lanka'); words and tune by A. Samarakone. There is a Tamil version, 'Sri Lanka thaaya, nam Sri Lanka'; words anonymous.

RECENT ELECTIONS
Presidential elections were held on 9 Nov. 1994. The incumbent Prime Minister, Chandrika Kumaratunga, was elected against 1 opponent by 62·28% of votes cast.

Parliamentary elections were held on 16 Aug. 1994. 1,449 candidates in 13 parties and 26 independent groups stood for office. The People's Alliance (a coalition of 9 parties) gained 105 seats, the United National Party 94, the Tamil party (EPDP) 9, the Sri Lanka Moslem Congress 7, the Tamil United Liberation Front 5 and the Democratic People's Liberation Front 3.

CURRENT ADMINISTRATION
In March 1999 the government comprised:

President, Minister of Finance and of Defence: Chandrika Bandaranaike Kumaratunga, b. 1945 (Sri Lanka Freedom Party; sworn in 12 Nov. 1994).

Prime Minister: Sirimavo Bandaranaike (b. 1916).

Minister of Agriculture and Lands: D. M. Jayaratna. *Buddha Sasana, Cultural and Religious Affairs:* Lakshman Jayakody. *Co-operative Development:* D. P. Wickremasinghe. *Education and Higher Education:* Richard Pathirana. *Ethnic Affairs and National Integration, Justice and Constitutional Affairs:* Gamini L. Peiris. *Fisheries and Aquatic Resources Development:* Mahinda Rajapakse. *Foreign Affairs:* Lakshman Kadirgamar. *Forestry and Environment:* Nandimithra Ekanayake. *Health and Indigenous Medicine:* Nimal Siripala de Silva. *Housing and Urban Development:* Indika Gunawardena. *Industrial Development:* Clement V. Gooneratne. *Internal and International Commerce and Food:* Kingsley Wickramaratne. *Irrigation and Power:* Gen. Anuruddha Ratwatte. *Labour:* John Seneviratne. *Livestock Development and Estate Infrastructure:* Sauvmiamoothy Thondaman. *Mahaweli Development:* Maithripala Sirsena. *Plan Implementation and Parliamentary Affairs:* Jeyaraj Fernandopulle. *Plantation Industries, and Public Administration and Home Affairs:* Ratnasiri Wickramanayake. *Posts and Telecommunications and Media:* Mangala Samaraweera. *Provincial Councils and Local Government:* S. Alavi Moulana. *Port Development, Rehabilitation and Reconstruction:* Mohamed H. M. Ashraff. *Samurdi, Youth Affairs and Sports:* D. M. Dissanayaka. *Science and Technology:* Batty Weerakoon. *Social Services:* Betty Premalal Dissanayake. *Tourism and Civil Aviation:* Dharmasiri Senanayake. *Transport and Highways:* A. H. M. Fowzie. *Women's Affairs:* Hema Ratnayake.

Local Government. Sri Lanka is divided into 25 districts, administered by government agents. There are 12 municipal councils, 39 urban councils and 257 *pradeshiya sabas*. There are 9 provincial councils, consisting of a governor, appointed by the President, a Chief Minister, a Board of Ministers and members elected for 5-year terms. Elections were held on 23 March 1997 for 238 local authorities. Some 18,000 candidates representing 12 parties stood.

DEFENCE
Defence expenditure in 1997 totalled US$898m. (US$49 per capita).

Army. The Army consists of 3 divisional and 4 task force headquarters, 1 independent special forces', 23 infantry, 1 mechanized infantry and 1 air-mobile brigade and 3 armoured reconnaissance, 4 field artillery and 1 armoured regiment. Equipment includes 25 T-54/-55 main battle tanks. Strength (1997), 95,000.

SRI LANKA

Paramilitary forces consist of the Ministry of Defence Police (80,000, including 1,000 women and a 3,000-strong anti-guerrilla force), the Home Guard (15,200) and the National Guard (some 15,000).

Navy. The naval force comprises 1 locally built coastal patrol craft, 38 inshore patrol craft of varying types as well as about 30 small fast patrol boats and service craft. There are 2 mechanized landing craft of 270 tonnes full load. The main naval base is at Trincomalee. Personnel in 1997 numbered 12,000, with a reserve of about 1,100.

Air Force. Air Force bases are at Anuradhapura, Katunayake, Ratmalana, Vavuniya and China Bay, Trincomalee. Equipment of 10 squadrons and wings comprises 4 F-7 and 8 Kfir fighters, 10 SF.260 and 2 Cessna 150 trainers, 1 Pucara light strike aircraft, 2 HS748, 8 Chinese-built Y-12s, 5 An-32, 1 Chinese-built Y-8 (An-12), 1 Super King Air, 5 Cessna Skymasters, 1 Cessna 421 and 12 Bell 212, 4 Bell 412, 10 Mi-17, 3 Mi-24 and 6 JetRanger helicopters for internal security operations. Total strength (1997) about 10,000 with 42 combat aircraft and 26 armed helicopters.

INTERNATIONAL RELATIONS
Sri Lanka is a member of the UN, the Commonwealth and the Colombo Plan.

ECONOMY
The conflict with the minority separatists, the Tamil Tigers, is estimated to be costing the country between 1 and 1·5% in growth per year.

Policy. The 1993–97 plan aimed at a 6·4% annual growth rate. Investment allocated was mainly for completion of projects in priority areas such as power, irrigation, road rehabilitation, water supply and telecommunications. Total public investment was about Rs 325,000m.

Performance. GDP growth in 1997 was estimated at 5·6%. Forecast for 1999, between 4·5 and 5%.

Budget. Revenue and expenditure of central government in Rs 1m. for financial years ending 31 Dec.:

Year	Revenue	Expenditure			
		Current	Capital	Total
1993	98,495	100,951	33,777	134,728
1994	110,038	127,085	30,391	157,476
1995	136,257	154,159	41,721	195,880
1996	146,280	175,148	37,639	212,787
1997[1]	164,866	184,746	44,168	228,914

[1]Provisional

The principal sources of revenue in 1992 were (in Rs 1m.): General sales and tax, 24,379; import levies, 21,391; export duties, 594; selective sales taxes, 14,550; property transfer taxes, 2,672; taxes on personal and corporate income, 11,561.

The principal items of recurrent expenditure in 1993 (in Rs 1m.): Finance, 32,365; defence, 15,441; public administration, 19,358; education, 5,994; agriculture, 564; health, 3,080. Capital expenditure on finance, 29,606; Mahaweli development, 5,219; power and energy, 5,955; transport and highways, 6,624.

Currency. The unit of currency is the *Sri Lankan rupee* (LKR) of 100 *cents*. Foreign exchange reserves were US$1,904m. and gold reserves were 60,000 troy oz. in Feb. 1998. Inflation was 10% in 1997. Total money supply in Jan. 1998 was Rs 85,527m.

Banking and Finance. The Central Bank of Sri Lanka is the bank of issue (*Governor* A. S. Jawardena). Two state-owned commercial banks, the Bank of Ceylon and the People's Bank, account for about 70% of bank lending. There are also 21 private banks (17 foreign). Total assets of commercial banks at 31 Dec. 1994, Rs 286,933m. Sri Lanka National Savings Bank at 31 Dec. 1994 had a balance to depositors' credit of Rs 53,278·1m. There are 5 main long-term credit institutions.

There is a stock exchange in Colombo.

Weights and Measures. The metric system has been established.

ENERGY AND NATURAL RESOURCES

Electricity. Installed capacity (1994), 1,409,000 kW. Energy produced, 4,364m. kWh; the main source was hydro-electric (2,900m. kWh). An 80 MW hydro-electricity station on the Kukule Ganga river (70 km south-east of Colombo) is to be constructed by a Swiss-German consortium. Consumption per capita in 1995 was estimated at 236 kWh.

Oil and Gas. Construction of a US$1·6bn. oil refinery at Hambantota in the south of the island began in 1999.

Water. The Mahaweli Ganga scheme irrigates 90,113 ha of new land and (1992) 100,653 ha of land already cultivated.

Minerals. Gems are among the chief minerals mined and exported. Graphite is also important; production in 1994 was 5,000 tonnes. Production of ilmenite, 1994, 60,400 tonnes. Some rutile is also produced (2,741 tonnes in 1992). Salt extraction is the oldest industry. The method is solar evaporation of sea-water. Production, 1992, 115,665 tonnes.

Agriculture. Agriculture accounted for 22% of GDP in 1996. About 2·5m. ha are under cultivation. Agriculture engages 47·5% of the labour force. Main crops in 1994: Paddy (2,684,000 tonnes from 929,621 ha), rubber (104,200 tonnes in 1993), tea (231,871 tonnes in 1993) and coconuts (2,628m. nuts). Tea plantations are being returned to the private sector after nationalization in 1975.

Livestock in 1996: 1,702,000 cattle, 87,000 pigs, 880,000 buffaloes (1995), 588,000 goats (1995), 10m. chickens (1995).

Agricultural output grew by 4% in 1997.

Forestry. The area under forests in 1995 was 1,796,000 ha, or 27·8% of the land area (1,897,000 and 29·4% in 1990). In 1995, 9·62m. cu. metres of roundwood were cut.

Fisheries. Production in 1995 was 235,829 tonnes (more than 93% from sea fishing). In 1992 there were 27,435 fishing craft, of which 15,637 were not motorized.

INDUSTRY

The main industries are the processing of rubber, tea, coconuts and other agricultural commodities, tobacco, textiles, clothing and leather goods, chemicals, plastics, cement, and petroleum refining. Industrial production grew by 7% in 1997.

Labour. The labour force in 1996 totalled 7,652,000 (65% males). In 1995 the unemployment rate was 12·5%. In 1994, 42% of the economically active population were engaged in agriculture, 40% in services and 18% in industry.

Trade Unions. In 1994 there were 1,304 registered trade unions.

INTERNATIONAL TRADE

Foreign debt in 1996 was US$7,995m., and in 1997 represented 54·4% of GDP. A free trade pact with India, signed in Dec. 1998, is expected to create growth in exports.

Imports and Exports. The values of total imports and exports (imports excluding bullion, specie and postal articles; exports, including re-exports and ship's stores) for calendar years (in US$1m.):

	1992	1993	1994	1995	1996
Imports	3,505	3,993	4,767	5,307	5,412
Exports	2,462	2,851	3,209	3,798	4,095

In 1997, total imports were US$5,748m. and exports US$4,522m. Principal exports in 1994 (in Rs 1m.): Tea, 20,964; rubber, 3,582; copra, coconut oil and desiccated coconut, 2,696; textiles and garments (1992), 52,588; precious stones, 12,159.

In 1996 the main export markets were the USA (34·1%), the UK (9·5%), Japan (6·2%), Germany (5·8%) and Belgium-Luxembourg (5·3%). The main import suppliers were India (11·2%), Japan (9·9%), Hong Kong (7%), South Korea (7%) and Singapore (7%).

COMMUNICATIONS

Roads. There were (1994) 25,952 km of motorable roads, of which 11,077 km were blacktopped, first-class nationally maintained roads. Number of motor vehicles, 31 Dec. 1995, 1,218,800, comprising 0·22m. passenger cars, 53,900 buses and coaches, 195,000 trucks and vans, 93,900 tractors and 656,000 motor cycles and mopeds.

Rail. In 1995 there were 1,459 km of railway (1,676 mm gauge). In 1995, 88m. passengers and 1·3m. tonnes of freight were carried.

Civil Aviation. There is an international airport at Colombo (Katunayake). The national carrier is Air Lanka. In 1998 services were also provided by Aeroflot, Air Maldives, AOM French Airlines, Balkan, Cathay Pacific Airways, Condor Flugdienst, Emirates, Gulf Air, Indian Airlines, Kuwait Airways, LTU International Airways, Lauda Air, Malaysia Airlines, Middle East Airlines, Oman Air, Pakistan International Airlines, Qatar Airways, Royal Jordanian, Saudia, Singapore Airlines and Thai Airways International. In 1995 Air Lanka flew 22m. km and carried 1,155,700 passengers (all on international flights). Colombo handled 2,148,578 passengers and 84,404 tonnes of freight in 1996.

Shipping. In 1996, the merchant marine comprised 26 ships (1,000 GRT or over) totalling 220,660 GRT, including 2 oil tankers. Colombo is a modern container port; Trincomalee and Galle are natural harbours. In 1994, 3,568 merchant vessels totalling 55m. GRT entered the ports: 9,588,000 tonnes of goods were unloaded and 5,892,000 tonnes loaded.

Telecommunications. Sri Lanka had 315,900 telehone main lines in 1997 (17 per 1,000 population). In 1995 there were 53,000 cellular phone subscribers, 20,000 PCs and 11,000 fax machines. There were approximately 14,000 Internet users in Sept. 1998.

Postal Services. In 1994 there were 557 post offices, 3,375 sub-post offices and 173 agency post offices.

SOCIAL INSTITUTIONS

Justice. The systems of law which are valid are Roman-Dutch, English, Tesawalamai, Islamic and Kandyan. Kandyan law applies in matters relating to inheritance, matrimonial rights and donations; Tesawalamai law applies in Jaffna as above and in sales of land. Islamic law is applied to all Moslems in respect of succession, donations, marriage, divorce and maintenance. These customary and religious laws have been modified by local enactments.

The courts of original jurisdiction are the High Court, Provincial Courts, District Courts, Magistrates' Courts and Primary Courts. District Courts have unlimited civil jurisdiction. The Magistrates' Courts exercise criminal jurisdiction. The Primary Courts exercise civil jurisdiction in petty disputes and criminal jurisdiction in respect of certain offences.

The Constitution of 1978 provided for the establishment of two superior courts, the Supreme Court and the Court of Appeal.

The Supreme Court is the highest and final superior court of record and exercises jurisdiction in respect of constitutional matters, jurisdiction for the protection of fundamental rights, final appellate jurisdiction in election petitions and jurisdiction in respect of any breach of the privileges of Parliament. The Court of Appeal has appellate jurisdiction to correct all errors in fact or law committed by any court, tribunal or institution.

Police. The strength of the police service in 1994 was 30,236.

Religion. In 1994 the population was 73% Buddhist, 15% Hinduist, 7% Moslem and 5% Christian.

Education. Education is free and is compulsory from age 5 to 14 years. Literacy rate, 1995, 90·2% (male, 93·4%; female, 87·2%).

In 1995 there were 9,657 primary schools with 70,537 teachers for 1·9m. pupils. There were 2·3m. secondary pupils with 103,572 teachers and 63,660 students in higher education with 2,636 staff. There are 9 universities, 1 open (distance) university and 1 Buddhist and Pali university.

In 1994 total expenditure on education came to 3·2% of GNP and represented 9·4% of total government expenditure.

Health. In 1993 there were 426 hospitals, including 84 maternity homes, and 350 central dispensaries. The hospitals had 48,948 beds. There were 3,713 Department of Health doctors. Total state budget expenditure on health, 1993, Rs 7,160m.

Welfare. The activities of the Department of Social Services include: Payment of Public Assistance, monthly allowance, financial assistance to needy tuberculosis, leprosy and cancer patients and their dependants; relief of those affected by widespread distress, such as floods, drought, cyclone; custodial care and welfare services to the elderly and infirm; vocational training, aids and appliances for the physically and mentally handicapped; custodial care, vocational training and rehabilitation for socially handicapped persons; community-based rehabilitation of treated drug addicts; registration of and financial assistance to voluntary organizations which engage in social welfare activities.

The government's Poverty Alleviation ('Janasaviya') Programme targets 0·35m. of the neediest families, who received a monthly Rs 1,458 (in 1992) in return for 20 days' community service. Total budget was Rs 4,900m. in 1992.

CULTURE

Broadcasting. Broadcasting is provided by the Sri Lanka Broadcasting Corporation. In 1995 there were 3·7m. radio and 915,000 TV sets (colour by PAL).

Cinema. In 1995 there were 259 cinemas and 27·2m. admissions.

Press. In 1995 there were 9 daily newspapers with a combined circulation of 0·45m. and 43 weekly newspapers, in Sinhalese, Tamil and English.

Tourism. In 1996 there were 302,000 foreign tourists, bringing revenue of US$168m.

DIPLOMATIC REPRESENTATIVES

Of Sri Lanka in Great Britain (13 Hyde Park Gdns, London, W2 2LU)
High Commissioner: Sarath Kusum Wickremesinghe.

Of Great Britain in Sri Lanka (190 Galle Rd., Kollupitiya, Colombo 3)
High Commissioner: David E. Tatham, CMG.

Of Sri Lanka in the USA (2148 Wyoming Ave., NW, Washington, D.C., 20008)
Ambassador: Warnasena Rasaputram.

Of the USA in Sri Lanka (210 Galle Rd., Kollupitiya, Colombo 3)
Ambassador: Shaun E. Donnelly.

Of Sri Lanka to the United Nations
Ambassador: John de Saram.

Of Sri Lanka to the European Union
Ambassador: Christopher Casie Chetty.

FURTHER READING

De Silva, C. R., *Sri Lanka: a History.* Delhi, 1991
Johnson, B. L. C. and Scrivenor, M. le M., *Sri Lanka: Land, People and Economy.* London, 1981
Manogaran, C., *Ethnic Conflict and Reconciliation in Sri Lanka.* Univ. Hawaii Press, 1987
Manor, J., *Sri Lanka: In Change and Crisis.* London, 1984
McGowan, W., *Only Man is Vile: the Tragedy of Sri Lanka.* New York, 1992
Moore, M., *The State and Peasant Politics in Sri Lanka.* CUP, 1985
Samaraweera, V., *Sri Lanka.* [Bibliography] Oxford and Santa Barbara (CA), 1987
Schwarz, W., *The Tamils of Sri Lanka.* London, 1983
Tambiah, S. J., *Sri Lanka: Ethnic Fratricide and the Dismantling of Democracy.* London, 1986
Wilson, A. J., *The Break-Up of Sri Lanka: The Sinhalese-Tamil Conflict.* London, 1988

National statistical office: Department of Census and Statistics, POB 563, Colombo 7.

SUDAN

Jamhuryat es-Sudan
(Republic of Sudan)

Capital: Khartoum
Population estimate, 2000: 29·82m.
Estimated GDP: $26·6bn.
HDI/world rank: 0·343/157

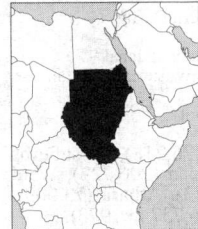

KEY HISTORICAL EVENTS

In 1821 the area that is now Sudan was conquered by the Egyptians. In 1881 Muhammad Ahmad, proclaiming himself the Mahdi, led an uprising and gained control until, in 1899, an Anglo–Egyptian army defeated the Mahdi and established an Anglo–Egyptian condominium.

On 19 Dec. 1955 the Sudanese parliament passed unanimously a declaration that a fully independent state should be established forthwith and that a Council of State should assume the duties of head of state. The UK and Egypt gave their assent on 31 Dec. 1955 and on 1 Jan. 1956 Sudan was proclaimed a sovereign independent republic. In 1958 there was a coup that established a military government until the end of 1964 when a civilian government was re-established. On 8 July 1965 the Constituent Assembly elected Ismail al-Azhari as President of the Supreme Council but the government was faced with constant difficulties from the southern provinces which considered themselves dominated by the north. Rebellions began in 1965.

On 23 April 1969 the prime minister, Muhammad Ahmed Mahgoub, resigned; and on 25 May the government was taken over by a 10-man Revolutionary Council under Col. Jaafar al-Nemery. The Council was dissolved in 1972 and a new constitution was introduced in 1973. Legislative power was placed with a National Assembly, an elected body; and some measure of self-government was granted to the southern provinces. However, discontent in these latter provinces continued and in addition Nemery met considerable opposition in his attempts to make Sudan a formal Islamic state. On 6 April 1985 he was deposed in a military coup led by Gen. Abel-Rahman Swar al-Dahab, who established a Military Council to which the Cabinet was responsible prior to the promised re-establishment of civilian rule. Elections were held, although they were suspended in parts of the southern provinces, in April 1986. On 30 June 1989 Brig.-Gen. (later Lieut.-Gen.) Omar Hassan Ahmad al-Bashir overthrew the civilian government in a military coup.

The rebel Sudan People's Liberation Army (SPLA), consisting of non-Moslem southerners, maintains guerrilla activities in the south while the National Democratic Alliance (NDA), northern Moslems opposed to the ruling National Islamic Front, and non-Moslem southerners of the SPLA fight on in the north. Fighting also erupted in Jan. 1997 along the border with Ethiopia. On 9 July 1997 at a meeting attended by representatives of Djibouti, Eritrea, Ethiopia, Kenya and Uganda the Sudanese government accepted a 'Declaration of Principles' as a framework for negotiations to end the civil war, including the separation of state and religion and self-determination for the south of Sudan.

After 14 years Sudan's civil war has killed some 1·3m. people and reduced the south to a level barely above subsistence. Some 12,000 tons of food were airlifted between mid-April and the end of July 1998 as famine hit southern areas of the country. The severe shortage of food was made even worse by the late arrival of the rains which affected the harvest of Oct. 1998. On 20 Aug. 1998 the USA launched cruise missile attacks against a plant in Khartoum which the USA claimed was being used to make nerve gas ingredients. The attacks were carried out in response to the bombings of the US embassies in Kenya and Tanzania earlier in the month in which 263 people had been killed.

TERRITORY AND POPULATION

Sudan is bounded in the north by Egypt, north-east by the Red Sea, east by Eritrea and Ethiopia, south by Kenya, Uganda and the Democratic Republic of the Congo, west by the Central African Republic and Chad, and north-west by Libya. Its area is 967,500 sq. miles (2,505,813 sq. km). Population (1993 census), 24,940,683; estimate, 1997, 27,953,000, giving a density of 11 per sq. km.

SUDAN

The UN gives a projected population for 2000 of 29·82m.
An estimated 68·6% of the population were rural in 1995.
In Feb. 1994 the former 9 regions were subdivided to form 26 federal states as follows:

Former region	New states
Khartoum	Khartoum
Bahr al-Ghazal	Western Bahr al-Ghazal; Northern Bahr al-Ghazal; Warab
Central	Gezira; White Nile; Sinnar; Blue Nile
Darfur	Northern Darfur; Southern Darfur; Western Darfur
Eastern	Red Sea; Gedaref; Kassala
Equatoria	Eastern Equatoria; Western Equatoria; Bahr al-Jabal
Kurdufan	Northern Kurdufan; Southern Kurdufan; Western Kurdufan
Northern	Nile; Northern State
Upper Nile	Upper Nile; Unity State; Jonglei; Buheyrat

The chief cities (census, 1983) are the capital, Khartoum (476,218), its suburbs Omdurman (526,287) and Khartoum North (341,146), Port Sudan (206,727), Wadi Medani (141,065), al-Obeid (140,024), Kassala (98,751 in 1973), Atbara (73,009), al-Qadarif (66,465 in 1973), Kosti (65,257 in 1973) and Juba (56,737 in 1973).
The northern and central thirds of the country are populated by Arab and Nubian peoples, while the southern third is inhabited by Nilotic and Bantu peoples.
Arabic, the official language, is spoken by 60% of inhabitants.

SOCIAL STATISTICS
1997 births, 1,323,000; deaths, 365,000. Rates, 1997 estimates (per 1,000 population). Births, 40·6; deaths, 11·2. Infant mortality (per 1,000 live births), 74·3. Expectation of life in 1997 was 55·5 years (54·6 for males and 56·5 for females). Growth rate, 3·06% per annum. Fertility rate, 1990–95, 5·0 births per woman.

CLIMATE
Lying wholly within the tropics, the country has a continental climate and only the Red Sea coast experiences maritime influences. Temperatures are generally high throughout the year, with May and June the hottest months. Winters are virtually cloudless and night temperatures are consequently cool. Summer is the rainy season inland, with amounts increasing from north to south, but the northern areas are virtually a desert region. On the Red Sea coast, most rain falls in winter. Khartoum, Jan. 74°F (23·3°C), July 89°F (31·7°C). Annual rainfall 6" (157 mm). Juba, Jan. 83°F (28·3°C), July 78°F (25·6°C). Annual rainfall 39" (968 mm). Port Sudan, Jan. 74°F (23·3°C), July 94°F (34·4°C). Annual rainfall 4" (94 mm). Wadi Halfa, Jan. 60°F (15·6°C), July 90°F (32·2°C). Annual rainfall 0·1" (2·5 mm).

CONSTITUTION AND GOVERNMENT
The constitution was suspended after the 1989 coup and a 12-member Revolutionary Council then ruled. A 300-member Provisional National Assembly was appointed in Feb. 1992 as a transitional legislature pending elections. These were held in March 1996. The President is elected for a 5-year term by the people. The National Assembly (Majlis Watani) now has 400 members, 275 of whom are directly elected for 4 years in single-seat constituencies, 125 indirectly elected by national conference.

National Anthem. 'Nahnu Djundullah' ('We are God's army'); words by A. M. Salih, tune by A. Murjan.

RECENT ELECTIONS
Presidential elections were held in March 1996. President Hassan Ahmed el-Bashir was re-elected by 75·7% of votes cast.
At the National Assembly elections held on 2 and 17 March 1996, no parties were allowed to participate—main opposition parties boycotted the elections. The Government is dominated by the National Islamic Front and other fundamentalist-islamist members.

CURRENT ADMINISTRATION
President: Lieut.-Gen. Omar Hassan Ahmad al-Bashir (app. 1989, re-elected March 1996).

SUDAN

First Vice-President: Ali Osman Mohammed Taha. *Second Vice-President:* Maj.-Gen. George Kongor Arop.

In March 1999 the government comprised:

Minister of the Interior: Brig. Abdul Rahim Mohamed Hussein. *Presidential Affairs:* Brig. Bakri Hassan Salih. *Federal Relations:* Dr Ali Alhaj Mohammed. *Cabinet Affairs:* Brig. Salah Eddin Karrar. *Foreign Affairs:* Dr Mustafa Osman Ismail. *Defence:* Maj.-Gen. Ibrahim Suleiman. *Justice and Attorney General:* Ali Muhammad Uthman Yasin. *Culture and Information:* Ghazi Salah Al-Din. *Agriculture and Forests:* Dr Nafi Ali Nafi. *Irrigation:* Sherif Tuhami. *Energy and Mining:* Dr Awad al-Jaz. *Industry:* Badr Eddin Mohammed Suleiman. *Social Planning:* Brig. al-Tayeb Ibrahim Mohammed Khair. *Higher Education and Scientific Research:* Ahmed Omer Ibrahim. *Tourism and Environment:* Mohammed Tahir Eila. *Commerce:* Osman Alhadi Ibrahim. *Education:* Kabshur Kuku. *Aviation:* Torain Hamid. *Transport and Communications:* Lam Akhol Ajawin. *Communications and Roads:* Maj.-Gen. Alhadi Bushra. *Public Services:* Angelo Beda. *Health:* Lt.-Gen. Mahdi Babou Nimir. *Animal Resources:* Musa al-Muk Kur. *Finance and National Economy:* Dr Abdul Wahab Osman. *Survey and Architectural Development:* Col. Galwak Deng. *National Assembly Relations:* Abul Gasim Mohammed Ibrahim; *Labour:* Agnes Lukudu; *International Co-operation and Investment:* Abdalla Hassan Ahmed.

Local Government. In Feb. 1994 a federal system of 26 states was set up, each under a governor, a deputy governor and a cabinet of ministers. The states are subdivided into 66 provinces and 218 districts.

DEFENCE
There is conscription for 3 years. Defence expenditure totalled US$418m. in 1997 (US$14 per capita).

Army. The army is organized in 1 armoured, 1 engineer, 1 airborne and 6 infantry divisions, 1 mechanized infantry, 24 infantry, 10 artillery, 1 reconnaissance and 12 air defence artillery brigades and 3 artillery regiments. Equipment includes 250 T-54/T-55, 20 M-60A3 and 10 Ch Type-59 main battle tanks. Strength (1997) 75,000 (20,000 conscripts). There is a paramilitary People's Defence Force of about 15,000.

Navy. The navy operates in the Red Sea and also on the River Nile. It comprises 2 inshore patrol craft, 4 riverine patrol craft, 7 ex-Yugoslav landing craft and some armed boats. The flotilla suffers from lack of maintenance and spares. Personnel in 1997 were believed to number 1,700.

Air Force. 2 combat squadrons are equipped with 12 F-7 (Chinese-built MiG-21s) fighters, 8 F-6 (Chinese-built MiG-19) fighter-bombers. There is 1 transport squadron with 3 C-130H Hercules, 6 Aviocars, 2 Y-8 and 2 DHC-5D Buffalo turboprop transports; 2 helicopter squadrons have 6 AB.212s, 9 Romanian-built Pumas, 5 Mi-8s; there are 3 F-7B conversion trainers. Personnel totalled (1996) about 3,000, with 20 combat aircraft. Effectiveness is reduced by economic problems and insurgency.

INTERNATIONAL RELATIONS
Sudan is a member of the UN, OAU, the Arab League and is an ACP member state of the ACP-EU relationship.

ECONOMY

Policy. Subsidies on consumer staples including sugar and fuel were abolished in Oct. 1991.

Performance. Real GDP growth was 4·7% in 1996.

Budget. In 1996 revenues were US$482m. and expenditures US$1·5bn., including capital expenditures of US$30m.

Currency. Until 1992 the monetary unit was the *Sudanese pound* (SDP) of 100 *piastres* and 1,000 *milliemes*. This was replaced in May 1992 by the *dinar* at a rate of 1 dinar = £S10. Sudanese pounds remain legal tender. Inflation was 118% in March 1997 (150% in 1996). Foreign exchange reserves were US$100m. in July 1997.

SUDAN

Banking and Finance. The bank of Sudan opened in Feb. 1960 with an authorized capital of £S1·5m. as the central bank and bank of issue. Banks were nationalized in 1970 but in 1974 foreign banks were allowed to open branches. The application of Islamic law from 1 Jan. 1991 put an end to the charging of interest in official banking transactions, and 7 banks are run on Islamic principles. Mergers of 7 local banks in 1993 resulted in the formation of the Khartoum Bank, the Industrial Development Bank and the Savings Bank. In 1994 there were 27 commercial and private banks.

A stock exchange opened in 1995.

Weights and Measures. The metric system is in use.

ENERGY AND NATURAL RESOURCES

Electricity. Installed capacity was 500 MW in 1994. Production in 1994 was 1,300m. kWh, with consumption per capita in 1994 estimated at 37 kWh.

Oil and Gas. Main production figures for 1994 (in tonnes) were: Distillate fuel oils, 327,000; residual fuel oils, 316,000; motor spirit (petrol), 95,000 jet fuels, 90,000. In June 1998 Sudan began exploiting its oil reserves, with the aim of having a 1,540 km pipeline in operation by April 1999. By June 1999 it was envisaged that some 150,000 bbls. per day would be exported. An oil refinery with a capacity of 2·5m. tonnes is under construction at Al-Jayli.

Minerals. Mineral deposits include graphite, sulphur, chromium, iron, manganese, copper, zinc, fluorspar, natron, gypsum and anhydrite, magnesite, asbestos, talc, halite, kaolin, white mica, coal, diatomite (kieselguhr), limestone and dolomite, pumice, lead, wollastonite, black sands and vermiculite pyrites. Chromite and gold are mined.

Agriculture. 80% of the population depends on agriculture. Land tenure is based on customary rights; land is ultimately owned by the government.

Production (1995 estimates) in 1,000 tonnes: Sugar-cane, 4,800; sorghum, 2,600; millet, 650; groundnuts, 630; wheat, 520; seed cotton, 400; cottonseed, 260; sesame seed, 195; tomatoes, 165.

One of the largest sugar complexes in the world was opened at Kenana in March 1981. Production in 1992 was 513,000 tonnes.

Livestock (1995): Cattle, 22m.; sheep, 23m.; goats, 16·5m.; poultry, 37m.

Forestry. Forests covered 41·61m. ha in 1995, or 17·5% of the total land area (43·38m. ha and 18·3% of the land area in 1990). The loss of 1·77m. ha of forests between 1990 and 1995 was exceeded among African nations only in the Democratic Republic of the Congo. In 1995, 25·41m. cu. metres of roundwood were cut.

Fisheries. In 1995 the total catch was 45,000 tonnes, of which 41,000 tonnes were marine fish.

INDUSTRY
About 17% of GDP came from industry in 1992, 9% from manufacturing.

Labour. The total workforce in 1996 was 10,652,000 (71% males). There was a monthly minimum wage of 15,000 dinars in 1996. Approximately 68% of the economically active population in 1995 were engaged in agriculture, fisheries and forestry.

INTERNATIONAL TRADE
Foreign debt was US$20,000m. in March 1997.

Imports and Exports. Imports and exports in 1996 (1995 in brackets) totalled respectively an estimated US$1,344m. (US$1,185m.) and US$600m. (US$556m.).

The main exports are cotton, sesame, gum arabic, sorghum, livestock, gold and sugar. Main imports are petroleum products, machinery and equipment, foodstuffs, manufactured goods, medicines and chemicals. The main import sources in 1994-95 were Saudi Arabia (13·5%), UK (12·1%), Egypt (5·8%) and Germany (4·4%). Principal export markets in 1994-95 were Saudi Arabia (19·7%), UK (9·7%), Italy (9·0%) and China (7·5%).

COMMUNICATIONS

Roads. In 1995 there were 11,610 km of roads, of which 4,203 km were paved, and 45,000 km of tracks. There were an estimated 285,000 passenger cars and 53,000 trucks and vans in 1996.

Rail. The total length of the railways is 5,516 km, of which 4,800 km is of 1,067 mm gauge and 716 km of 1,610 mm gauge. In 1994 the railways carried 0·6m. passengers and 1·9m. tonnes of freight.

Civil Aviation. There is an international airport at Khartoum. The national carrier is the government-owned Sudan Airways, which operates domestic and international services. In 1998 Sudan was also served by Air Djibouti, Egyptair, Gulf Air, Kenya Airways, Lufthansa, Qatar Airways, SAS, Saudia, Syrian Arab Airlines and Yemenia Yemen Airways. In 1995 scheduled airline traffic of Sudan-based carriers flew 12·9m. km, carrying 497,000 passengers (344,000 on international flights).

Shipping. Supplementing the railways are regular steamer services of the Sudan Railways. Port Sudan is the major seaport; another port at Suakin was opened in 1991. Traffic on the River Nile has ceased owing to the civil war. Sea-going shipping totalled 72,752 GRT in 1995, including oil tankers, 1,222 GRT.

Telecommunications. In 1997 Sudan had 112,500 main telephone lines (4 per 1,000 persons). In 1995 there were 5,800 fax machines and in Jan. 1998 around 300 Internet users.

Postal Services. In 1995 there were 411 post offices.

SOCIAL INSTITUTIONS

Justice. The judiciary is a separate independent department of state, directly and solely responsible to the President of the Republic. The general administrative supervision and control of the judiciary is vested in the High Judicial Council.

Civil Justice is administered by the courts constituted under the Civil Justice Ordinance, namely the High Court of Justice—consisting of the Court of Appeal and Judges of the High Court, sitting as courts of original jurisdiction—and Province Courts—consisting of the Courts of Province and District Judges. The law administered is 'justice, equity and good conscience' in all cases where there is no special enactment. Procedure is governed by the Civil Justice Ordinance.

Justice for the Moslem population has always been administered by the Islamic law courts, which form the Sharia Divisions of the Court of Appeal, High Courts and Kadis Courts; President of the Sharia Division is the Grand Kadi. In Dec. 1990 the government announced that Sharia would be applied in the non-Moslem southern parts of the country as well.

Criminal Justice is administered by the courts constituted under the Code of Criminal Procedure, namely major courts, minor courts and magistrates' courts. Serious crimes are tried by major courts, which are composed of a President and 2 members and have the power to pass the death sentence. Major Courts are, as a rule, presided over by a Judge of the High Court appointed to a Provincial Circuit or a Province Judge. There is a right of appeal to the Chief Justice against any decision or order of a Major Court, and all its findings and sentences are subject to confirmation by him.

Lesser crimes are tried by Minor Courts consisting of 3 Magistrates and presided over by a Second Class Magistrate, and by Magistrates' Courts.

Religion. Islam is the state religion. In 1992 there were 21·9m. Sunni Moslems, concentrated in the north, and 2·4m. Christians and some 5m. traditionalist animists in the south.

Education. In 1995 there were 10,636 pre-primary schools with 11,992 teachers for 537,395 pupils and 12,187 primary schools with 83,306 teachers for 3·02m. pupils. In 1992 there were 718,298 secondary level pupils with 30,642 teachers. In 1996 there were 17 universities, 2 Islamic universities, 1 university of science and technology, and an institute of advanced banking. There were also 14 colleges or other institutions of higher education. Adult literacy rate, 1995, 46·1% (male, 57·7%; female, 34·6%).

Health. In 1994 there were 2,600 doctors, equivalent to 1 for every 11,300 persons. Hospital bed provision in 1986 was 8 per 10,000 population.

CULTURE

Broadcasting. Broadcasting is controlled by the Sudan National Broadcasting Corporation and Sudan Television (colour by PAL). There are also 2 regional TV stations, in the centre and in the north of the country. In 1995 there were some 7·2m. radio and 2·2m. TV sets.

Press. In 1995 there were 5 daily newspapers with a combined circulation of 650,000.

Tourism. In 1996 there were 65,000 foreign tourists, bringing revenue of US$7m.

DIPLOMATIC REPRESENTATIVES

Of Sudan in Great Britain (3 Cleveland Row, London, SW1A 1DD)
Ambassador: Vacant.

Of Great Britain in Sudan (off Sharia Al Baladia, Khartoum East)
Ambassador: Alan F. Goulty, CMG.

Of Sudan in the USA (2210 Massachusetts Ave., NW, Washington, D.C., 20008)
Ambassador: Mahdi Ibrahim Mohamed.

Of the USA in Sudan (Sharia Ali Abdul Latif POB 699, Khartoum)
Ambassador: Vacant.

Of Sudan to the United Nations
Ambassador: Elfatih Mohamed Ahmed Erwa.

Of Sudan to the European Union
Ambassador: Galal Hassan Atabani.

FURTHER READING

Craig, G. M. (ed.) *Agriculture of the Sudan.* OUP, 1991
Daly, M. W., *Sudan.* [Bibliography] Oxford and Santa Barbara (CA), 1983
Gurdon, C., *Sudan in Transition: A Political Risk Analysis.* London, 1986
Halasa, A., et al. *The Return to Democracy in Sudan.* Geneva, 1986
Holt, P. M., *A Modern History of the Sudan.* New York, 3rd ed. 1979
Khalid, M., *The Government They Deserve: the Role of the Elite in Sudan's Political Evolution.* London, 1990
Woodward, P., *Sudan, 1898-1989: the Unstable State.* London, 1991

SURINAME

Republic of Suriname

Capital: Paramaribo
Population estimate, 2000: 452,000
GNP per capita: (PPP$) 2,630
HDI/world rank: 0·796/65

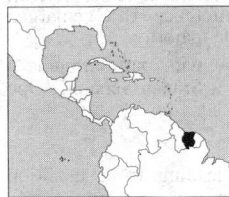

KEY HISTORICAL EVENTS

The first Europeans to reach the area were the Spanish in 1499 but it was the British who established a colony in 1650. At the peace of Breda (1667) between Great Britain and the United Netherlands, the area known as Suriname was assigned to the Netherlands in exchange for the colony of New Netherland in North America. This was confirmed by the treaty of Westminster of Feb. 1674. Suriname was twice in British possession during the Napoleonic Wars in 1799-1802 (when it was restored to the Batavian Republic at the peace of Amiens) and 1804-16, when it was returned to the Netherlands.

On 25 Nov. 1975 Suriname gained full independence and was admitted to the UN on 4 Dec. 1975. On 25 Feb. 1980 the government was ousted in a *coup* and a National Military Council (NMC) established. A further *coup* on 13 Aug. replaced several members of the NMC and the State President. Other attempted *coups* took place in 1981 and 1982, with the NMC retaining control. In Oct. 1987 a new constitution was approved by referendum; following elections in Nov. Suriname returned to democracy in Jan. 1988 but on 24 Dec. 1990 a further military coup deposed the government. Ronald Venetiaan was elected President in Sept. 1991.

The government and rebel guerrilla groups reached a peace agreement in Aug. 1992 and after the elections of May 1996 Jules Wijdenbosch, a candidate of the National Democratic Party, was elected President.

TERRITORY AND POPULATION

Suriname is located on the northern coast of South America between 2-6° North latitude and 54-59° West longitude. It is bounded in the north by the Atlantic Ocean, east by French Guiana, west by Guyana, and south by Brazil. Area, 163,820 sq. km. Census population (1995), 407,000. Estimate, Jan. 1997, 417,000; density, 3 per sq. km.

The UN gives a projected population for 2000 of 452,000.

In 1995, 50·8% lived in rural areas. The capital, Paramaribo, had (1997 estimate) 289,000 inhabitants.

Suriname is divided into 10 districts. They are (with 1992 population estimate and chief town): Brokopondo, population 7,554 (Brokopondo); Commewijne, 22,822 (Nieuw Amsterdam); Coronie, 3,151 (Totness); Marowijne, 18,339 (Albina); Nickerie, 37,200 (Nieuw Nickerie); Para, 13,693 (Onverwacht); Paramaribo, 240,000—representing 66% of Suriname's total population (Paramaribo); Saramacca, 12,320 (Groningen); Sipaliwini, 26,458 (local authority in Paramaribo); Wanica, 69,114 (Lelydorp).

Major ethnic groups in percentages of the population in 1991: Creole, 35%; Indian, 33%; Javanese, 16%; Bushnegroes (Blacks),10%; Amerindian, 3%.

The official language is Dutch. English is widely spoken next to Hindi, Javanese and Chinese as inter-group communication. A vernacular, called 'Sranan' or 'Surinamese', is used as a lingua franca. In 1976 it was decided that Spanish was to become the nation's principal working language.

SOCIAL STATISTICS

Births, 1995, 10,100; deaths, 2,400. 1995 rates per 1,000 population: Birth rate, 23·6; death rate, 5·6. Annual growth rate, 1990–95, 0·9%. Expectation of life, 1990–95, was 67·8 years for males and 72·8 for females. Infant mortality, 1990–95, 28 per 1,000 live births; fertility rate, 2·7 births per woman.

CLIMATE

The climate is equatorial, with uniformly high temperatures and rainfall. The temperature is an average of 27°C throughout the year; there are 2 rainy seasons

1473

(May–July and Nov.–Jan.) and 2 dry seasons (Aug.–Oct. and Feb.–April). Paramaribo, Jan. 21°C, July 32·4°C. Average rainfall 182·3 mm.

CONSTITUTION AND GOVERNMENT
Parliament is a 51-member *National Assembly*. The head of state is the *President*, elected for a 5-year term by a two-thirds majority by the National Assembly, or, failing that, by an electoral college, the United People's Conference (UPC) enlarged by the inclusion of regional and local councillors, by a simple majority.

National Anthem. 'God zij met ons Suriname' ('God be with our Suriname'); words by C. A. Hoekstra, tune by J. C. de Puy. There is a Sranan version, 'Opo kondreman oen opo'; words by H. de Ziel.

RECENT ELECTIONS
Parliamentary elections were held on 23 May 1996, leading to a coalition government headed by the National Democratic Party.

CURRENT ADMINISTRATION
President: Jules Wijdenbosch (NDP; elected by the UPC on 5 Sept. 1996, sworn in 14 Sept. 1996).
   Vice-President: Pretaapnarain Radhakisun.
   In March 1999 the government comprised:
   Minister of Foreign Affairs: Errol Snijders. *Defence:* Ramon Dwarka-Panday. *Finance:* Tjan Gobardhan. *Justice and Police:* Paul Sjak Shie. *Public Works:* Rudolf Vishnudath Mangal. *Regional Affairs and Development:* Yvonne Raveles-Resida. *Transport, Communication and Tourism:* Dick De Bie. *Public Health:* Theo Vishnudath. *Social Affairs:* Soewarto Moestadja. *Labour:* M. A. Faried Pierkhan. *Natural Resources:* Errol Alibuks. *Education and Human Development:* Karan Ramsundersingh. *Planning and Development Co-operation:* Waldi Nain. *Agriculture and Fisheries:* Saimin Redjosentono. *Interior and Home Affairs:* Sonny Kertowidjojo. *Trade and Industry:* Robby Dragman.

DEFENCE
Defence expenditure totalled US$15m. in 1997 (US$36 per capita).

Army. The armed forces consist of 1 infantry and 1 military police battalion and 1 mechanized cavalry squadron with a total strength of about 1,800 in 1997. Officers' ranks were abolished in Feb. 1986.

Navy. The flotilla comprises 5 inshore patrol craft, as well as 3 river patrol boats, all built in the Netherlands. In 1997 personnel totalled 240.

Air Force. Personnel (1997): 160.

INTERNATIONAL RELATIONS
Suriname is a member of the UN, OAS, CARICOM and is an ACP member state of the ACP-EU relationship.

ECONOMY
Performance. Real GDP growth was 4·0% in 1995 (–0·8% in 1994).

Budget. 1996 revenue (in 1m. Sf) was 90,874·6 (68,918·0 in 1995), made up of direct taxes, 38,371·4; indirect taxes, 29,285·9; bauxite levy and other revenues, 22,697·4; aid, 519·9.
   Total expenditure was 96,957·5 (94,900·7 in 1995), made up of wages and salaries, 27,598·4; transfers and subsidies, 13,235·3; interest, 1,659·5; social securities, 994·1; material cost, 595·1; other current expenditures, 52,463·2; development expenditure, 411·9.

Currency. The unit of currency is the *Suriname guilder* (SRG; written as Sf[lorin]) of 100 *cents*. Foreign exchange reserves totalled US$103m. and gold reserves were 210,000 troy oz. in Feb. 1998. Total money supply in May 1997 was 61,792m. Sf.

Banking and Finance. The Central Bank of Suriname is a bankers' bank and also the bank of issue. There are 3 commercial banks; the Suriname People's Credit Bank operates under the auspices of the Government. There is a post office savings bank, a mortgage bank, an investment bank, a long-term investments agency, a National Development Bank and an Agrarian Bank.

Weights and Measures. The metric system is in use.

ENERGY AND NATURAL RESOURCES

Electricity. Installed capacity in 1995 was 425,000 kW. Production (1994) 1,332m. kWh. Consumption per capita was an estimated 2,929 kWh in 1995.

Oil and Gas. Crude petroleum production (1996), 3m. bbls.

Minerals. Bauxite is the most important mineral. Production (1995), 3,596,000 tonnes.

Agriculture. Agriculture is restricted to the alluvial coastal zone; in 1994 there were 57,000 ha of arable land, 11,000 ha of permanent cropland and 21,000 ha of pasture. The staple food crop is rice. Production (1996, in 1,000 tonnes): Paddy, 228·6; rice (white), 86·4; oranges, 10·3; grapefruit, 1·0; other citrus fruit, 2·1; bananas, 12·9; plantains, 41·7; vegetables, 32·2; coconuts, 12·3; cassava, 5·0; root crops, 6·2.

Livestock (1996): Cattle, 97,800; sheep, 9,000; goats, 9,000 (1995); pigs, 21,100; poultry, 2·7m.

Forestry. Forests covered 14·72m. ha in 1995, or 94·8% of the land area (14·78m. ha in 1990). In terms of percentage coverage, Suriname and Guyana were the world's most heavily forested countries in 1995. Production in 1996 was 213,657 cu. metres of roundwood and an estimated 34,600 cu. metres of sawn logs.

Fisheries. The catch in 1995 amounted to 13,000 tonnes, of which 12,860 tonnes were from marine waters.

INDUSTRY

There are aluminium smelting, food-processing and wood-using industries. Production, 1994: Cement, 24,665 tonnes (estimate); palm oil, 1,051,000 litres (estimate); beer 3,456,000 litres; alumina, 1,498,000 tonnes; aluminium, 26,700 tonnes; cigarettes, 443m.; shoes, 98,990 pairs (estimate); plywood, 6,864 cu. metres.

Labour. Out of 77,900 people in employment in 1994, 35,700 were in community, social and personal services, 13,400 in trade, restaurants and hotels and 6,300 in manufacturing. There were 11,300 unemployed persons, or 12·7% of the workforce.

INTERNATIONAL TRADE

Imports and Exports. In 1995 (provisional) imports totalled 258,916·7m. Sf and exports, 211,020·6m. Sf. Principal imports, 1995 (in 1m. Sf): Raw materials and semi-manufactured goods, 94,254·3; investment goods, 65,128·7; fuels and lubricants, 28,629·4; foodstuffs, 24,987·6; cars and motor cycles, 9,244·8; textiles, 3,986·0. Principal exports, 1994 (in 1m. Sf): Alumina, 42,358·2; aluminium, 5,278·2; shrimps, 5,257·4; rice, 3,402·3; bananas and plantains, 1,274·3; wood and wood products, 261·4.

In 1995 (provisional) exports, including re-exports, (in 1m. Sf) were mainly to Netherlands (58,963·3), Norway (52,587·8), USA (47,126·1), Japan (12,835·7) and Brazil (10,889·0); imports were mainly from the USA (109,068·9), Netherlands (51,337·3), Trinidad and Tobago (19,071·5), Netherlands Antilles (6,582·5), Japan (5,513·7), UK (2,580·3).

COMMUNICATIONS

Roads. The road network covered 4,530 km in 1996, of which 1,200 km were paved. In 1996 there were 46,408 passenger cars, 16,738 goods vehicles, 2,517 buses, 833 motor cycles and 26,735 mopeds.

Rail. There are 2 single-track railways.

Civil Aviation. There is an international airport at Paramaribo (Johan Adolf Pengel). The national carrier is Surinam Airways, which in 1998 had flights to Amsterdam, Aruba, Barbados, Belem, Cayenne, Curaçao, Georgetown, Macapa, Miami and Port of Spain. In 1998 services were also provided by ALM and KLM. In 1995 Surinam Airways flew 5m. km, carrying 161,800 passengers. In 1996 there were 89,438 passenger arrivals and 91,151 departures.

Shipping. The Royal Netherlands Steamship Co. operates services to the Netherlands, the USA, and regionally. The Suriname Navigation Co. maintains services from Paramaribo to Georgetown, Cayenne and the Caribbean area. Merchant shipping in 1995 totalled 8,000 GRT. In 1995 vessels totalling 1,167,000 net registered tons entered ports and vessels totalling 1,926,000 NRT cleared.

Telecommunications. Main telephone lines numbered 63,900 in 1997, equivalent to 146·2 for every 1,000 persons. There were 3,752 cellular phone subscribers in 1996 and 300 fax machines in 1995.

SOCIAL INSTITUTIONS

Justice. Members of the court of justice are nominated by the President. There are 3 cantonal courts.

Religion. In 1997 there were estimated to be 116,000 Hindus, 89,000 Roman Catholics, 83,000 Moslems, 69,000 Protestants and 67,000 followers of other religions.

Education. Adult literacy was 93% in 1995 (male, 95·1%; female, 91%). In 1995–96 there were 304 primary schools with 3,611 teachers and 75,585 pupils. 104 secondary schools had 2,286 teachers and 31,918 pupils. In 1995–96 the university had 1,335 students and 155 academic staff. There is a teacher training college with (1995–96) 1,462 students.

Health. There were (1995) 1,805 general hospital beds and 227 physicians.

CULTURE

Broadcasting. The government controls the partly commercial Stichting Radio Omroep Suriname and Radio Suriname Internationaal, and Surinaamse Televisie Stichting. In 1995 there were 290,000 radio and 60,000 TV sets (colour by NTSC). There are 13 broadcasting and 3 television stations.

Cinema. There were (1998) 2 cinemas in Paramaribo.

Press. There were 3 daily newspapers in 1995, with a combined circulation of 43,000, equivalent to 101 per 1,000 inhabitants.

Tourism. In 1996 there were 19,130 tourist arrivals by air. Receipts totalled US$14m. Tourism is a relatively new industry in Suriname.

Festivals. The people of Suriname celebrate Chinese New Year (Jan.); Phagwa, a Hindu celebration (March–April); Id-Ul-Fitre, the sugar feast at the end of Ramadan (May); Avondvierdaagse, a carnival (during the Easter holidays); Suriflora, a celebration of plants and flowers (April–May); Keti koti, an Afro-Surinamese holiday to commemorate the abolition of slavery (1 July); Suri-pop, a popular music festival (July); Nationale Kunstbeurs, arts and crafts (Oct.–Nov.); Divali, the Hindu ceremony of light (Nov.); Djaran Kepang, a Javanese dance held on feast days; Winti-prey, a ceremony for the Winti gods.

Museums and Galleries. The main museums (1998) were: Surinaams Museum and Fort Zeelandia in Paramaribo; the Open Air Museum at Nieuw Amsterdam. Art Galleries include: Suriname Art 2000; the Academy for Higher Arts and Cultural Education; and the Ready Tex Art Boutique, all in Paramaribo; and Nola Hatterman Instituut at Fort Zeelandia.

DIPLOMATIC REPRESENTATIVES
Of Suriname in Great Britain
Ambassador: Evert Guillaume Azimullah (resides in The Hague).

Of Great Britain in Suriname
Ambassador: Vacant.

Of Suriname in the USA (4301 Connecticut Ave., NW, Washington, D.C., 20008)
Ambassador: Arnold T. Halfhide.

Of the USA in Suriname (Dr Sophie Redmondstraat 129, Paramaribo)
Ambassador: Dennis K. Hays.

Of Suriname to the United Nations
Ambassador: Subhas Chandra Mungra.

Of Suriname to the European Union
Ambassador: Ewald Leeflang.

FURTHER READING
Dew, E. M., *Trouble in Suriname, 1975–1993.* New York, 1995
Hoefte, R. A. L., *Suriname* [Bibliography]. Oxford and Santa Barbara (CA), 1990

National statistical office: Algemeen Bureau voor de Statistiek, POB244, Paramaribo.

SWAZILAND

Umbuso weSwatini—

Kingdom of Swaziland

Capital: Mbabane
Population estimate, 2000: 984,000
GNP per capita: (PPP$) 3,320
HDI/world rank: 0·597/115

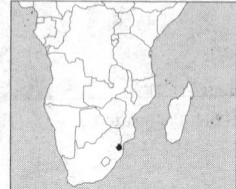

KEY HISTORICAL EVENTS

The Swazi migrated into the country to which they have given their name in the last half of the 18th century. They settled first in what is now southern Swaziland, but moved northwards under their chief, Sobhuza—known also to the Swazi as Somhlolo. Sobhuza died in 1838 and was succeeded by ·Mswati. The further order of succession has been Mbandzeni and Bhunu, whose son, Sobhuza II, was installed as King of the Swazi nation in 1921 after a long minority.

The independence of the Swazis was guaranteed in the conventions of 1881 and 1884 between the British Government and the Government of the South African Republic. In 1890, soon after the death of Mbandzeni, a provisional government was established with representatives of the Swazis, the British and the South African Republic Governments. In 1894 the South African Republic was given powers of protection and administration. In 1902, after the conclusion of the Boer War, a special commissioner took charge, and under an order-in-council in 1903 the Governor of the Transvaal administered the territory, through the special commissioner. Swaziland became independent on 6 Sept. 1968.

On 25 April 1967 the British Government gave the country internal self-government, changing the country's status to that of a protected state. The Ngwenyama, Sobhuza II, was recognized as King of Swaziland and head of state. King Sobhuza died on 21 Aug. 1982. On 25 April 1986, King Mswati III was installed as King of Swaziland. Despite a secret pact with the Republic of South Africa concluded in 1982 and providing for joint operations against guerrillas fighting apartheid, the South Africans launched an armed raid into Swaziland in Aug. 1986, aimed at the (South African) African National Congress. There is conflict within the Swazi government over the role of the royal family and relations with the Republic of South Africa.

TERRITORY AND POPULATION

Swaziland is bounded in the north, west and south by South Africa, and in the east by Mozambique. The area is 6,705 sq. miles (17,400 sq. km). Population (census 1986), 681,059. Estimate, 1997, 966,000; density, 55 per sq. km. In 1993, 53·3% of the population were females. More than 50% of the population is under 18 years of age.

The UN gives a projected population for 2000 of 984,000.

In 1995 an estimated 68·9% of the population were rural. Main urban areas with 1986 census populations: Mbabane, the administrative capital (38,290); Manzini (18,084); Big Bend (9,676); Mhlume (6,509); Havelock Mine (4,850); Nhlangano (4,107). The legislative capital is Lobamba.

A census was held in 1996.

The population is 84% Swazi and 10% Zulu. The official languages are Swazi and English.

SOCIAL STATISTICS

1996 births, 33,000; deaths, 9,000. Birth rate, 1996 (per 1,000 population), 35·4; death rate, 9·8. Life expectancy, 1997, 59·8 years for women and 52·8 for men. Infant mortality, 1990–95, 75 per 1,000 live births; fertility rate, 4·9 births per woman.

CLIMATE

A temperate climate with two seasons. Nov. to March is the wet season, when temperatures range from mild to hot, with frequent thunderstorms. The cool, dry season from May to Sept. is characterized by clear, bright sunny days. Mbabane, Jan. 68°F (20°C), July 54°F (12·2°C). Annual rainfall 56" (1,402 mm).

CONSTITUTION AND GOVERNMENT
The reigning King is **Mswati III** (b. 1968; crowned 25 April 1986), who succeeded his father, King Sobhuza II (reigned 1921–82). The King rules in conjunction with the Queen Mother (his mother, or a senior wife).

There is a *House of Assembly* of 65 members, 55 of whom are elected each from 1 constituency (*inkhundla*), and 10 appointed by the King; and a *House of Senators* of 30 members, 10 of whom are elected by the House of Assembly and 20 appointed by the King. Elections are held in 2 rounds, the second being a run-off between the 5 candidates who come first in each constituency.

There is also a traditional *Swazi National Council* headed by the King and Queen Mother at which all Swazi men are entitled to be heard.

A commission has been established to review the constitution.

National Anthem. 'Nkulunkulu mnikati wetibuso temaSwati' ('O Lord our God bestower of blessings upon the Swazi'); words by A. E. Simelane, tune by D. K. Rycroft.

RECENT ELECTIONS
At the elections of 19 Sept. and 24 Oct. 1998 the electorate was approximately 200,000. Only non-partisans were elected.

CURRENT ADMINISTRATION
In March 1999 the Cabinet was composed as follows:
Prime Minister: Dr Barnabas Sibusiso Dlamini.
Deputy Prime Minister: Arthur R. V. Khoza. *Foreign Affairs, Defence and Trade:* Albert H. N. Shabangu. *Enterprise and Employment:* Lutfo E. Dlamini. *Agriculture and Co-operatives:* Roy Fanourakis. *Public Works and Transport:* Peter Dlamini. *Education:* Rev. Abednego Ntshangase. *Health and Social Welfare:* Dr Phetsile Dlamini. *Justice and Constitutional Affairs:* Chief Maweni Simelane. *Home Affairs:* Prince Sobandla. *Natural Resources and Energy:* HRH Prince Guduza. *Tourism, Environment and Communications:* Dr George Soze Vilakazi. *Public Service and Information:* Magwagwa Buhlebzitha. *Economic Planning and Development:* Majozi Sithole. *Finance:* John P. Carmichael. *Housing and Urban Development:* Stella Lukhele.

Local Government. The country is divided into the 4 regions: Shiselweni, Lubombo, Manzini and Hhohho. They are administered by Regional Administrators.

DEFENCE
Army Air Wing. There are 2 Israeli-built Arava light twin-turboprop transports with underwing weapon attachments for light attack duties.

INTERNATIONAL RELATIONS
Swaziland is a member of the UN, OAU, SADC, the Commonwealth and is an ACP member state of the ACP-EU relationship.

ECONOMY
At the core of Swazi society is Tibiyo Taka Ngwane. Created in 1968 by Royal Charter, Tibiyo is a national development fund which operates outside the government and falls directly under the King, who holds it in trust for the nation. Its money derives from its stake in virtually every sector of Swazi commerce and industry, from sugar plantations to the media, tourism to finance.

Performance. Real GDP growth was 3·0% in 1997.

Budget. Revenue and expenditure (in 1m. emalangeni) for financial years ending 31 March:

	1991–92	1992–93	1993–94	1994–95
Revenue	816·1	890·3	1,089·4	1,200·1
Expenditure	794·9	932·6	1,209·3	1,397·5

Currency. The unit of currency is the *lilangeni* (plural *emalangeni*) (SZL) of 100 *cents* but Swaziland remains in the Common (formerly Rand) Monetary Area and the South African rand is legal tender. The average annual inflation rate over the period 1990–96 was 10·6% and in 1997 inflation stood at 9·5%. In Feb. 1998 foreign exchange reserves were US$335m. Total money supply in Feb. 1998 was 446m. emalangeni.

Banking and Finance. The central bank and bank of issue is the Central Bank of Swaziland, established in 1974. There were 24 commercial banks in 1992. Foreign banks include Nedbank, Standard Chartered, Stanbic and First National. The Swaziland Development and Savings Bank concentrates on agricultural and housing loans. Total assets of the above were 1·05m. emalangeni in 1992. The Swaziland Building Society had assets of 84·6m. emalangeni in 1990–91.

In 1990 Swaziland Stock Brokers was established to trade in stocks and shares for institutional and private clients.

ENERGY AND NATURAL RESOURCES

Electricity. Installed capacity was 50,000 kW in 1993. Production was 568m. kWh in 1994. Consumption per capita was 612 kWh in 1993.

Minerals. Output (in tonnes) in 1995: Coal, 171,666; asbestos, 28,591; quarry stone, 117,175 cu. metres. Diamond production was worth 15·2m. emalangeni in 1990 (20m. in 1989).

Agriculture. Agriculture accounted for 12% of GDP in 1996. In 1994 there were 187,000 ha of arable land, 4,000 ha of permanent cropland and 1·07m. ha of pasture. Production (1993–94, in tonnes): Sugar-cane, 3,647,244; citrus, 88,263; pineapples, 19,700; tobacco, 394; seed cotton, 6,294; maize, 85,748; sorghum, 1,830; tomatoes, 242.

Livestock (1996): Cattle, 646,000; goats (1995), 435,000; pigs, 31,000; chickens (1995), 1m.

Forestry. Forests covered 146,000 ha in 1995, or 8·5% of the land area. In 1995 timber production was 1·42m. cu. metres.

Fisheries. Estimated total catch, 1995, 115 tonnes, entirely from inland waters.

INDUSTRY

Most industries are based on processing agricultural products and timber. Footwear and textiles are also manufactured, and some engineering products.

Labour. The formal labour force numbered 88,290 in 1994; 15,892 Swazis worked in gold mines in South Africa. Unemployment in 1995 was 22%.

Trade Unions. In 1998 there were 20 unions grouped in the Swaziland Federation of Trade Unions and 4 unions grouped in the Swaziland Federation of Labour.

INTERNATIONAL TRADE

Swaziland has a customs union with South Africa and receives a pro rata share of the dues collected. External debt was US$220m. in 1996.

Imports and Exports. In 1996 exports were valued at US$893m., and imports at US$1·1bn. Main export commodities are soft drink concentrates, sugar, wood pulp and cotton yarn; main import products are motor vehicles, machinery, transport equipment, foodstuffs, petroleum products and chemicals. By far the most significant trading partner is South Africa, followed by the UK.

COMMUNICATIONS

Roads. Total length of roads (1995), 2,886 km, of which 828 km were tarred. There were 29,700 passenger cars in 1996 (32 per 1,000 inhabitants) plus 28,420 trucks and vans.

Rail. In 1997 the system comprised 301 km of route, and carried 4,129,000 tonnes of freight in 1995–96.

Civil Aviation. There is an international airport at Manzini (Matsapha). The national carrier, Royal Swazi National Airways Corporation, is 50% state-owned. It had flights in 1998 to Dar es Salaam, Harare, Johannesburg, Lusaka, Maputo and Nairobi. Services were also provided in 1998 by Metavia Airlines. In 1995 Royal

Swazi National Airways Corporation flew 1·4m. km and carried 49,300 passengers, and Manzini handled 66,000 passengers.

Telecommunications. Swaziland had 25,400 telephone main lines in 1997, or 28·1 for every 1,000 persons. In 1995 there were 20,611 exchange connections, 155 telex exchange connections and 900 fax machines. There were around 900 Internet users in Jan. 1998.

Postal Services. There were 65 post offices in 1995, or 1 for every 14,900 persons.

SOCIAL INSTITUTIONS

Justice. The constitutional courts practice Roman-Dutch law. The judiciary is headed by the Chief Justice. There is a High Court and various Magistrates and Courts. A Court of Appeal with a President and 3 Judges deals with appeals from the High Court. There are 16 courts of first instance. There are also traditional Swazi National Courts.

Religion. There are about 0·12m. Christians and about 30,000 of other faiths.

Education. In 1998 there were 446 pre-schools with 19,000 children, and 543 primary schools with 212,292 children and 5,347 teachers. The teacher/pupil ratio has decreased from 40/1 in the 1970s to 33/1. About half the children of secondary school age attend school. There are also private schools. In 1998 there were 69,009 children in secondary and high school classes. Many secondary and high schools teach agricultural activities.

The University of Swaziland, at Matsapha, had 2,533 students in 1996–97. There are 3 teacher training colleges (total enrolment in 1994–95, 857) and 8 vocational institutions (1,150 students and 147 teachers in 1991). There is also an institute of management.

Rural education centres offer formal education for children and adult education geared towards vocational training. The adult literacy rate in 1995 was 76·7% (78% among males and 75·6% among females).

Health. In 1998 there were 176 hospitals, clinics and health centres.

CULTURE

Broadcasting. The Broadcasting Corporation and Swaziland Television Authority are government-owned. Swaziland Broadcasting Services run on a semi-commercial basis. In 1995 there were some 140,000 radio and 18,000 television receivers (colour by PAL).

Press. In 1995 there were 2 daily newspapers, both in English.

Tourism. There were 305,000 foreign tourists in 1996, bringing revenue of US$38m.

Libraries. There is the government-subsidized National Library Service, which comprises 2 libraries at Mbabane and Manzini with 11 branches throughout the country.

DIPLOMATIC REPRESENTATIVES

Of Swaziland in Great Britain (20 Buckingham Gate, London, SW1E 6LB)
High Commissioner: Rev. Percy S. Mngomezulu.

Of Great Britain in Swaziland (Allister Miller St., Mbabane)
High Commissioner: John F. Doble, OBE.

Of Swaziland in the USA (3400 International Dr., NW, Washington, D.C., 20008)
Ambassador: Mary M. Kanya.

Of the USA in Swaziland (PO Box 199, Mbabane)
Ambassador: Alan McKee.

Of Swaziland to the United Nations
Ambassador: Moses Mathedele Dlamini.

Of Swaziland to the European Union

Ambassador: Thambayena Annastasia Dlamini.

FURTHER READING

Booth, A., *Swaziland: Tradition and Change in a Southern African Kingdom.* Aldershot and Boulder (CO), 1984

Funnell, D. C., *Under the Shadow of Apartheid: Agrarian Transformation in Swaziland.* Avebury, 1991

Grotpeter, J. J., *Historical Dictionary of Swaziland.* Metuchen, 1975

Matsebula, J. S. M., *A History of Swaziland.* 3rd ed. London, 1992

Nyeko, B., *Swaziland.* [Bibliography] 2nd ed. Oxford and Santa Barbara (CA), 1994

National statistical office: Central Statistical Office, POB 456, Mbabane.

SWEDEN

Konungariket Sverige

(Kingdom of Sweden)

Capital: Stockholm
Population estimate, 2000: 8·9m.
GNP per capita: (PPP$) 18,770
HDI/world rank: 0·936/10

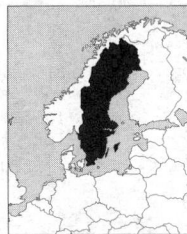

KEY HISTORICAL EVENTS

Sweden was organized as an independent unified state in the 10th century when the Swedes in the north of the country and the Goths in the south were united by Olof. Finland was acquired in the 13th century. In the 14th century Sweden was joined with Norway and Denmark in the Kalmar Union; however, under Gustavus Vasa, Sweden regained her independence in 1523. Under Gustavus Adolphus (1611-32) Sweden became a first rank military power and, at the close of the Thirty Years War in 1648, was in possession of Pomerania and of extensive territories on the eastern shores of the Baltic. But war with Russia and her allies in the early 18th century ended disastrously for Sweden. By the treaty of Nystad (1721) Sweden lost her Baltic empire. In 1810 the French marshal, Bernadotte, was made crown prince. With the fall of Napoleon, Norway was taken from Denmark and attached to Sweden. Bernadotte became King in 1818. Sweden became a constitutional monarchy in 1809, in which year she also ceded Finland to Russia. Norway became independent in 1905. Sweden remained neutral during the two world wars of 1914-18 and 1939-45.

From 1932 to 1976, Sweden was governed by the Social Democratic Party which set the model for welfare reform, combined with rapid economic growth. But high taxation brought a reaction in the 1970s when the Centre Party (representing chiefly small farmers and traders) and the Conservatives staged a comeback which brought them to power in coalition with the Liberal Party in 1976. However, in 1981 the Social Democrat leader, Olaf Palme, became prime minister with support from the Communist Party. On 28 Feb. 1986 Palme was assassinated in Stockholm by unknown assailants; Ingvar Carlsson succeeded him as prime minister.

In 1991 a Conservative-led coalition took over the government at a time of recession. Austerity measures helped in the revival of the Social Democrats who returned to power in 1994 but with a commitment to economic stringency. Although the Social Democrats won the 1998 election, they saw their support fall to its lowest level since the First World War.

TERRITORY AND POPULATION

Sweden is bounded in the west and north-west by Norway, east by Finland and the Gulf of Bothnia, south-east by the Baltic Sea and south-west by the Kattegat. The area is 449,964 sq. km. At the 1990 census the population was 8,587,353. Estimate, July 1997, 8,865,051; density 20 per sq. km.

The UN gives a projected population for 2000 of 8·9m.

In 1995, 83·1% of the population lived in urban areas.

Area, population and population density of the counties (*län*):

	Land area (in sq. km)	Population (1990 census)	Population 31 Dec 1996	Density per sq. km 31 Dec. 1996
Stockholm	6,490	1,640,389	1,744,330	269
Uppsala	6,989	268,503	289,153	41
Södermanland	6,062	255,546	257,153	42
Östergötland	10,562	402,849	415,659	39
Jönköping	9,944	308,294	311,765	31
Kronoberg	8,458	177,880	179,655	21
Kalmar	11,171	241,149	241,896	22
Gotland	3,140	57,132	57,971	18
Blekinge	2,941	150,615	151,972	52
Skåne	11,027	1,068,587	1,114,368	101
Kristianstad	1,250	289,251	294,709	48

	Land area (in sq. km)	Population (1990 census)	Population 31 Dec 1996	Density per sq. km 31 Dec. 1996
Malmöhus	4,938	778,939	817,022	165
Halland	5,454	254,568	270,060	50
Göteborg and Bohus	5,141	739,863	775,638	151
Älvsborg	11,395	441,031	448,074	39
Skaraborg	7,937	276,698	278,263	35
Värmland	17,586	283,148	282,147	16
Örebro	8,517	272,474	275,855	32
Västmanland	6,302	258,544	259,987	41
Kopparberg	28,193	288,919	288,171	10
Gävleborg	18,192	289,346	286,789	16
Västernorrland	21,678	261,099	256,587	12
Jämtland	49,443	135,724	134,561	3
Västerbotten	55,401	251,846	259,895	5
Norrbotten	98,911	263,546	264,320	3

There are some 17,000 Sami (Lapps).

On 31 Dec. 1996 aliens in Sweden numbered 433,174. Of these, 121,069 were from Nordic countries; 157,392 from Northern Europe; 24,862 from Africa; 12,371 from North America; 18,826 from South America; 94,474 from Asian countries; 2,410 from USSR; 1,695 from Oceania; and 75 Country unknown.

Immigration: 1995, 45,887; 1996, 39,895. Emigration: 1995, 33,984; 1996, 33,884.

Population of the 50 largest communities, 31 Dec. 1996:

Stockholm	718,462	Södertälje	82,589	Sollentuna	55,476
Göteborg	454,016	Karlstad	79,469	Falun	55,005
Malmö	248,007	Huddinge	78,873	Solna	54,644
Uppsala	184,507	Skellefteå	74,684	Mölndal	54,492
Linköping	131,898	Kristianstad	73,726	Trollhättan	52,338
Västerås	124,084	Växjö	73,089	Varberg	52,134
Norrköping	123,531	Luleå	71,238	Norrtälje	50,767
Örebro	120,774	Nacka	71,213	Hässleholm	49,681
Jönköping	115,636	Botkyrka	70,700	Skövde	49,643
Helsingborg	114,866	Haninge	66,100	Uddevalla	49,167
Umeå	102,487	Kungsbacka	61,477	Nyköping	48,730
Lund	97,208	Karlskrona	60,388	Borlänge	48,457
Borås	96,246	Östersund	59,497	Motala	42,754
Sundsvall	94,440	Täby	59,445	Piteå	40,859
Gävle	90,678	Järfälla	58,772	Västervik	39,256
Eskilstuna	88,688	Gotland	57,971	Falkenberg	39,010
Halmstad	83,549	Örnsköldsvik	57,742		

A fixed link with Denmark will be created in 2000 when the Öresund motorway and railway bridge between Malmö and Copenhagen is completed.

The official language is Swedish.

SOCIAL STATISTICS
Statistics for calendar years:

	Total living births	To mothers single, divorced or widowed	Stillborn	Marriages	Divorces	Deaths exclusive of still-born
1994	112,257	57,927	348	34,203	22,740	91,844
1995	103,422	54,769	350	33,642	22,885	93,955
1996	95,297	51,348	330	33,484	21,612	94,133

Rates, 1996, per 1,000 population: Births, 10·8; deaths, 10·6; marriages, 3·8. Sweden has the highest rate of births outside marriage in Europe, at nearly 54% in 1996. In 1994 the most popular age range for marrying was 25–29 for both males and females, followed by 30–34 for both males and females. Expectation of life in 1997 (estimate): Males, 76·4 years; females, 81·9. Infant mortality, 1990–95, 5 per

1,000 live births. Fertility rate, 1990–95, 2·0 births per woman, up from 1·6 in 1980–85. Sweden and Denmark are the only European countries where the rate went up by such an extent over the same period—in most of Europe it went down.

CLIMATE
The north has severe winters, with snow lying for 4–7 months. Summers are fine but cool, with long daylight hours. Further south, winters are less cold, summers are warm and rainfall well distributed throughout the year, with a slight summer maximum. Stockholm, Jan. 3·2°C, July 18·4°C. Annual rainfall 385 mm.

CONSTITUTION AND GOVERNMENT
The reigning King is **Carl XVI Gustaf**, b. 30 April 1946, succeeded on the death of his grandfather Gustaf VI Adolf, 15 Sept. 1973, married 19 June 1976 to *Silvia* Renate Sommerlath, b. 23 Dec. 1943 (Queen of Sweden). *Daughter* and *Heir Apparent:* Crown Princess Victoria Ingrid Alice Désirée, Duchess of Västergötland, b. 14 July 1977; *son:* Prince Carl Philip Edmund Bertil, Duke of Värmland, b. 13 May 1979; *daughter:* Princess Madeleine Thérèse Amelie Josephine, Duchess of Hälsingland and Gästrikland, b. 10 June 1982. *Sisters of the King.* Princess Margaretha, b. 31 Oct. 1934, married 30 June 1964 to John Ambler; Princess Birgitta (Princess of Sweden), b. 19 Jan. 1937, married 25 May 1961 (civil marriage) and 30 May 1961 (religious ceremony) to Johann Georg, Prince of Hohenzollern; Princess Désirée, b. 2 June 1938, married 5 June 1964 to Baron Niclas Silfverschiöld; Princess Christina, b. 3 Aug. 1943, married 15 June 1974 to Tord Magnuson. *Uncles of the King.* Count Sigvard Bernadotte of Wisborg, b. on 7 June 1907; Count Carl Johan, Bernadotte of Wisborg, b. on 31 Oct. 1916. *Aunt of the King.* Princess Ingrid (Princess of Sweden, Dowager Queen of Denmark), b. 28 March 1910, married 24 May 1935 to Frederik, Crown Prince of Denmark (King Frederik IX), died 14 Jan. 1972.

Under the 1975 Constitution Sweden is a representative and parliamentary democracy. The King is Head of State, but does not participate in government. Parliament is the single-chamber *Riksdag* of 349 members elected for a period of 4 years in direct, general elections.

The manner of election to the *Riksdag* is proportional. The country is divided into 29 constituencies. In these constituencies 310 members are elected. The remaining 39 seats constitute a nationwide pool intended to give absolute proportionality to parties that receive at least 4% of the votes. A party receiving less than 4% of the votes in the country is, however, entitled to participate in the distribution of seats in a constituency, if it has obtained at least 12% of the votes cast there.

A parliament, the *Sameting*, was instituted for the Sami (Lapps) in 1993.

National Anthem. 'Du gamla, du fria' ('Thou ancient, thou free'); words by R. Dybeck; folk-tune.

RECENT ELECTIONS
At the elections of 20 Sept. 1998 turn-out was 81·4%. A total of 5,374,588 votes were cast of which 5,261,122 were valid votes. The Social Democratic Party (SDP) won 131 seats with 36·6% of votes cast (162 with 45·3% in 1994), the Moderate Party 82 with 22·7% (80 with 22·4%), the Left Party (ex-Communists) 43 with 12·0% (22 with 6·2%), the Christian Democratic Party 42 with 11·8% (14 with 4·1%), the Centre Party 18 with 5·1% (27 with 7·7%), the Liberal Party 17 with 4·7% (26 with 7·2%) and the Green Party 16 with 4·5% (18 with 5%). Of the 349 Members of Parliament there are 200 men (57·3%) and 149 women (42·7%), the highest percentage of women for any parliament in the world.

CURRENT ADMINISTRATION
A minority Social Democratic government was formed in Oct. 1998, which comprised in March 1999:
  Prime Minister: Göran Persson (b. 1949).
  Deputy Prime Minister: Lena Hjelm-Wallén.
  Minister of Justice: Laila Freivalds. *Foreign Affairs:* Anna Lindh. *Agriculture and Lapp Affairs:* Margareta Winberg. *Culture:* Marita Ulvskog. *Defence:* Björn von

Sydow. *Education:* Thomas Östros. *Environment:* Kjell Larsson. *Finance:* Erik Åsbrink. *Social Affairs:* Lars Engqvist. *Trade and Industry:* Björn Rosengren.

The *Speaker* is Birgitta Dahl.

Local Government. The country is divided into 21 counties *(län)* subdivided into 288 municipalities, each with an elected council. The Government appoints a Governor to each county who is chair of a 14-member board, elected from the county by the county council for a 4-year period.

Gotland consists of only one municipality. The parishes, 2,528 in 1997, are the local units of the Swedish Lutheran Church and have the same status as municipalities. The publicly elected parochial church council is the supreme decision-making body in larger parishes. Small parishes have the parish meeting, a form of direct democracy.

Regional and local elections took place simultaneously with the parliamentary elections on 20 Sept. 1998.

DEFENCE

The Supreme Commander is, under the Government, in command of the three services. He is assisted by the Swedish Armed Forces HQ.

There is conscription of 7–15 months for males. Refresher training (3–34 days) is obligatory. Females have the possibility to serve on a voluntary basis. Conscription is due to be scaled down in 2002.

In 1997 military expenditure totalled US$5,481m. (US$619 per capita), representing 2·4% of GDP. Defence spending is to be cut by more than 10% (4bn. kr.) per year following a decline in possible military threats in the Nordic and Baltic Sea region since the collapse of Soviet communism. A reduction in army brigades, airforce divisions and naval vessels is due to come into effect in 2002.

Army. The peace-time Army consists for training purposes of 38 mechanized, cavalry, infantry, artillery and other units. On mobilization to a war footing the Field Army comprises 3 divisional HQs, 4 infantry, 3 Arctic, 1 mechanized Arctic and 5 mechanized brigades and 3 artillery regiments. Anti-aircraft units, engineers and supply are included as well as units to support command and control. There are also Territorial Defence units. Equipment includes 70 Centurion, 160 Strv 121 Leopard and 120 Strv 122 Leopard main battle tanks. The Army Aviation operate 20 anti-tank helicopters and 50 transport helicopters. Army strength, 1998, 36,000 (26,000 conscripts and active reservists). The Army can mobilize about 350,000.

Navy. Naval forces are divided between 2 branches: the Fleet and Coastal Artillery. There are 4 Naval Command Areas, covering southern, eastern, western and northern coasts. The Fleet is organised in flotillas covering different branches. The branches are: surface and under-water warfare (2 flottilas), mine warfare (2 flottilas) and submarine (1 flottila). Each branch is represented in Sweden's different coastal areas. The Coastal Artillery have 2 main tasks: Fixed coastal defence and mobile coastal defence. The fixed coastal defence is organized in Coast Artillery Regiments consisting of artillery up to 120-mm calibre and land-sea missiles. The mobile element consists of 2 Mobile Coastal Artillery Battalions, 1 Heavy Coastal Missile Battery and 6 Amphibious Battalions. The Coastal Artillery operates 8 coastal and 12 small patrol craft and some 140 small amphibious craft. The Naval Air Arm comprises 14 Boeing Vertol Kawasaki KV 107 helicopters and 10 AB-206 Jet-Ranger helicopters, and 1 Aviocar for anti-submarine warfare and electronic surveillance.

The personnel of the Navy in 1998 totalled 12,700 (including 3,100 reservists and 4,000 conscripts). The Navy can mobilize about 45,000.

A separate civil Coast Guard, 600-strong, operates some 70 inshore cutters, patrol boats and service craft, and 4 aircraft.

Air Force. There are 3 Air Commands. After mobilization to a war footing, the Air Force consists of 8 fighter squadrons, 2 medium attack/reconnaissance squadrons, 2 multi-role squadrons, 4 central transport and 4 regional transport squadrons, 16 combat air-bases and 6 combat command, and control and air surveillance battalions. Combat aircraft include JAS 39 Gripens, JA 37 Viggens and AJS 37 Viggens.

Strength (1998) 10,000 (3,150 conscripts), with approximately 250 combat aircraft. The Air Force can mobilize about 70,000.

During peace-time all the helicopters of the Army, Navy and Air Force are organized into a joint Helicopter Wing with a staff and 4 helicopter battalions.

INTERNATIONAL RELATIONS
Sweden is a member of the UN, EU and the NATO Partnership for Peace, and is a signatory to the Schengen Accord, which abolishes border controls between Austria, Belgium, Denmark, Finland, France, Germany, Greece, Iceland, Italy, Luxembourg, the Netherlands, Norway, Portugal, Spain and Sweden.

ECONOMY
Performance. Real GDP growth was 1·3% in 1996 and 1·8% in 1997. It was forecast to rise to 3·0% in 1998. In 1997 the state debt amounted to 1,432,076m. kr.

Budget. Revenue and expenditure of the total budget (Current and Capital) for financial years ending 30 June (in 1m. kr.):

	Revenue	Expenditure		Revenue	Expenditure
1992–93	377,743	565,548	1994–95	423,183	579,421
1993–94	376,925	554,023	1995–96	787,570	985,852

Revenue and expenditure for 1998 (1,000 kr.):

Revenue	
Taxes on income	34,205
Tax on income—legal entities	57,884
Other revenue	5,765
Social security fees	208,777
Estate tax	24,240
Other taxes on property	10,865
VAT	154,884
Excise duties	83,430
Compensation for municipalities and county councils	20,966
Income from government activities	39,704
Income from sale of assets	15,001
Loans repaid	2,691
Computed revenue	5,337
Contributions, etc., from the EU	10,979
Total revenue	676,077

Expenditure	
The Swedish political system	3,977
Economy and fiscal administration	2,063
Tax administration and collection	5,662
Justice	21,034
Foreign policy administration and international co-operation	2,811
Total defence	41,244
International development assistance	11,434
Immigrants and refugees	3,864
Health care, medical care, social services	22,500
Financial security in the event of illness and disability	37,192
Financial security in old age	62,701
Financial security for families and children	35,814
Financial security in the event of unemployment	42,723
The labour market and working life	47,542
Study support	21,334
Education and university research	27,051
Culture, the media, religious organizations and leisure	7,335
Planning, housing supply and construction	22,826
Regional balance and development	3,605
General environment and conservation	1,178
Energy	1,583
Communications	24,101
Agriculture and forestry, fisheries, etc.	13,726
Business sector	2,698
General grants to municipalities	93,049
Interest on Central Government Debt, etc.	109,125
Contribution to the European Community	19,645
Total areas of expenditure	687,815
Take-up of funds previously allocated	5,000
Total Expenditure	692,815

VAT is 25% (reduced rate, 12%).

Currency. The unit of currency is the *krona* (SEK), of 100 *öre*. Inflation was 0·8% in 1996, and by June 1998 had dropped to 0·6%. Foreign exchange reserves were US$8,013m. and gold reserves 4·72m. troy oz. in Feb. 1998.

Banking and Finance. The central bank and bank of issue is the *Sveriges Riksbank*, whose *Governor* is appointed for 5 years by 8 trustees, 7 of whom are appointed by Parliament. The *Governor* is Urban Backström. On 31 Dec. 1996 there were 37 commercial banks. Their total deposits amounted to 771,476m. kr.; advances to the public amounted to 724,278m. kr. On 31 Dec. 1996 there were 87 savings banks. The largest banks are Svenska Handelsbanken, MeritaNordbanken (formed in 1997 when Nordbanken of Sweden merged with Merita of Finland), FöreningsSparbanken and Skandinavska Enskilda Banken.

There is a stock exchange in Stockholm.

Weights and Measures. The metric system is obligatory.

ENERGY AND NATURAL RESOURCES

Electricity. Sweden is rich in hydro-power resources. Installed capacity was 35,559 MW in 1995, of which 16,593 MW was in hydro-electric plants, 10,409 MW in nuclear plants and 8,557 MW in thermal plants. Electricity net production in 1995 was 143,316m. kWh. Consumption per capita in 1995 was an estimated 14,862 kWh. A referendum of 1980 called for the phasing out of nuclear power by 2010. In Feb. 1997 the government began denuclearization by designating one of the 10 reactors for decommissioning. The state corporation Vattenfall was given the responsibility of financing and overseeing the transition to the use of non-fossil fuel alternatives.

Minerals. Sweden is a leading producer of iron ore. There are also deposits of copper, lead, zinc and alum shale containing oil and uranium. Iron ore produced, 1996, 20·3m. tonnes; copper ore, 1994, 297,999 tonnes.

Agriculture. In 1996 the total area of land given over to farms of 2 ha or more was 8,134,160 ha; of this 2,811,534 was arable land, 446,458 natural pasture, 4,077,481 forest and 798,689 other. Of the land used for arable farming, 2–5 ha holdings covered a total area of 55,858 ha; 5·1–10 ha holdings covered 132,551 ha; 10·1–20 ha, 278,256; 20·1–30 ha, 271,369; 30·1–50 ha, 490,386; 50·1–100 ha, 773,512 and holdings larger than 100 ha covered 809,602 ha. There were 90,488 agricultural enterprises in 1996 compared to 150,014 in 1971 and 282,187 in 1951. Around 40% of the enterprises were between 5 and 20 ha.

Agriculture accounts for 0·4% of GDP (the lowest of any EU member country), 5·8% of exports and 7·9% of imports. The agricultural sector employs 3% of the workforce.

	Area (1,000 ha)			Production (1,000 tonnes)		
Chief crops	1994	1995	1996	1994	1995	1996
Wheat	251·8	261·4	334·6	1,345	1,554	2,029·9
Rye	38·96	39·7	33·6	173	206	165·7
Barley	473·0	453·4	468·6	1,661	1,793	2,113·4
Oats	341·4	278·3	283·6	991	947	1,199·8
Potatoes	33·0	35·0	36·6	763	792	853·2
Sugarbeet	53·4	57·5	59·2	2,350	2,479	2,430·0
Tame hay	780·0	782·0	772·4	3,156	3,378	3,365·2
Oil linseed	128·5	104·6	72·8	...	...	9·9

Milk production (in 1,000 tonnes) 1996 (1995): 3,304 (3,316). Butter production (in 1,000 tonnes): 57 (57); cheese: 127 (129).

Livestock 1996: Cattle, 1,790,240; sheep and lambs, 469,035; pigs, 2,348,754; poultry, 7,897,240. There were 279,869 reindeer in Sami villages in 1994. Harvest of moose during open season 1996: 91,079.

Forestry. Forests form one of the country's greatest natural assets. The growing stock includes 45% Norway spruce, 39% Scots pine and 15% deciduous trees. In 1995 forests covered 24,425,000 ha (59·3% of the land area). Municipal and state ownership accounts for 37% of the forests, companies own 13% and the remaining half is in private hands. Sweden is the largest producer of roundwood in Europe. In 1996, 56·4m. cu. metres of wood was felled, of which 30·8m. cu. metres were sawlogs, 20·9m. cu. metres pulpwood, 3·8m. cu. metres fuelwood and 0·9 cu. metres other.

Fisheries. In 1996 the total catch of the sea fisheries was 361,693 tonnes. In 1995, 5,047 tonnes were caught from inland waters.

INDUSTRY

Manufacturing is mainly based on metals and forest resources. Chemicals (especially petro-chemicals), building materials and decorative glass and china are also important.

Industry groups	No. of establishments 1996	Average no. of wage-earners 1996	Sales value of production (gross) in 1m. kr. 1996
Mines and quarries	149	5,328	9,780
Manufacturing industry	8,707	405,790	931,782
Food products, beverages and tobacco	842	41,518	102,694
Textiles and textile products, leather and leather products	270	8,450	9,765
Wood and wood products	714	23,747	41,015
Pulp, paper and paper products publishers and printers	1,197	54,253	132,481
Coke, refined petroleum products and nuclear fuel	16	1,228	26,373
Chemicals, chemical products and man-made fibres	317	14,339	65,778
Rubber and plastic products	407	15,656	23,115
Other non-metallic mineral products	357	11,543	16,234
Basic metals	159	23,913	67,848
Fabricated metal products, machinery and equipment	4,018	196,655	427,358
Other manufacturing industries	410	14,488	19,116

Labour. In 1997 there were 3,922,000 persons in the labour force, employed as follows: 763,000 in health and social work; 800,000 in manufacturing, mining, quarrying, electricity and water services; 761,000 in trade and communication; 446,000 in financial services and business activities; 306,000 in education, research and development; 305,000 in personal services and cultural activities, and sanitation; 211,000 in public administration; 109,000 in agriculture, forestry and fishing. The unemployment rate in 1996 of 8·1% declined slightly in 1997 to 8·0%, with a forecast of a further drop to 6·7% for 1998.

Trade Unions. At 31 Dec. 1997 the Swedish Trade Union Confederation (LO) had 20 member unions with a total membership of 2,129,504; the Central Government Organization of Salaried Employees (TCO) had 20, with 1,252,020; the Swedish Confederation of Professional Associations (SACO) had 26, with 426,234; the Central Organization of Swedish Workers had 8,798 members.

In March 1997 employers' organizations and trade unions signed an agreement on the conduct of wage negotiations in 1998. The agreement involved 0·8m. workers, and provided for the establishment of an Industrial Committee to promote the development of industry.

INTERNATIONAL TRADE

Imports and Exports. Imports and exports (in 1m. kr.):

	1992	1993	1994	1995	1996
Imports	290,929	334,257	399,152	460,578	446,508
Exports	326,031	388,290	471,602	567,836	566,480

Breakdown by Standard International Trade Classification (SITC, revision 3) categories (value in 1m. kr.; 1996 figures are estimates):

	Imports		Exports	
	1995	1996	1995	1996
0. Food and live animals	26,232	26,866	11,182	12,004
1. Beverages and tobacco	2,897	3,940	1,553	1,777
2. Raw materials	17,795	14,070	43,905	35,754
3. Fuels and lubricants	28,522	38,203	11,923	15,161
4. Animal and vegetable oils	1,276	932	789	686
5. Chemicals	52,161	47,740	51,032	49,936
6. Manufactured materials	77,836	68,954	137,200	129,494
7. Machinery and transport equipment	189,899	184,985	260,609	271,294
8. Manufactured items	63,736	60,699	48,583	49,134
9. Other	224	119	1,059	1,240

Principal exports in 1996 (in tonnes): Paper and board, 4,494,688; lumber, sawn and planed, 10,962,00 sq. metres; power-generating non-electrical machinery, 13,390; chemical wood pulp, 2,744,532; newsprint, 1,958,019; mechanical handling equipment, 149,964; flat-rolled products of iron, 1,236,008; pumps and centrifuges, 61,265.

Imports and exports by countries (in 1m. kr.):

	Imports from		Exports to	
	1994	1996	1994	1996
Belgium	13,905	16,268	23,224	25,033
Denmark	27,032	33,422	32,621	34,783
Finland	25,104	25,183	22,547	28,865
France	22,278	25,014	24,125	26,313
Germany	73,607	83,818	62,777	66,284
Italy	15,339	14,312	17,833	18,304
Netherlands	16,279	33,483	24,941	31,331
Norway	24,341	34,828	38,358	47,910
Switzerland	7,643	8,420	9,120	10,083
UK	38,306	44,621	48,042	53,659
USA	34,167	25,880	37,624	46,982

COMMUNICATIONS

Roads. On 1 Jan. 1996 there were 0·21m. km of public roads comprising: State administered roads, 97,908 km; municipal, 38,300 km; private roads with subsidies, 73,913 km. A total of 74,642 km were surfaced. Motor vehicles on 31 Dec. 1995 included 3,631,000 passenger cars, 323,000 buses and trucks and 117,000 motor cycles.

Rail. Total length of railways at 31 Dec. 1996 was 10,939 km (7,469 km electrified). The state railway operator SJ carried 99m. passengers and 54m. tonnes of freight in 1996. Some lines are run under contract by private operators. There is a metro in Stockholm (108 km), and tram/light rail networks in Stockholm, Göteborg (81 km) and Norrköping.

Civil Aviation. The main international airports are at Stockholm (Arlanda), Göteborg (Landvetter) and Malmö (Sturup). The principal carrier is Scandinavian Airlines System (SAS), of which SAS Sverige AB is the Swedish partner (SAS Denmark A/S and SAS Norge ASA being the other two). SAS has a joint paid-up capital of 14,241m. Sw. kr. Capitalization of SAS Sverige AB, 5,560m. Sw. kr., of which 50% is owned by the Government and 50% by private enterprises.

In 1997, the total distance flown was 109·0m. km; passenger-km, 8,893·7m.; goods, 294·7m. tonne-km. These figures represent the Swedish share of the SAS traffic (Swedish domestic and three-sevenths of international traffic). Malmö Aviation and Skyways AB, both Sweden-based carriers, operate some international as well as domestic flights. In 1998 services were also provided by Aer Lingus, Aeroflot, Air Baltic, Air Canada, Air China, Air Express, Air France, Air Lithuania, Air Malta, Air Ukraine, Airborne of Sweden, Alitalia, American Airlines, Austrian Airlines, Balkan, Belavia, Braathens, British Airways, Continental Airlines, Croatia Airlines, Czech Airlines, Delta Air Lines, Deutsche BA, Egyptair, El Al, Estonia Air, Falcon Air, Finnair, Flying Enterprise, Guard Air, Iberia, Icelandair, Interimpex-Avioimpex, Iran Air, JAT, Kenya Airways, KLM, KLM UK, Lithuanian Airlines, LOT, Lufthansa, Maersk Air, Malév, Minskavia, Muk Air, Royal Air Maroc, Ryanair, SABENA, Skargardsflyg, Swedeways Air Lines, Swissair, Syrian Arab Airlines, TAP, Thai Airways International, Trans Travel Airlines, Turkish Airlines, Tyrolean Airways, United Airlines, West Air Sweden and Wideroe's Flyveselskap.

In 1996 Stockholm (Arlanda) handled 13,881,559 passengers (8,232,122 on international flights) and 112,497 tonnes of freight. Göteborg (Landvetter) was the second busiest airport in 1996, handling 3,211,345 passengers (2,079,516 on international flights) and 32,044 tonnes of freight.

Shipping. There are major ports at Helsingborg, Malmö, Stockholm and Göteborg. The mercantile marine consisted on 31 Dec. 1996 of 450 vessels of 2·95m. GRTs. Vessels to and from foreign countries (exclusive of passenger liners and ferries) with cargoes and in ballast, in 1995: With cargoes, 27,995 with a gross tonnage of 155·53m.; in ballast, 16,241 with a gross tonnage of 68·53m.

Telecommunications. There were 6,010,000 main telephone lines in 1997, or 678 per 1,000 population. In 1995 there were 6,830 telephone exchanges. 3·8m. cellular phones were in use in 1998. More than 43% of Swedes are mobile telephone subscribers—a penetration rate only exceeded in Finland. There were 1,700,000 PCs in 1995 (193 per 1,000 population) and 329,000 fax machines. In Nov. 1998 there were 2·9m. Internet users, or nearly a third of the total population.

Postal Services. There were 1,853 post offices at the end of 1995. A total of 4,533m. pieces of mail were processed in 1995, equivalent to 513 per person.

SOCIAL INSTITUTIONS

Justice. The administration of justice is independent. The Attorney-General (appointed by the Government) and 3 Ombudsmen exercise a check on judicial affairs administration. In 1995–96 the Ombudsmen received altogether 5,121 cases, of which 125 were instituted on their own initiative.

Sweden has no constitutional court. However, in each particular case the courts do have a certain right to ascertain whether a statute meets the standards set out by superordinate provisions.

The courts can be divided into general or ordinary courts and special courts. There are 2 general court organizations: the courts of general jurisdiction and the administrative courts. These organizations are, in all essentials, parallel and are structured as a triple instance system. The general courts handle criminal cases and civil disputes between individuals. The general administrative courts primarily deal with cases which relate to matters between the community at large and a private individual. A number of courts of special jurisdiction exist beside the courts, such as the labour court.

There is a 3-tier hierarchy of courts: The Supreme Court; 6 intermediate courts of appeal; and 97 district courts. Of the district courts 27 also serve as real estate courts and 6 as water rights courts. When a permanent judge is appointed by the government, he cannot, in principle, be dismissed.

District courts are courts of first instance and deal with both civil and criminal cases. Petty cases are tried by 1 judge. Civil and criminal cases are tried as a rule by 3 to 4 judges or in minor cases by 1 judge. Disputes of greater consequence relating to the Marriage Code or the Code relating to Parenthood and Guardianship are tried by a judge and a jury of 3–4 lay assessors. More serious criminal cases are tried by a judge and a jury of 5 members (lay assessors) in felony cases, and of 3 members in misdemeanour cases. The cases in courts of appeal are generally tried by 4 or 5 judges.

Those with low incomes can receive free legal aid out of public funds. In criminal cases a suspected person has the right to a defence counsel, paid out of public funds.

The Attorney-General and the Judicial Commissioner for the Judiciary and Civil Administration (Ombudsman) supervise the application in the public sector of acts of Parliament and regulations.

There were 76 penal and correctional institutions for offenders in 1996 with an average population of 6,000 inmates (including offenders in remand prison).

Religion. The national church is the Swedish Lutheran Church, due to be disestablished in 2000. It is headed by Archbishop Karl Gustaf Hammar (b. 1943) and has its metropolitan see at Uppsala. In 1996 there were 13 bishoprics and 2,544 parishes. The clergy are chiefly supported from the parishes and the proceeds of the church lands. Other denominations, in 1996: Pentecostal Movement, 91,939 members; The Mission Covenant Church of Sweden, 70,072; Salvation Army, 26,089; Orebo Missionary Society, 22,801; Swedish Evangelical Mission, 26,089; The Baptist Union of Sweden, 18,548; Swedish Alliance Missionary Society, 12,846; Holiness Mission, 6,393. There were also 164,015 Roman Catholics (under a Bishop resident at Stockholm).

Education. In 1995–96 there were 640,797 pupils in primary education (grades 1–6 in compulsory comprehensive schools); secondary education at the lower stage (grades 7–9 in compulsory comprehensive schools) comprised 297,743 pupils. In secondary education at the higher stage (the integrated upper secondary school), there were 66,561 pupils in Oct. 1995 (excluding pupils in the fourth year of the technical course regarded as third-level education). The folk high schools, 'people's colleges', had 37,148 pupils in courses of more than 10 weeks in 1994–95.

In municipal adult education there were 155,971 students in 1995.

There are also special schools for pupils with visual and hearing handicaps (766 pupils in 1995) and for those who are mentally retarded (13,417 pupils).

In 1994–95 there were in integrated institutions for higher education 269,815 students enrolled for undergraduate studies. The number of students enrolled for postgraduate studies in 1995 was 16,079.

In 1995 total expenditure on education came to 8·1% of GNP and represented 11·6% of total government expenditure.

Health. In 1996 there were 23,000 doctors, 14,300 dentists, 73,600 nurses and midwives and 38,139 hospital beds. In 1994 the total cost of healthcare was 112,983m. kr., representing 7% of GDP.

Welfare. Social insurance benefits are granted mainly according to uniform statutory principles. All persons resident in Sweden are covered, regardless of citizenship. All schemes are compulsory, except for unemployment insurance. Benefits are usually income-related. Most social security schemes are at present undergoing extensive discussion and changes. Recent proposals include the introduction of a new pension scheme.

Type of scheme	Beneficiaries	Expenditure 1995 (in 1m. kr.)
Sickness and parental insurance	All residents	53,352
Work injury insurance	All gainfully occupied persons	6,793
Unemployment insurance	Members of unemployment insurance societies	36,068
Basic and supplementary pensions (old-age, disability, survivors)	All resident or gainfully occupied persons (2,448,397)	182,894
Partial pensions	All gainfully occupied persons between 61 and 64 (38,000)	2,370
Child allowance	All children below 16 (1,770,000)	16,959

The total social insurance expenditure amounted to 309,000m. kr. in 1995, representing 19% of GDP.

CULTURE

Broadcasting. 3,368,000 combined radio and TV reception fees were paid in 1995. There were an estimated 8m. radio and 4·4m. television receivers in 1996. *Sveriges Radio AB* is a non-commercial semi-governmental corporation, transmitting 3 national programmes and regional programmes. It also broadcasts 2 TV programmes (colour by PAL). There are 3 commercial satellite channels (TV3, TV4 and Nordic), and a land-based commercial channel.

Cinema. In 1996 there were 1,169 cinemas. Total attendances in 1995 were 15·2m.

Press. In 1996 there were 168 daily newspapers with an average weekday net circulation of 4,284,000.

Tourism. There were 2,376,000 foreign tourists in 1996, bringing revenue of US$3·68bn. In 1996 (1995) foreign visitors stayed 3,930,464 (3,693,727) nights in hotels and 899,292 (1,014,027) in holiday villages and youth hostels.

Libraries. In 1996 there were 1 national library, 1,656 public libraries, 31 university libraries and 42 special libraries.

Museums and Galleries. Sweden had 228 museums in 1997 with a combined total of 15,061,412 visits.

DIPLOMATIC REPRESENTATIVES
Of Sweden in Great Britain (11 Montagu Pl., London, W1H 2AL)
Ambassador: Mats Bergquist, CMG.

SWEDEN

Of Great Britain in Sweden (Skarpögatan 6-8, S-115 93 Stockholm)
Ambassador: Roger Bone, CMG.

Of Sweden in the USA (1501 M Street, NW, Suite 900, Washington, D.C., 20005-1702)
Ambassador: Rolf Ekéus.

Of the USA in Sweden (Strandvägen 101, S-115 89 Stockholm)
Ambassador: Lyndon L. Olson, Jr.

Of Sweden to the United Nations
Ambassador: Hans Dahlgren.

FURTHER READING
Statistics Sweden. *Statistik Årsbok/Statistical Yearbook of Sweden.—Historisk statistik för Sverige* (Historical Statistics of Sweden). 1955 ff.—*Allmän månadsstatistik* (Monthly Digest of Swedish Statistics).—*Statistiska meddelanden* (Statistical Reports). From 1963

Andersson, L., *A History of Sweden.* Stockholm, 1962
Grosskopf, G., *The Swedish Tax System.* Stockholm, 1986
Gustafsson, A., *Local Government in Sweden.* Stockholm, 1988
Hadenius, S., *Swedish Politics during the Twentieth Century.* Stockholm, 1988
Heelo, H. and Madsen, H., *Policy and Politics in Sweden: Principled Pragmatism.* Philadelphia, 1987
Henrekson, M., *An Economic Analysis of Swedish Government Expenditure.* Aldershot, 1992
Lindström, E., *The Swedish Parliamentary System.* Stockholm, 1983
Olsson, S. E., *Social Policy and Welfare State in Sweden.* Lund, 1990
Peterson, C.-G., *Local Self-Government and Democracy in Transition.* Stockholm, 1989
Petersson, O., *Swedish Government and Politics.* Stockholm, 1994
Sather, L. B. and Swanson, A., *Sweden.* [Bibliography] Oxford and Santa Barbara (CA), 1987
Scott, F. D., *Sweden: the Nation's History.* Univ. of Minnesota Press, 1983
Sveriges statskalender. Published by Vetenskapsakademien. Annual, from 1813

National library: Kungliga Biblioteket, Stockholm.
National statistical office: Statistics Sweden, S-11581 Stockholm.
Website: http://www.scb.se/
Swedish Institute Website: http://www.si.se

SWITZERLAND

Schweizerische
Eidtgenossenschaft—
Confédération Suisse—
Confederazione Svizzera[1]

Capital: Berne
Population estimate, 2000: 7·41m.
GNP per capita: (PPP$) 26,340
HDI/world rank: 0·930/16

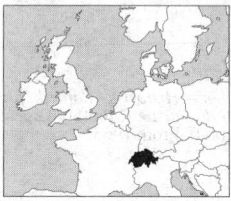

KEY HISTORICAL EVENTS

The history of Switzerland can be traced back to Aug. 1291 when the Uri, Schwyz and Unterwalden entered into a defensive league. In 1353 the league included 8 members and in 1515, 13. Various territories were acquired either by single cantons or by several in common and in 1648 the league became formally independent of the Holy Roman Empire. No addition was made to the number of cantons until 1798 in which year, under the influence of France, the unified Helvetic Republic was formed. This failed to satisfy the Swiss and in 1803 Napoleon, in the Act of Mediation, granted a new constitution and increased the number of cantons to 19. In 1815 the perpetual neutrality of Switzerland and the inviolability of her territory were guaranteed by Austria, France, Great Britain, Portugal, Prussia, Spain and Sweden, and the Federal Pact, which included 3 new cantons, was accepted by the Congress of Vienna. In 1848 a new constitution was passed. The 22 cantons set up a federal government (consisting of a federal parliament and a federal council) and a federal tribunal. This constitution, in turn, was on 29 May 1874 superseded by the present constitution, which also combines the federal principle with a national and local use of referendums. Female franchise dates only from Feb. 1971. In a national referendum held in Sept. 1978, 69·9% voted in favour of the establishment of a new canton, Jura, which was established on 1 Jan. 1979.

Switzerland was neutral in both world wars. After the First World War, it joined the League of Nations, which was based in Geneva. But after the Second World War neutrality was thought to conflict with membership of the UN, though Switzerland participates in its agencies, and since 1948 has been a contracting party to the Statute of the International Court of Justice.

TERRITORY AND POPULATION

Switzerland is bounded in the west and north-west by France, north by Germany, east by Austria and south by Italy. Area and population by canton (with date of establishment), according to the census held on 1 Dec. 1980 and estimates of 31 Dec. 1994 and 31 Dec. 1997:

Canton	Area (sq. km)	Census 1 Dec. 1980	Estimate (in 1,000) 31 Dec. 1994	Estimate (in 1,000) 31 Dec. 1997
Zürich (1351)	1,729	1,122,839	1,167·6	1,175·5
Berne (1553)	6,050	912,022	943·6	942·0
Lucerne (1332)	1,493	296,159	337·7	340·5
Uri (1291)	1,077	33,883	35·9	35·9
Schwyz (1291)	908	97,354	120·6	122·4
Obwalden (1291)	490	25,865	31·1	31·3
Nidwalden (1291)	276	28,617	36·0	36·5
Glarus (Glaris) (1352)	685	36,718	39·3	39·4
Zug (1352)	239	75,930	90·3	92·4
Fribourg (Freiburg) (1481)	1,671	185,246	222·1	224·6
Solothurn (Soleure) (1481)	791	218,102	237·1	239·3
Basel-Town (Bâle-V.) (1501)	37	203,915	197·7	195·8
Basel-Country (Bâle-C.) (1501)	428	219,822	251·4	252·3
Schaffhausen (Schaffhouse) (1501)	299	69,413	74·0	74·0
Appenzell-Outer Rhoden (1513)	243	47,611	54·4	54·1

[1]The Latin 'Confoederatio Helvetica' is also in use.

1494

	Area	Census	Estimate (in 1,000)	Estimate (in 1,000)
Canton	(sq. km)	1 Dec. 1980	31 Dec. 1994	31 Dec. 1997
Appenzell-Inner Rhoden (1513)	173	12,844	14·7	14·8
St Gallen (St Gall) (1803)	2,026	391,995	440·7	442·4
Graubünden (Grisons) (1803)	7,105	164,641	184·3	185·1
Aargau (Argovie) (1803)	1,404	453,442	524·1	528·9
Thurgau (Thurgovie) (1803)	991	183,795	220·4	223·4
Ticino (Tessin) (1803)	2,812	265,899	302·4	305·2
Vaud (Waadt) (1803)	3,212	528,747	601·6	605·7
Valais (Wallis) (1815)	5,225	218,707	269·6	271·3
Neuchâtel (Neuenburg) (1815)	803	158,368	164·5	165·3
Geneva (1815)	282	349,040	391·1	395·5
Jura (1979)	836	64,986	69·0	69·2
Total	41,129	6,365,960	7,021·2	7,062·4

In 1994 there were 3,591,600 females and 1,331,600 resident foreign nationals. In 1995, 61% of the population lived in urban areas. Population density in 1997 was 172 per sq. km.

The UN gives a projected population for 2000 of 7·41m.

German, French and Italian are the official languages; Romansch (spoken mostly in Graubünden), hitherto a national language, was upgraded to 'semi-official' in 1996. German is spoken by the majority of inhabitants in 19 of the 26 cantons, French in Fribourg, Vaud, Valais, Neuchâtel, Jura and Geneva, and Italian in Ticino. At the 1990 census 63·6% of the population gave German as their mother tongue, 19·2% French, 7·6% Italian, 0·6% Romansch and 8·9% other languages. 1997 statistics are 65% German, 18·4% French, 9·8% Italian, and 0·8% Romansch.

At the end of 1994 the 5 largest cities were Zürich (353,361); Basle (179,639); Geneva (174,363); Berne (134,129); Lausanne (123,266). At the end of 1990 the population figures of conurbations were: Zürich, 841,100; Geneva, 394,800; Basle, 360,400; Berne, 299,500; Lausanne, 263,600; other towns 1994, (and their conurbations 1992), Winterthur, 88,168 (109,800); St Gallen, 75,541 (127,400); Lucerne, 61,656 (161,000); Biel, 52,197 (83,000).

SOCIAL STATISTICS
Statistics for calendar years:

	Live births	Marriages	Divorces	Deaths
1992	86,900	45,000	14,500	62,300
1993	83,762	43,257	15,053	62,512
1994	82,900	42,400	15,600	61,800
1995	82,203	40,820	15,703	63,387
1996	83,000	41,000	16,200	62,600

Rates (1996, per 1,000 population): Birth, 11·7; death, 8·8; marriage, 5·7; divorce, 2·3. In 1994 the most popular age range for marrying was 25–29 for both males and females. Expectation of life, 1997 est.: Males, 75·6 years; females, 82·1. Over the period 1990–95 the suicide rate per 100,000 population was 22·7 (men, 34·3; women, 11·6). Infant mortality, 1990–95, 5 per 1,000 live births; fertility rate, 1·5 births per woman.

CLIMATE
The climate is largely dictated by relief and altitude, and includes continental and mountain types. Summers are generally warm, with quite considerable rainfall; winters are fine, with clear, cold air. Berne, Jan. 32°F (0°C), July, 65°F (18·5°C). Annual rainfall 39·4" (986 mm).

CONSTITUTION AND GOVERNMENT
The Constitution dates from 29 May 1879. Switzerland is a republic. The highest authority is vested in the electorate, i.e., all Swiss citizens over 18. This electorate, besides electing its representatives to the Parliament has the voting power on amendments to, or on the revision of, the Constitution. It also takes decisions on laws and international treaties if requested by 50,000 voters or 8 cantons (facultative referendum), and it has the right of initiating constitutional amendments, the support

required for such demands being 100,000 voters (popular initiative). The Swiss vote in more referendums—3 or 4 a year—than any other nation. Between 1971 and 1997, 68 initiatives were put to the vote; but only 5 were adopted. Turn-out has dropped from a peak of 80% in 1947 to 42% in 1999.

The Federal Government is supreme in matters of peace, war and treaties; it regulates the army, the railway, telecommunication systems, the coining of money, the issue and repayment of banknotes and weights and measures. It also legislates on matters of copyright, bankruptcy, patents, sanitary policy in dangerous epidemics, and it may create and subsidize, besides the Polytechnic School at Zürich and at Lausanne, 2 federal universities and other educational institutions. There has also been entrusted to it the authority to decide on matters concerning public works for the whole or great part of Switzerland, such as those relating to rivers, forests and the construction of national highways and railways. By referendum of 13 Nov. 1898 it is also the authority in the entire spheres of common law. In 1957 the Federation was empowered to legislate on atomic energy matters and in 1961 on the construction of pipelines of petroleum and gas.

The legislative authority is vested in a parliament of 2 chambers: the Council of States (*Ständerat/Conseil des États*) and the National Council (*Nationalrat/Conseil National*). The Council of States is composed of 46 members, chosen and paid by the 23 cantons of the Confederation, 2 for each canton. The mode of their election and the term of membership depend on the canton. 3 of the cantons are politically divided–Basle into Town and Country, Appenzell into Outer-Rhoden and Inner-Rhoden, and Unterwalden into Obwalden and Nidwalden. Each of these 'half-cantons' sends 1 member to the State Council.

The National Council has 200 members directly elected for 4 years, in proportion to the population of the cantons, with the proviso that each canton or half-canton is represented by at least 1 member. The members are paid from federal funds. The parliament sits for 16 three-day sessions annually.

The 200 members are distributed among the cantons as follows:

Zürich	35	Appenzell—Outer- and Inner-Rhoden	3
Berne	29	St Gallen (St Gall)	12
Lucerne	9	Graubünden (Grisons)	5
Uri	1	Aargau (Argovie)	14
Schwyz	3	Thurgau (Thurgovie)	6
Unterwalden—Upper and Lower	2	Ticino (Tessin)	8
Glarus (Glaris)	1	Vaud (Waadt)	17
Zug	2	Valais (Wallis)	7
Fribourg (Freiburg)	6	Neuchâtel (Neuenburg)	5
Solothurn (Soleure)	7	Geneva	11
Basel (Bâle)—town and country	13	Jura	2
Schaffhausen (Schaffhouse)	2		

A general election takes place by ballot every 4 years. Every citizen of the republic who has entered on his 18th year is entitled to a vote, and any voter who is not a clergyman may be elected a deputy. Laws passed by both chambers may be submitted to direct popular vote, when 50,000 citizens or 8 cantons demand it; the vote can be only 'Yes' or 'No'. This principle, called the *referendum*, is frequently acted on.

The chief executive authority is deputed to the *Bundesrat*, or Federal Council, consisting of 7 members, elected from 7 different cantons for 4 years by the *United Federal Assembly*, i.e., joint sessions of both chambers. On 7 Feb. 1999 there was a referendum to decide whether to eliminate the condition that each cabinet minister come from a different one of the 26 cantons. 74·7% of votes cast were in favour of the proposal to change the conditions. The members of this council must not hold any other office in the Confederation or cantons, nor engage in any calling or business. In the Federal Parliament legislation may be introduced either by a member, or by either chamber, or by the Federal Council (but not by the people). Every citizen who has a vote for the National Council is eligible to become a member of the executive.

The *President* of the Federal Council (called President of the Confederation) and the Vice-President are the first magistrates of the Confederation. Both are elected by the United Federal Assembly for 1 calendar year from among the Federal Councillors, and are not immediately re-eligible to the same offices. The Vice-

President, however, may be, and usually is, elected to succeed the outgoing President.

The 7 members of the Federal Council act as ministers, or chiefs of the 7 administrative departments of the republic. The city of Berne is the seat of the Federal Council and the central administrative authorities.

National Anthem. 'Trittst im Morgenrot daher'/'Sur nos monts quand le soleil'/'Quando il ciel' di porpora' ('Step into the rosy dawn'); German words by Leonard Widmer, French by C. Chatelanat, Italian by C. Valsangiacomo, tune by Alberik Zwyssig.

RECENT ELECTIONS
On 22 Oct. 1995 elections were held for both chambers of the federal parliament; turn-out was 42%. In the Council of States, the Radical Democratic Party (RDP) gained 17 seats (18 in 1991); the Christian Democratic Party (CDP), 16 (16); the Swiss Socialist Party (SSP), 5 (nil); the Swiss People's Party or Democratic Centre Union (SPPDCU), 5 (4); others, 3. In the National Council, SSP gained 54 seats (41 in 1991); RDP, 45 (44); CDP, 34 (35); SPPDCU, 29 (25); others, 38. Parliamentary elections are scheduled for Oct. 1999.

At the presidential election held in the United Federal Assembly on 9 Dec. 1998, Ruth Dreifuss was elected, thus becoming Switzderland's first female president.

CURRENT ADMINISTRATION
President of the Confederation and Chief of the Department of the Interior, 1999: Ruth Dreifuss, b. 1940 (SSP).

Vice President and Chief of the Department of Military Affairs: Adolf Ogi (SPPDCU).

In March 1999 the Federal Council comprised:
Minister of Foreign Affairs: Flavio Cotti (CDP). *Justice and Police:* Arnold Koller (CDP). *Finance:* Kaspar Villiger (RDP). *Public Economy:* Pascal Couchepin. *Transport, Communications and Energy:* Moritz Leuenberger (SSP).

Local Government. Each of the 26 cantons and demi-cantons is sovereign, so far as its independence and legislative powers are not restricted by the federal constitution; all cantonal governments, though different in organization (membership varies from 5 to 11, and terms of office from 1 to 5 years), are based on the principle of sovereignty of the people.

In 21 cantons a body chosen by universal suffrage, usually called the *Great Council*, or *Canton Council*, exercises the functions of a parliament. In all the cantonal constitutions except those of the 5 cantons which have a *Landsgemeinde*, the referendum has a place. By this principle, where it is most fully developed, as in Zürich, all laws and concordats, or agreements with other cantons, and the chief matters of finance, as well as all revisions of the Constitution, must be submitted to the popular vote. In the 5 cantons of Appenzell, Glarus and Unterwalden the people exercise their powers direct in the *Landsgemeinde*, i.e., the assembly in the open air of all citizens of full age. In all the cantons the *popular initiative* for constitutional affairs, as well as for legislation, has been introduced, except in Lucerne, where the *initiative* exists only for constitutional affairs. In most cantons there are districts (*Amtsbezirke*) consisting of a number of communes grouped together, each district having a Prefect (*Regierungsstatthalter*) representing the cantonal government. In the larger communes, for local affairs, there is an Assembly (legislative) and a Council (executive) with a president, mayor or syndic, and not less than 4 other members. In the smaller communes there is a council only, with its officials.

DEFENCE
There are fortifications in all entrances to the Alps and on the important passes crossing the Alps and the Jura. Large-scale destruction of bridges, tunnels and defiles are prepared for an emergency.

In 1997 military expenditure totalled US$3,837m. (US$544 per capita), representing 1·5% of GDP.

Army. There are about 3,400 regular soldiers, but some 360,000 conscripts undergo training annually in the following phases: At 20 years of age, 15 weeks recruit training; between 21 and 32, reservist refresher training (*Auszug*); between 33 and

42, 39 days training for the Militia (*Landwehr*). Proposals ('Army 95') implemented in 1995 envisaged a more flexible army to protect the population against military or natural catastrophes, combat terrorism and take part in international peacekeeping. The conscript sign-off age was reduced to 42 years, the number of conscripts reduced to 360,000, and the number of regular soldiers (including women) increased.

The Army is divided into 3 field corps, each of 1 armoured and 2 infantry divisions and support groups, a corps with 3 mountain divisions, and independent redoubt-, fortress- and territorial-brigades. The administration of the Swiss Army is partly in the hands of the Cantonal authorities, who can promote officers up to the rank of captain. But the Federal Government is concerned with all general questions and makes all the higher appointments. In peace-time the Army has no general; in time of war the Federal Assembly in joint session of both Houses appoints a general. Equipment includes about 370 Leopard, 186 Pz-68 and 186 Pz-68/88 main battle tanks.

Air Corps. The Air Corps is part of the Army. It has 3 flying regiments. The fighter squadrons are equipped with Swiss-built F-5E Tiger IIs (6 squadrons), Mirage IIIS supersonic interceptor/ground-attack (2 squadrons), Mirage IIIRS fighter/reconnaissance (3 squadrons); and Bloodhound surface-to-air missile batteries are operational. Training aircraft are Pilatus PC-7 Turbo-Trainers and Hawks; there are also communications and transport aircraft and helicopters. Personnel (1996), 32,600 on mobilization, with 150 combat aircraft.

INTERNATIONAL RELATIONS
Switzerland is a member of OECD, EFTA, the Council of Europe and the NATO Partnership for Peace, and applied to join the EU on 26 May 1992. In referendums in 1986 the electorate voted against joining the UN, and in Dec. 1992 the European Economic Area.

ECONOMY
Performance. Total GDP was US$292,500m. in 1996, a decline of 0·7% on 1995. Real GDP growth in 1998 was 2·1%. In 1998 the current account surplus was US$18,200m.

Budget. Revenue and expenditure of the Confederation, in 1m. Swiss francs, for calendar years:

	1991	1992	1993	1994	1995	1996
Revenue	31,564	32,846	31,497	34,794	35,837	37,563
Expenditure	34,916	37,283	38,035	39,830	40,185	42,466

Main sources of revenue, 1995 (in 1m. Swiss francs): Direct federal taxes, 8,650; VAT, 7,700; corporation tax, 3,000; settlement taxes, 2,900; stamp duty, 1,850. Expenditure: Social security, 10,955; defence, 5,952; transport, 6,351; agriculture, 3,461; education and research, 3,233.

Currency. The unit of currency is the *Swiss franc* (CHF) of 100 *centimes* or *Rappen*. Foreign exchange reserves were US$32,257m. and gold reserves 83·28m. troy oz. in Feb. 1998. Inflation was zero in 1998. Total money supply in Jan. 1998 was 143bn. Swiss francs.

Banking and Finance. The National Bank, with headquarters divided between Berne and Zürich, opened on 20 June 1907. It has the exclusive right to issue banknotes. The *Chairman* is Hans Meyer (b. 1936).

On 31 Dec. 1996 there were 370 banks with total assets of 1,467,459m. Swiss francs. They included 24 cantonal banks, 4 big banks, 119 regional and saving banks, 1 *Raiffeisen* (consisting of 962 member banks in 1996) and 222 other banks. The number of banks has come down from over 600 in 1990. In 1997 the 3 largest banks in order of capitalization were: Union Bank of Switzerland, Crédit Suisse, Swiss Bank Corporation. In June 1998 the Union Bank of Switzerland and Swiss Bank Corporation merged, resulting in the formation of UBS AG, the world's largest private bank, with assets of nearly US$600bn. (£360bn.).

Money laundering was made a criminal offence in Aug. 1990. Complete secrecy about clients' accounts remains intact, but anonymity was abolished in July 1991.

The stock exchange system has been reformed under federal legislation of 1990 on securities trading and capital market services. The 4 smaller exchanges have been closed and activity concentrated on the major exchanges of Zürich, Basle and Geneva, which harmonized their operations with the introduction of the Swiss Electronic Exchange (EBS) in Dec. 1995. Zürich is a major international insurance centre.

In Aug. 1998 Crédit Suisse and UBS AG agreed a deal to pay US$1·25bn. (£750m.) to Holocaust survivors over a 3-year-period in an out-of-court settlement. The deal brought to an end the issue of money left in Holocaust victims' Swiss Bank accounts which were allowed to remain dormant after the war.

Weights and Measures. The metric system is legal.

ENERGY AND NATURAL RESOURCES

Electricity. The Energy 2000 programme aims to stabilize consumption. Installed capacity was 14·27m. kW in 1994. Production was 55·1bn. kWh in 1996. 43% of energy produced was nuclear, 21·9 hydro-electric from storage power stations, 24·8% hydro-electric from turbine power stations and 3·1% from conventional thermal. In Sept. 1990 54% of citizens voted for a 10-year moratorium on the construction of new nuclear plants. Consumption per capita in 1995 was an estimated 6,810 kWh.

Minerals. Salt is mined. Approximately 6,000 people work in mining and quarrying.

Agriculture. The country is self-sufficient in wheat and meat. Agriculture is protected by subsidies, price guarantees and import controls. Farmers are guaranteed an income equal to industrial workers. Agriculture occupied 5·1% of the total workforce in 1995. In 1997 there were 300,738 ha of arable land, 113,865 ha of cultivated grassland and and 623,457 ha of pasture. In 1997 there were 20,255 ha of vineyards. In 1991 there were 108,296 farms (40% in mountain or hill regions), of which 23,493 were under 1 ha, 13,953 over 20 ha, and 45,492 in part-time use.

Area harvested, 1995 (in 1,000 ha): Cereals, 215; coarse grains, 102; potatoes, 17; sugar-beet, 14. Production, 1995 (in 1,000 tonnes): Sugar-beet, 825; potatoes, 680; wheat, 623; barley, 298; maize, 243; tobacco, 1. Fruit production (in 1,000 tonnes) in 1995 was: Apples, 262; pears, 91; plums, 10; walnuts, 3·2. Wine is produced in 18 of the cantons. In 1995 vineyards produced 119 tonnes of wine.

Livestock, 1996: Cattle, 1,772,000; pigs, 1,580,000; horses, 55,000; sheep, 442,000; goats (1995), 52,000; chickens (1995), 6m.

Forestry. The forest area was 1,130,000 ha in 1995 (28·6% of the land area). In 1995, 4·75m. cu. metres of roundwood were cut (74% coniferous and 26% broadleaved).

Fisheries. Total catch, 1995, 2,749 tonnes, exclusively freshwater fish.

INDUSTRY

There were 347,500 firms in 1991, of which 84·9% employed fewer than 10 persons. The chief food producing industries, based on Swiss agriculture, are the manufacture of cheese, butter, sugar and meat. Among the other industries, the manufacture of textiles, clothing and footwear, chemicals and pharmaceutical products, the production of machinery (including electrical machinery and scientific and optical instruments) and watch and clock making are the most important.

Labour. In 1995, the total working population was 3,783,000, of whom 1,089,000 people were in community, social and personal services, 782,000 in manufacturing and 733,000 in trade, restaurants and hotels. 141,700 persons were registered unemployed in Feb. 1999—a rate of 3·9% (3·575% for males, 4·25% for females), up from 0·5% in 1990.

The foreign labour force with permit of temporary residence was 939,000 in Aug. 1995 (326,600 women). Of these 261,400 were Italian, 146,700 Yugoslav, 108,600 French, 103,400 Portuguese and 89,600 German. In 1997 approximately 800,000 EU citizens worked in Switzerland.

Trade Unions. The Swiss Federation of Trade Unions had about 419,000 members in 1996.

INTERNATIONAL TRADE

Legislation of 1991 increased the possibilities of foreign ownership of domestic companies.

Imports and Exports. Imports and exports, excluding gold (bullion and coins) and silver (coins), were (in 1m. Swiss francs):

	1991	1992	1993	1994	1995	1996	1997
Imports	95,032	92,330	89,830	92,608	94,483	96,664	103,088
Exports	87,947	92,142	93,289	95,827	96,236	98,589	105,133

In 1997 the EU accounted for 77·1% of imports (84·8bn. Swiss francs) and 60·0% of exports (65·9bn. Swiss francs). Main import suppliers in 1997 (share of total trade): Germany, 30·2%; France, 11·0%; Italy, 9·8%; USA, 7·9%; UK, 6·5%. Main export markets: Germany, 22·4%; USA, 10·3%; France, 9·0%; Italy, 7·5%; UK, 5·8%.

Main imports in 1994 (in 1m. Swiss francs): Raw materials and semi-manufactures, 31,952; consumer goods, 35,263; producers' goods, 22,349. Exports: Machinery and apparatus, 26,123; chemicals, 23,492; precision instruments, clocks and watches and jewellery, 19,994; metals, 7,780; textiles, clothing and shoes, 4,292.

COMMUNICATIONS

Roads. In 1996 there were 71,117 km of roads, including 1,594 km of national highways, 18,326 km of cantonal roads and 51,197 km of local roads. Motor vehicles in 1997 (in 1,000): Passenger cars, 3,323; commercial vehicles, 264; buses, 15 (1996); motor cycles, 382 (1996). Goods transport by road, 1993, totalled 10,378m. tonne-km. There were 89,098 road accidents in 1995, with 692 fatalities. In 1990 there had been 79,436 road accidents, but 954 fatalities.

Rail. In 1995 the length of the general traffic railways was 5,040 km, and of special lines (funiculars etc.), 814 km. In 1995 the Federal Railway carried 253m. passengers and 47·3m. tonnes of freight. There are tram/light rail networks in Basle, Berne, Bex, Geneva, Lausanne, Neuchâtel and Zürich. There are many other lines, the most important of which are the Berne–Lötschberg–Simplon (115 km) and Rhaetian (363 km) networks.

Civil Aviation. There are international airports at Basle (which also serves Mulhouse in France), Berne (Belp), Geneva, Lugano and Zürich. Swissair is the national carrier. In 1995 it flew 136·7m. km, carrying 7,146,600 passengers (6,492,100 on international flights). Crossair is the second largest airline, flying 26·3m. km in 1995 and carrying 1,213,700 passengers (921,600 on international flights). Services were also provided in 1998 by over 80 foreign airlines. In 1996 Zürich was the busiest airport, handling 15,795,624 passengers (14,783,473 on international flights) and 322,541 tonnes of freight. Geneva was the second busiest airport in 1996, with 5,955,821 passengers and 63,871 tonnes of freight.

Shipping. In 1989 there were 1,208 km of navigable waterways. 13·3m. tonnes of freight were transported. A merchant marine was created in 1941, the place of registry of its vessels being Basle. In 1995 it consisted of 174 vessels with a total of 4·36m. DWT. GRT totalled 0·38m.

Telecommunications. Switzerland had 4,688,000 main telephone lines in 1997 (660·9 per 1,000 persons). In 1995 there were 2,450,000 PCs, equivalent to 348 per 1,000 population—the highest rate in the world. Cellular phone subscribers numbered 447,000 in 1995 and there were 207,000 fax machines in 1996. There were 1·2m. Internet users in Sept. 1998.

Postal Services. In 1995 there were 3,674 post offices, or 1 for every 1,920 persons.

SOCIAL INSTITUTIONS

Justice. The Federal Court, which sits at Lausanne, consists of 30 judges, 15 supplementary judges and 15 temporary supplementary judges, elected by the Federal Assembly for 6 years and eligible for re-election; the President and Vice-President serve for 2 years and cannot be re-elected. The Tribunal has original and final jurisdiction in suits between the Confederation and cantons; between different cantons; between the Confederation or cantons and corporations or individuals;

between parties who refer their case to it; in such suits as the constitution or legislation of cantons places within its authority; and in many classes of railway suits. It is a court of appeal against decisions of other federal authorities, and of cantonal authorities applying federal laws. The Tribunal comprises 2 courts of public law, 2 civil courts, a chamber of bankruptcy, a chamber of prosecution, a court of criminal appeal, a court of extraordinary appeal, a federal criminal court, and a criminal chamber for cases of treason (sits very rarely). The jurors who serve in the Assize Courts are elected by the people, and are paid a daily allowance.

A Federal Insurance Court sits in Lucerne, and comprises 9 judges and 9 supplementary judges elected for 6 years by the Federal Assembly.

A federal penal code replaced cantonal codes in 1942. It abolished capital punishment except for offences in wartime; this latter proviso was abolished in 1991.

There were 64,151 adult criminal convictions in 1992 (13·4% female; 44·4% foreign).

Religion. There is liberty of conscience and of creed. At the 1990 census 47·3% of the population were Protestant, 46·2% Roman Catholic and 7·4% without religion. In 1997 the figures were estimated to be: Roman Catholics, 3,280,000; Protestants, 2,850,000; other, 990,000.

Education. Education is administered by the cantons and communes and is free and compulsory for 9 years. Compulsory education consists of 4 (Berne, Basel-Town, Jura, Vaud), 5 (Aargau, Basel-Country, Neuchâtel) or 6 (other cantons except Ticino, which has 9) years of primary education, and the balance in Stage I secondary education. This may be followed by 5 years of Stage II secondary education of general or vocational schools. Tertiary education is at universities, higher vocational schools and advanced vocational training institutes.

In 1995–96 there were 158,200 children in nursery schools. There were 777,100 pupils in compulsory education (452,800 at primary, 280,500 at lower secondary and 43,700 at special schools), 87,500 in Stage II general secondary education, 192,700 in Stage II vocational secondary education, and 148,000 students in higher education, including 88,200 at universities.

There are 7 universities (date of foundation and students in 1989–90): Basle (1460, 6,763), Berne (1528, 9,511), Fribourg (1889, 5,814), Geneva (1559, 12,028), Lausanne (1537, 6,942), Neuchâtel (1866, 2,512), Zürich (1523, 20,690); and 5 institutions of equivalent status: Lucerne Theological Faculty (199), St Gallen PHS (171), St Gallen School of Economics and Social Science (3,952), Lausanne Federal Institute of Technology (3,495), Zürich Federal Institute of Technology (11,200).

In 1995 total expenditure on education came to 20,498m. Swiss francs, or 5·6% of GNP, and represented 14·7% of total government expenditure.

Health. In 1994 there were an estimated 21,700 doctors (1 for every 323 persons) and 1,591 pharmacies. There were 4,400 dentists in 1992. Hospital bed provision in 1994 was 69 for every 10,000 persons.

New cases of infectious diseases, 1992: Tuberculosis, 987; malaria, 261; AIDS (1996), 322.

Welfare. The Federal Insurance Law against illness and accident, of 13 June 1911, entitles all citizens to insurance against illness; foreigners may be admitted to the benefits. Compulsory insurance against illness does not exist, but cantons and communities are entitled to declare insurance obligatory for certain classes or to establish public benefit (sick fund) associations, and to make employers responsible for the payment of the premiums of their employees.

Unemployment insurance is compulsory for all wage-earners. Insurance against accident is compulsory for all officials, employees and workmen of all the factories, trades, etc., which are under the federal liability law.

Old-age and widows/widowers' insurance has been compulsory since 1948.

The following amounts (in 1m. Swiss francs) were paid in social security benefits:

	1993	1994	1995
Federal Old-Age Pensions	23,047	23,363	24,503
Supplementary Benefits	1,541	1,567	1,575
Federal Disability Insurance	5,987	6,396	6,826
Loss of Earnings Insurance	831	810	621
Unemployment Insurance	5,986	5,921	5,240
Family Allowances	1,144	3,872	3,920

SWITZERLAND

CULTURE
Unlike most other countries, Switzerland is not planning to celebrate the Millennium officially until 1 Jan 2001.

Broadcasting. Schweizerische Radio- und Fernsehgesellschaft/Société Suisse de Radiodiffusion et Télévision/Società Svizzera di Radiotelevisione is a non-profit-making company responsible for radio and television services. There are German, French and Italian radio and TV networks (colour by PAL). The German radio service has 3 programmes, local programmes and also broadcasts in Romansch; the French service ('Suisse Romande') has 3 programmes, as does the Italian. There is an external service, Swiss Radio International (Arabic, English, Spanish) and 4 city-based private stations. The UN and the Red Cross have radio stations. In 1995 there were 6·1m. radio and 3m. TV sets in use.

Cinema. There were 431 cinemas in 1994; total attendance for the year was 16·2m. 37 films were produced in 1995.

Press. There were 88 daily newspapers in 1996 with a total circulation of 2,383,000 (330 per 1,000 population). There were 131 non-daily papers with a combined circulation of 1,314,000 (182 per 1,000 population). 15,371 book titles were published in 1996.

Tourism. Tourism is an important industry. In 1996 there were 10,600,000 foreign tourists, bringing revenue of US$8·89bn. In 1994, overnight stays by tourists totalled 74,788,000. 9·56m. Swiss citizens travelled abroad in 1993.

Festivals. Switzerland will be holding Expo 2001 in the Three Lakes District in the west of the country. The exposition will be focusing on new ways of communicating, and on the future of transport in the 21st century.

Libraries. In 1995 there was 1 National library with 2,582,000 volumes and 6,298 registered users, and 34 non-specialized libraries with 8,442,000 volumes and 447,386 users. In 1993 there were 9 higher education libraries with 14,427,000 volumes and 200,711 users; and in 1990, 2,555 public libraries with 27,674 volumes and 351,444 users.

Museums and Galleries. In 1993 there were 776 museums, visited by around 8,800,000 people.

DIPLOMATIC REPRESENTATIVES
Of Switzerland in Great Britain (16–18 Montagu Pl., London, W1H 2BQ)
Ambassador: François Nordmann.

Of Great Britain in Switzerland (Thunstrasse 50, 3005 Berne)
Ambassador: C. Hulse, CMG, OBE.

Of Switzerland in the USA (2900 Cathedral Ave., NW, Washington, D.C., 20008)
Ambassador: Alfred Defago.

Of the USA in Switzerland (Jubilaeumstrasse 93, 3005, Bern)
Ambassador: Madeleine Kunin.

Of Switzerland to the European Union
Ambassador: Alexis Lautenberg.

FURTHER READING
Office Fédéral de la Statistique. *Annuaire Statistique de la Suisse.*

Hilowitz, J. E., (ed.) *Switzerland in Perspective.* New York, 1991
Meier, H. K. and Meier, R. A., *Switzerland.* [Bibliography] London and Santa Barbara (CA), 1990
New, M., *Switzerland Unwrapped: Exposing the Myths.* London, 1997
Wildblood, R., *What makes Switzerland tick?* London, 1988

National library: Bibliothèque Nationale Suisse, Hallwylstr. 15, 3003 Berne.
National statistical office: Office Fédéral de la Statistique, Schwarztorstr. 96, 3003 Berne.
SFSO Information Service e-mail: *information@bfs.admin.ch*
Website: http://www.admin.ch/bfs/

SYRIA

Jumhuriya al-Arabya
as-Suriya

(Syrian Arab Republic)

Capital: Damascus
Population estimate, 2000: 16·13m.
GNP per capita: (PPP$) 3,020
HDI/world rank: 0·749/81

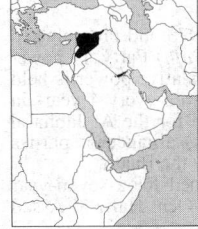

KEY HISTORICAL EVENTS

Syria was under Turkish control from the 12th century, and part of the Ottoman Empire from the 16th century until the First World War. Following the defeat of the Turks in that war, the League of Nations granted to France a mandate for Syria from 1920. On 27 Sept. 1941, Gen. Catroux, the Free French C.-in-C., in the name of the Allies, proclaimed the independence of Syria at Damascus. On 27 Dec. 1943 an agreement was signed between representatives of the French National Committee of Liberation and of Syria, by which most of the powers and capacities exercised hitherto by France under mandate were transferred as from 1 Jan. 1944 to the Syrian government. The evacuation of all foreign troops in April 1946 marked the complete independence of Syria, but the political situation was unsettled and military *coups* were staged in Dec. 1949 and in Feb. 1954.

Syria merged with Egypt to form the United Arab Republic from 2 Feb. 1958 until 29 Sept. 1961, when Syrian independence was resumed following a *coup* the previous day. Following the fifth *coup* of the decade, Lieut.-Gen. Hafez al-Assad became prime minister on 13 Nov. 1970, and assumed the presidency on 22 Feb. 1971.

A new constitution, approved by plebiscite on 12 March 1973, confirmed the Arab Socialist Renaissance (Ba'ath) Party as the 'leading party in the state and society'.

TERRITORY AND POPULATION

Syria is bounded by the Mediterranean and Lebanon in the west, by Israel and Jordan in the south, by Iraq in the east and by Turkey in the north. The frontier between Syria and Turkey was settled by the Franco-Turkish agreement of 22 June 1929. The area is 185,180 sq. km (71,498 sq. miles). The census of 1994 gave a population of 13,782,000. Estimate (1997), 14,972,000 (52% urban); density, 81 per sq. km.

The UN gives a projected population for 2000 of 16·13m.

Area and population (1996 estimate, in 1,000) of the 14 districts *(mohafaza)*:

	Sq. km	Population		Sq. km	Population
Damascus (City)	105	1,347	Idlib	6,097	1,270
Damascus (District)	18,032	1,237	Hasakah	23,334	1,013
Aleppo	18,500	3,694	Raqqah	19,616	592
Homs	42,223	1,471	Suwaydá	5,550	380
Hama	8,883	1,415	Dará	3,730	689
Lattakia	2,297	936	Tartous	1,892	730
Deir Ez-Zor	33,060	994	Qunaytirah	1,861	330

Principal towns (population, 1994 in 1,000): Damascus (the capital), 1,444; Aleppo, 1,542; Homs, 558; Lattakia, 303; Hama, 273; Al-Kamishli, 165; Raqqah, 138; Deir Ez-Zor, 133.

Arabic is the official language, spoken by 89% of the population, while 6% speak Kurdish (chiefly Hasakah governorate), 3% Armenian and 2% other languages.

SOCIAL STATISTICS

1997 births, estimate, 625,000; deaths, 92,000. Rates, 1997 estimate (per 1,000 population): Birth, 38·7; death, 5·7; infant mortality (per 1000 live births), 39. Expectation of life, 1990–95, was 65·2 years for males and 69·2 for females. Population growth (1997 estimate) 3·3%. Fertility rate, 1990–95, 4·7 births per woman.

SYRIA

CLIMATE
The climate is Mediterranean in type, with mild wet winters and dry, hot summers, though there are variations in temperatures and rainfall between the coastal regions and the interior, which even includes desert conditions. The more mountainous parts are subject to snowfall. Damascus, Jan. 38·1°F (3·4°C), July 77·4°F (25·2°C). Annual rainfall 8·8" (217 mm). Aleppo, Jan. 36·7°F (2·6°C), July 80·4°F (26·9°C). Annual rainfall 10·2" (258 mm). Homs, Jan. 38·7°F (3·7°C), July 82·4°F (28°C). Annual rainfall 3·4" (86·7 mm).

CONSTITUTION AND GOVERNMENT
A new Constitution was approved by plebiscite on 12 March 1973 and promulgated on 14 March. It confirmed the Arab Socialist Renaissance *(Ba'ath)* Party, in power since 1963, as the 'leading party in the State and society'. Legislative power is held by a 250-member People's Assembly *(Majlis al-Sha'ab)*, renewed every 4 years in 15 multi-seat constituencies, in which 167 seats are guaranteed for the Al Jabha al Watniyah at Wahdwamiyah (JWW/National Progressive Front) alliance of parties (i.e. the Baath party and partners). The government is formed by the Baath.

The President is appointed by the Parliament and is confirmed for a seven-year term in a referendum. At a referendum on 10 Feb. 1999, Lieut.-Gen. Hafiz al-Assad (b. 1930) was confirmed as *President* for a fifth term.

National Anthem. 'Humata al Diyari al aykum salaam' ('Defenders of the Realm, on you be peace'); words by Khalil Mardam Bey, tune by M. S. and A. S. Flayfel.

RECENT ELECTIONS
Elections were held on 30 Nov. and 1 Dec. 1998. The Baath party won 135 seats; its partners won: HSS 8 seats, IIA 7, HTI 7, HIA 6, HDTI 4. This gave the JWW alliance 167 seats. Non-partisan candidates gained 83 seats.

CURRENT ADMINISTRATION
President: Lieut.-Gen. Hafiz al-Assad (appointed 1971; re-appointed for a fifth term in Feb. 1999).

First Vice-President: Abd al-Halim ibn Said Khaddam. *Second Vice-President:* Mohammed Zuhayr Mashariqa.

A government was formed in Dec. 1998, which in March 1999 comprised:
Prime Minister: Mahmud Zubi.

Deputy Prime Minister and Minister of Defence: Lieut.-Gen. Mustafa Talas; *Deputy Prime Minister for Economic Affairs:* Dr Salim Yasin; *Deputy Prime Minister for Services Affairs:* Rashid Akhtarini.

Minister of Education: Ghassan Halabi. *Higher Education:* Saliha Sanqar. *Interior:* Mohammad Harbar. *Information:* Mohammad Salman. *Local Administration:* Yahya Abu Asali. *Supply and Internal Trade:* Nadim Akkash. *Transport:* Mufid Abd al-Karim. *Labour and Social Welfare:* Ali Khalil. *Economy and Foreign Trade:* Mohammad al-Imadi. *Culture and National Guidance:* Najah al-Attar. *Foreign Affairs:* Farouk al-Shara. *Tourism:* Danhu Dawud. *Health:* Dr Iyad al-Shatti. *Irrigation:* Abd al-Rahman Madani. *Electricity:* Munib Saim al-Dahar. *Oil and Mineral Resources:* Muhammad Maher Hosni Jamal. *Construction:* Majid Izzu Ruhaybani. *Housing and Utilities:* Hussam al-Safadi. *Agriculture and Agrarian Reform:* Assad Mustafa. *Finance:* Khalid al-Mahayni. *Communications:* Radwan Martini. *Justice:* Hussein Hassun. *Industry:* Ahmad Nizam al-Din. *Religious Trusts:* Abdul-Raouf Ziada. *Presidential Affairs:* Wahib Fadil.

Local Government. Syria is administratively divided into 14 districts *(mohafaza)*. These are divided into 59 *mantika*, which are subdivided into 179 smaller administrative units *(nahia)*, each covering a number of villages.

DEFENCE
Military service is compulsory for a period of 30 months. Defence expenditure in 1997 totalled US$2,217m. (US$145 per capita), representing 6·3% of GDP.

Army. The Army is organized into 6 armoured and 3 mechanized divisions, a Republican Guard division, 1 special forces division, 8 independent special forces regiments, 3 independent infantry brigades, 2 independent artillery, 3 surface-to-surface missile, 2 independent anti-tank and 1 coastal defence surface-to-surface missile brigade and 1 independent tank regiment. Equipment includes 2,100 T-54/-55, 1,000 T-62 and 1,500 T-72/-72M main battle tanks. Strength (1997) about 215,000 (including conscripts).

Navy. The Navy includes 1 ex-Soviet 'Romeo'-class diesel submarine, 2 small frigates, 14 fast-missile craft, 11 inshore patrol craft, 2 coastal and 5 inshore minesweepers, and 3 medium landing ships (all ex-Soviet). A small naval aviation branch of the Air Force operates 18 Soviet-built anti-submarine helicopters. Personnel in 1997 numbered 5,000. The main base is at Tartus.

Air Force. The Air Force, including Air Defence Command, had (1997) about 40,000 personnel, over 500 combat aircraft and 60 armed helicopters, including about 180 MiG-21, 80 MiG-23, 20 MiG-25 and 40 MiG-29 supersonic interceptors, 60 MiG-23, 60 Su-22 and 20 Su-24 fighter-bombers, as well as some MiG-25 reconnaissance aircraft. Training units have Spanish-built Flamingo and Pakistani-built Mushshak piston-engined primary trainers and Czechoslovakian L-29 Delfin and L-39 jet basic trainers. There are also transport units with Il-76, An-12, An-24/26 and other types, and helicopter units with Soviet-built Mi-8/17s and Mi-24s and French-built Gazelles. 'Guideline', 'Goa', 'Gainful' and 'Gaskin' surface-to-air missiles are widely deployed in Syria by Air Defence Command, and 'Gammon' long-range surface-to-air missiles in Lebanon.

INTERNATIONAL RELATIONS

A Treaty of Brotherhood, Co-operation and Co-ordination with Lebanon of May 1991 provides for close relations in the fields of foreign policy, the economy, military affairs and security. By the treaty the Lebanese government's decisions are subject to review by 6 joint Syrian-Lebanese bodies.

Syria is a member of the UN and Arab League.

ECONOMY

Policy. The relaxation of state control and foreign exchange regulations in response to the 1980s' recession has led to a consumer boom. Since 1991, the proportion of the economy in private hands has risen from 35% to 70%, but further reforms have been stalled.

Performance. Economic growth for 1997 was estimated at 3·4%.

Budget. In 1996 revenues were £Syr.152,231m. and expenditures £Syr.155,596m.

Currency. The monetary unit is the *Syrian pound* (SYP) of 100 *piastres*. Inflation was 12% in 1992. Gold reserves were 830,000 troy oz. in Nov. 1997. Total money supply in Dec. 1995 was £Syr.228,123m.

Banking and Finance. The Central Bank is the bank of issue. Commercial banks were nationalized in 1963. The *Governor* of the Central Bank is Hisham Mutawalli.

Weights and Measures. The metric system is legal, though former weights and measures may still be in use: 1 *okiya* = 0·47 lb; 6 *okiyas* = 1 *oke* = 2·82 lb; 2 *okes* = 1 *rottol* = 5·64 lb; 200 *okes* = 1 *kantar*.

ENERGY AND NATURAL RESOURCES

Electricity. Installed capacity was 4·16m. kW in 1994. Production in 1995 was 15,549m. kWh and consumption per capita in 1995 was estimated at 902 kWh.

Oil and Gas. Estimated crude oil production (1995), 28m. tonnes. Reserves 1,521m. bbls. Gas reserves (1997), 235,000m. cu. metres. Natural gas production (1995), 4,412m. cu. metres.

Water. In 1992 there were 5 main dams and 127 surface dams. Production of drinking water, 1995, 608·86m. cu. metres.

Minerals. Phosphate deposits have been discovered. Production, 1995, 1,598,000 tonnes; other minerals were salt, 111,000 tonnes and gypsum 336,000 tonnes. There are indications of lead, copper, antimony, nickel, chrome and other minerals widely distributed. Sodium chloride and bitumen deposits are being worked.

Agriculture. In 1994 agriculture accounted for 28·4% of GDP. The arable area in 1995 was 5,979,000 ha, there were 4,982,000 ha of cropland and 8,287,000 ha of pasture. In 1995 there were 82,603 tractors.

Production of principal crops, 1995 (in 1,000 tonnes): Wheat, 4,184; barley, 1,705; maize, 199; seed cotton, 600; olives, 423; lentils, 148; millet, 5; sugar-beet, 1,406; potatoes, 471; tomatoes, 427; grapes, 384.

Production of animal products, 1995 (in tonnes): Milk, 1,414,000; butter, 14,007; cheese, 65,512; honey, 889; 2,136m. eggs.

Livestock (1995, in 1,000): Cattle, 775; asses, 200; sheep, 12,075; goats, 1,063; poultry, 18,746.

Forestry. In 1995 there were 219,000 ha of forest (1·2% of the land area). Timber production in 1995 was 55,000 cu. metres.

Fisheries. The total catch in 1995 was 11,639 tonnes (81% freshwater fish).

INDUSTRY
Public-sector industrial production in 1995 included (in tonnes): Cotton yarn, 40,417; cotton and mixed textiles, 16,597; mixed woollen yarn, 1,442; manufactured tobacco, 9,699; iron bars, 36,675; asbestos, 15,623; vegetable oil, 33,435; 77,001 electrical engines; 69,163 refrigerators; 80,010 water meters; woollen carpets, 538,000 sq. metres.

Labour. In 1996 the labour force totalled 4,396,000 (74% males).

Trade Unions. In 1995 there were 199 trade unions with 460,967 members.

INTERNATIONAL TRADE
Legislation of 1991 permits foreign investors a 10-year tax-exemption duty-free import of equipment and repatriation of profits. Foreign debt was US$21,420m. in 1996.

Imports and Exports. Imports in 1996 totalled US$5,244m.; exports, US$3,999m.

Main imports, 1995 (in £Syr.1) included: Petroleum and products, 318,463; iron and steel bars and rods, 3,269,247; cane sugar, 1,014,390; yarn of continuous synthetic fibres, 1,627,972; alternating current motors and generators, 185,388; passenger transport motor vehicles, 374,583. Main exports included: Petroleum and products, 27,862,627; raw cotton, 2,390,774; printed woven cotton fabrics, 34,418; natural phosphate, 251,061.

In 1995 imports came mainly from Germany, Italy, USA, China, Turkey, Japan and Romania. Exports went mainly to Italy, France, Lebanon and Spain.

COMMUNICATIONS
Roads. In 1995 there were 27,769 km of asphalted roads, 9,327 km of paved non-asphalted road and 2,237 km of earth roads. There were 486,776 motor vehicles in 1995, including 136,160 cars and taxis, 5,239 buses, 25,145 mini-buses, 58,717 goods vehicles and 89,038 motor cycles.

Rail. In 1995 the network totalled 2,423 km of 1,435 mm gauge (Syrian Railways) and 327 km of 1,050 mm gauge (Hedjaz-Syrian Railway). In 1995 Syrian Railways carried 2m. passengers and 4·3m. tonnes of freight.

Civil Aviation. The main international airport is at Damascus, with some international traffic at Aleppo, Lattakia and Deir Ez-Zor. The national carrier is the state-owned Syrian Arab Airlines. In 1998 services were also provided by Aeroflot, Air Algérie, Air France, Air Malta, Air Ukraine, Alitalia, Austrian Airlines, Balkan, British Airways, Cyprus Airways, Czech Airlines, Egyptair, Emirates, Gulf Air, Iberia, Iran Air, JAT, KLM, Kuwait Airways, Lufthansa, Malév, Middle East Airlines, Pakistan International Airlines, Qatar Airways, Royal Jordanian, SAS, Saudia, Sudan Airways, Tarom, Tunis Air, Turkish Airlines and Yemenia Yemen Airways. In 1995 Syrian Arab Airlines flew 10·4m. km, carrying 563,100 passengers (515,300 on international flights). Damascus handled 1,399,680 passengers in 1996 (1,329,618 on international flights) and 21,054 tonnes of freight. Aleppo was the second busiest airport in 1996, handling 195,054 passengers (164,453 on international flights) and 27,083 tonnes of freight.

Shipping. In 1995 the merchant marine totalled 0·45m. GRT. Vessels totalling 2,884,000 net registered tons entered ports and vessels totalling 2,701,000 NRT cleared in 1995.

Telecommunications. Number of main telephone lines (1997), 1,312,600. Mobile phones and the Internet are banned. There were 10,000 PCs and 5,000 fax machines in 1995.

Postal Services. There were 650 post offices in 1995.

SOCIAL INSTITUTIONS

Justice. Syrian law is based on both Islamic and French jurisprudence. There are 2 courts of first instance in each district, one for civil and 1 for criminal cases. There is also a Summary Court in each sub-district, under Justices of the Peace. There is a Court of Appeal in the capital of each governorate, with a Court of Cassation in Damascus. The death penalty is in force, and executions may be held in public.

Religion. In 1997 there were an estimated 12·91m. Moslems (namely Sunni with some Shi'ites and Ismailis). There are also Druzes and Alawites. Christians (830,000 in 1997) include Greek Orthodox, Greek Catholics, Armenian Orthodox, Syrian Orthodox, Armenian Catholics, Protestants, Maronites, Syrian Catholics, Latins, Nestorians and Assyrians. There are also Jews and Yezides.

Education. In 1995 there were 1,037 kindergartens with 90,681 children; 10,420 primary schools with 113,384 teachers and 2,651,247 pupils; 2,526 intermediate and secondary schools with 50,779 teachers and 841,964 pupils. In 1995, 14 teacher colleges had 766 teachers and 4,989 students; 292 schools for technical education had 10,105 teachers and 72,859 students. Adult literacy, 1995, 70·8% (male, 85·7%; female, 55·8%).

In 1995–96 there were 4 universities and 1 higher institution of political science, with 161,185 students and 4,806 academic staff.

Health. In 1995 there were 17,623 beds in 294 hospitals, and 795 health centres. In 1995 there were 15,391 doctors, 8,025 dentists, 5,919 pharmacists, 6,063 midwives and 23,151 nursing personnel.

CULTURE

Broadcasting. Broadcasting is controlled by the government-owned Syrian Broadcasting and Television Organization. There are 2 national radio programmes and an external service and 2 TV programmes (colour by SECAM and PAL). In 1995 there were 3·75m. radio and 950,000 TV sets.

Cinema. In 1994 there were 49 cinemas with 25,111 seats.

Press. In 1995 there were 8 national daily newspapers with a combined circulation of 274,000.

Tourism. In 1996 there were 888,000 foreign tourists, bringing revenue of US$1·48bn.

DIPLOMATIC REPRESENTATIVES
Of Syria in Great Britain (8 Belgrave Sq., London, SW1X 8PH)
Ambassador: Vacant.

Of Great Britain in Syria (Kotob Building, 11 Mohammad Kurd Ali St., Malki, Damascus POB 37)
Ambassador: Basil S. T. Eastwood, CMG.

Of Syria in the USA (2215 Wyoming Ave., NW, Washington, D.C., 20008)
Ambassador: Walid Al-Moualem.

Of the USA in Syria (Abu Rumaneh, Al Mansur St. No. 2, Damascus)
Ambassador: Christopher W. S. Ross.

Of Syria to the United Nations
Ambassador: Mikhail Wehbe.

Of Syria to the European Union
Ambassador: Vacant.

FURTHER READING

Choueiri, Y., *State and Society in Syria and Lebanon.* Exeter Univ. Press, 1994
Devlin, J. F., *Syria: Modern State in an Ancient Land.* Boulder, 1983
Maoz, M. and Yaniv, A., *Syria under Assad.* New York, 1986
Seale, P., *The Struggle for Syria.* London, 1986.—*Asad of Syria: the Struggle for the Middle East.* London, 1989
Seccombe, I. J., *Syria.* [Bibliography] Oxford and Santa Barbara (CA), 1987

National statistical office: Central Bureau of Statistics, Office of the Prime Minister, Damascus.

TAJIKISTAN

Jumkhurii Tojikiston

Capital: Dushanbe
Population estimate, 2000: 6·4m.
GNP per capita: (PPP$) 900
HDI/world rank: 0·575/118

KEY HISTORICAL EVENTS
The Tajik Soviet Socialist Republic was formed from those regions of Bokhara and Turkestan where the population consisted mainly of Tajiks. It was admitted as a constituent republic of the Soviet Union on 5 Dec. 1929. In Aug. 1990 the Tajik Supreme Soviet adopted a declaration of republican sovereignty, and in Dec. 1991 the republic became a member of the CIS. After demonstrations and fighting the Communist government was replaced by a Revolutionary Coalition Council on 7 May 1992. Following further demonstrations President Nabiev was ousted on 7 Sept. Civil war broke out, and the government resigned on 10 Nov. On 30 Nov. it was announced that a CIS peacekeeping force would be sent to Tajikistan. A state of emergency was imposed in Jan. 1993. On 23 Dec. 1996 a ceasefire was signed in the presence of the Russian prime minister between President Rakhmonov and insurgent leader Sayed Abdullo Nuri. A further agreement on 8 March 1997 provided for the disarmament of the insurgents and their eventual integration into the regular armed forces.

A peace agreement brokered by Iran and Russia was signed in Moscow on 27 June 1997 stipulating that the opposition should have 30% of ministerial posts, in a Commission of National Reconciliation

TERRITORY AND POPULATION
Tajikistan is bordered in the north and west by Uzbekiston (formerly Uzbekistan) and Kyrgyzstan, in the east by China and in the south by Afghanistan. Area, 143,100 sq. km (55,240 sq. miles). It includes 2 provinces (Khudzand and Khatlon) and 43 rural districts, 18 towns and 49 urban settlements, together with the Gorno-Badakhshan Autonomous Region. Of the 1989 census population of 5,092,603, 62·3% were Tajik, 23·5% Uzbek and 7·6% Russian. Population (1997 estimate), 5,945,900 (1,234,700 female); density, 41·6 per sq. km.

The UN gives a projected population for 2000 of 6·4m.

In 1995, 67·8% of the population lived in rural areas, making it the most rural of the former Soviet republics.

The capital is Dushanbe (1991 population estimate, 592,000). Other large towns are Khudzand (formerly Leninabad), Kurgan-Tyube and Kulyab.

The official language is Tajik, written in Arabic script until 1930 and after 1992 (the Roman alphabet was used 1930–40; the Cyrillic, 1940–92).

SOCIAL STATISTICS
1997 births, estimate, 166,000; deaths, 46,000. Rates, 1997 estimate (per 1,000 population): Births, 27·9; deaths, 7·7. Life expectancy, 1997, 66·8 years. Population growth, 1997, 1·18%. Infant mortality, 1990–95, 56 per 1,000 live births; fertility rate, 4·3 births per woman.

CLIMATE
Considering its altitude, Tajikistan is a comparatively dry country. July to Sept. are particularly dry months. Winters are cold but spring comes earlier than farther north. Dushanbe, Jan. –10°C, July 25°C. Annual rainfall 375 mm.

CONSTITUTION AND GOVERNMENT
In Nov. 1994 a new Constitution was approved by a 90% favourable vote by the electorate, which enhanced the President's powers. The head of state is the *President*, elected by universal suffrage for 5 years. Parliament is the 181-member National Assembly (*Majlisi Oli*), elected for a 5-year term in single-seat constituencies.

TAJIKISTAN

RECENT ELECTIONS
At presidential elections on 6 Nov. 1994 the electorate was 2·6m.; turn-out was 90%. President Rakhmonov was re-elected by 58·3% of votes cast against 1 opponent. The next presidential election is due in Nov. 1999.

At the elections of 26 Feb. and 12 March 1995 to the National Assembly, the electorate was 2·6m.; turn-out was officially put at 84%. 40% of the seats were uncontested. The next parliamentary election is scheduled for Feb. 2000.

CURRENT ADMINISTRATION
President: Emomali Rakhmonov (as Speaker elected by the former Supreme Soviet 19 Nov. 1992; re-elected 6 Nov. 1994).

In March 1999 the government comprised:
Prime Minister: Yakhiye Azimov.

First Deputy Prime Minister: Hajji Akbar Turajonzoda. *Deputy Prime Ministers:* Abdurakhman Azimov; Bozqul Dodkhodoeva; Jalol Mansurov; Kholisj Timurjonov; Ramazan Mirzoyev; Abdurakhman Nazimov.

Minister of Agriculture: Shodi Kabirov. *Culture, Press and Information:* Bobkhan Makhmadov. *Defence:* Maj.-Gen. Sherali Khairullaev. *Economy and Foreign Economic Relations:* Davlat Usmon. *Education:* Munira Inoyatova. *Protection of the Environment:* Ismail Davlatov. *Finance:* Anvarsho Muzafarov. *Internal Affairs:* Khomiddin Sharipov. *Justice:* Shavkat Ismailov. *Foreign Affairs:* Talbak Nasarov. *Transport and Roads:* Khayriddin Mukhiddinov. *Grain Products:* Bekmurod Urokov. *Health:* Alamkhon Akhmedov. *Labour and Employment:* Khudoiberdi Kholiknazarov. *Land Improvement and Water Resources:* Davlatbek Makhsudov. *Security:* Maj.-Gen. Saidamir Zukhurov. *Social Security:* Abdusattor Jabborov.

DEFENCE
In 1997 the Army had a strength of 7,000 and comprised 2 motor rifle (1 training) and 1 special forces brigade and 1 surface-to-air missile regiment. Equipment included 40 T-72 main battle tanks. There is a para-military Border Guard (mainly Russian) of 1,200. 25,000 Russian troops and some Air Force units are stationed in the country.

Defence expenditure in 1997 totalled US$132m. (US$22 per capita).

INTERNATIONAL RELATIONS
Tajikistan is a member of the UN and CIS.

ECONOMY
Performance. Real GDP growth was −12·4% in 1995 and −12·0% in 1994. Between 1990 and 1996 the average annual real growth in GNP per capita was −18·5%.

Budget. Income, 1993, 406,800m. roubles; expenditure 329,100m. roubles.

Currency. The unit of currency is the *Tajik rouble* (TJR) of 100 *tanga*, which replaced the Russian rouble on 10 May 1995 at 1 Tajik rouble = 100 Russian roubles. The average annual inflation rate during the period 1990–96 was 394%. Inflation for Feb. 1997 was 3%, the reduction coming about as a result of a US$22m. IMF loan in 1996 and maintenance of a tight monetary regime.

Banking and Finance. The central bank and bank of issue is the National Bank (*Chair*, Murodali Alimordonov). In 1996, there were 8 commercial banks, 1 commercial savings bank and 1 state-owned bank for economic affairs.

ENERGY AND NATURAL RESOURCES
Electricity. Installed capacity in 1994 was 4·44m. kW and production was 16bn. kWh. Consumption per capita in 1995 was estimated to be 2,135 kWh.

Oil and Gas. In 1995 oil production (including gas concentrate) was 64,000 tonnes; natural gas, 50m. cu. metres.

Minerals. There are deposits of brown coal, lead, zinc, iron ore, antimony, mercury, gold silver tungsten and uranium. Coal production, 1993, 150,000 tonnes. Aluminium production, 1996, 198,000 tonnes.

Agriculture. Area under cultivation in 1997 was 9·6m. ha, mainly in the hands of state and collective farms. Cotton, the major cash crop, accounts for around two-thirds of total production (315,000 tonnes in 1996–97). Various fruits, sugarcane, jute, silk, rice and millet are also grown. There are rich pasture lands. Livestock, 1996: 1·15m. cattle, 1·78m. sheep; 826,000 goats (1995) and 5m. chickens (1995).

Output of main agricultural products (in 1,000 tonnes) in 1993: Grain, 254; potatoes, 147; vegetables, 485; fruit and berries, 148; meat, 69; milk, 432; and 154m. eggs.

Forestry. Forests covered 410,000 ha in 1995, or 2·9% of the land area.

Fisheries. The 1995 catch was 3,900 tonnes, exclusively from inland waters.

INDUSTRY
Major industries: aluminium, electro-chemical plants, textile machinery, carpet weaving, silk mills, refrigerators, hydroelectric power. Output, 1993 (in tonnes unless otherwise stated): Mineral fertilizer, 20,000; cement, 0·3m.; fabrics, 114m. cu. metres; footwear, 3·9m. pairs; 1,100 lathes; 18,000 refrigerators and freezers.

Labour. The labour force in 1996 totalled 2,238,000 (56% males). In 1993, 55·3% of the economically active population worked in the state sector, 25·1% in the private sector and 18·4% in co-operatives. In Jan. 1994 there were 21,500 registered unemployed. In 1995 the monthly minimum wage was 14,400 roubles.

INTERNATIONAL TRADE
External debt was US$707m. in 1996.

Imports and Exports. In 1996 imports were estimated to be valued at US$657m. and exports at US$768m. Main imports: petroleum products, grain, manufactured consumer goods; main exports: cotton and aluminium. The main trading partners are former Soviet republics, most notably Russia and Uzbekiston.

COMMUNICATIONS

Roads. In 1996 there were estimated to be 13,700 km of roads (11,300 km surfaced). In 1993, 139·9m. passengers and 12·3m. tonnes of freight were carried.

Rail. Length of railways, 1990, 480 km. Passenger-kilometres travelled in 1995 came to 124m. and freight tonne-kilometres to 2·11bn.

Civil Aviation. There is an international airport at Dushanbe. In 1998 there was a weekly flight to Samara, in Russia, with Samara Airlines. In 1995 scheduled airline traffic of Tajikistan-based carriers flew 8·1m. km, carrying 3,000 passengers.

Telecommunications. There were 227,600 main telephone lines in 1997, or 37·5 for every 1,000 persons. In 1995 there were 1,300 fax machines.

Postal Services. In 1995 there were 736 post offices.

SOCIAL INSTITUTIONS

Justice. In 1994, 14,279 crimes were reported, including 636 murders or attempted murders.

Religion. The Tajiks are predominantly Sunni Moslems (80%); Shi'a Moslems, 5%.

Education. The adult literacy rate is over 99%. In 1994–95 there were 593,526 pupils and 25,698 teachers at (1993) 625 primary schools, and 724,056 pupils at secondary schools, plus 108,203 students at higher education institutions. In Jan. 1992, 14% of eligible children were attending pre-school institutions.

There is 1 university, which had 7,220 students in 1994–95.

Health. There were 374 hospitals in Jan. 1994 with 60,000 beds, 13,000 doctors and 42,800 junior medical personnel.

Welfare. In Jan. 1994 there were 0·41m. age pensioners and 0·2m. other pensioners.

CULTURE

Broadcasting. Broadcasting is controlled by the State Teleradio Broadcasting Company. Tajik Radio broadcasts 3 national programmes, a Radio Moscow relay and a foreign service (Dari, Iranian).

Cinema. In 1995 there were 159 cinemas with a seating capacity of 39,000 and an annual attendance of 400,000.

Press. There were 2 daily newspapers in 1995 with a combined circulation of 80,000, equivalent to 14 per 1,000 inhabitants.

DIPLOMATIC REPRESENTATIVES
Of Great Britain in Tajikistan
Ambassador: B. Hay (resides in Toshkent).

Of the USA in Tajikistan (Oktyabrskaya Hotel, 105A Prospekt Rudaki, Dushanbe)
Ambassador: R. Grant Smith.

Of Tajikistan to the United Nations
Ambassador: Rashid Alimov.

BADAKHSHAN AUTONOMOUS REPUBLIC

Comprising the Pamir massif along the borders of Afghanistan and China, the province was set up on 2 Jan. 1925, initially as the Special Pamir Province. Area, 63,700 sq. km (24,590 sq. miles). The population at the 1989 census was 161,000 (89·5% Tajik, 6·7% Kirghiz). Estimate, 1990, 164,300. Capital, Khorog (14,800). The inhabitants are predominantly Ismaili Moslems.

Mining industries are developed (gold, rock-crystal, mica, coal, salt). Wheat, fruit and fodder crops are grown, and cattle and sheep are bred in the western parts. In 1990 there were 74,200 cattle and 329,500 sheep and goats. Total area under cultivation, 18,400 ha.

In 1990-91 there were 47,600 students at all levels of education. There were 140 doctors and 1,400 junior medical personnel in 1991.

TANZANIA

Jamhuri ya Muungano
wa Tanzania—United
Republic of Tanzania

Capital: Dodoma
Population estimate, 2000: 33·69m.
Estimated GDP: $18·9bn.
HDI/world rank: 0·358/150

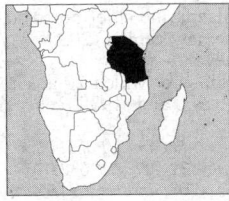

KEY HISTORICAL EVENTS

At the end of the 17th century the inhabitants of Zanzibar drove out the Portuguese with the assistance of the Arabs of Oman. Thereafter an Arab governor from Oman was sent to Zanzibar but the government of the interior remained in the hands of a local ruler. In 1832 Seyyid Said bin Sultan, ruler of Oman, established his capital at Zanzibar. Arab merchants explored the mainland in search of slaves and ivory, and soon the whole of that island and the island of Pemba together with a large strip of the east African mainland coast came under his effective rule. Seyyid Said died in 1856. Five years later his former African possessions were subject to an arbitration award made by the British Governor-General of India and declared to be independent of Oman. In 1887 the Sultan of Zanzibar handed over the administration of his possessions to the north of Vanga on the African continent to the British East Africa Association. These territories eventually passed to the British government and are now part of Kenya. In 1888 a similar concession was granted to the German East Africa Association of the Sultan's mainland territories between the River Umba and Cape Delgado. In 1890 the German government bought these territories outright for 4m. German marks. In 1892 the administration of the Benadir Ports (which had in 1889 been conceded to the British East Africa Association) was, with the consent of the Sultan, transferred to the Italian government in consideration of a quarterly payment of Rs 40,000. In 1886 the Sultan renounced in favour of Portugal all claims to the coast to the south of Cape Delgado.

German East Africa was conquered by the Allies in the First World War and subsequently divided between the Belgians, the Portuguese and the British. Ruanda and Urundi went to the Belgians, the Kionga triangle to Portugal, and Tanganyika to Britain. The country was administered as a League of Nations mandate until 1946, and then as a UN trusteeship territory until 9 Dec. 1961.

Tanganyika achieved responsible government in Sept. 1960 and full self-government on 1 May 1961. On 9 Dec. 1961 Tanganyika became a sovereign independent member state of the Commonwealth of Nations. The first prime minister, Dr Julius Nyerere, resigned in Jan. 1962; but on 9 Dec 1962 the country adopted a republican form of government (still within the British Commonwealth), and Dr Nyerere was elected as the first president.

On 24 June 1963 Zanzibar became an internal self-governing state which achieved independence on 9 Dec. 1963. On 12 Jan. 1964 her sultanate was overthrown by a revolt of the Afro-Shirazi Party leaders who established the People's Republic of Zanzibar. Also in Jan. 1964 there was an attempted *coup* against Nyerere who had to seek British military help. On 26 April 1964 Tanganyika, Zanzibar and Pemba combined to form the United Republic of Tanzania.

Before independence the East Africa High Commission had been administering services of an inter-territorial nature for Kenya, Tanzania and Uganda, and this continued for the East African Community. The Community practically ceased to function after 30 June 1977, chiefly because of the failure to agree a budget and the refusal of President Nyerere to negotiate with President Idi Amin of Uganda. In 1978 Amin attacked Tanzania and the following year Tanzania invaded Uganda, overthrew the Amin régime and remained in occupation until 1981.

In 1991 a presidential commission recommended a multi-party political system. In 1993 regional parliaments for Zanzibar and mainland Tanzania (Tanganyika) were set up. The first multi-party elections were held in 1995.

TERRITORY AND POPULATION
Tanzania is bounded in the north-east by Kenya, north by Lake Victoria and Uganda, north-west by Rwanda and Burundi, west by Lake Tanganyika, south-west by Zambia and Malawi, and south by Mozambique. Total area 945,037 sq. km (364,881 sq. miles), including the offshore islands of Zanzibar (1,660 sq. km) and Pemba (984 sq. km) and inland water surfaces (59,050 sq. km). The total population was estimated in July 1997 to be 29,460,800; density, 31·2 per sq. km.

The UN gives a projected population for 2000 of 33·69m.

75·8% of the population lived in rural areas in 1995. 0·5m. Hutu refugees were forcibly repatriated to Rwanda in Dec. 1996.

The chief towns (1988 census populations) are Dar es Salaam, the chief port and former capital (1,360,850), Mwanza (223,013), Dodoma, the new capital (203,833), Tanga (187,634), Zanzibar Town (157,634), Tabora and Mbeya.

The United Republic is divided into 25 administrative regions of which 20 are in mainland Tanzania, 3 in Zanzibar and 2 in Pemba. Areas and 1988 census populations of the regions:

Region	Sq. km	Population	Region	Sq. km	Population
Arusha	82,306	1,351,675	Pwani (Coast)	32,407	638,015
Dar es Salaam	1,393	1,360,850	Rukwa	68,635	694,974
Dodoma	41,311	1,237,819	Ruvuma	63,498	783,327
Iringa	56,864	1,208,914	Shinyanga	50,781	1,772,549
Kagera	28,388	1,326,183	Singida	49,341	791,814
Kigoma	37,037	854,817	Tabora	76,151	1,036,293
Kilimanjaro	13,309	1,108,699	Tanga	26,808	1,283,636
Lindi	66,046	646,550	Zanzibar and Pemba	2,460	640,578
Mara	19,566	970,942	Pemba North	574	137,399
Mbeya	60,350	1,476,199	Pemba South	332	127,640
Morogoro	70,799	1,222,737	Zanzibar North	470	97,028
Mtwara	16,707	889,494	Zanzibar South	854	70,184
Mwanza	19,592	1,878,271	Zanzibar West	230	208,327

The official languages are English and Swahili (spoken as a mother tongue by only 8·8% of the population, but used as a lingua franca by 90%).

SOCIAL STATISTICS
1997 births, estimate, 1,208,000; deaths, 583,000. 1997 rates per 1,000 population: Birth, 41·0; death, 19·8. The population growth rate was estimated in 1997 at 1·6%. Life expectancy in 1997 was estimated at 41·7 years (40·3 for men and 43·1 for women). 45% of the population was below 15 years old in 1997. Infant mortality, 1990–95, 86 per 1,000 live births; fertility rate, 5·9 births per woman.

CLIMATE
The climate is very varied and is controlled very largely by altitude and distance from the sea. There are three climatic zones: the hot and humid coast, the drier central plateau with seasonal variations of temperature, and the semi-temperate mountains. Dodoma, Jan. 75°F (23·9°C), July 67°F (19·4°C). Annual rainfall 23" (572 mm). Dar es Salaam, Jan. 82°F (27·8°C), July 74°F (23·3°C). Annual rainfall 43" (1,064 mm).

CONSTITUTION AND GOVERNMENT
The *President* is head of state, chairman of the party and commander-in-chief of the armed forces. The second Vice-President is head of the executive in Zanzibar. The Prime Minister and first Vice-President is also the leader of government business in the National Assembly.

The *Bunge (National Assembly)* is composed of 232 Members of Parliament elected from the Constituencies, 5 delegates from the Zanzibar House of Representatives, the Attorney General, 42 co-opted members and 1 ex officio member.

In Dec. 1979 a separate Constitution for Zanzibar was approved. Although at present under the same Constitution as Tanzania, Zanzibar has, in fact, been ruled by decree since 1964.

TANZANIA

National Anthem. 'God Bless Africa/Mungu ibariki Afrika'; words collective, tune (same as that for Zambia and Zimbabwe) by M. E. Sontanga.

RECENT ELECTIONS

Presidential and parliamentary elections were held on 29 Oct. 1995, in many places postponed or extended because of administrative problems or faults. On 11 Nov. all opposition candidates withdrew from the presidential elections because of alleged irregularities. Benjamin Mkapa was elected President with 61·8% of votes cast. His party, Chama Cha Mapinduzi, gained 214 seats.

CURRENT ADMINISTRATION

President: Benjamin Mkapa (Chama Cha Mapinduzi; sworn in 30 Nov. 1995).
 Vice-President: Dr Omar Ali Juma.
 In March 1999 the Government consisted of:
 Prime Minister: Frederick Sumaye.
 President of Zanzibar: Salmin Amour.
 Minister of Home Affairs: Ali Ameir Mohammed. *Finance:* Daniel Yona. *Justice and Constitutional Affairs:* Bakari Mwapachu. *Defence:* Edgar Maokola Majogo. *Industries and Trade:* Iddi Simba. *Communications and Transport:* Ernest Nyanda. *Agriculture and Co-operatives:* William Kusila. *Health:* Dr Aaron Chiduo. *Foreign Affairs and International Co-operation:* Jakaya Kikwete. *Education:* Juma Athumani Kapuya. *Energy and Mineral Resources:* Abdallah Kigoda. *Water and Livestock Development:* Mussa Nkhangaa. *Tourism, Natural Resources and Environment:* Zakhia Meghji. *Lands, Housing and Urban Development:* Gideon Cheyo. *Science, Technology and Higher Education:* Pius Ng'wandu. *Works:* Anna Abdallah. *Labour and Youth Development:* Paul Kimiti. *Community Development, Women's Affairs and Children:* Mary Nagu; *Regional Affairs and Local Government:* Kingunge Ngombale-Mwiru.

Local Government. There are regional parliaments for Zanzibar and mainland Tanzania (Tanganyika); and Zanzibar has a President, who is ex officio a Vice-President of Tanzania.
 Elections were held on 22 Oct. 1995. Salmin Amour (Chama Cha Mapinduzi) was elected President of Zanzibar by 50·2% of votes cast against 1 opponent. Chama Cha Mapinduzi gained 26 seats; the Civic United Front, 24.

DEFENCE

Conscription is for 2 years, which may include civilian service. Defence expenditure totalled US$123m. in 1997 (US$4 per capita).

Army. The Army consists of 5 infantry and 1 tank brigade and 2 artillery, 2 anti-aircraft, 2 mortar, 2 anti-tank and 1 engineer battalion. Equipment includes 30 Chinese Type-59 and 35 T-54 main battle tanks. Strength (1997), 30,000. There is also a Citizen's Militia of 80,000.

Navy. There are 4 ex-Chinese torpedo-armed hydrofoils and 12 inshore patrol craft of mixed Chinese and North Korean origins. 2 further British-built inshore patrol craft are based permanently in Zanzibar and 4 armed patrol boats on Lake Victoria Nyanza. Personnel in 1997 totalled about 1,000.

Air Force. The Tanzanian People's Defence Force Air Wing was built up initially with the help of Canada, but combat equipment has been acquired from China. Personnel totalled 3,600 in 1997 (including some 2,600 air defence troops), with about 10 F-7 (MiG-21) and 10 F-6 (MiG-19) combat aircraft, mostly in store; 4 Buffalo twin-engined short-take-off-and-land transports; 1 HS 748 turboprop transport; 2 Chinese-built Y-12 transports; 2 Cessna 404 liaison aircraft; 6 Agusta-Bell AB.205 transport helicopters, and 2 JetRanger helicopters.

INTERNATIONAL RELATIONS

Tanzania is a member of the UN, OAU, the Commonwealth, SADC, and is an ACP member state of the ACP-EU relationship.

ECONOMY

Policy. Tanzania's economy has been hard hit by a series of natural disasters—drought in 1996, floods in 1997 and early 1998—which slowed real economic growth to 3·3% in 1997, from 4·2% in 1996. Gradual recovery is expected and a modest economic growth of 3·5% is projected. Headline inflation rate is down to 12·2%, compared with a high of 29·8% in 1995. The central bank aimed to reduce headline inflation to 7·5% by the end of the 1998–99 fiscal year. After more than 30 years of a centrally planned economy, the government has privatized or sold about 150 companies.

Performance. Real GDP growth was 27·5% in 1995, up from 3·0% in 1994.

Budget. The fiscal year ends 30 June. Total revenues in 1996–97 were an estimated US$959m. and expenditure US$1·1bn.

Currency. The monetary unit is the *Tanzanian shilling* (TZS) of 100 *cents*. Foreign exchange reserves were US$568m. in Feb. 1998. The average annual inflation rate during the period 1990–96 was 25·9%. Total money supply in Feb. 1998 was Sh. 486,920m.

Banking and Finance. The central bank is the Bank of Tanzania (*Governor*, Idris Rashid).

On 6 Feb. 1967 all commercial banks with the exception of National Co-operative Banks were nationalized, and their interests vested in the National Bank of Commerce on the mainland and the Peoples' Bank in Zanzibar. However, in 1993 private-sector commercial banks were allowed to open. In 1997 the National Commercial Bank, which controls 70% of the country's banking and has 172 branches, was split into a trade bank, a regional rural bank and a micro-finance bank.

A stock exchange opened in Dar es Salaam in 1996.

Weights and Measures. The metric system is in use.

ENERGY AND NATURAL RESOURCES

Electricity. Installed capacity was 440,000 kW in 1994. Production in 1994 was 1·91bn. kWh, with consumption per capita in 1994 an estimated 60 kWh. In 1998, only 10% of the population had access to electricity.

Oil and Gas. A number of international companies are exploring for both gas and oil.

Minerals. Tanzania's mineral resources include gold, nickel, cobalt and diamonds. International funds injected to improve Tanzania's economy have resulted in notable increases, particularly in gold production. Large deposits of coal and tin exist but mining is on a small scale.

Agriculture. 90% of the workforce are engaged in agriculture, chiefly in subsistence farming. Agricultural produce accounted for 48% of GDP in 1996, and contributes around 85% of exports. Production of main agricultural crops in 1992 (in 1,000 tonnes) was: Sisal, 35; seed cotton, 218; sugarcane, 1,410; coffee, 56; tobacco, 17; maize, 2,226; millet, 263; sorghum, 587; wheat, 64; cashew nuts, 40; citrus, 34. Zanzibar is a major producer of cloves.

Livestock (1996): 13·36m. cattle, 3·95m. sheep, 9·68m. goats (1995), 27m. chickens (1995). Livestock products (1995): Honey, 24,500 tonnes.

Forestry. Forests covered 32·51m. ha in 1995 (36·8% of the total land area), down from 34·12m. ha and 38·6% of the land area in 1990. In 1995, 36·75m. cu. metres of roundwood were cut.

Fisheries. Catch (1995) 360,000 tonnes, of which inland waters, 317,000 tonnes.

INDUSTRY

Industry is limited, accounting for 17% of GDP, and is mainly textiles, petroleum and chemical products, food processing, tobacco, brewing and paper manufacturing.

INTERNATIONAL TRADE

Foreign debt was estimated at US$7,412m. in 1996.

TANZANIA

Imports and Exports. Total trade (in US$1m.):

	1995	1996	1997
Imports	1,679	1,386	1,337
Exports	685	758	719

Principal exports, 1991 (in US$1m.): Coffee, 77·3; manufactures, 70·3; cotton, 63·3; minerals, 41·6; tea, 21·7; tobacco, 16·7; cashew nuts, 16·7; petroleum products, 7·3. Principal imports: Machinery, 254·2; transport equipment, 247·7; crude oil and products, 168·5; building materials, 110·7. Main export markets, 1995: Germany, 9·6%; Japan, 8·5%; India, 8·4% and UK, 5·7%. Main import suppliers: UK, 9·7%; Kenya, 9·1%; Japan, 7·2% and China, 4·9%.

COMMUNICATIONS

Roads. In 1996 there were 88,200 km of roads, of which 3,700 km were tarred. Passenger cars in use in 1996 numbered 26,000, and there were 81,000 buses and coaches, and 27,720 trucks and vans.

Rail. In 1977 the independent Tanzanian Railway Corporation was formed. The network totals 2,600 km (metre-gauge), excluding the joint Tanzanian Zambian (Tazara) railway's 969 km in Tanzania (1,067 mm gauge) operated by a separate administration. In 1994, the state railway carried 1·2m. passengers and 1·2m. tonnes of freight, and the Tazara carried 1·8m. passengers and 0·6m. tonnes of freight.

In Oct. 1998 a transshipment facility for containers opened at Kidatu, south-west of Dar es Salaam, providing a link between the 1,067-mm gauge railways of the southern part of Africa and the 1,000-mm gauge lines of the north.

Civil Aviation. There are 3 international airports (Dar es Salaam, Zanzibar and Kilimanjaro). Air Tanzania Corporation, the state-owned national carrier, provides domestic services and in 1998 had flights to the Democratic Republic of the Congo, Kenya, Oman, Rwanda, Saudi Arabia, South Africa, Uganda, Yemen, Zambia and Zimbabwe. Tanzania is a partner with Uganda and South African Airways in Alliance Airlines. In 1998 services were also provided by Air Djibouti, Air India, Air Malaŵi, Air Zimbabwe, Alliance Air, British Airways, Egyptair, Emirates, Ethiopian Airlines, Gulf Air, Kenya Airways, KLM, Royal Swazi National Airways Corporation, South African Airways and Swissair. In 1995 Air Tanzania Corporation flew 3·6m. km, carrying 236,400 passengers (84,700 on international flights). Dar es Salaam handled 434,322 passengers in 1996 (255,603 on international flights) and 10,744 tonnes of freight. Kilimanjaro was the second busiest airport, handling 110,221 passengers (53,132 on international flights) and 1,824 tonnes of freight.

Shipping. In 1996, the merchant marine totalled 30,371 GRT, including oil tankers, 7,173 GRT. The main seaports are Dar es Salaam, Mtwara, Tanga and Zanzibar. There are also ports on the lakes. In 1991, 1m. tonnes of freight were loaded, and 2·9m. unloaded.

Telecommunications. Tanzania had 105,100 main telephone lines in 1997 (3·3 per 1,000 inhabitants). There were 3,500 cellular phone subscribers and around 100 fax machines in 1995, and 2,500 Internet users in Jan. 1998.

Postal Services. In 1995 there were 525 post offices.

SOCIAL INSTITUTIONS

Justice. The Judiciary is independent in both judicial and administrative matters and is composed of a 4-tier system of Courts: Primary Courts; District and Resident Magistrates' Courts; the High Court and the Court of Appeal. The Chief Justice is head of the Court of Appeal and the Judiciary Department. The Court's main registry is at Dar es Salaam; its jurisdiction includes Zanzibar. The Principal Judge is head of the High Court, also headquartered at Dar es Salaam, which has resident judges at 7 regional centres.

Religion. In 1992 there were 8·4m. Roman Catholics, Anglicans and Lutherans, and 9m. Moslems. Moslems are concentrated in the coastal towns; Zanzibar is 99% Moslem. Some 23% follow traditional religions.

Education. In 1995 there were 10,927 primary schools with 105,280 teachers for 3·8m. pupils. At secondary level there were 212,763 pupils with 12,198 teachers, and at university level there were 12,776 students with 1,650 staff.

Technical and vocational education is provided at several secondary and technical schools, and at the Dar es Salaam Technical College. There are 42 teacher training colleges, including the college at Chang'ombe for secondary-school teachers.

There is 1 university, 1 university of agriculture and 1 open university. There are also 9 other institutions of higher education.

Adult literacy rate (1995): 67·8% (79·4% of men; 56·8% of women).

Health. In 1993 there were 1,365 doctors, and in 1991, 173 hospitals with 24,130 beds. In the period 1990–96 only 38% of the population had access to safe drinking water.

CULTURE

Broadcasting. The government-controlled Radio Tanzania and Sauti ya Tanzania Zanzibar are responsible for radio broadcasting on the mainland and on Zanzibar respectively. On the mainland there is a national service and a commercial programme in Swahili and an external service in English. There is television only on Zanzibar provided by the government-run Television Zanzibar (colour by PAL). There were about 8·3m. radio and 70,000 TV sets in 1995.

Cinema. In 1995 there were 27 cinemas with a seating capacity of 10,000 and an annual attendance of 1·8m.

Press. In 1995 there were 3 dailies (1 in English), with a combined circulation of 364,000.

Tourism. There are (1999) 12 national parks in Tanzania. In 1998 there were 359,000 foreign tourists, bringing revenue of US$393m. compared to 153,000 visitors in 1990. The government aims to raise the number of tourists to half a million by 2000, with tourism the country's largest foreign exchange earner.

DIPLOMATIC REPRESENTATIVES

Of Tanzania in Great Britain (43 Hertford St., London, W1Y 8DB)
High Commissioner: Dr Abdul-Kader A. Shareef.

Of Great Britain in Tanzania (Social Security Hse., Samora Ave., Dar es Salaam)
High Commissioner: B. Dinwiddy.

Of Tanzania in the USA (2139 R. St., NW, Washington, D.C., 20008)
Ambassador: Mustafa Salim Nyang'anyi.

Of the USA in Tanzania (36 Laibon Rd., Dar es Salaam)
Ambassador: Vacant.

Of Tanzania to the United Nations
Ambassador: Daudi Ngelautwa Mwakawago.

Of Tanzania to the European Union
Ambassador: Ali Abeid Aman Karume.

FURTHER READING
Ayany, S. G., *A History of Zanzibar.* Nairobi, 1970
Coulson, A., *Tanzania: A Political Economy.* OUP, 1982
Darch, C., *Tanzania.* [Bibliography] 2nd ed. Oxford and Santa Barbara (CA), 1996
Hood, M., (ed.) *Tanzania and Nyerere.* London, 1988
Nyerere, J., *Freedom and Development.* New York, 1976
Resnick, I. N., *The Long Transition: Building Socialism in Tanzania.* New York and London, 1981
Yeager, R., *Tanzania: An African Experiment.* Aldershot, 1982

National statistical office: Bureau of Statistics, Dar es Salaam.

THAILAND

Prathet Thai

(Kingdom of Thailand)

Capital: Bangkok
Population estimate, 2000: 60·49m.
GNP per capita: (PPP$) 6,700
HDI/world rank: 0·838/59

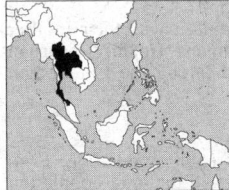

KEY HISTORICAL EVENTS

The Thais migrated to the present territory from Nan Chao in the Yunnan area of China in the 8th and 9th centuries. Thais today look back to the state of Sukhothai, a Buddhist kingdom which grew up in the central plain of Thailand in the 13th century, as their first historical state. A hundred years later Sukhothai was succeeded by the new kingdom of Ayutthaya, which served until the Burmese invasion of 1767. After some years of confusion Thailand's leading general, Chao Phraya Chakkri, assumed the throne in 1782, thus establishing the dynasty which still heads the Thai state.

Siam, as Thailand was called until 1939, remained an independent state ruled by an absolute monarchy until 24 June 1932. Discontented with the social, political and economic stagnation of the country, a group of rebels calling themselves the People's Party and headed by a young lawyer, Pridi Phanomyong, precipitated a bloodless *coup*. The rebels seized control of the army, imprisoned many royal officials and persuaded the king to accept the introduction of constitutional monarchy.

When, the following year, the king tried to dissolve the newly appointed General Assembly, the army moved to prevent him, thus becoming the dominant force behind the government, which they have remained ever since. Nationalism dominated political life through the 1930s. In 1939 Field Marshal Pibul Songgram became premier and embarked on a pro-Japanese irridentist policy that eventually brought Thailand into the Second World War on Japan's side.

After 1945 political life was characterized by periods of military rule interspersed with short attempts at democratic, civilian government. Thus, three years of civilian rule from 1945 to 1948 were brought to an end when Songgram came back to power for a nine-year period. In 1957 power was seized from him by another army leader, Sarit Thanarat, who abolished the constitution and ruled without outside interference until his death in 1963, when he was replaced by the new Commander-in-Chief, Thano Kittikachon. Democratic government was reintroduced for a short time after 1963, when 100 students were killed in clashes with the army, and again from 1969 to 1971 when another successful military *coup* was staged, aimed at checking the high crime rate and the growth of Communist insurgence. A new, moderately democratic constitution was introduced in 1978.

On 23 Feb. 1991 a military junta seized power, deposing the prime minister. Following the appointment of Gen. Suchinda Kraprayoon as Prime Minister on 17 April 1992 there were massive anti-government demonstrations over several weeks in the course of which many demonstrators were killed. Gen. Suchinda resigned, and in May the legislative assembly voted that future prime ministers should be elected by its members rather than appointed by the military. A new government was elected on 13 Sept. led by Chuan Leekpai of the Democratic Party (DP). The 1995 election was fought against a background of political and financial corruption. The result was a coalition government which proved as ineffective as its predecessor in coming to grips with fundamental problems in the country. After the 1996 election a new constitution was drafted allowing for the separation of the executive, legislative and judicial branches of government.

TERRITORY AND POPULATION

Thailand is bounded in the west by Myanmar, north and east by Laos and south-east by Cambodia. In the south it becomes a peninsula bounded in the west by the Indian Ocean, south by Malaysia and east by the Gulf of Thailand. Area is 513,115 sq. km (198,114 sq. miles).

At the census taken in 1990 the total population was 54,548,530, of whom 17,947,700 lived in the Central region, 19,037,300 in the North-East region,

6,964,000 in the South region, 10,583,300 in the North region. Estimated population, 1997: 59,450,818; density, 116 per sq. km.

The UN gives a projected population for 2000 of 60·49m.

In 1995, 80·0% of the population lived in rural areas.

Thailand is divided into 4 regions, 76 provinces and Bangkok, the capital. Population of Bangkok (1993 census), 5,572,712. Other towns (1991 estimate): Nonthaburi (264,201), Nakhon Ratchasima (202,503), Chiangmai (161,541), Hat Yai (142,351), Khon Kaen, (131,478), Nakhon Sawan (108,569).

Thai is the official language, spoken by 53% of the population as their mother tongue. 27% speak Lao (mainly in the north-east), 12% Chinese (mainly in urban areas), 3·7% Malay (mainly in the south) and 2·7% Khmer (along the Cambodian border).

SOCIAL STATISTICS
1995 births, 1,013,000; deaths, 373,000. 1995 birth rate per 1,000 population, 17·4; death rate, 6·4. Estimate of population growth rate, 1997, 1%. Of the total population in 1997, 25% were under 15 years, 69% between 15 and 64 years, and 6% aged 65 and over. Expectation of life (1997): 68·8 years (65·1 for men; 72·2 for women). Infant mortality, 1990–95, 32 per 1,000 live births; fertility rate, 1·9 births per woman.

CLIMATE
The climate is tropical, with high temperatures and humidity. Over most of the country, 3 seasons may be recognized. The rainy season is June to Oct., the cool season from Nov. to Feb. and the hot season is March to May. Rainfall is generally heaviest in the south and lightest in the north-east. Bangkok, Jan. 78°F (25·6°C), July 83°F (28·3°C). Annual rainfall 56" (1,400 mm).

CONSTITUTION AND GOVERNMENT
The reigning King is **Bhumibol Adulyadej,** born 5 Dec. 1927. King Bhumibol married on 28 April 1950 Princess Sirikit, and was crowned 5 May 1950. *Offspring:* Princess Ubol Ratana (born 5 April 1951, married Aug. 1972 Peter Ladd Jensen); Crown Prince Vajiralongkorn (born 28 July 1952, married 3 Jan. 1977 Soamsawali Kitiyakra); Princess Maha Chakri Sirindhorn (born 2 April 1955); Princess Chulabhorn (born 4 July 1957, married 7 Jan. 1982 Virayudth Didyasarin).

Parliament consists of a 270-member *Senate,* appointed by the King, and a 393-member *House of Representatives,* elected for 4-year terms by universal suffrage of citizens over 17 years. A constitutional amendment in 1995 restricted to two-thirds the proportion of the military in the House of Representatives. The *Prime Minister* is elected by the House of Representatives.

National Anthem. 'Prathet Thai ruam nua chat chua Thai' ('Thailand, cradle of Thais wherever they may be'); words by Luang Saranuprapan, tune by Phrachen Duriyang.

RECENT ELECTIONS
At the elections of 17 Nov. 1996, 11 parties fielded candidates. New Aspiration (NA) gained 125 seats; the Democratic Party 123; National Development 52; Thai Nation 39; Social Action Party 20; Thai Citizens' Party 18. 5 other parties gained fewer than 10 seats each. Parliamentary elections were scheduled to take place by June 1999 at the latest.

CURRENT ADMINISTRATION
Following a reshuffle on 5 Oct. 1998, the government comprised in March 1999:

Prime Minister and Minister of Defence: Chuan Leekpai (DP).

Deputy Prime Ministers: Bhichai Rattakul, Supachai Panitchpakdi (*Minister of Commerce*), Panja Kesornthong (*Education*), Suwit Khunkitti (*Science, Technology and Environment*), Sanan Kachonprasart (*Interior*), Korn Dabbaransi (*Public Health*).

Ministers to the Prime Minister's Office: Khunving Supatra Massdit, Savit Bhodivihok, Jurin Laksanawisit, Abhisit Vejjajiva, Somboon Rahong, Pitak

THAILAND

Intrawithayanunt. *Minister of Finance:* Tarrin Nimmanhaeminda. *Foreign Affairs:* Surin Pitsuwan. *Agriculture and Co-operatives:* Pongpol Adireksarn. *Transport and Communications:* Suthep Thaugsuban. *Justice:* Sutasn Ngenmune. *Labour and Social Welfare:* Sompong Amornvivat. *Industry:* Suwat Liptapallop. *University Affairs:* Prachuab Chaiyasarn.

Local Government. Thailand is divided into 76 provinces (*changwads*), each under the control of a *changwad* governor. The *changwads* are subdivided into 744 districts (*amphurs*) and 81 sub-districts (*king amphurs*), 7,307 communes (*tambons*) and 65,277 villages (*moobans*).

DEFENCE
Conscription is for 2 years. In 1997 defence expenditure totalled US$3,248m. (US$52 per capita).

Army. The Army is organized in 4 regions and includes 1 armoured, 1 cavalry, 1 mechanized infantry, 7 infantry (including the Royal Guard), 2 special forces and 1 artillery division; 19 engineer and 8 independent infantry battalions; 1 independent cavalry and 1 armoured air cavalry regiment and 3 reconnaissance companies. Equipment includes 150 M-48A5, 53 M-60A1 and about 50 Chinese Type-69 main battle tanks. There is also an Army Aviation force including more than 100 UH-1 and Bell 212 transport helicopters, and over 60 O-1 Bird Dog observation aircraft, and about 20 fixed-wing transports as well as 4 AH-1 armed helicopters. Strength (1997) 150,000 (80,000 conscripts).

Navy. The Royal Thai Navy is, next to the Chinese, the most significant naval force in the South China Sea. The combatant fleet includes 2 ex-US Knox class, 5 missile-armed and 5 other frigates, 2 modern missile-armed 950-tonne corvettes and 3 anti-submarine corvettes, 6 German and Italian-built fast missile craft, 9 coastal and 40 inshore patrol craft, and about 40 riverine patrol boats. There is 1 mine counter-measures support vessel, 2 coastal minehunters and 2 coastal minesweepers. Amphibious capability is provided by 7 tank landing ships and 2 medium landing ships as well as 50 landing craft. Major auxiliaries are 1 small tanker, 3 surveying ships and 3 training ships. Minor auxiliaries and service craft number about 12. The new small Spanish-built vertical/short-take-off-and-land carrier *Chakrinareubet* entered service in 1997 and operates 8 ex-Spanish AV-8A Harrier aircraft and helicopters.

The Naval air element includes 3 P-3T Orion, 6 F-27 Maritime and 3 DO228 for maritime patrol, 4 F-27 Friendship transports, 9 Cessna T-337 armed light transports and 16 Bell anti-submarine, and 14 utility and search-and-rescue helicopters. 18 A-7 Corsair II strike aircraft were delivered in 1997.

Naval personnel in 1997 totalled 73,000, including 22,000 marines and 1,700 Naval Air Arm. The main bases are at Bangkok, Sattahip, Songkla and Phang Nga, with the riverine forces based at Nakhon Phanom.

A separate coastguard force, the Royal Thai Marine Police, numbers 2,500 and operates 3 offshore, 3 coastal patrol, 32 riverine and inshore craft, and numerous boats.

Air Force. The Royal Thai Air Force had a strength (1997) of 43,000 personnel and 210 combat aircraft, and is made up of a headquarters and Combat, Logistics Support, Training and Special Services Groups. Combat units comprise 2 squadrons of F-16s, 3 squadrons of F-5E/F interceptors, 4 squadrons with L-39 light strike aircraft, 1 with OV-10 Bronco light reconnaissance/attack aircraft, 2 with AU-23A Peacemakers and 1 with Nomads for security duties. 3 Aravas are used for electronic intelligence gathering and 3 Learjets for combat support. There are transport units equipped with a total of about 70 C-130H/H-30 Hercules, HS 748, C-47, G.222 and smaller aircraft, including Australian-built Missionmasters; there are 30 UH-1H and 14 S-58T helicopters; training units with Airtrainer CT/4 primary trainers built in New Zealand, Italian-built SF.260MTs, and PC-9 and intermediate trainers.

INTERNATIONAL RELATIONS
Thailand is a member of the UN, ASEAN and the Colombo Plan.

ECONOMY

Policy. The financial crisis that spread across south-east Asia in 1997 started as a result of the devaluation of the baht (the Thai currency) in July and hit Thailand with particular force. Over 50 finance companies suspended business, the Thai stock exchange lost 82% of its 1995 peak value and the baht devalued by 40% in the second half of 1997. An IMF rescue package of US$17·2bn. gained time to put reforms in place, including tighter budgetary control, the merging of banks, and the restructuring of the country's outmoded financial system.

In May 1998 the government agreed to adopt a strategy for the eventual privatization of the four commercial banks nationalized earlier in the year.

Performance. Real GDP growth was 7·8% in 1996 (8·6% in 1995). In 1997 and 1998 it was estimated to be –1% and –8% respectively.

Budget. The fiscal year starts in Oct. Total revenues and expenditures (in 1m. baht):

	1993-94	1994-95	1995-96	1996-97[1]
Revenue	653,217	761,819	851,178	846,384
Expenditure	578,331	645,272	739,756	881,492

[1]Provisional.

Principle expenditure in 1996 (in 1m. baht) was on: defence (95,601), public order and safety (46,615), education (159,035), health (59,205) and social security and welfare (28,637).

Currency. The unit of currency is the *baht* (THB) of 100 *satang*. After being pegged to the US dollar, the baht was devalued and allowed to float on 2 July 1997. It was the devaluation of the baht that sparked the financial turmoil throughout the world. Foreign exchange reserves were US$24,906m. and gold reserves 2·47m. troy oz. in Feb. 1998. Inflation was 5·5% in 1996. Total money supply in Dec. 1997 was 430bn. baht.

Banking and Finance. The Bank of Thailand (founded in 1942) is the central bank and bank of issue, an independent body although its capital is government-owned. Its assets and liabilities in Dec. 1991 were 580,844·5m. baht. Its *Governor* is Rerngchai Marakanonda (b. 1942). In 1997 there were 21 domestic commercial banks, 14 foreign banks with branch licences and 22 foreign banks with representative offices. Total credits of commercial banks, Dec. 1995, 4,144,000m. baht. Deposits, Dec. 1995, 3,141,500m. baht. There is a Government Savings Bank.

There is a stock exchange (SET) in Bangkok.

Weights and Measures. The metric system was made compulsory in 1923. Traditional units are also widely used.

ENERGY AND NATURAL RESOURCES

Electricity. Installed capacity, 1994, was 15·84m. kW. Output: 70·21bn. kWh. Consumption per capita was an estimated 1,205 kWh in 1995. Privatization of the Electricity Generating Authority (EGAT) was set to start during 1999.

Oil and Gas. Proven crude petroleum reserves in 1997 were 295m. bbls. Estimated production of crude petroleum (1996), 22m. bbls. Thailand and Vietnam settled an offshore dispute in 1997 which stretched back to 1973. Demarcation allowed for petroleum exploration in the Gulf of Thailand, with each side required to give the other some revenue if an underground reservoir is discovered which straddles the border. Privatization of the Petroleum Authority (PTT) was due to start in 1999.

Production of natural gas (1995) 10,477m. cu. metres. Estimated reserves, 1997, 202bn. cu. metres. In April 1998 Thailand and Malaysia agreed to share equally the natural gas jointly produced in an offshore area which both countries claim as their own territory. It is expected that from 2001 around 640m. cu. ft of natural gas will be produced in the area every day.

Minerals. The mineral resources include cassiterite (tin ore), wolfram, scheelite, antimony, coal, copper, gold, iron, lead, manganese, molybdenum, rubies, sapphires, silver, zinc and zircons. Production, 1995 (in tonnes): Iron ore, 34,500; tin concentrates, 2,200; lead concentrates, 22,800; antimony ore, 500; zinc ore, 135,200; lignite, 18·4m.; gypsum, 8·5m.; tungsten concentrates, 100; fluorite ore, 24,100; marl, 563·7.

Agriculture. In 1994 there were 17·6m. ha of arable land, 3·2m. ha of permanent cropland and 800,000 ha of pasture; 4·8m. ha were irrigated in 1994. In 1996 agriculture produced an estimated 10·5% of GDP. The chief produce is rice, a staple of the national diet. Output of the major crops in 1995 was (in 1,000 tonnes): paddy (rice) (21,130); cassava (manioc/tapioca) (18,164); sugar cane (50,597); maize (3,965); bananas (1,700); rubber latex (1,721); pineapples (2,370); sorghum (228); dried beans (240); soybeans (528); groundnuts (150); watermelons (400); kenaf fibre (132); dried onions (250).

Livestock, 1995: buffaloes, 4,807,000; cattle, 7,593,000; pigs, 4,507,000; sheep, 130,000; goats, 78,000; chickens and ducks, 101m.

Forestry. Forests covered 11·63m. ha in 1995, or 22·8% of the land area (down from 13·28m. ha in 1990). Teak and other hardwoods grow in the deciduous forests of the north; elsewhere tropical evergreen forests are found, with the timber yang the main crop (a source of yang oil). In 1995, 39·3m. cu. metres of roundwood were cut. Rubber production in 1993: 1·58m. tonnes.

Fisheries. In 1995 the catch of sea fish was 3,501,772 tonnes, including marine prawns, shrimps and other shellfish. Fish caught from inland waters in 1995 totalled 279,672 tonnes. Thailand is the leading exporter of fishery commodities in the world, with exports in 1995 totalling US$4·45bn.

INDUSTRY

In 1996 industry produced 30·5% and services 59% of GDP. Production of manufactured goods in 1994 included: 29·9m. tonnes of cement, 5·2m. hectolitres of beer, 9,363 tonnes of tin plate (1993), 126,000 automobiles and 324,000 commercial vehicles, 2m. tonnes of synthetic fibre (non-cellolosic continuous filaments), 1·8m. tonnes of petroleum products, 4,168,000 tonnes of raw sugar and 100,000 tonnes of crude steel.

Labour. In 1996 the total labour force (aged 13 and over) was 34m., of whom 57% were in agriculture, 17% in industry, 11% in commerce and 15% in services industries (including government). The unemployment rate was 2·6%. A minimum wage is set by the National Wages Committee. It was 157 baht per day in Sept. 1996.

INTERNATIONAL TRADE
Foreign debt was US$90,824m. in 1996.

Imports and Exports. Tariffs on raw materials and semi-manufactures were reduced on 1 Jan. 1995. Total exports in 1996 were valued at US$57·3bn.; total imports at US$72·4bn.

Main exports by category in 1994, in US$1m.: machinery and transport equipment (25,449·9), road vehicles and parts (excluding tyres, engines and electrical parts) (4,034·9), electrical apparatus (6,873·2), chemicals and chemical products (5,506·8), manufactures (10,313·4). Imports: machinery (15,039), manufactured articles (10,980), manufactures (5,506), food and live animals (9,291), seafood (4,181), clothing and accessories (4,531), office machinery (4,123) and other electrical machinery (4,913).

The main import sources in 1995 were Japan (30·5%), USA (12·0%), Singapore (5·9%) and Germany (5·3%). Principal export destinations were USA (17·8%), Japan (16·8%), Singapore (14·0%) and Hong Kong (5·2%).

COMMUNICATIONS

Roads. In 1996 there were 64,600 km of highways. Vehicles in use in 1996 comprised: 1·56m. passenger cars, 2·83m. commercial vehicles and 10·7m. motor cycles.

Rail. The State Railway totals 4,623 km. In 1994 it carried 87m. passengers and 7·6m. tonnes of freight.

Civil Aviation. There are international airports at Bangkok, Chiangmai, Phuket and Hat Yai. The national carrier is Thai Airways International, which is 92·85% state-owned. In 1998 services were also provided by Aeroflot, Air China, Air France, Air India, Air Koryo, Air Lanka, Air Macau, Air Mandalay, Air New Zealand, Alitalia,

All Nippon Airways, Asiana Airlines, Balkan, Bangkok Airways, Biman Bangladesh Airlines, British Airways, Canadian Airlines International, Cathay Pacific Airways, China Airlines, China Eastern Airlines, China Southern Airlines, China Southwest Airlines, China Yunnan Airlines, Condor Flugdienst, Czech Airlines, Delta Air Lines, Dragonair, Druk-Air, Egyptair, El Al, Emirates, Ethiopian Airways, EVA Airways, Finnair, Garuda Indonesia, Gulf Air, Indian Airlines, JAL, Kampuchea Airlines, KLM, Korean Air, Kuwait Airways, Lao Aviation, Lauda Air, LOT, LTU International Airways, Lufthansa, Malaysia Airlines, Malév, Myanma Airways International, Northwest Airlines, Olympic Airways, Pakistan International Airlines, Philippine Airlines, Qantas Airways, Qatar Airways, Royal Air Cambodge, Royal Brunei Airlines, Royal Jordanian, Royal Nepal Airlines, SABENA, SAN Air Company, SAS, Saudia, Silk Air, Singapore Airlines, South African Airways, Swissair, TAP, Trans Pacific Air, Turkish Airlines, United Airlines, Uzbekiston Airways, Varig and Vietnam Airlines. Bangkok handled 22,910,996 passengers in 1996 (16,380,434 on international flights) and 701,268 tonnes of freight. Phuket was the second busiest airport in 1996 for passenger traffic, with 2,723,365 (1,875,519 on domestic flights), and Chiangmai the second busiest for freight, with 17,617 tonnes.

Shipping. In 1996 Thailand had registered a total of 540 vessels with a total of 2·04 GRT, including 49 oil tankers, 154 cargo ships (10 refrigerated) and 15 liquefied gas tankers. In 1995, 2,524 vessels of 21·7m. NRT entered the port of Bangkok, where 17·9 tonnes of cargo were loaded.

Telecommunications. Main telephone lines numbered 4,826,700 in 1997 (79·6 per 1,000 population). There were 1,088,000 cellular phone subscribers in 1995, 900,000 PCs and 60,000 fax machines. Thailand had approximately 131,000 Internet users in Jan. 1998.

Postal Services. There were 4,264 post offices in 1994, or 1 for every 13,900 persons.

SOCIAL INSTITUTIONS

Justice. The judicial power is exercised in the name of the King, by *(a)* courts of first instance, *(b)* the court of appeal *(Uthorn)* and *(c)* the Supreme Court *(Dika)*. The King appoints, transfers and dismisses judges, who are independent in conducting trials and giving judgment in accordance with the law.

Courts of first instance are subdivided into 20 magistrates' courts *(Kwaeng)* with limited civil and minor criminal jurisdiction; 85 provincial courts *(Changwad)* with unlimited civil and criminal jurisdiction; the criminal and civil courts with exclusive jurisdiction in Bangkok; the central juvenile courts for persons under 18 years of age in Bangkok.

The court of appeal exercises appellate jurisdiction in civil and criminal cases from all courts of first instance. From it appeals lie to Dika Court on any point of law and, in certain cases, on questions of fact.

The Supreme Court is the supreme tribunal of the land. Besides its normal appellate jurisdiction in civil and criminal matters, it has semi-original jurisdiction over general election petitions. The decisions of Dika Court are final. Every person has the right to present a petition to the Government who will deal with all matters of grievance.

Religion. In 1993 there were 54·53m. Buddhists, 2·31m. Moslems, 0·29m. Christians and 0·69m. others.

Education. Education is compulsory for children for 9 years and is free in local municipal schools. In 1996 there were 34,001 primary schools with 5·9m. pupils. There were 3·7m. secondary school pupils with (in 1994) 151,008 teachers. In higher education there were 1·2m. students (481,936 at university level). In 1996 there were 13 universities, 2 open (distance) universities, 4 institutes of technology and 1 institute of development administration in the public sector, and 9 universities and 1 institute of technology in the private sector.

The adult literacy rate in 1995 was 93·8% (96·9% among males and 91·6% among females).

In 1994 total expenditure on education came to 3·8% of GNP and represented 18·9% of total government expenditure.

THAILAND

Health. In 1992 there were 1,097 hospitals, with a provision of 17 beds per 10,000 population. In 1994 there were 14,098 doctors, 2,984 dentists, 5,575 pharmacists, 94,103 nurses and 10,342 midwives.

CULTURE

Broadcasting. The Radio and Television Executive Committee controls the administrative, legal, technical and programming aspects of broadcasting, and consists of representatives of various government bodies. All radio stations are operated by, or under the supervision of, government agencies. Radio Thailand broadcasts 3 national programmes, provincial programmes, an educational service and an external service (9 languages), and the Voice of Free Asia. Television of Thailand is the state service (colour by PAL). There are 3 commercial channels and an Army service. In 1995 there were 11m. radio and 11m. TV sets in use.

Cinema. In 1993 there were 600 cinemas with a seating capacity of 380,011.

Press. In 1995 there were 35 daily newspapers, including 2 in English and 7 in Chinese, with a combined circulation of about 2·7m.

Tourism. In 1996, 7·19m. foreigners visited Thailand. Tourist revenue was estimated at 215,000m. baht.

DIPLOMATIC REPRESENTATIVES

Of Thailand in Great Britain (29–30 Queen's Gate, London, SW7 5JB)
Ambassador: Vidhya Rayananonda, KCVO.

Of Great Britain in Thailand (Wireless Rd., Bangkok 10330)
Ambassador: Sir James Hodge, KCVO, CMG.

Of Thailand in the USA (2300 Kalorama Rd., NW, Washington, D.C., 20008)
Ambassador: Nitya Pibulsonggram.

Of the USA in Thailand (120 Wireless Rd., Bangkok 10330)
Ambassador: William Itoh.

Of Thailand to the United Nations
Ambassador: Asda Jayanama.

Of Thailand to the European Union
Ambassador: Somkiati Ariyapruchya.

FURTHER READING

National Statistical Office *Thailand Statistical Yearbook.*

Girling, J. I. S., *Thailand: Society and Politics.* Cornell Univ. Press, 1981
Krongkaew, M. (ed.) *Thailand's Industrialization and its Consequences.* London, 1995
Kulick, E. and Wilson, D., *Thailand's Turn: Profile of a New Dragon.* London and New York, 1993 (NY, 1994)
Watts, M., *Thailand.* [Bibliography] Oxford and Santa Barbara (CA), 1986

National statistical office: National Statistical Office, Thanon Lan Luang, Bangkok 10100.

TOGO

République Togolaise

Capital: Lomé
Population estimate, 2000: 4·68m.
GNP per capita: (PPP$) 1,650
HDI/world rank: 0·380/144

KEY HISTORICAL EVENTS

The Africans of Togo are of several tribes, including the Ewes of the south (also living in Ghana and Benin), and the Kabres, Dagombas, Tyokossis and others in the north. They had small pre-colonial states but were dominated by the powerful kingdoms of Ashanti to the west and Dahomey to the east. Europeans, beginning with the Portuguese who first visited the area in 1471-72, traded on the coast for centuries, especially in slaves, but the area between the Gold Coast forts and Whydah was for long relatively unimportant for them. In the 19th century, however, palm oil exports flourished at Anecho, Agoue and Porto Seguro, where British, French and German traders operated. Several prominent Togolese families of partly Brazilian or Portuguese origin, still important among the coastal African élite, arose at that time. Protestant and Catholic missions began working before the establishment of colonial rule. Despite the important rival influences of Britain and France in the area, it was Germany that established colonial rule on the coast in 1884.

German control was then extended inland but encountered strong resistance from the Kabres, Konkombas and other peoples, and only in 1912 was the colony fully subdued.

German Togo was overrun by the Allies in 1914. It was partitioned in 1919 into British and French Mandated Territories under the League of Nations. After the Second World War French Togo and British Togoland became Trust Territories under the United Nations. In British Togoland a referendum was held on 9 May 1956, in which a majority voted for union with Gold Coast, although most people in the south voted for union with French Togo. The whole territory was merged with what soon afterwards became independent Ghana, but many Togolese objected. In French Togo partial self-government was granted in 1956. On 27 April 1960 the country became independent and Sylvanus Olympio was elected president.

On 13 Jan. 1963 the President Olympio was murdered by soldiers. His successor, Nicolas Grunitzky, was deposed in a bloodless military coup in Jan. 1967 and on 14 April 1967, Gen. (then Col.) Gnassingbé Eyadéma assumed the Presidency. Following a general strike in June 1991 the government agreed to hold a National Conference, and this elected an interim Supreme Republican Council. A new constitution was approved in 1992.

TERRITORY AND POPULATION

Togo is bounded in the west by Ghana, north by Burkina Faso, east by Benin and south by the Gulf of Guinea. The area is 56,785 sq. km. The population of Togo in 1981 (census) was 2,700,982; 1997 (estimate) 4·32m.; density, 76 per sq. km.

The UN gives a projected population for 2000 of 4·68m.

In 1997, 79% of the population lived in rural areas, and 46% were below the age of 15. The capital is Lomé (population in 1997, 375,000), other towns being Sokodé (51,000), Lama-Kara (35,000), Kpalimé (30,000), Atakpamé (30,000), Bassar (22,000), Dapaong (22,000) and Mango (20,000).

Area, population and chief town of the 5 regions:

Region	Area in sq. km	Population (1981 census)	Population (1984 estimate)	Chief town
Des Savanes	8,602	326,826	358,700	Dapaong
De La Kara	11,630	432,626	444,200	Lama-Kara
Centrale	13,182	269,174	310,500	Sokodé
Des Plateaux	16,975	561,656	708,100	Atakpamé
Maritime	6,396	1,039,700	1,147,800	Lomé

There are 37 ethnic groups. The south is largely populated by Ewe-speaking peoples (forming 44% of the population) and related groups, while the north is mainly inhabited by Hamitic groups speaking Kabre (27%), Gurma (14%) and Tem (4%). The official language is French but Ewe and Kabre are also taught in schools.

SOCIAL STATISTICS
Births, 1996, 197,000; deaths, 55,000. 1996 birth rate (per 1,000 population), 45·5; death rate, 12·8. Expectation of life (1995) was 54 years for males and 56 for females. Infant mortality, 1990–95, 91 per 1,000 live births; fertility rate, 6·6 births per woman. The growth rate in 1997 was 2·7%.

CLIMATE
The tropical climate produces wet seasons from March to July and from Oct. to Nov. in the south. The north has one wet season, from April to July. The heaviest rainfall occurs in the mountains of the west, south-west and centre. Lomé, Jan. 81°F (27·2°C), July 76°F (24·4°C). Annual rainfall 35" (875 mm).

CONSTITUTION AND GOVERNMENT
A referendum on 27 Sept. 1992 approved a new constitution by 98·11% of votes cast. Under this the *President* and the *National Assembly* are directly elected for 5-year terms. The latter has 81 seats and is elected for a 5-year term in single-seat constituencies.

National Anthem. 'Terre de nos aïeux' ('Land of our forefathers').

RECENT ELECTIONS
In the presidential elections held on 21 June 1998, it was clear that the chief opposition candidate Gilchrist Olympio, son of the country's first president, was going to win, but the paramilitary police intervened and prevented the count in the capital city, Lomé, from being completed; it was also reported that ballot boxes were seized and burnt. The head of the electoral commission resigned in protest along with 4 of its members and the EU and American observers declared the election to be fraudulent. The interior minister pronounced Gen. Gnassingbé Eyadéma the winner, enabling him to continue as the country's ruler, having already been in power since 1967.

At the parliamentary elections in Feb. 1994, the electorate was 2m. 352 candidates stood. The Togolese People's Assembly (RPT, the former sole party) gained 38 seats, the Action Committee for Renewal (CAR) 36 and the Togolese Union for Democracy (UTD) 7. Following by-elections on 4 and 20 Aug. 1996, the Assembly composition changed to: Action Committee for Renewal (CAR) 36; the Togolese People's Assembly (RPT) 35; Togolese Union for Democracy (UTD) 7; Union for Justice and Democracy (UJD) 2; Co-ordination of New Forces (CDN) 1.

At the last parliamentary elections on 21 March 1999, the main opposition parties to the RPT boycotted the election. Turn-out was 66%; the RPT won 79 seats, ind 2.

CURRENT ADMINISTRATION
President: Gen. Gnassingbé Eyadéma (since 1967, most recently re-elected on 21 June 1998; RPT).

A new cabinet was in the process of being formed by the RPT following the election of 21 March 1999.

Local Government. There are 5 regions, each under an inspector appointed by the President; they are divided into 31 prefectures and the capital Lomé, each administered by a district chief assisted by an elected district council.

DEFENCE
There is selective conscription which lasts for 2 years. Defence expenditure totalled US$29m. in 1997 (US$6 per capita).

Army. In 1997 the army consisted of 2 infantry, 1 Presidential Guard, 1 parachute commando and 1 support regiment. Equipment included 2 T-54/-55 main battle tanks. Strength (1997) 6,500, with a further 750 in a paramilitary gendarmerie.

Navy. In 1996 the Naval wing of the armed forces operated 2 inshore patrol craft from the naval base at Lomé. Naval personnel numbered 150.

Air Force. In 1997 the Air Force—established with French assistance—had 4 Brazilian-built EMB-326 Xavante (Aermacchi MB.326) armed jet trainers; 5 Alpha Jet advanced trainers, with strike capability, 1 turboprop Buffalo transport; 2 Beech King Air 200s and 1 Cessna 337 for liaison; 3 Epsilon armed trainers; 2 Lama helicopters. Personnel (1997), 250, with 9 combat aircraft.

INTERNATIONAL RELATIONS
Togo is a member of the UN, OAU and ECOWAS, and is an ACP member state of the ACP-EU relationship.

ECONOMY
Policy. After civil and economic turmoil in the early 1990s, a structural redevelopment programme, launched in 1994, resulted in positive growth after 2 years of negative growth and 2 years of growth at less than 1% prior to that. Private-sector development is encouraged and there are plans to privatize some 20 state companies.

Performance. Real GDP growth was estimated at 4·8% in 1997.

Budget. In 1997 revenues were an estimated US$232m. and expenditures US$252m.

Currency. The unit of currency is the *franc CFA* with a parity rate of 100 francs CFA to 1 French franc. Foreign exchange reserves were US$119m. in Dec. 1997. The inflation rate in 1995 was 15·7%; average inflation rate during the period 1990–96 was 9·4%. Total money supply in Dec. 1997 was 123bn. francs CFA.

Banking and Finance. The bank of issue is the Central Bank of West African States (BCEAO). 10 commercial and 2 development banks were based in Lomé in 1997. Bank deposits totalled 168,700m. francs CFA in 1989.

Weights and Measures. The metric system is in use.

ENERGY AND NATURAL RESOURCES
Electricity. Installed capacity in 1995 was 34,000 kW, and 90m. kWh of electricity were produced. Additional electricity is imported from Ghana.

Minerals. Output of phosphate rock (1995) 2,500,000 tonnes. Other minerals are limestone, iron ore (550m. tonnes in 1992) and marble.

Agriculture. Agriculture supports about 80% of the population and produced 35% of GDP in 1996. Most food production comes from individual holdings under 3 ha. Inland, the country is hilly; dry plains alternate with arable land. There are considerable plantations of oil and cocoa palms, coffee, cacao, kola, cassava and cotton. Production, 1995 (in 1,000 tonnes): Cassava, 469; tomatoes, 9; yams, 375; maize, 296; sorghum, 109; millet, 82; seed cotton, 44; rice, 26; groundnuts, 32; coffee, 16.

Livestock (1995, in 1,000): Cattle, 248; sheep, 1,200; pigs, 850; goats, 1,900.

Forestry. Forests covered 1,245,000 ha in 1995, or 22·9% of the land area (compared to 1,338,000 ha in 1990). Teak plantations covered 8,600 ha. In 1995, 2·4m. cu. metres of roundwood were cut.

Fisheries. The catch in 1995 totalled 13,723 tonnes (11,203 tonnes marine fish).

INDUSTRY
Industry is small-scale. Cement and textiles are produced and food processed.

Labour. In 1996 the workforce was 1,739,000 (60% males). Around 62% of the economically active population in 1995 were engaged in agriculture, fisheries and forestry. In 1994 the statutory minimum wage was 75·60 francs CFA per hour.

Trade Unions. With the abandonment of single-party politics, the former monolithic Togo National Workers Confederation (CNTT) has split into several federations and independent trade unions.

INTERNATIONAL TRADE

A free trade zone was established in 1990. Foreign debt was US$1,463m. in 1996.

Imports and Exports. (in US$1m.):

	1994	1995	1996
Imports	222	385	404
Exports	162	209	239

The main import suppliers in 1994 were France (24·0%), Germany (9·9%) and Côte d'Ivoire (6·3%). Principal export destinations were Canada (17·0%), Bolivia (7·6%) and Indonesia (5·7%).

COMMUNICATIONS

Roads. There were, in 1996, 7,520 km of roads, of which 2,380 km were paved. In 1995 there were 74,662 passenger cars, 54,902 motor cycles and 32,514 commercial vehicles.

Rail. There are 4 metre-gauge railways connecting Lomé, with Aného (continuing to Cotonou in Benin), Kpalimé, Tabligbo and (via Atakpamé) Blitta; total length 525 km. In 1994 the railways carried 5·7 tonne-km and 0·6m. passengers.

Civil Aviation. Togo is a member of the multinational Air Afrique. In 1998 it had flights from Tokoin airport, near Lomé, to Abidjan, Accra, Bamako, Bangui, Brazzaville, Cotonou, Dakar, Douala, Libreville, N'Djaména, Ouagadougou, Paris and Pointe Noire. Services were also provided in 1998 by Air Burkina, Ethiopian Airlines, Air France, Air Gabon, Air Guinée, Ghana Airways, KLM, Nigeria Airways, Nouvelles Frontières, SABENA, Aeroflot and Tap Air Portugal. Air Burkina also provided an internal service from Lomé to Niamtougou in 1998, and had flights from Niamtougou to Ouagadougou.

In 1995, 3,068 tonnes of freight (import, 1,450; export, 1,618) was transported, and scheduled airline traffic of Togo-based carriers flew 2·6m. km, carrying 74,000 passengers.

Shipping. In 1995 merchant shipping totalled 1,000 GRT.

Telecommunications. Togo had 25,100 main telephone lines in 1997 (5·8 per 1,000 population). In 1995 there were 10,000 fax machines, and in Jan. 1998 approximately 300 Internet users.

Postal Services. In 1995 there were 50 post offices.

SOCIAL INSTITUTIONS

Justice. The Supreme Court and two Appeal Courts are in Lomé, one for criminal cases and one for civil and commercial cases. Each receives appeal from a series of local tribunals.

Religion. In 1997, 60% of the population followed traditional animist religions; 28·5% were Christian and 12% Moslem.

Education. The adult literacy rate in 1995 was 51·7% (67% among males and 37% among females). In 1995-96 there were 824,626 pupils and 16,217 teachers in 3,283 primary schools; in 1994-95 there were 153,348 pupils and 4,847 teachers in secondary schools, and 11,172 students in higher education institutions. In 1990 about 50% of children of school age were attending school. The University of Benin at Lomé (founded in 1970) had 9,139 students and 134 academic staff in 1994-95. An estimated 23,800m. francs CFA was spent on education in 1995.

Health. In 1990 hospital bed provision was 16 per 10,000 population. In 1991 there were 319 doctors, 22 dentists, 65 pharmacists, 222 midwives and 1,187 nursing staff. Government expenditure on health in 1995 was estimated at 5,900m. francs CFA.

CULTURE

Broadcasting. Broadcasting is provided by the government-controlled Radiodiffusion-Télévision Togolaise. There were 880,000 radio and 50,000 TV receivers (colour by SECAM) in 1995.

Press. There is 1 government-controlled daily newspaper (circulation 10,000).

Tourism. In 1996 there were 58,000 foreign tourists, bringing revenue of US$8m.

DIPLOMATIC REPRESENTATIVES
The Embassy of Togo in Great Britain closed on 30 Sept. 1991.

Of Great Britain in Togo
Ambassador: Ian W. Mackley, CMG (resides in Ghana).

Of Togo in the USA (2208 Massachusetts Ave., NW, Washington, D.C., 20008)
Ambassador: Akoussouleou Bodjona.

Of the USA in Togo (Rue Pelletier Caventou and Rue Vauban, Lomé)
Ambassador: Brenda Schoonover.

Of Togo to the United Nations
Ambassador: Roland Yao Kpotsra.

Of Togo to the European Union
Ambassador: Elliott Latévi-Atcho Lawson.

FURTHER READING
Cornevin, R., *Histoire du Togo.* 3rd ed., Paris, 1969
Decalo, S., *Togo.* [Bibliography] Oxford and Santa Barbara (CA), 1995
Feuillet, C., *Le Togo en Général.* Paris, 1976

TONGA

Kingdom of Tonga

Capital: Nuku'alofa
Population estimate, 2000: 110,000
Estimated GDP: $228m.

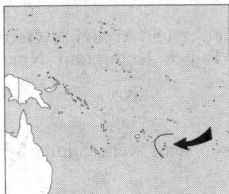

KEY HISTORICAL EVENTS

The Tongatapu group of islands in the south western Pacific Ocean was discovered by Tasman in 1643. The Kingdom of Tonga attained unity under Taufa'ahau Tupou (George I) who became ruler of his native Ha'apai in 1820, of Vava'u in 1833 and of Tongatapu in 1845. By 1860 the kingdom had become converted to Christianity (George himself having been baptized in 1831). In 1862 the king granted freedom to the people from arbitrary rule of minor chiefs and gave them the right to the allocation of land for their own needs. These institutional changes, together with the establishment of a parliament of chiefs, paved the way towards the democratic constitution under which the kingdom is now governed.

The kingdom continued up to 1899 as a neutral region in accordance with the Declaration of Berlin of 6 April 1886. By the Anglo-German Agreement of 14 Nov. 1899, subsequently accepted by the USA, the Tonga Islands were left under the Protectorate of Great Britain. A protectorate was proclaimed on 18 May 1900 and a British Agent and Consul appointed. The Protectorate was dissolved on 4 June 1970 when Tonga, the only ancient kingdom surviving from the pre-European period in Polynesia, achieved complete independence within the Commonwealth.

TERRITORY AND POPULATION

The Kingdom consists of some 169 islands and islets with a total area of 289 sq. miles (748 sq. km; including inland waters), and lies between 15° and 23° 30' S. lat and 173° and 177° W. long, its western boundary being the eastern boundary of the Fiji Islands. The islands are split up into the following groups (reading from north to south): The Niuas, Vava'u, Ha'apai, Tongatapu and 'Eua. The 3 main groups, both from historical and administrative significance, are Tongatapu in the south, Ha'apai in the centre and Vava'u in the north.

Census population (1996) 97,000. July 1997 estimate, 107,335; density, 144 per sq. km. In 1995, 59% of the population lived in rural areas.

The capital is Nuku'alofa on Tongatapu, population (1986) 29,018.

There are 5 divisions comprising 23 districts:

Division	Sq. km	Census 1986	Capital
Niuas	72	2,368	Hihifo
Vava'u	119	15,175	Neiafu
Ha'apai	110	8,919	Pangai
Tongatapu	261	63,794	Nuku'alofa
'Eua	87	4,393	Ohonua

In 2000 the population is projected to be 110,000.

Tongan and English are both spoken.

SOCIAL STATISTICS

Annual growth rate, 1990–95, 0·3%.

CLIMATE

Generally a healthy climate, although Jan. to March hot and humid, with temperatures of 90°F (32·2°C). Rainfall amounts are comparatively high, being greatest from Dec. to March. Nuku'alofa, Jan. 25·8°C, July 21·3°C. Annual rainfall 1,643 mm. Vava'u, Jan. 27·3°C, July 23·4°C. Annual rainfall 2,034 mm.

CONSTITUTION AND GOVERNMENT

The reigning King is **Taufa'ahau Tupou IV**, GCVO, GCMG, KBE, born 4 July 1918, succeeded on 16 Dec. 1965 on the death of his mother, Queen Salote Tupou III.

TONGA

The present Constitution is almost identical with that granted in 1875 by King George Tupou I. There is a Privy Council, Cabinet, Legislative Assembly and Judiciary. The 30-member *Legislative Assembly*, which meets annually, is composed of the King, 9 nobles elected by their peers, 9 elected representatives of the people and the Privy Councillors (numbering 11); the King appoints one of the 9 nobles to be the Speaker. The elections are held triennially.

National Anthem. 'E 'Otua, Mafimafi, ko ho mau 'eiki Koe' ('Oh Almighty God above, thou art our Lord and sure defence'); words by Prince Uelingtoni Ngu Tupoumalohi, tune by K. G. Schmitt.

RECENT ELECTIONS
Elections were held on 11 March 1999 for the 9 elected seats. 5 seats were gained by the Human Rights and Democracy Movement.

CURRENT ADMINISTRATION
In March 1999 the government comprised:
Prime Minister: Baron Vaea.
Deputy Prime Minister, Minister of Education, of Public Works, Civil Aviation and Disaster Relief: Dr S. Langi Kavaliku.
Minister of Agriculture and Marine Affairs: Prince Fatafehi Tu'ipelehake. *Labour, Commerce, Industries and Tourism:* Dr Hulioo Tukikolongahau Paunga. *Foreign Affairs and Defence:* HRH The Crown Prince Lavaka ata Ulukalala. *Health:* Dr Vailami Tangi. *Justice:* Tevita Tupou. *Police and Immigration:* Clive Edwards. *Finance:* Tutoatasi Fakafanua. *Lands, Surveys and Natural Resources and Governor of Vava'u:* Tu'i'afitu.

DEFENCE
A naval force some 125-strong in 1996 operated 3 inshore patrol craft and 1 ex-Australian amphibious craft base at Tuliki, Nuku'alofa. An Air Force was created in 1996 and operates 3 Beech 18s for maritime patrol.

INTERNATIONAL RELATIONS
Tonga is a member of the Commonwealth, the Pacific Community and the South Pacific Forum, and is an ACP member state of the ACP-EU relationship.

ECONOMY
Performance. Real GDP growth was 5·4% in 1995 and 0·3% in 1994.

Budget. Revenues were estimated to be US$44m. in 1995, with expenditures US$86m.

Currency. The unit of currency is the *pa'anga* (TOP) of 100 *seniti*. The average annual inflation rate over the period 1990–96 was 3·7%. In Jan. 1998 foreign exchange reserves were US$25m. In Dec. 1997 total money supply was T$23,801,000.

Banking and Finance. The National Reserve Bank of Tonga was established in 1989 as a bank of issue and to manage foreign reserves. The Bank of Tonga and the Tonga Development Bank are both situated in Nuku'alofa with branches in the main islands.

ENERGY AND NATURAL RESOURCES
Electricity. Production (1994) 30m. kWh. Capacity (1995) 7,000 kW.

Agriculture. Agriculture accounted for 37% of GDP in 1996. Production (1992, in 1,000 tonnes): Coconuts, 25; fruit and vegetables, 28; copra, 2; cassava, 15.
Livestock (1996): Cattle, 9,000; horses, 11,000; pigs, 81,000; goats, 16,000.

Forestry. Timber production in 1995 was 5,000 cu. metres.

Fisheries. In 1995 the catch totalled 2,596 tonnes.

INTERNATIONAL TRADE

Imports and Exports. In 1996 imports were valued at US$75m. and exports at US$11m. Main exports are coconut oil, vanilla beans, dessicated coconut and water melons. The leading import suppliers in 1995-96 were New Zealand (36·1%), Australia (28·9%), USA (11·5%) and Japan (8·0%). Principal export markets in 1995-96 were Japan (51·8%), USA (27·7%), New Zealand (8·3%) and Australia (4·0%).

COMMUNICATIONS

Roads. In 1996 there were 680 km of roads (184 km paved). Vehicles in use in 1996 numbered approximately 1,140 passenger cars, 740 trucks and vans, and 40 buses and coaches.

Civil Aviation. There is an international airport at Tongatapu (Fua'Amotu International). The national carrier is the state-owned Royal Tongan Airlines, which in 1998 provided domestic services and had flights to Auckland, the Fiji Islands, Honolulu, Los Angeles, Niue, Samoa and Sydney. Services were also provided in 1998 by Air New Zealand, Air Pacific and Polynesian Airlines. In 1996 Fua'Amotu International handled 127,382 passengers (86,953 on international flights) and 968 tonnes of freight.

Shipping. In 1995 sea-going shipping totalled 12,307 GRT. 2 shipping lanes provide monthly services to American Samoa, Australia, the Fiji Islands, Kiribati, New Caledonia, New Zealand, Samoa and Tuvalu.

Telecommunications. The operation of the International Telecommunication Services is undertaken by Cable and Wireless, under an agreement between the Company and the Government. The operation and development of the National Telecommunication Network and Services are the responsibilities of the Tonga Telecommunication Commission. There were 7,800 main telephone lines in 1996, or 79 per 1,000 population. In 1995 cellular phone subscribers numbered around 100 and there were approximately 200 fax machines.

SOCIAL INSTITUTIONS

Justice. The judiciary is presided over by the Chief Justice. The enforcement of justice is the responsibility of the Attorney-General and the Minister of Police. In 1994 the UK ceased appointing Tongan judges and subsidizing their salaries.

Religion. The Tongans are mainly Christian adherents of the Free Wesleyan Church. Some 40% are Latter-day Saints (Mormons).

Education. In 1993 there were 115 primary schools, with a total of 17,000 pupils. There were 7 government and 32 mission schools, and 1 private school offering secondary education, with a total roll of 15,000. There is an extension centre of the University of the South Pacific at Nuku'alofa, a teacher training college and 3 technical institutes.

In 1993 total expenditure on education came to 4·8% of GNP and represented 17·3% of total government expenditure.

Health. There were 4 hospitals in 1993, and 45 doctors, 9 dentists and 292 nurses.

CULTURE

Broadcasting. The Tonga Broadcasting Commission is an independent statutory board which operates 2 programmes. There is also a religious service. There were 56,000 radio sets in 1995. There are 2 television channels, and in 1995 an estimated 2,000 TV receivers.

Press. In 1995 there was 1 daily newspaper with a circulation of 7,000.

Tourism. There were 100,000 visitors in 1996. Receipts totalled US$100m.

DIPLOMATIC REPRESENTATIVES

Of Tonga in Great Britain (36 Molyneux St., London, W1H 6AB)
High Commissioner: 'Akosita Fineanganofo.

Of Great Britain in Tonga (POB 56 Nuku'alofa)
High Commissioner: B. Connelly.

Of Tonga in the USA
Ambassador: 'Akosita Fineanganofo (resides in London).

Of the USA in Tonga
Ambassador: Don Gevirtz (resident in the Fiji Islands).

Of Tonga to the European Union
Ambassador: 'Akosita Fineanganofo.

FURTHER READING

Campbell, I. C., *Island Kingdom: Tonga, Ancient and Modern.* Canterbury (NZ) Univ. Press, 1994

TRINIDAD AND TOBAGO

Republic of Trinidad
and Tobago

Capital: Port-of-Spain
Population estimate, 2000: 1·34m.
GNP per capita: (PPP$) 6,100
HDI/world rank: 0·880/40

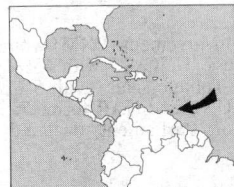

KEY HISTORICAL EVENTS

Trinidad and Tobago lie just off the coast of Venezuela in the Caribbean Sea. When Columbus visited Trinidad in 1498 the island was inhabited by Arawak Indians. Tobago was occupied by the Caribs. Trinidad remained a neglected Spanish possession for almost 300 years until it was surrendered to a British naval expedition in 1797. The main crop on the island was tobacco.

The British first attempted to settle Tobago in 1721 but the French captured the island in 1781 and transformed it into a sugar-producing colony. In 1802 the British acquired Tobago and in 1899 it was administratively combined with Trinidad. When slavery was abolished in the late 1830s, the British subsidized immigration from India to replace plantation labourers. Sugar and cocoa declined towards the end of the 19th century. Oil and asphalt became the dominant sources of income.

On 31 Aug. 1962 Trinidad and Tobago became an independent member state of the Commonwealth. A Republican Constitution was adopted on 1 Aug. 1976.

During an attempted coup in July 1990 by a Moslem sect, the prime minister was taken hostage and wounded.

TERRITORY AND POPULATION

The island of Trinidad is situated in the Caribbean Sea, about 12 km off the north-east coast of Venezuela; several islets, the largest being Chacachacare, Huevos, Monos and Gaspar Grande, lie in the Gulf of Paria which separates Trinidad from Venezuela. The smaller island of Tobago lies 30·7 km further to the north-east. Altogether, the islands cover 5,124 sq. km (1,978 sq. miles), of which Trinidad (including the islets) has 4,821 sq. km (1,861 sq. miles) and Tobago 303 sq. km (117 sq. miles). Population (census 1995) 1,259,972 (Trinidad, 1,208,625; Tobago, 51,347). Estimate, 1996, 1,272,500; density, 248 per sq. km.

The UN gives a projected population for 2000 of 1·34m.

An estimated 71·7% of the population were urban in 1995. Capital, Port-of-Spain (1995 census, 45,284); other important towns, San Fernando (55,784), Arima (24,874) and Point Fortin (20,084). The main town on Tobago is Scarborough. Those of African descent are (1990 census) 39·6% of the population, Indians, 40·3%, mixed races, 18·4%, European, Chinese and others, 1·2%.

English is the official language.

SOCIAL STATISTICS

1997 birth rate (per 1,000 population), 14·0; death rate, 7·2; growth rate, 0·7%. Births, 1997, 18,300; deaths, 9,400. Expectation of life, 1990–95, was 70·5 years for males and 75·2 for females. Infant mortality, 1990–95, 16 per 1,000 live births; fertility rate, 2·3 births per woman.

CLIMATE

A tropical climate cooled by the north-east trade winds. The dry season runs from Jan. to June, with a wet season for the rest of the year. Temperatures are uniformly high the year round. Port-of-Spain, Jan. 76·3°F (24·6°C), July 79·2°F (26·2°C). Annual rainfall 1,869·8 mm.

CONSTITUTION AND GOVERNMENT

The 1976 Constitution provides for a bicameral legislature of a *Senate* and a *House of Representatives*, who elect the *President*, who is head of state. The *Senate* consists of 31 members, 16 being appointed by the President on the advice of the

Prime Minister, 6 on the advice of the Leader of the Opposition and 9 at the discretion of the President.

The *House of Representatives* consists of 36 (34 for Trinidad and 2 for Tobago) elected members and a Speaker elected from within or outside the House.

Executive power is vested in the Prime Minister, who is appointed by the President, and the Cabinet.

National Anthem. 'Forged from the love of liberty'; words and music by P. Castagne.

RECENT ELECTIONS

At the general election of 6 Nov. 1995 the People's National Movement (PNM) won 17 seats with 50% of votes cast, the United National Congress (UNC) 17 with 45%, and the National Alliance for Reconstruction (NAR) 2 (the Tobago seats) with 5%. In 1995 the PNM became the official Opposition, while the UNC and NAR formed a coalition government. In 1997, two PNM members of Parliament declared themselves independents.

CURRENT ADMINISTRATION

President: HE Arthur Napoleon Raymond Robinson.

In March 1999 the Cabinet comprised:

Prime Minister: Basdeo Panday (b. 1933; UNC).

Finance: Brian Kuei Tung. *Legal Affairs:* Kamla Persad-Bissessar. *Energy and Energy Industries:* Finbar K. Gangar. *Public Utilities:* Ganga Singh. *Trade and Industry, Consumer Affairs and Tourism:* Mervyn Assam. *National Security:* Brig.-Gen. Joseph Theodore. *Foreign Affairs:* Ralph Maraj. *Public Administration:* Mark Wade. *Sport and Youth Affairs, Social and Community Development:* Manohar Ramsaran. *Local Government:* Dhanraj Singh. *Works and Transport:* Sadiq Baksh. *Education:* Dr Adesh Nanan. *Health:* Dr Hamza Rafeeq. *Planning and Development:* Trevor Sudama. *Labour and Co-operatives:* Harry Partap. *Culture and Gender Affairs:* Dr Daphne Phillips. *Agriculture, Land and Marine Resources:* Dr Reeza Mohammed. *Housing and Settlements:* John Humphrey. *Tobago Affairs:* Dr Morgan Job. *Information, Communications, Training and Distance Learning:* Dr Rupert Griffith.

There is a Minister in the Ministry of Planning and Development with responsibility for the Environment, Dr Vincent Lasse, and 4 Parliamentary Secretaries: Chandresh Sharma (*Works and Transport*), Carol Cuffy-Dowlat (*Housing*), Vimala Tota-Maharaj (*Agriculture, Lands and Marine Resources*) and Nizam Baksh (*Social and Community Development*).

The *Speaker* of the House of Representatives is Hector McClean.

Leader of the Opposition: Patrick Manning.

President of the Senate: Ganesh Ramdial.

Local Government. Trinidad is divided into 9 regional corporations, 2 city corporations, 3 borough corporations. Tobago has a 15-member elected House of Assembly with limited powers of self-government. Local elections were held on 24 June 1996. The electorate was 816,809; turn-out was 43·95%. The PNM gained 43·95% of the votes cast, the UNC 49·92%, the NAR 5·81% and the independents 0·59%.

DEFENCE

The Defence Force has 2 infantry battalions and 1 support battalion. The small air element was disbanded in 1994. Security aircraft are operated by the police. Personnel in 1996 totalled 2,100.

The Coast Guard of 700 (1996) operates 8 inshore patrol craft, a number of boats, and has 2 Cessna light aircraft for patrol duties.

The paramilitary police has 4,800 personnel.

In 1997 defence expenditure totalled US$83m. (US$63 per capita).

INTERNATIONAL RELATIONS

Trinidad and Tobago is a member of the UN and many of its specialized agencies including WIPO, IMF, World Bank, IDA, IFC, IOB and ILO; and of the

Commonwealth, OAS, CARICOM, Association of Caribbean States (ACS), Caribbean Development Bank, Andean Development Bank, and is an ACP member state of the ACP-EU relationship.

ECONOMY

Performance. Real GDP growth was 3·2% in 1997. The forecast for 1998 was 4·5%.

Budget. The fiscal year for the Budget is 1 Oct. to 30 Sept. In 1997 total government revenue was TT$10,024·3m. (TT$11,547m. in 1996) and total expenditure was TT$9,775·9m. (TT$11,010m. in 1996). The budget envisaged total recurrent expenditure of TT$8,727·6m. (TT$7,837m. in 1996) and total capital expenditure of TT$1,048·3m. (TT$2,269·1m. in 1996).

Currency. The unit of currency is the *Trinidad and Tobago dollar* (TTD) of 100 *cents*. The average annual inflation rate over the period 1990–96 was 6·5%, and 3·5% in Oct. 1996. In April 1994 the TT dollar was floated and managed by the Central Bank at TT$6·06 to US$1·00. In Nov. 1997, the TT dollar depreciated to an all-time low of TT$6·29 to US$1·00. Foreign exchange reserves in Oct. 1997 were US$652m. Total money supply in Nov. 1997 was TT$3,805m.

Banking and Finance. A Central Bank began operations in 1964 (*Governor*, Winston Dookeran). Its net reserves were US$507·4m. in Dec. 1996. There are 6 commercial banks. Government savings banks are established in 69 offices, with a head office in Port-of-Spain. The stock exchange in Port-of-Spain participates in the regional Caribbean exchange.

ENERGY AND NATURAL RESOURCES

Electricity. Installed capacity was 1·25m. kW in 1995. In 1997, 4,481m. kWh was generated. Consumption per capita in 1995 was estimated to be 2,885 kWh.

Oil and Gas. Oil production is one of Trinidad's leading industries. Commercial production began in 1909; production of crude oil in 1996 was 47,951,000 bbls. Crude oil is also imported for refining. Oil accounted for 30% of GDP and 75% of revenues in 1996, but dependence on the oil industry is declining.

In 1997 production of natural gas was 4,111,000 bbls. Proven reserves of natural gas were 19,000bn. cu. ft in 1998, compared to 8,000bn. cu. ft in 1993. Production was 850m. cu. ft per day in 1998, but a proposed US$3bn. investment plan by a consortium of US, European and local companies was to increase production to an estimated 1,500m. cu. ft per day in 1999.

Agriculture. Sugar production in 1997 was 137,000 tonnes; cocoa, 1,740,000 kg; coffee, 1,101,000kg. In 1994 there were 75,000 ha of arable land, 47,000 ha of permanent cropland and 11,000 ha of pasture; 22,000 ha were irrigated in 1994.

Livestock (1995): Cattle 36,000; sheep, 12,000; goats, 59,000; pigs, 45,000; chickens, 10m. Livestock products, 1995: Beef, 1,175 tonnes; pork, 1,585 tonnes (2,808 tonnes in 1997); broilers, 15,532 (13,986 in 1997).

Forestry. Forests covered 161,000 ha in 1995, or 31·4% of the land area (down from 174,000 ha in 1990). Timber production in 1995 was 68,000 cu. metres.

Fisheries. The catch in 1997 was 14,046 tonnes.

INDUSTRY

In 1997, 2,548,800 tonnes of iron and steel were produced. Other manufacturing includes ammonia and urea (production, 1997, 2,690,700 tonnes), methanol (1997, 1,520,000 tonnes), cement (1997, 652,000 tonnes), rum (1997, 4,726,000 proof gallons), beer (1997, 36,937,000 litres), cigarettes (1997, 1,043,000 kg), sugar (1997, 137,000 tonnes), fertilizer (1997, 2,691,000 tonnes). Trinidad and Tobago is set to become the world's largest producer of ammonia and methanol.

Labour. The working population in 1997 was 541,000. The number of unemployed was 81,200. In 1995, 133,000 people worked in community, social and personal services, 81,000 in trade, restaurants and hotels, and 46,000 in agriculture, fishing and forestry.

Trade Unions. About 30% of the labour force belong to unions, which are grouped under the National Trade Union Centre.

INTERNATIONAL TRADE

The Foreign Investment Act of 1990 permits foreign investors to acquire land and shares in local companies, and to form companies. External debt was TT$10,105·1m. in Dec. 1996.

Imports and Exports. Exports in 1996 were TT$15,014m. of which TT$7,546m. was mineral fuels and products. Imports totalled TT$12,867m. of which TT$3,945m. was for machinery and transport equipment. Exports in 1997 were TT$15,903m.; imports were TT$18,934·5m. The principal import sources in 1995 were USA (50·4%), UK (6·8%), Germany (6·2%) and Canada (5·2%). The main export markets in 1995 were USA (43·3%), Jamaica (8·4%), Guyana (3·1%) and Barbados (also 3·1%).

COMMUNICATIONS

Roads. In 1996 there were 9,586 km of main and local roads. Motor vehicles registered in 1997 totalled 237,299.

Civil Aviation. There is an international airport at Port-of-Spain (Piarco) and in Tobago (Crown Point). The national carrier is BWIA International Trinidad and Tobago Airways, which was privatized in March 1995 by the Acker group of companies. In 1998 it flew to Antigua, Barbados, Caracas, Georgetown , Grenada, Kingston, London, Miami, New York, St Lucia, St Maarten, Tobago and Toronto. Services were also provided in 1998 by Aeropostal Alas de Venezuela, Air Canada, Air Caribbean, ALM, American Airlines, British Airways, Caledonian Airways, Guyana Airways Corporation, Helenair Corporation, LIAT, Regional Air Caribbean and Surinam Airways.

Shipping. Sea-going shipping totalled 17,037 GRT in 1995 and 11,703,768 tonnes of cargo were handled. A deep-water harbour at Scarborough (Tobago) was opened in 1991. The other main harbours are Point Lisas and Port-of-Spain.

Telecommunications. International and domestic communications are provided by Telecommunications Services of Trinidad and Tobago (TSTT) by means of a satellite earth station and various high-quality radio circuits. The marine radio service is also maintained by TSTT. Number of telephone main lines, 1997, 243,400 (190·1 per 1,000 population). There were 5,600 cellular phone subscribers, 25,000 PCs and 2,600 fax machines in 1995.

Postal Services. Number of post offices (1998), 75; postal agencies, 167.

SOCIAL INSTITUTIONS

Justice. The High Court consists of the Chief Justice and 11 puisne judges. In criminal cases a judge of the High Court sits with a jury of 12 in cases of treason and murder, and with 9 jurors in other cases. The Court of Appeal consists of the Chief Justice and 7 Justices of Appeal. In hearing appeals, the Court is comprised of 3 judges sitting together except when the appeal is from a Summary Court or from a decision of a High Court judge in chambers. In such cases 2 judges would comprise the Court. There is a limited right of appeal from it to the Privy Council. There are 3 High Courts and 12 magistrates' courts. There is an *Ombudsman*. The death penalty is authorized.

Religion. In 1997, 14·4% of the population were Anglicans (under the Bishop of Trinidad and Tobago), 32·2% Roman Catholics (under the Archbishop of Port-of-Spain), 24·3% Hindus and 6% Moslems.

Education. In 1996–97 there were 181,003 pupils enrolled in 476 primary schools, 16,321 in government secondary schools, 20,103 in assisted secondary schools, 35,192 in junior secondary schools, 24,102 in senior comprehensive schools, 8,148 in composite schools and 4,221 in technical and vocational schools. The University of the West Indies campus in St Augustine (1996–97) had 4,580 students and 509 academic staff. 693 of the students were from other countries.

Adult literacy was 97·9% in 1995 (male, 98·8%; female, 97%).

In 1994 total expenditure on education came to 4·5% of GNP.

Health. In 1997 there were 949 physicians, 141 dentists, 518 pharmacists and 77 hospitals and nursing homes with 4,771 beds. There were 1,378 nurses and midwives and 1,369 nursing assistants in government institutions.

CULTURE

Broadcasting. Radio programmes are overseen by the Telecommunications Authority. There are 16 commercial stations. There are 3 TV stations, as well as community and cable services. In 1995 there were 650,000 radio and 415,000 television receivers.

Cinema. In 1996 there were 19 cinemas and 1 drive-in cinema.

Press. As at Oct. 1996 there were 4 daily newspapers with a total daily circulation of 219,000, 4 Sunday newspapers with a total circulation of 224,000, 6 weekly and 1 bi-weekly newspaper.

Tourism. There were 324,293 visitors in 1997. There were 48,145 cruise ship visitors in 1996.

Festivals. Religious festivals: The Feast of La Divina Pastora, or Sipari Mai, a Catholic and Hindu celebration of the Holy Mother Mary; Saint Peter's Day Celebration, the Patron Saint of Fishermen; Hosein, or Hosay, a Shiite Moslem festival; Phagwah, a Hindu spring festival; Santa Rosa, celebrated on 30 Aug.; Eid-ul-Fitr, a Moslem festival at the end of Ramadan; Divali, the Hindu festival of light; Christmas.

Cultural festivals: Carnival (on 6 and 7 March in 2000); Spiritual Baptist Shouter Liberation Day (30 March), a recognition of the Baptist religion; Indian Arrival Day (30 May), commemorating the arrival of the first East Indian labourers; Sugar and Energy Festival; Pan Ramajay, a music festival of all types; Emancipation (1 Aug.), a recognition of the period of slavery; Tobago Heritage Festival, celebrating Tobago's traditions and customs; Parang Festival, traditional folk music of Christmas; Pan Jazz Festival; Music Festival, predominantly classical music but Indian and Calypso are included.

Museums and Galleries. Port-of-Spain has a National Museum and Art Gallery, the Aquarela Galleries, the 101 Art Gallery, and Gallery 1.2.3.4. The Chaguaramas Military History and Aviation Museum is at Chaguaramas; Art Creators is at Saint Ann's; Okazions is in Westmoorings; and On Location is at St James.

DIPLOMATIC REPRESENTATIVES
Of Trinidad and Tobago in Great Britain (42 Belgrave Sq., London, SW1X 8NT)
High Commissioner: Sheelagh M. de Osuna.

Of Great Britain in Trinidad and Tobago (19 St Clair Ave., Port-of-Spain)
High Commissioner: Gregory Faulkner.

Of Trinidad and Tobago in the USA (1708 Massachusetts Ave., NW, Washington, D.C., 20036)
Ambassador: Michael Arneaud.

Of the USA in Trinidad and Tobago (15 Queen's Park West, Port-of-Spain)
Ambassador: Edward Shumaker III.

Of Trinidad and Tobago to the United Nations
Ambassador: George Winston McKenzie.

Of Trinidad and Tobago to the European Union
Ambassador: Lingston Cumberbatch.

FURTHER READING
Chambers, F., *Trinidad and Tobago.* [Bibliography] Oxford and Santa Barbara (CA), 1986
Cooper, St G. C. and Bacon, P. R. (eds.) *The Natural Resources of Trinidad and Tobago.* London, 1981
Central library: The Central Library of Trinidad and Tobago, Queen's Park East, Port-of-Spain.

National statistical office: Central Statistical Office, 2 Edward St., Port-of-Spain.

TUNISIA

Jumhuriya at-Tunisiya

(Republic of Tunisia)

Capital: Tunis
Population estimate, 2000: 9·84m.
GNP per capita: (PPP$) 4,550
HDI/world rank: 0·744/83

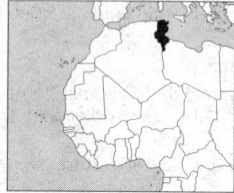

KEY HISTORICAL EVENTS

Settled by the Phoenicians, this area of the north African coast developed into the Carthaginian Empire and was later incorporated into the Roman Empire. It became a powerful state under the dynasty of the Berber Hafsids (1207-1574).

Tunisia was nominally a part of the Ottoman Empire from the end of the 17th century and descendants of the original Ottoman ruler remained Beys of Tunis until the modern state of Tunisia was established. A French protectorate since 1883, Tunisia saw considerable anti-French activity in the late 1930s including a general strike in 1938 led by the *Néo-Destour* party (renamed *Parti Socialiste Destourien*—PSD—in 1964) under Habib Bourguiba. Tunisia did, however, support the Allies in the Second World War and was the scene of heavy fighting.

France granted internal self-government in 1955 and Tunisia became fully independent on 20 March 1956. A constitutional assembly was established and Habib Bourguiba became prime minister. A republic was established in 1957, the Bey deposed and the monarchy was abolished; Bourguiba became president. In 1975 the constitution was changed so that Bourguiba could be made President-for-life.

Tunisia was a one-party (PSD) state until 1981. When elections were held on 2 Nov. 1986 all seats in the national assembly were won by *Front National*, an alliance of the PSD and the *Union générale des travailleurs tunisiens*. All other parties boycotted the elections.

Bourguiba was overthrown in a bloodless *coup* in 1987. His successor as president, Zine El Abidine Ben Ali, introduced democratic reforms but a long running struggle with Islamic fundamentalists has been marked by sporadic violence, and the suspension of political rights.

TERRITORY AND POPULATION

Tunisia is bounded in the north and east by the Mediterranean Sea, west by Algeria and south by Libya. The area is 154,530 sq. km. The 1996 official estimate put the total population at 9,092,000; density, 59 per sq. km.

The UN gives a projected population for 2000 of 9·84m.

In 1995 some 62% of the population were urban.

The 1984 census populations of the 23 governorates:

	Area in sq. km	Population		Area in sq. km	Population
Aryanah	1,558	374,192	Qasrayn (Kassérine)	8,066	297,959
Bajah (Béja)	3,558	274,706	Qayrawan (Kairouan)	6,712	421,607
Banzart (Bizerta)	3,685	394,670	Qibili (Kebili)	22,084	95,371
Bin Arus	761	246,193	Safaqis (Sfax)	7,545	577,992
Jundubah (Jendouba)	3,102	359,429	Sidi Bu Zayd		
Kaf (Le Kef)	4,965	247,672	(Sidi Bouzid)	6,994	288,528
Madaniyin (Médénine)	8,588	295,889	Silyanah (Siliana)	4,631	222,038
Mahdiyah (Mahdia)	2,966	270,435	Susah (Sousse)	2,621	322,491
Munastir (Monastir)	1,019	278,478	Tatawin (Tataouine)	38,889	100,329
Nabul (Nabeul)	2,788	461,405	Tawzar (Tozeur)	4,719	67,943
Qabis (Gabès)	7,175	240,016	Tunis	346	774,364
Qafsah (Gafsa)	8,990	235,723	Zaghwan (Zaghouan)	2,768	118,743

Tunis, the capital, had (1994 census, in 1,000) 674·1 inhabitants: Sfax, 230·9; Aryanah, 152·7; Ettadhamen, 149·2; Sousse, 125; Kairouan, a holy city of the Moslems, 102·6; Gabès, 98·9; Bizerta, 98·9; Bardo, 72·7; Gafsa, 71·1.

The official language is Arabic but French is the main language in the media, commercial enterprise and government departments. Berber-speaking people form less than 1% of the population.

TUNISIA

SOCIAL STATISTICS
Births, 1995, 223,000; deaths, 55,000; marriages, 53,726. Rates (1995): Birth, 24·8 per 1,000 population; death, 6·1. Annual growth rate, 1990–95, 1·9%. In 1996 the most popular age range for marrying was 25–29 for males and 20–24 for females. Expectation of life, 1990–95, was 66·9 years for males and 68·7 for females. Infant mortality, 1990–95, 43 per 1,000 live births; fertility rate, 3·3 births per woman.

CLIMATE
The climate ranges from warm temperate in the north, where winters are mild and wet and the summers hot and dry, to desert in the south. Tunis, Jan. 48°F (8·9°C), July 78°F (25·6°C). Annual rainfall 16" (400 mm). Bizerta, Jan. 52°F (11·1°C), July 77°F (25°C). Annual rainfall 25" (622 mm). Sfax, Jan. 52°F (11·1°C), July 78°F (25·6°C). Annual rainfall 8" (196 mm).

CONSTITUTION AND GOVERNMENT
The Constitution was promulgated on 1 June 1959 and reformed in 1988. The office of President-for-life was abolished and Presidential elections were to be held every 5 years. The *President* and the *National Assembly* are elected simultaneously by direct universal suffrage for a period of 5 years. The President cannot be re-elected more than 3 times consecutively.

The National Assembly has 163 seats, 144 directly elected by the first-past-the-post system and 19 distributed nationally by proportional representation to parties that fail to win seats under the first-past-the-post system.

National Anthem. 'Humata al Hima' ('Defenders of the Homeland'); words by Mustapha al Rafi, tune by M. A. Wahab.

RECENT ELECTIONS
Presidential and parliamentary elections were held on 20 March 1994; turn-out was 93%. President Zine El Abidine Ben Ali, the sole candidate, was re-elected by 99·8% of votes cast. The Constitutional Democratic Assembly (CDA) won all 144 of the directly elected National Assembly seats with 97·73% of votes cast. The next presidential and parliamentary elections are due to take place in Oct. 1999. The Islamist opposition movement (al-Nahda) was defeated in 1991; it is no longer seen as a threat to the Western-leaning government.

CURRENT ADMINISTRATION
President: Zine El Abidine Ben Ali (appointed 2 April 1989, re-elected 20 March 1994).

The Cabinet in March 1999 comprised:
Prime Minister: Hamed Karoui.
Minister, Head of the Presidential Cabinet: Mohamed Jegham. *Secretary General of the Government:* Ridha Grira. *Minister of Justice:* Abdullah Kallel. *Foreign Affairs:* Said Ben Mustapha. *Defence:* Habib Ben Yahia. *Interior:* Ali Chaouch. *International Co-operation and Foreign Investment:* Mohamed Ghannouchi. *Finance:* Mohamed Jeri. *Development:* Taoufik Baccar. *Transport:* Hassine Chouk. *Equipment and Housing:* Slaheddine Belaid. *Tourism and Handicrafts:* Slaheddine Maaoui. *Social Affairs:* Chedli Neffati. *Education:* Abderrahim Zouari. *Higher Education and Scientific Research:* Daly Jazi. *Employment and Professional Training:* Moncer Rouissi. *Public Health:* Hedi Mhenni. *Youth and Children:* Raouf Najjar. *Culture:* Abdelbaki Hermassi. *Environment and Land Use Management:* Mohamed Mehdi Mlika. *Agriculture:* Sadok Rabha. *State Landed Property:* Mustapha Bouaziz. *Communications:* Ahmed Friaa. *Religious Affairs:* Ali Chebbi. *Industry:* Moncef Ben Abdallah. *Commerce:* Mondher Znaidi. *Family and Women's Affairs:* Neziha Zarrouk.

The *Speaker* is Habib Boulares.

Local Government. The country is divided into 23 governorates, sub-divided into 199 districts and then into communes and *imadas*. On 21 May 1995 elections were held for the 3,774 seats on the 257 local councils. The CDA gained control of all councils.

TUNISIA

DEFENCE
Selective conscription is 1 year. Defence expenditure in 1997 totalled US$334m. (US$35 per capita), representing 1·8% of GDP.

Army. The Army consists of 3 mechanized, 1 Sahara and 1 special forces brigade; and 1 engineer regiment. Equipment includes 54 M-60A3 and 30 M-60A1 main battle tanks. Strength (1997) 27,000 (22,000 conscripts). There are also the paramilitary Police (13,000) and National Guard (10,000).

Navy. The Navy includes 3 French-built 380-tonne fast missile craft and 3 smaller craft with short range missiles. In 1996 naval personnel totalled 4,500. Forces are based at Bizerta, Sfax and Kelibia.

The Coast Guard operates 4 coastal and 19 inshore patrol craft.

Air Force. Equipment of the Air Force includes 1 squadron of Aermacchi M.B.326K/L; 1 squadron of L-59 jet light attack aircraft; 1 squadron of F-5E/F Tiger II fighters. Personnel (1996) about 3,500 (700 conscripts), with 44 combat aircraft.

INTERNATIONAL RELATIONS
Tunisia is a member of the UN, OAU, the Islamic Conference and the Arab League.

ECONOMY
Policy. The ninth 5-year development plan runs from 1997 to 2001. Growth is to reach 6% per annum; inflation is to be held at 4·1%.

Performance. Real GDP growth was 3·5% in 1995 and 3·3% in 1994.

Budget. The fiscal year is the calendar year. Revenue and expenditure in 1m. dinars:

	1993	1994	1995	1996
Revenue	3,845·7	4,089·7	4,214·9	4,854·3
Expenditure	3,995·8	4,227·1	4,603·2	4,930·1

Currency. The unit of currency is the *Tunisian dinar* (TND) of 1,000 *millimes*. The currency was made convertible on 6 Jan. 1993. Foreign exchange reserves were US$1,884m. in Jan. 1998 and gold reserves were 220,000 troy oz. Inflation was 3·7% in 1996. Total money supply was 4,329m. dinars in Jan. 1998.

Banking and Finance. The Central Bank of Tunisia is the bank of issue. In 1988 there were 9 development banks, 10 deposit banks and 9 off-shore banks.

There is a small stock exchange (16 companies trading in 1993).

Weights and Measures. The metric system is legal. Some traditional weights are still in use: 12 *sa* = 1 *wiba* = 1 bushel; 16 *wiba* = 1 *kfiz*; 1 *ounce* = 31·487 grammes.

ENERGY AND NATURAL RESOURCES
Electricity. Installed capacity was estimated to be 1·7m. kW in 1995. Production in 1996 was 7·55bn. kWh. Consumption per capita in 1995 was an estimated 678 kWh.

Oil and Gas. Crude petroleum production (1996) was 32m. bbls. Natural gas production (1995) 337m. cu. metres.

Water. In 1993 there were 20 large dams, 250 hillside dams and some 1,000 artificial lakes.

Minerals. Mineral production (in 1,000 tonnes) in 1995: Calcium phosphate, 6,302; iron ore, 225; lead ore (concentrated), 11·0; zinc ore (concentrated), 80·0; sea salt, 319.

Agriculture. Agriculture provided 14% of GDP in 1996. There are 5 agricultural regions: The *north*, mountainous with large fertile valleys; the *north-east*, with the peninsula of Cap Bon, suited for the cultivation of oranges, lemons and tangerines; the *Sahel*, where olive trees abound; the *centre*, a region of high tablelands and pastures; and the *desert* of the south, where dates are grown.

Some 23% of the population are employed in agriculture, which contributed 16·1% of GDP in 1992. Large estates predominate; smallholdings are tending to fragment, partly owing to inheritance laws. There were some 0·4m. farms in 1990 (0·32m. in 1960). Of the total area of 15,583,000 ha, about 9m. ha are productive, including 2m. under cereals, 3·6m. used as pasturage, 0·9m. forests and 1·3m. uncultivated. In 1994, 385,000 ha were irrigated. The main crops are cereals, citrus fruits, tomatoes, melons, olives, dates, grapes and olive oil. Production, 1995 (in

1,000 tonnes): Wheat, 530; barley, 80; olives, 630 (unofficial figure); dates, 84; almonds, 35; potatoes, 199 (unofficial figure); tomatoes, 452; peppers, 170; melons, including watermelons, 354; apples, 75; apricots, 24; citrus fruits, 271; pears, 42; peaches and nectarines, 59; plums 11; chickpeas, 27; sugar-beet, 246; tobacco, 6; grapes, 108; wine, 237,000 hectolitres.

Livestock, 1995 (in 1,000): Horses, 56; asses, 231; mules, 81; cattle, 659; sheep, 7,110; goats, 1,417; camels, 231; pigs, 6. Livestock products, 1995 (in 1,000 tonnes): Meat, 141; milk, 565; eggs, 62·5.

Forestry. In 1995 there were 555,000 ha of forests (3·6% of the land area). Timber production in 1995 was 3·56m. cu. metres.

Fisheries. In 1995 the catch amounted to 95,000 tonnes, almost exclusively from marine waters.

INDUSTRY
Production, 1996 (in 1,000 tonnes): phosphoric acid, 1,063; cement, 4,560; lime, 464. 2,010 cars, 450 lorries, 1,240 vans, 220 buses and coaches, 330 tractors.

Labour. The labour force in 1996 totalled 3,459,000 (69% males). Unemployment was 15·0% in 1996.

Trade Unions. The Union Générale des Travailleurs Tunisiens won 27 seats in the parliamentary elections of 1 Nov. 1981. There are also the Union Tunisienne de l'Industrie, du Commerce et de l'Artisanat (UTICA, the employers' union) and the Union National des Agriculteurs (UNA, farmers' union).

INTERNATIONAL TRADE
In Feb. 1989 Tunisia signed a treaty of economic co-operation with the other countries of Maghreb: Algeria, Libya, Mauritania and Morocco. Foreign debt was US$9,887m. in 1996.

Tunisia was the first country to sign a partnership agreement with the European Union. The agreement aims at creating a non-agricultural free trade zone by 2008.

Imports and Exports. Imports and exports for calendar years (US$1m.):

	1992	1993	1994	1995	1996
Imports	6,431	6,214	6,581	7,903	7,745
Exports	4,019	3,802	4,657	5,475	5,517

Main exports in 1991 (in 1,000 tonnes): Crude oil, 3,993; textiles, 90; olive oil, 158; phosphates, 808; fertilizers, 1,471; fruit, 48; leather and shoes, 5·7; fishery products, 13·6; machinery and electrical appliances, 13·1.

Main imports in 1991 (in 1,000 tonnes): Oil and by-products, 2,404; natural gas, 639; vegetable oil, 136; dairy products, 20; coffee, tea and spices, 21; cereals, 922; sugar, 168.

The main import suppliers in 1995 were France (25·6%), Italy (15·4%) and Germany (12·5%). Main export markets in 1995 were France (28·1%), Italy (18·7%) and Germany (15·7%).

COMMUNICATIONS
Roads. In 1996 there were 23,100 km of roads (18,200 km surfaced). Vehicles in 1996 numbered 581,000 (269,000 passenger cars and 312,000 trucks and vans).

Rail. In 1994 there were 2,152 km of railways (468 km of 1,435 mm gauge and 1,684 km of metre-gauge), of which 110 km were electrified. 28·3m. passengers and 11·8m. tonnes of freight were carried in 1994. There is a light rail network in Tunis (33 km).

Civil Aviation. The national carrier, Tunis Air, is 84·86% state-owned. There are 6 international airports, the main one at Tunis-Carthage. In 1998 services were also provided by Aeroflot, Air Algérie, Air France, Air Malta, Air Ukraine, Alitalia, Balkan, British Airways, Egyptair, Iberia, JAT, Kuwait Airways, Lufthansa, Royal Air Maroc, Royal Jordanian, Saudia, Swissair, Syrian Arab Airlines and Turkish Airlines. In 1996 Tunis handled 2,935,315 passengers (2,584,752 on international flights) and 23,739 tonnes of freight. Monastir (Habib Bourguiba) was the second busiest airport for passenger traffic in 1996, with 2,602,082 (2,583,120 on international flights), and Djerba the second busiest for freight, with 2,539 tonnes.

Shipping. The main port is Tunis, and its outer port is Tunis-Goulette. These two ports, and Sfax, Sousse and Bizerta, are directly accessible to ocean-going vessels. The ports of La Skhirra and Gabès are used for the shipping of Algerian and Tunisian oil. In 1995, sea-going shipping totalled 0·18m. GRT, including oil tankers, 9,976 GRT.

Telecommunications. Tunisia had 654,200 main telephone lines in 1997, or 70·2 per 1,000 persons. Cellular phone subscribers numbered 3,200 in 1995, there were 60,000 PCs and 25,000 fax machines. In Jan. 1998 there were approximately 3,500 Internet users.

Postal Services. In 1995 there were 955 post offices. A total of 117m. pieces of mail were processed in 1995.

SOCIAL INSTITUTIONS

Justice. There are 51 magistrates' courts, 13 courts of first instance, 3 courts of appeal (in Tunis, Sfax and Sousse) and the High Court in Tunis.

A Personal Status Code was promulgated on 13 Aug. 1956 and applied to Tunisians from 1 Jan. 1957. This raised the status of women, made divorce subject to a court decision, abolished polygamy and decreed a minimum marriage age.

Religion. The constitution recognizes Islam as the state religion. In 1992 there were 8·36m. Sunni Moslems. There are about 20,000 Roman Catholics, under the Prelate of Tunis.

Education. The adult literacy rate in 1995 was 66·4% (78·6% among males and 54·6% among females). All education is free from primary schools to university. In 1994 there were 4,286 primary schools with 58,279 teachers and 1,472,844 pupils; 712 secondary schools with 27,785 teachers and 662,222 pupils.

Higher education includes 6 universities, 3 of them being specialized by faculty, a teacher training college, a school of law, 2 centres of economic studies, 2 schools of engineering, 2 medical schools, a faculty of agriculture, 2 institutes of business administration and 1 school of dentistry.

Health. There were 163 government hospitals in 1994, with provision of 18 beds per 10,000 population. In 1994 there were 5,344 doctors, 1,004 dentists, 12,195 nurses and 1,685 pharmacists.

Welfare. A system of social security was set up in 1950 (amended 1963, 1964 and 1970).

CULTURE

Broadcasting. The government-controlled Radiodiffusion-Télévision Tunisienne provides a national radio programme, an international service—Radio Tunisie Internationale (French and Italian)—and 2 regional programmes. There are Arabic and French TV networks (colour by SECAM). In 1995 there were 1·8m. radio and 800,000 TV sets.

Press. In 1995 there were 7 daily newspapers with a combined circulation of 400,000, giving a rate of 45 per 1,000 inhabitants. Press freedom is severely limited.

Tourism. In 1996 there were 3,885,000 foreign tourists, bringing revenue of US$1·44bn. Revenues doubled between 1991 (US$685m.) and 1996, and tourism now accounts for 10% of GDP.

DIPLOMATIC REPRESENTATIVES
Of Tunisia in Great Britain (29 Prince's Gate, London, SW7 1QG)
Ambassador: Mohamed Ben Ahmed.

Of Great Britain in Tunisia (5 Place de la Victoire, Tunis)
Ambassador and Consul-General: I. Rawlinson, OBE.

Of Tunisia in the USA (1515 Massachusetts Ave., NW, Washington, D.C., 20005)
Ambassador: Noureddine Mejdoub.

Of the USA in Tunisia (144 Ave. de la Liberté, 1002 Tunis-Belvedere)
Ambassador: Robin L. Raphel.

Of Tunisia to the United Nations
Ambassador: Ali Hachani.

Of Tunisia to the European Union
Ambassador: Tahar Sioud.

FURTHER READING
Lawless R. I. et al., *Tunisia.* [Bibliography] Oxford and Santa Barbara (CA), 1982
Pazzanita, A. G., *The Maghreb.* [Bibliography] Oxford and Santa Barbara (CA), 1998
Salem, N., *Habib Bourguiba, Islam and the Creation of Tunisia.* London, 1984

National statistical office: Institut National de la Statistique, 27 Rue de Liban, Tunis.

TURKEY

Türkiye Çumhuriyeti

(Republic of Turkey)

Capital: Ankara
Population estimate, 2000: 65·73m.
GNP per capita: (PPP$) 6,060
HDI/world rank: 0·782/69

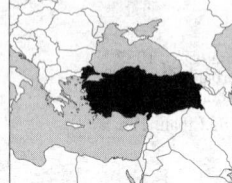

KEY HISTORICAL EVENTS

In the 13th century the kingdom of Othman I became the dominant power in Asia Minor (now the Asian part of Turkey). In 1453 the Turks captured Constantinople and destroyed the Eastern Roman Empire. Thereafter, the Ottoman Empire expanded to include an area from Morocco to Persia and westwards into the Balkans. From the 17th century, however, the Empire began to decline, its power weakening rapidly in the 19th century.

The Turkish War of Independence (1919-22), following the disintegration of the Ottoman Empire, was led and won by Mustafa Kemal (Atatürk) on behalf of the Grand National Assembly which first met in Ankara on 23 April 1920. On 20 Jan. 1921 the Grand National Assembly voted a constitution which declared that all sovereignty belonged to the people, and vested all power, both executive and legislative, in the Grand National Assembly. The name 'Ottoman Empire' was later replaced by 'Turkey'. On 1 Nov. 1922 the Grand National Assembly abolished the office of Sultan, and Turkey became a republic on 29 Oct. 1923. Religious courts were abolished in 1924, Islam ceased to be the official state religion in 1928, women were given the franchise and western-style surnames were adopted in 1934.

On 27 May 1960 the Turkish Army, directed by a National Unity Committee under the leadership of Gen. Cemal Gürsel, overthrew the government of the Democratic Party. The Grand National Assembly was dissolved and party activities were suspended. Party activities were legally resumed on 12 Jan. 1961. A new constitution was approved in a referendum held on 9 July 1961 and general elections were held the same year.

On 12 Sept. 1980, the Turkish armed forces overthrew the Demirel Government (Justice Party). Parliament was dissolved and all activities of political parties were suspended. The Constituent Assembly was convened in Oct. 1981, and prepared a new constitution which was enforced after a national referendum on 7 Nov. 1982.

In the face of mounting Islamicization of government policy, the Supreme National Security Council convened on 28 Feb. 1997 and reaffirmed its commitment to the secularity of the state. On 6 March Prime Minister Neçmettin Erbakan, leader of the pro-Islamist Welfare Party, agreed to sign a list of measures to combat Moslem fundamentalism. In June he was forced to resign by a campaign led by the Army. On 16 Jan. 1998 a Constitutional Court ruling ordered the closure of the Welfare Party. In Feb. Neçmettin Erbakan and 5 other party members were expelled from parliament and banned from political office for 5 years.

There are quarrels with Greece over the division of Cyprus, oil rights under the Aegean and ownership of uninhabited islands close to the Turkish coast.

Kurdish rebels are active in the south-east, occupying a large part of the Turkish army.

TERRITORY AND POPULATION

Turkey is bounded in the west by the Aegean Sea and Greece, north by Bulgaria and the Black Sea, east by Georgia, Armenia and Iran, and south by Iraq, Syria and the Mediterranean. The area (including lakes) is 779,452 sq. km (300,947 sq. miles). At the 1990 census the population was 56,473,035. A census is scheduled for 2000. Population estimate (July 1997), 63,528,225; density, 82 per sq. km.

The UN gives a projected population for 2000 of 65·73m.

In 1995, 69·2% of the population lived in urban areas.

Turkish is the official language. Kurdish and Arabic are also spoken.

Some 12m. Kurds live in Turkey. Limited use of the Kurdish language (not in schools or publications) was sanctioned in Feb. 1991.

TURKEY

Area and population of the 73 provinces[1] at the 1990 census:

	Area in sq.km.	Population	Density per sq.km.
Adana	17,562	1,934,907	111
Adiyaman	7,423	513,131	70
Afyonkarahisar	14,295	739,223	52
Ağri	11,066	437,093	40
Aksaray	7,626	326,399	43
Amasya	5,452	357,191	66
Ankara	25,614	3,236,626	126
Antalya	20,815	1,132,211	55
Artvin	7,436	212,833	29
Aydin	7,870	824,816	105
Balikesir	14,456	973,314	68
Batman	4,694	344,669	74
Bayburt	3,652	107,330	30
Bilecik	4,321	175,526	40
Bingöl	8,319	250,966	30
Bitlis	8,010	330,115	41
Bolu	10,575	536,869	51
Burdur	7,167	254,899	36
Bursa	10,990	1,603,137	146
Çanakkale	9,950	432,263	44
Çankırı	8,659	279,129	33
Çorum	12,729	609,863	49
Denizli	11,874	750,882	64
Diyarbakir	4,908	1,094,996	73
Edirne	6,174	404,599	65
Elazığ	9,455	498,225	53
Erzincan	11,413	299,251	27
Erzurum	25,133	848,201	34
Eskişehir	13,477	641,057	48
Gaziantep	8,015	1,140,594	153
Giresun	6,965	499,087	75
Gümüşhane	6,748	169,375	25
Hakkâri	7,121	172,479	25
Hatay	5,570	1,109,754	204
İsparta	8,847	434,771	49
İçel	15,448	1,266,995	82
İstanbul	5,591	7,309,190	1,330
İzmir	12,263	2,694,770	220
Karaman	9,163	217,536	24
Kars	18,841	662,155	35
Kastamonu	12,982	423,611	33
Kayseri	16,537	943,484	57
Kırıkkale	4,365	349,396	84
Kırklareli	6,378	309,512	49
Kirşehir	6,501	256,862	40
Kocaeli	3,578	936,163	260
Konya	40,451	1,750,303	43
Kütahya	11,661	578,020	51
Malatya	11,752	702,055	57
Manisa	13,237	1,154,418	87
K. Maraş	14,680	892,952	61
Mardin	8,594	557,727	65
Muğla	12,504	562,809	45
Muş	8,413	376,543	45
Nevşehir	5,540	289,509	52
Niğde	7,831	305,861	39
Ordu	6,142	830,105	137
Rize	3,920	348,776	91
Sakarya	4,821	683,061	140
Samsun	9,739	1,158,400	120
Siirt	6,176	243,435	40
Sinop	5,657	265,153	48

Şırnak	7,172	262,006	40
	Area in sq.km.	Population	Density per sq.km.
Sivas	28,568	767,481	28
Tekirdağ	6,333	468,842	74
Tokat	9,869	719,251	73
Trabzon	4,498	795,849	180
Tunceli	7,954	133,143	17
Urfa	19,271	1,001,455	52
Uşak	5,389	290,283	54
Van	21,095	637,433	30
Yozgat	13,597	579,150	43
Zonguldak	8,560	1,073,560	126

[1]In 1995 there were 79 provinces.

Population of urban areas and towns of over 120,000 inhabitants in 1990:

	Urban area	Town		Urban area	Town
İstanbul	6,407,215	6,293,397	Erzurum	409,095	297,544
Ankara	3,022,236	2,541,899	Kahramanmaraş	395,872	237,456
İzmir	2,665,105	2,319,188	Zonguldak	381,824	124,862
Adana	1,429,677	972,318	Malatya	367,765	304,760
Bursa	1,030,737	775,388	Sivas	350,564	219,949
Konya	1,015,415	543,460	Trabzon	288,118	173,354
Gaziantep	759,893	573,968	Denizli	285,836	199,360
İçel	700,851	414,308	Elazığ	275,342	218,121
Kayseri	587,793	461,415	Kırıkkale	267,379	233,008
Diyarbakır	560,347	371,038	Sakarya	255,112	170,231
Manisa	556,787	158,426	Kütahya	232,632	135,432
Şanlıurfa	520,533	239,604	Van	217,442	126,010
Antalya	514,264	353,149	İsparta	204,311	113,693
Kocaeli	498,646	271,132	İskenderun	· · ·	175,998
Hatay	481,560	118,443	Tarsus	· · ·	168,654
Samsun	462,836	277,222	Batman	· · ·	131,812
Balıkesir	461,618	172,570	Osmaniye	· · ·	121,188
Eskişehir	455,478	415,831			

SOCIAL STATISTICS
Births, 1995, 1,369,000; deaths, 408,000. 1995 birth rate per 1,000 population, 22·5; death rate, 6·7. 1994 marriages, 462,415; divorces, 28,041. Annual growth rate, 1990–95, 1·9%. Expectation of life, 1990–95, was 65·0 years for males and 69·6 for females. Infant mortality, 1990–95, was 53 per 1,000 live births, down from 102 in 1980–85. The rate dropped more in Turkey than in any other country over the same period. Fertility rate, 1990–95, 2·7 births per woman.

CLIMATE
Coastal regions have a Mediterranean climate, with mild, moist winters and hot, dry summers. The interior plateau has more extreme conditions, with low and irregular rainfall, cold and snowy winters, and hot, almost rainless summers. Ankara, Jan. 32·5°F (0·3°C), July 73°F (23°C). Annual rainfall 14·7" (367 mm). İstanbul, Jan. 41°F (5°C), July 73°F (23°C). Annual rainfall 28·9" (723 mm). İzmir, Jan. 46°F (8°C), July 81°F (27°C). Annual rainfall 28" (700 mm).

CONSTITUTION AND GOVERNMENT
On 7 Nov. 1982 a referendum established that 98% of the electorate were in favour of a new Constitution. The *President* is elected for 7-year terms. The Presidency is not an executive position, and the President may not be linked to a political party. There is a 550-member *Grand National Assembly*, elected by universal suffrage (at 18 years and over) for 5-year terms by proportional representation. There is a *Constitutional Court* consisting of 15 regular and 5 alternating members.

National Anthem. 'Korkma! Sönmez bu şafaklarda yüzen al sancak' ('Be not afraid! Our flag will never fade'); words by Mehmed Akif Ersoy, tune by Zeki Güngör.

TURKEY

RECENT ELECTIONS
Elections were held on 24 Dec. 1995. The electorate was 34,155,981; turn-out was 85·2%. The Welfare Party (pro-Islamist) gained 158 seats with 21·38% of votes cast (62 with 16·9% in 1991); the True Path Party, 135 with 19·18% (178 with 27%); the Motherland Party (MP), 132 with 19·65% (115 with 27%); the Democratic Left Party (DLP), 76 with 14·64% (7 with 10·8%); and the Republican Populist Party, 49 with 10·71%.

In June 1997 a minority 3-party (MP/DLP/Democratic Turkey Party) coalition government was formed, but it collapsed in Nov. 1998 over corruption allegations. Turkey was without an established government until Jan. 1999 when President Suleyman Demirel accepted Bülent Ecevit's minority government. On 22 March 1999 he survived a no-confidence vote in parliament. The next general election was brought forward a year to 18 April 1999.

CURRENT ADMINISTRATION
President: Suleyman Demirel (b. 1924; sworn in 16 May 1993).

In Jan. 1999 a minority government was formed, comprising in March 1999:
Prime Minister: Bülent Ecevit.
Deputy Prime Ministers: Husamettin Ozkan, Hikmet Ulugbay.
Minister of Agriculture: Mahmut Erdir. *Culture:* Istemihan Talay. *Education:* Metin Bostancioğlu. *Energy and National Resources:* Ziya Aktas. *Environment:* Fevzi Aytekin. *Finance:* Nami Cagan. *Foreign Affairs:* Ismail Cem. *Forestry:* Arif Sezer. *Health:* Mustafa Guven Karahan. *Industry and Commerce:* Metin Sahin. *Interior:* Cahit Bayar. *Justice:* Selcuk Oztek. *Labour and Social Security:* Hakan Tartan. *National Defence:* Sami Hikmet Turk. *Public Works and Housing:* Ali Iliksov. *Tourism:* Ahmet Tan. *Transportation and Communications:* Hasan Basri Aktan.

The *Speaker* is Hikmet Citin.

Local Government. The 79 provinces have elected councils, as do municipalities. Mayors (of metropolitan areas and municipalities) and village heads and councils of elders are also elected. At partial municipal elections on 4 June 1995 the TPP gained 22 of 36 seats with 39·6% of votes cast, the Republican Populist Party gained 20·36%, the Prosperity Party 17·4%.

DEFENCE
The *Supreme Council of National Security*, chaired by the Prime Minister and comprising military leaders and the ministers of defence and the economy, also functions as a *de facto* constitutional watchdog.

Conscription is 18 months.

In 1997 defence expenditure totalled US$8,110m., up from US$3,269m. in 1985. Spending per capita in 1997 was US$131, up from US$65 per capita in 1985. The 1997 expenditure represented 4·2% of GDP.

Army. The Army consists of 1 mechanized divisional HQ, 1 mechanized and 1 infantry division, 9 infantry, 14 armoured, 17 mechanized and 4 commando brigades, 1 armoured, 1 Presidential Guard and 5 coastal defence regiments, and 26 frontier defence battalions. Equipment includes 75 M-47, 2,876 M-48, 932 M-60 and 397 Leopard main battle tanks. Army Aviation has some 400 aircraft and helicopters. Strength (1997) 525,000 (462,000 conscripts). There is also a paramilitary gendarmerie-cum-national guard of 180,000.

Navy. Current strength includes 15 diesel submarines (8 reasonably modern, of German design and 7 very old ex-US built 1944–45), 5 ex-US destroyers (1943–46), 16 frigates of which 6 are modern German MEKO-type, 8 ex-US Knox class and 2 locally built in the 1970s. Light forces comprise 18 fast missile craft, 11 coastal and 21 inshore patrol craft. Mine warfare forces include 3 minelayers, 17 coastal and 4 inshore minesweepers. Amphibious lift is provided by 8 tank landing ships and about 60 landing craft. Major auxiliaries in service are 1 replenishment and 5 support tankers, 5 depot ships, 3 salvage/rescue ships, 2 survey ships and 1 training ship. Minor auxiliaries, coastal freighters and service craft number about 120. The main naval base is at Gölcük in the Gulf of İzmit. There are others at İskenderun, Eregli, Aksaz Karaağaç Mersin and İzmir. There are 3 naval shipyards: Gölcük, Taşkizak and İzmir.

TURKEY

The naval air component operates 10 S-2 mixed Air Force and Naval-manned Tracker anti-submarine aircraft and 20 helicopters for anti-submarine and patrol duties. There is a Marine Regiment some 3,000-strong with 18 artillery pieces.

Personnel in 1997 totalled 51,000 (34,500 conscripts) including marines.

The separate Coast Guard numbers about 2,000 and performs coastal police duties with a force of 40 inshore patrol vessels, 4 transports and numerous boats.

Air Force. The Air Force is organized as 2 tactical air forces, with headquarters at Eskisehir and Diyarbakir, each having a flight of UH-1H helicopters. Combat aircraft comprise F-5As in 3 squadrons; F-16A/Bs in 8 squadrons; F-4E and RF-4E Phantoms in 8 squadrons; plus Nike-Hercules surface-to-air missile batteries. The 4 transport squadrons are equipped with Transall C-160, C-130 Hercules, Citation, Gulfstream and CN-235 aircraft, and UH-1H helicopters. Training types include T-37 and T-38 advanced trainers, SF.260 basic and T-41 primary trainers. Personnel strength (1997), 63,000 (31,500 conscripts).

INTERNATIONAL RELATIONS

In Oct. 1998 Turkish troops were mobilized on the border with Syria amidst concern that differences between the 2 countries had reached the stage of undeclared war. Turkey had threatened to invade Syria unless Syria withdraw its support for Kurdish rebels operating from its territory.

Turkey is a member of the UN, OECD, NATO and Council of Europe and an Associate Member of the WEU.

ECONOMY

Policy. Privatization is co-ordinated by the Public Participation Fund. The government expected to raise between US$9bn. and US$12bn. in privatization revenues in 1998.

Performance. Real GDP growth was forecast at 5·5% in 1997 and 3·6% in 1998.

Budget. Budgets (in TL1,000m.):

	1993	1994	1995	1996
Revenue	349,248	741,557	1,380,356	2,683,175
Expenditure	416,381	795,331	1,524,762	3,546,114

Tax revenues were TL2,244,094,000m. in 1996.

Currency. The unit of currency is the *Turkish lira* (TRL) notionally of 100 *kuruş*. In Feb. 1998 gold reserves were 3·75m. troy oz. and foreign exchange reserves US$19,482m. Inflation in 1997 was 99·1%, down from 125% in 1994, and was expected to fall to around 70% in 1998. Total money supply in Nov. 1997 was TL1,145bn.

Banking and Finance. The Central Bank (Merkez Bankası; *Governor*, Gazi Erçel) is the bank of issue. In 1997 there were 57 commercial banks (7 state-owned, 29 private, 21 foreign), and 12 development and investment banks. The Central Bank's assets were TL1,486,927,500m. in 1995. The assets and liabilities of deposit money banks were TL3,673,689,800m. Foreign investment in 1995 was US$1·1bn. compared to US$150m. in 1985.

There is a stock exchange in İstanbul (ISE).

Weights and Measures. The metric system is in use. The Gregorian calendar has been in exclusive use since 26 Dec. 1925.

ENERGY AND NATURAL RESOURCES

Electricity. In 1996 installed capacity was 21,246·9 MW (9,862·8 MW hydro-electric in 1995). Production was 90,354·5m. kWh in 1996; consumption per capita in 1996 was 1,161 kWh.

Oil and Gas. Crude oil production (1996) was 3,498,633 tonnes. Total refining capacity (1995) was 24m. tonnes. 22,915,817 tonnes of crude petroleum were imported in 1994. 198·63m. cu. metres of natural gas were produced in 1994.

Minerals. Turkey is rich in minerals, and is a major producer of chrome.

Production of principal minerals (in 1,000 tonnes) was:

	1992	1993	1994	1995

Coal	4,791	4,609	4,211	3,377
Lignite	54,458	51,359	55,038	51,185
Chrome	1,446	767	1,270	2,080
	1992	1993	1994	1995
Copper concentrate	139	140	140	114
Bauxite	859	538	373	232
Iron	5,917	6,480	5,773	4,931
Boron	1,796	1,892	2,088	1,769
Salt	1,418	1,526	1,353	1,442

Agriculture. Agriculture accounted for 17% of GDP in 1996. At the 1991 census of agriculture there were 4,091,530 households engaged in farming, of which 148,190 were engaged purely in animal farming. Holdings are increasingly fragmented by the custom of dividing land equally amongst sons. There are government price supports to cereal growers. The sown area in 1995 was 18,475,000 ha; 5,124,000 ha was fallow; vineyards, orchards and olive groves occupied 2,461,000 ha.

Production (in 1,000 tonnes) of principal crops:

	1992	1993	1994	1995	1996
Wheat	19,300	21,000	17,500	18,000	18,500
Barley	6,900	7,500	7,000	7,500	8,000
Maize	2,225	2,500	1,850	1,900	2,000
Rye	230	235	195	240	245
Tobacco	334	339	187	210	232
Oats	240	245	230	250	275
Rice	129	135	120	150	168

Other produce, 1995 (in 1,000 tonnes): dry beans, 225; lentils, 665; chick peas, 730; cotton lint, 837; sugar-beet, 11,171; sunflower seeds, 900; cotton seed, 1,263; soya beans, 75; onions, 2,850; potatoes, 4,750; pears, 410; apples, 2,100; figs, 300; apricots, 281; grapes, 3,550; oranges, 846; tangerines, 453; lemons, 418; nuts, 715; tea, 103; olives, 515; olive oil (1992), 121.

Livestock, 1996 (in 1,000): horses, 391; mules, 154; asses, 689; cattle, 11,886; sheep, 33,072; goats (including Angora), 8,951. Livestock products, 1995 (in 1,000 tonnes): total meat, 415; milk, 10,602; greasy wool, 51; goat hair and mohair, 4,200 tonnes; 10,268,668 eggs; honey, 69.

Forestry. There were 8·86m. ha of forests in 1995 (11·5% of the land area). Timber production was 19·28m. cu. metres in 1995.

Fisheries. Catch (1995): Sea fish, 557,138 tonnes; crustaceans and molluscs, 25,472 tonnes; freshwater fish, 44,983 tonnes. Aquaculture production, 1995, 21,607 tonnes (mainly carp and trout). There were (1996) 1,165 sea fishing boats.

INDUSTRY

In 1990, 55 state enterprises accounted for about 30% of production. In 1993 there were 10,567 industrial enterprises. Production in 1995 (in 1,000 tonnes unless otherwise stated): ammonia, 586; sulphuric acid, 630; PVC, 181; polyethylene, 300; ethylene, 411; fertilizers, 5,022; cotton yarn, 388; woollen yarn, 53; cotton textiles, 489·89m. metres; woollen textiles, 30·5m. metres; carpets, 16,215,974 sq. metres; paper, 515; cement, 33,153; pig-iron, 330; crude iron, 4,363; crude steel, 12,798; coke, 3,021; iron and steel bars, 1,426; sugar, 1,290; lorries, 19,172 units; motor cars, 222,145 units.

Labour. In Oct. 1995 the labour force was 22·9m. (6,956,000 females) of whom 21,378,000 (6,486,000) were employed: 10,226,000 were engaged in agriculture, forestry and fishing, 2,947,000 in manufacturing, 2,780,000 in services and 2,612,000 in trade, restaurants and hotels. 1,522,000 were unemployed in Oct. 1995.

Trade Unions. There are 4 national confederations (including Türk-İş and Disk) and 6 federations. There are 35 unions affiliated to Türk-İş and 17 employers' federations affiliated to Disk, whose activities were banned on 12 Sept. 1980. In 1995, labour unions totalled 109 and employers' unions, 54. Some 2·2m. workers belonged to unions in 1990. Membership is forbidden to civil servants (including schoolteachers). There were 120 strikes in 1995, with 4,838,241 working days lost, and 5 lock-outs, with 162,512 working days lost.

INTERNATIONAL TRADE

Total foreign debt in 1996 was US$79,789m. A customs union with the EU came into force on 1 Jan. 1996.

Imports and Exports. Imports and exports (in US$1m.) for calendar years:

	1992	1993	1994	1995	1996
Imports	22,879	28,291	23,262	35,709	42,901
Exports	14,022	15,274	18,102	21,637	23,070

Chief exports (1996) in US$1m.: wearing apparel, 5,714·6; iron and steel, 1,746·5; electrical machinery and apparatus, 1,317·7; fruits and nuts, 1,134·2. Chief imports: nuclear reactor machinery, 8,286·5; electrical machinery and apparatus, 2,925·7; iron and steel, 2,685·2; road vehicles, 2,682·9.

The main export markets in 1996 (in US$1m.) were: Germany, 5,168·8; USA, 1,615·7; Russia, 1,494·5; Italy, 1,438·3; UK, 1,246·8; France, 1,040·6. Main import suppliers: Germany, 7,583·2; Italy, 4,245·1; USA, 3,287·8; France, 2,739·5; UK, 2,486·3; Russia, 1,900·5; Saudi Arabia, 1,706·2.

COMMUNICATIONS

Roads. In 1996 there were an estimated 31,412 km of state highways (including 125 km of motorway) and 28,813 km of provincial roads. In 1996 there were 3,274,156 cars, 776,057 trucks and pick-ups, 94,978 buses, 182,694 minibuses and 854,150 motor cycles. There were 344,643 road accidents in 1996, with 5,428 fatalities (279,663 accidents with 6,004 fatalities in 1995).

Rail. Total length of railway lines in 1996 was 8,607 km (1,435 mm gauge), of which 1,524 km were electrified; 98·3m. passengers and 15·8m. tonnes of freight were carried.

Civil Aviation. There are international airports at İstanbul (Atatürk), Dalaman (Muğla), Ankara (Esenboga), İzmir (Adnan Menderes), Adana and Antalya. The national carrier is Turkish Airlines, which is 98·2% state-owned. In 1996 it flew 8,450,120 passengers (3,346,428 on international flights) and carried 797,176 tonnes (350,728 international) of freight. In 1998 services were also provided by Aeroflot, Air Algérie, Air Bosna, Air France, Air Kazakhstan, Air Malta, Air Moldova, Air Ukraine, Air Urga, Aircompany Karat, Albanian Airlines, Alitalia, Armenian Airlines, Asiana Airlines, Austrian Airlines, Aviacompany Turkmenistan, Azerbaijan Airlines, Balkan, Belavia, British Airways, Cathay Pacific Airways, Condor Flugdienst, Crimea Air, Croatia Airlines, Cubana, Czech Airlines, Delta Air Lines, Dneproavia Joint Stock Aviation Co, Donavia, Egyptair, El Al, Emirates, Finnair, Gulf Air, Hapag Lloyd, Iberia, Interimpex-Avioimpex, Iran Air, Istanbul Airlines, JAL, JAT, KLM, Kuwait Airways, Kyrgyzstan Airlines, Lithuanian Airlines, LOT, LTU International Airways, Lufthansa, Malaysia Airlines, Malév, Middle East Airlines, MIAT-Mongolian Airlines, Olympic Airways, Pakistan International Airlines, Royal Air Maroc, Royal Jordanian, SABENA, SAS, Saudia, Singapore Airlines, Sudan Airways, Swissair, Syrian Arab Airlines, TAP, Tarom, Tavrey Aircompany, TCH of Russian Airlines, Transavia Airlines, Trans European Airlines, Tunis Air, Tyumen Airlines, Uzbekiston Airways and VIP Air.

In 1996 İstanbul handled 13,394,666 passengers (9,255,296 on international flights) and 134,782 tonnes of freight. Antalya was the second busiest airport for passenger traffic in 1996, with 5,586,905 (4,949,089 on international flights), and Ankara the second busiest for freight, with 17,568 tonnes.

Shipping. In 1996 there were 1,592 cargo ships totalling 5,476,774 GRT, 277 tankers totalling 1,043,883 GRT and 628 passenger ships totalling 209,037 GRT. The main ports are: İstanbul, İzmir, Samsun, Mersin, İskenderun and Trabzon.

Coastal shipping, 1996: 19,057 vessels handled; 225,318 passengers entered, and 251,742 cleared; 17·0m. tonnes of goods entered, 12·9m. cleared. International shipping: 22,595 vessels handled; 615,838 passengers entered, 595,476 cleared; 55·2m. tonnes of goods entered, 19·0m. cleared.

Telecommunications. In 1997 main telephone lines numbered 15,744,000 (250·4 for every 1,000 persons). There were 770,000 PCs in 1995, 437,000 cellular phone subscribers and 99,000 fax machines. Turkey had 600,000 Internet users in May 1997.

Postal Services. In 1996 there were 24,860 post, telegraph and telephone offices.

SOCIAL INSTITUTIONS

Justice. The unified legal system consists of: (1) justices of the peace (single judges with limited but summary penal and civil jurisdiction); (2) courts of first instance (single judges, dealing with cases outside the jurisdiction of (3) and (4)); (3) central criminal courts (a president and 2 judges, dealing with cases where the crime is punishable by imprisonment over 5 years); (4) commercial courts (3 judges); (5) state security courts, to prosecute offences against the integrity of the state (a president and 4 judges, 2 of the latter being military).

The civil and military High Courts of Appeal sit at Ankara. The Council of State is the highest administrative tribunal; it consists of 5 chambers. Its 31 judges are nominated from among high-ranking personalities in politics, economy, law, the army, etc. The Military Administrative Court deals with the judicial control of administrative acts and deeds concerning military personnel. The Court of Jurisdictional Disputes is empowered to resolve disputes between civil, administrative and military courts. The Supreme Council of Judges and Public Prosecutors appoints judges and prosecutors to the profession and has disciplinary powers.

The Civil Code and the Code of Obligations have been adapted from the corresponding Swiss codes. The Penal Code is largely based upon the Italian Penal Code, and the Code of Civil Procedure closely resembles that of the Canton of Neuchâtel. The Commercial Code is based on the German.

Prison population (1995), 26,501 (683 females; 530 juveniles).

Religion. Islam ceased to be the official religion in 1928. The Constitution guarantees freedom of religion but forbids its political exploitation or any impairment of the secular character of the republic.

In 1992 there were 58·12m. Moslems, two-thirds Sunni and one-third Shi'ite (Alevis). The administration of the Sunni Moslem religious organizations is the responsibility of the Department of Religious Affairs. The Greek Orthodox, Gregorian Armenian, Armenian Apostolic and Roman Catholic Churches are represented in İstanbul, and there are small Uniate, Protestant and Jewish communities.

Education. Adult literacy was 82·3% (male 91·7%; female 72·4%) in 1995. Primary education from 6 to 14 is compulsory and co-educational and, in state schools, free. Religious instruction (Sunni Moslem) in state schools is now compulsory. In 1991 there were 5,197 religious secondary schools with 0·29m. pupils up to 14 years.

Statistics for 1995–96	Number	Teachers	Students
Pre-school institutions	5,600	9,771	158,354
Primary schools	49,240	231,900	6,403,000
Junior high schools	8,493	70,345	2,296,000
High schools	2,196	71,105	1,201,000
Vocational and technical junior high schools	892	316	349,054
Vocational and technical high schools	2,791	74,136	961,727
Higher education institutes	817	50,259	1,161,000

In 1994–95 there were 54 universities. A total of 1,160,688 students enrolled at 817 establishments of higher education (1995–96); teaching staff numbered 50,259. In 1996, 27,452 students were studying abroad.

In 1994 total expenditure on education came to 3·3% of GNP.

Health. In 1995 there were 39,503 general practitioners, 29,846 specialist doctors, 11,717 dentists, 19,090 pharmacists and 64,243 nurses. In 1996 there were 883 hospitals (including maternity hospitals) and 151 health centres.

Welfare. In 1995, 1,001,216 beneficiaries received TL89,871,844m. from the Government Employees Retirement Fund; 2,337,755 beneficiaries received TL69,740,150m. from the Social Insurance Institution; and (1992) 664,621 beneficiaries received TL3,369,195m. from the Independent Insurance System.

CULTURE

Broadcasting. Broadcasting is regulated by the 9-member Radio and Television Council. The government monopoly of broadcasting was abolished in 1994 and in 1997 there were 35 national, 109 regional and 990 local radio stations; and 16 national, 15 regional and 304 local TV stations (colour by PAL). The Turkish Radio Television Corporation (TRT) broadcasts tourist radio programmes and a foreign service, Voice of Turkey. In 1995 there were 10m. radio and 11·5m. TV sets in use.

Cinema. In 1996 there were 300 cinemas; attendances totalled 9,454,596.

Press. In 1995 there were 400 daily newspapers with a combined circulation of 7m. and 1,321 non-daily newspapers with a combined circulation of 2m. 5,172 book titles were published in 1995.

Tourism. The number of foreign visitors was 8,614,085 in 1996. Earnings from tourism in 1996, US$5·97bn. 4,045,143 Turks travelled abroad in 1995. There were 0·6m. tourist beds in 1993.

Libraries. There were 1,806 libraries serving a readership of 22,478,681 in 1995.

National Theatre and Opera. In 1995–96 there were 6 opera and ballet theatres, where 77 shows (64 foreign) were attended by 254,158 spectators.

Museums and Galleries. Approximately 17·8m. persons visited the 167 museums and ruins maintained by museums in 1996.

DIPLOMATIC REPRESENTATIVES

Of Turkey in Great Britain (43 Belgrave Sq., London, SW1X 8PA)
Ambassador: Özdem Sanberk.

Of Great Britain in Turkey (Sehit Ersan Caddesi 46/A, Cankaya, Ankara)
Ambassador: David B. C. Logan, CMG.

Of Turkey in the USA (1606 23rd St., NW, Washington, D.C., 20008)
Ambassador: Baki Ilkin.

Of the USA in Turkey (110 Atatürk Blvd., Ankara)
Ambassador: Mark R. Parris.

Of Turkey to the United Nations
Ambassador: Volkan Vural.

Of Turkey to the European Union
Ambassador: Nihat Akyol.

FURTHER READING

State Institute of Statistics. *Türkiye İstatistik Yilliği/Statistical Yearbook of Turkey.—Diş Ticaret İstatistikleri/Foreign Trade Statistics* (Annual).—*Aylik İstatistik Bülten* (Monthly).

Ahmad, F., *The Making of Modern Turkey.* London, 1993
Birand, M. A., *Shirts of Steel: an Anatomy of the Turkish Armed Forces.* London, 1991
Güclü, M., *Turkey.* [Bibliography] Oxford and Santa Barbara (CA), 1981
Hale, W., *The Political and Economic Development of Modern Turkey.* London, 1981
Kedourie, S., *Turkey: Identity, Democracy, Politics.* London, 1996
Pettifer, J., *The Turkish Labyrinth: Atatürk and the new Islam.* London, 1997
Pope, N. and Pope, H., *Turkey Unveiled: Atatürk and After.* London, 1997
Zürcher, E. J., *Turkey: a Modern History.* London and New York, 1993 (NY, 1994)

National statistical office: State Institute of Statistics Prime Ministry, Necatibey Caddesi no. 114, 06100 Ankara.
Website: http//:www.die.gov.tr

TURKMENISTAN

Capital: Ashgabat
Population estimate, 2000: 4·48m.
GNP per capita: (PPP$) 2,010
HDI/world rank: 0·660/103

KEY HISTORICAL EVENTS
Descended from the Oghuz tribes who migrated to Central Asia in the 10th century, the Turkmen were conquered by the Russians in the 1860s. In 1866 Tashkent (now Toshkent) was occupied and in 1868 Samarkand (now Samarqand) and subsequently further territory was conquered and united with Russian Turkestan. In the 1870s Bokhara was subjugated, the emir, by an agreement of 1873, recognizing the suzerainty of Russia. In the same year Khiva became a vassal state to Russia. Until 1917 Russian Central Asia was divided politically into the Khanate of Khiva, the Emirate of Bokhara and the Governor-Generalship of Turkestan.

In the summer of 1919 the authority of the Soviet Government became definitely established in these regions. The Khan of Khiva was deposed in Feb. 1920 and a People's Soviet Republic was set up, the medieval name of Khorezm being revived. In Aug. 1920 the Emir of Bokhara suffered the same fate, and a similar regime was set up in Bokhara. The former Governor-Generalship of Turkestan was constituted an Autonomous Soviet Socialist Republic within the RSFSR on 11 April 1921.

In the autumn of 1924 the Soviets of the Turkestan, Bokhara and Khiva Republics decided to redistribute the territories of these republics on a nationality basis; at the same time Bokhara and Khiva became Socialist Republics. The redistribution was completed in May 1925 when the new states of Uzbekistan (now Uzbekiston), Turkmenistan and Tadzhikistan were accepted into the USSR as Union Republics.

Following the break-up of the Soviet Union, Turkmenistan declared independence in Oct. 1991. It became a member of the CIS in Dec. 1991.

TERRITORY AND POPULATION
Turkmenistan is bounded in the north by Kazakhstan, in the north and north-east by Uzbekiston (formerly Uzbekistan), in the south-east by Afghanistan, in the south-west by Iran and in the west by the Caspian Sea. Area, 448,100 sq. km (186,400 sq. miles). In 1995, 77% of the population were Turkmen, 9·2% Uzbek, 6·7% Russian, 2% Kazakh, and 5·1% other. The population was estimated at 4,229,200 in July 1998; density, 9 per sq. km.

The UN gives a projected population for 2000 of 4·48m.

In 1995, 55·1% of the population lived in rural areas.

There are 5 regions: Chardzhou, Mary, Ashgabat, Dashauz and Bafkan, comprising 42 rural districts, 15 towns and 74 urban settlements. The capital is Ashgabat (formerly Ashkhabad; 1990 population, 411,000); other large towns are Chardzhou, Mary (Merv), Nebit-Dag and Dashhouz.

Languages spoken include Turkmen, 72%; Russian, 12%; Uzbek, 9%; other, 7%.

There is a dual citizenship agreement with Russia.

SOCIAL STATISTICS
1997 births, estimate, 112,000; deaths, 36,000. Rates per 1,000 population, 1997: Birth, 26·6; death, 8·6. 1997 population growth 1·61%. Life expectancy: 61·5 years. Infant mortality, 1990–95, 57 per 1,000 live births; fertility rate, 4·0 births per woman.

CLIMATE
The summers are warm to hot but the humidity is relatively low. The winters are cold but generally dry and sunny over most of the country. Ashgabat, Jan. −1°C, July 25°C. Annual rainfall 375 mm.

CONSTITUTION AND GOVERNMENT
A new constitution was adopted in 1992. It provides for an executive head of state, the *Turkmenbashi* (*Leader of Turkmens*). At a referendum on 16 Jan. 1994, 99·99%

of votes cast were in favour of prolonging President Niyazov's term of office to 2002.

National Anthem. A competition for a new text and tune was announced in 1996.

RECENT ELECTIONS

At the presidential elections of June 1992, the electorate was 1·86m. Saparmurad Niyazov was re-elected unopposed by 99·5% of votes cast.

Parliament is the 50-member *Majlis*. Parliamentary elections were held on 11 Dec. 1994. The only party standing was the Democratic Party (DP; former Communists). 1 candidate stood in each constituency, but to be elected had to receive 51% of the vote. Turn-out was said to be 99·8%.

CURRENT ADMINISTRATION

President: Saparmurad Niyazov, b. 1940 (DP; re-elected June 1992).

In March 1999 the government comprised:

Head of State and Prime Minister: Saparmurad Niyazov.

Minister of Agriculture: Kurbanmurad Rozyev. *Culture:* Orazgeldy Aydogdoiyev. *Defence:* Kurban Kasimov. *Economics and Finance:* Matkarim Rajapov. *Education:* Ashir Orazov. *Energy and Industry:* Saparmurat Nuriyev. *Environment:* Pirdjan Kurbanov. *Foreign Affairs:* Boris Shikhmuradov. *Foreign and Economic Relations:* Toili Kurbanov. *Health and Medical Industry:* Gurganguly Berdimukhamedov. *Industry and Construction:* Mukhammetnazar Hudayguliyev. *Internal Affairs:* Poran Berdiyev. *Justice:* Tagandurdy Khalliyev. *Oil and Gas Industries and Mineral Resources:* Rejepbay Arazov. *Trade and Resources:* Khalnazar Agakhanov. *Transportation and Communication:* Khudykuly Khalykov.

Chairman, Supreme Council (Mejlis): Sakhat Muradov.

Deputy Chairmen to the Cabinet: Kurbanmurad Rozyev *(Agriculture)*, Orazgeldy Aydogdyyev *(Culture and Mass Media)*, Yolly Gurbanmuradov *(Banking, Currency Affairs and Exchange)*, Mukhamed Abalakov *(Education, Health, Sciences)*, Saparmurat Nuryyev *(Electrical Power, Machine-Building, Chemical Industry, Construction)*, Batyr Sarjayev *(Energy)*, Rejep Saparov *(Foreign Economic Relations, Business Development, Light Industry)*, Hudayguly Halykov *(Transport, Telecommunications)*, Aleksandr Dadonov *(Water Management and Irrigation)*.

DEFENCE

Defence expenditure in 1997 totalled US$107m. (US$23 per capita).

Army. In 1997 the Army was 16,000-strong and organized in 4 motor rifle divisions, 1 artillery and 1 engineer brigade and 1 multiple rocket launcher, 1 anti-tank and 3 engineer regiments. Equipment includes 570 T-72 main battle tanks.

Air Force. The Air Force, with 3,000 personnel, had 65 Su-17s and 2 air defence regiments of 48 MiG-23s and 24 MiG-25s.

INTERNATIONAL RELATIONS

Turkmenistan is a member of the UN, OSCE, CIS and the NATO Partnership for Peace.

ECONOMY

Policy. A privatization programme was launched on 1 June 1994. Enterprises with fewer than 100 employees are being sold to the employees or auctioned to citizens or foreign nationals. Large enterprises are to become joint stock companies, with the state retaining a controlling number of shares. But economic reform moves slowly. Citizens enjoy free gas and electricity, and heavily subsidized bread and transport.

Performance. GNP in 1995 was US$11,900m. Real GDP growth was −12·0% in 1995 and −18·8% in 1994.

Budget. Revenues were an estimated US$521m. in 1996 and expenditure US$548m.

Currency. The unit of currency is the *manat* (TMM) of 100 *tenesi*. Foreign exchange reserves were US$300m. in 1993. Inflation was estimated to be 600% in 1996. The manat was devalued in 1994 to an official rate of US$1 = 230 manat.

Banking and Finance. The *governor* of the Central Bank is Khudayberdy Ozarov. In 1996 there were 7 joint stock banks, the State Bank for Foreign Economic Affairs, the state savings bank, 4 joint venture banks and 2 foreign banks.

ENERGY AND NATURAL RESOURCES

Electricity. Installed capacity in 1994 was 3·95m. kW. Production was 11,200m. kWh in 1995, with consumption per capita in 1995 estimated at 1,855 kWh.

Oil and Gas. Turkmenistan possesses the world's fifth largest reserves of natural gas, and substantial oil resources, but disputes with Russia have held up development. So far, Turkmenistan has been unable to get its gas to world markets. Pipeline plans exist only on paper. Moreover, ownership of offshore oil reserves is disputed by Iran and Azerbaijan.

In 1997 gas reserves were estimated at 21,000,000m. cu. metres and oil reserves at 700m. tonnes. In 1996 crude petroleum production was 32m. bbls.; natural gas (1995), 43,000m. cu. metres.

Turkmenistan's biggest oil development deal was signed in July 1998 when Mobil of the USA and Monument Oil of the UK, in co-operation with the state oil group Turkmeneft, agreed to spend some US$100m. over 3 years. In 1998 the two companies were producing 14,000 bbls. a day in western Turkmenistan but it was hoped that expansion and development of the Garashsyzlyk area could lead to production of approaching 500,000 bbls. a day by 2007.

Minerals. There are reserves of coal, sulphur, magnesium, potassium, lead, barite, viterite, bromine, iodine and salt.

Agriculture. Cotton and wheat account for two-thirds of agricultural production. Barley, maize, corn, rice, wool, silk and fruit are also produced. Cotton production was 11·5m. tonnes in 1995. 1998 produced a bumper wheat harvest.

Livestock, 1996: Cattle, 1·2m.; sheep, 6·15m.; goats, 314,000 (1995); pigs, 82,000; chickens, 7m.

Forestry. There were 3·75m. ha of forests (8% of the land area) in 1995.

Fisheries. There are fisheries in the Caspian Sea. The total catch in 1995 was 15,000 tonnes, exclusively freshwater fish.

INDUSTRY

Main industries: oil refining, gas extraction, chemicals, manufacture of machinery, fertilizers, textiles and clothing. Output, 1993 (in tonnes): Cement, 1·1m.; mineral fertilizer, 0·13m.; fabrics, 48·3m. sq. metres; footwear, 3·4m. pairs.

Labour. The labour force in 1996 totalled 1,750,000 (55% males). In 1993, 53·8% of the economically active population were engaged in the state sector, 19·7% in the private sector and 25·9% in co-operatives. Average monthly wage in 1994 was 1,000 manat.

INTERNATIONAL TRADE
External debt was US$825m. in 1996.

Imports and Exports. Exports, 1995, US$2,000m.; imports, US$1,600m. Main imports: light manufactured goods, processed food, metalwork, machinery and parts. Main exports: gas, oil and cotton. The main import suppliers in 1995 were USA (25·8%), Ukraine (17·4%), Turkey (13·1%) and Russia (10·1%). The leading export markets in 1995 were Russia (62·5%), Switzerland (6·5%), Hong Kong (6·2%) and Turkey (4·7%).

COMMUNICATIONS

Roads. Length of roads in 1996, 24,000 km (9,500 km hard surface). In 1993, 273·1m. passengers and 46·3m. tonnes of freight were carried.

Rail. Length of railways in 1995, 2,164 km of 1,520 mm gauge. A rail link to Iran was opened in May 1996, and there are plans to build a futher 2,000 km of rail network. In 1995, 5·5m. passengers and 22·2m. tonnes of freight were carried.

Civil Aviation. The national carrier is Avia Company Turkmenistan. In 1998 it operated flights from Ashgabat to Abu Dhabi, Almaty, Birmingham, Delhi, Istanbul, Karachi, Kiev, London, Moscow and Toshkent. Services were also provided in 1998 by Aerosweet Airlines, Armenian Airlines, Azerbaijan Airlines, British Airways, Iran Air, Lufthansa, MDA Airlines, Turkish Airlines, United Airlines and Uzbekiston Airways. In 1995 scheduled airline traffic of Turkmenistan-based carriers flew 21·5m. km, carrying 748,000 passengers.

Shipping. In 1995, sea-going shipping totalled 15,812 GRT, including oil tankers, 1,621 GRT. In 1993, 1·1m. tonnes of freight were carried by inland waterways.

Telecommunications. Main telephone lines numbered 363,000 in 1997 (78 per 1,000 population).

SOCIAL INSTITUTIONS

Justice. In 1994, 14,824 crimes were reported, including 308 murders and attempted murders. There were over 100 executions in 1996.

Religion. Approximately 90% of the population are Sunni Moslems.

Education. In 1993-94 there were 1,900 primary and secondary schools with 874,000 pupils, 11 higher educational institutions with 38,900 students, 41 technical colleges with 29,000 students, and 11 music and art schools.

In Jan. 1994, 0·2m. children (29·5% of those eligible) were attending pre-school institutions. In 1995 adult literacy was over 99%.

Health. There were 14,000 doctors in Jan. 1994, 43,000 junior medical personnel and 368 hospitals with 46,100 beds.

Welfare. In Jan. 1994 there were 0·3m. old-age, and 0·16m. other, pensioners.

CULTURE

Broadcasting. Turkmen Radio is government-controlled. It broadcasts 2 national and 1 regional programme, a Moscow Radio relay and a foreign service, Voice of Turkmen. There is 1 state-run TV station. In 1995 there were 330,000 radio receivers and 735,000 televisions.

Press. In 1995 there were 130 newspapers and periodicals.

DIPLOMATIC REPRESENTATIVES

Of Turkmenistan in Great Britain (2nd Floor, St George's Hse., 14-17 Wells St, London, W1P 3FP)
Ambassador: Murad Chariev.

Of Great Britain in Turkmenistan (3rd Floor, Office Building, Ak Atin Plaza Hotel, Ashgabat)
Ambassador: Frazer Wilson, OBE.

Of Turkmenistan in the USA (2207 Massachusetts Ave., NW, Washington, D.C., 20008)
Ambassador: Halil Ugar.

Of the USA in Turkmenistan (9 Puskin St., Ashgabat)
Ambassador: Vacant.

Of Turkmenistan to the United Nations
Ambassador: Aksoltan T. Ataeva.

Of Turkmenistan to the European Union
Ambassador: Niyazklych Nurklychev.

TUVALU

Capital: Fongafale
Population estimate, 2000: 11,000
Estimated GDP: $7·8m.

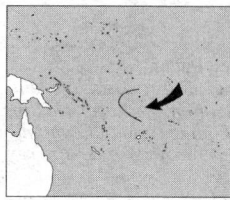

KEY HISTORICAL EVENTS
Formerly known as the Ellice Islands, Tuvalu is a group of nine islands in the western central Pacific. Traditions recorded by missionaries in the 19th century indicate Samoa or Tonga as the original home of Tuvalu's first Polynesian settlers. Tuvaluan language supports this and genealogical data suggests settlement dates back to 1325. A number of castaways and beachcombers settled and intermarried with the Tuvuluans during 1820–70, when whalers frequented the surrounding seas.

In 1892 when the British established the Gilbert Islands Protectorate, the Tuvalu islanders were encouraged to join. They became the Gilbert and Ellice Islands colony in 1916.

After the Japanese occupied the Gilbert Islands in 1942, US forces occupied the Ellice Islands and built airstrips on 3 islands. Many Tuvaluans emigrated to Tarawa in the Gilberts after the Second World War for employment; rivalry between them and the Kiribatians set the stage for separation. On the recommendation of a commissioner, appointed by the British Government to consider requests that the island group be separated from the Gilbert islands, a referendum was held in 1974. There was a large majority in favour of separation and this took place in Oct. 1975. Independence was achieved on 1 Oct. 1978. Early in 1979 the USA signed a treaty of friendship with Tuvalu and relinquished its claim to the four southern islands in return for access to its Second World War bases, and the right to veto any other nation's request to use any of Tuvalu's islands for military purposes.

TERRITORY AND POPULATION
Tuvalu lies between 5° 30' and 11° S. lat. and 176° and 180° E. long. and comprises Nanumea, Nanumanga, Niutao, Nui, Vaitupu, Nukufetau, Funafuti (administrative centre; 1991 population, 3,432), Nukulaelae and Niulakita. Population (census 1991) 9,043, excluding an estimated 1,500 who were working abroad, mainly in Nauru and Kiribati. Estimate, 1995, 10,500, of whom 1,000 were working abroad. Area approximately 9½ sq. miles (24 sq. km). Density, 1995, 396 per sq. km.

In 2000 the population is projected to be 11,000.

In 1995 an estimated 53·2% of the population lived in rural areas. The population is of a Polynesian race.

Both Tuvaluan and English are spoken.

SOCIAL STATISTICS
1996 births (approx.), 250; deaths, 90. Rates, 1996 (per 1,000 population): Births, 24; deaths, 9; infant mortality (per 1,000 live births), 28. Expectation of life: Males, 62 years; females, 65.

CLIMATE
A pleasant but monotonous climate with temperatures averaging 86°F (30°C), though trade winds from the east moderate conditions for much of the year. Rainfall ranges from 120" (3,000 mm) to over 160" (4,000 mm). Funafuti, Jan. 84°F (28·9°C), July 81°F (27·2°C). Annual rainfall 160" (4,003 mm). Although the islands are north of the recognized hurricane belt they have been badly hit by hurricanes in the 1990s, raising fears for the long-term future of Tuvalu as the sea level continues to rise.

CONSTITUTION AND GOVERNMENT
The Constitution provides for a Prime Minister and 4 other Ministers to be elected from among the 12 elected members of the *House of Parliament.*

National Anthem. 'Tuvalu mo te Atua' ('Tuvalu for the Almighty'); words and tune by A. Manoa.

RECENT ELECTIONS
Elections were held on 26 March 1998. Only non-partisans were elected as there are no political parties.

CURRENT ADMINISTRATION
Governor-General: HE Dr Tomasi Puapua.
  In March 1999 the Cabinet comprised:
  Prime Minister and Minister for Foreign Affairs: Bikenibeu Paeniu.
  Deputy Prime Minister, Minister for Home Affairs and Rural Development, Natural Resources and Environment: Kokeiya Malua. *Education, Culture, Health, Women's and Community Affairs:* Ionatana Ionatana. *Finance and Economic Planning, Tourism, Trade and Commerce:* Alesana Kleis Seluka. *Works, Energy and Communications:* Otinielu Tauteleimalae Tausi.

Local Government. There is a town council on Funafuti and island councils on the 7 other atolls, each consisting of 6 elected members including a president. Since 1966 Members of Parliament have been ex-officio members of Island Councils. The island of Niulakita is administered as part of Niutao.

INTERNATIONAL RELATIONS
Tuvalu is a member of the Commonwealth, the Pacific Community and the South Pacific Forum, and is an ACP member state of the ACP-EU relationship.

ECONOMY
Performance. Real GDP growth was 2·5% in 1995 and 1·8% in 1994.

Budget. In 1994 the budget envisaged revenue of $A9·4m.

Currency. The unit of currency is the Australian *dollar* although Tuvaluan coins up to $A1 are in local circulation.

Banking and Finance. The Tuvalu National Bank was established at Funafuti in 1980, and is a joint venture between the Tuvalu Government and Wespac International.

ENERGY AND NATURAL RESOURCES
Electricity. Installed capacity was 2,600 kW in 1995. Production in 1995 was 3m. kWh.

Agriculture. Coconut palms are the main crop. Production of coconuts (1991), 4,000 tonnes. Fruit and vegetables are grown for local consumption. Livestock, 1996: Pigs, 13,000.

Fisheries. Sea fishing is excellent, particularly for tuna. Total catch, 1995, 399 tonnes. A seamount was discovered in Tuvaluan waters in 1991 and is an excellent location for deep-sea fish. The sale of fishing licences to American and Japanese fleets provides a significant source of income.

INTERNATIONAL TRADE
Imports and Exports. Commerce is dominated by co-operative societies, the Tuvalu Co-operative Wholesale Society being the main importer. Main sources of income are copra, stamps, handicrafts and remittances from Tuvaluans abroad. 1991 imports, $A6·7m.; 1991 exports, $A0·3m. The leading import supplier is the Fiji Islands, and the leading export destination South Africa.

COMMUNICATIONS
Roads. In 1996 there were 8 km of roads.

Civil Aviation. In 1998 Air Marshall Islands had flights from Funafuti International to Majuro (Marshall Islands), Nadi and Suva (Fiji Islands), and Tarawa (Kiribati).

Shipping. Funafuti is the only port and a deep-water wharf was opened in 1980. In 1995 merchant shipping totalled 64,000 GRT.

TUVALU

SOCIAL INSTITUTIONS

Justice. There is a High Court presided over by the Chief Justice of the Fiji Islands. A Court of Appeal is constituted if required. There are also 8 Island Courts with limited jurisdiction.

Religion. The majority of the population are Christians, mainly Protestant, but with small groups of Roman Catholics, Seventh Day Adventists, Jehovah's Witnesses and Latter-day Saints (Mormons). There are some Moslems and Baha'is.

Education. There were 1,906 pupils at 11 primary schools in 1994, and 345 pupils at 2 secondary schools in 1990. There is a Maritime Training School at Funafuti, and the University of the South Pacific, based in the Fiji Islands, has an extension centre at Funafuti.

Health. In 1993 there was 1 central hospital situated at Funafuti. There were 8 doctors and 39 nurses in 1993.

CULTURE

Broadcasting. The Tuvalu Broadcasting Service transmits daily, and all islands have daily radio communication with Funafuti. There were about 3,000 radio receivers in 1995.

Press. The Government Broadcasting and Information Division produces *Tuvalu Echoes*, a fortnightly publication, and *Te Lama*, a monthly religious publication.

Tourism. There were 639 visitor arrivals in 1995.

DIPLOMATIC REPRESENTATIVES
Of Great Britain in Tuvalu
High Commissioner: M. A. C. Dibben (resides in the Fiji Islands).

Of Tuvalu in the USA
Ambassador: Vacant.

Of the USA in Tuvalu
Ambassador: Don Gevirtz (resides in the Fiji Islands).

UGANDA

Republic of Uganda

Capital: Kampala
Population estimate, 2000: 22·21m.
GNP per capita: (PPP$) 1,030
HDI/world rank: 0·340/160

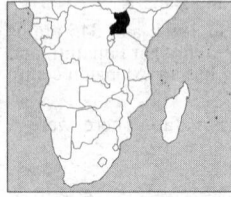

KEY HISTORICAL EVENTS

The Luo (a Nilotic-speaking people) invaded the territory of present-day Uganda in the late 15th and 16th centuries and while assimilating with the existing Bantu-speaking inhabitants, also founded several strong centralized kingdoms. Buganda was the most prominent of these and prospered through the 19th century, assisting British forces in the conquest of its neighbours. Uganda became a British Protectorate in 1894, the province of Buganda being recognized as a native kingdom under its Kabaka. In 1961, Uganda was granted internal self-government with federal status for Buganda.

Uganda became a fully independent member of the Commonwealth on 9 Oct. 1962 after nearly 70 years of British rule. Full sovereign status was granted by the Ugandan Independence Act 1962. The post of Governor-General was on 9 Oct. 1963 replaced by that of President as head of state, elected by the National Assembly for a five-year term. Uganda became a republic on 8 Sept. 1967. President Milton Obote set about returning land given to the Buganda by the British in 1900 to its original Bunyoro owners. He also abolished Buganda's federal status and autonomy in the country. A rebellion by Buganda was quelled, but in 1971 Obote was overthrown by troops under Gen. Idi Amin. Amin's rule was characterized by widespread repression and in 1972, the expulsion of Asian residents. In April 1979, a force of the Tanzanian Army and Ugandan exiles advanced into Uganda, taking Kampala on 11 April. Amin fled into exile. On 14 April, Dr Yusuf Lule was sworn in as president and the country was administered, initially, by the Uganda National Liberation Front.

The former Attorney-General, Godfrey Lukonwa Binaisa QC, was appointed president by the National Consultative Council on 20 June 1979. Dr Lule subsequently left the country. Dr Binaisa was overthrown in May 1980 by the Military Commission, the military arm of the Uganda National Liberation Front. In Dec. 1980, following elections, Dr Obote again became president, but on 27 July 1985 was overthrown. The constitution was suspended and the borders closed. Lieut. Gen. Tito Okello became head of state on 29 July but on the following day the National Resistance Army (NRA) was not prepared to co-operate with the new régime. After an abortive ceasefire between the NRA and government forces on 17 Dec. 1985, the NRA, later known more usually as the National Resistance Movement, fought its way into Kampala, and Yoweri Museveni was installed as President on 27 Jan. 1986.

There is insurgent activity near Gulu and Kitgun in Northern Uganda. Rebels belonging to a religious sect, the Lords Resistance Army, are covertly supported by Sudan.

Many of the Asians expelled by Gen. Idi Amin in 1972 returned to Uganda in the second half of the 1990s, bringing with them both capital and much-needed skills.

TERRITORY AND POPULATION

Uganda is bounded in the north by Sudan, in the east by Kenya, in the south by Tanzania and Rwanda, and the west by the Democratic Republic of the Congo. Total area 241,038 sq. km, including 43,938 sq. km of water.

In 1999 the population was estimated to be 21,619,700 (10,708,000 male, 10,911,000 female); density, 90 per sq. km. The largest towns are Kampala, the capital (890,800), Jinja (397,600), Mbale (931,500), Masaka (1,038,400), Gulu (455,400), Soroti (657,000) and Mbarara (1,012,400).

The projected population for 2000 is 22·21m.

An estimated 84·5% of the population lived in rural areas in 1999.

UGANDA

The country is administratively divided into 39 districts, which are grouped in 4 geographical regions (which do not have administrative status). Area and estimated population of the regions in 1999:

Region	Area in sq. km	Population in 1,000
Central Region	61,510	6,046·0
Eastern Region	39,953	5,469·5
Western Region	54,917	5,997·7
Northern Region	84,658	4,106·5

The official language is English, but Kiswahili is used as a lingua franca. About 70% of the population speak Bantu languages; Nilotic languages are spoken in the north and east.

Uganda is host to around 500,000 refugees from a number of neighbouring countries, and internally displaced people. Probably in excess of 100,000 southern Sudanese fled to Uganda during 1996.

SOCIAL STATISTICS
Births, 1995, 1,004,000; deaths, 421,000. Rates per 1,000 population, 1995: Birth, 51·0; death, 21·4. Uganda's life expectancy at birth in 1998 was 41 years, down from 47 in 1985. It had last been 41 in the late 1950s. The sharp decline is largely attributed to the huge number of people in the country with HIV. Population growth in 1996–97 was an estimated 2·8%. Infant mortality, 1990–95, 122 per 1,000 live births; fertility rate, 7·1 births per woman.

CLIMATE
Although in equatorial latitudes, the climate is more tropical, because of its elevation, and is characterized by 2 distinct rainy seasons, March-May and Sept.-Nov. June-Aug. and Dec.-Feb. are comparatively dry. Temperatures vary little over the year. Kampala, Jan. 74°F (23·3°C), July 70°F (21·1°C). Annual rainfall 46·5" (1,180 mm). Entebbe, Jan. 72°F (22·2°C), July 69°F (20·6°C). Annual rainfall 63·9" (1,624 mm).

CONSTITUTION AND GOVERNMENT
The *President* is head of state and head of government, and is elected for a 5-year term by adult suffrage.

Having lapsed in 1966, the kabakaship was revived as a ceremonial office in 1993. Ronald Muwenda Mutebi (b. 13 April 1955) was crowned Mutebi II, 36th Kabaka, on 31 July 1993.

Until 1994 the national legislature was the 278-member National Resistance Council, but this was replaced by a 276-member *Constituent Assembly* in March 1994, 214 of whose members are elected in single-seat constituencies, 39 (women) indirectly elected by women's associations, and 23 set aside for indirectly elected representatives of the army (10), the disabled (5), youth (5) and trade unions (3). A new constitution was adopted on 8 Oct. 1995. The return of multiparty democracy is promised for the year 2000.

National Anthem. 'Oh, Uganda, may God uphold thee'; words and tune by G. W. Kakoma.

RECENT ELECTIONS
Presidential elections were held on 9 May 1996 for the first time by universal suffrage. Turn-out was 72·6%. President Museveni was re-elected by 74·2% of votes cast. He had two opponents.

Parliamentary elections were held on 27 June 1996. The electorate was 8·5m. The National Resistance Movement is reported to have obtained 156 seats.

CURRENT ADMINISTRATION
President: H. E. Yoweri K. Museveni (b. 1945; sworn in 27 Jan. 1986, re-elected 1996).

In March 1999 the government comprised:

Vice-President, Minister of Agriculture, Animal Industry and Fisheries: Dr Specîosa Wandira Kazibwe.

Prime Minister: Kintu Musoke.
First Deputy Prime Minister and Minister of Foreign Affairs: Eriya Kategaya.
Second Deputy Prime Minister and Minister of Tourism, Trade and Industry: Brig.
Moses Ali. *Third Deputy Prime Minister and Minister of Disaster Preparedness and
Refugees:* Paul Etiang. *Minister of Defence:* Yoweri Kaguta Museveni. *Education
and Sports:* Dr Apollo Nsibambi. *Energy and Minerals:* Richard Kaijuka. *Finance,
Planning and Economic Growth:* Gerald Ssendaula. *Health:* Dr Crispus Kiyonga.
Gender, Labour and Social Development: Janati Mukwaya. *Justice and
Constitutional Affairs:* J. Mayanja Nkangi. *Local Government:* Jaberi Bidandi Ssali.
Internal Affairs: Maj. Tom Butime. *Public Services:* Amanya Mushega. *Water,
Lands and Environment:* Kajura Henry Muganwa. *Works, Housing and
Communications:* John Nasasira.

Local Government. The 43 districts are divided into 150 counties, which are in turn
divided into sub-counties, which form the basic administrative units.

DEFENCE
In 1997 defence expenditure totalled US$166m. (US$8 per capita).

Army. The Uganda Peoples Defence Forces had a strength of about 50,000 in 1997.
Equipment includes 20 T-54/-55 main battle tanks. There is a Border Defence Unit
about 600-strong.

Navy. A Marine unit of the police (400-strong in 1996) operates 8 small patrol craft.

Air Force. The Air Wing in 1997 had 5 SF-260 light strike aircraft, 9 Bell and Mi 1
transport helicopters, 4 communications helicopters and 5 AS-202 and 3 L-39
trainers.

INTERNATIONAL RELATIONS
Uganda is a member of UN, OAU, Islamic Conference Organization, the
Commonwealth, and is an ACP state of EU.

ECONOMY
Policy. A privatization programme was instituted in 1991 managed by the Public
Enterprise Reform and Divestiture Secretariat. The state is to retain ownership of
certain utilities, national parks and the development bank. About 100 enterprises
were in state ownership, but most had been privatized by 1997.

Performance. Real GDP growth was 7% in 1996 (10% in 1995). In spite of growth
rates which averaged 6·4% over 10 years to 1998, per capita income is only just
approaching the levels of 1971, when Gen. Idi Amin came to power.

Budget. The estimated total expenditure for the financial year 1998–99 is 1,448 bn.
Uganda Sh., compared to 1997–98 actual expenditure of 1,232 bn. Uganda Sh. The
economy registered a 5·5% growth in real terms in 1997–98 compared to 1996–97.
In 1994–95 revenue (excluding grants) was 522,390m. Uganda Sh., and expenditure
(1991–92), 410,310m. Uganda Sh. Sources of revenue included (in 1m. Uganda
Sh.): Tax, 213,609; export duties, 14,412; customs duties, 190,905. Expenditures (in
1991–92) included: Agriculture, animal industry and fisheries, 8,192; education,
38,009; health, 3,306; defence, 63,421.

Currency. The monetary unit is the *Uganda shilling* (UGS) notionally divided into
100 *cents.* In 1987 the currency was devalued by 77% and a new 'heavy' shilling
was introduced worth 100 old shillings. Annualized inflation in 1996 was 5%.
Foreign exchange reserves in Feb. 1998 were US$662m. Total money supply in
Dec. 1997 was 533m. Uganda Sh.

Banking and Finance. The Bank of Uganda (established 1966) is the central bank
and bank of issue. The Uganda Credit and Savings Bank, established in 1950, was
on 9 Oct. 1965 reconstituted as the Uganda Commercial Bank, with its capital fully
owned by the Government. In 1992 it had 188 branches. In addition there are 4
foreign, 2 private and 2 development banks and 1 co-operative bank.

UGANDA

ENERGY AND NATURAL RESOURCES

Electricity. Installed capacity in 1995 was 155 MW, about 95% of which was provided by the Owen Falls Extension Project (a hydroelectric scheme). Production (1995) 807m. kWh.

Oil and Gas. Heritage Oil, an Australian company, was exploring for oil in Western Uganda in early 1999.

Minerals. In Nov. 1997 extraction started of the first of an estimated US$400m. worth of cobalt from pyrites. Tungsten and tin concentrates are also mined. There are also significant quantities of clay and gypsum.

Agriculture. 80% of the workforce is involved with agriculture. In 1994 the agricultural area included 5·06m. ha of arable land, 1·74m. ha of permanent crops and 1·8m. ha of pasture. Agriculture is one of the priority areas for increased production, with many projects funded both locally and externally. In 1996 it recorded 24·2% growth. It accounted for 46% of GDP in 1996 and contributes 90% of exports. Production (1995) in 1,000 tonnes: Tobacco, 7; coffee, 200; cotton lint, 12; tea, 15; sugar-cane, 1,450; plantains, 9,519; millet, 143; maize, 950; sorghum, 398; cassava, 2,625; dry beans, 387. Coffee is the mainstay of the economy.

Livestock (1995): Cattle, 5·2m.; sheep, 0·9m.; goats, 5·5m.; pigs, 1·3m.; chickens, 23m. Livestock products, 1995 (in 1,000 tonnes): Beef and veal, 90; pork, 51; poultry meat, 36; eggs, 18; honey, 250; milk, 455.

Forestry. In 1995 the area under forests was 6·1m. ha, or 30·6% of the total land area (6·4m. ha and 32·1% in 1990). Exploitable forests consist almost entirely of hardwoods. 17·23m. cu. metres of wood were cut in 1995. Uganda has great potential for timber-processing for export, manufacture of high-quality furniture and wood products, and various packaging materials.

Fisheries. Uganda possesses one of the largest freshwater fisheries in the world. In 1996 fish production was 222,000 tonnes. Fish farming (especially carp and tilapia) is a growing industry. Uganda's fish-processing industry has greatly expanded in recent years, and by 1998 export earnings were in excess of US$100m. per year

INDUSTRY
Production (in 1,000 tonnes) in 1995: Cement, 88·5; soap, 55·7; sugar, 70·1; beer, 51·2m. litres. The manufacturing sector is growing by around 14% annually.

Labour. The labour force in 1996 totalled 10,084,000 (52% males). Around 80% of the workforce are involved in the coffee business.

INTERNATIONAL TRADE
Foreign debt was US$3,674m. in 1996. Over the period 1981–96 foreign investment totalled US$850m.

Imports and Exports. In 1995–96 imports were US$866·7m. and exports US$548·9m. Coffee, cotton, tea and tobacco are the principal exports. Coffee accounts for nearly 70% of exports. Timber and fish exports are increasingly important. In 1996 the main export markets were Spain (21·1%), France (11·1%) and Germany (8·8%). Main import suppliers in 1996 were Kenya (29·4%), UK (11·8%) and India (6·1%).

COMMUNICATIONS

Roads. In 1994 there were 6,727 km of highways and 2,105 km of secondary roads. There were 35,000 passenger cars in 1996, and 50,000 commercial vehicles.

In 1997 the Government embarked upon a 10-year road-improvement programme, costing US$1·5bn., funded by international loans.

Rail. The Uganda Railways network totals 1,241 km (metre gauge). In 1996 railways carried 184,000 passengers and 877,000 tonnes of freight.

A US$20m. project is under way to establish a direct rail link between Kampala and Johannesburg, South Africa.

Civil Aviation. There is an international airport at Entebbe, 40 km from Kampala. The national carrier is the state-owned Uganda Airlines, which in 1998 flew to Dar es Salaam, Dubai, Harare, Johannesburg, Kigali, Lusaka and Nairobi. Uganda and Tanzania are partners with South African Airways, in Alliance Air. In 1998 services were also provided by Air Tanzania Corporation, British Airways, Delta Air Lines, Egyptair, Ethiopian Airlines, Gulf Air, Inter Air, Iran Air, Kenya Airways, KLM and SABENA. Uganda Airlines flew 1·9m. km in 1995, carrying 94,600 passengers. In 1996 Entebbe handled 324,760 passengers (296,867 on international flights) and 27,296 tonnes of freight.

Telecommunications. There were 46,000 telephone main lines in 1998 (2·2 per 1,000 persons); there had been 100,000 in 1971 when Idi Amin seized power. There were 10,000 PCs in 1995, 2,500 fax machines and 1,700 cellular phone subscribers. In Jan. 1998 Uganda had approximately 2,000 Internet users.

Postal Services. In 1995 there were 306 post offices.

SOCIAL INSTITUTIONS

Justice. The Supreme Court of Uganda, presided over by the Chief Justice, is the highest court. There is a Court of Appeal and a High Court below that. Subordinate courts, presided over by Chief Magistrates and Magistrates of the first, second and third grade, are established in all areas: Jurisdiction varies with the grade of Magistrate. Chief and first-grade Magistrates are professionally qualified; second- and third-grade Magistrates are trained to diploma level at the Law Development Centre, Kampala. Chief Magistrates exercise supervision over and hear appeals from second- and third-grade courts, and village courts.

Religion. In 1992 there were 8·53m. Roman Catholics, 4·5m. Anglicans and 1·13m. Moslems.

Education. In 1995 there were 2,636,400 pupils in 7,905 primary schools (of which 7,420 were Government-aided schools and 485 private schools); 255,158 students in 774 secondary schools; 13,174 students in 94 primary teacher training colleges; 13,360 students in 24 technical institutes and colleges; 22,703 students in 10 national teachers colleges; 1,628 students in 5 colleges of commerce; 504 students in the Uganda Polytechnic, Kyambogo; 800 students in the National College of Business Studies, Nakawa. In 1995–96 there was 1 university and 1 university of science and technology in the public sector, and 2 universities, 1 Christian, 1 Roman Catholic and 1 Islamic university in the private sector, catering for 29,343 students. The adult literacy rate was 61·8% in 1995 (73·7% among males and 50·2% among females).

Health. In 1988 there were 980 health centres (217 private), and in 1989 there were 81 hospitals and 20,136 hospital beds. In 1993 there were 840 doctors and 2,782 nurses. In the period 1990–96 only 38% of the population had access to safe drinking water.

CULTURE

Broadcasting. The government runs Radio Uganda, which has 10 stations and transmits 3 regional programmes, and Uganda Television with 9 stations and 1 programme. Colour is by PAL. There were about 2·3m. radio receivers and about 250,000 television sets in 1995. There are 3 private television operators.

Press. There were 2 daily newspapers in 1994 with a fluctuating circulation of 45,000-55,000, and 12 weekly, 1 bi-weekly and 5 monthly newspapers and magazines.

Tourism. In 1996 there were 205,000 foreign tourists, bringing revenue of US$100m.

Festivals. The main festivals are for Islamic holidays (March and June), Martyrs' Day (3 June), Heroes' Day (9 June) and Independence Day (9 Oct.).

Libraries. In 1992 there were 17 libraries in Uganda with 53,476 registered users.

National Theatre and Opera. There is a National Theatre at Kampala.

Museums and Galleries. The Nommo Gallery houses famous works of art, and is involved in educational and other cultural programmes.

DIPLOMATIC REPRESENTATIVES

Of Uganda in Great Britain (Uganda Hse., 58/59 Trafalgar Sq., London, WC2N 5DX)
High Commissioner: George Kirya.

Of Great Britain in Uganda (10/12 Parliament Ave., Kampala)
High Commissioner: M. E. Cook.

Of Uganda in the USA (5909 16th St., NW, Washington, D.C., 20011)
Ambassador: Edith Ssempala.

Of the USA in Uganda (Parliament Ave., Kampala)
Ambassador: Nancy J. Powell.

Of Uganda to the United Nations
Ambassador: Matia Mulumba Semakula Kiwanuka.

Of Uganda to the European Union
Ambassador: Kakima Ntambi.

FURTHER READING

Jørgensen, J. J., *Uganda: A Modern History.* London, 1981
Museveni, Y., *What is Africa's Problem?* London, 1993.—*The Mustard Seed.* London, 1997
Mutibwa, P., *Uganda since Independence: a Story of Unfulfilled Hopes.* London, 1992
Nyeko, B., *Uganda.* [Bibliography] 2nd ed. Oxford and Santa Barbara (CA), 1996

National statistical office: Statistical Department, Ministry of Finance and Economic Planning, Kampala.

UKRAINE

Ukraina

Capital: Kyiv (formerly Kiev)
Population estimate, 2000: 50·8m.
GNP per capita: (PPP$) 2,230
HDI/world rank: 0·665/102

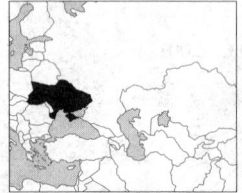

KEY HISTORICAL EVENTS

Kyiv (formerly Kiev) was the centre of the Rus principality in the 11th and 12th centuries and is still known as the Mother of Russian cities. In the 13th century the area was invaded by Tatar-Mongols and the western Ukraine principality of Galicia was annexed by Poland in the 14th century. At about the same time, Kyiv and the Ukrainian principality of Volhynia were conquered by Lithuania, before being absorbed by Poland. Poland, however, could not subjugate the Ukrainian cossacks, who allied themselves with Russia. The lands east of the Dnepr River were ceded to Russia in 1667 (some parts of Ukraine had been annexed by Muscovy much earlier), and the remainder of Ukraine, except for Galicia (part of the Austrian Empire, 1772-1919), was incorporated into the Russian Empire after the second partition of Poland in 1793.

The Ukrainians under Austrian rule in Galicia and Bukovina, and in the region of Hungary known as the Carpatho-Ukraine, preserved their identity as a separate group and engendered a forceful nationalist movement. In 1917, following the Bolshevik revolution, the Ukrainians in Russia established an independent republic. Austrian Ukraine proclaimed itself a republic in 1918 and was federated with its Russian counterpart. The Allies ignored Ukrainian claims to Galicia, however, and in 1918 awarded that area to Poland. In 1919 the Russian Ukrainian republic, under the leader Simon Petlyura, declared war on Poland. In the same year Ukrainian Communists established a second government and declared the existence of the Ukrainian SSR. In 1920 the advance of the Russian Bolshevik armies caused the Petlyura government and Poland to become allies but they were unable to prevent the Soviet government from taking control of the country.

From 1922 to 1932, drastic efforts were made by the USSR to suppress Ukrainian nationalism. Ukraine suffered from the forced collectivization of agriculture and the expropriation of foodstuffs; the result was the famine of 1932-33 when more than 7m. people died.

Following the Soviet seizure of eastern Poland in Sept. 1939, Polish Galicia was incorporated into the Ukrainian SSR. When the Germans invaded Ukraine in 1941 hopes that an autonomous or independent Ukrainian republic would be set up under German protection were disappointed. Ukraine was re-taken by the USSR in 1944. Parts of Bessarabia and northern Bukovina were added to Ukraine together with the Ruthenian region of Czechoslovakia. The Crimean region was joined to Ukraine in 1954.

On 5 Dec. 1991 the Supreme Soviet unanimously repudiated the 1922 Treaty of Union and declared Ukraine's independence. Ukraine was one of the founder members of the CIS in Dec. 1991. After independence, political tension developed in Ukraine over several domestic and international issues. Crimea, which was part of Russia until 1954, became a source of contention between Moscow and Kyiv. Shortly after Ukrainian independence in 1991, a Russian-led movement to secede from Ukraine was formed in Crimea, which succeeded in changing the status of the Crimean *oblast* to an autonomous republic. Crimea also issued a declaration of independence, which was rescinded in May 1992. In the same month, however, the Supreme Soviet of Russia declared the 1954 transfer of Crimea null and void. The Russian Supreme Soviet laid claim to the Crimean port city of Sevastopol, the home port of the 350-ship Black Sea Fleet, despite an agreement to divide the fleet which was signed by President Kravchuk and Russian President Boris Yeltsin in Aug. 1992. Conflict between Ukraine and Russia also developed over possession and transfer of nuclear weapons, delivery of Russian fuel to Ukraine, the division of Soviet assets, and military and political integration within the CIS.

A second separatist movement developed in eastern Ukraine, where coal miners and other workers went on strike in June 1993 to protest against the poor state of the

1568

economy. A political crisis developed within the government over the pace of economic reform in 1993. In May 1993, Prime Minister Leonid Kuchma threatened to resign if he was not granted additional powers. In response, President Kravchuk urged the Ukrainian parliament to submit. But parliament rejected Kuchma's resignation and most of Kravchuk's proposals, although it did grant Kravchuk the power to rule by decree on some economic issues. Leonid Kuchma was elected President in 1994.

TERRITORY AND POPULATION

Ukraine is bounded in the east by the Russian Federation, north by Belarus, west by Poland, Slovakia, Hungary, Romania and Moldova, and south by the Black Sea and Sea of Azov. Area, 603,700 sq. km (231,990 sq. miles). The 1995 census population was 51·7m., of whom 73% were Ukrainians, 22% Russians, 1% Jews and 4% other—Belarusians, Moldovans, Hungarians, Bulgarians, Poles and Crimean Tatars (most of the Tatars were forcibly transported to Central Asia in 1944 for anti-Soviet activities during the Second World War). Estimate, 1998, 51·37m. (70% urban); density, 85 per sq. km.

The UN gives a projected population for 2000 of 50·8m.

Ukraine is divided into 24 provinces and the Autonomous Republic of Crimea. Area (1991) and population of the provinces (1 Jan. 1998):

	Area (sq. km)	Population (in 1,000)		Area (sq. km)	Population (in 1,000)
Cherkaska	20,900	1,478·7	Lvivska	21,800	2,739·6
Chernihivska	31,900	1,318·5	Mykolaïvska	24,600	1,322·5
Chernivetska	8,100	938·5	Odeska	33,300	2,547·8
Dnipropetrovska	31,000	3,775·4	Poltavska	28,800	1,708·3
Donetska	26,500	5,064·4	Rivnenska	20,100	1,192·2
Ivano-Frankivska	13,900	1,463·6	Sumska	23,800	1,369·8
Kharkivska	31,400	3,024·4	Ternopilska	13,800	1,168·4
Khersonska	28,500	1,246·8	Vinnytska	26,500	1,847·1
Khmelnytska	20,600	1,485·7	Volynska	20,200	1,067·9
Kyivska	28,900	4,493·3	Zakarpatska	12,800	1,288·2
Kirovohradska	24,600	1,197·8	Zaporizhska	27,200	2,042·5
Luhanska	26,700	2,706·4	Zhytomyrska	29,900	1,457·1

The capital is Kyiv (population 2·6m. in 1998). Other towns with 1998 populations over 0·2m. are:

	Population (in 1,000)		Population (in 1,000)		Population (in 1,000)
Kharkiv	1,521	Makiïvka	395	Zhytomyr	298
Dnipropetrovsk	1,122	Vinnytsya	389	Dniprodzerzhynsk	275
Donetsk	1,065	Kherson	359	Kirovohrad	270
Odesa	1,027	Sevastopol	356	Chernivtsi	259
Zaporizhzhya	863	Simferopol	341	Rivne	245
Lviv	794	Poltava	317	Kremenchuk	241
Kryvy Rih	715	Cherkasy	311	Ivano-Frankivsk	237
Mykolaïv	518	Chernihiv	311	Ternopil	235
Mariupol	500	Horlivka	309	Lutsk	218
Luhansk	475	Sumy	300	Bila Tserkva	215

The 1996 Constitution made Ukrainian the sole official language. Russian, Romanian, Polish and Hungarian are also spoken. Additionally, the 1996 Constitution abolished dual citizenship, previously available if there was a treaty with the other country (there was no such treaty with Russia). Anyone resident in Ukraine since 1991 may be naturalized.

SOCIAL STATISTICS

1997 births, 442,600; deaths, 754,200; 1995 marriages, 431,731. Rates (per 1,000 population), 1997 estimate: Births, 8·7; deaths, 14·9. Annual rate of increase, 1997, −6·2%. Life expectancy, 1996–97 estimate: Males, 62 years, females, 73. In 1995 the most popular age range for marrying was 20–24 for both males and females. Infant mortality, 1997, 14 per 1,000 live births; fertility rate, 1·3 births per woman.

CLIMATE

Temperate continental with a subtropical Mediterranean climate prevalent on the southern portions of the Crimean Peninsula. The average monthly temperature in winter ranges from 17·6°F to 35·6°F (−8°C to 2°C), while summer temperatures average 62·6°F to 77°F (17°C to 25°C). The Black Sea coast is subject to freezing, and no Ukrainian port is permanently ice-free. Precipitation generally decreases from north to south; it is greatest in the Carpathians where it exceeds more than 58·5" (1500 mm) per year, and least in the coastal lowlands of the Black Sea where it averages less than 11·7" (300 mm) per year.

CONSTITUTION AND GOVERNMENT

In a referendum on 1 Dec. 1991, 90·3% of votes cast were in favour of independence. Turn-out was 83·7%.

A new Constitution was adopted on 28 June 1996. It defines Ukraine as a sovereign, democratic, unitary state governed by the rule of law and guaranteeing civil rights. The head of state is the *President*. Parliament is the 450-member unicameral *Supreme Council*, elected by universal suffrage for 4-year terms. For an election to be valid, turn-out in an electoral district must reach 50%. The Prime Minster is nominated by the President with the agreement of more than half the Supreme Council. There is an 18-member *Constitutional Court*, 6 members being appointed by the President, 6 by parliament and 6 by a panel of judges. Constitutional amendments may be initiated at the President's request to parliament, or by at least one third of parliamentary deputies. The Communist part was officially banned in the country in 1990, but was renamed the Socialist party of Ukraine and has retained political control. Hard-line Communists protested the ban, which was rescinded by the Supreme Council in May 1993. Several important democratic institutions have recently appeared in Ukraine, however, including a free press, a new constitution, and several popular opposition groups, such as Rukh and New Ukraine.

National Anthem. 'Shche ne vmerla, Ukraïna' ('Thou hast not perished, Ukraine'); words by P. Chubynsky, tune by M. Verbytsky.

RECENT ELECTIONS

Parliamentary elections were held on 29 March 1998. The Communist Party of Ukraine emerged as by far the largest single party, winning more seats than the next 2 most successful parties combined, although around 1 in 4 of the 450 seats went to candidates with no party affiliation.

Presidential elections were held in 2 rounds on 26 June and 10 July 1994. At the first round, turn-out was 69%. President Leonid Kravchuk gained 37·8% of votes cast against 6 opponents. At the second round, turn-out was 71·6%. Leonid Kuchma was elected against President Kravchuk by 51·5% of votes cast. The next presidential elections are to be held in Oct. 1999.

CURRENT ADMINISTRATION

President: Leonid Kuchma (sworn in 19 July 1994).

In March 1999 the government comprised:

Prime Minister: Valeriy Pustovoitenko.

First Deputy Prime Minister: Volodymyr Kuratchenko; *Deputy Prime Ministers:* Serhiy Tyhypko; Mykola Biloblotsyy; Mykhaylo Hladiy; Valeriy Smoliy.

Minister of Foreign Affairs: Borys Tarasyuk. *Defence:* Col.-Gen. Oleksandr Kuzmuk. *Foreign Economic Relations and Trade:* Andriy Honcharuk. *Interior:* Yuri Kravchenko. *Economy:* Vasyl Rohovyy. *Culture:* Dmytro Ostapenko. *Environmental Protection and Nuclear Safety:* Vasyl Shevchuk. *Finance:* Ihor Metyukiv. *Justice:* Suzanna Stanik. *Industrial Policy, Fuel and Energy:* Vasyl Hureyev. *Power and Energy:* Ivan Plachkov. *Education:* Valentin Zaychuk. *Coal Industry:* Serhiy Tulub. *Agriculture:* Borys Supikhanov. *Press and Information:* Zinoviy Kulyk. *Family and Youth Affairs:* Valentyna Dovzhenko. *Health:* Raisa Bohatyryova. *Labour:* Ivan Sakhan. *Science and Technology:* Stanislov Dovhyy. *Transport:* Arkadiy Demydenko. *Minister of the Cabinet:* Anatoliy Tolstoukhov.

Speaker: Oleksandr Moroz.

Local Government. The 24 provincial councils are subordinate to the President. Lower-level councils are subordinate to the provincial authorities. Elections were held on 4 March 1990.

DEFENCE

The 1996 Constitution bans the stationing of foreign troops on Ukrainian soil, but permits Russia to retain naval bases. Conscription is for 18 months. On 31 May 1997 the presidents of Ukraine and Russia signed a Treaty of Friendship and Co-operation which provided *inter alia* for the division of the former Soviet Black Sea Fleet and shore installations.

Military expenditure in 1997 totalled US$1,324m. (US$26 per capita), representing 2·7% of GDP.

Army. In 1997 ground forces numbered about 187,800 organized as follows: Ministry of Defence troops comprised 1 training tank brigade, 1 training artillery division, 1 artillery, 1 anti-tank and 3 engineer brigades; Western Operations Command comprised 1 artillery division, 1 training tank division, 1 surface-to-surface missile brigade and 1 engineer regiment, and 3 corps (1 with 2 motor rifle divisions, 2 mechanized, 1 artillery and 1 engineer brigade, 1 multiple rocket launcher and 1 anti-tank regiment; 1 with 2 mechanized divisions, 1 mechanized and 1 artillery brigade, 1 reserve anti-tank and 1 reserve multiple rocket launcher regiment; and 1 with 1 tank division and 1 anti-tank regiment); Southern Operations Command comprised 2 mechanized, 1 air mobile and 1 artillery division, 1 surface-to-surface missile, 2 surface-to-air missile and 2 artillery brigades, and 3 corps (1 with 2 mechanized and 1 artillery brigade and 1 anti-tank, 1 multiple rocket launcher and 2 reserve artillery brigades; 1 with 1 reserve motor rifle and 1 mechanized division, and 1 multiple rocket launcher and 1 reserve anti-tank regiment; and 1 with 1 tank and 2 mechanized divisions, 1 artillery brigade and 1 anti-tank and 1 multiple rocket launcher regiment); and 2 special forces units. Equipment includes 4,026 main battle tanks (182 T-55, 1 T-62, 2,216 T-64, 1,305 T-72 and 322 T-80), 636 medium-range launchers and 132 surface-to-surface missiles.

Navy. The former Soviet Black Sea Fleet continues to be the object of wrangling between Russia and Ukraine, and is financially and operationally paralyzed by the dispute. In 1996, the undisputed Ukrainian elements numbered 16,000, including 7,000 Naval Aviation and 4,000 in coastal defence, with fleet units based at Sevastopol and Odesa. The operational forces include 3 submarines, 2 Krivak-3 frigates, 2 smaller frigates and some 40 patrol craft and 6 amphibious units.

The aviation forces of the former Soviet Black Sea Fleet under Ukrainian command constitute about 40 bombers and about 40 anti-submarine and maritime reconnaissance aircraft. Main bomber types are Tu-26 'Backfire' and Tu-16 'Badger', armed principally with stand-off anti-ship missiles. There are also some 50 armed helicopters, most of seagoing types. The personnel of the Ukrainian Naval Aviation Force numbered (1996) about 7,000.

Air Force. Ukraine has taken over more than 2,000 ex-Soviet aircraft, nearly 1,500 of them combat equipment. It is limited to 1,090 combat aircraft and 330 armed helicopters under the Conventional Forces in Europe Agreement, and will have to dispose of some materiel. Equipment includes 190 MiG-29 and 60 Su-27 interceptors, several hundred MiG-23/27 and Su-17 fighter-bombers, 200 Su-24 strike aircraft, Tu-22M strategic bombers and 30 Il-76 tankers. Support equipment includes 200 Il-76 transports, and 250 armed Mi-24 and 400 transport helicopters. Personnel (including Air Defence), 1996, 124,000.

INTERNATIONAL RELATIONS

Ukraine is a member of the UN, CIS, the Council of Europe, the Central European Initiative and the NATO Partnership for Peace.

ECONOMY

Policy. After considerable delay, the process of economic reform began in Ukraine. Prices on food, transportation and other services were deregulated in Jan. 1993, although food prices remained low in comparison to prices in neighbouring countries. The government issued privatization certificates and set up the western city of Lviv as a model for future privatization. The country's leadership attempted to re-establish close economic ties with former Soviet republics, supporting economic co-operation between the member states of the CIS. In July 1993 Ukraine also agreed in principle to establish an economic and customs union with Russia and Belarus. Although privatization began in 1994, foreign participation has been very limited and the larger industrial sector enterprises are still for the most part state-owned. In Feb. 1998 a 10-year economic agreement was signed between Ukraine and Russia; but economic crisis in Russia inevitably had its impact on Ukraine. The hryvna lost half of its value in Sept. 1998 and though the IMF, EU and World Bank advanced more than US$700m., interest rates were pushed up to 82%.

Performance. Real GDP growth was −3·2% in 1997.

Budget. 1997 budget (in 1,000m. hryvna): Revenue, 28,112·0; expenditure, 34,312·7. Sources of revenue included: VAT, 8,242·3; profits tax, 5,792·1. Expenditure included: Welfare, 15,949·3; population social protection, 5,607·7; defence, 1,738·9; administration, 2,974·9.

Currency. The unit of currency is the *hryvna* of 100 *kopiykas*, which replaced karbovanets on 2 Sept. 1996 at 100,000 karbovanets = 1 hryvna. Inflation was 16% in 1997, down from 80% in 1996. Foreign exchange reserves in Feb. 1998 were US$2,023m. and gold reserves 60,000 troy oz.

Banking and Finance. A National Bank was founded in March 1991. It operates under government control, its Governor being appointed by the President with the approval of parliament. Its *governor* is Viktor Yushchenko. There were 219 banks in all in 1996.

There is a stock exchange in Kyiv.

ENERGY AND NATURAL RESOURCES

Electricity. Installed capacity was 53·9m. kW in 1997. In 1997 production was 178bn. kWh and consumption per capita 3,487 kWh. In 1997 there were 5 nuclear power stations producing 44·6% of output. A Soviet programme to greatly expand nuclear power-generating capacity in the country was abandoned in the wake of the 1986 accident at Chernobyl.

Oil and Gas. In 1997 output of crude oil and gas concentrate was 4·1m. tonnes, and of natural gas 18,100m. cu. metres.

Water. In 1997 water consumption totalled 15,623m. cu. metres.

Minerals. Ukraine's industrial economy, accounting for more than a quarter of total employment, is based largely on the republic's vast mineral resources. The Donetsk Basin contains huge reserves of coal, and the nearby iron-ore reserves of Kryvy Rih are equally rich. Among Ukraine's other mineral resources are manganese, bauxite, nickel, titanium and salt. Coal accounts for roughly 30% of the country's energy production. Coal and lignite production, 1994, 94·4m. tonnes; iron ore production, 1996, 48·0m. tonnes.

Agriculture. Agriculture accounted for 13% of GDP in 1996. Ukraine has extremely fertile black-earth soils in the central and southern portions, totalling nearly two-thirds of the territory. The original vegetation of the area formed three broad belts that crossed the territory of Ukraine latitudinally. Mixed forest vegetation occupied the northern third of the country, forest-steppe the middle portion and steppe the southern third of the country. Now, however, much of the original vegetation has been cleared and replaced by cultivated crops. Ukraine is a major producer and exporter of a wide variety of agricultural products, including wheat and sugar-beets. Other crops include potatoes, vegetables, fruit, sunflowers, flax, buckwheat, cotton, tobacco, soya, hops and the rubber plant kok-sagyz. Livestock raising is also important. Agricultural production has suffered greatly since independence, however, and domestic food consumption has decreased. In 1997 there were 41·8m. ha of land under cultivation.

State farm members may leave and receive a portion of land free; the land may be resold.

Output (in 1,000 tonnes) in 1997: Grain, 35,472; sugar-beet, 17,633; potatoes, 16,701; vegetables, 5,168; fruit and berries, 2,793; meat, 1,875; milk, 13,800. 8,242m. eggs were produced. At 1 Jan. 1998 there were 12·3m. cattle, 9·5m. pigs, 2·4m. sheep and goats, 136m. chickens (1995) and 20m. ducks (1995).

Forestry. The area of forestry fund of Ukraine in 1995 was 10·78m. ha. In 1991, 7·8m. cu. metres of timber were produced. In 1997 there were 24 national parks and reservations with a total area of 761,800 ha.

Fisheries. In 1995 the catch totalled 424,812 tonnes, of which 372,474 tonnes were from sea fishing. The total catch in 1988 was 1,144,339 tonnes.

INDUSTRY
In 1997 there were 9,989 industrial enterprises. Output, 1997 (in tonnes unless otherwise stated): Rolled ferrous metals, 21m.; mineral fertilizer, 3·9m.; synthetic fibre, 10,600; paper, 8·7m.; cement, 5,101; sugar, 2·0m.; milk products, 661,000; processed meats, 558,000; butter, 117,000. Fabrics, 82m. sq. metres; footwear, 10·4m. pairs; TV sets, 5·0m.; refrigerators, 380,000; lathes, 2,300 units; motor cars, 2,000 units; tractors, 4,600 units.

Labour. At 1 Jan. 1997 the labour force totalled 28·4m. In 1997, 22·6m. were employed in business activity (37·9% in the state sector, 22·9% in the private sector and 39·2% in the collective sector). In Oct. 1996, according to the International Labour Organization, unemployment stood at 7·6%.

Trade Unions. There are 13 trade unions grouped in a Trades Union Federation (*Chair*, Oleksandr Stoyan).

INTERNATIONAL TRADE
At 1 Jan. 1998 total foreign debt was US$9,526m.

Imports and Exports. Total foreign trade by year (in US$1m.):

	1996	1997
Imports	17,603·4	17,128·0
Exports	14,440·8	14,231·9

During 1997 Ukraine traded with 189 different countries. 40·8% of exports went to CIS countries and 59·2% to the rest of the world. 60% of all imports came from CIS countries. In 1996 Russia accounted for 47% of all imports, followed by Turkmenistan with 8·8%. 38% of exports in 1996 went to Russia, with China the second biggest export destination, at 5·3%.

Main exports, 1997 (% share of trade): Ferrous metals and ferrous alloy products, 31·6%; chemical and associated products, 10·6%; machinery and equipment, 9·6%. Main imports: mineral fuel, oil and its processed products, 45·6%; machinery and equipment, 15·2%.

COMMUNICATIONS

Roads. In 1997 there were 164,097 km of hard-surfaced motor roads. There were 4·9m. passenger cars in 1997 and 3m. motor cycles and mopeds (1996).

Rail. Total length was 22,701·5 km in 1997, of which 8,711 km were electrified. In 1997 railways carried 501m. passengers and 293m. tonnes of freight. There are metros in Kyiv, Kharkiv and Dnipropetrovsk.

Civil Aviation. The main international airport is Kyiv (Boryspil), and there are international flights from 7 other airports. There are 2 Ukrainian carriers. Air Ukraine operates domestic services and had international flights in 1998 to Beijing, Bratislava, Bucharest, Budapest, Cairo, Damascus, Delhi, Dubai, Istanbul, Moscow, Murmansk, New York, Novosibirsk, Prague, Sharjah, Sofia, Tbilisi, Toronto, Toshkent, Tunis, Tyumen and Warsaw. Ukraine International Airlines also operated on some domestic routes, with international flights in 1998 to Amsterdam, Barcelona, Berlin, Brussels, Frankfurt, London, Omsk, Paris, Rome, Rostov, Vienna and Zürich. Services were also provided in 1998 by Aeroflot, Aerosweet Airlines, Air Baltic, Air Canada, Air Enterprise Pulkovo, Air France, Air Khors, Air Moldova International, Austrian Airlines, Aviacompany Turkmenistan, Azerbaijan Airlines, Balkan, British Airways, Czech Airlines, Delta Air Lines, Dneproavia Joint Stock Aviation Co, Egyptair, El Al, Estonian Air, Iberia, Icar, JAT, Khabarovsk Aviation, KLM, Lithuanian Airlines, LOT, Lufthansa, Malév, Olympic Airways, Royal Air Maroc, SK Air, Swissair, Tarom, Tavrey Aircompany, Transaero Airlines, Turkish Airlines, United Airlines and Uzbekiston Airways. In 1996 Kyiv handled 1,273,764 passengers (880,213 on international flights) and 16,003 tonnes of freight.

Simferopol was the second busiest airport for passenger traffic in 1996, with 501,862 (427,786 on international flights), and Odesa the second busiest for freight, with 6,197 tonnes.

Shipping. In 1997, 2m. passengers and 9m. tonnes of freight were carried by inland waterways. In 1995 there were 649 ocean-going vessels, totalling 5·83m. DWT. 38 vessels (5·09% of total tonnage) were registered under foreign flags. GRT totalled 5·29m., including oil tankers, 84,276 GRT, and container ships, 139,187 GRT. The main seaports are Mariupol, Odesa, Kherson and Mykolaïv. Odesa is the leading port, and takes 30m. tonnes of cargo annually. In 1995 vessels totalling 4,270,000 NRT entered ports and vessels totalling 21,916,000 NRT cleared.

Telecommunications. In 1997 main telephone lines numbered 9,410,000 (185·6 per 1,000 persons). There were 290,000 PCs in 1995, 14,000 cellular phone subscribers and 1,500 fax machines.

Postal Services. In 1995 there were 16,421 post offices. In 1997, 359m. letters, 17m. telegrams and 2m. packages were handled.

SOCIAL INSTITUTIONS

Justice. The death penalty is authorized. Over the period 1991–95, 642 death sentences were awarded and 442 carried out; there were 169 executions in 1996. In March 1997, death penalties were still being awarded but not carried out. 589,200 crimes were reported in 1997. A new civil code was voted into law in June 1997.

Religion. The majority faith is the Orthodox Church, which in 1996 was split into 3 factions: The Ukrainian Orthodox Church, which owes obedience to the Russian Orthodox Church in Moscow, and is headed by Volodymyr, Patriarch of Kyiv and All Rus-Ukraine; the Autocephalous Ukrainian Orthodox Church, which served émigrés and dissidents during the Soviet era, headed by Patriarch Mstyslav; and the Kyiv Patriarchate Ukrainian Orthodox Church, headed by Metropolitan Filaret, which was unified with the Autocephalous Church in the period 1991–92. Filaret was excommunicated by the Ukrainian Orthodox Church in Feb. 1997. Catholicism is strong in the western half of the country.

The hierarchy of the Uniate Church (*head*, Cardinal Myroslav Lubachivsky, b. 1914) was restored by the Pope's confirmation of 10 bishops in Jan. 1991.

Education. In 1997 the number of pupils in 22,100 primary and secondary schools was 7m.; 280 further education establishments had 1,110,000 students, and 660 technical colleges, 526,400 students; 1,172,000 children were attending pre-school institutions.

In 1995–96 there were 7 universities and an international university of science and technology.

Adult literacy rate, 1995, 98·8% (male, 98·2%; female, 99·3%).

In 1994 total expenditure on education came to 8·2% of GNP.

Health. Doctors and dentists numbered 227,000 in 1997 and junior medical personnel, 566,000. There were 503,000 beds in 3,400 hospitals.

Welfare. There were 10·6m. old-age pensioners in 1997 and 3·7m. other pensioners.

CULTURE

Broadcasting. Broadcasting is administered by the government State Teleradio Company of Ukraine. The state-controlled Ukrainian Radio broadcasts 3 national and various regional programmes, a shared relay with Radio Moscow, and a foreign service (Ukrainian, English, German and Romanian). There were 4 independent stations in 1993 and 44·3m. radio receivers in 1995. The state-controlled Ukrainian Television broadcasts on 2 channels (colour by SECAM). In 1995 there were 17·5m. television receivers.

Cinema. In 1997 there were 10,800 cinemas.

Press. As at June 1996, 5,325 periodicals were registered, including 3,953 newspapers and 1,025 journals. In 1997, 1,270m. newspapers and magazines were sold.

Tourism. There were 337,000 foreign tourists and 1,375 hotels in 1997. 631,000 Ukrainian citizens travelled to foreign countries.

Libraries. In 1997 there were 21,504 libraries with 355·7m. copies of books and magazines.

DIPLOMATIC REPRESENTATIVES

Of Ukraine in Great Britain (60 Holland Park, London, W11 3SJ)
Ambassador: Vlodymyr Vassylenko.

Of Great Britain in Ukraine (252025 Kyiv, 9 Desyatinna)
Ambassador: Roy S. Reeve, CMG.

Of Ukraine in the USA (L Street, NW, Washington, D.C., 20036)
Ambassador: Anton Buteyko.

Of the USA in Ukraine (10 Yuria Kotsyubinskoho, 254053 Kyiv 53)
Ambassador: Steven K. Pifer.

Of Ukraine to the United Nations
Ambassador: Volodymyr Yu Yel'chenko.

Of Ukraine to the European Union
Ambassador: Igor Mitiukov.

FURTHER READING

Encyclopedia of Ukraine, 5 vols. Toronto, 1984–93
Koropeckyj, I. S., *The Ukrainian Economy: Achievements, Problems, Challenges.* Harvard Univ. Press, 1993
Kuzio, T., *Ukraine under Kuchma: Political Reform, Economic Transformation and Security Policy in Independent Ukraine.* London, 1997
Kuzio, T. and Wilson, A., *Ukraine: Perestroika to Independence.* London, 1994
Magocsi, P. R., *A History of Ukraine.* Toronto Univ. Press, 1997
Marples, D., *Ukraine under Perestroika: Ecology, Economics and the Workers' Revolt.* London, 1991
Motyl, A. J., *Dilemmas of Independence: Ukraine after Totalitarianism.* New York, 1993
Nahaylo, B., *Ukrainian Resurgence.* Farnborough, 1993
Reid, A., *Borderland: A Journey through the History of Ukraine.* Weidenfeld, London, 1997.
Solchanyk, R., (ed.) *Ukraine: from Chernobyl to Sovereignty.* London, 1991
Subtelny, O., *Ukraine: a History.* Toronto, 1989

CRIMEA

The Crimea is a peninsula extending southwards into the Black Sea with an area of 25,881 sq. km. Population (1991 estimate), 2,549,800 (Ethnic groups, Sept. 1993: Russians, 61·6%; Ukrainians, 23·6%; Tatars, 9·6%). The capital is Simferopol.

It was occupied by Tatars in 1239, conquered by Ottoman Turks in 1475 and retaken by Russia in 1783. In 1921 after the Communist revolution it became an autonomous republic, but was transformed into a province (*oblast*) of the Russian Federation in 1945, after the deportation of the Tatar population in 1944 for alleged collaboration with the German invaders in the Second World War. It was transferred to Ukraine in 1954 and became an autonomous republic in 1991. About half the surviving Tatar population of 0·4m. had returned from exile by mid-1992.

At elections held in 2 rounds on 16 and 30 Jan. 1994 Yuri Meshkov was elected *President* for a 4-year term by 38·5% and 72% of votes cast against 5 opponents. The electorate was 1·8m. There is a 94-member local parliament. Parliamentary elections were held on 27 March 1994. The Russia Bloc gained 54 seats, Kurultai (Tatars) 14, ind 21.

On 2 Nov. 1995 parliament adopted a new constitution which defines the Crimea as 'an autonomous republic forming an integral part of Ukraine'. The status of 'autonomous republic' was confirmed by the 1996 Ukrainian Constitution, which provides for Crimea to have its own constitution as approved by its parliament. The Prime Minister is appointed by the Crimean parliament with the approval of the Ukrainian parliament.

The *Prime Minister* is Anatoliy Franchuk.

UNITED ARAB EMIRATES

(UAE)

Imarat al-Arabiya al-Muttahida

Capital: Abu Dhabi
Population estimate, 2000: 2·44m.
GNP per capita: (PPP$) 17,000
HDI/world rank: 0·855/48

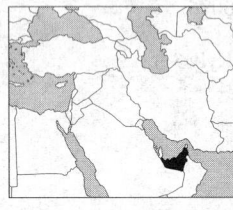

KEY HISTORICAL EVENTS

From Sha'am, 35 miles south-west of Ras Musam dam, for nearly 400 miles to Khor al Odeid at the south-eastern end of the peninsula of Qatar, the coast, formerly known as the Trucial Coast, of the Gulf (together with 50 miles of the coast of the Gulf of Oman) belongs to the rulers of the 7 Trucial States. In 1820 these rulers signed a treaty prescribing peace with the British Government. This treaty was followed by further agreements providing for the suppression of the slave trade, and by a series of other engagements, of which the most important were the Perpetual Maritime Truce (May 1853) and the Exclusive Agreement (March 1892). Under the latter, the sheikhs, on behalf of themselves, their heirs and successors, undertook that they would on no account enter into any agreement or correspondence with any power other than the British Government, receive foreign agents, or cede, sell or give for occupation any part of their territory save to the British Government.

British forces withdrew from the Gulf at the end of 1971 and the treaties whereby the UK had been responsible for the defence and foreign relations of the Trucial States were terminated, being replaced on 2 Dec. 1971 by a treaty of friendship between the UK and the United Arab Emirates. The United Arab Emirates (formed 2 Dec. 1971) consists of the former Trucial States: Abu Dhabi, Dubai, Sharjah, Ajman, Umm al Qaiwain, Ras al-Khaimah (joined in Feb. 1972) and Fujairah. The small state of Kalba was merged with Sharjah in 1952.

TERRITORY AND POPULATION

The Emirates are bounded in the north by the Persian (Arabian) Gulf, north-east by Oman, east by the Gulf of Oman and Oman, south and west by Saudi Arabia, and north-west by Qatar. Their area is approximately 32,300 sq. miles (83,657 sq. km), excluding over 100 offshore islands. The total population at census (1995, preliminary) was 2,377,453 (797,710 females). About one-tenth are nomads. Population density, 28 per sq. km.

The UN gives a projected population for 2000 of 2·44m.

In 1995, 83·8% of the population lived in urban areas.

Populations of the 7 Emirates, 1995 census: Abu Dhabi, 928,360; Ajman, 118,812; Dubai, 674,101; Fujairah, 76,254; Ras al-Khaimah, 144,430; Sharjah, 400,339; Umm al Qaiwain, 35,157.

The chief cities are Abu Dhabi, the federal capital, Dubai, Sharjah and Ras al-Khaimah.

The official language is Arabic; English is widely spoken.

SOCIAL STATISTICS

1997 births, 42,000; deaths, 7,000. 1997 birth rate (per 1,000 population), 18·4; death rate, 3·0; infant mortality rate (per 1,000 live births), 15·5; life expectancy, 74·6 years. 90% of the population are migrants, the highest percentage in any country in the world. Annual growth rate, 1997, 1·8%. Fertility rate, 1990–95, 3·8 births per woman.

CLIMATE

The country experiences desert conditions, with rainfall both limited and erratic. The period May to Sept. is generally rainless. Dubai, Jan. 74°F (23·4°C), July 108°F (42·3°C). Annual rainfall 2·4" (60 mm). Sharjah, Jan. 64°F (17·8°C), July 91°F (32°C). Annual rainfall 4·2" (105 mm).

CONSTITUTION AND GOVERNMENT

The Emirates is a federation, headed by a *Supreme Council of Rulers* which is composed of the 7 rulers which elects from among its members a *President* and *Vice-President* for 5-year terms, and appoints a *Council of Ministers.* The Council of Ministers drafts legislation and a federal budget; its proposals are submitted to a *Federal National Council* of 40 elected members which may propose amendments but has no executive power. There is a *National Consultative Council* made up of citizens.

National Anthem. There are no words, tune by M. A. Wahab.

CURRENT ADMINISTRATION

President: HH Sheikh Zayed bin Sultan al-Nahyan, Ruler of Abu Dhabi.
   Members of the Supreme Council of Rulers:
   President: HH Sheikh Zayed bin Sultan al-Nahyan (re-elected Oct. 1996).
   Vice-President and Prime Minister: HH Sheikh Maktoum bin Rashid al-Maktoum, Ruler of Dubai.
   HH Dr Sheikh Sultan bin Mohammed al-Qassimi, Ruler of Sharjah.
   HH Sheikh Saqr bin Mohammed al-Qassimi, Ruler of Ras al-Khaimah.
   HH Sheikh Hamad bin Mohammed al-Sharqi, Ruler of Fujairah.
   HH Sheikh Humaid bin Rashid al-Nuaimi, Ruler of Ajman.
   HH Sheikh Rashid bin Ahmed al-Mualla, Ruler of Umm al Qaiwain.

   The Council of Ministers (appointed March 1997) was in March 1999:
   Prime Minister: HH Sheikh Maktoum bin Rashid al-Maktoum.
   Deputy Prime Minister: HH Sheikh Sultan bin Zayed al-Nahyan.
   Minister of the Interior: Lieut.-Gen. Dr Mohammed Saeed al-Badi. *Finance and Industry:* HH Sheikh Hamdan bin Rashid al-Maktoum. *Defence:* Gen. Sheikh Mohammed bin Rashid al-Maktoum. *Economy and Commerce:* Sheikh Fahim bin Sultan al-Qassimi. *Information and Culture:* Sheikh Abdullah bin Zayed al-Nahyan. *Communications:* Ahmed Humaid al-Tayer. *Public Works and Housing:* Rakad bin Salem al-Rakad. *Education and Youth:* Dr Abdul Aziz al-Sharhan. *Petroleum and Mineral Resources:* Obeid bin Saif al-Nassiri. *Electricity and Water:* Humaid bin Nasser al-Owais. *Labour and Social Affairs:* Mattar Humaid al-Tayer. *Planning:* HH Sheikh Humaid bin Ahmed al-Mualla. *Agriculture and Fisheries:* Saeed Mohammed al-Ragabani. *Justice, Islamic Affairs and Endowments:* Mohammed Mukhaira al-Dhahiri. *Foreign Affairs:* Rashid Abdullah al-Nuaimi. *Higher Education and Scientific Research:* Sheikh Nahyan bin Mubarak al-Nahyan. *Health:* Hamad Abdul Rahman al-Madfa.

Local Government. Each Emirate has its own local institutions, whose nature depends on size and population. Abu Dhabi has an Executive Council chaired by the Crown Prince.

DEFENCE

In 1997 defence expenditure totalled US$2,424m. (US$978 per capita), representing 5·5% of GDP.

Army. The Army consists of 1 Royal Guard, 1 armoured, 1 mechanized infantry, 2 infantry and 1 artillery brigade. There are also 2 unintegrated infantry brigades in Dubai. Equipment includes 95 AMX-30 and 36 Lion OF-40 Mk 2 main battle tanks. The strength was (1997) 59,000.

Navy. The combined naval flotilla of the Emirates includes 1 leased ex-US guided missile frigate, 2 German-built missile corvettes, 8 German-built fast missile craft, 9 British-built inshore patrol craft, 3 tank landing craft, 2 transports, 1 maintenance ship and 3 service craft. Personnel in 1997 numbered 1,500. The main base is at Taweela (Sharjah), with minor bases in the other Emirates.
   The Coast Guard flotilla comprises 40 inshore patrol craft and some 30 boats.

Air Force. Current equipment of the Abu Dhabi component of the service includes 21 Mirage 2000 and 23 Mirage 5 supersonic fighter-bombers, 8 Mirage 2000R and 3 Mirage 5R tactical reconnaissance aircraft, 5 Mirage 2000D and 3 Mirage 5D 2-seat trainers; 4 Hercules turboprop transports; 4 CASA C-212 Aviocar electronic countermeasures and intelligence aircraft; 30 Apache armed helicopters; about 50

Gazelle, Alouette III, Puma, Super Puma and Ecureuil transport and liaison helicopters; 23 PC-7 Turbo-Trainers and 40 Hawk light attack/trainers. Current equipment of the Dubai component comprises 3 Aermacchi MB 326K jet light attack aircraft, 5 SF.260TP turboprop trainers, and 2 MB 326L, 4 MB 339 and 8 Hawk jet trainers, 6 Bell 205A-1, 3 Bell 212, 8 Bell 214 and 6 JetRanger helicopters, as well as 2 L-100-30 Hercules transports and a variety of other types for VIP and transport use. Personnel (1997) 4,000, with 102 combat aircraft and 42 armed helicopters.

INTERNATIONAL RELATIONS
The UAE is a member of the UN, OPEC, the Gulf Co-operation Council and the Arab League.

ECONOMY
Performance. GDP was DH 164,000m. in 1996 (non-oil sector DH 114,000m.). Growth in 1996, 2·9%.

Budget. Revenue is principally derived from oil-concession payments. Revenues in 1997 were an estimated US$5·1bn. and expenditure US$5·4bn. Expenditure in 1994 (in DH 1m.) included: Defence, 5,827; education, 2,692; public order and safety, 2,021; health, 1,153; social security and welfare, 527.

Currency. The unit of currency is the *dirham* (AED) of 100 *fils*. Gold reserves in Nov. 1997 were 790,000 troy oz. and foreign exchange reserves US$8,244m. Inflation was 3% in Sept. 1994. Total money supply in Nov. 1997 was DH 24,702m.

Banking and Finance. The UAE Central Bank was established in 1980 (*Governor*, Sultan al-Suweidi). In 1994 there were 47 local and foreign banks with 349 branches, and deposits of DH 13,200m. Foreign banks are restricted to 8 branches each.

ENERGY AND NATURAL RESOURCES
Electricity. Installed capacity was 5·29m. kW in 1994. Production in 1994 was 23,402m. kWh. Consumption per capita was estimated to be 5,724 kWh in 1995.

Oil and Gas. Oil and gas provided about 33·4% of GDP in 1994. Production, 1995, 103m. tonnes. The UAE produced 3·5% of the world total oil output in 1996, and had reserves amounting to 97·8bn. bbls. in 1996.

Abu Dhabi. Proven reserves (1988) 31,000m. bbls. Estimated oil production is 85% of the UAE's total.

Dubai. In 1975 Dubai took control of foreign oil and gas operations, and a Dubai producing group was set up to comprise the foreign interests. Estimated oil production, 1995, 0·3m. bbls. a day.

Sharjah. Oil production, 1992, 1·92m. tonnes.

Ras al-Khaimah. Oil production (1990) 0·4m. tonnes.
   Abu Dhabi has reserves of natural gas, nationalized in 1976. There is a gas liquefaction plant on Das Island. Gas proven reserves (1994) were 6,130,000m. cu. metres. Gas production, 1995, 1,113 petajoules.

Water. Production of drinking water by desalination of sea water (1994) was 117,000m. gallons.

Agriculture. The fertile Buraimi Oasis, known as Al Ain, is largely in Abu Dhabi territory. By 1994, 21,194 farms had been set up on land reclaimed from sand dunes. Owing to lack of water and good soil, there are few natural opportunities for agriculture, but there is a programme of fostering agriculture by desalination of water, dam-building and tree-planting; and strawberries, flowers and dates are now cultivated for export. The total area under cultivation in 1994 was 72,370 ha. In 1994 there were 29,000 ha of arable land, 10,000 ha of cropland and 200,000 ha of pasture. Output, 1995 (in 1,000 tonnes): Dates, 240; tomatoes, 245; aubergines, 69; cucumbers and gherkins, 14; melons, 11; cereals, 7. Livestock products, 1995 (in 1,000 tonnes): Mutton and lamb, 31; poultry meat, 23; eggs, 12; goats' milk, 20.
   Livestock (1995): Cattle, 65,000; camels, 155,000; sheep, 350,000; goats, 862,000; chickens, 11m.

Forestry. The area under forests in 1995 was 60,000 ha, or 0·7% of the total land area.

Fisheries. In 1994 there were 4,000 fishing boats and (1992) 11,074 fishermen. Catch, 1995, 105,554 tonnes (exclusively marine fish).

INDUSTRY

In 1993 there were 904 industrial firms. Products include aluminium, cable, cement, chemicals, fertilizers (Abu Dhabi), rolled steel and plastics (Dubai, Sharjah), and tools and clothing (Dubai).

Labour. Males constituted 86% of the labour force in 1996. The labour force totalled 1,289,654 in 1995.

INTERNATIONAL TRADE

There are free trade zones at Jebel Ali (administered by Dubai), Sharjah and Fujairah. Foreign companies may set up wholly owned subsidiaries. In 1994 there were 650 companies in the Jebel Ali zone.

Imports and Exports. Imports in 1996 totalled US$22,300m.; exports US$31,300m., of which crude oil 66%. Oil and gas exports accounted for DH 44,480m. in 1994.

Main import suppliers, 1995: Japan (9%), USA (8%), UK (8%), Germany (7%) and South Korea (5%). Main export markets: Japan (38%), India (6%), South Korea (6%), Singapore (5%), Iran (4%) and Oman (4%).

COMMUNICATIONS

Roads. In 1996 there were 6,550 km of paved roads, and in 1994, 447,000 vehicles.

Civil Aviation. There are international airports at Abu Dhabi, Al Ain, Dubai, Fujairah, Ras al-Khaimah and Sharjah. 7,946,000 passengers were handled in 1994. Gulf Air is owned equally by Abu Dhabi, Bahrain, Oman and Qatar. For details *see* BAHRAIN: Civil Aviation. Dubai set up its own airline, Emirates Air, in 1985. It now operates internationally, and in 1995 flew 52m. km, carrying 2,478,000 passengers. In 1998 services were also provided by Aero Asia, Aeroflot, Air Afrique, Air Algérie, Air Djibouti, Air France, Air India, Air Khors, Air Lanka, Air Malawi, Air Maldives, Air Malta, Air Seychelles, Air Tanzania Corporation, Air Ukraine, Airzena Georgia Airlines, Alitalia, American Airlines, Ariana Afghan Airlines, Armenian Airlines, Austrian Airlines, Aviacompany Turkmenistan, Azerbaijan Airlines, Balkan, Bhoja Air, Biman Bangladesh Airlines, British Airways, Cathay Pacific Airways, China Airlines, China Southern Airlines, Condor Flugdienst, Cyprus Airways, Czech Airlines, Daallo Airlines, Delta Air Lines, Donavia, Egyptair, Ethiopian Airlines, EVA Airways, Garuda Indonesia, Imair Airline, Indian Airlines, Iran Air, JAT, Kenya Airways, KLM, Kuwait Airways, Kyrgyzstan Airlines, Lithuanian Airlines, Lufthansa, Malaysia Airlines, Mandarin Airlines, Middle East Airlines, Olympic Airways, Oman Air, Pakistan International Airlines, Qantas Airways, Qatar Airways, Royal Air Maroc, Royal Brunei Airlines, Royal Jordanian, Royal Nepal Airlines, SAS, Saudia, Shaheen Air International, Shuttle Air Cargo, Siberia Airlines, Singapore Airlines, Sochi Airlines-Aviaprima, South African Airways, Sudan Airways, Swissair, Syrian Arab Airlines, Tarom, Tavrey Aircompany, Thai Airways International, Transavia Airlines, Tunis Air, Turkestan Airlines, Turkish Airlines, Uganda Airlines, United Airlines, Uzbekiston Airways, Vietnam Airlines, VIP Air and Yemenia Yemen Airways.

Shipping. There are 15 commercial seaports, of which 5 major ports are on the Persian (Arabian) Gulf (Zayed in Abu Dhabi, Rashid and Jebel Ali in Dubai, Khalid in Sharjah, and Saqr in Ras al-Khaimah) and 2 on the Gulf of Oman: Fujairah and Khor Fakkan. Rashid and Fujairah are important container terminals. 45m. tonnes of cargo were handled in 1994. In 1996, the merchant marine comprised 60 ships (1,000 GRT or over) totalling 1,128,495 GRT, including 22 oil tankers and 6 container ships.

Telecommunications. Main telephone lines numbered 835,100 in 1997 (350·9 per 1,000 persons). In 1995 there were 129,000 cellular phone subscribers, 115,000 PCs and 25,000 fax machines. There were approximately 89,000 Internet users in Jan. 1998.

Postal Services. In 1995 there were 180 post offices.

SOCIAL INSTITUTIONS

Justice. The basic principles of the law are Islamic. Legislation seeks to promote the harmonious functioning of society's multi-national components while protecting the interests of the indigenous population. Each Emirate has its own penal code. A federal code takes precedence and ensures compatibility. There are federal courts with appellate powers, which function under federal laws. Emirates have the option to merge their courts with the federal judiciary.

The death penalty for drug smuggling was introduced in April 1995.

Religion. Nearly all the inhabitants are Moslem of the Sunni, and a small minority of the Shi'ite, sects.

Education. In 1996 there were 19,290 pre-primary pupils with 1,128 teachers, 152,741 primary pupils with 10,123 teachers, and 121,736 secondary pupils with 9,832 teachers. In 1995 there were 11,576 students at the Emirates University and 2,324 students in 3 higher colleges of technology. The adult literacy rate in 1995 was 79·2% (78·9% among males and 79·8% among females).

Health. In 1996 there were 36 government hospitals with 4,344 beds. In 1994 there were 14 private hospitals, 128 government health centres, a herbal medicine centre, 752 private clinics, 4,095 doctors, 563 dentists and 8,506 nurses.

CULTURE

Broadcasting. There are several government authorities providing broadcasting nationally (Voice of the United Arab Emirates, Capital Radio, which is partly commercial, and United Arab Emirates Television Service), and regionally (UAE Radio and Television-Dubai, Ras al-Khaimah Broadcasting, Umm al Qaiwain Broadcasting, and Sharjah TV). In 1995 there were 600,000 radio and 230,000 TV sets (colour by PAL).

Press. In 1996 there were 9 daily newspapers (5 Arabic and 4 English) with a combined circulation of 0·3m.

Tourism. In 1996 there were 1,768,000 foreign tourists.

DIPLOMATIC REPRESENTATIVES
Of the UAE in Great Britain (30 Prince's Gate, London, SW7 1PT)
Ambassador: Easa Saleh Al Gurg, CBE.

Of Great Britain in the UAE (POB 248, Abu Dhabi)
Ambassador: P. Nixon, CMG, OBE.

Of the UAE in the USA (3000 K St., NW, Washington, D.C., 20007)
Ambassador: Mohammad Bin Hussein Al-Shaali.

Of the USA in the UAE (POB 4009, Abu Dhabi)
Ambassador: David C. Litt.

Of the UAE to the United Nations
Ambassador: Mohammed Jassim Samhan.

Of the UAE to the European Union
Ambassador: Salem Rached Salem Al-Agroobi.

FURTHER READING
Alkim, H. al.-, *The Foreign Policy of the UAE.* Saqi, 1989
Clements, F. A., *United Arab Emirates.* [Bibliography] Oxford and Santa Barbara (CA), (rev. ed.) 1998
Heard-Bey, F., *From Trucial States to United Arab Emirates.* London, 1982
Taryam, A. O., *The Establishment of the United Arab Emirates.* London, 1987

UNITED KINGDOM OF GREAT BRITAIN AND NORTHERN IRELAND

Capital: London
Population estimate, 2000: 59·45m.
GNP per capita: (PPP$) 19,960
HDI/world rank: 0·932/14

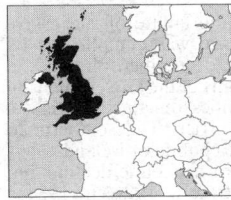

KEY HISTORICAL EVENTS

The United Kingdom may be said to date from 1707 when the parliament of England and Scotland were united but the name was not adopted until 1800 when the government of Ireland was incorporated. Ireland was governed by English law through a nominally independent parliament. The people, mainly Catholic, rebelled in 1798. The settlement proposed was legislative union and Catholic emancipation; the latter was delayed until 1828–29 (when Nonconformists also received full civic rights) but the union took effect in 1801, as the United Kingdom of Great Britain and Ireland.

With the accession of the Hanoverian George I (1714), the system of Parliamentary party government took hold. In 1721 Sir Robert Walpole began his long spell in office as Britain's first prime minister, adopting a peace policy that stressed the benefits of trade.

Walpole left office in 1742 and for the next 40 years none of his successors, with the exception of Lord North, enjoyed long periods of power. The greatest of them was William Pitt. In the Seven Years War with France which broke out in 1756, Pitt put new life into the military, and his policy contributed greatly to substantial imperial gains, notably Canada and much of India.

Relations between Parliament and Crown went through an unsettled period in the reign of George III. He and Lord North, as prime minister, took the blame for the loss of the American colonies. The War of Independence ended with Britain's recognition of American right to self-government in 1783. The humiliation was softened by economic development at home where the Industrial Revolution was in full swing.

In 1793 revolutionary France declared war, and was not finally defeated until 1815. The demands of war stimulated the new, steam-powered industries. After 1815 there was frequent unrest as an increasingly urban and industrial society found its interests poorly represented by a parliament composed chiefly of landowners.

The Reform Act of 1832 improved representation in Parliament, and further acts (1867, 1884, 1918 and 1928) led gradually to universal adult suffrage.

The accession of Victoria in 1837 was the beginning of an era of unprecedented material progress. There were many causes but the most potent were the creation of a modern banking system, new means of communication, railways and steamships, and the use of the same power, steam, to build a factory system to produce consumer goods on an enormous scale.

Early industrial development produced great national wealth but its distribution was extremely uneven and the condition of the poor improved slowly. Legislation to improve working conditions, education and public health did not keep pace with the growth of industrial cities. The 1840s saw much immigration from Ireland (where there was famine) and from areas of political unrest in continental Europe; a second wave of immigration from the continent occurred after 1880, including Jewish refugees.

Abroad, there was war with Russia in the Crimea (1854–56); most wars, however, were fought to conquer or pacify colonies. The 19th-century empire included India, Canada, Australasia, and vast territories in Africa and Eastern Asia. After 1870 the Suez Canal enabled Britain to control the empire more efficiently; she became a 40% shareholder in 1875 and the controlling power in Egypt in 1882.

The most serious imperial wars were the Boer Wars of 1881 and 1899–1902. British opinion was deeply divided, and the Liberal government elected in 1905 negotiated a Union of South Africa, by which South Africa enjoyed the same autonomy which had been agreed for Canada (1867), Australia (1901) and later New Zealand (1907). The 'dominion status' of these countries was clarified by the Statute of Westminster (1931).

Whereas early Victorian reforms were responses to obvious distress, governments after 1868 were more inclined towards preventive state action. The budget of 1910 was designed largely to finance a programme of welfare; its rejection in Parliament by the House of Lords led to the Parliament Act (1911) which ended the Lords' power to veto bills.

On 3 Aug. 1914 Germany invaded Belgium, and Britain was obliged by treaty to retaliate by declaring war.

At this time, a rebellion was staged in Ireland, born of the failure of successive attempts to agree a formula for Irish Home Rule. The issue was complicated by factional disagreement in southern Ireland and the wish of northern Ireland to remain in the United Kingdom. In 1920 after four years' conflict the Government of Ireland Act partitioned the country. The northern six counties remained British, a parliament was created and a Unionist government took office. The southern 26 counties moved by stages to complete independence as the Republic of Ireland.

After the First World War there followed a long period of economic decline and industrial difficulty. There was an unsuccessful General Strike in 1926. In 1931 a coalition National Government was formed to deal none too successfully with the impact of world depression.

Germany revived as a military power in the 1930s, and invaded Poland on 1 Sept. 1939. Britain, bound once more by treaty, declared war.

The Second World War ended with German and Japanese defeat in 1945. It was a time of great social upheaval. In the 1945 election a Labour government was returned with a large majority, and a socialist programme which emphasized wealth distribution above wealth creation. Subsequent governments modified but generally accepted the changes then introduced. After 1979, however, Conservative governments reversed much of this legislation before Labour regained power in 1997 on a free-market manifesto which promised better economic management and job creation.

Beginning with the independence and partition of India and Pakistan in 1947, there was rapid progress to independence for all the colonies. The new concept was of a Commonwealth of freely associated states, recognizing the British monarch as symbolic Commonwealth head (some states chose to retain the monarch as head of state).

The Second World War all but bankrupted Britain, but it was at least a decade before her politicians began to realize that they could no longer play the world stage on a par with leaders from the USA and USSR. The option of joining other European countries in moves towards unity was resisted in favour of a 'special relationship' with the USA. It was not until 1961 that economic reality persuaded Britain of the need to join the European Economic Community. The application was rebuffed by France where President Charles de Gaulle was suspicious of 'Anglo-Saxon' motives. A second application was successful in 1973. Membership of the Community was endorsed by referendum in 1975.

GREAT BRITAIN

TERRITORY AND POPULATION
Area (in sq. km) and population (present on census night) at the census taken on 21 April 1991:

Divisions	Area	Population
England	130,423	46,382,050
Wales	20,766	2,811,865
Scotland	78,133	4,998,567
	229,322	54,192,482

GREAT BRITAIN

Population (present on census night) at the 4 previous decennial censuses:

Divisions	1951	1961	1971	1981
England[1]	41,159,213	43,460,525	46,018,371	46,226,100[2]
Wales	2,598,675	2,644,023	2,731,204	2,790,500[2]
Scotland	5,096,415	5,179,344	5,228,963	5,130,735
Great Britain	48,854,303	51,283,892	53,978,538	54,147,300[2]

[1]Areas now recognised as part of Gwent, Wales, formed the English county of Monmouthshire until 1974. [2]The final counts for England and Wales are believed to be overstated as a result of an error in processing. The preliminary counts presented here rounded to the nearest hundred are thought to be more accurate.

UK population estimate, 1998, 59,128,000 (30,064,000 females); density, 244 per sq. km. In 1995, 89·2% of the population lived in urban areas.

Population (usually resident) at the census of 1991:

Divisions	Males	Females	Total
England	22,812,889	24,242,315	47,055,204
Wales	1,370,104	1,464,969	2,835,073
Scotland	2,391,961	2,606,606	4,998,567
Great Britain	26,574,954	28,313,890	54,888,844

In 1991 in Wales 508,098 persons were able to speak Welsh. In Scotland in 1991, 65,978 of the usually resident population could speak Gaelic (79,297 in 1981).

Private households at the 1991 census: England, 19,984,500; Wales, 1,201,700; Scotland, 2,036,136.

The age distribution in 1991 of the 'usually resident' population of England and Wales, and Scotland, was as follows (in 1,000):

Age-group		England and Wales	Scotland	Great Britain
Under	5	3,316	317	3,633
5 and under	10	3,123	318	3,440
10 ,,	15	2,988	312	3,299
15 ,,	20	3,205	332	3,547
20 ,,	25	3,731	375	4,106
25 ,,	35	7,594	768	8,361
35 ,,	45	6,970	695	7,665
45 ,,	55	5,793	578	6,372
55 ,,	65	5,126	537	5,663
65 ,,	70	2,491	247	2,737
70 ,,	75	2,014	193	2,208
75 ,,	85	2,776	259	3,035
85 and upwards		763	68	831

England and Wales: The census population (present on census night) of England and Wales 1801 to 1991:

Date of enumeration	Population	Pop. per sq. mile	Date of enumeration	Population	Pop. per sq. mile[1]
1801	8,892,536	152	1901	32,527,843	558
1811	10,164,256	174	1911	36,070,492	618
1821	12,000,236	206	1921	37,886,699	649
1831	13,896,797	238	1931	39,952,377	685
1841	15,914,148	273	1951	43,757,888	750
1851	17,927,609	307	1961	46,104,548	791
1861	20,066,224	344	1971	48,749,575	323
1871	22,712,266	389	1981	49,016,600	325
1881	25,974,439	445	1991	49,193,915	330
1891	29,002,525	497			

[1]Per sq. km from 1971.

Estimated population of England and Wales, mid-1998, 52,495,000 (26,635,000 females and 25,860,000 males; 2,937,000 in Wales).

The birthplaces of the 1991 'usually resident' UK population were: England, 42,897,179; Wales, 2,747,790; Scotland, 5,221,038; Northern Ireland, 244,914; Ireland, 592,020; Commonwealth, 1,865,751; foreign countries, 1,287,821.

Ethnic Groups. The 1991 census was the first to include a question on ethnic status. Ethnic groups as enumerated:

	Total	Females	Total born in UK
White	51,873,794	26,807,415	49,703,681
Indian	840,225	417,364	352,448
Black Caribbean	499,964	260,480	268,318
Pakistani	476,555	230,983	240,552
Black African	212,362	105,562	77,315
Black Other	178,401	90,888	150,638
Bangladeshi	162,835	77,891	56,678
Chinese	156,938	79,269	44,635
Other Asian	197,534	103,929	43,265
Other	290,206	140,109	173,518

11 'Standard Regions' (also classified as 'level 1 regions' for EU purposes) are identified in the UK as economic planning regions. They have no administrative significance. They are: Northern Ireland, Scotland, Wales, and 8 regions of England. Estimated population of the regions (in 1,000), 1995, East Anglia, 2,123; East Midlands, 4,124; West Midlands, 5,306; North, 3,095; North West, 6,410; South East, 17,989 (including Greater London, 7,007); South West, 4,827; Yorkshire and Humberside, 5,029.

England is divided (apart from Greater London) into 35 counties and 50 unitary authorities with a single administrative tier, of which 36 are metropolitan boroughs and 27 unitary authorities established since 1995. The 35 counties are subdivided into 274 districts and the Isles of Scilly. Wales is divided into 22 unitary authorities (counties and county boroughs). Greater London comprises 32 boroughs and the City of London.

Area in sq. km of counties and usually resident population at the 1991 census:

	Area sq. km	Population		Area sq. km	Population
Metropolitan counties					
ENGLAND					
Greater Manchester	1,286	2,499,441	Isle of Wight (IOW)	380	124,577
Merseyside	655	1,403,642	Kent	3,735	1,508,873
South Yorkshire	1,559	1,262,630	Lancashire (Lancs)	3,070	1,383,998
Tyne and Wear	537	1,095,152	Leicestershire (Leics)	2,551	867,521
West Midlands	899	2,551,671	Lincolnshire (Lincs)	5,921	584,536
West Yorkshire	2,034	2,013,693	Norfolk	5,372	745,613
			Northamptonshire		
Non-metropolitan counties			(Northants)	2,367	578,807
ENGLAND			Northumberland	5,026	304,694
Avon	1,332	932,674	North Yorkshire		
Bedfordshire (Beds)	1,236	524,105	(N. Yorks)	8,309	702,161
Berkshire (Berks)	1,256	734,246	Nottinghamshire		
Buckinghamshire			(Notts)	2,160	993,872
(Bucks)	1,877	632,487	Oxfordshire (Oxon)	2,583	547,584
Cambridgeshire			Shropshire (Salop)	3,488	406,387
(Camb)	3,400	645,125	Somerset (Som)	3,452	460,368
Cheshire	2,331	956,616	Staffordshire (Staffs)	2,715	1,031,135
Cleveland	597	550,293	Suffolk	3,798	632,266
Cornwall and Isles			Surrey	1,677	1,018,003
of Scilly	3,530	468,425	Warwickshire	1,979	484,247
Cumbria	6,817	483,163	West Sussex	1,988	702,290
Derbyshire	2,629	928,636	Wiltshire (Wilts)	3,476	564,471
Devon	6,703	1,009,950			
Dorset	2,653	645,166	WALES		
Durham	2,429	593,430	Clwyd	2,430	408,090
East Sussex	1,794	690,447	Dyfed	5,766	343,543
Essex	3,675	1,528,577	Gwent	1,377	442,212
Gloucestershire			Gwynedd	3,863	235,452
(Gloucs)	2,653	528,370	Mid Glamorgan		
Hampshire (Hants)	3,779	1,541,547	(M. Glam)	1,017	534,101
Hereford and			Powys	5,072	117,647
Worcester	3,923	676,747	South Glamorgan		
Hertfordshire (Herts)	1,639	975,829	(S. Glam)	416	392,780
Humberside (Humb)	3,508	858,040	West Glamorgan		
			(W. Glam)	820	361,428

GREAT BRITAIN

Changes in the above administrative structure following the Local Government Act 1992 comprised the following as at 1 April 1997:

The Welsh counties, and the English counties of Avon, Cleveland, Humberside and the Isle of Wight had been abolished, and new unitary authorities had been established: in England (Bath and North East Somerset, Bournemouth, Brighton and Hove, Bristol, Darlington, Derby, East Riding of Yorkshire, Hartlepool, Isle of Wight, Kingston-upon-Hull, Leicester, Luton, Middlesbrough, Milton Keynes, North East Lincolnshire, North Lincolnshire, North Somerset, Poole, Portsmouth, Redcar and Cleveland, Rutland, South Gloucestershire, Southampton, Stockton-on-Tees, Stoke-on-Trent, Thamesdown and York); in Wales: (*Counties:* Carmarthenshire, Ceredigion, Denbighshire, Flintshire, Gwynedd, Isle of Anglesey, Monmouthshire, Pembrokeshire, Powys; *County Boroughs:* Blaenau Gwent, Bridgend, Caerphilly, Cardiff, Conwy, Merthyr Tydfil, Neath Port Talbot, Newport, Rhondda Cynon Taff, Swansea, Torfaen, Vale of Glamorgan, Wrexham).

In 1996 London had an estimated population of 7,074,000. Populations of next largest cities in 1996 was: Birmingham, 1,021,000; Leeds, 727,000; Glasgow, 616,000; Sheffield, 530,000; Bradford (1995), 483,000; Liverpool, 468,000; Edinburgh, 449,000; Manchester, 431,000; Bristol (1995), 401,000.

The following table shows the distribution of the urban and rural population of England and Wales (persons present) in 1951, 1961, 1971, and 1981:

		Population		Percentage	
	England and Wales	Urban districts[1]	Rural districts[1]	Urban	Rural
1951	43,757,888	35,335,721	8,422,167	80·8	19·2
1961	46,071,604	36,838,442	9,233,162	80·0	20·0
1971	48,755,000	38,151,000	10,598,000	78·2	21·5
1981	49,011,417	37,686,863	11,324,554	76·9	23·1

[1]As existing at each census.

Urban and rural areas were re-defined for the 1981 and 1991 censuses on a land use basis. In Scotland 'localities' correspond to urban areas. The 1981 census gave the usually resident population of England and Wales as 48,521,596, of which 43,599,431 were in urban areas; and of Scotland as 5,035,315, of which 4,486,140 were in localities.

Greater London Boroughs. Total area 1,580 sq. km. Usually resident total population at the 1991 census, 6,679,699 (inner London, 2,504,451). 1996 estimate, 7,074,000. By borough (1991):

Barking and Dagenham	143,681	Hammersmith and Fulham[1]	148,502	Lewisham[1]	230,983
Barnet	293,564	Haringey[1]	202,204	Merton	168,470
Bexley	215,615	Harrow	200,100	Newham[1]	212,170
Brent	243,025	Havering	229,492	Redbridge	226,218
Bromley	290,609	Hillingdon	231,602	Richmond upon Thames	160,732
Camden[1]	170,444	Hounslow	204,397	Southwark[1]	218,541
Croydon	313,510	Islington[1]	164,686	Sutton	168,880
Ealing	275,257	Kensington and Chelsea[1]	138,394	Tower Hamlets[1]	161,064
Enfield	257,417	Kingston upon Thames	132,996	Waltham Forest	212,033
Greenwich	207,650	Lambeth[1]	244,834	Wandsworth[1]	252,425
Hackney[1]	181,248			Westminster, City of [1]	174,718

[1]Inner London borough.

The City of London (677 acres) is administered by its Corporation which retains some independent powers. Resident population (1991 census) 4,142.

Scotland: Area 78,133 sq. km, including its islands, 186 in number, and inland water, 1,580 sq. km.

Population (including military in the barracks and seamen on board vessels in the harbours) at the dates of each census:

Date of enumeration	Population	Pop. per sq. mile[1]	Date of enumeration	Population	Pop. per sq. mile[1]
1811	1,805,864	60	1851	2,888,742	97
1821	2,091,521	70	1861	3,062,294	100
1831	2,364,386	79	1871	3,360,018	113
1841	2,620,184	88	1881	3,735,573	125

Date of enumeration	Population	Pop. per sq. mile[1]	Date of enumeration	Population	Pop. per sq. mile[1]
1891	4,025,647	135	1951	5,096,415	171
1901	4,472,103	150	1961	5,179,344	174
1911	4,760,904	160	1971	5,229,963	68
1921	4,882,497	164	1981	5,130,735	66
1931	4,842,980	163	1991	4,998,567	60

[1]Per sq. km from 1971.

The 1991 census population included 2,606,606 males.

Until April 1996 Scotland was divided into 9 regions (subdivided into 53 districts) and 3 island authority areas.

Area of regions and usually resident population figures of regions and districts at the 1991 census:

Regions (area sq. km) and Districts	Population	Regions (area sq. km) and Districts	Population
Borders (4,713)	*103,881*	*Lothian (1,716)*	*726,010*
Berwickshire	19,174	East Lothian	84,114
Ettrick and Lauderdale	34,038	Edinburgh City	418,914
Roxburgh	35,346	Midlothian	78,845
Tweeddale	15,323	West Lothian	144,137
Central (2,635)	*267,492*	*Strathclyde (13,503)*	*2,248,706*
Clackmannan	47,679	Argyll and Bute	65,140
Falkirk	140,980	Bearsden and Milngavie	40,612
Stirling	78,833	Clydebank	45,717
		Clydesdale	57,588
Dumfries and Galloway (6,396)	*147,805*	Cumbernauld and Kilsyth	62,412
Annandale and Eskdale	37,087	Cumnock and Doon Valley	42,594
Nithsdale	57,012	Cunninghame	136,875
Stewartry	23,629	Dumbarton	77,173
Wigtown	30,077	East Kilbride	82,777
		Eastwood	59,959
Fife (1,312)	*341,199*	Glasgow City	662,853
Dunfermline	127,258	Hamilton	105,202
Kirkcaldy	147,053	Inverclyde	90,103
North East Fife	66,888	Kilmarnock and Loudoun	79,861
		Kyle and Carrick	112,658
Grampian (8,698)	*503,888*	Monklands	102,379
Aberdeen City	204,885	Motherwell	142,632
Banff and Buchan	85,303	Renfrew	196,980
Gordon	76,642	Strathkelvin	85,191
Kincardine and Deeside	53,442		
Moray	83,616	*Tayside (7,942)*	*383,848*
		Angus	94,480
Highland (25,398)	*204,004*	Dundee City	165,873
Badenoch and Strathspey	11,008	Perth and Kinross	123,495
Caithness	26,710		
Inverness	62,186	*Island Authority Areas*	
Lochaber	19,310	Orkney Islands (976)	19,612
Nairn	10,623	Shetland Islands (1,433)	22,522
Ross and Cromarty	49,197	Western Isles (2,898)	29,600
Skye and Lochalsh	11,754		
Sutherland	13,216		

In April 1996, 29 new unitary authority areas came into being: Aberdeen City, Aberdeenshire, Angus, Argyll and Bute, Clackmannanshire, Dumfries and Galloway, Dundee City, East Ayrshire, East Dunbartonshire, East Lothian, East Renfrewshire, City of Edinburgh, Falkirk, Fife, Glasgow City, Highland, Inverclyde, Midlothian, Moray, North Ayrshire, North Lanarkshire, Perth and Kinross, Renfrewshire, Scottish Borders, South Ayrshire, South Lanarkshire, Stirling, West Dunbartonshire, West Lothian. The Island Authority Areas (Orkney, Shetland, Western Isles) remained as they were.

The birthplaces of the 1991 usually resident population in Scotland were: Scotland, 4,454,065; England, 354,268; Wales, 4,710; Northern Ireland, 26,393; Ireland 22,773; Commonwealth, 59,134; foreign countries, 148,987.

British Citizenship. Under the British Nationality Act 1981 there are 3 main forms of citizenship: Citizenship for persons closely connected with the UK; British Dependent Territories citizenship; British Overseas citizenship. British citizenship is acquired automatically at birth by a child born in the UK if his or her mother or father is a British citizen or is settled in the UK. A child born abroad to a British citizen is a British citizen by descent. British citizenship may be acquired by registration for stateless persons, and for children not automatically acquiring such citizenship or born abroad to parents who are citizens by descent; and, for other adults, by naturalization. Requirements for the latter include 5 years' residence (3 years for applicants married to a British citizen). The Hong Kong (British Nationality) Order 1986 created the status of British National (Overseas) for citizens connected with Hong Kong before 1997, and the British Nationality (Hong Kong) Act 1990 made provision for up to 50,000 selected persons to register as British citizens.

In 1995, 40,500 persons were granted citizenship and a further 26,000 under the Hong Kong Act.

Emigration and Immigration. Immigration is mainly governed by the Immigration Act 1970 and Immigration Rules made under it. British and Commonwealth citizens with the right of abode before 1983 are not subject to immigration control, nor are citizens of European Economic Area countries. Other persons seeking to work or settle in the UK must obtain a visa or entry clearance.

Migration statistics are derived from the government's International Passenger Survey, and exclude the Republic of Ireland.

Immigrants (in 1,000) by sex and occupation:

	Total	Females	Professional	Manual/ Clerical	Non-Employed
1992	216	99	62	44	111
1993	213	101	66	43	105
1994	253	126	82	56	115
1995	245	130	86	46	113

Emigrants (in 1,000) by sex and occupation:

	Total	Females	Professional	Manual/ Clerical	Non-Employed
1992	227	114	82	47	98
1993	216	103	70	45	101
1994	191	98	55	48	87
1995	192	90	62	42	88

In 1996 (and 1995) there were 61,730 (55,480) acceptances for settlement in the UK, including from: European Economic Area, 120 (220); rest of Europe, 7,370 (4,030), notably Turkey 3,720 (1,170); Pakistan, 6,250 (6,310); India, 4,620 (4,860); Bangladesh, 2,720 (3,280); USA, 4,030 (3,960); Nigeria, 3,220 (3,260); Sri Lanka, 2,180 (1,370); Australia, 2,120 (2,020); Ghana, 1,970 (1,820); Japan, 1,780 (1,870); Iran, 1,720 (1,120); Iraq, 1,580 (540).

Asylum. In 1996 there were 29,640 applications for asylum (2,905 applications in 1984). While respecting its obligations to political refugees under the UN Convention and Protocol relating to the status of Refugees, the Government has powers under the Asylum and Immigration Act 1996 to weed out applicants seeking entry for non-political reasons and to designate certain countries as not giving risk of persecution. 6% of applicants were accepted in 1995.

Coleman, D. and Salt, J., *The British Population: Patterns, Trends and Processes.* OUP, 1992

SOCIAL STATISTICS

UK statistics: Births, 1996, 733,000 (260,000 outside marriage); deaths, 636,000; marriages, 322,000 (1995); divorces, 170,100 (1995); abortions, 1993, 179,783. Life expectancy, 1994–96: Males, 74·1 years; females, 79·4. Annual growth rate, 1990–95, 0·2%. Over 1990–95, suicide rates per 100,000 population were 7·9 (men, 12·4; women, 3·6). Infant mortality, 1996, 4,500; rate of 6·1 per 1,000 live births. Fertility rate, 1990–95, 1·8 births per woman. Of the estimated 800,000 pregnancies in 1997, around half were to unmarried women, up from a third 10 years earlier. Birth rates (per 1,000 population), 1996, 12·5; death, 10·9. 36% of births in 1996 were outside marriage.

In 1997, 15·7% of the total population was over 65, up from 11·7% in 1960.

In 1998 the average household in Great Britain consisted of 2·4 people, down from 3·1 in 1961.

England and Wales statistics (in 1,000), 1996 (and 1995): Births, 649 (648); deaths, 560 (570); marriages, (283); divorces, (155).

Scotland statistics:

	Estimated resident population at 30 June[1]	Total births	Live births outside marriage	Deaths	Marriages	Divorces, annulments and dissolutions
1991	5,107,000	67,024	19,517	61,041	33,762	12,399
1992	5,111,200	65,789	19,950	60,937	35,057	12,479
1993	5,120,200	63,337	19,855	64,049	33,366	12,787
1994	5,132,400	61,656	19,224	59,328	31,480	13,133
1995	5,136,600	60,051	20,266	60,500	30,663	12,249
1996	5,128,000	59,440	21,361	60,671	30,242	11,123

[1]Includes merchant navy at home and forces stationed in Scotland.

Birth rate for Scotland, 1996, per 1,000 population, 11·6; death rate, 11·8; marriage, 5·9; infant mortality per 1,000 live births, 6·2; sex ratio, 1,061 male births to 1,000 female. Average age of marriage in 1996: Males, 29·1 years, females, 27·4. Expectation of life, 1996: Males, 72·0 years, females, 77·7.

CLIMATE
The climate is cool temperate oceanic, with mild conditions and rainfall evenly distributed over the year, though the weather is very changeable because of cyclonic influences. In general, temperatures are higher in the west and lower in the east in winter and rather the reverse in summer. Rainfall amounts are greatest in the west, where most of the high ground occurs.

London, Jan. 39°F (3·9°C), July 64°F (17·8°C). Annual rainfall 25" (635 mm).
Aberdeen, Jan. 38°F (3·3°C), July 57°F (13·9°C). Annual rainfall 32" (813 mm).
Belfast, Jan. 40°F (4·4°C), July 61°F (16·1°C). Annual rainfall 34·6" (879 mm).
Birmingham, Jan. 38°F (3·3°C), July 61°F (16·1°C). Annual rainfall 30" (749 mm).
Cardiff, Jan. 40°F (4·4°C), July 61°F (16·1°C). Annual rainfall 42·6" (1,065 mm).
Edinburgh, Jan. 38°F (3·3°C), July 58°F (14·5°C). Annual rainfall 27" (686 mm).
Glasgow, Jan. 39°F (3·9°C), July 59°F (15°C). Annual rainfall 38" (965 mm).
Manchester, Jan. 39°F (3·9°C), July 61°F (16·1°C). Annual rainfall 34·5" (876 mm).

CONSTITUTION AND GOVERNMENT
The reigning Queen, Head of the Commonwealth, is **Elizabeth II** Alexandra Mary, b. 21 April 1926, daughter of King George VI and Queen Elizabeth; married on 20 Nov. 1947 Lieut. Philip Mountbatten (formerly Prince Philip of Greece), created Duke of Edinburgh, Earl of Merioneth and Baron Greenwich on the same day and created Prince Philip, Duke of Edinburgh, 22 Feb. 1957; succeeded to the crown on the death of her father, on 6 Feb. 1952.

Offspring: Prince Charles Philip Arthur George, Prince of Wales (Heir Apparent), b. 14 Nov. 1948; married Lady Diana Frances Spencer on 29 July 1981; after divorce, 28 Aug. 1996, Diana, Princess of Wales. She died in Paris in a road accident on 31 Aug. 1997. *Offspring:* William Arthur Philip Louis, b. 21 June 1982; Henry Charles Albert David, b. 15 Sept. 1984. Princess Anne Elizabeth Alice Louise, the Princess Royal, b. 15 Aug. 1950; married Mark Anthony Peter Phillips on 14 Nov. 1973; divorced, 1992; married Cdr Timothy Laurence on 12 Dec. 1992. *Offspring of first marriage:* Peter Mark Andrew, b. 15 Nov. 1977; Zara Anne Elizabeth, b. 15 May 1981. Prince Andrew Albert Christian Edward, created Duke of York, 23 July 1986, b. 19 Feb. 1960; married Sarah Margaret Ferguson on 23 July 1986; after divorce, 30 May 1996, Sarah, Duchess of York. *Offspring:* Princess Beatrice Mary, b. 8 Aug. 1988; Princess Eugenie Victoria Helena, b. 23 March 1990. Prince Edward Antony Richard Louis, b. 10 March 1964.

The Queen Mother: Queen Elizabeth Angela Marguerite, b. 4 Aug. 1900, daughter of the 14th Earl of Strathmore and Kinghorne; married the Duke of York, afterwards King George VI, on 26 April 1923.

Widow of the Uncle of the Queen: Princess Alice Christabel, Duchess of Gloucester, b. 25 Dec. 1901, married the late Duke of Gloucester 6 Nov. 1935.

Sister of the Queen: Princess Margaret Rose, Countess of Snowdon, b. 12 Aug. 1930; married Antony Armstrong-Jones (created Earl of Snowdon, 3 Oct. 1961) on 6 May 1960; divorced, 1978. *Offspring:* David Albert Charles (Viscount Linley), b. 3 Nov. 1961, married Serena Alleyne Stanhope on 8 Oct. 1993. Lady Sarah Frances Elizabeth Chatto, b. 1 May 1964; married Daniel Chatto on 14 July 1994. *Offspring:* Samuel David Benedict Chatto, b. 28 July 1996.

Cousins of the Queen: Richard Alexander Walter George, Duke of Gloucester, b. 26 Aug. 1944; married Birgitte van Deurs on 8 July 1972 (*offspring:* Alexander Patrick Gregers Richard, Earl of Ulster, b. 24 Oct. 1974; Lady Davina Elizabeth Alice Benedikte Windsor, b. 19 Nov. 1977; Lady Rose Victoria Birgitte Louise Windsor, b. 1 March 1980). Edward George Nicholas Paul Patrick, Duke of Kent, b. 9 Oct. 1935; married Katharine Worsley on 8 June 1961 (*offspring:* George Philip Nicholas, Earl of St Andrews, b. 26 June 1962; married Sylvania Tomaselli on 9 Jan. 1988 (*offspring:* Edward Edmund Maximilian George, Baron Downpatrick, b. 2 Dec. 1988; Lady Marina Charlotte Alexandra Katharine Windsor, b. 30 Sept. 1992); Lady Helen Marina Lucy Windsor, b. 28 April 1964; married 18 July 1992 Timothy Verner Taylor (*offspring:* Columbus George Donald Taylor, b. 6 Aug. 1994; Cassius Edward Taylor, b. 26 Dec. 1996); Lord Nicholas Charles Edward Jonathan Windsor, b. 25 July 1970). Princess Alexandra Helen Elizabeth Olga Christabel, the Hon. Lady Ogilvy b. 25 Dec. 1936; married 24 April 1963 Sir Angus Ogilvy (*offspring:* James Robert Bruce, b. 29 Feb. 1964; married 30 July 1988, Julia Rawlinson; Lady Marina Victoria Alexandra, Mrs Mowatt, b. 31 July 1966, married 2 Feb. 1990 Paul Mowatt (*offspring:* Zenouska May Mowatt, b. 26 May 1990; Christian Alexander Mowatt, b. 4 June 1993); separated, 11 April 1996. Prince Michael George Charles Franklin, b. 4 July 1942; married Baroness Marie-Christine von Reibnitz on 30 June 1978 (*offspring:* Lord Frederick Michael George David Louis Windsor, b. 6 April 1979; Lady Gabriella Marina Alexandra Ophelia Windsor, b. 23 April 1981).

The Queen's legal title rests on the statute of 12 and 13 Will. III, ch. 3, by which the succession to the Crown of Great Britain and Ireland was settled on the Princess Sophia of Hanover and the 'heirs of her body being Protestants'. By proclamation of 17 July 1917 the royal family became known as the House and Family of Windsor. On 8 Feb. 1960 the Queen issued a declaration varying her confirmatory declaration of 9 April 1952 to the effect that while the Queen and her children should continue to be known as the House of Windsor, her descendants, other than descendants entitled to the style of Royal Highness and the title of Prince or Princess, and female descendants who marry and their descendants should bear the name of Mountbatten-Windsor.

Lineage to the throne: 1) Prince of Wales. 2) Prince William of Wales. 3) Prince Henry of Wales. 4) Duke of York. 5) Princess Beatrice of York. 6) Princess Eugenie of York.

For the Royal Style and Titles of Queen Elizabeth *see* Commonwealth section. By letters patent of 30 Nov. 1917 the titles of Royal Highness and Prince or Princess are restricted to the Sovereign's children, the children of the Sovereign's sons and the eldest living son of the eldest son of the Prince of Wales.

Provision is made for the support of the royal household, after the surrender of hereditary revenues, by the settlement of the Civil List soon after the beginning of each reign. The Civil List Act of 1 Jan. 1972 provided for a decennial, and the Civil List (Increase of Financial Provision) Order 1975 for an annual review of the List, but in July 1990 it was again fixed for one decade.

The Civil List of 1991–2000 provided for an annuity of £7,900,000 to the Queen; £360,000 to Prince Philip; £640,500 to Queen Elizabeth (the Queen Mother); £230,500 to the Princess Royal; £220,000 to the Princess Margaret; £250,000 to the Duke of York; £100,000 to Prince Edward; £90,000 to Princess Alice. However, since April 1993 only the Queen, Prince Philip and the Queen Mother have received payments from the Civil List. The income of the Prince of Wales derives from the Duchy of Cornwall. The Civil List was exempted from taxation in 1910. The Queen has paid income tax on her private income since April 1993.

The supreme legislative power is vested in Parliament, which consists of the Crown, the House of Lords and the House of Commons, and dates in its present form from the middle of the 14th century. A Bill which is passed by both Houses and receives Royal Assent becomes an Act of Parliament and part of statute law.

Parliament is summoned, and a General Election is called, by the sovereign on the advice of the Prime Minister. A Parliament may last up to 5 years, normally divided into annual sessions. A session is ended by prorogation, and all Public Bills which have not been passed by both Houses then lapse. A Parliament ends by dissolution, either by will of the sovereign or by lapse of the 5-year period.

Under the Parliament Acts 1911 and 1949, all Money Bills (so certified by the Speaker of the House of Commons), if not passed by the Lords without amendment, may become law without their concurrence within 1 month of introduction in the Lords. Public Bills, other than Money Bills or a Bill extending the maximum duration of Parliament, if passed by the Commons in 2 successive sessions and rejected each time by the Lords, may become law without being passed by the Lords provided that 1 year has elapsed between Commons second reading in the first session and third reading in the second session, and that the Bill reaches the Lords at least 1 month before the end of the second session. The Parliament Acts have only been used twice since 1949, in 1991 for the War Crimes Act and for the European Parliamentary Elections Act of 1999.

Peerages are created by the sovereign, with no limits on their number. There are 4 types of Lord: 1) *Lords Spiritual*, comprising 2 archbishops and 24 diocesan bishops of the Church of England, who leave the House when they retire; 2) *hereditary peers*—in Jan. 1999 there were 750 peers who had succeeded to a peerage on the death of a relative and 9 who had themselves been granted a hereditary peerage; 3) *life peers*—there were 480 lords who had been given a peerage for their own lifetime only under the Life Peerages Act 1958; 4) *Lords of Appeal* (both active and retired)—there were 29 peers, granted a peerage for life under the Appellate Jurisdiction Act 1876, in order to enable them to hear appeal cases in the House of Lords. The full House thus consists of 1,294 lords, of whom 103 are women. The average attendance at each sitting of the House is approximately 417.

In Jan. 1999 the Government brought forward a Bill to fulfill its election manifesto pledge to remove the voting and sitting rights of the hereditary peers.

The House of Commons consists of members (of both sexes) representing constituencies determined by the Boundary Commissions. Persons under 21 years of age, Clergy of the Church of England and of the Scottish Episcopal Church, Ministers of the Church of Scotland, Roman Catholic clergymen, civil servants, members of the regular armed forces, policemen, most judicial officers and other office-holders named in the House of Commons (Disqualification) Act are disqualified from sitting in the House of Commons. No peer eligible to sit in the House of Lords can be elected to the House of Commons unless he has disclaimed his title, but Irish peers and holders of courtesy titles, who are not members of the House of Lords, are eligible.

The Representation of the People Act 1948 abolished the business premises and University franchises, and the only persons entitled to vote at Parliamentary elections are those registered as residents or as service voters. No person may vote in more than one constituency at a general election. Persons may apply on certain grounds to vote by post or by proxy. Elections are held on the first-past-the-post system, in which the candidate who receives the most votes is elected.

All persons over 18 years old and not subject to any legal incapacity to vote and who are either British subjects or citizens of Ireland are entitled to be included in the register of electors for the constituency containing the address at which they were residing on the qualifying date for the register, and are entitled to vote at elections held during the period for which the register remains in force.

Members of the armed forces, Crown servants employed abroad, and the wives accompanying their husbands, are entitled, if otherwise qualified, to be registered as 'service voters' provided they make a 'service declaration'. To be effective for a particular register, the declaration must be made on or before the qualifying date for that register. In certain circumstances, British subjects living abroad may also vote.

The Parliamentary Constituencies Act 1986, as amended by the Boundary Commissions Act 1992, provided for the setting up of Boundary Commissions for England, Wales, Scotland and Northern Ireland. The Commissions' last reports were made in 1995, and thereafter reports are due at intervals of not less than 8 and not more than 12 years; and may be submitted from time to time with respect to the area comprised in any particular constituency or constituencies where some change appears necessary. Any changes giving effect to reports of the Commissions are to be made by Orders in Council laid before Parliament for approval by resolution of each House. The Parliamentary electorate of the United Kingdom and Northern Ireland in the register in 1998 numbered 44,296,793, of whom 36,885,805 were in England, 2,230,451 in Wales, 3,992,502 in Scotland and 1,188,034 in Northern Ireland. In 1991 it was officially estimated that 7·1% of eligible voters failed to register on the electoral roll.

At the UK general election held in 1997, 659 members were returned, 529 from England, 72 from Scotland, 40 from Wales and 18 from Northern Ireland. Every constituency returns a single member.

One of the main aspects of the Labour Government's programme of constitutional reform is Scottish and Welsh devolution. In the referendum on Scottish devolution on 11 Sept. 1997, 1,775,045 votes (74·3%) were cast in favour of a Scottish parliament and 614,400 against (25·7%). The turn-out was 60·4%, so around 44·8% of the total electorate voted in favour. For the second question, on the Parliament's tax-raising powers, 1,512,889 votes were cast in favour (63·5%) and 870,263 against (36·5%). This represented 38·4% of the total electorate.

On 18 Sept. 1997 in Wales there were 559,419 votes cast in favour of a Welsh assembly (50·3%) and 552,698 against (49·7%). The turn-out was 51·3%.

In Aug. 1911 provision was first made for the payment of a salary of £400 per annum to members of the Commons, other than those already in receipt of salaries as officers of the House, as Ministers or as officers of Her Majesty's household. For current salaries *see below*. Members of the House of Lords are unsalaried but may recover expenses incurred in attending sittings of the House within maxima for each day's attendance of £33·50 for day subsistence, £75·50 for night subsistence and £32·50 for secretarial and research assistance and office expenses. Additionally, Members of the House who are disabled may recover the extra cost of attending the House incurred by reason of their disablement. In connection with attendance at the House and parliamentary duties within the UK, Lords may also recover the cost of travelling to and from home.

The executive government is vested nominally in the Crown, but practically in a committee of Ministers, called the Cabinet, which is dependent on the support of a majority in the House of Commons. The head of the Cabinet is the *Prime Minister*, a position first constitutionally recognized in 1905. The Prime Minister's colleagues in the Cabinet are appointed on his recommendation.

Governments and Prime Ministers since the Second World War (Con = Conservative Party; Lab = Labour Party):

1945–51	Lab	Clement Attlee	1970–74	Con	Edward Heath
1951–55	Con	Winston Churchill	1974–76	Lab	Harold Wilson
1955–57	Con	Anthony Eden	1976–79	Lab	James Callaghan
1957–63	Con	Harold Macmillan	1979–90	Con	Margaret Thatcher
1963–64	Con	Alec Douglas-Home	1990–97	Con	John Major
1964–70	Lab	Harold Wilson	1997–	Lab	Tony Blair

Salaries: Members of Parliament receive an annual parliamentary salary of £45,066. The salaries of Ministers who are MPs include this as a component in addition to their ministerial salary. Total salaries accepted for 1998–99: Prime Minister, £105,233; Cabinet Ministers, £90,267 (Cabinet Ministers in the House of Lords, £60,495); Lord Chancellor, £151,002; Ministers of State, £77,047 (in the Lords £53,264); Parliamentary Under-Secretaries, £69,339 (in the Lords, £44,832); Chief Whip, £82,686; Leader of the Opposition, £101,579 (in the Lords, £44,832); Speaker, £106,716; Attorney-General, £110,575; Lord Advocate, £80,219; Solicitor-General, £80,219; Solicitor General in Scotland, £68,648. In addition to pay, MPs are entitled to Office Costs, Supplementary London, Additional Costs, Motor Mileage, Temporary Secretarial and Winding Up Allowances, reimbursement of costs due to recall during a recess and a Resettlement Grant. Ministers receive a severance payment of 3 months' salary.

The Prime Minister is entitled to a salary of £102,750 in addition to the parliamentary salary of £45,066, but decided to accept the pre-election salary of £60,167 (giving the total of £105,233). Cabinet ministers are entitled to salaries of £61,650 (Commons) and £80,107 (Lords), but they also decided to accept the pre-election rates of £45,201 and £60,495. Cabinet ministers in the Commons receive the parliamentary salary of £45,066, to give a total of £90,267; those in the Lords do not receive the parliamentary salary.

The Privy Council: Before the development of the Cabinet System, the Privy Council was the chief source of executive power, but now its functions are largely formal. It advises the monarch to approve Orders in Council and on the issue of royal proclamations, and has some independent powers such as the supervision of the registration of the medical profession. It consists of all Cabinet members, the Archbishops of Canterbury and York, the Speaker of the House of Commons and senior British and Commonwealth statesmen. There are a number of advisory Privy Council committees. The Judicial Committee is the final court of appeal from courts of the UK dependencies, the Channel Islands and the Isle of Man, and some Commonwealth countries.

Boulton, C. J. (ed.) *Erskine May's Treatise on the Law Privileges, Proceedings and Usage of Parliament.* 21st ed. London, 1990

Bruce, A., et al. *The House of Lords: 1,000 Years of British Tradition.* London, 1994

Butler, D. and Butler, G., *British Political Facts, 1900–1994.* London, 1994

Dod's Parliamentary Companion. London [published after elections]

Drewry, G. (ed.) *The New Select Committees.* OUP, 1985

Griffith, J. A. G. and Ryle, M., *Parliament: Functions, Practices and Procedures.* London, 1990

Hanson, A. H. and Walles, M., *Governing Britain: a Guidebook to Political Institutions.* 5th ed. London, 1990

Harrison, B., *The Transformation of British Politics, 1860–1995.* OUP, 1996

Hennessy, P., *Whitehall.* London, 1989

King, A. (ed.) *The British Prime Minister.* Rev. ed. London, 1985

Norris, P., *Electoral Change in Britain since 1945.* Oxford, 1996

Parker, F. K., *Conduct of Parliamentary Elections.* London, 1983

Shell, D., *The House of Lords.* 2nd ed. Hemel Hempstead, 1992

Silk, E. P., *How Parliament Works.* London, 1987

The Times Guide to the House of Commons. London, [published after elections]

Waller, R., *The Almanac of British Politics.* 4th ed. London, 1991

National Anthem. 'God Save the Queen' (King) (words and tune anonymous; earliest known printed source, 1744).

RECENT ELECTIONS

At the general election of 1 May 1997, 31,286,597 votes were cast, a turn-out of 71·4%. The Labour Party won 418 seats with 43·2% of votes cast (271 with 32% in 1992); the Conservative Party 165 with 30·7% (336 with 42·8%); the Liberal Democratic Party 46 with 17·2% (20 with 18·3%); ind 1 (nil); 1 seat went to the Speaker. Regional parties (Scotland): the Scottish National Party gained 6 seats (3 in 1992); (Wales): Plaid Cymru 4 (4); (Northern Ireland): the Ulster Unionist Party 10 (9); the Democratic Unionist Party 2 (3); the Social and Democratic Labour Party 3 (4); Sinn Féin 2 (nil); the United Kingdom Unionist 1 (replaced the Ulster Popular Unionist Party, 1 seat in 1992). Labour gained 146 seats and lost none; the Conservatives gained no seats and lost 178; the Liberal Democrats gained 30 seats and lost 2.

European Parliament: The United Kingdom has 87 representatives. At the June 1994 elections turn-out was 36·4%. The Labour Party won 62 seats with 44·2% of votes cast (group in European Parliament: European Socialist Party); the Conservative Party, 18 with 27·8% (Popular European Party); the Liberal Democratic Party, 2 with 16·7% (Liberal, Democratic and Reformist Group); the Scottish National Party, 2 with 3·2% (European Radical Alliance). Voting for these parties was on the first-past-the-post system. Voting in Northern Ireland was by the single transferable vote system: the Democratic Ulster Unionist Party, the Social Democrat and Labour Party (European Socialist Party) and the Official Ulster Union Party (Popular European Party) gained 1 seat each.

CURRENT ADMINISTRATION

In March 1999 the Government consisted of the following ('Rt Hon.'—Right Honourable—signifies a member of the Privy Council):

(a) 22 MEMBERS OF THE CABINET

Prime Minister, First Lord of the Treasury and Minister for the Civil Service: Rt Hon. Tony Blair, MP, b. 1953.

Deputy Prime Minister and Secretary of State for the Environment, Transport and the Regions: Rt Hon. John Prescott, MP, b. 1938.

Chancellor of the Exchequer: Rt Hon. Gordon Brown, MP, b. 1951.

Secretary of State for Foreign and Commonwealth Affairs: Rt Hon. Robin Cook, MP, b. 1946.

Lord Chancellor: Rt Hon. Lord Irvine of Lairg, QC, b. 1940.

Minister for the Cabinet Office and Chancellor of the Duchy of Lancaster: Rt Hon. Jack Cunningham, MP, b. 1939.

Secretary of State for the Home Department: Rt Hon. Jack Straw, MP, b. 1946.

Secretary of State for Education and Employment: Rt Hon. David Blunkett, MP, b. 1947.

Secretary of State for Defence: Rt Hon. George Robertson, MP, b. 1946.

President of the Council and Leader of the House of Commons: Rt Hon. Margaret Beckett, MP, b. 1943.

Leader of the House of Lords, Minister for Women and Lord Privy Seal: Rt Hon Baroness Jay of Paddington CBE, MP, b. 1939.

Secretary of State for Trade and Industry: Rt Hon. Stephen Byers, MP, b. 1953.

Secretary of State for Social Security: Rt Hon. Alistair Darling, MP, b. 1953.

Secretary of State for Health: Rt Hon. Frank Dobson, MP, b. 1940.

Secretary of State for Culture, Media and Sport: Rt Hon. Chris Smith, MP, b. 1951.

Minister of Agriculture, Fisheries and Food: Rt Hon. Nick Brown, MP, b. 1950.

Secretary of State for International Development: Rt Hon. Clare Short, MP, b. 1946.

Secretary of State for Northern Ireland: Rt Hon. Marjorie ('Mo') Mowlam MP, b. 1949.

Secretary of State for Wales: Rt Hon. Alun Michael, MP, b. 1943.

Secretary of State for Scotland: Rt Hon. Donald Dewar, MP, b. 1937.

Chief Secretary to the Treasury: Rt Hon. Alan Milburn, MP, b. 1958.

Parliamentary Secretary HM Treasury (Chief Whip): Rt Hon. Ann Taylor, MP, b. 1947.

(b) LAW OFFICERS

Attorney-General: Rt Hon. John Morris, QC, MP, b. 1931.

Lord Advocate: Andrew Hardie, QC, b. 1946.

Solicitor-General: Ross Cranston, MP, b. 1948.

Solicitor-General for Scotland: Colin Boyd, QC.

(c) MINISTERS OF STATE (BY DEPARTMENT)

Ministry of Agriculture, Fisheries and Food: Jeff Rooker, MP, b. 1941.

Minister of State, Cabinet Office: Lord Falconer of Thoroton, QC, b. 1951.

Department of Culture, Media and Sport: Rt Hon. Tom Clarke, CBE, MP, b. 1941, *Minister for Film and Tourism.*

Ministry of Defence: Rt Hon. Dr John Gilbert, b. 1927, *Minister for Defence Procurement;* Doug Henderson, MP, b. 1949, *Minister for the Armed Forces.*

Department for Education and Employment: Rt Hon. Andrew Smith, MP, b. 1951, *Minister for Employment and Disability Rights;* Estelle Morris, b. 1952, *Minister for School Standards;* Baroness Blackstone, b. 1942; *Minister for Education and Employment.*

Department of the Environment, Transport and the Regions: Rt Hon. Michael Meacher, MP, b. 1939, *Minister for the Environment;* Hilary Armstrong, MP, b. 1945, *Minister for Local Government and Housing;* Richard Caborn, MP, b. 1943, *Minister for Regions, Regeneration and Planning;* Rt Hon. Dr John Reid, MP, b. 1947, *Minister for Transport.*

Foreign and Commonwealth Affairs Office: Tony Lloyd, MP, b. 1950; Rt Hon. Joyce Quin, MP, b. 1944, *Minister for Europe.*

Department of Health: John Denham, MP, b. 1953; Rt Hon. Tessa Jowell, MP, b. 1947, *Minister for Public Health.*

Home Office: Paul Boateng, MP, b. 1951, *Minister for Criminal Policy;* Lord Williams of Mostyn, MP, b. 1941, *Minister for Prisons, Probation and Europe.*

Lord Chancellor's Department: Geoff Hoon, MP, b. 1953.

Northern Ireland Office: Rt Hon. Adam Ingram, MP, b. 1947, *Minister for Security, Police, Criminal Justice, Prisons and Economic Development*; Rt Hon. Paul Murphy, MP, b. 1948, *Minister for Political Development, Finance, Personnel and Information.*

Scottish Office: Henry McLeish, MP, b. 1948, *Minister for Home Affairs and Devolution;* Rt Hon. Helen Liddell, MP, b. 1950, *Minister for Education and Industry.*

Department of Social Security: Stephen Timms, MP, b. 1955, *Minister for Welfare Reform.*

Department of Trade and Industry: Lord Simon of Highbury CBE, b. 1939, *Minister for Trade and Competitiveness in Europe;* Brian Wilson, MP, b. 1948, *Minister for Trade;* John Battle, MP, b. 1951, *Minister for Industry, Energy, Science and Technology;* Ian McCartney, MP, b. 1951, *Minister for Competitiveness.*

Treasury: Barbara Roche, MP, b. 1954, *Financial Secretary;* Dawn Primarolo, MP, b. 1954, *Paymaster-General.*

(d) PARLIAMENTARY SECRETARIES (BY DEPARTMENT)

Ministry of Agriculture, Fisheries and Food: Elliott Morley, MP, b. 1952, *Minister for Fisheries and the Countryside;* Lord Donoghue, b. 1934, *Minister for Farming and Food Industry.*

There are also 34 Parliamentary Under-Secretaries of State.

Leader of the Opposition in the House of Commons: Rt Hon. William Hague, MP, b. 1961.

Leader of the Opposition in the House of Lords: Rt Hon. Lord Strathclyde, b. 1960.

The *Speaker* of the House of Commons is Betty Boothroyd (Labour), elected for a second term on 7 May 1997.

Local Government. Local Administration is carried out by 4 different types of bodies, namely: (i) local branches of some central ministries, such as the Departments of Health and Social Security; (ii) local sub-managements of nationalized industries; (iii) specialist authorities such as the National Rivers Authority; and (iv) the system of local government described below. The phrase 'local government' has come to mean that part of the local administration conducted by elected councils. There are separate systems for England, Wales and Scotland.

The Local Government Act 1992 established a Local Government Commission, which completed its report in 1996 on whether the two-tier local government structure should be replaced by unitary authorities in some areas. Following its recommendations, 27 new unitary councils had been established by April 1997. The Commission is currently reviewing electoral arrangements.

Local authorities have statutory powers and claims on public funds. Relations with central government are maintained through the Department of the Environment in England, and through the Welsh and Scottish Offices. In England the Home Office and the Department of Education and Employment are also concerned with some local government functions. (These are performed by departments within the Welsh and Scottish Offices). Ministers have powers of intervention to protect individuals' rights and safeguard public health, and the Government has power to cap (i.e. limit) local authority budgets.

Local government is conducted by elected councils at different levels of administration. England, Wales and Scotland have different systems. See under 'Local Government' in England, Scotland and Wales for more details.

Resident citizens of the UK, Ireland, a Commonwealth country or an EU country may (at age 18) vote and (at age 21) stand for election. In England, councils are elected for 4 years, except that in the metropolitan and other districts, one-third of councillors are elected in each of the 3 years that no county council election is held. Counties are divided into electoral divisions and districts into wards. In Wales, elections for the full councils are held every 4 years, and in Scotland every 3 years. The chair of the council is one of the councillors elected by the rest. In boroughs and cities his or her title is Mayor. Mayors of cities may have the title of Lord Mayor conferred on them. 51 towns in England and Wales and 4 in Scotland have the status of city. This status is granted by the personal command of the monarch and confers no special privileges or powers. In Scotland, the chair of city councils is deemed Lord Provost, and is elsewhere known as Convenor or Provost. In Wales, the chair is called Chairman in counties and Mayor in county boroughs. Any parish or community council can by simple resolution adopt the style 'town council' and the status of town for the parish or community. Basic and other allowances are payable to councillors (except Scottish community councillors).

Functions. Legislation in the 1980s initiated a trend for local authorities to arrange for the provision of services by, or in collaboration with, commercial or voluntary bodies rather than provide them directly. Savings in expenditure are encouraged by compulsory competitive tendering. In England, county councils are responsible for strategic planning, transport planning, non-trunk roads and regulation of traffic, personal social services, consumer protection, disposal of waste, the fire and library services, and partially for education. District councils are responsible for environmental health, housing, local planning applications (in the first instance) and refuse collection. Unitary authorities combine the functions of both levels.

Finance. Revenue is derived from the Council Tax, which supports about one-fifth of current expenditure, the remainder being funded by central government grants and by the redistribution of revenue from the national non-domestic rate (property tax). Capital expenditure is financed by borrowing within government-set limits and sales of real estate.

Election Results. Elections for one third of the seats on the councils of the 32 London boroughs, 36 metropolitan districts and 118 non-metropolitan districts were held on 5 May 1994. The Labour Party gained control of 93 councils; the Liberal Democratic Party, 19; the Conservative Party, 15; ind, 5. There was no overall majority in 54 councils.

Elections were held outside the metropolitan areas ('the shires') on 4 May 1995. Labour made a net gain of 155 councils, the Liberal Democrats 45 and the Conservatives lost 51.

At the elections of 2 May 1996 for 32 metropolitan and 114 non-metropolitan and unitary councils, Labour took control of 84 councils and gained 431 seats, the Liberal Democrats took control of 23 councils and gained 142 seats, the Conservatives took control of 3 councils and lost 534 seats, and independents took control of 3 councils and lost 29 seats. In 33 councils no party gained an absolute majority.

On 6 April 1995 elections were held for the 29 newly-created unitary councils. 1,161 seats were contested. Labour won 614 seats with 47% of votes cast, and gained control of 20 of the councils; the Scottish National Party won 181 seats with 26% and gained 3 councils; the Liberal Democrats won 123 seats with 10%; the Conservative Party won 81 seats with 11%. Independents gained control of 3 councils, and 3 councils had no overall control.

County council elections and those for 19 further new unitary authorities took place on 1 May 1997. Elections for the 1,014 seats on the unitary authorities created shadow councils whose job was to prepare the area for transfer to the new status in April 1998. Councillors for these areas did not stand for election but stepped down in April 1998 leaving those elected on 1 May 1997 in charge.

The next local government elections were scheduled for 6 May 1999.

DEFENCE

The Defence Council was established on 1 April 1964 under the chairmanship of the Secretary of State for Defence, who is responsible to the Sovereign and Parliament for the defence of the realm. Vested in the Defence Council are the functions of commanding and administering the Armed Forces. The Secretary of State heads the Department of Defence. There are 3 subordinate Ministers; 2 Ministers of State and 1 Parliamentary Under-Secretary of State.

Defence Council membership comprises the Secretary of State, the 3 Ministers mentioned above, the Chief of the Defence Staff, the 3 single Service Chiefs of Staff, the Vice-Chief of Defence Staff, the Chief of Defence Procurement, the Chief

Scientific Adviser, the Permanent Under-Secretary of State and the Second Permanent Under Secretary of State.

There are 3 Service Boards, each of which enjoys delegated powers for the administration of matters relating to the naval, military and air forces respectively.

Defence policy decision-making is a collective Governmental responsibility. Important matters of policy are considered by the full Cabinet or, more frequently, by the Defence and Overseas Policy Committee under the chairmanship of the Prime Minister. Other members of this Committee include the Secretary of State for Defence, the Foreign and Commonwealth Secretary and the Home Secretary.

The Procurement Executive is responsible for procurement of equipment and supplies.

The ban on homosexuals serving in the armed forces was upheld by a House of Commons vote in May 1996.

Defence Budget: 1996–97, £21,425m. Estimates for 1997–98, £21,923m.; 1998–99, £22,624m. In 1997 per capita defence expenditure totalled US$611 (US$803 per capita in 1985). As a percentage of GDP, spending was 2·8% in 1997, down from 5·2% in 1985).

Nuclear weapons: Having carried out its first test in 1952, there have been 45 tests in all. The nuclear arsenal consisted of approximately 260 warheads in Jan. 1998 according to the Stockholm International Peace Research Institute.

Arms Trade: The UK is the world's second largest exporter of arms after the USA, with sales in 1997 worth US$8·5bn., or 18·5% of the world total. In 1987 sales had been worth US$7·4bn., but had only represented 8·3% of the total. The UK is the third largest importer of arms, after Saudi Arabia and Taiwan, spending US$2·5bn. in 1997, up from US$2·4bn. in 1996.

Army. Control of the British Army is vested in the Defence Council and is exercised through the Army Board. The Secretary of State for Defence is Chairman of the Army Board. The other civilian members are the 3 subordinate Ministers and the Second Permanent Under Secretary of State.

The Military members of the Army Board are the Chief of the General Staff, the Adjutant General, the Quartermaster General, the Master General of the Ordnance, the C.-in-C. Land Command and the Assistant Chief of General Staff. The Chief of the General Staff is the professional head of his Service and the professional adviser to Ministers on the Army aspects of military matters. He is responsible for the fighting efficiency of his Service; for Army advice on the conduct of operations; and for the issuing of such single Service operational orders as may be appropriate resulting from defence policy decisions. He is also responsible for the Territorial Army. The Chief of the General Staff is a member of the Chiefs of Staff Committee which is chaired by the Chief of the Defence Staff, who is responsible to HM Government for professional advice on strategy and military operations, and on the military implication of defence policy. The Adjutant-General is responsible for recruiting and selection of army manpower; for the administration and individual training of military personnel; for the discipline of the Army; for pay and allowances and pensions; for legal services; for the veterinary and remount services; for the Army Cadet Forces; for questions of Army welfare and education including school children overseas; and for resettlement and sports. The Quartermaster-General is responsible for logistic planning for the Army; for the storage, distribution, maintenance, repair and inspection of equipment, stores and ammunition; for development of stores; for supply, transport and accommodation; for the development, production and inspection of clothing; for military movements and transportation; for the Army postal, catering, salvage and fire services; and for questions connected with canteens, institutes and military labour. The Master General of the Ordnance is a member of both the Army Board and of the Procurement Executive Management Board. He is responsible to the Chief of Defence Procurement for the financial and technical management of the approved programme for the procurement of service equipment for the Armed Services, and to the Army Board for the co-ordination of the Army's total equipment programme.

The Field Army is run from Headquarters Land Command, based at Wilton. This consists of 2 operational divisions, 3 reserve divisions, 2 districts and United Kingdom Support Command (Germany) (UKSC(G)). 1 (UK) Armoured Division, based in Germany, has 3 armoured brigades each consisting of 2 tank regiments, 2 armoured infantry battalions, and supported by artillery, engineers, aviation, air defence and logistics units. 3 (UK) Division, based in the UK, consists of 2 mechanized and 1 airborne brigade, together with artillery, engineers, aviation, air defence and logistics units. Other forces assigned to NATO's Rapid Reaction Corps (ARRC) include 24 Airmobile Brigade, a reconnaissance Brigade, intelligence and Electronic Warfare units, signals regiments, a depth artillery brigade, air defence regiments, engineers and some general duty infantry battalions.

The Ministry of Defence retains direct control of units in Northern Ireland, although day-to-day military responsibility is given to the Chief of the General Staff. The Permanent Joint Headquarters, recently formed at Northwood, is responsible for overseas garrisons, which include the Falkland Islands, Cyprus and Brunei.

The established strength of the Regular Army in 1998 was 114,000, which includes soldiers under training and Gurkhas. In addition there were some 4,000 Royal Irish Home Service soldiers. The strengths of the Regular Reserves was 212,000 in 1998.

The role of the Territorial Army (TA) is to act as a general Reserve for the Army by reinforcing it as required, with individuals, sub-units and other units, either in the UK or overseas; and by providing the framework and basis for regeneration and reconstruction to cater for the unforeseen in times of national emergency. The TA also provides a nationwide link between the military and civil communities. Strength, 1997, 57,700. In addition, men who have completed service in the Regular Army normally have some liability to serve in the Regular Reserve. All members of the TA and Regular Reserve may be called out by a Queen's Order in time of emergency of imminent national danger, and most of the TA and a large proportion of the Regular Reserve may be called out by a Queen's Order when warlike operations are in preparation or in progress. The Home Service Battalions of the Royal Irish Regiment are only liable for service in Northern Ireland.

Men, women and juniors enlist in the Army for up to 22 years' active service and reserve service up to 45 years of age. Soldiers enlist for a minimum of 3 years and can leave active service thereafter on one year's notice. Bonuses are paid to those who serve for certain periods and there are manning control points at which the Army may require soldiers to terminate their service, again on one year's notice. Those enlisting in certain technical trades must agree to serve for a minimum of 3 years. Recruits under the age of 17½ on reaching the age of 18 are entitled either to confirm their original engagement or to reduce their period of service to 3 years.

Equipment includes 426 Challenger, 36 Challenger 2 and 79 Chieftain main battle tanks, 8 Scorpion light tanks, 1,225 armoured fighting vehicles, 524 artillery pieces, 63 multiple rocket launchers, 880 anti-tank guided weapons and 562 surface-to-air missiles.

Women serve throughout the Army in the same regiments and corps as men. There are only a few roles in which they are not employed such as the Infantry and Royal Armoured Corps.

Brereton, J. M., *The British Soldier*. London, 1985

The Oxford Illustrated History of the British Army. OUP, 1995

Strawson, J., *Gentlemen in Khaki: the British Army, 1890–1990*. London, 1985

Navy. Control of the Royal Navy is vested in the Defence Council and is exercised through the Admiralty Board, chaired by the Secretary of State for Defence. The other civilian members are the Ministers of State for the Armed Forces and Defence Procurement, the Parliamentary Under Secretary for Defence and the Second Permanent Under Secretary of State. The naval members are the Chief of Naval Staff (First Sea Lord) responsible for management, fighting efficiency, planning and operational advice; the combined Second Sea Lord and C.-in-C. Naval Home Command, responsible for the manning of the Fleet and all personnel aspects; the Controller of the Navy, responsible for procurement of ships, their weapons and equipment; the Chief of Fleet Support, responsible for logistic support, stores, fuels and transport, naval dockyards and the auxiliary services; the C.-in-C. Fleet, and the Assistant Chief of Naval Staff, responsible for co-ordinating advice on certain policy and operational matters. The Navy Board, an executive sub-committee of the Admiralty Board, is responsible for the professional management of the service.

In 1996, the changes in management structure, reductions in strength, base closures and rationalization initiated in 1994 began to approach completion. The

Chief of Fleet Support and Controller of the Navy are now located in the Bristol area and their various support agencies rationalized. The naval bases at Rosyth and Portland closed in 1995. Although the dockyards at Rosyth and Devonport remain largely committed to naval refit work, both yards have now been sold to commercial operators.

The C.-in-C. Fleet, headquartered at Northwood, is responsible for the command of the fleet, while command of naval establishments in the UK is exercised by the C.-in-C. Naval Home Command from Portsmouth. Main naval bases are at Devonport, Portsmouth and Faslane, with a minor base overseas at Gibraltar.

The Royal Naval Reserve (RNR) and the Royal Marines Reserve (RMR) are volunteer forces which together in 1996 numbered 3,450. The RNR provides trained personnel in war to supplement regular forces. The main roles of the RMR are reinforcement and other specialist tasks with the UK-Netherlands Amphibious Force. In addition, men who have completed service in the Royal Navy and the Royal Marines have a commitment to serve in the Royal Fleet Reserve, currently 23,000-strong.

Royal Navy and Queen Alexandra's Royal Naval Nursing Service (QARNNS) ratings, both male and female, and Royal Marine ranks enlist on the 'Open Engagement' to complete 22 years active service with the option to leave at 18 months notice on completion of a minimum of 2½ years productive service. Those who leave before completing 22 years have a liability for up to 3 years service in the Royal Fleet Reserve.

The roles of the Royal Navy are first, to deploy the national strategic nuclear deterrent, second to provide maritime defence of the UK and its dependent territories, third to contribute to the maritime elements of NATO's force structure and fourth to meet national maritime objectives outside the NATO area. Personnel strength has reduced steadily over the past 5 years and is now stabilizing at about 47,500 (including Royal Marines) in 1997, with operational strength at 12 nuclear attack submarines, 2 aircraft carriers and about 35 destroyers and frigates.

The strategic deterrent is now borne principally by the new Trident submarines, of which the first 3 of 4, *Vanguard, Victorious* and *Vigilant*, each of 15,250 tonnes, and deploying 16 US-built Trident-2 D5 UGM-133A missiles with up to 96 British warheads per operational load, are now operational. The fourth ship, *Vengeance*, is scheduled to be operational in 1999. The last missile submarine of the Resolution class, *Renown*, deploying Polaris missiles, decommissioned in Aug. 1996.

The strength of the fleet's major units at the end of the respective years:

	1991	1992	1993	1994	1995	1996
Strategic Submarines	4	4	4	3	3	3
Nuclear Submarines	15	13	13	12	12	12
Diesel Submarines	6	4	4	nil	nil	nil
Aircraft Carriers	2[1]	2[1]	2[1]	2[1]	2[1]	2[1]
Destroyers	12	12	12	12	12	12
Frigates	33	30	25	24	23	23

[1]Following Government policy, of the 3 Carriers held, only 2 are kept in operational status.

The nuclear-powered submarine force numbers 12, of 2 classes, armed with torpedoes and Harpoon anti-ship missiles. There are 7 Trafalgar class, (5,300 tonnes) completed 1983–1991 and 5 Swiftsure (4,900 tonnes) completed 1973–79. The 4 diesel-electric submarines of the Upholder class were decommissioned in 1994 but remain serviceable awaiting a possible purchaser.

The principal surface ships are the Light vertical/short take-off and landing Aircraft Carriers of the Invincible class (*Invincible, Illustrious* and *Ark Royal*), 20,900 tonnes, completed 1980–85, embarking an air group of 8 Sea Harrier vertical/short take-off and landing fighters, 9 anti-submarine Sea King and 3 radar early-warning Sea King helicopters, armed with 1 twin Sea Dart surface-to-air missile system. 2 of these ships are maintained in the operational fleet, with the third (currently *Ark Royal*) either in refit or reserve.

The 12 destroyers are all Type 42 (completed 1976–85), armed with 1 twin Sea Dart surface-to-air missile system. Frigates comprise 10 Type 22 (completed 1979–89) and 13 Norfolk class (Type 23) completed 1989–96.

The lightly armed patrol force comprises 1 ice patrol ship, 16 other offshore patrol vessels and 16 inshore patrol craft mostly employed in training. Mine countermeasures capability is provided by 13 offshore hunter/sweepers and 5 coastal minehunters. Amphibious lift for the Royal Marines is provided by 1 dock landing ship (with a second in reserve) and 5 tank landing ships (civil manned, and in peacetime employed on army freighting), supported by about 32 small amphibious craft. A new Helicopter Carrier, specifically designed for amphibious operations, *HMS Ocean*, 16,000 tonnes, has completed initial sea trials and was due to fit out for entry into service in 1998.

Comprehensive support to the fleet is provided by 27 major auxiliaries including 5 replenishment and 4 support tankers, 2 multi-purpose fuel and ammunition ships, 3 ammunition and stores ships, 1 repair ship, 2 ocean tugs, 5 survey ships, 1 trials ship, 1 aviation training ship, 2 armament transports and the Royal Yacht. Second-line support is provided by about 200 harbour and coastal service craft and minor auxiliaries.

The Fleet Air Arm, 5,500-strong in 1996, has some 300 aircraft, in 19 operational, training and search-and-rescue squadrons, including 40 Sea Harrier vertical/short take-off and landing fighter aircraft, 70 Sea King and 76 Lynx anti-submarine helicopters, 10 Sea King airborne early-warning helicopters and 36 Sea King (commando transports) and 70 miscellaneous support and training craft.

The Royal Marines corps, 6,750-strong in 1996, provides a commando brigade comprising 3 commando groups, each approximately 1,000-strong with artillery, air defence, engineering and logistic support, and three light utility helicopter squadrons. The Special Boat Squadron and specialist defence units complete the operational strength. Equipment includes 15 helicopters and 30 light assault craft.

The total number of male and female personnel (including Royal Marines) was (in 1,000) on 31 March: 1993, 59·4; 1994, 55·8; 1995, 50·9; 1996, 48·5 and 1997 (estimated), 47·5.

Jane's Fighting Ships. London, annual
The Oxford Illustrated History of the Royal Navy. OUP, 1996

Air Force. In May 1912 the Royal Flying Corps first came into existence with military and naval wings, of which the latter became the independent Royal Naval Air Service in July 1914. On 2 Jan. 1918 an Air Ministry was formed, and on 1 April 1918 the Royal Flying Corps and the Royal Naval Air Service were amalgamated, under the Air Ministry, as the Royal Air Force (RAF).

In 1937 the units based on aircraft carriers and naval shore stations again passed to the operational and administrative control of the Admiralty, as the Fleet Air Arm. In 1964 control of the RAF became a responsibility of the Ministry of Defence.

The RAF is administered by the Air Force Board, of which the Secretary of State for Defence is Chairman. The Minister of State for the Armed Forces is Vice-Chairman, and normally acts as Chairman on behalf of the Secretary of State. Other members of the Board are the Minister of State for Defence Procurement, the Under-Secretary of State for Defence, the Chief of the Air Staff, Air Member for Personnel, Air Member for Logistics, Air Officer Commanding-in-Chief Strike Command, Controller of Aircraft and the Second Permanent Under Secretary of State.

The RAF is organized into 3 commands: Strike Command, Personnel and Training Command, and Logistics Command.

Strike Command is responsible for all of the RAF's frontline forces, although day-to-day control of most operations is delegated to its 3 Groups. No 1 Group is responsible for strike/attack, offensive air support, support helicopters and reconnaissance. Tornado GR1s, Tornado GR1As and Tornado GR4s are used in the attack and reconnaissance roles, while Tornado GR1Bs also maintain a maritime attack role. Jaguars are used in the attack, reconnaissance and light anti-shipping roles. Battlefield support forces comprise Harrier GR7s, as well as Chinook, Puma and Wessex helicopters. No 1 Group also operates Canberra aircraft in the strategic photographic reconnaissance role. No 11/18 Group controls the air defence forces, Tornado F3 fighters and Boeing E-3D Airborne Early-Warning aircraft, together with ground environment radars, associated communications systems and the Ballistic Missile Early-Warning System at Fylingdales. Maritime air operations, together with the RAF's search and rescue flights, are also under the operational control of No 11/18 Group. A maritime patrol and anti-submarine warfare capability is provided by Nimrod aircraft, which also have a capability against surface ships.

The search and rescue flights are equipped with Sea King helicopters. Additionally No 11/18 Group operates Nimrod Reconnaissance aircraft. No 38 Group is responsible for air-to-air refuelling and strategic air transport, which is carried out by VC10, Tristar and Hercules aircraft. No 38 Group also controls the aircraft of No 32 (The Royal) Squadron, comprising British Aerospace 146 and 125 aircraft and Wessex and Twin Squirrel helicopters. RAF forces in Germany, which are made up of Tornado GR1s, Harrier GR7s and Chinook and Puma helicopters, are under the day-to-day control of No 1 Group. The Military Air Traffic Operations organization also has the status of a Group.

The RAF Regiment, which is under the control of No 38 Group, has field squadrons in service with No 1 Group and short-range air defence squadrons armed with Rapier in service with No 1 Group and No 11/18 Group.

As well as the forces in Germany, the RAF has a flight of Tornado F3s, a flight of Hercules and a combined squadron comprising RAF Chinooks and Royal Navy Sea King helicopters based in the Falkland Islands, and a squadron of Wessex helicopters in Cyprus. In addition, Strike Command forces are deployed overseas in support of UN/WEU, NATO and Coalition operations.

Headquarters RAF Strike Command is based at RAF High Wycombe.

Personnel and Training Command was formed at RAF Innsworth, Gloucester, on 1 April 1994.

Two agencies fall under the Command, the Training Group Defence Agency and the Personnel Management Agency.

The Personnel Management Agency was formed on 1 Feb. 1997 and is responsible for the deployment of manpower throughout the RAF and for developing RAF personnel policy.

The main RAF units within the Command are, for Ground Training: RAF Cosford, RAF Cranwell and RAF Halton; for Flying Training: RAF Cranwell (where the Red Arrows are based), RAF Linton-on-Ouse, RAF Shawbury and RAF Valley. Initial Officer Training for commissioned candidates is undertaken at the RAF College, Cranwell. Further command and staff training for officers takes place at the Joint Service Command and Staff College Bracknell. Airmen aircrew are trained at RAF Cranwell, while recruit training for ground airmen is undertaken at RAF Halton. A single, tri-Service Defence Helicopter Flying School is located at RAF Shawbury.

Personnel and Training Command is equipped with the following aircraft types: Bulldog and Slingsby Firefly as primary trainers, Tucano as basic trainers for fast jet crew, Hawk as advanced fast jet trainers, Jetstreams for multi-engined pilot training, and Dominies for training navigators and other non-pilot aircrew. The Defence Helicopter Training School uses Squirrel and Griffin helicopters.

Logistics Command was formed on 1 April 1994, with its headquarters at RAF Brampton and nearby RAF Wyton. The Command is responsible for providing the full range of logistics support activities to all RAF units worldwide and Joint Service support to Royal Navy and Army units for rationalized equipment ranges. It is responsible for: Support chain management, including the provisioning, storage, distribution and disposal of equipment; repair, overhaul, maintenance and modification programmes at 3rd and 4th line; provision and management of communications and information systems; RAF catering.

RAF personnel, 1 Dec. 1998, 55,523 (including 4,537 women); total trained personnel, 51,891. Since Dec. 1991 women have been eligible to fly combat aircraft.
McIntosh, M., *Managing British Defence*. London, 1990

INTERNATIONAL RELATIONS
The UK is a member of the UN, Commonwealth, the EU, OECD, the Council of Europe, the Pacific Community, WEU and NATO.

ECONOMY
The economy is expected to grow by 1·25 % in 1999 and 2·5% in 2000.

Although the overall growth forecast was unchanged from the Pre-Budget Report (PBR) of Nov. 1998, the Treasury was expecting in March 1999 that manufacturers and exporters would be hit harder than had been envisaged.

Manufacturing output was forecast to decline by 1·25% in 1999. Export growth in 1999 was projected in the March 1999 budget to be 0·5%, compared with 3% in the PBR. The balance of payments deficit is forecast to widen from £2bn. in 1998 to £10bn. in 1999. In Nov. 1998 the Treasury was forecasting a current account deficit of £7·5bn. These more pessimistic projections reflect the deterioration in European growth prospects and the fragility of many world markets.

Central government transactions (in £1bn.).

	1997–98 Outturn	1998–99 Estimate	1999–2000 Forecast
Total cash receipts	287·0	303·8	307·9
Inland Revenue	117·6	127·5	130·3
Customs and Excise	89·8	93·4	96·2
Social Security	49·3	53·3	54·0
Interest and Dividends	9·5	9·4	8·7
Other	20·9	20·2	18·7
Total cash outlays	289·6	299·8	312·8
Investment Payments	27·7	27·1	24·6
Privatization Proceeds	−1·8	−0·1	−0·4
Net Departmental Outlays	263·7	272·7	288·5

Current Receipts (in £1bn.).

	1997–98 Outturn	1998–99 Estimate	1999–2000 Forecast
Total Inland Revenue (net of tax credits)	117·5	127·3	128·9
Total Customs and Excise	89·8	93·4	96·2
Net Taxes and Social Security Contributions	297·2	315·2	321·8
Current Receipts	315·7	334·2	344·3

Surplus on Current Budget (in £1bn.).

1997–98 Outturn	1998–99 Estimate	1999–2000 Forecast
−5·1	4·1	2·0

Departmental Expenditure Limits (Current Budget, in £1bn.).

	1997–98 Estimate	1998–99 Estimate	1999–2000 Planned
Education and Employment	14·0	13·7	14·5
Health	35·1	37·6	39·9
Environment, Transport and the Regions	35·2	36·5	38·3
Home Office	6·2	6·6	7·4
Legal Departments	2·6	2·6	2·7
Defence	20·1	20·9	20·8
Foreign and Commonwealth Office	1·0	1·0	1·0
International Development	1·9	2·1	2·0
Trade and Industry	2·7	2·7	2·9
Agriculture, Fisheries and Food	1·4	1·2	1·1
Culture, Media and Sport	0·8	0·8	0·9
Social Security (administration)	3·4	3·5	3·3
Scotland	11·5	11·7	12·2
Wales	5·6	5·9	6·3
Northern Ireland	4·9	5·2	5·3
Chancellor's Department	2·7	2·9	3·0
Cabinet Office	0·8	1·2	1·2

Performance. Real GDP growth in 1997 was 3·1%. Depending on an improvement in labour market performance, GDP was forecast to grow 2–2·5% in 1998. The outlook for exports in the traded goods sector was problematic, with the effect of sterling's 25% appreciation compounded by financial developments in Asia. Consumer spending was forecast to grow 3·75–4% in 1998. Growth in 1999 was projected at 1·75–2·25%. The savings ratio is assumed to decline to 9% by 2000.

Currency. The unit of currency is the *pound sterling* (£; GBP) of 100 *pence* (p.). (Before decimalization on 15 Feb. 1971 £1 = 20 shillings (*s*) of 12 pence (*d*). A gold standard was adopted in 1816, the sovereign or twenty-shilling piece weighing 7·98805 grammes 0·916²/₃ fine. Currency notes for £1 and 10*s*. were first issued by the Treasury in 1914, replacing the circulation of sovereigns. The issue of £1 and 10*s*. notes was taken over by the Bank of England in 1928. 10*s*. notes were withdrawn in 1970 and £1 notes (in England and Wales) in 1988. The UK is a member of the EU European Monetary System (EMS), but on 16 Sept. 1992 it suspended its membership of the Exchange Rate Mechanism (ERM), which it had entered on 8 Oct. 1990.

Inflation. Inflation was 2·8% in Dec. 1998 (3·6% in Dec. 1997). The average annual inflation rate over the period 1990–96 was 3·3%.

The Treasury envisaged in March 1999 that the inflation target, set for the retail price index less mortgage interest payments (RPIX), will be met for both the final quarters of 1999 and 2000. In 1999, RPIX inflation will dip below the target of 2·5% as import prices remain weak and domestically generated inflation moderates. However, the Treasury expected import prices to recover gradually in the latter part of 1999, offsetting the reduction in home-grown inflation.

Coinage. Coins in circulation at 31 Dec. 1997: £1, 1,142m.; 50p, 581m.; 20p, 1,687m.; 10p, 1,464m.; 5p, 3,216m.; 2p, 4,609m.; 1p, 7,496m.

Banknotes. The Bank of England issues notes in denominations of £5, £10, £20 and £50 up to the amount of the fiduciary issue. Under the provisions of the Currency Act 1983 the amount of the fiduciary issue is limited, but can be altered by direction of HM Treasury on the advice of the Bank of England. Since Nov. 1998 the limit has been £34,300m.

All current series Bank of England notes are legal tender in England and Wales. Some banks in Scotland (Bank of Scotland, Clydesdale Bank and the Royal Bank of Scotland) and Northern Ireland (Bank of Ireland, First Trust Bank, Northern Bank and Ulster Bank) have note-issuing powers.

The total amount of Bank of England notes issued at 30 Dec. 1998 was £25,730m., of which £25,722m. represented notes with other banks and the public, and £8m. notes in the Banking Department of the Bank of England.

Foreign exchange reserves in Jan. 1998 were US$27,001m. and gold reserves 18·42m. troy oz.

Banking and Finance. The Bank of England, Threadneedle Street, London, is the Government's banker and the 'banker's bank'. It has the sole right of note issue in England and Wales and manages the National Debt. It was founded by Royal Charter in 1694 and nationalized in 1946. The capital stock has, since 1 March 1946, been held by HM Treasury. The *Governor* (appointed for 5-year terms) is Eddie George (b. 1938; took office 1993).

The statutory Bank Return is published weekly. End-Dec. figures for the past 4 years are as follows (in £1m.):

	Notes in circulation	Notes and coin in Banking Department	Public deposits (government)	Other deposits[1]
1995	21,717	3	1,281	5,281
1996	22,609	11	203	5,691
1997	24,100	10	223	9,750
1998	25,722	8	229	8,022

[1]Including Special Deposits.

The value of paper-based credit transfers for 1993 was 432·2m. (volumes); of paperless credit transfers, 935·7m. (volumes); of direct debits, 1,046m. (volumes).

Major British Banking Groups' statistics at 31 Dec. 1998: Total deposits (sterling and currency), £901,176m.; sterling market loans, £179,877m.; market loans (sterling and currency), £255,765m.; advances (sterling and currency), £586,180m.; sterling investments, £56,196m.

In 1996 there were 520 overseas banks from 76 countries.

In May 1997 the power to set base interest rates was transferred from the Treasury to the Bank of England. The government continues to set the inflation target but the bank has responsibility for setting interest rates to meet the target. Base rates are now set by a 9-member Monetary Policy Committee at the Bank; members include the Governor. Membership of the Court (the governing body) was widened. Responsibility for supervising banks was transferred from the Bank to the Financial Services Authority (FSA).

National Savings Bank. Statistics for 1996 and 1997 (provisional):

	Ordinary accounts		Investment accounts	
	1996	*1997*	*1996*	*1997*
Accounts opened at 31 Dec.	16,039,050[1]	16,086,719[1]	4,507,525	4,361,992
Amounts—	*in £1,000*	*in £1,000*	*in £1,000*	*in £1,000*
Received	647,040	651,609	1,508,928	1,378,885
Interest credited	32,976[2]	30,302[2]	499,566	494,753
Paid	688,491	703,170	1,846,771	2,106,729
Due to depositors at 31 Dec.	1,410,308	1,389,049	9,468,900	9,236,809
Average amount due to each depositor (in £1)	£87·93	£86·35	£2,100·69	£2,117·56

[1]Excluding non-computerized accounts, amounting to £102m. in 1996 and £103m. in 1997. [2]The interest credited to depositors for the Ordinary account for 1997 was calculated on the same basis as 1996. The interest rate was increased during the year; from 2·5% to 3·0%, payable to accounts with a minimum balance of £500, and from 1·5% to 2·0% on accounts with a minimum balance of less than £500. Interest is earned on each whole pound on deposit for complete calendar months.

The amount due to depositors on Ordinary Accounts on 1 Jan. 1998 was £1,416,556,595 and in Investment Accounts £9,220,546,660.

There are stock exchanges in Belfast, Birmingham, Glasgow and Manchester which function mainly as representative offices for the London Stock Exchange (called International Stock Exchange until May 1991). In July 1991 the 91 shareholders voted unanimously for a new memorandum and articles of association which devolves power to a wider range of participants in the securities industry, and replaces the Stock Exchange Council with a 14-member board.

Roberts, R. and Kynaston, D. (eds.) *The Bank of England: Money, Power and Influence, 1694– 1994.* OUP, 1995

Weights and Measures. Conversion to the metric system, which replaced the imperial system, became obligatory on 1 Oct. 1995. The use of the pint for milk deliveries and bar sales, and use of miles and yards in road signs, is exempt indefinitely, and the use of the pound (weight) in selling greengrocery is exempt until 1999.

ENERGY AND NATURAL RESOURCES

Electricity. The Electricity Act of 1989 implemented the restructuring and transfer to the private sector of the electricity supply industry.

The Office of Electricity Regulation ('Offer') was set up under the Act to protect consumer interests following privatization.

Generators. Under the provisions of the 1989 Electricity Act, National Power and PowerGen took over the fuel-fired and hydro-electric power stations, and were privatized in 1991. Nuclear Electric, responsible for operating the 12 nuclear power stations, and Scottish Nuclear, were merged as a single holding company in 1996 with 2 new operating subsidiaries, Magnox Electric and British Energy. These were privatized in 1996. Under licence, generating companies may also be involved in electricity supply.

A levy (Non-Fossil Fuel Obligation) is being imposed on generators until 1998 to fund the decommissioning of ageing nuclear plant and finance renewable energy sources, mainly wind generation, which in 1995 supplied 2% of demand.

Suppliers. The 12 Area Electricity Boards were replaced under the 1989 Electricity Act by 12 successor companies which were privatized in 1990. These are Eastern

Electricity; East Midlands Electricity; London Electricity; Manweb; Midlands Electricity; Northern Electric; NORWEB; SEEBOARD; Southern Electric; SWALEC; South Western Electricity; Yorkshire Electricity. The companies are responsible for maintaining and operating their local distribution networks, and have a statutory duty to supply electricity to their tariff customers. Their main business, therefore, is in electricity supply. Some of the companies are involved in the retailing of electrical goods and electrical contracting. Some have diversified into other business activities.

The *Electricity Association* is the trade association of the UK electricity companies, providing a forum for members to discuss matters of common interest, a collective voice for the electricity industry when needed, and specialist research and professional services. It publishes an annual *Electricity Industry Review*, which contains detailed information on the development of the industry during the previous year.

The National Grid Company is responsible for operating the transmission system and for co-ordinating the operation of power stations connected to it. The company also operates the cross-Channel link with France and the interconnection with the Scottish power system.

In Scotland there are 3 main electricity companies. ScottishPower and Scottish Hydro-Electric are vertically integrated companies carrying out generation, transmission, distribution and supply of electricity within their areas. Scottish Nuclear, responsible for operating the 2 Scottish nuclear power stations, was merged with Nuclear Electric in 1996.

The electricity industry contributes about 1·7% of the UK's Gross Domestic Product. The installed capacity of all UK power stations as at the end of March 1998 was 72,498 MW. 34% of electricity generated was coal-fired, 25% was nuclear, 30% was gas and 2% was hydro-electric and other renewables. Imports accounted for the remaining 9%. 301,300 GWh were supplied to 27m. customers in 1997, of which domestic users took 35%, industrial users 31% and commercial and other users 34%. The net total electricity supplied in 1997 was 317,486 GWh. The average domestic consumption per capita in 1997 was 4,250 kWh.

Electricity Association. *Electricity Industry Review.* Annual

Surrey, J. (ed.) *The British Electricity Experience: Privatization – the Record, the Issues, the Lessons.* London, 1996

Oil and Gas. Production in 1,000 tonnes, in 1997: Throughput of crude and process oils, 97,024; refinery use, 6,572. Refinery output: Gases, 2,089; naphtha, 2,854; motor spirit, 28,260; kerosene, 11,678; diesel oil, 28,778; fuel oil, 11,747; lubricating oils, 1,231; bitumen, 2,258. Total output of refined products, 90,366. Crude oil production, 128·2m. tonnes. Estimated production, 1997, 2,634,349 bbls. a day. The UK had proven oil reserves of 5·2bn. bbls. in Dec. 1997.

The reform of the old nationalized gas industry began with the Gas Act of 1986, which paved the way for the privatization later that year of the British Gas Corporation, and established the Director General of Gas Supply (DGSS) as the independent regulator. This had a limited effect on competition, as Britsh Gas retained a monopoly on tariff (domestic) supply. Competition progressively developed in the industrial and commercial (non-tariff) market.

The Gas Act 1995 amended the 1986 Act to prepare the way for full competition, including the domestic market. It created 3 separate licences—for Public Gas Transporters who operate pipelines, for Shippers (wholesalers) who contract for gas to be transported through the pipelines, and for Suppliers (retailers) who then market gas to consumers. It also placed the DGSS under a statutory duty to secure effective competition.

The domestic market was progressively opened to full competition from 1996 until May 1998. Over 2m. customers have taken the opportunity to change supplier.

In 1997 British Gas took a commercial decision to de-merge its trading business. Centrica plc (a new company) was formed to handle the gas sales, gas trading, services and retail businesses of BG, together with the gas production businesses of the North and South Morecambe Field. The remaining parts of the business, including transportation and storage and the international downstream activities, remain part of BG plc.

In 1998 a new Director General of Gas Supply (Callum McCarthy) was appointed for a 5-year term. In recognition of the increasing convergence between the gas and

GREAT BRITAIN

electricity markets, he was also appointed as Director General of Electricity Supply from Jan. 1999.

A European Directive introducing rules for the internal market in natural gas entered into force in Aug. 1998 (98/80/EC). Member states have 2 years to give effects to its provisions. A pipeline linking the UK and European gas grids opened in Oct. 1998. It has an export capacity of 20bn. cu. metres a year and an import capacity of 8·5bn. cu. metres a year.

Gas reserves are some 765,000m. cu. metres. Production was 1,000,700 GWh in 1997, 39% of which was used by domestic users and 27% by electricity generators.

The *Office of Gas Supply ('Ofgas')* is the regulator charged with protecting gas consumers' interests.

Wind. In 1997 there were 55 wind farms with a capacity of 132·29 MW for electricity generation.

Water. The Water Act of Sept. 1989 privatized the 10 water authorities in England and Wales: Anglian; North West; Northumbrian; Severn Trent; South West; Southern; Thames; Welsh; Wessex; Yorkshire. The Act also inaugurated the National Rivers Authority, with environmental and resource management responsibilities, and the 'regulator' *Office of Water Services ('Ofwat')*, charged with protecting consumer interests.

In Scotland water supply is the responsibility of the Regional and Island local authorities. 7 river purification boards are responsible for environmental management.

Minerals. Legislation to privatize the coal industry was introduced in 1994 and a new Coal Authority has taken over from British Coal. The Coal Authority is the owner of coal reserves; it licenses private coal-mining and deals with claims in former mining areas and disposes of unworked assets. In 1995 there were 15 British Coal collieries and 32 large deep mines in the private sector, employing some 13,500 mineworkers. Total production from deep mines was 32·2m. tonnes in 1996 (35·2m. in 1995). 91 opencast sites were operating in 1996. Output, 1996, 16·3m. tonnes; 1995, 16·4m. tonnes. In 1996 inland coal consumption was 71·4m. tonnes, of which 54·9m. tonnes was used by electricity generators, 8·6m. tonnes by coke ovens and 2·7m. tonnes by domestic consumers.

Output of non-fuel minerals in Great Britain, 1996 (in 1,000 tonnes): Limestone, 82,442; sandstone, 12,581; igneous rock, 43,731; clay and shale, 11,804; industrial sand, 4,861; chalk, 9,239; china clay, 2,654; sand and gravel, 81,997.

Steel and metals. There were 33 steel furnaces in 1997. Steel production in recent years (in 1m. tonnes):

1993	16·6
1994	17·3
1995	17·6
1996	18·0
1997	18·5
1998	17·3

Deliveries of finished steel products from UK mills in 1998 were worth £7bn. in product sales and comprised 8·6m tonnes to the UK domestic market and 8·0m. tonnes for export. About two-thirds of UK steel exports go to other EU countries. Exports have grown from 20% of total mill output to nearly 50% over the last 20 years. UK steel imports in 1998 were about 6·9m. tonnes. The UK steel industry's main markets are construction (31%), automotive (21%), engineering (17%) and metal goods (14%). British Steel is the UK's largest steel producer (and the fourth largest steel company in the world) and produces about 85% of UK crude steel. The UK steel industry has improved productivity nearly 5-fold over the past 20 years and invests about £350m. a year on new technology and a further £65m. a year on employee training and development.

Agriculture. Land use in 1996: Agriculture, 77%; urban, 10%; forests, 10%; other, 3%. In 1996 (and 1995) agricultural land in the UK totalled (in 1,000 ha) 18,401 (18,406), comprising common grazing, 1,237 (1,248), and agricultural holdings, 17,164 (17,158). Land use of the latter (in 1,000 ha): All grasses 6,665 (6,697); crops, 4,721 (4,544); rough grazing, 4,489 (4,516); bare fallow, 35 (40); other, 745

UNITED KINGDOM OF GREAT BRITAIN AND NORTHERN IRELAND

(729). Area sown to crops (in 1,000 ha): Cereals, 3,357 (3,180); other arable crops, 1,003 (1,005); horticultural crops, 189 (187); fruit, 40 (40).

Farmers receiving financial support under the EU's Common Agricultural Policy are obliged to 'set-aside' land in order to control production. In 1995 such set-aside totalled 633,000 ha (728,000 ha in 1994).

The number of workers employed in agriculture in the UK was, in June 1995 (in 1,000), 243·4. Of these, 159·4 (12·9 females) were engaged full-time, 56·2 (24·3 females) part-time, and 84 (27·2 females) were seasonal or casual workers. In addition, there were in 1995, 170,000 full-time and 112,000 part-time farmers, partners, directors, and 75,000 of their spouses, engaged in farm work. There were some 234,900 farm holdings in 1995, about 66% owner-occupied. Average size of holdings, 72·4 ha.

Agriculture accounts for 1% of GDP, 7·3% of exports and 11·4% of imports.

Area given over to principal crops in the UK (1996 figures are provisional):

	Wheat	Barley	Oats	Potatoes	Sugar beet	Oilseed rape
			Area (1,000 ha)			
1993	1,759	1,164	92	170	197	377
1994	1,811	1,106	109	164	195	404
1995	1,859	1,192	112	171	196	354
1996	1,976	1,267	96	177	199	356

Production of principal crops in the UK (1996 figures are provisional):

	Wheat	Barley	Oats	Potatoes	Sugar beet	Oilseed rape
		Total product (1,000 tonnes)				
1993	12,890	6,038	479	7,065	9,666	1,100
1994	13,314	5,945	597	6,531	8,720	1,253
1995	14,310	6,834	617	6,398	8,431	1,235
1996	16,102	7,784	589	7,220	9,555	1,410

Horticultural crops. 1996 output (in 1,000 tonnes): Cabbage, 353; carrots, 617; onions, 288; tomatoes, 116; apples, 223·5; soft fruit, 80·6.

Livestock in the UK as at June in each year (in 1,000):

	1992	1993	1994	1995	1996
Cattle	11,804	11,729	11,834	11,733	11,913
(dairy)	(2,682)	(2,667)	(2,175)	(2,602)	(2,587)
(beef)	(1,699)	(1,751)	(1,775)	(1,805)	(1,829)
Sheep	43,998	43,901	43,295	42,771	41,530
Pigs	7,609	7,754	7,797	7,534	7,496
Poultry	124,013	130,175	125,718	125,981	...

Livestock products, 1996 (1,000 tonnes): Hens' eggs, 554; poultry meat, 1,532; beef and veal, 813; mutton and lamb, 501; pork, 968; bacon and ham, 502; milk, 13,950m. litres (1995).

In March 1996 the Government acknowledged the possibility that bovine spongiform encephalopathy (BSE) might be transmitted to humans as a form of Creutzfeldt-Jakob disease via the food chain. Cases of BSE in cattle in the UK: 1988, 1,954; 1989, 6,955; 1990, 13,042; 1991, 22,939; 1992, 35,269; 1993, 37,020; 1994, 26,087; 1995, 15,600. British beef has been widely banned overseas. Government preventive measures include bans on sales of older meat and the use of meat in animal feed and fertilizer, and compensation schemes.

Forestry. The area under forests in Britain in 1996–97 was 2·42m. ha. On 31 March 1997 the area of productive woodland was 2,212,000 ha, of which the Forestry Commission managed 795,000 ha and the private sector 1,417,000 ha. The Forestry Commission employed 6,650 staff in 1995. In addition a further 10,400 were employed in private forestry, with an estimated 11,215 engaged in the wood-processing industry. In 1995 a total of 8·7m. cu. metres of roundwood was produced.

New planting (1996–97), 16,900 ha (500, Forestry Commission; 16,400, private woodlands).

Forestry Commission. *Forestry Facts and Figures.* Annual
James, N. D. G., *A History of English Forestry.* London, 1981

Fisheries. Quantity (in 1,000 tonnes) and value (in £1,000) of fish of British taking, landed in Great Britain (excluding salmon and sea-trout):

Quantity	1991	1992	1993	1994	1995
Wet fish	477·7	505·6	536·2	576·5	601·0
Shell fish	84·6	108·0	102·5	111·1	124·6
	562·3	613·7	638·7	687·6	725·6
Value					
Wet fish	310,042	309,470	317,800	326,720	333,174
Shell fish	86,427	95,743	107,163	127,746	145,035
	396,469	405,213	423,963	454,466	478,209

In Dec. 1996 the fishing fleet comprised 8,073 registered vessels. Major fishing ports: (England) Fleetwood, Grimsby, Hull, Lowestoft, North Shields; (Wales) Milford Haven; (Scotland) Aberdeen, Mallaig, Lerwick, Peterhead.

In the period 1991–93 the average person in the UK consumed nearly 19 kg of fish and fishery products a year, compared to the European Union average of just over 22 kg.

INDUSTRY

In 1995 there were 156,310 manufacturing firms, of which 475 employed 1,000 or over persons, and 110,350, 9 or fewer. 1996 output (in 1,000 tonnes): Fertilizers, 2,688; cement, 11,287; man-made fibres, 183·7; woollen yarn, 62·6; cars, 1,686,134 units; bricks, 3,046m.; cotton, 83m. metres.

Engineering. Manufacturers' sales (in £1m.) for 1996 (and 1995): Motor vehicles, 20,760 (20,440); railway and tramway vehicles, 1,011 (911); lifting and handling equipment, 2,531 (2,310); earth-moving equipment, 897 (898); agricultural tractors, 1,124 (949); machine tools, 1,823 (1,688).

Electrical Goods. Manufacturers' sales (in £1m.) for 1996 (and 1995): Radio and electronic capital goods, 2,051 (2,144); domestic electrical appliances, 1,984 (1,874); telephone and telegraph apparatus and equipment, 2,854 (2,514); lighting equipment, 1,186 (1,048).

Foodstuffs, etc. Manufacturers' sales (in £1m.) for 1996 (and 1995): Meat production and preservation, 3,811 (3,855); fish processing and preservation, 1,486 (1,308); cocoa, chocolate and sugar confectionery, 3,195 (3,024); tea and coffee, 1,496 (1,426); beer, 2,976 (2,940); tobacco products, 2,588 (2,420).

Textiles. Manufacturers' sales (in £1m.) in 1996 (and 1995): Preparation and spinning, 1,596 (1,412); weaving, 1,323 (1,341); carpets, 1,183 (1,096); men's outerwear and underwear, 1,570 (1,510); women's outerwear and underwear, 2,711 (2,776).

Wood products, furniture, pulp and paper. Manufacturers' sales (in £1m.) in 1996 (and 1995): Wood products except furniture, 4,354 (3,955); furniture of whatever construction, 6,568 (6,325); paper and paper board, 4,112 (4,075); containers, 3,524 (3,414); stationery, 1,022 (983).

Chemicals. Manufacturers' sales, (in £1m.) in 1996 (and 1995): Dyes, 1,250 (1,134); other inorganic chemicals, 1,560 (1,358); organic chemicals, 4,532 (4,849); fertilizers, 933 (930); primary plastics, 4,166 (4,257); pesticides, 1,646 (1,562); paints, etc., 2,569 (2,771); pharmaceuticals, 5,987 (5,768); soap, polish and detergents, 2,318 (2,247); rubber products, 3,159 (2,909).

Construction. Total value (in £1m.) of constructional work in Great Britain in 1994 (and 1995) was 49,439 (52,643), including new work, 25,086 (26,672), of which housing, 7,417 (7,135).

Labour. In June 1997 the UK workforce (i.e. all persons in employment plus the claimant unemployed) totalled (in 1,000) 28,107 (12,592 females), of whom 26,507 (12,215 females) were in employment, 22,792 (11,285 females) as employees, 3,338 (851 females) as self-employed and 210 (15 females) in HM Forces. UK employees by form of employment in 1997 (in 1,000): Agriculture, forestry and fishing, 279; energy and water supply, 148; manufacturing industry, 4,106; construction, 885;

wholesale and retail trade, repair of motor vehicles, motor cycles and household goods, 3,930; hotels and restaurants, 1,307; transport and communications, 1,328; finance, 1,031; estate agency, 2,929; public administration and defence, compulsory social security, 1,362; education, 1,852; health and social work, 2,566. Registered unemployed in UK as at July (in 1,000; figures adjusted for seasonality and discontinuities): 1992, 2,723 (634); 1993, 2,912 (674); 1994, 2,632; 1995, 2,311; 1996, 2,126; 1997, 1,545. In Dec. 1996 the Government headline unemployment figure was 1,884,700. In Dec. 1992, 955,600 persons (165,200 females) had been unemployed for more than a year. In July 1997 there were 285,000 vacancies at Jobcentres.

In 1998 there were 3·7m. businesses in the UK of which 1·32m. were registered at Companies House. 12,000 were public limited companies and just 2,450 had their shares listed on the Stock Exchange. The sector comprising the most companies was property and business services with 23·3% of the total number, followed by retail with 13·1%, construction 10·6% and production 10·1%. Over 200,000 new companies were created in 1998, up from just 100,000 in 1984.

Workers (in 1,000) involved in industrial stoppages (and working days lost): 1992, 148 (0·53m.); 1993, 385 (0·69m.); 1994, 107 (0·28m.); 1995, 174 (0·42m.); 1996, 364 (1·3m.).

The Wages Councils set up in 1909 to establish minimum rates of pay (in 1992 of 2·5m. workers) were abolished in 1993. The Labour Government, elected in May 1997, was committed to the introduction of a National Minimum Wage and established a Low Pay Commission to advise on its implementation. It was fixed at £3.20 an hour in 1999.

Trade Unions. In Jan. 1998 there were 76 unions affiliated to the Trades Union Congress (TUC) with a total membership of 6,754,245 (6,756,544 in 1997) (2·6m. of them women). The unions affiliated to the TUC in 1998 ranged in size from UNISON with 1·3m. members, to the Sheffield Wool Shear Workers' Union with 11 members. The 4 largest unions, however, account for more than half the total membership. In 1997, 61% of public-sector employees and 21% of private-sector employees were unionized. 46% of employees were in workplaces where trade unions were recognized for collective bargaining.

The TUC's executive body, the General Council, is elected at the annual Congress. Congress consists of representatives of all unions according to the size of the organization, and is the principal policy-making body.

The General Secretary (John Monks, b. 1945) is elected by the Congress but is not subject to annual re-election. The TUC draws up policies and promotes and publicizes them. It makes representations to government, employers and international bodies. The TUC also carries out research and campaigns, and provides a range of services to unions including courses for union representatives.

The TUC is affiliated to the International Confederation of Free Trade Unions, the Trade Union Advisory Committee of OECD, the Commonwealth Trade Union Council and the European Trade Union Confederation. The TUC provides a service of trade union education. It provides members to serve, with representatives of employers, on the managing boards of such bodies as the Health and Safety Commission and the Advisory, Conciliation and Arbitration Service.

Clegg, H. A., *A History of British Trade Unions since 1889* [until 1951]. 3 vols. Oxford, 1994
Pelling, H., *A History of British Trade Unionism.* 5th ed. London, 1992.
Willman, P. et al., *Union Business: Trade Union Organization and Financial Reform in the Thatcher Years.* CUP, 1993

INTERNATIONAL TRADE

Imports and Exports. Value of the imports and exports of merchandise, excluding bullion and specie (in US$1m.):

	Total imports	Total exports
1996	23,930·7	21,850·2
1997	25,611·4	23,410·6
1998	26,156·0	22,572·3

Until 1992 all overseas trade statistics were compiled from Customs declarations. With the inception of the Single Market on 1 Jan. 1993, however, the requirement for Customs declarations in intra-EU trade was removed.

GREAT BRITAIN

In 1998 the UK's trade with non-EU countries was: Imports, US$12,202·6m.; exports, US$9,559·3m. (1997 figures were imports US$12,015·6m. and exports US$10,510·9m.).

In 1996 other European Union members accounted for 51·2% of the UK's foreign trade, compared with 25·2% in 1956. Asia accounted for 14·2%, down from 21·3% in 1956, the USA 12·4%, up from 9·1% in 1956, and the rest of the world 22·2%, down from 44·4% in 1956.

Figures for trade by countries and groups of countries (in US$1m.):

	Imports from		Exports to	
EU countries	1997	1998	1997	1998
EU	13,395·8	13,953·4	12,899·7	13,013·0
Austria	188·3	187·7	153·4	161·4
Belgium and Luxembourg	1,242·3	1,305·3	1,137·5	1,148·6
Denmark and Faroe Islands	315·1	293·8	280·6	275·6
Finland	350·3	326·4	211·2	195·4
France	2,421·8	2,424·1	2,236·4	2,239·6
Germany	3,504·9	3,473·2	2,771·2	2,804·2
Greece	53·8	49·4	141·4	141·8
Ireland	987·8	1,066·8	1,241·8	1,298·1
Italy	1,289·3	1,331·5	1,109·6	1,174·7
Netherlands	1,675·1	1,854·3	1,876·1	1,767·4
Portugal, Azores and Madeira	238·3	245·3	236·2	233·4
Spain	692·9	794·9	908·3	975·6
Sweden	635·8	600·7	596·1	597·1
Other foreign countries	*1997*	*1998*	*1997*	*1998*
Europe—				
Baltic States	88·5	83·4	35·1	37·3
Czech Republic	64·2	79·6	96·8	98·6
Hungary	66·3	77·1	59·5	69·0
Iceland	33·2	36·6	21·7	22·6
Norway	670·9	500·1	363·0	377·8
Poland	84·8	94·4	185·0	166·9
Romania	28·0	32·2	29·0	32·6
Russia	202·2	202·3	168·4	128·9
Slovakia	10·0	10·4	18·1	14·5
Switzerland and Liechtenstein	668·9	696·7	412·6	412·2
Turkey	142·5	160·9	241·3	221·8
Other in Europe	95·7	106·1	205·5	193·9
Africa—				
Algeria	11·6	11·3	12·3	15·6
Egypt	36·8	40·1	68·0	70·4
Morocco	47·3	50·7	48·8	48·3
Nigeria	16·8	19·3	58·2	64·7
South Africa	192·3	199·9	225·1	214·0
Tunisia	8·1	10·6	14·5	14·0
Other in Africa	210·1	198·3	251·9	220·3
Asia and Oceania—				
Australia	187·6	197·1	335·0	310·0
China	340·8	408·8	125·7	119·8
Hong Kong	593·8	637·4	438·7	372·2
Japan	1,284·5	1,318·3	570·4	443·1
Korea (South)	305·7	318·1	166·7	94·2
India	221·6	200·7	215·1	173·4
Indonesia	140·4	133·4	95·7	52·6
Malaysia	276·6	275·4	164·4	94·2
New Zealand	78·9	74·8	55·6	47·8
Pakistan	51·8	49·4	36·6	31·9
Philippines	103·8	124·2	81·9	41·9
Singapore	370·4	340·2	278·9	222·6
Taiwan	319·6	321·7	141·4	120·8

	Imports from		Exports to	
Asia and Oceania (contd)—	*1997*	*1998*	*1997*	*1998*
Other in Asia and Oceania	186·9	167·8	154·2	92·8
Middle East—				
Iran	5·0	5·0	54·0	46·6
Israel	120·0	126·8	160·9	150·3
Kuwait	27·4	25·6	68·7	46·3
Saudi Arabia	136·0	123·3	519·1	370·9
United Arab Emirates	70·4	77·2	211·4	215·5
Other Middle East	32·6	40·0	223·0	167·7
America—				
Argentina	36·8	28·8	66·5	63·6
Brazil	130·3	128·3	140·5	125·5
Canada	348·7	359·6	294·3	300·4
Chile	53·7	47·9	28·7	23·7
Colombia	25·3	28·8	23·2	24·4
Mexico	52·2	52·2	58·5	72·4
USA	3,431·5	3,557·9	2,916·7	2,999·8
Venezuela	21·4	16·9	27·9	33·8
Other in America	151·8	150·0	147·8	151·0
Total, foreign countries (including some not specified above)	25,611·4	26,156·0	23,410·6	22,572·3

In 1998 machinery and transport equipment accounted for 44·8% of the UK's imports and 47·8% of exports; chemicals, manufactured goods classified chiefly by material and miscellaneous manufactured articles 40·5% of imports and 40·2% of exports; food, live animals, beverages and tobacco 8·9% of imports and 6·2% of exports; crude materials, inedible, animal and vegetable oil and fats 3·3% of imports and 1·5% of exports; and mineral fuels, lubricants and related materials 2·5% of imports and 4·2% of exports.

COMMUNICATIONS

Roads. Responsibility for the construction and maintenance of trunk roads belongs to central government (in England, the Department of Transport; in Wales the Welsh Office; and in Scotland the Scottish Office). Roads not classified as trunk roads are the responsibility of county or unitary councils.

In 1996 there were 368,820 km of public roads, classified as: Motorways, 3,225 km; trunk roads, 12,359 km; principal roads, 35,856 km; others, 317,380 km.

Motor vehicles for which licences were current at 31 Dec. 1996, numbered (in 1,000) 26,302, including 21,172 private cars, 609 mopeds, scooters and motor cycles, 77 public transport vehicles and 413 goods vehicles. The average distance travelled by a passenger car in the year 1995 was 15,000 km. New vehicle registrations in 1996, 2,410. Driving tests, 1996 (in 1,000): Applications, 1,741·3; tests held, 1,685·4; tests passed, 748·4; pass rate, 44%. The driving test was extended in 1996 to include a written examination.

Road casualties in Great Britain, 1994, 315,189 including 3,650 killed; in 1995, 310,506 including 3,621 killed; in 1996, 320,302 including 3,598 killed (the lowest figure since records began in 1926).

Inter- and intra-urban bus and coach journeys average 44,000m. passenger-km annually. Passenger journeys by public road transport, 1994–95, 5,050m., including 4,420m. by local bus services. For London buses *see* London Transport *under* RAILWAYS, *below.*

Rail. In 1994 the nationalized railway network was restructured to allow for privatization. Ownership of the track, stations and infrastructure was vested in a government-owned company, Railtrack, which was privatized in May 1996.

Passenger operations were reorganized into 25 train-operating companies, wholly owned subsidiaries of the British Railways Board, and all had been transferred to the private sector by Feb. 1997. These pay Railtrack for access to the rail network, and lease their rolling stock from 3 private-sector companies. All freight operations have

GREAT BRITAIN

also now been privatized. Eurotunnel PLC holds a concession from the government to operate the Channel Tunnel (49·4 km), through which vehicle-carrying and Eurostar passenger trains are run in conjunction with French and Belgian railways. A new dedicated high-speed line is planned to connect the Channel Tunnel to London St Pancras. This line will be used by both international and domestic trains. Construction is being undertaken in 2 sections and the line should be completed in 2007.

In 1997 total route length was 16,666 km (5,176 km electrified). For the year 1997–98, passenger journeys totalled 845·7m. (34,200m. passenger km). Freight moved in 1997–98 amounted to 16·9bn. freight tonne-km, an increase of 12% over the previous year.

London Transport is responsible to the Secretary of State for the Environment, Transport and the Regions for the operations of the capital's metro, London Underground, and for the planning and procurement of bus services. In 1998, London Underground, its wholly owned subsidiary, carried 2·8m. passengers a day to and from 267 stations (including 21 managed by Railtrack) on 12 lines. Some 6,000 buses, run under contract to London Transport by independent companies, carried 3·8m. passengers a day on some 800 routes.

The privately franchised Docklands Light Railway is operated in east inner London.

There are metros in Glasgow and Newcastle, and light rail systems in Manchester and Sheffield.

Civil Aviation. All UK airports handled a total of more than 114·6m. passengers during 1997. Of those, 82·8m. were handled by London area airports (Heathrow, Gatwick, London City, Luton and Stansted). The busiest airport in 1996 was Heathrow, which handled 55,731,864 passengers (48,275,300 on international flights) and 1,040,486 tonnes of freight. Gatwick was the second busiest, with 24,101,735 passengers (22,028,832 on international flights) and 267,326 tonnes of freight. More international passengers use Heathrow than any other airport in the world.

Following the Civil Aviation Act 1971, the Civil Aviation Authority (CAA) was established as an independent public body responsible for the economic and safety regulation of British civil aviation. A CAA wholly owned subsidiary, National Air Traffic Services, operates air traffic control. Highlands and Islands Airports Ltd is owned by the Scottish Office and operates 8 airports.

Operating and traffic statistics of UK airlines on scheduled services during the calendar year 1997 (and 1996): Aircraft–km flown, 809m. (735m.); revenue passengers carried, 56·3m. (51·1m.); cargo (freight and mail) carried 782,855 (690,806) tonnes. Air transport movements between UK airports and international destinations in 1997 (and 1996) on all services totalled 1,081,605 (1,019,267).

There were 15,594 civil aircraft registered in the UK at 31 Dec. 1997.

British Airways is the largest UK airline, with a total of 226 aircraft at 31 Dec. 1997. It operates long- and short-haul international services, as well as an extensive domestic network. British Airways also has franchise agreements with other UK operators: British Mediterranean, British Regional Airways, Brymon Airways, City Flyer Express, GB Airways, Loganair and Maersk Air. Other airlines operating scheduled flights in 1997 (with numbers of aircraft): Air Belfast (3); Air UK (39); British Midland Airways (33); British World Airlines (19); Channel Express (13); Jersey European Airways (18); Manx and British Regional Airways (40); Monarch Airlines (17); Virgin Atlantic Airways (20). In 1997 British Airways flew 478·67m. km and carried 29,466,683 passengers (24,273,681 on international flights). British Midland flew 44·91m. km in 1997 and carried 5,671,971 passengers (3,152,072 on international flights). British Airways carried more passengers on international flights in 1997 than any other airline.

Shipping. The UK-owned merchant fleet (trading vessels over 100 GT) in June 1998 totalled 617 ships of 10·1m. DWT and 7·7m. GT. The UK-owned and registered fleet totalled 347 ships of 2·2m. DWT.

The average age of the UK-owned fleet was 17·8 years, while that of the world fleet was 14·3 years. Total gross international revenue in 1997 was £4,815m. The net contribution to the UK balance of payments was £910m.; there were import savings of £1,247m., giving a total contribution of £2,157m. The container and roll-on-roll-off (RoRo) shipping sectors are the leading revenue earners. The net output of the UK water transport sector was £1·9bn. in 1996.

The principal ports are (with 1m. tonnes of cargo handled in 1997): London (55·7), Grimsby and Immingham (48·0), Forth (43·1), Milford Haven (34·5), Southampton (33·1), Sullom Voe (32·1), Liverpool (30·8), Felixstowe (28·9), Dover (19·1), Medway (13·8), Port Talbot (13·1), Belfast (12·3), Orkneys (10·5) and Hull (10·0). All ports in the UK carried 558·5m. tonnes.

Inland Waterways. There are approximately 3,500 miles of navigable canals and river navigations in Great Britain. Of these, the publicly-owned British Waterways (BW) is responsible for some 385 miles (620 km) of commercial waterways (maintained for freight traffic) and some 1,160 miles (1,868 km) of cruising waterways (maintained for pleasure cruising, fishing and amenity). BW is also responsible for a further 450 miles (732 km) of canals, some of which are not navigable. BW's external turnover for the year to 31 March 1997 was £46·8m. This comprised principally: Freight Activities (£2·1m.), Leisure (£10·9m.), the Estate (£19·5m.) and Water Charges (£3·4m.). Additionally, British Waterways was in receipt of Department of the Environment grants of £51·8m.

River navigations and canals managed by other authorities include the Thames, Great Ouse and Nene, Norfolk Broads and Manchester Ship Canal.

Telecommunications. In 1997 there were 148 licensed telecommunications operators: 125 cable operators, 19 national and regional public telecommunications operators and 4 mobile telephone (cellular) operators. Fixed-link telephone services were offered by BT, Mercury Communications, Kingston Communications (Hull), most of the cable operators and the public telecommunications operators. BT (then British Telecom) was established in 1981 to take over the management of telecommunications from the Post Office. In 1984 it was privatized as British Telecommunications plc, changing its trading name from British Telecom to BT in 1991.

In 1998, all of the BT system was served by digital exchanges. Almost 3·5m. km of optical fibre have been installed. In 1997 there were 31,878,000 main telehone lines (equivalent to 540 peer 1,000 population). In 1996, 76% of the lines were residential and 24% business. There were 138,000 public payphones, 200,000 private rented payphones and 20,000 UK telex connections in 1996. BT handles a daily average of 103m. telephone calls a day and 22m. calls to emergency fire, police or ambulance services a year. In 1995 there were 1·8m. fax receivers. Electronic services include electronic mail ('email') and a complete corporate global messaging network. BT telephone, television and business services are carried by 15–20 satellites. In 1995 BT had some 20 offices worldwide and employed 137,561 persons.

In 1997 there were more than 7m. mobile telephone users.

Telecommunications services are regulated by OFTEL in the interests of consumers.

Internet. In Oct 1998 there were 7·5m. Internet users in the UK, or nearly 13% of the total population. 42% of users were at home and 38% at work. In 1995 there were 10·9m. PCs (186 per 1,000 persons) and by 1999 around 27% of homes in the UK had a PC.

Postal Services. The Post Office operates as a group of 4 distinct businesses: Royal Mail (letter delivery), Parcelforce Worldwide (parcel delivery), Post Office Counters Ltd (retailing and agency services) and SSL (telemarketing). Every area of the country is served by regional offices for each of the businesses. Royal Mail collects and delivers 75m. letters a day to the 26m. UK addresses. Other services include electronic mail, guaranteed mail deliveries (same-day and overnight to UK addresses), and Swiftair deliveries to 140 other countries and territories. The British Postal Consultancy Service provides advice to administrations abroad.

In 1998 there were almost 19,000 post offices, over 600 operated directly by The Post Office, the remainder (sub-post offices) on a franchise or agency basis; and 120,000 posting points. Staff numbered 193,000 in 1997–98. 18·4bn. letters were posted in 1997–98.

The Post Office has a monopoly on the carriage of letters within the UK, but the government has suspended this, subject to a minimum delivery charge of £1, and licensed mail transferred between document exchanges. Private services are permitted to handle door-to-door deliveries subject to the minimum fee of £1.

SOCIAL INSTITUTIONS

Justice. England and Wales. The legal system of England and Wales, divided into civil and criminal courts has at the head of the superior courts, as the ultimate court of appeal, the House of Lords, which hears each year a number of appeals in civil matters, including a certain number from Scotland and Northern Ireland, as well as some appeals in criminal cases. In order that civil cases may go from the Court of Appeal to the House of Lords, it is necessary to obtain the leave of either the Court of Appeal or the House itself, although in certain cases an appeal may lie direct to the House of Lords from the decision of the High Court. An appeal can be brought from a decision of the Court of Appeal or the Divisional Court of the Queen's Bench Division of the High Court in a criminal case provided that the Court is satisfied that a point of law 'of general public importance' is involved, and either the Court or the House of Lords is of the opinion that it is desirable in the public interest that a further appeal should be brought. As a judicial body, the House of Lords consists of the Lord Chancellor, the Lords of Appeal in Ordinary, commonly called Law Lords, and such other members of the House as hold or have held high judicial office. The final court of appeal for certain of the Commonwealth countries is the Judicial Committee of the Privy Council which, in addition to Privy Counsellors who are or have held high judicial office in the UK, includes others who are or have been Chief Justices or Judges of the Superior Courts of Commonwealth countries.

Civil Law. The main courts of original civil jurisdiction are the High Court and county courts.

The High Court has exclusive jurisdiction to deal with specialist classes of case e.g. Judicial Review. It has concurrent jurisdiction with county courts in cases involving contract and tort although it will only hear those cases where the issues are complex or important. The High Court also has appellate jurisdiction to hear appeals from lower tribunals.

The judges of the High Court are attached to one of its 3 divisions: Chancery, Queen's Bench and Family; each with its separate field of jurisdiction. The Heads of the 3 divisions are the Lord Chief Justice (Queen's Bench), the Vice-Chancellor (Chancery) and the President of the Family Division. In addition there are 99 High Court judges (92 men and 7 women). For the hearing of cases at first instance, High Court judges sit singly. Appellate jurisdiction is usually exercised by Divisional Courts consisting of 2 (sometimes 3) judges, though in certain circumstances a judge sitting alone may hear the appeal. High Court business is dealt with in the Royal Courts of Justice and by over 130 District Registries outside London.

County courts can deal with all contract and tort cases, and recovery of land actions, regardless of value. They have upper financial limits to deal with specialist classes of business such as equity and Admiralty cases. Certain county courts have been designated to deal with family, bankruptcy, patents and discrimination cases.

There are about 260 county courts located throughout the country each with its own district. A case may be heard by a Circuit Judge or by a District Judge, (the latter generally being restricted to cases valued at £5,000 or less). County courts have a small claims jurisdiction for actions for money worth £3,000 or less; this is an informal procedure where parties are encouraged to present cases without the need for legal representation.

The Restrictive Practices Court was set up in 1956 under the Restrictive Trade Practices Act and is responsible for deciding whether a restrictive trade agreement is in the public interest. It is presided over by a High Court judge, but laymen sit on the bench also. Another specialist court is the Employment Appeal Tribunal, with similar composition, which hears appeals in employment cases from lower tribunals.

The Court of Appeal (Civil Division) hears appeals in civil actions from the High Court and county courts, and certain special courts such as the Restrictive Practice Court and Employment Appeal Tribunal. Its President is the Master of the Rolls, aided by up to 35 Lords Justices of Appeal (as at 1 Jan. 1999) sitting in 6 or 7 divisions of 2 or 3 judges each.

Civil proceedings are instituted by the aggrieved person, but as they are a private matter, they are frequently settled by the parties through their lawyers before the matter comes to trial. In very limited classes of dispute (e.g. libel and slander), a party may request a jury to sit to decide questions of fact and the award of damages.

Criminal Law. At the base of the system of criminal courts in England and Wales are the magistrates' courts which deal with over 97% of criminal cases. In general, in exercising their summary jurisdiction, they have power to pass a sentence of up to six months imprisonment and to impose a fine of up to £5,000 on any one offence. They also deal with the preliminary hearing of cases triable at the Crown Court. In addition to dealing summarily with over 2·3m. cases, which include thefts, assaults, drug abuse, etc, they also have a limited civil and family jurisdiction.

Magistrates' courts normally sit with a bench of 3 lay justices. Although unpaid they are entitled to loss of earnings and travel and subsistence allowance. They undergo training after appointment and they are advised by a professional justices' clerk. In central London and in some provincial areas full-time stipendiary magistrates have been appointed. Generally they possess the same powers as the lay bench, but they sit alone. On 1 Jan. 1999 the total strength of the lay magistracy was 30,260 including 14,699 women. Justices are appointed on behalf of the Queen by the Lord Chancellor, except in Greater Manchester, Merseyside and Lancashire, where they are appointed by the Chancellor of the Duchy of Lancaster.

Justices are selected and trained specially to sit in Youth and Family Proceedings Courts. Youth Courts deal with cases involving children and young persons up to the age of 18 charged with criminal offences (other than homicide and other grave offences). These courts normally sit with 3 justices, including at least one man and one woman, and are accommodated separately from other courts.

Family Proceedings Courts deal with matrimonial applications, Children Act matters, including care, residence and contact and adoption. These courts normally sit with three justices including at least one man and one woman.

Above the magistrates' courts is the Crown Court. This was set up by the Courts Act 1971 to replace quarter sessions and assizes. Unlike quarter sessions and assizes, which were individual courts, the Crown Court is a single court which is capable of sitting anywhere in England and Wales. It has power to deal with all trials on indictment and has inherited the jurisdiction of quarter sessions to hear appeals, proceedings on committal of persons from the magistrates' courts for sentence, and certain original proceedings on civil matters under individual statutes.

The jurisdiction of the Crown Court is exercisable by a High Court judge, a Circuit judge or a Recorder or Assistant Recorder (part-time judges) sitting alone, or, in specified circumstances, with justices of the peace. The Lord Chief Justice has given directions as to the types of case to be allocated to High Court judges (the more serious cases) and to Circuit judges or Recorders respectively.

Appeals from magistrates' courts go either to a Divisional Court of the High Court (when a point of law alone is involved) or to the Crown Court where there is a complete re-hearing on appeals against conviction and/or sentence. Appeals from the Crown Court in cases tried on indictment lie to the Court of Appeal (Criminal Division). Appeals on questions of law go by right, and appeals on other matters by leave. The Lord Chief Justice or a Lord Justice sits with judges of the High Court to constitute this court. Thereafter, appeals in England and Wales can be made to the House of Lords.

There remains as a last resort the invocation of the royal prerogative exercised on the advice of the Home Secretary. In 1965 the death penalty was abolished for murder.

All contested criminal trials, except those which come before the magistrates' courts, are tried by a judge and a jury consisting of 12 members. The prosecution or defence may challenge any potential juror for cause. The jury decides whether the accused is guilty or not. The judge is responsible for summing up on the facts and explaining the law; he sentences convicted offenders. If, after at least 2 hours and 10 minutes of deliberation, a jury is unable to reach a unanimous verdict it may, on the judge's direction, provided that in a full jury of 12 at least 10 of its members are agreed, bring in a majority verdict. The failure of a jury to agree on a unanimous verdict or to bring in a majority verdict may involve the retrial of the case before a new jury.

GREAT BRITAIN

The Employment Appeal Tribunal. The Employment Appeal Tribunal which is a superior Court of Record with the like powers, rights, privileges and authority of the High Court, was set up in 1976 to hear appeals on questions of law against decisions of employment tribunals and of the Certification Officer. The appeals are heard by a High Court Judge sitting with 2 members (in exceptional cases 4) appointed for their special knowledge or experience of industrial relations either on the employer or the trade union side, with always an equal number on each side. The great bulk of their work is concerned with the problems which can arise between employees and their employers.

Military Courts. Offences committed by persons subject to service law under the Army Act 1955, the Air Force Act 1955 or the Naval Discipline Act 1957 may be dealt with either summarily or by courts-martial.

The Personnel of the Law. All judicial officers are independent of Parliament and the Executive. They are appointed by the Crown on the advice of the Prime Minister or the Lord Chancellor, and hold office until retiring age. Under the Judicial Pensions and Retirement Act 1993 judges normally retire by age 70 years.

The legal profession is divided; barristers, who advise on legal problems and can conduct cases before all courts, usually act for the public only through solicitors, who deal directly with the legal business brought to them by the public and have rights to present cases before certain courts. The distinction between the 2 branches of the profession has been weakened since the passing of the Courts and Legal Services Act 1990, which has enabled solicitors to obtain the right to appear as advocates before all courts. Long-standing members of both professions are eligible for appointment to most judicial offices.

For all judicial appointments up to and including the level of Circuit Judge (except for Recordership, which is achieved on promotion from assistant Recordership), it is necessary to apply in writing to be considered for appointment. Vacancies are advertised. A panel consisting of a judge, an official and a lay member decide whom to invite for interview and also interview the shortlisted applicants. They make recommendations to the Lord Chancellor, who retains the right of final recommendation to the Sovereign or appointment, as appropriate.

Legal Aid. Broadly there are 3 kinds of legal aid available in England and Wales. Firstly there is legal advice and assistance, otherwise known as the 'Green Form' scheme. This includes advice and assistance on almost any question of English law, both civil and criminal, but does not normally cover any form of representation before a court or tribunal. Qualification for 'Green Form' is dependent on the means of the applicant. As an extension of the scheme, however, assistance by way of representation is available for certain proceedings, chiefly family matters, in magistrates' courts. Assistance by way of representation is also means-tested. In 1997–98 there were 1·6m. payments under the Legal Advice and Assistance Scheme. The net cost to the Legal Aid Fund of this part was £186·4m., of which £12·2m. was accounted for by assistance by way of representation. Legal advice and assistance also provides for duty solicitor schemes at magistrates' courts and police stations. Under the magistrates' courts scheme, initial advice, and representation where necessary, is available to unrepresented defendants at court from duty solicitors either in attendance at courts or on call. The scheme covers advice to a defendant in custody, making a bail application, representing a defendant in custody on a guilty plea, and certain other cases. The advice and assistance at police stations scheme enables any person who has been arrested and taken to a police station, or who is assisting the police with their enquiries, to receive advice and assistance, from either a duty solicitor or the person's own solicitor. The cost of these schemes, which are not subject to means test or contribution, is met from the Legal Aid Fund and in 1997–98 amounted to £115·1m. Secondly, under Part IV of the Legal Aid Act 1988, there is legal aid for civil court proceedings. Under regulations, aid is available to those of low or moderate means either free or subject to a contribution, depending on means. In 1997–98, 319,432 civil legal aid certificates were issued. The cost of legal aid is met from *(a)* contributions from assisted persons; *(b)* the operation of the statutory charge which gives the Legal Aid Board a first charge on money or property recovered or preserved for an assisted person; *(c)* costs recovered from opposing parties and *(d)* a grant from the Exchequer. The net cost of civil legal aid to the state (excluding administration costs of the scheme) in 1997–98 amounted to £634m. Thirdly under Part V of the Legal Aid Act 1988 a court dealing with criminal proceedings may order legal aid to be given if it considers it is desirable in the interests of justice and if it also considers that the defendant (or appellant) requires financial assistance in meeting the costs he or she may incur. The factors to be taken into account when determining whether it is in the interests of justice that criminal legal aid be granted are defined by statute to include cases where, for example, the defendant is likely to be deprived of his or her liberty, consideration of a substantial question of law may be involved, or the defendant may be unable to understand the proceedings or to state his or her case due to inadequate knowledge of English, mental illness or other mental or physical disability. Legal aid must be granted, subject to means, in the following circumstances: Where a person is committed for trial on a charge of murder, where the prosecutor appeals or applies for leave to appeal from the criminal division of the Court of Appeal or the Courts-Martial Appeal Court to the House of Lords, and in certain circumstances where the court is considering depriving a defendant of his liberty.

The costs of legal aid in criminal proceedings are paid by the central government, but courts have power to require legally aided persons to contribute towards the cost of legal aid given to them. The net cost of legal aid in criminal proceedings in 1997–87 was £591m. Of this total, £349m. was for legal aid in the higher courts which is paid for out of the Lord Chancellor's vote, and £242m. for legal aid in the magistrates' courts which is paid from the Legal Aid Fund.

Legislation is currently before Parliament (the Access to Justice Bill) which will bring changes to legal aid. The proposed reforms will create a Legal Services Commission, which will replace the Legal Aid Board. The Commission will establish a Community Legal Service which will fund civil and family cases, and a Criminal Defence Service for all criminal matters.

Police. In England and Wales, excluding London, there are 41 police forces each maintained by a police authority typically comprising 9 local councillors, 3 magistrates and 5 independent members. London is policed by the Metropolitan Police Service (responsible to the Home Secretary) and the City of London Police. In April 1995 the Home Office gave up central control of police manpower and authorized establishments of police no longer exist. Instead, chief constables recruit according to their budgets. The Home Office collates police strength in March and Sept. each year. Provisional figures show that the total strength of the police service in England and Wales at 30 Sept. 1998 was 126,266 (including 19,876 women). In addition there were 17,296 special constables (including 5,965 women). The net total revenue expenditure on the police service for 1997–98 was £6,870m.

See also SCOTLAND.

CIVIL JUDICIAL STATISTICS

ENGLAND AND WALES	1995	1996
Appellate Courts		
Judicial Committee of the Privy Council	82	80
House of Lords	72	65
Court of Appeal	1,853	1,804
High Court of Justice (appeals and special cases from inferior courts)	4,674	4,891
Courts of First Instance (excluding Magistrates' Courts and Tribunals)		
High Court of Justice:		
Chancery Division	42,251	40,500
Queen's Bench Division	154,186	143,033
Official Referee's	1,804	1,564
County courts: Matrimonial suits	178,196	181,467
County courts: Other	2,472,637	2,363,017
Restrictive Practices Court	2	6

CRIMINAL STATISTICS

ENGLAND AND WALES

	Total number of offenders		Indictable offences	
	1996	1997	1996	1997
Aged 10 and over				
Proceeded against in magistrates' courts	1,919,494	1,855,333	464,677	486,701

	Total number of offenders		Indictable offences	
	1996	1997	1996	1997
Aged 10 and over				
Found guilty at magistrates' courts	1,368,942	1,312,479	233,854	249,171
Found guilty at the Crown Court	69,085	73,343	66,726	70,881
Cautioned	286,198	282,093	190,811	189,359
Aged 10 and under 18				
Proceeded against in magistrates' courts	119,937	122,595	74,813	75,635
Found guilty at magistrates' courts	71,184	74,809	40,991	42,133
Found guilty at the Crown Court	3,491	4,342	3,392	4,225
Cautioned	113,065	104,520	79,858	73,712

In 1997 the average prison population in England and Wales was 61,114 (55,281 in 1996).

See also SCOTLAND.

Religion. The Anglican Communion has originated from the Church of England and parallels in its fellowship of autonomous churches the evolution of British influence beyond the seas from colonies to dominions and independent nations. The Archbishop of Canterbury presides as *primus inter pares* at the decennial meetings of the bishops of the Anglican Communion at the Lambeth Conference and at the biennial meetings of the Primates and the Anglican Consultative Council. The last Conference was held in Canterbury in 1998 and was attended by 743 bishops.

The Anglican Communion consists of 41 member Churches or Provinces. These are: The Anglican Church of Aotearoa, New Zealand and Polynesia; The Anglican Church of Australia; The Church of Bangladesh; The Episcopal Anglican Church of Brazil; The Church of the Province of Burundi; The Anglican Church of Canada; The Church of the Province of Central Africa; The Anglican Church of the Central America Region; The Church of Ceylon (Sri Lanka) Extra Provincial; The Province of the Anglican Church of the Congo; The Church of England; Hong Kong Sheng Kung Hui; The Church of the Province of the Indian Ocean; The Church of Ireland; The Holy Catholic Church in Japan; The Episcopal Church in Jerusalem and the Middle East; The Church of the Province of Kenya; The Anglican Church of Korea; The Church of the Province of Melanesia; The Anglican Church of Mexico; The Church of the Province of Myanmar (Burma); The Church of the Province of Nigeria; The Church of North India; The Church of Pakistan; The Anglican Church of Papua New Guinea; The Philippine Episcopal Church; The Lusitanian Church of Portugal; The Province of the Episcopal Church of Rwanda; The Scottish Episcopal Church; The Spanish Reformed Episcopal Church; The Church of the Province of South East Asia; The Church of the Province of Southern Africa; The Anglican Church of the Southern Cone of America; The Church of South India; The Episcopal Church of the Sudan; The Church of the Province of Tanzania; The Church of the Province of Uganda; The Episcopal Church in the United States of America; The Church in Wales; The Church of the Province of West Africa; and The Church in the Province of the West Indies. There are Extra Provincial Dioceses of Bermuda, Cuba, Puerto Rico and Venezuela, and new provinces are also currently in formation. Churches in Communion include the Mar Thoma Syrian Church, the Philippine Independent Church, and some Lutheran and Old Catholic Churches in Europe. The Church in China is known as a 'post denominational' Church whose formation included Anglicans in the Holy Catholic Church in China.

England and Wales. The established Church of England, which baptizes about 25% of the children born in England (i.e. excluding Wales but including the Isle of Man and the Channel Islands), is Anglican. Civil disabilities on account of religion do not attach to any class of British subject. Under the Welsh Church Acts, 1914 and 1919, the Church in Wales and Monmouthshire was disestablished as from 1 April 1920, and Wales was formed into a separate Province.

The Queen is, under God, the supreme governor of the Church of England, with the right, regulated by statute, to nominate to the vacant archbishoprics and bishoprics. The Queen, on the advice of the First Lord of the Treasury, also appoints to such deaneries, prebendaries and canonries as are in the gift of the Crown, while a large number of livings and also some canonries are in the gift of the Lord Chancellor.

There are 2 archbishops (at the head of the 2 Provinces of Canterbury and York), and 42 diocesan bishops including the bishop of the diocese in Europe, which is part of the Province of Canterbury. Dr George Carey was enthroned as *Archbishop of Canterbury* in April 1991. Each archbishop has also his own particular diocese, wherein he exercises episcopal, as in his Province he exercises metropolitan, jurisdiction. In Dec. 1997 there were 68 suffragan and assistant bishops, 40 deans and provosts of cathedrals and 110 archdeacons. The *General Synod*, which replaced the Church Assembly in 1970 in England, consists of a House of Bishops, a House of Clergy and a House of Laity, and has power to frame legislation regarding Church matters. Each House has a veto over the others. The first two Houses consist of the members of the Convocations of Canterbury and York, each of which consists of the diocesan bishops and elected representatives of the suffragan bishops, 6 for Canterbury province and 3 for York (forming an Upper House); deans, provosts, and archdeacons, and a certain number of proctors elected as the representatives of the inferior clergy, together with, in the case of Canterbury Convocation, 4 representatives of the Universities of Oxford, Cambridge, London and the Southern Universities, and in the case of York 2 representatives for the Universities of Durham and Newcastle and the other Northern Universities, and 3 archdeacons to the Armed Forces, the Chaplain General of Prisons and 2 representatives of the Religious Communities (forming the Lower House). The House of Laity is elected by the lay members of the Deanery Synods but also includes 3 representatives of the Religious Communities and *ex-officio* appointed members of the Archbishops' Council, Church Commissioners and Ecclesiastical Judges. Every Measure passed by the General Synod must be submitted to the Ecclesiastical Committee, consisting of 15 members of the House of Lords nominated by the Lord Chancellor and 15 members of the House of Commons nominated by the Speaker. This committee reports on each Measure to Parliament, and the Measure receives the Royal Assent and becomes law if each House of Parliament resolves that the Measure be presented to the Queen.

Parochial affairs are managed by annual parochial church meetings and parochial church councils. At 30 June 1996 there were 12,982 ecclesiastical parishes, inclusive of the Isle of Man and the Channel Islands. These parishes do not, in many cases, coincide with civil parishes. Although most parishes have their own churches, not every parish nowadays can have its own incumbent or priest. Over 2,000 non-stipendiary clergy hold a bishop's licence to officiate at services.

In Dec. 1997 there were 5,590 beneficed clergy excluding dignitaries, 1,881 other clergy of incumbent status and 1,661 assistant curates working in the parishes.

Women have been admitted to Holy Orders (but not the Episcopate) as deacons since 1987 and as priests since 1994. At 31 Dec. 1997 there were 919 full-time stipendiary women clergy, 871 of whom were in the parochial ministry. In July 1995 the General Synod stated that 304 clergymen had left the Church of England because they disagreed with the ordination of women, and that perhaps 75% of these had joined the Roman Catholic Church.

Private persons possess the right of presentation to over 2,000 benefices; the patronage of the others belongs mainly to the Queen, the bishops and cathedrals, the Lord Chancellor, and the colleges of the universities of Oxford and Cambridge. In addition to the dignitaries and parochial clergy already identified there were, in 1997, 119 cathedral and 285 non-parochial clergy working within the diocesan framework, giving a total of 9,798 full-time stipendary clergy working as at Dec. 1997. Although these figures account for the majority of active clergy in England, there are many others serving in parishes and institutions who cannot be quantified with any certainty. They include some 1,300 full-time hospital, Forces, prison, industrial, and school and college chaplains.

Of the 40,397 buildings registered for the solemnization of marriages at 30 June 1994, (statistics from the Office of Population Censuses and Surveys) 16,538 belonged to the Established Church and the Church in Wales, and 23,859 to other religious denominations (Methodist, 6,739; Roman Catholic, 3,331; Baptist, 3,109; United Reformed, 1,689; Congregational, 1,264; Calvinistic Methodist, 1,093; Jehovah's Witnesses, 786; Brethren, 744; Salvation Army, 737; Unitarians, 165; other Christian, 3,857; Sikhs, 129; Moslems, 90; other non-Christian, 126). Of the 283,012 marriages celebrated in 1995 (291,069 in 1994), 83,685 were in the

GREAT BRITAIN

Established Church and the Church in Wales, 43,837 in other denominations, and 155,490 were civil marriages in Register Offices.

Roman Catholics in England and Wales were estimated at 4,174,418 in 1997. There are 22 dioceses in 5 provinces. There are 5 archbishops, 17 diocesan bishops and 8 auxiliary or assistant bishops. There are 5,178 priests in active ministry and 2,843 parish churches. There are 1,295 convents of female religious, who number 9,655.

Membership of other denominations in the UK in 1991 (and 1975): Presbyterians, 1,291,672 (1·65m.); Methodists, 483,387 (0·61m.); Baptists, 241,842 (0·27m.); other Protestants, 123,677; independent churches, 408,999; Orthodox, 265,258 (0·2m.); Afro-Caribbean churches, 69,658; Latter-day Saints (Mormons) (1997), 170,500; Jehovah's Witnesses, 0·12m.; Spiritualists, 60,000; Moslems, 0·99m. (0·4m.); Sikhs, 0·39m. (0·12m.); Hindus, 0·14m. (0·1m.); Jews, 108,400 (0·11m.).

The Salvation Army is established in 94 countries. In 1991 in the UK and Ireland it had 1,792 ministers, 55,000 members and 837 churches.

There is a 400-member Board of Deputies of British Jews.

There were approximately 2·5m. visits to Westminster Abbey in 1997, 2m. to both St Paul's Cathedral and York Minster, and 1·6m. to Canterbury Cathedral.

See also SCOTLAND.

Bradley, I., *Marching to the Promised Land: Has the Church a Future?* London, 1992.
De La Noy, M., *The Church of England: a Portrait.* London, 1993.

Education. (England and Wales). *The Publicly Maintained System of Education:* Compulsory schooling begins at the age of 5 and the minimum leaving age for all pupils is 16. No tuition fees are payable in any publicly maintained school (but it is open to parents, if they choose, to pay for their children to attend other schools). The post-school or tertiary stage, which is voluntary, includes universities, further education establishments and other higher education establishments (including those which provide courses for the training of teachers), as well as adult education centres and the youth service. Financial assistance (grants and loans) is generally available to students on higher education courses in the university and non-university sectors, and to some students on other courses in further education.

National Curriculum. The Education Reform Act 1988 established a National Curriculum for gradual introduction into primary and secondary schools. It was revised in 1995. Statutory subjects at 5 to 11 years: English (and Welsh in Wales), mathematics, science (core subjects); design and technology, information technology, geography, history, physical education, art and music. At 11 to 14 years a foreign language is added. Statutory subjects at 14 to 16: English, mathematics, science, technology, a foreign language and physical education. Religious education and, at secondary level, sex education, are not prescribed in the curriculum but are requirements; parents may withdraw their children from these lessons. Careers education is also statutory at secondary level.

Nursery Education. Provision for children under 5 is made in either nursery schools or in nursery or infant classes in primary schools. In the public sector no fees are payable.

Primary Schools. These provide for pupils from the age of 5 up to the age of 11. In 1997–98 there were 23 pupils per teacher at primary schools in the United Kingdom as a whole.

Middle Schools. A number of local education authorities operate a middle school system. These provide for pupils from the age of 8, 9 or 10 up to the age of 12, 13 or 14.

Secondary Schools. These usually provide for pupils from the age of 11 upwards. In Jan. 1998 there were 3,190 secondary schools in England and 229 in Wales. In England some local authorities have retained selection at age 11 for entry to grammar schools, of which there were 157 in 1998. There were a small number of technical schools in 1998 which specialise in technical studies. There were 113 secondary modern schools in 1998 providing a general education up to the minimum school leaving age of 16, although exceptionally some pupils stay on beyond that age.

Almost all local education authorities operate a system of comprehensive schools to which pupils are admitted without reference to ability or aptitude. In Jan. 1997 there were 2,882 such schools in England with over 2·6m. pupils. With the development of comprehensive education, various patterns of secondary schools have come into operation. Principally these are: 1) All-through schools with pupils aged 11 to 18 or 11 to 16; pupils over 16 being able to transfer to an 11 to 18 school or a sixth form college providing for pupils aged 16 to 19. (There were 115 sixth form colleges in England in 1992). 2) Local education authorities operating a three-tier system involving middle schools where transfer to secondary school is at ages 12, 13 or 14. These correspond to 12 to 18, 13 to 18 and 14 to 18 comprehensive schools respectively. 3) In areas where there are no middle schools a two-tier system of junior and senior comprehensive schools for pupils aged 11 to 18, with optional transfer to these schools at age 13 or 14.

Grant Maintained Schools. Local education authority maintained secondary, middle and primary schools can apply for Grant Maintained (GM) status as self-governing state schools. Under GM status, schools receive funding directly from the Funding Agency for Schools or, in Wales, from the Welsh Office. Their governing bodies are responsible for all aspects of school management, including the deployment of funds, employment of staff and provision of most of the educational support services for staff and pupils. The first GM primary schools were incorporated in 1991.

Specialist Schools. Technology Colleges, Language Colleges, Art Colleges and Sports Colleges. A programme to help existing maintained secondary schools to specialize in a particular area of the curriculum, while continuing to cover the full National Curriculum. To be included in the programme, schools must raise sponsorship and then prepare development plans, in competition with other schools, to seek extra government funding. They must demonstrate how they will share their resources and expertise with local schools and the wider community. The first Technology Colleges operated from Sept. 1994. By Sept. 2001 the government expect there to be 500 Specialist Schools.

City Technology Colleges. 15 independent all-ability secondary schools established in partnership between government and business sponsors, under the Education Reform Act 1988. They teach the full National Curriculum but give special emphasis to technology, science and mathematics. Government meets all recurrent costs.

Assisted Places Scheme. The Government is phasing out the assisted places scheme and is using the money saved to reduce infant class sizes in the maintained sector. The Education (Schools) Act 1997, which came into force on 1 Sept. 1997, has the effect of preventing any further intakes to assisted places after the start of the 1997–98 school year. However, the Government has made a commitment to provide continued support for existing assisted pupils for the remainder of the current phase of their education. Children in receipt of secondary education will continue to hold their assisted places until the completion of their secondary education. Children in receipt of primary education will normally hold their place until the completion of their primary education.

Music and Ballet Scheme. The 'Aided Pupil Scheme' for boys and girls with outstanding talent in music or ballet helps parents with the fees and boarding costs at seven specialist private schools. This scheme provides a specialist provision not readily available in the maintained sector and will therefore continue to operate.

Special Education. Under the Education Act 1996 children have special educational needs if they have a learning difficulty which calls for special educational provision to be made for them. It has been estimated that, nationally, some 20% of the school population will have special educational needs at some time during their school career. In a minority of cases, perhaps just over 2% of children, the Local Education Authority will need to make a statutory assessment of special educational needs under the Education Act 1996, which may ultimately lead to a 'statement'.

The Education Act 1996 and regulations made thereunder build upon the principles and practices first set out in the 1981 Education Act. They place duties and responsibilities on Local Education Authorities and schools, and all those who help them work with children with special educational needs. Maintained schools must use their best endeavours to make provision for such pupils. The Code of Practice on the Identification and Assessment of Special Educational Needs, which came into force on 1 Sept. 1994, gives practical guidance to these bodies as to how they fulfill their duties. Provision for all children with special educational needs will be made by the most appropriate agency, which in most cases will be the child's mainstream school. The Code of Practice recognizes that there is a continuum of needs and a continuum of provision, which may be made in a variety of different forms. However, even before reaching statutory school age, a child may have special educational needs requiring the intervention of the Local Education as well as the Health Authority.

Some pupils with 'statements' remain in school after the age of 16. Local Education Authorities remain responsible for such pupils until they are 19. Others with statements leave school at 16, moving perhaps to a college within the further education sector, or to social services provision.

Ancillary Services. Local Education Authorities (LEAs) and the governing bodies of GM schools may provide registered pupils at schools maintained by them with meals, milk and other refreshment and make such charges as they think fit. However, they must charge the same price for the same quantity of the same item. It is for LEAs and GM schools to decide on the presentation and content of school meals. They must provide meals free of charge to pupils whose parents receive income support or income-based jobseekers' allowance, or to pupils who receive income support in their own right. Where LEAs or GM schools decide to provide milk, it must be free to these categories of pupils. The provision of free meals and milk must be made in the middle of the day.

Further Education (Non-University). The Further Education Funding Council (FEFC) is statutorily required to secure the provision of: sufficient facilities for the full-time education of 16–18 year olds; and adequate facilities for part-time education of those over 16; and for the full-time education of those over 18, where such education falls within schedule 2 of the Further and Higher Education Act 1992.

The Council funds further education at 435 further education (FE) sector colleges (including sixth form colleges) and certain other designated institutions. Provision of further education is also funded at other institutions that have been franchised or sponsored by FE sector colleges. In 1997–98 some 3·5m. students, funded by the FEFC, were attending colleges and institutions in England, studying for a total of 5·8m. qualifications.

Local education authorities are required to secure and keep under review the adequate provision of those categories of further education outside the Council's duty.

The Youth Service. The Youth Service forms part of the education system and is mainly concerned with the provision of personal and social education for young people to enable them to become responsible citizens. The Youth Service is chiefly provided by Local Education Authorities (the statutory sector) and a wide range of voluntary organizations. The priority age group for the service is usually regarded as 13-19 years old but this target age group extends to 11–25-year-olds. A duty is laid upon Local Education Authorities by the provision of the (Consolidation) Education Act 1996 which has superseded earlier Education Acts, to secure adequate provision of further education which includes the Youth Service. Provision is usually in the form of a wide range of leisure-time activities or through 'detached' or outreach work aimed at young people at risk. The Department for Education and Employment awards grants to the headquarters of national voluntary youth organizations through its Grant Scheme. The 1999–2000 Scheme has 2 main aims: to combat social exclusion and inequality through targeting priority groups; and to raise the standard and quality of youth work undertaken by youth organizations. Some 60 organizations are being funded to pursue approved programmes of work concerned with the social and personal education of young people, particularly those aged 13-19. The Scheme aims to widen access to the youth services especially for those who are disadvantaged, who have disabilities, who come from minority ethnic groups or inner city or rural areas, and for girls and young women. It also places priority on work which aims to contribute to crime prevention and health education, and to encourage the involvement of volunteers.

Independent/State School Partnerships Grant Scheme. The aim of this scheme is to promote collaborative working between the independent and state school sectors to raise standards in education. In its first year, 47 projects worth almost £600,000 were funded. £250,000 of this was provided by the Sutton Trust, an educational charity established to provide educational opportunities for young people from non-privileged backgrounds. A further £1·2m. is available for 1999–2001, including £200,000 from the Sutton Trust, and schools have been invited to apply for funding.

Awards to Students. Local Education Authorities in England and Wales are currently responsible for making mandatory awards to eligible students enrolled on designated full-time or sandwich courses leading to a first degree or comparable qualification, and on certain courses of initial teacher-training for existing students. These awards cover fees and maintenance but the maintenance grants are subject to the income of the student and his or her parents or spouse. For new students in 1998–99, awards to cover both fees (up to £1,000 a year) and maintenance will depend on income. In addition studentships may be available both from universities and other sources. The authorities may also give discretionary awards to students who are not eligible for mandatory awards including those taking non-degree level courses. In 1998–99 loans will form about three-quarters and grants about a quarter of the grant and loan package. Loans will not be available to help contribute towards tuition fees. Support for students through grants and loans rose in line with inflation, resulting in a 2·5% increase over the 1996–97 levels. In 1996–97 the Government provided further and higher education institutions with £27·7m. in Access Funds to help students with severe financial difficulties.

The Student Loans scheme was introduced by the Government in 1990 to supplement mandatory awards. Eligible students apply for loans to the Student Loans Company which is funded wholly by the Government. On leaving higher education former students begin to repay loans over a 5-year period when they reach an income threshold of 85% of average earnings. New students in 1998–99 will have new repayment arrangements once they have graduated and their income is at least £10,000 a year. They will begin to pay back their loans on an income-contingent basis. In the academic year 1997–98 about 64% of those estimated to be eligible took out a student loan; average loan was £1,530.

Awards known as state studentships are offered on a competitive basis by the British Academy and the Students Awards Agency for Scotland to candidates considered by the universities and other higher education institutions to be qualified for postgraduate studies in the humanities; similar awards, tenable at universities or other higher education institutions are offered by the Research Councils to students studying topics within the broad spectrum of agriculture and food; the biological sciences; man's natural environment; science and engineering, and the social sciences at postgraduate level.

In the academic year 1996–97, the latest year for which data are available, the 6 Research Councils made over 16,000 awards, of which 7,000 were new awards. In the same year the British Academy made almost 2,000 awards (of which just under half were new awards) and the Department for Education and Employment made almost 800 awards (of which just under 100 were new awards).

Career Development Loans (CDLs) were introduced by the Government in 1988 to provide wider opportunities for adults to acquire and improve vocational skills. The loans are aimed at those who would otherwise not have reasonable or adequate access to the funds required to train. Loans of between £300 and £8,000 can support up to 2 years of education or training, plus up to 1 year's practical work experience where it forms part of the course. Loans to pay for training are available through 4 high street banks (Barclays, The Co-operative, Clydesdale and the Royal Bank of Scotland). The Department of Education and Employment pays the interest on the loan for the period of the training and for 1 month afterwards. Borrowers may apply to the bank to defer payments for up to a further 18 months after completing their course if they are unemployed, employed and receiving certain benefits, or need to extend their training.

By March 1998 nearly £325m. had been advanced to over 102,000 applicants since the programme began.

Teachers. In order to teach in a maintained school or a non-maintained special school in England or Wales, it is first necessary to achieve qualified teacher status. This is generally achieved by successfully completing an undergraduate or postgraduate course of initial teacher training.

Those who are recognized as qualified teachers in Scotland or Northern Ireland are also entitled to qualified teacher status. Teachers who are nationals of participating member states of the European Economic Area who are recognized as qualified in their own countries may also be entitled to qualified teacher status if they meet the requirements on the mutual recognition of qualifications.

Those who have trained overseas in a country outside of the European Economic Area or candidates over 24 who have successfully completed two or more years of higher education may be eligible to train on the job through what are known as 'employment-based' routes. These are the Graduate Teacher Programme (for graduates) and the Registered Teacher Programme (for those with two years of higher education).

In 1997–98 there were about 53,700 students on initial teacher training courses; this figure includes students on the Open University and school-centred courses.

On 1 Jan. 1997, 420,908 full-time equivalent teachers were employed by Local Education Authorities in maintained (including grant-maintained) nursery, primary and secondary schools in England and Wales.

Finance. Total current and capital expenditure on education in England from public funds is estimated at £28,111m. for 1994–95. In 1993–94 total expenditure on education came to 5·2% of GDP.

See also SCOTLAND.

Independent Schools. All independent schools in England (and Wales) are required to be registered by the Department for Education and Employment (and the Welsh Office). Just over half of all independent schools belong to an association affiliated to the Independent Schools Council (ISC). Independent schools which belong to an association affiliated to the Independent Schools Council are now subject to a new inspection regime agreed between the Government and the ISC. These arrangements provide for inspections which are broadly comparable with the OFSTED framework for inspections of maintained schools and to the same 6-year cycle. They result in publicly available reports which enable parents and others to have information about the general quality and standards achieved in ISC schools. Independent schools which belong to an association account for approximately 80% of the total independent school pupil population. Non-association schools will continue to be inspected by HM inspectors from OFSTED on a 5–6 year cycle.

The earliest of the schools were founded by, and attached to, medieval churches. Many were founded as 'grammar' (classical) schools in the 16th century, receiving charters from the reigning sovereign. Reformed mainly in the middle of the 19th century, among the best-known are Eton College, founded in 1440 by Henry VI; Winchester College (1394), founded by William of Wykeham, Bishop of Winchester; Harrow School, founded in 1560 as a grammar school by John Lyon, a yeoman; and Charterhouse (1611). Among the earliest foundations are King's School, Canterbury, founded 600; King's School, Rochester (604) and St Peter's, York, (627).

Higher Education. Higher education has been through considerable changes over the last 30 years. There are now over 1·7m. students studying in higher education institutions in the UK; they study at 111 universities and 60 higher education colleges. The number of male and female students is roughly equal.

Total revenue for higher education institutions was around £11·1bn. in 1996–97. Approximately 63% of this comes from UK or European Union governments. Higher education institutions are funded by 4 UK funding bodies, one each for England, Scotland, Wales and Northern Ireland. They are responsible to Parliament for higher education. Their roles include: allocating funds for teaching and research; promoting high-quality education and research; advising Government on the needs of higher education; informing students about the quality of higher education available; and ensuring the proper use of public funds.

The *Open University* received its Royal Charter on 1 June 1969 and is an independent, self-governing institution, awarding its own degrees at undergraduate and postgraduate level. It is financed by the Government through the HEFCE and by the receipt of students' fees. Tuition is by means of correspondence textbooks, audio and video cassettes, radio and television broadcasts and, for some courses, residential schools and access to a personal computer. There are also 311 local study centres where face-to-face tutorials may be offered. No formal qualifications are required for entry to undergraduate courses. Residents from most countries of Western Europe aged 18 or over may apply, though some courses are not available outside the UK. There are over 130 undergraduate courses; many are available on a one-off basis. In 1998 there were over 112,000 undergraduates, and over 29,000 postgraduate level students, The university has some 3,000 full-time staff working at its Milton Keynes headquarters, and in 13 regional centres throughout the country. There are over 6,000 part-time associate lecturers.

One university is independent of the state system, the *University of Buckingham*, which opened in 1976 and received a Royal charter in 1983. It offers 2-year courses towards its own honours degrees, the academic year commencing in Jan. or July and consisting of four 10-week terms. There are 4 areas of study: Business; Humanities; Law; and Sciences. In 1999 there were 583 full-time and 45 part-time undergraduate students and 79 full-time and 14 part-time postgraduate students. There were 75 teachers (3 part-time).

All universities charge fees, but financial help is available to students from several sources (*see Awards to Students* above), and the majority of students receive some form of financial assistance.

The British Council. The British Council promotes cultural, educational and technical co-operation between Britain and other countries. Established in 1934 and incorporated by Royal Charter in 1940, it is Britain's principal agency for cultural relations overseas. An independent, non-political organization, it is represented in 109 countries, running a mix of offices, libraries, resource centres and English-teaching operations. Its headquarters are in London and Manchester, with further centres in Belfast, Cardiff and Edinburgh.

The British Council's total expenditure in 1997–98 was £413·9m. This was made up of government grants (£133·9m.), revenues from English-language teaching and client-funded education services (£141·3m.), and development programmes, principally in education and training, which are managed on behalf of the British Government and other clients (£136·0m.).

The purpose of the British Council is to enhance the reputation of the UK as a forward-looking democracy, to advance the use of the English language and to reinforce the country's role in the international community.

Chairman: Baroness Helena Kennedy QC.

Acting Director-General: Dr David Drewry.

Headquarters: 10 Spring Gdns., London, SW1A 2BN.

Donaldson, F., *The British Council: the First Fifty Years.* London, 1984.

Health. The National Health Service (NHS) in England and Wales started on 5 July 1948 under the National Health Service Act, 1946. There is a separate Act for Scotland.

The NHS is a charge on the national income in the same way, e.g., as the armed forces. Every person normally resident in the UK is entitled to use any complete part of the services, and no insurance qualification is necessary.

Since 1948 a weekly NHS contribution has been payable by employees and the self-employed. In 1957 this contribution was extended to employers. For convenience this contribution is collected with the National Insurance contribution and amounts to 1·05% of the latter for employees and 0·9% for employers. The NHS is funded 12·1% by these contributions, 82% by general taxation and 2·3% by charges for drugs and dental treatment, and the rest from other receipts. Health authorities may raise funds from voluntary sources; hospitals may take private, paying patients.

Organization. The National Health Service and Community Care Act, 1990, provided for a major restructuring of the NHS. From 1 April 1991 health authorities became the purchasers of healthcare, concentrating on their responsibilities to plan and obtain services for their local residents by the placement of health service contracts with the appropriate units. Day-to-day management tasks became the responsibility of hospitals and other units, with whom the contracts are placed, in their capacity as providers of care.

In April 1996 the Regional Health Authorities were replaced by 8 regional offices of the NHS Executive. The District Health Authorities and Family Health Service Authorities were replaced by comprehensive Health Authorities directly financed by central governments Hospital and Community Health Services funds. The budget for 1996–97 was £2,260m.

The key responsibility of Health Authorities is to ensure that the health needs of their local communities are met. They have the purchasing power to commission hospital and community health services for their residents. In doing so they have a duty to ensure that high standards are maintained and that they are securing the best possible value for money.

The Health Authorities manage the Family Doctor (or General Medical) Service and also organize the general dental, pharmaceutical and ophthalmic services for their areas. Any doctor may take part in the Family Doctor Service, and are paid for their NHS work; they may also take private fee-paying patients.

NHS Trusts are established as self-governing units within the NHS. Trusts are responsible for the ownership and management of the hospitals or other establishments or facilities vested in them, and for carrying out the individual functions set out in their establishment orders. In April 1996 there were 520 Trusts, representing most hospitals.

General practitioners (GPs) may apply for fundholding status, responsible for their own NHS budget for a specified range of goods and services. There are 2 types of fundholder: Standard fundholders for practices with at least 5,000 patients in England and 4,000 in Wales and Scotland, who purchase the full range of in- and out-patient services; and Community fundholders, for smaller practices of at least 3,000 patients, who purchase only community nursing services and diagnostic tests. In 1996 there were some 14,000 fundholding GPs in 3,300 practices, covering 47% of the population.

Services. The NHS broadly consists of hospital and specialist services, general medical, dental and ophthalmic services, pharmaceutical services, community health services and school health services. All these services are free of charge except for such things as prescriptions, spectacles, dental and optical examination, dentures and dental treatment, amenity beds in hospitals, and for some of the community services, for which charges are made with certain exemptions.

The total cost of the NHS was estimated at £42,600m. for 1996–97.

In 1996 there were 26,855 GPs in England with an average of 1,885 patients each, 1,736 in Wales with 1,724 patients and 3,573 in Scotland with 1,488. There were 15,280 general dental practitioners in England, 834 in Wales and 1,772 in Scotland. In hospitals in Great Britain, in 1996, there were 59,592 medical staff and 356,109 nurses and midwives (excluding agency staff). In 1996 provision of beds in the UK was 47 per 10,000 population.

In the UK in 1995 there were 193 public and private hospices for the terminally ill with 2,982 beds.

Personal Social Services. Under the Local Authority Social Services Act, 1970, and in Scotland the Social Work (Scotland) Act, 1968, the welfare and social work services provided by local authorities were made the responsibility of a new local authority department—the Social Services Department in England and Wales, and Social Work Departments in Scotland headed by a Director of Social Work, responsibility in Scotland passing in 1975 to the local authorities. The social services thus administered include: the fostering, care and adoption of children, welfare services and social workers for people with learning difficulties and the mentally ill, the disabled and the aged, and accommodation for those needing residential care services. Legislation of 1996 permits local authorities to make cash payments as an alternative to community care. In Scotland the Social Work Departments' functions also include the supervision of persons on probation, of adult offenders and of persons released from penal institutions or subject to fine supervision orders.

Personal Social Services staff numbered 233,655 in 1996. The total cost of these services was estimated at £8,849m. for 1995–96. Expenditure is reviewed by the

Social Services Inspectorate and the Audit Commission (in Scotland by the Social Work Services Inspectorate and the Accounts Commission).

Welfare. The National Insurance Act 1946 came into operation on 5 July 1948, repealing the existing schemes of health, pensions and unemployment insurance. This Act, along with later legislation, was consolidated as the National Insurance Act 1965. The scheme now operates under the Social Security Contributions and Benefits Act 1992 and the Social Security Administration Act 1992.

Since 1975 Class 1 contributions have been related to the employee's earnings and are collected with PAYE income tax, instead of by affixing stamps to a card. Class 2 and Class 3 contributions remain flat-rate, but, in addition to Class 2 contributions, those who are self-employed may be liable to pay Class 4 contributions, which for the year 1997–98 are at the rate of 6% on profits or gains between £7,010 and £24,180, which are assessable for income tax under Schedule D. The non-employed and others whose contribution record is not sufficient to give entitlement to benefits are able to pay a Class 3 contribution of £6·05 per week in 1997–98 voluntarily, to qualify for a limited range of benefits. Class 2 weekly contributions for 1997–98 for men and women are £6·15. Class 1A contributions are paid by employers who provide employees with a car and fuel for their private use.

From 6 April 1978 the Social Security Pensions Act 1975 introduced earnings-related retirement, invalidity and widows' pensions. Members of occupational pension schemes may be contracted out of the earnings-related part of the state scheme relating to retirement and widows' benefits. Employee's national insurance contribution liability depends on whether he/she is in contracted-out or not contracted-out employment.

Full-rate contributions for non-contracted-out employment in 1997–98:

Weekly Earnings (in £1)	Yearly earnings (in £1)	Employee pays	Employer pays
Nil–62	Nil–3,223	Nil	Nil
62–109	3,223–5,719	10%[1]	3%
110–154	5,720–8,059	10%[1]	5%
155–209	8,060–10,919	10%[1]	7%
210–464	10,920–24,180	10%[1]	10%
Over 465	Over 24,180	£41·54	10%

[1]Plus 2% of £62.

Where earnings exceed £62 per week the employee contributes 2% of earnings up to £62 and 10% thereafter.

For contracted-out employment the employees' contributions are as above, but 8·2% on weekly earnings of £62–£465. The employer's rates are reduced by 3%.

From April 1996 employers who engage a trainee, or a person who has been unemployed for at least 2 years are eligible for a year's rebate of contributions.

Contributions together with interest on investments form the income of the *National Insurance Fund* from which benefits are paid. A Treasury grant was instituted in 1993. 24,810,000 persons (10,780,000 women) paid contributions in 1994–95, including 21,790,000 employees at standard rate.

Receipts, 1995–96 (in £1m.), 52,756, including: Contributions, 40,874·58; compensation from Consolidated Fund for recoveries, 474·7; investment income, 459·22. Disbursements (in £1m.), 37,088·12, including: Unemployment Benefit, 1,131·37; Sickness Benefit, 14·71; Invalidity Benefit, 599·83; Maternity Allowances, 29·9; Widow's Benefit, 1,050·69; Guardian's Allowances, 1·84; Retirement Pensions, 32,619·57; Pensioners' Lump Sums, 127·19; Redundancy Payments, 155·07; transfers to Northern Ireland, 125; administration, 1,218·77. Total benefit expenditure, 1995–96, £88,787m.

Statutory Sick Pay (SSP). Employers are responsible for paying statutory sick pay (SSP) to their employees who are absent from work through illness or injury for up to 28 weeks in any 3-year period. Basically, all employees aged between 16 and 65 (60 for women) with earnings above the Lower Earnings Limit are covered by the scheme whenever they are sick for 4 or more days consecutively. The weekly rate is £54·55. For most employees SSP completely replaces their entitlement to state incapacity benefit which is not payable as long as any employer's responsibility for SSP remains.

Pregnant working women may be eligible to receive statutory maternity pay directly from their employer for a maximum of 18 weeks. There are 2 rates: Where a woman has been working for the same employer for at least 26 weeks, she is entitled to 90% of her average weekly earnings for the first 6 weeks and to the lower rate of £54·55 a week for the remaining 12 weeks. Employers are reimbursed by the state for 92% of the amount they pay.

Women who are not eligible for statutory maternity pay, those who are self-employed, have recently changed jobs or given up their job, may qualify for a weekly maternity allowance of £54·55 for employees and £47·35 for the self- or non-employed, which is payable for up to 18 weeks.

All pregnant employees have the right to take 14 weeks' maternity leave.

A payment of £100 from the Social Fund may be available if the mother or her partner are receiving income support, family credit or disability working allowance. It is also available if a woman adopts a baby.

Contributory benefits. Qualification for these depends upon fulfilment of the appropriate contribution conditions, except that persons who are incapable of work as the result of an industrial accident may receive incapacity benefit followed by invalidity benefit without having to satisfy the contributions conditions.

Jobseekers' Allowance. This replaced unemployment benefit on 7 Oct. 1996. Unemployed persons claiming the allowance must sign a 'Jobseekers' Agreement' setting out a plan of action to find work. The allowance is not payable to persons who left their job voluntarily or through misconduct. Claimants with sufficient National Insurance contributions are entitled to the allowance for 6 months regardless of their means; otherwise, recipients qualify through a means test and the allowance is fixed according to family circumstances, at a rate corresponding to Income Support for an indefinite period. In 1996, there were some 397,800 recipients of Unemployment Benefit at any one time.

Incapacity benefit. This replaced the former sickness benefit and invalidity benefit on 13 April 1995. Entitlement begins when entitlement to SSP (if any) ends. There are 3 rates: A lower rate for the first 28 weeks; a higher rate between the 29th and 52nd week; and a long-term rate from the 53rd week of incapacity. It also comprises certain age additions and increases for adult and child dependants. A more objective medical test of incapacity for work was introduced for incapacity benefit as well as for other social security benefits paid on the basis of incapacity for work. This test applies after 28 weeks' incapacity for work and assesses ability to perform a range of work-related activities rather than the ability to perform a specific job. Benefit is taxable after 28 weeks. Some 1,910,000 claims were being met at any one time in 1996.

Maternity Benefit. Women who do not qualify for statutory maternity pay may be entitled to maternity allowance if they satisfy a test of recent work and contributions paid. Maternity allowance can be paid for up to 18 weeks. Payment can start at the earliest 11 weeks before the expected week of confinement but the woman has some choice in deciding when to give up work and still retains title to the full 18 weeks. There were some 12,000 beneficiaries in 1995–96.

Widow's Benefits. From 11 April 1988 the three main widow's benefits are: Widow's payment, widowed mother's allowance, widow's pension.

A widow cannot get any widow's benefits based on her husband's National Insurance contributions (NIC) if: She had been divorced from the man who has died; or she was living with the man as if she were married to him, but without being legally married to him; or she is living with another man as if she is married to him; or she was in prison or held in legal custody. A widow can only get widow's benefits if her husband has paid enough NIC. *Widow's Payment* is a single tax-free payment of £1,000. A widow may be able to get this benefit if her husband has paid enough NIC and she was under 60 when her husband died; or her husband was not getting a State Retirement Pension when he died. *Widowed Mother's Allowance:* A widow may be able to get a widowed mother's allowance if her husband has paid enough NIC and she is receiving child benefit for one of her children, or her husband was receiving child benefit, or she is expecting her husband's baby, or if she was widowed before 11 April 1988 and has a young person under 19 living with her for whom she was receiving Child Benefit. A widow entitled to a widowed mother's allowance will get an amount based on her husband's NIC. She will also get benefit for her eldest dependent child and further higher benefit for each subsequent child, and she may also get an additional pension based on her husband's earnings since 1978. Widowed mother's allowance is usually paid as long as the widow is getting child benefit. It is taxable. *Widow's Pension:* A widow may be able to get a widow's pension if her husband has paid enough NIC. She must be 45 or over (40 or over if widowed before 11 April 1988) when her husband died or when her widowed mother's allowance ends. A widow cannot get a widow's pension at the same time as a widowed mother's allowance. A widow who is entitled to a widow's pension will get an amount that depends on her age when her husband died or when her widowed mother's allowance ends. If she was 55 or over (50 or over if widowed before 11 April 1988) she will get the full rate of widow's pension. She may also get an additional pension based on her husband's earnings since 1978. If her late husband was a member of a contracted-out occupational scheme or a personal pension scheme, that scheme is responsible for paying the whole or part of the additional pensions. Widow's pension is usually paid until the widow is entitled to state retirement pension, when she is 60 or older. Widow's pension is taxable. There were some 311,600 pensioners in 1996 at any one time.

Retirement Pension. The state retirement ('old-age') pension scheme has 2 components: A basic pension and an earnings-related pension (State Earnings Related Pension—SERPS). The amount of the first is subject to National Insurance contributions made; SERPS is 1·25% of average earnings between the lower weekly earnings limit for Class I contribution liability and the upper earnings limit for each year of such earnings, building up to 25% in 20 years. For individuals reaching pensionable age after 6 April 1999, changes in the way pensions are calculated will be phased in over 10 years to include a lifetime's earnings with an accrual rate of 20%. Pensions are payable to women at 60 years of age and men at 65, but the age differential will be progressively phased out starting in April 2010. Women born before 6 April 1950 will be unaffected; women born after 5 March 1955 will receive their pension at 65; pension age for women between these dates will move up gradually from 60 to 65. There are standard rates for single persons and for married couples, the latter being 159% of 2 single-person rates. Proportionately reduced pensions are payable where contribution records are deficient.

Employees in an occupational scheme may be contracted out of SERPS provided that the occupational scheme provides a pension not less than the 'guaranteed minimum pension'. Self-employed persons, and also employees, may substitute personal pension schemes for SERPS. An independent statutory body, the Occupational Pension Board, is responsible for supervising contracted-out schemes.

Self- and non-employed persons may contribute voluntarily for retirement pension.

Persons who defer claiming their pension during the 5 years following retirement age are paid an increased amount, as do men and women who had paid graduated contributions. Although no further graduated contributions have been paid after April 1975, pension already earned will be paid along with the basic pension in the normal way. In 1996 some 10,814,600 persons were receiving pensions at any one time. Since 1 Oct. 1989 the pension for which a person has qualified may be paid in full whether a person continues in work or not irrespective of the amount of earnings.

At the age of 80 a small age addition is payable. In addition non-contributory pensions are now payable, subject to residence conditions, to persons aged 80 and over who do not qualify for a retirement pension or qualify for one at a low rate. These pensions are financed by Exchequer funds.

Pensioners whose pension is insufficient to live on may qualify for Income Support.

Non-Contributory Benefits.

Child Benefit. Child benefit is a tax-free cash allowance for children normally paid to the mother. The weekly rates are highest for the eldest qualifying child and less

GREAT BRITAIN

for each other child. Child benefit is payable for children under 16, for 16- and 17-year-olds registered for work or training, and for those under 19 receiving full-time non-advanced education. Some 12,993,000 children in 7,251,600 families received benefit in 1995–96 at any one time.

One Parent Benefit is a tax-free cash allowance for certain people bringing up children alone. It is payable for the first or only child in the family in addition to child benefit. There were some 1,067,000 beneficiaries in 1995–96.

Child Support Agency. The Agency, which started work in April 1993, is gradually replacing the court system for obtaining maintenance for children being brought up by single parents. The Agency is responsible for assessing, collecting and enforcing child maintenance payments and for tracing absent parents. Assessments are made using a formula which takes into account each parent's income and essential outgoings. Changes to the child support arrangements were introduced in Feb. 1994 to take account of concerns raised by members of the public and MPs. These are designed to reduce the amount of child maintenance that many absent parents are required to pay, and to give some families more time to adjust to increased bills. Legislation of 1995 introduced the possibility of fixing maintenance alongside the formula-assessment method. Appeals on points of law may be made to the Child Support Commissioners. In 1994–95 the Agency took on 398,584 new cases and completed 568,149 assessments.

Family Credit. Family Credit is a tax-free benefit for working families with children. To be able to get Family Credit there must be at least one child under 16 in the family (or under 19 if in full-time education up to, and including, A level or equivalent standard). The claimant or partner (if there is one) must be working at least 16 hours a week to qualify. They may be employed or self-employed, a lone parent or a couple. The claim should be made by the woman in two-parent families. The amount of Family Credit payable depends on the income of the claimant and partner, how many children there are in the family and their ages. The same rates of benefit are paid for one-parent families as for two-parent families. There are adult rates as well as a rate for each child varying with age, payable if the family's income does not exceed a certain limit. The award is reduced by £0·70 for each extra £1 earned. Family Credit is not payable if the claimant (or claimant and partner together) have savings or capital of over £8,000. Benefit is reduced if savings or capital of more than £3,000 is held. Family Credit is paid at the same rate for 26 weeks. The amount of the award will usually stay the same even if earnings, or other circumstances, change during that period. There were some 716,300 recipients in 1996 at any one time.

Earnings Top-up. This was introduced in Oct. 1996 on a pilot basis in 8 areas. Wages for workers with dependent children are topped up. There are different rates for couples and single persons.

Guardian's Allowance. A person responsible for an orphan child may be entitled to a guardian's allowance in addition to child benefit. Normally, both the child's parents must be dead but when they never married or were divorced, or one is missing, or serving a long sentence of imprisonment, the allowance may be paid on the death of one parent only. In 1996 there were 2,300 recipients at any one time.

Attendance Allowance. This is a tax-free Social Security benefit for disabled people over 65 who need help with personal care. The rates are increased for the terminally ill. There were some 1,161,000 recipients in 1996 at any one time.

Invalid Care Allowance. This is a taxable benefit which may be paid to those who forgo the opportunity of full-time work to care for a person who is receiving attendance allowance, constant attendance allowance or the highest or middle-core component of Disability Living Allowance. There is a weekly rate, with increases for dependants. There were some 339,000 recipients in 1995–96.

Disability Living Allowance. This is a non-taxable benefit available to people disabled before the age of 65, who need help with getting around or with personal care for at least 3 months. The mobility component has 2 weekly rates, the care component has 3. There were some 1,786,000 recipients in 1996 at any one time.

UNITED KINGDOM OF GREAT BRITAIN AND NORTHERN IRELAND

Disability Working Allowance. This is a tax-free benefit for people with an illness or disability which puts them at a disadvantage in getting a job. It is income-related and is intended for people who are starting work or already working at least 16 hours a week. The allowance is not payable if assets exceed £16,000. About 8,000 people received the allowance in 1995–96.

Industrial Injuries Disablement and Death Benefits. The Industrial Injuries Act, which also came into operation on 5 July 1948, with its later amending Acts, was consolidated as the National Insurance (Industrial Injuries) Act, 1965. This legislation was incorporated in the Social Security Act, 1975. The scheme provides a system of insurance against 'personal injury by accident arising out of and in the course of employment' and against certain prescribed diseases and injuries due to the nature of the employment. It takes the place of the Workmen's Compensation Acts and covers persons who are employed earners under the Social Security Act. There are no contribution conditions for the payment of benefit. There were 244,800 recipients in 1996 at any one time. Three types of benefit are provided:

Disablement benefit. This is payable where, as the result of an industrial accident or prescribed disease, there is a loss of physical or mental faculty. The loss of faculty will be assessed as a percentage by comparison with a person of the same age and sex whose condition is normal. If the assessment is between 14–100% benefit will be paid as weekly pension; 14–19% are payable at the 20% rate. The rates vary from 20% disabled to 100% disablement. Assessments of less than 14% do not normally attract basic benefit except for certain progressive chest diseases. Pensions for persons under 18 are at a reduced rate. When injury benefit was abolished for industrial accidents occurring and prescribed diseases commencing on or after 6 April 1983, a common start date was introduced for the payment of disablement benefit 90 days (excluding Sundays) after the date of the relevant accident or onset of the disease. The following increases can be paid with disablement benefit: *Constant attendance allowance* – where the disability for which the claimant is receiving disablement benefit is assessed at 100% and is so severe that they need constant care and attention. There are 4 rates depending on the amount of attendance needed. *Exceptionally severe disablement allowance* – where the claimant is in receipt of constant attendance allowance at one of the two higher rates and the need for attendance is likely to be permanent. *Reduced earnings allowance* (REA) is a separate benefit. Entitlement exists if the claimant has not retired and cannot go back to their normal job or do another job for the same pay because of the effects of the disability caused by an accident or disease which occurred on or before 30 Sept. 1990. It can be paid whether or not disablement benefit is paid, providing the disablement benefit assessment is 1% or more (e.g. where disablement is assessed at less than 14%) and on top of 100% disablement benefit. From 1 Oct. 1989, if a claimant is of pensionable age (60 for a woman, 65 for a man) they can continue to receive REA if they are in regular employment, or in some cases if they are receiving Sickness Benefit, Invalidity Benefit or Unemployment Benefit. It will not matter whether or not they receive State Retirement Pension. If they are not in regular employment, then entitlement to REA will cease. In most cases it will be replaced by Retirement Allowance.

Death Benefit. This is payable to the widow of a person who died before 11 April 1988 as the result of an industrial accident or a prescribed disease. Deaths which occurred on or after 11 April 1988—a widow is entitled to full widow's benefits even if her late husband did not satisfy the contribution condition, if he died as a result of an industrial accident or prescribed disease.

Allowances may be paid to people who are suffering from pneumoconiosis or byssinosis or certain other slowly developing diseases due to employment before 5 July 1948. They must not at any time have been entitled to benefit for the disabled under the Industrial Injuries provision of the Social Security Act, or compensation under Workmen's Compensation Acts, or have received damages through the courts.

In certain cases supplementation allowances are payable to people who are getting or are entitled to compensation under the Workmen's Compensation Acts.

War Pensions. Pensions are payable for disablement or death as a result of service in the armed forces, Merchant Navy or Civil Defence during war, or to civilians injured by enemy action. The amount depends on the degree of disablement. Various supplements may apply. There were some 303,000 recipients in 1996 at any one time.

Severe Disablement Allowance. A severe disablement allowance as well as an age-related addition may be payable to people under pensionable age who have been continuously incapable of work for at least 28 weeks, but who do not qualify for incapacity benefit. Those over 20 who are unable to work and are 80% disabled but do not qualify for the National Insurance invalidity pension because they have not paid sufficient contributions may be entitled to severe disablement allowance. Additions for adult dependants and for children may also be paid. There were some 368,000 beneficiaries in 1995–96.

Housing Benefit. The housing benefit scheme assists persons who need help to pay their rent, using general assessment rules and benefit levels similar to those for the income support scheme. People whose net income is below certain specified levels qualify for housing benefit of up to 100% of their rent. The scheme sets a limit of £16,000 on the amount of capital a person may have and still remain entitled. Restrictions on the granting of benefit to persons under 25 were introduced in 1995. In 1996 some 2,898,300 claims for rent rebate and 1,877,500 for rent allowance were being made at any one time.

Council Tax Benefit. The scheme offers help to those claiming income support and others with low incomes. Subject to rules broadly similar to those governing the provision of income support and housing benefit, people may receive rebates of up to 100% of their council tax. In 1996 some 5,614,200 households received such help at any one time. A person who is liable for the council tax may also claim benefit (called 'second adult rebate') for a second adult who is not liable to pay the council tax and who is living in the home on a non-commercial basis.

Income Support. Under the Social Security Act, 1986, benefit was payable to any persons aged 18 years or over not in full-time work who were without adequate resources. Since 7 Oct. 1996, Income Support has been payable only to persons not required to be available for work whose resources are below a certain level. These include single parents, pensioners, long-term sick or disabled persons, and those caring for them who qualify for the invalid care allowance. Income Support is not payable if the claimant (or claimant and partner together) have savings or capital over £8,000. Benefit is reduced if savings or capital of more than £3,000 is held. A person who is excluded from benefit under the normal rules may receive payments to meet urgent need. Additional sums, known as premiums, are available. There were some 5,778,300 recipients in 1996 (under the 1986 Act) at any one time.

The Social Fund. The Fund makes payments and loans to help recipients meet intermittent expenses. 'Regulated payments' comprise: *Maternity Payments* (a payment of up to £100 for each baby expected, born or adopted, payable to persons receiving income support, income-based jobseekers' allowance, disability working allowance or family credit); *Funeral Payments* (a payment of reasonable funeral expenses up to £500 incurred by persons receiving income support, income-based jobseekers' allowance, housing benefit, Council Tax benefit, disability working allowance or family credit; recoverable from the estate of the deceased); *Cold Weather Payments* (a payment of £8·50 for any consecutive 7 days when the temperature is below freezing to persons receiving income support who are pensioners, disabled or have a child under 5). 'Discretionary Payments' comprise: *Community Care Grants* (payments to help persons receiving income support to move into the community or avoid institutional care); *Budgeting Loans* (interest-free loans to persons receiving income support for expenses difficult to budget for); *Crisis Loans* (interest-free loans to anyone without resources in an emergency where there is no other means of preventing serious risk to health or safety). Savings over £500 (£1,000 for persons aged 60 or over) are taken into account before payments are made.

Barr, N., et al. *The State of Welfare: the Welfare State in Britain since 1974.* Oxford, 1990
Hill, M., *The Welfare State in Britain: a Political History since 1945.* Aldershot, 1993
Timmins, N., *The Five Giants: a Biography of the Welfare State.* London, 1995

CULTURE

Millennium celebrations will be focused on London, where there will be the Millennium Dome, a Millennium Wheel, a Millennium Bridge and a Millennium Village. Over £4bn. (US$6·5bn.) is being invested in leisure industries in the capital in the run-up to 2000, with some 50 hotels under construction. The Millennium Dome in Greenwich, the 'official home of world time', opens on 31 Dec. 1999. The scale and ambition of the Dome dwarfs any other monument to the millennium built anywhere on the planet. The Dome's translucent canopy, 1 km in circumference, is suspended by a web of twelve vast steel masts. The interior has an enormous 50m-high canopy creating a vast canvas for special effects.

In Cardiff a Millennium Stadium has been constructed at Cardiff Arms Park in time to host the Rugby World Cup in 1999. Scotland's only landmark project for the millennium is the rebuilding of Glasgow's Hampden Park Stadium.

Broadcasting. Radio and television services are provided by the British Broadcasting Corporation (BBC), by licensees of the Radio Authority and the Independent Television Commission (ITC) and by the Welsh-language Sianel Pedwar Cymru (S4C, Channel 4 Wales). The BBC, constituted by Royal Charter until 31 Dec. 1996, has responsibility for providing domestic and external broadcast services, the former financed from the television licence revenue, the latter by Government grant. The domestic services include 2 national television services, 5 national radio network services and a network of local radio stations. Government proposals for the future of the BBC after 1996 were published in July 1994.

The ITC is responsible for licensing and regulating all non-BBC TV services (except S4C), provided in and from the UK whether analogue or digital. These include ITV (regional and breakfast-time licensees), Channel 4, Channel 5, cable and satellite and additional services, such as teletext, carried on the spare capacity of TV signals. The Radio Authority is responsible for licensing and regulating independent national and local radio services. S4C is transmitted in Wales, and is funded by the government. It acts as both broadcaster and regulator.

The BBC's domestic radio services are available on Long Wave, FM and VHF; those of the Radio Authority on FM and VHF. Television services other than those only on cable and satellite are broadcast at UHF in 625-line definition and in colour (by PAL). The BBC World Service, which started life in 1932 as the Empire Service, broadcast in 42 languages to an audience estimated at 140m. in 1997. As the self-financed BBC Worldwide TV, the BBC is also involved in commercial joint ventures to provide international television services.

The broadcasting authorities, whose governing bodies are appointed (by HM the Queen in the case of the BBC and by the Secretary of State for National Heritage in the case of the ITC, the Radio Authority and S4C) as trustees for the public interest in broadcasting, are independent of government and are publicly accountable to Parliament for the discharge of their responsibilities. Their duties and powers are laid down in the BBC Royal Charter and the Broadcasting Act 1990.

All independent (non-BBC) radio and television services other than S4C are financed by the sale of broadcasting advertising time, commercial sponsorship, or, in some cable and satellite services, by subscription.

The Broadcasting Standards Commission (BSC) was established on 1 April 1997 by the Broadcasting Act 1996, through the merger of the Broadcasting Standards Council and Broadcasting Complaints Commission. Combining the functions of the two predecessor bodies, it acts as a forum for public concern about fairness and taste and decency on television and radio. The Commission considers and reaches findings on taste and decency complaints received from the public and adjudicates upon complaints of unfair or unjust treatment in broadcast programmes, and of unwarranted infringement of privacy in programmes or in their preparation. It also undertakes and commissions research and the monitoring of public attitudes, and must draw up a code of practice on both broadcasting standards and fairness which the broadcasters and regulators are required to reflect in their own programming guidelines. The Commission is half-funded by the Department, half by contributions from the BBC, ITC, Radio Authority and S4C.

The number of television receiving licences in force on 31 March 1997 was 21,305,000, including 20,849,000 for colour. There were 779,461 cable television subscribers in 1994. In 1995 there were 83·2m. radio receivers, or 1,428 per 1,000 inhabitants—a figure only exceeded in the USA, with 2,122 per 1,000 inhabitants.

Cinema. In 1996 cinemas had 1,744 screens. By 2000 this will have increased to around 2,800. Admissions were 112·1m. in 1996. 127 full-length films were made in 1996.

Press. In 1996 there were 10 national dailies with a combined average daily circulation in June of 13,202,574, and 9 national Sunday newspapers (15,174,032). There were also about 100 morning, evening and Sunday regional newspapers and 2,000 weeklies (about 1,000 of these for free distribution). There were about 6,500 other commercial periodicals and 4,000 professional and business journals. In 1996, an average of 18·3m. newspapers were sold per day, down from over 23m. in 1980.

In Jan. 1991 the Press Complaints Commission replaced the former Press Council. It has 15 members and a chair (Lord Wakeham), including 7 editors. It is funded by the newspaper industry.

In 1996, 101,504 book titles were published, including 89,984 non-fiction. 95,064 titles were published in 1995.

Tourism. In 1997, 133·6m. UK residents made trips within the UK, passing 474m. nights in accommodation and spending £15,075m. Of these, 70·8m. were holiday-makers spending £10,355m. There were 25·5m. overseas visitors in 1997 passing 223m. nights in accommodation and spending £12,244m. UK residents made 46·0m. trips abroad in 1997. The main countries of origin for foreign visitors in 1997 were: France (3·59m.), USA (3·43m.), Germany (2·91m.), Ireland (2·23m.) and the Netherlands (1·65m.).

The leading attraction in 1997 was Blackpool Pleasure Beach, Lancs, with an estimated 7·8m. visits. The leading tourist attractions charging admission in 1997 were Madame Tussaud's in London, with 2,798,801 visits; Alton Towers in Staffordshire, with 2,701,945 visits; and the Tower of London, with 2,615,170 visits.

Festivals. Among the most famous music festivals are the Promenade Concerts or 'Proms', which take place at the Royal Albert Hall in London every year from July to Sept, culminating in the Last Night of the Proms; the Glyndebourne Festival in Sussex (May to Aug.); the Aldeburgh Festival in Suffolk (June); and the Buxton Festival in Derbyshire (July). The annual London Film Festival takes place in Nov. There are major literary festivals at Hay-on-Wye in Powys (late May/early June) and Cheltenham in Gloucestershire (Oct.). The multicultural Notting Hill Carnival in London takes place at the end of Aug.

Museums and Galleries. The museums with the highest number of visitors are all in London. In 1997 there were 6,056,633 visits to the British Museum, 4,809,063 to the National Gallery, 1,793,400 to the Natural History Museum, 1,757,735 to the Tate Gallery and 1,537,151 to the Science Museum.

DIPLOMATIC REPRESENTATIVES
Of the USA in Great Britain (24/31 Grosvenor Sq., London, W1A 1AE)
Ambassador: Philip Lader.

Of Great Britain in the USA (3100 Massachusetts Ave., NW, Washington, D.C., 20008)
Ambassador: Sir Christopher. J. R. Meyer, KCMG.

Of Great Britain to the United Nations
Ambassador: Sir Jeremy Greenstock, KCMG.

Great Britain's permanent representative to the European Union
Ambassador: Sir Stephen Wall, KCMG, LVO.

FURTHER READING
Government publications are published by HM Stationery Office (HMSO).
Office for National Statistics. *Annual Abstract of Statistics.* HMSO.—*Monthly Digest of Statistics.* HMSO.—*Social Trends.* HMSO.—*Regional Statistics.* HMSO
Central Office of Information. *Britain: An Official Handbook.* HMSO, annual.—*The Monarchy.* 1992

Directory of British Associations. Beckenham, annual

Beloff, M., *Britain and the European Union: Dialogue of the Deaf.* London, 1997

Cairncross, A., *The British Economy since 1945: Economic Policy and Performance, 1945–1995.* 2nd ed. London, 1995

Catterall, P., *British History, 1945–1987: an Annotated Bibliography.* Oxford, 1991

Gascoigne, B. (ed.) *Encyclopedia of Britain.* London, 1994

Harbury, C. D. and Lipsey, R. G., *Introduction to the UK Economy.* 4th ed. Oxford, 1993

Institute of Contemporary British History. *Contemporary Britain: an Annual Review.* Oxford, from 1990

Irwin, J. L., *Modern Britain: an Introduction.* 3rd ed. London, 1994

Leventhal, F. M. (ed.) *20th-Century Britain: an Encyclopedia.* New York, 1995

Marr, A., *Ruling Britannia: the Failure and Future of British Democracy.* London, 1995

Morgan, K.O., *The People's Peace: British History, 1945–89.* OUP, 1990

Oakland, J., *British Civilization: an Introduction.* 3rd ed. London, 1995

Oxford History of England. 16 vols. OUP, 1936–91

Palmer, A. and Palmer, V., *The Chronology of British History.* London, 1995

Penguin History of Britain. 9 vols. London, 1996–

Sked, A. and Cook, C., *Post-War Britain: a Political History.* 4th ed. London, 1993

Strong, R., *The Story of Britain.* London, 1996

Thompson, F. M. L. (ed.) *The Cambridge Social History of Britain, 1750–1950.* 3 vols. CUP, 1990

Other more specialized titles are listed under TERRITORY AND POPULATION; CONSTITUTION AND GOVERNMENT; DEFENCE; ELECTRICITY; FORESTRY; TRADE UNIONS; RELIGION; THE BRITISH COUNCIL; *and* WELFARE, *above. See also Further Reading in England, Scotland and Wales.*

Website: http://www.ons.gov.uk

National Statistical Office: Office for National Statistics (ONS), 1 Drummond Gate, London SW1V 2QQ. ONS was formed from a merger of the former Central Statistical Office and the Office of Population Censuses and Surveys on 1 April 1996. *Director:* Dr Tim Holt.

ENGLAND

KEY HISTORICAL EVENTS

After the withdrawal of the Roman legions, 5th century Celtic Britain was invaded by Scandinavian and Teutonic tribes, collectively called the English. In the course of the next 150 years the English conquered the east and centre of the country, pinning down the Celtic Britons on the higher lands to the west. More than 200 years passed before the prevailing tribes recognized one king.

Then came the Danish invasion, their incomplete defeat by Alfred the Great, the consolidation of the kingdom under Alfred's successors and the Norman Conquest led by William, duke of Normandy, who was crowned king in 1066. When William died in 1087, he left Normandy to his eldest son Robert, thus separating it from England. The French dialect known as Anglo Norman was spoken by the ruling class in England for two centuries after the Conquest.

The Norman heritage was preserved also in the overlap between French and English feudal lords. Henry II, the founder of the Plantagenet dynasty, was feudatory lord of half France. But most of the French possessions were lost by Henry's son John. Thereafter, the Norman baronage came to regard themselves as English.

The ambitions of Edward III began and those of Henry V renewed the Hundred Years War (1338-1453) with France, which ended with the loss of all the remaining French possessions except Calais.

The dynastic struggle between the rival houses of York and Lancaster culminated in the Tudor ascendancy over political and clerical factions. Henry VII was a unifying monarch preparing the way for Henry VIII who forced the Church to submit to lay rule. Tudor power reached its zenith with Elizabeth I when England, allied with other Protestant powers, humbled the Spanish Armada.

Elizabeth's death brought on a great struggle for supremacy between Crown and Parliament. There followed the Civil War, the execution of Charles I, the rule by Protector Cromwell by military dictatorship, and the restoration of the Stuart monarchy on terms which conceded financial authority and thus decision-making power to Parliament.

The attempt of James II to restore the royal prerogative led to the intervention of William of Orange. James fled the country and the crown was taken by William and his wife Mary as Queen. The accession of William involved England in a protracted war against France but before peace was achieved, the 1688 revolution was confirmed by the Hanoverian succession, and the history of England was merged with that of Great Britain by the union with Scotland in 1707.

TERRITORY AND POPULATION

At the census taken on 21 April 1991 the area of England was 130,423 sq. km and the population 46,382,050. Population density (persons per ha), 1991 census: 3·6. Private households at the 1991 census: 19,984,500. Estimated population of England, mid-1998, 49,558,000 (25,131,000 females and 24,427,000 males), giving a density of 3·8 per ha.

Population (present on census night) at the 4 previous decennial censuses:

1951	1961	1971	1981
41,159,213[1]	43,460,525[1]	46,018,371[1]	46,226,100[2]

[1]Areas now recognized as part of Gwent, Wales, formed the English county of Monmouthshire until 1974. [2]The final count is believed to be over-stated as a result of an error in processing. The preliminary counts presented here rounded to the nearest hundred are thought to be more accurate.

Population (usually resident) at the census of 1991:

Males	Females	Total
22,812,889	24,242,315	47,055,204

For further statistical information, see under Territory and Population, Great Britain.

England is divided (apart from Greater London) into 35 counties and 50 unitary authorities with a single administrative tier, of which 36 are metropolitan boroughs and 27 unitary authorities established since 1995. The 35 counties are subdivided into 274 districts and the Isles of Scilly. Greater London comprises 32 boroughs and the City of London.

Area in sq. km of counties and usually resident population at the 1991 census:

	Area sq. km	Population		Area sq. km	Population
Metropolitan counties			*Non-metropolitan counties*		
Greater Manchester	1,286	2,499,441	Hampshire (Hants)	3,779	1,541,547
Merseyside	655	1,403,642	Hereford and		
South Yorkshire	1,559	1,262,630	Worcester	3,923	676,747
Tyne and Wear	537	1,095,152	Hertfordshire (Herts)	1,639	975,829
West Midlands	899	2,551,671	Humberside (Humb)	3,508	858,040
West Yorkshire	2,034	2,013,693	Isle of Wight (IOW)	380	124,577
			Kent	3,735	1,508,873
Non-metropolitan counties			Lancashire (Lancs)	3,070	1,383,998
Avon	1,332	932,674	Leicestershire (Leics)	2,551	867,521
Bedfordshire (Beds)	1,236	524,105	Lincolnshire (Lincs)	5,921	584,536
Berkshire (Berks)	1,256	734,246	Norfolk	5,372	745,613
Buckinghamshire			Northamptonshire		
(Bucks)	1,877	632,487	(Northants)	2,367	578,807
Cambridgeshire			Northumberland	5,026	304,694
(Camb)	3,400	645,125	North Yorkshire		
Cheshire	2,331	956,616	(N. Yorks)	8,309	702,161
Cleveland	597	550,293	Nottinghamshire		
Cornwall and Isles			(Notts)	2,160	993,872
of Scilly	3,530	468,425	Oxfordshire (Oxon)	2,583	547,584
Cumbria	6,817	483,163	Shropshire (Salop)	3,488	406,387
Derbyshire	2,629	928,636	Somerset (Som)	3,452	460,368
Devon	6,703	1,009,950	Staffordshire (Staffs)	2,715	1,031,135
Dorset	2,653	645,166	Suffolk	3,798	632,266
Durham	2,429	593,430	Surrey	1,677	1,018,003
East Sussex	1,794	690,447	Warwickshire	1,979	484,247
Essex	3,675	1,528,577	West Sussex	1,988	702,290
Gloucestershire			Wiltshire (Wilts)	3,476	564,471
(Gloucs)	2,653	528,370			

Changes in the above administrative structure following the Local Government Act 1992 comprised the following as at 1 April 1997:

The counties of Avon, Cleveland, Humberside and the Isle of Wight had been abolished, and new unitary authorities had been established in England (Bath and North East Somerset, Bournemouth, Brighton and Hove, Bristol, Darlington, Derby, East Riding of Yorkshire, Hartlepool, Isle of Wight, Kingston-upon-Hull, Leicester, Luton, Middlesbrough, Milton Keynes, North East Lincolnshire, North Lincolnshire, North Somerset, Poole, Portsmouth, Redcar and Cleveland, Rutland, South Gloucestershire, Southampton, Stockton-on-Tees, Stoke-on-Trent, Thamesdown and York).

In 1996 London had an estimated population of 7,074,000. Populations of next largest cities in 1996 was: Birmingham, 1,021,000; Leeds, 727,000; Sheffield, 530,000; Bradford (1995), 483,000; Liverpool, 468,000; Manchester, 431,000; Bristol (1995), 401,000.

Greater London Boroughs. Total area 1,580 sq. km. Usually resident total population at the 1991 census, 6,679,699 (inner London, 2,504,451). 1996 estimate, 7,074,000. By borough (1991):

Barking and		Hammersmith		Lewisham[1]	230,983
Dagenham	143,681	and Fulham[1]	148,502	Merton	168,470
Barnet	293,564	Haringey[1]	202,204	Newham[1]	212,170
Bexley	215,615	Harrow	200,100	Redbridge	226,218
Brent	243,025	Havering	229,492	Richmond upon	
Bromley[1]	290,609	Hillingdon	231,602	Thames	160,732
Camden[1]	170,444	Hounslow	204,397	Southwark[1]	218,541
Croydon	313,510	Islington[1]	164,686	Sutton	168,880
Ealing	275,257	Kensington and		Tower Hamlets[1]	161,064
Enfield	257,417	Chelsea[1]	138,394	Waltham Forest	212,033
Greenwich	207,650	Kingston upon		Wandsworth[1]	252,425
Hackney[1]	181,248	Thames	132,996	Westminster,	
		Lambeth[1]	244,834	City of[1]	174,718

[1]Inner London borough.

The City of London (677 acres) is administered by its Corporation which retains some independent powers. Resident population (1991 census) 4,142.

CLIMATE

For more detailed information, see under Climate, Great Britain.

London, Jan. 39°F (3·9°C), July 64°F (17·8°C). Annual rainfall 25" (635 mm). Birmingham, Jan. 38°F (3·3°C), July 61°F (16·1°C). Annual rainfall 30" (749 mm). Manchester, Jan. 39°F (3·9°C), July 61°F (16·1°C). Annual rainfall 34·5" (876 mm).

CONSTITUTION AND GOVERNMENT

The Parliamentary electorate of England in the register numbered 36,885,805 in 1998.

RECENT ELECTIONS

At the UK general election held in May 1997, 529 members were returned from England.

See also Constitution and Government, Recent Elections and Current Administration in Great Britain.

CURRENT ADMINISTRATION

Local Government. Local authorities have statutory powers and claims on public funds. Relations with central government are maintained through the Department of the Environment. Changes introduced by the Local Government Commission set up in 1992 included the introduction of single-tier unitary authorities alongside the previous two-tier county and district administrations. By 1997 there were (*two-tier*) 35 non-metropolitan county councils under which were 274 district councils and the Scilly Isles, and (*single-tier*) 27 unitary authorities, 36 metropolitan district councils and 32 Greater London borough councils. Greater London and the 6 metropolitan counties no longer have councils, the former county functions having devolved to the boroughs and districts, but some services (e.g. fire services) are administered by joint authorities nominated by the latter. There are also some 10,000 parishes, of which about 800 have elected councils. About 300 are former small boroughs or urban districts which became successor parishes. Parish councils manage local facilities and may act as agents for district council functions.

Resident citizens of the UK, Ireland, a Commonwealth country or an EU country may (at age 18) vote and (at age 21) stand for election. Councils are elected for 4 years, except that in the metropolitan and one-third of the other districts, one-third of councillors are elected in each of the 3 years that no county council election is held. Counties are divided into electoral divisions and districts into wards.

Functions. County councils are responsible for strategic planning, transport planning, non-trunk roads and regulation of traffic, personal social services, consumer protection, disposal of waste, the fire and library services and partially for education. District councils are responsible for environmental health, housing, local planning applications (in the first instance) and refuse collection. Unitary authorities combine the functions of both levels.

Election Results. Across the UK to 1 May 1997: Elections for one third of the seats on the councils of the 32 London boroughs, 36 metropolitan districts and 118 non-metropolitan districts were held on 5 May 1994. The Labour Party gained control of 93 councils; the Liberal Democratic Party, 19; the Conservative Party, 15; ind, 5. There was no overall majority in 54 councils.

Elections were held outside the metropolitan areas ('the shires') on 4 May 1995. Labour made a net gain of 155 councils, the Liberal Democrats 45 and the Conservatives lost 51.

At the elections of 2 May 1996 for 32 metropolitan and 114 non-metropolitan and unitary councils, Labour took control of 84 councils and gained 431 seats, the Liberal Democrats took control of 23 councils and gained 142 seats, the Conservatives took control of 3 councils and lost 534 seats, and independents took control of 3 councils and lost 29 seats. In 33 councils no party gained an absolute majority.

On 6 April 1995 elections were held for the 29 newly-created unitary councils. 1,161 seats were contested. Labour won 614 seats with 47% of votes cast, and gained control of 20 of the councils.

County council elections and those for 19 further new unitary authorities took place on 1 May 1997. Elections for the 1,014 seats on the unitary authorities created shadow councils whose job was to prepare the area for transfer to the new status in April 1998. Councillors for these areas did not stand for election but stepped down in April 1998 leaving those elected on 1 May 1997 in charge.

Local elections were due to take place on 6 May 1999.

DEFENCE
For information on defence, see Great Britain.

ECONOMY
For information on the economy, see Great Britain.

ENERGY AND NATURAL RESOURCES
For information on energy and natural resources, see Great Britain.

Water. The Water Act of Sept. 1989 privatized the 9 water authorities in England: Anglian; North West; Northumbrian; Severn Trent; South West; Southern; Thames; Wessex; Yorkshire. The Act also inaugurated the National Rivers Authority, with environmental and resource management responsibilities, and the 'regulator' Office of Water Services (Ofwat), charged with protecting consumer interests.

INTERNATIONAL TRADE
For information on international trade, see Great Britain.

COMMUNICATIONS
For information on communications, see Great Britain.

SOCIAL INSTITUTIONS

Education. For details on the nature and types of school, see under Education, Great Britain.

In Jan. 1997 there were 544 public-sector nursery and 5,793 primary schools with nursery classes in England; in addition, there were 1,538 independent schools with provision for children under 5. In 1997 there were 50,734 pupils under 5 attending nursery schools and 662,775 pupils under 5 in nursery and infant classes in primary schools. About 48% of all these children were attending part-time.

In Jan. 1998 there were 4,398,381 pupils at 18,117 primary schools in England, of which 2,274 were infant schools providing for pupils up to the age of about 7, the remainder mainly taking pupils from age 5 through to 11. Nearly all primary schools take both boys and girls. 15·2% of primary schools had 100 full-time pupils or less.

In Jan. 1998 there were 572 middle schools in England deemed either primary or secondary according to the age range of the school concerned.

In Jan. 1998 there were 3,190 secondary schools in England. Some local authorities have retained selection at age 11 for entry to grammar schools, of which there were 157 in 1998. There were a small number of technical schools in 1998 which specialize in technical studies. There were 113 secondary modern schools in 1998, providing a general education up to the minimum school leaving age of 16, although exceptionally some pupils stay on beyond that age.

Almost all local education authorities operate a system of comprehensive schools to which pupils are admitted without reference to ability or aptitude. In Jan. 1997 there were 2,882 such schools in England with over 2·6m. pupils. With the development of comprehensive education, various patterns of secondary schools have come into operation. Principally these are: 1) All-through schools with pupils aged 11 to 18 or 11 to 16; pupils over 16 being able to transfer to an 11 to 18 school or a sixth form college providing for pupils aged 16 to 19. (There were 115 sixth form colleges in England in 1992). 2) Local education authorities operating a three-tier system involving middle schools where transfer to secondary school is at ages 12, 13 or 14. These correspond to 12 to 18, 13 to 18 and 14 to 18 comprehensive schools respectively; or 3) In areas where there are no middle schools a two-tier system of junior and senior comprehensive schools for pupils aged 11 to 18 with optional transfer to these schools at age 13 or 14.

Local education authority-maintained secondary, middle and primary schools can apply for Grant Maintained (GM) status as self-governing state schools. By Sept. 1997 there were 1,196 GM schools in England (507 primary, 668 secondary and 21 special schools).

Under the Education Act 1996 children have special educational needs if they have a learning difficulty which calls for special educational provision to be made for them. In a minority of cases, perhaps just over 2% of children, the Local Education Authority will need to make a statutory assessment of special educational needs under the Education Act 1996, which may ultimately lead to a 'statement'. In England the total number of pupils with statements in 1997 was over 234,000. In 1997 there were 1,171 maintained special schools and 68 non-maintained special schools.

Outside the state system of education there were in England about 2,250 independent schools in Jan. 1999, ranging from large prestigious schools to small local ones. Some provide boarding facilities but the majority include non-resident day pupils. There are about 550,000 pupils in these schools, which represent about 7% of the total pupil population in England.

Further Education (Non-University). In 1997–98 some 3·5m. students, funded by the Further Education Funding Council (FEFC), were attending colleges and institutions in England, studying for a total of 5·8m. qualifications.

Higher Education. Polytechnics made into universities by the 1992 Further and Higher Education Act (P = Polytechnic): Anglia P became Anglia P Univ.; Birmingham P, Univ. of Central England in Birmingham; Bournemouth P, Bournemouth Univ.; Brighton P, Univ. of Brighton; Bristol P, Univ. of the West of England, Bristol; City of London P, London Guildhall Univ.; Coventry P, Coventry Univ.; Derby P, Univ. of Derby; Hatfield P, Univ. of Hertfordshire; Huddersfield P, Univ. of Huddersfield; Humberside P, Univ. of Humberside (since re-named Univ.

of Lincolnshire and Humberside); Kingston P, Kingston Univ.; Leeds P, Leeds Metropolitan Univ.; Lancashire P, Univ. of Central Lancashire; Leicester P, De Montfort Univ.; Liverpool P, Liverpool John Moores Univ.; Manchester P, Manchester Metropolitan Univ.; Middlesex P, Middlesex Univ.; Newcastle P, Univ. of Northumbria at Newcastle; Nottingham P, Nottingham Trent Univ.; Oxford P, Oxford Brookes Univ.; P of Central London, Univ. of Westminster; P of East London, Univ. of East London; P of North London, Univ. of North London; P South West, Univ. of Plymouth; P of West London, Thames Valley Univ.; Portsmouth P, Univ. of Portsmouth; Sheffield City P, Sheffield Hallam Univ.; South Bank P, South Bank Univ.; Staffordshire P, Staffordshire Univ.; Sunderland P, Univ. of Sunderland; Teesside P, Univ. of Teesside; Thames P, Univ. of Greenwich; Wolverhampton P, Univ. of Wolverhampton.

In England in 1995–96 there were 137 institutions of higher education directly funded by the HEFCE (Higher Education Funding Council for England), of which 70 were universities. The HEFCE allocates public funds for teaching and research to universities and colleges. It works in partnership with the higher education sector and advises the Government on higher education policy. In 1998–99 the HEFCE distributed £3·87bn. in funding: £2,694m. for teaching, £829m. for research, £334m. to special funding and £10m. to flexibility. There were 1,137,000 students in funded institutions, including 727,000 full-time.

a) *Universities*

Name (Location)	No. of students (1996–97)	No. of academic staff (1996–97)
Anglia Polytechnic Univ. (Chelmsford)	18,480	734
Aston Univ. (Birmingham)	5,626	377
Univ. of Bath	8,266	798
Univ. of Birmingham	22,967	2,441
Bournemouth Univ. (Poole)	10,522	538
Univ. of Bradford	10,694	672
Univ. of Brighton	14,271	780
Univ. of Bristol	17,916	2,041
Brunel Univ. (Uxbridge)	14,077	787
Univ. of Cambridge	19,603	3,865
Univ. of Central England in Birmingham	20,406	892
Univ. of Central Lancashire (Preston)	19,790	770
City Univ. (London)	11,913	673
Coventry Univ.	15,603	940
Cranfield Univ. (Bedford)	3,594	750
De Montfort Univ. (Leicester)	28,664	1,406
Univ. of Derby	12,027	513
Univ. of Durham	11,376	978
Univ. of East Anglia (Norwich)	10,554	842
Univ. of East London (London)	12,034	697
Univ. of Essex (Colchester)	7,292	577
Univ. of Exeter	11,091	871
Univ. of Greenwich (London)	16,962	1,052
Univ. of Hertfordshire (Hatfield)	18,649	945
Univ. of Huddersfield	14,874	658
Univ. of Hull	11,702	887
Univ. of Keele	12,813	593
Univ. of Kent at Canterbury	10,728	746
Kingston Univ. (Kingston-upon-Thames)	14,853	870
Univ. of Lancaster	10,829	848
Univ. of Leeds	24,222	2,630
Leeds Metropolitan Univ.	19,498	792
Univ. of Leicester	14,870	1,365
Univ. of Lincolnshire and Humberside (Hull)	12,036	450
Univ. of Liverpool	18,154	1,890
Liverpool John Moores Univ.	19,580	1,058
Univ. of London	101,576[1]	7,414[2]
London Guildhall Univ.	13,223	452

Name (Location)	No. of students (1996–97)	No. of academic staff (1996–97)
Loughborough Univ. of Technology	10,834	1,050
Luton Univ.	12,604	676
Univ. of Manchester	23,132	2,898
Univ. of Manchester Institute of Science and Technology	7,102	970
Manchester Metropolitan Univ.	28,761	1,442
Middlesex Univ. (London)	21,589	952
Univ. of Newcastle upon Tyne	16,096	2,061
Univ. of North London	14,368	595
Univ. of Northumbria at Newcastle	19,722	1,178
Univ. of Nottingham	22,152	2,046
Nottingham Trent Univ.	23,869	989
Univ. of Oxford	19,805	3,805
Oxford Brookes Univ.	11,722	828
Univ. of Plymouth	20,487[2]	1,266
Univ. of Portsmouth	18,414	1,062
Univ. of Reading	13,936	1,288
Univ. of Salford	18,049	695
Univ. of Sheffield	21,863	2,316
Sheffield Hallam Univ.	22,328	1,232
Univ. of Southampton	18,354	2,010
South Bank Univ. (London)	18,223	1,010
Staffordshire Univ. (Stoke on Trent)	14,987	823
Univ. of Sunderland	15,526	771
Univ. of Surrey (Guildford)	11,679	946
Univ. of Sussex (Brighton)	12,132	981
Univ. of Teesside (Middlesbrough)	11,996	596
Thames Valley Univ. (London)	21,851	546
Univ. of Warwick (Coventry)	17,507	1,488
Univ. of Westminster (London)	19,441	1,124
Univ. of the West of England, Bristol	21,506	1,263
Univ. of Wolverhampton	22,090	894
Univ. of York	7,534[1]	933

[1]1997–98: Internal students only; also 26,000 external students.
[2]1997–98: Teachers, readers and professors only.

b) *Other Institutions*

Bath College of Higher Education[1]; Bishop Grosseteste College (Lincoln); Bolton Institute of Higher Education[1]; Bretton Hall (Wakefield); Buckinghamshire Chilterns University College[1] (High Wycombe); Central School of Speech and Drama (London); Canterbury Christ Church University College; Cheltenham and Gloucester College of Higher Education[1]; Chester College of Higher Education; College of Guidance Studies (Swanley); College of Ripon and York St. John (York); College of St. Mark and St. John (Plymouth); Dartington College of Arts (Totnes); Edge Hill College of Higher Education (Ormskirk); Falmouth College of Arts; Harper Adams University College[1] (Newport); Homerton College (Cambridge); Institute of Advanced Nursing Education (London); Kent Institute of Art and Design (Maidstone); King Alfred's College, Winchester; Liverpool Hope; London Business School; The London Institute[1]; Loughborough College of Art and Design; University College, Northampton[1]; Newman College (Birmingham); North Riding College (Scarborough); Ravensbourne College of Design and Communication (Bromley); Roehampton Institute[1] (London); Rose Bruford College of Speech and Drama (Sidcup); Royal Academy of Music (London); Royal College of Art[1] (London); Royal College of Music[1] (London); Royal Northern College of Music (Manchester); St. Martin's College (Lancaster); St. Mary's College (Twickenham); Southampton Institute; Trinity and All Saints (Leeds); Trinity College of Music (London); Westhill College (Birmingham); Westminster College, Oxford; Surrey Institute of Art and Design University College (Farnham)[1]; Chichester Institute of Higher Education[1]; Wimbledon School of Art; University College, Worcester[1].

[1]May award degrees

The Teaching and Higher Education Act 1998 made provision for colleges of higher education with degree-awarding powers to adopt the title 'university college'.

CULTURE

Millennium celebrations will be focused on London, where there will be the Millennium Dome, a Millennium Wheel, a Millennium Bridge and a Millennium Village. Over £4bn. (US$6·5bn.) is being invested in leisure industries in the capital in the run-up to 2000, with some 50 hotels under construction. The Millennium Dome in Greenwich, the 'official home of world time', opens on 31 Dec. 1999. The scale and ambition of the Dome dwarfs any other monument to the millennium built anywhere on the planet. The Dome's translucent canopy, 1 km in circumference, is suspended by a web of twelve vast steel masts. The interior has an enormous 50m-high canopy creating a vast canvas for special effects.

Tourism. The leading attraction in 1997 was Blackpool Pleasure Beach, Lancs, with an estimated 7·8m. visits in 1997. The leading tourist attractions charging admission in 1997 were Madame Tussaud's in London, with 2,798,801 visits; Alton Towers in Staffordshire, with 2,701,945 visits; and the Tower of London, with 2,615,170 visits.

FURTHER READING
Day, A., *England* [Bibliography]. Oxford and Santa Barbara (CA), 1993
Lloyd, T. O., *Empire, Welfare State, Europe: English History, 1906–1992*. 4th ed. OUP, 1993

SCOTLAND

KEY HISTORICAL EVENTS

Earliest evidence of human settlement in Scotland dates from the Middle Stone Age. Hunters and fishermen on the west coast were succeeded by farming communities who made homes as far north as Shetland. The Romans were active in the first century AD but made so little impact on hostile tribes they built Hadrian's Wall between the Tyne and Solway Firth as their northern frontier. At this time, the Picts with their own language and culture consolidated their strength beyond the Firth of Clyde, but it was the southern Scots, a Celtic people from Ireland, who gave their name to the land.

In 843 Kenneth MacAlpine united the Scots and the Picts to found the kingdom of Scotland. A legal and administrative uniformity was established by David I whose 29-year reign ended in 1153. His successors maintained an understanding with England which allowed for two centuries of peace, but in 1286 Edward I of England asserted his claim as overlord of Scotland and appointed his son nominee to succeed to the crown.

Resistance to English rule was led by Robert Bruce, who turned back the English at Bannockburn. His son, David II, was less successful in the battlefield, but defended independence by clever diplomacy. He died in 1371 and was succeeded by his nephew Robert, the first king of the Stuart line.

The reigns of five James's occupied the century and a half between the death of Robert III in 1406 and the accession of Mary. This was the time when the alliance between France and Scotland was cemented by common hostility to England.

James IV reinforced a peace agreement with Henry VII by marrying his daughter Margaret in 1503. Religious differences put a strain on the alliance, and when Henry VIII invaded France, James attacked England only to be killed in the Battle of Flodden.

The young James V was assailed by conflicting pressures from pro-French and pro-English factions but having secured his personal rule, he entered into two successive French marriages. His second wife, Mary, was the mother of Mary, Queen of Scots, who married the Dauphin in 1558. Protestant opposition to French influence was bolstered by Elizabeth I of England who sent troops. Mary was then in France. Returning to Scotland after her husband's death in 1561 she was beset by religious enemies and forced to take refuge in England, where she was the nearest heir to Elizabeth. Her son James VI survived the animosity between his own and his mother's followers to make an alliance with England. With the execution of his mother by a nervous Protestant establishment in England, James became heir to the English throne to which he succeeded in 1603.

The crowns of England and Scotland were now worn by the same monarch but for a century more the two countries remained independent. Reflecting the religious and political divisions of the Civil War in England, which led to the execution of Charles I, Scottish armies fought for both sides. The Scots soon united, however, to accept Charles II as their king. Having established dominance in England, Cromwell moved against Scotland forcing Charles II into exile. His restoration in 1660 was welcomed in both kingdoms. His successor James VII of Scotland and James II of Great Britain and Ireland was less astute in managing religious and political differences. The collapse of his regime in 1688 and the arrival of William of Orange confirmed the Protestant ascendency in Scotland and England.

The union of parliament, which followed in 1707, brought Scotland more directly under English authority but in many respects the country retained its own system of government.

The remaining supporters of James VII, the Jacobites, led two abortive risings on behalf of James's son and grandson (the old and new Pretenders) but were defeated decisively at Culloden in 1746.

TERRITORY AND POPULATION

The total area of Scotland is 78,133 sq. km (census of 21 April 1991), including its islands, 186 in number, and inland water 1,580 sq. km.

Population (including military in the barracks and seamen on board vessels in the harbours) at the dates of each census:

Date of enumeration	Population	Pop. per sq. mile[1]	Date of enumeration	Population	Pop. per sq. mile[1]
1811	1,805,864	60	1901	4,472,103	150
1821	2,091,521	70	1911	4,760,904	160
1831	2,364,386	79	1921	4,882,497	164
1841	2,620,184	88	1931	4,842,980	163
1851	2,888,742	97	1951	5,096,415	171
1861	3,062,294	100	1961	5,179,344	174
1871	3,360,018	113	1971	5,229,963	68
1881	3,735,573	125	1981	5,130,735	66
1891	4,025,647	135	1991	4,998,567	60

[1]Per sq. km from 1971.

Population (usually resident) at the census of 1991:

Males	Females	Total
2,391,961	2,606,606	4,998,567

Population density (persons per ha), 1991 census: 0·6. Estimated 1998 population, 5,119,000, giving a density of 0·66 per ha.

In 1991, 65,978 of the usually resident population could speak Gaelic (79,297 in 1981). Private households at the 1991 census: 2,036,136.

The age distribution in 1991 of the 'usually resident' population of Scotland was as follows (in 1,000):

Age-group		
Under	5	317
5 and under	10	318
10 ,,	15	312
15 ,,	20	332
20 ,,	25	375
25 ,,	35	768
35 ,,	45	695
45 ,,	55	578
55 ,,	65	537
65 ,,	70	247
70 ,,	75	193
75 ,,	85	259
85 and upwards		68

Until April 1996 Scotland was divided into 9 regions (subdivided into 53 districts) and 3 island authority areas. Area of regions and usually resident population figures of regions and districts at the 1991 census:

Regions (area sq. km) and Districts	Population	Regions (area sq. km) and Districts	Population
Borders (4,713)	103,881	Lothian (1,716)	726,010
Berwickshire	19,174	East Lothian	84,114
Ettrick and Lauderdale	34,038	Edinburgh City	418,914
Roxburgh	35,346	Midlothian	78,845
Tweeddale	15,323	West Lothian	144,137
Central (2,635)	267,492	Strathclyde (13,503)	2,248,706
Clackmannan	47,679	Argyll and Bute	65,140
Falkirk	140,980	Bearsden and Milngavie	40,612
Stirling	78,833	Clydebank	45,717
		Clydesdale	57,588
Dumfries and Galloway (6,396)	147,805	Cumbernauld and Kilsyth	62,412
Annandale and Eskdale	37,087	Cumnock and Doon Valley	42,594
Nithsdale	57,012	Cunninghame	136,875
Stewartry	23,629	Dumbarton	77,173
Wigtown	30,077	East Kilbride	82,777
		Eastwood	59,959
Fife (1,312)	341,199	Glasgow City	662,853
Dunfermline	127,258	Hamilton	105,202
Kirkcaldy	147,053	Inverclyde	90,103
North East Fife	66,888	Kilmarnock and Loudoun	79,861
		Kyle and Carrick	112,658
Grampian (8,698)	503,888	Monklands	102,379
Aberdeen City	204,885	Motherwell	142,632
Banff and Buchan	85,303	Renfrew	196,980
Gordon	76,642	Strathkelvin	85,191
Kincardine and Deeside	53,442		
Moray	83,616	Tayside (7,942)	383,848
		Angus	94,480
Highland (25,398)	204,004	Dundee City	165,873
Badenoch and Strathspey	11,008	Perth and Kinross	123,495
Caithness	26,710		
Inverness	62,186	Island Authority Areas	
Lochaber	19,310	Orkney Islands (976)	19,612
Nairn	10,623	Shetland Islands (1,433)	22,522
Ross and Cromarty	49,197	Western Isles (2,898)	29,600
Skye and Lochalsh	11,754		
Sutherland	13,216		

In April 1996, 29 new unitary authority areas came into being: Aberdeen City, Aberdeenshire, Angus, Argyll and Bute, Clackmannanshire, Dumfries and Galloway, Dundee City, East Ayrshire, East Dunbartonshire, East Lothian, East Renfrewshire, City of Edinburgh, Falkirk, Fife, Glasgow City, Highland, Inverclyde, Midlothian, Moray, North Ayrshire, North Lanarkshire, Perth and Kinross, Renfrewshire, Scottish Borders, South Ayrshire, South Lanarkshire, Stirling, West Dunbartonshire, West Lothian. The Island Authority Areas (Orkney, Shetland, Western Isles) remained as they were.

Glasgow is Scotland's largest city, with an estimated population of 616,000 in 1996, followed by Edinburgh, the capital (estimated 1996 population of 449,000), and Aberdeen, with 217,000.

The birthplaces of the 1991 usually resident population were: Scotland, 4,454,065; England, 354,268; Wales, 4,710; Northern Ireland, 26,393; Ireland 22,773; Commonwealth, 59,134; foreign countries, 148,987.

SOCIAL STATISTICS

	Estimated resident population at 30 June[1]	Total births	Live births outside marriage	Deaths	Marriages	Divorces, annulments and dissolutions
1991	5,107,000	67,024	19,517	61,041	33,762	12,399
1992	5,111,200	65,789	19,950	60,937	35,057	12,479
1993	5,120,200	63,337	19,855	64,049	33,366	12,787

	Estimated resident population at 30 June[1]	Total births	Live births outside marriage	Deaths	Marriages	Divorces, annulments and dissolutions
1994	5,132,400	61,656	19,224	59,328	31,480	13,133
1995	5,136,600	60,051	20,266	60,500	30,663	12,249
1996	5,128,000	59,440	21,361	60,671	30,242	11,123

[1]Includes merchant navy at home and forces stationed in Scotland.

Birth rate, 1997, per 1,000 population, 11·6; death rate, 11·6; marriage, 5·9 (1996); infant mortality per 1,000 live births, 5·3; sex ratio, 1,061 male births to 1,000 female (1996). Average age of marriage in 1996: Males, 29·1, females, 27·4. Expectation of life, 1997: Males, 72·6 years, females, 78·01.

CLIMATE
For more detailed information, see under Climate, Great Britain.

Aberdeen, Jan. 38°F (3·3°C), July 57°F (13·9°C). Annual rainfall 32" (813 mm). Edinburgh, Jan. 38°F (3·3°C), July 58°F (14·5°C). Annual rainfall 27" (686 mm). Glasgow, Jan. 39°F (3·9°C), July 59°F (15°C). Annual rainfall 38" (965 mm).

CONSTITUTION AND GOVERNMENT
One of the main aspects of the British Labour Government's programme of constitutional reform is devolution. In the referendum on Scottish devolution on 11 Sept. 1997, 1,775,045 votes (74·3%) were cast in favour of a Scottish parliament and 614,400 against (25·7%). The turn-out was 60·4%, so around 44·8% of the total electorate voted in favour. For the second question, on the Parliament's tax-raising powers, 1,512,889 votes were cast in favour (63·5%) and 870,263 against (36·5%). This represented 38·4% of the total electorate.

The Parliamentary electorate of Scotland in the register numbered 3,992,502 in 1998.

RECENT ELECTIONS
At the UK general election held in May 1997, 72 members were returned from Scotland. The Scottish National Party gained 6 seats (3 in 1992). At the June 1994 European Parliament elections the Scottish National Party won 2 seats with 3·2% of the votes cast (European Radical Alliance).

The first elections for a Scottish Parliament were scheduled for 6 May 1999.

See also Constitution and Government, Recent Elections and Current Administration in Great Britain.

CURRENT ADMINISTRATION
Local Government. Local authorities have statutory powers and claims on public funds. Relations with central government are maintained through the Scottish Office. The Local Government (Scotland) Act 1994 set up 29 unitary authorities alongside the existing 3 Island Authority Areas. There are about 1,000 community councils, but unlike their English and Welsh counterparts, they do not have statutory powers.

Resident citizens of the UK, Ireland, a Commonwealth country or an EU country may (at age 18) vote and (at age 21) stand for election. Elections for the full councils are held every 3 years. Mayors of cities may have the title of Lord Mayor conferred on them. 4 towns in Scotland have the status of city (Aberdeen, Dundee, Edinburgh and Glasgow). This status is granted by the personal command of the monarch and confers no special privileges or powers. The chair of city councils is deemed Lord Provost, and is elsewhere known as Convenor or Provost. Basic and other allowances are payable to councillors (except Scottish community councillors).

On 6 April 1995 elections were held for the 29 newly-created unitary councils. 1,161 seats were contested. The Scottish National Party won 181 seats with 26% and gained 3 councils.

The next local government elections were scheduled for 6 May 1999.

DEFENCE
For information on defence, see Great Britain.

ECONOMY

Performance. A deceleration in Scottish GDP growth was predicted for 1999 of between 1·4% and 1·7%, but growth was expected to recover to between 1·9% and 2·9% in 2000.

Budget. Government expenditure in Scotland came to £24,748m. in 1996–97, of which £9,142m. went on social security, £5,225m. on health and personal social services and £4,026m. on education.

Currency. The Bank of Scotland, Clydesdale Bank and the Royal Bank of Scotland have note-issuing powers. The underlying inflation rate rose to 2·6% in Dec. 1998.

Banking and Finance. There is a stock exchange in Glasgow.

ENERGY AND NATURAL RESOURCES

Water. Water supply is the responsibility of the Regional and Island local authorities. 7 river purification boards are responsible for environmental management.

Agriculture. In 1997 total agricultural area was 6,122,000 ha, of which 3,494,000 ha were used for rough grazing and 1,809,000 ha for crops and grass.

Selected crop production, 1997 (1,000 tonnes): Barley, 1,813; potatoes, 1,149; wheat, 821; oats,121.

Livestock, 1997 (in 1,000): Cattle, 2,079; sheep, 9,563; pigs, 645; poultry, 14,725.

Forestry. Total forest area in 1997 was 1,189,000 ha, of which 503,000 ha was state-owned.

Fisheries. The major fishing ports are Aberdeen, Mallaig, Lerwick and Peterhead. In 1997 there were 2,770 fishing vessels that landed 686,400 tonnes of fish worth £278·7m.

INDUSTRY

Labour. In 1997 the economically active population numbered 2,490,000 (1,126,000 females), of whom 212,000 (78,000) were unemployed. This equates to an unemployment rate of 8·5% for men and 7·0% for women. There were 24,600 notified job vacancies at Dec. 1996.

COMMUNICATIONS

Roads. Responsibility for the construction and maintenance of trunk roads belongs to the Scottish Office. Roads not classified as trunk roads are the responsibility of county or unitary councils. In 1997 there were 53,100 km of public roads, of which 329 km were motorways. There were 1,779,000 licenced private and light goods vehicles.

Rail. Total railway length in 1997 was 2,696 km. There is a metro in Glasgow.

Civil Aviation. There are major airports at Aberdeen, Edinburgh, Glasgow and Prestwick. In 1997, 14,429,000 passengers and 63,100 tonnes of freight were carried.

Shipping. The principal Scottish port is Forth, which handled 43·1m. tonnes of cargo in 1997.

SOCIAL INSTITUTIONS

Justice. The High Court of Justiciary is the supreme criminal court in Scotland and has jurisdiction in all cases of crime committed in any part of Scotland, unless expressly excluded by statute. It consists of the Lord Justice General, the Lord Justice Clerk and 24 other Judges, who are the same Judges who preside in the Court of Session, the Scottish Supreme Civil Court. One Judge is seconded to the Scottish Law Commission. The Court is presided over by the Lord Justice General, whom failing, by the Lord Justice Clerk, and exercises an appellate jurisdiction as well as being a court of first instance. The home of the High Court is Edinburgh, but the court visits other towns and cities in Scotland on circuit and indeed the busiest High Court sitting is in Glasgow. The court sits in Edinburgh both as a Court of Appeal (the *quorum* being 2 judges if the appeal is against sentence or other disposals, and 3 in all other cases) and on circuit as a court of first instance. Although the decisions of the High Court are not subject to review by the House of Lords, with the Scotland Act 1998 coming into force on 20 May 1999, there is a limited right of appeal against the termination of a devolution issue to the Judicial Committee of the Privy Council. One Judge sitting with a Jury of 15 persons can, and usually does, try cases, but 2 or more Judges (with a Jury) may do so in important or complex cases. The court has a privative jurisdiction over cases of treason, murder, rape, breach of duty by Magistrates and certain statutory offences under the Official Secrets Act 1911 and the Geneva Conventions Act 1957. It also tries the most serious crimes against person or property and those cases in which a sentence greater than imprisonment for 3 years is likely to be imposed. Once the Human Rights Act 1998 comes into force in mid-2000, the court will no longer be able to exercise its declaratory power to try and to punish all acts which are plainly criminal though previously unknown to law.

The appellate jurisdiction of the High Court of Justiciary extends to all cases tried on indictment, whether in the High Court or the Sheriff Court, and persons so convicted may appeal to the court against conviction or sentence, or both, except where the sentence is fixed by law. In such an appeal, a person may bring under review any alleged miscarriage of justice including an alleged miscarriage of justice based on the existence and significance of evidence not heard at the original proceedings provided there is reasonable explanation of why it was not heard and an alleged miscarriage of justice where the Jury returned a verdict which no reasonable Jury, properly directed, could have returned. It is also a court of review from courts of summary jurisdiction, and on the final termination of any summary prosecution the convicted person may appeal to the court by way of stated case on questions of law, but not on questions of fact, except in relation to a miscarriage of justice alleged by the person accused on the basis of the existence and significance of additional evidence not heard at the original proceedings provided that there is a reasonable explanation of why it was not heard. Before cases proceed to a full hearing, leave of appeal must first be granted. Grounds of appeal and any relevant reports are sifted by a Judge sitting alone in chambers, who will decide if there are arguable grounds of appeal. Should leave of appeal be refused, this decision may be appealed to the High Court within 14 days, when the matter will be reviewed by 3 Judges. The Lord Advocate is entitled to appeal to the High Court against any sentence passed on indictment on the ground that it is unduly lenient, or on a point of law. Both the prosecution and defence, at any time in solemn and summary proceedings, may appeal by way of Bill of Advocation in order to correct irregularities in the preliminary stages of a case. In summary proceedings the accused may appeal by Bill of Suspension, where he desires to bring under review a warrant, conviction or judgement issued by an inferior Judge. In summary proceedings the accused can also appeal against sentence alone by way of Stated Case. In summary proceedings the Crown can appeal against a sentence on the grounds that it is unduly lenient. The court also hears appeals under the Courts-Martial (Appeals) Act 1951.

The Sheriff Court has an inherent universal criminal jurisdiction (as well as an extensive civil one), limited in general to crimes and offences committed within a sheriffdom (a specifically defined region), which has, however, been curtailed by statute or practice under which the High Court of Justiciary has exclusive jurisdiction in relation to the crimes mentioned above. The Sheriff Court is presided over by a Sheriff Principal or a Sheriff, who when trying cases on indictment sits with a Jury of 15 people. His powers of awarding punishment involving imprisonment are restricted to a maximum of 3 years, but he may under certain statutory powers remit the prisoner to the High Court for sentence if this is felt to be insufficient. The Sheriff also exercises a wide summary criminal jurisdiction and when doing so sits without a Jury; and he has concurrent jurisdiction with every other court within his Sheriff Court district in regard to all offences competent for trial in summary courts. The great majority of offences which come before courts are of a more minor nature and as such are disposed of in the Sheriff Summary Courts or in the District Courts (*see* below). Where a case is to be tried on indictment either in the High Court of Justiciary or in the Sheriff Court, the Judge may, before the trial, hold a preliminary or first diet to decide questions of a preliminary nature, whether relating to the competency or relevancy of proceedings

SCOTLAND

or otherwise. Any decision at a preliminary diet (other than a decision to adjourn the first or preliminary diet or discharge trial diet) can be the subject of an appeal to the High Court of Justiciary prior to the trial. The High Court also has the exclusive power to provide a remedy for all extraordinary occurrences in the course of criminal business where there is no other mode of appeal available. This is known as the Nobile Officium powers of the High Court and all petitions to the High Court as the Nobile Officium must be heard before at least 3 judges.

In cases to be tried on indictment in the Sheriff Court a first diet is mandatory before the trial diet to decide questions of a preliminary nature and to identify cases which are unlikely to go to trial on the date programmed. Likewise in summary proceedings, an intermediate diet is again mandatory before trial. In High Court cases such matters may be dealt with at a preliminary diet.

District Courts have jurisdiction in more minor offences occurring within a district which before recent local government reorganization corresponded to district council boundaries. These courts are presided over by Lay Magistrates, known as Justices, who have limited powers for fine and imprisonment. In Glasgow District there are also Stipendiary Magistrates, who are legally qualified, and who have the same sentencing powers as Sheriffs.

The Court of Session, presided over by the Lord President (the Lord Justice General in criminal cases), is divided into an inner-house comprising 2 divisions of 4 judges each with a mainly appellate function, and an outer-house comprising 18 single Judges sitting individually at first instance; it exercises the highest civil jurisdiction in Scotland, with the House of Lords as a Court of Appeal.

Police. In Scotland, the unitary councils have the role of police authorities. Establishment levels throughtthe UK home office were abolished in Scotland on 1 April 1996. The actual strength at 31 March 1998 was 12,652 men and 2,227 women. There were 1,723 special constables. The total police net expenditure in Scotland for 1996–97 was £655·7m.

CIVIL JUDICIAL STATISTICS

	1996	1997
House of Lords (Appeals from Court of Session)	15	6
Court of Session—		
General Department	3,638	3,397
Petition Department	1,045	1,116
Sheriff Courts—Ordinary Cause	45,660	44,366
Sheriff Courts—Summary Cause	30,078	33,447
Small Claims	59,009	56,551

CRIMINAL STATISTICS

	All Crimes and Offences		Crimes[1]	
	1994	1995	1994	1995
All persons and companies				
Cautioned	120,561	113,065	90,643	79,858
Proceeded against in all courts	178,292	176,420	62,432	61,859
Charge proved	158,119	156,707	51,265	51,073
Children (aged 8–15)				
Proceeded against in all courts	237	244	182	194

[1]Crimes are generally the more serious criminal acts and offences the less serious. 'Crimes' are not equivalent in coverage to 'indictable/triable either way offences'.

In 1997 there were 421,000 crimes reported, of which 19,000 were violent. There were 48,000 criminal convictions in 1997 and an average prison population in Scotland of 6,084.

Religion. The Church of Scotland, which was reformed in 1560, subsequently developed a presbyterian system of church government which was established in 1690 and has continued to the present day.

The supreme court is the General Assembly, which now consists of some 800 members, ministers and elders in equal numbers, together with members of the diaconate commissioned by presbyteries. It meets annually in May, under the presidency of a Moderator appointed by the Assembly. The Queen is normally represented by a Lord High Commissioner, but has occasionally attended in person. The royal presence in a special throne gallery in the hall but outside the Assembly symbolizes the independence from state control of what is nevertheless recognized as the national Church in Scotland.

There are also 46 presbyteries in Scotland, roughly co-terminous with District Councils, together with 1 presbytery of England, 1 presbytery of Europe, and 1 presbytery of Jerusalem. At the base of this conciliar structure of Church courts are the kirk sessions, of which there were 1,601 on 31 Dec. 1997. The total communicant membership of the Church at that date was 664,237.

The Episcopal Church of Scotland is a province of the Anglican Church and is one of the historic Scottish churches. It consists of 7 dioceses. As at 31 Dec. 1998 it had 313 churches and missions, 351 clergy and 52,641 members, of whom 32,218 were communicants.

There are in Scotland some small outstanding Presbyterian bodies and also Baptists, Congregationalists, Methodists and Unitarians.

The Roman Catholic Church which celebrated the centenary of the restoration of the Hierarchy in 1978, had in Scotland (1998) 1 cardinal archbishop, 1 archbishop, 5 bishops, 20 permanent deacons, 907 clergy, 463 parishes, and 705,650 adherents.

The proportion of marriages in Scotland according to the rites of the various Churches in 1995 was: Church of Scotland, 36·5%; Roman Catholic, 9·6%; Episcopal, 1·5%; others, 6%; civil, 46·4%.

Education. In Sept. 1997 there were 3,869 publicly funded (education authority, grant-aided and self-governing) schools. All teachers employed in these schools require to be qualified; all figures on teaching relate to Sept. 1996 and are full-time equivalents.

Nursery Education. There were 1,010 publicly funded nursery schools and classes, with a total enrolment of 53,260 pupils in Sept. 1997.

Primary Education. In Sept. 1997 there were 2,300 publicly funded primary schools with 440,594 pupils and 21,187 teachers.

Secondary Education. In Sept. 1997 there were 401 publicly funded secondary schools with 314,916 pupils and 2,044 adults. All but 26 schools provided a full range of Scottish Certificate of Education courses and non-certificate courses. Pupils who start their secondary education in schools which do not cater for a full range of courses may be transferred at the end of their second or fourth year to schools where a full range of courses is provided. There were 23,875 full-time equivalent teachers in secondary schools.

Independent schools. There were 209 independent schools in Sept. 1997, with a total of 32,782 pupils. A small number of the Scottish independent schools are of the 'public school' type, but they are not known as 'public schools' since in Scotland this term is used to denote education authority (i.e., state) schools.

Special Education. In Sept. 1997 there were 158 publicly funded special schools with 8,056 pupils.

Further Education. Under the Further and Higher Education (Scotland) Act 1992 funding of further education colleges was transferred to central government on 1 April 1993.

There are 43 incorporated colleges as well as the education centres in Orkney and Shetland, which are run by the education authorities but funded by direct payments from the Scottish Office Education and Industry Department. The colleges offer training in a wide range of vocational areas and co-operate with the Scottish Qualifications Authority and the Scottish Office Education and Industry Department in the development of new courses. Scottish Vocational Qualifications (SVQs) were introduced in 1989 and General SVQs were piloted in 1993. Both qualifications aim to improve the skills of the nation's workforce and increase the country's competitiveness. The colleges benefit from co-operation with industry, both by the involvement of Industry Lead Bodies and National Training Organizations in developing SVQs, and by membership of the college boards of management.

In 1996–97 there were 334,365 students enrolled at the 43 colleges on vocational courses (61,495 full-time and sandwich). The full-time equivalent staff number in the colleges was 6,865.

SCOTLAND

A student support system is administered by the Student Awards Agency for Scotland. The Agency offers means-tested awards to eligible Scottish-domiciled students undertaking courses of Higher Education. The arrangements described above for new students in 1998–99 will also apply to Scottish students. The Agency also administers the Postgraduate Students' Allowance Scheme and the Scottish Studentship Scheme (SSS) which offer means-tested awards to students studying at postgraduate and advanced postgraduate levels respectively. 75 new awards are offered each year under the SSS for study in the field of Arts and Humanities.

Awards known as state studentships are offered on a competitive basis by the Students Awards Agency for Scotland to candidates considered by the universities and other higher education institutions to be qualified for postgraduate studies in the humanities; similar awards, tenable at universities or other higher education institutions are offered by the Research Councils to students studying topics within the broad spectrum of agriculture and food; the biological sciences; man's natural environment; science and engineering, and the social sciences at postgraduate level.

Higher Education. In Scotland in 1997 there were 21 institutions of higher education funded by the SHEFC, of which 5 were universities formed from former central institutions (cf. English polytechnics): Abertay Dundee Univ., Glasgow Caledonian Univ., Napier Univ. (Edinburgh), Univ. of Paisley, The Robert Gordon Univ. (Aberdeen); and 8 were already-existing universities:

a) *Universities*

Name (and Location)	Full-time and sandwich students (1996–97)	Full-time academic staff (1996–97)
Aberdeen Univ.	9,425	649
Abertay Dundee Univ.	3,698	247
Dundee Univ.	8,367	687
Edinburgh Univ.	15,880	1,232
Glasgow Univ.	15,270	1,339
Glasgow Caledonian Univ.	10,835	750
Heriot-Watt Univ. (Edinburgh)	4,550	331
Napier Univ. (Edinburgh)	8,437	618
Paisley Univ.	6,509	445
Robert Gordon Univ. (Aberdeen)	7,041	439
St Andrews Univ.	5,684	425
Stirling Univ.	6,466	402
Strathclyde Univ. (Glasgow)	14,980	913
Total	*117,412*	*8,477*

b) *Other Institutions*

Edinburgh College of Art, Glasgow School of Art, Moray House Institute of Education (Edinburgh), Northern College of Education (Aberdeen and Dundee), Queen Margaret College (Edinburgh), Royal Scottish Academy of Music and Drama (Glasgow), Scottish College of Textiles (Galashiels), St. Andrew's College of Education (Glasgow).

The Scottish Agricultural College (Perth) is funded by the Scottish Office Agriculture and Fisheries Department.

In 1996–97 there were 127,934 full-time and sandwich students at the institutions funded by SHEFC (67,095 female).

All the higher education institutions are independent and self-governing. In addition to funding through the higher education funding councils, they receive tuition fees through local education authorities for students domiciled in England and Wales, and from the Students Awards Agency for Scotland for students domiciled in Scotland. Institutions which carry out research may also receive funding through the 5 Research Councils administered by the Office of Science and Technology.

Health. At 1 Oct. 1997 there were 3,700 GPs with average patient list size of 1,468, and 1,800 dental practitioners with average list size of 2,800.

Welfare. In 1997 there were 861,600 recipients of National Insurance retirement pensions, 29,000 recipients of contribution-based Jobseeker's Allowance, and 74,000 families receiving family income supplement/family credit.

CULTURE
Scotland's landmark project for the millennium is the rebuilding of Glasgow's Hampden Park Stadium.

Tourism. There were 2,100,000 overseas visitors to Scotland in 1997. The tourist attraction receiving the most visitors was Edinburgh Castle, with 1,238,140 visits in 1997.

Festivals. The Edinburgh Festival and the Fringe Festival both take place in late-Aug./early-Sept. and are major international festivals of culture.

Museums and Galleries. The most visited museum is Glasgow Art Gallery and Museum, with 1,053,745 visits in 1997, followed by the Royal Museum of Scotland, in Edinburgh, with 591,152 visits.

FURTHER READING
Scottish Office. Scottish Economic Bulletin. HMSO (quarterly).—*Scottish Abstract of Statistics.* HMSO (annual)

Brown, A. et al., *Politics and Society in Scotland.* London, 1996
Bruce, D., *The Mark of the Scots.* Birch Lane Press, 1997
Dennistoun, R. and Linklater, M. (eds.) *Anatomy of Scotland.* Edinburgh, 1992
Devine, T. M. and Finlay, R. J. (eds.) *Scotland in the 20th Century.* Edinburgh Univ. Press, 1996
Donaldson, G. (ed.) *The Edinburgh History of Scotland.* 4 vols. Edinburgh, 1965–75
Grant, E., *Scotland.* [Bibliography] Oxford and Santa Barbara (CA), 1982
Harvie, C., *Scotland and Nationalism: Scottish Society and Politics, 1707–1994.* 2nd ed. London, 1994
Hunter, J., *A Dance Called America.* Edinburgh, 1997
Lynch, M., *Scotland: a New History.* London, 1991
Macleod, J., *Highlanders: A History of the Gaels.* London, 1997
McCaffrey, J. F., *Scotland in the Nineteenth Century.* London, 1998

WALES

KEY HISTORICAL EVENTS
After the Roman evacuation, Wales divided into tribal kingdoms. Cunedda Wledig, a prince from southern Scotland, founded a dynasty in the north-west district of Gwynedd to become the centrepoint for Welsh unity. Offa's Dyke, the defensive earthwork built in the time of King Offa of Mercia, was the dividing line between England and Wales but over the next two centuries a succession of Welsh kings deferred to the English monarchy.

With the accession of Llewelyn (1194-1240) the house of Gwynedd overcame rival claims from Powys and Deneubarth to forge a stable political state under English suzerainty. But when Llywelyn ap Gruffydd (1246-82) intrigued against Edward I, Wales was annexed and Edward's infant son, born at Caernarvon, was made Prince of Wales.

In the Tudor period, Welsh loyalty to Henry VIII, who was of Welsh descent, was fully reciprocated. The Act of Union in 1536 made English law general and admitted Welsh representatives to Parliament.

TERRITORY AND POPULATION
At the census taken on 21 April 1991 the area of Wales was 20,766 sq. km and the population 2,811,865.

Population ('usually resident') at the census of 1991:

Males	Females	Total
1,370,104	1,464,969	2,835,073

Population (present on census night) at the 4 previous decennial censuses:

1951	1961	1971	1981
2,598,675[1]	2,644,023[1]	2,731,204[1]	2,790,500[2]

[1]Areas now recognized as part of Gwent formed the English county of Monmouthshire until 1974. [2]The final count is believed to be over-stated as a result of an error in processing. The preliminary counts presented here rounded to the nearest hundred are thought to be more accurate.

Population density (persons per ha), 1991 census: 1·4. Estimated population, mid-1998, 2,937,000, giving a density of 1·41 per ha. Cardiff, the capital and largest city, had a population in 1996 of 315,000; Swansea, the second largest city, had a population of 230,000 in 1996.

In 1991 in Wales 508,098 persons were able to speak Welsh. Private households at the 1991 census: 1,201,700.

For further statistical information, see under Territory and Population, Great Britain.

Wales is divided into 22 unitary authorities (counties and county boroughs).

Areas (in sq. km) and usually resident population at the 1991 census:

	Area	Population		Area	Population
Clwyd	2,430	408,090	Powys	5,072	117,647
Dyfed	5,766	343,543	South Glamorgan		
Gwent	1,377	442,212	(S. Glam)	416	392,780
Gwynedd	3,863	235,452	West Glamorgan		
Mid Glamorgan			(W. Glam)	820	361,428
(M. Glam)	1,017	534,101			

As a result of the Local Government Act 1992 the following new unitary authorities were established: (*Counties:* Carmarthenshire, Ceredigion, Denbighshire, Flintshire, Gwynedd, Isle of Anglesey, Monmouthshire, Pembrokeshire, Powys; *County Boroughs:* Blaenau Gwent, Bridgend, Caerphilly, Cardiff, Conwy, Merthyr Tydfil, Neath Port Talbot, Newport, Rhondda Cynon Taff, Swansea, Torfaen, Vale of Glamorgan, Wrexham).

SOCIAL STATISTICS
1997: Births, 34,504 (60·5 per 1,000 women), of which 14,784 outside marriage; deaths, 34,640 (11·8 per 1,000 population); marriages, 14,548 (12·3 per 1,000 population); divorces, 8,702; still births, 176 (5 per 1,000 births); infant mortality, 203 (6 per 1,000 live births).

CLIMATE
For more detailed information, see under Climate, Great Britain.
Cardiff, Jan. 40°F (4·4°C), July 61°F (16·1°C). Annual rainfall 42·6" (1,065 mm).

CONSTITUTION AND GOVERNMENT
One of the main aspects of the British Labour Government's programme of constitutional reform is devolution. On 18 Sept. 1997 in the referendum there were 559,419 votes cast in favour of a Welsh assembly (50·3%) and 552,698 against (49·7%). The turn-out was 51·3%.

The Parliamentary electorate of Wales in the register in 1998 numbered 2,230,451.

RECENT ELECTIONS
At the UK general election of 1 May 1997, 40 members were returned from Wales. Labour won 34 seats (27 in 1992), Plaid Cymru, 4 seats (4), Liberals, 2 seats (1). There were 2,201,000 eligible voters, and turn-out was 73·5%. At the 1994 European Parliamentary elections, 5 Labour candidates were elected.

The first elections for the Welsh Assembly were scheduled for 6 May 1999.

See also Constitution and Government, Recent Elections and Current Administration in Great Britain.

CURRENT ADMINISTRATION
Local Government. Local authorities have statutory powers and claims on public funds. Relations with central government (pre-devolution) are maintained through the Welsh Office. The Local Government (Wales) Act 1994 set up 22 unitary authorities (9 counties and 13 county boroughs). 730 community councils manage local facilities and may act as agents for district council functions.

Resident citizens of the UK, Ireland, a Commonwealth country or an EU country may (at age 18) vote and (at age 21) stand for election. Elections for the full councils are held every 4 years. The chair is called Chairman in counties and Mayor in county boroughs.

The next local government elections were scheduled for 6 May 1999.

DEFENCE

For information on defence, see Great Britain.

ECONOMY

For information on the economy, see Great Britain.

Performance. GDP at factor cost in 1996 (provisional) was £25,995m.

Budget. General government expenditure in 1996–97 amounted to £4,620m.

ENERGY AND NATURAL RESOURCES

For information on energy and natural resources, see Great Britain.

Water. The Water Act of Sept. 1989 privatized Welsh Water, along with the 9 water authorities in England. Daily output, 1997, was 2,305 megalitres.

Agriculture. In 1997 there were 27,973 agricultural holdings. Of these, 916 were under 2 ha, 9,997 were between 2 and 19 ha, 5,671 were between 20 and 39 ha and 9,820 were over 40 ha. 1,569 were rough-grazing holdings. A total of 74,200 ha were used for crops, 76,000 ha for tillage and 1,900 ha left bare fallow. Major crops, 1997, (1,000 tonnes): Barley, 174; wheat, 107; potatoes, 58; oats, 18.

Livestock, 1997: Cattle, 1,323,000; sheep and lambs, 10,915,100; pigs, 98,600; poultry, 8,364,000.

Forestry. In 1998 there were 118,000 ha of Forestry Commission woodland and 129,000 ha of private woodland.

Fisheries. The major fishing port is Milford Haven. In 1997, in all ports, 19,211 tonnes of fish worth £12,835,600 were landed. There were 513 fishing vessels in all.

INDUSTRY

Selected industrial production, 1996 (£1m.): Basic metals and fabricated metal products, 1,656·7; electrical and optical equipment, 1,145·4; food products, beverages and tobacco, 877·6; chemicals, chemical products and man-made fibres, 736·3; transport equipment, 730·9.

Labour. At June 1998, the workforce numbered 1,227,000. There were 67,000 people claiming unemployment benefit and 172,000 people were self-employed. The largest employment sectors were: services, 699,000; production and construction industries, 265,000; manufacturing, 213,000.

INTERNATIONAL TRADE

For information on international trade, see Great Britain.

COMMUNICATIONS

Roads. Responsibility for the construction and maintenance of trunk roads belongs to the Welsh Office. Roads not classified as trunk roads are the responsibility of county or unitary councils. In 1998 there were 133 km of motorway, 1,585 km of trunk roads and 2,685 km of principal roads. 1,300,500 vehicles were registered, including 1,112,300 private and light goods vehicles. In 1997 there were 10,251 reported accidents which led to 14,835 casualties and 221 deaths.

Civil Aviation. Cardiff Airport handled 1,009,970 passengers in 1996 (917,034 on international flights) and 748 tonnes of freight.

Shipping. The principal ports are (with 1m. tonnes of cargo handled in 1997): Milford Haven (34·5) and Port Talbot (13·1).

Postal Services. In 1997–98, the Post Office handled 712m. letters and 3·4m. parcels.

SOCIAL INSTITUTIONS

Justice. In 1997 police strength amounted to 6,598. During that year there were 236,937 notable offences, including 17,387 violent and 1,874 sexual offences. The clear-up rate was 40·6%. 17,350 people were found guilty of indictable offences in Magistrates' Courts and 4,040 in Crown Courts. A total of 4,158 people were given custodial sentences.

Religion. Under the Welsh Church Acts, 1914 and 1919, the Church in Wales and Monmouthshire was disestablished as from 1 April 1920, and Wales was formed into a separate Province.

Education. There were 47 maintained nursery schools in 1997, and 66,972 pupils under 5 years provided for in nursery or infant classes in primary schools.

In Jan. 1998 there were 282,738 pupils at 1,672 primary schools. In those primary schools (and some secondary schools) which are in the predominantly Welsh-speaking areas, the main language of instruction is Welsh. There are also 'Welsh', or, more accurately, bilingual schools in mainly English-speaking parts of Wales. Generally, children transfer from primary to secondary schools at 11.

In Jan. 1998 there were 229 secondary schools. The majority of secondary schools are classified as comprehensive. In 1996, 67 schools used Welsh as a teaching medium.

Local education authority-maintained secondary, middle and primary schools can apply for Grant Maintained (GM) status as self-governing state schools. By Sept. 1997 there were 5 GM primary, 1 middle and 11 secondary schools.

Under the Education Act 1996 children have special educational needs if they have a learning difficulty which calls for special educational provision to be made for them. In a minority of cases, perhaps just over 2% of children, the Local Education Authority will need to make a statutory assessment of special educational needs under the Education Act 1996, which may ultimately lead to a 'statement'. The total number of pupils with statements in 1995 was 14,521.

In Nov. 1997 there were 29 institutions in the further education sector and 191,966 students.

In 1994, 10,672 full-time pupils attended 64 independent schools.

Higher Education. In 1998 there were 13 institutions of higher education funded directly by the HEFCW, including the University of Glamorgan and the colleges of the University of Wales. In 1997–98 the Council allocated £237m. for teaching, research and related activities. There were 84,687 students in the higher education sector in 1997–98, excluding those registered with the Open University, including 62,259 full-time, 1,084 students on their year out and 21,344 part-time students, including those enrolled on higher education provision at further education colleges.

Name	Full-time students (1997–98, provisional)[1]	No. of academic staff (1997–98)[2]
Univ. of Glamorgan (Pontypridd)	9,538	578
Univ. of Wales, Aberystwyth	6,195	536
Univ. of Wales, Bangor	6,145	673
Cardiff University	13,301	1,470
Univ. of Wales, Lampeter	1,547	119
Univ. of Wales, Swansea	8,185	866
Univ. of Wales College of Medicine	2,178	708
Univ. of Wales Institute, Cardiff	5,334	373
Univ. of Wales College, Newport	2,827	165
North East Wales Institute of Higher Education (Wrexham)	2,503	161
Swansea Institute of Higher Education	2,688	189
Trinity College Carmarthen	1,438	92
Welsh College of Music and Drama	485	104

[1]Sandwich year out counted as 0·5 full-time.
[2]Staff who meet the 25% full-time equivalent threshold.

Health. In 1997–98 there were 1,874 GPs, 924 dentists and 23,400 nurses, midwives and health visitors. The average daily number of hospital beds available was 15,200, of which 12,000 were occupied. 521,100 in-patient cases were reported, with stays lasting an average 8·4 days. 69,900 people were on hospital waiting lists.

Welfare. 230,000 people received some form of income support in 1997.

CULTURE

In Cardiff a Millennium Stadium has been constructed at Cardiff Arms Park in time to host the Rugby World Cup in 1999.

Broadcasting. Radio and television services are provided by the Welsh-language Sianel Pedwar Cymru (S4C, Channel 4 Wales). S4C is funded by the government. It acts as both broadcaster and regulator. In 1997–98, there were 1,260,900 television licences, of which 1,235,000 were colour.

Tourism. In 1997, there were 10,000,000 domestic trips (from elsewhere in the UK) into Wales. Visitors stayed 41,800,000 nights and spent £1,125m.

Festivals. Every year there are local and national *eisteddfods* (festivals for musical competitions, etc.).

Libraries. In 1996–97 there were 731 libraries with 6,128,000 books. 1,499,000 items were borrowed. The National Library is in Aberystwyth.

National Theatre and Opera. There is a Welsh National Opera and the BBC National Orchestra of Wales.

Museums and Galleries. The National Museum is in Cardiff.

FURTHER READING

Digest of Welsh Statistics. HMSO (annual)
Davies, J., *History of Wales.* London, 1993
History of Wales. vols. 3, 4 (1415–1780). 2nd ed. OUP, 1993
Huws, G. and Roberts, H., *Wales* [Bibliography]. Oxford and Santa Barbara (CA), 1990
Jenkins, G. H., *The Foundations of Modern Wales 1642–1780.* Oxford, 1988
Jenkins, P.A., *A History of Modern Wales, 1536–1990.* Harlow, 1991
Jones, G. E., *Modern Wales: a Concise History.* 2nd ed. CUP, 1994
May, J. (ed.) *Reference Wales.* Wales Univ. Press, 1994

NORTHERN IRELAND

KEY HISTORICAL EVENTS

Northern Ireland is part of the United Kingdom. The Government of Ireland Act 1920 granted Northern Ireland its own bicameral parliament (Stormont), and between 1921 and 1972 it had full responsibility for local affairs except for such matters as defence and the armed forces, foreign and trade policies, and taxation and customs. However, in the late 1960s a Civil Rights campaign and reactions to it escalated into serious rioting and sectarian violence involving the Irish Republican Army (IRA, an illegal organization aiming to unify Northern Ireland with the Republic of Ireland) and loyalist paramilitary organizations. The Northern Ireland government resigned and direct rule by the UK government began in 1972. The Northern Ireland parliament was abolished in 1973. The Northern Ireland Constitution Act 1973 provided for devolved government on a power-sharing basis, but this collapsed in May 1974.

Under the Northern Ireland Act 1974 the UK parliament approves all laws for Northern Ireland and the Northern Ireland departments are under the direction and control of a UK Cabinet Minister, the Secretary of State for Northern Ireland.

Attempts have been made by successive governments to find a means of restoring greater power to Northern Ireland's political representatives on a widely acceptable basis, including a Constitutional Convention (1975–76), a Constitutional Conference (1979–80) and 78-member Northern Ireland Assembly elected by proportional representation in 1982. This was dissolved in 1986, partly in response to Unionist reaction to the Anglo-Irish Agreement signed on 15 Nov. 1985, which established an Intergovernmental Conference of British and Irish ministers to monitor political, security, legal and other issues of concern to the nationalist community.

On 15 Dec. 1993 the Prime Ministers of the UK and the Republic of Ireland (John Major and Albert Reynolds) issued a joint declaration as a basis for all-party talks to achieve a political settlement, inviting Sinn Féin ('Ourselves Alone', pro-Republican nationalist party and the political wing of the IRA) to join the talks in an All-Ireland Forum 3 months after the cessation of terrorist violence.

The IRA announced 'a complete cessation of military operations' on 31 Aug. 1994. On 13 Oct. 1994 the anti-IRA Combined Loyalist Military Command also announced a ceasefire 'dependent upon the continued cessation of all nationalist republican violence'.

On 22 Feb. 1995 the British and Irish Prime Ministers (John Major and John Bruton) announced new joint UK-Irish proposals for a settlement in Northern Ireland contained in 2 documents: *A Framework for Accountable Government in Northern Ireland*, drawn up by the UK government, and *A New Framework for Agreement*, agreed by the UK and Irish governments.

The proposals envisaged an elected single-chamber 90-member Northern Ireland assembly with a north-south body comprising members of this assembly and representatives of the Irish government.

On 28 Nov. 1995, John Major and John Bruton agreed on a start to preliminary talks involving Northern Ireland's main political parties while a 3-member international body headed by former US Senator George Mitchell prepared a report on 'the arrangements necessary for the removal from the political equation' of paramilitary arms. The Mitchell report, published on 24 Jan. 1996, set out 6 principles to which all parties should adhere, including a commitment to renounce violence, verifiable disarmament of all paramilitaries and a pledge to adhere to any agreement reached through all-party negotiations. Concluding that the paramilitaries 'will not decommission any arms prior to all-party negotiations', the commission recommended that negotiations and decommissioning of weapons should proceed at the same time. However, John Major suggested that, 'In the absence of prior decommissioning, there may well be another way forward', proposing elections to a temporary body which could be used as a forum for negotiations.

On 9 Feb. 1996 the IRA exploded a bomb in the Docklands area of London (the first of several incidents) and announced the end of their ceasefire.

Elections were held on 30 May to constitute a 110-member forum to take part in talks with the British and Irish governments. Each of the 18 Northern Ireland constituencies returned 5 delegates. The 10 parties receiving the most votes received 2 extra delegates. The Ulster Unionist Party won 30 seats with 24·2% of votes cast; the Social Democratic and Labour Party, 21 with 21·4%; the Democratic Unionist Party, 24 with 18·8%; Sinn Féin, 17 with 15·5%; the Alliance Party, 7 with 6·5%; the United Kingdom Unionist Party, 3 with 3·7%; the Progressive Unionist Party, 2 with 3·5%; the Ulster Democratic Party, 2 with 2·2%; the Northern Ireland Women's Coalition, 2 with 1%; Labour, 2 with 0·8%. The electorate was 1·1m.

Opening Plenary talks, excluding Sinn Féin, began under the chairmanship of Senator Mitchell on 12 June 1996, with Gen. John de Chastelain (Canada) and Harri Holkeri (Finland) as deputies.

Talks resumed on 3 June 1997 under the newly elected Labour Government in which Dr Marjorie ('Mo') Mowlam was appointed as Secretary of State for Northern Ireland. The Government stated its intention that substantive negotiations should begin in September 1997, with a view to reaching a conclusion by May 1998, when the final outcome would be put to the people of Ireland, North and South, for approval in concurrent referendums.

A restoration of the IRA ceasefire was declared from 20 July 1997; the Government indicated it would assess whether it was genuine over a period of some six weeks. Sinn Féin was invited to enter the talks on 29 Aug. The talks resumed on 9 Sept. when Sinn Féin affirmed their commitment to the six Mitchell principles of democracy and non-violence.

Under the chairmanship of George Mitchell, a marathon negotiating struggle on 9–10 April 1998 led to agreement on a framework for sharing power designed to satisfy Protestant demands for a reaffirmation of their national identity as British, Catholic desires for a closer relationship with the predominantly Catholic Republic of Ireland and Britain's wish to return to Northern Ireland the powers London assumed in 1972 when the local Stormont legislature was disbanded.

Under the Good Friday Agreement, there is to be a democratically elected legislature in Belfast, a ministerial council giving the governments of Northern Ireland and Ireland joint responsibilities in areas like tourism, transportation and the environment, and a consultative council meeting twice a year to bring together ministers from the British and Irish parliaments, and the three assemblies being created in Northern Ireland and in Scotland and Wales.

The Irish government is moving to eliminate from its constitution its territorial claim on Northern Ireland.

The critical issues of police and judicial-system reform, the release of paramilitary prisoners, and the dismantling of the vast underground arsenals of weaponry in the province are the subject of further study and recommendations.

In the referendum on 22 May 1998, 71·12% of votes in Northern Ireland were cast in favour of the Good Friday peace agreement and 94·4% in the Republic of Ireland. As a consequence, in June, Northern Ireland's 1·2m. voters elected the first power-sharing administration since the collapse of the Sunningdale Agreement in 1974.

In Aug. 1998, a breakaway faction of the IRA exploded a bomb in the centre of Omagh, causing extensive mayhem. The outrage increased public demands for a workable peace. In Sept., Gerry Adams, leader of Sinn Féin, declared that violence must be 'a thing of the past'. But IRA blockage on the decommissioning of arms continues to hold up the transfer of powers from London to Belfast.

TERRITORY AND POPULATION
Area (revised by the Ordnance Survey Department) and population were as follows:

District	Population (usually resident) 1991 Census	Population present on 21 April 1991	Area in ha. (including inland water)
Antrim	44,516	44,322	57,793
Ards	64,764	64,026	38,067
Armagh	51,817	51,331	67,128
Ballymena	56,641	56,032	63,195
Ballymoney	24,198	23,984	41,855
Banbridge	33,482	33,102	44,556
Belfast	279,237	283,746	11,489
Carrickfergus	32,750	32,439	8,193
Castlereagh	60,799	60,649	8,500
Coleraine	50,438	51,062	48,555
Cookstown	31,082	30,808	62,171
Craigavon	74,986	74,494	37,925
Derry (Londonderry)	95,371	94,918	38,742
Down	58,008	57,511	64,953
Dungannon	45,428	45,322	78,323
Fermanagh	54,033	54,062	187,677
Larne	29,419	29,181	33,646
Limavady	29,57	29,201	58,635
Lisburn	99,458	99,162	44,638
Magherafelt	36,293	35,874	57,239
Moyle	14,789	14,617	49,440
Newry and Mourne	82,943	82,288	90,937
Newtownabbey	74,035	73,832	15,069
North Down	71,832	70,308	8,158
Omagh	45,809	45,343	112,990
Strabane	36,141	35,668	86,165
Northern Ireland	*1,577,836*	*1,573,282*	*1,416,039*

Chief town (population present on 21 April 1991): Belfast, 283,746.

SOCIAL STATISTICS
In 1997 there were 8,071 marriages, 2,176 deaths, 24, 277 births and 14,971 deaths.

CLIMATE
For more detailed information, see under Climate, Great Britain.

Belfast. Jan. 40°F (4·5°C), July 61°F (15°C). Annual rainfall 34·7" (885 mm).

CONSTITUTION AND GOVERNMENT
Under the Northern Ireland Act 1974 the UK parliament approves all laws for Northern Ireland and the Northern Ireland departments are under the direction and control of a UK Cabinet Minister, the Secretary of State for Northern Ireland.

NORTHERN IRELAND

The Parliamentary electorate of Northern Ireland in the register in 1998 numbered 1,188,034.

Secretary of State for Northern Ireland: Rt Hon. Marjorie ('Mo') Mowlam, MP.

RECENT ELECTIONS

At the general election of 1 May 1997, 18 members were returned from Northern Ireland. The Ulster Unionist Party gained 10 seats (9 in 1992); the Democratic Unionist Party 2 (3); the Social and Democratic Labour Party 3 (4); Sinn Féin 2 (nil); the United Kingdom Unionist 1 (replaced the Ulster Popular Unionist Party, 1 seat in 1992).

In the Northern Ireland Assembly elections on 25 June 1998, the Ulster Unionist Party (UUP) won 28 of the 108 seats, the Social Democratic and Labour Party 24, the Democratic Unionist Party 20, Sinn Féin 18, Alliance 6, United Kingdom Unionist Party 5, Independent Unionists 3, Popular Unionist Party 2 and Women's Coalition also 2.

At the June 1994 European Parliament elections, voting was by the single transferable vote system: the Democratic Ulster Unionist Party, the Social Democrat and Labour Party (European Socialist Party) and the Official Ulster Union Party (Popular European Party) gained 1 seat each.

CURRENT ADMINISTRATION

David Trimble (Ulster Unionist Party) was elected as the Northern Ireland Assembly's 'first minister' on 25 June 1998.

Local Government. Northern Ireland has a single-tier system of 26 district councils based on main centres of population. Elections were held on 19 May 1993 for the 582 council seats. The Ulster Unionist Party gained 201 seats with 34·5% of votes cast, the Social Democratic and Labour Party 127 with 21·8%, the Democratic Unionist Party 102 with 17·5%, Sinn Féin 51 with 8·8%, the Alliance 44 with 7·6%, the Conservative Party 6 with 1·8%, others 22. Independents gained 29 seats with 5%.

ECONOMY

Policy. The main Northern Ireland government department concerned with economic development is the Department of Economic Development (DED). The department and its agencies have responsibility for the promotion of inward investment and the development of larger home industry (Industrial Development Board, IDB); promotion of enterprise and small business (Local Enterprise Development Unit, LEDU); training and employment matters (Training and Employment Agency, T&EA); promotion of industrially relevant research and development and technology transfer (Industrial Research and Technology Unit, IRTU); promotion and development of tourism (Northern Ireland Tourist Board, NITB); energy matters; mineral development; company regulation; consumer protection; health and safety at work; industrial relations; equality of opportunity in employment; and better regulation.

IDB's overall objective is to encourage the development of internationally competitive companies in the manufacturing and tradeable service sectors in Northern Ireland, and to attract new inward investment, contributing to growth in durable employment.

During 1996–97, IDB secured 35 investment projects by externally owned companies, promoting 4,641 new jobs and safeguarding a further 3,345 jobs. In addition, IDB assisted 56 projects by locally owned companies, promoting 1,364 new jobs and safeguarding a further 2,232 jobs.

The *LEDU* is the small business agency (for companies employing fewer than 50 people). It aims to strengthen the economy by encouraging enterprise and new business start-ups, and by helping established small businesses achieve export-orientated, profitable growth.

In 1996–97 LEDU assisted 1,545 new business start-ups. As a result, LEDU achieved 3,425 new jobs and a further 755 among existing businesses.

The *T&EA* is an Executive Agency within DED. It assists economic development and helps people find work through training and employment services delivered on the basis of equality of opportunity. It works closely with employers and business interests, and with the other economic development agencies in making training relevant to local needs.

In 1996–97 T&EA placed 46,018 people into employment. At the end of 1996–97, 290 companies were receiving assistance to train and develop their management and workforce through the Company Development Programme. Jobskills, which commenced across Northern Ireland in April 1995, achieved its interim target for 1996–97 of 35% attainment of National Vocational Qualification (NVQ) at Level 2 or above, and the Agency is confident that the 1997–98 target of 45% will be achieved.

The *IRTU*, an Executive Agency within DED, provides the focus for all aspects of industry-related technology and innovation policy, including grants for industrial research and development, information, advice, scientific testing and analysis services.

In 1996–97, IRTU disbursed £13·1m. of Government funding to Research and Development projects; in addition, IRTU enabled companies to obtain support under EU programmes.

Currency. Banknotes are issued by Allied Irish Banks, Bank of Ireland, First Trust Bank, Northern Bank and Ulster Bank.

Banking and Finance. The Finance Department is responsible for control of the expenditure of Northern Ireland departments, liaison with HM Treasury and the Northern Ireland Office on financial matters, economic and social research and analysis, Citizens Charter Unit, the Valuation and Lands Agency, the Government Purchasing Service (Northern Ireland) and the Legal Services.

Income of the Northern Ireland Consolidated Fund (in £1,000 sterling):

	1995–96	1996–97	1997–98
Attributed share of UK taxes	3,903,450	3,960,600	4,581,501
Grant in Aid from UK Government	2,129,000	2,394,300	1,536,400
Regional and district rates	245,967	222,00	245,000
Other receipts	300,600	323,00	276,868
Total	6,234,870	6,579,018	6,639,769

The public debt at 31 March 1998 was as follows: Ulster Savings Certificates, £85,316,120; Ulster Development Bonds, £13,845; borrowing from UK Government, £1,681,126,864; borrowing from Northern Ireland Government Funds, £98,158,461; European Investment Bank Loan, £1,653,845. Excess of public income over public expenditure at 31 March 1998: –£222,790,334. Net assets available for debt repayment: £99,850,404.

The above amount of public debt is offset by equal assets in the form of loans from Government to public and local bodies, and of cash balances.

ENERGY AND NATURAL RESOURCES

Electricity. There are 4 power stations with an installed capacity of some 2,200 MW.

Oil and Gas. An undersea pipeline from Scotland was completed in 1996 to bring natural gas to Northern Ireland for the first time. Ballylumford Power Station is now operating on natural gas, and gas is currently being systematically made available to industrial, commercial and domestic consumers in the Greater Belfast and Larne areas.

Minerals. Output of minerals (in 1,000 tonnes), 1996: Basalt and igneous rock (other than granite), 6,974; sandstone, 4,941; limestone, 4,122; sand and gravel, 7,684; other minerals (rocksalt, fireclay, diatomite, granite, chalk, clay and shale), 1,392. There are lignite deposits of 1,000m. tonnes which have not yet been developed.

NORTHERN IRELAND

Agriculture. Provisional gross output in 1998:

	Quantity	Value (£1m.)			Quantity	Value (£1m.)
Finished cattle and calves	575,700	317·7	Other crops ⎫		...	7·5
Finished sheep and lambs	1,326,600	93·6	Fruit ⎬ 1,000 tonnes	24·1	5
Finished pigs	1,179,000	66·8	Vegetables ⎬	35·8	10·6
Poultry (1,000 tonnes)	165·9	91·3	Mushrooms ⎭	26	29·9
Eggs (including export of			Flowers		...	10·2
hatching eggs (m. dozen)	80·6	37·2	Quota leasing		...	5·5
Milk (m. litres)	1,509	286	Secondary activities			3·7
Other livestock products	...	14·9	Agricultural contracting			31·5
Potatoes ⎫	240·4	21·9	Gross fixed capital			
Barley ⎬ 1,000 tonnes	167·9	19·3	formation		...	44·1
Wheat ⎬	48	5·9				
Oats ⎭	12·3	1·5				
			Gross output			1,104·15

Area (in 1,000 ha) of crops at June census:

	1996	1997	1998[1]		1996	1997	1998[1]
Barley	34·2	36·4	34·8	Fruit	1·7	1·6	1·7
Wheat	6·9	6·9	7·1	Other crops	2·9	3·1	4
Oats	2·2	2·4	2·6	Grass	819·3	825·1	830·8
Potatoes	8·8	7·8	7·5	Rough grazing	169	164·1	159·1
Vegetables	1·4	1·4	1·4				

Livestock (in 1,000 heads) at June census:

	1997	1998[1]		1997	1998[1]
Cattle	1,731·0	1,763·3	Pigs	618·8	653·4
Dairy	279·2	287·7	Sows	63·8	66·9
Beef	323·9	344·7	Poultry	15,507·6	15,170·6
Sheep	2,880·1	2,986·6	Laying hens	2,848·9	2,562·1
Ewes	1,384·1	1,449·8	Broilers	8,994·9	8,854·1

[1]Provisional.

INDUSTRY

Labour. The main sources of employment statistics are the Census of Employment, conducted every 2 years, and the Quarterly Employment Survey. In June 1997 there were 585,290 employees, of whom 289,910 were males. Employment in manufacturing and construction amounted to 128,680, 22% of the total employees in employment. 19,740 of these jobs were in the food, drink and tobacco industries, 12,750 in the manufacture of wearing apparel, 10,640 in textiles, 24,240 in construction and 61,590 in other sectors of manufacturing.

COMMUNICATIONS

Roads. At 1 April 1993 the total mileage of roads was 15,060, graded for administrative purposes as follows: Motorway, 70 miles; Class I dual carriageway, 95 miles; Class I single carriageway, 1,287 miles; Class II, 1,770 miles; Class III, 2,935 miles; unclassified, 8,903 miles.

Ulsterbus and Citybus subsidiaries of N.I. Transport Holding Company (NITHC) provide co-ordinated services with N.I. Railways (NIR) Ltd under the service brand name of Translink.

At 31 March 1997 there were 1,893 professional hauliers and 4,827 vehicles licensed to engage in road haulage.

The number of motor vehicles licensed at 31 Dec. 1996 was 639,286, comprising private light goods, 540,083; motor cycles, scooters and mopeds, 10,026; buses, 2,090; goods vehicles, 17,401; other vehicles, 6,930. In addition, there were 62,756 vehicles which were not subject to licence duty.

Rail. NIR, a subsidiary of NITHC, provide rail services within Northern Ireland and cross-border services to Dublin, jointly with Irish Rail. The number of track-km operated is 478·8. In 1996–97 railways carried 6·2m. passengers.

Civil Aviation. There are scheduled air services to 3 airports in Northern Ireland. Belfast International Airport is the main one of these. Scheduled services are provided by British Airways and its franchise partners British Regional Airlines &

Maersk, British Midland, Jersey European Airways, Aer Lingus and Air UK. Belfast International is also Northern Ireland's holiday airport with holiday flights operated direct to European and transatlantic destinations by a wide range of local and UK tour operators. In the year to 31 March 1997, the airport handled 2·4m. passengers and 38,000 tonnes of freight and mail.

Belfast City Airport offers commuter services to 14 regional airports in Great Britain as well as services to London Gatwick and Luton, the Isle of Man, Channel Islands and Cork. A 'feeder' service operates between Belfast City and City of Derry Airports. In 1994 Belfast City Airport handled 1·35m. passengers. The City of Derry Airport is situated 14 km from Londonderry and provides services from the north-west of Ireland to 14 United Kingdom destinations (Aberdeen, Belfast, Birmingham, Blackpool, Bristol, Glasgow, Guernsey, Isle of Man, Jersey, Leeds/Bradford, Liverpool, London Gatwick, Manchester, Newcastle) and 4 European destinations (Amsterdam, Brussels, Frankfurt and Paris). In 1996 the City of Derry Airport handled 68,000 passengers. There are two other licensed airfields at St Angelo and Newtownards, the latter of which is used principally by flying clubs, private owners and air taxi businesses. St Angelo has commercial flights operated by Brymon Airways to Jersey, and by Crossair to Zürich. It handled 3,500 passengers in 1996.

Shipping. There are passenger services from Belfast to Liverpool and Stranraer, and from Larne to Cairnryan. Drive-on/drive-off cargo services operate from Belfast and Larne to other UK ports. Belfast, Londonderry and Warrenpoint offer conventional cargo services. A new port at Londonderry opened in 1993. A new car ferry service between Ballycastle and Campbeltown, in Scotland, commenced operations on 1 July 1997. It is hoped the season will be extended in future years.

SOCIAL INSTITUTIONS

Justice. The Lord Chancellor has responsibility for the administration of all courts through the Northern Ireland Court Service and for the appointment of judges and magistrates. The court structure has 3 tiers: The Supreme Court of Judicature of Northern Ireland (comprising the Court of Appeal, the High Court and the Crown Court), the County Courts and the Magistrates' Courts. There are 21 Petty Sessions districts which when grouped together for administration purposes form 7 County Court Divisions and 4 Crown Court Circuits.

The County Court has general civil jurisdiction subject to an upper monetary limit. Appeals from the Magistrates' Courts lie to the County Court, or to the Court of Appeal on a point of law, while appeals from the County Court lie to the High Court or, on a point of law, to the Court of Appeal.

Police. The police force consists of the Royal Ulster Constabulary, supported by the Royal Ulster Constabulary Reserve, a mainly part-time force.

Religion. According to the census of 1991 there were: Roman Catholics, 605,639; Presbyterians, 336,891; Church of Ireland, 279,280; Methodists, 59,517. Those belonging to other denominations numbered 122,448; to none, 59,234. 114,827 persons did not answer the voluntary question on religion.

Education. Public education, other than university education, is presently administered centrally by the Department of Education for Northern Ireland and locally by 5 Education and Library Boards. The Department is concerned with the whole range of education from nursery education through to higher education and continuing education; for sport and recreation; for youth services; for the arts and culture (including libraries) and for the development of community relations within and between schools.

Each Education and Library Board is the local education authority for its area. Boards were first appointed in 1973, the year of local government reorganization, and are normally reappointed every 4 years following the District Council elections. The membership of each Board consists of District councillors, representatives of transferors of schools, representatives of trustees of maintained schools and other persons who are interested in the service for which the Board is responsible. Boards have a duty, amongst other things, to ensure that there are sufficient schools of all kinds to meet the needs of their areas. The Boards are responsible for costs associated with capital works at controlled schools. Voluntary schools, including maintained and voluntary grammar schools, can receive grant-aid from the Department of Education toward capital works of up to 85%, or 100% if they have opted to change their management structures so that no single interest group has a majority of nominees. Most voluntary grammar schools can receive the same rate of grant on the purchase of equipment. The Boards award university and other scholarships; they provide school milk and meals; free books and transport for pupils; they enforce school attendance; provide a curriculum advisory and support service to all schools in their area; regulate the employment of children and young people; and secure the provision of youth and recreational facilities. They are also required to develop a comprehensive and efficient library service for their area. Board expenditure is funded at 100% by the Department of Education. Integrated schools receive 100% funding for recurrent costs from the Department of Education, and, where long-term viability has been established, for capital works.

The Education Reform (NI) Order 1989 made provision for the setting up of a Council for Catholic Maintained Schools with effect from April 1990. The Council has responsibility for all maintained schools under Roman Catholic Management which are under the auspices of the diocesan authorities and of religious orders. The main objective of the Council is to promote high standards of education in the schools for which it is responsible. Its functions include providing advice on matters relating to its schools, the employment of teaching staff and administration of appointment procedures, the promotion of effective management, and the promotion and co-ordination of effective planning and rationalization of school provision in the Catholic Maintained sector. The membership of the Council consists of trustee representatives appointed by the Northern Roman Catholic Bishops, parents, teachers, and persons appointed by the Head of the Department of Education in consultation with the Bishops.

Integrated Schools. In recent years a small number of integrated schools have been established at primary and post-primary levels with the aim of providing education for Roman Catholic and Protestant children together. These schools began as independent schools and qualified for public funding (on the same basis as other non-state schools) when their longer-term viability had been adequately demonstrated. The Education Reform (NI) Order 1989 introduced new measures whereby new integrated schools may receive public funding right from the start. Grant Maintained Integrated schools are eligible for grants on capital works, including purchase of sites and buildings and equipment, at the rate of 100%. At Oct. 1998 there were 40 integrated schools with total enrolments of some 11,381 pupils, about 3·3% of all pupils.

Pre-school Education is provided in nursery schools and nursery or reception classes in primary schools. There were 91 nursery schools in 1998–99 with 5,501 pupils, and 173 teachers in 1997–98. A further 3,377 nursery pupils and 2,521 reception pupils were situated in primary schools.

Primary Education is from 4 to 11 years. In 1998–99 there were 916 primary schools with 175,885 pupils. There were also 24 preparatory departments of grammar schools with 3,167 pupils. In 1997–98 there were 9,367 primary school teachers and 181 preparatory school teachers.

Secondary Education is from 11 to 18 years. In 1998–99 there were 72 grammar schools with 62,192 pupils and 165 secondary schools with 91,758 pupils. In 1997–98 there were 6,567 secondary school teachers and 3,980 grammar school teachers.

Further Education. There were 17 institutions of further education in 1998–99 with 1,974 full-time and 2,867 part-time teachers and in 1997–98 an enrolment of 24,968 full-time, 29,922 part-time day and 30,779 evening students on vocational courses; and about 60,000 students on non-vocational (mostly evening) courses.

Special Education. The Education and Library Boards provide for children with special educational needs up to the age of 19. This provision may be made in ordinary classes in primary or secondary schools or in special units attached to those schools, or in special schools. In 1998–99 there were 47 special schools with 4,675 pupils. This includes 3 hospital schools.

Universities. There are 2 universities: The Queen's University of Belfast (founded in 1849 as a college of the Queen's University of Ireland and reconstituted as a separate university in 1908) had 20,462 students, 1,402 full-time and 70 part-time academic staff in 1997–98. The University of Ulster, formed on 1 Oct. 1984, has campuses in Belfast, Coleraine, Jordanstown and Londonderry. In the 1997–98 academic year it had 20,158 students, 1,162 full-time and 65 part-time academic staff.

Teacher training takes place at both universities and at 2 colleges of education: Stranmillis, and St. Mary's, the latter mainly for the primary school sector, in respect of which 4-year (Hons) BEd courses and one-year Postgraduate Certificate in Education (PGCE) courses are available. The training of teachers for secondary schools is provided, in the main, in the education departments of the 2 universities, but 4-year (Hons) BEd courses are also available in the colleges for intending secondary teachers of religious education, business studies and craft, design and technology. Part-time PGCE courses (primary and secondary) are available through the Open University. There were a total of 1,547 students (1,231 women) in training at the 2 colleges and the 2 universities during 1997–98. The principal initial teacher-training courses are the Bachelor of Education (4-year honours), BA (Hons) with education (4-year) and the one-year Certificate of Education for graduates.

Gross expenditure by the Department of Education (1997–98) was £1,436m.

Health. The Department of Health and Social Services is responsible for the provision of integrated health and personal social services. 4 Health and Social Services Boards are responsible for assessing the requirements of their resident populations and for purchasing appropriate services. Since 1 April 1996 services have been delivered exclusively by HSS Trusts (similar to NHS Trusts in the rest of the UK) established under the Health and Personal Social Services (NI) Order 1991.

A total of 20 HSS Trusts are fully operational. 8 HSS Trusts based on acute hospitals and the regional Northern Ireland Ambulance Service are identical in structure and management to NHS Trusts in Great Britain. Of the remaining 11, 6 provide community-based health and personal social services and the other 5 provide both hospital and community-based health and personal social services, reflecting the integrated nature of these services in Northern Ireland.

Welfare. Social security schemes are similar to those in Great Britain.

National Insurance. During the year ended 31 March 1998 the expenditure of the National Insurance Fund at £1,202m. exceeded contributions by £186·7m. The shortfall in income was made up by a Treasury Grant, investment income and a transfer from the Great Britain Fund. Total benefit expenditure was £1,130·9m., excluding £2·7m. which was subsequently recovered from damages paid to recipients of National Insurance Fund Benefits. Employers received £1m. reimbursement in respect of Statutory Sick Pay paid to their employees. £14·6m. was paid in Jobseekers Allowance contributions. Widows Benefit amounted to £33·7m. and Retirement Pensions to £751·2m. Incapacity Benefits totalled £327·3m. Maternity Allowance of £1m. was paid and employers were reimbursed £18·5m. in respect of Statutory Maternity Pay. £36·5m. was given to personal pension plan providers.

Child Benefit: During the year ended 31 March 1998, £252·4m. was paid. *Income Support:* In 1997–98, £499·7m. was paid. *Family Credit:* In 1997–98, £891·3m. was paid.

CULTURE

Tourism. 1,415,000 visitors came to Northern Ireland in 1997, contributing £208m. to the economy. The Northern Ireland Tourist Board is responsible for encouraging tourism. 9 Areas of Outstanding Natural Beauty and 45 Statutory Nature Reserves have been declared, and there are many country and regional parks.

FURTHER READING

Arthur, P. and Jeffery, K., *Northern Ireland since 1968.* Oxford, 1988

Aughey, A. and Morrow, D. (eds.) *Northern Ireland Politics.* Harlow, 1996

Bloomfield, D., *Peacemaking Strategies in Northern Ireland.* London, 1998

Bow, P. and Gillespie, G., *Northern Ireland: a Chronology of the Troubles, 1968–1993.* Dublin, 1993

Cormack, R. J. and Osborne, R. D. (eds.) *Discrimination and Public Policy in Northern Ireland.* OUP, 1991

NORTHERN IRELAND

Cunningham, M. J., *British Government Policy in Northern Ireland, 1969–89*. Manchester Univ. Press, 1991

Hennessey, T., *A History of Northern Ireland 1920–96*. London, 1998

Irvine, M., *Northern Ireland: Faith and Faction*. London, 1991

Kennedy–Pipe, C., *The Origins of the Present Troubles in Northern Ireland*. Harlow, 1997

Keogh, D. and Haltzel, M. (eds.) *Northern Ireland and the Politics of Reconciliation*. CUP, 1994

McGarry, J. and O'Leary, B. (eds.) *The Future of Northern Ireland*. Oxford, 1991.—*Explaining Northern Ireland: Broken Images*. Oxford, 1995

Roche, P. J. and Barton, B. (eds.) *The Northern Ireland Question: Myth and Reality*. London, 1991

Ruane, J. and Todd, J., *The Dynamics of Conflict in Northern Ireland: Power, Conflict and Emancipation*. CUP, 1997

Shannon, M. O., *Northern Ireland*. [Bibliography] Oxford and Santa Barbara (CA), 1991

Whyte, J., *Interpreting Northern Ireland*. Oxford Univ. Press, 1990

STILL IN SEARCH OF AN ANSWER

David Trimble

Named as The Statesman's Yearbook's Statesman of the Year for 1998, David Trimble, First Minister elect of the Northern Ireland Assembly went on to receive the Nobel Peace Prize which he shared with John Hume, leader of the Social Democrat and Labour Party. Speaking in Oslo at the prize-giving ceremony, he told his audience that no single conflict can be used as a model to find the solution to other conflicts.

In fact if anything, the opposite is true. I believe that a sense of the unique is the first indispensable step to solving problems. It was the eighteenth century Irish political philosopher and British Parliamentarian, Edmund Burke, who taught us this essential truth.

Burke was the most powerful and prophetic political intellect of his century. He anticipated and welcomed the American revolution. He foresaw the dark side of the French revolution. He delved deep into the roots of that political violence, based on a false notion of the perfectibility of man, which has plagued us since the French revolution. He is admired by conservatives and liberals. He can be claimed by Britain and Ireland, by Catholic and Protestant, and indeed by the world. For Burke's belief in the rule of law and in parliamentary democracy is not our monopoly, but the birthright of men and women of all countries, all colours and all creeds.

But, of course, Burke has special significance for us in Ireland. The son of a Protestant father and a Catholic mother, he was a man who, in honouring both religious traditions, recognized and respected his Irish roots and the British Parliamentary system which nursed him to the full flowering of his genius.

Burke believed that the source of political, religious and racial violence is the Platonic pursuit of abstract perfection. I say Platonic because that savage pursuit of abstract perfection starts in the Western world with Plato's Republic. It rises to a plateau with the French and Russian revolutions. It descended to new depths with the Nazis and is present in all the national, ethnic and religious conflicts current after the collapse of communism, itself the most determined and ruthless Platonic experiment in perfecting the economic system whatever the cost in human life.

Burke challenged the Platonic perfectibility doctrine proclaimed by Rousseau. Rousseau regarded man as perfect and society as corrupt. Burke believed man was flawed and that society was redemptive. The revolution tested these theories and it was Burke who proved to have the measure of practical politics. At the end of Rousseau's road, Burke predicted, we would find not the perfectibility of man but the gibbet and the guillotine. And so it proved when Stalin set out to perfect the new Soviet man. So it proved with Mao in China and Pol Pot in Cambodia. So it will prove in every conflict when perfection is sought at the point of a gun.

Amos Oz, the distinguished Israeli writer, has arrived at the same conclusion. Recently he was asked to define a political fanatic. 'A political fanatic,' he said, 'is someone who is more interested in you than in himself.' A political fanatic is not someone who wants to perfect himself, he wants to perfect you.

In Northern Ireland we have a few fanatics who dream of forcing the Ulster British people into a Utopian Irish state, more ideologically Irish than its own inhabitants actually want. We also have fanatics who dream of suppressing northern nationalists in a state more supposedly British than its inhabitants actually want.

But a few fanatics are containable. The problem arises when they bury themselves within a morally legitimate political movement. Then there is a double danger. The first is that we might dismiss legitimate claims for reform because of the barbarism of terrorist groups bent on revolution. In this situation experience would suggest that the best way forward is for democrats to carry out what the Irish writer, Eoghan Harris calls acts of good authority. Thus each reformist group has a moral obligation to deal with its own fanatics. The Serbian democrats must take on the Serbian fascists. The PLO must take on Hamas. In Northern Ireland, constitutional nationalists must take on republican dissident terrorists and constitutional Unionists must confront Protestant terrorists.

There is a second danger. Sometimes in our search for a solution, we deny the darker side of human nature. We cannot ignore the existence of evil. It has many faces. Some look suspiciously like the leaders of the Serbian forces wanted for massacres such as that at Srebenica, some like those wielding absolute power in Baghdad, some like those wanted for the Omagh bombing.

It worries me that there is tendency in Western politics to hope that things are not as bad as they look, that the fanatics can be weaned away from terror. I prefer George Keenan's hardheaded advice, based on his years as US Ambassador in Moscow. 'Don't act chummy with terrorists; don't assume a community of aims with them which does not really exist; don't make fatuous gestures of goodwill.'

Here again we come to Burke's belief that politics proceeds not by abstract notions or by simple appeal to the past, but by close attention to detail and circumstance. 'Circumstances,' says Burke, 'give reality to every political principle, its distinguishing colour and discriminating effect. The circumstances are what render every civil and political scheme beneficial or noxious to mankind.'

Having taken this first step away from abstraction towards reality, we need space to explore possibilities. This is what I have tried to do in Northern Ireland. Critics say that concessions are a sign of weakness. Burke, however, says, 'Magnanimity in politics is not seldom the truest wisdom; and a great empire and little minds go ill together.' Prophetic words when we think of the history of the British Empire.

But the achievement of peace depends on a willingness not to be too precise or pedantic. Burke says, 'It is the nature of greatness not to be exact.' Amos Oz agrees, 'Inconsistency is the basis of coexistence. The heroes of tragedy, driven by consistency and by righteousness, destroy each other. He who seeks total supreme justice seeks death.' Again, the warning is not to aim for abstract perfection. In Ulster, what I have looked for is a peace within the realms of the possible. We can only start from where we are, not from where we would like to be.

And we have started. We will go on all the better if we put aside fantasy and accept the flawed nature of human enterprises. For this reason, I have not pressed the paramilitaries on the details of decommissioning. Although I am under pressure from my own political community I have not insisted on precise dates, quantities and manner of decommissioning. All I have asked for is a credible beginning, a common agreement that the 'war' is over. That is not too much to ask. But common sense dictates that I cannot convince society that real peace is at hand if there is not soon a beginning to the decommissioning of weapons.

Both communities must put sectarianism behind them for both helped to create it. Each thought it had good reason to fear the other. As Namier says, the irrational is not necessarily unreasonable. Ulster Unionists, fearful of being isolated on the island, built a solid house but it was a cold house for Catholics. And Catholic nationalists, although they had a roof over their heads, seemed to us as if they meant to burn the house down.

None of us are entirely innocent. But thanks to our strong sense of civil society, thanks to the knowledge that none of us are perfect, thanks to the thousands of people from both sides who have made countless acts of good authority, thanks to a tradition of parliamentary democracy which has meant that paramilitarism has never displaced politics, thanks to all these specific, concrete circumstances we, thank God, have stopped short of the abyss that is Bosnia, Kosovo, Somalia and Rwanda.

We have a peace of sorts in Northern Ireland. The paramilitaries are finished. But politics is not finished. It is the bedrock to which all societies return. The work that politicians do may be grubby and without glamour. But it has one saving grace. It is grounded on reality and reason. What is the nature of that reason? Let Burke answer.

'Political reason is a computing principle: adding, subtracting, multiplying and dividing, morally—and not metaphysically or mathematically—true moral denominations.'

There are two traditions in Northern Ireland. There are two religious denominations. But there is only one true moral denomination. And it wants peace.

ISLE OF MAN

KEY HISTORICAL EVENTS

The Isle of Man was first inhabited by the Celts and the Island became attached to Norway in the 9th century. In 1266 it was ceded to Scotland, but it came under English control in 1406 when possession was granted to the Stanley family (the Earls of Derby), and was later purchased by the British.

The Isle of Man has been a British Crown Possession since 1828, with the British government responsible for its defence and foreign policy. Otherwise it has extensive right of self-government.

A special relationship exists between the Isle of Man and the European Union providing for free trade, and adoption by the Isle of Man of the EU's external trade policies with third countries. The Island remains free to levy its own system of taxes.

TERRITORY AND POPULATION

Area, 221 sq. miles (572 sq. km); resident population census April 1996, 71,714, giving a density of 125 per sq. km. In 1996 an estimated 73% of the population lived in urban areas. The principal towns are Douglas (population, 23,487), Onchan (adjoining Douglas; 8,656), Ramsey (6,874), Peel (3,819), Castletown (2,958). The Island is divided into 6 sheadings—Ayre, Garff, Glenfaba, Michael, Middle and Rushen. Garff is further subdivided into 2 parishes and the others each have 3 parishes.

SOCIAL STATISTICS

1997: Births, 870; deaths, 950; marriages, 409. Annual growth rate, 1991–96, 1·6%.

CLIMATE

Lying in the Irish Sea, the Island's climate is temperate and lacking in extremes. Thunderstorms, snow and frost are infrequent, although the Island tends to be windy. July and Aug. are the warmest months with an average daily maximum temperature of around 17·6°C (63°F).

CONSTITUTION AND GOVERNMENT

As a result of Revestment in 1765, the Isle of Man became a dependency of the British Crown. The UK Government is responsible for the external relations of the Island, including its defence and international affairs, and the Island makes a financial contribution to the cost of these services. The Isle of Man has a special relationship with the European Union. It neither contributes funds to, nor receives money from, the EU. The Isle of Man is not represented in either the UK or European Parliaments.

The Island is administered in accordance with its own laws by the High Court of *Tynwald*, consisting of the President of Tynwald, the *Legislative Council* and the *House of Keys*. The Legislative Council is composed of the Lord Bishop of Sodor and Man, 8 members selected by the House of Keys and the Attorney General, who has no vote. The House of Keys is an assembly of 24 members chosen by adult suffrage. The President of Tynwald is chosen by the Legislative Council and the House of Keys, sitting together as Tynwald. An open-air Tynwald ceremony is held in early July each year at St Johns. Until 1990 the Lieutenant-Governor, appointed by the UK Government, presided over Tynwald.

A Council of Ministers was instituted in 1990, replacing the Executive Council which had acted as an advisory body to the Lieutenant-Governor. The Council of Ministers consists of the Chief Minister (elected for a 5-year term) and the ministers of the 9 major departments, being the Treasury; Agriculture, Fisheries and Forestry; Education; Health and Social Security; Home Affairs; Local Government and the Environment; Tourism and Leisure; Trade and Industry; and Transport.

RECENT ELECTIONS

The last election for the House of Keys was held on 21 Nov. 1996. 52 candidates stood, mostly independents. Turn-out was 62%.

CURRENT ADMINISTRATION

Lieut.-Governor: Sir Timothy Daunt.
  President: Sir Charles Kerruish (elected July 1990).
  In Dec. 1998 the *Chief Minister* was Donald Gelling. *Finance Minister:* Richard Corkill.

Local Government. There are 24 local authorities in the Isle of Man, each of which has elections.

ECONOMY

Policy. The Isle of Man's economic policy is the pursuit of manageable and sustainable growth based on a diversified economy with the aims of raising the standard of living of the whole population, securing future prosperity and providing the resources needed to sustain public services.

Performance. In 1996-97, GNP was £713m. and GDP was £645m. Just over 80% of national income is generated from services with the finance sector being the single largest contributor (37%). Around 67% of national income is personal incomes and the remainder is company income.

Budget. The Isle of Man is statutorily required to budget for a surplus of estimated revenue over expenditure. Revenue is raised from income tax, taxes on expenditure, health and social security contributions, and fees and charges for services.

  The standard rate of tax is 15% for personal income, and there is a higher rate of 20%. Companies are liable at 20% on their taxable income.

  There is a Customs and Excise Agreement with the UK, and rates of tax on expenditure are the same as those in the UK with very few exceptions. In addition, there is a reciprocal agreement on social security with the UK, and the rates of health and social security (National Insurance) contributions are the same as in the UK.

  In 1998-99 the Isle of Man Government budgeted for expenditure of £458m. and revenue of £461m.

Currency. The Isle of Man Government issues its own notes and coin on a par with £ sterling. Various commemorative coins have been minted. Inflation was around 3% at the end of 1998.

Banking and Finance. The banking sector is regulated by the Financial Supervision Commission which is responsible for the licensing and supervision of banks, deposit-takers and financial intermediaries giving financial advice, and receiving client monies for investment and management. A compensation fund to protect investors was set up in 1991 under the Commission.

  In late 1998, the deposit base was £21bn., and there were 67 licensed banks, 81 investment businesses and 3 building societies with Isle of Man licences.

  The insurance industry is regulated by the Insurance and Pensions Authority. In Dec. 1998 there were almost 200 insurance companies.

Weights and Measures. Both metric and avoirdupois are used.

ENERGY AND NATURAL RESOURCES

Electricity. The Manx Electricity Authority generates most of the Island's electricity by oil-fired power stations although there is a small hydroelectric plant. There are plans for a cable link with the UK power grid.

Oil and Gas. At present, all oil and gas needs are met from imports, although there has been exploration for petroleum in the Manx territorial waters, and a gas pipe link with either Eire or the UK is under consideration. The Island's gas suppliers and distributors are in the private sector.

Water. The Isle of Man Water Authority is the statutory body for supply of water in the Island.

Minerals. Although lead and tin mining industries were major employers in the past, they have long since shut down and the only mining activity in the Island is now for aggregates. The Lady Isabella, built in 1854 to drain the mines above Laxey, is one of the largest waterwheels in Europe.

Agriculture. The area farmed is about 113,000 acres, being 80% of a total land area of around 141,500 acres. 65,000 acres are grassland with a further 36,000 acres for rough grazing. There are approximately 174,000 sheep, 34,000 cattle, 18,000 poultry and 6,000 pigs on the Island's 778 farms. Just over 300 people are employed in agriculture, which now contributes less than 2% of the Island's GDP.

Forestry. The Department of Agriculture, Fisheries and Forestry has a forestry estate of some 6,800 acres. Commercial forestry is directed towards softwood production. The Manx National Glens and other amenity areas are maintained for public use by the Department, which owns some 18,000 acres of the Island's hills and uplands open for public use.

Fisheries. The Isle of Man is noted for the Manx kipper, a gutted smoked herring. Scallops and the related queen scallops (queenies) are the economic mainstay of the Manx fishing fleet.

INDUSTRY
Labour. The economically active population in 1996 was 34,811, of whom 5,695 were self-employed and 1,234 were unemployed. Employment by sector: Professional services, 18%; finance, 18%; construction, 10%; manufacturing, 11%; distributive services, 11%.

At the end of 1998, there were less than 400 persons on the unemployment register giving an unemployment rate of around 1%.

INTERNATIONAL TRADE
The Isle of Man forms part of the customs union of the European Union, although the Island is not part of the EU itself. The relationship with the EU provides for free trade and the adoption of the EU's external trade policies and tariffs with non-EU countries.

COMMUNICATIONS
Roads. There are 500 miles of good roads. At the end of March 1998 there were 49,688 licensed vehicles, with 40,168 of these being private cars. Omnibus services operate to all parts of the Island. The TT (Tourist Trophy) motor cycle races take place annually on the 37·75-mile Mountain Circuit.

Rail. Several novel transport systems operate on the Island during the summer season from May to Sept. Horse-drawn trams run along Douglas promenade, and the Manx Electric Railway links Douglas, Laxey, Ramsey and Snaefell Mountain (2,036 ft) in the north. The Isle of Man Steam Railway also operates between Douglas and Port Erin in the south.

Civil Aviation. Ronaldsway Airport in the south handles scheduled services linking the Island with London, Manchester, Dublin, Belfast, Glasgow, Liverpool, Blackpool, Birmingham, Leeds, Luton, Newcastle, Cardiff and Jersey. Air taxi services also operate.

Shipping. Car ferries run between Douglas and the UK and the Irish Republic. The Island has a shipping register.

Telecommunications. Manx Telecom Limited, a wholly owned subsidiary of British Telecom, holds the telecommunications licence issued by the Communications Commission for the Isle of Man.

Postal Services. The Isle of Man Post Office Authority operates the Island's mail system and issues various commemorative stamps.

SOCIAL INSTITUTIONS
Justice. The First Deemster is the head of the Isle of Man's judiciary. The Isle of Man Constabulary numbered 212 all ranks in 1997.

Religion. The Island has a rich heritage of Christian associations, and the Diocese of Sodor and Man, one of the oldest in the British Isles, has existed since 476.

Education. Education is compulsory between the ages of 5 and 16. In 1998 there were 6,210 pupils in the 33 primary schools and 4,732 pupils in the 5 secondary schools operated by the Department of Education. The Department also runs a college of further education and a special school. Government expenditure on education totalled £51m. in 1998-99. The Island has a private primary school and a private secondary school.

Health. The Island has had its own National Health Service since 1948, providing medical, dental and ophthalmic services. In 1998-99 Government expenditure on the NHS was £67m. There are 2 hospitals and a further hospital was under construction in 1999.

Welfare. Numbers receiving certain benefits at July 1997: Retirement Pension, 15,079; Unemployment Benefit, 233; Sick and Disablement Benefit, 4,570; Child Benefit, 8,613; Supplementary Benefit, 4,154. Total Government expenditure on the social security system in 1997-98 was £114m., with almost 60% of this sum going to the elderly.

CULTURE

Broadcasting. Manx Radio is a commercial broadcaster operated by the Government from Douglas.

Cinema. There are 2 cinemas in Douglas, 1 of which is owned and operated by the Isle of Man Government.

Press. In 1998 there were 3 weekly newspapers, 2 bi-weekly newspapers and 1 monthly newspaper. There are also various magazines concentrating on Manx issues.

Tourism. During the late 19th century through to the middle of the 20th century, tourism was one of the Island's main sources of income and employment. Tourism now contributes around 6% of the Island's GDP; there were 250,000 visitors during 1997.

Festivals. There is a Manx language festival—Feailley Ghaelgagh; and a Manx cultural festival—Yn Chruinnaght.

Libraries. The Manx Museum Library in Douglas has an extensive collection relating to all aspects of the Island's history, culture and folklore. The Central Reference Library in Government Office specializes in the central administration of the Island.

National Theatre and Opera. The main theatre is the Government-owned Gaiety in Douglas, staging a wide variety of drama, musicals and opera throughout the year. Designed by Frank Matcham and opened in 1900, the theatre has undergone extensive restoration to its Victorian decor. A larger concert hall, the Villa Marina, is owned and operated by the local authority for Douglas.

Museums and Galleries. The Manx Museum is the Island's major museum and houses the National Art Gallery. Castle Rushen in Castletown is one of Britain's best-preserved medieval castles and Peel Castle on St. Patrick's Isle dates back to the 11th century. There is also the Nautical Museum in Castletown, Cregneash Village Folk Museum and the Grove Rural Life Museum in Ramsey. The House of Mannannan in Peel explores various aspects of the Island's history and culture. Small private museums include the Motor Cycle Museum, the Manx Regiment Museum and the T. E. Leece Museum.

FURTHER READING

Additional information is available from: Economic Affairs Division, 2 Circular Rd, Douglas, Isle of Man IM1 1PQ. *e-mail: economics@gov.im*
Government website: http://www.gov.im
Isle of Man Digest of Economic and Social Statistics, Isle of Man Government, annual

Kermode, D. G., *Devolution at Work: A Case Study of the Isle of Man*, Saxon House, 1979
Kinvig, R. H., *The Isle of Man: A Social, Cultural and Political History*. Liverpool Univ. Press, 1975
Moore, A. W., *A History of the Isle of Man*, London, 1900; reprinted Manx National Heritage, 1992
Robinson, V. and McCarroll, D. (eds.) *The Isle of Man: Celebrating a Sense of Place*. Liverpool Univ. Press, 1990
Solly, M., *Government and Law in the Isle of Man*. London, 1994
Young, G. V. C., *A Brief History of the Isle of Man*. The Manx-Svenska Publishing Co. Ltd., 1983

Manx National Heritage publishes a series of booklets including *Early Maps of the Isle of Man*, *The Art of the Manx Crosses*, *The Ancient & Historic Monuments of the Isle of Man*, *Prehistoric Sites in the Isle of Man*.

CHANNEL ISLANDS

KEY HISTORICAL EVENTS

The Channel Islands consist of Jersey, Guernsey and the following dependencies of Guernsey: Alderney, Brechou, Great Sark, Little Sark, Herm, Jethou and Lihou. They were an integral part of the Duchy of Normandy at the time of the Norman Conquest of England in 1066. Since then they have belonged to the British Crown and are not part of the UK. The islands have created their own form of self-government, with the British government at Westminster being responsible for defence and foreign policy. The Lieut.-Governors of Jersey and Guernsey, appointed by the Crown, are the personal representatives of the Sovereign as well as being the commanders of the armed forces. The legislature of Jersey is 'The States of Jersey', and that of Guernsey is 'The States of Deliberation'.

From 1940 to 1945 the islands were left undefended and were the only British territory to fall to the Germans.

TERRITORY AND POPULATION

The Channel Islands cover a total of 75 sq. miles (194 sq. km), and in 1996 had a population of approximately 147,000.

The official languages are French and English, but English is now the main language.

CLIMATE

The climate is mild, with an average temperature for the year of 11·5°C. Average yearly rainfall totals: Jersey, 862·9 mm; Guernsey, 858·9 mm. The wettest months are in the winter. Highest temperatures recorded: Jersey, 34·8°C; Guernsey, 31·7°C. Maximum temperatures usually occur in July and Aug. (daily maximum 20·8°C in Jersey, slightly lower in Guernsey). Lowest temperatures recorded: Jersey, 10·3°C; Guernsey, −7·4°C Jan. and Feb. are the coldest months (mean temperature approximately 6°C).

CONSTITUTION AND GOVERNMENT

The Lieut.-Governors and Cs.-in-C. of Jersey and Guernsey are the personal representatives of the Sovereign, the Commanders of the Armed Forces of the Crown, and the channel of communication between the Crown and the insular governments. They are appointed by the Crown and have a voice but no vote in the islands' legislatures. The Secretaries to the Lieut.-Governors are their staff officers.

EXTERNAL ECONOMIC RELATIONS

The Channel Islands are not members of the EU, but participate in ERM through their monetary union with the UK. Trade with the UK is classed as domestic.

COMMUNICATIONS

Civil Aviation. Scheduled air services are maintained by Aer Lingus, Air Corbière, Air UK, Aurigny Air Services, British Airways, British Midland, Crossair, Delta, Gill Aviation, Jersey European Airways, KLM, Loganair, Lufthansa and Manx Airlines.

Shipping. Passenger and cargo services between Jersey, Guernsey and England (Poole) are maintained by Condor Ltd hydrofoil; between Guernsey, Jersey and England and St Malo by the Commodore Shipping Co. Emeraude Ferries connect Jersey and Guernsey with St Malo; local companies run between Guernsey, Alderney and England, and between Guernsey and Sark by .

SOCIAL INSTITUTIONS

Justice. Justice is administered by the Royal Courts of Jersey and Guernsey, each of which consists of the Bailiff and 12 Jurats, the latter being elected by an electoral college. There is an appeal from the Royal Courts to the Courts of Appeal of Jersey and of Guernsey. A final appeal lies to the Privy Council in certain cases. A stipendiary magistrate in each, Jersey and Guernsey, deals with minor civil and criminal cases.

Religion. Jersey and Guernsey each constitutes a deanery under the jurisdiction of the Bishop of Winchester. The rectories (12 in Jersey; 10 in Guernsey) are in the gift of the Crown. The Roman Catholic and various Nonconformist Churches are represented.

FURTHER READING
Coysh, V., *The Channel Islands: A New Study*. Newton Abbot, 1977
Lemprière, R., *History of the Channel Islands*. Rev. ed. London, 1980
Uttley, J., *The Story of the Channel Islands*. London, 1966

JERSEY

TERRITORY AND POPULATION
The area is 116·2 sq. km (44·9 sq. miles). Resident population (1991 census), 84,082 (43,220 females); density, 724 per sq. km. 1996 population, 85,150 (733 per sq. km). The projected population for 2000 is 90,000. The chief town is St Helier on the south coast. The official language is English (French until 1960).

SOCIAL STATISTICS
In 1998 there were 1,200 births (rate, 14·1 per 1,000 population) and 781 deaths (9·2). Infant mortality rate, 1995 (per 1,000 live births), 6·5. In 1998 there were 824 marriages and, in 1996, 285 divorces. Life expectancy, 1996: Males, 75·1 years; females, 80·2.

CONSTITUTION AND GOVERNMENT
The island parliament is the *States of Jersey*. The States comprises the Bailiff, the Lieut.-Governor, the Dean of Jersey, the Attorney-General and the Solicitor-General, and 53 members elected by universal suffrage: 12 Senators (elected for 6 years, 6 retiring every third year), the Constables of the 12 parishes (every third year) and 29 Deputies (every third year). They all have the right to speak in the Assembly, but only the 53 elected members have the right to vote; the Bailiff has a casting vote. Except in specific instances, enactments passed by the States require the sanction of The Queen-in-Council. The Lieut.-Governor has the power of veto on certain forms of legislation.

Administration is carried out by Committees of the States.

CURRENT ADMINISTRATION
Lieut.-Governor and C.-in-C. of Jersey: Gen. Sir Michael Wikes, KCB, CBE.

Secretary and ADC to the Lieut.-Governor: Lieut.-Colonel C. Woodrow, OBE, MC, QGM.

Bailiff of Jersey and President of the States: Sir Philip Bailhache.

ECONOMY

Performance. GDP grew by an estimated 5·5% in 1996.

Budget. 1997: Revenue, £291m.; expenditure, £245m. Income from taxation was £268·0m. The standard rate of income tax is 20p in the pound.

Parochial rates are payable by owners and occupiers.

Currency. The States issue banknotes in denominations of £50, £20, £10, £5 and £1. Coinage from 1p to 50p is struck in the same denominations as the UK. £32·1m. were in circulation in 1991. Inflation in Sept. 1998 was running at an annualized 4·3%.

Banking and Finance. Financial services contributed 55% of GDP in 1996. In 1998 there were 79 banks, with combined deposits of £103·7bn. (£31bn. in 1988). 30,232 companies were registered at the end of 1995.

ENERGY AND NATURAL RESOURCES

Agriculture. Total output (1988), £36·4m.; and total exports, £30·7m. 54% of the island's land area was farmed commercially in 1995. 48% of cropland was sown to potatoes. In 1995 there were 455 commercial farms. Livestock, 1995: Cattle, 6,934 (milch cows, 4,281).

Fisheries. There were 65 fishing vessels in 1995. The total catch in 1995 was 782 tonnes.

INDUSTRY
Principal activities: Light industry, mainly electrical goods, textiles and clothing.

Labour. At the 1996 census 46,992 persons were economically active (20,975 females). 1,549 persons were identified as unemployed but seeking work. 367 persons were registered unemployed in June 1996. Financial services was the largest employment sector, followed by distributive trades, construction, and then hotels and restaurants.

INTERNATIONAL TRADE

Imports and Exports. Since 1980 the Customs have ceased recording imports and exports. Principal imports: Machinery and transport equipment, manufactured goods, food, mineral fuels, and chemicals. Principal exports: Machinery and transport equipment, food, and manufactured goods.

COMMUNICATIONS

Roads. In 1995 there were 50,796 private cars, 7,638 hire cars, 5,973 vans, 3,301 lorries, 811 buses and coaches, and 5,177 motor cycles and scooters.

Civil Aviation. Jersey airport is situated at St Peter. It covers approximately 375 acres. Number of aircraft movements excluding local flying (1990) 60,107; number of passengers: 1,890,714; cargo and mail, 8,792 tonnes.

Shipping. (1990). All vessels arriving in Jersey from outside Jersey waters report at St Helier or Gorey on first arrival. There is a harbour of minor importance at St Aubin. Number of commercial vessels entering St Helier in 1990, 26,472; number of visiting yachts (1990), 12,097. Passengers arrived in 1990, 491,145.

Telecommunications. Postal, and overseas telephone and telegraph services, are maintained by the Postal Administration of Jersey. The local telephone service is maintained by the Insular Authority. In 1997 main telephone lines numbered 65,500 (730·4 for every 1,000 persons). There were 4,400 cellular phone subscribers and 700 fax machines in 1995.

Postal Services. In 1993 there were 23 post offices. A total of 50m. pieces of mail were processed in 1993, or 594 items per person.

SOCIAL INSTITUTIONS

Justice. Justice is administered by the Royal Court, consisting of the Bailiff and 12 Jurats (magistrates). There is a final appeal in certain cases to the Sovereign in Council. There is also a Court of Appeal, consisting of the Bailiff and 2 judges. Minor civil and criminal cases are dealt with by a stipendiary magistrate.

Education. In 1996 there were 5 States secondary schools and 1 high school, and 24 States primary schools; 6,906 pupils attended the primary schools, 4,924 the secondary schools. These figures include 8 private primary schools with 1,250 pupils and 8 private secondary schools with 843 pupils. There were 1,298 full-time students at the further education college.

Health. Expenditure on public health in 1995 was £73·2m. In 1995 there were 5 hospitals with 651 beds. There were 95 doctors (general practitioners).

Welfare. A contributory Health Insurance Scheme is administered by the Social Security Department. In 1994–95 income was £67·1m. Benefits paid totalled £71·2m. (long-term benefits, £53·2m.; sickness, £6·6m.; invalidity, £6·9m.). 2,672 families totalling 4,783 children were receiving family allowances as at Sept. 1995.

CULTURE

Tourism. Total number of hotel and guesthouse bedrooms (1990), 23,069. In 1996 tourism accounted for 24% of GDP. 798,000 leisure visitors came to the island in 1995, with a spend of £266m.

FURTHER READING

Balleine, G. R., *Biographical Dictionary of Jersey.* London, 1948.—*A History of the Island of Jersey.* Rev. ed. Chichester, 1981.—*The Bailiwick of Jersey.* 3rd ed. London, 1970
Bois, F. de L., *The Constitutional History of Jersey.* Jersey, 1970

States of Jersey Library: Halkett Place, St Helier.

GUERNSEY

TERRITORY AND POPULATION

The area is 63·4 sq. km. Census population (1996) 58,681. The main town is St Peter Port.

English and French are spoken, as is a Norman-French dialect in country areas.

SOCIAL STATISTICS

Births during 1997 were 672; deaths, 583.

CONSTITUTION AND GOVERNMENT

The States of Deliberation, the Parliament of Guernsey, is composed of the following members: The Bailiff, who is President *ex officio;* 12 Conseillers elected by popular franchise; H.M. Procureur and H.M. Comptroller (Law Officers of the Crown), who have a voice but no vote; 33 People's Deputies elected by popular franchise; 10 Douzaine Representatives elected by their Parochial Douzaines; 2 representatives of the States of Alderney.

The States of Election, an electoral college, elects the Jurats. It is composed of the following members: The Bailiff (President *ex officio*); the 12 Jurats or 'Jurés-Justiciers'; the 12 Conseillers; H.M. Procureur and H.M. Comptroller; the 33 People's Deputies and 34 Douzaine Representatives.

Since Jan. 1949 all legislative powers and functions (with minor exceptions) formerly exercised by the Royal Court have been vested in the States of Deliberation. Projets de Loi (Bills) require the sanction of The Queen-in-Council.

RECENT ELECTIONS

Elections for People's Deputies were held on 20 April 1994.

CURRENT ADMINISTRATION

Lieut.-Governor and C.-in-C. of Guernsey and its Dependencies: Vice-Admiral Sir John Coward, KCB, DSO.
Secretary and Aide-de-Camp to the Lieut.-Governor: Colonel R. H. Graham.
Bailiff of Guernsey and President of the States: Sir Graham Dorey.
Deputy Bailiff of Guernsey: de V. G. Carey.

ECONOMY

Budget. (year ended 31 Dec. 1996). Revenue, including Alderney, £233,765,000; expenditure, including Alderney, £212,062,000. The standard rate of income tax is

20p in the pound. States and parochial rates are very moderate. No super-tax or death duties are levied.

Banking and Finance. There were 78 banks in 1997.
Financial services account for about 55% of total income.

INDUSTRY

Trade Unions. There is a Transport & General Workers' Union.

INTERNATIONAL TRADE

Imports and Exports. (1997). Principal imports: Petrol and oils, 176,634,000 litres. Principal exports: Tomatoes, £3·43m.; flowers and fern, £21·7m.; flowers by post, £4·7m.; vegetables, £2·35m.; plants, £8·3m.; manufacturing, £52m.; services £60m.

Trade Fairs. There are several trade fairs each year.

COMMUNICATIONS

Rail. There is no rail system.

Civil Aviation. The airport is situated at La Villiaze. In 1997 passenger arrivals totalled 870,869.

Shipping. The principal port is St Peter Port. There is also a harbour at St Sampson's (mainly for commercial shipping). In 1996 passenger arrivals totalled 322,222. Ships registered at 31 Dec. 1997 numbered 2,125 and 302 fishing vessels. In 1997, 12,656 yachts visited Guernsey.

Telecommunications. There were 44,000 main telephone lines in 1996, or 716 per 1,000 population. Cellular phone subscribers numbered 2,400 in 1995 and there were 700 fax machines.

SOCIAL INSTITUTIONS

Education. There are 2 public schools, 1 grammar school, and modern secondary and primary schools, and a College of Further Education. The total number of schoolchildren was (1997) 8,787. Facilities are available for the study of art, domestic science, and many other subjects of a technical nature.

Health. Guernsey is not covered by the UK National Health Service. Public health is overseen by the States of Guernsey Insurance Authority and Board of Health. A private medical insurance scheme to provide specialist cover for all residents was implemented by the States on 1 Jan. 1996.

CULTURE

Broadcasting. Guernsey is served by BBC Radio Guernsey, Island FM and Channel Television.

Cinema. There are 2 cinemas.

Press. The *Guernsey Evening Press* is published daily except Sundays.

Tourism. There were 297,000 visitors in 1997. In 1996 tourism generated revenue of £176m., and in 1995, £157m.

Festivals. Liberation Day is on 9 May.

Libraries. The two principal libraries are the Guille-Alles Library and the Priaulx Library.

Museums and Galleries. The island is home to the Guernsey Museum and Art Gallery, Victor Hugo House and several small museums.

FURTHER READING

Le Huray, C. P., *The Bailiwick of Guernsey*. London, 1952
Marr, L. J., *A History of Guernsey*. Chichester, 1982

ALDERNEY

Population (1986 census, 2,130; 1994 estimate, 2,375). The main town is St Anne's. The island has an airport.

The Constitution of the island (reformed 1987) provides for its own popularly elected President and States (12 members), and its own Court. Elections were held for the President and 4 members of the States in Dec. 1993. Alderney levies its taxes at Guernsey rates and passes the revenue to Guernsey, which charges for the services it provides.

President of the States: Jon Kay-Mouat, OBE.
Clerk of the States: D. V. Jenkins.
Clerk of the Court: A. Johnson.

FURTHER READING
Coysh, V., *Alderney*. Newton Abbot, 1974

SARK

Population (1986 estimate, 550). The Constitution is a mixture of feudal and popular government with its Chief Pleas (parliament), consisting of 40 tenants and 12 popularly elected deputies, presided over by the Seneschal. The head of the island is the Seigneur. Sark has no income tax. Motor vehicles, except tractors, are not allowed.

Seigneur: J. M. Beaumont.
Seneschal: L. P. de Carteret.

FURTHER READING
Carteret, A. R. de, *The Story of Sark*. London, 1956
Hathaway, S., *Dame of Sark: An Autobiography*. London, 1961

UNITED KINGDOM OVERSEAS TERRITORIES

After the retrocession of Hong Kong to China on 1 July 1997, 13 territories remained under British sovereignty as a legacy of the former Empire. 3 of these (British Antarctic Territory, British Indian Ocean Territory and South Georgia and the South Sandwich Islands) have no resident populations and are administered by a commissioner instead of a governor.

Gibraltar is an enclave in Spain; the remainder are islands in the Caribbean and South Atlantic. Gibraltar and the Falkland Islands are the subjects of territorial claims by Spain and Argentina respectively.

Governors of Overseas Territories are appointed by the Queen, and are responsible for external affairs, internal security and the public service. Territories have their own elected legislatures and ministers, but final responsibility for government belongs to the Foreign and Commonwealth Office in London. For the Caribbean Territories some aspects of administration are carried out by the United Kingdom Overseas Territories Regional Secretariat in Barbados. The citizenship status of residents is defined in the British Nationality Act 1981.

ANGUILLA

KEY HISTORICAL EVENTS

Anguilla was probably given its name by the Spaniards or the French because of its eel-like shape. It was inhabited by Arawaks for several centuries before the arrival of Europeans. Anguilla was colonized in 1650 by English settlers from neighbouring St Kitts. In 1688 the island was attacked by a party of Irishmen who then settled. Anguilla was subsequently administered as part of the Leeward Islands, and from 1825 became even more closely associated with St Kitts. In 1875 a petition sent to London requesting separate status and direct rule from Britain met with a negative response. Again in 1958 the islanders formally petitioned the Governor requesting a dissolution of the political and administrative association with St Kitts, but this too failed. From 1958 to 1962 Anguilla was part of the Federation of the West Indies.

Opposition to rule from St Kitts erupted on 30 May 1967 when St Kitts policemen were evicted from the island and Anguilla refused to recognize the authority of the State Government any longer. During 1968–69 the British Government maintained a 'Senior British Official' to advise the local Anguilla Council and devise some solution to the problem. In March 1969, following the ejection from the island of a high-ranking British civil servant, British security forces occupied Anguilla. A Commissioner was installed, and in 1969 Anguilla became *de facto* a separate dependency of Britain, a situation rendered *de jure* on 19 Dec. 1980 under the Anguilla Act 1980 when Anguilla formally separated from the state of St Kitts, Anguilla-Nevis. A new constitution came into effect in 1982 providing for a large measure of internal autonomy under the Crown.

TERRITORY AND POPULATION

Anguilla is the most northerly of the Leeward Islands, some 70 miles (112 km) to the north-west of St Kitts and 5 miles (8 km) to the north of St Martin/Sint Maarten. The territory also comprises the island of Sombrero and several other off-shore islets or cays. The total area of the territory is about 60 sq. miles (155 sq. km). Census population (1984) was 6,897. Population estimate, 1997, 10,663. The projected population for 2000 is 12,000. The capital is The Valley. In 1995 an estimated 89% of the population lived in rural areas.

The official language is English.

SOCIAL STATISTICS

Annual growth rate, 1990–95, 2·7%.

CLIMATE

Tropical oceanic climate with rain throughout the year, particularly between May and Dec. Tropical storms and hurricanes may occur between July and Nov. Generally summers are hotter than winters although there is little variation in temperatures.

CONSTITUTION AND GOVERNMENT

A set of amendments to the constitution came into effect in 1990, providing for a Deputy Governor, a Parliamentary Secretary and an Opposition Leader. The *House of Assembly* consists of a Speaker, Deputy Speaker, 7 directly elected members for 5-year terms, 2 nominated members and 2 *ex-officio* members: the Deputy Governor and the Attorney-General. The Governor discharges his executive powers on the advice of an Executive Council comprising a Chief Minister, 3 Ministers and 2 *ex-officio* members: the Deputy Governor, Attorney-General and the Secretary to the Executive Council.

RECENT ELECTIONS

Elections were held on 4 March 1999 for the House of Assembly. The Anguilla National Alliance gained 3 seats, the Anguilla United Party, 2 and the Anguilla Democratic Party (ADP), 2.

CURRENT ADMINISTRATION

Governor: Alan Hoole, OBE.
  Deputy-Governor: Robert Malcolm Harris.
  Chief Minister and Minister of Lands, Tourism, Agriculture and Fisheries: Hubert Hughes (ADP).

ECONOMY

Performance. Real GDP growth was –4·3% in 1995 and 7·0% in 1994.

Budget. In 1997 current revenue was EC$52·7m. and expenditure, EC$50·2m. The main sources of revenue are custom duties, tourism and bank licence fees. There is little taxation. A 'Policy Plan' with the UK provided for £10·5m. of aid in 1994-97.

Currency. The *Eastern Caribbean dollar* (*see* ANTIGUA AND BARBUDA).

Banking and Finance. The East Caribbean Central Bank based in St Kitts-Nevis functions as a central bank. There is a small offshore banking sector. In 1996 there were 2 domestic and 2 foreign commercial banks.

ENERGY AND NATURAL RESOURCES

Electricity. Production (1996) 28·5m. kWh.

Agriculture. Because of low rainfall, agriculture potential is limited. About 1,200 ha are cultivable. Main crops are pigeon peas, maize and sweet potatoes. Livestock consists of sheep, goats, cattle and poultry. The island relies on imports for food.

Fisheries. Fishing is a thriving industry (mainly lobster). The total catch in 1995 was 350 tonnes.

COMMUNICATIONS

Roads. There are about 40 miles of tarred roads and 25 miles of secondary roads. In 1991 there were 2,450 passenger cars and 733 commercial vehicles.

Civil Aviation. Wallblake is the airport for The Valley. Anguilla is linked to neighbouring islands by services operated by Air Anguilla, LIAT, Tyden Air, WINAIR and American Eagle.

Shipping. The main seaports are Sandy Ground and Blowing Point, the latter serving passenger and cargo traffic to and from St Martin. In 1995 merchant shipping totalled 2,000 GRT.

Telecommunications. There is a modern internal telephone service with (1992) 2,923 exchange lines; and international telegraph, telex, fax and internet services.

SOCIAL INSTITUTIONS

Justice. Based on UK common law as exercised by the Eastern Caribbean Supreme Court on St Lucia. Final appeal lies to the UK Privy Council.

Religion. There were in 1992 Anglicans, Roman Catholics, Methodists, Seventh Day Adventists, Church of God and Baptists.

Education. Adult literacy was 80% in 1995. Education is free and compulsory between the ages of 5 and 16 years. There are 6 government primary schools with (1996) 1,540 pupils and 1 comprehensive school with (1996) 1,060 pupils. Higher education is provided at regional universities and similar institutions.

Health. In 1996 there was 1 hospital with a total of 60 beds, 4 health centres and a government dental clinic. There were 5 government-employed and 3 private doctors.

Welfare. A social security system was instituted in 1982 to provide age and disability pensions, and sickness and maternity benefits.

CULTURE

Broadcasting. There is 1 government (Radio Anguilla) and 2 other radio broadcasters. TV is privately owned; there are 2 channels and a cable system. In 1995 there were 3,000 radio and 1,000 television receivers.

Press. In 1995 there were 1 daily, 2 weeklies and a quarterly periodical.

Tourism. Tourism accounts for 50% of GDP. In 1996 there were 86,239 visitor arrivals (66% from the USA), bringing revenue of US$48m. in 1995.

FURTHER READING
Petty, C. L., *Anguilla: Where there's a Will, there's a Way.* Anguilla, 1984.—*A Handbook History of Anguilla.* Anguilla, 1991.

BERMUDA

KEY HISTORICAL EVENTS
The islands were discovered by Juan Bermúdez, probably in 1503, but were uninhabited until British colonists were wrecked there in 1609. A plantation company was formed; in 1684 the Crown took over the government. A referendum in Aug. 1995 rejected independence from the UK.

TERRITORY AND POPULATION
Bermuda consists of a group of 138 islands and islets (about 20 inhabited), situated in the western Atlantic (32° 18' N. lat., 64° 46' W. long.); the nearest point of the mainland, 940 km distant, is Cape Hatteras (North Carolina). The area is 20·59 sq. miles (53·3 sq. km). In June 1995 the USA surrendered its lease on land used since 1941 for naval and air force bases. At the 1991 census the population (excluding British military personnel) numbered 58,460. Estimate, 1996, 60,144; density, 1,128 per sq. km. The projected population for 2000 is 63,000. Chief town, Hamilton; population, 1994, 1,100.

The official language is English.

SOCIAL STATISTICS
In 1996 there were 833 live births, 944 marriages and 444 deaths. Annual growth rate, 1990–95, 0·8%.

Bermuda limits cars to one per household and bans hire vehicles. There are heavy fines for breaking the 20 m.p.h. speed limit. Bermuda is the only country in the world where McDonald's restaurants are banned by law.

CLIMATE
A pleasantly warm and humid climate, with up to 60" (1,500 mm) of rain spread evenly throughout the year. Hamilton, Jan. 63°F (17·2°C), July 79°F (26·1°C). Annual rainfall 58" (1,463 mm).

CONSTITUTION AND GOVERNMENT
The electorate was 38,000; turn-out was 58%. Under the 1968 constitution the *Governor*, appointed by the Crown, is normally bound to accept the advice of the Cabinet in matters other than external affairs, defence, internal security and the police, for which he retains special responsibility. The legislature consists of a Senate of 11 members, 5 appointed by the Governor on the recommendation of the Premier, 3 by the Governor on the recommendation of the Opposition Leader and 3 by the Governor in his own discretion. The 40 members of the *House of Assembly* are elected, 2 from each of 20 constituencies by universal suffrage.

At a referendum on 17 Aug. 1995, 16,369 votes were cast against the option of independence, and 5,714 were in favour.

RECENT ELECTIONS
A general election was held on 10 Nov. 1998. Turn-out was 81%. The Progressive Labour Party (PLP) won 26 of the 40 seats in parliament, with 54·2% of votes cast, throwing out the United Bermuda Party (UBP) government which had dominated politics for 35 years. The PLP is largely representative of the black population, while the UBP membership is mostly white.

CURRENT ADMINISTRATION
Governor: John Thorold Masefield, CMG.
  Premier: Jennifer Smith.

Local Government. The City of Hamilton and the Town of St. George's have local government authority.

DEFENCE
The Bermuda Regiment numbered 684 in 1996.

ECONOMY
Bermuda is the world's third largest insurance market after London and New York. Reserves of insurance companies total $39bn.

Performance. GNP per capita was US$29,900 in 1995–96. Real GDP growth was 2·0% in 1995 and 0·7% in 1994. GDP for 1998 was $30,000.

Budget. The fiscal year ends on 31 March. The 1997–98 budget envisaged revenue of BD$488m. and current expenditure of BD$448m. The estimated chief sources of revenue (in BD$1m.) in 1997–98: Customs duties, 144; payroll tax, 133; companies fees, 38; land tax, 24; passenger tax, 20; vehicle licences, 17.

Currency. The unit of currency is the *Bermuda dollar* (BMD) of 100 *cents* at parity with the US dollar. The Bermuda Monetary Authority issues notes in denominations of BD$100, 50, 20, 10, 5 and 2, and coins in values of BD$5, 1, 50c, 25c, 10c, 5c and 1c. Inflation averaged 2·5% in 1996.

Banking and Finance. Bermuda is an offshore financial centre with tax exemption facilities. At 31 Dec. 1996, 9,252 international companies were registered in Bermuda, with insurers the most important category. There are 3 commercial banks, with total assets of BD$8,475m. in 1995. At the end of the first quarter of 1997 there were 8,703 exempted companies, 292 exempted partnership companies, 520 non-resident companies and 26 non-resident insurance companies on the Bermuda register. Bermuda is now the world's third largest insurance market after London and New York.

Weights and Measures. Metric, except that US and Imperial (British) measures are used in certain fields.

ENERGY AND NATURAL RESOURCES
Electricity. Installed capacity was 145,000 kW in 1996. Production in 1996 was 527·5m. kWh, with consumption per capita 7,856 kWh.

Agriculture. The chief products are fresh vegetables, bananas and citrus fruit. In 1995, 839 acres were being used for production of vegetables, fruit and flowers as well as for pasture, forage and fallow. In 1996, 503 persons were employed in agriculture, fishing and quarrying. In 1995 the total value of agricultural products was BD$5,989,000. Livestock, 1996: 1,000 cattle, 1,000 horses, 1,000 pigs, 1,000 goats.

Fisheries. In 1996 there were 194 fishing vessels and 274 registered fishermen. The total catch in 1995 was 444 tonnes. Fishing is centred on reef-dwelling species such as groupers and lobsters.

INDUSTRY
Labour. The labour force numbered 34,633 in 1996. Unemployment was less than 1·5% of the working population.

Trade Unions. There are 9 trade unions with a total membership (1995) of 8,728.

INTERNATIONAL TRADE
Foreign firms conducting business overseas only are not subject to a 60% Bermuda ownership requirement. In 1996, over 8,200 international companies had a physical presence in Bermuda.

Imports and Exports. The visible adverse balance of trade is more than compensated for by invisible exports, including tourism and off-shore insurance business.

Merchandise imports and exports in BD$1m.:

	1992	1993	1994	1995	1996
Imports	483	519	551	551	569
Exports	84	35	51	57	...

Imports in 1996: from USA, BD$416·6m.; UK, BD$28·8m.; Canada, BD$25·3m.; Caribbean, BD$31·8m.

In 1992 the principal imports (in BD$1m.) were: food, beverages and tobacco (106); machinery (68); chemicals (67); clothing (36); fuels (31); transport equipment (22). The bulk of exports comprise sales of fuel to aircraft and ships, and re-exports of pharmaceuticals.

COMMUNICATIONS

Roads. There are 140 miles of public highway and 138 miles of private roads. There are approximately 21,100 private cars, 22,100 motor cycles, scooters and mopeds, 700 buses, taxis and limousines, and 3,600 lorries and tank wagons.

Civil Aviation. The Bermuda International Airport is 19 km from Hamilton. Bermuda is served on a regularly scheduled basis by Air Canada, American Airlines, British Airways, Continental Airlines, Delta Airlines, Northwest Airlines and US Air.

Shipping. There are 3 ports, Hamilton, St George's and Dockyard. There is an open shipping registry. In 1995, ships registered totalled 4·49m. DWT, all foreign-owned.

Telecommunications. Main telephone lines numbered 51,900 in 1997, equivalent to 803·9 for every 1,000 inhabitants—the highest penetration rate in the world.

Postal Services. There were 15 post offices in 1995.

SOCIAL INSTITUTIONS

Justice. There are 4 magistrates' courts, 3 Supreme Courts and a Court of Appeal. The police had a strength of about 500 men and women in 1996.

Religion. Many religions are represented, but the larger number of worshippers are attracted to the Anglican, Roman Catholic, Seventh Day Adventist, African Methodist Episcopal, Methodist and Baptist faiths.

Education. Education is compulsory between the ages of 5 and 16, and government assistance is given by the payment of grants and, where necessary, school fees. In 1995–96 there were 6,362 pupils in state schools and 3,179 in independent schools. There were 515 full-time students attending the Bermuda College in 1995. A restructuring of secondary education has resulted in the construction of a new state-of-the-art secondary school, Cedarbridge Academy, which opened in September 1997.

Health. In 1996 there were 2 hospitals, 100 physicians and surgeons, 49 dentists and dental hygienists, 6 optometrists, 27 pharmacists, 8 dieticians and 553 nurses.

CULTURE

Broadcasting. Radio and television broadcasting are commercial; there are 2 broadcasting companies which offer a choice of 5 AM and 3 FM radio stations and 3 TV channels. A cable TV service also offers some 40 channels. In 1995 there were 81,000 radio and 59,000 TV receivers, or 978 per 1,000 inhabitants—more than anywhere else in the world. The USA ranked second, with 816 per 1,000 inhabitants.

Press. In 1996 there was 1 daily newspaper with a circulation of about 17,000 and 2 weeklies with a combined circulation of about 15,000.

Tourism. In 1996, 570,631 tourists, including cruise ship passengers, visited Bermuda. Visitor expenditure in 1995 was BD$487m.

BRITISH INDIAN OCEAN TERRITORY

FURTHER READING
Government Statistical Department. *Bermuda Facts and Figures.* Annual.
Ministry of Finance. *Bermuda Digest of Statistics.* Annual.

Boultbee, P. and Raine, D., *Bermuda* [Bibliography]. Oxford and Santa Barbara (CA), 1998
Zuill, W. S., *The Story of Bermuda and Her People.* 2nd ed. London, 1992

National library: The Bermuda Library, Hamilton.
National statistical office: Government Statistical Department, Hamilton.

BRITISH ANTARCTIC TERRITORY

KEY HISTORICAL EVENTS
The British Antarctic Territory was established on 3 March 1962, as a consequence of the entry into force of the Antarctic Treaty, to separate those areas of the then Falkland Islands Dependencies which lay within the Treaty area from those which did not (i.e. South Georgia and the South Sandwich Islands).

TERRITORY AND POPULATION
The territory encompasses the lands and islands within the area south of 60°S latitude lying between 20°W and 80°W longitude (approximately due south of the Falkland Islands and the Dependencies). It covers an area of some 660,000 sq. miles, and its principal components are the South Orkney and South Shetland Islands, the Antarctic Peninsula (Palmer Land and Graham Land), the Filchner and Ronne Ice Shelves and Coats Land.

There is no indigenous or permanently resident population. There is however an itinerant population of scientists and logistics staff of about 300, manning a number of research stations.

CURRENT ADMINISTRATION
Commissioner: Anthony J. Longrigg (non-resident).
Administrator: Dr. M. G. Richardson (non-resident)

BRITISH INDIAN OCEAN TERRITORY

KEY HISTORICAL EVENTS
This territory was established to meet UK and US defence requirements by an Order in Council on 8 Nov. 1965, consisting then of the Chagos Archipelago (formerly administered from Mauritius) and the islands of Aldabra, Desroches and Farquhar (all formerly administered from Seychelles). The latter islands became part of Seychelles when that country achieved independence on 29 June 1976.

TERRITORY AND POPULATION
The group, with a total land area of 23 sq. miles (60 sq. km) comprises 5 coral atolls (Diego Garcia, Peros Banhos, Salomon, Eagle and Egmont), of which the largest and southernmost, Diego Garcia, covers 17 sq. miles (44 sq. km) and lies 450 miles (724 km) south of the Maldives. A US Navy support facility has been established on Diego Garcia. There is no permanent population.

CURRENT ADMINISTRATION
Commissioner: Bruce Dinwiddy (non-resident).
Administrator: Margaret Savill (non-resident).
Commissioner's Representative: Cdr S. Jackson.

BRITISH VIRGIN ISLANDS

KEY HISTORICAL EVENTS
Discovered by Columbus on his second voyage in 1493, British Virgin Islands were first settled by the Dutch in 1648 and taken over in 1666 by a group of English planters. The islands were annexed to the British Crown in 1672. Constitutional government was granted in 1773, but was later surrendered in 1867. A Legislative Council formed in that year was abolished in 1902. In 1950 a partly nominated and partly elected Legislative Council was restored. A ministerial system of government was introduced in 1967.

TERRITORY AND POPULATION
The Islands form the eastern extremity of the Greater Antilles and number 70, of which 16 are inhabited. The largest, with population (1991 census), are Tortola, 13,568, Virgin Gorda, 2,495, Anegada, 156 and Jost Van Dyke, 141. Other islands had a total population (estimate 1990) of 183; marine population (estimate 1989), 124. Total area 59 sq. miles (130 sq. km); total population (1991 census), 16,749. The most recent estimate of the population of the British Virgin Islands was 19,107 in 1997. The projected population for 2000 is 20,000. In 1995 an estimated 56% of the population were urban. The capital, Road Town, on the south-east of Tortola, is a port of entry; population (estimate, 1991), 6,330.

The official language is English. Spanish and Creole are also spoken.

SOCIAL STATISTICS
Annual growth rate, 1996–97, 1·96%.

CLIMATE
A pleasantly healthy sub-tropical climate with summer temperatures lowered by sea breezes and cool nights. Road Town, Jan. 26°C, July 23°C. 1997 rainfall, 1091 mm.

CONSTITUTION AND GOVERNMENT
The Constitution dates from 1967 but was amended in 1977 and 1994. The Executive Council consists of the Governor, the Chief Minister, the Attorney-General *ex officio* and 3 ministers. The ministers are appointed by the Governor from among the elected members of the Legislative Council. The *Legislative Council* consists of the 4 ministers, 5 directly elected members from constituencies and 4 members from 'at large' seats covering the territory as a whole. The Speaker is elected from outside the Council.

RECENT ELECTIONS
At the elections of Feb. 1995 the Virgin Islands Party gained 6 seats, the Independent People's Movement, 3, the United Party, 2, and the Concerned Citizens' Movement, 2. Parliamentary elections were scheduled for May 1999.

CURRENT ADMINISTRATION
Governor: Francis Savage, CMG, OBE, LVO.
   Chief Minister: Ralph T. O'Neal (Virgin Islands Party; sworn in 25 May 1995).

INTERNATIONAL RELATIONS
The Islands are an associate member of CARICOM, OECS, UNESCO and ECLAC.
   The UK Government is responsible for the international relations of the Territory. Through this link, the Territory is party to a large number of treaties and international covenants.

ECONOMY
The economy is based on tourism and international financial services.

Performance. In 1994 GNP per capita was US$16,755. Real GDP growth was 3·7% in 1995 and 3·5% in 1994.

Budget. In 1998 revenue was US$127·31m and expenditure US$108·36m. (projected).

BRITISH VIRGIN ISLANDS

Currency. The official unit of currency is the US dollar.

Banking and Finance. In 1998 there were 13 banks and 189 trust companies. As of 30 Sept. 1998 total deposits were a recorded US$2bn. Financial Services has surpassed the performance of the tourism industry to become the largest contributor to the GDP. As of 11 Jan. 1999, 307,970 International Business Companies were registered in the British Virgin Islands.

ENERGY AND NATURAL RESOURCES

Electricity. Production, 1997–98, 99·039m. kWh.

Water. The major part of the water supplied in the public mains is from wells and sea water produced by reverse osmosis desalination plants.

Agriculture. The value of agricultural production in 1997 was US$1·52m. despite 3 destructive hurricanes in the course of the year. In 1994: Total land suitable for agriculture, 5,324 acres; crops, 1,767 acres; and pastures, 3,557 acres. Agricultural production is limited, with the chief products being livestock (including poultry), fish, fruit and vegetables. Production, 1994, in tonnes: Fruits, 525; vegetables/root crop, 153; beef, 172; mutton, 29; pork, 39; and 1,535 cases of eggs.

Livestock (1996): Cattle, 2,000; pigs, 2,000; sheep, 5,000 and goats (1995), 10,000.

Forestry. The area under forests in 1995 was 4,000 ha, or 26·7% of the total land area.

Fisheries. The total catch was estimated to be 1,000 tonnes in 1995.

INDUSTRY

The construction industry is a significant employer. There are a rum distillery, ice-making plants and cottage industries producing tourist items.

EXTERNAL ECONOMIC RELATIONS

Imports and Exports.

There is a very small export trade, almost entirely with the Virgin Islands of the USA. In 1997 imports were US$166·4m. while 1996 exports were US$5·9m.

COMMUNICATIONS

Roads. In 1997 there were 132 km of paved roads and there were 7,944 registered vehicles.

Civil Aviation. Beef Island Airport, about 16 km from Road Town, is capable of receiving 80-seat short-take-off-and-landing jet aircraft. American Eagle and LIAT provide scheduled flights to Puerto Rico and the Eastern Caribbean.

Shipping. There are 2 deep-water harbours: Port Purcell and Road Town. There are services to the Netherlands, UK, USA and other Caribbean islands. Merchant shipping totalled 5,000 GRT in 1995.

Telecommunications. There were (1995) 9,282 telephones, 21 telex subscribers, 582 fax machine subscribers, and an external telephone service links Tortola with Bermuda and the rest of the world.

SOCIAL INSTITUTIONS

Justice. Law is based on UK common law. There are courts of first instance. The appeal court is in the UK.

Religion. There are Anglican, Methodist, Seventh-Day Adventist, Roman Catholic, Baptist, Pentecostal and other Christian churches in the Territory. There are also Jehovah's Witness and Hindu congregations.

Education. In 1995 adult literacy was 95%. Primary education is provided in 16 government schools, 3 with secondary divisions, and 16 private schools. Total number of pupils in primary and pre-primary schools (31 Dec. 1994) 2,855.

Secondary education to GCSE level and Caribbean Examination Council level is provided by the BVI High School, and the secondary divisions of the schools on

Virgin Gorda and Anegada. Total number of secondary level pupils (31 Dec. 1994) 1,363. In 1996 the total number of classroom teachers in all Government schools was 116.

In 1986 a branch of the Hull University (England) School of Education was established.

Government expenditure, 1995 (estimate), US$4·3m.

Health. As of 31 Dec. 1995 there were 17 doctors, 67 nurses, 50 public hospital beds and 1 private hospital with 10 beds. Expenditure, 1994 (estimate) was US$5·3m.

CULTURE

Broadcasting. Radio ZBVI transmits 10,000 watts; and British Virgin Islands Cable TV operates a cable system of 19 television channels and 8 pay-per-view channels.

Press. In 1994 there were 2 weekly newspapers and a periodical.

Tourism. Tourism is the most important industry and accounts for some 75% of economic activity. In 1995 there were 364,147 visitor arrivals, of whom 122,054 were cruise ship visitors, and 23,712 day visitors. Total tourist expenditure for 1994 was US$197·7m.

FURTHER READING

Dookham, I., *A History of the British Virgin Islands.* Epping, 1975
Harrigan, N. and Varlack, P., *The Virgin Islands Story.* Road Town, 1975
Moll, V. P., *Virgin Islands.* [Bibliography] Oxford and Santa Barbara (CA), 1991
Pickering, V. W., *Early History of the British Virgin Islands.* London, 1983

CAYMAN ISLANDS

KEY HISTORICAL EVENTS

The islands were discovered by Columbus on 10 May 1503 and (with Jamaica) were recognized as British possessions by the Treaty of Madrid in 1670. Grand Cayman was settled in 1734 and the other islands in 1833. They were administered by Jamaica from 1863, but remained under British sovereignty when Jamaica became independent on 6 Aug. 1962.

TERRITORY AND POPULATION

The Islands consist of Grand Cayman, Little Cayman and Cayman Brac. Situated in the Caribbean Sea, about 200 miles north-west of Jamaica. Area, 100 sq. miles (260 sq. km). Census population of 1989, 25,355 (13,202 Caymanians by birth). Estimate, 1996, 35,000; density, 135 per sq. km. The projected population for 2000 is 41,000. The spoken language is English. The chief town is George Town, census (1989) 12,921.

The areas and populations of the islands are:

	Sq. km	Census 1979	Census 1989	Estimate 1996
Grand Cayman	197	15,000	23,881	33,584
Cayman Brac	36	1,607	1,441	1,300
Little Cayman	26	70	33	116

SOCIAL STATISTICS

1996: Births, 561; marriages, 300; deaths, 125. Annual growth rate, 1990–95, 3·3%.

CLIMATE

The climate is tropical maritime, with a cool season from Nov. to March and temperatures some 10°F warmer for the remaining months. Rainfall averages 56" (1,400 mm) a year at George Town. Hurricanes may be experienced between July and Nov.

CAYMAN ISLANDS

CONSTITUTION AND GOVERNMENT

The 1972 Constitution provides for a *Legislative Assembly* consisting of the Speaker, 3 official members and 15 elected members. The *Executive Council* consists of the Governor (as Chairman), the 3 official members and 5 members elected by the elected members of the Legislative Assembly.

RECENT ELECTIONS

At the Legislative Assembly elctions on 22 Nov. 1996, National Team won 9 seats, Democratic Alliance 2, Team Cayman 1 and Non-partisans 3.

CURRENT ADMINISTRATION

Governor: John W. Owen, MBE.

ECONOMY

Performance. Real GDP growth was 5·0% in 1995 and 1·0% in 1994.

Budget. Estimated revenue 1998, CI$248·2m.; expenditure, CI$204m. Public debt (Dec. 1994), CI$37m.; total reserves (Dec. 1997), CI$8·9m.

Currency. The unit of currency is the *Cayman Island dollar* (KYD) of 100 *cents*. There are coins of 1, 5, 10, 25 and 50 cents and CI$1, 2 and 5, and notes of CI$1, 5, 10, 25, 50 and 100.

Banking and Finance. A Monetary Authority was inaugurated in Jan. 1997. 576 commercial banks and trust companies held licences at Dec. 1996, which permit the holders to offer services to the public, 29 domestically. Financial services are the Islands' chief industry. 37,919 companies, almost all offshore, were registered at the end of 1996.

ENERGY AND NATURAL RESOURCES

Electricity. Installed capacity was 71,000 kW in 1994. Production in 1994 was 281m. kWh, with consumption per capita 8,800 kWh.

Agriculture. Livestock, 1996: 1,000 cattle.

Fisheries. In 1995 the total catch was 612 tonnes.

EXTERNAL ECONOMIC RELATIONS

Imports and Exports.

Exports, 1995, totalled US$4m.; imports, US$399m.

COMMUNICATIONS

Roads. There were (1996) about 252 miles of motorable road, of which about 200 miles were surfaced with tarmac, and (1996) 19,164 motor vehicles.

Civil Aviation. There is an international airport at Grand Cayman. CAL provides a regular inter-island service. Cayman Airways operates a service to Cayman Brac, and also flies to Miami, Orlando, Houston, Tampa, Honduras and Jamaica. American Airlines and Northwest Airlines provide services to Miami; US Air to Baltimore and North Carolina; American Airlines to Raleigh/Durham; Air Jamaica to Jamaica; and British Airways to Gatwick, London.

Shipping. Motor vessels ply regularly between the Cayman Islands, Jamaica, Costa Rica and Florida. In 1995 merchant shipping totalled 368,000 GRT.

Telecommunications. There were 20,731 telephone lines in 1996 serving 29,500 stations and 2,900 cellular customers.

SOCIAL INSTITUTIONS

Justice. There is a Grand Court, sitting 6 times a year for criminal sessions at George Town under a Chief Justice and 2 puisne judges. There are 2 Magistrates presiding over the Summary Court.

Religion. There are Anglican, Roman Catholic, Presbyterian and other Christian communities represented in the islands.

Education. In 1996 there were 10 government primary schools with 1,739 pupils and 9 private schools. Post-primary education at the 3 government high schools was attended by 1,626 pupils. There is also a private institution for tertiary education; a government school for special educational needs; a government-operated community college offering technical, vocational and business studies, and a 2-year programme in arts and sciences, as well as adult, educational and recreational courses; and a centre for training of handicapped persons.

Health. In 1996 there was a general hospital in George Town with 59 beds, a dental clinic, 4 district clinics; and a hospital in Cayman Brac with specialist services (18 beds). There were 28 doctors in the government service and 26 in private practice.

CULTURE

Broadcasting. There are 4 radio broadcasting stations in the Islands, with (1997) an estimated 20,000 receivers. There are 2 local commercial TV companies.

Press. The *Caymanian Compass* is published 5 days a week.

Tourism. Tourism is the chief industry after financial services, and there were (1994) 3,880 beds in hotels and 3,162 in apartments, guest houses and cottages. In 1996 there were 373,000 foreign tourists, bringing revenue of US$394m.

FURTHER READING
Compendium of Statistics of the Cayman Islands, 1994. Cayman Islands Government Statistics Office, 1995
Cayman Islands Annual Report 1996. Cayman Islands Government Information Services, 1996
Boultbee, P. G., *Cayman Islands.* [Bibliography]. Oxford and Santa Barbara (CA), 1996

FALKLAND ISLANDS

KEY HISTORICAL EVENTS
France established a settlement in 1764 and Britain a second settlement in 1765. In 1770 Spain bought out the French and drove off the British. This action on the part of Spain brought that country and Britain to the verge of war. The Spanish restored the settlement to the British in 1771, but the settlement was withdrawn on economic grounds in 1774. In 1806 Spanish rule was overthrown in Argentina, and the Argentine claimed to succeed Spain in the French and British settlements in 1820. The British objected and reclaimed their settlement in 1832 as a Crown Colony.

On 2 April 1982 Argentine forces occupied the Falkland Islands. On 3 April the UN Security Council called, by 10 votes to 1, for Argentina's withdrawal. After a military campaign, but without a formal declaration of war, the UK regained possession on 14–15 June after Argentina surrendered.

In April 1990 Argentina's Congress declared the Falkland and other British-held South Atlantic islands part of the new Argentine province of Tierra del Fuego.

TERRITORY AND POPULATION
The Territory comprises numerous islands situated in the South Atlantic Ocean about 480 miles north-east of Cape Horn covering 4,700 sq. miles. The main East Falkland Island, 2,610 sq. miles; the West Falkland, 2,090 sq. miles, including the adjacent small islands. The population at the census of 1996 was 2,607. The only town is Stanley, in East Falkland, with a population of 1,636. The population is nearly all of British descent, with 1,267 born in the Islands (1996 census figures) and 885 in the UK. In 1995, 84·1% lived in urban areas. A British garrison of about 2,000 servicemen, stationed in East Falkland in 1991, is not included in the 1996 census figures, but the 483 civilians employed there are.

The official language is English.

FALKLAND ISLANDS

CLIMATE
A cool temperate climate, much affected by strong winds, particularly in spring. Stanley, Jan. 49°F (9·4°C), July 35°F (1·7°C). Annual rainfall 27" (681 mm).

CONSTITUTION AND GOVERNMENT
A new Constitution came into force on 3 Oct. 1985. This incorporated a chapter protecting fundamental human rights, and in the preamble recalled the provisions on the right of self-determination contained in international covenants.

Executive power is vested in the Governor who must consult the Executive Council except on urgent or trivial matters. He must consult the Commander British Forces on matters relating to defence and internal security (except police).

There is a *Legislative Council* consisting of 8 elected members and 2 *ex officio* members, the Chief Executive and Financial Secretary. Only elected members have a vote. The Commander British Forces has a right to attend and take part in its proceedings but has no vote. The Attorney General also has a similar right to take part in proceedings with the consent of the person presiding. The Governor presides over sittings. He also presides over sittings of the Executive Council which consists of 3 elected members (elected by and from the elected members of Legislative Council) and the Chief Executive and Financial Secretary (*ex officio*). The Commander British Forces and Attorney General have a right to attend but may not vote.

British citizenship was withdrawn by the British Nationality Act 1981, but restored after the Argentine invasion of 1982.

CURRENT ADMINISTRATION
Governor: Richard Ralph, CVO.
 Chief Executive: Andrew Gurr.

DEFENCE
Since 1982 the Islands have been defended by a 2,000-strong garrison of British servicemen. In addition there is a local volunteer defence force.

ECONOMY
Policy. The Falkland Islands Development Corporation began operations in 1984. Projects assisted include a spinning mill dairy, hydroponic market garden, tourist lodges, agricultural supply co-operatives, and research into seabird populations and their diets.

Budget. Revenue and expenditure (in £ sterling) for fiscal years ending 30 June:

	1990–91	1991–92	1992–93	1993–94	1994–95	1995–96
Revenue	41,940,000	40,270,000	40,452,000	32,690,000	33,812,000	42,351,679
Expenditure	45,967,000	39,145,000	30,452,000	24,535,000	33,614,000	42,351,953

Currency. The unit of currency is the *Falkland Islands pound* (FKP) of 100 *pence*, at parity with £1 sterling.

Banking and Finance. The only bank is Standard Chartered Bank, which had assets of £31m. in 1997.

ENERGY AND NATURAL RESOURCES
Oil and Gas. The UK government authorized exploration for oil in Nov. 1991 in the 200-mile economic exclusion zone, except where it overlapped Argentina's zone in the west. An Anglo-Argentine agreement of 27 Sept. 1995 establishes 2 legal frameworks for marine oil exploration areas without prejudice to either country's claim to sovereignty over the Falkland Islands. The first, close to the Islands, is to have licensing terms which give companies 22 years to explore and complete drilling. The second extends between the Islands and Argentina wherein licensing will be overseen by a joint Anglo-Argentine commission. Argentina may bid for licences in the first area, and draws revenue directly from the second.

Agriculture. The economy was formerly based solely on agriculture, principally sheep farming. Following a programme of sub-division, much of the land is divided into family-size units. There were 100 farms in 1997, averaging 33,600 acres and

8,200 sheep. During 1991 the Falklands Islands Co. sold its agricultural holdings to the Falkland Island government. Less than 5% of the total land area is owned outside the islands. Wool is the principal product; output was 2,521 tonnes in 1991.

Livestock: In 1997 there were over 700,000 sheep. 1996: cattle, 4,000; horses, 1,000.

Fisheries. Since the establishment of a 150-mile interim conservation and management zone around the Islands in 1986 and the consequent introduction, on 1 Feb. 1987, of a licensing regime for vessels fishing within the zone, income from the associated fishing activities is now the largest source of revenue. Licences raised £25m. in 1992. Some 0·2m. tonnes of illex squid are caught annually. In 1994 Argentina's quota was raised to 0·22m. tonnes; that of the Falkland Islands remained at 0·15m. tonnes. 79,803 tonnes were caught in the Falklands zone in 1996. 61,360 tonnes of Patagonian squid and 23,515 tonnes of blue whiting were also caught.

As recently as 1986 the annual catch was just 8 tonnes. Nowhere else in the world has there been such a rapid rate of growth in the annual fish catch since the mid 1980s.

On 26 Dec. 1990 the Falklands outer conservation zone was introduced which extends beyond the 150-mile zone out to 200 miles from baselines. In Nov. 1992 commercial fishing in the outer zone was banned, the zone was reopened to fishing in 1994. A UK-Argentine South Atlantic Fisheries Commission was set up in 1990; it meets at least twice a year.

EXTERNAL ECONOMIC RELATIONS
90% of trade is with the UK, the rest with Latin America, mainly Chile. In 1995 imports totalled £17m.; exports (mainly wool), £3·5m.

COMMUNICATIONS
Roads. There are 27 km of made-up roads in and around Stanley, and another 54 km of all-weather road between Stanley and Mount Pleasant Airport. Other settlements outside Stanley are linked by tracks. There were about 1,100 private cars in 1996.

Civil Aviation. Air communication is currently via Ascension Island. An airport, completed in 1986, is sited at Mount Pleasant on East Falkland. RAF Tristar aircraft operate a twice-weekly service between the Falklands and the UK. Internal air links are provided by the government-operated air service, which carries passengers, mail, freight and medical patients between the settlements and Stanley on non-scheduled flights in Islander aircraft. A Chilean airline runs a weekly service to Punta Arenas.

Shipping. A charter vessel calls 4 or 5 times a year to/from the UK. Vessels of the Royal Fleet Auxiliary run regularly to South Georgia. Sea links with Chile and Uruguay began in 1989. In 1995 merchant shipping totalled 20,000 GRT.

Telecommunications. Number of telephones (Sept. 1991) 1,180. International direct dialling is available, as are international telex and facsimile links. There is a government-operated radio and TV station at Stanley.

SOCIAL INSTITUTIONS
Justice. There is a Supreme Court, and a Court of Appeal sits in the UK; appeals may go from that court to the judicial committee of the Privy Council. Judges may only be removed for inability or misbehaviour on the advice of the judicial committee of the Privy Council. The senior resident judicial officer is the Senior Magistrate. There is an Attorney General and a Senior Crown Counsel.

Education. Education is compulsory between the ages of 5 and 15 years. In 1992 there were 350 children receiving education in the Islands. 60 of these were of primary school age, living on isolated farms and receiving teacher visits and radio lessons. There is a primary school in Stanley, and a community school opened in 1992 with secondary study and sport facilities. Estimated recurrent expenditure on education and training from own funds in 1994–95, £2,041,440.

Health. The Government Medical Department is responsible for all medical services to civilians. Estimated expenditure (1994–95), £2,092,490. A new hospital and some sheltered accommodation was completed in March 1987. Services include all primary care for Stanley, and the flying doctor service for outlying farm settlements.

CULTURE

Tourism. There are about 200 tourists and 5,000 cruise ship visitors a year.

FURTHER READING

Day, A., *The Falkland Islands*. [Bibliography]. Oxford and Santa Barbara (CA), 1995
Gough, B., *The Falkland Islands/Malvinas: the Contest for Empire in the South Atlantic*. London, 1992
Smith, W. S. (ed.) *Towards Resolution? The Falklands/Malvinas Dispute*. London, 1991

GIBRALTAR

KEY HISTORICAL EVENTS

The Rock of Gibraltar was settled by Moors in 711. In 1462 it was taken by the Spaniards, from Granada. It was captured by Admiral Sir George Rooke on 24 July 1704, and ceded to Great Britain by the Treaty of Utrecht, 1713. The cession was confirmed by the treaties of Paris (1763) and Versailles (1783).

On 10 Sept. 1967, in pursuance of a UN resolution on the decolonization of Gibraltar, a referendum was held to ascertain whether the people of Gibraltar wished to retain their link with the UK or pass under Spanish sovereignty. Out of an electorate of 12,762, 12,138 voted to retain the British connection.

The border was closed by Spain in 1969, opened to pedestrians in 1982 and fully opened in 1985.

In 1973 Gibraltar joined the European Community, as a dependent territory of the United Kingdom.

TERRITORY AND POPULATION

Gibraltar is situated in latitude 36°07' N and longitude 05°21' W. Area, 2½ sq. miles (6·5 sq. km) including port and harbour. Highest point is 1,396ft. Total population, (census, 1991), 28,074. Estimate (1997) 27,086 (of whom 20,608 were British Gibraltarian, 3,908 Other British and 2,570 Non-British); density, 4,167 per sq. km. The projected population for 2000 is 29,000. The population is mostly of Genoese, Portuguese and Maltese and Spanish descent.

The official language is English. Spanish, Italian and Portuguese are also spoken.

SOCIAL STATISTICS

Statistics (1997): Births, 440; marriages, 722; deaths, 238. Annual growth rate, 1990–95, –1·9%.

CLIMATE

The climate is warm temperate, with westerly winds in winter bringing rain. Summers are pleasantly warm and rainfall is low. Mean maximum temperatures: Jan. 16°C, July 28°C. Annual rainfall 722 mm.

CONSTITUTION AND GOVERNMENT

A new Constitution was introduced in 1969. The Legislative and City Councils were merged to produce an enlarged legislature known as the *Gibraltar House of Assembly*. Executive authority is exercised by the Governor, who is also Commander-in-Chief. The Governor retains direct responsibility for matters relating to defence, external affairs and internal security. He has the power to intervene in the conduct of domestic affairs in support of this responsibility and has certain powers of intervention in the interests of maintaining financial and economic stability. However, he is normally required to act in accordance with the advice of the Gibraltar Council, which consists of 4 *ex-officio* members (the Deputy Governor, the Deputy Fortress Commander, the Attorney-General and the Financial and Development Secretary) together with 5 elected members of the House of Assembly appointed by the Governor after consultation with the Chief Minister. Matters of primarily domestic concern are devolved to elected Ministers. There is a Council of Ministers presided over by the Chief Minister.

The House of Assembly consists of a Speaker appointed by the Governor, 15 elected and 2 *ex-officio* members (the Attorney-General and the Financial and Development Secretary). No more than 8 of the elected seats may go to the winning party at elections.

Gibraltarians have full UK citizenship.

A Mayor of Gibraltar is elected by the elected members of the Assembly.

RECENT ELECTIONS
At the elections of May 1996 the electorate was 18,437; turn-out was 88%. The Gibraltar Social Democratic Party (GSD) gained 8 seats with 48% of votes cast. The Gibraltar Socialist and Labour Party gained 7 with 39%. The Gibraltar National Party gained 13% of the vote but won no seats. All of the parties advocate self-determination.

CURRENT ADMINISTRATION
Governor and C.-in-C.: Sir Richard Luce.
   Chief Minister: Peter Caruana (b. 1956; GSD).
   Deputy Chief Minister and Minister for Trade and Industry: Peter Montegriffo.
Education, Training, Culture and Youth: Dr Bernard Linares. *Government Services and Sport:* Ernest Britto. *Tourism and Transport:* Joe Holliday. *Social Affairs:* Hubert Corby. *Employment and Buildings and Works:* Jaime Netto. *Environment and Health:* Keith Azzopardi.
   The Speaker (House of Assembly): John E Alcantara.

DEFENCE
The Ministry of Defence presence consists of a tri-service garrison numbering approximately 900 uniformed personnel. Supporting the garrison are approximately 1,100 locally-employed civilian personnel. In addition to the defence of the Rock, the garrison supports a NATO Headquarters, provides and operates communications and surveillance facilities, operates the airfield and provides berthing facilities for naval vessels in the harbour.

ECONOMY
Policy. The economy is primarily dependent upon service industries and port facilities, with income derived from tourism, transshipment and, perhaps most importantly in terms of growth, the provision of financial services.

Performance. In 1994–95 Gibraltar's provisional GDP was £326·6m., equivalent to £11,263 per head.

Budget. Revenue and expenditure (in £1,000 sterling):

	1992–93	1993–94	1994–95	1995–96	1996–97
Revenue	72,735	73,443	69,808	70,688	72,017
Expenditure	77,915	74,697	73,215	73,255	73,304

The main sources of Consolidated Fund revenues were Income Tax and General Rates. Main items of expenditure (as % of total expenditure): Education and sport, 20·4%; environment/housing, 14·1%; police, 11·5%; electricity undertaking, 8·2%; support services, 7·2%.

Currency. The legal tender currency is UK sterling. Also legal tender are Government of Gibraltar Currency notes and coins for the *Gibraltar pound* (GIP) of 100 *pence*, at parity with the UK £1 sterling. The total of Government of Gibraltar notes in circulation at 31 March 1997 was £10·3m.

Banking and Finance. In Dec. 1997 there were 26 banks and 4 building societies. The annual rate of inflation was 1·5% in 1997. The financial sector employs 12% of the working population. In 1989 the Financial Services Commission was established to regulate financial activities.

ENERGY AND NATURAL RESOURCES

Electricity. Installed capacity was 33,000 kW in 1993. Production in 1994 was 90m. kWh.

Oil and Gas. Gibraltar is dependent on imported petroleum for its energy supplies.

Water. There are no permanent natural water supplies in Gibraltar. The main sources of water supply are the distillation plants which purify sea water.

Minerals. Mineral fuels comprised around 25% of the value of total imports in 1996.

Agriculture. Gibraltar lacks agricultural land and natural resources; the territory is dependent on imports of foodstuffs and fuels.

INDUSTRY

The industrial sector (including manufacturing, construction and power) employed around 15% of the working population in 1996. There is a bottling plant and a floppy diskette manufacturer.

Labour. The total insured labour force at April 1996 was 12,980 (males, 8,130; females, 4,850). Principal areas of employment (April 1996): Community, social and personal services, 6,192; trade, restaurants and hotels, 2,939; construction, 1,349; manufacturing, 452; electricity and water, 238; other, 1,810. (Figures cover only non-agricultural activities, excluding mining and quarrying). An estimated 13% of the labour force were unemployed in 1996.

Trade Unions. In 1991 there were 8 registered trade unions.

EXTERNAL ECONOMIC RELATIONS

Gibraltar has a special status within the EU which exempts it from the latter's fiscal policy.

Imports and Exports. Imports and exports (in £1,000 sterling):

	1991	1992	1993	1994	1995
Imports	278,866	327,536	370,884	420,192	379,919
Exports	70,102	92,971	161,400	175,643	172,599

Britain and the Commonwealth provide the bulk of imports, but fresh vegetables and fruit come mainly from the Netherlands and Spain. Foodstuffs accounted for 14% of total imports in 1996 (excluding petroleum products); about 51% of non-fuel imports originated from the UK. Other sources include Japan, Spain and the Netherlands. Value of non-fuel imports, 1995, £276·2m. Exports are mainly re-exports of petroleum and petroleum products supplied to shipping, and include manufactured goods, wines, spirits, malt and tobacco. Gibraltar depends largely on tourism, offshore banking and other financial sector activity, the entrepôt trade and the provision of supplies to visiting ships. Exports of local produce are negligible. In 1996 Gibraltar recorded a visible trade deficit of £258m.

COMMUNICATIONS

Roads. There are 33 miles of roads including 4·25 miles of pedestrian way. In 1995 there were 18,400 passenger cars and 1,000 commercial vehicles.

Civil Aviation. There is an international airport, Gibraltar North Front. Scheduled flights were operated in 1998 by British Airways to London (Gatwick), Manchester and Casablanca, and by Monarch Airlines to London (Luton). 89,300 passengers arrived by air in 1995.

Shipping. A total of 4,222 merchant ships of 79·2m. GRT entered port during 1996, including 3,411 deep-sea ships of 78·2m. GRT. 5,042 calls were made by yachts of 191,613 GRT. 139 cruise liners called during 1996 involving 96,684 passengers. In 1995 merchant shipping totalled 307,000 GRT.

Telecommunications. The telephone service is operated by Gibraltar Nynex Communications, a joint venture company between the Government of Gibraltar and Nynex Worldwide Systems from the USA. The number of telephone stations (1996) was 21,466. A new Digital System X Exchange became operational in 1990, with capacity for 25,800 lines in 1996. A Fibre Optic Network became operational in 1991. International direct dialling is available to over 150 countries via the Gibraltar Telecommunications Ltd (Gibtel) Earth Satellite Station and other international circuits. Gibtel began operating a mobile system in 1994.

SOCIAL INSTITUTIONS

Justice. The judicial system is based on the English system. There is a Court of Appeal, a Supreme Court, presided over by the Chief Justice, a Court of First Instance and a Magistrates' Court.

Religion. The population are mostly Roman Catholic. In 1997 there were 7 Roman Catholic and 3 Anglican churches, 1 Presbyterian and 1 Methodist church and 4 synagogues, and a mosque is currently under construction. Annual subsidy to each communion, £500.

Education. Free compulsory education is provided between ages 5 and 15 years. The medium of instruction is English. The comprehensive system was introduced in Sept. 1972. There were (1996) 12 primary and 2 comprehensive schools. Primary schools are mixed and divided into first schools for children aged 4-8 years and middle schools for children aged 8-12 years. The comprehensives are single-sex. In addition, there is 1 Services primary school and 1 private primary school. A new purpose-built Special School for severely handicapped children aged 2-16 years was opened in 1977, and there are 4 Special Units for children with special educational needs (1 attached to a first school, 1 to a middle school and 1 at each secondary school), 3 nurseries for children aged 3-4 years, and an occupational therapy centre for handicapped adults. Technical and vocational education and training is available at the Gibraltar College of Further Education managed by the Gibraltar Government. In Sept. 1996, there were 2,810 pupils at government primary schools, 200 at private and 294 at the Services school; 19 at the special school; 929 at the boys' comprehensive school and 878 at the girls' comprehensive. There were 165 full-time and 297 part-time students in the Gibraltar College of Further Education in Sept. 1996. Scholarships are made available for universities, teacher training and other higher education in the UK. Government expenditure on education in the year ended 31 March 1996 was £11·5m.

Health. In 1994 there were 2 hospitals with 244 beds and 29 doctors. Total expenditure on medical and health services during year ended 31 March 1995 was £19,354,653.

CULTURE

Gibraltar's main events are organized by the Ministry of Culture.

Broadcasting. Radio Gibraltar broadcasts for 24 hours daily, in English and Spanish; and GBC Television operates for 24 hours daily in English. Number of TV licences as at 31 Dec. 1996, 7,014. In 1995 there were 36,000 radios.

Press. There were (1997) 1 daily and 3 weeklies.

Tourism. In 1996 more than 6m. tourists visited Gibraltar (including day-visitors).

Festivals. The main festivals (1999) are: Gibraltar Spring Festival, 26 April to 5 June; 27th Gibraltar Open Art Exhibition, 12 July to 19 Aug.; Gibraltar National Week Festivities, 4 Sept. to 12 Sept.; 55th Annual Drama Festival, 29 Nov. to 4 Dec.

Museums and Galleries. The Gibraltar Museum documents the island's 200m. year history with an audio-visual presentation and several galleries.

FURTHER READING
Gibraltar Year Book. Gibraltar, (Annual)
Ellicott, D., *Our Gibraltar.* Gibraltar, 1975
Green, M. M., *A Gibraltar Bibliography.* London, 1980.—*Supplement.* London, 1982
Hills, G., *Rock of Contention: a History of Gibraltar.* London, 1974
Jackson, W. G. F., *The Rock of the Gibraltarians.* Farleigh Dickinson Univ. Press, 1987
Magauran, H. C., *Rock Siege: the Difficulties with Spain 1964–85.* Gibraltar, 1986
Morris, D. S. and Haigh, R. H., *Britain, Spain and Gibraltar, 1945–90: the Eternal Triangle.* London, 1992
Shields, G. J., *Gibraltar.* [Bibliography] Oxford and Santa Barbara (CA), 1988

MONTSERRAT

KEY HISTORICAL EVENTS

Montserrat was discovered by Columbus in 1493 and colonized by Britain in 1632, who brought Irish settlers to the island. Montserrat formed part of the federal colony of the Leeward Islands from 1871 until 1958, when it became a separate colony following the dissolution of the Federation.

On 18 July 1995 the Soufriere Hills volcano erupted for the first time in recorded history, which led to over half the inhabitants being evacuated to the north of the island, and the relocation of the chief town, Plymouth. Another major eruption on 25 June 1997 caused a number of deaths and led to further evacuation.

TERRITORY AND POPULATION

Montserrat is situated in the Caribbean Sea, 27 miles south-west of Antigua. The area is 39·5 sq. miles (102 sq. km). Population, 1991, 11,957; estimate, Aug. 1998, 4,008. What was previously the capital, Plymouth, is now deserted as a result of the continuing activity of the Soufriere Hills volcano. The safe area is in the north of the island.

The official language is English.

CLIMATE

A tropical climate with an average annual rainfall of 60" (1,500 mm) the wettest months being Sept.–Dec., with a hurricane season June–Nov. Plymouth, Jan. 76°F (24·4°C), July 81°F (27·2°C).

CONSTITUTION AND GOVERNMENT

Montserrat is a British Overseas Territory. The Constitution dates from the 1989 Montserrat Constitutional Order. The head of state is Queen Elizabeth II, represented by a *Governor* who heads an Executive Council, comprising also the Chief Minister, the Financial Secretary, the Attorney-General and 3 other ministers. The *Legislative Council* consists of 7 elected members, 2 civil service officials (the Attorney-General and Financial Secretary) and 2 nominated members; it sits for 5-year terms.

RECENT ELECTIONS

Following elections to the Legislative Council on 11 Nov. 1996, a coalition government was formed, comprising 2 members of the Movement for National Reconstruction, 1 member of the National Progressive Party and 1 independent.

CURRENT ADMINISTRATION

Governor: Tony Abbott.
  Chief Minister: David Brandt.

INTERNATIONAL RELATIONS

Montserrat is a member of CARICOM and the OECS.

ECONOMY

Performance. Real GDP growth was –2·9% in 1995 and 0·8% in 1994.

Budget. In 1998 the estimated expenditure was EC$60·6m. compared with actual expenditure of EC$63·5m. in 1997, a reduction of 5%. It was estimated that the government would collect EC$16·5m. during 1998—a decline of 38% when compared with 1997.

Currency. The *Eastern Caribbean dollar* (*see* ANTIGUA AND BARBUDA: Currency).

Banking and Finance. In 1996 there were 3 commercial and 21 offshore banks. Responsibility for overseeing offshore banking rests with the Governor. In late 1998 there were 2 commercial banks on the island.

Weights and Measures. Both metric and imperial weights and measures are in use.

ENERGY AND NATURAL RESOURCES

Electricity. Production (1995) 19·23m. kWh. With the reduction in habitable area, it is anticipated that the general production will be considerably less.

Agriculture. 3,700 ha are normally suitable for agriculture, with about half in use, but only 1,000 ha were available in 1996 because of the volcanic crisis. Potatoes, tomatoes, onions, mangoes and limes were produced in recent times. Meat production began in 1994 and the island soon became self-sufficient in chicken, mutton and beef.

Livestock (1996); Cattle, 10,000; pigs, 1,000; sheep, 5,000; goats, 7,000.

Forestry. The area under forests in 1995 was 3,000 ha, or 30% of the total land area.

Fisheries. Total catch, 1995, 175 tonnes.

INDUSTRY

Manufacturing has in recent years contributed about 6% to GDP and accounted for 10% of employment, but has been responsible for about 80% of exports. It has been limited to rice milling and the production of light consumer goods such as electronic components, light fittings, plastic bags and leather goods. The volcanic activity has put a halt to the milling of rice in the exclusion zone and curtailed the production of light consumer goods.

Trade Unions. There is 1 trade union, the Montserrat Allied Workers Union (MAWU).

EXTERNAL ECONOMIC RELATIONS

Imports and Exports. Imports in 1995 totalled US$80m.; exports, US$5m. The USA was the main trading partner. Chief exports were milled rice, electronic parts, lighting fittings, plastic bags and leather goods.

COMMUNICATIONS

Roads. In 1995 there were 205 km of paved roads, 25 km of unsurfaced roads and 50 km of tracks. In 1995 there were 2,700 cars and 400 commercial vehicles registered. These figures have changed since then, but the government, through the Ministry of Communications and Works, is focusing its road developments in the north of the island, and in 1998 and 1999 a number of road work projects were under way.

Civil Aviation. At the W. H. Bramble airport LIAT used to provide services to Antigua with onward connections to the rest of the Eastern Caribbean, but it was closed in June 1997 as volcanic activity increased.

Shipp

ing. Plymouth is the port of entry, but alternative anchorage was provided at Old Bay Road during the volcanic crisis.

Telecommunications. Number of telephones, 1995, 4,783. With the migration of people to the north and overseas, and the subsequent destruction of the southern part of the island, the number of telephones has shrunk to 2,100.

SOCIAL INSTITUTIONS

Justice. Law is based on UK common law as exercised by the Eastern Caribbean Supreme Court. Final appeal lies to the UK Privy Council. Law is administered by the West Indies Associated States Court, a Court of Summary Jurisdiction and Magistrate's Courts.

Religion. In 1997, 25% of the population were Anglican, 20% Methodist, 15% Pentecostal, 10% Roman Catholic and 10% Adventist.

Education. In 1996–97 there were 11 primary schools (only 4 open), a comprehensive secondary school with 3 campuses, and a technical college. Schools are run by the Government, the churches and the private sector. There is a medical school, the American University of the Caribbean.

Health. In 1996 there were 4 medical officers, 1 surgeon, 1 dentist and 1 hospital with 69 beds.

CULTURE

Broadcasting. There is a government-owned radio station (ZJB) and 2 commercial stations (Radio Antilles and GEM Radio). There is a commercial cable TV company.

Press. In 1996 there was 1 weekly newspaper.

Tourism. Tourism has in recent years contributed about 30% of GDP; earnings in 1993 were EC$40m. There were 36,077 visitors including 11,636 cruise ship arrivals in 1994. However, since the volcanic eruptions the tourist industry has become practically non-existent.

FURTHER READING

Fergus, H.A., *Montserrat: History of a Caribbean Colony.* London, 1994

PITCAIRN ISLAND

KEY HISTORICAL EVENTS

Pitcairn was discovered by Carteret in 1767, but remained uninhabited until 1790, when it was occupied by 9 mutineers of HMS *Bounty*, with 12 women and 6 men from Tahiti. Nothing was known of their existence until the island was visited in 1808.

TERRITORY AND POPULATION

Pitcairn Island (1·75 sq. miles; 4·6 sq. km) is situated in the Pacific Ocean, nearly equidistant from New Zealand and Panama (25° 04' S. lat., 130° 06' W. long.). Adamstown is the only settlement. The population in Dec. 1996 was 42. The uninhabited islands of Henderson (12 sq. miles), Ducie (1½ sq. miles) and Oeno (2 sq. miles) were annexed in 1902. Henderson is a World Heritage Site.

CLIMATE

An equable climate, with average annual rainfall of 80" (2,000 mm) spread evenly throughout the year. Mean monthly temperatures range from 75°F (24°C) in Jan. to 66°F (19°C) in July.

CONSTITUTION AND GOVERNMENT

The Local Government Ordinance of 1964 constitutes a *Council* of 10 members, of whom 6 are elected, 3 are nominated (1 by the 6 elected members and 2 by the Governor), and the Island Secretary is an *ex-officio* member. The Island Magistrate, who is elected triennially, presides over the Council; other members hold office for only 1 year. Liaison between Governor and Council is through a Commissioner in the Auckland, New Zealand, office of the British Consulate-General.

CURRENT ADMINISTRATION

Governor: Martin Williams.
   Island Magistrate: Jay Warren (re-elected Dec. 1996).

ECONOMY

Budget. For the year to 31 March 1997 revenue was $604,234 and expenditure $601,665.

Currency. New Zealand currency is used.

ENERGY AND NATURAL RESOURCES

Fisheries. The catch in 1995 was approximately 7 tonnes.

COMMUNICATIONS

Roads. There were (1997) 6 km of roads. In 1997 there were 29 motor cycles.

SOCIAL INSTITUTIONS

Justice. The Island Court consists of the Island Magistrate and 2 assessors.

Education. In Aug. 1997 there was 1 teacher and 8 pupils.

FURTHER READING

A Guide to Pitcairn. Pitcairn Island Administration, Auckland, revised ed. 1990
Ball, I., *Pitcairn: Children of the Bounty.* London, 1973
Murray, S., *Pitcairn Island: the First 200 Years.* La Canada (CA), 1992

ST HELENA

KEY HISTORICAL EVENTS

The island was uninhabited when discovered by the Portuguese in 1502. It was administered by the East India Company from 1659 and became a British colony in 1834. Napoleon died here in exile in 1821.

Public demonstrations took place in April 1997 against government spending cuts and the Governor's imposition of his own, instead of the elected, head of social services.

TERRITORY AND POPULATION

St Helena, of volcanic origin, is 1,200 miles from the west coast of Africa. Area, 47 sq. miles (121·7 sq. km), with a cultivable area of 243 ha. The projected population for 2000 is 7,000. In 1995 an estimated 62·6% of the population were urban. The capital and port is Jamestown, population (1992) 1,500.

The official language is English.

SOCIAL STATISTICS

Annual growth rate, 1990–95, 0·6%.

CLIMATE

A mild climate, with little variation. Temperatures range from 75–85°F (24–29°C) in summer to 65–75°F (18–24°C) in winter. Rainfall varies between 13" (325 mm) and 37" (925 mm) according to altitude and situation.

CONSTITUTION AND GOVERNMENT

The *Legislative Council* consists of the Governor, 2 *ex-officio* members (the Government Secretary and the Treasurer) and 12 elected members. The Governor is assisted by an *Executive Council* consisting of the 2 *ex-officio* members and the chairs of the 6 Council Committees.

St Helenians do not have British citizenship.

CURRENT ADMINISTRATION

Governor and C.-in-C.: D.L. Smallman, LVO.
Chief Secretary: J. G. Perrott.

ENERGY AND NATURAL RESOURCES

Fisheries. The total catch in 1995 was 818 tonnes.

INDUSTRY

Labour. In 1995 there were 300 registered unemployed persons.

INTERNATIONAL TRADE

The economy is dependent on UK and EU aid of £8·5m. a year.

COMMUNICATIONS

There were (1988) 94 km of all-weather motor roads. There were 1,301 vehicles in 1987.

Shipping. There is a service from Cardiff (UK) 6 times a year, and links with South Africa and neighbouring islands. In 1995 vessels entered totalling 55,000 net registered tons.

SOCIAL INSTITUTIONS

Justice. Police force, 32; cases are dealt with by a police magistrate.

Religion. There are 10 Anglican churches, 4 Baptist chapels, 3 Salvation Army halls, 1 Seventh Day Adventist church and 1 Roman Catholic church.

Education. 3 pre-school playgroups, 7 primary and 1 comprehensive school controlled by the Government had 1,188 pupils in 1987. The Prince Andrew School (opened in 1989) offers vocational courses leading to British qualifications.

Health. There were 3 doctors, 1 dentist and 1 hospital in 1992.

CULTURE

Broadcasting. The Cable & Wireless Ltd cable connects St Helena with Cape Town and Ascension Island. The government run Radio St Helena, broadcasts daily and relays BBC programmes. Number of radio receivers (1993), 2,500. Television reception was introduced in 1996 from the BBC World Service, South African M-Net and a US Satellite channel.

Ascension is a small island of volcanic origin, of 34 sq. miles (88 sq. km), 700 miles north-west of St Helena. There are 120 ha providing fresh meat, vegetables and fruit. Population (1993), was 1,117 (excluding military personnel).

The island is the resort of sea turtles, rabbits, the sooty tern or 'wideawake', and feral donkeys.

A cable station connects the island with St Helena, Sierra Leone, St Vincent, Rio de Janeiro and Buenos Aires. There is an airstrip (Miracle Mile) near the settlement of Georgetown; the Royal Air Force maintains an air link with the Falkland Islands.

Administrator: Roger Huxley.

Tristan da Cunha is the largest of a small group of islands in the South Atlantic, lying 1,320 miles (2,124 km) south-west of St Helena, of which they became dependencies on 12 Jan. 1938. Tristan da Cunha has an area of 98 sq. km and a population (1988) of 313, all living in the settlement of Edinburgh. Inaccessible Island (10 sq. km) lies 20 miles west, and the 3 Nightingale Islands (2 sq. km) lie 20 miles south of Tristan da Cunha; they are uninhabited. Gough Island (90 sq. km) is 220 miles south, of Tristan and has a meteorological station.

Tristan consists of a volcano rising to a height of 6,760 ft, with a circumference at its base of 21 miles. The volcano, believed to be extinct, erupted unexpectedly early in Oct. 1961. The whole population was evacuated without loss and settled temporarily in the UK; in 1963 they returned to Tristan. Potatoes remain the chief crop. Cattle, sheep and pigs are now reared, and fish are plentiful. Poulation in 1996, 292. The original inhabitants were shipwrecked sailors and soldiers who remained behind when the garrison from St Helena was withdrawn in 1817.

At the end of April 1942 Tristan da Cunha was commissioned as HMS *Atlantic Isle*, and became an important meteorological and radio station. In Jan. 1949 a South African company commenced crawfishing operations. An Administrator was appointed at the end of 1948 and a body of basic law brought into operation. The Island Council, which was set up in 1932, consists of a Chief Islander, 3 nominated and 8 elected members (including 1 woman), under the chairmanship of the Administrator.

Administrator: B. G. Dalley.

FURTHER READING

Crawford, A., *Tristan da Cunha and the Roaring Forties.* Edinburgh, 1982

Cross, A., *Saint Helena.* Newton Abbot, 1980

Day, A., *St. Helena, Ascension and Tristan da Cunha.* [Bibliography]. Oxford and Santa Barbara (CA), 1997

SOUTH GEORGIA AND THE SOUTH SANDWICH ISLANDS

KEY HISTORICAL EVENTS

The first landing and exploration was undertaken by Captain James Cook, who formally took possession in the name of George III on 17 Jan. 1775. British sealers arrived in 1788 and American sealers in 1791. Sealing reached its peak in 1800. A German team was the first to carry out scientific studies there in 1882–83. Whaling began in 1904 and ceased in 1966, and the civil administration was withdrawn. Argentine forces invaded South Georgia on 3 April 1982. A British naval task force recovered the Island on 25 April 1982.

TERRITORY AND POPULATION

South Georgia lies 800 miles south-east of the Falkland Islands and has an area of 1,450 sq. miles. The South Sandwich Islands are 470 miles south-east of South Georgia and have an area of 130 sq. miles. In 1993 crown sovereignty and jurisdiction were extended from 12 to 200 miles around the islands. There is no permanent population. There is a small military garrison. The British Antarctic Survey have a biological station on Bird Island. The South Sandwich Islands are uninhabited.

CLIMATE

The climate is wet and cold, with strong winds and little seasonal variation. 15°C is occasionally reached on a windless day. Temperatures below –15°C at sea level are unusual.

CONSTITUTION AND GOVERNMENT

Under the new Constitution which came into force on 3 Oct. 1985 the Territories ceased to be dependencies of the Falkland Islands. Executive power is vested in a Commissioner who is the officer for the time being administering the Government of the Falkland Islands. The Commissioner is obliged to consult the officer for the time being commanding Her Majesty's British Forces in the South Atlantic on matters relating to defence and internal security (except police). The Commissioner, whenever practicable, consults the Executive Council of the Falkland Islands on the exercise of functions that in his opinion might affect the Falkland Islands. There is no Legislative Council. Laws are made by the Commissioner (Richard Ralph, CVO, resident in the Falkland Islands).

ECONOMY

Budget. The total revenue of the Territories (estimate, 1988–89) £268,240, mainly from philatelic sales and investment income. Expenditure (estimate), £194,260.

COMMUNICATIONS

There is occasional communication by sea with the Falkland Islands by means of research and ice patrol ships. Royal Fleet Auxiliary ships, which serve the garrison, run regularly to South Georgia.

Mail is dropped from military aircraft.

SOCIAL INSTITUTIONS

Justice. There is a Supreme Court for the Territories and a Court of Appeal in the United Kingdom. Appeals may go from that court to the Judicial Committee of the Privy Council. There is no magistrate permanently in residence. The Officer Commanding the garrison is usually appointed a magistrate.

FURTHER READING

Headland, R. K., *The Island of South Georgia.* CUP, 1985

THE TURKS AND CAICOS ISLANDS

KEY HISTORICAL EVENTS
After a long period of rival French and Spanish claims the islands were eventually secured to the British Crown in 1766, and became a separate colony in 1973 after association at various times with the colonies of the Bahamas and Jamaica.

TERRITORY AND POPULATION
The Islands are situated between 21° and 22°N. lat. and 71° and 72°W. long., about 50 miles east of the Bahamas, of which they are geographically an extension. There are over 40 islands, covering an estimated area of 192 sq. miles (497 sq. km). Only 8 are inhabited: Grand Caicos, the largest, is 30 miles long by 2 to 3 miles broad; Grand Turk, the capital and main political and administrative centre, is 7 miles long by 1·25 broad. Population, 1990 census, 12,350; Grand Turk, 3,761; Providenciales, 5,586; South Caicos, 1,220; Middle Caicos, 275; North Caicos, 1,305; Salt Cay, 213. The projected population for 2000 is 17,000. An estimated 56·4% of the population were rural in 1995.

The official language is English.

SOCIAL STATISTICS
Vital statistics (1997): Births, 160; deaths, 58. Annual growth rate, 1990–95, 3·1%.

CLIMATE
An equable and healthy climate as a result of regular trade winds, though hurricanes are sometimes experienced. Grand Turk, Jan. 76°F (24·4°C), July 83°F (28·3°C). Annual rainfall 21".

CONSTITUTION AND GOVERNMENT
A new Constitution was introduced in 1988 and amended in 1992. The Executive Council comprises 2 official members: The Chief Secretary and the Attorney-General; a Chief Minister and 5 other ministers from among the elected members of the Legislative Council; and is presided over by the Governor. The Legislative Council consists of a Speaker, the 2 official members of the Executive Council, 13 elected members and 3 appointed members.

RECENT ELECTIONS
At general elections held on 4 March 1999 for the 13 elective seats on the Legislative Council, the People's Democratic Movement gained 9 seats and the People's National Party 5.

CURRENT ADMINISTRATION
Governor: John P. Kelly, LVO, MBE.
  Chief Minister: Derek Taylor.

INTERNATIONAL RELATIONS
The Islands are a member of CARICOM.

ECONOMY

Policy. The economy is based on free-market private sector-led development. The government plays a supplementary role by providing the necessary legislature, infrastructure, and resources to aid development. The government development trust is aimed at promoting orderly development of the islands, considering the available resources. The focus is on the service sector, but tourism and finance are still the dominant industries. Diversification is also emphasized which is mainly centred around fishing and agriculture.

Performance. The annual rates of growth in GDP are as follows: 1993, 14·6; 1994, 14·2; 1995, 16·7; 1996, 8·1.

Budget. 1996–97 recurrent revenue was US$41·2m. and expenditure US$38·8m.

Currency. The US dollar is the official currency.

Banking and Finance. There are 4 commercial banks. Offshore finance is a major industry.

Weights and Measures. Ounces and pounds are generally used as weights, and feet and yards are the measures.

ENERGY AND NATURAL RESOURCES

Electricity. Electrical services are provided to all of the inhabited islands. For all US appliances, 110 volts, 60 cycles, are suitable.

Oil and Gas. Both oil and gas are imported.

Water. Fresh water receptacles are commonly used; there is also piped potable supply.

Agriculture. Farming is done on a small scale mainly for subsistence.

Fisheries. In 1995 the total catch was approximately 1,400 tonnes.

INDUSTRY

Labour. In 1989, out of a total population of 4,885 aged 14 or over, 4,043 were working, 573 unemployed and 269 economically inactive.

EXTERNAL ECONOMIC RELATIONS

Imports and Exports.

Exports, 1992–93, US$6·47m.; imports, US$39,835,000. The main export is dried, frozen and processed fish.

COMMUNICATIONS

Civil Aviation. The international airports are on Grand Turk and Providenciales. Turks and Caicos Airways had 2 aircraft in 1995. Services are also provided by American Airlines and Carnival Airlines. An internal air service provides regular daily flights between the inhabited islands.

Shipping. The main ports are at Grand Turk, Cockburn Harbour and Providenciales. There is a service to Miami. In 1995 the merchant fleet totalled 2,000 GRT.

Telecommunications. There are internal and international cable, telephone, telex, telegraph and fax services.

Postal Services. Postal services are provided on all of the inhabited islands by the government. Postal agencies such as UPS and Federal Express also exist.

SOCIAL INSTITUTIONS

Justice. Laws are a mixture of Statute and Common Law. There is a Magistrates Court and a Supreme Court. Appeals lie from the Supreme Court to the Court of Appeal which sits in Nassau, Bahamas. There is a further appeal in certain cases to the Privy Council in London.

Religion. There are Anglican, Methodist, Baptist and evangelists groups.

Education. Education is free between the ages of 5 and 14 in the 10 government primary schools; there are also 4 private primary schools. In March 1993 the average number of pupils in the 4 government secondary schools was 1,075.

Health. In 1995 there were 6 doctors, 1 dentist, 56 nurses and midwives, and 36 hospital beds.

CULTURE

Broadcasting. The Government operates the semi-commercial Radio Turks and Caicos. There are also 2 commercial and 1 religious station. In 1995 there were about 7,000 radio sets. There is cable and satellite TV.

Press. There is 1 weekly and 1 bi-weekly newspaper.

Tourism. Number of visitors, 1994, 70,946.

FURTHER READING

Boultbee, P. G., *Turks & Caicos Islands*. [Bibliography]. Oxford and Santa Barbara (CA), 1991

UNITED STATES OF AMERICA

Capital: Washington, D.C.
Population estimate, 2000: 274·63m.
GNP per capita: (PPP$) 28,020
HDI/world rank: 0·943/4

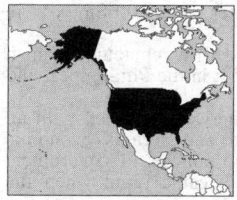

KEY HISTORICAL EVENTS

The first white settlers in north America were Spaniards who made their home in Florida. In 1607 some English settled at Jamestown around which the colony of Virginia grew. In 1620 others landed at Plymouth Rock to found the colony of Massachusetts. Other colonies followed. One group, inhabited chiefly by Puritan exiles was called New England. The South attracted religionists of less rigid views including the Roman Catholics who established Maryland. Between the two were Dutch settlements and Pennsylvania, the Quaker colony founded by William Penn. The Dutch settlements became British after a war in 1664 and the name of the chief town was changed to New York. In 1775 white settlement in America was located in 13 British colonies on the east coast and in Spanish colonial territory in the south and south-west. The rest was Indian land, where former French claims to control had been given up in 1763. Spain succeeded to those claims in land west of the Mississippi and Britain in land east of it. Britain designated such land as Indian territory and forbade colonial expansion west of the Appalachians.

Britain's colonial subjects rebelled against her taxation and trading exploitation. The colonies declared their independence on 4 July 1776, provoking war with Britain which lasted until 1783 when Britain acknowledged the independent United States of America.

The Union extended south to the border of Florida (Spanish) and west to the Mississippi. A permanent constitution came into force in 1789, providing for a federal government. The rights of states to nullify federal laws if they contradicted state policies became a source of dispute, especially in relation to the slave-owning southern states which feared the Union preference for abolition.

In 1800 France bought back from Spain her title to 'Louisiana', the territory west of the Mississippi. In 1803 the USA bought it from France.

In 1812–14 the USA fought an inconclusive war with Britain on the grounds that Britain, operating from Canada, was encouraging Indian resistance; at sea, Britain was using her conduct of the Napoleonic War to harass American shipping.

Westward movement began almost with independence, increasing after the Homestead Act of 1832 and the removal of Indians to reservations during the 1830s.

The Spanish empire in the Americas had ended in 1821, and the north American territories had passed to Mexico, except for Florida which the USA acquired. In 1836 Texas broke away from Mexico, surviving as an independent republic until 1845 when the US, seeing strategic danger in its vulnerability, annexed it. This provoked war with Mexico which the US won in 1848, receiving the Mexican territories in the south-west including the present states of California, Arizona, Colorado, Utah, Nevada and New Mexico.

In the north-west, the Oregon Trail attracted thousands of migrants in the 1840s. In 1846 a long dispute with Britain was resolved, confirming the US title to the Oregon Territory. Westward migration was further stimulated by the California gold rush of 1848.

In the east and mid-west, tension over the question of slavery led to the secession of the southern states in 1860–61, and their formation as the Confederacy. Civil war broke out, ending in northern victory in 1865. Slavery was abolished and a period of radical reconstruction began for the South. Many reforms then implemented were cancelled after 1877, when the northern military presence was withdrawn and southern whites regained their political power, enforcing segregation and curtailing black civil and political rights.

During the late 19th century eastern and mid-western industrialization expanded rapidly. Growing cities attracted thousands of poor European immigrants, many of whom were escaping religious or political persecution as well as looking for work. This inward flow of labour continued into the 1930s and was matched by a flow of

UNITED STATES OF AMERICA

Asians to the west coast. A similar northward movement of Spanish speakers from the Caribbean and Mexico, and of black workers from southern states, continues.

In the west there were Indian wars. The Apache and Navajo wars of the south-west lasted intermittently from 1861 until 1886. The Comanche fought for decades to protect their hunting grounds on the plains from settlement, as did the Cheyenne and Sioux. The latter's victory under Sitting Bull in 1876 only produced an increase in military action against them. Indian resistance ended after some 200 Sioux were shot at Wounded Knee in 1890.

In the Spanish-American war of 1898 the USA succeeded in replacing Spanish influence in the Caribbean with her own. She also replaced it in the Philippines, and acquired Guam in the western Pacific as a strategic base.

The USA entered the First World War in 1917, and afterwards reacted with an isolationist policy. In 1929 the stock market collapsed and serious economic depression lasted through the 1930s. The country turned to policies of government intervention in the economy; recovery began, but only became rapid when the Second World War necessitated a huge increase in production.

The war and subsequent victory led to active participation in the affairs of Europe and to a state of 'cold war' mistrust between the USA and the USSR. The US Marshall Plan financed the recovery of much of European industry. At the same time it appeared prudent to aid other nations where instability might admit Communist influence; this policy governed relations with Caribbean and Central American countries, and involved the USA in war against Communist forces in Korea (1950–53) and Vietnam (1961–73).

Following President Kennedy's assassination in 1963, US military involvement in Vietnam was intensified, but opposition at home led to withdrawal of forces in 1973.

In 1974 President Nixon was forced to resign amidst charges of corruption known collectively as Watergate. A revival of Republican fortunes came with the election of Ronald Reagan in the 1980 presidential race. In international affairs, Reagan was resolutely anti-Communist, raising fears of confrontation with the Soviet Union over his Strategic Defense Initiative, otherwise known as his 'Star Wars' system of defence. However, relations between the two super powers improved in the mid-eighties with successful negotiations on nuclear arms limitations. The collapse of the Soviet empire in 1990 extended US economic aid to Eastern Europe.

The Democrats regained control of the White House with the election of Bill Clinton, who combined economic recovery at home with an active foreign policy which underlined America's role as the only super power. But in his second term, Bill Clinton was dogged by sexual scandal. The Lewinsky affair, leading to an impeachment trial, all but robbed the President of his moral authority.

TERRITORY AND POPULATION

The United States is bounded in the north by Canada, east by the North Atlantic, south by the Gulf of Mexico and Mexico, and west by the North Pacific Ocean. It covers an area of 3,536,278 sq. miles, of which 181,518 sq. miles is made up of water (comprising Great Lakes, inland and coastal water).

Population at each census from 1790 to 1990 (including Alaska and Hawaii from 1960). Figures do not include Puerto Rico, Guam, American Samoa or other Pacific islands, or the US population abroad. Residents of Indian reservations not included before 1890.

	White	Black	Other races	Total
1790	3,172,464	757,208	—	3,929,672
1800	4,306,446	1,002,037	—	5,308,483
1810	5,862,073	1,377,808	—	7,239,881
1820	7,866,797	1,771,562	—	9,638,359
1830	10,537,378	2,328,642	—	12,866,020
1840	14,195,805	2,873,648	—	17,069,453
1850	19,553,068	3,638,808	—	23,191,876
1860	26,922,537	4,441,830	78,954	31,443,321
1870	34,337,292	5,392,172	88,985	39,818,449
1880	43,402,970	6,580,793	172,020	50,155,783
1890	55,101,258	7,488,676	357,780	62,947,714
1900	66,868,508	8,834,395	509,265	76,212,168

	White	Black	Other races	Total
1910	81,812,405	9,828,667	587,459	92,228,531
1920	94,903,540	10,463,607	654,421	106,021,568
1930	110,395,753	11,891,842	915,065	123,202,660
1940	118,357,831	12,865,914	941,384	132,165,129
1950	135,149,629	15,044,937	1,131,232	151,325,798
1960	158,831,732	18,871,831	1,619,612	179,323,175
1970	177,748,975	22,580,289	2,882,662	203,211,926
1980	188,371,622	26,495,025	11,679,158	226,545,805
1990	199,686,070	29,986,060	19,037,743	248,709,873

Subsequent revised mid-year estimates have been:-

	White	Black	Other races	Total
1991	210,979,000	31,107,000	10,020,000	252,106,000
1992	212,910,000	31,654,000	10,447,000	255,011,000
1993	214,760,000	32,168,000	10,867,000	257,795,000
1994	216,480,000	32,647,000	11,245,000	260,372,000
1995	218,149,000	33,095,000	11,646,000	262,890,000
1996	219,749,000	33,503,000	12,032,000	265,284,000
1997	221,334,000	33,947,000	12,355,000	267,636,000
1998	221,242,000	33,924,000	14,863,000	270,029,000

1997 density, 29 per sq. km (76 per sq. mile). Urban population (persons living in places with at least 2,500 inhabitants) at the 1990 census was 187,053,487 (75·2%); rural, 61,656,386. By 1995 the urban population was estimated to have risen to 76·2%. In 1980 it was 73·7%; in 1970, 73·6%.

The projected population for 2000 is 274,634,000.

Sex distribution by race of the population at the 1990 census:

	Total population	White	Black	American Indian	Asian or Pacific	Other
Males:	121,239,418	97,475,880	14,170,151	967,186	3,558,038	5,068,163
Females:	127,470,455	102,210,190	15,815,909	992,048	3,715,624	4,736,684

Alongside these racial groups, and applicable to all of them, a category of 'Hispanic origin' comprised 22,354,059 persons (11,388,059 males; 10,966,000 females).

Among 5-year age groups the 30–34 age group contained most people according to the 1990 census, with a total of 21,862,887 (10,985,954 females and 10,876,933 males), followed by 25–29, with 21,313,045 (10,617,109 females and 10,695,936 males).

The US population abroad at the time of the 1990 census was 925,845.

At the 1990 census there were 91,947,410 households. By 1996 this figure is estimated to have risen to 98,751,000.

Population in July 1998 as estimated by the US Bureau of the Census (females in parentheses):

Total, 270,029,000 (137,766,000); white, 221,242,000 (112,374,000); black, 33,924,000 (17,816,000); American Indian, Eskimo, Aleut, 2,322,000 (1,170,000); Asian and Pacific Islander, 10,086,000 (5,210,000); Hispanic origin, 29,240,000 (14,209,000). The July 1998 estimates included a figure of 63,000 people aged 100 or over, compared to 37,000 in 1990. Of the 63,000, an estimated 52,000 were female, and of the 37,000 in 1990, 29,000 were female.

The 1990 census showed that 31·8m. persons 5 years and over spoke a language other than English in the home, including Spanish by 17·3m.; French, 1·7m.; German, 1·5m.; Italian, 1·3m.; Chinese, 1·2m.

The following table includes population statistics, the year in which each of the original 13 states (Connecticut, Delaware, Georgia, Maryland, Massachusetts, New Hampshire, New Jersey, New York, North Carolina, Pennsylvania, Rhode Island, South Carolina, Virginia) ratified the constitution, and the year when each of the other states was admitted into the Union. Traditional abbreviations for the names of the states are shown in brackets with postal codes for use in addresses. The area of the USA is 3,717,796 sq. miles (9,629,091 sq. km), of which 3,536,278 sq. miles (9,158,960 sq. km) are land.

The USA is divided into 4 geographic regions comprised of 9 divisions. These are, with their 1990 census populations: Northeast (comprised of the New England and Middle Atlantic divisions), 50,809,229; Midwest (East North Central, West

UNITED STATES OF AMERICA

North Central), 59,668,632; South (South Atlantic, East South Central, West South Central), 85,445,930; West (Mountain, Pacific), 52,786,082.

Geographic divisions and states		Land area: sq. miles 1990	Census population 1 April 1990	Pop. per sq. mile, 1990
United States		3,536,278	248,709,873	70·3
New England		62,812	13,206,943	210·3
Maine (1820)	*(Me./ME)*	30,865	1,227,928	39·8
New Hampshire (1788)	*(N.H./NH)*	8,969	1,109,252	123·7
Vermont (1791)	*(Vt./VT)*	9,249	562,758	60·8
Massachusetts (1788)	*(Mass./MA)*	7,838	6,016,425	767·6
Rhode Island (1790)	*(R.I./RI)*	1,045	1,003,464	960·3
Connecticut (1788)	*(Conn./CT)*	4,845	3,287,116	678·4
Middle Atlantic		99,462	37,602,286	378·1
New York (1788)	*(N.Y./NY)*	47,224	17,990,455	381·0
New Jersey (1787)	*(N.J./NJ)*	7,419	7,730,188	1,042·0
Pennsylvania (1787)	*(Pa./PA)*	44,820	11,881,643	265·1
East North Central		243,539	42,008,942	172·5
Ohio (1803)	*(Oh./OH)*	40,953	10,847,115	264·9
Indiana (1816)	*(Ind./IN)*	35,870	5,544,159	154·6
Illinois (1818)	*(Ill./IL)*	55,593	11,430,602	205·6
Michigan (1837)	*(Mich./MI)*	56,809	9,295,297	163·6
Wisconsin (1848)	*(Wis./WI)*	54,314	4,891,769	90·1
West North Central		504,981	17,659,690	35·0
Minnesota (1858)	*(Minn./MN)*	79,617	4,375,099	55·0
Iowa (1846)	*(Ia./IA)*	55,875	2,776,755	49·7
Missouri (1821)	*(Mo./MO)*	68,898	5,117,073	74·3
North Dakota (1889)	*(N.D./ND)*	68,994	638,800	9·3
South Dakota (1889)	*(S.D./SD)*	75,896	696,004	9·2
Nebraska (1867)	*(Nebr./NE)*	76,878	1,578,385	20·5
Kansas (1861)	*(Kans./KS)*	81,823	2,477,574	30·3
South Atlantic		266,160	43,566,853	163·2
Delaware (1787)	*(Del./DE)*	1,955	666,168	340·8
Maryland (1788)	*(Md./MD)*	9,775	4,781,468	489·2
Dist. of Columbia (1791)	*(D.C./DC)*	61	606,900	9,884·4
Virginia (1788)	*(Va./VA)*	39,598	6,187,358	156·3
West Virginia (1863)	*(W. Va./WV)*	24,087	1,793,477	74·5
North Carolina (1789)	*(N.C./NC)*	48,718	6,628,637	136·1
South Carolina (1788)	*(S.C./SC)*	30,111	3,486,703	115·8
Georgia (1788)	*(Ga./GA)*	57,919	6,478,216	111·9
Florida (1845)	*(Fla./FL)*	53,937	12,937,926	239·9
East South Central		178,616	15,176,284	85·0
Kentucky (1792)	*(Ky./KY)*	39,732	3,685,296	92·8
Tennessee (1796)	*(Tenn./TN)*	41,220	4,877,185	118·3
Alabama (1819)	*(Al./AL)*	50,750	4,040,587	79·6
Mississippi (1817)	*(Miss./MS)*	46,914	2,573,216	54·8
West South Central		426,234	26,702,793	62·6
Arkansas (1836)	*(Ark./AR)*	52,075	2,350,725	45·1
Louisiana (1812)	*(La./LA)*	43,566	4,219,973	96·9
Oklahoma (1907)	*(Okla./OK)*	68,679	3,145,585	45·8
Texas (1845)	*(Tex./TX)*	261,914	16,986,510	64·9

Geographic divisions and states		Land area: sq. miles 1990	Census population 1 April 1990	Pop. per sq. mile, 1990
Mountain		856,121	13,658,776	16·0
Montana (1889)	*(Mont./MT)*	145,556	799,065	5·5
Idaho (1890)	*(Id./ID)*	82,751	1,006,749	12·2
Wyoming (1890)	*(Wyo./WY)*	97,105	453,588	4·7
Colorado (1876)	*(Colo./CO)*	103,729	3,294,394	31·8
New Mexico (1912)	*(N. Mex./NM)*	121,365	1,515,069	12·5
Arizona (1912)	*(Ariz./AZ)*	113,642	3,665,228	32·3
Utah (1896)	*(Ut./UT)*	82,168	1,722,850	21·0
Nevada (1864)	*(Nev./NV)*	109,806	1,201,833	10·9
Pacific		895,354	39,127,306	43·7
Washington (1889)	*(Wash./WA)*	66,581	4,866,692	73·1
Oregon (1859)	*(Oreg./OR)*	96,003	2,842,321	29·6
California (1850)	*(Calif./CA)*	155,973	29,760,021	190·8
Alaska (1959)	*(Ak./AK)*	570,374	550,043	1·0
Hawaii (1960)	*(Hi./HI)*	6,423	1,108,229	172·5

Geographic divisions and states	Land area: sq. miles 1990	Census population 1 April 1990	Pop. per sq. mile, 1990
Outlying Territories, total	4,691	3,862,431	760
Puerto Rico (1898)	3,427	3,522,037	1,028
Virgin Islands (1917)	134	101,809	761
American Samoa (1900)	77	46,773	607
Guam (1898)	209	133,152	637
Northern Marianas (1947)	184	43,345	235
Palau (1947)	192	15,122	79
Midway Islands (1867)	3	13	5
Wake Island (1898)	3	7	3
Johnston Atoll (1858)	1	173	157

Palau became an independent country on 1 Oct. 1994.

The 1990 census showed 19,767,316 foreign-born persons. In 1996 the 9 countries contributing the largest numbers who were foreign-born were: Mexico, 6,679,000; Philippines, 1,164,000; China, 801,000; Cuba, 772,000; India, 757,000; Vietnam, 740,000; El Salvador, 701,000; Canada, 660,000; UK, 579,000. By 1997 the total of foreign-born persons had increased to an estimated 25,779,000 (9·7% of the total population), of whom an estimated 7,000,000 were born in Mexico.

Increase or decrease of native White, and foreign-born White, population from 1870 to 1990, by decades:

	Native White			Foreign-born White		
	Total	Increase	Per cent increase	Total	Increase or decrease (−)	Per cent. change
1870	28,095,665	5,269,881	23·1	5,493,712	1,396,959	34·1
1880	36,843,291	8,747,626	31·1	6,559,679	1,065,967	19·4
1890	45,979,391	9,018,732[1]	24·5	9,121,867	2,562,188	39·1
1900	56,595,379	10,615,988	23·1	10,213,817	1,091,950	12·0
1910	68,386,412	11,791,033	20·8	13,345,545	3,131,728	30·7
1920	81,108,161	12,721,749	18·6	13,712,754	367,209	2·8
1930	96,303,335	15,195,174	18·7	13,983,405	270,651	2·0
1940	106,795,732	10,492,397	10·9	11,419,138	−2,564,267	−18·3
1950	124,780,860	17,985,128	16·8	10,161,168	−1,257,970	−11·0
1960	149,543,638	24,762,778	19·8	9,293,992	−867,176	−8·5
1970	169,385,451	19,841,813	13·3	8,733,770	−560,222	−6·0
1980	179,711,066	10,325,615	6·0	9,323,946	590,176	6·7
1990	189,663,258	9,952,192	5·5	10,022,812	698,866	7·5

[1]Exclusive of population specially enumerated in 1890 in Indian Territory and on Indian reservations.

Population of cities with over 100,000 inhabitants at the census of 1990 and as estimated on 1 July 1996:

Cities	Census 1990	Estimate 1996	Cities	Census 1990	Estimate 1996
New York, NY	7,322,564	7,380,906	Louisville, KY	269,555	260,689
Los Angeles, CA	3,485,557	3,553,638	St. Paul, MN	272,235	259,606
Chicago, IL	2,783,726	2,721,547	Birmingham, AL	265,347	258,543
Houston, TX	1,637,859	1,744,058	Riverside, CA	226,546	255,069
Philadelphia, PA	1,585,577	1,478,002	Aurora, CO	222,103	252,341
San Diego, CA	1,110,623	1,171,121	Anchorage, AK	226,338	250,505
Phoenix, AZ	984,310	1,159,014	Raleigh, NC	212,092	243,835
San Antonio, TX	959,295	1,067,816	Lexington-Fayette, KY	225,366	239,942
Dallas, TX	1,007,618	1,053,292	St. Petersburg, FL	240,318	235,988
Detroit, MI	1,027,974	1,000,272	Norfolk, VA	261,250	233,430
San Jose, CA	782,224	838,744	Stockton, CA	210,943	232,660
Indianapolis, IN	731,278	746,737	Jersey City, NJ	228,517	229,039
San Francisco, CA	723,959	735,315	Rochester, NY	230,356	221,594
Jacksonville, FL	635,230	679,792	Akron, OH	223,019	216,882
Baltimore, MD	736,014	675,401	Baton Rouge, LA	219,531	215,882
Columbus, OH	632,945	657,053	Lincoln, NE	191,972	209,192
El Paso, TX	515,342	599,865	Bakersfield, CA	176,264	205,508
Memphis, TN	618,652	596,725	Hialeah, FL	188,008	204,684
Milwaukee, WI	628,088	590,503	Mobile, AL	196,263	202,581
Boston, MA	574,283	558,394	Richmond, VA	202,798	198,267
Washington, DC	606,900	543,213	Madison, WI	190,766	197,630
Austin, TX	472,020	541,278	Montgomery, AL	190,350	196,363
Seattle, WA	516,259	524,704	Greensboro, NC	183,894	195,426
Nashville-Davidson, TN	488,366	511,263	Lubbock, TX	186,206	193,565
Cleveland, OH	505,616	498,246	Des Moines, IA	193,189	193,422
Denver, CO	467,610	497,840	Jackson, MS	202,062	192,923
Portland, OR	463,634	480,824	Chesapeake, VA	151,982	192,342
Fort Worth, TX	447,619	479,716	Plano, TX	127,885	192,280
New Orleans, LA	496,938	476,625	Shreveport, LA	198,525	191,558
Oklahoma City, OK	444,724	469,852	Huntington Beach, CA	181,519	190,751
Tucson, AZ	411,480	449,002	Yonkers, NY	188,082	190,316
Charlotte, NC	419,539	441,297	Garland, TX	180,635	190,055
Kansas City, MO	434,829	441,259	Grand Rapids, MI	189,126	188,242
Virginia Beach, VA	393,089	430,385	Fremont, CA	173,339	187,800
Honolulu, HI	377,059	423,475	Spokane, WA	177,165	186,562
Long Beach, CA	429,321	421,904	Fort Wayne, IN	191,839	184,783
Albuquerque, NM	384,915	419,681	Glendale, CA	180,038	184,321
Atlanta, GA	393,929	401,907	San Bernardino, CA	170,036	183,474
Fresno, CA	354,091	396,011	Columbus, GA	178,683	182,828
Tulsa, OK	367,302	378,491	Glendale, AZ	147,864	182,219
Las Vegas, NV	258,204	376,906	Tacoma, WA	176,664	179,114
Sacramento, CA	369,365	376,243	Scottsdale, AZ	130,075	179,012
Oakland, CA	372,242	367,230	Modesto, CA	164,746	178,559
Miami, FL	358,648	365,127	Irving, TX	155,037	176,993
Omaha, NE	342,862	364,253	Newport News, VA	171,439	176,122
Minneapolis, MN	368,383	358,785	Little Rock, AR	175,727	175,752
St. Louis, MO	396,685	351,565	Arlington, VA	170,897	175,334
Pittsburgh, PA	369,879	350,363	Orlando, FL	164,674	173,902
Cincinnati, OH	364,114	345,816	Dayton, OH	182,005	172,947
Colorado Springs, CO	280,430	345,127	Salt Lake City, UT	159,928	172,575
Mesa, AZ	289,199	344,764	Huntsville, AL	159,880	170,424
Wichita, KS	304,017	320,395	Amarillo, TX	157,571	169,588
Toledo, OH	332,943	317,606	Knoxville, TN	169,761	167,535
Buffalo, NY	328,175	310,548	Worcester, MA	169,759	166,350
Santa Ana, CA	293,827	302,419	Laredo, TX	122,899	164,899
Arlington, TX	261,717	294,816	Tempe, AZ	141,993	162,701
Anaheim, CA	266,406	288,945	Syracuse, NY	163,860	155,865
Tampa, FL	280,015	285,206	Reno, NV	133,850	155,499
Corpus Christi, TX	257,453	280,260	Winston-Salem, NC	150,958	153,541
Newark, NJ	275,221	268,510	Boise City	126,685	152,737

Cities	Census 1990	Estimate 1996	Cities	Census 1990	Estimate 1996
Providence, RI	160,728	152,558	Escondido, CA	108,648	116,184
Chula Vista, CA	135,160	151,963	Lancaster, CA	97,300	115,675
Fort Lauderdale, FL	149,238	151,805	Concord, CA	111,308	114,850
Oxnard, CA	142,560	151,009	Cedar Rapids, IA	108,772	113,482
Chattanooga, TN	152,393	150,425	Thousand Oaks, CA	104,381	113,368
Paterson, NJ	140,891	150,270	Macon, GA	107,365	113,352
Springfield, MA	156,983	149,948	Sioux Falls, SD	100,836	113,223
Durham, NC	138,894	149,799	Springfield, IL	105,417	112,921
Garden Grove, CA	142,965	149,208	Columbia, SC	110,734	112,773
Oceanside, CA	128,090	145,941	Peoria, IL	113,513	112,306
Ontario, CA	133,179	144,854	Mesquite, TX	101,484	111,947
Rockford, IL	141,787	143,531	Salinas, CA	108,777	111,757
Springfield, MO	140,494	143,407	Beaumont, TX	114,323	111,224
Chandler, AZ	89,862	142,918	Inglewood, CA	109,602	111,040
Kansas City, KS	151,521	142,654	Gary, IN	116,646	110,975
Moreno Valley, CA	118,779	140,932	Independence, MO	112,301	110,303
Hampton, VA	133,811	138,757	Elizabeth, NJ	110,002	110,149
Warren, MI	144,864	138,078	Stamford, CT	108,056	110,056
Bridgeport, CT	141,686	137,990	El Monte, CA	106,162	110,026
Tallahassee, FL	124,773	136,812	Vallejo, CA	109,199	109,593
Savannah, GA	137,812	136,262	Grand Prairie, TX	99,606	109,231
Torrance, CA	133,107	136,183	Ann Arbor, MI	109,608	108,758
Lakewood, CO	126,475	134,999	Abilene, TX	106,707	108,476
Flint, MI	140,925	134,881	Waco, TX	103,590	108,412
Pomona, CA	131,700	134,706	Naperville, IL	85,806	107,001
Pasadena, CA	131,586	134,116	Simi Valley, CA	100,218	106,974
Hartford, CT	139,739	133,086	Palmdale, CA	70,262	106,540
Brownsville, TX	107,027	132,091	Waterbury, CT	108,961	106,412
Pasadena, TX	119,604	131,620	Coral Springs, FL	78,864	105,275
Overland Park, KS	111,790	131,053	Erie, PA	108,718	105,270
Hollywood, FL	121,720	127,894	Livonia, MI	100,850	105,099
Irvine, CA	110,330	127,873	Lafayette, LA	101,852	104,899
Lansing, MI	127,321	125,736	Fort Collins, CO	87,491	104,196
Sunnyvale, CA	117,324	125,156	Fontana, CA	87,535	104,124
Santa Clarita, CA	120,050	125,153	Albany, NY	100,031	103,564
New Haven, CT	130,474	124,655	McAllen, TX	84,021	103,352
Eugene, OR	112,733	123,718	Berkeley, CA	102,724	103,243
Evansville, IN	126,272	123,456	Allentown, PA	105,301	102,211
Salem, OR	107,793	122,566	South Bend, IN	105,511	102,100
Henderson, NV	64,948	122,339	Green Bay, WI	96,466	102,076
Santa Rosa, CA	113,261	121,879	West Covina, CA	96,226	101,526
Hayward, CA	114,705	121,631	Portsmouth, VA	103,910	101,308
Fullerton, CA	114,144	120,188	Lowell, MA	103,439	100,973
Orange, CA	110,658	119,890	Manchester, NH	99,332	100,967
Topeka, KS	119,883	119,658	Costa Mesa, CA	96,357	100,938
Sterling Heights, MI	117,810	118,698	Pembroke Pines, FL	65,566	100,662
Alexandria, VA	111,182	117,586	Norwalk, CA	94,279	100,209
Rancho Cucamonga, CA	101,409	116,613	Corona, CA	75,943	100,208
Aurora, IL	99,672	116,405	Wichita Falls, TX	96,259	100,138
			Clearwater, FL	98,669	100,132

Of all the American cities with more than 100,000 inhabitants, Phoenix saw the greatest increase in its population between 1990 and 1996, with an additional 174,704 people based on the above estimates, and Henderson the highest percentage increase, with an 88·4% rise. Philadelphia's population saw the greatest decline, dropping by 107,575 based on these estimates, and St Louis the highest percentage fall, with an 11·4% drop.

Immigration and naturalization: The Immigration and Nationality Act, as amended, provides for the numerical limitation of most immigration. The Immigration Act of 1990 established major revisions in the numerical limits and preference system regulating legal immigration. The numerical limits are imposed on visas issued and not admissions. The maximum number of visas allowed to be issued under the preference categories in 1996 was 451,819: 311,819 for family-sponsored immigrants and 140,000 for employment-based immigrants. Within the overall limitations the per-country limit for independent countries is set to 7% of the total family and employment limits, while dependent areas are limited to 2% of the total. The 1996 limit allowed no more than 31,627 preference visas for any independent country and 9,036 for any dependency. Immigrants not subject to any numerical limitation are spouses, children, and parents of US citizens who are 21 years of age or older; certain former US citizens; ministers of religion; certain long-term US government employees; refugees and asylum-seekers adjusting to immigrant status; and certain other groups of immigrants.

Immigration data for 1996 include 4,635 aliens who were admitted as permanent residents under the legalization programme created by the Immigrant Reform and Control Act of 1986. These aliens have resided in the USA since before 1982 or were agricultural workers on perishable crops and have qualified as temporary residents under the first phase of the legalization programme; in the fiscal year 1989, they began qualifying for permanent status.

Immigrant aliens admitted to the USA for permanent residence, by country or region of birth, for fiscal years:

Country or region of birth	1991	*Immigrants admitted* 1992	1995	1996
All countries	1,827,167	973,977	720,500	915,900
Europe	135,234	145,392	128,200	147,581
Germany	6,509	9,888	6,200	6,748
Greece	2,079	1,858	1,300	1,452
Italy	2,619	2,592	2,200	2,501
Poland	19,199	25,504	13,800	15,772
Portugal	4,524	2,748	2,600	2,984
Spain	1,849	1,631	1,300	1,659
UK	13,903	19,973	12,400	13,624
Yugoslavia	2,713	2,604	8,300	11,854
Other Europe	81,839	78,594	80,100	90,987
Asia	358,533	356,955	267,900	307,807
China and Taiwan	46,299	55,251	44,900	55,129
Hong Kong	10,427	10,452	7,200	7,834
India	45,064	36,755	34,700	44,859
Japan	5,049	11,028	4,800	6,011
Korea (North and South)	26,518	19,359	16,000	18,185
Philippines	63,596	61,022	51,000	55,876
Thailand	7,397	7,090	5,100	4,310
Other Asia	154,183	155,998	104,200	115,603
North America	1,210,981	384,047	231,500	340,540
Canada	13,504	15,205	12,900	15,825
Mexico	946,167	213,802	89,900	163,572
Cuba	10,349	11,791	17,900	26,466
Dominican Republic	41,405	41,969	38,500	39,604
Haiti	47,527	11,002	14,000	18,386
Jamaica	23,828	18,915	16,400	19,089
Trinidad and Tobago	8,407	7,008	5,400	7,344
Other Caribbean	8,623	6,728	4,100	5,912
Central America	111,093	57,558	31,800	44,289
Other North America	78	69	60	53
South America	79,934	55,308	45,700	61,769
Colombia	19,702	13,201	10,800	14,283
Ecuador	9,958	7,286	6,400	8,321
Other South America	50,274	34,821	28,500	39,165
Africa	36,179	27,086	42,500	52,889
Australia and New Zealand	2,471	3,205	2,478	2,750
Other countries	3,835	1,984	2,219	2,564

The total number of immigrants admitted from 1820 up to 30 Sept. 1996 was 63,140,227; this included 7,142,593 from Germany, and 5,427,298 from Italy.

Aliens coming to the USA for temporary periods of time are classified as non-immigrants. During fiscal year 1996, a total of 24,842,503 non-immigrants were admitted. This total included multiple entries but excluded border crossers, crewmen and insular travellers. There were 1,641,455 aliens expelled during the fiscal year 1996. Of this number, 68,657 were removed with a formal order from an immigration judge and 1,572,798 were required to depart without orders of deportation.

During fiscal year 1996, 1,044,689 persons became US citizens through naturalization, including 890,949 naturalized under the general provisions of 5-year residence in the USA, 35,449 spouses and children of US citizens and 6,948 members of the US Armed Forces. The new citizens included 43,087 from China and Taiwan, 62,168 from Cuba, 4,617 from Italy, 24,270 from Jamaica, 24,693 from Korea, 217,418 from Mexico, 45,210 from the Philippines and 47,625 from Vietnam.

The refugee admissions ceiling for the fiscal year 1996 was fixed at 90,000, including 45,000 from Eastern Europe and the former Soviet Union and 29,000 from south-east Asia.

SOCIAL STATISTICS
Figures include Alaska beginning with 1959 and Hawaii beginning with 1960.

	Live births	Deaths	Marriages	Divorces	Deaths under 1 year
1900	—	343,217	709,000	56,000	—
1910	2,777,000	696,856	948,000	83,000	—
1920	2,950,000	1,118,070	1,274,476	170,505	170,911
1930	2,618,000	1,327,240	1,126,856	195,961	143,201
1940	2,559,000	1,417,269	1,595,879	264,000	110,984
1950	3,632,000	1,452,454	1,667,231	385,144	103,825
1960	4,257,850	1,711,982	1,523,000	393,000	110,873
1970	3,731,386	1,921,031	2,158,802	708,000	74,667
1980	3,612,258	1,989,841	2,390,252	1,189,000	45,526
1990	4,148,000	2,155,000	2,448,000	1,182,000	38,351
1991	4,111,000	2,170,000	2,371,100	1,189,000	36,766
1992	4,065,000	2,176,000	2,362,000	1,215,000	34,628
1993	4,000,000	2,269,000	2,334,000	1,187,000	33,000[1]
1994	3,953,000	2,279,000	2,362,000	1,191,000	31,000[1]
1995[2]	3,900,000	2,312,000	2,336,000	1,169,000	30,000
1996[2]	3,915,000	2,332,000	2,344,000	1,151,000	28,000

[1]Estimate. [2]Preliminary

Rates (per 1,000 population):

	Birth	Death	Marriage	Divorce
1991	16·3	8·6	9·4	4·7
1992	15·9	8·5	9·3	4·8
1993	15·5	8·8	9·0	4·6
1994	15·2	8·8	9·1	4·6
1995	14·8	8·8	9·0	4·5
1996	14·5	8·9	8·9	4·4

Rate of natural increase per 1,000 population: 7·7 in 1991; 5·6 in 1996.

Even though the marriage rate shows a gradual decline, it remains much higher than in most other industrial countries. The most popular age range for marrying is 25–29 for males and 20–24 for females. Estimated number of births to unmarried women in 1995 was 1,254,000 (32·2% of all births), compared to 666,000 in 1980.

Infant mortality rates, per 1,000 live births: 29·2 in 1950; 12·9 in 1980; 7·4 in 1996. Fertility rate, 1996, 2·0 births per woman.

Expectation of life, 1970: males, 67·1 years; females, 74·7 years; 1996: males, 73·0 years; females, 79·0 years.

Numbers of deaths by principal causes, 1995 (and as a percentage of all deaths): heart disease, 738,781 (32·0%); cancer, 537,969 (23·3%); stroke, 158,061 (6·8%); obstructive lung disease, 104,756 (4·5%); accidents, 89,703 (3·9%); pneumonia and influenza, 83,528 (3·6%); diabetes mellitus, 59,085 (2·6%); AIDS, 42,506 (1·8%); suicide, 30,893 (1·3%); liver disease, 24,848 (1·1%).

UNITED STATES OF AMERICA

In 1995 there were 35,957 deaths caused by firearms; 14,218 from drug-induced causes; and 20,231 from alcohol-induced causes.

The number of Americans living below the poverty line in 1997 was 35·6m. or 13·3% of the total population, down from 13·7% in 1996.

CLIMATE

For temperature and rainfall figures, *see* entries on individual states as indicated by regions, below, of mainland USA.

Pacific Coast. The climate varies with latitude, distance from the sea and the effect of relief, ranging from polar conditions in North Alaska through cool to warm temperate climates further south. The extreme south is temperate desert. Rainfall everywhere is moderate. *See* Alaska, California, Oregon, Washington.

Mountain States. Very varied, with relief exerting the main control; very cold in the north in winter, with considerable snowfall. In the south, much higher temperatures and aridity produce desert conditions. Rainfall everywhere is very variable as a result of rain-shadow influences. *See* Arizona, Colorado, Idaho, Montana, Nevada, New Mexico, Utah, Wyoming.

High Plains. A continental climate with a large annual range of temperature and moderate rainfall, mainly in summer, although unreliable. Dust storms are common in summer and blizzards in winter. *See* Nebraska, North Dakota, South Dakota.

Central Plains. A temperate continental climate, with hot summers and cold winters, except in the extreme south. Rainfall is plentiful and comes at all seasons, but there is a summer maximum in western parts. *See* Mississippi, Missouri, Oklahoma, Texas.

Mid-West. Continental, with hot summers and cold winters. Rainfall is moderate, with a summer maximum in most parts. *See* Indiana, Iowa, Kansas.

Great Lakes. Continental, resembling that of the Central Plains, with hot summers but very cold winters because of the freezing of the lakes. Rainfall is moderate with a slight summer maximum. *See* Illinois, Michigan, Minnesota, Ohio, Wisconsin.

Appalachian Mountains. The north is cool temperate with cold winters, the south warm temperate with milder winters. Precipitation is heavy, increasing to the south but evenly distributed over the year. *See* Kentucky, Pennsylvania, Tennessee, West Virginia.

Gulf Coast. Conditions vary from warm temperate to sub-tropical, with plentiful rainfall, decreasing towards the west but evenly distributed over the year. *See* Alabama, Arkansas, Florida, Louisiana.

Atlantic Coast. Temperate maritime climate but with great differences in temperature according to latitude. Rainfall is ample at all seasons; snowfall in the north can be heavy. *See* Delaware, District of Columbia, Georgia, Maryland, New Jersey, New York, North Carolina, South Carolina, Virginia.

New England. Cool temperate, with severe winters and warm summers. Precipitation is well distributed with a slight winter maximum. Snowfall is heavy in winter. *See* Connecticut, Maine, Massachusetts, New Hampshire, Rhode Island, Vermont. *See* also Hawaii and Outlying Territories.

CONSTITUTION AND GOVERNMENT

The form of government of the USA is based on the constitution of 17 Sept. 1787.

By the constitution the government of the nation is composed of three co-ordinate branches, the executive, the legislative and the judicial.

The Federal Government has authority in matters of general taxation, treaties and other dealings with foreign countries, foreign and inter-state commerce, bankruptcy, postal service, coinage, weights and measures, patents and copyright, the armed forces (including, to a certain extent, the militia), and crimes against the USA; it has sole legislative authority over the District of Columbia and the possessions of the USA.

The 5th article of the constitution provides that Congress may, on a two-thirds vote of both houses, propose amendments to the constitution, or, on the application of the legislatures of two-thirds of all the states, call a convention for proposing amendments, which in either case shall be valid as part of the constitution when ratified by the legislatures of three-fourths of the several states, or by conventions in three-fourths thereof, whichever mode of ratification may be proposed by Congress. Ten amendments (called collectively 'the Bill of Rights') to the constitution were added 15 Dec. 1791; two in 1795 and 1804; a 13th amendment, 6 Dec. 1865, abolishing slavery; a 14th in 1868, including the important 'due process' clause; a 15th, 3 Feb. 1870, establishing equal voting rights for white and black; a 16th, 3 Feb. 1913, authorizing the income tax; a 17th, 8 April 1913, providing for popular election of senators; an 18th, 16 Jan. 1919, prohibiting alcoholic liquors; a 19th, 18 Aug. 1920, establishing woman suffrage; a 20th, 23 Jan. 1933, advancing the date of the President's and Vice-President's inauguration and abolishing the 'lameduck' sessions of Congress; a 21st, 5 Dec. 1933, repealing the 18th amendment; a 22nd, 26 Feb. 1951, limiting a President's tenure of office to 2 terms, or to 2 terms plus 2 years in the case of a Vice-President who has succeeded to the office of a President; a 23rd, 30 March 1961, granting citizens of the District of Columbia the right to vote in national elections; a 24th, 4 Feb. 1964, banning the use of the poll-tax in federal elections; a 25th, 10 Feb. 1967, dealing with Presidential disability and succession; a 26th, 22 June 1970, establishing the right of citizens who are 18 years of age and older to vote; a 27th, 7 May 1992, providing that no law varying the compensation of Senators or Representatives shall take effect until an election has taken place.

National motto: 'In God we trust'; formally adopted by Congress 30 July 1956.

Presidency. The executive power is vested in a president, who holds office for 4 years, and is elected, together with a vice-president chosen for the same term, by electors from each state, equal to the whole number of senators and representatives to which the state may be entitled in the Congress.

The President must be a natural-born citizen, resident in the country for 14 years, and at least 35 years old.

The presidential election is held every fourth (leap) year on the Tuesday after the first Monday in November. Technically, this is an election of presidential electors, not of a president directly; the electors thus chosen meet and give their votes (for the candidate to whom they are pledged, in some states by law, but in most states by custom and prudent politics) at their respective state capitals on the first Monday after the second Wednesday in December next following their election; and the votes of the electors of all the states are opened and counted in the presence of both Houses of Congress on the sixth day of January. The total electorate vote is one for each senator and representative. Electors may not be a member of Congress or hold federal office. If no candidate secures the minimum 270 college votes needed for outright victory, the 12th Amendment to the Constitution applies, and the House of Representatives chooses a president from among the first 3 finishers in the electoral college. (This last happened in 1824).

If the successful candidate for President dies before taking office the Vice-President-elect becomes President; if no candidate has a majority or if the successful candidate fails to qualify; then, by the 20th amendment, the Vice-President acts as President until a president qualifies. The duties of the Presidency, in absence of the President and Vice-President by reason of death, resignation, removal, inability or failure to qualify, devolve upon the Speaker of the House under legislation enacted on 18 July 1947. In case of absence of a Speaker for like reason, the presidential duties devolve upon the President *pro tem.* of the Senate and successively upon those members of the cabinet in order of precedence, who have the constitutional qualifications for President.

The presidential term, by the 20th amendment to the constitution, begins at noon on 20 Jan. of the inaugural year. This amendment also installs the newly elected Congress in office on 3 Jan. instead of—as formerly—in the following December. The President's salary is $200,000 per year (taxable), with in addition $50,000 to assist in defraying expenses resulting from official duties. Also he may spend up to $100,000 non-taxable for travel and $20,000 for official entertainment. The office of Vice-President carries a salary of $171,500 and $10,000 allowance for expenses, all taxable. The Vice-President is *ex-officio* President of the Senate, and in the case of 'the removal of the President, or of his death, resignation, or inability to discharge the powers and duties of his office', he becomes the President for the remainder of the term.

PRESIDENTS OF THE USA

Name	From state	Term of service	Born	Died
George Washington	Virginia	1789–97	1732	1799
John Adams	Massachusetts	1797–1801	1735	1826
Thomas Jefferson	Virginia	1801–09	1743	1826
James Madison	Virginia	1809–17	1751	1836
James Monroe	Virginia	1817–25	1759	1831
John Quincy Adams	Massachusetts	1825–29	1767	1848
Andrew Jackson	Tennessee	1829–37	1767	1845
Martin Van Buren	New York	1837–41	1782	1862
William H. Harrison	Ohio	Mar.–Apr. 1841	1773	1841
John Tyler	Virginia	1841–45	1790	1862
James K. Polk	Tennessee	1845–49	1795	1849
Zachary Taylor	Louisiana	1849–July 1850	1784	1850
Millard Fillmore	New York	1850–53	1800	1874
Franklin Pierce	New Hampshire	1853–57	1804	1869
James Buchanan	Pennsylvania	1857–61	1791	1868
Abraham Lincoln	Illinois	1861–Apr. 1865	1809	1865
Andrew Johnson	Tennessee	1865–69	1808	1875
Ulysses S. Grant	Illinois	1869–77	1822	1885
Rutherford B. Hayes	Ohio	1877–81	1822	1893
James A. Garfield	Ohio	Mar.–Sept. 1881	1831	1881
Chester A. Arthur	New York	1881–85	1830	1886
Grover Cleveland	New York	1885–89	1837	1908
Benjamin Harrison	Indiana	1889–93	1833	1901
Grover Cleveland	New York	1893–97	1837	1908
William McKinley	Ohio	1897–Sept. 1901	1843	1901
Theodore Roosevelt	New York	1901–09	1858	1919
William H. Taft	Ohio	1909–13	1857	1930
Woodrow Wilson	New Jersey	1913–21	1856	1924
Warren Gamaliel Harding	Ohio	1921–Aug. 1923	1865	1923
Calvin Coolidge	Massachusetts	1923–29	1872	1933
Herbert C. Hoover	California	1929–33	1874	1964
Franklin D. Roosevelt	New York	1933–Apr. 1945	1882	1945
Harry S Truman	Missouri	1945–53	1884	1972
Dwight D. Eisenhower	New York	1953–61	1890	1969
John F. Kennedy	Massachusetts	1961–Nov. 1963	1917	1963
Lyndon B. Johnson	Texas	1963–69	1908	1973
Richard M. Nixon	California	1969–74	1913	1994
Gerald R. Ford	Michigan	1974–77	1913	—
James Earl Carter	Georgia	1977–81	1924	—
Ronald W. Reagan	California	1981–89	1911	—
George H. Bush	Texas	1989–93	1924	—
Bill (William J.) Clinton	Arkansas	1993–	1946	—

VICE-PRESIDENTS OF THE USA

Name	From state	Term of service	Born	Died
John Adams	Massachusetts	1789–97	1735	1826
Thomas Jefferson	Virginia	1797–1801	1743	1826
Aaron Burr	New York	1801–05	1756	1836
George Clinton	New York	1805–12[1]	1739	1812
Elbridge Gerry	Massachusetts	1813–14[1]	1744	1814
Daniel D. Tompkins	New York	1817–25	1774	1825
John C. Calhoun	South Carolina	1825–32[1]	1782	1850
Martin Van Buren	New York	1833–37	1782	1862
Richard M. Johnson	Kentucky	1837–41	1780	1850
John Tyler	Virginia	Mar.–Apr.1841[1]	1790	1862
George M. Dallas	Pennsylvania	1845–49	1792	1864
Millard Fillmore	New York	1849–50[1]	1800	1874
William R. King	Alabama	Mar.–Apr. 1853[1]	1786	1853
John C. Breckinridge	Kentucky	1857–61	1821	1875
Hannibal Hamlin	Maine	1861–65	1809	1891
Andrew Johnson	Tennessee	Mar.–Apr. 1865[1]	1808	1875
Schuyler Colfax	Indiana	1869–73	1823	1885
Henry Wilson	Massachusetts	1873–75[1]	1812	1875
William A. Wheeler	New York	1877–81	1819	1887
Chester A. Arthur	New York	Mar.–Sept. 1881[1]	1830	1886

Thomas A. Hendricks	Indiana	Mar.–Nov. 1885[1]	1819	1885
Levi P. Morton	New York	1889–93	1824	1920
Adlai Stevenson	Illinois	1893–97	1835	1914
Garret A. Hobart	New Jersey	1897–99[1]	1844	1899
Theodore Roosevelt	New York	Mar.–Sept. 1901[1]	1858	1919
Charles W. Fairbanks	Indiana	1905–09	1855	1920
James S. Sherman	New York	1909–12[1]	1855	1912
Thomas R. Marshall	Indiana	1913–21	1854	1925
Calvin Coolidge	Massachusetts	1921–Aug. 1923[1]	1872	1933
Charles G. Dawes	Illinois	1925–29	1865	1951
Charles Curtis	Kansas	1929–33	1860	1935
John N. Garner	Texas	1933–41	1868	1967
Henry A. Wallace	Iowa	1941–45	1888	1965
Harry S Truman	Missouri	1945–Apr. 1945[1]	1884	1972
Alben W. Barkley	Kentucky	1949–53	1877	1956
Richard M. Nixon	California	1953–61	1913	1994
Lyndon B. Johnson	Texas	1961–Nov. 1963[1]	1908	1973
Hubert H. Humphrey	Minnesota	1965–69	1911	1978
Spiro T. Agnew	Maryland	1969–73	1918	1996
Gerald R. Ford	Michigan	1973–74	1913	—
Nelson Rockefeller	New York	1974–77	1908	1979
Walter Mondale	Minnesota	1977–81	1928	—
George Bush	Texas	1981–89	1924	—
Danforth Quayle	Indiana	1989–93	1947	—
Albert Gore	Tennessee	1993–	1948	—

[1]Position vacant thereafter until commencement of the next presidential term.

Cabinet. The administrative business of the nation has been traditionally vested in several executive departments, the heads of which, unofficially and *ex officio*, formed the President's cabinet. Beginning with the Interstate Commerce Commission in 1887, however, an increasing amount of executive business has been entrusted to some 60 so-called independent agencies, such as the Housing and Home Finance Agency, Tariff Commission, etc.

All heads of departments and of the 60 or more administrative agencies are appointed by the President, but must be confirmed by the Senate.

Congress. The legislative power is vested by the Constitution in a Congress, consisting of a Senate and House of Representatives.

Electorate. By amendments of the constitution, disqualification of voters on the ground of race, colour or sex is forbidden. The electorate consists of all citizens over 18 years of age. Literacy tests have been banned since 1970. In 1972 durational residency requirements were held to violate the constitution. In 1973 US citizens abroad were enfranchised.

With limitations imposed by the constitution, it is the states which determine voter eligibility. In general states exclude from voting: persons who have not established residency in the jurisdiction in which they wish to vote; persons who have been convicted of felonies whose civil rights have not been restored; persons declared mentally incompetent by a court.

Illiterate voters are entitled to receive assistance in marking their ballots. Minority-language voters in jurisdictions with statutorily prescribed minority concentrations are entitled to have elections conducted in the minority language as well as English. Disabled voters are entitled to accessible polling places. Voters absent on election days or unable to go to the polls are generally entitled under state law to vote by absentee ballot.

The Constitution guarantees citizens that their votes will be of equal value under the 'one person, one vote' rule.

Senate. The Senate consists of 2 members from each state (but not from the District of Columbia), chosen by popular vote for 6 years, approximately one-third retiring or seeking re-election every 2 years. Senators must be no less than 30 years of age; must have been citizens of the USA for 9 years, and be residents in the states for which they are chosen. The Senate has complete freedom to initiate legislation, except revenue bills (which must originate in the House of Representatives); it may, however, amend or reject any legislation originating in the lower house. The Senate is also entrusted with the power of giving or withholding its 'advice and consent' to the ratification of all treaties initiated by the President with foreign powers, a two-thirds majority of senators present being required for approval. (However, it has no control over 'international executive agreements' made by the President with foreign governments; such 'agreements' cover a wide range and are more numerous than formal treaties.) It also has the power of confirming or rejecting major appointments to office made by the President, but it has no direct control over the appointment by the President of 'personal representatives' or 'personal envoys' on missions abroad. Members of the Senate constitute a High Court of Impeachment, with power, by a two-thirds vote, to remove from office and disqualify any civil officer of the USA impeached by the House of Representatives, which has the sole power of impeachment.

The Senate has 17 Standing Committees to which all bills are referred for study, revision or rejection. The House of Representatives has 19 such committees. In both Houses each Standing Committee has a chairman and a majority representing the majority party of the whole House; each has numerous sub-committees. The jurisdictions of these Committees correspond largely to those of the appropriate executive departments and agencies. Both Houses also have a few select or special Committees with limited duration.

House of Representatives. The House of Representatives consists of 435 members elected every second year. The number of each state's representatives is determined by the decennial census, in the absence of specific Congressional legislation affecting the basis. In 1997 the states had the following numbers of representatives:

Alabama	7	Indiana	10	Nebraska	3	South Carolina	6
Alaska	1	Iowa	5	Nevada	2	South Dakota	1
Arizona	6	Kansas	4	New Hampshire	2	Tennessee	9
Arkansas	4	Kentucky	6	New Jersey	13	Texas	30
California	52	Louisiana	7	New Mexico	3	Utah	3
Colorado	6	Maine	2	New York	31	Vermont	1
Connecticut	6	Maryland	8	North Carolina	12	Virginia	11
Delaware	1	Massachusetts	10	North Dakota	1	Washington	9
Florida	23	Michigan	16	Ohio	19	West Virginia	3
Georgia	11	Minnesota	8	Oklahoma	6	Wisconsin	9
Hawaii	2	Mississippi	5	Oregon	5	Wyoming	1
Idaho	2	Missouri	9	Pennsylvania	21		
Illinois	20	Montana	1	Rhode Island	2		

The constitution requires congressional districts within each state to be substantially equal in population. Final decisions on congressional district boundaries are taken by the state legislatures and governors. By custom the representative lives in the district from which he is elected. Representatives must be not less than 25 years of age, citizens of the USA for 7 years and residents in the state from which they are chosen.

In addition, 5 delegates (1 each from the District of Columbia, American Samoa, Guam, the US Virgin Islands and Puerto Rico) are also members of Congress. They have a voice but no vote, except in committees. The delegate from Puerto Rico is the resident commissioner. Puerto Ricans vote at primaries, but not at national elections. Each of the two Houses of Congress is sole 'judge of the elections, returns and qualifications of its own members'; and each of the Houses may, with the concurrence of two-thirds, expel a member. The period usually termed 'a Congress' in legislative language continues for 2 years, terminating at noon on 3 Jan.

The salary of a senator is $133,600 per annum, with tax-free expense allowance and allowances for travelling expenses and for clerical hire. The salary of the Speaker of the House of Representatives is $171,500 per annum, with a taxable allowance. The salary of a Member of the House is $133,600 ($148,400 for the Majority Leader and Minority Leader).

No senator or representative can, during the time for which he is elected, be appointed to any *civil* office under authority of the USA which shall have been created or the emoluments of which shall have been increased during such time; and no person holding *any* office under the USA can be a member of either House during his continuance in office. No religious text may be required as a qualification to any office or public trust under the USA or in any state.

Indians. By an Act passed on 2 June 1924 full citizenship was granted to all Indians born in the USA, though those remaining in tribal units were still under special federal jurisdiction. The Indian Reorganization Act of 1934 gave the tribal Indians, at their own option, substantial opportunities of self-government and the establishment of self-controlled corporate enterprises empowered to borrow money and buy land, machinery and equipment; these corporations are controlled by democratically elected tribal councils. Recently a trend towards releasing Indians from federal supervision has resulted in legislation terminating supervision over specific tribes. In 1988 the federal government recognized that it had a special relationship with, and a trust responsibility for, federally recognized Indian entities in continental USA and tribal entities in Alaska. In 1993 the Bureau of Indian Affairs listed 552 'Indian Entities Recognized and Eligible to Receive Services'. Indian lands (1991) amounted to 52,092,247 acres, of which 41,868,582 was tribally owned and 10,233,665 in trust allotments. Indian lands are held free of taxes. Total Indian population at the 1990 census was 1,959,000, of which Oklahoma, Arizona, California and New Mexico accounted for 832,466.

The **District of Columbia**, ceded by the State of Maryland for the purposes of government in 1791, is the seat of the US Government. It includes the city of Washington, and embraces a land area of 61 sq. miles. The Reorganization Plan No. 3 of 1967 instituted a Mayor Council form of government with appointed officers. In 1973 an elected Mayor and elected councillors were introduced; in 1974 they received power to legislate in local matters. Congress retains power to enact legislation and to veto or supersede the Council's acts. Since 1961 citizens have had the right to vote in national elections. On 23 Aug. 1978 the Senate approved a constitutional amendment giving the District full voting representation in Congress. This has still to be ratified.

The **Commonwealth of Puerto Rico, American Samoa, Guam and the Virgin Islands** each have a local legislature, whose acts may be modified or annulled by Congress, though in practice this has seldom been done. Puerto Rico, since its attainment of commonwealth status on 25 July 1952, enjoys practically complete self-government, including the election of its governor and other officials. The conduct of foreign relations, however, is still a federal function and federal bureaux and agencies still operate in the island.

General supervision of territorial administration is exercised by the Office of Territories in the Department of Interior.

National Anthem. The Star-spangled Banner, 'Oh say, can you see by the dawn's early light'; words by F. S. Key, 1814, tune by J. S. Smith; formally adopted by Congress 3 March 1931.

RECENT ELECTIONS

At the presidential election on 5 Nov. 1996 turn-out was 49% (55·9% in 1992). Bill Clinton (D.) received 45,590,703 votes (49%), Bob Dole (R.) 37,816,307 (41%) and Ross Perot (Reform Party) 7,866,284 (8%). Electoral college votes: Clinton, 379; Dole, 159; Perot, nil.

Voting percentages and electoral college votes by state:

a) Majority for Clinton

State	Clinton (%)	Dole (%)	Perot (%)	Electoral College (votes)
Arizona	47	44	8	8
Arkansas	53	37	8	6
California	51	38	7	54
Connecticut	52	36	10	8
Delaware	52	37	11	3
DC	85	9	2	3
Florida	48	42	9	25
Hawaii	58	38	8	4
Illinois	54	37	8	22
Iowa	50	40	8	7
Kentucky	46	45	9	8
Louisiana	52	40	7	9
Maine	52	31	14	4
Maryland	54	36	7	10
Massachusetts	62	28	9	12
Michigan	51	39	9	18

State	Clinton (%)	Dole (%)	Perot (%)	Electoral College (votes)
Minnesota	51	35	12	10
Missouri	48	41	10	11
Nevada	44	42	9	4
New Hampshire	50	40	10	4
New Jersey	53	36	9	15
New Mexico	49	41	6	5
New York	59	31	8	33
Ohio	47	41	11	21
Oregon	47	37	11	7
Pennsylvania	49	40	10	23
Rhode Island	60	27	11	4
Tennessee	48	46	6	11
Vermont	54	31	12	3
Washington	51	36	9	11
West Virginia	51	37	11	5
Wisconsin	49	39	10	11

b) Majority for Dole

	Dole	Clinton	Perot	
Alabama	50	43	6	9
Alaska	51	33	11	3
Colorado	46	45	7	8
Georgia	47	46	6	13
Idaho	52	34	13	4
Indiana	48	41	10	12
Kansas	54	36	9	6
Mississippi	49	44	6	7
Montana	44	41	14	3
Nebraska	53	35	11	5
North Carolina	49	44	7	14
North Dakota	47	40	12	3
Oklahoma	48	40	11	8
South Carolina	50	44	6	8
South Dakota	46	43	10	3
Texas	49	44	7	32
Utah	54	33	10	5
Virginia	47	45	7	13
Wyoming	50	37	12	3

Following the mid-term elections of 4 Nov. 1998, the 106th Congress (1999–2001) was constituted as follows: Senate—55 Republicans and 45 Democrats (no change); House of Representatives—223 Republicans (–5 seats), 211 Democrats (+5 seats), 1 Independent. For the first time since 1934 the party of the President had not lost any House seats in mid-term elections.

The *Speaker* of the House of Representatives is Dennis Hastert (R.). The *Majority Leader* of the Senate is Trent Lott (R).

CURRENT ADMINISTRATION

President of the United States: William (Bill) Jefferson Blythe IV Clinton, of Arkansas, b. 1946. (Governor of Arkansas, 1979–81, 1983–92).

Vice President: Albert Gore, of Tennessee, b. 1948 (House of Representatives, 1977–85; Senate, 1985–).

The cabinet consisted of the following in March 1999:

1. *Secretary of State* (created 1789). Madeleine Albright, b. Czechoslovakia, 1938. Professor of International Affairs; Head, Center for National Policy; Legislative aide to Democrat Senator Muskie; member of National Security Council staff; 1993–96 US Permanent Representative to the UN.

2. *Secretary of the Treasury* (1789). Robert Rubin, b. New York, 1938. Economist, investment banker; head of the National Economic Council; Economic Adviser to the President.

3. *Secretary of Defense* (1947). William Cohen, b. Maine, 1940. Lawyer, author; local government, mayor; basketball Hall of Fame team; Congress, 1973–96; Republican Senator.

4. *Attorney-General* (Department of Justice, 1870). Janet Reno, b. Florida, 1938. Lawyer; State Attorney of Dade County (FL), 1978–92.

5. *Secretary of the Interior* (1849). Bruce Babbitt, b. California, 1938. Lawyer, Attorney-General of Arizona, 1975–78; Governor of Arizona, 1978–87.

6. *Secretary of Agriculture* (1889). Dan Glickman, b. Kansas, 1944. Lawyer; Congress, 1977–94; member of House Agriculture, Judiciary and Science, Space and Technology Committees, chair Select Committee on Intelligence, 1993–94.

7. *Secretary of Commerce* (1903). William Daley, b. Illinois, 1949. Lawyer, Chicago politician, President Clinton's campaign manager, 1992; negotiator of the North American Free Trade Agreement, 1993.

8. *Secretary of Labor* (1913). Alexis Herman, b. Alabama, 1948. Director, Women's Bureau, Department of Labor; deputy chair, Democratic National Convention Commission; deputy chair, Presidential Transition Office; Director, White House Office of Public Liaison.

9. *Secretary of Health and Human Services* (1953). Dr Donna Shalala b. Ohio, 1941. Political scientist, educator; US Housing Department, 1977–81; President of Hunter College (NY), Chancellor of the Univ. of Wisconsin, 1988–92.

10. *Secretary of Housing and Urban Development* (1966). Andrew Cuomo, b. Alabama, 1958. Lawyer, Assistant District Attorney, Manhattan; chair, New York Commission on Homeless; Assistant Secretary, County Planning, Department of Housing and Urban Development; Assistant Housing Secretary.

11. *Secretary of Transportation* (1967). Rodney Slater, b. Mississippi, 1955. Lawyer, Assistant Attorney-General, Arkansas; Arkansas state government; Federal Highways Administrator. President Clinton's deputy campaign manager.

12. *Secretary of Energy* (1977). Bill Richardson. US Ambassador to United Nations, 1997–98; member of US Congress representing New Mexico.

13. *Secretary of Education* (1979). Richard Riley, b. South Carolina, 1933. Lawyer; South Carolina state representative, 1963–66; state senator, 1966–76; Governor of South Carolina, 1979–87.

14. *Secretary of Veterans' Affairs* (1989). Togo D. West, Jr, b. North Carolina, 1942. Lawyer; Special Assistant to the Secretary of Defense and the Deputy Secretary of Defense, 1979; appointed General Counsel of the Department of Defense, 1980.

Each of the above cabinet officers receives an annual salary of $148,400 and holds office during the pleasure of the President.

A number of administrators also have honorary cabinet status.

Key White House Posts: White House Chief of Staff: Erskine Bowles; National Security Adviser: Samuel Berger; Director of the National Economic Council: Gene Sperling; Chair, Council of Economic Advisers: Janet Yellen.

Local Government. The Union comprises 13 original states, 7 states which were admitted without having been previously organized as territories, and 30 states which had been territories—50 states in all. Each state has its own constitution (which the USA guarantees shall be republican in form), deriving its authority, not from Congress, but from the people of the state. Admission of states into the Union has been granted by special Acts of Congress, either (1) in the form of 'enabling Acts' providing for the drafting and ratification of a state constitution by the people, in which case the territory becomes a state as soon as the conditions are fulfilled, or (2) accepting a constitution already framed, and at once granting admission.

Each state is provided with a legislature of two Houses (except Nebraska, which since 1937 has had a single-chamber legislature), a governor and other executive officials, and a judicial system. Both Houses of the legislature are elective, but the senators (having larger electoral districts usually covering 2 or 3 counties compared with the single county or, in some states, the town, which sends 1 representative to the Lower House) are less numerous than the representatives, while in 38 states their terms are 4 years; in 12 states the term is 2 years. Of the 4-year senates, Illinois, Montana and New Jersey provide for two 4-year terms and one 2-year term in each decade. Terms of the lower houses are usually shorter; in 45 states, 2 years.

Members of both Houses are paid at the same rate, which varies from $200 a year in New Hampshire to $57,500 a year in New York. The trend is towards annual sessions of state legislatures; most meet annually now whereas in 1939 only 4 did.

The Governor has power to summon an extraordinary session, but not to dissolve or adjourn. The duties of the two Houses are similar, but in many states money bills must be introduced first in the Lower House. The Senate sits as a court for the trial of officials impeached by the other House, and often has power to confirm or reject appointments made by the Governor.

State legislatures are competent to deal with all matters not reserved for the federal government by the federal constitution nor specifically prohibited by the federal or state constitutions. Among their powers are the determination of the qualifications for the right of suffrage, and the control of all elections to public office, including elections of members of Congress and electors of President and Vice-President; the criminal law, both in its enactment and in its execution, with unimportant exceptions, and the administration of prisons; the civil law, including all matters pertaining to the possession and transfer of, and succession to, property; marriage and divorce, and all other civil relations; the chartering and control of all manufacturing, trading, transportation and other corporations, subject only to the right of Congress to regulate commerce passing from one state to another; labour; education; charities; licensing; fisheries within state waters, and game laws (apart from the hunting of migratory birds, which is a federal concern under treaties with Canada and Mexico). Taxes on income were left to the states until 1913, when the 16th amendment authorized the imposition of federal taxes on income without regard to apportionment.

The Governor is elected by direct vote of the people over the whole state for a term of office ranging in the various states from 2 to 4 years, and with a salary ranging from $60,000 (Arkansas) to $130,000 (New York). His duty is to see to the faithful administration of the law, and he has command of the military forces of the state. He may recommend measures but does not present bills to the legislature. In some states he presents estimates. In all but one of the states (North Carolina) the Governor has a veto upon legislation, which may, however, be overridden by the two Houses, in some states by a simple majority, in others by a three-fifths or two-thirds majority. In some states the Governor, on his death or resignation, is succeeded by a Lieut.-Governor who was elected at the same time and has been presiding over the state Senate. In several states the Speaker of the Lower House succeeds the Governor.

There were elections for 36 governors' seats on 4 Nov. 1998: Republicans won 23, Democrats 11 and Independents 2. As a result there were 31 Republican, 17 Democrat and 2 Independent Governors in total.

The chief officials by whom the administration of state affairs is carried on (secretaries, treasurers, members of boards of commissioners, etc.) are usually chosen by the people at the general state elections for terms similar to those for which governors hold office.

The chief unit of local government is the county, of which there were (1997) 2,994 with definite functions; in addition, Rhode Island has 5 'counties' which have no functions; Alaska does not have counties but 25 divisions and, since Oct. 1960, there has been no active county government in Connecticut. Louisiana has 64 'parishes'. The counties maintain public order through the sheriff and his deputies, who may, in a crisis, be drawn temporarily from willing citizens; in many states the counties maintain the smaller local highways; other functions are the granting of licences and the apportionment and collection of taxes. In a few states they also manage the schools.

The unit of local government in New England is the rural township, governed directly by the voters, who assemble annually or more often if necessary, and legislate in local affairs, levy taxes, make appropriations and appoint and instruct the local officials. Townships are grouped to form counties. Where cities exist, the township government is superseded by the city government.

Local elections and 94 referendums were held on 5 Nov. 1996.

DEFENCE

The President is C.-in-C. of the Army, Navy and Air Force.

The National Security Act of 1947 provides for the unification of the Army, Navy and Air Forces under a single Secretary of Defense with cabinet rank. The President is also advised by a National Security Council and the Office of Civil and Defense Mobilization.

The major components of the Department of Defense are the Office of the Secretary of Defense and the Joint Chiefs of Staff, who provide immediate staff assistance and advice to the Secretary; the departments of the Army, Navy and Air

Force, each separately organized under a civilian head (not of cabinet rank); and the unified and specified commands.

Defence expenditure in 1997 totalled US$272,955m. (US$1,018 per capita), representing 3·4% of GDP. The USA spent more on defence in 1997 than the next 7 biggest spenders combined. In 1997 the Quadrennial Defense Review (QDR) was implemented—a plan to transform US defence strategy and military forces. The 1999 defence budget continues to support the plan by funding relevant new technologies.

The USA is the world's largest exporter of arms, with sales in 1997 worth $20·9bn., or 45% of the world total. In 1987 sales had been worth more, at $23·6bn., but had only represented 26·7% of the total. The estimated number of active military personnel in 1998 was 1,483,000.

In accordance with START I—the treaty signed by the US and USSR in 1991 to reduce strategic offensive nuclear capability—the number of nuclear warheads (intercontinental ballistic missiles, submarine-launched ballistic missiles and bombers) in Jan. 1998 was approximately 7,250. In 1990 the number of warheads had been 12,718. Strategic nuclear delivery vehicles were made up as follows:

Intercontinental ballistic missiles: 500 Minuteman III; 50 Peacekeeper (MX).

Submarine-launched ballistic missiles: 192 Trident I (C-4); 240 Trident II (D-5).

Bombers: 71 B-52H; 21 B-2.

Army. *Secretary of the Army:* Louis Caldera.

Central Administration. The Secretary of the Army is the head of the Department of the Army. Subject to the authority of the President as C.-in-C. and of the Secretary of Defense, he is responsible for all affairs of the Department.

The Secretary of the Army is assisted by the Under Secretary of the Army, 5 Assistant Secretaries of the Army (Civil Works, Financial Management, Installations, Logistics and Environment, Manpower and Reserve Affairs, Research, Development and Acquisition), General Counsel, Administrative Assistant, Director for Information Systems for Command, Control, Communications and Computers, Inspector General, Auditor General, Chief of Legislative Liaison, Chief of Public Affairs, Director for Small and Disadvantaged Business Utilization, Chairman of the Army Reserve Forces Policy Committee and the Army Staff headed by the Chief of Staff, US Army. The Office of the Under Secretary of the Army includes a Deputy Under Secretary (Operations Research).

The Chief of Staff, Army, in his role as a member of the Joint Chiefs of Staff, takes part in the planning and supervision of the operational forces under the command of the Commanders-in-Chief. The Vice Chief of Staff assists and advises the Chief of Staff.

The Army General Staff is the principal element of the Army Staff and includes the Offices of the Chief of Staff, Deputy Chief of Staff for Operations and Plans, Deputy Chief of Staff for Personnel, Deputy Chief of Staff for Logistics, and Deputy Chief of Staff for Intelligence. Other elements of the Army Staff are the offices of the Judge Advocate General, Surgeon General, Chief of Chaplains, Chief, Army Reserve, Chief, National Guard Bureau, and Chief of Engineers.

The Army consists of the Active Army, the Army National Guard of the US, the Army Reserve and civilian workforce; and all persons appointed to or enlisted into the Army without component; and all persons serving under call or conscription, including members of the National Guard of the States, etc., when in the service of the US. The strength of the Active Army was (1 Aug. 1996) 495,000 (including 67,100 women).

The US Army Forces Command, with headquarters at Fort McPherson, Georgia, commands the Third US Army; 4 continental US Armies, and all assigned Active Army and US Army Reserve troop units in the continental US, the Commonwealth of Puerto Rico, and the Virgin Islands of the USA. The headquarters of the continental US Armies are: First US Army, Fort George G. Meade, Maryland; Second US Army, Fort Gillem, Georgia; Fifth US Army, Fort Sam Houston, Texas; Sixth US Army, Presidio of San Francisco, California. The US Army Training and Doctrine Command, with headquarters at Fort Monroe, Virginia, co-ordinates and integrates the total combat development effort of the Army as well as developing, managing, establishing and verifying the training of individuals of the US Army and authorized foreign nationals. The US Army Health Services Command, with headquarters at Fort Sam Houston, Texas, provides health services in the continental US for the US Army and provides professional education and training for medical personnel of the US Army and authorized foreign national personnel. The US Army Materiel Command, with headquarters in Alexandria, Virginia, is responsible for US Army activities dealing with equipment development, procurement, delivery, supply and maintenance. The US Army Information Systems Communications Command, with headquarters at Fort Huachuca, Arizona, provides worldwide communication automation support to the Department of the Army and supports the Defense Communications Systems. The US Army Military District of Washington, with headquarters at Fort McNair, Washington, D.C., provides support to the Department of the Army and the Department of Defense at the seat of Government. The US Army Space Command, with headquarters in Colorado Springs (CO), is the Army component to the US Space Command.

Approximately 32% of the Active Army is deployed outside the continental USA. Several divisions, which are located in the USA, keep equipment in Germany and can be flown there in 48–72 hours. Headquarters of US Seventh and Eighth Armies are in Europe and Korea respectively.

Operational Commands and Weapons. The larger commands are the theater army and corps. The typical theater army may consist of a variable number of corps composed of combat forces of armour, infantry, air defense artillery, aviation and field artillery units; combat support forces of aviation, engineer, intelligence and signal elements; and combat service support forces. A typical corps consists of a variable number and mixture of infantry, mechanized infantry, armoured, air assault, or airborne divisions; one or more separate infantry, mechanized infantry or armoured brigades; one or more armoured cavalry regiments; corps artillery (155-mm howitzer, 203-mm howitzer, multiple launch rocket system (MLRS); corps air defense brigade *(Hawk, Chaparral, Patriot* and *Avenger battalions),* corps aviation brigade and combat support and combat service support forces.

US Army Divisions have a common base (containing command, divisional artillery, air defense artillery, combat support and combat service support units) aviation brigade, and a varying mixture of combat manoeuvre battalions (usually 9 or 10 in number in 3 brigades) to make up airborne, infantry, armoured, mechanized infantry and air assault divisions. Divisions can in this way be 'tailored' to fit a variety of strategic or tactical situations. A mechanized infantry division, with about 17,300 soldiers, may have 5 mechanized infantry battalions and 4 armoured battalions; an armoured division, with about 17,300 soldiers, may have 4 mechanized infantry battalions and 5 armoured battalions; an airborne division, with 13,100 soldiers, may have 9 infantry (airborne) battalions. The air assault division is a highly specialized force capable of battlefield helicopter operations for infantry, field artillery, air defense artillery and necessary support forces.

The 10,800-man light infantry divisions consist of 9 infantry battalions and offer rapid strategic force projection. Light divisions can operate in all environments and are general-purpose forces. Special operations forces consist of special forces, rangers, special operations aviation psychological operations, and civil affairs units. The units are designed, equipped, and trained for special missions.

Small arms include the M-9 (9mm pistol), the M-16 series rifle and the M-249 Squad Automatic Weapon both of which fire a 5·56-mm cartridge. The standard generalpurpose machine-gun is the M-60 (23 lb; 550 rounds of 7·62-mm per minute). Infantry weapons also include M-203 grenade launcher attachment for the M-16A1 rifle, which fire a 40-mm grenade up to 400 metres, the *TOW* and *Dragon* anti-tank missile systems, and the M-72 rocket, a light anti-tank weapon.

Combat vehicles of the US Army are the tank, armoured personnel carrier, infantry fighting vehicle, and the armoured command vehicle. The first-line tanks are the M1A1 Abrams tank with a 120mm main gun, and the M1 Abrams. The standard armoured infantry personnel carrier is the M2 Bradley Fighting Vehicle (BFV), which is replacing the older M113. Both carry a mechanized infantry squad, but the BFV mounts a 25-mm Bushmaster gun and *TOW* missile launchers. The M3 version of the BFV is being used as the ground scout vehicle in armoured cavalry regiments, armoured and mechanized infantry divisional cavalry squadrons and in scout platoons of armoured and mechanized infantry battalions.

The approved calibres of artillery are: light, 105-mm howitzer; medium, 155-mm howitzer; heavy, 203-mm howitzer. The Multiple Launch Rocket System (MLRS) is

UNITED STATES OF AMERICA

a 227-mm rapid firerocket system used in a non-nuclear counterfire, reinforcing and deep fire roles. The 107-mm mortar, the 81-mm mortar and the 60-mm mortar are used by the combat manoeuvre elements. The 120-mm mortar will replace the 107-mm mortar. The *TOW* is the primary anti-tank weapon. Forward-area air-defence weapons, including the *Chaparral, Stinger* and *Avenger* 20-mm gun, provide the capability of low-altitude defence against high-performance aircraft.

The Army has three categories of missiles—surface-to-surface (field artillery) and surface-to-air (air defence artillery) and anti-tank. Surface-to-surface missiles are now limited to the Army Tactical Missile System (ATACMS; fielded) and the Tri-Service Stand-Off Attack Missile (TSSAM; EMD). ATACMS is a semi-ballistic missile capable of carrying a variety of warheads to ranges in excess of 150 km. Planned improvements include an extended range variant with a range of 300+ km. TSSAM is a joint Army, Air Force, Navy cruise missile programme. TSSAM carries the Bat submunition (anti-tank) to distances in excess of 200 km. Planned improvements modify Bat submunition for targets other than armour. Surface-to-air missiles, for air defence, are: *Patriot*, guided, conventional warhead, operational; *Hawk*, homing type, low-to-mid-altitude, field operational (product improvements continue to improve the effectiveness of the system); *Chaparral*, infra-red homing, low-altitude, forward area, operational (improvements to the basic system are under development); *Stinger*, hand-held or mobile-launched, infra-red homing, low-altitude, forward area, operational. Anti-tank missiles are: *TOW*, tube launched, optically tracked, wire guided, anti-armour, forward area, operational; *Hellfire*, laser-guided, anti-armour, operational and *Dragon*, wire-guided, medium anti-armour, forward area, operational.

The Army employs rotary- and fixed-wing aircraft as organic elements of its ground formations where their use is required on a full-time basis and their immediate and constant availability is essential. The front line commander exploits the benefits of aviation technology to perform traditional land battle tasks in the third dimension. This concept of airmobility for ground formation utilizes aerial vehicles as a highly integrated team to perform all five functions of land combat: reconnaissance, command and control, logistics and that inseparable combination, firepower and manoeuvre.

The Army has some 7,000 aircraft, all but about 400 of them helicopters. The principal types are 1,000 UH-1 Iroquois Huey and 1,600 UH-60 Black Hawk utility helicopters, 1,000 OH-58 Kiowa observation helicopters, 600 AH-1 Cobra and 700 AH-64 Apache attack helicopters, and 450 CH-47 Chinook cargo helicopters.

Enlistment, Terms of Service. Since 1974 the Army has operated an 'all volunteer' system making it, in effect, an all-regular force both regular and reserve components. Terms of service may be 2, 3, 4, 5 or 6 years. Men and women who enlist incur an 8-year obligation and must serve in the reserve components any part of the period not served on active duty. Over 95% of recruits enlisting in the Army have a high-school education and over 50% of the Army is married. Women serve in both combat support and combat service support units.

The National Guard is a reserve military component with both a state and a federal role. Enlistment is voluntary. The members are recruited by each state, but are equipped and paid by the federal government (except when performing state missions). Training is supervised by the active Army (FORSCOM), and unit organization parallels that for the active Army; training facilities are made available by the USA and each state. As the organized militia of the several states, the District of Columbia, Puerto Rico and the Territories of the Virgin Islands and Guam, the Guard may be called into service for local emergencies by the chief executives in those jurisdictions; and may be called into federal service by the President to thwart invasion or rebellion or to enforce federal law. In its role as a reserve component of the Army, the Guard is subject to the order of the President in the event of national emergency. In 1996 it numbered 499,800 (Army, 387,100; Air Force, 112,700).

The Army Reserve is designed to supply qualified and experienced units and individuals in an emergency. US Army Forces Command is charged with the command, support and training supervision of US Army Reserve units. Members of units are assigned to the Ready Reserve, which is subject to call by the President in case of national emergency without declaration of war by Congress. The Standby Reserve and the Retired Reserve may be called only after declaration of war or national emergency by Congress. In 1996 the Army Reserve numbered 596,700 (114,000 women).

1721

UNITED STATES OF AMERICA

Navy. *Secretary of the Navy:* John Dalton.

The Department of the Navy is administered under the Defense Secretary by the Secretary of the Navy, assisted by the Under Secretary and 4 Assistant Secretaries (for Financial Management; Installation and Environment; Manpower and Reserve Affairs; and Research, Development and Acquisition). Other divisions of the Department of the Navy are those of: Legislative Affairs, Information and the Judge Advocate General of the Navy.

The professional head of the Navy is the Chief of Naval Operations, whose staff includes the Vice Chief, 4 Deputy Chiefs responsible for Manpower and Personnel; Plans, Policy and Operations; Logistics; and Resources, Warfare Requirements and Assessments. There are 3 major staff directorates for Intelligence; Training; and Space and electronic warfare and 5 specialist divisions.

The Operating Forces include the Atlantic Fleet, divided between the 2nd fleet (home waters) and 6th fleet (Mediterranean) and the Pacific Fleet, similarly divided between the 3rd fleet (home waters), the 7th fleet (West Pacific) and the 5th fleet (Indian Ocean), which was formally activated in 1995 and maintained by units from both Pacific and Atlantic. All fleets include associated Fleet Marine Forces. Other operational commands include the Military Sealift Command, US Naval Forces Europe, the Mine Warfare Command and the Operational Test and Evaluation Force.

The authorized budget for the Department of the Navy (which includes funding both for the Navy and Marine Corps) for current and recent fiscal years: 1995, $78,200m.; 1996, $76,400m.; 1997, $79,370m.; 1998, $79,340m.

Personnel and fleet strength declined during the mid-1990s but are now stabilizing. The '600-ship battle force' planned in the late 1980s has reduced to such an extent that the eventual figure is likely to be about 335. In late 1997 it was 347. The Navy personnel total in 1997 was 388,760, including 52,178 women who are eligible to serve at sea in support ships.

The operational strength of the Navy at the end of the year indicated:

Category	1992	1993	1994	1995	1996	1997
Strategic Submarines	23	22	16	17	17	18
Nuclear Attack Submarines	87	86	85	78	76	67
Aircraft Carriers	12	13	12	13[1]	12[1]	11[1]
Amphibious Carriers	13	14	13	11	11	11
Cruisers	46	49	44	31	31	30
Destroyers	51	40	39	46	52	56
Frigates	90	67	59	46	45	31

[1]Includes the USS *John F. Kennedy* as 'operational and training reserve carrier' in the Naval Reserve Force.

Ships in the inactive reserve are not included in the table, but those serving as Naval Reserve Force training ships are. Amphibious Carriers are those ships of the WASP, Tarawa, and Iwo Jima classes capable of operating AV-8 Harrier-type aircraft as well as helicopters.

Submarine Forces. A principal part of the US naval task is to deploy the seaborne strategic deterrent from nuclear-powered ballistic missile-carrying submarines (SSBN), of which there were, in 1997, 18, all of the Ohio class. These ships, the first of which entered service in 1981, are of 18,700 tons submerged displacement, and capable of speeds in excess of 25 knots. 10 of the 18 submarines are designed to deploy the Trident-2 D-5 missile, with a range of 4,000 nautical miles, carrying as many as 24 warheads with substantially improved targeting accuracy over the Trident-1 C-4 missile, which is deployed in the first 8 ships of the class, also with up to 24 warheads. The first submarine deployed the Trident-2 operationally in 1990. Pending ratification of the START II treaty, 4 of the first 8 ships may be retrofitted with the Trident-2. The remaining 4 ships will be removed from strategic service and may be employed in a non-strategic role. The last of the Benjamin Franklin class previous generation SSBNs was withdrawn in 1995.

The listed total of 67 nuclear-powered attack submarines (SSN) includes the first of 3 new Seawolf class and 54 of the Los Angeles class (7,040 tons) in 3 major batches: a basic design (23 ships) completed 1976–85, a small group of 8 ships additionally equipped with vertical-launch missile tubes for Tomahawk cruise missiles completed 1985–89, and the remaining 23 ships, the last of which was completed in 1996. These latter are known as the 'Improved' Los Angeles class

(6881), incorporating vertical-launch cruise missile tubes, a new combat control system, and several important additional technical modifications. There are also 9 Sturgeon class (5,040 tons) completed 1967–75, and 3 other submarines.

Surface Combatant Forces. The surface combatant forces are comprised of modern cruisers, destroyers and frigates equipped with standoff strike weapons, anti-air missiles, guns and anti-submarine torpedoes. These ships provide multi-mission capabilities to achieve maritime dominance in the crowded and complex littoral warfare environment.

The cruiser force consists of 27 Ticonderoga class ships. These vessels, commissioned between 1983 and 1993, are 9,600 tons, capable of in excess of 30 knots, equipped with the highly capable Aegis weapon system and armed with medium range Standard Missile (SM2-MR) surface-to-air missiles (SAM). They have two 127mm guns, 8 Harpoon anti-surface ship missiles and 2 SH-60B Seahawk, Light Airborne Multipurpose System (LAMPS-III) helicopters. All but the first 5 ships of the class are equipped with two 61-cell vertical launch systems, designed to launch the Standard Missile (SM2-MR), Vertical Launched Anti-Submarine Rocket (ASROC) and Tomahawk land attack cruise missile.

There are 24 guided-missile Arleigh Burke Aegis class destroyers, 24 Spruance class destroyers, and 38 (28 active and 10 in the reserve force) Oliver Hazard Perry class guided missile frigates.

The surface combatant force is undergoing a 'measured' revolution into the 21st century. Fundamental changes are occurring in Land Attack and Theatre Ballistic Missile Defence missions. The Extended Range Guided Munition (ERGM) will increase naval fires from 21 km to a precise 113 km. In the final testing stages are new land attack missiles, some of which are hypersonic. The Tomahawk missile system has been completely reconfigured since the Gulf War. The Tactical Tomahawk extends naval fires beyond the littoral. Area theatre ballistic missile defence will be achieved through the evolution of the SM-2 block IV standard missile and deployment of a theatre-wide capability is on the near horizon with the SM-3. Through these developments, and those which are dramatically increasing network capacity, the Navy's ability to mass volume precision fires from distributed sources is now a reality.

Aircraft carriers. There are 7 Nimitz class carriers of about 90,000 tons completed between 1975 and 1995, nuclear-powered and capable of 33 knots. The USS *Enterprise*, completed in 1961, displacing 76,000 tons, was the prototype nuclear-powered carrier and is also capable of 33 knots. The 2 ships of the Kitty Hawk and 1 of the John F. Kennedy classes are about 80,000 tons, were completed between 1961 and 1968, and represent the last oil-fuelled carriers built by the US Navy. The force is completed by the remaining ship of the Forrestal class, USS *Independence*, completed in 1959, of about 82,000 tons full load. All carriers deploy an air group which comprises on average 2 squadrons each of 10 F-14 Tomcat fighters and 3 squadrons each of 12 F/A-18 Hornet fighter/ground attack aircraft. They also carry a squadron of 4 E-2C Hawkeye early warning aircraft, 4 KA-6 airborne tankers, 4 EA-6B Prowler electronic combat aircraft, 6 S-3B Viking anti-submarine aircraft and 6 SH-3D Sea King or SH-60F Oceanhawk anti-submarine helicopters.

Amphibious Warfare. Amphibious capability comprises 42 specialist ships. The 5 Wasp (LHD-1) class and the 5 Tarawa (LHA-1) class ships are in many respects similar to the vertical/short take-off and landing carriers in other principal navies and are capable of sea control tasks. The Wasp class, completed from 1989 to 1995 and still building, are of 41,200 tons, capable of 23 knots, equipped with an air group of some 6-8 Harrier AV-8B aircraft, and up to 42 mixed helicopters, and accommodating 1,900 troops. The 5 ships of the Tarawa class are of 40,000 tons, were completed between 1976 and 1981, deploy a similar air group and carry 1,700 troops. The 1 remaining Iwo Jima class ship is also capable of operating vertical/short take-off and landing aircraft but does not normally do so. Dating from the 1960s, it is of 18,800 tons, is capable of 21 knots and normally carries 20 mixed helicopters and accommodates 1,740 troops. Additionally there are 2 amphibious command ships, 16 dock-landing ships, 11 transport dock ships and 2 tank-landing ships. There are 129 amphibious craft including 91 air-cushion landing craft (hovercraft) and 38 others, and several hundred minor personnel and vehicle transports. The total oceanic lift capability of the amphibious forces amounts to over

50,000 personnel, 1,000 main battle tank equivalents, and operating facilities for about 180 helicopters.

Underway Support. The ships of Military Sealift Command's Naval Fleet Auxiliary Force—composed of 3 ammunition ships, 6 combat stores ships, 2 hospital ships, 12 underway replenishment oilers and 7 ocean-going tugs—provide underway replenishment services to US Navy ships worldwide, alleviating the need for them to return to port for supplies. Providing fuel, food, ammunition, mail, spare parts and other supplies, these NFAF ships enable the Navy fleet to operate at the highest operational tempo possible.

Military Sealift Command also provides operating platforms and service for unique US military and federal government missions. Both civil service and contractor-employed mariners operate an acoustic survey ship, a cable repair ship; 3 counter-drug surveillance ships; 1 missile range instrumentation ship; 3 navigation test/launch area support ships; 8 oceanographic surveillance ships; and 9 oceanographic surveying ships. Technical work, research and communications are conducted by embarked military personnel, civilian scientists and related technicians.

In addition, Military Sealift Command operates 34 prepositioning ships—which include tankers, freighters, large, medium-speed, roll-on/roll-off ships (LMSRs)—which improve US capabilities to deploy forces in any area of conflict or contingency. The Prepositioning Program provides support to the US Marine Corps, Navy, Army, Air Force and the Defense Logistics Agency around the globe.

Sealift support for deployment, supplies and redeployment to Joint Forces around the world is routinely provided through MSC's surge sealift capability, employing 8 fast sealift ships and 96 Ready Reserve Force ships. MSC's ability to quickly contract for unique shipping requirements allows MSC to be responsive to contingencies in every region of the world.

Military Sealift Command employs approximately 7,500 people worldwide, the vast majority of whom are assigned to seagoing jobs. MSC's workforce consists mainly of civil service personnel, but includes military and contractor personnel.

Shipbuilding. Major warship building yards involved in the current building programme are located at Groton, Conn. (submarines), Newport News, Va. (submarines and aircraft carriers), Pascagoula, Miss. (destroyers and amphibious ships), Bath, Me. (destroyers), New Orleans, La. (amphibious and auxiliary ships) and San Diego, Ca. (auxiliary ships).

Naval Aviation. The principal function of the naval aviation organization (72,500 strong in 1997) is to train and provide combat ready aviation forces (both sea and shore-based consisting of 10 Air Wings maintained for service in Aircraft Carriers; maritime patrol and helicopter forces; and support and training aircraft). Carrier Air Wings usually consist of 70 fixed-wing and 6 rotary-wing aircraft. In addition, 1 reserve carrier air wing is available. The main carrier-borne combat aircraft in the current inventory are 230 F-14 fighters, 770 F/A-18 Hornet dual-purpose fighter/attack aircraft, 117 S-3B Viking anti-submarine aircraft and 126 EA-6B Prowler electronic warfare aircraft. Combat support roles are performed by 70 E-2C Hawkeye airborne early-warning aircraft, 16 ES-3 electronic warfare/intelligence aircraft and 115 SH-60F Seahawk helicopters for inner-zone anti-submarine defence. SH-60B Seahawk helicopters are routinely embarked on various surface combatants. The SH-60B force consists of approximately 165 aircraft. The principal tasks of the shore-based elements of US naval aviation are maritime reconnaissance and patrol, and anti-submarine warfare, for which there are 12 active and 8 reserve P-3C Orion squadrons (240 aircraft). Additional sea/shore-based tasks include electronic warfare (12 EP-3 aircraft) and mine countermeasures accomplished by a force of 40 MH-53 helicopters. Finally there are some 700 training aircraft (both fixed-wing and helicopters) and other aircraft for transport and other miscellaneous duties.

The Marine Corps. While administratively part of the Department of the Navy, the Corps ranks as a separate armed service, with the Commandant serving in his own right as a member of the Joint Chiefs of Staff, and responsible directly to the Secretary of the Navy. Its strength had stabilized at 174,000 by late 1997.

The role of the Marine Corps is to provide specially trained and equipped amphibious expeditionary forces. It is organized into Marine Forces Atlantic,

Marine Forces Pacific and Marine Forces Reserve. Nearly 65% of the active duty force is assigned to Marine Forces Atlantic and Marine Forces Pacific. The commanders of Marine Forces Atlantic and Pacific provide the regional Commanders-in-Chief with versatile forces with which to respond to their respective needs. In peacetime, Marine Expeditionary Units are permanently deployed afloat in the Eastern Atlantic/Mediterranean and the West Pacific/Indian Ocean. The principal equipment of the Corps consists of 420 M-1A1 Abrams tanks, 747 Light Armoured Vehicles, primarily of the LAV-25 variant which mounts a 25 mm chain gun, 1,320 amphibious assault vehicles and about 800 artillery pieces of calibres between 105 mm and 155 mm. Additional heavy equipment for US-based Marine forces units, beyond that which can be embarked in the amphibious shipping, is provided in 3 squadrons each of 13 large cargo ships prepositioned at Diego Garcia (Indian Ocean), the Pacific, and in the Mediterranean. In addition the Corps includes an autonomous aviation element numbering 34,000 in 1998 with some 400 combat aircraft and 515 helicopters. There are 280 F/A 18 Hornet, 180 AV-8B Harriers, 25 EA-6B electronic warfare aircraft, 75 KC-130 tankers, and a miscellany of other support and training aircraft. Helicopters include 240 CH-46E and 175 CH-53 transport, as well as 180 AH-1W Cobra attack helicopters of various types. Harriers and helicopters are normally employed afloat on amphibious assault ships. The Hornets and other fixed-wing aircraft are normally based ashore, but may be embarked on aircraft carriers, given the operational need.

Under development is the MV-22 Osprey, a tilt-rotor aircraft which can take off and land vertically like a helicopter, but whose twin engines tilt completely to the front for forward flight. It is intended to replace the Corps' fleet of CH-46E medium transport helicopters. Estimated cost of the development programme was $36bn. and the delivery date for the aircraft is 2001.

The US Coast Guard. The Coast Guard operates under the Department of Transportation in time of peace and as a part of the Navy in time of war or when directed by the President. The act of establishment stated the Coast Guard 'shall be a military service and branch of the armed forces of the United States at all times'. It comprises 250 ships including cutters of destroyer, frigate, corvette and patrol vessel types, 2 large Polar class icebreakers, and various auxiliaries and tenders, as well as over 1,400 rescue and utility craft. It also maintains 74 fixed-wing aircraft and 137 helicopters. The workforce, in 1996, was made up of over 34,000 active duty personnel augmented by 7,340 reserve and 35,638 auxiliary members.

The Coast Guard missions include maintenance of aids to navigation, boating safety, defence operations, environmental response (oil spills), ice operations, maritime law enforcement, marine inspection, marine licensing, marine science, port safety and security, search and rescue and waterways management.

On an average Coast Guard day, the service saves 12 lives, conducts 142 Search and Rescue cases and 128 maritime law-enforcement boardings, responds to 34 oil or hazardous chemical spills, seizes over $8m. in illegal contraband, interdicts 22 illegal immigrants and services 150 aids to navigation.

Air Force. *Secretary of the Air Force:* Dr Sheila E. Widnall.

The Department of the Air Force was activated within the Department of Defense on 18 Sept. 1947, under the terms of the National Security Act of 1947. It is administered by the Secretary of the Air Force, assisted by an Under Secretary, a Deputy for International Affairs and 4 Assistant Secretaries (Acquisition; Space; Manpower, Reserve Affairs, Installations and Environment; and Financial Management and Comptroller). The USAF, under the administration of the Department of the Air Force, is supervised by a Chief of Staff, who is a member of the Joint Chiefs of Staff. He is assisted by a Vice Chief of Staff, Assistant Vice Chief of Staff, 4 Deputy Chiefs of Staff (Personnel; Plans and Operations; Logistics; Communications and Information) and an Assistant Chief of Staff for Intelligence.

The USAF consists of active duty Air Force officers and enlisted personnel, civilian employees, the Air National Guard and the Air Force Reserve. The USAF has the mission to defend the USA through control and exploitation of air and space. For operational purposes the service is divided into 8 major commands, 37 field operating agencies and 3 direct-reporting units. Under these organizations there are 88 major and 89 minor facilities worldwide including National Guard and Reserve bases.

Major commands are organized on a functional basis in the USA and a geographic basis overseas. They accomplish designated phases of Air Force worldwide activities. They also organize, administer, equip and train their subordinate elements for the accomplishment of assigned missions. Major commands are generally assigned specific responsibilities based on functions. In descending order of command, elements of major commands include numbered air forces, wings, groups, squadrons and flights.

The bulk of the combat forces are grouped under the Air Combat Command, which controls strategic bombing, tactical strike, air defence and reconnaissance assets in the USA. The Air Mobility Command provides air lift, air refuelling, special air mission and aeromedical evacuation for US forces. The newest major command is the Air Education and Training Command which provides a wide variety of training from initial to advanced degree-granting education.

The other major commands are the Air Force Materiel Command, Air Force Special Operations Command, Air Force Space Command, Pacific Air Forces and United States Air Forces in Europe. The Pacific (PACAF) and European (USAFE) are responsible for offensive and defensive air operations in the Pacific and Asia, and Europe and the Mediterranean, respectively.

The field operating agencies are (AF = Air Force): the AF Audit Agency, AF Base Disposal Agency, AF Center for Environmental Excellence, AF Civil Engineering Support Agency, AF Civilian Personnel Management Center, AF Combat Operations Staff, AF Command, Control, Communications and Computer Agency, AF Cost Analysis Agency, AF Flight Standards Agency, AF Frequency Management Agency, AF Historical Research Agency, AF Inspection Agency, AF Intelligence Command, AF Intelligence Support Agency, AF Legal Services Agency, AF Logistics Management Agency, AF Management Engineering Agency, AF Medical Operations Agency, AF Medical Support Agency, AF Military Personnel Center, AF Morale, Welfare, Recreation and Services Agency, AF News Agency, AF Office of Special Investigations, AF Program Executive Office, AF Real Estate Agency, AF Review Boards Agency, AF Safety Agency, AF Security Police Agency, AF Studies and Analyses Agency, AF Technical Applications Center, Air Reserve Personnel Center, Air Weather Service, Center for Air Force History, Joint Services Survival, Evasion, Resistance and Escape Agency, and 7th Communications Group.

The direct-reporting units are: AF Academy, AF District of Washington and AF Operational Test and Evaluation Center.

Air Force aircraft are categorized as bombers, fighters, attack and observation aircraft, reconnaissance and special duty aircraft, transports and tankers, trainers and helicopters. The bombers are the B-1B Lancer, a supersonic inter-continental, nuclear and conventional aircraft; the B-2A, a subsonic, multi-role strategic bomber; and the B-52G/H Stratofortress, which has been the primary manned strategic bomber for over 35 years.

In the fighter category are the F-15 Eagle for air superiority tactical missions; the F-16 Fighting Falcon, a compact, multi-role fighter and attack aircraft; the F-117A, the world's first operational aircraft to exploit low-observable stealth technology; the A-10/OA-10 Thunderbolt II attack aircraft; and the AC-130H/U for counter-insurgency.

Under the reconnaissance and special duty heading are the U-2R/S for reconnaissance; the EC-130E/H Commando/Compass Call and the EF-111A Raven for electronic countermeasures; the E-3B/C Sentry, the E-4B and E-8 Joint Surveillance and Target Attack Radar System for command and control functions; the E-9A for telemetry relay; and the WC-130E/H for weather reconnaissance.

The primary transporters are the C-5A/B Galaxy for long-range heavy loads; the C-9A/C Nightingale for aeromedical evacuation; the C-17A Globemaster III for cargo and tactical air lift, the C-141B Starlifter for long-range troop and cargo; and the C-130 Hercules for theatre tactical air lift. The 2 refuelling aircraft types are the KC-135 Stratotanker and the KC-10A Extender.

Strategic missiles in the Air Force's inventory include the LGM-30G Minuteman, the LGM-118A Peacekeeper, the AGM-69A Short-Range Attack Missile and the AGM-86B/C Air-Launched Cruise Missile.

In 1996 the Air Force had approximately 390,000 military personnel. Approximately 60,000 Air Force members are women. Since 1991 women have been authorized to fly combat aircraft, but not until 1993 were they allowed to fly fighters.

INTERNATIONAL RELATIONS
The USA is a member of the UN, OAS, NATO, OECD, the Pacific Community and the Colombo Plan.

ECONOMY
Performance. Real GDP growth was 2·4% in 1996, 2·0% in 1995 and 3·5% in 1994.

Budget. The budget covers virtually all the programmes of federal government, including those financed through trust funds, such as for social security, Medicare and highway construction. Receipts of the Government include all income from its sovereign or compulsory powers; income from business-type or market-orientated activities of the Government is offset against outlays. The fiscal year ends on 30 Sept. (before 1977 on 30 June). Budget receipts and outlays (in $1m.):

Fiscal year ending in	Receipts	Outlays	Surplus (+) or deficit (−)
1950	39,443	42,562	−3,119
1960	92,492	92,191	+301
1970	192,807	195,649	−2,842
1980	517,112	590,947	−73,835
1990	1,031,969	1,253,163	−221,194
1995	1,351,830	1,515,729	−163,899
1996	1,453,062	1,560,212	−107,450
1997	1,579,292	1,601,232	−21,940
1998	1,721,798	1,652,552	+69,246
1999[1]	1,806,334	1,727,071	+79,263
2000[1]	1,882,992	1,765,687	+117,305

[1]Estimates.

In the fiscal year 1998 the federal budget had a surplus of $69bn., the first surplus in nearly 30 years.

Budget and off-budget receipts, by source, for fiscal years (in $1m.):

Source	1997	1998	1999[1]
Individual income taxes	737,466	828,586	868,945
Corporation income taxes	182,293	188,677	182,210
Social insurance and retirement receipts	539,371	571,831	608,824
Excise taxes	56,924	57,673	68,075
Other	63,238	75,031	78,280
Total	1,579,292	1,721,798	1,806,334

[1]Estimates.

Budget and off-budget outlays, by function, for fiscal years (in $1m.):

Function	1997	1998	1999[1]
National defence	270,505	268,456	276,730
International affairs	15,228	13,109	15,474
General science, space and technology	17,174	18,219	18,529
Energy	1,475	1,270	49
Natural resources and environment	21,369	22,396	24,261
Agriculture	9,032	12,206	21,449
Commerce and housing credit	−14,624	1,014	452
Transportation	40,767	40,332	42,640
Community and regional development	11,005	9,720	10,428
Education, training, employment and social service	53,008	54,919	60,065
Health	123,843	131,440	143,095
Medicare	190,016	192,822	204,982
Income security	230,899	233,202	243,130
Social Security	365,257	379,225	392,608
Veterans' benefits and services	39,313	41,781	43,526
Administration of justice	20,173	22,832	24,467
General government	12,749	13,444	14,852
Net interest	244,016	243,359	227,244
Allowances	—	—	3,118
Undistributed offsetting receipts	−49,973	−47,194	−40,028
Total	1,601,232	1,652,552	1,727,071

[1]Estimates.

Budget and off-budget outlays, by agency, for fiscal years (in $1m.):

Agency	1997	1998	1999[1]
Legislative branch	2,363	2,600	2,850
The Judiciary	3,259	3,467	3,913
Executive Office of the President	221	237	374
International assistance programmes	10,126	8,974	10,130
Agriculture	52,547	53,947	63,412
Commerce	3,783	4,046	4,767
Corps of engineers	3,598	3,845	4,209
Defence—Military functions	258,322	256,122	263,556
Defence—Civil	30,282	31,216	32,311
Education	30,009	31,463	34,360
Energy	14,467	14,438	15,544
Health and Human Services	339,535	350,568	375,532
Housing and Urban Development	27,527	30,227	32,324
Interior	6,720	7,218	8,426
Justice	14,310	16,168	16,458
Labor	30,458	30,007	34,923
State	6,033	5,382	6,791
Transportation	39,832	39,463	41,873
Treasury	379,342	390,140	385,976
Veterans Affairs	39,280	41,773	43,474
Environmental Protection Agency	6,164	6,284	6,667
General Services Administration	1,084	1,091	328
National Aeronautics and Space Administration	14,360	14,206	14,043
Office of Personnel Management	45,404	46,305	48,266
Small Business Administration	333	−77	−866
Social Security Administration	393,311	408,203	422,438
Other independent agencies	3,531	16,274	12,268
Allowances	—	—	3,118
Undistributed offsetting receipts	−154,969	−161,035	−160,394
Total	1,601,232	1,652,552	1,727,071

[1]Estimates.

National Debt: Federal debt held by the public (in $1m.), and per capita debt (in $1) on 30 June to 1976 and on 30 Sept. since then:

	Public debt	Per capita		Public debt	Per capita
1920	24,299	228	1992	2,998,834	11,742
1930	16,185	132	1993	3,247,471	12,581
1940	42,772	325	1994	3,432,117	13,166
1950	219,023	1,438	1995	3,603,373	13,692
1960	236,840	1,311	1996	3,732,968	14,057
1970	283,198	1,381	1997	3,771,148	14,153
1980	709,838	3,117	1998	3,719,878	13,838
1990	2,410,722	9,646	1999[1]	3,669,737	13,533
1991	2,688,137	10,641	2000[1]	3,571,830	13,061

[1]Estimates.

National Income. The Bureau of Economic Analysis of the Department of Commerce prepares detailed estimates on the national income and product. In Jan. 1996, the Bureau revised these accounts back to 1959 (eventually 1929), notably by introducing a new featured measure of real output and prices. The principal tables are published monthly in *Survey of Current Business;* the complete set of national income and product tables are published in the *Survey* normally each Aug., showing data for recent years. *The National Income and Product Accounts of the United States* (1929–94, 2 vols.) were published in 1998. The conceptual framework and statistical methods underlying the accounts are described in National Income and Product Account (NIPA) Methodology Papers 1–6. Subsequent limited changes are described in the Jan.–Feb. 1996, Aug. 1997, Aug. 1998, and Sept. 1998 *Surveys.*

	Gross Domestic Product (in $1,000m.)				
	1993	1994	1995	1996	1997
Gross Domestic Product	6,558·1	6,947·0	7,269·6	7,661·6	8,110·9
Personal consumption expenditures	4,459·2	4,717·0	4,953·9	5,215·7	5,493·7
Durable goods	530·2	579·5	611·0	643·3	673·0
Nondurable goods	1,370·7	1,428·4	1,473·6	1,539·2	1,600·6
Services	2,558·4	2,709·1	2,869·2	3,033·2	3,220·1

Gross Domestic Product (in $1,000m.)

Gross private domestic investment	876·2	1,007·9	1,043·2	1,131·9	1,256·0
Fixed investment	855·7	946·6	1,012·5	1,099·8	1,188·6
Nonresidential	604·1	660·6	727·7	787·9	860·7
Structures	176·4	184·5	201·3	216·9	240·2
Producers' durable equipment	427·7	476·1	526·4	571·0	620·5
Residential	251·6	286·0	284·8	311·8	327·9
Change in business inventories	20·5	61·2	30·7	32·1	67·4
Net exports of goods and services	−60·7	−90·9	−83·9	−91·2	−93·4
Exports	658·6	721·2	819·4	873·8	965·4
Goods	459·7	509·6	583·8	618·3	688·3
Services	198·9	211·6	235·6	255·5	277·1
Imports	719·3	812·1	903·3	965·0	1,058·8
Goods	592·8	676·8	757·6	809·0	888·3
Services	126·5	135·3	145·7	156·0	170·4
Government consumption expenditures and gross investment	1,283·4	1,313·0	1,356·4	1,405·2	1,454·6
Federal	518·3	510·2	509·1	518·4	520·2
National defence	360·7	349·2	344·4	351·0	346·0
Nondefence	157·7	161·0	164·7	167·4	174·3
State and local	765·0	802·8	847·3	886·8	934·4

Relation of Gross Domestic Product, Gross National Product, Net National Product, National Income, and Personal Income

(in $1,000m.)

	1993	1994	1995	1996	1997
Gross domestic product	6,558·1	6,947·0	7,269·6	7,661·6	8,110·9
Plus: Receipts of factor income from the rest of the world	150·8	176·5	225·2	235·5	265·5
Less: Payments of factor income to the rest of the world	132·1	168·3	207·6	223·1	273·5
Equals: Gross national product	6,576·8	6,955·2	7,287·1	7,674·0	8,102·9
Less: Consumption of fixed capital	727·9	777·5	800·8	832·0	871·8
Private	594·5	638·6	657·0	684·3	720·2
Capital consumption allowances	599·1	647·3	677·1	719·7	760·5
Less: Capital consumption adjustment	4·6	8·7	20·1	35·4	40·4
Government	133·4	138·8	143·8	147·7	151·6
General government	114·3	118·2	122·4	125·3	128·3
Government enterprises	19·1	20·6	21·4	22·4	23·4
Equals: Net national product	5,848·9	6,177·7	6,486·3	6,842·0	7,231·1
Less: Indirect business tax and non-tax liability	532·5	568·5	581·2	606·4	627·2
Business transfer payments	28·2	30·5	32·9	33·8	35·1
Statistical discrepancy	52·6	14·6	−26·5	−32·2	−55·8
Plus: Subsidies less current surplus of government enterprises	31·1	26·6	25·1	22·0	21·9
Equals: National income	5,266·8	5,590·7	5,923·7	6,256·0	6,646·5
Less: Corporate profits with inventory valuation and capital consumption adjustments	492·8	570·5	672·4	750·4	817·9
Net interest	402·5	412·3	420·6	418·6	432·0
Contributions for social insurance	596·0	630·5	658·9	688·0	727·0
Wage accruals less disbursements	4·4	13·3	13·4	9·3	3·7
Plus: Personal interest income	651·0	668·1	704·9	719·4	747·3
Personal dividend income	147·1	171·0	192·8	248·2	260·3
Government transfer payments to persons	889·8	930·9	990·1	1,041·5	1,083·3
Business transfer payments to persons	22·1	23·7	25·8	26·4	27·2
Equals: Personal income	5,481·0	5,757·9	6,072·1	6,425·2	6,784·0
Addenda:					
Gross domestic income	6,505·5	6,932·4	7,296·1	7,693·8	8,166·7
Gross national income	6,524·2	6,940·6	7,313·6	7,706·2	8,158·7
Net domestic product	5,830·2	6,169·5	6,468·8	6,829·6	7,239·1

UNITED STATES OF AMERICA

National Income by Type of Income

(in $1,000m.)

	1993	1994	1995	1996	1997
National income	5,266·8	5,590·7	5,923·7	6,256·0	6,646·5
Compensation of employees	3,814·9	4,012·0	4,208·9	4,409·0	4,687·2
Wage and salary accruals	3,094·0	3,254·0	3,441·9	3,640·4	3,893·6
Government	584·3	602·2	622·7	640·9	664·2
Other	2,509·7	2,651·8	2,819·2	2,999·5	3,229·4
Supplements to wages and salaries	720·8	758·0	767·0	768·6	793·7
Employer contributions for social insurance	335·7	353·0	365·3	381·7	400·7
Other labour income	385·1	405·0	401·6	387·0	392·9
Proprietors' income with inventory valuation and capital consumption adjustments	450·8	471·6	488·1	527·7	551·2
Farm	32·4	36·9	22·4	38·9	35·5
Proprietors' income with inventory valuation adjustment	40·4	44·8	30·3	46·7	43·0
Capital consumption adjustment	–8·0	–7·9	–7·9	–7·8	–7·5
Nonfarm	418·4	434·7	465·6	488·8	515·8
Proprietors' income	392·7	415·0	442·7	461·6	485·3
Inventory valuation adjustment	–1·1	–0·6	–1·6	–0·6	0·6
Capital consumption adjustment	26·8	20·4	24·6	27·8	29·9
Rental income of persons with capital consumption adjustment	105·7	124·4	133·7	150·2	158·2
Rental income of persons	148·5	172·0	181·8	198·4	208·6
Capital consumption adjustment	–42·8	–47·6	–48·0	–48·1	–50·4
Corporate profits with inventory valuation and capital consumption adjustments	492·8	570·5	672·4	750·4	817·9
Corporate profits with inventory valuation adjustment	456·9	519·1	613·0	679·0	741·2
Profits before tax	465·4	535·1	635·6	680·2	734·4
Profits tax liability	165·2	186·6	211·0	226·1	246·1
Profits after tax	300·2	348·5	424·6	454·1	488·3
Dividends	157·6	182·4	205·3	261·9	275·1
Undistributed profits	142·6	166·1	219·3	192·3	213·2
Inventory valuation adjustment	–8·5	–16·1	–22·6	–1·2	6·9
Capital consumption adjustment	36·0	51·4	59·4	71·4	76·6
Net interest	402·5	412·3	420·6	418·6	432·0
Addenda:					
Corporate profits after tax with inventory valuation and capital consumption adjustments	327·6	383·8	461·4	524·3	571·8
Net cash flow with inventory valuation and capital consumption adjustments	558·5	613·8	687·2	714·4	774·1
Undistributed profits with inventory valuation and capital consumption adjustments	170·1	201·4	256·1	262·4	296·7
Consumption of fixed capital	388·4	412·3	431·1	452·0	477·3
Less: Inventory valuation adjustment	–8·5	–16·1	–22·6	–1·2	6·9
Equals: Net cash flow	567·0	629·8	709·8	715·7	767·2

Real Gross Domestic Product

(in 1,000m. chained [1992] dollars[1])

	1993	1994	1995	1996	1997
Gross domestic product	6,389·6	6,610·7	6,761·7	6,994·8	7,269·8
Personal consumption expenditures	4,343·6	4,486·0	4,605·6	4,752·4	4,913·5
Durable goods	523·8	561·2	589·1	626·1	668·6
Nondurable goods	1,351·0	1,389·9	1,417·6	1,450·9	1,486·3
Services	2,468·9	2,535·5	2,599·6	2,676·7	2,761·5
Gross private domestic investment	863·6	975·7	996·1	1,084·1	1,206·4
Fixed investment	842·8	915·5	966·0	1,050·6	1,138·0
Nonresidential	600·2	648·4	710·6	776·6	859·4
Structures	170·8	172·5	180·7	189·7	203·2
Producers' durable equipment	429·6	476·8	531·7	589·8	660·9
Residential	242·6	267·0	256·8	275·9	282·8
Change in business inventories	22·1	60·6	27·7	30·0	63·2
Net exports of goods and services	–70·2	–104·6	–96·5	–111·2	–136·1

UNITED STATES OF AMERICA

Real Gross Domestic Product

(in 1,000m. chained [1992] dollars[1])

Exports	658·2	712·4	792·6	860·0	970·0
Goods	463·7	509·8	573·7	629·4	726·5
Services	194·5	202·9	219·5	231·8	247·0
Imports	728·4	817·0	889·0	971·2	1,106·1
Goods	602·0	684·1	749·7	824·7	945·7
Services	126·5	133·2	139·7	147·3	161·8
Government consumption expenditures and gross investment	1,252·1	1,252·3	1,254·5	1,268·2	1,285·0
Federal	505·7	486·6	470·6	465·6	458·0
National defence	354·4	336·9	323·5	319·1	308·9
Non-defence	151·2	149·5	146·9	146·2	148·6
State and local	746·4	765·7	783·9	802·7	827·1
Residual	−0·9	−0·3	0·4	−1·5	−7·3

[1]In 1996 the chain-weighted method of estimating GDP replaced that of constant base-year prices. In chain-weighting the weights used to value different sectors of the economy are continually updated to reflect changes in relative prices.

Currency. The unit of currency is the *dollar* (USD) of 100 *cents*. Notes are issued by the 12 Federal Reserve Banks, which are denoted by a branch letter (A = Boston, MA; B = New York, NY; C = Philadelphia, PA; D = Cleveland, OH; E = Richmond, VA; F = Atlanta, GA; G = Chicago, IL; H = St Louis, MO; I = Minneapolis, MN; J = Kansas City, MO; K = Dallas, TX; L = San Francisco, CA).

Inflation was 2·3% in 1997 and was forecast to drop to 1·6% in 1998. Foreign exchange reserves in Feb. 1998 were US$31,230m. Gold reserves in Feb. 1998 were 261·7m. troy oz. The USA has the most gold reserves of any country, and more than the combined reserves of the next three (Germany, Switzerland and France). Total money supply in Dec. 1997 was $1,281bn.

Banking and Finance. The Federal Reserve System, established under The Federal Reserve Act of 1913, comprises the Board of 7 Governors, the 12 regional Federal Reserve Banks with their 25 branches, and the Federal Open Market Committee. The 7 members of the Board of Governors are appointed by the President with the consent of the Senate. Each Governor is appointed to a full term of 14 years or an unexpired portion of a term, one term expiring every 2 years. The Board exercises broad supervisory authority over the operations of the 12 Federal Reserve Banks, including approval of their budgets and of the appointments of their presidents and first vice presidents; it designates 3 of the 9 directors of each Reserve Bank including the Chairman and Deputy Chairman. The *Chairman* of the Federal Reserve Board is appointed by the President for 4-year terms. The Chairman for 1996–2000 is Alan Greenspan. The Board has supervisory and regulatory responsibilities over banks that are members of the Federal Reserve System, bank holding companies, bank mergers, Edge Act and agreement corporations, foreign activities of member banks, international banking facilities in the USA, and activities of the US branches and agencies of foreign banks. Legislation of 1991 requires foreign banks to prove that they are subject to comprehensive consolidated supervision by a regulator at home, and have the Board's approval to establish branches, agencies and representative offices. The Board also assures the smooth functioning and continued development of the nation's vast payments system. Another area of the Board's responsibilities involves the implementation by regulation of major federal laws governing consumer credit.

The 12 members of the Federal Open Market Committee (FOMC) include the 7 members of the Board of Governors and 5 of the 12 Federal Reserve Bank presidents. The latter serve 1-year terms on the FOMC in rotation except for the President of the Federal Reserve Bank of New York, who is a permanent member. The FOMC has an essential role in the formulation of monetary policy. It influences credit market conditions, money and bank credit, by buying or selling US Government securities; and it also oversees system operations in foreign currencies for the purpose of helping to safeguard the value of the dollar in international exchange markets and facilitating co-operation and efficiency in the international monetary system. The Board of Governors also influences credit conditions through powers to set reserve requirements, to approve discount rates at Federal Reserve Banks, and to fix margin requirements on stock-market credit.

The Reserve Banks advance funds to depository institutions, issue Federal Reserve notes (the only form of currency apart from coins), act as fiscal agent for the Government, and afford nationwide cheque-clearing and fund transfer arrangements. They may increase or reduce the country's supply of reserve funds by buying or selling Government securities and other obligations at the direction of the FOMC. The purchase and sale of securities in the open market is conducted by the Federal Reserve Bank of New York. Their capital stock is held by the member banks, but it carries no voting rights except in the election of directors.

From 1968, the Congress passed a number of consumer financial protection acts, the first of which was the Truth in Lending Act, for which it has directed the Board to write implementing regulations and assume partial enforcement responsibility. Others include the Equal Credit Opportunity Act, Home Mortgage Disclosure Act, Consumer Leasing Act, Fair Credit Billing Act, Truth in Savings Act and Electronic Fund Transfer Act. To manage these responsibilities the Board has established a Division of Consumer and Community Affairs. To assist it, the Board consults with a Consumer Advisory Council, established by the Congress in 1976 as a statutory part of the Federal Reserve System.

Another statutory body, the Federal Advisory Council, consists of 12 members (one from each district); it meets in Washington four times a year to advise the Board of Governors on economic and banking developments. Following the passage of the Monetary Control Act of 1980, the Board of Governors established the Thrift Institutions Advisory Council to provide information and views on the special needs and problems of thrift institutions. The group is comprised of representatives of mutual savings banks, savings and loan associations, and credit unions.

All depository institutions (commercial and savings banks, savings and loan associations, credit unions, US agencies and branches of foreign banks, and Edge Act and agreement corporations) must meet reserve requirements set by the Federal Reserve and hold the reserves in the form of vault cash or deposits at Federal Reserve Banks.

Banks which participate in the federal deposit insurance fund have their deposits insured against loss up to $100,000 for each account. The fund is administered by the Federal Deposit Insurance Corporation established in 1933; it obtains resources through annual assessments on participating banks. All members of the Federal Reserve System are required to insure their deposits through the Corporation, and non-member banks may apply and qualify for insurance.

The Federal Deposit Insurance Corporation Improvement Act of 1992 originated with bank reform initiatives. It imposed new capital rules on banks, new reporting requirements and a code of 'safety and soundness' standards. The main aim of the Act is to reduce risk through rigorous enforcement of capital requirements. Regulators are required to take action where banks fail to observe these standards.

In June 1997 the 10 major banks in terms of assets ($1,000m.) were: Chase Manhattan, 281; Citibank, 254; Bank of America, 224; Morgan Guaranty, 189; NationsBank, 159; Bankers Trust, 99; Wells Fargo, 92; First Union, 84; Keybank, 66; BankBoston; 57.

The key stock exchanges are the New York Stock Exchange (NYSE), the Nasdaq Stock Exchange (NASDAQ) and the American Stock Exchange (ASE). There are several other stock exchanges, in Philadelphia, Boston, San Francisco (Pacific Stock Exchange) and Chicago, although trading is very limited in them.

Weights and Measures. The US Customary System derives from the British Imperial System. It differs in respect of the *gallon* (= 0·83268 Imperial gallon); *bushel* (= 0·969 Imperial bushel); *hundredweight* (= 100 lbs); and the *short* or *net ton* (= 2,000 lbs).

ENERGY AND NATURAL RESOURCES

Electricity. Installed capacity in 1997 was 709·9m. kW. In 1997, 20·1% of electricity was produced by 107 nuclear reactors. (The last one to begin commercial operation was in 1996.) Electricity production in 1997 was the highest in the world, at 3,122,522m. kWh. Consumption per capita in 1996 was an estimated 11,681 kWh.

UNITED STATES OF AMERICA

Oil and Gas. Crude oil production (includes natural gas plant liquids and other liquids):1995, 8,626,000 bbls. a day; 1996, 8,607,000 bbls. a day; 1997, 8,611,000 bbls. a day. Proven reserves were 22,546m. bbls. at 31 Dec. 1997. Output (1997, preliminary) was valued at $40·34bn. Dry natural gas production, 1997, was 18,901,423m. cu. ft with marketed production 19,865,182m. cu. ft, valued at $48·13bn. (provisional). The USA produced 9·7% of the world total oil output in 1997.

Coal. Demonstrated coal reserves were 507·7bn. short tons at 1 Jan. 1997. Output in 1997 (in 1m. short tons): 1,089·9 including bituminous coal, 653·8; sub-bituminous coal, 345·1; lignite, 86·3; anthracite, 4·7. Output from opencast workings, 669·3; underground mines, 420·7. Value of total output, 1997 (preliminary), $19·80bn.

Water. The total area covered by water is approximately 181,518 sq. miles: comprising 78,937 sq. miles inland; 42,528 sq. miles coastal; 60,052 great lakes.

Non-Fuel Minerals. The USA is wholly dependent upon imports for columbium, bauxite, mica sheet, manganese, strontium and graphite, and imports over 80% of its requirements of industrial diamonds, fluorspar, platinum, tantalum, tungsten, chromium and tin.

Total value of non-fuel minerals produced in 1995 was $38,500m. ($33,464m. in 1990). Details of some of the main minerals produced are given in the following tables.

Production of metals:

	Unit	Quantity 1990	1995	Value ($1m.) 1990	1995
Copper	1,000 tonnes	1,590	1,850	4,311	5,640
Gold	tonnes	294	320	3,650	3,990
Iron ore	1m. tonnes	57	61	1,741	1,710
Lead	1,000 tonnes	497	386	491	359
Magnesium metal	1,000 tonnes	139	142	433	476
Silver	tonnes	2,121	1,640	329	271
Zinc	1,000 tonnes	515	614	847	756
Total metals				12,442	14,100

Precious metals are mined mainly in Nevada, California and Utah; (gold) and Nevada, Arizona and Idaho (silver).

Production of non-metals:

	Unit	Quantity 1990	1995	Value ($1m.) 1990	1995
Barite	1,000 tonnes	430	543	16	17
Boron	1,000 tonnes	1,094	796	436	372
Bromine	1,000 tonnes	177	218	173	186
Cement	1m. short tons	78·9	77·3	3,908	5,227
Clays	1,000 tonnes	42,904	43,100	1,620	1,730
Diatomite	1,000 tonnes	631	687	138	171
Feldspar	1,000 tonnes	630	882	28	37
Garnet (industrial)	1,000 tonnes	47·0	53·0	7	10
Gypsum	1m. tonnes	16·4	17·0	100	121
Lime	1m. short tons	17·5	18·5	902	1,100
Phosphate rock	1m. tonnes	46·3	44	1,075	945
Pumice	1,000 tonnes	443	529	11	13
Salt	1m. tonnes	36·9	41·0	827	1,000
Sand and gravel	1m. tonnes	852	938	3,686	4,410
Sodium sulphate	1,000 tonnes	349	327	34	29
Stone (crushed)	1m. tonnes	1,109	1,260	5,591	6,750
Sulphur (all forms)	1,000 tonnes	3,676	3,070	335	207

Production estimates for 1997: (in 1m. tonnes) iron ore, 60; gypsum, 17; phosphate rock, 46·3; salt, 41·4; sand and gravel, 989; stone (crushed), 1,396: (in 1m. short tons) cement, 77·3; lime, 19·3: (in 1,000 tonnes) copper, 1,920; lead, 441; magnesium metal, 120; zinc, 607; barite, 700; boron, 1,200; bromine, 250; clays, 43,900; diatomite, 705; feldspar, 930; garnet (industrial), 71; pumice, 538; sodium sulphate, 320; sulphur (all forms), 2,900: (in tonnes) gold, 325; silver, 1,600.

Agriculture. Agriculture in the USA is characterized by its ability to adapt to widely varying conditions, and still produce an abundance and variety of agricultural products. From colonial times to about 1920 the major increases in farm production were brought about by adding to the number of farms and the amount of land under cultivation. During this period nearly 320m. acres of virgin forest were converted to crop land or pasture, and extensive areas of grasslands were ploughed. Improvident use of soil and water resources was evident in many areas.

During the next 20 years the number of farms reached a plateau of about 6·5m., and the acreage planted to crops held relatively stable around 330m. acres. The major source of increase in farm output arose from the substitution of power-driven machines for horses and mules. Greater emphasis was placed on development and improvement of land, and the need for conservation of basic agricultural resources was recognized. A successful conservation programme, highly co-ordinated and on a national scale—to prevent further erosion, to restore the native fertility of damaged land and to adjust land uses to production capabilities and needs—has been in operation since early in the 1930s.

Since the Second World War the uptrend in farm output has been greatly accelerated by increased production per acre and per farm animal. These increases are associated with a higher degree of mechanization; greater use of lime and fertilizer; improved varieties, including hybrid maize and grain sorghums; more effective control of insects and disease; improved strains of livestock and poultry; and wider use of good husbandry practices, such as nutritionally balanced feeds, use of superior sites and better housing. During this period land included in farms decreased slowly, crop land harvested declined somewhat more rapidly, but the number of farms declined sharply.

All land in farms totalled less than 500m. acres in 1870, rose to a peak of over 1,200m. acres in the 1950s and declined to 968m. acres in 1997, even with the addition of the new States of Alaska and Hawaii in 1960. The number of farms declined from 6·35m. in 1940 to 2·06m. in 1997, as the average size of farms doubled. The average size of farms in 1997 was 471 acres, but ranged from a few acres to many thousand acres. In 1997 the total value of land and buildings was $912,344m. The average value of land and buildings per acre in 1998 was $1,000.

At the 1990 census 66,964,000 persons (22·5% of the population) were rural, of whom 4,591,000 (under 2%) lived on farms. In 1997 there were an estimated 1,317,000 farm operators and managers and 2,030,000 persons in other agricultural and related occupations, of which 796,000 were farm workers.

Cash receipts from farm marketings and government payments (in $1bn.):

	Crops	Livestock and livestock products	Government payments	Total
1993	87·5	90·2	13·4	191·1
1994	92·6	88·1	7·9	188·6
1995	98·9	86·8	7·3	193·0
1996	109·4	92·9	7·3	209·6

Gross farm income (including government payments), was $219·9bn. in 1996 compared to $198·2bn. in 1990. Net farm income was $52·2bn. compared to $44·8bn. in 1990.

Acreage and specified values of farms (area in 1m. acres; value in $1m.):

	Farm area	Crop land used for crops	Value of land and buildings
1990	987	341	671,419
1991	982	337	...
1992	979	337	687,432
1993	976	330	682,039
1994	973	339	725,711
1995	972	332	807,017
1996	968	346	859,711
1997	968	353	912,344

The harvest area and production of the principal crops for 1996 and 1997 were:

	1996			1997		
	Harvested 1m. acres	Produc- tion 1m.	Yield per acre	Harvested 1m. acres	Produc- tion 1m.	Yield per acre
Corn for grain (bu.)	73·1	9,293	127	73·7	9,366	127
Soybeans (bu.)	63·4	2,382	37·6	69·9	2,727	39·0
Wheat (bu.)	62·9	2,282	36·3	63·6	2,527	39·7
Cotton (bales)[1]	12·9	19·0	707	13·3	19·0	686
Tobacco (lbs.)	0·7	1,565	2,133	0·8	1,679	2,106
Potatoes (cwt.)	1·4	497	349	1·3	460	347
Sorghum for grain (bu.)	11·9	803	67·5	9·4	653	69·5
Rice (cwt.)[1]	2·8	171	6,121	3·0	179	5,896

[1]Yield in lbs.

UNITED STATES OF AMERICA

Fruit. Utilized production:

	1995	1996	1997
Apples (1m. lbs)	10,390	10,392	10,227
Oranges and tangerines (1m. boxes[1])	278	280	306
Grapes (1,000 tons)	5,913	5,529	6,833

[1]Average net weight per box 75–95 lbs.

The farm value of the above crops in 1997 was: apples, $1,688m.; oranges and tangerines, $2,055m.; and grapes, $2,691m.

Dairy produce. In 1997 production of milk was 156,602m. lbs; cheese, 7,329m. lbs; butter, 1,151m. lbs; ice cream, 906m. gallons; non-fat dry milk, 1,223m. lbs; yoghurt, 1,574m. lbs.

Livestock. In 1997 there were 7,660m. broilers and 301m. turkeys. Eggs produced, 1997, 77·4bn.

Value of production (in $1m.) was:

	1995	1996	1997
Cattle and calves	24,830	22,259	24,900
Hogs and pigs	9,829	11,997	12,600
Broilers	11,762	13,906	14,153
Turkeys	2,776	3,102	2,880
Eggs	3,880	4,757	4,531

Livestock numbered, in 1998 (1m.): cattle and calves (including milch cows), 99·5; sheep and lambs, 7·6; hogs and pigs, 60·9. Approximate value of livestock (in $1bn.), 1998: cattle, 59·9; hogs and pigs, 5·0; sheep and lambs (in $1m.), 776.

Forestry. Forests covered a total area of 525m. acres (212m. ha) in 1995, or 23% of the land area. The gross area of national forest was 231·7 acres in 1996, of which 191·6m. acres were federally owned ('National Forest system'). Between 1990 and 1995 new planting resulted in the total area under forests growing by 7·2m. acres (2·9m. ha), the largest increase in any country in the world over the same period. In 1992 there were 490m. acres of timberland (97m. acres federally owned or managed, 35m. acres state, county or municipality owned, 358m. acres private). Timber production was 503·41m. cu. metres (17,777·76m. cu. ft) in 1995. The USA is both the world's largest producer of roundwood (15% of the world total in 1995) and the largest exporter (17% of the world total in 1995). Lumber consumption in 1996 reached its highest level since 1987 with just over 9·2bn. cu. ft being consumed, including 2·6bn. cu. ft of imports.

There are 624 designated wilderness areas throughout the USA, covering a total of 104m. acres (42m. ha). More than half of the areas are in Alaska (56%), followed by California (13%), Arizona, Washington and Idaho.

Fisheries. In 1996 the domestic catch was 9,565m. lbs (4,338,588 tonnes), valued at $3,487m. (including 1,292m. lbs of shellfish valued at $1,695·7m.). Main species landed in terms of value ($1m.): shrimp, 509; crab, 426·7; salmon, 368·7; Alaska pollock, 238·1; flounder, 154. Disposition of the domestic catch (1m. lbs): fresh or frozen, 7,054; tinned, 678; cured, 93; reduced to meal or oil, 1,740. The USA's imports of fishery commodities in 1995 ($7·14bn.) were exceeded only by those of Japan, and exports in 1995 ($3·38bn.) were exceeded only by those of Thailand.

In the period 1991–93 the average American citizen consumed 47·2 lbs (21·4 kg) of fish and fishery products a year, compared to an average 28·7 lbs (13 kg) for the world as a whole. In 1996 per capita consumption of fish and shellfish was 14·7 lbs (6·7kg).

Tennessee Valley Authority. Established by Act of Congress, 1933, the TVA is a multiple-purpose federal agency which carries out its duties in an area embracing some 41,000 sq. miles in the 7 Tennessee River Valley states: Tennessee, Kentucky, Mississippi, Alabama, North Carolina, Georgia and Virginia. In addition, 76 counties outside the Valley are served by TVA power distributors. Its 3 directors are appointed by the President, with the consent of the Senate; headquarters are in Knoxville (TN). Under a policy announced in Dec. 1994 the TVA is subject to a debt ceiling of $30,000m. Total debt in 1994 was $26,000m.

The primary task of the TVA was the multipurpose development of the Tennessee River for flood control, navigation, and electric power production. In 1994 three nuclear reactors were in operation.

The TVA has also contributed to controlling erosion on the land, introducing better fertilizers and new farming practices, eradicating malaria, demonstrating ways electricity could lighten the burdens in the home and increase production on the farm, and the creation of potential job-producing enterprises.

INDUSTRY
The following table presents industry statistics of manufactures as reported at various censuses from 1909 to 1987 and from the Annual Survey of Manufactures for years in which no census was taken.

The annual Surveys of Manufactures carry forward the key measures of manufacturing activity which are covered in detail by the Census of Manufactures. The large plants in the surveys account for approximately two-thirds of the total employment in operating manufacturing establishments in the USA.

	Number of establish-ments	Production workers (average for year)	Production workers' wages total ($1,000)	Value added by manufacture ($1,000)
1909	264,810	3,261,736	3,205,213	8,160,075
1919	270,231	9,464,916	9,664,009	23,841,624
1929	206,663	8,369,705	10,884,919	30,591,435
1933	139,325	5,787,611	4,940,146	14,007,540
1939	173,802	7,808,205	8,997,515	24,487,304
1950	260,000	11,778,803	34,600,025	89,749,765
1960	...	12,209,514	55,555,452	163,998,531
1970	...	13,528,000	91,609,000	300,227,600
1980	...	13,900,100	198,164,000	773,831,300
1982	358,061	12,400,600	204,787,200	824,117,700
1984	...	12,572,800	231,783,900	983,227,700
1986	...	11,800,000	237,000,000	1,035,000,000
1988	...	12,400,000	264,000,000	1,262,000,000
1989	...	12,300,000	269,000,000	1,308,000,000
1990	...	12,100,000	272,000,000	1,326,000,000
1991	...	11,500,000	266,000,000	1,314,000,000
1992	382,000	11,641,000	282,000,000	1,428,707,000
1993	...	11,700,000	290,000,000	1,483,000,000
1994	...	11,900,000	304,000,000	1,598,000,000
1995	...	12,300,000	317,000,000	1,709,000,000
1996	...	12,168,000	420,490,000	1,749,662,000

The number of employees in the manufacturing industry in 1997 was approximately 18,657,000. Employees worked an average of 42 hours per week for an average weekly income of $533.

The leading industries in 1995 in terms of value added by manufacture (in $1m.) were: motor vehicles and car bodies, 55,696; semiconductors and related devices, 51,272; motor vehicle parts, 43,084; pharmaceutical preparations, 41,186.

In 1997 principal commodities produced (by value of shipments, in $1m.) included: industrial machinery and equipment, 408,860; electronic components and accessories, 351,554; motor vehicles and parts, 346,606; petroleum and coal products, 177,314.

Net profits (1997) for manufacturing corporations reached a record $335bn. before tax ($247bn. after tax).

Iron and Steel: Output of the iron and steel industries (in 1m. net tons of 2,000 lb.), according to figures supplied by the American Iron and Steel Institute, was:

	Pig-iron (including ferro-alloys)	Raw steel	Steel by method of production[1] Electric	Basic Oxygen
1993	53·1	97·9	38·5	59·3
1994	54·4	100·6	39·6	61·0
1995	56·1	104·9	42·4	62·5
1996	54·5	105·3	44·9	60·4
1997	54·7	108·6	47·5	61·1

[1]The sum of these 2 items should equal the total in the preceding column; any difference is due to rounding.

In 1997 companies comprising 65% of raw steel production employed 83,466 wage-earners who worked an average of 42·7 hours per week and earned an average

UNITED STATES OF AMERICA

of $23·90 per hour: total employment costs were $6,465m. and total employment costs for 28,359 salaried employees were $2,378m.

Labour. The Bureau of Labor Statistics estimated that in 1998 the civilian labour force was 137,673,000 (67·1% of those 16 years and over), of whom 131,463,000 were employed and 6,210,000 (4·5%) were unemployed. Employment by industry in 1998:

Industry Group	Male	Female	Total	Percentage distribution
Employed (1,000 persons):	70,693	60,771	131,463	100·0
Agriculture, forestry and fisheries	2,657	852	3,509	2·7
Mining	535	85	620	0·5
Construction	7,721	798	8,518	6·5
Manufacturing:				
Durable goods	9,140	3,426	12,566	9·6
Non-durable (including not specified)	4,998	3,169	8,168	6·2
Transportation, communication and other				
public utilities	6,598	2,709	9,307	7·1
Wholesale and retail trade	14,367	12,836	27,203	20·7
Finance, insurance and real estate	3,552	5,053	8,605	6·5
Services	17,906	29,306	47,212	35·9
Private households	90	877	967	0·7
Other services	17,816	28,428	46,244	35·2
Professional services	9,568	21,824	31,392	23·9
Public administration	3,323	2,564	5,887	4·5

A total of 29 strikes and lockouts of 1,000 workers or more occurred in 1997, involving 339,000 workers and 4·5m. idle days; the number of idle days was 0·01% of the year's total working time of all workers.

The Federal Mediation and Conciliation Service, the National Labor Relations Board, the National Mediation Board and the National Railroad Adjustment Board provide formal machinery for the settlement of labour disputes.

On 1 Sept. 1997 the federal hourly minimum wage was raised from $4·75 to $5·15 an hour. On 1 Oct. 1996 it had been raised from $4·25 to $4·75 an hour, the first time it had been raised since 1991.

Labour relations are legally regulated by the National Labor Relations Act, amended by the Labor–Management Relations (Taft–Hartley) Act, 1947 as amended by the Labor–Management Reporting and Disclosure Act, 1959, again amended in 1974, and the Railway Labor Act of 1926, as amended in 1934 and 1936.

Trade Unions. The labour movement comprises 78 national and international labour organizations plus a large number of small independent local or single-firm labour organizations. The American Federation of Labor and the Congress of Industrial Organizations merged into one organization, the AFL–CIO, in 1955, with 13m. members in 1995. Its president is John Sweeney, elected 1995.

Unaffiliated or independent labour organizations, inter-state in scope, had an estimated total membership excluding all foreign members (1993) of about 3m.

Labour organizations represented 15·4% (17·9m.) of wage and salary workers in 1998; a newly developing 'associative unionism' is not based on the workplace, but provides representation for employees which is portable throughout their work history; 13·9% (16·2m.) were actual members of unions. 37% of employees in the public sector, and 10% in the private sector, were members of unions in 1998. Strongholds of organized labour are, industry-wise, iron and steel, railways, coal mining and car building; region-wise, East coast cities and the mid-West industrial belt.

INTERNATIONAL TRADE

The North American Free Trade Agreement (NAFTA) between the USA, Canada and Mexico was signed on 7 Oct. 1992 and came into effect on 1 Jan. 1994. The UK has had 'most-favoured-nation' status since 1815. In 1997 foreign direct investment totalled $681,651m., the leading investor still being the United Kingdom.

Imports and Exports. Total value of exports and imports (in $1m.):

	Exports	Imports
1993	464,773	603,438
1994	512,627	689,215
1995	584,743	770,852
1996	625,073	822,025
1997	689,184	898,590

Exports and imports (in $1m.), 1997:

	Exports	Imports
Agricultural commodities	55,639	35,164
Animal feeds	4,621	648
Bulbs	106[1]	312[1]
Cereal flour	1,241	1,328
Cocoa	111[1]	962[1]
Coffee	7	3,575
Corn	5,426	103
Cotton, raw and linters	2,716	2,791
Dairy products, eggs	713[1]	717[1]
Fur skins, raw	181[1]	74[1]
Grains, unmilled	800[1]	212[1]
Hides and skins	1,503	130
Live animals	685	1,655
Meat and preparations	6,885	2,656
Oil/fats, animal	613[1]	43[1]
Oils/fats, vegetables	1,398	1,381
Plants	94[1]	145[1]
Rice	933	217
Seeds	355[1]	200[1]
Soybeans	7,479	86
Sugar	3	956
Tobacco, unmanufactured	1,548	1,129
Vegetables and fruit	7,472	7,752
Wheat	4,196	359
Other agricultural	9,526	13,169

[1]1996 data

	Exports	Imports
Manufactured goods	550,529	728,928
ADP equipment, office machinery	43,698	74,993
Airplanes	25,552	4,557
Airplane parts	13,266	4,917
Aluminium	3,768	4,558
Artwork/antiques	1,120	3,587
Basketware, etc.	2,494	3,364
Chemicals – cosmetics	4,873	2,677
Chemicals – dyeing	3,294	2,485
Chemicals – fertilizers	3,123	1,374
Chemicals – inorganic	5,264	5,132
Chemicals – medicinal	8,087	8,748
Chemicals – organic	14,744	14,820
Chemicals – plastics	15,467	7,443
Chemicals – other	11,160	4,821
Clothing	8,396	48,408
Copper	1,441	3,254
Electrical machinery	65,816	80,370
Footwear	800	14,026
Furniture and parts	3,942	11,144
Gem diamonds	108	7,595
General industrial machinery	30,603	26,321
Glass	1,814	1,679
Glassware	813	1,553
Gold, non-monetary	5,673	3,035
Iron and steel mill products	5,637	14,285
Lighting, plumbing	1,535	2,944
Metal manufactures	10,309	12,242
Metalworking machinery	5,702	7,325
Motorcycles, bicycles	1,009[1]	2,150[1]
Nickel	347	1,144

	Exports	Imports
Optical goods	1,697	2,493
Paper and paperboard	10,283	11,697
Photographic equipment	3,865	5,759
Plastic articles	5,092	5,676
Platinum	437	1,973
Pottery	101	1,683
Power generating machinery	27,221	24,601
Printed materials	4,605	2,871
Records/magnetic media	6,815	4,137
Rubber articles	1,256	1,553
Rubber tyres and tubes	2,394	3,417
Scientific instruments	24,039	13,969
Ships, boats	1,366	875
Silver and bullion	641	472
Spacecraft	994	239
Specialized industrial machinery	29,162	21,182
Television VCR, etc.	24,093	36,771
Textile yarn, fabric	8,975	11,951
Toys/games/sporting goods	3,827	17,374
Travel goods	330	3,841
Vehicles/new cars – Canada	7,899[1]	25,351[1]
Vehicles/new cars – Japan	2,327[1]	20,134[1]
Vehicles/new cars – other	6,021[1]	21,574[1]
Vehicles/trucks	5,991[1]	11,355[1]
Vehicles/chassis/bodies	516[1]	499[1]
Vehicles/parts	24,628[1]	20,859[1]
Watches/clocks/parts	310	2,838
Wood manufactures	1,958	4,668
Other manufactured goods	92,222	170,087

[1]1996 data

	Exports	Imports
Mineral fuel	12,682	78,277
Coal	3,586	655
Crude oil	1,040	54,226
Petroleum preparations	3,899	13,904
Liquefied propane/butane	298	1,158
Natural gas	275	5,477
Electricity	69[1]	402[1]
Other mineral fuels	3,584	2,857

[1]1996 data

	Exports	Imports
Selected commodities		
Fish and preparations	2,624	7,687
Cork, wood, lumber	5,146	8,179
Pulp and waste paper	3,868	2,639
Metal ores, scrap	4,662	4,156
Crude fertilizers	1,621	1,334
Cigarettes	4,417	75
Alcoholic beverages, distilled	385	2,186
All other (including re-exports)	46,135[1]	1,726[1]

[1]1996 figures

Imports and exports by selected countries for the calendar years 1996 and 1997 (in $1m.):

Country	General imports		Exports incl. re-exports	
	1996	1997	1996	1997
UK	28,978	32,659	30,962	36,425
France	18,645	20,636	14,456	15,965
Germany	38,945	43,122	23,495	24,458
Italy	18,325	19,408	8,797	8,995
Netherlands	6,583	7,293	16,663	19,827
Russia	3,577	4,319	3,346	3,365
Canada	155,893	168,201	134,210	151,767
Mexico	74,297	85,938	56,792	71,388
China	51,513	62,558	11,993	12,862
Japan	115,187	121,663	67,607	65,549
South Korea	22,655	23,173	26,621	25,046
Taiwan	29,907	32,629	18,460	20,366
Australia	3,869	4,602	12,008	12,063
Hong Kong	9,865	10,288	13,966	15,117
Singapore	20,341	20,075	16,720	17,696

COMMUNICATIONS

Roads. On 31 Dec. 1996 the total public road mileage was 3,933,985 miles (urban, 833,623; rural, 3,100,362), of which an estimated 60·8% was paved. Of the urban roads, 113,000 were state controlled and 719,000 under local control. 693,000 miles of rural roads were controlled by the states, about 2,238,000 miles of rural roads were under local control, and there were about 169,000 miles of federal park and forest roads. State highway funds were $71,736m. in 1996.

Motor vehicles registered in 1996: 206,365,000, including 138,203,000 automobiles, 701,000 buses and coaches, 64,756,000 trucks and 3,816,000 motor cycles and mopeds. There were 179,539,000 licensed drivers in 1996 (177·43m. in 1995 of which 87·2m. were females). The average distance travelled by a passenger car in the year 1995 was 11,330 miles. There were 41,907 deaths in road accidents in 1996 (39,250 in 1992). 1996 was the 4th consecutive year in which the number of road deaths went up.

Rail. Freight service is provided by 12 major independent railroad companies and several hundred smaller operators. Long-distance passenger trains are run by the National Railroad Passenger Corporation (Amtrak), which is federally assisted. Amtrak was set up in 1971 to maintain a basic network of long-distance passenger trains, and is responsible for almost all non-commuter services over some 38,000 route-km, of which it owns only 1,256 km (555 km electrified). Outside the major conurbations, there are almost no regular passenger services other than those of Amtrak, which carried 19,700,000 passengers in 1996. Passenger revenue for Amtrak (1996) was $756·2m.; revenue passenger miles, 5,066m.

Civil Aviation. There were 39 airports with more than 100,000 international enplanements in 1997. These were, in descending order: New York (John F. Kennedy), Miami, Los Angeles, Honolulu, San Francisco, Chicago (O'Hare), New York (Newark), Houston (George Bush), Guam, Atlanta (Hartsfield), Dallas/Fort Worth, Boston (Logan), Washington, D.C. (Dulles International), Detroit (Metropolitan-Wayne County), San Juan (Luis Muñoz Marin International), Orlando (Orlando International), Philadelphia, Anchorage, Saipan, Seattle-Tacoma, Minneapolis/St Paul, Fort Lauderdale (Hollywood), New York (La Guardia), Orlando (Sanford), Las Vegas (McCarran), Cincinnati (Northern Kentucky), Phoenix (Sky Harbor), Bangor, Baltimore (Baltimore/Washington), Charlotte, Portland, Denver, Tampa, San Jose, Pittsburgh, St Petersburg/Clearwater, San Diego (Lindbergh Field) and Kahului.

In 1995 Delta Air Lines carried the most passengers of any airline in the world, with 86,909,000 (7,810,000 on international flights), ahead of American Airlines, with 79,511,000 (16,638,000 on international flights) and United Airlines, with 78,665,000 (11,409,700 on international flights). American Airlines carried the most international passengers of any US carrier, ahead of United Airlines. American Airlines also flew the furthest of any carrier in the world in 1995, covering 1,479·8m. km, ahead of United Airlines, with 1,311·3m. km.

The busiest airport in 1996 was Chicago (O'Hare), which handled 69,154,000 passengers (61,935,000 on domestic flights). The second busiest was Atlanta, Hartsfield International, with 62,885,000 passengers (59,825,000 on domestic flights), followed by Los Angeles International, with 57,975,000 passengers (43,974,000 on domestic flights). As well as being the 3 busiest airports in the USA for passenger traffic in 1996, they are also the 3 busiest in the world. New York (John F. Kennedy) was the busiest airport in the USA for international passengers in 1996, with 17,453,000 (9th in the world), ahead of Miami International, with 14,913,000. The leading domestic routes for 1996 were New York to/from Los Angeles (3,149,020 passengers), New York to/from Chicago (2,996,460) and New York to/from Miami (2,777,610).

The leading airports in 1997 on the basis of aircraft departures completed were Dallas/Fort Worth (451,500); Chicago, O'Hare (446,300); Atlanta, Hartsfield International (392,900). The leading domestic routes for 1997 based on enplanements were New York to/from Los Angeles, Chicago to/from New York, Boston to/from New York, Honolulu to/from Kahului, and New York to/from Orlando.

US flag carriers in scheduled service had 594·7m. revenue passengers enplaned in 1997, with 599,300m. revenue passenger miles.

Shipping. On 1 Oct. 1994 US merchant ocean-going vessels were employed as follows: Active, 345 of 15·2m. DWT, of which 132 of 4·7m. DWT were foreign trade, 129 of 7·3m. DWT in domestic trade and 24 of 1·8m. DWT in foreign to foreign operations. Inactive vessels totalled 4·7m. DWT; 26 of 1·4m. DWT privately owned were laid up and 136 of 2·7m. DWT were Government-owned National Defense reserve fleet. Of the total vessels in the US fleet, 333 of 15·1m. DWT were privately owned.

US exports and imports carried on dry cargo and tanker vessels in 1994 totalled 899·1m. long tons, of which 35m. long tons were carried in US flag vessels. In 1995, 55,184 vessels entered, and 52,772 cleared, all US ports.

On 1 Oct. 1998 the US merchant marine included 473 ocean-going self-propelled merchant vessels of 1,000 gross tons or over, with an aggregate 16·8m. DWT. This included 156 tankers of 9·4m. DWT.

Telecommunications. Regional private companies formed from the American Telephone and Telegraph Co. after its dissolution in 1995 ('Baby Bells') operate the telephone, telegraph, telex and electronic transmission services system at the national and local levels. In 1997 main telephone lines numbered 172,452,500 (or 643·7 per 1,000 persons); there were 55,312,000 subscribers to cellular phones. There were 86·3m. PCs in 1995 (328 for every 1,000 persons) and 14,052,000 fax machines.

Legislation on the media and telecommunications of 1996 coming into force on 31 March 1999 aimed at deregulating the market while preserving safeguards against over-concentration of individual ownership: a single company may not control a network reaching more than 35% of TV viewers, or produce a newspaper and a television service in the same market. Local companies are now permitted to operate long-distance telephone services and also cable TV services. There were estimated to be 73m. Internet users in Oct. 1998, or 27% of the population.

Postal Services. The US Postal Service superseded the Post Office Department on 1 July 1971.

Postal business for the years ended 30 Sept. included the following items:

	1995	1996	1997	1998
Number of post offices	39,749	38,212	38,019	37,941
Operating revenue ($1,000)	54,293,000	56,402,000	58,132,600	54,873,000
Expenditures ($1,000)	50,730,200	53,112,500	60,192,256	58,385,426

SOCIAL INSTITUTIONS

Justice. Legal controversies may be decided in two systems of courts: The federal courts, with jurisdiction confined to certain matters enumerated in Article III of the Constitution, and the state courts, with jurisdiction in all other proceedings. The federal courts have jurisdiction exclusive of the state courts in criminal prosecutions for the violation of federal statutes, in civil cases involving the government, in bankruptcy cases and in admiralty proceedings, and have jurisdiction concurrent with the state courts over suits between parties from different states, and certain suits involving questions of federal law.

The highest court is the Supreme Court of the US, which reviews cases from the lower federal courts and certain cases originating in state courts involving questions of federal law. It is the final arbiter of all questions involving federal statutes and the Constitution; and it has the power to invalidate any federal or state law or executive action which it finds repugnant to the Constitution. This court, consisting of 9 justices appointed by the President who receive salaries of $164,100 a year (the Chief Justice, $171,500), meets from Oct. until June every year. For the term ended June 1996 it disposed of 6,692 cases, deciding 129 on their merits. In the remainder of cases it either summarily affirms lower court decisions or declines to review. A few suits, usually brought by state governments, originate in the Supreme Court, but issues of fact are mostly referred to a master.

The US courts of appeals number 13 (in 11 circuits composed of 3 or more states and 1 circuit for the District of Columbia and 1 Court of Appeals for the Federal Circuit); the 179 circuit judges receive salaries of $141,700 a year. Any party to a suit in a lower federal court usually has a right of appeal to one of these courts. In addition, there are direct appeals to these courts from many federal administrative agencies. In the year ending 30 June 1997, 53,742 appeals were filed in the courts of appeals, including 1,417 in the Federal Circuit.

UNITED STATES OF AMERICA

The trial courts in the federal system are the US district courts, of which there are 89 in the 50 states, 1 in the District of Columbia and 1 each in the Commonwealth of Puerto Rico and the Territories of the Virgin Islands, Guam and the Northern Marianas. Each state has at least 1 US district court, and 3 states have 4 apiece. Each district court has from 1 to 28 judgeships. There are 649 US district judges ($133,600 a year), who received 265,151 civil cases and 68,307 criminal defendants from 1 July 1996 to 30 June 1997.

In addition to these courts of general jurisdiction, there are special federal courts of limited jurisdiction. The US Court of Federal Claims (16 judges at $133,600 a year) decides claims for money damages against the federal government in a wide variety of matters; the Court of International Trade (9 judges at $133,600) determines controversies concerning the classification and valuation of imported merchandise.

The judges of all these courts are appointed by the President with the approval of the Senate; to assure their independence, they hold office during good behaviour and cannot have their salaries reduced. This does not apply to judges in the Territories, who hold their offices for a term of 10 years or to judges of the US Court of Federal Claims. The judges may retire with full pay at the age of 70 years if they have served a period of 10 years, or at 65 if they have 15 years of service, but they are subject to call for such judicial duties as they are willing to undertake. 11 US judges up to 1997 have been involved in impeachment proceedings, of whom 7 were convicted and removed from office.

In 1997, of the 265,151 civil cases filed in the district courts, 167,807 arose under various federal statutes (such as labour, social security, tax, patent, securities, antitrust and civil rights laws); 52,710 involved personal injury or property damage claims; 38,858 dealt with contracts; and 5,761 were actions concerning real property.

Among the 69,052 criminal defendants (48,682 criminal cases) filed in 1997 in the district courts, 25,090 persons were charged with alleged infractions of drug laws; 11,832 persons were charged with miscellaneous general offences; 11,664 with embezzlement and fraud; 4,089 for larceny and theft; 7,016 were charged with immigration violations; 1,763 with robbery; and 1,663 with forgery and counterfeiting and fraud.

Persons convicted of federal crimes may be fined, released on probation under the supervision of the probation officers of the federal courts, confined in prison, or confined in prison with a period of supervised release to follow, also under the supervision of probation officers of the federal courts. Federal prisoners are confined in 87 institutions incorporating various security levels that are operated by the Bureau of Prisons. Prisoners confined in Federal and State Prisons at June 1996, numbered 1,136,819 (6·1% women). In 1996 there were 615 inmates in prisons and jails per 100,000 population. By 1998 the figure had risen to 668 per 100,000.

The state courts have jurisdiction over all civil and criminal cases arising under state laws, but decisions of the state courts of last resort as to the validity of treaties or of laws of the USA, or on other questions arising under the Constitution, are subject to review by the Supreme Court of the US. The state court systems are generally similar to the federal system, to the extent that they generally have a number of trial courts and intermediate appellate courts, and a single court of last resort. The highest court in each state is usually called the Supreme Court or Court of Appeals with a Chief Justice and Associate Justices, usually elected but sometimes appointed by the Governor with the advice and consent of the State Senate or other advisory body; they usually hold office for a term of years, but in some instances for life or during good behaviour. The lowest tribunals are usually those of Justices of the Peace; many towns and cities have municipal and police courts, with power to commit for trial in criminal matters and to determine misdemeanours for violation of the municipal ordinances; they frequently try civil cases involving limited amounts of damages.

There were no executions from 1968 to 1976. The US Supreme Court had held the death penalty, as applied in general criminal statutes, to contravene the eighth and fourteenth amendments of the US constitution, as a cruel and unusual punishment when used so irregularly and rarely as to destroy its deterrent value. The death penalty was reinstated by the Supreme Court in 1976, but has not been authorized in Alaska, the District of Columbia, Hawaii, Iowa, Kansas, Maine, Massachusetts, Michigan, Minnesota, North Dakota, Rhode Island, Vermont, West

Virginia and Wisconsin. There were, in 1996, 3,219 prisoners under sentence of death. In 1997 there were 74 executions (45 in 1996).

Religion. The Yearbook of American and Canadian Churches, published by the National Council of the Churches of Christ in the USA, New York, gave the following figures available from official statisticians of church bodies: The principal religions (numerically or historically) or groups of religious bodies (in 1995) are shown below:

Protestant Churches	No. of churches	Membership (in 1,000)
Baptist bodies		
Southern Baptist Convention	40,039	15,663
National Baptist Convention, USA	33,000	8,200
National Baptist Convention of America, Inc.	2,500	3,500
American Baptist Churches in the USA	5,823	1,517
American Baptist Association	1,705	250
Conservative Baptist Association of America	1,084	200
Free Will Baptists	2,496	208
Baptist Missionary Association of America	1,355	231
Christian Church (Disciples of Christ)	4,036	930
Christian Churches and Churches of Christ	5,579	1,071
Church of the Nazarene	5,135	602
Churches of Christ	13,020	1,655
The Episcopal Church	7,415	2,537
Jehovah's Witnesses	10,541	966
Latter-Day Saints:		
Church of Jesus Christ of Latter-day Saints (Mormons)	10,417	4,923
Reorganized Church of Jesus Christ of Latter-day Saints	1,160	178
Lutheran bodies		
Evangelical Lutheran Church in America	10,955	5,190
The Lutheran Church-Missouri Synod	6,154	2,595
Wisconsin Evangelical Lutheran Synod	1,252	412
Mennonite churches:		
Mennonite Church	986	91
Old Order Amish	898	81
Methodist bodies:		
United Methodist Church	36,361	8,539
African Methodist Episcopal Church	8,000	3,500
African Methodist Episcopal Zion Church	3,098	1,231
Wesleyan Church (USA)	1,609	117
Pentecostal bodies:		
The Church of God in Christ	15,300	5,500
Assemblies of God	11,764	2,325
Church of God (Cleveland, Tenn.)	5,918	723
United Pentecostal Church International	3,730	550
Presbyterian bodies:		
Presbyterian Church (USA)	11,399	3,698
Presbyterian Church in America	1,263	258
Reformed Churches:		
Reformed Church in America	915	309
Christian Reformed Church in North America	737	211
The Salvation Army	1,222	443
United Church of Christ	6,264	1,555
Seventh-day Adventist Church	4,303	775
Roman Catholic Church	19,723	60,191
Orthodox Churches	1,750	5,302
Non-Christian Religions:		
Hindus	–	910
Baha'i	–	300
Islam[1]	–	5,100
Jews	2,876	4,300

[1]Figures include Canada.

Education. Elementary and secondary education is mainly a state responsibility. Each state and the District of Columbia has a system of free public schools, established by law, with courses covering 12 years plus kindergarten. There are 3 structural patterns in common use; the K8-4 plan, meaning kindergarten plus 8 elementary grades followed by 4 high school grades; the K6-3-3 plan, or kindergarten plus 6 elementary grades followed by a 3-year junior high school and a 3-year senior high school; and the K5-3-4 plan, kindergarten plus 5 elementary grades followed by a 3-year middle school and a 4-year high school. All plans lead to high-school graduation, usually at age 17 or 18. Vocational education is an integral part of secondary education. Some states also have 2-year colleges in which education is provided at a nominal cost. Each state has delegated a large degree of control of the educational programme to local school districts (numbering 14,883 in school year 1995–96), each with a board of education (usually 3 to 9 members) selected locally and serving mostly without pay. The school policies of the local school districts must be in accord with the laws and the regulations of their state Departments of Education. While regulations differ from one jurisdiction to another, in general it may be said that school attendance is compulsory from age 7 to 16.

'Charter schools' are legal entities outside the school boards administration. They retain the basics of public school education, but may offer unconventional curricula and hours of attendance. Founders may be parents, teachers, public bodies or commercial firms. Organization and conditions depend upon individual states' legislation. The first charter schools were set up in Minnesota in 1991.

The Census Bureau estimates that in Nov. 1979 only 1m. or 0·6% of the 170m. persons who were 14 years of age or older were unable to read and write; in 1930 the percentage was 4·8. In 1940 a new category was established—the 'functionally illiterate', meaning those who had completed fewer than 5 years of elementary schooling; for persons 25 years of age or over this percentage was 1·8 in March 1996 (for the Black population it was 2·3%); it was 0·9% for white and 0·4% for Blacks in the 25–29-year-old group. The Bureau reported that in March 1998, 82·8% of all persons 25 years old and over had completed 4 years of high school or more, and that 24·4% had completed 4 or more years of college. In the age group 25 to 29, 88·1% had completed 4 years of high school or more, and 27·3% had completed 4 or more years of college.

In the autumn of 1996, 14,300,000 students (7,956,000 women) were enrolled in 3,647 colleges and universities; 2,193,000 were first-time students. 35·5% of the population between the ages of 18 and 24 were enrolled in colleges and universities.

Public elementary and secondary school revenue is supplied from the county and other local sources (45·9% in 1995–96), state sources (47·5%) and federal sources (6·6%). In 1996–97 expenditure for public elementary and secondary education totalled about $310,200m., including $274,500m. for current operating expenses, $29,100m. for capital outlay and $6,600m. for interest on school debt. The current expenditure per pupil in average daily attendance was about $6,390. The total cost per pupil, also including capital outlay and interest, amounted to about $7,230.

In 1996–97 total expenditure on education came to about 7·3% of GDP. Estimated total expenditures for private elementary and secondary schools in 1996–97 were about $25,800m. In 1996–97 college and university spending totalled about $223,500m., of which about $140,000m. was spent by institutions under public control. The federal government contributed about 12% of total current-fund revenue; state governments, 23%; student tuition and fees, 28%; and all other sources, 37%.

Vocational education below college grade, including the training of teachers to conduct such education, has been federally aided since 1918. Federal support for vocational education in 1996–97 amounted to about $1,115m. Many public high schools offer vocational courses in addition to their usual academic programmes.

Summary of statistics of regular schools (public and private), teachers and pupils for 1996–97 (compiled by the US National Center for Education Statistics):

Schools by level	Number of schools[1]	Teachers (in 1,000)	Enrolment (in 1,000)
Elementary schools:			
Public	64,785	1,582	29,732
Private	25,153[2]	274	4,486
Secondary schools:			
Public	24,287	1,084	15,860
Private	10,942[2]	113	1,297

Schools by level	Number of schools[1]	Teachers (in 1,000)	Enrolment (in 1,000)
Higher education:			
Public	1,644	657	11,090
Private	2,003	278	3,210
Total	128,814	3,988	65,675

[1]Schools with both elementary and secondary grades are counted twice, once with the elementary and once with the secondary schools. [2]Data for 1995–96.

In the autumn of 1996 there were 18·8 pupils per teacher in public elementary schools in the USA and 14·6 pupils per teacher in public secondary schools.

Most of the private elementary and secondary schools are affiliated with religious denominations. In 1996–97 there were 7,005 Roman Catholic elementary schools with 1,885,000 pupils and 107,500 teachers, and 1,226 secondary schools with 612,000 pupils and 45,700 teachers.

During the school year 1996–97 high-school graduates numbered about 2,573,000 (of whom about 2,306,000 were from public schools). Institutions of higher education conferred about 1,166,000 bachelor's degrees during the year 1996–97, 528,000 associate's degrees; 402,000 master's degrees; 45,000 doctorates; and 80,000 first professional degrees. In 1996–97 the federal government provided $8,983m. in grants and work-study programmes and $27,081m. in loans and other financial assistance to students.

During the academic year 1997–98, 481,000 foreign students were enrolled in American colleges and universities. The countries with the largest numbers of students in American colleges were: Japan, 47,100; China, 47,000; South Korea, 42,900; India, 33,800; Taiwan, 30,900; Canada, 22,100.

In 1996–97, 99,400 US students were enrolled at colleges and universities abroad. The country attracting the most students from the USA was the United Kingdom, with 22,800.

School enrolment, Oct. 1996, embraced 94·0% of the children who were 5 and 6 years old; 97·7% of the children aged 7–13 years; 98·0% of those aged 14–15, 92·8% of those aged 16–17 and 61·5% of those aged 18–19.

The US National Center for Education Statistics estimates the total enrolment in the autumn of 1998 at all of the country's elementary, secondary and higher educational institutions (public and private) at 67·3m. (66·2m. in the autumn of 1997).

The number of teachers in regular public and private elementary and secondary schools in the autumn of 1998 was expected to increase slightly to 3,126,000. The average annual salary of public school teachers was $39,400 in 1997–98.

Health. Admission to the practice of medicine (for both doctors of medicine and doctors of osteopathic medicine) is controlled in each state by examining boards directly representing the profession and acting with authority conferred by state law. Although there are a number of variations, the usual time now required to complete training is 8 years beyond the secondary school with up to 3 or more years of additional graduate training. Certification as a specialist may require between 3 and 5 more years of graduate training plus experience in practice. In Jan. 1994 the estimated number of active physicians (MD and DO—in all forms of practice) in the USA, Puerto Rico and outlying US areas was 684,400.

Active dentists in Dec. 1994 numbered 190,000.

Number of hospitals listed by the American Hospital Association in 1996 was 6,201, with 1,062,000 beds (equivalent to 4 beds per 1,000 population). Of the total, 290 hospitals with 73,000 beds were operated by the federal government; 1,330 with 155,000 beds by state and local government; 3,045 with 598,000 beds by non-profit organizations (including church groups); 759 with 109,000 beds were investor-owned. The categories of non-federal hospitals were (1996): 5,143 short-term general and special hospitals with approximately 864,000 beds; 112 non-federal long-term general and special hospitals with 19,000 beds; 653 psychiatric hospitals with approximately 106,000 beds; 3 tuberculosis hospitals with (in 1995) 214 beds.

Patient admissions to community hospitals (1996) were 31,099,000; average daily census was 530,800. There were 505·5m. outpatient visits and 97·6m. emergencies.

Personal health-care costs in 1996 totalled $907,200m., distributed as follows: hospital care, $358,500m.; doctors, $202,100m.; nursing-home care, $78,500m.;

UNITED STATES OF AMERICA

drugs, $91,400m.; dentists, $47,600m.; medical durables, $13,300m.; home health care, $30,200m.; other personal health care, $27,600m. Total national health expenditure in 1996 amounted to $1,035·1bn.

Welfare. Social welfare legislation was chiefly the province of the various states until the adoption of the Social Security Act of 14 Aug. 1935. This as amended provides for a federal system of old-age, survivors and disability insurance; health insurance for the aged and disabled; supplemental security income for the aged, blind and disabled; federal state unemployment insurance; and federal grants to states for public assistance (medical assistance for the aged and aid to families with dependent children generally and for maternal and child health and child welfare services).

Legislation of Aug. 1996 began the transfer of aid administration back to the states, restricted the provision of aid to a maximum period of 5 years, and abolished benefits to immigrants (both legal and illegal) for the first 5 years of their residence in the USA. The Social Security Administration (formerly part of the Department of Health and Human Services but an independent agency since March 1995) has responsibility for the programmes—old-age, survivors and disability insurance and supplemental security income. The Administration for Children and Families (ACF), an agency of the Department of Health and Human Services, is responsible for federal programmes which promote the economic and social wellbeing of families, children, individuals and communities. ACF has federal responsibility for the following programmes: The Aid to Families with Dependent Children Program (providing cash assistance to family and children in the 50 states, the District of Columbia, Guam, Puerto Rico and the Virgin Islands); low income energy assistance; Head Start; child care; child protective services; and a community services block grant. The ACF also has federal responsibility for social service programmes for children, youth, native Americans and persons with developmental disabilities.

The Administration of Aging (AOA), an agency of the Department of Health and Human Services, serves older persons and their families with social, nutritional, education, and aging-related research and demonstration projects through the administration of the Older Americans Act. In addition, AOA is the focal point for aging policy within the Federal government. The Assistant Secretary for Aging is the primary advocate for the elderly in the USA. In 1995–96, $830m. was expended through a network of 57 State Units on Aging, 661 Area Agencies on Aging, 228 tribal organizations, 6,000 senior centres, and more than 27,000 service providers. More than 250m. meals were also provided through this programme.

The Health Care Financing Administration, an agency of the Health and Human Services Department, has federal responsibility for health insurance for the aged and disabled. Unemployment insurance is the responsibility of the Department of Labor.

In 1996 an average of 4,166,000 families were receiving payments under Aid to Families with Dependent Children (average monthly payment, $383 per family). Total payments under Aid to Families with Dependent Children were $20,411m. in 1996. The role of Child Support Enforcement is to ensure that children are supported by their parents. Money collected is for children who live with only one parent because of divorce, separation or out-of-wedlock birth. In 1996 approximately $12,020m. was collected on behalf of these children.

The Social Security Act provides for protection against the cost of medical care through Medicare, a two-part programme of health insurance for people age 65 and over, people of any age with permanent kidney failure, and for certain disabled people under age 65 who receive Social Security disability benefits. In 1995, payments totalling $116,400m. were made under the hospital portion of Medicare on behalf of 37m. people. During the same period, $65,000m. was paid under the voluntary medical insurance portion of Medicare on behalf of 36m. people.

In 1996 about 43·3m. beneficiaries were on the rolls; the average paid to a retired worker (not counting any benefits paid to his/her dependants) was about $724 per month. Full retirement benefits are now payable at age 65, with reduced benefits available as early as age 62. Beginning in 2000, the age for full retirement benefits will gradually increase until it reaches 67 in 2027.

In Dec. 1995, 6·5m. persons were receiving Supplementary Security Income payments, including 1·4m. persons aged 65 or over and over 5·1m. disabled or blind persons, of whom nearly 1m. were children. Payments, including supplemental amounts from various states, totalled $27,600m. in 1995.

In 1996 a total of $367,712m. was spent on cash and non-cash benefits (such as food stamps) for persons with limited incomes: 1,413,000 old-age persons received $28,792m. in benefits; 82,000 blind people received $4,507m.; and 5,119,000 disabled people received $23,906m. In 1997 the food stamp programme helped 22,799,000 persons at a cost of $19,504m.; and 25,903,000 persons received help from the national school lunch programme at a cost of $4,814m.

CULTURE

To mark the new Millennium, a non-stop three-day Party 2000 will take place on 6 sq. miles (16 sq. km) of land in southern California between Palm Springs and the Arizona border. It has described itself as ''The Biggest Concert and Party ever held on Planet Earth'' with ''the largest fireworks' display ever held in the world''. The projected budget is $1·1bn (£675m.).

In Times Square in New York City giant video screens will be positioned around the square, broadcasting footage of celebrations taking place around the world, beginning with the Fiji Islands at 7 a.m. EST.

Boston has developed the concept of the First Night alcohol-free celebrations, which have won support in well over 100 communities across the USA.

Broadcasting. The licensing agency for broadcasting stations is the Federal Communications Commission, an independent federal body composed of 5 Commissioners appointed by the President. Its regulatory activities comprise: allocation of spectrum space; consideration of applications to operate individual stations; and regulation of their operations. In 1996 there were 12,313 commercial radio stations, 1,174 commercial TV stations, 352 non-commercial TV stations and 11,119 cable TV systems. Programming is targeted to appeal to a given segment of the population or audience taste. There are 5 national TV networks (3 commercial; colour by NTSC) with 46 national cable networks. All major cities have network affiliates and additional commercial stations.

Legislation on the media and telecommunications of 1996 came into force on 31 March 1999 deregulating the market while preserving safeguards against over-concentration of individual ownership: a single company may not control a network reaching more than 35% of TV viewers, or produce a newspaper and a television service in the same market. Local companies are now permitted to operate long-distance telephone services and also cable TV services.

Broadcasting to countries abroad is conducted by The Voice of America, which functions under a 7-member council nominated by the President and reviewed by Congress. In 1996 Voice of America had 126m. listeners.

In 1996 there were 570m. radio receivers in use, equivalent to 2,115 per 1,000 inhabitants. No other country averaged more than 1,500 radios per 1,000. There were 217m. TV receivers in 1996, or 805 per 1,000 inhabitants—a figure only exceeded in Bermuda, with 1,041 per 1,000 in 1996.

Cinema. In Jan. 1994 there were 25,737 screens, including 850 drive-ins. 420 full-length films were made in 1995. An estimated 66% of adults went to the cinema in 1997.

Press. In 1997 there were 1,509 daily newspapers with a combined daily circulation of 56·7m., the second highest in the world behind Japan. These included 705 morning papers and 816 evening papers, and there were also 903 Sunday papers (circulation, 60·5m.). Unlike Japan, where circulation is rising, in the USA it has fallen since 1980, when daily circulation was 62·2m.

New books and editions published in 1996, 68,175.

Tourism. In 1996 the USA received 46,489,000 visitors, of whom 19,110,004 were classified as tourists. Of the 46,489,000 visitors, 15,301,000 were from Canada and 8,530,000 from Mexico. Tourists came mainly from Japan (3·62m.), the UK (2·49m.) and Germany (1·62m.). Nearly 40% of all tourists were from Europe.

In 1997 an estimated 46,216,000 visitors spent approximately $68,043m. (excluding transportation paid to US international carriers). The USA has the highest annual revenue from tourists of any country (more than twice as much as Italy, which with $28,673m. received the second most in 1996). Expenditure by US travellers in foreign countries for 1997 was an estimated $53,991m. (excluding transportation paid to foreign flag international carriers).

DIPLOMATIC REPRESENTATIVES
Of the USA in Great Britain (24/31 Grosvenor Sq., London, W1A 1AE)
Ambassador: Philip Lader.

Of Great Britain in the USA (3100 Massachusetts Ave., NW, Washington, D.C., 20008)
Ambassador: Sir Christopher. J. R. Meyer, KCMG.

Of the United States to the United Nations
Chargé d'Affaires a.i.: A. Peter Burleigh.

Of the United States to the European Union
Ambassador: Vernon Weaver.

FURTHER READING
OFFICIAL STATISTICAL INFORMATION
The Office of Management and Budget, Washington, D.C., 20503 is part of the Executive Office of the President; it is responsible for co-ordinating all the statistical work of the different Federal Government agencies. The Office does not collect or publish data itself. The main statistical agencies are as follows:

(1) Data User Services Division, Bureau of the Census, Department of Commerce, Washington, D.C., 20233. Responsible for decennial censuses of population and housing, quinquennial census of agriculture, manufactures and business; current statistics on population and the labour force, manufacturing activity and commodity production, trade and services, foreign trade, state and local government finances and operations. (*Statistical Abstract of the United States*, annual, and others).

(2) Bureau of Labor Statistics, Department of Labor, 441 G Street NW, Washington, D.C., 20212. (*Monthly Labor Review* and others).

(3) Information Division, Economic Research Service, Department of Agriculture, Washington, D.C., 20250. (*Agricultural Statistics*, annual, and others).

(4) National Center for Health Statistics, Department of Health and Human Services, 3700 East-West Highway, Hyattsville, MD 20782. (*Vital Statistics of the United States*, monthly and annual, and others).

(5) Bureau of Mines Office of Technical Information, Department of the Interior, Washington, D.C., 20241. (*Minerals Yearbook*, annual, and others).

(6) Office of Energy Information Services, Energy Information Administration, Department of Energy, Washington, D.C., 20461.

(7) Statistical Publications, Department of Commerce, Room 5062 Main Commerce, 14th St and Constitution Avenue NW, Washington, D.C., 20230; the Department's Bureau of Economic Analysis and its Office of Industry and Trade Information are the main collectors of data.

(8) Center for Education Statistics, Department of Education, 555 New Jersey Avenue NW, Washington, D.C., 20208.

(9) Public Correspondence Division, Office of the Assistant Secretary of Defense (Public Affairs P.C.), The Pentagon, Washington, D.C., 20301-1400.

(10) Bureau of Justice Statistics, Department of Justice, 633 Indiana Avenue NW, Washington, D.C., 20531.

(11) Public Inquiry, APA 200, Federal Aviation Administration, Department of Transportation, 800 Independence Avenue SW, Washington, D.C., 20591.

(12) Office of Public Affairs, Federal Highway Administration, Department of Transportation, 400 7th St. SW, Washington, D.C., 20590.

(13) Statistics Division, Internal Revenue Service, Department of the Treasury, 1201 E St. NW, Washington, D.C., 20224.

Statistics on the economy are also published by the Division of Research and Statistics, Federal Reserve Board, Washington, D.C., 20551; the Congressional Joint Committee on the Economy, Capitol; the Office of the Secretary, Department of the Treasury, 1500 Pennsylvania Avenue NW, Washington, D.C., 20220.

STATES AND TERRITORIES

OTHER OFFICIAL PUBLICATIONS

Economic Report of the President. Annual. Bureau of the Census. *Statistical Abstract of the United States*. Annual. *Historical Statistics of the United States, Colonial Times to 1970*.
United States Government Manual. Washington. Annual.

The official publications of the USA are issued by the US Government Printing Office and are distributed by the Superintendent of Documents, who issued in 1940 a cumulative *Catalog of the Public Documents of the. . . Congress and of All the Departments of the Government of the United States*. This *Catalog* is kept up to date by *United States Government Publications, Monthly Catalog* with annual index and supplemented by *Price Lists*. Each *Price List* is devoted to a special subject or type of material.

Treaties and other International Acts of the United States of America (Edited by Hunter Miller), 8 vols. Washington, 1929–48. This edition stops in 1863. It may be supplemented by *Treaties, Conventions. . . Between the US and Other Powers, 1776–1937* (Edited by William M. Malloy and others). 4 vols. 1909–38. A new Treaty Series, *US Treaties and Other International Agreements* was started in 1950.

Writings on American History. Washington, annual from 1902 (except 1904–5 and 1941–47).

NON-OFFICIAL PUBLICATIONS

The Cambridge Economic History of the United States. vol. 1–. CUP, 1996–

Brogan, H., *The Longman History of the United States of America*. London, 1985

Fawcett, E. and Thomas, T., *America and the Americans*. London, 1983

Foner, E. and Garraty, J. A. (eds.) *The Reader's Companion to American History*. New York, 1992

Haass, Richard, *The Reluctant Sheriff: The United States After the Cold War*. New York, 1998

Herstein, S. R. and Robbins, N., *United States of America*. [Bibliography] Oxford and Santa Barbara (CA), 1982

Lord, C. L. and E. H., *Historical Atlas of the US*. Rev. ed. New York, 1969

Jentleson, B. W. and Paterson, T. G. (eds.) *Encyclopedia of US Foreign Relations*. 4 vols. OUP, 1997

Merriam, L. A. and Oberly, J. (eds.) *United States History: an Annotated Bibliography*. Manchester Univ. Press, 1995

Morison, S. E. with Commager, H. S., *The Growth of the American Republic*. 2 vols. 5th ed. OUP, 1962–63

Norton, M. B., *People and Nation: the History of the United States*. 4th ed. 2 vols. New York, 1994

Pfucha, F. P., *Handbook for Research in American History: a Guide to Bibliographies and Other Reference Works*. 2nd ed. Nebraska Univ. Press, 1994

Who's Who in America. Annual

National library: The Library of Congress, Independence Ave. SE, Washington, D.C., 20540.
Librarian: James H. Billington.
National statistical office: Bureau of the Census, Washington, D.C., 20233.
Website: http://www.census.gov

STATES AND TERRITORIES

See also the section 'Local Government' under UNITED STATES.

Against the names of the Governors, Lieutenant-Governors and the Secretaries of State, (D.) stands for Democrat and (R.) for Republican.

Figures for the revenues, expenditures and debt outstanding of the various states are those of the Federal Bureau of the Census, which takes the original state figures and arranges them on a common pattern so that those of one state can be compared with those of any other.

FURTHER READING

Official publications of the various states and insular possessions are listed in the *Monthly Check-List of State Publications*, issued by the Library of Congress since 1910.

The Book of the States. Biennial. Council of State Governments, Lexington, 1953 ff.

State Government Finances. Annual. Dept. of Commerce, 1966 ff.

Bureau of the Census. *State and Metropolitan Area Data Book*. Irregular.—*County and City Data Book*. Irregular.

Hill, K. Q., *Democracy in the 50 States*. Nebraska Univ. Press, 1995

ALABAMA

KEY HISTORICAL EVENTS
The first European explorers were Spanish, including Hernando de Soto in 1540, but the first permanent European settlement was French, as part of French Louisiana after 1699. During the 17th and 18th centuries the British, Spanish and French all fought for control of the territory; it passed to Britain in 1763 and thence to the USA in 1783, except for a Spanish enclave on Mobile Bay, which lasted until 1813. Alabama was organized as a Territory in 1817 and was admitted to the Union as a state on 14 Dec. 1819.

The economy was then based on cotton, grown in white-owned plantations by black slave labour imported since 1719. Alabama seceded from the Union at the beginning of the Civil War (1861) and joined the Confederate States of America; its capital Montgomery became the Confederate capital. After the defeat of the Confederacy the state was readmitted to the Union in 1878. Attempts made during the reconstruction period to find a role for the newly freed black slaves—who made up about 50% of the population—largely failed, and when whites regained political control in the 1870s a strict policy of segregation came into force.

At the same time Birmingham began to develop as an important centre of iron- and steel-making. Most of the state was still rural. In 1915 a boll-weevil epidemic attacked the cotton and forced diversification into other farm produce. More industries developed from the power schemes of the Tennessee Valley Authority in the 1930s.

The black population remained mainly rural, poor and without political power, until the 1960s when confrontations on the issue of civil rights produced reforms.

TERRITORY AND POPULATION
Alabama is bounded in the north by Tennessee, east by Georgia, south by Florida and the Gulf of Mexico and west by Mississippi. Land area, 50,750 sq. miles (131,443 sq. km). Census population, 1 April 1990, 4,040,587 (60·4% urban), an increase of 3·87% since 1980. Population estimate (1997), 4,319,000 (of the total population in 1995, 48·0% were male).

Population in 5 census years was:

	White	Black	Indian	Asiatic	Total	Per sq. mile
1930	1,700,844	944,834	465	105	2,646,248	51·3
1960	2,283,609	980,271	1,726	915	3,266,521	64·0
			All others			
1970	2,533,831	903,467	6,867		3,444,165	66·7
1980	2,872,621	996,335	24,932		3,893,888	74·9
1990	2,975,797	1,020,705	44,085		4,040,587	79·6

Of the total population in 1990, 47·9% were male, 60·4% were urban and 68·7% were 21 years or older.

The large cities (1994 estimate) were: Birmingham, 264,527 (metropolitan area, 872,834); Mobile, 204,490 (512,657); Montgomery (the capital), 195,471 (312,141); Huntsville, 170,984 (316,909); Tuscaloosa, 79,797 (156,422).

SOCIAL STATISTICS
Births, 1995, 60,264 (14·7 per 1,000 population); deaths, 42,321 (10·3); infant deaths (under 1 year), 592 (9·8 per 1,000 live births); marriages, 42,234 (10·3); divorces, 25,813 (6·3).

CLIMATE
Birmingham, Jan. 46°F (7·8°C), July 80°F (26·7°C). Annual rainfall 54" (1,346 mm). Mobile, Jan. 52°F (11·1°C), July 82°F (27·8°C). Annual rainfall 63" (1,577 mm). Montgomery, Jan. 49°F (9·4°C), July 81°F (27·2°C). Annual rainfall 53" (1,321 mm). The growing season ranges from 190 days (north) to 270 days (south). Alabama belongs to the Gulf Coast climate zone (see UNITED STATES: Climate).

CONSTITUTION AND GOVERNMENT
The present constitution dates from 1901; it has had 658 amendments (as at Nov. 1998). The legislature consists of a Senate of 35 members and a House of

ALABAMA

Representatives of 105 members, all elected for 4 years. The Governor and Lieut.-Governor are elected for 4 years.

The state is represented in Congress by 7 representatives. Applicants for registration must take an oath of allegiance to the United States and fill out a questionnaire to the satisfaction of the registrars.

Montgomery is the capital.

RECENT ELECTIONS
In the 1996 presidential election Dole polled 769,044 votes; Clinton, 662,165; Perot, 92,149.

CURRENT ADMINISTRATION
Governor: Don Siegelman (D.), 1999–2003 ($87,643).
  Lieut.-Governor: Steve Windom (R.), ($3,780).
  Secretary of State: Jim Bennett (R.), ($61,779).

ECONOMY
Budget. In 1996 total revenue was $12,741m. Total expenditure was $12,127m. (education, $4,872m.; public welfare, $2,325m.; health and hospitals, $1,330m.; highways, $881m.; police protection, $87m.) Debt outstanding (1996) amounted to $3,645m.

Per capita income (1997, preliminary) was $20,842.

ENERGY AND NATURAL RESOURCES
Water. The total area covered by water is approximately 1,486 sq. miles.

Minerals. Principal minerals, 1995 (in net 1,000 tons): limestone, 30,484; coal, 24,640; sand and gravel, 10,039. Value of non fuel mineral production (1997) was $805m.

Agriculture. The number of farms in 1995 was some 47,000, covering 10·2m. acres; the average farm had 217 acres and was valued at $1,262 per acre in 1995.

Cash receipts from farm marketings, 1996: crops, $815m.; livestock and poultry products, $2,363m.; and total, $3,178m. Principal sources: broilers, cattle and calves, eggs, hogs, dairy products, greenhouses and nurseries, peanuts, soybeans, cotton and vegetables. In 1994 broilers accounted for the largest percentage of cash receipts from farm marketings; cattle and calves were second, eggs third, cotton fourth.

Forestry. Area of national forest lands, 1996, 663,000 acres. Area of commercial timberland, 1990, 21,931,600 acres, of which 1,161,700 acres were public forests and 20,769,900 acres private forests. Harvest volumes in 1995, 294·12m. cu. ft softwood saw timber, 78·63m. cu. ft hardwood saw timber, 744·47m. cu. ft paper fibre and 11·74m. cu. ft poles. Total harvest, 1994, was 1,128·9m. cu. ft. The estimated delivered timber value of forest products in 1994 was $1,359m.

INDUSTRY
Alabama is both an industrial and service-oriented state. The chief industries are paper, lumber and wood products, primary metals, fabricated metal products, industrial machinery and equipment, transportation equipment, and electronic and electric equipment.

Labour. In 1997, 1,863,200 were employed in non-agricultural sectors, of which 345,700 were in government; 427,200 in trade; 427,900 in services; 91,000 in transport and public utilities; 380,100 in manufacturing; 96,800 in construction.

COMMUNICATIONS
Roads. Paved roads of all classes in 1996 totalled 70,255 miles; total highways, 93,337 miles. Registered motor vehicles, 1996, 4,315,381.

Rail. At Sept. 1997 the railways had a length of 5,072 miles including side and yard tracks.

Civil Aviation. In 1997 the state had 98 public-use airports. Eight airports are for commercial service, three are relief airports for Birmingham and the rest, general aviation.

Shipping. There are 1,600 miles of navigable inland water and 50 miles of Gulf Coast. The only deep-water port is Mobile, with a large ocean-going trade; total tonnage (1997), 36·3m. tons. The Alabama State Docks also operates a system of 10 inland docks; there are several privately run inland docks.

SOCIAL INSTITUTIONS

Justice. In 1997 there were 374 law enforcement agencies and 5 state agencies employing 9,855 sworn and 4,861 civilian people. There were 207,509 offences reported of which 21% were cleared by arrest. Total property value stolen was $193,865,821 of which 21% was recovered. In total, for past and present felony and misdemeanour crimes, there were 35,442 people arrested for Part I offences, 189,447 for Part II offences, 16,345 for drug violations, and 42,206 for alcohol violations. As of 30 Sept. 1997 there were 22,240 people in prison or community-based facilities; 32,664 people on probation and/or parole; and 158 were on death row awaiting execution. Following the reinstatement of the death penalty by the US Supreme Court in 1976, death sentences have been awarded since 1983.

In 41 counties the sale of alcoholic beverage is permitted, and in 26 counties it is prohibited; but it is permitted in 8 cities within those 26 counties. Draught beverages are permitted in 22 counties.

Religion. Membership in selected religious bodies (in 1993): Southern Baptist Convention (1,049,441), Black Baptist (estimated 315,331), United Methodist Church (264,968), African Methodist Episcopal Zion Church (134,305), Roman Catholic (137,834 adherents), Churches of Christ (91,660), Assemblies of God (38,442).

Education. In the school year 1995–96 the 1,333 public elementary and high schools required 43,796 teachers to teach 735,912 students enrolled in grades K-12. The average salary of public school teachers (1994–95) was $31,144. In 1995–96 there were 16 public senior institutions with 127,465 students and 4,887 faculty members. As of autumn 1997–98 the 19 community colleges had 74,070 students and 3,805 faculty members; 2 public junior colleges had 3,467 students and 180 faculty members; 10 public technical colleges had 9,274 students and 550 faculty members.

Health. In 1996 there were 123 hospitals licensed by the State Board of Health, 7 exempt from licensure with a total of 20,663 beds. In 1992 there were 5,281 patients in hospitals for mental illness and 1,449 residents in facilities for the mentally retarded.

Welfare. In June 1997 Alabama paid supplements (to federal welfare payments) to 684 recipients of old-age assistance, receiving an average of $49·52 each; 772 permanently and totally disabled, $55·68; 19 blind, $48·79. Combined state–federal aid to dependent children was paid to 31,981 families, average $139·96 per family.

CULTURE

Tourism. In 1997 tourists spent approximately $5bn. in Alabama, representing an increase of 4% over 1996 spending.

FURTHER READING

Alabama Official and Statistical Register. Montgomery. Quadrennial
Alabama County Data Book. Alabama Dept. of Economic and Community Affairs. Annual
Directory of Health Care Facilities. Alabama State Board of Health
Economic Abstract of Alabama. Center for Business and Economic Research, Univ. of Alabama, 1992
McCurley, R. L., Jr., ed., *The Legislative Process.* Alabama Law Institute, 3rd ed., 1984
Thigpen, R. A., *Alabama Government Manual.* Alabama Law Institute, 7th ed., 1986
Wiggins, S. W., (ed.) *From Civil War to Civil Rights, 1860–1960.* Univ. of Alabama Press, 1987

ALASKA

KEY HISTORICAL EVENTS
Discovered in 1741 by Vitus Bering, Alaska's first settlement, on Kodiak Island, was in 1784. The area known as Russian America with its capital (1806) at Sitk was ruled by a Russo-American fur company and vaguely claimed as a Russian colony. Alaska was purchased by the United States from Russia under the treaty of 30 March 1867 for $7·2m. Settlement was boosted by gold workers in the 1880s. In 1884 Alaska became a 'district' governed by the code of the state of Oregon. By Act of Congress approved 24 Aug. 1912 Alaska became an incorporated Territory; its first legislature in 1913 granted votes to women, 7 years in advance of the Constitutional Amendment.

During the Second World War the Federal Government acquired large areas for defence purposes and for the construction of the strategic Alaska Highway. In the 1950s oil was found. Alaska became the 49th state of the Union on 3 Jan. 1959.

In the 1970s new oilfields were discovered and the Trans-Alaska pipeline was opened in 1977. The state obtained most of its income from petroleum by 1985.

Questions of land-use predominate; there are large areas with valuable mineral resources, other large areas held for the native peoples and some still held by the Federal Government. The population increased by over 400% between 1940 and 1980.

TERRITORY AND POPULATION
Alaska is bounded north by the Beaufort Sea, west and south by the Pacific and east by Canada. The land area is 570,374 sq. miles (1,477,268 sq. km). Census population, 1 April 1990, was 550,043 (67·5% urban), including military personnel, an increase of 37·4% over 1980. Population estimate (1997), 609,000.

Population in 5 census years was:

	White	Black	All Others	Total	Per sq. mile
1950	92,808	...	35,835	128,643	0·23
1960	174,649	...	51,518	226,167	0·40
1970	236,767	8,911	54,704	300,382	0·53
1980	309,728	13,643	78,480	401,851	1·00
1990	415,492	22,451	112,100	550,043	1·00

Of the total population in 1990, 52·7% were male, 67·5% were urban and 68·7% were aged 18 years or over.

The largest city is in the borough of Anchorage, which had a 1990 census population of 226,338 and an estimated 1994 population of 254,000. Census populations of the other 13 boroughs, 1990: Aleutians East, 2,464; Bristol Bay, 1,410; Fairbanks North Star, 77,720; Haines, 2,117; Juneau, 26,751; Kenai Peninsula, 40,802; Ketchikan Gateway, 13,828; Kodiak Island, 13,309; Lake and Peninsula, 1,668; Matanuska-Susitna 39,683; North Slope, 5,979; Northwest Arctic, 6,113; Sitka, 8,588. Other Census Area populations, 1990: Aleutians West, 9,478; Bethel, 13,656; Dillingham, 4,012; Nome, 8,288; Prince of Wales-Outer Ketchikan, 6,278; Skagway-Yakutat-Angoon, 4,385; Southeast Fairbanks, 5,913; Valdez-Cordova, 9,952; Wade Hampton, 5,791; Wrangell-Petersburg, 7,042; Yukon-Koyukuk, 8,478. In 1995 there were 16 boroughs and 145 incorporated cities.

SOCIAL STATISTICS
Births, 1995, 10,244 (17 per 1,000 population); deaths, 3,000 (4·2); infant mortality rate, 7·7 per 1,000 live births. Marriages (1996, provisional), 5,400; divorces, 2,800.

CLIMATE
Anchorage, Jan. 12°F (−11·1°C), July 57°F (13·9°C). Annual rainfall 15" (371 mm). Fairbanks, Jan. −11°F (−23·9°C), July 60°F (15·6°C). Annual rainfall 12" (300 mm). Sitka, Jan. 33°F (0·6°C), July 55°F (12·8°C). Annual rainfall 87" (2,175 mm). Alaska belongs to the Pacific Coast climate zone (see UNITED STATES: Climate).

CONSTITUTION AND GOVERNMENT
The state has the right to select 103·55m. acres of vacant and unappropriated public lands in order to establish 'a tax basis'; it can open these lands to prospectors for

minerals, and the state is to derive the principal advantage in all gains resulting from the discovery of minerals. In addition, certain federally administered lands reserved for conservation of fisheries and wild life have been transferred to the state. Special provision is made for federal control of land for defence in areas of high strategic importance.

The constitution of Alaska was adopted by public vote, 24 April 1956. The state legislature consists of a Senate of 20 members (elected for 4 years) and a House of Representatives of 40 members (elected for 2 years). The state sends 1 representative to Congress. The franchise may be exercised by all citizens over 18.

The capital is Juneau.

RECENT ELECTIONS

In the 1996 presidential election Dole polled 101,234 votes; Clinton, 66,508; Perot, 21,536.

CURRENT ADMINISTRATION

Governor: Tony Knowles (D.), 1998–2002 ($81,648).
   Lieut.-Governor: Fran Ulmer (D.), ($76,188).

ECONOMY

Budget. In 1996 total revenue was $8,254m. Total expenditure was $5,630m. (education, $1,236m.; public welfare, $713m.; health and hospitals, $191m.; highways, $623m.; police protection, $53m.) Outstanding debt (1996) stood at $3,177m.

Per capita personal income (1997, preliminary) was $25,305.

ENERGY AND NATURAL RESOURCES

Oil and Gas. Commercial production of crude petroleum began in 1959 and by 1961 had become the most important mineral by value. Production: 1997, 473m. bbls. (of US gallons). Proven reserves at 31 Dec. 1997 were 5,161m. bbls. Oil comes mainly from Prudhoe Bay, the Kuparuk River field and several Cook Inlet fields. Revenue to the state from petroleum in 1993 was $2,684·8m. (87% of general fund revenues). General fund unrestricted revenues, 1993: Severance taxes, 33%; oil and gas royalties, 25%; investment earnings, 2%; other oil and gas, 27%; non-petroleum, 13%. In 1996, 9,294bn. cu. ft of natual gas was produced. Natural gas (liquid) production, 1997, 35m. bbls. Proven reserves as at 31 Dec. 1997, 631m. bbls.

Oil from the Prudhoe Bay Arctic field is now carried by the Trans-Alaska pipeline to Prince William Sound on the south coast, where a tanker terminal has been built at Valdez.

Water. The total area covered by water is approximately 44,856 sq. miles.

Minerals. Estimated value of production, 1994, in $1,000: Gold, 70,291; silver, 10,391; lead, 25,513; zinc, 296,103; industrial minerals (including sand, gravel and building stone), 68,009; coal, 36,750; peat, 439·5. Total 1994 value, $507·5m. Value of nonfuel mineral production (1997), $827m.

Agriculture. In some parts of the state the climate during the brief spring and summer (about 100 days in major areas and 152 days in the south-eastern coastal area) is suitable for agricultural operations, thanks to the long hours of sunlight, but Alaska is a food-importing area. In 1995 about 1m. acres was farmland and there were (in 1994) 520 farms and ranches with annual sales of $1,000 or more; crops covered 28,940 acres. In 1997 the average farm had 1,804 acres.

Total value of agricultural products in 1994: $27,766,000 of which $2,828,000 was from feed crops, $2,738,000 from vegetables (including potatoes), $6·1m. from livestock and poultry, $2,465,000 from dairy products and $15,833,000 from greenhouse and nursery industries. Net income from farms in 1996 was $10m.

At 1 Jan. 1995 there were 9,900 cattle and calves and 1,700 sheep and lambs; at 1 Dec. 1994, 2,000 hogs and pigs and 2,000 poultry. There were about 33,000 reindeer in western Alaska in 1994. Sales of reindeer meat and by-products in 1994 were valued at $1,366,000.

Forestry. Of the 129m. forested acres of Alaska, 24m. acres are classified as timberland or commercial forest. The interior forest covers 115m. acres; more than

ALASKA

13m. acres are considered commercial forest, of which 3·4m. acres are in designated parks or wilderness and unavailable for harvest. The coastal rain forests provide the bulk of commercial timber volume; of their 13·6m. acres, 7·6m. acres support commercial stands, of which 1·9m. acres are in parks or wilderness and unavailable for harvest. In 1992, 590m. bd ft of timber were harvested from private land for a total value of $548·9m., and in 1993, 9·38m. bd ft from state land for $342·6m.

There are 624 designated wilderness areas throughout the USA, covering a total of 104m. acres (42m. ha). Nearly 56% of the system is in Alaska (58·18m acres or 23·54m. ha).

Fisheries. The catch for 1993 was 2·7m. lbs of fish and shellfish having a value to fishermen of $905m. The most important species are salmon, crab, herring, halibut and pollock.

INDUSTRY
The largest manufacturing sectors are wood processing, seafood products and printing and publishing.

Labour. Total non-agricultural employment, 1995, 280,000. Employees by branch, 1995 (in 1,000): government service, 69; trade, 58·1; services, 63·4; construction, 15·5; manufacturing, 26·2; mining including oil and gas, 9·9; transport, communication and utilities, 25·3; finance, insurance and property, 12·6.

COMMUNICATIONS
Roads. Alaska's highway and road system, 1996, totalled 13,255 miles. Registered motor vehicles, 1996, 531,000.

The Alaska Highway extends 1,523 miles from Dawson Creek, British Columbia, to Fairbanks, Alaska. It was built by the US Army in 1942, at a cost of $138m. The greater portion of it, because it lies in Canada, is maintained by Canada.

Rail. There is a railway of 111 miles from Skagway to the town of Whitehorse, the White Pass and Yukon route, in the Canadian Yukon region (this service operates seasonally). The government-owned Alaska Railroad runs from Seward to Fairbanks, a distance of 471 miles. This is a freight service with only occasional passenger use. A passenger service operates from Anchorage to Fairbanks via Denali National Park in the tourist season.

Civil Aviation. Commercial passengers by air from Alaska's largest international airports Anchorage and Fairbanks in fiscal year 1994 numbered 4,358,437 at Anchorage and 721,496 at Fairbanks. General aviation aircraft in the state per 1,000 population is about 10 times the US average.

Shipping. Regular shipping services to and from the USA are furnished by 2 steamship and several barge lines operating out of Seattle and other Pacific coast ports. A Canadian company also furnishes a regular service from Vancouver, BC. Anchorage is the main port.

A 1,435 nautical-mile ferry system for motor cars and passengers (the 'Alaska Marine Highway') operates from Bellingham, Washington and Prince Rupert (British Columbia) to Juneau, Haines (for access to the Alaska Highway) and Skagway. A second system extends throughout the south-central region of Alaska linking the Cook Inlet area with Kodiak Island and Prince William Sound.

SOCIAL INSTITUTIONS
Justice. There is no death penalty in Alaska. In 1996 there were 3,716 prisoners in state and federal institutions.

Religion. Many religions are represented, including the Russian Orthodox, Roman Catholic, Episcopalian, Presbyterian, Methodist and other denominations.

Education. Total expenditure on public schools in fiscal year 1994 was $896,307,252. In 1994 there were 7,195 teachers; average salary, fiscal year 1994, $46,263. In 1994 there were 121,396 pupils enrolled at public schools. The University of Alaska (founded in 1922) main campuses had (autumn 1993) 33,087 students. Other colleges had 2,718 students in autumn 1993.

Health. In 1993 there were 27 acute care hospitals with 1,892 beds, of which 7 were federal public health hospitals and 1 mental hospital. Many hospitals offer mental health services and most communities have mental health services and/or centres.

Welfare. Old-age assistance was established under the Federal Social Security Act; in 1993 aid to dependent children covered a monthly average of 11,300 households; payments, an average of $834 per month; aid to the disabled was given to a monthly average of 4,698 persons receiving on average $348 per month. An average of 3,666 aged per month received $351.

CULTURE

Tourism. About 1·05m. tourists visited the state in 1993.

FURTHER READING

Statistical Information: Department of Commerce and Economic Development, Economic Analysis Section, POB 110804, Juneau 99811. Publishes *The Alaska Economy Performance Report.*

Alaska Industry–Occupation Outlook to 1995, Department of Labor, Juneau.
Annual Financial Report, Department of Administration, Juneau.
Falk, M., *Alaska.* [Bibliography]. Oxford and Santa Barbara (CA), 1995
Gardey, J., *Alaska: The Sophisticated Wilderness.* London, 1976
Hulley, Clarence C., *Alaska Past and Present.* Portland, Oregon, 1970
Hunt, W. R., *Alaska: a Bicentennial History.* New York, 1976
Naske, C.-M. and Slotnick, H. E., *Alaska: a History of the 49th State.* 2nd ed. Univ. of Oklahoma Press, 1995
Thomas, L., Jr., *Alaska and the Yukon.* New York, 1983
Tourville, M., *Alaska: a Bibliography, 1570–1970.* 1971

State library: POB 110571, Juneau, Alaska 99811-0571.

ARIZONA

KEY HISTORICAL EVENTS

Spaniards looking for sources of gold or silver entered Arizona in the 16th century, finding there people from several Native American groups, including Tohono O'odham, Navajo, Hopi and Apache. The first Spanish Catholic mission was founded in the early 1690s by Father Eusebio Kino, settlements were made in 1752 and a Spanish army headquarters was set up at Tucson in 1776. The area was governed by Mexico after the collapse of Spanish colonial power. Mexico ceded it to the USA in the Treaty of Guadelupe Hidalgo after the Mexican-American war (1848). Arizona was then part of New Mexico; the Gadsden Purchase (of land south of the Gila River) was added to it in 1853. The whole was organized as the Arizona Territory on 24 Feb. 1863.

Miners and ranchers began settling in the 1850s. Conflicts between Indian and immigrant populations intensified when troops were withdrawn to serve in the Civil War. The Navajo surrendered in 1865, but the Apache continued to fight, under Geronimo and other leaders, until 1886. Arizona was admitted to the Union as the 48th state in 1912.

Large areas of the state have been retained as Indian reservations and as parks to protect the exceptional desert and mountain landscape. In recent years this landscape and the Indian traditions have been used to attract tourist income.

TERRITORY AND POPULATION

Arizona is bounded north by Utah, east by New Mexico, south by Mexico, west by California and Nevada. Area, 114,006 sq. miles (295,276 sq. km), including 364 sq. miles (943 sq. km) of inland water. Of the total area in 1992, 28% was Indian Reservation, 17% was in individual or corporate ownership, 19% was held by the US Bureau of Land Management, 15% by the US Forest Service, 13% by the State and 8% by others. Census population on 1 April 1990 was 3,665,228 (87·5% urban), an increase of 34·92% over 1980. Population estimate (1996), 4,462,300.

Population in 5 census years:

	White	Black	Indian	Chinese	Japanese	Total	Per sq. mile
1910	171,468	2,009	29,201	1,305	371	204,354	1·8
1930	378,551	10,749	43,726	1,110	879	435,573	3·8
	White	Black	Indian	Chinese	Japanese	Total	Per sq. mile
1960	1,169,517	43,403	83,387	2,937	1,501	1,302,161	11·3
				All others			
1980	2,260,288	74,159	162,854	383,768		2,718,215	23·9
1990	2,963,186	110,524	203,527	387,991		3,665,228	32·3

Of the population in 1990, 1,810,691 (49·4%) were male, 3,206,973 (87·5%) were urban and 2,684,109 (73·2%) were aged 18 and over.

The 1996 estimated population of Phoenix was 1,180,740; Tucson, 449,635; Mesa, 343,710; Glendale, 186,697; Scottsdale, 178,525; Tempe, 156,000; Chandler, 141,735; Peoria, 78,310; Gilbert, 67,440; Yuma, 63,150.

SOCIAL STATISTICS
In 1996: births, 75,094; deaths, 36,579; infant deaths, 576; marriages, 39,611; dissolutions of marriages, 26,483.

CLIMATE
Phoenix, Jan. 53·6°F (12°C), July 93·5°F (34°C). Annual rainfall 7·66" (194 mm). Yuma, Jan. 56·5°F (13·6°C), July 93·7°F (34·3°C). Annual rainfall 3·17" (80 mm). Flagstaff, Jan. 38·3°F (3·5°C), July 82·7°F (27·8°C). Annual rainfall 15·72" (396 mm). Arizona belongs to the Mountain States climate zone (*see* UNITED STATES: Climate).

CONSTITUTION AND GOVERNMENT
The state constitution (1911, with 129 amendments) placed the government under direct control of the people through the initiative, referendum and the recall provisions. The state Senate consists of 30 members, and the House of Representatives of 60, all elected for 2 years. Arizona sends to Congress 6 representatives.

The state capital is Phoenix. The state is divided into 15 counties.

RECENT ELECTIONS
In the 1996 presidential election Clinton polled 653,288 votes; Dole, 622,073; Perot, 112,072.

CURRENT ADMINISTRATION
Governor: Jane Dee Hull (R.), 1999–2003 ($95,000).
   Secretary of State: Betsey Bayless (R.), ($70,000).

ECONOMY
Budget. In 1996 total revenue was $12,594m. Total expenditure was $11,898m. (education, $3,788m.; public welfare, $2,605m.; health and hospitals, $600m.; highways, $1,143m.; police protection, $120m.) Debt outstanding (1996) was $2,936m.
   Per capita personal income (1997, preliminary) was $22,364.

ENERGY AND NATURAL RESOURCES
Water. The total area covered by water is approximately 364 sq. miles.

Minerals. The mining industry historically has been and continues to be a significant part of the economy. By value the most important mineral produced is copper. Production (1996) 1,356,000 tons. Most of the state's silver and gold are recovered from copper ore. Other minerals include sand and gravel, molybdenum, coal and gemstones. Total value of minerals mined in 1996 was $4,487m.

Agriculture. Arizona, despite its dry climate, is well suited for agriculture along the water-courses and where irrigation is practised on a large scale from great reservoirs constructed by the USA as well as by the state government and private interests. Irrigated area, 1992, 956,454 acres. The wide pasture lands are favourable for the rearing of cattle and sheep, but numbers are either stationary or declining compared with 1920.

In 1996 Arizona contained 7,500 farms and ranches and the total farm and pastoral area was 35·4m. acres. In 1992 there were 1,344,091 acres of crop land. The average farm was estimated in 1996 at 4,720 acres. Farming is highly commercialized and mechanized and concentrated largely on cotton picked by machines operated by Indian, Mexican and migratory workers.

Area under cotton (1995): Upland cotton, 365,000 acres (793,000 bales harvested); American Pima cotton, 48,600 acres (72,200 bales harvested).

Cash income, 1995, from crops, $1,445,568,000; from livestock and products, $810,318,000. Most important cereals are wheat, corn and barley; most important crops include cotton, citrus fruit, lettuce, broccoli, grapes, cauliflower, melons, onions, potatoes and carrots. In 1995 there were 850,000 cattle, 135,000 sheep, 125,000 hogs, 52,000 goats and 330,000 chickens.

Forestry. The national forests in the state had an area (1997) of 11,250,000 acres.

INDUSTRY

In the first quarter of 1997 the state had an average of 4,903 manufacturing employers with an average of 202,812 employees earning total wages of $2,022,035,640 for the quarter.

COMMUNICATIONS

Roads. As of 31 Dec. 1996 there were 54,895 miles of public roads and streets and 3,476,893 motor vehicles were registered.

Civil Aviation. Registered landing facilities, 1997, numbered 294, of which 83 were for public use; 5,347 aircraft were registered.

SOCIAL INSTITUTIONS

Justice. A 'right-to-work' amendment to the constitution, adopted 5 Nov. 1946, makes illegal any concessions to trade-union demands for a 'closed shop'.

The Arizona state prison held 21,725 male and 1,555 female prisoners on 30 June 1997. Chain gangs were reintroduced into prisons in 1995. The death penalty is authorized; the last execution was on 25 June 1997.

Religion. The leading religious bodies are Roman Catholics and Latter-day Saints (Mormons); others include United Methodists, Presbyterians, Baptists, Lutherans, Episcopalians, Eastern Orthodox, Jews and Moslems.

Education. School attendance is compulsory between the ages of 6 and 16. In 1995–96 K-12 enrolment numbered 761,410 students. There are 227 school districts containing 964 elementary schools and 183 high schools. Charter schools first opened their doors in 1995. There are 46 charter schools providing parents and students with expanded educational choices. In 1995–96 the total funds appropriated by the state legislature for all education, including the Board of Regents and community colleges, was $2,511,527,000. The state maintains 3 universities: the University of Arizona (Tucson) with an enrolment of 30,740 in autumn 1997; Arizona State University (3 campuses) with 43,105; Northern Arizona University (Flagstaff) with 17,183.

Health. In 1996 there were 87 hospitals; capacity 12,311 beds; 14,179 licensed physicians and 3,029 dentists, 67,217 registered nurses and 20,669 licensed practical nurses.

Welfare. Old-age assistance (maximum depending on the programme) is given to needy citizens 65 years of age or older through the federal supplemental security income (SSI) programme. In March 1997, SSI payments went to 13,534 aged (average $234·01 each), 61,486 disabled (average $388·41 each) and 993 blind people (average $375·85 each). In Sept. 1997, 134,827 people (average $104·87 each) in 49,201 families (average $287·37 each) received Aid for Families with Dependent Children.

CULTURE

Tourism. In 1995, 27·2m. tourists visited Arizona; tourism-related jobs, direct and indirect (1995), 300,001; total taxes attributed to tourism for 1995, $228,332,135.

FURTHER READING

Statistical information: College of Business and Public Administration, Univ. of Arizona, Tucson 85721. Publishes *Arizona Statistical Abstract.*
Arizona Commission of Indian Affairs. *Resource Directory, 1997/98.* Phoenix, 1998
Arizona Department of Commerce. *Community Profiles.* Phoenix, 1998
Arizona Department of Health Services, Center for Health Statistics. *Arizona Health Status and Vital Statistics, 1996.* Phoenix, 1997
Arizona Historical Society. *Official Directory, Arizona Historical Museums and Related Support Organizations.* Tucson, 1997
Goff, J., *Arizona: an Illustrated History of Grand Canyon State.* Northridge (CA), 1988
Office of the Secretary of State. *Arizona Blue Book, 1997–98.* 1998
Public Sector Information, Inc. *1997–98 Arizona Yearbook: A Guide to Government in the Grand Canyon State.* Eugene (OR); 1997
Richards, J. M., *History of the Arizona State Legislature, 1912–1967.* Phoenix, 1990
Trimble, M., *Arizona: A Cavalcade of History.* Tucson, 1989

State Government Web Site: http://www.state.az.us
Department of Library, Archives and Public Records Web Site: http://www.dlapr.lib.az.us

ARKANSAS

KEY HISTORICAL EVENTS

In the 16th and 17th centuries, French and Spanish explorers entered Arkansas, finding there tribes of Chaddo, Osage and Quapaw. The first European settlement was French, at Arkansas Post in 1686, and the area became part of French Louisiana. The USA bought Arkansas from France as part of the Louisiana Purchase in 1803, it was organized as a Territory in 1819 and entered the Union on 15 June 1836 as the 25th state.

The eastern plains by the Mississippi were settled by white plantation-owners who grew cotton with black slave labour. The rest of the state attracted a scattered population of small farmers. The plantations were the centre of political power. Arkansas seceded from the Union in 1861 and joined the Confederate States of America. At that time the slave population was about 25% of the total.

In 1868 the state was readmitted to the Union. Attempts to integrate the black population into state life achieved little, and a policy of segregation was rigidly adhered to until the 1950s.

In 1957 federal law ordered that segregation in a public high school must end. The state governor ordered the state militia to prevent desegregation; there was rioting, and federal troops were called to Little Rock, the capital, to restore order. School segregation ended within the following 10 years.

The main industrial development followed the discovery of large reserves of bauxite.

TERRITORY AND POPULATION

Arkansas is bounded north by Missouri, east by Tennessee and Mississippi, south by Louisiana, south-west by Texas and west by Oklahoma. Area, 53,187 sq. miles (137,754 sq. km), 1,107 sq. miles being inland water. Census population on 1 April 1990 was 2,350,725 (53·5% urban), an increase of 2·8% from that of 1980. Population estimate (1997), 2,523,000.

Population in 5 census years was:

	White	Black	Indian	Asiatic	Total	Per sq. mile
1910	1,131,026	442,891	460	472	1,574,449	30·0
1930	1,375,315	478,463	408	296	1,854,482	35·2
1960	1,395,703	388,787	580	1,202	1,786,272	34·0
			All others			
1980	1,890,332	373,768	22,335		2,286,435	43·9
1990	1,944,744	373,912	32,069		2,350,725	45·1

UNITED STATES OF AMERICA

Of the total population in 1990, 48·2% were male and 68·9% were 21 years of age or older.

Little Rock (capital) had a population of 175,795 in 1990; Fort Smith, 72,798; North Little Rock, 61,741; Pine Bluff, 57,140; Fayetteville, 42,099; Hot Springs, 32,462; Jonesboro, 46,535; West Memphis, 28,259. The population of the largest standard metropolitan statistical areas: Little Rock–North Little Rock, 513,117; Fayetteville, 113,409; Fort Smith (Arkansas portion), 142,083; Pine Bluff, 85,487; Memphis (Arkansas portion), 49,939; Texarkana (Arkansas portion), 38,467.

SOCIAL STATISTICS
Births, 1995, were 35,175; deaths, 27,000; infant mortality rate (per 1,000 live births), 8·8. Marriages (1996, provisional), 36,200; divorces 15,200.

CLIMATE
Little Rock, Jan. 39·9°F, July 84°F. Annual rainfall 52·4". Arkansas belongs to the Gulf Coast climate zone (*see* UNITED STATES: Climate).

CONSTITUTION AND GOVERNMENT
The General Assembly consists of a Senate of 35 members elected for 4 years, partially renewed every 2 years, and a House of Representatives of 100 members elected for 2 years. The sessions are biennial and usually limited to 60 days. The Governor and Lieut.-Governor are elected for 4 years. The state is represented in Congress by 4 representatives.

The state is divided into 75 counties; the capital is Little Rock.

RECENT ELECTIONS
In the 1996 presidential election Clinton polled 465,362 votes; Dole, 320,323; Perot, 67,245.

CURRENT ADMINISTRATION
Governor: Mike Huckabee (R.), 1999–2003 ($87,000).
  Lieut.-Governor: Vacant. ($29,000).
  Secretary of State: Sharon Priest (D.) ($37,500).

ECONOMY
Budget. In 1996 total revenue was $8,653m. Total expenditure was $7,050m. (education, $2,509m.; public welfare, $1,583m.; health and hospitals, $589m; highways, $698m.; police protection, $52m.) Outstanding debt (1996) was $2,142m.
  Per capita personal income (1997, preliminary) was $19,585.

Banking and Finance. In 1993–94 total bank deposits were $22,107·8m.

ENERGY AND NATURAL RESOURCES
Oil and Gas. 1997 production of crude oil was 6m. bbls.; natural gas, 190bn. cu. ft.

Water. The total area covered by water is approximately 1,107 sq. miles.

Minerals. The U.S. Bureau of Mines estimated Arkansas' mineral value in 1992 at $287m. Mining employment totalled 3,600 in Oct. 1992. Crushed stone was the leading mineral commodity produced, in terms of value, followed by bromine. Value of domestic non-fuel mineral production in 1997 was $535m.

Agriculture. In 1995, 44,000 farms had a total area of 15·0m. acres; average farm was 341 acres. 8·2m. acres were harvested cropland (1993). In the same year Arkansas ranked first in the production of broilers (1,050m. birds) and in the acreage and production of rice (40% of US total production) and third in turkeys (25m. birds).

Total farm income, 1996, $5,887m.

Forestry. The national forests had a total area of 3,495,232 acres in 1997.

INDUSTRY

In 1996 total employment averaged 1,234,000 (including 254,000 manufacturing, 247,000 wholesale and retail trade, 179,000 government). The Arkansas Department of Labor estimated that 196,700 factory production workers earned an average $370.77 per week (41·8 hours). In the manufacturing group, food and kindred products employed 52,400, electric and electronic equipment, 20,500 and lumber and wood products, 21,500. In Aug. 1994 estimated employment was 1,153,700, including 1,025,300 non-agricultural waged and salaried jobs.

COMMUNICATIONS

Roads. Total road mileage (1996), 77,746 miles—urban, 7,698; rural, 70,048. In 1996 there were 1,633,000 registered motor vehicles.

Rail. In 1991 there were in the state 3,169 miles of commercial railway. In 1994 rail service was provided by 4 Class I and 23 short-line railways.

Civil Aviation. In Oct. 1994, 7 air carriers and 2 commuter airlines served the state; there were 175 airports (96 public-use and 79 private).

Shipping. There are about 1,000 miles of navigable rivers, including the Mississippi, Arkansas, Red, White and Ouachita Rivers. The Arkansas River/Kerr-McClellan Channel flows diagonally eastward across the state and gives access to the sea via the Mississippi River.

SOCIAL INSTITUTIONS

Justice. There were, in 1996, 9,407 state and federal prisoners. In 1996, 524,000 violent crimes were committed and a total of 4,175,000 property crimes. The death penalty is authorized. The last execution took place in 1994.

Religion. Main Protestant churches in 1990: Southern Baptist (617,524), United Methodist (197,402), Church of Christ (86,502), Assembly of God (55,438). Roman Catholics (1990), 72,952.

Education. In the school year 1992–93 public elementary and secondary schools had 440,682 enrolled pupils and 25,771 classroom teachers. Average salary of teachers in elementary schools was $25,771, junior high $27,492 and high $27,760.

Higher education is provided at 34 institutions: 9 state universities, 1 medical college, 12 private or church colleges, 12 community or 2-year branch colleges and 12 technical colleges. Total enrolment in institutions of higher education in the autumn of 1993 was 99,344.

In the autumn of 1993 there were 2 vocational-training schools and 9 technical institutes with 28,261 students.

Health. There were 99 licensed hospitals (13,329 beds) in 1994, and 273 nursing facilities (25,888 licensed beds), excluding private facilities.

Welfare. In Dec. 1993, 481,910 persons drew social security payments; 271,510 were retired workers; 53,240 were disabled workers; 68,920 were widows and widowers; 36,050 were spouses. Monthly payments were $251·5m., including $159·6m. to retired workers and their dependants and $31·6m. to disabled workers.

CULTURE

Broadcasting. An educational TV network provides a full 18-hour-day telecasting; it has 5 stations (1994).

FURTHER READING

Statistical information: Arkansas Institute for Economic Advancement, Univ. of Arkansas at Little Rock, Little Rock 72204. Publishes *Arkansas State and County Economic Data.*
Agricultural Statistics for Arkansas. Arkansas Agricultural Statistics Service, Little Rock, 1993
Current Employment Developments. Dept. of Labor, Little Rock, 1994
Statistical Summary for the Public Schools of Arkansas. Dept. of Education, Little Rock, 1990-92

CALIFORNIA

KEY HISTORICAL EVENTS

There were many small Indian tribes, but no central power, when the area was discovered in 1542 by the Spanish navigator Juan Cabrillo. The Spaniards did not begin to establish missions until the 18th century, when the Franciscan friar Junipero Serra settled at San Diego in 1769. The missions became farming and ranching villages with large Indian populations. When the Spanish empire collapsed in 1821, the area was governed from newly independent Mexico.

The first wagon-train of American settlers arrived from Missouri in 1841. In 1846, during the war between Mexico and the USA, Americans in California proclaimed it to be part of the USA. The territory was ceded by Mexico on 2 Feb. 1848 and became the 31st state of the Union on 9 Sept. 1850.

Gold was discovered in 1848–49 and there was an immediate influx of population. The state remained isolated, however, until the development of railways in the 1860s. From then on the population doubled on average every 20 years. The sunny climate attracted fruit-growers, market-gardeners and wine producers. In the early 20th century the bright light and cheap labour attracted film-makers to Hollywood, Los Angeles.

Southern California remained mainly agricultural with an Indian or Spanish-speaking labour force until after the Second World War. Now more than 90% of the population is urban, with the main manufacture being hi-technology equipment, much of it for the aerospace, computer and office equipment industries.

TERRITORY AND POPULATION

Land area, 155,973 sq. miles (403,971 sq. km). Census population, 1 April 1990, 29,760,021 (92·6% urban), an increase of 25·7% over 1980. Population estimate (1998), 33,252,000.

Population in 5 census years was:

	White	Black	Japanese	Chinese	Total (incl. all others)	Per sq. mile
1910	2,259,672	21,645	41,356	36,248	2,377,549	15·0
1930	5,408,260	81,048	97,456	37,361	5,677,251	35·8
1960	14,455,230	883,861	157,317	95,600	15,717,204	99·0
	White	Black	Asian/other	Hispanic	Total	Per sq. mile
1980	15,763,992	1,783,810	1,575,769	4,544,331	23,667,902	149·1
1990	17,029,126	2,092,446	2,950,511	7,687,938	29,760,021	190·8

Of the 1990 population 50·1% were male, 92·6% were urban and 69% were 21 years old or older.

The largest cities with 1998 estimated population are:

Los Angeles	3,772,500	San Bernadino	182,600	Orange	125,100
San Diego	1,224,800	Chula Vista	162,000	Fullerton	125,100
San Jose	894,000	Oxnard	156,000	Escondido	123,100
San Francisco	789,600	Garden Grove	154,400	Inglewood	118,500
Long Beach	446,200	Oceanside	153,900	Rancho	
Fresno	411,600	Santa Clarita	143,800	Cucamonga	118,400
Oakland	396,300	Ontario	143,800	Palmdale	117,300
Sacramento	392,800	Torrance	143,600	El Monte	116,400
Santa Ana	311,200	Pomana	143,200	Thousand Oaks	115,700
Anaheim	301,200	Pasadena	140,400	Concord	113,400
Riverside	250,800	Moreno Valley	137,200	Corona	111,500
Stockton	241,100	Santa Rosa	136,100	Vallejo	111,400
Bakersfield	221,700	Irvine	133,200	Berkeley	107,800
Fremont	198,700	Sunnyvale	131,100	Fontana	107,600
Glendale	197,600	Salinas	128,300	Simi Valley	106,000
Huntington Beach	192,400	Lancaster	127,100	West Covina	104,800
Modesto	182,700	Hayward	126,500	Costa Mesa	104,200

Urbanized areas (1990 census): Los Angeles, 11,402,946; San Francisco–Oakland, 3,629,516; San Diego, 2,348,417; San Jose, 1,435,019; Sacramento, 1,097,005; Riverside–San Bernardino, 1,170,196; Oxnard–Ventura, 480,482; Fresno, 453,388.

CALIFORNIA

SOCIAL STATISTICS
Births in 1997, 544,000 (16·6 per 1,000 population); deaths, 228,000 (6·9 per 1,000 population); infant deaths (1995), approximately 3,480 (6·3 per 1,000 live births). Marriages (1996, provisional), 202,800 (in 1990, 236,693); divorces (1990), 127,967.

CLIMATE
Los Angeles, Jan. 58°F (14·4°C), July 74°F (23·3°C). Annual rainfall 15" (381 mm). Sacramento, Jan. 45°F (7·2°C), July 76°F (24·4°C). Annual rainfall 18" (457 mm). San Diego, Jan. 57°F (13·9°C), July 71°F (21·7°C). Annual rainfall 10" (259 mm). San Francisco, Jan. 51°F (10·6°C), July 59°F (15°C). Annual rainfall 20" (508 mm). Death Valley, Jan. 52°F (11°C), July 100°F (38°C). Annual rainfall 1·6" (40 mm). California belongs to the Pacific Coast climate zone (see UNITED STATES: Climate).

CONSTITUTION AND GOVERNMENT
The present constitution became effective from 4 July 1879; it has had numerous amendments since 1962. The Senate is composed of 40 members elected for 4 years—half being elected every 2 years—and the Assembly, of 80 members, elected for 2 years. Two-year regular sessions convene in Dec. of each even numbered year. The Governor and Lieut.-Governor are elected for 4 years.

California is represented in Congress by 52 representatives.

The capital is Sacramento. The state is divided into 58 counties.

RECENT ELECTIONS
In the 1996 presidential election Clinton polled 5,119,835 votes; Dole, 3,828,380; Perot, 667,702.

CURRENT ADMINISTRATION
Governor: Gray Davis (D.), 1999–2002 ($165,000).
Lieut.-Governor: Cruz Bustamante (D.) ($124,000).
Secretary of State: Bill Jones (R.) ($123,750).
Attorney General: Bill Lockyer (D.) ($140,250).

ECONOMY
Performance. California's economy continued to expand in 1998. Non-farm employment growth averaged 3·2% and personal income was up more than 6%. The unemployment rate was below 6% for most of the year. Non-residential construction activity remained quite strong, with building permit value up almost 18%. Homebuilding continued on a moderate recovery path with permits for new houses reaching 126,000 units, a 13·5% increase over 1997.

Budget. In 1996 total revenue was $123·3bn. Total expenditure was $113·4bn. (education, $34·8bn.; public welfare, $28·8bn.; health and hospitals, $8·3bn.; highways, $4·5bn.; police protection, $1bn.) Debt outstanding (1996) $45·9bn.

Per capita personal income (1997, preliminary) was $26,570.

Banking and Finance. In 1992 there were 11,079 establishments of depository institutions which included 5,746 commercial banks, 2,982 savings institutions and 1,293 credit unions.

In 1996 savings and loan associations had deposits of $166,833m. Total real-estate loans were $177,707m. On 31 Dec. 1997 all insured commercial banks had demand deposits of $84,651m. and time and savings deposits of $224,400m. Total loans reached $301,975m., of which real-estate loans were $133,781m.

ENERGY AND NATURAL RESOURCES
Electricity. 75% of electricity is derived from in-state resources. In 1996 total consumption amounted to 258,801m. kWh.

Oil and Gas. Total onshore and offshore production was 341m. bbls. in 1997; crude oil output was estimated at 286m. bbls. Net natural gas production (1997) was 291bn. cu. ft; natural gas liquids from wells (1996) was 71,369 bbls.

UNITED STATES OF AMERICA

Water. The total area covered by water is approximately 2,895 sq. miles.

Minerals. Gold output was 23,000 kg in 1997. Asbestos, boron minerals, diatomite, tungsten, sand and gravel, lime, salt, magnesium compounds, clays, cement, copper, silver, gypsum, calcium chloride and iron ore are also produced.

Non-fuel mineral production in 1997 accounted for approximately 7% of US total production. The value of non-fuel minerals produced (1997) was $2,864m.; the mining industry employed 29,400 persons.

Agriculture. In 1997 there were some 87,000 farms, comprising 29m. acres; average farm, 330 acres. Cash receipts, 1996, were $24,789m. Nuts and fruit remained the most significant cash crop (1996), accounting for 26% of agriculture's gross income. Livestock and poultry accounted for 25%; vegetables and melons, 21%; field crops, 13%; greenhouse products and Christmas trees, 9%. The state's leading billion-dollar agricultural products included milk and cream with receipts of $3·7bn.; grapes, $2·2bn.; nursery products, $1·6bn.; cattle and calves, $1·2bn.; cotton lint, $1·1bn.; and almonds, $1·0bn.

Production of cotton lint, 1996, was 667,200 short tons; other field and seed crops included (in 1m. short tons): sugar-beet, 2; hay and alfalfa, 8; rice, 1·9; wheat, 1·6. Principal fruit, nut and vegetable crops in 1996 (in 1,000 short tons): wine, table and raisin grapes, 5,003; tomatoes, 11,145; lettuce, 3,142; almonds, 255; oranges, 2,175; lemons, 798; grapefruit, 271.

On 1 Jan. 1997 the farm animals were: 1·3m. milk cows; 4·6m. all cattle; 0·48m. sheep; and 0·24m. swine.

Forestry. There are about 16·6m. acres of productive forest land, from which about 2,900m. bd ft are harvested annually. Total value of timber harvest, 1996, $921m. Lumber production, 1997, 2,400m. bd ft.

Fisheries. The catch in 1997 was 491m. lbs; leading species in landings were squid, sardine, mackerel, tuna, herring, urchin, rockfish, sole and shrimp.

INDUSTRY

In 1998 the fastest-growing industries were business services, construction, and engineering and management consulting.

Labour. In 1998 the civilian labour force was 16·22m., of whom 15·35m. were employed (1·93m. in manufacturing, 0·62m. in construction, and 4·32m. in services).

INTERNATIONAL TRADE

Imports and Exports. Estimated total foreign exports were $165bn. in 1997.

Agricultural exports grew to $9·3bn. in 1997—a 4% increase on the previous year. California's top markets included Japan, the EU, Canada, Mexico, Hong Kong and Korea.

COMMUNICATIONS

Roads. In 1997 California had 68,490 miles of roads inside cities and 102,110 miles outside; there were about 16·9m. registered cars and about 5·6m. commercial vehicles. Road accident fatalities (1996) numbered 41,900.

Rail. In addition to Amtrak's long-distance trains, local and medium-distance passenger trains run in the San Francisco Bay area sponsored by the California Department of Transportation, and a network of commuter trains around Los Angeles opened in 1992. There are metro and light rail systems in San Francisco and Los Angeles, and light rail lines in Sacramento, San Diego and San Jose.

Civil Aviation. In 1996 there were a total of 933 public and private airports, heliports, stolports and seaplane bases.

A total of 57,975,000 passengers (14,033,000 international; 43,942,000 domestic) embarked/disembarked at Los Angeles airport (1996). The airport handled approximately 1,538,900 tonnes of freight (694,450 international; 844,450 domestic). At San Francisco airport, in 1996, 38,560,000 passengers (6,644,000 international; 31,916,000 domestic) embarked/disembarked, and 564,300 tonnes of freight (338,400 tonnes international; 225,900 tonnes domestic) were handled.

Shipping. The chief ports are San Francisco and Los Angeles.

SOCIAL INSTITUTIONS

Justice. A '3 strikes law', making 25-years-to-life sentences mandatory for third felony offences was adopted in 1994 after an initiative (i.e. referendum) was 72% in favour. However, the state's Supreme Court ruled in June 1996 that judges may disregard previous convictions in awarding sentences. In 1997 there were 33 adult prisons. State prisons, 1 Jan. 1997, had 135,481 male and 10,084 female inmates. In Jan. 1997 there were some 9,572 juveniles in custody. As of 30 June 1998 there were 4,368 adults serving '3 strikes' sentences. The death penalty has been authorized following its reinstatement by the US Supreme Court in 1976. Death sentences have been passed since 1980. The last execution was in 1993.

Religion. There is a strong Roman Catholic presence. There were 733,000 Latter-day Saints (Mormons) in 1997.

Education. Full-time attendance at school is compulsory for children from 6 to 18 years of age for a minimum of 175 days per annum. In autumn 1998 there were 6·3m. pupils enrolled in both public and private elementary and secondary schools. Total state expenditure on public education, 1997–98, was $29,447m.

Community colleges had 1,407,335 students in autumn 1996.

California has two publicly supported higher education systems: The University of California (1868) and the California State University and Colleges. In autumn 1997 the University of California, with campuses for resident instruction and research at Berkeley, Los Angeles, San Francisco and 6 other centres, had 169,862 students. California State University and Colleges with campuses at Sacramento, Long Beach, Los Angeles, San Francisco and 15 other cities had 343,779 students. In addition to the 28 publicly supported institutions for higher education there are 117 private colleges and universities which had a total estimated enrolment of 217,968 in the autumn of 1997.

Health. In 1996 there were 500 general acute care hospitals; capacity, 105,096 beds. On 30 June 1998 state hospitals for the mentally disabled had 4,458 patients.

Welfare. On 1 Jan. 1974 the federal government (Social Security Administration) assumed responsibility for the Supplemental Security Income/State Supplemental Program which replaced the State Old-Age Security. The SSI/SSP provides financial assistance for needy aged (65 years or older), blind or disabled persons. An individual recipient may own assets up to $2,000; a couple up to $3,000, subject to specific exclusions. In 1997–98 fiscal year an average of 127,399 cases per month were receiving an average of $213·65 in assistance in the general relief programme.

CULTURE

Tourism. Visitors in 1996 spent $61·2bn. and tax revenues relating to tourism were $330m. California was the state most visited by overseas travellers (1996), with 6,004,000 overseas visitors—25·5% of the market share. In 1997 there were 260m. tourists, 249·5m. from within the United States and 10·5m. from abroad.

Libraries. The California State Library is in Sacramento.

FURTHER READING

California Almanac. Pacific Data Resources, Santa Barbara
California Government and Politics. Hoeber, T. R., et al, (eds.) Sacramento, Annual
California Statistical Abstract. 38th ed. Dept. of Finance, Sacramento, 1997
Economic Report of the Governor. Dept. of Finance, Sacramento, Annual
Bean, W. and Rawls, J. J., *California: an Interpretive History.* 6th ed. New York, 1993
Gerston, L. N. and Christensen, T., *California Politics and Government: a Practical Approach.* 3rd ed. New York, 1995
Lavender, D. S., *California.* New York, 1976
State Library: The California State Library, Library-Courts Bldg, Sacramento 95814.

COLORADO

KEY HISTORICAL EVENTS

Spanish explorers claimed the area for Spain in 1706; it was then the territory of the Arapaho, Cheyenne, Ute and other Plains and Great Basin Indians. Eastern

Colorado, the hot, dry plains, passed to France in 1802 and then to the USA as part of the Louisiana Purchase in 1803. The rest remained Spanish, becoming Mexican when Spanish power in the Americas ended. In 1848, after war between Mexico and the USA, Mexican Colorado was ceded to the USA. A gold rush in 1859 brought a great influx of population, and in 1861 Colorado was organized as a Territory. The Territory officially supported the Union in the Civil War of 1861–65, but its settlers were divided and served on both sides.

Colorado became a state in 1876. Mining and ranching were the mainstays of the economy. In the 1920s the first large projects were undertaken to exploit the Colorado River. The Colorado River Compact was agreed in 1922, and the Boulder Dam (now Hoover Dam) was authorized in 1928. Since then irrigated agriculture has overtaken mining as an industry and is as important as ranching. In 1945 the Colorado-Big Thompson project diverted water by tunnel beneath the Rocky Mountains to irrigate 700,000 acres (284,000 ha) of northern Colorado. Now more than 80% of the population is urban, and most engaged in telecommunications, aerospace and computer technology.

TERRITORY AND POPULATION
Colorado is bounded north by Wyoming, north-east by Nebraska, east by Kansas, south-east by Oklahoma, south by New Mexico and west by Utah. Land area, 103,729 sq. miles (268,658 sq. km).

Population, 1 July 1997, was 3,892,644 (83·1% urban). Population estimate (2000), 4,175,003.

Population in 5 census years was:

	White	Black	Indian	Asiatic	Total	Per sq. mile
1910	783,415	11,453	1,482	2,674	799,024	7·7
1930	1,018,793	11,828	1,395	3,775	1,035,791	10·0
1950	1,296,653	20,177	1,567	5,870	1,325,089	12·7
			All others			
1980	2,571,498	101,703	216,763		2,889,964	27·9
1990	2,658,945	128,057	22,068	56,773	3,294,394	31·8

Of the total population in 1995, 1,858,346 were male and 1,888,272 were female. Large cities with 1997 estimated population: Denver City, 504,704; Colorado Springs, 338,016; Aurora, 249,907; Lakewood, 139,966; Pueblo, 102,723; Fort Collins, 107,563; Boulder, 92,446.

Main metropolitan areas (1995): Denver, 1,826,468; Colorado Springs, 462,711; Boulder, 255,156; Fort Collins, 215,774; Greeley, 147,524; Pueblo, 129,332; Front Range Urban Area, 3,037,013.

SOCIAL STATISTICS
Births, 1995, were 53,748 (14·5 per 1,000 population); deaths, 24,898 (6·6); infant deaths, 352 (6·5 per 1,000 live births); marriages, 34,296 (9·2); divorces, 18,844.

CLIMATE
Denver, Jan. 31°F (–0·6°C), July 73°F (22·8°C). Annual rainfall 14" (358 mm). Pueblo, Jan. 30°F (–1·1°C), July 83°F (28·3°C). Annual rainfall 12" (312 mm). Colorado belongs to the Mountain States climate zone (*see* UNITED STATES: Climate).

CONSTITUTION AND GOVERNMENT
The constitution adopted in 1876 is still in effect with (1989) 115 amendments. The General Assembly consists of a Senate of 35 members elected for 4 years, one-half retiring every 2 years, and of a House of Representatives of 65 members elected for 2 years. Sessions are annual, beginning 1951. Qualified as electors are all citizens, male and female (except convicted, incarcerated criminals), 18 years of age, who have resided in the state and the precinct for 32 days immediately preceding the election.

The state sends 6 representatives to Congress.

The capital is Denver. There are 63 counties.

RECENT ELECTIONS
In the 1996 presidential election Dole polled 691,290 votes; Clinton, 670,854; Perot, 99,510.

COLORADO

CURRENT ADMINISTRATION
Governor: Bill Owens (D.), 1999–2003 ($90,000).
Lieut.-Governor: Joe Rogers (D.) ($65,500).
Secretary of State: Vicky Buckley (R.) ($68,500).

ECONOMY

Budget. In 1996 total state revenue was $11,866m. Total expenditure was $10,312m. (education, $3,945m.; public welfare, $2,081m.; health and hospitals, $381m.; highways, $796m.; police protection, $52m.) Outstanding debt was $3,577m. in 1996.
Per capita personal income (1997, preliminary) was $27,051.

ENERGY AND NATURAL RESOURCES

Water. The Rocky Mountains of Colorado form the headwaters for 4 major American rivers: the Colorado, Rio Grande, Arkansas and Platte. The total area covered by water is approximately 371 sq. miles.

Minerals. Colorado has a variety of mineral resources. Among the most important are crude oil and coal and gas. Coal (1997) 27·4m. short tons; crude oil, 25·6m. barrels; natural gas, 309,368,163m. cu. ft. In 1996 there were 13,619 people employed in mining, including 7,782 in extracting oil and natural gas.

Agriculture. In 1998 farms and ranches numbered 25,500, with a total of 34m. acres of agricultural land. 5,748,610 acres were harvested crop land; average farm, 1,327 acres. Average value of farmland and buildings per acre in 1996 was $558. Farm income 1995: from crops, $1,361m.; from livestock, $2,624m.

Production of principal crops in 1990: corn for grain, 128·65m. bu.; wheat for grain, 84·95m. bu.; barley for grain, 12m. bu.; hay, 3,805,000 tons; dry beans, 4,275,000 cwt; oats and sorghum, 12·59m. bu.; sugar beets, 944,000 tons; potatoes, 24,032,000 cwt; vegetables, 10,683 tons; fruits, 39,000 tons.

In 1995 the number of farm animals was: 3,100,000 cattle, 83,000 milch cows, 580,000 swine. In 1991 there were 708,070 sheep.

Forestry. In 1997 there were 15m. acres of national forest.

INDUSTRY

In 1996, 1,847,591 were employed in non-agricultural sectors, of which 466,411 were in trade; 536,084 in services; 293,698 in government; 196,517 in manufacturing; 111,064 in construction; 115,345 in transportation; 13,619 in mining; 114,561 in finance and insurance. In manufacturing in 1996 the biggest employers were 30,919 in non-electrical machinery; 26,916 in printing and publishing; 25,863 in food products.

COMMUNICATIONS

Roads. In 1995 there were 84,447 miles of road and 2,811,790 motor vehicle registrations.

Rail. There were 3,439 miles of railway in 1995.

Civil Aviation. There were (1990) 81 airports open to the public; 14 with commercial service, 53 public non-commercial (general aviation) and 14 private non-commercial.

Telecommunications. Colorado is headquarters to US West and TCI Cable. Other major communications employers are AT&T and MCI.

SOCIAL INSTITUTIONS

Justice. In 1996 there were 11,742 federal and state prisoners. The death penalty is authorized.

Religion. In 1984 the Roman Catholic Church had 550,300 members; the ten main Protestant denominations had 350,900 members; the Jewish community had 45,000 members. Buddhism is among other religions represented.

Education. In 1995 the public elementary and secondary schools had 656,279 pupils, 35,364 teachers; teachers' salaries averaged $35,364. Enrolments in 4-year state universities and colleges were: University of Colorado (Boulder), 24,440 students; University of Colorado (Denver), 10,538; University of Colorado (Colorado Springs), 5,871; Colorado State University (Fort Collins), 21,393; Colorado School of Mines (Golden), 3,083; University of Northern Colorado (Greeley), 10,488; University of Southern Colorado (Pueblo), 4,331; Western State College (Gunnison), 2,473; Adams State College (Alamosa), 2,419; Mesa College (Grand Junction), 4,721; Fort Lewis College (Durango), 4,363; Metropolitan State College (Denver), 16,351; University of Colorado Health Sciences Centre (Denver), 2,281. 1994 total enrolments: Private 4-year universities and colleges, 27,899; 2-year colleges, 65,882; all universities and colleges, 207,039.

Health. Community hospitals, 1995, numbered 69.

Welfare. In 1995 total beneficiaries numbered 495,320 and total payments $3,694m.

CULTURE
Tourism. Skiing is a major tourist attraction.

Festivals. Cherry Creek Arts Festival takes place in July.

National Theatre and Opera. The main venue is the Denver Performing Arts Center.

FURTHER READING
Statistical information: Business Research Division, Univ. of Colorado, Boulder 80309. Publishes *Statistical Abstract of Colorado.*
Griffiths, M. and Rubright, L., *Colorado: a Geography.* Boulder, 1983
Sprague, M., *Colorado: A History.* New York, 1976

State Library: Colorado State Library, State Capitol, Denver 80203.

CONNECTICUT

KEY HISTORICAL EVENTS
Formerly territory of Algonquian-speaking Indians, Connecticut was first colonized by Europeans during the 1630s, when English Puritans moved there from Massachusetts Bay. Settlements were founded in the Connecticut River Valley at Hartford, Saybrook, Wethersfield and Windsor in 1635. They formed an organized commonwealth in 1637. A further settlement was made at New Haven in 1638 and was united to the commonwealth under a royal charter in 1662. The charter confirmed the commonwealth constitution, drawn up by mutual agreement in 1639 and called the Fundamental Orders of Connecticut.

The area was agricultural and its population of largely English descent until the early 19th century. After the War of Independence Connecticut was one of the original 13 states of the Union. Its state constitution came into force in 1818 and survived with amendment until 1965 when a new one was adopted.

In the early 1800s a textile industry was established using local water power. By 1850 the state had more employment in industry than in agriculture, and immigration from the continent of Europe (and especially from southern and eastern Europe) grew rapidly throughout the 19th century. Some immigrants worked in whaling and iron-mining, both now extinct, but most sought industrial employment. Settlement was spread over a large number of relatively small cities, with no single dominant culture.

Yale University was founded at New Haven in 1701. The US Coastguard Academy was founded in 1876 at New London, a former whaling port.

TERRITORY AND POPULATION
Connecticut is bounded in the north by Massachusetts, east by Rhode Island, south by the Atlantic and west by New York. Land area, 4,844 sq. miles (12,547 sq. km).

CONNECTICUT

Census population, 1 April 1990, 3,287,116 (79·1% urban), an increase of 5·78% since 1980. Population estimate (1997), 3,270,000.

Population in 4 census years was:

	White	Black	Indian	Asian		Total	Per sq. mile
1910	1,098,897	15,174	152	533		1,114,756	231·3
1930	1,576,700	29,354	162	687		1,606,903	328·0
1980	2,799,420	217,433	4,533	18,970		3,107,576	634·3
	White	Black	Indian	Asian	Others	Total	Per sq. mile
1990	2,859,353	274,269	6,654	50,698	96,142	3,287,116	678·6

Of the total population in 1993, 242,572 persons (of any race) were of Hispanic origin, 1,589,000 persons were male. Those 18 years old or older numbered 2,497,836. There were 183 residents in 5 Indian Reservations.

The chief cities and towns are (1994 state estimates):

Bridgeport	141,686	Stamford	108,056	Bristol	60,640
Hartford	139,739	Norwalk	78,331	West Hartford	60,110
New Haven	130,474	New Britain	75,491	Meriden	59,479
Waterbury	108,961	Danbury	65,585	Greenwich	58,441

SOCIAL STATISTICS
Births (1995) were 44,334 (13·5 per 1,000 population); deaths, 29,000 (9·0); infant mortality rate (per 1,000 live births), 7·2. Marriages (1996, provisional), 21,400; divorces, 10,500.

CLIMATE
New Haven: Jan. 25°F (−3·8°C), July 74°F (23·4°C). Annual rainfall 45" (1,143 mm). Connecticut belongs to the New England climate zone (*see* UNITED STATES: Climate).

CONSTITUTION AND GOVERNMENT
The 1818 Constitution was revised in 1955. On 30 Dec. 1965 a new constitution went into effect, having been framed by a constitutional convention in the summer of 1965 and approved by the voters in Dec. 1965.

The General Assembly consists of a Senate of 36 members and a House of Representatives of 151 members. Members of each House are elected for the term of 2 years. Legislative sessions are annual.

The state sends 6 representatives to Congress.

There are 8 counties.

RECENT ELECTIONS
In the 1996 presidential election Clinton polled 712,603 votes; Dole, 481,047; Perot, 137,784. The state capital is Hartford.

CURRENT ADMINISTRATION
Governor: John G. Rowland (R.), 1999–2002 ($78,000).
Lieut.-Governor: M. Jodi Rell (R.) ($71,500).
Secretary of State: Susan Bysiewicz (D.) ($65,000).

ECONOMY
Budget. In 1996 total revenue was $14,349m. Total expenditure was $13,530m. (education, $2,888m.; public welfare, $2,815m.; health and hospitals, $1,340m.; highways, $712m.; police protection, $105m.) Outstanding debt (1996) was $16,415m.
Per capita personal income (1997, preliminary) was $36,263.

ENERGY AND NATURAL RESOURCES
Water. The total area covered by water is approximately 698 sq. miles.

Minerals. The state has some mineral resources: crushed stone, sand, gravel, clay, dimension stone, feldspar and quartz; total production in 1995 was valued at $81m.

Agriculture. In 1997 the state had 4,000 farms with a total area (1995) of 358,743 acres; the average farm size was 108 acres, valued at $7,800 per acre in 1998. Farm income (1996): crops $252m., and livestock and products $237m. Principal crops are grains, hay, tobacco, vegetables, maize, melons, fruit, nuts, berries and greenhouse and nursery products.

Livestock (1993): 77,000 all cattle (value $59·3m.), 10,900 sheep ($1·1m.), 6,000 swine ($630,000) and 4·6m. poultry ($11·5m.).

Forestry. The state has 144,464 acres of state forest land.

INDUSTRY

Total non-agricultural employment in Sept. 1997 was 1,629,100. The main employers are manufacturers (275,000 workers mainly in transport equipment, machinery, computer, electronic and electrical equipment and fabricated metals); retail trade (273,000 workers); services (504,700) and government (225,800). There were 79,300 unemployed.

COMMUNICATIONS

Roads. The total length of highways in 1996 was 20,600 miles. Motor vehicles registered in 1996 numbered 2,609,000.

Rail. In 1994 there were 570 miles (912 km) of railway route miles.

Civil Aviation. In 1995 there were 61 airports (20 commercial, 6 state-owned and 35 private), 63 heliports and 8 seaplane bases.

SOCIAL INSTITUTIONS

Justice. In 1995 there were 14,246 inmates in 19 state correctional institutions and centres. There were 57,000 adults under state correctional supervision. The death penalty for murder has been authorized.

Religion. The leading religious denominations (1990) in the state are the Roman Catholic (1,374,000 members), United Churches of Christ (135,000), Protestant Episcopal (78,000), Jewish (115,000), Methodist (56,000), Black Baptist (64,000), Presbyterian and Greek Orthodox.

Education. Elementary instruction is free for all children between the ages of 4 and 16 years, and compulsory for all children between the ages of 7 and 16 years. In 1993 there were 978 public local schools, 3 academies, 17 state vocational-technical schools, 30 state or state-aided schools, 6 regional educational service centres and 334 non-public schools. In 1994 there were 507,825 pupils and 39,816 public elementary and secondary teachers. Expenditure of the state on public schools, 1994, $4,000m. Average salary of teachers in public schools, 1993, $48,300. In 1997 expenditure per pupil (public elementary and secondary) was $8,845.There were an estimated 26,600 public high-school graduates in 1997.

Connecticut had 42 colleges (1995), of which one state university, 4 state colleges and 12 community-technical colleges are state funded. Total enrolment, 1995, was 155,000 students. The University of Connecticut at Storrs, founded 1881, had 1,502 faculty and 23,649 students in 1994. Yale University, New Haven, founded in 1701, had 2,358 faculty and 10,916 students; Wesleyan University, Middletown, founded 1831, 261 faculty and 3,270 students; Trinity College, Hartford, founded 1823, 166 faculty and 2,146 students; Connecticut College, New London, founded 1915, 175 faculty and 1,919 students; The University of Hartford, founded 1877, 331 faculty and 7,241 students. The state colleges faculty was 1,087 and the number of students was 35,111. The technical colleges had 718 faculty and 45,542 students. There were 18 independent (4-year course) colleges with 4,219 faculty and 55,234 students; 6 independent (2-year course) colleges and 74 faculty and 1,790 students and 1 US Coastguard Academy with 43 faculty and 930 students.

Health. Hospitals listed by the American Hospital Association, 1993, numbered 62. The state operated 1 general hospital (252 beds), 7 hospitals for the mentally ill (891 patients), 1 training school for the mentally retarded, and 6 regional centres (5,705 clients in residential settings). In 1996 there were 33 community hospitals with approximately 7,300 beds; 11,015 non-federal physicians; and 33,400 nurses.

Welfare. Disbursements in 1992 amounted to $42m. in aid to the aged and disabled (with an average payment per month of $664·82). In other areas of welfare, there was an average of 57,000 cases for aid to families with dependent children comprising 162,000 recipients. In 1996 there were a total of 596,000 beneficiaries; annual payments amounted to $5,003m.

CULTURE

Broadcasting. In 1994 there were 75 broadcasting stations and 11 television stations.

Press. In 1994 there were 141 daily, Sunday, weekly and monthly newspapers.

FURTHER READING

State Register and Manual. Secretary of State. Hartford (CT). Annual
The Structure of Connecticut's State Government. Connecticut Public Expenditure Council. Hartford, 1973
Halliburton, W. J., *The People of Connecticut.* Norwalk, 1985
Van Dusen, Albert E., *Connecticut.* New York, 1961

State Library: Connecticut State Library, 231 Capitol Avenue, Hartford (CT) 06105; Tel. 860-566-4971.
State Book Store: Dept. of Environmental Protection, 79 Elm St., Hartford (CT) 06106; Tel. 860-424-3555.
Business Incentives: Connecticut Economic Resource Center, 805 Brook St., Rocky Hill (CT) 06067; Tel. 860-571-7136.
Connecticut Tourism: Dept. of Economic and Community Development, 865 Brook St., Rocky Hill (CT) 06067; Tel. 860-258-4355.

DELAWARE

KEY HISTORICAL EVENTS

Delaware was the territory of Algonquian-speaking Indians who were displaced by European settlement in the 17th century. The first settlers were Swedes who came in 1638 to build Fort Christina (now Wilmington), and colonize what they called New Sweden. Their colony was taken by the Dutch from New Amsterdam in 1655. In 1664 the British took the whole New Amsterdam colony, including Delaware, and called it New York.

In 1682 Delaware was granted to William Penn, who wanted access to the coast for his Pennsylvania colony. Union of the two colonies was unpopular, and Delaware gained its own government in 1704, although it continued to share a royal governor with Pennsylvania until the War of Independence. Delaware then became one of the 13 original states of the Union and the first to ratify the federal constitution (on 7 Dec. 1787).

The population was of Swedish, Finnish, British and Irish extraction. The land was low-lying and fertile, and the use of slave labour was legal. There was a significant number of black slaves, but Delaware was a border state during the Civil War (1861–65) and did not leave the Union.

The main 19th-century immigrants were European Jews, Poles, Germans and Italians. The north became industrial and densely populated, becoming more so after the Second World War with the rise of the petrochemical industry. Industry in general profited from the opening of the Chesapeake and Delaware Canal in 1829; it was converted to a toll-free deep channel for ocean-going ships in 1919.

TERRITORY AND POPULATION

Delaware is bounded in the north by Pennsylvania, north-east by New Jersey, east by Delaware Bay, south and west by Maryland. Land area 1,982 sq. miles (5,133 sq. km). Census population, 1 April 1990 was 666,168 (73% urban), an increase of 12·1% since 1980. Population estimate (1998), 743,603.

Population in 5 census years was:

	White	Black	Indian	Asiatic	Total	Per sq. mile
1910	171,102	31,181	5	34	202,322	103·0
1930	205,718	32,602	5	55	238,380	120·5
1960	384,327	60,688	597	410	446,292	224·0
			All others			
1980	488,002	96,157	10,179		594,338	290·8
1990	535,094	112,460	18,614		666,168	325·9

Of the total population in 1990, 48·5% were male and 70·4% were 21 years old or older.

The 1990 census figures show Wilmington with a population of 71,529; Newark, 25,098; Dover, 27,630; Elsmere Town, 5,935; Milford City, 6,040; Seaford City, 5,089.

SOCIAL STATISTICS
Births in 1996, 10,152 (14·0 births per 1,000 population); deaths, 6,506 (9·0 per 1,000 population); infant deaths, 77 (7·9 per 1,000 live births); marriages, 5,209 (7·3 per 1,000 population); divorces, 3,405 (4·8).

CLIMATE
Wilmington, Jan. 32°F (0°C), July 75°F (23·9°C). Annual rainfall 43" (1,076 mm). Delaware belongs to the Atlantic Coast climate zone (*see* UNITED STATES: Climate).

CONSTITUTION AND GOVERNMENT
The present constitution (the fourth) dates from 1897, and has had 51 amendments; it was not ratified by the electorate but promulgated by the Constitutional Convention. The General Assembly consists of a Senate of 21 members elected for 4 years and a House of Representatives of 41 members elected for 2 years.

The state sends 1 representative to Congress.

The state capital is Dover. Delaware is divided into 3 counties.

RECENT ELECTIONS
In the 1996 presidential election Clinton polled 140,209 votes; Dole, 98,906; Perot, 28,693.

CURRENT ADMINISTRATION
Governor: Thomas R. Carper (D.), 1997–2001 ($107,100).
  Lieut.-Governor: Ruth Ann Minner (D.), ($46,300).
  Secretary of State: Edward J. Freel (D.) ($93,000).

ECONOMY
Budget. In 1996 total revenue was $3,619m. Total expenditure was $3,248m. (education, $962m.; public welfare, $463m.; health and hospitals, $211m.; highways, $257m.; police protection, $48m.) Debt outstanding, in 1996, was $4,279m.

Per capita personal income (1997, preliminary) was $29,022.

ENERGY AND NATURAL RESOURCES
Electricity. Net generation of electric energy, 1995, 8·3bn. kWh.

Water. The total area covered by water is approximately 442 sq. miles.

Minerals. The mineral resources of Delaware are not extensive, consisting chiefly of clay products, stone, sand and gravel and magnesium compounds.

Agriculture. Delaware is mainly an industrial state, with agriculture as its principal industry. There were 565,000 acres in 2,400 farms in 1997; 407,000 acres of this is harvested annually. The average farm was valued (land and buildings) at $745,000. The major product is broilers, accounting for $529,875m. in cash receipts, out of total farm cash receipts of $748,933m. in 1997.

The chief field crops are soybeans and corn for feed.

INDUSTRY

In 1996 manufacturing establishments employed 56,600 people; main manufactures were chemicals, transport equipment and food.

COMMUNICATIONS

Roads. The state in 1997 maintained 5,054 miles of roads and streets, including 321·04 miles of roads in the National Highway System. There were also 667·22 miles of municipally maintained streets. Vehicles registered in the year ended 31 Dec. 1997, 672,449.

Rail. In 1997 the state had 288·5 miles of active rail line, 23·2 miles of which is part of Amtrak's high-speed Northeast corridor. In 1996 there were 1,058,067 passenger trips beginning or ending in Delaware—581,285 intercity (Amtrak) and 476,782 commuter. An important component of Delaware's freight infrastructure is the rail access to the Port of Wilmington.

Civil Aviation. In 1997 Delaware had 11 public use airports and one helistop.

SOCIAL INSTITUTIONS

Justice. State prisons over the period 1 Jan. 1997–31 Dec. 1998 had a daily average of 5,283 inmates. The death penalty has been authorized; the last execution was in 1996.

Religion. The leading religious denominations are Roman Catholics, Methodists, Episcopalians and Lutherans.

Education. The state has free public schools and compulsory school attendance. In Sept. 1997 the elementary and secondary public schools had 111,960 enrolled pupils and 6,794 classroom teachers. Another 25,497 children were enrolled in private and parochial schools. State appropriation for public schools (financial year 1997–98) was about $649m. Average salary of classroom teachers (financial year 1997–98), $42,439. The state supports the University of Delaware at Newark (1834) which had 935 full-time faculty members and 20,517 students in Sept. 1997, Delaware State University, Dover (1892), with 174 full-time faculty members and 3,320 students, and the 4 campuses of Delaware Technical and Community College (Wilmington, Stanton, Dover and Georgetown) with 302 full-time faculty members and 43,535 students.

Health. In 1997 there were 7 short-term general hospitals. During the fiscal year 1997 the average daily census in state mental hospitals was 308.

Welfare. In 1974 the federal Supplemental Security Income (SSI) programme lessened state responsibility for the aged, blind and disabled. Total SSI payments in Delaware from Oct. 1996 through Sept. 1997 were $144,969,349. Provisions are also made for the care of dependent children; in the same period there were 2,882 children under the age of 20 receiving SSI payments totalling $39,679,812.

FURTHER READING

Statistical information: Delaware Economic Development Office POB 1401, Dover 19903. Publishes *Delaware Data Book.*

State Manual, Containing Official List of Officers, Commissions and County Officers. Secretary of State, Dover. Annual

Hoffecker, C. E., *Delaware: a Bicentennial History.* New York, 1977

Smeal, L., *Delaware Historical and Biographical Index.* New York, 1984

Weslager, C. A., *Delaware Indians, a History.* Rutgers Univ. Press, 1972

Topical History of Delaware. Division of Historical and Cultural Affairs. Dover, 1977

DISTRICT OF COLUMBIA

KEY HISTORICAL EVENTS

The District of Columbia, organized in 1790, is the seat of the Government of the USA, for which the land was ceded by the states of Maryland and Virginia to the USA as a site for the national capital. It was established under Acts of Congress in 1790 and 1791. Congress first met in it in 1800 and federal authority over it became vested in 1801. In 1846 the land ceded by Virginia (about 33 sq. miles) was given back.

TERRITORY AND POPULATION

The District forms an enclave on the Potomac River, where the river forms the south-west boundary of Maryland. The land area of the District of Columbia is 61 sq. miles (159 sq. km).

Census population, 1 April 1990, was 606,900 (100% urban), a decrease of 4·82% from that of 1980. Metropolitan statistical area of Washington, D.C.–Md–Va. (1980), 3m. Density of population in the District, 1990, 9,884 per sq. mile. Population estimate (1997), 529,000.

Population in 5 census years was:

	White	Black	Indian	Chinese and Japanese	Total	Per sq. mile
1910	236,128	94,446	68	427	331,069	5,517·8
1930	353,981	132,068	40	780	486,869	7,981·5
1960	345,263	411,737	587	3,532	763,956	12,523·9
				All others		
1970	209,272	537,712		9,526	756,510	12,321·0
1980	171,768	448,906		17,659	638,333	10,184·0

SOCIAL STATISTICS

Births, 1995, were 9,014 (16·3 per 1,000 population); deaths, 7,000 (11·6); infant mortality rate (per 1,000 live births), 16·2. Marriages (1996, provisional), 3,400 (6·4 per 1,000 population in 1995); divorce rate (1995), 3·4.

CLIMATE

Washington, Jan. 34°F (1·1°C), July 77°F (25°C). Annual rainfall 43" (1,064 mm). The District of Columbia belongs to the Atlantic Coast climate zone (*see* UNITED STATES: Climate).

CONSTITUTION AND GOVERNMENT

Local government, from 1 July 1878 until Aug. 1967, was that of a municipal corporation administered by a board of 3 commissioners, of whom 2 were appointed from civil life by the President, and confirmed by the Senate, for a term of 3 years each. The other commissioner was detailed by the President from the Engineer Corps of the Army. The Commission form of government was abolished in 1967 and a new Mayor Council instituted with officers appointed by the President with the advice and consent of the Senate. On 24 Dec. 1973 the appointed officers were replaced by an elected Mayor and councillors, with full legislative powers in local matters as from 1974. Congress retains the right to legislate, to veto or supersede the Council's acts. The 23rd amendment to the federal constitution (1961) conferred the right to vote in national elections. The District has 2 delegates in Congress who may vote in committees but not on the House floor.

RECENT ELECTIONS

In the 1996 presidential election Clinton polled 152,031 votes; Dole, 16,637; Perot, 3,479.

CURRENT ADMINISTRATION

Governor: Anthony Williams (D.), 1998–2002.

ECONOMY

Budget. The District's revenues are derived from a tax on real and personal property, sales taxes, taxes on corporations and companies, licences for conducting various businesses and from federal payments. The District of Columbia has no bonded debt not covered by its accumulated sinking fund.

ENERGY AND NATURAL RESOURCES

Water. The total area covered by water is approximately 7 sq. miles.

INDUSTRY

The main industries are government service, service, wholesale and retail trade, finance, real estate, insurance, communications, transport and utilities.

COMMUNICATIONS

Roads. Within the District are 340 miles of bus routes. There are 1,102 miles of streets maintained by the District; of these, 673 miles are local streets, 262 miles are major arterial roads. In 1996, 237,000 motor vehicles were registered.

Rail. There is a metro in Washington extending to 130 km, and 2 commuter rail networks.

Civil Aviation. The District is served by 3 general airports; across the Potomac River in Arlington, Va., is National Airport, in Chantilly, Va., is Dulles International Airport and in Maryland is Baltimore–Washington International Airport.

SOCIAL INSTITUTIONS

Justice. The death penalty was declared unconstitutional in the District of Columbia on 14 Nov. 1973. In 1996 there were 9,376 prisoners in state correctional institutions.

The District's Court system is the Judicial Branch of the District of Columbia. It is the only completely unified court system in the United States, possibly because of the District's unique city-state jurisdiction. Until the District of Columbia Court Reform and Criminal Procedure Act of 1970, the judicial system was almost entirely in the hands of Federal Government. Since that time, the system has been similar in most respects to the autonomous systems of the states.

Religion. The largest churches are the Protestant and Roman Catholic Christian churches; there are also Jewish, Eastern Orthodox and Islamic congregations.

Education. In 1996 there were an estimated 105,700 pupils enrolled at elementary and secondary public schools. Average expenditure per pupil in 1997 was $8,167.

Higher education is given through the Consortium of Universities of the Metropolitan Washington Area, which consists of six universities and three colleges: Georgetown University, founded in 1795 by the Jesuit Order; George Washington University, non-sectarian founded in 1821; Howard University, founded in 1867; Catholic University of America, founded in 1887; American University (Methodist) founded in 1893; University of D.C., founded 1976; Gallaudet College, founded 1864; Trinity College, founded 1897. There are altogether 18 institutes of higher education.

Health. The District government provides primary health care for residents, mainly through its Department of Human Services. In 1994 there were 12 community hospitals with 4,000 beds.

Welfare. There were 77,000 beneficiaries of social security in 1996 including 53,000 retired workers and dependants, 15,000 survivors of deceased workers and 9,000 disabled workers and dependants. Total annual payments were $539m.

CULTURE

Tourism. About 17m. visitors stay in the District every year and spend about $1,000m.

FURTHER READING

Statistical Information: The Metropolitan Washington Board of Trade publications.
Reports of the Commissioners of the District of Columbia. Annual. Washington
Bowling, K. R., *The Creation of Washington D.C.: the Idea and the Location of the American Capital.* Washington (D.C.), 1991

UNITED STATES OF AMERICA

FLORIDA

KEY HISTORICAL EVENTS

There were French and Spanish settlements in Florida in the 16th century, of which the Spanish, at St Augustine in 1565, proved permanent. Florida was claimed by Spain until 1763 when it passed to Britain. Although regained by Spain in 1783, the British used it as a base for attacks on American forces during the war of 1812. Gen. Andrew Jackson captured Pensacola for the USA in 1818. In 1819 a treaty was signed which ceded Florida to the USA with effect from 1821 and it became a Territory of the USA in 1822.

Florida had been the home of the Apalachee and Timucua Indians. After 1770 groups of Creek Indians began to arrive as refugees from the European-Indian wars. These 'Seminoles' or runaways attracted other refugees including slaves, the recapture of whom was the motive for the first Seminole War of 1817–18. A second war followed in 1835–42, when the Seminoles retreated to the Everglades swamps. After a third war in 1855–58 most Seminoles were forced or persuaded to move to reserves in Oklahoma.

Florida became a state in 1845. About half of the population were black slaves. At the outbreak of Civil War in 1861 the state seceded from the Union.

During the 20th century Florida continued to grow fruit and vegetables, but real-estate development (often for retirement) and the growth of tourism and the aerospace industry set it apart from other ex-plantation states.

TERRITORY AND POPULATION

Florida is a peninsula bounded in the west by the Gulf of Mexico, south by the Straits of Florida, east by the Atlantic, north by Georgia and north-west by Alabama. Land area, 53,937 sq. miles (139,697 sq. km). Census population, 1 April 1990, 12,937,926, an increase of 32·8% since 1980. Estimate (1997), 14,654,000.

Population in 5 federal census years was:

	White	Black	All Others	Total	Per Sq. mile
1950	2,166,051	603,101	2,153	2,771,305	51·1
1960	4,063,881	880,168	7,493	4,952,788	91·5
1970	5,719,343	1,041,651	28,449	6,789,443	125·6
1980	8,319,448	1,342,478	84,398	9,746,324	180·1
1990	10,749,285	1,759,534	429,107	12,937,926	238·9

Of the population in 1990, 84·8% were urban, 48·4% male and 73·8% were 20 years of age or over.

The largest cities in the state, 1990 census (and 1994) are: Jacksonville, 672,971 (676,718); Miami, 358,548 (365,498); Tampa, 280,015 (285,153); St Petersburg, 238,629 (241,563); Hialeah, 188,004 (203,911); Orlando, 164,693 (170,307); Fort Lauderdale, 149,377 (149,491); Tallahassee, 124,773 (137,057); Hollywood, 121,697 (125,342); Clearwater, 98,784 (101,162); Gainesville, 84,770 (96,052); Coral Springs, 79,443 (93,439); Miami Beach, 92,639 (91,775); Pembroke Pines, 65,452 (87,948); Cape Coral, 74,991 (85,807); West Palm Beach, 67,764 (76,418); Plantation, 66,814 (75,484); Lakeland, 70,576 (74,626); Pompano Beach, 72,411 (73,950).

Population of the largest metropolitan areas (1994): Tampa-St Petersburg-Clearwater, 2,163,509; Miami, 1,990,445; Orlando, 1,359,001; Fort Lauderdale, 1,340,220.

SOCIAL STATISTICS

Births in 1995 were 192,537; deaths, 148,000; in 1994, infant deaths, 1,567; marriages, 142,895; divorces and other dissolutions, 81,628.

CLIMATE

Jacksonville, Jan. 55°F (12·8°C), July 81°F (27·2°C). Annual rainfall 54" (1,353 mm). Key West, Jan. 70°F (21·1°C), July 83°F (28·3°C). Annual rainfall 39" (968 mm). Miami, Jan. 67°F (19·4°C), July 82°F (27·8°C). Annual rainfall 60" (1,516 mm). Tampa, Jan. 61°F (16·1°C), July 81°F (27·2°C). Annual rainfall 51" (1,285 mm). Florida belongs to the Gulf Coast climate zone (see UNITED STATES: Climate).

FLORIDA

CONSTITUTION AND GOVERNMENT
The 1968 Legislature revised the constitution of 1885. The state legislature consists of a Senate of 40 members, elected for 4 years, and House of Representatives with 120 members elected for 2 years. Sessions are held annually, and are limited to 60 days.

The state sends 23 representatives to Congress.

The state capital is Tallahassee. The state is divided into 67 counties.

RECENT ELECTIONS
In the 1996 presidential election Clinton polled 2,533,502 votes; Dole, 2,226,117; Perot, 482,237.

CURRENT ADMINISTRATION
Governor: Jeb Bush (R.), 1999–2003 ($114,070).
Lieut.-Governor: Frank Brogan (R.), ($109,245).
Secretary of State: Katherine Harris (R.), ($112,895).

ECONOMY

Budget. In 1996 total revenue was $41,680m. Total expenditure was 36,454m. (education, $10,872m.; public welfare, $7,318m.; health and hospitals, $2,606m.; highways, $3,241m.; police protection, $295m.)

Outstanding debt, 1996, amounted to $15,515m.

Per capita personal income (1997, preliminary) was $25,255.

ENERGY AND NATURAL RESOURCES

Oil and Gas. In 1996, 6bn. bbls. of crude oil was produced; natural gas production was 6bn. cu. ft.

Water. The total area covered by water is approximately 5,991 sq. miles.

Minerals. Chief mineral is phosphate rock, of which marketable production in 1992 was 36·2m. tonnes. This was approximately 75% of US and 25% of the world supply of phosphate in 1992.

Agriculture. In 1997 there were 10m. acres of farmland; 40,000 farms with an average of 258 acres per farm. The total value of land and buildings was $23,690m.; average value (1998) of land and buildings per acre, $2,300.

Farm income from crops and livestock (1996) was $6,131m., of which crops provided $4,942m. Major crop contributors were oranges, grapefruit, tomatoes, peppers, other winter vegetables, indoor and landscaping plants and sugar-cane. In 1994 poultry farms produced 132·7m. chickens, 2,538m. eggs and (in 1997) 596m. lbs of broilers. On 1 Jan. 1995 the state had 2·02m. cattle, including 176,000 milch cows (1994), and about 0·1m. swine.

Forestry. The national forests covered an area of 1·1m. acres in 1997. There were 16,548,922 acres of commercial forest and 33 state forests of 596,137 acres.

Fisheries. Florida has extensive fisheries for oysters, shrimp, red snapper, crabs, mackerel and mullet. Catch (1990), 180m. lbs, valued at $203m.

INDUSTRY
In 1994 there were 15,831 manufacturers. They employed 483,754 persons. Main industries included: printing and publishing, machinery and computer equipment, apparel and finished products, fabricated metal products, and lumber and wood products.

COMMUNICATIONS

Roads. The state (1996) had 114,422 miles of highways, roads, and streets all of which were in the state and local system (66,083 miles being rural roads); there were 10,889,000 vehicle registrations.

Rail. In 1993 there were 2,988 miles of railway and 14 rail companies. There is a metro of 20 miles (33 km), a peoplemover and a commuter rail route in Miami.

Civil Aviation. In 1993 Florida had 133 public use airports (12 international) of which 20 have scheduled commercial service, and 28 seaplane bases.

SOCIAL INSTITUTIONS

Justice. The death penalty is authorized; there have been over 30 executions since 1979. In 1996 there were 63,763 prisoners under jurisdiction of state and federal correction authorities. Chain gangs were introduced in 1995.

Religion. The main Christian churches are Roman Catholic, Baptist, Methodist, Presbyterian and Episcopalian. There were 105,000 Latter-day Saints (Mormons) in 1997.

Education. Attendance at school is compulsory between 7 and 16. In the 1994–95 school year the public elementary and secondary schools had 2,107,514 pupils enrolled in grades K-12. Total expenditure on public schools (1994) was $17,035m. The state maintains 28 community colleges, with a full-time equivalent enrolment of 192,698 in 1995.

There are 9 universities in the state system, with a total of 207,812 students in 1995: The University of Florida at Gainesville (founded 1853) with 39,417 students; the Florida State University (founded at Tallahassee in 1857) with 30,268; the University of South Florida at Tampa (founded 1960) with 36,146; Florida A. & M. University at Tallahassee (founded 1887) with 10,267; Florida Atlantic University (founded 1964) at Boca Raton with 18,240; the University of West Florida at Pensacola with 8,250; the University of Central Florida at Orlando with 26,555; the University of North Florida at Jacksonville with 10,463; Florida International University at Miami with 28,206.

Health. In 1994 there were 218 community hospitals with 51,400 beds.

Welfare. From 1974 aid to the aged, blind and disabled became a federal responsibility. The state continued to give aid to families with dependent children and general assistance. In 1996 there were 3,034,000 beneficiaries, including: 2,269,000 retired workers and dependants; 428,000 widows and widowers; 337,000 disabled workers and dependants. Total annual payments (1996), $24,195m.

CULTURE

Tourism. During 1994, 39·8m. tourists visited Florida. They spent $33,390m., making tourism one of the biggest industries in the state. In 1996 Florida was the second most visited state by overseas travellers (behind California) with 5,710,000 visitors (25·2% of the market). There are 148 state parks, 33 state forests, 3 national parks, 8 national memorials, monuments, seashores and preserves and 3 national forests.

FURTHER READING

Statistical information: Bureau of Economic and Business Research, Univ. of Florida, Gainesville 32611. Publishes *Florida Statistical Abstract.*
Denslow, D. A. *et al., The Economy of Florida.* Florida Univ. Press, 1990
Fernald, E. A. (ed.) *Atlas of Florida.* Florida State Univ., 1981
Huckshorn, R. J. (ed.) *Government and Politics in Florida.* Florida Univ. Press, 1991
Morris, A., *The Florida Handbook.* Tallahassee. Biennial
Shermyen, A. H. (ed.), *1991 Florida Statistical Abstract.* Florida Univ. Press, 1991

State Library: Gray Building, Tallahassee.

GEORGIA

KEY HISTORICAL EVENTS

Originally the territory of Creek and Cherokee tribes, Georgia was first settled by Europeans in the 18th century. James Oglethorpe founded Savannah in 1733, intending it as a colony which offered a new start to debtors, convicts and the poor. Settlement was slow until 1783, when growth began in the cotton-growing areas west of Augusta. The Indian population was cleared off the rich cotton land and moved beyond the Mississippi. Georgia became one of the original 13 states of the Union.

A plantation economy developed rapidly, using slave labour. In 1861 Georgia seceded from the Union and became an important source of supplies for the Confederate cause, although some northern areas never accepted secession and continued in sympathy with the Union during the Civil War. At the beginning of the war 56% of the population were white, descendants of British, Austrian and New England immigrants; the remaining 44% were black slaves.

The city of Atlanta, which grew as a railway junction, was destroyed during the war but revived to become the centre of southern states during the reconstruction period. Atlanta was confirmed as state capital in 1877. Also in Atlanta were developed successive movements for black freedom in social, economic and political life. The Southern Christian Leadership Conference, led by Martin Luther King (assassinated in 1968), was based in King's native city of Atlanta.

TERRITORY AND POPULATION
Georgia is bounded north by Tennessee and North Carolina, north-east by South Carolina, east by the Atlantic, south by Florida and west by Alabama. Land area, 58,910 sq. miles (152,577 sq. km). Census population, 1 April 1990, was 6,478,216 (63·2% urban), an increase of 18·56% since 1980. Population estimate (1997), 7,486,000.

Population in 5 census years was:

	White	Black	Indian	Asiatic	Total	Per sq. mile
1910	1,431,802	1,176,987	95	237	2,609,121	44·4
1930	1,837,021	1,071,125	43	317	2,908,506	49·7
			All others			
1970	3,391,242	1,187,149	11,184		4,589,575	79·0
1980	3,948,007	1,465,457	50,801		5,464,265	92·7
1990	4,600,148	1,746,565	131,507		6,478,216	110·0

Of the 1990 population, 3,144,503 were male, 4,097,339 were urban and those 20 years of age and over numbered 4,534,963.

The largest cities are: Atlanta (capital), with population, 1994 estimate, of 396,000; Columbus, 186,000; Savannah, 141,000; Macon, 109,000.

SOCIAL STATISTICS
Births, 1995, were 112,246 (15·8 per 1,000 population); deaths, 58,433 (8·2); infant deaths, 1,058 (9·4 per 1,000 live births); marriages, 61,908 (8·7 per 1,000 population); divorces and annulments, 37,070 (5·2).

CLIMATE
Atlanta, Jan. 43°F (6·1°C), July 78°F (25·6°C). Annual rainfall 49" (1,234 mm). Georgia belongs to the Atlantic Coast climate zone (*see* UNITED STATES: Climate).

CONSTITUTION AND GOVERNMENT
A new constitution was ratified in the general election of 2 Nov. 1976, proclaimed on 22 Dec. 1976 and became effective on 1 Jan. 1977. The General Assembly consists of a Senate of 56 members and a House of Representatives of 180 members, both elected for 2 years. Legislative sessions are annual, beginning the 2nd Monday in Jan. and lasting for 40 days.

Georgia was the first state to extend the franchise to all citizens 18 years old and above.

The state sends 11 representatives to Congress.

The state capital is Atlanta. Georgia is divided into 159 counties.

RECENT ELECTIONS
At the 1996 presidential election Dole polled 1,078,837 votes; Clinton, 1,052,928; Perot, 146,039.

CURRENT ADMINISTRATION
Governor: Roy Barnes, 1999–2003.
Secretary of State: Cathy Cox.

ECONOMY

Budget. In 1996 total state revenue was $22,409m. Total expenditure was $20,013m. (education, $7,933m.; public welfare, $4,623m.; health and hospitals, $1,289m.; highways, $1,228m.; police protection, $150m.) Debt outstanding (1996), $6,200m.

Per capita personal income (1997, preliminary) was $24,061.

ENERGY AND NATURAL RESOURCES

Water. The total area covered by water is approximately 1,058 sq. miles.

Minerals. Georgia is the leading producer of kaolin. The state ranks first in production of crushed and dimensional granite, and second in production of fuller's earth and marble (crushed and dimensional).

Agriculture. In 1996, 43,000 farms covered 11·8m. acres; the average farm was of 274 acres. In 1995 the average value of farmland and buildings was $1,256 per acre. For 1995 cotton output was 1,941m. bales (of 480 lbs). Other major crops include tobacco, corn, wheat, soybeans, peanuts and pecans. Cash income, 1996, $5,687m.: from crops, $2,408m.; from livestock and products, $3,279m.

In 1996 farm animals included 1·56m. all cattle, 0·90m. swine and 1,070m. (1995) poultry.

Forestry. The forested area in 1996 was 23·6m. acres.

INDUSTRY

In 1996 the state's 10,598 manufacturing establishments had 583,314 workers; the main groups were textiles, apparel, food and transport equipment. Trade employed 887,466, services 826,165 and government 558,753.

COMMUNICATIONS

Roads. In 1996 there were 111,746 miles of public roads, including 1,241 miles of interstate highways; there were 6,283,000 motor vehicles registered.

Rail. In 1996 there were 4,962 miles of railways and a metro in Atlanta.

Civil Aviation. In 1997 there were 106 public airports, 9 with scheduled commercial service.

Shipping. There are deepwater ports at Savannah, the principal port, and Brunswick.

SOCIAL INSTITUTIONS

Justice. In 1996 state prisons had 35,139 inmates. The death penalty is authorized for capital offences.

Under a Local Option Act, the sale of alcoholic beverages is prohibited in some counties.

Religion. An estimated 57·6% of the population are church members. Of the total population, 45·6% are Protestant, 3·2% are Roman Catholic and 1·1% are Jewish.

Education. Since 1945 education has been compulsory; tuition is free for pupils between the ages of 6 and 18 years. In 1996 there were 1,799 public elementary and public secondary schools with 1·3m. pupils and 81,058 teachers. Teachers' salaries averaged $33,869 in 1996. Expenditure on public schools (1995–96), $7,781m. or $1,080 per capita and $4,589 per pupil.

The University of Georgia (Athens) was founded in 1785 and was the first chartered State University in the USA (29,404 students in 1996–97). Other institutions of higher learning include Georgia Institute of Technology, Atlanta (12,985); Emory University, Atlanta (11,308); Georgia State University, Atlanta (23,410); and Georgia Sourheev University, Statesboro (14,312). The Atlanta University Center, devoted primarily to Black education, includes Clark Atlanta University (5,230) and Morris Brown College (2,169) co-educational; Morehouse (2,884), a liberal arts college for men; Interdenominational Theological Center (419), a co-educational theological school; and Spelman College (1,961), the first liberal arts college for Black women in the USA. Atlanta University serves as the graduate school centre for the complex. Wesleyan College (445) near Macon is the oldest chartered women's college in the world.

Health. In 1995 general hospitals licensed by the Department of Human Resources numbered 158 with 24,756 beds.

Welfare. In Dec. 1995, 43,666 persons were receiving Supplemental Security Income old-age assistance and 126,662 receiving benefits for blind and disabled persons. In 1996 a total of 1,027,000 beneficiaries received $7,677m., of which there were 132,625 families receiving aid to dependant children.

CULTURE

Tourism. In 1996 tourists spent $14,775m. There are 44 state parks.

FURTHER READING

Statistical information: Selig Center for Economic Growth, Univ. of Georgia, Athens 30602. Publishes *Georgia Statistical Abstract.*

Rowland, A. R., *A Bibliography of the Writings on Georgia History.* Hamden, Conn., 1978

State Library: Judicial Building, Capital Sq., Atlanta.

HAWAII

KEY HISTORICAL EVENTS

The islands of Hawaii were settled by Polynesian immigrants, probably from the Marquesas Islands, about AD 400. A second major immigration, from Tahiti, occurred around 800–900. In the late 18th century all the islands of the group were united into one kingdom by Kamehameha I. Western exploration began in 1778, and Christian missions were established after 1820. Europeans called Hawaii the Sandwich Islands. The main foreign states interested were the USA, Britain and France. Because of the threat imposed by their rivalry, Kamehameha III placed Hawaii under US protection in 1851. US sugar-growing companies became dominant in the economy and in 1887 the USA obtained a naval base at Pearl Harbour. A struggle developed between forces for and against annexation by the USA. In 1893 the monarchy was overthrown. The republican government agreed to be annexed to the USA in 1898, and Hawaii became a US Territory in 1900.

The islands and the naval base were of great strategic importance during the Second World War, when the Japanese attack on Pearl Harbour brought the USA into the war.

Hawaii became the 50th state of the Union in 1959. The 19th-century plantation economy led to much immigration of workers, especially from China and Japan. At the same time the Hawaiian laws, religions and culture were gradually adapted to foreign models.

TERRITORY AND POPULATION

The Hawaiian Islands lie in the North Pacific Ocean, between 18° 56' and 28° 25' N. lat. and 154° 49' and 178° 22' W. long., about 2,090 nautical miles south-west of San Francisco. There are 136 named islands and islets in the group, of which 7 major and 8 minor islands are inhabited. Land area, 6,423 sq. miles (16,636 sq. km). Census population, 1 April 1990, 1,108,229 (51% male, 89% urban), an increase of 14·84% since 1980; density was 172·5 per sq. mile. Estimated population (1997), 1,186,602.

The principal islands are Hawaii, 4,028 sq. miles, population 1990, 120,317; Maui, 727 sq. miles, population 91,361; Oahu, 600 sq. miles, population 836,231; Kauai, 552 sq. miles, population 50,947; Molokai, 260 sq. miles, population 6,717; Lanai, 141 sq. miles, population 2,426; Niihau, 70 sq. miles, population 230; Kahoolawe, 45 sq. miles (uninhabited). The capital Honolulu—on the island of Oahu—had a population in 1980 of 365,048, and Hilo—on the island of Hawaii—37,808 in 1990.

UNITED STATES OF AMERICA

Estimated figures in 1996 for racial groups (excluding persons in institutions or military barracks) were: 254,421 white; 233,435 Japanese; 114,717 Filipinos; 237,128 Hawaiian; 35,682 Chinese; 8,862 Korean; 16,314 black; 248,117 all others.

Inter-marriage between the races is common. Of the 19,589 marriages in 1996, 45·6% were between partners of different race.

SOCIAL STATISTICS
Births, 1996, were 18,378 (15·5 per 1,000 population); deaths, 7,803 (6·6). Infant deaths were at a rate of 5·8 per 1,000 live births. There were 19,589 marriages (7·6 per 1,000 population), and divorces and annulments numbered 4,903 (4·1 per 1,000 population) in 1996.

CLIMATE
All the islands have a tropical climate, with an abrupt change in conditions between windward and leeward sides, most marked in rainfall. Temperatures vary little. Average temperatures in Honolulu in 1997: warmest month 81·4°F, coolest month 72·9°F. Annual rainfall in Honolulu (1997) 22·02".

CONSTITUTION AND GOVERNMENT
The constitution took effect on 21 Aug. 1959; amended 1968 and 1978. The Legislature is bicameral consisting of a Senate of 25 members elected from the state's 25 single-member districts for 4 years, and a House of Representatives of 51 members elected for 2 years. The constitution provides for annual meetings of the legislature with 60-day regular sessions.

The state sends 2 representatives to Congress.

The state capital is Honolulu. There are 5 counties.

RECENT ELECTIONS
In the 1996 presidential election Clinton polled 205,012 votes; Dole, 113,943; Perot, 27,358.

CURRENT ADMINISTRATION
Governor: Benjamin Cayetano (D.), 1999–2003 ($94,780).
   Lieut.-Governor: Mazie Hirono (D.) ($90,041).

ECONOMY
Budget. Revenue is derived mainly from taxation of sales and gross receipts, real property, corporate and personal income, and inheritance taxes, licences, public land sales and leases.

In 1996 total state revenue was $6,383m. Total expenditure was $5,947m. (education, $1,548m.; public welfare, $915m.; health and hospitals, $487m.; highways, $270m.; police protection, $9m.) Outstanding debt, 1996, amounted to $5,117m.

Estimated *per capita* personal income (1997, preliminary) was $26,034.

Banking and Finance. In 1997 there were 5 state-chartered banks with assets of $21,468·4m., and 1 federal bank.

ENERGY AND NATURAL RESOURCES
Electricity. Installed capacity in 1995 was 1,714,729 kW; total power consumed (1997) was 9,345·3m. kWh.

Oil and Gas. In 1997, $51·2m. was generated by gas sales.

Water. The total area covered by water is approximately 36 sq. miles. Water consumption in 1997 amounted to 71,810m. gallons.

Minerals. Total value of non-fuel mineral production, 1996, $112m.; mainly crushed stone (7·8m. tonnes, value $77·2m.) and cement (310,000 tonnes, value $30·8m.).

Agriculture. Farming is highly commercialized and highly mechanized. In 1996 there were about 4,600 farms covering an area of 1·59m. acres; average number of acres per farm, 346; paid workforce totalled 10,100.

HAWAII

Sugar and pineapples are the staple crops. Farm income, 1996, from crop sales was $422·6m., and from livestock $65·7m. The sugar crop was valued at $108·1m.; pineapples, $95·9m.; other crops, $218·6m. in 1996.

Forestry. In 1997 conservation district forest land amounted to 971,876 acres (of which 328,742 was privately owned); there were 46,191 acres of planted forest; and 109,164 acres of natural area.

Fisheries. In 1997 the commercial fish catch was 25·3m. lbs with a value of $53·3m. to primary producers. There were (1991) 4,043 fishermen.

INDUSTRY
In 1996 manufacturing establishments employed 17,100 production workers. Defence is the second-largest industry.

Labour. The labour force amounted to 592,000 in 1997; 6·4% (37,900) were unemployed.

Trade Unions. In 1996, 16% of workers in the private sector belonged to a union: 51·1% in the public sector.

INTERNATIONAL TRADE

Imports and Exports. Sugar exports brought in $168·8m. in 1996; pineapple exports, $147m.

COMMUNICATIONS

Roads. In 1996 there were 4,133 miles of roads (2,293 miles rural). There were, in 1997, 906,964 registered motor vehicles (704,693 passenger vehicles; 158,457 trucks; 22,697 trailers; 3,226 buses; and 17,160 motor cycles).

Civil Aviation. There were 9 commercial airports in 1997. Passengers arriving from overseas numbered 7·79m., and there were 10·45m. passengers between the islands.

Shipping. Several lines of steamers connect the islands with the mainland USA, Canada, Australia, the Philippines, China and Japan. In the year ended 30 June 1997, 1,604 overseas and 2,679 inter-island vessels entered the port of Honolulu carrying a total of 18,262 overseas and 46,825 inter-island passengers.

Telecommunications. There were 703,879 telephone access lines in 1996.

SOCIAL INSTITUTIONS

Justice. There is no capital punishment in Hawaii. In 1997 there were 3,450 prisoners in federal and state prisons.

Religion. The residents are mainly Christians, though there are many Buddhists.

Education. Education is free, and compulsory for children between the ages of 6 and 18. The language in the schools is English. In 1994–95 there were 242 public schools and 132 private schools. There were 183,795 pupils and 11,602 teachers in public elementary and secondary schools. In 1994–95, $1058·6m. was spent on education; average amount spent on each pupil, $5,794; average annual salary for teachers, $35,532. In 1997 the number of students to enrol at college or university was 70,450.

Health. In 1996 there were 71 state-approved hospitals (acute care/long-term/speciality care) with 7,433 beds.

Welfare. In 1996 there were 81,774 individuals (33,232 cases) in receipt of state assistance, receiving on average $225 per month.

CULTURE

Broadcasting. There were (1995) 55 radio and television stations. In 1997 there were, in addition, 3 cable television companies.

Cinema. In 1995 there were 41 cinemas.

Press. A total of 27 newspapers were in circulation in 1995.

Tourism. Tourism is outstanding in Hawaii's economy. Tourist arrivals numbered only 1·1m. in 1967, but reached 6·9m. in 1997. Tourist expenditure ($380m. in 1967) contributed $10,381m. to the state's economy in 1997.

Libraries. There were 49 libraries employing a total of 512 people in 1997.

FURTHER READING

Statistical information: Hawaii State Department of Business, POB 2359, Honolulu 96804. Publishes *The State of Hawaii Data Book.*
Legislative Reference Bureau. *Guide to Government in Hawaii.* 8th ed. Honolulu, 1989
Atlas of Hawaii. Rev. ed. Hawaii Univ. Press, 1983
Bell, R. J., *Last Among Equals: Hawaiian Statehood and American Politics.* Honolulu, 1984
Kuykendall, R. S. and Day, A. G., *Hawaii: a History.* Rev. ed. New Jersey, 1961
Morgan, J. R., *Hawaii.* Boulder, 1982
Morris, N. J. and Dean, L. *Hawai'i* [Bibliography]. Santa Barbara (CA) and Oxford, 1992

IDAHO

KEY HISTORICAL EVENTS

The original people of Idaho were Kutenai, Kalispel, Nez Percé and other tribes, living on the Pacific watershed of the northern Rocky Mountains. European exploration began in 1805, and after 1809 there were trading posts and small settlements, with fur-trapping as the primary economic activity. The area was disputed between Britain and the USA until 1846 when British claims were dropped. In 1860 gold and silver were found, and there was a rush of immigrant prospectors. The newly enlarged population needed organized government. An area including that which is now Montana was created a Territory in March 1863. Montana was separated from it in 1864. Population growth continued, stimulated by refugees from the Confederate states after the Civil War and by settlements of Mormons from Utah.

Fur-trapping and mining gave way to farming, especially of grains, as the main economic activity. Idaho became a state in 1890, with its capital at Boise. The Territory capital, Idaho City, had been a gold-mining boom town in the 1860s whose population (about 40,000 at its height) was the largest in the Pacific Northwest. The population declined to 1,000 by 1869.

During the 20th century the Indian population shrunk to nearly 1%. The Mormon community has grown to include much of south-eastern Idaho and more than half the church-going population of the state.

Industrial history has been influenced by the development of the Snake River of southern Idaho for hydro-electricity and irrigation, especially at the American Falls and reservoir. Processing food, minerals and timber are important to the economy. The population, however, remains mainly sparse and rural. Rapid growth of high technology companies in Idaho's metropolitan areas has prompted economic diversification and rapid population growth. Between 1990 and 1998, the Idaho rate of population change of 22% has been the third highest in the United States. The two county Boise metropolitan area population exceeds 400,000.

TERRITORY AND POPULATION

Idaho is bounded north by Canada, east by the Rocky Mountains of Montana and Wyoming, south by Nevada and Utah, west by Oregon and Washington. Land area, 82,751 sq. miles (214,325 sq. km). Census population, 1 April 1990, 1,006,749 (57·4% urban), an increase of 6·65% since 1980. Population estimate (1998), 1,228,684.

Population in 5 census years was:

	White	Black	Indian	Asiatic	Total	Per sq. mile
1910	319,221	651	3,488	2,234	325,594	3·9
1930	438,840	668	3,638	1,886	445,032	5·4
1960	657,383	1,502	5,231	2,958	667,191	8·1
1980	901,641	2,716	10,521	5,948	943,935	11·3
1990	950,451	3,370	13,780	9,365	1,006,749	12·2

IDAHO

Of the total 1990 population, 500,956 were male, 578,214 were urban and those 20 years of age or older 665,889.

The largest cities are: Boise City, with 1996 census population of 152,737; Pocatello, 51,344; Idaho Falls, 48,079; Nampa, 37,558; Twin Falls, 31,989; Coeur d'Alene, 31,076; Lewiston, 30,271.

SOCIAL STATISTICS
Births (1997), 18,537 (15·3 per 1,000 population); deaths, 8,952 (7·4); marriages, 15,114 (12·5); divorces, 6,961 (5·8); infant deaths, 127; infant mortality rate, 6·9 (per 1,000 live births).

CLIMATE
Boise City, Jan. 29°F (–1·7°C), July 74°F (23·3°C). Annual rainfall 12" (303 mm). Idaho belongs to the Mountain States climate zone (*see* UNITED STATES: Climate).

CONSTITUTION AND GOVERNMENT
The constitution adopted in 1890 is still in force; it has had 105 amendments. The Legislature consists of a Senate of 35 members and a House of Representatives of 70 members, all the legislators being elected for 2 years. It meets annually.

The state sends 2 representatives to Congress.

The state is divided into 44 counties. The capital is Boise City.

RECENT ELECTIONS
In the 1996 presidential election Dole polled 256,406 votes; Clinton, 165,545; Perot, 62,506.

CURRENT ADMINISTRATION
Governor: Dirk Kempthorne (R.), 1999–2003 ($92,500).
Lieut.-Governor: C. L. 'Butch' Otter (R.), 1999–2003 ($24,500).
Secretary of State: Pete T. Cenarrusa (R.), 1999–2003 ($75,000).

Local Government. Idaho has 44 counties and 201 cities.

ECONOMY
Budget. In 1996 total revenue was $4,384m. Total expenditure was $3,501m. (education, $1,361m.; public welfare, $528m.; health and hospitals, $106m.; highways, $346m.; police protection, $30m.).

Per capita personal income (1997) was $20,380.

ENERGY AND NATURAL RESOURCES
Electricity. Idaho's rivers provide dependable and low-cost electrical power. Almost two-thirds of Idaho's electrical needs come from this resource, resulting in electricity rates much lower than those found in the East and Midwest.

Water. The total area covered by water is approximately 823 sq. miles. Much of Idaho's surface water flows out of the high mountains and is generally of high quality. High quality groundwater is pumped for agricultural, industrial and residential use. Idaho is second only to California in the amount of water used for irrigating crops.

Minerals. Principal non-fuel minerals are phosphate rock, silver, gold, and sand and gravel. The estimated value of total mineral output, 1997, was $477m.

Agriculture. Agriculture is the leading industry, although a great part of the state is naturally arid. Extensive irrigation works have been carried out, bringing an estimated 4m. acres under irrigation, and there are over 50 soil conservation districts.

In 1997 there were 22,000 farms with a total area of 13·5m. acres; average value per acre (1997), $1,017. In 1997 the average farm was 614 acres.

Farm income, 1997, from crops, $1,944m., and livestock, $1,408m. The most important crops are potatoes and wheat. Other crops are sugar-beet, alfalfa, barley, field peas and beans, onions and apples. In 1997 there were 1·75m. cattle, 285,000 sheep, 33,000 hogs and 1·19m. poultry. The dairy industry is the fastest growing sector in Idaho agriculture.

Forestry. In 1997 a total of 21,598,522 acres was forest.

Fisheries. 75% of the commercial trout processed in the USA is produced in Idaho.

INDUSTRY

Labour. In 1997, 128,700 people were employed in trade, 99,300 in government, 121,800 in services and 74,400 in manufacturing. The workforce totalled 619,000 in 1996. In 1997 state unemployment was running at 5·3%.

Trade Unions. Idaho has a right-to-work law. In 1997, 43,400 people were union members.

COMMUNICATIONS

Roads. In 1998 there were 59,897 miles of roads (56,435 miles rural) and 1,187,000 registered non-commercial vehicles.

Rail. The state had (1991) 1,910 miles of railways (including 1 Amtrak route).

Civil Aviation. There were 68 municipally owned airports in 1991.

Shipping. Water transport is provided from the Pacific to the port of Lewiston, by way of the Columbia and Snake rivers, a distance of 464 miles.

Telecommunications. In 1990, 94% of state households had telephones. Telephone penetration is lowest in remote rural areas.

Postal Services. Idaho is served by the United States Postal Service. Major carriers, including UPS, Federal Express, Airborne Express and DHL Worldwide Express, provide Idaho residents with global shipping access. There are numerous local mailing and shipping services available in Idaho's larger cities.

SOCIAL INSTITUTIONS

Justice. The death penalty may be imposed for first degree murder or aggravated kidnapping, but the judge must consider mitigating circumstances before imposing a sentence of death. The last execution was in 1994. The state prison system had an average 4,111 inmates in March 1999.

Religion. The leading religious denominations are the Church of Jesus Christ of Latterday Saints (Mormons; 333,000 adherents in 1997), Roman Catholics, Methodists, Presbyterians, Episcopalians and Lutherans.

Education. In 1997–98 public elementary schools (grades K to 6) had 130,080 pupils and 6,811 teachers; secondary schools had 114,323 pupils and 6,394 classroom teachers. Average base salary (1996–97) of elementary and secondary teachers was $31,820.

The University of Idaho, founded at Moscow in 1889, in 1998 had 519 full-time instructional faculty, and a total enrolment of 11,437. There were 9 other higher education institutions, 5 of them public institutions. College and university enrolment in the autumn of 1998 was 63,138.

Health. In 1999 there were 3,087 hospital beds in 48 licensed facilities.

Welfare. Old-age survivor disability insurance (OASDI) is granted to persons if they meet needs qualifications. 1996: total beneficiaries, 181,160 with annual benefit payments of $1,395m.

CULTURE

Broadcasting. In 1998 there were 90 radio stations and 15 television stations.

Cinema. There were 80 movie theatres in 1998.

Press. Idaho has 12 daily newspapers and 53 weekly papers.

Tourism. Money spent by travellers in 1997 was about $1,700m.

Festivals. Idaho hosts Ballet Idaho, the Idaho Shakespeare Festival, the Lionel Hampton Jazz Festival, the International Folk Dance Festival, the Boise River Festival and the National Old Time Fiddler's Contest.

Libraries. 83% of the population had access to library services in 1997.

Museums and Galleries. Amongst Idaho's many museums and galleries are the Boise Art Museum, the Idaho State Historical Museum and the Nez Percé National Historic Park and Museum.

FURTHER READING

Statistical information: Department of Commerce, 700 West State St., Boise 83720. Publishes *Idaho Facts.*

Schwantes, C. A. *In Mountain Shadows: a History of Idaho.* Nebraska Univ. Press, 1996

ILLINOIS

KEY HISTORICAL EVENTS

Territory of a group of Algonquian-speaking tribes, Illinois was explored first by the French in 1673. France claimed the area until 1763 when, after the French and Indian War, it was ceded to Britain along with all the French land east of the Mississippi. In 1783 Britain recognized the US' title to Illinois, which became part of the North West Territory of the USA in 1787, and of Indiana Territory in 1800. Illinois became a Territory in its own right in 1809, and a state in 1818.

Settlers from the eastern states moved on to the fertile farmland, immigration increasing greatly with the opening in 1825 of the Erie Canal from New York along which settlers could move west and their produce back east for sale. Chicago was incorporated as a city in 1837 and quickly became the transport, trading and distribution centre of the middle west. Once industrial growth had begun there, a further wave of immigration took place in the 1840s, mainly of European refugees looking for work. This movement continued with varying force until the 1920s, when it was largely replaced by immigration of black work-seekers from the southern states.

During the 20th century the population became largely urban and heavy industry was established along an intensive network of rail and waterway routes. Chicago recovered from a destructive fire in 1871 to become the hub of this network and at one time the second largest American city.

TERRITORY AND POPULATION

Illinois is bounded north by Wisconsin, north-east by Lake Michigan, east by Indiana, south-east by the Ohio River (forming the boundary with Kentucky), and west by the Mississippi River (forming the boundary with Missouri and Iowa). Land area 55,646 sq. miles (144,123 sq. km). Census population, 1990, 11,430,602 (84·6% urban), an increase of 0·36% since 1980. Population estimate (1997), 11,895,849.

Population in 5 census years was:

	White	Black	Indian	All others	Total	Per sq. mile
1910	5,526,962	109,049	188	2,392	5,638,591	100·6
1930	7,266,361	328,972	469	35,321	7,630,654	136·4

	White	Black		All others	Total	Per sq. mile
1970	9,600,381	1,425,674		87,921	11,113,976	199·4
1980	9,233,327	1,675,398		517,793	11,426,518	203·0

	White	Black	American Indian, Eskimo or Aleut	Asian or Pacific Islander	Other	Total	Per sq. mile
1990	8,952,978	1,694,273	21,836	285,311	476,204	11,430,602	205·6

Of the total population in 1980, 5,537,737 were male, 9,518,039 persons were urban and 5,597,360 were 18 years of age or older.

The most populous cities (1996 population estimate) are: Chicago, 2,721,547; Rockford, 143,531; Aurora, 116,405; Springfield, 112,921; Peoria, 112,306; Naperville,107,001; Joliet, 86,749; Elgin, 86,034; Decatur, 81,369; Arlington Heights, 76,740.

Primary Metropolitan Statistical Area population, 1990 census: Chicago, 6,069,974; East St Louis, 588,995; Peoria, 339,172; Rockford, 283,719; Springfield, 189,550; Decatur, 117,206.

SOCIAL STATISTICS
Births in 1997 were 180,647; deaths, 102,404; infant deaths under 1 year, 1,476; marriages, 94,574; divorces and annulments, 39,981.

CLIMATE
Chicago, Jan. 25·2°F (–3·8°C), July 79·9°F (26·6°C) average mean. Average annual rainfall 39·8". In Jan. 1998 total rainfall was 2·67"; in July total rainfall was 1·38" (O'Hare International Airport). Illinois belongs to the Great Lakes climate zone (*see* UNITED STATES: Climate).

CONSTITUTION AND GOVERNMENT
The present constitution became effective on 1 July 1971. The General Assembly consists of a House of Representatives of 118 members elected for 2 years, and a Senate of 59 members who are divided into 3 groups; in one, they are elected for terms of 4 years, 4 years, and 2 years; in the next, for terms of 4 years, 2 years, and 4 years; and in the last, for terms of 2 years, 4 years, and 4 years. Sessions are annual. The state is divided into legislative districts, in each of which 1 senator is chosen; each district is divided into 2 representative districts, in each of which 1 representative is chosen.

The state sends 20 representatives to Congress.

The capital is Springfield.

RECENT ELECTIONS
In the 1996 presidential election Clinton polled 2,341,744 votes; Dole, 1,587,021; Perot, 346,408.

CURRENT ADMINISTRATION
Governor: George H. Ryan (R.), 1999–2001 ($135,524).
  Lieut.-Governor: Corrine Woods (R). ($103,636).
  Secretary of State: Jessie White (D.) ($119,580).

Local Government. The state has 102 counties. The forms of government include mayor-council and council-manager.

ECONOMY
Important industries include financial services, manufacturing, retail and transportation.

Performance. In 1997 gross state product was estimated at $394bn. (ranked 4th in the USA).

Budget. In 1996 total state revenue was $36,991m. Total expenditure was $34,111m. (education, $8,773m.; public welfare, $9,377m.; health and hospitals, $2,310m.; highways, $2,435m.; police protection, $295m.) Outstanding debt, 1996, amounted to $22,676m.

Per capita personal income (1997, preliminary) was $28,202.

Banking and Finance. There were 788 banks (head offices) and 2,108 branches in 1998; assets were $262·4bn.

ENERGY AND NATURAL RESOURCES
Electricity. Electricity consumption 1996, 125·9bn. kWh. There were 13 nuclear plants (1996).

Oil and Gas. Gas utility revenues 1996, $3,177m.; crude petroleum revenues, $325m.

Water. The total area covered by water is approximately 2,325 sq. miles. In 1997 there were 26,443 miles of streams.

Minerals. Chief mineral product is coal; 23 operative mines had an output (1997) of 41,247,632 tons (clean). Mineral production also includes: fluorspar, tripoli, lime, sand, gravel and stone. Value of nonfuel mineral production in 1997 was $880m.

Agriculture. In 1997 there were 73,051 farms. The 77,000 farms in 1995 covered an area of 28m. acres with the average farm having 365 acres. In 1998 the average value of farmland and buildings per acre was $1,020.

Farm income, 1996, $9,050m. Illinois is a large producer of maize and soybeans, the state's leading cash commodities. Output, 1997: soybeans, 427·9m. bu.; corn, 1·42m. bu.; wheat (1994), 50m. bu.; maize (1994), 1,786m. bu. In Jan. 1993 there were 186,000 milch cows; and in Jan. 1997, 1·68m. cattle and calves, 79,000 sheep and lambs and 4·75m. swine. The wool clip was 639,000 lbs in 1994.

Forestry. The gross forest area in 1997 was 714,890 acres of which 264,018 acres was National Forest Land.

INDUSTRY

Largest industry, in 1994, was services; gross state product, $333,200m. In 1996 there were 297,386 establishments with 4,978,371 employees. The annual payroll was $151·9bn.

Labour. In 1996 there were 4,978,371 employees including: agricultural services, forestry and fishing, 23,428; mining, 13,008; construction, 210,394; manufacturing, 998,132; transportation and public utilities, 309,926; wholesale trade, 376,601; retail trade, 955,595; finance, insurance and real estate, 412,281; services, 1,677,677.

Trade Unions. Labour union membership in 1997 was 1,063,800.

INTERNATIONAL TRADE

Imports and Exports. For the third quarter of 1997 direct exports were $7,954m.

Trade Fairs. There were 14 international trade shows in 1998.

COMMUNICATIONS

Roads. In 1996 there were 137,577 miles of roads, which included (31 Dec. 1997) 16,090 miles of state highways. In 1997 there were 6,780,496 passenger cars, 1,183,155 pickup trucks, 250,075 recreational vehicles, buses and trucks, and 189,267 motor cycles in the state, and 170,104 Interstate Registration Plan vehicles.

Rail. There were, in 1990, more than 7,000 miles of Class I railway. Chicago is served by Amtrak long-distance trains on several routes, and by a metro (CTA) system, and by 7 groups of commuter railways controlled by the Northeast Illinois Railroad Corporation (now called METRA). In 1997 there were 46 rail companies operating in the state.

Civil Aviation. There were (1996) 136 public airports, 629 restricted landing areas and 283 heliports.

Shipping. In 1996 the seaport of Chicago handled 27,866,169 tons of cargo.

Telecommunications. 1,890 telecommunications establishments had a total annual payroll of $2,502,192m. in 1996.

Postal Services. In 1998 there were approximately 800 post offices.

SOCIAL INSTITUTIONS

Justice. In Jan. 1999 the adult inmate population in state prisons was 43,172. The death penalty is authorized, and executions began in 1990 following the US Supreme Courts reinstatement of capital punishment in 1976. The last execution took place on 21 Jan. 1998.

A Civil Rights Act (1941), as amended, bans all forms of discrimination by places of public accommodation, including inns, restaurants, retail stores, railroads, aeroplanes, buses, etc., against persons on account of 'race, religion, colour, national ancestry or physical or mental handicap'; another section similarly mentions 'race or colour'.

UNITED STATES OF AMERICA

The Fair Employment Practices Act of 1961, as amended, prohibits discrimination in employment based on race, colour, sex, religion, national origin or ancestry, by employers, employment agencies, labour organizations and others. These principles are embodied in the 1971 constitution.

The Illinois Human Rights Act (1979) prevents unlawful discrimination in employment, real property transactions, access to financial credit, and public accommodations, by authorizing the creation of a Department of Human Rights to enforce, and a Human Rights Commission to adjudicate, allegations of unlawful discrimination.

Religion. Among the larger religious denominations are: Roman Catholic (3·6m.), Jewish (268,000), Presbyterian Church, USA (0·2m.), Lutheran Church in America (0·2m.), Lutheran Church Missouri Synod (325,000), American Baptist (105,000), Disciples of Christ (75,000), United Methodist (505,000), Southern Baptist (265,000), United Church of Christ (192,000), Assembly of God (63,000), Church of Nazarene (50,000).

Education. Education is free and compulsory for children between 7 and 16 years of age. In 1996–97 public school enrolments were 1,973,040; total public school teachers (including special education teachers), 118,594. Enrolment (1996–97) in non-public schools was 320,880; total non-public school teachers (including special education teachers), 18,129. Teachers' salaries (1996–97): median salary for elementary was $37,259, mean salary $39,421; median for secondary, $43,451; mean $47,845. In 1997, 181 higher education institutions had a total enrolment of 728,805.

Major colleges and universities (autumn 1997):

Founded	Name	Place	Control	Enrolment
1851	Northwestern University	Evanston	Independent	17,478
1857	Illinois State University	Normal	Public	20,331
1867	University of Illinois	Urbana/Champaign	Public	38,070
		Springfield		4,463
		Chicago		24,921
1867	Chicago State University	Chicago	Public	8,772
1869	Southern Illinois University	Carbondale	Public	21,908
		Edwardsville		11,207
1890	Loyola University	Chicago	Roman Catholic	13,604
1891	University of Chicago	Chicago	Independent	11,849
1895	Eastern Illinois University	Charleston	Public	11,777
1895	Northern Illinois University	DeKalb	Public	22,082
1897	Bradley University	Peoria	Independent	5,861
1899	Western Illinois University	Macomb	Public	12,200
1940	Illinois Institute of Technology	Chicago	Independent	6,100
1945	Roosevelt University	Chicago	Independent	6,605
1961	Northeastern Illinois University	Chicago	Public	10,224

Health. In 1997 there were 207 community hospitals with 45,800 beds. Total admissions in 1996 were 1,443,619.

Welfare. In fiscal year 1997 there were 42,121 participating providers in the state and 24,117,000 medical claims processed. Child support enforcement collections totalled $88m. and total non-assistance child support collections were $207·8m.

CULTURE

In 1996 there were approximately 273 theatres.

Broadcasting. There were 303 radio and broadcasting establishments (in 1996), and 194 cable and other pay TV services establishments.

Press. 422 newspapers and 277 periodicals were in circulation in 1996.

Tourism. Tourism revenue in 1997 was $19·5bn.

Festivals. In 1998 there were more than 100 festivals, parades and special celebrations.

Libraries. There were, in 1998, 637 public libraries, 180 college and university libraries, 2,399 school library media centres and 540 special libraries.

FURTHER READING

Statistical information: Department of Commerce and Community Affairs, 620 Adams St., Springfield 62701. Publishes *Illinois State and Regional Economic Data Book.* Bureau of Economic and Business Research, Univ. of Illinois, 1206 South 6th St., Champaign 61820. Publishes *Illinois Statistical Abstract.*

Blue Book of the State of Illinois. Edited by Secretary of State. Springfield. Biennial

Angle, P. M. and Beyer, R. L., *A Handbook of Illinois History.* Illinois State Historical Society, Springfield, 1943

Clayton, J., *The Illinois Fact Book and Historical Almanac 1673–1968.* Southern Illinois Univ., 1970

Howard, R. P., *Illinois: A History of the Prairie State.* Grand Rapids, 1972.—*Mostly Good and Competent Men: Illinois Governors, 1818–1988.* Springfield, 1989

Pease, T. C., *The Story of Illinois.* 3rd ed. Chicago, 1965

The Illinois State Library: Springfield, IL 62756.

INDIANA

KEY HISTORICAL EVENTS

The area was inhabited by Algonquian-speaking tribes when the first European explorers (French) laid claim to it in the 17th century. They established some fortified trading posts but there was little settlement. In 1763 the area passed to Britain, with other French-claimed territory east of the Mississippi. In 1783 Indiana became part of the North West Territory of the USA; it became a separate territory in 1800 and a state in 1816. Until 1811 there had been continuing conflict with the Indian inhabitants, who were then defeated at Tippecanoe.

Early farming settlement was by families of British and German descent, including Amish and Mennonite communities. Later industrial development offered an incentive for more immigration from Europe, and, later, from the southern states. In 1906 the town of Gary was laid out by the United States Steel Corporation and named after its chairman, Elbert H. Gary. The industry flourished on navigable water midway between supplies of iron ore and of coal. Trade and distribution in general benefited from Indiana Port on Lake Michigan, especially after the opening of the St Lawrence Seaway in 1959. The Ohio River was also exploited for carrying freight.

Indianapolis was laid out after 1821 and became the state capital in 1825. Natural gas was discovered in the neighbourhood in the late 19th century, and this stimulated the growth of a motor industry, celebrated with the Indianapolis 500 race, held annually since 1911.

TERRITORY AND POPULATION

Indiana is bounded west by Illinois, north by Michigan and Lake Michigan, east by Ohio and south by Kentucky across the Ohio River. Land area, 35,870 sq. miles (92,903 sq. km). Census population, 1 April 1990, was 5,544,159 (64·9% urban), an increase of 0·98% since 1980. Population estimate (1997), 5,864,108.

Population in 5 census years was:

	White	Black	Indian	Asiatic	Total	Per sq. mile
1930	3,125,778	111,982	285	458	3,238,503	89·4
1960	4,388,554	269,275	948	2,447	4,662,498	128·9
			All others			
1970	4,820,324	357,464	15,881		5,193,669	143·9
1980	5,004,394	414,785	71,045		5,490,224	152·8
1990	5,020,700	432,092	91,367		5,544,159	154·6

Of the total in 1990, 2,688,281 were male and 3,545,431 were 21 years of age or older.

The largest cities with census population, 1990, are: Indianapolis (capital), 741,952; Fort Wayne, 173,072; Evansville, 126,272; Gary, 116,646; South Bend, 105,511; Hammond, 84,236; Muncie, 71,035; Bloomington, 60,633; Anderson, 59,459; Terre Haute, 57,483.

SOCIAL STATISTICS
1995 statistics: births, 82,835 (14·3 per 1,000 population); deaths, 53,000 (9·2); infant mortality rate, 8·4 (per 1,000 live births). Marriages (1996, provisional), 49,200.

CLIMATE
Indianapolis, Jan. 29°F (−1·7°C), July 76°F (24·4°C). Annual rainfall 41" (1,034 mm). Indiana belongs to the Mid-West climate zone (*see* UNITED STATES: Climate).

CONSTITUTION AND GOVERNMENT
The present constitution (the second) dates from 1851; it has had (as of Nov. 1983) 34 amendments. The General Assembly consists of a Senate of 50 members elected for 4 years, and a House of Representatives of 100 members elected for 2 years. It meets annually.

The state sends 10 representatives to Congress.

The state capital is Indianapolis. The state is divided into 92 counties and 1,008 townships.

RECENT ELECTIONS
In the 1996 presidential election Dole polled 995,082 votes; Clinton, 874,668; Perot, 218,739.

CURRENT ADMINISTRATION
Governor: Frank O'Bannon (D.), 1997–2001 ($77,200).
   Lieut.-Governor: Joseph E. Kernan (D.) ($64,000).
   Secretary of State: Sue Anne Gilroy (R.) ($46,000).

ECONOMY
Budget. In the fiscal year 1996 total revenue was $16,550m.; total expenditure was $15,368m. ($6,142m. for education; $3,155m. for public welfare; 608m. for health and hospitals; $1,532m. for highways; and $146m. for police protection).

Debt outstanding (1996) was $6,117m.

Per capita personal income (1997, preliminary) was $23,604.

ENERGY AND NATURAL RESOURCES
Oil and Gas. Production of crude oil in 1996 was 3m. bbls., value $52m.; $1m. worth of natural gas was produced.

Water. The total area covered by water is approximately 550 sq. miles.

Minerals. The state produced 36,862,000 metric tons of crushed stone and 155·62m. metric tons of dimension stone in 1993. Total reserves of coal (1996), 9,991m. short tons. Value of domestic nonfuel mineral production, in 1997, $669m.

Agriculture. Indiana is largely agricultural, about 75% of its total area being in farms. In 1997, 62,000 farms had 16m. acres (average, 256 acres). The average value of land and buildings per acre was $2,170 in 1998. Acreage harvested in 1997 was 12·8m., with a market value of $4,031m.

Farm income 1996, $5,558m.: crops were $3,663m.; livestock and products, $1,895m. The 4 most important products were corn, soybeans, hogs and chicken eggs. The livestock on 1 Jan. 1992 included 1,113,473 all cattle, 144,532 milch cows, 72,386 sheep and lambs, 4,618,663 hogs and pigs, 22,256,785 chickens, 12,648,219 turkeys. In 1992 the wool clip yielded 440,768 lbs of wool from 65,775 sheep and lambs.

Forestry. In 1997 there were 644,000 acres of forest including Hoosier National Forest (192,000 acres).

INDUSTRY
In 1993, 9,440 manufacturing establishments employed 636,495 workers, earning $20,690,996,000. The steel industry is the largest in the country.

Labour. In 1997, of the 3,093,900 labour force, 108,600 persons (3·5% of the population) were unemployed.

INTERNATIONAL TRADE

Imports and Exports. Exports valued $12,029m. in 1997.

COMMUNICATIONS

Roads. In 1996 there were 92,970 miles of road (73,326 miles rural); there were 5,216,000 registered motor vehicles.

Rail. In 1989 there were 3,796 miles of mainline railway and 861·5 miles of secondary track.

Civil Aviation. Of airports, 1990, 115 were for public use and 486 were for private use.

SOCIAL INSTITUTIONS

Justice. Following the US Supreme Court's reinstatement of the death penalty in 1976, death sentences have been awarded since 1980. 16,960 prisoners were under the jurisdiction of state and federal correctional authorities in 1996.

The Civil Rights Act of 1885 forbids places of public accommodation to bar any persons on grounds not applicable to all citizens alike; no citizen may be disqualified for jury service 'on account of race or colour'. An Act of 1947 makes it an offence to spread religious or racial hatred.

A 1961 Act provided 'all . . . citizens equal opportunity for education, employment and access to public conveniences and accommodations' and created a Civil Rights Commission.

Religion. Religious denominations include Methodists, Roman Catholic, Disciples of Christ, Baptists, Lutheran, Presbyterian churches, Society of Friends, Episcopal.

Education. School attendance is compulsory from 7 to 16 years. In 1995 there were an estimated 684,000 pupils attending elementary schools and 293,000 at secondary schools. The average expenditure per pupil was $6,411. Teachers' salaries averaged $36,516 (1994–95). Total expenditure for public schools, 1997, $6,885m.

The principal institutions for higher education were (1989–90):

Founded	Institution	Control	Students (full-time)
1801	Vincennes University	State	10,139
1824	Indiana University, Bloomington	State	34,863
1837	De Pauw University, Greencastle	Methodist	2,415
1842	University of Notre Dame	R.C.	9,700
1850	Butler University, Indianapolis	Independent	4,187
1859	Valparaiso University, Valparaiso	Evangelical Lutheran Church	3,858
1870	Indiana State University, Terre Haute	State	12,005
1874	Purdue University, Lafayette	State	35,817
1898	Ball State University, Muncie	State	18,993
1902	University of Indianapolis, Indianapolis	Methodist	3,119
1963	Indiana Vocational Technical College, Indianapolis	State	5,117
1985	University of Southern Indiana	State	5,713

Health. There were 114 community hospitals with 19,900 beds in 1994. In 1993 there were 3,568 patients in state mental hospitals.

Welfare. In 1994, under the Federal Supplemental Security Income programme and federally administered State Supplementary programme, payments to 15,546 aged persons, 56,502 disabled adults and 18,305 disabled children totalled $27·97m. In 1996, 967,000 beneficiaries received an annual total of $8,055m.

CULTURE

Broadcasting. In 1992 there were 34 television stations and 43 cable television systems. There were (1992) 208 radio stations: 81 AM; 127 FM.

Press. There were 70 dailies and 21 Sunday newspapers in circulation in 1997.

Tourism. Tourists—60% of whom travelled from outside the state—spent $5·93bn. in 1996.

Festivals. Over 750 festivals were held in Indiana in 1998.

Libraries. In 1997 there were 238 public libraries (with 3,177,716 registered borrowers) and 78 college and university libraries.

Museums and Galleries. There were over 300 museums listed in 1996. The first Cine Dome theatre in the country is attached to the Children's Museum of Indianapolis.

FURTHER READING

Statistical information: Indiana Business Research Center, Indiana Univ., Indianapolis 46202. Publishes *Indiana Factbook.*

Gray, R. D. (ed.) *Indiana History: a Book of Readings.* Indiana Univ. Press, 1994

Martin, J. B., *Indiana: an Interpretation.* Indiana Univ. Press, 1992

State Library: Indiana State Library, 140 North Senate, Indianapolis 46204.

IOWA

KEY HISTORICAL EVENTS

Originally the territory of the Iowa Indians, the area was explored by the Frenchmen Marquette and Joliet in 1673. French trading posts were set up, but there was little other settlement. In 1803 the French sold their claim to Iowa to the USA as part of the Louisiana Purchase. The land was still occupied by Indians but, in the 1830s, the tribes sold their land to the US government and migrated to reservations. Iowa became a US Territory in 1838 and a state in 1846.

The state was settled by immigrants drawn mainly from neighbouring states to the east. Later there was more immigration from Protestant states of northern Europe. The land was extremely fertile and most immigrants came to farm. Not all the Indian population had accepted the cession and there were some violent confrontations, notably the murder of settlers at Spirit Lake in 1857.

The population is still mainly rural and farming predominates, especially livestock farming with its associated stockfeed crops. Most industry is based on agriculture, either as food-processing or agricultural engineering.

The capital, Des Moines, was founded in 1843 as a fort to protect Indian rights. It expanded rapidly with the growth of a local coal field after 1910.

TERRITORY AND POPULATION

Iowa is bounded east by the Mississippi River (forming the boundary with Wisconsin and Illinois), south by Missouri, west by the Missouri River (forming the boundary with Nebraska), north-west by the Big Sioux River (forming the boundary with South Dakota) and north by Minnesota. Land area, 55,875 sq. miles (144,716 sq. km). Census population, 1 April 1990, 2,776,755 (60·6% urban), a decrease of 4·7% since 1980. Population estimate (1998), 2,862,447.

Population in 6 census years was:

	White	Black	Indian	Asiatic	Total	Per sq. mile
1870	1,188,207	5,762	48	3	1,194,020	21·5
1930	2,452,677	17,380	660	222	2,470,939	44·1
1960	2,728,709	25,354	1,708	1,022	2,757,537	49·2
			All others			
1970	2,782,762	32,596	10,010		2,825,368	50·5
1980	2,839,225	41,700	32,882		2,913,808	51·7
1990	2,683,090	48,090	45,575		2,776,755	49·7

At the census of 1990, 1,344,802 were male, 1,683,065 were urban and 2,057,875 were 18 years of age or older.

The largest cities in the state, with their estimated population in 1996, are: Des Moines (capital), 193,422; Cedar Rapids, 113,482; Davenport, 97,010; Sioux City, 83,791; Waterloo, 65,022; Iowa City, 60,923; Dubuque, 57,312; Council Bluffs,

55,569; Ames, 47,698; West Des Moines, 40,380; Cedar Falls, 34,884; Bettendorf, 31,015; Mason City, 28,972; Clinton, 28,323; Urbandale, 26,902.

SOCIAL STATISTICS
1997 statistics: births, 36,641; deaths, 27,669; infant deaths, 229; marriages, 21,909; dissolutions of marriages, 9,712.

CLIMATE
Cedar Rapids, Jan. 23·7°F, July 72·6°F. Annual rainfall 34". Des Moines, Jan. 22·6°F, July 72·4°F. Annual rainfall 32·1". Iowa belongs to the Mid-West climate zone (see UNITED STATES: Climate).

CONSTITUTION AND GOVERNMENT
The constitution of 1857 still exists; it has had 45 amendments. The General Assembly comprises a Senate of 50 and a House of Representatives of 100 members, meeting annually for an unlimited session. Senators are elected for 4 years, half retiring every second year: Representatives for 2 years. The Governor and Lieut.-Governor are elected for 4 years. The state is represented in Congress by 5 representatives. Iowa is divided into 99 counties; the capital is Des Moines.

RECENT ELECTIONS
In the 1996 presidential election Clinton polled 615,499 votes; Dole, 488,776; Perot, 104,401.

CURRENT ADMINISTRATION
Governor: Tom Vilsack (D.), 1999–2003 ($102,039).
   Lieut.-Governor: Sally Pederson (D.) ($71,396).
   Secretary of State: Chet Culver (D.) ($81,114).

ECONOMY
Budget. In 1996 total state revenue was $9,245m. Total expenditure was $8,853m. (education, $3,263m.; public welfare, $1,710m.; health and hospitals, $698m.; highways, $1,046m.; police protection, $61m.)
   Debt outstanding in 1996 was $2,065m.
   Per capita personal income (1998) was $23,743.

ENERGY AND NATURAL RESOURCES
Water. The total area covered by water is approximately 401 sq. miles.

Minerals. Production in 1997: crushed stone, 37·0m. tons; sand and gravel, 12·5m. tons; gypsum, 2,030,000 tonnes; cement, 2,440,000 tonnes; coal (1994), 33,173 short tons. The value of domestic nonfuel mineral products in 1997 was $493m.

Agriculture. Iowa is the wealthiest of the agricultural states, partly because nearly the whole area (92·8%) is arable and included in farms. Large-scale commercial farming has not developed; the average farm at 1 June 1997 was 339 acres. The average value of buildings and land per acre was, in 1998, $1,800.
   Farm income (1997), $12,840m.: from livestock, $5,530m., and from crops, $7,830m. Production of corn was 1,656m. bu.[1], value $4,140m. and (in 1996) soybeans, 415·8m. bu.[1], value $2,800m. In 1997 livestock included: swine, 14·6m.; milch cows, 225,000; all cattle, 3·75m.; sheep and lambs, 235,000. The wool clip (1997 estimate) yielded 1·6m. lbs.

[1]More than any other state.

INDUSTRY
Labour. In 1997 manufacturing establishments employed 251,600 people; trade, 346,800; services, 380,300.

COMMUNICATIONS
Roads. On 1 Jan. 1998 there were 113,084 miles of streets and highways. There were (1998) 1·96m. licensed drivers and 3,421,633 registered vehicles.

Rail. The state, as of 1 Jan. 1998, had 4,296 miles of track, 3 Class I, 4 Class II and 10 Class III railways.

Civil Aviation. Airports numbered 216 in 1998, consisting of 103 publicly owned, 103 privately owned and 10 commercial facilities. As of 31 Dec. 1995 there were 2,250 private aircraft registered.

SOCIAL INSTITUTIONS

Justice. There is no longer capital punishment in Iowa. In 1998 the 9 state prisons had 7,415 inmates.

Religion. Chief religious bodies: Roman Catholic, (1998) 516,101 members; United Methodists, (1998) 202,750; Evangelical Lutheran in America, (1997) 266,250 baptized members; USA Presbyterians, (1997) 60,098; United Church of Christ, (1997) 41,076.

Education. School attendance is compulsory for 24 consecutive weeks annually during school age (7–16). In 1997–98, 505,094 pupils were attending primary and secondary schools; 43,737 pupils attending non-public schools; classroom teachers numbered 33,137 for public schools with an average salary of $34,084. In 1997 the state spent an average of $5,037 on each elementary and secondary school student.

Leading institutions for higher education enrolment figures (autumn 1998) were:

Founded	Institution	Control	Professors	Full-time Students
1843	Clarke College, Dubuque	Independent	27	1,023
1846	Grinnell College, Grinnell	Independent	43	1,323
1847	University of Iowa, Iowa City	State	1,645	25,924
1851	Coe College, Cedar Rapids	Independent	28	1,156
1852	Wartburg College, Waverly	Evangelical Lutheran	27	1,499
1853	Cornell College, Mount Vernon	Independent	37	1,018
1858	Iowa State University, Ames	State	1,103	23,457
1876	Univ. of Northern Iowa, Cedar Falls	State	162	12,075
1881	Drake University, Des Moines	Independent	267	4,342
1894	Morningside College, Sioux City	Methodist	41	1,043

Health. In 1997 the state had 117 community hospitals (12,675 beds).

Welfare. Iowa has a Civil Rights Act (1939) which makes it a misdemeanour for any place of public accommodation to deprive any person of 'full and equal enjoyment' of the facilities it offers the public.

Supplemental Security Income (SSI) assistance is available for the aged (65 or older), the blind and the disabled. As of June 1998, 5,020 elderly persons were drawing an average of $169·55 per month, 806 blind persons $290·24 per month, and 34,455 disabled persons $320·45 per month. As of July 1998 temporary assistance to needy families (TANF) was received by 23,907 cases representing 73,329 recipients.

CULTURE

There were a total of 60 venues for live performances (1997).

Broadcasting. In 1997 there were 213 radio stations, and 26 television stations (comprising 17 commercial and 9 educational).

Cinema. There were 115 cinemas in 1997.

Press. In 1997 there were a total of 334 newspapers.

Tourism. In 1997 there were over 17m. visitors; value of industry, $3·6bn.

Festivals. There were over 1,300 events in 1998, including music festivals, fairs, concerts, antique shows and art festivals.

Libraries. In 1997 there were 563 public libraries and 186 special libraries.

Museums and Galleries. There were 13 art museums and 4 history museums in 1997.

FURTHER READING

Statistical Information: Iowa Department of Economic Development Research Bureau, 200 East Grand Ave., Des Moines 50309. Publishes *Statistical Profile of Iowa.*

Annual Survey of Manufactures. US Department of Commerce
Government Finance. US Department of Commerce
Official Register. Secretary of State. Des Moines. Biennial
Petersen, W. J., *Iowa History Reference Guide.* Iowa City, 1952
Smeal, L., *Iowa Historical and Biographical Index.* New York, 1984
Vexler, R. I., *Iowa Chronology and Factbook.* Oceana, 1978
State Library of Iowa: Des Moines 50319.

KANSAS

KEY HISTORICAL EVENTS
The area was explored from Mexico in the 16th century, when Spanish travellers
found groups of Kansa, Wichita, Osage and Pawnee tribes. The French claimed
Kansas in 1682 and they established a valuable fur trade with local tribes in the 18th
century. In 1803 the area passed to the USA as part of the Louisiana Purchase and
became a base for pioneering trails further west. After 1830 it was 'Indian Territory'
and a number of tribes displaced from eastern states were settled there. In 1854 the
Kansas Territory was created and opened for white settlement. The early settlers
were farmers from Europe or New England, but the Territory's position brought it
into contact with southern ideas also. Until 1861 there were frequent outbursts of
violence over the issue of slavery. Slavery had been excluded from the future
Territory by the Missouri Compromise of 1820, but the 1854 Kansas-Nebraska Act
had affirmed the principle of 'popular sovereignty' to settle the issue, which was
then fought out by opposing factions throughout 'Bleeding Kansas'.
  Kansas finally entered the Union (as a non-slavery state) in 1861; the part of
Colorado which had formed part of the Kansas Territory was then separated from it.
  The economy developed through a combination of cattle-ranching and railways.
Herds were driven to the railheads and shipped from vast stockyards, or slaughtered
and processed in railhead meat-packing plants. Wheat and sorghum also became
important once the plains could be ploughed on a large scale.

TERRITORY AND POPULATION
Kansas is bounded north by Nebraska, east by Missouri, with the Missouri River as
boundary in the north-east, south by Oklahoma and west by Colorado. Land area,
81,823 (211,922 sq. km). Census population, 1 April 1990, 2,477,574 (69·1%
urban), an increase of 4·84% since 1980. Population estimate (1997), 2,595,000.
  Population in 5 federal census years was:

	White	Black	Indian	Asiatic	Total	Per sq. mile
1870	346,377	17,108	914	—	364,399	4·5
1930	1,811,997	66,344	2,454	204	1,880,999	22·9
1960	2,078,666	91,445	5,069	2,271	2,178,611	26·3
			All others			
1970	2,122,068	106,977	17,533		2,249,071	27·5
1980	2,168,221	126,127	69,888		2,364,236	28·8

  Of the total population in 1980, 1,156,941 were male, 1,575,899 were urban and
those 20 years of age or older numbered 1,620,368.
  Cities, with 1990 census population: Wichita, 304,011; Kansas City, 149,767;
Topeka (capital), 119,883; Overland Park, 111,790; Lawrence, 65,608; Olathe,
63,352.

SOCIAL STATISTICS
Vital statistics 1995: births, 37,201 (14·5 per 1,000 population); deaths, 24,000 (9·3);
1992, infant deaths, 316 (8·6 per 1,000 live births). Marriages (1996, provisional),
20,600; divorces 11,700.

CLIMATE
Dodge City, Jan. 29°F (−1·7°C), July 78°F (25·6°C). Annual rainfall 21" (518 mm).
Kansas City, Jan. 30°F (−1·1°C), July 79°F (26·1°C). Annual rainfall 38" (947 mm).
Topeka, Jan. 28°F (−2·2°C), July 78°F (25·6°C). Annual rainfall 35" (875 mm).

UNITED STATES OF AMERICA

Wichita, Jan. 31°F (–0·6°C), July 81°F (27·2°C). Annual rainfall 31" (777 mm). Kansas belongs to the Mid-West climate zone (*see* UNITED STATES: Climate).

CONSTITUTION AND GOVERNMENT
The year 1861 saw the adoption of the present constitution; it has had 78 amendments. The Legislature includes a Senate of 40 members, elected for 4 years, and a House of Representatives of 125 members, elected for 2 years. Sessions are annual.

The state sends 4 representatives to Congress.

The capital is Topeka. The state is divided into 105 counties.

RECENT ELECTIONS
In the 1996 presidential election Dole polled 578,572 votes; Clinton, 384,439; Perot, 92,093.

CURRENT ADMINISTRATION
Governor: Bill Graves (R.), 1999–2003 ($88,639.72).
Lieut.-Governor: Gary Sherrer (R.) ($26,946.66).
Secretary of State: Ron Thornburgh (R.) ($68,859.70).

ECONOMY
Budget. In 1996 total state revenue was $7,864m. Total expenditure was $7,276m. (education, $2,961m.; public welfare, $1,102m.; health and hospitals, $565m.; highways, $996m.; police protection, $40m.). Debt outstanding, in 1996, $1,161m.

Per capita income (1997, preliminary) was $24,379.

ENERGY AND NATURAL RESOURCES
Water. The total area covered by water is approximately 459 sq. miles.

Minerals. Important fuel minerals are coal, petroleum and natural gas. Non-fuel minerals, mainly cement, salt and crushed stone, were worth $547m. in 1997.

Agriculture. Kansas is pre-eminently agricultural, but sometimes suffers from lack of rainfall in the west. In 1996 there were some 66,000 farms with a total acreage of 48m. Average number of acres per farm was 724. Average value of farmland and buildings per acre, in 1996, was $553. Farm income, 1996, from livestock and products, $4,570m.; from crops, $3,299m. Chief crops: wheat, sorghum, maize, hay. Wheat production was 472m. bu. in 1990. There is an extensive livestock industry, comprising, in 1990, 5·7m. cattle, 887,000 sheep, 1·45m. pigs and 1·4m. poultry.

Forestry. In 1997 Kansas had 108,000 acres of National Forest System Land.

INDUSTRY
Employment distribution (1996): Total non-farm workforce 1,228,000, of which 303,000 were in wholesale and retail; 301,000 in services; 235,000 in government; 196,000 in manufacturing; 70,000 in transport and utilities; 59,000 in finance, insurance and real estate; 57,000 in construction. The slaughtering industry, other food processing, aircraft, the manufacture of transport equipment and petroleum refining are also important.

COMMUNICATIONS
Roads. In 1996 there were 133,386 miles of roads (123,629 miles rural); and 2,110,000 registered motor vehicles.

Rail. There were 7,273 miles of railway in Jan. 1982.

Civil Aviation. There is an international airport at Wichita.

SOCIAL INSTITUTIONS
Justice. There were 7,756 prisoners in state institutions in 1996. The death penalty is authorized for capital murder, although as of Dec. 1994 no prisoner was under sentence of death.

Religion. The most numerous religious bodies are Roman Catholic, Methodists and Disciples of Christ.

Education. In 1995 there were approximately 463,000 public elementary and secondary pupils enrolled and (1994–95) 30,588 teachers.

Kansas has 6 state-supported institutions of higher education: Kansas State University, Manhattan (1863); The University of Kansas, Lawrence, founded in 1865; Emporia State University, Emporia; Pittsburg State University, Pittsburg; Fort Hays State University, Hays; and Wichita State University, Wichita. The state also supports a two-year technical school, Kansas Technical Institute, at Salina.

Education expenditure by state and local governments in 1997 was $2,874m.

Health. In 1995 Kansas had 132 community hospitals with 10,800 beds.

Welfare. In 1996, 436,000 people received social security benefit totalling $3,545m. Average monthly payment to retired workers was $764.

FURTHER READING

Statistical information: Institute for Public Policy and Business Research, Univ. of Kansas, 607 Blake Hall, Lawrence 66045. Publishes *Kansas Statistical Abstract*.

Annual Economic Report of the Governor. Topeka

Drury, J. W., *The Government of Kansas.* Lawrence, Univ. of Kansas, 1970

Zornow, W. F., *Kansas: A History of the Jayhawk State.* Norman, Okla., 1957

State Library: Kansas State Library, Topeka.

KENTUCKY

KEY HISTORICAL EVENTS

Lying west of the Appalachians and south of the Ohio River, the area was the meeting place and battleground for the eastern Iroquois and the southern Cherokees. Northern Shawnees also penetrated. The first successful white settlement took place in 1769 when Daniel Boone reached the Bluegrass plains from the eastern, trans-Appalachian, colonies. After 1783 immigration from the east was rapid, settlers travelling by river or crossing the mountains by the Cumberland Gap. The area was originally attached to Virginia but became a separate state in 1792.

Large plantations dependent on slave labour were established, as were small farms worked by white owners. The state became divided on the issue of slavery, although plantation interests (mainly producing tobacco) dominated state government. In the event the state did not secede in 1861, and the majority of citizens supported the Union. Public opinion swung round in support of the south during the difficulties of the reconstruction period.

The eastern mountains became an important coal-mining area, tobacco-growing continued and the Bluegrass plains produced livestock, including especially fine thoroughbred horses.

TERRITORY AND POPULATION

Kentucky is bounded in the north by the Ohio River (forming the boundary with Illinois, Indiana and Ohio), north-east by the Big Sandy River (forming the boundary with West Virginia), east by Virginia, south by Tennessee and west by the Mississippi River (forming the boundary with Missouri). Land area, 39,732 sq. miles (102,907 sq. km). Census population, 1990, 3,685,296 (51·8% urban), an increase of 0·7% since 1980. Population estimate (1997), 3,686,892.

Population in 5 census years was:

	White	Black	All others	Total	Per sq. mile
1930	2,388,364	226,040	185	2,614,589	65·1
1950	2,742,090	201,921	795	2,944,806	73·9
1960	2,820,083	215,949	2,124	3,038,156	76·2
1980	3,379,006	259,477	22,294	3,660,777	92·3
1990	3,391,832	262,907	30,557	3,685,296	92·8

Of the total population in 1990, 1,785,235 were male and 1,136,272 were 21 years old or older.

The principal cities with census population in 1990 are: Louisville, 269,555 (urbanized area, 654,870); Lexington-Fayette, 225,336; Owensboro, 53,577; Covington, 43,646; Bowling Green, 41,688; Hopkinsville, 29,818; Paducah, 27,256; Frankfort (capital), 25,535; Henderson, 25,945.

SOCIAL STATISTICS
Births in 1996, 52,509 (13·5 per 1,000 population); deaths, 37,193 (9·6); infant deaths, 385 (7·3 per 1,000 live births); marriages, 43,910 (11·3); divorces, 21,192 (5·5).

CLIMATE
Kentucky is in the Appalachian Mountains climatic zone (*see* UNITED STATES: Climate). It has a temperate climate. Temperatures are moderate during both winter and summer, precipitation is ample without a pronounced dry season, and winter snowfall amounts are variable. Mean annual temperatures range from 52°F in the northeast to 58°F in the south-west. Annual rainfall averages at about 45". Snowfall ranges from 5 to 10" in the south-west of the state, to 25" in the north-east, and 40" at higher altitudes in the south-east.

CONSTITUTION AND GOVERNMENT
The constitution dates from 1891; there had been 3 preceding it. The 1891 constitution was promulgated by convention and provides that amendments be submitted to the electorate for ratification. The General Assembly consists of a Senate of 38 members elected for 4 years, one half retiring every 2 years, and a House of Representatives of 100 members elected for 2 years. It has biennial sessions. All citizens of 18 or over are qualified as electors. Registered voters, Oct. 1996, 2,490,674.

The state sends 6 representatives to Congress.

The capital is Frankfort. The state is divided into 120 counties.

RECENT ELECTIONS
In the 1996 presidential election Clinton polled 635,451 votes; Dole, 621,842; Perot, 120,243.

CURRENT ADMINISTRATION
Governor: Paul E. Patton (D.), 1995–99 ($97,067.52).
  Lieut.-Governor: Steve D. Henry (D.) ($82,834).
  Secretary of State: John Y. Brown III (D.) ($82,834).

ECONOMY
Budget. In 1996 total state revenue was $13,788m. Total expenditure was $11,842m. (education, $4,263m.; public welfare, $2,770m.; health and hospitals, $638m.; highways, $1,059m.; police protection, $115m.). Debt outstanding, in 1996, $7,030m.

Per capita personal income (1997) was $20,657.

ENERGY AND NATURAL RESOURCES
Electricity. In 1997 production was 91,558m. kWh, of which 87,875m. kWh was from coal.

Oil and Gas. Production of crude oil in 1997 was 3m. bbls. (of 42 gallons); natural gas, 79,547m. cu. ft.

Water. Kentucky has 12 major river basins that contain nearly 90,000 miles of streams. Virtually all of these streams form part of the larger Ohio River basin. The state's surface water includes more than 2,700 natural and artificial impoundments, of which roughly one-third are larger than 10 acres in size. Kentucky has two major ground water regions—the alluvial valley along the Ohio River and beach and gravel deposits located west of Kentucky Lake. The total area covered by water is approximately 679 sq. miles.

KENTUCKY

Minerals. The principal mineral is coal: 155·8m. short tons were mined in 1997, value $3,696·8m.; stone, 64m. short tons, value $272m.; clay, 0·8m. tonnes, value $9·9m.; sand and gravel, 7·9m. short tons, value $28·3m. Total value of non-fuel mineral products in 1997 was $476m. Other minerals include fluorspar, ball clay, gemstones, dolomite, cement and lime.

Agriculture. In 1997, 88,000 farms covered an area of 13·9m. acres. The average farm was 158 acres. In 1998 the average value of farmland and buildings per acre was $1,550.

Farm income, 1997, from crops, $1,654·9m., and from livestock, $1,978·1m. The chief crop is tobacco: production, in 1997, 498·3m. lbs. Other principal crops include corn, soybeans, wheat, hay, fruit and vegetables, sorghum grain and barley.

Stock-raising is important in Kentucky, which has long been famous for its horses. The livestock in 1998 included 140,000 milch cows, 2·4m. cattle and calves, 17,000 sheep, 0·6m. swine.

Forestry. State forest area, 1997, 264,000 acres.

Fisheries. Cash receipts from catfish farming totalled $0·9m. in 1997.

INDUSTRY
In 1997 the state's approximately 4,500 manufacturing plants had 244,700 production workers; value added by manufacture in 1996 was $35,040·2m. The leading manufacturing industries (by employment) are transportation equipment, industrial machinery, electronic equipment, food products and apparel.

Labour. The 1997 the civilian labour force was 1,928,061. Of the 1,824,260 persons employed, 316,100 were engaged in manufacturing, 28,921 in agriculture, 410,300 in wholesale and retail trade, 424,600 in service industries, and 635,339 in other employment. The unemployment rate in 1997 was 5·4%.

Trade Unions. In 1996, 198,800 (12·7%) workers were union members.

INTERNATIONAL TRADE
Imports and Exports. Exports in 1997 totalled almost $8·7bn. with manufactured goods accounting for 95% of total exports. Transportation equipment, industrial machinery and chemicals were important manufactured exports. Livestock and coal were major non-manufactured goods exported.

COMMUNICATIONS
Roads. In 1996 the state had about 73,000 miles of federal, state and local roads. There were almost 2·9m. motor vehicle registrations in 1996.

Rail. In 1997 there were 2,892 miles of railway.

Civil Aviation. There were (1996) 70 publicly used airports and (1992) 2,294 registered aircraft. Commercial airports providing scheduled airline services in Kentucky are located in Erlanger (Covington/Cincinnati area), Louisville, Lexington, Owensboro and Paducah.

Shipping. There is barge traffic on the 1,100 miles of navigable rivers. There are 6 public river ports, 30 contract terminal facilities and 150 private terminal operations. Kentucky's waterways have access to the junction of the upper and lower Mississippi, Ohio and Tennessee-Tombigbee navigation corridors.

SOCIAL INSTITUTIONS
Justice. There are 12 adult prisons within the Department of Corrections Adult Institutions and 3 privately run adult institutions; average daily population (1997–98), 10,816 in prisons, 1,064 in jails awaiting incarceration, and 2,510 in local community centres. There were also 16,130 individuals on parole.

The death penalty is authorized for murder and kidnap. As of Nov. 1998 there were 36 persons under sentence of death. The last execution was in 1997.

Religion. The chief religious denominations in 1990 were: Southern Baptists, with 770,425 members, Roman Catholic (365,270), United Methodists (182,302),

Christian Churches and Church of Christ (90,520) and Christian (Disciples of Christ) (66,798).

Education. Attendance at school between the ages of 5 and 15 years (inclusive) is compulsory, the normal term being 175 days. In 1997–98, 38,647 teachers were employed in public elementary and secondary schools. In 1997–98 there were 623,475 pupils in public elementary and secondary schools. Public school classroom teachers' salaries (1997–98) averaged $34,453. The average total expenditure per pupil was $4,652.

There were also 4,143 teachers working in private elementary and secondary schools with some 63,000 students in 1995–96.

The state has 28 universities and senior colleges, 1 junior college and 14 community colleges, with a total (autumn 1997) of 173,147 students. Of these universities and colleges, 22 are state-supported, and the remainder are supported privately. The largest of the institutions of higher learning are (autumn 1997): University of Kentucky, with 24,171 students; University of Louisville, 20,894; Eastern Kentucky University, 15,425; Western Kentucky University, 14,543; Northern Kentucky University, 11,785; Morehead State University, 8,208; Murray State University, 8,811; Kentucky State University, 2,288. Five of the several privately endowed colleges of standing are Berea College, Berea; Centre College, Danville; Transylvania University, Lexington; Georgetown College, Georgetown; and Bellarmine College, Louisville.

Health. In 1998 the state had 123 licensed hospitals (18,624 beds). There were 421 licensed long-term care facilities (35,125 beds), 311 family care homes, 127 home health agencies and 2,073 miscellaneous health facilities.

Welfare. In the all-state-funded Supplementation programme, payments were made in Sept. 1998 to 5,186 persons, of whom 2,402 were senior citizens, 48 blind and 2,736 disabled. The average State Supplementation payment was $293·08 to senior citizens, $170·08 to blind and $284·64 to disabled.

In the Kentucky Transitional Assistance Program (as of Sept. 1998) aid was given to 112,666 persons in 47,410 families. The average payment per person was $92·76, per family $220·43.

In addition to money payments, medical assistance, food stamps and social services are available.

CULTURE
The Kentucky Center for the Arts hosts productions by the Kentucky Opera Association, the Louisville Ballet, the Louisville Orchestra and Broadway touring productions.

Tourism. In 1997 tourist expenditure was $7,440m., producing over $1,807m. in tax revenues and generating 146,738 jobs. The state had (1997) 1,022 hotels and motels, 240 camping grounds and 50 state parks.

Libraries. There were, in 1998, 189 public libraries, 83 academic libraries, 128 institutional and special libraries, and 1,254 school libraries.

FURTHER READING
Kentucky Deskbook of Economic Statistics, Decker, R. (ed.), Kentucky Cabinet for Economic Development, Frankfort
Lee, L. G., *A Brief History of Kentucky and its Counties*. Berea, 1981
Miller, P. M., *Kentucky Politics and Government: Do We Stand United?* Nebraska Univ. Press, 1994

LOUISIANA

KEY HISTORICAL EVENTS
Originally the Territory of Choctaw and Caddo tribes, the whole area was claimed for France in 1682. The French founded New Orleans in 1718 and it became the centre of a crown colony in 1731. During the wars which the European powers fought over their American interests, the French ceded the area west of the

LOUISIANA

Mississippi (most of the present state) to Spain in 1762 and the eastern area, north of New Orleans, to Britain in 1763. The British section passed to the USA in 1783, but France bought back the rest from Spain in 1800, including New Orleans and the mouth of the Mississippi. The USA, fearing to be excluded from a strategically important and commercially promising shipping area, persuaded France to sell Louisiana again in 1803. The present states of Missouri, Arkansas, Iowa, North Dakota, South Dakota, Nebraska and Oklahoma were included in the purchase.

The area became the Territory of New Orleans in 1804 and was admitted to the Union as a state in 1812. The economy at first depended on cotton and sugar-cane plantations. The population was of French, Spanish and black descent, with a growing number of American settlers. Plantation interests succeeded in achieving secession in 1861, but New Orleans was occupied by the Union in 1862. Planters re-emerged in the late 19th century and imposed rigid segregation of the black population, denying them their new rights.

The state has become mainly urban industrial, with the Mississippi ports growing rapidly. There is petroleum and natural gas, and a strong tourist industry based on the French culture and Caribbean atmosphere of New Orleans.

TERRITORY AND POPULATION
Louisiana is bounded north by Arkansas, east by Mississippi, south by the Gulf of Mexico and west by Texas. Land area, 43,566 sq. miles (112,836 sq. km). Census population, 1 April 1990, 4,219,973 (68·1% urban), an increase of 0·38% since 1980. Population estimate (1997), 4,351,769.

Population in 5 census years was:

	White	Black	Indian	Asiatic	Total	Per sq. mile
1930	1,322,712	776,326	1,536	1,019	2,101,593	46·5
1960	2,211,715	1,039,207	3,587	2,004	3,257,022	72·2
			All others			
1970	2,541,498	1,086,832	12,976		3,641,306	81·1
1980	2,911,243	1,237,263	55,466		4,205,900	93·5
1990	2,839,138	1,299,281	81,554		4,219,973	96·9

Of the 1990 total, 2,031,386 were male, 2,872,038 were urban; those 20 years of age or older numbered 2,852,363.

The largest cities with their 1990 census population are: New Orleans, 496,938; Baton Rouge, 219,531; Shreveport, 198,525; Lafayette, 94,440; Kenner, 72,033; Lake Charles, 70,580; Monroe, 54,909; Bossier City, 52,721.

SOCIAL STATISTICS
Statistics 1995: births, 65,574 (15·1 per 1,000 population); deaths, 40,000 (9·1); infant deaths, 639 (9·8); marriages, 40,516; divorces, 15,097.

CLIMATE
New Orleans, Jan. 54°F (12·2°C), July 83°F (28·3°C). Annual rainfall 58" (1,458 mm). Louisiana belongs to the Gulf Coast climate zone (see UNITED STATES: Climate).

CONSTITUTION AND GOVERNMENT
The present constitution dates from 1974. The Legislature consists of a Senate of 39 members and a House of Representatives of 105 members, both chosen for 4 years. Sessions are annual; a fiscal session is held in even years.

The state sends 7 representatives to Congress.

Louisiana is divided into 64 parishes (corresponding to the counties of other states). The capital is Baton Rouge.

RECENT ELECTIONS
In the 1996 presidential election Clinton polled 928,983 votes; Dole, 710,240; Perot, 122,981.

CURRENT ADMINISTRATION
Governor: Murphy J. Foster (R.), 1996–2000 ($95,000).
Lieut.-Governor: Kathleen Blanco (D.), ($85,000).
Secretary of State: W. Fox McKeithen (R.), ($85,000).

ECONOMY

Budget. In 1996 total revenue was $14,296m. Total expenditure was $14,030m. (education, $4,348m.; public welfare, $2,976m.; health and hospitals, $1,494m.; highways, $858m.; police protection, $166m.). Debt outstanding (1996), $7,452m.

Per capita personal income (1997, provisional) was $20,680.

ENERGY AND NATURAL RESOURCES

Electricity. 65,555m. kWh of electricity were produced in 1996.

Oil and Gas. Production (1995) of crude oil was 82·6m. bbls.; production of natural gas, 1,456·9m. cu. ft.

Water. The area covered by water is approximately 6,085 sq. miles.

Minerals. Principal non-fuel minerals are sulphur, salt and sand, and gravel.

Agriculture. The state is divided into two parts, the uplands and the alluvial and swamp regions of the coast. A delta occupies about one-third of the total area. Manufacturing is the leading industry, but agriculture is important. The number of farms in 1997 was some 27,000 covering 9m. acres; the average farm had 321 acres. Average value of farmland and buildings per acre in 1998 was $1,280.

Principal crops, 1996 production, were: soyabeans, 28·8m. bu.; sugar-cane, 2,405·9m. lbs sugar and 65·7m. gallons molasses; rice, 28·6m. cwt; corn, 49·7m. bu.; cotton, 463·4m. lbs lint and 741·8m. lbs seed; sweet potatoes, 7·2m. bu.; pecans, 12·6m. lbs; grain sorghum, 3·4m. cwt.

Forestry. State forests, 1m. acres in 1997. Income from manufactured products exceeds $2,500m. annually. Production 1996: sawtimber, 1,359,007,504 bd ft; pulpwood, 5,435,872 standard cords.

Fisheries. The value of the 1996 catch of marine and freshwater fish was $689·6m.; of aquaculture, $263·2m.

INDUSTRY

The manufacturing industries are chiefly those associated with petroleum, chemicals, lumber, food and paper. In 1996, 10·4% of the workforce were employed in manufacturing, 23·4% in trade and 26·8% in service industries.

Labour. In 1997 the civilian labour force totalled 2,024,000; there were 123,800 persons (6·1% of the population) unemployed.

INTERNATIONAL TRADE

In 1997 exports were valued at $18,732m. Foreign investment amounted to $1,774m. (gross book value).

COMMUNICATIONS

Roads. In 1997 there were 60,021 miles of public roads (46,702 miles rural in 1996) and, in Oct. 1996, 5,800,961 registered motor vehicles.

Rail. In 1998 there were approximately 2,786 miles of main-line track in the state. There is a tramway in New Orleans.

Civil Aviation. In 1996 there were 73 public airports.

Shipping. There are ports at New Orleans, Baton Rouge, St Bernard, Plaquemines and Lake Charles. The Mississippi and other waterways provide 7,500 miles of navigable water.

SOCIAL INSTITUTIONS

Justice. There were 26,779 prisoners in state correctional institutions in 1996. The death penalty is authorized; the last execution was in 1996.

Religion. The Roman Catholic Church is the largest denomination in Louisiana. The leading Protestant Churches are Southern Baptist and Methodist.

Education. School attendance is compulsory between the ages of 7 and 15, both inclusive. In 1996–97 there were 1,447 public elementary and secondary schools with 781,450 registered pupils, and 48,047 teachers paid an average salary of $28,315. There are 20 four-year and 5 two-year public colleges and universities and 12 non-public four-year institutions of higher learning. There are 44 state trade and vocational technical schools.

In 1996, 204,000 students enrolled at colleges. Enrolment, 1996, in Louisiana State University, Baton Rouge was 22,667; University of Southwestern Louisiana, 13,878; University of New Orleans, 10,758; Southeastern Louisiana University, 12,323; Northeast Louisiana University, 10,002; Tulane University, 11,000; Southern University, Baton Rouge, 9,692; Northwestern State University, 7,922; McNeese State University, 6,985; Grambling State University, 6,461; Nicholls State University, 6,005; Loyola University (1995), 5,634; Louisiana State University in Shreveport, 910; Southern University of New Orleans, 3,518; Xavier University (1995), 3,419; Dillard University (1995), 1,566.

Health. In 1996 there were 129 hospitals with 19,300 beds.

Welfare. In 1996 assistance was given to 701,000 persons and their dependants at a total cost of $5,117m.

CULTURE

Broadcasting. In 1996 there were 175 radio stations (81 AM; 94 FM) and 32 television stations.

Press. In 1996 there were 120 newspapers in circulation.

Tourism. Tourism is the second most important industry for state income; travellers spent an estimated $5,900m. in 1994. In 1996 there were 25·1m. visitors from within the USA, and 600,000 from foreign countries.

Libraries. There were 232 libraries in 1996—65 public, 35 academic, 26 institutional and 106 special libraries.

Museums and Galleries. Museums and galleries include: Louisiana Arts and Sciences Center, Baton Rouge; Rural Life Museum, Baton Rouge; New Orleans Museum of Art; Louisiana State Museum.

FURTHER READING

1997 Statistical Abstract of Louisiana, 10th Edition, New Orleans, LA: Division of Business and Economic Research, College of Business Administration, Univ. of New Orleans, 1997.
Davis, E. A., *Louisiana, the Pelican State.* Louisiana State Univ. Press, 1975
Kniffen, F. B., *Louisiana, its Land and People.* Louisiana State Univ. Press, 1968
Wilds, J. *et al.* (eds), *Louisiana Yesterday and Today: a Historical Guide to the State.* Louisiana State Univ. Press, 1996

State Library: The State Library of Louisiana, Baton Rouge, Louisiana.

MAINE

KEY HISTORICAL EVENTS

Originally occupied by Algonquian-speaking tribes, the Territory was disputed between different groups of British settlers, and between the British and French, throughout the 17th and most of the 18th centuries. After 1652 it was governed as part of Massachusetts, and French claims finally failed in 1763. Most of the early settlers were English and Protestant Irish, with many Quebec French.

The Massachusetts settlers had gained control when the original colonist, Sir Ferdinando Gorges, supported the losing royalist side in the English civil war. Their control was questioned during the English-American war of 1812, when Maine residents claimed that the Massachusetts government did not protect them against British raids. Maine was separated from Massachusetts and entered the Union as a state in 1820.

Maine is a mountainous state and even the coastline is rugged, but the coastal belt is where most settlement has developed. In the 19th century there were manufacturing towns making use of cheap water-power, and the rocky shore supported a shell-fish industry. The latter still flourishes, together with intensive horticulture, producing potatoes and fruit. The other main economic development has been in exploiting the forests for timber, pulp and paper.

The capital is Augusta, a river trading post which was fortified against Indian attacks in 1754, incorporated as a town in 1797 and chosen as capital in 1832.

TERRITORY AND POPULATION
Maine is bounded west, north and east by Canada, south-east by the Atlantic, south and south-west by New Hampshire. Land area, 30,865 sq. miles (79,931 sq. km). Census population, 1 April 1990, 1,127,928 (44·6% urban), an increase of 9·18% since 1980. Population estimate (1997), 1,242,000.

Population for 5 census years was:

	White	Black	Indian	Asiatic	Total	Per sq. mile
1910	739,995	1,363	992	121	742,371	24·8
1930	795,185	1,096	1,012	130	797,423	25·7
1950	910,846	1,221	1,522	185	913,774	29·4
				All others		
1970	985,276	2,800		3,972	992,048	31·0
1980	1,109,850	3,128		12,049	1,125,027	36·3

Of the total population in 1980, 48·5% were male, 40·7% were urban and 60·5% were 21 years or older.

The largest city in the state is Portland with a census population of 61,572 in 1980. Other cities (with population in 1980) are: Lewiston, 40,481; Bangor, 31,643; Auburn, 23,128; South Portland, 22,712; Augusta (capital), 21,819; Biddeford, 19,638; Waterville, 17,779.

SOCIAL STATISTICS
Births, 1995, 13,896 (11·2 per 1,000 population); deaths, 12,000 (9·5); infant mortality rate, 6·5 (per 1,000 live births). Marriages (1994), 11,077 (8·8 per 1,000 population); divorces 5,816 (4·6).

CLIMATE
Average maximum temperatures range from 56·3°F in Waterville to 48·3°F in Caribou, but record high (since c. 1950) is 103°F. Average minimum ranges from 36·9°F in Rockland to 28·3°F in Greenville, but record low (also in Greenville) is −42°F. Average annual rainfall ranges from 48·85" in Machias to 36·09" in Houlton. Average annual snowfall ranges from 118·7" in Greenville to 59·7" in Rockland. Maine belongs to the New England climate zone (see UNITED STATES: Climate).

CONSTITUTION AND GOVERNMENT
The constitution of 1820 is still in force, but it has been amended 153 times. In 1951, 1965 and 1973 the Legislature approved recodifications of the constitution as arranged by the Chief Justice under special authority.

The Legislature consists of the Senate with 35 members and the House of Representatives with 151 members, both Houses being elected simultaneously for 2 years. Sessions are annual.

The state sends 2 representatives to Congress.

The capital is Augusta. The state is divided into 16 counties.

RECENT ELECTIONS
In the 1996 presidential election Clinton polled 326,217 votes; Dole, 190,711; Perot, 88,082.

CURRENT ADMINISTRATION
Governor: Angus S. King, Jr (ind.), 1999–2003 ($69,992).
  Secretary of State: Dan Gwadosky (D.), 1999–2001 ($60,000).

ECONOMY
Budget. In 1996 total state revenue was $4,267m. Total expenditure was $4,240m. (education, $1,080m.; public welfare, $1,256m.; health and hospitals, $235m.;

MAINE

highways, \$362m.; police protection, \$34m.). Debt outstanding, in 1996, was \$3,160m.

Per capita income (1997, preliminary) was \$22,078.

ENERGY AND NATURAL RESOURCES

Water. The total area covered by water is approximately 2,876 sq. miles.

Minerals. Minerals include sand and gravel, stone, lead, clay, copper, peat, silver and zinc. Domestic non-fuel mineral output, 1997, was valued at \$88m.

Agriculture. In 1997, some 7,000 farms occupied 1m. acres; the average farm was 184 acres. Average value of farmland and buildings per acre in 1998 was \$1,320. Farm income, 1996: crops, \$224m.; livestock and products, \$262m. Principal commodities are potatoes, dairy products, chicken eggs and aquaculture.

Forestry. There are some 17·5m. acres of commercial forest, mainly pine, spruce and fir. Wood products industries are of great economic importance.

Fisheries. In 1990 the commercial catch was valued at \$129·9m.

INDUSTRY

Total non-agricultural workforce, 1996, 540,000. Services employed 150,000; wholesale and retail, 136,000; government, 93,000; manufacturing, 88,000; the main manufacture is paper at 47 plants, producing about 34% of manufacturing value added.

COMMUNICATIONS

Roads. In 1996 there were 22,577 miles of roads (19,962 miles rural). There were 959,000 registered motor vehicles.

Rail. In 1984 there were 1,516 miles of mainline railway tracks.

Civil Aviation. There are international airports at Portland and Bangor.

SOCIAL INSTITUTIONS

Justice. In 1996 there were 1,426 prisoners in state and federal correctional institutions. There is no capital punishment.

Religion. The largest religious bodies are Roman Catholics, Baptists and Congregationalists.

Education. Education is free for pupils from 5 to 21 years of age, and compulsory from 7 to 17. In 1994–95 there were 212,322 pupils and 15,398 teachers in public elementary and secondary schools. Education expenditure by state and local government in 1997, \$1,494m.

The state University of Maine, founded in 1865, has 7 locations; Bowdoin College, founded in 1794 at Brunswick; Bates College at Lewiston; Colby College at Waterville; Husson College, Bangor; Westbrook College at Westbrook; Unity College at Unity; and the University of New England (formerly St Francis College) at Biddeford.

Health. In 1995 there were 39 community hospitals with 4,000 beds.

Welfare. Supplemental Security Income (SSI) is administered by the Social Security Administration. It became effective on 1 Jan. 1974 and replaces former aid to the aged, blind and disabled, administered by the state with state and federal funds. SSI is supplemented by Medicaid for nursing home patients or hospital patients. Aid to families with dependent children is granted where one or both parents are disabled or absent and income is insufficient. There is a programme of assistance for catastrophic illness. Child welfare services include basic child protective services, enforcing child support, establishing paternity and finding missing parents, foster home placements, adoptions; services in divorce cases and licensing of foster homes, day care and residential treatment services, and public guardianship. There are also protective services for adults. In 1996, 242,000 persons received a total of \$1,777m. in welfare assistance.

FURTHER READING

Statistical information: Maine Department of Economic and Community Development, State House Station 59, Augusta 04333. Publishes *Maine: a Statistical Summary.*
Maine Register, State Year-Book and Legislative Manual. Tower Publishing, Portland. Annual
Banks, R., *Maine Becomes A State.* Wesleyan U.P., 1970
Clark, C., *Maine.* New York, 1977
Palmer, K. T. *et al., Maine Politics and Government.* Univ. of Nebraska Press, 1993

MARYLAND

KEY HISTORICAL EVENTS

The first European visitors found groups of Algonquian-speaking tribes, often under attack by Iroquois from further north. The first white settlement was made by the Calvert family, British Roman Catholics, in 1634. The settlers received some legislative rights in 1638. In 1649 their assembly passed the Act of Toleration, granting freedom of worship to all Christians. A peace treaty was signed with the Iroquois in 1652, after which it was possible for farming settlements to expand north and west. The capital (formerly at St Mary's City) was moved to Annapolis in 1694. Baltimore, which became the state's main city, was founded in 1729.

The first industry was tobacco-growing, which was based on slave-worked plantations. There were also many immigrant British small farmers, tradesmen and indentured servants.

At the close of the War of Independence the treaty of Paris was ratified in Annapolis. Maryland became a state of the Union in 1788. In 1791 the state ceded land for the new federal capital, Washington, and its economy has depended on the capital's proximity ever since. Baltimore also grew as a port and industrial city, attracting much European immigration in the 19th century. Although strong sympathy for the south was expressed, Maryland remained within the Union in the Civil War albeit under the imposition of martial law.

TERRITORY AND POPULATION

Maryland is bounded north by Pennsylvania, east by Delaware and the Atlantic, south by Virginia and West Virginia, with the Potomac River forming most of the boundary, and west by West Virginia. Chesapeake Bay almost cuts off the eastern end of the state from the rest. Land area, 9,775 sq. miles (25,316 sq. km). Census population, 1 April 1990, 4,781,468 (81·3% urban), an increase since 1980 of 564,535 or 13·4%. Population estimate (1998), 5,134,800.

Population for 4 federal censuses was:

	White	Black	Indian	Asiatic	Total	Per sq. mile
1920	1,204,737	244,479	32	400	1,449,661	145·8
1930	1,354,226	276,379	50	857	1,631,526	165·0
1960	2,573,919	518,410	1,538	5,700	3,100,689	314·0
			All others			
1990	3,438,985	1,202,070	156,621		4,797,676	490·8

Of the total population in 1990, 2,318,671 were male, 3,888,429 persons were urban and those 20 years old or older numbered 3,484,455.

The largest city in the state (containing 15·4% of the population) is Baltimore, with 675,401 (1996 est.); Baltimore metropolitan area, 2·4m. Maryland residents in the Washington, D.C., metropolitan area total more than 1·8m. Other cities (1990) are Dundalk (65,800); Towson (49,445); Silver Spring (76,046); Columbia (75,883) and Bethesda (62,936). Incorporated places, 1994: Rockville, 47,078; Frederick, 46,630; Gaithersburg, 43,259; Bowie, 39,345; Hagerstown, 38,510; Annapolis, 35,169; Cumberland, 23,901; Salisbury, 22,204; College Park, 21,320; Greenbelt, 20,711 and Cambridge, 11,673.

SOCIAL STATISTICS

In 1997 births were 70,267 (13·8 per 1,000 population); deaths, 41,810 (8·2 per 1,000); infant deaths (1996), 8·5 (per 1,000 live births). Marriages (1996, provisional), 41,800; divorces, 16,300.

MARYLAND

CLIMATE
Baltimore, Jan. 36°F (2·2°C), July 79°F (26·1°C). Annual rainfall 42" (1,066 mm). Maryland belongs to the Atlantic Coast climate zone (*see* UNITED STATES: Climate).

CONSTITUTION AND GOVERNMENT
The present constitution dates from 1867; it has had 125 amendments. Amendments are proposed and considered annually by the General Assembly and must be ratified by the electorate. The General Assembly consists of a Senate of 47, and a House of Delegates of 141 members, both elected for 4 years, as are the Governor and Lieut.-Governor. Voters are citizens who have the usual residential qualifications.

Maryland sends to Congress 8 representatives.

The state capital is Annapolis. The state is divided into 23 counties and Baltimore City.

RECENT ELECTIONS
At the 1996 presidential election Clinton polled 924,284 votes; Dole, 651,682; Perot, 219,525.

CURRENT ADMINISTRATION
Governor: Parris N. Glendening (D.), 1999–2003 ($120,000).
  Lieut.-Governor: Kathleen K. Townsend (D.) ($100,000).
  Secretary of State: John Willis (D.) ($70,000).

ECONOMY
Budget. In 1996 total state revenue was $16,041m. Total expenditure was $15,554m. (education, $4,050m.; public welfare, $2,923m.; health and hospitals, $1,072m.; highways, $1,220m.; police protection, $274m.). Debt outstanding in 1996 was $9,691m.

Per capita income (1997, preliminary) was $22,078.

ENERGY AND NATURAL RESOURCES
Electricity. The territory is served by 4 investor-owned utilities, 5 municipal systems and 4 rural co-operatives. 86·6% of electricity comes from fossil fuels and 17·6% from nuclear power.

Oil and Gas. Natural gas is produced from 1 field in Garrett County; 25·9m. cu. ft in 1994. A second gas field is used for natural gas storage. No oil is produced and there are no major reserves located in Maryland.

Water. The total area covered by water is approximately 2,522 sq. miles. Abundant fresh water resources allow water withdrawals for neighbouring states and the District of Columbia. The state straddles the upper portions of the world's largest freshwater estuary, Chesapeake Bay.

Minerals. Value of non-fuel mineral production, 1996, was $324m. Sand and gravel (9·75m. tonnes) and stone (35·6m. tonnes) account for 70% of the total value. Stone is the leading mineral commodity by value followed by coal, Portland cement, and sand and gravel. Output of stone was about 31m. tonnes, valued at $158m.; coal output was 3·36m. short tons, valued at $95·6m.

Agriculture. In 1997 there were approximately 13,000 farms with an area of 2·1m. acres (33% of the land area). The average number of acres per farm was 162. The average value per acre was $4,000. In 1997, 26,600 people were employed in agriculture.

Farm animals, Jan. 1998 were: milch cows 86,000; all cattle, 265,000; swine, 73,000 and sheep, 33,000. As of Dec. 1997, chickens (not broilers), 4·1m. Farm income cash receipts, 1997: $1,570m.; from livestock and livestock products, $915m.; and crops, $655m. Milk (1997 value $182m.) and broilers ($532m.) are important products.

Fisheries. In 1997 the wholesale value of aquafarm-raised products totalled nearly $21·4m. Estimates for 1997 indicated that Maryland aquafarmers produced 285,000 lbs of hybrid striped bass; 50,000 lbs of catfish; 1,340,000 lbs of tilapia; and 20,000 lbs of trout. Nearly 11m. individual ornamental fish and 8m. oysters were harvested.

INDUSTRY

In 1998 manufacturers had a workforce of 174,700. Total value added by manufacture in 1996 was $17,454·6m. Chief industries included food processing ($2,728·7m.), instruments ($1,266·6m.), chemicals and products ($2,306·8m.), printing and publishing (2,175·6m.), primary metal industries ($1,465·7m.) and machinery and equipment ($1,429·7m.).

Total non-agricultural employment, 1998: 2,317,500.

Labour. In 1996, 24% of the workforce were professional and technical workers, more than any other state in the USA. The workforce is well educated with 32% of the population over age 25 holding a bachelor's or higher degree in 1997; it has the second highest concentration of PhD degrees in the sciences of US states—with 389 per 100,000 of the population.

COMMUNICATIONS

Roads. In 1997 the state highway maintained 5,242 miles of highways, of which 89 miles were toll roads. The counties maintained 19,700 miles of highways, and the municipalities (including the city of Baltimore) maintained 4,332 miles of streets and alleys. Total mileage of public highways, streets and alleys (1997), 29,265 miles. In March 1996 an estimated 3·8m. automobiles were registered.

Rail. Maryland is served by CSX Transportation, Norfolk Southern Railroad as well as by six short-line railroads. Metro lines also serve Maryland in suburban Washington D.C. Amtrak provides passenger service linking Baltimore and BWI Airport to major cities on the Atlantic Coast. MARC commuter rail serves the Baltimore–Washington metropolitan area.

Civil Aviation. There were (1998) 38 public-use airports, and 45 commercial airlines at BWI Airport. The airport serves an average of 14m. passengers annually. A newly opened passenger pier serves the airport's increasing numbers of international customers. Air cargo throughput has grown rapidly to over 350m. tons per annum, with increases planned.

Shipping. In 1997 Baltimore was the 9th largest US seaport in value of imports, and 12th largest in value of exports; in 1996 it ranked 16th in annual tonnage handled. It is located as much as 200 miles further inland than any other Atlantic seaport.

SOCIAL INSTITUTIONS

Justice. Prisons in Jan. 1999 held 22,900 inmates; 446 per 100,000 population. Maryland's prison system has conducted a work-release programme for selected prisoners since 1963. All institutions have academic and vocational training programmes. The death penalty is authorized.

Religion. Maryland was the first US state to give religious freedom to all who came within its borders. Present religious affiliations of the population are approximately: Protestant, 32%; Roman Catholic, 24%; Jewish, 10%; remaining 34% is non-related and other faiths.

Education. Education is compulsory from 6 to 16 years of age. In 1997–98 public schools (including pre-kindergarten through secondary schools) had 830,744 pupils; teachers numbered 62,503; average salary was $41,404. Expenditure on education, 1997–98, was $5·6bn., of which the state's contribution was $2,645m. Per pupil cost (1997–98) was $6,584.

There are 54 institutions of higher learning (34 four-year and 20 two-year). The largest is the Maryland University system, with 130,000 students (Sept. 1996), consisting of 11 campuses, 2 major research institutions, and over 250 learning centres in Europe and the Far East. Career and technical education is available through a network of community colleges and in some 200 secondary schools.

Health. In May 1997 there were 76 hospitals (with 18,618 beds) licensed by the State Department of Health and Mental Hygiene.

The Maryland State Department of Health, organized in 1874, was in 1969 made part of the Department of Health and Mental Hygiene which performs its functions through its central office, 23 county health departments and the Baltimore City Health Department. For the fiscal year 1998 the department's budget was $3,464m., of which $1,934·2m. were general funds and $118·7m. special funds appropriated by the General Assembly. The balance of the budget, $1,411·1m., is derived from federal funds.

During fiscal year 1998 Maryland's programme of medical care for indigent and medically indigent patients covered 441,448 persons. The programme, which covers in-patient and out-patient hospital services, laboratory services, skilled nursing home care, physician services, pharmacy services, dental services and home health services, cost approximately $2,047·7m.

Welfare. Under the supervision of the Department of Human Resources, local departments of social services administer Temporary Assistance to Needy Families, which amounted to $121,419,676 in 1998; an average monthly amount of $117·85 for the 136,005 beneficiaries. General Public Assistance—called Transitional Emergency Medical and Housing Assistance (TEMHA)—cost the state $14,896,100 (1998), assisting 12,414 persons with an average monthly payment of $100.

CULTURE
Cultural venues include: Frostburg Performing Arts Center, Strathmore Hall Arts Center, and Center Stage. Performing arts institutions include the Baltimore Opera Company, Peabody Music Conservatory and Arena Players.

Broadcasting. There are 15 TV stations, 22 cable television stations, 48 FM radio, and 31 AM radio stations.

Cinema. Maryland is a popular filming location. Recent films include *Washington Square*, *Enemy of the State*, *Pecker*, *Runaway Bride*, and *Species II*. The economic impact of film making on the state in 1998 was $77m.

Tourism. Tourism is one of the state's leading industries. In 1996 tourists spent over $6,064m. Direct employment in tourism (1996) was 89,900.

Festivals. The Rossborough Festival is hosted in Maryland every 4 years.

National Theatre and Opera. The main venues are the Lyric Opera House and Meyerhoff Symphony Hall.

Museums and Galleries. Galleries include the Walter's Art Gallery, the Baltimore Museum of Art, and the American Visionary Art Museum. Specialized museums cover historical and cultural aspects of life, from the B&O Railroad Museum to the US Naval Academy Museum, from battlefields to the Goddard Space Flight Center, from colonial life to baseball. Baltimore's Inner Harbor is home to 4 floating museums, 3 ships and a submarine.

FURTHER READING
Statistical Information: Maryland Department of Economic and Employment Development, 217 East Redwood St., Baltimore 21202.
DiLisio, J. E., *Maryland.* Boulder, 1982
Rollo, V. F., *Maryland's Constitution and Government.* Maryland Hist. Press, Rev. ed., 1982

State Library: Maryland State Library, Annapolis.

MASSACHUSETTS

KEY HISTORICAL EVENTS
The first European settlement was at Plymouth, when the *Mayflower* landed its company of English religious separatists in 1620. In 1626–30 more colonists arrived, the main body being a large company of English Puritans who founded a Puritan commonwealth. This commonwealth, of about 1,000 colonists led by John Winthrop, became the Massachusetts Bay Colony and was founded under a company charter. Following disagreement between the English government and the

colony the charter was withdrawn in 1684, but in 1691 a new charter united a number of settlements under the name of Massachusetts Bay. The colony's government was rigidly theocratic.

Shipbuilding, iron-working and manufacturing were more important than farming from the beginning, the land being poor. The colony was Protestant and of English descent until the War of Independence. The former colony adopted its present constitution in 1780. In the struggle which ended in the separation of the American colonies from the mother country, Massachusetts took the foremost part, and on 6 Feb. 1788 became the 6th state to ratify the US constitution. The state acquired its present boundaries (having previously included Maine) in 1820.

During the 19th century industrialization and immigration from Europe both increased while Catholic Irish and Italian immigrants began to change the population's character. The main inland industry was textile manufacture, the main coastal occupation was whaling; both have now gone. Boston has remained the most important city of New England, attracting a large black population since 1950.

TERRITORY AND POPULATION
Massachusetts is bounded north by Vermont and New Hampshire, east by the Atlantic, south by Connecticut and Rhode Island and west by New York. Land area, 7,838 sq. miles (20,300 sq. km). Population estimate (1997), 6,118,000.

Population at 5 federal census years was:

	White	Black	Other	Total	Per sq. mile
1950	4,611,503	73,171	5,840	4,690,514	598·4
1960	5,023,144	111,842	13,592	5,148,578	656·8
1970	5,477,624	175,817	35,729	5,689,170	725·8
1980	5,362,836	221,279	152,922	5,737,037	732·0
1990	...	...	...	6,016,425	767·6

Of the total population in 1980, 47·6% were male, 83·8% were urban and 32% were 21 years old or older.

Population of the largest cities at the 1990 census: Boston, 574,283; Lowell, 103,439; Springfield, 156,983; Worcester, 169,759; New Bedford, 99,922; Cambridge, 95,802; Brockton, 92,788; Fall River, 92,703; Quincy, 84,985; Newton, 82,585; Lynn, 81,245.

SOCIAL STATISTICS
1995: births, 81,648 (13·4 per 1,000 population); deaths, 55,000 (9·1); infant deaths in 1992, 529 (6·0 per 1,000 live births; 5·2 in 1995). Marriages (1996, provisional), 40,600; divorces, 12,400.

CLIMATE
Boston, Jan. 28°F (–2·2°C), July 71°F (21·7°C). Annual rainfall 41" (1,036 mm). Massachusetts belongs to the New England climate zone (see UNITED STATES: Climate).

CONSTITUTION AND GOVERNMENT
The constitution dates from 1780 and has had 116 amendments. The legislative body, styled the General Court of the Commonwealth of Massachusetts, meets annually, and consists of the Senate with 40 members and the House of Representatives of 160 members, both elected for 2 years.

The state sends 10 representatives to Congress.

The capital is Boston. The state has 14 counties.

RECENT ELECTIONS
At the 1996 presidential election Clinton polled 1,532,917 votes; Dole, 693,866; Perot, 219,525.

CURRENT ADMINISTRATION
Governor: A. Paul Cellucci (R.), 1999–2002 ($75,000).
Lieut.-Governor: Jane M. Swift (R.) ($75,000).
Secretary of State: William F. Galvin (D.) ($75,000).

ECONOMY

Budget. In 1996 total state revenue was \$25,197m. Total expenditure was \$24,950m. (education, \$4,492m.; public welfare, \$5,999m.; health and hospitals, \$2,182m.; highways, \$1,803m.; police protection, \$287m.). Debt outstanding in 1996 was \$29,295m.

Per capita income (1997, preliminary) was \$31,524.

ENERGY AND NATURAL RESOURCES

Water. The total area covered by water is approximately 1,403 sq. miles.

Minerals. Total domestic non-fuel mineral output in 1997 was valued at \$213m., of which most came from sand, gravel, crushed stone and lime.

Agriculture. In 1996 there were approximately 6,000 farms with an average area of 92 acres and a total area of 1m. acres. Average value per acre in 1998 was \$6,450. Farm income in 1996: crops, \$369m.; livestock and products, \$109m. Principal crops included cranberries and greenhouse products.

Forestry. About 68% of the state is forest. State forests cover about 256,000 acres. Total forest land covers about 3m. acres. Commercially important hardwoods are sugar maple, northern red oak and white ash; softwoods are white pine and hemlock.

Fisheries. The 1990 catch totalled 328m. lbs and was valued at \$303m.

INDUSTRY

In 1996 the total non-agricultural workforce was 3,036,000. Manufacturing establishments employed an average of 444,000 workers, service industries employed 1,063,000 and wholesale and retail 697,000.

COMMUNICATIONS

Roads. In 1996 there were 34,725 miles of public roads (12,050 miles rural) and 4,702,000 registered motor vehicles.

Rail. In 1984 there were 1,310 miles of mainline railway. There are metro, light rail, tramway and commuter networks in and around Boston.

Civil Aviation. There is an international airport at Boston.

Shipping. The state has 3 deep-water harbours, the largest of which is Boston. Other ports are Fall River and New Bedford.

SOCIAL INSTITUTIONS

Justice. In 1996 state and federal correctional institutions held 11,796 prisoners. The death penalty is not authorized.

Religion. The principal religious bodies are the Roman Catholics, Jewish Congregations, Methodists, Episcopalians and Unitarians.

Education. School attendance is compulsory for ages 6–16. In 1994–95 there were 58,893 classroom teachers and 890,240 pupils.

Some leading higher education institutions are:

Year opened	Name and location of universities and colleges	Students 1988
1636	Harvard University, Cambridge[1]	16,871
1839	Framingham State College	4,303
1839	Westfield State College	6,053
1840	Bridgewater State College	6,539
1852	Tufts University, Medford[1,3]	6,297
1854	Salem State College	6,364
1861	Mass. Institute of Technology, Cambridge[1]	9,158
1863	University of Massachusetts, Amherst[1]	26,233
1863	Boston College (RC), Chestnut Hill[1]	12,858
1865	Worcester Polytechnic Institute, Worcester[1]	4,022
1869	Boston University, Boston[1]	22,373
1874	Worcester College	4,899
1894	Fitchburg State College	5,212

Year opened	Name and location of universities and colleges	Students 1988
1894	University of Lowell[1]	10,445
1895	Southeastern Massachusetts University	5,031
1898	Northeastern University, Boston[1,4]	20,618
1899	Simmons College, Boston[2]	2,594
1905	Wentworth Institute of Technology	3,350
1906	Suffolk University	5,978
1917	Bentley College	5,611
1919	Western New England College	3,686
1919	Babson College	3,163
1947	Merrimack College	2,300
1948	Brandeis University, Waltham[1]	3,484
1964	University of Massachusetts, Boston	8,027

[1]Co-educational.   [2]For women only.
[3]Includes Jackson College for women.   [4]Includes Forsyth Dental Center School.

Health. In 1995 there were 96 community hospitals with 18,900 beds and 106,000 personnel.

Welfare. In 1996, 1,052,000 persons received welfare totalling $8,548m.: including 746,000 retired workers and dependants who received on average $748 per month; and 154,000 disabled workers and dependants who received on average $697 per month.

FURTHER READING

Hart, Albert B., (ed.) *Commonwealth History of Massachusetts, Colony, Province and State.* 5 vols., New York, 1966

Levitan, D. with Mariner, E. C., *Your Massachusetts Government.* Newton, Mass., 1984

MICHIGAN

KEY HISTORICAL EVENTS

The French were the first European settlers, establishing a fur trade with the local Algonquian Indians in the late 17th century. They founded Sault Ste Marie in 1668 and Detroit in 1701. In 1763 Michigan passed to Britain, along with other French territory east of the Mississippi, and from Britain it passed to the USA in 1783. Britain, however, kept a force at Detroit until 1796, and recaptured Detroit in 1812. Regular American settlement did not begin until later. The Territory of Michigan (1805) had its boundaries extended after 1818 and 1834. It was admitted to the Union as a state (with its present boundaries) in 1837.

During the 19th century there was rapid industrial growth, especially in mining and metalworking. The largest groups of immigrants were British, German, Irish and Dutch. Other significant groups came from Scandinavia, Poland and Italy. Many groups of immigrants came to settle as miners, farmers and industrial workers. The motor industry became dominant, especially in Detroit. Lake Michigan ports shipped bulk cargo, especially iron ore and grain.

Detroit was the capital until 1847, when that function passed to Lansing. Detroit remained, however, an important centre of flour-milling and shipping and, after the First World War, of the motor industry.

TERRITORY AND POPULATION

Michigan is divided into two by Lake Michigan. The northern part is bounded south by the lake and by Wisconsin, west and north by Lake Superior, east by the North Channel of Lake Huron; between the two latter lakes the Canadian border runs through straits at Sault Ste Marie. The southern part is bounded in the west and north by Lake Michigan, east by Lake Huron, Ontario and Lake Erie, south by Ohio and Indiana. Area, 58,110 sq. miles (150,544 sq. km). Census population, 1 April 1990, 9,295,297 (70·5% urban), an increase of 0·4% since 1980. Population estimate (1998), 9,817,242.

Population of 5 federal census years was:

	White	Black	Indian	Asiatic	Total	Per sq. mile
1910	2,785,247	17,115	7,519	292	2,810,173	48·9
1930	4,663,507	69,453	7,080	2,285	4,842,325	84·9
1960	7,085,865	717,581	9,701	10,047	7,823,194	137·2
			All others			
1980	7,872,241	1,199,023	190,814		9,262,078	162·6
1990	7,756,086	1,291,706	247,505		9,295,297	160·0

Of the total population in 1990, 4,512,781 were male, 6,554,846 persons were urban and those 20 years old or older numbered 6,540,323. 201,596 were Hispanic.

Populations of the chief cities (1996 estimates) were: Detroit, 1,000,272; Grand Rapids, 188,242; Warren, 138,078; Flint, 134,881; Lansing, 125,736; Sterling Heights, 118,698; Ann Arbor, 108,758; Livonia, 105,099.

SOCIAL STATISTICS
In 1997 births were 133,621; deaths, 83,620; infant deaths, 1,085 (8·1 per 1,000 live births); marriages, 66,817; divorces, 38,623.

CLIMATE
Detroit, Jan. 22·9°F (–5·1°C), July 72·3°F (22·4°C). Annual rainfall 32·6" (828 mm). Grand Rapids, Jan. 21·8°F (–5·7°C), July 71·6°F (22·0°C). Annual rainfall 36·0" (914 mm). Lansing, Jan. 20·9°F (–6·2°C), July 70·8°F (21·6°C). Annual rainfall 30·6" (777 mm). Michigan belongs to the Great Lakes climate zone (*see* UNITED STATES: Climate).

CONSTITUTION AND GOVERNMENT
The present constitution became effective on 1 Jan. 1964. The Senate consists of 38 members, elected for 4 years, and the House of Representatives of 110 members, elected for 2 years.

The state sends 16 representatives to Congress.

The capital is Lansing. The state is organized in 83 counties.

RECENT ELECTIONS
At the 1996 presidential election Clinton polled 1,989,653 votes; Dole, 1,481,212; Perot, 336,670.

CURRENT ADMINISTRATION
Governor: John Engler (R.), 1999–2003 ($127,300).
  Lieut.-Governor: Richard Posthumus (R.) ($93,978).
  Secretary of State: Candice Miller (R.) ($112,000).

ECONOMY
Performance. New business incorporations for 1996 totalled 32,027. Personal income grew by 5·9% *per capita* from 1994 to 1995.

Budget. In 1996 total state revenue was $38,047m. Total expenditure was $35,080m. (education, $13,812m.; public welfare, $6,440m.; health and hospitals, $3,406m.; highways, $1,936m.; police protection, $229m.). Total debt outstanding was $13,668m. in 1996.

  Per capita income (1997, preliminary) was $25,560.

ENERGY AND NATURAL RESOURCES
Electricity. Electricity sales for 1997 were 97,354m. kWh.

Oil and Gas. Natural gas production 1997, 277bn. cu. ft; demand, 937·2bn. cu. ft. Production of crude oil averaged 25,000 bbls. a day in 1998.

Water. The total area covered by water is approximately 39,895 sq. miles. Total freshwater withdrawn (1995) was 667m. gallons per day; 1,260 gallons *per capita*.

Minerals. Domestic non-fuel mineral output in 1996 was valued at $1,540m., mainly iron ore, cement, crushed stone, sand and gravel.

Agriculture. The state, formerly agricultural, is now chiefly industrial. It contained 51,000 farms (1997) with a total area of 10·5m. acres; the average farm was 206 acres. In 1997, 6,893,000 acres were harvested. Average value per acre in 1998 was $1,720. Principal crops are corn, oats, wheat, sugar-beets, soybeans, hay and dry beans. Total crop cash receipts for 1997, $2·24bn. Principal fruit crops are apples, cherries (tart and sweet) and blueberries. In 1996 there were 328,000 milch cows, 122,000 beef cows and 6·56m. chickens. Farm income, 1996: crops, $3,195m.; livestock and products, $1,448m.

Forestry. The forests in 1993 covered 19·3m. acres. About 18·6m. acres of this total is timberland acreage. Three-quarters of the timber volume is hardwoods, principally hard and soft maples, aspen, oak and birch. Christmas trees are another important forest crop. Sawtimber harvests in 1990 totalled 1bn. bd feet.

Fisheries. In 1996 recreational fishing licences were purchased by 1·4m. residents and 129,000 non-residents. Recreational fishing revenue (1996) was approximately $2bn.

INDUSTRY
Manufacturing is important; among principal products are motor vehicles and trucks, machinery, fabricated metals, primary metals, cement, chemicals, furniture, paper, foodstuffs, rubber, plastics and pharmaceuticals.

Labour. Total non-agricultural labour force, 1997, 4,446,000, of which 967,200 were in manufacturing.

COMMUNICATIONS

Roads. In 1996 there were 119,113 miles of roads (9,583 miles of state highways, 89,129 miles of county roads and 20,401 miles of municipal roads). In 1997 there were 9,275,870 registered motor vehicles.

Rail. In 1996 there were 3,876 miles of railway.

Civil Aviation. There are international airports at Detroit, Flint, Grand Rapids, Kalamazoo, Port Huron, Saginaw and Sault Ste Marie. In 1996 there were 4,174,743 aircraft operations at Michigan's 239 public-use airports. 24 carriers provided passenger service at 19 airports.

Shipping. There are over 100 commercial and recreational ports spanning the state's 3,200 miles of shoreline. In 1997, 40 of these ports served commercial cargoes. The 20 ferry services carried 722,804 passengers and 437,697 vehicles in 62,369 crossings in 1996. Stone, sand, iron ore and coal accounted for 88% of approximately 94m. tons of traffic in 1995.

SOCIAL INSTITUTIONS

Justice. A Civil Rights Commission was established, and its powers and duties were implemented by legislation in the extra session of 1963. Statutory enactments guaranteeing civil rights in specific areas date from 1885. The legislature has a unique one-person grand jury system. The Michigan Supreme Court consists of 7 non-partisan elected justices. In 1996, 2,898 cases were completed and at the close of the year 2,051 cases were pending. In 1997 there were 42,570 prisoners in state correctional institutions. Michigan has no capital punishment statute.

Religion. Roman Catholics make up the largest body; largest Protestant denominations, Lutherans, United Methodists, United Presbyterians and Episcopalians.

Education. Education is compulsory for children from 6 to 16 years of age. Education expenditure by state and local governments in 1996–97 was $11,071m. In 1996–97 there were 1,678,288 pupils and 86,985 teachers in public elementary and secondary schools.

In 1996 there were 110 institutes of higher education with (autumn 1994) 551,307 students.

Universities and students (autumn 1998):

Founded	Name	Students
1817	University of Michigan, Ann Arbor	37,197
	University of Michigan, Dearborn	8,335[1]
	University of Michigan, Flint	6,408[1]
1849	Eastern Michigan University	23,558
1855	Michigan State University	43,189
1884	Ferris State University	9,651
1885	Michigan Technological University	6,302
1868	Wayne State University	30,729[1]
1892	Central Michigan University	25,595
1899	Northern Michigan University	7,670
1903	Western Michigan University	26,132[1]
1946	Lake Superior State University	3,264
1957	Oakland University	14,289
1960	Grand Valley State College	16,751
1963	Saginaw Valley College	8,054

[1] 1997 data

Health. There were, in 1998, 183 Medicare and Medicaid certified hospitals (34,724 beds); 13 psychiatric hospitals (1,519 beds) and 8 rehabilitation hospitals (442 beds).

In the fiscal year 1996 the Medicaid programme disbursed (with federal support) $5,180m. in medical assistance payments to 1,171,622 persons.

Welfare. Old-age assistance is provided for persons 65 years of age or older who have resided in Michigan for one year before application; assets must not exceed various limits. In 1974 federal Supplementary Security Income (SSI) replaced the adults' programme. A monthly average of 99,599 families received $360 per month in 1998 through the Family Independence Program.

CULTURE

Tourism. In 1996, 372,000 overseas visitors (1·6% of the market share) visited Michigan.

Libraries. There were in 1998, 384 public libraries. Total public library operating expenditures were $205·5m.; $22 *per capita*.

FURTHER READING

Michigan Manual. Dept of *Management and Budget*. Lansing. Biennial

Michigan Employment Security Commission. *Michigan Statistical Abstract, 1996*. Univ of Michigan Press

Bald, F. C., *Michigan in Four Centuries*. 2nd ed. New York, 1961

Browne, W. P. and Verburg, K., *Michigan Politics and Government: Facing Change in a Complex State*. Nebraska Univ. Press, 1995

Catton. B., *Michigan: A Bicentennial History*. Norton, New York, 1976

Lewis, F. E., *State and Local Government in Michigan*. 9th ed. Hillsdale, 1984

Dunbar, W. F. and May, G. S., *Michigan: A History of the Wolverine State*. 3rd ed. Grand Rapids, 1995

Sommers, L. (ed.), *Atlas of Michigan*. East Lansing, 1977

State Library Services: Library of Michigan, Lansing 48909.

MINNESOTA

KEY HISTORICAL EVENTS

Minnesota remained an Indian territory until the middle of the 19th century, the main groups being Chippewa and Sioux, many of whom are still there. In the 17th century there had been some French exploration, but no permanent settlement. After passing under the nominal control of France, Britain and Spain, the area became part of the Louisiana Purchase and so was sold to the USA in 1803.

Fort Snelling was founded in 1819. Early settlers came from other states, especially New England, to exploit the great forests. Lumbering gave way to homesteading, and the American settlers were joined by Germans, Scandinavians and Poles. Agriculture, mining and forest industries became the mainstays of the economy. Minneapolis, founded as a village in 1856, grew first as a lumber centre, processing the logs floated down the Minnesota River, and then as a centre of flour-milling and grain marketing. St Paul, its twin city across the river, became Territorial capital in 1849 and state capital in 1858. St Paul also stands at the head of navigation on the Mississippi, which rises in Minnesota.

The Territory (1849) included parts of North and South Dakota, but at its admission to the Union in 1858, the state of Minnesota had its present boundaries.

TERRITORY AND POPULATION

Minnesota is bounded north by Canada, east by Lake Superior and Wisconsin, with the Mississippi River forming the boundary in the south-east, south by Iowa, west by South and North Dakota, with the Red River forming the boundary in the north-west. Land area, 79,617 sq. miles (206,207 sq. km). Census population, 1 April 1990, 4,375,099 (69·9% urban), an increase of 7·31% since 1980. Population estimate (1997), 4,686,000.

Population in 5 census years was:

	White	Black	Indian	Asiatic	Total	Per sq. mile
1910	2,059,227	7,084	9,053	344	2,075,708	25·7
1930	2,542,599	9,445	11,077	832	2,563,953	32·0
			All others			
1970	3,736,038	34,868	34,163		3,805,069	47·6
1980	3,935,770	53,344	86,856		4,075,970	51·4
1990	4,130,395	94,944	149,760		4,375,099	55·0

Of the 1990 population, 2,145,183 were male; 3,056,474 were urban; those 21 years of age or older numbered 3,015,507.

The largest cities (with 1990 census population) are Minneapolis (368,383), St Paul (272,253), Bloomington (86,335) and Duluth (85,931).

SOCIAL STATISTICS

Births in 1995, 63,258 (13·7 per 1,000 population); deaths, 37,429 (8·1); infant deaths, 494 (7·4 per 1,000 live births); marriages, 32,878 (7·1); divorces, 15,486 (3·3).

CLIMATE

Duluth, Jan. 8°F (−13·3°C), July 63°F (17·2°C). Annual rainfall 29" (719 mm). Minneapolis-St. Paul, Jan. 12°F (−11·1°C), July 71°F (21·7°C). Annual rainfall 26" (656 mm). Minnesota belongs to the Great Lakes climate zone (*see* UNITED STATES: Climate).

CONSTITUTION AND GOVERNMENT

The original constitution dated from 1857; it was extensively amended and given a new structure in 1974. The Legislature consists of a Senate of 67 members, elected for 4 years, and a House of Representatives of 134 members, elected for 2 years. It meets for 120 days within each 2 years.

The state sends 8 representatives to Congress.

The capital is St Paul. There are 87 counties.

RECENT ELECTIONS

In the 1996 presidential election Clinton polled 1,911,553 votes; Dole 1,413,812; Perot, 319,095.

CURRENT ADMINISTRATION

Governor: Jesse Ventura, 1999–2003.
  Lieut.-Governor: Mae Schunk.
  Secretary of State: Mary Kiffmeyer.

ECONOMY

Budget. In 1996 total state revenue was $20,525m. Total expenditure was $17,325m. (education, $5,783m.; public welfare, $4,129m.; health and hospitals, $1,117m.; highways, $1,214m.; police protection, $89m.)

Debt outstanding in 1996, $4,858m.
Per capita income (1997, preliminary) was $26,797.

ENERGY AND NATURAL RESOURCES

Water. The total area covered by water is approximately 7,327 sq. miles.

Minerals. The iron ore and taconite industry is the most important in the USA. Production of usable iron ore in 1996 was 46m. tons, value $1,390m. Other important minerals are sand and gravel, crushed and dimension stone, clays and peat. Total value of mineral production, 1996, $1,800m.

Agriculture. In 1995 there were some 87,000 farms with a total area of 29·8m. acres; the average farm was of 343 acres. Average value of land and buildings per acre, 1995, $936. Farm income, 1996, from crops, $4,641m.; from livestock and products, $4,168m. Important products: sugar-beet, spring wheat, processing sweet corn, oats, dry milk, cheese, mink, turkeys, wild rice, butter, eggs, flaxseed, milch cows, milk, corn, barley, swine, cattle for market, soybeans, honey, potatoes, rye, chickens, sunflower seed and dry edible beans. In 1996 there were 2·9m. cattle (0·6m. milch cows) and 4·9m. hogs and pigs. In 1995 the wool clip amounted to 1·15m. lb of wool from 170,000 sheep.

Forestry. Forests of commercial timber cover 14·7m. acres, of which 55% is government-owned. The value of forest products in 1994 was $7,500m.: $2,250m. from primary processing, of which $1,687m. was from pulp and paper; and $3,100m. from secondary manufacturing. Logging, pulping, saw-mills and associated industries employed 57,200 in 1995.

INDUSTRY

In 1996 manufacturing establishments employed 429,000 workers; value added by manufacture in 1995 was $32,600m. Largest manufacturing industry is computers and non-electric machinery (74,000 employees); then food products and kindred products (55,000) and printing and publishing (also 55,000).

COMMUNICATIONS

Roads. In 1996 there were 130,613 miles of roads (115,232 miles rural); 3·7m. motor vehicles were registered.

Rail. There are 3 Class I and 16 Class II and smaller railroads operating, with total mileage of 4,650.

Civil Aviation. In 1989 there were 138 airports for public use and 8 public seaplane bases.

SOCIAL INSTITUTIONS

Justice. In 1996 there were 5,158 prisoners in state correctional institutions. There is no death penalty.

Religion. The chief religious bodies are: Lutheran with 1,126,008 members in 1990; Roman Catholic, 1,110,071; Methodist, 142,771. Total membership of all denominations, 2,837,415.

Education. In 1992, there were 775,567 students and 44,200 teachers in public elementary and secondary schools. In 1988 there were 1,511 public schools, and 82,165 kindergarten, elementary, and secondary students enrolled in 572 private schools. The University of Minnesota, chartered in 1851 and opened in 1869, had a total enrolment in 1988 of 54,515 students on all campuses. The 18 public community colleges (2-year) had a total enrolment of 49,589. There are seven state universities (4-year) at Bemidji, Mankato, Marshall, Moorhead, St Cloud, Winona, Minneapolis and St Paul. Enrolment in all institutions of higher education, 1988, 251,304.

Health. In 1989 the state had 163 general acute hospitals with 19,229 beds. Patients resident in institutions under the Department of Human Services in Sept. 1997 included 977 people with mental illness, 231 people with mental retardation, 178 with chemical dependency and 232 in state nursing homes.

Welfare. Programmes of old age assistance, aid to the disabled, and aid to the blind are administered under the federal Supplemental Security Income (SSI) Programme. Minnesota has a supplementary programme, Minnesota Supplemental Aid (MSA) to cover individuals not eligible for SSI, to supplement SSI benefits for others whose income is below state standards, and to provide one-time payments for emergency needs such as major home repair, essential furniture or appliances, moving expenses, fuel, food and shelter.

CULTURE

Tourism. In 1995, travellers spent about $8,699m. The industry employed about 162,800.

FURTHER READING

Statistical Information: Department of Trade and Economic Development, 500 Metro Square, St Paul 55101. Publishes *Compare Minnesota: an Economic and Statistical Factbook.— Economic Report to the Governor.*
Legislative Manual. Secretary of State. St Paul. Biennial
Minnesota Agriculture Statistics. Dept. of Agric., St Paul. Annual

MISSISSIPPI

KEY HISTORICAL EVENTS

Mississippi was one of the territories claimed by France after the 17th century and ceded to Britain in 1763. The indigenous people were Choctaw and Natchez. French settlers at first traded amicably with them, but in the course of three wars (1716, 1723 and 1729) the French allied with the Choctaw to drive the Natchez out. During hostilities the Natchez massacred the settlers of Fort Rosalie, which the French had founded in 1716 and which was later renamed Natchez.

In 1783 the area became part of the USA except for Natchez which was under Spanish control until 1798. The United States then made it the capital of the Territory of Mississippi. The boundaries of the Territory were extended in 1804 and again in 1812. In 1817 it was divided into two territories, with the western part becoming the state of Mississippi. (The eastern part became the state of Alabama in 1819.) The city of Jackson was laid out in 1822 as the new state capital.

A cotton plantation economy developed, based on black slave labour, and by 1860 the majority of the population was black. Mississippi joined the Confederacy during the Civil War. After defeat and reconstruction there was a return to rigid segregation and denial of black rights. This situation lasted until the 1960s. There was a black majority until the Second World War, when out-migration began to change the pattern. By 1990 about 35% of the population was black, and manufacture (especially clothing and textiles) had become the largest single employer of labour.

TERRITORY AND POPULATION

Mississippi is bounded in the north by Tennessee, east by Alabama, south by the Gulf of Mexico and Louisiana, west by the Mississippi River forming the boundary with Louisiana and Arkansas. Area, 47,689 sq. miles (123,515 sq. km), 457 sq. miles (1,184 sq. km) being inland water. Census population, 1 July 1990, 2,573,216 (47·1% urban), an increase of 2·09% since 1980. Population estimate (1997), 2,731,644.

Population of 5 federal census years was:

	White	Black	Indian	Asiatic	Total	Per sq. mile
1910	786,111	1,009,487	1,253	263	1,797,114	38·8
1930	998,077	1,009,718	1,458	568	2,009,821	42·4
1950	1,188,632	986,494	2,502	1,286	2,178,914	46·1
			All others			
1980	1,615,190	887,206	18,242		2,520,638	53·0
1990	1,633,461	915,057	24,698		2,573,216	54·8

Of the population in 1990, 1,230,617 were male, 1,211,271 were urban and 1,729,749 were 20 years old or older.

The largest city (1996 estimate) is Jackson, 192,923. Others (1996 estimates) are: Gulfport, 64,829; Biloxi, 48,414; Hattiesburg, 47,803; Greenville, 42,993; Meridian, 40,835; Tupelo, 35,194; Vicksburg, 27,056; Pascagoula, 27,026; Columbus, 22,724; Clinton, 21,992.

SOCIAL STATISTICS
Births occurring in the state, 1997, were 40,612; deaths, 26,741; infant deaths, 399; marriages, 21,338; divorces, 13,860.

CLIMATE
Jackson, Jan. 47°F (8·3°C), July 82°F (27·8°C). Annual rainfall 49" (1,221 mm). Vicksburg, Jan. 48°F (8·9°C), July 81°F (27·2°C). Annual rainfall 52" (1,311 mm). Mississippi belongs to the Central Plains climate zone (see UNITED STATES: Climate).

CONSTITUTION AND GOVERNMENT
The present constitution was adopted in 1890 without ratification by the electorate; 103 amendments by 1990.

The Legislature consists of a Senate (52 members) and a House of Representatives (122 members), both elected for 4 years. The state is represented in Congress by 2 senators and 5 representatives. Electors are all citizens who have resided in the state 1 year, in the county 1 year, in the election district 6 months before the election and have been registered according to law.

The capital is Jackson; there are 82 counties.

RECENT ELECTIONS
In the 1996 presidential election Dole polled 434,547 votes; Clinton, 385,005; Perot, 51,500.

CURRENT ADMINISTRATION
Governor: Kirk Fordice (R.), 1996–2000 ($83,160).
   Lieut.-Governor: Ronnie Musgrove (D.) ($40,800).
   Secretary of State: Eric Clark (D.) ($75,000).

ECONOMY
Budget. In 1996 total state revenue was $8,865m. Total expenditure was $8,217m. (education, $2,724m.; public welfare, $1,658m.; health and hospitals, $623m.; highways, $718m.; police protection, $52m.)

   Debt outstanding, in 1996, $2,232m.

Per capita income (1997, preliminary) was $18,272.

ENERGY AND NATURAL RESOURCES
Oil and Gas. Petroleum and natural gas account for about 90% (by value) of mineral production. Output of petroleum, 1997, was 20,996,623 bbls. and of natural gas 126,452m. cu. ft. There are 4 oil refineries. Taxable value of oil and gas products sold in fiscal year 1998 was $423,591,249.

Water. The total area covered by water is approximately 1,372 sq. miles.

Minerals. The total value of domestic non-fuel mineral production in 1997 was $137m.

Agriculture. Agriculture is the leading industry of the state because of the semi-tropical climate and a rich productive soil. In 1998 there were 82 soil and water conservation districts representing 53,725 co-operators on 12·5m. acres. In 1997 farms numbered 43,000 with an area of 12·5m. acres. Average size of farm was 291 acres. This compares with an average farm size of 138 acres in 1960. Average value of farm per acre in 1997 was $950.

Cash income from all crops and livestock during 1997, including government payments, was $3,653,023,000. Cash income from crops was $1,470,003,000, and from livestock and products, $2,006,387,000. The chief product is cotton, cash income (1997) $569,900,000 from 930,000 acres producing 1,821,000 bales of 480 lbs. Soybeans, rice, corn, hay, wheat, oats, sorghum, peanuts, pecans, sweet potatoes, peaches, other vegetables, nursery and forest products continue to contribute.

On 1 Jan. 1998 there were 1·3m. head of cattle and calves on Mississippi farms. In Jan. 1998 milk cows totalled 44,000, beef cows, 666,000; (1997) hogs and pigs, 240,000. Of cash income from livestock and products, 1997, $195,608,000 was credited to cattle and calves. Cash income from poultry and eggs, 1997, totalled $1,376,662,000; dairy products, $90,720,000; swine, $64,809,000.

Forestry. In 1997 income from forestry amounted to $1·3bn.; output of logs, lumber, etc., was 2·13bn. bd ft; pulpwood, 7·8m. cords. There are about 18·6m. acres of forest (62% of the state's area). National forest area, 1998, 1·1m. acres.

INDUSTRY
In 1997 the 3,758 manufacturing establishments employed 241,618 workers, earning $6,181,542,440. The average annual wage was $25,584.

COMMUNICATIONS
Roads. The state as of 31 Dec. 1997 maintained 10,651 miles of highways, all paved. In fiscal year 1998, 2,484,364 passenger vehicles and pick-ups were registered.

Rail. The state in 1998 had 2,841 main-line miles of railway.

Civil Aviation. There were 76 public airports in 1998, 69 of them general aviation airports. There were also 3 privately owned airports.

SOCIAL INSTITUTIONS
Justice. The death penalty is authorized. As of Nov. 1998, the state prison system had 16,649 inmates.

Religion. Southern Baptists in Mississippi (1997), 696,279 members; United Methodists (1997) 188,910; Roman Catholics (1998), 110,932 in Biloxi and Jackson dioceses.

Education. Attendance at school is compulsory as laid down in the Education Reform Act of 1982. The public elementary and secondary schools in 1997–98 had 504,792 pupils and 29,574 classroom teachers.

In 1997–98, teachers' average salary was $28,691. The expenditure per pupil in average daily attendance, 1997–98, was $4,491.

There are 20 universities and senior colleges, of which 8 are state-supported. In 1997–98, the University of Mississippi, Oxford had 1,279 instructors and 11,301 students; Mississippi State University, Starkville, 1,238 instructors and 15,645 students; Mississippi University for Women, Columbus, 198 instructors and 3,309 students; University of Southern Mississippi, Hattiesburg, 758 instructors and 14,593 students; Jackson State University, Jackson, 424 instructors and 6,333 students; Delta State University, Cleveland, 292 instructors and 4,085 students; Alcorn State University, Lorman, 216 instructors and 2,847 students; Mississippi Valley State University, Itta Bena, 160 instructors and 2,253 students. State support for the universities (1997–98) was $278,527,948.

Junior colleges had (1997–98) 63,596 full-time equivalent students and 3,049 full-time instructors. The state appropriation for junior colleges, 1997–98, was $152,469,084.

Health. In 1997 the state had 102 acute general hospitals (11,715 beds) listed by the State Department of Health; 18 hospitals with facilities for the care of the mentally ill had 658 licensed beds. In addition, 1 rehabilitation hospital had 100 beds.

Welfare. The Division of Medicaid paid (fiscal year 1998) $1,444,761,824 for medical services, including $224,419,498 for drugs, $311,090,613 for skilled nursing home care, and $349,593,778 for hospital services. There were 57,964 persons eligible for Aged Medicaid benefits as of 30 June 1998 and 125,114 persons eligible for Disabled Medicaid benefits. In June 1998, 20,897 families with 39,759 dependent children received $2,117,921 in the Temporary Assistance to Needy Families programme. The average monthly payment was $101·93 per family or $41·32 per recipient.

CULTURE
In 1998, 45,000 persons attended the only professional theatre in Mississippi, the New Stage Theatre in Jackson.

Tourism. Total receipts in 1998 amounted to $5·1bn.; an estimated 9m. overnight tourists visited the state in 1997.

Festivals. The Neshoba County Fair, Philadelphia (estimated attendance in 1998, 150,000); Choctaw Indian Fair, Philadelphia (approximate attendance in 1998, 22,000); USA International Ballet Competition, held in Jackson every 4 years (approximate attendance in 1998, 39,700); Mississippi Delta Blues and Heritage Festival, Greenville (approximate attendance in 1998, 10,000).

Libraries. There are 48 public library systems with 241 branches. As of 30 Sept. 1997, 1,209,691 persons were registered with public libraries.

Museums and Galleries. The main attractions are the Mississippi Agriculture and Forestry Museum, Jackson (132,256 visitors in 1998); Mississippi Museum of Art, Jackson (81,453 visitors in 1998); Mississippi Museum of Natural Science, Jackson (67,555 visitors in 1998); Delta Blues Museum, Clarksdale (15,222 visitors in 1998).

FURTHER READING
Statistical information: College of Business and Industry, Mississippi State Univ., Mississippi State 39762. Publishes *Mississippi Statistical Abstract.*
Secretary of State. *Mississippi Official and Statistical Register.* Biennial
Bettersworth, J. K., *Mississippi: A History.* Rev. ed. Austin, Tex., 1964

Mississippi Library Commission: PO Box 10700 Jackson, MS 39289–0700. *Executive Director:* John A. Pritchard

MISSOURI

KEY HISTORICAL EVENTS
Territory of several Indian groups, including the Missouri, the area was not settled by European immigrants until the 18th century. The French founded Ste Genevieve in 1735, partly as a lead-mining community. St Louis was founded as a fur-trading base in 1764. The area was nominally under Spanish rule from 1770 until 1800 when it passed back to France. In 1803 the USA bought it as part of the Louisiana Purchase.

St Louis was made the capital of the whole Louisiana Territory in 1805, and of a new Missouri Territory in 1812. In that year American immigration increased markedly. The Territory became a state in 1821, but there had been bitter disputes between slave-owning and anti-slavery factions, with the former succeeding in obtaining statehood without the prohibition of slavery required of all other new states north of latitude 36°30'; this was achieved by the Missouri Compromise of 1820. The Compromise was repealed in 1854 and declared unconstitutional in 1857. During the Civil War the state held to the Union side, although St Louis was placed under martial law.

With the development of steamboat traffic on the Missouri and Mississippi rivers, and the expansion of railways, the state became the transport hub of all western movement. Lead and other mining remained important, as did livestock farming. European settlers came from Germany, Britain and Ireland.

TERRITORY AND POPULATION
Missouri is bounded north by Iowa, east by the Mississippi River forming the boundary with Illinois and Kentucky, south by Arkansas, south-east by Tennessee,

south-west by Oklahoma, west by Kansas and Nebraska, with the Missouri River forming the boundary in the north-west. Land area, 68,898 sq. miles (178,446 sq. km).

Census population, 22 April 1990, 5,117,073 (68·7% urban), an increase since 1980 of 4·1%. Population estimate (1997), 5,402,000.

Population of 5 federal census years was:

	White	Black	Indian	Asiatic	Total	Per sq. mile
1930	3,403,876	223,840	578	1,073	3,629,367	52·4
1960	3,922,967	390,853	1,723	3,146	4,319,813	62·5
			All others			
1970	4,177,495	480,172	19,732		4,677,399	67·0
1980	4,345,521	514,276	56,889		4,916,686	71·3
1990	4,486,228	548,208	82,637		5,117,073	74·3

Of the total population in 1990, 2,464,315 were male. In 1990, 3,515,882 persons were urban and those 18 years of age or older numbered 3,939,284.

The principal cities at the 1990 census are:

Kansas City	435,146	Columbia	69,101
St Louis	396,685	St Charles	54,555
Springfield	140,494	Florissant	51,206
Independence	112,301	Joplin	40,961
St Joseph	71,852	University City	40,087

Metropolitan areas, 1990: St Louis, 2,444,099; Kansas City, 1,566,280.

SOCIAL STATISTICS
Births, 1995, were 73,028 (13·7 per 1,000 population); deaths, 54,000 (10·2). 1994 statistics: infant deaths, 597 (8·1 per 1,000 live births); marriages, 45,070 (8·5 per 1,000 population); divorces, 26,441 (5).

CLIMATE
Kansas City, Jan. 30°F (−1·1°C), July 79°F (26·1°C). Annual rainfall 38" (947 mm). St Louis, Jan. 32°F (0°C), July 79°F (26·1°C). Annual rainfall 40" (1,004 mm). Missouri belongs to the Central Plains climate zone (*see* UNITED STATES: Climate).

CONSTITUTION AND GOVERNMENT
A new constitution, the fourth, was adopted on 27 Feb. 1945; it has been revised 9 times with over 100 amendments. The General Assembly consists of a Senate of 34 members elected for 4 years (half for re-election every 2 years), and a House of Representatives of 163 members elected for 2 years. The Governor and Lieut.-Governor are elected for 4 years.

The state sends 9 representatives to Congress.

Jefferson City is the state capital. The state is divided into 114 counties and the city of St Louis.

RECENT ELECTIONS
In the 1996 presidential election Clinton polled 1,024,679 votes; Dole, 889,684; Perot, 217,101.

CURRENT ADMINISTRATION
Governor: Mel Carnahan (D.), 1997–2001 ($107,269).
  Lieut.-Governor: Roger Wilson (D.) ($64,823).
  Secretary of State: Rebecca McDowell Cook (D.) ($86,046).

ECONOMY
Budget. In 1996 total state revenue was $17,051m. Total expenditure was $12,841m. (education, $4,387m.; public welfare, $2,898m.; health and hospitals, $1,032m.; highways, $1,152m.; police protection, $130m.). Debt outstanding was $7,128m. in 1996.

Per capita income (1997, preliminary) was $24,001.

MISSOURI

ENERGY AND NATURAL RESOURCES

Water. The total area covered by water is approximately 811 sq. miles.

Minerals. The 3 leading mineral commodities are lead, portland cement and crushed stone. Value of domestic non-fuel mineral production (1997) $1,320m.

Agriculture. In 1996 there were 104,000 farms in Missouri producing crops and livestock on 30m. acres; the average farm had 288 acres and in 1994 was valued at $762 per acre. Production of principal crops, 1994: corn, 273·7m. bu.; soybeans, 173·3m. bu.; wheat, 49·5m. bu.; sorghum grain, 49·5m. bu.; oats, 1·77m. bu.; rice, 6·5m. cwt; cotton, 615,000 bales (of 480 lbs). Farm income 1996: $4,950m. (from crops, $2,500m.; from livestock and products, $2,450m.)

Forestry. Forest land area, 1997, 3·06m. acres.

INDUSTRY

The largest employer in 1996 was manufacturing, with 414,000 employees. Other large industries are food and kindred products, electronics and other electronic equipment, apparel and other textile products, industrial machinery and equipment, leather products, chemicals, paper, primary metal industries and metal products, printing and publishing, stone, clay, glass, rubber and plastic products, instruments, lumber and wood products. Wholesale and retail trade employed 561,001 as of March 1992.

Labour. The State Board of Mediation has jurisdiction in labour disputes involving only public utilities. The Prevailing Wage Law (1959) provides that no less than the local hourly rate of wages for work of a similar character shall be paid to any workmen engaged in public works. The Industrial Commission has authority to inspect records and to institute actions for penalties described in the Act. There is a state programme for industrial safety in hand, under the Federal Occupational and Health Act. In 1994 the annual average number of employed was 2,564,000, and 131,000 were unemployed; the unemployment rate was 4·9%.

COMMUNICATIONS

Roads. In 1995 there were 122,616 miles of roads (106,306 miles rural) and 4,255,000 registered motor vehicles.

Rail. The state has 8 Class I railways; approximate total mileage, 6,645. There are 9 Class II and Class III railways (switching, terminal or short-line), total mileage 435, in 1993. There is a light rail line in St Louis.

Civil Aviation. In 1994 there were 114 public airports and 359 private airports.

Shipping. Two major barge lines (1993) operated on about 1,050 miles of navigable waterways including the Missouri and Mississippi Rivers. Boat shipping seasons: Missouri River, April–end Nov.; Mississippi River, all seasons.

SOCIAL INSTITUTIONS

Justice. State prisons in 1994 had an average of 18,346 inmates including 886 females. The median age was 33·3 in 1994. The death penalty was reinstated in 1978. The last execution was in 1996. The Missouri Law Enforcement Assistance Council was created in 1969 for law reform. With reorganization of state government in 1974 the duties of the Council were delegated to the Department of Public Safety. The Dept. of Corrections was organized as a separate department of State by an Act of the Legislature in 1981.

Religion. Chief religious bodies (1990) are Catholic, with 802,434 members, Southern Baptists (789,183), United Methodists (255,111), Christian Churches (166,412), Lutheran (142,824), Presbyterian (45,341). Total membership, all denominations, about 2·3m. in 1990.

Education. School attendance is compulsory for children from 7 to 16 years for the full term. In the 1993–94 school year, public schools (kindergarten through grade 12) had 851,086 pupils. Total expenditure for public schools in 1993–94, $3,563,419,000. Salaries for teachers (kindergarten through grade 12), 1993–94, averaged $30,227. Institutions for higher education include the University of Missouri, founded in 1839 with campuses at Columbia, Rolla, St Louis and Kansas City, with 3,469 accredited teachers and 48,072 students in 1994–95. Washington University at St Louis, founded in 1857, is an independent co-ed university with 11,655 students in 1994–95. St Louis University (1818) is an independent Roman Catholic co-ed university with 10,365 students in 1994–95. Seventeen state colleges had 129,466 students in 1994–95. Private colleges had (1994–95) 34,548 students. Church-affiliated colleges (1994–95) had 41,420 students. Public junior colleges had 66,853 students. There are about 90 secondary and post-secondary institutions offering vocational courses, and about 294 private career schools. There were 265,186 students in higher education in autumn 1994.

Health. In 1995 there were 126 community hospitals with 21,900 beds.

Welfare. The number of actual recipients of medicaid for the last 5 months of 1994 averaged 346,873; eligible to receive medicaid, 559,331. The number of recipients of Aid to Families with Dependent Children was 259,048 with an average monthly payment per family of $264·79.

CULTURE

Broadcasting. There were 196 commercial radio stations and 29 TV stations in 1995.

Press. There were (1995) 46 daily and 260 weekly newspapers.

FURTHER READING
Statistical information: Business and Public Administration Research Center, Univ. of Missouri, Columbia 65211. Publishes *Statistical Abstract for Missouri.*
Missouri Area Labor Trends, Department of Labor and Industrial Relations, monthly
Missouri Farm Facts, Department of Agriculture, annual
Report of the Public Schools of Missouri. State Board of Education, annual

MONTANA

KEY HISTORICAL EVENTS
Originally the territory of many groups of Indian hunters including the Sioux, Cheyenne and Chippewa, Montana was not settled by American colonists until the 19th century. The area passed to the USA with the Louisiana Purchase of 1803, but the area west of the Rockies was disputed with Britain until 1846. Trappers and fur-traders were the first immigrants, and the fortified trading post at Fort Benton (1846) became the first permanent settlement. Colonization increased when gold was found in 1862. Montana was created a separate Territory (out of Idaho and Dakota Territories) in 1864. In 1866 large-scale grazing of sheep and cattle was allowed, and this provoked violent confrontation with the indigenous people whose hunting lands were invaded. Indian wars led to the defeat of federal forces at Little Bighorn in 1876 and at Big Hole Basin in 1877, but the Indians could not continue the fight and they had been moved to reservations by 1880. Montana became a state in 1889.

Helena, the capital, was founded as a mining town in the 1860s. In the early 20th century there were many European immigrants who settled as farmers or in the mines, especially in copper-mining at Butte.

TERRITORY AND POPULATION
Montana is bounded north by Canada, east by North and South Dakota, south by Wyoming and west by Idaho and the Bitterroot Range of the Rocky Mountains. Land area, 145,556 sq. miles (336,991 sq. km). US Bureau of Indian Affairs (1990) administered 5,574,835 acres, of which 2,663,385 were allotted to tribes. Census population, 1 April 1990, 799,065 (52·5% urban), an increase of 2% since 1980. Population estimate (1997), 879,000.

MONTANA

Population in 5 census years was:

	White	Black	Indian	Asiatic	Total	Per sq. mile
1910	360,580	1,834	10,745	2,870	376,053	2·6
1930	519,898	1,256	14,798	1,239	537,606	3·7
1950	572,038	1,232	16,606	—	591,024	4·1
1980	740,148	1,786	37,270	2,503	786,690	5·3
1990	741,111	2,381	47,679	4,259	799,065	5·4

Of the total population in 1990, 395,769 were male, 419,826 persons were urban. Persons 18 years of age or older numbered 576,961. Median age, 33·8 years. Households, 306,163.

The largest cities, 1990, are Billings, 81,151; Great Falls, 55,097. Others: Missoula, 42,918; Butte-Silver Bow, 33,336; Helena (capital), 24,569; Bozeman, 22,660; Kalispell, 11,917; Anaconda-Deer Lodge County, 10,278; Havre, 10,201.

SOCIAL STATISTICS
Births in 1995, 11,142 (12·8 per 1,000 population); deaths, 8,000 (8·6); infant mortality rate, 7·0 (per 1,000 live births). Marriages (1996, preliminary), 6,600; divorces, 4,300.

CLIMATE
Helena, Jan. 18°F (−7·8°C), July 69°F (20·6°C). Annual rainfall 13" (325 mm). Montana belongs to the Mountain States climate zone (*see* UNITED STATES: Climate).

CONSTITUTION AND GOVERNMENT
A new constitution came into force on 1 July 1973. The Senate consists of 50 senators, elected for 4 years, one half at each biennial election. The 100 members of the House of Representatives are elected for 2 years.

The state sends 1 representative to Congress.

The capital is Helena. The state is divided into 56 counties.

RECENT ELECTIONS
In the 1996 presidential election Dole polled 178,957 votes; Clinton, 167,169; Perot, 55,017.

CURRENT ADMINISTRATION
Governor: Marc Racicot (R.), 1997–2001 ($78,246).
Lieut.-Governor: Judy Martz (R.), ($53,407).
Secretary of State: Mike Cooney (D.), ($58,658).

ECONOMY
Budget. In 1996 total state revenue was $3,476m. Total expenditure was $3,136m. (education, $1,014m.; public welfare, $510m.; health and hospitals, $168m.; highways, $340m.; police protection, $30m.). Total debt outstanding in 1996 was $2,244m.

Per capita income (1997, preliminary) was $20,046.

ENERGY AND NATURAL RESOURCES
Water. The total area covered by water is approximately 1,490 sq. miles.

Minerals. 1997 domestic non-fuel mineral production value was $4,983m. Principal minerals include copper, gold, platinum-group metals, molybdenum and silver.

Agriculture. In 1996 there were 22,000 farms and ranches (50,564 in 1935) with an area of 60m. acres (47,511,868 acres in 1935). Large-scale farming predominates; in 1996 the average size per farm was 2,714 acres, and in 1998 the average value per acre was $320. In 1997 a total of 13,267,000 acres were harvested; including

5,930,000 acres of wheat. The farm population in 1991, was 67,546 (2·8% people per farm).

The chief crops are wheat, barley, oats, sugar-beet, hay, potatoes, corn, dry beans and cherries. Farm income, 1996: crops, $1,230m.; livestock and products, $797m. In 1998 there were 2·6m. cattle and calves; value, $716m.

Forestry. In 1997 there were 19,106,569 acres within 11 national forests.

INDUSTRY

In 1996 manufacturing had 24,000 production workers.

Labour. In 1996 the total number of non-agricultural workers was 359,000. Workers employed by major industry group, 1991; mining, 5,900 (average net weekly earnings, $592·18); construction, 7,700 ($499·56); manufacturing, 20,200 ($442·37); transport and public utilities, 20,000 ($468·43); trade industry, 76,500 ($388·90); finance/insurance/real estate, 13,270; services, 75,500 ($258·34); government, 71,400 (no income figures available). Average weekly earnings for all workers in private non-agricultural industries, $295·45.

COMMUNICATIONS

Roads. In 1995 there were a total of 69,537 miles of roads and 968,000 registered motor vehicles.

Rail. In Feb. 1992 there were 3,329 route miles of railway in the state.

Civil Aviation. There were 122 publicly owned airports in 1992.

Telecommunications. In 1992 there were 51 radio stations, 18 TV stations and 10 cable systems.

SOCIAL INSTITUTIONS

Justice. In 1996 there were 2,293 prison inmates. The death penalty is authorized, but there have been no executions since 1943.

Religion. The leading religious bodies are Roman Catholic, followed by Lutheran and Methodist.

Education. In 1995 (preliminary) public elementary and secondary schools had 165,000 pupils and (in 1994) 10,079 teachers. Expenditure on public school education by state and local governments in 1997 was $986m.

In 1996 there were 43,000 students enrolled at 26 higher education institutions. The Montana University system consists of the Montana State University, at Bozeman (autumn 1992 enrolment: 10,111 students); the University of Montana, at Missoula, founded in 1895 (10,788); the Montana College of Mineral Science and Technology, at Butte (1,881); Northern Montana College, at Havre (1,973); Eastern Montana College, at Billings (3,631); and Western Montana College, at Dillon (1,106).

Health. In 1995 there were 55 community hospitals with 4,200 beds.

Welfare. In 1994 there were 150,000 beneficiaries receiving $1,078 annual payments.

CULTURE

Broadcasting. In 1992 there were 51 radio stations, 18 TV stations and 10 cable systems.

Press. There were 11 daily newspapers and 7 Sunday papers in 1997.

FURTHER READING

Statistical information. Census and Economic Information Center, Montana Department of Commerce, 1425 9th Ave., Helena 59620.

Lang, W, L. and Myers, R. C., *Montana, Our Land and People.* Pruett, 1979

Malone, M. P. and Roeder, R. B., *Montana, A History of Two Centuries.* Univ. of Washington Press, 1976

Spence, C. C., *Montana: a History.* New York, 1978

NEBRASKA

KEY HISTORICAL EVENTS
The Nebraska region was first reached by Europeans from Mexico under the Spanish general Coronado in 1541. It was ceded by France to Spain in 1763, retroceded to France in 1801, and sold by Napoleon to the USA as part of the Louisiana Purchase in 1803. During the 1840s the Platte River valley became an established trail for thousands of pioneers' wagons heading for Oregon and California. The need to serve and protect the trail led to the creation of Nebraska as a Territory in 1854. In 1862 the Homestead Act opened the area for settlement, but colonization was not very rapid until the Union Pacific Railroad was completed in 1869. The largest city, Omaha, developed as the starting point of the Union Pacific and became one of the largest railway towns in the country.

Nebraska became a state in 1867, with approximately its present boundaries except that it later received small areas from the Dakotas. Many early settlers were from Europe, brought in by railway-company schemes, but from the late 1880s eastern Nebraska suffered catastrophic drought. Crop and stock farming recovered, but crop growing was only established in the west by means of irrigation.

TERRITORY AND POPULATION
Nebraska is bounded in the north by South Dakota, with the Missouri River forming the boundary in the north-east and the boundary with Iowa and Missouri to the east; south by Kansas, south-west by Colorado and west by Wyoming. Land area, 76,878 sq. miles (199,113 sq. km). Population estimate (1997), 1,657,000.

Population in 5 census years was:

	White	Black	Indian	Asiatic	Total	Per sq. mile
1910	1,180,293	7,689	3,502	730	1,192,214	15·5
1920	1,279,219	13,242	2,888	1,023	1,296,372	16·9
1960	1,374,764	29,262	5,545	1,195	1,411,330	18·3
			All others			
1980	1,490,381	48,390	31,054		1,569,825	20·5
1990	1,480,558	57,409	40,423		1,578,385	20·5

Of the total population in 1990, 796,439 were male, 66·1% were urban, 1,102,135 were 20 years of age or older. The largest cities in the state are: Omaha, with a census population, 1990, of 335,795; Lincoln, 191,972; Grand Island, (1986 estimate) 39,100; North Platte, 22,490; Fremont, 23,780; Hastings, 22,990; Bellevue, 32,200; Kearney, 22,770; Norfolk, 20,260.

The Bureau of Indian Affairs in 1990 administered 64,932 acres, of which 21,742 acres were allotted to tribal control.

SOCIAL STATISTICS
Births, 1995, were 23,221 (14·4 per 1,000 population); deaths, 15,216 (9·5); marriages, 12,351 (7·7); divorces, 6,262 (3·9); infant mortality rate, 7·4 (per 1,000 live births).

CLIMATE
Omaha, Jan. 22°F (−5·6°C), July 77°F (25°C). Annual rainfall 29" (721 mm). Nebraska belongs to the High Plains climate zone (*see* UNITED STATES: Climate).

CONSTITUTION AND GOVERNMENT
The present constitution was adopted in 1875; it has been amended 184 times. By an amendment of 1934 Nebraska has a single-chambered legislature (elected for 4 years) of 49 members elected on a non-party ballot and classed as senators—the only state in the USA to have one. It meets annually.

The state sends 3 representatives to Congress.

The capital is Lincoln. The state has 93 counties.

RECENT ELECTIONS
In the 1996 presidential election Dole polled 355,562 votes; Clinton, 231,863; Perot, 76,103.

CURRENT ADMINISTRATION

Governor: Mike Johanns (R.), 1999–2002 ($65,000).
  Lieut.-Governor: Dave Maurstad (R.) ($47,000).
  Secretary of State: Scott Moore (R.) ($52,000).

ECONOMY

Budget. In 1996 total state revenue was $4,999m. Total expenditure was $4,490m. (education, $1,514m.; public welfare, $976m.; health and hospitals, $503m.; highways, $574m.; police protection, $43m.). Total debt outstanding in 1996 was $1,402m.

  Per capita income (1997, preliminary) was $23,803.

ENERGY AND NATURAL RESOURCES

Oil and Gas. Petroleum output, 1995: 15,934·3m. gallons; gas, 683m. cu. ft.

Water. The total area covered by water is approximately 481 sq. miles.

Minerals. Output of non-fuel minerals, 1995 (in 1,000 short tons) and value (in $1,000): Clays, 243 (1,025); sand and gravel for construction, 17,637 (55·2); stone, 7,275 (39·6). Other minerals include limestone, potash, pumice, slate and shale.

Agriculture. Nebraska is one of the most important agricultural states. In 1996 it contained approximately 55,000 farms, with a total area of 47m. acres. The average farm area was 854 acres. In 1997 the total acreage harvested was 18,696,000 acres.

  In 1994, net farm income was $2,264·2m. Farm income from crops (1996), $4,177m., and from livestock and products, $5,277m. Principal crops were maize, sorghum for grain, soybeans and wheat. Livestock, 1990: cattle, 6m.; pigs, 4·2m.; sheep, 0·16m.; chickens, 2·1m.; turkeys, 2·1m. Value: 1994, $656m.; Dairy products, 1994: $14·3m.

Forestry. There were 346,485 acres of national forest in 1997.

INDUSTRY

In 1995 there were 2,071 manufacturing establishments with 112,951 employees, with an annual payroll of $3,121,427,000. Value added by manufacturing was $9,452·1m. The chief industry is meat-packing. Pork products were worth $878m. in 1991.

  Total labour force, 1996, 912,900. 207,500 workers were employed in trade, 220,300 in services, 151,500 in government, 113,800 in manufacturing, 53,100 in finance, insurance and real estate, 49,400 in transport, communication and utilities and 37,900 in construction and mining. 27,000 were unemployed; the average unemployment rate was 2·9%.

COMMUNICATIONS

Roads. In 1995 there were 95,933 miles of roads (90,826 miles rural). In 1996 there were 1,703,434 registered motor vehicles.

Rail. In 1996 there were 4,000 miles of railway.

Civil Aviation. Airports (1996) numbered 384 which were publicly owned.

SOCIAL INSTITUTIONS

Justice. A 'Civil Rights Act' revised in 1969 provides that all people are entitled to a full and equal enjoyment of public facilities. In 1996 there were 3,287 prisoners in state correctional institutions. The death penalty is authorized. The last execution was in 1996.

Religion. The Roman Catholics had 337,855 members in 1985; Protestant Churches, 737,361; Jews, 7,865 members. Total, all denominations, 1,083,081.

Education. School attendance is compulsory for children from 7 to 16 years of age. Public elementary and secondary schools, in 1995 (preliminary), had 265,000 enrolled pupils and (in 1993–94) 19,465 teachers. Total enrolment in institutions of higher education, autumn 1994, was 95,560 students in public and 19,872 in independent institutions.

Opened	Institution	Students 1997
	University of Nebraska (State)	46,565
1869	Lincoln	22,827
1908	Omaha	13,710
	Medical Center	2,618
	College of Technology, Agriculture, Curtis	277
1905	Kearney	7,133
1911	Chardon State College	2,939
1867	Peru State College	1,814
1910	Wayne State College	3,839
	Nebraska Community Colleges (Local government)	34,442
	Central Area	6,743
	Metropolitan Area	11,213
	Mid Plains Area	2,825
	Northeast Area	4,573
	Southeast Area	7,080
	Western Area	2,008
1966	Bellevue College (Private)	2,928
	Clarkson College (Private)	597
1923	College of St. Mary (Roman Catholic)	1,001
1894	Concordia Teachers' College, Seward (Lutheran)	1,214
1878	Creighton University, Omaha (Roman Catholic)	6,424
	Dana College (American Lutheran)	594
1872	Doane College, Crete (United Church of Christ)	1,809
	Grace College of the Bible (Private)	519
1882	Hastings College (Presbyterian)	1,059
1883	Midland Lutheran College, Fremont (Lutheran Church of America)	1,038
	Nebraska Christian College (Church of Christ)	152
	Nebraska Methodist College (Private)	223
1887	Nebraska Wesleyan University (Private)	1,719
	Platt Valley Bible College (Private)	75
1891	Union College, Lincoln (Seventh Day Adventist)	630
	York College[1] (Private)	497
	Nebraska Indian Community College	(1994) 320

[1]Two-year college.

Health. There were 106 community hospitals in 1997.

Welfare. In 1996 public welfare provided financial aid and/or services as follows (figures and total expenditure): aid to dependent children, 14,717 families/month and $55·2m. total expenditure; aged, blind and disabled, 6,059 persons/month and $6·0m., food stamps, 102,053 recipients/month and $77·9m.; medicaid, 120,012 recipients/month and $645·1m.

CULTURE

Tourism. In 1995 there were an estimated 16·1m. visits. Travellers and tourists spent over $2,000m.

FURTHER READING

Statistical information: Department of Economic Development, Box 94666, Lincoln 68509.
Agricultural Atlas of Nebraska. Univ. of Nebraska Press, 1977
Climatic Atlas of Nebraska. Univ. of Nebraska Press, 1977
Economic Atlas of Nebraska. Univ. of Nebraska Press, 1977
Nebraska. A Guide to the Cornhusker State. Univ. of Nebraska Press, 1979
Nebraska Blue-Book. Legislative Council. Lincoln. Biennial
Olson, J. C., *History of Nebraska.* 3rd ed. Univ. of Nebraska Press, 1997

State Library: State Law Library, State House, Lincoln.

NEVADA

KEY HISTORICAL EVENTS

The area was part of Spanish America until 1821, when it became part of the newly independent state of Mexico. Following a war between Mexico and the USA, Nevada was ceded to the USA as part of California in 1848. Settlement began in 1849, and the area was separated from California and joined with Utah Territory in 1850. In 1859 a rich deposit of silver was found in the Comstock Lode. Virginia City was founded as a mining town and immigration increased rapidly. Nevada Territory was formed in 1861. During the Civil War the Federal Government, allegedly in order to obtain the wealth of silver for the Union cause, agreed to admit Nevada to the Union in 1864 as the 36th state. Areas of Arizona and Utah Territories were added to it in 1866–67.

The mining boom lasted until 1882, by which time cattle ranching had become equally important in the valleys where the climate is less arid. Carson City, the capital, developed in association with the nearby mining industry. The largest cities, Las Vegas and Reno, grew most in the 20th century with the building of the Hoover dam, the introduction of legal gambling and of easily obtained divorce.

After 1950 much of the desert area was adopted by the Federal Government for weapons testing and other military purposes.

TERRITORY AND POPULATION

Nevada is bounded north by Oregon and Idaho, east by Utah, south-east by Arizona, with the Colorado River forming most of the boundary, south and west by California. Land area, 109,889 sq. miles (284,613 sq. km). The federal government (fiscal year 1995) owned 54,159,458 acres, or 77·1% of the land area.

Census population on 1 April 1990, 1,201,833 (88·3% urban), an increase of 401,325 since 1980. Population estimate (1999), 1,961,670.

Population in 5 census years was:

	White	Black	Indian	All others	Total	Per sq. mile
1910	74,276	513	5,240	1,846	81,875	0·7
1930	84,515	516	4,871	1,156	91,058	0·8
1970	449,850	27,579	7,329	3,980	488,738	4·4
1980	700,360	50,999	13,308	35,841	800,508	7·2
1990	1,012,695	78,771	19,637	90,730	1,201,833	10·9

Of the total population in 1990, 611,880 were male, 1,061,312 were urban and 364,109 were under 21 years of age. Nevada's population rise has made it the fastest-growing state in the USA every year since 1986.

The largest cities (with 1998 estimated population) are: Las Vegas, 441,230; Reno, 165,940; Henderson, 159,380; North Las Vegas, 106,660; Sparks, 61,560; Carson City (the capital), 51,860.

SOCIAL STATISTICS

Births, 1997, were 26,977; deaths, 12,985; infant mortality rate, in 1995, 5·7 per 1,000 live births. Marriages (1996, provisional), 141,200; divorces, 15,900.

CLIMATE

Las Vegas, Jan. 44°F (6·7°C), July 85°F (29·4°C). Annual rainfall 4·13" (105 mm). Reno, Jan. 32°F (0°C), July 69°F (20·6°C). Annual rainfall 7·53" (191 mm). Nevada belongs to the Mountain States climate zone (see UNITED STATES: Climate).

CONSTITUTION AND GOVERNMENT

The constitution adopted in 1864 is still in force, with 119 amendments by 1994. The Legislature meets biennially (and in special sessions) and consists of a Senate of 21 members elected for 2 years, half their number retiring every 2 years, and an Assembly of 42 members elected for 4 years. The Governor may be elected for 2 consecutive 4-year terms.

The state sends 2 representatives to Congress.

The state capital is Carson City. There are 16 counties, 18 incorporated cities and 49 unincorporated communities and 1 city-county (the Capitol District of Carson City).

RECENT ELECTIONS
In the 1996 presidential election Clinton polled 231,863 votes; Dole, 198,775; Perot, 43,855.

CURRENT ADMINISTRATION
Governor: Kenny C. Guinn (R.), 1999–2003 ($117,000).
  Lieut.-Governor: Lorraine Hunt (R.) ($50,000).
  Secretary of State: Dean Heller (R.) ($80,000).

ECONOMY
Budget. In 1996 total state revenue was $5,997m. Total expenditure was $4,831m. (education, $1,539m.; public welfare, $653m.; health and hospitals, $140m.; highways, $400m.; police protection, $39m.). Outstanding debt (1996) was $2,259m.
  Per capita personal income (1997, provisional) was $26,791.

ENERGY AND NATURAL RESOURCES
Electricity. There are (1997) 14 geothermal electric plants in 10 locations with a total plant capacity of approximately 236,000 kW. Gross sales in 1997 totalled 1,348m. kWh, which is enough to provide for the electricity needs of more than 46,000 households.

Oil and Gas. In 1997 over 980,200 bbls. of crude oil were produced from oil fields located in Nye and Eureka.

Water. The total area covered by water is approximately 761 sq. miles.

Minerals. Nevada led the nation in precious metal production in 1997, producing 69·5% of the domestic gold (9·9% of total produced worldwide) and 46·3% of the nation's silver. 1997 production: gold, 7·85m. troy oz.; silver, 24·7m. troy oz. Estimated geologic gold reserves (1997), 103m. troy oz. with an approximate value of $30·9bn.
  1995 value and production: sand and gravel, $126m., 88m. short tons (includes stone); barite, $23m., 467,000 short tons. In 1997 Nevada was the nation's leading producer of barite, lithium, carbonate and mined magnesite, and was second in the production of diatomite. Other minerals include iron ore, mercury, lime, gemstones, lead, molybdenum, fluorspar, perlite, pumice, clays, talc, salt, tungsten, gypsum and zinc. Total value of domestic non-fuel mineral production in 1997 was $3,030m.; there were 14,700 persons employed directly in the mineral industry with an average annual salary of $49,742.

Agriculture. In 1997 there were an estimated 2,500 farms with a total area of 8·8m. acres. Farms averaged 3,520 acres. Average value per acre in 1998 was $365. Area under irrigation (1992) was 556,000 acres compared with 542,976 acres in 1959.
  Total farm income, 1996, from crops, $133m.; and from livestock and products, $153m. In 1993 cattle, hay, dairy products, potatoes and sheep were the principal commodities in order of cash receipts. Crop production (in 1,000 tons) and value (in $1,000) 1995: hay, 1,505 ($142,275); potatoes, 139 ($23,302); alfalfa seed, 10·35m. lbs ($12,213); onions, 43·7 ($11,362); garlic, 12·7 ($4,447) and all grain crops, 1,170 ($4,361). 469,000 lbs of wool were produced (1996) with a total value of $462,000, and 426m. lbs of milk, total receipts $62,310.
  In 1998 there were 529,000 cattle and 80,000 sheep.

Forestry. The national forests covered an area of 6,275,313 acres in 1997.

INDUSTRY
The main industry is the service industry (43·2% of employment in 1996), especially tourism and legalized gambling. In 1996 there were 1,814 manufacturing establishments with 38,742 employees, and 4,708 construction firms with 75,499 employees.
  Gaming industry gross revenue for 1998 was $7,873·8m. In 1994 there were 361 non-restricted licensed casinos and 2,468 licences in force.

UNITED STATES OF AMERICA

Labour. In 1998 industries employed an annual average total of 956,900 workers. Main industries and employees, 1998: service industries, 809,800 (including gaming and tourism, 228,300); retail trade, 157,300; government, 116,100; finance, insurance and real estate, 43,900; transport, communications and public utilities, 48,500; mining, 13,600; manufacturing, 42,900. There were 31,400 unemployed in 1998.

COMMUNICATIONS

Roads. State maintained road mileage totalled 5,164 in 1996; motor vehicle registrations in 1997 numbered 1,145,656.

Rail. In 1995 there were 1,272 miles of main-line railway. Nevada is served by the Southern Pacific, Union Pacific and Burlington Northern BPH Nevada Railroad railways, and Amtrak passenger service for Las Vegas, Elko, Reno, Caliente, Lovelock, Stateline, Winnemucca and Sparks.

Civil Aviation. There were 98 civil airports and 24 heliports in Jan. 1996. During 1997 McCarran International Airport (Las Vegas) handled 30,305,822 passengers and Reno-Tahoe International Airport handled 6,279,133 passengers.

Telecommunications. In Sept. 1998 there were 62 telephone exchanges, and 1,131,810 telephones in service (not including cellular).

SOCIAL INSTITUTIONS

Justice. Capital punishment was reintroduced in 1978, and executions began in 1979. In 1998 there were 9,530 prisoners in state and federal prisons.

Religion. Roman Catholics are the most numerous religious group, followed by members of the Church of Jesus Christ of Latter-day Saints (Mormons) and various Protestant churches.

Education. School attendance is compulsory for children from 7 to 17 years of age. Numbers of pupils in public schools, 1998–99: pre-kindergarten, 2,140; kindergarten, 23,986; elementary, 155,486; secondary grades 7–9, 70,167; secondary grades 10–12, 58,586; special education, 698. Numbers of teachers in public schools, 1994–95: elementary, 6,642; secondary, 4,605; special education, 17,434; occupational, 239. Numbers of pupils in private schools, 1995–96: Kindergartens, 1,875; elementary, 5,922; secondary grades 7–9, 2,313; secondary grades 10–12, 1,376; multi-grades, 496.

The University of Nevada System comprises campuses at Las Vegas and Reno and 3 community colleges. In 1997–98 it had 71,925 students and (in 1994–95) 1,710 academic staff.

Health. In 1996 the state had 20 hospitals and medical centres (2,600 beds); and 36 nursing units (3,676 beds). There were (1996) 2,602 physicians, 618 dentists and 9,900 registered nurses.

Welfare. In 1996 benefits were paid to 241,000 persons: 161,000 retired (aged 62 and over) workers (average payment $750 per month); 22,600 widows and widowers ($716); 25,400 disabled workers ($741).

FURTHER READING

Statistical information: Budget and Planning Division, Department of Administration, Capitol Complex, Carson City, Nevada 89710. Publishes *Nevada Statistical Abstract* (Biennial).
Bushnell, E. and Driggs, D. W., *The Nevada Constitution: Origin and Growth.* 5th ed. Univ. of Nevada Press, 1980
Hulse, J. W., *The Nevada Adventure: a History.* 6th ed. Univ. of Nevada Press, 1990
Laxalt, R., *Nevada: a History.* New York, 1977
Mack, E. M. and Sawyer, B. W., *Here is Nevada: a History of the State.* Sparks, 1965
Paher, S. W., *Nevada: an Annotated Bibliography.* Carson City, 1980

State Library: Nevada State Library, Carson City.

NEW HAMPSHIRE

KEY HISTORICAL EVENTS
The area was part of a grant by the English crown made to John Mason and fellow-colonists, and was first settled in 1623. In 1629 an area between the Merrimack and Piscataqua rivers was called New Hampshire. More settlements followed, and in 1641 they were taken under the jurisdiction of the governor of Massachusetts. New Hampshire became a separate colony in 1679.

After the War of Independence New Hampshire became one of the 13 original states of the Union, drawing up its constitution in 1784 and revising it on accession to the Union in 1792.

The settlers were Protestants from Britain and Northern Ireland. They developed manufacturing industries, especially shoe-making, textiles and clothing, to which large numbers of French Canadians were attracted after the Civil War.

Portsmouth, originally a fishing settlement, was the colonial capital and is the only seaport. In 1808 the state capital was moved to Concord (having had no permanent home since 1775); Concord produced the Concord Coach which was widely used on the stagecoach routes of the West until at least 1900.

TERRITORY AND POPULATION
New Hampshire is bounded in the north by Canada, east by Maine and the Atlantic, south by Massachusetts and west by Vermont. Land area, 8,993 sq. miles (23,292 sq. km). Census population, 1 April 1990, 1,109,252 (51% urban), an increase of 20·49% since 1980. Estimated population (1997), 1,173,000.

Population at 5 federal censuses was:

	White	Black	Indian	Asiatic	Total	Per sq. mile
1910	429,906	564	34	68	430,572	47·7
1960	604,334	1,903	135	549	606,921	65·2
			All others			
1970	733,106	2,505	2,070		737,681	81·7
1980	910,099	3,990	6,521		920,610	101·9
1990	1,087,433	7,198	14,621		1,109,252	123·7

The largest city in the state is Manchester, with an estimated 1996 population of 102,675. The capital is Concord, with 37,850. Other cities are: Nashua, 82,785; Rochester, 28,726; Dover, 26,200; Keene, 22,872; Portsmouth, 22,830; Laconia, 17,053; Claremont, 13,980; Lebanon, 12,662; Berlin, 11,923; Somersworth, 11,623; Franklin, 8,394. There are also 221 towns.

SOCIAL STATISTICS
Births, 1995, were 14,665 (12·8 per 1,000 population); deaths, 9,000 (8·0); infant mortality rate, 5·5 (per 1,000 live births); marriages, 9,863; divorces, 4,949.

CLIMATE
New Hampshire is in the New England climate zone (*see* UNITED STATES: Climate). Manchester, Jan. 22°F (–5·6°C), July 70°F (21·1°C). Annual rainfall 40" (1,003 mm).

CONSTITUTION AND GOVERNMENT
While the present constitution dates from 1784, it was extensively revised in 1792 when the state joined the Union. Since 1775 there have been 16 state conventions with 49 amendments adopted to amend the constitution.

The Legislature (called the General Court) consists of a Senate of 24 members, elected for 2 years, and a House of Representatives, of 400 members, elected for 2 years. It meets annually. The Governor and 5 administrative officers called 'Councillors' are also elected for 2 years.

The state sends 2 representatives to Congress.

The capital is Concord. The state is divided into 10 counties.

RECENT ELECTIONS
In the 1996 presidential election Clinton polled 245,260 votes; Dole, 196,740; Perot, 48,140.

UNITED STATES OF AMERICA

CURRENT ADMINISTRATION
Governor: Jeanne Shaheen (D.), 1999–2001 ($86,235).
Secretary of State: William M. Gardner (D.) ($68,768).

ECONOMY
Budget. New Hampshire has no general sales tax or state income tax but does have local property taxes. Other government revenues come from rooms and meals tax, business profits tax, motor vehicle licences, fuel taxes, fishing and hunting licences, state-controlled sales of alcoholic beverages, cigarette and tobacco taxes.

In 1996 total state revenue was $3,561m. Total expenditure was $3,240m. (education, $579m.; public welfare, $988m.; health and hospitals, $146m.; highways, $224m.; police protection, $27m.). Total debt outstanding (1996), $5,883m.

Per capita income (1997, preliminary) was $28,047.

ENERGY AND NATURAL RESOURCES
Water. The total area covered by water is approximately 314 sq. miles.

Minerals. Minerals are little worked; they consist mainly of sand and gravel, stone, and clay for building and highway construction. Value of domestic non-fuel mineral production, 1996, $60m.

Agriculture. In 1996 there were some 2,000 farms covering nearly 500,000 acres; average farm was 179 acres. Average value per acre in 1995, $2,486. Farm income 1996: from crops, $89m.; from livestock and products, $72m.

The chief field crops are hay and vegetables; the chief fruit crop is apples. Livestock, 1992: Cattle, 48,419; pigs, 4,458; sheep, 8,052; poultry, 212,748.

Forestry. In 1997 there were 798,397 acres of national forest.

Fisheries. The 1990 catch was worth $10m.

INDUSTRY
Principal manufactures: Electrical and electronic goods, machinery, and metal products.

Labour. In 1996, 560,000 persons were in employment (excluding agriculture), of whom 162,000 worked in services, 145,000 in retail and 105,000 in manufacturing.

COMMUNICATIONS
Roads. In 1995 there were 15,086 miles of roads (12,173 miles rural). There were 1,122,000 registered motor vehicles.

Rail. In 1993 the length of operating railway in the state was 540 miles.

Civil Aviation. In 1997 there were 26 public and 21 private airports.

Telecommunications. Across the state there were 49 radio and 6 TV stations in 1997.

SOCIAL INSTITUTIONS
Justice. The Department of Corrections held 2,180 persons on 1 July 1997. The death penalty is authorized, but there have been no executions since 1939.

Religion. The Roman Catholic Church is the largest single body. The largest Protestant churches are Congregational, Episcopal, Methodist and United Baptist Convention of N.H.

Education. School attendance is compulsory for children from 6 to 14 years of age during the whole school term, or to 16 if their district provides a high school. Employed illiterate minors between 16 and 21 years of age must attend evening or special classes, if provided by the district.

In 1995 the public elementary and secondary schools had 209,150 pupils and 12,300 teachers. Public school salaries, 1995, averaged $35,792. An average of $6,449 was spent on education per pupil.

Of the 4-year colleges, the University of New Hampshire (founded in 1866) had 12,000 students in 1992–93; New Hampshire College (1932), 5,300; Keene State

College (1909), 4,900; Plymouth State College (1871), 4,228; Dartmouth College (1769), 5,180. Total enrolment, 1995–96, in the 30 institutions of higher education, was 64,406.

Health. In 1995 the state had 29 community hospitals with 3,400 beds.

Welfare. The Division of Human Services handles public assistance for (1) aged citizens 65 years or over, (2) needy aged aliens, (3) needy blind persons, (4) needy citizens between 18 and 64 years inclusive, who are permanently and totally disabled, (5) needy children under 18 years, (6) Medicaid and the medically needy not eligible for a monthly grant.

In 1995 the annual average number of welfare cases were: 65 years or over, 8,446; disabled, 8,305; families with dependent children, 12,798.

CULTURE

Broadcasting. Across the state there were 49 radio and 6 TV stations in 1997.

Press. In 1997 there were 12 daily and 8 Sunday newspapers in circulation.

FURTHER READING

Delorme, D. (ed.) *New Hampshire Atlas and Gazetteer.* Freeport, 1983
Morison, E. E. and E. F., *New Hampshire.* New York, 1976
Squires, J. D., *The Granite State of the United States: A History of New Hampshire from 1623 to the present.* 4 vols. New York, 1956

NEW JERSEY

KEY HISTORICAL EVENTS

Originally the territory of Delaware Indians, the area was first settled by immigrant colonists in the early 17th century, when Dutch and Swedish traders established fortified posts on the Hudson and Delaware Rivers. The Dutch took control but lost it to the English in 1664. In 1676 the English divided the area in two; the eastern portion was assigned to Sir George Carteret and the western granted to Quaker settlers. This division lasted until 1702 when New Jersey was united as a colony of the Crown and placed under the jurisdiction of the governor of New York. It became a separate colony in 1738.

During the War of Independence crucial battles were fought at Trenton, Princeton and Monmouth. New Jersey became the 3rd state of the Union in 1787. Trenton, the state capital since 1790, began as a Quaker settlement and became an iron-working town. Industrial development grew rapidly, there and elsewhere in the state, after the opening of canals and railways in the 1830s. Princeton, also a Quaker settlement, became an important post on the New York road; the college of New Jersey (Princeton University) was transferred there from Newark in 1756.

The need for supplies in the Civil War stimulated industry and New Jersey became a manufacturing state. The growth beyond its borders of New York and Philadelphia, however, produced a pattern of commuting to employment in both centres. By 1980 about 60% of the state's population lived within 30 miles of New York.

TERRITORY AND POPULATION

New Jersey is bounded north by New York, east by the Atlantic with Long Island and New York City to the north-east, south by Delaware Bay and west by Pennsylvania. Land area, 7,419 sq. miles (19,210 sq. km). Census population, 1 April 1990, 7,730,188 (89·4% urban), an increase of 4·96% since 1980. Population density, 1990, 1,042·2 per sq. mile. Population estimate (1997), 8,053,000.

Population at 5 federal censuses was:

	White	Black	Indian	Asiatic	Others	Total
1910	2,445,894	89,760	168	1,345	—	2,537,167
1930	3,829,663	208,828	213	2,630	—	4,041,334
1960	5,539,003	514,875	1,699	8,778	2,427	6,066,782
1980	6,127,467	925,066	8,394	103,848	200,048	7,364,823
1990	6,130,465	1,036,825	14,970	272,521	275,407	7,730,188

Of the population in 1990, 3,735,685 were male, 6,910,220 persons were urban, 5,718,136 were 20 years of age or older and 739,861 were Hispanic.

Census population of the larger cities and towns in 1990 was:

Newark	275,221	East Orange	73,552	Vineland	54,780
Jersey City	228,537	Clifton	71,742	Gloucester	53,797
Paterson	140,891	Cherry Hill	69,348	Union Township	50,024
Elizabeth	110,002	Middletown	68,183	Parsippany-	
Woodbridge	93,086	Brick	66,473	Troy Hills	48,478
Edison	88,680	Bayonne	61,444	North Bergen	48,414
Trenton (capital)	88,675	Irvington	61,018	Piscataway	47,089
Camden	87,492	Passaic	58,041	Wayne	47,025
Hamilton	86,553	Union City	58,012	Plainfield	46,567
Dover	76,371	Old Bridge	56,475	Bloomfield	45,061

Largest metropolitan areas (1990) were: Newark, 1,824,321; Bergen-Passaic, 1,278,440; Jersey City, 553,099; Trenton, 325,824.

SOCIAL STATISTICS
1995 (rates per 1,000 population): births, 114,828 (14·5); deaths, 74,000 (9·3); infant deaths in 1993, 989 (8·2 per 1,000 live births; 6·6 in 1995). Marriages (1996, provisional), 51,700; divorces, 25,000.

CLIMATE
Jersey City, Jan. 31°F (–0·6°C), July 75°F (23·9°C). Annual rainfall 41" (1,025 mm). Trenton, Jan. 32°F (0°C), July 76°F (24·4°C). Annual rainfall 40" (1,003 mm). New Jersey belongs to the Atlantic Coast climate zone (*see* UNITED STATES: Climate).

CONSTITUTION AND GOVERNMENT
The present constitution, ratified by the registered voters on 4 Nov. 1947, has been amended 45 times. There is a 40-member Senate and an 80-member General Assembly. Assembly members serve 2 years, senators 4 years, except those elected at the election following each census, who serve for 2 years. Sessions are held throughout the year.

The state sends 13 representatives to Congress.

The capital is Trenton. The state is divided into 21 counties, which are subdivided into 567 municipalities—cities, towns, boroughs, villages and townships.

RECENT ELECTIONS
In the 1996 presidential election Clinton polled 1,588,811 votes; Dole, 1,067,274; Perot, 254,941.

CURRENT ADMINISTRATION
Governor: Christine Todd Whitman (R.), 1998–2002 ($85,000).
Secretary of State: Lonna R. Hooks ($100,225).

ECONOMY
Budget. In 1996 total state revenue was $35,857m. Total expenditure was $32,315m. (education, $7,750m.; public welfare, $6,744m.; health and hospitals, $1,588m.; highways, $1,812m.; police protection, $259m.). Debt outstanding in 1996 was $25,602m.

Per capita income (1997, preliminary) was $32,654.

ENERGY AND NATURAL RESOURCES
Water. The total area covered by water is approximately 796 sq. miles.

Minerals. In 1992 the chief minerals were stone (17·1m. short tons, value $126m.) and sand and gravel (17·9m. short tons, value $105m.); others are clays, peat and gemstones. New Jersey is a leading producer of greensand marl, magnesium compounds and peat. Total value of domestic non-fuel mineral products, 1997, was $296m.

Agriculture. Livestock raising, market-gardening, fruit-growing, horticulture and forestry are pursued. In 1997 there were some 8,000 farms with a total acreage of

1m., averaging 88 acres. Average value per acre in 1998 was $8,370—making it the most valuable land per acre in the USA.

Farm income 1996: crops, $605m.; livestock and products, $196m.

Leading crops are tomatoes (value, $18·9m., 1993), corn for grain ($15·1m.), peaches ($25·3m.), blueberries ($26·4m.), soybeans ($25·7m.), sweet corn ($15·9m.), peppers ($21·8m.), cranberries ($18·8m.). Livestock, 1993: 25,000 milch cows, 75,000 all cattle, 13,000 sheep and lambs and (Dec. 1992) 28,000 swine.

INDUSTRY

The unemployment rate in Oct. 1998 was 4·5%, falling below the US average for the first time since Dec. 1991. In Oct. 1998 there were 3,816,600 employees on non-agricultural payrolls; 1,800 in mining, 138,100 in construction, 474,100 in manufacturing, 264,300 in transportation and public utilities, 894,100 in wholesale and retail trade, 1,228,000 in services, 570,700 in government.

COMMUNICATIONS

Roads. In 1997 there were 35,921 miles of public roads, and 5,278,282 motor vehicle registrations.

Rail. NJ Transit provides a rail service to 93,950 weekday passengers on 12 rail lines, with 848·3 track miles. The state is also served by 13 shortline freight railroads, 2 Class 1 rail carriers and a statewide terminal railroad.

There is a metro link to New York (22 km), a light rail line (7 km), and extensive commuter railways around Newark.

Civil Aviation. There is an international airport at Newark.

In total there are an estimated 72,000 jobs in New Jersey that are linked to the general aviation airport system. The annual payroll associated with these jobs is estimated at $2·4bn. The annual value of goods and services purchased by airport tenants, visitors and general aviation-dependent businesses exceeds $4·6bn.

SOCIAL INSTITUTIONS

Justice. State prisons in Aug. 1996 had 27,490 inmates. The death penalty is authorized.

Religion. In 1994 the Roman Catholic population of New Jersey was 3·25m., and there were 436,000 Jews. Among Protestant sects were United Methodists, 132,000; United Presbyterians (1993), 106,700; Episcopalians, 64,200; Lutherans, 82,200; American Baptists (1992), 66,000.

Education. Elementary instruction is compulsory for all from 6 to 16 years of age and free to all from 5 to 20 years of age. In 1993–94 public elementary schools had 830,628 and secondary schools had 320,982 enrolled pupils; public colleges in autumn 1993 had 278,306 students, including 139,915 in community colleges; independent colleges had 63,051. Average salary of 83,289 elementary and secondary classroom teachers in public schools in 1993–94 was $45,880. In 1997 school expenditure totalled $12,240m.; approximately $10,284 per pupil.

In autumn 1993: Rutgers, the State University (founded as Queen's College in 1766), had 48,062 students; Princeton (founded in 1746) had 6,592; Fairleigh Dickinson (1941), had 10,751; Montclair State College, 13,214; Rowan College (formerly Glassboro State College), 9,368; Trenton State College, 7,063.

Health. In 1995 there were 92 community hospitals with 29,900 beds.

Welfare. In 1996, 1,314,000 beneficiaries received a total annual payment of $11,614m. Retired workers received an average monthly payment of $820; disabled workers and dependants, $744; widows and widowers, $780.

FURTHER READING

Statistical information: New Jersey State Data Center, Department of Labor, CN 388, Trenton 08625. Publishes *New Jersey Statistical Factbook.*
Legislative District Data Book. Bureau of Government Research. Annual
Manual of the Legislature of New Jersey. Trenton. Annual
Boyd, J. P. (ed.) *Fundamentals and Constitutions of New Jersey, 1664–1954.* Princeton, 1964
Cunningham, J. T., *New Jersey: America's Main Road.* Rev. ed. New York, 1976
Kull, I. Stoddard (ed.) *New Jersey: a History.* New York, 1930

State Library: 185 W. State Street, Trenton, CN 520. N.J. 08625.

NEW MEXICO

KEY HISTORICAL EVENTS

The first European settlement was established in 1598. Until 1771 New Mexico was the Spanish kings' 'Kingdom of New Mexico'. In 1771 it was annexed to the northern province of New Spain. When New Spain won its independence in 1821, it took the name of Republic of Mexico and established New Mexico as its northernmost department. Ceded to the USA in 1848 after war between the USA and Mexico, the area was organized as a Territory in 1850, by which time its population was Spanish and Indian. There was frequent conflict, especially between new settlers and raiding parties of Navajo and Apaches. The Indian war lasted from 1861 until 1866, and from 1864–68 about 8,000 Navajo were imprisoned at Bosque Redondo.

The boundaries were altered several times when land was taken into Texas, Utah, Colorado and lastly (1863) Arizona. New Mexico became a state in 1912.

Settlement proceeded by means of irrigated crop-growing and Mexican-style ranching. During the Second World War the desert areas were brought into use as testing zones for atomic weapons. Mineral extraction also developed, especially after the discovery of uranium and petroleum.

TERRITORY AND POPULATION

New Mexico is bounded north by Colorado, north-east by Oklahoma, east by Texas, south by Texas and Mexico and west by Arizona. Land area, 121,365 sq. miles (314,334 sq. km). Public lands, administered by federal agencies (1975) amounted to 26·7m. acres or 34% of the total area. The Bureau of Indian Affairs held 7·3m. acres; the State of New Mexico held 9·4m. acres; 34·4m. acres were privately owned.

Census population, 1 April 1990, 1,515,069 (73% urban), an increase of 211,767 or 16·2% since 1980. Population estimate (1997), 1,736,931.

The population in 5 census years was:

	White	Black	Indian	Asian and Pacific Island	Other	Total	Per sq. mile
1910	304,594	1,628	20,573	506	...	327,301	2·7
1940	492,312	4,672	34,510	324	...	531,818	4·4
1960	875,763	17,063	56,255	1,942	...	951,023	7·8
1980	977,587	24,020	106,119	6,825	188,343	1,302,894	10·7
1990	1,146,028	30,210	134,355	14,124	190,352	1,515,069	12·5

Of the 1990 total, 745,253 were male, 1,068,328 were 18 years of age or older, 163,062 were 65 years of age or older.

Before 1930 New Mexico was largely a Spanish-speaking state, but since 1945 an influx of population from other states has reduced the percentage of persons of Spanish origin or descent to 40·0% (1997 estimate).

The largest cities are Albuquerque, with estimated population, 1996, 419,681; Las Cruces, 74,779; Santa Fé, 66,522; Roswell, 47,559; Rio Rancho, 46,565.

SOCIAL STATISTICS

Statistics 1996: births, 27,216 (15·9 per 1,000 population); deaths, 12,456 (7·3); infant deaths, 169 (6·2 per 1,000 live births); marriages, 16,026 (9·4 per 1,000 population); divorces, 10,945 (6·4).

CLIMATE

Santa Fé, Jan. 26·4°F (−3·1°C), July 68·4°F (20°C). Annual rainfall 15·2" (386 mm). New Mexico belongs to the Mountain States climate zone (*see* UNITED STATES: Climate).

CONSTITUTION AND GOVERNMENT

The constitution of 1912 is still in force with 137 amendments. The state Legislature, which meets annually, consists of 42 members of the Senate, elected for 4 years, and 70 members of the House of Representatives, elected for 2 years.

The state sends 3 representatives to Congress.

The state capital is Santa Fé. The state is divided into 33 counties.

RECENT ELECTIONS

In the 1996 presidential election Clinton polled 252,215 votes; Dole, 210,791; Perot, 30,978.

CURRENT ADMINISTRATION

Governor: Gary Johnson (R.), 1999–2002 ($90,000).
  Lieut.-Governor: Walter Bradley (R.) ($65,000).
  Secretary of State: Rebecca Vigil-Giron (D.) ($65,000).

ECONOMY

Budget. In 1996 total state revenue was $8,129m. Total expenditure was $6,740m. (education, $2,457m.; public welfare, $1,118m.; health and hospitals, $577m.; highways, $651m.; police protection, $56m.). Debt outstanding in 1996 was $2,147m.

  Per capita income (1997, preliminary) was $19,587.

ENERGY AND NATURAL RESOURCES

Oil and Gas. 1995 production: petroleum, 64,508,000 bbls. (of 42 gallons); natural gas, 1,426,000m. cu. ft. An average of 10,000 persons were employed in oil and gas extraction in 1995.

Water. The total area covered by water is approximately 234 sq. miles.

Minerals. New Mexico is one of the largest energy producing states in the USA. Production in 1995: potash, 2,568,000 short tons; copper, 276,000 short tons; coal, 26,813,000 short tons. The value of the total mineral output (1995) was $4,897m. An average of 15,900 persons were employed in the mining industry in 1995.

  The mining industry was expected to lose 700–800 jobs in 1999.

Agriculture. New Mexico produces grains, vegetables, fruit, livestock, cotton and nuts. Dry farming and irrigation have proved profitable in periods of high prices. In 1992 there were 14,279 farms covering 46·8m. acres; average farm size, 3,281 acres. In 1995 average value of farmland and buildings per acre was $225.

  Cash receipts, 1996, from crops, $512m., and from livestock products, $1,197m. Principal crops are wheat (4·0m. bu. from 0·11m. acres), hay (1·6m. tons from 0·35m. acres) and sorghum/grains (7·4m. bu. from 0·225m. acres). Farm animals in 1997 included 197,000 milch cows, 1·5m. all cattle, 235,000 sheep and 5,000 swine.

Forestry. There were 10m. acres of national forest in 1997.

INDUSTRY

Average monthly non-agricultural employment during 1997 was 707,200: 46,400 were employed in manufacturing, 177,200 in government. Value of manufactures shipments, 1992, $9,491·5m.; leading industries, food and kindred products, electrical and electronic equipment, petroleum and coal products.

Labour. Civilian workforce in 1997 was 820,469; 51,257 persons (6·2%) were unemployed.

COMMUNICATIONS

Roads. In 1995 there were 61,289 miles of roads and (1996) 1,683,243 registered motor vehicles.

Rail. In 1994 there were 1,868 miles of railway in operation.

Civil Aviation. There were 64 public-use airports in Nov. 1995.

SOCIAL INSTITUTIONS

Justice. The number of state prison inmates in Oct. 1998 was 4,661, and there was an average of 602 in state-operated juvenile centres in the fiscal year 1996. The death penalty is authorized.

  Since 1949 the denial of employment by reason of race, colour, religion, national origin or ancestry has been forbidden. A law of 1955 prohibits discrimination in public places because of race or colour. An 'equal rights' amendment was added to the constitution in 1972.

Religion. There were (1990) approximately 883,000 Christian Church adherents (421,868 Roman Catholics in 1996).

Education. Elementary education is free, and compulsory between 6 and 17 years or high-school graduation age. In 1995–96 the 89 school districts had an enrolment of 348,543 students in elementary and secondary schools of which private, parochial and state supported schools had 31,112. In 1994–95 there were 18,500 FTE teachers receiving an average salary of $29,074. Total revenue for public elementary and secondary schools was $1,702m. (1994–95).

In autumn 1997 there were 47,017 students attending universities and 52,736 students attending community colleges.

The state-supported 4-year institutes of higher education are (autumn 1996[1]):

	Students
University of New Mexico, Albuquerque	30,534
New Mexico State University, Las Cruces	22,313
Eastern New Mexico University, Portales	7,008
New Mexico Highlands University, Las Vegas	2,787
Western New Mexico University, Silver City	2,533
New Mexico Institute of Mining and Technology, Socorro	1,467

[1]Figures include branches outside main campus in cities listed.

Health. In 1995 there were 36 community hospitals with 3,700 beds. The state had 2,009 active non-federal physicians.

Welfare. In fiscal year 1997 a monthly average of 30,280 cases received $140·4m. from aid to families with dependent children funds and 79,610 cases received $181·6m. in food stamp funds. In 1995 a total of 44,755 persons in the state were receiving federally administered payment totalling $165·6m. Among these 9,844 were receiving aid for the aged ($21·7m.), 644 were receiving aid to the blind ($2·3m.) and 34,267 were receiving aid for the disabled ($141·5m.).

CULTURE

Tourism. In 1995 there were 47,200 travel-generated jobs; total travel expenditure (domestic and international), $3,045·7m.

Festivals. In 1996, 1·7m. persons attended the New Mexico Arts and Crafts Fair, Albuquerque; and 1·5m. attended the annual Albuquerque International Balloon Fiesta.

National Theatre and Opera. There is an indoor/outdoor theatre at the Santa Fé Opera in the capital.

Museums and Galleries. There were more than 150 art galleries in 1998.

FURTHER READING

Bureau of Business and Economic Research, Univ. of New Mexico—*Census in New Mexico* (Continuing series. Vols. 1–5, 1992–).—*Economic Census: New Mexico* (Continuing series. Vols. 1–3). *–New Mexico Business.* Monthly; annual review in Jan.–Feb. issue.

Beck, W., *New Mexico: a History of Four Centuries.* Univ. of Oklahoma Press, 1979

Etulain. R., *Contemporary New Mexico, 1940–1990.* Univ. of New Mexico Press, 1994

Garcia, C., Haine, P. and Rhodes, H., *State and Local Government in New Mexico.* Albuquerque, 1979

Jenkins, M. and Schroeder, A., *A Brief History of New Mexico.* Univ. of New Mexico Press, 1974

Muench, D. and Hillerman, T., *New Mexico.* Portland (OR), 1974

Williams, J. L., *New Mexico in Maps.* Univ. of New Mexico Press, 1986

NEW YORK STATE

KEY HISTORICAL EVENTS

The first European immigrants came in the 17th century, when there were two powerful Indian groups in rivalry: the Iroquois confederacy (Mohawk, Oneida, Onondaga, Cayuga and Seneca) and the Algonquian-speaking Mohegan and

Munsee. The Dutch made settlements at Fort Orange (now Albany) in 1624 and at New Amsterdam in 1625, trading with the Indians for furs. In the 1660s there was conflict between the Dutch and the British in the Caribbean; as part of the concluding treaty the British in 1664 received Dutch possessions in the Americas, including New Amsterdam, which they renamed New York.

In 1763 the Treaty of Paris ended war between the British and the French in North America (in which the Iroquois had allied themselves with the British). Settlers of British descent in New England then felt confident enough to expand westward into the area. The climate of northern New York being severe, most settled in the Hudson river valley. After the War of Independence New York became the 11th state of the Union (1778), having first declared itself independent of Britain in 1777.

The economy depended on manufacturing, shipping and other means of distributing goods, and trade. During the 19th century New York became the most important city in the USA. Its manufacturing industries, especially clothing, attracted thousands of European immigrants. Industrial development spread along the Hudson-Mohawk valley, which was made the route of the Erie Canal (1825) linking New York with Buffalo on Lake Erie and thus with the developing farmlands of the middle west.

TERRITORY AND POPULATION

New York is bounded west and north by Canada with Lake Erie, Lake Ontario and the St Lawrence River forming the boundary; east by Vermont, Massachusetts and Connecticut, south-east by the Atlantic, south by New Jersey and Pennsylvania. Land area, 47,224 sq. miles (122,310 sq. km). Census population, 1 April 1990, 17,990,455 (84·3% urban), an increase of 2·47% since 1980. Population estimate (1997), 18,137,000.

Population in 5 census years was:

	White	Black	Indian	Asiatic	Total	Per sq. mile
1910	8,966,845	134,191	6,046	6,532	9,113,614	191·2
1930	12,143,191	412,814	6,973	15,088	12,588,066	262·6
1960	15,287,071	1,417,511	16,491	51,678	16,782,304	350·2
			All others			
1980	13,961,106	2,401,842	1,194,340		17,557,288	367·0
1990	12,460,189	2,569,126	2,961,140		17,990,455	381·0

Of the 1990 population, 8,625,673 were male, 14,857,202 (1980) were urban; those 20 years of age or older numbered 13,186,381. Aliens registered in Jan. 1980 numbered 801,411.

The population of New York City, by boroughs, census of 1 April 1990 was: Manhattan, 1,487,536; Bronx, 1,203,789; Brooklyn, 2,291,664; Queens, 1,951,598; Staten Island, 378,977; total, 7,322,564. The New York metropolitan statistical area had, in 1990, 8,546,846.

Population of other large cities and incorporated places census, April 1990, was:

Buffalo	328,123	Troy	54,269	Auburn	31,258
Rochester	231,636	Binghampton	53,008	Waterdown	29,429
Yonkers	188,082	Hempstead	49,453	Poughkeepsie	28,844
Syracuse	163,860	White Plains	48,718	Lindenhurst	26,879
Albany (capital)	101,082	Rome	44,350	Newburgh	26,454
Utica	68,637	Freeport	39,894	Rockville Centre	24,727
New Rochelle	67,265	N. Tonawanda	34,989	Garden City	21,686
Mount Vernon	67,153	Jamestown	34,681	Massapequa Park	18,044
Schenectady	65,566	Valleystream	33,946		
Niagara Falls	61,840	Elmira	33,724		

Other large urbanized areas, census 1990; Buffalo, 968,532; Rochester, 1,002,410; Albany–Schenectady–Troy, 874,304.

SOCIAL STATISTICS

Births in 1995 were 271,369 (15·0 per 1,000 population); deaths, 168,000 (9·3); infant mortality rate, 7·7 (per 1,000 live births). Marriages in 1996 (provisional), 152,300; divorces, 60,800.

CLIMATE

Albany, Jan. 24°F (−4·4°C), July 73°F (22·8°C). Annual rainfall 34" (855 mm). Buffalo, Jan. 24°F (−4·4°C), July 70°F (21·1°C). Annual rainfall 36" (905 mm).

New York, Jan. 30°F (–1·1°C), July 74°F (23·3°C). Annual rainfall 43" (1,087 mm). New York belongs to the Atlantic Coast climate zone (*see* UNITED STATES: Climate).

CONSTITUTION AND GOVERNMENT

The present constitution dates from 1894; a later constitutional convention, 1938, is now legally considered merely to have amended the 1894 constitution, which has now had 93 amendments. A proposed new constitution in 1967 was rejected by the electorate. The Senate consists of 60 members, and the Assembly of 150 members, both elected every 2 years. The state capital is Albany. For local government the state is divided into 62 counties, 5 of which constitute the city of New York. There were state parks and recreation areas covering 260,198 acres in 1990.

Each of the state's 62 cities is incorporated by charter, under special legislation. The government of New York City is vested in the mayor (David Dinkins), elected for 4 years, and a city council, whose president and members are elected for 4 years. The council has a President and 51 members, each elected from a district wholly within the city. The mayor appoints all the heads of departments, except the comptroller, who is elected. Each of the 5 city boroughs (Manhattan, Bronx, Brooklyn, Queens and Staten Island) has a president, elected for 4 years. Each borough is also a county bearing the same name except Manhattan borough, which, as a county, is called New York, and Brooklyn, which is Kings County.

The state sends 31 representatives to Congress.

RECENT ELECTIONS

In the 1996 presidential election Clinton polled 3,513,191 votes; Dole, 1,861,198; Perot, 485,547.

CURRENT ADMINISTRATION

Governor: George E. Pataki (R.), 1999–2003 ($130,000).
  Lieut.-Governor: Elizabeth McGaughey (D.) ($110,000).
  Secretary of State: Alexander F. Treadwell (D.) ($87,338).

ECONOMY

Budget. In 1996 total state revenue was $94,277m. Total expenditure was $82,420m. (education, $17,326m.; public welfare, $26,146m.; health and hospitals, $6,433m.; highways, $2,841m.; police protection, $353m.). Debt outstanding in 1996 was $73,122m.
  Per capita income (1997, preliminary) was $30,752.

ENERGY AND NATURAL RESOURCES

Water. The total area covered by water is approximately 6,766 sq. miles.

Minerals. Principal minerals are: sand and gravel, salt, titanium concentrate, talc, abrasive garnet, wollastonite and emery. Quarry products include trap rock, slate, marble, limestone and sandstone. Value of domestic non-fuel mineral output in 1997, $904m.

Agriculture. New York has large agricultural interests. In 1996 it had some 36,000 farms, with a total area of 8m. acres; average farm was 214 acres. Average value per acre in 1998 was $1,390.

Farm income, 1996, from crops $998m. and livestock $2,045m. Dairying is an important type of farming. Field crops comprise maize, winter wheat, oats and hay. New York ranks second in USA in the production of apples and maple syrup. Other products are grapes, tart cherries, peaches, pears, plums, strawberries, raspberries, cabbages, onions, potatoes, maple sugar. Estimated farm animals, 1990, included 1,540,000 all cattle, 966,000 milch cows, 92,000 sheep and lambs, 124,000 swine and 5·1m. chickens.

INDUSTRY

The main employers (1996) are service industries (2,610,000), retail and wholesale (1,621,000) and manufacture (922,000). Leading industries were clothing, non-electrical machinery, printing and publishing, electrical equipment, instruments, food and allied products and fabricated metals.

COMMUNICATIONS

Roads. In 1995 there were 112,193 miles of roads (71,873 miles rural). The New York State Thruway extends 559 miles from New York City to Buffalo. The Northway, a 176-mile toll-free highway, is a connecting road from the Thruway at Albany to the Canadian border at Champlain, Quebec.

Motor vehicle registrations in 1991 were 9,771,437.

Rail. There were in 1981, 3,891 miles of Class I railways. New York City has NYCTA and PATH metro systems, and commuter railways run by Metro-North, New Jersey Transit and Long Island Rail Road.

Civil Aviation. There were 489 airports and landing areas in 1989.

Shipping. The canals of the state, combined in 1918 in what is called the Improved Canal System, have a length of 524 miles, of which the Erie or Barge canal has 340 miles.

SOCIAL INSTITUTIONS

Justice. The State Human Rights Law was approved on 12 March 1945, effective on 1 July 1945. The State Division of Human Rights is charged with the responsibility of enforcing this law. The division may request and utilize the services of all governmental departments and agencies; adopt and promulgate suitable rules and regulations; test, investigate and pass judgment upon complaints alleging discrimination in employment, in places of public accommodation, resort or amusement, education, and in housing, land and commercial space; hold hearings, subpoena witnesses and require the production for examination of papers relating to matters under investigation; grant compensatory damages and require repayment of profits in certain housing cases among other provisions; apply for court injunctions to prevent frustration of orders of the Commissioner.

In 1996, 69,709 prisoners were in state correctional institutions.

The death penalty is authorized.

Religion. The main religious denominations are Roman Catholics, Jews and Protestant Episcopal.

Education. Education is compulsory between the ages of 7 and 16. In 1994–95 the public elementary and secondary schools had 2,790,700 pupils and 193,000 teachers. Expenditure on education in 1996 was $27,621m.

The state's educational system, including public and private schools and secondary institutions, universities, colleges, libraries, museums, etc., constitutes (by legislative act) the 'University of the State of New York', which is governed by a Board of Regents consisting of 15 members appointed by the Legislature. Within the framework of this 'University' was established in 1948 a 'State University' which controls 64 colleges and educational centres, 30 of which are locally operated community colleges. The 'State University' is governed by a board of 16 Trustees, appointed by the Governor with the consent and advice of the Senate.

Higher education in the state is conducted in 311 institutions (1,028,000 students enrolled in 1996).

In autumn 1990 the institutions of higher education in the state included:

Founded	Name and place	Teachers	Students
1754	Columbia University, New York	2,305	18,242
1795	Union University, Schenectady and Albany	228	2,877
1824	Rensselaer Polytechnic Institute, Troy	375	6,692
1831	New York University, New York	2,386	32,813
1846	Colgate University, New York	255	2,710
1846	Fordham University, New York	703	13,158
1847	University of the City of New York, New York	9,065	200,700
1848	University of Rochester, Rochester	1,250	9,291
1854	Polytechnic Institute of New York	261	3,701
1856	St Lawrence University, Canton	189	2,091
1857	Cooper Union Institute of Technology, New York	108	1,036
1861	Vassar College, Poughkeepsie	235	2,453
1863	Manhattan College, New York	234	3,794
1865	Cornell University, Ithaca	1,779	17,171
1870	Syracuse University, Syracuse	990	21,900
1948	State University of New York	18,852	403,028

The Saratoga Performing Arts Centre (5,100 seats), a non-profit, tax-exempt organization, which opened in 1966, is the summer residence of the New York City Ballet and the Philadelphia Orchestra—two groups which present special educational programmes for students and teachers.

Health. In 1995 the state had 230 community hospitals (73,900 beds).

Welfare. The federal Supplemental Security Income programme covered aid to the needy aged, blind and disabled from 1 Jan. 1975. In 1996 there were 2,968,000 persons in receipt of welfare assistance: 2,103,000 retired workers received an average of $794 per month. Total annual cost for welfare assistance, in 1996, $25,268m.

FURTHER READING

Statistical information: Nelson Rockefeller Institute of Government, 411 State St., Albany 12203. Publishes *New York State Statistical Yearbook.*

Governing the Empire State: an Insider's Guide. Albany, Rockefeller Institute, 1988

New York Red Book. Albany. Biennial.

Legislative Manual. Department of State. Biennial.

Managing Modern New York: the Carey Era. Albany, Rockefeller Institute, 1985

The Modern New York State Legislature: Redressing the Balance. Albany, Rockefeller Institute, 1991

Rockefeller in Retrospect: the Governor's New York Legacy. Albany, Rockefeller Institute, 1987

Connery, R. and G. B., *Governing New York State: The Rockefeller Years.* New York, 1974

Ellis, D. M., *History of New York State.* Cornell Univ. Press, 1967

Flick, A. (ed.) *History of the State of New York.* Columbia Univ. Press, 1933–37

Zimmerman, J. F., *The Government and Politics of New York.* New York Univ. Pres, 1981

State Library: The New York State Library, Albany 12230.

NORTH CAROLINA

KEY HISTORICAL EVENTS

The early inhabitants were Cherokees. European settlement was attempted in 1585–87, following an exploratory visit by Sir Walter Raleigh, but this failed. Settlers from Virginia came to the shores of Albemarle Sound after 1650, and in 1633 Charles II chartered a private colony of Carolina. In 1691 the north was put under a deputy governor who ruled from Charleston in the south. The colony was formally separated into North and South Carolina in 1712. In 1729 control was taken from the private proprietors and vested in the Crown, whereupon settlement grew, and the boundary between north and south was finally fixed (1735).

After the War of Independence North Carolina became one of the original 13 states of the Union. The city of Raleigh was laid out as the new capital. Having been a plantation colony North Carolina continued to develop as a plantation state, growing tobacco with black slave labour. It was also an important source of gold before the western gold-rushes of 1848.

In 1861 at the outset of the Civil War North Carolina seceded from the Union, but General Sherman occupied the capital unopposed. A military governor was admitted in 1862, and civilian government restored with readmission to the Union in 1868.

TERRITORY AND POPULATION

North Carolina is bounded north by Virginia, east by the Atlantic, south by South Carolina, south-west by Georgia and west by Tennessee. Land area, 48,718 sq. miles (126,180 sq. km). Census population, 1 April 1990, 6,628,637 (50·4% urban), an increase of 12·84% since 1980. Population estimate (1997), 7,425,000.

Population in 5 census years was:

	White	Black	Indian	Asiatic	Total	Per sq. mile
1910	1,500,511	697,843	7,851	82	2,206,287	45·3
1930	2,234,958	918,647	16,579	92	3,170,276	64·5
1950	2,983,121	1,047,353	3,742	—	4,061,929	82·7

NORTH CAROLINA

	White	Black	All others	Total	Per sq. mile
1970	3,901,767	1,126,478	53,814	5,082,059	104·1
1980	4,453,010	1,316,050	105,369	5,874,429	111·5

Of the total population in 1980, 2,852,012 were male, 2,818,794 were urban and 3,976,359 were 20 years old or older.

The principal cities (with census population in 1990) are: Charlotte, 395,934; Raleigh, 207,951; Greensboro, 183,521; Winston-Salem, 143,485; Durham, 136,611; Fayetteville, 75,695; High Point, 69,496; Asheville, 61,607; Wilmington, 55,530.

SOCIAL STATISTICS
Births, 1995, were 101,592 (14·1 per 1,000 population); deaths, 65,000 (9·0); infant mortality rate, 9·2 (per 1,000 live births). Marriages (1996 provisional), 61,900; divorces, 35,900.

CLIMATE
Climate varies sharply with altitude; the warmest area is in the south-east near Southport and Wilmington; the coldest is Mount Mitchell (6,684 ft). Raleigh, Jan. 42°F (5·6°C), July 79°F (26·1°C). Annual rainfall 46" (1,158 mm). North Carolina belongs to the Atlantic Coast climate zone (*see* UNITED STATES: Climate).

CONSTITUTION AND GOVERNMENT
The present constitution dates from 1971 (previous constitution, 1776 and 1868/76); it has had 19 amendments. The General Assembly consists of a Senate of 50 members and a House of Representatives of 120 members; all are elected by districts for 2 years. It meets in odd-numbered years in Jan.

The Governor and Lieut.-Governor are elected for 4 years. The Governor may succeed himself but has no veto. There are 19 other executive heads of department, 8 elected by the people and 9 appointed by the Governor.

The state sends 12 representatives to Congress.

The capital is Raleigh. There are 100 counties.

RECENT ELECTIONS
In the presidential election of 1996 Dole polled 1,211,655 votes; Clinton, 1,099,123; Perot, 164,512.

CURRENT ADMINISTRATION
Governor: James B. Hunt Jr (D.), 1997–2001 ($103,012).
   Lieut.-Governor: Dennis Wicker (D.) ($90,915).
   Secretary of State: Janice H. Faulkner (D.) ($90,915).

ECONOMY
Budget. In 1996 total state revenue was $23,387m. Total expenditure was $21,221m. (education, $8,051m.; public welfare, $4,419m.; health and hospitals, $1,577m.; highways, $1,733m.; police protection, 195m.). Debt outstanding (1996) $4,513m.

   Per capita income (1997, preliminary) was $23,345.

ENERGY AND NATURAL RESOURCES
Water. The total area covered by water is approximately 3,954 sq. miles.

Minerals. Principal minerals are stone, sand and gravel, phosphate rock, feldspar, lithium minerals, olivine, kaolin and talc. North Carolina is a leading producer of bricks, making more than 1,000m. bricks a year. Value of domestic non-fuel mineral production in 1997 was $758m.

Agriculture. In 1996 there were some 58,000 farms covering 9m. acres; average size of farms was 159 acres and average value per acre in 1995 was $1,749.

   Farm income, 1991, from crops, $2,272m. and from livestock and products $2,554m. Main crop production: flue-cured tobacco, maize, soybeans, peanuts, wheat, sweet potatoes and apples.

   Livestock, 1990: Cattle, 0·9m.; pigs, 2·6m.; chickens, 19·6m.

Forestry. Commercial forest covered 18,891,000 acres in 1990. Main products are hardwood veneer and hardwood plywood, furniture woods, pulp, paper and lumber.

Fisheries. Commercial fish catch, 1990, had a value of approximately $71·5m. The catch is mainly of menhaden, crabmeat, bay scallops, flounder, croaker, shrimps, sea trout, spots and clams.

INDUSTRY
North Carolina's manufacturing establishments in 1996 had 847,000 workers. The leading industries by employment are textiles, clothing, furniture, electrical machinery and equipment, non-electrical machinery, and food processing.

COMMUNICATIONS

Roads. In 1995 there were 96,809 miles of roads (74,660 miles rural). In 1995 there were 5,682,000 registered motor vehicles.

Rail. The state in 1986 contained 3,682 miles of railway operating in 91 of the 100 counties. There are 22 Class I, II and III rail companies.

Civil Aviation. In 1986 there were 82 public airports of which 14 are served by major airlines.

Shipping. There are 2 ocean ports, Wilmington and Morehead City.

SOCIAL INSTITUTIONS

Justice. Following the US Supreme Court's reinstatement of the death penalty in 1976, capital punishment has been authorized. There was an execution in 1986. In 1996 there were 30,647 prisoners in state correctional institutions.

Religion. Leading denominations are the Baptists (48·9% of church membership), Methodists (20·7%), Presbyterians (7·7%), Lutherans (3%) and Roman Catholics (2·7%). Total estimate of all denominations in 1983 was 2·6m.

Education. School attendance is compulsory between 6 and 16. In 1994–95 there were 1,146,639 pupils and 71,070 teachers. State and local government expenditure in 1996 was $7,094m.; an average of $5,623 per pupil. There were (1997) an estimated 58,000 high-school graduates.

In 1996, 373,000 students enrolled at the 121 higher education institutions. The 16 senior universities are all part of the University of North Carolina system, the largest campus being North Carolina State University and Raleigh. The university system was founded in 1789 at Chapel Hill and first opened in 1792.

Health. In 1995 the state had 119 community hospitals with 22,700 beds.

Welfare. In 1995 there were 1,232,000 persons receiving $893·4m. in social security benefits. Of that number 819,000 were retired (receiving $682 a month); 206,000 were disabled ($651 a month); and there were 206,000 others.

CULTURE

Tourism. Total receipts of the travel industry, $6,400m. in 1990.

FURTHER READING
Statistical information: Office of State Planning, 116 West Jones St., Raleigh 27603. Publishes *Statistical Abstract of North Carolina Counties.*
North Carolina Manual. Secretary of State. Raleigh. Biennial
Clay, J. W. *et al* (eds.), *North Carolina Atlas: Portrait of a Changing Southern State.* Univ. of North Carolina Press, 1975
Corbitt, D. L., *The Formation of the North Carolina Counties.* Raleigh, 1969
Fleer, J. D., *North Carolina: Government and Population.* Univ. of Nebraska Press, 1995
Lefler, H. T. and Newsome, A. R., *North Carolina: The History of a Southern State.* Univ. of North Carolina Press, 1973

NORTH DAKOTA

KEY HISTORICAL EVENTS

The original inhabitants were various groups of Plains Indians. French explorers and traders were active among them in the 18th century, often operating from French possessions in Canada. France claimed the area until 1803, when it passed to the USA as part of the Louisiana Purchase, except for the north-eastern part which was held by the British until 1818.

Trading with the Indians, mainly for furs, continued until the 1860s, with American traders succeeding the French. In 1861 the Dakota Territory (North and South) was established. In 1862 the Homestead Act was passed (allowing 160 acres of public land free to any family who had worked and lived on it for 5 years) and this greatly stimulated settlement. Farming settlers came on to the wheat lands in great numbers, many of them from Canada, Norway and Germany.

Bismarck, the capital, began as a crossing-point on the Missouri and was fortified in 1872 to protect workers building the Northern Pacific Railway. There followed a gold-rush nearby, and the town became a service centre for prospectors. In 1899 North and South Dakota were admitted to the Union as separate states, and Bismarck became the Northern capital. The largest city is Fargo which was also a railway town, named after William George Fargo the express-company founder.

The population grew rapidly until 1890 and steadily until 1930 by which time it was about one-third European in parentage. Between 1930 and 1970 there was a steady population drain, increasing whenever farming was affected by the extremes of the continental climate. The state is still mainly agricultural although oil was discovered in 1951.

TERRITORY AND POPULATION

North Dakota is bounded north by Canada, east by the Red River (forming a boundary with Minnesota), south by South Dakota and west by Montana. Land area, 68,994 sq. miles (178,695 sq. km). The Federal Bureau of Indian Affairs administered (1992) 841,295 acres, of which 214,006 acres were assigned to tribes. Census population, 1 April 1990, 638,800 (53·3% urban), a decrease of 2·13% since 1980. Population estimate (1996), 643,539.

Population at 5 census years was:

	White	Black	Indian	Asiatic	Total	Per sq. mile
1910	569,855	617	6,486	98	577,056	8·2
1930	671,851	377	8,617	194	680,845	9·7
			All others			
1970	599,485	2,494	15,782		617,761	9·0
1980	625,557	2,568	24,692		652,717	9·5
1990	604,142	3,524	31,134		638,800	9·3

Of the total population in 1990, 318,201 were male, 340,490 were urban and 436,665 were 21 years old or older. Estimated outward migration, 1980–90, 110 per 1,000 population.

The largest cities are Fargo with population, census 1990, of 74,111; Grand Forks, 49,425; Bismarck (capital), 49,256, and Minot, 34,544.

SOCIAL STATISTICS

Births in 1995 were 8,476 (13·2 per 1,000 population); deaths, 6,000 (9·3); infant mortality rate, 7·2 (per 1,000 live births). Marriages (1996, provisional), 5,000; divorces, 2,200.

CLIMATE

Bismarck, Jan. 8°F (−13·3°C), July 71°F (21·1°C). Annual rainfall 16" (402 mm). Fargo, Jan. 6°F (−14·4°C), July 71°F (21·1°C). Annual rainfall 20" (503 mm). North Dakota belongs to the High Plains climate zone (see UNITED STATES: Climate).

CONSTITUTION AND GOVERNMENT

The present constitution dates from 1889; it has had 95 amendments. The Legislative Assembly consists of a Senate of 53 members elected for 4 years, and a

House of Representatives of 106 members elected for 4 years. The Governor and Lieut.-Governor are elected for 4 years.

The state sends 1 representative to Congress.

The capital is Bismarck. The state has 53 organized counties.

RECENT ELECTIONS

In the 1996 presidential election Dole polled 125,050 votes; Clinton, 106,905; Perot, 32,515.

CURRENT ADMINISTRATION

Governor: Edward Schafer (R.), 1997–2001 ($75,372).
  Lieut.-Governor: Rosemarie Myrdal (R.) ($61,944).
  Secretary of State: Alvin A. Jaeger (R.) ($57,120).

ECONOMY

Budget. In 1996 total state revenue was $2,569m. Total expenditure was $2,064m. (education, $705m.; public welfare, $361m.; health and hospitals, $84m.; highways, $209m.; police protection, $6m.). Debt outstanding was $819m. in 1996.

Per capita income (1997, preliminary) was $20,721.

ENERGY AND NATURAL RESOURCES

Oil and Gas. The mineral resources of North Dakota consist chiefly of oil, which was discovered in 1951. Production of crude petroleum in 1996 was 32m. bbls. (value, $629m.); of natural gas, 50bn. cu. ft.

Water. The total area covered by water is approximately 1,710 sq. miles.

Minerals. Output of lignite coal in 1994 was 32m. tons. Total value of domestic nonfuel mineral production, 1997, $32m.

Agriculture. Agriculture is the chief pursuit of the population. In 1997 there were some 31,000 farms (61,963 in 1954) with an area of 40·3m. acres. In 1998 the average value of farmland and buildings per acre was $415.

In 1994 (per farm) net farm income was $26,838. Farm income, 1996, from crops, $2,996m. and from livestock, $537m. Production 1995: wheat (durum), 77·8m bu.; barley, 101·3m. bu.; oats, 21·6m. bu.; flaxseed, 1·7m. bu.; dry edible beans, 7,182 cwt; sunflower (all), 17,462 cwt. Other important products are all beans, all wheat, rye and honey.

The state has also an active livestock industry, chiefly cattle raising. Livestock, 1996: cattle, 1·9m.; pigs, 0·28m.; sheep, 125,000; poultry, 270,000.

Forestry. Forest area, 1990, 0·46m. acres.

INDUSTRY

In Oct. 1996, 43,700 persons were employed in production and 272,900 in services.

COMMUNICATIONS

Roads. In 1996 there were 86,808 miles of highway, of which 84,985 were rural. Motor vehicle registrations (1996) numbered 679,000.

Rail. In 1994 there were 4,143 miles of railway.

Civil Aviation. In 1994 there were 100 public airports and 350 private airports.

SOCIAL INSTITUTIONS

Justice. The state penitentiary had an average population of 722 inmates in 1996. The Missouri River Correctional Center is a minimum custody institution. There is no death penalty.

Religion. Church membership totalled 484,628 in 1990. The leading religious denominations were: Combined Lutherans, 179,711 members; Roman Catholics, 173,432; Methodists, 23,850; Presbyterians, 11,960.

Education. School attendance is compulsory between the ages of 7 and 16, or until the 17th birthday if the eighth grade has not been completed. In 1995–96 the public

OHIO

elementary schools had 81,798 pupils; secondary schools, 36,755 pupils. State expenditure per pupil in elementary and secondary schools, 1997, $5,016. Teachers (4,208 in elementary and 2,208 in secondary schools in 1994) earned an average $25,506 in 1993–94 school year.

The University of North Dakota in Grand Forks, founded in 1883, had 10,392 students in autumn 1998; North Dakota State University in Fargo, 9,688 students (1996). Total enrolment in the 11 public institutions of higher education, autumn 1995, 35,199; in the 2 private, 2,911.

Health. In 1994 the state had 46 general hospitals (3,571 beds), and 86 nursing facilities (7,125 beds).

Welfare. In 1996, 116,000 people received $864m. in Supplemental Security Income payments.

CULTURE

Press. There were, in 1997, 10 daily and 7 Sunday newspapers in circulation.

FURTHER READING

Statistical information: Bureau of Business and Economic Research, Univ. of North Dakota, Grand Forks 58202. Publishes *Statistical Abstract of North Dakota.*
North Dakota Blue Book. Secretary of State. Bismarck
Glaab, C. L. et al, *The North Dakota Political Tradition.* Iowa State Univ. Press, 1981
Jelliff, T. B., *North Dakota: A Living Legacy.* Fargo, 1983
Robinson, E. B., *History of North Dakota.* Univ. of Nebraska Press, 1966

OHIO

KEY HISTORICAL EVENTS

The land was inhabited by Delaware, Miami, Shawnee and Wyandot Indians. It was explored by French and British traders in the 18th century and confirmed as part of British North America in 1763. After the War of Independence it became part of the Northwest Territory of the new United States. Former American soldiers of the war came in from New England in 1788 and made the first permanent white settlement at Marietta, at the confluence of the Ohio and Muskingum rivers. In 1803 Ohio was separated from the rest of the Territory and admitted to the Union as the 17th state.

During the early 19th century there was steady immigration from Europe, mainly of Germans, Swiss, Irish and Welsh. Industrial growth began from the processing of local farm, forest and mining products; it increased rapidly with the need to supply the Union armies in the Civil War of 1861–65.

As the industrial cities grew, so immigration began again, with many whites from eastern Europe and the Balkans and blacks from the southern states looking for work in Ohio.

Cleveland, which developed rapidly as a Lake Erie port after the opening of commercial waterways to the interior and the Atlantic coast (1825, 1830 and 1855), became an iron-and-steel town during the Civil War.

TERRITORY AND POPULATION

Ohio is bounded north by Michigan and Lake Erie, east by Pennsylvania, south-east and south by the Ohio River (forming a boundary with West Virginia and Kentucky) and west by Indiana. Land area, 40,952 sq. miles (106,067 sq. km). Census population, 1 April 1990, 10,847,115 (74·1% urban), an increase of 89,695 or 0·8% since 1980. Population estimate (1997), 11,186,331.

Population at 6 census years was:

	White	Black	Indian	Asiatic	Total	Per sq. mile
1910	4,654,897	111,452	127	645	4,767,121	117·0
1930	6,335,173	309,304	435	1,785	6,646,697	161·6
1960	8,909,698	786,097	1,910	8,692	9,706,397	236·9
			All others			
1970	9,646,997	970,477	34,543		10,652,017	260·0
1980	9,597,458	1,076,748	123,424		10,797,630	263·2
1990	9,521,756	1,154,826	170,533		10,847,115	264·5

Of the total population in 1990, 5,226,340 were male. Those 18 years old or older numbered 8,047,371 in 1990.

Census population of chief cities on 1 April 1990 was:

Columbus	632,910	Hamilton	61,368	Middletown	46,022
Cleveland	505,616	Kettering	60,569	Lima	45,549
Cincinnati	364,040	Lakewood	59,718	Newark	44,389
Toledo	332,943	Elyria	56,746	Lancaster	34,507
Akron	223,019	Euclid	54,875	North Olmsted	34,204
Dayton	182,044	Cleveland Heights	54,052	Upper Arlington	34,128
Youngstown	95,753	Warren	50,793	Marion	34,075
Parma	87,876	Mansfield	50,627	East Cleveland	33,096
Canton	84,161	Cuyahoga Falls	48,950	Garfield Heights	31,793
Lorain	71,245	Mentor	47,358	Zanesville	26,788
Springfield	70,487				

Urbanized areas, 1990 census: Cleveland, 1,831,122; Cincinnati, 1,452,645; Columbus (the capital), 1,377,419; Dayton, 951,270; Akron, 657,575; Toledo, 614,128; Youngstown-Warren, 492,619; Canton, 394,106.

SOCIAL STATISTICS
Statistics 1996 (per 1,000 population): births 151,545 (14·0); deaths, 104,856 (9·7); infant deaths 1,188 (7·8 per 1,000 live births); stillbirths, 1,604 (10·6 per 1,000 live births); marriages, 83,851 (7·7 per 1,000 population); divorces, 44,918 (4·1).

CLIMATE
Average temperatures and rainfall in 1997: Cincinnati, Jan. 28·5°F, July 75·0°F, annual rainfall 41·13"; Cleveland, Jan. 25·7°F, July 70·6°F, annual rainfall 35·36"; Columbus, Jan. 28·1°F, July 74·2°F, annual rainfall 38·16". Ohio belongs to the Great Lakes climate zone (*see* UNITED STATES: Climate).

CONSTITUTION AND GOVERNMENT
The question of a general revision of the constitution drafted by an elected convention is submitted to the people every 20 years. The constitution of 1851 had 142 amendments by 1994.

The Senate consists of 33 members and the House of Representatives of 99 members. The Senate is elected for 4 years, half every 2 years; the House is elected for 2 years; the Governor, Lieut.-Governor and Secretary of State for 4 years. Qualified as electors are (with necessary exceptions) all citizens 18 years of age who have the usual residential qualifications. Ohio sends 19 representatives to Congress.

The capital (since 1816) is Columbus. Ohio is divided into 88 counties.

RECENT ELECTIONS
In the 1996 presidential election Clinton polled 2,099,395 votes; Dole, 1,821,750; Perot, 470,461.

CURRENT ADMINISTRATION
Governor: Bob Taft (R.), 1999–2003 ($115,763).
   Lieut.-Governor: Maureen O'Connor (R.), ($59,861).
   Secretary of State: J. Kenneth Blackwell (R.), ($85,517).

ECONOMY
Budget. In 1996 total state revenue was $43,823m. Total expenditure was $35,517m. (education, $10,315m.; public welfare, $7,392m.; health and hospitals, $2,268m.; highways, $2,203m.; police protection, $192m.). Debt outstanding was $12,628m. in 1996.
   Per capita income (1997, preliminary) was $24,661.

ENERGY AND NATURAL RESOURCES
Oil and Gas. In 1997 an estimated 8·6m. bbls. of crude oil was produced with a value of $151,887,623; production of gas was estimated at 117,408·4m. cu. ft.

OHIO

Water. Lake Erie supplies Ohio with its water. In 1996 there were 31 lake-fed water treatment plants and on average 437m. gallons of water is withdrawn every day. The total area covered by water is approximately 3,875 sq. miles.

Minerals. Ohio has extensive mineral resources, of which coal is the most important by value: Estimated production (1997) 30,635,239 short tons. Production of other minerals (in short tons), 1996: Limestone and dolomite, 69,098,412; sand and gravel, 52,767,008; salt, 4,885,957.

Agriculture. Ohio is extensively devoted to agriculture. In 1997 about 73,000 farms covered 15·1m. acres; average farm value per acre, $2,110. The average size of a farm in 1997 was 207 acres.

Cash income 1996 from crop and livestock and products, $5,063·5m. Estimated crop production 1996–97: corn for grain (463m. bu.), wheat (68·67m. bu.), oats (7·8m. bu.), soybeans (197·56m. bu.). In 1997 there were 1·5m. pigs, 1·47m. cattle and 130,000 sheep.

Forestry. State forest area, 1998, 182,223 acres. In 1998 there were 72 state parks covering 293,293 acres.

INDUSTRY
In 1996, 18,726 manufacturing establishments employed 1,083,429 persons out of a total workforce of 4,640,371. The largest industries were manufacturing of transport equipment, industrial machinery and equipment, and fabricated metal products.

COMMUNICATIONS

Roads. In 1995 there were 114,563 miles of roads. There were 11·2m. registered motor vehicles in 1997.

Rail. In 1994 there were 6,458 miles of track used by 4 Class I freight railways, 1 regional railway and several short line railways. Amtrak also serves parts of Ohio.

Civil Aviation. In 1994 there were 8 major passenger airports and 1 cargo airport. There were also 177 public use general aviation airports and 28 heliports. There were 13·4m. passenger emplanements in 1991.

Shipping. In 1995 Lake Erie ports generated over $1bn. in revenue.

SOCIAL INSTITUTIONS

Justice. In 1997 there were 47,166 inmates (44,298 males; 2,868 females) in the 24 adult correctional institutions. The death penalty is authorized; the last execution was in 1963. There were 173 death-row inmates in 1997: 84 were white; 84 black; 4 Hispanic and 1 Native Indian.

Religion. Many religious faiths are represented, including (but not limited to) the Baptist, Jewish, Lutheran, Methodist, Moslem, Orthodox, Presbyterian and Roman Catholic.

Education. School attendance during full term is compulsory for children from 6 to 18 years of age. In 1994–95 public schools had 1,827,624 enrolled pupils (1,846,644 in 1997–98) and 103,929 full-time equivalent classroom teachers. Teachers' salaries (1997–98) averaged $39,092. Estimated expenditure on elementary and secondary schools for 1998 was $5,007m.; 32·1% of the total state budget.

State universities and colleges had a total enrolment (1998) of 411,446 students. Estimated annual operating budget for higher education institutions in 1998 was $4·4m. Average annual charge (for undergraduates in 1995) at 4-year institutions: $3,405 (state); $11,782 (private).

Main campuses, 1996:

Founded	Institutions	Enrolments
1804	Ohio University, Athens (State)	19,729
1809	Miami University, Oxford (State)	15,723
1819	University of Cincinnati (State)	22,795
1826	Case Western Reserve University, Cleveland	9,569
1850	University of Dayton (R.C.)	1,709
1870	University of Akron (State)	15,847
1870	Ohio State University, Columbus (State)	44,428

Founded	Institutions	Enrolments
1872	University of Toledo (State)	17,029
1908	Youngstown University (State)	9,547
1910	Bowling Green State University (State)	15,147
1910	Kent State University (State)	16,243
1964	Cleveland State University (State)	10,905
1964	Wright State University (State)	10,958
1986	Shawnee State University, Portsmouth (State)	2,778

(Figures for Case Western Reserve University and University of Dayton are for 1994 enrolments).

Health. In 1997 the state had 210 hospitals listed by the American Hospital Association with 43,317 beds. State facilities for the severely mentally retarded had 12 developmental centres serving 1,431 residents.

Welfare. Public assistance is administered through 7 basic programmes (with number of recipients as at June 1996): Aid to dependent children (518,395), family emergency assistance (8,449), Medicaid, 1995 (807,523), food stamps (1,009,599) and foster care (18,590).

In the fiscal year 1994–95 Medicaid cost \$5,417·2m. Aid to dependent children cost \$856m. Food stamps cost \$1,029·6m. General assistance cost \$57m. Optional State Supplement is paid to aged, blind or disabled adults. Free social services are available to those eligible by income or circumstances.

CULTURE

Museums and Galleries. The Ohio Historical Center showcases pre-European history, and Ohio's history from the Ice Age to 1970.

FURTHER READING

Official Roster: Federal, State, County Officers and Department Information. Secretary of State, Columbus. Biennial

Rosebloom, E. H. and Weisenburger, F. P., *A History of Ohio.* Columbus, State Archive and Historical Society, 1953

Shkurti, W. J. and Bartle, J. (eds.) *Benchmark Ohio.* Ohio State Univ. Press, 1991

OKLAHOMA

KEY HISTORICAL EVENTS

Francisco Coronado led a Spanish expedition in 1541, claiming the land for Spain. There were several Indian groups, but no strong political unit. In 1714 Juchereau de Saint Denis made the first French contact. During the 18th century French fur-traders were active, and France and Spain struggled for control, a struggle which was resolved by the French withdrawal in 1763. France returned briefly in 1800–03, and the territory then passed to the USA as part of the Louisiana Purchase.

In 1828 the Federal Government set aside the area of the present state as Indian Territory, that is, a reservation and sanctuary for Indian tribes who had been driven off their lands elsewhere by white settlement. About 70 tribes came, among whom were Creeks, Choctaws and Cherokees from the south-eastern states, and Plains Indians.

In 1889 the government took back about 2·5m. acres of the Territory and opened it to white settlement. About 10,000 homesteaders gathered at the site of Oklahoma City on the Santa Fe Railway in the rush to stake their land claims. The settlers' area, and others subsequently opened to settlement, were organized as the Oklahoma Territory in 1890. In 1907 the Oklahoma and Indian Territories were combined and admitted to the Union as a state. Indian reservations were established within the state.

The economy first depended on ranching and farming, with packing stations on the railways. A mining industry grew in the 1870s attracting foreign immigration, mainly from Europe. In 1901 oil was found near Tulsa, and the industry grew rapidly.

OKLAHOMA

TERRITORY AND POPULATION
Oklahoma is bounded north by Kansas, north-east by Missouri, east by Arkansas, south by Texas (the Red River forming part of the boundary) and, at the western extremity of the 'panhandle', by New Mexico and Colorado. Land area, 68,679 sq. miles (177,877 sq. km). Census population, 1 April 1990, 3,189,456 (67·7% urban), an increase of 5·42% since 1980. Population estimate (1997), 3,317,000.

The population at 5 federal censuses was:

	White	Black	Indian	Other	Total	Per sq. mile
1930	2,130,778	172,198	92,725	339	2,396,040	34·6
1960	2,107,900	153,084	68,689	1,414	2,328,284	33·8
1970	2,280,362	171,892	97,179	10,030	2,559,253	37·2
1980	2,597,783	204,658	169,292	53,557	3,025,486	43·2
1990	2,583,512	233,801	252,420	119,723	3,189,456	44·5

In 1980, 1,476,719 were male, 2,035,082 were urban and those 20 years of age or older numbered 2,052,729. The US Bureau of Indian Affairs is responsible for 1,097,004 acres (1990), of which 96,839 acres were allotted to tribes.

The most important cities with population, 1990, are Oklahoma City (capital), 444,719; Tulsa, 367,302; Lawton, 80,561; Norman, 80,071; Broken Arrow, 58,043; Edmond, 52,315; Midwest City, 52,267; Enid, 45,309; Moore, 40,318; Muskogee, 37,708; Stillwater, 36,676; Bartlesville, 34,252.

SOCIAL STATISTICS
Births, 1995, 45,672 (13·9 per 1,000 population); deaths, 33,000 (10·0); infant mortality rate, 8·3 (per 1,000 live births). Marriages (1996, provisional), 26,700; divorces, 19,300.

CLIMATE
Oklahoma City, Jan. 34°F (1°C), July 81°F (27°C). Annual rainfall 31·9" (8,113 mm). Tulsa, Jan. 34°F (1°C), July 82°F (28°C). Annual rainfall 33·2" (8,438 mm). Oklahoma belongs to the Central Plains climate zone (*see* UNITED STATES: Climate).

CONSTITUTION AND GOVERNMENT
The constitution, dating from 1907, provides for amendment by initiative petition and legislative referendum; it has had 155 amendments (as of Jan. 1995).

The Legislature consists of a Senate of 48 members, who are elected for 4 years, and a House of Representatives elected for 2 years and consisting of 101 members. The Governor and Lieut.-Governor are elected for 4-year terms; the Governor can only be elected for two terms in succession. Electors are (with necessary exceptions) all citizens 18 years or older, with the usual qualifications.

The state sends 6 representatives to Congress.

The capital is Oklahoma City. The state has 77 counties.

RECENT ELECTIONS
In the 1996 presidential election Dole polled 582,310 votes; Clinton, 488,102; Perot, 130,788.

CURRENT ADMINISTRATION
Governor: Frank Keating (R.), 1999–2003 ($70,000).
Lieut.-Governor: Mary Fallin (R.) ($62,500).
Secretary of State: Tom J. Cole (R.) ($43,700).

ECONOMY
Budget. In 1996 total state revenue was $10,609m. Total expenditure was $9,265m. (education, $3,476m.; public welfare, $1,658m.; health and hospitals, $593m.; highways, $832m.; police protection, $51m.). Outstanding debt in 1996, $3,889m.
Per capita income (1997, preliminary) was $20,556.

ENERGY AND NATURAL RESOURCES
Oil and Gas. Production 1996: crude oil, 85m. bbls.; natural gas,1,735bn. cu. ft. In 1993 there were 122,094 oil and gas wells in production.

UNITED STATES OF AMERICA

Water. The total area covered by water is approximately 1,224 sq. miles.

Minerals. Coal production (1993), 1,796,000m. tons. Principal minerals are: crushed stone, cement, sand and gravel, iodine, glass sand, gypsum. Other minerals are helium, clay and sand, zinc, lead, granite, tripoli, bentonite, lime and volcanic ash. Total value of domestic non-fuel minerals produced in 1997 was $411m.

Agriculture. In 1996 the state had some 72,000 farms and ranches with a total area of 34m. acres; average size was 472 acres; average value per acre was $494. Area harvested, 1992, 8,272,889 acres. Livestock, 1992: Cattle, 4,736,594; sheep and lambs, 103,732; hogs and pigs, 260,682.

Farm income 1996: crops, $1,126m.; livestock and products, $2,439m. The major cash grain is winter wheat (value, 1997, $579m.): 1,579m. bu. of wheat for grain were harvested from 5,400,000 acres. Other crops include barley, oats, rye, grain, corn, soybeans, grain sorghum, cotton, peanuts and peaches. Value of cattle and calves produced, 1990, $3,080m.; catfish, $1m.; racehorses, $63m.

The Oklahoma Conservation Commission works with 91 conservation districts, universities, state and federal government agencies. The early work of the conservation districts, beginning in 1937, was limited to flood and erosion control: since 1970, they include urban areas also.

Irrigated production has increased in the Oklahoma 'panhandle'. The Ogalala aquifer is the primary source of irrigation water there and in western Oklahoma, a finite source because of its isolation from major sources of recharge. Declining groundwater levels necessitate the most effective irrigation practices.

Forestry. There are 7·5m. acres of forest, one half considered commercial. The forest products industry is concentrated in the 118 eastern counties. There are 3 forest regions: Ozark (oak, hickory); Ouachita highlands (pine, oak); Cross-Timbers (post oak, black jack oak). Southern pine is the chief commercial species, at almost 80% of saw-timber harvested annually. Replanting is essential.

INDUSTRY

In 1994 there were 3,858 industrial firms: Major commodities produced include transportation equipment (accounting for 15·3% of manufactured goods), petroleum and coal products (14·1%), non-electrical machinery (12·2%), food products (9·7%), electronic and electrical equipment (9·2%).

Labour. Total non-agricultural labour force, 1996, 1,354,000, including: manufacturing, 174,000; construction, 50,000.

COMMUNICATIONS

Roads. In 1995 there were 112,035 miles of roads and in 1991, 2,669,312 registered motor vehicles.

Rail. In 1995 Oklahoma had 3,867 miles of railway operated by 21 companies.

Civil Aviation. Airports, 1995, numbered 421, of which 127 were publicly owned. 5 cities were served by commercial airlines.

Shipping. The McClellan-Kerr Arkansas Navigation System provides access from east central Oklahoma to New Orleans through the Verdigris, Arkansas and Mississippi rivers. In 1991, 63m. tons were shipped inbound and outbound on the Oklahoma Segment. Commodities shipped, 1are mainly chemical fertilizer, farm produce, petroleum products, iron and steel, coal, sand and gravel.

SOCIAL INSTITUTIONS

Justice. There were 19,593 prisoners in state correctional institutions in 1996. In 1990 there were 15 penal institutions, 8 community treatment centres and 7 probation and parole centres. The death penalty was suspended in 1966 and re-imposed in 1976. The last execution was in 1995.

Religion. The chief religious bodies are: Baptists, followed by United Methodists, Roman Catholics, Churches of Christ, Assembly of God, Disciples of Christ, Presbyterian, Lutheran, Nazarene and Episcopal.

Education. In 1994–95 there were 609,800 pupils and 39,290 teachers at public elementary and secondary school. The average teacher salary per annum was

$28,928. In 1997 total expenditure on the 3,257 schools was $3,033m. There were 177,000 students enrolled at the 45 higher education establishments in 1996.

Institutions of higher education include:

Founded	Name	Place	1994 Enrolment
1890	University of Oklahoma	Norman	21,373
1890	Oklahoma State University	Stillwater	18,290
1890	University of Central Oklahoma	Edmond	16,039
1894	The University of Tulsa	Tulsa	4,579
1897	Northeastern State University	Tahlequah	9,374
1897	Northwestern Oklahoma State University	Alva	1,870
1897	Southwestern Oklahoma State University	Weatherford	5,289
1908	Cameron University	Lawton	5,863
1909	East Central University	Ada	4,468
1909	Southeastern Oklahoma State University	Durant	4,104
1909	Rogers State College	Claremore	3,404
1950	Oklahoma Christian University of Science and Arts	Oklahoma City	1,505
1969	Rose State College	Midwest City	9,234
1970	Tulsa Junior College	Tulsa	21,055
1972	Oklahoma City Community College	Oklahoma City	11,185

Health. In 1995 there were 110 community hospitals with 11,500 beds.

Welfare. In 1996 there were 580,000 persons receiving welfare assistance. Of this total: 395,000 retired workers received an average of $711 per month; 106,000 widows and widowers received $680 per month; and 79,000 disabled workers and their dependants received $688 per month.

CULTURE

Broadcasting. In 1995 there were 172 radio and 25 television broadcasting stations, and 16 cable-TV companies.

Press. In 1995 there were 49 daily and, in 1990, 190 weekly newspapers.

Tourism. There are 72 state parks and 10 museums and monuments. Tourists spend some $3,000m. annually.

FURTHER READING

Center for Economic and Management Research, Univ. of Oklahoma, 307 West Brooks St., Norman 73019. *Statistical Abstract of Oklahoma.*
Oklahoma Department of Libraries. *Oklahoma Almanac.* Biennial
Gibson, A. M., *The History of Oklahoma.* Rev. ed. Oklahoma Univ. Press, 1984
Morris, J. W. *et al.*, *Historical Atlas of Oklahoma.* 3rd ed. Oklahoma Univ. Press, 1986
Strain, J. W., *Outline of Oklahoma Government.* Rev. ed. Central State Univ., 1983

State library: Oklahoma Department of Libraries, 200 Northeast 18th Street, Oklahoma City 73105.

OREGON

KEY HISTORICAL EVENTS

The area was divided between many Indian groups including the Chinook, Tillamook, Cayuse and Modoc. In the 18th century English and Spanish visitors tried to establish national claims, based on explorations of the 16th century. The USA also laid claim by right of discovery when an expedition entered the mouth of the Columbia River in 1792.

Oregon was disputed between Britain and the USA. An American fur company established a trading settlement at Astoria in 1811, which the British took in 1812. The Hudson Bay Company were the most active force in Oregon until the 1830s when American pioneers began to migrate westwards along the Oregon Trail. The dispute between Britain and the USA was resolved in 1846 with the boundary fixed at 49°N. lat. Oregon was organized as a Territory in 1848 but with wider boundaries; it became a state with its present boundaries in 1859.

Early settlers were mainly American. They came to farm in the Willamette Valley and to exploit the western forests. Portland developed as a port for ocean-going traffic, although it was 100 miles inland at the confluence of the Willamette and Columbia rivers. Industries followed when the railways came and the rivers were exploited for hydro-electricity. The capital of the Territory from 1851 was Salem, a mission for Indians on the Willamette river; it was confirmed as state capital in 1864. Salem became the processing centre for the farming and market-gardening Willamette Valley.

TERRITORY AND POPULATION
Oregon is bounded in the north by Washington, with the Columbia River forming most of the boundary, east by Idaho, with the Snake River forming most of the boundary, south by Nevada and California and west by the Pacific. Land area, 97,060 sq. miles (251,385 sq. km). The federal government owned (1994) 32,132,581 acres (51·73% of the state area). Census population, 1 April 1990, 2,842,321 (70·5% urban), an increase of 8% since 1980. Population estimate (1997), 3,243,000.

Population at 5 federal censuses was:

	White	Black	Indian	Asiatic	Total	Per sq. mile
1930	938,598	2,234	4,776	8,179	953,786	9·9
1960	1,732,037	18,133	8,026	9,120	1,768,687	18·4
1970	2,032,079	26,308	13,510	13,290	2,091,385	21·7
1980	2,490,610	37,060	27,314	34,775	2,633,105	27·3
1990	2,636,787	48,178	38,496	69,269	2,842,321	29·6

Of the total population in 1990, 1,397,073 were male. In 1980, 1,788,354 persons lived in urban areas, and those 18 years and older numbered 1,910,048.

The US Bureau of Indian Affairs (area headquarters in Portland) administers (1994) 783,227·13 acres, of which 627,615·54 acres are held by the USA in trust for Indian tribes and 138,950·05 acres for individual Indians, and 16,661·54 acres of mineral tracts.

The largest cities according to 1998 figures are: Portland, 509,610: Eugene, 133,460; Salem (the capital), 126,635; Gresham, 83,595; Beaverton, 68,050; Hillsboro, 65,110; Medford, 58,895; Springfield, 51,700; Corvallis, 49,630; Albany, 38,925. Primary statistical (metropolitan) areas: Portland-Vancouver (Wash.), 1,815,300; Salem, 331,400; Eugene-Springfield, 313,000.

SOCIAL STATISTICS
In 1995 births numbered 42,811 (13·6 per 1,000 population); deaths, 28,000 (9·0); infant mortality rate, 6·1 (per 1,000 live births). Marriages (1996, provisional), 25,600, and divorces, 15,000.

CLIMATE
Jan. 32°F (0°C), July 66°F (19°C). Annual rainfall 28" (710 mm). Oregon belongs to the Pacific coast climate zone (see UNITED STATES: Climate).

CONSTITUTION AND GOVERNMENT
The present constitution dates from 1859; some 250 items in it have been amended. The Legislative Assembly consists of a Senate of 30 members, elected for 4 years (half their number retiring every 2 years), and a House of 60 representatives, elected for 2 years. The Governor is elected for 4 years. The constitution reserves to the voters the rights of initiative and referendum and recall.

The state sends 5 representatives to Congress.

The capital is Salem. There are 36 counties in the state.

RECENT ELECTIONS
In the 1996 presidential election Clinton polled 325,225 votes; Dole, 255,452; Perot, 73,011.

CURRENT ADMINISTRATION

Governor: John Kitzhaber (D.), 1999–2003 ($80,000).
Secretary of State: Phil Keisling (D.), 1997–2001 ($61,500).

ECONOMY

Budget. In 1996 total state revenue was $15,432m. Total expenditure was $11,858m. (education, $3,473m.; public welfare, $2,116m.; health and hospitals, $809m.; highways, $933m.; police protection, $120m.). Outstanding debt in 1996, $6,086m.

Per capita income (1997, preliminary) was $20,556.

ENERGY AND NATURAL RESOURCES

Water. The total area covered by water is approximately 1,129 sq. miles.

Minerals. Mineral resources include gold, silver, nickel copper, lead, mercury, chromite, sand and gravel, stone, clays, lime, silica, diatomite, expansible shale, scoria, pumice and uranium. There is geothermal potential. Domestic non-fuel mineral production value (1997), $272m.

Agriculture. Oregon, which has an area of 61,557,184 acres, is divided by the Cascade Range into two distinct zones as to climate. West of the Cascade Range there is a good rainfall and almost every variety of crop common to the temperate zone is grown; east of the Range stock-raising and wheat-growing are the principal industries and irrigation is needed for row crops and fruits. In 1993 the monthly average employed in agriculture was 22,500.

There were, in 1996, 39,000 farms with an acreage of 18m.; average farm size was 455 acres; most are family-owned corporate farms. Average value per acre (1998), $1,030.

Farm income in 1996: from crops, $2,320m.; from livestock and products, $657m., of which cattle made most. Principal crops: Greenhouse and nursery products ($415·8m.), hay ($104·4m.), farmforest products, wheat, potatoes, grass seed (ryegrass and fescue), Christmas trees, pears, onions ($255·8m.).

Livestock, 1 Jan. 1993: milch cows (1992), 0·1m.; cattle and calves, 1·4m.; sheep and lambs, 415,000; swine (1992), 75,000.

Forestry. About 28·2m. acres is forested, almost half of the state. Of this amount, 22·4m. is commercial forest land suitable for timber production; ownership is as follows (acres): US Forestry Service, 13·1m.; US Bureau of Land Management, 2·7m.; other federal, 165,000; State of Oregon, 907,000; other public (city, county), 123,000; private owners, 10·8m., of which the forest industry owns 5·8m., non-industrial private owners, 4·6m., Indians, 399,000. Oregon's commercial forest lands provided a 1992 harvest of 5,742m. bd ft of logs, as well as the benefits of recreation, water, grazing, wildlife and fish. Trees vary from the coastal forest of hemlock and spruce to the state's primary species, Douglas-fir, throughout much of western Oregon. In eastern Oregon, ponderosa pine, lodgepole pine and true firs are found. Here, forestry is often combined with livestock grazing to provide an economic operation. Along the Cascade summit and in the mountains of north-east Oregon, alpine species are found.

Total covered payroll in lumber and wood products industry in 1991 was $1,475m.

Fisheries. All food and shellfish landings in the calendar year 1992 amounted to a value of $74·4m. The most important are: Ground fish, shrimp, crab, tuna, salmon.

INDUSTRY

Forest products manufacturing is Oregon's leading industry, and in 1992 employed 64,000. The second most important industry is high technology. Gross State product, 1991, $50,618m. Manufacturing employed 208,831 in 1992; trade, 328,824; services, 295,006; government, 214,659.

COMMUNICATIONS

Roads. There were 83,944 miles of highway in 1995, of which 73,789 miles were rural. Registered vehicles, also 1995, totalled 2,785,000.

Rail. The state had (1994) 21 railways with a total mileage of 2,572 (4,115 km). There is a light rail network in Portland.

Civil Aviation. In 1994 there were 1 public-use and 93 personal-use heliports; 248 personal-use and 101 public-use airports of which 34 were state-owned airports, and 2 sea-plane bases, 1 public-use and 1 personal-use.

Shipping. Portland is a major seaport for large ocean-going vessels and is 101 miles inland from the mouth of the Columbia River. In 1993 Portland handled 11·7m. short tons of cargo and other Columbia River ports 13·7m. short tons, the main commodities being grain, petroleum and wood products; the ports of Coos Bay and Newport handled 2·7m. short tons of cargo, chiefly logs, lumber and wood products.

SOCIAL INSTITUTIONS

Justice. There are 12 correctional institutions in Oregon. Total inmates, in 1996, 8,661, including those in treatment in mental hospitals. The sterilization law, originally passed in 1917, was amended in 1967 and abolished in 1993. Some categories of euthanasia were legalized in Dec. 1994.

The death penalty is authorized.

Religion. The chief religious bodies are Catholic, Baptist, Lutheran, Methodists, Presbyterian and Latter-day Saints (Mormons).

Education. School attendance is compulsory from 7 to 18 years of age if the twelfth year of school has not been completed; those between the ages of 16 and 18 years, if legally employed, may attend part-time or evening schools. Others may be excused under certain circumstances. In 1994–95 the public elementary and secondary schools had 521,000 students and 27,000 teachers; average salary for teachers (1993–94), $37,589. Total expenditure on elementary and secondary education (1997) was $3,769m.

Leading state-supported institutions of higher education (1993–94) included:

	Students
University of Oregon, Eugene	16,680
Oregon Health Sciences University	1,396
Oregon State University, Corvallis	14,131
Portland State University, Portland	14,428
Western Oregon State College, Monmouth	3,871
Southern Oregon State College, Ashland	4,535
Eastern Oregon State College, La Grande	1,931
Oregon Institute of Technology, Klamath Falls	2,444

Enrolment in state colleges and universities, in autumn 1996, was approximately 165,000 students. Largest of the privately endowed universities are Lewis and Clark College, Portland, with 3,132 students (1993–94); University of Portland, 2,700 students; Willamette University, Salem, 2,451 students; Reed College, Portland, 1,277 students; Linfield College, McMinnville, 2,354 students; Marylhurst College, 1,183 students; and George Fox College, 1,557 students. In 1993–94 there were 314,926 students (full-time equivalent) in community colleges.

Health. In 1995 there were 73 licensed hospitals, 2 state hospitals for the mentally ill (798 beds), 1 for the mentally retarded (400) and 1 with both programmes (133). There were 64 community hospitals with 7,200 beds.

Welfare. The State Adult and Family Services Division provides cash payments, medical care, food stamps, day care and help in finding jobs. As of July 1994 there were an estimated 495,000 people on low incomes. Many of them were children in single-parent families, benefiting from the Aid to Families with Dependent Children Programme; 282,500 people were receiving food stamps; an estimated 376,000 were below the poverty level. There is also a Children's Services Division.

A system of unemployment benefit payments, financed by employers, with administrative allotments made through a federal agency, started in 1938.

CULTURE

Broadcasting. In 1996 there were 194 commercial radio stations and 37 educational radio stations. There were 24 commercial television stations and 26 educational television stations. There were also 24 cable companies.

Cinema. The Portland Art Museum Northwest Film Center is a regional media arts resource organization. Programmes include: the Portland International Film Festival (Feb.), a survey of new world cinema; the Northwest Film and Video Festival (Nov.), a juried showcase of new work by regional artists; and the Young People's Film and Video Festival (June), featuring new work by students.

Press. In 1996 there were 21 daily newspapers with a circulation of more than 676,000 and 111 non-daily newspapers.

Tourism. The total income from tourism in 1992 was estimated to be $3,100m.

FURTHER READING

Oregon Blue Book. Issued by the Secretary of State. Salem. Biennial

Carey, C. H., *General History of Oregon, prior to 1861.* 2 vol. (1 vol. reprint, 1971) Portland, 1935

Conway, F. D. L., *Timber in Oregon: History and Projected Trends.* Oregon State Univ., 1993

Corning, H. M. (ed.), *Dictionary of Oregon History.* Rev. ed. New York, 1989

Dicken, E. F. and S. N., *Oregon Divided: A Regional Geography.* Portland, 1982

Dodds, G. B., *Oregon: A Bicentennial History.* New York, 1977.—*American North-West: a History of Oregon and Washington.* Arlington Heights, (Ill.), 1986

Friedman, R., *The Other Side of Oregon.* Caldwell (ID), 1993

Highsmith, R. M. Jr. (ed.), *Atlas of the Pacific Northwest.* Rev. ed. Corvallis, 1985

McArthur, L. A., *Oregon Geographic Names.* 6th ed., rev. and enlarged. Portland, 1992

Orr, E. L. *et al., Geology of Oregon.* Dubuque (IA), 1992

Patton, Clyde P., *Atlas of Oregon.* Univ. Oregon Press, Eugene, 1976

Ronda, J. P., *Astoria and Empire.* Univ. of Nebraska Press, 1990

State Library: The Oregon State Library, Salem.

PENNSYLVANIA

KEY HISTORICAL EVENTS

Pennsylvania was occupied by 4 powerful tribes in the 17th century: Delaware, Susquehannock, Shawnee and Iroquois. The first white settlers were Swedish, arriving in 1643. The British became dominant in 1664, and in 1681 William Penn, an English Quaker, was given a charter to colonize the area as a sanctuary for his fellow Quakers. Penn's ideal was peaceful co-operation with the Indians and religious toleration within the colony. Several religious groups were attracted to Pennsylvania because of this policy, including Protestant sects from Germany and France. During the 18th century, co-operation with the Indians failed as the settlers pushed into more territory and the Indians resisted.

During the War of Independence the Declaration of Independence was signed in Philadelphia, the main city. Pennsylvania became one of the original 13 states of the Union. In 1812 the state capital was moved to its current location in Harrisburg, which began as a trading post and ferry point on the Susquehanna River in the south-central part of the state. The Mason-Dixon line, the state's southern boundary, became the dividing line between free and slave states during the conflict leading to the Civil War. During the war crucial battles were fought in the state, including the battle of Gettysburg. Industrial growth was rapid after the war. Pittsburgh, founded as a British fort in 1761 during war with the French, had become an iron-making town by 1800 and grew rapidly when canal and railway links opened in the 1830s. The American Federation of Labor was founded in Pittsburgh in 1881, by which time the city was of national importance in producing coal, iron, steel and glass.

At the beginning of the 20th century, industry attracted immigration from Italy and eastern Europe. In farming areas the early sect communities survive, notably Amish and Mennonites. (The Pennsylvania 'Dutch' are of German extraction.)

TERRITORY AND POPULATION

Pennsylvania is bounded north by New York, east by New Jersey, south by Delaware and Maryland, south-west by West Virginia, west by Ohio and north-west by Lake Erie. Land area, 44,820 sq. miles (116,083 sq. km). Census population, 1

April 1990, 11,881,643, an increase of 0·13% since 1980. Population estimate (1998), 12,001,451.

Population at 5 census years was:

	White	Black	Indian	All others	Total	Per sq. mile
1910	7,467,713	193,919	1,503	1,976	7,665,111	171·0
1930	9,196,007	431,257	523	3,563	9,631,350	214·8
1960	10,454,004	852,750	2,122	10,490	11,319,366	252·5
				All others		
1980	10,652,320	1,046,810		164,765	11,863,895	264·7
1990	10,520,201	1,089,795		271,647	11,881,643	265·1

Of the total population in 1990, 47·9% were male, 68·9% were urban and 76·5% were 21 years of age or older.

The population of the large cities and townships, 1996 estimate, was:

Philadelphia	1,478,002	Scranton	77,189	Lancaster	53,597
Pittsburgh	350,363	Reading	75,723	Harrisburg	50,886
Erie	105,270	Bethlehem	71,153	Altoona	50,101
Allentown	102,211				

SOCIAL STATISTICS
Births, 1996, 147,890 (12·3 per 1,000 population); deaths, 128,028 (10·6); infant deaths, 1,145 (7·7 per 1,000 live births); marriages, 70,929 (5·9 per 1,000 population); divorces, 38,217 (3·2).

CLIMATE
Philadelphia, Jan. 32°F (0°C), July 77°F (25°C). Annual rainfall 40" (1,006 mm). Pittsburgh, Jan. 31°F (–0·6°C), July 74°F (23·3°C). Annual rainfall 37" (914 mm). Pennsylvania belongs to the Appalachian Mountains climate zone (*see* UNITED STATES: Climate).

CONSTITUTION AND GOVERNMENT
The present constitution dates from 1968. The General Assembly consists of a Senate of 50 members chosen for 4 years, one-half being elected biennially, and a House of Representatives of 203 members chosen for 2 years. The Governor and Lieut.-Governor are elected for 4 years. Every citizen 18 years of age, with the usual residential qualifications, may vote. Registered voters in Nov. 1998, 7,258,822.

The state sends 21 representatives to Congress.

The state capital is Harrisburg. The state is organized in counties (numbering 67), cities, boroughs, townships and school districts.

RECENT ELECTIONS
In the 1996 presidential election Clinton polled 2,206,241 votes; Dole, 1,793,568; Perot, 430,082.

CURRENT ADMINISTRATION
Governor: Tom Ridge (R.), 1999–2003 ($132,382).
  Lieut.-Governor: Mark Schweiker (R.), ($111,201).
  Secretary of the Commonwealth: Yvette Kane (R.), ($95,315).

ECONOMY
Budget. In 1996 total state revenue was $42,796m. Total expenditure was $38,699m. (education, $10,526m.; public welfare, $9,835m.; health and hospitals, $3,005m.; highways, $2,427m.; police protection, $625m.). Outstanding debt in 1996, $15,046m.

Per capita income (1997, preliminary) was $26,058.

ENERGY AND NATURAL RESOURCES
Oil and Gas. 1997 production: crude petroleum, 1·32m. bbls.; natural gas, 80,000m. cu. ft.

Water. The total area covered by water is approximately 1,239 sq. miles.

PENNSYLVANIA

Minerals. Pennsylvania is almost the sole producer of anthracite coal. Production, 1997: anthracite coal, 8,934,325 tons, bituminous coal, 73,491,175 tons; industrial minerals (shale, limestone, sandstone, clay, dolomite, sand and gravel), 120,883,881 tons. Non-fuel mineral production was worth $1,240m. in 1997.

Agriculture. Agriculture, market-gardening, fruit-growing, horticulture and forestry are pursued within the state. In 1997 there were 50,000 farms with a total farm area of 7·7m. acres (4·5m. acres in crops in 1988). Average number of acres per farm in 1997 was 154 and the average value per acre in 1998 was $2,760. Cash receipts, 1997, from crops, $1338·9m., and from livestock and products, $2,788·8m.

In 1997, Pennsylvania ranked first in the production of mushrooms (361m. lbs, value $258·8m.). Other production figures include: corn for grain (97·5m. bu., value $312·0m.); sweet corn (0·9m. cwt, value $24·9m.) and tomatoes (0·5m. cwt, value $12·4m.). Pennsylvania is also a major fruit producing state; in 1997 apples totalled 535m. lbs (value $69·8m.), peaches, 75m. lbs (value $25·3m.) and grapes, 0·6m. tons (value $14·5m.). Pennsylvania ranked fourth in milk production in 1997 with 10,740m. lbs. Egg production totalled 5,788m., value $315m.; chicken production (excluding broilers) was 26·9m., value $45·8m. in chicken inventory, and chicken production of broilers was 135·2m., value $259m. Other products included turkey (11·6m. poults, value $96·5m.) and cheese (343m. lbs).

On 1 Jan. 1998 there were on farms: 1·75m. cattle and calves, 94,000 sheep, and 1m. hogs and swine.

Forestry. In 1998 state forest land totalled 2,100,113 acres; state park land, 282,500 acres; state game lands, 1,382,412 acres.

INDUSTRY
In Nov. 1998 manufacturing employed 927,400 workers; services, 1,755,400; trade, 1,232,400; government, 723,500. The total workforce was 5,484,800.

COMMUNICATIONS
Roads. Highways and roads in the state (federal, local and state combined) totalled (1997) 119,128 miles. Registered motor vehicles (31 Dec.1997) numbered 9,692,499.

Rail. In Jan. 1999 there were 70 freight railways operating within the state with a line mileage of 5,379. There are metro, light rail and tramway networks in Philadelphia and Pittsburgh, and commuter networks around Philadelphia.

Civil Aviation. In Jan. 1999 there were 139 public airports, 312 private and 8 public heliports, 349 airports for personal use (includes seaplane bases).

Shipping. Trade at the ports of the Philadelphia area (Chester, Marcus Hook and Philadelphia) for 1997: imports, 41,917,676 short tons of cargo (includes bulk and general cargo); exports, 723,808 short tons of cargo.

SOCIAL INSTITUTIONS
Justice. The death penalty is authorized. The last execution was in 1995. There were 36,377 prisoners in state correctional institutions as of 30 Dec. 1998.

Religion. The principal religious bodies in 1990 were the Roman Catholics (3,675,250 members), Protestant (3,615,450) and Jewish (325,000 in 1996). The 5 largest Protestant denominations by adherents were the Evangelical Lutheran Church in America (682,800), the United Methodist Church (678,700), the Presbyterian Church (USA) (388,747), the United Church of Christ (286,500), and the Episcopal Church (140,050).

Education. School attendance is compulsory for children 8–17 years of age. In 1997–98 there were 1,815,151 pupils and 106,687 teachers in public elementary and secondary schools. The public kindergartens and elementary schools (Grades K-6) had 990,351 pupils and public secondary schools (Grades 7–12) had 824,800 pupils. Non-public elementary schools had 249,753 pupils and non-public secondary had 82,872 pupils. Average salary for public school professional personnel was $48,949; classroom teachers $47,542. In fiscal year 1996–97 state and local government revenues for elementary and secondary schools totalled $12,936m. Total expenditures from all funding sources (state, local, federal government, and other financing sources) totalled $13,347m.

Leading senior academic institutions included:

Founded	Institutions	Faculty[1] (Autumn 1997)	Students[2] (Autumn 1997)
1740	University of Pennsylvania (non-sect.)	6,634	21,643
1787	University of Pittsburgh (all campuses)	6,142	31,776
1832	Lafayette College, Easton (Presbyterian)	264	2,185
1833	Haverford College	121	1,147
1842	Villanova University (R.C.)	1,079	10,020
1846	Bucknell University (Baptist)	285	3,537
1851	St Joseph's University, Philadelphia (R.C.)	474	7,027
1852	California University of Pennsylvania	332	5,783
1855	Pennsylvania State University (all campuses)	9,017	73,494
1855	Millersville University of Pennsylvania	440	7,564
1863	LaSalle University, Philadelphia (R.C.)	391	5,452
1864	Swarthmore College	228	1,370
1866	Lehigh University, Bethlehem (non-sect.)	909	6,316
1871	West Chester University of Pennsylvania	711	11,430
1875	Indiana University of Pennsylvania	824	13,736
1878	Duquesne University, Pittsburgh (R.C.)	1,124	9,500
1884	Temple University, Philadelphia	3,697	27,652
1885	Bryn Mawr College	283	1,825
1888	University of Scranton (R.C.)	452	4,816
1891	Drexel University, Philadelphia	1,117	10,632
1900	Carnegie-Mellon University, Pittsburgh	1,235	7,858

[1]Includes full-time and part-time
[2]Includes undergraduate, graduate and first professional students

Health. In June 1997 the state had 200 general/acute care hospitals with 46,528 beds licensed and approved by the Department of Health. In addition there were 80 speciality (federal, psychiatric, and rehabilitation) hospitals with a licensed capacity of 10,094 beds.

Welfare. During the year ending 30 June 1998 the monthly average number of cases receiving public assistance was 463,745, including: Temporary Assistance for Needy Families (formerly Aid to Families with Dependent Children), 395,013; general assistance, 67,609; State Blind Pension, 1,123.

Payments for medical assistance (state and federal) in fiscal year 1997–98 included: outpatient care, $1,442m.; inpatient care, $980m.; capitation, $1,925m.; and long-term care, $2,790m.

CULTURE

Broadcasting. Broadcasting stations in 1998 included 44 television stations and 362 radio stations.

Press. There were (1998) 84 daily and 273 weekly newspapers.

Festivals. The leading festivals are the Festival of Fountains, Longwood; Gettysburg Civil War Heritage Days, Gettysburg; Bethlehem Musikfest, Bethlehem; and the Philadelphia Flower Show.

National Theatre and Opera. Pennsylvania has an Opera Company of Philadelphia and the Pittsburgh Ballet Theatre.

Museums and Galleries. The main attractions are the Philadelphia Museum of Art; Andy Warhol Museum, Pittsburgh; and the Carnegie Museums of Art and Natural History, Pittsburgh.

FURTHER READING

Statistical information: Pennsylvania State Data Center, 777 West Harrisburg Pike, Midelleton 17057. Publishes *Pennsylvania Statistical Abstract.*
Encyclopaedia of Pennsylvania, New York, 1984
Cochran, T. C., *Pennsylvania*, New York, 1978
Downey, D. B. and Bremer, F. (eds.) *Guide to the History of Pennsylvania.* London, 1994
Klein, P. S. and Hoogenboom, A., *A History of Pennsylvania.* New York, 1973
Majumdar, S. K. and Miller, E. W., *Pennsylvania Coal: Resources, Technology and Utilisation.* Pennsylvania Science, 1983
Weigley, R. F., (ed.) *Philadelphia: A 300-year History.* New York, 1984
Wilkinson, N. B., *Bibliography of Pennsylvania History.* Harrisburg, 1957

RHODE ISLAND

KEY HISTORICAL EVENTS
The earliest white settlement was founded by Roger Williams, an English Puritan who was expelled from Massachusetts because of his dissident religious views and his insistence on the land-rights of the Indians. At Providence he bought land from the Narragansetts and founded a colony there in 1636. A charter was granted in 1663. The colony was governed according to policies of toleration, which attracted Jewish and nonconformist settlers; later there was French Canadian settlement also.

Shipping and fishing developed strongly, especially at Newport and Providence; these two cities were twin capitals until 1900, when the capital was fixed at Providence.

Significant actions took place in Rhode Island during the War of Independence. In 1790 the state accepted the federal constitution and was admitted to the Union.

Early farming development was most successful in dairying and poultry. Early industrialization was mainly in textiles, beginning in the 1790s, and flourishing on abundant water power. Textiles dominated until the industry began to decline after the First World War. British, Irish, Polish, Italian and Portuguese workers settled in the state, working in the mills or in the shipbuilding, shipping, fishing and naval ports. The crowding of a new population into cities led to the abolition of the property qualification for the franchise in 1888.

TERRITORY AND POPULATION
Rhode Island is bounded north and east by Massachusetts, south by the Atlantic and west by Connecticut. Land area, 1,045 sq. miles (2,707 sq. km). Census population, 1 April 1990, 1,003,464 (86% urban), a decrease of 5·95% since 1980. Population estimate (1997), 987,000.

Population of 5 census years was:

	White	Black	Indian	Asiatic	Total	Per sq. mile
1910	532,492	9,529	284	305	542,610	508·5
1930	677,026	9,913	318	240	687,497	649·3
1960	838,712	18,332	932	1,190	859,488	812·4
			All others			
1980	896,692	27,584	22,878		947,154	903·0
1990	917,375	38,861	4,071	18,325	1,003,164	960·3

Of the total population in 1990, 481,496 were male, 777,474 were 18 years of age or older and 45,752 were of Hispanic origin. 824,004 were urban in 1980.

The chief cities and their population (census, 1990) are Providence, 160,728; Warwick, 85,427; Cranston, 76,060; Pawtucket, 72,644; East Providence, 50,380.

SOCIAL STATISTICS
Births, 1995, were 12,776 (12·9 per 1,000 population); deaths, 10,000 (9·8); infant mortality rate, 7·2 (per 1,000 live births). Marriages (1996, provisional), were 7,800; divorces, 3,700.

CLIMATE
Providence, Jan. 28°F (−2·2°C), July 72°F (22·2°C). Annual rainfall 43" (1,079 mm). Rhode Island belongs to the New England climate zone (see UNITED STATES: Climate).

CONSTITUTION AND GOVERNMENT
The present constitution dates from 1843; it has had 42 amendments. The General Assembly consists of a Senate of 50 members and a House of Representatives of 100 members, both elected for 2 years. The Governor and Lieut.-Governor are now elected for 4 years. Every citizen, 18 years of age, who has resided in the state for 30 days, and is duly registered, is qualified to vote.

The state sends 2 representatives to Congress.

The capital is Providence. The state has 5 counties but no county governments. There are 39 municipalities, each having its own form of local government.

RECENT ELECTIONS

At the 1996 presidential election Clinton polled 220,592 votes; Dole, 198,325; Perot, 39,965.

CURRENT ADMINISTRATION

Governor: Lincoln C. Almond (R.), 1999–2003 ($69,900).
  Lieut.-Governor: Vacant ($52,000).
  Secretary of State: James R. Langerin (D.) ($52,000).

ECONOMY

Budget. In 1996 total state revenue was $4,271m. Total expenditure was $4,061m. (education, $886m.; public welfare, $882m.; health and hospitals, $332m.; highways, $210m.; police protection, $30m.). Outstanding debt in 1996, $5,506m.
  Per capita income (1997, preliminary) was $25,760.

ENERGY AND NATURAL RESOURCES

Water. The total area covered by water is approximately 186 sq. miles.

Minerals. The small non-fuel mineral output—mostly stone, sand and gravel—was valued (1997) at $23m.

Agriculture. In 1997 there were 1,000 farms with an area (1991) of some 66,000 acres. The average size of a farm (1997) was 90 acres. In 1998 the average value of land and buildings per acre was $8,200—land per acre in Rhode Island was the second most valuable in the USA, after New Jersey. Farm income 1996: from crops, $72m.; livestock and products, $11m.

Fisheries. In 1990 the catch was 13·2m. lb (mainly lobster and quahang) valued at $72·9m.

INDUSTRY

Manufacturing is the chief source of income and the largest employer. Total non-agricultural employment in 1996 was 442,000, of which 82,000 were manufacturing (99,500 in 1990). Average weekly earnings for production workers in 1989 was $359·99. Principal industries are jewellery and silverware, electrical machinery, electronics, plastics, metal products, instruments, chemicals and boat building.

COMMUNICATIONS

Roads. In 1995 there were 5,893 miles of roads (1,321 miles rural). There were 699,000 registered motor vehicles.

Rail. Amtrak's New York-Boston route runs through the state, serving Providence.

Civil Aviation. In 1988 there were 6 state-owned airports. Theodore Francis Green airport at Warwick, near Providence, is served by 9 airlines, and handled over 2m. passengers and 37m. lb of freight in 1995.

Shipping. Waterborne freight through the port of Providence (1988) totalled 10·6m. tons.

SOCIAL INSTITUTIONS

Justice. The state's correctional institutions had 3,271 prisoners in 1996. The death penalty is illegal, except that it is mandatory in the case of murder committed by a prisoner serving a life sentence.

Religion. Chief religious bodies are Roman Catholic, Protestant Episcopal (baptized persons), Jewish, Baptist, Congregational and Methodist.

Education. In 1996 there were 149,802 pupils in public elementary and secondary schools. There were 219 public elementary schools with 85,691 pupils; about 24,941 pupils were enrolled in private and parochial schools. The 38 public senior and vocational high schools had 64,111 pupils. State and local government expenditure for schools in 1991 totalled $1,212·7m. The total expenditure per pupil in 1995 was $6,634.

SOUTH CAROLINA

There are 11 institutions of higher learning (3 public and 8 private). The state maintains Rhode Island College, at Providence, with over 350 faculty members, and 8,900 students (2,594 part-time, 1,816 graduates), and the University of Rhode Island, at South Kingstown, with over 650 faculty members and 13,707 students (2,198 part-time, 3,176 graduates). Brown University, at Providence, founded in 1764, is now non-sectarian; in 1996 it had over 500 faculty members and 7,458 students (1,786 part-time or graduate). Providence College, at Providence, founded in 1917 by the Order of Preachers (Dominican), had (1996) 300 faculty members and 5,520 students (1,911 part-time or graduate). The largest of the other colleges are Bryant College, at Smithfield, with over 200 faculty members and 3,310 students (1,100 part-time or graduate), and the Rhode Island School of Design, in Providence, with over 250 faculty members and 1,830 students (170 graduates) in 1996.

Health. In 1995 there were 11 community hospitals with 2,700 beds.

Welfare. In 1995, 190,000 people were receiving benefit totalling $1,478m. including 140,000 retired workers and dependants and 25,000 disabled workers and dependants.

CULTURE

Broadcasting. There are 24 radio stations and 5 television stations; there are 8 cable television companies.

FURTHER READING

Statistical information: Rhode Island Economic Development Corporation, 1 West Exchange Street, Providence, RI 02903. Publishes *Rhode Island Basic Economic Statistics.*
Rhode Island Manual. Prepared by the Secretary of State. Providence
Providence Journal Almanac: A Reference Book for Rhode Islanders. Providence. Annual
McLoughlin, W. G., *Rhode Island: a History.* Norton, 1978
Wright, M. I. and Sullivan, R. J., *Rhode Island Atlas.* Rhode Island Pubs., 1983

State Library: Rhode Island State Library, State House, Providence 02908.

SOUTH CAROLINA

KEY HISTORICAL EVENTS
Originally the territory of Yamasee Indians, the area attracted French and Spanish explorers in the 16th century. There were attempts at settlement on the coast, none of which lasted. Charles I of England made a land grant in 1629, but the first permanent white settlement began at Charles Town in 1670, moving to Charleston in 1680. This was a proprietorial colony including North Carolina until 1712; both passed to the Crown in 1729.

The coastlands developed as plantations worked by slave labour. In the hills there were small farming settlements and many trading posts, dealing with Indian suppliers.

After active campaigns during the War of Independence, South Carolina became one of the original states of the Union in 1778.

In 1793 the cotton gin was invented, enabling the speedy mechanical separation of seed and fibre. This made it possible to grow huge areas of cotton and meet the rapidly growing needs of new textile industries. Plantation farming spread widely, and South Carolina became hostile to the anti-slavery campaign which was strong in northern states. The state first attempted to secede from the Union in 1847, but was not supported by other southern states until 1860, when secession led to civil war.

At that time the population was about 730,000, of whom 413,000 were black. During the reconstruction periods there was some political power for black citizens, but control was back in white hands by 1876. The constitution was amended in 1895 to disenfranchise most black voters, and they remained with hardly any voice in government until the Civil Rights movement of the 1960s. Columbia became the capital in 1786.

TERRITORY AND POPULATION

South Carolina is bounded in the north by North Carolina, east and south-east by the Atlantic, south-west and west by Georgia. Land area, 30,111 sq. miles (77,988 sq. km). Census population, 1 April 1990, 3,486,703 (54·6% urban), an increase of 11·73% since 1980. Population estimate (1997), 3,760,000.

The population in 5 census years was:

	White	Black	Indian	Asiatic	Total	Per sq. mile
1910	679,161	835,843	331	65	1,515,400	49·7
1930	944,049	793,681	959	76	1,738,765	56·8
			All others			
1970	1,794,432	789,040	3,588		2,587,060	83·2
1980	2,150,507	948,623	22,703		3,121,833	100·3
1990	2,406,974	1,039,884	39,845		3,486,703	115·8

Of the total population in 1990, 1,905,378 (54·6%) were urban and 2,159,970 (61·9%) were 25 years old or older. Median age, 32.

Population estimate of large towns in 1994: Columbia (capital), 112,800; Charleston, 71,100; North Charleston, 58,100; Greenville, 57,100; Rock Hill, 44,100; Spartanburg, 42,100.

SOCIAL STATISTICS

Births, 1996, were 50,105 (13·8 per 1,000 population); deaths, 34,035 (9·2); marriages, 43,439 (11·7); divorces and annulments, 15,323 (4·1); infant deaths, 424 (8·3 per 1,000 live births).

CLIMATE

Columbia, Jan. 44·7°F (7°C), Aug. 80·2°F (26·9°C). Annual rainfall 49·12" (1,247·6 mm). South Carolina belongs to the Atlantic Coast climate zone (*see* UNITED STATES: Climate).

CONSTITUTION AND GOVERNMENT

The present constitution dates from 1895, when it went into force without ratification by the electorate. The General Assembly consists of a Senate of 46 members, elected for 4 years, and a House of Representatives of 124 members, elected for 2 years. It meets annually. The Governor and Lieut.-Governor are elected for 4 years.

The state sends 6 representatives to Congress.

The capital is Columbia. There are 46 counties.

RECENT ELECTIONS

At the 1996 presidential election Dole polled 573,339 votes; Clinton 506,152; Perot, 64,377.

CURRENT ADMINISTRATION

Governor: Jim Hodges (D.), 1999–2003.
Lieut.-Governor: Robert L. Peeler (R.).
Secretary of State: Jim Miles (R.).

ECONOMY

Budget. In 1996 total state revenue was $12,602m. Total expenditure was $12,400m. (education, $3,832m.; public welfare, $2,554m.; health and hospitals, $1,308m.; highways, $616m.; police protection, $140m.). Outstanding debt in 1996, $5,324m.

Per capita income (1997, preliminary) was $20,755.

ENERGY AND NATURAL RESOURCES

Water. The total area covered by water is approximately 1,078 sq. miles.

Minerals. Gold is found, though non-metallic minerals are of chief importance: Value of non-fuel mineral output in 1997 was $507m., chiefly from cement (Portland), stone and gold. Production of kaolin, vermiculite, scrap mica and fuller's earth is also important.

SOUTH CAROLINA

Agriculture. In 1996 there were 21,500 farms covering a farm area of 5m. acres. The average farm was of 233 acres. The average value of farmland and buildings per acre was $1,363 in 1996.

Farm income in 1995, $817·8m. for crops and $611m. for livestock and products. Chief crops are tobacco, soybeans, wheat, cotton, peanuts and corn. Production, 1996: Cotton, 455,000 bales; peanuts, 32·5m. lb; soybeans, 13·5m. bu.; tobacco, 117·8m. lb; corn, 30m. bu.; wheat, 12·2m. bu. Livestock on farms, Jan. 1997: 520,000 all cattle, 300,000 swine (Dec. 1996).

Forestry. The forest industry is important; total forest land (1993), 12·6m. acres. National forests amounted to 609,000 acres in 1993.

INDUSTRY

A monthly average of 1,618,313 were employed in 1995, with 377,246 workers in manufacturing and 331,350 in service. Major sectors are textiles (23·9%), apparel (8·6%), chemicals (10·2%), business service (26·8%) and health service (22·6%). Tourism is important.

COMMUNICATIONS

Roads. Total highway mileage in the combined highway system in Dec. 1996 was 41,502·91 miles. Motor vehicle registrations numbered 2,852,990 in 1995.

Rail. In 1994 the length of railway in the state was 2,306·76 miles.

Civil Aviation. In 1995 there were 1,496,680 general aviation aircraft operations in South Carolina, 112,438 taxi and commuter aircraft operations, 88,766 air carrier aircraft operations and 80,948 military aircraft operations.

Shipping. The state has 3 deep-water ports.

SOCIAL INSTITUTIONS

Justice. In 1997 there were on average 20,146 prisoners in state correctional institutions. The death penalty is authorized. The last execution was in 1997.

Education. In 1995–96 there were 648,677 pupils and 46,073 teachers in public elementary and secondary schools. In 1995–96 the average teaching salary was $31,622.

For higher education the state operates the University of South Carolina (USC), founded at Columbia in 1801, with (autumn 1996), 20,380 enrolled students; USC Aiken, with 2,292 students; USC Spartanburg, with 2,292 students; USC 2-year regional campuses, with 2,696 students; Clemson University, founded in 1889, with 14,978 students; The Citadel, at Charleston, with 3,046 students; Winthrop University, Rock Hill, with 4,293 students; Medical University of S. Carolina, at Charleston, with 2,293 students; S. Carolina State University, at Orangeburg, with 4,364 students; and Francis Marion University, at Florence, with 3,076 students; the College of Charleston has 8,948 students and Lander University, Greenwood, 2,217. There are 16 technical institutions (35,454).

There are also 387 private kindergartens, elementary and high schools with total enrolment (1996–97) of 49,534 pupils, and 23 private and denominational colleges and 5 junior colleges with (autumn 1996) enrolments of 27,280 and 1,314 students respectively.

Health. In 1996 the state had 464 non-federal health facilities with 35,714 beds licensed by the South Carolina Department of Health and Environmental Control. There were 6,846 physicians and 25,589 registered nurses in 1996.

Welfare. In 1995 there were 363,362 recipients of social security benefits. The annual payment in benefits was $2,968·7m. and the average monthly benefit was $658.

CULTURE

Press. In 1997 there were 15 daily and 14 Sunday newspapers in circulation.

FURTHER READING

Statistical information: Budget and Control Board, R.C. Dennis Bldg., Columbia 29201. Publishes *South Carolina Statistical Abstract.*

South Carolina Legislative Manual. Columbia. Annual

Edgar, W. B., *South Carolina in the Modern Age.* Univ. of South Carolina Press, 1992

Graham, C. B. and Moore, W. V., *South Carolina Politics and Government.* Univ. of Nebraska Press, 1995

Jones, L., *South Carolina: A Synoptic History for Laymen.* Lexington, 1978

State Library: South Carolina State Library, Columbia.

SOUTH DAKOTA

KEY HISTORICAL EVENTS

The area was part of the hunting grounds of nomadic Dakota (Sioux) Indians. French explorers visited the site of Fort Pierre in 1742–43, and claimed the area for France. In 1763 the claim fell and, together with French claims to all land west of the Mississippi, passed to Spain. Spain held the Dakotas until defeated by France in the Napoleonic Wars, when France regained the area and sold it to the USA as part of the Louisiana Purchase in 1803.

Fur-traders were active, but there was no settlement until Fort Randall was founded on the Missouri river in 1856. In 1861 North and South Dakota were organized as the Dakota Territory, and the Homestead Act of 1862 stimulated settlement, mainly in the south-east until there was a gold-rush in the Black Hills of the west in 1875–76. Colonization developed as farming communities in the east, miners and ranchers in the west. Livestock farming predominated, attracting European settlers from Scandinavia, Germany and Russia.

In 1899 the North and South were separated and admitted to the Union as states. The capital of South Dakota is Pierre, founded as a railhead in 1880, chosen as a temporary capital and confirmed as permanent capital in 1904. It faces Fort Pierre, the former centre of the fur trade, across the Missouri river. During the 20th century there have been important schemes to exploit the Missouri for power and irrigation.

TERRITORY AND POPULATION

South Dakota is bounded in the north by North Dakota, east by Minnesota, south-east by the Big Sioux River (forming the boundary with Iowa), south by Nebraska (with the Missouri River forming part of the boundary) and west by Wyoming and Montana. Land area, 75,898 sq. miles (196,576 sq. km). Area administered by the Bureau of Indian Affairs, 1985, covered 5m. acres (10% of the state), of which 2·6m. acres were held by tribes. The federal government, 1994, owned 2,698,000 acres.

Census population, 1 April 1990, 696,004 (50% urban), an increase of 2·4% since 1980. Population estimate (1997), 738,000.

Population in 5 federal censuses was:

	White	Black	American Indian	Asiatic	Total	Per sq. mile
1910	563,771	817	19,137	163	583,888	7·6
1930	669,453	646	21,833	101	692,849	9·0
1960	653,098	1,114	25,794	336	680,514	8·9
			All others			
1980	638,955	2,144	49,079		690,178	9·0
				Asian/ other		
1990	637,515	3,258	50,575	4,656	696,004	9·2

Of the total population in 1990, 497,942 were 18 years of age and over and 5,252 were of Hispanic origin. A total of 342,498 were male and 347,903 were urban.

Population of the chief cities (census of 1990) was: Sioux Falls, 100,814; Rapid City, 54,523; Aberdeen, 24,927; Watertown, 17,592; Brookings, 16,270; Mitchell, 13,798; Pierre, 12,906; Yankton, 12,703; Huron, 12,448; Vermillion, 10,034; Spearfish, 6,996; Madison, 6,257; Sturgis, 5,330; Belle Fourche, 4,335; Hot Springs, 4,325.

SOUTH DAKOTA

SOCIAL STATISTICS
In 1996: births, 10,469 (15·0 per 1,000 population); deaths, 6,793 (9·8); infant deaths, 60 (5·7 per 1,000 live births); marriages, 6,991 (10·0 per 1,000 population); divorces, 2,749 (3·9).

CLIMATE
Rapid City, Jan. 25°F (−3·9°C), July 73°F (22·8°C). Annual rainfall 19" (474 mm). Sioux Falls, Jan. 14°F (−10°C), July 73°F (22·8°C). Annual rainfall 25" (625 mm). South Dakota belongs to the High Plains climate zone (*see* UNITED STATES: Climate).

CONSTITUTION AND GOVERNMENT
Voters are all citizens 18 years of age or older. The people reserve the right of the initiative and referendum. The Senate has 35 members, and the House of Representatives 70 members, all elected for 2 years; the Governor and Lieut.-Governor are elected for 4 years.

The state sends 1 representative to Congress.

The capital is Pierre. The state is divided into 66 organized counties.

RECENT ELECTIONS
In the 1996 presidential election Dole polled 150,508 votes; Clinton, 139,295; Perot, 31,248.

CURRENT ADMINISTRATION
Governor: William J. Janklow, (R.), 1999–2003 ($87,277).
   Lieut.-Governor: Carole Hillard, (R.) ($63,378).
   Secretary of State: Joyce Hazeltine, (R.) ($59,301).

ECONOMY
Budget. In 1996 total state revenue was $2,284m. Total expenditure was $1,975m. (education, $529m.; public welfare, $393m.; health and hospitals, $107m.; highways, $265m.; police protection, $20m.). Outstanding debt in 1996, $1,704m.

Per capita income (1997, preliminary) was $21,447.

ENERGY AND NATURAL RESOURCES
Water. The total area covered by water is approximately 1,225 sq. miles.

Minerals. In 1996 the mineral products included gold, 17·4 tonnes (fourth largest yield of all states); silver, 7 tonnes. Domestic non-fuel mineral products, 1997, were valued at $340m., including gold and silver.

Agriculture. In 1996 there were 32,500 farms, average size 1,354 acres. Average value of farmland and buildings per acre in 1998 was $350. Farm income, 1996: crops, $2,051m.; livestock and products, $1,633m.

South Dakota is a major producer of rye (1·5m. bu. in 1996), sunflower oil (1,056·2m. lb), flaxseed (126,000 bu.), and oats (21·6m. bu.). The other important crops are all wheat (139,270,000 bu.), sorghum for grain (7,975,000 bu.), corn for grain (370m. bu.) and soybeans (90,780,000 bu.). The farm livestock on 1 Jan. 1997 included 3·8m. cattle, 0·45m. sheep and lambs, and 1·13m. hogs (1 March 1997). In 1996, 23,280,000 lb of honey were produced.

Forestry. National forest area, 1992, 2,013,000 acres.

INDUSTRY
In 1996, 1,044 manufacturing establishments had 47,750 employees. Industrial machinery and computer equipment had 160 establishments with 13,559 workers; food and kindred products had 115 establishments with 8,590 workers. Construction had 2,925 companies with 14,646 workers. Also significant were transportation, communications and public utilities (1,811 establishments employing 15,576 workers). Mining establishments were 83 and employed 2,270 workers.

COMMUNICATIONS

Roads. In 1996 there were 83,358 miles of roads. There were 706,984 registered cars and trucks, 133,677 trailers, 24,704 motor cycles and 6,979 snowmobiles.

Rail. In 1997 there were 1,855 miles of track of which 811 miles were state-owned.

Civil Aviation. In 1996 there were 73 general aviation airports, of which 9 were 'air carrier' airports with regular passenger services utilizing turbo-prop or jet aircraft.

SOCIAL INSTITUTIONS

Justice. On 30 Nov. 1997 there were 2,232 adults in state prisons. The death penalty is authorized.

Religion. The chief religious bodies are: Lutherans, Roman Catholics, Methodist, United Church of Christ, Presbyterian, Baptist and Episcopal.

Education. Elementary and secondary education are free from 6 to 21 years of age. Between the ages of 6 and 16, attendance is compulsory. In 1997 there were 133,723 PK-12 public school students and 16,792 PK-12 non-public students.

Teachers' salaries (1997) averaged $27,072. Total expenditure on public schools (1995–96), $588,200,564.

Higher education (autumn 1997): The School of Mines at Rapid City, established 1885, had 2,210 students; South Dakota State University at Brookings, 8,162; the University of South Dakota, founded at Vermillion in 1882, 6,535; Northern State University, Aberdeen, 2,464; Black Hills State University at Spearfish, 2,773; Dakota State University at Madison, 1,326. There were 7,436 students at 12 of the 13 private colleges including 2 of 3 Indian colleges in the spring of 1996.

Health. In 1997 there were 60 licensed hospitals (3,478 beds).

Welfare. In fiscal year 1996, under Supplemental Security Income, there were on average 10,731 disabled persons receiving $42,965,196 in benefits; 131 blind persons received $505,556 and 2,462 aged persons received $4,378,038. Aid to Families with Dependent Children distributed $21,582,846 to 6,056 cases (average) involving 16,461 recipients (average) and 11,971 children (average).

FURTHER READING

Statistical information: State Data Center, Univ. of South Dakota, Vermillion 57069.
Governor's Budget Report. South Dakota Bureau of Finance and Management. Annual
South Dakota Historical Collections. 1902–82
South Dakota Legislative Manual. Secretary of State, Pierre, S.D. Biennial
Berg, F. M., *South Dakota: Land of Shining Gold.* Hettinger, 1982
Karolevitz, R. F., *Challenge: the South Dakota Story.* Sioux Falls, 1975
Milton, John R., *South Dakota; a Bicentennial History.* New York, 1977
Schell, H. S., *History of South Dakota.* 3rd ed. Lincoln, Neb., 1975
Vexler, R. I., *South Dakota Chronology and Factbook.* New York, 1978

State Library: South Dakota State Library, 800 Governor's Drive, Pierre, S.D. 57501–2294.

TENNESSEE

KEY HISTORICAL EVENTS

Bordered on the west by the Mississippi, Tennessee was part of an area inhabited by Cherokee. French, Spanish and British explorers penetrated the area up the Mississippi and traded with the Cherokee in the late 16th and 17th centuries. French claims were abandoned in 1763, colonists from the British colonies of Virginia and Carolina then began to cross the Appalachians westwards, but there was no organized Territory until after the War of Independence. In 1784 there was a short-lived, independent state called Franklin. In 1790 the South West Territory (including Tennessee) was formed, and Tennessee entered the Union as a state in 1796.

The state was active in the war against Britain in 1812. After the American victory, colonization increased and pressure for land mounted. The Cherokee were forcibly removed during the 1830s and taken to Oklahoma, a journey on which many died.

Tennessee was a slave state and seceded from the Union in 1861, although eastern Tennessee was against secession. There were important battles at Shiloh, Chattanooga, Stone River and Nashville. In 1866 Tennessee was readmitted to the Union.

Nashville, the capital since 1843, Memphis, Knoxville, and Chattanooga all developed as river towns, Memphis becoming an important cotton and timber port. Growth was greatly accelerated by the creation of the Tennessee Valley Authority in the 1930s, producing power for a manufacturing economy. Industry increased to the extent that, by 1970, the normal southern pattern of emigration and population loss had been reversed.

TERRITORY AND POPULATION
Tennessee is bounded north by Kentucky and Virginia, east by North Carolina, south by Georgia, Alabama and Mississippi and west by the Mississippi River (forming the boundary with Arkansas and Missouri). Land area, 41,220 sq. miles (106,759 sq. km). Census population, 1 April 1990, 4,877,185 (60·9% urban), an increase of 6·2% since 1980. Population estimate (1997), 5,368,000.

Population in 5 census years was:

	White	Black	Indian	Asiatic	Total	Per sq. mile
1910	1,711,432	473,088	216	53	2,184,789	52·4
1930	2,138,644	477,646	161	105	2,616,556	62·4
			All others			
1970	3,293,930	621,261	8,496		3,923,687	95·3
1980	3,835,452	725,942	29,726		4,591,120	111·6
1990	4,048,068	778,035	51,082		4,877,185	115·7

Of the population in 1990, 2,348,928 were male, 2,969,948 were urban and those 21 years of age or older numbered 3,421,633.

The cities, with population (1996) are Memphis, 596,725; Nashville (capital), 511,263; Knoxville, 167,535; Chattanooga, 150,425; Clarksville, 94,879; Johnson City, 55,542; Murfreesboro, 53,996; Jackson, 50,406; Kingsport, 41,335; Oak Ridge, 27,742. Metropolitan Statistical Areas, 1996 (1992): Memphis, 1,048,684 (1,033,183); Nashville, 1,117,178 (1,023,315); Knoxville, 649,277 (610,482); Chattanooga, 446,096 (430,848); Johnson City–Kingsport–Bristol, 458,229 (444,625); Clarksville, 186,368 (178,155); Jackson, 98,489 (80,230).

SOCIAL STATISTICS
Statistics 1996: births, 73,710 (13·9 per 1,000 population); deaths, 51,367 (9·7); infant deaths, 626 (8·5 per 1,000 live births); marriages, 82,031; divorces, 33,161.

CLIMATE
Memphis, Jan. 41°F (5°C), July 82°F (27·8°C). Annual rainfall 49" (1,221 mm). Nashville, Jan. 39°F (3·9°C), July 79°F (26·1°C). Annual rainfall 48" (1,196 mm). Tennessee belongs to the Appalachian Mountains climate zone (*see* UNITED STATES: Climate).

CONSTITUTION AND GOVERNMENT
The state has operated under 3 constitutions, the last of which was adopted in 1870 and has been since amended 22 times (first in 1953). Voters at an election may authorize the calling of a convention limited to altering or abolishing one or more specified sections of the constitution. The General Assembly consists of a Senate of 33 members and a House of Representatives of 99 members, senators elected for 4 years and representatives for 2 years. Qualified as electors are all citizens (usual residential and age (18) qualifications). Tennessee sends 9 representatives to Congress.

The capital is Nashville. The state is divided into 95 counties.

RECENT ELECTIONS
In the 1996 presidential election Clinton polled 905,999 votes; Dole, 860,809; Perot, 105,577.

CURRENT ADMINISTRATION
Governor: Don Sundquist (R.), 1999–2001 ($85,000).
  Lieut.-Governor: John Wilder (D.), ($49,500).
  Secretary of State: Riley C. Darnell (D.), ($80,700).

ECONOMY
Budget. For 1996 total state revenue was $14,749m.; general expenditure, $13,829m. (education, $4,383m.; public welfare, $3,958m.; health and hospitals, $1,058m.; highways, $1,233m.; police protection, $87m.). Outstanding debt in 1996, $3,069m.
  Per capita personal income (1997, preliminary) was $23,018.

ENERGY AND NATURAL RESOURCES
Water. The total area covered by water is approximately 926 sq. miles.

Minerals. Domestic non-fuel mineral production was worth $786m. in 1996.

Agriculture. In 1996, 80,000 farms covered 11·8m. acres. The average farm was of 148 acres, valued (land and buildings) at $225,088.
  Farm income (1996) from crops was $1,374m.; from livestock, $998m. Main crops were cotton, tobacco and soybeans.
  On 1 Jan. 1997 the domestic animals included 115,000 milch cows, 2·4m. all cattle, 13,500 sheep, 0·4m. swine.

Forestry. Forests occupy 13,258,000 acres. The forest industry and industries dependent on it employ about 0·04m. workers. Wood products are valued at over $500m. per year. National forest system land (1991) 626,000 acres.

INDUSTRY
The manufacturing industries include iron and steel working, but the most important products are chemicals, including synthetic fibres and allied products, electrical equipment and food. In 1995, manufacturing establishments employed 552,400 workers; value added by manufactures was $43,126m.

COMMUNICATIONS
Roads. In 1995 there were 85,599 miles of roads (65,793 miles rural). In 1994 there were 5,058,653 registered motor vehicles.

Rail. The state had (1995) 3,065 miles of track. There is a tramway in Memphis.

Civil Aviation. The state is served by 23 major and regional airlines. In 1997 Tennessee had 83 public airports; there were also 71 heliports and 2 military air bases.

SOCIAL INSTITUTIONS
Justice. The death penalty is authorized, but there has been no execution since 1960.
  Prison population, 30 June 1996, 13,817.

Religion. In 1990 there were 1,086,680 Southern Baptists, 320,724 United Methodists, 199,698 Black Baptists, 168,933 members of the Church of Christ, 137,203 Catholics and 18,377 members of the African Methodist Episcopal Zion.

Education. School attendance has been compulsory since 1925 and the employment of children under 16 years of age in workshops, factories or mines is illegal.
  In 1995–96 there were 1,562 public schools with a net enrolment of 948,217 pupils; 49,627 teachers earned an average salary of $33,646. Total expenditure for operating schools was $4,266m. Tennessee has 49 accredited colleges and universities, 16 2-year colleges and 27 vocational schools. The universities include the University of Tennessee, Knoxville (founded 1794), with 25,337 students in 1996–97, Vanderbilt University, Nashville (1873) with 10,253, Tennessee State University (1912) with 8,643, the University of Tennessee at Chattanooga (1886) with 8,296, University of Memphis (1912) with 19,271 and Fisk University (1866) with 812.

Health. In 1994 the state had 127 hospitals with 26,018 beds. State facilities for the mentally retarded had 1,290 resident patients and mental hospitals had 1,003 in 1996.

Welfare. In 1995 Tennessee paid $6,672m. to retired workers and their survivors and to disabled workers. Total beneficiaries: 587,940 retired; 172,110 survivors; 166,060 disabled. 1·5m. people received $2,772m. in Medicaid. Supplemental Security Income ($648m.) was paid to 179,676. In 1994, 294,733 people received aid to dependent children ($212m.).

CULTURE

Tourism. In 1994, 29·9m. out-of-state tourists spent $5,900m.

FURTHER READING

Statistical information: Center for Business and Economic Research, Univ. of Tennessee, Knoxville 37996. Publishes *Tennessee Statistical Abstract*

Tennessee Blue Book. Secretary of State, Nashville

Corlew, R. E., *Tennessee: a Short History.* 2nd ed. Univ. of Tennessee, 1981

Davidson, D., *Tennessee: Vol. I, The Old River Frontier to Secession,* Univ. of Tennessee, 1979

Dykeman, W., *Tennessee.* Rev. ed., New York, 1984

State Library: State Library and Archives, Nashville.

TEXAS

KEY HISTORICAL EVENTS

A number of Indian tribes occupied the area before French and Spanish explorers arrived in the 16th century. In 1685 La Salle established a colony at Fort St Louis, but Texas was confirmed as Spanish in 1713. Spanish missions increased during the 18th century with San Antonio (1718) as their headquarters.

In 1820 a Virginian colonist, Moses Austin, obtained permission to begin a settlement in Texas. In 1821 the Spanish empire in the Americas came to an end, and Texas, together with Coahuila, formed a state of the newly independent Mexico. The Mexicans agreed to the Austin venture, and settlers of British and American descent came in.

The settlers became discontented with Mexican government and declared their independence in 1836. Warfare, including the siege of the Alamo fort, ended with the foundation of the independent Republic of Texas, which lasted until 1845. During this period the Texas Rangers were organized as a policing force and border patrol. Texas was annexed to the Union in Dec. 1845, as the Federal Government feared its vulnerability to Mexican occupation. This led to war between Mexico and the USA from 1845 to 1848. In 1861 Texas left the Union and joined the southern states in the Civil War, being readmitted in 1869. Ranching and cotton-growing were the main activities before the discovery of oil in 1901.

TERRITORY AND POPULATION

Texas is bounded north by Oklahoma, north-east by Arkansas, east by Louisiana, south-east by the Gulf of Mexico, south by Mexico and west by New Mexico. Land area, 261,914 sq. miles (678,358 sq. km). Census population, 1990, 16,986,510 (80·3% urban). Population estimate (1997), 19,439,000.

Population for 5 census years was:

	White	Black	American Indian	Asian	Total	Per sq. mile
1910	3,204,848	690,049	702	943	3,896,542	14·8
1930	4,967,172	854,964	1,001	1,578	5,824,715	22·1
			All others			
1970	9,717,128	1,399,005	80,597		11,196,730	42·7
1980	11,197,663	1,710,250	1,320,470		14,228,383	54·2
				Asian/ other		
1990	12,774,762	2,021,632	65,877	2,124,239	16,986,510	64·9

Of the population in 1980, 6,998,301 were male, 11,327,159 persons were urban. Persons of Hispanic origin were also identified in the last 2 censuses, numbering 2,985,643 in 1980 and 4,339,905 in 1990.

The largest cities, with census population in 1993, are:

Houston	1,700,672	Garland	187,439	Mesquite	108,960
Dallas	1,036,309	Irving	166,523	Waco	107,191
San Antonio	991,861	Amarillo	163,569	Grand Prairie	103,913
El Paso	554,496	Plano	153,624	Wichita Falls	98,356
Austin (capital)	501,637	Laredo	140,688	Midland	95,003
Fort Worth	459,085	Pasadena	127,843	Odessa	92,257
Arlington	277,939	Beaumont	118,289	McAllen	91,184
Corpus Christi	266,958	Brownsville	117,326	Carollton	90,934
Lubbock	193,194	Abilene	100,661	San Angelo	87,980

Metropolitan statistical areas, 1993: Houston, 3,544,601; Dallas, 2,731,503; Fort Worth-Arlington, 1,379,539; San Antonio, 1,387,618.

SOCIAL STATISTICS
Statistics 1996: births, 330,238 (17·4 per 1,000 population); deaths, 139,678 (7·4); infant deaths, 2,079 (6·3 per 1,000 live births); marriages, 178,659 (9·4 per 1,000 population); divorces, 95,185 (5·0).

CLIMATE
Dallas, Jan. 45°F (7·2°C), July 84°F (28·9°C). Annual rainfall 38" (945 mm). El Paso, Jan. 44°F (6·7°C), July 81°F (27·2°C). Annual rainfall 9" (221 mm). Galveston, Jan. 54°F (12·2°C), July 84°F (28·9°C). Annual rainfall 46" (1,159 mm). Houston, Jan. 52°F (11·1°C), July 83°F (28·3°C). Annual rainfall 48" (1,200 mm). Texas belongs to the Central Plains climate zone (see UNITED STATES: Climate).

CONSTITUTION AND GOVERNMENT
The present constitution dates from 1876; it has been amended 364 times since. The Legislature consists of a Senate of 31 members elected for 4 years (half their number retire every 2 years), and a House of Representatives of 150 members elected for 2 years. It meets in odd-numbered years in Jan. The Governor and Lieut.-Governor are elected for 4 years.

The state sends 30 representatives to Congress.

The capital is Austin. The state has 254 counties.

RECENT ELECTIONS
In the 1996 presidential election Dole polled 2,736,167 votes; Clinton, 2,459,683; Perot, 377,530.

CURRENT ADMINISTRATION
Governor: George W. Bush (R.), 1999–2003 ($99,122).
  Lieut.-Governor: Bob Bullock (D.) ($7,200).
  Secretary of State: Antonio Garza (D.) ($76,966).

ECONOMY
Budget. For 1996 total state revenue was $51,118m.; general expenditure, $46,082m. (education, $17,049m.; public welfare, $10,636m.; health and hospitals, $3,079m.; highways, $3,563m.; police protection, $292m.). Outstanding debt in 1996, $14,576m.

Per capita personal income (1997, preliminary) was $23,656.

ENERGY AND NATURAL RESOURCES
Oil and Gas. Production, 1996: crude petroleum, 543m. bbls. (value, $11,035m.); natural gas 6,449bn. cu. ft (value, $14,768m.). Natural gasoline, butane and propane gases are also produced.

Water. The total area covered by water is approximately 5,363 sq. miles.

Minerals. Minerals include helium, crude gypsum, granite and sandstone, salt and cement. Total value of domestic non-fuel mineral products in 1997 was $1,700m.

TEXAS

Agriculture. Texas is one of the most important agricultural states. In 1995 it had 205,000 farms covering 127m. acres; average farm was of 620 acres. In 1995, land and buildings were valued at $550 per acre. Large-scale commercial farms, highly mechanized, dominate in Texas; farms of 1,000 acres or more in number far exceed that of any other state, but small-scale farming persists. Soil erosion is serious in some parts. For some 97,297,000 acres drastic curative treatment has been indicated, and for 51,164,000 acres, preventive treatment.

Production: corn, barley, beans, cotton, hay, oats, peanuts, rye, sorghum, soybeans, sunflowers, wheat, oranges, grapefruit, peaches, sweet potatoes. Farm income, 1996, from crops was $5,295m.; from livestock, $7,758m.

The state has an important livestock industry, leading in the number of all cattle (15·1m.) and sheep (1·7m.), both figures for 1995; it also had 0·4m. milch cows and 0·58m. swine in 1994.

Forestry. There were (1993) 22,032,000 acres of forested land.

INDUSTRY

In 1994 manufacturing establishments employed 1,015,800 workers; trade employed 1,889,400; government, 1,438,200; services, 2,014,500; construction, 393,000; finance, insurance and real estate, 445,300; transport and public utilities, 466,100. Chemical industries along the Gulf Coast, such as the production of synthetic rubber and of primary magnesium (from sea-water), are increasingly important.

Texas has a labour code (adopted 1993) which includes laws concerning protection of labourers, employer-employee relations, employment services and unemployment, and workers' compensation.

COMMUNICATIONS

Roads. In 1995 there were 296,186 miles of highways (including 4,474 miles of inter-state highways). In 1996 there were 15,274,000 registered motor vehicles.

Civil Aviation. In 1993 there were 307 public and 1,308 private airports.

Shipping. The port of Houston, connected by the Houston Ship Channel (50 miles long) with the Gulf of Mexico, is a large cotton market. Total cargo handled by all ports, 1990, 335,311,608 short tons.

SOCIAL INSTITUTIONS

Justice. In 1996 there were 132,383 men and women in state prisons. There have been more than 100 executions since 1982, and most recently in 1998.

Religion. Religious bodies represented include Roman Catholics, Baptists, Methodists, Churches of Christ, Lutherans, Presbyterians and Episcopalians.

Education. School attendance is compulsory from 6 to 18 years of age.

In 1995–96 public elementary and secondary schools had over 3,740,260 students; there were 240,371 teachers whose salaries averaged $31,400. State and Federal support for public schools, 1994–95, $11,256m.

In 1994 there were 138 higher education institutions (35 public, 38 independent colleges and universities, 50 public community college districts and 15 others). The largest institutions with student enrolment, 1995–96, were:

Founded	Institutions	Control	Students
1845	Baylor University, Waco	Baptist	12,202
1852	St Mary's University, San Antonio	R.C.	4,202
1869	Trinity University, San Antonio	Presb.	2,482
1873	Texas Christian University, Fort Worth	Christian	7,050
1876	Texas A. and M. Univ., College Station	State	38,636
1878	Prairie View Agr. and Mech. Coll., Prairie View	State	5,999
1879	Sam Houston State University	State	12,439
1883	University of Texas System (every campus)	State	136,597
1890	University of North Texas, Denton	State	25,122
1891	Hardin-Simmons University, Abilene	Baptist	2,373
1889	East Texas State University, Commerce	State	7,629
1899	South West Texas State University, San Marcos	State	20,929

Founded	Institutions	Control	Students
1901	Texas Woman's University, Denton	State	9,827
1906	Abilene Christian University, Abilene	Church of Christ	4,436
1911	Southern Methodist University, Dallas	Methodist	8,986
1912	Rice University	Independent	4,099
1923	Lamar University, Beaumont	State	8,419
1923	Stephen F. Austin State University	State	11,781
1923	Texas Technical University, Lubbock	State	24,185
1925	Texas A&M University, Kingsville	State	6,061
1927	University of Houston, Houston	State	30,358
1947	Texas Southern University, Houston	State	9,458

Health. In 1995, the state had 498 hospitals (70,881 beds) listed by the American Hospital Association. In the fiscal year 1989, the average daily census of patients was: State hospitals, 3,629; state schools, 7,265 and state centres, 331.

Welfare. Aid is from state and federal sources. Number of Social Security beneficiaries in 1996 was 2,498,000, who received an average of $722 (for retired workers), $697 (for disabled workers) and $687 (for widows/widowers) per month.

FURTHER READING
Texas Almanac. Dallas. Biennial
Cruz, G. R. and Irby, J. A. (eds.) *Texas Bibliography.* Austin, 1982
Fehrenbach, T. R., *Lone Star: A History of Texas and the Texans.* London, 1986
Jordan, T. G. and Bean, J. L., Jr., *Texas.* Boulder, 1983
Kingston, M. *Texas Almanac's Political History of Texas.* Austin, 1992
Kraemer, R. and Newell, C. *Essentials of Texas Politics.* 5th ed. Austin, 1992
MacCorkle, S. A. and Smith, D., *Texas Government.* 7th ed. New York, 1974
Marten, J., *Texas* [Bibliography]. Santa Barbara and Oxford (CA), 1992

Legislative Reference Library: Box 12488, Capitol Station, Austin, Texas 78711-2488.

UTAH

KEY HISTORICAL EVENTS
Spanish Franciscan missionaries explored the area in 1776, finding Shoshoni Indians. Spain laid claim to Utah and designated it part of Spanish Mexico. As such it passed into the hands of the Mexican Republic when Mexico rebelled against Spain and gained independence in 1821.

In 1848, at the conclusion of war between the USA and Mexico, the USA received Utah along with other south-western territory. Settlers had already arrived in 1847 when the Mormons (the Church of Jesus Christ of Latter-day Saints) arrived, having been driven on by local hostility in Ohio, Missouri and Illinois. Led by Brigham Young, they entered the Great Salt Valley and colonized it. In 1849 they applied for statehood but were refused. In 1850 Utah and Nevada were joined as one Territory. The Mormon community continued to ask for statehood but this was only granted in 1896, after they had renounced polygamy and disbanded their People's Party.

Mining, especially of copper, and livestock farming were the base of the economy. Settlement had to adapt to desert conditions, and the main centres of population were in the narrow belt between the Wasatch Mountains and the Great Salt Lake. Salt Lake City, the capital, was founded in 1847 and laid out according to Joseph Smith's plan for the city of Zion. It was the centre of the Mormons' provisional 'State of Desert' and Territorial capital from 1856 until 1896, except briefly in 1858 when federal forces occupied it during conflict between territorial and Union governments.

TERRITORY AND POPULATION
Utah is bounded north by Idaho and Wyoming, east by Colorado, south by Arizona and west by Nevada. Land area, 82,168 sq. miles (212,816 sq. km). The Bureau of Indian Affairs in 1990 administered 2,317,604 acres, 2,284,766 acres of which were allotted to Indian tribes.

UTAH

Census population, 1 April 1990, 1,722,850 (87% urban), an increase of 17·92% since 1980. Population estimate (1997), 2,059,000.

Population at 5 federal censuses was:

	White	Black	Indian	Asiatic	Total	Per sq. mile
1910	366,583	1,144	3,123	2,501	373,851	4·5
1930	499,967	1,108	2,869	3,903	507,847	6·2
1960	873,828	4,148	6,961	5,207	890,627	10·8
1970	1,031,926	6,617	11,273	6,230	1,059,273	12·9
1980	1,382,550	9,225	19,256	15,076	1,461,037	17·7

Of the total in 1980, 724,501 were male, 1,232,908 persons were urban; 860,304 were 20 years of age or older.

The largest cities are Salt Lake City, with a population (census, 1990) of 159,936; West Valley City, 86,976; Provo, 86,835; Sandy City, 75,058; Orem, 67,561; Ogden, 63,905.

SOCIAL STATISTICS
Births in 1995 were 39,577 (20·3 per 1,000 population); deaths, 11,000 (5·6); infant mortality rate, 5·4 (per 1,000 live births). Marriages (1996, provisional), 22,000; divorces, 9,300.

CLIMATE
Salt Lake City, Jan. 29°F (−1·7°C), July 77°F (25°C). Annual rainfall 16" (401 mm). Utah belongs to the Mountain States climate region (*see* UNITED STATES: Climate).

CONSTITUTION AND GOVERNMENT
Utah adopted its present constitution in 1896 (now with 61 amendments). The Legislature consists of a Senate (in part renewed every 2 years) of 29 members, elected for 4 years, and of a House of Representatives of 75 members elected for 2 years. It sits annually in Jan. The Governor is elected for 4 years. The constitution provides for the initiative and referendum.

The state sends 3 representatives to Congress.

The capital is Salt Lake City. There are 29 counties in the state.

RECENT ELECTIONS
In the 1996 presidential election Dole polled 359,394 votes; Clinton, 220,197; Perot, 66,100.

CURRENT ADMINISTRATION
Governor: Mike Leavitt (R.), 1996–2000 ($77,250).
Lieut.-Governor and Secretary of State: Olene S. Walker (R.) ($60,000).

ECONOMY
Budget. In 1996 total state revenue was $6,773m. Total expenditure was $6,172m. (education, $2,751m.; public welfare, $952m.; health and hospitals, $440m.; highways, $357m.; police protection, $44m.). Debt outstanding was $2,464m.
Per capita income (1997, preliminary) was $20,432.

ENERGY AND NATURAL RESOURCES
Water. The total area covered by water is approximately 2,736 sq. miles.

Minerals. The principal minerals are: Copper, gold, magnesium, petroleum, lead, silver and zinc. The state also has natural gas, clays, tungsten, molybdenum, uranium and phosphate rock. The value of domestic non-fuel mineral production in 1997 was $1,760m.

Agriculture. In 1996 Utah had some 13,300 farms covering 11m. acres. Of the total surface area, 9% is severely eroded and only 9·4% is free from erosion; the balance is moderately eroded. In 1985 about 2m. acres were crop land, and about 300,000 acres pasture and about 1m. acres had irrigation. In 1996 the average farm was of 821 acres and the average value per acre in 1995 was $606.

Farm income, 1996, from crops, $227m. and from livestock, $646m. The principal crops are: barley, wheat (spring and winter), oats, potatoes, hay (alfalfa, sweet clover and lespedeza), maize. Livestock, 1990: cattle, 855,000; pigs, 34,000; Sheep 0·6m.; poultry, 3·8m.

Forestry. Area of national forests, 1991, was 9,128,000 acres, of which 8,014,000 acres were under forest service administration.

INDUSTRY
In 1996 manufacturing establishments had 129,000 workers. Leading manufactures by value added are primary metals, ordinances and transport, food, fabricated metals and machinery, and petroleum products. Service industries employed 256,000; trade, 231,000; government, 167,000.

COMMUNICATIONS
Roads. In 1995 there were 41,044 miles of roads (34,817 miles rural). In 1995 there were 1,447,000 registered motor vehicles.

Rail. On 1 July 1974 the state had 1,734 miles of railways.

Civil Aviation. There is an international airport at Salt Lake City.

SOCIAL INSTITUTIONS
Justice. In 1996 there were 3,471 prisoners in state correctional institutions. The death penalty is authorized.

Religion. Latter-day Saints (Mormons) numbered 1,551,000 in 1997. World membership was 9,025,000. The President of the Mormon Church is Howard Hunter (born 1908). The Roman Catholic church and most Protestant denominations are represented.

Education. School attendance is compulsory for children from 6 to 18 years of age. There are 40 school districts. Teachers' salaries, 1994–95, averaged $29,672. There were 471,557 pupils and 21,778 teachers in public elementary and secondary schools in the same year. In 1994 education expenditure by state and local government was $2,251·2m.

In 1994 there were 146,196 enrolled in colleges and universities. The University of Utah (1850) (24,770 students in 1985–86) is in Salt Lake City; the Utah State University (1890) (11,804) is in Logan. The Mormon Church maintains the Brigham Young University at Provo (1875) with 26,894 students. Other colleges include: Westminster College, Salt Lake City (1,302); Weber State College, Ogden (11,117); Southern Utah State College, Cedar City (2,587); College of Eastern Utah, Price (1,132); Snow College, Ephraim (1,328); Dixie College, St George (2,234).

Health. In 1995 the state had 42 community hospital facilities (4,200 beds).

Welfare. In 1996, 228,000 beneficiaries received $1,782m. annual benefit payments.

FURTHER READING
Statistical information: Bureau of Economic and Business Research, Univ. of Utah, 401 Kendall D. Garff Bldg., Salt Lake City 84112. Publishes *Statistical Abstract of Utah.*
Utah Foundation. *Statistical Review of Government in Utah.* Salt Lake City, 1991
Arrington, L., *Great Basin Kingdom: An Economic History of the Latter-Day Saints, 1830–1900.* Cambridge, Mass., 1958
Petersen, C. S., *Utah: a History.* New York, 1977

VERMONT

KEY HISTORICAL EVENTS
The original Indian hunting grounds of the Green Mountains and lakes was explored by the Frenchman Samuel de Champlain in 1609 who reached Lake Champlain on the north-west border. The first attempt at permanent settlement was also French, on Isle la Motte in 1666. In 1763 the British gained the area from the French by the

VERMONT

Treaty of Paris. The Treaty, which also brought peace with the Indian allies of the French, opened the way for settlement, but in a mountain state transport was slow and difficult. Montpelier, the state capital from 1805, was chartered as a township site in 1781 to command the main pass through the Green Mountains.

During the War of Independence Vermont declared itself an independent state, to avoid being taken over by New Hampshire and New York. In 1791 it became the 14th state of the Union.

Most early settlers were New Englanders of British and Protestant descent. After 1812 a granite-quarrying industry grew around the town of Barre, attracting immigrant workers from Italy and Scandinavia. French Canadians also settled in Winooski. When textile and engineering industries developed in the 19th century these brought more European workers.

Vermont saw the only Civil War action north of Pennsylvania, when a Confederate raiding party attacked from Canada in 1864.

During the 20th century the textile and engineering industries have declined but paper and lumber industries flourish. Settlement is still mainly rural or in small towns, and farming is pastoral.

TERRITORY AND POPULATION

Vermont is bounded in the north by Canada, east by New Hampshire, south by Massachusetts and west by New York. Land area, 9,614 sq. miles (23,955 sq. km). Census population, 1 April 1990, 562,758 (32·2% urban), an increase of 10% since 1980. Population estimate (1997), 589,000.

Population at 5 census years was:

	White	Black	Indian	Asiatic	Total	Per sq. mile
1910	354,298	1,621	26	11	355,956	39·0
1930	358,966	568	36	41	359,611	38·8
1960	389,092	519	57	172	389,881	42·0
1980	506,736	1,135	984	1,355	511,456	55·1
1990	555,088	1,951	1,696[1]	3,215[2]	562,758	60·8

[1]Includes Eskimo and Aleut. [2]Includes Pacific Islander.

Of the population in 1990, 275,492 were male; 180,904 were urban; those 20 years of age or older numbered 400,019. The largest cities are Burlington, with a population (1996 estimate) of 39,004; Rutland, 17,605; Essex, 16,498 (1994 estimate); Colchester, 16,400.

SOCIAL STATISTICS

Births, 1995, were 6,783 (11·6 per 1,000 population); deaths, 4,949 (8·5); infant deaths, 41 (6·0 per 1,000 live births); marriages, 6,000 (10·3 per 1,000 population); divorces, 2,520 (4·3).

CLIMATE

Burlington, Jan. 17°F (−8·3°C), July 70°F (21·1°C). Annual rainfall 33" (820 mm). Vermont belongs to the New England climate zone (*see* UNITED STATES: Climate).

CONSTITUTION AND GOVERNMENT

The constitution was adopted in 1793 and has since been amended. Amendments are proposed by two-thirds vote of the Senate every 4 years, and must be accepted by two sessions of the legislature; they are then submitted to popular vote. The state Legislature, consisting of a Senate of 30 members and a House of Representatives of 150 members (both elected for 2 years), meets in Jan. every year. The Governor and Lieut.-Governor are elected for 2 years. Electors are all citizens who possess certain residential qualifications and have taken the freeman's oath set forth in the constitution.

The state sends 1 representative to Congress.

The capital is Montpelier (8,254 in 1990). There are 14 counties and 251 cities, towns and other administrative divisions.

RECENT ELECTIONS

In the 1996 presidential election Clinton polled 137,030 votes; Dole, 79,675; Perot, 30,491.

UNITED STATES OF AMERICA

CURRENT ADMINISTRATION
Governor: Howard Dean (D.), 1998–2000 ($80,724).
  Lieut.-Governor: Douglas Racine (D.) ($33,654).
  Secretary of State: Deborah Markowitz (D.) ($50,794).

ECONOMY
Budget. In 1996 total state revenue was $2,146m. Total expenditure was $2,061m. (education, $623m.; public welfare, $516m.; health and hospitals, $60m.; highways, $189m.; police protection, $34m.). Debt outstanding in 1996 was $1,718m.
  Per capita income (1997, preliminary) was $23,401.

Banking and Finance. In 1998 there were 29 banking institutions domiciled in Vermont, and 4 out-of-state banks operating.

ENERGY AND NATURAL RESOURCES
Water. The total area covered by water is approximately 366 sq. miles. There are 46 utility-owned hydro-sites and 35 independently owned sites providing about 10% of Vermont's energy.

Minerals. Stone, chiefly granite, marble and slate, is the leading mineral produced in Vermont, contributing about 60% of the total value of mineral products. Other products include asbestos, talc, sand and gravel. Value of domestic non-fuel mineral products, 1997, approximately $68m.

Agriculture. Agriculture is the most important industry. In 1996 the state had some 6,000 farms covering 1m. acres; the average farm was of 225 acres in 1996 and in 1995 the average value per acre was $1,479. Farm income, 1995, from livestock and products, $380m.; from crops, $35m. The dairy farms produced about 2,538,000 lbs of milk in 1995. The chief agricultural crops are hay, apples and silage. In 1995 Vermont had 290,000 cattle and calves, 19,500 sheep and lambs, 2,800 hogs and pigs, and 134,000 chickens and turkeys.

Forestry. In 1994 the harvest was 251,159m. bd ft, of which 50,663m. bd ft was veneer logs, and 415,985 cords of pulpwood and boltwood.
  The state is 76% forest, with 10% in public ownership. National forests area (1996), 350,000 acres. State-owned forests, parks, fish and game areas, 250,000 acres; municipally owned, 38,500 acres.

INDUSTRY
In 1996 service industries employed 82,000; trade, 65,000; manufacturing, 46,000; government, 45,000; construction, 13,000.

COMMUNICATIONS
Roads. The state had 13,991 miles of roads in 1998, including 7,376 miles of gravel, graded and drained, or unimproved roads. Motor vehicle registrations, 1996, 724,846 (including motor cycles and mopeds).

Rail. There were, in 1988, 793 miles of railway, 291 of which was leased by the state to private operators.

Civil Aviation. There were 18 airports in 1990, of which 11 were state operated, 1 municipally owned and 6 private. Some are only open in summer.

Telecommunications. In 1997, 11 telephone companies provided 426,199 access lines. Total net income, $35,785,373.

SOCIAL INSTITUTIONS
Justice. As of midnight on 11 Sept. 1997, prisons and centres had 1,238 inmates. The death penalty is not authorized.

Religion. The principal denominations are Roman Catholic, United Church of Christ, United Methodist, Protestant Episcopal, Baptist and Unitarian–Universalist.

Education. School attendance during the full school term is compulsory for children from 7 to 16 years of age, unless they have completed the 10th grade or undergo approved home instruction. In 1994–95 the public elementary and secondary schools had 101,045 pupils and 7,410 teachers. Average teacher's salary was $36,681. State and local governments expenditure on public schools, 1994, $569·2m.

In the autumn of 1997 there were 36,239 students in higher education. The University of Vermont (1791) had 10,368 students in 1997–98; Norwich University (1834, founded as the American Literary, Scientific and Military Academy in 1819), had 2,791; St Michael's College (1904), 2,729; there are 5 state colleges.

Health. In 1995 the state had 14 community hospitals (1,800 beds).

Welfare. Old-age assistance (Supplemental Security Income) was being granted in 1993 to 3,654 (including aged, blind and disabled) persons, drawing an average of $320·42 per month; aid to dependent children was being granted to 26,986 persons, drawing an average of $194·25 per month; and aid to the permanently and totally disabled was being granted to 10,177 persons, drawing an average of $355·36.

CULTURE

Broadcasting. In 1998 there were 55 radio stations, 7 television stations and 8 cable TV stations.

Press. There were 9 dailies and 23 weekly newspapers in 1998.

Festivals. Of particular importance are the Marlboro Music Festival (Marlboro) and the Vermont Maple Festival (St Albans).

Libraries. In 1996 there were approximately 573 libraries.

FURTHER READING
Statistical information: Office of Policy Research and Coordination, Montpelier 05602
Legislative Directory. Secretary of State, Montpelier. Biennial
Vermont Annual Financial Report. Auditor of Accounts, Montpelier. Annual
Vermont Year-Book, formerly *Walton's Register.* Chester. Annual
Bassett T. (ed.) *Vermont: A Bibliography of its History,* Boston, 1981
Vermont Atlas and Gazetteer, Rev. ed., Freeport, 1983
Morrissey, C. T., *Vermont,* New York, 1981

State Library: Vermont Dept. of Libraries, Montpelier.

VIRGINIA

KEY HISTORICAL EVENTS
In 1607 a British colony was founded at Jamestown, on a peninsula in the James River, to grow tobacco. The area was marshy and unhealthy but the colony survived and in 1619 introduced a form of representative government. The tobacco plantations expanded and African slaves were imported. Jamestown was later abandoned, but tobacco-growing continued and spread through the eastern part of the territory.

In 1624 control of the colony passed from the Virginia Company of London to the Crown. Growth was rapid during the 17th and 18th centuries. The movement for American independence was strong in Virginia; George Washington and Thomas Jefferson were both Virginians, and crucial battles of the War of Independence were fought there.

When the Union was formed, Virginia became one of the original states, but with reservations regarding the constitution because of its attachment to slave-owning. In 1831 there was a slave rebellion. The tobacco plantations began to decline, and plantation owners turned to the breeding of slaves. While the eastern plantation lands seceded from the Union in 1861, the small farmers and miners of the western hills refused to secede and remained in the Union as West Virginia.

Richmond, the capital, became the capital of the Confederacy. Much of the Civil War's decisive conflict took place in Virginia, with considerable damage to the economy. After the war the position of the black population was little improved. Blacks remained without political or civil rights until the 1960s.

TERRITORY AND POPULATION
Virginia is bounded north-west by West Virginia, north-east by Maryland, east by the Atlantic, south by North Carolina and Tennessee and west by Kentucky. Land area, 39,598 sq. miles (102,558 sq. km). Census population, 1 April 1990, 6,187,358 (69·4% urban), an increase of 15·73% since 1980. Population estimate (1997), 6,734,000.

Population for 5 federal census years was:

	White	Black	Indian	Asian/Other	Total	Per sq. mile
1910	1,389,809	671,096	539	168	2,061,612	51·2
1930	1,770,441	650,165	779	466	2,421,851	60·7
1960	3,142,443	816,258	2,155	4,725	3,966,949	99·3
				All others		
1980	4,230,000	1,008,311		108,517	5,346,818	134·7
1990	4,791,739	1,162,994	15,282	217,343	6,187,358	155·9

Of the total population in 1990, 49% were male, 69·4% were urban and 70·7% were 21 years of age or older.

The population (census of 1990) of the principal cities was: Virginia Beach, 393,069; Norfolk, 261,229; Richmond, 203,056; Newport News, 170,045; Chesapeake, 151,976; Hampton, 133,793; Alexandria, 111,183; Portsmouth, 103,907.

SOCIAL STATISTICS
In 1995 there were 91,286 births (13·9 per 1,000 population), 52,507 deaths (9), 712 infant deaths under 1 year (7·8 per 1,000 live births), 67,858 marriages (10·3 per 1,000 population) and 29,629 divorces (4·5).

CLIMATE
Average temperatures in Jan. are 41°F in the Tidewater coastal area and 32°F in the Blue Ridge mountains; July averages, 78°F and 68°F respectively. Precipitation averages 36" in the Shenandoah valley and 44" in the south. Snowfall is 5-10" in the Tidewater and 25-30" in the western mountains. Norfolk, Jan. 41°F (5°C), July 79°F (26·1°C). Annual rainfall 46" (1,145 mm). Virginia belongs to the Atlantic Coast climate zone (*see* UNITED STATES: Climate).

CONSTITUTION AND GOVERNMENT
The present constitution dates from 1971. The General Assembly consists of a Senate of 40 members, elected for 4 years, and a House of Delegates of 100 members, elected for 2 years. It sits annually in Jan. The Governor and Lieut.-Governor are elected for 4 years.

The state sends 11 representatives to Congress.

The state capital is Richmond; the state contains 95 counties and 40 independent cities.

RECENT ELECTIONS
In the 1996 presidential election Dole polled 1,119,974 votes; Clinton, 1,070,990; Perot, 158,707.

CURRENT ADMINISTRATION
Governor: James S. Gilmore, III (R.), 1998–2002 ($124,855).
  Lieut.-Governor: John H. Hager (R.) ($36,321).
  Secretary of the Commonwealth: Anne P. Petera (R.).

ECONOMY
Budget. In 1996 total state revenue was $20,072m. Total expenditure was $17,717m. (education, $6,430m.; public welfare, $2,916m.; health and hospitals, $1,613m.; highways, $2,011m.; police protection, $313m.). The outstanding debt in 1996 stood at $8,793m.

Per capita personal income (1997, preliminary) was $26,438.

ENERGY AND NATURAL RESOURCES

Water. The total area covered by water is approximately 2,729 sq. miles.

Minerals. Coal is the most important mineral, with output (1994) of 37,129,301 short tons. Lead and zinc ores, stone, sand and gravel, lime and titanium ore are also produced. Total domestic non-fuel mineral output was valued at $600m. in 1997.

Agriculture. In 1996 there were 48,000 farms with an area of 8·6m. acres; the average farm had 179 acres, and the average value per acre was $1,771 in 1995. Farm income, 1995, from field crops, $556·2m.; from greenhouse, nursery and tree produce, $138·63m.; from vegetables, $87·8m.; from fruits, $52·19m. and from livestock and livestock products, $1,393·18m. The chief crops are tobacco, soybeans, peanuts, winter wheat, maize, tomatoes, apples, potatoes and sweet potatoes. Livestock, 1 Jan. 1996: Cattle and calves, 1·8m.; milch cows, 128,000; sheep and lambs, 84,000; 1 Dec. 1995: Hogs and pigs, 0·38m.; 1995: Turkeys, 23·5m.; broilers, 260·1m.

Forestry. Forests covered 16,026,874 acres in 1992 (63·1% of the total land area).

INDUSTRY

The manufacture of cigars and cigarettes and of rayon and allied products and the building of ships lead in value of products. In 1996 manufacturing employed 399,000 people out of a total non-agricultural workforce of 3,130,000.

COMMUNICATIONS

Roads. In 1995 there were 67,155 miles of roads (52,848 miles rural in 1993). In 1994 there were 5,383,500 registered motor vehicles.

Rail. In 1992 there were 3,295 miles of Class I track including commuter services to Washington.

Civil Aviation. There are international airports at Norfolk, Dulles, Richmond and Newport News.

SOCIAL INSTITUTIONS

Justice. Prison population, June 1996, 25,242 in federal and state prisons. The death penalty is authorized. The last execution was in 1997.

Religion. The principal churches are the Baptist, Methodist, Protestant-Episcopal, Roman Catholic and Presbyterian.

Education. Elementary and secondary instruction is free, and for ages 6–17 attendance is compulsory.

In 1994–95 the 133 school districts had, in primary schools, 684,000 pupils and 43,000 teachers and in public high schools, 377,000 pupils and 28,000 teachers. Teachers' salaries averaged $32,700 (primary school) and $35,300 (high school). Total expenditure on education, 1994–95, was $6,435m.

In 1993–94 there were 87 higher education institutions (48 private) including:

Founded	Name and place of college	Staff 1994–95	Students 1994
1693	College of William and Mary, Williamsburg (State)	479	7,547
1749	Washington and Lee University, Lexington	166	1,990
1776	Hampden-Sydney College, Hampden-Sydney (Pres.)	84	970
1819	University of Virginia, Charlottesville (State)	987	21,421
1832	Randolph-Macon College, Ashland (Methodist)	79	1,093
1832	University of Richmond, Richmond (Baptist)	228	4,258
1838	Virginia Commonwealth University, Richmond	777	21,523
1839	Virginia Military Institute Lexington (State)	97	1,179
1865	Virginia Union University, Richmond	83	1,525
1868	Hampton University	303	5,769
1872	Virginia Polytechnic Institute and State University	1,466	25,842
1882	Virginia State University, Petersburg	168	4,007
1908	James Madison University, Harrisonburg	520	11,680
1910	Radford University (State)	394	9,105
1930	Old Dominion University, Norfolk	634	16,49
1956	George Mason University (State)	677	21,774

Health. In 1994 the state had 123 hospitals listed by the American Hospital Association.

Welfare. In 1993 there were 901,000 Social Security beneficiaries (average monthly grant $642); 118,000 Supplemental Security Income beneficiaries (average monthly grant $279); 779,000 Medicare beneficiaries (average monthly grant $259); 576,000 recipients of Medicaid; 195,000 recipients of aid to families with dependent children (average monthly payment per family $262); 11,399 persons receiving Black Lung benefits (average monthly payment $373), and 10,650 children enrolled in the Head Start programme. In 1994 there were 232,000 households (547,000 persons) participating in the federal Food Stamp programme and 601,000 students participating in the National School Lunch programme; a total of 210,116 persons received some form of state-sponsored public assistance.

Total annual payments to beneficiaries in 1996 were $7,372m.

CULTURE

Tourism. Domestic tourists spent about $9,076m. in 1993.

FURTHER READING

Statistical information: Cooper Center for Public Service, Univ. of Virginia, 918 Emmet St. N., Suite 300, Charlottesville 22903-4832. Publishes *Virginia Statistical Abstract.—Population Estimates of Virginia Cities and Counties.*

Dabney, V., *Virginia, the New Dominion.* 1971

Gottmann, J., *Virginia in our Century.* Charlottesville, 1969

Morton, R. L., *Colonial Virginia.* 2 vols. Univ. Press of Virginia, 1960

Rouse, P. *Virginia: a Pictorial History.* New York, 1975

Rubin, L. D. Jr., *Virginia: a Bicentennial History.* Norris, 1977

State Library: Virginia State Library, Richmond 23219.

WASHINGTON

KEY HISTORICAL EVENTS

The strongest Indian tribes in the 18th century were Chinook, Nez Percé, Salish and Yakima. The area was designated by European colonizers as part of the Oregon Country. Between 1775 and 1800 it had been claimed by explorers for Spain, Britain and the USA; the dispute between the two latter nations was not settled until 1846.

The first small white settlements were Indian missions and fur-trading posts. In the 1840s American settlers began to push westwards along the Oregon Trail, making a speedy solution of the dispute with Britain necessary. When this was achieved the whole area was organized as the Oregon Territory in 1848, and Washington was made a separate Territory in 1853.

Apart from trapping and fishing, the important industry was logging, mainly to supply building timbers to the new settlements of California. After 1870 the westward extension of railways helped to stimulate settlement. Statehood was granted in 1889. The early population was composed mainly of Americans from neighbouring states to the east, and Canadians. Scandinavian immigrants followed. Seattle, the chief city, was laid out in 1853 as a saw-milling town and named after the Indian chief who had ceded the land and befriended the settlers. It grew as a port during the Alaskan and Yukon gold-rushes of the 1890s. The economy thrived on exploiting the Columbia River for hydro-electric power.

TERRITORY AND POPULATION

Washington is bounded north by Canada, east by Idaho, south by Oregon with the Columbia River forming most of the boundary, and west by the Pacific. Land area, 66,582 sq. miles (172,447 sq. km). Lands owned by the federal government, 1993, were 12·7m. acres or 29·8% of the total area. Census population, 1 April 1990, 4,866,663 (76·4% urban), an increase of 17·83% since 1980. Population estimate (1997), 5,606,800.

WASHINGTON

Population in 5 federal census years was:

	White	Black	Indian	Asian/Other	Total	Per sq. mile
1910	1,109,111	6,058	10,997	15,824	1,141,990	17·1
1930	1,521,661	6,840	11,253	23,642	1,563,396	23·3
1960	2,751,675	48,738	21,076	31,725	2,853,214	42·8
1980	3,779,170	105,574	60,804	186,608	4,132,156	62·1
1990	4,308,937	149,801	81,483	326,471	4,866,663	73·1

Of the total population in 1990, 2,413,747 were male; 3,387,546 were 20 years of age or older.

There are 27 Indian reservations. Indian reservations in 1990 covered 2,718,516 acres, of which 2,250,731 acres were tribal lands.

Leading cities are Seattle, with a population in 1990 (and 1997 estimate) of 516,259 (536,600); Spokane, 177,165 (188,300); Tacoma, 176,664 (185,600); Vancouver, 46,380 (127,900); Bellevue, 86,872 (104,800). Others: Everett, 84,130; Federal Way, 75,960; Yakima, 63,510; Lakewood, 62,240; Kent, 62,006; Bellingham, 61,240; Shoreline, 50,380; Kennewick, 49,090; Renton, 45,920; Kirkland, 43,720; Redmond, 42,230.

SOCIAL STATISTICS
Births, 1997, were 77,000; deaths, 41,500; infant mortality rate (1995), 5·9 (per 1,000 live births). Marriages, 1996, were 41,537 (7·5 per 1,000 population); divorces, 28,012 (5·1).

CLIMATE
Seattle, Jan. 40°F (4·4°C), July 63°F (17·2°C). Annual rainfall 34" (848 mm). Spokane, Jan. 27°F (−2·8°C), July 70°F (21·1°C). Annual rainfall 14" (350 mm). Washington belongs to the Pacific Coast climate zone (*see* UNITED STATES: Climate).

CONSTITUTION AND GOVERNMENT
The constitution, adopted in 1889, has had 63 amendments. The Legislature consists of a Senate of 49 members elected for 4 years, half their number retiring every 2 years, and a House of Representatives of 98 members, elected for 2 years. The Governor and Lieut.-Governor are elected for 4 years.

The state sends 9 representatives to Congress.

The capital is Olympia. The state contains 39 counties.

RECENT ELECTIONS
In the 1996 presidential election Clinton polled 899,645 votes; Dole, 639,743; Perot, 161,642.

CURRENT ADMINISTRATION
Governor: Gary Locke (D.), 1997–2001 ($121,000).

ECONOMY
Budget. In 1996 total state revenue was $24,700m. General expenditure was $21,086m.: (education, $2,079m.; public welfare, $1,588m.; health and hospitals, $203m.; highways, $705m.; police protection, $39m.). Outstanding debt in 1996, $8,991m.

Per capita personal income (1997, preliminary) was $26,718.

ENERGY AND NATURAL RESOURCES
Water. The total area covered by water is approximately 4,055 sq. miles.

Minerals. Mining and quarrying are not as important as forestry, agriculture or manufacturing.

Agriculture. Agriculture is constantly growing in value because of more intensive and diversified farming, and because of the 1m.-acre Columbia Basin Irrigation Project.

In 1997 there were 36,000 farms with an acreage of 15·7m.; the average farm was 436 acres. Average value of farmland and buildings per acre in 1996 was $1,117. Apples, milk, wheat, potatoes, and cattle and calves are the top five commodities.

UNITED STATES OF AMERICA

On 1 Jan. 1997 livestock included 266,000 milch cows, 294,000 beef cows, and 50,000 sheep and lambs. Hogs and pigs as of 1 Dec. 1996 totalled 35,000 head.

Value of agricultural production in 1996 (in $1m.): Field crops, 2,046·3; fruit, 1,263·7; vegetables, 299·5; livestock, poultry and their products, 1,464·8.

Forestry. Forests cover 21,856,000 acres, of which 9m. acres are national forest. In 1995, timber harvested was an estimated 4,393m. bd ft. Acres planted or seeded, 1993, 163,442, not including natural re-seeding. Production of wood residues, 1992, included 2,671,000 tons of pulp and board.

Fisheries. Salmon and shellfish are important; total fish catch, 1995, was worth an estimated $170,597,000.

INDUSTRY

In 1996 manufacturing employed 344,100 workers, of whom 86,100 were in aerospace and 52,400 in the forest products industry. Principal manufactures: Aircraft, pulp and paper, lumber and plywood, aluminium, processed fruit and vegetables. In 1996 trade employed 590,900, service industries 649,200, and government 450,400.

COMMUNICATIONS

Roads. In 1996 there were 79,555 miles of roads and 5,383,000 registered motor vehicles.

Rail. In 1996 there were 3,090 route miles.

Civil Aviation. There are international airports at Seattle/Tacoma, Spokane and Boeing Field.

SOCIAL INSTITUTIONS

Justice. The adult inmates in state prisons on 30 June 1997 numbered 12,735. The death penalty is authorized. The last execution was in 1994.

Religion. Religious faiths represented include the Roman Catholic, United Methodist, Lutheran, Presbyterian and Episcopalian. There were 219,000 Latter-day Saints (Mormons) in 1997.

Education. Education is given free to all children between the ages of 5 and 21 years, and is compulsory for children from 8 to 15 years of age. In Oct. 1997 there were 990,389 pupils in elementary and secondary schools. In Oct. 1995 there were 46,883 classroom teachers, average salary, $39,900.

The University of Washington, founded 1861, at Seattle, had, autumn 1997, 36,355 students; and Washington State University at Pullman, founded 1890, for science and agriculture, had 20,020 students. Eastern Washington University had 7,537; Central Washington University, 8,438; The Evergreen State College, 4,084; Western Washington University, 11,476. All counts are state-funded enrolment students. Community colleges had (1996) a total of 172,643 state-funded and excess enrolment students.

Health. In fiscal year 1997 the 2 state hospitals for mental illness, the 1 mental health facility and the child study and treatment centre had, together, a daily average of 1,278 patients.

In 1997 there were 93 accredited acute hospitals (11,484 beds) and 4 psychiatric hospitals (215 beds). In Sept. 1997 there were 16,790 doctors, 4,860 dentists, 58,120 registered nurses and 5,855 pharmacists.

Welfare. Old-age assistance is provided for persons 65 years of age or older without adequate resources (and not in need of continuing home care) who are residents of the state. In July 1997 the following assistance was provided: 916 blind persons received a monthly average of $362·07; 13,305 aged, $302·06; 80,251 disabled, $377·99. Aid was also given to 156,995 children in 88,266 families, averaging $376·90 per family monthly.

FURTHER READING

Statistical information: State Office of Financial Management, POB 43113, Olympia 98504-3113. Publishes *Washington State Data Book*
Dodds, G.B., *American North-West: a History of Oregon and Washington.* Arlington (Ill), 1986
Swanson, T., *Political Life in Washington.* Pullman, 1985

WEST VIRGINIA

KEY HISTORICAL EVENTS

In 1861 the state of Virginia seceded from the Union over the issue of slave-owning. The 40 western counties of the state were composed of hilly country, settled by miners and small farmers who were not slave-owners. In 1862 these counties ratified an ordinance providing for the creation of a new state. On 20 June 1863 West Virginia became the 35th state of the Union.

The capital, Charleston, was an 18th-century fortified post on the early westward migration routes across the Appalachians. In 1795 local brine wells were tapped and the city grew as a salt town. Coal, oil, natural gas and a variety of salt brines were all found in due course. Huntington, the next largest town, developed as a railway terminus serving the same industrial area, and also providing transport on the Ohio river.

Three-quarters of the state is forest and settlement has been concentrated in the mineral-bearing Kanawha valley, along the Ohio river and in the industrial Monongahela valley of the north. More than half of the population is still classified as rural. The traditional small firms and small hill-mines, however, support few, and the majority of rural dwellers commute to industrial employment.

TERRITORY AND POPULATION

West Virginia is bounded in north by Pennsylvania and Maryland, east and south by Virginia, south-west by the Big Sandy River (forming the boundary with Kentucky) and west by the Ohio River (forming the boundary with Ohio). Total area, 24,232 sq. miles (62,761 sq. km). Census population, 1 April 1990, 1,793,477 (36·1% urban), a decrease of 8·01% since 1980. Population estimate (1997), 1,828,754.

Population in 6 federal census years was:

	White	Black	Indian	Asiatic	Total	Per sq. mile
1910	1,156,817	64,173	36	93	1,221,119	50·8
1940	1,614,191	114,893	18	103	1,729,205	71·8
1960	1,770,133	89,378	181	419	1,860,421	77·3
1970	1,673,480	67,342	751	1,463	1,744,237	71·8
1980	1,874,751	65,051	1,610	5,194	1,949,644	80·3
1990	1,725,523	56,295	2,458	7,459	1,793,477	74·0

Of the total population in 1990, 861,536 were male, and 647,853 lived in urban areas; those 19 years of age or older numbered 1,349,900.

The 1990 census population of the principal cities was: Charleston, 57,287; Huntington, 54,844. Others: Wheeling, 34,882; Parkersburg, 33,862; Morgantown, 25,879; Weirton, 22,124; Fairmont, 20,210; Clarksburg, 18,059.

SOCIAL STATISTICS

Statistics 1996: births, 20,744 (11·4 per 1,000 population); deaths, 20,314 (11·1); infant deaths, 150 (7·2 per 1,000 live births); marriages, 10,997 (6·0 per 1,000 population); divorces, 9,023 (4·9).

CLIMATE

Charleston, Jan. 34°F (1·1°C), July 76°F (24·4°C). Annual rainfall 40" (1,010 mm). West Virginia belongs to the Appalachian Mountains climate zone (see UNITED STATES: Climate).

CONSTITUTION AND GOVERNMENT

The present constitution was adopted in 1872; it has had 69 amendments. The Legislature consists of the Senate of 34 members elected for a term of 4 years, one-half being elected biennially, and the House of Delegates of 100 members, elected biennially. The Governor is elected for 4 years and may serve 1 successive term.

The state sends 3 representatives to Congress.

The state capital is Charleston. There are 55 counties.

RECENT ELECTIONS

In the 1996 presidential election Clinton polled 327,812 votes; Dole, 233,946; Perot, 71,639.

UNITED STATES OF AMERICA

CURRENT ADMINISTRATION

Governor: Cecil Underwood (R.), 1997–2001 ($90,000).
  Secretary of State: Ken Hechler (D.) ($65,000).

ECONOMY

Budget. In 1996 total state revenue was $6,866m.; general expenditure, $6,970m. (education, $2,079m.; public welfare, $1,588m.; health and hospitals, $203m.; highways, $705m.; police protection, $39m.). Outstanding debt in 1996, $2,830m.
  Estimated *per capita* personal income (1997) was $18,957.

Banking and Finance. There were 75 state banks and 38 national banks with a total of $18,011m. in deposits in 1996.

ENERGY AND NATURAL RESOURCES

Oil and Gas. Petroleum output (1997), 1·5m. bbls.; natural gas production, 181,641m. cu. ft.

Water. The total area covered by water is approximately 145 sq. miles.

Minerals. 38% of the state is underlain with mineable coal; 181·9m. short tons of coal were produced in 1997. Salt, sand and gravel, sandstone and limestone are also produced. The total non-fuel mineral output in 1997 was 17m. tons.

Agriculture. In 1997 the state had 20,000 farms with an area of 3·7m. acres; average size of farm was 185 acres and valued at $100 per acre. Livestock farming predominates.
  Cash income, 1995, from crops was $74·3m.; from government payments, $5·2m., and from livestock and products, $312·1m. Main crops harvested, 1997: hay (1·06m. tons); all corn (3·5m. bu.); tobacco (3·06m. lbs). Area of main crops, 1997: hay, 0·56m. acres; corn, 65,000 acres. Apples (105m. lbs) and peaches (13m. lbs) are important fruit crops (1997 figures).
  Livestock on farms, 1997, included 0·42m. cattle, of which 18,000 were milch cows; sheep, 40,000; hogs, 14,000; chickens, 1·79m. excluding broilers. Production (1997) included 381·4m. lbs broilers, 20·4m. doz. eggs; 87·3m. lbs turkey.

Forestry. State forests, 1997, covered 79,385 acres; national forests, 1,032,000 acres; 79% of the state is woodland.

Fisheries. In 1997, 6 state fish hatcheries and 2 federal hatcheries sold 236,000 lbs food-size trout and stocked 752,305 lbs trout, in addition to other types of fish.

INDUSTRY

In 1997, 2,065 manufactories had 81,559 production workers. Leading manufactures are primary and fabricated metals, glass, chemicals, wood products, textiles and apparel, machinery, plastics, speciality chemicals, aerospace, electronics, medical and related technologies and industrial products recycling.
  In Oct. 1997 non-agricultural employment was 710,600 of whom 164,000 were in trade, 134,000 in government and 199,000 in service industries. In 1998, 731,500 persons were employed in non-agricultural jobs.

INTERNATIONAL TRADE

Imports and Exports. The state's major export markets are the EU and Canada, with coal being a major export commodity. West Virginia staffs trade offices in Nagoya, Japan; Taipei, Taiwan; and Munich, Germany.

COMMUNICATIONS

Roads. In 1997 there were 37,662 miles of roads (34,928 miles rural) and 1,453,616 registered motor vehicles.

Rail. In 1997 the state had 2,633 miles of railway.

Civil Aviation. There were 37 public airports in 1997.

Shipping. There are some 300 miles of navigable rivers.

Postal Services. In 1997 there were 1,048 post offices.

SOCIAL INSTITUTIONS

Justice. The state court system consists of a Supreme Court, 31 circuit courts, and magistrate courts in each county. The Supreme Court of Appeals, exercising original and appellate jurisdiction, has 5 members elected by the people for 12-year terms. Each circuit court has from 1 to 7 judges (as determined by the Legislature on the basis of population and case-load) chosen by the voters within each circuit for 8-year terms.

There were 11 penal and correctional institutions which had, in Dec. 1998, 2,830 inmates. There were also (1998) 6 regional jails housing 1,398 county, state and federal inmates, and 7 juvenile facilities housing 76 juveniles. Capital punishment was abolished in 1965. The last execution was in 1959.

Religion. Chief denominations in 1997 were: United Methodists (119,648 members), Roman Catholics (98,224), Baptists American (86,000) and Southern (34,000).

Education. Public school education is free for all from 5 to 21 years of age, and school attendance is compulsory for all between the ages of 7 and 16 (school term, 200 days—180–185 days of actual teaching). The public schools are non-sectarian. In 1996–97 public elementary and secondary schools had 299,557 pupils and 20,888 classroom teachers. Average salary of teachers was $33,258. Total 1995–96 education expenditures, including higher education, $2,131·2m.

Leading institutions of higher education in the autumn of 1997:

Founded		Full-time students
1837	Marshall University, Huntington	13,596
1837	West Liberty State College, West Liberty	2,397
1867	Fairmont State College, Fairmont	6,619
1868	West Virginia University, Morgantown	22,238
1872	Concord College, Athens	2,780
1872	Glenville State College, Glenville	2,288
1872	Shepherd College, Shepherdstown	4,025
1891	West Virginia State College, Institute	4,603
1895	West Virginia Univ. Inst. of Technology, Montgomery	2,554
1895	Bluefield State College, Bluefield	2,496
1901	Potomac State College of West Virginia Univ., Keyser	1,209
1961	West Virginia Univ. at Parkersburg, Parkersburg	3,443
1972	West Virginia Graduate College, Institute	2,094
1976	School of Osteopathic Medicine, Lewisburg	261

In addition to the universities and state-supported schools, there are 2 community colleges (5,317 students in 1997), 10 denominational and private institutions of higher education (10,271 students in 1997) and 11 business colleges.

Health. In 1997 the state had 65 licensed hospitals and 54 licensed personal care homes, 141 skilled-nursing homes and 3 mental hospitals.

Welfare. The Department of Health Human Resources, originating in the 1930s as the Department of Public Assistance, is both state and federally financed. In 1997 expenditures for medical services totalled $602m., of which $441m. came from federal funds and $160m. from state funds. 6,240 payments totalling $1,019,837 were given as aid to families with dependant children (average award, $163·44 per month).

CULTURE

Broadcasting. In 1997 there were 165 commercial and public radio stations. Television stations numbered 13 commercial and 3 public.

Press. In 1997 daily newspapers numbered 23, weekly and college newspapers 86.

Tourism. There are 34 state parks, 8 state forests, 4 wildlife management areas and 2 state trails. Visitors are attracted to the area by whitewater rafting, hiking, skiing and biking.

Festivals. There are over 100 fairs and festivals throughout the year including: the Mountain State Art and Craft Fair, Cedar Lakes; West Virginia State Folk Festival, Glenville; and Preston County Buckwheat Festival, Kingwood.

Libraries. In 1997 there were 177 public libraries, 28 college and university libraries, and 46 special libraries.

Museums and Galleries. The main museums are Huntington Museum of Art, Huntington; Oglebay Institute, Wheeling; and Virginia State Museum, Charleston.

FURTHER READING

West Virginia Blue Book. Legislature, Charleston. Annual, since 1916

Statistical Handbook, 1997. West Virginia Research League, Charleston, 1997

West Virginia History. Archives and History. Charleston. Quarterly, from 1939. Annual, from 1985

Doherty, W. T., *West Virginia: Our Land, Our People.* Charleston, 1990

Forbes, H. M., *West Virginia History: A Bibliography and Guide to Research.* Morgantown, 1981

Lewis, R. L. and Hennen, J. C., *West Virginia History: Critical Essays on the Literature.* Kendall/Hunt Publishing, Dubuque, IA, 1993.

Rice, O. K., *West Virginia: A History.* 2nd ed. Univ. Press of Kentucky, Lexington, 1994

Williams, J. A., *West Virginia: A Bicentennial History.* New York, 1976

State Library: Archives and History, Division of Culture and History, Charleston.

WISCONSIN

KEY HISTORICAL EVENTS

The French were the first European explorers of the territory; Jean Nicolet landed at Green Bay in 1634, a mission was founded in 1671 and a permanent settlement at Green Bay followed. In 1763 French claims were surrendered to Britain. In 1783 Britain ceded them to the USA, which designated the Northwest Territory, of which Wisconsin was part. In 1836 a separate Territory of Wisconsin was organized, including the present Iowa, Minnesota and parts of the Dakotas.

Territorial organization was a great stimulus to settlement. In 1836 James Duane Dooty founded the town site of Madison and successfully pressed its claim to be the capital of the Territory even before it was inhabited. In 1848 Wisconsin became a state, with its present boundaries.

The city of Milwaukee was founded, on Lake Michigan, when Indian tribes gave up their claims to the land in 1831–33. It grew rapidly as a port and industrial town, attracting Germans in the 1840s, Poles and Italians 50 years later. The Lake Michigan shore was developed as an industrial area; the rest of the south proved suitable for dairy farming; the north, mainly forests and lakes, has remained sparsely settled except for tourist bases.

There is a Menominee Indian reservation in the north-east, where many of the 29,000 remaining Indians live. Since the Second World War there has been black immigration from the southern states to the industrial lake-shore cities.

TERRITORY AND POPULATION

Wisconsin is bounded north by Lake Superior and the Upper Peninsula of Michigan, east by Lake Michigan, south by Illinois, and west by Iowa and Minnesota, with the Mississippi River forming most of the boundary. Area, 56,154 sq. miles (145,439 sq. km), including 1,439 sq. miles of inland water, but excluding any part of the Great Lakes. Census population, 1 April 1990, 4,891,769 (65·7% urban), an increase of 4% since 1980. Estimated population (1997), 5,192,298.

Population in 5 census years was:

	White	*Black*	*All others*	*Total*	*Per sq. mile*
1910	2,320,555	2,900	10,405	2,333,860	42·2
1930	2,916,255	10,739	12,012	2,939,006	53·7
1960	3,858,903	74,546	18,328	3,951,777	72·2
1980	4,443,035	182,592	80,015	4,705,642	86·4
1990	4,512,523	244,539	134,767	4,891,769	90·1

Of the total population in 1990, 49% were male, 65·7% were urban and 73·7% were 18 years old or older.

WISCONSIN

Population of the large cities, 1990 census, was as follows:

Milwaukee	628,088	Waukesha	56,958	Fond du Lac	37,757
Madison	191,262	Eau Claire	56,856	Wausau	37,060
Green Bay	96,466	Oshkosh	55,006	Beloit	35,573
Racine	84,298	Janesville	52,133	Brookfield	35,184
Kenosha	80,352	La Crosse	51,003	Neenah	33,592
Appleton	65,695	Sheboygan	49,676	Greenfield	33,403
West Allis	63,221	Wauwatosa	49,366		

Population of larger metropolitan areas, 1990 census: Milwaukee, 1,432,149; Madison, 367,085; Appleton–Neenah, 315,121; Duluth–Superior (Minn.–Wis.), 239,971; Green Bay, 194,594; Racine, 175,034.

SOCIAL STATISTICS
Births in 1997 were 66,490 (13·0 per 1,000 population); deaths in 1996 were 45,107 (8·7); infant deaths (1996), 492 (7·3 per 1,000 live births). In 1997 there were 35,546 marriages (6·8 per 1,000 population); divorces and annulments, 17,289 (3·4).

CLIMATE
Milwaukee, Jan. 19°F (−7·2°C), July 70°F (21·1°C). Annual rainfall 29" (727 mm). Wisconsin belongs to the Great Lakes climate zone (*see* UNITED STATES: Climate).

CONSTITUTION AND GOVERNMENT
The constitution, which dates from 1848, has 138 amendments. The legislative power is vested in a Senate of 33 members elected for 4 years, one-half elected alternately, and an Assembly of 99 members all elected simultaneously for 2 years. The Governor and Lieut.-Governor are elected for 4 years.

The state sends 9 representatives to Congress.

The capital is Madison. The state has 72 counties.

RECENT ELECTIONS
In the 1996 presidential election Clinton polled 1,058,059 votes; Dole, 832,458; Perot, 218,043.

CURRENT ADMINISTRATION
Governor: Tommy G. Thompson (R.), 1999–2000 ($115,699).
  Lieut.-Governor: Scott McCallum (R.) ($60,183).
  Secretary of State: Douglas La Follette (D.) ($54,610).

Local Government. Wisconsin's 72 counties are governed by an elected county board. 9 counties elect a county executive and 6 appoint a county administrator. Most of the state's 189 cities elect a mayor and a common council. 10 cities hire a city manager. Other local units include villages, which elect a board and a board president, and towns which are governed by an elected town board.

ECONOMY

Policy. Wisconsin has a graduated individual income tax which ranges from 4·77% to 6·77% of gross income. Among the tax credits allowed are ones for school property tax, working families, married couples and 60% of capital gains. In 1997–98 corporate income tax was 7·9% of net income. The state levied a 5% sales tax on most goods. The gasoline tax was 25·4 cents per gallon. A shared revenue programme distributes money to municipalities and the state pays for two-thirds of public school costs. The state's Department of Commerce budgeted $63·8m. for various business assistance, loan and grant programmes in 1997–98.

Budget. In 1996 total state revenue was $24,365m.; general expenditure, $16,990m. (education, $5,324m.; public welfare, $3,193m.; health and hospitals, $969m.; highways, $1,172m.; police protection, $61m.). Outstanding debt, in 1996, $9,127m.
  Per capita personal income in 1997 was $24,199.

Banking and Finance. On 30 June 1998 there were 295 state chartered banks with assets of $56·6bn., and 61 federally chartered banks with $20·3bn. in assets. In 1997, 33 state chartered savings institutions had $9·3bn. in assets. As of 30 June 1998 there were 363 state chartered credit unions with $7·7bn. in assets.

ENERGY AND NATURAL RESOURCES

Electricity. 48,596m. kWh of electricity were produced in 1997; an additional 11,377m. kWh were imported. Fossil fuel plants accounted for 85·6% of state production, nuclear 6·1%, and hydropower 4·6%. Coal accounted for 69·6% of utility energy use in 1997; nuclear fuel 6·4%; renewable sources 13·2%; natural gas 2·4%; and electricity imports 19·4%.

Oil and Gas. Petroleum accounted for 30% of the total energy consumed in 1997 and natural gas 24%. Transportation accounted for 82% of petroleum consumption. Natural gas accounted for 53% of residential end use and petroleum 15%. There are no known petroleum or natural gas reserves in Wisconsin.

Water. The total area covered by water is approximately 11,186 sq. miles.

Minerals. Construction sand and gravel, crushed stone, industrial or specialty sand, lime, copper, gold and silver are the chief mineral products. Mineral production in 1997 was valued at over $389m. This value included $64m. of copper, gold and silver from the Flambeau Mine in Rusk County (which ceased operations in 1997), $111m. for construction sand and gravel, $128m. for crushed stone, $34m. for industrial or specialty sand and $32m. for lime. The value of all other minerals including crushed trap rock, silica stone, peat and gemstones was around $18m.

Agriculture. On 1 Jan. 1997 there were 79,000 farms (27,000 dairy farms) with a total acreage of 16·8m. acres and an average size of 213 acres, compared with 142,000 farms with a total acreage of 22·4m. acres and an average of 158 acres in 1959. In 1997 the average value per acre was $1,413. Cash receipts from products sold by Wisconsin farms in 1997, $5,755m.; $4,070m. from livestock and livestock products; and $1,684m. from crops.

Dairy farming is important, with 1·38m. milch cows. Production of cheese accounted for 29% of the USA's total. Production of the principal field crops in 1997 included: corn for grain, 402·6m. bu.; corn for silage, 10·95m. tons; oats, 20·8m. bu.; all hay, 5·9m. tons. Other crops of importance: 27·9m. cwt of potatoes, 5·7m. lbs of tobacco, 2·3m. bbls. of cranberries, 69·1m. tons of carrots and the processing crops of 717,700 tons of sweet corn, 104,400 tons of green peas, 195,000 tons of snap beans, 27,700 tons of cucumbers for pickles,10·5m. lbs of tart cherries, 50,100 tons of beets for canning, 80,100 tons of cabbage for kraut and 1·4m. cwt of cabbage for fresh market.

Wisconsin is also a major producer of mink pelts.

Forestry. Wisconsin has an estimated 16·0m. acres of forest land. Of 15·7m. acres of timberland (Oct. 1997), national forests covered 1·4m. acres; state forests, 0·7m.; county and municipal forests, 2·3m.; forest industry, 1·1m.; private land, 10·1m.

Growing stock (1996), 18,500m. cu. ft, of which 14,100m. cu. ft is hardwood and 4,400m. cu. ft softwood. Main hardwoods are maple, oak, aspen and basswood; main softwoods are red pine, white pine, northern white cedar and balsam fir. The timber industry employs 99,000, has a payroll of $3,400m. and shipments valued at $19,700m. (1996).

INDUSTRY

Wisconsin has much heavy industry, particularly in the Milwaukee area. Three-fifths of manufacturing employees work on durable goods. Industrial machinery is the major industrial group (17% of all manufacturing employment) followed by fabricated metals, food and kindred products, printing and publishing, paper and allied products, electrical equipment and transportation equipment. Manufacturing establishments in 1996 provided 23% of non-farm wage and salary workers, 29% of all earnings. The total number of establishments was 10,454 in 1994; the biggest concentration is in the south-east. In 1998 manufacturing employed 631,000 people out of a total non-agricultural workforce of 2,927,400.

Labour. Average annual pay per worker (1996) was $26,021 ($29,079 in Milwaukee metropolitan area). Median household income (1995–97) was $40,400. Women were 47% of the workforce in 1998. Workforce participation rates for people over 16 (1996) were 79·9% for males and 69·6% for females. Average weekly earnings ranged from $200 in the service sector to $580 in manufacturing in 1998. Average unemployment was 3·3% in 1998.

Trade Unions. Labour union membership numbered 468,000 in 1997 compared to 465,500 in 1983. In 1997 union members were 18·8% of the workforce whereas they were 23·8% of the workforce in 1983. Union membership declined from 36% of workers in the manufacturing sector in 1983 to 21·4% in 1997.

COMMUNICATIONS

Roads. The state had, on 1 Jan. 1997, 111,500 miles of highway. 77% of all roads in the state have a bituminous (or similar) surface. There are 11,813 miles of state trunk roads and 19,621 miles of county trunk roads.

On 1 July 1997 Wisconsin registered 4,339,088 motor vehicles.

Rail. On 31 Dec. 1996 the state had 5,403 track-miles of railway.

Civil Aviation. There were, in 1998, 100 publicly operated airports. 9 scheduled air carrier airports were served by 15 regional and national air carriers.

Shipping. Lake Superior and Lake Michigan ports handled 47·9m. tons of freight in 1994; 87% of it at Superior, one of the world's biggest grain ports, and much of the rest at Milwaukee and Green Bay.

SOCIAL INSTITUTIONS

Justice. The state's penal, reformatory and correctional system on 4 Dec. 1998 held 16,707 men and 1,107 women in 12 prisons, 17 community facilities and other institutions for adult offenders, including contract beds in county jails, federal facilities, 699 males in Texas county jails, and 1,553 males in private prisons in Oklahoma and Tennessee. The probation and parole system was supervising 65,820 adults (31 Aug. 1998), and 622 males and 101 females were being supervised under intensive sanctions (which is being phased out). Parole for new convictions will officially end 31 Dec. 1999. Average daily population in the state's 5 juvenile institutions as at 4 Dec. 1998 was 909 males and 84 females.

Religion. Wisconsin church affiliation, as a percentage of the 1990 population, was estimated at 31·8% Catholic, 20·1% Lutheran, 3·2% Methodist, 9·5% other churches and 35·4% un-affiliated.

Education. All children between the ages of 6 and 18 are required to attend school full-time to the end of the school term in which they become 18 years of age. In 1997–98 the public school grades kindergarten-12 had 861,784 pupils and 56,564 (full-time equivalent) teachers. Private schools enrolled 135,727 students grades kindergarten-12. Public pre-schools enrolled 19,464 children, and private, 11,617. Children taught in home schools numbered 18,712. Public elementary teachers' salaries, 1995–96, averaged $38,043; secondary, $39,424.

In 1995–96 vocational, technical and adult schools had an enrolment of 431,405 and 4,351 (full-time and part-time) teachers and 2 Indian tribe community colleges enrolled 670 (autumn 1996). There is a school for the visually handicapped and a school for the deaf.

The University of Wisconsin, established in 1848, was joined by law in 1971 with the Wisconsin State Universities System to become the University of Wisconsin System with 13 degree granting campuses, thirteen 2-year campuses in the Center System, and the University Extension. The system had, in 1997–98, 6,611 full-time professors and instructors. In autumn 1997, 150,818 students enrolled (10,486 at Eau Claire, 5,419 at Green Bay, 9,086 at La Crosse, 40,196 at Madison, 22,251 at Milwaukee, 10,960 at Oshkosh, 4,537 at Parkside, 4,843 at Platteville, 5,441 at River Falls, 8,458 at Stevens Point, 7,145 at Stout, 2,557 at Superior, 10,564 at Whitewater and 8,875 at the Center System freshman-sophomore centres).

UW-Extension enrolled 251,651 students in its continuing education programmes in 1996–97. There are also several independent institutions of higher education. These (with autumn 1997 enrolment) include 3 universities (16,226), 16 colleges (28,461), 4 technical and professional schools (4,991), and 5 theological seminaries (449). The state's educational and broadcasting service is licensed through the UW Board of Regents.

The total expenditure, 1995–96, for all public education (except capital outlay and debt service) was $9,075m. ($1,779 per capita).

Health. In fiscal year 1996 the state had 123 general medical and surgical hospitals (13,967 beds), 13 psychiatric hospitals (789 beds), 2 treatment centres for alcohol and drug abuse (60 beds) and 1 physical rehabilitation hospital (69 beds). There were 2 state mental hospitals (587 beds) and 3 US Veterans' Administration hospitals. Patients in state mental hospitals and institutions for the developmentally disabled averaged 1,795 in 1995. On 31 Dec. 1997 the state had 466 licensed nursing homes with 44,613 residents.

Welfare. On 1 Jan. 1974 the US Social Security administration assumed responsibility for financial aid (Supplemental Security Income) to persons 65 years old and over, blind persons and totally disabled persons, who satisfy requirements as to need. Recipients receive a federal payment plus a federally administered state supplementary payment, except for those who reside in a medical institution. In Dec. 1997, there were 108,328 SSI recipients in the state; payments (1998) were $578 for a single individual, $624 for an eligible individual with an ineligible spouse, and $873 for an eligible couple. A special payment level of $674 for an individual and $1,218 for a couple may be paid with special approval for SSI recipients who are developmentally disabled or chronically mentally ill, living in a non-medical living arrangement not his or her own home. All SSI recipients receive state medical assistance coverage.

Wisconsin completed its conversion to the W-2 (Wisconsin Works) programme on 31 March 1998, ending the 62-year-old Aid to Families with Dependent Children (AFDC) programme. W-2 clients (31 Dec. 1998) totalled 13,093 with 9,078 receiving cash assistance. W-2 clients must be working, seeking employment, or be enrolled in job-training programmes. Recipients are limited to 60 months of financial assistance (consecutive or non-consecutive). Participants are eligible for child care assistance, a state subsidized health plan, job and transportation assistance and food stamps. In Dec. 1998 there were 71,382 food stamp recipients and 144,874 medical assistance (medicaid) clients.

CULTURE
There are 2 professional opera companies in Wisconsin: the Madison Opera, and the Florentine Opera in Milwaukee.

Broadcasting. In 1998 there were 32 commercial TV stations; 8 educational TV stations; 255 commercial radio stations; and 49 non-commercial.

Press. There were 36 daily newspapers in 1998.

Tourism. The tourist-vacation industry ranks among the first three in economic importance with an estimated $6,735m. spent in 1996. The Department of Tourism budgeted $13,101,800 to promote tourism in 1998–99.

Festivals. Summer music festivals include: the Great River Jazz Fest; the River Folk Fest (both take place in La Crosse, Milwaukee); and the Peninsula Music Festival, Door County.

Museums and Galleries. Attractions include the Madison and Milwaukee Art Museums; Leigh Yawkey Woodson Art Museum, Wausau; and Wisconsin Veterans' Museum, Madison.

FURTHER READING
Dictionary of Wisconsin Biography. Wisconsin Historical Society, Madison, 1960
Wisconsin Blue Book. Wisconsin Legislative Reference Bureau, Madison. Biennial
Current, R. N., *Wisconsin, a History.* New York, 1977
Danziger, S. and Witte, J. F., *State Policy Choices: The Wisconsin Experience.* Univ. Wisconsin Press, 1988
Martin, L., *The Physical Geography of Wisconsin.* Univ. Wisconsin Press, 3rd ed., 1965
Nesbit, R. C., *Wisconsin, A History.* State Historical Society of Wisconsin, Madison, rev. ed., 1989
Robinson, A. H. and Culver, J. B., (eds.) *The Atlas of Wisconsin.* Univ. Wisconsin Press, 1974
Vogeler, I., *Wisconsin: A Geography.* Boulder, 1986
State Historical Society of Wisconsin: *The History of Wisconsin.* Vol. I [Alice E. Smith], Madison, 1973.—Vol. II [R. N. Current], Madison, 1976.—Vol. III [R. C. Nesbit], Madison, 1985.—Vol. IV [W. F. Thompson], Madison, 1988.—Vol. V (P. W. Glad), Madison, 1990

State Information Agency: Legislative Reference Bureau, 100 N. Hamilton St., P.O. Box 2037, Madison, WI 53701-2037. *Chief:* Stephen R. Miller.

WYOMING

KEY HISTORICAL EVENTS
The territory was inhabited by Plains Indians (Arapahoes, Sioux and Cheyenne) in the early 19th century. There was some trading between them and white Americans, but very little white settlement. In the 1840s the great western migration routes, the Oregon and the Overland Trails, ran through the territory, Wyoming offering mountain passes accessible to wagons. Once migration became a steady flow it was necessary to protect the route from Indian attack, and forts were built.

In 1867 coal was discovered. In 1868 Wyoming was organized as a separate Territory, and in 1869 the Sioux and Arapaho were confined to reservations. At the same time the route of the Union Pacific Railway was laid out, and working settlements and railway towns grew up in southern Wyoming. Settlement of the north was delayed until after the final defeat of hostile Indians in 1876.

The economy of the settlements at first depended on ranching. Cheyenne had been made Territorial capital in 1869, and also functioned as a railway town moving cattle. Casper, on the site of a fort on the Pony Express route, was also a railway town on the Chicago and North Western. Laramie started as a Union Pacific construction workers' shanty town in 1868. In 1890 oil was discovered at Casper, and Wyoming became a state in the same year. Subsequently, mineral extraction became the leading industry, as natural gas, uranium, bentonite and trona were exploited as well as oil and coal.

TERRITORY AND POPULATION
Wyoming is bounded north by Montana, east by South Dakota and Nebraska, south by Colorado, south-west by Utah and west by Idaho. Land area, 97,105 sq. miles (251,501 sq. km). The Yellowstone National Park occupies about 2·22m. acres; the Grand Teton National Park has 307,000 acres. The federal government in 1986 owned 49,838 sq. miles (50·9% of the total area of the state). The Federal Bureau of Land Management administers 17,546,188 acres.

Census population, 1 April 1990, 453,588 (65% urban), a decrease of 3·66% since 1980. Population estimate (1997), 480,000.

Population in 5 census years was:

	White	Black	American Indian	Asiatic	Total	Per sq. mile
1910	140,318	2,235	1,486	1,926	145,965	1·5
1930	221,241	1,250	1,845	1,229	225,565	2·3

	White	Black	All others	Total	Per sq. mile
1970	323,619	2,568	6,229	332,416	3·4
1980	446,488	3,364	19,705	469,557	4·8

	White	Black	American Indian	Asian/ Pacific Islands	Other	Total	Per sq. mile
1990	427,061	3,606	9,479	2,806	10,636	453,588	4·7

Of the total population in 1990, 227,007 were male and those over 18 years of age numbered 318,063.

The largest towns (with 1990 census population) are Cheyenne, 50,008; Casper, 46,742; Laramie, 26,687; Rock Springs, 19,050; Gillette, 17,635; Sheridan, 13,900; Green River, 12,711.

SOCIAL STATISTICS
Births in 1995 were 6,261; deaths, 3,720; marriages, 5,037; divorces, 3,149; infant deaths, 48 (7·7 per 1,000 live births).

CLIMATE
Cheyenne, Jan. 25°F (−3·9°C), July 66°F (18·9°C). Annual rainfall 15" (376 mm). Yellowstone Park, Jan. 18°F (−7·8°C), July 61°F (16·1°C). Annual rainfall 18" (444 mm). Wyoming belongs to the Mountain States climate region (see UNITED STATES: Climate).

CONSTITUTION AND GOVERNMENT
The constitution, drafted in 1890, has since had 43 amendments. The Legislature consists of a Senate of 30 members elected for 4 years, 15 retiring every 2 years, and a House of Representatives of 60 members elected for 2 years. It sits annually in Jan. or Feb. The Governor is elected for 4 years.

The state sends 1 representative to Congress.

The capital is Cheyenne. The state contains 23 counties.

RECENT ELECTIONS
In the 1996 presidential election Dole polled 105,347 votes; Clinton, 77,807; Perot, 25,854.

CURRENT ADMINISTRATION
Governor: Jim Geringer (R.), 1999–2003 ($95,000).
Secretary of State: Joseph B. Meyer (R.) ($77,000).

ECONOMY

Budget. In 1996 total state revenue was $2,348m. General expenditure was $2,062m. (education, $659m.; public welfare, $253m.; health and hospitals, $118m.; highways, $270m.; police protection, $12m.). Outstanding debt, in 1996, $799m.

Average income *per capita* (1997, provisionally) was $22,648.

Banking and Finance. In June 1997 there were 21 national and 37 state banks with a total of $6,789,441,000 deposits.

ENERGY AND NATURAL RESOURCES

Oil and Gas. Wyoming is largely an oil-producing state. In 1995 the output of oil was 75·6m. bbls.; natural gas, 994,300m. cu. ft.

Water. The total area covered by water is approximately 714 sq. miles.

Minerals. In 1992 there were 620 mining establishments. 1995 production: Coal, 263·9m. short tons; trona, 18·1m. short tons; uranium, 1·3m. lbs; bentonite, 4·3m. short tons. Total value of non-fuel mineral production, 1996, $316·7m.

Agriculture. Wyoming is semi-arid, and agriculture is carried on by irrigation and dry farming. In 1996 there were 9,100 farms and ranches; total farm area in 1996 was 34·6m. acres; average size of farm in 1996 was 3,802 acres, and average value per acre in 1995 was $192. In 1995, 12,594 people were employed on farms.

Total value, 1996, of crops produced, $297m.; of livestock and products, $411m. Crop production in 1996 (1,000 bushels): Corn for grain, 6,150; wheat, 7,110; oats, 1,696; barley, 10,320; sugar-beet, 1,074 tons. Animals on farms in 1996 included 1·49m. cattle, 0·72m. sheep and 35,000 hogs and pigs. Total egg production in 1996 was 2·4m.

Forestry. In 1992 there were 9,704 acres of gross forest land.

Fisheries. In 1991 the production of fish hatchery was 522,388 lbs.

INDUSTRY
In 1995 there were 604 manufacturing establishments. In 1995 there were 620 mining establishments. A large portion of the manufacturing in the state is based on natural resources, mainly oil and farm products. Leading industries are food, wood products (except furniture) and machinery (except electrical). The Wyoming Industrial Development Corporation assists in the development of small industries by providing credit.

Labour. In June 1997 the mining industry employed 15,700 wage and salary workers; construction, 15,500; manufacturing, 10,900; transportation and public utilities, 13,900. The total civilian labour force in June 1997 was 262,643, of whom 255,077 were employed; non-agricultural wage and salary employment, 231,300.

WYOMING

The unemployment rate was 4·3% in June 1997. Total wages paid in covered employment in 1990, $3,825m.

Trade Unions. There were 21,694 working members in trade unions (10·2% of total employment) in 1989.

COMMUNICATIONS

Roads. In 1995 there were 2,298 miles of urban roads and 32,911 miles of rural roads, the latter including (1990, in miles): Federal, 3,882; state, 6,226; county, 13,636. There were 590,750 motor vehicle registrations in 1994.

Rail. In 1995, 1,795 miles of Class I railway were operated.

Civil Aviation. There were 10 towns with commuter air services and 2 towns on jet routes in 1995.

SOCIAL INSTITUTIONS

Justice. In the third quarter of 1995 there were 1,190 prisoners in state adult correctional institutions. The death penalty is authorized.

Religion. Chief religious bodies in 1990 were the Roman Catholic (with 59,565 members), Latter-day Saints (Mormons) (54,000 in 1997) and Protestant churches (110,375). There were 5,000 members of the Eastern Orthodox Church in 1972.

Education. In 1996–97 public elementary and secondary schools had 98,777 pupils and 6,690 teachers. In 1990–91 enrolment in the parochial elementary and secondary schools was about 3,500. The average expenditure per pupil for 1996–97 was $5,638. State and local government expenditure in 1991 was $839·2m.

The University of Wyoming, founded at Laramie in 1887, had in academic year 1996–97, 11,251 students. There were 7 community colleges in 1991–92 with 20,517 students.

Health. In 1993 the state had 29 general hospitals with 1,998 beds, and 37 registered nursing homes with 2,899 beds.

Welfare. In the fiscal year 1995, $24·6m. was distributed in food stamps; $19·6m. in aid to families with dependent children; and $129m. in Medicaid. Total expenditure on public assistance and social services programmes, fiscal year 1992, $190·1m.

CULTURE

Broadcasting. In 1995 there were 29 AM, 35 FM radio stations and 9 television stations.

Press. In 1995 there were 9 daily newspapers.

Tourism. There are over 7m. tourists annually, mainly outdoor enthusiasts. The state has large elk and pronghorn antelope herds, 10 fish hatcheries and numerous wild game. In 1995, 7,933,493 people visited the 6 national areas; 2,147,633 people visited state parks and historic sites. In 1990, 811,183 fishing, game and bird licences were sold. There were (1994) 9 operational ski areas.

FURTHER READING

Statistical information: Department of Administration and Information, 327 E. Emerson Bldg., Cheyenne 82002. Publishes *Wyoming Data Handbook*
Equality State Almanac. Wyoming Department of Administration and Information, Cheyenne, WY 82002
Wyoming Official Directory. Secretary of State. Cheyenne, annual
Wyoming Data Handbook. Dept. of Administration and Information. Division of Economic Analysis. Cheyenne, annual
Brown, R. H., *Wyoming: A Geography.* Boulder, 1980
Larsen, T. A., *History of Wyoming.* Rev. ed. Univ. of Nebraska, 1979
Treadway, T., *Wyoming.* New York, 1982

OUTLYING TERRITORIES

GUAM

KEY HISTORICAL EVENTS

Magellan is said to have discovered the island in 1521; it was ceded by Spain to the USA by the Treaty of Paris (10 Dec. 1898). The island was captured by the Japanese on 10 Dec. 1941, and retaken by American forces from 21 July 1944. Guam is of great strategic importance; substantial numbers of naval and air force personnel occupy about one-third of the usable land.

TERRITORY AND POPULATION

Guam is the largest and most southern island of the Marianas Archipelago, in 13° 26' N. lat., 144° 43' E. long. Total area, 209 sq. miles (541 sq. km). Agaña, the seat of government is about 8 miles from the anchorage in Apra Harbor. The census on 1 April 1990 showed a population of 133,152, an increase of 27,173 since 1980 (62,207 female). Estimate, 1996, 157,000; density, 290 per sq. km. In 1995 an estimated 61·7% of the population lived in rural areas. In 1990 those of Guamanian ancestry numbered 63,504. The Malay strain is predominant. The native language is Chamorro; English is the official language and is taught in all schools.

SOCIAL STATISTICS

1996: birth rate, 24·2 per 1,000 population; death rate, 3·9 per 1,000 population; infant mortality rate, 15·7 per 1,000 live births. Life expectancy, 1990–95, was 72·2 years for males and 76·0 years for females. Fertility rate, 1990–95, 3·4 births per woman.

CLIMATE

Tropical maritime, with little difference in temperatures over the year. Rainfall is copious at all seasons, but is greatest from July to Oct. Agaña, Jan. 81°F (27·2°C), July 81°F (27·2°C). Annual rainfall 93" (2,325 mm).

CONSTITUTION AND GOVERNMENT

Guam's constitutional status is that of an 'unincorporated territory' of the USA. Entry of US citizens is unrestricted; foreign nationals are subject to normal regulations. In 1949–50 the President transferred the administration of the island from the Navy Department (who held it from 1899) to the Interior Department. The transfer conferred full citizenship on the Guamanians, who had previously been 'nationals' of the USA. There was a referendum on status on 30 Jan. 1982. 38% of eligible voters voted; 48·5% of those favoured Commonwealth status.

The Governor and his staff constitute the executive arm of the government. The legislature is a 21-member Senate; its powers are similar to those of an American state legislature.

RECENT ELECTIONS

At the election of 3 Nov. 1998 for the Guam Legislature the Republican Party won 12 seats. Guam returns 1 non-voting delegate to the House of Representatives.

CURRENT ADMINISTRATION

Governor: Carl Gutierrez (D.), 1999–2003.
Lieut.-Governor: Madeleine Bordallo.

ECONOMY

Budget. Total revenue (1991) $525m.; expenditure $395m.

Banking and Finance. Banking law makes it possible for foreign banks to operate in Guam.

ENERGY AND NATURAL RESOURCES

Electricity. Installed capacity was 302,000 kW in 1993. Production was 750m. kWh in 1994. Consumption per capita in 1995 was estimated at 4,566 kWh.

Water. The total area covered by water is approximately 7 sq. miles. Supplies are from springs, reservoirs and groundwater; 65% comes from water-bearing limestone in the north. The Navy and Air Force conserve water in reservoirs. The Water Resources Research Centre is at Guam University.

Agriculture. The major products of the island are sweet potatoes, cucumbers, water melons and beans. In 1994 there were approximately 15,000 acres of arable land, 15,000 acres of permanent cropland and 20,000 acres of pasture. Livestock (1996) included 1,000 goats and 4,000 pigs. Commercial productions (1983) amounted to 6·6m. lbs of fruit and vegetables ($3·4m.), 567,000 doz. eggs ($811,093). There is an agricultural experimental station at Inarajan.

Fisheries. In 1995 total catches were 919,300 lbs (417 tonnes), of which 54% were marine fish.

INDUSTRY

Guam Economic Development Authority controls three industrial estates: Cabras Island (32 acres); Calvo estate at Tamuning (26 acres); Harmon estate (16 acres). Industries include textile manufacture, cement and petroleum distribution, warehousing, printing, plastics and ship-repair. Other main sources of income are construction and tourism.

Labour. In 1990 there were 90,990 persons of employable age, of whom 66,138 were in the workforce (54,186 civilian). 2,042 were unemployed.

INTERNATIONAL TRADE

Guam is the only American territory which has complete 'free trade'; excise duties are levied only upon imports of tobacco, liquid fuel and liquor. In 1984 imports were valued at $493m. and exports at $34m.

COMMUNICATIONS

Roads. There are 674 km of all-weather roads. In 1995 there were 79,800 passenger cars and 34,700 commercial vehicles.

Civil Aviation. There is an international airport at Tamuning. 7 commercial airlines serve Guam.

Shipping. There is a port at Apra Harbor.

Telecommunications. Overseas telephone and radio dispatch facilities are available. Main telephone lines numbered 71,100 in 1997 (453·1 per 1,000 inhabitants). Cellular phone subscribers numbered 5,000 in 1995.

SOCIAL INSTITUTIONS

Justice. The Organic Act established a District Court with jurisdiction in matters arising under both federal and territorial law; the judge is appointed by the President subject to Senate approval. There is also a Supreme Court and a Superior Court; all judges are locally appointed except the Federal District judge. Misdemeanours are under the jurisdiction of the police court. The Spanish law was superseded in 1933 by 5 civil codes based upon California law.

Religion. About 98% of the Guamanians are Roman Catholics; the other 2% are Baptists, Episcopalians, Bahais, Lutherans, Latter-day Saints (Mormons), Presbyterians, Jehovah's Witnesses and members of the Church of Christ and Seventh Day Adventists.

Education. 8 years of primary education to the age of 16 are compulsory. There are Chamorro Studies courses and bi-lingual teaching programmes to integrate the Chamorro language and culture into elementary and secondary school courses. In 1988-89 there were 18,713 pupils in primary schools and 7,223 in secondary schools. There were 1,403 teachers in 1986. There is a University of Guam.

Welfare. There is a hospital, 8 nutrition centres, a school health programme and an extensive immunization programme. Emphasis is on disease prevention, health education and nutrition. In 1990, $83·2m. was paid in Federal direct payments for individuals, including $1·91m. Medicare, $1·91m. disability insurance and $11·37m. retirement insurance.

CULTURE

Broadcasting. There are 4 commercial stations, a commercial television station, a public broadcasting station and a cable television station with 24 channels. In 1995 there were 211,000 radio and 100,000 TV sets (colour by NTSC).

Press. There is 1 daily newspaper, a twice-weekly paper, and 4 weekly publications (all of which are of military or religious interest only).

Tourism. There were 1,361,830 tourist arrivals in 1995, bringing in revenue of US$1·27bn.

FURTHER READING

Report (Annual) of the Governor of Guam to the US Department of Interior
Guam Annual Economic Review. Economic Research Center, Agaña

Carano, P. and Sanchez, P. C., *Complete History of Guam.* Rutland, VT, 1964
Rogers, R. F., *Destiny's Landfall: a History of Guam.* Hawaii Univ. Press, 1995
Wuerch, W. L. and Ballendorf, D. A., *Historical Dictionary of Guam and Micronesia.* Metuchen, NJ, 1995

COMMONWEALTH OF THE NORTHERN MARIANA ISLANDS

KEY HISTORICAL EVENTS

In 1889 Spain ceded Guam (largest and southernmost of the Marianas Islands) to the USA and sold the rest to Germany. Occupied by Japan in 1914, the islands were administered by Japan under a League of Nations mandate until occupied by US forces in August 1944. In 1947 they became part of the US-administered Trust Territory of the Pacific Islands. On 17 June 1975 the electorate adopted a covenant to establish a Commonwealth in association with the USA; this was approved by the US government in April 1976 and came into force on 1 Jan. 1978. In Nov. 1986 the islanders were granted US citizenship. The UN terminated the Trusteeship status on 22 Dec. 1990.

TERRITORY AND POPULATION

The Northern Marianas form a single chain of 16 mountainous islands extending north of Guam for about 560 km, with a total area of 5,050 sq. km (1,950 sq. miles) of which 464 sq. km (179 sq. miles) are dry land, and with a population (1990 Census) of 43,345 (urban, 12,151; female, 20,543). 16,752 persons were born in the Islands. The projected population for 2000 is 72,000. In 1995 an estimated 53·6% of the population lived in urban areas.

The areas and populations of the islands are as follows:

Island(s)	Sq. km	1980 Census	1990 Census
Northern Group[1]	171	·104	36
Saipan	122	14,585	38,896
Tinian (with Aguijan)	101[2]	899	2,118
Rota	83	1,274	2,295

[1]Pagan, Agrihan, Alamagan and 9 uninhabited islands.   [2]Including uninhabited Aguijan.

In 1980, 55% spoke Chamorro, 11% Woleaian and 13% Filipino languages, but English remains the official language. The largest town is Chalan Kanoa on Saipan.

COMMONWEALTH OF THE NORTHERN MARIANA ISLANDS

SOCIAL STATISTICS

In 1996 the birth rate was 33 per 1,000 population and the death rate 4·6 per 1,000 population. Infant mortality was 38 per 1,000 live births.

CONSTITUTION AND GOVERNMENT

The Constitution was approved by a referendum on 6 March 1977 and came into force on 9 Jan. 1978. The legislature comprises a 9-member *Senate*, with 3 Senators elected from each of the main 3 islands for a term of 4 years, and an 18-member *House of Representatives*, elected for a term of 2 years.

The Commonwealth is administered by a Governor and Lieut.-Governor, elected for 4 years.

RECENT ELECTIONS

At the elections of Nov. 1997 the Republican Party won 8 seats and the Democratic Party 1 in the Senate; the Republicans won 13 and the Democrats 5 in the House of Representatives.

CURRENT ADMINISTRATION

Governor: Pedro Pangelinan Trenorio (R.), 1998–2002.
Lieut.-Governor: Juan Babauta.

ENERGY AND NATURAL RESOURCES

Water. The total area covered by water is approximately 10 sq. miles.

Fisheries. In 1995 total catches were 423,300 lbs (192 tonnes), almost entirely from marine waters.

INDUSTRY

Labour. In 1990 there were 7,476 workers from the indigenous population and 21,188 were foreign workers; 2,699 were unemployed.

INTERNATIONAL TRADE

Imports and Exports. In 1991 imports totalled $392·4m.; exports were $263·4m.

COMMUNICATIONS

Roads. There are about 381 km of roads.

Civil Aviation. Air Micronesia provides inter-island services. There are 5 airports in all.

Telecommunications. There were 21,000 main telephone lines in 1996, or 428·1 for every 1,000 persons.

SOCIAL INSTITUTIONS

Religion. The population is predominantly Roman Catholic.

Education. In 1989 there were 18 primary schools with 4,882 pupils and 9 secondary schools with 2,075 pupils. The tertiary college on Saipan had 1,097 students.

Health. In 1986 there were 23 doctors, 4 dentists, 103 nursing personnel, 2 pharmacists and 2 midwives. In 1988 there was 1 hospital with 70 beds.

CULTURE

Broadcasting. In 1989 there were 10,500 radio and 4,100 television receivers, 3 radio stations and a 15-channel cable TV station in Saipan.

Tourism. In 1995 there were 676,161 visitors.

AMERICAN SAMOA

KEY HISTORICAL EVENTS

The Samoan Islands were first visited by Europeans in the 18th century; the first recorded visit was in 1722. On 14 July 1889 a treaty between the USA, Germany and Great Britain proclaimed the Samoan islands neutral territory, under a 4-power government consisting of the 3 treaty powers and the local native government. By the Tripartite Treaty of 7 Nov. 1899, ratified 19 Feb. 1900, Great Britain and Germany renounced in favour of the USA all rights over the islands of the Samoan group east of 171° long. west of Greenwich, the islands to the west of that meridian being assigned to Germany (now the independent state of Samoa). The islands of Tutuila and Aunu'u were ceded to the USA by their High Chiefs on 17 April 1900, and the islands of the Manu'a group on 16 July 1904. Congress accepted the islands under a Joint Resolution approved 20 Feb. 1929. Swain's Island, 210 miles north of the Samoan Islands, was annexed in 1925 and is administered as an integral part of American Samoa.

TERRITORY AND POPULATION

The islands (Tutuila, Aunu'u, Ta'u, Olosega, Ofu and Rose) are approximately 650 miles east-north-east of the Fiji Islands. The total area is 1,511 sq. km (583 sq. miles), of which 200 sq. km (77 sq. miles) are dry land; population (1990 Census), 46,773, nearly all Polynesians or part-Polynesians, of whom 25,573 were born in American Samoa (female, 22,750); estimate (July 1996), 59,566, giving a density of 298 per sq. km (774 per sq. mile). The projected population for 2000 is 65,000.

In 1995 an estimated 50·3% of the population lived in urban areas. The island's 3 Districts are Eastern (population, 1980, 17,311), Western (13,227) and Manu'a (1,732). There is also Swain's Island, with an area of 1·9 sq. miles and 100 inhabitants (1994), which lies 210 miles to the north-west. Rose Island (uninhabited) is 0·4 sq. mile in area. In 1990 some 85,000 American Samoans lived in the USA.

Samoan and English are spoken.

SOCIAL STATISTICS

In 1996 the birth rate was 35·6 per 1,000 population and the death rate 4·0 per 1,000 population. Infant mortality was 18·8 per 1,000 live births. Annual growth rate, 1990–95, 3·5%.

CLIMATE

A tropical maritime climate with a small annual range of temperature and plentiful rainfall. Pago Pago, Jan. 83°F (28·3°C), July 80°F (26·7°C). Annual rainfall 194" (4,850 mm).

CONSTITUTION AND GOVERNMENT

American Samoa is constitutionally an unorganized unincorporated territory of the USA administered under the Department of the Interior. Its indigenous inhabitants are US nationals and are classified locally as citizens of American Samoa with certain privileges under local laws not granted to non-indigenous persons. Polynesian customs (not inconsistent with US laws) are respected.

Fagatogo is the seat of the Government.

The islands are organized in 15 counties grouped in 3 districts; these counties and districts correspond to the traditional political units. On 25 Feb. 1948 a bicameral legislature was established, at the request of the Samoans, to have advisory legislative functions. With the adoption of the Constitution of 22 April 1960, and the revised Constitution of 1967, the legislature was vested with limited law-making authority. The lower house, or House of Representatives, is composed of 20 members elected by universal adult suffrage and 1 non-voting member for Swain's Island. The upper house, or Senate, is comprised of 18 members elected, in the traditional Samoan manner, in meetings of the chiefs. The Governor and Lieut.-Governor have been popularly elected since 1978.

RECENT ELECTIONS

At elections on 3 Nov. 1998 only non-partisans were elected.

CURRENT ADMINISTRATION
Governor: A. P. Lutati (D.).
  Lieut.-Governor: Tauese P. Sunia.

ECONOMY
Policy. The first formal Economic Development and Planning Office completed its first year in 1971. Much has been done to promote economic expansion within the Territory and a large amount of outside investment interest has been stimulated.

The Office initiated the first Territorial Comprehensive Plan. This plan when completed will, with periodic updating, provide a guideline to territorial development for 20 years. The planning programme was made possible under a Housing and Urban Development '701' grant programme, and Economic Development Administration '302' planning programmes.

The focus will be on physical development and the problems of a rapidly increasing population with severely limited labour resources.

Budget. The chief sources of revenue are annual federal grants from the USA, and local revenues from taxes, and duties, and receipts from commercial operations (enterprise and special revenue funds), utilities, rents and leases and liquor sales. In 1990–91 revenues were $97m. ($43m. in local revenue and $54m. in grant revenue).

Banking and Finance. The American Samoa branch of the Bank of Hawaii and the American Samoa Bank offer all commercial banking services. The Development Bank of American Samoa, government-owned, is concerned primarily through loans and guarantees with the economic advancement of the Territory.

ENERGY AND NATURAL RESOURCES
Electricity. Installed capacity was 33,000 kW in 1993. Production in 1994 was 100m. kWh. Per capita consumption in 1995 was an estimated 1,743 kWh. All the Manu'a islands have electricity.

Water. The total area covered by water is approximately 13 sq. miles.

Agriculture. Of the 48,640 acres of land area, 11,000 acres are suitable for tropical crops; most commercial farms are in the Tafuna plains and west Tutuila. Principal crops are taro, bread-fruit, yams, bananas and coconuts.

Livestock (1996): Pigs, 11,000.

Fisheries. Total catches in 1995 were 385,800 lbs (175 tonnes).

INDUSTRY
Fish canning is important, employing the second largest number of people (after government). Attempts are being made to provide a variety of light industries. Tuna fishing and local inshore fishing are both expanding. In 1990 there were 27,991 persons of employable age, of whom 14,400 were in the workforce. The unemployment rate in 1991 was 12%.

INTERNATIONAL TRADE
Imports and Exports. In 1989 American Samoa exported goods valued at $306m. and imported goods valued at $360·3m. Chief exports are canned tuna, watches, pet foods and handicrafts. Chief imports are building materials, fuel oil, food, jewellery, machines and parts, alcoholic beverages and cigarettes.

COMMUNICATIONS
Roads. There are about 150 km of paved roads and 200 km of unpaved roads in all. Motor vehicles in use, 1995, 5,900 (5,300 passenger cars and 600 commercial vehicles).

Civil Aviation. South Pacific Island Airways and Polynesian Airlines operate daily services between American Samoa and Samoa. South Pacific Island Airways also operates between Pago Pago and Honolulu, and between Pago Pago and Tonga. The islands are also served by Air Nauru which operates between Pago Pago, Tahiti and Auckland, and Air Pacific (Fiji Islands and westward). South Pacific and Manu'a Air Transport run local services. There are 3 airports.

Shipping. The harbour at Pago Pago, which nearly bisects the island of Tutuila, is the only good harbour for large vessels in American Samoa. By sea there is a twice-monthly service between the Fiji Islands, New Zealand and Australia and regular services between the USA, South Pacific ports, Honolulu and Japan. In 1993-94 vessels entering totalled 581,000 net registered tons.

Telecommunications. A commercial radiogram service is available to all parts of the world. Commercial phone and telex services are operated to all parts of the world. Number of telephones (1996), 8,399.

SOCIAL INSTITUTIONS

Justice. Judicial power is vested firstly in a High Court. The trial division has original jurisdiction of all criminal and civil cases. The probate division has jurisdiction of estates, guardianships, trusts and other matters. The land and title division decides cases relating to disputes involving communal land and Matai title court rules on questions and controversy over family titles. The appellate division hears appeals from trial, land and title and probate divisions as well as having original jurisdiction in selected matters. The appellate court is the court of last resort. Two American judges sit with 5 Samoan judges permanently. In addition there are temporary judges or assessors who sit occasionally on cases involving Samoan customs. There is also a District Court with limited jurisdiction and there are 69 village courts.

Religion. In 1997 about 56% of the population belonged to the Congregational Church and 19% were Roman Catholics. Methodists and Latter-day Saints (Mormons) are also represented.

Education. Education is compulsory between the ages of 6 and 18. In 1991-92 there were 7,884 pupils and 524 teachers at 30 elementary schools and 3,643 pupils and 266 teachers at secondary schools.

Welfare. In 1990 federal direct payments to individuals totalled $14·62m., of which $2·41m. were disability, and $4·33m. were retirement, insurance.

CULTURE

Broadcasting. In 1995 there were 54,000 radio and 12,000 TV (colour by NTSC) sets in use.

Tourism. In 1996 there were 19,000 tourist arrivals; receipts totalled US$9m.

FURTHER READING
Hughes, H. G. A., *Samoa: American Samoa, Western Samoa, Samoans Abroad* [Bibliography]. Oxford and Santa Barbara (CA), 1997

OTHER PACIFIC TERRITORIES

Johnston Atoll. Two small islands 1,150 km south-west of Hawaii, administered by the US Air Force. Area, under 1 sq. mile; population (1996) totalled 1,200 US military and civilian contractor personnel.

Midway Islands. Two small islands at the western end of the Hawaiian chain, administered by the US Navy. Area, 2 sq. miles; population (1995) was 453 US military personnel.

Wake Island. Three small islands 3,700 km west of Hawaii, administered by the US Air Force. Area, 3 sq. miles; population (1995) numbered 302 US military and contract personnel.

COMMONWEALTH OF PUERTO RICO

KEY HISTORICAL EVENTS

A Spanish dependency since the 16th century, Puerto Rico was ceded to the USA in 1898 after the Spanish defeat in the Spanish-American war. In 1917 US citizenship was conferred and in 1932 there was a name change from Porto Rico to Puerto Rico. In 1952 Puerto Rico was proclaimed a commonwealth with a representative government and a directly elected governor.

TERRITORY AND POPULATION

Puerto Rico is the most easterly of the Greater Antilles and lies between the Dominican Republic and the US Virgin Islands. The total area is 13,791 sq. km (5,325 sq. miles), of which 8,875 sq. km (3,427 sq. miles) are dry land; population, according to the census of 1990, of 3,522,037 (1,816,395 females), an increase of 10·2% over 1980. Urban population (1995), 73·3%. Population estimate (1996), 3·82m.; density, 1,115 per sq. mile.

A law of April 1991 making Spanish the sole official language (which replaced a law of 1902 establishing Spanish and English as joint official languages) was reversed in 1993.

Chief towns, 1996 estimates, are: San Juan, 433,705; Bayamón, 231,845; Ponce, 189,988; Carolina, 188,427; Caguas, 140,114; Guaynabo, 104,927; Mayaguez, 100,937; Arecibo, 100,755.

The Puerto Rican island of Vieques, 10 miles to the east, has an area of 51·7 sq. miles and 9,503 (1996) inhabitants. The island of Culebra, between Puerto Rico and St Thomas, has an area of 10 sq. miles and 1,632 (1996) inhabitants. It has a good harbour.

SOCIAL STATISTICS

1996: births, 64,000 (17·2 per 1,000 population); deaths, 29,000 (7·9); marriages (1994), 33,200; infant mortality rate, 12·4 per 1,000 live births. Annual growth rate, 1990–95, 0·8%. In 1994 the most popular age range for marrying was 20–24 for both males and females. Fertility rate, 1990–95, 2·2 births per woman.

CLIMATE

Warm, sunny winters with hot summers. The north coast experiences more rainfall than the south coast and generally does not have a dry season as rainfall is evenly spread throughout the year. San Juan, Jan. 25°C, July 28°C. Annual rainfall 1,246 mm.

CONSTITUTION AND GOVERNMENT

Puerto Rico has representative government, the franchise being restricted to citizens 18 years of age or over, residence (1 year) and such additional qualifications as may be prescribed by the Legislature of Puerto Rico, but no property qualification may be imposed. Puerto Ricans vote in presidential primary elections but not in US general elections. They have one non-voting representative in Washington and do not pay federal taxes. The island is given billions of dollars each year in food stamps and other federal aid from Washington and although Puerto Ricans fight in the US army, the island sends its own teams to the Olympic Games. The executive power resides in a Governor, elected directly by the people every 4 years. 22 heads of departments form the Governor's Council of Secretaries. The legislative functions are vested in a Senate, composed of 28 members, and the House of Representatives, composed of 54 members. Both houses meet annually in Jan. Puerto Rican men are subject to conscription in US services.

A new constitution was drafted by a Puerto Rican Constituent Assembly and approved by the electorate at a referendum on 3 March 1952. It was then submitted to Congress, which struck out Section 20 of Article 11 covering the 'right to work' and the 'right to an adequate standard of living'; the remainder was passed and proclaimed by the Governor on 25 July 1952.

UNITED STATES OF AMERICA

RECENT ELECTIONS

At the election on 5 Nov. 1996 the New Progressive Party, headed by Dr Pedro Rosselló, polled 978,263 votes (49·6% of the total); the Popular Democratic Party, headed by Hector L. Acevedo, polled 862,166 votes (43·7% of the total); the Puerto Rican Independence Party, headed by David Noriega, polled 70,516 votes (3·6% of the total).

At a plebiscite on 14 Nov. 1993 on Puerto Rico's future status, 48·6% of votes cast were for Commonwealth (status quo), 46·3% for Statehood (51st State of the USA) and 4·4% for full independence. In a further plebiscite in Dec. 1998, some 52·2% of voters backed the opposition's call for no change, while 46·5% supported statehood. Independence was supported by 2·5%, while free association received 0·3%.

CURRENT ADMINISTRATION

Governor: Dr Pedro Rosselló (New Progressive Party), 1997–2001 ($70,000).

ECONOMY

Performance. Real GDP growth was 3·4% in 1995 and 4·3% in 1994.

Budget. Total consolidated budget balance as of 30 June 1996: consolidated revenues total, $16,844·6m.; consolidated budget total, $16,385·2m.; balance, $459·4m. GNP, 1996, $30,253·7m. GDP, 1996, $45,504·8m. Per capita GNP, 1996, $8,119. Per capita GDP, 1996, $12,212.

Bonded indebtedness for the commonwealth and municipalities, 30 June 1996, was $4,968·7m.

The USA administers and finances the postal service and maintains air and naval bases. Net US federal government payments in Puerto Rico, including direct expenditures (mainly military), grants-in-aid and other payments to individuals and to business totalled: 1994, $5,998·3m.; 1995, $6,314·4m.; 1996, $6,976·7m.

Per capita personal income (1996) was $7,882.

Banking and Finance. Banks on 30 June 1996 had total deposits of $27,502·2m. Bank loans were $17,940·5m. This includes 15 commercial banks, 3 government banks and 1 trust company.

ENERGY AND NATURAL RESOURCES

Electricity. Installed capacity was 4·47m. kW in 1994. Production in 1995 was 18,143·6m. kWh. Consumption per capita in 1995 was estimated to be 4,231 kWh.

Water. The total area covered by water is approximately 81 sq. miles.

Minerals. There is stone, and some production of cement (1·54m. tons in 1995).

Agriculture. Gross income in agriculture in 1996 was $662·6m., of which $387·2m. consisted of livestock products and $71·2m. traditional crops, including: coffee, 12·0m. kg; raw sugar, 96 degrees basis, 33,484 tons. Livestock (1996): cattle, 370,546; pigs, 182,247; poultry, 12,433,834.

Forestry. In 1995 the area under forests was 275,000 ha, or 31% of the total land area (down from 287,000 ha in 1990).

Fisheries. The total catch in 1995 was 5,795,900 lbs (2,629 tonnes), of which nearly 96% were sea fish.

INDUSTRY

Labour. In 1996 the total labour force was 1,268,000, with 1,092,000 employed. In 1995, 500,000 people were employed in community, social and personal services (including hotels), 216,000 in trade and restaurants and 170,000 in manufacturing industries. 175,000 persons were unemployed in 1996.

INTERNATIONAL TRADE

Imports and Exports. In 1997 imports amounted to $21,387·4m., of which $13,317·8m. came from the USA; exports were valued at $23,946·8m., of which $21,187·3m. went to the USA.

In 1997 main exports (in $1m.) were: chemical products, 10,627·8; machinery (except electrical), 3,490·0; food, 3,386·4. Main imports were: chemical products, 5,416·3; electrical machinery, 2,423·8; transportation equipment, 2,241·2.

Puerto Rico is not permitted to levy taxes on imports.

COMMUNICATIONS

Roads. The Department of Public Works had 23,291 km of paved road under maintenance on 31 Dec. 1994. Motor vehicles registered, 30 June 1996, 2,163,787.

Rail. There are 96 km of railway, although no passenger service.

Shipping. In 1996, 9,931 US and foreign vessels of 81,961,309 gross tons entered and cleared Puerto Rico.

Telecommunications. In 1997 there were 1,322,500 main telephone lines, or 350·7 for every 1,000 persons. Cellular phone subscribers numbered 171,000 in 1995 and there were 543,000 fax machines.

SOCIAL INSTITUTIONS

Justice. The Commonwealth judiciary system is headed by a Supreme Court of 7 members, appointed by the Governor, and consists of a First Instance Court and an Appellative Court, all appointed by the Governor. The First Instance Court consists of a Superior Tribunal with 78 judges and a municipal Tribunal of 70 judges. The Appellative Court has 33 judges.

Religion. In 1996 about 75% of the population were Roman Catholic.

Education. Education was made compulsory in 1899. The percentage of literacy in 1990 was 89·4% of those 10 years of age or older. Total enrolment in public day schools, Aug. 1995, was 627,620 (first school month). All private schools had a total enrolment of 148,610 pupils in 1995. All instruction below senior high school standard is given in Spanish only.

The University of Puerto Rico, in Río Piedras, 7 miles from San Juan, had 62,340 students in 1996. Higher education is also available in the Inter-American University of Puerto Rico (39,319 students in 1996), the Pontifical Catholic University of Puerto Rico (11,786), the Sacred Heart University (5,001) and the Fundación Ana G. Méndez (16,983). Other private colleges and universities had 35,717 students.

Health. There were 72 hospitals in 1994, with a hospital bed provision of 26 per 10,000 population.

CULTURE

Broadcasting. In 1995 there were 118 radio and 21 television stations, 2,636,000 radio receivers and 1m. TV receivers.

Press. In 1995 there were 3 main newspapers: *El Nuevo Día* had a daily circulation of 227,661; *El Vocero*, 206,125; *San Juan Star,* 33,353.

Tourism. There were 3,065,000 tourist arrivals in 1996, bringing in revenue of $1·9bn.

FURTHER READING
Statistical Information: The Area of Economic Research and Social Planning of the Puerto Rico Planning Board publishes: *(a)* annual *Economic Report to the Governor; (b) External Trade Statistics* (annual report); *(c) Reports on national income and balance of payments; (d) SocioEconomic Statistics* (since 1940); *(e) Puerto Rico Monthly Economic Indicators.*
Annual Reports. Governor of Puerto Rico. Washington
Bloomfield, R. J., *Puerto Rico: the Search for a National Policy.* Boulder (Colo.), 1985
Carr, R., *Puerto Rico: a Colonial Experiment.* New York Univ. Press, 1984
Cevallos, E., *Puerto Rico* [Bibliography]. Oxford and Santa Barbara (CA), 1985
Crampsey, R. A., *Puerto Rico.* Newton Abbot, 1973
Dietz, J. L., *Economic History of Puerto Rico: Institutional Change and Capital Development.* Princeton Univ. Press, 1987
Falk, P. S., (ed.) *The Political Status of Puerto Rico.* Lexington, Mass., 1986

Commonwealth Library: Univ. of Puerto Rico Library, Rio Piedras.

VIRGIN ISLANDS OF THE UNITED STATES

KEY HISTORICAL EVENTS

The Virgin Islands of the United States, formerly known as the Danish West Indies, were named and claimed for Spain by Columbus in 1493. They were later settled by Dutch and English planters, invaded by France in the mid-17th century and abandoned by the French c. 1700, by which time Danish influence had been established. St Croix was held by the Knights of Malta between two periods of French rule.

The Virgin Islands were purchased by the United States from Denmark for $25m. in a treaty ratified by both nations and proclaimed on 31 March 1917. Their value was wholly strategic, inasmuch as they commanded the Anegada Passage from the Atlantic Ocean to the Caribbean Sea and the approach to the Panama Canal. Although the inhabitants were made US citizens in 1927, the islands are, constitutionally, an 'unincorporated territory'.

TERRITORY AND POPULATION

The Virgin Islands group, lying about 40 miles due east of Puerto Rico, comprises the islands of St Thomas (31 sq. miles), St Croix (83 sq. miles), St John (20 sq. miles) and 65 small islets or cays, mostly uninhabited. The total area is 1,910 sq. km (738 sq. miles), of which 346 sq. km (134 sq. miles) are dry land.

The population, according to the census of 1 April 1990, was 101,809, a decrease of 8,991 since 1985 (52,599 females); population estimate, 1996, 97,120, giving a density of 725 per sq. mile. An estimated 54·9% of the population were rural in 1995.

Population (1990 census) of St Croix, 50,139; St Thomas, 48,166; St John, 3,504. About 45% (1990) were native-born, 29% from other Caribbean islands, 13% from mainland USA and 5% from Puerto Rico. St Croix has over 40% of Puerto Rican origin or extraction, Spanish speaking.

The capital and only city, Charlotte Amalie, on St Thomas, had a population (1990 census) of 12,331. There are two towns on St Croix: Christiansted (2,555) and Frederiksted (1,064).

SOCIAL STATISTICS

1996: birth rate, 17·6 per 1,000 population; death rate, 5·2; infant mortality rate, 12·5 per 1,000 live births.

CLIMATE

Average temperatures vary from 77°F to 82°F throughout the year; humidity is low. Average annual rainfall, about 45". The islands lie in the hurricane belt; tropical storms with heavy rainfall can occur in late summer, but hurricanes rarely.

CONSTITUTION AND GOVERNMENT

The Organic Act of 22 July 1954 gives the US Department of the Interior full jurisdiction; some limited legislative powers are given to a single-chambered legislature, composed of 15 senators elected for 2 years representing the two legislative districts of St Croix and St Thomas-St John.

The Governor is elected by the residents. Since 1954 there have been four attempts to redraft the Constitution, to provide for greater autonomy. Each has been rejected by the electorate. The latest was defeated in a referendum in Nov. 1981, 50% of the electorate participating.

For administration, there are 14 executive departments, 13 of which are under commissioners and the other, the Department of Justice, under an Attorney-General. The US Department of the Interior appoints a Federal Comptroller of government revenue and expenditure.

The franchise is vested in residents who are citizens of the United States, 18 years of age or over. In 1986 there were 34,183 voters, of whom 26,377 participated in the local elections that year. They do not participate in the US presidential election but they have a non-voting representative in Congress.

The capital is Charlotte Amalie, on St Thomas Island.

RECENT ELECTIONS

In the elections for governor held on 3 Nov. 1998 Charles Turnbull II (Democrat) gained 58·9% of the votes against Roy Schneider (Independent Citizens' Movement). In the Senate election on the same day the Democrats won 6 seats, Non-partisans also 6, Republicans 2 and the Independent Citizens' Movement 1.

CURRENT ADMINISTRATION

Governor: Charles Turnbul II (D), 1999–2003.

    Administrator St Croix: Richard Roebuck, Jr.

    Administrator St John: William Lomax.

    Administrator St Thomas: Harold Robinson.

ECONOMY

Budget. Under the 1954 Organic Act finances are provided partly from local revenues—customs, federal income tax, real and personal property tax, trade tax, excise tax, pilotage fees, etc.—and partly from Federal Matching Funds, being the excise taxes collected by the federal government on such Virgin Islands products transported to the mainland as are liable.

    Per capita income, 1990, \$8,717.

    Budget for financial year 1990: revenues, \$364·4m.; expenditures, \$364·4m.

Currency. United States currency became legal tender on 1 July 1934.

Banking and Finance. Banks are the Chase Manhattan Bank; the Bank of Nova Scotia; the First Federal Savings and Loan Association of Puerto Rico; Barclays Bank International; Citibank; First Pennsylvania Bank; Banco Popular de Puerto Rico, and the First Virgin Islands Federal Savings Bank.

ENERGY AND NATURAL RESOURCES

Electricity. The Virgin Islands Water and Power Authority provides electric power from generating plants on St Croix and St Thomas; St John is served by power cable and emergency generator. Production in 1994 was 990m. kWh. Per capita consumption in 1995 was an estimated 9,565 kWh.

Water. There are 6 de-salinization plants with maximum daily capacity of 8·7m. gallons of fresh water. Rainwater remains the most reliable source. Every building must have a cistern to provide rainwater for drinking, even in areas served by mains (10 gallons capacity per sq. ft of roof for a single-storey house).

    The total area covered by water is approximately 37 sq. miles.

Agriculture. Land for fruit, vegetables and animal feed is available on St Croix, and there are tax incentives for development. Sugar has been terminated as a commercial crop and over 4,000 acres of prime land could be utilized for food crops.

    Livestock (1996): cattle, 8,000; goats, 4,000; pigs, 3,000; sheep, 3,000.

Fisheries. There is a fishermen's co-operative with a market at Christiansted. There is a shellfish-farming project at Rust-op-Twist, St Croix. The total catch in 1995 was approximately 2,028,300 lbs (920 tonnes).

INDUSTRY

The main occupations on St Thomas are tourism and government service; on St Croix manufacturing is more important. Manufactures include rum (the most valuable product), watches, pharmaceuticals and fragrances. Industries in order of revenue: tourism, refining oil, watch assembly, rum distilling, construction.

Labour. In 1990 the total labour force was 45,990, of whom 13,640 were employed in government, 8,450 in retail trades, 9,030 in hotels and other lodgings, 3,550 self-employed and unpaid family workers, 2,290 in transportation and public utilities, 2,420 in manufacturing, 4,140 in construction, 930 in banking, 2,090 in finance, insurance and real estate, 970 in wholesale trades, 920 in business services, 350 in legal services, and 2,330 in gift shops. In 1995 there were 2,700 registered unemployed persons, or 5·7% of the workforce.

INTERNATIONAL TRADE

Imports and Exports. Exports, calendar year 1990, totalled $2,820·7m. and imports $3,294·6m. The main import is crude petroleum, while the principal exports are petroleum products.

COMMUNICATIONS

Roads. In 1996 the Virgin Islands had 856 km of roads.

Civil Aviation. There is a daily cargo and passenger service between St Thomas and St Croix. Alexander Hamilton Airport on St Croix can take all aircraft except Concorde. Cyril E. King Airport on St Thomas takes 727-class aircraft. There are air connections to mainland USA, other Caribbean islands, Latin America and Europe. In 1991, 1,023,055 passengers were handled.

Shipping. The whole territory has free port status. There is an hourly boat service between St Thomas and St John.

Telecommunications. All three Virgin Islands have a dial telephone system. Main telephone lines numbered 62,100 in 1997 (580·7 per 1,000 population). Direct dialling to Puerto Rico and the mainland, and internationally, is now possible. Worldwide radio telegraph service is also available.

Postal Services. In 1994 there were 9 post offices.

SOCIAL INSTITUTIONS

Religion. There are churches of the Protestant, Roman Catholic and Jewish faiths in St Thomas and St Croix and Protestant and Roman Catholic churches in St John.

Education. In 1992–93 there were 14,544 pupils and 790 teachers in 62 elementary schools, and 12,502 pupils and 723 teachers (1988) in secondary schools; 33 non-public schools had 5,079 pupils in 1988. In autumn 1991 the University of the Virgin Islands had 924 full-time students, 1,538 part-time students and 254 graduate students. The College is part of the United States land-grant network of higher education. The Virgin Islands has the highest proportion of female students in higher education anywhere in the world, at 74% in 1992–93.

Welfare. In 1990 Federal direct payments for individuals totalled $95·4m., including: Medicare, $4·98m.; supplemental medical insurance, $3·72m.; disability insurance, $5·69m.; retirement insurance, $31·6m.; food Stamps, $18·4m.

CULTURE

Broadcasting. There are 8 radio stations and 1 public and 1 commercial TV station. In 1995 there were 105,000 radio and 67,000 TV (colour by NTSC) receivers in use.

Press. In 1991 there were 2 dailies, 1 fortnightly paper and 1 magazine.

Tourism. Tourism accounts for 70% of GDP. There were 375,000 foreign tourists in 1996, bringing revenue of $811m.

FURTHER READING
Boyer, W. W., *America's Virgin Islands*. Durham, (NC), 1983
Dookhan, I., *A History of the Virgin Islands of the United States*. Caribbean Univ. Press, 1974
Moll, V. P., *Virgin Islands* [Bibliography]. Oxford and Santa Barbara (CA), 1991

URUGUAY

República Oriental
del Uruguay

Capital: Montevideo
Population estimate, 2000: 3·27m.
GNP per capita: (PPP$) 7,760
HDI/world rank: 0·885/38

KEY HISTORICAL EVENTS

Uruguay was the last colony settled by Spain in the Americas. Part of the Spanish viceroyalty of Rio de la Plata until revolutionaries expelled the Spanish in 1811, and subsequently a province of Brazil, Uruguay declared its independence on 25 Aug. 1825 which was recognized by the treaty between Argentina and Brazil signed at Rio de Janeiro on 27 Aug. 1828. The first constitution was adopted on 18 July 1830. In the 1830s two political parties, the *blancos* (conservatives) and the *colorados* (liberals), emerged and conflict between the parties in 1865-70 precipitated the War of the Triple Alliance. In 1903, peace and prosperity were restored under President José Battle y Ordónezo. Since 1904 Uruguay has been unique in her constitutional innovations, all designed to protect her from the emergence of a dictatorship. The favourite device of the group known as the 'Batllistas' (a *colorado* faction) which, until defeated at the 1958 elections, held a parliamentary majority for over 90 years, has been the collegiate system of government, in which the two largest political parties were represented.

The early part of the 20th century saw the development of a welfare state in Uruguay which encouraged extensive immigration. In 1919 a new constitution was adopted providing for a *colegiado*—plural executive based on the Swiss pattern. However, the system was abolished in 1933 and replaced by presidential government, with quadrennial elections. From 1951 to 1966 a collective form of leadership again replaced the presidency. During the 1960s, following a series of strikes and riots, the Army became increasingly influential, repressive measures such as censorship of the press were adopted and presidential government was restored in 1967. The Tupamaro, Marxist urban guerrillas, sought violent revolution but were finally defeated by the Army in 1972. In 1984 the military permitted presidential elections, although several candidates were banned.

The return to civilian rule came on 12 Feb. 1985 when Gen. Alvarez resigned as president and was succeeded by Dr Julio Maria Sanguinetti, who established a government of National Unity and ordered the release of all political prisoners.

TERRITORY AND POPULATION

Uruguay is bounded on the north-east by Brazil, on the south-east by the Atlantic, on the south by the Río de la Plata and on the west by Argentina. The area is 176,215 sq. km (68,037 sq. miles). The following table shows the area and the population of the 19 departments at census 1985:

Departments	Sq. km	Census 1985	Capital	Census 1985
Artigas	11,928	68,400	Artigas	34,551
Canelones	4,536	359,700	Canelones	17,316
Cerro-Largo	13,648	78,000	Melo	42,329
Colonia	6,106	112,100	Colonia	19,077
Durazno	11,643	54,700	Durazno	27,602
Flores	5,144	24,400	Trinidad	18,271
Florida	10,417	65,400	Florida	28,560
Lavalleja	10,016	61,700	Minas	34,634
Maldonado	4,793	93,000	Maldonado	33,498
Montevideo	530	1,309,100	Montevideo	1,247,920
Paysandú	13,922	104,500	Paysandú	75,081
Río Negro	9,282	47,500	Fray Bentos	20,431
Rivera	9,370	88,400	Rivera	56,335
Rocha	10,551	68,500	Rocha	23,910
Salto	14,163	107,300	Salto	80,787
San José	4,992	91,900	San José	31,732
Soriano	9,008	77,500	Mercedes	37,110
Tacuarembó	15,438	82,600	Tacuarembó	40,470
Treinta y Tres	9,529	45,500	Treinta y Tres	30,956

Total population, census (1996) 3,137,668 (89·3% urban). Population density, 17·8 per sq. km.

The UN gives a projected population for 2000 of 3·27m.

In 1996, Montevideo (the capital) accounted for 44·5% of the total population. Uruguay has the highest percentage of urban population in South America, with 90·3% living in urban areas in 1995.

16·5% of the population are over 60; 27% are under 17½; 66·1% are between 15 and 60.

The official language is Spanish.

SOCIAL STATISTICS
1996 births, 55,000; deaths, 30,000. Rates (per 1,000 population), 1996: Birth, 17·6; death, 9·7. Population growth rate, growth, 0·7%. Infant mortality (per 1,000 live births), 14·7. Life expectancy was 72·4 years in 1996. Fertility rate, 1990–95, 2·3 births per woman, the lowest rate in South America.

CLIMATE
A warm temperate climate, with mild winters and warm summers. The wettest months are March to June, but there is really no dry season. Montevideo, Jan. 72°F (22·2°C), July 50°F (10°C). Annual rainfall 38" (950 mm).

CONSTITUTION AND GOVERNMENT
Congress consists of a *Senate* of 31 members and a *Chamber of Deputies* of 99 members, both elected by proportional representation for 5-year terms. The electoral system provides that the successful presidential candidate be a member of the party which gains a parliamentary majority. Electors vote for deputies on a first-past-the-post system, and simultaneously vote for a presidential candidate of the same party. The winners of the second vote are credited with the number of votes obtained by their party in the parliamentary elections. Referendums may be called at the instigation of 10,000 signatories. A referendum was held on 8 Dec. 1996 to prohibit parties from presenting more than 1 candidate in presidential elections, and to provide for 2 rounds of voting if no candidate gained an absolute majority in the first round. 50·2% of votes cast were in favour.

National Anthem. 'Orientales, la patria o la tumba' ('Easterners, the fatherland or the tomb'); words by F. Acuña de Figueroa, tune by F. J. Deballi.

RECENT ELECTIONS
Presidential, parliamentary and gubernatorial elections were held on 27 Nov. 1994. The electorate was 2·4m. Julio Sanguinetti was elected President with 31·36% of votes cast against 18 opponents. In the elections to the Chamber of Deputies 31 seats were won by both the Colorado Party (PC) and the National Party-Whites (PN), 17 by Uruguay Assembly (AU), 7 by the Socialist Party of Uruguay (PS) and 5 by New Space (NE), with other parties winning either 1 or 2 seats. A coalition government was formed between PC, PN and PGP, which won a single seat. In the Senate election, PC won 11 seats, PN 10, AU 4, PS 2 with other parties winning 1 seat each.

CURRENT ADMINISTRATION
President: Dr Julio Maria Sanguinetti, b. 1939 (Colorado Party; sworn in on 1 March 1995).

Vice-President: Hugo Fernandez Faingold.

The government in March 1999 comprised:

Minister of the Interior: Luis Hierro Lopez. *Foreign Affairs:* Didier Opertti. *Finance and Economy:* Luis Mosca Sobrero. *Transport and Public Works:* Lucio Cáceres Behrens. *Health:* Dr José Raúl Bustos Alonso. *Labour and Social Security:* Dr Ana Lia Piñeyrua. *Agriculture, Livestock and Fisheries:* Sergio Chiesa. *Education and Culture:* Samuel Lichtensztejn. *Defence:* Juan Luis Storace. *Industry and Energy:* Dr Julio Herrera. *Tourism:* Benito Stern Prac. *Housing and Environment:* Juan A. Chiruchi Fuentes.

Local Government. The 19 departments are each administered by a governor, elected for 5-year terms simultaneously with the presidential and parliamentary elections.

DEFENCE
Defence expenditure totalled US$307m. in 1997 (US$96 per capita).

Army. The Army consists of volunteers who enlist for 1-2 years service. There are 4 military regions with divisional headquarters. The Army is organized in 5 infantry, 1 engineer, 1 artillery and 3 cavalry brigades and 3 artillery and 4 combat engineer battalions. Equipment includes 17 M-24, 29 M-3A1 and 22 M-41A1 light tanks. Strength (1997) 17,600.

Navy. The navy consists of 3 ex-French frigates, 3 fast inshore patrol craft, 7 other inshore patrol vessels and 4 ex-German inshore minesweepers. Auxiliaries comprise 1 freighting tanker, 1 sail training ship, 1 ex-German support ship, 1 salvage ship and 2 service vessels. There are 4 small landing craft.

A naval aviation service 300 strong operates 6 S-2 Tracker anti-submarine aircraft, 1 King Air for maritime reconnaissance, 6 training aircraft and 6 general purpose helicopters. Personnel in 1997 totalled 5,000 including 400 naval infantry. The main base is at Montevideo.

An integrated coastguard operates 8 inshore patrol craft.

Air Force. Organized with US aid, the Air Force had (1997) about 3,000 personnel and 20 combat aircraft, including 2 counter-insurgency squadrons with 5 IA 58 Pucara, 4 AT-33 armed jet trainers and 10 A-37B light strike aircraft, a reconnaissance and training squadron with 6 PC-7 Turbo-Trainers, 3 transport squadrons with 1 turboprop F.27 Friendship, 3 turbo-prop C-130s, 3 Brazilian-built EMB-110 Bandeirantes (1 equipped for photographic duties), 2 CASA C-212 Aviocars and 5 Queen Airs, a search and rescue squadron with Cessna U-17A aircraft and Bell helicopters, and a number of Cessna 182 light aircraft for liaison duties. Basic training types are the T-41 and T-34.

INTERNATIONAL RELATIONS
Uruguay is a member of the UN, OAS, Mercosur and LAIA.

ECONOMY
Policy. Uruguay's small economy benefits from a favourable climate for agriculture and substantial hydropower potential. Economic development has been restrained in recent years by high—though declining—inflation and extensive government regulation. The Sanguinetti government's conservative monetary and fiscal policies are aimed at continuing to reduce inflation, at 24·3% at year end 1996; other priorities include extensive reform of the social security system and increased investment in education. Uruguayan trade continued to expand and the potential for new markets continued to open through the negotiations of Mercosur (Southern Cone Common Market) with neighbouring countries and the EU.

Performance. Uruguay recovered from recession in 1996—partly due to the recovery in Argentina—and ended the year with a rise in GDP of nearly 5%. In 1997 the economy grew by almost 6%.

Budget. Central government finance (millions of pesos):

	1992	1993	1994	1995	1996	1997
Revenue	6,695	10,030	15,095	21,141	28,845	38,180
Expenditure	4,661	9,039	13,968	15,657	19,628	25,535

Components of 1995 revenue: VAT, 44·9%; customs duties, 5·7%; fuel tax, 7·9%; income tax, 10%; capital gains tax, 5·7%. Expenditure included: Social welfare and salaries, 60·8%; interest on public debt, 7%; capital expenditure, 10·9%.

Standard rate of VAT is 23%.

Currency. The unit of currency is the *Uruguayan peso* (UYP), of 100 *centésimos*, which replaced the nuevo peso in March 1993 at 1 Uruguayan peso = 1,000 nuevos pesos. Foreign exchange reserves were US$1,540m. and gold reserves 1·76m. troy oz. in Jan. 1998. Inflation, which was over 100% in 1990, was down to 20% by the end of 1997. Total money supply in Oct. 1997 was 9,436m. pesos.

Banking and Finance. The Central Bank was inaugurated on 16 May 1967. It is the bank of issue and supreme regulatory authority. In 1994 there were 22 commercial banks, 3 state-supported and 18 foreign-owned. Savings banks deposits were 1,993,029m. pesos in 1995.

The State Insurance Bank has a monopoly of new insurance business. There is a stock exchange in Montevideo.

Weights and Measures. The metric system is in use.

ENERGY AND NATURAL RESOURCES

Electricity. Installed capacity was 2·14m. kW in 1995. Production in 1995 was 6,167m. kWh, with consumption per capita in 1995 estimated at 1,568 kWh.

Agriculture. Uruguay is primarily a pastoral country. In 1996, 9% of GDP was produced by agriculture. Rising investment has helped agriculture, which has given a major boost to the country's economy. Some 41m. acres are devoted to farming, of which 90% to livestock and 10% to crops. Some large *estancias* have been divided up into family farms; the average farm is about 250 acres.

Livestock, 1996: cattle, 10·68m.; sheep, 19·86m.; pigs, 270,000; goats, 15m. (1995); horses, 480,000; chickens, 10m. (1995).

Livestock products, 1993 (in 1,000 tonnes): Beef and veal, 317; cow's milk (1995), 1·3m; wool, 83.

Main crops (in 1,000 tonnes), 1995: Rice, 804; maize, 108; 1993: Barley, 140; oats, 35; sugar-beet, 40; wheat, 300; sugar-cane, 350; potatoes, 170. Wine is produced for domestic consumption (107,000 tonnes in 1993). The country has some 6m. fruit trees, principally peaches, oranges, tangerines and pears.

Forestry. In 1995 the area under forests was 814,000 ha (mainly eucalyptus and pine), representing 4·7% of the total land area. In 1995, 4·1m. cu. metres of roundwood were cut.

Fisheries. The total catch in 1995 was 126,514 tonnes, almost entirely marine fish.

INDUSTRY

In 1995 services accounted for 20·9% of GDP, and manufacturing and building 22·4%. Industries include meat packing, oil refining, cement manufacture, foodstuffs, beverages, leather and textile manufacture, chemicals, light engineering and transport equipment. 1991 output (in 1,000 tonnes): Cement, 436; sugar, 86; motor cars, 11,794 units; lorries, 567 units; meat-packing, 1,132,000 head (1,408,000 head in 1990); petroleum, 1,587,000 cu. metres.

Labour. In 1996 the retirement age was raised from 55 to 60 for women; it remains 60 for men. The labour force in 1996 totalled 1,444,000 (59% males). In 1991, 40·2% of the workforce was engaged in services, 21·8% in manufacturing, 16·7% in trade, 6·9% in building and 5·6% in transport and communications.

INTERNATIONAL TRADE
External debt was US$5,899m. in 1996.

Imports and Exports. The foreign trade (officially stated in US dollars, with the figure for imports based on the clearance permits granted and that for exports on export licences utilized) was as follows (in US$1m.):

	1991	1992	1993	1994	1995	1996
Imports	1,636·5	2,045	2,324	2,786	2,867	3,300
Exports	1,604·7	1,702	1,645	1,913	2,106	2,400

Principal exports in 1995 (in US$1,000): Textiles, 421·3 (including washed wool, 25·8); meat, live animals and by-products, 561·8; agricultural produce, 304·1 (including rice, 163·0); leather, hides and manufactures, 250·7; footwear, 17·8.

The main import suppliers in 1996 were Brazil (22·4%), Argentina (20·8%), USA (12·0%) and Italy (5·2%). Leading export destinations in 1996 were Brazil (34·7%), Argentina (11·3%), USA (7·0%) and Germany (4·7%).

COMMUNICATIONS

Roads. In 1995, it was estimated that there were about 50,900 km of roads including 12,000 km of motorways. Passenger cars in 1996 numbered 484,000 (153 per 1,000 inhabitants).

Rail. The total railway system open for traffic was (1992) 2,073 km of 1,435 mm gauge, which carried 1m. tonnes of freight in 1994. Passenger service, which had been abandoned in 1988, was resumed on a limited basis in 1993.

Civil Aviation. There is an international airport at Montevideo (Carrasco). The national carrier is Pluna. In 1998 it operated domestic services and maintained routes to Argentina, Bolivia, Brazil, Chile, Cuba and Paraguay, Spain and the USA. In 1998 services were also provided by Aerolíneas Argentinas, Air France, ALTA, American Airlines, Cubana, Iberia, Lan-Chile, Lloyd Aéreo Boliviano, Transportes Aereos del Mercosur, United Airlines and Varig. There are 60 airports (1996), 45 with paved runways and 15 with unpaved runways. In 1996 Montevideo handled 1,102,000 passengers (568,000 on domestic flights) and 26,500 tonnes of freight.

Shipping. In 1995, sea-going shipping totalled 150,296 GRT; including oil tankers 93,297 GRT, and container ships 28,153 GRT. Navigable inland waterways total 1,270 km.

Telecommunications. The telephone system in Montevideo is controlled by the State; small companies operate in the interior. Uruguay had 761,100 main telephone lines in 1997 (232 for every 1,000 persons). In 1995 there were 70,000 PCs, 40,000 cellular phone subscribers and 11,000 fax machines. There were approximately 9,000 Internet users in Oct. 1997.

Postal Services. In 1995 there were 295 post offices.

SOCIAL INSTITUTIONS

Justice. The Supreme Court is elected by Congress; it appoints all other judges. There are 4 courts of appeal, each with 3 judges. There are civil and criminal courts. Each department has its court, and there are 224 lower courts.

Religion. State and Church are separated, and there is complete religious liberty. In 1992 there were 1·83m. Roman Catholics.

Education. Adult literacy in 1995 was 97·3% (male, 96·9%; female, 97·7%). The female literacy rate is the highest in South America. Primary education is obligatory; both primary and secondary education are free. In 1995 there were 1,693 pre-primary schools with 2,707 teachers for 69,464 pupils; 2,424 primary schools with 16,991 teachers for 341,197 pupils and at secondary level 263,616 pupils.

There is 1 state university, 1 independent Roman Catholic university and 1 private institute of technology. In 1995 there were 71,379 students and 6,683 academic staff.

In 1994 total expenditure on education came to 2·5% of GNP and represented 13·3% of total government expenditure.

Health. In 1994 there were 11,241 doctors, 3,740 dentists, 2,139 nurses, 922 pharmacists and 554 midwives. There were 112 hospitals in 1993, with a provision of 45 beds for every 10,000 persons.

Welfare. The welfare state dates from the beginning of the 1900s. In 1994 there were 0·5m. recipients of pensions and benefits. A private pension scheme inaugurated in 1996 had 315,000 members at 31 Dec. 1996. State spending on social security has been capped at 15% of GDP.

CULTURE

Broadcasting. There were (1995) 1·94m. radio and 750,000 television receivers (colour by PAL). There are 4 TV networks (3 commercial) and about 100 radio stations.

Press. In 1995 there were 32 daily newspapers with a combined circulation of 750,000. There were also 30 provincial newspapers, many bi-weekly.

Tourism. There were 2m. tourists in 1996, mainly from Argentina. Receipts totalled US$599m.

DIPLOMATIC REPRESENTATIVES
Of Uruguay in Great Britain (2nd Floor, 140 Brompton Rd., London, SW3 1HY)
Ambassador: Dr. Augustín Espinosa Lloveras.

URUGUAY

Of Great Britain in Uruguay (Calle Marco Bruto 1073, 11300 Montevideo)
Ambassador: A. R. Murray.

Of Uruguay in the USA (2715 M. St., NW, Washington, D.C., 20007)
Ambassador: Dr Alvaro Mario Diez de Medina.

Of the USA in Uruguay (Lauro Muller 1776, Montevideo)
Ambassador: Christopher C. Ashby.

Of Uruguay to the United Nations
Ambassador: Dr Jorge Pérez Otermín.

Of Uruguay to the European Union
Ambassador: Guillermo Valles Galmes.

FURTHER READING
Finch, H., *Uruguay* [Bibliography]. Oxford and Santa Barbara (CA), 1989
González, L. E., *Political Structures and Democracy in Uruguay.* Univ. of Notre Dame Press, 1992
Sosnowski, S. (ed.) *Repression, Exile and Democracy: Uruguayan Culture.* Duke Univ. Press, 1993
Weinstein, M., *Uruguay: Democracy at the Crossroads.* Boulder (CO), 1988

National library: Biblioteca Nacional del Uruguay, Guayabo 1793, Montevideo.

UZBEKISTON

Uzbekiston Respublikasy

Capital: Toshkent
Population estimate, 2000: 25·02m.
GNP per capita: (PPP$) 2,450
HDI/world rank: 0·659/104

KEY HISTORICAL EVENTS

Descended from nomadic Mongol tribes who settled in Central Asia in the 13th century, the Uzbeks came under Russian control in the late 19th century. In Oct. 1917 the Tashkent Soviet assumed authority and in the following years established its power throughout Turkestan. The semi-independent Khanates of Khiva and Bokhara were first (1920) transformed into People's Republics, then (1923–24) into Soviet Socialist Republics, and finally merged in the Uzbek SSR and other republics.

The Uzbek Soviet Socialist Republic was formed on 27 Oct. 1924 from lands formerly included in Turkestan. It included a large part of the Samarqand (formerly Samarkand) region, the southern part of the Syr Darya, Western Ferghana, the western plains of Bukhara, the Karakalpak ASSR and the Uzbek regions of Khorezm. In 1963, 40,000 sq. km were transferred from Kazakhstan. On 20 June 1990 the Supreme Soviet adopted a declaration of sovereignty, and in Aug. 1991, following an unsuccessful coup, declared independence as the 'Republic of Uzbekistan'. This was confirmed by referendum in Dec. In Dec. 1991 Uzbekistan became a member of the CIS. In the meantime it changed spelling to 'Uzbekiston'.

TERRITORY AND POPULATION

Uzbekiston is bordered in the north by Kazakhstan, in the east by Kyrgyzstan and Tajikistan, in the south by Afghanistan and in the west by Turkmenistan. Area, 447,400 sq. km (172,741 sq. miles). At the 1989 census the population was 19,810,077 (71·4% Uzbek, 8·4% Russian, 4·7% Tajik, 4·1% Kazakh, 3·2% Tatar and 2·1% Karakalpak). The population in 1997 was 23,467,700 (11,842,800 females); density, 52·5 per sq. km.

The UN gives a projected population for 2000 of 25·02m.

In 1995, 58·9% of the population lived in rural areas.

The areas and populations of the 12 Regions and the Autonomous Republic of Qoraqalpoghiston (formerly Karkalpakstan) are as follows (former spellings in brackets):

Region	Area (in sq. km)	Population (1994 estimate)	Capital	Population (1994 estimate)
Andijon (Andizhan)	4,200	1,899,000	Andijon	303,000
Bukhoro (Bukhara)	39,400	1,262,000	Bukhoro	236,000
Farghona (Ferghana)	7,100	2,338,000	Farghona	191,000
Jizzakh (Dzhizak)	20,500	831,000	Jizzakh	116,000
Khorazm (Khorezm)	6,300	1,135,000	Urganch (Urgench)	135,000
Namangan	7,900	1,652,000	Namangan	341,000
Nawoiy (Navoi)	110,800	715,000	Nawoiy	115,000
Qashqadaryo (Kashkadar)	28,400	715,000	Qarshi (Karshi)	177,000
Qoralpoghiston (Karakalpakstan Autonomous Republic)	164,900	1,343,000	Nuqus (Nukus)	185,000
Samarqand (Samarkand)	16,400	2,322,000	Samarqand	368,000
Sirdaryo (Syr-Darya)	5,100	600,000	Guliston	...
Surkhondaryo (Surkhan-Darya)	20,800	1,437,000	Termiz	...
Toshkent (Tashkent)	15,600	4,357,000	Toshkent	2,121,000

The capital is Toshkent; other large towns are Samarqand, Andijon and Namangan. There are 124 towns, 97 urban settlements and 155 rural districts.

The Roman alphabet (in use 1929–40) was reintroduced in 1994 and is to be completely phased in by 2000. Arabic script was in use prior to 1929, and Cyrillic, 1940–94.

Uzbek, Russian and Tajik are all spoken.

SOCIAL STATISTICS
Births, 1997, 563,000; deaths, 178,000; marriages, 1994, 176,287. Rates, 1997: Birth (per 1,000 population), 24·0; death, 7·6. Life expectancy, 1997, 64·3 years. Annual growth rate, 1990–95, 2·1%. In 1994 the most popular age range for marrying was 20–24 for both males and females. Infant mortality, 1990–95, 43 per 1,000 live births; fertility rate, 3·8 births per woman.

CLIMATE
The summers are warm to hot but the heat is made more bearable by the low humidity. The winters are cold but generally dry and sunny. Toshkent, Jan. –1°C, July 25°C. Annual rainfall 14·76" (375 mm).

CONSTITUTION AND GOVERNMENT
A new constitution was adopted on 8 Dec. 1992 stating that Uzbekistan (now Uzbekiston) is a pluralist democracy. Parliament is the 250-member *Oliy Majlis* (Supreme Assembly).

RECENT ELECTIONS
Presidential elections were held on 29 Dec. 1991. Islam Karimov was elected against a single opponent with over 80% of the vote. A referendum on 26 March 1995 proposed the cancellation of elections due in 1997 and the extension of President Karimov's term of office to 2000. The electorate was 11m.; turn-out was reported to be 99·3%, with 99·62% of votes cast in favour.

Parliamentary elections were held in Dec. 1994 and Jan. 1995. The electorate was 11m. The People's Democratic Party (former Communists) won 69 seats; the Progress of the Fatherland won 14; and the remaining 167 seats were split between the Social Democratic Party (47) and a bloc of MPs elected from representative executive bodies.

CURRENT ADMINISTRATION
President: Islam Karimov (b. 1938).
In March 1999 the government comprised:
Prime Minister: Utkur Sultanov.
Deputy Prime Ministers: Rustam Yunusov; Bakhtiar Hamidov; Mirabror Usmanov; Hamidulla Karamatov; Viktor Chzen; Dilbar Ghulomova; Bakhtiar Alimdjanov; Akhmetov Lerik; Anatoliy Isaev.
Minister of the Interior: Zokirjon Almatov. *Foreign Economic Relations:* Elyor Ghaniev. *Finance:* Rustam Azimov. *Defence:* Maj.-Gen. Hikmatulla Tursunov. *Foreign Affairs:* Abdulaziz Komilov. *Justice:* Srojiddin Mirsafoev. *Power and Electrification:* Valeri Otaev. *Communications:* Abduvokhid Jurabaev. *Education:* Jura Yuldoshev. *Higher and Secondary Specialized Education:* Saidahror Guljamov. *Cultural Affairs:* Hairulla Juraev. *Health:* Feruz Nazirov. *Social Security:* Bakhodir Umurzakov. *Labour:* Oqiljon Obidov. *Housing and Municipal Economy:* Gofurjon Muhamedov. *Emergency Situations:* Bahodir Kacimov. *Agriculture and Water Utilization*: Islom Babajanov. *Macroeconomics and Statistics:* Bakhtiar Hamidov.

Local Government. Local authorities are headed by governors appointed by the President of the Republic and directly responsible to him. Local elections were held on 25 Dec. 1994.

DEFENCE
Conscription is for 18 months. Defence expenditure in 1997 totalled US$447m. (US$19 per capita).

Army. The Army comprises 4 motor rifle, 1 airborne, 1 artillery and 1 special forces brigade, and 2 tank and 3 artillery regiments. Equipment includes 179 T-62 main battle tanks. Personnel, 1997, 45,000. There are paramilitary forces totalling 16,000.

Air Force. Aviation units include a regiment of MiG-27 fighter-bombers and a regiment of An-12 transports, as well as some armed helicopters. Personnel, 1997, 4,000.

INTERNATIONAL RELATIONS
A major concern is a possible spillover of fighting from the troubles in Afghanistan.
Uzbekiston is a member of the UN, CIS and the NATO Partnership for Peace.

ECONOMY

Performance. Real GDP growth was –1·2% in 1995 and –4·0% in 1994.

Budget. The 1997 budget provided for revenue of 123,600m. soums and expenditure of 150,400m. soums.

Currency. A coupon for a new unit of currency, the *soum* (UKS), was introduced alongside the rouble on 15 Nov. 1993. This was replaced by the *soum* proper at 1 soum = 1,000 coupons on 1 July 1994. The average annual inflation rate over the period 1990–96 was 546%. In 1996 it was only 40%. Exchange controls were abolished on 1 July 1995.

Banking and Finance. The Central Bank is the bank of issue (*Governor*, Dr Faizulla Mulladjanov). In 1996 there were 10 commercial banks, the National Bank for Foreign Economic Affairs (state-owned), 3 specialized commercial banks and 1 co-operative bank. 2 foreign banks had representative offices.

ENERGY AND NATURAL RESOURCES

Electricity. Installed capacity was 11·82m. kW in 1994; production was 45,150m. kWh. Consumption per capita (1995 estimate), 1,970 kWh. In 1997, 3,615 km of power transmission lines were conducted.

Oil and Gas. Crude oil production (including gas concentrate) was 8m. tonnes in 1995; natural gas, 1,703 petajoules. In 1997, 9 oil wells, 18 gas wells and 320·4 km of gas mains lines came into operation.

Minerals. 3·8m. tonnes of coal were produced in 1993. Some 70 tonnes of gold are produced annually. There are also large reserves of silver, uranium, copper, lead, zinc and tungsten; all uranium mined is exported.

Agriculture. Agriculture accounted for 26% of GDP in 1996. Farming is intensive and based on irrigation. In 1994 there were 4·1m. ha of arable land, 0·4m. ha of permanent cropland and 20·8m. ha of pasture; 4m. ha were irrigated in 1994.

By 1996 some 97% of the 715 state farms were co-operative, private or otherwise owned, and accounted for over 98% of agricultural production. The contribution of individual land holdings to the development of food provision for the population has increased in recent years. In 1997 their share in the production of potatoes was 68·7%; of grapes and fruits, 45%; vegetables, 70·1%; meat, 87·3%; milk, 90·9%; and eggs, 69·5%.

Cotton is the main crop, accounting for more than 40% of the value of total agricultural production. In 1997, more than 3·6m. tonnes of raw cotton was laid. Fruit, vegetables and rice are also grown; sericulture and the production of astrakhan wool are also important.

Output of main agricultural products (1993, in 1,000 tonnes): Grain, 2,098; cotton, 4,234; potatoes, 463; vegetables, 2,941; fruit and berries, 486; meat, 452; milk, 3,566; and 1,663m. eggs.

Livestock, 1996: 5·2m. cattle, 8·35m. sheep, 968,000 goats (1995), 208,000 pigs and 30m. chickens (1995).

Forestry. In 1995 the area under forests was 9·12m. ha, accounting for 22% of the total land area (up from 7·99m. ha and 19·3% of the land area in 1990). This is due to new planting between 1990 and 1995, which resulted in an increase of 1·13m. ha of forest—a figure exceeded only in the USA over the same period.

Environment. Irrigation of arid areas has caused the drying up of the Aral Sea.

Fisheries. The total catch in 1995 was 24,004 tonnes of freshwater fish.

INDUSTRY

Industrial production increased by 6·5% in 1997 owing to the growth of industrial investment in previous years. The production of consumer goods increased by 11·2%. Major industries include fertilizers, agricultural and textile machinery, aircraft, metallurgy and chemicals. Output, 1993 (in tonnes): Rolled ferrous metals, 0·6m.; cement, 5·3m.; mineral fertilizer, 1·3m.; chemical fibre, 22,600; paper, 13,100; fabrics, 632m. sq. metres; footwear, 39·6m. pairs; 11,500 tractors; 10,000 TV sets; 81,700 refrigerators and freezers; 10,300 washing machines.

Labour. In 1995 the labour force was 8·2m.: agriculture and forestry, 44%; industry and construction, 20%; other, 36%. In 1997 there were 28,800 people officially registered as unemployed. Average monthly salary in 1997 was 3,681·3 soums. A minimum wage of 70,000 soum-coupons a month was imposed on 1 June 1994.

INTERNATIONAL TRADE

In Jan. 1994 an agreement to create a single economic zone was signed with Kazakhstan and Kyrgyzstan. Foreign investors are entitled to a 2-year tax holiday and repatriation of hard currency. External debt was US$2,319m. (17% of GDP) in 1996. In 1997 external trade turnover was US$8,910·5m.

Imports and Exports. In 1997 imports were valued at US$3,200m. and exports at US$2,878·9m. Principal imports, 1996, were machinery (35% of the total), light industrial goods, food and raw materials; principal exports were cotton (38% of the total), textiles, machinery, chemicals, food and energy products.

The main import sources in 1996 were Russia (24·9%), South Korea (11·8%), Germany (11·0%) and USA (8·1%). Principal export markets in 1996 were Russia (22·4%), Italy (8·8%), Tajikistan (6·8%), China (5·1%) and Ukraine (also 5·1%).

COMMUNICATIONS

Roads. Length of roads, 1995, was 80,000 km (hard surface, 69,760 km). In 1993, 2,347m. passengers and 217·2m. tonnes of freight were carried.

Rail. The total length of railway in 1993 was 3,483 km of 1,520 mm gauge (432 km electrified). In 1994, 22·4m. passengers and 40m. tonnes of freight were carried.

Civil Aviation. The main international airport is in Toshkent (Vostochny). Andijon and Namangan also have airports. The national carrier is the state-owned Uzbekiston Airways, which in 1998 operated domestic services and flew to Almaty, Amsterdam, Ashgabat, Athens, Baku, Bangkok, Beijing, Chelyabinsk, Delhi, Ekaterinburg, Frankfurt, Istanbul, Kazan, Khabarovsk, Krasnoyarsk, Kuala Lumpur, London, Mineralnye Vody, Moscow, New York, Novosibirsk, Omsk, Rostov, St Petersburg, Samara, Seoul, Sharjah, Simferopol, Tel Aviv, Tyumen, Ufa and Vientiane. In 1998 services were also provided by Air Enterprise Pulkovo, Air Kazakhstan, Air Lines of Kuban, Air Ukraine, Airzena Georgian Airlines, Armenian Airlines, Arax Airways, Asiana Airlines, Avia Company Turkmenistan, Baïkal Airlines, Bashkir Airlines, Belavia, Crimea Air, Domodedovo Airlines, Donavia, Imair, Iran Air, Kaliningrad Air Enterprise, Kavminvodyavia, Khabarovsk Aviation, Kyrgyzstan Airlines, Lufthansa, Novosibirsk Airlines, Pakistan International Airlines, Samara Airlines, Siberia Airlines, Transaero Airlines, Turkish Airlines, United Airlines and Xinjiang Airways. In 1995 scheduled airline traffic of Afghanistan-based carriers flew 32·1m. km, carrying 4,855,000 passengers.

Shipping. The total length of inland waterways in 1990 was 1,100 km.

Telecommunications. In 1997 main telephone lines numbered 1,490,000 (63 per 1,000 population). Cellular phone subscribers numbered 3,700 in 1995 and there were 1,900 fax machines.

SOCIAL INSTITUTIONS

Justice. In 1994, 73,561 crimes were reported, including 1,219 murders and attempted murders.

Religion. The Uzbeks are predominantly Sunni Moslems.

Education. In 1995 there were 1·07m. pre-primary pupils with 96,100 teachers, 1·9m. primary pupils with 92,400 teachers, and 3·31m. secondary pupils with 340,200 teachers. There were (1998) 55 higher educational establishments with 272,300 students, and 248 technical colleges with 240,100 students. There are universities and medical schools in Toshkent and Samarqand. Adult literacy rate in 1995 was over 99%.

Health. In 1995 there were 76,200 doctors, 249,600 nurses and 192 hospitals, with a provision of 84 beds per 10,000 population.

Welfare. In Jan. 1994 there were 1,726,000 old-age pensioners and 1,007,000 other pensioners.

CULTURE

Broadcasting. Broadcasting is under the aegis of the State Teleradio Broadcasting Company. The government-controlled Uzbek Radio transmits 2 national and several regional programmes, a Radio Moscow relay and a foreign service, Radio Toshkent (Uzbek, Arabic, English, Dari, Farsi, Hindi, Pushtu, Uighur). In 1996 there were 10·5m. radio and 6·25m. television receivers.

Cinema. In 1993 there were 2,365 cinemas with a seating capacity of 609,300 and an annual attendance of 27·4m.

Press. In 1995 there were 3 daily newspapers with a combined circulation of 140,000.

DIPLOMATIC REPRESENTATIVES

Of Uzbekiston in Great Britain (41 Holland Park, London, W11 2RP)
Ambassador: Fatih Gulyamovich Teshabaev.

Of Great Britain in Uzbekiston (Ul. Gogolya 67, Toshkent 700000)
Ambassador: Barbara L. Hay, MBE, CMG.

Of Uzbekiston in the USA (1746 Massachusetts Ave., NW, Washington, D.C., 20036)
Ambassador: Sodiq Safaev.

Of the USA in Uzbekiston (82 Chilanzarskaya, Toshkent)
Ambassador: Joseph Presel.

Of Uzbekiston to the United Nations
Ambassador: Alisher Vohidov.

Of Uzbekiston to the European Union
Ambassador: Alisher Faizullaev.

FURTHER READING

Kangas, R. D., *Uzbekistan in the Twentieth Century: Political Development and the Evolution of Power.* New York, 1994

QORAQALPOGH AUTONOMOUS REPUBLIC (QORAQALPOGHISTON)

Area, 164,900 sq. km (63,920 sq. miles); population (Jan. 1994), 1,343,000. Capital, Nukus (1989 census population, 174,000). The Qoraqalpoghs came under Russian rule in the second half of the 19th century. On 11 May 1925 the territory was constituted within the then Kazakh Autonomous Republic (of the Russian Federation) as an Autonomous Region. On 20 March 1932 it became an Autonomous Republic within the Russian Federation, and on 5 Dec. 1936 it became part of the Uzbek SSR. At the 1989 census Qoraqalpoghs were 32·1% of the population, Uzbeks, 32·8% and Kazakhs, 26·3%.

170 deputies were elected to its Supreme Soviet in Feb. 1990.

Its manufactures are in the field of light industry—bricks, leather goods, furniture, canning and wine. In Jan. 1990 cattle numbered 336,000, and sheep and goats 518,100. There were 38 collective and 124 state farms in 1987. The total cultivated area in 1985 was 350,400 ha.

In 1990–91 there were 313,500 pupils at schools, 22,100 student at technical colleges, and 7,800 at Nukus University. There is a branch of the Uzbek Academy of Sciences.

There were 2,600 doctors and 12,800 hospital beds in 1987.

VANUATU

Ripablik blong Vanuatu—

Republic of Vanuatu

Capital: Vila
Population estimate, 2000: 192,000
GNP per capita: (PPP$) 3,020
HDI/world rank: 0·559/124

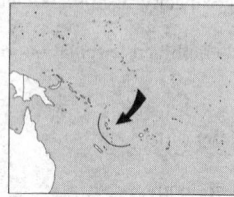

KEY HISTORICAL EVENTS

Vanuatu occupies the group of islands formerly known as the New Hebrides, in the south-western Pacific Ocean. Many of the northern islands have been inhabited by Melanesian peoples for at least 3,000 years. The islands which comprise the Republic of Vanuatu were first discovered in 1606 by the Portuguese. They were rediscovered by the French in 1768 and charted and named the New Hebrides by Captain Cook in 1774. Captain Bligh and his companions, cast adrift by the *Bounty* mutineers, sailed through part of the island group in 1789. Sandalwood merchants and European missionaries came to the islands in the mid 19th century and were then followed by cotton planters—mostly French and British—in 1868.

Complaints by missionaries regarding the activities of slave traders induced Britain to establish legislation to protect the islanders. Shortly thereafter British and French settlers began to arrive and French influence increased. In response to Australian calls to annexe the islands, Britain and France agreed on joint supervision, initially through an 1888 Joint Naval Commission and subsequently through a Condominium Government, established in 1906, which was superseded by an Anglo-French Protocol in 1914. Joint sovereignty was held over the indigenous Melanesia people, but each nation retained responsibility for its own nationals according to the protocol of 1914. The island group escaped Japanese invasion during the Second World War and became an Allied base.

In 1972, the New Hebrides National Party, now known as the Vanuaaku Pati, was formed. The Vanuaaku Pati was instrumental in winning agreement from the condominium powers for independence and on 30 July 1980 New Hebrides became an independent nation under the name of Vanuatu, meaning 'Our Land Forever'.

TERRITORY AND POPULATION

Vanuatu comprises 80 islands, which lie roughly 500 miles west of the Fiji Islands and 250 miles north-east of New Caledonia. The estimated land area is 4,706 sq. miles (12,190 sq. km). The larger islands of the group are: (Espiritu) Santo, Malekula, Epi, Pentecost, Aoba, Maewo, Paama, Ambrym, Efate, Erromanga, Tanna and Aneityum. They also claim Matthew and Hunter islands. 67 islands were inhabited in 1990. Population at the census (1989), 142,944, and estimated population in 1997, 181,400, giving a density of 15 per sq. km.

The UN gives a projected population for 2000 of 192,000.

In 1995 an estimated 81·1% of the population lived in rural areas. Vila (the capital) has a population of 31,800 (1996 estimate), and Luganville 10,000.

40% of the population is under 15 years of age, 57% between the ages of 15 and 64 and 3% 65 or over.

The national language is Bislama (spoken by 82% of the population): English and French are also official languages; about 50,000 speak French.

SOCIAL STATISTICS

Births, 1997, 5,400; deaths, 1,600. Rates per 1,000 population, 1997: Birth rate, 29·9; death rate, 8·6. 1997 population growth rate, 2·12%. Life expectancy, 1990–95, was 63·5 years for males and 67·3 years for females. Infant mortality, 1990–95, 47 per 1,000 live births; fertility rate, 4·7 births per woman.

CLIMATE

The climate is tropical, but moderated by oceanic influences and by trade winds from May to Oct. High humidity occasionally occurs and cyclones are possible. Rainfall ranges from 90" (2,250 mm) in the south to 155" (3,875 mm) in the north. Vila, Jan. 80°F (26·7°C), July 72°F (22·2°C). Annual rainfall 84" (2,103 mm).

CONSTITUTION AND GOVERNMENT

Legislative power resides in a 50-member unicameral Parliament elected for a term of 4 years. The President is elected for a 5-year term by an electoral college comprising Parliament and the presidents of the 11 regional councils. Executive power is vested in a Council of Ministers, responsible to Parliament, and appointed and led by a Prime Minister who is elected from and by Parliament.

There is also a *Council of Chiefs,* comprising traditional tribal leaders, to advise on matters of custom.

National Anthem. 'Yumi yumi yumi i glat blong talem se, yumi, yumi yumi i man blong Vanuatu' ('We we we are glad to tell, we we we are the people of Vanuatu'); words and tune by F. Vincent.

RECENT ELECTIONS

Parliamentary elections were held on 6 March 1998. The Party of Our Land (VP) gained 18 seats; the Union of Moderate Parties (UPM), 12; the National United Party (NUP), 11; others, 11.

CURRENT ADMINISTRATION

President: John Bani (elected on 24 March 1999).

A VP-NUP coalition government was formed following the March 1998 election, consisting in March 1999 of:

Prime Minister and Minister of Foreign Affairs: Donald Kalpokas (VP).

Deputy Prime Minister and Minister of Trade and Business Development: Willie Jimmy.

Minister of Internal Affairs: Vincent Boulekone. *Education, Youth and Sports:* Joe Natuman. *Finance and Economic Development:* Sela Molisa. *Infrastructure and Public Utilities:* Henry Taga. *Lands, Geology and Mines:* Silas Hakwa. *Agriculture, Forestry and Fisheries:* John Morrison Willie. *Health:* Jean Keasipai.

DEFENCE

There is a paramilitary force with about 300 personnel. The Vanuatu Police maritime service operates 1 inshore patrol craft, and a former motor yacht, both lightly armed. Personnel numbered about 50 in 1996.

INTERNATIONAL RELATIONS

Vanuatu is a member of the UN, the Commonwealth, the Pacific Community and the South Pacific Forum, and is an ACP member state of the ACP-EU relationship.

ECONOMY

Performance. Real GDP growth was 3·2% in 1995 and 3·0% in 1994.

Budget. Revenues totalled an estimated US$94·4m. and expenditures US$99·8m. in 1996.

Currency. The unit of currency is the *vatu* (VUV) with no minor unit. The average annual inflation rate over the period 1990–96 was 3·2%. Foreign exchange reserves in Feb. 1998 were US$25m. Total money supply in Jan. 1998 was 6,643m. vatu.

Banking and Finance. The Reserve Bank blong Vanuatu is the central bank and bank of issue. The Finance Centre in Vila consists of 4 international banks and 6 trust companies. Commercial banks' assets at 31 Dec. 1988, 20,900m. vatu.

Weights and Measures. The metric system is in force.

ENERGY AND NATURAL RESOURCES

Electricity. Electrical capacity in 1995 was 11,000 kW, with production in 1994 of 30m. kWh.

Agriculture. About 65% of the labour force are employed in agriculture. The main commercial crops are copra, coconuts, cocoa and coffee. Production (1995, in tonnes): copra, 30,000; coconuts, 280,000 (estimated); cocoa, 2,000. 80% of the population are engaged in subsistence agriculture; yams, taro, cassava, sweet potatoes and bananas are grown for local consumption. A large number of cattle are reared on plantations, and a beef industry is developing.

Livestock (1995): cattle, 151,000; goats, 12,000; pigs, 60,000; horses, 3,000; poultry, 158,000.

Forestry. There were 900,000 ha of forest in 1995 (73·8% of the land area), down from 738,000 ha in 1990. In 1995, 63,000 cu. metres of roundwood were cut.

Fisheries. The principal catch is tuna, mainly exported to the USA. The total catch in 1995 was 2,833 tonnes.

INDUSTRY
Industry in 1995 employed about 3% of the workforce, with 32% employed in services. Principal industries include copra processing, meat canning and fish freezing, a saw-mill, soft drinks factories and a print works. Building materials, furniture and aluminium are also produced, and in 1984 a cement plant opened.

Contributions to GDP in 1995 (in 1m. vatu) included: agriculture, forestry and fishing, 6,051; manufacturing, 1,386; electricity, gas and water, 462; construction, 1,721; wholesale and retail trade, restaurants and hotels, 8,611; transport, storage and communications, 2,247; finance and allied business services, 3,512; government services, 3,089.

INTERNATIONAL TRADE

Imports and Exports. In 1996 imports were valued at US$97m. and exports at US$30m. Main import markets (1995): Australia (37%), New Zealand (12%), Japan (9%), France (6%) and the Fiji Islands (6%). Main export suppliers: EU (37%), Japan (24%), Australia (10%) and Bangladesh (10%).

The main exports are copra, beef, timber and cocoa.

COMMUNICATIONS

Roads. There are 1,050 km of roads, about 250 km paved, mostly on Efate Island and Espiritu Santo. There were estimated to be 4,000 passenger cars and 2,300 commercial vehicles in use in 1996.

Civil Aviation. There is an international airport at Bauerfield Port Vila. In 1998 the state-owned Air Vanuatu provided domestic services and flew to Auckland, Brisbane, Honiara, Melbourne, Nadi, Nouméa and Sydney. Services were also provided in 1998 by Air Calédonie International, Air Pacific, Qantas Airways and Solomon Airlines. In 1995 Air Vanuatu flew 2·0m. km, carrying 65,600 passengers.

Shipping. Sea-going shipping totalled 2·57m. GRT in 1995, including oil tankers, 21,833 GRT, and container ships, 29,890 GRT. Several international shipping lines serve Vanuatu, linking the country with Australia, New Zealand, other Pacific territories, China (Hong Kong), Japan, North America and Europe. The chief ports are Vila and Santo. Small vessels provide frequent inter-island services.

Telecommunications. Services are provided by the Posts and Telecommunications and Radio Departments. There are automatic telephone exchanges at Vila and Santo; rural areas are served by a network of tele-radio stations. In 1996 there were 4,500 telephone main lines, equivalent to 25·7 per 1,000 population. Cellular phone subscribers numbered around 100 in 1995 and there were approximately 600 fax machines.

External telephone, telegram and telex services are provided by VANITEL, through their satellite earth station at Vila. There are direct circuits to Nouméa, Sydney, Hong Kong and Paris and communications are available on a 24-hour basis to most countries. Air radio facilities are provided. Marine coast station facilities are available at Vila and Santo.

SOCIAL INSTITUTIONS

Justice. A study was begun in 1980 which could lead to unification of the judicial system.

Religion. Over 80% of the population are Christians, but animist beliefs are still prevalent.

Education. In 1994 there were 252 pre-primary schools and 272 primary schools with 852 teachers for 26,267 pupils. There were 4,184 secondary pupils in 1991.

VANUATU

Tertiary education is provided at the Vanuatu Technical Institute and the Teachers College, while other technical and commercial training is through regional institutions in the Solomon Islands, the Fiji Islands and Papua New Guinea. The literacy rate (1979 estimates) is 53% (57% of men; 48% of women).

Health. In 1995 there were 12 doctors, 3 dentists, 259 nurses, 6 pharmacists and 33 midwives. There were 90 hospitals, with a provision of 22 beds per 10,000 population.

CULTURE

Broadcasting. The government-controlled Radio Vanuatu broadcasts in French, English and Bislama. In 1995 there were about 50,000 radio receivers and 2,000 televisions.

Tourism. In 1996 there were 46,123 visitors to Vanuatu. Receipts totalled US$50m.

DIPLOMATIC REPRESENTATIVES
Of Vanuatu in Great Britain
High Commissioner: Vacant.

Of Great Britain in Vanuatu (KPMG Hse., Rue Pasteur, Port Vila)
High Commissioner: Malcolm G. Hilson.

Of Vanuatu in the USA
Ambassador: Vacant.

Of the USA in Vanuatu
Ambassador: Richard W. Teare (resides in Papua New Guinea).

Of Vanuatu to the United Nations
Ambassador: Jean Ravou-Akii.

VATICAN CITY STATE

Population estimate, 2000: 900

Stato della Città del Vaticano

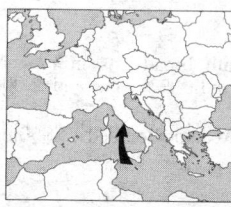

KEY HISTORICAL EVENTS

For many centuries the Popes bore temporal sway over a territory stretching across mid-Italy from sea to sea and comprising some 17,000 sq. miles, with a population finally of over 3m. In 1859–60 and 1870 the Papal States were incorporated into the Italian Kingdom. The consequent dispute between Italy and successive Popes was only settled on 11 Feb. 1929 by three treaties between the Italian Government and the Vatican: a political treaty, which recognized the full and independent sovereignty of the Holy See in the city of the Vatican; a concordat, to regulate the condition of religion and of the Church in Italy; and a financial convention, in accordance with which the Holy See received 750m. lire in cash and 1,000m. lire in Italian 5% state bonds. This sum was to be a definitive settlement of all the financial claims of the Holy See against Italy in consequence of the loss of its temporal power in 1870. The treaty and concordat were ratified on 7 June 1929 and embodied in the Constitution of the Italian Republic of 1947. A revised Concordat between the Italian Republic and the Holy See was negotiated and signed in 1984, and came into force on 3 June 1985. à

TERRITORY AND POPULATION

The area of the Vatican City is 44 ha (108·7 acres). It includes the Piazza di San Pietro (St Peter's Square), which is to remain normally open to the public and subject to the powers of the Italian police. It has its own railway station (for freight only), postal facilities, coins and radio. Twelve buildings in and outside Rome enjoy extra-territorial rights, including the Basilicas of St John Lateran, St Mary Major and St Paul without the Walls, the Pope's summer villa at Castel Gandolfo and a further Vatican radio station on Italian soil. *Radio Vaticana* broadcasts an extensive service in 34 languages from the transmitters in the Vatican City and in Italy.

The Vatican City has about 900 inhabitants.

CONSTITUTION AND GOVERNMENT

The Vatican City State is governed by a Commission appointed by the Pope. The reason for its existence is to provide an extra-territorial, independent base for the Holy See, the government of the Roman Catholic Church. The Pope exercises sovereignty and has absolute legislative, executive and judicial powers. The judicial power is delegated to a tribunal in the first instance, to the Sacred Roman Rota in appeal and to the Supreme Tribunal of the Signature in final appeal.

The Pope is elected by the College of Cardinals, meeting in secret conclave. The election is by scrutiny and requires a two-thirds majority.

CURRENT ADMINISTRATION

Supreme Pontiff: **John Paul II** (Karol Wojtyła), born at Wadowice near Kraków, Poland, 18 May 1920. Archbishop of Kraków 1964–78, created Cardinal in 1967; elected Pope 16 Oct. 1978, inaugurated 22 Oct. 1978.

Pope John Paul II was the first non-Italian to be elected since Pope Adrian VI (a Dutchman) in 1522.

Secretary of State: Cardinal Angelo Sodano.

Secretary for Relations with Other States: Jean-Louis Tauran.

ECONOMY

Performance. Real GDP growth was 3·0% in 1995 (2·2% in 1994 but –1·2% in 1993).

Budget. Revenues in 1994 were US$175·5m. and expenditures US$175m.

ROMAN CATHOLIC CHURCH

The Roman Pontiff (in orders a Bishop, but in jurisdiction held to be by divine right the centre of all Catholic unity, and consequently Pastor and Teacher of all Christians) has for advisers and coadjutors the Sacred College of Cardinals, consisting in Nov. 1996 of 167 Cardinals appointed by him from senior ecclesiastics who are either the bishops of important Sees or the heads of departments at the Holy See. In addition to the College of Cardinals, the Pope has created a 'Synod of Bishops'. This consists of the Patriarchs and certain Metropolitans of the Catholic Church of Oriental Rite, of elected representatives of the national episcopal conferences and religious orders of the world, of the Cardinals in charge of the Roman Congregations and of other persons nominated by the Pope. The Synod meets as and when decided by the Pope. The last Synod (on the formation of priests) met in Oct. 1990.

The central administration of the Roman Catholic Church is carried on by a number of permanent committees called Sacred Congregations, each composed of a number of Cardinals and diocesan bishops (both appointed for 5-year periods), with Consultors and Officials. Besides the Secretariat of State and the Second Section of the Secretariat of State (Section for Relations with States) there are now 9 Sacred Congregations, viz.: Doctrine, Oriental Churches, Bishops, the Sacraments and Divine Worship, Clergy, Religious, Catholic Education, Evangelization of the Peoples and Causes of the Saints. Pontifical Councils have replaced some of the previously designated Secretariats and Prefectures and now represent the Laity, Christian Unity, the Family, Justice and Peace, Cor Unum, Migrants, Health Care Workers, Interpretation of Legislative Texts, Inter-Religious Dialogue, Culture, Preserving the Patrimony of Art and History, and a new Commission, for Latin America. There are also various Offices. The Pontifical Academy of Sciences was revived in 1936. The director of the Vatican Bank (Istituto per le Opere di Religione) is Giovanni Bodio.

CULTURE

The Vatican is building some 25 new churches to mark The Great Jubilee. One of the most prominent will be the Church of the Year 2000. The Pope will usher in the new Millennium by banging on the Holy Door of St Peter's Basilica with a silver hammer in accordance with tradition.

DIPLOMATIC REPRESENTATIVES

In its diplomatic relations with foreign countries the Holy See is represented by its Secretariat of State and the Second Section (Relations with States) of the Council for Public Affairs of the Church. It maintains permanent observers to the UN.

Of the Holy See in Great Britain (54 Parkside, London, SW19 5NE)
Apostolic Nuncio: Archbishop Pablo Puente.

Of Great Britain at the Holy See (91 Via Dei Condotti, I–00187 Rome).
Ambassador: Mark E. Pellew, LVO.

Of the Holy See in the USA (3339 Massachusetts Ave., NW, Washington, D.C., 20008).
Apostolic Nuncio: Agostino Cacciavillan.

Of the USA at the Holy See (Villa Domiziana, Via Delle Terme Deciane 26, 00153 Rome).
Ambassador: Corinne C. Boggs.

FURTHER READING

Bull, G., *Inside the Vatican*. London, 1982
Cardinale, I., *The Holy See and the International Order*. Gerrards Cross, 1976
Mayer, F. *et al*, *The Vatican: Portrait of a State and a Community*. Dublin, 1980
Nichols, P., *The Pope's Divisions*. London, 1981
Reese. T., *Inside the Vatican*. Harvard Univ. Press, 1997
Walsh, M. J., *Vatican City State*. [Bibliography] Oxford and Santa Barbara (CA), 1983

VENEZUELA

República de Venezuela

Capital: Caracas
Population estimate, 2000: 24·17m.
GNP per capita: (PPP$) 8,130
HDI/world rank: 0·860/46

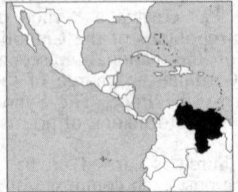

KEY HISTORICAL EVENTS

Columbus sighted Venezuela in 1498 and it was visited by Alonzo de Ojeda and Amerigo Vespucci in 1499 who named it Venezuela (Little Venice). It was part of the Spanish colony of New Granada until 1821 when it became independent, at first in union with Colombia and then as a separate independent republic from 1830.

Between 1830 and 1945 the country was governed mainly by dictators. In 1945 a three-day revolt against the reactionary government of Gen. Medina led to Romulo Betancourt assuming the presidency. Betancourt produced constitutional and economic reforms but he was replaced by Gen. Marcos Pérez Jiménez who seized power in 1952. Jiménez was himself overthrown by a military junta in a revolution in 1958, led by Adm. Wolfgang Larrazabal. Betancourt again became president.

In 1961 a new constitution was promulgated which provided for a presidential election every five years, a national congress, and state and municipal legislative assemblies.

Betancourt's progressive policies were continued by his successor, Dr Raúl Leoni. There was an abortive military uprising in 1966. In 1969 Dr Rafael Caldera Rodriguez became the first Christian Democratic president. In 1978 Dr Luis Herrera was chosen president but as his party, the *Partido Social-Christiano* (COPEI), failed to obtain an overall majority in congress he was forced to form alliances with smaller parties in order to make legislative progress.

Twenty political parties participated in the 1983 elections. Of 13 presidential candidates, Dr Jaime Lusinchi was elected with 57% of the votes. By now the economy was in crisis and social unrest was widespread. Corruption linked to drug trafficking led to further violence. In Feb. 1992 an attempt to overthrow the President by rebel troops was narrowly averted. There was another abortive coup in Nov. A state of emergency was declared. President Perez resisted demands for his resignation but he was later suspended from office. In Dec. 1993, Dr Rafael Caldera Rodriguez was returned to the presidency with 30·5% of the vote. Dr Caldera's election reflected disenchantment with the established political parties and concern over allegations of mismanagement and corruption. He took office in the early stages of a banking crisis which cost 15% of GDP to resolve. Fiscal tightening backed by the IMF brought rapid recovery.

TERRITORY AND POPULATION

Venezuela is bounded to the north by the Caribbean with a 2,813 km coastline, east by the Atlantic and Guyana, south by Brazil, and south-west and west by Colombia. The area is 916,490 sq. km (353,857 sq. miles) including 72 islands in the Caribbean. Population (1990) census, 19,455,429 (84% urban; estimate, 85·8% in 1995). Estimate (1997) 21·8m.; density, 23·9 per sq. km.

The UN gives a projected population for 2000 of 24·17m.

The official language is Spanish. English is taught as a mandatory second language in high schools.

Area, population and capitals of the 23 states and 1 federally-controlled area:

State	Sq. km	Census 1990	Capital	Density; inhabitants per sq. km
Federal District	1,930	2,265,874	Caracas	1,182·23
Amazonas	177,617	60,207	Puerto Ayacucho	0·55
Anzoátegui	43,300	924,074	Barcelona	24·88
Apure	76,500	305,132	San Fernando	5·43
Aragua	7,014	1,194,962	Maracay	202·30
Barinas	35,200	456,246	Barinas	15·48
Bolívar	240,528	968,695	Ciudad Bolívar	5·02

VENEZUELA

State	Sq. km	Census 1990	Capital	Density; inhabitants per sq. km
Carabobo	4,650	1,558,608	Valencia	443·00
Cojedes	14,800	196,526	San Carlos	16·31
Delta Amacuro	40,200	91,085	Tucupita	3·07
Falcón	24,800	632,513	Coro	29·01
Guárico	64,986	525,737	San Juan de los Morros	9·32
Lara	19,800	1,330,477	Barquisimeto	75·35
Mérida	11,300	639,846	Mérida	62·55
Miranda	7,950	2,026,229	Los Teques	305·01
Monagas	28,900	503,176	Maturín	19·86
Nueva Esparta	1,150	280,777	La Asunción	303·60
Portuguesa	15,200	625,576	Guanare	50·28
Sucre	11,800	772,707	Cumaná	67·79
Táchira	11,100	859,861	San Cristóbal	88·43
Trujillo	7,400	520,292	Trujillo	77·51
Yaracuy	7,100	411,980	San Felipe	68·65
Zulia	63,100	2,387,208	Maracaibo	50·21
Dependencias Federales	120	2,245		

84% of Venezuela's population lives in cities and towns with more than 2,500 inhabitants. 37·3% of all Venezuelans are under 15 years of age, 58·7% are between the ages of 15 and 64, and 4% are over the age of 65.

Caracas, Venezuela's largest city, is the political, financial, commercial, communications and cultural centre of the country. The population of metropolitan Caracas is approximately 3·1m. Maracaibo, the nation's second largest city, with an estimated population of 1·5m., is located near Venezuela's most important petroleum fields and richest agricultural areas.

SOCIAL STATISTICS
1995 births, 570,000; deaths, 103,000. 1995 birth rate per 1,000 population, 26·1; death rate, 4·7. Annual growth rate, 1993–97, 2·1%. Life expectancy, 1990–95, was 68·9 years for males and 74·7 years for females. Infant mortality, 1990–95, 23 per 1,000 live births; fertility rate, 3·3 births per woman.

CLIMATE
The climate ranges from warm temperate to tropical. Temperatures vary little throughout the year and rainfall is plentiful. The dry season is from Dec. to April. The hottest months are July and August. Caracas, Jan. 65°F (18·3°C), July 69°F (20·6°C). Annual rainfall 32" (833 mm). Ciudad Bolivar, Jan. 79°F (26·1°C), July 81°F (27·2°C). Annual rainfall 41" (1,016 mm). Maracaibo, Jan. 81°F (27·2°C), July 85°F (29·4°C). Annual rainfall 23" (577 mm).

CONSTITUTION AND GOVERNMENT
Venezuela is a federal republic, comprising 34 federal dependencies, 23 states and 1 federal district. Executive power is vested in the President. Re-elections can take place 10 years after the end of the first term. The ministers, who together constitute the Council of Ministers, are appointed by the President and head various executive departments. There are 17 ministries and 7 officials who also have the rank of Minister of State.

The Senate and Chamber of Deputies have similar legislative powers. For a bill to become law, it must be approved by a majority in both bodies. Differences between the 2 chambers are resolved through majority vote of the Congress, meeting in joint session. The constitution provides for procedures by which the President may reject bills passed by Congress, as well as provisions by which Congress may override such Presidential veto acts.

Main political organizations: the president's party, Movimiento Quinta República (MVR), which has 21 seats in the Chamber of Deputies and 12 in the Senate; Acción Democrática (AD); Comité de Organización Politica Electoral Independiente (Copei); Proyecto Venezuela (PVVZL); Movimiento al Socialismo (MAS); Patria Para Todos (PPT); La Causa R (LCR); Convergencia; Apertura.

National Anthem. 'Gloria al bravo pueblo' ('Glory to the brave people'); words by Vicente Salias, tune by Juan Landaeta.

RECENT ELECTIONS
Congressional elections were held on 8 Nov. 1998. Acción Democrático won 55 of the 189 seats in the Chamber of Deputies and 17 in the Senate, ahead of Movimiento Quinta República with 49 in the Chamber of Deputies and 14 in the Senate. Presidential elections were held on 6 Dec. 1998. Hugo Chávez Frías (MVR) was elected President against 2 other candidates with 56·5% of the vote.

CURRENT ADMINISTRATION
President: Hugo Chávez Frías; b. 1953 (ind; sworn in 2 Feb. 1999).

In March 1999 the government comprised:

Minister of the Interior, Justice and Decentralization: Luis Miquilena. *Foreign Affairs:* José Vicente Rangel. *Finance:* Maritza Izaguirre Porras. *Defence:* Raúl Salazar. *Transport and Communications, and Urban Development:* Luis Reyes Reyes. *Energy and Mines:* Alí Rodríguez. *Industry and Commerce:* Gustavo Márquez Marin. *Environment and Renewable Natural Resources:* Atalá Uriana Pocaterra. *Health and Social Security:* Gilberto Rodríguez. *Agriculture and Livestock:* Alejandro Riera. *Education:* Héctor Navarro. *Family, Labour and Social Development:* Leopoldo Puchi. *Presidential Secretariat:* Alfredo Peña. *Co-ordination and Planning:* Jorge Giordani. *Information:* Carmen Ramia.

Local Government. There are 23 states, each with an elected assembly and governor. The states are divided into 332 municipalities and 1,071 *parroquias* and the capital. The Federal District is administered by the President. Elections were held on 8 Nov. 1998 to elect 23 governors, 330 mayors and several thousand councillors. Turn-out was 40%. The Democratic Action Party gained 12 governorships.

DEFENCE
There is selective conscription for 30 months. Defence expenditure totalled US$962m. in 1997 (US$42 per capita).

Army. The Army consists of 6 infantry divisions, 7 infantry brigades, 1 airborne, 1 Ranger, 1 armoured and 1 cavalry brigade and 1 aviation regiment. Equipment includes 70 AMX-30 main battle tanks. Army aviation comprises 24 helicopters and 14 aircraft. Strength (1997) 34,000 (27,000 conscripts).

A 22,000-strong volunteer National Guard is responsible for internal security.

Navy. The combatant fleet comprises 2 German-built submarines, 2 ex-US Knox Class and 6 Italian-built Lupo class frigates, 6 fast missile craft, 4 tank landing ships and 12 craft. Auxiliaries comprise 1 logistic support, 1 survey ship, 2 transports, and a sail training ship, as well as a few harbour service craft.

The Naval Air Arm, 1,000 strong, comprises 6 shore-based C-212 Aviocars and 8 S-2 Trackers for maritime reconnaissance and transport, 9 AB-212 ship-borne anti-submarine helicopters and 7 miscellaneous transport and liaison aircraft.

Personnel in 1997 totalled 15,000 (4,000 conscripts) including the 5,000-strong Marine Corps and 1,000 in Naval Aviation. Main bases are at Caracas, Puerto Cabello and Punto Fijo.

The Coastguard, 1,000 strong in 1997, organizationally separate but under Naval operational control, is responsible for control of the economic exclusion zone.

Air Force. The Air Force was 7,000 strong in 1997, and had 80 combat aircraft and 15 armed helicopters. There are 6 combat squadrons. Two are equipped with 16 F-16A and 5 F-16B Fighting Falcons. Two have 9 Canadair CF-5A fighter-bombers and 9 two-seat CF-5Ds, and one has 12 Mirage 50 single-seaters and 3 Mirage 50 trainers. 2 other operational squadrons have 15 OV-10 Bronco twin-turboprop counter-insurgency aircraft and there is 1 squadron of armed Tucano trainers. A helicopter force consists of more than 40 Super Pumas, Bell 212s, 214STs and 412s, UH-1B/D/H Iroquois and Alouette IIIs.

INTERNATIONAL RELATIONS
Venezuela is a member of the UN, OAS, LAIA, OPEC, WTO, GATT, FAO, G-77, Interpol, Intelsat, IADB, IAEA, IMO, SELA, PAHO, UNCTAD, UNESCO, UPU, WHO and the Andean Community.

ECONOMY

Policy. A stabilization programme of April 1996 introduced market-oriented reforms, liberalizing interest rates and sextupling petrol prices. An ambitious programme of privatization has stalled.

Performance. GDP contracted by 1% in 1996 but grew by 5·1% in 1997. In 1998 it was forecast to grow slightly, by around 1%.

Budget. The fiscal year is the calendar year. Revenues and expenditures in Bs 1m. for the period 1994 to 1997 were:

	1994	1995	1996	1997
Revenue	1,481,533	2,144,214	5,661,252	9,985,506
Expenditure	1,566,229	2,413,543	4,775,871	8,473,305

The expected revenue and expenditure for 1999 is Bs 13,969,059.

Currency. The unit of currency is the *bolívar* (VEB) of 100 *céntimos*. Foreign exchange reserves were US\$14,849m. in Dec. 1998 and gold reserves 11·11m. troy oz. in Feb. 1998. Exchange controls were abolished in April 1996. The bolívar was devalued by 12·6% in 1998. Inflation rate in 1997 was 42·0%, in 1998, 29·9%, and predicted for 1999 to be 25·0%. Total money supply in Feb. 1998 was Bs 5,487m.

Banking and Finance. A law of Dec. 1992 provided for greater autonomy for the Central Bank. Its governor, currently Antonio Casas González, is appointed by the President for 5-year terms. Since 1993 foreign banks have been allowed a controlling interest in domestic banks.

There is a stock exchange in Caracas.

ENERGY AND NATURAL RESOURCES

Electricity. Installed capacity in 1997 was 19·59m. kW, production was 74·89bn. kWh and consumption per capita was estimated to be 2,550 kWh.

Oil and Gas. Proven resources of crude were 75bn. bbls. in 1997. The oil sector was nationalized in 1976, but private and foreign investment have again been permitted since 1992. Estimated crude oil production (1997) was 3,313,000 bbls. a day. Venezuela is the largest exporter of oil to the USA. Gas production (1997) 868bn. cu. feet. Oil provides about 40% of Venezuela's revenues.

Minerals. Output (in 1,000 tonnes) in 1997: iron ore, 18,359 (23,424 in 1995); coal, 3,097 (4,646 in 1995); gold, 19,661 kg (3,287 kg in 1995).

Agriculture. Coffee, cocoa, sugar-cane, maize, rice, wheat, tobacco, cotton, beans and sisal are grown. 50% of farmers are engaged in subsistence agriculture. There are government price supports and tax incentives.

Production in 1997 in 1,000 tonnes: Rice, 792·2 (643 in 1995); sugar-cane, 6,429 (6,900 in 1995); bananas, 504·1 (1,215 in 1995); oranges, 513·7 (440 in 1995); tomatoes, 261·5 (244 in 1995). In 1995, cassava, 285; potatoes, 215.

Livestock (1996): Cattle, 14·58m.; horses, 500,000; sheep, 1·2m.; pigs, 3·15m.; goats 2·96m. (1995); chickens, 95m. (1995).

Forestry. In 1995 the area under forests was 43·99m. ha, or 49·9% of the total land area (down from 46·51m. ha in 1990). Among South American countries only Brazil lost a larger area of forests over the same 5 years. Timber production 1995, 2,267,000 cu. metres.

Fisheries. In 1995 the total catch was 504,791 tonnes (88% from marine waters).

INDUSTRY

Production (1994, tonnes): Steel, 3·14m.; aluminium, 617,000; cement, 4·56m.

Labour. Out of 7,670,000 people in employment in 1995, 2,186,000 were in community, social and personal services, 1,739,000 in trade, restaurants and hotels, 1,047,000 in manufacturing and 1,012,000 in agriculture, fishing and forestry. Unemployment was 10·5% in 1997.

Trade Unions. The most powerful confederation of trade unions is the CTV (*Confederación de Trabajadores de Venezuela*, formed 1947).

INTERNATIONAL TRADE

The Group of Three free trade pact with Colombia and Mexico came into effect on 1 Jan. 1995. Foreign debt was US$35,344m. in 1996.

Imports and Exports. In 1997 imports were valued at US$12·7bn. and exports at US$21·4bn. Oil exports were valued at US$12·6bn. in 1991. The main import sources in 1995 were USA (42·6%), Colombia (7·6%), Germany (4·8%) and Japan (4·4%). Tha main markets for exports in 1995 were USA (51·3%), Brazil (9·0%), Colombia (7·6%) and Netherlands Antilles (4·9%).

COMMUNICATIONS

Roads. In 1996 there were 84,300 km of roads, of which 33,200 km were surfaced. There were 1,520,000 passenger cars in use in 1996 (69 per 1,000 inhabitants) plus 434,000 trucks and vans.

Rail. Railways (336 km—1,435 mm gauge) carried 31·3m. passenger-km and 259,000 tonnes of freight in 1994.

There is a metro in Caracas.

Civil Aviation. The main international airport is at Caracas (Simon Bolívar), with some international flights from Maracaibo. Servivensa and Aeropostal Alas de Venezuela are the main Venezuelan carriers. In 1998 services were also provided by Aerolíneas Argentinas, Aeroperú, Aeroservicios Carababo, Air Aruba, Air France, Alitalia, ALM, American Airlines, Avensa, Avianca, Aviones de Oriente C.A., British Airways, BWIA International, Continental Airlines, COPA, Cubana, Delta Air Lines, Ecuatoriana, Iberia, KLM, LACSA, Lan-Chile, LASER, Lloyd Aéreo Boliviano, Lufthansa, Mexicana, TAP, United Airlines and Varig. In 1995 scheduled airline traffic of Venezuela-based carriers flew 65·4m. km, carrying 4,446,000 passengers (1,604,000 on international flights).

Shipping. Ocean-going shipping totalled 1·37m. GRT in 1995, including oil tankers, 0·69m. GRT, and container ships, 1,180 GRT. La Guaira, Maracaibo, Puerto Cabello, Puerto Ordaz and Guanta are the chief ports. In 1995 vessels totalling 21,009,000 net registered tons entered ports and vessels totalling 8,461,000 NRT cleared. The principal navigable rivers are the Orinoco and its tributaries the Apure and Arauca.

Telecommunications. In 1997 there were 2,702,600 main telephone lines (116·4 per 1,000 population). Cellular phone subscribers numbered 400,000 in 1995, there were 370,000 PCs and 16,000 fax machines. There were approximately 12,000 Internet users in Oct. 1997.

Postal Services. In 1995 there were 444 post offices, or 1 for every 49,200 persons.

SOCIAL INSTITUTIONS

Justice. The Supreme Court, which operates in Divisions, each with 5 members, is elected by Congress for 5 years. The country is divided into 20 legal districts. The Federal Procurator-General is appointed for 5 years. There are lower federal courts. Each state has a Supreme Court with 3 members, a superior court, or superior tribunal, courts of first instance, district courts and municipal courts. In the territories there are civil and military judges of first instance, and also judges in the municipalities.

Religion. In 1992 there were 18·49m. Roman Catholics. There are 4 archbishops, 1 at Caracas, who is Primate of Venezuela, 2 at Mérida and 1 at Ciudad Bolívar. There are 19 bishops. Protestants number about 20,000.

Education. In 1994 there were 16,000 primary schools with 186,000 teachers and 4,200,000 pupils, 1,500 secondary schools with 34,000 teachers and 1,100,000 pupils.

In 1995–96 there were in the public sector 16 universities, 1 polytechnic university and 1 open (distance) university; and in the private sector, 12 universities, 2 Roman Catholic universities and 1 technological university.

Adult literacy was 91·1% in 1995 (male, 91·8%; female, 90·3%).

In 1994 total expenditure on education came to 5·1% of GNP and represented 22·4% of total government expenditure.

Health. In 1996 there were 42,725 doctors and 52,394 beds in hospitals and dispensaries.

CULTURE

Broadcasting. There are 2 government and 4 cultural radio stations; the remainder are commercial. There are 4 government, 3 commercial and 3 other TV channels (colour by NTSC). In 1997 there were 9·5m. radio and 3·5m. TV receivers.

Cinema. There were 213 cinemas in 1997.

Press. There are 25 leading daily newspapers with a circulation of over 1·7m.

Tourism. In 1997 there were 796,477 foreign tourists. In 1995, 769,000 tourists brought in a revenue of US$846m.

Libraries. Venezuela had 675 libraries in 1997.

Museums and Galleries. There were 144 museums in 1997.

DIPLOMATIC REPRESENTATIVES
Of Venezuela in Great Britain (1 Cromwell Rd., London, SW7 2HW)
Ambassador: Roy Chaderton Matos.

Of Great Britain in Venezuela (Edificio Torre Las Mercedes, piso 3, Av. La Estancia, Chuao, Caracas 1061)
Ambassador: Richard D. Wilkinson, CVO.

Of Venezuela in the USA (1099 30th St., NW, Washington, D.C., 20007)
Ambassador: Alfredo Toro Hardy.

Of the USA in Venezuela (Calle Suapure, con calle F. Colinas de Valle Arriba, Caracas)
Ambassador: John Maisto.

Of Venezuela to the United Nations
Ambassador: Ignacio Arcaya.

Of Venezuela to the European Union
Ambassador: Luis Xavier Grisanti.

FURTHER READING
*Dirección General de Estadística, Ministerio de Fomento, Boletín Mensual de Estadística.—
Anuario Estadístico de Venezuela.* Caracas, Annual
Ewell, J., *Venezuela: a Century of Change.* London, 1984
Hellinger, D.V., *Tarnished Democracy.* Boulder (CO), 1991
Naim, M., *Paper Tigers and Minotaurs: the Politics of Venezuela's Economic Reforms.*
Washington (D.C.), 1993

VIETNAM

Công Hòa Xã Hôi Chu Nghĩa

Viêt Nam

(Socialist Republic of Vietnam)

Capital: Hanoi
Population estimate, 2000: 80·55m.
GNP per capita: (PPP$) 1,570
HDI/world rank: 0·560/122

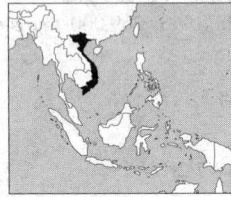

KEY HISTORICAL EVENTS

Vietnam was conquered by the Chinese in 111 BC, and though it broke free of Chinese domination in 939 AD, at many subsequent periods it was a nominal Chinese vassal.

By the end of the 15th century, the Vietnamese had conquered most of the Kingdom of Champa (now Vietnam's central area), and by the end of the 18th century had acquired Cochin-China (now its southern area). At the end of the 18th century, France helped to establish the Emperor Gia-Long (with whom Louis XVI had signed a treaty in 1787) as ruler of a unified Vietnam, known then as the Empire of Annam. French influence increased with a series of treaties between 1874 and 1884, the establishment of French protectorates over Tonkin and Annam, and the formation of the French colony of Cochin-China. By a Sino-French treaty of 1885, the Empire of Annam ceased to be a tributary to China. Cambodia had become a French protectorate in 1863, and in 1899 after the extension of French protection to Laos in 1893, the Indo Chinese Union was proclaimed.

In 1940, Vietnam was occupied by the Japanese. In 1941, a nationalist coalition of nationalist, revolutionary and Communist organizations, known as the Vietminh League, was founded by the Communists. On 9 March 1945, the Japanese interned the French authorities and proclaimed the independence of Indo-China. In Aug. 1945, they allowed the Vietminh movement to seize power, dethrone the Emperor of Annam and establish a republic known as Vietnam. On 6 March 1946, France recognized 'the Democratic Republic of Vietnam' as a 'Free State within the Indo-Chinese Federation'. On 19 Dec. Vietminh forces made a surprise attack on Hanoi, the signal for nearly eight years of hostilities. An agreement on the cessation of hostilities in Vietnam was reached on 20 July 1954 at the Geneva Conference. The French withdrew, and by the Paris Agreement of 29 Dec. 1954 completed the transfer of sovereignty to Vietnam.

The conference divided Vietnam along the 17th parallel into Communist North Vietnam and non-Communist South Vietnam. From 1959 the North promoted insurgency in the south, and from 1961 the USA came to the aid of the south and a full scale guerrilla war developed.

In 1963, the South Vietnamese president, Diem, was overthrown; Nguyen Van Thieu took power as chairman of a national leadership committee in 1965, becoming president in 1967.

In Paris on 27 Jan. 1973, an agreement was signed ending the war in Vietnam. After the US withdrawal in that year, however, hostilities continued between the North and the South until the latter's defeat in 1975. Between 150,000 and 200,000 South Vietnamese fled the country, including the former President Thieu.

After the collapse of Thieu's régime the provisional revolutionary government established an administration in Saigon. A general election was held on 25 April 1976 for a national assembly representing the whole country. Voting was by universal suffrage of all citizens of 18 or over, except former functionaries of South Vietnam undergoing 're-education'. The unification of North and South Vietnam into the Socialist Republic of Vietnam finally took place on 2 July 1976. Following the signing of a treaty of friendship with the USSR in 1978, relations with China correspondingly deteriorated. Vietnam invaded Cambodia in Dec. 1978 and China attacked Vietnam in consequence. Thailand's relations with Vietnam worsened considerably in view of Vietnam attacks on guerrilla bases along the Thai border. Many refugees escaped in small boats across the South China Sea.

In 1986, Vietnam implemented economic reforms, eliminating subsidies and gradually shifting to a multi-sectoral market economy under State regulation. On 11 July 1995, Vietnam and the USA officially normalized relations. On 28 July 1995, Vietnam became an official member of the Association of South East Asian Nations (ASEAN), and in the same month, signed a trade agreement with the European Union. At the present time, it has established diplomatic relations with more than 160 countries.

TERRITORY AND POPULATION

Vietnam is bounded in the west by Cambodia and Laos, north by China and east and south by the South China Sea. It has a total area of 331,690 sq. km and is divided into 60 provinces and a city under central government, grouped in 7 regions. Areas and populations (in 1,000):

Province/Region	Sq. km	Census, 1989	Estimate, 1992	Capital
Lai Chau	17,140	438	482	Lai Chau
Son La	14,210	682	754	Son La
Lao Cai	8,050		515	Lao Cai
Yen Bai	6,802		617	Yen Bai
Hoa Binh	4,612		699	Hoa Binh
Ha Giang	7,831	} 1,026	{ 506	Ha Giang
Tuyen Quang	7,801		614	Tuyen Quang
Cao Bang	8,445	566	614	Cao Bang
Lang Son	8,167	611	656	Lang Son
Bac Thai[1]	6,503	1,033	1,119	Thai Nguyen
Quang Ninh	5,939	814	874	Hai Duong
Vinh Phu[1]	4,836	1,806	2,164	Viet Tri
Ha Bac[1]	4,614	2,061	2,222	Bac Giang
North Mountain and Midland	102,949	11,909	11,823	
Hanoi	921	} 3,057	{ 2,106	Hanoi
Ha Tay	2,153		2,170	
Hai Phong	1,504	1,448	1,542	Hai Phong
Hai Hung[1]	2,552	2,440	2,612	Hai Duong
Thai Binh	1,524	1,632	1,738	Thai Binh
Nam Ha[1]	2,419	} 3,157	{ 2,531	Nam Ha
Ninh Binh	3,387		819	Ninh Binh
Red River Delta	12,457	11,734	13,518	
Nghe An	16,381	} 3,582	{ 2,623	Vinh
Ha Tinh	6,054		1,265	Ha Tinh
Thanh Hoa	11,168	2,991	3,233	Thanh Hoa
Quang Binh	7,983		716	Dong Hoi
Quang Tri	4,592	} 1,995	{ 505	Dong Ha
Thua Thien (Hue)	5,009		945	Hue
Central North Region Coast	51,187	8,568	9,287	
Quang Ngai	5,856	} 2,288	{ 1,120	Quang Ngai
Binh Dinh	6,076		1,137	Quy Nhon
Quang Nam (Da Nang)[1]	11,988	1,739	1,811	Da Nang
Phu Yen	5,223	} 1,463	{ 689	Tuy Hoa
Khanh Hoa	5,258		897	Nha Trang
Ninh Thuan	3,430	} 1,170	{ 438	
Binh Thuan	7,992		830	Phan Thiet
Central Coast of North Region	45,823	6,660	7,193	
Kon Tum	9,934	} 873	{ 241	Kon Tum
Gia Lai	15,662		708	Play Cu
Dac Lat	19,800	974	1,126	Buon Me Thoat
Lam Dong	10,173	639	729	Da Lat
Central Highlands	55,569	2,486	2,805	
Song Be[1]	9,546	939	1,046	Thu Dau Mot
Tay Ninh	4,024	791	856	Ho Chi Minh City
Thanh Pho Ho Chi Minh	2,090	3,934	4,145	Ho Chi Minh City
Dong Nai	5,865		1,721	Bien Hoa
Ba Ria (Vung Tau)	1,957		637	Ba Ria
North Eastern South Region	23,481	7,807	8,406	

Long An	4,338	1,121	1,197	Tan An
Dong Thap	3,276	1,337	1,433	Cao Lamh
Tien Giang	2,339	1,484	1,591	My Tho
Ben Tre	2,246	1,214	1,285	Ben Tre
Tra Vinh	2,247	} 1,812	{ 924	Tra Vinh
Vinh Long	1,487		1,025	Vinh Long
An Giang	3,424	1,793	1,896	Long Xuyen
Can Tho	3,054	} 2,682	{ 1,739	Can Tho
Soc Trang	3,107		1,152	Soc Trang
Kien Giang	4,243	1,198	1,299	Rach Gia
Minh Hai[1]	7,689	1,562	1,681	Bac Lieu
Mekong River Delta	39,575	14,203	15,221	

[1]8 provinces were split to produce 7 new provinces and a centrally-administered city (Da Nang) in 1997 as follows: Bac Thai became Bac Can and Thai Nguyen; Vinh Phu, Phu Tho and Vinh Phuc; Ha Bac, Bac Giang and Bac Ninh; Hai Hung, Hai Duong and Hung Yen; Nam Ha, Ha Nam and Nam Dinh; Quang Nam (Da Nang), Quang Nam Province and Da Nang City; Song Be, Binh Duong and Binh Phuoc; Minh Hai, Bac Lieu and Ca Mau.

At the 1989 census the population was 64,411,713; density, 195 per sq. km.

Estimated population (1992), 69,306,000 (33,555,000 females); 1998, approximately 76m. (51% women) consisting of 54 nationalities (Ho Chi Minh City, 4m.; Hanoi, 2m.). Density, 209 per sq. km.

The UN gives a projected population for 2000 of 80·55m.

In 1995, 19·4% of the population lived in urban areas.

Cities with over 0·2m. inhabitants at the 1989 census: Ho Chi Minh City (3,169,135), Hanoi (1,088,862), Hai Phong (456,049), Da Nang (370,670), Long Xuyen (217,171), Nha Trang (213,687), Hue (211,085), Can Tho (208,326).

87% of the population are Vietnamese (Kinh). There are also 53 minority groups thinly spread in the extensive mountainous regions. The largest minorities are: Tay, Khmer, Thai, Muong, Nung, Meo, Dao. The last remaining 'boat people' were repatriated from Hong Kong in 1997.

The official language is Vietnamese. Chinese, French and Khmer are also spoken.

SOCIAL STATISTICS
Births, 1995, 1,992,000; deaths, 553,000. Rates (1995 per 1,000 population); Birth rate, 27·0; death rate, 7·5. Life expectancy, 1990–95, was 62·9 years for males and 67·3 years for females. Annual rate of increase, 1990–95, 2·4%. Infant mortality, 1990–95, 42 per 1,000 live births; fertility rate, 3·4 births per woman. Sanctions are imposed on couples with more than two children.

CLIMATE
The humid monsoon climate gives tropical conditions in the south, with a rainy season from May to Oct., and sub-tropical conditions in the north, though near winter conditions can affect the north when polar air blows south over Asia. In general, there is little variation in temperatures over the year. Hanoi, Jan. 62°F (16·7°C), July 84°F (28·9°C). Annual rainfall 72" (1,830 mm).

CONSTITUTION AND GOVERNMENT
The National Assembly unanimously approved a new constitution on 15 April 1992. Under this the Communist Party retains a monopoly of power and the responsibility for guiding the state according to the tenets of Marxism-Leninism and Ho Chi Minh, but with certain curbs on its administrative functions. The powers of the National Assembly are increased. The 450-member *National Assembly* is elected for 5-year terms. Candidates may be proposed by the Communist Party or the Fatherland Front (which groups various social organizations), or they may propose themselves as individual Independents. The Assembly convenes 3 times a year and appoints a prime minister and cabinet. It elects the *President*, the head of state. The latter heads a *State Council* which issues decrees when the National Assembly is not in session.

The ultimate source of political power is the Communist Party of Vietnam, founded in 1930; it had 2·2m. members in 1996.

National Anthem. 'Doàn quân Viêt Nam di chung lòng cúú quóc' ('Soldiers of Vietnam, we are advancing'); words and tune by Van Cao.

RECENT ELECTIONS

At the National Assembly elections of 20 July 1997 the Fatherland Front (VVF) gained 447 seats of which 384 were won by members of the Communist Party of Vietnam (DCSV). 3 seats went to candidates not affiliated to the VVF.

CURRENT ADMINISTRATION

President (titular head of state): Tran Duc Luong (DCSV).

Vice-President: Nguyen Thi Binh, b. 1927 (DCSV; elected Sept. 1992).

Full members of the Politburo of the Communist Party of Vietnam: Gen. Le Kha Phieu (b. 1932; *Secretary General*); Gen. Le Duc Anh; Vo Van Kiet; Nguyen Van An; Pham Van Tra; Tran Duc Luong; Nguyen Thi Xuan My; Truong Tan Sang; Le Xuan Tung; Le Minh Huong; Nguyen Tan Dung; Gen. Doan Khue; Pham The Duyet; Nguyen Duc Binh; Nong Duc Manh; Phan Van Khai; Gen. Le Kha Phieu; Nguyen Manh Cam.

In March 1999 the government comprised:

Prime Minister: Phan Van Khai.

First Deputy Prime Minister: Nguyen Tan Dung. *Deputy Prime Ministers:* Nguyen Manh Cam, Nguyen Cong Tan, Ngo Xuan Loc, Pham Gia Khiem.

Minister of Foreign Affairs: Nguyen Manh Cam. *Defence:* Pham Van Tra. *Public Security:* Le Minh Huong. *Planning and Investment:* Tran Zuan Gia. *Justice:* Nguyen Dinh Loc. *Finance:* Nguyen Sinh Hung. *Trade:* Truong Dinh Tuyen. *Industry:* Dang Vu Chu. *Labour, War Invalids and Social Affairs:* Nguyen Thi Hang. *Construction:* Nguyen Manh Kiem. *Agriculture and Rural Development:* Le Huy Ngo. *Transport and Communications:* Le Ngoc Hoan. *Fisheries and Marine Products:* Ta Quang Ngoc. *Culture and Information:* Nguyen Khoa Diem. *Health:* Do Nguyen Phuong. *Education and Training:* Nguyen Minh Hien. *Science, Technology and the Environment:* Chu Tuan Nha.

Speaker of the National Assembly: Nong Duc Manh.

Local Government. Local Government is administered by people's councils, which appoint executive committees. Local elections were held with the National Assembly elections in July 1992.

DEFENCE

Conscription of men and women is for 2 years, specialists 3 years. Since 1989 troops have been permitted to engage in economic activity.

In 1997 defence expenditure totalled US$990m. (US$13 per capita). In 1985 defence expenditure had been US$3,418m.

Army. There are 8 military regions and 2 special areas. The Army consists of 14 corps headquarters, 50 infantry, 3 mechanized, 8 engineer and 10 to 16 economic construction divisions, 10 armoured, 10 field artillery and 20 independent engineer brigades and 15 independent infantry regiments. Special forces include an airborne brigade and a demolition engineer regiment. Equipment includes some 1,000 T-34/-54/-55, 200 T-62 and 100 Chinese Type-59 and M-48A3 main battle tanks. Strength, (1997), 0·5m. Paramilitary forces number 4·5m. and consist of the Peoples' Self-Defence Force (urban), a People's Militia (rural) and a rear force (reserves).

Navy. The fleet currently includes 5 ex-Soviet 'Petya' class frigates, 2 ex-US frigates (built 1943 and 1944), 2 ex-Soviet missile corvettes, 8 Soviet-built fast missile craft, 16 fast torpedo craft, 2 patrol hydrofoils, 21 inshore patrol craft, 6 coastal and 5 inshore minesweepers, 7 landing ships, and some 20 smaller amphibious craft.

In 1996 personnel were estimated to number 12,000 plus an additional Naval Infantry force of 30,000.

Air Force. In 1996 the Air Force had about 15,000 personnel and 196 combat aircraft and 33 armed helicopters. There are reported to be 3 squadrons of variable-geometry MiG-23s, 1 squadron of SU-27s, 3 squadrons of Su-22s, 12 squadrons of 150 MiG-21 interceptors; An-2, An-24 and An-26 transports; and a strong helicopter force with Ka-25, Mi-6, Mi-8/17 and Mi-24 helicopters. The 15,000 strong air defence force is organized in 14 divisions and deploys 66 surface-to-air missile sites.

INTERNATIONAL RELATIONS

Vietnam is a member of the UN and ASEAN.

ECONOMY

Policy. The sixth 5-year plan covers 1996–2000.

A reform programme (*Doi Moi*) injecting free enterprise principles and reducing central control has been implemented. The 'Draft Strategy for Socio-Economic Stabilization and Development to 2000' aims to double GDP through the 'socialist-oriented commodity economy, a market economy under state management' in which the state and collective sectors will play a 'predominant role'.

The 1992 constitution embodies the market-oriented reforms of recent years, recognizing citizens' right to engage in private business. A bankruptcy law was passed in Jan. 1994.

Performance. Real GDP growth was between 7 and 8% each year from 1994 to 1997, but was forecast to drop slightly to 5% in 1998.

Budget. Revenues in 1996 were an estimated US$5·6bn. and expenditures US$6·0bn.

Currency. The unit of currency is the *dong* (VND). In March 1989 the dong was brought into line with free market rates. The direct use of foreign currency was made illegal in Oct. 1994. Foreign exchange reserves were US$830m. at the end of 1995. Currency in circulation, 1991, 5,340,000m. dong. The average annual inflation rate over the period 1990–96 was 22·7%. Gold reserves were 98,300 troy oz. in June 1991.

Banking and Finance. The central bank and bank of issue is the National Bank of Vietnam (founded in 1951; *Governor*, Cao Sy Kiem). There are 52 commercial banks (4 state run and 48 shareholding), 19 foreign branches and 4 joint ventures set up with foreign capital. Vietcombank is the foreign trade bank. 50 foreign banks had branches in 1998.

ENERGY AND NATURAL RESOURCES

Electricity. Total capacity of power generation in 1995 was 4,400 MW. In 1994, 12,473m. kWh of electricity were produced (1995 estimated at 14,000m. kWh). Consumption per capita was an estimated 154 kWh in 1995. A hydro-electric power station with a capacity of 2m. kW was opened at Hoa-Binh in 1994.

Oil and Gas. Estimated crude oil production in 1995, 7·7m. tonnes. Natural gas reserves are estimated at 100bn. cu. metres. Vietnam and Thailand settled an offshore dispute in 1997 which stretched back to 1973. Demarcation allowed for petroleum exploration in the Gulf of Thailand, with each side required to give the other some revenue if an underground reservoir is discovered which straddles the border.

Minerals. Vietnam is endowed with an abundance of mineral resources such as coal (3·5bn. tonnes), bauxite (3bn. tonnes), iron ore (700m. tonnes), copper (600,000 tonnes), tin (70,000 tonnes), chromate (10m. tonnes) and apatite (1bn. tonnes): Coal production was 4·8m. tonnes in 1992. There are also deposits of manganese, titanium, a little gold and marble. 1992 output (in 1,000 tonnes): Sand, 13,260; limestone, 667; salt, 542.

Agriculture. Agriculture contributed 27% of GDP in 1996 and employs 70% of the workforce. Ownership of land is vested in the state, but since 1992 farmers may inherit and sell plots allocated on 20-year leases. The household is the basic production unit. Peasants may market their produce, or deal through the co-operatives.

Production in 1,000 tonnes in 1993: Coffee, 135; tea, 35; rubber, 76; coconut, 1,207; (1994) rice, 24,500. Other crops include sugar-cane and cotton. Total food output in 1995, 27·4m. tonnes.

Livestock, 1996: Cattle, 3·7m.; pigs, 16·90m.; buffaloes, 3m. (1995); goats, 305,000 (1995); chickens, 95m. (1995); ducks, 43m. (1995).

Livestock products (1993): Eggs, 115,000 tonnes; meat, 1,126,000 tonnes.

37,000 tractors were in use in 1994.

Forestry. In 1995 forests covered 9·12m. ha, or 28% of the land area (down from 9·79m. ha in 1990 and 13·5m. ha in 1943). Timber exports were prohibited in 1992. Timber production was 34,913,000 cu. metres in 1995, nearly all of it for fuel.

Fisheries. In 1992 there were 32 fishing vessels over 100 GRT with a total tonnage of 13,956 GRT. Total catch, 1995, approximately 1·2m. tonnes, of which 900,000 tonnes were marine fish.

INDUSTRY
The industrial sector generates about 30% (including construction) of GDP. 1992 production (in 1,000 tonnes): Crude steel, 175·2; cement, 3,727; fertilizers, 507; sulphuric acid, 8; dyestuffs, 4·3; glass and glassware, 32·3; textile fibre, 42·5; processed fish, 627·4; sugar, 304; tea, 20·1; (in units): Bricks, 3,675m.; tiles, 410m.; machine tools, 2,316; hydraulic pumps, 500; threshing machines, 40,125; diesel motors, 3,300; ventilators, 257,000; batteries, 68m.; lamps, 9·6m.; woven fabrics, 450m. metres (1995); knitting fabric, 15,000 tonnes (1995); beer, 162·1m. litres; cigarettes, 1,524m. packets.

Labour. In 1995 the workforce was estimated at 40m. In 1991 (in 1,000) agriculture accounted for 22,276 persons; forestry, 207; manufacturing, 3,394; building, 820; transport, 480; communications, 46; trade, 1,749; services, 296; research, 49; education, 804; culture, 46; health, social welfare and sport, 310; finance, 118; public administration, 240. In 1993, 32% of the workforce was female. In 1991, 58% of the workforce worked in co-operatives, 31% in the private sector and 11% in the state sector.

Trade Unions. There are 53 trade union associations.

INTERNATIONAL TRADE
In Feb. 1994 the USA lifted the trade embargo it had imposed in 1975. Foreign debt was US$26,764m. in 1996. The 1992 constitution regulates joint ventures with Western firms; full repatriation of profits and non-nationalization of investments are guaranteed. By May 1996 total foreign investment was US$19,925m., of which industry accounted for US$9,400m. services, US$6,700m.; oil and gas was US$1,200m., and transport and communications US$1,100m. 65% of Vietnam's trade is with Asian countries.

Imports and Exports. Trade is conducted through the state import-export agencies. Value of exports in 1996, US$7,256m.; imports, US$11,144m. Earnings in 1995 from seafood exports reached US$580m. and from textiles US$700m. The main import suppliers in 1995 were Singapore (17·0%), South Korea (12·9%) and Taiwan (9·6%). Principal export markets in 1995 were Japan (28·5%), Germany (9·4%) and Singapore (7·5%). Main exports are coal, farm produce, sea produce and livestock. Imports: Oil, steel, artificial fertilizers. Rice exports in 1992 were some 1·4m. tonnes, and coal 0·78m. tonnes (0·23m. in 1987), mainly to Japan and South Korea.

COMMUNICATIONS

Roads. There were about 105,000 km of roads in 1997, of which 15% are hard-surfaced. In 1995 there were 0·31m. 4-wheeled vehicles and around 3m. motor cycles. 373·7m. passengers (1994) and 39·57m. tonnes of freight (1991) were transported.

Rail. Route length is 2,600 km of single-track line covering seven routes. Rail links with China were reopened in Feb. 1996. 20% of trains were steam-hauled in 1992. In 1995, 1·92m. passengers and 3·5m. tonnes of freight were carried.

Civil Aviation. There are international airports at Hanoi (Noi Bai) and Ho Chi Minh City (Tan Son Nhat) and 13 domestic airports. The national carrier is Vietnam Airlines, which provides domestic services and in 1998 had international flights to Bangkok, Dubai, Guangzhou, Hong Kong, Kaohsiung, Kuala Lumpur, Manila, Melbourne, Moscow, Osaka, Paris, Phnom Pemh, Singapore, Sydney, Taipei, Vientiane and Zürich. Services were also provided in 1998 by Aeroflot, Air France, Asiana Airlines, Cathay Pacific Airways, China Airlines, China Southern Airlines, EVA Airways, JAL, Korean Air, Lao Aviation, Lauda Air, Lufthansa Malaysia Airlines, Pacific Airlines, Qantas Airways, Royal Air Cambodge, Singapore Airlines, Swissair and Thai International Airways. In 1995 scheduled airline traffic of Vietnam-based carriers flew 24·5m. km, carrying 2,290,000 passengers (1,031,000 on international flights).

Shipping. In 1995, sea-going vessels totalled 1·21m. GRT, including oil tankers 0·19m. GRT. The major ports are Hai Phong, which can handle ships of 10,000 tons, Ho Chi Minh City and Da Nang. There are regular services to Hong Kong, Singapore, Thailand, Cambodia and Japan. 0·7m. passengers and 4·88m. tonnes of freight were carried in 1991. There are some 19,500 km of navigable waterways.

Telecommunications. Vietnam Posts and Telecommunications and the military operate telephone systems with the assistance of foreign companies. Telephone main lines numbered 1,587,300 in 1997 (20·7 per 1,000 persons). In 1995 there were 30,000 PCs and 15,000 fax machines, and in 1996, 3 mobile phone networks with some 35,000 subscribers. There were around 6,000 Internet users in June 1998.

SOCIAL INSTITUTIONS

Justice. A new penal code came into force on 1 Jan. 1986 'to complete the work of the 1980 Constitution'. Penalties (including death) are prescribed for opposition to the people's power, and for economic crimes. The judicial system comprises the Supreme People's Court, provincial courts and district courts. The president of the Supreme Court is responsible to the National Assembly, as is the Procurator-General, who heads the Supreme People's Office of Supervision and Control.

Religion. Taoism is the traditional religion but Buddhism is widespread. At a Conference for Buddhist Reunification in Nov. 1981, 9 sects adopted a charter for a new Buddhist church under the Council of Sangha. The Hoa Hao sect, associated with Buddhism, claimed 1·5m. adherents in 1976. Caodaism, a synthesis of Christianity, Buddhism and Confucianism founded in 1926, has some 2m. followers. In 1992, there were 38·2m. Buddhists and 6m. Roman Catholics (1997). There is an Archbishopric of Hanoi and 13 bishops. There were 2 seminaries in 1989. In 1983 the Government set up a Solidarity Committee of Catholic Patriots.

Education. Adult literacy rate in 1995 was 93·7% (96·5% among males and 91·2% among females). Primary education consists of a 10-year course divided into 3 levels of 4, 3 and 3 years respectively. In 1993–94 there were 10,137 primary schools with 9,782,900 pupils and 278,000 teachers, and in 1995–96 there were 5,332,400 pupils and 193,814 teachers at secondary schools. In 1995–96 there were 7 universities, 2 open (distance) universities and 9 specialized universities (agriculture, 3; economics, 2; technology, 3; water resources, 1).

Health. In 1994 there were 29,700 doctors, and in 1993, 53,700 nurses, 12,000 midwives and 6,500 pharmacists. There were 12,500 hospitals in 1994.

CULTURE

Broadcasting. Broadcasting is controlled by the state Vietnam Radio and Television Committee. There are 2 national radio programmes from Hanoi and 1 from Ho Chi Minh City, 14 provincial programmes and an external service, the Voice of Vietnam (11 languages). There is a national and 2 provincial TV services. There were 7·8m. radio and 3·2m. TV sets in 1995 (colour by NTSC and SECAM).

Press. In 1994 there were some 350 newspaper and periodical titles. There are 2 national dailies, the Communist Party's *Nhan Dan* ('The People'), circulation, 0·2m., and the Army's *Quan Doi Nhan Dan*, 60,000. There are 3 major regional dailies with a combined circulation of 155,000. There were 10 titles in English, including 2 dailies in 1995. 3,043 book titles were published in 1991 totalling 62·4m. copies.

Tourism. There were 1,607,000 foreign tourists in 1996, bringing revenue of US$87m.

DIPLOMATIC REPRESENTATIVES
Of Vietnam in Great Britain (12–14 Victoria Rd., London, W8 5RD)
Ambassador: Vuong Thua Phong An.

Of Great Britain in Vietnam (Central Building, 31 Hai Ba Trung, Hanoi)
Ambassador: David W. Fall.

Of Vietnam in the USA (1233 20th Street, NW, Suite 400, Washington, D.C., 20036)
Ambassador: Bang Le.

Of the USA in Vietnam (7 Lang Ha, Ba Dinh District, Hanoi)
Ambassador: Douglas B. 'Pete' Peterson.

Of Vietnam to the United Nations
Ambassador: Ngo Quang Xuan.

Of Vietnam to the European Union
Ambassador: Huynh Anh Dzung.

FURTHER READING

Trade and Tourism Information Centre with the General Statistical Office. *Economy and Trade of Vietnam* [various 5-year periods]
Beresford, M., *National Unification and Economic Development in Vietnam.* London, 1989
Dellinger, D., *Vietnam Revisited.* Boston (Mass.), 1986
Ho Chi Minh, *Selected Writings, 1920–1969.* Hanoi, 1977
Karnow, S., *Vietnam: a History.* 2nd ed. London, 1992
Morley, J. W. and Nishihara M., *Vietnam Joins the World.* Armonk (NY), 1997
Norlund, I. (ed.) *Vietnam in a Changing World.* London, 1994
Harvie C. and Tran Van Hoa V., *Reforms and Economic Growth.* London, 1997
Post, K., *Revolution, Socialism and Nationalism in Vietnam.* vol. 1. Aldershot, 1989
Smith, R. B., *An International History of the Vietnam War.* London, 1983

National statistical office: General Statistical Office, Hanoi.

YEMEN

Jamhuriya al Yamaniya

(Republic of Yemen)

Capital: Sana'a
Commercial capital: Aden
Population estimate, 2000: 18·12m.
GNP per capita: (PPP$) 790
HDI/world rank: 0·356/151

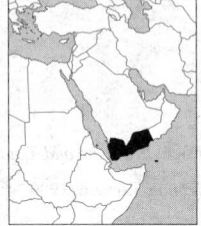

KEY HISTORICAL EVENTS

Following an agreement reached in Dec. 1989 on a constitution for a unified state, the (northern) Yemen Arab Republic and the (southern) People's Democratic Republic of Yemen were united as the Republic of Yemen on 22 May 1990.

In Aug. 1993 Vice-President Ali Salem Albidh withdrew to Aden and demanded the implementation of a reform programme as a condition of re-joining President Saleh in Sana'a. Albidh agreed to a modified reform programme at an agreement brokered by King Hussein of Jordan in Feb. 1994, but clashes between north and south escalated into full civil war at the beginning of May. Southern officials announced their secession from Yemen on 21 May 1994. Aden was captured by northern forces on 7 June 1994. The former vice-president and government went into exile.

TERRITORY AND POPULATION

Yemen is bounded in the north by Saudi Arabia, east by Oman, south by the Gulf of Aden and west by the Red Sea. The territory includes 112 islands including Kamaran (181 sq. km) and Perim (300 sq. km) in the Red Sea and Socotra (3,500 sq. km) in the Gulf of Aden. The islands of Greater and Lesser Hanish is claimed by both Yemen and Eritrea. On 15 Dec. 1995 Eritrean troops occupied it, and Yemen retaliated with aerial bombardments. A ceasefire was agreed at presidential level on 17 Dec. On 20 Dec. the UN resolved to send a good offices mission to the area. In an agreement of 21 May 1996 brokered by France, Yemen and Eritrea renounced the use of force to settle the dispute and agreed to submit it to arbitration. The area is 555,000 sq. km excluding the desert Empty Quarter (Rub Al-Khahi). A dispute with Saudi Arabia broke out in Dec. 1994 over some 1,500–2,000 km of undemarcated desert boundary. A memorandum of understanding signed on 26 Feb. 1995 reaffirmed the border agreement reached at Taif in 1934. An agreement of June 1995 completed the demarcation of the border with Oman.

The population was estimated at 15·8m. in 1995; density, 21 persons per sq. km.

The UN gives a projected population for 2000 of 18·12m.

In 1995, 33·5% of the population lived in urban areas. At the census of 1986 in the north and 1988 in the south the population was 9,664,939 (4,938,318 females). There were 1,168,199 citizens working abroad mainly in Saudi Arabia and the United Arab Emirates not included in the census total. Since 1990 Saudi Arabia has compulsorily repatriated almost all Yemeni workers. In 1988 there were 17 governorates:

	1986/88 census population		1986/88 census population
Sana'a (city)	427,502	Shabwah	192,324
Sana'a	1,237,016	Hajjah	720,000
Aden	326,919	Bayd	295,439
Ta'iz	1,419,708	Hadhrama	537,095
Hodeida	1,052,086	Sa'adah	323,124
Lahej	458,385	Mahwit	260,836
Ibb	1,254,128	Mahrah	44,225
Abyan	279,241	Marib	95,326
Dhamar	698,823	Jawf	42,762

The population of the capital, Sana'a, was estimated at 972,000 in 1995. The commercial capital is the port of Aden, with a population of (1995) 562,000. Other important towns are the port of Hodeida (population, 155,110), Mukalla (154,360), Ta'iz (178,043), Ibb and Abyan.

The national language is Arabic.

YEMEN

SOCIAL STATISTICS
Births, 1995, 724,000; deaths, 168,000. Birth rate, 1995, was 48·2 per 1,000 population; death rate, 11·2. Life expectancy, 1990–95, was 54·9 years for males and 55·9 years for females. Infant mortality, 1990–95, 92 per 1,000 live births. Fertility rate, 1990–95, 7·6 births per woman, the highest in any sovereign country and only exceeded by the rate in the Gaza Strip.

CLIMATE
A desert climate, modified by relief. Sana'a, Jan. 57°F (13·9°C), July 71°F (21·7°C). Aden, Jan. 75°F (24°C), July 90°F (32°C). Annual rainfall 20" (508 mm) in the north, but very low in coastal areas: 1·8" (46 mm).

CONSTITUTION AND GOVERNMENT
Parliament consists of a 301-member *Assembly of Representatives* (*Majlis al-Nuwaab*), elected for a 4-year term in single-seat constituencies.

On 28 Sept. 1994 the Assembly of Representatives unanimously adopted a new constitution founded on Islamic law. It abolished the former 5-member Presidential Council and installed a *President* elected by parliament for a 5-year term.

National Anthem. 'Raddidi Ayyatuha ad Dunya nashidi' ('Repeat, O World, my song'); words by A. Noman, tune by Ayub Tarish.

RECENT ELECTIONS
President: Ali Abdullah Saleh was elected on 1 Oct. 1994. Presidential elections are due to take place in Oct. 1999.

Parliamentary elections were held on 27 April 1997, in which the General People's Congress (MSA) gained 187 seats, Independents 55, Yemeni Congregation for Reform (Islah) 54, Nasserite Unionist People's Organization (NUPP) 3, and the Arab Socialist Rebirth Party (Baath) 2. There were 21 women candidates, of whom 2 were elected. The election was boycotted by the Yemeni Socialist Party (HIY).

CURRENT ADMINISTRATION
President: Ali Abdullah Saleh (GPC; sworn in 2 Oct. 1994).

Vice-President: Abd Rabbah Mansour Hadi.

In March 1999 the government comprised:

Prime Minister: Abdel Karim al-Iriani. *Deputy Prime Minister and Minister for Foreign Affairs:* Abd al-Qadir al-Ba Jamal.

Minister of Civil Service and Administrative Reform: Mohamed Ahmed Junayd. *Planning and Development:* Ahmed Mohamed Abdallah al-Sufan. *Oil and Mineral Resources:* Mohamed al-Khadem al-Wajeeh. *Legal and Parliamentary Affairs:* Abdullah Ahmed Ghanem. *Justice:* Ismael Ahmed al-Wazir. *Social Security and Social Affairs:* Mohamed Abdullah al-Batani. *Communications:* Ahmed Mohamed al-Anisi. *Local Administration:* Sadeq Amin Aburas. *Finance:* Alawi Salih al-Salami. *Fisheries:* Ahmed Musaed Hussein. *Transport:* Brig.-Gen. Abd al-Malik al-Sayani. *Interior:* Maj.-Gen. Hussein Mohamed al-Arab. *Trade and Provisions:* Abd al-Aziz al-Kumaim. *Information:* Abd al-Rahman al-Akwa. *Youth and Sports:* Abd al-Wahab al-Raweh. *Electricity and Water:* Ali Hamid al-Sharaf. *Agriculture and Water Resources:* Ahmed Salem Al-Gabali. *Industry:* Abd al-Rahman Mohamed Ali al-Uthman. *Culture and Tourism:* Abd al-Malek Mansour. *Construction, Housing and Urban Planning:* Abdullah Hussein Al-Dafee. *Defence:* Maj.-Gen. Mohamed Dhaifallah Mohamed. *Expatriate Affairs:* Ahmed Ali al-Bishari. *Labour and Vocational Training:* Mohamed Mohamed al-Tayeb. *Public Health:* Dr Abdullah Abd al-Wali Nasher. *Education:* Yahya Mohamed Abdullah Al-Shuaibi. *Minister of State for the Affairs of the Council of Ministers:* Ahmed Ali Al-Bushari. *Awqaf and Guidance:* Judge Ahmed Mohamed Al-Shami.

The *Speaker* is Sheikh Abdullah Al-Ahmar (Islah).

Local Government. The country is administratively divided into 27 governorates and the capital city.

DEFENCE
Conscription is for 3 years. Defence expenditure in 1997 totalled US$403m. (US$24 per capita), representing 7·0% of GDP.

Army. The Army comprises 7 armoured, 18 infantry, 5 mechanized, 2 airborne commando, 5 militia, 4 artillery, 1 special forces and 1 surface-to-surface missile brigade. Equipment includes 250 T-34, 675 T-54/-55, 150 T-62 and 50 M-60A1 main battle tanks. Strength (1997) 37,000 (some 25,000 conscripts) with 39,500 reserves. There are paramilitary tribal levies numbering at least 20,000 and a Ministry of Security force of 50,000.

Navy. The Navy comprises 3 Chinese-built and 4 ex-Soviet fast missile craft, 8 inshore patrol craft, 3 inshore minesweepers, 2 tank landing ships and 2 craft. Forces are based at Aden and Hodeida, with other facilities at Mokha, Mukalla and Perim. Personnel in 1997 were estimated at 1,800.

Air Force. The unified Air Forces of the former Arab Republic and People's Democratic Republic are now under one command, although this unity was broken by the attempted secession of the south in 1994 which resulted in heavy fighting between the air forces of Sana'a and Aden. There are 80 interceptors (60 MiG-21s, 10 MiG-29s and 10 F-5Es), 20 MiG-23s and 20 Su-22s for strike duties, 15 Mi-24 gunship helicopters, 5 An-24 and 8 An-26 twin-turboprop transports, 15 other transports (including 2 C-130H Hercules) and about 40 Mi-8 and 12 other helicopters. Personnel (1997) about 3,500.

INTERNATIONAL RELATIONS
Yemen is a member of the UN and the Arab League.

ECONOMY
Policy. A 5-year plan is running from 1996 to 2000. It includes some privatization proposals.

Performance. Real GDP growth was 8·2% in 1995 and –0·5% in 1994.

Budget. The fiscal year is the calendar year. Total revenues and expenditures (in 1m. riyals):

	1995	1996	1997[1]	1998[2]
Revenue	89,646	216,053	281,667	300,791
Expenditure	111,128	215,738	290,571	309,942

[1]Provisional. [2]Projected.

Currency. The unit of currency is the *riyal* (YER) of 100 *fils*. During the transitional period to north-south unification the northern *riyal* of 100 *fils* and the southern *dinar* of 1,000 *fils* co-existed. The average annual inflation rate during the period 1990–96 was 27·1%. There were 3 foreign exchange rates operating: an internal clearing rate, an official rate and a commercial rate. In 1996 the official rate was abolished. Total money supply in Nov. 1997 was 162,169m. riyals.

Banking and Finance. Total assets of the Central Bank were 109,497m. riyals in 1992. There were 6,616m. riyals in savings deposits.
   A stock exchange is scheduled to open in 1999.

ENERGY AND NATURAL RESOURCES
Electricity. Installed capacity was 810,000 kW in 1994. Production in 1994 was an estimated 1,958m. kWh and consumption per capita in 1995 an estimated 117 kWh.

Oil and Gas. The first large-scale oilfield and pipeline was inaugurated in 1987. There are reserves of 2,000m. bbls. on the former north-south border. Further major oil finds were announced in 1991. Crude oil production (1994): 16,005,000 tonnes. Gas reserves are some 7,000m. cu. metres.

Minerals. 107,000 tons of salt were produced in 1992. Reserves (estimate) 25m. tonnes. In 1992, 647,000 cu. metres of stone and 77,898 tons of gypsum were extracted.

Agriculture. Agriculture accounted for 18% of GDP in 1996. In 1994 there were 1·44m. ha of arable land, 105,000 ha of permanent cropland and 16·06m. ha of pasture; approximately 481,000 ha were irrigated in 1994. In the south, agriculture is largely of a subsistence nature, sorghum, sesame and millet being the chief crops, and wheat and barley widely grown at the higher elevations. Cash crops include cotton. Fruit is plentiful in the north.

Owing to the meagre rainfall, cultivation is largely confined to fertile valleys and flood plains on silt. Irrigation schemes with permanent installations are in progress. Estimate production (1995, in 1,000 tonnes): Wheat, 170; seed cotton, 8; sesame seeds, 13; millet, 60; maize, 80; sorghum, 450; barley, 65; pulses, 70; potatoes, 200; tomatoes, 192; onions, 57; watermelons, 102; melons, 31; alfalfa, 149,087 (1992 figure); coffee, 9; dates, 21; grapes, 147; bananas, 74.

Livestock in 1995: Cattle, 1·13m.; camels, 173,000; sheep, 3·71m.; goats, 3·23m.; poultry, 22m. Estimated livestock produce, 1995 (in 1,000 tonnes): Meat, 133; cows' milk, 155.

Forestry. There were 9,000 ha of forest in 1995. Timber production in 1995 was 324,000 cu. metres.

Fisheries. Fishing is a major industry. Total catch, 1995, 103,964 tonnes (102,964 tonnes from sea fishing).

INDUSTRY
In 1992 there were 211 industrial firms (142 private, 48 public, 13 mixed and 8 co-operative). 64 of these were producing foodstuffs, 50 chemicals and petroleum products, 27 textiles and leather goods and 27 metal goods. Output (in 1,000 tons), 1992: Edible oils, 102; flour, 247; cement, 820; cartons, 17; petrol, 947; fuel oil, 1,782; fuel gas, 160; jet fuel, 643; asphalt, 48.

Labour. The labour force in 1996 totalled 4,945,000 (71% males). Approximately 57% of the economically active population in 1995 were engaged in agriculture, fisheries and forestry. Unemployment was 36% at the end of 1993.

INTERNATIONAL TRADE
Foreign debt was US$6,356m. in 1996.

Imports and Exports. Trade (in US$1m.):

	1992	1993	1994
Exports	474	374	934
Imports	2,587	2,821	2,087

Main import suppliers, 1992 (in 1,000 riyals): USA, 2,858,220; UAE, 2,559,581; Saudi Arabia, 2,311,965; Japan, 2,172,044; UK, 1,713,618. Main export markets: USA, 1,396,053; Japan, 666,689; Germany, 470,723; Saudi Arabia, 268,769.

Cotton and fish are major exports, the largest imports being food and live animals. A large transhipment and entrepôt trade is centred on Aden, which was made a free trade zone in May 1991. Oil income (exports and concessions) was US$1,150m. in 1992.

COMMUNICATIONS
Roads. There were, in 1996, 64,725 km of roads, of which 5,240 km were paved. In 1995 there were 229,084 passenger cars, 2,835 buses and coaches, and 279,780 goods vehicles. In 1996 there were 7,303 road accidents with 1,267 fatalities.

Civil Aviation. There are international airports at Sana'a and Aden. The national carrier is Yemenia Yemen Airways, which operates internal services and in 1998 had international flights to Abu Dhabi, Addis Adaba, Amman, Bahrain, Beirut, Bombay, Cairo, Damascus, Djibouti, Doha, Dubai, Frankfurt, Jeddah, Karachi, Khartoum, London, Moroni, Nairobi, Paris, Riyadh, Rome and Sharjah. In 1998 services were also provided by Aeroflot, Air Tanzania Corporation, Egyptair, Emirates, Ethiopian Airlines, Gulf Air, KLM, Lufthansa, Royal Jordanian, Saudia, Sudan Airways and Syrian Arab Airlines. In 1995 scheduled airline traffic of Yemen-based carriers flew 5·8m. km, carrying 375,000 passengers (176,000 on international flights).

Shipping. In 1995, sea-going shipping totalled 26,431 GRT, including oil tankers, 3,185 GRT. There are ports at Aden, Mokha, Hodeida, Mukalla and Nashtoon. 449,621 tons of cargo were discharged in 1992, and 7,697 tonnes of oil at the Ras Issa terminal.

Telecommunications. Yemen had 220,300 main telephone lines in 1997, or 13·4 per 1,000 population. Cellular phone subscribers numbered 8,300 in 1995 and there were 2,000 fax machines. In Jan. 1998 there were approximately 2,400 Internet users.

Postal Services. In 1995 there were 451 post offices.

SOCIAL INSTITUTIONS

Justice. A civil code based on Islamic law was introduced in 1992.

Religion. In 1997 there were some 16·47m. Moslems (mostlySunnis) and approximately 20,000 followers of other religions.

Education. In 1994 there were 62 pre-primary schools with 680 teachers for 11,999 pupils. In 1993–94 there were 11,013 primary schools with 2,678,863 pupils and there were 212,129 pupils at secondary level. Yemen has the lowest proportion of female pupils enrolled at primary school in the world, at 28% in 1993. There are universities at Sana'a (founded 1974) and Aden (1975). The former had 3,520 students and 330 academic staff in 1994–95, the latter 4,800 and 470. The adult literacy rate in 1994 was estimated to be 37·3% (56·9% among males but only 17·2% among females). Yemen has the biggest difference in literacy rates between the sexes of any country in the world.

Health. In 1994 there were 2,785 doctors, 167 dentists, 5,772 nurses, 295 pharmacists and 385 midwives. There were 81 hospitals in 1994.

CULTURE

Broadcasting. Broadcasting is managed by the government-controlled Yemen Radio and Television Corporation. Programmes are transmitted from Sana'a and Aden. In 1995 there were 650,000 radio and 420,000 TV receivers (colour by PAL and NTSC).

Cinema. In 1992 there were 45 cinemas with 43,265 seats. Attendance was 8,319,805.

Press. In 1995 there were 3 daily (1 in English), 5 weekly and 4 monthly newspapers and 15 periodicals.

Tourism. There were 74,000 foreign tourists in 1996, bringing revenue of US$42m.

DIPLOMATIC REPRESENTATIVES
Of Yemen in Great Britain (57 Cromwell Rd., London, SW7 2ED)
Ambassador: Dr Hussein Abdullah Al-Amri.

Of Great Britain in Yemen (129 Haddah Rd., Sana'a)
Ambassador: V. J. Henderson.

Of Yemen in the USA (2600 Virginia Ave., NW, Washington, D.C., 20037)
Ambassador: Abdulwahab Al-Hajjiri.

Of the USA in Yemen (Dhahr Himyar Zone, Sheraton Hotel District, POB 22347, Sana'a)
Ambassador: Barbara K. Bodine.

Of Yemen to the United Nations
Ambassador: Abdalla Saleh Al-Ashtal.

Of Yemen to the European Union
Ambassador: Abdul Khaleq Al Aghbari.

FURTHER READING
Central Statistical Organization. *Statistical Year Book*
Auchterlonie, Paul, *Yemen.* [Bibliography] Oxford and Santa Barbara (CA), 1998
Bidwell, R., *The Two Yemens.* Boulder and London, 1983
El Mallakh, R., *The Economic Development of the Yemen Arab Republic.* London, 1986
Ismael, T. Y. and Ismael, J. S., *The People's Democratic Republic of Yemen.* London, 1986
Mackintosh-Smith, T., *Yemen—Travels in dictionary land.* London, 1997

National statistical office: Central Statistical Organization, Ministry of Planning and Development

YUGOSLAVIA

Savezna Republika Jugoslavija
(Federal Republic of Yugoslavia,
comprising the republics of Serbia and
Montenegro)

Capital: Belgrade
Population estimate, 2000: 10·5m.
Estimated GDP: $21bn.

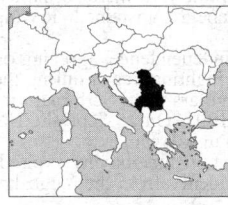

KEY HISTORICAL EVENTS

On 28 June 1914 Archduke Franz Ferdinand of Austria was assassinated in Bosnia by a young nationalist. Though Serbia complied with most of the terms of Austria's subsequent ultimatum, Austria declared war on 28 July, thus precipitating the First World War. In the winter of 1915–16 the Serbian army was forced to retreat to Corfu, where the government, under Prime Minister Pašić, was established. Montenegro capitulated in 1916 and its king fled. Exiles from Croatia and Slovenia had formed a Yugoslav Committee in 1914 whose aim was South Slav federation. This was not compatible with Pašić's goal of a centralized, Serb-run state, but the Committee and the government managed to contrive a joint 'Corfu Declaration' in July 1917 demanding a 'constitutional, democratic, parliamentary monarchy headed by the Karadjordevićs. This was accepted by the Allies as the basis for the new state. The Croats were forced by the pressure of events to join Serbia and Montenegro on 1 Dec. 1918. From 1918–29 the country was known as the Kingdom of the Serbs, Croats and Slovenes.

Boundary disputes with Italy and other neighbouring countries lasted into the 1920s. A constitution of 1921 established an assembly under King Alexander, but the trappings of parliamentarianism could not bridge the gulf between Serbs and Croats. The Croat peasant leader Radić was assassinated in 1928; his successor, Vlatko Maček, set up a separatist assembly in Zagreb. On 6 Jan. 1929 the king suspended the constitution and established a royal dictatorship, redrawing provincial boundaries without regard for ethnicity. In Oct. 1934 he was murdered by a Croat extremist while on an official visit to France.

During the 1930s Yugoslavia (southern Slavs) had become heavily dependent on the German economy. During the regency of Prince Paul, Prime Minister Stojadinović pursued a pro-fascist line. On 25 March 1941 Paul was induced to adhere to the Axis Tripartite Pact. On 27 March he was overthrown by military officers in favour of the boy king Peter. Germany invaded on 6 April. Within 10 days Yugoslavia surrendered; king and government fled to London. Two resistance movements came into being, a royalist group, under Draža Mihailović, and the communist-dominated partisans of Josip Broz, nicknamed Tito. The latter were imbued with revolutionary as well as liberationist aims. The movements often fought each other, and Mihailović collaborated to some extent with the Germans. Allied support was switched from him to Tito in 1944.

Tito succeeded in liberating Yugoslavia largely by his own efforts. The partisan Liberation Committee formed the nucleus of the post-war provisional government. A constituent assembly was elected in Nov. 1945 from a single list of People's Front candidates. A people's republic was proclaimed with a Soviet-type constitution. Tito embarked on a programme of enthusiastic Sovietization, but was too independent for Stalin, who sought to topple him by excommunicating Yugoslavia in 1948–49. However, Tito survived by the support of his people and a *rapprochement* with the west, and it was the Soviet Union under Khrushchev which had to extend the olive branch in 1956. As a spin-off from this schism Yugoslavia evolved its 'own road to socialism'. Collectivization of agriculture was abandoned; the principles of 'industrial self-management' were developed, and extended into the whole of the representative process; and Yugoslavia became a champion of international 'non-alignment'. A collective presidency came into being with the death of Tito in 1980.

Dissensions in Kosovo between Albanians and Serbs, and in parts of Croatia between Serbs and Croats, brought inter-ethnic tensions into prominence after 1988.

YUGOSLAVIA

With the election of new national assemblies in all 6 republics during 1990, several of the latter came increasingly into conflict with the federal government. At the end of 1990 both Croatia and Slovenia proclaimed their right to secede from federal Yugoslavia. In May 1991, following escalating Serb-Croat violence and demands for secession from predominantly Serb-inhabited areas of Croatia, the federal army was given powers to restrict the movement of unofficial armed groups. On 12 May the Krajina area held a self-styled referendum resulting, it was claimed, in an overwhelming vote for union with Serbia. Croatia rejected the poll.

On 15 May 1991 Croatia's representative in the federal presidency, Štipe Mesić, failed to secure the 5 votes needed to become president, hitherto a mere formality. Serbia, Kosovo and Vojvodina voted against and Montenegro abstained, leaving Yugoslavia without a head of state.

On 25 June Croatia and Slovenia made declarations of independence, agreeing on 30 June to an EU proposal to suspend them for 3 months. Fighting began during the summer in Croatia between Croatian forces and Serb irregulars from Serb-majority areas of Croatia. Federal forces had left Slovenia by July 1991. On 25 Sept. the UN Security Council imposed a mandatory arms embargo on Yugoslavia.

The 3-month moratorium agreed at the EU peace talks on 30 June having expired, both Slovenia and Croatia declared their complete independence from the Yugoslav federation on 8 Oct.

Trade sanctions on the whole of Yugoslavia were applied from 8 Nov., but restricted to Serbia after 2 weeks.

After 13 ceasefires had failed to be observed, a fourteenth was signed on 23 Nov. by the presidents of Croatia and Serbia and the federal defence minister, for the first time under UN auspices. Following a request on 26 Nov. from the federal government, a Security Council resolution of 27 Nov. proposed the deployment of a UN peace-keeping force if the ceasefire were kept. Fighting, however, continued.

On 15 Jan. 1992 the EU recognized Croatia and Slovenia as independent states. Bosnia-Hercegovina was recognized on 7 April 1992 and Macedonia on 8 April 1993. A UN delegation began monitoring the ceasefire on 17 Jan. and the UN Security Council on 21 Feb. voted unanimously to send a 14,000-strong peace-keeping force to Croatia and Yugoslavia.

On 27 April 1992 Serbia and Montenegro announced the formation of a federal republic of Yugoslavia constituted by themselves as the legal successor to the former Socialist Federal Republic of Yugoslavia (SFRY).

On 30 May, responding to further Serbian military activities in Bosnia and Croatia, the UN Security Council voted in favour of the imposition of sanctions.

In mid-1992 NATO countries began to commit air, sea and eventually land forces to enforce sanctions and protect humanitarian relief operations in Bosnia.

At a joint UN-EC peace conference on Yugoslavia held in London on 26–27 Aug. some 30 countries and all the former republics of Yugoslavia endorsed a plan to end the fighting in Croatia and Bosnia, install UN supervision of heavy weapons, recognize the borders of Bosnia-Hercegovina and return refugees. At a further conference at Geneva on 30 Sept. the Croatian and Yugoslav presidents agreed to make efforts to bring about a peaceful solution in Bosnia, but fighting continued.

On 22 Sept. the UN resolved (by 127 votes to 6 with 26 abstentions) that the self-proclaimed Federal Republic of Yugoslavia of Serbia and Montenegro could not automatically assume the seat of the former SFRY and excluded it from the General Assembly.

On 16 Nov. the UN Security Council voted for sanctions against Yugoslavia to be made more effective, and NATO agreed to lend naval support to their enforcement.

Further peace talks were held in Geneva in Jan. 1993, and transferred to the UN in Feb. On 22 Feb. the UN Security Council resolved to set up a war crimes tribunal for alleged violations of human rights in the former SFRY. A court was inaugurated at The Hague on 17 Nov. 1993. In 1995 the tribunal was merged into the International Penal Tribunal for Yugoslavia and Rwanda sitting at The Hague. The first sentence on a Yugoslav was delivered in Nov. 1996.

Following the Serbian President Milošević's announcement that Yugoslavia would no longer send supplies to Bosnian Serbs and would not accept international monitors on its borders, on 24 Sept. 1994 the UN Security Council lifted the non-trade sanctions against Yugoslavia affecting civil aviation, culture and sport. Following the Bosnian-Croatian-Yugoslav (Dayton) agreement all remaining UN sanctions were lifted in Nov. 1995.

Massive public anti-government demonstrations took place in Nov.–Dec. 1996 following the government's annulment of municipal election results where opposition candidates had been elected. An OSCE delegation investigated the disputed results and found that opposition candidates should have won in 22 municipalities. As demonstrations and protests from various quarters continued throughout Jan. 1997, Milošević conceded opposition victories in at first some, then finally on 7 Feb., all, the disputed municipalities.

In July 1997 Slobodan Milošević switched his power base to become president of federal Yugoslavia. Vojislav Seselj, leader of the ultra-nationalist Radical party, defeated his Socialist rival in the run-off for the Serbian presidency. But since the turn-out fell short of the 50% required by the constitution there was a further election in Dec. in which the former Yugoslav foreign minister, Milan Milutinović finally succeeded Milošević. Meanwhile, in Montenegro, the pro-western Milo Djukanović succeeded a pro-Milošević president despite violent demonstrations which raised fears that Montenegro might break away from Serbia to create an independent state.

In 1998 unrest in Kosovo led to a bid for outright independence. Violence flared resulting in what a US official described as 'horrendous human rights violations', including massive shelling of civilians and destruction of villages. A US-mediated agreement to allow negotiations to proceed during an interim period of autonomy allowed for food and medicine to be delivered to refugees and American support for a degree of autonomy (short of independence), accepted in principle by President Milošević, lifted the immediate threat of NATO air strikes. Further outbreaks of violence in early 1999 were followed by the departure of the 800-strong team of international 'verifiers' of the fragile peace. Peace talks in Paris broke down without a settlement though subsequently Albanian freedom fighters accepted terms allowing them broad autonomy. The sticking point on the Serbian side was the international insistence on having 28,000 NATO-led peacemakers in Kosovo to keep apart the warring factions. Meanwhile, the scale of Serbian repression in Kosovo persuaded the NATO allies to take direct action. On the night of 24 March, NATO aircraft began a bombing campaign against Yugoslavian military targets. Further Serbian provocation in Kosovo caused hundreds of thousands of ethnic Albanians to seek refuge in neighbouring countries.

TERRITORY AND POPULATION
Yugoslavia is bounded in the north by Hungary, north-east by Romania, east by Bulgaria, south by Macedonia and Albania, and west by the Adriatic Sea, Bosnia-Hercegovina and Croatia. Area, 102,173 sq. km. Population (1991 census), 10,394,026 (5,236,906 females). Estimate, 1997, 10,596,983; population density, 104 per sq. km.

The UN gives a projected population for 2000 of 10·5m.

In 1997 an estimated 51·5% of the population lived in urban areas.

Yugoslavia is a federation of 2 republics: Montenegro and Serbia, and 2 former autonomous provinces within Serbia: Kosovo and Metohija, and Vojvodina. The federal capital is Belgrade (Beograd); population estimate (1997), 1,597,599. Population (1991 census) of principal towns:

Belgrade	1,168,454	Subotica	100,386
Novi Sad	179,626	Zrenjanin	81,316
Niš	175,391	Pančevo	72,793
Kragujevac	147,305	Čačak	71,550
Podgorica	117,875	Smederevo	63,884

The 1991 census was not carried out in Kosovo and Metohija. 1991 estimated population: Priština, 155,499; Prizren 92,303; Peć 68,163; Kosovska Mitrovica, 64,323.

Ethnic groups at the 1991 census: Serbs, 6,504,048; Albanians, 1,714,768; Montenegrins, 519,766; Hungarians, 344,147; Moslems, 336,025; Gypsies, 143,519; Croats, 111,650; Slovaks, 66,863; Macedonians, 47,118; Romanians, 42,364; Bulgarians, 26,922; Valachians, 17,810; Turks, 11,263. At the 1991 census, 361,452 nationals worked abroad.

The official language is Serbian, the Eastern variant (Croatian is the Western) of Serbo-Croat, which was regarded as constituting one language in the Socialist Federal Republic of Yugoslavia. Serbian is written in the Cyrillic alphabet. There are also substantial Albanian and Hungarian-speaking minorities.

SOCIAL STATISTICS
1997 (provisional): Births, 132,602; deaths, 111,266; marriages, 56,004; divorces, 7,211. 1996 rates (per 1,000 population): Births, 12·5; death, 10·5; marriage, 5·3; natural increase, 1·9; infant mortality, 5·8 (per 1,000 live births). In 1994 the most popular age range for marrying was 25–29 for males and 20–24 for females. Expectation of life in 1996: Males, 69·9 years; females, 74·6. Annual growth rate, 1990–95, –0·1%. Infant mortality, 1990–95, 21 per 1,000 live births; fertility rate, 1·9 births per woman.

CLIMATE
Most parts have a central European type of climate, with cold winters and hot summers. Belgrade, Jan. 0·3°C, July 21·1°C. Annual rainfall 747 mm. Podgorica, Jan. 7·4°C, July 26·4°C. Annual rainfall 1,885 mm.

CONSTITUTION AND GOVERNMENT
The head of state is the *Federal President*, elected by both chambers of the federal parliament for a non-renewable 4-year term.

The federal parliament consists of 2 chambers: The *Chamber of the Republics* has 40 members, 20 each elected from the assemblies of Montenegro and Serbia. Its assent is necessary to all legislation. The *Chamber of Citizens* has 138 members, elected by universal suffrage.

National Anthem. 'Hej, Slaveni, jošte živi rečnaših dedova' ('O Slavs, our ancestors' words will live'); words by S. Tomašik, tune anonymous.

RECENT ELECTIONS
At the elections to the Chamber of Citizens on 3 Nov. 1996 the Coalition of the left gained 64 seats; Zajedno ('Together'; opposition party), 22; the Democratic Party of Socialists of Montenegro, 20; the Radical Serb Party, 16. The other 16 seats were shared among 6 parties.

CURRENT ADMINISTRATION
Federal President: Slobodan Milošević.

In March 1999 the government comprised:

Prime Minister: Momir Bulatović.

Deputy Prime Ministers: Vladan Kutlesić; Zoran Lilić; Nikola Sainović; Vuk Drasković, Danilo Vuksanović; Jovan Zebić.

Minister of Foreign Affairs: Zivadin Jovanović. *Interior:* Zoran Sokolović. *Defence:* Pavle Bulatović. *Domestic Trade:* Slobodan Nenadović. *Foreign Trade:* Borislav Vuković. *Trade and Tourism:* Djordje Siradović. *Telecommunications:* Dojcilo Radojević. *Transport:* Dejan Drobnjaković. *Labour, Health and Social Affairs*: Miroslav Ivanišević. *Science, Development and Environment:* Jagos Zelenović. *Agriculture:* Nedeljko Sipovać. *Sport:* Zoran Bingulać. *Justice*: Zoran Knezević. *Finance:* Bozidar Gazivoda. *Economy:* Rade Filipović. *Relations with International Relations:* Nebojsa Maljković.

The *Speaker* is Radoman Bozović.

Local Government. Within the federal framework of republics Yugoslavia is administratively divided into 29 districts, 210 communes, 7,401 localities, 233 urban localities and 4,819 local communities.

DEFENCE
Military service for 12 to 15 months is compulsory. Military expenditure totalled US$1,489m. in 1997 (US$140 per capita), representing 7·8% of GDP. In 1985 expenditure had been US$4,759m.

Army. The Army comprises 8 tank, 7 motorized infantry, 6 mixed artillery, 1 surface-to-air missile, 1 anti-tank artillery, 2 mechanized, 1 airborne and 1 special forces brigades, 9 air defence and 2 task forces. Equipment includes 785 T-55, 181 T-34, 65 T-72 and 239 M-84 main battle tanks. Personnel (1997) were about 90,000 (37,000 conscripts).

Navy. The Navy comprises 4 small diesel submarines, 5 midget submarines, 2 Soviet and 2 locally built missile-armed frigates, 10 fast missile craft, 6 inshore patrol craft, 4 inshore minesweepers and 18 small landing craft. Auxiliaries include 3 transports and 1 headquarters ship.

The Air Force operates 4 Mi-14, 4 Ka-25 Hormone and 2 Ka-27 Helix anti-submarine helicopters. A Marine force of 900 is divided into 2 'brigades'.

Personnel in 1997 totalled 7,500 including Coastal Defence and Marines. The force is based at Kotor.

Air Force. There are 2 fighter divisions equipped primarily with Russian-built MiG-21s and MiG-29s and 2 ground-attack divisions of locally-built Jastreb and Orao jet attack aircraft. Transport units fly An-26 twin-engined aircraft, 4-turboprop An-12s, and a few other types in small numbers, notably Turbo-Porters and Yak-40s, Falcon 50s and Learjets for VIP duties. Training types are the nationally-designed UTVA-75 primary trainer, Galeb jet basic trainer and the Super Galeb jet advanced trainer. About 120 Gazelle, Agusta-Bell 205 and Mi-8 helicopters are in service. 'Guideline' and 'Goa' surface-to-air missiles have been supplied by the USSR. Personnel (1997) 16,700 (3,000 conscripts), with 155 combat aircraft and 71 armed helicopters.

INTERNATIONAL RELATIONS

Relations with Croatia were established in Jan. 1994 with the opening of mutual representative offices.

The former Yugoslavia (SFRY) was a member of the UN but its self-proclaimed successor state (Federal Republic of Yugoslavia) is excluded from the General Assembly and related bodies such as the IMF and World Bank.

ECONOMY

Performance. Real GDP growth was 7·4% in 1997 (5·9% in 1996).

Budget. The federal budget for 1997 was set at 7,461,000,000 dinars; 72·1% of expenditure was on defence.

Currency. The unit of currency is the *dinar* (YUD) of 100 *paras*. On 24 Jan. 1994 a new convertible 'super-dinar' was introduced equivalent to 1,000m. previous dinars, at parity with, and pegged to, the Deutschmark, at 3·3 to the Deutschmark. This was devalued by 69·7% in Nov. 1995. In 1997 the unofficial rate of the dinar fell to 5·2 to the Deutschmark following a 50% increase in money supply. In Jan. 1998 foreign exchange reserves were estimated at less than US$200m., the equivalent of about 2 weeks of imports. A further official devaluation was anticipated. Inflation, which had been 93·1% in 1996, fell to 21·2% in 1997. Foreign exchange reserves were US$5,706m. in Feb. 1998. Total money supply in Feb. 1998 was 227,479bn. dinars.

Banking and Finance. The National Bank is the bank of issue. The Governor of the National bank is Dusan Vlatković. There are also republican banks. A reform programme which started in Feb. 1989 has transformed banks into shareholding companies, empowers the National Bank to impose solvency ratios on financial institutions and strengthens its control of the money supply. The National Bank's reserves were below US$200m. in Jan. 1998.

There is a stock exchange at Belgrade.

Weights and Measures. The metric weights and measures have been in use since 1883. The Gregorian calendar was adopted in 1919.

ENERGY AND NATURAL RESOURCES

Electricity. Installed capacity in 1994 was 11·78m. kW. Output in 1997, 40,312m. kWh, of which 27,453m. kWh were thermal and 12,860m. kWh hydro-electric. Consumption per capita was estimated at 2,798 kWh in 1995.

Oil and Gas. Crude oil production (1997), 979,000 tonnes; natural gas, 688 cu. metres.

Minerals. Lignite production (1997), 42,113,000 tonnes; coal, 38,429,000 tonnes; brown coal, 512,000 tonnes; copper ore, 20,507,000 tonnes.

Agriculture. In 1997 there were 6,222,000 ha of agricultural land, of which 3,708,000 ha were arable (2,397,000 ha cereals; 304,000 ha industrial crops), 789,000 ha meadow and 1,336,000 ha pasture. 4·79m. ha of land were in private farms and 1,459,000 ha in agricultural organizations. The economically active agricultural population was 1,061,488 in 1991.

Crop production, 1997 (in 1,000 tonnes): Maize, 6,939; sugar beet, 2,043; wheat, 2,920; potatoes, 1,066; grapes, 577; plums, 471; soya beans, 153.

Livestock, 1997 (in 1,000): Cattle, 1,899; pigs, 4,216; sheep, 2,566; horses, 90; poultry, 25,712.

Livestock products, 1997: Meat, 573,000 tonnes; milk, 2,064,000 litres; wool, 3,627,000 tonnes; eggs, 1,813m. 215,535,000 litres of wine were produced in 1997.

Forestry. The forest area is 8,258,000 ha, of which 1,341,000 ha are in private hands. 3·05m. cu. metres of timber were cut in 1997.

Fisheries. In 1997 the landings of fish were (in tonnes): Salt-water, 373; freshwater, 8,404; crustacea and shell, 13.

INDUSTRY
In Sept. 1998 there were 204,444 enterprises and institutions, including 134,275 private enterprises, 626 public enterprises, 190 co-operatives and 2,982 social enterprises.

Industrial output (in 1,000 tonnes) in 1997: Pig-iron, 907; crude steel, 979; steel castings, 21; tractors, 4,000 units; lorries, 1,269 units; passenger cars, 10,000 units; sugar, 240; TV sets, 25,000 units; refrigerators, 81,000 units; cement, 2,011; sulphuric acid, 177; artificial fertilizers, 831; plastics, 204.

Labour. In 1997 there were 2,044,774 workers in the social sector, including 820,167 in industry, 214,738 in trade, catering and tourism, 179,412 in education and culture, 140,461 in transport and communications, 93,055 in communities and organizations, 108,000 in agriculture, 74,625 in commercial services. In Oct. 1997 in the private sector there were 528,125 self-employed and employed, including 52,168 in arts and crafts, 42,545 in catering and tourism, 25,934 in transport and communications, 151,592 in trade. Average monthly wage in Dec. 1998 was 844 dinars. Unemployment is officially 25%.

INTERNATIONAL TRADE
In joint ventures the foreign partner may own up to 98% of the equity. 379 foreign-owned companies were operating in 1992. UN sanctions against Yugoslavia were lifted in Nov. 1995 following the Bosnian-Croatian-Yugoslav (Dayton) agreement on Bosnia. External debt was US$13,439m. in 1996.

Imports and Exports. Foreign trade, in US$1m., for calendar year:

	1991	1992	1996	1997
Imports	5,548	3,859	4,102	4,799
Exports	4,704	2,539	1,842	2,368

Exports, 1997 (in US$1m.): Manufactures and minerals (including machinery, 55; transport equipment, 71; electrical goods, 81; chemicals, 254; iron and steel, 212; textiles, 75; leather goods, 13); agricultural produce, 67; foodstuffs, 240. Imports: Transport equipment, 222; electrical goods, 331; machinery, 315; agricultural produce, 334; foodstuffs, 226; others, 3,358.

Main trading partners, 1997 (exports and imports in US$1m.): Germany, 339 and 650; Italy, 318 and 485; Rep. of Macedonia, 236 and 291; Russian Federation, 193 and 454.

COMMUNICATIONS
Roads. In 1997 there were 50,359 km of roads comprising 6,241 km of main roads, 12,636 km of regional roads and 31,482 km of local roads. In 1990 there were 1,903,149 registered motor vehicles, including 1,405,455 private cars, 92,874 trucks and 13,133 buses (1993). Passenger-km, 1997, 3,764,000; tonne-km of freight carried, 1,036,000. There were 2,031 deaths in road accidents in 1991.

Rail. In 1997 there were 4,069 km of railway, of which 1,384 km were electrified. 24,468,000 passengers and 10,878,000 tonnes of freight were carried.

Civil Aviation. There are 5 airports, the chief ones being at Belgrade and Tivat. The national carrier is JAT (Jugoslovenski Aero Transport) which operates internal flights and in 1998 flew to most major centres in Europe and the Middle East. In 1998 services were also provided by Aeroflot, Air Bosna, Air France, Alitalia, Austrian Airlines, Balkan, British Airways, Czech Airlines, Lufthansa, Macedonian Airlines, Olympic Airways, SAS, Swissair and Tarom.

Shipping. In 1997 Yugoslavia possessed 1 sea-going passenger vessel and 22 cargo vessels totalling 388,347 GRT.

Length of navigable waterways (1997), 1,419 km. In 1997 there were 499 cargo vessels and 542 tonnes of freight were transported.

Telecommunications. Main telephone lines numbered 2,182,000 in 1997 (205·8 for every 1,000 persons). In 1995 there were 125,000 PCs and 15,000 fax machines.

Postal Services. There were 1,694 post offices in 1997.

SOCIAL INSTITUTIONS

Justice. In 1997 there were 2 supreme courts, 32 district courts and 153 communal courts, with 1,982 judges and 7,621 lay assessors. There were also 18 economic courts with 237 judges.

In 1997, 44,092 criminal sentences were passed.

Religion. Religious communities are separate from the State and are free to perform religious affairs. All religious communities recognized by law enjoy the same rights.

Serbia has been traditionally Orthodox. Moslems are found in the south as a result of the Turkish occupation. The Serbian Orthodox Church with its seat in Belgrade has 27 bishoprics within the boundaries of former Yugoslavia and 12 abroad (5 in the USA and Canada, 5 in Europe and 2 in Australia). The Serbian Orthodox Church numbers about 2,000 priests. Its *Patriarch* is Pavle (enthroned 22 May 1994).

The Serbian Orthodox Church is the official church in Montenegro, the Montenegrin church having been banned in 1922, but in Oct. 1993 a breakaway Montenegrin church was set up under its own patriarch.

Relations with the Vatican are regulated by a 'Protocol' of 1966.

The Moslem Religious Union has Superiorates in Podgorica and Priština.

The Jewish religion has 9 communities making up a common league of Jewish Communities with its seat in Belgrade.

Education. Compulsory primary education lasts 8 years, secondary 3–4 years. In 1997 there were 1,799 nursery schools with 184,890 pupils and 8,503 teachers. In 1996–97 there were 4,460 primary schools with 895,188 pupils and 52,790 teachers and 566 secondary schools with 351,528 pupils and 27,335 teachers. There were 54 institutions of tertiary education with 31,745 students and 1,685 teachers and 93 institutes of higher education with 140,095 full-time students and 10,567 academic staff.

Adult literacy rate, 1995, 97·9% (male, 98·6%; female, 97·3%).

Health. In 1996 there were 21,697 doctors, 4,146 dentists, 2,005 pharmacists and 58,257 hospital beds.

Welfare. In 1997 there were 1,324,047 pensioners, including 561,325 old age, 445,807 disability and 316,915 survivors' pensioners. 10,966,547 working days were lost through sickness. In 1997 pensions and disability insurance totalled 16,485,181,000 dinars; old age pension, 5,743,293,000 dinars; and disability, 3,590,188,000 dinars. In 1994, 207m. dinars were paid in child allowances.

CULTURE

Broadcasting. Alongside the state-run Serbian Radio and Television and Montenegrin Radio and Television there were 3 independent radio and TV networks in 1993. 2 independent radio stations were shut down by the government in Dec. 1996. The state-run Kosovar Radio and Kosovar Television broadcast a few hours a week in Albanian. In 1997 there were 159 broadcasting and 51 TV stations. There were 2,692,000 TV and 1,384,000 radio receivers in use in 1997.

Cinema. In 1997 there were 186 cinemas. Cinema attendances were 5,353,000. 18 full-length films were made in 1997.

Press. In 1996 there were 18 dailies with a circulation of 1,128,000; 602 other newspapers with a circulation of 3,935,000; and 562 periodicals. 4,967 book titles (926 by foreign authors) were published in 1997 in a total of 11,931,000 copies.

Tourism. There were 2,826,000 foreign tourists in 1998.

Libraries. In 1995 there were 3 National, 800 public, 310 Higher Education and 11 non-specialized libraries with a combined 27,869,000 volumes and 8,546,509 registered users.

Museums and Galleries. In 1994 there were 21 museums with 208,000 visitors.

DIPLOMATIC REPRESENTATIVES
Of Yugoslavia in Great Britain (5 Lexham Gdns., London, W8 5JJ)
Ambassador: Dr Miloš Radulović.

Of Great Britain in Yugoslavia (Generala Zdanova 46, 11000 Belgrade)
Ambassador: Recalled in March 1999.

Of Yugoslavia in the USA (2410 California St., NW, Washington, D.C., 20008)
Chargé d'Affaires a.i.: Nebojsa Vujović.

Of the USA in Yugoslavia (Belgrade)
Ambassador: Vacant.

Of Yugoslavia to the United Nations
Ambassador: Vacant.

Of Yugoslavia to the European Union
Ambassador: Vacant.

FURTHER READING
Federal Statistical Office. *Statistical Yearbook of Yugoslavia.*

Bennett, C., *Yugoslavia's Bloody Collapse: Causes, Course and Consequences.* Farnborough, 1995
Bokovoy, M. K. et al (eds.) State-Society Relations in Yugoslavia 1945–1992. London, 1997
Cohen, L. J., *Broken Bonds: the Disintegration of Yugoslavia.* Boulder (CO), 1993
Djilas, A., *The Contested Country: Yugoslav Unity and Communist Revolution, 1919–1953.* Harvard Univ. Press, 1991
Dyker, D. and Vejvoda, I. (eds.) *Yugoslavia and After: a Study in Fragmentation, Despair and Rebirth.* Harlow, 1996
Friedman, F. (ed.) *Yugoslavia: a Comprehensive English-Language Bibliography.* London, 1993
Glenny, M., *The Fall of Yugoslavia.* London, 1992
Gow, J., *Triumph of the Lack of Will: International Diplomacy and the Yugoslav War.* London and Columbia University Press, 1997
Horton, J. J., *Yugoslavia.* [Bibliography] Oxford and Santa Barbara (CA), 1978
Judah, T., *The Serbs: History, Myth and the Destruction of Yugoslavia.* Yale, 1997
Magaš, B., *The Destruction of Yugoslavia: Tracking the Break-up, 1980–92.* London, 1993
Singleton, F., *Twentieth Century Yugoslavia.* London, 1976.—*A Short History of the Yugoslav Peoples.* CUP, 1985
Tito, J. B., *The Essential Tito.* New York, 1970
Udovicki, J., and Ridgeway, J. (eds.), *Burn This House: The Making and Unmaking of Yugoslavia.* Duke, 1997
Woodward, S. L., *Balkan Tragedy: Chaos and Dissolution after the Cold War.* Brookings Institution (Washington), 1995

National statistical office: Federal Statistical Office, Kneza Miloša 20, Belgrade. *Director:* Milovan Živković.

REPUBLICS AND PROVINCES

In Dec. 1992 the new self-styled Federal Republic of Yugoslavia comprised the 2 republics of Montenegro and Serbia, and the 2 formerly autonomous provinces of Kosovo and Metohija, and Vojvodina within Serbia.

MONTENEGRO

KEY HISTORICAL EVENTS
Montenegro emerged as a separate entity on the break-up of the Serbian Empire in 1355. Owing to its mountainous terrain, it was never effectively subdued by Turkey. It was ruled by Bishop Princes until 1851, when a royal house was founded. The Treaty of Berlin (1828) recognized the independence of Montenegro and doubled the size of the territory. The remains of King Nicholas I, who was deposed in 1918, were returned to Montenegro for reburial in Oct. 1989.

TERRITORY AND POPULATION
Montenegro is a mountainous region which opens to the Adriatic in the south-west. It is bounded in the west by Croatia, north-west by Bosnia-Hercegovina, in the north-east by Serbia and in the south-east by Albania. The capital is Podgorica (population, 1997 estimate, 162,172). Its area is 13,812, sq. km. Population at the 1991 census was 615,035, of which the predominating ethnic groups were Montenegrins (380,467), Moslems (89,614), Serbs (57,453) and Albanians (40,415). Population density per sq. km, 44·5. Estimate, 1997, 643,405; density, 46·6 per sq. km.

SOCIAL STATISTICS
Statistics for calendar years:

	Live births	Marriages	Deaths	Growth rate per 1,000
1994	8,887	3,753	4,660	6·7
1995	9,477	3,791	4,921	7·2
1996	9,193	3,869	5,029	6·5
1997	8,758	3,993	5,153	5·6

CONSTITUTION AND GOVERNMENT
There is an 85-member single-chamber National Assembly.

A referendum was held on 29 Feb.–1 March 1992 to determine whether Montenegro should remain within a common state, Yugoslavia, as a sovereign republic. The electorate was 412,000, of whom 66% were in favour.

RECENT ELECTIONS
In the general election on 31 May 1998, the party of Milo Djukanović, the Coalition for a Better Life, gained 49·5% of the vote and 40 seats (of 78) in defeating the Socialist People's Party, led by federal president Slobodan Milošević's ally, Momir Bulatović, Yugoslavia's prime minister, who gained about 30 seats with 36·1%. Montenegro had ceased to recognize federal Yugoslavia's government earlier in the month.

CURRENT ADMINISTRATION
President: Milo Djukanović; sworn in on 15 Jan. 1998.
  Prime Minister: Filip Vujanović.

ECONOMY
Budget. In 1997 the budget was set at 1,999,000,000 dinars.

ENERGY AND NATURAL RESOURCES
Electricity. Electricity production in 1997 was 2·27m. kWh.

Agriculture. In 1998 the cultivated area was 189,000 ha. Yields (in 1,000 tonnes): Wheat, 5; maize, 9; potatoes, 51. Livestock (1,000 head): Cattle, 180; sheep, 439; pigs, 22.

Forestry. Timber cut in 1997: 232,000 cu. metres.

INDUSTRY
Production (1997): Lignite, 1,282,194 tonnes; bauxite, 470,000 tonnes; heavy semi-manufactures, 24,807 tonnes; cotton carded yarn, 166 tonnes.

Labour. In 1997 there were 123,011 workers in the public sector, including 37,491 in industry, 18,589 in trade, catering and tourism, 13,827 in education and culture, 12,003 in transport and communications, 9,020 in communities and organizations, 3,400 in commercial services. In Oct. 1997 in the private sector there were 41,941 self-employed and employed, including 5,774 in catering and tourism, 3,466 in transport and communications, 15,150 in trade. Average monthly salary in Dec. 1998 was 1,556 dinars. Unemployment was running at 33%.

SOCIAL INSTITUTIONS

Justice. In 1997 there were 2 District Courts, 15 Communal Courts and 2 Economic courts of law with 222 judges.

Education. In 1997 there were: 69 nurseries with 10,269 pupils; 485 primary schools with 9,129 pupils; 43 secondary schools with 27,747 pupils; 1 high school with 79 students; 12 higher schools with 7,266 students.

SERBIA

KEY HISTORICAL EVENTS

The Serbs received Orthodox Christianity from the Byzantines in 891, but shook off the latter's suzerainty to form a prosperous state, firmly established under Stevan Nemanja (1167–96). A Serbian Patriarchate was established at Peć during the reign of Stevan Dušan (1331–55). Dušan planned the conquest of Constantinople, but he was forestalled by incursions of Turks. After he died many Serbian nobles accepted Turkish vassalage; the reduced Serbian state under Prince Lazar received the coup de grace at Kosovo on St Vitus day, 1389. Turkish preoccupations with a Mongol invasion and wars with Hungary, however, postponed the total incorporation of Serbia into the Ottoman Empire until 1459.

The Turks permitted the Orthodox church to practice, though the Patriarchate was abolished in 1776. The native aristocracy was eliminated and replaced by a system of fiefdoms held in return for military or civil service. Local self-government based on rural extended family units (*zadruga*) continued. In its heyday the Ottoman system probably bore no harder on the peasantry than the Christian feudalism it had replaced, but with the gradual decline of Ottoman power, corruption, oppression and reprisals led to economic deterioration and social unrest.

In 1804 murders carried out by mutinous Turkish infantry provoked a Serbian rising under Djordje Karadjordje. The Sultan's army disciplined the mutineers, but was then defeated by the intransigent Serbs. By the Treaty of Bucharest (1812), however, Russia agreed that Serbia, known as Servia until 1918, should remain Turkish. The Turks reoccupied Serbia with ferocious reprisals. A new rebellion broke out in 1815 under Miloš Obrenović which, this time with Russian support, won autonomy for Serbia within the Ottoman empire. Obrenović had Karadjordje murdered in 1817. In 1838 he was forced to grant a constitution establishing an appointed state council, and abdicated in 1839. In 1842 a coup overthrew the Obrenovićs and Alexander Karadjordjević was elected as ruler. He was deposed in 1858.

During the reign of the western-educated Michael Obrenović (1860 until his assassination in 1868) the foundations of a modern centralized and militarized state were laid, and the idea of a 'Great Serbia', first enunciated in Prime Minister Garašanin's *Draft Programme* of 1844, took root. Milan Obrenović, adopting the title of king, proclaimed formal independence in 1882. He suffered defeats against Turkey (1876) and Bulgaria (1885) and abdicated in 1889. Alexander Obrenović was assassinated in 1903, and replaced by Peter Karadjordjević, who brought in a period of stable constitutional rule.

In its foreign policy, Serbia's striving for an outlet to the sea was consistently thwarted by Austria. Annexing Bosnia in 1908, Austria forced the Serbs to withdraw from the Adriatic after the first Balkan war (1912).

Following the break-up of Yugoslavia, in March 1998 a coalition government was formed between the Socialist Party of Slobodan Milošević and the ultra-nationalist Radical Party.

TERRITORY AND POPULATION
Serbia is bounded in the north-west by Croatia, in the north by Hungary, in the north-east by Romania, in the east by Bulgaria, in the south by Macedonia and in the west by Albania, Montenegro and Bosnia-Hercegovina. It includes the 2 provinces (formerly autonomous) of Kosovo and Metohija in the south and Vojvodina in the north. With these Serbia's area is 88,361 sq. km; without, 55,968 sq. km. The capital is Belgrade (population estimate, 1997, 1,597,599). Population at the 1991 census was (with Kosovo and Vojvodina) 9,778,991, of which the predominating ethnic group was Serbs (6,446,595). Population density per sq. km, 110·7; (without Kosovo and Vojvodina), population estimate 5,808,906, of which the predominating ethnic group was Serbs (5,108,682). Population density per sq. km, 103·8. 1997 estimate (with Kosovo and Vojvodina), 9,956,662; density, 112·7 per sq. km; (without) 5,791,643; density, 103·5 per sq. km.

SOCIAL STATISTICS
Statistics for calendar years *(without Kosovo and Vojvodina):*

	Live births	*Marriages*	*Deaths*	*Growth rate per 1,000*
1995	63,737	32,295	66,756	−0·5
1996	60,924	29,703	69,218	−1·4
1997	59,071	29,638	69,422	−1·8

CONSTITUTION AND GOVERNMENT
In Sept. 1990 a new constitution was adopted by the National Assembly. It defines Serbia as a 'democratic' instead of a 'socialist' republic, lays down a framework for multi-party elections, and describes Serbia as 'united and sovereign on all its territory', thus stripping Kosovo and the Vojvodina of the attributes of autonomy granted by the 1974 federal constitution.

There is a 250-member single-chamber National Assembly. The *President* is elected by universal suffrage for not more than two 5-year terms.

RECENT ELECTIONS
At the elections on 20 Dec. 1992, Slobodan Milošević was re-elected *President* of Serbia with 56·32% of the votes cast against 34·05% for Milan Panić, the then prime minister. In July 1997 Milošević became President of Yugoslavia.

CURRENT ADMINISTRATION
President: Milan Milutinović; sworn in on 29 Dec. 1997.
  Prime Minister: Mirko Marjanović.

ECONOMY
Budget. In 1997 the budget was set at 13,820,000,000 dinars.

ENERGY AND NATURAL RESOURCES
Electricity. Electricity production in 1997 was 32·77m. kWh.

Agriculture. (Excluding Kosovo and Vojvodina). In 1997 the cultivated area was an estimated 2,614,000 ha. Yields in 1997 (in 1,000 tonnes): Wheat, 2,920; maize, 6,855; potatoes, 918; sugar-beet, 2,037; plums, 489; grapes, 397. Livestock estimates (in 1,000): Cattle, 402; sheep, 369; pigs, 74; poultry, 2,577.

Forestry. Timber cut in 1997: 1,614,000 cu. metres.

INDUSTRY
(1997, excluding Kosovo and Vojvodina). Lignite, 32,608,711 tonnes; steel, 862,944 tonnes; copper ore, 20,507,148 tonnes; lorries, 1,269 units; cars, 9,512 units; sulphuric acid, 150,371 tonnes; plastics, 27,220 tonnes; cement, 924,308 tonnes;

sugar, 14,682 tonnes; cotton fabrics, 17,228,000 sq. metres; woollen fabrics, 10,097,000 sq. metres.

Labour. In 1997 there were 1,921,763 workers in the public sector, including 782,676 in industry, 196,149 in trade, catering and tourism, 165,585 in education and culture, 128,458 in transport and communications, 84,035 in communities and organizations, 71,225 in commercial services. In Oct. 1997 in the private sector there were 486,183 self-employed and employed, including 51,553 in arts and crafts, 36,771 in catering and tourism, 18,468 in transport and communications, 136,443 in trade. Average monthly salary in Dec. 1998 was 1,313 dinars. Unemployment ran at 25%.

SOCIAL INSTITUTIONS

Justice. In 1997 there were 30 District Courts, 138 Communal Courts and 16 Economic courts of law with 1,997 judges.

Education. In 1997 there were: 1,730 nurseries with 174,621 pupils; 3,975 primary schools with 816,059 pupils; 523 secondary schools with 323,781 pupils; 53 high schools with 37,366 students; 83 higher schools with 144,330 students.

KOSOVO AND METOHIJA

KEY HISTORICAL EVENTS
Kosovo has a large ethnic Albanian majority. Following Albanian-Serb conflicts, the Kosovo and Serbian parliaments adopted constitutional amendments in March 1989 surrendering much of Kosovo's autonomy to Serbia. Renewed Albanian rioting broke out in 1990. The Prime Minister and 6 other ministers resigned in April 1990 over ethnic conflicts. In July 1990, 114 of the 130 Albanian members of the National Assembly voted for full republican status for Kosovo but the Serbian National Assembly declared this vote invalid and unanimously voted to dissolve the Kosovo Assembly. Direct Serbian rule was imposed causing widespread violence. Western demands for negotiations in granting Kosovo some kind of special status were rejected. Ibrahim Rugova, the leader of the main Albanian party, the Democratic League of Kosovo (LDK), has declared himself 'president' demanding talks on independence. In 1998 armed conflict between Yugoslavia and the Kosovo Liberation Army led to 200,000 people, or a tenth of the population of the whole province, fleeing the fighting. Further repression by Serbian forces led to the threat of NATO direct action. Air strikes against Yugoslavian military targets began on 24 March 1999. Retaliation against Albanian Kosovars led to a massive exodus of refugees.

TERRITORY AND POPULATION
Area: 10,887 sq. km. The capital is Priština. The 1991 census was not taken. Population estimate of Kosovo and Metohija, 1991, 1,956,196 (1,596,072 Albanians, 194,190 Serbs); density, 179·7 per sq. km; 1997 estimate, 2,188,083 and density 201·0 per sq. km. Population estimate of Priština, 1997, 241,565.

SOCIAL STATISTICS
Statistics for calendar years:

	Live births	Marriages	Deaths	Growth rate per 1,000
1994	43,450	11,959	7,667	17·2
1995	44,776	12,979	8,671	17·1
1996	45,343	12,309	8,142	17·3
1997	42,920	11,866	8,624	15·7

CURRENT ADMINISTRATION
The official *President* is Hisen Kajdomci.

ECONOMY
Budget. In 1997 the budget was set at 13,000,000 dinars.

ENERGY AND NATURAL RESOURCES
Electricity. Electricity production in 1997 was 4·87m. kWh.

Agriculture. The cultivated area in 1997 was an estimated 398,000 ha. Yields in 1997 (in 1,000 tonnes): Wheat, 272; maize, 296; potatoes, 92; plums, 15; grapes, 69. Livestock (in 1,000): Cattle, 402; sheep, 369; pigs, 74; poultry, 2,577. Timber cut in 1997, 130,000 cu. metres.

Forestry. Timber cut in 1997: 130,000 cu. metres.

INDUSTRY
Production (1997): Lignite, 8,421,991 tonnes; sulphuric acid, 26,900 tonnes; cement, 89,528 tonnes.

Labour. In 1997 there were 120,763 workers in the public sector, including 54,223 in industry, 9,245 in trade, catering and tourism, 10,471 in education and culture, 8,933 in transport and communications, 7,880 in communities and organizations, 1,526 in commercial services. In Oct. 1997 in the private sector there were 35,869 self-employed and employed, including 4,364 in arts and crafts, 5,023 in catering and tourism, 2,006 in transport and communications, 15,113 in trade. Average monthly salary in Dec. 1998 was 1,066 dinars.

SOCIAL INSTITUTIONS
Education. In 1997 there were: 111 nurseries with 8,179 pupils; 335 primary schools with 42,114 pupils; 55 secondary schools with 14,092 pupils; 4 high schools with 1,621 students; 15 higher schools with 12,725 students.

FURTHER READING
Vickers, M., *Between Serb and Albanian: A History of Kosovo.* Hurst, London, 1998

VOJVODINA

TERRITORY AND POPULATION
Area: 21,506 sq. km. The capital is Novi Sad. Population of Vojvodina at the 1991 census, 2,013,889 (1,143,723 Serbs, 339,491 Hungarians). Density, 93·6 per sq. km. Estimate, 1997, 1,976,936; density, 91·9 per sq. km. Population of Novi Sad, 1997, 266,808.

SOCIAL STATISTICS
Statistics for calendar years:

	Live births	Marriages	Deaths	Growth rate per 1,000
1994	21,595	11,048	27,518	−3·0
1995	22,499	11,260	27,177	−2·4
1996	20,483	11,112	28,832	−4·2
1997	20,645	10,706	28,646	−4·0

CONSTITUTION AND GOVERNMENT
The 1990 Serbian constitution deprived Vojvodina of its autonomy. Serbo-Croat was declared the only official language in 1991.

RECENT ELECTIONS
In March 1993 the provincial assembly comprised 7 members of the Socialist Party of Serbia and 5 of the Serbian Radical Party.

CURRENT ADMINISTRATION

The *Prime Minister* is Boško Perošević.

ECONOMY

Budget. In 1997 the budget was set at 68,000,000 dinars.

ENERGY AND NATURAL RESOURCES

Electricity. Electricity production in 1997 was 387m. kWh.

Agriculture. The cultivated area in 1997 was an estimated 1,649,000 ha. Yields (in 1,000 tonnes): Wheat, 1,423; maize, 3,847; potatoes, 255; sugar-beet, 1,805. Livestock estimates (in 1,000): Cattle, 231; sheep, 267; pigs, 1,691; poultry, 7,863.

Forestry. Timber cut in 1997: 548,000 cu. metres.

INDUSTRY

Production (1997): Crude petroleum, 965,655 tonnes; plastics, 212,352 tonnes; cement, 997,491 tonnes.

Labour. In 1997 there were 452,005 workers in the public sector, including 181,672 in industry, 38,382 in trade, catering and tourism, 38,000 in education and culture, 26,876 in transport and communications, 18,543 in communities and organizations, and 16,901 in commercial services. In Oct. 1997 in the private sector there were 86,320 self-employed and employed including 13,053 in arts and crafts, 5,436 in catering and tourism, 3,985 in transport and communications, and 39,612 in trade. Average monthly salary in Dec. 1998 was 1,493 dinars.

SOCIAL INSTITUTIONS

Education. In 1997 there were: 604 nurseries with 48,024 pupils; 535 primary schools with 212,453 pupils; 122 secondary schools with 81,893 pupils; 9 high schools with 7,790 students; and 15 higher schools with 25,505 students.

ZAMBIA

Republic of Zambia

Capital: Lusaka
Population estimate, 2000: 9·87m.
GNP per capita: (PPP$) 860
HDI/world rank: 0·378/146

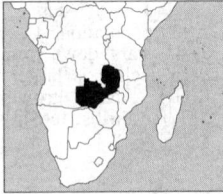

KEY HISTORICAL EVENTS

The early history of Zambia is obscure. The first expedition of real geographical value was Livingstone's missionary journey of 1851 during which he discovered the Victoria Falls.

The great majority of the present African population of the area is of Bantu origin, descended from invaders who swept over the country. There are more than 70 different tribes, the most important being the Bemba and the Bgoni in the north-east, and there are also about 30 different dialects in use. The chief invaders of the early 19th century were the Arabs from the north, the Ngoni Zulus fleeing from Shaka, and the Kololo, who fought their way from the south across the Zambezi and founded a kingdom with a high degree of social organization. One of the more successful of the invading tribes was the Lozi under Lewanika, who asked for and obtained the protection of the British government in 1891. In 1900 the chartered company acquired certain trading and mining rights over Lewanika's territory. These 2 territories were amalgamated in 1911 under the name of Northern Rhodesia, and in 1924 the Crown took over the administration of Northern Rhodesia from the British South Africa Company.

In 1953, following a referendum in Southern Rhodesia, the Federation of Rhodesia and Nyasaland, of which Northern Rhodesia was a component part, was created. Federation brought great economic benefits to Northern Rhodesia, but it was from the outset bitterly opposed by the African leaders there. Kenneth Kaunda led a sustained campaign against Federation, and after elections held under a new constitution of 1962, his United National Independence party gained wide success. In March 1963 Britain agreed in principle to Northern Rhodesia's right to secede from the Federation, which was duly dissolved at the end of the year. In Jan. 1964 full internal self-government was attained. On 24 Oct. Northern Rhodesia became an independent republic within the Commonwealth, changing its name to Zambia. Kaunda became its first president, and led the efforts to break the foreign hold on Zambia's mineral resources. He was ousted in the country's first multi-party elections in 1991.

A highly centralized one-party state was created which suffocated the emergent economy. Living standards fell sharply and the production of copper, Zambia's biggest foreign exchange earner, almost halved. In 1991 the Movement for Multiparty Democracy (MMD) was elected on a promise to transform the economy. Markets were liberalized and the budget deficit contained. Inflation fell from 46% in 1995 to around 20% in 1997. A Privatization Act was passed in 1992.

TERRITORY AND POPULATION

Zambia is bounded by the Democratic Republic of the Congo in the north, Tanzania in the north-east, Malaŵi in the east, Mozambique in the south-east and by Zimbabwe and Namibia in the south. The area is 290,586 sq. miles (752,614 sq. km). Population estimate (1997), 9·35m.; population density, 11·7 per sq. km.

The projected population for 2000 is 9·87m.

In 1995 an estimated 57% of the population were rural.

The republic is divided into 9 provinces. Area, population and chief towns:

Province	Area (in sq. kms)	Population (1991 census)	Chief Town
Central	94,395	697,000	Kabwe
Copperbelt	31,328	1,294,000	Ndola
Eastern	69,106	995,000	Chipata
Luapula	50,567	728,000	Mansa
Lusaka	21,898	1,327,000	Lusaka
Northern	147,826	972,000	Kasama
North-Western	125,827	415,000	Solwezi
Southern	85,283	944,000	Livingstone
Western	126,386	630,000	Mongu

Major towns (with estimated 1989 population in 1,000) are: Lusaka, 921; Kitwe, 495; Ndola, 467; Kabwe, 210; Mufulira, 206; Chingola, 201; Luanshya, 171; Livingstone, 102; Kalulushi, 100; Chililabombwe, 85.

The official language is English and the main ethnic groups are the Bemba (34%), Tonga (16%), Nyanja (14%) and Lozi (9%).

SOCIAL STATISTICS

Births, 1995, 351,000; deaths, 149,000. 1995 birth rate per 1,000 population, 43·4; death rate, 18·5. Zambia's life expectancy at birth in 1998 was 43 years, down from 50 in 1990. It had last been 43 in the mid 1960s. The sharp decline is largely attributed to the huge number of people in the country with HIV. Annual growth rate, 1990–95, 3·0%. Infant mortality, 1990–95, 111 per 1,000 live births; fertility rate, 6·0 births per woman.

CLIMATE

The climate is tropical, but has three seasons. The cool, dry one is from May to Aug., a hot dry one follows until Nov., when the wet season commences. Frosts may occur in some areas in the cool season. Lusaka, Jan. 70°F (21·1°C), July 61°F (16·1°C). Annual rainfall 33" (836 mm). Livingstone, Jan. 75°F (23·9°C), July 61°F (16·1°C). Annual rainfall 27" (673 mm). Ndola, Jan. 70°F (21·1°C), July 59°F (15°C). Annual rainfall 52" (1,293 mm).

CONSTITUTION AND GOVERNMENT

In Aug. 1991 the National Assembly adopted a new constitution by 107 votes to 15 permitting multi-party elections for a new wholly elected parliament of 150 members. Candidates for election as President must have both parents born in Zambia (this excludes ex-President Kaunda).

National Anthem. 'Stand and Sing of Zambia, Proud and Free'; words collective, tune (same as that for Tanzania and Zimbabwe) by M. E. Sontanga.

RECENT ELECTIONS

At the presidential and parliamentary elections on 18 Nov. 1996 the potential electorate was 6·4m., of whom only 60% registered. Turn-out was 40%. Frederick Chiluba was re-elected President by 70·2% of votes cast against 4 other candidates. In the National Assembly election the Movement for Multiparty Democracy (MMD) gained 127 of the 150 seats, receiving 60·8% of the vote.

CURRENT ADMINISTRATION

A state of emergency was imposed in Oct. 1997 after a failed coup, but President Chiluba lifted the emergency in March 1998.

President: Frederick Chiluba, b. 1943 (MMD; elected Oct. 1991, re-elected Nov. 1996).

Vice-President: Christon Tembo.

In March 1999 the government comprised:

Minister of Agriculture, Fisheries and Food Security: Suresh Desai. *Commerce, Trade and Industry:* David Mpamba. *Community Development and Social Welfare:* Dawson Lapunga. *Defence:* Chitalu Sampa. *Education:* Brig.-Gen. Godfrey Miyanda. *Energy and Water Development:* Benjamin Mwila. *Environment and Natural Resources:* William Harrington. *Finance:* Edith Nawakwi. *Foreign Affairs:* Sipakeli Walubita. *Health:* Nkandu Luo. *Home Affairs:* Katele Kalumba. *Information and Broadcasting:* Newstead Zimba. *Labour and Social Security:* Dr Peter Machungwa. *Lands:* Samuel Miyanda. *Legal Affairs:* Vincent Malambo. *Local Government and Housing:* Bennie Mwiinga. *Mines and Mineral Development:* Syamukayumbu Syamujaye. *Science, Technology and Vocational Training:* Alfeyo Hambayi. *State:* Eric Silwamba. *Tourism:* Anoshi Chipawa. *Transport and Communications:* David Saviye. *Works and Supply:* Godden Mandandi. *Youth, Sport and Child Development:* Abel Chambesi. *Without Portfolio:* Michael Sata.

Local Government. The 9 provinces (sub-divided into 61 districts) are administered by deputy ministers appointed by the President from elected or nominated members of parliament and with the Permanent Secretary as head of the civil service in each province. Elections are normally held every 3 years. Elections were held in Nov. 1992. Turn-out was 10%. The MMD won a majority of seats.

DEFENCE
In 1997 defence expenditure totalled US$59m. (US$6 per capita).

Army. The Army consists of 1 armoured and 1 artillery regiment and 1 engineer and 9 infantry battalions. Equipment includes 10 T-54/-55 and 20 Chinese Type-59 main battle tanks. Strength (1997) 20,000. There are also 2 paramilitary police units totalling 1,400.

Air Force. In 1996 the Air Force had 23 Aermacchi M.B.326G armed jet basic trainers (of which 12 remain in service), 8 SIAI-Marchetti SF.260M piston-engined trainers and 16 Agusta-Bell 47G, 10 AB.205 and 2 AB.212 helicopters. 12 F-6 (MiG-19) jet fighter-bombers have been acquired from China, a squadron of 12 MiG-21 fighters, 3 Yak-40 light jet transports, 4 An-26 twin-turboprop transports and 6 Mi-8 helicopters from the Soviet Union. Serviceability of most types is reported to be low. Personnel (1996) 1,600.

INTERNATIONAL RELATIONS
Zambia is a member of the UN, the Commonwealth, SADC, OAU and is an ACP member state of the ACP-EU relationship.

ECONOMY
Policy. The privatization programme of 235 state-owned companies (157 had been sold by 1996, raising K38,734m.) has created one of the most liberal economies in Africa. More than 80% of the economy is now in private hands.

Performance. Real GDP growth was 6·4% in 1996 and 5·5% in 1997.

Budget. 1997 budget: Expenditure, 1,427,100m. kwacha; revenue, 1,489,100m. kwacha.

Currency. The unit of currency is the *kwacha* (ZMK) of 100 *ngwee*. Foreign exchange reserves were US$170m. in May 1997. In Dec. 1992 the official and free market exchange rates were merged and the kwacha devalued 29%. Annualized inflation was 35% in 1996. Total money supply in Dec. 1997 was 355m. kwacha.

Banking and Finance. The central bank is the Bank of Zambia (*Governor,* Jacob Mwanza), which had deposits of K12,332m. in 1991 and assets of K33,393·4m. In 1996, 20 banks were operating. Total assets of domestic and foreign commercial banks were K71,216·6m. in 1991. Assets of the Zambia National Building Society were K1,683·2m.

Banks and building societies are governed by the Banking and Financial Services Act 1994. The Bank of Zambia monitors and supervizes the operations of financial institutions.

There is a stock exchange at Lusaka.

ENERGY AND NATURAL RESOURCES
Electricity. Installed capacity in 1994 was 2·44m. kW. Production in 1994 was 7·78bn. kWh. Consumption per capita was estimated to be 610 kWh in 1995.

Zambia is a net exporter of hydro-electric power and has huge potential for energy growth.

Minerals. Minerals produced (in 1,000 tonnes) in 1995: Copper, 307·8; cobalt, 2·93; silver, 7·88 tonnes; gold, 0·08 tonnes. Zambia is the world's fourth leading producer of copper and produces a fifth of the world's cobalt. It is well-endowed with gemstones, especially emeralds, amethysts, aquamarine, tourmaline and garnets. In 1990 the government freed the gemstones trade from restrictions.

Agriculture. 70% of the population is dependent on agriculture and 19·7% of GDP was provided by it and fishing in 1996. Principal agricultural products (1993, in 1,000 tonnes): Maize, 1,598; sugar-cane, 1,300; seed cotton, 58; tobacco, 7; groundnuts, 42.

Livestock (1996): Cattle, 2·6m.; pigs, 283,000; sheep, 65,000; goats, 620,000 (1995) and chickens, 22m. (1995).

ZAMBIA

Forestry. Forests covered 31·4m. ha in 1995, or 42·2% of the total land area (32·7m. ha and 44% in 1990). Roundwood removals in 1995 were 14·61m. cu. metres, most of it for fuel.

Fisheries. Total catch, 1995, 70,864 tonnes (exclusively from inland waters).

INDUSTRY
In 1996 manufacturing accounted for 25·5% of GDP.

Labour. The labour force totalled 3,454,000 in 1996 (55% males). Around 74% of the economically active population in 1995 were engaged in agriculture, fisheries and forestry.

Trade Unions. There is a Zambia Congress of Trade Unions.

INTERNATIONAL TRADE
In 1996 foreign debt was US$7,113m. Incentives contained in the 1993 Investment Act include tax holidays and exemptions, remittance of 75% of after-tax profits and guarantees against expropriation.

Imports and Exports. In 1996 exports were valued at US$1,010m. and imports at US$890m.

In 1997, copper provided 80% of all exports (by value), cobalt 10%, zinc 2%. Since 1990 non-copper exports have increased in value from US$50m. to US$230m. The main import sources in 1995 were South Africa (27·7%), UK (11·3%), Zimbabwe (9·2%) and Japan (8·6%). Principal export markets in 1995 were Japan (17·9%), Saudi Arabia (12·9%), Thailand (12·8%) and Taiwan (7·2%).

COMMUNICATIONS

Roads. There were, in 1996, 36,761 km of roads (6,476 km paved). 157,000 passenger cars were in use in 1996 (15 per 1,000 inhabitants) and there were 81,000 trucks and vans.

Rail. In 1993 there were 1,273 km of the state-owned Zambia Railways Ltd. (ZRL) and 891 km of the Tanzania-Zambia (Tazara) Railway, both on 1,067 mm gauge. ZRL carried 1·1m. passengers and 3·4m. tonnes of freight in 1993.

Civil Aviation. The national carrier, Zambia Airways, went into voluntary liquidation in 1995; some of its services have been taken over by Aero Zambia, which operates internal flights and in 1998 flew to Harare, Johannesburg and Nairobi. Lusaka is the principal international airport. In 1998 services were also provided by Air Malawi, Air Namibia, Air Tanzania Corporation, Air Zimbabwe, British Airways, Ethiopian Airlines, Inter Air, Kenya Airways, Royal Swazi National Airways Corporation, South African Airways and Uganda Airlines. In 1996 Lusaka International handled 284,000 passengers (219,000 on international flights) and 8,800 tonnes of freight.

Telecommunications. Main telephone lines numbered 77,300 in 1997, equivalent to 9·1 per 1,000 persons. In 1995 there were direct connections to 16 countries. Telecel (2) Ltd. has been licensed to run a cellular telecommunications service in addition to the Zambia Telecomms Company (ZAMTEL) since 1996. Cellular phone subscribers numbered 1,500 in 1995 and there were 600 fax machines. The telex network had 2,800 lines in 1995. Internet services are provided by Zambia Communications Systems (ZAMNET), a private company of ZAMTEL. There were approximately 2,000 Internet users in Jan. 1998.

Postal Services. In 1995 there were 203 post offices, or 1 for every 44,200 persons.

SOCIAL INSTITUTIONS

Justice. The Judiciary consists of the Supreme Court, the High Court and 4 classes of magistrates' courts; all have civil and criminal jurisdiction.

The Supreme Court hears and determines appeals from the High Court. Its seat is at Lusaka. The High Court exercises the powers vested in the High Court in England, subject to the High Court ordinance of Zambia. Its sessions are held where occasion requires, mostly at Lusaka and Ndola. All criminal cases tried by subordinate courts are subject to revision by the High Court.

Religion. In 1993 the President declared Zambia to be a Christian nation, but freedom of worship is a constitutional right. In 1992 there were 5·98m. Christians.

Education. Schooling is for 9 years. In 1996 there were 1·67m. pupils in 3,907 primary schools; secondary schools, 255,000 in 246 schools.

There are 2 universities, 3 teachers' colleges and 1 Christian college. In 1995–96 there were 4,470 university students and 640 academic staff.

The adult literacy rate in 1995 was 79·2% (85·6% among males and 71·3% among females).

Health. In 1990 there were 713 doctors, 26 dentists, 1,503 nurses, 24 pharmacists and 311 midwives. There were 42 state, 29 mission and 11 mining company hospitals in 1987, with a total of 15,846 beds and 912 health centres with 7,081 beds.

In the period 1990–96 only 27% of the population had access to safe drinking water.

CULTURE

Broadcasting. The Zambia National Broadcasting Corporation is an independent statutory body which oversees 4 radio networks. There is also a religious radio station. In 1996, 2 privately-owned radio stations also started operations. These were Radio Phoenix and Radio Ichengelo. In 1995 there were 800,000 radio and 260,000 TV receivers. Private broadcasting stations were licensed to operate in 1996. One such company was Multi Choice Kaleidoscope (2) Ltd. which commenced operations in Aug. 1995. By Oct. 1996 the number of subscribers was 6,617.

Press. There were (1996) 2 state-owned daily papers, *The Times of Zambia* and *Zambia Daily Mail*, and 3 weeklies. There were also 5 privately-owned newspapers in 1995.

Tourism. There were 48,589 international visitors in 1996. Revenue from international tourism was US$16·3m.

DIPLOMATIC REPRESENTATIVES
Of Zambia in Great Britain (2 Palace Gate, London, W8 5NG)
High Commissioner: Prof. Moses Musonda.

Of Great Britain in Zambia (Independence Ave., 15101 Lusaka)
High Commissioner: T. N. Young.

Of Zambia in the USA (2419 Massachusetts Ave., NW, Washington, D.C., 20008)
Ambassador: Dunstan Weston Kamana.

Of the USA in Zambia (PO Box 31617, Lusaka)
Ambassador: Arlene Render.

Of Zambia to the United Nations
Ambassador: Peter Lesa Kasanda.

Of Zambia to the European Union
Ambassador: Isaiah Chabala.

FURTHER READING
Central Statistical Office. *Monthly Digest of Statistics.*

Bliss, A. M. and Rigg, J. A., *Zambia.* [Bibliography] Oxford and Santa Barbara (CA), 1984
Burdette, M. M., *Zambia: between Two Worlds.* Boulder (CO), 1988
Chiluba, F., *Democracy: the Challenge of Change.* Lusaka, 1995
De Waal, V., *The Politics of Reconciliation: Zambia's First Decade.* London, 1990
Roberts, A., *A History of Zambia.* London, 1977

National statistical office: Central Statistical Office, Lusaka

ZIMBABWE

Republic of Zimbabwe

Capital: Harare
Population estimate, 2000: 12·39m.
GNP per capita: (PPP$) 2,200
HDI/world rank: 0·507/130

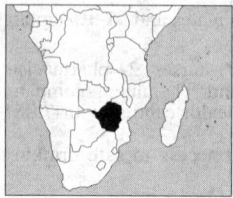

KEY HISTORICAL EVENTS

Shona-speaking people lived in Zimbabwe hundreds of years before the Europeans arrived. It was a major commercial centre in the 14th and 15th centuries, although the ruins of Great Zimbabwe date back to the 8th century. It became increasingly secondary of the Kingdom of Mwanamutapa which arose on the north. By backing rival kings, Portuguese traders managed to destroy Mwanamutapa by 1700. The Shona inhabitants were unable to repel the invasion of Ndebele people under Mzilikazi in 1870; the Ndebele had a very powerful state. However, it was not strong enough to defeat European settlers who forcibly aquired Shona lands in 1890 and turned to Ndebele territory in 1893. Revolts by both peoples several years later were also defeated.

The territory which now forms Zimbabwe was administered by the British South Africa Company from the beginning of European colonization in 1890 until 1923 when it was granted the status of a self-governing colony. In 1911 it had been divided into Southern and Northern Rhodesia (*see* Zambia).

In 1953 Southern and Northern Rhodesia were again united, along with Nyasaland to form the Federation of Rhodesia and Nyasaland. When this federation was dissolved on 31 Dec. 1963 Southern Rhodesia reverted to the status of a self-governing colony within the British Commonwealth.

Ian Smith, prime minister from April 1964, had discussions about independence on three occasions with two British prime ministers during 1964 and 1965. On 11 Nov. 1965 Smith and his government issued a unilateral declaration of independence (UDI). Thereupon the Governor dismissed Smith and his cabinet, and the British government reasserted its own formal responsibility for Rhodesia; but effective internal government was carried on by the Smith cabinet.

The UN Security Council on 20 Nov. called upon all member states to break off economic relations with Rhodesia. From 1-3 Dec. Harold Wilson, the British prime minister, and others met Smith on board H.M.S. *Tiger* and drafted a 'Working Document' on the procedure for progress towards legal independence. This statement was approved by the British cabinet, but rejected by the Smith government. As a result the Security Council voted for mandatory sanctions including oil: France and the USSR abstained. On 2 March 1970 the Smith government declared Rhodesia a republic and adopted a new constitution.

On 3 March 1978 Smith signed a constitutional agreement with the internationally-based black nationalist leaders. It decreed independence, as Zimbabwe, on 31 Dec. 1978. In Nov. 1978 the government considered it was impossible to meet the independence date. A draft constitution was published in Jan. 1979 and was accepted by the white electorate in a referendum. In April 1979 general elections were held for the 72 black seats in the 100-seat parliament. The United African National Council won 51 of the 72 seats and Bishop Abel Muzorewa became prime minister of Rhodesia-Zimbabwe on 1 June 1979.

At the Commonwealth Conference held in Lusaka in Aug. 1979 agreement was reached for a new constitutional conference to be held in London; elections took place in March 1980 resulting in a victory for the Zimbabwe African National Union (ZANU). Southern Rhodesia became the Republic of Zimbabwe, with Canaan Banana as president, and Robert Mugabe as prime minister. On 31 Dec. 1987 Robert Mugabe became the first executive president.

The state of emergency in force since 1965 was lifted in July 1990. In June 1991 the ZANU (PF) renounced Marxism.

Zimbabwe is currently beset by economic problems. A run on the currency in 1998 led to price rises on essential goods which caused widespread unrest. Hopes of IMF support have so far foundered on the government's reluctance to countenance radical economic reforms.

TERRITORY AND POPULATION
Zimbabwe is bounded in the north by Zambia, east by Mozambique, south by South Africa and west by Botswana and the Caprivi Strip of Namibia. The area is 150,872 sq. miles (390,759 sq. km). The population was (1992 census) 10,401,767 (51·2% female). Estimate, 1995, 11,536,000 (50·4% female); density, 29·5 per sq. km.

The UN gives a projected population for 2000 of 12·39m.

In 1995 an estimated 68·2% of the population were rural.

There are 8 provinces and 2 cities, Harare and Bulawayo, with provincial status.

Area and population (1992 census):

	Area (sq. km)	Population		Area (sq. km)	Population
Bulawayo	479	620,936	Mashonaland West	57,441	1,116,928
Harare	872	1,478,810	Masvingo	56,566	1,221,845
Manicaland	36,459	1,537,676	Matabeleland North	75,025	640,957
Mashonaland Central	28,374	857,318	Matebeleland South	54,172	591,747
Mashonaland East	32,230	1,033,336	Midlands	49,166	1,302,212

The chief cities (with 1992 census populations) were Harare, the capital (1,184,169), Bulawayo (620,936), Chitungwiza (274,035), Mutare (131,808) and Gweru (124,735). The main ethno-linguistic groups are the Shona (71%), Ndebele (16%) and Nyanja (3%).

The official language is English.

SOCIAL STATISTICS
1995 births, 434,000; deaths, 158,000. Rates, 1995: Birth, 38·8 per 1,000 population; death 14·1 per 1,000. Annual rate of increase, 1990–95, 4·1%. Zimbabwe's expectation of life at birth in 1998 was 49 years, down from 56 in 1990. The sharp decline is largely attributed to the huge number of people in the country with HIV. Life expectancy had last been 49 in the early 1970s. Researchers predict that by 2008 it will have dropped to 31. Infant mortality, 1990–95, 70 per 1,000 live births; fertility rate, 5·2 births per woman.

CLIMATE
Though situated in the tropics, conditions are remarkably temperate throughout the year because of altitude, and an inland position keeps humidity low. The warmest weather occurs in the three months before the main rainy season, which starts in Nov. and lasts till March. The cool season is from mid-May to mid-Aug. and, though days are mild and sunny, nights are chilly. Harare, Jan. 69°F (20·6°C), July 57°F (13·9°C). Annual rainfall 33" (828 mm). Bulawayo, Jan. 71°F (21·7°C), July 57°F (13·9°C). Annual rainfall 24" (594 mm). Victoria Falls, Jan. 78°F (25·6°C), July 61°F (16·1°C). Annual rainfall 28" (710 mm).

CONSTITUTION AND GOVERNMENT
The Constitution provides for a single-chamber 150-member Parliament (*House of Assembly*), universal suffrage for citizens over the age of 18, an *Executive President* (elected for a 6-year term of office by Parliament), an independent judiciary enjoying security of tenure and a Declaration of Rights, derogation from certain of the provisions being permitted, within specified limits, during a state of emergency. The House of Assembly is elected for 5 year terms: 120 members are elected by universal suffrage, 10 are chiefs elected by all the country's tribal chiefs, 12 are appointed by the President and 8 are provincial governors. The constitution can be amended by a two-thirds parliamentary majority.

National Anthem. 'Ngaikomborewe Nyika ye Zimbabwe' ('Blessed be the Land of Zimbabwe'); words by Dr Solomon M. Mutswairo; tune by Mr F. L. Changundega.

RECENT ELECTIONS
Presidential elections were held on 17 March 1996. The electorate was 4·9m.; turn-out was 35%. President Mugabe was re-elected unopposed.

At the elections of 8–9 April 1995, turn-out was 54%. ZANU-PF gained 118 seats of the electable seats with 82% of votes cast (55 seats were uncontested), ZANU (Ndonga) 2 with 6·5%. Parliamentary party composition: ZANU-PF, 147 seats; ZANU (Ndonga), 2; independents, 1. The next elections are due in March 2000.

CURRENT ADMINISTRATION

Executive President: Robert G. Mugabe (b. 1924; sworn in on 30 Dec. 1987, re-elected April 1990; re-elected again March 1996).

Following a reshuffle in July 1997, the council comprised in March 1999:

Vice-Presidents: Simon Muzenda, Dr Joshua Nkomo.

Minister of Foreign Affairs: Dr Stanislaus Mudenge. *Justice, Legal and Parliamentary Affairs:* Emmerson Mnangagwa. *Defence:* Moven Mahachi. *Home Affairs:* Dumiso Dabengwa. *Lands and Agriculture:* Kumbirai Kangai. *Information, Posts and Telecommunications:* Chen Chimutengwende. *Public Service, Labour and Social Welfare:* Florence Chitauro. *Industry and Commerce:* Dr Nathan Shamuyarira. *Mines and Environment:* Simon Moyo. *Transport and Energy:* Enos Chikowore. *Health and Child Welfare:* Dr Timothy Stamps. *Local Government and National Housing:* John Nkomo. *Higher Education and Technology:* Dr Ignatius Chombo. *Education, Sport and Culture:* Gabriel Machinga. *Finance:* Dr Herbert Murerwa. *National Affairs and Employment Creation:* Thenjiwe Lesabe. *Rural Resources and Water Development:* Joyce Mujuru.

DEFENCE

In 1997 military expenditure totalled US$304m. (US$26 per capita).

Army. The Army consists of 1 air defence, 1 engineer, 1 armoured and 1 field artillery regiment, 22 infantry battalions and 1 tank squadron. Equipment includes 30 Chinese T-59 and 10 Chinese T-69 main battle tanks. Strength in 1997 was 39,000, and there are a further 19,500 paramilitary police and a police support unit of 2,300.

Air Force. The Air Force (ZAF) has a strength of (1996) about 4,000 personnel and 58 combat aircraft. Headquarters ZAF and the main ZAF stations are in Harare; the second main base is at Gweru, with many secondary airfields throughout the country. Equipment includes 1 squadron of F-7 (MiG-21) interceptors, 1 squadron of Hunter fighter-bombers and 1 squadron of Hawk training and light attack aircraft, a transport squadron with 11 turbo-prop CASA Aviocars and 6 twin-engined Islanders; a squadron with 14 Reims/Cessna 337 Lynx attack aircraft; a squadron with 26 SIAI-Marchetti SF.260 trainers; a helicopter liaison/transport squadron with 20 Alouette IIIs; a helicopter casualty evacuation/transport squadron with 9 Bell 412s.

INTERNATIONAL RELATIONS

Zimbabwe is a member of UN, the Commonwealth, OAU and SADC and is an ACP member state of the ACP-EU relationship. Claiming to act on behalf of the 14 member Southern African Development Community (SADC), Zimbabwe has committed 10,000 troops to the campaign to support the Democratic Republic of the Congo's President Laurent Kabila.

ECONOMY

Policy. The second phase of structural adjustment dubbed Zimbabwe Programme for Economic and Social Transformation (ZIMPREST) was launched in early 1998. Its goals are similar to those of the first phase (1991–95), promoting a market economy by economic stabilization, liberalization of trade, deregulation, reform of the public sector and social reform. But confidence in the economy was undermined by promises to pay compensation (Z$365m.) to war veterans and to make compulsory purchase of 1,471 privately-owned farms for resettlement.

Performance. GDP is estimated to have grown by 5% in 1997. Agriculture contributes about 65% of GDP, which was left in tatters in 1992 after a severe drought cut it by about 12%. In 1996, on the other hand, thanks to favourable weather conditions in the 1995/96 growing season, agricultural production jumped 45% and GDP rose 8·1%. Manufacturing industry is estimated to have grown by 7% in 1997, against a 2·1% rise in 1996.

Budget. The 1999 budget forecasts a budget deficit of 6%.

Revenue and expenditure (in Z$1,000):

	1996–97	1997–98
Revenue	27,289	52,152
Expenditure	32,366	63,857

From Jan. 1998 the top rate of income tax was to be 55% for $80,000. Sales tax was cut from 17·5% to 15% and corporate tax from 39·4% to 35%.

Currency. The unit of currency is the *Zimbabwe dollar* (ZWD), divided into 100 *cents*. Gold reserves were 470,000 troy oz. in Feb. 1998 and foreign exchange reserves US$127m. The currency was devalued 17% in Jan. 1994 and made fully convertible. Its value dropped by 65% in 1998. Inflation doubled from 14·5% in 1997 to 35% by the end of 1998 and is expected to rise to 45% by the end of 1999. Total money supply was Z$21,320m. in Dec. 1997.

Banking and Finance. The Reserve Bank of Zimbabwe is the central bank (established 1965; *Governor*, Dr Leonard Tsumba). It acts as banker to the Government and to the commercial banks, is the note-issuing authority and co-ordinates the application of the Government's monetary policy. The Zimbabwe Development Bank, established in 1983 as a development finance institution, is 51% Government-owned. In 1997 there were 7 commercial and 5 merchant banks. There are 5 registered finance houses, 3 of which are subsidiaries of commercial banks.

The IMF announced in June 1998 that it was to lend Zimbabwe US$175m. in the form of a 13-month standby credit which would allow Harare to draw US$52m. immediately to replenish its depleted reserves.

There is a stock exchange.

Weights and Measures. The metric system is in use but the US short ton is also used.

ENERGY AND NATURAL RESOURCES

Electricity. Installed capacity was 2·15m. kW in 1994. In 1997 Zimbabwe Electricity Supply Authority's (Zesa) five power stations supplied 7,323·3 GWh, and a further 3,171·5 GWh was imported via the Southern African Power Pool (SAPP). Electricity sales during the financial year 1995/96 increased by 3·6% and revenues grew by 28% from US$2,222·7m. to US$2,852·7m. Consumption per capita in 1995 was estimated to be 747 kWh.

Minerals. The total value of all minerals produced in 1995 was Z$5,249·3m. 1995 production: gold, 23·9 tonnes, value Z$2,395m.; nickel, value (1993) Z$369·1m.; asbestos, 0·70m. tonnes; coal, some 5m. tonnes.

Agriculture. Current Land distribution Pattern: i) 4,000 large scale communal farmers (mainly white) on 11·2m. ha; ii) 1m. communal area families on 16·3m. ha; iii) 10,000 small scale commercial farmers on 1·2m. ha; iv) 60,000 resettlement families on 3·3m. ha; v) state farming sector on 0·5m. ha.

Agriculture contributes 30% of the country's annual production and 40% of its foreign-exchange earnings. It is also the largest employer, providing jobs for more than 320,000 labourers.

A constitutional amendment providing for the compulsory purchase of land for peasant resettlement came into force in March 1992. But dependence on IMF support has deterred the government from carrying out plans for the mass confiscation of white-owned farms. For the next two years the state will limit itself to buying land that farmers are willing to sell.

The staple food crop is maize. Tobacco is the most important cash crop. Production, 1993, in 1,000 tonnes: Maize, 2,562; tobacco, 205,000; sorghum, 90; barley, 24; millet, 95; soya beans, 65; groundnuts, 64; fruit, 153; vegetables and melons, 140; seed cotton, 187; wheat, 300; tea, 14; coffee, 4; sugar-cane, 700. Zimbabwe is the world's second largest exporter of flue-cured tobacco. In 1996 more than 201m. kg of tobacco were sold at nearly 3m. kg up on the previous year, fetching Z$5·8bn. More than 150,000 people work in the tobacco industry. Tobacco is a highly commercial crop, worth nearly 60 times as much as the same acreage planted with soya or maize.

Livestock (1996): Cattle, 5·44m.; pigs, 266,000; sheep, 530,000; goats (1995), 2·61m.; chickens (1995), 14m. Milk production (1993): 400,000 tonnes.

Forestry. In 1995 forests covered 8·71m. ha, or 22·5% of the total land area (down from 8·96m. ha in 1990). Timber production in 1995 was 8·1m. cu. metres.

Fisheries. Trout, prawns and bream are farmed to supplement supplies of fish caught in dams and lakes. The catch in 1995 was approximately 20,500 tonnes, entirely from inland waters.

INDUSTRY
Metal products account for over 20% of industrial output. Important agro-industries include food processing, textiles, furniture and other wood products.

Labour. The labour force in 1996 totalled 5,281,000 (56% males). Unemployment in Jan. 1998 was around 50%.

Trade Unions. There is a Zimbabwe Congress of Trade Unions.

INTERNATIONAL TRADE
Foreign debt was US$5,005m. in 1996. Since 1 Jan. 1995 foreign companies have been permitted to remit 100% of after-tax profits. The Customs Agreement with South Africa was extended in 1982.

Imports and Exports. In 1996 exports totalled US$2,403m.; imports, US$2,819m.

Principal exports in 1993 (in US$1m.): Tobacco, 365; ferrochrome, 142; clothing and textiles, 122; nickel, 56; cotton lint, 26; steel, 16.

Main import suppliers, 1996 (% of total trade): South Africa, 38·3%; UK, 7·9%; Japan, 5·1%; USA, 5·0%; Germany, 4·9%. Main export destinations: UK, 10·1%; South Africa, 9·6%; Germany, 7·9%; USA, 6·7%; Japan, 5·1%.

Recent estimates suggest a marked deterioration in balance of payments.

Trade Fairs. The highlight of the year is the Zimbabwe International Book Fair, held in Harare in August.

COMMUNICATIONS

Roads. In 1996 the road network covered 18,338 km, of which 8,700 km were paved. Number of vehicles, 1996: Passenger cars, 323,000; commercial vehicles, 32,000; motor cycles, 362,000; tractors, 7,520.

Rail. In 1995 the National Railways of Zimbabwe had 2,759 km (1,067 mm gauge) of route ways (313 km electrified). In 1995 the railways carried 12·2m. tonnes of freight and 1·9m. passengers.

Civil Aviation. There are 3 international airports: Harare (the main airport), Bulawayo and Victoria Falls. Air Zimbabwe, the state-owned national carrier, operates domestic services and in 1998 flew to the major centres in Africa and Europe. Zimbabwe Express Airlines likewise operates internal services, and had flights in 1998 to Johannesburg. Zimbabwe was also served in 1998 by Aero Zambia, Air Austral, Air Botswana, Air France, Air Malawi, Air Mauritius, Air Namibia, Air Tanzania Corporation, British Airways, Cameroon Airlines, Delta Air Lines, Egyptair, Ethiopian Airlines, Expedition Airways, Ghana Airways, Kenya Airways, KLM, LAM, Lufthansa, Royal Swazi National Airways Corporation, South African Airways, Swissair, TAAG and Uganda Airlines. In 1996 Harare handled 1,221,655 passengers (859,372 on international flights).

Shipping. Zimbabwe's outlets to the sea are Maputo and Beira in Mozambique, Dar es Salaam, Tanzania and the South African ports.

Telecommunications. Zimbabwe had 212,000 main telephone lines in 1997 (17·2 for every 1,000 persons). In 1995 there were 33,000 PCs and 10,000 fax machines, and in Jan. 1998, approximately 10,000 Internet users.

Postal Services. In Aug. 1995 there were 170 post offices, 47 postal telegraph agencies and 86 postal agencies. A total of 298m. pieces of mail were handled in 1995, or 26 items per person.

SOCIAL INSTITUTIONS

Justice. The general common law of Zimbabwe is the Roman Dutch law as it applied in the Colony of the Cape of Good Hope on 10 June 1891, as subsequently modified by statute. Provision is made by statute for the application of African customary law by all courts in appropriate cases.

The death penalty is authorized. The last execution took place in 1997.

The Supreme Court consists of the Chief Justice and at least 2 Supreme Court judges. It is the final court of appeal. It exercises appellate jurisdiction in appeals from the High Court and other courts and tribunals; its only original jurisdiction is that conferred on it by the Constitution to enforce the protective provisions of the Declaration of Rights. The Court's permanent seat is in Harare but it sits regularly in Bulawayo also.

The High Court is also headed by the Chief Justice, supported by the Judge President and an appropriate number of High Court judges. It has full original jurisdiction, in both Civil and Criminal cases, over all persons and all matters in Zimbabwe. The Judge President is in charge of the Court, subject to the directions of the Chief Justice. The Court has permanent seats in both Harare and Bulawayo and sittings are held three times a year in 3 other principal towns.

Regional courts, established in Harare and Bulawayo but also holding sittings in other centres, exercise a solely criminal jurisdiction which is intermediate between that of the High Court and the Magistrates' courts. Magistrates' courts, established in 20 centres throughout the country, and staffed by full-time professional magistrates, exercise both civil and criminal jurisdiction.

Primary courts consist of village courts and community courts. Village courts are presided over by officers selected for the purpose from the local population, sitting with two assessors. They deal with certain classes of civil cases only and have jurisdiction only where African customary law is applicable. Community courts are presided over by presiding officers in full-time public service who may be assisted by assessors. They have jurisdiction in all civil cases determinable by African customary law and also deal with appeals from village courts. They also have limited criminal jurisdiction in respect of petty offences.

Religion. Over a third of the population adhere to traditional animist religion. In 1997 approximately 2·42m. persons were Protestants, 1·54m. African Christians, 800,000 Roman Catholics and 2·03m. followers of other religions.

Education. Education is compulsory. 'Manageable' school fees were introduced in 1991; primary education had hitherto been free to all. All instruction is given in English. There are also over 3,800 private primary schools and over 950 private secondary schools, all of which must be registered by the Ministry of Education. In 1996 there were 2,499,381 pupils at primary schools and 760,572 pupils at secondary schools. In 1995 the adult literacy rate was 85·1% (90·4% among males and 79·9% among females). Both the overall rate and the rate for males are the highest in Africa.

There are 10 teachers' training colleges, 8 of which are in association with the University of Zimbabwe. In addition, there are 4 special training centres for teacher trainees in the Zimbabwe Integrated National Teacher Education Course. In 1990 there were 17,873 students enrolled at teachers' training colleges, 1,003 students at agricultural colleges and 20,943 students at technical colleges. There are 4 universities and 10 technical colleges.

Health. There were 1,378 government hospitals in 1993. All mission health institutions get 100% government grants-in-aid for recurrent expenditure. In 1993 there were 1,551 doctors, 194 dentists, 22,590 nurses, 411 pharmacists and 2,894 midwives. It is estimated that 1 in 5 adults are HIV infected.

Welfare. It is a statutory responsibility of the government in many areas to provide: Processing and administration of war pensions and old age pensions; protection of children; administration of remand, probation and correctional institutions; registration and supervision of welfare organizations.

CULTURE

Broadcasting. Zimbabwe Broadcasting Corporation is a statutory body broadcasting a general service in English, Shona, Ndebele, Nyanja, Tonga and Kalanga. There are 3 national semi-commercial services—Radio 1, 2 and 3, in English, Shona and Ndebele. Radio 4 transmits formal and informal educational programmes. Zimbabwe Television broadcasts on 2 channels (colour by PAL). In 1995 there were 320,000 TV and 1m. radio sets in use.

Press. In 1995 there were 2 daily newspapers with a combined circulation of 192,000, giving a rate of 17 per 1,000 inhabitants.

Tourism. There were 1,743,000 foreign tourists in 1996, bringing revenue of US$219m.

Festivals. Of particular importance are Amakhosi Inxusa Festival, a festival of soul, dance and theatre in Bulawayo (March); and Zimbabwe National Jazz Festival in Harare (Sept.–Nov.).

Libraries. There is a City Library in Harare.

National Theatre and Opera. Harare has a Repertory Theatre.

Museums and Galleries. The main attractions are the Queen Victoria Museum and the National Gallery of Zimbabwe.

DIPLOMATIC REPRESENTATIVES
Of Zimbabwe in Great Britain (Zimbabwe House, 429 Strand, London, WC2R 0SA)
High Commissioner: Vacant.

Of Great Britain in Zimbabwe (7th Floor, Corner House, Samora Machel Ave/Leopold Takawira Street, Harare, P.O. Box 4490)
High Commissioner: Peter Longworth.

Of Zimbabwe in the USA (1608 New Hampshire Ave., NW, Washington, D.C., 20009)
Ambassador: Vacant.

Of the USA in Zimbabwe (172 Herbert Chitepo Ave., Harare)
Ambassador: Tom Macdonald.

Of Zimbabwe to the United Nations
Ambassador: Vacant.

Of Zimbabwe to the European Union
Ambassador: Simbarashe Mumbengegwi.

FURTHER READING
Central Statistical Office. *Monthly Digest of Statistics.*

Caute, D., *Under the Skin: the Death of White Rhodesia.* London, 1983
Cliffe, L. and Stoneman, C., *Zimbabwe: Politics, Economy and Society.* London, 1989
Hatchard, J., *Individual Freedoms and State Security in the African Context: the Case of Zimbabwe.* Ohio Univ. Press, 1993
Herbst, J., *State Politics in Zimbabwe.* Univ. of California, 1990
Keppel-Jones, A., *Rhodes and Rhodesia: the White Conquest of Zimbabwe, 1884–1902.* Univ. of Natal Press, 1983
Morris-Jones, W. H., (ed.) *From Rhodesia to Zimbabwe.* London, 1980
Potts, D., *Zimbabwe* [Bibliography]. 2nd ed. Oxford and Santa Barbara (CA), 1993
Schatzberg, M. G., *The Political Economy of Zimbabwe.* New York, 1984
Skålnes, T., *The Politics of Economic Reform in Zimbabwe: Continuity and Change in Development.* London, 1995
Stoneman, C., *Zimbabwe's Inheritance.* London, 1982.—*Zimbabwe: Politics, Economics and Society.* London, 1988
Verrier, A., *The Road to Zimbabwe, 1890–1980.* London, 1986
Weiss, R. *Zimbabwe and the New Elite.* London, 1994
Zimmerman, Z., *Zimbabwe's First Decade of Independence, 1980–1990: a Select and Annotated Bibliography.* Johannesburg, 1991

National statistical office: Central Statistical Office, POB 8063, Causeway, Harare.

ABBREVIATIONS

ACP	African Caribbean Pacific
Adm.	Admiral
a.i.	ad interim
b.	born
bbls.	barrels
bd	board
bn.	billion (one thousand million)
Brig.	Brigadier
bu.	bushel
Cdr	Commander
CFA	Communauté Financière Africaine
CFP	Comptoirs Français du Pacifique
c.i.f.	cost, insurance, freight
C.-in-C.	Commander-in-Chief
CIS	Commonwealth of Independent States
cu.	cubic
CUP	Cambridge University Press
cwt	hundredweight
D.	Democratic Party
DWT	dead weight tonnes
ECOWAS	Economic Community of West African States
EEA	European Economic Area
EEZ	Exclusive Economic Zone
EMS	European Monetary System
EMU	European Monetary Union
ERM	Exchange Rate Mechanism
f.o.b.	free on board
ft	foot/feet
G8 Group	Canada, France, Germany, Italy, Japan, UK, USA, Russia
GDP	gross domestic product
Gen.	General
GNP	gross national product
GRT	gross registered tonnes
GW	gigawatt
GWh	gigawatt hours
ha	hectare(s)
HDI	Human Development Index
ind	independent(s)
K	kindergarten
kg	kilogramme(s)
kl	kilolitre(s)
km	kilometre(s)

kW	kilowatt
kWh	kilowatt hours
lb(s)	pound(s) (weight)
Lieut.	Lieutenant
m.	million
Maj.	Major
MW	megawatt
MWh	megawatt hours
NRT	net registered tonnes
OUP	Oxford University Press
oz.	ounce(s)
PAYE	Pay-As-You-Earn
PPP	Purchasing Power Parity
R.	Republican Party
Rt Hon.	Right Honourable
SADC	Southern African Development Community
SDR	Special Drawing Rights
sq.	square
SSI	Supplemental Security Income
TAFE	technical and further education
TEU	twenty-foot equivalent units
TV	television
Univ.	University
VAT	value-added tax
vfd	value for duty

PLACE AND INTERNATIONAL
ORGANIZATIONS INDEX

Italicised page numbers refer to extended entries.